BRITISH HIT SINGLES & ALBUMS

www.bibleofpop.com

ACKNOWLEDGEMENTS

Managing Editor:
David Roberts
Chief Consultant / Contributor:
Dave McAleer
Product Manager / Assistant Editor:
James Bradley
Researcher / Proofreader:
Matthew White
Desk Editor:
Mary Novakovich
Designer:
Yeung Poon
Picture Research:
Laura Jackson and Caroline Thomas
Production Director:
Patricia Langton
Business Consultant:
Matthias Bauss

WITH SPECIAL THANKS TO ...

The Official UK Charts Company, Billboard, BPI, Sam Fay, Nadine Causey, Nicky Boxall, Stuart Devoy, Alan Smith, Anthony Liu, Edmund Ip, Paul Rouse, James Herbert, Ryan Tunstall, Andy Gregory, Brian Southall, Stephen Thwaites, Scott Christie, Nicola Savage, Robin Tucker, Rob Bayston, Keith Badman, Peter Johnson, Andrew Ruffhead, Elliot Costi, Robert Dimery, Kate White, Sam Knights, Ceri Davies, Martin Downham, Mark Haden, Craig Glenday, Russtti Gaynor, Della Torra Howes, Janet Jones, Tony Upton, Ray Spiller, Tony Upton, Katie Havelock, Alan Jones, Tom Roberts, Mark Bennett, Bruno MacDonald, Steve Earnshaw, Ossie Dales, Neil Thompson, John Thomason, Pete Thomason, Alistair Richards, Ross Carter, Colin Hughes, Andy Butters, Kevin Ennis, Ian Evans, Dave Breese, Steve Hurst, Brian Griffiths, Paul Gilbert, Fred Bronson, Justin Lewis, Kirk McMillan, Ben Cook, Christopher Leah, Peter Berry, Matthew Rankin, Victor Aroldoss.

British Hit Singles & Albums 19th Edition

1st edition 1977, 2nd 1979, 3rd 1981, 4th 1983, 5th 1985, 6th 1987, 7th 1989, 8th 1991, 9th 1993, 10th 1995, 11th 1997, 12th 1999, 13th 2000, 14th 2001, 15th 2002, 16th 2003, 17th 2004, 18th 2005

Reprint 10 9 8 7 6 5 4 3 2 1 0

Printed and bound in Italy by Rotolito Lombarda SpA
Origination by Dot Gradations Ltd, Essex, UK

A catalogue record for this book is available from the British Library

ISBN-13 9781904994107
ISBN-10 1904994105

INTRODUCTION

Welcome to the 19th edition of our so-called Bible of Pop, the third to include every British hit single (now including downloads) and album.

It is our mission to make every annual edition of the book unmissable and collectable. With that in mind we unveil a brand new feature which literally stretches almost cover to cover, showing every No.1 single and album week by week, dating back to 1952. Use this No.1s timeline to find out the best-selling LP and single in the week you were born, started school, got married, celebrated an anniversary – in fact, any significant date at all. Elsewhere in the book you will see that we are celebrating the 50th anniversary of the albums chart with a series of special features, all carrying an Official UK Chart Company logo pictured on this page. There are many other new additions to the A-Z act listings in the book, which are explained in detail on page 10, and to help you to locate the 30 special feature articles and charts, turn to page 4.

One last reminder before you dive into the 720 pages. We'd love to hear from you, so keep in touch by writing, emailing or visiting our revamped website.

David Roberts
Managing Editor

KEEP IN TOUCH

We encourage your letters, emails and suggestions on anything connected to the book of British Hit Singles & Albums. There are three ways to do this.

Address your letters to:
The Editor: David Roberts
British Hit Singles & Albums
GUINNESS WORLD RECORDS
338 Euston Road
London NW1 3BD

Send your emails to
editor@bibleofpop.com

Join in the forum, play the quiz, find out what was No.1 on any day in the past 50 years, visit the shop, check out the latest reviews and remind yourself what was happening on this day in chart history at www.bibleofpop.com

CONTENTS

Use this page to go straight to the section of the book or individual feature you are searching for:

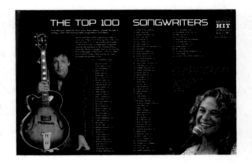

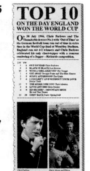

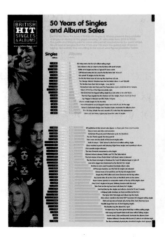

2005 REVIEW

The record of events, facts and statistics worth noting in a year when downloads made their first impact on the Official UK Singles Chart and the music making the charts was, perhaps, more varied than ever before. The antics of the much misunderstood and over-publicised Pete Doherty could have dominated the next few pages, but by dubbing him "Pop Celebrity of the Year" and acknowledging his determination to keep the genuine rock 'n' roll behaviour flag flying, we will leave it there and save a few trees.

JANUARY »

ITV's The X Factor winner Steve Brookstein tops the first singles chart of the new year with a former Phil Collins No.2, 'Against All Odds'. On the chart dated 22 January, the 1,000th No.1 single is fittingly by the No.1 chart star, Elvis. His double A-side 'One Night'/'I Got Stung' is one of a series of re-issues that will dominate the early charts of 2005. **Paul McCartney performs the half-time entertainment at the Super Bowl; 61,000 rock fans pack Cardiff's Millennium Stadium to watch Snow Patrol, Manic Street Preachers, Eric Clapton, Keane and Jools Holland help to raise cash for the tsunami relief fund.** Jamie Foxx gets rave reviews for his portrayal of Ray Charles following the release of the movie Ray.

MARCH Former Bad Company and Free front man Paul Rodgers makes his debut as Queen lead vocalist in a fans-only tour opener at Brixton Academy

50 Cent equals a Beatles record of three singles in the US Top Five and by the end of the year is officially the top male act of 2005 stateside

FEBRUARY »

Clash legend Joe Strummer has a Class 47 diesel locomotive named after him. At the Grammys, Ray Charles is given eight awards to add to the 12 he amassed during his lifetime. British and Irish winners are Rod Stewart (one), Annie Lennox (one) and U2 (three). **Lifetime Achievement Grammys are bestowed upon Eddy Arnold, Janis Joplin, Jerry Lee Lewis, Led Zeppelin and The Staple Singers.** Brian Wilson wins his first Grammy, not for his Beach Boys work but for an instrumental, 'Mrs O'Leary's Cow'. **Britain's first independent record producer, Joe Meek, is immortalised in a critically-acclaimed play, Telstar, in which actor Con O'Neil's performance of Meek is described as "sensational" by The Daily Telegraph.** To celebrate the singles chart reaching the magic 1,000 No.1s mark, record collector Larry Foster plays the entire 1,000 in a marathon for charity at City Limits, Romford, Essex, clocking up 59 hours and 17 minutes in five daytime sessions.

The single in its physical disc format is all but dead across the Atlantic as the sales chart (once a Top 100) is reduced to a meagre Top 20. Back in the UK cassette single sales hit an all-time low with just 22 recorded sales in one week. **An announcement is made that download sales will in future contribute to gold and platinum singles awards.** Pete Waterman is awarded an OBE. **High points of the BRIT awards are Bob Geldof's show-closing Outstanding Contribution to Music performance, and well-received live offerings from Joss Stone (best British female and urban act) and Scissor Sisters (best international group, international album and international breakthrough act).** Other winners include Franz Ferdinand (two awards), Keane (two) and The Streets, Will Young, Muse, McFly, Eminem and Gwen Stefani with one each. Robbie Williams accepts his 15th BRIT award for the best song from 25 years of the BRITs, 'Angels'.

MARCH »

The Queen invites 500 British music people (including the star-struck editor of this book) to Buckingham Palace for a reception. Soul men Bill Withers, Isaac Hayes (with David Porter) and Steve Cropper are inducted into the Songwriters' Hall of Fame. **The X Factor runners-up G4's self-titled album sells 244,671 in its first week – the fastest-selling debut album since Hear'Say.** The Ray Charles legacy lingers as he has reportedly sold 3.7 million albums in the US in nine months since his death. **His duets LP Genius Loves Company gives him his first US No.1 in more than 40 years.** 50 Cent becomes the first act since The Beatles to have three singles simultaneously in the US Top Five. **Fans at the Brixton Academy witness Paul Rodgers make his debut as Queen's new vocalist.** New Order are the recipients of the Godlike Genius award from the NME. **Digital TV channel Music Choice unveils the results of a survey to find out the UK's most appropriate funeral songs. 'Angels' by Robbie Williams tops the chart.** Radio 1 DJ Edith Bowman is crowned Comic Relief Does Celebrity Fame Academy queen. **U2, Percy Sledge, The Pretenders, The O'Jays and Buddy Guy are all inducted into the Rock and Roll Hall of Fame.** After performing with The Pretenders, Neil Young experiences "visual field disturbances" and later makes a full recovery from an aneurysm in his brain. **Husky-voiced broadcasting legend Tommy Vance dies.**

MARCH 'God' meets the Queen: Once dubbed guitar 'god', Eric Clapton meets the Queen at Buckingham Palace where she reportedly asked him: 'Have you been playing a long time?'

More copies of '(Is This Way to) Amarillo' were sold in the first week in the UK than there are people living in the Texas town (population 173,627).

APRIL »

For the first time, downloads are added to physical sales contributing to the Official UK Singles Chart dated 23 April. Physical sales of 392,882 plus 354,620 download singles make a total of 747,502 for the week. **R&B producer Scott Storch completes a record-equalling 18 successive weeks at the top of the US Hot 100.** A record-breaking three hours is all it takes to sell out all 112,000 Glastonbury tickets. **Cher's farewell tour ends and sets a female record, grossing $200m after 323 shows.**

MAY »

Cream reunite for four nights at the Royal Albert Hall and tickets are all gone in two hours. A frenzy on eBay sees some tickets reportedly change hands for more than £2,000. Oasis sell 250,000 tickets for their world tour on the opening day of sales. **As the band bag their seventh No.1 single they are recognised as the most successful chart act of the past decade (1995-2005) by British Hit Singles & Albums. Liam Gallagher graciously accepts an award for this achievement.** Elvis's series of 17 re-issued singles score three No.1s, eight No.2s, four No.3s, one No.4 and one No.5. This enables the King to become the third biggest-selling singles act of 2005. **Kylie Minogue is diagnosed with breast cancer.** The Beatles become the first act to earn six diamond discs in the US – a feat that requires 10 million sales. **The VE concert in Trafalgar Square features performances from the likes of Sir Cliff Richard, Dame Vera Lynn, Katherine Jenkins, Daniel Bedingfield, Katie Melua and Will Young.** Elton John's music contributes to a stunning review for the West End show Billy Elliot as The Daily Telegraph critic Charles Spencer proclaims it "the greatest British musical I have ever seen". **The Eurovision Song Contest is won by Greece.** Former East 17 singer Brian Harvey is crushed by his own car while reversing down a road in Walthamstow. After 3 weeks in intensive care, Harvey blames the accident on eating too many jacket potatoes, which caused him to open the car door to be sick. **Country star Kenny Chesney weds actress Renee Zellweger.**

MAY Oasis have a top year with another two No.1 singles from the chart-topping album Don't Believe the Truth

Live 8 Hyde Park statistics: 205,000 fans, 27 acts, 440 journalists and photographers, 12 giant TV screens, 200 toilets, 500 microphones trailing 8,000m of cable, 47 tonnes of lights, 2,100 security guards and stewards.

JUNE »

Coldplay's new X&Y album becomes the second highest seller in week one, shifting 464,471 copies. The band enjoy more success as the album tops the chart in no fewer than 22 countries, shipping five million copies worldwide. Jimmy Page (MBE), Brian May (CBE), Midge Ure (OBE) and John Mayall (OBE) are all suitably honoured. **Michael Jackson's jury brings in an innocent verdict.** James Blunt's 'You're Beautiful' makes the slowest climb to No.1 of any single in the 21st century. **'Axel F' by Crazy Frog is a huge hit around Europe.** Destiny's Child announce that they are splitting up.

JULY »

UK legitimate download sales are already treble those of 2004, and Apple announces that 500 million iTunes downloads have been banked in two years. However, piracy surveys suggest that illegal downloads are growing 10 times faster than legitimate purchases and that pirate CDs are outnumbering properly paid-for CDs in 31 countries. **A text message lottery provides 2,060,285 entries for free tickets to Live 8.** Ten concerts are staged around the world, allowing one million people to witness the biggest global music event since Live Aid. **A Hyde Park crowd of 205,000 is added to the BBC's estimate of half the UK population tuning in on TV and the internet at some point.** Paul McCartney and U2's Live 8 opening performance of 'Sgt. Pepper' is available to download just 46 minutes after they left the stage and knocks James Blunt off the top of the download chart.

The Christmas No.1 is The X Factor winner Shayne Ward's single 'That's My Goal', which sells 283,446 copies on its first day and 742,180 in four days, including a record-breaking 71,997 downloads in a week.

AUGUST »

Controversy on Top of the Pops as presenter Richard Bacon's "fat melting pot of talent" quip during rehearsal upsets The Magic Numbers, who walk off. Bacon's attempted apology to the Mercury Music Prize nominees is to no avail and Goldfrapp fill the breach. **Queen's 'Don't Stop Me Now' is voted the Greatest Driving Song by viewers of BBC2's Top Gear.** Iron Maiden are inducted into both the Kerrang! and the Hollywood Halls of Fame. **Fats Domino survives the New Orleans floods resulting from Hurricane Katrina.** Now 61! shows that there's still life in the compilation market as it amasses a staggering 310,230 sales in week one. **Elton John and Paul Anka make their respective debuts in the US country and jazz charts.** On her 47th birthday, Madonna falls off her horse, suffering a broken hand and collarbone and three cracked ribs.

SEPTEMBER »

Lemar wins two Mobo awards. Antony & The Johnsons win the Mercury Prize. **Kanye West makes a "George Bush doesn't care about black people" speech on an NBC Hurricane Katrina TV broadcast.** Status Quo are awarded a British Hit Singles & Albums certificate in recognition of their 60 hit singles, the most by any band in chart history. Francis Rossi and Rick Parfitt accept the award from Coronation Street actor Bruce Jones, aka Les Battersby. The band also celebrate their biggest hit single in 15 years. **The Rolling Stones' new album A Bigger Bang fails by just 11 copies to knock James Blunt from the top spot.** Rapper Lil' Kim starts a jail sentence. **A global search to find a new lead singer for INXS ends when a reality TV series of 11 shows provides the band with new Canadian front man Jason Dean Fortune.**

SEPTEMBER Coronation Street actor Bruce Jones (Les Battersby) presents Francis Rossi and Rick Parfitt with an award to mark their record of most hit singles by any band

OCTOBER »

A Sheffield four-piece band, Arctic Monkeys, have the first cyberspace No.1 single. A swiftly growing fanbase buys 'I Bet You Look Good on the Dancefloor' on the back of an internet buzz eschewing traditional band-breaking methods such as radio plays and record company marketing campaigns. **Gwen Stefani's 'Hollaback Girl' becomes the first track to reach one million paid downloads in the US.** For the first time since charts began, UK solo singers take the top five positions in the albums chart, and UK-signed acts top the chart for a record-breaking 25 weeks in a row. **Physical singles contribute just 38 per cent to the total number of singles sold as downloads pass the 600,000 mark for the first time in a week.** After 48 years Paul Anka finally gets an album to make the chart. **The US, not known for its love of British bands currently, hails Franz Ferdinand, as You Could Have It So Much Better makes the Top 10 in the albums chart.** The Prodigy score their fourth successive No.1 album – a record for a dance act. **An IFPI survey reveals that 6 per cent of the world's music sales are now via downloads.** More than 56,000 fans attend three sell-out shows at Madison Square Garden to see Cream gross $10.6m from ticket sales.

NOVEMBER »

UK Music Hall of Fame inductees include Pink Floyd, The Who, The Kinks, Bob Dylan, Jimi Hendrix, Aretha Franklin and Joy Division/New Order. Brit school R&B duo Floetry enter the US R&B albums chart at No.2 with Flo'ology, a record high for a new entry by a UK act. **Westlife score their 13th No.1 single when 'You Raise Me Up' hits the top spot.** Only, Elvis, Cliff and The Beatles have more. **This song also completes an unprecedented run of 18 Top Five hits and pushes their UK singles sales past the five million mark, with the boys' UK album sales breaking through the seven million barrier.** Twelve years after her last chart success, Kate Bush returns with a new single that delivers her highest ever chart entry position (No.4) and double album that makes No.3. **Kate is assisted on the album by, among others, Rolf Harris and her young son Bertie, who also designed the cover of mum's new single.** Green Day and Coldplay, with two awards each, are the top winners at the MTV Europe awards. **Madonna's 'Hung Up' gives her a 20-year span of chart-topping singles, while the album from which it comes, Confessions on a Dance Floor, is her ninth No.1, a feat by a solo artist bettered only by Elvis.** The 47-year-old mother also tops both charts simultaneously for the third time and is the oldest act to do this.

DECEMBER »

Billboard's list of top US tours of 2005 names U2's Vertigo tour as the highest grossing at $260,119,588. After a protracted legal battle over ownership of pop reality TV formats, Simon Cowell and Simon Fuller settle their differences out of court. **'Brown Eyed Girl' by Van Morrison, despite never being a hit single in the UK, is certified as having been played seven million times on US radio.** The Beatles sue EMI for £30m unpaid royalties. **For the fourth year running, American Idol artists notch up the best-selling single of the year in the US, and the top male, female and group acts of 2005 are 50 Cent, Kelly Clarkson and Green Day.** Just one behind Elvis, Mariah Carey registers her 17th US chart-topping single. **American download records of 2005 are smashed with just short of 20 million tracks purchased in one week, more than double the previous year's record.** 'Laffy Taffy' by D4L, with 175,000, becomes the top download for an individual track in one week. **John Lennon is remembered in celebrations of his life around the world 25 years to the day since his murder in New York City.** In the New Year's honours list, both Tom Jones and Johnny Dankworth are knighted.

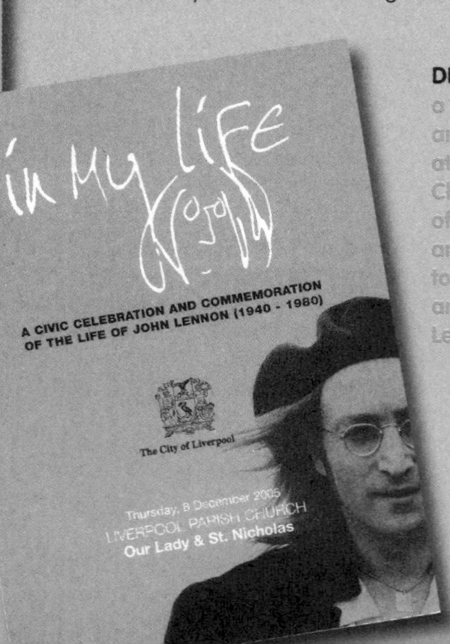

DECEMBER In My Life, a civic celebration and commemoration at Liverpool Parish Church, was just one of hundreds of events around the world to mark the 25th anniversary of John Lennon's murder

2005 BEST-SELLERS »

The most impressive sales fact of the year has to be that of James Blunt's 2,367,758-selling album Back to Bedlam. No other album in the history of British music has sold more copies in a calendar year than the former army reconnaissance officer's debut LP. A mention in dispatches should also go to Tony Christie, who sees his 2005 'Amarillo' re-issue bag enough sales not only to top the singles best-seller chart but also to enter the all-time best-sellers list at No.61.

TOP 10 BEST-SELLING SINGLES IN 2005

1. **(IS THIS THE WAY TO) AMARILLO** Tony Christie featuring Peter Kay – 1,100,233
2. **THAT'S MY GOAL** Shayne Ward – 874,444
3. **AXEL F** Crazy Frog – 525,123
4. **YOU'RE BEAUTIFUL** James Blunt – 474,455
5. **DON'T CHA** Pussycat Dolls featuring Busta Rhymes – 380,936
6. **ALL ABOUT YOU / YOU'VE GOT A FRIEND** McFly – 338,553
7. **LONELY** Akon – 334,413
8. **HUNG UP** Madonna – 327,504
9. **YOU RAISE ME UP** Westlife – 323,466
10. **PUSH THE BUTTON** Sugababes – 306,695

TOP 10 BEST-SELLING ALBUMS IN 2005

1. **BACK TO BEDLAM** James Blunt – 2,367,758
2. **X&Y** Coldplay – 1,999,260
3. **INTENSIVE CARE** Robbie Williams – 1,434,315
4. **EMPLOYMENT** Kaiser Chiefs – 1,312,122
5. **DEMON DAYS** Gorillaz – 1,198,202
6. **FACE TO FACE** Westlife – 1,142,563
7. **EYE TO THE TELESCOPE** KT Tunstall – 1,023,650
8. **BREAKAWAY** Kelly Clarkson – 952,225
9. **CURTAIN CALLS – THE HITS** Eminem – 926,012
10. **FOREVER FAITHLESS – THE GREATEST HITS** Faithless – 912,887

James Blunt's Back to Bedlam, although slow out of the blocks, eventually became the best-selling album in any calendar year since the albums chart began in 1956

A-Z BY ARTIST

The next 500-plus pages are devoted to every solo artist, band, duo, trio, orchestra, instrumentalist, glove puppet, choir, marching band, brass band, producer, comedian, DJ, actor, footballer, TV presenter and irritating amphibian that has registered one week or more in the world's most respected singles and albums charts.

The shelves of CDs and vinyl on this page illustrate just a tiny proportion of the massively comprehensive collection of every chart single and album stored by Broadchart in its London vaults

LISTEN TO THE BOOK

In addition to reading this book you will soon be able to listen to it! For more information about this Broadchart / British Hit Singles & Albums collaboration, check out our website **www.bibleofpop.com**

HOW TO USE THE A-Z

The following pages list, in alphabetical order, every act that has ever made the charts. All SINGLES in this section of the book are printed in BLACK and all ALBUMS in ORANGE. For the first time they appear together in chronological order. Other new features in this edition are the naming of lead vocalists for acts that have registered a Top 10 hit, a line in each biography adding up the totals of hits and weeks on chart, the addition of US million-selling singles (which are RIAA certified and additionally sourced from US trade papers and record company statistics) and NEW symbols for every brand new act in 2005. Also included are the real names of solo artists and duo members achieving a Top 40 entry and birth and death dates of deceased solo artists and duo members.

Use the key below to establish what all the book's various symbols stand for.

422 Top 500 = position in the British Hit Singles & Albums Top 500, our annual list calculated by total weeks on the singles and albums charts

NEW = indicates new act debuting in 2005 and in the book for the first time

(see also APHEX TWIN) = act connected to entry that is also listed in its own right elsewhere in the A-Z

1 ATB featuring York = footnote indicates change to act name for a particular single or album or collaboration with another artist

7 Feb 98 = date single or album first entered chart. Since 1969, this date has been a Saturday

Single		Album	
★	= No.1 single	★	= No.1 album
●	= Top 10 single	●	= Top 10 album
+	= single still on chart at end of 2005	+	= album still on chart at end of 2005
■	= single entered chart at No.1	■	= album entered chart at No.1
▲	= US No.1 single	▲	= US No.1 album
£	= UK million-selling single		
$	= US million-selling single		

BIOGRAPHICAL INFORMATION
Abbreviations: b. – born, d. – died, b – bass guitarist, d – drums, g – guitarist, k – keyboards, prc – percussion, sax – saxophone, syn – synthesizer, v – vocalist

ALPHABETICAL ORDERING
In keeping with traditional alphabetical ordering, artist names consisting of initials (e.g. ATB, BBMAK) appear at the beginning of each letter except when the names are acronyms (ie pronounceable as one word such as Abba). The exceptions to this rule are for acts appearing as DJs and MCs, whose actual names are listed in alphabetical order.

RE-ENTRIES, RE-MIXES, RE-ISSUES and RE-RECORDINGS
All singles that have re-entered the chart are indicated by (re), which shows that the single has re-entered once. Additional re-entries are listed (2re), (3re), etc. When a re-entry outperforms the original hit, the relevant information is given as a footnote. All weeks on chart for re-entries are added together with those of the original listing for that single. There is no re-entry data for albums. Albums re-entries are too numerous to record and all re-entry weeks are added to the original chart entry.

Re-mixes are updated different versions of a previous hit with a completely new catalogue number. Re-issues are new releases of an unaltered previous hit with a completely new catalogue number. Re-recordings are re-workings of a previous hit by the same act.

YOUR INTRODUCTION TO OUR NEW No.1s TIMELINE
The most exciting new feature in this year's book is the No.1s Timeline. Running across the bottom of virtually every page is this silver bar containing orange windows displaying the No.1 albums (startting on page 61) and black windows displaying the No.1 singles (starting on the page opposite) in chronological order, week by week.

To find out what was the No.1 single or album on a certain date, remember that the chart dates in the bar along the top indicate the 'week ending' date. For example, if the date you were interested in was 19 March 1976, you would find that on 20 March 'I Love to Love (But My Baby Loves to Dance)' by Tina Charles topped the singles chart and Blue for You by Status Quo was the No.1 album, which means that they were top for the entire week from 14 March to 20 March 1976.

Note that for the period between 28 July 1956 and 9 August 1969, the singles and albums charts are dated differently.

A *UK, male vocal (Jason Perry) / instrumental group (2 Albums: 10 Weeks, 12 Singles: 21 Weeks)*

7 Feb 98 **FOGHORN** *Tycoon TYCD 5* **63** 1
11 Apr 98 **NUMBER ONE** *Tycoon TYCD 6* **47** 1
27 Jun 98 **SING-A-LONG** *Tycoon TYCD 7* **57** 1
24 Oct 98 **SUMMER ON THE UNDERGROUND** *Tycoon TYCD 8* **72** 1
5 Jun 99 **OLD FOLKS** *Tycoon TYCD 9* **54** 1
21 Aug 99 **I LOVE LAKE TAHOE** *Tycoon TYCD 10* **59** 1
28 Aug 99 MONKEY KONG *Tycoon 3984276952* 62 1
2 Mar 02 ● **NOTHING** *London LONCD 463* **9** 6
16 Mar 02 HI-FI SERIOUS *London 927447762* 18 9
1 Jun 02 **STARBUCKS** *London LONCD 467* **20** 3
30 Nov 02 **SOMETHING'S GOING ON** *London LONCD 471* **51** 1
13 Sep 03 **GOOD TIME** *London LONCD 480* **23** 2
14 May 05 **RUSH SONG** *London LONCD 487* **35** 2
30 Jul 05 **BETTER OFF WITH HIM** *London LONCD 488* **52** 1

ABC (380 Top 500) *Glossy but witty pop group formed in 1980 in Sheffield, South Yorkshire, UK. Led by stylish vocalist Martin Fry, b. 9 Mar 1959. First UK group of the 1980s to prise four Top 20 hits off a debut album (1982's The Lexicon of Love) and they were equally successful Stateside (8 Albums: 91 Weeks, 19 Singles: 93 Weeks)*

31 Oct 81 **TEARS ARE NOT ENOUGH** *Neutron NT 101* **19** 8
20 Feb 82 ● **POISON ARROW** *Neutron NT 102* **6** 11
15 May 82 ● **THE LOOK OF LOVE (re)** *Neutron NT 103* **4** 12
3 Jul 82 ★ THE LEXICON OF LOVE *Neutron NTRS 1* ■ 1 50
4 Sep 82 ● **ALL OF MY HEART** *Neutron NT 104* **5** 8
5 Nov 83 **THAT WAS THEN THIS IS NOW** *Neutron NT 105* **18** 4
26 Nov 83 BEAUTY STAB *Neutron NTRL 2* 12 13
21 Jan 84 **S.O.S.** *Neutron NT 106* **39** 5
10 Nov 84 **HOW TO BE A MILLIONAIRE** *Neutron NT 107* **49** 4
6 Apr 85 **BE NEAR ME** *Neutron NT 108* **26** 4
15 Jun 85 **VANITY KILLS** *Neutron NT 109* **70** 1
26 Oct 85 HOW TO BE A ZILLIONAIRE *Neutron NTRH 3* 28 3
16 Jan 86 **OCEAN BLUE** *Neutron NT 110* **51** 3
6 Jun 87 **WHEN SMOKEY SINGS** *Neutron NT 111* **11** 10
5 Sep 87 **THE NIGHT YOU MURDERED LOVE** *Neutron NT 112* **31** 8
24 Oct 87 ● ALPHABET CITY *Neutron NTRH 4* 7 10
28 Nov 87 **KING WITHOUT A CROWN** *Neutron NT 113* **44** 3
27 May 89 **ONE BETTER WORLD** *Neutron NT 114* **32** 4
23 Sep 89 **THE REAL THING** *Neutron NT 115* **68** 1
28 Oct 89 UP *Neutron 8386461* 58 1
14 Apr 90 **THE LOOK OF LOVE** (re-mix) *Neutron NT 116* **68** 1
21 Apr 90 ● ABSOLUTELY *Neutron 8429671* 7 12
27 Jul 91 **LOVE CONQUERS ALL** *Parlophone R 6292* **47** 2
24 Aug 91 ABRACADABRA *Parlophone PCS 7355* 50 1
11 Jan 92 **SAY IT** *Parlophone R 6298* **42** 3
22 Mar 97 **STRANGER THINGS** *Blatant / Deconstruction 453632* **57** 1
4 Aug 01 THE LOOK OF LOVE – THE VERY BEST OF ABC *Mercury 5862372* 69 1

The act was a UK, male vocal / instrumental group for the first six hits, a UK / US, male / female vocal / instrumental group for the next four, a male duo from 1987-1992 and Martin Fry alone for 'Stranger Things'.

A.B.'S *Japan, male instrumental group*

14 Apr 84 DÉJA VU *Street Sounds XKHAN 503* 80 2

AC/DC (133 Top 500) *Internationally acclaimed Australia-based quintet: Angus Young (g), Malcolm Young (g), Bon Scott (v) (d. 1980), Cliff Williams (b), Phillip Rudd (d). Brian Johnson (ex-Geordie) replaced Scott in 1980. No act has had more hits (28) without a Top 10 than AC/DC. Inducted into the Rock and Roll Hall of Fame in 2003 (14 Albums: 255 Weeks, 28 Singles: 126 Weeks)*

5 Nov 77 LET THERE BE ROCK *Atlantic K 50366* 17 5
20 May 78 POWERAGE *Atlantic K 50483* 26 9
10 Jun 78 **ROCK 'N' ROLL DAMNATION** *Atlantic K 11142* **24** 9
28 Oct 78 IF YOU WANT BLOOD YOU'VE GOT IT *Atlantic K 50532* 13 58
18 Aug 79 ● HIGHWAY TO HELL *Atlantic K 50628* 8 32
1 Sep 79 **HIGHWAY TO HELL** *Atlantic K 11321* **56** 4
2 Feb 80 **TOUCH TOO MUCH** *Atlantic K 11435* **29** 9
28 Jun 80 **DIRTY DEEDS DONE DIRT CHEAP** *Atlantic HM 2* **47** 3
28 Jun 80 **HIGH VOLTAGE (LIVE VERSION)** *Atlantic HM 1* **48** 3
28 Jun 80 **IT'S A LONG WAY TO THE TOP (IF YOU WANNA ROCK 'N' ROLL)** *Atlantic HM 3* **55** 3
28 Jun 80 **WHOLE LOTTA ROSIE** *Atlantic HM 4* **36** 8
9 Aug 80 ★ BACK IN BLACK *Atlantic K 50735* ■ 1 40
13 Sep 80 **YOU SHOOK ME ALL NIGHT LONG** *Atlantic K 11600* **38** 6
29 Nov 80 **ROCK 'N' ROLL AIN'T NOISE POLLUTION** *Atlantic K 11630* **15** 8
5 Dec 81 ● FOR THOSE ABOUT TO ROCK WE SALUTE YOU *Atlantic K 50851* ▲ 3 29
6 Feb 82 **LET'S GET IT UP** *Atlantic K 11706* **13** 6
3 Jul 82 **FOR THOSE ABOUT TO ROCK (WE SALUTE YOU)** *Atlantic K 11721* **15** 6
3 Sep 83 ● FLICK OF THE SWITCH *Atlantic 7801001* 4 9
29 Oct 83 **GUNS FOR HIRE** *Atlantic A 9774* **37** 4
4 Aug 84 **NERVOUS SHAKEDOWN** *Atlantic A 9651* **35** 5
6 Jul 85 **DANGER** *Atlantic A 9532* **48** 4
13 Jul 85 ● FLY ON THE WALL *Atlantic 781263* 7 10
18 Jan 86 **SHAKE YOUR FOUNDATIONS** *Atlantic A 9474* **24** 5
24 May 86 **WHO MADE WHO** *Atlantic A 9425* **16** 5
7 Jun 86 WHO MADE WHO *Atlantic WX 57* 11 12
30 Aug 86 **YOU SHOOK ME ALL NIGHT LONG** (re-issue) *Atlantic A 9377* **46** 4
16 Jan 88 **HEATSEEKER** *Atlantic A 9136* **12** 6
13 Feb 88 ● BLOW UP YOUR VIDEO *Atlantic WX 144* 2 14
2 Apr 88 **THAT'S THE WAY I WANNA ROCK 'N' ROLL** *Atlantic A 9098* **22** 5
22 Sep 90 **THUNDERSTRUCK** *Atco B 8907* **13** 5
6 Oct 90 ● THE RAZOR'S EDGE *Atco WX 364* 4 18
24 Nov 90 **MONEYTALKS** *Atco B 8886* **36** 3
27 Apr 91 **ARE YOU READY** *Atco B 8830* **34** 3
17 Oct 92 **HIGHWAY TO HELL (LIVE)** *Atco B 8479* **14** 4
7 Nov 92 ● AC/DC LIVE *Atco 7567922152* 5 7
6 Mar 93 **DIRTY DEEDS DONE DIRT CHEAP (LIVE)** *Atco B 6073CD* **68** 1
10 Jul 93 **BIG GUN** *Atco B 8396CD* **23** 3
30 Sep 95 **HARD AS A ROCK** *Atlantic A 4368CD* **33** 2
7 Oct 95 ● BALLBREAKER *East West 7559617802* 6 8
11 May 96 **HAIL CAESAR** *East West 7559660512* **56** 1
11 Mar 00 STIFF UPPER LIP *EMI 5256672* 12 4
15 Apr 00 **STIFF UPPER LIP** *EMI CDSTIFF 100* **65** 1

A CAMP, A CERTAIN RATIO, A FLOCK OF SEAGULLS, A FLUX OF PINK INDIANS, A GUY CALLED GERALD, A HOMEBOY A HIPPIE AND A FUNKY DREDD, A HOUSE, A LOVE SUPREME, A PERFECT CIRCLE, A TASTE OF HONEY, A TRIBE CALLED QUEST, A VERY GOOD FRIEND OF MINE, A WAY OF LIFE, ETC – *See SECOND LETTER OF EACH ACT NAME TO LOCATE THESE ENTRIES*

A.D.A.M. featuring AMY *France, male / female vocal / instrumental duo – Andrea Bellicapelli and Amy*

1 Jul 95 **ZOMBIE** *Eternal YZ 951CD* **16** 11

AFI
US, male vocal / instrumental group (1 Album: 1 Week, 2 Singles: 4 Weeks)

22 Mar 03 SING THE SORROW *Dreamworks / Polydor 04504482* 52 1
21 Jun 03 **GIRL'S NOT GREY** *Dreamworks / Polydor 4504600* **22** 3
20 Sep 03 **THE LEAVING SONG PT.2** *Dreamworks / Polydor 4504625* **43** 1

AFX (see also APHEX TWIN; POLYGON WINDOW; POWERPILL)
UK, male instrumentalist / producer – Richard James

11 Aug 01 **2 REMIXES BY AFX** *MEN1 MEN 1CD* **69** 1

AKA *UK, male vocal group*

12 Oct 96 **WARNING** *RCA 74321360662* **43** 2

a1
UK / Norway, male vocal group (3 Albums: 19 Weeks, 9 Singles: 91 Weeks)

3 Jul 99 ● **BE THE FIRST TO BELIEVE** *Columbia 6674222* **6** 9
11 Sep 99 ● **SUMMERTIME OF OUR LIVES (re)** *Columbia 6678322* **5** 8

KEY UK No.1 ★ UK Top 10 ● Still on chart + UK entry at No.1 ■ US No.1 ▲ UK million seller £ US million seller $
Singles re-entries are listed as (re), (2re), (3re)... which signifies that the hit re-entered the chart once, twice or three times...
Peak Position / Weeks

20 Nov 99 ● **EVERYTIME / READY OR NOT** *Columbia 6681872* ... **3** 11
4 Dec 99 HERE WE COME *Columbia 4961362* ... 20 8
4 Mar 00 ● **LIKE A ROSE** *Columbia 6689032* ... **6** 12
9 Sep 00 ★ **TAKE ON ME (re)** *Columbia 6695902* ■ ... **1** 11
18 Nov 00 ★ **SAME OLD BRAND NEW YOU** *Columbia 6705202* ■ ... **1** 10
2 Dec 00 THE A LIST *Columbia 5011952* ... 14 9
3 Mar 01 ● **NO MORE (re)** *Columbia 6708742* ... **6** 13
2 Feb 02 ● **CAUGHT IN THE MIDDLE** *Columbia 6722322* ... **2** 12
25 May 02 **MAKE IT GOOD (re)** *Columbia 6726182* ... **11** 5
8 Jun 02 MAKE IT GOOD *Columbia 5082212* ... 15 2

A+ *US, male rapper – Andre Levins*

13 Feb 99 ● **ENJOY YOURSELF** *Universal UND 56230* ... **5** 9

A.R.E. WEAPONS *US, male vocal / instrumental group*

4 Aug 01 **STREET GANG** *Rough Trade RTRADSCD 022* ... **72** 1

ASAP
UK, male vocal / instrumental group (1 Album: 1 Week, 2 Singles: 4 Weeks)

14 Oct 89 **SILVER AND GOLD** *EMI EM 107* ... **60** 2
4 Nov 89 SILVER AND GOLD *EMI EMC 3566* ... 70 1
3 Feb 90 **DOWN THE WIRE** *EMI EM 131* ... **67** 2

ATB *Germany, male producer – Andre Tanneberger (1 Album: 3 Weeks, 9 Singles: 52 Weeks)*

13 Mar 99 **(9PM) TILL I COME** *Ministry of Sound DATA 1* ... **68** 1
22 May 99 **(9PM) TILL I COME (GERMAN IMPORT) (re)** (import) *Club Tools CLU 66066* ... **47** 5
19 Jun 99 **(9PM) TILL I COME (AUSTRALIAN IMPORT)** (import) *Dancenet DNET 131* ... **63** 1
3 Jul 99 ★ **9PM (TILL I COME)** *Sound of Ministry MOSCDS 132* ■ ... **1** 15
9 Oct 99 **DON'T STOP** (import) *Club Tools CLU 66406* ... **61** 2
23 Oct 99 ● **DON'T STOP (re)** *Sound of Ministry MOSCDS 134* ... **3** 13
25 Mar 00 ● **KILLER (re)** *Sound of Ministry MOSCDS 138* ... **4** 9
8 Apr 00 MOVIN MELODIES *Sound of Ministry ATBCDZ 1* ... 32 3
27 Jan 01 **THE FIELDS OF LOVE** *Club Tools / Edel 0124095 CLU* [1] ... **16** 4
30 Jun 01 **LET U GO** *Kontour 0117335 KTR* ... **34** 2

[1] ATB featuring York

ATC
Italy / New Zealand / UK / Australia, male / female vocal group

17 Aug 02 **AROUND THE WORLD (LA LA LA LA LA)** *EMI / Liberty CDATC 001* ... **15** 4

A.T.F.C. *UK, male producer – Aydin Hasirci (3 Singles: 10 Weeks)*

30 Oct 99 **IN AND OUT OF MY LIFE** *Defected DEFECT 8CDS* [1] ... **11** 5
16 Sep 00 **BAD HABIT** *Defected DFECT 19CDS* [2] ... **17** 3
9 Feb 02 **SLEEP TALK** *Defected DFECT 43CDS* [3] ... **33** 2

[1] ATFC presents Onephatdeeva [2] ATFC presents Onephatdeeva featuring Lisa Millett [3] ATFC featuring Lisa Millett

A.T.G.O.C. (see also FLICKMAN)
Italy, male instrumentalist / producer – Andrea Mazzali

21 Nov 98 **REPEATED LOVE** *Wonderboy WBOYD 012* ... **38** 2

A*TEENS *Sweden, male / female vocal group (4 Singles: 19 Weeks)*

4 Sep 99 **MAMMA MIA** *Stockholm 5613432* ... **12** 5
11 Dec 99 **SUPER TROUPER** *Stockholm 5615002* ... **21** 5
26 May 01 ● **UPSIDE DOWN** *Stockholm 1588492* ... **10** 7
27 Oct 01 **HALFWAY AROUND THE WORLD** *Stockholm 0153612* ... **30** 2

ATL *US, male vocal group (2 Singles: 9 Weeks)*

29 May 04 **CALLING ALL GIRLS** *Epic 6748272* ... **12** 5
28 Aug 04 **MAKE IT UP WITH LOVE** *Epic 6751102* ... **21** 4

A vs B *UK, male production duo*

9 May 98 **RIPPED IN 2 MINUTES** *Positiva CDTIV 89* ... **49** 1

AALIYAH *US, female vocalist – Aaliyah Haughton, b. 16 Jan 1979, d. 25 Aug 2001 (5 Albums: 59 Weeks, 18 Singles: 72 Weeks)*

2 Jul 94 **BACK AND FORTH** *Jive JIVECD 357* ... **16** 5
23 Jul 94 AGE AIN'T NOTHING BUT A NUMBER *Jive CHIP 149* ... 23 6
15 Oct 94 **(AT YOUR BEST) YOU ARE LOVE** *Jive JIVECD 359* ... **27** 2
11 Mar 95 **AGE AIN'T NOTHING BUT A NUMBER** *Jive JIVECD 369* ... **32** 2
13 May 95 **DOWN WITH THE CLIQUE** *Jive JIVECD 377* ... **33** 2
9 Sep 95 **THE THING I LIKE** *Jive JIVECD 382* ... **33** 2
3 Feb 96 **I NEED YOU TONIGHT** *Big Beat A 8130CD* [1] ... **66** 1
24 Aug 96 **IF YOUR GIRL ONLY KNEW** *Atlantic A 5669CD* ... **21** 2
7 Sep 96 ONE IN A MILLION *Atlantic 7567927152* ... 33 3
23 Nov 96 **GOT TO GIVE IT UP** *Atlantic A 5632CD* ... **37** 2
24 May 97 **IF YOUR GIRL ONLY KNEW / ONE IN A MILLION** (re-issue) *Atlantic A 5610CD* ... **15** 3
30 Aug 97 **4 PAGE LETTER** *Atlantic AT 0010CD1* ... **24** 2
22 Nov 97 **THE ONE I GAVE MY HEART TO / HOT LIKE FIRE** *Atlantic AT 0017CD* ... **30** 2
18 Apr 98 **JOURNEY TO THE PAST** *Atlantic AT 0026CD* ... **22** 3
12 Sep 98 **ARE YOU THAT SOMEBODY?** *Atlantic AT 0047CD* ... **11** 4
22 Jul 00 ● **TRY AGAIN (re)** *Virgin VUSCD 167* ▲ ... **5** 12
21 Jul 01 **WE NEED A RESOLUTION (re)** *Blackground VUSCD 206* [2] ... **20** 6
28 Jul 01 ● AALIYAH *Virgin CDVUS 199* ▲ ... 5 31
19 Jan 02 ★ **MORE THAN A WOMAN** *Blackground / Virgin VUSCD 230* ■ ... **1** 12
18 May 02 **ROCK THE BOAT** *Blackground / Virgin VUSCD 243* ... **12** 7
15 Feb 03 ● I CARE 4 U *Independiente / Blackground / Unique ISOM 37CDL* ... 4 16
26 Apr 03 **DON'T KNOW WHAT TO TELL YA** *Independiente / Blackground / Unique ISOM 73MS* ... **22** 3
16 Apr 05 ULTIMATE AALIYAH *Snapper Music SMADD 895X* ... 32 3

[1] Junior M.A.F.I.A. featuring Aaliyah [2] Aaliyah featuring Timbaland

ABBA (17 Top 500)

The most successful Swedish recording act ever amassed nine No.1 singles and achieved a run of eight consecutive chart-topping albums: Björn Ulvaeus (g/v), Benny Andersson (k/v), Agnetha Fältskog (v), Anni-Frid (Frida) Lyngstad (v). The video-genic quartet's 'Waterloo' was the first No.1 by a Scandinavian act in the UK and the biggest Eurovision Song Contest hit in the US. Their Gold - Greatest Hits topped the chart on two separate occasions, six years apart, selling over one million copies in 1999 alone. It returned to the top on its 218th chart week – a longevity record – and was the only album in the UK's Top 100 sellers every year between 1992 and 2000. Long after the group split in 1982 (following the divorces of Björn and Agnetha and Benny and Frida) they continued to collect awards and gold records on every continent. They have sold more than 300 million records, including over 10 million singles in the UK, and the Abba-based musical, Mamma Mia, has been internationally successful. They were given a star-studded tribute at the 1999 BRIT awards, which resulted in the hit single 'Thank Abba for the Music'. They were the first act from mainland Europe to become chart regulars in both the UK and US, and as such opened the doors to many later European artists. In 2005, Madonna sampled 'Gimme, Gimme, Gimme (A Man After Midnight)' on her No.1 single 'Hung Up' (16 Albums: 891 Weeks, 27 Singles: 255 Weeks)

20 Apr 74 ★ **WATERLOO** *Epic EPC 2240* ... **1** 9
8 Jun 74 WATERLOO *Epic EPC 80179* ... 28 2
13 Jul 74 **RING RING** *Epic EPC 2452* ... **32** 5
12 Jul 75 **I DO, I DO, I DO, I DO, I DO** *Epic EPC 3229* ... **38** 6
20 Sep 75 ● **SOS** *Epic EPC 3576* ... **6** 10
13 Dec 75 ★ **MAMMA MIA** *Epic EPC 3790* ... **1** 14
31 Jan 76 ABBA *Epic EPC 80835* ... 13 10
27 Mar 76 ★ **FERNANDO** *Epic EPC 4036* ... **1** 15
10 Apr 76 ★ GREATEST HITS *Epic EPC 69218* ... 1 130
21 Aug 76 ★ **DANCING QUEEN** *Epic EPC 4499* ▲ $ ... **1** 15
20 Nov 76 ● **MONEY, MONEY, MONEY** *Epic EPC 4713* ... **3** 12
27 Nov 76 ★ ARRIVAL *Epic EPC 86018* ... 1 92
26 Feb 77 ★ **KNOWING ME, KNOWING YOU** *Epic EPC 4955* ... **1** 13
22 Oct 77 ★ **THE NAME OF THE GAME** *Epic EPC 5750* ... **1** 12
4 Feb 78 ★ THE ALBUM *Epic EPC 86052* ■ ... 1 61
4 Feb 78 ★ **TAKE A CHANCE ON ME** *Epic EPC 5950* $ ... **1** 10
16 Sep 78 ● **SUMMER NIGHT CITY** *Epic EPC 6595* ... **5** 9
3 Feb 79 ● **CHIQUITITA** *Epic EPC 7030* ... **2** 9
5 May 79 ● **DOES YOUR MOTHER KNOW** *Epic EPC 7316* ... **4** 9

Date		Title / Label	Pos	Wks
19 May 79	★	VOULEZ-VOUS *Epic EPC 86086* ■	1	43
14 Jul 79	●	**ANGELEYES / VOULEZ-VOUS** *Epic EPC 7499*	**3**	11
20 Oct 79	●	**GIMME, GIMME, GIMME (A MAN AFTER MIDNIGHT)** *Epic EPC 7914*	**3**	12
10 Nov 79	★	GREATEST HITS VOL.2 *Epic EPC 10017*	1	63
15 Dec 79	●	**I HAVE A DREAM** *Epic EPC 8088*	**2**	10
2 Aug 80	★	**THE WINNER TAKES IT ALL** *Epic EPC 8835*	**1**	10
15 Nov 80	★	**SUPER TROUPER** *Epic EPC 9089*	**1**	12
22 Nov 80	★	SUPER TROUPER *Epic EPC 10022* ■	1	43
18 Jul 81	●	**LAY ALL YOUR LOVE ON ME** *Epic EPC A 131456*	**7**	7
12 Dec 81	●	**ONE OF US** *Epic EPC A 1740*	**3**	10
19 Dec 81	★	THE VISITORS *Epic EPC 10032* ■	1	21
20 Feb 82		**HEAD OVER HEELS** *Epic EPC A 2037*	**25**	7
23 Oct 82		**THE DAY BEFORE YOU CAME** *Epic EPC A 2847*	**32**	6
20 Nov 82	★	THE SINGLES – THE FIRST TEN YEARS *Epic ABBA 10*	1	22
11 Dec 82		**UNDER ATTACK** *Epic EPC A 2971*	**26**	8
12 Nov 83		**THANK YOU FOR THE MUSIC** *CBS A 3894*	**33**	6
19 Nov 83		THANK YOU FOR THE MUSIC *Epic EPC 10043*	17	12
19 Nov 88		ABSOLUTE ABBA *Telstar STAR 2329*	70	7
5 Sep 92		**DANCING QUEEN** (re-issue) *Polydor PO 231*	**16**	5
3 Oct 92	★	GOLD – GREATEST HITS *Polydor 5170072* ■	1	352
5 Jun 93		MORE ABBA GOLD – MORE ABBA HITS *Polydor 5193532*	13	23
7 Nov 98		LOVE STORIES *Polydor 5592212*	51	2
10 Nov 01		THE DEFINITIVE COLLECTION *Polydor 5499742*	17	8
29 May 04		**WATERLOO** (re-issue) *Polydor 9820539*	**20**	3

'Lay All Your Love on Me' was available only on 12-inch vinyl in the UK.
Gold – Greatest Hits peaked at No.4 when it re-entered the chart in Apr 2004 and was issued with a new catalogue number, Polydor 9818754. It returned to the chart in the final week of 2005.

ABBACADABRA *UK, male / female vocal / instrumental group*

Date		Title / Label	Pos	Wks
5 Sep 92		**DANCING QUEEN** *PWL International PWL 246*	**57**	1

Russ ABBOT *UK, male comedian / vocalist – Russell Roberts (2 Albums: 16 Weeks, 3 Singles: 22 Weeks)*

Date		Title / Label	Pos	Wks
6 Feb 82		**A DAY IN THE LIFE OF VINCE PRINCE (re)** *EMI 5249*	**61**	2
5 Nov 83		RUSS ABBOT'S MADHOUSE *Ronco RTL 2096*	41	7
29 Dec 84	●	**ATMOSPHERE** *Spirit FIRE 4*	**7**	13
13 Jul 85		**ALL NIGHT HOLIDAY** *Spirit FIRE 6*	**20**	7
23 Nov 85		I LOVE A PARTY *K-Tel ONE 1313*	12	9

Gregory ABBOTT *US, male vocalist*

Date		Title / Label	Pos	Wks
22 Nov 86	●	**SHAKE YOU DOWN** *CBS A 7326* ▲ $	**6**	13
10 Jan 87		SHAKE YOU DOWN *CBS 4500611*	53	5

Paula ABDUL *US, female vocalist (4 Albums: 51 Weeks, 12 Singles: 67 Weeks)*

Date		Title / Label	Pos	Wks
4 Mar 89	●	**STRAIGHT UP** *Siren SRN 111* ▲ $	**3**	13
15 Apr 89	●	FOREVER YOUR GIRL *Siren SRNLP 19* ▲	3	39
3 Jun 89		**FOREVER YOUR GIRL** *Siren SRN 112* ▲	**24**	6
19 Aug 89		**KNOCKED OUT** *Siren SRN 92*	**45**	3
2 Dec 89		**(IT'S JUST) THE WAY THAT YOU LOVE ME** *Siren SRN 101*	**74**	1
7 Apr 90	●	**OPPOSITES ATTRACT** *Siren SRN 124* [1] ▲	**2**	13
21 Jul 90		**KNOCKED OUT** (re-mix) *Virgin America VUS 23*	**21**	5
29 Sep 90		**COLD HEARTED** *Virgin America VUS 27* ▲	**46**	3
10 Nov 90		SHUT UP AND DANCE (THE DANCE MIXES) *Virgin America VUSLP 28*	40	2
22 Jun 91	●	**RUSH RUSH** *Virgin America VUS 38* ▲	**6**	11
27 Jul 91	●	SPELLBOUND *Virgin America VUSLP 33* ▲	4	9
31 Aug 91		**THE PROMISE OF A NEW DAY** *Virgin America VUS 44* ▲	**52**	2
18 Jan 92		**VIBEOLOGY** *Virgin America VUS 53*	**19**	6
8 Aug 92		**WILL YOU MARRY ME?** *Virgin America VUS 58*	**73**	1
17 Jun 95		**MY LOVE IS FOR REAL** *Virgin America VUSCD 91* [2]	**28**	3
1 Jul 95		HEAD OVER HEELS *Virgin America CDVUS 90*	61	1

[1] Paula Abdul with The Wild Pair [2] Paula Abdul featuring Ofra Haza

ABERFELDY *UK, male / female vocal / instrumental group (2 Singles: 2 Weeks)*

Date		Title / Label	Pos	Wks
28 Aug 04		**HELIOPOLIS BY NIGHT** *Rough Trade RTRADSCD 192*	**66**	1
26 Feb 05		**LOVE IS AN ARROW** *Rough Trade RTRADSCD 218*	**60**	1

ABI *UK, male vocalist*

Date		Title / Label	Pos	Wks
13 Jun 98		**COUNTING THE DAYS** *Kuku CDKUKU 1*	**44**	2

ABIGAIL *UK, female vocalist – Gayle Zsigmond*

Date		Title / Label	Pos	Wks
16 Jul 94		**SMELLS LIKE TEEN SPIRIT** *Klone CDKLONE 25*	**29**	4

Colonel ABRAMS *US, male vocalist (4 Singles: 35 Weeks)*

Date		Title / Label	Pos	Wks
17 Aug 85	●	**TRAPPED** *MCA MCA 997*	**3**	23
7 Dec 85		**THE TRUTH** *MCA MCA 1022*	**53**	3
8 Feb 86		**I'M NOT GONNA LET YOU** *MCA MCA 1031*	**24**	7
15 Aug 87		**HOW SOON WE FORGET** *MCA MCA 1179*	**75**	2

ABS (see also FIVE) *UK, male vocalist / rapper – Richard Breen (1 Album: 2 Weeks, 3 Singles: 24 Weeks)*

Date		Title / Label	Pos	Wks
31 Aug 02	●	**WHAT YOU GOT** *S 74321957192*	**4**	8
7 Jun 03	●	**STOP SIGN** *BMG 82876530392*	**10**	9
6 Sep 03	●	**MISS PERFECT** *BMG 82876556742* [1]	**5**	7
13 Sep 03		ABSTRACT THEORY *BMG 82876538802*	29	2

[1] Abs featuring Nodesha

ABSOLUTE *US, male production / instrumental duo – Mark Picchiotti and Craig Snider (2 Singles: 3 Weeks)*

Date		Title / Label	Pos	Wks
18 Jan 97		**I BELIEVE** *AM:PM 5820752* [1]	**38**	2
14 Mar 98		**CATCH ME** *AM:PM 5825032*	**69**	1

[1] Absolute featuring Suzanne Palmer

ACADEMY of ANCIENT MUSIC *UK, orchestra*

Date		Title / Label	Pos	Wks
16 Mar 85		VIVALDI'S THE FOUR SEASONS *L'Oiseau Lyre / London 4101261*	85	2

Conducted by Christopher Hogwood.

ACCEPT *Germany, male vocal / instrumental group (4 Albums: 5 Weeks)*

Date		Title / Label	Pos	Wks
7 May 83		RESTLESS AND WILD *Heavy Metal Worldwide HMILP 6*	98	2
30 Mar 85		METAL HEART *Portrait PRT 26358*	50	1
15 Feb 86		KAIZOKU-BAN *Portrait PRT 5916*	91	1
3 May 86		RUSSIAN ROULETTE *Portrait PRT 26893*	80	1

ACE *UK, male vocal / instrumental group – includes Paul Carrack*

Date		Title / Label	Pos	Wks
9 Nov 74		**HOW LONG** *Anchor ANC 1002*	**20**	10

Richard ACE *Jamaica, male vocalist*

Date		Title / Label	Pos	Wks
2 Dec 78		**STAYIN' ALIVE** *Blue Inc. INC 2*	**66**	2

ACE OF BASE *Sweden, male / female vocal / instrumental group (4 Albums: 45 Weeks, 13 Singles: 100 Weeks)*

Date		Title / Label	Pos	Wks
8 May 93	★	**ALL THAT SHE WANTS** *London 8612702* $	**1**	16
19 Jun 93	★	HAPPY NATION *London 5177492* ▲	1	38
28 Aug 93		**WHEEL OF FORTUNE** *London 8615452*	**20**	6
13 Nov 93		**HAPPY NATION** *London 8619272*	**42**	3
26 Feb 94	●	**THE SIGN** *London ACECD 1* ▲ $	**2**	16
11 Jun 94	●	**DON'T TURN AROUND** *London ACECD 2*	**5**	11
15 Oct 94		**HAPPY NATION** (re-issue) *London 8610972*	**40**	3
14 Jan 95		**LIVING IN DANGER** *London ACECD 3*	**18**	4
11 Nov 95		**LUCKY LOVE** *London ACECD 4*	**20**	5
2 Dec 95		THE BRIDGE *London 5296552*	66	1
27 Jan 96		**BEAUTIFUL LIFE** *London ACECD 5*	**15**	6
25 Jul 98	●	**LIFE IS A FLOWER** *London ACECD 7*	**5**	11
22 Aug 98		FLOWERS *London 5576912*	15	5
10 Oct 98	●	**CRUEL SUMMER** *London ACECD 8*	**8**	5
19 Dec 98		**ALWAYS HAVE, ALWAYS WILL** *London ACECD 9*	**12**	10
17 Apr 99		**EVERYTIME IT RAINS** *London ACECD 10*	**22**	4
27 Nov 99		SINGLES OF THE 90'S *Polydor 5432272*	62	1

Happy Nation changed catalogue number to 5214722 during its chart run.

ACEN *UK, male producer – Syed Ahsen Razvi (2 Singles: 4 Weeks)*

Date		Title / Label	Pos	Wks
8 Aug 92		**TRIP II THE MOON** *Production House PNT 042*	**38**	3
10 Oct 92		**TRIP II THE MOON** (re-mix) *Production House PNT 042RX*	**71**	1

ACT *UK / Germany, male / female vocal / instrumental group*

Date		Title / Label	Pos	Wks
23 May 87		**SNOBBERY AND DECAY** *ZTT ZTAS 28*	**60**	2

ACT ONE *US, male / female vocal / instrumental group*

Date		Title / Label	Pos	Wks
18 May 74		**TOM THE PEEPER** *Mercury 6008 005*	**40**	6

9 January 1953	16 January 1953	23 January 1953	30 January 1953
HERE IN MY HEART Al Martino	**YOU BELONG TO ME** Jo Stafford	**COMES A-LONG A-LOVE** Kay Starr	**OUTSIDE OF HEAVEN** Eddie Fisher

KEY
UK No.1 ★ UK Top 10 ● Still on chart + UK entry at No.1 ■
US No.1 ▲ UK million seller £ US million seller $
Singles re-entries are listed as (re), (2re), (3re)... which signifies that the hit re-entered the chart once, twice or three times...
Peak Position / Weeks

ACZESS *UK, male producer – Dave Birchard*

27 Oct 01 **DO WHAT WE WOULD** *INCredible 6719782* **65** 1

ADAM and The ANTS (255 Top 500)

Warpaint-wearing, colourfully-costumed 'Antmusic' innovators: included Stuart (Adam Ant) Goddard (v) and Marco Pirroni (g). The London-based act was 1981's top chart act with nine hits. Also in that year, they amassed 91 chart weeks – a total not bettered until 1996. Best-selling single: 'Stand and Deliver' 985,000 (4 Albums: 121 Weeks, 11 Singles: 130 Weeks)

2 Aug 80 ● **KINGS OF THE WILD FRONTIER (re)** *CBS 8877* **2** 18
11 Oct 80 ● **DOG EAT DOG** *CBS 9039* **4** 16
15 Nov 80 ★ KINGS OF THE WILD FRONTIER *CBS 84549* 1 66
6 Dec 80 ● **ANTMUSIC** *CBS 9352* **2** 18
27 Dec 80 ● **YOUNG PARISIANS** *Decca F13803* **9** 13
17 Jan 81 DIRK WEARS WHITE SOX *Do It RIDE 3* 16 29
24 Jan 81 **CARTROUBLE** *Do It DUN 10* **33** 9
24 Jan 81 **ZEROX** *Do It DUN 8* **45** 9
9 May 81 ★ **STAND AND DELIVER** *CBS A 1065* ■ **1** 15
12 Sep 81 ★ **PRINCE CHARMING** *CBS A 1408* **1** 12
14 Nov 81 ● PRINCE CHARMING *CBS 85268* 2 21
12 Dec 81 ● **ANT RAP** *CBS A 1738* **3** 10
27 Feb 82 **DEUTSCHER GIRLS** *Ego 5* **13** 6
13 Mar 82 **THE ANTMUSIC EP (THE B-SIDES)** *Do It DUN 20* **46** 4
3 Apr 99 THE VERY BEST OF ADAM AND THE ANTS *Columbia 4942292* 33 5

'Kings of the Wild Frontier' reached No.48 on its first visit to the chart, peaking at No.2 as a re-entry in Feb 1981. Tracks on The Antmusic EP (The B-sides): Friends / Kick / Physical. The Very Best of Adam and The Ants did not reach its peak position until 2004.

Arthur ADAMS *US, male vocalist*

24 Oct 81 **YOU GOT THE FLOOR** *RCA 146* **38** 5

Ben ADAMS NEW (see also a1) *UK, male vocalist*

11 Jun 05 **SORRY** *Phonogenic 82876699392* **18** 3

Bryan ADAMS (55 Top 500)

Globally successful rock singer / songwriter / guitarist who appeared at both Live Aid (US) and Live 8 (Canada) concerts, b. 5 Nov 1959, Kingston, Ontario. He has had more UK hits than any other Canadian artist and was the biggest-selling singles artist in the UK in 1991, when he was at No.1 for a record 16 consecutive weeks. Biggest-selling single: '(Everything I Do) I Do It for You' 1,527,824 (14 Albums: 409 Weeks, 36 Singles: 248 Weeks)

12 Jan 85 **RUN TO YOU** *A&M AM 224* **11** 12
2 Mar 85 ● RECKLESS *A&M AMA 5013* ▲ 7 115
16 Mar 85 **SOMEBODY** *A&M AM 236* **35** 7
25 May 85 **HEAVEN** *A&M AM 256* ▲ **38** 5
10 Aug 85 **SUMMER OF '69** *A&M AM 267* **42** 7
24 Aug 85 YOU WANT IT, YOU GOT IT *A&M AMLH 64864* 78 5
2 Nov 85 **IT'S ONLY LOVE** *A&M 285* [1] **29** 6
21 Dec 85 **CHRISTMAS TIME** *A&M AM 297* **55** 2
22 Feb 86 **THIS TIME** *A&M AM 295* **41** 7
15 Mar 86 CUTS LIKE A KNIFE *A&M AMLH 64919* 21 6
12 Jul 86 **STRAIGHT FROM THE HEART** *A&M AM 322* **51** 3
28 Mar 87 **HEAT OF THE NIGHT** *A&M ADAM 2* **50** 2
11 Apr 87 ● INTO THE FIRE *A&M AMA 3907* 10 21
20 Jun 87 **HEARTS ON FIRE** *A&M ADAM 3* **57** 3
17 Oct 87 **VICTIM OF LOVE** *A&M AM 407* **68** 2
29 Jun 91 ★ **(EVERYTHING I DO) I DO IT FOR YOU (re)** *A&M AM 789* ▲ £ $ **1** 25
14 Sep 91 **CAN'T STOP THIS THING WE STARTED** *A&M AM 612* **12** 6
5 Oct 91 ★ WAKING UP THE NEIGHBOURS *A&M 3971641* ■ 1 54
23 Nov 91 **THERE WILL NEVER BE ANOTHER TONIGHT** *A&M AM 838* **32** 3
22 Feb 92 ● **THOUGHT I'D DIED AND GONE TO HEAVEN** *A&M AM 848* **8** 7
18 Jul 92 **ALL I WANT IS YOU** *A&M AM 879* **22** 5
26 Sep 92 **DO I HAVE TO SAY THE WORDS?** *A&M AM 0068* **30** 3
30 Oct 93 ● **PLEASE FORGIVE ME** *A&M 5804232* **2** 16
20 Nov 93 ★ SO FAR SO GOOD *A&M 5401572* 1 55
15 Jan 94 ● **ALL FOR LOVE** *A&M 5804772* [2] ▲ $ **2** 13
6 Aug 94 LIVE! LIVE! LIVE! *A&M 3970942* 17 4
22 Apr 95 ● **HAVE YOU EVER REALLY LOVED A WOMAN** *A&M 5810282* ▲ **4** 9
11 Nov 95 **ROCK STEADY** *Capitol CDCL 763* [3] **50** 2
1 Jun 96 ● **THE ONLY THING THAT LOOKS GOOD ON ME IS YOU** *A&M 5813692* **6** 7
22 Jun 96 ★ 18 TIL I DIE *A&M 5405512* ■ 1 40
24 Aug 96 ● **LET'S MAKE A NIGHT TO REMEMBER** *A&M 5815672* **10** 8
23 Nov 96 **STAR** *A&M 5820252* **13** 4
8 Feb 97 ● **I FINALLY FOUND SOMEONE** *A&M 5820832* [4] **10** 7
19 Apr 97 **18 TIL I DIE** *A&M 5821852* **22** 3
13 Dec 97 UNPLUGGED *A&M 5408312* 19 19
20 Dec 97 **BACK TO YOU** *A&M 5824752* **18** 7
21 Mar 98 **I'M READY** *A&M 5825352* **20** 4
10 Oct 98 **ON A DAY LIKE TODAY** *Mercury MERCD 516* **13** 5
31 Oct 98 ON A DAY LIKE TODAY *Mercury / A&M 5410162* 11 35
12 Dec 98 ● **WHEN YOU'RE GONE** *A&M 5828212* [5] **3** 19
15 May 99 ● **CLOUD NUMBER 9** *A&M / Mercury 5828492* **6** 9
27 Nov 99 THE BEST OF ME *Mercury / A&M 4905222* 12 39
18 Dec 99 **THE BEST OF ME (re)** *Mercury / A&M 4971952* **47** 3
18 Mar 00 ★ **DON'T GIVE UP** *Xtravaganza XTRAV 9CDS* [6] ■ **1** 14
20 Jul 02 ● **HERE I AM** *A&M 4977442* **5** 8
27 Jul 02 ● SPIRIT – STALLION OF THE CIMARRON (FILM SOUNDTRACK) *A&M 4933042* 8 5
25 Sep 04 **OPEN ROAD** *Polydor 9869053* **21** 3
2 Oct 04 ● ROOM SERVICE *Polydor 9868245* 4 6
11 Dec 04 **FLYING** *Polydor 9869276* **39** 2
3 Dec 05 ANTHOLOGY *Polydor 9835827* 29 5+

[1] Bryan Adams and Tina Turner [2] Bryan Adams, Rod Stewart and Sting [3] Bonnie Raitt and Bryan Adams [4] Barbra Streisand and Bryan Adams [5] Bryan Adams featuring Melanie C [6] Chicane featuring Bryan Adams

Gayle ADAMS *US, female vocalist*

26 Jul 80 **STRETCH'IN OUT** *Epic EPC 8791* **64** 1

Oleta ADAMS *US, female vocalist / keyboard player* (3 Albums: 34 Weeks, 10 Singles: 36 Weeks)

24 Mar 90 **RHYTHM OF LIFE (re)** *Fontana OLETA 1* **52** 5
26 May 90 ★ CIRCLE OF ONE *Fontana 8427441* 1 26
12 Jan 91 ● **GET HERE** *Fontana OLETA 3* **4** 12
13 Apr 91 **YOU'VE GOT TO GIVE ME ROOM / RHYTHM OF LIFE** (re-issue) *Fontana OLETA 4* **49** 3
29 Jun 91 **CIRCLE OF ONE** *Fontana OLETA 5* **73** 1
28 Sep 91 **DON'T LET THE SUN GO DOWN ON ME** *Fontana TRIBO 1* **33** 5
25 Apr 92 **WOMAN IN CHAINS** (re-issue) *Fontana IDEA 16* [1] **57** 1
10 Jul 93 **I JUST HAD TO HEAR YOUR VOICE** *Fontana OLECD 6* **42** 3
7 Aug 93 ● EVOLUTION *Fontana 5149652* 10 7
7 Oct 95 **NEVER KNEW LOVE** *Fontana OLECD 9* **22** 3
4 Nov 95 MOVING ON *Fontana 5285302* 59 1
16 Dec 95 **RHYTHM OF LIFE** (re-mix) *Fontana OLECD 10* **38** 2
10 Feb 96 **WE WILL MEET AGAIN** *Mercury OLECD 11* **51** 1

[1] Tears for Fears featuring Oleta Adams

The original release of 'Woman in Chains' credits Tears for Fears only.

Ryan ADAMS

US, male vocalist (7 Albums: 17 Weeks, 5 Singles: 8 Weeks)

6 Oct 01 GOLD *Lost Highway 1702622* 20 9
8 Dec 01 **NEW YORK NEW YORK** *Lost Highway 1722232* **53** 1
20 Apr 02 **ANSWERING BELL** *Lost Highway 1722392* **39** 2
28 Sep 02 **NUCLEAR** *Lost Highway 1722592* **37** 1
5 Oct 02 DEMOLITION *Lost Highway 1703332* 22 2
15 Nov 03 ROCK N ROLL *Lost Highway 9861324* 41 1
15 Nov 03 LOVE IS HELL PT.1 (EP) *Lost Highway 9813666* 62 1
31 Jan 04 **SO ALIVE** *Lost Highway 9861610* **21** 2
15 May 04 LOVE IS HELL *Lost Highway 9862325* 68 1
10 Jul 04 **WONDERWALL** *Lost Highway 9863098* **27** 2
14 May 05 COLD ROSES *Lost Highway 9881827* [1] 20 2
8 Oct 05 JACKSONVILLE CITY NIGHTS *Lost Highway 9884907* [1] 59 1

[1] Ryan Adams & The Cardinals

Love is Hell Pt.1 is an eight-track EP. Love is Hell features tracks from Love is Hell Pt.1 and Love is Hell Pt.2, which failed to chart.

Cliff ADAMS SINGERS *UK, male / female vocal group – leader b. 21 Aug 1923, d. 22 Oct 2001 (4 Albums: 20 Weeks, 1 Single: 2 Weeks)*

16 Apr 60 SING SOMETHING SIMPLE *Pye MPL 28013*....15 4
28 Apr 60 **THE LONELY MAN THEME** *Pye International 7N 25056* [1] **39** 2
24 Nov 62 SING SOMETHING SIMPLE *Pye Golden Guinea GGL 0150*....15 2
20 Nov 76 SING SOMETHING SIMPLE '76 *Warwick WW 5016/17*....23 8
25 Dec 82 SING SOMETHING SIMPLE *Ronco RTD 2087*....39 6

[1] Cliff Adams Orchestra

Each of the Sing Something Simple albums have different track listings

ADAMSKI *UK, male instrumentalist /producer - Adam Tinley (2 Albums: 16 Weeks, 8 Singles: 39 Weeks)*

9 Dec 89 LIVEANDIRECT *MCA MCL 1900*....47 1
20 Jan 90 **N-R-G** *MCA MCA 1386*....**12** 6
7 Apr 90 ★ **KILLER** *MCA MCA 1400*....**1** 18
8 Sep 90 ● **THE SPACE JUNGLE** *MCA MCA 1435*....**7** 8
13 Oct 90 ● DOCTOR ADAMSKI'S MUSICAL PHARMACY *MCA MCG 6107*....8 5
17 Nov 90 **FLASHBACK JACK** *MCA MCA 1459*....**46** 2
9 Nov 91 **NEVER GOIN' DOWN / BORN TO BE ALIVE** *MCA MCS 1578* [1] **51** 2
4 Apr 92 **GET YOUR BODY** *MCA MCS 1613* [2] **68** 1
4 Jul 92 **BACK TO FRONT** *MCA MCS 1644*....**63** 1
11 Jul 98 **ONE OF THE PEOPLE** *ZTT ZTT 101CD* [3] **56** 1

[1] Adamski featuring Jimi Polo / Adamski featuring Soho [2] Adamski featuring Nina Hagen [3] Adamski's Thing

Featured vocalist on 'Killer' was Seal.

Barry ADAMSON *UK, male producer / bass guitarist*

10 Aug 96 OEDIPUS SCHMOEDIPUS *Mute CDSTUMM 134*....51 1

ADDAMS and GEE *UK, male instrumental duo*

20 Apr 91 **CHUNG KUO (REVISITED)** *Debut DEBT 3108*....**72** 1

ADDIS BLACK WIDOW *US, male rap duo*

3 Feb 96 **INNOCENT** *Mercury Black Vinyl MBVCD 1*....**42** 2

The ADDRISI BROTHERS *US, male vocal duo – Don, b. 14 Dec 1938, d. 13 Nov 1984, and Richard Addrisi*

6 Oct 79 **GHOST DANCER** *Scotti Brothers K 11361*....**57** 3

King Sunny ADE and his AFRICAN BEATS *Nigeria, male vocalist and vocal / instrumental group*

9 Jul 83 SYNCHRO SYSTEM *Island ILPS 9737*....93 1

ADEMA *US, male vocal / instrumental group (3 Singles: 3 Weeks)*

16 Mar 02 **GIVING IN** *Arista 74321924022*....**62** 1
10 Aug 02 **THE WAY YOU LIKE IT** *Arista 74321954712*....**61** 1
23 Aug 03 **UNSTABLE** *Arista 82876534512*....**46** 1

ADEVA *US, female vocalist – Patricia Daniels (1 Album: 24 Weeks, 18 Singles: 66 Weeks)*

14 Jan 89 **RESPECT** *Cooltempo COOL 179*....**17** 9
25 Mar 89 **MUSICAL FREEDOM (MOVING ON UP)** *Cooltempo COOL 182* [1] **22** 8
12 Aug 89 **WARNING** *Cooltempo COOL 185*....**17** 8
9 Sep 89 ● ADEVA *Cooltempo ICTLP 13*....6 24
21 Oct 89 **I THANK YOU** *Cooltempo COOL 192*....**17** 7
16 Dec 89 **BEAUTIFUL LOVE** *Cooltempo COOL 195*....**57** 5
28 Apr 90 **TREAT ME RIGHT** *Cooltempo COOL 200*....**62** 2
6 Apr 91 **RING MY BELL** *Cooltempo COOL 224* [2] **20** 5
19 Oct 91 **IT SHOULD'VE BEEN ME** *Cooltempo COOL 236*....**48** 3
29 Feb 92 **DON'T LET IT SHOW ON YOUR FACE** *Cooltempo COOL 248*....**34** 4
6 Jun 92 **UNTIL YOU COME BACK TO ME** *Cooltempo COOL 254*....**45** 3
17 Oct 92 **I'M THE ONE FOR YOU** *Cooltempo COOL 264*....**51** 2
11 Dec 93 **RESPECT** (re-mix) *Network NWKCD 79*....**65** 1
27 May 95 **TOO MANY FISH** *Virgin America VUSCD 89* [3] **34** 2
18 Nov 95 **WHADDA U WANT (FROM ME)** *Virgin America VUSCD 98* [3] **36** 2
6 Apr 96 **DO WATCHA DO** *Avex UK AVEXCD 24* [4] **54** 1
4 May 96 **I THANK YOU** (re-mix) *Cooltempo CDCOOLS 318*....**37** 2
12 Apr 97 **DO WATCHA DO** (re-mix) *Distinctive DISNCD 28* [4] **60** 1
26 Jul 97 **WHERE IS THE LOVE? / THE WAY THAT YOU FEEL** *Distinctive DISNCD 31*....**54** 1

[1] Paul Simpson featuring Adeva [2] Monie Love vs Adeva [3] Frankie Knuckles featuring Adeva [4] Hyper Go Go and Adeva

The ADICTS *UK, male vocal / instrumental group*

4 Dec 82 SOUND OF MUSIC *Razor RAZ 2*....99 1
14 May 83 **BAD BOY** *Razor RZS 104*....**75** 1

ADIEMUS *UK, male instrumental duo – Karl Jenkins and Mark Ratledge (3 Albums: 23 Weeks, 1 Single: 2 Weeks)*

1 Jul 95 SONGS OF SANCTUARY *Virgin CDVE 925*....35 13
14 Oct 95 **ADIEMUS** *Venture VEND 4*....**48** 2
1 Mar 97 ADIEMUS II – CANTATA MUNDI *Venture CDVE 932* [1] 15 9
24 Oct 98 ADIEMUS III – DANCES OF TIME *Venture CDVE 940* [2] 58 1

[1] Adiemus II [2] Adiemus III

All tracks on Songs of Sanctuary feature Miriam Stockley and the London Philharmonic Orchestra. The sleeve of Cantata Mundi contains the credit: 'Composed by Karl Jenkins'.

Larry ADLER *US, male harmonica player, b. 10 Feb 1914, d. 7 Aug 2001*

30 Jul 94 **THE MAN I LOVE** *Mercury MERCD 408* [1] **27** 2
6 Aug 94 ● THE GLORY OF GERSHWIN *Mercury 5227272*....2 18

[1] Kate Bush and Larry Adler

ADONIS featuring 2 PUERTO RICANS, A BLACK MAN AND A DOMINICAN *US, male vocal / instrumental group*

13 Jun 87 **NO WAY BACK / DO IT PROPERLY** *London LON 136*....**47** 4

ADORABLE *UK, male vocal / instrumental group*

13 Mar 93 AGAINST PERFECTION *Creation CRECD 138*....70 1

ADRENALIN M.O.D. *UK, male instrumental / production group*

8 Oct 88 **O-O-O** *MCA RAGAT 2*....**49** 5

ADULT NET *UK / US, male / female vocal / instrumental group*

10 Jun 89 **WHERE WERE YOU** *Fontana BRX 2*....**66** 2

The ADVENTURES *UK, male vocal / instrumental group (2 Albums: 11 Weeks, 6 Singles: 24 Weeks)*

15 Sep 84 **ANOTHER SILENT DAY** *Chrysalis CHS 2000*....**71** 2
1 Dec 84 **SEND MY HEART** *Chrysalis CHS 2001*....**62** 4
13 Jul 85 **FEEL THE RAINDROPS** *Chrysalis AD 1*....**58** 3
9 Apr 88 **BROKEN LAND** *Elektra EKR 69*....**20** 10
21 May 88 THE SEA OF LOVE *Elektra EKT 45*....30 10
2 Jul 88 **DROWNING IN THE SEA OF LOVE** *Elektra EKR 76*....**44** 4
17 Mar 90 TRADING SECRETS WITH THE MOON *Elektra EKT 63*....64 1
13 Jun 92 **RAINING ALL OVER THE WORLD** *Polydor PO 211*....**68** 1

The ADVENTURES OF STEVIE V *UK, male / female vocal / production group (4 Singles: 22 Weeks)*

21 Apr 90 ● **DIRTY CASH** *Mercury MER 311*....**2** 13
29 Sep 90 **BODY LANGUAGE** *Mercury MER 331*....**29** 5
2 Mar 91 **JEALOUSY** *Mercury MER 337*....**58** 3
27 Sep 97 **DIRTY CASH** (re-mix) *Avex Trax AVEXCDX 57*....**69** 1

The ADVERTS *UK, male / female vocal / instrumental group (1 Album: 1 Week, 2 Singles: 11 Weeks)*

27 Aug 77 **GARY GILMORE'S EYES** *Anchor ANC 1043*....**18** 7
4 Feb 78 **NO TIME TO BE 21** *Bright BR 1*....**34** 4
11 Mar 78 CROSSING THE RED SEA WITH THE ADVERTS *Bright BRL 201*....38 1

AEROSMITH (295 Top 500) *Godfathers of the contemporary heavy rock scene, formed 1970, New Hampshire, US. Multi-platinum album act's UK success came only after frontmen Steven Tyler (v) and Joe Perry (g) teamed with rappers Run-DMC on 'Walk This Way' (1986). Group's first US No.1 single (1998) came 25 years after chart debut. Best-selling single: 'I Don't Want to Miss a Thing' 572,900 (10 Albums: 137 Weeks, 19 Singles: 92 Weeks)*

5 Sep 87 PERMANENT VACATION *Geffen WX 126*....37 14

KEY
UK No.1 ★ UK Top 10 ● Still on chart + UK entry at No.1 ■
US No.1 ▲ UK million seller £ US million seller $
Singles re-entries are listed as (re), (2re), (3re)... which signifies that the hit re-entered the chart once, twice or three times...
Peak Position / Weeks

Date		Title / Label	Peak	Weeks
17 Oct 87		**DUDE (LOOKS LIKE A LADY)** *Geffen GEF 29*	45	5
16 Apr 88		**ANGEL** *Geffen GEF 34*	69	2
9 Sep 89		**LOVE IN AN ELEVATOR** *Geffen GEF 63*	13	8
23 Sep 89	●	**PUMP** *Geffen WX 304*	3	26
24 Feb 90		**DUDE (LOOKS LIKE A LADY)** (re-issue) *Geffen GEF 72*	20	5
14 Apr 90		**RAG DOLL** *Geffen GEF 76*	42	4
1 Sep 90		**THE OTHER SIDE** *Geffen GEF 79*	46	2
10 Apr 93		**LIVIN' ON THE EDGE** *Geffen GFSTD 35*	19	4
1 May 93	●	**GET A GRIP** *Geffen GED 24444* ▲	2	38
3 Jul 93		**EAT THE RICH** *Geffen GFSTD 46*	34	3
30 Oct 93		**CRYIN'** *Geffen GFSTD 56*	17	6
18 Dec 93		**AMAZING** *Geffen GFSTD 63*	57	3
2 Jul 94		**SHUT UP AND DANCE** *Geffen GFSTD 75*	24	4
20 Aug 94		**SWEET EMOTION** *Columbia 6604492*	74	1
5 Nov 94		**CRAZY / BLIND MAN** *Geffen GFSTD 80*	23	4
12 Nov 94	●	**BIG ONES** *Geffen GED 24546*	7	16
8 Mar 97		**FALLING IN LOVE (IS HARD ON THE KNEES)** *Columbia 6640752*	22	4
22 Mar 97	●	**NINE LIVES** *Columbia 4850206* ▲	4	11
21 Jun 97		**HOLE IN MY SOUL** *Columbia 66645012*	29	2
27 Dec 97		**PINK** *Columbia 6648722*	38	2
12 Sep 98	●	**I DON'T WANT TO MISS A THING** *Columbia 6664082* ▲	4	20
31 Oct 98		**A LITTLE SOUTH OF SANITY** *Geffen GED 25221*	36	2
26 Jun 99		**PINK** (re-issue) *Columbia 6675342*	13	6
17 Mar 01		**JADED** *Columbia 6709312*	13	7
24 Mar 01	●	**JUST PUSH PLAY** *Columbia 5015352*	7	5
8 Dec 01		**YOUNG LUST – THE AEROSMITH ANTHOLOGY** *UMTV 4931192*	32	14
3 Aug 02	●	**O YEAH – ULTIMATE HITS** *Columbia / UMTV 5084672*	6	8
10 Apr 04		**HONKIN' ON BOBO** *Columbia CK 92079*	28	3

Pump changed its catalogue number to GEF 24245 during its chart run.

The AFGHAN WHIGS
US, male vocal / instrumental group (2 Albums: 3 Weeks)

Date		Title / Label	Peak	Weeks
16 Oct 93		**GENTLEMEN** *Blast First BFFP 90CD*	58	1
23 Mar 96		**BLACK LOVE** *Mute CDSTUMM 143*	41	2

AFRICAN BUSINESS
Italy, male vocal / instrumental group

Date		Title / Label	Peak	Weeks
17 Nov 90		**IN ZAIRE** *Urban URB 64*	73	1

AFRO CELT SOUND SYSTEM *UK / Ireland / France / Guinea, male vocal / instrumental group (2 Albums: 5 Weeks, 1 Single: 1 Week)*

Date		Title / Label	Peak	Weeks
27 Jul 96		**VOLUME 1 – SOUND MAGIC** *Realworld CDRW 61*	59	2
8 May 99		**VOLUME 2 – RELEASE** *Realworld CDRW 76*	38	3
29 Apr 00		**RELEASE** *Realworld RWSCD 10*	71	1

AFRO MEDUSA *UK, male production duo – Patrick Cole and Nick Benneti and Spain, female vocalist – Isabel Fructuoso*

Date		Title / Label	Peak	Weeks
28 Oct 00		**PASILDA** *Rulin RULIN 6CDS*	31	2

AFROMAN *US, male vocalist – Joseph Foreman (3 Singles: 30 Weeks)*

Date		Title / Label	Peak	Weeks
6 Oct 01		**BECAUSE I GOT HIGH** (import) *Universal 0152822*	45	3
27 Oct 01	★	**BECAUSE I GOT HIGH (re)** *Universal MCSTD 40266* ■	1	19
2 Feb 02	●	**CRAZY RAP** *Universal MCSTD 40273*	10	8

AFTER DARK *UK, male saxophonist – Mornington Lockett*

Date		Title / Label	Peak	Weeks
3 Feb 96		**LATE NIGHT SAX** *EMI TV CDEMTV 108*	18	5

AFTER 7 *US, male vocal group*

Date		Title / Label	Peak	Weeks
3 Nov 90		**CAN'T STOP** *Virgin America VUS 31*	54	3

AFTER THE FIRE *UK, male vocal / instrumental group (3 Albums: 4 Weeks, 3 Singles: 12 Weeks)*

Date		Title / Label	Peak	Weeks
9 Jun 79		**ONE RULE FOR YOU** *CBS 7025*	40	6
8 Sep 79		**LASER LOVE** *CBS 7769*	62	2
13 Oct 79		**LASER LOVE** *CBS 83795*	57	1
1 Nov 80		**80'F** *Epic 84545*	69	1
3 Apr 82		**BATTERIES NOT INCLUDED** *CBS 85566*	82	2
9 Apr 83		**DER KOMMISSAR** *CBS A 2399*	47	4

AFTERSHOCK
US, male vocal / instrumental duo – Frost Rivera and Guy Routte

Date		Title / Label	Peak	Weeks
21 Aug 93		**SLAVE TO THE VIBE** *Virgin America VUSCD 75*	11	8

AGE OF CHANCE
UK, male / female vocal / instrumental group (3 Singles: 13 Weeks)

Date		Title / Label	Peak	Weeks
17 Jan 87		**KISS** *Fon AGE 5*	50	6
30 May 87		**WHO'S AFRAID OF THE BIG BAD NOISE!** *Fon VS 962*	65	2
20 Jan 90		**HIGHER THAN HEAVEN** *Virgin VS 1228*	53	5

AGE OF LOVE *Italy, male instrumental / production duo – Bruno Sanchioni and Guiseppe Cherchia (2 Singles: 6 Weeks)*

Date		Title / Label	Peak	Weeks
5 Jul 97		**THE AGE OF LOVE – THE REMIXES** *React CDREACT 100*	17	4
19 Sep 98		**AGE OF LOVE** *React CDREACT 135*	38	2

AGENT BLUE
UK, male vocal / instrumental group (3 Singles: 3 Weeks)

Date		Title / Label	Peak	Weeks
29 May 04		**SEX, DRUGS AND ROCKS THROUGH YOUR WINDOW** *Fierce Panda NING 153CD*	71	1
21 Aug 04		**SOMETHING ELSE** *Island TEMPTCD 001*	59	1
19 Mar 05		**CHILDREN'S CHILDREN** *Universal MMCSTD 40401*	62	1

AGENT 00 *UK, male production duo*

Date		Title / Label	Peak	Weeks
7 Mar 98		**THE MAGNIFICENT** *Inferno CDFERN 002*	65	1

AGENT PROVOCATEUR
UK, male / female vocal / production group

Date		Title / Label	Peak	Weeks
22 Mar 97		**AGENT DAN** *Epic AGENT 3CD*	49	1

AGENT SUMO *UK, male production duo – Steven Halliday and Martin Cole (2 Singles: 4 Weeks)*

Date		Title / Label	Peak	Weeks
9 Jun 01		**24 HOURS** *Virgin VSCDT 1806*	44	2
20 Apr 02		**WHY** *Virgin VSCDT 1819*	40	2

AGNELLI & NELSON *UK, male DJ duo – Chris Agnelli and Robbie Nelson (7 Singles: 17 Weeks)*

Date		Title / Label	Peak	Weeks
15 Aug 98		**EL NINO** *Xtravaganza 0091575 EXT*	21	4
11 Sep 99		**EVERYDAY** *Xtravaganza XTRAV 2CDS*	17	4
17 Jun 00		**EMBRACE** *Xtravaganza XTRAV 11CDS*	35	2
9 Sep 00		**HUDSON STREET** *Xtravaganza XTRAV 13CDS*	29	2
7 Apr 01		**VEGAS** *Xtravaganza XTRAV 23CDS*	48	1
15 Jun 02		**EVERYDAY** (re-mix) *Xtravaganza XTRAV 31CDS*	33	2
3 Apr 04		**HOLDING ON TO NOTHING** *Xtravaganza XTRAV 43CX* [1]	41	2

[1] Agnelli & Nelson featuring Aureus

Christina AGUILERA (227 Top 500) *Internationally successful photogenic pop vocalist, b. 18 Dec 1980, New York, US. She has had four US chart-toppers, was a winner of World Music Awards in 2000 and 2001 and won a Grammy in 2004 for 'Beautiful'. Best-selling single: 'Genie in a Bottle' 626,741 (2 Albums: 119 Weeks, 15 Singles: 158 Weeks)*

Date		Title / Label	Peak	Weeks
11 Sep 99		**GENIE IN A BOTTLE** (import) *RCA 701062*	50	5
16 Oct 99	★	**GENIE IN A BOTTLE** *RCA 74321705482* ■ ▲ $	1	19
30 Oct 99		**CHRISTINA AGUILERA** *RCA 7863676902* ▲	14	26
26 Feb 00	●	**WHAT A GIRL WANTS** *RCA 74321737522* ▲	3	13
22 Jul 00		**I TURN TO YOU** *RCA 74321765472*	19	6
11 Nov 00	●	**COME ON OVER BABY (ALL I WANT IS YOU) (re)** *RCA 74321799912* ▲	8	8
10 Mar 01	●	**NOBODY WANTS TO BE LONELY** *Columbia 6709462* [1]	4	12
30 Jun 01	★	**LADY MARMALADE** *Interscope / Polydor 4975612* [2] ■ ▲	1	16
9 Nov 02	●	**STRIPPED** *RCA 74321961252*	2	93
23 Nov 02	★	**DIRRTY** *RCA 74321962722* [3] ■	1	9
22 Feb 03		**BEAUTIFUL** (import) *Arista 74321983642*	51	2
8 Mar 03	★	**BEAUTIFUL** *RCA 82876502462* ■	1	10
21 Jun 03	●	**FIGHTER** *RCA 82876524292*	3	13
20 Sep 03	●	**CAN'T HOLD US DOWN** *RCA 87876556332* [4]	6	9

3 April 1953	10 April 1953	17 April 1953	24 April 1953
SHE WEARS RED FEATHERS Guy Mitchell	**BROKEN WINGS** The Stargazers	**(HOW MUCH IS) THAT DOGGIE IN THE WINDOW** Lita Roza	**I BELIEVE** Frankie Laine

◂◂ UK No.1 SINGLES ▸▸

20 Dec 03 ● **THE VOICE WITHIN** *RCA 82876584292* 9 10
13 Nov 04 ● **CAR WASH** *Dreamworks 986430* [5] 4 14
4 Dec 04 ● **TILT YA HEAD BACK** *Universal MCSTD 40396* [6] 5 12

[1] Ricky Martin and Christina Aguilera [2] Christina Aguilera, Lil' Kim, Mya and Pink [3] Christina Aguilera featuring Redman [4] Christina Aguilera featuring Lil' Kim [5] Christina Aguilera featuring Missy Elliott [6] Nelly & Christina Aguilera

A-HA 211 Top 500 *Norway's biggest-selling act: Morten Harket (v), Pal Waaktaar (g), Magna Furuholmen (k). This globally popular teen-targeted trio was noted for its innovative videos and stage shows (9 Albums: 156 Weeks, 19 Singles: 133 Weeks)*

28 Sep 85 ● **TAKE ON ME** *Warner Bros. W 9006* ▲ 2 19
9 Nov 85 ● HUNTING HIGH AND LOW *Warner Bros. WX 30* 2 78
28 Dec 85 ★ **THE SUN ALWAYS SHINES ON TV** *Warner Bros. W 8846* 1 12
5 Apr 86 ● **TRAIN OF THOUGHT** *Warner Bros. W 8736* 8 8
14 Jun 86 ● **HUNTING HIGH AND LOW** *Warner Bros. W 6663* 5 10
4 Oct 86 ● **I'VE BEEN LOSING YOU** *Warner Bros. W 8594* 8 7
18 Oct 86 ● SCOUNDREL DAYS *Warner Bros. WX 62* 2 29
6 Dec 86 ● **CRY WOLF** *Warner Bros. W 8500* 5 9
28 Feb 87 **MANHATTAN SKYLINE** *Warner Bros. W 8405* 13 6
4 Jul 87 ● **THE LIVING DAYLIGHTS** *Warner Bros. W 8305* 5 9
26 Mar 88 ● **STAY ON THESE ROADS** *Warner Bros. W 7936* 5 6
14 May 88 ● STAY ON THESE ROADS *Warner Bros. WX 166* 2 19
18 Jun 88 **THE BLOOD THAT MOVES THE BODY** *Warner Bros. W 7840* 25 4
27 Aug 88 **TOUCHY!** *Warner Bros. W 7749* 11 7
3 Dec 88 **YOU ARE THE ONE** *Warner Bros. W 7636* 13 10
13 Oct 90 **CRYING IN THE RAIN** *Warner Bros. W 9547* 13 7
2 Nov 90 EAST OF THE SUN WEST OF THE MOON *Warner Bros. WX 378* 12 4
15 Dec 90 **I CALL YOUR NAME** *Warner Bros. W 9462* 44 5
26 Oct 91 **MOVE TO MEMPHIS** *Warner Bros. W 0070* 47 2
16 Nov 91 HEADLINES AND DEADLINES – THE HITS OF A-HA *Warner Bros. WX 450* 12 12
5 Jun 93 **DARK IS THE NIGHT** *Warner Bros. W 0175CD* 19 4
26 Jun 93 MEMORIAL BEACH *Warner Bros. 9362452292* 17 3
18 Sep 93 **ANGEL** *Warner Bros. W 0195CD* 41 3
26 Mar 94 **SHAPES THAT GO TOGETHER** *Warner Bros. W 0236CD* 27 3
3 Jun 00 **SUMMER MOVED ON** *WEA WEA 275CD* 33 2
17 Jun 00 MINOR EARTH MAJOR SKY *WEA 8573821832* 27 2
22 Jun 02 LIFELINES *WEA 927448492* 67 1
23 Apr 05 THE DEFINITIVE SINGLES COLLECTION 1984-2004 *WEA 5046783242* 14 8

AHMAD *US, male rapper – Ahmad Lewis*

9 Jul 94 **BACK IN THE DAY** *Giant 74321212042* 64 2

AIDA *Holland, male production duo*

19 Feb 00 **FAR AND AWAY** *48K / Perfecto SPECT 03CDS* 58 1

AIM *UK, male DJ / producer – Andy Turner*

9 Feb 02 HINTERLAND *Grand Central GCCD 112* 47 1

AIR *France, male instrumental / production duo – Jean-Benoît Dunckel and Nicolas Godin (6 Albums: 85 Weeks, 6 Singles: 16 Weeks)*

31 Jan 98 ● MOON SAFARI *Virgin CDV 2848* 6 61
21 Feb 98 **SEXY BOY** *Virgin VSCDT 1672* 13 4
16 May 98 **KELLY WATCH THE STARS** *Virgin VSCDT 1690* 18 3
21 Nov 98 **ALL I NEED** *Virgin VSCDT 1702* 29 3
18 Sep 99 PREMIERS SYMPTOMES *Virgin CDV 2895* 12 7
26 Feb 00 **PLAYGROUND LOVE** *Virgin VSCDT 1764* 25 2
11 Mar 00 THE VIRGIN SUICIDES (FILM SOUNDTRACK) *Virgin CDV 2910* 14 4
2 Jun 01 **RADIO #1** *Virgin VSCDT 1803* 31 2
9 Jun 01 ● 10000 HZ LEGEND *Virgin CDV 2945* 7 5
2 Mar 02 EVERYBODY HERTZ *Virgin CDV 2956* 67 1
7 Feb 04 ● TALKIE WALKIE *Virgin CDVX2980* 2 7
21 Aug 04 **ALPHA BETA GAGA** *Source VSCDX 1880* 44 2

The sleeve of 'Playground Love' has the credit: 'Sung by Gordon Tracks'. The CD sleeve credits Moon Safari to Air – French Band.

AIR SUPPLY *Australia, male vocal / instrumental duo – Russell Hitchcock and Graham Russell (b. UK) (3 Singles: 17 Weeks)*

27 Sep 80 **ALL OUT OF LOVE** *Arista ARIST 362* $ 11 11
2 Oct 82 **EVEN THE NIGHTS ARE BETTER** *Arista ARIST 474* 44 4
20 Nov 93 **GOODBYE** *Giant 74321153462* 66 2

AIRHEAD *UK, male vocal / instrumental group (1 Album: 7 Weeks, 3 Singles: 10 Weeks)*

5 Oct 91 **FUNNY HOW** *Korova KOW 47* 57 3
21 Dec 91 **COUNTING SHEEP** *Korova KOW 48* 35 5
1 Feb 92 BOING! *Korova 9031746792* 29 7
7 Mar 92 **RIGHT NOW** *Korova KOW 49* 50 2

AIRHEADZ (see also DOUBLE TROUBLE) *UK, male DJ / production duo – Leigh Guest and Andrew Peach*

28 Apr 01 **STANLEY (HERE I AM)** *AM:PM CDAMPM 145* 36 2

AIRSCAPE (see also BALEARIC BILL; BLUE BAMBOO; CUBIC 22; Johan GIELEN presents ABNEA; SVENSON and GIELEN; TRANSFORMER 2) *Belgium / Holland, male instrumental / production duo – Johann Gielen and Sven Maes (3 Singles: 5 Weeks)*

9 Aug 97 **PACIFIC MELODY** *Xtravaganza 0091165* 27 2
29 Aug 98 **AMAZON CHANT** *Xtravaganza 0091605 EXT* 46 1
4 Dec 99 **L'ESPERANZA** *Xtravaganza EXTRAV 7CD* 33 2

Laurel AITKEN and The UNITONE *Jamaica (b Cuba), male vocalist and UK, male vocal / instrumental group*

17 May 80 **RUDI GOT MARRIED** *I-Spy SEE 6* 60 3

AKABU featuring Linda CLIFFORD (see also HED BOYS; IL PADRINOS featuring Jocelyn BROWN; JAKATTA; Li KWAN; Joey NEGRO; PHASE II; RAVEN MAIZE) *UK, male producer – Dave Lee and US, female vocalist*

15 Sep 01 **RIDE THE STORM** *NRK Sound Division NRKCD 053* 69 1

AKALA NEW *UK, male rapper*

28 May 05 **ROLL WID US** *Illa State ILLA 001CD2* 72 1

Jewel AKENS *US, male vocalist*

25 Mar 65 **THE BIRDS AND THE BEES** *London HLN 9954* 29 8

AKIN *UK, female vocal duo*

14 Jun 97 **STAY RIGHT HERE** *WEA WEA 117CD* 60 1

AKON *US (b. Senegal), male rapper – Aliaune Thiam (1 Album: 32 Weeks, 4 Singles: 40 Weeks)*

25 Dec 04 **LOCKED UP (re)** (import) *Universal AAB 224511* [1] 73 3
12 Feb 05 ★ TROUBLE *Universal 2103966* 1 32
5 Mar 05 ● **LOCKED UP** *Universal MSTD 40406* 5 13
14 May 05 ★ **LONELY** *Universal MCSTD 40415* ■ 1 16
20 Aug 05 ● **BELLY DANCER (BANANZA)** *Universal MCSXD 40426* 5 8

[1] Akon featuring Styles P

ALABAMA 3 *UK, male vocal / instrumental group (2 Singles: 3 Weeks)*

22 Nov 97 **SPEED OF THE SOUND OF LONELINESS** *Elemental ELM 42CDS 1721* 72 1
11 Apr 98 **AIN'T GOIN' TO GOA** *Elemental ELM 45CDS 1* 40 2

Roberto ALAGNA / Angela GHEORGIU *France, male vocalist and Romania, female vocalist*

18 May 96 DUETS & ARIAS *EMI Classics CDC 5561172* 42 5

The ALARM (see also The POPPY FIELDS) *UK, male vocal (Mike Peters) / instrumental group (7 Albums: 29 Weeks, 17 Singles: 65 Weeks)*

24 Sep 83 **68 GUNS** *IRS PFP 1023* 17 7
21 Jan 84 **WHERE WERE YOU HIDING WHEN THE STORM BROKE** *IRS IRS 101* 22 6
25 Feb 84 ● DECLARATION *IRS IRSA 7044* 6 11
31 Mar 84 **THE DECEIVER** *IRS IRS 103* 51 4
3 Nov 84 **THE CHANT HAS JUST BEGUN** *IRS IRS 104* 48 4
2 Mar 85 **ABSOLUTE REALITY** *IRS ALARM 1* 35 6
28 Sep 85 **STRENGTH** *IRS IRM 104* 40 4

KEY
UK No.1 ★ UK Top 10 ● Still on chart + UK entry at No.1 ■
US No.1 ▲ UK million seller £ US million seller $
Singles re-entries are listed as (re), (2re), (3re)… which signifies that the hit re-entered the chart once, twice or three times…
Peak Position / Weeks

Date	Title / Label	Peak	Wks
26 Oct 85	STRENGTH *IRS MIRF 1004*	18	6
18 Jan 86	SPIRIT OF '76 *IRS IRM 109*	22	5
26 Apr 86	KNIFE EDGE *IRS IRM 112*	43	3
17 Oct 87	RAIN IN THE SUMMERTIME *IRS IRM 144*	18	5
14 Nov 87	EYE OF THE HURRICANE *IRS MIRG 1023*	23	4
12 Dec 87	RESCUE ME *IRS IRM 150*	48	2
20 Feb 88	PRESENCE OF LOVE *IRS IRM 155*	44	3
5 Nov 88	ELECTRIC FOLKLORE LIVE *IRS MIRMC 5001*	62	2
16 Sep 89	SOLD ME DOWN THE RIVER *IRS EIRS 123*	43	3
30 Sep 89	CHANGE *IRS EIRSAX 1020*	13	3
4 Nov 89	A NEW SOUTH WALES / THE ROCK *IRS EIRS 129*	31	5
3 Feb 90	LOVE DON'T COME EASY *IRS EIRS 134*	48	3
27 Oct 90	UNSAFE BUILDING 1990 *IRS ALARM 2*	54	2
24 Nov 90	STANDARDS *IRS EIRSA 1043*	47	1
13 Apr 91	RAW *IRS ALARM 3*	51	2
4 May 91	RAW *IRS EIRSA 1055*	33	2
3 Jul 04	NEW HOME NEW LIFE *Snapper Music SMASCD 061*	45	1

'Sold Me Down the River' was joined by 'Yn Gymreag' for its first week on chart. 'A New South Wales' features The Morriston Orpheus Male Voice Choir.

Morris ALBERT *Brazil, male vocalist – Morris Kaisermann*

Date	Title / Label	Peak	Wks
27 Sep 75 ●	FEELINGS *Decca F 13591* $	4	10

ALBERTA *Sierra Leone, female vocalist – Alberta Sheriff*

Date	Title / Label	Peak	Wks
26 Dec 98	YOYO BOY *RCA 74321640602*	48	3

ALBERTO Y LOS TRIOS PARANOIAS
UK, male vocal / instrumental group

Date	Title / Label	Peak	Wks
23 Sep 78	HEADS DOWN NO NONSENSE MINDLESS BOOGIE *Logo GO 323*	47	5

ALBION (see also GOURYELLA; MOONMAN; STARPARTY; SYSTEM F; VERACOCHA) *Holland, male producer – Ferry Corsten*

Date	Title / Label	Peak	Wks
3 Jun 00	AIR 2000 *Platipus PLATCD 73*	59	1

ALCATRAZ (see also LITHIUM and Sonya MADAN; SUBMERGE featuring Jan JOHNSTON) *US, male instrumental / production duo – Jean-Philippe Aviance and Victor Imbres*

Date	Title / Label	Peak	Wks
17 Feb 96	GIV ME LUV *AM:PM 5814332*	12	4

ALCAZAR
Sweden, male / female vocal trio (3 Singles: 18 Weeks)

Date	Title / Label	Peak	Wks
8 Dec 01	CRYING AT THE DISCOTEQUE *Arista 74321893432*	13	11
16 Mar 02	SEXUAL GUARANTEE *Arista 74321920252*	30	2
2 Oct 04	THIS IS THE WORLD WE LIVE IN *RCA 82876652372*	15	5

ALDA *Iceland, female vocalist – Alda Olafsdottir (2 Singles: 14 Weeks)*

Date	Title / Label	Peak	Wks
29 Aug 98 ●	REAL GOOD TIME *Wildstar CDWILD 7*	7	7
26 Dec 98	GIRLS NIGHT OUT *Wildstar CDWILD 10*	20	7

ALENA *Jamaica, female vocalist – Alena Lova*

Date	Title / Label	Peak	Wks
13 Nov 99	TURN IT AROUND *Wonderboy WBOYD 16*	14	5

ALESSI *US, male vocal duo – Billy and Bobby Alessi*

Date	Title / Label	Peak	Wks
11 Jun 77 ●	OH, LORI *A&M AMS 7289*	8	11

ALEX PARTY (see also LIVIN' JOY) *Italy / UK, male / female vocal / instrumental group – leader Paolo Visnadi (4 Singles: 28 Weeks)*

Date	Title / Label	Peak	Wks
18 Dec 93	SATURDAY NIGHT PARTY (READ MY LIPS) (re) *Cleveland City Imports CCICD 17000*	29	10
18 Feb 95 ●	DON'T GIVE ME YOUR LIFE *Systematic SYSCD 7*	2	13
18 Nov 95	WRAP ME UP *Systematic SYSCD 22*	17	3
19 Oct 96	READ MY LIPS (re-mix) *Systematic SYSCD 30*	28	2

The ALEXANDER BROTHERS
UK, male vocal duo – Tom and Jack Alexander

Date	Title / Label	Peak	Wks
10 Dec 66	THESE ARE MY MOUNTAINS *Pye GGL 0375*	29	1

ALEXIA *Italy, female vocalist – Alessia Aquilani (3 Singles: 15 Weeks)*

Date	Title / Label	Peak	Wks
21 Mar 98 ●	UH LA LA LA *Dance Pool ALEX 1CD*	10	9
13 Jun 98	GIMME LOVE *Dance Pool ALEX 2CDZ*	17	4
10 Oct 98	THE MUSIC I LIKE *Dance Pool ALEX 3CD*	31	2

ALEXIA *UK, female vocalist*

Date	Title / Label	Peak	Wks
22 Feb 03	RING *Virgin VSCDT 1836*	48	1

ALFI and HARRY (see also The CHIPMUNKS; David SEVILLE)
US, male vocalist / instrumentalist – David Seville, b. 27 Jan 1919, d. 16 Jan 1972, under two false names

Date	Title / Label	Peak	Wks
23 Mar 56	TROUBLE WITH HARRY *London HLU 8242*	15	5

ALFIE
UK, male vocal / instrumental group (1 Album: 1 Week, 6 Singles: 6 Weeks)

Date	Title / Label	Peak	Wks
7 Apr 01	IF YOU HAPPY WITH YOU NEED DO NOTHING *Twisted Nerve TN 026CD*	62	1
8 Sep 01	YOU MAKE NO BONES *Twisted Nerve TN 033CD*	61	1
16 Mar 02	A WORD IN YOUR EAR *Twisted Nerve TN 037CD*	66	1
21 Jun 03	PEOPLE *Regal REG 84CD*	53	1
13 Sep 03	STUNTMAN *Regal REG 87CDS*	51	1
28 Feb 04	NO NEED *Regal REG 99CD*	66	1
13 Aug 05	YOUR OWN RELIGION *Regal REG 124CD*	61	1

John ALFORD
UK, male actor / vocalist – John Shannon (3 Singles: 12 Weeks)

Date	Title / Label	Peak	Wks
17 Feb 96	SMOKE GETS IN YOUR EYES *Love This LUVTHISCD 7*	13	5
25 May 96 ●	BLUE MOON / ONLY YOU *Love This LUVTHISCD 9*	9	4
23 Nov 96	IF / KEEP ON RUNNING *Love This LUVTHISCD 15*	24	3

ALI *UK, male vocalist – Ali Tennant (2 Singles: 2 Weeks)*

Date	Title / Label	Peak	Wks
23 May 98	LOVE LETTERS *Wild Card 5698092*	63	1
24 Oct 98	FEELIN' YOU *Wild Card 5676992*	63	1

Tatyana ALI *US, female vocalist (1 Album: 4 Weeks, 3 Singles: 18 Weeks)*

Date	Title / Label	Peak	Wks
14 Nov 98 ●	DAYDREAMIN' *Epic 6665462*	6	5
13 Feb 99 ●	BOY YOU KNOCK ME OUT (re) *MJJ / Epic 6669372* [1]	3	9
20 Feb 99	KISS THE SKY *Epic 4916519*	41	4
19 Jun 99	EVERYTIME *Epic / MJJ 674742*	20	4

[1] Tatyana Ali featuring Will Smith

ALI and FRAZIER *UK, female vocal duo – Kirsty Ali and Natasha Frazier*

Date	Title / Label	Peak	Wks
7 Aug 93	UPTOWN TOP RANKING *Arista 74321158842*	33	4

ALIBI *UK, male vocal duo (2 Singles: 2 Weeks)*

Date	Title / Label	Peak	Wks
15 Feb 97	I'M NOT TO BLAME *Urgent 74321434762*	51	1
7 Feb 98	HOW MUCH I FEEL *Urgent 74321548472*	58	1

The ALICE BAND *UK / Ireland / US, female vocal / instrumental group (1 Album: 1 Week, 2 Singles: 2 Weeks)*

Date	Title / Label	Peak	Wks
23 Jun 01	ONE DAY AT A TIME *Instant Karma KARMA 5CD*	52	1
27 Apr 02	NOW THAT YOU LOVE ME *Instant Karma KARMA 17CD*	44	1
25 May 02	THE LOVE JUNK STORE *Instant Karma KARMACD 4*	55	1

ALICE DEEJAY *Holland, male / female production / vocal (Judith Pronk) group (1 Album: 11 Weeks, 5 Singles: 50 Weeks)*

Date	Title / Label	Peak	Wks
31 Jul 99 ●	BETTER OFF ALONE *Positiva CDTIV 113* [1]	2	16
4 Dec 99 ●	BACK IN MY LIFE *Positiva CDTIV 121*	4	15
15 Jul 00 ●	WILL I EVER *Positiva CDTIV 134*	7	10
29 Jul 00 ●	WHO NEEDS GUITARS ANYWAY? *Positiva 5270010*	8	11
21 Oct 00	THE LONELY ONE *Positiva CDTIV 145*	16	5
10 Feb 01	CELEBRATE OUR LOVE *Positiva CDTIV 149*	17	4

[1] DJ Jurgen presents Alice Deejay

ALICE IN CHAINS *US, male vocal (Layne Staley, b. 22 Aug 1967, d. 5 Apr 2002) / instrumental group (4 Albums: 22 Weeks, 6 Singles: 14 Weeks)*

Date	Title / Label	Peak	Wks
24 Oct 92	DIRT *Columbia 4723302*	42	13

23 Jan 93 **WOULD?** *Columbia 6588882* **19** 3
20 Mar 93 **THEM BONES** *Columbia 6590902* **26** 3
5 Jun 93 **ANGRY CHAIR** *Columbia 6593652* **33** 2
23 Oct 93 **DOWN IN A HOLE** *Columbia 6597512* **36** 2
5 Feb 94 ● JAR OF FLIES / SAP *Columbia 4757132* ▲ 4 5
11 Nov 95 **GRIND** *Columbia 6626232* **23** 2
18 Nov 95 ALICE IN CHAINS *Columbia 4811149* ▲ 37 2
10 Feb 96 **HEAVEN BESIDE YOU** *Columbia 6628935* **35** 2
10 Aug 96 MTV UNPLUGGED *Columbia 4843002* 20 2

ALIEN ANT FARM *US, male vocal (Dryden Mitchell) / instrumental group (2 Albums: 24 Weeks, 5 Singles: 25 Weeks)*

30 Jun 01 **MOVIES** *Dreamworks / Polydor 4508992* **53** 1
18 Aug 01 ANTHOLOGY *Dreamworks 4502932* 11 23
8 Sep 01 **SMOOTH CRIMINAL** (import) *Dreamworks / Polydor 4508852* **74** 2
29 Sep 01 ● **SMOOTH CRIMINAL (re)** *Dreamworks / Polydor DRMDM 50887* **3** 13
16 Feb 02 ● **MOVIES** (re-issue) *Dreamworks / Polydor 4508492* **5** 8
25 May 02 **ATTITUDE** *Dreamworks / New Noize 4508292* **66** 1
30 Aug 03 TRUANT *Dreamworks / Polydor 4505014* 68 1

ALIEN SEX FIEND *UK, male / female vocal / instrumental group*

12 Oct 85 MAXIMUM SECURITY *Anagram GRAM 24* 100 1

ALIEN VOICES featuring The THREE DEGREES

(see also BOOGIE BOX HIGH; Andy G's STARSKY & HUTCH ALL STARS) *UK, male producer – Andros Georgiou and US, female vocal trio*

26 Dec 98 **LAST CHRISTMAS** *Wildstar CDWILD 15* **54** 2

ALISHA *US, female vocalist*

25 Jan 86 **BABY TALK** *Total Control TOCO 6* **67** 2

ALISHA'S ATTIC *UK, female vocal duo – Shellie and Karen Poole (3 Albums: 47 Weeks, 9 Singles: 47 Weeks)*

3 Aug 96 **I AM, I FEEL** *Mercury AATCD 1* **14** 10
2 Nov 96 **ALISHA RULES THE WORLD** *Mercury AATCD 2* **12** 6
23 Nov 96 ALISHA RULES THE WORLD *Mercury 5340272* 14 43
15 Mar 97 **INDESTRUCTIBLE** *Mercury AATCD 3* **12** 6
12 Jul 97 **AIR WE BREATHE** *Mercury AATCD 4* **12** 6
19 Sep 98 **THE INCIDENTALS** *Mercury AATCD 5* **13** 7
17 Oct 98 ILLUMINA *Mercury 5589912* 15 3
9 Jan 99 **WISH I WERE YOU** *Mercury AATCD 6* **29** 5
17 Apr 99 **BARBARELLA** *Mercury AATCD 7* **34** 2
24 Mar 01 **PUSH IT ALL ASIDE** *Mercury AATCD 8* **24** 4
28 Jul 01 **PRETENDER GOT MY HEART** *Mercury AATCD 9* **43** 1
4 Aug 01 THE HOUSE WE BUILT *Mercury 5428542* 55 1

ALIVE featuring D.D. KLEIN

Italy, male production trio and Antigua, female vocalist

27 Jul 02 **ALIVE** *Serious / Universal CDAMPM 153* **49** 1

ALIZÉE *France, female vocalist – Alizée Jacotet*

23 Feb 02 ● **MOI ... LOLITA** *Polydor 5705952* **9** 9

ALKALINE TRIO

US, male vocal / instrumental trio (2 Albums: 3 Weeks, 6 Singles: 8 Weeks)

2 Feb 02 **PRIVATE EYE** *B-Unique / Vagrant BUN 013CDS* **51** 1
30 Mar 02 **STUPID KID** *B-Unique / Vagrant BUN 016CD* **53** 1
24 May 03 GOOD MOURNING *Vagrant 9801238* 32 1
26 Jul 03 **WE'VE HAD ENOUGH** *Vagrant 9809023* **50** 1
18 Oct 03 **ALL ON BLACK** *Interscope 9811506* **60** 1
4 Jun 05 CRIMSON *Vagrant VRUK 012CD* 34 2
9 Jul 05 **TIME TO WASTE** *Vagrant VRUK 013CD* **32** 2
3 Dec 05 **MERCY ME** *Vagrant VRUK 024CDS* **30** 2

ALL ABOUT EVE *UK, female / male vocal (Julianne Regan) / instrumental group (4 Albums: 37 Weeks, 14 Singles: 48 Weeks)*

31 Oct 87 **IN THE CLOUDS** *Mercury EVEN 5* **47** 5
23 Jan 88 **WILD HEARTED WOMAN** *Mercury EVEN 6* **33** 4
27 Feb 88 ● ALL ABOUT EVE *Mercury MERH 119* 7 29
9 Apr 88 **EVERY ANGEL** *Mercury EVEN 7* **30** 5
30 Jul 88 ● **MARTHA'S HARBOUR** *Mercury EVEN 8* **10** 8
12 Nov 88 **WHAT KIND OF FOOL** *Mercury EVEN 9* **29** 4
30 Sep 89 **ROAD TO YOUR SOUL** *Mercury EVEN 10* **37** 4
28 Oct 89 ● SCARLET AND OTHER STORIES *Mercury 838965 1* 9 4
16 Dec 89 **DECEMBER** *Mercury EVEN 11* **34** 5
28 Apr 90 **SCARLET** *Mercury EVEN 12* **34** 2
15 Jun 91 **FAREWELL MR. SORROW** *Mercury EVEN 14* **36** 2
10 Aug 91 **STRANGE WAY** *Vertigo EVEN 15* **50** 3
7 Sep 91 TOUCHED BY JESUS *Vertigo 510461* 17 3
19 Oct 91 **THE DREAMER** *Vertigo EVEN 16* **41** 2
10 Oct 92 **PHASED (EP)** *MCA MCS 1688* **38** 2
7 Nov 92 ULTRAVIOLET *MCA MCD 10712* 46 1
28 Nov 92 **SOME FINER DAY** *MCA MCS 1706* **57** 1
5 Jun 04 **LET ME GO HOME** *Voiceprint AAEVP 10CD1* **52** 1

Tracks on Phased (EP): Phased / Mine / Infra Red / Ascent-Descent.

The ALL-AMERICAN REJECTS

US, male vocal / instrumental group (1 Album: 5 Weeks, 2 Singles: 6 Weeks)

2 Aug 03 **SWING, SWING** *Dreamworks 4504616* **13** 5
9 Aug 03 THE ALL-AMERICAN REJECTS *Dreamworks / Polydor 4504606* 50 5
22 Nov 03 **THE LAST SONG** *Dreamworks 4504641* **69** 1

ALL BLUE *UK, male vocal duo*

21 Aug 99 **PRISONER** *WEA WEA 213CD1* **73** 1

ALL EYES *UK, male vocal group*

13 Nov 04 **SHE'S A VISION** *Specsavers CXSPECS 1* **65** 1

ALL-4-ONE *US, male vocal group (1 Album: 5 Weeks, 4 Singles: 23 Weeks)*

2 Apr 94 **SO MUCH IN LOVE** *Atlantic A 7261CD* **60** 1
18 Jun 94 ● **I SWEAR** *Atlantic A 7255CD* ▲ $ **2** 18
23 Jul 94 ALL-4-ONE *Atlantic 7567825882* 25 5
19 Nov 94 **SO MUCH IN LOVE** (re-mix) *Atlantic A 7216CD* **49** 2
15 Jul 95 **I CAN LOVE YOU LIKE THAT** *Atlantic A 8193CD* **33** 2

ALL SAINTS 341 Top 500

(see also APPLETON; ARTFUL DODGER; OUTSIDAZ featuring Rah DIGGA and Melanie BLATT) *From All Saints Road, London, a cooler, R&B-motivated vocal girl group in the wake of the Spice Girls: Melanie Blatt, London, Shaznay Lewis, London, and sisters Nicole and Natalie Appleton, both Canada. Crowned Best Breakthrough Artists at the 1998 MTV Europe Music Awards. Group split in 2001. Biggest-selling single: 'Never Ever' 1,254,604 (3 Albums: 96 Weeks, 8 Singles: 109 Weeks)*

6 Sep 97 ● **I KNOW WHERE IT'S AT** *London LONCD 398* **4** 8
22 Nov 97 ★ **NEVER EVER** *London LONCD 407* £ **1** 24
6 Dec 97 ● ALL SAINTS *London 8289792* 2 71
9 May 98 ★ **UNDER THE BRIDGE / LADY MARMALADE** *London LONCD 408* ■ **1** 14
12 Sep 98 ★ **BOOTIE CALL** *London LONCD 415* ■ **1** 11
5 Dec 98 ● **WAR OF NERVES** *London LONCD 421* **7** 11
26 Feb 00 ★ **PURE SHORES** *London LONCD 444* ■ **1** 16
14 Oct 00 ★ **BLACK COFFEE (2re)** *London LONCD 454* ■ **1** 18
28 Oct 00 ★ SAINTS & SINNERS *London 8573852952* ■ 1 21
27 Jan 01 ● **ALL HOOKED UP (re)** *London LONCD 456* **7** 7
17 Nov 01 ALL HITS *London 927421522* 18 4

From 29 Apr 00 All Saints changed catalogue number to London 3984291362.

The ALL SEEING I *UK, male production / instrumental group (1 Album: 1 Week, 3 Singles: 17 Weeks)*

28 Mar 98 **BEAT GOES ON** *ffrr FCD 334* **11** 7
23 Jan 99 ● **WALK LIKE A PANTHER** *ffrr FCD 351* [1] **10** 7
18 Sep 99 **1ST MAN IN SPACE** *ffrr FCD 370* [2] **28** 3
2 Oct 99 PICKLED EGGS & SHERBET *ffrr 3984292412* 45 1

[1] The All Seeing I featuring Tony Christie [2] The All Seeing I featuring Phil Oakey

ALL SYSTEMS GO *UK, male vocal / instrumental group*

18 Jun 88 **POP MUZIK** *Unique NIQ 03* **63** 2

Richard ALLAN *UK, male vocalist*

24 Mar 60 **AS TIME GOES BY** *Parlophone R 4634* **43** 1

KEY
UK No.1 ★ UK Top 10 ● Still on chart + UK entry at No.1 ■
US No.1 ▲ UK million seller £ US million seller $
Singles re-entries are listed as (re), (2re), (3re)... which signifies that the hit re-entered the chart once, twice or three times...
Peak Position / Weeks

Steve ALLAN *UK, male vocalist*

Date		Title / Label	Peak	Weeks
27 Jan 79		**TOGETHER WE ARE BEAUTIFUL (re)** *Creole CR 164*	67	2

Donna ALLEN *US, female vocalist (4 Singles: 27 Weeks)*

Date		Title / Label	Peak	Weeks
18 Apr 87	●	**SERIOUS** *Portrait 650744 7*	8	12
3 Jun 89	●	**JOY AND PAIN** *BCM BCM 257*	10	10
21 Jan 95		**REAL** *Epic 6610992*	34	2
11 Oct 97		**SATURDAY** *AM:PM 5823752* [1]	29	3

[1] East 57th Street featuring Donna Allen

Ed ALLEYNE-JOHNSON *UK, male violinist*

Date		Title / Label	Peak	Weeks
18 Jun 94		ULTRAVIOLET *Equation EQCD 002*	68	1

Dot ALLISON (see also ONE DOVE) *UK, female vocalist*

Date		Title / Label	Peak	Weeks
17 Aug 02		**STRUNG OUT** *Mantra MNT 74CD*	67	1

Mose ALLISON *US, male vocalist / pianist*

Date		Title / Label	Peak	Weeks
4 Jun 66		MOSE ALIVE *Atlantic 587007*	30	1

The ALLISONS *UK, male vocal / instrumental duo – John (Brian Alford) and Bob Allison (Colin Day) (3 Singles: 27 Weeks)*

Date		Title / Label	Peak	Weeks
23 Feb 61	●	**ARE YOU SURE** *Fontana H 294*	2	16
18 May 61		**WORDS** *Fontana H 304*	34	5
15 Feb 62		**LESSONS IN LOVE** *Fontana H 362*	30	6

The ALLMAN BROTHERS BAND *US, male vocal / instrumental group (2 Albums: 4 Weeks)*

Date		Title / Label	Peak	Weeks
6 Oct 73		BROTHERS AND SISTERS *Warner Bros. K 47507* ▲	42	3
6 Mar 76		THE ROAD GOES ON FOREVER *Capricorn 2637 101*	54	1

ALLNIGHT BAND *UK, male instrumental group*

Date		Title / Label	Peak	Weeks
3 Feb 79		**THE JOKER (THE WIGAN JOKER)** *Casino Classics CC 6*	50	3

ALLSTARS *UK, female / male vocal group (1 Album: 2 Weeks, 4 Singles: 22 Weeks)*

Date		Title / Label	Peak	Weeks
23 Jun 01		**BEST FRIENDS (re)** *Island CID 775*	20	7
22 Sep 01		**THINGS THAT GO BUMP IN THE NIGHT / IS THERE SOMETHING I SHOULD KNOW** *Island CID 783*	12	4
26 Jan 02	●	**THE LAND OF MAKE BELIEVE (re)** *Island CID 791*	9	8
11 May 02		**BACK WHEN / GOING ALL THE WAY** *Island CID 796*	19	3
25 May 02		ALLSTARS *Island CID 8116*	43	2

ALLURE *US, female vocal group (2 Singles: 8 Weeks)*

Date		Title / Label	Peak	Weeks
14 Jun 97		**HEAD OVER HEELS** *Epic 6645942* [1]	18	3
10 Jan 98		**ALL CRIED OUT** *Epic 6652715* [2]	12	5

[1] Allure featuring Nas [2] Allure featuring 112

The ALMIGHTY *UK, male vocal (Ricky Warwick) / instrumental group (5 Albums: 13 Weeks, 11 Singles: 22 Weeks)*

Date		Title / Label	Peak	Weeks
30 Jun 90		**WILD AND WONDERFUL** *Polydor PO 75*	50	2
20 Oct 90		BLOOD, FIRE AND LOVE *Polydor 8471071*	62	1
2 Mar 91		**FREE 'N' EASY** *Polydor PO 127*	35	2
30 Mar 91		SOUL DESTRUCTION *Polydor 8479611*	22	4
11 May 91		**DEVIL'S TOY** *Polydor PO 144*	36	2
29 Jun 91		**LITTLE LOST SOMETIMES** *Polydor PO 151*	42	2
3 Apr 93		**ADDICTION** *Polydor PZCD 261*	38	2
17 Apr 93	●	POWERTRIPPIN' *Polydor 5191042*	5	4
29 May 93		**OUT OF SEASON** *Polydor PZCD 266*	41	2
30 Oct 93		**OVER THE EDGE** *Polydor PZCD 298*	38	2
24 Sep 94		**WRENCH** *Chrysalis CDCHS 5014*	26	2
8 Oct 94		CRANK *Chrysalis CDCHRZ 6086*	15	2
14 Jan 95		**JONESTOWN MIND** *Chrysalis CDCHS 5017*	26	3
16 Mar 96		**ALL SUSSED OUT** *Chrysalis CDCHS 5030*	28	2
30 Mar 96		JUST ADD LIFE *Chrysalis CDCHR 6112*	34	2
25 May 96		**DO YOU UNDERSTAND** *Raw Power RAWX 1022*	38	1

Marc ALMOND (see also SOFT CELL) *UK, male vocalist (9 Albums: 26 Weeks, 26 Singles: 112 Weeks)*

Date		Title / Label	Peak	Weeks
16 Oct 82		UNTITLED *Some Bizzare BZA 13* [1]	42	4
2 Jul 83		**BLACK HEART** *Some Bizzare BZS 19* [1]	49	3
20 Aug 83		TORMENT AND TOREROS *Some Bizzare BIZL 4* [1]	28	5
2 Jun 84		**THE BOY WHO CAME BACK** *Some Bizzare BZS 23*	52	5
1 Sep 84		**YOU HAVE** *Some Bizzare BZS 24*	57	3
10 Nov 84		VERMIN IN ERMINE *Some Bizzare BIZL 8*	36	2
20 Apr 85	●	**I FEEL LOVE (MEDLEY)** *Forbidden Fruit BITE 4* [2]	3	12
24 Aug 85		**STORIES OF JOHNNY** *Some Bizzare BONK 1*	23	5
5 Oct 85		STORIES OF JOHNNY *Some Bizzare FAITH 1*	22	3
26 Oct 85		**LOVE LETTER** *Some Bizzare BONK 2*	68	3
4 Jan 86		**THE HOUSE IS HAUNTED (BY THE ECHO OF YOUR LAST GOODBYE)** *Some Bizzare GLOW 1*	55	3
7 Jun 86		**A WOMAN'S STORY** *Some Bizzare GLOW 2* [3]	41	5
18 Oct 86		**RUBY RED** *Some Bizzare GLOW 3*	47	3
14 Feb 87		**MELANCHOLY ROSE** *Some Bizzare GLOW 4*	71	1
18 Apr 87		MOTHER FIST AND HER FIVE DAUGHTERS *Some Bizzare FAITH 2* [2]	41	2
3 Sep 88		**TEARS RUN RINGS** *Parlophone R 6186*	26	7
8 Oct 88		THE STARS WE ARE *Parlophone PCS 7324*	41	5
5 Nov 88		**BITTER SWEET** *Some Bizzare R 6194*	40	3
14 Jan 89	★	**SOMETHING'S GOTTEN HOLD OF MY HEART** *Parlophone R 6201* [4]	1	12
8 Apr 89		**ONLY THE MOMENT** *Parlophone R 6210*	45	2
3 Mar 90		**A LOVER SPURNED** *Some Bizzare R 6229*	29	4
19 May 90		**THE DESPERATE HOURS** *Some Bizzare R 6252*	45	2
16 Jun 90		ENCHANTED *Some Bizzare PCS 7344*	52	1
23 Mar 91		**SAY HELLO WAVE GOODBYE '91** (re-recording) *Mercury SOFT 1* [5]	38	3
18 May 91	●	**TAINTED LOVE** (re-issue) *Mercury SOFT 2* [5]	5	8
28 Sep 91		**JACKY** *Some Bizzare YZ 610*	17	6
26 Oct 91		TENEMENT SYMPHONY *Some Bizzare WX 442*	39	3
11 Jan 92		**MY HAND OVER MY HEART** *Some Bizzare YZ 633*	33	5
25 Apr 92	●	**THE DAYS OF PEARLY SPENCER** *Some Bizzare YZ 638*	4	7
27 Mar 93		**WHAT MAKES A MAN A MAN (LIVE)** *Some Bizzare YZ 720CD*	60	2
13 May 95		**ADORED AND EXPLORED** *Some Bizzare MERCD 431*	25	3
29 Jul 95		**THE IDOL** *Some Bizzare MERCD 437*	44	2
30 Dec 95		**CHILD STAR** *Some Bizzare MERCD 450*	41	1
9 Mar 96		FANTASTIC STAR *Some Bizzare 5286592*	54	1
28 Dec 96		**YESTERDAY HAS GONE (re)** *EMI Premier CDPRESX 13* [6]	58	2

[1] Marc and The Mambas [2] Bronski Beat and Marc Almond [3] Marc Almond and The Willing Sinners [4] Marc Almond featuring special guest star Gene Pitney [5] Soft Cell / Marc Almond [6] PJ Proby and Marc Almond featuring the My Life Story Orchestra [1] Marc and The Mambas [2] Marc Almond and The Willing Sinners

I Feel Love (medley): I Feel Love / Love to Love You Baby / Johnny Remember Me. Original hit versions of 'Tainted Love' (1981) and 'Say Hello Wave Goodbye' (1982) credited to Soft Cell alone.

ALOOF *UK, male vocal / instrumental group (5 Singles: 6 Weeks)*

Date		Title / Label	Peak	Weeks
19 Sep 92		**ON A MISSION** *Cowboy RODEO 5*	64	1
18 May 96		**WISH YOU WERE HERE ...** *East West EW 038CD*	61	1
30 Nov 96		**ONE NIGHT STAND** *East West EW 067CD*	30	2
1 Mar 97		**WISH YOU WERE HERE ...** (re-mix) *East West EW 083CD1*	43	1
29 Aug 98		**WHAT I MISS THE MOST** *East West EW 179CD1*	70	1

Herb ALPERT and The TIJUANA BRASS (112 Top 500)

Leader of the US's biggest-selling instrumental act, The Tijuana Brass, b. 31 Mar 1935, Los Angeles. The multi-talented trumpet-toting star's band had four albums simultaneously in the US Top 10 in the mid-1960s. He sold his A&M label for $300m in 1989 and his publishing company for $350m in 2000 (16 Albums: 312 Weeks, 11 Singles: 106 Weeks)

Date		Title / Label	Peak	Weeks
3 Jan 63		**THE LONELY BULL (EL SOLO TORRO)** *Stateside SS 138* [1]	22	9
9 Dec 65	●	**SPANISH FLEA** *Pye International 7N 25335*	3	20
29 Jan 66	●	GOING PLACES *Pye NPL 28065* ▲	4	138
24 Mar 66		**TIJUANA TAXI** *Pye International 7N 25352*	37	4
23 Apr 66	●	WHIPPED CREAM AND OTHER DELIGHTS *Pye NPL 28058* ▲	2	42
28 May 66		WHAT NOW MY LOVE *Pye NPL 28077* ▲	18	17
11 Feb 67	●	SRO *Pye NSPL 28088*	5	26
27 Apr 67		**CASINO ROYALE** *A&M AMS 700*	27	14
15 Jul 67		SOUNDS LIKE *A&M AMLS 900* ▲	21	10
3 Feb 68		NINTH *A&M AMLS 905*	26	9
29 Jun 68	●	BEAT OF THE BRASS *A&M AMLS 916* ▲	4	21
3 Jul 68	●	**THIS GUY'S IN LOVE WITH YOU (3re)** *A&M AMS 727* [2] ▲ $	3	19

18 Jun 69 **WITHOUT HER** *A&M AMS 755* 36 5
9 Aug 69 WARM *A&M AMLS 937* 30 4
14 Mar 70 THE BRASS ARE COMIN' *A&M AMLS 962* 40 1
30 May 70 ● GREATEST HITS *A&M AMLS 980* 8 27
27 Jun 70 DOWN MEXICO WAY *A&M AMLS 974* 64 1
12 Dec 70 **JERUSALEM (re)** *A&M AMS 810* 42 3
13 Nov 71 AMERICA *A&M AMLB 1000* 45 1
12 Nov 77 40 GREATEST *K-Tel NE 1005* 45 2
13 Oct 79 **RISE** *A&M AMS 7465* [2] ▲ $ 13 13
17 Nov 79 RISE *A&M AMLH 64790* [1] 37 7
19 Jan 80 **ROTATION** *A&M AMS 7500* [2] 46 3
21 Mar 87 **KEEP YOUR EYE ON ME** *Breakout USA 602* [2] 19 9
4 Apr 87 KEEP YOUR EYE ON ME *Breakout AMA 5125* [1] 79 3
6 Jun 87 **DIAMONDS** *Breakout USA 605* [2] 27 7
28 Sep 91 THE VERY BEST OF HERB ALPERT *A&M 3971651* [1] 34 3

[1] The Tijuana Brass [2] Herb Alpert [1] Herb Alpert

Alpert provides vocals on 'This Guy's in Love with You' and 'Without Her'. Janet Jackson and Lisa Keith provide uncredited vocals on 'Diamonds'. On 29 Jun 67 Going Places and What Now My Love changed labels and numbers to A&M AMLS 965 and AMLS 977 respectively.

ALPHAVILLE *Germany, male vocal (Marian Gold) / instrumental group*

18 Aug 84 ● **BIG IN JAPAN** *WEA Int. X 9505* 8 13

ALPINESTARS featuring Brian MOLKO

UK, male production duo and Belgium, male vocalist

22 Jun 02 **CARBON KID** *Riverman RMR 11CDS* 63 1

Glyn Thomas & Richard Woolgar

ALSOU *Russia, female vocalist – Alsou Tenisheva*

12 May 01 **BEFORE YOU LOVE ME** *Mercury 1589142* 27 3

Gerald ALSTON *US, male vocalist*

15 Apr 89 **ACTIVATED** *RCA ZB 42681* 73 1

ALT *Ireland / New Zealand / UK, male vocal / instrumental group*

24 Jun 95 ALTITUDE *Parlophone CDPCS 7377* 67 1

ALTER EGO

Germany, male production duo – Roman Flugel and Jorn Elling Wuttke

11 Dec 04 **ROCKER** *Skint SKINT 103CD* 32 6

ALTERED IMAGES *UK, male / female vocal (Claire Grogan) / instrumental group (3 Albums: 40 Weeks, 8 Singles: 60 Weeks)*

28 Mar 81 **DEAD POP STARS** *Epic EPC A 1023* 67 2
19 Sep 81 HAPPY BIRTHDAY *Epic EPC 84893* 26 21
26 Sep 81 ● **HAPPY BIRTHDAY** *Epic EPC A 1522* 2 17
12 Dec 81 ● **I COULD BE HAPPY** *Epic EPC A 1834* 7 12
27 Mar 82 **SEE THOSE EYES** *Epic EPC A 2198* 11 7
15 May 82 PINKY BLUE *Epic EPC 85665* 12 10
22 May 82 **PINKY BLUE** *Epic EPC A 2426* 35 6
19 Mar 83 ● **DON'T TALK TO ME ABOUT LOVE** *Epic EPC A 3083* 7 7
28 May 83 **BRING ME CLOSER** *Epic EPC A 3398* 29 6
25 Jun 83 BITE *Epic EPC 25413* 16 9
16 Jul 83 **LOVE TO STAY** *Epic EPC A 3582* 46 3

ALTERKICKS NEW *UK, male vocal / instrumental group*

26 Mar 05 **DO EVERYTHING I TAUGHT YOU** *Fierce Panda NING 162CD* 71 1

ALTERN 8 *UK, male instrumental / production duo – Mark Archer and Chris Peat (1 Album: 4 Weeks, 8 Singles: 34 Weeks)*

13 Jul 91 **INFILTRATE 202** *Network NWK 24* 28 7
16 Nov 91 ● **ACTIV 8 (COME WITH ME)** *Network NWK 34* 3 9
8 Feb 92 **FREQUENCY** *Network NWKT 37* 41 1
11 Apr 92 ● **EVAPOR 8** *Network NWK 38* [1] 6 6
4 Jul 92 **HYPNOTIC ST-8** *Network NWK 49* 16 4
25 Jul 92 FULL ON ... MASK HYSTERIA *Network TOPCD 1* 11 4
10 Oct 92 **SHAME** *Network NWKTEN 56* [2] 74 1
12 Dec 92 **BRUTAL-8-E** *Network NWK 59* 43 5
3 Jul 93 **EVERYBODY** *Network NWKCD 73* 58 1

[1] Guest vocal PP Arnold [2] Altern 8 vs Evelyn King

ALTHIA and DONNA

Jamaica, female vocal duo – Althea Forrest and Donna Reid

24 Dec 77 ★ **UPTOWN TOP RANKING** *Lightning LIG 506* 1 11

ALY-US *US, male vocal / instrumental group (2 Singles: 3 Weeks)*

21 Nov 92 **FOLLOW ME** *Cooltempo COOL 266* 43 2
25 May 02 **FOLLOW ME** (re-mix) *Strictly Rhythm SRUKCD 05* 54 1

Shola AMA *UK, female vocalist – Mathurin Campbell (1 Album: 32 Weeks, 9 Singles: 58 Weeks)*

19 Apr 97 ● **YOU MIGHT NEED SOMEBODY** *WEA WEA 097CD1* 4 14
30 Aug 97 ● **YOU'RE THE ONE I LOVE** *WEA WEA 121CD1* 3 8
13 Sep 97 ● MUCH LOVE *WEA 3984200202* 6 32
29 Nov 97 **WHO'S LOVING MY BABY** *WEA WEA 145CD1* 13 7
21 Feb 98 **MUCH LOVE** *WEA WEA 154CD1* 17 3
11 Apr 98 **SOMEDAY I'LL FIND YOU / I'VE BEEN TO A MARVELLOUS PARTY** *EMI CDTCB 001* [1] 28 3
17 Apr 99 ● **TABOO** *WEA WEA 203CD* [2] 10 8
6 Nov 99 **STILL BELIEVE** *WEA WEA 239CD1* 26 3
29 Apr 00 **IMAGINE** *WEA WEA 252CD* 24 4
11 Sep 04 ● **YOU SHOULD REALLY KNOW** *Relentless RELCD 9* [3] 8 8

[1] Shola Ama and Craig Armstrong / The Divine Comedy [2] Glamma Kid featuring Shola Ama [3] Pirates featuring Enya, Shola Ama, Naila Boss & Ishani

Eddie AMADOR *US, male DJ / producer (2 Singles: 5 Weeks)*

24 Oct 98 **HOUSE MUSIC** *Pukka CDPUKKA 18* 37 2
22 Jan 00 **RISE** *Defected DEFECT 9CDS* 19 3

Ruby AMANFU *US (b. Ghana), female vocalist*

15 Mar 03 **SUGAH** *Polydor 0658302* 32 2

AMAR *UK, female vocalist / instrumentalist – Amar Nagi*

9 Sep 00 **SOMETIMES IT SNOWS IN APRIL** *Blanco Y Negro NEG 129CD* 48 1

AMAZULU *UK, female / male vocal (Annie Ruddock) / instrumental group (1 Album: 1 Week, 6 Singles: 57 Weeks)*

6 Jul 85 **EXCITABLE** *Island IS 201* 12 13
23 Nov 85 **DON'T YOU JUST KNOW IT** *Island IS 233* 15 11
15 Mar 86 **THE THINGS THE LONELY DO** *Island IS 267* 43 6
31 May 86 ● **TOO GOOD TO BE FORGOTTEN** *Island IS 284* 5 13
13 Sep 86 **MONTEGO BAY** *Island IS 293* 16 9
10 Oct 87 **MONY MONY** *EMI EM 32* 38 5
6 Dec 88 AMAZULU *Island ILPS 9851* 97 1

AMBASSADOR *Holland, male DJ / producer*

12 Feb 00 **ONE OF THESE DAYS** *Platipus PLATCD 69* 67 1

AMBASSADORS OF FUNK featuring MC MARIO

UK, male DJ – Simon Harris and male rapper – Einstein

31 Oct 92 ● **SUPERMARIOLAND** *Living Beat SMASH 23* 8 8

AMBER *Holland, female vocalist – Marie Cremers*

24 Jun 00 **SEXUAL** *Substance SUBS 2CDS* 34 2

AMBULANCE LTD NEW

US, male vocal / instrumental group (2 Singles: 2 Weeks)

12 Mar 05 **STAY WHERE YOU ARE** *TVT TVTUKCD 5* 67 1
25 Jun 05 **PRIMITVE (THE WAY I TREAT YOU)** *TVT TVTUKCD 10* 72 1

AMEN *US, male vocal / instrumental group (3 Singles: 3 Weeks)*

17 Feb 01 **TOO HARD TO BE FREE** *Virgin VUSCD 191* 72 1
21 Jul 01 **THE WAITING 18** *Virgin VUSCD 207* 61 1
3 Apr 04 **CALIFORNIA'S BLEEDING** *Columbia 6746162* 52 1

AMEN CORNER (see also FAIR WEATHER)

UK, male vocal (Andy Fairweather-Low) / instrumental group (2 Albums: 8 Weeks, 7 Singles: 67 Weeks)

26 Jul 67 **GIN HOUSE BLUES** *Deram DM 136* 12 10
11 Oct 67 **THE WORLD OF BROKEN HEARTS** *Deram DM 151* 24 6

21 August 1953	28 August 1953	4 September 1953	11 September 1953
I BELIEVE Frankie Laine	**I BELIEVE** Frankie Laine	**I BELIEVE** Frankie Laine	**LOOK AT THAT GIRL** Guy Mitchell

KEY
UK No.1 ★ UK Top 10 ● Still on chart + UK entry at No.1 ■
US No.1 ▲ UK million seller £ US million seller $
Singles re-entries are listed as (re), (2re), (3re)... which signifies that the hit re-entered the chart once, twice or three times...
Peak Position / Weeks

17 Jan 68 ● **BEND ME, SHAPE ME** *Deram DM 172* ... 3 12
30 Mar 68 **ROUND AMEN CORNER** *Deram SML 1021* ... 26 7
31 Jul 68 ● **HIGH IN THE SKY** *Deram DM 197* ... 6 13
29 Jan 69 ★ **(IF PARADISE IS) HALF AS NICE** *Immediate IM 073* ... 1 11
25 Jun 69 ● **HELLO SUZIE** *Immediate IM 081* ... 4 10
1 Nov 69 **THE NATIONAL WELSH COAST LIVE EXPLOSION COMPANY** *Immediate IMSP 023* ... 19 1
14 Feb 76 **(IF PARADISE IS) HALF AS NICE** (re-issue) *Immediate IMS 103* ... 34 5

AMEN! UK *UK, male / female vocal / production group (3 Singles: 8 Weeks)*

8 Feb 97 **PASSION** *Feverpitch CDFVR 1015* ... 15 4
28 Jun 97 **PEOPLE OF LOVE** *Feverpitch CDFVR 18* ... 36 2
6 Sep 03 **PASSION** *Positiva CDTIV 195* ... 40 2

AMERICA *US / UK, male vocal / instrumental trio (4 Albums: 22 Weeks, 3 Singles: 20 Weeks)*

18 Dec 71 ● **A HORSE WITH NO NAME (re)** *Warner Bros. K 16128* ▲ $ ... 3 13
22 Jan 72 **AMERICA** *Warner Bros. K 46093* ▲ ... 14 13
25 Nov 72 **VENTURA HIGHWAY** *Warner Bros. K 16219* ... 43 4
9 Dec 72 **HOMECOMING** *Warner Bros. K 46180* ... 21 5
10 Nov 73 **HAT TRICK** *Warner Bros. K 56016* ... 41 3
7 Feb 76 **HISTORY – AMERICA'S GREATEST HITS** *Warner Bros. K 56169* ... 60 1
6 Nov 82 **YOU CAN DO MAGIC** *Capitol CL 264* ... 59 3

The AMERICAN BREED *US, male vocal / instrumental group*

7 Feb 68 **BEND ME SHAPE ME** *Stateside SS 2078* $ ... 24 6

AMERICAN HEAD CHARGE *US, male vocal / instrumental group*

8 Jun 02 **JUST SO YOU KNOW** *Mercury 5829622* ... 52 1

AMERICAN HI-FI *US, male vocal / instrumental group (2 Singles: 4 Weeks)*

8 Sep 01 **FLAVOR OF THE WEAK** *Mercury 5886722* ... 31 3
26 Apr 03 **THE ART OF LOSING** *Mercury 0779152* ... 75 1

AMERICAN MUSIC CLUB *US, male vocal / instrumental group (2 Albums: 3 Weeks, 2 Singles: 4 Weeks)*

27 Mar 93 **MERCURY** *Virgin CDV 2708* ... 41 2
24 Apr 93 **JOHNNY MATHIS' FEET** *Virgin VSCDG 1445* ... 58 2
10 Sep 94 **WISH THE WORLD AWAY** *Virgin VSCDX 1512* ... 46 2
24 Sep 94 **SAN FRANCISCO** *Virgin CDV 2752* ... 72 1

AMERIE *US, female vocalist – Amerie Rogers (1 Album: 6 Weeks, 4 Singles: 25 Weeks)*

9 Nov 02 **WHY DON'T WE FALL IN LOVE** *Columbia 6732212* [1] ... 40 2
22 Feb 03 **PARADISE** *Def Jam 0637032* [2] ... 18 5
14 May 05 **TOUCH** *Columbia 5201662* ... 28 6
4 Jun 05 ● **1 THING** *Columbia 6759402* ... 4 14
3 Sep 05 **TOUCH** *Columbia 6760612* ... 19 4

[1] Amerie featuring Ludacris [2] LL Cool J featuring Amerie

The AMES BROTHERS *US, male vocal group*

4 Feb 55 ● **THE NAUGHTY LADY OF SHADY LANE** *HMV B 10800* $ ... 6 6

With Hugo Winterhalter and his Orchestra.

AMICI FOREVER *UK / South Africa / New Zealand, male / female vocal group*

27 Sep 03 **THE OPERA BAND** *Victor / Arista Assoc 828765822* ... 39 9

AMILLIONSONS *UK, male production trio and US, female vocalist*

24 Aug 02 **MISTI BLU** *London LONCD 468* ... 39 2

Includes vocal by Taka Boom.

AMIRA *US, female vocalist – Amira McNiel (3 Singles: 7 Weeks)*

13 Dec 97 **MY DESIRE** *VC VCRD 27* ... 51 1
8 Aug 98 **MY DESIRE** (re-mix) *VC Recordings VCRD 36* ... 46 2
10 Feb 01 **MY DESIRE** (2nd re-mix) *VC Recordings VCRD 71* ... 20 4

Cherie AMORE *France, female vocalist*

15 Apr 00 **I DON'T WANT NOBODY (TELLIN' ME WHAT TO DO)** *Eternal / WEA WEA 262CD* ... 33 2

Vanessa AMOROSI *Australia, female vocalist*

23 Sep 00 ● **ABSOLUTELY EVERYBODY** *Mercury 1582972* ... 7 10

AMORPHOUS ANDROGYNOUS (see also FUTURE SOUND OF LONDON) *UK, male instrumental / production duo – Brian Dougans and Gary Cobain*

17 Aug 02 **FSOL PRESENTS AMORPHOUS ANDROGYNOUS: THE ISNESS** *Artful FSOLCD 101* ... 68 1

Amorphous Androgynous is Future Sound Of London under a different name.

AMOS (see also Jeremy HEALY and AMOS) *UK, male vocalist / rapper / producer – Amos Pizzey (5 Singles: 12 Weeks)*

3 Sep 94 **ONLY SAW TODAY – INSTANT KARMA** *Positiva CDTIV 16* ... 48 2
25 Mar 95 **LET LOVE SHINE** *Positiva CDTIV 24* ... 31 2
7 Oct 95 **CHURCH OF FREEDOM** *Positiva CDTIV 38* ... 54 1
12 Oct 96 **STAMP!** *Positiva CDTIV 65* ... 11 5
31 May 97 **ARGENTINA** *Positiva CDTIV 74* ... 30 2

Tori AMOS *US, female vocalist / pianist – Myra Amos (9 Albums: 55 Weeks, 17 Singles: 66 Weeks)*

23 Nov 91 **SILENT ALL THESE YEARS** *East West YZ 618* ... 51 3
18 Jan 92 **LITTLE EARTHQUAKES** *East West 7567823582* ... 14 23
1 Feb 92 **CHINA** *East West YZ 7531* ... 51 2
21 Mar 92 **WINTER** *East West A 7504* ... 25 4
20 Jun 92 **CRUCIFY** *East West A 7479* ... 15 6
22 Aug 92 **SILENT ALL THESE YEARS** (re-issue) *East West A 7433* ... 26 4
22 Jan 94 ● **CORNFLAKE GIRL** *East West A 7281CD* ... 4 6
12 Feb 94 ★ **UNDER THE PINK** *East West 7567825672* ■ ... 1 13
19 Mar 94 ● **PRETTY GOOD YEAR** *East West A 7263CD* ... 7 4
28 May 94 **PAST THE MISSION** *East West YZ 7257CD* ... 31 3
15 Oct 94 **GOD** *East West A 7251CD* ... 44 2
13 Jan 96 **CAUGHT A LITE SNEEZE** *East West A 5524CD1* ... 20 3
3 Feb 96 ● **BOYS FOR PELE** *East West 7567828622* ... 2 6
23 Mar 96 **TALULA** *East West A 8512CD1* ... 22 2
3 Aug 96 **HEY JUPITER / PROFESSIONAL WIDOW** *East West A 5494CD* ... 20 9
9 Nov 96 **BLUE SKIES** *Perfecto PERF 130CD1* [1] ... 26 2
11 Jan 97 ★ **PROFESSIONAL WIDOW (IT'S GOT TO BE BIG)** (re-mix) *East West A 5450CD* ... 1 10
2 May 98 **SPARK** *Atlantic AT 0031CD* ... 16 3
16 May 98 ● **FROM THE CHOIRGIRL HOTEL** *Atlantic 7567830952* ... 6 5
2 Oct 99 **TO VENUS AND BACK** *Atlantic 7567832422* ... 22 2
13 Nov 99 **GLORY OF THE 80'S** *Atlantic AT 0077CD1* ... 46 1
29 Sep 01 **STRANGE LITTLE GIRLS** *Atlantic 7567834862* ... 16 2
26 Oct 02 **A SORTA FAIRYTALE** *Epic 6730432* ... 41 2
9 Nov 02 **SCARLET'S WALK** *Epic 5087829* ... 26 1
29 Nov 03 **TALES OF A LIBRARIAN** *Atlantic 7567932232* ... 74 1
5 Mar 05 **THE BEEKEEPER** *Epic 5194259* ... 24 2

[1] BT featuring Tori Amos

'Past the Mission' features guest vocals by Trent Reznor of Nine Inch Nails.

AMOURE *UK, male production duo – Rod Edwards and Nick Magnus*

27 May 00 **IS THAT YOUR FINAL ANSWER? (WHO WANTS TO BE A MILLIONAIRE – THE SINGLE)** *Celador MILLION 2* ... 33 2

AMP FIDDLER *US, male producer / instrumentalist – Joseph 'Amp' Fiddler (2 Singles: 2 Weeks)*

20 Mar 04 **I BELIEVE IN YOU** *Genuine GEN 022CD* ... 72 1
19 Jun 04 **DREAMIN'** *Genuine GEN 025CDM* ... 71 1

The AMPS *US, male / female vocal / instrumental group*

21 Oct 95 **TIPP CITY** *4AD BAD 5015CD* ... 61 1
11 Nov 95 **PACER** *4AD CAD 5016CD* ... 60 1

AMSTERDAM NEW

UK, male / female vocal / instrumental group (2 Singles: 2 Weeks)

5 Feb 05 **THE JOURNEY / STOP KNOCKING THE WALLS DOWN** *Beat Crazy BEAT 001CD* [1] 32 1
11 Jun 05 **DOES THIS TRAIN STOP ON MERSEYSIDE?** *Beat Crazy BEAT 002CD2* 53 1

[1] Amsterdam / Ricky

AN EMOTIONAL FISH *Ireland, male vocal / instrumental group*

23 Jun 90 **CELEBRATE** *East West YZ 489* 46 5
25 Aug 90 AN EMOTIONAL FISH *East West WX 359* 40 3

ANASTACIA (244 Top 500)

Unique, powerhouse vocalist who has sold more than 20 million albums world-wide but remains little known in her homeland, b. Anastacia Newkirk, 17 Sep 1975, Chicago, US. Her first three albums went triple-platinum in the UK (4 Albums: 161 Weeks, 13 Singles: 99 Weeks)

30 Sep 00 ● **I'M OUTTA LOVE** *Epic 6695782* 6 17
14 Oct 00 ● NOT THAT KIND *Epic 4974122* 2 65
3 Feb 01 **NOT THAT KIND (re)** *Epic 6707632* 11 8
2 Jun 01 **COWBOYS & KISSES** *Epic 6712622* 28 5
25 Aug 01 **MADE FOR LOVIN' YOU** *Epic 6717172* 27 3
1 Dec 01 **PAID MY DUES** *Epic 6721252* 14 9
8 Dec 01 ● FREAK OF NATURE *Epic 5047572* 4 42
6 Apr 02 **ONE DAY IN YOUR LIFE** *Epic 6724562* 11 9
21 Sep 02 **WHY'D YOU LIE TO ME (re)** *Epic 6731112* 25 5
7 Dec 02 **YOU'LL NEVER BE ALONE** *Epic 6733802* 31 3
3 Apr 04 ● **LEFT OUTSIDE ALONE** *Epic 6747482* 3 20
10 Apr 04 ★ ANASTACIA *Epic 5134717* ■ 1 47
14 Aug 04 ● **SICK AND TIRED** *Epic 6751092* 4 11
27 Nov 04 **WELCOME TO MY TRUTH** *Epic 6754922* 25 5
23 Apr 05 **HEAVY ON MY HEART** *Epic 6758402* 21 3
19 Nov 05 ● PIECES OF A DREAM *Epic 82876731962* ....6 7+
3 Dec 05 **PIECES OF A DREAM** *Epic 82876738082* 48 1

AND WHY NOT?

UK, male vocal / instrumental group (1 Album: 3 Weeks, 3 Singles: 18 Weeks)

14 Oct 89 **RESTLESS DAYS (SHE SCREAMS OUT LOUD)** *Island IS 426* 38 7
13 Jan 90 **THE FACE** *Island IS 444* 13 8
10 Mar 90 MOVE YOUR SKIN *Island ILPS 9935* 24 3
21 Apr 90 **SOMETHING YOU GOT** *Island IS 452* 39 3

... AND YOU WILL KNOW US BY THE TRAIL OF DEAD

US, male vocal / instrumental group (1 Album: 1 Week, 2 Singles: 2 Weeks)

11 Nov 00 **MISTAKES AND REGRETS** *Domino RUG 114CD* 69 1
16 Mar 02 SOURCE TAGS AND CODES *Interscope 4932492* 73 1
11 May 02 **ANOTHER MORNING STONER** *Interscope / Polydor 4977162* ...54 1

Angry ANDERSON *Australia, male vocalist – Gary Anderson*

19 Nov 88 ● **SUDDENLY (THE WEDDING THEME FROM NEIGHBOURS)** *Food For Thought YUM 113* 3 13

Carl ANDERSON *US, male vocalist*

8 Jun 85 **BUTTERCUP** *Streetwave KHAN 45* 49 4

Carleen ANDERSON (see also The BRAND NEW HEAVIES; Paul WELLER) *US, female vocalist (3 Albums: 7 Weeks, 6 Singles: 17 Weeks)*

13 Nov 93 DUSKY SAPPHO (EP) *Circa YRCDG 108* 38 1
12 Feb 94 **NERVOUS BREAKDOWN** *Circa YRCDG 112* 27 4
28 May 94 **MAMA SAID** *Circa YRCD 114* 26 4
18 Jun 94 TRUE SPIRIT *Circa CIRCDX 30* 12 4
13 Aug 94 **TRUE SPIRIT** *Circa YRCD 118* 24 3
14 Jan 95 **LET IT LAST** *Circa YRCD 119* 16 3
7 Feb 98 **MAYBE I'M AMAZED** *Circa YRCD 128* 24 2
25 Apr 98 **WOMAN IN ME** *Circa YRCD 129* 74 1
2 May 98 BLESSED BURDEN *Circa CIRCD 35* 51 2

Ian ANDERSON (see also JETHRO TULL) *UK, male vocalist / flute*

26 Nov 83 WALK INTO LIGHT *Chrysalis CDL 1443* 78 1

John ANDERSON BIG BAND *UK, big band*

21 Dec 85 **GLENN MILLER MEDLEY (re)** *Modern GLEN 1* 61 5

Glenn Miller Medley comprises the following tracks: In the Mood / American Patrol / Little Brown Jug / Pennsylvania 65000.

John ANDERSON ORCHESTRA

Ireland, orchestra

25 Nov 95 PAN PIPES – ROMANCE OF IRELAND *MCA MCD 60004* 56 5

Jon ANDERSON (see also ANDERSON BRUFORD WAKEMAN HOWE; JON and VANGELIS; YES) *UK, male vocalist (3 Albums: 19 Weeks)*

24 Jul 76 ● OLIAS OF SUNHILLOW *Atlantic K 50261* 8 10
15 Nov 80 SONG OF SEVEN *Atlantic K 50756* 38 3
5 Jun 82 ANIMATION *Polydor POLD 5044* 43 6

Laurie ANDERSON *US, female vocalist / multi-instrumentalist (2 Albums: 8 Weeks, 1 Single: 6 Weeks)*

17 Oct 81 ● **O SUPERMAN** *Warner Bros. K 17870* 2 6
1 May 82 BIG SCIENCE *Warner Bros. K 57002* 29 6
10 Mar 84 MISTER HEARTBREAK *Warner Bros. 9250771* 93 2

LC ANDERSON vs PSYCHO RADIO

UK, male vocalist and Italy, male production duo

26 Jul 03 **RIGHT STUFF** *Faith & Hope FHCD 039* 45 2

Leroy ANDERSON and his POP CONCERT ORCHESTRA

US, orchestra – leader b. 29 Jun 1908, d. 18 May 1975

28 Jun 57 **FORGOTTEN DREAMS (2re)** *Brunswick 05485* 24 4

Lynn ANDERSON *US, female vocalist*

20 Feb 71 ● **ROSE GARDEN** *CBS 5360* $ 3 20
17 Apr 71 ROSE GARDEN *CBS 64333* 45 1

Moira ANDERSON

UK, female vocalist (2 Albums: 6 Weeks, 1 Single: 2 Weeks)

27 Dec 69 **THE HOLY CITY** *Decca F 12989* 43 2
20 Jun 70 THESE ARE MY SONGS *Decca SKL 5016* 50 1
5 Dec 81 GOLDEN MEMORIES *Warwick WW 5107* [1] 46 5

[1] Harry Secombe and Moira Anderson

Sunshine ANDERSON

US, female vocalist (1 Album: 6 Weeks, 2 Singles: 8 Weeks)

26 May 01 YOUR WOMAN *Atlantic 7567930112* 39 6
2 Jun 01 ● **HEARD IT ALL BEFORE** *Atlantic AT 0100CD* 9 7
22 Sep 01 **LUNCH OR DINNER** *Atlantic AT 0109CD* 57 1

ANDERSON BRUFORD WAKEMAN HOWE (see also Jon ANDERSON; Steve HOWE; Rick WAKEMAN; YES) *UK, male vocal / instrumental group*

24 Jun 89 **BROTHER OF MINE** *Arista 112379* 63 2
8 Jul 89 ANDERSON BRUFORD WAKEMAN HOWE *Arista 209970* 14 6

Peter ANDRE

UK, male vocalist – Peter Andrea (3 Albums: 28 Weeks, 15 Singles: 106 Weeks)

10 Jun 95 **TURN IT UP** *Mushroom D 1000* 64 1
16 Sep 95 **MYSTERIOUS GIRL** *Mushroom D 11921* 53 2
16 Mar 96 **ONLY ONE (re)** *Mushroom D 1307* 16 4
1 Jun 96 ● **MYSTERIOUS GIRL** (re-issue) *Mushroom D 2000* [1] 2 18
14 Sep 96 ★ **FLAVA** *Mushroom D 2003* ■ 1 9
12 Oct 96 ★ NATURAL *Mushroom D 2005* ■ 1 23
7 Dec 96 ★ **I FEEL YOU (2re)** *Mushroom D 1521* ■ 1 11
8 Mar 97 ● **NATURAL (2re)** *Mushroom DX 1577* 6 11
9 Aug 97 ● **ALL ABOUT US (re)** *Mushroom MUSH 5CD* 3 9
8 Nov 97 ● **LONELY (re)** *Mushroom MUSH 16CD* 6 9
29 Nov 97 TIME *Mushroom MUSH 18CD* 28 4
24 Jan 98 **ALL NIGHT ALL RIGHT** *Mushroom MUSH 21CD* [2] 16 4
25 Jul 98 ● **KISS THE GIRL** *Mushroom MUSH 34CDSX* 9 5
6 Mar 04 ★ **MYSTERIOUS GIRL** (2nd re-issue) *A&E PA 01CD* ■ 1 11
12 Jun 04 ● **INSANIA (re)** *East West PA 0002CD* 3 7
19 Jun 04 THE LONG ROAD BACK *East West 5046738102* 44 1
18 Sep 04 **THE RIGHT WAY** *Atlantic ATUK 001CD* 14 5

[1] Peter Andre featuring Bubbler Ranx [2] Peter Andre featuring Warren G

KEY
UK No.1 ★ UK Top 10 ● Still on chart + UK entry at No.1 ■
US No.1 ▲ UK million seller £ US million seller $
Singles re-entries are listed as (re), (2re), (3re)… which signifies that the hit re-entered the chart once, twice or three times…
Peak Position / Weeks

Chris ANDREWS *UK, male vocalist (5 Singles: 36 Weeks)*

7 Oct 65 ● **YESTERDAY MAN** *Decca F 12236*.....3 15
2 Dec 65 **TO WHOM IT CONCERNS** *Decca F 22285*.....13 10
14 Apr 66 **SOMETHING ON MY MIND (re)** *Decca F 22365*.....41 3
2 Jun 66 **WHAT'CHA GONNA DO NOW?** *Decca F 22404*.....40 4
25 Aug 66 **STOP THAT GIRL** *Decca F 22472*.....36 4

Eamonn ANDREWS
Ireland, male vocalist / TV presenter, b. 19 Dec 1922, d. 5 Nov 1987

20 Jan 56 **THE SHIFTING WHISPERING SANDS (PARTS 1 & 2)** *Parlophone R 4106*.....18 3

Hit is credited: 'with Ron Goodwin and his Orchestra and Chorus'.

Julie ANDREWS *UK, female vocalist / actor – Julia Wells*

16 Jul 83 LOVE ME TENDER *Peach River JULIE 1*.....63 5

Michael ANDREWS featuring Gary JULES
US, male producer and male vocalist

27 Dec 03 ★ **MAD WORLD** *Adventures in Music / Sanctuary SANXD 250* ■.....1 15

The ANDROIDS *Australia, male vocal / instrumental group*

17 May 03 **DO IT WITH MADONNA** *Universal MCSTD 40321*.....15 5

ANEKA *UK, female vocalist – Mary Sandeman (2 Singles: 16 Weeks)*

8 Aug 81 ★ **JAPANESE BOY** *Hansa HANSA 5*.....1 12
7 Nov 81 **LITTLE LADY** *Hansa HANSA 8*.....50 4

Dave ANGEL *UK, male DJ / producer – Dave Gooden*

2 Aug 97 **TOKYO STEALTH FIGHTER** *Fourth & Broadway BRCD 355*.....58 1

Simone ANGEL *Holland, female vocalist*

13 Nov 93 **LET THIS FEELING** *A&M 5803652*.....60 1

ANGEL CITY (see also NIGHTBREED) *Holland, male production duo – Aldwin Oomen and Hugo Zentveld (1 Album: 2 Weeks, 4 Singles: 23 Weeks)*

8 Nov 03 **LOVE ME RIGHT (OH SHEILA) (re)** *Data DATA 59CDS* [1].....11 8
3 Jul 04 **TOUCH ME** *Data DATA 73CDS*.....18 4
16 Oct 04 ● **DO YOU KNOW (I GO CRAZY)** *Data DATA 76CDS*.....8 7
26 Feb 05 ● **SUNRISE** *Data DATA 84CDS*.....9 4
12 Mar 05 LOVE ME RIGHT *Data DATACD 5X*.....44 2

[1] Angel City featuring Lara McAllen

Lara McAllen is the uncredited vocalist on the last three singles.

The ANGELETTES *UK, female vocal group*

13 May 72 **DON'T LET HIM TOUCH YOU** *Decca F 13284*.....35 5

ANGELHEART
UK, female DJ / producer – Angel Johnson (2 Singles: 2 Weeks)

6 Apr 96 **COME BACK TO ME** *Hi-Life 5776312* [1].....68 1
22 Mar 97 **I'M STILL WAITING** *Hi-Life 5735452* [2].....74 1

[1] Angelheart featuring Rochelle Harris [2] Angelheart featuring Aletia Bourne

ANGELIC (see also CITIZEN CANED; DT8 PROJECT; ORION; Jurgen VRIES) *UK, male / female production / vocal duo – Amanda O'Riordan and Darren Tate (3 Singles: 16 Weeks)*

17 Jun 00 **IT'S MY TURN** *Serious MCSTD 40235*.....11 10
24 Feb 01 **CAN'T KEEP ME SILENT** *Serious SERR 023CD*.....12 4
10 Nov 01 **STAY WITH ME** *Serious SERR 35CD*.....36 2

ANGELIC UPSTARTS *UK, male vocal / instrumental group (4 Albums: 20 Weeks, 7 Singles: 30 Weeks)*

21 Apr 79 **I'M AN UPSTART** *Warner Bros. K 17354*.....31 8
11 Aug 79 **TEENAGE WARNING** *Warner Bros. K 17426*.....29 6
18 Aug 79 TEENAGE WARNING *Warner Bros. K 50634*.....25 7
3 Nov 79 **NEVER 'AD NOTHIN'** *Warner Bros. K 17476*.....52 4
9 Feb 80 **OUT OF CONTROL** *Warner Bros. K 17558*.....58 3
22 Mar 80 **WE GOTTA GET OUT OF THIS PLACE** *Warner Bros. K 17576*.....65 2
12 Apr 80 WE'VE GOTTA GET OUT OF THIS PLACE *Warner Bros. K 56806*.....54 3
2 Aug 80 **LAST NIGHT ANOTHER SOLDIER** *Zonophone Z 7*.....51 4
7 Feb 81 **KIDS ON THE STREET** *Zonophone Z 16*.....57 3
7 Jun 81 2,000,000 VOICES *Zonophone ZONO 104*.....32 3
26 Sep 81 ANGELIC UPSTARTS *Zonophone ZEM 102*.....27 7

ANGELLE
UK, female vocalist – Sarah Davies

17 Aug 02 **JOY AND PAIN** *Innovation CDINNOV 1*.....43 1

Bobby ANGELO and The TUXEDOS
UK, male vocal / instrumental group

10 Aug 61 **BABY SITTIN'** *HMV POP 892*.....30 6

The ANGELS *US, female vocal trio*

3 Oct 63 **MY BOYFRIEND'S BACK** *Mercury AMT 1211* ▲ $.....50 1

ANGELS REVERSE *Germany, male production duo*

31 Aug 02 **DON'T CARE** *Inferno CDFERN 46*.....71 1

ANGELWITCH *UK, male vocal / instrumental group*

7 Jun 80 **SWEET DANGER** *EMI 5064*.....75 1

ANIMAL (see also The MUPPETS)
US, male puppet vocalist / drums

23 Jul 94 **WIPE OUT** *BMG Kidz 74321219532*.....38 3

ANIMAL NIGHTLIFE *UK, male / female vocal / instrumental group (1 Album: 6 Weeks, 4 Singles: 22 Weeks)*

13 Aug 83 **NATIVE BOY (UPTOWN)** *Innervision A3584*.....60 3
18 Aug 84 **MR. SOLITAIRE** *Island IS 193*.....25 12
6 Jul 85 **LOVE IS JUST THE GREAT PRETENDER** *Island IS 200*.....28 6
24 Aug 85 SHANGRI-LA *Island ILPS 9830*.....36 6
5 Oct 85 **PREACHER, PREACHER** *Island IS 245*.....67 1

ANIMALHOUSE *UK, male vocal / instrumental group*

15 Jul 00 **READY TO RECEIVE** *Boilerhouse / Arista 74321771072*.....61 1

The ANIMALS (287 Top 500)
Ground-breaking Newcastle band: Eric Burdon (v), Alan Price (k), Brian 'Chas' Chandler (b) (d. 1996), Hilton Valentine (g), John Steel (d). They were the first hit act produced by Mickie Most, who reportedly helped them to record 'The House of the Rising Sun' in 15 minutes at a cost of £1 10 shillings. After The Tornados and The Beatles, they were the third UK group to top the US singles chart (5 Albums: 86 Weeks, 16 Singles: 146 Weeks)

16 Apr 64 **BABY LET ME TAKE YOU HOME** *Columbia DB 7247*.....21 8
25 Jun 64 ★ **THE HOUSE OF THE RISING SUN** *Columbia DB 7301* ▲ $.....1 12
17 Sep 64 ● **I'M CRYING** *Columbia DB 7354*.....8 10
14 Nov 64 ● THE ANIMALS *Columbia 33SX 1669*.....6 20
4 Feb 65 ● **DON'T LET ME BE MISUNDERSTOOD** *Columbia DB 7445*.....3 9
8 Apr 65 ● **BRING IT ON HOME TO ME** *Columbia DB 7539*.....7 11
22 May 65 ● ANIMAL TRACKS *Columbia 33SX 1708*.....6 26
15 Jul 65 ● **WE'VE GOTTA GET OUT OF THIS PLACE** *Columbia DB 7639*.....2 12
28 Oct 65 ● **IT'S MY LIFE** *Columbia DB 7741*.....7 11
17 Feb 66 **INSIDE – LOOKING OUT** *Decca F 12332*.....12 8
16 Apr 66 ● THE MOST OF THE ANIMALS *Columbia 33SX 6035*.....4 20
28 May 66 ● ANIMALISMS *Decca LK 4797*.....4 17
2 Jun 66 ● **DON'T BRING ME DOWN** *Decca F 12407*.....6 8
27 Oct 66 **HELP ME GIRL** *Decca F 12502* [1].....14 9
15 Jun 67 **WHEN I WAS YOUNG** *MGM 1340* [2].....45 3
6 Sep 67 **GOOD TIMES** *MGM 1344* [2].....20 11
18 Oct 67 ● **SAN FRANCISCAN NIGHTS** *MGM 1359* [2].....7 10
14 Feb 68 **SKY PILOT** *MGM 1373* [2].....40 3
15 Jan 69 **RING OF FIRE** *MGM 1461* [2].....35 5

25 Sep 71 THE MOST OF THE ANIMALS (re-issue) *MFP 5218* 18 3
7 Oct 72 **THE HOUSE OF THE RISING SUN (re)** (re-issue) *RAK RR 1* 11 16

[1] Eric Burdon and session musicians billed as The Animals [2] Eric Burdon and The Animals

'The House of the Rising Sun' (re-issue) peaked at No.11 as a re-entry in 1982.

ANIMOTION
US / UK, male / female vocal (Astrid Plane) / instrumental group

11 May 85 ● **OBSESSION** *Mercury PH 34* 5 12

Paul ANKA
Canada, male vocalist (1 Album: 4 Weeks, 15 Singles: 134 Weeks)

9 Aug 57 ★ **DIANA** *Columbia DB 3980* ▲ £ $ 1 25
8 Nov 57 ● **I LOVE YOU, BABY** *Columbia DB 4022* 3 15
8 Nov 57 **TELL ME THAT YOU LOVE ME** *Columbia DB 4022* 25 2
31 Jan 58 ● **YOU ARE MY DESTINY** *Columbia DB 4063* 6 13
30 May 58 **CRAZY LOVE** *Columbia DB 4110* 26 1
26 Sep 58 **MIDNIGHT** *Columbia DB 4172* 26 1
30 Jan 59 ● **(ALL OF A SUDDEN) MY HEART SINGS** *Columbia DB 4241* 10 13
10 Jul 59 ● **LONELY BOY** *Columbia DB 4324* ▲ $ 3 17
30 Oct 59 ● **PUT YOUR HEAD ON MY SHOULDER** *Columbia DB 4355* 7 12
26 Feb 60 **IT'S TIME TO CRY (re)** *Columbia DB 4390* 28 2
31 Mar 60 **PUPPY LOVE (re)** *Columbia DB 4434* $ 33 7
15 Sep 60 **HELLO YOUNG LOVERS** *Columbia DB 4504* 44 1
15 Mar 62 **LOVE ME WARM AND TENDER** *RCA 1276* 19 11
26 Jul 62 **A STEEL GUITAR AND A GLASS OF WINE** *RCA 1292* 41 4
28 Sep 74 ● **(YOU'RE) HAVING MY BABY** *United Artists UP 35713* [1] ▲ $ 6 10
15 Oct 05 ● ROCK SWINGS *Globe Records 9885933* 9 4

[1] Paul Anka featuring Odia Coates

Ana ANN *UK, female vocalist – Ana Petrovic (2 Singles: 3 Weeks)*

23 Feb 02 **RIDE** *LL RIDELLR 100* 24 2
6 Mar 04 **CHILDREN OF THE WORLD** *Century Vista LLR 104* [1] 44 1

[1] Ana Ann & the London Community Choir

ANNIE
Norway, female vocalist – Annie Lilia Berge Strand (2 Singles: 4 Weeks)

25 Sep 04 **CHEWING GUM** *679 Recordings 679L 075CD1* 25 3
12 Mar 05 **HEARTBEAT** *679 Recordings 679L 091CD2* 50 1

ANNIHILATOR *Canada, male vocal / instrumental group*

11 Aug 90 NEVER NEVERLAND *Roadrunner RR 93741* 48 1

ANOTHER LEVEL
UK, male vocal group (2 Albums: 40 Weeks, 8 Singles: 81 Weeks)

28 Feb 98 ● **BE ALONE NO MORE** *Northwestside 74321551982* 6 9
18 Jul 98 ★ **FREAK ME** *Northwestside 74321582362* ■ 1 12
7 Nov 98 ● **GUESS I WAS A FOOL** *Northwestside 74321621202* 5 13
21 Nov 98 ANOTHER LEVEL *Northwestside 74321582412* 13 25
23 Jan 99 ● **I WANT YOU FOR MYSELF** *Northwestside 7432164632* [1] 2 8
10 Apr 99 **BE ALONE NO MORE** *Northwestside 74321658472* [2] 11 9
12 Jun 99 ● **FROM THE HEART (re)** *Northwestside 74321673012* 6 11
4 Sep 99 ● **SUMMERTIME** *Northwestside 74321694672* [3] 7 7
25 Sep 99 ● NEXUS … *Northwestside 74321694572* 7 15
13 Nov 99 ● **BOMB DIGGY** *Northwestside 74321712212* 6 12

[1] Another Level / Ghostface Killah [2] Another Level featuring Jay-Z [3] Another Level featuring TQ

ANOTHERSIDE (see also HONEYZ)
UK, female duo – Alani Gibbon and Celena Cherry

5 Jul 03 **THIS IS YOUR NIGHT** *V2 / J-Did JAD 5023293* 41 1

Adam ANT (see also ADAM and The ANTS)
Innovative and flamboyant pop idol, b. Stuart Goddard, 3 Nov 1954, London. He left Adam and The Ants at their peak, immediately topped the UK chart and scored his first ever US hit. He later made his mark as an actor (6 Albums: 39 Weeks, 11 Singles: 69 Weeks)

22 May 82 ★ **GOODY TWO SHOES** *CBS A 2367* 1 11
18 Sep 82 ● **FRIEND OR FOE** *CBS A 2736* 9 8
23 Oct 82 ● FRIEND OR FOE *CBS 25040* 5 12
27 Nov 82 **DESPERATE BUT NOT SERIOUS** *CBS A 2892* 33 7
29 Oct 83 ● **PUSS 'N BOOTS** *CBS A 3614* 5 11
19 Nov 83 STRIP *CBS 25705* 20 8
10 Dec 83 **STRIP** *CBS A 3589* 41 6
22 Sep 84 **APOLLO 9** *CBS A 4719* 13 8
13 Jul 85 **VIVE LE ROCK** *CBS A 6367* 50 4
14 Sep 85 VIVE LE ROCK *CBS 26583* 42 3
17 Feb 90 **ROOM AT THE TOP** *MCA MCA 1387* 13 7
24 Mar 90 MANNERS AND PHYSIQUE *MCA MCG 6068* 19 3
28 Apr 90 **CANT SET RULES ABOUT LOVE** *MCA MCA 1404* 47 2
28 Aug 93 ● ANTMUSIC – THE VERY BEST OF ADAM ANT *Arcade ARC 3100052* 6 11
11 Feb 95 **WONDERFUL** *EMI CDEMS 366* 32 3
15 Apr 95 WONDERFUL *EMI CDEMC 3687* 24 2
3 Jun 95 **GOTTA BE A SIN** *EMI CDEMS 379* 48 2

ANT & DEC *UK, male actors / TV presenters / vocal duo – Anthony McPartlin and Declan Donnelly (aka PJ & Duncan) (3 Albums: 31 Weeks, 15 Singles: 92 Weeks)*

18 Dec 93 **TONIGHT I'M FREE** *Telstar CDSTAS 2706* [1] 62 3
23 Apr 94 **WHY ME** *Telstar CDSTAS 2719* [1] 27 4
23 Jul 94 ● **LET'S GET READY TO RHUMBLE** *XSrhythm CDANT 1* [1] 9 11
8 Oct 94 **IF I GIVE YOU MY NUMBER** *XSrhythm CDANT 2* [1] 15 7
19 Nov 94 ● PSYCHE – THE ALBUM *XSrhythm TCD 2746* [1] 5 20
3 Dec 94 **ETERNAL LOVE** *XSrhythm CDANT 3* [1] 12 9
25 Feb 95 **OUR RADIO ROCKS** *XSrhythm CDANT 4* [1] 15 5
29 Jul 95 **STUCK ON U** *XSrhythm CDANT 5* [1] 12 5
14 Oct 95 **U KRAZY KATZ** *XSrhythm CDANT 6* [1] 15 4
18 Nov 95 TOP KATZ – THE ALBUM *XSrhythm TCD 2793* [1] 46 8
2 Dec 95 **PERFECT** *Telstar CDANT 7* [1] 16 7
20 Mar 96 **STEPPING STONE** *Telstar CDANT 8* [1] 11 5
24 Aug 96 ● **BETTER WATCH OUT** *Telstar CDANT 9* 10 4
23 Nov 96 **WHEN I FALL IN LOVE** *Telstar CDANT 10* 12 8
15 Mar 97 ● **SHOUT** *Telstar CDDEC 11* 10 5
10 May 97 **FALLING** *Telstar CDDEC 12* 14 4
24 May 97 THE CULT OF ANT & DEC *Telstar TCD 2887* 15 3
8 Jun 02 ● **WE'RE ON THE BALL** *Columbia 6727312* 3 11

[1] PJ & Duncan [1] PJ & Duncan

ANTARCTICA
Australia, male producer – Steve Gibbs (2 Singles: 2 Weeks)

29 Jan 00 **RETURN TO REALITY** *React CDREACT 173* 53 1
8 Jul 00 **ADRIFT (CAST YOUR MIND)** *React CDREACT 172* 72 1

Billie ANTHONY *UK, female vocalist – Philomena Brown, b. 1933, d. 1991*

15 Oct 54 ● **THIS OLE HOUSE** *Columbia DB 3519* 4 16

Hit credits Eric Jupp and his Orchestra.

Marc ANTHONY (see also Louie VEGA)
US, male vocalist – Marco Antonio Muniz

13 Nov 99 **I NEED TO KNOW** *Columbia 6683612* 28 3

Miki ANTHONY *UK, male vocalist*

3 Feb 73 **IF IT WASN'T FOR THE REASON THAT I LOVE YOU** *Bell 1275* 27 7

Ray ANTHONY & his ORCHESTRA *US, orchestra – leader Ray Antonini*

4 Dec 53 ● **DRAGNET (re)** *Capitol CL 13983* 7 2

Richard ANTHONY
France, male vocalist – Richard Anthony Bush (2 Singles: 15 Weeks)

12 Dec 63 **WALKING ALONE** *Columbia DB 7133* 37 5
2 Apr 64 **IF I LOVED YOU (re)** *Columbia DB 7235* 18 10

ANTHRAX *US, male vocal / instrumental group*
(6 Albums: 23 Weeks, 10 Singles: 37 Weeks)

28 Feb 87 **I AM THE LAW** *Island IS LAW 1* 32 5
18 Apr 87 AMONG THE LIVING *Island ILPS 9865* 18 5
27 Jun 87 **INDIANS** *Island IS 325* 44 4
5 Dec 87 **I'M THE MAN** *Island IS 338* 20 6
10 Sep 88 **MAKE ME LAUGH** *Island IS 379* 26 3

11 December 1953	18 December 1953	25 December 1953	1 January 1954
ANSWER ME / ANSWER ME Frankie Laine / David Whitfield (tied at No.1)	ANSWER ME Frankie Laine	ANSWER ME Frankie Laine	ANSWER ME Frankie Laine

KEY
UK No.1 ★ UK Top 10 ● Still on chart + UK entry at No.1 ■
US No.1 ▲ UK million seller £ US million seller $
Singles re-entries are listed as (re), (2re), (3re)… which signifies that the hit re-entered the chart once, twice or three times…
Peak Position / Weeks

Date	Title / Label	Peak	Weeks
24 Sep 88	STATE OF EUPHORIA *Island ILPS 9916*	12	4
18 Mar 89	ANTI-SOCIAL *Island IS 409*	44	3
1 Sep 90	IN MY WORLD *Island IS 470*	29	2
8 Sep 90	PERSISTENCE OF TIME *Island ILPS 9967*	13	5
5 Jan 91	GOT THE TIME *Island IS 476*	16	4
6 Jul 91	BRING THE NOISE *Island IS 490* [1]	14	5
20 Jul 91	ATTACK OF THE KILLER B'S *Island ILPS 9980*	13	5
8 May 93	ONLY *Elektra EKR 166CD*	36	3
29 May 93	SOUND OF WHITE NOISE *Elektra 7559614302*	14	3
11 Sep 93	BLACK LODGE *Elektra EKR 171CD*	53	2
1 Aug 98	VOLUME 8 – THE THREAT IS REAL! *Ignition IGN 740343*	73	1

[1] Anthrax featuring Chuck D

ANTI-NOWHERE LEAGUE *UK, male vocal / instrumental group (2 Albums: 12 Weeks, 3 Singles: 10 Weeks)*

Date	Title / Label	Peak	Weeks
23 Jan 82	STREETS OF LONDON *WXYZ ABCD 1*	48	5
20 Mar 82	I HATE … PEOPLE *WXYZ ABCD 2*	46	3
22 May 82	WE ARE … THE LEAGUE *WXYZ LMNOP 1*	24	11
3 Jul 82	WOMAN *WXYZ ABCD 4*	72	2
5 Nov 83	LIVE IN YUGOSLAVIA *I.D. NOSE 3*	88	1

ANTI-PASTI *UK, male vocal / instrumental group*

Date	Title / Label	Peak	Weeks
15 Aug 81	THE LAST CALL *Rondelet ABOUT 5*	31	7
5 Dec 81	DON'T LET 'EM GRIND YOU DOWN *Superville EXP 1003* [1]	70	1

[1] Exploited and Anti-Pasti

ANTICAPPELLA *Italy / UK, male / female vocal / instrumental group (5 Singles: 12 Weeks)*

Date	Title / Label	Peak	Weeks
16 Nov 91	THE SQUARE ROOT OF 231 *PWL Continental PWL 205*	24	4
18 Apr 92	EVERYDAY *PWL Continental PWL 220*	45	2
25 Jun 94	MOVE YOUR BODY *Media MCSTD 1980* [1]	21	3
1 Apr 95	EXPRESS YOUR FREEDOM *Media MCSTD 2048*	31	2
25 May 96	THE SQUARE ROOT OF 231 (re-mix) / MOVE YOUR BODY *Media MCSTD 40037*	54	1

[1] Anticappella featuring MC Fixx It

ANTONY & The JOHNSONS NEW *UK / US / Canada / Russia, male / female vocal / instrumental group – leader Antony Hegarty (1 Album: 5 Weeks, 2 Singles: 6 Weeks)*

Date	Title / Label	Peak	Weeks
28 May 05	HOPE THERE'S SOMEONE (re) *Rough Trade RTRADSCD 229*	44	3
17 Sep 05	I AM A BIRD NOW *Rough Trade RTRADCD 223*	16	5
3 Dec 05	YOU ARE MY SISTER *Rough Trade RTRADSCDX 276*	39	3

I Am a Bird Now was released in Feb 2005 but only charted after winning the 2005 Nationwide Mercury Prize.

APACHE INDIAN *UK, male vocalist – Steven Kapur (1 Album: 2 Weeks, 10 Singles: 33 Weeks)*

Date	Title / Label	Peak	Weeks
28 Nov 92	FE REAL *Ten TEN 416* [1]	33	3
2 Jan 93	ARRANGED MARRIAGE *Island CID 544*	16	6
6 Feb 93	NO RESERVATIONS *Island CID 8001*	36	2
27 Mar 93	CHOK THERE *Island CID 555*	30	4
14 Aug 93 ●	NUFF VIBES (EP) *Island CID 560*	5	10
22 Oct 93	MOVIN' ON *Island CID 580*	48	2
7 May 94	WRECKX SHOP *MCA MCSTD 1969* [2]	26	2
11 Feb 95	MAKE WAY FOR THE INDIAN *Island CID 586* [3]	29	2
22 Apr 95	RAGGAMUFFIN GIRL *Island CID 606* [4]	31	2
29 Mar 97	LOVIN' (LET ME LOVE YOU) *Coalition COLA 002CD*	53	1
18 Oct 97	REAL PEOPLE *Coalition COLA 019CD*	66	1

[1] Maxi Priest featuring Apache Indian [2] Wreckx-N-Effect featuring Apache Indian [3] Apache Indian and Tim Dog [4] Apache Indian with Frankie Paul

The listed flip side of 'Fe' Real' was 'Just Wanna Know' by Maxi Priest. Tracks on Nuff Vibes (EP): Boom Shack a Lak / Fun / Caste System / Warning.

APARTMENT NEW *UK, male vocal / instrumental group*

Date	Title / Label	Peak	Weeks
19 Feb 05	EVERYONE SAYS I'M PARANOID / JUNE JULY *Fierce Panda NING 160CD*	67	1

APHEX TWIN (see also AFX; POLYGON WINDOW; POWERPILL) *UK, male instrumentalist / producer – Richard James (6 Albums: 11 Weeks, 6 Singles: 12 Weeks)*

Date	Title / Label	Peak	Weeks
9 May 92	DIGERIDOO *R&S RSUK 12*	55	2
27 Nov 93	ON *Warp WAP 39CD*	32	3
19 Mar 94	SELECTED AMBIENT WORKS VOLUME II *Warp WARPCD 21*	11	3
11 Feb 95	CLASSICS *R&S RS 94035CD*	24	2
8 Apr 95	VENTOLIN *Warp WAP 60CD*	49	1
6 May 95	… I CARE BECAUSE YOU DO *Warp WARPCD 30*	24	2
26 Oct 96	GIRL / BOY (EP) *Warp WAP 78CD*	64	1
16 Nov 96	RICHARD D JAMES ALBUM *Warp WARPCD 43*	62	1
18 Oct 97	COME TO DADDY *Warp WAP 94CD*	36	2
3 Apr 99	WINDOWLICKER *Warp WAP 105CD*	16	3
3 Nov 01	DRUKQS *Warp WARPCD 2*	22	2
5 Apr 03	26 MIXES FOR CASH *Warp WARPCD 102*	63	1

Tracks on Girl / Boy (EP): Girl / Boy Song / Milkman / Inkey $ / Beatles Under My Carpet. The EP was incorrectly listed in the singles chart and, because of its length, should have been considered an album.

APHRODITE featuring WILDFLOWER (see also URBAN SHAKEDOWN) *UK, male producer (Gavin King) and female rapper / vocalist*

Date	Title / Label	Peak	Weeks
16 Nov 02	SEE THRU IT *V2 VVR 5020983*	68	1

APHRODITE'S CHILD *Greece, male vocal / instrumental group – includes Demis Roussos and Vangelis*

Date	Title / Label	Peak	Weeks
6 Nov 68	RAIN AND TEARS *Mercury MF 1039*	29	7

APOLLO FOUR FORTY *UK, male instrumental / production group (2 Albums: 4 Weeks, 12 Singles: 53 Weeks)*

Date	Title / Label	Peak	Weeks
22 Jan 94	ASTRAL AMERICA *Stealth Sonic SSXCD 2* [1]	36	2
5 Nov 94	LIQUID COOL *Stealth Sonic SSXCD 3* [1]	35	2
25 Mar 95	(DON'T FEAR) THE REAPER *Stealth Sonic SSXCD 4* [1]	35	2
27 Jul 96	KRUPA (re) *Stealth Sonic SSXCD 5*	23	8
15 Feb 97 ●	AIN'T TALKIN' 'BOUT DUB *Stealth Sonic SSXCDX 6*	7	7
15 Mar 97	ELECTRO GLIDE IN BLUE *Stealth Sonic SSX 2440CD*	62	1
5 Jul 97	RAW POWER *Stealth Sonic SSXCD 7*	32	3
11 Jul 98	RENDEZ-VOUS 98 *Epic 6661102* [2]	12	6
8 Aug 98 ●	LOST IN SPACE (THEME) *Stealth Sonic SSX 9CD*	4	9
28 Aug 99 ●	STOP THE ROCK *Epic SSX 10CD*	10	6
18 Sep 99	GETTIN' HIGH ON YOUR OWN SUPPLY *Epic SSX 3440CD*	20	3
27 Nov 99	HEART GO BOOM *Epic SSX 11CD*	57	1
9 Dec 00	CHARLIE'S ANGELS 2000 *Epic SSX 13CD*	29	6
21 Jun 03	DUDE DESCENDING A STAIRCASE *Stealth / SONY SSX 14CD* [3]	58	1

[1] Apollo 440 [2] Jean-Michel Jarre and Apollo 440 [3] Apollo 440 featuring The Beatnuts

APOLLO presents HOUSE OF VIRGINISM *Sweden, male instrumentalist and vocal / instrumental group*

Date	Title / Label	Peak	Weeks
17 Feb 96	EXCLUSIVE *Logic 74321324102*	67	1

APOLLO 2000 *UK, male instrumentalist / producer – Gordon Smith*

Date	Title / Label	Peak	Weeks
27 Apr 96	OUT OF THIS WORLD *Telstar TCD 2816*	43	3

Fiona APPLE *US, female vocalist – Fiona Apple Maggart*

Date	Title / Label	Peak	Weeks
26 Feb 00	FAST AS YOU CAN *Columbia 6689962*	33	2
11 Mar 00	WHEN THE PAWN HITS THE CONFLICTS HE THINKS LIKE A KING WHAT HE KNOWS THROWS THE BLOWS WHEN HE GOES TO THE FIGHT AND HE'LL WIN THE WHOLE THING 'FORE HE ENTERS THE RING THERE'S NOBODY TO BATTER WHEN YOUR MIND IS YOUR MIGHT SO WHEN YOU GO SOLO, YOU HOLD YOUR OWN HAND AND REMEMBER THAT DEPTH IS THE GREATEST OF HEIGHTS AND IF YOU KNOW WHERE YOU STAND, THEN YOU KNOW WHERE TO LAND, AND IF YOU FALL IT WON'T MATTER, CUZ YOU'LL KNOW THAT YOU'RE RIGHT *Columbia 4964282*	46	1

Album title frequently shortened to When the Pawn ….

Kim APPLEBY (see also MEL and KIM) *UK, female vocalist (1 Album: 13 Weeks, 7 Singles: 31 Weeks)*

Date	Title / Label	Peak	Weeks
3 Nov 90 ●	DON'T WORRY *Parlophone R 6272*	2	10

8 Dec 90		KIM APPLEBY *Parlophone PCS 7348*	23	13
9 Feb 91	●	**G.L.A.D.** *Parlophone R 6281*	**10**	6
29 Jun 91		**MAMA** *Parlophone R 6291*	**19**	8
19 Oct 91		**IF YOU CARED** *Parlophone R 6297*	**44**	3
31 Jul 93		**LIGHT OF THE WORLD** *Parlophone CDR 6352*	**41**	2
13 Nov 93		**BREAKAWAY** *Parlophone CDR 6362*	**56**	1
12 Nov 94		**FREE SPIRIT** *Parlophone CDR 6397*	**51**	1

The APPLEJACKS *UK, male / female vocal (Al Jackson) / instrumental group (3 Singles: 29 Weeks)*

5 Mar 64	●	**TELL ME WHEN** *Decca F 11833*	**7**	13
11 Jun 64		**LIKE DREAMERS DO** *Decca F 11916*	**20**	11
15 Oct 64		**THREE LITTLE WORDS (I LOVE YOU)** *Decca F 11981*	**23**	5

APPLES *UK, male vocal / instrumental group*

23 Mar 91		**EYE WONDER** *Epic 6566717*	**75**	1

APPLETON (see also ALL SAINTS) *Canada, female vocal duo – Nicole and Natalie Appleton (1 Album: 6 Weeks, 3 Singles: 22 Weeks)*

14 Sep 02	●	**FANTASY** *Polydor 5709842*	**2**	10
22 Feb 03	●	**DON'T WORRY** *Polydor 0658182*	**5**	10
8 Mar 03	●	EVERYTHING'S EVENTUAL *Polydor 0651992*	9	6
26 Jul 03		**EVERYTHING EVENTUALLY** *Polydor 9808278*	**38**	2

Charlie APPLEWHITE *US, male vocalist, b. 1933, d. 27 Apr 2001*

23 Sep 55		**BLUE STAR** *Brunswick 05416*	**20**	1

Hit credits Victor Young, his Orchestra and Chorus.

APRIL WINE *Canada, male vocal / instrumental group (2 Albums: 8 Weeks, 2 Singles: 9 Weeks)*

15 Mar 80		HARDER ... FASTER *Capitol EST 12013*	34	5
15 Mar 80		**I LIKE TO ROCK** *Capitol CL 16121*	**41**	5
24 Jan 81		THE NATURE OF THE BEAST *Capitol EST 12125*	48	3
11 Apr 81		**JUST BETWEEN YOU AND ME** *Capitol CL 16184*	**52**	4

AQUA *Denmark / Norway, male / female vocal / production group (2 Albums: 49 Weeks, 7 Singles: 85 Weeks)*

25 Oct 97	★	**BARBIE GIRL (re)** *Universal UMD 80413* £	**1**	26
15 Nov 97	●	AQUARIUM *Universal UMD 85020*	6	47
7 Feb 98	★	**DOCTOR JONES** *Universal UMD 80457* ■	**1**	14
16 May 98	★	**TURN BACK TIME** *Universal UMD 80490* ■	**1**	10
1 Aug 98	●	**MY OH MY (re)** *Universal UMD 85058*	**6**	11
26 Dec 98		**GOOD MORNING SUNSHINE** *Universal UMD 85086*	**18**	7
26 Feb 00	●	**CARTOON HEROES (re)** *Universal MCSTD 40226*	**7**	11
11 Mar 00		AQUARIUS *Universal 1538102*	24	2
10 Jun 00		**AROUND THE WORLD** *Universal MCSTD 40234*	**26**	6

AQUAGEN *Germany, male production duo – Olaf Dieckman and Gino Montesano (2 Singles: 11 Weeks)*

9 Dec 00	●	**PHATT BASS** *Nulife / Arista 74321817102* [1]	**9**	8
1 Mar 03		**HARD TO SAY I'M SORRY** *All Around the World CDGLOBE 265*	**33**	3

[1] Warp Brothers vs Aquagen

AQUALUNG *UK, male vocalist / instrumentalist / producer – Matt Hales (1 Album: 6 Weeks, 4 Singles: 10 Weeks)*

28 Sep 02	●	**STRANGE AND BEAUTIFUL (I'LL PUT A SPELL ON YOU)** *B-Unique BUN 032CDS*	**7**	6
12 Oct 02		AQUALUNG *B-Unique 5046606982*	15	6
14 Dec 02		**GOOD TIMES GONNA COME** *B-Unique BUN 043CDS*	**71**	1
25 Oct 03		**BRIGHTER THAN SUNSHINE** *B-Unique BUN 072CDS*	**37**	2
27 Mar 04		**EASIER TO LIE** *B-Unique WEA 373CD*	**60**	1

AQUANUTS *US / Argentina, male production / instrumental duo*

4 May 02		**DEEP SEA** *Data DATA 34T*	**74**	1

AQUARIAN DREAM *US, male / female vocal / instrumental group*

24 Feb 79		**YOU'RE A STAR** *Elektra LV 7*	**67**	1

ARAB STRAP *UK, male vocal / instrumental duo – Aiden Moffat and Malcolm Middleton (1 Album: 2 Weeks, 4 Singles: 4 Weeks)*

13 Sep 97		**THE GIRLS OF SUMMER (EP)** *Chemikal Underground CHEM 017CD*	**74**	1
4 Apr 98		**HERE WE GO / TRIPPY** *Chemikal Underground CHEM 20CD*	**48**	1
2 May 98		PHILOPHOBIA *Chemikal Underground CHEM 21CD*	37	2
10 Oct 98		**(AFTERNOON) SOAPS** *Chemikal Underground CHEM 27CD*	**74**	1
10 Feb 01		**LOVE DETECTIVE** *Chemikal Underground CHEM 049CD*	**66**	1

Tracks on The Girls of Summer (EP): Hey! Fever / Girls of Summer / The Beautiful Barmaids of Dundee / One Day After School.

ARCADE FIRE NEW *Canada, male / female vocal / instrumental group (1 Album: 9 Weeks, 5 Singles: 9 Weeks)*

12 Mar 05		FUNERAL *Rough Trade RTRADCD 219*	42	9
9 Apr 05		**NEIGHBOURHOOD #2 (LAIKA)** *Rough Trade RTRADSCD 225*	**30**	2
4 Jun 05		**NEIGHBOURHOOD #3 (POWER OUT)** *Rough Trade RTRADSCD 232*	**26**	2
13 Aug 05		**COLD WIND** *Rough Trade RTRADSCD 254*	**52**	1
17 Sep 05		**REBELLION (LIES)** *Rough Trade RTRADSCD 252*	**19**	2
26 Nov 05		**WAKE UP** *Rough Trade RTRADSCD 286*	**29**	2

ARCADIA (see also DURAN DURAN) *UK, male vocal / instrumental group (1 Album: 10 Weeks, 3 Singles: 13 Weeks)*

26 Oct 85	●	**ELECTION DAY** *Odeon NSR 1*	**7**	7
7 Dec 85		SO RED THE ROSE *Parlophone Odeon PCSD 101*	30	10
25 Jan 86		**THE PROMISE** *Odeon NSR 2*	**37**	4
26 Jul 86		**THE FLAME** *Odeon NSR 3*	**58**	2

Arcadia was a Duran Duran sideline band featuring Simon Le Bon, Nick Rhodes and Roger Taylor.

Tasmin ARCHER *UK, female vocalist (1 Album: 42 Weeks, 6 Singles: 37 Weeks)*

12 Sep 92	★	**SLEEPING SATELLITE (re)** *EMI EM 233*	**1**	17
31 Oct 92	●	GREAT EXPECTATIONS *EMI CDEMC 3624*	8	42
20 Feb 93		**IN YOUR CARE** *EMI CDEMS 260*	**16**	6
29 May 93		**LORDS OF THE NEW CHURCH** *EMI CDEM 266*	**26**	4
21 Aug 93		**ARIENNE** *EMI CDEM 275*	**30**	4
8 Jan 94		**SHIPBUILDING** *EMI CDEM 302*	**40**	4
23 Mar 96		**ONE MORE GOOD NIGHT WITH THE BOYS** *EMI CDEM 401*	**45**	2

The ARCHIES (see also The CUFF LINKS) *US, male / female cartoon vocal (Ron Dante) group*

11 Oct 69	★	**SUGAR, SUGAR** *RCA 1872* ▲ $	**1**	26

ARCHITECHS *UK, male production duo and female vocalist (2 Singles: 19 Weeks)*

7 Oct 00	●	**BODY GROOVE** *Go Beat / Polydor GOBCD 33* [1]	**3**	14
7 Apr 01		**SHOW ME THE MONEY (re)** *Go Beat GOBCD 38*	**20**	5

[1] Architechs featuring Nana

ARCTIC MONKEYS NEW *UK, male vocal / instrumental group*

29 Oct 05	★	**I BET YOU LOOK GOOD ON THE DANCEFLOOR** *Domino Recordings RUG 212CD* ■	**1**	10+

Jann ARDEN *Canada, female vocalist – Jann Arden Richards*

13 Jul 96		**INSENSITIVE** *A&M 5812652*	**40**	2

Tina ARENA *Australia, female vocalist – Philopina Arena (1 Album: 15 Weeks, 9 Singles: 33 Weeks)*

15 Apr 95	●	**CHAINS** *Columbia 6611255*	**6**	11
20 May 95		DON'T ASK *Columbia 4778862*	11	15
12 Aug 95		**HEAVEN HELP MY HEART** *Columbia 6620975*	**25**	5
2 Dec 95		**SHOW ME HEAVEN** *Columbia 6626975*	**29**	3
3 Aug 96		**SORRENTO MOON (I REMEMBER)** *Columbia 6635435*	**22**	4
27 Jun 98		**WHISTLE DOWN THE WIND** *Really Useful 5672192*	**24**	5
24 Oct 98		**IF I WAS A RIVER** *Columbia 6665605*	**43**	2
13 Mar 99		**BURN** *Columbia 6667442*	**47**	1
20 May 00		**LIVE FOR THE ONE I LOVE** *Columbia 6691332*	**63**	1
12 Apr 03		**NEVER (PAST TENSE)** *Illustrious CDILL 010* [1]	**42**	1

[1] ROC Project featuring Tina Arena

5 February 1954	12 February 1954	19 February 1954	26 February 1954
OH, MEIN PAPA Eddie Calvert	**OH, MEIN PAPA** Eddie Calvert	**OH, MEIN PAPA** Eddie Calvert	**OH, MEIN PAPA** Eddie Calvert

THE FIRST BRITISH No.1 ALBUM

On 20 July 1957, The Tommy Steele Story became the first LP by a British act to top the UK albums chart. It went on to spend four weeks at No.1 and 21 weeks in the top five.

British Hit Singles & Albums caught up with the pop music legend that is Tommy Steele in late 2005 to present him with an award to mark this milestone. Tommy was, in his words, "flabbergasted" by the award, as he had not realised that he held this record. He went on to explain the background to the album's release.

"Film producers Nat Cohen and Stuart Levy asked me to write some songs for a proposed film. After approving the songs they said, 'We now need a story to link them together.' After some thought my co-writers, Lionel Bart and Michael Pratt, and I decided that my own life story – about a kid who goes away to sea, learns guitar, entertains his shipmates, comes back to Britain, performs in coffee bars and becomes a star – would be ideal. So within just four months of first making the charts, I was filming my own life story."

Tommy's pop career, he admits, was most influenced by Hank Williams and, later, Buddy Holly, who Tommy saw performing in early 1956, in Virginia, when he was in the navy. "What I was playing at the time we called rock country. What I most definitely was not was a skiffle act. I remember a Royal Variety performance in front of the Royal Family when compère Bob Monkhouse introduced me as representing skiffle music – I could have punched him!"

The US country music scene might have had a big say in the shaping of Tommy's style of delivery back in the 1950s, but he identifies Robbie Williams as a performer he admires from the 21st-century music scene. "He has charisma." Quite a compliment from Britain's first No.1 album act.

Tommy Steele with his British Hit Singles & Albums special award, backstage at the Palladium, London, December 2005

◂◂ UK No.1 SINGLES ▸▸

5 March 1954	12 March 1954	19 March 1954	26 March 1954
OH, MEIN PAPA Eddie Calvert	**I SEE THE MOON** The Stargazers	**I SEE THE MOON** The Stargazers	**I SEE THE MOON** The Stargazers

ARGENT
(see also SAN JOSE featuring Rodriguez ARGENTINA; SILSOE; The ZOMBIES) *UK, male vocal instrumental group - Russ Ballard and Rod Argent (2 Albums: 9 Weeks, 3 Singles: 27 Weeks)*

4 Mar 72 ● HOLD YOUR HEAD UP *Epic EPC 7786* 5 12
29 Apr 72 ALL TOGETHER NOW *Epic EPC 64962* 13 8
10 Jun 72 TRAGEDY *Epic EPC 8115* 34 7
24 Mar 73 GOD GAVE ROCK AND ROLL TO YOU *Epic EPC 1243* 18 8
31 Mar 73 IN DEEP *Epic EPC 65475* 49 1

india.arie *US, female vocalist – India.Arie Simpson (1 Album: 3 Weeks, 3 Singles: 6 Weeks)*

30 Jun 01 VIDEO *Motown TMGCD 1505* 32 3
7 Jul 01 ACOUSTIC SOUL *Motown 137702* 55 3
20 Oct 01 BROWN SKIN *Motown TMGCD 1507* 29 2
12 Apr 03 LITTLE THINGS *Motown TMGCD 1509* 62 1

ARIEL *UK, male production group*

27 Mar 93 LET IT SLIDE *Deconstruction 74321134512* 57 2

ARIEL *Argentina, male DJ / producer – Ariel Belloso (2 Singles: 4 Weeks)*

21 Jun 97 DEEP (I'M FALLING DEEPER) *Wonderboy WBOYD 005* 47 1
17 Jun 00 A9 *Essential Recordings ESCD 15* 28 3

ARIZONA featuring ZEITIA
UK, male production / instrumental duo and female vocalist

12 Mar 94 I SPECIALIZE IN LOVE *Union City UCRCD 27* 74 1

Ship's Company and Royal Marine Band of HMS ARK ROYAL
UK, male choir and marine band

23 Dec 78 THE LAST FAREWELL *BBC RESL 61* 46 6

ARKARNA
UK, male vocal / instrumental / production group (2 Singles: 3 Weeks)

25 Jan 97 HOUSE ON FIRE *WEA WEA 088CD1* 33 2
2 Aug 97 SO LITTLE TIME *WEA WEA 108CD1* 46 1

Joan ARMATRADING (261 Top 500) *Highly acclaimed singer-songwriter / guitarist, b. 9 Dec 1950, St. Kitts, West Indies, and raised in Birmingham, UK. Her debut album was issued in 1972, and she has twice been nominated at both the BRIT and Grammy Awards. She won an Ivor Novello award in 1996 (15 Albums: 196 Weeks, 10 Singles: 53 Weeks)*

4 Sep 76 JOAN ARMATRADING *A&M AMLH 64588* 12 27
16 Oct 76 ● LOVE AND AFFECTION *A&M AMS 7249* 10 9
1 Oct 77 ● SHOW SOME EMOTION *A&M AMLH 68433* 6 11
14 Oct 78 TO THE LIMIT *A&M AMLH 64732* 13 10
23 Feb 80 ROSIE *A&M AMS 7506* 49 5
24 May 80 ● ME MYSELF I *A&M AMLH 64809* 5 23
14 Jun 80 ME MYSELF I *A&M AMS 7527* 21 11
6 Sep 80 ALL THE WAY FROM AMERICA *A&M AMS 7552* 54 3
12 Sep 81 ● WALK UNDER LADDERS *A&M AMLH 64876* 6 29
12 Sep 81 I'M LUCKY *A&M AMS 8163* 46 5
16 Jan 82 NO LOVE *A&M AMS 8179* 50 5
19 Feb 83 DROP THE PILOT *A&M AMS 8306* 11 10
12 Mar 83 ● THE KEY *A&M AMLX 64912* 10 14
26 Nov 83 TRACK RECORD *A&M JA 2001* 18 32
16 Feb 85 SECRET SECRETS *A&M AMA 5040* 14 12
16 Mar 85 TEMPTATION *A&M AM 238* 65 2
24 May 86 SLEIGHT OF HAND *A&M AMA 5130* 34 6
16 Jul 88 THE SHOUTING STAGE *A&M AMA 5211* 28 10
26 May 90 MORE THAN ONE KIND OF LOVE *A&M AM 561* 75 1
16 Jun 90 HEARTS AND FLOWERS *A&M 3952981* 29 4
16 Mar 91 ● THE VERY BEST OF JOAN ARMATRADING *A&M 3971221* 9 11
23 May 92 WRAPPED AROUND HER *A&M AM 877* 56 2
20 Jun 92 SQUARE THE CIRCLE *A&M 3953882* 34 2
10 Jun 95 WHAT'S INSIDE *RCA 74321272692* 48 2
4 Sep 04 LOVE AND AFFECTION: JOAN ARMATRADING CLASSICS (1975-1983) *Universal TV 9823506* 24 3

ARMOURY SHOW
UK, male vocal / instrumental group (1 Album: 1 Week, 3 Singles: 6 Weeks)

25 Aug 84 CASTLES IN SPAIN *Parlophone R 6079* 69 2
26 Jan 85 WE CAN BE BRAVE AGAIN *Parlophone R 6087* 66 1
21 Sep 85 WAITING FOR THE FLOODS *Parlophone ARM 1* 57 1
17 Jan 87 LOVE IN ANGER *Parlophone R 6149* 63 3

Craig ARMSTRONG (see also Shola AMA) *UK, male musical director*

27 Apr 02 AS IF TO NOTHING *Melankolic CDSAD 13* 61 1

Louis ARMSTRONG *US, male vocalist / trumpeter, b. 4 Aug 1901, d. 6 Jul 1971 (10 Albums: 32 Weeks, 10 Singles: 93 Weeks)*

19 Dec 52 ● TAKES TWO TO TANGO *Brunswick 04995* 6 10
13 Apr 56 ● A THEME FROM THE THREEPENNY OPERA (MACK THE KNIFE) *Philips PB 574* [1] 8 11
15 Jun 56 TAKE IT SATCH (EP) *Philips BBE 12035* [1] 29 1
13 Jul 56 THE FAITHFUL HUSSAR *Philips PB 604* [1] 27 2
28 Jul 56 ● AT THE CRESCENDO *Brunswick LAT 8084* 4 1
6 Nov 59 MACK THE KNIFE (A THEME FROM THE THREEPENNY OPERA) *Philips PB 967* [1] 24 1
22 Oct 60 SATCHMO PLAYS KING OLIVER *Audio Fidelity AFLP 1930* 20 1
28 Oct 61 JAZZ CLASSICS *Ace of Hearts AH 7* 20 1
4 Jun 64 ● HELLO, DOLLY! *London HLR 9878* [2] ▲ $ 4 14
27 Jun 64 HELLO, DOLLY! *London HAR 8190* ▲ 11 6
7 Feb 68 ★ WHAT A WONDERFUL WORLD / CABARET *HMV POP 1615* [3] 1 29
26 Jun 68 THE SUNSHINE OF LOVE *Stateside SS 2116* 41 7
16 Nov 68 WHAT A WONDERFUL WORLD *Stateside SSL 10247* 37 3
20 Feb 82 THE VERY BEST OF LOUIS ARMSTRONG *Warwick WW 5112* 30 3
16 Apr 88 WHAT A WONDERFUL WORLD (re-issue) *A&M AM 435* [3] 53 5
21 May 94 THE ULTIMATE COLLECTION *Bluebird 74321197062* 48 3
19 Nov 94 ● WE HAVE ALL THE TIME IN THE WORLD (re) *EMI CDEM 357* 3 13
17 Dec 94 ● WE HAVE ALL THE TIME IN THE WORLD – THE VERY BEST OF LOUIS ARMSTRONG *EMI CDEMTV 89* 10 12
25 Oct 03 AT HIS VERY BEST *UCJ 9812425* 75 1
18 Sep 04 ELLA AND LOUIS TOGETHER ... *UCJ 9867768* [1] 43 1

[1] Louis Armstrong and his All-Stars [2] Louis Armstrong and The All Stars
[3] Louis Armstrong Orchestra & Chorus [1] Ella Fitzgerald and Louis Armstrong

Take It Satch (EP) tracks: Tiger Rag / Mack the Knife / The Faithful Hussar / Back O'Town Blues. 'Mack the Knife' is a re-issue of 'Theme from the Threepenny Opera' under a different title. 'Cabaret' was not listed with 'What a Wonderful World' until 14 Feb 1968.

ARMY OF LOVERS *Sweden / France, male / female vocal / instrumental group (4 Singles: 12 Weeks)*

17 Aug 91 CRUCIFIED *Ton Son Ton WOK 2007* 47 5
28 Dec 91 OBSESSION *Ton Son Ton WOK 2009* 67 1
15 Feb 92 CRUCIFIED (re-issue) *Ton Son Ton WOK 2017* 31 5
18 Apr 92 RIDE THE BULLET *Ton Son Ton WOK 2018* 67 1

ARNEE and The TERMINATERS *UK, male vocal / instrumental group*

24 Aug 91 ● I'LL BE BACK *Epic 6574177* 5 7

ARNIE'S LOVE *US, male / female vocal / instrumental group*

26 Nov 83 I'M OUT OF YOUR LIFE *Streetwave WAVE 9* 67 3

David ARNOLD
UK, male composer (2 Albums: 10 Weeks, 4 Singles: 14 Weeks)

23 Oct 93 PLAY DEAD *Island CID 573* [1] 12 6
17 Aug 96 INDEPENDENCE DAY (FILM SOUNDTRACK) *RCA Victor 9026685642* 71 1
18 Oct 97 ● ON HER MAJESTY'S SECRET SERVICE *East West EW 136CD* [2] 7 5
1 Nov 97 SHAKEN AND STIRRED *East West 3984207382* 11 9
22 Nov 97 DIAMONDS ARE FOREVER *East West EW 141CD* [3] 39 2
29 Apr 00 THEME FROM RANDALL & HOPKIRK (DECEASED) *Island CID 762* [4] 49 1

[1] Bjork and David Arnold [2] Propellerheads / David Arnold
[3] David McAlmont / David Arnold [4] Nina Persson and David Arnold

Eddy ARNOLD *US, male vocalist (3 Singles: 21 Weeks)*

17 Feb 66 ● MAKE THE WORLD GO AWAY *RCA 1496* 8 17

2 April 1954	9 April 1954	16 April 1954	23 April 1954
I SEE THE MOON The Stargazers	I SEE THE MOON The Stargazers	SECRET LOVE Doris Day	I SEE THE MOON The Stargazers

KEY	
UK No.1 ★★ UK Top 10 ●● Still on chart ++ UK entry at No.1 ■■	Peak Position
US No.1 ▲▲ UK million seller £ US million seller $	Weeks
Singles re-entries are listed as (re), (2re), (3re)... which signifies that the hit re-entered the chart once, twice or three times...	

26 May 66 **I WANT TO GO WITH YOU (re)** *RCA 1519* 46 3
28 Jul 66 **IF YOU WERE MINE MARY** *RCA 1529* 49 1

PP ARNOLD *US, female vocalist – Patricia Arnold (5 Singles: 37 Weeks)*

4 May 67 **THE FIRST CUT IS THE DEEPEST** *Immediate IM 047* 18 10
2 Aug 67 **THE TIME HAS COME** *Immediate IM 055* 47 2
24 Jan 68 **(IF YOU THINK YOU'RE) GROOVY** *Immediate IM 061* 41 4
10 Jul 68 **ANGEL OF THE MORNING** *Immediate IM 067* 29 11
24 Sep 88 **BURN IT UP** *Rhythm King LEFT 27* [1] 14 10

[1] The Beatmasters with PP Arnold

ARPEGGIO *US, male / female vocal group*

31 Mar 79 **LOVE AND DESIRE (PART 1)** *Polydor POSP 40* 63 3

ARRESTED DEVELOPMENT *US, male / female vocal / instrumental / rap group (3 Albums: 40 Weeks, 5 Singles: 39 Weeks)*

16 May 92 **TENNESSEE (re)** *Cooltempo COOL 253* 46 7
24 Oct 92 ● **PEOPLE EVERYDAY** *Cooltempo COOL 265* 2 14
31 Oct 92 ● 3 YEARS 5 MONTHS AND 2 DAYS IN THE LIFE OF ... *Cooltempo CCD 1929* 3 34
9 Jan 93 ● **MR WENDAL / REVOLUTION** *Cooltempo CDCOOL 268* 4 9
3 Apr 93 **TENNESSEE** (re-issue) *Cooltempo CDCOOL 270* 18 6
10 Apr 93 UNPLUGGED *Cooltempo CTCD 33* 40 3
28 May 94 **EASE MY MIND** *Cooltempo CDCOOL 293* 33 3
18 Jun 94 ZINGALAMDUNI *Cooltempo CTCD 42* 16 3

Steve ARRINGTON *US, male vocalist (1 Album: 11 Weeks, 2 Singles: 19 Weeks)*

13 Apr 85 DANCIN' IN THE KEY OF LIFE *Atlantic 781245* 41 11
27 Apr 85 ● **FEEL SO REAL** *Atlantic A 9576* 5 10
6 Jul 85 **DANCIN' IN THE KEY OF LIFE (re)** *Atlantic A 9534* 21 9

ARRIVAL *UK, male / female vocal / instrumental group (2 Singles: 20 Weeks)*

10 Jan 70 ● **FRIENDS** *Decca F 12986* 8 9
6 Jun 70 **I WILL SURVIVE** *Decca F 13026* 16 11

ARROW *Montserrat, male vocalist – Alphonsus Cassell (3 Singles: 15 Weeks)*

28 Jul 84 **HOT HOT HOT** *Cooltempo ARROW 1* 59 5
13 Jul 85 **LONG TIME** *London LON 70* 30 7
3 Sep 94 **HOT HOT HOT** (re-mix) *The Hit Label HLC 7* 38 3

The ARROWS *US / UK, male vocal (Alan Merrill) / instrumental trio (2 Singles: 16 Weeks)*

25 May 74 ● **A TOUCH TOO MUCH** *RAK 171* 8 9
1 Feb 75 **MY LAST NIGHT WITH YOU** *RAK 189* 25 7

ARSENAL FC *UK, male football team vocal group (4 Singles: 16 Weeks)*

8 May 71 **GOOD OLD ARSENAL** *Pye 7N 45067* [1] 16 7
15 May 93 **SHOUTING FOR THE GUNNERS** *London LONCD 342* [2] 34 3
23 May 98 ● **HOT STUFF** *Grapevine AFCCD 1* 9 5
3 Jun 00 **ARSENAL NUMBER ONE / OUR GOAL** *Grapevine CDGPS 280* . 46 1

[1] Arsenal FC First Team Squad [2] Arsenal FA Cup Squad featuring Tippa Irie and Peter Hunnigale

ART BRUT *UK, male vocal / instrumental group (4 Singles: 4 Weeks)*

10 Apr 04 **FORMED A BAND** *Rough Trade RTRADSCD 174* 52 1
18 Dec 04 **MODERN ART / MY LITTLE BROTHER** *Fierce Panda NING 164CD* 49 1
14 May 05 **EMILY KANE** *Fierce Panda NING 167CD* 41 1
8 Oct 05 **GOOD WEEKEND** *Fierce Panda NING 173CD* 56 1

ART COMPANY *Holland, male vocal / instrumental group*

26 May 84 **SUSANNA** *Epic A 4174* 12 11

ART OF NOISE *UK, male / female instrumental / production trio (4 Albums: 37 Weeks, 12 Singles: 65 Weeks)*

3 Nov 84 (WHO'S AFRAID OF?) THE ART OF NOISE! *ZTT ZTTIQ 2* 27 17
24 Nov 84 ● **CLOSE (TO THE EDIT)** *ZTT ZTPS 01* 8 19
13 Apr 85 **MOMENTS IN LOVE / BEAT BOX** *ZTT ZTPS 02* 51 4
9 Nov 85 **LEGS** *China WOK 5* 69 1
22 Mar 86 ● **PETER GUNN** (re-recording) *China WOK 6* [1] 8 9
26 Apr 86 IN VISIBLE SILENCE *Chrysalis WOL 2* 18 15
21 Jun 86 **PARANOIMIA** *China WOK 9* [2] 12 9
18 Jul 87 **DRAGNET** *China WOK 14* 60 4
10 Oct 87 IN NO SENSE/NONSENSE *China WOL 4* 55 2
29 Oct 88 ● **KISS** *China CHINA 11* [3] 5 7
3 Dec 88 THE BEST OF THE ART OF NOISE *China 837 367 1* 55 3
12 Aug 89 **YEBO!** *China CHINA 18* [4] 63 3
16 Jun 90 **ART OF LOVE** *China CHINA 23* 67 1
11 Jan 92 **INSTRUMENTS OF DARKNESS (ALL OF US ARE ONE PEOPLE)** *China WOK 2012* 45 5
29 Feb 92 **SHADES OF PARANOIMIA** *China WOK 2014* 53 2
26 Jun 99 **METAFORCE** *ZTT ZTT 129CD* 53 1

[1] Art of Noise featuring Duane Eddy [2] Art of Noise featuring Max Headroom [3] Art of Noise featuring Tom Jones [4] Art of Noise featuring Mahlathini and The Mahotella Queens

Act was a male / female instrumental group for first two albums.

ART OF TRANCE (see also POLTERGEIST; VICIOUS CIRCLES) *UK, male instrumentalist / producer – Simon Berry (4 Singles: 6 Weeks)*

31 Oct 98 **MADAGASCAR** *Platipus PLAT 43CD* 69 1
7 Aug 99 **MADAGASCAR** (re-mix) *Platipus PLAT 58CD* 48 2
15 Jun 02 **MADAGASCAR** (2nd re-mix) *Platipus PLATCD 102* 41 2
10 Aug 02 **LOVE WASHES OVER** *Platipus PLATCD 98* 60 1

ARTEMESIA (see also ETHICS; MOVIN' MELODIES; SUBLIMINAL CUTS) *Holland, male producer – Patrick Prinz (2 Singles: 4 Weeks)*

15 Apr 95 **BITS + PIECES (re)** *Hooj Choons HOOJ 31CD* 46 3
12 Aug 00 **BITS AND PIECES** (re-mix) *Tidy Trax TIDT 141CD* 51 1

ARTFUL DODGER *UK, male production / instrumental duo – Mark Hill and Peter Devereux (1 Album: 27 Weeks, 7 Singles: 71 Weeks)*

11 Dec 99 ● **RE-REWIND THE CROWD SAY BO SELECTA** *Public Demand / Relentless RELENT 1CDS* [1] 2 17
4 Mar 00 ● **MOVIN TOO FAST (re)** *Locked On XL LOX 117CD* [2] 2 12
15 Jul 00 ● **WOMAN TROUBLE** *Public Demand / ffrr FCD 380* [3] 6 10
25 Nov 00 ● **PLEASE DON'T TURN ME ON** *Public Demand / ffrr FCD 388* [4] 4 10
2 Dec 00 IT'S ALL ABOUT THE STRAGGLERS *ffrr 8573859092* 18 27
17 Mar 01 **THINK ABOUT ME** *ffrr FCD 394* [5] 11 8
15 Sep 01 ● **TWENTYFOURSEVEN** *ffrr / Public Demand FCD 400* [6] 6 9
15 Dec 01 **IT AIN'T ENOUGH** *ffrr / Public Demand FCD 401* [7] 20 5

[1] Artful Dodger featuring Craig David [2] Artful Dodger and Romina Johnson [3] Artful Dodger and Robbie Craig featuring Craig David [4] Artful Dodger featuring Lifford [5] Artful Dodger featuring Michelle Escoffery [6] Artful Dodger featuring Melanie Blatt [7] Dreem Teem vs Artful Dodger featuring MZ May and MC Alistair

Neil ARTHUR (see also BLANCMANGE) *UK, male vocalist*

5 Feb 94 **I LOVE I HATE** *Chrysalis CDCHSS 5005* 50 2

ARTIFICIAL FUNK featuring Nellie ETTISON *Denmark, male producer – Rune Kolsch and female vocalist*

22 Mar 03 **TOGETHER** *Skint SKINT 82CD* 40 1

ARTIFICIAL INTELLIGENCE *UK, male production duo*

21 Aug 04 **UPRISING / THROUGH THE GATE** *V Recordings VRECS 001UK* 73 1

ARTISTS AGAINST AIDS WORLDWIDE *US / Ireland, all-star male / female vocal ensemble*

17 Nov 01 ● **WHAT'S GOING ON** *Columbia 6721172* 6 12

ARTISTS UNITED AGAINST APARTHEID

International, male / female vocal / instrumental charity assembly

23 Nov 85 **SUN CITY** *Manhattan MT 7* **21** 8

ASCENSION (see also CHAKRA; ESSENCE; LUSTRAL; OXYGEN featuring Andrea BRITTON; SPACE BROTHERS)

UK, male production duo – Ricky Simmons and Steve Jones (3 Singles: 4 Weeks)

5 Jul 97 **SOMEONE** *Perfecto PERF 141CD* **55** 1
15 Jul 00 **SOMEONE** (re-mix) *Code Blue BLU 011CD1* **43** 2
23 Mar 02 **FOR A LIFETIME** *Xtravaganza XTRAV 20CDS* [1] **45** 1

[1] Ascension featuring Erin Lordan

ASH

UK, male / female vocal / instrumental group (5 Albums: 73 Weeks, 17 Singles: 69 Weeks)

1 Apr 95 **KUNG FU** *Infectious INFECT 21CD* **57** 1
12 Aug 95 **GIRL FROM MARS** *Infectious INFECT 24CD* **11** 5
21 Oct 95 **ANGEL INTERCEPTOR** *Infectious INFECT 27CD* **14** 4
27 Apr 96 ● **GOLDFINGER** *Infectious INFECT 39CD* **5** 5
18 May 96 ★ 1977 *Infectious INFECT 40CD* ■ 1 27
6 Jul 96 ● **OH YEAH (re)** *Infectious INFECT 41CD* **6** 8
25 Oct 97 ● **A LIFE LESS ORDINARY** *Infectious INFECT 50CD* **10** 5
3 Oct 98 **JESUS SAYS** *Infectious INFECT 59CD* **15** 4
17 Oct 98 ● NU-CLEAR SOUNDS *Infectious INFECT 60CD* 7 4
5 Dec 98 **WILD SURF** *Infectious INFECT 61CDS* **31** 2
10 Feb 01 ● **SHINING LIGHT** *Infectious INFECT 98CD* **8** 4
14 Apr 01 **BURN BABY BURN** *Infectious INFECT 99CDS* **13** 6
5 May 01 ★ FREE ALL ANGELS *Infectious INFECT 100CD* ■ 1 28
21 Jul 01 **SOMETIMES** *Infectious INFECT 101CDS* **21** 6
13 Oct 01 **CANDY** *Infectious INFECT 106CDS* **20** 3
12 Jan 02 **THERE'S A STAR** *Infectious INFECT 112CDS* **13** 3
7 Sep 02 **ENVY** *Infectious INFECT 119CDS* **21** 2
21 Sep 02 ● INTERGALACTIC SONIC 7"S – SINGLES COLLECTION 1994-2002 *Infectious INFEC 120CDB* 3 6
15 May 04 **ORPHEUS** *Infectious ASH 01CD* **13** 4
29 May 04 ● MELTDOWN *Infectious 5046732462* 5 8
31 Jul 04 **STARCROSSED** *Infectious ASH 02CD* **22** 5
18 Dec 04 **RENEGADE CAVALCADE** *Infectious ASH 03CD* **33** 2

Act was a male trio before 1997 hit.

ASHA

Italy, female vocalist

8 Jul 95 **J.J. TRIBUTE** *Ffrreedom TABCD 228* **38** 2

ASHANTI

US, female vocalist – Ashanti Douglas (3 Albums: 51 Weeks, 12 Singles: 94 Weeks)

2 Feb 02 ● **ALWAYS ON TIME** *Def Jam 5889462* [1] ▲ **6** 13
20 Apr 02 ● ASHANTI *Mercury 5868302* ▲ 3 36
25 May 02 ● **WHAT'S LUV?** *Atlantic AT 0128CD* [2] **4** 8
8 Jun 02 **FOOLISH (re)** (import) *Mercury 5829362* **68** 3
20 Jul 02 ● **FOOLISH** *Murder Inc / Mercury 0639942* ▲ **4** 10
12 Oct 02 ● **DOWN 4 U (2re)** *Murder Inc 0639002* [3] **4** 10
23 Nov 02 **HAPPY** *Murder Inc / Mercury 0638242* **13** 8
29 Mar 03 **MESMERIZE** *Murder Inc / Mercury 0779582* [1] **12** 8
28 Jun 03 ● **ROCK WIT U (AWWW BABY)** *Murder Inc / Mercy 9808431* **7** 10
12 Jul 03 ● CHAPTER II *Murder Inc / Mercury 9808434* ▲ 5 8
1 Nov 03 **RAIN ON ME** *Murder Inc / Mercury 9813176* **19** 4
6 Nov 04 ★ **WONDERFUL** *Def Jam 9864605* [4] ■ **1** 10
15 Jan 05 CONCRETE ROSE *Mercury / The Inc 2103261* 25 7
5 Feb 05 ● **ONLY U** *The Inc / Mercury 2103785* **2** 8
18 Jun 05 **DON'T LET THEM** *The Inc / Mercury 9882725* **38** 2

[1] Ja Rule featuring Ashanti [2] Fat Joe featuring Ashanti [3] Irv Gotti presents Ja Rule, Ashanti, Charli Baltimore and Vita [4] Ja Rule featuring R Kelly & Ashanti

ASHAYE

UK, male vocalist – Trevor Ashaye

15 Oct 83 **MICHAEL JACKSON MEDLEY** *Record Shack SOHO 10* **45** 3

Tracks on Michael Jackson Medley: Don't Stop Til You Get Enough / Wanna Be Startin' Something / Shake Your Body Down to the Ground / Blame It on the Boogie.

Richard ASHCROFT (see also The VERVE)

UK, male vocalist (2 Albums: 30 Weeks, 6 Singles: 30 Weeks)

15 Apr 00 ● **A SONG FOR THE LOVERS (re)** *Hut / Virgin HUTCD 128* **3** 11
24 Jun 00 **MONEY TO BURN** *Hut / Virgin HUTCD 136* **17** 4
8 Jul 00 ★ ALONE WITH EVERYBODY *Hut CDHUTX 63* ■ 1 20
23 Sep 00 **C'MON PEOPLE (WE'RE MAKING IT NOW)** *Hut / Virgin HUTCD 138* **21** 3
19 Oct 02 **CHECK THE MEANING (re)** *Hut / Virgin HUTCD 161* **11** 6
2 Nov 02 ● HUMAN CONDITIONS *Hut / Virgin CDHUT 77* 3 10
18 Jan 03 **SCIENCE OF SILENCE** *Hut / Virgin HUTCD 163* **14** 4
19 Apr 03 **BUY IT IN BOTTLES** *Hut / Virgin HUTCD 167* **26** 2

John ASHER

UK, male vocalist / TV presenter

15 Nov 75 **LET'S TWIST AGAIN** *Creole CR 112* **14** 6

ASHFORD and SIMPSON

US, male / female vocal duo – Nickolas Ashford and Valerie Simpson (1 Album: 6 Weeks, 3 Singles: 22 Weeks)

18 Nov 78 **IT SEEMS TO HANG ON** *Warner Bros. K 17237* **48** 4
5 Jan 85 ● **SOLID** *Capitol CL 345* **3** 15
16 Feb 85 SOLID *Capitol SASH 1* 42 6
20 Apr 85 **BABIES** *Capitol CL 355* **56** 3

ASHTON, GARDNER AND DYKE

UK, male vocal (Tony Ashton) / instrumental trio

16 Jan 71 ● **THE RESURRECTION SHUFFLE** *Capitol CL 15665* **3** 14

ASIA (see also Steve HOWE)

UK, male vocal (John Wetton) / instrumental group (3 Albums: 50 Weeks, 3 Singles: 13 Weeks)

10 Apr 82 ASIA *Geffen GEF 85577* ▲ 11 38
3 Jul 82 **HEAT OF THE MOMENT** *Geffen GEF A2494* **46** 5
18 Sep 82 **ONLY TIME WILL TELL** *Geffen GEF A2228* **54** 3
13 Aug 83 **DON'T CRY** *Geffen A 3580* **33** 5
20 Aug 83 ● ALPHA *Geffen GEF 25508* 5 11
14 Dec 85 ASTRA *Geffen GEF 26413* 68 1

ASIA BLUE

UK, female vocal group

27 Jun 92 **ESCAPING** *Atomic WNR 882* **50** 2

ASIAN DUB FOUNDATION

UK, male vocal / instrumental group (2 Albums: 6 Weeks, 6 Singles: 8 Weeks)

21 Feb 98 **FREE SATPAL RAM** *ffrr FCD 326* **56** 1
2 May 98 **BUZZIN'** *ffrr FCD 335* **31** 2
23 May 98 RAFI'S REVENGE *ffrr 5560062* 20 3
4 Jul 98 **BLACK WHITE** *ffrr FCD 337* **52** 1
18 Mar 00 **REAL GREAT BRITAIN** *ffrr FCD 376* **41** 2
1 Apr 00 COMMUNITY MUSIC *ffrr 8573820422* 20 3
3 Jun 00 **NEW WAY, NEW LIFE** *ffrr FCD 378* **49** 1
1 Feb 03 **FORTRESS EUROPE** *Virgin DINSDX 253* **57** 1

The ASSEMBLY

(see also ERASURE; KINKY; The UNDERTONES; YAZOO) *UK, male vocal / instrumental group – includes Feargal Sharkey and Vince Clarke*

12 Nov 83 ● **NEVER NEVER** *Mute TINY 1* **4** 10

ASSOCIATES

UK, male vocal / instrumental group – leader Billy MacKenzie, b. 27 Mar 1957, d. 22 Jan 1997 (3 Albums: 28 Weeks, 7 Singles: 47 Weeks)

20 Feb 82 ● **PARTY FEARS TWO** *Associates ASC 1* **9** 10
8 May 82 **CLUB COUNTRY** *Associates ASC 2* **13** 10
22 May 82 ● SULK *Associates ASCL 1* 10 20
7 Aug 82 **18 CARAT LOVE AFFAIR / LOVE HANGOVER** *Associates ASC 3* **21** 8
16 Jun 84 **THOSE FIRST IMPRESSIONS** *WEA YZ 6* **43** 6
1 Sep 84 **WAITING FOR THE LOVEBOAT** *WEA YZ 16* **53** 4
19 Jan 85 **BREAKFAST** *WEA YZ 28* **49** 6
16 Feb 85 PERHAPS *WEA WX 9* 23 7
17 Sep 88 **HEART OF GLASS** *WEA YZ 310* **56** 3
31 Mar 90 WILD AND LONELY *Circa CIRCA 11* 71 1

'18 Carat Love Affair' listed until 28 Aug only. The act was a duo on their 1982 hits and their first album.

The ASSOCIATION

US, male vocal / instrumental group

22 May 68 **TIME FOR LIVIN'** *Warner Bros. WB 7195* **23** 8

28 May 1954	4 June 1954	11 June 1954	18 June 1954
SECRET LOVE Doris Day	**SECRET LOVE** Doris Day	**SECRET LOVE** Doris Day	**SECRET LOVE** Doris Day

KEY
UK No.1 ★ UK Top 10 ● Still on chart + UK entry at No.1 ■
US No.1 ▲ UK million seller £ US million seller $
Singles re-entries are listed as (re), (2re), (3re)... which signifies that the hit re-entered the chart once, twice or three times...
Peak Position / Weeks

Rick ASTLEY (445 Top 500)

Soulful-voiced pop vocalist, b. 6 Feb 1966, Warrington, UK. His BRIT award-winning, US chart-topping debut hit was 1987's best-selling UK single. No British solo male can match his seven consecutive (mostly Stock Aitken Waterman produced) Top 10 hits in the 1980s (5 Albums: 69 Weeks, 12 Singles: 91 Weeks)

Date	Title	Label	Pos	Wks
8 Aug 87 ★	NEVER GONNA GIVE YOU UP	*RCA PB 41447* ▲ $	1	18
31 Oct 87 ●	WHENEVER YOU NEED SOMEBODY	*RCA PB 41567*	3	12
28 Nov 87 ★	WHENEVER YOU NEED SOMEBODY	*RCA PL 71529* ■	1	34
12 Dec 87 ●	WHEN I FALL IN LOVE / MY ARMS KEEP MISSING YOU	*RCA PB 41683*	2	10
27 Feb 88 ●	TOGETHER FOREVER	*RCA PB 41817* ▲	2	9
24 Sep 88 ●	SHE WANTS TO DANCE WITH ME	*RCA PB 42189*	6	10
26 Nov 88 ●	TAKE ME TO YOUR HEART	*RCA PB 42573*	8	10
10 Dec 88 ●	HOLD ME IN YOUR ARMS	*RCA PL 71932*	8	19
11 Feb 89 ●	HOLD ME IN YOUR ARMS	*RCA PB 42615*	10	8
26 Jan 91 ●	CRY FOR HELP	*RCA PB 44247*	7	7
2 Mar 91 ●	FREE	*RCA PL 74896*	9	9
30 Mar 91	MOVE RIGHT OUT	*RCA PB 44407*	58	2
29 Jun 91	NEVER KNEW LOVE	*RCA PB 44737*	70	1
4 Sep 93	THE ONES YOU LOVE	*RCA 74321160142*	48	2
13 Nov 93	HOPELESSLY	*RCA 74321175642*	33	2
14 Sep 02	GREATEST HITS	*BMG 74321955122*	16	4
29 Oct 05	PORTRAIT	*RCA 82876734312*	26	3

Before 9 Jan 1988, 'When I Fall in Love' was listed by itself. After that date 'My Arms Keep Missing You' was the side listed.

ASTRO TRAX

UK, male / female vocal / production trio

Date	Title	Label	Pos	Wks
24 Oct 98	THE ENERGY (FEEL THE VIBE)	*Satellite 74321622052*	74	1

ASWAD

UK, male vocal (Brinsley Forde) / instrumental group (10 Albums: 61 Weeks, 17 Singles: 81 Weeks)

Date	Title	Label	Pos	Wks
24 Jul 82	NOT SATISFIED	*CBS 85666*	50	6
10 Dec 83	LIVE AND DIRECT	*Island IMA 6*	57	16
3 Mar 84	CHASING FOR THE BREEZE	*Island IS 160*	51	3
6 Oct 84	54-46 (WAS MY NUMBER)	*Island IS 170*	70	3
3 Nov 84	REBEL SOULS	*Island ILPS 9780*	48	2
28 Jun 86	TO THE TOP	*Simba SIMBALP 2*	71	3
27 Feb 88 ★	DON'T TURN AROUND	*Mango IS 341*	1	12
9 Apr 88 ●	DISTANT THUNDER	*Mango ILPS 9895*	10	15
21 May 88	GIVE A LITTLE LOVE	*Mango IS 358*	11	8
24 Sep 88	SET THEM FREE	*Mango IS 383*	70	2
3 Dec 88	RENAISSANCE	*Stylus SMR 866*	52	8
1 Apr 89	BEAUTY'S ONLY SKIN DEEP	*Mango MNG 105*	31	6
22 Jul 89	ON AND ON	*Mango MNG 708*	25	8
18 Aug 90	NEXT TO YOU	*Mango MNG 753*	24	6
22 Sep 90	TOO WICKED	*Mango MLPS 1054*	51	2
17 Nov 90	SMILE	*Mango MNG 767* [1]	53	2
30 Mar 91	TOO WICKED (EP)	*Mango MNG 771*	61	2
31 Jul 93	HOW LONG	*Polydor PZCD 252* [2]	31	5
9 Oct 93	DANCEHALL MOOD	*Bubblin' CDBUBB 1*	48	2
18 Jun 94 ●	SHINE	*Bubblin' CDBUBB 3*	5	14
9 Jul 94	RISE AND SHINE	*Bubblin' BUBBCD 1*	38	5
17 Sep 94	WARRIORS	*Bubblin' CDBUBB 4*	33	3
18 Feb 95	YOU'RE NO GOOD	*Bubblin' CDBUBB 5*	35	3
5 Aug 95	IF I WAS	*Bubblin' CDBUBB 6*	58	1
12 Aug 95	GREATEST HITS	*Bubblin' BUBBCD 4*	20	3
24 Aug 02	COOL SUMMER REGGAE	*UMTV 643762*	54	1
31 Aug 02	SHY GUY	*Universal TV 0192632* [3]	62	1

[1] Aswad featuring Sweetie Irie [2] Yazz and Aswad [3] Aswad featuring Easther Bennett

Tracks on Too Wicked (EP): Best of My Love / Warrior Re-Charge / Fire / I Shot the Sheriff.

AT THE DRIVE-IN

US, male vocal / instrumental group (1 Album: 2 Weeks, 3 Singles: 3 Weeks)

Date	Title	Label	Pos	Wks
19 Aug 00	ONE ARMED SCISSOR	*Grand Royal GR 091CD*	64	1
30 Sep 00	RELATIONSHIP OF COMMAND	*Grand Royal CDVUS 184*	33	2
16 Dec 00	ROLODEX PROPAGANDA	*Grand Royal / Virgin VUSCD 189*	54	1
24 Mar 01	INVALID LITTER DEPT	*Grand Royal / Virgin VUSCD 193*	50	1

The ATARIS

US, male vocal / instrumental group

Date	Title	Label	Pos	Wks
11 Oct 03	THE BOYS OF SUMMER	*Columbia 6743402*	49	1

ATEED

Germany, female vocalist

Date	Title	Label	Pos	Wks
4 Oct 03	COME TO ME	*Better the Devil BTD 4CD*	56	1

ATHLETE

UK, male vocal (Joel Pott) / instrumental group (2 Albums: 61 Weeks, 9 Singles: 32 Weeks)

Date	Title	Label	Pos	Wks
29 Jun 02	YOU GOT THE STYLE	*Parlophone CDATH 001*	37	2
16 Nov 02	BEAUTIFUL	*Parlophone CDATH 002*	41	1
5 Apr 03	EL SALVADOR	*Parlophone CDATHS 003*	31	2
19 Apr 03	VEHICLES & ANIMALS	*Parlophone 5842112*	19	32
5 Jul 03	WESTSIDE	*Parlophone CDATHS 005*	42	1
4 Oct 03	YOU GOT THE STYLE (re-issue)	*Parlophone CDATH 006*	42	1
29 Jan 05 ●	WIRES (re)	*Parlophone CDATHS 007*	4	15
12 Feb 05 ★	TOURIST	*Parlophone 5637040* ■	1	29
7 May 05	HALF LIGHT	*Parlophone CDATHS 008*	16	7
27 Aug 05	TOURIST	*Parlophone CDATH 009*	43	1
26 Nov 05	TWENTY FOUR HOURS	*Parlophone CDATH 010*	42	2

ATHLETICO SPIZZ 80

UK, male vocal / instrumental group

Date	Title	Label	Pos	Wks
26 Jul 80	DO A RUNNER	*A&M AMLE 68514*	27	5

Chet ATKINS

US, male guitarist – Chester Atkins, b. 20 Jun 1924, d. 30 Jun 2001 (4 Albums: 16 Weeks, 1 Single: 2 Weeks)

Date	Title	Label	Pos	Wks
17 Mar 60	TEENSVILLE (re)	*RCA 1174*	46	2
18 Mar 61	THE OTHER CHET ATKINS	*RCA RD 27194*	20	1
17 Jun 61	CHET ATKINS' WORKSHOP	*RCA RD 27214*	19	1
20 Feb 63	CARIBBEAN GUITAR	*RCA RD 7519*	17	3
24 Nov 90	NECK AND NECK	*CBS 4674351* [1]	41	11

[1] Chet Atkins and Mark Knopfler

Rowan ATKINSON

(see also MR BEAN and SMEAR CAMPAIGN featuring Bruce DICKINSON; NOT THE 9 O'CLOCK NEWS CAST) *UK, male comedian / actor*

Date	Title	Label	Pos	Wks
7 Feb 81	LIVE IN BELFAST	*Arista SPART 1150*	44	9

ATLANTA RHYTHM SECTION

US, male vocal / instrumental group

Date	Title	Label	Pos	Wks
27 Oct 79	SPOOKY	*Polydor POSP 74*	48	4

ATLANTIC OCEAN

Holland, male instrumental duo – Rene van der Weyde and Lex van Coeverden (4 Singles: 14 Weeks)

Date	Title	Label	Pos	Wks
19 Feb 94	WATERFALL	*Eastern Bloc BLOCCD 001*	22	6
2 Jul 94	BODY IN MOTION	*Eastern Bloc BLOCCD 009*	15	4
26 Nov 94	MUSIC IS A PASSION	*Eastern Bloc BLOCCDX 017*	59	1
30 Nov 96	WATERFALL (re-mix)	*Eastern Bloc BLOC 104CD*	21	3

ATLANTIC STARR

US, male / female vocal / instrumental group (2 Albums: 15 Weeks, 8 Singles: 48 Weeks)

Date	Title	Label	Pos	Wks
9 Sep 78	GIMME YOUR LUVIN'	*A&M AMS 7380*	66	3
15 Jun 85	AS THE BAND TURNS	*A&M AMA 5019*	64	3
29 Jun 85	SILVER SHADOW	*A&M AM 260*	41	6
7 Sep 85	ONE LOVE	*A&M AM 273*	58	4
15 Mar 86 ●	SECRET LOVERS	*A&M AM 307*	10	12
24 May 86	IF YOUR HEART ISN'T IN IT	*A&M AM 319*	48	4
13 Jun 87 ●	ALWAYS	*Warner Bros. W 8455* ▲	3	14
11 Jul 87	ALL IN THE NAME OF LOVE	*WEA WX 115*	48	12
12 Sep 87	ONE LOVER AT A TIME	*Warner Bros. W 8327*	57	3
27 Aug 94	EVERYBODY'S GOT SUMMER	*Arista 74321228072*	36	2

ATLANTIS vs AVATAR featuring Miriam STOCKLEY

UK, male production group and female vocalist

Date	Title	Label	Pos	Wks
28 Oct 00	FIJI	*Inferno CDFERN 34*	52	2

ATMOSFEAR

UK, male instrumental group

Date	Title	Label	Pos	Wks
17 Nov 79	DANCING IN OUTER SPACE	*MCA 543*	46	7

ATOMIC KITTEN 284 Top 500

The Liverpool ladies were the first female trio to amass three No.1 singles. Line-up is Natasha Hamilton, Elizabeth McClarnon and Jenny Frost (who replaced Kerry Katona in 2001). The girls have sold over seven million albums and had many international hits. Best-selling single: 'Whole Again' 940,000 (5 Albums: 87 Weeks, 14 Singles: 148 Weeks)

11 Dec 99 ● **RIGHT NOW** *Innocent SINCD 15*......10 9
8 Apr 00 ● **SEE YA (re)** *Innocent SINCD 17*......6 7
15 Jul 00 ● **I WANT YOUR LOVE** *Innocent SINCD 18*......10 5
21 Oct 00 **FOLLOW ME** *Innocent SINCD 22*......20 5
4 Nov 00 RIGHT NOW *Innocent CDSIN 6*......39 4
10 Feb 01 ★ **WHOLE AGAIN (re)** *Innocent SINDX 24* ■......1 23
4 Aug 01 ★ **ETERNAL FLAME (re)** *Innocent SINCD 27* ■......1 15
18 Aug 01 ★ RIGHT NOW (re-issue) *Innocent CDSINY 6* ■......1 37
1 Jun 02 ● **IT'S OK!** *Innocent SINCD 36*......3 13
7 Sep 02 ★ **THE TIDE IS HIGH (GET THE FEELING)** *Innocent SINCD 38* ■...1 16
21 Sep 02 ★ FEELS SO GOOD *Innocent CDSIN 10* ■......1 27
7 Dec 02 ● **THE LAST GOODBYE / BE WITH YOU** *Innocent SINDX 42*......2 12
12 Apr 03 ● **LOVE DOESN'T HAVE TO HURT** *Innocent SINCD 45*......4 10
8 Nov 03 ● **IF YOU COME TO ME** *Innocent SINCD 50*......3 10
22 Nov 03 ● LADIES NIGHT *Innocent CDSIN 14*......5 11
27 Dec 03 ● **LADIES NIGHT** *Innocent SINCD 53* [1]......8 11
10 Apr 04 ● **SOMEONE LIKE ME / RIGHT NOW 2004** (re-recording) *Innocent SINDX 60*......8 8
17 Apr 04 ● THE GREATEST HITS *Innocent CDSIN 16*......5 8
26 Feb 05 ● **CRADLE** *Innocent SINDX 72*......10 4

[1] Atomic Kitten featuring Kool and The Gang

ATOMIC ROOSTER *UK, male vocal / instrumental group (3 Albums: 13 Weeks, 2 Singles: 25 Weeks)*

13 Jun 70 ATOMIC ROOSTER *B&C CAS 1010*......49 1
16 Jan 71 DEATH WALKS BEHIND YOU *Charisma CAS 1026*......12 8
6 Feb 71 **TOMORROW NIGHT** *B&C CB 131*......11 12
10 Jul 71 ● **DEVIL'S ANSWER** *B&C CB 157*......4 13
21 Aug 71 IN HEARING OF ATOMIC ROOSTER *Pegasus PEG 1*......18 4

Winifred ATWELL *Trinidad, female pianist, b. 27 Apr 1914, d. 28 Feb 1983 (15 Singles: 117 Weeks)*

12 Dec 52 ● **BRITANNIA RAG (re)** *Decca F 10015*......5 6
15 May 53 ● **CORONATION RAG (re)** *Decca F 10110*......5 6
25 Sep 53 ● **FLIRTATION WALTZ (2re)** *Decca F 10161*......10 3
4 Dec 53 ● **LET'S HAVE A PARTY (re)** *Philips PB 213*......2 15
23 Jul 54 ● **RACHMANINOFF'S 18TH VARIATION ON A THEME BY PAGANINI (THE STORY OF THREE LOVES) (re)** *Philips PB 234*..9 9
26 Nov 54 ★ **LET'S HAVE ANOTHER PARTY** *Philips PB 268*......1 8
4 Nov 55 ● **LET'S HAVE A DING DONG** *Decca F 10634*......3 10
16 Mar 56 ★ **THE POOR PEOPLE OF PARIS** *Decca F 10681*......1 16
18 May 56 **PORT-AU-PRINCE** *Decca F 10727* [1]......18 6
20 Jul 56 **LEFT BANK (C'EST A HAMBOURG)** *Decca F 10762*......14 7
26 Oct 56 ● **MAKE IT A PARTY** *Decca F 10796*......7 12
22 Feb 57 **LET'S ROCK 'N' ROLL (re)** *Decca F 10852*......24 4
6 Dec 57 ● **LET'S HAVE A BALL** *Decca F 10956*......4 6
7 Aug 59 **THE SUMMER OF THE SEVENTEENTH DOLL** *Decca F 11143*...24 2
27 Nov 59 ● **PIANO PARTY** *Decca F 11183*......10 7

[1] Winifred Atwell and Frank Chacksfield

Various hits listed above were medleys as follows: Let's Have a Party: If You Knew Suzie / The More We Are Together / That's My Weakness Now / Knees Up Mother Brown / Daisy Bell / Boomps a Daisy / She Was One of the Early Birds / Three O'Clock in the Morning. Let's Have Another Party: Somebody Stole My Gal / I Wonder Where My Baby Is Tonight / When the Red Red Robin / Bye Bye Blackbird / Sheik of Araby / Another Little Drink / Lilly of Laguna / Honeysuckle and the Bee / Broken Doll / Nellie Dean. Let's Have a Ding Dong: Ain't She Sweet / Oh Johnny Oh Johnny Oh / Oh You Beautiful Doll / Yes We Have No Bananas / Happy Days Are Here Again / I'm Forever Blowing Bubbles / I'll Be Your Sweetheart / If These Lips Could Only Speak / Who's Taking You Home Tonight. Make It a Party: Who Were You With Last Night / Hello Hello Who's Your Lady Friend / Yes Sir That's My Baby / Don't Dilly Dally on the Way / Beer Barrel Polka / After the Ball / Peggy O'Neil / Meet Me Tonight in Dreamland / I Belong to Glasgow / Down at the Old Bull and Bush. Let's Rock 'n' Roll: Singin' The Blues / Green Door / See You Later Alligator / Shake Rattle and Roll / Rock Around the Clock / Razzle Dazzle. Let's Have a Ball: Music Music Music / This Ole House / Heartbreaker / Woody Woodpecker / Last Train to San Fernando / Bring a Little Water Sylvie / Puttin' on the Style / Don't You Rock Me Daddy-O. Piano Party: Baby Face / Comin' Thru' The Rye / Annie Laurie / Little Brown Jug / Let Him Go Let Him Tarry / Put Your Arms Around Me Honey / I'll Be With You in Apple Blossom Time / Shine on Harvest Moon / Blue Skies / I'll Never Say 'Never Again' Again / I'll See You in My Dreams. 'Let's Have A Party' re-entered for a second visit peaking at No.14 in Nov 1954.

AU PAIRS *UK, female / male vocal / instrumental group (2 Albums: 10 Weeks)*

6 Jun 81 PLAYING WITH A DIFFERENT SEX *Human HUMAN 1*......33 7
4 Sep 82 SENSE AND SENSUALITY *Kamera KAM 010*......79 3

AUDIO BULLYS *UK, male vocal / production duo – Simon Franks and Tom Dinsdale (2 Albums: 5 Weeks, 5 Singles: 28 Weeks)*

18 Jan 03 **WE DON'T CARE** *Source SOURCD 061*......15 3
31 May 03 **THE THINGS / TURNED AWAY** *Source SOURCD 084*......22 3
14 Jun 03 EGO WAR *Source CDSOUR 073*......19 3
26 Jun 04 **BREAK DOWN THE DOORS** *Subliminal SUB 124CD* [1]......44 2
4 Jun 05 ● **SHOT YOU DOWN** *Source SOURCDX 111* [2]......3 17
5 Nov 05 **I'M IN LOVE** *Source SOURCDX 113*......27 3
12 Nov 05 GENERATION *Source CDSOUR 107*......33 2

[1] Morillo featuring Audio Bullys [2] Audio Bullys featuring Nancy Sinatra

AUDIOSLAVE *US, male vocal / instrumental group (2 Albums: 25 Weeks, 2 Singles: 4 Weeks)*

30 Nov 02 AUDIOSLAVE *Epic / Interscope 5101302*......19 20
1 Feb 03 **COCHISE** *Epic / Interscope 6732762*......24 3
4 Jun 05 ● OUT OF EXILE *Epic / Interscope 9882468* ▲......5 5
18 Jun 05 **BE YOURSELF** *Epic / Interscope 9882599*......40 1

AUDIOWEB *UK, male vocal / instrumental group (1 Album: 1 Week, 9 Singles: 12 Weeks)*

14 Oct 95 **SLEEPER** *Mother MUMCD 69*......74 1
9 Mar 96 **YEAH?** *Mother MUMCD 72*......73 1
15 Jun 96 **INTO MY WORLD** *Mother MUMCD 76*......42 1
19 Oct 96 **SLEEPER** (re-mix) *Mother MUMCD 78*......50 2
9 Nov 96 AUDIOWEB *Mother MUMXD 9604*......70 1
15 Feb 97 **BANKROBBER** *Mother MUMCD 85*......19 2
24 May 97 **FAKER** *Mother MUMCD 91*......70 1
25 Apr 98 **POLICEMAN SKANK … (THE STORY OF MY LIFE)** *Mother MUMCD 100*......21 2
4 Jul 98 **PERSONAL FEELING** *Mother MUMCD 104*......65 1
20 Feb 99 **TEST THE THEORY** *Mother MUMCD 110*......56 1

AUF DER MAUR *Canada, female vocalist / bass guitarist – Melissa Auf Der Maur (1 Album: 2 Weeks, 3 Singles: 5 Weeks)*

28 Feb 04 **FOLLOWED THE WAVES** *EMI CDEM 635*......35 2
13 Mar 04 AUF DER MAUR *EMI 5943082CD*......31 2
15 May 04 **REAL A LIE** *EMI CDEMS 642*......33 2
9 Oct 04 **TASTE YOU** *EMI CDEM 650*......51 1

AURORA (see also DIVE) *UK, male production duo – Sacha Collisson and Simon Greenaway (5 Singles: 19 Weeks)*

5 Jun 99 **HEAR YOU CALLING** *Additive 12AD 040*......71 1
5 Feb 00 **HEAR YOU CALLING** (re-issue) *Positiva CDTIV 124*......17 4
23 Sep 00 ● **ORDINARY WORLD** *Positiva CDTIV 139* [1]......5 7
13 Apr 02 **DREAMING** *EMI CDEM 611*......24 4
6 Jul 02 **THE DAY IT RAINED FOREVER** *EMI CDEMS 613*......29 3

[1] Aurora featuring Naimee Coleman

AURRA *US, male / female vocal / instrumental group (3 Singles: 18 Weeks)*

4 May 85 **LIKE I LIKE IT** *10 TEN 45*......51 5
19 Apr 86 **YOU AND ME TONIGHT** *10 TEN 71*......12 8
21 Jun 86 **LIKE I LIKE IT** (re-issue) *10 TEN 126*......43 5

Adam AUSTIN *UK, male vocalist*

13 Feb 99 **CENTERFOLD** *Media PSRCA 0107*......41 1

David AUSTIN *UK, male vocalist*

21 Jul 84 **TURN TO GOLD** *Parlophone R 6068*......68 3

Patti AUSTIN *US, female vocalist (1 Album: 1 Week, 2 Singles: 11 Weeks)*

26 Sep 81 EVERY HOME SHOULD HAVE ONE *Qwest K 56931*......99 1
12 Feb 83 **BABY COME TO ME** *Qwest K 15005* [1] ▲ $......11 10
5 Sep 92 **I'LL KEEP YOUR DREAMS ALIVE** *Ammi AMMI 101* [2]......68 1

[1] Patti Austin and James Ingram [2] George Benson and Patti Austin

KEY
UK No.1 ★★ UK Top 10 ●● Still on chart ++ UK entry at No.1 ■■
US No.1 ▲▲ UK million seller £ US million seller $
Singles re-entries are listed as (re), (2re), (3re)... which signifies that the hit re-entered the chart once, twice or three times...
Peak Position / Weeks

AUTECHRE *UK, male production / instrumental duo*

7 May 94 **BASSCAD EP** *Warp WAP 44CD* 56 1

Tracks on Basscad EP: BCDTMX / Beaumonthannattwomx / Seefeelmx / Tazmx / Basscaddubmx

The AUTEURS *UK, male / female vocal / instrumental group (3 Albums: 4 Weeks, 5 Singles: 9 Weeks)*

6 Mar 93 NEW WAVE *Hut CDHUT 7* 35 2
27 Nov 93 **LENNY VALENTINO** *Hut HUTCD 36* 41 2
23 Apr 94 **CHINESE BAKERY** *Hut HUTDX 41* 42 2
21 May 94 NOW I'M A COWBOY *Hut CDHUT 16* 27 1
6 Jan 96 **BACK WITH THE KILLER AGAIN EP** *Hut HUTCD 65* 45 3
24 Feb 96 **LIGHT AIRCRAFT ON FIRE** *Hut HUTCD 66* 58 1
16 Mar 96 AFTER MURDER PARK *Hut CDHUT 33* 53 1
3 Jul 99 **THE RUBETTES** *Hut HUTCD 113* 66 1

Tracks on Back With The Child Killer Again EP: Back With The Child Killer Again / Unsolved Child Murder

AUTUMN *UK, male vocal / instrumental group*

16 Oct 71 **MY LITTLE GIRL** *Pye 7N 45090* 37 6

Peter AUTY and the SINFONIA OF LONDON conducted by Howard BLAKE (see also DIGITAL DREAM BABY) *UK, male vocalist with orchestra (2 Singles: 9 Weeks)*

14 Dec 85 **WALKING IN THE AIR** *Stiff LAD 1* 42 5
19 Dec 87 **WALKING IN THE AIR** (re-issue) *CBS GA 3950* 37 4

The AVALANCHES *Australia, male production group (1 Album: 25 Weeks, 2 Singles: 12 Weeks)*

7 Apr 01 **SINCE I LEFT YOU** *XL Recordings XLS 128CD* 16 7
28 Apr 01 ● SINCE I LEFT YOU *XL Recordings XLCD 138* 8 25
21 Jul 01 **FRONTIER PSYCHIATRIST** *XL Recordings XLS 134CD* 18 5

Frankie AVALON *US, male vocalist – Francis Avallone (4 Singles: 15 Weeks)*

10 Oct 58 **GINGERBREAD** *HMV POP 517* 30 1
24 Apr 59 **VENUS** *HMV POP 603* ▲ $ 16 6
22 Jan 60 **WHY** *HMV POP 688* ▲ $ 20 4
28 Apr 60 **DON'T THROW AWAY ALL THOSE TEARDROPS** *HMV POP 727* 37 4

AVENGED SEVENFOLD NEW *US, male vocal / instrumental group*

18 Jun 05 CITY OF EVIL *Warner Bros. 9362486132* 63 1

AVERAGE WHITE BAND *UK, male vocal / instrumental group (6 Albums: 50 Weeks, 8 Singles: 47 Weeks)*

22 Feb 75 ● **PICK UP THE PIECES** *Atlantic K 10489* ▲ $ 6 9
1 Mar 75 ● AVERAGE WHITE BAND *Atlantic K 50058* ▲ 6 14
26 Apr 75 **CUT THE CAKE** *Atlantic K 10605* 31 4
5 Jul 75 CUT THE CAKE *Atlantic K 50146* 28 4
31 Jul 76 SOUL SEARCHING TIME *Atlantic K 50272* 60 1
9 Oct 76 **QUEEN OF MY SOUL** *Atlantic K 10825* 23 7
10 Mar 79 I FEEL NO FRET *RCA XL 13063* 15 15
28 Apr 79 **WALK ON BY** *RCA XC 1087* 46 5
25 Aug 79 **WHEN WILL YOU BE MINE** *RCA XB 1096* 49 5
26 Apr 80 **LET'S GO ROUND AGAIN** *RCA AWB 1* 12 11
31 May 80 SHINE *RCA XL 13123* 14 13
26 Jul 80 **FOR YOU FOR LOVE** *RCA AWB 2* 46 4
26 Mar 94 **LET'S GO ROUND AGAIN** (re-mix) *The Hit Label HLC 5* 56 2
2 Apr 94 LET'S GO ROUND AGAIN – THE BEST OF THE AVERAGE WHITE BAND *The Hit Label AHLCD 15* 38 3

Kevin AVIANCE *US, male vocalist*

13 Jun 98 **DIN DA DA** *Distinctive DISNCD 42* 65 1

The AVONS *UK, male / female vocal trio (4 Singles: 22 Weeks)*

13 Nov 59 ● **SEVEN LITTLE GIRLS SITTING IN THE BACK SEAT** *Columbia DB 4363* 3 13
7 Jul 60 **WE'RE ONLY YOUNG ONCE (re)** *Columbia DB 4461* 45 2
27 Oct 60 **FOUR LITTLE HEELS (re)** *Columbia DB 4522* 45 3
26 Jan 61 **RUBBER BALL** *Columbia DB 4569* 30 4

AWESOME *UK, male vocal group (2 Singles: 2 Weeks)*

8 Nov 97 **RUMOURS** *Universal MCSTD 40145* 58 1
21 Mar 98 **CRAZY** *Universal MCSTD 40195* 63 1

AWESOME 3 *UK, male / female vocal / instrumental group (4 Singles: 8 Weeks)*

8 Sep 90 **HARD UP** *A&M AM 591* 55 3
3 Oct 92 **DON'T GO** *Citybeat CBE 1271* 75 1
4 Jun 94 **DON'T GO** (re-mix) *XL Recordings CBX 771CD* 45 2
26 Oct 96 **DON'T GO** (2nd re-mix) *XL Recordings XLS 78CD* [1] 27 2

[1] Awesome 3 featuring Julie McDermott

Hoyt AXTON *US, male vocalist, b. 25 Mar 1938, d. 26 Oct 1999*

7 Jun 80 **DELLA AND THE DEALER** *Young Blood YB 82* 48 4

AXUS *Canada, male DJ / producer*

26 Sep 98 **ABACUS (WHEN I FALL IN LOVE)** *INCredible INCRL 8CD* 62 1

AXWELL NEW *Sweden, male producer – Axel Hedfors*

20 Aug 05 **FEEL THE VIBE (TIL THE MORNING COMES)** *Data DATA 85CDS* 16 4

Roy AYERS *US, male vocalist / instrumentalist – vibraphone (1 Album: 2 Weeks, 4 Singles: 13 Weeks)*

21 Oct 78 **GET ON UP, GET ON DOWN** *Polydor AYERS 7* 41 4
13 Jan 79 **HEAT OF THE BEAT** *Polydor POSP 16* [1] 43 5
2 Feb 80 **DON'T STOP THE FEELING** *Polydor STEP 6* 56 3
26 Oct 85 YOU MIGHT BE SURPRISED *CBS 26653* 91 2
16 May 98 **EXPANSIONS** *Soma Recordings SOMA 65CDS* [2] 68 1

[1] Roy Ayers and Wayne Henderson [2] Scott Grooves featuring Roy Ayers

AYLA *Germany, male producer – Ingo Kunzi*

4 Sep 99 **AYLA** *Positiva CDTIV 117* 22 3

Pam AYRES *UK, female poet (2 Albums: 29 Weeks)*

27 Mar 76 SOME OF ME POEMS AND SONGS *Galaxy GAL 6003* 13 23
11 Dec 76 SOME MORE OF ME POEMS AND SONGS *Galaxy GAL 6010* 23 6

AZ *US, male rapper – Anthony Cruz*

30 Mar 96 **SUGARHILL** *Cooltempo CDCOOL 315* 67 1

AZ YET *US, male vocal group (2 Singles: 10 Weeks)*

1 Mar 97 **LAST NIGHT** *LaFace 74321423202* 21 3
21 Jun 97 ● **HARD TO SAY I'M SORRY** *LaFace 74321481482* [1] $ 7 7

[1] Az Yet featuring Peter Cetera

Charles AZNAVOUR *France, male vocalist – Shanaur Aznavourian (3 Albums: 21 Weeks, 2 Singles: 29 Weeks)*

22 Sep 73 **THE OLD FASHIONED WAY (LES PLAISIRS DEMODES) (2re)** *Barclay BAR 20* 38 15
22 Jun 74 ★ **SHE** *Barclay BAR 26* 1 14
29 Jun 74 AZNAVOUR SINGS AZNAVOUR VOLUME 3 *Barclay 80472* 23 7
7 Sep 74 ● A TAPESTRY OF DREAMS *Barclay 90003* 9 13
2 Aug 80 HIS GREATEST LOVE SONGS *K-Tel NE 1078* 73 1

'The Old Fashioned Way (Les Plaisirs Demodes)' re-entered the chart in Oct 1973 (at its peak position) and Jul 1974.

20 August 1954	27 August 1954	3 September 1954	10 September 1954

◂◂ UK No.1 SINGLES ▸▸

CARA MIA David Whitfield	CARA MIA David Whitfield	CARA MIA David Whitfield	LITTLE THINGS MEAN A LOT Kitty Kallen

AZTEC CAMERA (481 Top 500)

Sensitive, tuneful pop band formed in 1980 and centred around teenage singer / songwriter Roddy Frame, b. 29 Jan 1964, East Kilbride, Scotland. Album Love was among the nominations for Best British Album at the 1989 BRIT awards (6 Albums: 80 Weeks, 12 Singles: 74 Weeks)

Date	Title / Label	Pos	Wks
19 Feb 83	**OBLIVIOUS** *Rough Trade RT 122*	47	6
23 Apr 83	HIGH LAND HARD RAIN *Rough Trade ROUGH 47*	22	18
4 Jun 83	**WALK OUT TO WINTER** *Rough Trade RT 132*	64	4
5 Nov 83	**OBLIVIOUS** (re-issue) *WEA AZTEC 1*	18	11
1 Sep 84	**ALL I NEED IS EVERYTHING / JUMP** *WEA AC 1*	34	6
29 Sep 84	KNIFE *WEA WX 8*	14	6
21 Nov 87 ●	LOVE *WEA WX 128*	10	43
13 Feb 88	**HOW MEN ARE** *WEA YZ 168*	25	9
23 Apr 88 ●	**SOMEWHERE IN MY HEART** *WEA YZ 181*	3	14
6 Aug 88	**WORKING IN A GOLDMINE** *WEA YZ 199*	31	5
8 Oct 88	**DEEP & WIDE & TALL** *WEA YZ 154*	55	3
16 Jun 90	STRAY *WEA WX 350*	22	7
7 Jul 90	**THE CRYING SCENE** *WEA YZ 492*	70	3
6 Oct 90	**GOOD MORNING BRITAIN** *WEA YZ 521* [1]	19	8
18 Jul 92	**SPANISH HORSES** *WEA YZ 688*	52	3
1 May 93	**DREAM SWEET DREAMS** *WEA YZ 740CD1*	67	2
29 May 93	DREAMLAND *WEA 4509924922*	21	2
7 Aug 99	THE BEST OF AZTEC CAMERA *Warner.esp 3984289842*	36	4

[1] Aztec Camera and Mick Jones

'Jump' listed only from 22 Sep 1984 to end of chart run.

AZURE

Italy / US, male / female vocal / DJ duo

Date	Title / Label	Pos	Wks
25 Apr 98	**MAMA USED TO SAY** *Inferno CDFERN 005*	56	1

AZYMUTH *Brazil, male instrumental group*

Date	Title / Label	Pos	Wks
12 Jan 80	**JAZZ CARNIVAL** *Milestone MRC 101*	19	8

Bob AZZAM and his ORCHESTRA and CHORUS

Egypt, male bandleader and orchestra

Date	Title / Label	Pos	Wks
26 May 60	**MUSTAPHA** *Decca F 21235*	23	14

Derek B

UK, male rapper – Derek Boland (1 Album: 9 Weeks, 3 Singles: 15 Weeks)

Date	Title / Label	Pos	Wks
27 Feb 88	**GOODGROOVE** *Music of Life 7NOTE 12*	16	6
7 May 88	**BAD YOUNG BROTHER** *Tuff Audio DRKB 1*	16	6
28 May 88	BULLET FROM A GUN *Tuff Audio DRKLP 1*	11	9
2 Jul 88	**WE'VE GOT THE JUICE** *Tuff Audio DRKB 2*	56	3

Eric B and RAKIM *US, male DJ / rap duo – Eric Barrier and William Griffin Jr (4 Albums: 10 Weeks, 6 Singles: 26 Weeks)*

Date	Title / Label	Pos	Wks
12 Sep 87	PAID IN FULL *Fourth & Broadway BRLP 514*	85	4
7 Nov 87	**PAID IN FULL** *Fourth & Broadway BRW 78*	15	6
20 Feb 88	**MOVE THE CROWD** *Fourth & Broadway BRW 88*	53	2
12 Mar 88	**I KNOW YOU GOT SOUL** *Cooltempo COOL 146*	13	6
2 Jul 88	**FOLLOW THE LEADER** *MCA MCA 1256*	21	5
6 Aug 88	FOLLOW THE LEADER *MCA MCG 6031*	25	4
19 Nov 88	**MICROPHONE FIEND** *MCA MCA 1300*	74	1
12 Aug 89	**FRIENDS** *MCA MCA 1352* [1]	21	6
7 Jul 90	LET THE RHYTHM HIT 'EM *MCA MCG 6097*	58	1
11 Jul 92	DON'T SWEAT THE TECHNIQUE *MCA MCAD 10594*	73	1

[1] Jody Watley with Eric B and Rakim

Howie B *UK, male instrumentalist / producer – Howard Bernstein (1 Album: 1 Week, 3 Singles: 4 Weeks)*

Date	Title / Label	Pos	Wks
19 Jul 97	**ANGELS GO BALD: TOO** *Polydor 5711672*	36	2
9 Aug 97	TURN THE DARK OFF *Polydor 5379342*	58	1
18 Oct 97	**SWITCH** *Polydor 5717112*	62	1
11 Apr 98	**TAKE YOUR PARTNER BY THE HAND** *Polydor 5693272* [1]	74	1

[1] Howie B featuring Robbie Robertson

John B *UK, male producer*

Date	Title / Label	Pos	Wks
22 Jun 02	**UP ALL NIGHT / TAKE CONTROL** *Metalheadz METH 041CD*	58	1

Jon B *US, male vocalist – Jonathan Buck (3 Singles: 6 Weeks)*

Date	Title / Label	Pos	Wks
17 Oct 98	**THEY DON'T KNOW** *Epic 6663975* $	32	2
26 May 01	**DON'T TALK** *Epic 6712792*	29	3
19 Mar 05	**LATELY** *Sanctuary Urban SANXS 357*	68	1

Lisa B *US, female vocalist – Lisa Barbuscia (3 Singles: 9 Weeks)*

Date	Title / Label	Pos	Wks
12 Jun 93	**GLAM** *ffrr FCD 210*	49	2
25 Sep 93	**FASCINATED** *ffrr FCD 218*	35	3
8 Jan 94	**YOU AND ME** *ffrr FCD 226*	39	4

Lorna B *UK, female vocalist – Lorna Bannon (3 Singles: 6 Weeks)*

Date	Title / Label	Pos	Wks
28 Jan 95	**DO YOU WANNA PARTY** *Steppin' Out SPONCD 2* [1]	36	3
1 Apr 95	**SWEET DREAMS** *Steppin' Out SPONCD 3* [1]	37	2
15 Mar 97	**FEELS SO GOOD** *Avex UK AVEXCD 53*	69	1

[1] DJ Scott featuring Lorna B

Mark B *UK, male rapper / producer – Mark Barnes (3 Singles: 5 Weeks)*

Date	Title / Label	Pos	Wks
10 Feb 01	**THE UNKNOWN** *Wordplay WORDCDS 011* [1]	49	1
26 May 01	**YA DON'T SEE THE SIGNS** *Wordplay WORDCDSE 019* [1]	23	3
25 Sep 04	**MOVE NOW** *Genuine GEN 033CD* [2]	61	1

[1] Mark B & Blade [2] Mark B featuring Tommy Evans

Melanie B (see also SPICE GIRLS) *UK, female vocalist – Melanie Brown (1 Album: 2 Weeks, 6 Singles: 37 Weeks)*

Date	Title / Label	Pos	Wks
26 Sep 98 ★	**I WANT YOU BACK** *Virgin VSCDT 1716* [1] ■	1	9
10 Jul 99	**WORD UP** (re) *Virgin VSCDT 1735* [2]	14	8
7 Oct 00 ●	**TELL ME** *Virgin VSCDT 1777*	4	7
21 Oct 00	HOT *Virgin CDVX 2918*	28	2
3 Mar 01 ●	**FEELS SO GOOD** *Virgin VSCDT 1787*	5	8
16 Jun 01	**LULLABY** *Virgin VSCDT 1798*	13	4
25 Jun 05	**TODAY** *Amber Cafe AMBER 003* [3]	41	1

[1] Melanie B featuring Missy 'Misdemeanor' Elliott [2] Melanie G [3] Melanie Brown

Sandy B *US, female vocalist – Sandy Barber (6 Singles: 11 Weeks)*

Date	Title / Label	Pos	Wks
20 Feb 93	**FEEL LIKE SINGIN'** *Nervous SANCD 1*	60	1
18 May 96	**MAKE THE WORLD GO ROUND** *Champion CHAMPCD 322*	73	1
24 May 97	**MAKE THE WORLD GO ROUND** (re-mix) *Champion CHAMPCD 327*	35	2
8 Nov 97	**AIN'T NO NEED TO HIDE** *Champion CHAMPCD 331*	60	1
28 Feb 98	**MAKE THE WORLD GO ROUND** (re-mix) *Champion CHAMPCD 333*	20	3
1 May 04	**MAKE THE WORLD GO ROUND 2004 (re)** *Champion CHAMPCD 780*	51	3

Stevie B *US, male vocalist – Steven Hill*

Date	Title / Label	Pos	Wks
23 Feb 91 ●	**BECAUSE I LOVE YOU (THE POSTMAN SONG)** *Polydor PO 126* ▲	6	9

Tairrie B *US, female rapper*

Date	Title / Label	Pos	Wks
1 Dec 90	**MURDER SHE WROTE** *MCA MCA 1455*	71	2

B B and Q BAND

US, male vocal / instrumental group (4 Singles: 15 Weeks)

Date	Title / Label	Pos	Wks
18 Jul 81	**ON THE BEAT** *Capitol CL 202*	41	5
6 Jul 85	**GENIE** *Cooltempo COOL 110* [1]	40	4
20 Sep 86	**DREAMER** *Cooltempo COOL 132*	35	5
17 Oct 87	**RICOCHET** *Cooltempo COOL 154*	71	1

[1] Brooklyn Bronx and Queens

17 September 1954	24 September 1954	1 October 1954	8 October 1954
THREE COINS IN THE FOUNTAIN Frank Sinatra	**THREE COINS IN THE FOUNTAIN** Frank Sinatra	**THREE COINS IN THE FOUNTAIN** Frank Sinatra	**HOLD MY HAND** Don Cornell

KEY
UK No.1 ★★ UK Top 10 ●● Still on chart ++ UK entry at No.1 ■■
US No.1 ▲▲ UK million seller £ US million seller $
Singles re-entries are listed as (re), (2re), (3re)... which signifies that the hit re-entered the chart once, twice or three times...
Peak Position / Weeks

BBC CONCERT ORCHESTRA, BBC SYMPHONY CHORUS cond. Stephen JACKSON *UK, orchestra, chorus and conductor*

22 Jun 96 **ODE TO JOY (FROM BEETHOVEN'S SYMPHONY NO.9)** *Virgin VSCDT 1591* 36 3

BBC SYMPHONY ORCHESTRA SINGERS and CHORUS
(see also Andrew DAVIS; Colin DAVIS)
UK, orchestra / choir and audience (3 Albums: 7 Weeks)

4 Oct 69 LAST NIGHT OF THE PROMS *Philips SFM 23033* [1] 36 1
11 Dec 82 HIGHLIGHTS – LAST NIGHT OF THE PROMS '82 *K-Tel NE 1198* [2] 69 5
28 Feb 98 ELGAR / PAYNE – SYMPHONY NO.3 *NMCD 053* [3] 44 1

[1] BBC Symphony Orchestra Singers and Chorus conducted by Colin Davis [2] BBC Symphony Orchestra Singers and Symphony Chorus conducted by James Loughran [3] BBC Symphony Orchestra conducted by Andrew Davis

B.B.E. *France / Italy, male instrumental group*
(1 Album: 2 Weeks, 4 Singles: 20 Weeks)

28 Sep 96 ● **SEVEN DAYS AND ONE WEEK** *Positiva CDTIV 67* 3 9
29 Mar 97 ● **FLASH** *Positiva CDTIV 73* 5 5
14 Feb 98 **DESIRE** *Positiva CDTIV 87* 19 3
28 Feb 98 GAMES *Positiva 4934932* 60 2
30 May 98 **DEEPER LOVE (SYMPHONIC PARADISE)** *Positiva CDTIV 93* 19 3

BBG *UK, male vocal / instrumental trio (5 Singles: 10 Weeks)*

28 Apr 90 **SNAPPINESS** *Urban URB 54* [1] 28 5
11 Aug 90 **SOME KIND OF HEAVEN** *Urban URB 59* 65 2
23 Mar 96 **LET THE MUSIC PLAY** *MCA MCSTD 40029* [2] 46 1
18 May 96 **SNAPPINESS** (re-mix) *Hi-Life 5762972* 50 1
5 Jul 97 **JUST BE TONIGHT** *Hi-Life 5738972* [2] 45 1

[1] BBG featuring Dina Taylor [2] BBG featuring Erin

BBM (see also Ginger BAKER'S AIR FORCE; BAKER-GURVITZ ARMY; Gary MOORE) *UK, male vocal / instrumental trio*

18 Jun 94 ● AROUND THE NEXT DREAM *Virgin CDV 2745* 9 4
6 Aug 94 **WHERE IN THE WORLD** *Virgin VSCD 1495* 57 2

BBMAK *UK, male vocal trio (1 Album: 3 Weeks, 4 Singles: 18 Weeks)*

28 Aug 99 **BACK HERE** *Telstar CDSTAS 3053* 37 2
24 Feb 01 ● **BACK HERE** (re-issue) *Telstar CDSTAS 3166* 5 10
26 May 01 ● **STILL ON YOUR SIDE** *Telstar CDSTAS 3185* 8 4
9 Jun 01 SOONER OR LATER *Telstar TCD 3179* 16 3
16 Nov 02 **OUT OF MY HEART** *Telstar CDSTAS 3281* 36 2

B BOYS *US, male vocal / instrumental group*

28 Jan 84 CUTTIN' HERBIE *Streetwave X KHAN 501* 90 1

BEF featuring Lalah HATHAWAY *US, male production duo – Martyn Ware and Ian Craig Marsh and female vocalist*

27 Jul 91 **FAMILY AFFAIR** *Ten TEN 369* 37 5

B-15 PROJECT featuring Crissy D and Lady G
UK / Jamaica, male production duo and female vocalists

17 Jun 00 ● **GIRLS LIKE US (re)** *Ministry of Sound RELENT 3CDS* 7 10

The B-52's *US, male / female vocal / instrumental group (9 Albums: 69 Weeks, 11 Singles: 61 Weeks)*

4 Aug 79 B-52'S *Island ILPS 9580* 22 12
11 Aug 79 **ROCK LOBSTER** *Island WIP 6506* 37 5
9 Aug 80 **GIVE ME BACK MY MAN** *Island WIP 6579* 61 3
13 Sep 80 WILD PLANET *Island ILPS 9622* 18 4
11 Jul 81 THE PARTY MIX ALBUM *Island IPM 1001* 36 5
27 Feb 82 MESOPOTAMIA *EMI ISSP 4006* 18 6
7 May 83 **SONG FOR A FUTURE GENERATION** *Island IS 107* 63 2
21 May 83 WHAMMY! *Island ILPS 9759* 33 4
10 May 86 **ROCK LOBSTER / PLANET CLAIRE** (re-issue) *Island BFT 1* 12 7
8 Aug 87 BOUNCING OFF THE SATELLITES *Island ILPS 9871* 74 2
29 Jul 89 ● COSMIC THING *Reprise WX 283* 8 27
3 Mar 90 ● **LOVE SHACK** *Reprise W 9917* 2 13
19 May 90 **ROAM** *Reprise W 9827* 17 7
14 Jul 90 THE BEST OF THE B-52'S – DANCE THIS MESS AROUND *Island ILPS 9959* 36 3
18 Aug 90 **CHANNEL Z** *Reprise W 9737* 61 2
20 Jun 92 **GOOD STUFF** *Reprise W 0109* 21 6
11 Jul 92 ● GOOD STUFF *Reprise 7599269432* 8 6
12 Sep 92 **TELL IT LIKE IT T-I-IS** *Reprise W 0130* 61 3
9 Jul 94 ● **(MEET) THE FLINTSTONES** *MCA MCSTD 1986* [1] 3 12
30 Jan 99 **LOVE SHACK 99** *Reprise W 0461CD* 66 1

[1] The BC-52's

'Planet Claire' listed only from 17 May 1986.

BG THE PRINCE OF RAP
Germany (b. US), male rapper – Bernard Greene

18 Jan 92 **TAKE CONTROL OF THE PARTY** *Columbia 6576330* 71 2

BK *UK, male producer – Ben Keen (6 Singles: 11 Weeks)*

25 Nov 00 **HOOVERS AND HORNS** *Nukleuz NUKC 0185* [1] 57 2
8 Dec 01 **FLASH** *Nukleuz NUKP 0361* [2] 67 1
26 Jan 02 **ERECTION (TAKE IT TO THE TOP)** *Nukleuz NUKC 0352* [3] 48 1
9 Feb 02 **FLASH** (re-mix) *Nukleuz NUKC 0361* [2] 61 1
7 Dec 02 **REVOLUTION** *Nukleuz NUKC 0437* 42 2
16 Aug 03 **KLUB KOLLABORATIONS (re)** *Nukleuz 0524 FNUK* 43 4

[1] Fergie and BK [2] BK and Nick Sentience [3] Cortina featuring BK and Madam Friction

BM DUBS present MR RUMBLE featuring BRASSTOOTH and KEE *UK, male production group*

17 Mar 01 **WHOOMP THERE IT IS** *Incentive CENT 16CDS* 32 2

B M EX *UK, male production / instrumental group*

30 Jan 93 APPOLONIA *Union City UCRCD 14* 17 2

B.M.R. featuring FELICIA
Germany, male producer – Michi Lange and female vocalist

1 May 99 **CHECK IT OUT (EVERYBODY)** *AM:PM CDAMPM 120* 29 2

B.M.U. *US / UK, male vocal group*

18 Feb 95 **U WILL KNOW** *Mercury MERCD 420* 23 2

B REAL / BUSTA RHYMES / COOLIO / LL COOL J / METHOD MAN
US, male rappers

5 Apr 97 ● **HIT 'EM HIGH (MONSTARS' ANTHEM)** *Atlantic A 5449CD* 8 6

BT *US, male producer – Brian Transeau*
(2 Albums: 5 Weeks, 13 Singles: 29 Weeks)

18 Mar 95 **EMBRACING THE SUNSHINE** *East West YZ 895CD* 34 2
16 Sep 95 **LOVING YOU MORE** *Perfecto PERF 110CD* [1] 28 2
21 Oct 95 IMA *Perfecto 0630123452* 45 4
10 Feb 96 **LOVING YOU MORE** (re-mix) *Perfecto PERF 117CD* [1] 14 3
9 Nov 96 **BLUE SKIES** *Perfecto PERF 130CD1* [2] 26 2
19 Jul 97 **FLAMING JUNE** *Perfecto PERF 145CD1* 19 4
4 Oct 97 ESCM *Perfecto 3984200652* 35 1
29 Nov 97 **LOVE, PEACE & GREASE** *Perfecto PERF 153CD1* 41 1
10 Jan 98 **FLAMING JUNE** (re-mix) *Perfecto PERF 157CD1* 28 4
18 Apr 98 **REMEMBER** *Perfecto PERF 160CD1* 27 2
21 Nov 98 **GODSPEED** *Renaissance RENCD 002* 54 1
9 Oct 99 **MERCURY AND SOLACE** *Headspace HEDSCD 001* 38 2
24 Jun 00 **DREAMING** *Headspace HEDSCD 002* [3] 38 2
23 Jun 01 **NEVER GONNA COME BACK DOWN** *Ministry of Sound MOSBT CDS1* 51 1
15 May 04 **LOVE COMES AGAIN** *Nebula NEBCD 058* [4] 30 3

[1] BT featuring Vincent Covello [2] BT featuring Tori Amos [3] BT featuring Kirsty Hawkshaw [4] Tiesto featuring BT

BT EXPRESS *US, male instrumental / vocal group (3 Singles: 11 Weeks)*

29 Mar 75 **EXPRESS** *Pye International 7N 25674* $ **34** 6
26 Jul 80 **DOES IT FEEL GOOD / GIVE UP THE FUNK (LET'S DANCE)** *Calibre CAB 503* **52** 4
23 Apr 94 **EXPRESS** (re-mix) *PWL International PWCD 285* **67** 1

B BUMBLE and The STINGERS
US, male instrumental group (2 Singles: 26 Weeks)

19 Apr 62 ★ **NUT ROCKER** *Top Rank JAR 611* **1** 15
3 Jun 72 **NUT ROCKER** (re-issue) *Stateside SS 2203* **19** 11

B-CREW *US, female vocal group*

20 Sep 97 **PARTAY FEELING** *Positiva CDTIV 78* **45** 1

B-MOVIE
UK, male vocal / instrumental group (2 Singles: 7 Weeks)

18 Apr 81 **REMEMBRANCE DAY** *Deram DM 437* **61** 3
27 Mar 82 **NOWHERE GIRL** *Some Bizzare B258* **67** 4

B-TRIBE *Spain, male / female vocal / instrumental group*

25 Sep 93 **¡FIESTA FATAL!** *East West YZ 770CD* **64** 4

B2K
US, male vocal group (1 Album: 12 Weeks, 5 Singles: 20 Weeks)

24 Aug 02 **UH HUH** *Epic 6729512* **35** 2
29 Mar 03 **BUMP, BUMP, BUMP** *Epic 6732762* [1] ▲ **24** 3
5 Apr 03 PANDEMONIUM *Epic 5105342* 35 12
21 Jun 03 ● **GIRLFRIEND** *Epic 6739332* **10** 8
18 Oct 03 **UH HUH 2003** *Epic 6744012* **31** 2
20 Mar 04 **BADABOOM** *Epic 6747512* [2] **26** 5

[1] B2K featuring P Diddy [2] B2K featuring Fabolous

BVSMP *US, male rap / vocal group*

23 Jul 88 ● **I NEED YOU** *Debut DEBT 3044* **3** 12

B*WITCHED
Ireland, female vocal group (2 Albums: 48 Weeks, 8 Singles: 98 Weeks)

6 Jun 98 ★ **C'EST LA VIE** *Glow Worm / Epic 6660532* ■ **1** 19
3 Oct 98 ★ **ROLLERCOASTER** *Glow Worm / Epic 6664752* ■ **1** 15
24 Oct 98 ● B*WITCHED *Epic 4917042* 3 36
19 Dec 98 ★ **TO YOU I BELONG (re)** *Glow Worm / Epic 6667712* ■ **1** 14
27 Mar 99 ★ **BLAME IT ON THE WEATHERMAN** *Glow Worm / Epic 6670335* ■ **1** 9
10 Apr 99 ● **THANK ABBA FOR THE MUSIC** *Epic ABCD 1* [1] **4** 13
16 Oct 99 ● **JESSE HOLD ON (re)** *Glow Worm / Epic 6679612* **4** 12
30 Oct 99 ● AWAKE AND BREATHE *Epic 4960792* 5 12
18 Dec 99 **I SHALL BE THERE** *Glow Worm / Epic 683332* [2] **13** 9
8 Apr 00 **JUMP DOWN (re)** *Glow Worm / Epic 6691282* **16** 7

[1] Steps, Tina Cousins, Cleopatra, B*Witched, Billie [2] B*Witched featuring Ladysmith Black Mambazo

BABE INSTINCT *UK, female vocal group*

16 Jan 99 **DISCO BABES FROM OUTER SPACE** *Positiva CDTIV 103* **21** 2

BABE TEAM *UK, female vocal group*

8 Jun 02 **OVER THERE** *Edel 0140655 ERE* **45** 2

BABES IN TOYLAND
US, female vocal / instrumental group (2 Albums: 3 Weeks)

5 Sep 92 FONTANELLE *Southern 185012* 24 2
3 Jul 93 PAINKILLERS *Southern 185122* 53 1

Alice BABS *Sweden, female vocalist – Alice Nilsson*

15 Aug 63 **AFTER YOU'VE GONE** *Fontana TF 409* **43** 1

BABY ANIMALS
Australia, male vocal / instrumental group

14 Mar 92 BABY ANIMALS *Imago PD 90580* 70 1

BABY BUMPS *UK, male / female vocal / instrumental duo – Sean Casey and Lisa Millett (2 Singles: 6 Weeks)*

8 Aug 98 **BURNING** *Delirious DELICD 10* **17** 4
26 Feb 00 **I GOT THIS FEELING** *Sound of Ministry MOSCDS 137* **22** 2

BABY D *UK, male / female vocal (Dee Galdes / Fearon) / instrumental group (1 Album: 5 Weeks, 7 Singles: 45 Weeks)*

18 Dec 93 **DESTINY** *Production House PNC 057* **69** 1
23 Jul 94 **CASANOVA** *Production House PNC 065* **67** 1
19 Nov 94 ★ **LET ME BE YOUR FANTASY** *Systematic SYSCD 4* **1** 14
3 Jun 95 ● **(EVERYBODY'S GOT TO LEARN SOMETIME) I NEED YOUR LOVING** *Systematic SYSCD 11* **3** 12
13 Jan 96 ● **SO PURE** *Systematic SYSCD 21* **3** 7
10 Feb 96 ● DELIVERANCE *Systematic 8287202* 5 5
6 Apr 96 **TAKE ME TO HEAVEN** *Systematic SYSCD 26* **15** 5
2 Sep 00 **LET ME BE YOUR FANTASY** (re-mix) *Systematic SYSCD 35* **16** 5

BABY DC featuring IMAJIN
US, male rapper – Derrick Coleman Jr and vocal group

24 Apr 99 **BOUNCE, ROCK, SKATE, ROLL** *Jive 0522142* **45** 1

BABY FORD
UK, male DJ / producer – Peter Ford (4 Singles: 16 Weeks)

10 Sep 88 **OOCHY KOOCHY (F.U. BABY YEAH YEAH)** *Rhythm King 7BFORD 1* **58** 6
24 Dec 88 **CHIKKI CHIKKI AHH AHH (re)** *Rhythm King 7BFORD 2* **54** 4
17 Jun 89 **CHILDREN OF THE REVOLUTION** *Rhythm King 7BFORD 4* **53** 4
17 Feb 90 **BEACH BUMP** *Rhythm King 7BFORD 6* **68** 2

BABY JUNE *UK, male vocalist – Tim Hegarty*

15 Aug 92 **HEY! WHAT'S YOUR NAME** *Arista 115271* **75** 1

BABY O *US, male / female vocal / instrumental group*

26 Jul 80 **IN THE FOREST** *Calibre CAB 505* **46** 5

BABY ROOTS *UK, male vocalist*

1 Aug 92 **ROCK ME BABY** *ZYX ZYX 68027* **71** 1

BABY SHAMBLES (see also The LIBERTINES; LITTLE'ANS featuring Peter DOHERTY) *UK, male / female vocal / instrumental group – leader Peter Doherty (1 Album: 2 Weeks, 3 Singles: 17 Weeks)*

11 Dec 04 ● **KILLAMANGIRO** *Rough Trade RTRADSCD 201* **8** 8
27 Aug 05 ● **FUCK FOREVER** *Rough Trade RTRADSCDX 210* **4** 5
26 Nov 05 ● DOWN IN ALBION *Rough Trade RTRADCD 240* [1] 10 2
10 Dec 05 ● **ALBION** *Rough Trade RTRADCDX 260* [1] ..... **8** 4+

[1] Babyshambles [1] Babyshambles

BABYBIRD *UK, male vocal (Stephen Jones) / instrumental group (2 Albums: 14 Weeks, 9 Singles: 35 Weeks)*

10 Aug 96 **GOODNIGHT** *Echo ECSCD 24* **28** 2
12 Oct 96 ● **YOU'RE GORGEOUS** *Echo ECSD 26* **3** 16
2 Nov 96 ● UGLY BEAUTIFUL *Echo ECHCD 11* 9 12
1 Feb 97 **CANDY GIRL** *Echo ECSCD 31* **14** 3
17 May 97 **CORNERSHOP** *Echo ECSCD 33* **37** 2
9 May 98 **BAD OLD MAN** *Echo ECSCD 60* **31** 2
22 Aug 98 **IF YOU'LL BE MINE** *Echo ECSCX 65* **28** 4
5 Sep 98 THERE'S SOMETHING GOING ON *Echo ECHCD 24* 28 2
27 Feb 99 **BACK TOGETHER** *Echo ECSCD 73* **22** 3
25 Mar 00 **THE F-WORD** *Echo ECSCD 92* **35** 2
3 Jun 00 **OUT OF SIGHT** *Echo ECSCD 97* **58** 1

BABYFACE *US, male vocalist / producer – Kenneth Edmonds (1 Album: 5 Weeks, 6 Singles: 23 Weeks)*

9 Jul 94 **ROCK BOTTOM** *Epic 6601832* **50** 4
1 Oct 94 **WHEN CAN I SEE YOU** *Epic 6606592* **35** 3
9 Nov 96 **THIS IS FOR THE LOVER IN YOU** *Epic 6639352* $ **12** 5
16 Nov 96 THE DAY *Epic 4853682* 34 5
8 Mar 97 **EVERYTIME I CLOSE MY EYES** *Epic 6642492* **13** 4
19 Jul 97 ● **HOW COME, HOW LONG** *Epic 6646202* [1] **10** 5
25 Oct 97 **SUNSHINE** *Northwestside 74321528702* [2] **25** 2

[1] Babyface featuring Stevie Wonder [2] Jay-Z featuring Babyface and Foxy Brown

KEY UK No.1 ★ UK Top 10 ● Still on chart + UK entry at No.1 ■ US No.1 ▲ UK million seller £ US million seller $
Singles re-entries are listed as (re), (2re), (3re)… which signifies that the hit re-entered the chart once, twice or three times…
Peak Position / Weeks

BABYLON ZOO *UK, male vocalist / multi-instrumentalist – Jas Mann (1 Album: 5 Weeks, 4 Singles: 20 Weeks)*

27 Jan 96 ★ **SPACEMAN** *EMI CDEM 416* ■ £ 1 14
17 Feb 96 ● THE BOY WITH THE X-RAY EYES *EMI CDEMC 3742* 6 5
27 Apr 96 **ANIMAL ARMY** *EMI CDEM 425* 17 3
5 Oct 96 **THE BOY WITH THE X-RAY EYES** *EMI CDEMS 440* 32 2
6 Feb 99 **ALL THE MONEY'S GONE** *EMI CDEM 519* 46 1

The BABYS
US / UK, male vocal / instrumental group – includes John Waite

21 Jan 78 **ISN'T IT TIME** *Chrysalis CHS 2173* 45 3

BACCARA *Spain, female vocal duo – Maria Mendiola and Mayte Mateos (1 Album: 6 Weeks, 2 Singles: 25 Weeks)*

17 Sep 77 ★ **YES SIR, I CAN BOOGIE** *RCA PB 5526* 1 16
14 Jan 78 ● **SORRY I'M A LADY** *RCA PB 5555* 8 9
4 Mar 78 BACCARA *RCA PL 28316* 26 6

Burt BACHARACH
US, male pianist (5 Albums: 47 Weeks, 2 Singles: 12 Weeks)

20 May 65 ● **TRAINS AND BOATS AND PLANES** *London HL 9968* [1] 4 11
22 May 65 ● HIT MAKER – BURT BACHARACH *London HAR 8233* 3 18
28 Nov 70 REACH OUT *A&M AMLS 908* 52 3
27 Mar 71 ● PORTRAIT IN MUSIC *A&M AMLS 2010* 5 23
10 Oct 98 PAINTED FROM MEMORY *Mercury 5380022* [1] 32 2
1 May 99 **TOLEDO** *Mercury 8709652* [2] 72 1
5 Nov 05 AT THIS TIME *Sony BMG 82876734112* 60 1

[1] Burt Bacharach, his Orchestra and Chorus [2] Elvis Costello / Burt Bacharach
[1] Elvis Costello with Burt Bacharach

The BACHELORS (212 Top 500)
Irish vocal / instrumental trio from Dublin who were one of the few popular non-rock groups of the 1960s: brothers Declan and Con Cluskey and John Stokes. The first trio to top the UK singles chart, they had hits on both sides of the Atlantic with revivals of popular pre-rock ballads (8 Albums: 102 Weeks, 17 Singles: 187 Weeks)

24 Jan 63 ● **CHARMAINE** *Decca F 11559* 6 19
4 Jul 63 **FARAWAY PLACES** *Decca F 11666* 36 3
29 Aug 63 **WHISPERING** *Decca F 11712* 18 10
23 Jan 64 ★ **DIANE** *Decca F 11799* 1 19
19 Mar 64 ● **I BELIEVE** *Decca F 11857* 2 17
4 Jun 64 ● **RAMONA** *Decca F 11910* 4 13
27 Jun 64 ● THE BACHELORS AND 16 GREAT SONGS *Decca LK 4614* 2 44
13 Aug 64 ● **I WOULDN'T TRADE YOU FOR THE WORLD** *Decca F 11949* 4 16
3 Dec 64 ● **NO ARMS CAN EVER HOLD YOU** *Decca F 12034* 7 12
1 Apr 65 **TRUE LOVE FOR EVER MORE** *Decca F 12108* 34 6
20 May 65 ● **MARIE** *Decca F 12156* 9 12
9 Oct 65 MORE GREAT SONG HITS FROM THE BACHELORS *Decca LK 4721* 15 6
28 Oct 65 **IN THE CHAPEL IN THE MOONLIGHT** *Decca F 12256* 27 10
6 Jan 66 **HELLO, DOLLY!** *Decca F 12309* 38 4
17 Mar 66 ● **THE SOUND OF SILENCE** *Decca F 12351* 3 13
7 Jul 66 **CAN I TRUST YOU** *Decca F 12417* 26 7
9 Jul 66 HITS OF THE SIXTIES *Decca TXL 102* 12 9
5 Nov 66 BACHELORS' GIRLS *Decca LK 4827* 24 7
1 Dec 66 **WALK WITH FAITH IN YOUR HEART** *Decca F 22523* 21 9
6 Apr 67 **OH HOW I MISS YOU** *Decca F 22592* 30 8
1 Jul 67 GOLDEN ALL TIME HITS *Decca SKL 4849* 19 7
5 Jul 67 **MARTA** *Decca F 22634* 20 9
14 Jun 69 ● WORLD OF THE BACHELORS *Decca SPA 2* 8 18
23 Aug 69 WORLD OF THE BACHELORS VOLUME 2 *Decca SPA 22* 11 7
22 Dec 79 25 GOLDEN GREATS *Warwick WW 5068* 38 4

Tal BACHMAN *Canada, male vocalist / guitarist*

30 Oct 99 **SHE'S SO HIGH** *Columbia 6679932* 30 2

BACHMAN-TURNER OVERDRIVE (see also Randy BACHMAN) *Canada, male vocal / instrumental group (1 Album: 13 Weeks, 2 Singles: 18 Weeks)*

16 Nov 74 ● **YOU AIN'T SEEN NOTHING YET** *Mercury 6167 025* ▲ $ 2 12
14 Dec 74 NOT FRAGILE *Mercury 9100 007* ▲ 12 13
1 Feb 75 **ROLL ON DOWN THE HIGHWAY** *Mercury 6167 071* 22 6

BACK TO THE PLANET *UK, male / female vocal / instrumental group (1 Album: 2 Weeks, 2 Singles: 2 Weeks)*

10 Apr 93 **TEENAGE TURTLES** *Parallel LLLCD 3* 52 1
4 Sep 93 **DAYDREAM** *Parallel LLLCD 8* 52 1
18 Sep 93 MIND AND SOUL COLLABORATORS *Parallel ALLCD 2* 32 2

BACKBEAT BAND *US, male vocal / instrumental group (1 Album: 2 Weeks, 2 Singles: 5 Weeks)*

26 Mar 94 **MONEY (re)** *Virgin VSCDX 1489* 48 4
16 Apr 94 BACKBEAT (FILM SOUNDTRACK) *Virgin CDV 2729* 39 2
14 May 94 **PLEASE MR POSTMAN** *Virgin VSCDX 1502* 69 1

BACKSTREET BOYS (172 Top 500) *American boy band who have sold over 70 million records: Brian Littrell, Nick Carter, A J McLean, Howie Dorough, Kevin Richardson. They created teen hysteria in Europe before becoming 1999's top-selling act in their homeland. Their 13 consecutive UK Top 10 entries are a record for a US group. Act reformed successfully in 2005 after a five year break (6 Albums: 151 Weeks, 21 Singles: 172 Weeks)*

28 Oct 95 **WE'VE GOT IT GOIN' ON** *Jive JIVECD 386* 54 1
16 Dec 95 **I'LL NEVER BREAK YOUR HEART** *Jive JIVECD 389* 42 3
1 Jun 96 **GET DOWN (YOU'RE THE ONE FOR ME)** *Jive JIVECD 394* 14 8
24 Aug 96 ● **WE'VE GOT IT GOIN' ON** (re-issue) *Jive JIVECD 400* 3 7
21 Sep 96 BACKSTREET BOYS *Jive CHIP 169* 12 19
16 Nov 96 ● **I'LL NEVER BREAK YOUR HEART** (re-issue) *Jive JIVECD 406* 8 8
18 Jan 97 ● **QUIT PLAYING GAMES (WITH MY HEART)** *Jive JIVECD 409* $ 2 10
29 Mar 97 ● **ANYWHERE FOR YOU (2re)** *Jive JIVECD 416* 4 8
2 Aug 97 ● **EVERYBODY (BACKSTREET'S BACK)** *Jive JIVECD 426* $ 3 11
23 Aug 97 ● BACKSTREET'S BACK *Jive CHIP 186* 2 44
11 Oct 97 ● **AS LONG AS YOU LOVE ME** *Jive JIVECD 434* 3 19
14 Feb 98 ● **ALL I HAVE TO GIVE** *Jive JIVECD 445* $ 2 12
15 May 99 ★ **I WANT IT THAT WAY** *Jive 0523392* ■ 1 14
29 May 99 ● MILLENNIUM *Jive 523222* ▲ 2 56
30 Oct 99 ● **LARGER THAN LIFE** *Jive 0550562* 5 14
26 Feb 00 **SHOW ME THE MEANING OF BEING LONELY** (import) *Jive IMPORT 9250082* 66 1
4 Mar 00 ● **SHOW ME THE MEANING OF BEING LONELY (re)** *Jive 9250082* 3 11
24 Jun 00 ● **THE ONE (re)** *Jive 9250662* 8 8
18 Nov 00 ● **SHAPE OF MY HEART** *Jive 9251442* 4 9
2 Dec 00 BLACK & BLUE *Jive 9221172* ▲ 13 9
24 Feb 01 ● **THE CALL** *Jive 9251702* 8 5
7 Jul 01 **MORE THAN THAT** *Jive 9252342* 12 5
10 Nov 01 ● GREATEST HITS – CHAPTER ONE *Jive 9222672* 5 18
12 Jan 02 ● **DROWNING** *Jive 9252882* 4 7
25 Jun 05 NEVER GONE *Jive 82876702652* 11 5
9 Jul 05 ● **INCOMPLETE** *Jive 82876699282* 8 8
5 Nov 05 ● **JUST WANT YOU TO KNOW** *Jive 82876733802* 8 3

Never Gone was available only as a CD and DVD package.

BACKYARD DOG *UK, male vocal / production group*

7 Jul 01 **BADDEST RUFFEST (re)** *East West EW 233CD* 15 6

BAD BOYS INC
UK, male vocal group (1 Album: 6 Weeks, 6 Singles: 31 Weeks)

14 Aug 93 **DON'T TALK ABOUT LOVE** *A&M 5803412* 19 5
2 Oct 93 **WHENEVER YOU NEED SOMEONE** *A&M 5804032* 26 3
11 Dec 93 **WALKING ON AIR** *A&M 5804692* 24 6
21 May 94 ● **MORE TO THIS WORLD** *A&M 5806072* 8 7
18 Jun 94 BAD BOYS INC *A&M 5402002* 13 6
23 Jul 94 **TAKE ME AWAY (I'LL FOLLOW YOU)** *A&M 5806912* 15 6
17 Sep 94 **LOVE HERE I COME** *A&M 5807752* 26 4

BAD COMPANY (see also QUEEN) *UK, male vocal (Paul Rodgers) / instrumental group (6 Albums: 87 Weeks, 3 Singles: 23 Weeks)*

1 Jun 74 **CAN'T GET ENOUGH** *Island WIP 6191* 15 8

15 Jun 74 ● BAD COMPANY *Island ILPS 9279* ▲ 3 25
22 Mar 75 **GOOD LOVIN' GONE BAD** *Island WIP 6223* **31** 6
12 Apr 75 ● STRAIGHT SHOOTER *Island ILPS 9304* 3 27
30 Aug 75 **FEEL LIKE MAKIN' LOVE** *Island WIP 6242* **20** 9
21 Feb 76 ● RUN WITH THE PACK *Island ILPS 9346* 4 12
19 Mar 77 BURNIN' SKY *Island ILPS 9441* 17 8
17 Mar 79 ● DESOLATION ANGELS *Swansong SSK 59408* 10 9
28 Aug 82 ROUGH DIAMONDS *Swansong SSK 59419* 15 6

BAD COMPANY (see also DJ FRESH; FRESH BC)
UK, male production group (3 Singles: 5 Weeks)

9 Mar 02 **SPACEHOPPER / TONIGHT** *Ram RAMM 37* **56** 1
4 May 02 **RUSH HOUR / BLIND** *BC Recordings BCRUK 002CD* **59** 1
15 Mar 03 **MO' FIRE** *BC Recordings BCRUK 003CD* **24** 3

BAD ENGLISH *UK / US, male vocal / instrumental group (2 Albums: 2 Weeks, 1 Single: 3 Weeks)*

16 Sep 89 BAD ENGLISH *Epic 4634471* 74 1
25 Nov 89 **WHEN I SEE YOU SMILE** *Epic 655347 1* ▲ **61** 3
19 Oct 91 BACKLASH *Epic 4685691* 64 1

BAD HABIT BOYS *Germany, male production duo*

1 Jul 00 **WEEKEND** *Inferno CDFERN 28* **41** 1

BAD MANNERS (474 Top 500)
Good-time ska band fronted by shaven-headed Buster Bloodvessel, b. Douglas Trendle, 6 Sep 1958, London, UK. They spent more weeks on the UK chart in 1980 (45) than anyone bar Madness. Even after the hits, they remained a popular live attraction (5 Albums: 44 Weeks, 12 Singles: 111 Weeks)

1 Mar 80 **NE-NE NA-NA NA-NA NU-NU** *Magnet MAG 164* **28** 14
26 Apr 80 SKA 'N' B *Magnet MAG 5033* 34 13
14 Jun 80 **LIP UP FATTY** *Magnet MAG 175* **15** 14
27 Sep 80 ● **SPECIAL BREW** *Magnet MAG 180* **3** 13
29 Nov 80 LOONEE TUNES *Magnet MAG 5038* 36 12
6 Dec 80 **LORRAINE** *Magnet MAG 181* **21** 12
28 Mar 81 **JUST A FEELING** *Magnet MAG 187* **13** 9
27 Jun 81 ● **CAN CAN** *Magnet MAG 190* **3** 13
26 Sep 81 ● **WALKING IN THE SUNSHINE** *Magnet MAG 197* **10** 9
24 Oct 81 GOSH IT'S BAD MANNERS *Magnet MAGL 5043* 18 12
21 Nov 81 **THE R'N'B PARTY FOUR (EP)** *Magnet MAG 211* **34** 9
1 May 82 **GOT NO BRAINS** *Magnet MAG 216* **44** 5
31 Jul 82 ● **MY GIRL LOLLIPOP (MY BOY LOLLIPOP)** *Magnet MAG 232* **9** 7
30 Oct 82 **SAMSON AND DELILAH** *Magnet MAG 236* **58** 3
27 Nov 82 FORGING AHEAD *Magnet MAGL 5050* 78 1
7 May 83 THE HEIGHT OF BAD MANNERS *Telstar STAR 2229* 23 6
14 May 83 **THAT'LL DO NICELY** *Magnet MAG 243* **49** 3

Tracks on The R'n'B Party Four (EP): Bueno Sera / Don't Be Angry / No Respect / The New One

BAD MEETS EVIL featuring EMINEM & ROYCE DA 5'9" (see also EMINEM) *US, male producer and rappers*

1 Sep 01 **SCARY MOVIES** *Mole UK MOLEUK 045* **63** 1

BAD NEWS *UK, male vocal group*

12 Sep 87 **BOHEMIAN RHAPSODY** *EMI EM 24* **44** 5
24 Oct 87 BAD NEWS *EMI EMC 3535* 69 1

BAD RELIGION
US, male vocal / instrumental group (2 Singles: 3 Weeks)

11 Feb 95 **21ST CENTURY (DIGITAL BOY)** *Columbia 6611435* **41** 2
21 Aug 04 **LOS ANGELES IS BURNING** *Epitaph 11692* **67** 1

Angelo BADALAMENTI with Julee CRUISE and VARIOUS ARISTS (see also BOOTH and The BAD ANGEL; ORBITAL)
US, male composer and female vocalist

17 Nov 90 MUSIC FROM 'TWIN PEAKS' *Warner Bros. 7599263161* 27 25

Wally BADAROU *France, male keyboard player*

19 Oct 85 **CHIEF INSPECTOR** *Fourth & Broadway BRW 37* **46** 6

BADDIEL and SKINNER and The LIGHTNING SEEDS
UK, male vocal group – David Baddiel, Frank Skinner (Christopher Collins) and The Lightning Seeds (3 Singles: 34 Weeks)

1 Jun 96 ★ **THREE LIONS (THE OFFICIAL SONG OF THE ENGLAND FOOTBALL TEAM)** *Epic 6632732* [1] ■ **1** 15
20 Jun 98 ★ **THREE LIONS '98** *Epic 6660982* [1] ■ **1** 13
15 Jun 02 **THREE LIONS '98 (re)** (re-issue) *Epic 6728152* [2] **16** 6

[1] Baddiel and Skinner and The Lightning Seeds [2] Baddiel, Skinner and The Lightning Seeds

BADFELLAS featuring CK
UK, male production group and Kenya, female vocalist

15 Feb 03 **SOC IT TO ME** *Serious SER 053CD* **55** 1

BADFINGER *UK, male vocal / instrumental group (3 Singles: 34 Weeks)*

10 Jan 70 ● **COME AND GET IT** *Apple 20* **4** 11
9 Jan 71 ● **NO MATTER WHAT** *Apple 31* **5** 12
29 Jan 72 ● **DAY AFTER DAY** *Apple 40* $ **10** 11

BADLANDS *UK, male vocal / instrumental group (2 Albums: 3 Weeks)*

24 Jun 89 BADLANDS *WEA 7819661* 39 2
22 Jun 91 VOODOO HIGHWAY *Atlantic 7567822511* 74 1

BADLY DRAWN BOY *UK, male vocalist / producer / instrumentalist – Damon Gough (4 Albums: 89 Weeks, 11 Singles: 28 Weeks)*

4 Sep 99 **ONCE AROUND THE BLOCK** *Twisted Nerve / XL Recordings TNXL 003CD* **46** 2
17 Jun 00 **ANOTHER PEARL** *Twisted Nerve / XL Recordings TNXL 004CD* **41** 1
8 Jul 00 THE HOUR OF BEWILDERBEAST *XL Recordings TNXLCD 133* 13 47
16 Sep 00 **DISILLUSION** *Twisted Nerve / XL Recordings TNXL 005CD* **26** 2
25 Nov 00 **ONCE AROUND THE BLOCK** (re-issue) *Twisted Nerve / XL Recordings TNXL 009CD* **27** 2
19 May 01 **PISSING IN THE WIND** *Twisted Nerve / XL Recordings TNXL 010CD* **22** 2
6 Apr 02 **SILENT SIGH** *Twisted Nerve / XL Recordings TNXL 012CD* **16** 7
20 Apr 02 ● ABOUT A BOY – ORIGINAL SOUNDTRACK *Twisted Nerve TNXLCD 152* 6 18
22 Jun 02 **SOMETHING TO TALK ABOUT** *Twisted Nerve / XL Recordings TNXL 014CD* **28** 2
26 Oct 02 ● **YOU WERE RIGHT** *Twisted Nerve / XL Recordings TNXL 015CD* **9** 3
16 Nov 02 ● HAVE YOU FED THE FISH? *XL Recordings TNXLCD 156* 10 20
18 Jan 03 **BORN AGAIN** *Twisted Nerve / XL Recordings TNXL 016CD* **16** 3
3 May 03 **ALL POSSIBILITIES** *Twisted Nerve / XL Recordings TNXL 017CD* **24** 2
3 Jul 04 ● ONE PLUS ONE IS ONE *Twisted Nerve / XL Recordings TNXLCD 179* 9 4
31 Jul 04 **YEAR OF THE RAT** *XL Recordings TNXL 018CD* **38** 2

BADMAN *UK, male producer – Julian Brettle*

2 Feb 91 **MAGIC STYLE** *Citybeat CBE 759* **61** 3

Erykah BADU *US, female vocalist – Erica Wright (1 Album: 25 Weeks, 6 Singles: 17 Weeks)*

1 Mar 97 BADUIZM *MCA UD 530272* 17 25
19 Apr 97 **ON & ON** *Universal UND 561117* **12** 4
14 Jun 97 **NEXT LIFETIME** *Universal UND 56132* **30** 3
29 Nov 97 **APPLE TREE** *Universal UND 56150* **47** 1
11 Jul 98 **ONE** *Elektra E 3833CD 1* [1] **23** 3
6 Mar 99 **YOU GOT ME** *MCA MCSTD 48110* [2] **31** 2
15 Sep 01 **SWEET BABY** *Epic 6718822* [3] **23** 4

[1] Busta Rhymes featuring Erykah Badu [2] Roots featuring Erykah Badu
[3] Macy Gray featuring Erykah Badu

Joan BAEZ
US, female vocalist / guitarist (6 Albums: 88 Weeks, 6 Singles: 47 Weeks)

18 Jul 64 ● JOAN BAEZ IN CONCERT VOLUME 2 *Fontana TFL 6033* 8 19
6 May 65 **WE SHALL OVERCOME** *Fontana TF 564* **26** 10
15 May 65 ● JOAN BAEZ 5 *Fontana TFL 6043* 3 27
19 Jun 65 ● JOAN BAEZ *Fontana TFL 6002* 9 13

7 January 1955	14 January 1955	21 January 1955	28 January 1955
THE FINGER OF SUSPICION Dickie Valentine with The Stargazers	**MAMBO ITALIANO** Rosemary Clooney and The Mellomen	**THE FINGER OF SUSPICION** Dickie Valentine with The Stargazers	**THE FINGER OF SUSPICION** Dickie Valentine with The Stargazers

KEY UK No.1 ★ UK Top 10 ● Still on chart + UK entry at No.1 ■ US No.1 ▲ UK million seller £ US million seller $
Singles re-entries are listed as (re), (2re), (3re)... which signifies that the hit re-entered the chart once, twice or three times...
Peak Position / Weeks

8 Jul 65 ● **THERE BUT FOR FORTUNE** *Fontana TF 587*....8 12
2 Sep 65 **IT'S ALL OVER NOW, BABY BLUE** *Fontana TF 604*....22 8
27 Nov 65 ● FAREWELL ANGELINA *Fontana TFL 6058*....5 23
23 Dec 65 **FAREWELL ANGELINA (re)** *Fontana TF 639*....35 4
28 Jul 66 **PACK UP YOUR SORROWS** *Fontana TF 727*....50 1
19 Jul 69 JOAN BAEZ ON VANGUARD *Vanguard SVXL 100*....15 5
3 Apr 71 FIRST TEN YEARS *Vanguard 6635 003*....41 1
9 Oct 71 ● **THE NIGHT THEY DROVE OLD DIXIE DOWN** *Vanguard VS 35138* $....6 12

BAHA MEN *Bahamas, male vocal group (3 Singles: 35 Weeks)*

14 Oct 00 ● **WHO LET THE DOGS OUT** *Edel 0115425 ERE*....2 23
3 Feb 01 **YOU ALL DAT** *Edel 0124855 ERE*....14 5
13 Jul 02 **MOVE IT LIKE THIS** *S-Curve / EMI CDEM 615*....16 7

'You All Dat' features vocal by Imani Coppola.

Carol BAILEY *UK, female vocalist*

25 Feb 95 **FEEL IT** *Multiply CDMULTY 3*....41 2

Philip BAILEY (see also EARTH WIND AND FIRE) *US, male vocalist (1 Album: 17 Weeks, 2 Singles: 20 Weeks)*

9 Mar 85 ★ **EASY LOVER** *CBS A 4915* [1] $....1 12
30 Mar 85 CHINESE WALL *CBS 26161*....29 17
18 May 85 **WALKING ON THE CHINESE WALL** *CBS A 6202*....34 8

[1] Philip Bailey (duet with Phil Collins)

Corinne BAILEY RAE NEW *UK, female vocalist*

19 Nov 05 **LIKE A STAR** *EMI CDEM 678*....34 2

Merril BAINBRIDGE *Australia, female vocalist*

7 Dec 96 **MOUTH** *Gotham 74321431012*....51 1

Adrian BAKER and The TONICS (see also GIDEA PARK) *UK, male vocalist*

19 Jul 75 ● **SHERRY** *Magnet MAG 34*....10 8

Anita BAKER *US, female vocalist (5 Albums: 83 Weeks, 5 Singles: 22 Weeks)*

3 May 86 RAPTURE *Elektra EKT 37*....13 47
15 Nov 86 **SWEET LOVE** *Elektra EKR 44*....13 10
31 Jan 87 **CAUGHT UP IN THE RAPTURE** *Elektra EKR 49*....51 5
8 Oct 88 **GIVING YOU THE BEST THAT I GOT** *Elektra EKR 79*....55 3
29 Oct 88 ● GIVING YOU THE BEST THAT I GOT *Elektra EKT 49* ▲....9 20
30 Jun 90 **TALK TO ME** *Elektra EKR 111*....68 2
14 Jul 90 ● COMPOSITIONS *Elektra EKT 72*....7 9
17 Sep 94 **BODY & SOUL** *Elektra EKR 190CD*....48 2
24 Sep 94 RHYTHM OF LOVE *Elektra 7559615552*....14 5
1 Jun 02 SWEET LOVE – THE VERY BEST OF ANITA BAKER *Atlantic 8122736032*....49 2

Arthur BAKER
(see also Wally JUMP Jr and The CRIMINAL ELEMENT; Jack E MAKOSSA)
US, male producer / multi-instrumentalist (3 Singles: 8 Weeks)

20 May 89 **IT'S YOUR TIME** *Breakout USA 654* [1]....64 2
21 Oct 89 **THE MESSAGE IS LOVE** *Breakout USA 668* [2]....38 5
30 Nov 02 **CONFUSION** *Whacked WACKT 002CD* [3]....64 1

[1] Arthur Baker featuring Shirley Lewis [2] Arthur Baker and The Backbeat Disciples featuring Al Green [3] Arthur Baker vs New Order

George BAKER SELECTION
Holland, male / female vocal / instrumental group

6 Sep 75 ● **PALOMA BLANCA** *Warner Bros. K 16541*....10 10

Hylda BAKER and Arthur MULLARD *UK, female, b. 4 Feb 1905, d. 1 May 1986 / male, b. 10 Nov 1913, d. 11 Dec 1995, actors / vocal duo*

9 Sep 78 **YOU'RE THE ONE THAT I WANT** *Pye 7N 46121*....22 6

Ginger BAKER'S AIR FORCE (see also BBM; BAKER-GURVITZ ARMY; BLIND FAITH) *UK, male vocal / instrumental group*

13 Jun 70 GINGER BAKER'S AIR FORCE *Polydor 266 2001*....37 1

BAKER-GURVITZ ARMY (see also BBM; Ginger BAKER'S AIR FORCE; BLIND FAITH) *UK, male vocal / instrumental group*

22 Feb 75 BAKER-GURVITZ ARMY *Vertigo 9103 201*....22 5

BAKSHELF DOG *UK, male bulldog vocalist – Churchill*

21 Dec 02 **NO LIMITS** *WVC CDCHURCH 1*....51 2

BALAAM and The ANGEL *UK, male vocal / instrumental group*

29 Mar 86 **SHE KNOWS** *Virgin VS 842*....70 2
16 Aug 86 THE GREATEST STORY EVER TOLD *Virgin V 2377*....67 2

Long John BALDRY
UK, male vocalist, b. 12 Jan 1941, d. 21 Jul 2005 (4 Singles: 36 Weeks)

8 Nov 67 ★ **LET THE HEARTACHES BEGIN** *Pye 7N 17385*....1 13
28 Aug 68 **WHEN THE SUN COMES SHINING THRU** *Pye 7N 17593*....29 7
23 Oct 68 **MEXICO** *Pye 7N 17563*....15 8
29 Jan 69 **IT'S TOO LATE NOW** *Pye 7N 17664*....21 8

BALEARIC BILL (see also AIRSCAPE; BLUE BAMBOO; CUBIC 22; SVENSON and GIELEN; TRANSFORMER 2)
Belgium / Holland, male production duo – Johan Gielen and Sven Maes

2 Oct 99 **DESTINATION SUNSHINE** *Xtravaganza XTRAV 3CDS*....36 2

Edward BALL *UK, male vocalist (2 Singles: 2 Weeks)*

20 Jul 96 **THE MILL HILL SELF HATE CLUB** *Creation CRESCD 233*....57 1
22 Feb 97 **LOVE IS BLUE** *Creation CRESCD 244*....59 1

Kenny BALL and his JAZZMEN 375 Top 500
Top UK trad jazz bandleader, b. 22 May 1930, Essex. His Dixieland band was at the forefront of the early 1960s jazz revival. Their biggest hit, 'Midnight in Moscow', reached the runner-up spot on both sides of the Atlantic (2 Albums: 50 Weeks, 14 Singles: 136 Weeks)

23 Feb 61 **SAMANTHA** *Pye Jazz Today 7NJ 2040* [1]....13 15
11 May 61 **I STILL LOVE YOU ALL** *Pye Jazz 7NJ 2042*....24 6
31 Aug 61 **SOMEDAY (YOU'LL BE SORRY)** *Pye Jazz 7NJ 2047*....28 6
9 Nov 61 ● **MIDNIGHT IN MOSCOW** *Pye Jazz 7NJ 2049*....2 21
15 Feb 62 ● **MARCH OF THE SIAMESE CHILDREN** *Pye Jazz 7NJ 2051*....4 13
17 May 62 ● **THE GREEN LEAVES OF SUMMER** *Pye Jazz 7NJ 2054*....7 14
23 Aug 62 **SO DO I** *Pye Jazz 7NJ 2056*....14 8
25 Aug 62 ★ THE BEST OF BALL, BARBER AND BILK *Pye Golden Guinea GGL 0131* [1]....1 24
18 Oct 62 **THE PAY-OFF (AMOI DE PAYER)** *Pye Jazz 7NJ 2061* [2]....23 6
17 Jan 63 ● **SUKIYAKI** *Pye Jazz 7NJ 2062*....10 13
25 Apr 63 **CASABLANCA** *Pye Jazz 7NJ 2064*....21 11
13 Jun 63 **RONDO** *Pye Jazz 7NJ 2065*....24 8
22 Aug 63 **ACAPULCO 1922** *Pye Jazz 7NJ 2067*....27 6
7 Sep 63 ● KENNY BALL'S GOLDEN HITS *Pye Golden Guinea GGL 0209* [2]....4 26
11 Jun 64 **HELLO, DOLLY!** *Pye Jazz 7NJ 2071*....30 7
19 Jul 67 **WHEN I'M SIXTY FOUR** *Pye 7N 17348*....43 2

[1] Lonnie Donegan presents Kenny Ball and his Jazz Band [2] Clarinet – Dave Jones [1] Kenny Ball, Chris Barber and Acker Bilk [2] Kenny Ball

Michael BALL 500 Top 500
UK, male vocalist / actor (13 Albums: 109 Weeks, 10 Singles: 39 Weeks)

28 Jan 89 ● **LOVE CHANGES EVERYTHING** *Really Useful RUR 3*....2 14
28 Oct 89 **THE FIRST MAN YOU REMEMBER** *Really Useful RUR 6* [1]....68 2
10 Aug 91 **IT'S STILL YOU** *Polydor PO 160*....58 2
25 Apr 92 **ONE STEP OUT OF TIME** *Polydor PO 206*....20 7
30 May 92 ★ MICHAEL BALL *Polydor 5113302* ■....1 10
12 Dec 92 **IF I CAN DREAM (EP) (re)** *Polydor PO 248*....51 2
17 Jul 93 ● ALWAYS *Polydor 5196662*....3 11
11 Sep 93 **SUNSET BOULEVARD** *Polydor PZCD 293*....72 1
30 Jul 94 **FROM HERE TO ETERNITY** *Columbia 6606905*....36 3
13 Aug 94 ● ONE CAREFUL OWNER *Columbia 4772802*....7 6
17 Sep 94 **THE LOVERS WE WERE** *Columbia 6607972*....63 2

◄◄ UK No.1 SINGLES ►►

4 February 1955	11 February 1955	18 February 1955	25 February 1955
MAMBO ITALIANO Rosemary Clooney and The Mellomen	MAMBO ITALIANO Rosemary Clooney and The Mellomen	SOFTLY, SOFTLY Ruby Murray	SOFTLY, SOFTLY Ruby Murray

19 Nov 94 THE BEST OF MICHAEL BALL *PolyGram TV 5238912*....25 7
9 Dec 95 **THE ROSE** *Columbia 6614535*....42 4
27 Jan 96 ● FIRST LOVE *Columbia 4835992*....4 6
17 Feb 96 **(SOMETHING INSIDE) SO STRONG** *Columbia 6629005*....40 2
16 Nov 96 THE MUSICALS *PolyGram TV 5338922*....20 10
7 Nov 98 THE MOVIES *PolyGram TV 5592412*....13 17
20 Nov 99 THE VERY BEST OF MICHAEL BALL – IN CONCERT AT THE ROYAL ALBERT HALL / CHRISTMAS *Universal Music TV 5421952*....18 7
11 Nov 00 THIS TIME ... IT'S PERSONAL *Universal Music TV 1597282*....20 8
29 Sep 01 CENTRE STAGE *Universal Music TV 160712*....11 7
1 Nov 03 A LOVE STORY *Liberty 5919492*....41 1
6 Nov 04 LOVE CHANGES EVERYTHING – THE ESSENTIAL MICHAEL BALL *Universal TV 9825039*....21 9
29 Oct 05 MUSIC *UMTV 9874241*....11 10+

[1] Michael Ball and Diana Morrison

Tracks on If I Can Dream (EP): If I Can Dream / You Don't Have to Say You Love Me / Always on My Mind / Tell Me There's a Heaven.

Steve BALSAMO *UK, male vocalist*

16 Mar 02 **SUGAR FOR THE SOUL** *Columbia 6718552*....32 2

BALTIMORA

Ireland, male vocalist – Jimmy McShane, b. 23 May 1957, d. 14 Dec 2002

10 Aug 85 ● **TARZAN BOY** *Columbia DB 9102*....3 12

Charli BALTIMORE

US, female rapper – Tiffany Lane (2 Singles: 14 Weeks)

1 Aug 98 **MONEY** *Epic 6662272*....12 4
12 Oct 02 ● **DOWN 4 U (2re)** *Murder Inc 0639002* [1] 4 10

[1] Irv Gotti presents Ja Rule, Ashanti, Charli Baltimore and Vita

BAM BAM *US, male vocalist / instrumentalist – Chris Westbrook*

19 Mar 88 **GIVE IT TO ME** *Serious 70US 10*....65 2

Afrika BAMBAATAA

US, male DJ / producer / rapper – Kevin Donovan (9 Singles: 34 Weeks)

28 Aug 82 **PLANET ROCK** *21 POSP 497* [1] 53 3
10 Mar 84 **RENEGADES OF FUNK** *Tommy Boy AFR 1* [1] 30 4
1 Sep 84 **UNITY (PART 1 – THE THIRD COMING)** *Tommy Boy AFR 2* [2] .49 5
27 Feb 88 **RECKLESS** *EMI EM 41* [3] 17 8
12 Oct 91 **JUST GET UP AND DANCE** *EMI USA MT 100*....45 3
17 Oct 98 **GOT TO GET UP** *Multiply CDMULTY 42*....22 4
18 Sep 99 ● **AFRIKA SHOX** *Hard Hands HAND 057CD1* [4] 7 5
25 Aug 01 **PLANET ROCK** *Tommy Boy TBCD 2266* [5] 47 1
13 Mar 04 **D-FUNKTIONAL** *Wall of Sound WALLD 092* [6] 72 1

[1] Afrika Bambaataa and The Soul Sonic Force [2] Afrika Bambaataa and James Brown [3] Afrika Bambaataa and Family featuring UB40 [4] Leftfield / Bambaataa [5] Paul Oakenfold presents Afrika Bambaataa and Soulsonic Force [6] Mekon featuring Afrika Bambaataa

BAMBOO (see also HED BOYS)

UK, male producer – Andrew Livingstone (2 Singles: 12 Weeks)

17 Jan 98 ● **BAMBOOGIE** *VC Recordings VCRD 29*....2 10
4 Jul 98 **THE STRUTT** *VC Recordings VCRD 35*....36 2

BANANARAMA (189 Top 500) *Britain's most charted female group: Sarah Dallin, Keren Woodward, Siobhan Fahey. The London-based trio was also a best-selling act in the US, where 'Venus' topped the chart. Fahey, who married Eurythmic Dave Stewart, left in 1988 to form Shakespear's Sister and was replaced by Jacqui O'Sullivan, who left prior to the act's 2005 comeback (8 Albums: 99 Weeks, 29 Singles: 208 Weeks)*

13 Feb 82 ● **IT AIN'T WHAT YOU DO IT'S THE WAY THAT YOU DO IT** *Chrysalis CHS 2570* [1] 4 10
10 Apr 82 ● **REALLY SAYING SOMETHING** *Deram NANA 1* [2] 5 10
3 Jul 82 ● **SHY BOY** *London NANA 2*....4 11
4 Dec 82 **CHEERS THEN** *London NANA 3*....45 7
26 Feb 83 ● **NA NA HEY HEY KISS HIM GOODBYE** *London NANA 4*....5 10
19 Mar 83 ● DEEP SEA SKIVING *London RAMA 1*....7 16
9 Jul 83 ● **CRUEL SUMMER** *London NANA 5*....8 10
3 Mar 84 ● **ROBERT DE NIRO'S WAITING** *London NANA 6*....3 11
28 Apr 84 BANANARAMA *London RAMA 2*....16 11
26 May 84 **ROUGH JUSTICE** *London NANA 7*....23 7
24 Nov 84 **HOTLINE TO HEAVEN** *London NANA 8*....58 2
24 Aug 85 **DO NOT DISTURB** *London NANA 9*....31 6
31 May 86 ● **VENUS** *London NANA 10* ▲ 8 13
19 Jul 86 TRUE CONFESSIONS *London RAMA 3*....46 5
16 Aug 86 **MORE THAN PHYSICAL** *London NANA 11*....41 5
14 Feb 87 **TRICK OF THE NIGHT** *London NANA 12*....32 5
11 Jul 87 **I HEARD A RUMOUR** *London NANA 13*....14 9
19 Sep 87 WOW! *London RAMA 4*....26 26
10 Oct 87 ● **LOVE IN THE FIRST DEGREE / MR. SLEAZE** *London NANA 14*...3 12
9 Jan 88 **I CAN'T HELP IT** *London NANA 15*....20 6
9 Apr 88 ● **I WANT YOU BACK** *London NANA 16*....5 10
24 Sep 88 **LOVE, TRUTH AND HONESTY** *London NANA 17*....23 8
22 Oct 88 ● THE GREATEST HITS COLLECTION *London RAMA 5*....3 37
19 Nov 88 **NATHAN JONES** *London NANA 18*....15 9
25 Feb 89 ● **HELP** *London LON 222* [3] 3 9
10 Jun 89 **CRUEL SUMMER** (re-mix) *London NANA 19*....19 6
28 Jul 90 **ONLY YOUR LOVE** *London NANA 21*....27 4
5 Jan 91 **PREACHER MAN** *London NANA 23*....20 6
20 Apr 91 **LONG TRAIN RUNNING** *London NANA 24*....30 5
25 May 91 POP LIFE *London 8282461*....42 1
29 Aug 92 **MOVIN' ON** *London NANA 25*....24 5
28 Nov 92 **LAST THING ON MY MIND** *London NANA 26*....71 2
20 Mar 93 **MORE, MORE, MORE** *London NACPD 27*....24 4
10 Apr 93 PLEASE YOURSELF *London 8283572*....46 1
10 Nov 01 THE VERY BEST OF BANANARAMA *London 927414992*....43 2
6 Aug 05 **MOVE IN MY DIRECTION** *A& G Productions CXAGO 003*....14 4
19 Nov 05 **LOOK ON THE FLOOR (HYPNOTIC TANGO)** *A&G Productions CXAG 004*....26 2

[1] Fun Boy Three and Bananarama [2] Bananarama with Fun Boy Three [3] Bananarama / La Na Nee Nee Noo Noo

The flip side of 'Love in the First Degree', 'Mr Sleaze' by Stock Aitken Waterman, was listed from 24 Oct and shown as the 'A' side from 28 Nov. Act was a duo for last three hits.

BANCO DE GAIA

UK, male multi-instrumentalist – Toby Marks (2 Albums: 4 Weeks)

12 Mar 94 MAYA *Planet Dog BARKCD 3*....34 2
13 May 95 LAST TRAIN TO LHASA *Planet Dog BARKCD 0115*....31 2

The BAND (see also Bob DYLAN; Robbie ROBERTSON) *Canada / US, male vocal / instrumental group (4 Albums: 26 Weeks, 2 Singles: 18 Weeks)*

18 Sep 68 **THE WEIGHT** *Capitol CL 15559*....21 9
31 Jan 70 THE BAND *Capitol EST 132*....25 12
4 Apr 70 **RAG MAMA RAG** *Capitol CL 15629*....16 9
3 Oct 70 STAGE FRIGHT *Capitol EA SW 425*....15 6
27 Nov 71 CAHOOTS *Capitol EAST 651*....41 1
13 Jul 74 ● BEFORE THE FLOOD *Asylum IDBD 1* [1] 8 7

[1] Bob Dylan / The Band

BAND AID *International, male / female vocal / instrumental charity assembly (3 Singles: 37 Weeks)*

15 Dec 84 ★ **DO THEY KNOW IT'S CHRISTMAS? (re)** *Mercury FEED 1* ■ £ $....1 20
23 Dec 89 ★ **DO THEY KNOW IT'S CHRISTMAS?** *PWL / Polydor FEED 2* [1] ■....1 6
11 Dec 04 ★ **DO THEY KNOW IT'S CHRISTMAS? (re)** *Mercury 9869413* [2] ■ £....1 11

[1] Band Aid II [2] Band Aid 20

BAND AID: Adam Clayton, Bono (U2); Bob Geldof, Johnny Fingers, Simon Crowe, Peter Briquette (Boomtown Rats); David Bowie; Paul McCartney; Holly Johnson (Frankie Goes To Hollywood); Midge Ure, Chris Cross (Ultravox); Simon Le Bon, Nick Rhodes, Andy Taylor, John Taylor, Roger Taylor (Duran Duran); Paul Young; Tony Hadley, Martin Kemp, John Keeble, Gary Kemp, Steve Norman (Spandau Ballet); Martyn Ware, Glenn Gregory (Heaven 17); Francis Rossi, Rick Parfitt (Status Quo); Sting; Boy George, Jon Moss (Culture Club); Marilyn; Keren Woodward, Sarah Dallin, Siobhan Fahey (Bananarama); Jody Watley (Shalamar); Paul Weller; Robert "Kool" Bell, James Taylor, Dennis Thomas (Kool and The Gang); George Michael and Phil Collins. Band Aid's 1984 'Do They Know It's Christmas?' re-entered the chart and peaked at No.3 in Dec 1985

BAND AID II: Bananarama, Big Fun, Bros, Cathy Dennis, D Mob, Jason Donovan, Kevin Godley, Glen Goldsmith, Kylie Minogue, The Pasadenas, Chris Rea, Cliff Richard, Jimmy Somerville, Sonia, Lisa Stansfield, Technotronic, Wet Wet Wet

4 March 1955	11 March 1955	18 March 1955	25 March 1955
SOFTLY, SOFTLY Ruby Murray	GIVE ME YOUR WORD Tennessee Ernie Ford	GIVE ME YOUR WORD Tennessee Ernie Ford	GIVE ME YOUR WORD Tennessee Ernie Ford

KEY UK No.1 ★ UK Top 10 ● Still on chart + UK entry at No.1 ■ US No.1 ▲ UK million seller £ US million seller $ Singles re-entries are listed as (re), (2re), (3re)... which signifies that the hit re-entered the chart once, twice or three times... Peak Position / Weeks

BAND AID 20: Keane, Sir Paul McCartney, Sugababes, Skye, Robbie Williams, Dido, Bono (U2), Jamelia, Justin Hawkins (The Darkness), Chris Martin (Coldplay), Fran Healy (Travis), Beverley Knight, Busted, Ms Dynamite, Danny Goffey (Supergrass), Katie Melua, Will Young, Natasha Bedingfield, Snow Patrol, Shaznay Lewis, Joss Stone, Daniel Bedingfield, Rachel Stevens, The Thrills, Roisin Murphy (Moloko), Lemar, Estelle, Neil Hannon (The Divine Comedy), Feeder, Dizzee Rascal

BAND AKA *US, male vocal / instrumental group (2 Singles: 12 Weeks)*

15 May 82 **GRACE** *Epic EPC A 2376* **41** 5
5 Mar 83 **JOY** *Epic EPC A 3145* **24** 7

BAND OF GOLD *Holland, male / female vocal / instrumental group*

14 Jul 84 **LOVE SONGS ARE BACK AGAIN (MEDLEY)** *RCA 428* **24** 11

BANDA SONORA *UK, male producer – Gerald Elms (2 Singles: 3 Weeks)*

6 Oct 01 **GUITARRA G** *Defected DFECT 36CDS* **50** 2
19 Oct 02 **PRESSURE COOKER** *Defected DFTD 060CDS* [1] **46** 1

[1] G Club Presents Banda Sonora

BANDERAS *UK, female vocal / instrumental duo – Sally Herbert and Caroline Buckley (1 Album: 3 Weeks, 2 Singles: 16 Weeks)*

23 Feb 91 **THIS IS YOUR LIFE** *London LON 290* **16** 10
13 Apr 91 RIPE *London 8282471* 40 3
15 Jun 91 **SHE SELLS** *London LON 298* **41** 6

The BANDITS *UK, male vocal / instrumental group (2 Singles: 2 Weeks)*

28 Jun 03 **TAKE IT AND RUN** *B-Unique BUN 055CDS* **32** 1
20 Sep 03 **2 STEP ROCK** *B-Unique BUN 065CDS* **35** 1

Honey BANE *UK, female vocalist – Donna Boylan (2 Singles: 8 Weeks)*

24 Jan 81 **TURN ME ON TURN ME OFF** *Zonophone Z 15* **37** 5
18 Apr 81 **BABY LOVE** *Zonophone Z 19* **58** 3

BANG *UK, male vocal duo*

6 May 89 **YOU'RE THE ONE** *RCA PB 42715* **74** 2

The BANGLES (348 Top 500) *Originally named the Supersonic Bangs, then The Bangs, this melodic pop-rock quartet formed in 1981, in Los Angeles, California, US and comprised Susanna Hoffs (v), sisters Vicki (g) and Debbi Peterson (d) and Michael Steele (b). They split in 1989, having become the most successful all-female rock band in chart history, but reformed for a tour in 2000 (6 Albums: 105 Weeks, 13 Singles: 96 Weeks)*

16 Mar 85 ALL OVER THE PLACE *CBS 26015* 86 1
15 Feb 86 ● **MANIC MONDAY** *CBS A 6796* **2** 12
15 Mar 86 ● DIFFERENT LIGHT *CBS 26659* 3 47
26 Apr 86 **IF SHE KNEW WHAT SHE WANTS** *CBS A 7062* **31** 7
5 Jul 86 **GOING DOWN TO LIVERPOOL** *CBS A 7255* **56** 3
13 Sep 86 ● **WALK LIKE AN EGYPTIAN** *CBS 650071 7* ▲ $ **3** 19
10 Jan 87 **WALKING DOWN YOUR STREET** *CBS BANGS 1* **16** 6
18 Apr 87 **FOLLOWING** *CBS BANGS 2* **55** 3
6 Feb 88 **HAZY SHADE OF WINTER** *Def Jam BANGS 3* **11** 10
5 Nov 88 **IN YOUR ROOM** *CBS BANGS 4* **35** 6
10 Dec 88 ● EVERYTHING *CBS 4629791* 5 26
18 Feb 89 ★ **ETERNAL FLAME** *CBS BANGS 5* ▲ **1** 18
10 Jun 89 **BE WITH YOU** *CBS BANGS 6* **23** 8
14 Oct 89 **I'LL SET YOU FREE** *CBS BANGS 7* **74** 1
9 Jun 90 ● GREATEST HITS *CBS 4667691* 4 23
9 Jun 90 **WALK LIKE AN EGYPTIAN** (re-issue) *CBS BANGS 8* **73** 1
4 Aug 01 ETERNAL FLAME – THE BEST OF THE BANGLES *Columbia STVCD 121* 15 7
15 Mar 03 **SOMETHING THAT YOU SAID** *Down Kiddie / EMI / Liberty BANGLES 003* **38** 2
29 Mar 03 DOLL REVOLUTION *EMI / Liberty 5815102* 62 1

Devendra BANHART NEW *US, male vocalist / guitarist*

17 Sep 05 **I FEEL JUST LIKE A CHILD** *XL Recordings XLS 217CD* **68** 1
1 Oct 05 CRIPPLE CROW *XL Recordings XLCD 192* 69 1

Lloyd BANK$ (see also G-UNIT) *US, male rapper*

10 Jul 04 THE HUNGER FOR MORE *Interscope 9863026* ▲ 15 10
21 Aug 04 **ON FIRE** *Interscope 9863485* **19** 6

Tony BANKS (see also GENESIS) *UK, male vocalist / keyboard player (2 Albums: 7 Weeks, 1 Single: 1 Week)*

20 Oct 79 A CURIOUS FEELING *Charisma CAS 1148* 21 5
25 Jun 83 THE FUGITIVE *Charisma TBLP 1* 50 2
18 Oct 86 **SHORTCUT TO SOMEWHERE** *Charisma CB 426* [1] **75** 1

[1] Fish and Tony Banks

BANNED *UK, male vocal / instrumental group*

17 Dec 77 **LITTLE GIRL** *Harvest HAR 5145* **36** 6

Buju BANTON *Jamaica, male vocalist*

7 Aug 93 **MAKE MY DAY** *Mercury BUJCD 2* **72** 1

Pato BANTON *UK, male vocalist – Patrick Murray (5 Singles: 37 Weeks)*

1 Oct 94 ★ **BABY COME BACK** *Virgin VSCDT 1522* **1** 18
11 Feb 95 **THIS COWBOY SONG** *A&M 5809652* [1] **15** 6
8 Apr 95 **BUBBLING HOT** *Virgin VSCDT 1530* [2] **15** 7
20 Jan 96 **SPIRITS IN THE MATERIAL WORLD** *MCA MCSTD 2113* [3] **36** 2
27 Jul 96 **GROOVIN'** *IRS CDEIRS 195* [4] **14** 4

[1] Sting featuring Pato Banton [2] Pato Banton with Ranking Roger [3] Pato Banton with Sting [4] Pato Banton and The Reggae Revolution

The sleeve of 'Baby Come Back' credits Ali and Robin Campbell.

BAR CODES featuring Alison BROWN *UK, male / female vocal group*

17 Dec 94 **SUPERMARKET SWEEP** *Blanca Casa BC 101CD* **72** 1

Chris BARBER *UK, male jazz band – leader Chris Barber – trombone (7 Albums: 91 Weeks, 3 Singles: 30 Weeks)*

13 Feb 59 ● **PETITE FLEUR (re)** *Pye Nixa NJ 2026* [1] $ **3** 24
9 Oct 59 **LONESOME (SI TU VOIS MA MERE)** *Columbia DB 4333* [2] **27** 2
24 Sep 60 CHRIS BARBER BAND BOX NO. 2 *Columbia 33SCX 3277* 17 1
5 Nov 60 ELITE SYNCOPATIONS *Columbia 33SX 1245* 18 1
12 Nov 60 THE BEST OF CHRIS BARBER *Ace of Clubs ACL 1037* 17 1
27 May 61 ● THE BEST OF BARBER AND BILK VOLUME 1 *Pye Golden Guinea GGL 0075* [1] 4 43
11 Nov 61 ● THE BEST OF BARBER AND BILK VOLUME 2 *Pye Golden Guinea GGL 0096* [1] 8 18
4 Jan 62 **REVIVAL (re)** *Columbia SCD 2166* [3] **43** 4
25 Aug 62 ★ THE BEST OF BALL, BARBER AND BILK *Pye Golden Guinea GGL 0131* [2] 1 24
29 Jan 00 THE SKIFFLE SESSIONS – LIVE IN BELFAST *Venture CDVE 945* [3] 14 3

[1] Clarinet solo – Monty Sunshine [2] Chris Barber featuring Monty Sunshine [3] Chris Barber's Jazz Band [1] Chris Barber and Acker Bilk [2] Kenny Ball, Chris Barber and Acker Bilk [3] Van Morrison / Lonnie Donegan / Chris Barber

BARCLAY JAMES HARVEST *UK, male vocal / instrumental group (10 Albums: 42 Weeks, 4 Singles: 9 Weeks)*

14 Dec 74 BARCLAY JAMES HARVEST LIVE *Polydor 2683 052* 40 2
18 Oct 75 TIME HONOURED GHOST *Polydor 2383 361* 32 3
23 Oct 76 OCTOBERON *Polydor 2442 144* 19 4
2 Apr 77 **LIVE (EP) (re)** *Polydor 2229 198* **49** 2
1 Oct 77 GONE TO EARTH *Polydor 2442 148* 30 7
21 Oct 78 BARCLAY JAMES HARVEST XII *Polydor POLD 5006* 31 2
26 Jan 80 **LOVE ON THE LINE** *Polydor POSP 97* **63** 2
22 Nov 80 **LIFE IS FOR LIVING** *Polydor POSP 195* **61** 3
23 May 81 TURN OF THE TIDE *Polydor POLD 5040* 55 2
24 Jul 82 A CONCERT FOR THE PEOPLE (BERLIN) *Polydor POLD 5052* 15 11
21 May 83 **JUST A DAY AWAY** *Polydor POSP 585* **68** 2
28 May 83 RING OF CHANGES *Polydor POLH 3* 36 4
14 Apr 84 VICTIMS OF CIRCUMSTANCE *Polydor POLD 5135* 33 6
14 Feb 87 FACE TO FACE *Polydor POLD 5209* 65 1

Tracks on Live (EP): Rock 'n' Roll Star / Medicine Man (Parts 1 & 2).

BARDO
UK, male / female vocal duo – Sally Ann Triplett and Stephen Fischer

10 Apr 82 ● **ONE STEP FURTHER** *Epic EPC A2265* **2** 8

BARDOT *Australia, female vocal group*

14 Apr 01 **POISON** *East West EW 229CD* **45** 1

BAREFOOT MAN *Germany, male vocalist – George Nowak*

5 Dec 98 **BIG PANTY WOMAN** *Plaza PZACD 082* **21** 7

BARENAKED LADIES *Canada, male vocal (Steven Page) / instrumental group (3 Albums: 18 Weeks, 4 Singles: 12 Weeks)*

27 Aug 94 **MAYBE YOU SHOULD DRIVE** *Reprise 9362457092* **57** 1
20 Feb 99 ● **ONE WEEK** *Reprise W 468CD* ▲ **5** 8
6 Mar 99 **STUNT** *Reprise 9362469632* **20** 16
15 May 99 **IT'S ALL BEEN DONE** *Reprise W 476CD* **28** 2
24 Jul 99 **CALL AND ANSWER** *Reprise W 498CD1* **52** 1
11 Dec 99 **BRIAN WILSON** *Reprise W 511CD1* **73** 1
30 Sep 00 **MAROON** *Reprise 9362478912* **64** 1

The BAR-KAYS
US, male vocal / instrumental group (3 Singles: 15 Weeks)

23 Aug 67 **SOUL FINGER** *Stax 601 014* $ **33** 7
22 Jan 77 **SHAKE YOUR RUMP TO THE FUNK** *Mercury 6167 417* **41** 4
12 Jan 85 **SEXOMATIC** *Club JAB 10* **51** 4

The BARKIN BROTHERS featuring Johnnie FIORI
UK, male production group and US, female vocalist

15 Apr 00 **GONNA CATCH YOU** *Brothers Organisation BRUVCD 15* **51** 2

Gary BARLOW (see also TAKE THAT)
UK, male vocalist (2 Albums: 27 Weeks, 6 Singles: 47 Weeks)

20 Jul 96 ★ **FOREVER LOVE** *RCA 74321397922* ■ **1** 16
10 May 97 ★ **LOVE WON'T WAIT (2re)** *RCA 74321470842* ■ **1** 9
7 Jun 97 ★ **OPEN ROAD** *RCA 74321417202* ■ **1** 26
26 Jul 97 **SO HELP ME GIRL (re)** *RCA 74321501202* **11** 11
15 Nov 97 ● **OPEN ROAD** *RCA 74321518292* **7** 5
17 Jul 99 **STRONGER** *RCA 74321682002* **16** 4
9 Oct 99 **FOR ALL THAT YOU WANT** *RCA 74321701012* **24** 2
23 Oct 99 **TWELVE MONTHS ELEVEN DAYS** *RCA 74321707662* **35** 1

BARNBRACK *UK, male vocal / instrumental group*

16 Mar 85 **BELFAST** *Homespun HS 092* **45** 7

BARNDANCE BOYS
UK, male production duo – John Matthews and Darren Simpson

13 Sep 03 **YIPPIE-I-OH** *Concept CDCON 41* **32** 2

Jimmy BARNES and INXS *Australia (b. UK), male vocalist – James Swan and vocal / instrumental group*

26 Jan 91 **GOOD TIMES** *Atlantic A 7751* **18** 8

Richard BARNES *UK, male vocalist (2 Singles: 10 Weeks)*

23 May 70 **TAKE TO THE MOUNTAINS** *Philips BF 1840* **35** 6
24 Oct 70 **GO NORTH (re)** *Philips 6006 039* **38** 4

BARON *UK, male producer – Piers Bailey (3 Singles: 4 Weeks)*

7 Feb 04 **THE WAY IT WAS / REDHEAD** *Virus VRS 012* **71** 1
12 Feb 05 **SUPERNATURE** *Breakbeat BBK 006* [1] **59** 2
30 Apr 05 **GUNS AT DAWN** *Breakbeat Kaos BBK 008* [2] **71** 1

[1] Baron & Fresh [2] DJ Baron featuring Pendulum

The BARRACUDAS *UK / US, male vocal / instrumental group*

16 Aug 80 **SUMMER FUN** *Zonophone Z 5* **37** 6

Syd BARRETT (see also PINK FLOYD) *UK, male vocalist / guitarist*

7 Feb 70 **THE MADCAP LAUGHS** *Harvest SHVL 765* **40** 1

Amanda BARRIE and Johnny BRIGGS
UK, female / male actors / vocal duo

16 Dec 95 **SOMETHING STUPID** *EMI Premier CDEMS 411* **35** 3

The listed flip side of 'Something Stupid' was 'Always Look on the Bright Side of Life' by the Coronation Street Cast.

JJ BARRIE *Canada, male vocalist – Barrie Authors*

24 Apr 76 ★ **NO CHARGE** *Power Exchange PX 209* **1** 11

Featured vocalist is Vicki Brown.

Ken BARRIE *UK, male vocalist*

10 Jul 82 **POSTMAN PAT (2re)** *Post Music PP 001* **44** 15

Re-entries at Christmas 1982 and 1983.

The BARRON KNIGHTS *UK, male vocal / instrumental group – leader Duke D'Mond (Richard Palmer) (3 Albums: 22 Weeks, 13 Singles: 94 Weeks)*

9 Jul 64 ● **CALL UP THE GROUPS** *Columbia DB 7317* [1] **3** 13
22 Oct 64 **COME TO THE DANCE** *Columbia DB 7375* [1] **42** 2
25 Mar 65 ● **POP GO THE WORKERS** *Columbia DB 7525* [1] **5** 13
16 Dec 65 ● **MERRY GENTLE POPS** *Columbia DB 7780* [1] **9** 7
1 Dec 66 **UNDER NEW MANAGEMENT** *Columbia DB 8071* [1] **15** 9
23 Oct 68 **AN OLYMPIC RECORD** *Columbia DB 8485* **35** 4
29 Oct 77 ● **LIVE IN TROUBLE** *Epic EPC 5752* **7** 10
2 Dec 78 **NIGHT GALLERY** *Epic EPC 83221* **15** 13
2 Dec 78 ● **A TASTE OF AGGRO** *Epic EPC 6829* **3** 10
1 Dec 79 **TEACH THE WORLD TO LAUGH** *Epic EPC 83891* **51** 4
8 Dec 79 **FOOD FOR THOUGHT** *Epic EPC 8011* **46** 6
4 Oct 80 **THE SIT SONG** *Epic EPC 8994* **44** 4
6 Dec 80 **NEVER MIND THE PRESENTS** *Epic EPC 9070* **17** 8
13 Dec 80 **JUST A GIGGLE** *Epic EPC 84550* **45** 5
5 Dec 81 **BLACKBOARD JUMBLE** *CBS A 1795* **52** 5
19 Mar 83 **BUFFALO BILL'S LAST SCRATCH** *Epic EPC A 3208* **49** 3

[1] The Barron Knights with Duke D'Mond

Joe BARRY *US, male vocalist – Joe Barrios*

24 Aug 61 **I'M A FOOL TO CARE** *Mercury AMT 1149* **49** 1

John BARRY *UK, male composer – John Prendergast (3 Albums: 18 Weeks, 11 Singles: 79 Weeks)*

4 Mar 60 ● **HIT AND MISS (re)** *Columbia DB 4414* [1] **10** 14
28 Apr 60 **BEAT FOR BEATNIKS** *Columbia DB 4446* [2] **40** 2
14 Jul 60 **NEVER LET GO** *Columbia DB 4480* [2] **49** 1
18 Aug 60 **BLUEBERRY HILL** *Columbia DB 4480* [2] **34** 3
8 Sep 60 **WALK DON'T RUN (re)** *Columbia DB 4505* [3] **11** 14
8 Dec 60 **BLACK STOCKINGS** *Columbia DB 4554* [3] **27** 9
2 Mar 61 **THE MAGNIFICENT SEVEN (3re)** *Columbia DB 4598* [3] **45** 5
26 Apr 62 **CUTTY SARK** *Columbia DB 4806* [3] **35** 2
1 Nov 62 **THE JAMES BOND THEME** *Columbia DB 4898* [2] **13** 11
21 Nov 63 **FROM RUSSIA WITH LOVE (re)** *Ember S 181* [2] **39** 3
11 Dec 71 **THEME FROM 'THE PERSUADERS'** *CBS 7469* **13** 15
29 Jan 72 **THE PERSUADERS** *CBS 64816* **18** 9
20 Apr 91 **DANCES WITH WOLVES (FILM SOUNDTRACK)** *Epic 4675911* **45** 8
8 May 99 **THE BEYONDNESS OF THINGS** *Decca 4600092* [1] **67** 1

[1] John Barry Seven plus Four [2] John Barry Orchestra [3] John Barry Seven
[1] English Chamber Orchestra conducted by John Barry

Len BARRY *US, male vocalist – Leonard Borisoff (2 Singles: 24 Weeks)*

4 Nov 65 ● **1-2-3** *Brunswick 05942* **3** 14
13 Jan 66 ● **LIKE A BABY** *Brunswick 05949* **10** 10

Michael BARRYMORE *UK, male vocalist / comedian – Michael Parker*

16 Dec 95 **TOO MUCH FOR ONE HEART** *EMI CDEM 412* **25** 4

Lionel BART *UK, male vocalist, b. 1 Aug 1930, d. 3 Apr 1999*

25 Nov 89 **HAPPY ENDINGS (GIVE YOURSELF A PINCH) (re)** *EMI EM 121* **68** 3

BARTHEZZ *Holland, male producer – Bart Claessen (2 Singles: 8 Weeks)*

22 Sep 01 **ON THE MOVE** *Positiva CDTIV 158* **18** 4
20 Apr 02 **INFECTED** *Positiva CDTIVS 168* **25** 4

29 April 1955	6 May 1955	13 May 1955	20 May 1955
CHERRY PINK AND APPLE BLOSSOM WHITE Perez 'Prez' Prado and his Orchestra	**CHERRY PINK AND APPLE BLOSSOM WHITE** Perez 'Prez' Prado and his Orchestra	**STRANGER IN PARADISE** Tony Bennett	**STRANGER IN PARADISE** Tony Bennett

KEY UK No.1 ★ UK Top 10 ● Still on chart + UK entry at No.1 ■ US No.1 ▲ UK million seller £ US million seller $ Singles re-entries are listed as (re), (2re), (3re)... which signifies that the hit re-entered the chart once, twice or three times... Peak Position / Weeks

BAS NOIR *US, female vocal duo*

11 Feb 89 **MY LOVE IS MAGIC** *10 TEN 257* ... **73** 1

Rob BASE and DJ E-Z ROCK *US, male rap / DJ duo – Robert Ginyard and Rodney Bryce (3 Singles: 19 Weeks)*

16 Apr 88 **IT TAKES TWO (re)** *Citybeat CBE 724* $ ... **24** 9
14 Jan 89 **GET ON THE DANCE FLOOR** *Supreme SUPE 139* ... **14** 7
22 Apr 89 **JOY AND PAIN** *Supreme SUPE 143* ... **47** 3

The BASEMENT *UK, male vocal / instrumental group*

14 Jun 03 **SLAIN THE TRUTH (AT THE ROADHOUSE)** *Deltasonic DLTCD 012* ... **48** 1

BASEMENT BOYS present Ultra NATÉ *US, male production group and female vocalist*

23 Feb 91 **IS IT LOVE?** *Eternal YZ 509* ... **71** 1

BASEMENT JAXX (316 Top 500) *Boundary-stretching "punk garage" production duo from South London: Felix Buxton and Simon Ratcliffe. They surfaced from the underground house scene, are regular transatlantic club chart-toppers and won the BRIT award for Best Dance Act in 2002 and 2004 (4 Albums: 119 Weeks, 16 Singles: 98 Weeks)*

31 May 97 **FLY LIFE** *Multiply CDMULTY 21* ... **19** 3
1 May 99 ● **RED ALERT** *XL Recordings XLS 100CD* ... **5** 10
22 May 99 ● REMEDY *XL Recordings XLCD 129* ... 4 45
14 Aug 99 ● **RENDEZ-VU** *XL Recordings XLS 110CD* ... **4** 8
6 Nov 99 **JUMP 'N SHOUT** *XL Recordings XLS 116CD* ... **12** 5
15 Apr 00 **BINGO BANGO** *XL Recordings XLS 120CD* ... **13** 4
16 Jun 01 ● **ROMEO** *XL Recordings XLS 132CD* ... **6** 10
7 Jul 01 ● ROOTY *XL Recordings XLCD 143* ... 5 26
6 Oct 01 **JUS 1 KISS (re)** *XL Recordings XLS 136CD* ... **23** 4
8 Dec 01 ● **WHERE'S YOUR HEAD AT?** *XL Recordings XLS 140CD* ... **9** 8
29 Jun 02 **GET ME OFF** *XL Recordings XLS 146CD* ... **22** 3
1 Nov 03 KISH KASH *XL Recordings XLCD 174* ... 17 16
22 Nov 03 **LUCKY STAR** *XL Recordings XLS 172CD* [1] ... **23** 4
17 Jan 04 **GOOD LUCK** *XL Recordings XLS 178CD* [2] ... **12** 8
10 Apr 04 **PLUG IT IN** *XL Recordings XLS 180CD* [3] ... **22** 4
10 Jul 04 **GOOD LUCK** (re-issue) *XL Recordings XLS 190CD* [2] ... **14** 7
26 Mar 05 ● **OH MY GOSH** *XL Recordings XLS 209CD1* ... **8** 12
2 Apr 05 ★ THE SINGLES *XL Recordings XLCD 187X* ... 1 32
25 Jun 05 **U DON'T KNOW ME** *XL Recordings XLS 215CD1* [2] ... **26** 3
8 Oct 05 **DO YOUR THING** *XL Recordings XLS 220CD* ... **32** 5

[1] Basement Jaxx featuring Dizzee Rascal [2] Basement Jaxx featuring Lisa Kekaula [3] Basement Jaxx featuring JC Chasez

'Good Luck' was re-issued after the BBC adopted it for their coverage of the Euro 2004 football championships.

BASIA (see also MATT BIANCO) *Poland, female vocalist – Basia Trzetrzelewska (2 Albums: 4 Weeks, 3 Singles: 9 Weeks)*

23 Jan 88 **PROMISES** *Epic BASH 4* ... **48** 4
13 Feb 88 TIME AND TIDE *Portrait 4502631* ... 61 3
28 May 88 **TIME AND TIDE** *Epic BASH 5* ... **61** 3
3 Mar 90 LONDON WARSAW NEW YORK *Epic 4632821* ... 68 1
14 Jan 95 **DRUNK ON LOVE** *Epic 6611582* ... **41** 2

Count BASIE (see also Frank SINATRA) *US, orchestra – leader William Basie, b. 21 Aug 1904, d. 26 Mar 1984 (2 Albums: 24 Weeks)*

16 Apr 60 CHAIRMAN OF THE BOARD *Columbia 33SX 1209* ... 17 1
23 Feb 63 ● SINATRA – BASIE *Reprise R 1008* [1] ... 2 23

[1] Frank Sinatra and Count Basie

Toni BASIL *US, female vocalist – Antonia Basilotta (1 Album: 16 Weeks, 2 Singles: 16 Weeks)*

6 Feb 82 WORD OF MOUTH *Radialchoice BASIL 1* ... 15 16
6 Feb 82 ● **MICKEY** *Radialchoice TIC 4* ▲ $ ... **2** 12
1 May 82 **NOBODY** *Radialchoice TIC 2* ... **52** 4

Olav BASOSKI *Holland, male producer (2 Singles: 2 Weeks)*

26 Aug 00 **OPIUM SCUMBAGZ** *Defected DFECT 20CDS* ... **56** 1
29 Oct 05 **WATERMAN** *Positiva CDTIVS 224* [1] ... **45** 1

[1] Olav Basoski featuring Michie One

Fontella BASS *US, female vocalist (2 Singles: 15 Weeks)*

2 Dec 65 **RESCUE ME** *Chess CRS 8023* ... **11** 10
20 Jan 66 **RECOVERY** *Chess CRS 8027* ... **32** 5

Norman BASS *Germany, male producer – Uwe Taubert*

21 Apr 01 **HOW U LIKE BASS** *Substance SUBS 10CDS* ... **17** 4

BASS BOYZ (see also PIANOMAN) *UK, male producer – James Sammon*

28 Sep 96 **GUNZ AND PIANOZ** *Polydor 5753432* ... **74** 1

BASS BUMPERS *Germany / UK, male / female vocal / instrumental group (2 Singles: 4 Weeks)*

25 Sep 93 **RUNNIN'** *Vertigo VERCD 78* ... **68** 1
5 Feb 94 **THE MUSIC'S GOT ME** *Vertigo VERCD 84* ... **25** 3

BASS JUMPERS *Holland, male producer and female vocalist*

13 Feb 99 **MAKE UP YOUR MIND** *Pepper 0530112* ... **44** 1

Shirley BASSEY (58 Top 500) *Internationally acclaimed vocalist and cabaret entertainer, b. 8 Jan 1937, Cardiff, Wales. With 31 hit singles (spanning a record 42-year period for a female) and 36 hit albums, she is Britain's most successful female chart artist. Honoured with a damehood in 2000 (36 Albums: 294 Weeks, 31 Singles: 326 Weeks)*

15 Feb 57 ● **THE BANANA BOAT SONG** *Philips PB 668* ... **8** 10
23 Aug 57 **FIRE DOWN BELOW** *Philips PB 723* ... **30** 1
6 Sep 57 **YOU YOU ROMEO** *Philips PB 723* ... **29** 2
19 Dec 58 ★ **AS I LOVE YOU (re)** *Philips PB 845* ... **1** 19
26 Dec 58 ● **KISS ME, HONEY HONEY, KISS ME** *Philips PB 860* ... **3** 17
31 Mar 60 **WITH THESE HANDS (2re)** *Columbia DB 4421* ... **38** 6
4 Aug 60 ● **AS LONG AS HE NEEDS ME** *Columbia DB 4490* ... **2** 30
28 Jan 61 FABULOUS SHIRLEY BASSEY *Columbia 33SX 1178* ... 12 2
25 Feb 61 ● SHIRLEY *Columbia 33SX 1286* ... 9 10
11 May 61 ● **YOU'LL NEVER KNOW** *Columbia DB 4643* ... **6** 17
27 Jul 61 ★ **REACH FOR THE STARS / CLIMB EV'RY MOUNTAIN (re)** *Columbia DB 4685* ... **1** 18
23 Nov 61 ● **I'LL GET BY (AS LONG AS I HAVE YOU)** *Columbia DB 4737* ... **10** 8
15 Feb 62 **TONIGHT** *Columbia DB 4777* ... **21** 8
17 Feb 62 SHIRLEY BASSEY *Columbia 33SX 1382* ... 14 11
26 Apr 62 **AVE MARIA** *Columbia DB 4816* ... **31** 4
31 May 62 **FAR AWAY** *Columbia DB 4836* ... **24** 13
30 Aug 62 ● **WHAT NOW MY LOVE?** *Columbia DB 4882* ... **5** 17
15 Dec 62 LET'S FACE THE MUSIC *Columbia 33SX 1454* [1] ... 12 7
28 Feb 63 **WHAT KIND OF FOOL AM I?** *Columbia DB 4974* ... **47** 2
26 Sep 63 ● **I (WHO HAVE NOTHING)** *Columbia DB 7113* ... **6** 20
23 Jan 64 **MY SPECIAL DREAM** *Columbia DB 7185* ... **32** 7
9 Apr 64 **GONE** *Columbia DB 7248* ... **36** 5
15 Oct 64 **GOLDFINGER** *Columbia DB 7360* ... **21** 9
20 May 65 **NO REGRETS** *Columbia DB 7535* ... **39** 4
4 Dec 65 SHIRLEY BASSEY AT THE PIGALLE *Columbia 33SX 1787* ... 15 7
27 Aug 66 I'VE GOT A SONG FOR YOU *United Artists ULP 1142* ... 26 1
11 Oct 67 **BIG SPENDER** *United Artists UP 1192* ... **21** 15
17 Feb 68 TWELVE OF THOSE SONGS *Columbia SCX 6204* ... 38 3
7 Dec 68 GOLDEN HITS OF SHIRLEY BASSEY *Columbia SCX 6294* ... 28 40
20 Jun 70 ● **SOMETHING (re)** *United Artists UP 35125* ... **4** 22
11 Jul 70 LIVE AT THE TALK OF THE TOWN *United Artists UAS 29095* ... 38 6
29 Aug 70 ● SOMETHING *United Artists UAS 29100* ... 5 20
2 Jan 71 **THE FOOL ON THE HILL** *United Artists UP 35156* ... **48** 1
27 Mar 71 **(WHERE DO I BEGIN) LOVE STORY** *United Artists UP 35194* ... **34** 9
15 May 71 ● SOMETHING ELSE *United Artists UAG 29149* ... 7 9
7 Aug 71 ● **FOR ALL WE KNOW (re)** *United Artists UP 35267* ... **6** 24

2 Oct 71 BIG SPENDER *Sunset SLS 50262*.....27 8
30 Oct 71 IT'S MAGIC *Starline SRS 5082*.....32 1
6 Nov 71 THE FABULOUS SHIRLEY BASSEY *MFP 1398*.....48 1
4 Dec 71 WHAT NOW MY LOVE *MFP 5230*.....17 5
8 Jan 72 THE SHIRLEY BASSEY COLLECTION *United Artists UAD 60013/4*.....37 1
15 Jan 72 **DIAMONDS ARE FOREVER** *United Artists UP 35293*.....**38** 6
19 Feb 72 I CAPRICORN *United Artists UAS 29246*.....13 11
29 Nov 72 AND I LOVE YOU SO *United Artists UAS 29385*.....24 9
3 Mar 73 ● **NEVER, NEVER, NEVER (GRANDE, GRANDE, GRANDE) (re)** *United Artists UP 35490*.....**8** 19
2 Jun 73 ● NEVER NEVER NEVER *United Artists UAG 29471*.....10 10
15 Mar 75 ● THE SHIRLEY BASSEY SINGLES ALBUM *United Artists UAS 29728*.....2 23
1 Nov 75 GOOD BAD BUT BEAUTIFUL *United Artists UAS 29881*.....13 7
15 May 76 LOVE LIFE AND FEELINGS *United Artists UAS 29944*.....13 5
4 Dec 76 THOUGHTS OF LOVE *United Artists UAS 30011*.....15 9
25 Jun 77 YOU TAKE MY HEART AWAY *United Artists UAS 30037*.....34 5
4 Nov 78 ● 25TH ANNIVERSARY ALBUM *United Artists SBTV 601 4748*.....3 12
12 May 79 THE MAGIC IS YOU *United Artists UATV 30230*.....40 5
17 Jul 82 LOVE SONGS *Applause APKL 1163*.....48 5
20 Oct 84 I AM WHAT I AM *Towerbell TOWLP 7*.....25 18
22 Aug 87 **THE RHYTHM DIVINE** *Mercury MER 253* [1].....**54** 2
18 May 91 KEEP THE MUSIC PLAYING *Dino DINTV 21*.....25 7
5 Dec 92 THE BEST OF SHIRLEY BASSEY *Dino DINCD 49*.....27 5
4 Dec 93 SHIRLEY BASSEY SINGS ANDREW LLOYD WEBBER *Premier CDDPR 114*.....34 5
11 Nov 95 SHIRLEY BASSEY SINGS THE MOVIES *PolyGram TV 5293992*.....24 9
9 Nov 96 THE SHOW MUST GO ON *PolyGram TV 5337122*.....47 8
16 Nov 96 **'DISCO' LA PASSIONE** *East West EW 072CD* [2].....**41** 1
20 Dec 97 **HISTORY REPEATING** *Wall of Sound WALLD 036* [3].....**19** 7
23 Oct 99 **WORLD IN UNION** *Universal TV 4669402* [4].....**35** 3
9 Sep 00 THE REMIX ALBUM ... DIAMONDS ARE FOREVER *EMI 5258732*.....62 1
25 Nov 00 THE GREATEST HITS – THIS IS MY LIFE *Liberty 5258742*.....54 4
7 Jun 03 THANK YOU FOR THE YEARS *Citrus 5122722*.....19 4

[1] Yello featuring Shirley Bassey [2] Chris Rea and Shirley Bassey [3] Propellerheads featuring Miss Shirley Bassey [4] Shirley Bassey / Bryn Terfel
[1] Shirley Bassey with the Nelson Riddle Orchestra

BASSHEADS
UK, male / female vocal / instrumental group (5 Singles: 19 Weeks)

16 Nov 91 ● **IS THERE ANYBODY OUT THERE?** *Deconstruction R 6303*.....**5** 8
30 May 92 **BACK TO THE OLD SCHOOL** *Deconstruction R 6310*.....**12** 4
28 Nov 92 **WHO CAN MAKE ME FEEL GOOD?** *Deconstruction R 6326*.....**38** 2
28 Aug 93 **START A BRAND NEW LIFE (SAVE ME)** *Deconstruction CDR 6353*.....**49** 2
15 Jul 95 **IS THERE ANYBODY OUT THERE?** (re-mix) *Deconstruction 74321293882*.....**24** 3

BASS-O-MATIC
(see also William ORBIT) *UK, male multi-instrumentalist / producer – William Orbit (1 Album: 2 Weeks, 4 Singles: 19 Weeks)*

12 May 90 **IN THE REALM OF THE SENSES** *Virgin VS 1265*.....**66** 3
1 Sep 90 ● **FASCINATING RHYTHM** *Virgin VS 1274*.....**9** 11
13 Oct 90 SET THE CONTROLS FOR THE HEART OF THE BASS *Virgin V 2641*.....57 2
22 Dec 90 **EASE ON BY** *Virgin VS 1295*.....**61** 4
3 Aug 91 **FUNKY LOVE VIBRATIONS** *Virgin VS 1355*.....**71** 1

BASSTOY
(see also ABSOLUTE, SANDSTORM) *US, male producer – Mark Picchiotti (2 Singles: 6 Weeks)*

27 May 00 **RUNNIN** *Neo NEOCD 029*.....**62** 1
19 Jan 02 **RUNNIN'** (re-recording) *Black & White NEOCD 073* [1].....**13** 5

[1] Mark Picchiotti presents Basstoy featuring Dana

BATES
Germany, male vocal / instrumental group

3 Feb 96 **BILLIE JEAN** *Virgin International DINSD 151*.....**67** 1

Mike BATT with The NEW EDITION
(see also Justin HAYWARD; The WOMBLES) *UK, male vocalist and male / female vocal group*

16 Aug 75 ● **SUMMERTIME CITY** *Epic EPC 3460*.....**4** 8

28 Oct 89 CLASSIC BLUE *Trax MODEM 1040* [1].....47 7

[1] Justin Hayward, Mike Batt and the London Philharmonic Orchestra

BAUHAUS
(see also Peter MURPHY) *UK, male vocal / instrumental group (5 Albums: 24 Weeks, 8 Singles: 35 Weeks)*

15 Nov 80 IN THE FLAT FIELD *4AD CAD 13*.....72 1
18 Apr 81 **KICK IN THE EYE** *Beggars Banquet BEG 54*.....**59** 3
4 Jul 81 **THE PASSION OF LOVERS** *Beggars Banquet BEG 59*.....**56** 2
24 Oct 81 MASK *Beggars Banquet BEGA 29*.....30 5
6 Mar 82 **KICK IN THE EYE (SEARCHING FOR SATORI) (EP)** *Beggars Banquet BEG 74*.....**45** 4
19 Jun 82 **SPIRIT** *Beggars Banquet BEG 79*.....**42** 5
9 Oct 82 **ZIGGY STARDUST** *Beggars Banquet BEG 83*.....**15** 7
30 Oct 82 ● THE SKY'S GONE OUT *Beggars Banquet BEGA 42*.....4 6
22 Jan 83 **LAGARTIJA NICK** *Beggars Banquet BEG 88*.....**44** 4
9 Apr 83 **SHE'S IN PARTIES** *Beggars Banquet BEG 91*.....**26** 6
23 Jul 83 BURNING FROM THE INSIDE *Beggars Banquet BEGA 45*.....13 10
29 Oct 83 **THE SINGLES 1981-83** *Beggars Banquet BEG 100E*.....**52** 4
30 Nov 85 1979-1983 *Beggars Banquet BEGA 64*.....36 2

Tracks on Kick in the Eye (Searching For Satori) (EP): Kick in the Eye (Searching for Satori) / Harry / Earwax. The Singles 1981-83 was an EP: The Passion of Lovers / Kick in the Eye / Spirit / Ziggy Stardust / Lagartija Nick / She's in Parties.

Les BAXTER, his Chorus and Orchestra
US, chorus and orchestra – leader b. 14 Mar 1922, d. 15 Jan 1996

13 May 55 ● **UNCHAINED MELODY** *Capitol CL 14257* **$**.....**10** 9

Tom BAXTER
UK, male vocalist

31 Jul 04 **THIS BOY** *Sony Music 6751692*.....**65** 1
14 Aug 04 FEATHER & STONE *Columbia 5174689*.....65 3

BAY CITY ROLLERS
250 Top 500 *Tartan teen sensations from Edinburgh: Leslie McKeown (v), Eric Faulkner (g), Stuart Wood (g), Alan Longmuir (b), Derek Longmuir (d). They were the first of many acts heralded as the 'Biggest Group Since The Beatles' and one of the most screamed-at teeny-bopper acts of the 1970s (6 Albums: 136 Weeks, 12 Singles: 117 Weeks)*

18 Sep 71 ● **KEEP ON DANCING** *Bell 1164*.....**9** 13
9 Feb 74 ● **REMEMBER (SHA-LA-LA)** *Bell 1338*.....**6** 12
27 Apr 74 ● **SHANG-A-LANG** *Bell 1355*.....**2** 10
27 Jul 74 ● **SUMMERLOVE SENSATION** *Bell 1369*.....**3** 10
12 Oct 74 ★ ROLLIN' *Bell BELLS 244* ■.....1 62
12 Oct 74 ● **ALL OF ME LOVES ALL OF YOU** *Bell 1382*.....**4** 10
8 Mar 75 ★ **BYE BYE BABY** *Bell 1409*.....**1** 16
3 May 75 ★ ONCE UPON A STAR *Bell SYBEL 8001* ■.....1 37
12 Jul 75 ★ **GIVE A LITTLE LOVE** *Bell 1425*.....**1** 9
22 Nov 75 ● **MONEY HONEY** *Bell 1461*.....**3** 9
13 Dec 75 ● WOULDN'T YOU LIKE IT *Bell SYBEL 8002*.....3 12
10 Apr 76 ● **LOVE ME LIKE I LOVE YOU** *Bell 1477*.....**4** 10
11 Sep 76 ● **I ONLY WANNA BE WITH YOU** *Bell 1493*.....**4** 9
25 Sep 76 ● DEDICATION *Bell SYBEL 8005*.....4 12
7 May 77 **IT'S A GAME** *Arista 108*.....**16** 6
30 Jul 77 **YOU MADE ME BELIEVE IN MAGIC** *Arista 127*.....**34** 3
13 Aug 77 IT'S A GAME *Arista SPARTY 1009*.....18 4
17 Apr 04 THE VERY BEST OF BAY CITY ROLLERS *Bell / Arista 82876608192*.....11 9

Duke BAYSEE
UK, male vocalist – Kevin Rowe (2 Singles: 6 Weeks)

3 Sep 94 **SUGAR SUGAR** *Bell 74321228702*.....**30** 4
21 Jan 95 **DO YOU LOVE ME?** *Double Dekker CDDEK 1*.....**46** 2

BAZ
UK, female vocalist – Baz Gooden (2 Singles: 3 Weeks)

15 Dec 01 **BELIEVERS** *One Little Indian 313TP 7CD1*.....**36** 2
30 Mar 02 **SMILE TO SHINE** *One Little Indian 316TP 7CD*.....**58** 1

BE BOP DELUXE
(see also Bill NELSON) *UK, male vocal / instrumental group (4 Albums: 28 Weeks, 2 Singles: 13 Weeks)*

31 Jan 76 SUNBURST FINISH *Harvest SHSP 4053*.....17 12
21 Feb 76 **SHIPS IN THE NIGHT** *Harvest HAR 5104*.....**23** 8
25 Sep 76 MODERN MUSIC *Harvest SHSP 4058*.....12 6
13 Nov 76 **HOT VALVES (EP)** *Harvest HAR 5117*.....**36** 5
6 Aug 77 ● LIVE! IN THE AIR AGE *Harvest SHVL 816*.....10 5
25 Feb 78 DRASTIC PLASTIC *Harvest SHSP 4091*.....22 5

Tracks on Hot Valves (EP): Maid in Heaven / Blazing Apostles / Jet Silver and the Dolls of Venus / Bring Back the Spark.

24 June 1955	1 July 1955	8 July 1955	15 July 1955
UNCHAINED MELODY Jimmy Young	UNCHAINED MELODY Jimmy Young	UNCHAINED MELODY Jimmy Young	DREAMBOAT Alma Cogan

BRITISH **HIT** SINGLES & ALBUMS

www.bibleofpop.com

She's a model and she's looking good. Naomi Campbell, pictured left, heads a glamorous list of supermodels who have fashioned secondary careers as video stars. Naomi has strutted her stuff in five music videos for other artists, not to mention appearing in her own video for her single 'Love and Tears'. Kate Moss, pictured right, has catwalked her way into second place, while five supermodels have each starred in two videos. We've endeavoured to make this fun list as comprehensive as possible, including all the supermodels and videos that have kept teenage boys (and their dads) glued to MTV over the past couple of decades.

The models are ranked according to who has starred in the most videos associated with a Top 75 single, with the peak position of the best performing single, then total weeks on chart separating any ties.

VITAL STATISTICS

★ **George Michael** has used at least 14 different supermodels in his videos.

★ **Caprice** and **Naomi Campbell** have both recorded hits, and thus appeared in the videos, in their own right.

★ Supermodels who have dated or married pop stars: **Kate Moss** (Pete Doherty), **Heidi Klum** (Seal), **Iman** (David Bowie), **Rachel Hunter** (Rod Stewart).

Visit **www.bibleofpop.com** for information on how to view some of the classic videos listed on these pages

Supermodels Caprice, Rachel Hunter and Heidi Klum with Rod and Seal in close attendance

MOST APPEARANCES BY SUPERMODELS IN MUSIC VIDEOS

Pos / **SUPERMODEL / No of Videos**
MOST SUCCESSFUL SINGLE

1. **NAOMI CAMPBELL 5**
EROTICA Madonna No.3
Plus: IN THE CLOSET Michael Jackson
FREEDOM! George Michael
CHANGE CLOTHES Jay-Z
SEXUAL REVOLUTION Macy Gray

2. **KATE MOSS 4**
SOMETHING ABOUT THE WAY YOU LOOK TONIGHT
Elton John No.1
Plus: KOWALSKI Primal Scream
I JUST DON'T KNOW WHAT TO DO WITH MYSELF
The White Stripes
SOME VELVET MORNING
Primal Scream featuring Kate Moss

3. **CLAUDIA SCHIFFER 2**
UPTOWN GIRL Westlife No.1
Plus: SAY IT ISN'T SO Bon Jovi

4. **TYRA BANKS 2**
BLACK OR WHITE Michael Jackson No.1
Plus: TOO FUNKY George Michael

5. **LINDA EVANGELISTA 2**
TOO FUNKY George Michael No.4
Plus: FREEDOM! George Michael

6. **CINDY CRAWFORD 2**
PLEASE COME HOME FOR CHRISTMAS Bon Jovi No.7
Plus: FREEDOM! George Michael

7. **CHRISTY TURLINGTON 2**
NOTORIOUS Duran Duran No.7
Plus: FREEDOM! George Michael

8. **CHRISTIE BRINKLEY 1**
UPTOWN GIRL Billy Joel No.1

9. **IMAN 1**
REMEMBER THE TIME Michael Jackson No.3

10. **HELENA CHRISTENSEN 1**
WICKED GAME Chris Isaak No.10

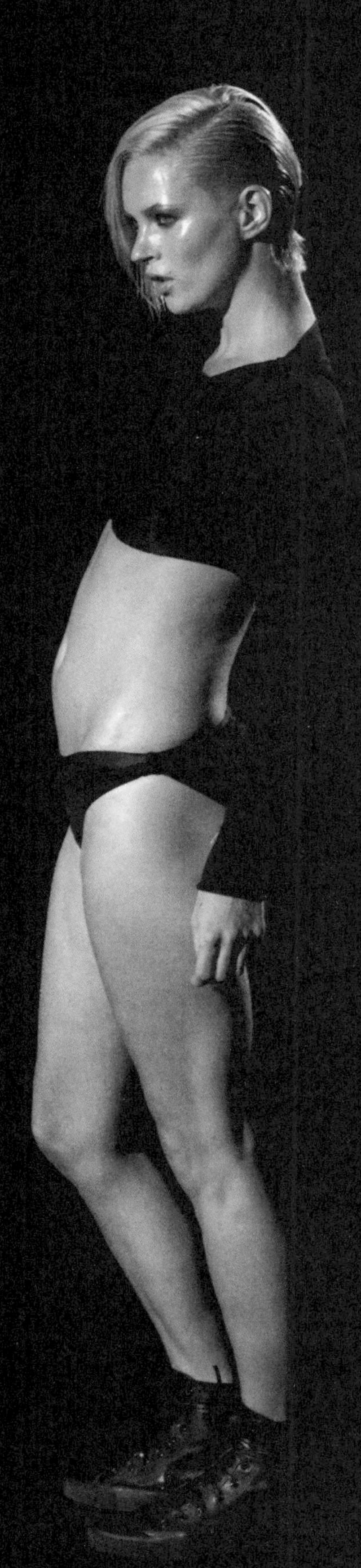

KEY
UK No.1 ★ UK Top 10 ● Still on chart + UK entry at No.1 ■ US No.1 ▲ UK million seller £ US million seller $
Singles re-entries are listed as (re), (2re), (3re)... which signifies that the hit re-entered the chart once, twice or three times...
Peak Position / Weeks

BE YOUR OWN PET NEW
US, male / female vocal / instrumental group (2 Singles: 2 Weeks)

		Peak	Wks
26 Mar 05	**DAMN DAMN LEASH** *XL Recordings XLS 212CD*	**68**	1
2 Jul 05	**FIRE DEPARTMENT** *Rough Trade RTRADSCD 238*	**59**	1

The BEACH BOYS 28 Top 500
California family band famous for their harmonies. The most successful and consistently popular US group of the rock era: Brian Wilson (b/k/v), Mike Love (v), Carl Wilson (g/v) (d. 1998), Al Jardine (g/v), Dennis Wilson (d/v) (d. 1983) (32 Albums: 574 Weeks, 32 Singles: 281 Weeks)

		Peak	Wks
1 Aug 63	**SURFIN' U.S.A.** *Capitol CL 15305* $	**34**	7
9 Jul 64 ●	**I GET AROUND** *Capitol CL 15350* ▲ $	**7**	13
29 Oct 64	**WHEN I GROW UP (TO BE A MAN) (re)** *Capitol CL 15361*	**27**	7
21 Jan 65	**DANCE, DANCE, DANCE** *Capitol CL 15370*	**24**	6
3 Jun 65	**HELP ME, RHONDA** *Capitol CL 15392* ▲ $	**27**	10
2 Sep 65	**CALIFORNIA GIRLS** *Capitol CL 15409*	**26**	8
25 Sep 65	SURFIN' USA *Capitol T 1890*	17	7
17 Feb 66 ●	**BARBARA ANN** *Capitol CL 15432* $	**3**	10
19 Feb 66 ●	BEACH BOYS PARTY *Capitol T 2398*	3	14
16 Apr 66 ●	BEACH BOYS TODAY *Capitol T 2269*	6	25
21 Apr 66 ●	**SLOOP JOHN B** *Capitol CL 15441*	**2**	15
9 Jul 66 ●	PET SOUNDS *Capitol T 2458*	2	39
16 Jul 66 ●	SUMMER DAYS (AND SUMMER NIGHTS!!) *Capitol T 2354*	4	22
28 Jul 66 ●	**GOD ONLY KNOWS** *Capitol CL 15459*	**2**	14
3 Nov 66 ★	**GOOD VIBRATIONS** *Capitol CL 15475* ▲ $	**1**	13
12 Nov 66 ●	BEST OF THE BEACH BOYS *Capitol T 20865*	2	142
11 Mar 67	SURFER GIRL *Capitol T 1981*	13	14
4 May 67 ●	**THEN I KISSED HER** *Capitol CL 15502*	**4**	11
23 Aug 67 ●	**HEROES AND VILLAINS** *Capitol CL 15510*	**8**	9
21 Oct 67 ●	BEST OF THE BEACH BOYS VOLUME 2 *Capitol ST 20956*	3	39
18 Nov 67 ●	SMILEY SMILE *Capitol ST 9001*	9	8
22 Nov 67	**WILD HONEY** *Capitol CL 15521*	**29**	6
17 Jan 68	**DARLIN'** *Capitol CL 15527*	**11**	14
16 Mar 68 ●	WILD HONEY *Capitol ST 2859*	7	15
8 May 68	**FRIENDS** *Capitol CL 15545*	**25**	7
24 Jul 68 ★	**DO IT AGAIN** *Capitol CL 15554*	**1**	14
21 Sep 68	FRIENDS *Capitol ST 2895*	13	8
23 Nov 68 ●	BEST OF THE BEACH BOYS VOLUME 3 *Capitol ST 21142*	9	12
25 Dec 68	**BLUEBIRDS OVER THE MOUNTAIN** *Capitol CL 15572*	**33**	5
26 Feb 69 ●	**I CAN HEAR MUSIC** *Capitol CL 15584*	**10**	13
29 Mar 69 ●	20/20 *Capitol EST 133*	3	10
11 Jun 69 ●	**BREAK AWAY** *Capitol CL 15598*	**6**	11
16 May 70 ●	**COTTONFIELDS** *Capitol CL 15640*	**5**	17
19 Sep 70 ●	GREATEST HITS *Capitol T 21628*	5	22
5 Dec 70	SUNFLOWER *Stateside SSL 8251*	29	6
27 Nov 71	SURF'S UP *Stateside SLS 10313*	15	7
24 Jun 72	CARL AND THE PASSIONS / SO TOUGH *Reprise K 44184*	25	1
17 Feb 73	HOLLAND *Reprise K 54008*	20	7
3 Mar 73	**CALIFORNIA SAGA – CALIFORNIA** *Reprise K 14232*	**37**	5
3 Jul 76	**GOOD VIBRATIONS** (re-issue) *Capitol CL 15875*	**18**	7
10 Jul 76 ★	20 GOLDEN GREATS *Capitol EMTV 1*	1	86
10 Jul 76	**ROCK AND ROLL MUSIC** *Reprise K 14440*	**36**	4
24 Jul 76	15 BIG ONES *Reprise K 54079*	31	3
7 May 77	THE BEACH BOYS LOVE YOU *Reprise K 54087*	28	1
31 Mar 79	**HERE COMES THE NIGHT** *Caribou CRB 7204*	**37**	8
21 Apr 79	LA (LIGHT ALBUM) *Caribou CRB 86081*	32	6
16 Jun 79 ●	**LADY LYNDA** *Caribou CRB 7427*	**6**	11
29 Sep 79	**SUMAHAMA** *Caribou CRB 7846*	**45**	4
12 Apr 80	KEEPING THE SUMMER ALIVE *Caribou CRB 86109*	54	3
29 Aug 81	**THE BEACH BOYS MEDLEY** *Capitol CL 213*	**47**	4
30 Jul 83 ★	THE VERY BEST OF THE BEACH BOYS *Capitol BBTV 1867193*	1	17
22 Jun 85	THE BEACH BOYS *Caribou CRB 26378*	60	2
22 Aug 87 ●	**WIPEOUT** *Urban URB 5* [1]	**2**	12
19 Nov 88	**KOKOMO** *Elektra EKR 85* ▲ $	**25**	9
2 Jun 90	**WOULDN'T IT BE NICE** *Capitol CL 579*	**58**	1
23 Jun 90 ●	SUMMER DREAMS – 28 CLASSIC TRACKS *Capitol EMTVD 51*	2	27
29 Jun 91	**DO IT AGAIN** (re-issue) *Capitol EMCT 1*	**61**	2
1 Jul 95	THE BEST OF THE BEACH BOYS *Capitol CDESTVD 3*	25	6
16 Sep 95	PET SOUNDS (re-issue) *Fame CDFA 3298*	59	6
2 Mar 96	**FUN FUN FUN** *PolyGram TV 5762972* [2]	**24**	4
11 Jul 98	GREATEST HITS *EMI 4956962*	28	4
19 Sep 98	ENDLESS HARMONY SOUNDTRACK *Capitol 4963912*	56	1
21 Jul 01	THE VERY BEST OF THE BEACH BOYS *Capitol 5326152*	31	9
11 Jun 05	THE PLATINUM COLLECTION *Capitol 5713452*	30	5

[1] Fat Boys and The Beach Boys [2] Status Quo with The Beach Boys

The Beach Boys Medley comprised Good Vibrations / Help Me, Rhonda / I Get Around / Shut Down / Surfin' Safari / Barbara Ann / Surfin' USA / Fun, Fun, Fun. The two Best of The Beach Boys, Greatest Hits and The Very Best of The Beach Boys albums are different. The re-issued Pet Sounds (1995) features the album's original tracks in a different order plus bonus tracks 'Hang on to Your Ego' and 'Trombone Dixie'. The album returned to the chart in 2005 with the catalogue number Capitol 5262662 and peaked at No.62.

Walter BEASLEY *US, male vocalist*

		Peak	Wks
23 Jan 88	**I'M SO HAPPY** *Urban URB 14*	**70**	3

BEASTIE BOYS 430 Top 500
Scourge of the tabloids in the late 1980s: MCA (Adam Yauch, v/b), Mike D (Michael Diamond, v/d) and Ad-Rock (Adam Horowitz, v/g). This New York rap trio turned their backs on their early image to become dedicated campaigners for a free Tibet. Known for their innovative videos, they founded a record label and magazine, both called Grand Royal (9 Albums: 95 Weeks, 15 Singles: 73 Weeks)

		Peak	Wks
31 Jan 87 ●	LICENCE TO ILL *Def Jam 450062* ▲	7	40
28 Feb 87	**(YOU GOTTA) FIGHT FOR YOUR RIGHT (TO PARTY)** *Def Jam 650418 7*	**11**	11
30 May 87	**NO SLEEP TILL BROOKLYN** *Def Jam BEAST 1*	**14**	7
18 Jul 87 ●	**SHE'S ON IT** *Def Jam BEAST 2*	**10**	8
3 Oct 87	**GIRLS / SHE'S CRAFTY** *Def Jam BEAST 3*	**34**	4
5 Aug 89	PAUL'S BOUTIQUE *Capitol EST 2102*	44	2
11 Apr 92	**PASS THE MIC** *Capitol 12CL 653*	**47**	2
4 Jul 92	**FROZEN METAL HEAD (EP)** *Capitol 12CL 665*	**55**	1
4 Jun 94 ●	ILL COMMUNICATION *Capitol CDEST 2229* ▲	10	15
9 Jul 94	**GET IT TOGETHER / SABOTAGE** *Capitol CDCL 716*	**19**	4
26 Nov 94	**SURE SHOT** *Capitol CDCL 726*	**27**	3
10 Jun 95	ROOT DOWN EP *Capitol CDEST 2262*	23	2
6 Apr 96	THE IN SOUND FROM WAY OUT! *Grand Royal CDEST 2281*	45	1
4 Jul 98 ●	**INTERGALACTIC** *Grand Royal CDCL 803*	**5**	7
18 Jul 98 ★	HELLO NASTY *Grand Royal 4957232* ■ ▲	1	21
7 Nov 98	**BODY MOVIN' (re)** *Grand Royal CDCL 809*	**15**	5
29 May 99	**REMOTE CONTROL / 3 MCS & 1 DJ** *Grand Royal CDCL 812*	**21**	3
4 Dec 99	ANTHOLOGY – THE SOUNDS OF SCIENCE *Grand Royal 5236642*	36	7
18 Dec 99	**ALIVE** *Grand Royal CDCL 818*	**28**	4
12 Jun 04 ●	**CH-CHECK IT OUT** *Capitol CDCLS 857*	**8**	7
26 Jun 04 ●	TO THE 5 BOROUGHS *Capitol 4733390* ▲	2	6
25 Sep 04	**TRIPLE TROUBLE** *Capitol CDCLS 859*	**37**	3
18 Dec 04	**AN OPEN LETTER TO NYC** *Capitol CDCLS 867*	**38**	4
19 Nov 05	SOLID GOLD HITS *Parlophone 3440492*	71	1

Tracks on Frozen Metal Head (EP): Jimmy James / Jimmy James (Original) / Drinkin' Wine / The Blue Nun.

The BEAT 437 Top 500
Birmingham, UK-based band, formed in 1978, who married ska and new wave influences: Dave Wakeling (v/g), Ranking Roger (v), Andy Cox (g) and David Steele (b). After their 1983 break-up, the former two launched General Public and the latter pair formed Fine Young Cannibals (5 Albums: 73 Weeks, 14 Singles: 92 Weeks)

		Peak	Wks
8 Dec 79 ●	**TEARS OF A CLOWN / RANKING FULL STOP** *2 Tone CHSTT 6*	**6**	11
23 Feb 80 ●	**HANDS OFF – SHE'S MINE** *Go Feet FEET 1*	**9**	9
3 May 80 ●	**MIRROR IN THE BATHROOM** *Go Feet FEET 2*	**4**	9
31 May 80 ●	I JUST CAN'T STOP IT *Go Feet BEAT 001*	3	32
16 Aug 80	**BEST FRIEND / STAND DOWN MARGARET (DUB)** *Go Feet FEET 3*	**22**	9
13 Dec 80 ●	**TOO NICE TO TALK TO** *Go Feet FEET 4*	**7**	11
18 Apr 81	**DROWNING / ALL OUT TO GET YOU** *Go Feet FEET 6*	**22**	8
16 May 81 ●	WHA'PPEN *Go Feet BEAT 3*	3	18
20 Jun 81	**DOORS OF YOUR HEART** *Go Feet FEET 9*	**33**	6
5 Dec 81	**HIT IT** *Go Feet FEET 11*	**70**	2
17 Apr 82	**SAVE IT FOR LATER** *Go Feet FEET 333*	**47**	4
18 Sep 82	**JEANETTE** *Go Feet FEET 15*	**45**	3
9 Oct 82	SPECIAL BEAT SERVICE *Go Feet BEAT 5*	21	6
4 Dec 82	**I CONFESS** *Go Feet FEET 16*	**54**	3
30 Apr 83 ●	**CAN'T GET USED TO LOSING YOU** *Go Feet FEET 17*	**3**	11

11 Jun 83 ● WHAT IS BEAT? (THE BEST OF THE BEAT) *Go Feet BEAT 6*.....10 13
2 Jul 83 **ACKEE 1-2-3** *Go Feet FEET 18*.....54 4
27 Jan 96 **MIRROR IN THE BATHROOM** (re-mix) *Go Feet 74321232062*....44 2
10 Feb 96 B.P.M. … THE VERY BEST OF THE BEAT *Go Feet 74321231952*.....13 4

BEAT RENEGADES (see also DREAM FREQUENCY; QUAKE featuring Marcia RAE; RED) *UK, male production duo – Ian Bland and Paul Fitzpatrick*

19 May 01 **AUTOMATIK** *Slinky Music SLINKY 014CD*.....73 1

BEAT SYSTEM *UK, male vocal / instrumental group (2 Singles: 3 Weeks)*

3 Mar 90 **WALK ON THE WILD SIDE** *Fourth & Broadway BRW 163*.....63 2
18 Sep 93 **TO A BRIGHTER DAY (O' HAPPY DAY)** *ffrr FCD 217*.....70 1

The BEAT UP *UK, male vocal / instrumental group (2 Singles: 2 Weeks)*

4 Dec 04 **MESSED UP** *Fantastic Plastic FPS 043*.....62 1
5 Mar 05 **ALRIGHT** *Fantastic Plastic FPS 045*.....58 1

The Beat Up are The Beatings under a different name.

BEATCHUGGERS featuring Eric CLAPTON
Denmark, male producer – Michael Linde and UK, male vocalist / guitarist

18 Nov 00 **FOREVER MAN (HOW MANY TIMES)** *ffrr FCD 386*.....26 2

The BEATINGS (see also The BEAT UP)
UK, male vocal / instrumental group

26 Oct 02 **BAD FEELING** *Fantastic Plastic FPS 034*.....68 1

The Beatings changed their name to The Beat Up.

The BEATLES 4 Top 500

The world's most successful group: John Lennon (v/g), b. 9 Oct 1940, Liverpool, d. 8 Dec 1980, New York, Paul McCartney (v/b), b. 18 Jun 1942, Liverpool, George Harrison (v/g), b. 25 Feb 1943, Liverpool, d. 29 Nov 2001, Ringo Starr (Richard Starkey) (v/d), b. 7 Jul 1940, Liverpool. This legendary group changed the face of popular music. Achievements include the most No.1 albums in the UK and US. Within three months of their US chart debut in 1964, they held all the Top 5 single chart places, had a record 14 simultaneous entries in the Billboard Top 100 and had the two top-selling albums. During those 12 weeks they earned six gold singles and sold four million albums. Sgt. Pepper's Lonely Hearts Club Band is the biggest-selling album ever in the UK. The group is the No.1 all-time US best-selling album act and the only act to earn six diamond albums (sales of 10 million) in the US. They split on 9 Apr 1970, since when Lennon, McCartney and Harrison have all had No.1 singles; Starr reached No.2. Their 1 collection (2000) is the world's fastest-selling album, with 23.5 million copies shipped in the first month, and was the top-selling album of 2000 in the UK. The Beatles, who were made MBEs in 1965 and, in 2004, were honoured as founder members of the UK Music Hall of Fame, representing the 1960s, have sold an estimated one billion records, including 20,799,632 UK singles. Best-selling single: 'She Loves You' 1,890,000 (49 Albums: 1293 Weeks, 32 Singles: 456 Weeks)

11 Oct 62 ● **LOVE ME DO (2re)** *Parlophone R 4949* ▲ $.....4 26
17 Jan 63 ● **PLEASE PLEASE ME (re)** *Parlophone R 4983* $.....2 22
6 Apr 63 ★ PLEASE PLEASE ME *Parlophone PMC 1202*.....1 70
18 Apr 63 ★ **FROM ME TO YOU (re)** *Parlophone R 5015*.....1 25
6 Jun 63 **MY BONNIE** *Polydor NH 66833* [1].....48 1
29 Aug 63 ★ **SHE LOVES YOU (2re)** *Parlophone R 5055* ▲ £ $.....1 36
30 Nov 63 ★ WITH THE BEATLES *Parlophone PMC 1206*.....1 51
5 Dec 63 ★ **I WANT TO HOLD YOUR HAND (2re)** *Parlophone R 5084* ▲ £ $.....1 24
26 Mar 64 ★ **CAN'T BUY ME LOVE (2re)** *Parlophone R 5114* ▲ £ $.....1 17
11 Jun 64 **AIN'T SHE SWEET** *Polydor 52 317*.....29 6
16 Jul 64 ★ **A HARD DAY'S NIGHT (re)** *Parlophone R 5160* ▲ $.....1 15
18 Jul 64 ★ A HARD DAY'S NIGHT *Parlophone PMC 1230* ▲.....1 38
3 Dec 64 ★ **I FEEL FINE (re)** *Parlophone R 5200* ▲ £ $.....1 14
12 Dec 64 ★ BEATLES FOR SALE *Parlophone PMC 1240* ▲.....1 46
15 Apr 65 ★ **TICKET TO RIDE (re)** *Parlophone R 5265* ▲ $.....1 14
29 Jul 65 ★ **HELP! (re)** *Parlophone R 5305* ▲ $.....1 17
14 Aug 65 ★ HELP! *Parlophone PMC 1255* ■ ▲.....1 37
9 Dec 65 ★ **DAY TRIPPER / WE CAN WORK IT OUT** *Parlophone R 5389* ▲ £ $.....1 12
11 Dec 65 ★ RUBBER SOUL *Parlophone PMC 1267* ▲.....1 42
16 Jun 66 ★ **PAPERBACK WRITER (re)** *Parlophone R 5452* ▲ $.....1 16
11 Aug 66 ★ **YELLOW SUBMARINE / ELEANOR RIGBY (re)** *Parlophone R 5493* $.....1 14
13 Aug 66 ★ REVOLVER *Parlophone PMC 7009* ■ ▲.....1 34
10 Dec 66 ● A COLLECTION OF BEATLES OLDIES *Parlophone PMC 7016*.....7 34
23 Feb 67 ● **PENNY LANE / STRAWBERRY FIELDS FOREVER (2re)** *Parlophone R 5570* ▲ $.....2 16
3 Jun 67 ★ SGT. PEPPER'S LONELY HEARTS CLUB BAND *Parlophone PCS 7027* ▲.....1 149
12 Jul 67 ★ **ALL YOU NEED IS LOVE (re)** *Parlophone R 5620* ▲ $.....1 16
29 Nov 67 ★ **HELLO, GOODBYE (re)** *Parlophone R 5655* ▲ $.....1 13
13 Dec 67 ● **MAGICAL MYSTERY TOUR (DOUBLE EP)** *Parlophone SMMT / MMT 1*.....2 12
13 Jan 68 MAGICAL MYSTERY TOUR (import) *Capitol SMAL 2835* ▲.....31 2
20 Mar 68 ★ **LADY MADONNA (re)** *Parlophone R 5675* $.....1 9
4 Sep 68 ★ **HEY JUDE (2re)** *Apple R 5722* ▲ $.....1 25
7 Dec 68 ★ THE BEATLES (WHITE ALBUM) *Apple PCS 7067/8* ■ ▲.....1 22
1 Feb 69 ● YELLOW SUBMARINE *Apple PCS 7070*.....3 10
23 Apr 69 ★ **GET BACK (2re)** *Apple R 5777* [2] ■ ▲ $.....1 23
4 Jun 69 ★ **THE BALLAD OF JOHN AND YOKO** *Apple R 5786* $.....1 14
4 Oct 69 ★ ABBEY ROAD *Apple PCS 7088* ■ ▲.....1 81
8 Nov 69 ● **SOMETHING / COME TOGETHER** *Apple R 5814* ▲ $.....4 12
14 Mar 70 ● **LET IT BE (re)** *Apple R 5833* ▲ $.....2 10
23 May 70 ★ LET IT BE *Apple PCS 7096* ■ ▲.....1 59
16 Jan 71 A HARD DAY'S NIGHT (re-issue) *Parlophone PCS 3058*.....30 1
24 Jul 71 HELP! (re-issue) *Parlophone PCS 3071*.....33 2
5 May 73 ● THE BEATLES 1962-1966 *Apple PCSP 717*.....3 148
5 May 73 ● THE BEATLES 1967-1970 *Apple PCSP 718* ▲.....2 115
13 Mar 76 ● **YESTERDAY** *Apple R 6013* ▲ $.....8 7
26 Jun 76 ROCK 'N' ROLL MUSIC *Parlophone PCSP 719*.....11 15
10 Jul 76 **BACK IN THE U.S.S.R.** *Parlophone R 6016*.....19 6
21 Aug 76 THE BEATLES TAPES *Polydor 2683 068*.....45 1
21 May 77 ★ THE BEATLES AT THE HOLLYWOOD BOWL *Parlophone EMTV 4*.....1 17
17 Dec 77 ● LOVE SONGS *Parlophone PCSP 721*.....7 17
7 Oct 78 **SGT. PEPPER'S LONELY HEARTS CLUB BAND – WITH A LITTLE HELP FROM MY FRIENDS** *Parlophone R 6022*.....63 3
3 Nov 79 RARITIES *Parlophone PCM 1001*.....71 1
15 Nov 80 BEATLES BALLADS *Parlophone PCS 7214*.....17 16
5 Jun 82 ● **BEATLES MOVIE MEDLEY** *Parlophone R 6055*.....10 9
30 Oct 82 ● 20 GREATEST HITS *Parlophone PCTC 260*.....10 30
7 Mar 87 A HARD DAY'S NIGHT (2nd re-issue) *Parlophone CDP 746 4372*.....30 4
7 Mar 87 BEATLES FOR SALE (re-issue) *Parlophone CDP 746 4382*.....45 2
7 Mar 87 PLEASE PLEASE ME (re-issue) *Parlophone CDP 746 4352*.....32 4
7 Mar 87 WITH THE BEATLES (re-issue) *Parlophone CDP 746 4362*.....40 3
9 May 87 HELP! (2nd re-issue) *Parlophone CDP 746 4392*.....61 2
9 May 87 REVOLVER (re-issue) *Parlophone CDP 746 4412*.....46 12
9 May 87 RUBBER SOUL (re-issue) *Parlophone CDP 746 4402*.....60 5
6 Jun 87 ● SGT. PEPPER'S LONELY HEARTS CLUB BAND (re-issue) *Parlophone CDP 746 4422*.....3 49
5 Sep 87 THE BEATLES (WHITE ALBUM) (re-issue) *Parlophone CDS 746 4439*.....18 2
5 Sep 87 YELLOW SUBMARINE (re-issue) *Parlophone CDP 746 4452*.....60 1
3 Oct 87 MAGICAL MYSTERY TOUR (re-issue) *Parlophone PCTC 255*.....52 1
31 Oct 87 ABBEY ROAD (re-issue) *Parlophone CDP 746 4462*.....30 11
31 Oct 87 LET IT BE (re-issue) *Parlophone CDP 746 4472*.....50 1
19 Mar 88 PAST MASTERS – VOLUME ONE *Parlophone CDBPM 1*.....49 1
19 Mar 88 PAST MASTERS – VOLUME TWO *Parlophone CDBPM 2*.....46 1
2 Oct 93 ● THE BEATLES 1962-1966 (re-issue) *Parlophone BEACD 2511*.3 24
2 Oct 93 ● THE BEATLES 1967-1970 (re-issue) *Parlophone BEACD 2512*.4 21
10 Dec 94 ★ LIVE AT THE BBC *Apple CDS 8317962* ■.....1 20
1 Apr 95 ● **BABY IT'S YOU (re)** *Apple CDR 6406*.....7 7
2 Dec 95 ● ANTHOLOGY 1 *Apple CDPCSP 727* ▲.....2 10
16 Dec 95 ● **FREE AS A BIRD** *Apple CDR 6422*.....2 8
16 Mar 96 ● **REAL LOVE** *Apple CDR 6425*.....4 7
30 Mar 96 ★ ANTHOLOGY 2 *Apple CDPCSP 728* ■ ▲.....1 12
9 Nov 96 ● ANTHOLOGY 3 *Apple CDPCSP 729* ▲.....4 11
25 Sep 99 ● YELLOW SUBMARINE – SONGTRACK (FILM SOUNDTRACK) *Parlophone 5214812*.....8 5
25 Nov 00 ★ 1 *Apple 5299702* ■ ▲.....1 46
29 Nov 03 ● LET IT BE – NAKED *Apple 5957132*.....7 7

[1] Tony Sheridan and The Beatles [2] The Beatles with Billy Preston

Tracks on Magical Mystery Tour (EP): Magical Mystery Tour / Your Mother Should Know / I Am the Walrus / Fool on the Hill / Flying / Blue Jay Way. 'We Can Work It Out' and 'Penny Lane' were the tracks from the double A-sides that topped the

KEY
UK No.1 ★ UK Top 10 ● Still on chart + UK entry at No.1 ■
US No.1 ▲ UK million seller £ US million seller $
Singles re-entries are listed as (re), (2re), (3re)... which signifies that the hit re-entered the chart once, twice or three times...
Peak Position / Weeks

US chart. 'Beatles Movie Medley' (A-side): Magical Mystery Tour / All You Need Is Love / You've Got To Hide Your Love Away / I Should Have Known Better / A Hard Day's Night / Ticket To Ride / Get Back. B-side: I'm Happy Just To Dance With You. Many Beatles hits re-entered the chart, including a large number on the original Parlophone label between 1982 and 1992. The best performing re-entry was 'Love Me Do', which made No.4 in 1982 but only peaked at No.17 on its release in 1962.

The BEATMASTERS

UK, male / female production group (1 Album: 10 Weeks, 7 Singles: 47 Weeks)

9 Jan 88 ● **ROK DA HOUSE** *Rhythm King LEFT 11* [1] 5 11
24 Sep 88 **BURN IT UP** *Rhythm King LEFT 27* [2] 14 10
22 Apr 89 ● **WHO'S IN THE HOUSE** *Rhythm King LEFT 31* [3] 8 9
1 Jul 89 ANYWAYAWANNA *Rhythm King LEFTLP 10* 30 10
12 Aug 89 ● **HEY DJ – I CAN'T DANCE (TO THAT MUSIC YOU'RE PLAYING) / SKA TRAIN** *Rhythm King LEFT 34* [4] 7 11
2 Dec 89 **WARM LOVE** *Rhythm King LEFT 37* [5] 51 2
21 Sep 91 **BOULEVARD OF BROKEN DREAMS** *Rhythm King 6573617* 62 1
16 May 92 **DUNNO WHAT IT IS (ABOUT YOU)** *Rhythm King 6580017* [6] 43 3

[1] The Beatmasters featuring The Cookie Crew [2] The Beatmasters with PP Arnold [3] The Beatmasters with Merlin [4] The Beatmasters featuring Betty Boo [5] The Beatmasters featuring Claudia Fontaine [6] The Beatmasters featuring Elaine Vassell

The BEATNUTS

US, male rap duo (3 Singles: 2 Weeks)

14 Jul 01 **NO ESCAPIN' THIS** *Epic 6713412* 47 1
21 Jun 03 **DUDE DESCENDING A STAIRCASE** *Stealth / SONY SSX 14CD* [1] 58 1

[1] Apollo 440 featuring The Beatnuts

BEATS INTERNATIONAL (see also FATBOY SLIM; FREAKPOWER; The HOUSEMARTINS; MIGHTY DUB KATZ; PIZZAMAN; URBAN ALL STARS)

UK, male / female vocal / instrumental group – leader Norman Cook (Quentin Cook) (1 Album: 15 Weeks, 6 Singles: 30 Weeks)

10 Feb 90 ★ **DUB BE GOOD TO ME** *Go Beat GOD 39* [1] 1 13
14 Apr 90 LET THEM EAT BINGO *Go Beat 8421961* 17 15
12 May 90 ● **WON'T TALK ABOUT IT** *Go Beat GOD 43* 9 7
15 Sep 90 **BURUNDI BLUES** *Go Beat GOD 45* 51 3
2 Mar 91 **ECHO CHAMBER** *Go Beat GOD 51* 60 2
21 Sep 91 **THE SUN DOESN'T SHINE** *Go Beat GOD 59* 66 2
23 Nov 91 **IN THE GHETTO** *Go Beat GOD 64* 44 3

[1] Beats International featuring Lindy Layton

BEAUTIFUL PEOPLE *UK, male instrumental / production group*

28 May 94 **IF 60'S WERE 90'S** *Essential ESSX 2037* 74 1

The BEAUTIFUL SOUTH (95 Top 500)

Ex-Housemartins Paul Heaton (v/g) and Dave Hemingway (v) (from the beautiful north of England) formed the band that featured Briana Corrigan (v) (replaced by Jacqui Abbot 1994-2000). Heaton and Dave Rotheray (g) write the witty and ironic songs (11 Albums: 291 Weeks, 31 Singles: 161 Weeks)

3 Jun 89 ● **SONG FOR WHOEVER** *Go Discs GOD 32* 2 11
23 Sep 89 ● **YOU KEEP IT ALL IN** *Go Discs GOD 35* 8 8
4 Nov 89 ● WELCOME TO THE BEAUTIFUL SOUTH *Go Discs AGOLP 16* 2 26
2 Dec 89 **I'LL SAIL THIS SHIP ALONE** *Go Discs GOD 38* 31 8
6 Oct 90 ★ **A LITTLE TIME** *Go Discs GOD 47* 1 14
10 Nov 90 ● CHOKE *Go Discs 8282331* 2 22
8 Dec 90 **MY BOOK** *Go Discs GOD 48* 43 6
16 Mar 91 **LET LOVE SPEAK UP ITSELF** *Go Discs GOD 53* 51 2
11 Jan 92 **OLD RED EYES IS BACK** *Go Discs GOD 66* 22 6
14 Mar 92 **WE ARE EACH OTHER** *Go Discs GOD 71* 30 3
11 Apr 92 ● 0898 BEAUTIFUL SOUTH *Go Discs 8283102* 4 17
13 Jun 92 **BELL BOTTOMED TEAR** *Go Discs GOD 78* 16 5
26 Sep 92 **36D** *Go Discs GOD 88* 46 2
12 Mar 94 **GOOD AS GOLD** *Go Discs GODCD 110* 23 5
9 Apr 94 ● MIAOW *Go Discs 8285072* 6 24
4 Jun 94 **EVERYBODY'S TALKIN'** *Go Discs GODCD 113* 12 8
3 Sep 94 **PRETTIEST EYES** *Go Discs GODCD 119* 37 3
12 Nov 94 **ONE LAST LOVE SONG** *Go Discs GODCD 122* 14 5
19 Nov 94 ★ CARRY ON UP THE CHARTS – THE BEST OF THE BEAUTIFUL SOUTH *Go Discs 8285722* 1 89
18 Nov 95 **PRETENDERS TO THE THRONE** *Go Discs GODCD 134* 18 4
12 Oct 96 ● **ROTTERDAM** *Go Discs GODCD 155* 5 9
2 Nov 96 ★ BLUE IS THE COLOUR *Go Discs 8288452* ■ 1 46
14 Dec 96 ● **DON'T MARRY HER** *Go Discs GODCD 158* 8 10
29 Mar 97 **BLACKBIRD ON THE WIRE** *Go Discs 5821252* 23 5
5 Jul 97 **LIARS' BAR** *Go Discs 5822492* 43 1
3 Oct 98 ● **PERFECT 10** *Go Discs 5664832* 2 14
24 Oct 98 ★ QUENCH *Go Discs 5381662* ■ 1 37
19 Dec 98 **DUMB (re)** *Go Discs 5667532* 16 8
20 Mar 99 **HOW LONG'S A TEAR TAKE TO DRY?** *Go Discs 8708212* 12 6
10 Jul 99 **THE TABLE** *Go Discs 5621652* 47 2
7 Oct 00 **CLOSER THAN MOST** *Go Discs / Mercury 5629672* 22 4
21 Oct 00 ● PAINTING IT RED *Go Discs / Mercury 5483352* 2 11
23 Dec 00 **THE RIVER / JUST CHECKIN'** *Go Discs / Mercury 5727552* 59 1
17 Nov 01 **THE ROOT OF ALL EVIL** *Go Discs / Mercury 5888702* 50 1
24 Nov 01 ● SOLID BRONZE – GREAT HITS *Go Discs / Mercury 5864442* 10 13
25 Oct 03 **JUST A FEW THINGS THAT I AIN'T** *Go Discs / Mercury 981308* 30 2
8 Nov 03 GAZE *Go Discs 9865694* 14 3
13 Dec 03 **LET GO WITH THE FLOW** *Go Discs / Mercury 9815083* 47 2
23 Oct 04 **LIVIN' THING** *Sony Music 6753712* 24 2
6 Nov 04 GOLDDIGGAS HEADNODDERS & PHOLK SONGS *Sony Music 5186329* 11 3
18 Dec 04 **THIS OLD SKIN** *Sony Music 6756842* 43 2
19 Feb 05 **THIS WILL BE OUR YEAR** *Sony Music 6757464* 36 2

Gilbert BECAUD

France, male vocalist – Francois Silly, b. 24 Oct 1927, d. 18 Dec 2001

29 Mar 75 ● **A LITTLE LOVE AND UNDERSTANDING** *Decca F 13537* 10 12

BECK *US, male vocalist – David Campbell (6 Albums: 81 Weeks, 11 Singles: 31 Weeks)*

5 Mar 94 **LOSER** *Geffen GFSTD 67* 15 6
2 Apr 94 MELLOW GOLD *Geffen GED 24634* 41 4
29 Jun 96 **WHERE IT'S AT** *Geffen GFSTD 22156* 35 2
6 Jul 96 ODELAY *Geffen GED 24926* 17 51
16 Nov 96 **DEVIL'S HAIRCUT** *Geffen GFSTD 22183* 22 2
8 Mar 97 **THE NEW POLLUTION** *Geffen GFSTD 22205* 14 5
24 May 97 **SISSYNECK** *Geffen GFSTD 22253* 30 2
8 Nov 97 **DEADWEIGHT** *Geffen GFSTD 22293* 23 3
14 Nov 98 MUTATIONS *Geffen GED 25184* 24 6
19 Dec 98 **TROPICALIA** *Geffen GFSTD 22365* 39 2
20 Nov 99 **SEXX LAWS** *Geffen 4971812* 27 3
4 Dec 99 MIDNITE VULTURES *Geffen 4905272* 19 14
8 Apr 00 **MIXED BIZNESS** *Geffen 4973002* 34 2
5 Oct 02 SEA CHANGE *Geffen / Polydor 4933932* 20 3
26 Mar 05 **E-PRO** *Interscope 9880052* 38 2
2 Apr 05 GUERO *Interscope 9880288* 15 3
16 Jul 05 **GIRL** *Interscope 9882469* 45 2

Jeff BECK (see also The YARDBIRDS)

UK, male vocalist / guitarist (6 Albums: 15 Weeks, 7 Singles: 57 Weeks)

23 Mar 67 **HI-HO SILVER LINING** *Columbia DB 8151* 14 14
2 Aug 67 **TALLYMAN** *Columbia DB 8227* 30 3
28 Feb 68 **LOVE IS BLUE (L'AMOUR EST BLEU)** *Columbia DB 8359* 23 7
9 Jul 69 **GOO GOO BARABAJAGAL (LOVE IS HOT)** *Pye 7N 17778* [1] 12 9
13 Sep 69 BECK-OLA *Columbia SCX 6351* 39 1
4 Nov 72 **HI-HO SILVER LINING (re)** (re-issue) *RAK RR 3* 17 15
28 Apr 73 JEFF BECK, TIM BOGERT AND CARMINE APPICE *Epic EPC 65455* [1] 28 3
5 May 73 **I'VE BEEN DRINKING** *RAK RR 4* [2] 27 6
24 Jul 76 WIRED *CBS 86012* 38 5
19 Jul 80 THERE AND BACK *Epic EPC 83288* 38 4
17 Aug 85 FLASH *Epic EPC 26112* 83 1
7 Mar 92 **PEOPLE GET READY** *Epic 6577567* [2] 49 3
27 Mar 99 WHO ELSE! *Epic 4930412* 74 1

[1] Donovan with the Jeff Beck Group [2] Jeff Beck and Rod Stewart
[1] Jeff Beck, Tim Bogert and Carmine Appice

Robin BECK *US, female vocalist*

22 Oct 88 ★ **THE FIRST TIME** *Mercury MER 270*....1 13

Victoria BECKHAM (see also SPICE GIRLS) *UK, female vocalist – Victoria Adams (1 Album: 3 Weeks, 4 Singles: 46 Weeks)*

26 Aug 00 ● **OUT OF YOUR MIND (re)** *Nulife 74321782942* [1] 2 20
29 Sep 01 ● **NOT SUCH AN INNOCENT GIRL (2re)** *Virgin VSCDT 1816*....6 11
13 Oct 01 ● **VICTORIA BECKHAM** *Virgin CDV 2942*....10 3
23 Feb 02 ● **A MIND OF ITS OWN** *Virgin VSCDT 1824*....6 7
10 Jan 04 ● **THIS GROOVE / LET YOUR HEAD GO** *19 / Telstar CDVB 1*....3 8

[1] True Steppers and Dane Bowers featuring Victoria Beckham

BEDAZZLED *UK, male vocal / instrumental group*

4 Jul 92 **SUMMER SONG** *Columbia 6581627*....73 1

Daniel BEDINGFIELD (391 Top 500)

Highly talented musical chameleon, b. New Zealand, 3 Dec 1979, and raised in South London. This singer / songwriter / producer, who recorded his first hits in his bedroom, was voted Best British Male Solo Artist at the 2004 BRITs (2 Albums: 94 Weeks, 9 Singles: 87 Weeks)

8 Dec 01 ★ **GOTTA GET THRU THIS** *Relentless RELENT 27CD* ■....1 18
24 Aug 02 ● **JAMES DEAN (I WANNA KNOW)** *Polydor 5709342*....4 8
7 Sep 02 ● **GOTTA GET THRU THIS** *Polydor 651252*....2 81
7 Dec 02 ★ **IF YOU'RE NOT THE ONE** *Polydor 0658632* ■....1 21
19 Apr 03 ● **I CAN'T READ YOU** *Polydor 0657132*....6 11
2 Aug 03 ★ **NEVER GONNA LEAVE YOUR SIDE** *Polydor CDATH 006* ■....1 11
1 Nov 03 **FRIDAY** *Polydor 9812919*....28 2
6 Nov 04 ● **NOTHING HURTS LIKE LOVE** *Polydor 9868820*....3 7
20 Nov 04 ● **SECOND FIRST IMPRESSION** *Polydor 9868637*....8 13
19 Feb 05 **WRAP MY WORDS AROUND YOU** *Polydor 987019*....12 7
4 Jun 05 **THE WAY** *Polydor 9871535*....41 2

Natasha BEDINGFIELD

UK, female vocalist (1 Album: 37 Weeks, 4 Singles: 42 Weeks)

15 May 04 ● **SINGLE** *Phonogenic / BMG 82876615232*....3 10
28 Aug 04 ★ **THESE WORDS** *Phonogenic / BMG 82876639182* ■....1 13
18 Sep 04 ★ **UNWRITTEN** *Arista / Phonogenic 82876637022* ■....1 37
11 Dec 04 ● **UNWRITTEN** *Phonogenic 82876663522*....6 12
16 Apr 05 **I BRUISE EASILY** *Phonogenic 82876681532*....12 7

BEDLAM (see also DIDDY)

UK, male DJ / production duo – Alan Thomson and Richard 'Diddy' Dearlove

6 Feb 99 **DA-FORCE** *Playola 0091695 PLA*....68 1

BEDLAM AGO GO

UK, male vocal / instrumental group

4 Apr 98 **SEASON NO.5** *Sony S2 BDLM 2CD*....57 1

BEDOUIN SOUNDCLASH NEW

Canada, male vocal / instrumental trio

8 Oct 05 **WHEN THE NIGHT FEELS MY SONG** *B-Unique / Polydor BUN 098CD*....24 4

BEDROCK *UK, male vocal / instrumental duo – John Digweed and Nick Muir (4 Singles: 9 Weeks)*

1 Jun 96 **FOR WHAT YOU DREAM OF** *Stress CDSTR 23* [1] 25 3
12 Jul 97 **SET IN STONE / FORBIDDEN ZONE** *Stress CDSTR 80*....71 1
6 Nov 99 **HEAVEN SCENT** *Bedrock BEDRCDS 001*....35 3
8 Jul 00 **VOICES** *Bedrock BEDRCDS 005*....44 2

[1] Bedrock featuring KYO

BEDROCKS

UK, male vocal / instrumental group

18 Dec 68 **OB-LA-DI, OB-LA-DA** *Columbia DB 8516*....20 7

Celi BEE and The BUZZY BUNCH

US, male / female vocal / instrumental group

17 Jun 78 **HOLD YOUR HORSES, BABE** *TK TKR 6032*....72 1

The BEE GEES (32 Top 500)

All-time top family recording act, who are members of the exclusive 100 million-plus sales club, are Isle of Man, UK, born and Australian raised Barry, Robin and Maurice Gibb, b. 22 Dec 1949, d. 12 Jan 2003. As composers, they have penned hits for many top acts and had 10 UK No.1s. In 1978 they wrote four consecutive US chart-toppers (three of which they also produced). Their Saturday Night Fever album is the world's biggest selling soundtrack and they were the first group to have UK Top 20s in five decades. This distinctive trio has won countless trophies including the World Music Legend Award (1997) and BRITs Outstanding Contribution to British Music (1997) (20 Albums: 417 Weeks, 38 Singles: 354 Weeks)

27 Apr 67 **NEW YORK MINING DISASTER 1941** *Polydor 56 161*....12 10
12 Jul 67 **TO LOVE SOMEBODY (re)** *Polydor 56 178*....41 5
12 Aug 67 ● **BEE GEES FIRST** *Polydor 583012*....8 27
20 Sep 67 ★ **(THE NIGHT THE LIGHTS WENT OUT IN) MASSACHUSETTS** *Polydor 56 192*....1 17
22 Nov 67 ● **WORLD** *Polydor 56 220*....9 16
31 Jan 68 ● **WORDS** *Polydor 56 229*....8 10
24 Feb 68 **HORIZONTAL** *Polydor 582020*....16 15
27 Mar 68 **JUMBO / THE SINGER SANG HIS SONG** *Polydor 56 242*....25 7
7 Aug 68 ★ **I'VE GOTTA GET A MESSAGE TO YOU** *Polydor 56 273*....1 15
28 Sep 68 ● **IDEA** *Polydor 583036*....4 18
19 Feb 69 ● **FIRST OF MAY** *Polydor 56 304*....6 11
5 Apr 69 ● **ODESSA** *Polydor 583049/50*....10 1
4 Jun 69 **TOMORROW, TOMORROW** *Polydor 56 331*....23 8
16 Aug 69 ● **DON'T FORGET TO REMEMBER** *Polydor 56 343*....2 15
8 Nov 69 ● **BEST OF THE BEE GEES** *Polydor 583063*....7 22
28 Mar 70 **I.O.I.O.** *Polydor 56 377*....49 1
9 May 70 **CUCUMBER CASTLE** *Polydor 2383010*....57 2
5 Dec 70 **LONELY DAYS** *Polydor 2001 104* $....33 9
29 Jan 72 **MY WORLD** *Polydor 2058 185*....16 9
22 Jul 72 ● **RUN TO ME** *Polydor 2058 255*....9 10
28 Jun 75 ● **JIVE TALKIN'** *RSO 2090 160* ▲ $....5 11
31 Jul 76 ● **YOU SHOULD BE DANCING** *RSO 2090 195* ▲ $....5 10
13 Nov 76 **LOVE SO RIGHT** *RSO 2090 207* $....41 4
29 Oct 77 ● **HOW DEEP IS YOUR LOVE** *RSO 2090 259* ▲ $....3 15
4 Feb 78 ● **STAYIN' ALIVE (re)** *RSO 2090 267* ▲ $....4 18
15 Apr 78 ★ **NIGHT FEVER** *RSO 002* ▲ $....1 20
25 Nov 78 ● **TOO MUCH HEAVEN** *RSO 25* ▲ $....3 13
17 Feb 79 ★ **SPIRITS HAVING FLOWN** *RSO RSBG 001* ▲....1 33
17 Feb 79 ★ **TRAGEDY** *RSO 27* ▲ $....1 10
14 Apr 79 **LOVE YOU INSIDE OUT** *RSO 31* ▲ $....13 9
10 Nov 79 ● **BEE GEES GREATEST** *RSO RSDX 001* ▲....6 25
5 Jan 80 **SPIRITS (HAVING FLOWN)** *RSO 52*....16 7
7 Nov 81 **LIVING EYES** *RSO RSBG 002*....73 8
17 Sep 83 **SOMEONE BELONGING TO SOMEONE** *RSO 96*....49 4
26 Sep 87 ★ **YOU WIN AGAIN** *Warner Bros. W 8351*....1 15
3 Oct 87 ● **E.S.P.** *Warner Bros. WX 83*....5 24
12 Dec 87 **E.S.P.** *Warner Bros. W 8139*....51 5
15 Apr 89 **ORDINARY LIVES** *Warner Bros. W 7523*....54 3
29 Apr 89 **ONE** *Warner Bros. WX 252*....29 3
24 Jun 89 **ONE** *Warner Bros. W 2916*....71 1
17 Nov 90 ● **THE VERY BEST OF THE BEE GEES** *Polydor 8473391*....6 108
2 Mar 91 ● **SECRET LOVE** *Warner Bros. W 0014*....5 11
6 Apr 91 **HIGH CIVILISATION** *Warner Bros. WX 417*....24 5
21 Aug 93 **PAYING THE PRICE OF LOVE** *Polydor PZCD 284*....23 5
25 Sep 93 **SIZE ISN'T EVERYTHING** *Polydor 5199452*....23 13
27 Nov 93 ● **FOR WHOM THE BELL TOLLS** *Polydor PZCD 299*....4 14
16 Apr 94 **HOW TO FALL IN LOVE PART 1** *Polydor PZDD 311*....30 4
1 Mar 97 ● **ALONE** *Polydor 5735272*....5 9
22 Mar 97 ● **STILL WATERS** *Polydor 5373022*....2 19
21 Jun 97 **I COULD NOT LOVE YOU MORE** *Polydor 5712232*....14 3
8 Nov 97 **STILL WATERS (RUN DEEP)** *Polydor 5718892*....18 3
18 Jul 98 ● **IMMORTALITY** *Epic 6661682* [1] 5 12
19 Sep 98 ● **ONE NIGHT ONLY** *Polydor 5592202*....4 44
7 Apr 01 **THIS IS WHERE I CAME IN** *Polydor 5879772*....18 5
14 Apr 01 ● **THIS IS WHERE I CAME IN** *Polydor 5494582*....6 6
24 Nov 01 ● **THEIR GREATEST HITS – THE RECORD** *Polydor 5894492*....5 33
13 Nov 04 ● **NUMBER ONES** *Polydor 9868840*....7 10
10 Dec 05 **LOVE SONGS** *Polydor 9874225*....51 1

[1] Celine Dion with special guests the Bee Gees

KEY
UK No.1 ★ UK Top 10 ● Still on chart + UK entry at No.1 ■
US No.1 ▲ UK million seller £ US million seller $
Singles re-entries are listed as (re), (2re), (3re)... which signifies that the hit re-entered the chart once, twice or three times...

Peak Position / Weeks

Sir Thomas BEECHAM (see also ORCHESTRE NATIONALE DE LA RADIO DIFFUSION FRANÇAISE) *UK, conductor, b. 29 Apr 1879, d. 8 Mar 1961*

26 Mar 60		CARMEN *HMV ALP 1762/4*	18	2

Full credit on sleeve reads 'Orchestre National de la Radio Diffusion Française conducted by Sir Thomas Beecham'.

BEENIE MAN *Jamaica, male vocalist / toaster / rapper – Anthony Moses David (10 Singles: 51 Weeks)*

20 Sep 97		DANCEHALL QUEEN *Island Jamaica IJCD 2018* [1]	70	1
7 Mar 98	●	WHO AM I "SIM SIMMA" *Greensleeves GRECD 588*	10	5
8 Aug 98		FOUNDATION *Shocking Vibes SVJCDS1*	69	1
4 Mar 00	●	MONEY *Parlophone Rhythm Series CDRHYTHM 27* [2]	5	9
24 Mar 01		GIRLS DEM SUGAR *Virgin VUSCD 173* [3]	13	5
28 Sep 02	●	FEEL IT BOY (re) *Virgin VUSCD 258* [4]	9	7
14 Dec 02		DIRTY HARRY'S REVENGE *Kaos KAOS 004* [5]	50	2
8 Feb 03		STREET LIFE *Virgin VUSCD 260*	13	5
13 Mar 04	●	DUDE *Virgin VUSCD 282* [6]	7	11
21 Aug 04		KING OF THE DANCEHALL *Virgin VUSCD 293*	14	5

[1] Chevelle Franklyn / Beenie Man [2] Jamelia featuring Beenie Man [3] Beenie Man featuring Mya [4] Beenie Man featuring Janet [5] Adam F featuring Beenie Man [6] Beenie Man featuring Ms Thing

The BEES
UK, male vocal / instrumental group (1 Album: 3 Weeks, 3 Singles: 8 Weeks)

1 May 04		WASH IN THE RAIN *Virgin VSCDT 1868*	31	3
26 Jun 04		HORSEMEN *Virgin VSCDX 1869*	41	2
10 Jul 04		FREE THE BEES *Virgin CDV 2983*	26	3
16 Apr 05		CHICKEN PAYBACK *Virgin VSCDX 1884*	28	3

Lou BEGA *Germany, male vocalist – David Lubega (1 Album: 2 Weeks, 3 Singles: 21 Weeks)*

7 Aug 99		MAMBO NO.5 (A LITTLE BIT OF ...) (import) *Ariola 74321658012*	31	4
4 Sep 99	★	MAMBO NO.5 (A LITTLE BIT OF ...) *RCA 74321696722* ■	1	15
18 Sep 99		A LITTLE BIT OF MAMBO *RCA 74321688612*	50	2
18 Dec 99		I GOT A GIRL *RCA 74321720642*	55	2

BEGGAR and CO
UK, male vocal / instrumental group (2 Singles: 15 Weeks)

7 Feb 81		(SOMEBODY) HELP ME OUT *Ensign ENY 201*	15	10
12 Sep 81		MULE (CHANT NO.2) *RCA 130*	37	5

BEGINERZ *UK, male production duo – Ibi Tijani and Euen MacNeil*

13 Jul 02		RECKLESS GIRL *Cheeky / Arista 74321942232*	28	3

BEGINNING OF THE END *US, male vocal / instrumental group*

23 Feb 74		FUNKY NASSAU *Atlantic K 10021*	31	6

BEIJING SPRING
UK, female vocal duo (2 Singles: 5 Weeks)

23 Jan 93		I WANNA BE IN LOVE AGAIN *MCA MCSTD 1709*	43	3
8 May 93		SUMMERLANDS *MCA MCSTD 1761*	53	2

BEL AMOUR *France, male / female vocal / production trio*

12 May 01		BEL AMOUR *Credence CDCRED 010*	23	3

BEL CANTO *UK, male vocal / instrumental group*

14 Oct 95		WE'VE GOT TO WORK IT OUT *Good Groove CDGG 2*	65	1

Harry BELAFONTE
US, male vocalist / actor (7 Singles: 87 Weeks)

1 Mar 57	●	BANANA BOAT SONG (DAY-O) *HMV POP 308* [1] $	2	18
14 Jun 57	●	ISLAND IN THE SUN *RCA 1007*	3	25
6 Sep 57		SCARLET RIBBONS *HMV POP 360* [2]	18	6
1 Nov 57	★	MARY'S BOY CHILD (2re) *RCA 1022* £	1	19
22 Aug 58		LITTLE BERNADETTE *RCA 1072* [3]	16	7
12 Dec 58		THE SON OF MARY *RCA 1084*	18	4
21 Sep 61		THERE'S A HOLE IN MY BUCKET (re) *RCA 1247* [4]	32	8

[1] Harry Belafonte with Tony Scott's Orchestra and Chorus and Millard Thomas, Guitar [2] Harry Belafonte and Millard Thomas [3] Belafonte [4] Harry Belafonte and Odetta

'Mary's Boy Child' re-entered twice, peaking at No.10 in 1958 and No.30 in 1959.

Andy BELL NEW (see also ERASURE) *UK, male vocalist*

8 Oct 05		CRAZY *Sanctuary SANXD 396*	35	2

Freddie BELL and The BELLBOYS *US, male vocal / instrumental group*

28 Sep 56	●	GIDDY-UP-A DING DONG *Mercury MT 122*	4	10

Archie BELL and The DRELLS
US, male vocal / instrumental group (5 Singles: 33 Weeks)

7 Oct 72		HERE I GO AGAIN *Atlantic K 10210*	11	10
27 Jan 73		(THERE'S GONNA BE A) SHOWDOWN *Atlantic K 10263*	36	5
8 May 76		THE SOUL CITY WALK *Philadelphia International PIR 4250*	13	10
11 Jun 77		EVERYBODY HAVE A GOOD TIME *Philadelphia International PIR 5179*	43	4
28 Jun 86		DON'T LET LOVE GET YOU DOWN *Portrait A 7254*	49	4

Maggie BELL (see also STONE THE CROWS)
UK, female vocalist (2 Singles: 12 Weeks)

15 Apr 78		HAZELL (re) *Swansong SSK 19412*	37	4
17 Oct 81		HOLD ME *Swansong BAM 1* [1]	11	8

[1] B A Robertson and Maggie Bell

William BELL
US, male vocalist – William Yarborough (3 Singles: 22 Weeks)

29 May 68		A TRIBUTE TO A KING *Stax 601 038*	31	7
20 Nov 68	●	PRIVATE NUMBER *Stax 101* [1]	8	14
26 Apr 86		HEADLINE NEWS *Absolute LUTE 1*	70	1

[1] Judy Clay and William Bell

BELL and JAMES *US, male vocal duo*

31 Mar 79		LIVIN' IT UP (FRIDAY NIGHT) (re) *A&M AMS 7424* $	59	3

BELL & SPURLING *UK, male vocal duo – Martin Bellamy and John Spurling (2 Singles: 10 Weeks)*

13 Oct 01	●	SVEN SVEN SVEN *Eternal WEA 336CD*	7	6
8 Jun 02		GOLDENBALLS (MR BECKHAM TO YOU) *Eternal WEA 350CD*	25	4

BELL BIV DEVOE (see also NEW EDITION)
US, male vocal group (1 Album: 5 Weeks, 4 Singles: 29 Weeks)

30 Jun 90		POISON *MCA MCA 1414* $	19	11
1 Sep 90		POISON *MCA MCG 6094*	35	5
22 Sep 90		DO ME *MCA MCA 1440*	56	3
15 Aug 92	●	THE BEST THINGS IN LIFE ARE FREE *Perspective PERSS 7400* [1]	2	13
9 Oct 93		SOMETHING IN YOUR EYES *MCA MCSTD 1934*	60	2

[1] Luther Vandross and Janet Jackson with special guests BBD and Ralph Tresvant

BELL BOOK & CANDLE
Germany, male / female vocal / instrumental group

17 Oct 98		RESCUE ME *Logic 74321616882*	63	1

BELL X1 *Ireland, male vocal / instrumental group*

26 Jun 04		EVE, THE APPLE OF MY EYE *Island CID 856*	65	1

The BELLAMY BROTHERS *US, male vocal duo – Howard and David Bellamy (1 Album: 6 Weeks, 3 Singles: 29 Weeks)*

17 Apr 76	●	LET YOUR LOVE FLOW *Warner Bros. / Curb K 16690* ▲	7	12

◂◂ UK No.1 SINGLES ▸▸

11 November 1955	18 November 1955	25 November 1955	2 December 1955
HERNANDO'S HIDEAWAY The Johnston Brothers	HERNANDO'S HIDEAWAY The Johnston Brothers	ROCK AROUND THE CLOCK Bill Haley and his Comets	ROCK AROUND THE CLOCK Bill Haley and his Comets

19 Jun 76	BELLAMY BROTHERS *Warner Bros. K 56242*	21	6
21 Aug 76	**SATIN SHEETS** *Warner Bros. / Curb K 16775*	**43**	3
11 Aug 79 ●	**IF I SAID YOU HAVE A BEAUTIFUL BODY WOULD YOU HOLD IT AGAINST ME** *Warner Bros. / Curb K 17405*	**3**	14

BELLATRIX *Iceland, male / female vocal / instrumental group*

16 Sep 00	**JEDI WANNABE** *Fierce Panda NING 101CD*	**65**	1

Regina BELLE
US, female vocalist (2 Albums: 5 Weeks, 2 Singles: 13 Weeks)

1 Aug 87	ALL BY MYSELF *CBS 450 9981*	53	4
16 Sep 89	STAY WITH ME *CBS 465 1321*	62	1
21 Oct 89	**GOOD LOVIN'** *CBS 655230*	**73**	1
11 Dec 93	**A WHOLE NEW WORLD (ALADDIN'S THEME)** *Columbia 6599002* [1] ▲	**12**	12

[1] Regina Belle and Peabo Bryson

BELLE & SEBASTIAN *UK, male / female vocal / instrumental group (6 Albums: 19 Weeks, 9 Singles: 21 Weeks)*

24 May 97	**DOG ON WHEELS** *Jeepster JPRCDS 001*	**59**	1
9 Aug 97	**LAZY LINE PAINTER JANE** *Jeepster JPRCDS 002*	**41**	2
25 Oct 97	**3 … 6 … 9 SECONDS OF LIGHT (EP)** *Jeepster JPRCDS 003*	**32**	2
19 Sep 98	THE BOY WITH THE ARAB STRAP *Jeepster JPRCD 003*	12	6
24 Jul 99	TIGERMILK *Jeepster JPRCD 007*	13	4
3 Jun 00	**LEGAL MAN** *Jeepster JPRCD 018*	**15**	3
17 Jun 00 ●	FOLD YOUR HANDS CHILD YOU WALK LIKE A PEASANT *Jeepster JPRMD 010*	10	3
30 Jun 01	**JONATHAN DAVID** *Jeepster JPRCDS 022*	**31**	2
8 Dec 01	**I'M WAKING UP TO US** *Jeepster JPRCDS 023*	**39**	2
15 Jun 02	STORYTELLING *Jeepster JPRCD 014*	26	2
18 Oct 03	DEAR CATASTROPHE WAITRESS *Rough Trade RTRADCD 080*	21	3
29 Nov 03	**STEP INTO MY OFFICE, BABY** *Rough Trade RTRADSCD 128*	**32**	2
28 Feb 04	**I'M A CUCKOO** *Rough Trade RTRADSCD 157*	**14**	4
3 Jul 04	**BOOKS** *Rough Trade RTRADSCD 180*	**20**	3
4 Jun 05	PUSH BARMAN TO OPEN OLD WOUNDS *Jeepster JPRDP 015*	40	1

Tracks on 3 … 6 … 9 Seconds of Light (EP): A Century of Fakers / Le Pastie de la Bourgeoisie / Beautiful / Put the Book Back on the Shelf. The album track 'Wrapped Up in Books' was abbreviated to 'Books' for the single release.
Group billed as Belle and Sebastian on Tigermilk, Storytelling and Push Barman to Open Old Wounds. The latter is a two-CD collection of the band's Jeepster EP and single releases, available for the first time on an album

BELLE and The DEVOTIONS *UK, female vocal group*

21 Apr 84	**LOVE GAMES** *CBS A 4332*	**11**	8

The BELLE STARS *UK, female vocal / instrumental group (1 Album: 12 Weeks, 7 Singles: 42 Weeks)*

5 Jun 82	**IKO IKO** *Stiff BUY 150*	**35**	6
17 Jul 82	**THE CLAPPING SONG** *Stiff BUY 155*	**11**	9
16 Oct 82	**MOCKINGBIRD** *Stiff BUY 159*	**51**	3
15 Jan 83 ●	**SIGN OF THE TIMES** *Stiff BUY 167*	**3**	11
5 Feb 83	THE BELLE STARS *Stiff SEEZ 45*	15	12
16 Apr 83	**SWEET MEMORY** *Stiff BUY 174*	**22**	9
13 Aug 83	**INDIAN SUMMER** *Stiff BUY 185*	**52**	3
14 Jul 84	**80'S ROMANCE** *Stiff BUY 200*	**71**	1

BELLEFIRE *Ireland, female vocal group (4 Singles: 12 Weeks)*

14 Jul 01	**PERFECT BLISS** *Virgin VSCDT 1807*	**18**	4
18 May 02	**ALL I WANT IS YOU** *Virgin VSCDT 1820*	**18**	4
24 Apr 04	**SAY SOMETHING ANYWAY** *East West EW 287CD*	**26**	3
16 Oct 04	**SPIN THE WHEEL** *East West EW 293CD1*	**67**	1

BELLINI *Germany, male vocal / production group*

27 Sep 97 ●	**SAMBA DE JANEIRO** *Virgin DINSD 165*	**8**	7

The BELLRAYS *US, male / female vocal / instrumental group*

18 May 02	MEET THE BELLRAYS *Poptones MC 5069CD*	73	1
20 Jul 02	**THEY GLUED YOUR HEAD ON UPSIDE DOWN** *Poptones MC 5073SCD*	**75**	1

BELLY (see also Tanya DONELLY) *US, male / female vocal / instrumental group (2 Albums: 13 Weeks, 4 Singles: 9 Weeks)*

23 Jan 93	**FEED THE TREE** *4AD BAD 3001CD*	**32**	3
13 Feb 93 ●	STAR *4AD 3002CD*	2	10
10 Apr 93	**GEPETTO** *4AD BAD 2018CD*	**49**	2
4 Feb 95	**NOW THEY'LL SLEEP** *4AD BAD 5003CD*	**28**	2
25 Feb 95 ●	KING *4AD CADD 5004CD*	6	3
22 Jul 95	**SEAL MY FATE** *4AD BAD 5007CD*	**35**	2

Pierre BELMONDE (see also Jeff JARRATT and Don REEDMAN)
France, male instrumentalist – panpipes – Jeff Jarrett

7 Jun 80	THEMES FOR DREAMS *K-Tel ONE 1077*	13	10

The BELOVED *UK, male / female vocal / instrumental duo (4 Albums: 31 Weeks, 11 Singles: 47 Weeks)*

21 Oct 89	**THE SUN RISING** *WEA YZ 414*	**26**	7
27 Jan 90	**HELLO** *WEA YZ 426*	**19**	7
3 Mar 90	HAPPINESS *East West WX 299*	14	14
24 Mar 90	**YOUR LOVE TAKES ME HIGHER** *East West YZ 463*	**39**	3
9 Jun 90	**TIME AFTER TIME** *East West YZ 482*	**46**	4
10 Nov 90	**IT'S ALRIGHT NOW** *East West YZ 541*	**48**	3
1 Dec 90	BLISSED OUT *East West WX 383*	38	2
23 Jan 93 ●	**SWEET HARMONY** *East West YZ 709CD*	**8**	10
20 Feb 93 ●	CONSCIENCE *East West 4509914832*	2	12
10 Apr 93	**YOU'VE GOT ME THINKING** *East West YZ 738CD*	**23**	4
14 Aug 93	**OUTERSPACE GIRL** *East West YZ 726CD*	**38**	2
30 Mar 96	**SATELLITE** *East West EW 034CD*	**19**	3
20 Apr 96	X *East West 630133162*	25	3
10 Aug 96	**EASE THE PRESSURE** *East West EW 058CD*	**43**	2
30 Aug 97	**THE SUN RISING** (re-issue) *East West EW 122CD1*	**31**	2

The act was male only before 1993.

BELTRAM (see also SECOND PHASE)
US, male producer – Joey Beltram (2 Singles: 4 Weeks)

28 Sep 91	**ENERGY FLASH (EP)** *R&S RSUK 3*	**52**	2
7 Dec 91	**THE OMEN** *R&S RSUK 7* [1]	**53**	2

[1] Program 2 Beltram

Tracks on Energy Flash (EP): Energy Flash / Psycho Bass / My Sound / Sub-Base Experience.

Benny BENASSI presents the BIZ
Italy, male producer (2 Singles: 13 Weeks)

26 Jul 03 ●	**SATISFACTION** *Data / MoS DATA 58CDS*	**2**	11
14 Feb 04	**NO MATTER WHAT YOU DO** *Data / MoS DATA 66CDS*	**40**	2

Pat BENATAR *US, female vocalist – Patricia Andrzejewski (9 Albums: 84 Weeks, 10 Singles: 53 Weeks)*

25 Jul 81	PRECIOUS TIME *Chrysalis CHR 1346* ▲	30	7
13 Nov 82	GET NERVOUS *Chrysalis CHR 1396*	73	6
15 Oct 83	LIVE FROM EARTH *Chrysalis CHR 1451*	60	5
21 Jan 84	**LOVE IS A BATTLEFIELD** *Chrysalis CHS 2747* **$**	**49**	5
17 Nov 84	TROPICO *Chrysalis CHR 1471*	31	25
12 Jan 85	**WE BELONG** *Chrysalis CHS 2821*	**22**	9
23 Mar 85	**LOVE IS A BATTLEFIELD** (re-issue) *Chrysalis PAT 1*	**17**	10
15 Jun 85	**SHADOWS OF THE NIGHT** *Chrysalis PAT 2*	**50**	4
24 Aug 85	IN THE HEAT OF THE NIGHT *Chrysalis CHR 1236*	98	1
19 Oct 85	**INVINCIBLE (THEME FROM 'THE LEGEND OF BILLIE JEAN')** *Chrysalis PAT 3* **$**	**53**	3
7 Dec 85	SEVEN THE HARD WAY *Chrysalis CHR 1507*	69	4
15 Feb 86	**SEX AS A WEAPON** *Chrysalis PAT 4*	**67**	3
7 Nov 87 ●	BEST SHOTS *Chrysalis PATV 1*	6	19
2 Jul 88	**ALL FIRED UP** *Chrysalis PAT 5*	**19**	10
16 Jul 88	WIDE AWAKE IN DREAMLAND *Chrysalis CDL 1628*	11	14
1 Oct 88	**DON'T WALK AWAY** *Chrysalis PAT 6*	**42**	5
14 Jan 89	**ONE LOVE** *Chrysalis PAT 7*	**59**	3
4 May 91	TRUE LOVE *Chrysalis CHR 1805*	40	3
30 Oct 93	**SOMEBODY'S BABY** *Chrysalis CDCHS 5001*	**48**	1

David BENDETH
Canada, male vocalist / multi-instrumentalist

8 Sep 79	**FEEL THE REAL** *Sidewalk SID 113*	**44**	5

KEY UK No.1 ★★ UK Top 10 ●● Still on chart ++ UK entry at No.1 ■■ US No.1 ▲▲ UK million seller £ US million seller $
Singles re-entries are listed as (re), (2re), (3re)... which signifies that the hit re-entered the chart once, twice or three times...
Peak Position / Weeks

BENELUX and Nancy DEE
Belgium / Holland / Luxembourg, female vocal group

25 Aug 79 **SWITCH** *Scope SC 4* 52 4

Eric BENET
US, male vocalist – Eric Bennet Jordan
(1 Album: 1 Week, 3 Singles: 5 Weeks)

22 Mar 97 **SPIRITUAL THANG** *Warner Bros. W 0390CD* 62 1
1 May 99 **GEORGY PORGY** *Warner Bros. W 478CD 2* [1] 28 3
15 May 99 A DAY IN THE LIFE *Warner Bros. 9362473702* 67 1
5 Feb 00 **WHY YOU FOLLOW ME** *Warner Bros. W 491CD* 48 1

[1] Eric Benet featuring Faith Evans

BENNET *UK, male vocal / instrumental group (2 Singles: 3 Weeks)*

22 Feb 97 **MUM'S GONE TO ICELAND** *Roadrunner RR 22853* 34 2
3 May 97 **SOMEONE ALWAYS GETS THERE FIRST** *Roadrunner RR 22983* 69 1

Boyd BENNETT and his ROCKETS *US, male vocalist, b. 7 Dec 1924, d. 2 Jun 2002, and vocal / instrumental group*

23 Dec 55 **SEVENTEEN** *Parlophone R 4063* 16 2

Cliff BENNETT and The REBEL ROUSERS *UK, male vocal / instrumental group (1 Album: 3 Weeks, 3 Singles: 23 Weeks)*

1 Oct 64 ● **ONE WAY LOVE** *Parlophone R 5173* 9 9
4 Feb 65 **I'LL TAKE YOU HOME** *Parlophone R 5229* 42 3
11 Aug 66 ● **GOT TO GET YOU INTO MY LIFE** *Parlophone R 5489* 6 11
22 Oct 66 DRIVIN' ME WILD *MFP 1121* 25 3

Peter E BENNETT with the CO-OPERATION CHOIR *UK, male vocalist and choir*

7 Nov 70 **THE SEAGULL'S NAME WAS NELSON** *RCA 1991* 45 1

Tony BENNETT *US, male vocalist – Anthony Benedetto (8 Albums: 70 Weeks, 8 Singles: 61 Weeks)*

15 Apr 55 ★ **STRANGER IN PARADISE** *Philips PB 420* 1 16
16 Sep 55 **CLOSE YOUR EYES** *Philips PB 445* 18 1
13 Apr 56 **COME NEXT SPRING** *Philips PB 537* 29 1
5 Jan 61 **TILL** *Philips PB 1079* 35 2
18 Jul 63 **THE GOOD LIFE** *CBS AAG 153* 27 13
6 May 65 **IF I RULED THE WORLD** *CBS 201735* 40 5
27 May 65 **(I LEFT MY HEART) IN SAN FRANCISCO (2re)** *CBS 201730* 25 14
29 May 65 I LEFT MY HEART IN SAN FRANCISCO *CBS BPG 62201* 13 14
23 Dec 65 **THE VERY THOUGHT OF YOU** *CBS 202021* 21 9
19 Feb 66 ● A STRING OF TONY'S HITS *CBS DP 66010* 9 13
10 Jun 67 TONY'S GREATEST HITS *CBS SBPG 62821* 14 24
23 Sep 67 TONY MAKES IT HAPPEN *CBS SBPG 63055* 31 3
23 Mar 68 FOR ONCE IN MY LIFE *CBS SBPG 63166* 29 5
26 Feb 77 THE VERY BEST OF TONY BENNETT – 20 GREATEST HITS *Warwick PA 5021* 23 4
28 Nov 98 THE ESSENTIAL TONY BENNETT *Columbia 4928222* 49 4
5 Jul 03 A WONDERFUL WORLD *Columbia 5098702* [1] 33 3

[1] Tony Bennett & kd lang

Brendan BENSON NEW *US, male vocalist / guitarist*

26 Mar 05 THE ALTERNATIVE TO LOVE *V2 VVR 1031212* 70 1
9 Apr 05 **SPIT IT OUT** *V2 VVR 5031203* 75 1

Gary BENSON *UK, male vocalist – Harry Hyams*

9 Aug 75 **DON'T THROW IT ALL AWAY** *State STAT 10* 20 8

George BENSON (101 Top 500)
Grammy-winning guitarist / vocalist, b. 22 Mar 1943, Pennsylvania, US. This one-time child prodigy topped the US chart in 1976 with the triple-platinum album 'Breezin'. He was also a major live attraction in Britain during the 1980s (17 Albums: 299 Weeks, 22 Singles: 143 Weeks)

25 Oct 75 **SUPERSHIP** *CTI CTSP 002* [1] 30 6
19 Mar 77 IN FLIGHT *Warner Bros. K 56237* 19 23
4 Jun 77 **NATURE BOY** *Warner Bros. K 16921* 26 6
24 Sep 77 **THE GREATEST LOVE OF ALL** *Arista 133* 27 7
18 Feb 78 WEEKEND IN L.A. *Warner Bros. K 66074* 47 1
24 Mar 79 LIVING INSIDE YOUR LOVE *Warner Bros. K 66085* 24 14
31 Mar 79 **LOVE BALLAD** *Warner Bros. K 17333* 29 9
26 Jul 80 ● GIVE ME THE NIGHT *Warner Bros. K 56823* 3 40
26 Jul 80 ● **GIVE ME THE NIGHT** *Warner Bros. K 17673* 7 10
4 Oct 80 ● **LOVE X LOVE** *Warner Bros. K 17699* 10 8
7 Feb 81 **WHAT'S ON YOUR MIND** *Warner Bros. K 17748* 45 5
19 Sep 81 **LOVE ALL THE HURT AWAY** *Arista ARIST 428* [2] 49 3
14 Nov 81 THE GEORGE BENSON COLLECTION *Warner Bros. K 66107* 19 35
14 Nov 81 **TURN YOUR LOVE AROUND** *Warner Bros. K 17877* 29 11
23 Jan 82 **NEVER GIVE UP ON A GOOD THING** *Warner Bros. K 17902* 14 10
21 May 83 **LADY LOVE ME (ONE MORE TIME)** *Warner Bros. W 9614* 11 10
11 Jun 83 ● IN YOUR EYES *Warner Bros. 9237441* 3 53
16 Jul 83 **FEEL LIKE MAKIN' LOVE** *Warner Bros. W 9551* 28 7
24 Sep 83 ● **IN YOUR EYES** *Warner Bros. W 9487* 7 10
17 Dec 83 **INSIDE LOVE (SO PERSONAL)** *WEA Int. W 9427* 57 5
19 Jan 85 **20 / 20** *Warner Bros. W 9120* 29 9
26 Jan 85 ● 20/20 *Warner Bros. 9251781* 9 19
20 Apr 85 **BEYOND THE SEA (LA MER)** *Warner Bros. W 9014* 60 3
19 Oct 85 ★ THE LOVE SONGS *K-Tel NE 1308* 1 26
16 Aug 86 **KISSES IN THE MOONLIGHT** *Warner Bros. W 8640* 60 4
6 Sep 86 WHILE THE CITY SLEEPS ... *Warner Bros. WX 55* 13 27
29 Nov 86 **SHIVER** *Warner Bros. W 8523* 19 9
14 Feb 87 **TEASER** *Warner Bros. W 8437* 45 4
11 Jul 87 COLLABORATION *Warner Bros. WX 91* [1] 47 6
27 Aug 88 **LET'S DO IT AGAIN** *Warner Bros. W 7780* 56 3
10 Sep 88 TWICE THE LOVE *Warner Bros. WX 160* 16 10
8 Jul 89 TENDERLY *Warner Bros. WX 263* 52 3
26 Oct 91 MIDNIGHT MOODS – THE LOVE COLLECTION *Telstar STAR 2450* 25 12
5 Sep 92 **I'LL KEEP YOUR DREAMS ALIVE** *Ammi AMMI 101* [3] 68 1
29 Jun 96 THAT'S RIGHT *GRP GRP 98242* 61 1
25 Apr 98 ● ESSENTIALS ... THE VERY BEST OF GEORGE BENSON *Warner.esp / Jive 9548362292* 8 10
11 Jul 98 **SEVEN DAYS** *MCA MCSTD 48083* [4] 22 3
5 Jul 03 ● THE VERY BEST OF GEORGE BENSON – THE GREATEST HITS OF ALL *WSM 8122736932* 4 18
27 Mar 04 IRREPLACEABLE *GRP 9861996* 58 1

[1] George "Bad" Benson [2] Aretha Franklin and George Benson [3] George Benson and Patti Austin [4] Mary J Blige featuring George Benson [1] George Benson and Earl Klugh

Rhian BENSON *Ghana, female vocalist*

23 Oct 04 **SAY HOW I FEEL** *DKG 10071002* 27 2

BENT *UK, male production duo*

12 Jul 03 **STAY THE SAME** *Sport SPORT 9CDS* 59 1

BENTLEY RHYTHM ACE *UK, male instrumental duo – Mike Stokes and Richard March (2 Albums: 6 Weeks, 3 Singles: 7 Weeks)*

24 May 97 BENTLEY RHYTHM ACE *Skint BRASSIC 5CD* 13 5
6 Sep 97 **BENTLEY'S GONNA SORT YOU OUT!** *Parlophone CDRS 6476* 17 4
27 May 00 **THEME FROM GUTBUSTER** *Parlophone CDRS 6537* 29 2
10 Jun 00 FOR YOUR EARS ONLY *Parlophone 5257322* 48 1
2 Sep 00 **HOW'D I DO DAT???** *Parlophone CDRS 6543* 57 1

Brook BENTON *US, male vocalist – Benjamin Peay, b. 19 Sep 1931, d. 9 Apr 1988 (4 Singles: 18 Weeks)*

10 Jul 59 **ENDLESSLY** *Mercury AMT 1043* 28 2
6 Oct 60 **KIDDIO (re)** *Mercury AMT 1109* 41 6
16 Feb 61 **FOOLS RUSH IN** *Mercury AMT 1121* 50 1
13 Jul 61 **THE BOLL WEEVIL SONG** *Mercury AMT 1148* $ 30 9

BENZ *UK, male rap / vocal group (5 Singles: 9 Weeks)*

16 Dec 95 **BOOM ROCK SOUL** *Hacktown 74321329652* 62 2
16 Mar 96 **URBAN CITY GIRL** *Hacktown 74321348732* 31 3
25 May 96 **MISS PARKER** *Hacktown 74321377292* 35 2

29 Mar 97 **IF I REMEMBER** *Hendricks CDBENZ 1* ...59 1
9 Aug 97 **ON A SUN-DAY** *Hendricks CDBENZ 2* ...73 1

BERLIN *US, male / female vocal (Terri Nunn) / instrumental group (1 Album: 11 Weeks, 4 Singles: 39 Weeks)*

25 Oct 86 ★ **TAKE MY BREATH AWAY (LOVE THEME FROM 'TOP GUN') (re)** *CBS A 7320* ▲ $ ...1 18
17 Jan 87 **COUNT THREE AND PRAY** *Mercury MER 101* ...32 11
17 Jan 87 **YOU DON'T KNOW** *Mercury MER 237* ...39 6
14 Mar 87 **LIKE FLAMES** *Mercury MER 240* ...47 3
13 Oct 90 ● **TAKE MY BREATH AWAY** (re-issue) *CBS 656361 7* ...3 12

'Take My Breath Away' re-entered the chart in 1988, peaking at No.52.

BERLIN PHILHARMONIC ORCHESTRA / Herbert Von KARAJAN *Germany, orchestra and Austria, male conductor*

13 Apr 96 **ADAGIO 2** *Deutsche Grammophon 4495152* ...63 1

Shelley BERMAN *US, male comedian*

19 Nov 60 **INSIDE SHELLEY BERMAN** *Capitol CLP 1300* ...12 4

Elmer BERNSTEIN *US, orchestra – leader b. 4 Apr 1922, d. 19 Aug 2004*

18 Dec 59 ● **STACCATO'S THEME (re)** *Capitol CL 15101* ...4 11

Leonard BERNSTEIN *US, orchestra and chorus – leader b. 25 Aug 1918, d. 14 Oct 1990*

10 Feb 90 **BERNSTEIN IN BERLIN – BEETHOVEN'S 9TH** *Deutsche Grammophon 42986* ...54 2
2 Jul 94 **AMERICA – WORLD CUP THEME 1994** *Deutsche Grammophon USACD 1* [1] ...44 4

[1] Leonard Bernstein, Orchestra and Chorus

BERRI *UK, female vocalist – Rebecca Sleight (3 Singles: 22 Weeks)*

26 Nov 94 **THE SUNSHINE AFTER THE RAIN** *Ffrreedom TABCD 223* [1] 26 6
2 Sep 95 ● **THE SUNSHINE AFTER THE RAIN** (re-mix) *Ffrreedom TABCD 232* ...4 11
2 Dec 95 **SHINE LIKE A STAR** *Ffrreedom TABCD 239* ...20 5

[1] New Atlantic / U4EA featuring Berri

LaKiesha BERRI *US, female vocalist*

5 Jul 97 **LIKE THIS AND LIKE THAT** *Adept ADPTCD 7* ...54 1

Chuck BERRY *US, male vocalist / guitarist (6 Albums: 53 Weeks, 11 Singles: 91 Weeks)*

21 Jun 57 **SCHOOL DAY (re)** *Columbia DB 3951* $ ...24 4
25 Apr 58 **SWEET LITTLE SIXTEEN** *London HLM 8585* $ ...16 5
25 May 63 **CHUCK BERRY** *Pye International NPL 28024* ...12 16
11 Jul 63 **GO GO GO** *Pye International 7N 25209* ...38 6
5 Oct 63 ● **CHUCK BERRY ON STAGE** *Pye International NPL 28027* ...6 11
10 Oct 63 ● **LET IT ROCK / MEMPHIS TENNESSEE** *Pye International 7N 25218* ...6 13
7 Dec 63 ● **MORE CHUCK BERRY** *Pye International NPL 28028* ...9 8
19 Dec 63 **RUN RUDOLPH RUN** *Pye International 7N 25228* ...36 6
13 Feb 64 **NADINE (IS IT YOU) (re)** *Pye International 7N 25236* ...27 7
7 May 64 ● **NO PARTICULAR PLACE TO GO** *Pye International 7N 25242* ...3 12
30 May 64 ● **THE LATEST AND THE GREATEST** *Pye NPL 28037* ...8 7
20 Aug 64 **YOU NEVER CAN TELL** *Pye International 7N 25257* ...23 8
3 Oct 64 **YOU NEVER CAN TELL** *Pye NPL 29039* ...18 2
14 Jan 65 **THE PROMISED LAND** *Pye International 7N 25285* ...26 6
28 Oct 72 ★ **MY DING-A-LING** *Chess 6145 019* ▲ $ ...1 17
3 Feb 73 **REELIN' AND ROCKIN'** *Chess 6145 020* ...18 7
12 Feb 77 ● **MOTORVATIN'** *Chess 9288 690* ...7 9

Dave BERRY *UK, male vocalist – Dave Grundy (8 Singles: 77 Weeks)*

19 Sep 63 **MEMPHIS TENNESSEE** *Decca F 11734* [1] ...19 13
9 Jan 64 **MY BABY LEFT ME (re)** *Decca F 11803* [1] ...37 9
30 Apr 64 **BABY IT'S YOU** *Decca F 11876* ...24 6
6 Aug 64 ● **THE CRYING GAME** *Decca F 11937* ...5 12
26 Nov 64 **ONE HEART BETWEEN TWO (re)** *Decca F 12020* ...41 3
25 Mar 65 ● **LITTLE THINGS** *Decca F 12103* ...5 12
22 Jul 65 **THIS STRANGE EFFECT** *Decca F 12188* ...37 6
30 Jun 66 ● **MAMA** *Decca F 12435* ...5 16

[1] Dave Berry and The Cruisers

Mike BERRY *UK, male vocalist – Michael Bourne (1 Album: 3 Weeks, 6 Singles: 51 Weeks)*

12 Oct 61 **TRIBUTE TO BUDDY HOLLY** *HMV POP 912* [1] ...24 6
3 Jan 63 ● **DON'T YOU THINK IT'S TIME** *HMV POP 1105* [1] ...6 12
11 Apr 63 **MY LITTLE BABY** *HMV POP 1142* [1] ...34 7
2 Aug 80 ● **THE SUNSHINE OF YOUR SMILE** *Polydor 2059 261* ...9 12
29 Nov 80 **IF I COULD ONLY MAKE YOU CARE** *Polydor POSP 202* ...37 9
24 Jan 81 **THE SUNSHINE OF YOUR SMILE** *Polydor 2383 592* ...63 3
5 Sep 81 **MEMORIES** *Polydor POSP 287* ...55 5

[1] Mike Berry and The Outlaws

Nick BERRY *UK, male actor / vocalist (2 Albums: 8 Weeks, 3 Singles: 24 Weeks)*

4 Oct 86 ★ **EVERY LOSER WINS (re)** *BBC RESL 204* ...1 13
20 Dec 86 **NICK BERRY** *BBC REB 618* ...99 1
13 Jun 92 ● **HEARTBEAT** *Columbia 6581517* ...2 8
31 Oct 92 **LONG LIVE LOVE** *Columbia 6587597* ...47 3
21 Nov 92 **NICK BERRY** *Columbia 4727182* ...28 7

The two identically titled albums are different.

BEST COMPANY *UK, male vocal duo*

27 Mar 93 **DON'T YOU FORGET ABOUT ME** *ZYX ZYX 69468* ...65 1

BEST SHOT *UK, male rap group*

5 Feb 94 **UNITED COLOURS** *East West YZ 795CD* ...64 2

The BETA BAND *UK, male vocal / instrumental group (4 Albums: 9 Weeks, 5 Singles: 7 Weeks)*

10 Oct 98 **THE THREE EP'S** *Regal Recordings 4973852* ...35 1
3 Jul 99 **THE BETA BAND** *Regal Recordings REG 30CD* ...18 2
14 Jul 01 **BROKE / WON** *Regal Recordings REG 60CD* ...30 2
28 Jul 01 **HOT SHOTS II** *Regal Recordings REG 59CD* ...13 3
27 Oct 01 **HUMAN BEING** *Regal Recordings REG 65CD* ...57 1
16 Feb 02 **SQUARES** *Regal Recordings REG 69CD* ...42 1
24 Apr 04 **ASSESSMENT** *Regal Recordings REG 012CDS* ...31 2
8 May 04 **HEROES TO ZEROS** *Regal Recordings REG 101CD* ...18 3
24 Jul 04 **OUT-SIDE** *Regal Recordings REG 110CDS* ...54 1

The BEVERLEY SISTERS *UK, female vocal trio (6 Singles: 34 Weeks)*

27 Nov 53 ● **I SAW MOMMY KISSING SANTA CLAUS (re)** *Philips PB 188* ...6 5
13 Apr 56 **WILLIE CAN** *Decca F 10705* ...23 4
1 Feb 57 **I DREAMED** *Decca F 10832* ...24 2
13 Feb 59 ● **LITTLE DRUMMER BOY** *Decca F 11107* ...6 13
20 Nov 59 **LITTLE DONKEY** *Decca F 11172* ...14 7
23 Jun 60 **GREEN FIELDS (re)** *Columbia DB 4444* ...29 3

BEVERLEY-PHILLIPS ORCHESTRA *UK, orchestra*

9 Oct 76 **GOLD ON SILVER** *Warwick WW 5018* ...22 9

BEYONCÉ (see also DESTINY'S CHILD) *US, female vocalist – Beyoncé Knowles (1 Album: 51 Weeks, 6 Singles: 64 Weeks)*

27 Jul 02 ● **WORK IT OUT (re)** *Columbia 6729822* ...7 11
1 Feb 03 ● **'03 BONNIE & CLYDE** *Roc-A-Fella 0770102* [1] ...2 12
5 Jul 03 ★ **DANGEROUSLY IN LOVE** *Columbia 5093952* ■ ▲ ...1 51
12 Jul 03 ★ **CRAZY IN LOVE** *Columbia 6740672* ■ ▲ ...1 15
18 Oct 03 ● **BABY BOY (re)** *Columbia 6744082* [2] ▲ ...2 11
24 Jan 04 **ME, MYSELF AND I** *Columbia 6745442* ...11 7
17 Apr 04 ● **NAUGHTY GIRL** *Columbia 6748282* ...10 8

[1] Jay-Z featuring Beyoncé Knowles [2] Beyoncé featuring Sean Paul

BEYOND *UK, male vocal / instrumental group*

21 Sep 91 **RAGING (EP)** *Harvest HARS 530* ...68 1

Tracks on Raging (EP): Great Indifference / Nail / Eve of My Release.

KEY UK No.1 ★ UK Top 10 ● Still on chart + UK entry at No.1 ■ US No.1 ▲ UK million seller £ US million seller $
Singles re-entries are listed as (re), (2re), (3re)... which signifies that the hit re-entered the chart once, twice or three times...
Peak Position / Weeks

BHANGRA KNIGHTS vs HUSAN
UK, male production trio and Holland, male production duo – Jeroen Den Hengst and Niels Zuiderhoek

17 May 03 ● **HUSAN** *Positiva CDTIV 188* 7 7

BHOYS FROM PARADISE
UK, male vocal group – Celtic fans

3 Jul 04 **DIRTY OLD TOWN / THE ROAD TO PARADISE** *Lord of the Wing LWSP 7* 46 2

The BIBLE
UK, male vocal / instrumental group (2 Albums: 2 Weeks, 2 Singles: 8 Weeks)

2 Jan 88 EUREKA *Cooltempo CHR 1646* 71 1
20 May 89 **GRACELAND** *Chrysalis BIB 4* 51 4
26 Aug 89 **HONEY BE GOOD** *Ensign BIB 5* 54 4
7 Oct 89 THE BIBLE *Ensign CHEN 12* 67 1

BIDDU ORCHESTRA
UK, orchestra – leader Biddu Appaiah (3 Singles: 13 Weeks)

2 Aug 75 **SUMMER OF '42** *Epic EPC 3318* 14 8
17 Apr 76 **RAIN FOREST** *Epic EPC 4084* 39 4
11 Feb 78 **JOURNEY TO THE MOON** *Epic EPC 5910* 41 1

BIFFY CLYRO
UK, male vocal / instrumental trio (2 Albums: 2 Weeks, 6 Singles: 11 Weeks)

16 Feb 02 **57** *Beggars Banquet BBQ 358CD* 61 1
5 Apr 03 **THE IDEAL HEIGHT** *Beggars Banquet BBQ 365CD* 46 1
7 Jun 03 **QUESTIONS & ANSWERS** *Beggars Banquet BBQ 368CD* 26 2
28 Jun 03 THE VERTIGO OF BLISS *Beggars Banquet BBQCD 233* 48 1
21 Aug 04 **GLITTER AND TRAUMA** *Beggars Banquet BBQ 377CD* 21 3
2 Oct 04 **MY RECOVERY INJECTION** *Beggars Banquet BBQ 379CD* 24 2
16 Oct 04 INFINITY LAND *Beggars Banquet BBQCD 238* 47 1
26 Feb 05 **ONLY ONE WORD COMES TO MIND** *Beggars Banquet BBQ 384CD* 27 2

BIG ANG featuring SIOBHAN NEW
UK, female producer and vocalist – Siobhan Gallagher

10 Sep 05 **IT'S OVER NOW** *All Around the World CDGLOBE 298* 29 3

BIG AUDIO DYNAMITE
UK / US, male vocal / instrumental group (6 Albums: 43 Weeks, 6 Singles: 27 Weeks)

16 Nov 85 THIS IS BIG AUDIO DYNAMITE *CBS 26714* 27 27
22 Mar 86 **E=MC2** *CBS A 6963* 11 9
7 Jun 86 **MEDICINE SHOW** *CBS A 7181* 29 5
18 Oct 86 **C'MON EVERY BEATBOX** *CBS 650147* 51 3
8 Nov 86 NO. 10 UPPING STREET *CBS 4501371* 11 8
21 Feb 87 **V. THIRTEEN** *CBS BAAD 2* 49 5
28 May 88 **JUST PLAY MUSIC!** *CBS BAAD 4* 51 3
9 Jul 88 TIGHTEN UP VOL. 88 *CBS 4611991* 33 3
16 Sep 89 MEGATOP PHOENIX *CBS 4657901* 26 3
2 Nov 90 **KOOL-AID** *CBS 4674661* 55 1
17 Aug 91 THE GLOBE *Columbia 4677061* 63 1
12 Nov 94 **LOOKING FOR A SONG** *Columbia 6610182* [1] 68 2

[1] Big Audio

BIG BAM BOO
UK / Canada, male vocal / instrumental duo

28 Jan 89 **SHOOTING FROM MY HEART** *MCA MCA 1281* 61 2

BIG BAND
UK, male instrumental group

16 Nov 02 SWINGIN' WITH THE BIG BAND *Columbia STVCD 157* 62 1

BIG BANG THEORY
UK, male producer – Seamus Haji

2 Mar 02 **GOD'S CHILD** *Defected DFECT 45CDS* 51 1

BIG BASS vs Michelle NARINE
Canada, male production group and female vocalist

2 Sep 00 **WHAT YOU DO** *Stonebridge / Edel 0110965 ERE* 67 1

BIG BEN
UK, clock bell

1 Jan 00 **MILLENNIUM CHIMES** *London BIGONE 2000* 53 2

BIG BEN BANJO BAND
UK, male instrumental group – leader Norrie Paramor, b. 1913, d. 9 Sep 1979 (1 Album: 1 Week, 2 Singles: 6 Weeks)

10 Dec 54 ● **LET'S GET TOGETHER NO.1** *Columbia DB 3549* 6 4
9 Dec 55 **LET'S GET TOGETHER AGAIN NO.1 (re)** *Columbia DB 3676* 18 2
17 Dec 60 MORE MINSTREL MELODIES *Columbia 33SX 1254* 20 1

Both singles were medleys, as follows: Let's Get Together No.1: I'm Just Wild About Harry / April Showers / Rock-a-Bye Your Baby / Swanee / Darktown Strutters Ball / For Me and My Gal / Oh You Beautiful Doll / Yes Sir That's My Baby / Let's Get Together.

The BIG BOPPER
US, male vocalist – JP Richardson, b. 24 Oct 1930, d. 3 Feb 1959

26 Dec 58 **CHANTILLY LACE (re)** *Mercury AMT 1002* 12 8

BIG BOSS STYLUS presents RED VENOM
UK, male production duo and male rapper – Mike Neilson

31 Jul 99 **LET'S GET IT ON** *All Around the World CDGLOBE 195* 72 1

BIG BROVAZ
UK, male / female vocal / rap / production group (1 Album: 35 Weeks, 7 Singles: 65 Weeks)

26 Oct 02 ● **NU FLOW (re)** *Epic 6730282* 3 18
16 Nov 02 ● NU FLOW *Epic 5099402* 6 35
15 Feb 03 ● **OK** *Epic 6735212* 7 9
17 May 03 ● **FAVOURITE THINGS** *Epic 6738072* 2 11
13 Sep 03 ● **BABY BOY** *Epic 6743092* 4 12
20 Dec 03 **AIN'T WHAT YOU DO** *Epic 6745102* 15 7
17 Apr 04 **WE WANNA THANK YOU (THE THINGS YOU DO)** *Epic 6748602* 17 4
9 Oct 04 **YOURS FATALLY** *Epic 6753542* 15 4

BIG COUNTRY 254 Top 500
Distinctively Scottish-sounding rock quartet from Dunfermline, Scotland: Stuart Adamson (v/g), b. 11 Apr 1958, d. 16 Dec 2001 (ex-Skids), Bruce Watson (g), Tony Butler (b), Mark Brzezicki (d). These frequent early-1980s chart visitors achieved five Top 10 albums, including the 1984 No.1 'Steeltown', and were well known for Watson and Adamson's twin guitar bagpipe-like sound (11 Albums: 149 Weeks, 23 Singles: 103 Weeks)

26 Feb 83 ● **FIELDS OF FIRE (400 MILES)** *Mercury COUNT 2* 10 12
28 May 83 **IN A BIG COUNTRY** *Mercury COUNT 3* 17 7
6 Aug 83 ● THE CROSSING *Mercury MERH 27* 3 80
3 Sep 83 ● **CHANCE** *Mercury COUNT 4* 9 9
21 Jan 84 ● **WONDERLAND** *Mercury COUNT 5* 8 8
29 Sep 84 **EAST OF EDEN** *Mercury MER 175* 17 6
27 Oct 84 ★ STEELTOWN *Mercury MERH 49* ■ 1 21
1 Dec 84 **WHERE THE ROSE IS SOWN** *Mercury MER 185* 29 7
19 Jan 85 **JUST A SHADOW** *Mercury BCO 8* 26 4
12 Apr 86 ● **LOOK AWAY** *Mercury BIGC 1* 7 8
21 Jun 86 **THE TEACHER** *Mercury BIGC 2* 28 4
12 Jul 86 ● THE SEER *Mercury MERH 87* 2 16
20 Sep 86 **ONE GREAT THING** *Mercury BIGC 3* 19 6
29 Nov 86 **HOLD THE HEART** *Mercury BIGC 4* 55 2
20 Aug 88 **KING OF EMOTION (re)** *Mercury BIGC 5* 16 6
8 Oct 88 ● PEACE IN OUR TIME *Mercury MERH 130* 9 6
5 Nov 88 **BROKEN HEART (THIRTEEN VALLEYS)** *Mercury BIGC 6* 47 4
4 Feb 89 **PEACE IN OUR TIME** *Mercury BIGC 7* 39 3
12 May 90 **SAVE ME** *Mercury BIGC 8* 41 3
26 May 90 ● THROUGH A BIG COUNTRY – GREATEST HITS *Mercury 8460221* 2 17
21 Jul 90 **HEART OF THE WORLD** *Mercury BIGC 9* 50 2
31 Aug 91 **REPUBLICAN PARTY REPTILE (EP)** *Vertigo BIC 1* 37 2
28 Sep 91 NO PLACE LIKE HOME *Vertigo 5102301* 28 2
19 Oct 91 **BEAUTIFUL PEOPLE** *Vertigo BIC 2* 72 1
13 Mar 93 **ALONE** *Compulsion CDPULSS 4* 24 3
3 Apr 93 THE BUFFALO SKINNERS *Compulsion CDNOIS 2* 25 2
1 May 93 **SHIPS (WHERE WERE YOU?)** *Compulsion CDPULSS 6* 29 3
18 Jun 94 WITHOUT THE AID OF A SAFETY NET (LIVE) *Compulsion CDNOIS 5* 35 1
10 Jun 95 **I'M NOT ASHAMED** *Transatlantic TRAX 1009* 69 1
24 Jun 95 WHY THE LONG FACE *Transatlantic TRACD 109* 48 2

9 Sep 95 **YOU DREAMER** *Transatlantic TRAD 1012* 68 1
24 Aug 96 ECLECTIC *Transatlantic TRACD 234* 41 1
21 Aug 99 **FRAGILE THING** *Track TRACK 0004A* [1] 69 1
8 Jun 02 THE GREATEST HITS OF BIG COUNTRY AND THE SKIDS – THE BEST OF STUART ADAMSON *UMTV 5869892* [1] 71 1

[1] Big Country featuring Eddi Reader [1] Big Country and The Skids

Tracks on Republican Party Reptile (EP): Republican Party Reptile / Comes a Time / You Me and the Truth.

BIG DADDY *US, male vocal group*

9 Mar 85 **DANCING IN THE DARK (EP)** *Making Waves SURF 1033* 21 8

Tracks on Dancing in the Dark (EP): I Write The Songs / Bette Davis Eyes / Dancing In The Dark / Eye Of The Tiger – Making Waves.

BIG DADDY KANE
US, male rapper – Antonio Hardy (1 Album: 3 Weeks, 3 Singles: 6 Weeks)

13 May 89 **RAP SUMMARY / WRATH OF KANE** *Cold Chillin' W 2973* 52 2
26 Aug 89 **SMOOTH OPERATOR** *Cold Chillin' W 2804* 65 1
30 Sep 89 IT'S A BIG DADDY THING *Cold Chillin' WX 305* 37 3
13 Jan 90 **AIN'T NO STOPPIN' US NOW** *Cold Chillin' W 2635* 44 3

BIG DISH
UK, male vocal / instrumental group (2 Albums: 3 Weeks, 1 Single: 5 Weeks)

11 Oct 86 SWIMMER *Virgin V 2374* 85 1
12 Jan 91 **MISS AMERICA** *East West YZ 529* 37 5
23 Feb 91 SATELLITES *East West WX 400* 43 2

BIG FUN *UK, male vocal group (1 Album: 11 Weeks, 5 Singles: 33 Weeks)*

12 Aug 89 ● **BLAME IT ON THE BOOGIE** *Jive JIVE 217* 4 11
25 Nov 89 ● **CAN'T SHAKE THE FEELING** *Jive JIVE 234* 8 9
17 Mar 90 **HANDFUL OF PROMISES** *Jive JIVE 243* 21 6
12 May 90 ● A POCKETFUL OF DREAMS *Jive FUN 1* 7 11
23 Jun 90 **YOU'VE GOT A FRIEND** *Jive CHILD 90* [1] 14 6
4 Aug 90 **HEY THERE LONELY GIRL** *Jive JIVE 251* 62 1

[1] Big Fun and Sonia featuring Gary Barnacle

BIG MOUNTAIN *US, male / female vocal (James McWhinney) / instrumental group (2 Singles: 15 Weeks)*

4 Jun 94 ● **BABY I LOVE YOUR WAY** *RCA 74321198062* 2 14
24 Sep 94 **SWEET SENSUAL LOVE** *Giant 74321234642* 51 1

BIG RON *UK, male producer – Aaron Gilbert (aka Jules Verne)*

11 Mar 00 **LET THE FREAK** *48k SPECT 06CDS* 57 1

BIG ROOM GIRL featuring Darryl PANDY
(see also RHYTHM MASTERS) *UK, male production / instrumental duo – Robert Chetcutti and Steve McGuinness and US, male vocalist*

20 Feb 99 **RAISE YOUR HANDS** *VC Recordings VCRD 44* 40 2

BIG SOUND AUTHORITY
UK, male / female vocal / instrumental group (2 Singles: 12 Weeks)

19 Jan 85 **THIS HOUSE (IS WHERE YOUR LOVE STANDS)** *Source BSA 1* 21 9
8 Jun 85 **A BAD TOWN** *Source BSA 2* 54 3

BIG SUPREME *UK, male vocal group (2 Singles: 5 Weeks)*

20 Sep 86 **DON'T WALK** *Polydor POSP 809* 58 3
14 Mar 87 **PLEASE YOURSELF** *Polydor POSP 840* 64 2

The BIG THREE *UK, male vocal / instrumental group (2 Singles: 17 Weeks)*

11 Apr 63 **SOME OTHER GUY** *Decca F 11614* 37 7
11 Jul 63 **BY THE WAY** *Decca F 11689* 22 10

BIG TIME CHARLIE (see also BIG RON) *UK, male DJ / production duo – Aaron Gilbert and Les Sharma (2 Singles: 4 Weeks)*

23 Oct 99 **ON THE RUN** *Inferno CDFERN 18* 22 2
18 Mar 00 **MR DEVIL** *Inferno CDFERN 24* [1] 39 2

[1] Big Time Charlie featuring Soozy Q

BIGFELLA featuring Noel McCALLA
US, male production duo and UK, male vocalist

17 Aug 02 **BEAUTIFUL** *Nulife 74321942282* 52 1

Barry BIGGS *Jamaica, male vocalist (6 Singles: 46 Weeks)*

28 Aug 76 **WORK ALL DAY** *Dynamic DYN 101* 38 5
4 Dec 76 ● **SIDESHOW** *Dynamic DYN 118* 3 16
23 Apr 77 **YOU'RE MY LIFE** *Dynamic DYN 127* 36 4
9 Jul 77 **THREE RING CIRCUS** *Dynamic DYN 128* 22 8
15 Dec 79 **WHAT'S YOUR SIGN GIRL** *Dynamic DYN 150* 55 7
20 Jun 81 **WIDE AWAKE IN A DREAM** *Dynamic DYN 10* 44 6

Ivor BIGGUN *UK, male vocalist – Doc Cox (2 Singles: 15 Weeks)*

2 Sep 78 **THE WINKER'S SONG (MISPRINT)** *Beggars Banquet BOP 1* [1] 22 12
12 Sep 81 **BRAS ON 45 (FAMILY VERSION)** *Dead Badger BOP 6* [2] 50 3

[1] Ivor Biggun & the Red-Nosed Burglars [2] Ivor Biggun and The D Cups

BILBO *UK, male vocal / instrumental group*

26 Aug 78 **SHE'S GONNA WIN** *Lightning LIG 548* 42 7

Acker BILK (166 Top 500)
First UK act to top the US chart in the 1960s, b. 28 Jan 1929, Somerset, UK. Band leader / clarinettist / vocalist was at the forefront of the UK trad-jazz revival. 'Stranger on the Shore' spent more than one year on the chart, selling 1,130,000, and was voted No.1 instrumental of 1962 in the US. Made an MBE in the 2001 honours list (12 Albums: 161 Weeks, 12 Singles: 172 Weeks)

22 Jan 60 ● **SUMMER SET** *Columbia DB 4382* [1] 5 20
19 Mar 60 ● SEVEN AGES OF ACKER *Columbia 33SX 1205* 6 6
9 Apr 60 ACKER BILK'S OMNIBUS *Pye NJL 22* 14 3
9 Jun 60 **GOODNIGHT SWEET PRINCE** *Melodisc MEL 1547* [1] 50 1
18 Aug 60 **WHITE CLIFFS OF DOVER** *Columbia DB 4492* [1] 30 9
8 Dec 60 ● **BUONA SERA** *Columbia DB 4544* [1] 7 18
4 Mar 61 ACKER *Columbia 33SX 1248* 17 1
1 Apr 61 GOLDEN TREASURY OF BILK *Columbia 33SX 1304* 11 6
27 May 61 ● THE BEST OF BARBER AND BILK VOLUME 1 *Pye Golden Guinea GGL 0075* [1] 4 43
13 Jul 61 ● **THAT'S MY HOME** *Columbia DB 4673* [1] 7 17
2 Nov 61 **STARS AND STRIPES FOREVER / CREOLE JAZZ** *Columbia SCD 2155* [1] 22 10
11 Nov 61 ● THE BEST OF BARBER AND BILK VOLUME 2 *Pye Golden Guinea GGL 0096* [1] 8 18
30 Nov 61 ● **STRANGER ON THE SHORE** *Columbia DB 4750* [2] ▲ £ $ 2 55
15 Mar 62 **FRANKIE AND JOHNNY** *Columbia DB 4795* [1] 42 2
26 May 62 ● STRANGER ON THE SHORE *Columbia 33SX 1407* 6 28
26 Jul 62 **GOTTA SEE BABY TONIGHT** *Columbia SCD 2176* [1] 24 9
25 Aug 62 ★ THE BEST OF BALL, BARBER AND BILK *Pye Golden Guinea GGL 0131* [2] 1 24
27 Sep 62 **LONELY** *Columbia DB 4897* [2] 14 11
24 Jan 63 **A TASTE OF HONEY** *Columbia DB 4949* [2] 16 9
4 May 63 A TASTE OF HONEY *Columbia 33SX 1493* 17 4
21 Aug 76 ● **ARIA** *Pye 7N 45607* [3] 5 11
9 Oct 76 THE ONE FOR ME *Pye NSPX 41052* 38 6
4 Jun 77 ● SHEER MAGIC *Warwick WW 5028* 5 8
11 Nov 78 EVERGREEN *Warwick PW 5045* 17 14

[1] Mr Acker Bilk and his Paramount Jazz Band [2] Mr Acker Bilk with the Leon Young String Chorale [3] Acker Bilk, his Clarinet and Strings
[1] Chris Barber and Acker Bilk [2] Kenny Ball, Chris Barber and Acker Bilk

BILL *UK, male vocalist*

23 Oct 93 **CAR BOOT SALE** *Mercury MINCD 1* 73 1

BILL & BEN
UK, male flowerpot-dwelling vocalists – voiced by John Thomson

13 Jul 02 **FLOBBADANCE** *BBC Music WMSS 60552* 23 4

BILLY TALENT
Canada, male vocal / instrumental group (3 Singles: 3 Weeks)

13 Sep 03 **TRY HONESTLY** *Atlantic AT 0160CD* 68 1
10 Apr 04 **THE EX** *Atlantic AT 0173CD* 61 1
17 Jul 04 **RIVER BELOW** *Atlantic AT 0178CD* 70 1

KEY
UK No.1 ★ UK Top 10 ● Still on chart + UK entry at No.1 ■
US No.1 ▲ UK million seller £ US million seller $
Singles re-entries are listed as (re), (2re), (3re)... which signifies that the hit re-entered the chart once, twice or three times...
Peak Position / Weeks

BIMBO JET *France, male / female vocal / instrumental group*

26 Jul 75 **EL BIMBO** *EMI 2317* 12 10

BINARY FINARY

UK, male production duo – Matt Lawes and Ricky Grant (2 Singles: 9 Weeks)

10 Oct 98 **1998** *Positiva CDTIV 98* 24 3
28 Aug 99 **1999** *Positiva CDTIV 118* 11 6

Umberto BINDI

Italy, male vocalist, b. 12 May 1933, d. May 2002

10 Nov 60 **IL NOSTRO CONCERTO** *Oriole CB 1577* 47 1

BINI & MARTINI

(see also ECLIPSE; GOODFELLAS featuring Lisa MILLETT; HOUSE OF GLASS)
Italy, male production duo – Gianni Bini and Paolo Martini (2 Singles: 2 Weeks)

4 Mar 00 **HAPPINESS (MY VISION IS CLEAR)** *Azuli AZNYCDX 113* 53 1
10 Mar 01 **BURNING UP** *Azuli AZNY 137* 65 1

BIOHAZARD *US, male vocal / instrumental group (2 Albums: 2 Weeks, 2 Singles: 4 Weeks)*

14 May 94 STATE OF THE WORLD ADDRESS *Warner Bros. 9362455952* 72 1
9 Jul 94 **TALES FROM THE HARD SIDE** *Warner Bros. W 0254CD* 47 2
20 Aug 94 **HOW IT IS** *Warner Bros. W 0259CD* 62 2
8 Jun 96 MATA LEAO *Warner Bros. 9362462082* 72 1

La BIONDA

Italy, male / female vocal group

7 Oct 78 **ONE FOR YOU ONE FOR ME** *Philips 6198 227* 54 4

BIOSPHERE

Norway, male producer / keyboard player – Ger Jenssen

5 Mar 94 PATASHNIK *Apollo AMB 3927CDX* 50 1
29 Apr 95 **NOVELTY WAVES** *Apollo APOLLO 20CDX* 51 2

BIRDLAND

UK, male vocal / instrumental group (1 Album: 1 Week, 5 Singles: 7 Weeks)

1 Apr 89 **HOLLOW HEART** *Lazy LAZY 13* 70 1
8 Jul 89 **PARADISE** *Lazy LAZY 14* 70 1
3 Feb 90 **SLEEP WITH ME** *Lazy LAZY 17* 32 3
22 Sep 90 **ROCK 'N' ROLL NIGGER** *Lazy LAZY 20* 47 1
2 Feb 91 **EVERYBODY NEEDS SOMEBODY** *Lazy LAZY 24* 44 1
2 Mar 91 BIRDLAND *Lazy LAZY 25* 44 1

The BIRDS *UK, male vocal / instrumental group*

27 May 65 **LEAVING HERE** *Decca F 12140* 45 1

Zoe BIRKETT *UK, female vocalist*

25 Jan 03 **TREAT ME LIKE A LADY** (re) *19 / Universal 0196822* 12 6

Jane BIRKIN and Serge GAINSBOURG

UK / France, female / male vocal duo – Serge Gainsbourg (Lucien Ginsberg), b. 2 Apr 1928, d. 2 Mar 1991 (3 Singles: 34 Weeks)

30 Jul 69 ● **JE T'AIME ... MOI NON PLUS** *Fontana TF 1042* 2 11
4 Oct 69 ★ **JE T'AIME ... MOI NON PLUS** (re-issue) *Major Minor MM 645* 1 14
7 Dec 74 **JE T'AIME ... MOI NON PLUS** (2nd re-issue) *Antic K 11511* 31 9

BIRTHDAY PARTY (see also Nick CAVE & The BAD SEEDS)

Australia, male vocal / instrumental group

24 Jul 82 JUNKYARD *4AD CAD 207* 73 3

BIS *UK, male / female vocal / instrumental group (1 Album: 1 Week, 7 Singles: 9 Weeks)*

30 Mar 96 **THE SECRET VAMPIRE SOUNDTRACK (EP)** *Chemikal Underground CHEM 003CD* 25 2
22 Jun 96 **BIS VS THE DIY CORPS (EP)** *Teen-C SKETCH 001CD* 45 1
9 Nov 96 **ATOM POWERED ACTION! (EP)** *Wiiija WIJ 55CD* 54 1
15 Mar 97 **SWEET SHOP AVENGERZ** *Wiiija WIJ 67CD* 46 1
19 Apr 97 THE NEW TRANSISTOR HEROES *Wiiija WIJCD 1064* 55 1
10 May 97 **EVERYBODY THINKS THAT THEY'RE GOING TO GET THEIRS** *Wiiija WIJ 69CD* 64 1
14 Nov 98 **EURODISCO** *Wiiija WIJ 86CD* 37 2
27 Feb 99 **ACTION AND DRAMA** *Wiiija WIJ 95CD* 50 1

Tracks on The Secret Vampire Soundtrack (EP): Kandy Pop / Secret Vampires / Teen-C Power / Diska. Tracks on Bis vs the DIY Corps (EP): This Is Fake DIY / Burn the Suit / Dance to the Disco Beat. Tracks on Atom Powered Action (EP): Starbright Boy / Wee Love / Team Theme / Cliquesuck.

BISCUIT BOY *UK, male vocal / instrumental trio*

15 Sep 01 **MITCH** *Mercury 5887582* 75 1

Elvin BISHOP *US, male guitarist*

15 May 76 **FOOLED AROUND AND FELL IN LOVE** *Capricorn 2089 024* $ 34 4

Hit has uncredited vocal by Mickey Thomas of Starship.

Stephen BISHOP *US, male pianist*

1 Apr 72 GRIEG AND SCHUMANN PIANO CONCERTOS *Philips 6500 166* 34 3

BIZARRE (see also D12) NEW *US, male rapper – Rufus Johnson*

2 Jul 05 **ROCKSTAR** *Sanctuary Urban SANXD 379* 17 4
9 Jul 05 HANNICAP CIRCUS *Sanctuary Urban SANCD 363* 43 1

BIZARRE INC *UK, male / female vocal / instrumental group (1 Album: 2 Weeks, 9 Singles: 49 Weeks)*

16 Mar 91 **PLAYING WITH KNIVES** *Vinyl Solution STORM 25R* 43 5
14 Sep 91 **SUCH A FEELING** *Vinyl Solution STORM 32S* 13 9
23 Nov 91 ● **PLAYING WITH KNIVES** (re-issue) *Vinyl Solution STORM 38S* 4 8
3 Oct 92 ● **I'M GONNA GET YOU** (re) *Vinyl Solution STORM 46S* [1] 3 13
7 Nov 92 ENERGIQUE *Vinyl Solution STEAM 47CD* 41 2
27 Feb 93 **TOOK MY LOVE** *Vinyl Solution STORM 60CD* [1] 19 5
23 Mar 96 **KEEP THE MUSIC STRONG** *Some Bizzare MERCD 451* 33 2
6 Jul 96 **SURPRISE** *Some Bizzare MERCD 462* 21 3
14 Sep 96 **GET UP SUNSHINE STREET** *Some Bizzare MERCD 471* 45 2
13 Mar 99 **PLAYING WITH KNIVES** (re-mix) *Vinyl Solution VC 01CD1* 30 2

[1] Bizarre Inc featuring Angie Brown

BIZZ NIZZ *US / Belgium, male / female vocal / instrumental group*

31 Mar 90 ● **DON'T MISS THE PARTYLINE** *Cooltempo COOL 203* 7 11

BIZZI *UK, male vocalist – Basil Dixon*

6 Dec 97 **BIZZI'S PARTY** *Parlophone Rhythm CDRHYTHM 7* 62 1

BJÖRK (330 Top 500)

Captivating, eccentric, uncompromising female singer / songwriter, b. Björk Gudmundsdottir, 21 Nov 1965, Reykjavik, Iceland. Formerly a member of The Sugarcubes, she was a double BRITs winner in 1994 (Best International Female and Best International Newcomer) and sang at the 2004 Olympics opening ceremony (7 Albums: 130 Weeks, 22 Singles: 81 Weeks)

27 Apr 91 **OOOPS** *ZTT ZANG 19* [1] 42 3
19 Jun 93 **HUMAN BEHAVIOUR** *One Little Indian 112TP 7CD* 36 2
17 Jul 93 ● DEBUT *One Little Indian TPLP 31CD* 3 69
4 Sep 93 **VENUS AS A BOY** *One Little Indian 122TP 7CD* 29 4
23 Oct 93 **PLAY DEAD** *Island CID 573* [2] 12 6
4 Dec 93 **BIG TIME SENSUALITY** *One Little Indian 132TP 7CD* 17 8
19 Mar 94 **VIOLENTLY HAPPY** *One Little Indian 142TP 7CD* 13 4
6 May 95 ● **ARMY OF ME** *One Little Indian 162TP 7CD* 10 5
24 Jun 95 ● POST / TELEGRAM *One Little Indian TPLP 51CD* 2 38
26 Aug 95 **ISOBEL** *One Little Indian 172TP 7CD* 23 3
25 Nov 95 ● **IT'S OH SO QUIET** *One Little Indian 182TP 7CD* 4 15

24 Feb 96 ● **HYPERBALLAD** *One Little Indian 192TP 7CD* 8 4
9 Nov 96 **POSSIBLY MAYBE** *One Little Indian 193TP 7CD* 13 3
1 Mar 97 **I MISS YOU** *One Little Indian 194TP 7CDL* 36 2
4 Oct 97 ● HOMOGENIC *One Little Indian TPLP 71CD* 4 13
20 Dec 97 **BACHELORETTE** *One Little Indian 212TP 7CD* 21 5
17 Oct 98 **HUNTER** *One Little Indian 222TP 7CD* 44 1
12 Dec 98 **ALARM CALL** *One Little Indian 232TP 7CDL* 33 2
19 Jun 99 **ALL IS FULL OF LOVE** *One Little Indian 242TP 7CD* 24 2
30 Sep 00 SELMA SONGS (FILM SOUNDTRACK) *One Little Indian TPLP 151CD* 34 1
18 Aug 01 **HIDDEN PLACE** *One Little Indian 332TP 7CD* 21 2
8 Sep 01 ● VESPERTINE *One Little Indian TPLP 101CD* 8 4
17 Nov 01 **PAGAN POETRY** *One Little Indian 352TP 7CD* 38 2
23 Mar 02 **COCOON** *One Little Indian 322TP 7CD* 35 2
16 Nov 02 GREATEST HITS *One Little Indian TPLP 359CD* 53 2
7 Dec 02 **IT'S IN OUR HANDS** *One Little Indian 366TP 7CD* 37 2
11 Sep 04 ● MEDULLA *One Little Indian TPLP 358CD* 9 3
30 Oct 04 **WHO IS IT** *One Little Indian 446TPT 7CD2* 26 2
12 Mar 05 **TRIUMPH OF A HEART** *One Little Indian 447 TP 7CD2* 31 2

[1] 808 State featuring Björk [2] Björk and David Arnold

Telegram, a re-mix album, was listed with Post from 7 Dec 96 and sales were combined.

BJÖRN AGAIN
Australia, male / female vocal / instrumental group (3 Singles: 8 Weeks)

24 Oct 92 **ERASURE-ISH (A LITTLE RESPECT / STOP!)** *M&G MAGS 32* 25 3
12 Dec 92 **SANTA CLAUS IS COMING TO TOWN** *M&G MAGS 35* 55 4
27 Nov 93 **FLASHDANCE … WHAT A FEELING** *M&G MAGCD 50* 65 1

BLACK *UK, male vocalist – Colin Vearncombe (3 Albums: 29 Weeks, 9 Singles: 35 Weeks)*

27 Sep 86 **WONDERFUL LIFE** *Ugly Man JACK 71* 72 1
27 Jun 87 ● **SWEETEST SMILE** *A&M AM 394* 8 10
22 Aug 87 ● **WONDERFUL LIFE** (re-recording) *A&M AM 402* 8 9
26 Sep 87 ● WONDERFUL LIFE *A&M AMA 5165* 3 23
16 Jan 88 **PARADISE** *A&M AM 422* 38 3
24 Sep 88 **THE BIG ONE** *A&M AM 468* 54 4
29 Oct 88 COMEDY *A&M AMA 5222* 32 4
21 Jan 89 **NOW YOU'RE GONE** *A&M AM 491* 66 2
4 May 91 **FEEL LIKE CHANGE** *A&M AM 780* 56 2
1 Jun 91 BLACK *A&M 3971261* 42 2
15 Jun 91 **HERE IT COMES AGAIN** *A&M AM 753* 70 1
5 Mar 94 **WONDERFUL LIFE** (re-issue) *PolyGram TV 5805552* 42 3

Cilla BLACK (246 Top 500)
Undoubtedly one of Britain's favourite female vocalists / entertainers of the past 50 years, b. Priscilla White, 27 May 1943, Liverpool. After handing in her Top 20 season ticket, she has become an award-winning and extremely popular TV presenter (8 Albums: 64 Weeks, 21 Singles: 194 Weeks)

17 Oct 63 **LOVE OF THE LOVED** *Parlophone R 5065* 35 6
6 Feb 64 ★ **ANYONE WHO HAD A HEART** *Parlophone R 5101* 1 17
7 May 64 ★ **YOU'RE MY WORLD** *Parlophone R 5133* 1 17
6 Aug 64 ● **IT'S FOR YOU** *Parlophone R 5162* 7 10
14 Jan 65 ● **YOU'VE LOST THAT LOVIN' FEELIN'** *Parlophone R 5225* 2 9
13 Feb 65 ● CILLA *Parlophone PMC 1243* 5 11
22 Apr 65 **I'VE BEEN WRONG BEFORE** *Parlophone R 5269* 17 8
13 Jan 66 ● **LOVE'S JUST A BROKEN HEART** *Parlophone R 5395* 5 11
31 Mar 66 ● **ALFIE** *Parlophone R 5427* 9 12
14 May 66 ● CILLA SINGS A RAINBOW *Parlophone PMC 7004* 4 15
9 Jun 66 ● **DON'T ANSWER ME** *Parlophone R 5463* 6 10
20 Oct 66 **A FOOL AM I (DIMMELO PARLAME)** *Parlophone R 5515* 13 9
8 Jun 67 **WHAT GOOD AM I?** *Parlophone R 5608* 24 7
29 Nov 67 **I ONLY LIVE TO LOVE YOU** *Parlophone R 5652* 26 11
13 Mar 68 ● **STEP INSIDE LOVE** *Parlophone R 5674* 8 9
13 Apr 68 ● SHER-OO *Parlophone PCS 7041* 7 11
12 Jun 68 **WHERE IS TOMORROW** *Parlophone R 5706* 39 3
30 Nov 68 THE BEST OF CILLA BLACK *Parlophone PCS 7065* 21 11
12 Feb 69 ● **SURROUND YOURSELF WITH SORROW** *Parlophone R 5759* 3 12
9 Jul 69 ● **CONVERSATIONS** *Parlophone R 5785* 7 12
13 Dec 69 **IF I THOUGHT YOU'D EVER CHANGE YOUR MIND** *Parlophone R 5820* 20 9
25 Jul 70 SWEET INSPIRATION *Parlophone PCS 7103* 42 4
20 Nov 71 ● **SOMETHING TELLS ME (SOMETHING IS GONNA HAPPEN TONIGHT)** *Parlophone R 5924* 3 14
2 Feb 74 **BABY WE CAN'T GO WRONG** *EMI 2107* 36 6
29 Jan 83 THE VERY BEST OF CILLA BLACK *Parlophone EMTV 38* 20 9
18 Sep 93 **THROUGH THE YEARS** *Columbia 6596982* 54 1
2 Oct 93 THROUGH THE YEARS *Columbia 4746502* 41 2
30 Oct 93 **HEART AND SOUL** *Columbia 6598562* [1] 75 1
4 Oct 03 BEGINNINGS … GREATEST HITS AND NEW SONGS *EMI 5931812* 68 1

[1] Cilla Black with Dusty Springfield

Frank BLACK *US, male vocalist – Charles Thompson (4 Albums: 8 Weeks, 3 Singles: 4 Weeks)*

20 Mar 93 ● FRANK BLACK *4AD CAD 3004CD* 9 3
21 May 94 **HEADACHE** *4AD BAD 4007CD* 53 1
4 Jun 94 TEENAGER OF THE YEAR *4AD CAD 4009CD* 21 2
20 Jan 96 **MEN IN BLACK** *Dragnet 6627862* 37 2
3 Feb 96 THE CULT OF RAY *Dragnet 4816472* 39 2
27 Jul 96 **I DON'T WANT TO HURT YOU (EVERY SINGLE TIME)** *Dragnet 6634635* 63 1
16 May 98 FRANK BLACK AND THE CATHOLICS *Play It Again Sam BIAS 370CD* [1] 61 1

[1] Frank Black and The Catholics

Jeanne BLACK *US, female vocalist – Gloria Jeanne Black*

23 Jun 60 **HE'LL HAVE TO STAY** *Capitol CL 15131* **$** 41 4

Mary BLACK *Ireland, female vocalist (4 Albums: 10 Weeks)*

3 Jul 93 THE HOLY GROUND *Grapevine GRACD 11* 58 2
16 Sep 95 CIRCUS *Grapevine GRACD 014* 16 4
29 Mar 97 SHINE *Grapevine GRACD 015* 33 3
28 Aug 99 SPEAKING WITH THE ANGEL *Grapevine GRACD 264* 63 1

BLACK & WHITE ARMY *UK, 250 Newcastle United football fan vocalists*

23 May 98 **BLACK & WHITE ARMY (BRINGING THE PRIDE BACK HOME)** *Toon TOON 1CD* 26 2

BLACK BOX *Italy, male / female vocal / instrumental / production group (1 Album: 30 Weeks, 11 Singles: 74 Weeks)*

12 Aug 89 ★ **RIDE ON TIME** *Deconstruction PB 43055* 1 22
17 Feb 90 ● **I DON'T KNOW ANYBODY ELSE** *Deconstruction PB 43479* 4 8
5 May 90 DREAMLAND *Deconstruction PL 74572* 14 30
2 Jun 90 **EVERYBODY EVERYBODY** *Deconstruction PB 43715* 16 5
3 Nov 90 ● **FANTASY** *Deconstruction PB 43895* 5 11
15 Dec 90 **THE TOTAL MIX** *Deconstruction PB 44235* 12 8
6 Apr 91 **STRIKE IT UP** *Deconstruction PB 44459* 16 8
14 Dec 91 **OPEN YOUR EYES** *Deconstruction PB 45053* 48 4
14 Aug 93 **ROCKIN' TO THE MUSIC** *Deconstruction 74321158122* 39 2
24 Jun 95 **NOT ANYONE** *Mercury MERCD 434* 31 2
20 Apr 96 **I GOT THE VIBRATION / A POSITIVE VIBRATION** *Manifesto MERCD 459* [1] 21 3
22 Feb 97 **NATIVE NEW YORKER** *Manifesto FESCD 18* [1] 46 1

[1] Blackbox

BLACK BOX RECORDER *UK, male / female vocal / instrumental group (1 Album: 1 Week, 2 Singles: 4 Weeks)*

22 Apr 00 **THE FACTS OF LIFE** *Nude NUD 48CD1* 20 3
13 May 00 THE FACTS OF LIFE *Nude NUDE 16CD* 37 1
15 Jul 00 **THE ART OF DRIVING** *Nude NUD 51CD1* 53 1

BLACK CONNECTION
Italy, male / female vocal / production group (2 Singles: 3 Weeks)

14 Mar 98 **GIVE ME RHYTHM** *Xtravaganza / Edel 0091465 EXT* 32 2
24 Oct 98 **I'M GONNA GET YA BABY** *Xtravaganza 0091615 EXT* 62 1

The BLACK CROWES *US, male vocal (Chris Robinson) / instrumental group (7 Albums: 33 Weeks, 12 Singles: 28 Weeks)*

1 Sep 90 **HARD TO HANDLE** *Def American DEFA 6* 45 5
12 Jan 91 **TWICE AS HARD** *Def American DEFA 7* 47 3
22 Jun 91 **JEALOUS AGAIN / SHE TALKS TO ANGELS** *Def American DEFA 8* 70 1
24 Aug 91 SHAKE YOUR MONEY MAKER *Def American 8425151* 36 11
24 Aug 91 **HARD TO HANDLE** (re-issue) *Def American DEFA 10* 39 4
26 Oct 91 **SEEING THINGS** *Def American DEFA 13* 72 1
2 May 92 **REMEDY** *Def American DEFA 16* 24 3

25 May 1956	1 June 1956	8 June 1956	15 June 1956
NO OTHER LOVE Ronnie Hilton	**NO OTHER LOVE** Ronnie Hilton	**NO OTHER LOVE** Ronnie Hilton	**I'LL BE HOME** Pat Boone

KEY UK No.1 ★ UK Top 10 ● Still on chart + UK entry at No.1 ■ US No.1 ▲ UK million seller £ US million seller $
Singles re-entries are listed as (re), (2re), (3re)... which signifies that the hit re-entered the chart once, twice or three times...
Peak Position / Weeks

23 May 92 ● THE SOUTHERN HARMONY AND MUSICAL COMPANION Def American 5122632 ▲ ... 2 7
26 Sep 92 STING ME Def American DEFA 21 ... 42 2
28 Nov 92 HOTEL ILLNESS Def American DEFA 23 ... 47 3
12 Nov 94 ● AMORICA American 74321241942 ... 8 4
11 Feb 95 HIGH HEAD BLUES / A CONSPIRACY American 74321258492 ... 25 2
22 Jul 95 WISER TIME American 74321298272 ... 34 2
27 Jul 96 ONE MIRROR TOO MANY American 74321398572 ... 51 1
3 Aug 96 THREE SNAKES AND ONE CHARM American Recordings 74321384842 ... 17 3
7 Nov 98 KICKING MY HEART AROUND American Recordings 6666665 ... 55 1
23 Jan 99 BY YOUR SIDE Columbia 4916992 ... 34 2
22 Jul 00 LIVE AT THE GREEK SPV Recordings SPV 09172022 [1] ... 39 4
19 May 01 LIONS V2 VVR 1015672 ... 37 2

[1] Jimmy Page and The Black Crowes

BLACK DIAMOND
US, male vocalist – Charles Diamond

17 Sep 94 LET ME BE Systematic SYSCD 1 ... 56 1

BLACK DOG *UK, male instrumentalist / producer – Ken Downie*

28 Jan 95 SPANNERS Warp PUPCD 1 ... 30 2
3 Apr 99 BABYLON Warner.esp WESP 006CD1 [1] ... 65 1

[1] Black Dog featuring Ofra Haza

BLACK DUCK *UK, male rapper – Blair Mackichan*

17 Dec 94 WHIGGLE IN LINE Flying South CDDUCK 1 ... 33 5

The BLACK EYED PEAS 378 Top 500
The world's biggest selling hip-hop group includes Will Adams (Will.I.Am) and Stacy Ferguson. Grammy-winning act, who appeared at US Live 8 show, sold eight million copies of 'Elephunk' and became a global phenomenon (2 Albums: 97 Weeks, 9 Singles: 87 Weeks)

10 Oct 98 JOINTS & JAMS Interscope IND 95604 ... 53 1
12 May 01 REQUEST LINE Interscope 4970532 [1] ... 31 3
30 Aug 03 ● ELEPHUNK A&M / Mercury 9860365 ... 3 67
13 Sep 03 ★ WHERE IS THE LOVE? A&M 9810996 ■ ... 1 19
13 Dec 03 ● SHUT UP A&M 9814501 ... 2 12
20 Mar 04 ● HEY MAMA A&M 9861976 ... 6 10
10 Jul 04 LET'S GET IT STARTED A&M 9863032 ... 11 10
28 May 05 ● DON'T PHUNK WITH MY HEART Interscope 9882331 ... 3 16
11 Jun 05 ● MONKEY BUSINESS A&M 9882184 ... 4 30+
3 Sep 05 ● DON'T LIE Interscope / A&M 9884362 ... 6 10
26 Nov 05 ● MY HUMPS A&M 9887259 ... 3 6+

[1] The Black Eyed Peas featuring Macy Gray

Act were male only on first two singles.

BLACK GORILLA *UK, male / female vocal / instrumental group*

27 Aug 77 GIMME DAT BANANA Response SR 502 ... 29 6

BLACK GRAPE *UK, male vocal / instrumental group (2 Albums: 46 Weeks, 7 Singles: 25 Weeks)*

10 Jun 95 ● REVEREND BLACK GRAPE Radioactive RAXTD 16 ... 9 5
5 Aug 95 ● IN THE NAME OF THE FATHER Radioactive RAXTD 19 ... 8 4
19 Aug 95 ★ IT'S GREAT WHEN YOU'RE STRAIGHT ... YEAH Radioactive RAD 11224 ■ ... 1 39
2 Dec 95 KELLY'S HEROES Radioactive RAXTD 22 ... 17 5
25 May 96 ● FAT NECK Radioactive RAXTD 24 ... 10 3
29 Jun 96 ● ENGLAND'S IRIE Radioactive RAXTD 25 [1] ... 6 4
1 Nov 97 GET HIGHER Radioactive RAXTD 32 ... 24 3
22 Nov 97 STUPID STUPID STUPID Radioactive RARD 11716 ... 11 7
7 Mar 98 MARBLES Radioactive RAXTD 33 ... 46 1

[1] Black Grape featuring Joe Strummer and Keith Allen

The BLACK KEYS
US, male vocal / instrumental duo (1 Album: 1 Week, 2 Singles: 2 Weeks)

11 Sep 04 10 A.M. AUTOMATIC Epitaph 11732 ... 66 1
18 Sep 04 RUBBER FACTORY Fat Possum 03792 ... 62 1
11 Dec 04 TILL I GET MY WAY / GIRL IS ON MY MIND Fat Possum 11832 ... 62 1

BLACK LACE
UK, male vocal / instrumental duo – Alan Barton, b. 16 Sep 1953, d. 23 Mar 1995, and Colin Routh (3 Albums: 26 Weeks, 11 Singles: 83 Weeks)

31 Mar 79 MARY ANN EMI 2919 ... 42 4
24 Sep 83 ● SUPERMAN (GIOCA JOUER) Flair FLA 105 ... 9 18
30 Jun 84 ● AGADOO Flair FLA 107 ... 2 30
24 Nov 84 ● DO THE CONGA Flair FLA 108 ... 10 9
8 Dec 84 ● PARTY PARTY – 16 GREAT PARTY ICEBREAKERS Telstar STAR 2250 ... 4 14
1 Jun 85 EL VINO COLLAPSO Flair LACE 1 ... 42 5
7 Sep 85 I SPEAKA DA LINGO Flair LACE 2 ... 49 4
7 Dec 85 PARTY PARTY 2 Telstar STAR 2266 ... 18 6
7 Dec 85 HOKEY COKEY Flair LACE 3 ... 31 6
20 Sep 86 WIG WAM BAM Flair LACE 5 ... 63 3
6 Dec 86 PARTY CRAZY Telstar STAR 2288 ... 58 6
26 Aug 89 I AM THE MUSIC MAN Flair LACE 10 ... 52 3
22 Aug 98 AGADOO (re-recording) NOW CDWAG 260 ... 64 1

Black Lace was a group for first hit.

BLACK LEGEND *Italy, male production duo – Ciro Sasso and Enrico Ferrari (3 Singles: 22 Weeks)*

20 May 00 YOU SEE THE TROUBLE WITH ME (import) Rise RISECD 072 ... 52 5
24 Jun 00 ★ YOU SEE THE TROUBLE WITH ME Eternal WEA 282CD ■ ... 1 15
4 Aug 01 SOMEBODY WEA WEA 328CD [1] ... 37 2

[1] Shortie vs Black Legend

No.1 version features a 'karaoke' re-recording of the original Barry White vocal by UK vocalist Spoonface.

BLACK MACHINE *France / Nigeria, male vocal / instrumental duo – Herry Iyere Innocent and Alasson Wat*

9 Apr 94 HOW GEE London LONCD 348 ... 17 5

BLACK MAGIC (see also LIL' LOUIS) *US, male producer – Marvin Burns*

1 Jun 96 FREEDOM (MAKE IT FUNKY) Positiva CDTIV 51 ... 41 2

BLACK REBEL MOTORCYCLE CLUB *US, male vocal / instrumental group (3 Albums: 25 Weeks, 6 Singles: 12 Weeks)*

26 Jan 02 B.R.M.C. Virgin CDVUS 207 ... 25 17
2 Feb 02 LOVE BURNS Virgin VUSCD 234 ... 37 2
1 Jun 02 SPREAD YOUR LOVE Virgin VUSCD 245 ... 27 2
28 Sep 02 WHATEVER HAPPENED TO MY ROCK 'N' ROLL (PUNK SONG) Virgin VUSCD 257 ... 46 2
30 Aug 03 STOP Virgin VUSCD 273 ... 19 3
6 Sep 03 ● TAKE THEM ON, ON YOUR OWN Virgin CDVUS 245 ... 3 4
29 Nov 03 WE'RE ALL IN LOVE Virgin VUSCDX 279 ... 45 1
27 Aug 05 AIN'T NO EASY WAY Echo ECSCX 175 ... 21 2
3 Sep 05 HOWL Echo ECHCD 67 ... 14 4

BLACK RIOT (see also The GYPSYMEN; ROYAL HOUSE; SWAN LAKE; Todd TERRY) *US, male producer – Todd Terry*

3 Dec 88 WARLOCK / A DAY IN THE LIFE Champion CHAMP 75 ... 68 3

'A Day in the Life' listed only from 17 Dec 1988.

BLACK ROB *US, male rapper – Robert Ross (3 Singles: 8 Weeks)*

12 Aug 00 WHOA Puff Daddy / Arista 74321782732 ... 44 2
6 Oct 01 BAD BOY FOR LIFE Bad Boy / Arista 74321889982 [1] ... 13 6

[1] P Diddy, Black Rob and Mark Curry

22 June 1956	29 June 1956	6 July 1956	13 July 1956
UK No.1 SINGLES			
I'LL BE HOME Pat Boone	I'LL BE HOME Pat Boone	I'LL BE HOME Pat Boone	I'LL BE HOME Pat Boone
UK No.1 ALBUMS			

BLACK, ROCK and RON *US, male rap group*

22 Apr 89 STOP THE WORLD *Supreme SU 5* ... 72 1

BLACK ROCK featuring Debra Andrew NEW
Germany, male production duo and UK, female vocalist

7 May 05 **BLUE WATER** *Positiva CDTIVS 217* ... **36** 2

BLACK SABBATH 217 Top 500 (see also GILLAN)
Macabre Birmingham, UK-based seminal heavy metal outfit first fronted by Ozzy (John) Osbourne (v) and Tommy Iommi (g). Later vocalists included Ronnie James Dio and Ian Gillan. Voted Act of The Millennium by Kerrang! in 1999, and elected into the Rock & Roll Hall of Fame in 2006 (25 Albums: 214 Weeks, 10 Singles: 70 Weeks)

7 Mar 70 ● BLACK SABBATH *Vertigo VO 6* ... 8 42
29 Aug 70 ● **PARANOID** *Vertigo 6059 010* ... **4** 18
26 Sep 70 ★ PARANOID *Vertigo 6360 011* ... 1 20
21 Aug 71 ● MASTER OF REALITY *Vertigo 6360 050* ... 5 13
30 Sep 72 ● BLACK SABBATH VOL 4 *Vertigo 6360 071* ... 8 10
8 Dec 73 ● SABBATH BLOODY SABBATH *WWA WWA 005* ... 4 11
27 Sep 75 ● SABOTAGE *NEMS 9119 001* ... 7 7
7 Feb 76 WE SOLD OUR SOUL FOR ROCK 'N' ROLL *NEMS 6641 335* ... 35 5
6 Nov 76 TECHNICAL ECSTASY *Vertigo 9102 750* ... 13 6
3 Jun 78 **NEVER SAY DIE** *Vertigo SAB 001* ... **21** 8
14 Oct 78 NEVER SAY DIE *Vertigo 9102 751* ... 12 6
14 Oct 78 **HARD ROAD** *Vertigo SAB 002* ... **33** 4
26 Apr 80 ● HEAVEN AND HELL *Vertigo 9102 752* ... 9 22
5 Jul 80 ● BLACK SABBATH LIVE AT LAST *NEMS BS 001* ... 5 15
5 Jul 80 **NEON KNIGHTS** *Vertigo SAB 3* ... **22** 9
16 Aug 80 **PARANOID** (re-issue) *Nems BSS 101* ... **14** 12
27 Sep 80 PARANOID (re-issue) *NEMS NEL 6003* ... 54 2
6 Dec 80 **DIE YOUNG** *Vertigo SAB 4* ... **41** 7
7 Nov 81 **MOB RULES** *Vertigo SAB 5* ... **46** 4
14 Nov 81 MOB RULES *Mercury 6V02119* ... 12 14
13 Feb 82 **TURN UP THE NIGHT** *Vertigo SAB 6* ... **37** 5
22 Jan 83 LIVE EVIL *Vertigo SAB 10* ... 13 11
24 Sep 83 ● BORN AGAIN *Vertigo VERL 8* ... 4 7
1 Mar 86 SEVENTH STAR *Vertigo VERH 29* [1] ... 27 5
28 Nov 87 THE ETERNAL IDOL *Vertigo VERH 51* ... 66 1
15 Apr 89 **HEADLESS CROSS** *IRS EIRS 107* ... **62** 1
29 Apr 89 HEADLESS CROSS *IRS EIRSA 1002* ... 31 2
1 Sep 90 TYR *IRS EIRSA 1038* ... 24 3
13 Jun 92 **TV CRIMES** *IRS EIRSP 178* ... **33** 2
4 Jul 92 DEHUMANIZER *IRS EIRSCD 1064* ... 28 2
12 Feb 94 CROSS PURPOSES *IRS EIRSCD 1067* ... 41 1
17 Jun 95 FORBIDDEN *IRS EIRSCD 1072* ... 71 1
31 Oct 98 REUNION *Epic 4919549* ... 41 1
17 Jun 00 THE BEST OF BLACK SABBATH *Metal Is RAWDD 145* ... 24 6
6 Jul 02 PARANOID (2nd re-issue) *Castle Music CMTCD 004* ... 63 1

[1] Black Sabbath featuring Tony Iommi

Group UK only for first three hits and re-issue of 'Paranoid'.

BLACK SCIENCE ORCHESTRA *UK, male production group*

3 Aug 96 WALTERS ROOM *Junior Boy's Own JBOCD 5* ... 68 1

BLACK SHEEP *US, male rap duo*

19 Nov 94 **WITHOUT A DOUBT** *Mercury MERCD 417* ... **60** 1

BLACK SLATE *UK / Jamaica, male vocal (Keith Drummond) / instrumental group (2 Singles: 15 Weeks)*

20 Sep 80 ● **AMIGO** *Ensign ENY 42* ... **9** 9
6 Dec 80 **BOOM BOOM** *Ensign ENY 47* ... **51** 6

BLACK STAR LINER
UK, male / female vocal / instrumental group

7 Sep 96 YEMEN CUTTA CONNECTION *EXP EXPCD 006* ... 66 1

BLACK UHURU *Jamaica, male vocal / instrumental group (4 Albums: 22 Weeks, 2 Singles: 9 Weeks)*

13 Jun 81 RED *Island ILPS 9625* ... 28 13
22 Aug 81 BLACK UHURU *Virgin VX 1004* ... 81 2
19 Jun 82 CHILL OUT *Island ILPS 9701* ... 38 6
25 Aug 84 ANTHEM *Island ILPS 9773* ... 90 1
8 Sep 84 **WHAT IS LIFE?** *Island IS 150* ... **56** 6
31 May 86 **THE GREAT TRAIN ROBBERY** *Real Authentic Sound RAS 7018* ... **62** 3

The BLACK VELVETS NEW
UK, male vocal / instrumental group (2 Singles: 3 Weeks)

26 Mar 05 **3345** *Vertigo 9870472* ... **34** 2
17 Sep 05 **ONCE IN A WHILE** *Vertigo 9873237* ... **75** 1

Band of the BLACK WATCH
UK, military band (1 Album: 13 Weeks, 2 Singles: 22 Weeks)

30 Aug 75 ● **SCOTCH ON THE ROCKS** *Spark SRL 1128* ... **8** 14
13 Dec 75 **DANCE OF THE CUCKOOS (THE 'LAUREL AND HARDY' THEME)** *Spark SRL 1135* ... **37** 8
7 Feb 76 SCOTCH ON THE ROCKS *Spark SRLM 503* ... 11 13

BLACK WIDOW *UK, male vocal / instrumental group*

4 Apr 70 SACRIFICE *CBS 63948* ... 32 2

Tony BLACKBURN
UK, male vocalist / radio DJ – Kenneth Blackburn (2 Singles: 7 Weeks)

24 Jan 68 **SO MUCH LOVE** *MGM 1375* ... **31** 4
26 Mar 69 **IT'S ONLY LOVE** *MGM 1467* ... **42** 3

The BLACKBYRDS *US, male vocal / instrumental group*

31 May 75 **WALKING IN RHYTHM** *Fantasy FTC 114* ... **23** 6

BLACKFOOT *US, male vocal / instrumental group (4 Albums: 22 Weeks, 2 Singles: 5 Weeks)*

18 Jul 81 MARAUDER *Atco K 50799* ... 38 12
6 Mar 82 **DRY COUNTY** *Atco K 11686* ... **43** 4
11 Sep 82 HIGHWAY SONG BLACKFOOT LIVE *Atco K 50910* ... 14 6
21 May 83 SIOGO *Atco 7900801* ... 28 3
18 Jun 83 **SEND ME AN ANGEL** *Atco B 9880* ... **66** 1
29 Sep 84 VERTICAL SMILES *Atco 790218* ... 82 1

J BLACKFOOT
US, male vocalist – John Colbert

17 Mar 84 **TAXI** *Allegiance ALES 2* ... **48** 4

BLACKFOOT SUE
UK, male vocal (Tom Farmer) / instrumental group (2 Singles: 15 Weeks)

12 Aug 72 ● **STANDING IN THE ROAD** *Jam 13* ... **4** 10
16 Dec 72 **SING DON'T SPEAK** *Jam 29* ... **36** 5

BLACKGIRL *US, female vocal group*

16 Jul 94 **90'S GIRL** *RCA 74321217882* ... **23** 3

BLACKNUSS *Sweden, male / female vocal / instrumental group*

28 Jun 97 **DINAH** *Arista 74321479762* ... **56** 1

BLACKOUT
UK, male production / instrumental duo – Marc Dillon and Pat Dickins

27 Mar 99 **GOTTA HAVE HOPE** *Multiply CDMULTY 47* ... **46** 1

BLACKOUT *UK, male / female vocal / rap group (2 Singles: 8 Weeks)*

31 Mar 01 **MR DJ** *Independiente ISOM 48MS* ... **19** 7
6 Oct 01 **GET UP** *Independiente ISOM 52MS* ... **67** 1

20 July 1956	27 / 28 July 1956	3 / 4 August 1956	10 / 11 August 1956
WHY DO FOOLS FALL IN LOVE? Teenagers featuring Frankie Lymon	WHY DO FOOLS FALL IN LOVE? Teenagers featuring Frankie Lymon	WHY DO FOOLS FALL IN LOVE? Teenagers featuring Frankie Lymon	WHATEVER WILL BE, WILL BE (QUE SERA, SERA) Doris Day
	SONGS FOR SWINGIN' LOVERS Frank Sinatra	SONGS FOR SWINGIN' LOVERS Frank Sinatra	CAROUSEL Soundtrack

KEY: UK No.1 ★ UK Top 10 ● Still on chart + UK entry at No.1 ■ US No.1 ▲ UK million seller £ US million seller $
Singles re-entries are listed as (re), (2re), (3re)... which signifies that the hit re-entered the chart once, twice or three times...
Peak Position / Weeks

Bill BLACK'S COMBO *US, male instrumental group – leader b. 17 Sep 1926, d. 21 Oct 1965 (2 Singles: 8 Weeks)*

8 Sep 60 **WHITE SILVER SANDS** *London HLU 9090* $ 50 1
3 Nov 60 **DON'T BE CRUEL** *London HLU 9212* 32 7

BLACKSTREET *US, male vocal group – includes Teddy Riley (3 Albums: 36 Weeks, 16 Singles: 72 Weeks)*

19 Jun 93 **BABY BE MINE** *MCA MCSTD 1772* [1] 37 3
9 Jul 94 BLACKSTREET *Interscope 6544923512* 35 6
13 Aug 94 **BOOTI CALL** *Interscope A 8250CD* 56 1
11 Feb 95 **U BLOW MY MIND** *Interscope A 8222CD* 39 2
27 May 95 **JOY** *Interscope A 8195CD* 56 2
21 Sep 96 ANOTHER LEVEL *Interscope INTD 90071* 26 26
19 Oct 96 ● **NO DIGGITY** *Interscope IND 95003* [2] ▲ $ 9 7
8 Mar 97 **GET ME HOME** *Def Jam DEFCD 32* [3] 11 5
26 Apr 97 ● **DON'T LEAVE ME** *Interscope IND 95534* 6 10
27 Sep 97 ● **FIX** *Interscope IND 97521* 7 5
13 Dec 97 **(MONEY CAN'T) BUY ME LOVE** *Interscope IND 95563* 18 6
4 Apr 98 ● **I GET LONELY** *Virgin VSCDT 1683* [4] 5 7
27 Jun 98 **THE CITY IS MINE** *Northwestside 74321588012* [5] 38 2
12 Dec 98 ● **TAKE ME THERE** *Interscope IND 95620* [6] 7 9
3 Apr 99 FINALLY *Interscope IND 90323* 27 4
17 Apr 99 **GIRLFRIEND / BOYFRIEND** *Interscope IND 95640* [7] 11 7
10 Jul 99 **GET READY** *Puff Daddy / Arista 74321682602* [8] 32 4
8 Feb 03 **WIZZY WOW** *Dreamworks 4507902* 37 2

[1] BLACKstreet featuring Teddy Riley [2] BLACKstreet featuring Dr Dre [3] Foxy Brown featuring BLACKstreet [4] Janet featuring BLACKstreet [5] Jay-Z featuring BLACKstreet [6] BLACKstreet and Mya featuring Ma$e and Blinky Blink [7] BLACKstreet with Janet [8] Ma$e featuring BLACKstreet

The BLACKWELLS *US, male vocal duo – Dewayne and Ronald Blackwell*

18 May 61 **LOVE OR MONEY** *London HLW 9334* 46 2

Richard BLACKWOOD *UK, male comedian / rapper (1 Album: 2 Weeks, 3 Singles: 16 Weeks)*

17 Jun 00 ● **MAMA – WHO DA MAN?** *East West MICKY 01CD1* 3 7
16 Sep 00 ● **1.2.3.4. GET WITH THE WICKED** *East West MICKY 05CD1* 10 6
30 Sep 00 YOU'LL LOVE TO HATE THIS *Hopefield / East West 8573844882* 35 2
25 Nov 00 **SOMEONE THERE FOR ME** *Hopefield / East West MICKY 06CD* 23 3

BLAGGERS I.T.A. *UK, male vocal / instrumental group (3 Singles: 7 Weeks)*

12 Jun 93 **STRESS** *Parlophone CDITA 1* 56 2
9 Oct 93 **OXYGEN** *Parlophone CDITA 2* 51 2
8 Jan 94 **ABANDON SHIP** *Parlophone CDITA 3* 48 3

BLAHZAY BLAHZAY *US, male rapper*

2 Mar 96 **DANGER** *Mercury Black Vinyl MBVCD 2* 56 1

Vivian BLAINE *US, female actor / vocalist – Vivienne Stapleton, b. 21 Nov 1921, d. 13 Dec 1995*

10 Jul 53 **BUSHEL AND A PECK** *Brunswick 05100* 12 1

BLAIR *UK, male vocalist – Blair Mackichan (2 Singles: 5 Weeks)*

2 Sep 95 **HAVE FUN, GO MAD!** *Mercury MERCD 443* 37 3
6 Jan 96 **LIFE?** *Mercury MERCD 447* 44 2

BLAK TWANG *UK, male rapper – Tony Rotton (2 Singles: 2 Weeks)*

29 Jun 02 **TRIXSTAR** *Bad Magic MAGICD 24* [1] 54 1
26 Oct 02 **SO ROTTEN** *Bad Magic MAGICD 25* [2] 48 1

[1] Blak Twang featuring Est'Elle [2] Blak Twang featuring Jahmali

Howard BLAKE conducting the SINFONIA OF LONDON *UK, conductor and orchestra*

22 Dec 84 THE SNOWMAN *CBS 71116* 54 12

Narration by Bernard Cribbins.

Peter BLAKE *UK, male vocalist*

8 Oct 77 **LIPSMACKIN' ROCK 'N' ROLLIN'** *Pepper UP 36295* 40 4

BLAME *UK, male instrumental / production duo*

11 Apr 92 **MUSIC TAKES YOU** *Moving Shadow SHADOW 11* 48 2

BLAMELESS *UK, male vocal / instrumental group (3 Singles: 5 Weeks)*

4 Nov 95 **TOWN CLOWNS** *China WOKCD 2046* 56 1
23 Mar 96 **BREATHE (A LITTLE DEEPER)** *China WOKCD 2070* 27 3
1 Jun 96 **SIGNS ...** *China WOKCD 2077* 49 1

BLANCMANGE (see also Neil ARTHUR) *UK, male vocal / instrumental duo (3 Albums: 57 Weeks, 10 Singles: 71 Weeks)*

17 Apr 82 **GOD'S KITCHEN / I'VE SEEN THE WORD** *London BLANC 1* 65 2
31 Jul 82 **FEEL ME** *London BLANC 2* 46 5
9 Oct 82 HAPPY FAMILIES *London SH 8552* 30 38
30 Oct 82 ● **LIVING ON THE CEILING** *London BLANC 3* 7 14
19 Feb 83 **WAVES** *London BLANC 4* 19 9
7 May 83 ● **BLIND VISION** *London BLANC 5* 10 8
26 Nov 83 **THAT'S LOVE, THAT IT IS** *London BLANC 6* 33 8
14 Apr 84 ● **DON'T TELL ME** *London BLANC 7* 8 10
26 May 84 ● MANGE TOUT *London SH 8554* 8 17
21 Jul 84 **THE DAY BEFORE YOU CAME** *London BLANC 8* 22 8
7 Sep 85 **WHAT'S YOUR PROBLEM** *London BLANC 9* 40 5
26 Oct 85 BELIEVE YOU ME *London LONLP 10* 54 2
10 May 86 **I CAN SEE IT** *London BLANC 11* 71 2

Bobby BLANCO & Mikki MOTO *UK, male production duo*

29 May 04 **3 AM** *Defected DFTD 088* 70 1

Billy BLAND *US, male vocalist*

19 May 60 **LET THE LITTLE GIRL DANCE** *London HL 9096* 15 10

BLANK & JONES *Germany, production duo – Piet Blank and Jaspa Jones (5 Singles: 9 Weeks)*

26 Jun 99 **CREAM** *Devia DVNT 31CDS* 24 3
27 May 00 **AFTER LOVE** *Nebula NEBCDS 3* 57 1
30 Sep 00 **THE NIGHTFLY** *Nebula NEBCD 010* 55 1
3 Mar 01 **BEYOND TIME** *Gang Go / Edel 01245115 GAG* 53 2
29 Jun 02 **DJS FANS & FREAKS** *Incentive CENT 42CDS* 45 2

BLAQUE IVORY *US, female vocal group*

3 Jul 99 **808** *Columbia 6674962* 31 3

BLAST featuring VDC *Italy, male / female vocal / instrumental group (2 Singles: 5 Weeks)*

18 Jun 94 **CRAYZY MAN** *UMM MCSTD 1982* 22 3
12 Nov 94 **PRINCES OF THE NIGHT** *UMM MCSTD 2011* 40 2

Melanie BLATT (see also ALL SAINTS) *UK, female vocalist (3 Singles: 14 Weeks)*

15 Sep 01 ● **TWENTYFOURSEVEN** *ffrr / Public Demand FCD 400* [1] 6 9
2 Mar 02 **I'M LEAVIN'** *Rufflife RLCDM 03* [2] 41 2
6 Sep 03 **DO ME WRONG** *London LONCD 479* [3] 18 3

[1] Artful Dodger featuring Melanie Blatt [2] Outsidaz featuring Rah Digga and Melanie Blatt [3] Mel Blatt

17 / 18 August 1956	24 / 25 August 1956	31 August / 1 September 1956	7 / 8 September 1956
UK No.1 SINGLES			
WHATEVER WILL BE, WILL BE (QUE SERA, SERA) Doris Day	**WHATEVER WILL BE, WILL BE (QUE SERA, SERA)** Doris Day	**WHATEVER WILL BE, WILL BE (QUE SERA, SERA)** Doris Day	**WHATEVER WILL BE, WILL BE (QUE SERA, SERA)** Doris Day
UK No.1 ALBUMS			
CAROUSEL Soundtrack	SONGS FOR SWINGIN' LOVERS Frank Sinatra	CAROUSEL Soundtrack	CAROUSEL Soundtrack

BLAZE *US, male production duo and vocalist (3 Singles: 6 Weeks)*

Date	Title / Label	Pos	Wks
10 Mar 01	**MY BEAT** *Black & Blue / Kickin' NEOCD 053* [1]	53	2
21 Sep 02	**DO YOU REMEMBER HOUSE** *Slip 'n' Slide SLIPCD 151* [1]	55	1
14 May 05	**MOST PRECIOUS LOVE** *Defected DFTD 100CDS* [2]	44	3

[1] Blaze featuring Palmer Brown [2] Blaze presents Uda featuring Barbara Tucker

BLAZIN' SQUAD (see also FRIDAY HILL)
UK, male vocal / rap group (2 Albums: 8 Weeks, 10 Singles: 58 Weeks)

Date	Title / Label	Pos	Wks
31 Aug 02 ★	**CROSSROADS** *East West SQUAD 01CD* ■	1	13
23 Nov 02 ●	**LOVE ON THE LINE** *East West SQUAD 02CD1*	6	13
7 Dec 02	IN THE BEGINNING *East West 5046610792*	33	6
8 Feb 03 ●	**REMINISCE / WHERE THE STORY ENDS** *East West SQUAD 003CD1*	8	8
5 Jul 03 ●	**WE JUST BE DREAMIN'** *East West SQUAD 04CD*	3	9
15 Nov 03 ●	**FLIP REVERSE** *East West SQUAD 05CD1*	2	10
29 Nov 03	NOW OR NEVER *East West 5046703662*	37	2
14 Feb 04 ●	**HERE 4 ONE** *East West SQUAD 06CD*	6	5

BLEACHIN' *UK, male vocal / instrumental group*

Date	Title / Label	Pos	Wks
22 Jul 00	**PEAKIN' (re)** *Boiler House / Arista 74321774812*	32	4

BLESSID UNION OF SOULS
US, male vocal / instrumental group (2 Singles: 6 Weeks)

Date	Title / Label	Pos	Wks
27 May 95	**I BELIEVE** *EMI CDEM 374*	29	5
23 Mar 96	**LET ME BE THE ONE** *EMI CDEM 387*	74	1

The BLESSING *UK, male vocal / instrumental group (3 Singles: 13 Weeks)*

Date	Title / Label	Pos	Wks
11 May 91	**HIGHWAY 5** *MCA MCS 1509*	42	6
18 Jan 92	**HIGHWAY 5** (re-mix) *MCA MCS 1603*	30	6
19 Feb 94	**SOUL LOVE** *MCA MCSTD 1940*	73	1

Mary J BLIGE (270 Top 500) *Original queen of hip hop and R&B, b. 11 Jan 1971, the Bronx, New York, US. Transatlantic chart regular since platinum-selling debut album 'What's the 411?' (1992). She won Grammy Awards in both 2003 and 2004 (7 Albums: 107 Weeks, 31 Singles: 137 Weeks)*

Date	Title / Label	Pos	Wks
28 Nov 92	**REAL LOVE** *Uptown MCS 1721*	68	2
27 Feb 93	**REMINISCE** *Uptown MCSTD 1731*	31	4
20 Mar 93	WHAT'S THE 411? *Uptown UPTD 10681*	53	1
12 Jun 93	**YOU REMIND ME** *Uptown MCSTD 1770*	48	3
28 Aug 93	**REAL LOVE** (re-mix) *Uptown MCSTD 1922*	26	4
4 Dec 93	**YOU DON'T HAVE TO WORRY** *Uptown MCSTD 1948*	36	2
14 May 94	**MY LOVE** *Uptown MCSTD 1972*	29	3
10 Dec 94	**BE HAPPY** *Uptown MCSTD 2033*	30	4
17 Dec 94	MY LIFE *Uptown UPTD 11156*	59	3
15 Apr 95	**I'M GOIN' DOWN** *Uptown MCSTD 2053*	12	4
29 Jul 95 ●	**I'LL BE THERE FOR YOU – YOU'RE ALL I NEED TO GET BY** *Def Jam DEFDX 11* [1] $	10	5
30 Sep 95	**MARY JANE (ALL NIGHT LONG)** *Uptown MCSTD 2088*	17	4
16 Dec 95	**(YOU MAKE ME FEEL LIKE A) NATURAL WOMAN** *Uptown MCSTD 2108*	23	3
30 Mar 96	**NOT GON' CRY** *Arista 74321358252* $	39	2
1 Mar 97	**CAN'T KNOCK THE HUSTLE** *Northwestside 74321447192* [2]	30	2
26 Apr 97 ●	SHARE MY WORLD *MCA MCD 11619* ▲	8	32
17 May 97	**LOVE IS ALL WE NEED** *Uptown MCSTD 48053*	15	4
16 Aug 97 ●	**EVERYTHING** *MCA MCSTD 48059*	6	9
29 Nov 97	**MISSING YOU (2re)** *MCA MCSTD 48071*	19	5
11 Jul 98	**SEVEN DAYS** *MCA MCSTD 48083* [3]	22	3
13 Mar 99 ●	**AS** *Epic 6670122* [4]	4	10
21 Aug 99	**ALL THAT I CAN SAY** *MCA MCSTD 40215*	29	3
28 Aug 99 ●	MARY *MCA MCD 11976*	5	6
11 Dec 99	**DEEP INSIDE** *MCA MCSTD 40224*	42	2
29 Apr 00	**GIVE ME YOU** *MCA MCSTD 40230*	19	4
16 Dec 00 ●	**911** *Columbia 6706122* [5]	9	10
8 Sep 01 ●	NO MORE DRAMA *MCA 1126322*	4	58
6 Oct 01 ●	**FAMILY AFFAIR** *MCA MCSTD 40267* ▲	8	16
9 Feb 02	**DANCE FOR ME** *MCA MCSTD 40274* [6]	13	7
11 May 02 ●	**NO MORE DRAMA** *MCA MCSTD 40281*	9	7
24 Aug 02	**RAINY DAYZ** *MCA MCSTD 40288* [7]	17	5
6 Sep 03 ●	LOVE & LIFE *Geffen / Island 9860700* ▲	8	5
27 Sep 03	**LOVE @ 1ST SIGHT** *Geffen / Island MCSTD 40338* [8]	18	5
6 Dec 03	**NOT TODAY** *Geffen MCSTD 40349* [9]	40	2
20 Dec 03	**WHENEVER I SAY YOUR NAME** *A&M 9815394* [10]	60	1
18 Dec 04	**I TRY** *Island MCSTD 40390* [11]	59	1
24 Dec 05	THE BREAKTHROUGH *Geffen 9889349*	43	2+
31 Dec 05	**BE WITHOUT YOU** *Geffen MCSTD 40445*	32	1+

[1] Method Man featuring Mary J Blige [2] Jay-Z featuring Mary J Blige [3] Mary J Blige featuring George Benson [4] George Michael and Mary J Blige [5] Wyclef Jean featuring Mary J Blige [6] Mary J Blige featuring Common [7] Mary J Blige featuring Ja Rule [8] Mary J Blige featuring Method Man [9] Mary J Blige featuring Eve [10] Sting and Mary J Blige [11] Talib Kweli featuring Mary J Blige

BLIND FAITH *UK, male vocal / instrumental group – Ginger Baker, Eric Clapton, Steve Winwood, Rick Grech*

Date	Title / Label	Pos	Wks
13 Sep 69 ★	BLIND FAITH *Polydor 583059* ▲	1	10

BLIND MELON *US, male vocal / instrumental group (2 Albums: 4 Weeks, 4 Singles: 13 Weeks)*

Date	Title / Label	Pos	Wks
12 Jun 93	**TONES OF HOME (EP)** *Capitol CDCL 687*	62	2
11 Dec 93	**NO RAIN** *Capitol CDCL 699*	17	6
22 Jan 94	BLIND MELON *Capitol CDEST 2188*	53	3
9 Jul 94	**CHANGE** *Capitol CDCL 717*	35	3
5 Aug 95	**GALAXIE** *Capitol CDCLS 755*	37	2
19 Aug 95	SOUP *Capitol CDEST 2261*	48	1

Tracks on the Tones of Home (EP): Tones Of Home / No Rain / Drive / Sock The Sin (last three are live)

BLINK *Ireland, male vocal / instrumental group*

Date	Title / Label	Pos	Wks
16 Jul 94	**HAPPY DAY** *Lime CDR 6385*	57	1

BLINK-182 *US, male vocal / instrumental group (5 Albums: 91 Weeks, 10 Singles: 53 Weeks)*

Date	Title / Label	Pos	Wks
2 Oct 99	**WHAT'S MY AGE AGAIN?** *MCA MCSTD 40219*	38	2
11 Mar 00	ENEMA OF THE STATE *MCA MCD 11950*	15	32
25 Mar 00 ●	**ALL THE SMALL THINGS** *MCA MCSTD 40223*	2	10
8 Jul 00	**WHAT'S MY AGE AGAIN?** (re-issue) *MCA MCSZD 40219*	17	6
18 Nov 00	THE MARK, TOM & TRAVIS SHOW – THE ENEMA STRIKES BACK *MCA 1123792*	69	1
23 Jun 01 ●	TAKE OFF YOUR PANTS AND JACKET *MCA 1126712* ▲	4	24
14 Jul 01	**THE ROCK SHOW** *MCA MCSTD 40259*	14	7
6 Oct 01	**FIRST DATE (re)** *MCA MCSTD 40264*	31	4
29 Nov 03	BLINK-182 *Geffen / Polydor 9861408*	22	26
6 Dec 03	**FEELING THIS** *Geffen MCSTD 40347*	15	5
13 Mar 04 ●	**I MISS YOU** *Geffen MCSTD 40359*	8	10
3 Jul 04	**DOWN** *Geffen MCSTD 40366*	24	3
25 Dec 04	**ALWAYS** *Geffen MCSTD 40400*	36	4
12 Nov 05 ●	GREATEST HITS *Geffen 9886987*	6	8+
10 Dec 05	**NOT NOW** *Geffen MCSTD 40440*	30	2

BLITZ *UK, male vocal / instrumental group*

Date	Title / Label	Pos	Wks
6 Nov 82	VOICE OF A GENERATION *No Future PUNK 1*	27	3

BLOC PARTY *UK, male vocal (Kele Okereke) / instrumental group (2 Albums: 24 Weeks, 7 Singles: 22 Weeks)*

Date	Title / Label	Pos	Wks
15 May 04	**BANQUET / STAYING FAT** *Moshi Moshi MOSH 10CD*	51	1
24 Jul 04	**LITTLE THOUGHTS / TULIPS** *Wichita WEBB 067SCD*	38	2
6 Nov 04	**HELICOPTER** *Wichita WEBB 070SCD*	26	2
12 Feb 05 ●	**SO HERE WE ARE / POSITIVE TENSION** *Wichita WEBB 076SCD*	5	4
26 Feb 05 ●	SILENT ALARM *Wichita WEBB 075CD*	3	23
7 May 05	**BANQUET** (re-issue) *Wichita WEBB 078SCD*	13	3
30 Jul 05	**THE PIONEERS** *Wichita WEBB 088SCD*	18	2
10 Sep 05	SILENT ALARM REMIXED *Wichita WEBB 090CD*	54	1
15 Oct 05 ●	**TWO MORE YEARS** *Wichita WEBB 095SCDX*	7	8

14 / 15 September 1956	21 / 22 September 1956	28 / 29 September 1956	5 / 6 October 1956
WHATEVER WILL BE, WILL BE (QUE SERA, SERA) Doris Day	**LAY DOWN YOUR ARMS** Anne Shelton	**LAY DOWN YOUR ARMS** Anne Shelton	**LAY DOWN YOUR ARMS** Anne Shelton
CAROUSEL Soundtrack	**CAROUSEL** Soundtrack	**OKLAHOMA!** Soundtrack	**OKLAHOMA!** Soundtrack

KEY UK No.1 ★ UK Top 10 ● Still on chart + UK entry at No.1 ■ US No.1 ▲ UK million seller £ US million seller $
Singles re-entries are listed as (re), (2re), (3re)... which signifies that the hit re-entered the chart once, twice or three times...
Peak Position / Weeks

The BLOCKHEADS (see also Ian DURY and The BLOCKHEADS)
UK, male vocal / instrumental group

21 Apr 01 BRAND NEW BOOTS AND PANTIES *East Central One NEWBOOTS 2CD* 44 3

BLOCKSTER
UK / Italy, male production group (2 Singles: 11 Weeks)

16 Jan 99 ● **YOU SHOULD BE ...** *Sound of Ministry MOSCDS 128* 3 9
24 Jul 99 **GROOVELINE** *Sound of Ministry MOSCDS 131* 18 2

BLODWYN PIG (see also JETHRO TULL)
UK, male vocal (Mick Abrahams) / instrumental group (2 Albums: 11 Weeks)

16 Aug 69 ● AHEAD RINGS OUT *Island ILPS 9101* 9 4
25 Apr 70 ● GETTING TO THIS *Island ILPS 9122* 8 7

Kristine BLOND
Denmark, female vocalist (3 Singles: 7 Weeks)

11 Apr 98 **LOVE SHY** *Reverb BNOISE 1CD* 22 3
11 Nov 00 **LOVE SHY** (re-mix) *Relentless RELENT 4CDS* 28 2
4 May 02 **YOU MAKE ME GO OOOH** *WEA WEA 343CD* 35 2

BLONDIE 72 Top 500
Influential New York-based quintet, fronted by ex-Bunny Girl Deborah Harry (v) (b. 1 Jul 1945, Miami) and Chris Stein (g). Few acts can match the 20-year span of No.1 hits of the group who were inducted into the Rock & Roll Hall of Fame in 2006. Best-selling single: 'Heart of Glass' 1,180,000 (15 Albums: 358 Weeks, 22 Singles: 172 Weeks)

18 Feb 78 ● **DENIS (DENEE)** *Chrysalis CHS 2204* 2 14
4 Mar 78 ● PLASTIC LETTERS *Chrysalis CHR 1166* 10 54
6 May 78 ● **(I'M ALWAYS TOUCHED BY YOUR) PRESENCE DEAR** *Chrysalis CHS 2217* 10 9
26 Aug 78 **PICTURE THIS** *Chrysalis CHS 2242* 12 11
23 Sep 78 ★ PARALLEL LINES *Chrysalis CDL 1192* 1 108
11 Nov 78 ● **HANGING ON THE TELEPHONE** *Chrysalis CHS 2266* 5 12
27 Jan 79 ★ **HEART OF GLASS** *Chrysalis CHS 2275* ▲ £ $ 1 12
10 Mar 79 BLONDIE *Chrysalis CHR 1165* 75 1
19 May 79 ★ **SUNDAY GIRL** *Chrysalis CHS 2320* 1 13
29 Sep 79 ● **DREAMING** *Chrysalis CHS 2350* 2 8
13 Oct 79 ★ EAT TO THE BEAT *Chrysalis CDL 1225* ■ 1 38
24 Nov 79 **UNION CITY BLUE** *Chrysalis CHS 2400* 13 10
23 Feb 80 ★ **ATOMIC** *Chrysalis CHS 2410* 1 9
12 Apr 80 ★ **CALL ME** *Chrysalis CHS 2414* ▲ $ 1 9
8 Nov 80 ★ **THE TIDE IS HIGH** *Chrysalis CHS 2465* ▲ $ 1 12
29 Nov 80 ● AUTOAMERICAN *Chrysalis CDL 1290* 3 16
24 Jan 81 ● **RAPTURE** *Chrysalis CHS 2485* ▲ $ 5 8
31 Oct 81 ● THE BEST OF BLONDIE *Chrysalis CDLTV 1* 4 40
8 May 82 **ISLAND OF LOST SOULS** *Chrysalis CHS 2608* 11 9
5 Jun 82 ● THE HUNTER *Chrysalis CDL 1384* 9 12
24 Jul 82 **WAR CHILD** *Chrysalis CHS 2624* 39 4
3 Dec 88 **DENIS** (re-mix) *Chrysalis CHS 3328* 50 3
17 Dec 88 ONCE MORE INTO THE BLEACH *Chrysalis CJB 2* [1] 50 4
11 Feb 89 **CALL ME** (re-mix) *Chrysalis CHS 3342* 61 2
16 Mar 91 ● THE COMPLETE PICTURE – THE VERY BEST OF DEBORAH HARRY AND BLONDIE *Chrysalis CHR 1817* [1] 3 22
10 Sep 94 **ATOMIC** (re-mix) *Chrysalis CDCHS 5013* 19 4
8 Jul 95 **HEART OF GLASS** (re-mix) *Chrysalis CSCHS 5023* 15 3
29 Jul 95 BEAUTIFUL – THE REMIX ALBUM *Chrysalis CDCHR 6105* 25 2
28 Oct 95 **UNION CITY BLUE** (re-mix) *Chrysalis CDCHS 5027* 31 2
25 Jul 98 ATOMIC – THE VERY BEST OF BLONDIE / ATOMIX *EMI 4949962* 12 34
13 Feb 99 ★ **MARIA** *Beyond 74321645632* ■ 1 12
27 Feb 99 ● NO EXIT *Beyond Music 74321641142* 3 15
12 Jun 99 **NOTHING IS REAL BUT THE GIRL** *Beyond 74321669472* 26 3
2 Nov 02 GREATEST HITS *Chrysalis 5431052* 38 4
18 Oct 03 **GOOD BOYS** *Epic 6743992* 12 3
25 Oct 03 THE CURSE OF BLONDIE *Epic 5119219* 36 1
19 Nov 05 GREATEST HITS *EMI 3450542* ..... 48 7+

[1] Deborah Harry and Blondie

The re-mix album Atomix was listed with Atomic – The Very Best of Blondie from 20 Feb 99. Parallel Lines changed catalogue number to Fame CD 25CR 01 when it charted in 2004. The two Greatest Hits album are different – the 2005 compilation is sub-titled Sight & Sound and comes with a videos DVD

The BLOOD ARM NEW *US, male vocal / instrumental group*

11 Jun 05 **SAY YES** *City Rockers ROCKERS 29CD* 52 1

BLOOD SWEAT & TEARS *US / Canada, male vocal / instrumental group (3 Albums: 21 Weeks, 1 Single: 6 Weeks)*

13 Jul 68 CHILD IS FATHER TO THE MAN *CBS 63296* 40 1
12 Apr 69 BLOOD SWEAT & TEARS *CBS 63504* ▲ 15 8
30 Apr 69 **YOU'VE MADE ME SO VERY HAPPY** *CBS 4116* $ 35 6
8 Aug 70 BLOOD SWEAT & TEARS 3 *CBS 64024* ▲ 14 12

The BLOODHOUND GANG *US, male vocal (Jimmy Pop Ali) / instrumental group (1 Album: 7 Weeks, 4 Singles: 22 Weeks)*

23 Aug 97 **WHY'S EVERYBODY ALWAYS PICKIN' ON ME?** *Geffen GFSTD 22252* 56 1
15 Apr 00 ● **THE BAD TOUCH** *Geffen 4972672* 4 14
6 May 00 HOORAY FOR BOOBIES *Geffen 4904552* 37 7
2 Sep 00 **THE BALLAD OF CHASEY LAIN** *Geffen 4973812* 15 6
1 Oct 05 **FOXTROT UNIFORM CHARLIE KILO** *Geffen 9885038* 47 1

The act were male / female for their 1997 hit.

BLOODSTONE *US, male vocal / instrumental group*

18 Aug 73 **NATURAL HIGH** *Decca F 13382* $ 40 4

Bobby BLOOM
US, male vocalist, b. 1945, d. 28 Feb 1974 (2 Singles: 24 Weeks)

29 Aug 70 ● **MONTEGO BAY (2re)** *Polydor 2058 051* 3 19
9 Jan 71 **HEAVY MAKES YOU HAPPY** *Polydor 2001 122* 31 5

BLOOMSBURY SET *UK, male vocal / instrumental group*

25 Jun 83 **HANGING AROUND WITH THE BIG BOYS** *Stiletto STL 13* 56 3

Tanya BLOUNT *US, female vocalist*

11 Jun 94 **I'M GONNA MAKE YOU MINE** *Polydor PZCD 315* 69 1

Kurtis BLOW *US, male rapper – Kurtis Walker (6 Singles: 23 Weeks)*

15 Dec 79 **CHRISTMAS RAPPIN'** *Mercury BLOW 7* 30 6
11 Oct 80 **THE BREAKS** *Mercury BLOW 8* 47 4
16 Mar 85 **PARTY TIME (THE GO-GO EDIT)** *Club JAB 12* 67 1
15 Jun 85 **SAVE YOUR LOVE (FOR #1)** *Club JAB 14* [1] 66 2
18 Jan 86 **IF I RULED THE WORLD** *Club JAB 26* 24 8
8 Nov 86 **I'M CHILLIN'** *Club JAB 42* 64 2

[1] René and Angela featuring Kurtis Blow

The BLOW MONKEYS *UK, male vocal (Bruce 'Dr Robert' Howard) / instrumental group (4 Albums: 27 Weeks, 11 Singles: 46 Weeks)*

1 Mar 86 **DIGGING YOUR SCENE** *RCA PB 40599* 12 10
19 Apr 86 ANIMAL MAGIC *RCA PL 70910* 21 8
17 May 86 **WICKED WAYS** *RCA MONK 2* 60 2
31 Jan 87 ● **IT DOESN'T HAVE TO BE THIS WAY** *RCA MONK 4* 5 8
28 Mar 87 **OUT WITH HER** *RCA MONK 5* 30 6
25 Apr 87 SHE WAS ONLY A GROCER'S DAUGHTER *RCA PL 71245* 20 8
30 May 87 **(CELEBRATE) THE DAY AFTER YOU** *RCA MONK 6* [1] 52 2

	12 / 13 October 1956	19 / 20 October 1956	26 / 27 October 1956	2 / 3 November 1956
UK No.1 SINGLES	LAY DOWN YOUR ARMS Anne Shelton	A WOMAN IN LOVE Frankie Laine	A WOMAN IN LOVE Frankie Laine	A WOMAN IN LOVE Frankie Laine
UK No.1 ALBUMS	THE KING AND I Soundtrack	THE KING AND I Soundtrack	ROCK 'N' ROLL STAGE SHOW Bill Haley	THE KING AND I Soundtrack

15 Aug 87 **SOME KIND OF WONDERFUL** *RCA MONK 7* 67 1
6 Aug 88 **THIS IS YOUR LIFE** *RCA PB 42149* 70 2
11 Feb 89 **WHOOPS! THERE GOES THE NEIGHBOURHOOD** *RCA PL 71858* 46 2
8 Apr 89 **THIS IS YOUR LIFE** (re-mix) *RCA PB 42695* 32 5
15 Jul 89 **CHOICE?** *RCA PB 42885* [2] 22 6
26 Aug 89 ● **CHOICES – THE SINGLES COLLECTION** *RCA PL 74191* 5 9
14 Oct 89 **SLAVES NO MORE** *RCA PB 43201* [2] 73 2
26 May 90 **SPRINGTIME FOR THE WORLD** *RCA PB 43623* 69 2

[1] The Blow Monkeys with Curtis Mayfield [2] The Blow Monkeys featuring Sylvia Tella

BLOWING FREE (see also HYPNOSIS; IN TUNE; The JAMES BOYS; RAINDANCE; SCHOOL OF EXCELLENCE)

UK, male instrumental duo – Stewart and Bradley Palmer (2 Albums: 14 Weeks)

29 Jul 95 ● **SAX MOODS** *Dino DINCD 106* 6 13
30 Nov 96 **SAX MOODS – VOLUME 2** *Dino DINCD 118* 70 1

BLU PETER *UK, male DJ / producer – Peter Harris*

21 Mar 98 **TELL ME WHAT YOU WANT / JAMES HAS KITTENS** *React CDREACT 285* 70 1

BLUE *UK, male vocal / instrumental group*

30 Apr 77 **GONNA CAPTURE YOUR HEART** *Rocket ROKN 522* 18 8

BLUE (266 Top 500)

One of Britain's top global sellers this century: Duncan James, Antony Costa, Lee Ryan and Simon Webbe. The London based boy band, who have won countless awards, including Best Pop Act at the 2003 BRITs, saw their first three albums top the chart. In 2005, the group split and all the members recorded solo projects (4 Albums: 119 Weeks, 12 Singles: 125 Weeks)

2 Jun 01 ● **ALL RISE** *Innocent SINCD 28* 4 13
8 Sep 01 ★ **TOO CLOSE** *Innocent SINCD 30* ■ 1 13
24 Nov 01 ★ **IF YOU COME BACK** *Innocent SINCD 32* ■ 1 13
8 Dec 01 ★ **ALL RISE** *Innocent CDSIN 8* 1 63
30 Mar 02 ● **FLY BY II** *Innocent SINCD 33* 6 12
2 Nov 02 ● **ONE LOVE** *Innocent SINCD 41* 3 12
21 Dec 02 ★ **SORRY SEEMS TO BE THE HARDEST WORD** *Innocent SINDX 43* [1] ■ 1 17
16 Nov 02 ★ **ONE LOVE** *Innocent CDSIN 11* ■ 1 29
29 Mar 03 ● **U MAKE ME WANNA** *Innocent SINCD 44* 4 10
1 Nov 03 ● **GUILTY** *Innocent SINCD 51* 2 11
15 Nov 03 ★ **GUILTY** *Innocent CDSIN 13* ■ 1 16
27 Dec 03 **SIGNED, SEALED, DELIVERED, I'M YOURS** *Innocent SINCD 50* [2] 11 10
3 Apr 04 ● **BREATHE EASY** *Innocent SINCD 58* 4 12
10 Jul 04 ● **BUBBLIN'** *Innocent SINDX 64* 9 8
20 Nov 04 ● **CURTAIN FALLS** *Innocent SINDX 67* 4 11
27 Nov 04 ● **BEST OF BLUE** *Innocent CDSINX 18* 6 11

[1] Blue featuring Elton John [2] Blue featuring Stevie Wonder and Angie Stone

Babbity BLUE *UK, female vocalist*

11 Feb 65 **DON'T MAKE ME (FALL IN LOVE WITH YOU)** *Decca F 12053* ...48 2

Barry BLUE

(see also CRY SISCO!) *UK, male vocalist – Barry Green (5 Singles: 48 Weeks)*

28 Jul 73 ● **DANCIN' (ON A SATURDAY NIGHT)** *Bell 1295* 2 15
3 Nov 73 ● **DO YOU WANNA DANCE?** *Bell 1336* 7 12
2 Mar 74 **SCHOOL LOVE** *Bell 1345* 11 9
3 Aug 74 **MISS HIT AND RUN** *Bell 1364* 26 7
26 Oct 74 **HOT SHOT** *Bell 1379* 23 5

BLUE ADONIS featuring LIL' MISS MAX *Belgium, male production duo – Dirk de Boeck and Wim Perdaen and female vocalist*

17 Oct 98 **DISCO COP** *Serious SERR 002CD* 27 3

TOP 10

ON THE DAY OF THE FALL OF THE BERLIN WALL IN 1989

As midnight approached on 9 November 1989, after months of protests from both sides of the wall and the international community 'All Around the World', the authorities finally gave in to the inevitable under pressure from tens of thousands of East Germans. Bewildered officials looked on as East and West joined in jubilation and partied hard. On the following Christmas Day, a united Berlin celebrated with an enormous festival of soft rock – notably including the Scorpions, whose 'Wind of Change' became the event's unofficial anthem, and David Hasselhoff. He later claimed that his performance of 'Looking for Freedom' had helped to unite Germany.

LW	TW	
3	1	**ALL AROUND THE WORLD** Lisa Stansfield
2	2	**GIRL I'M GONNA MISS YOU** Milli Vanilli
1	3	**THAT'S WHAT I LIKE** Jive Bunny and the Mastermixers
17	4	**NEVER TOO LATE** Kylie Minogue
4	5	**STREET TUFF** Rebel MC and Double Trouble
5	6	**ROOM IN YOUR HEART** Living in a Box
12	7	**I FEEL THE EARTH MOVE** Martika
22	8	**ANOTHER DAY IN PARADISE** Phil Collins
6	9	**LEAVE A LIGHT ON** Belinda Carlisle
7	10	**IF I COULD TURN BACK TIME** Cher

Lisa Stansfield

East meets West as the wall comes down

9 / 10 November 1956	16 / 17 November 1956	23 / 24 November 1956	30 November / 1 December 1956
A WOMAN IN LOVE Frankie Laine	**JUST WALKING IN THE RAIN** Johnnie Ray	**JUST WALKING IN THE RAIN** Johnnie Ray	**JUST WALKING IN THE RAIN** Johnnie Ray
ROCK 'N ROLL Elvis Presley	**THE KING AND I** Soundtrack	**THE KING AND I** Soundtrack	**THE KING AND I** Soundtrack

KEY
UK No.1 ★ UK Top 10 ● Still on chart + UK entry at No.1 ■
US No.1 ▲ UK million seller £ US million seller $
Singles re-entries are listed as (re), (2re), (3re)... which signifies that the hit re-entered the chart once, twice or three times...
Peak Position / Weeks

The BLUE AEROPLANES *UK, male / female vocal / instrumental group (3 Albums: 5 Weeks, 2 Singles: 3 Weeks)*

17 Feb 90	**JACKET HANGS** *Ensign ENY 628*	72	1
24 Feb 90	SWAGGER *Ensign CHEN 13*	54	1
26 May 90	**... AND STONES** *Ensign ENY 632*	63	2
17 Aug 91	BEATSONGS *Ensign CHEN 21*	33	3
12 Mar 94	LIFE MODEL *Beggars Banquet BBQCD 143*	59	1

BLUE AMAZON

UK, male production duo and female vocalist (2 Singles: 2 Weeks)

17 May 97	**AND THEN THE RAIN FALLS** *Sony S2 BAS 301CD*	53	1
1 Jul 00	**BREATHE** *Subversive SUB 61D*	73	1

BLUE BAMBOO (see also AIRSCAPE; BALEARIC BILL; CUBIC 22; Johan GIELEN presents ABNEA; SVENSON and GIELEN; TRANSFORMER 2)

Belgium, male producer – Johan Gielen

3 Dec 94	**ABC AND D ...** *Escapade CDJAPE 6*	23	4

BLUE BOY *UK, male producer – Alexis Blackmore (2 Singles: 16 Weeks)*

1 Feb 97 ●	**REMEMBER ME** *Pharm CDPHARM 1*	8	13
23 Aug 97	**SANDMAN** *Sidewalk CDSWALK 001*	25	3

BLUE FEATHER *Holland, male vocal / instrumental group*

3 Jul 82	**LET'S FUNK TONIGHT** *Mercury MER 109*	50	4

BLUE HAZE *UK, male vocal / instrumental group*

18 Mar 72	**SMOKE GETS IN YOUR EYES** *AMS 891*	32	6

BLUE MELONS *UK, male / female vocal / instrumental group*

8 Jun 96	**DO WAH DIDDY DIDDY** *Fundamental FUNDCD 1*	70	1

BLUE MERCEDES *UK, male vocal / instrumental duo – Duncan Millar and David Titlow (3 Singles: 18 Weeks)*

10 Oct 87	**I WANT TO BE YOUR PROPERTY** *MCA BONA 1*	23	11
13 Feb 88	**SEE WANT MUST HAVE** *MCA BONA 2*	57	2
23 Jul 88	**LOVE IS THE GUN** *MCA BONA 3*	46	5

BLUE MINK (see also DAVID and JONATHAN; The PIPKINS)

UK / US, male vocal (Roger Cook & Madeline Bell) / instrumental group (7 Singles: 83 Weeks)

15 Nov 69 ●	**MELTING POT** *Philips BF 1818*	3	15
28 Mar 70 ●	**GOOD MORNING FREEDOM** *Philips BF 1838*	10	10
19 Sep 70	**OUR WORLD** *Philips 6006 042*	17	9
29 May 71 ●	**BANNER MAN** *Regal Zonophone RZ 3034*	3	14
11 Nov 72	**STAY WITH ME (re)** *Regal Zonophone RZ 3064*	11	15
3 Mar 73	**BY THE DEVIL (I WAS TEMPTED)** *EMI 2007*	26	9
23 Jun 73 ●	**RANDY** *EMI 2028*	9	11

BLUE MURDER *UK, male vocal / instrumental group*

6 May 89	BLUE MURDER *Geffen WX 245*	45	3

BLUE NILE *UK, male vocal (Paul Buchanan) / instrumental group (4 Albums: 13 Weeks, 4 Singles: 5 Weeks)*

19 May 84	A WALK ACROSS THE ROOFTOPS *Linn LKH 1*	80	2
30 Sep 89	**THE DOWNTOWN LIGHTS** *Linn LKS 3*	67	1
21 Oct 89	HATS *Linn LKH 2*	12	4
29 Sep 90	**HEADLIGHTS ON THE PARADE** *Linn LKS 4*	72	1
19 Jan 91	**SATURDAY NIGHT** *Linn LKS 5*	50	2

22 Jun 96	PEACE AT LAST *Warner Bros. 9362458482*	13	4
4 Sep 04	**I WOULD NEVER** *Sanctuary SANXD 305*	52	1
11 Sep 04 ●	HIGH *Sanctuary SANDP 285*	10	3

BLUE ÖYSTER CULT *US, male vocal / instrumental group (8 Albums: 40 Weeks, 1 Single: 14 Weeks)*

3 Jul 76	AGENTS OF FORTUNE *CBS 81385*	26	10
4 Feb 78	SPECTRES *CBS 86050*	60	1
20 May 78	**(DON'T FEAR) THE REAPER** *CBS 6333*	16	14
28 Oct 78	SOME ENCHANTED EVENING *CBS 86074*	18	4
18 Aug 79	MIRRORS *CBS 86087*	46	5
19 Jul 80	CULTOSAURUS ERECTUS *CBS 86120*	12	7
25 Jul 81	FIRE OF UNKNOWN ORIGIN *CBS 85137*	29	7
22 May 82	EXTRATERRESTRIAL LIVE *CBS 22203*	39	5
19 Nov 83	THE REVOLUTION BY NIGHT *CBS 25686*	95	1

BLUE PEARL *UK / US, male / female vocal (Carol 'Durga' McBroom) / instrumental group (1 Album: 2 Weeks, 6 Singles: 29 Weeks)*

7 Jul 90 ●	**NAKED IN THE RAIN** *Big Life BLR 23*	4	13
3 Nov 90	**LITTLE BROTHER** *Big Life BLR 32*	31	5
1 Dec 90	NAKED *Big Life BLR LP4*	58	2
11 Jan 92	**(CAN YOU) FEEL THE PASSION** *Big Life BLR 67*	14	6
25 Jul 92	**MOTHER DAWN** *Big Life BLR 73*	50	2
27 Nov 93	**FIRE OF LOVE** *Logic 74321170292* [1]	71	1
4 Jul 98	**NAKED IN THE RAIN '98** (re-recording) *Malarky MLKD 7*	22	2

[1] Jungle High with Blue Pearl

BLUE RONDO A LA TURK *UK, male vocal / instrumental group (1 Album: 2 Weeks, 2 Singles: 9 Weeks)*

14 Nov 81	**ME AND MR SANCHEZ** *Virgin VS 463*	40	4
13 Mar 82	**KLACTOVEESEDSTEIN** *Diable Noir VS 476*	50	5
6 Nov 82	CHEWING THE FAT *Diable Noir V 2240*	80	2

BLUE ZOO *UK, male vocal / instrumental group (3 Singles: 17 Weeks)*

12 Jun 82	**I'M YOUR MAN** *Magnet MAG 224*	55	3
16 Oct 82	**CRY BOY CRY** *Magnet MAG 234*	13	10
28 May 83	**(I JUST CAN'T) FORGIVE AND FORGET** *Magnet MAG 241*	60	4

The BLUEBELLS *UK, male vocal (Ken McCluskey) / instrumental group (2 Albums: 15 Weeks, 7 Singles: 49 Weeks)*

12 Mar 83	**CATH / WILL SHE ALWAYS BE WAITING** *London LON 20*	62	2
9 Jul 83	**SUGAR BRIDGE (IT WILL STAND)** *London LON 27*	72	1
24 Mar 84	**I'M FALLING** *London LON 45*	11	12
23 Jun 84 ●	**YOUNG AT HEART** *London LON 49*	8	12
11 Aug 84	SISTERS *London LONLP 1*	22	10
1 Sep 84	**CATH** (re-issue) *London LON 54*	38	7
9 Feb 85	**ALL I AM (IS LOVING YOU)** *London LON 58*	58	3
27 Mar 93 ★	**YOUNG AT HEART** (re-issue) *London LONCD 338*	1	12
17 Apr 93	THE SINGLES COLLECTION *London 8284052*	27	5

The BLUES BAND *UK, male vocal / instrumental group (3 Albums: 18 Weeks, 1 Single: 2 Weeks)*

8 Mar 80	OFFICIAL BOOTLEG ALBUM *Arista BBBP 101*	40	9
12 Jul 80	**BLUES BAND (EP)** *Arista BOOT 2*	68	2
18 Oct 80	READY *Arista BB 2*	36	6
17 Oct 81	ITCHY FEET *Arista BB 3*	60	3

Tracks on Blues Band (EP): Maggie's Farm / Ain't it Tuff / Diddy Wah Diddy / Back Door Man.

The BLUES BROTHERS *US / Canada, male actors / vocal duo – John Belushi, b. 24 Jan 1949, d. 5 Mar 1982, and Dan Ackroyd*

7 Apr 90	**EVERYBODY NEEDS SOMEBODY TO LOVE** *East West A 7591*	12	8
4 Dec 04	THE DEFINITIVE BLUES BROTHERS COLLECTION *Atlantic 7567808405*	64	3

For the first two weeks, the flip side of 'Everybody Needs Somebody to Love' – 'Think' by Aretha Franklin - was listed.

7 / 8 December 1956	14 / 15 December 1956	21 / 22 December 1956	28 / 29 December 1956
UK No.1 SINGLES			
JUST WALKING IN THE RAIN Johnnie Ray	JUST WALKING IN THE RAIN Johnnie Ray	JUST WALKING IN THE RAIN Johnnie Ray	JUST WALKING IN THE RAIN Johnnie Ray
UK No.1 ALBUMS			
THE KING AND I Soundtrack	THE KING AND I Soundtrack	THE KING AND I Soundtrack	THE KING AND I Soundtrack

The BLUESKINS *UK, male vocal / instrumental group (2 Singles: 2 Weeks)*

21 Feb 04 **CHANGE MY MIND / I WANNA KNOW** *Domino RUG 174CD*......56 1
5 Jun 04 **THE STUPID ONES** *Domino RUG 175CD*......61 1

The BLUETONES *UK, male vocal (Mark Morriss) / instrumental group (5 Albums: 50 Weeks, 13 Singles: 46 Weeks)*

17 Jun 95 **ARE YOU BLUE OR ARE YOU BLIND?** *Superior Quality BLUE 001CD*......31 2
14 Oct 95 **BLUETONIC** *Superior Quality BLUE 002CD*......19 3
3 Feb 96 ● **SLIGHT RETURN** *Superior Quality BLUE 003CD*......2 8
24 Feb 96 ★ EXPECTING TO FLY *Superior Quality BLUECD 004* ■......1 25
11 May 96 ● **CUT SOME RUG / CASTLE ROCK (re)** *Superior Quality BLUE 005CD*......7 6
28 Sep 96 ● **MARBLEHEAD JOHNSON** *Superior Quality BLUE 006CD*......7 6
21 Feb 98 ● **SOLOMON BITES THE WORM** *Superior Quality BLUED 007*......10 3
21 Mar 98 ● RETURN TO THE LAST CHANCE SALOON *Superior Quality BLUED 008*......10 16
9 May 98 **IF ...** *Superior Quality BLUED 009*......13 5
8 Aug 98 **SLEAZY BED TRACK** *Superior Quality BLUED 010*......35 2
4 Mar 00 **KEEP THE HOME FIRES BURNING** *Superior Quality BLUED 012*......13 3
20 May 00 **AUTOPHILIA** *Superior Quality BLUED 013*......18 3
27 May 00 ● SCIENCE & NATURE *Superior Quality BLUECD 014*......7 4
6 Apr 02 **AFTER HOURS** *Superior Quality BLUED 016*......26 2
20 Apr 02 THE SINGLES *Superior Quality BLUECD 017*......14 4
3 May 03 **FAST BOY / LIQUID LIPS** *Superior Quality BLUE 18CDS*......25 2
24 May 03 LUXEMBOURG *Superior Quality BLUE 019CD*......49 1
23 Aug 03 **NEVER GOING NOWHERE** *Superior Quality BLUE 020CDS*......40 1

Colin BLUNSTONE (see also Neil MacARTHUR; The ZOMBIES) *UK, male vocalist (6 Singles: 30 Weeks)*

12 Feb 72 **SAY YOU DON'T MIND** *Epic EPC 7765*......15 9
11 Nov 72 **I DON'T BELIEVE IN MIRACLES** *Epic EPC 8434*......31 6
17 Feb 73 **HOW COULD WE DARE TO BE WRONG** *Epic EPC 1197*......45 2
14 Mar 81 **WHAT BECOMES OF THE BROKEN HEARTED** *Stiff BROKEN 1* [1]......13 10
29 May 82 **TRACKS OF MY TEARS** *PRT 7P 236*......60 2
15 Jan 83 **OLD AND WISE** *Arista ARIST 494* [2]......74 1

[1] Dave Stewart: Guest vocals: Colin Blunstone [2] Alan Parsons Project: Lead vocals by Colin Blunstone

James BLUNT NEW *UK, male vocalist / guitarist (1 Album: 38 Weeks, 5 Singles: 52 Weeks)*

19 Mar 05 **WISEMEN (3re)** *Atlantic AT 0198CD*......44 9
26 Mar 05 ★ BACK TO BEDLAM *Atlantic 7567837525*......1 38+
11 Jun 05 ★ **YOU'RE BEAUTIFUL** *Atlantic AT 0207CDX*......1 30+
8 Oct 05 **HIGH** *Atlantic AT 0184CD*......74 1
15 Oct 05 **HIGH** (re-issue) *Atlantic AT 022CDX*......16 11
31 Dec 05 **GOODBYE MY LOVER** *Atlantic AT 0230CDX*......11 1+

BLUR (94 Top 500) (see also FAT LES) *Prime movers of Britpop: Damon Albarn (v/k), Graham Coxon (g) (left 2002), Alex James (b), Dave Rowntree (d). They won a record four BRIT awards in 1995, and their first No.1 caused a media storm when it outpaced 'Roll With It' by Britpop rivals Oasis to become their best-selling single at 640,000. Albarn is now a prime mover in muti-platinum band Gorillaz (8 Albums: 308 Weeks, 26 Singles: 146 Weeks)*

27 Oct 90 **SHE'S SO HIGH / I KNOW** *Food FOOD 26*......48 3
27 Apr 91 ● **THERE'S NO OTHER WAY** *Food FOOD 29*......8 8
10 Aug 91 **BANG** *Food FOOD 31*......24 4
7 Sep 91 ● LEISURE *Food FOODLP 6*......7 12
11 Apr 92 **POPSCENE** *Food FOOD 37*......32 2
1 May 93 **FOR TOMORROW** *Food CDFOODS 40*......28 4
22 May 93 MODERN LIFE IS RUBBISH *Food FOODCD 9*......15 14
10 Jul 93 **CHEMICAL WORLD** *Food CDFOODS 45*......28 4
16 Oct 93 **SUNDAY SUNDAY** *Food CDFOOD 46*......26 3
19 Mar 94 ● **GIRLS AND BOYS** *Food CDFOODS 47*......5 7
7 May 94 ★ PARKLIFE *Food FOODCD 10* ■......1 106
11 Jun 94 **TO THE END** *Food CDFOODS 50*......16 5
3 Sep 94 ● **PARKLIFE** *Food CDFOOD 53*......10 7
19 Nov 94 **END OF A CENTURY** *Food CDFOOD 56*......19 3
26 Aug 95 ★ **COUNTRY HOUSE (re)** *Food FOODS 63* ■......1 12
23 Sep 95 ★ THE GREAT ESCAPE *Food FOODCD 14* ■......1 47
25 Nov 95 ● **THE UNIVERSAL** *Food CDFOODS 69*......5 9
24 Feb 96 ● **STEREOTYPES** *Food CDFOOD 73*......7 5
11 May 96 ● **CHARMLESS MAN** *Food CDFOOD 77*......5 6
1 Feb 97 ★ **BEETLEBUM (re)** *Food CDFOODS 89* ■......1 7
22 Feb 97 ★ BLUR *Food FOODCD 19* ■......1 65
19 Apr 97 ● **SONG 2** *Food CDFOODS 93*......2 5
28 Jun 97 ● **ON YOUR OWN** *Food CDFOOD 98*......5 5
27 Sep 97 **MOR** *Food CDFOOD 107*......15 3
6 Mar 99 ● **TENDER** *Food CDFOODS 117*......2 10
27 Mar 99 ★ 13 *Food FOODCD 29* ■......1 27
10 Jul 99 **COFFEE + TV** *Food CDFOODS 122*......11 7
27 Nov 99 **NO DISTANCE LEFT TO RUN (re)** *Food CDFOOD 123*......14 4
28 Oct 00 ● **MUSIC IS MY RADAR (re)** *Food / Parlophone CDFOODS 135*......10 9
11 Nov 00 ● THE BEST OF *Food FOODCD 33*......3 29
26 Apr 03 ● **OUT OF TIME** *Parlophone CDR 6606*......5 9
17 May 03 ★ THINK TANK *Parlophone 5829972* ■......1 8
19 Jul 03 **CRAZY BEAT** *Parlophone CDR 6610*......18 3
18 Oct 03 **GOOD SONG** *Parlophone CDR 6619*......22 2

Chart rules allow for a maximum of three formats; the 7-inch of 'Country House', already available on two CDs and cassette, was therefore listed separately.

BO SELECTA (see also MERRION, McCALL & KENSIT) *UK, male rubber-faced comedian / vocalist – Avid Merrion (Leigh Francis)*

27 Dec 03 ● **PROPER CRIMBO** *BMG 82876581412*......4 9

BOARDS OF CANADA *UK, male instrumental / production duo – Michael Sandison and Marcus Eoin (2 Albums: 3 Weeks)*

2 Mar 02 GEOGADDI *Warp WARPCD 101*......21 2
29 Oct 05 THE CAMPFIRE HEADPHASE *Warp WARPCD 123*......41 1

BOB and EARL *US, male vocal duo – Bobby Relf and Earl Nelson*

12 Mar 69 ● **HARLEM SHUFFLE** *Island WIP 6053*......7 13

BOB and MARCIA *Jamaica, male / female vocal duo – Bob Andy and Marcia Griffiths (2 Singles: 25 Weeks)*

14 Mar 70 ● **YOUNG, GIFTED AND BLACK** *Harry J HJ 6605*......5 12
5 Jun 71 **PIED PIPER** *Trojan TR 7818*......11 13

BOB THE BUILDER *UK, male silicone puppet building contractor – voice of Neil Morrissey (1 Album: 12 Weeks, 2 Singles: 41 Weeks)*

16 Dec 00 ★ **CAN WE FIX IT? (2re)** *BBC Music WMSS 60372* £......1 22
15 Sep 01 ★ **MAMBO NO.5** *BBC Music WMSS 60442* ■......1 19
13 Oct 01 ● THE ALBUM *BBC Music WMSF 60472*......4 12

The BOBBYSOCKS *Norway / Sweden, female vocal duo*

25 May 85 **LET IT SWING** *RCA PB 40127*......44 4

Andrea BOCELLI (425 Top 500) *Blind Italian operatic tenor who has sold more than 50 million albums worldwide, b. 22 Sep 1958, Lajatico. 'Sogno' topped the European chart and at times he held the top 3 places on the US classical chart (9 Albums: 146 Weeks, 3 Singles: 24 Weeks)*

24 May 97 ● **TIME TO SAY GOODBYE (CON TE PARTIRO)** *Coalition COLA 003CD* [1]......2 14
31 May 97 ● ROMANZA *Philips 4564562*......6 25
9 May 98 ARIA – THE OPERA ALBUM *Philips 4620332*......33 9+
13 Feb 99 VIAGGIO ITALIANO *Philips 4621962*......24 10
10 Apr 99 ● SOGNO *Polydor 5472212*......4 42
25 Sep 99 **CANTO DELLA TERRA (re)** *Polydor / Sugar 5613192*......24 9
20 Nov 99 SACRED ARIAS *Philips 4626002*......20 12
18 Dec 99 **AVE MARIA** *Philips 4644852*......65 1
23 Sep 00 VERDI *Philips 4646002*......17 10
27 Oct 01 ● CIELI DI TOSCANA *Polydor 5892452*......3 16

KEY: UK No.1 ★ UK Top 10 ● Still on chart + UK entry at No.1 ■ US No.1 ▲ UK million seller £ US million seller $
Singles re-entries are listed as (re), (2re), (3re)... which signifies that the hit re-entered the chart once, twice or three times...
Peak Position / Weeks

16 Nov 02 ●	SENTIMENTO *Philips 4734102*	7	15
13 Nov 04	ANDREA *Universal 9867973*	19	7

[1] Sarah Brightman and Andrea Bocelli

'Canto Della Terra' was originally No.25 before re-entering and peaking one place higher in Jul 2000. Viaggio Italiano stalled at No.55 in 1999 and reached its peak position in 2003 after the album was repackaged with bonus tracks. Sentimento features the London Symphony Orchestra and Lorin Maazel. A repackaged version of Aria – The Opera Album reached No.38 in 2005.

Karen BODDINGTON and Mark WILLIAMS
Australia / New Zealand, female / male vocal duo

2 Sep 89	HOME AND AWAY *First Night SCORE 19*	73	1

The BODINES *UK, male vocal / instrumental group*

29 Aug 87	PLAYED *Pop BODL 2001*	94	1

BODY COUNT (see also ICE-T)
US, male rap / instrumental group (1 Album: 2 Weeks, 2 Singles: 4 Weeks)

17 Sep 94	BORN DEAD *Rhyme Syndicate RSYND 2*	15	2
8 Oct 94	BORN DEAD *Rhyme Syndicate SYNDG 4*	28	2
17 Dec 94	NECESSARY EVIL *Virgin VSCDX 1529*	45	2

BODYROCKERS NEW *UK / Australia, vocal / instrumental / production duo – Dylan Burns and Kaz James*

30 Apr 05 ●	I LIKE THE WAY (re) *Mercury 987115*	3	35+

BODYSNATCHERS
UK, female vocal / instrumental group (2 Singles: 12 Weeks)

15 Mar 80	LET'S DO ROCK STEADY *2 Tone CHSTT 9*	22	9
19 Jul 80	EASY LIFE *2 Tone CHSTT 12*	50	3

Suzy BOGGUSS *US, female vocalist*

25 Sep 93	SOMETHING UP MY SLEEVE *Liberty CDEST 221*	69	1

Hamilton BOHANNON
US, male vocalist / drums (6 Singles: 38 Weeks)

15 Feb 75	SOUTH AFRICAN MAN *Brunswick BR 16*	22	8
24 May 75 ●	DISCO STOMP *Brunswick BR 19*	6	12
5 Jul 75	FOOT STOMPIN' MUSIC *Brunswick BR 21*	23	6
6 Sep 75	HAPPY FEELING *Brunswick BR 24*	49	3
26 Aug 78	LET'S START THE DANCE *Mercury 6167 700*	56	4
13 Feb 82	LET'S START TO DANCE AGAIN *London HL 10582*	49	5

BOILING POINT *US, male vocal / instrumental group*

27 May 78	LET'S GET FUNKTIFIED *Bang BANG 1312*	41	6

CJ BOLLAND
(see also RAVESIGNAL III; SONIC SOLUTION) *Belgium, male producer – Christian Jay Bolland (1 Album: 2 Weeks, 3 Singles: 10 Weeks)*

5 Oct 96	SUGAR IS SWEETER *Internal LIECD 35*	11	5
26 Oct 96	THE ANALOGUE THEATRE *Internal TRUCD 13*	43	2
17 May 97	THE PROPHET *ffrr FCD 300*	19	3
3 Jul 99	IT AIN'T GONNA BE ME *Essential Recordings ESCD 5*	35	2

BOLSHOI *UK, male vocal / instrumental group*

3 Oct 87	LINDY'S PARTY *Beggars Banquet BEGA 86*	100	1

Michael BOLTON 156 Top 500 *Soulful rock balladeer / songwriter who initially recorded under his real name, Michael Bolotin (b. 26 Feb 1953, Connecticut, US), and fronted recording groups The Nomads and Blackjack (12 Albums: 240 Weeks, 18 Singles: 113 Weeks)*

17 Feb 90 ●	HOW AM I SUPPOSED TO LIVE WITHOUT YOU *CBS 655397 7* ▲	3	10
17 Mar 90 ●	SOUL PROVIDER *CBS 4653431*	4	72
28 Apr 90 ●	HOW CAN WE BE LOVERS *CBS 655918 7*	10	10
21 Jul 90	WHEN I'M BACK ON MY FEET AGAIN *CBS 656077 7*	44	5
11 Aug 90	THE HUNGER *CBS 4601631*	44	5
20 Apr 91	LOVE IS A WONDERFUL THING *Columbia 6567717*	23	8
18 May 91 ●	TIME, LOVE AND TENDERNESS *Columbia 4678121* ▲	2	57
27 Jul 91	TIME LOVE AND TENDERNESS *Columbia 6569897*	28	7
9 Nov 91 ●	WHEN A MAN LOVES A WOMAN *Columbia 6574887* ▲	8	9
8 Feb 92	STEEL BARS *Columbia 6577257*	17	6
9 May 92	MISSING YOU NOW *Columbia 6579917* [1]	28	4
10 Oct 92 ●	TIMELESS – THE CLASSICS *Columbia 4723022* ▲	3	24
31 Oct 92	TO LOVE SOMEBODY *Columbia 6584557*	16	6
26 Dec 92	DRIFT AWAY *Columbia 6588657*	18	5
13 Mar 93	REACH OUT I'LL BE THERE *Columbia 6588972*	37	4
13 Nov 93	SAID I LOVED YOU BUT I LIED *Columbia 6598762*	15	8
27 Nov 93 ●	THE ONE THING *Columbia 4743552*	4	24
26 Feb 94	SOUL OF MY SOUL *Columbia 6601772*	32	3
14 May 94	LEAN ON ME *Columbia 6604132*	14	7
9 Sep 95 ●	CAN I TOUCH YOU ... THERE *Columbia 6624385*	6	9
30 Sep 95 ●	GREATEST HITS 1985-1995 *Columbia 4810022*	2	30
2 Dec 95	A LOVE SO BEAUTIFUL *Columbia 6627092*	27	5
16 Mar 96	SOUL PROVIDER *Columbia 6629812*	35	3
8 Nov 97	THE BEST OF LOVE / GO THE DISTANCE *Columbia 6652802*	14	4
22 Nov 97	ALL THAT MATTERS *Columbia 4885312*	20	7
2 May 98	MY SECRET PASSION – THE ARIAS *Sony Classical SK 63077*	25	5
4 Dec 99	TIMELESS – THE CLASSICS – VOL.2 *Columbia 4960782*	50	2
6 Apr 02	ONLY A WOMAN LIKE YOU *Jive 9223522*	19	2
27 Mar 04	VINTAGE *Universal TV 9817973*	23	2
29 Oct 05	THE VERY BEST OF MICHAEL BOLTON *Columbia 82876747942*	18	10+

[1] Michael Bolton featuring Kenny G

BOMB THE BASS *UK, male producer – Tim Simenon (3 Albums: 16 Weeks, 10 Singles: 50 Weeks)*

20 Feb 88 ●	BEAT DIS *Mister-ron DOOD 1*	2	9
27 Aug 88 ●	MEGABLAST / DON'T MAKE ME WAIT *Mister-ron DOOD 2* [1]	6	9
22 Oct 88	INTO THE DRAGON *Rhythm King DOOD 1*	18	10
26 Nov 88 ●	SAY A LITTLE PRAYER *Rhythm King DOOD 3* [2]	10	10
27 Jul 91 ●	WINTER IN JULY *Rhythm King 6572757*	7	9
31 Aug 91	UNKNOWN TERRITORY *Rhythm King 4687740*	19	4
9 Nov 91	THE AIR YOU BREATHE *Rhythm King 6575387*	52	3
2 May 92	KEEP GIVING ME LOVE *Rhythm King 6579887*	62	2
1 Oct 94	BUG POWDER DUST *Stoned Heights BRCD 300* [3]	24	3
17 Dec 94	DARKHEART *Stoned Heights BRCD 305* [4]	35	3
1 Apr 95	1 TO 1 RELIGION *Stoned Heights BRCD 313* [5]	53	1
15 Apr 95	CLEAR *Fourth & Broadway BRCD 611*	22	2
16 Sep 95	SANDCASTLES *Fourth & Broadway BRCD 324* [6]	54	1

[1] Bomb the Bass featuring Merlin and Antonia / Bomb the Bass featuring Lorraine and Lose [2] Bomb the Bass featuring Maureen [3] Bomb the Bass featuring Justin Warfield [4] Bomb the Bass featuring Spikey Tee [5] Bomb the Bass featuring Carlton [6] Bomb the Bass featuring Bernard Fowler

BOMBALURINA featuring Timmy MALLETT
UK, male / female vocal group and male vocalist / TV presenter (1 Album: 5 Weeks, 2 Singles: 20 Weeks)

28 Jul 90 ★	ITSY BITSY TEENY WEENY YELLOW POLKA DOT BIKINI *Carpet CRPT 1* [1]	1	13
24 Nov 90	SEVEN LITTLE GIRLS SITTING IN THE BACKSEAT *Carpet CRPT 2* [2]	18	7
15 Dec 90	HUGGIN' AN' A KISSIN' *Polydor 8476481*	55	5

[1] Bombalurina [2] Bombalurina featuring Timmy Mallett

1 / 2 February 1957	8 / 9 February 1957	15 / 16 February 1957	22 / 23 February 1957
UK No.1 SINGLES			
SINGING THE BLUES Guy Mitchell / THE GARDEN OF EDEN Frankie Vaughan (tied at No.1)	THE GARDEN OF EDEN Frankie Vaughan	THE GARDEN OF EDEN Frankie Vaughan	YOUNG LOVE Tab Hunter
UK No.1 ALBUMS			
THE KING AND I Soundtrack	THE KING AND I Soundtrack	THE KING AND I Soundtrack	THE KING AND I Soundtrack

The BOMBERS

Canada, male / female vocal / instrumental group (2 Singles: 10 Weeks)

5 May 79 **(EVERYBODY) GET DANCIN'** *Flamingo FM 1* 37 7
18 Aug 79 **LET'S DANCE** *Flamingo FM 4* 58 3

BOMFUNK MC'S

Finland, male DJ / rap duo – Raymond Ebanks and DJ Gismo (1 Album: 2 Weeks, 2 Singles: 21 Weeks)

5 Aug 00 ● **FREESTYLER** *Dancepool DPS 2CD* 2 12
26 Aug 00 IN STEREO *INCredible 4943092* 33 2
2 Dec 00 **UP ROCKING BEATS** *INCredible 6706132* 11 9

BON

Germany, male vocal duo – Guy Gross and Claus Capek

3 Feb 01 **BOYS** *Epic 6707092* 15 5

BON GARÇON NEW

(see also LONYO) *UK, male production / vocal / instrumental duo – Lonyo Engele and Kevin McPherson*

18 Jun 05 **FREEK U** *Eye Industries / UMTV 9871395* 42 2

BON JOVI 50 Top 500

Globally popular New Jersey band: Jon Bon Jovi (John Bongiovi Jr) (v), Richie Sambora (g), David Bryan (k), Alec John Such (b), Tico Torres (d). The UK's biggest-selling album act of 1994. They have sold 100 million albums worldwide and appeared at the US Live 8 concert. Legendary fact: At one of their gigs a pig's head was thrown on stage. Best-selling single: 'Always' 560,500 (12 Albums: 435 Weeks, 33 Singles: 236 Weeks)

28 Apr 84 BON JOVI *Vertigo VERL 14* 71 3
11 May 85 7800 FAHRENHEIT *Vertigo VERL 24* 28 12
31 Aug 85 **HARDEST PART IS THE NIGHT** *Vertigo VER 22* 68 1
9 Aug 86 **YOU GIVE LOVE A BAD NAME** *Vertigo VER 26* ▲ 14 10
20 Sep 86 ● SLIPPERY WHEN WET *Vertigo VERH 38* ▲ 6 123
25 Oct 86 ● **LIVIN' ON A PRAYER** *Vertigo VER 28* ▲ 4 15
11 Apr 87 **WANTED DEAD OR ALIVE** *Vertigo JOV 1* 13 7
15 Aug 87 **NEVER SAY GOODBYE** *Vertigo JOV 2* 21 5
24 Sep 88 **BAD MEDICINE** *Vertigo JOV 3* ▲ 17 7
1 Oct 88 ★ NEW JERSEY *Vertigo VERH 62* ■ ▲ 1 47
10 Dec 88 **BORN TO BE MY BABY** *Vertigo JOV 4* 22 7
29 Apr 89 **I'LL BE THERE FOR YOU** *Vertigo JOV 5* ▲ 18 7
26 Aug 89 **LAY YOUR HANDS ON ME** *Vertigo JOV 6* 18 6
9 Dec 89 **LIVING IN SIN** *Vertigo JOV 7* 35 6
24 Oct 92 ● **KEEP THE FAITH** *Jambco JOV 8* 5 6
14 Nov 92 ★ KEEP THE FAITH *Jambco 5141972* ■ 1 70
23 Jan 93 **BED OF ROSES** *Jambco JOVCD 9* 13 6
15 May 93 ● **IN THESE ARMS** *Jambco JOVCD 10* 9 7
7 Aug 93 **I'LL SLEEP WHEN I'M DEAD** *Jambco JOVCD 11* 17 5
2 Oct 93 **I BELIEVE** *Jambco JOVCD 12* 11 6
26 Mar 94 ● **DRY COUNTY** *Jambco JOVCD 13* 9 6
24 Sep 94 ● **ALWAYS** *Jambco JOVCD 14* $ 2 18
22 Oct 94 ★ CROSS ROAD – THE BEST OF BON JOVI *Jambco 5229362* ■ 1 68
17 Dec 94 ● **PLEASE COME HOME FOR CHRISTMAS (re)** *Jambco JOVCD 16* 7 10
25 Feb 95 ● **SOMEDAY I'LL BE SATURDAY NIGHT** *Jambco JOVDD 15* 7 7
10 Jun 95 ● **THIS AIN'T A LOVE SONG** *Mercury JOVCD 17* 6 9
1 Jul 95 ★ THESE DAYS *Mercury 5282482* ■ 1 50
30 Sep 95 ● **SOMETHING FOR THE PAIN** *Mercury JOVCD 18* 8 7
25 Nov 95 ● **LIE TO ME** *Mercury JOVCD 19* 10 8
9 Mar 96 ● **THESE DAYS** *Mercury JOVCD 20* 7 6
6 Jul 96 **HEY GOD** *Mercury JOVCD 21* 13 5
10 Apr 99 **REAL LIFE** *Reprise W 479CD* 21 5
3 Jun 00 ● **IT'S MY LIFE** *Mercury 5627682* 3 13
10 Jun 00 ★ CRUSH *Mercury 5425622* ■ 1 29
9 Sep 00 ● **SAY IT ISN'T SO (re)** *Mercury 5688972* 10 7
9 Dec 00 **THANK YOU FOR LOVING ME** *Mercury 5727302* 12 6
19 May 01 ● **ONE WILD NIGHT** *Mercury 5729502* 10 7
26 May 01 ● ONE WILD NIGHT – LIVE 1985-2001 *Mercury 5488652* 2 9
28 Sep 02 ● **EVERYDAY (re)** *Mercury 0639362* 5 6
5 Oct 02 ● BOUNCE *Mercury 0633952* 2 9
21 Dec 02 **MISUNDERSTOOD (re)** *Mercury 0638152* 21 5
24 May 03 ● **ALL ABOUT LOVIN' YOU (re)** *Mercury 9800242* 9 6
15 Nov 03 ● THIS LEFT FEELS RIGHT *Mercury 9861391* 4 8
24 Sep 05 ● **HAVE A NICE DAY** *Mercury 9884894* 6 4
1 Oct 05 ● HAVE A NICE DAY *Mercury 2103556* 2 7

Jon BON JOVI

(see also BON JOVI) *US, male vocalist / guitarist – John Bongiovi Jr (2 Albums: 41 Weeks, 5 Singles: 27 Weeks)*

4 Aug 90 **BLAZE OF GLORY** *Vertigo JBJ 1* ▲ $ 13 8
25 Aug 90 ● BLAZE OF GLORY / YOUNG GUNS II (FILM SOUNDTRACK) *Vertigo 8464731* 2 23
10 Nov 90 **MIRACLE** *Vertigo JBVJ 2* 29 5
14 Jun 97 ● **MIDNIGHT IN CHELSEA** *Mercury MERCD 488* 4 7
28 Jun 97 ● DESTINATION ANYWHERE *Mercury 5360112* 2 18
30 Aug 97 ● **QUEEN OF NEW ORLEANS** *Mercury MERCD 493* 10 4
15 Nov 97 **JANIE, DON'T TAKE YOUR LOVE TO TOWN** *Mercury 5749872* 13 3

BOND

Australia / UK, female instrumental group (3 Albums: 23 Weeks)

14 Oct 00 BORN *Decca 4670912* 16 18
16 Nov 02 SHINE *Decca 4734602* 26 3
18 Sep 04 CLASSIFIED *Decca 4756301* 32 2

Graham BOND

UK, male vocalist / keyboard player, b. 28 Oct 1937, d. 8 May 1974

20 Jun 70 SOLID BOND *Warner Bros. WS 3001* 40 2

Ronnie BOND

UK, male vocalist

31 May 80 **IT'S WRITTEN ON YOUR BODY** *Mercury MER 13* 52 5

Gary 'U.S.' BONDS

US, male vocalist – Gary Anderson (2 Albums: 8 Weeks, 6 Singles: 39 Weeks)

19 Jan 61 **NEW ORLEANS** *Top Rank JAR 527* [1] 16 11
20 Jul 61 ● **QUARTER TO THREE** *Top Rank JAR 575* [1] ▲ $ 7 13
30 May 81 **THIS LITTLE GIRL** *EMI America EA 122* 43 6
22 Aug 81 DEDICATION *EMI America AML 3017* 43 3
22 Aug 81 **JOLE BLON** *EMI America EA 127* 51 3
31 Oct 81 **IT'S ONLY LOVE** *EMI America EA 128* 43 3
10 Jul 82 ON THE LINE *EMI America AML 3022* 55 5
17 Jul 82 **SOUL DEEP** *EMI America EA 140* 59 3

[1] US Bonds

BONE

UK, male vocal / instrumental duo

2 Apr 94 **WINGS OF LOVE** *Deconstruction 74321176282* 55 1

BONE THUGS-N-HARMONY

US, male rap group (2 Albums: 4 Weeks, 6 Singles: 26 Weeks)

4 Nov 95 **1ST OF THA MONTH** *Epic 6625172* 32 2
10 Aug 96 ● **THA CROSSROADS** *Epic 6635502* ▲ $ 8 11
31 Aug 96 E.1999 ETERNAL *Epic 4810382* ▲ 39 3
9 Nov 96 **1ST OF THA MONTH** (re-issue) *Epic 6638505* 15 4
15 Feb 97 **DAYS OF OUR LIVEZ** *East West A 3982CD* 37 2
26 Jul 97 **LOOK INTO MY EYES** *Epic 6647862* $ 16 3
9 Aug 97 THE ART OF WAR *Epic 4880802* ▲ 42 1
24 May 03 **HOME** *Epic 6738302* [1] 19 4

[1] Bone Thugs-N-Harmony featuring Phil Collins

Elbow BONES and The RACKETEERS

US, male vocalist and female backing group

14 Jan 84 **A NIGHT IN NEW YORK** *EMI America EA 165* 33 9

BONEY M 182 Top 500

Internationally successful West Indian vocal group: Bobby Farrell, Marcia Barrett, Liz Mitchell, Maisie Williams. This German-based quartet, assembled by producer Frank Farian, are the only act to have two singles in the Top 10 all-time best sellers. Best-selling single: 'Rivers of Babylon' / 'Brown Girl in the Ring' 1,985,000 (8 Albums: 142 Weeks, 19 Singles: 171 Weeks)

18 Dec 76 ● **DADDY COOL** *Atlantic K 10827* 6 13
12 Mar 77 ● **SUNNY** *Atlantic K 10892* 3 10

1 / 2 March 1957	8 / 9 March 1957	15 / 16 March 1957	22 / 23 March 1957
YOUNG LOVE Tab Hunter	YOUNG LOVE Tab Hunter	YOUNG LOVE Tab Hunter	YOUNG LOVE Tab Hunter
THIS IS SINATRA! Frank Sinatra	THE KING AND I Soundtrack	THIS IS SINATRA! Frank Sinatra	THE KING AND I Soundtrack

KEY
UK No.1 ★★ UK Top 10 ●● Still on chart ++ UK entry at No.1 ■■
US No.1 ▲▲ UK million seller £ US million seller $
Singles re-entries are listed as (re), (2re), (3re)... which signifies that the hit re-entered the chart once, twice or three times...

Peak Position / Weeks

23 Apr 77	TAKE THE HEAT OFF ME *Atlantic K 50314*	40	5
25 Jun 77 ●	**MA BAKER** *Atlantic K 10965*	2	13
6 Aug 77	LOVE FOR SALE *Atlantic K 50385*	13	10
29 Oct 77 ●	**BELFAST** *Atlantic K 11020*	8	13
29 Apr 78 ★	**RIVERS OF BABYLON / BROWN GIRL IN THE RING** *Atlantic / Hansa K 11120* £	1	40
29 Jul 78 ★	NIGHT FLIGHT TO VENUS *Atlantic / Hansa K 50498*	1	65
7 Oct 78 ●	**RASPUTIN** *Atlantic / Hansa K 11192*	2	10
2 Dec 78 ★	**MARY'S BOY CHILD – OH MY LORD** *Atlantic / Hansa K 11221* £	1	8
3 Mar 79 ●	**PAINTER MAN** *Atlantic / Hansa K 11255*	10	6
28 Apr 79 ●	**HOORAY HOORAY, IT'S A HOLI-HOLIDAY** *Atlantic / Hansa K 11279*	3	9
11 Aug 79	**GOTTA GO HOME / EL LUTE** *Atlantic / Hansa K 11351*	12	11
29 Sep 79 ★	OCEANS OF FANTASY *Atlantic / Hansa K 50610* ■	1	18
15 Dec 79	**I'M BORN AGAIN** *Atlantic / Hansa K 11410*	35	7
12 Apr 80 ★	THE MAGIC OF BONEY M – 20 GOLDEN HITS *Atlantic / Hansa BMTV 1*	1	26
26 Apr 80	**MY FRIEND JACK** *Atlantic / Hansa K 11463*	57	5
14 Feb 81	**CHILDREN OF PARADISE** *Atlantic / Hansa K 11637*	66	2
21 Nov 81	**WE KILL THE WORLD (DON'T KILL THE WORLD)** *Atlantic / Hansa K 11689*	39	5
6 Sep 86	THE BEST OF 10 YEARS – 32 SUPERHITS *Stylus SMR 621*	35	5
24 Dec 88	**MEGAMIX / MARY'S BOY CHILD** (re-mix) *Ariola 111947*	52	3
5 Dec 92 ●	**BONEY M MEGAMIX** *Arista 74321125127*	7	9
27 Mar 93	THE GREATEST HITS *Telstar TCD 2656*	14	10
17 Apr 93	**BROWN GIRL IN THE RING** (re-mix) *Arista 74321137052*	38	3
8 May 99	**MA BAKER / SOMEBODY SCREAM** *Logic 74321653872* [1]	22	2
15 Dec 01	THE GREATEST HITS *BMG 74321896142*	66	3
29 Dec 01	**DADDY COOL 2001** (re-mix) *BMG 74321913512*	47	2

[1] Boney M vs Horny United

'Brown Girl in the Ring' listed with 'Rivers of Babylon' only from 5 Aug 1978, peaking at No.2. 'El Lute' listed with 'Gotta Go Home' only from 29 Sep 1979. The 1988 and 1992 megamixes are different. The two The Greatest Hits albums are different.

BONFIRE *Germany, male vocal / instrumental group*

21 Oct 89	POINT BLANK *MSA ZL 74249*	74	1

BONIFACE *Seychelles, male vocalist – Bruce Boniface*

31 Aug 02	**CHEEKY** *Columbia 6729902*	25	3

Guest vocal by Lady Luck.

Graham BONNET (see also The MARBLES; RAINBOW) *UK, male vocalist (1 Album: 3 Weeks, 2 Singles: 15 Weeks)*

21 Mar 81 ●	**NIGHT GAMES** *Vertigo VER 1*	6	11
13 Jun 81	**LIAR** *Vertigo VER 2*	51	4
7 Nov 81	LINE UP *Mercury 6302151*	62	3

Graham BONNEY *UK, male vocalist – Graham Bradley*

24 Mar 66	**SUPERGIRL** *Columbia DB 7843*	19	8

BONNIE 'PRINCE' BILLY *US, male vocalist / guitarist – Will Oldham (2 Albums: 2 Weeks, 1 Single: 1 Week)*

8 Feb 03	MASTER AND EVERYONE *Domino WIGCD 121*	48	1
3 Apr 04	BONNIE 'PRINCE' BILLY SINGS GREATEST PALACE MUSIC *Domino WIGCD 140*	63	1
4 Sep 04	**AGNES, QUEEN OF SORROW** *Domino RUG 185CD*	69	1

BONO (see also PASSENGERS; U2) *Ireland, male vocalist – Paul Hewson (5 Singles: 25 Weeks)*

25 Jan 86	**IN A LIFETIME** *RCA PB 40535* [1]	20	5
10 Jun 89	**IN A LIFETIME** (re-issue) *RCA PB 42873* [1]	17	7
4 Dec 93 ●	**I'VE GOT YOU UNDER MY SKIN** *Island CID 578* [2]	4	9
9 Apr 94	**IN THE NAME OF THE FATHER** *Island CID 593* [3]	46	2
23 Oct 99	**NEW DAY** *Columbia 6682122* [4]	23	2

[1] Clannad featuring Bono [2] Frank Sinatra with Bono
[3] Bono and Gavin Friday [4] Wyclef Jean featuring Bono

'I've Got You Under My Skin' was the listed B-side of 'Stay (Faraway So Close)' by U2.

The BONZO DOG DOO-DAH BAND *UK, male vocal (Viv Stanshall) / instrumental group (3 Albums: 4 Weeks, 1 Single: 14 Weeks)*

6 Nov 68 ●	**I'M THE URBAN SPACEMAN** *Liberty LBF 15144*	5	14
18 Jan 69	DOUGHNUT IN GRANNY'S GREENHOUSE *Liberty LBS 83158*	40	1
30 Aug 69	TADPOLES *Liberty LBS 83257*	36	1
22 Jun 74	THE HISTORY OF THE BONZOS *United Artists UAD 60071*	41	2

Betty BOO *UK, female rapper – Alison Clarkson (2 Albums: 25 Weeks, 7 Singles: 55 Weeks)*

12 Aug 89 ●	**HEY DJ – I CAN'T DANCE (TO THAT MUSIC YOU'RE PLAYING) / SKA TRAIN** *Rhythm King LEFT 34* [1]	7	11
19 May 90 ●	**DOIN' THE DO** *Rhythm King LEFT 39*	7	12
11 Aug 90 ●	**WHERE ARE YOU BABY?** *Rhythm King LEFT 43*	3	10
22 Sep 90 ●	BOOMANIA *Rhythm King LEFTLP 12*	4	24
1 Dec 90	**24 HOURS** *Rhythm King LEFT 45*	25	8
8 Aug 92	**LET ME TAKE YOU THERE** *WEA YZ 677*	12	8
3 Oct 92	**I'M ON MY WAY** *WEA YZ 693*	44	3
24 Oct 92	GRRR! IT'S BETTY BOO *WEA 4509909082*	62	1
10 Apr 93	**HANGOVER** *WEA YZ 719CD*	50	3

[1] The Beatmasters featuring Betty Boo

The BOO RADLEYS *UK, male vocal (Simon Rowbottom) / instrumental group (5 Albums: 29 Weeks, 12 Singles: 27 Weeks)*

4 Apr 92	EVERYTHING'S ALRIGHT FOREVER *Creation CRECD 120*	55	1
20 Jun 92	**DOES THIS HURT / BOO! FOREVER** *Creation CRE 128*	67	1
28 Aug 93	GIANT STEPS *Creation CRECD 149*	17	4
23 Oct 93	**WISH I WAS SKINNY** *Creation CRESCD 169*	75	1
12 Feb 94	**BARNEY (... AND ME)** *Creation CRESCD 178*	48	2
11 Jun 94	**LAZARUS** *Creation CRESCD 187*	50	2
11 Mar 95 ●	**WAKE UP BOO!** *Creation CRESCD 191*	9	8
8 Apr 95 ★	WAKE UP! *Creation CRECD 179* ■	1	21
13 May 95	**FIND THE ANSWER WITHIN** *Creation CRESCD 202*	37	3
29 Jul 95	**IT'S LULU** *Creation CRESCD 211*	25	2
7 Oct 95	**FROM THE BENCH AT BELVIDERE** *Creation CRESCD 214*	24	2
17 Aug 96	**WHAT'S IN THE BOX? (SEE WATCHA GOT)** *Creation CRESCD 220*	25	2
21 Sep 96	C'MON KIDS *Creation CRECD 194*	20	2
19 Oct 96	**C'MON KIDS** *Creation CRESCD 236*	18	2
1 Feb 97	**RIDE THE TIGER** *Creation CRESCD 248X*	38	1
17 Oct 98	**FREE HUEY** *Creation CRESCD 299X*	54	1
31 Oct 98	KINGSIZE *Creation CRECD 228*	62	1

BOO-YAA T.R.I.B.E. *US, male rap group (1 Album: 1 Week, 2 Singles: 6 Weeks)*

14 Apr 90	NEW FUNKY NATION *Fourth & Broadway BRCD 5448423962*	74	1
30 Jun 90	**PSYKO FUNK** *Fourth & Broadway BRW 179*	43	3
6 Nov 93	**ANOTHER BODY MURDERED** *Epic 6597942* [1]	26	3

[1] Faith No More and Boo-Yaa TRIBE

BOOGIE BOX HIGH (see also Andy G's STARSKY & HUTCH ALL STARS) *UK, male vocal / instrumental group – leader Andros Georgiou*

4 Jul 87 ●	**JIVE TALKIN'** *Hardback 7BOSS 4*	7	11

29 / 30 March 1957	5 / 6 April 1957	12 / 13 April 1957	19 / 20 April 1957
UK No.1 SINGLES			
YOUNG LOVE Tab Hunter	YOUNG LOVE Tab Hunter	CUMBERLAND GAP Lonnie Donegan and his Skiffle Group	CUMBERLAND GAP Lonnie Donegan and his Skiffle Group
UK No.1 ALBUMS			
THIS IS SINATRA! Frank Sinatra	THE KING AND I Soundtrack	THE KING AND I Soundtrack	THE KING AND I Soundtrack

BOOGIE DOWN PRODUCTIONS
US, male rap / production group (3 Albums: 9 Weeks, 1 Single: 2 Weeks)

18 Jan 88 BY ALL MEANS NECESSARY *Jive HIP 63* 38 3
4 Jun 88 MY PHILOSOPHY / STOP THE VIOLENCE *Jive JIVEX 170* 69 2
22 Jul 89 GHETTO MUSIC: THE BLUEPRINT OF HIP HOP *Jive HIP 80* 32 4
25 Aug 90 EDUTAINMENT *Jive HIP 100* 52 2

BOOGIE PIMPS
Germany, male DJ / production / instrumental duo – Mark J. Klak and Mirko Jacob (2 Singles: 21 Weeks)

17 Jan 04 ● SOMEBODY TO LOVE *Data DATA 61CDS* 3 15
8 May 04 ● SUNNY *Data DATA 67CDX* 10 6

BOOKER T and The MG's
US, male instrumental group (2 Albums: 5 Weeks, 4 Singles: 43 Weeks)

25 Jul 64 GREEN ONIONS *London HAK 8182* 11 4
11 Dec 68 SOUL LIMBO *Stax 102* 30 9
7 May 69 ● TIME IS TIGHT *Stax 119* 4 18
30 Aug 69 SOUL CLAP '69 *Stax 127* 35 4
11 Jul 70 MCLEMORE AVENUE *Stax SXATS 1031* 70 1
15 Dec 79 ● GREEN ONIONS *Atlantic K 10109* $ 7 12

BOOM!
UK, male / female vocal group

27 Jan 01 FALLING *London LONCD 458* 11 5

BOOM BOOM ROOM
UK, male vocal / instrumental group

8 Mar 86 HERE COMES THE MAN *Fun After All FUN 101* 74 1

BOOMKAT
US, male / female vocal / instrumental / production duo – Kellin and Taryn Mann

31 May 03 THE WRECKONING *Dreamworks 4504580* 37 2

The BOOMTOWN RATS (305 Top 500)
New wave group named after a band in a Woody Guthrie novel. Fronted by the charismatic Bob Geldof, b. 5 Oct 1954, Dublin, Ireland. Organised Live Aid (and Live 8), was knighted and won an Outstanding Contribution to Music award at the 2005 BRITs. The Mutt Lange-produced 'Rat Trap' was the first new wave No.1 (7 Albums: 101 Weeks, 15 Singles: 123 Weeks)

27 Aug 77 LOOKING AFTER NO.1 *Ensign ENY 4* 11 9
17 Sep 77 BOOMTOWN RATS *Ensign ENVY 1* 18 11
19 Nov 77 MARY OF THE 4TH FORM *Ensign ENY 9* 15 9
15 Apr 78 SHE'S SO MODERN *Ensign ENY 13* 12 11
17 Jun 78 ● LIKE CLOCKWORK *Ensign ENY 14* 6 13
8 Jul 78 ● A TONIC FOR THE TROOPS *Ensign ENVY 3* 8 44
14 Oct 78 ★ RAT TRAP *Ensign ENY 16* 1 15
21 Jul 79 ★ I DON'T LIKE MONDAYS *Ensign ENY 30* 1 12
3 Nov 79 ● THE FINE ART OF SURFACING *Ensign ENROX 11* 7 26
17 Nov 79 DIAMOND SMILES *Ensign ENY 33* 13 10
26 Jan 80 ● SOMEONE'S LOOKING AT YOU *Ensign ENY 34* 4 9
22 Nov 80 ● BANANA REPUBLIC *Mercury BONGO 1* 3 11
24 Jan 81 ● MONDO BONGO *Mercury 6359 042* 6 7
31 Jan 81 THE ELEPHANT'S GRAVEYARD (GUILTY) *Mercury BONGO 2* 26 6
12 Dec 81 NEVER IN A MILLION YEARS *Mercury MER 87* 62 4
20 Mar 82 HOUSE ON FIRE *Mercury MER 91* 24 8
3 Apr 82 V DEEP *Mercury 6359 082* 64 5
18 Feb 84 TONIGHT *Mercury MER 154* 73 1
19 May 84 DRAG ME DOWN *Mercury MER 163* 50 3
2 Jul 94 I DON'T LIKE MONDAYS (re-issue) *Vertigo VERCD 87* 38 2
9 Jul 94 ● LOUDMOUTH – THE BEST OF BOB GELDOF & THE BOOMTOWN RATS *Vertigo 5222852* [1] 10 3
8 May 04 THE BEST OF THE BOOMTOWN RATS *Universal TV 9819145* 43 5

[1] The Boomtown Rats and Bob Geldof

The Best of The Boomtown Rats reached its peak position in Feb 2005.

The Clint BOON EXPERIENCE
UK, male / female vocal / instrumental group (3 Singles: 3 Weeks)

6 Nov 99 WHITE NO SUGAR *Artful CDARTFUL 32* 61 1
5 Feb 00 BIGGEST HORIZON *Artful CDARTFUL 33* 70 1
5 Aug 00 DO WHAT YOU DO (EARWORM SONG) *Artful CDARTFUL 34* 63 1

Daniel BOONE
UK, male vocalist – Peter Lee Stirling (2 Singles: 25 Weeks)

14 Aug 71 DADDY DON'T YOU WALK SO FAST *Penny Farthing PEN 764* 17 15
1 Apr 72 BEAUTIFUL SUNDAY (re) *Penny Farthing PEN 781* 21 10

Debby BOONE
US, female vocalist

24 Dec 77 YOU LIGHT UP MY LIFE *Warner Bros. / Curb K 17043* ▲ $ 48 2

Pat BOONE (173 Top 500)
Major rival to Elvis in the late 1950s, b. Charles Boone, 1 Jun 1934, Florida, US. This clean-cut vocalist was voted the World's Outstanding Male Singer in the UK in 1957. He was seldom absent from the UK or US charts during the early rock 'n' roll years (4 Albums: 12 Weeks, 27 Singles: 311 Weeks)

18 Nov 55 ● AIN'T THAT A SHAME (re) *London HLD 8172* $ 7 11
27 Apr 56 ★ I'LL BE HOME (re) *London HLD 8253* $ 1 24
27 Jul 56 LONG TALL SALLY (re) *London HLD 8291* 18 7
17 Aug 56 I ALMOST LOST MY MIND *London HLD 8303* $ 14 7
7 Dec 56 ● FRIENDLY PERSUASION (THEE I LOVE) *London HLD 8346* $ 3 21
1 Feb 57 ● DON'T FORBID ME *London HLD 8370* $ 2 16
26 Apr 57 WHY BABY WHY *London HLD 8404* $ 17 7
5 Jul 57 ● LOVE LETTERS IN THE SAND *London HLD 8445* ▲ $ 2 21
27 Sep 57 ● REMEMBER YOU'RE MINE / THERE'S A GOLDMINE IN THE SKY *London HLD 8479* $ 5 18
6 Dec 57 ● APRIL LOVE *London HLD 8512* ▲ $ 7 23
13 Dec 57 WHITE CHRISTMAS *London HLD 8520* 29 1
4 Apr 58 ● A WONDERFUL TIME UP THERE *London HLD 8574 (A)* $ 2 17
11 Apr 58 ● IT'S TOO SOON TO KNOW *London HLD 8574 (B)* 7 12
27 Jun 58 ● SUGAR MOON *London HLD 8640* 6 12
29 Aug 58 IF DREAMS CAME TRUE *London HLD 8675* 16 11
22 Nov 58 ● STARDUST *London HAD 2127* 10 1
5 Dec 58 GEE, BUT IT'S LONELY *London HLD 8739* 30 1
16 Jan 59 I'LL REMEMBER TONIGHT (2re) *London HLD 8775* 18 9
10 Apr 59 WITH THE WIND AND THE RAIN IN YOUR HAIR *London HLD 8824* 21 3
22 May 59 FOR A PENNY (re) *London HLD 8855* 19 9
31 Jul 59 'TWIXT TWELVE AND TWENTY (re) *London HLD 8910* 18 7
28 May 60 HYMNS WE HAVE LOVED *London HAD 2228* 12 2
23 Jun 60 WALKING THE FLOOR OVER YOU (re) *London HLD 9138* 39 8
25 Jun 60 HYMNS WE LOVE *London HAD 2092* 14 1
6 Jul 61 MOODY RIVER *London HLD 9350* ▲ $ 18 10
7 Dec 61 ● JOHNNY WILL *London HLD 9461* 4 13
15 Feb 62 I'LL SEE YOU IN MY DREAMS *London HLD 9504* 27 9
24 May 62 QUANDO, QUANDO, QUANDO *London HLD 9543* 41 4
12 Jul 62 ● SPEEDY GONZALES *London HLD 9573* 2 19
15 Nov 62 THE MAIN ATTRACTION *London HLD 9620* 12 11
24 Apr 76 PAT BOONE ORIGINALS *ABC ABSD 301* 16 8

'There's a Goldmine in the Sky' was listed only for the week of 27 Sep 1957. It peaked at No.23. 'A Wonderful Time Up There' and 'It's Too Soon to Know' were both on the same single release.

BOOTH and The BAD ANGEL (see also JAMES)
UK / US, male vocal / instrumental duo – Tim Booth and Angelo Badalamenti (1 Album: 2 Weeks, 2 Singles: 4 Weeks)

22 Jun 96 I BELIEVE *Fontana BBCD 1* 25 3
13 Jul 96 BOOTH AND THE BAD ANGEL *Fontana 5268522* 35 2
11 Jul 98 FALL IN LOVE WITH ME *Mercury MERCD 503* 57 1

Tim BOOTH
(see also BOOTH and The BAD ANGEL; JAMES) *UK, male vocalist*

10 Jul 04 DOWN TO THE SEA *Sanctuary SANXS 279* 68 1

Ken BOOTHE
Jamaica, male vocalist (2 Singles: 22 Weeks)

21 Sep 74 ★ EVERYTHING I OWN *Trojan TR 7920* 1 12
14 Dec 74 CRYING OVER YOU *Trojan TR 7944* 11 10

BOOTHILL FOOT-TAPPERS
UK, male / female vocal / instrumental group

14 Jul 84 GET YOUR FEET OUT OF MY SHOES *Go Discs TAP 1* 64 3

KEY UK No.1 ★ UK Top 10 ● Still on chart + UK entry at No.1 ■ US No.1 ▲ UK million seller £ US million seller $
Singles re-entries are listed as (re), (2re), (3re)... which signifies that the hit re-entered the chart once, twice or three times...
Peak Position / Weeks

BOOTSY'S RUBBER BAND *US, male vocal / instrumental group*

8 Jul 78 **BOOTZILLA** *Warner Bros. K 17196*......43 3

BOSS (see also David MORALES; PULSE featuring Antoinette ROBERSON)
US, male producer – David Morales

27 Aug 94 **CONGO** *Cooltempo CDCOOL 296*......54 1

Naila BOSS *UK, female rapper / vocalist (3 Singles: 16 Weeks)*

22 May 04 ● **IT CAN'T BE RIGHT** *2PSL / Inferno 2PSLCD 04* [1] 8 7
10 Jul 04 **LA LA LA** *LaBoss NBCD 1*......65 1
11 Sep 04 ● **YOU SHOULD REALLY KNOW** *Relentless RELCD 9* [2] 8 8

[1] 2Play featuring Raghav & Naila Boss [2] Pirates featuring Enya, Shola Ama, Naila Boss & Ishani

BOSTON *US, male vocal (Brad Delp) / instrumental group (5 Albums: 44 Weeks, 2 Singles: 13 Weeks)*

29 Jan 77 **MORE THAN A FEELING** *Epic EPC 4658*......22 8
5 Feb 77 BOSTON *Epic EPC 81611*......11 20
9 Sep 78 ● DON'T LOOK BACK *Epic EPC 86057* ▲......9 10
7 Oct 78 **DON'T LOOK BACK** *Epic EPC 6653*......43 5
4 Apr 81 BOSTON (re-issue) *Epic EPC 32038*......58 2
18 Oct 86 THIRD STAGE *MCA MCG 6017* ▲......37 11
25 Jun 94 WALK ON *MCA MCD 10973*......56 1

Eve BOSWELL
Hungary, female vocalist – b. Eva Keleti, 11 May 1924, d. 13 Aug 1998

30 Dec 55 ● **PICKIN' A-CHICKEN (2re)** *Parlophone R 4082*......9 13

Hit credits Glen Somers and his Orchestra.

Judy BOUCHER
St Vincent, female vocalist (1 Album: 1 Week, 2 Singles: 23 Weeks)

4 Apr 87 ● **CAN'T BE WITH YOU TONIGHT** *Orbitone OR 721*......2 14
25 Apr 87 CAN'T BE WITH YOU TONIGHT *Orbitone OLP 024*......95 1
4 Jul 87 **YOU CAUGHT MY EYE** *Orbitone OR 722*......18 9

BOUNCING CZECKS *UK, male vocal / instrumental group*

29 Dec 84 **I'M A LITTLE CHRISTMAS CRACKER** *RCA 463*......72 1

BOUNTY KILLER *Jamaica, male rapper – Rodney Price*

27 Feb 99 **IT'S A PARTY** *Edel 0066135 BLA*......65 1

BOURGEOIS TAGG
US, male vocal / instrumental duo – Brent Bourgeois and Larry Tagg

6 Feb 88 **I DON'T MIND AT ALL** *Island IS 353*......35 6

BOURGIE BOURGIE *UK, male vocal / instrumental group*

3 Mar 84 **BREAKING POINT** *MCA BOU 1*......48 4

Toby BOURKE with George MICHAEL *UK, male vocalists*

7 Jun 97 ● **WALTZ AWAY DREAMING** *Aegean AECD 01*......10 4

BOW WOW *US, male rapper – Rashad Moss (4 Singles: 26 Weeks)*

14 Apr 01 ● **BOW WOW (THAT'S MY NAME)** *So So Def / Columbia 6709832* [1] 6 9
27 Nov 04 ● **BABY IT'S YOU** *Mercury 9869056* [2] 8 9
8 Oct 05 **LET ME HOLD YOU** (import) *Sony BMG 6760602* [3] 64 2
22 Oct 05 **LET ME HOLD YOU** *Columbia 6760601* [3] 27 6

[1] Lil Bow Wow [2] JoJo featuring Bow Wow [3] Bow Wow featuring Omarion

BOW WOW WOW
UK / Burma, female / male vocal (Myant Myant Awe aka Annabella Lwin) / instrumental group (2 Albums: 38 Weeks, 10 Singles: 54 Weeks)

26 Jul 80 **C'30, C'60, C'90, GO** *EMI 5088*......34 7
6 Dec 80 **YOUR CASSETTE PET (EP)** *EMI WOW 1*......58 6
28 Mar 81 **W.O.R.K. (N.O. NAH NO NO MY DADDY DON'T)** *EMI 5153*......62 3
15 Aug 81 **PRINCE OF DARKNESS** *RCA 100*......58 4
24 Oct 81 SEE JUNGLE! SEE JUNGLE! GO JOIN YOUR GANG YEAH! CITY ALL OVER GO APE CRAZY *RCA RCALP 00273000*......26 32
7 Nov 81 **CHIHUAHUA** *RCA 144*......51 4
30 Jan 82 ● **GO WILD IN THE COUNTRY** *RCA 175*......7 13
1 May 82 **SEE JUNGLE! (JUNGLE BOY) / (I'M A) TV SAVAGE** *RCA 220*......45 3
5 Jun 82 ● **I WANT CANDY** *RCA 238*......9 8
31 Jul 82 **LOUIS QUATORZE** *RCA 263*......66 2
7 Aug 82 I WANT CANDY *EMI EMC 3416*......26 6
12 Mar 83 **DO YOU WANNA HOLD ME?** *RCA 314*......47 4

'Your Cassette Pet' listed as 'Louis Quatorze' on 6 Dec 1980 only. Tracks on Your Cassette Pet (available on cassette only): Louis Quatorze / Gold He Said / Umo-Sex-Al Apache / I Want My Baby on Mars / Sexy Eiffel Towers / Giant Sized Baby Thing / Fools Rush In / Radio G String. RCA 263 is disc version of track on EMI WOW 1.

BOWA featuring MALA *US, male / female vocal / instrumental duo*

7 Dec 91 **DIFFERENT STORY** *Dead Dead Good GOOD 8*......64 1

David BOWIE (10 Top 500) (see also TIN MACHINE)
Chameleon-like singer / songwriter / entertainer, b. David Jones, 8 Jan 1947, Brixton, London. Noted for his changes of character and fashion, he became Ziggy Stardust, Aladdin Sane and The Thin White Duke. His striking appearance was enhanced by an unfortunate school playground incident that changed the colour of one of his blue eyes to green after being stabbed by a compass. Among his many accolades and awards, for both recording and songwriting, is the 1996 BRIT Award for Outstanding Contribution to British Music and being voted most influential artist in an NME poll in 2000. He is the only act to reject induction into the Rock and Roll Hall of Fame. No UK act can better the 10 albums he charted with simultaneously in the Top 100 in 1983 and no British male can match his eight No.1 albums. This often sampled performer has starred in movies, acted on Broadway, painted and recorded music with many of the world's leading acts. In 1999 he released the first virtual album and became the first major act to make a full album available for download, released the first enhanced CD single (1995) and became the first singer / songwriter to go to the stock market selling interest in his back catalogue, raising $55 million in the process. Bowie, who was awarded a Lifetime Achievement Grammy in 2006, has sold more than nine million singles in the UK (60 Albums: 1006 Weeks, 70 Singles: 454 Weeks)

6 Sep 69 ● **SPACE ODDITY (re)** *Philips BF 1801*......5 14
24 Jun 72 ● **STARMAN** *RCA 2199*......10 11
1 Jul 72 ● THE RISE AND FALL OF ZIGGY STARDUST AND THE SPIDERS FROM MARS *RCA Victor SF 8287*......5 106
16 Sep 72 **JOHN, I'M ONLY DANCING** *RCA 2263*......12 10
23 Sep 72 ● HUNKY DORY *RCA Victor SF 8244*......3 69
25 Nov 72 SPACE ODDITY *RCA Victor LSP 4813*......17 37
25 Nov 72 THE MAN WHO SOLD THE WORLD *RCA Victor LSP 4816*......26 22
9 Dec 72 ● **THE JEAN GENIE** *RCA 2302*......2 13
14 Apr 73 ● **DRIVE-IN SATURDAY** *RCA 2352*......3 10
5 May 73 ★ ALADDIN SANE *RCA Victor RS 1001* ■......1 48
30 Jun 73 ● **LIFE ON MARS?** *RCA 2316*......3 13
15 Sep 73 ● **THE LAUGHING GNOME** *Deram DM 123*......6 12
20 Oct 73 ● **SORROW** *RCA 2424*......3 15
3 Nov 73 ★ PINUPS *RCA Victor RS 1003* ■......1 21
23 Feb 74 ● **REBEL REBEL** *RCA LPBO 5009*......5 7
20 Apr 74 **ROCK 'N' ROLL SUICIDE** *RCA LPBO 5021*......22 7
8 Jun 74 ★ DIAMOND DOGS *RCA Victor APLI 0576* ■......1 17
22 Jun 74 **DIAMOND DOGS** *RCA APBO 0293*......21 6
28 Sep 74 ● **KNOCK ON WOOD** *RCA 2466*......10 6
16 Nov 74 ● DAVID LIVE *RCA Victor APL 20771*......2 12
1 Mar 75 **YOUNG AMERICANS** *RCA 2523*......18 7
5 Apr 75 ● YOUNG AMERICANS *RCA Victor RS 1006*......2 12
2 Aug 75 **FAME** *RCA 2579* ▲ $......17 8

24 / 25 May 1957	31 May / 1 June 1957	7 / 8 June 1957	14 / 15 June 1957
UK No.1 SINGLES			
BUTTERFLY Andy Williams	BUTTERFLY Andy Williams	YES TONIGHT, JOSEPHINE Johnnie Ray	YES TONIGHT, JOSEPHINE Johnnie Ray
UK No.1 ALBUMS			
THE KING AND I Soundtrack	THE KING AND I Soundtrack	THE KING AND I Soundtrack	OKLAHOMA! Soundtrack

11 Oct 75 ★ **SPACE ODDITY** (re-issue) *RCA 2593* **1** 10
29 Nov 75 ● **GOLDEN YEARS** *RCA 2640* **8** 10
7 Feb 76 ● STATION TO STATION *RCA Victor APLI 1327* 5 16
22 May 76 **TVC 15** *RCA 2682* **33** 4
12 Jun 76 ● CHANGESONEBOWIE *RCA Victor RS 1055* 2 28
29 Jan 77 ● LOW *RCA Victor PL 12030* 2 18
19 Feb 77 ● **SOUND AND VISION** *RCA PB 0905* **3** 11
15 Oct 77 **HEROES** *RCA PB 1121* **24** 8
29 Oct 77 ● HEROES *RCA Victor PL 12522* 3 18
21 Jan 78 **BEAUTY AND THE BEAST** *RCA PB 1190* **39** 3
14 Oct 78 ● STAGE *RCA Victor PL 02913* 5 10
2 Dec 78 **BREAKING GLASS (EP)** *RCA BOW 1* **54** 7
5 May 79 ● **BOYS KEEP SWINGING** *RCA BOW 2* **7** 10
9 Jun 79 ● LODGER *RCA Victor BOW LP 1* 4 17
21 Jul 79 **D.J.** *RCA BOW 3* **29** 5
15 Dec 79 **JOHN, I'M ONLY DANCING (AGAIN) (1975) / JOHN, I'M ONLY DANCING (1972)** *RCA BOW 4* **12** 8
1 Mar 80 **ALABAMA SONG** *RCA BOW 5* **23** 5
16 Aug 80 ★ **ASHES TO ASHES** *RCA BOW 6* **1** 10
27 Sep 80 ★ SCARY MONSTERS AND SUPER CREEPS *RCA Victor BOW LP 2* ■ 1 32
1 Nov 80 ● **FASHION** *RCA BOW 7* **5** 12
10 Jan 81 ● THE VERY BEST OF DAVID BOWIE *K-Tel NE 1111* 3 20
10 Jan 81 **SCARY MONSTERS (AND SUPER CREEPS)** *RCA BOW 8* **20** 6
17 Jan 81 HUNKY DORY (re-issue) *RCA International INTS 5064* 32 51
31 Jan 81 THE RISE AND FALL OF ZIGGY STARDUST AND THE SPIDERS FROM MARS (re-issue) *RCA International INTS 5063* 33 62
28 Mar 81 **UP THE HILL BACKWARDS** *RCA BOW 9* **32** 6
14 Nov 81 ★ **UNDER PRESSURE** *EMI 5250* [1] **1** 11
28 Nov 81 CHANGESTWOBOWIE *RCA BOW LP 3* 24 17
28 Nov 81 **WILD IS THE WIND** *RCA BOW 10* **24** 10
6 Mar 82 ALADDIN SANE (re-issue) *RCA International INTS 5067* 49 24
6 Mar 82 **BAAL (EP)** *RCA BOW 11* **29** 5
10 Apr 82 **CAT PEOPLE (PUTTING OUT FIRE)** *MCA 770* **26** 6
27 Nov 82 ● **PEACE ON EARTH – LITTLE DRUMMER BOY** *RCA BOW 12* [2] .. **3** 8
14 Jan 83 RARE *RCA PL 45406* 34 11
26 Mar 83 ★ **LET'S DANCE** *EMI America EA 152* ▲ $ **1** 14
23 Apr 83 ★ LET'S DANCE *EMI America AML 3029* ■ 1 56
30 Apr 83 PIN-UPS (re-issue) *RCA International INTS 5236* 57 15
30 Apr 83 THE MAN WHO SOLD THE WORLD (re-issue) *RCA International INTS 5237* 64 8
14 May 83 DIAMOND DOGS (re-issue) *RCA International INTS 5068* 60 14
11 Jun 83 HEROES (re-issue) *RCA International INTS 5066* 85 5
11 Jun 83 LOW (re-issue) *RCA International INTS 5065* 75 8
11 Jun 83 ● **CHINA GIRL** *EMI America EA 157* **2** 8
20 Aug 83 GOLDEN YEARS *RCA BOWLP 4* 33 5
24 Sep 83 ● **MODERN LOVE** *EMI America EA 158* **2** 8
5 Nov 83 ZIGGY STARDUST – THE MOTION PICTURE *RCA PL 84862* 17 6
5 Nov 83 **WHITE LIGHT, WHITE HEAT** *RCA 372* **46** 3
28 Apr 84 FAME AND FASHION (BOWIE'S ALL TIME GREATEST HITS) *RCA PL 84919* 40 6
19 May 84 LOVE YOU TILL TUESDAY *Deram BOWIE 1* 53 4
22 Sep 84 ● **BLUE JEAN** *EMI America EA 181* **6** 8
6 Oct 84 ★ TONIGHT *EMI America DB 1* ■ 1 19
8 Dec 84 **TONIGHT** *EMI America EA 187* **53** 4
9 Feb 85 **THIS IS NOT AMERICA (THE THEME FROM 'THE FALCON AND THE SNOWMAN')** *EMI America EA 190* [3] **14** 7
8 Jun 85 **LOVING THE ALIEN (re)** *EMI America EA 195* **19** 7
7 Sep 85 ★ **DANCING IN THE STREET** *EMI America EA 204* [4] ■ **1** 12
15 Mar 86 ● **ABSOLUTE BEGINNERS** *Virgin VS 838* **2** 9
21 Jun 86 **UNDERGROUND** *EMI America EA 216* **21** 6
8 Nov 86 **WHEN THE WIND BLOWS** *Virgin VS 906* **44** 4
4 Apr 87 **DAY-IN DAY-OUT** *EMI America EA 230* **17** 6
2 May 87 ● NEVER LET ME DOWN *EMI America AMLS 3117* 6 16
27 Jun 87 **TIME WILL CRAWL** *EMI America EA 237* **33** 4
29 Aug 87 **NEVER LET ME DOWN** *EMI America EA 239* **34** 6
24 Mar 90 ★ CHANGESBOWIE *EMI DBTV 1* 1 29
7 Apr 90 **FAME** (re-mix) *EMI-USA FAME 90* **28** 4
14 Apr 90 HUNKY DORY (2nd re-issue) *EMI EMC 3572* 39 5
14 Apr 90 SPACE ODDITY (re-issue) *EMI EMC 3571* 39 2
14 Apr 90 THE MAN WHO SOLD THE WORLD (2nd re-issue) *EMI EMC 3573* 64 1
23 Jun 90 THE RISE AND FALL OF ZIGGY STARDUST AND THE SPIDERS FROM MARS (2nd re-issue) *EMI EMC 3577* 25 4
28 Jul 90 ALADDIN SANE (2nd re-issue) *EMI EMC 3579* 43 1
28 Jul 90 PIN-UPS (2nd re-issue) *EMI EMC 3580* 52 1
27 Oct 90 DIAMOND DOGS (2nd re-issue) *EMI EMC 3584* 67 3
4 May 91 STATION TO STATION (re-issue) *EMI EMD 1020* 54 1
4 May 91 YOUNG AMERICANS (re-issue) *EMI EMD 1021* 57 1
7 Sep 91 LOW (2nd re-issue) *EMI EMD 1027* 64 1
22 Aug 92 **REAL COOL WORLD** *Warner Bros. W 0127* **53** 1
27 Mar 93 ● **JUMP THEY SAY** *Arista 74321139422* **9** 6
17 Apr 93 ★ BLACK TIE WHITE NOISE *Arista 74321136972* ■ 1 11
12 Jun 93 **BLACK TIE WHITE NOISE** *Arista 74321148682* [5] **36** 2
23 Oct 93 **MIRACLE GOODNIGHT** *Arista 74321162262* **40** 2
20 Nov 93 ● THE SINGLES COLLECTION *EMI CDEM 1512* 9 16
4 Dec 93 **BUDDHA OF SUBURBIA** *Arista 74321177052* [6] **35** 3
7 May 94 SANTA MONICA '72 *Trident GY 002* 74 1
23 Sep 95 **THE HEART'S FILTHY LESSON** *RCA 74321307032* **35** 2
7 Oct 95 ● OUTSIDE *RCA 74321310662* 8 4
2 Dec 95 **STRANGERS WHEN WE MEET / THE MAN WHO SOLD THE WORLD (LIVE)** *RCA 74321329402* **39** 2
2 Mar 96 **HALLO SPACEBOY** *RCA 74321353842* **12** 4
8 Feb 97 **LITTLE WONDER** *RCA 74321452072* **14** 3
15 Feb 97 ● EART HL I NG *RCA 74321449442* 6 4
26 Apr 97 **DEAD MAN WALKING** *RCA 74321475852* **32** 2
30 Aug 97 **SEVEN YEARS IN TIBET** *RCA 74321512542* **61** 1
8 Nov 97 THE BEST OF DAVID BOWIE 1969/1974 *EMI 8218492* 13 17
21 Feb 98 **I CAN'T READ** *Velvet ZYX 87578* **73** 1
2 May 98 THE BEST OF DAVID BOWIE 1974/1979 *EMI 4943002* 39 2
2 Oct 99 **THURSDAY'S CHILD** *Virgin VSCDT 1753* **16** 3
16 Oct 99 ● HOURS ... *Virgin CDV 2900* 5 5
18 Dec 99 **UNDER PRESSURE** (re-mix) *Parlophone CDQUEEN 28* [1] **14** 7
5 Feb 00 **SURVIVE** *Virgin VSCDT 1767* **28** 2
29 Jul 00 **SEVEN** *Virgin VSCDT 1776* **32** 2
7 Oct 00 ● BOWIE AT THE BEEB – THE BEST OF THE BBC RADIO SESSIONS 68-72 *EMI 5289582* 7 4
11 May 02 **LOVING THE ALIEN** (re-mix) *Positiva CDTIV 172* [7] **41** 1
22 Jun 02 ● HEATHEN *Columbia 5082222* 5 18
20 Jul 02 THE RISE AND FALL OF ZIGGY STARDUST AND THE SPIDERS FROM MARS (3rd re-issue) *EMI 5398262* 36 2
28 Sep 02 **EVERYONE SAYS "HI"** *Columbia 6731342* **20** 3
16 Nov 02 BEST OF BOWIE *EMI 5398212* 11 36
12 Jul 03 **JUST FOR ONE DAY (HEROES)** *Virgin DINST 263* [8] **73** 1
27 Sep 03 ● REALITY *Columbia 5125552* 3 4
26 Jun 04 **REBEL NEVER GETS OLD** *Columbia 6750406* **47** 2
9 Oct 04 THE RISE AND FALL OF ZIGGY STARDUST AND THE SPIDERS FROM MARS (4th re-issue) *EMI CDP 7944002* 17 2
19 Nov 05 THE PLATINUM COLLECTION *EMI 3313042* 55 1

[1] Queen and David Bowie [2] David Bowie and Bing Crosby [3] David Bowie and The Pat Metheny Group [4] David Bowie and Mick Jagger [5] David Bowie featuring Al B Sure! [6] David Bowie featuring Lenny Kravitz [7] Scumfrog vs Bowie [8] David Guetta vs Bowie

The 1975 reissue of 1969's 'Space Oddity' was part of a three track single which also included 'Changes' and 'Velvet Goldmine'. Tracks on Breaking Glass (EP): Breaking Glass / Art Decade / Ziggy Stardust. All three versions of 'John, I'm Only Dancing' are different. Tracks on Baal (EP): Baal's Hymn / Remembering Marie A. / Ballad of the Adventurers / The Drowned Girl / Dirty Song.

BOWLING FOR SOUP

US, male vocal / instrumental group (2 Albums: 5 Weeks, **4 Singles: 12 Weeks**)

17 Aug 02 ● **GIRL ALL THE BAD GUYS WANT** *Music for Nations CDKUT 194* **8** 8
7 Sep 02 DRUNK ENOUGH TO DANCE *Music for Nations JIV 418192* 14 4
16 Nov 02 **EMILY** *Music for Nations CDKUT 198* **67** 1
6 Sep 03 **PUNK ROCK 101** *Music for Nations CDKUT 203* **43** 1
25 Sep 04 A HANGOVER YOU DON'T DESERVE *Jive 82876643652* 64 1
16 Oct 04 **1985** *Jive 82876647472* **35** 2

George BOWYER *UK, male vocalist*

22 Aug 98 **GUARDIANS OF THE LAND** *Boys BYSCD 01* **33** 2

21 / 22 June 1957	28 / 29 June 1957	5 / 6 July 1957	12 / 13 July 1957
YES TONIGHT, JOSEPHINE Johnnie Ray	**GAMBLIN' MAN / PUTTIN' ON THE STYLE** Lonnie Donegan and his Skiffle Group	**GAMBLIN' MAN / PUTTIN' ON THE STYLE** Lonnie Donegan and his Skiffle Group	**ALL SHOOK UP** Elvis Presley with The Jordanaires
THE KING AND I Soundtrack	**THE KING AND I** Soundtrack	**THE KING AND I** Soundtrack	**THE KING AND I** Soundtrack

KEY UK No.1 ★ UK Top 10 ● Still on chart + UK entry at No.1 ■ US No.1 ▲ UK million seller £ US million seller $
Singles re-entries are listed as (re), (2re), (3re)... which signifies that the hit re-entered the chart once, twice or three times...
Peak Position / Weeks

BOX CAR RACER
US, male vocal / instrumental group

8 Jun 02 BOX CAR RACER *MCA 1129472* 27 3
6 Jul 02 I FEEL SO *MCA MCSTD 40290* 41 1

The BOX TOPS
US, male vocal (Alex Chilton) / instrumental group (3 Singles: 33 Weeks)

13 Sep 67 ● THE LETTER *Stateside SS 2044* ▲ $ 5 12
20 Mar 68 CRY LIKE A BABY *Bell 1001* $ 15 12
23 Aug 69 SOUL DEEP *Bell 1068* 22 9

BOXCAR WILLIE
US, male vocalist – Lecil Martin, b. 1 Sep 1931, d. 12 Apr 1999

31 May 80 ● KING OF THE ROAD *Warwick WW 5084* 5 12

BOXER REBELLION
UK, male vocal / instrumental group (2 Singles: 2 Weeks)

10 Apr 04 IN PURSUIT *Poptones MC 5088SCD* 57 1
9 Oct 04 CODE RED *Vertigo 9867001* 61 1

BOY GEORGE (see also CULTURE CLUB) *UK, male vocalist – George O'Dowd (5 Albums: 15 Weeks, 13 Singles: 46 Weeks)*

7 Mar 87 ★ EVERYTHING I OWN *Virgin BOY 100* 1 9
6 Jun 87 KEEP ME IN MIND *Virgin BOY 101* 29 4
27 Jun 87 SOLD *Virgin V 2430* 29 6
18 Jul 87 SOLD *Virgin BOY 102* 24 5
21 Nov 87 TO BE REBORN *Virgin BOY 103* 13 7
5 Mar 88 LIVE MY LIFE *Virgin BOY 105* 62 2
18 Jun 88 NO CLAUSE 28 *Virgin BOY 106* 57 3
8 Oct 88 DON'T CRY *Virgin BOY 107* 60 2
4 Mar 89 DON'T TAKE MY MIND ON A TRIP *Virgin BOY 108* 68 2
13 Apr 91 THE MARTYR MANTRAS *More Protein CUMLP 1* [1] 60 1
19 Sep 92 THE CRYING GAME *Spaghetti CIAO 6* 22 4
12 Jun 93 MORE THAN LIKELY *Gee Street GESCD 49* [1] 40 3
2 Oct 93 AT WORST ... THE BEST OF BOY GEORGE AND CULTURE CLUB *Virgin VTCD 19* [2] 24 5
12 Mar 94 THE DEVIL IN SISTER GEORGE *Virgin VSCDG 1490* 26 2
1 Apr 95 FUNTIME *Virgin VSCDG 1538* 45 2
3 Jun 95 CHEAPNESS AND BEAUTY *Virgin CDV 2780* 44 1
1 Jul 95 IL ADORE *Virgin VSCDX 1543* 50 2
21 Oct 95 SAME THING IN REVERSE *Virgin VSCDT 1561* 56 1

[1] PM Dawn featuring Boy George [1] Jesus Loves You [2] Boy George and Culture Club

BOY MEETS GIRL
US, male / female vocal duo – Shannon Rubicam and George Merrill

3 Dec 88 ● WAITING FOR A STAR TO FALL *RCA PB 49519* 9 13
4 Feb 89 REEL LIFE *RCA PL 88414* 74 1

MAX BOYCE
UK, male comedian / vocalist (8 Albums: 105 Weeks)

5 Jul 75 LIVE AT TREORCHY *One Up OU 2033* 21 32
1 Nov 75 ★ WE ALL HAD DOCTORS' PAPERS *EMI MB 101* 1 17
20 Nov 76 ● THE INCREDIBLE PLAN *EMI MB 102* 9 12
7 Jan 78 THE ROAD AND THE MILES *EMI MB 103* 50 3
11 Mar 78 LIVE AT TREORCHY (re-issue) *One Up OU 54043* 42 6
27 May 78 ● I KNOW COS I WAS THERE *EMI MAX 1001* 6 14
13 Oct 79 NOT THAT I'M BIASED *EMI MAX 1002* 27 13
15 Nov 80 ME AND BILLY WILLIAMS *EMI MAX 1003* 37 8

Jimmy BOYD *US, male vocalist (2 Singles: 22 Weeks)*

8 May 53 ● TELL ME A STORY (re) *Philips PB 126* [1] 5 16
27 Nov 53 ● I SAW MOMMY KISSING SANTA CLAUS *Columbia DB 3365* ▲ 3 6

[1] Jimmy Boyd – Frankie Laine

Jacqueline BOYER *France, female vocalist*

28 Apr 60 TOM PILLIBI *Columbia DB 4452* 33 2

The BOYS *UK, male vocal group*

1 Oct 77 THE BOYS *NEMS NEL 6001* 50 1

BOYS TOWN GANG *US, male / female vocal group (3 Singles: 20 Weeks)*

22 Aug 81 AIN'T NO MOUNTAIN HIGH ENOUGH – REMEMBER ME (MEDLEY) *WEA DICK 1* 46 6
31 Jul 82 ● CAN'T TAKE MY EYES OFF YOU *ERC 101* 4 11
9 Oct 82 SIGNED SEALED DELIVERED (I'M YOURS) *ERC 102* 50 3

BOYSTEROUS *UK, male vocal group*

22 Nov 03 UP & DOWN *Square Biz SBR 4* 53 1

BOYZ II MEN
US, male vocal group (6 Albums: 46 Weeks, 12 Singles: 81 Weeks)

5 Sep 92 ★ END OF THE ROAD *Motown TMG 1411* ▲ $ 1 21
31 Oct 92 ● COOLEYHIGHHARMONY *Motown 5300892* 7 18
19 Dec 92 MOTOWNPHILLY *Motown TMG 1402* $ 23 6
27 Feb 93 IN THE STILL OF THE NITE (I'LL REMEMBER) *Motown TMGCD 1415* $ 27 4
3 Sep 94 ● I'LL MAKE LOVE TO YOU (re) *Motown TMGCD 1431* ▲ $ 5 15
24 Sep 94 II *Motown 5304312* ▲ 17 5
26 Nov 94 ON BENDED KNEE *Motown TMGCD 1433* ▲ $ 20 3
22 Apr 95 THANK YOU *Motown TMGCD 1438* 26 3
8 Jul 95 WATER RUNS DRY *Motown TMGCD 1443* 24 3
9 Dec 95 ● ONE SWEET DAY *Columbia 6626035* [1] ▲ $ 6 11
20 Jan 96 HEY LOVER *Def Jam DEFCD 14* [2] $ 17 4
20 Sep 97 ● 4 SEASONS OF LONELINESS *Motown 8606992* ▲ $ 10 6
4 Oct 97 EVOLUTION *Motown 5308222* ▲ 12 5
6 Dec 97 A SONG FOR MAMA *Motown 8607372* $ 34 2
25 Jul 98 CAN'T LET HER GO *Motown 8607952* 23 3
23 Sep 00 NATHAN MICHAEL SHAWN WANYA *Universal 1592812* 54 1
16 Feb 02 ● LEGACY – THE GREATEST HITS COLLECTION *UMTV 168882* 2 15
3 Aug 02 FULL CIRCLE *Arista 7822147412* 56 2

[1] Mariah Carey and Boyz II Men [2] LL Cool J featuring Boyz II Men

BOYZONE 113 Top 500 (see also CHILDLINERS; KEITH 'N' SHANE)
Irish boy band vocal quintet who became international teen idols and the UK's best-selling boyband with total single sales of 6,435,711: Ronan Keating, Stephen Gately, Mikey Graham, Keith Duffy, Shane Lynch. They broke the record for best chart start when they amassed 16 consecutive Top 5 singles. Best-selling single: 'No Matter What' 1,074,192 (5 Albums: 203 Weeks, 16 Singles: 213 Weeks)

10 Dec 94 ● LOVE ME FOR A REASON *Polydor 8512802* 2 13
29 Apr 95 ● KEY TO MY LIFE *Polydor PZCD 342* 3 8
12 Aug 95 ● SO GOOD *Polydor 5797732* 3 6
2 Sep 95 ★ SAID AND DONE *Polydor 5278012* ■ 1 58
25 Nov 95 ● FATHER AND SON *Polydor 5775762* 2 16
9 Mar 96 ● COMING HOME NOW *Polydor 5775702* 4 9
19 Oct 96 ★ WORDS *Polydor 5755372* ■ 1 14
9 Nov 96 ★ A DIFFERENT BEAT *Polydor 5337422* ■ 1 24
14 Dec 96 ★ A DIFFERENT BEAT (2re) *Polydor 5732052* ■ 1 15
22 Mar 97 ● ISN'T IT A WONDER (re) *Polydor 5735472* 2 14
2 Aug 97 ● PICTURE OF YOU *Polydor 5713112* 2 18
6 Dec 97 ● BABY CAN I HOLD YOU / SHOOTING STAR *Polydor 5691672* 2 14
2 May 98 ★ ALL THAT I NEED (re) *Polydor 5698732* ■ 1 14
6 Jun 98 ★ WHERE WE BELONG *Polydor 5573982* ■ 1 55
15 Aug 98 ★ NO MATTER WHAT *Polydor 5675672* ■ £ 1 15
5 Dec 98 ● I LOVE THE WAY YOU LOVE ME *Polydor 5631992* 2 13

	19 / 20 July 1957	26 / 27 July 1957	2 / 3 August 1957	9 / 10 August 1957
UK No.1 SINGLES	ALL SHOOK UP Elvis Presley with The Jordanaires	ALL SHOOK UP Elvis Presley with The Jordanaires	ALL SHOOK UP Elvis Presley with The Jordanaires	ALL SHOOK UP Elvis Presley with The Jordanaires
UK No.1 ALBUMS	THE TOMMY STEELE STORY Tommy Steele	THE TOMMY STEELE STORY Tommy Steele	THE TOMMY STEELE STORY Tommy Steele	THE KING AND I Soundtrack

13 Mar 99 ★ **WHEN THE GOING GETS TOUGH (re)** *Polydor 5699132* ■ 1 16
22 May 99 ★ **YOU NEEDED ME (re)** *Polydor 5639332* ■ 1 15
12 Jun 99 ★ **... BY REQUEST** *Polydor 5475992* ■ 1 57
4 Dec 99 ● **EVERY DAY I LOVE YOU** *Polydor 5615802* 3 13
29 Mar 03 ● **BALLADS – THE LOVE SONG COLLECTION** *Universal TV 0760742* 6 9

BRAD *US, male vocal / instrumental group*

15 May 93 **SHAME** *Epic 4735962* 72 1
26 Jun 93 **20TH CENTURY** *Epic 6592482* 64 1

Scott BRADLEY *UK, male vocalist*

15 Oct 94 **ZOOM** *Hidden Agenda HIDDCD 1* 61 1

Paul BRADY *UK, male vocalist*

6 Apr 91 **TRICK OR TREAT** *Fontana 8484541* 62 1
13 Jan 96 **THE WORLD IS WHAT YOU MAKE IT** *Mercury PBCD 5* 67 1

Billy BRAGG

UK, male vocalist / guitarist (14 Albums: 89 Weeks, 14 Singles: 58 Weeks)

21 Jan 84 **LIFE'S A RIOT WITH SPY VS SPY** *Utility UTIL 1* 30 30
20 Oct 84 **BREWING UP WITH BILLY BRAGG** *Go Discs AGOLP 4* 16 21
16 Mar 85 **BETWEEN THE WARS (EP)** *Go Discs AGOEP 1* 15 6
28 Dec 85 **DAYS LIKE THESE** *Go Discs GOD 8* 43 5
28 Jun 86 **LEVI STUBBS' TEARS** *Go Discs GOD 12* 29 6
4 Oct 86 ● **TALKING WITH THE TAXMAN ABOUT POETRY** *Go Discs AGOLP 6* 8 8
15 Nov 86 **GREETINGS TO THE NEW BRUNETTE** *Go Discs GOD 15* [1] 58 2
13 Jun 87 **BACK TO BASICS** *Go Discs AGOLP 8* 37 4
14 May 88 ★ **SHE'S LEAVING HOME** *Childline CHILD 1* [2] 1 11
10 Sep 88 **WAITING FOR THE GREAT LEAP FORWARDS** *Go Discs GOD 23* 52 3
1 Oct 88 **WORKERS PLAYTIME** *Go Discs AGOLP 15* 17 4
8 Jul 89 **WON'T TALK ABOUT IT** *Go Beat GOD 33* [3] 29 6
12 May 90 **THE INTERNATIONALE** *Utility UTIL 11* 34 4
6 Jul 91 **SEXUALITY** *Go Discs GOD 56* 27 5
7 Sep 91 **YOU WOKE UP MY NEIGHBOURHOOD** *Go Discs GOD 60* 54 2
28 Sep 91 ● **DON'T TRY THIS AT HOME** *Go Discs 8282791* 8 6
29 Feb 92 **ACCIDENT WAITING TO HAPPEN (EP)** *Go Discs GOD 67* 33 3
31 Aug 96 **UPFIELD** *Cooking Vinyl FRYCD 051* 46 1
21 Sep 96 **WILLIAM BLOKE** *Cooking Vinyl COOKCD 100* 16 3
17 May 97 **THE BOY DONE GOOD** *Cooking Vinyl FRYCD 064* 55 1
28 Jun 97 **BLOKE ON BLOKE** *Cooking Vinyl COOKCD 127* 72 1
11 Jul 98 **MERMAID AVENUE** *Elektra 7559622042* [1] 34 2
11 Sep 99 **REACHING TO THE CONVERTED** *Cooking Vinyl COOKCD 186* 41 2
10 Jun 00 **MERMAID AVENUE – VOL.2** *Elektra 7559625222* [1] 61 1
16 Mar 02 **ENGLAND HALF ENGLISH** *Cooking Vinyl COOKCD 222* [2] 51 2
1 Jun 02 **TAKE DOWN THE UNION JACK** *Cooking Vinyl FRYCD 131* [4] 22 2
18 Oct 03 **MUST I PAINT YOU A PICTURE** *Cooking Vinyl COOKCD 266X* 49 1
12 Nov 05 **WE LAUGHED** *Cooking Vinyl FRYCD 252* [5] 11 5

[1] Billy Bragg with Johnny Marr and Kirsty MacColl [2] Billy Bragg with Cara Tivey [3] Norman Cook featuring Billy Bragg [4] Billy Bragg and The Blokes [5] Rosetta Life featuring Billy Bragg [1] Billy Bragg and Wilco [2] Billy Bragg and The Blokes

Tracks on Between the Wars (EP): Between the Wars / Which Side Are You On / World Turned Upside Down / It Says Here. Tracks on Accident Waiting to Happen (EP): Accident Waiting to Happen / Revolution / Sulk / The Warmest Room. 'She's Leaving Home' was listed with the flip side, 'With a Little Help from My Friends' by Wet Wet Wet. 'Won't Talk About It' was listed with the flip side, 'Blame It on the Bassline' by Norman Cook featuring MC Wildski.

The BRAIDS *US, female vocal duo – Zoe Ellis and Caitlin Cornwell*

2 Nov 96 **BOHEMIAN RHAPSODY** *Atlantic A 5640CD* 21 3

BRAIN BASHERS *UK, male / female DJ / production duo*

1 Jul 00 **DO IT NOW** *Tidy Trax TIDY 137CD* 64 1

BRAINBUG *Italy, male producer – Alberto Bertapelle (3 Singles: 8 Weeks)*

3 May 97 **NIGHTMARE** *Positiva CDTIV 76* 11 5
22 Nov 97 **BENEDICTUS / NIGHTMARE** *Positiva CDTIV 86* 24 2
4 Sep 04 **NIGHTMARE** *Positiva 12TIV 200* 63 1

BRAINCHILD (see also CYGNUS X; VERNON'S WONDERLAND)

Germany, male producer – Matthias Hoffmann

30 Oct 99 **SYMMETRY C** *Multiply CDMULTY 55* 31 2

The BRAKES NEW *UK, male vocal / instrumental group*

25 Jun 05 **ALL NIGHT DISCO PARTY** *Rough Trade RTRADSCD 241* 67 1

Wilfrid BRAMBELL and Harry H. CORBETT *UK, male vocal / TV comedy duo – Wilfrid Brambell, b. 22 Mar 1912, d. 18 Jan 1985, and Harry Corbett, b. 28 Feb 1925, d. 21 Mar 1982 (3 Albums: 34 Weeks, 1 Single: 12 Weeks)*

23 Mar 63 ● **STEPTOE AND SON** *Pye NPL 18081* 4 28
28 Nov 63 **STEPTOE AND SON AT BUCKINGHAM PALACE (PARTS 1 & 2)** *Pye 7N 15588* 25 12
11 Jan 64 **STEPTOE AND SON** *Pye GGL 0217* 14 5
14 Mar 64 **MORE JUNK** *Pye NPL 18090* 19 1

The two Steptoe and Son albums are different.

BRAN VAN 3000

Canada, male / female vocal / instrumental group (3 Singles: 15 Weeks)

6 Jun 98 **DRINKING IN L.A.** *Capitol CDCL 802* 34 2
21 Aug 99 ● **DRINKING IN L.A. (re-issue)** *Capitol CDCL 811* 3 11
16 Jun 01 **ASTOUNDED** *Virgin VUSCD 194* [1] 40 2

[1] Bran Van 3000 featuring Curtis Mayfield

BRANCACCIO & AISHER

UK, male production duo – Luke Brancaccio and Bruce Aisher

16 Mar 02 **IT'S GONNA BE ... (A LOVELY DAY)** *Credence CDCRED 017* 40 2

Michelle BRANCH

US, female vocalist (2 Albums: 5 Weeks, 4 Singles: 18 Weeks)

13 Apr 02 **EVERYWHERE** *Maverick W 577CDX* 18 6
27 Apr 02 **THE SPIRIT ROOM** *Maverick 9362480972* 54 2
3 Aug 02 **ALL YOU WANTED** *Maverick W 585CDX* 33 2
23 Nov 02 **THE GAME OF LOVE** *Arista 74321959442* [1] 16 8
12 Jul 03 **ARE YOU HAPPY NOW?** *Maverick W 613CD* 31 2
19 Jul 03 **HOTEL PAPER** *Maverick / Warner Bros. MAV 484262* 35 3

[1] Santana featuring Michelle Branch

BRAND NEW *US, male vocal / instrumental group (2 Singles: 3 Weeks)*

14 Feb 04 **SIC TRANSIT GLORIA GLORY FADES** *Sore Point SORE 011CDS* 37 2
29 May 04 **THE QUIET THINGS THAT NO ONE EVER KNOWS** *Sore Point SORE 014CDS* 39 1

The BRAND NEW HEAVIES 419 Top 500

Sophisticated funk / 'acid jazz' band, formed 1985 in London, UK. Remaining original members Simon Bartholomew (g), Andrew Levy (b) and Jan Kincaid (d/v) had vocal assistance on their hits from US females N'dea Davenport (1991-95), Siedah Garrett (1997-98) and Carleen Anderson (1999-2000) (6 Albums: 103 Weeks, 17 Singles: 69 Weeks)

5 Oct 91 **NEVER STOP** *ffrr F 165* 43 3
15 Feb 92 **DREAM COME TRUE** *ffrr F 180* 24 4
14 Mar 92 **BRAND NEW HEAVIES** *London 8283002* 25 16
18 Apr 92 **ULTIMATE TRUNK FUNK (EP)** *ffrr F 185* 19 6
1 Aug 92 **DON'T LET IT GO TO YOUR HEAD** *ffrr BNH 1* 24 4
5 Sep 92 **HEAVY RHYME EXPERIENCE: VOL.1** *Acid Jazz 8283352* 38 2
19 Dec 92 **STAY THIS WAY** *ffrr BNH 2* 40 5
26 Mar 94 **DREAM ON DREAMER** *ffrr BNHCD 3* 15 4
16 Apr 94 ● **BROTHER SISTER** *ffrr 8284902* 4 48

16 / 17 August 1957	23 / 24 August 1957	30 / 31 August 1957	6 / 7 September 1957
ALL SHOOK UP Elvis Presley with The Jordanaires	**ALL SHOOK UP** Elvis Presley with The Jordanaires	**DIANA** Paul Anka	**DIANA** Paul Anka
THE KING AND I Soundtrack	**THE KING AND I** Soundtrack	**THE TOMMY STEELE STORY** Tommy Steele	**LOVING YOU (Soundtrack)** Elvis Presley

KEY: UK No.1 ★ UK Top 10 ● Still on chart + UK entry at No.1 ■ US No.1 ▲ UK million seller £ US million seller $
Singles re-entries are listed as (re), (2re), (3re)... which signifies that the hit re-entered the chart once, twice or three times...
Peak Position / Weeks

Date	Title / Label	Peak	Weeks
11 Jun 94	**BACK TO LOVE** *ffrr BNHCD 4*	23	4
13 Aug 94	**MIDNIGHT AT THE OASIS** *ffrr BNHCD 5*	13	6
5 Nov 94	**SPEND SOME TIME** *ffrr BNHCD 6*	26	4
12 Nov 94	ORIGINAL FLAVA *Acid Jazz JAZIDCD 114*	64	1
11 Mar 95	**CLOSE TO YOU** *ffrr BNHCD 7*	38	3
12 Apr 97	**SOMETIMES** *ffrr BNHCD 8*	11	5
3 May 97 ●	SHELTER *ffrr 8288872*	5	33
28 Jun 97	**YOU ARE THE UNIVERSE** *ffrr GNHCD 9*	21	4
18 Oct 97 ●	**YOU'VE GOT A FRIEND** *London BNHCD 10*	9	8
10 Jan 98	**SHELTER** *London BNHCD 11*	31	4
11 Sep 99	**SATURDAY NITE** *ffrr BNHCD12*	35	2
25 Sep 99	TRUNK FUNK – THE BEST OF THE BRAND NEW HEAVIES *ffrr 3984291642*	13	3
29 Jan 00	**APPARENTLY NOTHING** *ffrr BNHCD 13*	32	2
23 Oct 04	**BOOGIE** *Onetwo TBNHCDS 001* [1]	66	1

[1] The Brand New Heavies featuring Nicole Russo

The first 10 hits are credited 'featuring N'Dea Davenport' on either the sleeve or the label. Tracks on Ultimate Trunk Funk (EP): Never Stop / Stay This Way / Mr Tanaka. 'Stay This Way' is a re-mixed version of the track on the Ultimate Trunk Funk EP.

BRAND X *UK, male vocal / instrumental group (2 Albums: 6 Weeks)*

Date	Title / Label	Peak	Weeks
21 May 77	MOROCCAN ROLL *Charisma CAS 1126*	37	5
11 Sep 82	IS THERE ANYTHING ABOUT? *CBS 85967*	93	1

Johnny BRANDON with The PHANTOMS
UK, male vocalist and instrumental group (2 Singles: 12 Weeks)

Date	Title / Label	Peak	Weeks
11 Mar 55 ●	**TOMORROW (re)** *Polygon P 1131* [1]	8	8
1 Jul 55	**DON'T WORRY** *Polygon P 1163*	18	4

[1] Johnny Brandon with The Phantoms and The Norman Warren Music

BRANDY (460 Top 500) *US, female vocalist / actor – Brandy Norwood (4 Albums: 54 Weeks, 14 Singles: 104 Weeks)*

Date	Title / Label	Peak	Weeks
10 Dec 94	**I WANNA BE DOWN** *Atlantic A 7217CD*	44	3
3 Jun 95	**I WANNA BE DOWN** (re-mix) *Atlantic A 7186CD*	36	3
3 Feb 96	**SITTIN' UP IN MY ROOM** *Arista 74321344012* $	30	4
6 Jun 98 ●	**THE BOY IS MINE** *Atlantic AT 0036CD* [1] ▲ $	2	20
20 Jun 98	NEVER S-A-Y NEVER *Atlantic 7567830392*	19	31
10 Oct 98 ●	**TOP OF THE WORLD (re)** *Atlantic AT 0046CD* [2]	2	9
12 Dec 98	**HAVE YOU EVER?** *Atlantic AT 0058CD* ▲	13	8
19 Jun 99	**ALMOST DOESN'T COUNT** *Atlantic AT 0068CD1*	15	5
16 Jun 01 ●	**ANOTHER DAY IN PARADISE** *WEA WEA 327CD1* [3]	5	10
23 Feb 02 ●	**WHAT ABOUT US? (re)** *Atlantic AT 0125CD*	4	11
9 Mar 02 ●	FULL MOON *Atlantic 7567931102*	9	15
15 Jun 02	**FULL MOON** (import) *Atlantic 7567853092*	72	1
29 Jun 02	**FULL MOON** *Atlantic AT 130CD*	15	9
26 Jun 04 ●	**TALK ABOUT OUR LOVE** *Atlantic AT 017CD* [4]	6	10
10 Jul 04	AFRODISIAC *Atlantic 7567836332*	32	4
16 Oct 04	**AFRODISIAC** *Atlantic AT 0183CD*	11	8
2 Apr 05	**WHO IS SHE 2 U** *Atlantic AT 0192CD*	50	3
9 Apr 05	THE BEST OF BRANDY *Atlantic 8122746612*	24	4

[1] Brandy and Monica [2] Brandy featuring Ma$e [3] Brandy and Ray J [4] Brandy featuring Kanye West

Laura BRANIGAN *US, female vocalist, b. 3 Jul 1957, d. 26 Aug 2004 (2 Albums: 18 Weeks, 3 Singles: 33 Weeks)*

Date	Title / Label	Peak	Weeks
18 Dec 82 ●	**GLORIA** *Atlantic K 11759* $	6	13
7 Jul 84 ●	**SELF CONTROL** *Atlantic A 9676*	5	17
18 Aug 84	SELF CONTROL *Atlantic 780147*	16	14
6 Oct 84	**THE LUCKY ONE** *Atlantic A 9636*	56	3
24 Aug 85	HOLD ME *Atlantic 7812651*	64	4

BRASS CONSTRUCTION *US, male vocal / instrumental group (2 Albums: 12 Weeks, 9 Singles: 35 Weeks)*

Date	Title / Label	Peak	Weeks
20 Mar 76 ●	BRASS CONSTRUCTION *United Artists UAS 29923*	9	11
3 Apr 76	**MOVIN'** *United Artists UP 36090*	23	6
5 Feb 77	**HA CHA CHA (FUNKTION)** *United Artists UP 36205*	37	5
26 Jan 80	**MUSIC MAKES YOU FEEL LIKE DANCING** *United Artists UP 615*	39	6
28 May 83	**WALKIN' THE LINE** *Capitol CL 292*	47	3
16 Jul 83	**WE CAN WORK IT OUT** *Capitol CL 299*	70	2
30 Jun 84	RENEGADES *Capitol EJ 240160*	94	1
7 Jul 84	**PARTYLINE** *Capitol CL 335*	56	4
27 Oct 84	**INTERNATIONAL** *Capitol CL 341*	70	2
9 Nov 85	**GIVE AND TAKE** *Capitol CL 377*	62	3
28 May 88	**MOVIN' 1988** (re-mix) *Syncopate SY 11*	24	4

BRAT *UK, male vocalist – Roger Kitter*

Date	Title / Label	Peak	Weeks
10 Jul 82	**CHALK DUST – THE UMPIRE STRIKES BACK** *Hansa SMASH 1*	19	8

BRATZ ROCK ANGELZ NEW
US, female doll vocal / instrumental group

Date	Title / Label	Peak	Weeks
15 Oct 05	**SO GOOD** *Universal 9885280*	23	7
22 Oct 05	BRATZ ROCK ANGELZ *Universal 9884259*	42	4

BRAUND REYNOLDS NEW *UK, male vocal / instrumental group*

Date	Title / Label	Peak	Weeks
17 Dec 05	**ROCKET (A NATURAL GAMBLER)** *Virgin TENCDX 504*	27	3+

BRAVADO *UK, male / female vocal / instrumental group*

Date	Title / Label	Peak	Weeks
18 Jun 94	**HARMONICA MAN** *Peach PEACHCD 5*	37	3

The BRAVERY NEW *US, male vocal (Sam Endicott) / instrumental group (1 Album: 11 Weeks, 3 Singles: 12 Weeks)*

Date	Title / Label	Peak	Weeks
12 Mar 05 ●	**AN HONEST MISTAKE (re)** *Loog 9880300*	7	10
26 Mar 05 ●	THE BRAVERY *Loog 9880499*	5	11
4 Jun 05	**FEARLESS** *Loog 9882338*	43	1
10 Sep 05	**UNCONDITIONAL** *Loog 9885197*	49	1

BRAVO ALL STARS
UK / US, male / female vocal / instrumental group

Date	Title / Label	Peak	Weeks
29 Aug 98	**LET THE MUSIC HEAL YOUR SOUL** *Edel 0039335 ERE*	36	2

Artists featured: Backstreet Boys, Aaron Carter, Scooter, 'N Sync, Caught in the Act, The Boyz, Blumchen, Gil, Squeezer, Mr President, Touche, R'N'G and The Moffatts.

Alan BRAXE and Fred FALKE *France, male production duo*

Date	Title / Label	Peak	Weeks
25 Nov 00	**INTRO** *Vulture / Credence CDCRED 006*	35	3

Dhar BRAXTON *US, female vocalist*

Date	Title / Label	Peak	Weeks
31 May 86	**JUMP BACK (SET ME FREE)** *Fourth & Broadway BRW 47*	32	8

Toni BRAXTON (309 Top 500) *Sultry, sexy soul / R&B vocalist, b. 7 Oct 1968, Maryland, US, who won Best New Artist Grammy in 1993 and was one of America's top-selling pop and R&B artists of the 1990s. Her biggest hits have been ballads from the pens of top writers Babyface, Diane Warren, R Kelly and Rodney Jerkins. Biggest-selling single: 'Un-Break My Heart' 770,000 (4 Albums: 136 Weeks, 11 Singles: 86 Weeks)*

Date	Title / Label	Peak	Weeks
18 Sep 93	**ANOTHER SAD LOVE SONG** *LaFace 74321163502*	51	2
15 Jan 94 ●	**BREATHE AGAIN** *LaFace 74321185442*	2	12
29 Jan 94 ●	TONI BRAXTON *LaFace 74321162682* ▲	4	33
2 Apr 94	**ANOTHER SAD LOVE SONG** (re-issue) *LaFace 74321196682*	15	8
9 Jul 94	**YOU MEAN THE WORLD TO ME** *LaFace 74321214702*	30	5
3 Dec 94	**LOVE SHOULDA BROUGHT YOU HOME** *LaFace 74321249412*	33	3
29 Jun 96 ●	SECRETS *LaFace 73008260202*	10	81
13 Jul 96 ●	**YOU'RE MAKIN' ME HIGH** *LaFace 74321395402* ▲ $	7	11
2 Nov 96 ●	**UN-BREAK MY HEART** *LaFace 74321410632* ▲ $	2	19
24 May 97 ●	**I DON'T WANT TO** *LaFace 74321468612*	9	8

	13 / 14 September 1957	20 / 21 September 1957	27 / 28 September 1957	4 / 5 October 1957
UK No.1 SINGLES	DIANA Paul Anka	DIANA Paul Anka	DIANA Paul Anka	DIANA Paul Anka
UK No.1 ALBUMS	LOVING YOU (Soundtrack) Elvis Presley	A SWINGIN' AFFAIR! Frank Sinatra	A SWINGIN' AFFAIR! Frank Sinatra	A SWINGIN' AFFAIR! Frank Sinatra

8 Nov 97	HOW COULD AN ANGEL BREAK MY HEART *LaFace 74321531982* [1]	22	4
29 Apr 00 ●	HE WASN'T MAN ENOUGH *LaFace 74321757852*	5	11
6 May 00 ●	THE HEAT *LaFace 73008260692*	3	19
8 Mar 03	HIT THE FREEWAY *LaFace / Arista 82876506372*	29	3
15 Nov 03	ULTIMATE *Arista 82876574852*	23	3

[1] Toni Braxton with Kenny G

The BRAXTONS *US, female vocal group (3 Singles: 7 Weeks)*

1 Feb 97	SO MANY WAYS *Atlantic A 5469CD*	32	2
29 Mar 97	THE BOSS *Atlantic A 5441CD*	31	3
19 Jul 97	SLOW FLOW *Atlantic AT 0001CD*	26	2

BREAD 269 Top 500

Internationally popular soft-rock group whose initial line-up was David Gates (v/g/k), James Griffin (g) (d. 2005), Robb Royner (g) and Jim Gordon (d). Los Angeles formed quartet wrote and orignally recorded No.1 hits 'If' and 'Everything I Own' (8 Albums: 198 Weeks, 5 Singles: 46 Weeks)

1 Aug 70 ●	MAKE IT WITH YOU *Elektra 2101 010* ▲ $	5	14
26 Sep 70	ON THE WATERS *Elektra 2469005*	34	5
15 Jan 72	BABY I'M-A WANT YOU *Elektra K 12033* $	14	10
18 Mar 72 ●	BABY I'M-A WANT YOU *Elektra K 42100*	9	19
29 Apr 72	EVERYTHING I OWN *Elektra K 12041*	32	6
30 Sep 72	THE GUITAR MAN *Elektra K 12066*	16	9
28 Oct 72 ●	THE BEST OF BREAD *Elektra K 42115*	7	100
27 Jul 74	THE BEST OF BREAD VOLUME 2 *Elektra K 42161*	48	1
25 Dec 76	LOST WITHOUT YOUR LOVE *Elektra K 12241*	27	7
29 Jan 77	LOST WITHOUT YOUR LOVE *Elektra K 52044*	17	6
5 Nov 77 ★	THE SOUND OF BREAD *Elektra K 52062*	1	46
28 Nov 87	THE VERY BEST OF BREAD *Telstar STAR 2303*	84	2
5 Jul 97 ●	ESSENTIALS *Jive 9548354082* [1]	9	19

[1] David Gates and Bread

BREAK MACHINE
US, male vocal group (1 Album: 16 Weeks, 3 Singles: 32 Weeks)

4 Feb 84 ●	STREET DANCE *Record Shack SOHO 13*	3	14
12 May 84 ●	BREAK DANCE PARTY (re) *Record Shack SOHO 20*	9	10
9 Jun 84	BREAK MACHINE *Record Shack SOHOLP 3*	17	16
11 Aug 84	ARE YOU READY? *Record Shack SOHO 24*	27	8

BREAKBEAT ERA *UK, male / female drum and bass trio (1 Album: 2 Weeks, 3 Singles: 5 Weeks)*

18 Jul 98	BREAKBEAT ERA *XL Recordings XLS 95CD*	38	2
21 Aug 99	ULTRA – OBSCENE *XL Recordings XLS 107CD*	48	2
11 Sep 99	ULTRA OBSCENE *XL Recordings XLCD 130*	31	2
11 Mar 00	BULLITPROOF *XL Recordings XLS 115CD*	65	1

BREAKFAST CLUB
US, male vocal / instrumental group

27 Jun 87	RIGHT ON TRACK *MCA MCA 1146*	54	3

Julian BREAM *UK, male instrumentalist – guitarist / lute*

27 Apr 96	THE ULTIMATE GUITAR COLLECTION *RCA Victor 74321337052*	66	2

BREATHE *UK, male vocal (David Glasper) / instrumental group (1 Album: 5 Weeks, 4 Singles: 27 Weeks)*

30 Jul 88 ●	HANDS TO HEAVEN *Siren SRN 68*	4	12
8 Oct 88	ALL THAT JAZZ *Siren SRNLP 12*	22	5
22 Oct 88	JONAH *Siren SRN 95*	60	3
3 Dec 88	HOW CAN I FALL? *Siren SRN 102*	48	7
11 Mar 89	DON'T TELL ME LIES *Siren SRN 109*	45	5

Freddy BRECK *Germany, male vocalist*

13 Apr 74	SO IN LOVE WITH YOU *Decca F 13481*	44	4

The BRECKER BROTHERS
US, male vocal / instrumental duo – Randy and Michael Brecker

4 Nov 78	EAST RIVER *Arista ARIST 211*	34	5

BREED 77 *Gibraltar, male vocal / instrumental group (1 Album: 1 Week, 3 Singles: 5 Weeks)*

1 May 04	THE RIVER *Albert Productions JASCDUK 007*	39	2
15 May 04	CULTURA *Albert Productions JASCDUK 008*	61	1
7 Aug 04	WORLD'S ON FIRE *Albert Productions JASCDUK 011*	43	2
5 Feb 05	SHADOWS *Albert Productions JASCDUK 013*	42	1

The BREEDERS (see also PIXIES; THROWING MUSES) *US / UK, female / male vocal / instrumental group (3 Albums: 9 Weeks, 5 Singles: 7 Weeks)*

9 Jun 90	POD *4AD CAD 0006*	22	3
18 Apr 92	SAFARI (EP) *4AD BAD 2003*	69	1
21 Aug 93	CANNONBALL (EP) *4AD BAD 3011CD*	40	3
11 Sep 93 ●	LAST SPLASH *4AD CAD 3014CD*	5	5
6 Nov 93	DIVINE HAMMER *4AD BAD 3017CD*	59	1
23 Jul 94	HEAD TO TOE (EP) *4AD BADD 4012*	68	1
1 Jun 02	TITLE TK *4AD CAD 2205CD*	51	1
14 Sep 02	SON OF THREE *4AD BAD 2213CD*	72	1

Tracks on Safari (EP): Do You Love Me Now / Don't Call Home / Safari / So Sad About Us. Tracks on Cannonball (EP): Cannonball / Cro-Aloha / Lord of the Thighs / 900. Tracks on Head to Toe (EP): Head to Toe / Shocker in Gloom Town / Freed Pig.

BREEKOUT KREW *US, male vocal duo*

24 Nov 84	MATT'S MOOD *London LON 59*	51	3

Ann BREEN *Ireland, female vocalist*

19 Mar 83	PAL OF MY CRADLE DAYS (re) *Homespun HS 052*	69	2

Jo BREEZER *UK, female vocalist*

13 Oct 01	VENUS AND MARS *Columbia 6717612*	27	2

BRENDON *UK, male vocalist – Brendon Dunning*

19 Mar 77	GIMME SOME *Magnet MAG 80*	14	9

Maire BRENNAN (see also CLANNAD)
Ireland, female vocalist (1 Album: 2 Weeks, 2 Singles: 12 Weeks)

16 May 92	AGAINST THE WIND *RCA PB 45399*	64	2
13 Jun 92	MAIRE *RCA PD 75358*	53	2
5 Jun 99 ●	SALTWATER *Xtravaganza XTRAV 1CDS* [1]	6	10

[1] Chicane featuring Maire Brennan of Clannad

Rose BRENNAN *Ireland, female vocalist*

7 Dec 61	TALL DARK STRANGER *Philips PB 1193*	31	9

Walter BRENNAN *US, male vocalist, b. 25 Jul 1894, d. 21 Sep 1974*

28 Jun 62	OLD RIVERS *Liberty LIB 55436*	38	3

Tony BRENT *UK, male vocalist – Reginald Bretagne, b. 26 Aug 1927, d. 19 Jun 1993 (8 Singles: 52 Weeks)*

19 Dec 52 ●	WALKIN' TO MISSOURI (re) *Columbia DB 3147*	7	7
2 Jan 53 ●	MAKE IT SOON (re) *Columbia DB 3187*	9	7
23 Jan 53	GOT YOU ON MY MIND *Columbia DB 3226*	12	1
30 Nov 56	CINDY, OH CINDY (re) *Columbia DB 3844*	16	7
28 Jun 57	DARK MOON *Columbia DB 3950*	17	14
28 Feb 58	THE CLOUDS WILL SOON ROLL BY (re) *Columbia DB 4066*	20	5
5 Sep 58	GIRL OF MY DREAMS *Columbia DB 4177*	16	7
24 Jul 59	WHY SHOULD I BE LONELY? *Columbia DB 4304*	24	4

Bernard BRESSLAW
(see also Michael MEDWIN, Bernard BRESSLAW, Alfie BASS and Leslie FYSON) *UK, male comedian / actor / vocalist, b. 25 Feb 1934, d. 11 Jun 1993*

5 Sep 58 ●	MAD PASSIONATE LOVE *HMV POP 522*	6	11

11 / 12 October 1957	18 / 19 October 1957	25 / 26 October 1957	1 / 2 November 1957
DIANA Paul Anka	DIANA Paul Anka	DIANA Paul Anka	THAT'LL BE THE DAY The Crickets
A SWINGIN' AFFAIR! Frank Sinatra	A SWINGIN' AFFAIR! Frank Sinatra	A SWINGIN' AFFAIR! Frank Sinatra	A SWINGIN' AFFAIR! Frank Sinatra

KEY
UK No.1 ★ UK Top 10 ● Still on chart + UK entry at No.1 ■
US No.1 ▲ UK million seller £ US million seller $
Singles re-entries are listed as (re), (2re), (3re)... which signifies that the hit re-entered the chart once, twice or three times...

Peak Position / Weeks

Adrian BRETT *UK, male flute player*

10 Nov 79 ECHOES OF GOLD *Warwick WW 5062* ... 19 11

Paul BRETT *UK, male guitarist*

19 Jul 80 ROMANTIC GUITAR *K-Tel ONE 1079* ... 24 7

Teresa BREWER
US, female vocalist – Theresa Breuer (5 Singles: 53 Weeks)

11 Feb 55 ● **LET ME GO LOVER** *Vogue / Coral Q 72043* [1] ... 9 10
13 Apr 56 ● **A TEAR FELL** *Vogue / Coral Q 72146* ... 2 15
13 Jul 56 ● **A SWEET OLD FASHIONED GIRL** *Vogue / Coral Q 72172* ... 3 15
10 May 57 **NORA MALONE** *Vogue / Coral Q 72224* ... 26 2
23 Jun 60 **HOW DO YOU KNOW IT'S LOVE** *Coral Q 72396* ... 21 11

[1] Teresa Brewer with The Lancers

BRIAN and MICHAEL
UK, male vocal duo – Kevin Parrott and Michael Coleman

25 Feb 78 ★ **MATCHSTALK MEN AND MATCHSTALK CATS AND DOGS (LOWRY'S SONG)** *Pye 7N 46035* ... 1 19

Hit features backing vocals by St Winifred's School Choir.

BRICK *US, male vocal / instrumental group*

5 Feb 77 **DAZZ** *Bang 004* ... 36 4

Edie BRICKELL and The NEW BOHEMIANS *US, female / male vocal / instrumental group (3 Albums: 19 Weeks, 3 Singles: 10 Weeks)*

4 Feb 89 SHOOTING RUBBERBANDS AT THE STARS *Geffen WX 215* ... 25 17
4 Feb 89 **WHAT I AM** *Geffen GEF 49* ... 31 7
27 May 89 **CIRCLE** *Geffen GEF 51* ... 74 1
10 Nov 90 GHOST OF A DOG *Geffen WX 386* ... 63 1
3 Sep 94 PICTURE PERFECT MORNING *Geffen GED 24715* [1] ... 59 1
1 Oct 94 **GOOD TIMES** *Geffen GFSTD 78* [1] ... 40 2

[1] Edie Brickell [1] Edie Brickell

Alicia BRIDGES *US, female vocalist (2 Singles: 11 Weeks)*

11 Nov 78 **I LOVE THE NIGHTLIFE (DISCO 'ROUND)** *Polydor 2066 936* $ .. 32 10
8 Oct 94 **I LOVE THE NIGHTLIFE (DISCO 'ROUND)** (re-mix) *Mother MUMCD 57* ... 61 1

The BRIGHOUSE and RASTRICK BRASS BAND
UK, male brass band

12 Nov 77 ● **THE FLORAL DANCE** *Transatlantic BIG 548* ... 2 13
28 Jan 78 ● FLORAL DANCE *Logo 1001* ... 10 11

Bette BRIGHT *UK, female vocalist*

8 Mar 80 **HELLO, I AM YOUR HEART** *Korova KOW 3* ... 50 5

BRIGHT EYES NEW *US, male vocalist / guitarist – Conor Oberst (2 Albums: 4 Weeks, 2 Singles: 4 Weeks)*

5 Feb 05 I'M WIDE AWAKE IT'S MORNING *Saddle Creek SCE 72CD* ... 23 3
5 Feb 05 DIGITAL ASH IN A DIGITAL URN *Saddle Creek SCE 73CD* ... 43 1
2 Apr 05 **FIRST DAY OF MY LIFE** *Saddle Creek SCE 79CD* ... 37 3
6 Aug 05 **EASY / LUCKY / FREE** *Saddle Creek SCE 84CD* ... 42 1

Sarah BRIGHTMAN
UK, female vocalist (5 Albums: 31 Weeks, 13 Singles: 98 Weeks)

11 Nov 78 ● **I LOST MY HEART TO A STARSHIP TROOPER** *Ariola / Hansa AHA 527* [1] ... 6 14
7 Apr 79 **THE ADVENTURES OF THE LOVE CRUSADER** *Ariola / Hansa AHA 538* [2] ... 53 5
30 Jul 83 **HIM** *Polydor POSP 625* [3] ... 55 4
23 Mar 85 ● **PIE JESU** *HMV WEBBER 1* [4] ... 3 8
11 Jan 86 ● **THE PHANTOM OF THE OPERA** *Polydor POSP 800* [5] ... 7 10
4 Oct 86 ● **ALL I ASK OF YOU** *Polydor POSP 802* [6] ... 3 16
10 Jan 87 ● **WISHING YOU WERE SOMEHOW HERE AGAIN** *Polydor POSP 803* ... 7 11
17 Jun 89 THE SONGS THAT GOT AWAY *Really Useful 839116 1* ... 48 2
11 Jul 92 **AMIGOS PARA SIEMPRE (FRIENDS FOR LIFE)** *Really Useful RUR 10* [7] ... 11 11
8 Aug 92 AMIGOS PARA SIEMPRE *East West 4509902562* [1] ... 53 4
11 Nov 95 THE UNEXPECTED SONGS – SURRENDER *Really Useful 5277022* ... 45 2
24 May 97 ● **TIME TO SAY GOODBYE (CON TE PARTIRO)** *Coalition COLA 003CD* [8] ... 2 14
14 Jun 97 ● TIMELESS *Coalition 630191812* ... 2 21
23 Aug 97 **WHO WANTS TO LIVE FOREVER** *Coalition COLA 014CD* ... 45 1
6 Dec 97 **JUST SHOW ME HOW TO LOVE YOU** *Coalition COLA 035CD* [9] ... 54 2
14 Feb 98 **STARSHIP TROOPERS** *Coalition COLA 040CD* ... 58 1
13 Feb 99 **EDEN** *Coalition COLA 065CD* ... 68 1
20 Jan 01 LA LUNA *East West 8573859152* ... 37 2

[1] Sarah Brightman and Hot Gossip [2] Sarah Brightman and the Starship Troopers [3] Sarah Brightman and the London Philharmonic [4] Sarah Brightman and Paul Miles-Kingston [5] Sarah Brightman and Steve Harley [6] Cliff Richard and Sarah Brightman [7] José Carreras and Sarah Brightman [8] Sarah Brightman and Andrea Bocelli [9] Sarah Brightman and the LSO featuring José Cura
[1] José Carreras and Sarah Brightman

The listed flip side of 'Wishing You Were Somehow Here Again' was 'The Music of the Night' by Michael Crawford. COLA 040CD is a dance re-mix of AHA 527.

BRIGHTON AND HOVE ALBION FC
UK, male football team vocalists

28 May 83 **THE BOYS IN THE OLD BRIGHTON BLUE** *Energy NRG 2* ... 65 2

BRILLIANT *UK, male / female vocal / instrumental group (1 Album: 1 Week, 3 Singles: 13 Weeks)*

19 Oct 85 **IT'S A MAN'S MAN'S MAN'S WORLD** *Food FOOD 5* ... 58 5
22 Mar 86 **LOVE IS WAR** *Food FOOD 6* ... 64 4
2 Aug 86 **SOMEBODY** *Food FOOD 7* ... 67 4
20 Sep 86 KISS THE LIPS OF LIFE *Food BRILL 1* ... 83 1

Danielle BRISEBOIS *US, female vocalist*

9 Sep 95 **GIMME LITTLE SIGN** *Epic 6610782* ... 75 1

Johnny BRISTOL *US, male vocalist, b. 3 Feb 1939, d. 21 Mar 2004 (1 Album: 7 Weeks, 2 Singles: 16 Weeks)*

24 Aug 74 ● **HANG ON IN THERE BABY** *MGM 2006 443* ... 3 11
5 Oct 74 HANG ON IN THERE BABY *MGM 2315 303* ... 12 7
19 Jul 80 **MY GUY – MY GIRL (MEDLEY)** *Atlantic / Hansa K 11550* [1] ... 39 5

[1] Amii Stewart and Johnny Bristol

BRIT PACK *UK / Ireland, male vocal group*

12 Feb 00 **SET ME FREE** *When! WENX 2000* ... 41 2

BRITISH SEA POWER
UK, male vocal / instrumental group (2 Albums: 5 Weeks, 4 Singles: 7 Weeks)

14 Jun 03 THE DECLINE OF BRITISH SEA POWER *Rough Trade RTRADCD 065* ... 54 1
12 Jul 03 **CARRION / APOLOGIES TO INSECT LIFE** *Rough Trade RTRADSCD 092* ... 36 1
1 Nov 03 **REMEMBER ME** *Rough Trade RTRADSCD 125* ... 30 2
2 Apr 05 **IT ENDED ON AN OILY STAGE** *Rough Trade RTRADSCDX 220* .. 18 3
16 Apr 05 OPEN SEASON *Rough Trade RTRADCD 200* ... 13 4
4 Jun 05 **PLEASE STAND UP** *Rough Trade RTRADSCDX 242* ... 34 1

BRITISH WHALE NEW (see also The DARKNESS)
UK, male vocalist / instrumentalist – Justin Hawkins

27 Aug 05 ● **THIS TOWN AIN'T BIG ENOUGH FOR BOTH OF US** *Atlantic ATUK 011CD* 6 4

BROCK LANDARS
UK, male vocal / production duo

11 Jul 98 **S.M.D.U.** *Parlophone CDBLUE 001* 49 2

BROCKIE & ED SOLO *UK, male producers*

24 Apr 04 **SYSTEM CHECK** *Undiluted UD 010* 68 1

BROKEN ENGLISH (see also John WAITE)
UK, male vocal / instrumental group (2 Singles: 13 Weeks)

30 May 87 **COMIN' ON STRONG** *EMI EM 5* 18 10
3 Oct 87 **LOVE ON THE SIDE** *EMI EM 55* 69 3

June BRONHILL and Thomas ROUND
Australia / UK, female / male vocal duo

18 Jun 60 LILAC TIME *HMV CLP 1248* 17 1

BRONSKI BEAT (see also The COMMUNARDS) *UK, male vocal (Jimmy Somerville) / instrumental group (4 Albums: 69 Weeks, 8 Singles: 78 Weeks)*

2 Jun 84 ● **SMALLTOWN BOY** *Forbidden Fruit BITE 1* 3 13
22 Sep 84 ● **WHY?** *Forbidden Fruit BITE 2* 6 10
20 Oct 84 ● THE AGE OF CONSENT *Forbidden Fruit BITLP 1* 4 53
1 Dec 84 **IT AIN'T NECESSARILY SO** *Forbidden Fruit BITE 3* 16 11
20 Apr 85 ● **I FEEL LOVE (MEDLEY)** *Forbidden Fruit BITE 4* [1] 3 12
21 Sep 85 HUNDREDS AND THOUSANDS *Forbidden Fruit BITLP 2* 24 6
30 Nov 85 ● **HIT THAT PERFECT BEAT** *Forbidden Fruit BITE 6* 3 14
29 Mar 86 **COME ON, COME ON** *Forbidden Fruit BITE 7* 20 7
10 May 86 TRUTHDARE DOUBLEDARE *Forbidden Fruit BITLP 3* 18 6
1 Jul 89 **CHA CHA HEELS** *Arista 112331* [2] 32 7
2 Feb 91 **SMALLTOWN BOY** (re-mix) *London LON 287* [3] 32 4
22 Sep 01 THE VERY BEST OF JIMMY SOMERVILLE, BRONSKI BEAT AND THE COMMUNARDS *London 927412582* [1] 29 4

[1] Bronski Beat and Marc Almond [2] Eartha Kitt and Bronski Beat [3] Jimmy Somerville with Bronski Beat [1] Jimmy Somerville, Bronski Beat and The Communards

Tracks on I Feel Love (medley): I Feel Love / Love to Love You Baby / Johnny Remember Me.

The BRONX
US, male vocal / instrumental group (2 Singles: 2 Weeks)

24 Apr 04 **THEY WILL KILL US ALL** *Wichita Recordings WEBB 0603CD* 65 1
17 Jul 04 **FALSE ALARM** *Wichita Recordings WEBB 062SCD* 73 1

Jet BRONX and The FORBIDDEN
UK, male vocal / instrumental group – featuring TV presenter Loyd Grossman

17 Dec 77 **AIN'T DOIN' NOTHIN'** *Lightning LIG 50* 49 1

The BROOK BROTHERS
UK, male vocal duo – Geoff and Ricky Brook (5 Singles: 35 Weeks)

30 Mar 61 ● **WARPAINT** *Pye 7N 15333* 5 14
24 Aug 61 **AIN'T GONNA WASH FOR A WEEK** *Pye 7N 15369* 13 10
25 Jan 62 **HE'S OLD ENOUGH TO KNOW BETTER** *Pye 7N 15409* 37 1
16 Aug 62 **WELCOME HOME BABY** *Pye 7N 15453* 33 6
21 Feb 63 **TROUBLE IS MY MIDDLE NAME** *Pye 7N 15498* 38 4

BROOKLYN BOUNCE
Germany, male production duo and male / female vocal group

30 May 98 **THE MUSIC'S GOT ME** *Club Tools 0064795 CLU* 67 1

Elkie BROOKS 181 Top 500 *Husky-voiced female vocalist, professional at age 15, b. Elaine Bookbinder, 25 Feb 1945, Salford, UK. Blues, jazz then rock phases (in Vinegar Joe with Robert Palmer) followed by a solo career which featured an impressive 20-year run of 15 hit albums from 1977 (15 Albums: 223 Weeks, 13 Singles: 91 Weeks)*

2 Apr 77 ● **PEARL'S A SINGER** *A&M AMS 7275* 8 9
18 Jun 77 TWO DAYS AWAY *A&M AMLH 68409* 16 20
20 Aug 77 ● **SUNSHINE AFTER THE RAIN** *A&M AMS 7306* 10 9
25 Feb 78 **LILAC WINE** *A&M AMS 7333* 16 7
13 May 78 SHOOTING STAR *A&M AMLH 64695* 20 13
3 Jun 78 **ONLY LOVE CAN BREAK YOUR HEART** *A&M AMS 7353* 43 5
11 Nov 78 **DON'T CRY OUT LOUD** *A&M AMS 7395* 12 11
5 May 79 **THE RUNAWAY** *A&M AMS 7428* 50 5
13 Oct 79 LIVE AND LEARN *A&M AMLH 68509* 34 6
14 Nov 81 ● PEARLS *A&M ELK 1981* 2 79
16 Jan 82 **FOOL IF YOU THINK IT'S OVER** *A&M AMS 8187* 17 10
1 May 82 **OUR LOVE** *A&M AMS 8214* 43 5
17 Jul 82 **NIGHTS IN WHITE SATIN** *A&M AMS 8235* 33 5
13 Nov 82 ● PEARLS II *A&M ELK 1982* 5 25
22 Jan 83 **GASOLINE ALLEY** *A&M AMS 8305* 52 5
14 Jul 84 MINUTES *A&M AML 68565* 35 7
8 Dec 84 SCREEN GEMS *EMI SCREEN 1* 35 11
22 Nov 86 ● **NO MORE THE FOOL** *Legend LM 4* 5 16
6 Dec 86 ● NO MORE THE FOOL *Legend LMA 1* 5 23
27 Dec 86 ● THE VERY BEST OF ELKIE BROOKS *Telstar STAR 2284* 10 18
4 Apr 87 **BREAK THE CHAIN** *Legend LM 8* 55 3
11 Jul 87 **WE'VE GOT TONIGHT** *Legend LM 9* 69 1
11 Jun 88 BOOKBINDER'S KID *Legend LMA 3* 57 3
18 Nov 89 INSPIRATIONS *Telstar STAR 2354* 58 3
13 Mar 93 ROUND MIDNIGHT *Castle Communications CTVCD 113* 27 4
16 Apr 94 NOTHIN' BUT THE BLUES *Castle Communications CTVCD 127* 58 2
13 Apr 96 AMAZING *Carlton Premiere 3036000282* [1] 49 2
15 Mar 97 THE VERY BEST OF ELKIE BROOKS *PolyGram TV 5407122* 23 7

[1] Elkie Brooks with the Royal Philharmonic Orchestra

The two The Very Best of Elkie Brooks albums are different.

Garth BROOKS
US, male vocalist – Troyal Brooks (6 Albums: 48 Weeks, 6 Singles: 15 Weeks)

1 Feb 92 **SHAMELESS** *Capitol CL 646* 71 1
15 Feb 92 ROPIN' THE WIND *Capitol CDESTU 2162* ▲ 41 2
22 Jan 94 **THE RED STROKES / AIN'T GOING DOWN** *Liberty CDCLS 704* 13 5
12 Feb 94 ● IN PIECES *Capitol CDEST 2212* ▲ 2 11
16 Apr 94 **STANDING OUTSIDE THE FIRE** *Liberty CDCL 712* 28 4
24 Dec 94 THE HITS *Capitol CDP 8320812* ▲ 11 21
18 Feb 95 **THE DANCE / FRIENDS IN LOW PLACES** *Capitol CDCL 735* 36 3
2 Dec 95 FRESH HORSES *Capitol CDGB 1* 22 6
17 Feb 96 **SHE'S EVERY WOMAN** *Capitol CDCL 767* 55 1
13 Dec 97 SEVENS *Capitol 8565992* ▲ 34 7
28 Nov 98 DOUBLE LIVE *Capitol 4974242* ▲ 57 1
13 Nov 99 **LOST IN YOU** *Capitol CDCL 814* 70 1

Mel BROOKS *US, male actor / rapper – Melvin Kaminsky*

18 Feb 84 **TO BE OR NOT TO BE (THE HITLER RAP)** *Island IS 158* 12 10

Meredith BROOKS
US, female vocalist / guitarist (1 Album: 10 Weeks, 3 Singles: 13 Weeks)

2 Aug 97 ● **BITCH** *Capitol CDCL 790* 6 10
23 Aug 97 ● BLURRING THE EDGES *Capitol CDEST 2298* 5 10
6 Dec 97 **I NEED** *Capitol CDCLS 794* 28 2
7 Mar 98 **WHAT WOULD HAPPEN** *Capitol CDCL 798* 49 1

Norman BROOKS *Canada, male vocalist – Norman Arie*

12 Nov 54 **A SKY-BLUE SHIRT AND A RAINBOW TIE** *London L 1228* 17 1

6 / 7 December 1957	13 / 14 December 1957	20 / 21 December 1957	27 / 28 December 1957
MARY'S BOY CHILD Harry Belafonte	MARY'S BOY CHILD Harry Belafonte	MARY'S BOY CHILD Harry Belafonte	MARY'S BOY CHILD Harry Belafonte
THE KING AND I Soundtrack	THE KING AND I Soundtrack	THE KING AND I Soundtrack	THE KING AND I Soundtrack

KEY: UK No.1 ★ UK Top 10 ● Still on chart + UK entry at No.1 ■ US No.1 ▲ UK million seller £ US million seller $
Singles re-entries are listed as (re), (2re), (3re)... which signifies that the hit re-entered the chart once, twice or three times...
Peak Position / Weeks

Nigel BROOKS SINGERS
UK, male / female vocal choir (2 Albums: 17 Weeks)

29 Nov 75 ● SONGS OF JOY *K-Tel NE 706*......5 16
5 Jun 76 20 ALL TIME EUROVISION FAVOURITES *K-Tel NE 712*......44 1

Steve BROOKSTEIN NEW *UK, male vocalist*

01 Jan 05 ★ AGAINST ALL ODDS *SyCo Music 82876672732*......1 10
21 May 05 ★ HEART & SOUL *SyCo Music 82876691852* ■......1 5

BROS 485 Top 500
Top teen appeal act; photogenic twins Matt (v) and Luke Goss (d), b. 29 Sep 1968, London, UK, and Craig Logan (b) (left 1989). They sold out tours, broke sales records, created hysteria and won the BRITs Best Newcomer of 1988 award. Matt had some solo success in the 21st century (3 Albums: 69 Weeks, 11 Singles: 84 Weeks)

5 Dec 87 ● WHEN WILL I BE FAMOUS? (re) *CBS ATOM 2*......2 15
19 Mar 88 ● DROP THE BOY *CBS ATOM 3*......2 10
9 Apr 88 ● PUSH *CBS 460629 1*......2 54
18 Jun 88 ★ I OWE YOU NOTHING *CBS ATOM 4*......1 11
17 Sep 88 ● I QUIT *CBS ATOM 5*......4 8
3 Dec 88 ● CAT AMONG THE PIGEONS / SILENT NIGHT *CBS ATOM 6*......2 8
29 Jul 89 ● TOO MUCH *CBS ATOM 7*......2 7
7 Oct 89 ● CHOCOLATE BOX *CBS ATOM 8*......9 6
28 Oct 89 ● THE TIME *CBS 465918 1*......4 13
16 Dec 89 ● SISTER *CBS ATOM 9*......10 6
10 Mar 90 MADLY IN LOVE *CBS ATOM 10*......14 4
13 Jul 91 ARE YOU MINE? *Columbia 6569707*......12 5
21 Sep 91 TRY *Columbia 6574047*......27 4
12 Oct 91 CHANGING FACES *Columbia 4688171*......18 2

Act was duo for last six hits.

BROTHER BEYOND *UK, male vocal (Nathan Moore) / instrumental group (2 Albums: 24 Weeks, 11 Singles: 58 Weeks)*

4 Apr 87 HOW MANY TIMES *EMI EMI 5591*......62 3
8 Aug 87 CHAIN-GANG SMILE *Parlophone R 6160*......57 3
23 Jan 88 CAN YOU KEEP A SECRET? *Parlophone R 6174*......56 4
30 Jul 88 ● THE HARDER I TRY *Parlophone R 6184*......2 14
5 Nov 88 ● HE AIN'T NO COMPETITION *Parlophone R 6193*......6 10
26 Nov 88 ● GET EVEN *Parlophone PCS 7327*......9 23
21 Jan 89 BE MY TWIN *Parlophone R 6195*......14 6
1 Apr 89 CAN YOU KEEP A SECRET (re-mix) *Parlophone R 6197*......22 5
28 Oct 89 DRIVE ON *Parlophone R 6233*......39 4
25 Nov 89 TRUST *Parlophone PCS 7337*......60 1
9 Dec 89 WHEN WILL I SEE YOU AGAIN *Parlophone R 6239*......43 5
10 Apr 90 TRUST *Parlophone R 6245*......53 2
19 Jan 91 THE GIRL I USED TO KNOW *Parlophone R 6265*......48 2

BROTHER BROWN featuring FRANK'EE
Denmark, male DJ / production duo and female vocalist (2 Singles: 5 Weeks)

2 Oct 99 UNDER THE WATER *ffrr FCD 367*......18 4
24 Nov 01 STAR CATCHING GIRL *Rulin / MoS RULIN 21CDS*......51 1

The BROTHERHOOD *UK, male rap group*

27 Jan 96 ONE SHOT / NOTHING IN PARTICULAR *Bite It BHOODD 3*......55 1
17 Feb 96 ELEMENTALZ *Bite It BHOODCD 1*......50 1

BROTHERHOOD OF MAN
UK, male / female vocal group (4 Albums: 40 Weeks, 10 Singles: 97 Weeks)

14 Feb 70 ● UNITED WE STAND *Deram DM 284*......10 9
4 Jul 70 WHERE ARE YOU GOING TO MY LOVE *Deram DM 298*......22 10
13 Mar 76 ★ SAVE YOUR KISSES FOR ME *Pye 7N 45569* £......1 16
24 Apr 76 LOVE AND KISSES FROM *Pye NSPL 18490*......20 8
19 Jun 76 MY SWEET ROSALIE *Pye 7N 45602*......30 7
26 Feb 77 ● OH BOY (THE MOOD I'M IN) *Pye 7N 45656*......8 12
9 Jul 77 ★ ANGELO *Pye 7N 45699*......1 12
14 Jan 78 ★ FIGARO *Pye 7N 46037*......1 11
27 May 78 BEAUTIFUL LOVER *Pye 7N 46071*......15 12
12 Aug 78 B FOR BROTHERHOOD *Pye NSPL 18567*......18 9
30 Sep 78 MIDDLE OF THE NIGHT *Pye 7N 46117*......41 6
7 Oct 78 ● BROTHERHOOD OF MAN *K-Tel BML 7980*......6 15
29 Nov 80 SING 20 NUMBER ONE HITS *Warwick WW 5087*......14 8
3 Jul 82 LIGHTNING FLASH *EMI 5309*......67 2

The BROTHERS *UK, male vocal group*

29 Jan 77 ● SING ME *Bus Stop Bus 1054*......8 9

The BROTHERS FOUR *US, male vocal group*

23 Jun 60 GREENFIELDS (re) *Philips PB 1009* $......40 2

BROTHERS IN RHYTHM *UK, male instrumental / production duo – Dave Seaman and Steve Anderson (3 Singles: 12 Weeks)*

16 Mar 91 SUCH A GOOD FEELING *Fourth & Broadway BRW 228*......64 2
14 Sep 91 SUCH A GOOD FEELING (re-issue) *Fourth & Broadway BRW 228 210*......14 8
30 Apr 94 FOREVER AND A DAY *Stress CDSTR 36* [1]......51 2

[1] Brothers in Rhythm present Charvoni

The BROTHERS JOHNSON *US, male vocal / instrumental duo – George and Louis Johnson (3 Albums: 22 Weeks, 6 Singles: 34 Weeks)*

9 Jul 77 STRAWBERRY LETTER 23 *A&M AMS 7297* $......35 5
19 Aug 78 BLAM!! *A&M AMLH 64714*......48 8
2 Sep 78 AIN'T WE FUNKIN' NOW *A&M AMS 7379*......43 6
4 Nov 78 RIDE-O-ROCKET *A&M AMS 7400*......50 4
23 Feb 80 LIGHT UP THE NIGHT *A&M AMLK 63716*......22 12
23 Feb 80 ● STOMP *A&M AMS 7509*......6 12
31 May 80 LIGHT UP THE NIGHT *A&M AMS 7526*......47 4
18 Jul 81 WINNERS *A&M AMLK 63724*......42 2
25 Jul 81 THE REAL THING *A&M AMS 8149*......50 3

BROTHERS LIKE OUTLAW featuring Alison EVELYN
UK, male / female vocal group

23 Jan 93 GOOD VIBRATIONS *Gee Street GESCD 44*......74 1

The Edgar BROUGHTON BAND
UK, male vocal / instrumental group (2 Albums: 6 Weeks, 2 Singles: 10 Weeks)

18 Apr 70 OUT DEMONS OUT *Harvest HAR 5015*......39 5
20 Jun 70 SING BROTHER SING *Harvest SHVL 772*......18 4
23 Jan 71 APACHE DROPOUT (3re) *Harvest HAR 5032*......33 5
5 Jun 71 THE EDGAR BROUGHTON BAND *Harvest SHVL 791*......28 2

Bobby BROWN 356 Top 500
Energetic swingbeat superstar, b. 5 Feb 1969, Massachusetts, US, who married Whitney Houston in 1992. He joined a re-formed New Edition in 1996, the vocal group in which he topped the chart with 'Candy Girl' as a 14-year-old (5 Albums: 65 Weeks, 19 Singles: 131 Weeks)

6 Aug 88 DON'T BE CRUEL *MCA MCA 1268* $......42 7
17 Dec 88 ● MY PREROGATIVE *MCA MCA 1299* ▲......6 17
28 Jan 89 ● DON'T BE CRUEL *MCA MCF 3425* ▲......3 41
25 Mar 89 DON'T BE CRUEL (re-issue) *MCA MCA 1310*......13 8
20 May 89 ● EVERY LITTLE STEP *MCA MCA 1338*......6 9
15 Jul 89 ● ON OUR OWN (FROM GHOSTBUSTERS II) *MCA MCA 1350* $......4 9
5 Aug 89 KING OF STAGE *MCA MCL 1886*......40 6
23 Sep 89 ROCK WIT'CHA *MCA MCA 1367*......33 6
25 Nov 89 RONI *MCA MCA 1384*......21 7
2 Dec 89 DANCE! ... YA KNOW IT! *MCA MCG 6074*......26 10
9 Jun 90 THE FREE STYLE MEGA-MIX *MCA MCA 1421*......14 7

3 / 4 January 1958	10 / 11 January 1958	17 / 18 January 1958	24 / 25 January 1958
UK No.1 SINGLES			
MARY'S BOY CHILD Harry Belafonte	GREAT BALLS OF FIRE Jerry Lee Lewis	GREAT BALLS OF FIRE Jerry Lee Lewis	JAILHOUSE ROCK Elvis Presley
UK No.1 ALBUMS			
THE KING AND I Soundtrack	THE KING AND I Soundtrack	THE KING AND I Soundtrack	THE KING AND I Soundtrack

Date	Title / Label	Pos	Wks
30 Jun 90	**SHE AIN'T WORTH IT** *London LON 265* [1] ▲	12	9
22 Aug 92	**HUMPIN' AROUND** *MCA MCS 1680*	19	6
5 Sep 92	BOBBY *MCA MCAD 10695*	11	5
17 Oct 92	**GOOD ENOUGH** *MCA MCS 1704*	41	4
19 Jun 93	**THAT'S THE WAY LOVE IS** *MCA MCSTD 1783*	56	2
22 Jan 94	**SOMETHING IN COMMON** *MCA MCSTD 1957* [2]	16	5
25 Jun 94 ●	**TWO CAN PLAY THAT GAME (re)** *MCA MCSTD 1973*	3	15
8 Jul 95 ●	**HUMPIN' AROUND** (re-mix) *MCA MCSTD 2073*	8	6
5 Aug 95	TWO CAN PLAY THAT GAME *MCA MCD 11334*	24	3
14 Oct 95	**MY PREROGATIVE** (re-mix) *MCA MCSTD 2094*	17	3
3 Feb 96	**EVERY LITTLE STEP** (re-mix) *MCA MCSTD 48004*	25	2
22 Nov 97	**FEELIN' INSIDE** *MCA MCSTD 48067*	40	1
21 Dec 02	**THUG LOVIN'** *Def Jam 0637872* [3]	15	8

[1] Glenn Medeiros featuring Bobby Brown [2] Bobby Brown and Whitney Houston [3] Ja Rule featuring Bobby Brown

'Two Can Play That Game' reached its peak position of No.3 only on its re-entry in Apr 1995.

Crazy World of Arthur BROWN

UK, male vocal / instrumental group – leader Arthur Wilton

Date	Title / Label	Pos	Wks
26 Jun 68 ★	**FIRE** *Track 604 022* **$**	1	14
6 Jul 68 ●	THE CRAZY WORLD OF ARTHUR BROWN *Track 612005*	2	16

Dennis BROWN

Jamaica, male vocalist – Clarence Brown, b. 1 Feb 1957, d. 1 Jul 1999 (1 Album: 6 Weeks, 3 Singles: 18 Weeks)

Date	Title / Label	Pos	Wks
3 Mar 79	**MONEY IN MY POCKET** *Lightning LV 5*	14	9
26 Jun 82	LOVE HAS FOUND ITS WAY *A&M AMLH 64886*	72	6
3 Jul 82	**LOVE HAS FOUND ITS WAY** *A&M AMS 8226*	47	6
11 Sep 82	**HALFWAY UP HALFWAY DOWN** *A&M AMS 8250*	56	3

Diana BROWN and Barrie K SHARPE

UK, female / male vocal duo (4 Singles: 11 Weeks)

Date	Title / Label	Pos	Wks
2 Jun 90	**THE MASTERPLAN** *ffrr F 133*	39	6
1 Sep 90	**SUN WORSHIPPERS (POSITIVE THINKING)** *ffrr F 144*	61	2
23 Mar 91	**LOVE OR NOTHING** *ffrr F 152*	71	1
27 Jun 92	**EATING ME ALIVE** *ffrr F 190*	53	2

Errol BROWN (see also HOT CHOCOLATE)

UK, male vocalist (1 Album: 2 Weeks, 3 Singles: 13 Weeks)

Date	Title / Label	Pos	Wks
4 Jul 87	**PERSONAL TOUCH** *WEA YZ 130*	25	8
28 Nov 87	**BODY ROCKIN'** *WEA YZ 162*	51	2
14 Feb 98	**IT STARTED WITH A KISS** *EMI CDHOT 101* [1]	18	3
9 Jun 01	STILL SEXY – THE ALBUM *Universal Music TV 138162*	44	2

[1] Hot Chocolate featuring Errol Brown

Foxy BROWN

US, female rapper – Inga Marchand (1 Album: 1 Week, 8 Singles: 25 Weeks)

Date	Title / Label	Pos	Wks
21 Sep 96	**TOUCH ME TEASE ME** *Def Jam DEFCD 18* [1]	26	3
8 Mar 97	**GET ME HOME** *Def Jam DEFCD 32* [2]	11	5
10 May 97	**AIN'T NO PLAYA** *Northwestside 74321474842* [3]	31	2
21 Jun 97 ●	**I'LL BE** *Def Jam 5710432* [4]	9	5
11 Oct 97	**BIG BAD MAMMA** *Def Jam 5749792* [5]	12	3
25 Oct 97	**SUNSHINE** *Northwestside 74321528702* [6]	25	2
6 Feb 99	CHYNA DOLL *Def Jam 5589332* ▲	51	1
13 Mar 99	**HOT SPOT** *Def Jam 8708352*	31	2
8 Sep 01	**OH YEAH** *Der Jam 5887312*	27	3

[1] Case featuring Foxxy Brown [2] Foxy Brown featuring BLACKstreet [3] Jay-Z featuring Foxy Brown [4] Foxy Brown featuring Jay-Z [5] Foxy Brown featuring Dru Hill [6] Jay-Z featuring Babyface and Foxy Brown

Gloria D BROWN

US, female vocalist

Date	Title / Label	Pos	Wks
8 Jun 85	**THE MORE THEY KNOCK, THE MORE I LOVE YOU** *10 TEN 52*	57	3

Horace BROWN

US, male vocalist (1 Album: 1 Week, 3 Singles: 7 Weeks)

Date	Title / Label	Pos	Wks
25 Feb 95	**TASTE YOUR LOVE** *Uptown MCSTD 2026*	58	1
18 May 96	**ONE FOR THE MONEY** *Motown 8605232*	12	4
6 Jul 96	HORACE BROWN *Motown 5306942*	48	1
12 Oct 96	**THINGS WE DO FOR LOVE** *Motown 8605712*	27	2

Howard BROWN NEW

UK, male vocalist

Date	Title / Label	Pos	Wks
19 Mar 05	**YOU'RE THE FIRST, THE LAST, MY EVERYTHING** *HBOS CDHALIFAX 1*	13	3

Ian BROWN (see also The STONE ROSES)

UK, male vocalist / instrumentalist (5 Albums: 49 Weeks, 13 Singles: 43 Weeks)

Date	Title / Label	Pos	Wks
24 Jan 98 ●	**MY STAR** *Polydor 5719872*	5	4
14 Feb 98 ●	UNFINISHED MONKEY BUSINESS *Polydor 5395652*	4	24
4 Apr 98	**CORPSES** *Polydor 5696552*	14	4
20 Jun 98	**CAN'T SEE ME** *Polydor 5440452*	21	3
20 Feb 99 ●	**BE THERE** *Mo Wax MW 108CD1* [1]	8	6
6 Nov 99	**LOVE LIKE A FOUNTAIN** *Polydor 5615162*	23	3
20 Nov 99	GOLDEN GREATS *Polydor 5431412*	14	6
19 Feb 00 ●	**DOLPHINS WERE MONKEYS** *Polydor 5616372*	5	4
17 Jun 00	**GOLDEN GAZE** *Polydor 5618442*	29	2
29 Sep 01	**F.E.A.R.** *Polydor 5872842*	13	4
13 Oct 01 ●	MUSIC OF THE SPHERES *Polydor 5891262*	3	5
23 Feb 02	**WHISPERS** *Polydor 5705382*	33	2
25 Sep 04 ●	SOLARIZED *Fiction 9867772*	7	6
2 Oct 04	**KEEP WHAT YA GOT** *Fiction 9868284*	18	3
27 Nov 04	**REIGN** *Mo Wax GUSIN 007CDS* [1]	40	2
29 Jan 05	**TIME IS MY EVERYTHING** *Fiction 9869960*	15	4
17 Sep 05	**ALL ABLAZE** *Fiction 9873252*	20	2
1 Oct 05 ●	THE GREATEST *Fiction 9872874*	5	8

[1] Unkle featuring Ian Brown

'Keep What Ya Got' features an uncredited Noel Gallagher.

James BROWN (463 Top 500)

'Soul Brother No.1', b. 3 May 1928, South Carolina, US. The most charted R&B performer of all time has influenced numerous musical styles since the mid-1950s. Only Elvis Presley has enjoyed more US pop chart entries (5 Albums: 54 Weeks, 23 Singles: 104 Weeks)

Date	Title / Label	Pos	Wks
23 Sep 65	**PAPA'S GOT A BRAND NEW BAG** *London HL 9990* [1]	25	7
24 Feb 66	**I GOT YOU (I FEEL GOOD)** *Pye International 7N 25350* [1] **$**	29	6
16 Jun 66	**IT'S A MAN'S MAN'S MAN'S WORLD** *Pye International 7N 25371* [1]	13	9
10 Oct 70	**GET UP I FEEL LIKE BEING A SEX MACHINE** *Polydor 2001 071*	32	7
27 Nov 71	**HEY AMERICA** *Mojo 2093 006*	47	3
18 Sep 76	**GET UP OFFA THAT THING** *Polydor 2066 687*	22	6
29 Jan 77	**BODY HEAT** *Polydor 2066 763*	36	4
10 Jan 81	**RAPP PAYBACK (WHERE IZ MOSES?)** *RCA 28*	39	5
2 Jul 83	**BRING IT ON ... BRING IT ON** *Sonet SON 2258*	45	4
1 Sep 84	**UNITY (PART 1 – THE THIRD COMING)** *Tommy Boy AFR 2* [2]	49	5
27 Apr 85	**FROGGY MIX** *Boiling Point FROG 1*	50	3
1 Jun 85	**GET UP I FEEL LIKE BEING A SEX MACHINE (re)** (re-issue) *Boiling Point POSP 751*	46	9
25 Jan 86 ●	**LIVING IN AMERICA** *Scotti Bros. A 6701*	5	10
18 Oct 86	GRAVITY *Scotti Bros. SCT 57108*	85	3
18 Oct 86	**GRAVITY** *Scotti Bros. 650059 7*	65	2
30 Jan 88	**SHE'S THE ONE** *Urban URB 13*	45	3
23 Apr 88	**THE PAYBACK MIX** *Urban URB 17*	12	6
4 Jun 88	**I'M REAL** *Scotti Bros. JSB 1* [3]	31	4
25 Jun 88	I'M REAL *Scotti Bros. POLD 5230*	27	5
23 Jul 88	**I GOT YOU (I FEEL GOOD)** (re-issue) *A&M AM 444*	52	3
10 Oct 88	THE BEST OF JAMES BROWN – GODFATHER OF SOUL *K-Tel NE 1376*	17	21
16 Nov 91	SEX MACHINE – THE VERY BEST OF JAMES BROWN *Polydor 8458281*	19	22
16 Nov 91	**GET UP (I FEEL LIKE BEING A) SEX MACHINE** (2nd re-issue) *Polydor PO 185*	69	2
24 Oct 92	**I GOT YOU (I FEEL GOOD)** (re-mix) *FBI FBI 9* [4]	72	1
17 Apr 93	**CAN'T GET ANY HARDER** *Polydor PZCD 262*	59	2
17 Apr 99	**FUNK ON AH ROLL** *Inferno / Eagle EAGXA 073*	40	2

KEY
UK No.1 ★ UK Top 10 ● Still on chart + UK entry at No.1 ■
US No.1 ▲ UK million seller £ US million seller $
Singles re-entries are listed as (re), (2re), (3re)… which signifies that the hit re-entered the chart once, twice or three times…

Peak Position | Weeks

22 Apr 00 **FUNK ON AH ROLL** (re-mix) *Eagle EAGXS 127*..........**63** 1
11 May 02 THE GODFATHER – THE VERY BEST OF JAMES BROWN *UMTV 5898412*..........30 3

[1] James Brown and the Famous Flames [2] Afrika Bambaataa and James Brown [3] James Brown featuring Full Force [4] James Brown vs Dakeyne

'Froggy Mix' is a medley of 12 James Brown songs. The listed flip side of 'I Got You (I Feel Good)' was 'Nowhere to Run' by Martha Reeves and the Vandellas.

Jennifer BROWN *Sweden, female vocalist*

1 May 99 **TUESDAY AFTERNOON** *RCA 74321604092*..........**57** 1

Jocelyn BROWN (see also MOTIV 8) *US, female vocalist (21 Singles: 79 Weeks)*

21 Apr 84 **SOMEBODY ELSE'S GUY** *Fourth & Broadway BRW 5*..........**13** 9
22 Sep 84 **I WISH YOU WOULD** *Fourth & Broadway BRW 14*..........**51** 3
15 Mar 86 **LOVE'S GONNA GET YOU** *Warner Bros. W 8889*..........**70** 1
29 Jun 91 ● **ALWAYS THERE** *Talkin Loud TLK 10* [1]..........**6** 9
14 Sep 91 **SHE GOT SOUL** *A&M AM 819* [2]..........**57** 3
7 Dec 91 ● **DON'T TALK JUST KISS** *Tug SNOG 2* [3]..........**3** 11
20 Mar 93 **TAKE ME UP** *A&M AMCD 210* [4]..........**61** 1
11 Jun 94 **NO MORE TEARS (ENOUGH IS ENOUGH)** *Bell 74321209032* [5]..........**13** 7
8 Oct 94 **GIMME ALL YOUR LOVIN'** *Bell 74321231322* [6]..........**22** 3
13 Jul 96 ● **KEEP ON JUMPIN'** *Manifesto FESCD 11* [7]..........**8** 6
10 May 97 **IT'S ALRIGHT, I FEEL IT!** *Talkin Loud TLCD 22* [8]..........**26** 2
12 Jul 97 ● **SOMETHING GOIN' ON** *Manifesto FESCD 25* [7]..........**5** 10
25 Oct 97 **I AM THE BLACK GOLD OF THE SUN** *Talkin Loud TLCD 26* [8]..........**31** 2
22 Nov 97 **HAPPINESS** *Sony S3 KAMCD 2* [9]..........**45** 1
2 May 98 **FUN** *INCredible INCRL 2CD*..........**33** 2
29 Aug 98 **AIN'T NO MOUNTAIN HIGH ENOUGH** *INCredible INCRL 7CD*...**35** 2
27 Mar 99 **I BELIEVE** *Playola 0091705 PLA* [2]..........**62** 1
3 Jul 99 **IT'S ALL GOOD** *INCredible INCRL 14CD*..........**54** 1
11 Mar 00 **BELIEVE** *Defected DFECT 14CD3* [10]..........**45** 2
27 Jan 01 **BELIEVE** (re-mix) *Defected DFECT 26CDS* [10]..........**42** 2
7 Sep 02 **THAT'S HOW GOOD YOUR LOVE IS** *Defected DFTD 057CDS* [11]..........**54** 1

[1] Incognito featuring Jocelyn Brown [2] Jamestown featuring Jocelyn Brown [3] Right Said Fred Guest vocals: Jocelyn Brown [4] Sonic Surfers featuring Jocelyn Brown [5] Kym Mazelle and Jocelyn Brown [6] Jocelyn Brown and Kym Mazelle [7] Todd Terry featuring Martha Wash and Jocelyn Brown [8] Nuyorican Soul featuring Jocelyn Brown [9] Kamasutra featuring Jocelyn Brown [10] Ministers De La Funk featuring Jocelyn Brown [11] Il Padrinos featuring Jocelyn Brown

Joe BROWN and The BRUVVERS *UK, male vocalist / guitarist and male group (2 Albums: 47 Weeks, 11 Singles: 92 Weeks)*

17 Mar 60 **THE DARKTOWN STRUTTERS' BALL** *Decca F 11207*..........**34** 6
26 Jan 61 **SHINE** *Pye 7N 15322* [1]..........**33** 6
11 Jan 62 **WHAT A CRAZY WORLD WE'RE LIVING IN** *Piccadilly 7N 35024*..........**37** 2
17 May 62 ● **A PICTURE OF YOU** *Piccadilly 7N 35047*..........**2** 19
1 Sep 62 ● A PICTURE OF YOU *Pye Golden Guinea GGL 0146* [1]..........3 39
13 Sep 62 **YOUR TENDER LOOK** *Piccadilly 7N 35058*..........**31** 6
15 Nov 62 ● **IT ONLY TOOK A MINUTE (re)** *Piccadilly 7N 35082*..........**6** 14
7 Feb 63 ● **THAT'S WHAT LOVE WILL DO** *Piccadilly 7N 35106*..........**3** 14
25 May 63 JOE BROWN – LIVE *Piccadilly NPL 38006* [1]..........14 8
27 Jun 63 **NATURE'S TIME FOR LOVE** *Piccadilly 7N 35129*..........**26** 6
26 Sep 63 **SALLY ANN** *Piccadilly 7N 35138*..........**28** 9
29 Jun 67 **WITH A LITTLE HELP FROM MY FRIENDS** *Pye 7N 17339* [1] .**32** 4
14 Apr 73 **HEY MAMA** *Ammo AMO 101* [1]..........**33** 6

[1] Joe Brown [1] Joe Brown

Kathy BROWN *US, female vocalist (6 Singles: 16 Weeks)*

25 Nov 95 **TURN ME OUT** *Stress CDSTR 40*..........**44** 2
20 Sep 97 **TURN ME OUT (TURN TO SUGAR)** (re-mix) *ffrr FCD* [1]..........**35** 3
10 Apr 99 **JOY** *Azuli AZNYCDX 094*..........**63** 1
5 May 01 **LOVE IS NOT A GAME** *Defected DFECT 31CDS* [2]..........**34** 2
2 Jun 01 **OVER YOU** *Defected DFECT 28CDS* [3]..........**42** 1
22 Jan 05 ● **STRINGS OF LIFE (STRONGER ON MY OWN)** *Defected DFTD 094CDS* [4]..........**6** 7

[1] Praxis featuring Kathy Brown [2] J Majik featuring Kathy Brown [3] Warren Clarke featuring Kathy Brown [4] Soul Central featuring Kathy Brown

Miquel BROWN *US, female vocalist (2 Singles: 7 Weeks)*

18 Feb 84 **HE'S A SAINT, HE'S A SINNER** *Record Shack SOHO 15*..........**68** 4
24 Aug 85 **CLOSE TO PERFECTION** *Record Shack SOHO 48*..........**63** 3

Peter BROWN *US, male vocalist (2 Singles: 9 Weeks)*

11 Feb 78 **DO YA WANNA GET FUNKY WITH ME** *TK TKR 6009* [1]..........**43** 4
17 Jun 78 **DANCE WITH ME** *TK TKR 6027*..........**57** 5

[1] special background vocals: Betty Wright

Polly BROWN (see also PICKETTYWITCH; SWEET DREAMS) *UK, female vocalist*

14 Sep 74 **UP IN A PUFF OF SMOKE** *GTO GT 2*..........**43** 5

Roy 'Chubby' BROWN *UK, male comedian / vocalist – Royston Vasey (2 Albums: 8 Weeks, 2 Singles: 22 Weeks)*

13 May 95 ● **LIVING NEXT DOOR TO ALICE (WHO THE F**K IS ALICE) (re)** *N.O.W. CDWAG 245* [1]..........**3** 19
25 Nov 95 TAKE FAT AND PARTY *PolyStar 5297842*..........29 7
7 Dec 96 FAT OUT OF HELL *PolyStar 5370602*..........67 1
21 Dec 96 **ROCKIN' GOOD CHRISTMAS** *PolyStar 5732612*..........**51** 3

[1] Smokie featuring Roy 'Chubby' Brown

Sam BROWN *UK, female vocalist (2 Albums: 30 Weeks, 5 Singles: 35 Weeks)*

11 Jun 88 ● **STOP (re)** *A&M AM 440*..........**4** 15
11 Mar 89 ● STOP! *A&M AMA 5195*..........4 18
13 May 89 **CAN I GET A WITNESS** *A&M AM 509*..........**15** 7
3 Mar 90 **WITH A LITTLE LOVE** *A&M AM 539*..........**44** 4
14 Apr 90 APRIL MOON *A&M AMA 9014*..........38 12
5 May 90 **KISSING GATE** *A&M AM 549*..........**23** 8
26 Aug 95 **JUST GOOD FRIENDS** *Dick Bros. DDICK 014CD1* [1]..........**63** 1

[1] Fish featuring Sam Brown

'Stop' reached its peak position of No.4 only on its re-entry in Feb 1989.

Sharon BROWN *US, female vocalist (2 Singles: 11 Weeks)*

17 Apr 82 **I SPECIALIZE IN LOVE** *Virgin VS 494*..........**38** 9
26 Feb 94 **I SPECIALIZE IN LOVE** (re-mix) *Deep Distraxion OILYCD 025*..........**62** 2

Sleepy BROWN *US, male rapper – Patrick Brown (2 Singles: 11 Weeks)*

27 Jul 02 **LAND OF A MILLION DRUMS** *Atlantic AT 0134CD* [1]..........**46** 1
3 Apr 04 ● **THE WAY YOU MOVE** *Arista 82876605602* [2] ▲..........**7** 10

[1] Outkast featuring Killer Mike and Sleepy Brown [2] Outkast featuring Sleepy Brown

BROWN SAUCE *UK, male / female vocal group*

12 Dec 81 **I WANNA BE A WINNER** *BBC RESL 101*..........**15** 12

Duncan BROWNE *UK, male vocalist (2 Singles: 8 Weeks)*

19 Aug 72 **JOURNEY** *RAK 135*..........**23** 6
22 Dec 84 **THEME FROM 'THE TRAVELLING MAN'** *Towerbell TOW 64*.....**68** 2

28 February / 1 March 1958	7 / 8 March 1958	14 / 15 March 1958	21 / 22 March 1958
UK No.1 SINGLES			
MAGIC MOMENTS Perry Como	MAGIC MOMENTS Perry Como	MAGIC MOMENTS Perry Como	MAGIC MOMENTS Perry Como
UK No.1 ALBUMS			
PAL JOEY Soundtrack	PAL JOEY Soundtrack	PAL JOEY Soundtrack	THE KING AND I Soundtrack

Jackson BROWNE
US, male vocalist (10 Albums: 41 Weeks, 3 Singles: 14 Weeks)

Date	Title / Label	Pos	Wks
4 Dec 76	THE PRETENDER *Asylum K 53048*	26	5
21 Jan 78	RUNNING ON EMPTY *Asylum K 53070*	28	7
1 Jul 78	**STAY** *Asylum K 13128*	**12**	11
12 Jul 80	HOLD OUT *Asylum K 52226* ▲	44	5
13 Aug 83	LAWYERS IN LOVE *Asylum 9602681*	37	7
8 Mar 86	LIVES IN THE BALANCE *Asylum EKT 31*	36	7
18 Oct 86	**IN THE SHAPE OF A HEART** *Elektra EKR 42*	**66**	2
17 Jun 89	WORLD IN MOTION *Elektra EKT 50*	39	2
6 Nov 93	I'M ALIVE *Elektra 7559615242*	35	3
25 Jun 94	**EVERYWHERE I GO** *Elektra EKR 184CD1*	**67**	1
9 Mar 96	LOOKING EAST *Elektra 7559618672*	47	1
26 Oct 02	THE NAKED RIDE HOME *Elektra EA 627932*	53	1
16 Oct 04	THE VERY BEST OF JACKSON BROWNE *Elektra / Rhino 8122780912*	53	3

Tom BROWNE
US, male trumpeter (4 Singles: 24 Weeks)

Date	Title / Label	Pos	Wks
19 Jul 80 ●	**FUNKIN' FOR JAMAICA (N.Y.)** *Arista ARIST 357*	**10**	11
25 Oct 80	**THIGHS HIGH (GRIP YOUR HIPS AND MOVE)** *Arista ARIST 367*	**45**	5
30 Jan 82	**FUNGI MAMA (BEBOPAFUNKADISCOLYPSO)** *Arista ARIST 450*	**58**	4
11 Jan 92	**FUNKIN' FOR JAMAICA** (re-mix) *Arista 114998*	**45**	4

The BROWNS
US, male / female vocal trio

Date	Title / Label	Pos	Wks
18 Sep 59 ●	**THE THREE BELLS** *RCA 1140* ▲ $	**6**	13

BROWNSTONE
US, female vocal group (2 Albums: 16 Weeks, 5 Singles: 24 Weeks)

Date	Title / Label	Pos	Wks
1 Apr 95 ●	**IF YOU LOVE ME** *MJJ 6614135*	**8**	12
29 Apr 95	FROM THE BOTTOM UP *MJJ 4773622*	18	13
15 Jul 95	**GRAPEVYNE** *MJJ 6620942*	**16**	4
23 Sep 95	**I CAN'T TELL YOU WHY** *MJJ 6623775*	**27**	2
17 May 97	**5 MILES TO EMPTY** *Epic 6640962*	**12**	4
31 May 97	STILL CLIMBING *Epic 4853882*	19	3
27 Sep 97	**KISS AND TELL** *Epic 6649852*	**21**	2

BROWNSVILLE STATION
US, male vocal / instrumental group

Date	Title / Label	Pos	Wks
2 Mar 74	**SMOKIN' IN THE BOYS' ROOM** *Philips 6073 834* $	**27**	6

Dave BRUBECK QUARTET
US, male instrumental group – leader David Warren (2 Albums: 17 Weeks, 3 Singles: 30 Weeks)

Date	Title / Label	Pos	Wks
25 Jun 60	TIME OUT *Fontana TFL 5085*	11	1
26 Oct 61 ●	**TAKE FIVE** *Fontana H 339*	**6**	15
8 Feb 62	**IT'S A RAGGY WALTZ** *Fontana H 352*	**36**	3
7 Apr 62	TIME FURTHER OUT *Fontana TFL 5161* [1]	12	16
17 May 62	**UNSQUARE DANCE** *CBS AAG 102*	**14**	12

[1] Dave Brubeck

Jack BRUCE (see also CREAM)
UK, male vocalist / bass guitarist – John Asher

Date	Title / Label	Pos	Wks
27 Sep 69 ●	SONGS FOR A TAILOR *Polydor 583058*	6	9

Tommy BRUCE and The BRUISERS
UK, male vocal / instrumental group (3 Singles: 21 Weeks)

Date	Title / Label	Pos	Wks
26 May 60 ●	**AIN'T MISBEHAVIN'** *Columbia DB 4453*	**3**	16
8 Sep 60	**BROKEN DOLL** *Columbia DB 4498*	**36**	4
22 Feb 62	**BABETTE** *Columbia DB 4776* [1]	**50**	1

[1] Tommy Bruce

Claudia BRÜCKEN
Germany, female vocalist (2 Singles: 2 Weeks)

Date	Title / Label	Pos	Wks
11 Aug 90	**ABSOLUT(E)** *Island IS 471*	**71**	1
16 Feb 91	**KISS LIKE ETHER** *Island IS 479*	**63**	1

The BRUISERS (see also Tommy BRUCE and The BRUISERS)
UK, male instrumental group

Date	Title / Label	Pos	Wks
8 Aug 63	**BLUE GIRL (re)** *Parlophone R 5042*	**31**	7

Frank BRUNO
UK, male boxer / vocalist

Date	Title / Label	Pos	Wks
23 Dec 95	**EYE OF THE TIGER** *RCA 74321336282*	**28**	4

Tyrone BRUNSON
US, male bass guitarist

Date	Title / Label	Pos	Wks
25 Dec 82	**THE SMURF** *Epic EPC A 3024*	**52**	5

Basil BRUSH featuring India BEAU
UK, male fox vocalist and female vocalist

Date	Title / Label	Pos	Wks
27 Dec 03	**BOOM BOOM / CHRISTMAS SLIDE** *Right RRBB 001*	**44**	3

Dora BRYAN
UK, female actor / vocalist – Dora Broadbent

Date	Title / Label	Pos	Wks
5 Dec 63	**ALL I WANT FOR CHRISTMAS IS A BEATLE** *Fontana TF 427*	**20**	6

Kéllé BRYAN (see also ETERNAL)
UK, female vocalist

Date	Title / Label	Pos	Wks
2 Oct 99	**HIGHER THAN HEAVEN** *1st Avenue / Mercury MERCD 522*	**14**	4

Anita BRYANT
US, female vocalist (2 Singles: 6 Weeks)

Date	Title / Label	Pos	Wks
26 May 60	**PAPER ROSES (2re)** *London HLL 9144*	**24**	4
6 Oct 60	**MY LITTLE CORNER OF THE WORLD** *London HLL 9171*	**48**	2

Peabo BRYSON
US, male vocalist – Robert Bryson (4 Singles: 35 Weeks)

Date	Title / Label	Pos	Wks
20 Aug 83 ●	**TONIGHT I CELEBRATE MY LOVE** *Capitol CL 302* [1]	**2**	13
16 May 92 ●	**BEAUTY AND THE BEAST** *Epic 6576607* [2] $	**9**	7
17 Jul 93	**BY THE TIME THIS NIGHT IS OVER** *Arista 74321157142* [3]	**56**	3
11 Dec 93	**A WHOLE NEW WORLD (ALADDIN'S THEME)** *Columbia 6599002* [4] ▲	**12**	12

[1] Peabo Bryson and Roberta Flack [2] Celine Dion and Peabo Bryson
[3] Kenny G with Peabo Bryson [4] Regina Belle and Peabo Bryson

Patrizio BUANNE NEW
Italy, male vocalist

Date	Title / Label	Pos	Wks
12 Mar 05 ●	THE ITALIAN *Globe Records 9868390*	10	12

Michael BUBLÉ
Canada, male vocalist (4 Albums: 59 Weeks, 2 Singles: 6 Weeks)

Date	Title / Label	Pos	Wks
18 Oct 03 ●	MICHAEL BUBLÉ *Reprise 9362485352*	6	26
29 May 04	COME FLY WITH ME *Reprise 9362486832*	52	2
20 Nov 04	MICHAEL BUBLÉ *Reprise 9362489162*	46	5
12 Feb 05 ●	IT'S TIME *Reprise 9362489962*	4	26+
9 Apr 05	**HOME** *Reprise W 668CD1*	**31**	4
3 Dec 05	**HOME** (re-issue) **/ SONG FOR YOU (re)** *Reprise W 693CD*	**63**	2

Michael Bublé (20 Nov 2004) is a limited edition version of the original Michael Bublé album with a bonus CD of Christmas songs.

Roy BUCHANAN
US, male guitarist, b. 23 Sep 1939, d. 14 Aug 1988

Date	Title / Label	Pos	Wks
31 Mar 73	**SWEET DREAMS** *Polydor 2066 307*	**40**	3

The BUCKETHEADS
US, male producer – Kenny Gonzalez (1 Album: 1 Week, 2 Singles: 16 Weeks)

Date	Title / Label	Pos	Wks
4 Mar 95 ●	**THE BOMB! (THESE SOUNDS FALL INTO MY MIND)** *Positiva CDTIV 33*	**5**	13
20 Jan 96	**GOT MYSELF TOGETHER** *Positiva CDTIV 48*	**12**	3
27 Jan 96	ALL IN THE MIND *Positiva CDTIVA 1010*	74	1

Lindsey BUCKINGHAM
(see also FLEETWOOD MAC) *US, male vocalist*

Date	Title / Label	Pos	Wks
16 Jan 82	**TROUBLE** *Mercury MER 85*	**31**	7
8 Aug 92	OUT OF THE CRADLE *Mercury 5126582*	51	1

28 / 29 March 1958	4 / 5 April 1958	11 / 12 April 1958	18 / 19 April 1958
MAGIC MOMENTS Perry Como	MAGIC MOMENTS Perry Como	MAGIC MOMENTS Perry Como	MAGIC MOMENTS Perry Como
PAL JOEY Soundtrack	PAL JOEY Soundtrack	PAL JOEY Soundtrack	PAL JOEY Soundtrack

11 Jan	**JAMES GRIFFIN** (Bread)
11 Jan	**SPENCER DRYDEN** (Jefferson Airplane)
20 Jan	**SOLOMON KING**
25 Jan	**RAY PETERSON**
28 Jan	**JIM CAPALDI**
8 Feb	**JIMMY SMITH**
8 Feb	**KEITH KNUDSEN** (The Doobie Brothers)
22 Feb	**HARRY SIMEONE**
28 Feb	**CHRIS CURTIS** (The Searchers)
8 Mar	**KATHIE KAY** (The Billy Cotton Band)
10 Mar	**DANNY JOE BROWN** (Molly Hatchet)
28 Mar	**PAUL HESTER** (Crowded House)
13 Apr	**JOHNNIE JOHNSON** (The Chuck Berry Band)
15 Apr	**JOHN FRED**
30 Apr	**NORMA-JEAN RICHARDSON** (The Duchess, The Bo Diddley Band)
17 Jun	**KARL MUELLER** (Soul Asylum)
1 Jul	**RENALDO 'OBIE' BENSON** (The Four Tops)
1 Jul	**LUTHER VANDROSS**
5 Jul	**SHIRLEY GOODMAN** (Shirley & Company)
5 Jul	**RAY DAVIS** (Funkadelic)
6 Jul	**DENNIS D'ELL** (The Honeycombs)
21 Jul	**LONG JOHN BALDRY**
22 Jul	**EUGENE RECORD** (The Chi-Lites)
31 Jul	**LES BRAID** (The Swinging Blue Jeans)
23 Aug	**HAL KALIN** (The Kalin Twins)
19 Sep	**WILLIE HUTCH**
10 Oct	**NICK HAWKINS** (Big Audio Dynamite)
23 Oct	**MEL WILLIAMS** (The Johnny Otis Show)
26 Oct	**DAVID TOWNSEND** (Surface)
22 Nov	**KEN MACKINTOSH**
29 Nov	**TONY MEEHAN** (The Shadows)
4 Dec	**DON CHARLES**
6 Dec	**DANNY WILLIAMS**

Two soul legends …

Smooth soul superstar Luther Vandross learned to play the piano aged three and achieved a significant career breakthrough 20 years later when David Bowie's musical director Carlos Alomar recommended him to his boss. This led to a backing singing role on Bowie's Young Americans. Before his untimely death he achieved a record-breaking 10 successive platinum albums.

Successful Sixties soul songwriter and Motown recording artist Willie Hutch first caught Berry Gordy's ear when he co-wrote the Jackson Five's 'I'll Be There'. The pinnacle of his career came with the 1973 release of his Blaxploitation movie soundtrack The Mack, which stands beside Shaft and Superfly as one of the finest of the genre.

	25 / 26 April 1958	2 / 3 May 1958	9 / 10 May 1958	16 / 17 May 1958
UK No.1 SINGLES	**WHOLE LOTTA WOMAN** Marvin Rainwater	**WHOLE LOTTA WOMAN** Marvin Rainwater	**WHOLE LOTTA WOMAN** Marvin Rainwater	**WHO'S SORRY NOW?** Connie Francis
UK No.1 ALBUMS	**THE DUKE WORE JEANS (Soundtrack)** Tommy Steele	**THE DUKE WORE JEANS (Soundtrack)** Tommy Steele	**MY FAIR LADY** Original London Cast	**MY FAIR LADY** Original London Cast

Jeff BUCKLEY *US, male vocalist, b. 17 Nov 1966, d. 29 May 1997 (4 Albums: 16 Weeks, 2 Singles: 3 Weeks)*

27 Aug 94 GRACE *Columbia 4759282* ... 42 8
27 May 95 **LAST GOODBYE** *Columbia 6620422* ... **54** 2
23 May 98 ● SKETCHES FOR MY SWEETHEART THE DRUNK *Columbia 4886616* ... 7 4
6 Jun 98 **EVERYBODY HERE WANTS YOU** *Columbia 6657912* ... **43** 1
20 May 00 ● MYSTERY WHITEBOY – LIVE '95-'96 *Columbia 4979722* ... 8 2
4 Sep 04 GRACE – LEGACY EDITION (re-issue) *Columbia 5174603* ... 44 2

Grace (1994) reached its peak position in 2005. Grace – Legacy Edition is a repackaged three-disc CD and DVD set commemorating the 10th anniversary of the Grace album.

BUCKS FIZZ 289 Top 500 *Chart-topping mixed quartet: Cheryl Baker, Mike Nolan, Jay Aston (replaced by Shelley Preston in 1985) and Bobby G (Gubby). Formed for the 1981 Eurovision Song Contest, they were the last UK winners for 16 years (6 Albums: 80 Weeks, 20 Singles: 150 Weeks)*

28 Mar 81 ★ **MAKING YOUR MIND UP** *RCA 56* ... **1** 12
6 Jun 81 **PIECE OF THE ACTION** *RCA 88* ... **12** 9
8 Aug 81 BUCKS FIZZ *RCA RCALP 5050* ... 14 28
15 Aug 81 **ONE OF THOSE NIGHTS** *RCA 114* ... **20** 10
28 Nov 81 ★ **THE LAND OF MAKE BELIEVE** *RCA 163* ... **1** 16
27 Mar 82 ★ **MY CAMERA NEVER LIES** *RCA 202* ... **1** 8
18 May 82 ● ARE YOU READY? *RCA RCALP 8000* ... 10 23
19 Jun 82 ● **NOW THOSE DAYS ARE GONE** *RCA 241* ... **8** 9
27 Nov 82 ● **IF YOU CAN'T STAND THE HEAT** *RCA 300* ... **10** 11
12 Mar 83 **RUN FOR YOUR LIFE** *RCA FIZ 1* ... **14** 7
19 Mar 83 HAND CUT *RCA RCALP 6100* ... 17 13
18 Jun 83 ● **WHEN WE WERE YOUNG** *RCA 342* ... **10** 8
1 Oct 83 **LONDON TOWN** *RCA 363* ... **34** 6
3 Dec 83 GREATEST HITS *RCA RCA PL 70022* ... 25 13
17 Dec 83 **RULES OF THE GAME** *RCA 380* ... **57** 6
25 Aug 84 **TALKING IN YOUR SLEEP** *RCA FIZ 2* ... **15** 9
27 Oct 84 **GOLDEN DAYS** *RCA FIZ 3* ... **42** 4
24 Nov 84 I HEAR TALK *RCA PL 70397* ... 66 2
29 Dec 84 **I HEAR TALK** *RCA FIZ 4* ... **34** 8
22 Jun 85 **YOU AND YOUR HEART SO BLUE** *RCA PB 40233* ... **43** 4
14 Sep 85 **MAGICAL** *RCA PB 40367* ... **57** 3
7 Jun 86 ● **NEW BEGINNING (MAMBA SEYRA)** *Polydor POSP 794* ... **8** 10
30 Aug 86 **LOVE THE ONE YOU'RE WITH** *Polydor POSP 813* ... **47** 3
15 Nov 86 **KEEP EACH OTHER WARM** *Polydor POSP 835* ... **45** 4
13 Dec 86 THE WRITING ON THE WALL *Polydor POHL 30* ... 89 1
5 Nov 88 **HEART OF STONE** *RCA PB 42035* ... **50** 3

BUCKSHOT LEFONQUE *US, male vocal / instrumental group*

6 Dec 97 **ANOTHER DAY** *Columbia 6653762* ... **65** 1

Roy BUDD *UK, male pianist*

19 Sep 98 GET CARTER (FILM SOUNDTRACK) *Cinephile CINCD 001* ... 68 1
10 Jul 99 **GET CARTER** *Cinephile CINX 1003* ... **68** 1

Harold BUDD / Liz FRASER / Robin GUTHRIE / Simon RAYMONDE (see also COCTEAU TWINS; Simon RAYMONDE) *UK, male / female vocal / instrumental group*

22 Nov 86 THE MOON AND THE MELODIES *4AD CAD 611* ... 46 2

Joe BUDDEN *US, male vocalist (1 Album: 1 Week, 3 Singles: 20 Weeks)*

28 Jun 03 JOE BUDDEN *Def Jam / Mercury 9807936* ... 55 1
19 Jul 03 **PUMP IT UP** *Def Jam / Mercury 9808879* ... **13** 7
20 Mar 04 **CLUBBIN'** *Elektra E 7544CD* [1] ... **15** 6
16 Oct 04 ● **WHATEVER U WANT** *Def Jam 9864266* [2] ... **9** 7

[1] Marques Houston featuring Joe Budden and Pied Piper [2] Christina Milian featuring Joe Budden

BUDGIE
UK, male vocal / instrumental group (4 Albums: 10 Weeks, 1 Single: 2 Weeks)

8 Jun 74 IN FOR THE KILL *MCA MCF 2546* ... 29 3
27 Sep 75 BANDOLIER *MCA MCF 2723* ... 36 4
3 Oct 81 **KEEPING A RENDEZVOUS** *RCA BUDGIE 3* ... **71** 2
31 Oct 81 NIGHT FLIGHT *RCA RCALP 6003* ... 68 2
23 Oct 82 DELIVER US FROM EVIL *RCA RCALP 6054* ... 62 1

BUFFALO G
Ireland, female vocal / rap duo – Olive Tucker and Naomi Lynch

10 Jun 00 **WE'RE REALLY SAYING SOMETHING (re)** *Epic 6694182* ... **17** 4

BUFFALO TOM
US, male vocal / instrumental group (3 Albums: 5 Weeks, 1 Single: 5 Weeks)

14 Mar 92 LET ME COME OVER *Situation Two SITU 36CD* ... 49 1
9 Oct 93 (BIG RED LETTER DAY) *Beggars Banquet BBQCD 142* ... 17 3
22 Jul 95 SLEEPY EYED *Beggars Banquet BBQCD 177* ... 31 1
23 Oct 99 ● **GOING UNDERGROUND / CARNATION** *Ignition IGNSCD 16* [1] **6** 5

[1] A-side: Buffalo Tom, B-side: Liam Gallagher / Steve Cradock

BUG KANN and The PLASTIC JAM
UK, male / female vocal / instrumental group (2 Singles: 2 Weeks)

31 Aug 91 **MADE IN TWO MINUTES** *Optimum Dance BKPJ 1S* [1] ... **70** 1
26 Feb 94 **MADE IN 2 MINUTES** (re-mix) *PWL International PWCD 286* ... **64** 1

[1] Bug Kann and the Plastic Jam featuring Patti Low and Doogie

The BUGGLES *UK, male vocal / instrumental duo – Trevor Horn and Geoff Downes (1 Album: 6 Weeks, 4 Singles: 28 Weeks)*

22 Sep 79 ★ **VIDEO KILLED THE RADIO STAR** *Island WIP 6524* ... **1** 11
26 Jan 80 **THE PLASTIC AGE** *Island WIP 6540* ... **16** 8
16 Feb 80 THE AGE OF PLASTIC *Island ILPS 9585* ... 27 6
5 Apr 80 **CLEAN, CLEAN** *Island WIP 6584* ... **38** 5
8 Nov 80 **ELSTREE** *Island WIP 6624* ... **55** 4

BUGZ IN THE ATTIC NEW
UK, male / female vocal / instrumental / production group

22 Jan 05 **BOOTY LA LA** *V2 VVR 5030093* ... **44** 2

LTJ BUKEM *UK, male DJ / producer – Danny Williamson*

8 Apr 00 JOURNEY INWARDS *Good Looking GLRAA 001* ... 40 3

James BULLER *UK, male vocalist*

6 Mar 99 **CAN'T SMILE WITHOUT YOU** *BBC Music WMSS 60092* ... **51** 1

BULLET FOR MY VALENTINE NEW
UK, male vocal / instrumental group (1 Album: 3 Weeks, 2 Singles: 3 Weeks)

9 Apr 05 **4 WORDS (TO CHOKE UPON)** *Visible Noise TORMENT 51* ... **40** 2
1 Oct 05 **SUFFOCATING UNDER WORDS OF SORROW (WHAT CAN I DO)** *Visible Noise TORMENT 58CD* ... **37** 1
15 Oct 05 THE POISON *Visible Noise TORMENT 50CD* ... 21 3

BULLETPROOF *UK, male producer – Paul Chambers*

10 Mar 01 **SAY YEAH / DANCE TO THE RHYTHM** *Tidy Trax TIDY 148CD* ... **62** 1

BUMP *UK, male instrumental / production duo – Marc Auerbach and Steve Travell (2 Singles: 5 Weeks)*

4 Jul 92 **I'M RUSHING** *Good Boy EDGE 71* ... **40** 4
11 Nov 95 **I'M RUSHING** (re-mix) *Deconstruction 74321320692* ... **45** 1

BUMP & FLEX *UK, male / female vocal / production duo*

23 May 98 **LONG TIME COMING** *Heat Recordings HEATCD 014* ... **73** 1

Emma BUNTON (see also SPICE GIRLS)
UK, female vocalist (2 Albums: 23 Weeks, 8 Singles: 68 Weeks)

13 Nov 99 ● **WHAT I AM** *VC Recordings VCRD 53* [1] ... **2** 12

KEY
UK No.1 ★ UK Top 10 ● Still on chart + UK entry at No.1 ■ US No.1 ▲ UK million seller £ US million seller $
Singles re-entries are listed as (re), (2re), (3re)... which signifies that the hit re-entered the chart once, twice or three times...
Peak Position / Weeks

14 Apr 01 ★ **WHAT TOOK YOU SO LONG** *Virgin VSCDT 1796* ■ 1 12
28 Apr 01 ● A GIRL LIKE ME *Virgin CDV 2935*........4 12
8 Sep 01 ● **TAKE MY BREATH AWAY** *Virgin VSCDT 1814*........5 9
22 Dec 01 **WE'RE NOT GONNA SLEEP TONIGHT** *Virgin VSCDT 1821*........20 5
7 Jun 03 ● **FREE ME** *19 / Universal 9807472* [2] 5 9
25 Oct 03 ● **MAYBE** *19 / Universal 9812785* [2] 6 9
7 Feb 04 ● **I'LL BE THERE (re)** *19 / Universal 9816267* [2] 7 8
21 Feb 04 ● FREE ME *19 / Universal 9866158* [1] 7 11
12 Jun 04 **CRICKETS SING FOR ANAMARIA** *19 9866826* [2] 15 4

[1] Tin Tin Out featuring Emma Bunton [2] Emma [1] Emma

Eric BURDON and WAR (see also The ANIMALS) *UK, male vocalist and US, male vocal / instrumental group (2 Albums: 4 Weeks)*

3 Oct 70 ERIC BURDON DECLARES WAR *Polydor 2310041*........50 2
20 Feb 71 BLACKMAN'S BURDON *Liberty LDS 8400*........25 2

Tim BURGESS (see also The CHEMICAL BROTHERS) *UK, male vocalist (1 Album: 1 Week, 2 Singles: 2 Weeks)*

6 Sep 03 **I BELIEVE IN THE SPIRIT** *PIAS Recordings PIASB 109CD*........44 1
20 Sep 03 I BELIEVE *PIAS PIASB 099CD*........38 1
15 Nov 03 **ONLY A BOY** *PIAS Recordings PIASB 119CD*........54 1

Geoffrey BURGON *UK, male orchestra leader*

26 Dec 81 **BRIDESHEAD THEME** *Chrysalis CHS 2562*........48 4

Keni BURKE *US, male vocalist (2 Singles: 4 Weeks)*

27 Jun 81 **LET SOMEBODY LOVE YOU** *RCA 93*........59 3
18 Apr 92 **RISIN' TO THE TOP** *RCA PB 49103*........70 1

BURN *UK, male vocal / instrumental group (2 Singles: 2 Weeks)*

8 Jun 02 **THE SMILING FACE** *Hut / Virgin HUTCD 155*........72 1
29 Mar 03 **DRUNKEN FOOL** *Hut / Virgin HUTCD 166*........54 1

Jean-Jacques BURNEL (see also Dave GREENFIELD) *UK, male vocalist / bass guitarist (2 Albums: 6 Weeks)*

21 Apr 79 EUROMAN COMETH *United Artists UAG 30214*........40 5
3 Dec 83 FIRE AND WATER *Epic EPC 25707* [1] 94 1

[1] Dave Greenfield and Jean-Jacques Burnel

Hank C BURNETTE *Sweden, male multi-instrumentalist – Sven-Ake Hogberg*

30 Oct 76 **SPINNING ROCK BOOGIE** *Sonet SON 2094*........21 8

Johnny BURNETTE *US, male vocalist, b. 25 Mar 1934, d. 1 Aug 1964 (5 Singles: 48 Weeks)*

29 Sep 60 ● **DREAMIN'** *London HLG 9172*........5 16
12 Jan 61 ● **YOU'RE SIXTEEN** *London HLG 9254*........3 12
13 Apr 61 **LITTLE BOY SAD** *London HLG 9315*........12 12
10 Aug 61 **GIRLS** *London HLG 9388*........37 5
17 May 62 **CLOWN SHOES** *Liberty LIB 55416*........35 3

Rocky BURNETTE *US, male vocalist – Jonathan Burnette*

17 Nov 79 **TIRED OF TOEIN' THE LINE** *EMI 2992*........58 7

Jerry BURNS *UK, female vocalist*

25 Apr 92 **PALE RED** *Columbia 6579467*........64 1

Pete BURNS (see also DEAD OR ALIVE) *UK, male vocalist*

19 Jun 04 **JACK AND JILL PARTY** *Olde English LKCDS 02*........75 1

Ray BURNS *UK, male vocalist (2 Singles: 19 Weeks)*

11 Feb 55 ● **MOBILE** *Columbia DB 3563* [1] 4 13
26 Aug 55 **THAT'S HOW A LOVE SONG WAS BORN** *Columbia DB 3640* [2] 14 6

[1] Ray Burns with Eric Jupp and his Orchestra [2] Ray Burns with The Coronets

Malandra BURROWS *UK, female vocalist / actor (3 Singles: 10 Weeks)*

1 Dec 90 **JUST THIS SIDE OF LOVE** *Yorkshire Television DALE 1*........11 8
18 Oct 97 **CARNIVAL IN HEAVEN** *Warner.esp WESP 001CD*........49 1
29 Aug 98 **DON'T LEAVE ME** *Warner.esp WESP 004CD*........54 1

Jenny BURTON *US, female vocalist*

30 Mar 85 **BAD HABITS** *Atlantic A 9583*........68 2

BURUNDI STEIPHENSON BLACK *Burundi, drummers and chanters and France, male instrumentalist – orchestral additions by Mike Steiphenson*

13 Nov 71 **BURUNDI BLACK** *Barclay BAR 3*........31 14

BUS STOP (see also FLIP & FILL) *UK, male production group (4 Singles: 19 Weeks)*

23 May 98 ● **KUNG FU FIGHTING** (re-recording) *All Around the World CDGLOBE 173* [1] 8 11
24 Oct 98 **YOU AIN'T SEEN NOTHIN' YET** *All Around the World CDGLOBE 187* [2] 22 4
10 Apr 99 **JUMP** *All Around the World CDGLOBE 186*........23 3
7 Oct 00 **GET IT ON** *All Around the World CDGLOBE 225* [3] 59 1

[1] Bus Stop featuring Carl Douglas [2] Bus Stop featuring Randy Bachman [3] Bus Stop featuring T. Rex

Lou BUSCH and his Orchestra *US, orchestra and chorus – leader aka Joe 'Fingers' Carr, b. 18 Jul 1910, d. 19 Sep 1979*

27 Jan 56 ● **ZAMBESI** *Capitol CL 14504*........2 17

BUSH *UK, male vocal (Gavin Rossdale) / instrumental group (4 Albums: 18 Weeks, 7 Singles: 13 Weeks)*

8 Jun 96 **MACHINEHEAD** *Interscope IND 95505*........48 2
15 Jun 96 SIXTEEN STONE *Interscope 6544925312*........42 3
1 Feb 97 ● RAZORBLADE SUITCASE *Interscope IND 90091* ▲ 4 12
1 Mar 97 ● **SWALLOWED** *Interscope IND 95528*........7 5
7 Jun 97 **GREEDY FLY** *Interscope IND 95536*........22 2
1 Nov 97 **BONE DRIVEN** *Interscope IND 95553*........49 1
6 Nov 99 THE SCIENCE OF THINGS *Trauma / Polydor 4904832*........28 2
4 Dec 99 **THE CHEMICALS BETWEEN US** *Trauma / Polydor 4972222*........46 1
18 Mar 00 **WARM MACHINE** *Trauma / Polydor 4972752*........45 1
3 Jun 00 **LETTING THE CABLES SLEEP** *Trauma / Polydor 4973352*........51 1
10 Nov 01 GOLDEN STATE *Atlantic 7567834882*........53 1

Kate BUSH (91 Top 500) *Unmistakable singer / songwriter with operatic vocal ability, b. 30 Jul 1958, Kent. Discovered by Dave Gilmour of Pink Floyd. First British female to top the singles chart with a self-composed song and the first to have a UK No.1 album. Her long-awaited new album in 2005 was typically inspirational with contributions from Rolf Harris and her son Bertie (9 Albums: 290 Weeks, 27 Singles: 174 Weeks)*

11 Feb 78 ★ **WUTHERING HEIGHTS (re)** *EMI 2719*........1 13
11 Mar 78 ● THE KICK INSIDE *EMI EMC 3223*........3 70
10 Jun 78 ● **THE MAN WITH THE CHILD IN HIS EYES** *EMI 2806*........6 11
11 Nov 78 **HAMMER HORROR** *EMI 2887*........44 6
25 Nov 78 ● LIONHEART *EMI EMA 787*........6 36
17 Mar 79 **WOW** *EMI 2911*........14 10
15 Sep 79 ● **ON STAGE (EP)** *EMI MIEP 2991*........10 9
26 Apr 80 **BREATHING** *EMI 5058*........16 7
5 Jul 80 ● **BABOOSHKA** *EMI 5085*........5 10

20 / 21 June 1958	27 / 28 June 1958	4 / 5 July 1958	11 / 12 July 1958
UK No.1 SINGLES			
WHO'S SORRY NOW? Connie Francis	**ON THE STREET WHERE YOU LIVE** Vic Damone	**ON THE STREET WHERE YOU LIVE** Vic Damone / **ALL I HAVE TO DO IS DREAM / CLAUDETTE** The Everly Brothers (tied at No.1)	**ALL I HAVE TO DO IS DREAM / CLAUDETTE** The Everly Brothers
UK No.1 ALBUMS			
MY FAIR LADY Original London Cast	**MY FAIR LADY** Original London Cast	**MY FAIR LADY** Original London Cast	**MY FAIR LADY** Original London Cast

20 Sep 80 ★ NEVER FOR EVER *EMI EMA 7964* ■ 1 23
4 Oct 80 ARMY DREAMERS *EMI 5106* 16 9
6 Dec 80 DECEMBER WILL BE MAGIC AGAIN *EMI 5121* 29 7
11 Jul 81 SAT IN YOUR LAP *EMI 5201* 11 7
7 Aug 82 THE DREAMING *EMI 5296* 48 3
25 Sep 82 ● THE DREAMING *EMI EMC 3419* 3 10
17 Aug 85 ● RUNNING UP THAT HILL *EMI KB 1* 3 11
28 Sep 85 ★ HOUNDS OF LOVE *EMI KAB 1* ■ 1 54
26 Oct 85 CLOUDBUSTING *EMI KB 2* 20 6
1 Mar 86 HOUNDS OF LOVE *EMI KB 3* 18 5
10 May 86 THE BIG SKY *EMI KB 4* 37 3
1 Nov 86 ● DON'T GIVE UP *Virgin PGS 2* [1] 9 11
8 Nov 86 EXPERIMENT IV *EMI KB 5* 23 4
22 Nov 86 ★ THE WHOLE STORY *EMI KBTV 1* 1 55
30 Sep 89 THE SENSUAL WORLD *EMI EM 102* 12 5
28 Oct 89 ● THE SENSUAL WORLD *EMI EMD 1010* 2 20
2 Dec 89 THIS WOMAN'S WORK *EMI EM 119* 25 5
10 Mar 90 LOVE AND ANGER *EMI EM 134* 38 3
7 Dec 91 ROCKET MAN (I THINK IT'S GOING TO BE A LONG LONG TIME) *Mercury TRIBO 2* 12 8
18 Sep 93 RUBBERBAND GIRL *EMI CDEM 280* 12 5
13 Nov 93 ● THE RED SHOES *EMI CDEMD 1047* 2 15
27 Nov 93 MOMENTS OF PLEASURE *EMI CDEM 297* 26 3
16 Apr 94 THE RED SHOES *EMI CDEMS 316* 21 3
30 Jul 94 THE MAN I LOVE *Mercury MERCD 408* [2] 27 2
19 Nov 94 AND SO IS LOVE *EMI CDEMS 355* 26 2
5 Nov 05 ● KING OF THE MOUNTAIN *EMI CDEM 674* 4 6
19 Nov 05 ● AERIAL *EMI 3439602* 3 7+

[1] Peter Gabriel and Kate Bush [2] Kate Bush and Larry Adler

Tracks on On Stage (EP): Them Heavy People / Don't Push Your Foot on the Heartbrake / James and the Cold Gun / L'Amour Looks Something Like You.

BUSTED (304 Top 500)

Talented pop punk trio who were the highest new entrants in the Top 500 acts in 2004: songwriter James Bourne (Southend), Charlie Simpson (Ipswich) and Mattie Jay (Surrey). Named Best Pop Act at the 2004 BRITs and 'Thunderbirds' was the ITV 'Record of the Year' in 2004. They split in early 2005, James started Son of Dork and Charlie formed Fightstar (3 Albums: 132 Weeks, 8 Singles: 92 Weeks)

28 Sep 02 ● WHAT I GO TO SCHOOL FOR *Universal MCSTD 40294* 3 12
12 Oct 02 ● BUSTED *Universal MCD 60084* 2 77
25 Jan 03 ● YEAR 3000 *Universal MCSTD 40306* 2 15
3 May 03 ★ YOU SAID NO *Universal MCSTD 40318* ■ 1 10
23 Aug 03 ● SLEEPING WITH THE LIGHT ON *Universal MCSTD 40327* 3 10
22 Nov 03 ★ CRASHED THE WEDDING *Universal MCSTD 40345* ■ 1 12
29 Nov 03 ● A PRESENT FOR EVERYONE *Universal MCD 60090* 2 43
28 Feb 04 ★ WHO'S DAVID *Universal MCSTD 40355* ■ 1 10
8 May 04 ● AIR HOSTESS (re) *Universal MCSXD 40361* 2 10
7 Aug 04 ★ THUNDERBIRDS / 3AM *Universal MCSXD 40375* 1 13
13 Nov 04 LIVE – A TICKET FOR EVERYONE *Universal MCD 60096* 11 12

BUSTER *UK, male vocal / instrumental group*

19 Jun 76 SUNDAY *RCA 2678* 49 1

Bernard BUTLER (see also McALMONT & BUTLER; SUEDE; The TEARS)

UK, male vocalist / guitarist (2 Albums: 9 Weeks, 4 Singles: 9 Weeks)

17 Jan 98 STAY *Creation CRESCD 281* 12 4
28 Mar 98 NOT ALONE *Creation CRESCD 289* 27 3
18 Apr 98 PEOPLE MOVE ON *Creation CCRE 221* 11 8
27 Jun 98 A CHANGE OF HEART *Creation CRESCD 297* 45 1
23 Oct 99 YOU MUST GO ON *Creation CRESCD 324* 44 1
6 Nov 99 FRIENDS AND LOVERS *Creation CRECD 248* 43 1

Jonathan BUTLER *South Africa, male vocalist / guitarist (2 Albums: 14 Weeks, 2 Singles: 18 Weeks)*

25 Jan 86 IF YOU'RE READY (COME GO WITH ME) *Jive JIVE 109* [1] 30 7
8 Aug 87 LIES *Jive JIVE 141* 18 11
12 Sep 87 JONATHAN BUTLER *Jive HIP 46* 12 11
4 Feb 89 MORE THAN FRIENDS *Jive HIP 70* 29 3

[1] Ruby Turner featuring Jonathan Butler

BUTTERSCOTCH *UK, male vocal group*

2 May 70 DON'T YOU KNOW (SHE SAID HELLO) *RCA 1937* 17 11

BUTTHOLE SURFERS

US, male vocal / instrumental group (2 Albums: 2 Weeks, 1 Single: 1 Week)

16 Mar 91 PIOUHGD *Rough Trade R 20812601* 68 1
3 Apr 93 INDEPENDENT WORM SALOON *Capitol CDEST 2192* 73 1
5 Oct 96 PEPPER *Capitol CDCL 778* 59 1

The BUZZCOCKS *UK, male vocal / instrumental group (3 Albums: 23 Weeks, 9 Singles: 53 Weeks)*

18 Feb 78 WHAT DO I GET? *United Artists UP 36348* 37 3
25 Mar 78 ANOTHER MUSIC IN A DIFFERENT KITCHEN *United Artists UAG 30159* 15 11
13 May 78 I DON'T MIND *United Artists UP 36386* 55 2
15 Jul 78 LOVE YOU MORE *United Artists UP 36433* 34 6
23 Sep 78 EVER FALLEN IN LOVE (WITH SOMEONE YOU SHOULDN'T'VE) *United Artists UP 36455* 12 11
7 Oct 78 LOVE BITES *United Artists UAG 30184* 13 9
25 Nov 78 PROMISES *United Artists UP 36471* 20 10
10 Mar 79 EVERYBODY'S HAPPY NOWADAYS *United Artists UP 36499* 29 6
21 Jul 79 HARMONY IN MY HEAD *United Artists UP 36541* 32 6
25 Aug 79 SPIRAL SCRATCH (EP) *New Hormones ORG 1* 31 6
6 Oct 79 A DIFFERENT KIND OF TENSION *United Artists UAG 30260* 26 3
6 Sep 80 ARE EVERYTHING / WHY SHE'S A GIRL FROM THE CHAINSTORE *United Artists BP 365* 61 3

Tracks on Spiral Scratch (EP): Breakdown / Time's Up / Boredom / Friends of Mine. Sleeve of EP (not the label) credits The Buzzcocks with Howard Devoto. 'Why She's a Girl from the Chainstore' listed from 13 Sep 1980.

BY ALL MEANS *US, male vocal group*

18 Jun 88 I SURRENDER TO YOUR LOVE *Fourth & Broadway BRW 102* 65 2
16 Jul 88 BY ALL MEANS *Fourth & Broadway BRLP 520* 80 1

Max BYGRAVES (188 Top 500)

One of Britain's best-loved entertainers, b. Walter Bygraves, 16 Oct 1922, London. The comedian / singer / songwriter was the only British male in the first UK singles chart. He had five Top 20 'sing-a-long' hit albums in just 15 months of the 1970s (12 Albums: 176 Weeks, 18 Singles: 131 Weeks)

14 Nov 52 ● COWPUNCHER'S CANTATA (3re) *HMV B 10250* 6 8
14 May 54 ● (THE GANG THAT SANG) HEART OF MY HEART *HMV B 10654* 7 8
10 Sep 54 ● GILLY GILLY OSSENFEFFER KATZENELLEN BOGEN BY THE SEA (re) *HMV B 10734* 7 8
21 Jan 55 MISTER SANDMAN *HMV B 10801* 16 1
18 Nov 55 ● MEET ME ON THE CORNER *HMV POP 116* 2 11
17 Feb 56 THE BALLAD OF DAVY CROCKETT *HMV POP 153* 20 1
25 May 56 OUT OF TOWN *HMV POP 164* 18 7
5 Apr 57 HEART *Decca F 10862* [1] 14 8
2 May 58 ● YOU NEED HANDS / TULIPS FROM AMSTERDAM *Decca F 11004* [2] 3 25
22 Aug 58 LITTLE TRAIN / GOTTA HAVE RAIN *Decca F 11046* 28 2
2 Jan 59 (I LOVE TO PLAY) MY UKULELE *Decca F 11077* 19 4
18 Dec 59 ● JINGLE BELL ROCK *Decca F 11176* 7 4
10 Mar 60 ● FINGS AIN'T WOT THEY USED T'BE *Decca F 11214* 5 15
28 Jul 60 CONSIDER YOURSELF *Decca F 11251* 50 1
1 Jun 61 THE BELLS OF AVIGNON *Decca F 11350* 36 5
19 Feb 69 YOU'RE MY EVERYTHING (re) *Pye 7N 17705* 34 4
23 Sep 72 ● SING ALONG WITH MAX *Pye NSPL 18361* 4 44
2 Dec 72 SING ALONG WITH MAX VOLUME 2 *Pye NSPL 18383* 11 23
5 May 73 ● SINGALONGAMAX VOLUME 3 *Pye NSPL 18401* 5 30
29 Sep 73 ● SINGALONGAMAX VOLUME 4 *Pye NSPL 18410* 7 12
6 Oct 73 DECK OF CARDS *Pye 7N 45276* 13 15
15 Dec 73 SINGALONGPARTY SONG *Pye NSPL 18419* 15 6
12 Oct 74 YOU MAKE ME FEEL LIKE SINGING A SONG *Pye NSPL 18436* 39 3
7 Dec 74 SINGALONGAXMAS *Pye NSPL 18439* 21 6
13 Nov 76 ● 100 GOLDEN GREATS *Ronco RTDX 2019* 3 21
28 Oct 78 LINGALONGAMAX *Ronco RPL 2033* 39 5

18 / 19 July 1958	25 / 26 July 1958	1 / 2 August 1958	8 / 9 August 1958
ALL I HAVE TO DO IS DREAM / CLAUDETTE The Everly Brothers	ALL I HAVE TO DO IS DREAM / CLAUDETTE The Everly Brothers	ALL I HAVE TO DO IS DREAM / CLAUDETTE The Everly Brothers	ALL I HAVE TO DO IS DREAM / CLAUDETTE The Everly Brothers
MY FAIR LADY Original London Cast	MY FAIR LADY Original London Cast	MY FAIR LADY Original London Cast	MY FAIR LADY Original London Cast

KEY
UK No.1 ★ UK Top 10 ● Still on chart + UK entry at No.1 ■
US No.1 ▲ UK million seller £ US million seller $
Singles re-entries are listed as (re), (2re), (3re)... which signifies that the hit re-entered the chart once, twice or three times...
Peak Position / Weeks

16 Dec 78 THE SONG AND DANCE MEN *Pye NSPL 18574*......67 1
19 Aug 89 ● SINGALONGAWARYEARS *Parkfield Music PMLP 5001*......5 19
25 Nov 89 SINGALONGAWARYEARS VOLUME 2 *Parkfield Music PMLP 5006*......33 6
9 Dec 89 **WHITE CHRISTMAS** *Parkfield PMS 5012*......**71** 4

[1] Max Bygraves with Malcolm Lockyer and his Orchestra [2] Max Bygraves with the Clark Bros and Eric Rodgers and his Orchestra / Max Bygraves with Eric Rodgers and his Orchestra

Cowpuncher's Cantata is a medley with the following songs: Cry of the Wild Goose / Riders in the Sky / Mule Train / Jezebel. 'Tulips from Amsterdam' was listed with 'You Need Hands' from 9 May 1958.

BYKER GROOOVE! *UK, female actors / vocal group*

24 Dec 94 **LOVE YOUR SEXY ... !!** *Groove GROVD 01*......**48** 3

Donald BYRD *US, male trumpeter*

26 Sep 81 **LOVING YOU / LOVE HAS COME AROUND** *Elektra K 12559*......**41** 6
10 Oct 81 LOVE BYRD *Elektra K 52301*......70 3

Gary BYRD and The GB EXPERIENCE
US, male rapper and male / female vocal / instrumental group

23 Jul 83 ● **THE CROWN** *Motown TMGT 1312*......**6** 9

Features uncredited vocals by Stevie Wonder.

The BYRDS *US, male vocal / instrumental group (10 Albums: 42 Weeks, 6 Singles: 52 Weeks)*

17 Jun 65 ★ **MR TAMBOURINE MAN** *CBS 201765* ▲ $......**1** 14
12 Aug 65 ● **ALL I REALLY WANT TO DO** *CBS 201796*......**4** 10
28 Aug 65 ● MR. TAMBOURINE MAN *CBS BPG 62571*......7 12
11 Nov 65 **TURN! TURN! TURN! (TO EVERYTHING THERE IS A SEASON)** *CBS 202008* ▲ $......**26** 8
9 Apr 66 TURN TURN TURN *CBS BPG 62652*......11 5
5 May 66 **EIGHT MILES HIGH** *CBS 202067*......**24** 9
1 Oct 66 5TH DIMENSION *CBS BPG 62783*......27 2
22 Apr 67 YOUNGER THAN YESTERDAY *CBS SBPG 62988*......37 4
4 May 68 THE NOTORIOUS BYRD BROTHERS *CBS 63169*......12 11
5 Jun 68 **YOU AIN'T GOING NOWHERE** *CBS 3411*......**45** 3
24 May 69 DR. BYRDS AND MR. HYDE *CBS 63545*......15 1
14 Feb 70 BALLAD OF EASY RIDER *CBS 63795*......41 1
28 Nov 70 (UNTITLED) / (UNISSUED) *CBS 66253*......11 4
13 Feb 71 **CHESTNUT MARE** *CBS 5322*......**19** 8
14 Apr 73 BYRDS *Asylum SYLA 8754*......31 1
19 May 73 HISTORY OF THE BYRDS *CBS 68242*......47 1

David BYRNE (see also TALKING HEADS) *UK, male vocalist / instrumentalist (5 Albums: 18 Weeks, 1 Single: 13 Weeks)*

21 Feb 81 MY LIFE IN THE BUSH OF GHOSTS *Polydor EGLP 48* [1]......29 8
21 Oct 89 REI MOMO *Warner Bros. WX 319*......52 2
14 Mar 92 UH-OH *Luaka Bop 7599267992*......26 5
4 Jun 94 DAVID BYRNE *Luaka Bop 9362455582*......44 2
19 May 01 LOOK INTO THE EYEBALL *Luaka Bop CDVUS 189*......58 1
20 Apr 02 ● **LAZY** *Skint SKINT 74CD* [1]......**2** 13

[1] X-Press 2 featuring David Byrne [1] Brian Eno and David Byrne

Edward BYRNES and Connie STEVENS *US, male / female actors / vocal duo – Edward Brietenberger and Concetta Ingolia*

5 May 60 **KOOKIE KOOKIE (LEND ME YOUR COMB)** *Warner Bros. WB 5* $......**27** 8

The BYSTANDERS *UK, male vocal / instrumental group*

9 Feb 67 **98.6** *Piccadilly 7N 35363*......**45** 1

C

Melanie C (422 Top 500) (see also SPICE GIRLS) *Former Sporty Spice (b. Melanie Chisholm, 12 Jan 1974, Liverpool, UK) has appeared on 11 No.1 hits. She is the only woman to top the UK chart solo and as part of a duo, quartet and quintet (3 Albums: 75 Weeks, 10 Singles: 95 Weeks)*

12 Dec 98 ● **WHEN YOU'RE GONE** *A&M 5828212* [1]......**3** 19
9 Oct 99 ● **GOIN' DOWN (re)** *Virgin VSCDT 1744*......**4** 6
30 Oct 99 ● NORTHERN STAR *Virgin CDVX 2893*......4 69
4 Dec 99 ● **NORTHERN STAR** *Virgin VSCDT 1748*......**4** 11
1 Apr 00 ★ **NEVER BE THE SAME AGAIN (re)** *Virgin VSCDT 1762* [2] ■......**1** 16
19 Aug 00 ★ **I TURN TO YOU** *Virgin VSCDT 1772* ■......**1** 12
9 Dec 00 **IF THAT WERE ME (re)** *Virgin VSCDT 1786*......**18** 10
8 Mar 03 ● **HERE IT COMES AGAIN (re)** *Virgin VSCDT 1842*......**7** 8
22 Mar 03 ● REASON *Virgin CDV 2969*......5 4
14 Jun 03 **ON THE HORIZON (re)** *Virgin VSCDT 1851*......**14** 7
22 Nov 03 **MELT / YEH YEH YEH** *Virgin VSCDX 1858*......**27** 2
16 Apr 05 ● **NEXT BEST SUPERSTAR** *Red Girl CXREDG 1*......**10** 4
23 Apr 05 BEAUTIFUL INTENTIONS *Red Girl REDGCD 1*......24 2

[1] Bryan Adams featuring Melanie C [2] Melanie C / Lisa 'Left Eye' Lopes

Roy C *US, male vocalist – Roy C Hammond (2 Singles: 24 Weeks)*

21 Apr 66 ● **SHOTGUN WEDDING** *Island WI 273*......**6** 11
25 Nov 72 ● **SHOTGUN WEDDING** (re-issue) *UK 19*......**8** 13

C & C MUSIC FACTORY *US, male instrumental / production duo – Robert Clivilles and David Cole, b. 3 Jun 1962, d. 24 Jan 1995, featuring male / female vocalists / rappers (2 Albums: 14 Weeks, 10 Singles: 53 Weeks)*

15 Dec 90 ● **GONNA MAKE YOU SWEAT (EVERYBODY DANCE NOW)** *CBS 6564540* [1] ▲ $......**3** 12
9 Feb 91 ● GONNA MAKE YOU SWEAT *Columbia 4678141* [1]......8 13
30 Mar 91 **HERE WE GO** *Columbia 6567557* [1]......**20** 7
6 Jul 91 ● **THINGS THAT MAKE YOU GO HMMM ...** *Columbia 6566907* [1]......**4** 11
23 Nov 91 **JUST A TOUCH OF LOVE (EVERYDAY)** *Columbia 6575247* [2]......**31** 3
18 Jan 92 **PRIDE (IN THE NAME OF LOVE)** *Columbia 6577017* [3]......**15** 5
14 Mar 92 **A DEEPER LOVE** *Columbia 6578497* [3]......**15** 5
28 Mar 92 GREATEST REMIXES VOLUME 1 *Columbia 4694462* [2]......45 1
3 Oct 92 **KEEP IT COMIN' (DANCE TILL YOU CAN'T DANCE NO MORE)** *Columbia 6584307* [4]......**34** 3
27 Aug 94 **DO YOU WANNA GET FUNKY** *Columbia 6607622*......**27** 3
18 Feb 95 **I FOUND LOVE / TAKE A TOKE** *Columbia 6612112* [5]......**26** 2
11 Nov 95 **I'LL ALWAYS BE AROUND** *MCA MCSTD 40001*......**42** 2

[1] C & C Music Factory (featuring Freedom Williams) [2] C & C Music Factory featuring Zelma Davis [3] Clivilles and Cole [4] C & C Music Factory featuring Q Unique and Deborah Cooper [5] C & C Music Factory / C & C Music Factory featuring Martha Wash [1] C&C Music Factory [2] Clivilles and Cole

C.C.S.
UK, male vocal / instrumental group (1 Album: 5 Weeks, 5 Singles: 55 Weeks)

31 Oct 70 **WHOLE LOTTA LOVE** *RAK 104*......**13** 13
27 Feb 71 ● **WALKIN'** *RAK 109*......**7** 16

15 / 16 August 1958	22 / 23 August 1958	29 / 30 August 1958	5 / 6 September 1958
UK No.1 SINGLES			
ALL I HAVE TO DO IS DREAM / CLAUDETTE The Everly Brothers	**WHEN** The Kalin Twins	**WHEN** The Kalin Twins	**WHEN** The Kalin Twins
UK No.1 ALBUMS			
MY FAIR LADY Original London Cast	**MY FAIR LADY** Original London Cast	**MY FAIR LADY** Original London Cast	**MY FAIR LADY** Original London Cast

4 Sep 71 ● **TAP TURNS ON THE WATER** *RAK 119* 5 13
4 Mar 72 **BROTHER** *RAK 126* 25 8
8 Apr 72 CCS *RAK SRAK 503* 23 5
4 Aug 73 **THE BAND PLAYED THE BOOGIE** *RAK 154* 36 5

CJ & CO *US, male vocal / instrumental group*

30 Jul 77 **DEVIL'S GUN** *Atlantic K 10956* 43 2

CK & SUPREME DREAM TEAM

Holland / Belgium / US, male production trio

11 Jan 03 **DREAMER** *Multiply CDMULTY 96* 23 3

CLS *US, male vocal / production duo*

30 May 98 **CAN YOU FEEL IT** *Satellite 74321580162* 46 1

CM2 featuring Lisa LAW *UK, male production group and female vocalist*

18 Jan 03 **FALL AT YOUR FEET** *Dance Pool 6732532* 66 1

C.O.D *US, male vocal / instrumental group*

14 May 83 **IN THE BOTTLE** *Streetwave WAVE 2* 54 2

CRW (see also R.A.F.)

Italy, male producer – Mauro Picotto (4 Singles: 8 Weeks)

26 Feb 00 **I FEEL LOVE** *VC Recordings VCRD 63* 15 4
25 Nov 00 **LOVIN'** *VC Recordings VCRD 77* 49 2
27 Apr 02 **LIKE A CAT** *BXR BXRC 0397* [1] 57 1
26 Oct 02 **PRECIOUS LIFE** *BXR BXRC 0395* [2] 57 1

[1] CRW featuring Veronika [2] CRW presents Veronika

C-SIXTY FOUR NEW *UK, male DJ / producer – Colin Hamilton*

19 Mar 05 **ON A GOOD THING** *Manifesto 9870564* 54 1

CZR featuring DELANO *US, male producer and vocalist*

30 Sep 00 **I WANT YOU** *Credence CDCRED 002* 57 1

ÇA VA ÇA VA *UK, male vocal / instrumental group (2 Singles: 8 Weeks)*

18 Sep 82 **WHERE'S ROMEO** *Regard RG 103* 49 5
19 Feb 83 **BROTHER BRIGHT** *Regard RG 105* 65 3

Montserrat CABALLÉ

Spain, female vocalist (2 Albums: 11 Weeks, 2 Singles: 17 Weeks)

7 Nov 87 ● **BARCELONA** *Polydor POSP 887* [1] 8 9
22 Oct 88 BARCELONA *Polydor POLH 44* [1] 15 8
8 Aug 92 FROM THE OFFICIAL BARCELONA GAMES CEREMONY *RCA Red Seal 09026612042* [2] 41 3
8 Aug 92 ● **BARCELONA** (re-issue) *Polydor PO 221* [1] 2 8

[1] Freddie Mercury and Montserrat Caballé [1] Freddie Mercury and Montserrat Caballé [2] Placido Domingo, José Carreras and Montserrat Caballé

CABANA *Brazil, male / female vocal / instrumental duo*

15 Jul 95 **BAILANDO CON LOBOS** *Hi-Life 5792512* 65 1

CABARET VOLTAIRE *UK, male vocal / instrumental group (5 Albums: 11 Weeks, 4 Singles: 8 Weeks)*

26 Jun 82 2 X 45 *Rough Trade ROUGH 42* 98 1
13 Aug 83 THE CRACKDOWN *Some Bizzare CV 1* 31 5
10 Nov 84 MICRO-PHONIES *Some Bizzare CV 2* 69 1
3 Aug 85 DRINKING GASOLINE *Some Bizzare CVM 1* 71 2
26 Oct 85 THE COVENANT THE SWORD AND THE ARM OF THE LORD *Some Bizzare CV 3* 57 2
18 Jul 87 **DON'T ARGUE** *Parlophone R 6157* 69 2
4 Nov 89 **HYPNOTISED** *Parlophone R 6227* 66 2
12 May 90 **KEEP ON** *Parlophone R 6250* 55 2
18 Aug 90 **EASY LIFE** *Parlophone R 6261* 61 2

CABIN CREW NEW

Australia, male production duo – Ben Garden and Rob Kittler

12 Mar 05 ● **STAR TO FALL** *Data DATA 87CDS* 4 8

CABLE *UK, male vocal / instrumental group*

14 Jun 97 **FREEZE THE ATLANTIC** *Infectious INFECT 38CD* 44 2

CACIQUE *UK, male / female vocal / instrumental group*

1 Jun 85 **DEVOTED TO YOU** *Diamond Duel DISC 1* 69 1

CACTUS WORLD NEWS *Ireland, male vocal / instrumental group (1 Album: 2 Weeks, 3 Singles: 7 Weeks)*

8 Feb 86 **YEARS LATER** *MCA MCA 1024* 59 3
26 Apr 86 **WORLDS APART** *MCA MCA 1040* 58 3
24 May 86 URBAN BEACHES *MCA MCG 6005* 56 2
20 Sep 86 **THE BRIDGE** *MCA MCA 1080* 74 1

CADETS with Eileen REID

Ireland, male / female vocal / instrumental group

3 Jun 65 **JEALOUS HEART** *Pye 7N 15852* 42 1

Susan CADOGAN

Jamaica, female vocalist – Alison Cadogan (2 Singles: 19 Weeks)

5 Apr 75 ● **HURT SO GOOD** *Magnet MAG 23* 4 12
19 Jul 75 **LOVE ME BABY** *Magnet MAG 36* 22 7

CAESARS *Sweden, male vocal (Caesar Vidal) / instrumental group (1 Album: 2 Weeks, 2 Singles: 11 Weeks)*

19 Apr 03 **JERK IT OUT** *Virgin DINSD 244* 60 1
30 Apr 05 ● **JERK IT OUT (remix)** *Virgin DINSD 274* 8 10
7 May 05 PAPER TIGERS *Virgin CDVIR 219* 40 2

Al CAIOLA *US, orchestra – leader Al Caiola – guitar*

15 Jun 61 **THE MAGNIFICENT SEVEN** *HMV POP 889 / LONDON HLT 9294* 34 6

CAKE

US, male vocal / instrumental group (1 Album: 2 Weeks, 4 Singles: 7 Weeks)

22 Mar 97 **THE DISTANCE** *Capricorn 5742212* 22 3
5 Apr 97 FASHION NUGGET *Capricorn 5328672* 53 2
31 May 97 **I WILL SURVIVE** *Capricorn 5744712* 29 2
1 May 99 **NEVER THERE** *Capricorn 8708112* 66 1
3 Nov 01 **SHORT SKIRT LONG JACKET** *Columbia 6720402* 63 1

J.J. CALE

US, male vocalist / guitarist – Jean Jacques Cale (6 Albums: 24 Weeks)

2 Oct 76 TROUBADOUR *Island ISA 5011* 53 1
25 Aug 79 5 *Shelter ISA 5018* 40 6
21 Feb 81 SHADES *Shelter ISA 5021* 44 7
20 Mar 82 GRASSHOPPER *Shelter IFA 5022* 36 5
24 Sep 83 #8 *Mercury MERL 22* 47 3
26 Sep 92 NUMBER 10 *Silvertone ORECD 523* 58 2

CALEXICO *US, male vocal / instrumental group (2 Albums: 2 Weeks)*

20 May 00 HOT RAIL *City Slang 201532* 57 1
22 Feb 03 FEAST OF WIRE *City Slang 5816932* 71 1

CALIFORNIA SUNSHINE

Israel / Italy, male / female DJ / production group

16 Aug 97 **SUMMER '89** *Perfecto PERF 143CD* 56 1

CALL *US, male vocal / instrumental group*

30 Sep 89 **LET THE DAY BEGIN** *MCA MCA 1362* 42 6

12 / 13 September 1958	19 / 20 September 1958	26 / 27 September 1958	3 / 4 October 1958
WHEN The Kalin Twins	WHEN The Kalin Twins	CAROLINA MOON / STUPID CUPID Connie Francis	CAROLINA MOON / STUPID CUPID Connie Francis
MY FAIR LADY Original London Cast	KING CREOLE (Soundtrack) Elvis Presley	KING CREOLE (Soundtrack) Elvis Presley	KING CREOLE (Soundtrack) Elvis Presley

KEY
UK No.1 ★ UK Top 10 ● Still on chart + UK entry at No.1 ■
US No.1 ▲ UK million seller £ US million seller $
Singles re-entries are listed as (re), (2re), (3re)... which signifies that the hit re-entered the chart once, twice or three times...
Peak Position / Weeks

Maria CALLAS *Greece, female vocalist – Cecilia Kalogeropoulou, b. 2 Dec 1923, d. 16 Sep 1978 (4 Albums: 19 Weeks)*

20 Jun 87 THE MARIA CALLAS COLLECTION *Stylus SMR 732*......50 7
24 Feb 96 DIVA – THE ULTIMATE COLLECTION *EMI CDEMTVD 113*......61 1
11 Nov 00 POPULAR MUSIC FROM TV FILM AND OPERA *EMI Classics CDC 5570502*......45 8
27 Oct 01 THE BEST OF – ROMANTIC CALLAS – A COLLECTION OF ROMANTIC ARIAS AND DUETS *EMI Classics CDC 5572112*...32 3

Terry CALLIER *US, male vocalist (2 Singles: 4 Weeks)*

13 Dec 97 BEST BIT (EP) *Heavenly HVN 72CD* [1] 36 3
23 May 98 LOVE THEME FROM SPARTACUS *Talkin Loud TLCD 32*......57 1

[1] Beth Orton featuring Terry Callier

Tracks on Best Bit (EP): Best Bit / Skimming Stone / Dolphins / Lean On Me.

The CALLING *US, male vocal (Alex Band) / instrumental group (2 Albums: 29 Weeks, 5 Singles: 21 Weeks)*

29 Jun 02 CAMINO PALMERO *RCA 74321916102*......12 25
29 Jun 02 WHEREVER YOU WILL GO (import) *RCA 74321912242*......64 1
6 Jul 02 ● WHEREVER YOU WILL GO *RCA 74321947652*......3 11
2 Nov 02 ADRIENNE *RCA 74321968352*......18 3
29 May 04 OUR LIVES *RCA 82876618642*......13 4
12 Jun 04 ● II *RCA 82876622622*......9 4
28 Aug 04 THINGS WILL GO MY WAY *RCA 82876637362*......34 2

Eddie CALVERT
UK, male trumpeter, b. 15 Mar 1922, d. 7 Aug 1978 (7 Singles: 80 Weeks)

18 Dec 53 ★ OH, MEIN PAPA *Columbia DB 3337*......1 21
8 Apr 55 ★ CHERRY PINK AND APPLE BLOSSOM WHITE *Columbia DB 3581*......1 21
13 May 55 STRANGER IN PARADISE *Columbia DB 3594*......14 4
29 Jul 55 ● JOHN AND JULIE *Columbia DB 3624*......6 11
9 Mar 56 ZAMBESI (re) *Columbia DB 3747*......13 7
7 Feb 58 ● MANDY (LA PANSE) *Columbia DB 3956*......9 14
20 Jun 58 LITTLE SERENADE *Columbia DB 4105*......28 2

CAMEL *UK, male vocal / instrumental group (8 Albums: 47 Weeks)*

24 May 75 THE SNOW GOOSE *Decca SKL 5207*......22 13
17 Apr 76 MOON MADNESS *Decca TXS 115*......15 6
17 Sep 77 RAIN DANCES *Decca TXS 124*......20 8
14 Oct 78 BREATHLESS *Decca TXS 132*......26 1
27 Oct 79 I CAN SEE YOUR HOUSE FROM HERE *Decca TXS 137*......45 3
31 Jan 81 NUDE *Decca SKL 5323*......34 7
15 May 82 THE SINGLE FACTOR *Decca SKL 5328*......57 5
21 Apr 84 STATIONARY TRAVELLER *Decca SKL 5334*......57 4

CAMEO *US, male vocal (Larry Blackmon) / instrumental group (3 Albums: 47 Weeks, 11 Singles: 71 Weeks)*

31 Mar 84 SHE'S STRANGE *Club JAB 2*......37 8
13 Jul 85 ATTACK ME WITH YOUR LOVE *Club JAB 16*......65 2
10 Aug 85 SINGLE LIFE *Club JABH 11*......66 12
14 Sep 85 SINGLE LIFE *Club JAB 21*......15 10
7 Dec 85 SHE'S STRANGE (re-issue) *Club JAB 25*......22 8
22 Mar 86 A GOODBYE *Club JAB 28*......65 2
30 Aug 86 ● WORD UP *Club JAB 38*......3 13
18 Oct 86 ● WORD UP *Club JABH 19*......7 34
29 Nov 86 CANDY *Club JAB 43*......27 9
25 Apr 87 BACK AND FORTH *Club JAB 49*......11 9
17 Oct 87 SHE'S MINE *Club JAB 57*......35 4
29 Oct 88 YOU MAKE ME WORK *Club JAB 70*......74 1
26 Nov 88 MACHISMO *Club 836002 1*......86 1
28 Jul 01 LOVERBOY (re) *Virgin VUSCD 211* [1] 12 5

[1] Mariah featuring Cameo

Andy CAMERON *UK, male vocalist*

4 Mar 78 ● ALLY'S TARTAN ARMY *Klub 03*......6 8

Tony CAMILLO'S BAZUKA *US, male instrumental / vocal group*

31 May 75 DYNOMITE (PART 1) *A&M AMS 7168*......28 5

CAMISRA (see also ESCRIMA; The GRIFTERS; PARTIZAN; TALL PAUL)
UK, male DJ / producer – 'Tall Paul' Newman (3 Singles: 12 Weeks)

21 Feb 98 ● LET ME SHOW YOU *VC Recordings VCRD 31*......5 8
11 Jul 98 FEEL THE BEAT *VC Recordings VCRD 39*......32 2
22 May 99 CLAP YOUR HANDS *VC Recordings VCRD 49*......34 2

CAMOUFLAGE featuring MYSTI
UK, male / female vocal / instrumental group

24 Sep 77 BEE STING *State STAT 58*......48 3

A CAMP *Sweden / US, female / male vocal / instrumental group – leader Nina Persson*

1 Sep 01 I CAN BUY YOU *Stockholm 0152162*......46 1

CAMP LO *US, male rap duo*

16 Aug 97 LUCHINI AKA (THIS IS IT) *ffrr FCD 305*......74 1

CAMPAG VELOCET *UK, male / female vocal / instrumental group*

19 Feb 00 VITO SATAN *Pias Recordings PIASX 010CD*......75 1

Ali CAMPBELL (see also Pato BANTON; UB40)
UK, male vocalist (1 Album: 11 Weeks, 3 Singles: 18 Weeks)

20 May 95 ● THAT LOOK IN YOUR EYE *Kuff KUFFDG 1*......5 10
17 Jun 95 ● BIG LOVE *Kuff CDV 2783*......6 11
26 Aug 95 LET YOUR YEAH BE YEAH *Kuff KUFFD 2*......25 4
9 Dec 95 SOMETHIN' STUPID *Kuff KUFFDG 5* [1] 30 4

[1] Ali and Kibibi Campbell

Danny CAMPBELL and SASHA
UK, male vocalist and DJ / producer

31 Jul 93 TOGETHER *ffrr FCD 212*......57 1

Ellie CAMPBELL *UK, female vocalist (3 Singles: 5 Weeks)*

3 Apr 99 SWEET LIES *Jive / Eastern Bloc 0519222*......42 1
14 Aug 99 SO MANY WAYS *Jive / Eastern Bloc 0519362*......26 3
9 Jun 01 DON'T WANT YOU BACK *Jive 9201302*......50 1

Ethna CAMPBELL *UK, female vocalist*

27 Dec 75 THE OLD RUGGED CROSS *Philips 6006 475*......33 11

Glen CAMPBELL 207 Top 500
Top session guitarist and singer who became one of the biggest selling country and easy listening artists of the 1960s, b. 22 Apr 1936, Arkansas, US. Other credits include part-time member of The Beach Boys and vocalist with The Crickets. In 2005, he was inducted into the Country Music Hall of Fame (10 Albums: 185 Weeks, 11 Singles: 106 Weeks)

29 Jan 69 ● WICHITA LINEMAN *Ember EMBS 261* $......7 13
7 May 69 GALVESTON *Ember EMBS 263* $......14 10
6 Dec 69 ● ALL I HAVE TO DO IS DREAM *Capitol CL 15619* [1] 3 14
31 Jan 70 GLEN CAMPBELL LIVE *Capitol SB 21444*......16 14
7 Feb 70 TRY A LITTLE KINDNESS *Capitol CL 15622*......45 2
28 Feb 70 BOBBIE GENTRY AND GLEN CAMPBELL *Capitol ST 2928* [1] 50 1

10 / 11 October 1958	17 / 18 October 1958	24 / 25 October 1958	31 October / 1 November 1958
UK No.1 SINGLES			
CAROLINA MOON / STUPID CUPID Connie Francis	CAROLINA MOON / STUPID CUPID Connie Francis	CAROLINA MOON / STUPID CUPID Connie Francis	CAROLINA MOON / STUPID CUPID Connie Francis
UK No.1 ALBUMS			
KING CREOLE (Soundtrack) Elvis Presley	KING CREOLE (Soundtrack) Elvis Presley	KING CREOLE (Soundtrack) Elvis Presley	KING CREOLE (Soundtrack) Elvis Presley

9 May 70 ● **HONEY COME BACK** *Capitol CL 15638*....4 19
30 May 70 **TRY A LITTLE KINDNESS** *Capitol ESW 389*....37 10
26 Sep 70 **EVERYTHING A MAN COULD EVER NEED** *Capitol CL 15653*....32 5
21 Nov 70 ● **IT'S ONLY MAKE BELIEVE** *Capitol CL 15663*....4 14
12 Dec 70 **THE GLEN CAMPBELL ALBUM** *Capitol ST 22493*....16 5
27 Mar 71 **DREAM BABY (HOW LONG MUST I DREAM)** *Capitol CL 15674*....39 3
27 Nov 71 ● **GLEN CAMPBELL'S GREATEST HITS** *Capitol ST 21885*....8 113
4 Oct 75 ● **RHINESTONE COWBOY** *Capitol CL 15824* ▲ $....4 12
25 Oct 75 **RHINESTONE COWBOY** *Capitol ESW 11430*....38 9
20 Nov 76 ★ **GLEN CAMPBELL'S TWENTY GOLDEN GREATS** *Capitol EMTV 2*....1 27
26 Mar 77 **SOUTHERN NIGHTS** *Capitol CL 15907* ▲ $....28 6
23 Apr 77 **SOUTHERN NIGHTS** *Capitol EST 11601*....51 1
22 Jul 89 **THE COMPLETE GLEN CAMPBELL** *Stylus SMR 979*....47 4
2 Oct 99 **MY HITS AND LOVE SONGS** *Capitol 5223002*....50 1
30 Nov 02 **RHINESTONE COWBOY (GIDDY UP GIDDY UP)** *Serious SER 059CD* [2]....12 8

[1] Bobbie Gentry and Glen Campbell [2] Rikki and Daz featuring Glen Campbell [1] Bobbie Gentry and Glen Campbell

Jo Ann CAMPBELL *US, female vocalist*

8 Jun 61 **MOTORCYCLE MICHAEL** *HMV POP 873*....41 3

Junior CAMPBELL (see also MARMALADE) *UK, male vocalist – William Campbell (2 Singles: 18 Weeks)*

14 Oct 72 ● **HALLELUJAH FREEDOM** *Deram DM 364*....10 9
2 Jun 73 **SWEET ILLUSION** *Deram DM 387*....15 9

Naomi CAMPBELL *UK, female vocalist*

24 Sep 94 **LOVE AND TEARS** *Epic 6608352*....40 3

Pat CAMPBELL *Ireland, male vocalist*

15 Nov 69 **THE DEAL** *Major Minor MM 648*....31 5

Stan CAMPBELL *UK, male vocalist*

6 Jun 87 **YEARS GO BY** *WEA YZ 127*....65 3

Tevin CAMPBELL *US, male vocalist*

18 Apr 92 **TELL ME WHAT YOU WANT ME TO DO** *Qwest W 0102*....63 2

Ian CAMPBELL FOLK GROUP *UK, male vocal / instrumental group*

11 Mar 65 **THE TIMES THEY ARE A-CHANGIN' (2re)** *Transatlantic SP 5*....42 5

CAM'RON *US, male rapper – Cameron Giles (5 Singles: 30 Weeks)*

19 Sep 98 **HORSE AND CARRIAGE** *Epic 6662612* [1]....12 4
17 Aug 02 **OH BOY** *Roc-A-Fella 0639642* [2]....13 7
8 Feb 03 ● **HEY MA** *Roc-A-Fella 0637242* [2]....8 10
5 Apr 03 **BOY (I NEED YOU)** *Def Jam 0779282* [3]....17 6
12 Feb 05 **GIRLS** *Roc-A-Fella 2103988* [4]....25 3

[1] Cam'ron featuring Ma$e [2] Cam'ron featuring Juelz Santana [2] Cam'Ron featuring Juelz Santana [3] Mariah Carey featuring Cam'ron [4] Cam'ron featuring Mona Lisa

CAN *Germany, male vocal / instrumental group*

28 Aug 76 **I WANT MORE** *Virgin VS 153*....26 10

CANDIDO *Cuba, male multi-instrumentalist – Candido Camero*

18 Jul 81 **JINGO** *Excalibur EXC 102*....55 3

CANDLEWICK GREEN *UK, male vocal / instrumental group*

23 Feb 74 **WHO DO YOU THINK YOU ARE?** *Decca F 13480*....21 8

CANDY FLIP *UK, male vocal / instrumental duo – Rick Peel and Danny 'Dizzy' Deo (2 Singles: 14 Weeks)*

17 Mar 90 ● **STRAWBERRY FIELDS FOREVER** *Debut DEBT 3092*....3 10
14 Jul 90 **THIS CAN BE REAL** *Debut DEBT 3099*....60 4

The CANDY GIRLS (see also CLERGY; DOROTHY; HI-GATE; Paul MASTERSON presents SUSHI; SLEAZESISTERS; YOMANDA) *UK, male / female instrumental / production duo – Rachel Auburn and Paul Masterson (3 Singles: 10 Weeks)*

30 Sep 95 **FEE FI FO FUM** *VC VCRD 1* [1]....23 4
24 Feb 96 **WHAM BAM** *VC VCRD 6* [1]....20 4
7 Dec 96 **I WANT CANDY** *Feverpitch CDFVR 1013* [2]....30 2

[1] Candy Girls featuring Sweet Pussy Pauline
[2] Candy Girls featuring Valerie Malcolm

CANDYLAND *UK, male vocal / instrumental group*

9 Mar 91 **FOUNTAIN O' YOUTH** *Non Fiction YES 4*....72 1

The CANDYSKINS *UK, male vocal / instrumental group (3 Singles: 4 Weeks)*

19 Oct 96 **MRS HOOVER** *Ultimate TOPP 051CD*....65 1
8 Feb 97 **MONDAY MORNING** *Ultimate TOPP 055CD*....34 2
3 May 97 **HANG MYSELF ON YOU** *Ultimate TOPP 059CD*....65 1

CANIBUS *US, male rapper – Germaine Williams (1 Album: 1 Week, 2 Singles: 3 Weeks)*

27 Jun 98 **SECOND ROUND KO** *Universal UND 56198*....35 2
19 Sep 98 **CAN-I-BUS** *Universal UND 53222*....43 1
10 Oct 98 **HOW COME** *Interscope IND 95598* [1]....52 1

[1] Youssou N'Dour and Canibus

CANNED HEAT *US, male vocal / instrumental group (4 Albums: 40 Weeks, 4 Singles: 41 Weeks)*

29 Jun 68 ● **BOOGIE WITH CANNED HEAT** *Liberty LBL 83103*....5 21
24 Jul 68 ● **ON THE ROAD AGAIN** *Liberty LBS 15090*....8 15
1 Jan 69 **GOING UP THE COUNTRY** *Liberty LBF 15169*....19 10
17 Jan 70 ● **LET'S WORK TOGETHER** *Liberty LBF 15302*....2 15
14 Feb 70 ● **CANNED HEAT COOKBOOK** *Liberty LBS 83303*....8 12
4 Jul 70 **CANNED HEAT '70 CONCERT** *Liberty LBS 83333*....15 3
11 Jul 70 **SUGAR BEE** *Liberty LBF 15350*....49 1
10 Oct 70 **FUTURE BLUES** *Liberty LBS 83364*....27 4

Freddy CANNON *US, male vocalist – Freddy Picariello (1 Album: 11 Weeks, 7 Singles: 54 Weeks)*

14 Aug 59 **TALLAHASSEE LASSIE** *Top Rank JAR 135*....17 8
1 Jan 60 ● **WAY DOWN YONDER IN NEW ORLEANS** *Top Rank JAR 247* $....3 18
27 Feb 60 ★ **THE EXPLOSIVE FREDDY CANNON** *Top Rank 25/108*....1 11
4 Mar 60 **CALIFORNIA HERE I COME (re)** *Top Rank JAR 309*....25 3
17 Mar 60 **INDIANA** *Top Rank JAR 309*....42 1
19 May 60 **THE URGE** *Top Rank JAR 369*....18 10
20 Apr 61 **MUSKRAT RAMBLE** *Top Rank JAR 548*....32 5
28 Jun 62 **PALISADES PARK** *Stateside SS 101* $....20 9

The CANTAMUS GIRLS CHOIR NEW *UK, female choir*

31 Dec 05 **EVERYBODY'S GOTTA LEARN SOMETIME** *EMI 3497582*....73 1+

Blu CANTRELL *US, female vocalist – Tiffany Cantrell (1 Album: 11 Weeks, 4 Singles: 32 Weeks)*

24 Nov 01 **HIT 'EM UP STYLE (OOPS!)** *Arista 74321891632*....12 9
19 Jul 03 **BREATHE** (import) *Arista 8786509842* [1]....59 3
9 Aug 03 **BITTERSWEET** *Arista 82876534042*....20 11
9 Aug 03 ★ **BREATHE** *Arista 82876545722* [1] ■....1 18
13 Dec 03 **MAKE ME WANNA SCREAM** *Arista 82876573382*....24 2

[1] Blu Cantrell featuring Sean Paul

7 / 8 November 1958	14 / 15 November 1958	21 / 22 November 1958	28 / 29 November 1958
IT'S ALL IN THE GAME Tommy Edwards	IT'S ALL IN THE GAME Tommy Edwards	IT'S ALL IN THE GAME Tommy Edwards	HOOTS MON Jack Good presents Lord Rockingham's XI
SOUTH PACIFIC Soundtrack	SOUTH PACIFIC Soundtrack	SOUTH PACIFIC Soundtrack	SOUTH PACIFIC Soundtrack

KEY
UK No.1 ★ UK Top 10 ● Still on chart + UK entry at No.1 ■
US No.1 ▲ UK million seller £ US million seller $
Singles re-entries are listed as (re), (2re), (3re)... which signifies that the hit re-entered the chart once, twice or three times...
Peak Position / Weeks

Jim CAPALDI (see also TRAFFIC)
UK, male vocalist, b. 2 Aug 1944, d. 28 Jan 2005 (2 Singles: 17 Weeks)

27 Jul 74 IT'S ALL UP TO YOU *Island WIP 6198* ... 27 6
25 Oct 75 ● LOVE HURTS *Island WIP 6246* ... 4 11

CAPERCAILLIE *UK / Ireland, male / female vocal / instrumental group (4 Albums: 8 Weeks, 2 Singles: 3 Weeks)*

23 May 92 A PRINCE AMONG ISLANDS (EP) *Survival ZB 45393* ... 39 2
25 Sep 93 SECRET PEOPLE *Arista 74321162742* ... 40 3
17 Sep 94 CAPERCAILLIE *Survival 74321229112* ... 61 1
17 Jun 95 DARK ALAN (AILEIN DUINN) *Survival SURCD 55* ... 65 1
4 Nov 95 TO THE MOON *Survival SURCD 019* ... 41 2
20 Sep 97 BEAUTIFUL WASTELAND *Survival SURCD 021* ... 55 2

Tracks on A Prince Among Islands (EP): Coisich a Ruin (Walk My Beloved) / Fagail Bhearnaraid (Leaving Bernaray) / The Lorn Theme / Gun Teann Mi Ris Na Ruinn Tha Seo (Remembrance).

CAPPADONNA (see also WU-TANG CLAN) *US, male rapper – Daryl Hill*

4 Apr 98 THE PILLAGE *Epic 4888502* ... 43 1

CAPPELLA (see also 49ers) *Italy, male / female production / vocal group (1 Album: 9 Weeks, 13 Singles: 68 Weeks)*

9 Apr 88 PUSH THE BEAT / BAUHAUS *Fast Globe FGL 1* ... 60 2
6 May 89 HELYOM HALIB *Music Man MMPS 7004* ... 11 9
23 Sep 89 HOUSE ENERGY REVENGE *Music Man MMPS 7009* ... 73 1
27 Apr 91 EVERYBODY *ffrr F158* ... 66 1
18 Jan 92 TAKE ME AWAY *PWL Continental PWL 210* [1] ... 25 5
3 Apr 93 ● U GOT 2 KNOW *Internal Dance IDC 1* ... 6 11
14 Aug 93 U GOT 2 KNOW (re-mix) *Internal Dance IDCR 2* ... 43 3
23 Oct 93 ● U GOT 2 LET THE MUSIC *Internal Dance IDC 3* ... 2 12
19 Feb 94 ● MOVE ON BABY *Internal Dance IDC 4* ... 7 7
26 Mar 94 ● U GOT 2 KNOW *Internal Dance CAPPC 1* ... 10 9
18 Jun 94 ● U & ME *Internal Dance IDCC 6* ... 10 7
15 Oct 94 MOVE IT UP / BIG BEAT *Internal Dance IDC 7* ... 16 6
16 Sep 95 TELL ME THE WAY *Systematic SYSCD 17* ... 17 3
6 Sep 97 BE MY BABY *Nukleuz PSNC 0072* ... 53 1

[1] Cappella featuring Loleatta Holloway

CAPRICCIO *UK, production duo*

27 Mar 99 EVERYBODY GET UP *Defected DEFECT 2CDS* ... 44 2

CAPRICE *US, female model / vocalist – Caprice Bourret (2 Singles: 5 Weeks)*

4 Sep 99 OH YEAH *Virgin VSCDT 1745* ... 24 3
10 Mar 01 ONCE AROUND THE SUN *Virgin VSCDT 1750* ... 24 2

CAPRICORN *Belgium, male DJ – Hans Weekhout*

29 Nov 97 20 HZ (NEW FREQUENCIES) *R&S RS 97126CD* ... 73 1

Tony CAPSTICK and The CARLTON MAIN / FRICKLEY COLLIERY BAND *UK, male vocalist, b. 27 Jul 1944, d. 23 Oct 2003, and instrumental band*

21 Mar 81 ● THE SHEFFIELD GRINDER / CAPSTICK COMES HOME *Dingles SID 27* ... 3 8

CAPTAIN BEEFHEART and his MAGIC BAND
(see also MAGIC BAND) *US, male vocal / instrumental group – leader Don Van Vliet (5 Albums: 8 Weeks)*

6 Dec 69 TROUT MASK REPLICA *Straight STS 1053* ... 21 1
23 Jan 71 LICK MY DECALS OFF BABY *Straight STS 1063* ... 20 2
29 May 71 MIRROR MAN *Buddah 2365 002* ... 49 1
19 Feb 72 THE SPOTLIGHT KID *Reprise K 44162* ... 44 2
18 Sep 82 ICE CREAM FOR CROW *Virgin V 2337* ... 90 2

CAPTAIN HOLLYWOOD PROJECT *US / Germany, male / female vocal / rap / instrumental group (16 Singles: 32 Weeks)*

22 Sep 90 ● I CAN'T STAND IT *BCM BCMR 395* [1] ... 7 10
24 Nov 90 ARE YOU DREAMING *BCM BCM 07504* [1] ... 17 10
27 Mar 93 ONLY WITH YOU *Pulse 8 CDLOSE 40* ... 67 1
6 Nov 93 MORE AND MORE *Pulse 8 CDLOSE 50* ... 23 6
5 Feb 94 IMPOSSIBLE *Pulse 8 CDLOSE 54* ... 29 3
11 Jun 94 ONLY WITH YOU (re-issue) *Pulse 8 CDLOSE 62* ... 61 1
1 Apr 95 FLYING HIGH *Pulse 8 CDLOSE 82* ... 58 1

[1] Twenty 4 Seven featuring Captain Hollywood

CAPTAIN SENSIBLE (see also The DAMNED)
UK, male vocalist – Ray Burns (1 Album: 3 Weeks, 5 Singles: 31 Weeks)

26 Jun 82 ★ HAPPY TALK *A&M CAP 1* ... 1 8
14 Aug 82 WOT! *A&M CAP 2* ... 26 7
11 Sep 82 WOMEN AND CAPTAIN FIRST *A&M AMLH 68548* ... 64 3
24 Mar 84 ● GLAD IT'S ALL OVER / DAMNED ON 45 *A&M CAP 6* ... 6 10
28 Jul 84 THERE ARE MORE SNAKES THAN LADDERS *A&M CAP 7* ... 57 5
10 Dec 94 THE HOKEY COKEY *Have a Nice Day CDHOKEY 1* ... 71 1

CAPTAIN and TENNILLE
US, male keyboard player – Daryl Dragon and female vocalist – Toni Tennille (1 Album: 6 Weeks, 4 Singles: 24 Weeks)

2 Aug 75 LOVE WILL KEEP US TOGETHER *A&M AMS 7165* ▲ $ ... 32 5
24 Jan 76 THE WAY I WANT TO TOUCH YOU *A&M AMS 7203* $ ... 28 6
4 Nov 78 YOU NEVER DONE IT LIKE THAT *A&M AMS 7384* ... 63 3
16 Feb 80 ● DO THAT TO ME ONE MORE TIME *Casablanca CAN 175* ▲ $ ... 7 10
22 Mar 80 MAKE YOUR MOVE *Casablanca CAL 2060* ... 33 6

Irene CARA *US, female actor / vocalist (3 Singles: 33 Weeks)*

3 Jul 82 ★ FAME *RSO 90* ... 1 16
4 Sep 82 OUT HERE ON MY OWN *RSO 66* ... 58 3
4 Jun 83 ● FLASHDANCE ... WHAT A FEELING *Casablanca CAN 1016* ▲ $ ... 2 14

CARAMBA *Sweden, male vocalist / multi-instrumentalist / dog impersonator – Michael Tretow*

12 Nov 83 FEDORA (I'LL BE YOUR DAWG) *Billco BILL 101* ... 56 6

CARAVAN *UK, male vocal / instrumental group (2 Albums: 2 Weeks)*

30 Aug 75 CUNNING STUNTS *Decca SKL 5210* ... 50 1
15 May 76 BLIND DOG AT ST. DUNSTAN'S *BTM BTM 1007* ... 53 1

The CARAVELLES
UK, female vocal duo – Lois Wilkinson and Andrea Simpson

8 Aug 63 ● YOU DON'T HAVE TO BE A BABY TO CRY *Decca F 11697* ... 6 13

CARCASS *UK, male vocal / instrumental group (2 Albums: 2 Weeks)*

6 Nov 93 HEARTWORK *Earache MOSH 097CD* ... 67 1
6 Jul 96 SWANSONG *Earache MOSH 160CD* ... 68 1

The CARDIGANS (see also A CAMP)
Sweden, female / male vocal / instrumental group – leader Nina Persson (4 Albums: 70 Weeks, 14 Singles: 70 Weeks)

17 Jun 95 CARNIVAL (re) *Trampolene PZCD 345* ... 35 3
8 Jul 95 LIFE *Stockholm 5235562* ... 51 9
30 Sep 95 SICK AND TIRED *Stockholm 5773112* ... 34 3
17 Feb 96 RISE AND SHINE *Trampolene 5778252* ... 29 2
21 Sep 96 LOVEFOOL *Stockholm 5752952* ... 21 4
12 Oct 96 FIRST BAND ON THE MOON *Stockholm 5331172* ... 18 10
7 Dec 96 BEEN IT *Stockholm 5759672* ... 56 1

5 / 6 December 1958	12 / 13 December 1958	19 / 20 December 1958	26 / 27 December 1958
UK No.1 SINGLES			
HOOTS MON Jack Good presents Lord Rockingham's XI	HOOTS MON Jack Good presents Lord Rockingham's XI	IT'S ONLY MAKE BELIEVE Conway Twitty	IT'S ONLY MAKE BELIEVE Conway Twitty
UK No.1 ALBUMS			
SOUTH PACIFIC Soundtrack	SOUTH PACIFIC Soundtrack	SOUTH PACIFIC Soundtrack	SOUTH PACIFIC Soundtrack

3 May 97 ● **LOVEFOOL** (re-issue) *Stockholm 5710502* **2** 13
6 Sep 97 **YOUR NEW CUCKOO** *Stockholm 5716632* **35** 2
17 Oct 98 **MY FAVOURITE GAME** *Stockholm 5679912* **14** 18
31 Oct 98 ● GRAN TURISMO *Stockholm 5590812* 8 49
6 Mar 99 ● **ERASE / REWIND** *Stockholm 5635332* **7** 9
24 Jul 99 **HANGING AROUND** *Stockholm 5612682* **17** 4
25 Sep 99 ● **BURNING DOWN THE HOUSE** *Gut CDGUT 26* [1] **7** 7
22 Mar 03 **FOR WHAT IT'S WORTH** *Stockholm 0657232* **31** 2
5 Apr 03 LONG GONE BEFORE DAYLIGHT *Stockholm / Polydor 0381092* 47 2
26 Jul 03 **YOU'RE THE STORM** *Stockholm 9809673* **74** 1
15 Oct 05 **I NEED SOME FINE WINE AND YOU, YOU NEED TO BE NICER** *Stockholm 9874124* **59** 1

[1] Tom Jones and The Cardigans

CARE *UK, male vocal / instrumental duo*

12 Nov 83 **FLAMING SWORD** *Arista KBIRD 2* **48** 4

Mariah CAREY (49 Top 500)

Record-shattering vocalist / songwriter, b. 27 Mar 1970, New York, US. Since her 1990 chart debut she has sold more than 150 million albums worldwide and has topped the US singles chart 16 times (only Elvis Presley has spent longer at the top). She had a brief $20m per album deal with Virgin in 2001 and performed at the Hyde Park Live 8 concert in 2005. Best-selling single: 'Without You' 559,200 (14 Albums: 355 Weeks, 35 Singles: 319 Weeks)

4 Aug 90 ● **VISION OF LOVE** *CBS 6559320* ▲ **9** 12
15 Sep 90 ● MARIAH CAREY *CBS 4668151* ▲ 6 40
10 Nov 90 **LOVE TAKES TIME** *CBS 6563647* ▲ **37** 8
26 Jan 91 **SOMEDAY** *Columbia 6565837* ▲ **38** 5
1 Jun 91 **THERE'S GOT TO BE A WAY** *Columbia 6569317* **54** 3
5 Oct 91 **EMOTIONS** *Columbia 6574037* ▲ **17** 9
26 Oct 91 ● EMOTIONS *Columbia 4688511* 4 40
11 Jan 92 **CAN'T LET GO** *Columbia 6576627* **20** 7
18 Apr 92 **MAKE IT HAPPEN** *Columbia 6579417* **17** 5
27 Jun 92 ● **I'LL BE THERE** *Columbia 6581377* ▲ **2** 9
18 Jul 92 ● MTV UNPLUGGED EP *Columbia 4718692* 3 10
21 Aug 93 ● **DREAMLOVER** *Columbia 6594445* ▲ $ **9** 10
11 Sep 93 ★ MUSIC BOX *Columbia 4742702* ■ ▲ 1 77
6 Nov 93 ● **HERO** *Columbia 6598122* ▲ $ **7** 15
19 Feb 94 ★ **WITHOUT YOU** *Columbia 6599192* ■ **1** 14
18 Jun 94 ● **ANYTIME YOU NEED A FRIEND** *Columbia 6603542* **8** 10
17 Sep 94 ● **ENDLESS LOVE (2re)** *Epic 6608062* [1] **3** 16
19 Nov 94 MERRY CHRISTMAS *Columbia 4773422* 32 7
10 Dec 94 ● **ALL I WANT FOR CHRISTMAS IS YOU (re)** *Columbia 6610702* **2** 8
23 Sep 95 ● **FANTASY** *Columbia 6624952* ▲ $ **4** 11
7 Oct 95 ★ DAYDREAM *Columbia 4813672* ■ ▲ 1 46
9 Dec 95 ● **ONE SWEET DAY** *Columbia 6626035* [2] ▲ $ **6** 11
17 Feb 96 ● **OPEN ARMS** *Columbia 6629772* **4** 6
22 Jun 96 ● **ALWAYS BE MY BABY** *Columbia 6633345* ▲ $ **3** 10
6 Sep 97 ● **HONEY** *Columbia 6650192* ▲ $ **3** 8
20 Sep 97 ● BUTTERFLY *Columbia 4885372* ▲ 2 27
13 Dec 97 **BUTTERFLY** *Columbia 6653365* **22** 6
13 Jun 98 ● **MY ALL** *Columbia 6660592* ▲ $ **4** 8
28 Nov 98 ● #1'S *Columbia 4926042* 10 32
19 Dec 98 ● **WHEN YOU BELIEVE (re)** *Columbia 6667522* [3] **4** 13
10 Apr 99 **I STILL BELIEVE** *Columbia 6670732* $ **16** 7
6 Nov 99 ● **HEARTBREAKER** *Columbia 6683012* [4] ▲ **5** 13
13 Nov 99 ● RAINBOW *Columbia 4950652* 8 15
11 Mar 00 ● **THANK GOD I FOUND YOU (re)** *Columbia 6690582* [5] ▲ **10** 10
30 Sep 00 ★ **AGAINST ALL ODDS (re)** *Columbia 6698872* [6] ■ **1** 12
28 Jul 01 **LOVERBOY (re)** *Virgin VUSCD 211* [7] **12** 5
22 Sep 01 ● GLITTER *Virgin CDVUS 201* 10 3
15 Dec 01 ● GREATEST HITS *Columbia 5054612* 7 15+
29 Dec 01 **NEVER TOO FAR / DON'T STOP (FUNKIN' 4 JAMAICA)** *Virgin VUSCD 228* [8] **32** 4
30 Nov 02 ● **THROUGH THE RAIN** *Mercury 0638072* **8** 8
14 Dec 02 CHARMBRACELET *Island US / Mercury 0633842* 52 3
5 Apr 03 **BOY (I NEED YOU)** *Def Jam 0779282* [9] **17** 6
7 Jun 03 ● **I KNOW WHAT YOU WANT** *J 82876528292* [10] **3** 13
18 Oct 03 THE REMIXES *Columbia 5107542* 35 2
9 Apr 05 ● **IT'S LIKE THAT** *Def Jam 9881337* **4** 11
16 Apr 05 ● THE EMANCIPATION OF MIMI *Def Jam 9881270* ▲ 7 38+
16 Jul 05 ● **WE BELONG TOGETHER** *Def Jam / Island 9883483* ▲ **2** 16
15 Oct 05 ● **GET YOUR NUMBER / SHAKE IT OFF** *Def Jam / Island 9886374* **9** 8
24 Dec 05 **DON'T FORGET ABOUT US** *Def Jam / Island 9889758* ▲ **11** 2+

[1] Luther Vandross and Mariah Carey [2] Mariah Carey and Boyz II Men [3] Mariah Carey & Whitney Houston [4] Mariah Carey featuring Jay-Z [5] Mariah Carey featuring Joe and 98 Degrees [6] Mariah Carey featuring Westlife [7] Mariah featuring Cameo [8] Mariah Carey / Mariah Carey featuring Mystikal [9] Mariah Carey featuring Cam'ron [10] Busta Rhymes and Mariah Carey featuring The Flipmode Squad

Although he is uncredited, 'I'll Be There' is a duet with Trey Lorenz. Greatest Hits peaked at No.46 on its initial chart run and reached its peak position in 2005.

Belinda CARLISLE (191 Top 500)

Lead vocalist of the first really successful all-girl rock group, The Go-Go's, b. 17 Aug 1958, Hollywood, US. She married the son of British-born film star James Mason in 1992 and her career fared even better in the UK than in her homeland. Joined a re-formed Go-Go's in 2001 (7 Albums: 160 Weeks, 23 Singles: 145 Weeks)

12 Dec 87 ★ **HEAVEN IS A PLACE ON EARTH** *Virgin VS 1036* ▲ **1** 14
2 Jan 88 ● HEAVEN ON EARTH *Virgin V 2496* 4 54
27 Feb 88 ● **I GET WEAK** *Virgin VS 1046* **10** 9
7 May 88 ● **CIRCLE IN THE SAND** *Virgin VS 1074* **4** 11
6 Aug 88 **MAD ABOUT YOU** *IRS IRM 118* **67** 3
10 Sep 88 **WORLD WITHOUT YOU** *Virgin VS 1114* **34** 6
10 Dec 88 **LOVE NEVER DIES ...** *Virgin VS 1150* **54** 5
7 Oct 89 ● **LEAVE A LIGHT ON** *Virgin VS 1210* **4** 10
4 Nov 89 ● RUNAWAY HORSES *Virgin V 2599* 4 39
9 Dec 89 **LA LUNA** *Virgin VS 1230* **38** 6
24 Feb 90 **RUNAWAY HORSES** *Virgin VS 1244* **40** 5
26 May 90 **VISION OF YOU (re)** *Virgin VS 1264* **41** 5
13 Oct 90 ● **(WE WANT) THE SAME THING** *Virgin VS 1319* **6** 10
22 Dec 90 **SUMMER RAIN** *Virgin VS 1323* **23** 10
28 Sep 91 **LIVE YOUR LIFE BE FREE** *Virgin VS 1370* **12** 7
26 Oct 91 ● LIVE YOUR LIFE BE FREE *Virgin V 2680* 7 16
16 Nov 91 **DO YOU FEEL LIKE I FEEL** *Virgin VS 1383* **29** 4
11 Jan 92 **HALF THE WORLD** *Virgin VS 1388* **35** 4
29 Aug 92 **LITTLE BLACK BOOK** *Virgin VS 1428* **28** 5
19 Sep 92 ★ THE BEST OF BELINDA VOLUME 1 *Virgin BELCD 1* 1 35
25 Sep 93 **BIGSCARYANIMAL** *Virgin VSCDT 1472* **12** 6
23 Oct 93 ● REAL *Virgin CDV 2725* 9 5
27 Nov 93 **LAY DOWN YOUR ARMS** *Virgin VSCDG 1476* **27** 6
13 Jul 96 ● **IN TOO DEEP** *Chrysalis CDCHS 5033* **6** 7
21 Sep 96 ● **ALWAYS BREAKING MY HEART** *Chrysalis CDCHS 5037* **8** 6
5 Oct 96 A WOMAN & A MAN *Chrysalis CDCHR 6115* 12 5
30 Nov 96 **LOVE IN THE KEY OF C** *Chrysalis CDCHS 5044* **20** 3
1 Mar 97 **CALIFORNIA** *Chrysalis CDCHSS 5047* **31** 2
13 Nov 99 A PLACE ON EARTH – THE GREATEST HITS *Virgin CDV 2901* 15 6
27 Nov 99 **ALL GOD'S CHILDREN** *Virgin VSCDT 1756* **66** 1

Bob CARLISLE *US, male vocalist*

30 Aug 97 **BUTTERFLY KISSES** *Jive JIVECD 249* **56** 2

Don CARLOS presents the SINGING DOGS

Denmark, canine vocal group

25 Nov 55 **THE SINGING DOGS (MEDLEY)** *Nixa N 15009* **13** 4

Medley songs: Pat-a-Cake / Three Blind Mice / Jingle Bells / Oh Susanna.

CARLTON

UK, male vocalist – Carlton McCarthy (2 Singles: 3 Weeks)

16 Feb 91 **LOVE AND PAIN** *Smith & Mighty SNM 4* **56** 2
1 Apr 95 **1 TO 1 RELIGION** *Stoned Heights BRCD 313* [1] **53** 1

[1] Bomb the Bass featuring Carlton

KEY UK No.1 ★ UK Top 10 ● Still on chart + UK entry at No.1 ■ US No.1 ▲ UK million seller £ US million seller $
Singles re-entries are listed as (re), (2re), (3re)... which signifies that the hit re-entered the chart once, twice or three times...
Peak Position / Weeks

Carl CARLTON *US, male vocalist*

18 Jul 81 **SHE'S A BAD MAMA JAMA (SHE'S BUILT, SHE'S STACKED)** *20th Century TC 2488* $ 34 8

Vanessa CARLTON

US, female vocalist (1 Album: 15 Weeks, 3 Singles: 23 Weeks)

27 Jul 02 ● BE NOT NOBODY *A&M 4933672* 7 15
3 Aug 02 ● **A THOUSAND MILES** *A&M 4977542* 6 13
30 Nov 02 **ORDINARY DAY** *A&M 4978132* 53 1
15 Feb 03 **BIG YELLOW TAXI** *Geffen 4978302* [1] 16 9

[1] Counting Crows featuring Vanessa Carlton

CARMEL *UK, female / male vocal / instrumental group (3 Albums: 11 Weeks, 3 Singles: 19 Weeks)*

6 Aug 83 **BAD DAY** *London LON 29* 15 9
1 Oct 83 CARMEL *Red Flame RFM 9* 94 2
11 Feb 84 **MORE, MORE, MORE** *London LON 44* 23 7
24 Mar 84 THE DRUM IS EVERYTHING *London SH 8555* 19 8
14 Jun 86 **SALLY** *London LON 90* 60 3
27 Sep 86 THE FALLING *London LONLP 17* 88 1

Eric CARMEN *US, male vocalist*

10 Apr 76 **ALL BY MYSELF** *Arista 42* $ 12 7
15 May 76 ERIC CARMEN *Arista ARTY 120* 58 1

Kim CARNEGIE *UK, female vocalist*

19 Jan 91 **JAZZ RAP** *Best ZB 44085* 73 1

Kim CARNES

US, female vocalist (1 Album: 16 Weeks, 3 Singles: 15 Weeks)

9 May 81 ● **BETTE DAVIS EYES** *EMI America EA 121* ▲ $ 10 9
20 Jun 81 MISTAKEN IDENTITY *EMI America AML 3018* ▲ 26 16
8 Aug 81 **DRAW OF THE CARDS** *EMI America EA 125* 49 4
9 Oct 82 **VOYEUR** *EMI America EA 143* 68 2

CARNIVAL featuring RIP vs RED RAT (see also RIP PRODUCTIONS)

UK, male production duo and Jamaica, male vocalist

12 Sep 98 **ALL OF THE GIRLS (ALL AI-DI GIRL DEM)** *Pepper 0530072* 51 1

Renato CAROSONE and his SEXTET *Italy, male vocalist, b. 2 Jan 1920, d. 27 Apr 2001, and instrumental backing group*

4 Jul 58 **TORERO – CHA CHA CHA** *Parlophone R 4433* 25 1

Mary-Chapin CARPENTER

US, female vocalist / guitarist (4 Albums: 9 Weeks, 3 Singles: 6 Weeks)

20 Nov 93 **HE THINKS HE'LL KEEP HER** *Columbia 6598632* 71 1
29 Oct 94 STONES IN THE ROAD *Columbia CK 64327* 26 5
7 Jan 95 **ONE COOL REMOVE** *Columbia 6611342* [1] 40 3
3 Jun 95 **SHUT UP AND KISS ME** *Columbia 6613675* 35 2
2 Nov 96 A PLACE IN THE WORLD *Columbia 4851822* 36 2
5 Jun 99 PARTY DOLL AND OTHER FAVOURITES *Columbia 4886592* 65 1
26 May 01 TIME*SEX*LOVE *Columbia 5023542* 57 1

[1] Shawn Colvin with Mary-Chapin Carpenter

The CARPENTERS (30 Top 500)

All-time biggest-selling brother / sister duo: Karen Carpenter (v/d), b. 2 Mar 1950, d. 4 Feb 1983, and Richard Carpenter (k/v). This Connecticut couple was among the world's most popular pop / MOR acts of the 1970s before Karen's anorexia-associated death (20 Albums: 609 Weeks, 21 Singles: 173 Weeks)

5 Sep 70 ● **(THEY LONG TO BE) CLOSE TO YOU** *A&M AMS 800* ▲ $ 6 18
9 Jan 71 **WE'VE ONLY JUST BEGUN** *A&M AMS 813* $ 28 7
23 Jan 71 CLOSE TO YOU *A&M AMLS 998* 23 75
18 Sep 71 **SUPERSTAR / FOR ALL WE KNOW** *A&M AMS 864* $ 18 13
30 Oct 71 CARPENTERS *A&M AMLS 63502* 12 36
1 Jan 72 **MERRY CHRISTMAS DARLING** *A&M AME 601* 45 1
15 Apr 72 TICKET TO RIDE *A&M AMLS 64342* 20 3
23 Sep 72 A SONG FOR YOU *A&M AMLS 63511* 13 37
23 Sep 72 ● **I WON'T LAST A DAY WITHOUT YOU / GOODBYE TO LOVE** *A&M AMS 7023* 9 16
7 Jul 73 ● NOW & THEN *A&M AMLH 63519* 2 65
7 Jul 73 ● **YESTERDAY ONCE MORE** *A&M AMS 7073* $ 2 17
20 Oct 73 ● **TOP OF THE WORLD** *A&M AMS 7086* ▲ $ 5 18
26 Jan 74 ★ THE SINGLES 1969-1973 *A&M AMLH 63601* ▲ 1 125
2 Mar 74 **JAMBALAYA (ON THE BAYOU) / MR GUDER** *A&M AMS 7098* 12 11
8 Jun 74 **I WON'T LAST A DAY WITHOUT YOU** (re-issue) *A&M AMS 7111* 32 5
18 Jan 75 ● **PLEASE MR POSTMAN** *A&M AMS 7141* ▲ $ 2 12
19 Apr 75 ● **ONLY YESTERDAY** *A&M AMS 7159* 7 10
28 Jun 75 ★ HORIZON *A&M AMLK 64530* 1 27
23 Aug 75 TICKET TO RIDE (re-issue) *Hamlet AMLP 8001* 35 2
30 Aug 75 **SOLITAIRE** *A&M AMS 7187* 32 5
20 Dec 75 **SANTA CLAUS IS COMIN' TO TOWN** *A&M AMS 7144* 37 4
27 Mar 76 **THERE'S A KIND OF HUSH (ALL OVER THE WORLD)** *A&M AMS 7219* 22 6
3 Jul 76 ● A KIND OF HUSH *A&M AMLK 64581* 3 15
3 Jul 76 **I NEED TO BE IN LOVE** *A&M AMS 7238* 36 5
8 Jan 77 LIVE AT THE PALLADIUM *A&M AMLS 68403* 28 3
8 Oct 77 PASSAGE *A&M AMLK 64703* 12 12
8 Oct 77 ● **CALLING OCCUPANTS OF INTERPLANETARY CRAFT (THE RECOGNISED ANTHEM OF WORLD CONTACT DAY)** *A&M AMS 7318* 9 9
11 Feb 78 **SWEET, SWEET SMILE** *A&M AMS 7327* 40 4
2 Dec 78 ● THE SINGLES 1974-1978 *A&M AMLT 19748* 2 27
27 Jun 81 MADE IN AMERICA *A&M AMLK 63723* 12 10
15 Oct 83 ● VOICE OF THE HEART *A&M AMLX 64954* 6 19
22 Oct 83 **MAKE BELIEVE IT'S YOUR FIRST TIME** *A&M AM 147* 60 3
20 Oct 84 ● YESTERDAY ONCE MORE *EMI / A&M SING 1* 10 26
13 Jan 90 LOVELINES *A&M AMA 3931* 73 1
31 Mar 90 ★ ONLY YESTERDAY – THEIR GREATEST HITS *A&M AMA 1990* 1 82
8 Dec 90 **MERRY CHRISTMAS DARLING / (THEY LONG TO BE) CLOSE TO YOU** (re-issue) *A&M AM 716* 25 5
13 Feb 93 **RAINY DAYS AND MONDAYS** *A&M AMCD 0180* $ 63 2
15 Oct 94 INTERPRETATIONS *A&M 5402512* 29 10
24 Dec 94 **TRYIN' TO GET THE FEELING AGAIN** *A&M 5807612* 44 2
22 Nov 97 LOVE SONGS *A&M 5408382* 47 8
9 Dec 00 ● GOLD – GREATEST HITS *A&M 4908652* 4 26

'I Won't Last a Day Without You' (AMS 7023) listed by itself on 23 Sep 1972 at No.49. 'Goodbye to Love', the other side, listed by itself from 30 Sep 1972 until the end of the record's chart run. 'Mr Guder' listed with 'Jambalaya' from 16 Mar 1974 until the end of its chart run. Gold – Greatest Hits reached its peak position in Mar 2005.

CARPET BOMBERS FOR PEACE

UK / US, male / female vocal / instrumental group

5 Apr 03 **SALT IN THE WOUND** *Jungle JUNG 066CD* 67 1

Joe 'Fingers' CARR *US, male pianist – Lou Busch under a false name, b. 18 Jul 1910, d. 19 Sep 1979*

29 Jun 56 **PORTUGUESE WASHERWOMAN** *Capitol CL 14587* 20 5

Linda CARR *US, female vocalist (2 Singles: 12 Weeks)*

12 Jul 75 **HIGHWIRE** *Chelsea 2005 025* [1] 15 8
5 Jun 76 **SOLD MY ROCK 'N' ROLL (GAVE IT FOR FUNKY SOUL)** *Spark SRL 1139* [2] 36 4

[1] Linda Carr and the Love Squad [2] Linda and the Funky Boys

Lucy CARR *UK, female vocalist (2 Singles: 3 Weeks)*

25 Jan 03 **MISSING YOU** *Lickin LICKINCD 001* 28 2
9 Aug 03 **THIS IS GOODBYE** *Lickin LICKINCD 002* 41 1

30 / 31 January 1959	6 / 7 February 1959	13 / 14 February 1959	20 / 21 February 1959
UK No.1 SINGLES			
ONE NIGHT / I GOT STUNG Elvis Presley	ONE NIGHT / I GOT STUNG Elvis Presley	ONE NIGHT / I GOT STUNG Elvis Presley	AS I LOVE YOU Shirley Bassey
UK No.1 ALBUMS			
SOUTH PACIFIC Soundtrack	SOUTH PACIFIC Soundtrack	SOUTH PACIFIC Soundtrack	SOUTH PACIFIC Soundtrack

Pearl CARR and Teddy JOHNSON
UK, female / male vocal duo (2 Singles: 19 Weeks)

20 Mar 59 **SING LITTLE BIRDIE** *Columbia DB 4275* 12 8
6 Apr 61 **HOW WONDERFUL TO KNOW** *Columbia DB 4603* [1] 23 11

[1] Teddy Johnson and Pearl Carr

Suzi CARR *US, female vocalist*

8 Oct 94 **ALL OVER ME** *Cowboy RODEO 947CD* 45 1

Valerie CARR *US, female vocalist*

4 Jul 58 **WHEN THE BOYS TALK ABOUT THE GIRLS (re)** *Columbia DB 4131* 29 2

Vikki CARR *US, female vocalist – Florencia Bisenta de Casillas Martinez Cardona (2 Albums: 12 Weeks, 3 Singles: 26 Weeks)*

1 Jun 67 ● **IT MUST BE HIM (SEUL SUR SON ETOILE)** *Liberty LIB 55917* 2 20
22 Jul 67 WAY OF TODAY *Liberty SLBY 1331* 31 2
12 Aug 67 IT MUST BE HIM *Liberty LBS 83037* 12 10
30 Aug 67 **THERE I GO** *Liberty LBF 15022* 50 1
12 Mar 69 **WITH PEN IN HAND (2re)** *Liberty LBF 15166* 39 5

Raffaella CARRA *Italy, female vocalist – Raffaella Pelloni*

15 Apr 78 ● **DO IT, DO IT AGAIN** *Epic EPC 6094* 9 12

Paul CARRACK (see also ACE; MIKE and The MECHANICS; SQUEEZE)
UK, male vocalist (3 Albums: 9 Weeks, 5 Singles: 18 Weeks)

16 May 87 **WHEN YOU WALK IN THE ROOM** *Chrysalis CHS 3109* 48 5
18 Mar 89 **DON'T SHED A TEAR** *Chrysalis CHS 3164* 60 3
6 Jan 96 **EYES OF BLUE** *IRS CDEIRS 192* 40 4
3 Feb 96 BLUE VIEWS *IRS EIRSCD 1075* 55 7
6 Apr 96 **HOW LONG** *IRS CDEIRS 193* 32 5
24 Aug 96 **EYES OF BLUE** (re-mix) *IRS CDEIRS 194* 45 1
24 Jun 00 SATISFY MY SOUL *Carrack-UK PCARCD 1* 63 1
19 Jun 04 REWIRED *Virgin CDVX 2984* [1] 61 1

[1] Mike and the Mechanics & Paul Carrack

José CARRERAS (420 Top 500)
One of the world's foremost opera singers, b. 5 Dec 1946, Barcelona, Spain. He is one of the world-acclaimed Three Tenors, the first chart-topping operatic act. His duet with Sarah Brightman was a No.1 single in Australia (13 Albums: 152 Weeks, 3 Singles: 19 Weeks)

1 Oct 88 JOSÉ CARRERAS COLLECTION *Stylus SMR 860* 90 4
23 Dec 89 JOSÉ CARRERAS SINGS ANDREW LLOYD WEBBER *WEA WX 325* 42 6
1 Sep 90 ★ IN CONCERT *Decca 4304331* [1] 1 78
23 Feb 91 THE ESSENTIAL JOSÉ CARRERAS *Philips 4326921* 24 9
6 Apr 91 HOLLYWOOD GOLDEN CLASSICS *East West WX 416* 47 3
11 Jul 92 **AMIGOS PARA SIEMPRE (FRIENDS FOR LIFE)** *Really Useful RUR 10* [1] 11 11
8 Aug 92 AMIGOS PARA SIEMPRE (FRIENDS FOR LIFE) *East West 4509902562* [3] 53 4
8 Aug 92 FROM THE BARCELONA GAMES CEREMONY *RCA Red Seal 09026612042* [2] 41 3
16 Oct 93 WITH A SONG IN MY HEART *Teldec 4509923692* 73 1
25 Dec 93 CHRISTMAS IN VIENNA *Sony Classical SK 53358* [4] 71 2
30 Jul 94 **LIBIAMO / LA DONNA E MOBILE** *Teldec YZ 843CD* [2] 21 4
10 Sep 94 ★ THE THREE TENORS IN CONCERT 1994 *Teldec 4509962002* [5] 1 26
3 Feb 96 PASSION *Erato 630125962* 21 8
25 Jul 98 **YOU'LL NEVER WALK ALONE** *Decca 4607982* [3] 35 4
29 Aug 98 THE THREE TENORS IN PARIS 1998 *Decca 4605002* [1] 14 6
23 Dec 00 THE THREE TENORS CHRISTMAS *Sony Classical SK 89131* [6] 57 2

[1] José Carreras and Sarah Brightman [2] José Carreras featuring Placido Domingo and Luciano Pavarotti with Mehta [3] José Carreras, Placido Domingo and Luciano Pavarotti with Mehta [1] José Carreras, Placido Domingo and Luciano Pavarotti [3] José Carreras and Sarah Brightman [2] Placido Domingo, José Carreras and Montserrat Caballe [4] Placido Domingo, Diana Ross and José Carreras [5] José Carreras, Placido Domingo and Luciano Pavarotti conducted by Zubin Mehta [6] José Carreras, Placido Domingo and Luciano Pavarotti featuring Zubin Mehta

Tia CARRERE *US, female actor / vocalist – Althia Janairo*

30 May 92 **BALLROOM BLITZ** *Reprise W 0105* 26 6

Jim CARREY *Canada, male actor / vocalist*

21 Jan 95 **CUBAN PETE** *Columbia 6606625* 31 3

CARRIE *US / UK, male vocal / instrumental group (2 Singles: 2 Weeks)*

14 Mar 98 **MOLLY** *Island CID 687* 56 1
9 May 98 **CALIFORNIA SCREAMIN'** *Island CID 694* 55 1

Dina CARROLL (400 Top 500)
BRIT award-winning Best Female Vocalist of 1994, b. 21 Aug 1968, Newmarket, UK. Soul / dance vocalist's So Close was the biggest-selling debut album by a British female artist in the 1990s, and she was the only UK woman to have two simultaneous Top 10 singles that decade (in 1993) (3 Albums: 80 Weeks, 14 Singles: 99 Weeks)

2 Feb 91 ● **IT'S TOO LATE** *Mercury ITM 3* [1] 8 14
15 Jun 91 **NAKED LOVE (JUST SAY YOU WANT ME)** *Mercury ITM 4* [2] 39 3
11 Jul 92 **AIN'T NO MAN** *A&M AM 0001* 16 8
10 Oct 92 **SPECIAL KIND OF LOVE** *A&M AM 0088* 16 5
5 Dec 92 **SO CLOSE** *A&M AM 0101* 20 8
30 Jan 93 ● SO CLOSE *A&M 5400342* 2 63
27 Feb 93 **THIS TIME** *A&M AMCD 0184* 23 6
15 May 93 **EXPRESS** *A&M 580262-7* 12 6
16 Oct 93 ● **DON'T BE A STRANGER** *A&M 5803892* 3 13
11 Dec 93 ● **THE PERFECT YEAR** *A&M 5804812* 5 11
28 Sep 96 ● **ESCAPING** *Mercury / First Avenue DCCD 1* 3 8
26 Oct 96 ● ONLY HUMAN *Mercury 5340962* 2 13
21 Dec 96 **ONLY HUMAN** *Mercury / First Avenue DCCD 2* 33 4
24 Oct 98 **ONE, TWO, THREE** *Mercury / First Avenue MERCD 514* 16 4
24 Jul 99 **WITHOUT LOVE** *Manifesto / First Avenue FESCD 57* 13 7
16 Jun 01 **SOMEONE LIKE YOU** *Mercury / First Avenue 5689062* 38 2
23 Jun 01 THE VERY BEST OF DINA CARROLL *Mercury 5489182* 15 4

[1] Quartz introducing Dina Carroll [2] Quartz and Dina Carroll

Ronnie CARROLL
Ireland, male vocalist – Ronald Cleghorn (7 Singles: 50 Weeks)

27 Jul 56 **WALK HAND IN HAND** *Philips PB 605* 13 8
29 Mar 57 **THE WISDOM OF A FOOL** *Philips PB 667* 20 2
31 Mar 60 **FOOTSTEPS** *Philips PB 1004* 36 3
22 Feb 62 **RING-A-DING GIRL** *Philips PB 1222* 46 3
2 Aug 62 ● **ROSES ARE RED** *Philips 326532 BF* 3 16
15 Nov 62 **IF ONLY TOMORROW** *Philips 326550 BF* 33 4
7 Mar 63 ● **SAY WONDERFUL THINGS** *Philips 326574 BF* 6 14

Jasper CARROTT *UK, male comedian / vocalist – Bob Davies (8 Albums: 66 Weeks, 1 Single: 15 Weeks)*

16 Aug 75 ● **FUNKY MOPED / MAGIC ROUNDABOUT** *DJM DJS 388* 5 15
18 Oct 75 ● RABBITS ON AND ON *DJM DJLPS 462* 10 7
6 Nov 76 CARROTT IN NOTTS *DJM DJF 20482* 56 1
25 Nov 78 THE BEST OF JASPER CARROTT *DJM DJF 20549* 38 13
20 Oct 79 THE UNRECORDED JASPER CARROTT *DJM DJF 20560* 19 15
19 Sep 81 BEAT THE CARROTT *DJM DJF 20575* 13 16
25 Dec 82 CARROTT'S LIB *DJM DJF 20580* 80 3
19 Nov 83 THE STUN (CARROTT TELLS ALL) *DJF 20582* 57 8
7 Feb 87 COSMIC CARROTT *Portrait LAUGH 1* 66 3

The CARS *US, male vocal (Ric Ocasek) / instrumental group (5 Albums: 72 Weeks, 5 Singles: 51 Weeks)*

11 Nov 78 ● **MY BEST FRIEND'S GIRL** *Elektra K 12301* 3 10

27 / 28 February 1959	6 / 7 March 1959	13 / 14 March 1959	20 / 21 March 1959
AS I LOVE YOU Shirley Bassey	AS I LOVE YOU Shirley Bassey	AS I LOVE YOU Shirley Bassey	SMOKE GETS IN YOUR EYES The Platters
SOUTH PACIFIC Soundtrack	SOUTH PACIFIC Soundtrack	SOUTH PACIFIC Soundtrack	SOUTH PACIFIC Soundtrack

KEY
UK No.1 ★ UK Top 10 ● Still on chart + UK entry at No.1 ■
US No.1 ▲ UK million seller £ US million seller $
Singles re-entries are listed as (re), (2re), (3re)... which signifies that the hit re-entered the chart once, twice or three times...
Peak Position / Weeks

2 Dec 78 CARS *Elektra K 52088* 29 15
17 Feb 79 **JUST WHAT I NEEDED** *Elektra K 12312* 17 10
7 Jul 79 CANDY-O *Elektra K 52148* 30 6
28 Jul 79 **LET'S GO** *Elektra K 12371* 51 4
5 Jun 82 **SINCE YOU'RE GONE** *Elektra K 13177* 37 4
29 Sep 84 ● **DRIVE (re)** *Elektra E 9706* 4 23
6 Oct 84 HEARTBEAT CITY *Elektra 960296* 25 30
9 Nov 85 THE CARS GREATEST HITS *Elektra EKT 25* 27 19
5 Sep 87 DOOR TO DOOR *Elektra EKT 42* 72 2

'My Best Friend's Girl' was the first picture disc to make the singles chart. 'Drive', originally a No.5 hit, re-entered and peaked one place higher in Aug 1985.

Alex CARTAÑA *Spain, female vocalist (2 Singles: 8 Weeks)*

6 Sep 03 **SHAKE IT (MOVE A LITTLE CLOSER)** *Credence CDCRED 039* [1] 16 6
8 May 04 **HEY PAPI** *EMI PAP 1CDS* 34 2

[1] Lee-Cabrera featuring Alex Cartaña

Aaron CARTER *US, male vocalist (1 Album: 8 Weeks, 7 Singles: 33 Weeks)*

29 Nov 97 ● **CRUSH ON YOU** *Ultra Pop 0099605 ULT* 9 8
7 Feb 98 ● **CRAZY LITTLE PARTY GIRL** *Ultra Pop 0099645 ULT* 7 6
28 Feb 98 AARON CARTER *Ultra Pop 0099572 ULT* 12 8
28 Mar 98 **I'M GONNA MISS YOU FOREVER** *Ultra Pop 0099725 ULT* 24 5
4 Jul 98 **SURFIN' USA** *Ultra Pop 0099805 ULT* 18 5
16 Sep 00 **I WANT CANDY** *Jive 9250892* 31 3
28 Oct 00 **AARON'S PARTY (COME GET IT)** *Jive 9251272* 51 2
13 Apr 02 **LEAVE IT UP TO ME** *Jive 9253262* 22 4

Brad CARTER (see also RUFF DRIVERZ) *UK, male producer / vocalist*

23 Oct 04 **MORNING ALWAYS COMES TOO SOON** *Positiva CDTIVS 210* 48 1

Clarence CARTER *US, male vocalist*

10 Oct 70 ● **PATCHES** *Atlantic 2091 030* $ 2 13

Nick CARTER (see also BACKSTREET BOYS) *US, male vocalist*

19 Oct 02 **HELP ME** *Jive 9254332* 17 3

CARTER – THE UNSTOPPABLE SEX MACHINE
UK, male vocal / instrumental duo – James 'Jim Bob' Morrison and Leslie 'Fruitbat' Carter (9 Albums: 40 Weeks, 13 Singles: 46 Weeks)

26 Jan 91 **BLOODSPORT FOR ALL** *Rough Trade R 20112687* 48 2
2 Mar 91 ● 30 SOMETHING *Rough Trade R 20112702* 8 9
22 Jun 91 **SHERIFF FATMAN** *Big Cat USM 1* 23 7
21 Sep 91 101 DAMNATIONS *Big Cat ABB 101* 29 6
26 Oct 91 **AFTER THE WATERSHED** *Big Cat USM 2* 11 5
11 Jan 92 **RUBBISH** *Big Cat USM 3* 14 5
1 Feb 92 30 SOMETHING (re-issue) *Chrysalis CHR 1897* 21 4
25 Apr 92 ● **THE ONLY LIVING BOY IN NEW CROSS** *Big Cat USM 4* 7 5
16 May 92 ★ 1992 – THE LOVE ALBUM *Chrysalis CCD 1946* ■ 1 9
4 Jul 92 **DO RE ME SO FAR SO GOOD** *Chrysalis USM 5* 22 3
28 Nov 92 **THE IMPOSSIBLE DREAM** *Chrysalis USM 6* 21 3
4 Sep 93 **LEAN ON ME I WON'T FALL OVER** *Chrysalis CDUSM 7* 16 3
18 Sep 93 ● POST HISTORIC MONSTERS *Chrysalis CDCHR 7090* 5 4
16 Oct 93 **LENNY AND TERENCE** *Chrysalis CDUSM 8* 40 2
12 Mar 94 **GLAM ROCK COPS** *Chrysalis CDUSMS 10* 24 3
26 Mar 94 STARRY EYED AND BOLLOCK NAKED *Chrysalis CDCHR 6069* 22 2
19 Nov 94 **LET'S GET TATTOOS** *Chrysalis CDUSMS 30* 30 3
4 Feb 95 **THE YOUNG OFFENDER'S MUM** *Chrysalis CDUSMS 12* 34 3
18 Feb 95 ● WORRY BOMB *Chrysalis CDCHRX 6096* 9 3
30 Sep 95 **BORN ON THE 5TH OF NOVEMBER** *Chrysalis CDUSM 13* 35 2
14 Oct 95 STRAW DONKEY ... THE SINGLES *Chrysalis CDCHR 6110* 37 2
5 Apr 97 A WORLD WITHOUT DAVE *Cooking Vinyl COOKCD 120* 73 1

CARTER TWINS *Ireland, male vocal duo*

8 Mar 97 **THE TWELFTH OF NEVER / TOO RIGHT TO BE** *RCA 74321453082* 61 1

Junior CARTIER *UK, male producer – Jon Carter*

6 Nov 99 **WOMEN BEAT THEIR MEN** *Nucamp CAMPD 3X* 70 1

CARTOONS *Denmark, male / female vocal / instrumental group (1 Album: 14 Weeks, 3 Singles: 30 Weeks)*

3 Apr 99 ● **WITCH DOCTOR** *Flex / EMI CDTOONS 001* 2 13
17 Apr 99 TOONAGE *EMI 4966922* 17 14
19 Jun 99 ● **DOODAH! (re)** *Flex / EMI CDTOON 002* 7 12
4 Sep 99 **AISY WAISY** *Flex/ EMI CDTOONS 003* 16 5

Richard CARTRIDGE *UK, male vocalist*

25 Sep 04 **I'VE FOUND LOVE AGAIN** *Springboard Media SMCDSRC 001* 50 1

CARVELLS *UK, male vocalist / instrumentalist – Alan Carvell*

26 Nov 77 **THE L.A. RUN** *Creole CR 143* 31 4

The CASCADES *US, male vocal (John Gummoe) group*

28 Feb 63 ● **RHYTHM OF THE RAIN** *Warner Bros. WB 88* $ 5 16

CASE *US, male rapper – Case Woodard (3 Singles: 15 Weeks)*

21 Sep 96 **TOUCH ME TEASE ME** *Def Jam DEFCD 18* [1] 26 3
10 Nov 01 **LIVIN' IT UP** *Def Jam 5888142* [2] 27 4
3 Aug 02 ● **LIVIN' IT UP** (re-issue) *Def Jam 0639782* [2] 5 8

[1] Case featuring Foxxy Brown [2] Ja Rule featuring Case

Ed CASE *UK, male producer – Edward Makromallies (3 Singles: 5 Weeks)*

21 Oct 00 **SOMETHING IN YOUR EYES** *Red Rose CDRROSE 003* 38 2
15 Sep 01 **WHO?** *Columbia 6718302* [1] 29 2
20 Jul 02 **GOOD TIMES** *Columbia 6727672* [2] 49 1

[1] Ed Case and Sweetie Irie [2] Ed Case featuring Skin

Natalie CASEY *UK, female actor / vocalist – youngest ever chart entrant at three years of age*

7 Jan 84 **CHICK CHICK CHICKEN** *Polydor CHICK 1* 72 1

Johnny CASH (163 Top 500)
Worldwide country music giant, b. J.R. Cash, 26 Feb 1932, Arkansas, US, d. 12 Sep 2003. He scored 136 country hits between 1956-2003. Elected to the Country Music Hall of Fame (1980) and Rock'n'Roll equivalent (1992) and enjoyed a renaissance late in his career, culminating in an MTV award for his version of Nine Inch Nails' 'Hurt' (20 Albums: 280 Weeks, 6 Singles: 62 Weeks)

3 Jun 65 **IT AIN'T ME BABE** *CBS 201760* 28 8
23 Jul 66 EVERYBODY LOVES A NUT *CBS BPG 62717* 28 1
4 May 68 FROM SEA TO SHINING SEA *CBS 62972* 40 1
6 Jul 68 OLD GOLDEN THROAT *CBS 63316* 37 2
24 Aug 68 ● JOHNNY CASH AT FOLSOM PRISON *CBS 63308* 8 45
23 Aug 69 ● JOHNNY CASH AT SAN QUENTIN *CBS 63629* ▲ 2 106
6 Sep 69 ● **A BOY NAMED SUE** *CBS 4460* $ 4 19
4 Oct 69 GREATEST HITS VOLUME 1 *CBS 63062* 23 25
7 Mar 70 ● HELLO I'M JOHNNY CASH *CBS 63796* 6 16
23 May 70 **WHAT IS TRUTH** *CBS 4934* 21 11
15 Aug 70 ● THE WORLD OF JOHNNY CASH *CBS 66237* 5 25
12 Dec 70 THE JOHNNY CASH SHOW *CBS 64089* 18 6
18 Sep 71 MAN IN BLACK *CBS 64331* 18 7
13 Nov 71 JOHNNY CASH *Hallmark SHM 739* 43 2
15 Apr 72 ● **A THING CALLED LOVE (re)** *CBS 7797* [1] 4 14

27 / 28 March 1959	3 / 4 April 1959	10 / 11 April 1959	17 / 18 April 1959
UK No.1 SINGLES			
SIDE SADDLE Russ Conway	SIDE SADDLE Russ Conway	SIDE SADDLE Russ Conway	SIDE SADDLE Russ Conway
UK No.1 ALBUMS			
SOUTH PACIFIC Soundtrack	SOUTH PACIFIC Soundtrack	SOUTH PACIFIC Soundtrack	SOUTH PACIFIC Soundtrack

20 May 72	●	A THING CALLED LOVE *CBS 64898*	8	11
14 Oct 72		STAR PORTRAIT *CBS 67201*	16	7
3 Jul 76		**ONE PIECE AT A TIME** *CBS 4287* [2]	**32**	7
10 Jul 76		ONE PIECE AT A TIME *CBS 81416*	49	3
9 Oct 76		THE BEST OF JOHNNY CASH *CBS 10000*	48	2
2 Sep 78		ITCHY FEET *CBS 10009*	36	4
27 Aug 94		THE MAN IN BLACK – THE DEFINITIVE COLLECTION *Columbia MOODCD 35*	15	5
9 Mar 02		MAN IN BLACK – THE VERY BEST OF JOHNNY CASH *Columbia 5063452*	39	4
10 May 03		**HURT / PERSONAL JESUS (re)** *American / Lost Highway 0779982*	**39**	3
6 Mar 04		AMERICAN RECORDINGS TV – THE MAN COMES AROUND *Lost Highway 0633392*	40	3
3 Dec 05		RING OF FIRE – THE LEGEND OF JOHNNY CASH *Columbia / UMTV 9887850*	43	5+

[1] Johnny Cash with the Evangel Temple Choir [2] Johnny Cash with the Tennessee Three

CA$HFLOW *US, male vocal / instrumental group*

24 May 86		**MINE ALL MINE / PARTY FREAK** *Club JAB 30*	**15**	8
28 Jun 86		CASHFLOW *Club JABH 17*	33	3

CASHMERE

US, male vocal / instrumental group (1 Album: 5 Weeks, 2 Singles: 11 Weeks)

19 Jan 85		**CAN I** *Fourth & Broadway BRW 19*	**29**	8
2 Mar 85		CASHMERE *Fourth & Broadway BRLP 503*	63	5
23 Mar 85		**WE NEED LOVE** *Fourth & Broadway BRW 22*	**52**	3

CASINO *UK, male vocal / production group (2 Singles: 2 Weeks)*

17 May 97		**SOUND OF EDEN** *Worx WORXCD 005*	**52**	1
10 Jul 99		**ONLY YOU** *Pow! CDPOW 006*	**72**	1

The CASINOS *US, male vocal group*

23 Feb 67		**THEN YOU CAN TELL ME GOODBYE** *President PT 123*	**28**	7

CASSIDY

US, male rapper – Barry Reese (2 Singles: 18 Weeks)

29 May 04	●	**HOTEL** *J 82876618532* [1]	**3**	14
25 Sep 04		**GET NO BETTER** *J 82876649282* [2]	**24**	4

[1] Cassidy featuring R Kelly [2] Cassidy featuring Mashonda

David CASSIDY (311 Top 500)

Top teen idol of the 1970s, b. 12 Apr 1950, New York, US. This photogenic singer / actor first found fame via the TV series The Partridge Family. His UK chart career took off as his US sales slowed down. He returned to the albums chart Top 5 in 2001 (8 Albums: 110 Weeks, 11 Singles: 109 Weeks)

8 Apr 72	●	**COULD IT BE FOREVER / CHERISH** *Bell 1224* $	**2**	17
20 May 72	●	CHERISH *Bell BELLS 210*	2	43
16 Sep 72	★	**HOW CAN I BE SURE** *Bell 1258*	**1**	11
25 Nov 72		**ROCK ME BABY** *Bell 1268*	**11**	9
24 Feb 73	●	ROCK ME BABY *Bell BELLS 218*	2	20
24 Mar 73	●	**I'M A CLOWN / SOME KIND OF A SUMMER** *Bell MABEL 4*	**3**	12
13 Oct 73	★	**DAYDREAMER / THE PUPPY SONG** *Bell 1334*	**1**	15
24 Nov 73	★	DREAMS ARE NOTHIN' MORE THAN WISHES *Bell BELLS 231*	1	13
11 May 74	●	**IF I DIDN'T CARE** *Bell 1350*	**9**	8
27 Jul 74		**PLEASE PLEASE ME** *Bell 1371*	**16**	6
3 Aug 74	●	CASSIDY LIVE *Bell BELLS 243*	9	7
5 Jul 75		**I WRITE THE SONGS / GET IT UP FOR LOVE** *RCA 2571*	**11**	8
9 Aug 75		THE HIGHER THEY CLIMB *RCA Victor RS 1012*	22	5
25 Oct 75		**DARLIN'** *RCA 2622*	**16**	8
23 Feb 85	●	**THE LAST KISS** *Arista ARIST 589*	**6**	9
11 May 85		**ROMANCE (LET YOUR HEART GO)** *Arista ARIST 620*	**54**	6
8 Jun 85		ROMANCE *Arista 206 983*	20	6
13 Oct 01	●	THEN AND NOW *Universal Music TV 160822*	5	15
15 Nov 03		A TOUCH OF BLUE *Universal TV 9812859*	61	1

Eva CASSIDY (442 Top 500)

Unique singer / songwriter / guitarist, whose fame came after her death, b. 2 Feb 1963, Maryland, US, d. 2 Nov 1996. Worldwide success started when her fourth album, Songbird, was 'discovered' by the BBC and 'Over the Rainbow' was shown on Top of the Pops 2. The only female singer to score three posthumous No.1 albums in the UK (5 Albums: 152 Weeks, 2 Singles: 10 Weeks)

3 Jun 00		TIME AFTER TIME *Blix Street G 210073*	25	14
10 Feb 01	★	SONGBIRD *Blix Street G 210045*	1	101
21 Apr 01		**OVER THE RAINBOW (3re)** *Blix Street / Hot HIT 16*	**42**	9
31 Aug 02	★	IMAGINE *Blix Street / Hot G 210075* ■	1	20
23 Aug 03	★	AMERICAN TUNE *Blix Street / Hot G 210079* ■	1	11
11 Oct 03		**YOU TAKE MY BREATH AWAY** *Blix Street / Hot HIT 27*	**54**	1
24 Jul 04		WONDERFUL WORLD *Blix Street G 210082*	11	6

CASSIUS *France, DJ / production duo – Philippe Zdar and Hubert Blanc-Francart (1 Album: 2 Weeks, 4 Singles: 13 Weeks)*

23 Jan 99	●	**CASSIUS 1999** *Virgin DINSD 177*	**7**	7
6 Feb 99		1999 *Virgin CDVIR 76*	28	2
15 May 99		**FEELING FOR YOU** *Virgin DINSD 181*	**16**	4
20 Nov 99		**LA MOUCHE** *Virgin DINSD 188*	**53**	1
5 Oct 02		**THE SOUND OF VIOLENCE** *Virgin DINSD 241*	**49**	1

CAST (421 Top 500)

The La's guitarist John Power, b. 14 Sep 1967, Liverpool, fronted this retro sounding Merseyside Britpop quartet, which featured Liam Tyson (g), Peter Wilkinson (b) and Keith O'Neill (d). Nominated for Best Newcomers at the 1995 BRIT awards (3 Albums: 116 Weeks, 12 Singles: 55 Weeks)

15 Jul 95		**FINETIME** *Polydor 5795072*	**17**	4
30 Sep 95		**ALRIGHT** *Polydor 5799272*	**13**	4
28 Oct 95	●	ALL CHANGE *Polydor 5293122*	7	67
20 Jan 96	●	**SANDSTORM** *Polydor 5778732*	**8**	5
30 Mar 96	●	**WALKAWAY** *Polydor 5762852*	**9**	7
26 Oct 96	●	**FLYING** *Polydor 5754772*	**4**	5
5 Apr 97	●	**FREE ME (re)** *Polydor 5736512*	**7**	7
26 Apr 97	●	MOTHER NATURE CALLS *Polydor 5375672*	3	42
28 Jun 97	●	**GUIDING STAR** *Polydor 5711732*	**9**	6
13 Sep 97	●	**LIVE THE DREAM** *Polydor 5716852*	**7**	5
15 Nov 97		**I'M SO LONELY** *Polydor 5690592*	**14**	3
8 May 99	●	**BEAT MAMA** *Polydor 5635932*	**9**	5
29 May 99	●	MAGIC HOUR *Polydor 5471762*	6	7
7 Aug 99		**MAGIC HOUR** *Polydor 5612272*	**28**	3
28 Jul 01		**DESERT DROUGHT** *Polydor 5871752*	**45**	1

CAST FROM CASUALTY *UK, male / female actors / vocal group*

14 Mar 98	●	**EVERLASTING LOVE** *Warner.esp WESP 003CD*	**5**	6

CAST OF THE NEW ROCKY HORROR SHOW

UK, male / female vocal group

12 Dec 98		**THE TIMEWARP** *Damn It Janet DAMJAN 1CD*	**57**	1

Roy CASTLE *UK, male vocalist, b. 31 Aug 1932, d. 2 Sep 1994*

22 Dec 60		**LITTLE WHITE BERRY** *Philips PB 1087*	**40**	3

The CASUALS *UK, male vocal / instrumental group (2 Singles: 26 Weeks)*

14 Aug 68	●	**JESAMINE** *Decca F 22784*	**2**	18
4 Dec 68		**TOY** *Decca F 22852*	**30**	8

The CAT *UK, male actor / vocalist – Danny John-Jules*

23 Oct 93		**TONGUE TIED** *EMI CDEM 286*	**17**	4

CATATONIA (408 Top 500)

(see also SPACE) *BRIT-nominated, chart-topping gregarious Welsh indie-pop band formed Cardiff 1991: Cerys Matthews (v), b. 11 Apr 1969, Swansea, Mark Roberts (g), Paul Jones (b), Owen Powell (g), Aled Richards (d). Group split in 2001 and Matthews launched her solo career (5 Albums: 125 Weeks, 13 Singles: 50 Weeks)*

3 Feb 96		**SWEET CATATONIA** *Blanco Y Negro NEG 85CD*	**61**	1

24 / 25 April 1959	1 / 2 May 1959	8 / 9 May 1959	15 / 16 May 1959
IT DOESN'T MATTER ANYMORE Buddy Holly	IT DOESN'T MATTER ANYMORE Buddy Holly	IT DOESN'T MATTER ANYMORE Buddy Holly	A FOOL SUCH AS I / I NEED YOUR LOVE TONIGHT Elvis Presley with The Jordanaires
SOUTH PACIFIC Soundtrack	SOUTH PACIFIC Soundtrack	SOUTH PACIFIC Soundtrack	SOUTH PACIFIC Soundtrack

KEY: UK No.1 ★ UK Top 10 ● Still on chart + UK entry at No.1 ■ US No.1 ▲ UK million seller £ US million seller $
Singles re-entries are listed as (re), (2re), (3re)... which signifies that the hit re-entered the chart once, twice or three times...
Peak Position / Weeks

4 May 96	**LOST CAT** *Blanco Y Negro NEG 88CD1*	41	1
7 Sep 96	**YOU'VE GOT A LOT TO ANSWER FOR** *Blanco Y Negro NEG 93CD1*	35	2
12 Oct 96	WAY BEYOND BLUE *Blanco Y Negro 630163052*	32	3
30 Nov 96	**BLEED** *Blanco Y Negro NEG 97CD1*	46	1
18 Oct 97	**I AM THE MOB** *Blanco Y Negro NEG 107CD*	40	2
31 Jan 98 ●	**MULDER AND SCULLY** *Blanco Y Negro NEG 109CD*	3	10
14 Feb 98 ★	INTERNATIONAL VELVET *Blanco Y Negro 3984208342*	1	93
2 May 98 ●	**ROAD RAGE** *Blanco Y Negro NEG 112CD*	5	8
1 Aug 98	**STRANGE GLUE** *Blanco Y Negro NEG 113CD*	11	6
7 Nov 98	**GAME ON** *WEA NEG 114CD*	33	2
10 Apr 99 ●	**DEAD FROM THE WAIST DOWN** *Blanco Y Negro NEG 115CD*	7	8
24 Apr 99 ★	EQUALLY CURSED AND BLESSED *Blanco Y Negro 3984270942* ■	1	23
24 Jul 99	**LONDINIUM** *Blanco Y Negro NEG 117CD*	20	3
13 Nov 99	**KARAOKE QUEEN** *Blanco Y Negro NEG 119CD*	36	2
4 Aug 01	**STONE BY STONE (re)** *Blanco Y Negro NEG 134CD*	19	4
18 Aug 01 ●	PAPER SCISSORS STONE *Blanco Y Negro 8573888482*	6	4
14 Sep 02	GREATEST HITS *Blanco Y Negro 0927491942*	24	2

CATCH
UK, male vocal / instrumental group (2 Singles: 6 Weeks)

11 Oct 97	**BINGO** *Virgin VSCDT 1656*	23	4
21 Feb 98	**DIVE IN** *Virgin VSCDT 1665*	44	2

CATCH *UK, male vocal / instrumental group*

17 Nov 90	**FREE (C'MON)** *ffrr F 147*	70	1

CATHERINE WHEEL *UK, male vocal / instrumental group (3 Albums: 3 Weeks, 10 Singles: 12 Weeks)*

23 Nov 91	**BLACK METALLIC (EP)** *Fontana CW 1*	68	1
8 Feb 92	**BALLOON** *Fontana CW 2*	59	1
29 Feb 92	FERMENT *Fontana 5109032*	36	1
18 Apr 92	**I WANT TO TOUCH YOU** *Fontana CW 3*	35	2
9 Jan 93	**30TH CENTURY MAN** *Fontana CWCD 4*	47	2
10 Jul 93	**CRANK** *Fontana CWCD 5*	66	1
31 Jul 93	CHROME *Fontana 5180392*	58	1
16 Oct 93	**SHOW ME MARY** *Fontana CWCDA 6*	62	1
5 Aug 95	**WAYDOWN** *Fontana CWCD 7*	67	1
13 Dec 97	**DELICIOUS** *Chrysalis CDCHS 5071*	53	1
28 Feb 98	**MA SOLITUDA** *Chrysalis CDCHS 5077*	53	1
2 May 98	**BROKEN NOSE** *Chrysalis CDCHS 5086*	48	1
16 May 98	ADAM AND EVE *Chrysalis 4930992*	53	1

Tracks on Black Metallic (EP): Black Metallic / Crawling Over Me / Let Me Down Again / Saccharine.

Lorraine CATO *UK, female vocalist (2 Singles: 3 Weeks)*

6 Feb 93	**HOW CAN YOU TELL ME IT'S OVER** *Columbia 6587662*	46	2
3 Aug 96	**I WAS MADE TO LOVE YOU** *MCA MCSTD 40055*	41	1

The CATS *UK, male instrumental group*

9 Apr 69	**SWAN LAKE (re)** *BAF 1*	48	2

CATS U.K. *UK, male instrumental group*

6 Oct 79	**LUTON AIRPORT** *WEA K 18075*	22	8

CAVE IN *US, male vocal / instrumental group*

29 Mar 03	ANTENNA *RCA 82876515552*	67	1
31 May 03	**ANCHOR** *RCA 82876522982*	42	1

Nick CAVE & The BAD SEEDS
(see also BIRTHDAY PARTY) *Australia / Germany, male vocal / instrumental group (15 Albums: 33 Weeks, 13 Singles: 17 Weeks)*

2 Jun 84	FROM HER TO ETERNITY *Mute STUMM 17*	40	3
15 Jun 85	THE FIRST BORN IS DEAD *Mute STUMM 21*	53	1
30 Aug 86	KICKING AGAINST THE PRICKS *Mute STUMM 28*	89	1
1 Oct 88	TENDER PREY *Mute STUMM 52*	67	1
28 Apr 90	THE GOOD SON *Mute STUMM 76*	47	1
11 Apr 92	**STRAIGHT TO YOU / JACK THE RIPPER** *Mute MUTE 140*	68	1
9 May 92	HENRY'S DREAM *Mute CDSTUMM 92*	29	2
12 Dec 92	**WHAT A WONDERFUL WORLD** *Mute MUTE 151* [1]	72	1
18 Sep 93	LIVE SEEDS *Mute CDSTUMM 122*	67	1
9 Apr 94	**DO YOU LOVE ME** *Mute CDMUTE 160*	68	1
30 Apr 94	LET LOVE IN *Mute LCDSTUMM 123*	12	2
14 Oct 95	**WHERE THE WILD ROSES GROW** *Mute CDMUTE 185* [2]	11	4
17 Feb 96 ●	MURDER BALLADS *Mute CDSTUMM 138*	8	5
9 Mar 96	**HENRY LEE** *Mute CDMUTE 189* [3]	36	1
22 Feb 97	**INTO MY ARMS** *Mute CDMUTE 192*	53	1
15 Mar 97	THE BOATMAN'S CALL *Mute CDSTUMM 142*	22	3
31 May 97	**(ARE YOU) THE ONE THAT I'VE BEEN ...** *Mute CDMUTE 206*	67	1
23 May 98	THE BEST OF NICK CAVE AND THE BAD SEEDS *Mute LCDMUTEL 4*	11	4
31 Mar 01	**AS I SAT SADLY BY HER SIDE** *Mute CDMUTE 249*	42	1
14 Apr 01	NO MORE SHALL WE PART *Mute CDSTUMM 164*	15	3
2 Jun 01	**FIFTEEN FEET OF PURE WHITE SNOW** *Mute CDMUTE 262*	52	1
15 Feb 03	NOCTURAMA *Mute LCDSTUMM 207*	20	2
8 Mar 03	**BRING IT ON** *Mute CDMUTE 265*	58	1
18 Sep 04	**NATURE BOY** *Mute CDMUTE 324*	37	2
2 Oct 04	ABATTOIR BLUES / THE LYRE OF ORPHEUS *Mute CDSTUMM 233*	11	3
27 Nov 04	**BREATHLESS / THERE SHE GOES, MY BEAUTIFUL WORLD** *Mute CDMUTE 329*	45	1
26 Mar 05	**GET READY FOR LOVE** *Mute CDMUTE 339*	62	1
9 Apr 05	B-SIDES & RARITIES *Mute CDMUTEL 11*	74	1

[1] Nick Cave and Shane MacGowan [2] Nick Cave and the Bad Seeds + Kylie Minogue [3] Nick Cave and the Bad Seeds and PJ Harvey

B-Sides & Rarities is a three-CD boxed set.

CAVEMAN *UK, male rap group*

9 Mar 91	**I'M READY** *Profile PROF 330*	65	2
13 Apr 91	POSITIVE REACTION *Profile FILER 406*	43	2

CECIL *UK, male vocal / instrumental group (2 Singles: 2 Weeks)*

25 Oct 97	**HOSTAGE IN A FROCK** *Parlophone CDRS 6471*	68	1
28 Mar 98	**THE MOST TIRING DAY** *Parlophone CDR 6490*	69	1

CELEDA *US, female vocalist – Victoria Sharpe (3 Singles: 5 Weeks)*

5 Sep 98	**MUSIC IS THE ANSWER (DANCIN' AND PRANCIN)** *Twisted UK TWCD 10038* [1]	36	3
12 Jun 99	**BE YOURSELF** *Twisted UK TWCD 10049*	61	1
23 Oct 99	**MUSIC IS THE ANSWER (DANCIN' AND PRANCIN)** *Twisted UK TWCD 10052* [2]	50	1

[1] Danny Tenaglia and Celeda [2] Celeda with Danny Tenaglia

CELETIA *UK, female vocalist – Celetia Martin (2 Singles: 3 Weeks)*

11 Apr 98	**REWIND** *Big Life BLRD 142*	29	2
8 Aug 98	**RUNAWAY SKIES** *Big Life BLRD 144*	66	1

CELTIC SPIRIT
Ireland / UK, male vocal / instrumental group (2 Albums: 1 Week)

31 Jan 98	CELTIC DREAMS *PolyGram TV 5399992*	62	1

CENOGINERZ *Holland, male producer – Michel Pollen*

2 Feb 02	**GIT DOWN** *Tripoli Trax TTRAX 081CD*	75	1

CENTORY *US, male rapper – Turbo B (Durron Butler)*

17 Dec 94	**POINT OF NO RETURN** *EMI CDEM 354*	67	1

22 / 23 May 1959	29 / 30 May 1959	5 / 6 June 1959	12 / 13 June 1959
UK No.1 SINGLES			
A FOOL SUCH AS I / I NEED YOUR LOVE TONIGHT Elvis Presley with The Jordanaires	A FOOL SUCH AS I / I NEED YOUR LOVE TONIGHT Elvis Presley with The Jordanaires	A FOOL SUCH AS I / I NEED YOUR LOVE TONIGHT Elvis Presley with The Jordanaires	A FOOL SUCH AS I / I NEED YOUR LOVE TONIGHT Elvis Presley with The Jordanaires
UK No.1 ALBUMS			
SOUTH PACIFIC Soundtrack	SOUTH PACIFIC Soundtrack	SOUTH PACIFIC Soundtrack	SOUTH PACIFIC Soundtrack

CENTRAL LINE
UK, male vocal / instrumental group (1 Album: 5 Weeks, 6 Singles: 30 Weeks)

31 Jan 81 **(YOU KNOW) YOU CAN DO IT** *Mercury LINE 7*..........67 3
15 Aug 81 **WALKING INTO SUNSHINE** *Mercury MER 78*..........42 10
30 Jan 82 **DON'T TELL ME** *Mercury MER 90*..........55 3
13 Feb 82 BREAKING POINT *Mercury MERA 001*..........64 5
20 Nov 82 **YOU'VE SAID ENOUGH** *Mercury MER 117*..........58 3
22 Jan 83 **NATURE BOY** *Mercury MER 131*..........21 8
11 Jun 83 **SURPRISE SURPRISE** *Mercury MER 133*..........48 3

CERRONE
France, male producer / multi-instrumentalist – Jean-Marc Cerrone (1 Album: 1 Week, 4 Singles: 21 Weeks)

5 Mar 77 **LOVE IN C MINOR** *Atlantic K 10895*..........31 4
29 Jul 78 ● **SUPERNATURE** *Atlantic K 11089*..........8 12
30 Sep 78 SUPERNATURE *Atlantic K 50431*..........60 1
13 Jan 79 **JE SUIS MUSIC** *CBS 6918*..........39 4
10 Aug 96 **SUPERNATURE** (re-mix) *Encore CDCOR 013*..........66 1

A CERTAIN RATIO
UK, male vocal / instrumental group

30 Jan 82 SEXTET *Factory FACT 55*..........53 3
16 Jun 90 **WON'T STOP LOVING YOU** *A&M ACR 540*..........55 3

Peter CETERA (see also CHICAGO)
US, male vocalist (1 Album: 4 Weeks, 2 Singles: 20 Weeks)

2 Aug 86 ● **GLORY OF LOVE** *Full Moon W 8662* ▲..........3 13
13 Sep 86 SOLITUDE / SOLITAIRE *Full Moon 9254741*..........56 4
21 Jun 97 ● **HARD TO SAY I'M SORRY** *LaFace 74321481482* [1] $..........7 7

[1] Az Yet featuring Peter Cetera

Frank CHACKSFIELD and his ORCHESTRA
UK, orchestra – leader b. 9 May 1914, d. 9 Jun 1995 (6 Singles: 41 Weeks)

3 Apr 53 ● **LITTLE RED MONKEY** *Parlophone R 3658* [1]..........10 3
22 May 53 ● **TERRY'S THEME FROM 'LIMELIGHT'** *Decca F 10106*..........2 24
12 Feb 54 ● **EBB TIDE** *Decca F 10122*..........9 2
24 Feb 56 **IN OLD LISBON** *Decca F 10689*..........15 4
18 May 56 **PORT-AU-PRINCE** *Decca F 10727* [2]..........18 6
31 Aug 56 **DONKEY CART** *Decca F 10743*..........26 2

[1] Frank Chacksfield's Tunesmiths, featuring Jack Jordan – clavioline [2] Winifred Atwell and Frank Chacksfield

The CHAIRMEN OF THE BOARD
US, male vocal (Norman Johnson) group (10 Singles: 77 Weeks)

22 Aug 70 ● **GIVE ME JUST A LITTLE MORE TIME** *Invictus INV 501* $..........3 13
14 Nov 70 ● **YOU'VE GOT ME DANGLING ON A STRING** *Invictus INV 504*..........5 13
20 Feb 71 **EVERYTHING'S TUESDAY** *Invictus INV 507*..........12 9
15 May 71 **PAY TO THE PIPER** *Invictus INV 511*..........34 7
4 Sep 71 **CHAIRMAN OF THE BOARD** *Invictus INV 516*..........48 2
15 Jul 72 **WORKING ON A BUILDING OF LOVE** *Invictus INV 519*..........20 8
7 Oct 72 **ELMO JAMES** *Invictus INV 524*..........21 7
16 Dec 72 **I'M ON MY WAY TO A BETTER PLACE (re)** *Invictus INV 527*..........30 6
23 Jun 73 **FINDERS KEEPERS** *Invictus INV 530*..........21 9
13 Sep 86 **LOVER BOY** *EMI EMI 5585* [1]..........56 3

[1] The Chairmen of the Board featuring General Johnson

The CHAKACHAS
Belgium, male / female vocal / instrumental group (2 Singles: 8 Weeks)

11 Jan 62 **TWIST TWIST** *RCA 1264*..........48 1
27 May 72 **JUNGLE FEVER** *Polydor 2121 064* $..........29 7

George CHAKIRIS
US, male vocalist / actor

2 Jun 60 **HEART OF A TEENAGE GIRL** *Triumph RGM 1010*..........49 1

CHAKKA BOOM BANG
Holland, male instrumental / production group

20 Jan 96 **TOSSING AND TURNING** *Hooj Choons HOOJCD 39*..........57 1

CHAKRA (see also ASCENSION; ESSENCE; LUSTRAL; OXYGEN featuring Andrea BRITTON; SPACE BROTHERS)
UK, male production duo – Ricky Simmons and Steve Jones and female vocalist (4 Singles: 5 Weeks)

18 Jan 97 **I AM** *WEA WEA 091CD*..........24 2
23 Aug 97 **HOME** *WEA WEA 116CD2*..........46 1
23 Oct 99 **LOVE SHINES THROUGH** *WEA WEA 227CD*..........67 1
26 Aug 00 **HOME** (re-mix) *WEA WEA 266CD*..........47 1

Sue CHALONER
UK, female vocalist

22 May 93 **MOVE ON UP** *Pulse 8 CDLOSE 41*..........64 1

Richard CHAMBERLAIN
US, male actor / vocalist – George Chamberlain (1 Album: 8 Weeks, 4 Singles: 36 Weeks)

7 Jun 62 **THEME FROM 'DR KILDARE' (THREE STARS WILL SHINE TONIGHT)** *MGM 1160*..........12 10
1 Nov 62 **LOVE ME TENDER** *MGM 1173*..........15 11
21 Feb 63 **HI-LILI, HI-LO** *MGM 1189*..........20 9
16 Mar 63 ● RICHARD CHAMBERLAIN SINGS *MGM C 923*..........8 8
18 Jul 63 **TRUE LOVE** *MGM 1205*..........30 6

CHAMELEON
UK, male vocal / instrumental group

18 May 96 **THE WAY IT IS** *Stress CDSTR 65*..........34 2

The CHAMELEONS (see also LORI and The CHAMELEONS)
UK, male vocal / instrumental group (2 Albums: 4 Weeks)

25 May 85 WHAT DOES ANYTHING MEAN? BASICALLY *Statik STATLP 22*..........60 2
20 Sep 86 STRANGE TIMES *Geffen 924 1191*..........44 2

CHAMPAIGN
US, male / female vocal (Pauli Carman) / instrumental group

9 May 81 ● **HOW 'BOUT US** *CBS A 1046*..........5 13
27 Jun 81 HOW 'BOUT US *CBS 84927*..........38 4

The CHAMPS
US, male instrumental group (2 Singles: 10 Weeks)

4 Apr 58 ● **TEQUILA** *London HLU 8580* ▲ $..........5 9
17 Mar 60 **TOO MUCH TEQUILA** *London HLH 9052*..........49 1

CHAMPS BOYS
France, male instrumental group

19 Jun 76 **TUBULAR BELLS** *Philips 6006 519*..........41 6

Gene CHANDLER
US, male vocalist – Eugene Dixon (4 Singles: 29 Weeks)

5 Jun 68 **NOTHING CAN STOP ME** *Soul City SC 102*..........41 4
3 Feb 79 **GET DOWN** *20th Century BTC 1040*..........11 11
1 Sep 79 **WHEN YOU'RE NUMBER 1** *20th Century TC 2411*..........43 5
28 Jun 80 **DOES SHE HAVE A FRIEND?** *20th Century TC 2451*..........28 9

CHANELLE
US, female vocalist – Charlene Munford (2 Singles: 9 Weeks)

11 Mar 89 **ONE MAN** *Cooltempo COOL 183*..........16 8
10 Dec 94 **ONE MAN** (re-mix) *Deep Distraxion OILYCD 031*..........50 1

CHANGE (see also Luther VANDROSS)
US, male / female vocal / instrumental group (2 Albums: 23 Weeks, 7 Singles: 43 Weeks)

28 Jun 80 **A LOVER'S HOLIDAY / THE GLOW OF LOVE** *WEA K 79141*..........14 8
6 Sep 80 **SEARCHING** *WEA K 79156*..........11 10
19 May 84 CHANGE OF HEART *WEA WX 5*..........34 17
2 Jun 84 **CHANGE OF HEART** *WEA YZ 7*..........17 10
11 Aug 84 **YOU ARE MY MELODY** *WEA YZ 14*..........48 4
16 Mar 85 **LET'S GO TOGETHER** *Cooltempo COOL 107*..........37 7
27 Apr 85 TURN ON THE RADIO *Cooltempo CHR 1504*..........39 6
25 May 85 **OH WHAT A FEELING** *Cooltempo COOL 109*..........56 2
13 Jul 85 **MUTUAL ATTRACTION** *Cooltempo COOL 111*..........60 2

CHANGING FACES
US, female vocal duo – Cassandra Lucas and Charisse Rose (5 Singles: 12 Weeks)

24 Sep 94 **STROKE YOU UP** *Big Beat A 8251CD* $..........43 3

KEY: UK No.1 ★ UK Top 10 ● Still on chart + UK entry at No.1 ■ US No.1 ▲ UK million seller £ US million seller $
Singles re-entries are listed as (re), (2re), (3re)... which signifies that the hit re-entered the chart once, twice or three times...
Peak Position / Weeks

26 Jul 97 ● **G.H.E.T.T.O.U.T.** *Atlantic AT 0003CD* $ 10 5
1 Nov 97 **I GOT SOMEBODY ELSE** *Atlantic AT 0014CD* 42 1
4 Apr 98 **TIME AFTER TIME** *Atlantic AT 0027CD* [1] 35 2
1 Aug 98 **SAME TEMPO** *A&M 5826952* 53 1

[1] Changing Faces featuring Jay-Z

Bruce CHANNEL *US, male vocalist (2 Singles: 28 Weeks)*

22 Mar 62 ● **HEY! BABY** *Mercury AMT 1171* ▲ $ 2 12
26 Jun 68 **KEEP ON** *Bell 1010* 12 16

CHANNEL X *Belgium, male / female vocal / instrumental group*

14 Dec 91 **GROOVE TO MOVE** *PWL Continental PWL 209* 67 1

CHANSON *US, male / female vocal group*

13 Jan 79 **DON'T HOLD BACK** *Ariola ARO 140* 33 7

The CHANTAYS *US, male instrumental group*

18 Apr 63 **PIPELINE** *London HLD 9696* 16 14

CHANTER SISTERS *UK, female vocal group*

17 Jul 76 **SIDESHOW** *Polydor 2058 735* 43 5

CHAOS *UK, male vocal group*

3 Oct 92 **FAREWELL MY SUMMER LOVE** *Arista 74321116397* 55 2

Harry CHAPIN *US, male vocalist, b. 7 Dec 1942, d. 16 Jul 1981*

11 May 74 **W.O.L.D.** *Elektra K 12133* 34 5

Beth Nielsen CHAPMAN *US, female vocalist*

12 Jun 04 LOOK *Sanctuary SANCD 269* 63 1

Michael CHAPMAN *UK, male vocalist*

21 Mar 70 FULLY QUALIFIED SURVIVOR *Harvest SHVL 764* 45 1

Tracy CHAPMAN (267 Top 500)

Modern folk vocalist / guitarist, whose socially conscious songs scored internationally, b. 20 Mar 1964, Ohio, US. Boosted by her appearance at Nelson Mandela's 70th Birthday Tribute show, her eponymous debut album sold more than 10 million copies and won the Grammy for Best New Act of 1988 (6 Albums: 229 Weeks, 2 Singles: 15 Weeks)

21 May 88 ★ TRACY CHAPMAN *Elektra EKT 44* ▲ 1 189
11 Jun 88 ● **FAST CAR** *Elektra EKR 73* 5 12
30 Sep 89 **CROSSROADS** *Elektra EKR 95* 61 3
14 Oct 89 ★ CROSSROADS *Elektra EKT 61* ■ 1 16
9 May 92 MATTERS OF THE HEART *Elektra 7559612152* 19 3
6 Oct 01 ● COLLECTION *Elektra 7559627002* 3 18
2 Nov 02 LET IT RAIN *Elektra 7559628362* 36 2
24 Sep 05 WHERE YOU LIVE *Elektra 7567838032* 43 1

CHAPTERHOUSE

UK, male vocal / instrumental group (1 Album: 3 Weeks, 2 Singles: 3 Weeks)

30 Mar 91 **PEARL** *Dedicated STONE 003* 67 1
11 May 91 WHIRLPOOL *Dedicated DEDLP 001* 23 3
12 Oct 91 **MESMERISE** *Dedicated HOUSE 001* 60 2

CHAQUITO ORCHESTRA *UK, orchestra – arranged and conducted by Johnny Gregory (2 Albums: 2 Weeks, 1 Single: 1 Week)*

27 Oct 60 **NEVER ON SUNDAY** *Fontana H 265* 50 1
24 Feb 68 THIS IS CHAQUITO *Fontana SFXL 50* [1] 36 1
4 Mar 72 THRILLER THEMES *Philips 6308 087* 48 1

[1] Chaquito and Quedo Brass

The CHARLATANS (351 Top 500)

North country boys from Northwich, Cheshire, UK, who came to prominence as part of the 'Madchester' scene: includes Tim Burgess (v), b. 30 May 1968, Manchester, and Rob Collins (k), b. 23 Feb 1963, d. 23 Jul 1996 (11 Albums: 114 Weeks, 24 Singles: 83 Weeks)

2 Jun 90 ● **THE ONLY ONE I KNOW** *Situation Two SIT 70T* 9 9
22 Sep 90 **THEN** *Situation Two SIT 74T* 12 5
20 Oct 90 ★ SOME FRIENDLY *Situation Two SITU 30* ■ 1 17
9 Mar 91 **OVER RISING** *Situation Two SIT 76* 15 5
17 Aug 91 **INDIAN ROPE** *Dead Dead Good GOOD 1T* 57 1
9 Nov 91 **ME. IN TIME** *Situation Two SIT 84* 28 3
7 Mar 92 **WEIRDO** *Situation Two SIT 88* 19 4
4 Apr 92 BETWEEN 10TH AND 11TH *Situation Two SITU 37CD* 21 4
18 Jul 92 **TREMELO SONG (EP)** *Situation Two SIT 97T* 44 2
5 Feb 94 **CAN'T GET OUT OF BED** *Beggars Banquet BBQ 27CD* 24 3
19 Mar 94 **I NEVER WANT AN EASY LIFE IF ME AND HE WERE EVER TO GET THERE** *Beggars Banquet BBQ 31CD* 38 1
2 Apr 94 ● UP TO OUR HIPS *Beggars Banquet BBQCD 147* 8 3
2 Jul 94 **JESUS HAIRDO** *Beggars Banquet BBQ 32CD1* 48 2
7 Jan 95 **CRASHIN' IN** *Beggars Banquet BBQ 44CD* 31 2
27 May 95 **JUST LOOKIN' / BULLET COMES** *Beggars Banquet BBQ 55CD* 32 3
26 Aug 95 **JUST WHEN YOU'RE THINKIN' THINGS OVER** *Beggars Banquet BBQ 60CD* 12 3
9 Sep 95 ★ THE CHARLATANS *Beggars Banquet BBQCD 174* ■ 1 13
7 Sep 96 ● **ONE TO ANOTHER** *Beggars Banquet BBQ 301CD* 3 6
5 Apr 97 ● **NORTH COUNTRY BOY (re)** *Beggars Banquet BBQ 309CD* 4 6
3 May 97 ★ TELLIN' STORIES *Beggars Banquet BBQCD 190* ■ 1 28
21 Jun 97 ● **HOW HIGH** *Beggars Banquet BBQ 312CD* 6 5
1 Nov 97 **TELLIN' STORIES** *Beggars Banquet BBQ 318CD* 16 3
7 Mar 98 ● MELTING POT *Beggars Banquet BBQCD 198* 4 25
16 Oct 99 **FOREVER** *Universal MCSTD 40220* 12 3
30 Oct 99 ● US AND US ONLY *Universal MCD 60069* 2 10
18 Dec 99 **MY BEAUTIFUL FRIEND** *Universal MCSTD 40225* 31 3
27 May 00 **IMPOSSIBLE** *Universal MCSTD 40231* 15 3
8 Sep 01 **LOVE IS THE KEY** *Universal MCSTD 40262* 16 3
22 Sep 01 ● WONDERLAND *Universal MCD 60076* 2 5
1 Dec 01 **A MAN NEEDS TO BE TOLD** *Universal MCSTD 40271* 31 2
1 Jun 02 SONGS FROM THE OTHER SIDE *Beggars Banquet BEGL 2032CD* 55 1
3 Aug 02 LIVE IT LIKE YOU LOVE IT *Universal MCD 60079* 40 2
22 May 04 **UP AT THE LAKE** *Universal MCSTD 40363* 23 3
29 May 04 UP AT THE LAKE *Universal MCD 60093* 13 6
7 Aug 04 **TRY AGAIN TODAY** *Universal MCSTD 40370* 24 3

Tracks on Tremelo Song (EP): Tremelo Song / Happen to Die / Normality Swing.

CHARLENE

US, female vocalist – Charlene Duncan

15 May 82 ★ **I'VE NEVER BEEN TO ME** *Motown TMG 1260* $ 1 12
17 Jul 82 I'VE NEVER BEEN TO ME *Motown STML 12171* 43 4

Don CHARLES

UK, male vocalist – Walter Scuffham, b. 12 Oct 1933, d. 4 Dec 2005

22 Feb 62 **WALK WITH ME MY ANGEL** *Decca F 11424* 39 5

Ray CHARLES (329 Top 500)

(see also INXS) *Rock era's first 'genius', b. Ray Charles Robinson, 23 Sep 1930, Georgia, US, d. 10 Jun 2004. This blind singer / songwriter / pianist and band leader had a US R&B chart career spanning seven decades. In 1994 he received a prestigious National Medal of Arts from US President Clinton. In 2004, his duet album and bio-pic, Ray, were huge international successes. He was a posthumous multi-Grammy winner in 2005 (10 Albums: 81 Weeks, 17 Singles: 130 Weeks)*

1 Dec 60 **GEORGIA ON MY MIND (re)** *HMV POP 792* ▲ $ 24 8

17 / 18 July 1959	24 / 25 July 1959	31 July / 1 August 1959	7 / 8 August 1959
UK No.1 SINGLES			
DREAM LOVER Bobby Darin	DREAM LOVER Bobby Darin	LIVING DOLL Cliff Richard and The Drifters	LIVING DOLL Cliff Richard and The Drifters
UK No.1 ALBUMS			
SOUTH PACIFIC Soundtrack	SOUTH PACIFIC Soundtrack	SOUTH PACIFIC Soundtrack	SOUTH PACIFIC Soundtrack

19 Oct 61 ● HIT THE ROAD JACK *HMV POP 935* ▲ $ 6 12
14 Jun 62 ★ I CAN'T STOP LOVING YOU *HMV POP 1034* ▲ $ 1 17
28 Jul 62 ● MODERN SOUNDS IN COUNTRY AND WESTERN MUSIC *HMV CLP 1580* ▲ 6 16
13 Sep 62 ● YOU DON'T KNOW ME *HMV POP 1064* 9 13
13 Dec 62 YOUR CHEATING HEART *HMV POP 1099* 13 8
23 Feb 63 MODERN SOUNDS IN COUNTRY AND WESTERN MUSIC VOLUME 2 *HMV CLP 1613* 15 5
28 Mar 63 DON'T SET ME FREE *HMV POP 1133* 37 3
16 May 63 ● TAKE THESE CHAINS FROM MY HEART *HMV POP 1161* 5 20
20 Jul 63 GREATEST HITS *HMV CLP 1626* 16 5
12 Sep 63 NO ONE *HMV POP 1202* 35 7
31 Oct 63 BUSTED *HMV POP 1221* 21 10
24 Sep 64 NO ONE TO CRY TO *HMV POP 1333* 38 3
21 Jan 65 MAKIN' WHOOPEE *HMV POP 1383* 42 4
10 Feb 66 CRYIN' TIME *HMV POP 1502* [1] 50 1
21 Apr 66 TOGETHER AGAIN *HMV POP 1519* 48 1
5 Jul 67 HERE WE GO AGAIN (re) *HMV POP 1595* 38 3
20 Dec 67 YESTERDAY *Stateside SS 2071* 44 4
31 Jul 68 ELEANOR RIGBY *Stateside SS 2120* 36 9
5 Oct 68 GREATEST HITS VOLUME 2 *Stateside SSL 10241* 24 8
19 Jul 80 HEART TO HEART – 20 HOT HITS *London RAY TV 1* 29 5
13 Jan 90 I'LL BE GOOD TO YOU *Qwest W 2697* [2] 21 7
24 Mar 90 THE COLLECTION *Arcade RCLP 101* 36 3
13 Mar 93 RAY CHARLES – THE LIVING LEGEND *Arcade ARC 94642* 48 3
25 Aug 01 THE DEFINITIVE RAY CHARLES *WSM 8122735562* 13 12
11 Sep 04 GENIUS LOVES COMPANY *Liberty 8665402* ▲ 18 16
29 Jan 05 RAY (FILM SOUNDTRACK) *Rhino 8122765402* 36 8

[1] With the Jack Halloran Singers and the Ray Charles Orchestra with the Raeletts [2] Quincy Jones featuring Ray Charles and Chaka Khan

'Ray' (film soundtrack) features original and live recordings by Ray Charles.

Suzette CHARLES *US, female vocalist*

21 Aug 93 FREE TO LOVE AGAIN *RCA 74321158372* 58 2

Tina CHARLES (see also 5000 VOLTS)

UK, female vocalist – Tina Hoskins (1 Album: 7 Weeks, 8 Singles: 63 Weeks)

7 Feb 76 ★ I LOVE TO LOVE (BUT MY BABY LOVES TO DANCE) *CBS 3937* ..1 12
1 May 76 LOVE ME LIKE A LOVER *CBS 4237* 28 7
21 Aug 76 ● DANCE LITTLE LADY DANCE *CBS 4480* 6 13
4 Dec 76 ● DR LOVE *CBS 4779* 4 10
14 May 77 RENDEZVOUS *CBS 5174* 27 6
29 Oct 77 LOVE BUG – SWEETS FOR MY SWEET (MEDLEY) *CBS 5680* 26 4
3 Dec 77 HEART 'N' SOUL *CBS 82180* 35 7
11 Mar 78 I'LL GO WHERE YOUR MUSIC TAKES ME *CBS 6062* 27 8
30 Aug 86 I LOVE TO LOVE (re-mix) *DMC DECK 1* 67 3

CHARLES and EDDIE

US, male vocal duo – Charles Pettigrew, b. 12 May 1963, d. 6 Apr 2001, and Eddie Chacon (1 Album: 15 Weeks, 4 Singles: 30 Weeks)

31 Oct 92 ★ WOULD I LIE TO YOU *Capitol CL 673* 1 17
12 Dec 92 DUOPHONIC *Capitol CDESTU 2186* 19 15
20 Feb 93 N.Y.C. (CAN YOU BELIEVE THIS CITY) *Capitol CDCL 681* 33 5
22 May 93 HOUSE IS NOT A HOME *Capitol CDCLS 688* 29 4
13 May 95 24-7-365 *Capitol CDCLS 747* 38 4

Dick CHARLESWORTH and his CITY GENTS

UK, male jazz band group – leader Dick Charlesworth – clarinet

4 May 61 BILLY BOY *Top Rank JAR 558* 43 1

CHARLOTTE *UK, female vocalist – Charlotte Kelly (4 Singles: 4 Weeks)*

12 Mar 94 QUEEN OF HEARTS *Big Life BLRD 106* 54 1
2 May 98 BE MINE *Parlophone Rhythm CDRHYTHM 10* 59 1
29 May 99 SKIN *Parlophone Rhythm Series CDRHYTHM 20* 56 1
4 Sep 99 SOMEDAY *Parlophone Rhythm Series CDRHYTHM 23* 74 1

CHARME *US, male / female vocal group*

17 Nov 84 GEORGY PORGY *RCA 464* 68 2

CHARO and the SALSOUL ORCHESTRA

US, female vocalist – Maria Martinez and orchestra

29 Apr 78 DANCE A LITTLE BIT CLOSER *Salsoul SSOL 101* 44 4

CHAS and DAVE 433 Top 500

(see also TOTTENHAM HOTSPUR FA CUP FINAL SQUAD) *Goodtime 'rockney' music duo: Chas Hodges (k/v), b. 28 Dec 1943, and Dave Peacock (b/v), b. 24 May 1945. Lovable Londoners who provide a mix of music hall, humorous 'knees-up' songs and early rock 'n' roll, songs which are ideal for pubs and parties (10 Albums: 101 Weeks, 10 Singles: 66 Weeks)*

11 Nov 78 STRUMMIN' / I'M IN TROUBLE *EMI 2874* [1] 52 3
26 May 79 GERTCHA *EMI 2947* 20 8
1 Sep 79 THE SIDEBOARD SONG (GOT MY BEER IN THE SIDEBOARD HERE) *EMI 2986* 55 3
29 Nov 80 ● RABBIT *Rockney 9* 8 11
5 Dec 81 CHAS AND DAVE'S CHRISTMAS JAMBOREE BAG *Warwick WW 5166* 25 15
12 Dec 81 STARS OVER 45 *Rockney KOR 12* 21 8
13 Mar 82 ● AIN'T NO PLEASING YOU *Rockney KOR 14* 2 11
17 Apr 82 MUSTN'T GRUMBLE *Rockney 909* 35 11
17 Jul 82 MARGATE *Rockney KOR 15* 46 4
8 Jan 83 JOB LOT *Rockney ROC 910* 59 15
19 Mar 83 LONDON GIRLS *Rockney KOR 17* 63 3
15 Oct 83 ● CHAS AND DAVE'S KNEES UP – JAMBOREE BAG NO. 2 *Rockney / Towerbell Roc 911* 7 17
3 Dec 83 MY MELANCHOLY BABY *Rockney KOR 21* 51 6
11 Aug 84 WELL PLEASED *Rockney ROC 912* 27 10
17 Nov 84 CHAS AND DAVE'S GREATEST HITS *Rockney ROC 913* 16 10
15 Dec 84 CHAS AND DAVE'S CHRISTMAS JAMBOREE BAG (re-issue) *Rockney ROCM 001* 87 1
9 Nov 85 JAMBOREE BAG NUMBER 3 *Rockney ROC 914* 15 13
3 May 86 ● SNOOKER LOOPY *Rockney POT 147* [2] 6 9
13 Dec 86 CHAS AND DAVE'S CHRISTMAS CAROL ALBUM *Telstar STAR 2293* 37 4
29 Apr 95 ● STREET PARTY *Telstar TCD 2765* 3 5

[1] Chas and Dave with Rockney [2] Matchroom Mob with Chas and Dave

JC CHASEZ (see also 'N SYNC)

US, male vocalist (1 Album: 2 Weeks, 2 Singles: 10 Weeks)

10 Apr 04 PLUG IT IN *XL Recordings XLS 180CD* [1] 22 4
24 Apr 04 SOME GIRLS (DANCE WITH WOMEN) / BLOWIN' ME UP (WITH HER LOVE) *Jive 82876605302* 13 6
8 May 04 SCHIZOPHRENIC *Jive JIV 537242* 46 2

[1] Basement Jaxx featuring JC Chasez

CHEAP TRICK *US, male vocal / instrumental group (3 Albums: 15 Weeks, 3 Singles: 14 Weeks)*

24 Feb 79 CHEAP TRICK AT BUDOKAN *Epic EPC 86083* 29 9
5 May 79 I WANT YOU TO WANT ME *Epic EPC 7258* $ 29 9
6 Oct 79 DREAM POLICE *Epic EPC 83522* 41 5
2 Feb 80 WAY OF THE WORLD *Epic EPC 8114* 73 2
5 Jun 82 ONE ON ONE *Epic EPC 85740* 95 1
31 Jul 82 IF YOU WANT MY LOVE *Epic EPC A 2406* 57 3

Oliver CHEATHAM *US, male vocalist (3 Singles: 22 Weeks)*

2 Jul 83 GET DOWN SATURDAY NIGHT *MCA 828* 38 5
5 Apr 03 ★ MAKE LUV *Positiva CDTIV 187* [1] ■ 1 15
6 Dec 03 MUSIC & YOU *Positiva CDTIV 197* [1] 38 2

[1] Room 5 featuring Oliver Cheatham

Chubby CHECKER

US, male vocalist – Ernest Evans, (2 Albums: 7 Weeks, 11 Singles: 112 Weeks)

22 Sep 60 THE TWIST (2re) *Columbia DB 4503* ▲ $ 14 12
30 Mar 61 PONY TIME *Columbia DB 4591* ▲ $ 27 6
17 Aug 61 ● LET'S TWIST AGAIN (3re) *Columbia DB 4691* $ 2 34
27 Jan 62 TWIST WITH CHUBBY CHECKER *Columbia 33SX 1315* 13 4

14 / 15 August 1959	21 / 22 August 1959	28 / 29 August 1959	4 / 5 September 1959
LIVING DOLL Cliff Richard and The Drifters	LIVING DOLL Cliff Richard and The Drifters	LIVING DOLL Cliff Richard and The Drifters	LIVING DOLL Cliff Richard and The Drifters
SOUTH PACIFIC Soundtrack	SOUTH PACIFIC Soundtrack	SOUTH PACIFIC Soundtrack	SOUTH PACIFIC Soundtrack

KEY: UK No.1 ★ UK Top 10 ● Still on chart + UK entry at No.1 ■ US No.1 ▲ UK million seller £ US million seller $
Singles re-entries are listed as (re), (2re), (3re)... which signifies that the hit re-entered the chart once, twice or three times...

Peak Position / Weeks

3 Mar 62 FOR TWISTERS ONLY *Columbia 33SX 1341* 17 3
5 Apr 62 SLOW TWISTIN' *Columbia DB 4808* $ 23 8
19 Apr 62 TEACH ME TO TWIST *Columbia DB 4802* [1] 45 1
9 Aug 62 DANCIN' PARTY *Columbia DB 4876* 19 13
1 Nov 62 LIMBO ROCK *Cameo Parkway P 849* $ 32 10
20 Dec 62 JINGLE BELL ROCK *Cameo Parkway C 205* [1] 40 3
31 Oct 63 WHAT DO YA SAY *Cameo Parkway P 806* 37 4
29 Nov 75 ● LET'S TWIST AGAIN / THE TWIST (re-issue) *London HLU 10512* 5 10
18 Jun 88 ● THE TWIST (YO, TWIST) *Urban URB 20* [2] 2 11

[1] Chubby Checker and Bobby Rydell [2] Fat Boys and Chubby Checker

'The Twist' first charted in Sep 1960 peaking at No.49, then re-entered making No.44 a month later and No.14 in Jan 1962. 'Let's Twist Again' first charted in Aug 1961 peaking at No.37, then No.2 in Dec 1961, No.46 in Aug 1962 and No.49 a month later.

CHECKMATES LTD *US, male vocal / instrumental group*

15 Nov 69 PROUD MARY *A&M AMS 769* 30 8

Judy CHEEKS *US, female vocalist (5 Singles: 15 Weeks)*

13 Nov 93 SO IN LOVE (THE REAL DEAL) *Positiva CDTIV 6* 27 3
7 May 94 REACH *Positiva CDTIV 12* 17 4
4 Mar 95 THIS TIME / RESPECT *Positiva CDTIV 28* 23 2
17 Jun 95 YOU'RE THE STORY OF MY LIFE / AS LONG AS YOU'RE GOOD TO ME *Positiva CDTIV 34* 30 3
13 Jan 96 REACH (re-mix) *Positiva CDTIV 42* 22 3

The CHEEKY GIRLS *Romania, female vocal duo – Monica and Gabriella Irimia (1 Album: 6 Weeks, 6 Singles: 41 Weeks)*

14 Dec 02 ● CHEEKY SONG (TOUCH MY BUM) *Multiply CDMULTY 97* 2 14
24 May 03 ● TAKE YOUR SHOES OFF *Multiply CDMULTY 101* 3 10
16 Aug 03 ● HOORAY HOORAY (IT'S A CHEEKY HOLIDAY) *Multiply CDMULTY 106* 3 7
23 Aug 03 PARTYTIME *Multiply MULTYCD 13* 14 6
20 Dec 03 ● HAVE A CHEEKY CHRISTMAS *Multiply CDMULTY 110* 10 5
9 Oct 04 CHEEKY FLAMENCO *XBN XBNCD 1* 29 2
18 Dec 04 BOYS AND GIRLS *XBN XBNCDS 001* [1] 50 3

[1] Cheeky Girls with Andy Newton-Lee

The CHEETAHS *UK, male vocal / instrumental group (2 Singles: 6 Weeks)*

1 Oct 64 MECCA *Philips BF 1362* 36 3
21 Jan 65 SOLDIER BOY *Philips BF 1383* 39 3

CHEF *US, male cartoon vocalist – Isaac Hayes*

26 Dec 98 ★ CHOCOLATE SALTY BALLS (PS I LOVE YOU) *Columbia 6667985* 1 13

CHELSEA FC *UK, male football team vocalists (4 Singles: 22 Weeks)*

26 Feb 72 ● BLUE IS THE COLOUR *Penny Farthing PEN 782* 5 12
14 May 94 NO ONE CAN STOP US NOW *RCA 74321210452* 23 3
17 May 97 BLUE DAY *WEA WEA 112CD* [1] 22 5
27 May 00 BLUE TOMORROW *Telstar TV CFCCD 2000* 22 2

[1] Suggs & Co featuring Chelsea Team

The CHEMICAL BROTHERS (277 Top 500) *Internationally successful Manchester formed (1992) dance production duo Tom Rowlands and Ed Simons, originally named The Dust Brothers (after their production heroes, who forced a name change). These BRIT and Grammy winners are the first contemporary dance act to achieve four successive No.1s with newly recorded albums (6 Albums: 151 Weeks, 16 Singles: 90 Weeks)*

17 Jun 95 LEAVE HOME *Junior Boy's Own CHEMSD 1* 17 4
8 Jul 95 ● EXIT PLANET DUST *Junior Boy's Own XDUSTCD 1* 9 41
9 Sep 95 LIFE IS SWEET *Junior Boy's Own CHEMSD 2* 25 3
27 Jan 96 LOOPS OF FURY (EP) *Junior Boy's Own CHEMSD 3* 13 1
12 Oct 96 ★ SETTING SUN *Junior Boy's Own CHEMSD 4* ■ 1 7
5 Apr 97 ★ BLOCK ROCKIN' BEATS (re) *Virgin CHEMSD 5* ■ 1 7
19 Apr 97 ★ DIG YOUR OWN HOLE *Virgin XDUSTCD 2* ■ 1 27
20 Sep 97 ELEKTROBANK *Virgin CHEMSD 6* 17 4
12 Jun 99 ● HEY BOY HEY GIRL *Virgin CHEMSD 8* 3 10
3 Jul 99 ★ SURRENDER *Virgin XDUSTCD 4* ■ 1 47
14 Aug 99 ● LET FOREVER BE *Virgin CHEMSD 9* 9 7
23 Oct 99 OUT OF CONTROL *Virgin CHEMSD 10* 21 4
22 Sep 01 ● IT BEGAN IN AFRIKA (re) *Virgin CHEMSD 12* 8 6
26 Jan 02 ● STAR GUITAR (re) *Virgin CHEMSD 14* 8 8
9 Feb 02 ★ COME WITH US *Virgin XDUSTCD 5* ■ 1 11
4 May 02 COME WITH US / THE TEST *Virgin CHEMSD 15* 14 3
27 Sep 03 THE GOLDEN PATH *Virgin CHEMSD 18* [1] 17 4
4 Oct 03 ● SINGLES 93-03 *Virgin XDUSTCD 6* 9 7
29 Jan 05 ● GALVANIZE (re) *Virgin CHEMSD 21* 3 16
5 Feb 05 ★ PUSH THE BUTTON *Virgin XDUSTCD 7* ■ 1 18
14 May 05 BELIEVE *Virgin CHEMSDX 22* 18 4
23 Jul 05 THE BOXER *Virgin CHEMSDX 23* 41 2

[1] The Chemical Brothers / The Flaming Lips

Tracks on Loops of Fury (EP): Loops of Fury / (The Best Part of) Breaking Up / Get Upon it Like This / Chemical Beats. Uncredited vocals on 'Setting Sun' and 'Let Forever Be' by Noel Gallagher and on 'Out of Control' by Bernard Sumner. Uncredited vocal on 'The Boxer' by Tim Burgess.

CHEQUERS *UK, male vocal / instrumental group (2 Singles: 10 Weeks)*

18 Oct 75 ROCK ON BROTHER *Creole CR 111* 21 5
28 Feb 76 HEY MISS PAYNE *Creole CR 116* 32 5

CHER (69 Top 500) (see also MEAT LOAF) *Perennially popular vocalist, b. Cherilyn Sarkisian LaPierre, 20 May 1946, California, US, who was half of the most successful husband / wife duo ever, Sonny and Cher. In 1998, at the age of 52, she became the oldest female solo singer to top the singles chart. Her 605 show Farewell Tour was seen by a record (for a female pop star) 5.88 million fans and grossed $394.6 million. Best-selling single: 'Believe' 1,672,108 (11 Albums: 310 Weeks, 42 Singles: 230 Weeks)*

19 Aug 65 ● ALL I REALLY WANT TO DO *Liberty LIB 66114* 9 10
2 Oct 65 ● ALL I REALLY WANT TO DO *Liberty LBY 3058* 7 9
31 Mar 66 ● BANG BANG (MY BABY SHOT ME DOWN) *Liberty LIB 66160* 3 12
7 May 66 SONNY SIDE OF CHER *Liberty LBY 3072* 11 11
4 Aug 66 I FEEL SOMETHING IN THE AIR *Liberty LIB 12034* 43 2
22 Sep 66 SUNNY *Liberty LIB 12083* 32 5
6 Nov 71 ● GYPSYS, TRAMPS AND THIEVES *MCA MU 1142* ▲ $ 4 13
16 Feb 74 DARK LADY (re) *MCA 101* ▲ $ 36 4
19 Dec 87 ● I FOUND SOMEONE *Geffen GEF 31* 5 10
16 Jan 88 CHER *Geffen WX 132* 26 22
2 Apr 88 WE ALL SLEEP ALONE *Geffen GEF 35* 47 5
22 Jul 89 ● HEART OF STONE *Geffen GEF 24239* 7 82
2 Sep 89 ● IF I COULD TURN BACK TIME *Geffen GEF 59* 6 14
13 Jan 90 JUST LIKE JESSE JAMES *Geffen GEF 69* 11 11
7 Apr 90 HEART OF STONE *Geffen GEF 75* 43 5
11 Aug 90 YOU WOULDN'T KNOW LOVE *Geffen GEF 77* 55 3
13 Apr 91 ★ THE SHOOP SHOOP SONG (IT'S IN HIS KISS) *Epic 6566737* 1 15
29 Jun 91 ★ LOVE HURTS *Geffen GEF 24427* ■ 1 51
13 Jul 91 ● LOVE AND UNDERSTANDING *Geffen GFS 5* 10 8
12 Oct 91 SAVE UP ALL YOUR TEARS *Geffen GFS 11* 37 5
7 Dec 91 LOVE HURTS *Geffen GFS 16* 43 5
18 Apr 92 COULD'VE BEEN YOU *Geffen GFS 19* 31 4
14 Nov 92 OH NO NOT MY BABY *Geffen GFS 29* 33 4
21 Nov 92 ★ GREATEST HITS 1965-1992 *Geffen GED 24439* ■ 1 33
16 Jan 93 MANY RIVERS TO CROSS *Geffen GFSTD 31* 37 3
6 Mar 93 WHENEVER YOU'RE NEAR *Geffen GFSTD 32* 72 1
15 Jan 94 I GOT YOU BABE *Geffen GFSTD 64* [1] 35 3
18 Mar 95 ★ LOVE CAN BUILD A BRIDGE *London COCD 1* [2] 1 8
28 Oct 95 WALKING IN MEMPHIS *WEA WEA 021CD1* 11 7
18 Nov 95 ● IT'S A MAN'S WORLD *WEA 0630126702* 10 18
20 Jan 96 ● ONE BY ONE *WEA WEA 032CD* 7 9

11 / 12 September 1959	18 / 19 September 1959	25 / 26 September 1959	2 / 3 October 1959
UK No.1 SINGLES			
ONLY SIXTEEN Craig Douglas	ONLY SIXTEEN Craig Douglas	ONLY SIXTEEN Craig Douglas	ONLY SIXTEEN Craig Douglas
UK No.1 ALBUMS			
SOUTH PACIFIC Soundtrack	SOUTH PACIFIC Soundtrack	SOUTH PACIFIC Soundtrack	SOUTH PACIFIC Soundtrack

27 Apr 96 **NOT ENOUGH LOVE IN THE WORLD** *WEA WEA 052CD*............**31** 2
17 Aug 96 **THE SUN AIN'T GONNA SHINE ANYMORE** *WEA WEA 071CD*..**26** 3
31 Oct 98 ★ **BELIEVE (re)** *WEA WEA 175CD* ■ ▲ £ $.........................**1** 28
7 Nov 98 ● BELIEVE *WEA 3984253192*......................................7 44
6 Mar 99 ● **STRONG ENOUGH** *WEA WEA 201CD1*...**5** 10
19 Jun 99 **ALL OR NOTHING** *WEA WEA 212CD1*...**12** 7
6 Nov 99 **DOVE L'AMORE** *WEA WEA 230CD1*..**21** 3
20 Nov 99 ● THE GREATEST HITS *WEA / Universal TV 8573804202*...............7 24
17 Nov 01 ● **THE MUSIC'S NO GOOD WITHOUT YOU** *WEA WEA 337CD*..........**8** 10
1 Dec 01 LIVING PROOF *WEA 927424632*..46 2
6 Dec 03 THE VERY BEST OF CHER *UMTV / WSM 5046685862*.................17 14

[1] Cher with Beavis and Butt-Head [2] Cher, Chrissie Hynde and Neneh Cherry with Eric Clapton

The catalogue number for Heart Of Stone changed from WX 262 during the album's chart run.

CHERI *Canada, female vocal duo – Rosalind Hunt and Lyn Cullerier*

19 Jun 82 **MURPHY'S LAW** *Polydor POSP 459*..**13** 9

The CHEROKEES *UK, male vocal / instrumental group*

3 Sep 64 **SEVEN DAFFODILS** *Columbia DB 7341*...**33** 5

CHERRELLE
US, female vocalist – Cheryl Norton (1 Album: 9 Weeks, 6 Singles: 26 Weeks)

28 Dec 85 ● **SATURDAY LOVE** *Tabu A 6829* [1] **6** 11
25 Jan 86 HIGH PRIORITY *Tabu TBU 26699*...17 9
1 Mar 86 **WILL YOU SATISFY?** *Tabu A 6927*..**57** 3
6 Feb 88 **NEVER KNEW LOVE LIKE THIS** *Tabu 6513827* [2] **26** 7
6 May 89 **AFFAIR** *Tabu 654673 7*..**67** 2
24 Mar 90 **SATURDAY LOVE** (re-mix) *Tabu 6558007* [1] **55** 2
2 Aug 97 **BABY COME TO ME** *One World OWECD 1* [2] **56** 1

[1] Cherrelle with Alexander O'Neal [2] Alexander O'Neal featuring Cherrelle

Don CHERRY *US, male vocalist, b. 11 Jan 1924, d. 19 Oct 1995*

10 Feb 56 ● **BAND OF GOLD** *Philips PB 549*...**6** 11

Eagle-Eye CHERRY
Sweden, male vocalist (2 Albums: 32 Weeks, 5 Singles: 28 Weeks)

4 Jul 98 ● **SAVE TONIGHT** *Polydor 5695952*...**6** 13
1 Aug 98 ● DESIRELESS *Polydor 5372262*...3 29
14 Nov 98 ● **FALLING IN LOVE AGAIN** *Polydor 5630252*...............................**8** 8
20 Mar 99 **PERMANENT TEARS** *Polydor 5636752*......................................**43** 1
29 Apr 00 **ARE YOU STILL HAVING FUN** *Polydor 5618032*.........................**21** 4
20 May 00 LIVING IN THE PRESENT FUTURE *Polydor 5437442*...................12 3
11 Nov 00 **LONG WAY AROUND** *Polydor 5677812* [1] **48** 2

[1] Eagle-Eye Cherry featuring Neneh Cherry

Neneh CHERRY
(see also RIP RIG AND PANIC) *UK (b. Sweden), female vocalist – Neneh Mariann Karlsson (3 Albums: 49 Weeks, 14 Singles: 98 Weeks)*

10 Dec 88 ● **BUFFALO STANCE** *Circa YR 21*...**3** 13
20 May 89 ● **MANCHILD** *Circa YR 30*..**5** 10
17 Jun 89 ● RAW LIKE SUSHI *Circa CIRCA 8*...2 43
12 Aug 89 **KISSES ON THE WIND** *Circa YR 33*..**20** 6
23 Dec 89 **INNA CITY MAMMA** *Circa YR 42*...**31** 7
29 Sep 90 **I'VE GOT YOU UNDER MY SKIN** *Circa YR 53*..............................**25** 5
3 Oct 92 **MONEY LOVE** *Circa YR 83*...**23** 4
7 Nov 92 HOMEBREW *Circa CIRCD 25*..27 2
16 Jan 93 **BUDDY X** *Circa YRCD 98*...**35** 3
25 Jun 94 ● **7 SECONDS (re)** *Columbia 6605082* [1] **3** 25
18 Mar 95 ★ **LOVE CAN BUILD A BRIDGE** *London COCD 1* [2] **1** 8
3 Aug 96 ● **WOMAN** *Hut HUTCD 70*...**9** 7
14 Sep 96 MAN *Hut CDHUT 38*...16 4
14 Dec 96 **KOOTCHI** *Hut HUTDG 75*..**38** 2
22 Feb 97 **FEEL IT** *Hut HUTCD 79*..**68** 1
6 Nov 99 **BUDDY X 99** *4 Liberty LIBTCD 33* [3] **15** 5
11 Nov 00 **LONG WAY AROUND** *Polydor 5677812* [4] **48** 2

[1] Youssou N'Dour (featuring Neneh Cherry) [2] Cher, Chrissie Hynde and Neneh Cherry with Eric Clapton [3] Dreem Teem vs Neneh Cherry [4] Eagle-Eye Cherry featuring Neneh Cherry

CHERRYFALLS *UK, male vocal / instrumental group (2 Singles: 2 Weeks)*

14 Aug 04 **STANDING WATCHING** *Island CID 868*..**64** 1
9 Apr 05 **MY DRUG** *Island CID 881*..**71** 1

The CHI-LITES
US, male vocal (Eugene Record, d. 2005) group (10 Singles: 89 Weeks)

28 Aug 71 **(FOR GOD'S SAKE) GIVE MORE POWER TO THE PEOPLE** *MCA MU 1138*...**32** 6
15 Jan 72 ● **HAVE YOU SEEN HER** *MCA MU 1146*...**3** 12
27 May 72 **OH GIRL** *MCA MU 1156* ▲ $...**14** 9
23 Mar 74 ● **HOMELY GIRL** *Brunswick BR 9*..**5** 13
20 Jul 74 **I FOUND SUNSHINE** *Brunswick BR 12*..**35** 5
2 Nov 74 ● **TOO GOOD TO BE FORGOTTEN** *Brunswick BR 13*......................**10** 11
21 Jun 75 ● **HAVE YOU SEEN HER / OH GIRL** (re-issue) *Brunswick BR 20*..**5** 9
13 Sep 75 ● **IT'S TIME FOR LOVE** *Brunswick BR 25*..**5** 10
31 Jul 76 ● **YOU DON'T HAVE TO GO** *Brunswick BR 34*..................................**3** 11
13 Aug 83 **CHANGING FOR YOU** *R&B RBS 215*...**61** 3

CHIC *US, male / female vocal / instrumental group – leaders Nile Rodgers and Bernard Edwards, b. 31 Oct 1952, d. 18 Apr 1996 (4 Albums: 47 Weeks, 11 Singles: 90 Weeks)*

26 Nov 77 ● **DANCE, DANCE, DANCE (YOWSAH, YOWSAH, YOWSAH)** *Atlantic K 11038* $..**6** 12
1 Apr 78 ● **EVERYBODY DANCE** *Atlantic K 11097*...**9** 11
18 Nov 78 ● **LE FREAK** *Atlantic K 11209* ▲ $...**7** 16
3 Feb 79 ● C'EST CHIC *Atlantic K 50565*...2 24
24 Feb 79 ● **I WANT YOUR LOVE** *Atlantic LV 16* $..**4** 11
30 Jun 79 ● **GOOD TIMES** *Atlantic K 11310* ▲ $..**5** 11
18 Aug 79 RISQUE *Atlantic K 50634*..29 12
13 Oct 79 **MY FORBIDDEN LOVER** *Atlantic K 11385*.....................................**15** 8
8 Dec 79 **MY FEET KEEP DANCING** *Atlantic K 11415*..................................**21** 9
15 Dec 79 THE BEST OF CHIC *Atlantic K 50686*...30 8
12 Mar 83 **HANGIN'** *Atlantic A 9898*..**64** 1
19 Sep 87 **JACK LE FREAK** *Atlantic A 9198*...**19** 6
5 Dec 87 FREAK OUT *Telstar STAR 2319* [1] 72 3
14 Jul 90 **MEGACHIC – CHIC MEDLEY** *East West A 7949*............................**58** 2
15 Feb 92 **CHIC MYSTIQUE** *Warner Bros. W 0083*..**48** 3

[1] Chic and Sister Sledge

Megachic was a medley of Le Freak / Everybody Dance / Good Times / I Want Your Love.

CHICAGO 324 Top 500 *Pioneering jazz-rock group included Peter Cetera (v/b), b. 13 Sep 1944. Group relocated from city of the same name to California, US, in 1967. Released longest numerical sequence of album titles (majority going platinum in the US) – the most recent being Chicago 26 (1999) (11 Albums: 132 Weeks, 7 Singles: 81 Weeks)*

27 Sep 69 ● CHICAGO TRANSIT AUTHORITY *CBS 66221* [1] 9 14
10 Jan 70 ● **I'M A MAN** *CBS 4715*..**8** 11
4 Apr 70 ● CHICAGO *CBS 66233*..6 27
18 Jul 70 ● **25 OR 6 TO 4** *CBS 5076*...**7** 13
6 Mar 71 ● CHICAGO 3 *CBS 66260*..9 5
30 Sep 72 CHICAGO 5 *CBS 69108* ▲..24 2
9 Oct 76 ★ **IF YOU LEAVE ME NOW** *CBS 4603* ▲ $...**1** 16
23 Oct 76 CHICAGO X *CBS 86010*..21 11
5 Nov 77 **BABY, WHAT A BIG SURPRISE** *CBS 5672*......................................**41** 3
21 Aug 82 ● **HARD TO SAY I'M SORRY** *Full Moon K 79301* ▲ $.........................**4** 15
2 Oct 82 CHICAGO 16 *Full Moon K 99235*..44 9
4 Dec 82 LOVE SONGS *TV TVA 6*..42 8
27 Oct 84 ● **HARD HABIT TO BREAK** *Full Moon W 9214*.................................**8** 13
1 Dec 84 CHICAGO 17 *Full Moon 925060*..24 20

9 / 10 October 1959	16 / 17 October 1959	23 / 24 October 1959	30 / 31 October 1959
HERE COMES SUMMER Jerry Keller	**MACK THE KNIFE** Bobby Darin	**MACK THE KNIFE** Bobby Darin	**TRAVELLIN' LIGHT** Cliff Richard and The Shadows
SOUTH PACIFIC Soundtrack	**SOUTH PACIFIC** Soundtrack	**SOUTH PACIFIC** Soundtrack	**SOUTH PACIFIC** Soundtrack

KEY UK No.1 ★ UK Top 10 ● Still on chart + UK entry at No.1 ■ US No.1 ▲ UK million seller £ US million seller $
Singles re-entries are listed as (re), (2re), (3re)... which signifies that the hit re-entered the chart once, twice or three times...
Peak Position | Weeks

26 Jan 85 **YOU'RE THE INSPIRATION** *Warner Bros. W 9126*..........14 10
25 Nov 89 ● THE HEART OF CHICAGO *Reprise WX 328*..........6 25
13 Feb 99 THE HEART OF CHICAGO – 1967-1997 *Reprise 9362465542*.....21 4
14 Sep 02 THE COMPLETE GREATEST HITS – THE CHICAGO STORY *Rhino 8122736302*..........11 7

[1] Chicago Transit Authority

CHICANE (see also DISCO CITIZENS) *UK, male producer / instrumentalist – Nick Bracegirdle (2 Albums: 9 Weeks, 12 Singles: 53 Weeks)*

21 Dec 96 **OFFSHORE** *Xtravaganza 0091005*..........14 7
14 Jun 97 **SUNSTROKE** *Xtravaganza 0091125*..........21 3
13 Sep 97 **OFFSHORE '97** (re-mix) *Xtravaganza 0091255 EXT* [1]..........17 4
1 Nov 97 FAR FROM THE MADDENING CROWDS *Xtravaganza 0093172 EXT*..........49 1
20 Dec 97 **LOST YOU SOMEWHERE** *Xtravaganza 0091415*..........35 3
10 Oct 98 **STRONG IN LOVE** *Xtravaganza 0091675 EXT* [2]..........32 2
5 Jun 99 ● **SALTWATER** *Xtravaganza XTRAV 1CDS* [3]..........6 10
18 Mar 00 ★ **DON'T GIVE UP** *Xtravaganza XTRAV 9CDS* [4] ■..........1 14
8 Apr 00 ● BEHIND THE SUN *Xtravaganza XTRAV 10CD*..........10 8
22 Jul 00 **NO ORDINARY MORNING / HALCYON** *Xtravaganza XTRAV 12CDS*..........28 3
28 Oct 00 **AUTUMN TACTICS** *Xtravaganza XTRAV 17CDS*..........44 2
8 Feb 03 **SALTWATER** (re-mix) *Xtravaganza XTRAV 35CDS*..........43 2
8 Mar 03 **LOVE ON THE RUN** *WEA WEA 361CD* [5]..........33 2
14 Feb 04 **DON'T GIVE UP 2004** *Xtravaganza XTRAV 44CDS*..........43 1

[1] Chicane with Power Circle [2] Chicane featuring Mason [3] Chicane featuring Maire Brennan of Clannad [4] Chicane featuring Bryan Adams [5] Chicane featuring Peter Cunnah

Chicane are Disco Citizens under another name.

CHICKEN SHACK (see also FLEETWOOD MAC) *UK, male / female vocal (Christine Perfect aka Christine McVie) / instrumental group (2 Albums: 9 Weeks, 2 Singles: 19 Weeks)*

22 Jul 68 40 BLUE FINGERS FRESHLY PACKED *Blue Horizon 763203*....12 8
15 Feb 69 ● OK KEN? *Blue Horizon 763209*..........9 1
7 May 69 **I'D RATHER GO BLIND** *Blue Horizon 57-3153*..........14 13
6 Sep 69 **TEARS IN THE WIND** *Blue Horizon 57-3160*..........29 6

CHICKEN SHED *UK, youth theatre company*

27 Dec 97 **I AM IN LOVE WITH THE WORLD** *Columbia 6654172*..........15 6

CHICKS ON SPEED (see also DAVE CLARKE) *Australia / Germany / US, female vocal / instrumental trio (3 Singles: 2 Weeks)*

21 Feb 04 **WHAT WAS HER NAME?** *Skint SKINT 94CD* [1]..........50 1
13 Mar 04 **WORDY RAPPINGHOOD** *Labels 5478360*..........66 1

[1] Dave Clarke featuring Chicks on Speed

CHICORY TIP *UK, male vocal (Peter Hewson) / instrumental group (3 Singles: 34 Weeks)*

29 Jan 72 ★ **SON OF MY FATHER** *CBS 7737*..........1 13
20 May 72 **WHAT'S YOUR NAME** *CBS 8021*..........13 8
31 Mar 73 **GOOD GRIEF CHRISTINA** *CBS 1258*..........17 13

The CHIEFTAINS *Ireland, male vocal / instrumental group (5 Albums: 27 Weeks, 2 Singles: 4 Weeks)*

28 Mar 87 JAMES GALWAY AND THE CHIEFTAINS IN IRELAND *RCA Red Seal RL 85798* [1]..........32 5
2 Jul 88 IRISH HEARTBEAT *Mercury MERH 124* [2]..........18 7
4 Feb 95 THE LONG BLACK VEIL *RCA 74321251672*..........17 9
18 Mar 95 **HAVE I TOLD YOU LATELY THAT I LOVE YOU** (re-recording) *RCA 74321271702* [1]..........71 1
6 Mar 99 TEARS OF STONE *RCA Victor 9026689682*..........36 4
12 Jun 99 **I KNOW MY LOVE** *RCA Victor 74321670622* [2]..........37 3
23 Mar 02 THE WIDE WORLD OVER *RCA Victor 9026639172*..........37 2

[1] The Chieftains with Van Morrison [2] The Chieftains featuring The Corrs
[1] James Galway and The Chieftains [2] Van Morrison and The Chieftains

The CHIFFONS *US, female vocal group (4 Singles: 40 Weeks)*

11 Apr 63 **HE'S SO FINE** *Stateside SS 172* ▲ $..........16 12
18 Jul 63 **ONE FINE DAY** *Stateside SS 202*..........29 6
26 May 66 **SWEET TALKIN' GUY** *Stateside SS 512*..........31 8
18 Mar 72 ● **SWEET TALKIN' GUY** (re-issue) *London HL 10271*..........4 14

CHIKINKI *UK, male vocal / instrumental group (4 Singles: 4 Weeks)*

29 Nov 03 **ASSASSINATOR 13** *Island CID 834*..........72 1
27 Mar 04 **LIKE IT OR LEAVE IT** *Island CID 848*..........65 1
19 Jun 04 **ETHER RADIO** *Island CID 860*..........50 1
6 Nov 04 **ALL EYES** *Island CIDX 875*..........74 1

CHILD *UK, male vocal / instrumental group (3 Singles: 22 Weeks)*

29 Apr 78 **WHEN YOU WALK IN THE ROOM** *Ariola Hansa AHA 511*..........38 5
22 Jul 78 ● **IT'S ONLY MAKE BELIEVE** *Ariola Hansa AHA 522*..........10 12
28 Apr 79 **ONLY YOU (AND YOU ALONE)** *Ariola Hansa AHA 536*..........33 5

Jane CHILD *Canada, female vocalist*

12 May 90 **DON'T WANNA FALL IN LOVE** *Warner Bros. W 9817*..........22 8

CHILDLINERS *UK / Australia, Ireland, male / female vocal group*

16 Dec 95 ● **THE GIFT OF CHRISTMAS** *London LONCD 376*..........9 6

Charity recording group included Dannii Minogue, Sean Maguire and members of East 17, Boyzone and Gemini.

CHILDREN FOR RWANDA *UK, male / female choir*

10 Sep 94 **LOVE CAN BUILD A BRIDGE** *East West YZ 849CD*..........57 2

CHILDREN OF THE NIGHT *UK, male vocalist / producer*

26 Nov 88 **IT'S A TRIP (TUNE IN, TURN ON, DROP OUT)** *Jive JIVE 189*..........52 2

Toni CHILDS *US, female vocalist*

25 Mar 89 **DON'T WALK AWAY** *A&M AM 462*..........53 4
29 Apr 89 UNION *A&M AMA 5175*..........73 1

CHILI HI FLY
Australia, male DJ / production duo – Simon Lewicki and Noel Burgess

18 Mar 00 **IS IT LOVE** *Ministry of Sound MOSCDS 141*..........37 2

CHILL FAC-TORR *US, male vocal / instrumental group*

2 Apr 83 **TWIST (ROUND 'N' ROUND)** *Phillyworld PWS 109*..........37 8

CHILLI featuring CARRAPICHO
US / Ghana / Brazil, male / female vocal / instrumental group

20 Sep 97 **TIC, TIC TAC** *Arista 74321511332*..........59 1

CHIMAIRA NEW *US, male vocal / instrumental group*

20 Aug 05 CHIMAIRA *Roadrunner RR 82622*..........62 1

The CHIMES *UK, male / female vocal (Pauline Henry) / instrumental group (1 Album: 19 Weeks, 6 Singles: 28 Weeks)*

19 Aug 89 **1-2-3** *CBS 655166 7*..........60 3
2 Dec 89 **HEAVEN** (re) *CBS 655432 7*..........66 5

6 / 7 November 1959	13 / 14 November 1959	20 / 21 November 1959	27 / 28 November 1959
UK No.1 SINGLES			
TRAVELLIN' LIGHT Cliff Richard and The Shadows	TRAVELLIN' LIGHT Cliff Richard and The Shadows	TRAVELLIN' LIGHT Cliff Richard and The Shadows	TRAVELLIN' LIGHT Cliff Richard and The Shadows
UK No.1 ALBUMS			
SOUTH PACIFIC Soundtrack	SOUTH PACIFIC Soundtrack	SOUTH PACIFIC Soundtrack	SOUTH PACIFIC Soundtrack

19 May 90 ● I STILL HAVEN'T FOUND WHAT I'M LOOKING FOR *CBS CHIM 1*....6 9
23 Jun 90 THE CHIMES *CBS 4664811*....17 19
28 Jul 90 TRUE LOVE *CBS CHIM 2*....48 3
29 Sep 90 HEAVEN (re-issue) *CBS CHIM 3*....24 6
1 Dec 90 LOVE COMES TO MIND *CBS CHIM 4*....49 2

CHIMIRA *South Africa, female vocalist*

6 Dec 97 SHOW ME HEAVEN *Neoteric NRDCD 11*....70 1

CHINA BLACK *UK, male vocal / instrumental duo – Errol Reid and Simon Fung (1 Album: 4 Weeks, 4 Singles: 35 Weeks)*

16 Jul 94 ● SEARCHING (re) *Wild Card CARDD 7*....4 20
29 Oct 94 STARS *Wild Card CARDD 9*....19 7
11 Feb 95 ALMOST SEE YOU (SOMEWHERE) *Wild Card CARDW 15*....31 2
11 Mar 95 BORN *Wild Card 5237552*....27 4
3 Jun 95 SWING LOW SWEET CHARIOT *PolyGram TV SWLOW 2* [1] 15 6

[1] Ladysmith Black Mambazo featuring China Black

CHINA CRISIS *UK, male vocal (Gary Daly) / instrumental group (6 Albums: 68 Weeks, 11 Singles: 66 Weeks)*

7 Aug 82 AFRICAN AND WHITE *Inevitable INEV 011*....45 5
20 Nov 82 DIFFICULT SHAPES & PASSIVE RHYTHMS SOME PEOPLE THINK IT'S FUN TO ENTERTAIN *Virgin V 2243*....21 18
22 Jan 83 CHRISTIAN *Virgin VS 562*....12 9
21 May 83 TRAGEDY AND MYSTERY *Virgin VS 587*....46 6
15 Oct 83 WORKING WITH FIRE AND STEEL *Virgin VS 620*....48 5
12 Nov 83 WORKING WITH FIRE AND STEEL – POSSIBLE POP SONGS VOLUME TWO *Virgin V 2286*....20 16
14 Jan 84 ● WISHFUL THINKING *Virgin VS 647*....9 8
10 Mar 84 HANNA HANNA *Virgin VS 665*....44 3
30 Mar 85 BLACK MAN RAY *Virgin VS 752*....14 9
11 May 85 ● FLAUNT THE IMPERFECTION *Virgin V 2342*....9 22
1 Jun 85 KING IN A CATHOLIC STYLE (WAKE UP) *Virgin VS 765*....19 9
7 Sep 85 YOU DID CUT ME *Virgin VS 799*....54 3
8 Nov 86 ARIZONA SKY *Virgin VS 898*....47 4
6 Dec 86 WHAT PRICE PARADISE *Virgin V 2410*....63 6
24 Jan 87 BEST KEPT SECRET *Virgin VS 926*....36 5
13 May 89 DIARY OF A HOLLOW HORSE *Virgin V 2567*....58 2
15 Sep 90 CHINA CRISIS COLLECTION *Virgin V 2613*....32 4

CHINA DRUM *UK, male vocal / instrumental group (1 Album: 1 Week, 4 Singles: 4 Weeks)*

2 Mar 96 CAN'T STOP THESE THINGS *Mantra MNT 8CD*....65 1
20 Apr 96 LAST CHANCE *Mantra MNT 10CD*....60 1
11 May 96 GOOSEFAIR *Mantra MNTCD 1002*....53 1
9 Aug 97 FICTION OF LIFE *Mantra MNT 21CD*....65 1
27 Sep 97 SOMEWHERE ELSE *Mantra MNT 022CD1*....74 1

Jonny CHINGAS *US, male instrumentalist*

19 Feb 83 PHONE HOME *CBS A 3121*....43 6

CHINGY *US, male rapper – Howard Bailey Jr. (1 Album: 1 Week, 5 Singles: 21 Weeks)*

25 Oct 03 RIGHT THURR *Capitol CDCLS 849*....17 5
21 Feb 04 HOLIDAE IN *Capitol CDCL 852* [1] 35 3
29 May 04 JACKPOT *Capitol 5818270*....73 1
29 May 04 ONE CALL AWAY *Capitol CDCL 856* [2] 26 4
18 Sep 04 I LIKE THAT *Capitol CDCL 861* [3] 11 6
13 Nov 04 BALLA BABY *Parlophone CDCLS 865*....34 3

[1] Chingy featuring Ludacris & Snoop Dogg [2] Chingy featuring J Weav [3] Houston featuring Chingy, Nate Dogg & I-20

The CHIPMUNKS *US, chipmunk vocal trio – David Seville (d. 1972) (3 Singles: 12 Weeks)*

24 Jul 59 RAGTIME COWBOY JOE *London HLU 8916* [1] 11 8
19 Dec 92 ACHY BREAKY HEART *Epic 6588837* [2] 53 3
14 Dec 96 MACARENA *Sony Wonder 6639981* [3] 65 1

[1] David Seville and The Chipmunks [2] Alvin and The Chipmunks featuring Billy Ray Cyrus [3] Los Del Chipmunks

The Chipmunk characters were created by David Seville. His son resurrected the act in 1980.

The CHIPPENDALES *UK / US, male vocal group*

31 Oct 92 GIVE ME YOUR BODY *XSrhythm XSR 3*....28 4

!!! (CHK CHK CHK) *US, male vocal / instrumental group*

21 Aug 04 HELLO? IS THIS THING ON? *Warp WAP 176CD*....74 1

CHOCOLATE MONDAY NEW *UK, female vocal group (2 Singles: 2 Weeks)*

12 Feb 05 YOUR PLACE OR MINE *DPI DPIBD 1*....49 1
29 Oct 05 MODEL LIFE *DPI CDCPIBD 2*....61 1

CHOCOLATE PUMA (see also GOODMEN; JARK PRONGO; RHYTHMKILLAZ; RIVA featuring Dannii MINOGUE; TOMBA VIRA) *Holland, male production duo – DJ Dobri and DJ Zki (Rene ter Horst and Gaston Steenkist)*

24 Mar 01 ● I WANNA BE U (re) *Cream / Parlophone CREAM 13CD*....6 9

THE CHOIRBOYS NEW *UK, male choristers*

10 Dec 05 THE CHOIRBOYS *UCJ 9874369*....25 4+
31 Dec 05 TEARS IN HEAVEN *UCJ 4763116*....22 1+

The Choirboys features the English Chamber Ensemble.

CHOO CHOO PROJECT (see also Jose NUNEZ featuring OCTAHVIA) *US, male / female production / instrumental / vocal duo – Harry Romero and Octahvia Lambert*

15 Jan 00 HAZIN' & PHAZIN' *Defected DEFECT 10CDS*....21 3

CHOPS-EMC + EXTENSIVE *UK, male instrumental group and rapper*

8 Aug 92 ME' ISRAELITES *Faze 2 FAZE 6*....60 1

The CHORDETTES *US, female vocal group (3 Singles: 25 Weeks)*

17 Dec 54 MR SANDMAN *Columbia DB 3553* ▲ $....11 8
31 Aug 56 ● BORN TO BE WITH YOU *London HLA 8302*....8 9
18 Apr 58 ● LOLLIPOP *London HLD 8584* $....6 8

The CHORDS *UK, male vocal / instrumental group (1 Album: 3 Weeks, 5 Singles: 17 Weeks)*

6 Oct 79 NOW IT'S GONE *Polydor 2059 141*....63 2
2 Feb 80 MAYBE TOMORROW *Polydor POSP 101*....40 5
26 Apr 80 SOMETHING'S MISSING *Polydor POSP 146*....55 3
24 May 80 SO FAR AWAY *Polydor POLS 1019*....30 3
12 Jul 80 THE BRITISH WAY OF LIFE *Polydor 2059 258*....54 3
18 Oct 80 IN MY STREET *Polydor POSP 185*....50 4

CHRIS and JAMES *UK, male instrumental / production duo (3 Singles: 3 Weeks)*

17 Sep 94 CALM DOWN (BASS KEEPS PUMPIN') *Stress 12STR 38*....74 1
4 Nov 95 FOX FORCE FIVE *Stress CDSTR 61*....71 1
7 Nov 98 CLUB FOR LIFE '98 *Stress CDSTR 85*....66 1

Neil CHRISTIAN *UK, male vocalist – Christopher Tidmarsh*

7 Apr 66 THAT'S NICE *Strike JH 301*....14 10

Roger CHRISTIAN *UK, male vocalist*

30 Sep 89 TAKE IT FROM ME *Island IS 427*....63 3

4 / 5 December 1959	11 / 12 December 1959	18 / 19 December 1959	25 / 26 December 1959
WHAT DO YOU WANT? Adam Faith	WHAT DO YOU WANT? Adam Faith	WHAT DO YOU WANT? Adam Faith / WHAT DO YOU WANT TO MAKE THOSE EYES AT ME FOR? Emile Ford and The Checkmates (tied at No.1)	WHAT DO YOU WANT? Adam Faith / WHAT DO YOU WANT TO MAKE THOSE EYES AT ME FOR? Emile Ford and The Checkmates (tied at No.1)
SOUTH PACIFIC Soundtrack	SOUTH PACIFIC Soundtrack	SOUTH PACIFIC Soundtrack	SOUTH PACIFIC Soundtrack

KEY
UK No.1 ★ UK Top 10 ● Still on chart + UK entry at No.1 ■
US No.1 ▲ UK million seller £ US million seller $
Singles re-entries are listed as (re), (2re), (3re)... which signifies that the hit re-entered the chart once, twice or three times...
Peak Position / Weeks

The CHRISTIANS 395 Top 500

Soul / gospel-influenced UK pop group: vocalist brothers Russell, Roger (who went solo in Autumn1987) and Garry Christian plus Henry Priestman (k/v). In 1974, the brothers appeared on TV talent show Opportunity Knocks. Their debut album went double platinum (4 Albums: 96 Weeks, 13 Singles: 84 Weeks)

31 Jan 87 **FORGOTTEN TOWN** *Island IS 291* 22 11
13 Jun 87 **HOOVERVILLE (AND THEY PROMISED US THE WORLD)** *Island IS 326* 21 10
26 Sep 87 **WHEN THE FINGERS POINT** *Island IS 335* 34 7
31 Oct 87 ● **THE CHRISTIANS** *Island ILPS 9876* 2 68
5 Dec 87 **IDEAL WORLD** *Island IS 347* 14 13
23 Apr 88 **BORN AGAIN** *Island IS 365* 25 7
15 Oct 88 ● **HARVEST FOR THE WORLD** *Island IS 395* 8 7
20 May 89 ★ **FERRY 'CROSS THE MERSEY** *PWL PWL 41* [1] ■ 1 7
23 Dec 89 **WORDS** *Island IS 450* 18 8
27 Jan 90 ★ **COLOUR** *Island ILPS 9948* ■ 1 17
7 Apr 90 **I FOUND OUT** *Island IS 453* 56 2
15 Sep 90 **GREENBANK DRIVE** *Island IS 466* 63 2
5 Sep 92 **WHAT'S IN A WORD** *Island IS 536* 33 5
10 Oct 92 **HAPPY IN HELL** *Island CID 9996* 18 3
14 Nov 92 **FATHER** *Island IS 543* 55 2
6 Mar 93 **THE BOTTLE** *Island CID 549* 39 3
20 Nov 93 **THE BEST OF THE CHRISTIANS** *Island CIDTV 6* 22 8

[1] The Christians, Holly Johnson, Paul McCartney, Gerry Marsden and Stock Aitken Waterman

CHRISTIE

UK, male vocal (Jeff Christie) / instrumental group (3 Singles: 37 Weeks)

2 May 70 ★ **YELLOW RIVER** *CBS 4911* 1 22
10 Oct 70 ● **SAN BERNADINO (re)** *CBS 5169* 7 14
25 Mar 72 **IRON HORSE** *CBS 7747* 47 1

David CHRISTIE *France, male vocalist*

14 Aug 82 ● **SADDLE UP** *KR KR 9* 9 12

John CHRISTIE *Australia, male vocalist*

25 Dec 76 **HERE'S TO LOVE (AULD LANG SYNE)** *EMI 2554* 24 6

Lou CHRISTIE *US, male vocalist – Lugee Sacco (4 Singles: 35 Weeks)*

24 Feb 66 **LIGHTNIN' STRIKES** *MGM 1297* ▲ $ 11 8
28 Apr 66 **RHAPSODY IN THE RAIN** *MGM 1308* 37 2
13 Sep 69 ● **I'M GONNA MAKE YOU MINE** *Buddah 201 057* 2 17
27 Dec 69 **SHE SOLD ME MAGIC** *Buddah 201 073* 25 8

Tony CHRISTIE

UK, male vocalist – Tony Fitzgerald (5 Albums: 33 Weeks, 9 Singles: 84 Weeks)

9 Jan 71 **LAS VEGAS** *MCA MK 5058* 21 9
8 May 71 ● **I DID WHAT I DID FOR MARIA** *MCA MK 5064* 2 17
24 Jul 71 **I DID WHAT I DID FOR MARIA** *MCA MKPS 2016* 37 1
20 Nov 71 **(IS THIS THE WAY TO) AMARILLO** *MCA MKS 5073* 18 13
10 Feb 73 **AVENUES AND ALLEYWAYS** *MCA MKS 5101* 37 4
17 Feb 73 **WITH LOVING FEELING** *MCA MUPS 468* 19 2
31 May 75 **TONY CHRISTIE – LIVE** *MCA MCF 2703* 33 3
17 Jan 76 **DRIVE SAFELY DARLIN'** *MCA 219* 35 4
6 Nov 76 **BEST OF TONY CHRISTIE** *MCA MCF 2769* 28 4
23 Jan 99 ● **WALK LIKE A PANTHER** *ffrr FCD 351* [1] 10 7
5 Mar 05 ★ **DEFINITIVE COLLECTION** *Universal TV 9827867* 1 23
26 Mar 05 ★ **(IS THIS THE WAY TO) AMARILLO (re) (re-issue)** *Universal TV 9828606* [2] ■ £ 1 26+
6 Aug 05 **AVENUES & ALLEYWAYS (re-issue)** *Universal TV 9831670* 26 3
17 Dec 05 **MERRY XMAS EVERYBODY** *Amarillo AMARILLO CD1* 49 1

[1] The All Seeing I featuring Tony Christie [2] Tony Christie featuring Peter Kay

Shawn CHRISTOPHER *US, female vocalist (3 Singles: 10 Weeks)*

4 May 91 **ANOTHER SLEEPLESS NIGHT** *Arista 114186* 50 4
21 Mar 92 **DON'T LOSE THE MAGIC** *Arista 115097* 30 5
2 Jul 94 **MAKE MY LOVE** *BTB BTBCD 502* 57 1

CHRON GEN *UK, male vocal / instrumental group*

3 Apr 82 **CHRONIC GENERATION** *Secret SEC 3* 53 3

The CHUCKS *UK, male / female vocal group*

24 Jan 63 **LOO-BE-LOO** *Decca F 11569* 22 7

CHUMBAWAMBA *UK, male / female vocal / instrumental group (3 Albums: 10 Weeks, 5 Singles: 31 Weeks)*

18 Sep 93 **ENOUGH IS ENOUGH** *One Little Indian 79TP 7CD* [1] 56 2
4 Dec 93 **TIMEBOMB** *One Little Indian 89TP 7CD* 59 1
7 May 94 **ANARCHY** *One Little Indian TPLP 46CD* 29 2
4 Nov 95 **SWINGIN' WITH RAYMOND** *One Little Indian TPLP 66CDS* 70 1
23 Aug 97 ● **TUBTHUMPING** *EMI CDEM 486* 2 20
13 Sep 97 **TUBTHUMPER** *EMI CDEMC 3773* 19 7
31 Jan 98 ● **AMNESIA** *EMI CDEM 498* 10 5
13 Jun 98 **TOP OF THE WORLD (OLE, OLE, OLE)** *EMI CDEM 511* 21 3

[1] Chumbawamba and Credit to the Nation

Chubby CHUNKS

UK, male instrumentalist / producer – Scott Tinsley (2 Singles: 2 Weeks)

4 Jun 94 **TESTAMENT 4** *Cleveland City CLECD 13017* [1] 52 1
29 May 99 **I'M TELLIN YOU (re-mix)** *Cleveland City CLECD 13052* [2] 61 1

[1] Chubby Chunks Volume II [2] Chubby Chunks featuring Kim Ruffin

'I'm Tellin You' is a re-mix of 'Testament 4' with a new title.

CHUPITO *Spain, male vocalist*

23 Sep 95 **AMERICAN PIE** *Eternal WEA 018CD* 54 2

Charlotte CHURCH *UK, female vocalist – Charlotte Reed (5 Albums: 68 Weeks, 5 Singles: 43 Weeks)*

21 Nov 98 ● **VOICE OF AN ANGEL** *Sony Classical SK 60957* 4 20
27 Nov 99 ● **CHARLOTTE CHURCH** *Sony Classical SK 89003* 8 10
25 Dec 99 **JUST WAVE HELLO** *Sony Classical 6685312* 31 4
2 Dec 00 **DREAM A DREAM** *Sony Classical SK 89459* 30 6
3 Nov 01 **ENCHANTMENT** *Sony Classical SK 89710* 24 9
1 Feb 03 ● **THE OPERA SONG (BRAVE NEW WORLD) (re)** *Direction 6734642* [1] 3 10
9 Jul 05 ● **CRAZY CHICK** *Sony BMG 6759542* 2 17
23 Jul 05 ● **TISSUES AND ISSUES** *Sony BMG 5203462* 5 23+
8 Oct 05 ● **CALL MY NAME** *Sony BMG 82876727642* 10 9
17 Dec 05 **EVEN GOD CAN'T CHANGE THE PAST** *Sony BMG 82876767052* 17 3+

[1] Jurgen Vries featuring CMC [Charlotte Church]

Sir Winston CHURCHILL

UK, male statesman, b. 30 Nov 1874, d. 24 Jan 1965

13 Feb 65 ● **THE VOICE OF CHURCHILL** *Decca LXT 6200* 6 8

CIARA NEW

US, female vocalist – Ciara Harris (1 Album: 20 Weeks, 7 Singles: 41 Weeks)

15 Jan 05 **GOODIES (import)** *Jive 82876648252* [1] 68 1
29 Jan 05 ★ **GOODIES** *LaFace 82876665882* [1] ■ ▲ 1 9
5 Feb 05 **GOODIES** *LaFace LFC 628192* 26 20
23 Apr 05 ● **1, 2 STEP** *LaFace 82876688192* [2] 3 11
2 Jul 05 ● **LOSE CONTROL** *Atlantic AT 0209CD* [3] 7 11
13 Aug 05 ● **OH** *LaFace 82876711372* [4] 4 9

[1] Ciara featuring Petey Pablo [2] Ciara featuring Missy Elliott [3] Missy Elliott featuring Ciara & Fat Man Scoop [4] Ciara featuring Ludacris

CICERO *UK, male vocalist – Dave Cicero (3 Singles: 12 Weeks)*

18 Jan 92 **LOVE IS EVERYWHERE** *Spaghetti CIAO 3*....19 8
18 Apr 92 **THAT LOVING FEELING** *Spaghetti CIAO 4*....46 3
1 Aug 92 **HEAVEN MUST HAVE SENT YOU BACK** *Spaghetti CIAO 5*....70 1

CINDERELLA
US, male vocal / instrumental group (2 Albums: 8 Weeks, 4 Singles: 7 Weeks)

23 Jul 88 LONG COLD WINTER *Vertigo VERH 59*....30 6
6 Aug 88 **GYPSY ROAD** *Vertigo VER 40*....54 2
4 Mar 89 **DON'T KNOW WHAT YOU GOT (TILL IT'S GONE)** *Vertigo VER 43*....54 2
17 Nov 90 **SHELTER ME** *Vertigo VER 51*....55 2
1 Dec 90 HEARTBREAK STATION *Vertigo 8480181*....36 2
27 Apr 91 **HEARTBREAK STATION** *Vertigo VER 53*....63 1

CINDY and The SAFFRONS *UK, female vocal group*

15 Jan 83 **PAST, PRESENT AND FUTURE** *Stiletto STL 9*....56 3

CINEMATIC ORCHESTRA *UK, male orchestra*

25 May 02 EVERY DAY *Ninja Tune ZENCD 59*....54 2

CINERAMA (see also The WEDDING PRESENT)
UK, male / female vocal / instrumental duo – David Gedge and Sally Murrell

18 Jul 98 **KERRY KERRY** *Cooking Vinyl FRYCD 072*....71 1

Gigliola CINQUETTI *Italy, female vocalist (2 Singles: 27 Weeks)*

23 Apr 64 **NON HO L'ETA PER AMARTI** *Decca F 21882*....17 17
4 May 74 ● **GO (BEFORE YOU BREAK MY HEART)** *CBS 2294*....8 10

CIRCA featuring DESTRY
UK, male production group and US, male vocalist

27 Nov 99 **SUN SHINING DOWN** *Inferno CDFERN 22*....70 1

CIRCUIT *UK, male / female vocal / instrumental group (2 Singles: 3 Weeks)*

20 Jul 91 **SHELTER ME** *Cooltempo COOL 237*....44 2
1 Apr 95 **SHELTER ME** (re-issue) *Pukka CDPUKA 2*....50 1

CIRCULATION *UK, male production duo*

1 Sep 01 **TURQUOISE** *Hooj Choons HOOJ 109*....64 1

CIRRUS *UK, male vocal group*

30 Sep 78 **ROLLIN' ON** *Jet 123*....62 1

CITIZEN CANED (see also ANGELIC; DT8 PROJECT; ORION; Jurgen VRIES) *UK, male producer – Darren Tate*

7 Apr 01 **THE JOURNEY** *Serious SERR 029CD*....41 2

CITY BOY
UK, male vocal (Lol Mason) / instrumental group (3 Singles: 20 Weeks)

8 Jul 78 ● **5.7.0.5.** *Vertigo 6059 207*....8 12
28 Oct 78 **WHAT A NIGHT** *Vertigo 6059 211*....39 5
15 Sep 79 **THE DAY THE EARTH CAUGHT FIRE** *Vertigo 6059 238*....67 3

CITY HIGH *US, male / female vocal / rap trio (2 Singles: 27 Weeks)*

6 Oct 01 ● **WHAT WOULD YOU DO?** *Interscope / Polydor IND 97617*....3 17
16 Mar 02 ● **CARAMEL** *Interscope / Polydor 4976742* [1] 9 10

[1] City High featuring Eve

Gary CLAIL ON-U SOUND SYSTEM (see also PRIMAL SCREAM) *UK, male vocal / instrumental group (1 Album: 2 Weeks, 5 Singles: 19 Weeks)*

14 Jul 90 **BEEF** *RCA PB 43843* [1] 64 2
30 Mar 91 ● **HUMAN NATURE** *Perfecto PB 44401*....10 9
4 May 91 THE EMOTIONAL HOOLIGAN *Perfecto PL 74965*....35 2
8 Jun 91 **ESCAPE** *Perfecto PB 44563*....44 3
14 Nov 92 **WHO PAYS THE PIPER** *Perfecto 74321117017*....31 3
22 May 93 **THESE THINGS ARE WORTH FIGHTING FOR** *Perfecto 74321147222*....45 2

[1] Gary Clail On-U Sound System featuring Bim Sherman

CLAIRE and FRIENDS
UK, female vocalist and young male / female friends

7 Jun 86 **IT'S 'ORRIBLE BEING IN LOVE (WHEN YOU'RE 8 1/2)** *BBC RESL 189*....13 11

The CLANCY BROTHERS and Tommy MAKEM
Ireland, male vocal / instrumental group and vocalist

16 Apr 66 ISN'T IT GRAND BOYS *CBS BPG 62674*....22 5

CLANNAD (386 Top 500)
Grammy-winning folk / new age / world music mainstays, formed in 1970 in Northern Ireland, included Brennan siblings Maire (Moya) (v/harp/k), Ciaran (g/k), Pol (k) and Eithne Ni Bhraonain, (Enya) (v/k) (1979-82). This Gaelic speaking group won a BAFTA for Best Soundtrack in 1985 for Robin of Sherwood (13 Albums: 154 Weeks, 6 Singles: 29 Weeks)

6 Nov 82 ● **THEME FROM 'HARRY'S GAME'** *RCA 292*....5 10
2 Apr 83 MAGICAL RING *RCA RCALP 6072*....26 21
2 Jul 83 **NEW GRANGE** *RCA 340*....65 1
12 May 84 LEGEND (MUSIC FROM ROBIN OF SHERWOOD) *RCA PL 70188*....15 40
12 May 84 **ROBIN (THE HOODED MAN)** *RCA HOOD 1*....42 5
2 Jun 84 MAGICAL RING (re-issue) *RCA PL 70003*....91 1
26 Oct 85 MACALLA *RCA PL 70894*....33 24
25 Jan 86 **IN A LIFETIME** *RCA PB 40535* [1] 20 5
7 Nov 87 SIRIUS *RCA PL 71513*....34 4
11 Feb 89 ATLANTIC REALM *BBC REB 727*....41 3
6 May 89 ● PASTPRESENT *RCA PL 74074*....5 26
10 Jun 89 **IN A LIFETIME** (re-issue) *RCA PB 42873* [1] 17 7
20 Oct 90 ANAM *RCA PL 74762*....14 7
10 Aug 91 **BOTH SIDES NOW** *MCA MCS 1546* [2] 74 1
15 May 93 ● BANBA *RCA 74321139612*....5 11
6 Apr 96 LORE *RCA 74321300802*....14 7
31 May 97 THE ULTIMATE COLLECTION *RCA 74321486742*....46 4
11 Apr 98 LANDMARKS *RCA 74321560072*....34 2
11 Oct 03 THE BEST OF – IN A LIFETIME *RCA 82876564022*....23 4

[1] Clannad featuring Bono [2] Clannad and Paul Young

Pastpresent changed its catalogue number to 74321289812 during its chart run.

Jimmy CLANTON *US, male vocalist*

21 Jul 60 **ANOTHER SLEEPLESS NIGHT** *Top Rank JAR 382*....50 1

CLAP YOUR HANDS SAY YEAH NEW
US, male vocal / instrumental group

17 Dec 05 **IS THIS LOVE** *Wichita Recordings WEBB 101S*....74 1

Eric CLAPTON (40 Top 500)
Rock and blues guitar player and vocalist, b. Eric Patrick Clapton (not Eric Clapp as previously thougth), 30 Mar 1945, Surrey, UK. "Clapton is God" was a description bestowed by fans and media alike in the 60s and 70s, he was also nicknamed 'Slowhand'. Prior to a long and lucrative solo career, he recorded with hitmakers The Yardbirds, Cream, Blind Faith and Derek and the Dominoes. The multi-Grammy-winning, mega-grossing live performer was awarded a CBE in 2004 (32 Albums: 558 Weeks, 27 Singles: 150 Weeks)

30 Jul 66 ● BLUES BREAKERS *Decca LK 4804* [1] 6 17
20 Dec 69 **COMIN' HOME** *Atlantic 584 308* [1] 16 9
5 Sep 70 ERIC CLAPTON *Polydor 2383021*....17 8
12 Aug 72 ● **LAYLA** *Polydor 2058 130* [2] 7 11
26 Aug 72 HISTORY OF ERIC CLAPTON *Polydor 2659 2478 027*....20 6
24 Mar 73 IN CONCERT *RSO 2659020* [2] 36 1

KEY
UK No.1 ★ UK Top 10 ● Still on chart + UK entry at No.1 ■ US No.1 ▲ UK million seller £ US million seller $
Singles re-entries are listed as (re), (2re), (3re)... which signifies that the hit re-entered the chart once, twice or three times...
Peak Position / Weeks

Date		Title / Label	Peak	Weeks
3 Nov 73		ERIC CLAPTON'S RAINBOW CONCERT *RSO 2394 116*	19	4
27 Jul 74	●	I SHOT THE SHERIFF *RSO 2090 132* ▲ $	9	9
24 Aug 74	●	461 OCEAN BOULEVARD *RSO 2479 118* ▲	3	19
12 Apr 75		THERE'S ONE IN EVERY CROWD *RSO 2479 132*	15	8
10 May 75		SWING LOW SWEET CHARIOT *RSO 2090 158*	19	9
16 Aug 75		KNOCKIN' ON HEAVEN'S DOOR *RSO 2090 166*	38	4
13 Sep 75		E.C. WAS HERE *RSO 2394 160*	14	6
11 Sep 76	●	NO REASON TO CRY *RSO 2479 179*	8	7
26 Nov 77		SLOWHAND *RSO 2479 201*	23	13
24 Dec 77		LAY DOWN SALLY *RSO 2090 264* $	39	6
21 Oct 78		PROMISES *RSO 21*	37	7
9 Dec 78		BACKLESS *RSO RSD 5001*	18	12
10 May 80	●	JUST ONE NIGHT *RSO RSDX 2*	3	12
7 Mar 81		ANOTHER TICKET *RSO RSD 5008*	18	8
6 Mar 82	●	LAYLA (re-issue) *RSO 87* [2]	4	10
24 Apr 82		TIMEPIECES – THE BEST OF ERIC CLAPTON *RSO RSD 5010*	20	14
5 Jun 82		I SHOT THE SHERIFF (re-issue) *RSO 88*	64	2
19 Feb 83		MONEY & CIGARETTES *Duck W 3773*	13	17
23 Apr 83		THE SHAPE YOU'RE IN *Duck W 9701*	75	1
9 Jun 84		BACKTRACKIN' *Starblend ERIC 1*	29	16
16 Mar 85		FOREVER MAN *Warner Bros. W 9069*	51	4
23 Mar 85	●	BEHIND THE SUN *Duck 9251661*	8	14
4 Jan 86		EDGE OF DARKNESS *BBC RESL 178* [3]	65	3
6 Dec 86	●	AUGUST *Duck WX 71*	3	46
17 Jan 87		BEHIND THE MASK *Duck W 8461*	15	11
20 Jun 87		TEARING US APART *Duck W 8299* [4]	56	3
26 Sep 87	●	THE CREAM OF ERIC CLAPTON *Polydor ECTV 1* [3]	3	109
18 Nov 89	●	JOURNEYMAN *Duck WX 322*	2	32
27 Jan 90		BAD LOVE *Duck W 2644*	25	7
14 Apr 90		NO ALIBIS *Duck W 9981*	53	3
26 Oct 91		24 NIGHTS *Duck WX 373*	17	7
16 Nov 91		WONDERFUL TONIGHT (LIVE) *Duck W 0069*	30	7
8 Feb 92	●	TEARS IN HEAVEN (re) *Reprise W 0081* $	5	12
1 Aug 92		RUNAWAY TRAIN *Rocket EJS 29* [5]	31	4
29 Aug 92		IT'S PROBABLY ME *A&M AM 883* [6]	30	5
12 Sep 92	●	UNPLUGGED *Duck 9362450242* ▲	2	90
3 Oct 92		LAYLA (ACOUSTIC) (re-recording) *Duck W 0134*	45	3
24 Sep 94	★	FROM THE CRADLE *Duck 9362457352* ■ ▲	1	18
15 Oct 94		MOTHERLESS CHILD *Duck W 0271CD*	63	1
18 Mar 95	★	LOVE CAN BUILD A BRIDGE *London COCD 1* [7]	1	8
20 Jul 96		CHANGE THE WORLD *Reprise W 0358CD*	18	5
21 Mar 98	●	PILGRIM *Duck 9362465772*	6	15
4 Apr 98		MY FATHER'S EYES *Duck W 0443CD*	33	2
4 Jul 98		CIRCUS *Duck W 0447CD*	39	2
26 Jun 99		BLUES *Polydor 5471782*	52	2
30 Oct 99	●	CLAPTON CHRONICLES – THE BEST OF ERIC CLAPTON *Duck 9362475642*	6	21
24 Jun 00		RIDING WITH THE KING *Reprise 9362476122* [4]	15	15
15 Jul 00		TIMEPIECES – THE BEST OF ERIC CLAPTON (re-issue) *Polydor 8000142*	73	2
18 Nov 00		FOREVER MAN (HOW MANY TIMES) *ffrr FCD 386*	26	2
17 Mar 01	●	REPTILE *Reprise 9362479662*	7	7
16 Nov 02		LIVE ON TOUR 2001 – ONE MORE CAR ONE MORE RIDER *Reprise 9362483972*	69	1
3 Apr 04	●	ME AND MR JOHNSON *Reprise 9362487302*	10	8
10 Sep 05		BACK HOME *Reprise 9362493952*	19	3

[1] Delaney and Bonnie and Friends featuring Eric Clapton [2] Derek and the Dominoes [3] Eric Clapton featuring Michael Kamen [4] Eric Clapton and Tina Turner [5] Elton John and Eric Clapton [6] Sting with Eric Clapton [7] Cher, Chrissie Hynde and Neneh Cherry with Eric Clapton [1] John Mayall and Eric Clapton [2] Derek and the Dominos [3] Eric Clapton and Cream [4] BB King and Eric Clapton

From 9 Jul 93 The Cream of Eric Clapton was repackaged and was available as The Best of Eric Clapton.

Dee CLARK *US, male vocalist – Delecta Clark, b. 7 Nov 1938, d. 7 Dec 1990 (2 Singles: 9 Weeks)*

Date		Title / Label	Peak	Weeks
2 Oct 59		JUST KEEP IT UP (AND SEE WHAT HAPPENS) *London HL 8915*	26	1
11 Oct 75		RIDE A WILD HORSE *Chelsea 2005 037*	16	8

Gary CLARK *UK, male vocalist (1 Album: 2 Weeks, 3 Singles: 8 Weeks)*

Date		Title / Label	Peak	Weeks
30 Jan 93		WE SAIL ON THE STORMY WATERS *Circa YRCDX 93*	34	4
3 Apr 93		FREEFLOATING *Circa YRCDX 94*	50	3
8 May 93		TEN SHORT SONGS ABOUT LOVE *Circa CIRCD 23*	25	2
19 Jun 93		MAKE A FAMILY *Circa YRCDX 105*	70	1

Loni CLARK *US, female vocalist (3 Singles: 6 Weeks)*

Date		Title / Label	Peak	Weeks
5 Jun 93		RUSHING *A&M 5802862*	37	2
22 Jan 94		U *A&M 5804752*	28	3
17 Dec 94		LOVE'S GOT ME ON A TRIP SO HIGH *A&M 5808872*	59	1

Petula CLARK (204 Top 500)

Britain's most consistently successful female vocalist, b. 15 Nov 1932, Surrey. Before her 48-year chart span, she starred in movies and was voted Britain's Top TV Personality. First UK female to win a Grammy and to be named Top Female Vocalist of the Year in the US in 1966 (7 Albums: 47 Weeks, 28 Singles: 247 Weeks)

Date		Title / Label	Peak	Weeks
11 Jun 54	●	THE LITTLE SHOEMAKER (re) *Polygon P 1117*	7	10
18 Feb 55		MAJORCA (re) *Polygon P 1146*	12	5
25 Nov 55	●	SUDDENLY THERE'S A VALLEY *Pye Nixa N 15013*	7	10
26 Jul 57	●	WITH ALL MY HEART *Pye Nixa N 15096*	4	18
15 Nov 57	●	ALONE *Pye Nixa N 15112*	8	12
28 Feb 58		BABY LOVER *Pye Nixa N 15126*	12	7
26 Jan 61	★	SAILOR *Pye 7N 15324*	1	15
13 Apr 61		SOMETHING MISSING *Pye 7N 15337*	44	1
13 Jul 61	●	ROMEO *Pye 7N 15361*	3	15
16 Nov 61	●	MY FRIEND THE SEA *Pye 7N 15389*	7	13
8 Feb 62		I'M COUNTING ON YOU *Pye 7N 15407*	41	2
28 Jun 62		YA YA TWIST (re) *Pye 7N 15448*	14	13
2 May 63		CASANOVA / CHARIOT *Pye 7N 15522*	39	7
12 Nov 64	●	DOWNTOWN *Pye 7N 15722* ▲ $	2	15
11 Mar 65		I KNOW A PLACE *Pye 7N 15772*	17	8
12 Aug 65		YOU'D BETTER COME HOME *Pye 7N 15864*	44	3
14 Oct 65		ROUND EVERY CORNER *Pye 7N 15945*	43	3
4 Nov 65		YOU'RE THE ONE *Pye 7N 15991*	23	9
10 Feb 66	●	MY LOVE *Pye 7N 17038* ▲ $	4	9
21 Apr 66		A SIGN OF THE TIMES *Pye 7N 17071*	49	1
30 Jun 66	●	I COULDN'T LIVE WITHOUT YOUR LOVE *Pye 7N 17133*	6	11
30 Jul 66		I COULDN'T LIVE WITHOUT YOUR LOVE *Pye NPL 18148*	11	10
2 Feb 67	★	THIS IS MY SONG *Pye 7N 17258*	1	14
4 Feb 67		HIT PARADE *Pye NPL 18159*	18	13
18 Feb 67		COLOUR MY WORLD *Pye NSPL 18171*	16	9
25 May 67		DON'T SLEEP IN THE SUBWAY *Pye 7N 17325*	12	11
7 Oct 67		THESE ARE MY SONGS *Pye NSPL 18197*	38	3
13 Dec 67		THE OTHER MAN'S GRASS (IS ALWAYS GREENER) *Pye 7N 17416*	20	9
6 Mar 68		KISS ME GOODBYE *Pye 7N 17466*	50	1
6 Apr 68		THE OTHER MAN'S GRASS IS ALWAYS GREENER *Pye NSPL 18211*	37	1
30 Jan 71		THE SONG OF MY LIFE (re) *Pye 7N 45026*	32	12
15 Jan 72		I DON'T KNOW HOW TO LOVE HIM (re) *Pye 7N 45112*	47	2
5 Feb 77		20 ALL TIME GREATEST *K-Tel NE 945*	18	7
19 Nov 88	●	DOWNTOWN '88 (re-mix) *PRT PYS 19*	10	11
27 Apr 02		THE ULTIMATE COLLECTION *Sanctuary SANDD 111*	18	4

The Dave CLARK FIVE (342 Top 500)

Beat Boom superstars from Tottenham, London, UK: Dave Clark (d), Mike Smith (v/k), Lenny Davidson (g), Denis Payton (s), Rick Huxley (g). In the first years of the 'British Invasion', this foot-stomping quintet was second only to The Beatles in the US (4 Albums: 31 Weeks, 23 Singles: 174 Weeks)

Date		Title / Label	Peak	Weeks
3 Oct 63		DO YOU LOVE ME *Columbia DB 7112*	30	6
21 Nov 63	★	GLAD ALL OVER *Columbia DB 7154*	1	19

26 / 27 February 1960	4 / 5 March 1960	10 / 12 March 1960	17 / 19 March 1960
UK No.1 SINGLES			
WHY – Anthony Newley	POOR ME – Adam Faith	POOR ME – Adam Faith	RUNNING BEAR – Johnny Preston
UK No.1 ALBUMS			
SOUTH PACIFIC – Soundtrack	SOUTH PACIFIC – Soundtrack	THE EXPLOSIVE FREDDIE CANNON – Freddy Cannon	SOUTH PACIFIC – Soundtrack

20 Feb 64	●	**BITS AND PIECES** *Columbia DB 7210*	**2**	11
18 Apr 64	●	A SESSION WITH THE DAVE CLARK FIVE *Columbia 33SX 1598*	3	8
28 May 64	●	**CAN'T YOU SEE THAT SHE'S MINE** *Columbia DB 7291*	**10**	11
13 Aug 64		**THINKING OF YOU BABY** *Columbia DB 7335*	**26**	4
22 Oct 64		**ANYWAY YOU WANT IT** *Columbia DB 7377*	**25**	5
14 Jan 65		**EVERYBODY KNOWS** *Columbia DB 7453*	**37**	4
11 Mar 65		**REELIN' AND ROCKIN'** *Columbia DB 7503*	**24**	8
27 May 65		**COME HOME** *Columbia DB 7580*	**16**	8
15 Jul 65	●	**CATCH US IF YOU CAN** *Columbia DB 7625*	**5**	11
14 Aug 65	●	CATCH US IF YOU CAN *Columbia 33SX 1756*	8	8
11 Nov 65		**OVER AND OVER** *Columbia DB 7744* ▲	**45**	4
19 May 66		**LOOK BEFORE YOU LEAP** *Columbia DB 7909*	**50**	1
16 Mar 67		**YOU GOT WHAT IT TAKES** *Columbia DB 8152*	**28**	8
1 Nov 67	●	**EVERYBODY KNOWS** *Columbia DB 8286*	**2**	14
28 Feb 68		**NO ONE CAN BREAK A HEART LIKE YOU** *Columbia DB 8342*	**28**	7
18 Sep 68	●	**THE RED BALLOON** *Columbia DB 8465*	**7**	11
27 Nov 68		**LIVE IN THE SKY** *Columbia DB 8505*	**39**	6
25 Oct 69		**PUT A LITTLE LOVE IN YOUR HEART** *Columbia DB 8624*	**31**	4
6 Dec 69	●	**GOOD OLD ROCK 'N' ROLL** *Columbia DB 8638*	**7**	12
7 Mar 70	●	**EVERYBODY GET TOGETHER** *Columbia DB 8660*	**8**	8
4 Jul 70		**HERE COMES SUMMER** *Columbia DB 8689*	**44**	3
7 Nov 70		**MORE GOOD OLD ROCK 'N' ROLL** *Columbia DB 8724*	**34**	6
4 Mar 78	●	25 THUMPING GREAT HITS *Polydor POLTV 7*	7	10
17 Apr 93		GLAD ALL OVER AGAIN *EMI CDEMTV 75*	28	5
1 May 93		**GLAD ALL OVER** (re-issue) *EMI CDEMCT 8*	**37**	3

'Everybody Knows' on DB 7453 and 'Everybody Knows' on DB 8286 are two different songs. The two Rock 'n' Roll titles are medleys, as follows: Good Old Rock 'n' Roll: Good Old Rock 'n' Roll / Sweet Little Sixteen / Long Tall Sally / Whole Lotta Shakin' Goin' On / Blue Suede Shoes / Lucille / Reelin' and Rockin' / Memphis Tennessee. More Good Old Rock 'n' Roll: More Good Old Rock 'n' Roll / Blueberry Hill / Good Golly Miss Molly / My Blue Heaven / Keep a Knockin' / Loving You / One Night / Lawdy Miss Clawdy.

Dave CLARKE

UK, male producer (1 Album: 2 Weeks, 9 Singles: 10 Weeks)

30 Sep 95		**RED THREE: THUNDER / STORM** *Deconstruction 74321306992*	**45**	2
3 Feb 96		**SOUTHSIDE** *Bush 74321335382*	**34**	2
17 Feb 96		ARCHIVE ONE *Bush 74321320672*	36	2
15 Jun 96		**NO ONE'S DRIVING** *Bush 74321380162*	**37**	2
8 Dec 01		**THE COMPASS** *Skint SKINT 73CD*	**46**	1
28 Dec 02		**THE WOLF** *Skint SKINT 78*	**66**	1
25 Oct 03		**WAY OF LIFE** *Skint SKINT 93CD*	**59**	1
21 Feb 04		**WHAT WAS HER NAME?** *Skint SKINT 94CD* [1]	**50**	1

[1] Dave Clarke featuring Chicks On Speed

Gilby CLARKE (see also GUNS N' ROSES) *US, male guitarist*

6 Aug 94		PAWNSHOP GUITARS *Virgin America CDVUS 76*	39	1

John Cooper CLARKE

UK, male vocalist (2 Albums: 9 Weeks, 1 Single: 3 Weeks)

10 Mar 79		**GIMMIX! PLAY LOUD** *Epic EPC 7009*	**39**	3
19 Apr 80		SNAP CRACKLE AND BOP *Epic EPC 84083*	26	7
5 Jun 82		ZIP STYLE METHOD *Epic EPC 85667*	97	2

Rick CLARKE *UK, male vocalist*

30 Apr 88		**I'LL SEE YOU ALONG THE WAY** *WA WA 1*	**63**	2

Stanley CLARKE *US, male vocalist / bass guitarist*

12 Jul 80		ROCKS PEBBLES AND SAND *Epic EPC 84342*	42	2

Warren CLARKE featuring Kathy BROWN

UK, male producer and US, female vocalist

2 Jun 01		**OVER YOU** *Defected DFECT 28CDS*	**42**	1

CLARKESVILLE *UK, male vocalist / guitarist – Michael Clarke*

7 Feb 04		**SPINNING** *Wildstar CDWILD 53*	**72**	1

Kelly CLARKSON

US, female vocalist (2 Albums: 27 Weeks, 5 Singles: 56 Weeks)

6 Sep 03		THANKFUL *S 82876540882* ▲	52	4
6 Sep 03	●	**MISS INDEPENDENT** *S 82876553642*	**6**	10
29 Nov 03		**LOW / THE TROUBLE WITH LOVE IS** *S 82876570702*	**35**	3
16 Jul 05	●	**SINCE U BEEN GONE** *RCA 82876700842*	**5**	25+
30 Jul 05	●	BREAKAWAY *RCA 82876690262*	6	23+
1 Oct 05	●	**BEHIND THESE HAZEL EYES** *RCA 82876730302*	**9**	14+
10 Dec 05	●	**BECAUSE OF YOU** *RCA 82876764542*	**7**	4+

The CLASH (257 Top 500)

Leading lights of the UK punk rock explosion: Joe Strummer (v/g), b. John Mellor, 21 Aug 1952, d. 23 Dec 2002, Mick Jones (g/v), Paul Simonon (b), Topper Headon (d). Their third LP, London Calling (first released in 1979), was voted Best Album of the 1980s by Rolling Stone magazine. The band were inducted into the Rock and Roll Hall of Fame in 2003 and Joe Strummer had a Class 47 Diesel locomotive named after him in 2005 (11 Albums: 116 Weeks, 23 Singles: 135 Weeks)

2 Apr 77		**WHITE RIOT** *CBS 5058*	**38**	3
30 Apr 77		THE CLASH *CBS 82000*	12	16
8 Oct 77		**COMPLETE CONTROL** *CBS 5664*	**28**	2
4 Mar 78		**CLASH CITY ROCKERS** *CBS 5834*	**35**	4
24 Jun 78		**(WHITE MAN) IN HAMMERSMITH PALAIS** *CBS 6383*	**32**	7
25 Nov 78	●	GIVE 'EM ENOUGH ROPE *CBS 82431*	2	14
2 Dec 78		**TOMMY GUN** *CBS 6788*	**19**	10
3 Mar 79		**ENGLISH CIVIL WAR (JOHNNY COMES MARCHING HOME)** *CBS 7082*	**25**	6
19 May 79		**THE COST OF LIVING (EP)** *CBS 7324*	**22**	8
15 Dec 79		**LONDON CALLING** *CBS 8087*	**11**	10
22 Dec 79	●	LONDON CALLING *CBS CLASH 3*	9	21
9 Aug 80		**BANKROBBER** *CBS 8323*	**12**	10
6 Dec 80		**THE CALL UP** *CBS 9339*	**40**	6
20 Dec 80		SANDINISTA! *CBS FSLN 1*	19	9
24 Jan 81		**HITSVILLE UK** *CBS 9480*	**56**	4
25 Apr 81		**THE MAGNIFICENT SEVEN** *CBS 1133*	**34**	5
28 Nov 81		**THIS IS RADIO CLASH** *CBS A 1797*	**47**	6
1 May 82		**KNOW YOUR RIGHTS** *CBS A 2309*	**43**	3
22 May 82	●	COMBAT ROCK *CBS FMLN 2*	2	23
26 Jun 82		**ROCK THE CASBAH** *CBS A 2429*	**30**	10
25 Sep 82		**SHOULD I STAY OR SHOULD I GO / STRAIGHT TO HELL** *CBS A 2646*	**17**	9
12 Oct 85		**THIS IS ENGLAND** *CBS A 6122*	**24**	5
16 Nov 85		CUT THE CRAP *CBS 26601*	16	3
12 Mar 88		**I FOUGHT THE LAW** *CBS CLASH 1*	**29**	5
2 Apr 88	●	THE STORY OF THE CLASH – VOLUME 1 *CBS 4602441*	7	21
7 May 88		**LONDON CALLING** (re-issue) *CBS CLASH 2*	**46**	3
21 Jul 90		**RETURN TO BRIXTON** *CBS 656072 7*	**57**	2
2 Mar 91	★	**SHOULD I STAY OR SHOULD I GO** (re-issue) *Columbia 6566677*	**1**	9
13 Apr 91		**ROCK THE CASBAH** (re-issue) *Columbia 6568147*	**15**	6
8 Jun 91		**LONDON CALLING** (re-issue) *Columbia 6569467*	**64**	2
16 Nov 91		THE SINGLES *Columbia 4689461*	68	2
16 Oct 99		FROM HERE TO ETERNITY *Columbia 4961832*	13	3
22 Mar 03		THE ESSENTIAL CLASH *Columbia 05109982*	18	3
2 Oct 04		LONDON CALLING – 25TH ANNIVERSARY EDITION *Columbia 5179283*	26	1

Tracks on The Cost of Living (EP): I Fought the Law / Groovy Times / Gates of the West / Capital Radio. CBS CLASH 1 is a re-issue of a track from 'The Cost of Living (EP)'.

CLASS ACTION featuring Chris WILTSHIRE

US, female vocal group

7 May 83		**WEEKEND** *Jive JIVE 35*	**49**	3

The CLASSICS IV *US, male vocal / instrumental group*

28 Feb 68		**SPOOKY** *Liberty LBS 15051* $	**46**	1

KEY UK No.1 ★★ UK Top 10 ●● Still on chart ++ UK entry at No.1 ■■ US No.1 ▲▲ UK million seller £ US million seller $
Singles re-entries are listed as (re), (2re), (3re)... which signifies that the hit re-entered the chart once, twice or three times...
Peak Position / Weeks

CLASSIX NOUVEAUX (see also Sal SOLO) *UK, male vocal / instrumental group (2 Albums: 6 Weeks, 7 Singles: 34 Weeks)*

28 Feb 81 **GUILTY** *Liberty BP 388* ... 43 7
16 May 81 **TOKYO** *Liberty BP 397* ... 67 3
30 May 81 NIGHT PEOPLE *Liberty LBG 30325* ... 66 2
8 Aug 81 **INSIDE OUTSIDE** *Liberty BP 403* ... 45 5
7 Nov 81 **NEVER AGAIN (THE DAYS TIME ERASED)** *Liberty BP 406* ... 44 4
13 Mar 82 **IS IT A DREAM** *Liberty BP 409* ... 11 9
24 Apr 82 LA VERITE *Liberty LBG 30346* ... 44 4
29 May 82 **BECAUSE YOU'RE YOUNG** *Liberty BP 411* ... 43 4
30 Oct 82 **THE END ... OR THE BEGINNING** *Liberty BP 414* ... 60 2

CLAWFINGER *Norway / Sweden, male vocal / instrumental group*

19 Mar 94 **WARFAIR** *East West YZ 804CD1* ... 54 1

Judy CLAY and William BELL
US, female / male vocal duo – Judy Clay, b. 12 Sep 1938, d. 19 Jul 2001

20 Nov 68 ● **PRIVATE NUMBER** *Stax 101* ... 8 14

Richard CLAYDERMAN (331 Top 500)
'The world's most successful pianist', according to Guinness World Records, b. Philippe Pagès (he adopted his great grandmother's surname), 28 Dec 1953, Paris, France. He has sold in excess of 70 million albums and earned 276 gold and 70 platinum albums (16 Albums: 211 Weeks)

13 Nov 82 ● RICHARD CLAYDERMAN *Decca SKL 5329* ... 2 64
8 Oct 83 THE MUSIC OF RICHARD CLAYDERMAN *Decca SKL 5333* ... 21 28
24 Nov 84 THE MUSIC OF LOVE *Decca SKL 5340* ... 28 21
1 Dec 84 CHRISTMAS *Decca SKL 5337* ... 53 5
23 Nov 85 THE CLASSIC TOUCH *Decca SKL 5343* ... 17 18
22 Nov 86 HOLLYWOOD AND BROADWAY *Decca SKL 5344* ... 28 9
28 Nov 87 SONGS OF LOVE *Decca SKL 5345* ... 19 13
3 Dec 88 A LITTLE NIGHT MUSIC *Decca Delphine 8281251* ... 52 5
25 Nov 89 THE LOVE SONGS OF ANDREW LLOYD WEBBER *Decca Delphine 8281751* ... 18 10
24 Nov 90 MY CLASSIC COLLECTION *Decca Delphine 8282281* ... 29 7
9 Nov 91 TOGETHER AT LAST *Delphine / Polydor 5115251* [1] ... 14 15
14 Nov 92 THE VERY BEST OF RICHARD CLAYDERMAN *Decca Delphine 8283362* [2] ... 47 5
19 Nov 94 IN HARMONY *Polydor 5238242* [1] ... 28 7
25 Nov 95 THE CARPENTERS COLLECTION *PolyGram TV 8286882* ... 65 2
20 Dec 97 THE BEST OF RICHARD CLAYDERMAN *Delphine DTVCD 700* ... 73 1
18 Sep 99 ... WITH LOVE *Music Club MCTVCD 002* ... 62 1

[1] Richard Clayderman and James Last [2] Richard Clayderman with the Royal Philharmonic Orchestra

Adam CLAYTON and Larry MULLEN
(see also U2) *Ireland, male instrumental duo*

15 Jun 96 ● **THEME FROM 'MISSION: IMPOSSIBLE'** *Mother MUMCD 75* ... 7 12

Merry CLAYTON *US, female vocalist – Mary Clayton*

21 May 88 **YES** *RCA PB 49563* ... 70 1

CLAYTOWN TROUPE *UK, male vocal / instrumental group (1 Album: 1 Week, 2 Singles: 3 Weeks)*

21 Oct 89 THROUGH THE VEIL *Island ILPS 9933* ... 72 1
16 Jun 90 **WAYS OF LOVE** *Island IS 464* ... 57 2
14 Mar 92 **WANTED IT ALL** *EMI USA MT 102* ... 74 1

CLEA *UK, female vocal group (3 Singles: 7 Weeks)*

4 Oct 03 **DOWNLOAD IT** *1967 CLEA 01CD* ... 21 3
28 Feb 04 **STUCK IN THE MIDDLE** *1967 CLEA 02CD* ... 23 2
29 Oct 05 **WE DON'T HAVE TO TAKE OUR CLOTHES OFF** *Upside UPSIDECD 02* [1] ... 35 2

[1] De Playaz vs Clea

Johnny CLEGG and SAVUKA (see also JULUKA)
UK / South Africa, male vocal / instrumental group

16 May 87 **SCATTERLINGS OF AFRICA** *EMI EMI 5605* ... 75 1

CLEOPATRA *UK, female vocal trio (1 Album: 4 Weeks, 6 Singles: 44 Weeks)*

14 Feb 98 ● **CLEOPATRA'S THEME** *WEA WEA 133CD* ... 3 10
16 May 98 ● **LIFE AIN'T EASY** *WEA WEA 159CD1* ... 4 7
6 Jun 98 COMIN' ATCHA! *WEA 3984233562* ... 20 4
22 Aug 98 ● **I WANT YOU BACK** *WEA WEA 172CD1* ... 4 7
6 Mar 99 **A TOUCH OF LOVE** *WEA WEA 199CD1* ... 24 4
10 Apr 99 ● **THANK ABBA FOR THE MUSIC** *Epic ABCD 1* [1] ... 4 13
29 Jul 00 **COME AND GET ME** *WEA WEA 216CD1* ... 29 3

[1] Steps, Tina Cousins, Cleopatra, B*Witched, Billie

CLEPTOMANIACS featuring Bryan CHAMBERS
UK, male production group and vocalist

3 Feb 01 **ALL I DO** *Defected DFECT 27CDS* ... 23 3

CLERGY (see also The CANDY GIRLS; DOROTHY; HI-GATE; Paul MASTERSON presents SUSHI; PRECOCIOUS BRATS featuring KEVIN and PERRY; SLEAZESISTERS; STIX 'N' STONED; YOMANDA)
UK, male production duo – Paul Masterson and Judge Jules

20 Jul 02 **THE OBOE SONG** *ffrr DFCD 005* ... 50 1

CLICK *US, male rap group*

29 Jun 96 **SCANDALOUS** *Jive JIVECD 393* ... 54 1

CLIENT *UK, female vocal / instrumental duo – Kate Holmes and Sarah Blackwood (3 Singles: 4 Weeks)*

26 Jun 04 **IN IT FOR THE MONEY** *Toast Hawaii CDTH 005* ... 51 1
2 Oct 04 **RADIO** *Toast Hawaii CDTH 006* ... 68 1
22 Jan 05 **PORNOGRAPHY** *Toast Hawaii CDTH 008* ... 22 2

Jimmy CLIFF
Jamaica, male vocalist – James Chambers (4 Singles: 33 Weeks)

25 Oct 69 ● **WONDERFUL WORLD, BEAUTIFUL PEOPLE** *Trojan TR 690* ... 6 13
14 Feb 70 **VIETNAM (re)** *Trojan TR 7722* ... 46 3
8 Aug 70 ● **WILD WORLD** *Island WIP 6087* ... 8 12
19 Mar 94 **I CAN SEE CLEARLY NOW** *Columbia 6601982* ... 23 5

Buzz CLIFFORD *US, male vocalist – Reese Clifford III*

2 Mar 61 **BABY SITTIN' BOOGIE** *Fontana H 297* ... 17 13

Linda CLIFFORD *US, female vocalist (3 Singles: 13 Weeks)*

10 Jun 78 **IF MY FRIENDS COULD SEE ME NOW** *Curtom K 17163* ... 50 5
5 May 79 **BRIDGE OVER TROUBLED WATER** *RSO 30* ... 28 7
15 Sep 01 **RIDE THE STORM** *NRK Sound Division NRKCD 053* [1] ... 69 1

[1] Akabu featuring Linda Clifford

The CLIMAX BLUES BAND *UK, male vocal / instrumental group*

9 Oct 76 ● **COULDN'T GET IT RIGHT** *BTM SBT 105* ... 10 9
13 Nov 76 GOLD PLATED *BTM 1009* ... 56 1

CLIMIE FISHER (see also NAKED EYES)
UK, male vocal / instrumental duo – Simon Climie and Rob Fisher, b. 5 Nov 1959, d. 25 Aug 1999 (2 Albums: 38 Weeks, 7 Singles: 44 Weeks)

5 Sep 87 **LOVE CHANGES (EVERYTHING)** *EMI EM 15* ... 67 2
12 Dec 87 ● **RISE TO THE OCCASION** *EMI EM 33* ... 10 11

13 Feb 88 EVERYTHING *EMI EMC 3538*....14 36
12 Mar 88 ● **LOVE CHANGES (EVERYTHING)** (re-mix) *EMI EM 47*....2 12
21 May 88 **THIS IS ME** *EMI EM 58*....22 5
20 Aug 88 **I WON'T BLEED FOR YOU** *EMI EM 66*....35 4
24 Dec 88 **LOVE LIKE A RIVER** *EMI EM 81*....22 7
23 Sep 89 **FACTS OF LOVE** *EMI EM 103*....50 3
21 Oct 89 COMING IN FOR THE KILL *EMI EMC 3565*....35 2

Simon CLIMIE (see also CLIMIE FISHER) *UK, male vocalist*

19 Sep 92 **SOUL INSPIRATION** *Epic 6582837*....60 2

Patsy CLINE *US, female vocalist – Virginia Hensley, b. 8 Sep 1932, d. 5 Mar 1963 (4 Albums: 28 Weeks, 3 Singles: 17 Weeks)*

26 Apr 62 **SHE'S GOT YOU** *Brunswick 05866*....43 1
29 Nov 62 **HEARTACHES** *Brunswick 05878*....31 5
8 Dec 90 **CRAZY** *MCA MCA 1465*....14 11
19 Jan 91 DREAMING *Platinum Music PLAT 303*....55 4
19 Jan 91 SWEET DREAMS *MCA MCG 6003*....18 10
5 Sep 92 THE DEFINITIVE PATSY CLINE *Arcade ARC 94992*....11 8
6 Jul 96 THE VERY BEST OF PATSY CLINE *MCA MCD 11483*....21 6

CLINIC *UK, male vocal / instrumental group (3 Singles: 3 Weeks)*

22 Apr 00 **THE RETURN OF EVIL BILL** *Domino RUG 093CD*....70 1
4 Nov 00 **THE SECOND LINE** *Domino RUG 116CD*....56 1
2 Mar 02 **WALKING WITH THEE** *Domino RUG 134CD*....65 1

George CLINTON (see also FUNKADELIC) *US, male vocalist (3 Singles: 10 Weeks)*

4 Dec 82 **LOOPZILLA** *Capitol CL 271*....57 5
26 Apr 86 **DO FRIES GO WITH THAT SHAKE** *Capitol CL 402*....57 2
27 Aug 94 **BOP GUN (ONE NATION)** *Fourth & Broadway BRCD 308* [1] ..22 3

[1] Ice Cube featuring George Clinton

CLIPSE *US, male rap duo – Gene and Terence Thornton (2 Singles: 5 Weeks)*

22 Feb 03 **WHEN THE LAST TIME** *Arista 82876502212*....41 2
24 May 03 **MA, I DON'T LOVE HER** *Arista 82876526482* [1] 38 3

[1] Clipse featuring Faith Evans

CLIPZ *UK, male producer (2 Singles: 2 Weeks)*

6 Mar 04 **COCOA / JIGGY** *Full Cycle FCY 064*....71 1
5 Mar 05 **SLIPPERY SLOPES / NASTY BREAKS** *Full Cycle FCY 075*....72 1

CLOCK *UK, male / female production / vocal / rap / instrumental group (2 Albums: 4 Weeks, 15 Singles: 70 Weeks)*

30 Oct 93 **HOLDING ON** *Media MRLCD 007*....66 1
21 May 94 **THE RHYTHM** *Media MCSTD 1971*....28 2
10 Sep 94 **KEEP THE FIRES BURNING** *Media MCSTD 1998*....36 3
4 Mar 95 ● **AXEL F / KEEP PUSHIN'** *Media MCSTD 2041*....7 9
1 Jul 95 ● **WHOOMPH! (THERE IT IS)** *Media MCSTD 2059*....4 9
26 Aug 95 ● **EVERYBODY** *Media MCSTD 2077*....6 5
23 Sep 95 IT'S TIME ... *Media MCD 11355*....27 2
18 Nov 95 **IN THE HOUSE** *Media MCSTD 40005*....23 3
24 Feb 96 **HOLDING ON 4 U** (re-mix) *Media MCSTD 40019*....27 2
7 Sep 96 **OH WHAT A NIGHT** *Power Station MCSTD 40057*....13 10
22 Mar 97 ● **IT'S OVER** *Media MCSTD 40100*....10 5
5 Apr 97 ABOUT TIME 2 *Media MCD 60032*....56 2
18 Oct 97 **U SEXY THING** *Media MCSTD 40138*....11 9
17 Jan 98 **THAT'S THE WAY (I LIKE IT)** *Media MCSTD 40148*....11 4
11 Jul 98 **ROCK YOUR BODY** *Media MCSTD 40160*....30 3
28 Nov 98 **BLAME IT ON THE BOOGIE** *Media MCSTD 40191*....16 4
31 Jul 99 **SUNSHINE DAY** *Media MCSTD 40208*....58 1

Rosemary CLOONEY *US, female vocalist, b. 23 May 1928, d. 29 Jun 2002 (7 Singles: 81 Weeks)*

14 Nov 52 ● **HALF AS MUCH** *Columbia DB 3129*....3 9
5 Feb 54 ● **MAN (UH-HUH)** *Philips PB 220*....7 5
8 Oct 54 ★ **THIS OLE HOUSE** *Philips PB 336* ▲....1 18
17 Dec 54 ★ **MAMBO ITALIANO** *Philips PB 382* [1] $....1 16
20 May 55 ● **WHERE WILL THE DIMPLE BE?** *Philips PB 428* [1] 6 13
30 Sep 55 ● **HEY THERE** *Philips PB 494* ▲ $....4 11
29 Mar 57 **MANGOS (re)** *Philips PB 671*....17 9

[1] Rosemary Clooney and the Mellomen

From 19 Feb 1954, the flip side of 'Man (Uh-Huh)' – 'Woman (Uh-Huh)' by José Ferrer – was also credited.

CLOR NEW *UK, male vocal / instrumental group (3 Singles: 3 Weeks)*

7 May 05 **LOVE & PAIN** *Regal Recordings REG 120CD*....48 1
23 Jul 05 **OUTLINES** *Regal Recordings REG 121CDS*....43 1
22 Oct 05 **GOOD STUFF** *Regal Recordings REG 128CD*....50 1

CLOUD *UK, male instrumental group*

31 Jan 81 **ALL NIGHT LONG / TAKE IT TO THE TOP** *UK Champagne FUNK 1*....72 1

CLOUT *South Africa, female vocal (Cindi Alter) / instrumental group*

17 Jun 78 ● **SUBSTITUTE** *Carrere EMI 2788*....2 15

CLUB NOUVEAU *US, male / female vocal / instrumental group*

21 Mar 87 ● **LEAN ON ME** *King Jay W 8430* ▲ $....3 12

CLUB 69 *Austria / US, male producer / instrumentalist – Peter Rauhofer (2 Singles: 6 Weeks)*

5 Dec 92 **LET ME BE YOUR UNDERWEAR** *ffrr F 204*....33 5
14 Nov 98 **ALRIGHT** *Twisted UK TWCD 10039* [1] 70 1

[1] Club 69 featuring Suzanne Palmer

CLUBHOUSE *Italy, male vocal / instrumental group (8 Singles: 40 Weeks)*

23 Jul 83 **DO IT AGAIN – BILLIE JEAN (MEDLEY)** *Island IS 132*....11 6
3 Dec 83 **SUPERSTITION – GOOD TIMES (MEDLEY)** *Island IS 147*....59 3
1 Jul 89 **I'M A MAN – YEKE YEKE (MEDLEY)** *Music Man MMPS 7003*....69 3
20 Apr 91 **DEEP IN MY HEART (re)** *ffrr F 157*....55 4
4 Sep 93 **LIGHT MY FIRE (2re)** *PWL Continental PWCD 272* [1] 45 12
30 Apr 94 ● **LIGHT MY FIRE** (re-mix) *PWL Continental PWCD 288* [1] 7 8
23 Jul 94 **LIVING IN THE SUNSHINE** *PWL Continental PWCD 309* [1] ...21 3
11 Mar 95 **NOWHERE LAND** *PWL International PWCD 318* [1] 56 1

[1] Clubhouse featuring Carl

CLUBZONE *UK / Germany, male vocal / instrumental group*

19 Nov 94 **HANDS UP** *Logic 74321236982*....50 1

CLUELESS *US, male / female vocal / production group*

5 Apr 97 **DON'T SPEAK** *ZYX ZYX 660738*....61 1

CLYDE VALLEY STOMPERS *UK, male instrumental group*

9 Aug 62 **PETER AND THE WOLF** *Parlophone R 4928*....25 8

CO-CO *UK, male / female vocal / instrumental group*

22 Apr 78 **BAD OLD DAYS** *Ariola Hansa AHA 513*....13 7

COAL CHAMBER *US, male vocal / instrumental group (2 Albums: 4 Weeks)*

18 Sep 99 CHAMBER MUSIC *Roadrunner RR 86592*....21 2
18 May 02 DARK DAYS *Roadrunner RR 84842*....43 2

COAST 2 COAST featuring DISCOVERY *Ireland, male production duo and female vocalist*

16 Jun 01 **HOME** *Religion RLG 0126955*....44 1

19 / 21 May 1960	26 / 28 May 1960	2 / 4 June 1960	9 / 11 June 1960
CATHY'S CLOWN The Everly Brothers	CATHY'S CLOWN The Everly Brothers	CATHY'S CLOWN The Everly Brothers	CATHY'S CLOWN The Everly Brothers
SOUTH PACIFIC Soundtrack	SOUTH PACIFIC Soundtrack	SOUTH PACIFIC Soundtrack	SOUTH PACIFIC Soundtrack

KEY UK No.1 ★ UK Top 10 ● Still on chart + UK entry at No.1 ■ US No.1 ▲ UK million seller £ US million seller $
Singles re-entries are listed as (re), (2re), (3re)... which signifies that the hit re-entered the chart once, twice or three times...

Peak Position / Weeks

COAST TO COAST
UK, male vocal (Sandy Fontaine) / instrumental group (2 Singles: 22 Weeks)

31 Jan 81 ● **(DO) THE HUCKLEBUCK** *Polydor POSP 214* **5** 15
23 May 81 **LET'S JUMP THE BROOMSTICK** *Polydor POSP 249* **28** 7

The COASTERS *US, male vocal group (5 Singles: 32 Weeks)*

27 Sep 57 **SEARCHIN'** *London HLE 8450* **$** **30** 1
15 Aug 58 **YAKETY YAK** *London HLE 8665* **$** **12** 8
27 Mar 59 ● **CHARLIE BROWN** *London HLE 8819* **$** **6** 12
30 Oct 59 **POISON IVY** *London HLE 8938* **$** **15** 7
9 Apr 94 **SORRY BUT I'M GONNA HAVE TO PASS** *Rhino A 4519CD* **41** 4

Luis COBOS *Spain, male orchestra conductor*

21 Apr 90 OPERA EXTRAVAGANZA *Epic MOOD 12* 72 1
16 Jun 90 **NESSUN DORMA FROM 'TURANDOT'** *Epic 656005 7* [1] **59** 2

[1] Luis Cobos featuring Placido Domingo

Eddie COCHRAN *US, male vocalist / guitarist, b. 3 Oct 1938, d. 17 Apr 1960 (8 Albums: 47 Weeks, 12 Singles: 90 Weeks)*

7 Nov 58 **SUMMERTIME BLUES** *London HLU 8702* **18** 6
13 Mar 59 ● **C'MON EVERYBODY** *London HLU 8792* **6** 13
16 Oct 59 **SOMETHIN' ELSE** *London HLU 8944* **22** 3
22 Jan 60 **HALLELUJAH, I LOVE HER SO (re)** *London HLW 9022* **22** 4
12 May 60 ★ **THREE STEPS TO HEAVEN** *London HLG 9115* **1** 15
30 Jul 60 SINGING TO MY BABY *London HAU 2093* 19 1
1 Oct 60 ● EDDIE COCHRAN MEMORIAL ALBUM *London HAG 2267* 9 12
6 Oct 60 **SWEETIE PIE** *London HLG 9196* **38** 3
3 Nov 60 **LONELY** *London HLG 9196* **41** 1
15 Jun 61 **WEEKEND** *London HLG 9362* **15** 16
30 Nov 61 **JEANNIE, JEANNIE, JEANNIE** *London HLG 9460* **31** 4
12 Jan 63 CHERISHED MEMORIES *Liberty LBY 1109* 15 3
20 Apr 63 EDDIE COCHRAN MEMORIAL ALBUM (re-issue) *Liberty LBY 1127* 11 18
25 Apr 63 **MY WAY** *Liberty LIB 10088* **23** 10
19 Oct 63 SINGING TO MY BABY (re-issue) *Liberty LBY 1158* 20 1
24 Apr 68 **SUMMERTIME BLUES** (re-issue) *Liberty LBF 15071* **34** 8
9 May 70 VERY BEST OF EDDIE COCHRAN *Liberty LBS 83337* 34 3
18 Aug 79 THE EDDIE COCHRAN SINGLES ALBUM *United Artists UAK 30244* 39 6
13 Feb 88 **C'MON EVERYBODY** (re-issue) *Liberty EDDIE 501* **14** 7
16 Apr 88 C'MON EVERYBODY *Liberty ECR 1* 53 3

Brenda COCHRANE *Ireland, female vocalist (2 Albums: 14 Weeks)*

14 Apr 90 THE VOICE *Polydor 8431411* 14 11
6 Apr 91 IN DREAMS *Polydor 8490341* 55 3

Tom COCHRANE *Canada, male vocalist*

27 Jun 92 **LIFE IS A HIGHWAY** *Capitol CL 660* **62** 2

COCK ROBIN *US, male / female vocal / instrumental group*

31 May 86 **THE PROMISE YOU MADE** *CBS A 6764* **28** 12

Joe COCKER (464 Top 500)

Throaty, emotive pop / rock singer, b. 20 May 1944, Sheffield, UK, whose first single was released in 1964. Remembered for a memorable performance at Woodstock, Cocker is still scoring Top 20 albums across Europe in the 21st century (10 Albums: 68 Weeks, 17 Singles: 89 Weeks)

22 May 68 **MARJORINE** *Regal-Zonophone RZ 3006* **48** 1
2 Oct 68 ★ **WITH A LITTLE HELP FROM MY FRIENDS** *Regal-Zonophone RZ 3013* **1** 13
27 Sep 69 ● **DELTA LADY** *Regal-Zonophone RZ 3024* **10** 11
4 Jul 70 **THE LETTER** *Regal-Zonophone RZ 3027* **39** 6
26 Sep 70 MAD DOGS AND ENGLISHMEN *A&M AMLS 6002* 16 8
6 May 72 JOE COCKER / WITH A LITTLE HELP FROM MY FRIENDS *Double Back TOOFA 1/2* 29 4
26 Sep 81 **I'M SO GLAD I'M STANDING HERE TODAY** *MCA 741* [1] **61** 3
15 Jan 83 ● **UP WHERE WE BELONG** *Island WIP 6830* [2] ▲ **$** **7** 13
30 Jun 84 A CIVILISED MAN *Capitol EJ 240139 1* 100 1
14 Nov 87 **UNCHAIN MY HEART** *Capitol CL 465* **46** 4
13 Jan 90 **WHEN THE NIGHT COMES** *Capitol CL 535* **65** 2
7 Mar 92 **(ALL I KNOW) FEELS LIKE FOREVER** *Capitol CL 645* **25** 5
11 Apr 92 NIGHT CALLS *Capitol CDESTU 2167* 25 14
9 May 92 **NOW THAT THE MAGIC HAS GONE** *Capitol CL 657* **28** 6
27 Jun 92 ● THE ESSENTIAL COLLECTION – THE LEGEND *PolyGram TV 5154112* 4 20
4 Jul 92 **UNCHAIN MY HEART** (re-issue) *Capitol CL 664* **17** 6
21 Nov 92 **WHEN THE NIGHT COMES** (re-issue) *Capitol CL 674* **61** 3
13 Aug 94 **THE SIMPLE THINGS** *Capitol CDCLS 722* **17** 5
17 Sep 94 ● HAVE A LITTLE FAITH *Capitol CDEST 2233* 9 15
22 Oct 94 **TAKE ME HOME** *Capitol CDCLS 729* [3] **41** 3
17 Dec 94 **LET THE HEALING BEGIN** *Capitol CDCLS 727* **32** 5
23 Sep 95 **HAVE A LITTLE FAITH** *Capitol CDCLS 744* **67** 2
12 Oct 96 **DON'T LET ME BE MISUNDERSTOOD** *Parlophone CDCLS 779* **53** 1
26 Oct 96 ORGANIC *Parlophone CDESTD 6* 49 1
20 Feb 99 GREATEST HITS *EMI 4977192* 24 2
23 Oct 99 NO ORDINARY WORLD *Parlophone 5230912* 63 1
15 Jun 02 RESPECT YOURSELF *Parlophone 5396432* 51 2

[1] The Crusaders, featured vocalist Joe Cocker [2] Joe Cocker and Jennifer Warnes [3] Joe Cocker featuring Bekka Bramlett

COCKEREL CHORUS
UK, male Tottenham Hotspur Football Club supporters vocal group

24 Feb 73 **NICE ONE CYRIL** *Youngblood YB 1017* **14** 12

COCKNEY REJECTS *UK, male vocal / instrumental group (3 Albums: 17 Weeks, 6 Singles: 22 Weeks)*

1 Dec 79 **I'M NOT A FOOL** *EMI 5008* **65** 2
16 Feb 80 **BADMAN** *EMI 5035* **65** 3
15 Mar 80 GREATEST HITS VOLUME 1 *Zonophone ZONO 101* 22 11
26 Apr 80 **THE GREATEST COCKNEY RIP-OFF** *Zonophone Z 2* **21** 7
17 May 80 **I'M FOREVER BLOWING BUBBLES** *Zonophone Z 4* **35** 5
12 Jul 80 **WE CAN DO ANYTHING** *Zonophone Z 6* **65** 2
25 Oct 80 GREATEST HITS VOLUME 2 *Zonophone ZONO 102* 23 3
25 Oct 80 **WE ARE THE FIRM** *Zonophone Z 10* **54** 3
18 Apr 81 GREATEST HITS VOLUME 3 (LIVE AND LOUD) *Zonophone ZEM 101* 27 3

COCO (see also FRAGMA)
UK, female vocalist – Sue Bryce

8 Nov 97 **I NEED A MIRACLE** *Positiva CDTIV 81* **39** 2

The COCONUTS (see also Kid CREOLE and The COCONUTS)
US, male / female vocal group (10 Singles: 3 Weeks)

11 Jun 83 **DID YOU HAVE TO LOVE ME LIKE YOU DID** *EMI America EA 156* **60** 3

COCTEAU TWINS (see also Harold BUDD / Liz FRASER / Robin GUTHRIE / Simon RAYMONDE) *UK, male / female vocal / instrumental group (8 Albums: 46 Weeks, 13 Singles: 25 Weeks)*

29 Oct 83 HEAD OVER HEELS *4AD CAD 313* 51 15
28 Apr 84 **PEARLY-DEWDROPS' DROPS** *4AD 405* **29** 5
24 Nov 84 TREASURE *4AD CAD 412* 29 8
30 Mar 85 **AIKEA-GUINEA** *4AD AD 501* **41** 3
23 Nov 85 **TINY DYNAMINE (EP)** *4AD BAD 510* **52** 2
7 Dec 85 **ECHOES IN A SHALLOW BAY (EP)** *4AD BAD 511* **65** 1
26 Apr 86 ● VICTORIALAND *4AD CAD 602* 10 7
25 Oct 86 **LOVE'S EASY TEARS** *4AD AD 610* **53** 1

16 / 18 June 1960	23 / 25 June 1960	30 June / 2 July 1960	7 / 9 July 1960
UK No.1 SINGLES			
CATHY'S CLOWN The Everly Brothers	THREE STEPS TO HEAVEN Eddie Cochran	THREE STEPS TO HEAVEN Eddie Cochran	GOOD TIMIN' Jimmy Jones
UK No.1 ALBUMS			
SOUTH PACIFIC Soundtrack	SOUTH PACIFIC Soundtrack	SOUTH PACIFIC Soundtrack	SOUTH PACIFIC Soundtrack

1 Oct 88 BLUE BELL KNOLL *4AD CAD 807*....15 4
8 Sep 90 **ICEBLINK LUCK** *4AD AD 0011*....**38** 3
22 Sep 90 ● HEAVEN OR LAS VEGAS *4AD CAD 0012*....7 5
2 Oct 93 **EVANGELINE** *Fontana CTCD 1*....**34** 2
30 Oct 93 FOUR-CALENDAR CAFÉ *Fontana 5182592*....13 3
18 Dec 93 **WINTER WONDERLAND / FROSTY THE SNOWMAN** *Fontana COCCD 1*....**58** 1
26 Feb 94 **BLUEBEARD** *Fontana CTCD 2*....**33** 2
7 Oct 95 **TWINLIGHTS (EP)** *Fontana CTCD 3*....**59** 1
4 Nov 95 **OTHERNESS (EP)** *Fontana CTCD 4*....**59** 1
30 Mar 96 **TISHBITE** *Fontana CTCD 5*....**34** 2
27 Apr 96 MILK & KISSES *Fontana 5145012*....17 3
20 Jul 96 **VIOLAINE** *Fontana CTCD 6*....**56** 1
28 Oct 00 STARS AND TOPSOIL – A COLLECTION (1982-1990) *4AD CAD 2K 019CD*....63 1

Tracks on Tiny Dynamine (EP): Pink Orange Red / Ribbed and Veined / Plain Tiger / Sultitan Itan. Tracks on Echoes in a Shallow Bay (EP): Great Spangled Fritillary / Melonella / Pale Clouded White / Eggs and Their Shells. Tracks on Twinlights (EP): Golden-Vein / Half-Gifts / Pink Orange Red / Rilkean Heart. Tracks on Otherness (EP): Cherry Coloured Funk / Feet Like Fins / Seekers Who Are Lovers / Violaine.

CODE RED *UK, male vocal group (5 Singles: 7 Weeks)*

6 Jul 96 **I GAVE YOU EVERYTHING** *Polydor 5763992*....**50** 1
16 Nov 96 **THIS IS OUR SONG** *Polydor 5756332*....**59** 1
14 Jun 97 **CAN WE TALK** *Polydor 5710992*....**29** 2
9 Aug 97 **IS THERE SOMEONE OUT THERE?** *Polydor 5714652*....**34** 2
4 Jul 98 **WHAT WOULD YOU DO IF ...?** *Polydor 569932*....**55** 1

COFFEE *US, female vocal group (2 Singles: 13 Weeks)*

27 Sep 80 **CASANOVA** *De-Lite MER 38*....**13** 10
6 Dec 80 **SLIP AND DIP / I WANNA BE WITH YOU** *De-Lite DE 1*....**57** 3

Alma COGAN
UK, female vocalist, b. 19 May 1932, d. 26 Oct 1966 (21 Singles: 110 Weeks)

19 Mar 54 ● **BELL BOTTOM BLUES** *HMV B 10653*....**4** 9
27 Aug 54 **LITTLE THINGS MEAN A LOT (2re)** *HMV B 10717*....**11** 5
3 Dec 54 ● **I CAN'T TELL A WALTZ FROM A TANGO** *HMV B 10786*....**6** 11
27 May 55 ★ **DREAMBOAT** *HMV B 10872*....**1** 16
23 Sep 55 **THE BANJO'S BACK IN TOWN** *HMV B 10917 (A)*....**17** 1
14 Oct 55 **GO ON BY** *HMV B 10917 (B)*....**16** 4
16 Dec 55 **TWENTY TINY FINGERS** *HMV POP 129 (A)*....**17** 1
23 Dec 55 ● **NEVER DO A TANGO WITH AN ESKIMO** *HMV POP 129 (B)*....**6** 5
30 Mar 56 **WILLIE CAN** *HMV POP 187* [1]....**13** 8
13 Jul 56 **THE BIRDS AND THE BEES** *HMV POP 223*....**25** 4
10 Aug 56 **WHY DO FOOLS FALL IN LOVE** *HMV POP 223*....**22** 3
2 Nov 56 **IN THE MIDDLE OF THE HOUSE (re)** *HMV POP 261*....**20** 4
18 Jan 57 **YOU, ME AND US** *HMV POP 284*....**18** 6
29 Mar 57 **WHATEVER LOLA WANTS (LOLA GETS)** *HMV POP 317*....**26** 2
31 Jan 58 **THE STORY OF MY LIFE** *HMV POP 433*....**25** 2
14 Feb 58 **SUGARTIME (re)** *HMV POP 450*....**16** 11
23 Jan 59 **LAST NIGHT ON THE BACK PORCH** *HMV POP 573*....**27** 2
18 Dec 59 **WE GOT LOVE** *HMV POP 670*....**26** 4
12 May 60 **DREAM TALK** *HMV POP 728*....**48** 1
11 Aug 60 **TRAIN OF LOVE** *HMV POP 760*....**27** 5
20 Apr 61 **COWBOY JIMMY JOE** *Columbia DB 4607*....**37** 6

[1] Alma Cogan with Desmond Lane – penny whistle

Shaye COGAN *US, female vocalist*

24 Mar 60 **MEAN TO ME** *MGM 1063*....**40** 1

Izhar COHEN and The ALPHA-BETA *Israel, male / female vocal group*

13 May 78 **A-BA-NI-BI** *Polydor 2001 781*....**20** 7

Leonard COHEN (469 Top 500)

Singer-songwriter and poet with a reputation for dark humour, b. 21 Sep 1934, Montreal, Canada, who was still charting worldwide at the age of 70. Jennifer Warnes devoted her 1987 set, Famous Blue Raincoat, entirely to his compositions (13 Albums: 156 Weeks)

31 Aug 68 SONGS OF LEONARD COHEN *CBS 63241*....13 71
3 May 69 ● SONGS FROM A ROOM *CBS 63587*....2 26
24 Apr 71 ● SONGS OF LOVE AND HATE *CBS 69004*....4 18
28 Sep 74 NEW SKIN FOR THE OLD CEREMONY *CBS 69087*....24 3
10 Dec 77 DEATH OF A LADIES' MAN *CBS 86042*....35 5
16 Feb 85 VARIOUS POSITIONS *CBS 26222*....52 6
27 Feb 88 I'M YOUR MAN *CBS 460642 1*....48 13
6 Aug 88 GREATEST HITS *CBS 32644*....99 1
5 Dec 92 THE FUTURE *Columbia 4724982*....36 3
6 Aug 94 COHEN LIVE – LEONARD COHEN IN CONCERT *Columbia 4771712*....35 4
20 Oct 01 TEN NEW SONGS *Columbia 5012022*....26 3
1 Feb 03 THE ESSENTIAL LEONARD COHEN *Columbia 4979952*....70 1
6 Nov 04 DEAR HEATHER *Columbia 5147682*....34 2

COHEN vs DELUXE (see also COHEN vs DELUXE; Tim DELUXE; DOUBLE 99; RIP PRODUCTIONS; SAFFRON HILL featuring Ben ONONO)
Brazil / UK, male producers – Renato Cohen and Tim Liken

13 Mar 04 **JUST KICK** *Intec INTEC 24XXX*....**70** 1

Marc COHN *US, male vocalist (2 Albums: 23 Weeks, 4 Singles: 15 Weeks)*

25 May 91 **WALKING IN MEMPHIS** *Atlantic A 7747*....**66** 4
29 Jun 91 MARC COHN *Atlantic 7567821781*....27 20
10 Aug 91 **SILVER THUNDERBIRD** *Atlantic A 7657*....**54** 3
12 Oct 91 **WALKING IN MEMPHIS** (re-issue) *Atlantic A 7585*....**22** 5
29 May 93 **WALK THROUGH THE WORLD** *Atlantic A 7340CD*....**37** 3
12 Jun 93 THE RAINY SEASON *Atlantic 7567824912*....24 3

COLA BOY *UK, male / female vocal / instrumental duo – Andrew Midgely and Janey Lee Grace*

6 Jul 91 ● **7 WAYS TO LOVE** *Arista 114526*....**8** 7

COLD JAM featuring GRACE
US, male / female vocal / instrumental group

28 Jul 90 **LAST NIGHT A DJ SAVED MY LIFE** *Big Wave BWR 39*....**64** 2

COLDCUT *UK, male production duo – Matt Black and Jonathan Moore (2 Albums: 5 Weeks, 10 Singles: 39 Weeks)*

20 Feb 88 ● **DOCTORIN' THE HOUSE** *Ahead of Our Time CCUT 27* [1]....**6** 9
10 Sep 88 **STOP THIS CRAZY THING** *Ahead of Our Time CCUT 4* [2]....**21** 7
25 Mar 89 **PEOPLE HOLD ON** *Ahead of Our Time CCUT 5* [3]....**11** 9
29 Apr 89 WHAT'S THAT NOISE *Ahead of Our Time CCUTLP 1*....20 4
3 Jun 89 **MY TELEPHONE** *Ahead of Our Time CCUT 6*....**52** 2
16 Dec 89 **COLDCUT'S CHRISTMAS BREAK** *Ahead of Our Time CCUT 7*....**67** 3
26 May 90 **FIND A WAY** *Ahead of Our Time CCUT 8* [4]....**52** 2
4 Sep 93 **DREAMER** *Arista 74321156642*....**54** 2
22 Jan 94 **AUTUMN LEAVES** *Arista 74321171052*....**50** 2
16 Aug 97 **MORE BEATS & PIECES** *Ninja Tune ZENCDS 58*....**37** 2
20 Sep 97 LET US PLAY! *Ninja Tune ZENCD 30*....33 1
16 Jun 01 **REVOLUTION** *Ninja Tune ZENCDS 88*....**67** 1

[1] Coldcut featuring Yazz and the Plastic Population [2] Coldcut featuring Junior Reid and the Ahead of Our Time Orchestra [3] Coldcut featuring Lisa Stansfield [4] Coldcut featuring Queen Latifah

COLDPLAY (151 Top 500)

Anthemic rock group with a social conscience: Chris Martin (v/k), Jonny Buckland (g), Guy Berryman (b) and Will Champion (d), who formed while attending University College, London. The only act to have won both a BRIT and a Grammy for each of their first two albums won the Record of the Year Grammy in 2004 for 'Clocks'. X&Y, which sold 464,471 in its first week in the UK, is the only UK album to top the US chart in 2005. The band were on the bill for Live 8 in London in 2005 (3 Albums: 274 Weeks, 9 Singles: 83 Weeks)

18 Mar 00 **SHIVER** *Parlophone CDR 6536*....**35** 3
8 Jul 00 ● **YELLOW** *Parlophone CDR 6538*....**4** 11
22 Jul 00 ★ PARACHUTES *Parlophone 5277832* ■....1 134
4 Nov 00 ● **TROUBLE** *Parlophone CDR 6549*....**10** 9
17 Aug 02 ● **IN MY PLACE** *Parlophone CDRS 6579*....**2** 10

14 / 16 July 1960	21 / 23 July 1960	28 / 30 July 1960	4 / 6 August 1960
GOOD TIMIN' Jimmy Jones	GOOD TIMIN' Jimmy Jones	PLEASE DON'T TEASE Cliff Richard and The Shadows	SHAKIN' ALL OVER Johnny Kidd and The Pirates
SOUTH PACIFIC Soundtrack	SOUTH PACIFIC Soundtrack	ELVIS IS BACK! Elvis Presley	SOUTH PACIFIC Soundtrack

KEY UK No.1 ★ UK Top 10 ● Still on chart + UK entry at No.1 ■ US No.1 ▲ UK million seller £ US million seller $
Singles re-entries are listed as (re), (2re), (3re)... which signifies that the hit re-entered the chart once, twice or three times...
Peak Position / Weeks

Date		Title	Peak	Weeks
7 Sep 02	★	A RUSH OF BLOOD TO THE HEAD *Parlophone 5405042* ■	1	111
23 Nov 02	●	**THE SCIENTIST** *Parlophone CDR 6588*	**10**	9
5 Apr 03	●	**CLOCKS** *Parlophone CDR 6594*	**9**	8
4 Jun 05	●	**SPEED OF SOUND** *Parlophone CDR 6664*	**2**	16
18 Jun 05	★	X&Y *Parlophone 4747862* ■ ▲	1	29+
17 Sep 05	●	**FIX YOU** *Parlophone CDRS 6671*	**4**	16+
31 Dec 05	●	**TALK** *Parlophone CDR 6679*	**10**	1+

Andy COLE *UK, male footballer / vocalist*

Date		Title	Peak	Weeks
18 Sep 99		**OUTSTANDING** *WEA WEA 224CD*	**68**	1

Cozy COLE

US, male instrumentalist – drums – William Cole, b. 17 Oct 1909, d. 9 Jan 1981

Date		Title	Peak	Weeks
5 Dec 58		**TOPSY (PARTS 1 AND 2)** *London HL 8750* $	**29**	1

Lloyd COLE (483 Top 500)

Introspective and inventive indie singer / songwriter / guitarist, b. 31 Jan 1961, Derbyshire, UK. He had most success with the Glasgow-based band The Commotions before he relocated to the US in 1990 (9 Albums: 92 Weeks, 15 Singles: 62 Weeks)

Date		Title	Peak	Weeks
26 May 84		**PERFECT SKIN (re)** *Polydor COLE 1* [1]	**26**	9
25 Aug 84		**FOREST FIRE** *Polydor COLE 2* [1]	**41**	6
20 Oct 84		RATTLESNAKES *Polydor LCLP 1* [1]	13	30
17 Nov 84		**RATTLESNAKES** *Poldor COLE 3* [1]	**65**	2
14 Sep 85		**BRAND NEW FRIEND** *Polydor COLE 4* [1]	**19**	8
9 Nov 85		**LOST WEEKEND** *Polydor COLE 5* [1]	**17**	7
30 Nov 85	●	EASY PIECES *Polydor LCLP 2* [1]	5	18
18 Jan 86		**CUT ME DOWN** *Polydor COLE 6* [1]	**38**	4
3 Oct 87		**MY BAG** *Polydor COLE 7* [1]	**46**	4
7 Nov 87	●	MAINSTREAM *Polydor LCLP 3* [1]	9	20
9 Jan 88		**JENNIFER SHE SAID** *Polydor COLE 8* [1]	**31**	5
23 Apr 88		**FROM THE HIP (EP)** *Polydor COLE 9* [1]	**59**	2
8 Apr 89		19841989 *Polydor 837736 1* [1]	14	7
3 Feb 90		**NO BLUE SKIES** *Polydor COLE 11*	**42**	4
3 Mar 90		LLOYD COLE *Polydor 8419071*	11	6
7 Apr 90		**DON'T LOOK BACK** *Polydor COLE 12*	**59**	3
31 Aug 91		**SHE'S A GIRL AND I'M A MAN** *Polydor COLE 14*	**55**	2
28 Sep 91		DON'T GET WEIRD ON ME BABE *Polydor 5110931*	21	3
25 Sep 93		**SO YOU'D LIKE TO SAVE THE WORLD** *Fontana VIBE D1*	**72**	2
23 Oct 93		BAD VIBES *Fontana 5183182*	38	2
16 Sep 95		**LIKE LOVERS DO** *Fontana LCDD 1*	**24**	3
7 Oct 95		LOVE STORY *Fontana 5285292*	27	2
2 Dec 95		**SENTIMENTAL FOOL** *Fontana LCDD 2*	**73**	1
23 Jan 99		THE COLLECTION *Mercury 5381042*	24	4

[1] Lloyd Cole and the Commotions [1] Lloyd Cole and the Commotions

Tracks on From the Hip (EP): From the Hip / Please / Lonely Mile / Love Your Wife.

MJ COLE

UK, male producer – Matt Coleman (1 Album: 4 Weeks, 5 Singles: 19 Weeks)

Date		Title	Peak	Weeks
23 May 98		**SINCERE** *AM:PM 5826912*	**38**	2
6 May 00	●	**CRAZY LOVE** *Talkin Loud TLCD 59*	**10**	7
12 Aug 00		**SINCERE** (re-mix) *Talkin Loud TLCD 60*	**13**	5
19 Aug 00		SINCERE *Talkin Loud 5425792*	14	4
2 Dec 00		**HOLD ON TO ME** *Talkin Loud TLCD 62* [1]	**35**	2
29 Mar 03		**WONDERING WHY** *Talkin Loud 0779522*	**30**	3

[1] MJ Cole featuring Elisabeth Troy

Nat 'King' COLE (117 Top 500)

One of the 20th century's most distinctive song stylists, b. Nathaniel Adams Coles, 17 Mar 1917, Montgomery, Alabama, US, d. 15 Feb 1965. His 50-year chart span, which includes an electronically recorded duet with his daughter, 26 years after his death, is proof that the highly regarded vocalist's recordings are timeless (14 Albums: 153 Weeks, 34 Singles: 249 Weeks)

Date		Title	Peak	Weeks
14 Nov 52	●	**SOMEWHERE ALONG THE WAY** *Capitol CL 13774*	**3**	7
19 Dec 52	●	**BECAUSE YOU'RE MINE (2re)** *Capitol CL 13811*	**6**	4
2 Jan 53	●	**FAITH CAN MOVE MOUNTAINS (2re)** *Capitol CL 13811*	**10**	4
24 Apr 53	●	**PRETEND** *Capitol CL 13878*	**2**	18
14 Aug 53	●	**CAN'T I (2re)** *Capitol CL 13937*	**6**	8
18 Sep 53	●	**MOTHER NATURE AND FATHER TIME** *Capitol CL 13912*	**7**	7
16 Apr 54	●	**TENDERLY** *Capitol CL 14061*	**10**	1
10 Sep 54	●	**SMILE** *Capitol CL 14149*	**2**	14
8 Oct 54		**MAKE HER MINE** *Capitol CL 14149*	**11**	2
25 Feb 55	●	**A BLOSSOM FELL** *Capitol CL 14235* $	**3**	10
26 Aug 55		**MY ONE SIN (re)** *Capitol CL 14327*	**17**	2
27 Jan 56	●	**DREAMS CAN TELL A LIE** *Capitol CL 14513*	**10**	9
11 May 56	●	**TOO YOUNG TO GO STEADY** *Capitol CL 14573*	**8**	14
14 Sep 56		**LOVE ME AS THOUGH THERE WERE NO TOMORROW (re)** *Capitol CL 14621*	**11**	15
19 Apr 57	●	**WHEN I FALL IN LOVE** *Capitol CL 14709*	**2**	20
18 May 57	★	LOVE IS THE THING *Capitol LCT 6129* ▲	1	14
5 Jul 57		**WHEN ROCK AND ROLL CAME TO TRINIDAD** *Capitol CL 14733*	**28**	1
18 Oct 57		**MY PERSONAL POSSESSION** *Capitol CL 14765* [1]	**21**	2
25 Oct 57		**STARDUST** *Capitol CL 14787*	**24**	2
29 May 59		**YOU MADE ME LOVE YOU** *Capitol CL 15017*	**22**	3
4 Sep 59		**MIDNIGHT FLYER (re)** *Capitol CL 15056*	**23**	4
12 Feb 60		**TIME AND THE RIVER (2re)** *Capitol CL 15111*	**23**	5
26 May 60	●	**THAT'S YOU** *Capitol CL 15129*	**10**	8
10 Nov 60		**JUST AS MUCH AS EVER** *Capitol CL 15163*	**18**	10
2 Feb 61		**THE WORLD IN MY ARMS** *Capitol CL 15178*	**36**	10
19 Aug 61		STRING ALONG WITH NAT 'KING' COLE *Encore ENC 102*	12	9
16 Nov 61		**LET TRUE LOVE BEGIN** *Capitol CL 15224*	**29**	10
22 Mar 62		**BRAZILIAN LOVE SONG (ANDORHINA PRETA)** *Capitol CL 15241*	**34**	4
31 May 62		**THE RIGHT THING TO SAY** *Capitol CL 15250*	**42**	4
19 Jul 62		**LET THERE BE LOVE** *Capitol CL 15257* [2]	**11**	14
27 Sep 62	●	**RAMBLIN' ROSE** *Capitol CL 15270* $	**5**	14
20 Oct 62	●	NAT 'KING' COLE SINGS AND THE GEORGE SHEARING QUINTET PLAYS *Capitol W 1675* [1]	8	7
20 Dec 62		**DEAR LONELY HEARTS** *Capitol CL 15280*	**37**	3
27 Mar 65		UNFORGETTABLE NAT 'KING' COLE *Capitol W 20664*	11	8
7 Dec 68	●	THE BEST OF NAT 'KING' COLE *Capitol ST 21139*	5	18
5 Dec 70		THE BEST OF NAT 'KING' COLE VOLUME 2 *Capitol ST 21687*	39	2
27 Nov 71		WHITE CHRISTMAS *MFP 5224* [2]	45	1
8 Apr 78	★	20 GOLDEN GREATS *Capitol EMTV 9*	1	37
20 Nov 82	●	GREATEST LOVE SONGS *Capitol EMTV 35*	7	26
12 Dec 87	●	**WHEN I FALL IN LOVE** (re-issue) *Capitol CL 15975*	**4**	7
26 Nov 88		CHRISTMAS WITH NAT 'KING' COLE *Stylus SMR 868*	25	9
22 Jun 91		**UNFORGETTABLE** *Elektra EKR 128* [3]	**19**	8
23 Nov 91		UNFORGETTABLE NAT 'KING' COLE *EMI EMTV 61*	23	9
14 Dec 91		**THE CHRISTMAS SONG** *Capitol CL 641*	**69**	2
19 Mar 94		**LET'S FACE THE MUSIC AND DANCE** *EMI CDEM 312*	**30**	3
20 Nov 99		THE ULTIMATE COLLECTION *EMI 4995752*	26	7
15 Feb 03		LOVE SONGS *Capitol 05815132*	20	3
5 Feb 05		THE WORLD OF NAT 'KING' COLE *Capitol 5606802*	51	3

[1] Nat 'King' Cole and the Four Knights [2] Nat 'King' Cole with George Shearing [3] Natalie Cole and Nat 'King' Cole [1] Nat 'King' Cole and the George Shearing Quintet [2] Nat 'King' Cole and Dean Martin

The two Unforgettable Nat 'King' Cole albums are different.

Natalie COLE (487 Top 500)

Daughter of the legendary Nat 'King' Cole who has a 20-year Grammy-winning span of her own, b. 6 Feb 1950, Los Angeles, US. The single 'Unforgettable' was an electronically recorded duet with her late father. Nat and Natalie are the only dad and daughter to have had No.1 albums in the US (6 Albums: 66 Weeks, 12 Singles: 87 Weeks)

Date		Title	Peak	Weeks
11 Oct 75		**THIS WILL BE** *Capitol CL 15834*	**32**	5
17 Sep 83	●	UNFORGETTABLE: A MUSICAL TRIBUTE TO NAT 'KING' COLE *CBS 10042* [1] ▲	5	16
8 Aug 87		**JUMP START** *Manhattan MT 22*	**44**	8

11 / 13 August 1960	18 / 20 August 1960	25 / 27 August 1960	1 / 3 September 1960
◂◂ UK No.1 SINGLES ▸▸			
PLEASE DON'T TEASE Cliff Richard and The Shadows	PLEASE DON'T TEASE Cliff Richard and The Shadows	APACHE The Shadows	APACHE The Shadows
◂◂ UK No.1 ALBUMS ▸▸			
SOUTH PACIFIC Soundtrack	SOUTH PACIFIC Soundtrack	SOUTH PACIFIC Soundtrack	SOUTH PACIFIC Soundtrack

26 Mar 88 ● **PINK CADILLAC** *Manhattan MT 35*..........5 12
7 May 88 EVERLASTING *Manhattan MTL 1012*..........62 4
25 Jun 88 **EVERLASTING** *Manhattan MT 46*..........28 6
20 Aug 88 **JUMP START** (re-issue) *Manhattan MT 50*..........36 5
26 Nov 88 **I LIVE FOR YOUR LOVE** *Manhattan MT 57*..........23 14
15 Apr 89 ● **MISS YOU LIKE CRAZY** *EMI-USA MT 63*..........2 15
20 May 89 ● GOOD TO BE BACK *EMI-USA MTL 1042*..........10 12
22 Jul 89 **REST OF THE NIGHT** *EMI-USA MT 69*..........56 2
16 Dec 89 **STARTING OVER AGAIN** *EMI-USA MT 77*..........56 4
21 Apr 90 **WILD WOMEN DO** *EMI-USA MT 81*..........16 7
22 Jun 91 **UNFORGETTABLE** *Elektra EKR 128* [1]..........19 8
27 Jul 91 UNFORGETTABLE – WITH LOVE *Elektra EKT 91*..........11 29
16 May 92 **THE VERY THOUGHT OF YOU** *Elektra EKR 147*..........71 1
26 Jun 93 TAKE A LOOK *Elektra 7559614962*..........16 4
30 Nov 02 ASK A WOMAN WHO KNOWS *Verve AA 3145897742*..........63 1

[1] Natalie Cole and Nat 'King' Cole [1] Johnny Mathis and Natalie Cole

Paula COLE

US, female vocalist (1 Album: 1 Week, 2 Singles: 9 Weeks)

28 Jun 97 **WHERE HAVE ALL THE COWBOYS GONE?** *Warner Bros. W 0406CD*..........15 8
26 Jul 97 THIS FIRE *Warner Bros. 9362464242*..........60 1
1 Aug 98 **I DON'T WANT TO WAIT** *Warner Bros. W 0422CD*..........43 1

COLLAGE

US / Canada / Philippines, male vocal / instrumental group

21 Sep 85 **ROMEO WHERE'S JULIET?** *MCA MCA 1006*..........46 5

COLLAPSED LUNG

UK, male vocal / instrumental group (2 Singles: 8 Weeks)

22 Jun 96 **LONDON TONIGHT / EAT MY GOAL** *Deceptive BLUFF 029CD*..31 3
30 May 98 **EAT MY GOAL** (re-issue) *Deceptive BLUFF 060CD*..........18 5

Dave and Ansil COLLINS

Jamaica, male vocal / instrumental duo – Dave Barker and Ansil Collins (1 Album: 2 Weeks, 2 Singles: 27 Weeks)

27 Mar 71 ★ **DOUBLE BARREL** *Technique TE 901*..........1 15
26 Jun 71 ● **MONKEY SPANNER** *Technique TE 914*..........7 12
7 Aug 71 DOUBLE BARREL *Trojan TBL 162*..........41 2

Edwyn COLLINS (see also ORANGE JUICE)

UK, male vocalist / guitarist (2 Albums: 9 Weeks, 7 Singles: 25 Weeks)

11 Aug 84 **PALE BLUE EYES** *Swamplands SWP 1* [1]..........72 2
12 Nov 94 **EXPRESSLY (EP)** *Setanta ZOP 001CD1*..........42 3
17 Jun 95 ● **A GIRL LIKE YOU** (re-issue) *Setanta ZOP 003CD*..........4 14
22 Jul 95 ● GORGEOUS GEORGE *Setanta AHOAON 058*..........8 8
2 Mar 96 **KEEP ON BURNING** *Setanta ZOP 004CD1*..........45 2
2 Aug 97 **THE MAGIC PIPER (OF LOVE)** *Setanta SETCDA 041*..........32 3
13 Sep 97 I'M NOT FOLLOWING YOU *Setanta SETCD 039*..........55 1
18 Oct 97 **ADIDAS WORLD** *Setanta SETCDB 045*..........71 1

[1] Paul Quinn and Edwyn Collins

The only track on all formats of Expressly (EP) was 'A Girl Like You'.

Jeff COLLINS *UK, male vocalist*

18 Nov 72 **ONLY YOU** *Polydor 2058 287*..........40 8

Judy COLLINS

US, female vocalist (3 Albums: 23 Weeks, 3 Singles: 86 Weeks)

17 Jan 70 **BOTH SIDES NOW** *Elektra EKSN 45043*..........14 11
5 Dec 70 ● **AMAZING GRACE (7re)** *Elektra 2101 020*..........5 67
27 Feb 71 WHALES AND NIGHTINGALES *Elektra EKS 75010*..........16 7
17 May 75 ● **SEND IN THE CLOWNS** *Elektra K 12177*..........6 8
31 May 75 ● JUDITH *Elektra K 52019*..........7 12
14 Dec 85 AMAZING GRACE *Telstar STAR 2265*..........34 4

'Amazing Grace' re-entered in Jul, Sep, Nov, Dec 1971 and Apr, Sep, Dec 1972.

Michelle COLLINS *UK, female actor / vocalist*

27 Feb 99 **SUNBURN** *BBC Music WMSS 60082*..........28 3

Phil COLLINS 19 Top 500

Continually popular singer / songwriter / drummer / actor, b. 31 Jan, 1951, Chiswick, London, UK. While at stage school he played the Artful Dodger in the West End production Oliver and was an extra in The Beatles' film A Hard Day's Night. He first recorded with art rock band Flaming Youth before joining Genesis in 1970 (taking over lead vocals when Peter Gabriel left in 1975). He first recorded solo in 1981 and until 1996 combined a successful solo career with fronting the hit group. He was one of the world's top artists in the 1980s and 1990s, during which time he collected numerous singing and songwriting awards, had transatlantic album chart-toppers No Jacket Required and ... But Seriously (which sold in excess of 13 million globally) and scored seven US No.1 singles. Known for his charitable work, he was the only act to appear on stage in both London and Philadelphia at Live Aid and played and sung on the original Band Aid single. The multi-talented artist became a household name, selling over 80 million copies of his first six albums by the time he left stadium-fillers Genesis in 1996. Only members of The Beatles have appeared on more UK No.1 albums than this Songwriters Hall of Fame member, who won an Oscar in 2000 for his music in Disney's Tarzan. He is one of the few British acts still selling well Stateside in the 21st century (11 Albums: 846 Weeks, 34 Singles: 235 Weeks)

17 Jan 81 ● **IN THE AIR TONIGHT** *Virgin VS102*..........2 10
21 Feb 81 ★ FACE VALUE *Virgin V 2185* ■..........1 274
7 Mar 81 **I MISSED AGAIN** *Virgin VS 402*..........14 8
30 May 81 **IF LEAVING ME IS EASY** *Virgin VS 423*..........17 8
23 Oct 82 **THRU' THESE WALLS** *Virgin VS 524*..........56 2
13 Nov 82 ● HELLO I MUST BE GOING *Virgin V 2252*..........2 163
4 Dec 82 ★ **YOU CAN'T HURRY LOVE** *Virgin VS 531*..........1 16
19 Mar 83 **DON'T LET HIM STEAL YOUR HEART AWAY** *Virgin VS 572*.....45 5
7 Apr 84 ● **AGAINST ALL ODDS (TAKE A LOOK AT ME NOW)** *Virgin VS 674* ▲ $..........2 14
26 Jan 85 **SUSSUDIO** *Virgin VS 736* ▲..........12 9
2 Mar 85 ★ NO JACKET REQUIRED *Virgin V 2345* ■ ▲..........1 176
9 Mar 85 ★ **EASY LOVER** *CBS A 4915* [1] $..........1 12
13 Apr 85 ● **ONE MORE NIGHT** *Virgin VS 755* ▲..........4 9
27 Jul 85 **TAKE ME HOME** *Virgin VS 777*..........19 9
23 Nov 85 ● **SEPARATE LIVES** *Virgin VS 818* [2] ▲..........4 13
18 Jun 88 ● **IN THE AIR TONIGHT** (re-mix) *Virgin VS 102*..........4 9
3 Sep 88 ★ **A GROOVY KIND OF LOVE** *Virgin VS 1117* ▲..........1 13
26 Nov 88 ● **TWO HEARTS** *Virgin VS 1141* ▲..........6 11
4 Nov 89 ● **ANOTHER DAY IN PARADISE** *Virgin VS 1234* ▲..........2 11
2 Dec 89 ★ ... BUT SERIOUSLY *Virgin V 2620* ■ ▲..........1 72
27 Jan 90 ● **I WISH IT WOULD RAIN DOWN** *Virgin VS 1240*..........7 9
28 Apr 90 **SOMETHING HAPPENED ON THE WAY TO HEAVEN** *Virgin VS 1251*..........15 7
28 Jul 90 **THAT'S JUST THE WAY IT IS** *Virgin VS 1277*..........26 5
6 Oct 90 **HANG IN LONG ENOUGH** *Virgin VS 1300*..........34 3
17 Nov 90 ● SERIOUS HITS ... LIVE! *Virgin PCLP 1*..........2 50
8 Dec 90 **DO YOU REMEMBER (LIVE)** *Virgin VS 1305*..........57 5
15 May 93 **HERO** *Atlantic A 7360* [3]..........56 3
30 Oct 93 ● **BOTH SIDES OF THE STORY (re)** *Virgin VSCDT 1500*..........7 6
20 Nov 93 ★ BOTH SIDES *Virgin CDV 2800* ■..........1 21
15 Jan 94 **EVERYDAY** *Virgin VSCDT 1505*..........15 5
7 May 94 **WE WAIT AND WE WONDER** *Virgin VSCDT 1510*..........45 2
5 Oct 96 ● **DANCE INTO THE LIGHT** *Face Value EW 066CD*..........9 6
2 Nov 96 ● DANCE INTO THE LIGHT *Face Value 630160002*..........4 13
14 Dec 96 **IT'S IN YOUR EYES** *Face Value EW 076CD1*..........30 4
12 Jul 97 **WEAR MY HAT** *Face Value EW 113CD*..........43 2
17 Oct 98 ★ ... HITS *Virgin CDV 2870* ■..........1 31
7 Nov 98 **TRUE COLORS** *Virgin VSCDT 1715*..........26 4
6 Nov 99 **YOU'LL BE IN MY HEART** *Edel / Walt Disney 0100735 DNY*.....17 6
22 Sep 01 **IN THE AIR TONITE** *WEA WEA 331CD* [4]..........26 2
16 Nov 02 **CAN'T STOP LOVING YOU** *Face Value EW 254CD*..........28 2
23 Nov 02 TESTIFY *Face Value / East West 5046614842*..........15 7
24 May 03 **HOME** *Epic 6738302* [5]..........19 4
29 Nov 03 **LOOK THROUGH MY EYES** *Walt Disney DISNEY 001*..........61 1
12 Jun 04 ● THE PLATINUM COLLECTION *Virgin PHILCD 1*..........4 18

8 / 10 September 1960	15 / 17 September 1960	22 / 24 September 1960	29 September / 1 October 1960
APACHE The Shadows	APACHE The Shadows	APACHE The Shadows	TELL LAURA I LOVE HER Ricky Valance
DOWN DRURY LANE TO MEMORY LANE 101 Strings	DOWN DRURY LANE TO MEMORY LANE 101 Strings	DOWN DRURY LANE TO MEMORY LANE 101 Strings	DOWN DRURY LANE TO MEMORY LANE 101 Strings

KEY: UK No.1 ★ UK Top 10 ● Still on chart + UK entry at No.1 ■ US No.1 ▲ UK million seller £ US million seller $
Singles re-entries are listed as (re), (2re), (3re)... which signifies that the hit re-entered the chart once, twice or three times...
Peak Position / Weeks

13 Nov 04 ● LOVE SONGS – A COMPILATION ... OLD AND NEW Virgin PHILCDX 2 ....9 21

[1] Philip Bailey (duet with Phil Collins) [2] Phil Collins and Marilyn Martin [3] David Crosby featuring Phil Collins [4] Lil' Kim featuring Phil Collins [5] Bone Thugs-N-Harmony featuring Phil Collins

Rodger COLLINS *US, male vocalist*

3 Apr 76 **YOU SEXY SUGAR PLUM (BUT I LIKE IT)** *Fantasy FTC 132* 22 6

Willie COLLINS *US, male vocalist*

14 Jun 86 WHERE YOU GONNA BE TONIGHT? *Capitol EST 2012* 97 1
28 Jun 86 **WHERE YOU GONNA BE TONIGHT?** *Capitol CL 410* 46 4

Willie COLON *US, male vocalist*

28 Jun 86 **SET FIRE TO ME** *A&M AM 330* 41 7

COLOR ME BADD
US, male vocal group (1 Album: 22 Weeks, 7 Singles: 31 Weeks)

18 May 91 ★ **I WANNA SEX YOU UP** *Giant W 0036* $ 1 14
3 Aug 91 ● **ALL 4 LOVE** *Giant W 0053* ▲ 5 10
24 Aug 91 ● CMB *Giant WX 425* 3 22
12 Oct 91 **I ADORE MI AMOR** *Giant W 0067* ▲ 44 2
9 Nov 91 **I ADORE MI AMOR** (re-issue) *Giant W 0076* 59 2
22 Feb 92 **HEARTBREAKER** *Giant W 0078* 58 1
20 Nov 93 **TIME AND CHANCE** *Giant 74321168992* 62 1
16 Apr 94 **CHOOSE** *Giant 74321199432* 65 1

COLORADO *UK, female vocal group*

21 Oct 78 **CALIFORNIA DREAMING** *Pinnacle PIN 67* 45 3

COLOSSEUM *UK, male vocal / instrumental group (4 Albums: 14 Weeks)*

17 May 69 THOSE WHO ARE ABOUT TO DIE *Fontana STL 5510* 15 1
22 Nov 69 VALENTYNE SUITE *Vertigo VO 1* 15 2
5 Dec 70 DAUGHTER OF TIME *Vertigo 6360 017* 23 5
26 Jun 71 COLOSSEUM LIVE *Bronze ICD 1* 17 6

COLOUR GIRL *UK, female vocalist – Rebecca Skingley (3 Singles: 5 Weeks)*

11 Mar 00 **CAN'T GET USED TO LOSING YOU** *4 Liberty LIBTCD 037* 31 3
9 Sep 00 **JOYRIDER (YOU'RE PLAYING WITH FIRE)** *4 Liberty LIBTCD 039* 51 1
3 Feb 01 **MAS QUE NADA** *4 Liberty LIBTCD 040* [1] 57 1

[1] Colour Girl featuring PSG

COLOURBOX *UK, male vocal / instrumental group*

24 Aug 85 COLOURBOX *4AD CAD 508* 67 2

The COLOURFIELD
UK, male vocal / instrumental group (2 Albums: 8 Weeks, 4 Singles: 18 Weeks)

21 Jan 84 **THE COLOURFIELD** *Chrysalis COLF 1* 43 4
28 Jul 84 **TAKE** *Chrysalis COLF 2* 70 1
26 Jan 85 **THINKING OF YOU** *Chrysalis COLF 3* 12 10
13 Apr 85 **CASTLES IN THE AIR** *Chrysalis COLF 4* 51 3
4 May 85 VIRGINS AND PHILISTINES *Chrysalis CHR 1480* 12 7
4 Apr 87 DECEPTION *Chrysalis CDL 1546* 95 1

COLOURS featuring EMMANUEL & ESKA
(see also EN-CORE featuring Stephen EMMANUEL & ESKA; Nitin SAWHNEY)
UK, male instrumentalist / producer and female vocalist

27 Feb 99 **WHAT U DO** *Inferno CDFERN 12* 51 1

COLOURSOUND *UK, male production duo*

28 Sep 02 **FLY WITH ME** *City Rockers ROCKERS 20CD* 49 2

COLUMBO featuring OOE *UK, male production duo*

15 May 99 **ROCKABILLY BOB** *V2 / Milkgems VVR 5006903* 59 1

Shawn COLVIN
US, female vocalist (1 Album: 1 Week, 7 Singles: 12 Weeks)

27 Nov 93 **I DON'T KNOW WHY** *Columbia 6598272* 62 1
12 Feb 94 **ROUND OF BLUES** *Columbia 6594282* 73 1
3 Sep 94 **EVERY LITTLE THING HE DOES IS MAGIC** *Columbia 6607742* ..65 2
17 Sep 94 COVER GIRL *Columbia 4772402* 67 1
7 Jan 95 **ONE COOL REMOVE** *Columbia 6611342* [1] 40 3
12 Aug 95 **I DON'T KNOW WHY** (re-issue) *Columbia 6622725* 52 1
15 Mar 97 **GET OUT OF THIS HOUSE** *Columbia 6638522* 70 1
30 May 98 **SUNNY CAME HOME** *Columbia 6648022* 29 3

[1] Shawn Colvin with Mary-Chapin Carpenter

COMIC RELIEF *UK, charity ensemble of comedians*

10 May 86 ● UTTERLY UTTERLY LIVE! *WEA WX 51* 10 8

COMING OUT CREW *US, male / female vocal duo*

18 Mar 95 **FREE, GAY AND HAPPY** *Out on Vinyl CDOOV 002* 50 1

COMMANDER TOM
Germany, male producer – Tom Weyer (2 Singles: 5 Weeks)

23 Dec 00 **EYE BEE M** *Tripoli Trax TTRAX 069CD* 75 1
5 Feb 05 **ATTENTION!** *Data DATA 81CDS* 23 4

The COMMENTATORS *UK, male impressionist – Rory Bremner*

22 Jun 85 **N-N-NINETEEN NOT OUT** *Oval 100* 13 7

The COMMITMENTS *Ireland, male / female vocal / instrumental group (2 Albums: 147 Weeks, 1 Single: 1 Week)*

26 Oct 91 ● THE COMMITMENTS (FILM SOUNDTRACK) *MCA MCA 10286* 4 136
30 Nov 91 **MUSTANG SALLY** *MCA MCS 1598* 63 1
25 Apr 92 THE COMMITMENTS VOLUME 2 *MCA MCAD 10506* 13 11

The COMMODORES (226 Top 500) *Top-notch US R&B combo:*
Lionel Richie (v/k), William King (t), Thomas McClary (g), Milan Williams (var), Ronald LaPread (b), Walter Orange (d). They were among the 1970s' biggest-selling groups, but lost ground when songwriter Richie went solo in 1982 (11 Albums: 157 Weeks, 17 Singles: 121 Weeks)

24 Aug 74 **MACHINE GUN** *Tamla Motown TMG 902* 20 11
23 Nov 74 **THE ZOO (THE HUMAN ZOO)** *Tamla Motown TMG 924* 44 2
2 Jul 77 ● **EASY** *Motown TMG 1073* $ 9 10
8 Oct 77 **SWEET LOVE / BRICK HOUSE** *Motown TMG 1086* 32 6
11 Mar 78 **TOO HOT TA TROT / ZOOM** *Motown TMG 1096* 38 4
13 May 78 LIVE! *Motown TMSP 6007* 60 1
10 Jun 78 ● NATURAL HIGH *Motown STML 12087* 8 23
24 Jun 78 **FLYING HIGH** *Motown TMG 1111* 37 7
5 Aug 78 ★ **THREE TIMES A LADY** *Motown TMG 1113* ▲ $ 1 14
25 Nov 78 **JUST TO BE CLOSE TO YOU** *Motown TMG 1127* 62 4
2 Dec 78 GREATEST HITS *Motown STML 12100* 19 16
18 Aug 79 MIDNIGHT MAGIC *Motown STMA 8032* 15 25
25 Aug 79 ● **SAIL ON** *Motown TMG 1155* 8 10
3 Nov 79 ● **STILL** *Motown TMG 1166* ▲ $ 4 11
19 Jan 80 **WONDERLAND** *Motown TMG 1172* 40 4
28 Jun 80 HEROES *Motown STMA 8034* 50 5
18 Jul 81 IN THE POCKET *Motown STML 12156* 69 5
1 Aug 81 **LADY (YOU BRING ME UP)** *Motown TMG 1238* 56 5
21 Nov 81 **OH NO** *Motown TMG 1245* 44 3
14 Aug 82 ● LOVE SONGS *K-Tel NE 1171* 5 28
26 Jan 85 ● **NIGHTSHIFT** *Motown TMG 1371* 3 14
23 Feb 85 NIGHTSHIFT *Motown ZL 72343* 13 10

6 / 8 October 1960	13 / 15 October 1960	20 / 22 October 1960	27 / 29 October 1960
UK No.1 SINGLES			
TELL LAURA I LOVE HER Ricky Valance	TELL LAURA I LOVE HER Ricky Valance	ONLY THE LONELY (KNOW HOW I FEEL) Roy Orbison	ONLY THE LONELY (KNOW HOW I FEEL) Roy Orbison
UK No.1 ALBUMS			
DOWN DRURY LANE TO MEMORY LANE 101 Strings	SOUTH PACIFIC Soundtrack	SOUTH PACIFIC Soundtrack	SOUTH PACIFIC Soundtrack

11 May 85 **ANIMAL INSTINCT** *Motown ZB 40097* **74** 1
9 Nov 85 ● THE VERY BEST OF THE COMMODORES *Telstar STAR 2249* 25 13
25 Oct 86 **GOIN' TO THE BANK** *Polydor POSPA 826* **43** 4
13 Aug 88 **EASY** (re-issue) *Motown ZB 41793* **15** 11
6 May 95 THE VERY BEST *Motown 5305472* 26 3
22 Nov 03 ● THE DEFINITIVE COLLECTION *Universal TV 9861394* [1] 10 28

[1] Lionel Richie & The Commodores

The group was US / UK for their 1985 and 1986 hits and US only for their first seven albums.

COMMON

US, male rapper – Rasheed Lynn (1 Album: 2 Weeks, 4 Singles: 10 Weeks)

8 Nov 97 **REMINDING ME (OF SEF)** *Relativity 6560762* [1] **59** 1
14 Oct 00 **THE LIGHT / THE 6TH SENSE (SOMETHING U FEEL)** *MCA MCSTD 40237* **56** 1
28 Apr 01 **GETO HEAVEN** *MCA MCSTD 40246* [2] **48** 1
9 Feb 02 **DANCE FOR ME** *MCA MCSTD 40274* [3] **13** 7
4 Jun 05 BE *Geffen 9882497* 38 2

[1] Common featuring Chantay Savage [2] Common featuring Macy Gray [3] Mary J Blige featuring Common

The COMMUNARDS (479 Top 500)

Controversial, melodic pop duo consisted of Bronski Beat's Jimmy Somerville (v), b. 22 Jun 1961, Glasgow, Scotland, and Richard Coles (k), b. 23 Jun 1962, Northampton, UK. Their No.1 cover marked the song's third Top 20 reading within a decade (3 Albums: 78 Weeks, 9 Singles: 76 Weeks)

12 Oct 85 **YOU ARE MY WORLD** *London LON 77* **30** 8
24 May 86 **DISENCHANTED** *London LON 89* **29** 5
2 Aug 86 ● COMMUNARDS *London LONLP 18* 7 45
23 Aug 86 ★ **DON'T LEAVE ME THIS WAY** *London LON 103* [1] **1** 14
29 Nov 86 ● **SO COLD THE NIGHT** *London LON 110* **8** 10
21 Feb 87 **YOU ARE MY WORLD (87)** (re-mix) *London LON 123* **21** 6
12 Sep 87 **TOMORROW** *London LON 143* **23** 7
17 Oct 87 ● RED *London LONLP 39* 4 29
7 Nov 87 ● **NEVER CAN SAY GOODBYE** *London LON 158* **4** 11
20 Feb 88 **FOR A FRIEND** *London LON 166* **28** 7
11 Jun 88 **THERE'S MORE TO LOVE** *London LON 173* **20** 8
22 Sep 01 THE VERY BEST OF JIMMY SOMERVILLE, BRONSKI BEAT AND THE COMMUNARDS *London 927412582* [1] 29 4

[1] The Communards with Sarah Jane Morris [1] Jimmy Somerville, Bronski Beat and The Communards

Perry COMO (75 Top 500)

One of the 20th century's most enduring entertainers, b. 18 May 1912, Pennsylvania, US, d. 12 May 2001. This easy-on-the-ear, relaxed balladeer launched his career in 1933, collected 150 US chart entries, hosted an Emmy-winning TV series and continued to score hits past the age of 60 (12 Albums: 203 Weeks, 26 Singles: 323 Weeks)

16 Jan 53 ★ **DON'T LET THE STARS GET IN YOUR EYES** *HMV B 10400* [1] ▲ **1** 15
4 Jun 54 ● **WANTED (re)** *HMV B 10691* ▲ **4** 15
25 Jun 54 ● **IDLE GOSSIP** *HMV B 10667* **3** 15
10 Dec 54 **PAPA LOVES MAMBO** *HMV B 10776* $ **16** 1
30 Dec 55 **TINA MARIE** *HMV POP 103* **24** 1
27 Apr 56 **JUKE BOX BABY** *HMV POP 191* **22** 6
25 May 56 ● **HOT DIGGITY (DOG ZIGGITY BOOM)** *HMV POP 212* $ **4** 13
21 Sep 56 ● **MORE (re)** *HMV POP 240* **10** 12
28 Sep 56 **GLENDORA** *HMV POP 240* **18** 6
7 Feb 58 ★ **MAGIC MOMENTS** *RCA 1036* **1** 17
7 Mar 58 ● **CATCH A FALLING STAR** *RCA 1036* $ **9** 10
9 May 58 ● **KEWPIE DOLL** *RCA 1055* **9** 7
30 May 58 **I MAY NEVER PASS THIS WAY AGAIN** *RCA 1062* **15** 8
28 Jun 58 ● WE GET LETTERS (VOL.2) *RCA RD 27070* 4 7
5 Sep 58 **MOON TALK** *RCA 1071* **17** 11
7 Nov 58 ● **LOVE MAKES THE WORLD GO ROUND** *RCA 1086* **6** 14
8 Nov 58 ● DEAR PERRY *RCA RD 27078* 6 5
21 Nov 58 **MANDOLINS IN THE MOONLIGHT** *RCA 1086* **13** 12
31 Jan 59 ● COMO'S GOLDEN RECORDS *RCA RD 27100* 4 5
27 Feb 59 ● **TOMBOY** *RCA 1111* **10** 12
10 Jul 59 **I KNOW** *RCA 1126* [2] **13** 16
26 Feb 60 ● **DELAWARE** *RCA 1170* **3** 14
10 May 62 **CATERINA (re)** *RCA 1283* **37** 6
30 Jan 71 ● **IT'S IMPOSSIBLE** *RCA 2043* **4** 23
10 Apr 71 IT'S IMPOSSIBLE *RCA Victor SF 8175* 13 13
15 May 71 **I THINK OF YOU** *RCA 2075* **14** 11
21 Apr 73 ● **AND I LOVE YOU SO (re)** *RCA 2346* **3** 35
7 Jul 73 ★ AND I LOVE YOU SO *RCA Victor SF 8360* 1 109
25 Aug 73 ● **FOR THE GOOD TIMES** *RCA 2402* **7** 27
8 Dec 73 **WALK RIGHT BACK** *RCA 2432* **33** 10
25 May 74 **I WANT TO GIVE** *RCA LPBO 7518* **31** 6
24 Aug 74 PERRY *RCA Victor APLI 0585* 26 3
19 Apr 75 MEMORIES ARE MADE OF HITS *RCA Victor RS 1005* 14 16
25 Oct 75 ★ 40 GREATEST HITS *K-Tel NE 700* 1 34
3 Dec 83 FOR THE GOOD TIMES *Telstar STAR 2235* 41 6
17 Nov 01 GOLD – GREATEST HITS *RCA 74321865542* 55 2
4 Oct 03 THE ESSENTIAL PERRY COMO *Jive / RCA 82876560172* 54 2
5 Jun 04 THE VERY BEST OF PERRY COMO – PAPA LOVES MAMBO *RCA 82876616572* 63 1

[1] Perry Como with the Ramblers [2] Perry Como with the Mitchell Ayers Orchestra and the Ray Charles Singers

LES COMPAGNONS DE LA CHANSON *France, male vocal group*

9 Oct 59 **THE THREE BELLS (THE JIMMY BROWN SONG) (re)** *Columbia DB 4358* **21** 3

COMPULSION *Ireland / Holland, male vocal / instrumental group*

9 Apr 94 COMFORTER *One Little Indian TPLP 59CDL* 59 1

COMSAT ANGELS

UK, male vocal / instrumental group (3 Albums: 9 Weeks, 1 Single: 2 Weeks)

5 Sep 81 SLEEP NO MORE *Polydor POLS 1038* 51 5
18 Sep 82 FICTION *Polydor POLS 1075* 94 2
8 Oct 83 LAND *Jive HIP 8* 91 2
21 Jan 84 **INDEPENDENCE DAY (re)** *Jive JIVE 54* **71** 2

CON FUNK SHUN *US, male vocal / instrumental group*

19 Jul 86 **BURNIN' LOVE** *Club JAB 32* **68** 2

CONCEPT *US, male vocalist / instrumentalist – Eric Reed*

14 Dec 85 **MR DJ** *Fourth & Broadway BRW 40* **27** 6

The CONCRETES

Sweden, male / female vocal / instrumental group (2 Singles: 2 Weeks)

26 Jun 04 **YOU CAN'T HURRY LOVE** *EMI LFS 011* **55** 1
2 Oct 04 **SEEMS FINE** *EMI LFS 013* **52** 1

CONDUCTOR & THE COWBOY

UK, male production duo – Lee Hallett and Adam Pracy

20 May 00 **FEELING THIS WAY** *Serious SERR 016CD* **35** 2

CONGREGATION *UK, male / female choir*

27 Nov 71 ● **SOFTLY WHISPERING I LOVE YOU** *Columbia DB 8830* **4** 14

CONGRESS *UK, male / female vocal / instrumental group*

26 Oct 91 **40 MILES** *Inner Rhythm 7HEART 01* **26** 4

CONJURE ONE *Canada, male producer – Rhys Fulber*

15 Feb 03 **SLEEP / TEARS FROM THE MOON** *Nettwerk 331792* **42** 1

'Tears from the Moon' features uncredited vocalist Sinead O'Connor.

Arthur CONLEY

US, male vocalist, b. 4 Jan 1946, d. 17 Nov 2003 (2 Singles: 15 Weeks)

27 Apr 67 ● **SWEET SOUL MUSIC** *Atlantic 584 083* $ **7** 14
10 Apr 68 **FUNKY STREET** *Atlantic 583 175* **46** 1

3 / 5 November 1960	10 / 12 November 1960	17 / 19 November 1960	24 / 26 November 1960
IT'S NOW OR NEVER Elvis Presley	IT'S NOW OR NEVER Elvis Presley	IT'S NOW OR NEVER Elvis Presley	IT'S NOW OR NEVER Elvis Presley
SOUTH PACIFIC Soundtrack	SOUTH PACIFIC Soundtrack	SOUTH PACIFIC Soundtrack	SOUTH PACIFIC Soundtrack

KEY
UK No.1 ★ UK Top 10 ● Still on chart + UK entry at No.1 ■
US No.1 ▲ UK million seller £ US million seller $
Singles re-entries are listed as (re), (2re), (3re)... which signifies that the hit re-entered the chart once, twice or three times...
Peak Position / Weeks

The CONNELLS *US, male vocal / instrumental group*

12 Aug 95 **74-75 (re)** *TVT LONCD 369* **14** 11
9 Sep 95 RING *London 8286602* 36 2

Harry CONNICK Jr *US, male vocalist / keyboard player (6 Albums: 73 Weeks, 3 Singles: 11 Weeks)*

22 Sep 90 ● WE ARE IN LOVE *CBS 4667361* 7 46
25 May 91 **RECIPE FOR LOVE / IT HAD TO BE YOU** *Columbia 6568907* **32** 6
3 Aug 91 **WE ARE IN LOVE** *Columbia 6572847* **62** 2
26 Oct 91 BLUE LIGHT *Columbia 4690871* 16 11
23 Nov 91 **BLUE LIGHT RED LIGHT (SOMEONE'S THERE)** *Columbia 6575367* **54** 3
30 Jan 93 25 *Columbia 4728092* 35 2
12 Jun 93 FOREVER FOR NOW *Columbia 4738732* 32 5
27 Aug 94 SHE *Columbia 4768162* 21 3
20 Mar 04 ● ONLY YOU *Columbia 5150462* 6 6

Ray CONNIFF *US, male orchestra leader, b. 6 Nov 1916, d. 12 Oct 2002 (13 Albums: 100 Weeks)*

28 May 60 IT'S THE TALK OF THE TOWN *Philips BBL 7354* 15 1
25 Jun 60 S'AWFUL NICE *Philips BBL 7281* 13 1
26 Nov 60 ● HI-FI COMPANION ALBUM *Philips BET 101* 3 44
20 May 61 MEMORIES ARE MADE OF THIS *Philips BBL 7439* 14 4
29 Dec 62 S WONDERFUL 'S MARVELLOUS *CBS DPG 66001* 18 3
29 Dec 62 WE WISH YOU A MERRY CHRISTMAS *CBS BPG 62092* 12 1
16 Apr 66 HI-FI COMPANION ALBUM (re-issue) *CBS DP 66011* 24 4
9 Sep 67 SOMEWHERE MY LOVE *CBS SBPG 62740* 34 3
21 Jun 69 ★ HIS ORCHESTRA, HIS CHORUS, HIS SINGERS, HIS SOUND *CBS SPR 27* ■ 1 16
23 May 70 BRIDGE OVER TROUBLED WATER *CBS 64020* 30 14
12 Jun 71 LOVE STORY *CBS 64294* 34 1
19 Feb 72 I'D LIKE TO TEACH THE WORLD TO SING *CBS 64449* 17 4
27 Oct 73 HARMONY *CBS 65792* 24 4

Billy CONNOLLY *UK, male comedian / vocalist / instrumentalist (8 Albums: 108 Weeks, 4 Singles: 31 Weeks)*

20 Jul 74 ● SOLO CONCERT *Transatlantic TRA 279* 8 33
18 Jan 75 ● COP YER WHACK OF THIS *Polydor 2383 310* 10 29
20 Sep 75 WORDS AND MUSIC *Transatlantic TRA SAM 32* 34 10
1 Nov 75 ★ **D.I.V.O.R.C.E.** *Polydor 2058 652* **1** 10
6 Dec 75 ● GET RIGHT INTAE HIM *Polydor 2383 368* 6 14
17 Jul 76 **NO CHANCE (NO CHARGE)** *Polydor 2058 748* **24** 5
11 Dec 76 ATLANTIC BRIDGE *Polydor 2383 419* 20 9
28 Jan 78 RAW MEAT FOR THE BALCONY *Polydor 2383 463* 57 3
25 Aug 79 **IN THE BROWNIES** *Polydor 2059 160* **38** 7
5 Dec 81 THE PICK OF BILLY CONNOLLY *Polydor POLTV 15* 23 8
9 Mar 85 **SUPER GRAN** *Stiff BUY 218* **32** 9
5 Dec 87 BILLY AND ALBERT *10 DIX 65* 81 2

Sarah CONNOR
(see also TQ) *Germany, female vocalist (2 Singles: 10 Weeks)*

13 Oct 01 **LET'S GET BACK TO BED ... BOY** *Epic 6718662* [1] **16** 5
5 Jun 04 **BOUNCE** *Epic 6749001* **14** 5

[1] Sarah Connor featuring TQ

CONQUERING LION *UK, male vocal group*

8 Oct 94 **CODE RED** *Mango CIDM 821* **53** 1

Leena CONQUEST and HIP HOP FINGER
US, female vocalist and male rapper

18 Jun 94 **BOUNDARIES** *Natural Response 74321208522* **67** 1

Jess CONRAD
UK, male vocalist / actor – Gerald James (3 Singles: 13 Weeks)

30 Jun 60 **CHERRY PIE** *Decca F 11236* **39** 1
26 Jan 61 **MYSTERY GIRL (re)** *Decca F 11315* **18** 10
11 Oct 62 **PRETTY JENNY** *Decca F 11511* **50** 2

CONSOLIDATED *US, male vocal / instrumental group*

30 Jul 94 BUSINESS OF PUNISHMENT *London 8285142* 53 1

CONSORTIUM *UK, male vocal group*

12 Feb 69 **ALL THE LOVE IN THE WORLD** *Pye 7N 17635* **22** 9

The CONTOURS *US, male vocal group*

24 Jan 70 **JUST A LITTLE MISUNDERSTANDING** *Tamla Motown TMG 723* **31** 6

CONTRABAND *Germany / US, male / female vocal / instrumental group*

20 Jul 91 **ALL THE WAY FROM MEMPHIS** *Impact American EM 195* **65** 2

CONTROL *UK, male / female vocal / instrumental group*

2 Nov 91 **DANCE WITH ME (I'M YOUR ECSTASY)** *All Around the World GLOBE 105* **17** 5

CONVERT (see also CUBIC 22; DECOY AND ROY)
Belgium, male instrumental / production duo – Peter Ramson and Danny Van Wauwe (3 Singles: 7 Weeks)

11 Jan 92 **NIGHTBIRD** *A&M AM 845* **39** 4
29 May 93 **ROCKIN' TO THE RHYTHM** *A&M 5802532* **42** 2
31 Jan 98 **NIGHTBIRD** (re-issue) *Wonderboy WBOYD 008* **45** 1

The CONWAY BROTHERS *US, male vocal group*

22 Jun 85 **TURN IT UP** *10 TEN 57* **11** 10

Russ CONWAY 260 Top 500
Popular pianist and composer, b. Trevor Stanford, 2 Sep 1925, Bristol, UK, d. 16 Nov 2000. Against the trends of the day, this MOR musician was the UK's top-selling artist in 1959 (7 Albums: 69 Weeks, 20 Singles: 180 Weeks)

29 Nov 57 **PARTY POPS** *Columbia DB 4031* **24** 5
29 Aug 58 **GOT A MATCH** *Columbia DB 4166* **30** 1
22 Nov 58 ● PACK UP YOUR TROUBLES *Columbia 33SX 1120* 9 5
28 Nov 58 ● **MORE PARTY POPS** *Columbia DB 4204* **10** 7
23 Jan 59 **THE WORLD OUTSIDE (re)** *Columbia DB 4234* **24** 4
20 Feb 59 ★ **SIDE SADDLE** *Columbia DB 4256* **1** 30
2 May 59 ● SONGS TO SING IN YOUR BATH *Columbia 33SX 1149* 8 10
15 May 59 ★ **ROULETTE** *Columbia DB 4298* **1** 19
21 Aug 59 ● **CHINA TEA** *Columbia DB 4337* **5** 13
19 Sep 59 ● FAMILY FAVOURITES *Columbia 33SX 1169* 3 16
13 Nov 59 ● **SNOW COACH** *Columbia DB 4368* **7** 9
20 Nov 59 ● **MORE AND MORE PARTY POPS** *Columbia DB 4373* **5** 8
19 Dec 59 ● TIME TO CELEBRATE *Columbia 33SX 1197* 3 7
4 Mar 60 **ROYAL EVENT** *Columbia DB 4418* **15** 9
26 Mar 60 ● MY CONCERTO FOR YOU *Columbia 33SX 1214* 5 17
21 Apr 60 **FINGS AIN'T WOT THEY USED T'BE** *Columbia DB 4422* **47** 1
19 May 60 **LUCKY FIVE** *Columbia DB 4457* **14** 9
29 Sep 60 **PASSING BREEZE** *Columbia DB 4508* **16** 10
24 Nov 60 **EVEN MORE PARTY POPS** *Columbia DB 4535* **27** 9
17 Dec 60 ● PARTY TIME *Columbia 33SX 1279* 7 11
19 Jan 61 **PEPE** *Columbia DB 4564* **19** 9
25 May 61 **PABLO** *Columbia DB 4649* **45** 2
24 Aug 61 **SAY IT WITH FLOWERS** *Columbia DB 4665* [1] **23** 10
30 Nov 61 ● **TOY BALLOONS** *Columbia DB 4738* **7** 11
22 Feb 62 **LESSON ONE** *Columbia DB 4784* **21** 7
29 Nov 62 **ALWAYS YOU AND ME (re)** *Columbia DB 4934* **33** 7
23 Apr 77 RUSS CONWAY PRESENTS 24 PIANO GREATS *Ronco RTL 2022* 25 3

[1] Dorothy Squires and Russ Conway

Several of the discs were medleys as follows: Party Pops: When You're Smiling /

1 / 3 December 1960	8 / 10 December 1960	15 / 17 December 1960	22 / 24 December 1960
UK No.1 SINGLES			
IT'S NOW OR NEVER Elvis Presley	IT'S NOW OR NEVER Elvis Presley	IT'S NOW OR NEVER Elvis Presley	IT'S NOW OR NEVER Elvis Presley
UK No.1 ALBUMS			
SOUTH PACIFIC Soundtrack	SOUTH PACIFIC Soundtrack	SOUTH PACIFIC Soundtrack	SOUTH PACIFIC Soundtrack

I'm Looking over a Four-Leafed Clover / When You Wore a Tulip / Row Row Row / For Me and My Girl / Shine on Harvest Moon / By the Light of the Silvery Moon / Side By Side. More Party Pops: Music Music Music / If You Were the Only Girl in the World / Nobody's Sweetheart / Yes Sir That's My Baby / Some of these Days / Honeysuckle and the Bee / Hello Hello Who's Your Lady Friend / Shanty in Old Shanty Town. More and More Party Pops: Sheik of Araby / Who Were You With Last Night / Any Old Iron / Tiptoe Through the Tulips / If You Were the Only Girl in the World / When I Leave the World Behind. Even More Party Pops: Ain't She Sweet / I Can't Give You Anything But Love / Yes We Have No Bananas / I May Be Wrong / Happy Days And Lonely Nights / Glad Rag Doll.

Ry COODER (see also Ali Farka TOURÉ)
US, male vocalist / guitarist – Ryland Cooder (8 Albums: 51 Weeks)

11 Aug 79 BOP TILL YOU DROP *Warner Bros. K 56691* 36 9
18 Oct 80 BORDER LINE *Warner Bros. K 56864* 35 6
24 Apr 82 THE SLIDE AREA *Warner Bros. K 56976* 18 12
14 Nov 87 GET RHYTHM *Warner Bros. WX 121* 75 3
9 Apr 94 TALKING TIMBUKTU *World Circuit WCD 040* [1] 44 3
5 Jul 97 BUENA VISTA SOCIAL CLUB *World Circuit WCD 050* 44 15
8 Feb 03 MAMBO SINUENDO *Nonesuch 75597969612* 40 1
25 Jun 05 CHAVEZ RAVINE *Nonesuch 7559798772* 35 2

[1] Ali Farka Touri and Ry Cooder

Norman COOK
(see also BEATS INTERNATIONAL; FATBOY SLIM; FREAKPOWER; The HOUSEMARTINS; MIGHTY DUB KATZ; PIZZAMAN; URBAN ALL STARS)
UK, male producer / multi-instrumentalist – Quentin Cook (2 Singles: 10 Weeks)

8 Jul 89 WON'T TALK ABOUT IT / BLAME IT ON THE BASSLINE *Go Beat GOD 33* [1] 29 6
21 Oct 89 FOR SPACIOUS LIES *Go Beat GOD 37* [2] 48 4

[1] Norman Cook featuring Billy Bragg / Norman Cook featuring MC Wildski
[2] Norman Cook featuring Lester

Peter COOK and Dudley MOORE
(see also DEREK AND CLIVE; Dudley MOORE) *UK, male comedy / vocal duo – Peter Cook, b. 17 Nov 1937, d. 9 Jan 1995, and Dudley Moore, b. 19 Apr 1935, d. 28 Mar 2002 (3 Albums: 34 Weeks, 3 Singles: 15 Weeks)*

17 Jun 65 GOODBYE-EE *Decca F 12158* 18 10
15 Jul 65 THE BALLAD OF SPOTTY MULDOON *Decca F 12182* [1] 34 5
21 May 66 ONCE MOORE WITH COOK *Decca LK 4785* 25 1
18 Sep 76 DEREK AND CLIVE LIVE *Island ILPS 9434* [1] 12 25
24 Dec 77 DEREK AND CLIVE COME AGAIN *Virgin V 2094* [1] 18 8

[1] Peter Cook [1] Derek and Clive

Brandon COOKE featuring Roxanne SHANTÉ
UK, male producer and US, female rapper – Lolita Gooden

29 Oct 88 SHARP AS A KNIFE *Club JAB 73* 45 3

Sam COOKE *US, male vocalist, b. 22 Jan 1931, d. 11 Dec 1964 (3 Albums: 47 Weeks, 10 Singles: 82 Weeks)*

17 Jan 58 YOU SEND ME *London HLU 8506* ▲ $ 29 1
14 Aug 59 ONLY SIXTEEN *HMV POP 642* 23 4
7 Jul 60 WONDERFUL WORLD *HMV POP 754* 27 8
29 Sep 60 ● CHAIN GANG *RCA 1202* $ 9 11
27 Jul 61 ● CUPID *RCA 1242* 7 14
8 Mar 62 ● TWISTIN' THE NIGHT AWAY *RCA 1277* 6 14
16 May 63 ANOTHER SATURDAY NIGHT *RCA 1341* 23 12
5 Sep 63 FRANKIE AND JOHNNY *RCA 1361* 30 6
22 Mar 86 ● WONDERFUL WORLD (re-issue) *RCA PB 49871* 2 11
26 Apr 86 ● THE MAN AND HIS MUSIC *RCA PL 87127* 8 27
10 May 86 ANOTHER SATURDAY NIGHT (re-issue) *RCA PB 49849* 75 1
25 Oct 03 PORTRAIT OF A LEGEND 1951-1964 *Universal TV 9807446* 30 5
2 Jul 05 PORTRAIT OF A LEGEND 1951-1964 (re-issue) *Abkco 9872418* 19 15

COOKIE NEW *UK, female vocal group*

16 Jul 05 DO IT AGAIN *The Bakery CXBAKERY 1* 52 1

The COOKIE CREW *UK, female rap duo – Susie Banfield and Debbie Pryce (1 Album: 4 Weeks, 5 Singles: 31 Weeks)*

9 Jan 88 ● ROK DA HOUSE *Rhythm King LEFT 11* [1] 5 11
7 Jan 89 BORN THIS WAY (LET'S DANCE) *ffrr FFR 19* 23 5
1 Apr 89 GOT TO KEEP ON *ffrr FFR 25* 17 9
6 May 89 BORN THIS WAY! *London 828134 1* 24 4
15 Jul 89 COME AND GET SOME *ffrr F 110* 42 3
27 Jul 91 SECRETS (OF SUCCESS) *ffrr F159* [2] 53 3

[1] The Beatmasters featuring The Cookie Crew [2] The Cookie Crew featuring Danny D

The COOKIES *US, female vocal group*

10 Jan 63 CHAINS *London HLU 9634* 50 1

COOL DOWN ZONE *UK, male / female vocal / instrumental group*

30 Jun 90 HEAVEN KNOWS *10 TEN 309* 52 4

COOL JACK *Italy, male instrumental / production duo*

9 Nov 96 JUS' COME *AM:PM 5819892* 44 1

The COOL NOTES *UK, male / female vocal / instrumental group (1 Album: 2 Weeks, 6 Singles: 28 Weeks)*

18 Aug 84 YOU'RE NEVER TOO YOUNG *Abstract Dance AD 1* 42 5
17 Nov 84 I FORGOT *Abstract Dance AD 2* 63 2
23 Mar 85 SPEND THE NIGHT *Abstract Dance AD 3* 11 9
13 Jul 85 IN YOUR CAR *Abstract Dance AD 4* 13 9
19 Oct 85 HAVE A GOOD FOREVER *Abstract Dance AD 5* 73 1
9 Nov 85 HAVE A GOOD FOREVER *Abstract Dance ADLP 1* 66 2
17 May 86 INTO THE MOTION *Abstract Dance AD 8* 66 2

COOL, The FAB, and The GROOVY present Quincy JONES *UK, male production duo, US, male band and US, male producer / instrumentalist*

1 Aug 98 SOUL BOSSA NOVA *Manifesto FESCD 48* 47 1

Rita COOLIDGE
US, female vocalist (4 Albums: 44 Weeks, 4 Singles: 24 Weeks)

25 Jun 77 ● WE'RE ALL ALONE *A&M AMS 7295* 6 13
6 Aug 77 ● ANYTIME ANYWHERE *A&M AMLH 64616* 6 28
15 Oct 77 (YOUR LOVE HAS LIFTED ME) HIGHER AND HIGHER (re) *A&M AMS 7315* $ 48 2
4 Feb 78 WORDS *A&M AMS 7330* 25 8
6 May 78 NATURAL ACT *A&M AMLH 64690* [1] 35 4
8 Jul 78 LOVE ME AGAIN *A&M AMLH 64699* 51 1
14 Mar 81 ● THE VERY BEST OF RITA COOLIDGE *A&M AMLH 68520* 6 11
25 Jun 83 ALL TIME HIGH *A&M AM 007* 75 1

[1] Kris Kristofferson and Rita Coolidge

COOLIO
US, male rapper – Artis Ivey Jr (3 Albums: 27 Weeks, 10 Singles: 62 Weeks)

23 Jul 94 FANTASTIC VOYAGE *Tommy Boy TB 0617CD* $ 41 2
15 Oct 94 I REMEMBER *Tommy Boy TBXCD 635* 73 1
29 Oct 94 IT TAKES A THIEF *Tommy Boy TBCD 1083* 67 1
28 Oct 95 ★ GANGSTA'S PARADISE *Tommy Boy MCSTD 2104* [1] ■ ▲ £ $ 1 20
18 Nov 95 GANGSTA'S PARADISE *Tommy Boy TBCD 1141* 18 24
20 Jan 96 ● TOO HOT *Tommy Boy TBCD 718* 9 6
6 Apr 96 1234 (SUMPIN' NEW) *Tommy Boy TBCD 7721* 13 7
17 Aug 96 IT'S ALL THE WAY LIVE (NOW) *Tommy Boy TBCD 7731* 34 2
5 Apr 97 ● HIT EM HIGH (THE MONSTARS' ANTHEM) *Atlantic A 5449CD* [2] 8 6
7 Jun 97 THE WINNER *Atlantic A 5433CD* 53 1

29 / 31 December 1960	5 / 7 January 1961	12 / 14 January 1961	19 / 21 January 1961
I LOVE YOU Cliff Richard and The Shadows	I LOVE YOU Cliff Richard and The Shadows	POETRY IN MOTION Johnny Tillotson	POETRY IN MOTION Johnny Tillotson
SOUTH PACIFIC Soundtrack	SOUTH PACIFIC Soundtrack	G.I. BLUES (Soundtrack) Elvis Presley	G.I. BLUES (Soundtrack) Elvis Presley

KEY UK No.1 ★ UK Top 10 ● Still on chart + UK entry at No.1 ■ US No.1 ▲ UK million seller £ US million seller $ — Peak Position — Weeks

Singles re-entries are listed as (re), (2re), (3re)... which signifies that the hit re-entered the chart once, twice or three times...

19 Jul 97 ●	**C U WHEN U GET THERE** *Tommy Boy TBCD 785* [3]	3	12
13 Sep 97	MY SOUL *Tommy Boy TBCD 1180*	28	2
11 Oct 97	**OOH LA LA** *Tommy Boy TBCD 799*	14	5

[1] Coolio featuring LV [2] B Real / Busta Rhymes / Coolio / LL Cool J / Method Man [3] Coolio featuring 40 Thevz

COOPER *Holland, male production trio*

11 Jan 03	**I BELIEVE IN LOVE** *Product PDT 05CDS*	50	2

Alice COOPER (265 Top 500)

The alter ego of shock-rock vocalist Vincent Furnier, b. 4 Feb 1948, Detroit, US. A transatlantic chart-topper whose group was voted World's Top Band in 1972 in the UK. In 2001 he received a Living Legend Award from the International Horror Guild (20 Albums: 141 Weeks, 19 Singles: 104 Weeks)

5 Feb 72	KILLER *Warner Bros. K 56005*	27	18
15 Jul 72 ★	**SCHOOL'S OUT** *Warner Bros. K 16188*	1	12
22 Jul 72 ●	SCHOOL'S OUT *Warner Bros. K 56007*	4	20
9 Sep 72	LOVE IT TO DEATH *Warner Bros. K 46177*	28	7
7 Oct 72 ●	**ELECTED** *Warner Bros. K 16214*	4	10
10 Feb 73 ●	**HELLO HURRAY** *Warner Bros. K 16248*	6	12
24 Mar 73 ★	BILLION DOLLAR BABIES *Warner Bros. K 56013* ■ ▲	1	23
21 Apr 73 ●	**NO MORE MR NICE GUY** *Warner Bros. K 16262*	10	10
4 Aug 73	SCHOOL DAYS *Warner Bros. 66021*	13	8
12 Jan 74	MUSCLE OF LOVE *Warner Bros. K 56018*	34	4
19 Jan 74	**TEENAGE LAMENT '74** *Warner Bros. K 16345*	12	7
15 Mar 75	WELCOME TO MY NIGHTMARE *Anchor ANCL 2011*	19	8
24 Jul 76	ALICE COOPER GOES TO HELL *Warner Bros. K 56171*	23	7
21 May 77	**(NO MORE) LOVE AT YOUR CONVENIENCE** *Warner Bros. K 16935*	44	2
28 May 77	LACE AND WHISKY *Warner Bros. K 56365*	33	3
23 Dec 78	FROM THE INSIDE *Warner Bros. K 56577*	68	3
23 Dec 78	**HOW YOU GONNA SEE ME NOW** *Warner Bros. K 17270*	61	6
17 May 80	FLUSH THE FASHION *Warner Bros. K 56805*	56	3
12 Sep 81	SPECIAL FORCES *Warner Bros. K 56927*	96	1
6 Mar 82	**SEVEN AND SEVEN IS (LIVE VERSION)** *Warner Bros. K 17924*	62	3
8 May 82	**FOR BRITAIN ONLY / UNDER MY WHEELS** *Warner Bros. K 17940*	66	2
12 Nov 83	DADA *Warner Bros. 9239691*	93	1
18 Oct 86	**HE'S BACK (THE MAN BEHIND THE MASK)** *MCA MCA 1090*	61	2
1 Nov 86	CONSTRICTOR *MCA MCF 3341*	41	2
7 Nov 87	RAISE YOUR FIST AND YELL *MCA MCF 3392*	48	3
9 Apr 88	**FREEDOM** *MCA MCA 1241*	50	3
29 Jul 89 ●	**POISON** *Epic 655061 7*	2	11
26 Aug 89 ●	TRASH *Epic 465130 1*	2	12
7 Oct 89	**BED OF NAILS** *Epic ALICE 3*	38	5
2 Dec 89	**HOUSE OF FIRE** *Epic ALICE 4*	65	2
22 Jun 91	**HEY STOOPID** *Epic 6569837*	21	6
13 Jul 91 ●	HEY STOOPID *Epic 4684161*	4	7
5 Oct 91	**LOVE'S A LOADED GUN** *Epic 6574387*	38	3
6 Jun 92	**FEED MY FRANKENSTEIN** *Epic 6580927*	27	3
28 May 94	**LOST IN AMERICA** *Epic 6603472*	22	3
18 Jun 94 ●	THE LAST TEMPTATION *Epic 4765949*	6	5
23 Jul 94	**IT'S ME** *Epic 6605632*	34	2
24 Jun 00	BRUTAL PLANET *Eagle EAGCD 115*	38	1
10 Mar 01	THE DEFINITIVE ALICE COOPER *Rhino 8122735342*	33	5

For the first five singles and albums, 'Alice Cooper' was the name of the entire group, not just of the lead vocalist. School Days is a double re-issue of earlier albums Pretties for You and Easy Action.

Tommy COOPER

UK, male comedian / vocalist, b. 19 Mar 1923, d. 15 Apr 1984

29 Jun 61	**DON'T JUMP OFF THE ROOF DAD (re)** *Palette PG 9019*	40	3

The COOPER TEMPLE CLAUSE *UK, male vocal (Ben Gautrey) / instrumental group (2 Albums: 5 Weeks, 5 Singles: 10 Weeks)*

29 Sep 01	**LET'S KILL MUSIC** *Morning MORNING 9*	41	1
9 Feb 02	**FILM MAKER / BEEN TRAINING DOGS** *Morning MORNING 15*	20	3
23 Feb 02	SEE THIS THROUGH AND LEAVE *Morning MORNING 18*	27	3
18 May 02	**WHO NEEDS ENEMIES?** *Morning MORNING 23*	22	2
13 Sep 03	**PROMISES PROMISES** *Morning MORNING 30*	19	2
20 Sep 03 ●	KICK UP THE FIRE, AND LET THE FLAMES BREAK LOOSE *Morning MORNING 36*	5	2
22 Nov 03	**BLIND PILOTS** *Morning MORNING 38*	37	2

Julian COPE (see also The TEARDROP EXPLODES)

UK, male vocalist (10 Albums: 35 Weeks, 16 Singles: 59 Weeks)

19 Nov 83	**SUNSHINE PLAYROOM** *Mercury COPE 1*	64	1
3 Mar 84	WORLD SHUT YOUR MOUTH *Mercury MERL 37*	40	4
31 Mar 84	**THE GREATNESS AND PERFECTION OF LOVE** *Mercury MER 155*	52	5
24 Nov 84	FRIED *Mercury MERL 48*	87	1
27 Sep 86	**WORLD SHUT YOUR MOUTH** *Island IS 290*	19	8
17 Jan 87	**TRAMPOLENE** *Island IS 305*	31	6
14 Mar 87	SAINT JULIAN *Island ILPS 9861*	11	10
11 Apr 87	**EVE'S VOLCANO (COVERED IN SIN)** *Island IS 318*	41	5
24 Sep 88	**CHARLOTTE ANNE** *Island IS 380*	35	6
29 Oct 88	MY NATION UNDERGROUND *Island ILPS 9918*	42	2
21 Jan 89	**5 O'CLOCK WORLD** *Island IS 399*	42	4
24 Jun 89	**CHINA DOLL** *Island IS 406*	53	2
9 Feb 91	**BEAUTIFUL LOVE** *Island IS 483*	32	6
16 Mar 91	PEGGY SUICIDE *Island ILPSD 9977*	23	7
20 Apr 91	**EAST EASY RIDER** *Island IS 492*	51	3
3 Aug 91	**HEAD** *Island IS 497*	57	2
8 Aug 92	**WORLD SHUT YOUR MOUTH** (re-issue) *Island IS 534*	44	3
15 Aug 92	FLOORED GENIUS – THE BEST OF JULIAN COPE AND THE TEARDROP EXPLODES 1979-91 *Island CID 8000* [1]	22	3
17 Oct 92	**FEAR LOVES THIS PLACE** *Island IS 545*	42	2
31 Oct 92	JEHOVAHKILL *Island 5140522*	20	2
16 Jul 94	AUTOGEDDON *Echo ECHCD 1*	16	3
12 Aug 95	**TRY TRY TRY** *Echo ECSCD 11*	24	3
9 Sep 95	JULIAN COPE PRESENTS 20 MOTHERS *Echo ECHCD 5*	20	2
27 Jul 96	**I COME FROM ANOTHER PLANET BABY** *Echo ECSCD 22*	34	2
5 Oct 96	**PLANETARY SIT-IN (EVERY GIRL HAS YOUR NAME)** *Echo ECSCD 25*	34	1
26 Oct 96	INTERPRETER *Echo ECHCD 12*	39	1

[1] Julian Cope and The Teardrop Explodes

Imani COPPOLA (see also BAHA MEN) *US, female vocalist / producer*

28 Feb 98	**LEGEND OF A COWGIRL** *Columbia 6656015*	32	3

The CORAL *UK, male vocal (James Skelly) / instrumental group (4 Albums: 51 Weeks, 8 Singles: 35 Weeks)*

27 Jul 02	**GOODBYE** *Deltasonic DLTCD 2005*	21	2
10 Aug 02 ●	THE CORAL *Deltasonic DLTCD 006*	5	34
19 Oct 02	**DREAMING OF YOU** *Deltasonic DLTCD 2008*	13	5
15 Mar 03 ●	**DON'T THINK YOU'RE THE FIRST (re)** *Deltasonic DLTCDC 010*	10	4
26 Jul 03 ●	**PASS IT ON** *Deltasonic DLTCD 013*	5	7
9 Aug 03 ★	MAGIC AND MEDICINE *Deltasonic DLTCDPS 014* ■	1	9
18 Oct 03	**SECRET KISS** *Deltasonic DLTCD 015*	25	2
6 Dec 03	**BILL MCCAI** *Deltasonic DLTCD 017*	23	2
7 Feb 04 ●	NIGHTFREAK AND THE SONS OF BECKER *Deltasonic DLTCD 018*	5	3
21 May 05 ●	**IN THE MORNING** *Deltasonic DLTCD 2033*	6	12
4 Jun 05 ●	THE INVISIBLE INVASION *Deltasonic DLTCDLE 036*	3	5
3 Sep 05	**SOMETHING INSIDE OF ME** *Deltasonic DLTCD 2039*	41	1

Frank CORDELL and his ORCHESTRA

UK, orchestra – leader b. 1918, d. 6 Jul 1980 (2 Singles: 4 Weeks)

24 Aug 56	**SADIE'S SHAWL** *HMV POP 229*	29	2
16 Feb 61	**THE BLACK BEAR** *HMV POP 824*	44	2

26 / 28 January 1961	2 / 4 February 1961	9 / 11 February 1961	16 / 18 February 1961
UK No.1 SINGLES			
ARE YOU LONESOME TO-NIGHT? Elvis Presley with The Jordanaires	ARE YOU LONESOME TO-NIGHT? Elvis Presley with The Jordanaires	ARE YOU LONESOME TO-NIGHT? Elvis Presley with The Jordanaires	ARE YOU LONESOME TO-NIGHT? Elvis Presley with The Jordanaires
UK No.1 ALBUMS			
G.I. BLUES (Soundtrack) Elvis Presley	G.I. BLUES (Soundtrack) Elvis Presley	G.I. BLUES (Soundtrack) Elvis Presley	G.I. BLUES (Soundtrack) Elvis Presley

Louise CORDET *UK, female vocalist – Louise Boisot*

5 Jul 62	**I'M JUST A BABY** *Decca F 11476*	**13**	13

CORDUROY *UK, male vocal / instrumental group*

8 Oct 94	OUT OF HERE *Acid Jazz JAZIDCD 107*	73	1

Billy CORGAN NEW
(see also The SMASHING PUMPKINS; ZWAN) *UK, male vocalist / guitarist*

18 Jun 05	**WALKING SHADE** *Reprise W 673DVD*	**74**	1

Chris CORNELL (see also SOUNDGARDEN) *US, male vocalist*

2 Oct 99	EUPHORIA MORNING *A&M 4904222*	31	1
23 Oct 99	**CAN'T CHANGE ME** *A&M 4971732*	**62**	1

Don CORNELL *US, male vocalist – Luigi Varlaro, b. 21 Apr 1919, d. 23 Feb 2004 (2 Singles: 23 Weeks)*

3 Sep 54 ★	**HOLD MY HAND** *Vogue Q 2013* $	**1**	21
22 Apr 55	**STRANGER IN PARADISE** *Vogue Q 72073*	**19**	2

Lynn CORNELL (see also The PEARLS) *UK, female vocalist*

20 Oct 60	**NEVER ON SUNDAY** *Decca F 11277*	**30**	9

CORNERSHOP *UK, male vocal (Tjinder Singh) / instrumental duo (2 Albums: 18 Weeks, 5 Singles: 19 Weeks)*

30 Aug 97	**BRIMFUL OF ASHA** *Wiiija WIJ 75CD*	**60**	1
20 Sep 97	WHEN I WAS BORN FOR THE 7TH TIME *Wiiija WIJCD 1065*	17	15
28 Feb 98 ★	**BRIMFUL OF ASHA** (re-mix) *Wiiija WIJ 81CD* ■	**1**	12
16 May 98	**SLEEP ON THE LEFT SIDE** *Wiiija WIJ 80CD*	**23**	3
16 Mar 02	**LESSONS LEARNED FROM ROCKY I TO ROCKY III** *Wiiija WIJ 129CD*	**37**	2
13 Apr 02	HANDCREAM FOR A GENERATION *Wiiija WIJCD 1115*	30	3
7 Aug 04	**TOPKNOT** *Rough Trade RTRADSCD 168* [1]	**53**	1

[1] Cornershop presents Bubbley Kaur

Hugh CORNWELL (see also The STRANGLERS) *UK, male vocalist / guitarist (1 Album: 1 Week, 3 Singles: 4 Weeks)*

24 Jan 87	**FACTS + FIGURES** *Virgin VS 922*	**61**	2
7 May 88	**ANOTHER KIND OF LOVE** *Virgin VS 945*	**71**	1
18 Jun 88	WOLF *Virgin V 2420*	98	1
12 Feb 05	**SPELL (UNDER HER)** *Track TRACK 0013B*	**62**	1

CORO DE MUNJES DEL MONASTERIO BENEDICTINO DE SANTO DOMINGO DE SILOS
(see also MONKS CHORUS SILOS) *Spain, monastic choir (2 Albums: 28 Weeks)*

5 Mar 94 ●	CANTO GREGORIANO *EMI Classics CMS 5652172*	7	25
17 Dec 94	CANTO NOEL *EMI Classics CDC 5552172*	53	3

CO-RO featuring TARLISA
Germany, male / female vocal / production group

12 Dec 92	**BECAUSE THE NIGHT** *ZYX ZYX 68227*	**61**	1

CORONA *Brazil, male producer and female vocalist – Francesco Bontempi and Olga de Souza (1 Album: 7 Weeks, 5 Singles: 44 Weeks)*

10 Sep 94 ●	**THE RHYTHM OF THE NIGHT (re)** *WEA YZ 837CD1*	**2**	18
8 Apr 95 ●	**BABY BABY** *Eternal YZ 919CD*	**5**	8
20 May 95	THE RHYTHM OF THE NIGHT *Eternal 0630103312*	18	7
22 Jul 95 ●	**TRY ME OUT** *Eternal YZ 955CD*	**6**	10
23 Dec 95	**I DON'T WANNA BE A STAR** *Eternal WEA 029CD*	**22**	6
22 Feb 97	**MEGAMIX** *Eternal WEA 092CD*	**36**	2

CORONATION STREET CAST featuring Bill WADDINGTON *UK, male / female actors and male actor / vocalist, b. 10 Jun 1916, d. 11 Sep 2000*

16 Dec 95	**ALWAYS LOOK ON THE BRIGHT SIDE OF LIFE** *EMI Premier CDEMS 411*	**35**	3

The listed flip side of 'Always Look on the Bright Side of Life' was 'Something Stupid' by Amanda Barrie and Johnny Briggs.

MOST No.1 ALBUMS

THE OFFICIAL UK ALBUM CHART 50 YEARS

The Fab Four are clear leaders in this list of chart-toppers, which is made up of acts with six No.1s or more.

15 THE BEATLES

10 ELVIS PRESLEY
10 THE ROLLING STONES

9 ABBA
9 MADONNA
9 QUEEN
9 U2

8 DAVID BOWIE
8 MICHAEL JACKSON
8 LED ZEPPELIN

7 PAUL McCARTNEY
7 R.E.M.
7 CLIFF RICHARD
7 THE SHADOWS
7 ROD STEWART
7 ROBBIE WILLIAMS

6 BOB DYLAN
6 GENESIS
6 ELTON JOHN
6 OASIS
6 THE POLICE
6 BRUCE SPRINGSTEEN

Robbie Williams holds the record for the fastest UK solo act to achieve seven No.1 albums. His solo seven have come in an eight-year period, preceded by an extra three No.1s with Take That.

23 / 25 February 1961	2 / 4 March 1961	9 / 11 March 1961	16 / 18 March 1961
SAILOR Petula Clark	**WALK RIGHT BACK / EBONY EYES** The Everly Brothers	**WALK RIGHT BACK / EBONY EYES** The Everly Brothers	**WALK RIGHT BACK / EBONY EYES** The Everly Brothers
G.I. BLUES (Soundtrack) Elvis Presley	**SOUTH PACIFIC** Soundtrack	**G.I. BLUES (Soundtrack)** Elvis Presley	**G.I. BLUES (Soundtrack)** Elvis Presley

KEY UK No.1 ★ UK Top 10 ● Still on chart + UK entry at No.1 ■ US No.1 ▲ UK million seller £ US million seller $
Singles re-entries are listed as (re), (2re), (3re)… which signifies that the hit re-entered the chart once, twice or three times… Peak Position / Weeks

The CORONETS *UK, male / female vocal group (2 Singles: 7 Weeks)*

26 Aug 55 **THAT'S HOW A LOVE SONG WAS BORN** *Columbia DB 3640* [1] ... 14 6
25 Nov 55 **TWENTY TINY FINGERS** *Columbia DB 3671* ... 20 1

[1] Ray Burns with The Coronets

The CORRIES *UK, male vocal / instrumental duo – Ronnie Browne and Roy Williamson (2 Albums: 5 Weeks)*

9 May 70 SCOTTISH LOVE SONGS *Fontana 6309004* ... 46 4
16 Sep 72 SOUND OF PIBROCH *Columbia SCX 6511* ... 39 1

Briana CORRIGAN (see also The BEAUTIFUL SOUTH) *UK, female vocalist*

11 May 96 **LOVE ME NOW** *East West EW 041CD1* ... 48 2

CORROSION OF CONFORMITY *US, male vocal / instrumental group*

14 Sep 96 WISEBLOOD *Columbia 4843282* ... 43 1

The CORRS (87 Top 500)
Internationally successful Irish sisters and brother group: Andrea, Caroline, Sharon and Jim Corr. The quartet, who have sold more than five million albums in the UK, was voted Best International Group at the 1999 BRITs and were awarded honorary MBE's. Talk on Corners was the best-selling UK album in 1998 (7 Albums: 367 Weeks, 19 Singles: 108 Weeks)

17 Feb 96 **RUNAWAY (re)** *Atlantic A 5727CD* ... 49 3
2 Mar 96 ● FORGIVEN NOT FORGOTTEN *Atlantic 7567926122* ... 2 113
1 Feb 97 **LOVE TO LOVE YOU / RUNAWAY** (re-issue) *Atlantic A 5621CD* ... 62 1
25 Oct 97 **ONLY WHEN I SLEEP** *Atlantic AT 0015CD* ... 58 1
1 Nov 97 ★ TALK ON CORNERS *Atlantic 7567830512* ... 1 142
20 Dec 97 **I NEVER LOVED YOU ANYWAY** *Atlantic AT 0018CD* ... 43 2
28 Mar 98 **WHAT CAN I DO** *Atlantic AT 0029CD* ... 53 1
16 May 98 ● **DREAMS** *Atlantic AT 0032CD* ... 6 10
29 Aug 98 ● **WHAT CAN I DO** (re-mix) *Atlantic AT 0044CD* ... 3 11
28 Nov 98 ● **SO YOUNG** *Atlantic AT 0057CD1* ... 6 13
27 Feb 99 ● **RUNAWAY** (re-mix) *Atlantic AT 0062CD* ... 2 11
12 Jun 99 **I KNOW MY LOVE** *RCA Victor 74321670622* [1] ... 37 3
27 Nov 99 ● UNPLUGGED *Atlantic 7567809862* ... 7 26
11 Dec 99 **RADIO** *Atlantic AT 0079CD* ... 18 9
15 Jul 00 ★ **BREATHLESS** *Atlantic AT 0084CD* ■ ... 1 13
29 Jul 00 ★ IN BLUE *Atlantic 7567833522* ■ ... 1 45
11 Nov 00 **IRRESISTIBLE (re)** *Atlantic AT 0089CD* ... 20 7
28 Apr 01 **GIVE ME A REASON** *Atlantic AT 0097CD* ... 27 2
10 Nov 01 **WOULD YOU BE HAPPIER?** *Atlantic AT 0115CD* ... 14 5
17 Nov 01 ● THE BEST OF THE CORRS *Atlantic 7567930732* ... 6 21
29 May 04 ● **SUMMER SUNSHINE** *Atlantic AT 0179CD1* ... 6 8
12 Jun 04 ● BORROWED HEAVEN *Atlantic 7567932432* ... 2 14
25 Sep 04 **ANGEL** *Atlantic AT 0182CD2* ... 16 4
18 Dec 04 **LONG NIGHT** *Atlantic AT 0190CD* ... 31 3
8 Oct 05 HOME *Atlantic 5101102932* ... 14 6
5 Nov 05 **HEART LIKE A WHEEL / OLD TOWN** *Atlantic ATUK 016CD* ... 68 1

[1] The Chieftains featuring The Corrs

CORRUPTED CRU featuring MC NEAT
(see also Scott GARCIA featuring MC STYLES) *UK, male rap / production duo – Scott Garcia and Michael Wood and male rapper*

2 Mar 02 **G.A.R.A.G.E.** *Red Rose CDRROSE 011* ... 59 1

Ferry CORSTEN
(see also ALBION; GOURYELLA; MOONMAN; STARPARTY; SYSTEM F; VERACOCHA) *Holland, male producer (3 Singles: 11 Weeks)*

8 Jun 02 **PUNK** *Positiva CDTIV 173* ... 29 3
21 Feb 04 **ROCK YOUR BODY ROCK (re)** *Positiva CDTIV 202* ... 11 6
10 Jul 04 **IT'S TIME** *Positiva CDTIVS 206* ... 51 2

CORTINA *UK, male producer – Ben Keen (2 Singles: 3 Weeks)*

24 Mar 01 **MUSIC IS MOVING** *Nukleuz NUKC 0159* ... 42 2
26 Jan 02 **ERECTION (TAKE IT TO THE TOP)** *Nukleuz NUKC 0352* [1] ... 48 1

[1] Cortina featuring BK and Madam Friction

Vladimir COSMA *Hungary, orchestra*

14 Jul 79 **DAVID'S SONG (MAIN THEME FROM 'KIDNAPPED')** *Decca FR 13841* ... 64 1

COSMIC BABY *Germany, male producer*

26 Feb 94 **LOOPS OF INFINITY** *Logic 74321191432* ... 70 1
23 Apr 94 THINKING ABOUT MYSELF *Logic 74321196052* ... 60 1

COSMIC GATE *Germany, male production trio (3 Singles: 12 Weeks)*

4 Aug 01 ● **FIRE WIRE** *Data DATA 24CDS* ... 9 7
11 May 02 **EXPLORATION OF SPACE** *Data DATA 30CDS* ... 29 3
25 Jan 03 **THE WAVE / RAGING** *Nebula NEBCD 036* ... 48 2

COSMIC ROUGH RIDERS
UK, male vocal / instrumental group (4 Singles: 4 Weeks)

4 Aug 01 **REVOLUTION (IN THE SUMMERTIME)** *Poptones MC 5047SCD* ... 35 1
29 Sep 01 **THE PAIN INSIDE** *Poptones MC 5052SCD* ... 36 1
5 Jul 03 **BECAUSE YOU** *Measured MRCOSMIC 2SC* ... 34 1
20 Sep 03 **JUSTIFY THE RAIN** *Measured MRCOSMIC 3SCD* ... 39 1

COSMOS (see also GLOBAL COMMUNICATION)
UK, male producer / instrumentalist – Tom Middleton (2 Singles: 3 Weeks)

18 Sep 99 **SUMMER IN SPACE** *Island Blue PFACD 3* ... 49 1
5 Oct 02 **TAKE ME WITH YOU** *Polydor 659952* ... 32 2

Don COSTA *US, orchestra – leader b. 10 Jun 1925, d. 19 Jan 1983*

13 Oct 60 **NEVER ON SUNDAY (re)** *London HLT 9195* ... 27 10

Nikka COSTA *US, female vocalist*

11 Aug 01 **LIKE A FEATHER** *Virgin VUSCD 199* ... 53 1

Elvis COSTELLO (115 Top 500)
ASCAP (US songwriter's body) Founders Award winner in 2003, b. Declan MacManus, 25 Aug 1954, Paddington, UK. He emerged during the punk explosion of 1976, but was soon accepted as a mainstream artist. Has clocked up 14 US Top 40 albums (27 Albums: 228 Weeks, 36 Singles: 180 Weeks)

6 Aug 77 MY AIM IS TRUE *Stiff SEEZ 3* ... 14 12
5 Nov 77 **WATCHING THE DETECTIVES** *Stiff BUY 20* ... 15 11
11 Mar 78 **(I DON'T WANT TO GO TO) CHELSEA** *Radar ADA 3* [1] ... 16 10
1 Apr 78 ● THIS YEAR'S MODEL *Radar RAD 3* [1] ... 4 14
13 May 78 **PUMP IT UP** *Radar ADA 10* [1] ... 24 10
28 Oct 78 **RADIO RADIO** *Radar ADA 24* [1] ... 29 7
20 Jan 79 ● ARMED FORCES *Radar RAD 14* [1] ... 2 28
10 Feb 79 ● **OLIVER'S ARMY** *Radar ADA 31* [1] ... 2 12
12 May 79 **ACCIDENTS WILL HAPPEN** *Radar ADA 35* [1] ... 28 8
16 Feb 80 ● **I CAN'T STAND UP FOR FALLING DOWN** *F-Beat XX 1* [1] ... 4 8
23 Feb 80 ● GET HAPPY!! *F. Beat XXLP 1* ... 2 14
12 Apr 80 **HIGH FIDELITY** *F-Beat XX 3* ... 30 5
7 Jun 80 **NEW AMSTERDAM** *F-Beat XX 5* ... 36 6
20 Dec 80 **CLUBLAND** *F-Beat XX 12* [1] ... 60 4
31 Jan 81 ● TRUST *F. Beat XXLP 11* [1] ... 9 7
3 Oct 81 ● **A GOOD YEAR FOR THE ROSES** *F-Beat XX 17* ... 6 11
31 Oct 81 ● ALMOST BLUE *F. Beat XXLP 13* ... 7 18
12 Dec 81 **SWEET DREAMS** *F-Beat XX 19* ... 42 8
10 Apr 82 **I'M YOUR TOY** *F-Beat XX 21* [2] ... 51 3
19 Jun 82 **YOU LITTLE FOOL** *F-Beat XX 26* ... 52 3
10 Jul 82 ● IMPERIAL BEDROOM *F. Beat XXLP 17* [1] ... 6 12

23 / 25 March 1961	30 March / 1 April 1961	6 / 8 April 1961	13 / 15 April 1961
UK No.1 SINGLES			
WOODEN HEART Elvis Presley	WOODEN HEART Elvis Presley	WOODEN HEART Elvis Presley	WOODEN HEART Elvis Presley
UK No.1 ALBUMS			
G.I. BLUES (Soundtrack) Elvis Presley	SOUTH PACIFIC Soundtrack	G.I. BLUES (Soundtrack) Elvis Presley	G.I. BLUES (Soundtrack) Elvis Presley

31 Jul 82	**MAN OUT OF TIME** *F-Beat XX 28*	58	2
25 Sep 82	**FROM HEAD TO TOE** *F-Beat XX 30*	43	4
11 Dec 82	**PARTY PARTY** *A&M AMS 8267* [3]	48	6
11 Jun 83	**PILLS AND SOAP** *Imp IMP 001* [4]	16	4
9 Jul 83	**EVERYDAY I WRITE THE BOOK** *F-Beat XX 32*	28	8
6 Aug 83 ●	PUNCH THE CLOCK *F. Beat XXLP 19* [1]	3	13
17 Sep 83	**LET THEM ALL TALK** *F-Beat XX 33*	59	2
28 Apr 84	**PEACE IN OUR TIME** *Imposter TRUCE 1* [4]	48	3
16 Jun 84	**I WANNA BE LOVED / TURNING THE TOWN RED** *F-Beat XX 35*	25	6
7 Jul 84 ●	GOODBYE CRUEL WORLD *F. Beat ZL 70317* [1]	10	10
25 Aug 84	**THE ONLY FLAME IN TOWN** *F-Beat XX 37*	71	2
20 Apr 85 ●	THE BEST OF ELVIS COSTELLO – THE MAN *Telstar STAR 2247* [1]	8	25
4 May 85	**GREEN SHIRT (re)** *F-Beat ZB 40085*	68	2
1 Feb 86	**DON'T LET ME BE MISUNDERSTOOD** *F-Beat ZB 40555* [5]	33	4
1 Mar 86	KING OF AMERICA *F. Beat ZL 70496* [2]	11	9
30 Aug 86	**TOKYO STORM WARNING** *Imp IMP 007*	73	1
27 Sep 86	BLOOD AND CHOCOLATE *Imp XFIEND 80*	16	5
18 Feb 89 ●	SPIKE *Warner Bros. WX 238*	5	16
4 Mar 89	**VERONICA** *Warner Bros. W 7558*	31	6
20 May 89	**BABY PLAYS AROUND (EP)** *Warner Bros. W 2949*	65	1
28 Oct 89	GIRLS GIRLS GIRLS *Demon DFIEND 160* [1]	67	1
4 May 91	**THE OTHER SIDE OF SUMMER** *Warner Bros. W 0025*	43	4
25 May 91 ●	MIGHTY LIKE A ROSE *Warner Bros. WX 419*	5	6
30 Jan 93	THE JULIET LETTERS *Warner Bros. 9362451802* [3]	18	3
5 Mar 94	**SULKY GIRL** *Warner Bros. W 0234CD*	22	3
19 Mar 94 ●	BRUTAL YOUTH *Warner Bros. 9362455352* [1]	2	5
30 Apr 94	**13 STEPS LEAD DOWN** *Warner Bros. W 0245CD*	59	1
12 Nov 94	THE VERY BEST OF ELVIS COSTELLO AND THE ATTRACTIONS *Demon DPAM 13* [1]	57	2
26 Nov 94	**LONDON'S BRILLIANT PARADE (EP)** *Warner Bros. W 0270CD1* [1]	48	2
27 May 95	KOJAK VARIETY *Warner Bros. 9362459032*	21	2
12 Aug 95	KING OF AMERICA (re-issue) *Demon DPAM 11*	71	1
11 May 96	**IT'S TIME** *Warner Bros. W 0348CD* [1]	58	1
25 May 96	ALL THIS USELESS BEAUTY *Warner Bros. 9362461982*	28	3
10 Oct 98	PAINTED FROM MEMORY *Mercury 5380022* [4]	32	2
1 May 99	**TOLEDO** *Mercury 8709652* [6]	72	1
31 Jul 99	**SHE (re)** *Mercury MERCD 521*	19	10
14 Aug 99 ●	THE VERY BEST OF ELVIS COSTELLO *Universal Music TV 5464902*	4	13
31 Mar 01	FOR THE STARS *Deutsche Grammophon 4695302* [5]	67	1
20 Apr 02	**TEAR OFF YOUR OWN HEAD (IT'S A DOLL REVOLUTION)** *Mercury 5828872*	58	1
27 Apr 02	WHEN I WAS CRUEL *Mercury 5868292*	17	4
27 Sep 03	NORTH *Deutsche Grammophon 9809656*	44	1
2 Oct 04	THE DELIVERY MAN *Lost Highway 9863727* [6]	73	1

[1] Elvis Costello and the Attractions [2] Elvis Costello and the Attractions with the Royal Philharmonic Orchestra [3] Elvis Costello and the Attractions with the Royal Horn Guards [4] Imposter [5] The Costello Show featuring The Confederates [6] Elvis Costello / Burt Bacharach [1] Elvis Costello and the Attractions [2] Costello Show [3] Elvis Costello and the Brodsky Quartet [4] Elvis Costello with Burt Bacharach [5] Anne von Otter Meets Elvis Costello [6] Elvis Costello & The Imposters

Tracks on Baby Plays Around (EP): Baby Plays Around / Poisoned Rose / Almost Blue / My Funny Valentine. Tracks on London's Brilliant Parade (EP): London's Brilliant Parade / Sweet Dreams / The Loved Ones / From Head To Toe

Billy COTTON and his BAND *UK, male bandleader / vocalist, b. 6 May 1899, d. 25 Mar 1969, with band and chorus (3 Singles: 25 Weeks)*

1 May 53 ●	**IN A GOLDEN COACH (THERE'S A HEART OF GOLD)** *Decca F 10058* [1]	3	10
18 Dec 53	**I SAW MOMMY KISSING SANTA CLAUS** *Decca F 10206* [2]	11	3
30 Apr 54 ●	**FRIENDS AND NEIGHBOURS (re)** *Decca F 10299* [3]	3	12

[1] Billy Cotton and his Band, vocals by Doreen Stephens [2] Billy Cotton and his Band, vocals by the Mill Girls and the Bandits [3] Billy Cotton and his Band, vocals by the Bandits

Mike COTTON'S JAZZMEN
UK, male instrumental band – leader Mike Cotton – trumpet

20 Jun 63	**SWING THAT HAMMER** *Columbia DB 7029*	36	4

The COUGARS *UK, male instrumental group*

28 Feb 63	**SATURDAY NITE AT THE DUCK-POND** *Parlophone R 4989*	33	8

Phil COULTER
Ireland, male orchestra leader / pianist (2 Albums: 15 Weeks)

13 Oct 84	SEA OF TRANQUILITY *K-Tel Ireland KLP 185*	46	14
18 May 85	PHIL COULTER'S IRELAND *K-Tel ONE 1296*	86	1

COUNCIL COLLECTIVE
UK / US, male / female vocal / instrumental group

22 Dec 84	**SOUL DEEP (PART 1)** *Polydor MINE 1*	24	6

COUNT INDIGO *UK, male vocalist – Bruce Marcus*

9 Mar 96	**MY UNKNOWN LOVE** *Cowboy RODEO 952CD*	59	1

COUNTING CROWS *US, male vocal (Adam Duritz) / instrumental group (6 Albums: 65 Weeks, 12 Singles: 29 Weeks)*

12 Mar 94	AUGUST AND EVERYTHING AFTER *Geffen GED 24528*	16	38
30 Apr 94	**MR JONES** *Geffen GFSTD 69*	28	2
9 Jul 94	**ROUND HERE** *Geffen GFSTD 74*	70	1
15 Oct 94	**RAIN KING** *Geffen GFSTD 82*	49	3
19 Oct 96	**ANGELS OF THE SILENCES** *Geffen GFSTD 22182*	41	1
26 Oct 96 ●	RECOVERING THE SATELLITES *Geffen GED 24975* ▲	4	4
14 Dec 96	**A LONG DECEMBER (re)** *Geffen GFSTD 22190*	62	2
31 May 97	**DAYLIGHT FADING** *Geffen GFSTD 22247*	54	1
25 Jul 98	ACROSS A WIRE – LIVE IN NEW YORK *Geffen GED 25226*	27	4
30 Oct 99	**HANGINAROUND** *Geffen 4971842*	46	1
13 Nov 99	THIS DESERT LIFE *Geffen 4904152*	19	3
29 Jun 02	**AMERICAN GIRLS** *Geffen 4977402*	33	2
20 Jul 02 ●	HARD CANDY *Geffen 4933662*	9	11
15 Feb 03	**BIG YELLOW TAXI** *Geffen 4978302* [1]	16	9
21 Jun 03	**IF I COULD GIVE ALL MY LOVE** *Geffen GED 9806830*	50	1
7 Feb 04	FILMS ABOUT GHOSTS – THE BEST OF ... *Geffen / Polydor 9861505*	15	5
27 Mar 04	**HANGINAROUND (re-recording)** *Geffen 9861994*	68	1
24 Jul 04	**ACCIDENTALLY IN LOVE** *Dreamworks 9862881*	28	5

[1] Counting Crows featuring Vanessa Carlton

The COUNTRYMEN *UK, male vocal group*

3 May 62	**I KNOW WHERE I'M GOING** *Piccadilly 7N 35029*	45	2

COURSE
Holland, male / female vocal / DJ / production group (3 Singles: 15 Weeks)

19 Apr 97 ●	**READY OR NOT** *The Brothers Organisation CDBRUV 2*	5	7
5 Jul 97 ●	**AIN'T NOBODY** *The Brothers Organisation CDBRUV 3*	8	6
20 Dec 97	**BEST LOVE** *The Brothers Organisation CDBRUV 6*	51	2

Tina COUSINS *UK, female vocalist (1 Album: 1 Week, 8 Singles: 43 Weeks)*

15 Aug 98 ●	**MYSTERIOUS TIMES** *Multiply CDMULTY 40* [1]	2	12
21 Nov 98	**PRAY** *Jive 0519162*	20	3
27 Mar 99	**KILLIN' TIME** *Jive / Eastern Bloc 0519232*	15	4
10 Apr 99 ●	**THANK ABBA FOR THE MUSIC** *ABCD 1 Epic* [2]	4	13
10 Jul 99	**FOREVER** *Jive 0519332*	45	2
24 Jul 99	KILLING TIME *Jive / Eastern Bloc 519342*	50	1
9 Oct 99	**ANGEL** *Ebul / Jive 0519432*	46	1
22 Apr 00 ●	**JUST AROUND THE HILL** *Multiply CDMULTY 62* [1]	8	7
10 Dec 05	**WONDERFUL LIFE** *All Around the World CDGLOBE 472*	58	1

[1] Sash! featuring Tina Cousins [2] Steps, Tina Cousins, Cleopatra, B*Witched, Billie

Don COVAY *US, male vocalist*

7 Sep 74	**IT'S BETTER TO HAVE (AND DON'T NEED)** *Mercury 6052 634*	29	6

20 / 22 April 1961	27 / 29 April 1961	4 / 6 May 1961	11 / 13 May 1961
WOODEN HEART Elvis Presley	WOODEN HEART Elvis Presley	BLUE MOON The Marcels	BLUE MOON The Marcels
G.I. BLUES (Soundtrack) Elvis Presley	G.I. BLUES (Soundtrack) Elvis Presley	G.I. BLUES (Soundtrack) Elvis Presley	G.I. BLUES (Soundtrack) Elvis Presley

KEY UK No.1 ★ UK Top 10 ● Still on chart + UK entry at No.1 ■ US No.1 ▲ UK million seller £ US million seller $
Singles re-entries are listed as (re), (2re), (3re)... which signifies that the hit re-entered the chart once, twice or three times...
Peak Position / Weeks

COVENTRY CITY CUP FINAL SQUAD *UK, male football team vocalists*

23 May 87 **GO FOR IT!** *Sky Blue SKB 1* 61 2

The COVER GIRLS *US, female vocal group*

1 Aug 92 **WISHING ON A STAR** *Epic 6581437* 38 4

David COVERDALE (see also COVERDALE PAGE; DEEP PURPLE; WHITESNAKE) *UK, male vocalist (2 Albums: 2 Weeks, 1 Single: 1 Week)*

27 Feb 82 NORTHWINDS *Purple TTS 3513* 78 1
7 Jun 97 **TOO MANY TEARS** *EMI CDEM 471* [1] 46 1
7 Oct 00 INTO THE LIGHT *EMI 5281242* 75 1

[1] David Coverdale and Whitesnake

COVERDALE PAGE *UK, male vocal / instrumental duo – David Coverdale and Jimmy Page (1 Album: 8 Weeks, 2 Singles: 3 Weeks)*

27 Mar 93 ● COVERDALE PAGE *EMI CDEMD 1041* 4 8
3 Jul 93 **TAKE ME FOR A LITTLE WHILE** *EMI CDEM 270* 29 2
23 Oct 93 **TAKE A LOOK AT YOURSELF** *EMI CDEM 279* 43 1

Julie COVINGTON *UK, female actor / vocalist (3 Singles: 35 Weeks)*

25 Dec 76 ★ **DON'T CRY FOR ME ARGENTINA (re)** *MCA 260* 1 18
21 May 77 ● **OK?** *Polydor 2001 714* [1] 10 6
3 Dec 77 **ONLY WOMEN BLEED** *Virgin VS 196* 12 11

[1] Julie Covington, Rula Lenska, Charlotte Cornwell and Sue Jones-Davies

COWBOY JUNKIES *US, male / female vocal / instrumental group (2 Albums: 7 Weeks)*

24 Mar 90 THE CAUTION HORSES *RCA PL 90450* 33 4
15 Feb 92 BLACK EYED MAN *RCA PD 90620* 21 3

Carl COX *UK, male producer (1 Album: 4 Weeks, 7 Singles: 19 Weeks)*

28 Sep 91 **I WANT YOU (FOREVER)** *Perfecto PB 44885* [1] 23 7
8 Aug 92 **DOES IT FEEL GOOD TO YOU** *Perfecto PB 74321102877* [1] 35 3
6 Nov 93 **THE PLANET OF LOVE** *Perfecto 74321161772* [2] 44 2
9 Mar 96 **TWO PAINTINGS AND A DRUM (EP)** *Edel 0090715 COX* 24 2
8 Jun 96 **SENSUAL SOPHIS-TI-CAT / THE PLAYER** *Ultimatum 0090875 COX* 25 2
15 Jun 96 AT THE END OF THE CLICHÉ *Ultimatum 0090752 COX* 23 4
12 Dec 98 **THE LATIN THEME** *Edel 0091685 COX* 52 1
22 May 99 **PHUTURE 2000** *Worldwide Ultimatum / Edel 0091715 COX* 40 2

[1] DJ Carl Cox [2] Carl Cox Concept

Tracks on Two Paintings and a Drum (EP): Phoebus Apollo / Yum Yum / Siberian Snow Storm.

Deborah COX *Canada, female vocalist (4 Singles: 8 Weeks)*

11 Nov 95 **SENTIMENTAL** *Arista 74321324962* 34 3
24 Feb 96 **WHO DO U LOVE** *Arista 74321337942* 31 3
31 Jul 99 **IT'S OVER NOW** *Arista 74321686942* 49 1
9 Oct 99 **NOBODY'S SUPPOSED TO BE HERE** *Arista 74321702102* $ 55 1

Michael COX *UK, male vocalist (2 Singles: 15 Weeks)*

9 Jun 60 ● **ANGELA JONES** *Triumph RGM 1011* 7 13
20 Oct 60 **ALONG CAME CAROLINE** *HMV POP 789* 41 2

Peter COX (see also GO WEST) *UK, male vocalist (1 Album: 1 Week, 3 Singles: 6 Weeks)*

2 Aug 97 **AIN'T GONNA CRY AGAIN** *Chrysalis CDCHS 5056* 37 2
15 Nov 97 **IF YOU WALK AWAY** *Chrysalis CDCHSS 5069* 24 2
29 Nov 97 PETER COX *Chrysalis CDCHR 6130* 64 1
20 Jun 98 **WHAT A FOOL BELIEVES** *Chrysalis CDCHS 5089* 39 2

Graham COXON (see also BLUR) *UK, male vocalist / guitarist (2 Albums: 5 Weeks, 4 Singles: 9 Weeks)*

22 Aug 98 THE SKY IS TOO HIGH *Transcopic TRAN 005CD* 31 2
20 Mar 04 **FREAKIN' OUT** *Transcopic R 6632* 37 1
15 May 04 **BITTERSWEET BUNDLE OF MISERY** *Transcopic CDRS 6637* 22 3
29 May 04 HAPPINESS IN MAGAZINES *Transcopic / Parlophone 5775192* 19 3
7 Aug 04 **SPECTACULAR** *Transcopic CDRS 6643* 32 2
6 Nov 04 **FREAKIN' OUT (re-issue) / ALL OVER ME** *Transcopic CDRS 6652* 19 3

CRACKER *US, male vocal / instrumental group (1 Album: 2 Weeks, 2 Singles: 9 Weeks)*

28 May 94 **LOW (re)** *Virgin America VUSDG 80* 43 6
25 Jun 94 KEROSENE HAT *Virgin America CDVUS 67* 44 2
23 Jul 94 **GET OFF THIS** *Virgin America VUSCD 83* 41 3

Sarah CRACKNELL (see also SAINT ETIENNE) *UK, female vocalist*

14 Sep 96 **ANYMORE** *Gut CDGUT 3* 39 1

CRACKOUT *UK, male vocal / instrumental group (3 Singles: 3 Weeks)*

22 Jun 02 **I AM THE ONE** *Hut / Virgin HUTCD 156* 72 1
9 Aug 03 **OUT OF OUR MINDS** *Hut / Virgin HUTCD 170* 63 1
13 Mar 04 **THIS IS WHAT WE DO** *Hut / Virgin HUTCD 174* 65 1

CRADLE OF FILTH *UK, male vocal / instrumental group (4 Albums: 4 Weeks, 1 Single: 2 Weeks)*

16 May 98 CRUELTY AND THE BEAST *Music for Nations CDMFN 242* 48 1
11 Nov 00 MIDIAN *Music for Nations CDMFN 666* 63 1
30 Jun 01 BITTER SUITES TO SUCCUBI *Snapper Music COF 001CD* 63 1
15 Mar 03 **BABALON A.D. (SO GLAD FOR THE MADNESS)** *Epic 6735549* 35 2
22 Mar 03 DAMNATION AND A DAY *Epic 5109632* 44 1

'Babalon A.D. (So Glad for the Madness)' was the first DVD-only single to reach the Top 40.

CRAIG *UK, male vocalist – Craig Phillips*

23 Dec 00 **AT THIS TIME OF YEAR (re)** *WEA WEA 321CD* 14 6

Floyd CRAMER *US, male pianist, b. 27 Oct 1933, d. 31 Dec 1997 (3 Singles: 24 Weeks)*

13 Apr 61 ★ **ON THE REBOUND** *RCA 1231* 1 14
20 Jul 61 **SAN ANTONIO ROSE** *RCA 1241* 36 8
23 Aug 62 **HOT PEPPER** *RCA 1301* 46 2

The CRAMPS *US, male / female vocal / instrumental group (4 Albums: 13 Weeks, 2 Singles: 4 Weeks)*

25 Jun 83 OFF THE BONE *Illegal ILP 012* 44 4
26 Nov 83 SMELL OF FEMALE *Big Beat NED 6* 74 2
9 Nov 85 **CAN YOUR PUSSY DO THE DOG?** *Big Beat NS 110* 68 1
1 Mar 86 A DATE WITH ELVIS *Big Beat WIKA 46* 34 6
10 Feb 90 **BIKINI GIRLS WITH MACHINE GUNS** *Enigma ENV 17* 35 3
24 Feb 90 STAY SICK! *Enigma ENVLP 1001* 62 1

The CRANBERRIES (274 Top 500)

Irish rock quartet with a feverish international following, formed in County Limerick in 1991 and fronted by Dolores O'Riordan (v). The group, who have sold over 40 million albums worldwide, spent longer on the UK charts in 1995 (96 weeks) than any other act (6 Albums: 193 Weeks, 11 Singles: 50 Weeks)

27 Feb 93 **LINGER** *Island CID 556* 74 1
13 Mar 93 ★ EVERYBODY ELSE IS DOING IT SO WHY CAN'T WE? *Island CID 8003* 1 86

18 / 20 May 1961	25 / 27 May 1961	1 / 3 June 1961	8 / 10 June 1961
UK No.1 SINGLES			
ON THE REBOUND Floyd Cramer	YOU'RE DRIVING ME CRAZY The Temperance Seven	SURRENDER Elvis Presley with The Jordanaires	SURRENDER Elvis Presley with The Jordanaires
UK No.1 ALBUMS			
G.I. BLUES (Soundtrack) Elvis Presley	G.I. BLUES (Soundtrack) Elvis Presley	G.I. BLUES (Soundtrack) Elvis Presley	G.I. BLUES (Soundtrack) Elvis Presley

12 Feb 94 **LINGER** (re-issue) *Island CID 559* **14** 11
7 May 94 **DREAMS** *Island CIDX 594* **27** 5
1 Oct 94 **ZOMBIE** *Island CID 600* **14** 6
15 Oct 94 ● NO NEED TO ARGUE *Island CID 8029* 2 78
3 Dec 94 **ODE TO MY FAMILY** *Island CIDX 601* **26** 6
11 Mar 95 **I CAN'T BE WITH YOU** *Island CID 605* **23** 5
12 Aug 95 **RIDICULOUS THOUGHTS** *Island CID 616* **20** 3
20 Apr 96 **SALVATION** *Island CID 633* **13** 5
11 May 96 ● TO THE FAITHFUL DEPARTED *Island CID 8048* 2 19
13 Jul 96 **FREE TO DECIDE** *Island CID 637* **33** 3
17 Apr 99 **PROMISES** *Island US / Mercury 5725912* **13** 4
1 May 99 ● BURY THE HATCHET *Island US / Mercury 5246442* 7 5
17 Jul 99 **ANIMAL INSTINCT** *Island US / Mercury 5621972* **54** 1
3 Nov 01 WAKE UP AND SMELL THE COFFEE *MCA 1127062* 61 1
28 Sep 02 STARS – THE BEST OF 1992-2002 *Universal TV 0633862* 20 4

Les CRANE *US, male vocalist*

19 Feb 72 ● **DESIDERATA** *Warner Bros. K 16119* **7** 14

The CRANES *UK, male / female vocal / instrumental group (2 Albums: 2 Weeks, 2 Singles: 2 Weeks)*

28 Sep 91 WINGS OF JOY *Dedicated DEDLP 003* 52 1
8 May 93 FOREVER *Dedicated DEDCD 009* 40 1
25 Sep 93 **JEWEL** *Dedicated CRANE 007CD* **29** 1
3 Sep 94 **SHINING ROAD** *Dedicated CRANE 008CD1* **57** 1

CRASH TEST DUMMIES *Canada, male / female vocal (Brad Roberts) / instrumental group (1 Album: 23 Weeks, 3 Singles: 20 Weeks)*

23 Apr 94 ● **MMM MMM MMM MMM** *RCA 74321201512* **2** 11
14 May 94 ● GOD SHUFFLED HIS FEET *RCA 74321201522* 2 23
16 Jul 94 **AFTERNOONS & COFFEESPOONS** *RCA 74321219622* **23** 5
15 Apr 95 **THE BALLAD OF PETER PUMPKINHEAD** *RCA 74321276772* [1] **30** 4

[1] Crash Test Dummies featuring Ellen Reid

CRASS *UK, male vocal / instrumental group*

28 Aug 82 CHRIST THE ALBUM *Crass BOLLOX 2U2* 26 2

Beverley CRAVEN *UK, female vocalist / keyboard player (3 Albums: 67 Weeks, 6 Singles: 33 Weeks)*

2 Mar 91 ● BEVERLEY CRAVEN *Columbia 4670531* 3 52
20 Apr 91 ● **PROMISE ME** *Epic 6559437* **3** 13
20 Jul 91 **HOLDING ON** *Epic 6565507* **32** 7
5 Oct 91 **WOMAN TO WOMAN** *Epic 6574647* **40** 5
7 Dec 91 **MEMORIES** *Epic 6576617* **68** 2
25 Sep 93 **LOVE SCENES** *Epic 6595952* **34** 4
9 Oct 93 ● LOVE SCENES *Epic 4745172* 4 13
20 Nov 93 **MOLLIE'S SONG** *Epic 6598132* **61** 2
12 Jun 99 MIXED EMOTIONS *Epic 4941502* 46 2

Billy CRAWFORD *US, male vocalist (3 Singles: 6 Weeks)*

10 Oct 98 **URGENTLY IN LOVE** *V2 VVR 5003063* **48** 2
3 May 03 **YOU DIDN'T EXPECT THAT** *V2 VVR 5022083* **35** 2
30 Aug 03 **TRACKIN'** *V2 VVR 5021753* **32** 2

Jimmy CRAWFORD *UK, male vocalist – Ronald Lindsey (2 Singles: 11 Weeks)*

8 Jun 61 **LOVE OR MONEY** *Columbia DB 4633* **49** 1
16 Nov 61 **I LOVE HOW YOU LOVE ME** *Columbia DB 4717* **18** 10

Michael CRAWFORD *UK, male actor / vocalist – Michael Dumble-Smith (8 Albums: 76 Weeks, 2 Singles: 14 Weeks)*

10 Jan 87 ● **THE MUSIC OF THE NIGHT** *Polydor POSP 803* [1] **7** 11
28 Nov 87 SONGS FROM THE STAGE AND SCREEN *Telstar STAR 2308* [1] 12 13
2 Dec 89 WITH LOVE *Telstar STAR 2340* 31 7
9 Nov 91 ● MICHAEL CRAWFORD PERFORMS ANDREW LLOYD WEBBER *Telstar STAR 2544* 3 36
13 Nov 93 A TOUCH OF MUSIC IN THE NIGHT *Telstar TCD 2676* 12 11
15 Jan 94 **THE MUSIC OF THE NIGHT** (re-recording) *Columbia 6597382* [2] **54** 3
19 Nov 94 THE LOVE SONGS ALBUM *Telstar TCD 2748* 64 3
21 Nov 98 ON EAGLE'S WINGS *Atlantic 7567830762* 65 2
25 Dec 99 THE MOST WONDERFUL TIME OF THE YEAR *Telstar TV TTVCD 3111* 69 1
4 Dec 04 THE VERY BEST OF MICHAEL CRAWFORD *Virgin / EMI VTCD 685* 54 3

[1] Michael Crawford with the Royal Philharmonic Orchestra, conducted by David Caddick [2] Barbra Streisand (duet with Michael Crawford) [1] Michael Crawford with the London Symphony Orchestra

The flip side of POSP 803 – 'Wishing You Were Somehow Here Again' by Sarah Brightman – was also listed.

Randy CRAWFORD 286 Top 500 (see also The CRUSADERS)

Soulful jazz-slanted song stylist, b. Veronica Crawford, 18 Feb 1952, Georgia, US, who has surprisingly proved more successful in Europe than her homeland, where she has yet to crack the pop Top 100. Winner of a BRIT in 1982 for Best Female Artist (11 Albums: 158 Weeks, 12 Singles: 75 Weeks)

21 Jun 80 **LAST NIGHT AT DANCELAND** *Warner Bros. K 17631* **61** 2
28 Jun 80 ● NOW WE MAY BEGIN *Warner Bros. K 56791* 10 16
30 Aug 80 ● **ONE DAY I'LL FLY AWAY** *Warner Bros. K 17680* **2** 11
16 May 81 ● SECRET COMBINATION *Warner Bros. K 56904* 2 60
30 May 81 **YOU MIGHT NEED SOMEBODY** *Warner Bros. K 17803* **11** 13
8 Aug 81 **RAINY NIGHT IN GEORGIA** *Warner Bros. K 17840* **18** 9
31 Oct 81 **SECRET COMBINATION** *Warner Bros. K 17872* **48** 3
30 Jan 82 **IMAGINE (re)** *Warner Bros. K 17906* **60** 2
5 Jun 82 **ONE HELLO** *Warner Bros. K 17948* **48** 4
12 Jun 82 ● WINDSONG *Warner Bros. K 57011* 7 17
19 Feb 83 **HE REMINDS ME** *Warner Bros. K 17970* **65** 2
8 Oct 83 **NIGHT LINE** *Warner Bros. W 9530* **51** 4
22 Oct 83 NIGHTLINE *Warner Bros. 9239761* 37 4
13 Oct 84 ● MISS RANDY CRAWFORD – THE GREATEST HITS *K-Tel NE 1281* 10 17
28 Jun 86 ABSTRACT EMOTIONS *Warner Bros. WX 46* 14 10
29 Nov 86 ● **ALMAZ** *Warner Bros. W 8583* **4** 17
10 Oct 87 THE LOVE SONGS *Telstar STAR 2299* 27 13
21 Oct 89 RICH AND POOR *Warner Bros. WX 308* 63 1
18 Jan 92 **DIAMANTE** *London LON 313* [1] **44** 7
27 Mar 93 ● THE VERY BEST OF RANDY CRAWFORD *Dino DINCD 58* 8 13
15 Nov 97 **GIVE ME THE NIGHT** *WEA WEA 142CD* **60** 1
12 Feb 00 LOVE SONGS – THE VERY BEST OF RANDY CRAWFORD *Warner.esp WMMCD 002* 22 4
18 Jun 05 THE ULTIMATE COLLECTION *WSM 5046787972* 31 3

[1] Zucchero with Randy Crawford

Robert CRAY BAND *US, male vocal / instrumental group (7 Albums: 53 Weeks, 2 Singles: 5 Weeks)*

12 Oct 85 FALSE ACCUSATIONS *Demon FIEND 43* 68 1
15 Nov 86 STRONG PERSUADER *Mercury MERH 97* 34 28
20 Jun 87 **RIGHT NEXT DOOR (BECAUSE OF ME)** *Mercury CRAY 3* **50** 4
3 Sep 88 DON'T BE AFRAID OF THE DARK *Mercury MERH 129* 13 12
22 Sep 90 MIDNIGHT STROLL *Mercury 8466521* 19 7
12 Sep 92 I WAS WARNED *Mercury 5127212* 29 3
16 Oct 93 SHAME AND SIN *Mercury 5185172* 48 1
20 May 95 SOME RAINY MORNING *Mercury 5269282* [1] 63 1
20 Apr 96 **BABY LEE** *Silvertone ORECD 81* [1] **65** 1

[1] John Lee Hooker with Robert Cray [1] Robert Cray

CRAZY ELEPHANT *US, male vocal group*

21 May 69 **GIMME GIMME GOOD LOVIN'** *Major Minor MM 609* **12** 13

15 / 17 June 1961	22 / 24 June 1961	29 June / 1 July 1961	6 / 8 July 1961
SURRENDER Elvis Presley with The Jordanaires	SURRENDER Elvis Presley with The Jordanaires	RUNAWAY Del Shannon	RUNAWAY Del Shannon
G.I. BLUES (Soundtrack) Elvis Presley	G.I. BLUES (Soundtrack) Elvis Presley	SOUTH PACIFIC Soundtrack	SOUTH PACIFIC Soundtrack

KEY UK No.1 ★★ UK Top 10 ●● Still on chart ++ UK entry at No.1 ■■ US No.1 ▲▲ UK million seller £ US million seller $
Singles re-entries are listed as (re), (2re), (3re)... which signifies that the hit re-entered the chart once, twice or three times...
Peak Position / Weeks

CRAZY FROG NEW *Germany, male producers and Sweden, computer animated amphibian vocalist (1 Album: 9 Weeks, 3 Singles: 25 Weeks)*

Date		Title	Peak	Weeks
4 Jun 05	★	**AXEL F** *Gusto CDGUS 17* ■	1	16
6 Aug 05	●	CRAZY HITS *Gusto GUSCD 03*	5	9
3 Sep 05		**POPCORN** *Gusto CDGUS 21*	12	7
24 Dec 05	●	**JINGLE BELLS / U CAN'T TOUCH THIS** *Gusto GDGUS 27*	5	2+

Crazy Hits re-entered the chart at Christmas 2005 as Crazy Hits – Crazy Christmas Edition with additional tracks. It peaked at No.75.

CRAZY TOWN (see also SHIFTY) *US, male vocal / rap / instrumental group (1 Album: 9 Weeks, 3 Singles: 19 Weeks)*

Date		Title	Peak	Weeks
7 Apr 01	●	**BUTTERFLY** *Columbia 6710012* ▲	3	13
21 Apr 01		THE GIFT OF GAME *Columbia 4952972*	15	9
11 Aug 01		**REVOLVING DOOR** *Columbia 6714942*	23	5
30 Nov 02		**DROWNING** *Columbia 6733262*	50	1

CRAZYHEAD *UK, male vocal / instrumental group (2 Singles: 4 Weeks)*

Date		Title	Peak	Weeks
16 Jul 88		**TIME HAS TAKEN ITS TOLL ON YOU** *Food FOOD 12*	65	2
25 Feb 89		**HAVE LOVE, WILL TRAVEL (EP)** *Food SGE 2025*	68	2

Tracks on Have Love, Will Travel (EP): Have Love, Will Travel / Out on a Limb (Live) / Baby Turpentine (Live) / Snake Eyes (Live).

CREAM 147 Top 500 *The first real 'supergroup' performed from 1966-1968: Eric Clapton (g/v), Jack Bruce (b/v) and Ginger Baker (d). Selling 35 million records, the innovative trio fused blues, jazz and rock, introduced long solos to popular music and were the prototype for 1970s progressive rock bands. Inducted into the Rock and Roll Hall of Fame in 1993 they played successful reunion gigs at the Albert Hall and Madison Square Gardens in 2005. The trio were awarded Lifetime Achievement Grammy status in 2006 (12 Albums: 299 Weeks, 9 Singles: 61 Weeks)*

Date		Title	Peak	Weeks
20 Oct 66		**WRAPPING PAPER** *Reaction 591 007*	34	6
15 Dec 66		**I FEEL FREE** *Reaction 591 011*	11	12
24 Dec 66	●	FRESH CREAM *Reaction 593001*	6	16
8 Jun 67		**STRANGE BREW** *Reaction 591 015*	17	9
18 Nov 67	●	DISRAELI GEARS *Reaction 594003*	5	42
5 Jun 68		**ANYONE FOR TENNIS (THE SAVAGE SEVEN THEME)** *Polydor 56 258*	40	3
17 Aug 68	●	WHEELS OF FIRE (DOUBLE) *Polydor 583-031/2* ▲	3	26
17 Aug 68	●	WHEELS OF FIRE (SINGLE) *Polydor 583033*	7	13
9 Oct 68		**SUNSHINE OF YOUR LOVE** *Polydor 56 286* $	25	7
15 Jan 69		**WHITE ROOM** *Polydor 56 300*	28	8
8 Feb 69	●	FRESH CREAM (re-issue) *Reaction 594001*	7	2
8 Mar 69	★	GOODBYE *Polydor 583053* ■	1	28
9 Apr 69		**BADGE** *Polydor 56 315*	18	10
8 Nov 69	●	THE BEST OF CREAM *Polydor 583060*	6	34
4 Jul 70	●	LIVE CREAM *Polydor 2383016*	4	15
24 Jun 72		LIVE CREAM VOLUME 2 *Polydor 2383 119*	15	5
28 Oct 72		**BADGE** (re-issue) *Polydor 2058 285*	42	4
26 Sep 87	●	THE CREAM OF ERIC CLAPTON *Polydor ECTV* [1]	3	109
14 May 05	●	I FEEL FREE – ULTIMATE CREAM *Polydor 9871362*	6	7
15 Oct 05		ROYAL ALBERT HALL – LONDON MAY 2-3-5-6 2005 *Reprise 9362494162*	61	2
26 Nov 05		**SUNSHINE OF YOUR LOVE** *Manifesto 9874942* [1]	46	2

[1] Cream vs The Hoxtons [1] Eric Clapton and Cream

From 9 Jul 1993 The Cream of Eric Clapton was repackaged and was available as The Best of Eric Clapton.

CREATION *UK, male vocal / instrumental group (2 Singles: 3 Weeks)*

Date		Title	Peak	Weeks
7 Jul 66		**MAKING TIME** *Planet PLF 116*	49	1
3 Nov 66		**PAINTER MAN** *Planet PLF 119*	36	2

The CREATURES (see also SIOUXSIE and The BANSHEES) *UK, male / female vocal / instrumental group (1 Album: 9 Weeks, 6 Singles: 28 Weeks)*

Date		Title	Peak	Weeks
3 Oct 81		**MAD EYED SCREAMER** *Polydor POSPD 354*	24	7
23 Apr 83		**MISS THE GIRL** *Wonderland SHE 1*	21	7
28 May 83		FEAST *Wonderland SHELP 1*	17	9
16 Jul 83		**RIGHT NOW** *Wonderland SHE 2*	14	10
14 Oct 89		**STANDING THERE** *Wonderland SHE 17*	53	2
27 Mar 99		**SAY** *Sioux SIOUX 6CD*	72	1
25 Oct 03		**GODZILLA** *Sioux SIOUX 14CD1*	53	1

CREDIT TO THE NATION *UK, male rap group (1 Album: 3 Weeks, 6 Singles: 11 Weeks)*

Date		Title	Peak	Weeks
22 May 93		**CALL IT WHAT YOU WANT** *One Little Indian 94TP 7CD*	57	3
18 Sep 93		**ENOUGH IS ENOUGH** *One Little Indian 79TP 7CD* [1]	56	2
12 Mar 94		**TEENAGE SENSATION** *One Little Indian 124TP 7CD*	24	3
9 Apr 94		TAKE DIS *One Little Indian TPLP 44CDH*	20	3
14 May 94		**SOWING THE SEEDS OF HATRED** *One Little Indian 134TP 7CD*	72	1
22 Jul 95		**LIAR LIAR** *One Little Indian 144TP 7CD*	60	1
12 Sep 98		**TACKY LOVE SONG** *Chrysalis CDCHS 5097*	60	1

[1] Chumbawamba and Credit to the Nation

CREED *US, male vocal / instrumental group (2 Albums: 21 Weeks, 5 Singles: 13 Weeks)*

Date		Title	Peak	Weeks
15 Jan 00		**HIGHER** *Epic 6683152*	47	1
20 Jan 01		**WITH ARMS WIDE OPEN** *Epic 6706952* ▲	13	5
3 Feb 01		HUMAN CLAY *Epic 4950276* ▲	29	4
29 Sep 01		**HIGHER** (re-issue) *Epic 6710642*	64	1
1 Dec 01		WEATHERED *Epic 5049792* ▲	44	17
16 Mar 02		**MY SACRIFICE** *Epic 6723162*	18	5
3 Aug 02		**ONE LAST BREATH / BULLETS** *Epic 6728262*	47	1

CREEDENCE CLEARWATER REVIVAL 452 Top 500 *Internationally successful combo who cleverly created original songs with a 50s rock 'n' roll feel, fronted by John Fogerty, b. 28 May 1945, California, US. Voted World's Top Group in UK Polls 1970/71 (beating The Beatles and The Rolling Stones) (7 Albums: 65 Weeks, 10 Singles: 94 Weeks)*

Date		Title	Peak	Weeks
28 May 69	●	**PROUD MARY** *Liberty LBF 15223* $	8	13
16 Aug 69	★	**BAD MOON RISING** *Liberty LBF 15230* $	1	15
15 Nov 69		**GREEN RIVER** *Liberty LBF 15250* $	19	11
24 Jan 70		GREEN RIVER *Liberty LBS 83273* ▲	20	6
14 Feb 70		**DOWN ON THE CORNER** *Liberty LBF 15283* $	31	6
28 Mar 70	●	WILLY AND THE POOR BOYS *Liberty LBS 83338*	10	24
4 Apr 70	●	**TRAVELLIN' BAND** (re) *Liberty LBF 15310* $	8	13
2 May 70		BAYOU COUNTRY *Liberty LBS 83261*	62	1
20 Jun 70	●	**UP AROUND THE BEND** *Liberty LBF 15354* $	3	12
5 Sep 70		**LONG AS I CAN SEE THE LIGHT** *Liberty LBF 15384* $	20	9
12 Sep 70	★	COSMO'S FACTORY *Liberty LBS 83388* ■ ▲	1	15
23 Jan 71	●	PENDULUM *Liberty LBG 83400*	8	12
20 Mar 71		**HAVE YOU EVER SEEN THE RAIN** *Liberty LBF 15440* $	36	6
24 Jul 71		**SWEET HITCH-HIKER** *United Artists UP 35261*	36	8
30 Jun 79		GREATEST HITS *Fantasy FT 558*	35	5
19 Oct 85		THE CREEDENCE COLLECTION *Impression IMDP 3*	68	2
2 May 92		**BAD MOON RISING** (re-issue) *Epic 6580047*	71	1

Kid CREOLE and The COCONUTS (see also The COCONUTS) *US, male vocalist – August Darnell Browder and female vocal group (4 Albums: 54 Weeks, 12 Singles: 58 Weeks)*

Date		Title	Peak	Weeks
13 Jun 81		**ME NO POP I** *Ze WIP 6711* [1]	32	7
15 May 82	●	**I'M A WONDERFUL THING, BABY** *Ze WIP 6756*	4	11
22 May 82	●	TROPICAL GANGSTERS *Ze ILPS 7016*	3	40
26 Jun 82		FRESH FRUIT IN FOREIGN PLACES *Ze ILPS 7014*	99	1
24 Jul 82	●	**STOOL PIGEON** *Ze WIP 6793*	7	9
9 Oct 82	●	**ANNIE I'M NOT YOUR DADDY** *Ze WIP 6801*	2	8
11 Dec 82		**DEAR ADDY** *Ze WIP 6840*	29	7
10 Sep 83		**THERE'S SOMETHING WRONG IN PARADISE** *Island IS 130*	35	5
17 Sep 83		DOPPELGANGER *Island ILPS 9743*	21	6

13 / 15 July 1961	20 / 22 July 1961	27 / 29 July 1961	3 / 5 August 1961
UK No.1 SINGLES			
RUNAWAY Del Shannon	TEMPTATION The Everly Brothers	TEMPTATION The Everly Brothers	WELL I ASK YOU Eden Kane
UK No.1 ALBUMS			
SOUTH PACIFIC Soundtrack	SOUTH PACIFIC Soundtrack	THE BLACK AND WHITE MINSTREL SHOW George Mitchell Minstrels	THE BLACK AND WHITE MINSTREL SHOW George Mitchell Minstrels

19 Nov 83	**THE LIFEBOAT PARTY** *Island IS 142*	**49**	4
15 Sep 84	**CRE-OLE (THE BEST OF KID CREOLE AND THE COCONUTS)** *Island IMA 13*	**21**	7
14 Apr 90	**THE SEX OF IT** *CBS 655698 7*	**29**	5
10 Apr 93	**I'M A WONDERFUL THING BABY** (re-mix) *Island CID 551*	**60**	2

1 Kid Creole and the Coconuts present Coati Mundi

CRESCENDO
UK / US, male / female vocal / instrumental duo – Serena and Steve Hitchcock

23 Dec 95	**ARE YOU OUT THERE** *ffrr FCD 270*	**20**	5

The CRESCENT *UK, male vocal / instrumental group (3 Singles: 3 Weeks)*

18 May 02	**ON THE RUN** *Hut / Virgin HUTCD 153*	**49**	1
27 Jul 02	**TEST OF TIME** *Hut / Virgin HUTCD 157*	**60**	1
28 Sep 02	**SPINNIN' WHEELS** *Hut / Virgin HUTCD 160*	**61**	1

The CREW CUTS *Canada, male vocal group (2 Singles: 29 Weeks)*

1 Oct 54	**SH-BOOM** *Mercury MB 3140* ▲	**12**	9
15 Apr 55 ●	**EARTH ANGEL** *Mercury MB 3202*	**4**	20

Bernard CRIBBINS (see also Howard BLAKE conducting the SINFONIA OF LONDON) *UK, male actor / vocalist (3 Singles: 29 Weeks)*

15 Feb 62 ●	**HOLE IN THE GROUND** *Parlophone R 4869*	**9**	13
5 Jul 62 ●	**RIGHT, SAID FRED** *Parlophone R 4923*	**10**	10
13 Dec 62	**GOSSIP CALYPSO** *Parlophone R 4961*	**25**	6

The CRIBS *UK, male vocal / instrumental trio (6 Singles: 9 Weeks)*

6 Mar 04	**YOU WERE ALWAYS THE ONE** *Wichita Recordings WEBB 059SCD*	**66**	1
29 May 04	**WHAT ABOUT ME** *Wichita Recordings WEBB 061SCD*	**75**	1
30 Apr 05	**HEY SCENESTERS!** *Wichita Recordings WEBB 074SCD*	**27**	2
25 Jun 05	**MIRROR KISSERS** *Wichita Recordings WEBB 080SCD*	**27**	2
3 Sep 05	**MARTELL** *Wichita Recordings WEBB 092SCD*	**39**	1
17 Dec 05	**YOU'RE GONNA LOSE US** *Wichita Recordings WEBB 097SCD*	**30**	2

The CRICKETS 438 Top 500
Band that originally featured Buddy Holly formed in Lubbock, Texas, US, its best known members being Jerry Allison (d), Joe B Mauldin (b) and Sonny Curtis (g/v). Without Holly they recorded original versions of Top 10 hits 'I Fought the Law', 'Someone Someone', 'When You Ask About Love' and 'More Than I Can Say' (6 Albums: 67 Weeks, 13 Singles: 97 Weeks)

27 Sep 57 ★	**THAT'LL BE THE DAY** (re) *Vogue Coral Q 72279* ▲ $	**1**	15
27 Dec 57 ●	**OH BOY** *Coral Q 72298*	**3**	15
14 Mar 58 ●	**MAYBE BABY** *Coral Q 72307*	**4**	10
19 Apr 58 ●	**THE "CHIRPING" CRICKETS** *Coral LVA 9081*	**5**	1
25 Jul 58	**THINK IT OVER** *Coral Q 72329*	**11**	7
24 Apr 59	**LOVE'S MADE A FOOL OF YOU** (re) *Coral Q 72365*	**26**	2
15 Jan 60	**WHEN YOU ASK ABOUT LOVE** *Coral Q 72382*	**27**	1
12 May 60	**MORE THAN I CAN SAY** *Coral Q 72395*	**42**	1
26 May 60	**BABY MY HEART** *Coral Q 72395*	**33**	4
25 Mar 61	**IN STYLE WITH THE CRICKETS** *Coral LVA 9142*	**13**	7
21 Jun 62 ●	**DON'T EVER CHANGE** *Liberty LIB 55441*	**5**	13
27 Oct 62 ●	**BOBBY VEE MEETS THE CRICKETS** *Liberty LBY 1086* 1	**2**	27
24 Jan 63	**MY LITTLE GIRL** *Liberty LIB 10067*	**17**	9
6 Jun 63	**DON'T TRY TO CHANGE ME** *Liberty LIB 10092*	**37**	4
14 May 64	**YOU'VE GOT LOVE** *Coral Q 72472* 1	**40**	6
2 Jul 64	**(THEY CALL HER) LA BAMBA** *Liberty LIB 55696*	**21**	10
11 Mar 78 ★	**20 GOLDEN GREATS** *MCA EMTV 8* 2	**1**	20
20 Feb 93 ★	**WORDS OF LOVE** *PolyGram TV 5144872* 2	**1**	9
28 Aug 99	**THE VERY BEST OF BUDDY HOLLY AND THE CRICKETS** *Universal Music TV 1120462* 2	**25**	3

1 Buddy Holly and The Crickets 1 Bobby Vee and The Crickets 2 Buddy Holly and The Crickets

Although not credited on the records, Buddy Holly was featured on the first four hits.

CRISPY AND COMPANY
US, male vocal / instrumental group (2 Singles: 11 Weeks)

16 Aug 75	**BRAZIL** *Creole CR 109*	**26**	5
27 Dec 75	**GET IT TOGETHER** *Creole CR 114* 1	**21**	6

1 Crispy & Co

The CRITTERS *US, male vocal / instrumental group*

30 Jun 66	**YOUNGER GIRL** *London HL 10047*	**38**	5

Tony CROMBIE and his ROCKETS *UK, male vocal / instrumental group – leader Tony Crombie – drums, b. 27 Aug 1925, d. 18 Oct 1999*

19 Oct 56	**TEACH YOU TO ROCK / SHORT'NIN' BREAD** *Columbia DB 3822*	**25**	2

Bing CROSBY *US, male vocalist – Harry Lillis Crosby, b. 3 May 1903, d. 14 Oct 1977 – "The King of the Crooners" with estimated sales of more than 400 million (including over of 30 million for 'White Christmas') (9 Albums: 45 Weeks, 15 Singles: 97 Weeks)*

14 Nov 52 ●	**THE ISLE OF INNISFREE** *Brunswick 04900*	**3**	12
5 Dec 52 ●	**ZING A LITTLE ZONG** *Brunswick 04981* 1	**10**	2
19 Dec 52 ●	**SILENT NIGHT, HOLY NIGHT** *Brunswick 03929*	**8**	2
19 Mar 54 ●	**CHANGING PARTNERS** (2re) *Brunswick 05244*	**9**	3
7 Jan 55	**COUNT YOUR BLESSINGS INSTEAD OF SHEEP** (re) *Brunswick 05339*	**11**	3
29 Apr 55	**STRANGER IN PARADISE** *Brunswick 05410*	**17**	2
27 Apr 56	**IN A LITTLE SPANISH TOWN** *Brunswick 05543*	**22**	3
23 Nov 56 ●	**TRUE LOVE** *Capitol CL 14645* 2 $	**4**	27
24 May 57 ●	**AROUND THE WORLD** *Brunswick 05674*	**5**	15
8 Oct 60 ●	**JOIN BING AND SING ALONG** *Warner Bros. WM 4021*	**7**	11
21 Dec 74	**WHITE CHRISTMAS** *MCA MCF 2568*	**45**	3
9 Aug 75	**THAT'S WHAT LIFE IS ALL ABOUT** *United Artists UP 35852*	**41**	4
20 Sep 75	**THAT'S WHAT LIFE IS ALL ABOUT** *United Artists UAG 2973*	**28**	6
5 Nov 77 ●	**LIVE AT THE LONDON PALLADIUM** *K-Tel NE 951*	**9**	2
5 Nov 77	**THE BEST OF BING** *MCA MCF 2540*	**41**	7
3 Dec 77 ●	**WHITE CHRISTMAS** *MCA 111* ▲ $	**5**	7
17 Dec 77	**SEASONS** *Polydor 2442 151*	**25**	7
5 May 79	**SONGS OF A LIFETIME** *Philips 6641 923*	**29**	3
27 Nov 82 ●	**PEACE ON EARTH – LITTLE DRUMMER BOY** *RCA BOW 12* 3	**3**	8
17 Dec 83	**TRUE LOVE** (re-issue) *Capitol CL 315* 2	**70**	3
21 Dec 85	**WHITE CHRISTMAS** (re-issue) *MCA BING 1*	**69**	2
14 Dec 91	**CHRISTMAS WITH BING CROSBY** *Telstar STAR 2468*	**66**	3
23 Nov 96	**THE BEST OF BING CROSBY** *MCA MCD 11561*	**59**	3
19 Dec 98	**WHITE CHRISTMAS** (2nd re-issue) *MCA MCSRD 48105*	**29**	4

1 Bing Crosby and Jane Wyman 2 Bing Crosby and Grace Kelly 3 David Bowie and Bing Crosby

David CROSBY (see also CROSBY, STILLS, NASH and YOUNG)
US, male vocalist / guitarist (2 Albums: 12 Weeks, 1 Single: 3 Weeks)

24 Apr 71	**IF I COULD ONLY REMEMBER MY NAME** *Atlantic 2401005*	**12**	7
13 May 72	**GRAHAM NASH DAVID CROSBY** *Atlantic K 50011* 1	**13**	5
15 May 93	**HERO** *Atlantic A 7360* 1	**56**	3

1 David Crosby featuring Phil Collins 1 Graham Nash David Crosby

CROSBY, STILLS, NASH and YOUNG (see also David CROSBY; Graham NASH; Stephen STILLS; Neil YOUNG) *US / UK / Canada, male vocal / instrumental group (7 Albums: 97 Weeks, 2 Singles: 12 Weeks)*

16 Aug 69	**MARRAKESH EXPRESS** *Atlantic 584 283* 1	**17**	9
23 Aug 69	**CROSBY, STILLS & NASH** *Atlantic 588189* 1	**25**	5
30 May 70 ●	**DEJA VU** *Atlantic 2401001* 2 ▲	**5**	60
22 May 71 ●	**4 WAY STREET** *Atlantic 2956 004* ▲	**5**	12
21 May 74	**SO FAR** *Atlantic K 50023* ▲	**25**	6
9 Jul 77	**CSN** *Atlantic K 50369* 1	**23**	9
21 Jan 89	**AMERICAN DREAM** *Atlantic A 9003*	**55**	3

10 / 12 August 1961	17 / 19 August 1961	24 / 26 August 1961	31 August / 2 September 1961
YOU DON'T KNOW Helen Shapiro	YOU DON'T KNOW Helen Shapiro	YOU DON'T KNOW Helen Shapiro	JOHNNY REMEMBER ME John Leyton
THE BLACK AND WHITE MINSTREL SHOW George Mitchell Minstrels	THE BLACK AND WHITE MINSTREL SHOW George Mitchell Minstrels	SOUTH PACIFIC Soundtrack	THE BLACK AND WHITE MINSTREL SHOW George Mitchell Minstrels

KEY	
UK No.1 ★	UK Top 10 ● Still on chart + UK entry at No.1 ■
US No.1 ▲	UK million seller £ US million seller $
Singles re-entries are listed as (re), (2re), (3re)... which signifies that the hit re-entered the chart once, twice or three times...	Peak Position / Weeks

6 Nov 99	LOOKING FORWARD Reprise 9362474362	54	1
12 Mar 05	GREATEST HITS Rhino 8122765372 [1]	38	4

[1] Crosby, Stills and Nash [1] Crosby, Stills & Nash

[2] Crosby, Stills, Nash & Young. Dallas Taylor & Greg Reeves

The CROSS *UK / US, male vocal / instrumental group*

17 Oct 87	**COWBOYS AND INDIANS** *Virgin VS 1007*	74	1
6 Feb 88	SHOVE IT *Virgin V 2477*	58	2

Christopher CROSS *US, male vocalist – Christopher Geppert (2 Albums: 93 Weeks, 4 Singles: 27 Weeks)*

19 Apr 80	**RIDE LIKE THE WIND** *Warner Bros. K 17582*	69	1
14 Feb 81	**SAILING** *Warner Bros. K 17695* ▲	48	6
21 Feb 81	CHRISTOPHER CROSS *Warner Bros. K 56789*	14	77
17 Oct 81 ●	**ARTHUR'S THEME (BEST THAT YOU CAN DO) (re)** *Warner Bros. K 17847* ▲ $	7	15
5 Feb 83	**ALL RIGHT** *Warner Bros. W 9843*	51	5
19 Feb 83 ●	ANOTHER PAGE *Warner Bros. W 3757*	4	16

It was not until 'Arthur's Theme' re-entered in Jan 1982 that it reached the peak position of No.7.

CROW *Germany, male production duo – David Rzenno and David Nothroff*

19 May 01	**WHAT YA LOOKIN' AT** *Tidy Trax TIDY 153CD*	60	1

Sheryl CROW (231 Top 500)

Singer, songwriter, guitarist and nine times Grammy winner, b. 11 Feb 1962, Missouri, US. The one-time backing singer for Michael Jackson and George Harrison became the first US female soloist to score six UK hits off a debut LP (6 Albums: 183 Weeks, 21 Singles: 91 Weeks)

12 Feb 94 ●	TUESDAY NIGHT MUSIC CLUB *A&M 5401262*	8	55
18 Jun 94	**LEAVING LAS VEGAS** *A&M 5806472*	66	1
5 Nov 94 ●	**ALL I WANNA DO** *A&M 5808452*	4	13
11 Feb 95	**STRONG ENOUGH** *A&M 5809212*	33	4
27 May 95	**CAN'T CRY ANYMORE** *A&M 5810552*	33	3
29 Jul 95	**RUN BABY RUN** *A&M 5811492*	24	4
11 Nov 95	**WHAT I CAN DO FOR YOU** *A&M 5812292*	43	1
21 Sep 96 ●	**IF IT MAKES YOU HAPPY** *A&M 5819032*	9	6
12 Oct 96 ●	SHERYL CROW *A&M 5405902*	5	70
30 Nov 96	**EVERYDAY IS A WINDING ROAD** *A&M 5820232*	12	6
29 Mar 97	**HARD TO MAKE A STAND** *A&M 5821492*	22	3
12 Jul 97 ●	**A CHANGE WOULD DO YOU GOOD** *A&M 5822092*	8	5
18 Oct 97	**HOME** *A&M 0440312*	25	2
13 Dec 97	**TOMORROW NEVER DIES** *A&M 5824572*	12	9
12 Sep 98 ●	**MY FAVORITE MISTAKE** *Polydor 5827632*	9	6
3 Oct 98 ●	THE GLOBE SESSIONS *A&M 5409742*	2	32
5 Dec 98	**THERE GOES THE NEIGHBORHOOD** *A&M 5828092*	19	7
6 Mar 99	**ANYTHING BUT DOWN** *A&M / Polydor 5828272*	19	4
11 Sep 99	**SWEET CHILD O' MINE** *Columbia 6678882*	30	3
13 Apr 02	**SOAK UP THE SUN** *A&M 4977042*	16	8
20 Apr 02 ●	C'MON C'MON *A&M 4932622*	2	8
13 Jul 02	**STEVE MCQUEEN** *A&M 4977422*	44	1
25 Oct 03 ●	THE VERY BEST OF SHERYL CROW *A&M / Mercury 9861092*	2	16
1 Nov 03	**THE FIRST CUT IS THE DEEPEST** *A&M 9813556*	37	3
3 Jul 04	**LIGHT IN YOUR EYES** *A&M 9862700*	73	1
1 Oct 05	**GOOD IS GOOD** *A&M 9885348*	75	1
8 Oct 05	WILDFLOWER *A&M 9884801*	25	2

The CROWD

International, male / female vocal / instrumental charity assembly

1 Jun 85 ★	**YOU'LL NEVER WALK ALONE** *Spartan BRAD 1*	1	11

CROWDED HOUSE (259 Top 500) (see also FINN; SPLIT ENZ)

Top Antipodean group who featured Split Enz featured New Zealanders Neil and Tim Finn (v/g/k). Formed in 1986, they received the Best International Group award at the 1993 BRITs and played their last show in 1996 to over 100,000 people on the steps of the Sydney Opera House (4 Albums: 186 Weeks, 14 Singles: 64 Weeks)

6 Jun 87	**DON'T DREAM IT'S OVER** *Capitol CL 438*	27	8
22 Jun 91	**CHOCOLATE CAKE** *Capitol CL 618*	69	2
13 Jul 91 ●	WOODFACE *Capitol EST 2144*	6	86
2 Nov 91	**FALL AT YOUR FEET** *Capitol CL 626*	17	7
29 Feb 92 ●	**WEATHER WITH YOU** *Capitol CL 643*	7	9
20 Jun 92	**FOUR SEASONS IN ONE DAY** *Capitol CL 655*	26	5
26 Sep 92	**IT'S ONLY NATURAL** *Capitol CL 661*	24	4
2 Oct 93	**DISTANT SUN** *Capitol CDCLS 697*	19	6
23 Oct 93 ●	TOGETHER ALONE *Capitol CDESTU 2215*	4	32
20 Nov 93	**NAILS IN MY FEET** *Capitol CDCLS 701*	22	4
19 Feb 94	**LOCKED OUT** *Capitol CDCLS 707*	12	4
11 Jun 94	**FINGERS OF LOVE** *Capitol CDCLS 715*	25	3
24 Sep 94	**PINEAPPLE HEAD** *Capitol CDCLS 723*	27	3
22 Jun 96	**INSTINCT** *Capitol CDCLS 774*	12	4
6 Jul 96 ★	RECURRING DREAM – THE VERY BEST OF CROWDED HOUSE *Capitol CDEST 2283* ■	1	66
17 Aug 96	**NOT THE GIRL YOU THINK YOU ARE** *Capitol CDCLS 776*	20	3
9 Nov 96	**DON'T DREAM IT'S OVER** (re-issue) *Capitol CDCL 780*	25	2
19 Feb 00	AFTERGLOW *Capitol 5237222*	18	2

CROWN HEIGHTS AFFAIR *US, male vocal (Phil Thomas) / instrumental group (1 Album: 3 Weeks, 5 Singles: 34 Weeks)*

19 Aug 78	**GALAXY OF LOVE** *Mercury 6168 801*	24	10
23 Sep 78	DREAM WORLD *Philips 6372 754*	40	3
11 Nov 78	**I'M GONNA LOVE YOU FOREVER** *Mercury 6168 803*	47	4
14 Apr 79	**DANCE LADY DANCE** *Mercury 6168 804*	44	4
3 May 80 ●	**YOU GAVE ME LOVE** *De-Lite MER 9*	10	12
9 Aug 80	**YOU'VE BEEN GONE** *De-Lite MER 28*	44	4

Julee CRUISE *US, female vocalist (3 Singles: 14 Weeks)*

10 Nov 90 ●	**FALLING** *Warner Bros. W 9544*	7	11
2 Mar 91	**ROCKIN' BACK INSIDE MY HEART** *Warner Bros. W 0004*	66	2
11 Sep 99	**IF I SURVIVE** *Distinctive DISNCD 55* [1]	52	1

[1] Hybrid featuring Julee Cruise

The CRUSADERS *US, male vocal / instrumental group – includes Wilton Felder (4 Albums: 30 Weeks, 3 Singles: 16 Weeks)*

21 Jul 79 ●	STREET LIFE *MCA MCF 3008*	10	16
18 Aug 79 ●	**STREET LIFE** *MCA 513*	5	11
19 Jul 80	RHAPSODY AND BLUES *MCA MCG 4010*	40	5
12 Sep 81	STANDING TALL *MCA MCF 3122*	47	5
26 Sep 81	**I'M SO GLAD I'M STANDING HERE TODAY** *MCA 741* [1]	61	3
7 Apr 84	GHETTO BLASTER *MCA MCF 3176*	46	4
7 Apr 84	**NIGHT LADIES** *MCA MCA 853*	55	2

[1] The Crusaders, featured vocalist Joe Cocker

Randy Crawford is the uncredited vocalist on 'Street Life'.

CRUSH *UK, female vocal duo (2 Singles: 3 Weeks)*

24 Feb 96	**JELLYHEAD** *Telstar CDSTAS 2809*	50	2
3 Aug 96	**LUV'D UP** *Telstar CDSTAS 2833*	45	1

Bobby CRUSH *UK, male pianist (2 Albums: 12 Weeks, 1 Single: 4 Weeks)*

4 Nov 72	**BORSALINO** *Philips 6006 248*	37	4
25 Nov 72	BOBBY CRUSH *Philips 6308 135*	15	7
18 Dec 82	THE BOBBY CRUSH INCREDIBLE DOUBLE DECKER *Warwick WW 5126/7*	53	5

CRY BEFORE DAWN *Ireland, male vocal / instrumental group*

17 Jun 89	**WITNESS FOR THE WORLD** *Epic GONE 3*	67	2

7 / 9 September 1961	14 / 16 September 1961	21 / 23 September 1961	28 / 30 September 1961
UK No.1 SINGLES			
JOHNNY REMEMBER ME John Leyton	**JOHNNY REMEMBER ME** John Leyton	**REACH FOR THE STARS / CLIMB EV'RY MOUNTAIN** Shirley Bassey	**JOHNNY REMEMBER ME** John Leyton
UK No.1 ALBUMS			
SOUTH PACIFIC Soundtrack	**THE BLACK AND WHITE MINSTREL SHOW** George Mitchell Minstrels	**THE SHADOWS** The Shadows	**THE SHADOWS** The Shadows

CRY OF LOVE *US, male / female vocal / instrumental group*

15 Jan 94 **BAD THING** *Columbia 6600462* **60** 1

CRY SISCO! *UK, male producer – Barry Blue*

2 Sep 89 **AFRO DIZZI ACT (re)** *Escape AWOL 1* **42** 9

The CRYIN' SHAMES *UK, male vocal / instrumental group*

31 Mar 66 **PLEASE STAY** *Decca F 12340* **26** 7

The CRYSTAL METHOD *US, male instrumental duo – Ken Jordan and Scott Kirkland (3 Singles: 4 Weeks)*

11 Oct 97 **(CAN'T YOU) TRIP LIKE I DO** *Epic 6650862* [1] **39** 2
7 Mar 98 **KEEP HOPE ALIVE** *Sony S2 CM 3CD* **71** 1
8 Aug 98 **COMIN' BACK** *Sony S2 CM 4CD* **73** 1

[1] Filter and The Crystal Method

CRYSTAL PALACE with The FAB FOUR *UK, male football team vocalists and vocal group*

12 May 90 **GLAD ALL OVER / WHERE EAGLES FLY** *Parkfield PMS 5019* **50** 2

The CRYSTALS *US, female vocal group (5 Singles: 54 Weeks)*

22 Nov 62 **HE'S A REBEL** *London HLU 9611* ▲ $ **19** 13
20 Jun 63 ● **DA DOO RON RON** *London HLU 9732* $ **5** 16
19 Sep 63 ● **THEN HE KISSED ME** *London HLU 9773* **2** 14
5 Mar 64 **I WONDER** *London HLU 9852* **36** 3
19 Oct 74 **DA DOO RON RON** (re-issue) *Warner Spector K 19010* **15** 8

CSILLA *Hungary, female vocalist*

13 Jul 96 **MAN IN THE MOON** *Worx WORXCD 001* **69** 1

Alex CUBA BAND featuring Ron SEXSMITH *Cuba, male instrumental group and Canada, male vocalist*

6 Nov 04 **LO MISMO QUE YO (IF ONLY)** *Shell GET 2CD* **52** 1

CUBAN BOYS *UK, male / female production group*

25 Dec 99 ● **COGNOSCENTI VS INTELLIGENTSIA (re)** *EMI CDCUBAN 001* **4** 9

CUBAN HEELS NEW *UK, male vocal / instrumental group*

19 Mar 05 **SHE'S ON FIRE** *Sugar Shack FOD 062* **72** 1

CUBIC 22 (see also AIRSCAPE; BALEARIC BILL; BLUE BAMBOO; CONVERT; DECOY AND ROY; Johan GIELEN presents ABNEA; SVENSON and GIELEN; TRANSFORMER 2) *Belgium, male instrumental / production duo – Peter Ramson and Danny Van Wauwe*

22 Jun 91 **NIGHT IN MOTION** *XL Recordings XLS 20* **15** 7

CUD *UK, male vocal / instrumental group (2 Albums: 2 Weeks, 8 Singles: 16 Weeks)*

19 Oct 91 **OH NO WON'T DO (EP)** *A&M AMB 829* **49** 2
28 Mar 92 **THROUGH THE ROOF** *A&M AM 857* **44** 2
30 May 92 **RICH AND STRANGE** *A&M AM 871* **24** 3
11 Jul 92 ASQUARIUS *A&M 3953902* 30 1
15 Aug 92 **PURPLE LOVE BALLOON** *A&M AM 0024* **27** 3
10 Oct 92 **ONCE AGAIN** *A&M AM 0081* **45** 1
12 Feb 94 **NEUROTICA** *A&M 5805172* **37** 2
2 Apr 94 **STICKS AND STONES** *A&M 5805472* **68** 1
23 Apr 94 SHOWBIZ *A&M 5402112* 46 1
3 Sep 94 **ONE GIANT LOVE** *A&M 5807292* **52** 2

Tracks on Oh No Won't Do (EP): Oh No Won't Do / Profession / Ariel / Price of Love.

The CUFF LINKS (see also The ARCHIES) *US, male vocal group – leader Ron Dante (2 Singles: 30 Weeks)*

29 Nov 69 ● **TRACY** *MCA MU 1101* **4** 16
14 Mar 70 ● **WHEN JULIE COMES AROUND** *MCA MU 1112* **10** 14

Jamie CULLUM *UK, male vocalist / pianist (3 Albums: 65 Weeks, 4 Singles: 16 Weeks)*

1 Nov 03 ● TWENTYSOMETHING *UCJ 9865574* 3 50
13 Mar 04 POINTLESS NOSTALGIC *Candid CCD 79782* 55 2
20 Mar 04 **THESE ARE THE DAYS / FRONTIN'** *UCJ 9866211* **12** 5
20 Nov 04 **EVERLASTING LOVE** *UCJ 9868834* **20** 9
1 Oct 05 **GET YOUR WAY** *UCJ 9873425* **44** 1
8 Oct 05 ● CATCHING TALES *UCJ 9873430* 4 13+
10 Dec 05 **MIND TRACK** *UCJ 9875047* **32** 1

The CULT 434 Top 500

UK gothic rock stars who became US heavy rock heroes. The West Yorkshire band's constant members are Ian Astbury (v) and Billy Duffy (g). The group, who previously recorded as Southern Death Cult and Death Cult, relocated to the US in 1988 and topped the UK album chart with their hits collection in 1993 (9 Albums: 86 Weeks, 17 Singles: 80 Weeks)

18 Jun 83 THE SOUTHERN DEATH CULT *Beggars Banquet BEGA 46* [1] 43 3
8 Sep 84 DREAMTIME *Beggars Banquet BEGA 57* 21 8
22 Dec 84 **RESURRECTION JOE** *Beggars Banquet BEG 122* **74** 2
25 May 85 **SHE SELLS SANCTUARY (re)** *Beggars Banquet BEG 135* **15** 19
5 Oct 85 **RAIN** *Beggars Banquet BEG 147* **17** 8
26 Oct 85 ● LOVE *Beggars Banquet BEGA 65* 4 22
30 Nov 85 **REVOLUTION** *Beggars Banquet BEG 152* **30** 7
28 Feb 87 **LOVE REMOVAL MACHINE** *Beggars Banquet BEG 182* **18** 7
18 Apr 87 ● ELECTRIC *Beggars Banquet BEGA 80* 4 27
2 May 87 **LIL' DEVIL** *Beggars Banquet BEG 188* **11** 7
22 Aug 87 **WILD FLOWER (DOUBLE SINGLE)** *Beggars Banquet BEG 195D* **24** 2
29 Aug 87 **WILD FLOWER** *Beggars Banquet BEG 195* **30** 4
1 Apr 89 **FIRE WOMAN** *Beggars Banquet BEG 228* **15** 4
22 Apr 89 ● SONIC TEMPLE *Beggars Banquet BEGA 98* 3 11
8 Jul 89 **EDIE (CIAO BABY)** *Beggars Banquet BEG 230* **32** 5
18 Nov 89 **SUN KING / EDIE (CIAO BABY)** (re-issue) *Beggars Banquet BEG 235* **39** 2
10 Mar 90 **SWEET SOUL SISTER** *Beggars Banquet BEG 241* **42** 4
14 Sep 91 **WILD HEARTED SON** *Beggars Banquet BEG 255* **40** 2
5 Oct 91 ● CEREMONY *Beggars Banquet BEGA 122* 9 4
29 Feb 92 **HEART OF SOUL** *Beggars Banquet BEG 260* **51** 1
30 Jan 93 **SHE SELLS SANCTUARY** (re-mix) *Beggars Banquet BEG 253CD* **15** 4
13 Feb 93 ★ PURE CULT *Beggars Banquet BEGACD 130* ■ 1 8
8 Oct 94 **COMING DOWN** *Beggars Banquet BBQ 40CD* **50** 1
22 Oct 94 THE CULT *Beggars Banquet BBQCD 164* 21 2
7 Jan 95 **STAR** *Beggars Banquet BBQ 45CD* **65** 1
23 Jun 01 BEYOND GOOD AND EVIL *Atlantic 7567834402* 69 1

[1] Southern Death Cult

Tracks on Wild Flower (double single): Wild Flower / Love Trooper / Outlaw (live) / Horse Nation (live).

CULTURE *Jamaica, male vocal / instrumental group*

1 Apr 78 TWO SEVENS CLASH *Lightning LIP 1* 60 1

Smiley CULTURE *UK, male vocalist – David Emanuel (3 Singles: 13 Weeks)*

15 Dec 84 **POLICE OFFICER** *Fashion FAD 7012* **12** 10
6 Apr 85 **COCKNEY TRANSLATION** *Fashion FAD 7028* **71** 1
13 Sep 86 **SCHOOLTIME CHRONICLE** *Polydor POSP 815* **59** 2

CULTURE BEAT *UK / US / Germany, male / female vocal / instrumental group (1 Album: 10 Weeks, 9 Singles: 47 Weeks)*

3 Feb 90 **CHERRY LIPS (DER ERDBEERMUND)** *Epic 6556337* **55** 3
7 Aug 93 ★ **MR VAIN** *Epic 6594682* **1** 15
25 Sep 93 SERENITY *Dance Pool 4741012* 13 10

5 / 7 October 1961	12 / 14 October 1961	19 / 21 October 1961	26 / 28 October 1961
KON-TIKI The Shadows	**MICHAEL** The Highwaymen	**WALKIN' BACK TO HAPPINESS** Helen Shapiro	**WALKIN' BACK TO HAPPINESS** Helen Shapiro
THE SHADOWS The Shadows	**THE SHADOWS** The Shadows	**THE BLACK AND WHITE MINSTREL SHOW** George Mitchell Minstrels	**THE SHADOWS** The Shadows

KEY: UK No.1 ★ UK Top 10 ● Still on chart + UK entry at No.1 ■ US No.1 ▲ UK million seller £ US million seller $
Singles re-entries are listed as (re), (2re), (3re)... which signifies that the hit re-entered the chart once, twice or three times...
Peak Position / Weeks

6 Nov 93 ● **GOT TO GET IT** *Epic 6597212*....4 11
15 Jan 94 ● **ANYTHING** *Epic 6600252*....5 8
2 Apr 94 **WORLD IN YOUR HANDS** *Epic 6602292*....20 4
27 Jan 96 **INSIDE OUT** *Epic 6626562*....32 2
15 Jun 96 **CRYING IN THE RAIN** *Epic 6633582*....29 2
28 Sep 96 **TAKE ME AWAY** *Epic 6637552*....52 1
20 Sep 03 **MR VAIN RECALL** *East West EW 270CD*....51 1

CULTURE CLUB (219 Top 500)

Internationally successful London-based quartet whose flamboyant lead singer, Boy George, b. George O'Dowd, 14 Jun 1961, Kent, attracted considerable media attention. In 1984, they won both BRIT (Best Group) and Grammy (Best New Artist) awards. Original members reunited for late 1990s tours. Best-selling single: 'Karma Chameleon' 1,405,000 (8 Albums: 163 Weeks, 13 Singles: 119 Weeks)

18 Sep 82 ★ **DO YOU REALLY WANT TO HURT ME** *Virgin VS 518*....1 18
16 Oct 82 ● KISSING TO BE CLEVER *Virgin V 2232*....5 59
27 Nov 82 ● **TIME (CLOCK OF THE HEART)** *Virgin VS 558*....3 12
9 Apr 83 ● **CHURCH OF THE POISON MIND** *Virgin VS 571*....2 9
17 Sep 83 ★ **KARMA CHAMELEON** *Virgin VS 612* ▲ £ $....1 20
22 Oct 83 ★ COLOUR BY NUMBERS *Virgin V 2285* ■....1 56
10 Dec 83 ● **VICTIMS** *Virgin VS 641*....3 10
24 Mar 84 ● **IT'S A MIRACLE** *Virgin VS 662*....4 9
6 Oct 84 ● **THE WAR SONG** *Virgin VS 694*....2 8
3 Nov 84 ● WAKING UP WITH THE HOUSE ON FIRE *Virgin V 2330*....2 13
1 Dec 84 **THE MEDAL SONG (re)** *Virgin VS 730*....32 5
15 Mar 86 ● **MOVE AWAY** *Virgin VS 845*....7 7
12 Apr 86 ● FROM LUXURY TO HEARTACHE *Virgin V 2380*....10 6
31 May 86 **GOD THANK YOU WOMAN** *Virgin VS 861*....31 5
18 Apr 87 ● THIS TIME *Virgin VTV 1*....8 10
2 Oct 93 AT WORST ... THE BEST OF BOY GEORGE AND CULTURE CLUB *Virgin VYCD 19* [1]....24 5
31 Oct 98 ● **I JUST WANNA BE LOVED** *Virgin VSCDT 1710*....4 10
21 Nov 98 GREATEST MOMENTS *Virgin CDVX 2865*....15 13
7 Aug 99 **YOUR KISSES ARE CHARITY** *Virgin VSCDT 1736*....25 4
27 Nov 99 **COLD SHOULDER / STARMAN** *Virgin VSCDT 1758*....43 2
4 Dec 99 DON'T MIND IF I DO *Virgin CDV 2887*....64 1

[1] Boy George and Culture Club

Larry CUNNINGHAM and The MIGHTY AVONS

Ireland, male vocal / instrumental group

10 Dec 64 **TRIBUTE TO JIM REEVES (re)** *King KG 1016*....40 11

CUPID'S INSPIRATION

UK, male vocal (Terry Rice-Milton) / instrumental group (2 Singles: 19 Weeks)

19 Jun 68 ● **YESTERDAY HAS GONE** *Nems 56 3500*....4 11
2 Oct 68 **MY WORLD** *Nems 56 3702*....33 8

The CURE (146 Top 500) (see also GLOVE)

Influential goth rock giants: Robert Smith (v/g), Lol Tolhurst (k), Simon Gallup (b), Porl Thompson (g) and Boris Williams (d), who went from UK cult heroes to stadium-packing supergroup. Voted Best Group at 1991 BRIT Awards (22 Albums: 212 Weeks, 31 Singles: 149 Weeks)

2 Jun 79 THREE IMAGINARY BOYS *Fiction FIX 001*....44 3
12 Apr 80 **A FOREST** *Fiction FICS 10*....31 8
3 May 80 17 SECONDS *Fiction FIX 004*....20 10
4 Apr 81 **PRIMARY** *Fiction FICS 12*....43 6
25 Apr 81 FAITH *Fiction FIX 6*....14 8
17 Oct 81 **CHARLOTTE SOMETIMES** *Fiction FICS 14*....44 4
15 May 82 ● PORNOGRAPHY *Fiction FIX D7*....8 9
24 Jul 82 **HANGING GARDEN** *Fiction FICS 15*....34 4
27 Nov 82 **LET'S GO TO BED (re)** *Fiction FICS 17*....44 5
9 Jul 83 **THE WALK** *Fiction FICS 18*....12 8
3 Sep 83 BOYS DON'T CRY *Fiction SPELP 26*....71 7
29 Oct 83 ● **THE LOVE CATS** *Fiction FICS 19*....7 11
24 Dec 83 JAPANESE WHISPERS *Fiction FIXM 8*....26 14
7 Apr 84 **THE CATERPILLAR** *Fiction FICS 20*....14 7
12 May 84 ● THE TOP *Fiction FIXS 9*....10 10
3 Nov 84 CONCERT – THE CURE LIVE *Fiction FIXH 10*....26 4
27 Jul 85 **IN BETWEEN DAYS** *Fiction FICS 22*....15 10
7 Sep 85 ● THE HEAD ON THE DOOR *Fiction FIXH 11*....7 13
21 Sep 85 **CLOSE TO ME** *Fiction FICS 23*....24 8
3 May 86 **BOYS DON'T CRY** *Fiction FICS 24*....22 6
31 May 86 ● STANDING ON A BEACH – THE SINGLES *Fiction FIXH 12*....4 35
18 Apr 87 **WHY CAN'T I BE YOU?** *Fiction FICS 25*....21 5
6 Jun 87 ● KISS ME KISS ME KISS ME *Fiction FIXH 13*....6 15
4 Jul 87 **CATCH** *Fiction FICS 26*....27 6
17 Oct 87 **JUST LIKE HEAVEN** *Fiction FICS 27*....29 5
20 Feb 88 **HOT HOT HOT!!!** *Fiction FICSX 28*....45 3
22 Apr 89 ● **LULLABY** *Fiction FICS 29*....5 6
13 May 89 ● DISINTEGRATION *Fiction FIXH 14*....3 26
2 Sep 89 **LOVESONG** *Fiction FICS 30*....18 7
31 Mar 90 **PICTURES OF YOU** *Fiction FICS 34*....24 6
29 Sep 90 **NEVER ENOUGH** *Fiction FICS 35*....13 5
3 Nov 90 **CLOSE TO ME** (re-mix) *Fiction FICS 36*....13 5
17 Nov 90 ● MIXED UP *Fiction 8470991*....8 17
6 Apr 91 ● ENTREAT *Fiction FIXH 17*....10 5
28 Mar 92 ● **HIGH** *Fiction FICS 39*....8 3
11 Apr 92 **HIGH** (re-mix) *Fiction FICSX 41*....44 1
2 May 92 ★ WISH *Fiction FIXCD 20* ■....1 13
23 May 92 ● **FRIDAY I'M IN LOVE** *Fiction FICS 42*....6 7
17 Oct 92 **A LETTER TO ELISE** *Fiction FICS 46*....28 2
25 Sep 93 SHOW *Fiction FIXCD 25*....29 2
6 Nov 93 PARIS *Fiction FIXCD 26*....56 1
4 May 96 **THE 13TH** *Fiction 5764692*....15 2
18 May 96 ● WILD MOOD SWINGS *Fiction FIXCD 28*....9 6
29 Jun 96 **MINT CAR** *Fiction FISCD 52*....31 2
14 Dec 96 **GONE** *Fiction FICD 53*....60 1
15 Nov 97 GALORE – THE SINGLES 1987-1997 *Fiction FIXCD 30*....37 2
29 Nov 97 **WRONG NUMBER** *Fiction FICD 54*....62 1
26 Feb 00 BLOODFLOWERS *Fiction FIXCD 31*....14 2
10 Nov 01 **CUT HERE** *Fiction 5873892*....54 1
24 Nov 01 GREATEST HITS *Fiction 5894352*....33 5
10 Jul 04 ● THE CURE *I Am / Geffen 9862890*....8 5
31 Jul 04 **THE END OF THE WORLD** *Geffen 9862976*....25 3
30 Oct 04 **TAKING OFF** *Geffen 9864491*....39 1

The CD version of Standing on a Beach – The Singles was titled Staring at the Sea.

CURIOSITY KILLED THE CAT

UK, male vocal (Ben Volpeliere-Pierrot) / instrumental group (2 Albums: 27 Weeks, 8 Singles: 58 Weeks)

13 Dec 86 ● **DOWN TO EARTH** *Mercury CAT 2*....3 18
4 Apr 87 **ORDINARY DAY** *Mercury CAT 3*....11 7
9 May 87 ★ KEEP YOUR DISTANCE *Mercury CATLP 1* ■....1 24
20 Jun 87 ● **MISFIT** *Mercury CAT 4*....7 9
19 Sep 87 **FREE** *Mercury CAT 5*....56 2
16 Sep 89 **NAME AND NUMBER** *Mercury CAT 6* [1]....14 9
4 Oct 89 GETAHEAD *Mercury 842010 1*....29 3
25 Apr 92 ● **HANG ON IN THERE BABY** *RCA PB 45377* [1]....3 10
29 Aug 92 **I NEED YOUR LOVIN'** *RCA 74321111377* [1]....47 2
30 Oct 93 **GIMME THE SUNSHINE** *RCA 74321168602* [1]....73 1

[1] Curiosity

Chantal CURTIS *France, female vocalist*

14 Jul 79 **GET ANOTHER LOVE** *Pye 7P 5003*....51 3

TC CURTIS *Jamaica, male vocalist / instrumentalist*

23 Feb 85 **YOU SHOULD HAVE KNOWN BETTER** *Hot Melt VS 754*....50 4

2 / 4 November 1961	9 / 11 November 1961	16 / 18 November 1961	23 / 25 November 1961
UK No.1 SINGLES			
WALKIN' BACK TO HAPPINESS Helen Shapiro	**(MARIE'S THE NAME) HIS LATEST FLAME / LITTLE SISTER** Elvis Presley	**(MARIE'S THE NAME) HIS LATEST FLAME / LITTLE SISTER** Elvis Presley	**(MARIE'S THE NAME) HIS LATEST FLAME / LITTLE SISTER** Elvis Presley
UK No.1 ALBUMS			
21 TODAY Cliff Richard, The Shadows and Norrie Paramor and Orchestra	**ANOTHER BLACK AND WHITE MINSTREL SHOW** George Mitchell Minstrels	**ANOTHER BLACK AND WHITE MINSTREL SHOW** George Mitchell Minstrels	**ANOTHER BLACK AND WHITE MINSTREL SHOW** George Mitchell Minstrels

CURVE *UK, male / female vocal / instrumental duo – Toni Halliday and Dean Garcia (3 Albums: 6 Weeks, 7 Singles: 14 Weeks)*

16 Mar 91 **THE BLINDFOLD (EP)** *AnXious ANX 27* **68** 1
25 May 91 **COAST IS CLEAR** *AnXious ANX 30* **34** 3
9 Nov 91 **CLIPPED** *AnXious ANX 35* **36** 2
7 Mar 92 **FAIT ACCOMPLI** *AnXious ANXT 36* **22** 3
21 Mar 92 DOPPELGANGER *AnXious ANXCD 77* 11 3
18 Jul 92 **HORROR HEAD (EP)** *AnXious ANXT 38* **31** 2
19 Jun 93 RADIO SESSIONS *AnXious ANXCD 80* 72 1
4 Sep 93 **BLACKERTHREETRACKER (EP)** *AnXious ANXCD 42* **39** 2
25 Sep 93 CUCKOO *AnXious ANXCD 81* 23 2
16 May 98 **COMING UP ROSES** *Universal UND 80489* **51** 1

Tracks on The Blindfold (EP): Ten Little Girls / I Speak Your Every Word / Blindfold / No Escape from Heaven. Tracks on Horror Head (EP): Horror Head / Falling Free / Mission from God / Today Is Not the Day. Tracks on Blackerthreetracker (EP): Missing Link (only track available on all formats of EP) / On the Wheel / Triumph.

CURVED AIR *UK, male / female vocal (Sonia Kristina) / instrumental group (3 Albums: 32 Weeks, 1 Single: 12 Weeks)*

5 Dec 70 ● AIR CONDITIONING *Warner Bros. WSX 3012* 8 21
7 Aug 71 ● **BACK STREET LUV** *Warner Bros. K 16092* **4** 12
9 Oct 71 CURVED AIR *Warner Bros. K 46092* 11 6
13 May 72 PHANTASMAGORIA *Reprise K 46158* 20 5

CUT 'N' MOVE
Denmark, male / female vocal / instrumental group (2 Singles: 4 Weeks)

2 Oct 93 **GIVE IT UP** *EMI CDEM 273* **61** 2
9 Sep 95 **I'M ALIVE** *EMI CDEM 375* **49** 2

Frankie CUTLASS *US, male rapper – Francis Parker*

5 Apr 97 **THE CYPHER: PART 3** *Epic 6641445* **59** 1

Jon CUTLER featuring E-MAN
US, male producer and vocalist – Eric Clark

19 Jan 02 **IT'S YOURS** *Direction 6720532* **38** 2

CUTTING CREW *UK / Canada, male vocal (Nick Van Eede) / instrumental group (1 Album: 6 Weeks, 5 Singles: 37 Weeks)*

16 Aug 86 ● **(I JUST) DIED IN YOUR ARMS** *Siren SIREN 21* ▲ **4** 12
25 Oct 86 **I'VE BEEN IN LOVE BEFORE (re)** *Siren SIREN 29* **31** 10
29 Nov 86 BROADCAST *Siren SIRENLP 7* 41 6
7 Mar 87 **ONE FOR THE MOCKINGBIRD** *Siren SIREN 40* **52** 5
21 Nov 87 **I'VE BEEN IN LOVE BEFORE** (re-mix) *Siren SRN 29* **24** 8
22 Jul 89 **(BETWEEN A) ROCK AND A HARD PLACE** *Siren SRN 108* **66** 2

CYBERSONIK *US, male instrumentalists / producers*

10 Nov 90 **TECHNARCHY** *Champion CHAMP 264* **73** 1

CYCLEFLY *Ireland, male vocal / instrumental group*

6 Apr 02 **NO STRESS** *Radioactive RAXTD 41* **68** 1

CYGNUS X (see also BRAINCHILD; VERNON'S WONDERLAND) *Germany, male producer – A C Bousten (aka Matthias Hoffmann) (2 Singles: 5 Weeks)*

11 Mar 00 **THE ORANGE THEME** *Hooj Choons HOOJ 88CD* **43** 2
18 Aug 01 **SUPERSTRING** *Xtravaganza XTRAV 28CDS* **33** 3

Johnny CYMBAL
Canada (b. UK), male vocalist, b. 3 Feb 1945, d. 16 Mar 1993

14 Mar 63 **MR BASS MAN** *London HLR 9682* **24** 10

CYPRESS HILL
US, male rap group (7 Albums: 68 Weeks, 14 Singles: 46 Weeks)

31 Jul 93 **INSANE IN THE BRAIN** *Ruff House 6595332* **32** 4
7 Aug 93 BLACK SUNDAY *Ruff House 4740752* ▲ 13 49
2 Oct 93 **WHEN THE SH.. GOES DOWN** *Ruff House 6596702* **19** 4
11 Dec 93 **I AIN'T GOIN' OUT LIKE THAT** *Ruff House 6596902* **15** 7
26 Feb 94 **INSANE IN THE BRAIN** (re-issue) *Ruff House 6601762* **21** 4
7 May 94 **LICK A SHOT** *Ruff House 6603192* **20** 3
7 Oct 95 **THROW YOUR SET IN THE AIR** *Ruff House 6623542* **15** 3
11 Nov 95 CYPRESS HILL III (TEMPLES OF BOOM) *Columbia 4781279* 11 5
17 Feb 96 **ILLUSIONS** *Columbia 6629052* **23** 2
24 Aug 96 UNRELEASED & REVAMPED (EP) *Columbia 4852302* 29 4
10 Oct 98 **TEQUILA SUNRISE** *Columbia 6664935* **23** 2
17 Oct 98 IV *Columbia 4916046* 25 3
10 Apr 99 **DR GREENTHUMB** *Columbia 6671202* **34** 2
26 Jun 99 **INSANE IN THE BRAIN** *INCredible INCRL 17CD* [1] **19** 3
29 Apr 00 **(RAP) SUPERSTAR / (ROCK) SUPERSTAR** *Columbia 6692642* **13** 5
6 May 00 ● SKULL & BONES *Columbia 4951832* 6 5
16 Sep 00 **HIGHLIFE / CAN'T GET THE BEST OF ME** *Columbia 6697892* **35** 2
8 Dec 01 **LOWRIDER / TROUBLE (re)** *Columbia 6721662* **33** 3
15 Dec 01 STONED RAIDERS *Columbia 5041719* 71 1
27 Mar 04 **WHAT'S YOUR NUMBER?** *Columbia 6746172* **44** 2
3 Apr 04 TILL DEATH DO U$ PART *Columbia 5150292* 53 1

[1] Jason Nevins vs Cypress Hill

Billy Ray CYRUS
US, male vocalist (1 Album: 10 Weeks, 4 Singles: 18 Weeks)

25 Jul 92 ● **ACHY BREAKY HEART** *Mercury MER 373* $ **3** 10
29 Aug 92 ● SOME GAVE ALL *Mercury 5106352* ▲ 9 10
10 Oct 92 **COULD'VE BEEN ME** *Mercury MER 378* **24** 4
28 Nov 92 **THESE BOOTS ARE MADE FOR WALKIN'** *Mercury MER 384* **63** 1
19 Dec 92 **ACHY BREAKY HEART** *Epic 6588837* [1] **53** 3

[1] Alvin and The Chipmunks featuring Billy Ray Cyrus

D

Asher D (see also SO SOLID CREW)
UK, male rapper – Ashley Walters (4 Singles: 2 Weeks)

4 Aug 01 **BABY, CAN I GET YOUR NUMBER** *East West EW 235CD* [1] **75** 1
8 Jun 02 **BACK IN THE DAY / WHY ME** *Independiente ISOM 57MS* **43** 1

[1] Obi Project featuring Harry, Asher D and DJ What?

Chuck D (see also PUBLIC ENEMY)
US, male rapper – Carlton Ridenhour (3 Singles: 9 Weeks)

6 Jul 91 **BRING THE NOISE** *Island IS 490* [1] **14** 5
26 Oct 96 **NO** *Mercury MERCD 476* **55** 1
23 Jun 01 **ROCK DA FUNKY BEATS** *Xtrahard / Xtravaganza X2H 3CDS* [2] **19** 3

[1] Anthrax featuring Chuck D [2] Public Domain featuring Chuck D

Dimples D *US, female rapper – Crystal Smith*

17 Nov 90 **SUCKER DJ** *FBI FBI 11* **17** 10

Juggy D (see also The RISHI RICH PROJECT) *UK, male vocalist*

4 Sep 04 JUGGY D *2point9 2POINT9 100CD* 70 1

Longsy D *UK, male instrumentalist / producer*

4 Mar 89 **THIS IS SKA** *Big One VBIG 13* **56** 7

30 November / 2 December 1961	7 / 9 December 1961	14 / 16 December 1961	21 / 23 December 1961
(MARIE'S THE NAME) HIS LATEST FLAME / LITTLE SISTER Elvis Presley	**TOWER OF STRENGTH** Frankie Vaughan	**TOWER OF STRENGTH** Frankie Vaughan	**TOWER OF STRENGTH** Frankie Vaughan
ANOTHER BLACK AND WHITE MINSTREL SHOW George Mitchell Minstrels	**ANOTHER BLACK AND WHITE MINSTREL SHOW** George Mitchell Minstrels	**ANOTHER BLACK AND WHITE MINSTREL SHOW** George Mitchell Minstrels	**ANOTHER BLACK AND WHITE MINSTREL SHOW** George Mitchell Minstrels

KEY
UK No.1 ★ UK Top 10 ● Still on chart + UK entry at No.1 ■
US No.1 ▲ UK million seller £ US million seller $
Singles re-entries are listed as (re), (2re), (3re)... which signifies that the hit re-entered the chart once, twice or three times...

Peak Position / Weeks

Maxwell D *UK, male rapper – Maxwell Donaldson*

15 Sep 01	**SERIOUS** *4 Liberty LIBTCD 046*	38	2

Nikki D *US, female rapper – Nichelle Strong (2 Singles: 6 Weeks)*

6 May 89	**MY LOVE IS SO RAW** *Def Jam 6548987* [1]	34	5
30 Mar 91	**DADDY'S LITTLE GIRL** *Def Jam 6567347*	75	1

[1] Alyson Williams featuring Nikki D

Vicky D *US, female vocalist*

13 Mar 82	**THIS BEAT IS MINE** *Virgin VS 486*	42	6

DB BOULEVARD (see also MOONY)
Italy, male production trio and female vocalist (Moony – Monica Bragato)

23 Feb 02 ●	**POINT OF VIEW** *Illustrious CDILL 002*	3	12

DBM *Germany, male / female vocal / instrumental group*

12 Nov 77	**DISCO BEATLEMANIA** *Atlantic K 11027*	45	3

D, B, M and T (see also Dave DEE, DOZY, BEAKY, MICK and TICH)
UK, male vocal / instrumental group

1 Aug 70	**MR PRESIDENT** *Fontana 6007 022*	33	8

The D4 *New Zealand, male vocal / instrumental group (3 Singles: 3 Weeks)*

28 Sep 02	**GET LOOSE** *Infectious INFEC 117CDS*	64	1
7 Dec 02	**COME ON!** *Infectious INFEC 121CDS*	50	1
29 Mar 03	**LADIES MAN** *Infectious INFECT 122CDS*	41	1

D.H.S. *UK, male producer – Ben Stokes*

9 Feb 02	**HOUSE OF GOD** *Club Tools 0135825 CLU*	72	1

DHT featuring EDMÉE NEW *Belgium, male / female production / vocal duo – Flor Theeuwes & Edmée Daenen*

17 Dec 05 ●	**LISTEN TO YOUR HEART** *Data 109CDS*	7	3+

D KAY & EPSILON featuring STAMINA MC
Austria / UK, male production / vocal trio

30 Aug 03	**BARCELONA** *Alphamagic / BC / BMG BCAU 001CD*	14	5

DMX *US, male rapper – Earl Simmons*
(2 Albums: 11 Weeks, 5 Singles: 27 Weeks)

15 May 99	**SLIPPIN'** *Def Jam 8707552*	30	2
3 Nov 01	THE GREAT DEPRESSION *Def Jam 5864502* ▲	20	3
15 Dec 01	**WHO WE BE** *Def Jam 5888512*	34	4
3 May 03 ●	**X GON' GIVE IT TO YA** *Def Jam 0779042*	6	12
27 Sep 03 ●	GRAND CHAMP *Def Jam / Mercury 9861021* ▲	6	8
11 Oct 03	**WHERE THE HOOD AT?** *Def Jam 9811251*	16	5
10 Jan 04	**GET IT ON THE FLOOR** *Def Jam 9815206* [1]	34	4

[1] DMX featuring Swizz Beatz

D MOB
UK, male producer – Danny Poku (1 Album: 11 Weeks, 7 Singles: 48 Weeks)

15 Oct 88 ●	**WE CALL IT ACIEED** *ffrr FFR 13* [1]	3	12
3 Jun 89 ●	**IT IS TIME TO GET FUNKY** *ffrr F 107* [2]	9	10
21 Oct 89	**C'MON AND GET MY LOVE** *ffrr F 117* [3]	15	10
11 Nov 89	A LITTLE BIT OF THIS A LITTLE BIT OF THAT *ffrr 8281591*	46	11
6 Jan 90 ●	**PUT YOUR HANDS TOGETHER** *ffrr F 124* [4]	7	8
7 Apr 90	**THAT'S THE WAY OF THE WORLD** *ffrr F 132* [3]	48	3
12 Feb 94	**WHY** *ffrr FCD 227* [3]	23	3
3 Sep 94	**ONE DAY** *ffrr FCDP 239*	41	2

[1] D Mob featuring Gary Haisman [2] D Mob featuring LRS [3] D Mob with Cathy Dennis [4] D Mob featuring Nuff Juice

DNA
UK, male production duo – Neal Slateford and Nick Bett (5 Singles: 29 Weeks)

28 Jul 90 ●	**TOM'S DINER** (re-mix) *A&M AM 592* [1]	2	10
18 Aug 90	**LA SERENISSIMA** *Raw Bass RBASS 006*	34	8
3 Aug 91	**REBEL WOMAN** *DNA 7DNA 001* [2]	42	4
1 Feb 92	**CAN YOU HANDLE IT** (re-recording) *EMI EM 219* [3]	17	5
9 May 92	**BLUE LOVE (CALL MY NAME)** *EMI EM 226* [4]	66	2

[1] DNA featuring Suzanne Vega [2] DNA featuring Jazzi P [3] DNA featuring Sharon Redd [4] DNA featuring Joe Nye

D*NOTE *UK, male producer – Matt Winn (3 Singles: 3 Weeks)*

12 Jul 97	**WAITING HOPEFULLY** *A&M 5822792*	46	1
15 Nov 97	**LOST AND FOUND** *VC VCRD 25*	59	1
27 Apr 02	**SHED MY SKIN** *Channel 4 Music C4M 00182*	73	1

D.O.N.S. featuring TECHNOTRONIC NEW
Germany, male production group and Belgium, male producer

5 Nov 05	**PUMP UP THE JAM** *Data DATA 94CDS*	22	3

D.O.P. *UK, male instrumental / production duo (2 Singles: 2 Weeks)*

3 Feb 96	**STOP STARTING TO START STOPPING (EP)** *Hi-Life 5779472*	58	1
13 Jul 96	**GROOVY BEAT** *Hi-Life 5750652*	54	1

Tracks on Stop Starting to Start Stopping (EP): Gusta / Dance to the House / Can You Feel It / How Do Y'All Feel.

D-RAIL NEW *UK, male vocal trio*

5 Feb 05	**HOW DO I SAY GOODBYE** *Silverword ECPCDS 1*	63	1

D:REAM *UK, male production / instrumental / vocal duo – Peter Cunnah and Al MacKenzie (left 1993) (2 Albums: 41 Weeks, 13 Singles: 74 Weeks)*

4 Jul 92	**U R THE BEST THING** *FXU FXU 3*	72	1
30 Jan 93	**THINGS CAN ONLY GET BETTER** *Magnet MAG 1010CD*	24	5
24 Apr 93	**U R THE BEST THING** (re-issue) *Magnet MAG 1011CD*	19	8
31 Jul 93	**UNFORGIVEN** *Magnet MAG 1016CD*	29	3
2 Oct 93	**STAR / I LIKE IT** *Magnet MAG 1019CD*	26	4
30 Oct 93 ●	D:REAM ON VOLUME 1 *Magnet 4509933712*	5	37
8 Jan 94 ★	**THINGS CAN ONLY GET BETTER** (re-issue) *Magnet MAG 1020CD*	1	16
26 Mar 94 ●	**U R THE BEST THING** (re-mix) *Magnet MAG 1021CD*	4	10
18 Jun 94	**TAKE ME AWAY** *Magnet MAG 1025CD*	18	5
10 Sep 94	**BLAME IT ON ME** *Magnet MAG 1027CD*	25	5
8 Jul 95 ●	**SHOOT ME WITH YOUR LOVE** *Magnet MAG 1034CD*	7	7
9 Sep 95	**PARTY UP THE WORLD** *Magnet MAG 1037CD*	20	6
30 Sep 95 ●	WORLD *Magnet 0630117962*	5	4
11 Nov 95	**THE POWER (OF ALL THE LOVE IN THE WORLD)** *Magnet MAG 1039CD*	40	1
3 May 97	**THINGS CAN ONLY GET BETTER** (2nd re-issue) *Magnet MAG 1050CD*	19	3

For second album D:Ream was just Peter Cunnah.

DSK *UK, male / female vocal / instrumental / production group (2 Singles: 4 Weeks)*

31 Aug 91	**WHAT WOULD WE DO / READ MY LIPS** *Boy's Own BOI 6*	46	3
22 Nov 97	**WHAT WOULD WE DO** (re-mix) *Fresh FRSHD 63*	55	1

DSM *US, male rap group*

7 Dec 85	**WARRIOR GROOVE** *10 DAZZ 45-7*	68	4

D-SHAKE *Holland, male producer – Adrianus De Mooy (2 Singles: 8 Weeks)*

2 Jun 90 **YAAAH / TECHNO TRANCE** *Cooltempo COOL 213*......20 6
2 Feb 91 **MY HEART THE BEAT** *Cooltempo COOL 228*......42 2

D-SIDE *Ireland, male vocal group (1 Album: 1 Week, 4 Singles: 25 Weeks)*

26 Apr 03 ● **SPEECHLESS** *WEA WEA 366CD1*......9 8
26 Jul 03 ● **INVISIBLE** *Blacklist / Edel / WEA WEA 369CD1*......7 6
13 Dec 03 ● **REAL WORLD** *Blacklist / Edel 9814017*......9 8
17 Jan 04 **STRONGER TOGETHER** *Blacklist / Edel 9866006*......62 1
12 Jun 04 **PUSHIN' ME OUT** *Blacklist / Edel 0155825 ERE*......21 3

DT8 PROJECT (see also ANGELIC; CITIZEN CANED; ORION; Jurgen VRIES)
UK, male producer – Darren Tate (3 Singles: 8 Weeks)

3 May 03 **DESTINATION** *ffrr DFCD 007* [1] 23 3
14 Aug 04 **THE SUN IS SHINING (DOWN ON ME)** *Mondo MNDO 19CD*......17 3
5 Mar 05 **WINTER** *Data DATA 80CDS* [2] 35 2

[1] DT8 featuring Roxanne Wilde [2] DT8 Project featuring Andrea Britton

DTI *US, male vocal / instrumental group*

16 Apr 88 **KEEP THIS FREQUENCY CLEAR** *Premiere UK ERE 501*......73 1

D-TEK *UK, male instrumental / production group*

6 Nov 93 **DROP THE ROCK (EP)** *Positiva 12TIV 5*......70 1

Tracks on Drop the Rock (EP): Drop the Rock / Chunkafunk / Drop the Rock (re-mix) / Don't Breathe.

D TRAIN *US, male vocal / instrumental duo – James Williams and Hubert Eaves III (1 Album: 4 Weeks, 6 Singles: 36 Weeks)*

6 Feb 82 **YOU'RE THE ONE FOR ME** *Epic EPC A 2016*......30 8
8 May 82 **D-TRAIN** *Epic EPC 85683*......72 4
8 May 82 **WALK ON BY** *Epic EPC A 2298*......44 6
7 May 83 **MUSIC PART 1** *Prelude A 3332*......23 7
16 Jul 83 **KEEP GIVING ME LOVE** *Prelude A 3497*......65 2
27 Jul 85 **YOU'RE THE ONE FOR ME** (re-mix) *Prelude ZB 40302*......15 11
12 Oct 85 **MUSIC** (re-mix) *Prelude ZB 40431*......62 2

D12 (see also BIZARRE; EMINEM)
US, male rap group (2 Albums: 37 Weeks, 5 Singles: 46 Weeks)

17 Mar 01 ● **SHIT ON YOU (re)** *Interscope 4974962*......10 8
30 Jun 01 ● **DEVILS NIGHT** *Interscope 4930792* ▲......2 17
21 Jul 01 ● **PURPLE PILLS** *Shady / Interscope 4975692*......2 12
17 Nov 01 **FIGHT MUSIC** *Shady / Interscope 4976522*......11 5
24 Apr 04 ● **MY BAND** *Shady / Interscope 9862352*......2 13
8 May 04 ★ **D12 WORLD** *Interscope 9862431* ■ ▲......1 20
7 Aug 04 ● **HOW COME** *Shady / Interscope 9863318*......4 8

Azzido DA BASS
Germany, male DJ / producer – Ingo Martens (3 Singles: 13 Weeks)

4 Mar 00 **DOOMS NIGHT (re)** *Club Tools 0067285 CLU*......46 3
21 Oct 00 ● **DOOMS NIGHT (re)** (re-mix) *Club Tools 0120285 CLU*......8 9
23 Mar 02 **SPEED (CAN YOU FEEL IT)** *Club Tools 0135815 CLU* [1] 68 1

[1] Azzido Da Bass featuring Roland Clark

DA BRAT *US, female rapper – Shawntae Harris (3 Singles: 3 Weeks)*

22 Oct 94 **FUNKDAFIED** *Columbia 6609212* $......65 1
29 Nov 97 **SOCKIT2ME** *East West E 3890CD* [1] 33 2

[1] Missy Elliott featuring Da Brat

DA CLICK *UK, male rap group and female vocalist (2 Singles: 8 Weeks)*

16 Jan 99 **GOOD RHYMES** *ffrr FCD 353*......14 6
29 May 99 **WE ARE DA CLICK** *ffrr FCD 363*......38 2

DA FOOL *US, male DJ / producer – Mike Stewart*

16 Jan 99 **NO GOOD** *ffrr FCD 352*......38 2

Ricardo DA FORCE (see also N-TRANCE)
UK, male rapper – Ricardo Lyte (3 Singles: 14 Weeks)

18 Mar 95 **PUMP UP THE VOLUME** *Stress CDSTR 49* [1] 51 2
16 Sep 95 ● **STAYIN' ALIVE** *All Around the World CDGLOBE 131* [2] 2 11
31 Aug 96 **WHY** *ffrr FCD 280*......58 1

[1] Greed featuring Ricardo Da Force [2] N-Trance featuring Ricardo Da Force

DA HOOL *Germany, male instrumentalist / producer – Frank Tomiczek (3 Singles: 13 Weeks)*

14 Feb 98 **MEET HER AT THE LOVE PARADE** *Manifesto FESCD 39*......15 4
22 Aug 98 **BORA BORA** *Manifesto FESCD 47*......35 3
28 Jul 01 **MEET HER AT THE LOVE PARADE 2001** *Manifesto FESCD 85*..11 6

DA LENCH MOB *US, male rap group*

20 Mar 93 **FREEDOM GOT AN A.K.** *East West America A 8431CD*......51 2

DA MOB featuring Jocelyn BROWN
US, male / female vocal / instrumental group (2 Singles: 3 Weeks)

2 May 98 **FUN** *INCredible INCRL 2CD*......33 2
3 Jul 99 **IT'S ALL GOOD** *INCredible INCRL 14CD*......54 1

DA MUTTZ (see also SHAFT)
UK, male production duo – Elliot Ireland and Alex Rizzo

9 Dec 00 **WASSUUP** *Eternal WEA 319CD*......11 10

DA PLAYAZ vs CLEA NEW
Sweden, male producers and UK, female vocal group

29 Oct 05 **WE DON'T HAVE TO TAKE OUR CLOTHES OFF** *Upside UPSIDECD 02*......35 2

Rui DA SILVA featuring CASSANDRA
Portugal, male producer and UK, female vocalist – Cassandra Fox

13 Jan 01 ★ **TOUCH ME** *Kismet / Arista 74321823992* ■......1 14

DA SLAMMIN' PHROGZ *France, male production duo*

29 Apr 00 **SOMETHING ABOUT THE MUSIC** *WEA WEA 251CD*......53 1

DA TECHNO BOHEMIAN (see also DRUNKENMUNKY; ITTY BITTY BOOZY WOOZY; KLUBBHEADS) *Holland, male production trio*

25 Jan 97 **BANGIN' BASS** *Hi-Life 5731772*......63 1

Paul DA VINCI (see also The RUBETTES) *UK, male vocalist – Paul Prewer*

20 Jul 74 **YOUR BABY AIN'T YOUR BABY ANYMORE** *Penny Farthing PEN 843*......20 8

Terry DACTYL and The DINOSAURS
UK, male vocal (Jona Lewie) / instrumental group (2 Singles: 16 Weeks)

15 Jul 72 ● **SEASIDE SHUFFLE** *UK 5*......2 12
13 Jan 73 **ON A SATURDAY NIGHT** *UK 21*......45 4

DADA *US, male vocal / instrumental group*

4 Dec 93 **DOG** *IRS CDEIRSS 185*......71 1

DADDY YANKEE NEW *Puerto Rico, male rapper – Raymond Ayala*

30 Jul 05 ● **GASOLINA** *Machete 9883425*......5 9

DADDY'S FAVOURITE
UK, male DJ / producer – James Harrigan (2 Singles: 3 Weeks)

21 Nov 98 **I FEEL GOOD THINGS FOR YOU** *Go Beat GONCD 12*......44 2
9 Oct 99 **I FEEL GOOD THINGS FOR YOU** (re-issue) *Go Beat GOBCD 22*......50 1

25 / 27 January 1962	1 / 3 February 1962	8 / 10 February 1962	15 / 17 February 1962
THE YOUNG ONES Cliff Richard and The Shadows	THE YOUNG ONES Cliff Richard and The Shadows	THE YOUNG ONES Cliff Richard and The Shadows	THE YOUNG ONES Cliff Richard and The Shadows
THE YOUNG ONES (Soundtrack) Cliff Richard - The Shadows with Grazina Frame	THE YOUNG ONES (Soundtrack) Cliff Richard - The Shadows with Grazina Frame	THE YOUNG ONES (Soundtrack) Cliff Richard - The Shadows with Grazina Frame	THE YOUNG ONES (Soundtrack) Cliff Richard - The Shadows with Grazina Frame

OSCAR-WINNING SONGS

Here are the Oscar-winning songs, their performers, writers and UK chart positions. Bing Crosby is the top performer. He's sung four Academy Award-winning songs from the movies he has starred in. Four writers have won the coveted award for original film songs four times. They are Sammy Cahn (nominated a record-breaking 26 times), Alan Menken, Johnny Mercer and James Van Heusen.

1934 **THE CONTINENTAL** Performed by Ginger Rogers in the movie The Gay Divorcee. Writers: Con Conrad (music), Herb Magidson (lyrics). UK hit single for Maureen McGovern (No.16 in 1976).

1935 **LULLABY OF BROADWAY** Performed by Dick Powell and Winifred Shaw in the movie Gold Diggers of 1935. Writers: Harry Warren (music), Al Dubin (lyrics). UK hit single (when re-issued) for Winifred Shaw (No.42 in 1976).

1936 **THE WAY YOU LOOK TONIGHT** Performed by Fred Astaire in the movie Swing Time. Writers: Jerome Kern (music), Dorothy Fields (lyrics). UK hit singles for The Lettermen (No.36 in 1961), Denny Seyton and The Sabres (No.48 in 1964), Edward Woodward (No.42 in 1971).

1937 **SWEET LEILANI** Performed by Bing Crosby in the movie Waikiki Wedding. Writer: Harry Owens (music and lyrics).

1938 **THANKS FOR THE MEMORY** Performed by Bob Hope and Shirley Ross in the movie The Big Broadcast. Writers: Ralph Rainger (music), Leo Robin (lyrics).

1939 **OVER THE RAINBOW** Performed by Judy Garland in the movie The Wizard of Oz. Writers: Harold Arlen (music), E Y Harburg (lyrics). UK hit singles for Matchbox (No.15 in 1980), Sam Harris (No.67 in 1985), Eva Cassidy (No.42 in 2001), and Cliff Richard (No.11 in 2001).

1940 **WHEN YOU WISH UPON A STAR** Performed by Cliff Edwards in the movie Pinocchio. Writers: Leigh Harline (music), Ned Washington (lyrics).

1941 **THE LAST TIME I SAW PARIS** Performed by Ann Southern in the movie Lady Be Good. Writers: Jerome Kern (music), Oscar Hammerstein II (lyrics).

1942 **WHITE CHRISTMAS** Performed by Bing Crosby in the movie Holiday Inn. Writer: Irving Berlin (music and lyrics). UK hit singles for Mantovani (No.6 in 1952), Pat Boone (No.29 in 1957), Freddie Starr (No.41 in 1975), Bing Crosby (No.5 in 1977 - re-issue hit in 1985 and 1998), Darts (No.48 in 1980), Jim Davidson (No.52 in 1980), Keith Harris and Orville (No.40 in 1985), Max Bygraves (No.71 in 1989).

1943 **YOU'LL NEVER KNOW** Performed by Alice Faye in the movie Hello, Frisco, Hello. Writers: Harry Warren (music), Mack Gordon (lyrics). UK hit single for Shirley Bassey (No.6 in 1961).

1944 **SWINGING ON A STAR** Performed by Bing Crosby, with the Williams Brothers Quartet, featuring a 15-year-old Andy Williams, in the movie Going My Way. Writers: James Van Heusen (music), Johnny Burke (lyrics). UK hit single for Big Dee Irwin (No.7 in 1963).

1945 **IT MIGHT AS WELL BE SPRING** Performed by Jeanne Crain in the movie State Fair. Writers: Richard Rodgers (music), Oscar Hammerstein II (lyrics).

1946 **ON THE ATCHISON, TOPEKA AND THE SANTA FE** Performed by Judy Garland in the movie The Harvey Girls. Writers: Harry Warren (music), Johnny Mercer (lyrics).

1947 **ZIP-A-DEE-DOO-DAH** Performed by James Baskett in the movie Song of the South. Writers: Allie Wrubel (music), Ray Gilbert (lyrics). UK hit single for Bob B Soxx and The Blue Jeans (No.45 in 1963).

1948 **BUTTONS AND BOWS** Performed by Bob Hope in the movie The Paleface. Writers: Jay Livingston, Ray Evans (music and lyrics).

1949 **BABY, IT'S COLD OUTSIDE** Performed by Esther Williams and Ricardo Montalban in the movie Neptune's Daughter. Writer: Frank Loesser (music and lyrics). UK hit single for Tom Jones and Cerys Matthews (No.17 in 1999).

1950 **MONA LISA** Performed by Nat 'King' Cole in the movie Captain Carey, USA. Writers: Ray Evans, Jay Livingston (music and lyrics). UK hit single for Conway Twitty (No.5 in 1959).

1951 **IN THE COOL, COOL, COOL OF THE EVENING** Performed by Bing Crosby in the movie Here Comes the Groom. Writers: Hoagy Carmichael (music), Johnny Mercer (lyrics).

1952 **HIGH NOON (DO NOT FORSAKE ME, OH MY DARLIN')** Performed by Tex Ritter in the movie High Noon. Writers Dmitri Tiomkin (music), Ned Washington (lyrics). UK hit single for Frankie Laine (No.7 in 1952).

	22 / 24 February 1962	1 / 3 March 1962	8 / 10 March 1962	15 / 17 March 1962
UK No.1 SINGLES	**ROCK-A-HULA BABY / CAN'T HELP FALLING IN LOVE** Elvis Presley with The Jordanaires	**ROCK-A-HULA BABY / CAN'T HELP FALLING IN LOVE** Elvis Presley with The Jordanaires	**ROCK-A-HULA BABY / CAN'T HELP FALLING IN LOVE** Elvis Presley with The Jordanaires	**ROCK-A-HULA BABY / CAN'T HELP FALLING IN LOVE** Elvis Presley with The Jordanaires
UK No.1 ALBUMS	**BLUE HAWAII (Soundtrack)** Elvis Presley	**BLUE HAWAII (Soundtrack)** Elvis Presley	**BLUE HAWAII (Soundtrack)** Elvis Presley	**BLUE HAWAII (Soundtrack)** Elvis Presley

Remarkably, father Rex Harrison and son Noel both sang Oscar-winning songs in consecutive years, 1967 and 1968

1953 SECRET LOVE Performed by Doris Day in the movie Calamity Jane. Writers: Sammy Fain (music), Paul Francis Webster (lyrics). UK hit singles for Doris Day (No.1 in 1953), Kathy Kirby (No.4 in 1963), Daniel O'Donnell (No.28 in 1995).

1954 THREE COINS IN THE FOUNTAIN Performed by Frank Sinatra in the movie Three Coins in the Fountain. Writers: Jule Styne (music), Sammy Cahn (lyrics). UK hit singles for Frank Sinatra (No.1 in 1954), The Four Aces (No.5 in 1954).

1955 LOVE IS A MANY SPLENDORED THING Performed by the chorus in the movie Love Is a Many Splendored Thing. Writers: Sammy Fain (music) Paul Francis Webster (lyrics). UK hit single for The Four Aces (No.2 in 1954).

1956 WHATEVER WILL BE, WILL BE (QUE SERA, SERA) Performed by Doris Day in the movie The Man Who Knew Too Much. Writers: Ray Evans, Jay Livingston (music and lyrics). UK hit singles for Doris Day (No.1 in 1956), Geno Washington (No.43 in 1966), Hermes House Band (No.53 in 2002).

1957 ALL THE WAY Performed by Frank Sinatra in the movie The Joker Is Wild. Writers: James Van Heusen (music), Sammy Cahn (lyrics). UK hit single for Frank Sinatra (No.3 in 1957).

1958 GIGI Performed by Maurice Chevalier in the movie Gigi. Writers: Frederick Loewe (music), Alan Jay Lerner (lyrics). UK hit single for Billy Eckstine (No.8 in 1959).

1959 HIGH HOPES Performed by Frank Sinatra in the movie A Hole in the Head. Writers: James Van Heusen (music), Sammy Cahn (lyrics). UK hit single for Frank Sinatra (No.6 in 1959).

1960 NEVER ON SUNDAY Performed by Melina Mercouri in the movie Pote Tin Kyriaki (Never on Sunday). Writers: Manos Hadjidakis (music and lyrics). 1960 UK hit single for Don Costa (No.27), Manuel and his Music of the Mountains (No.29), Lynn Cornell (No.30), Makadopoulos and his Greek Serenaders (No.36), Chaquito Orchestra (No.50).

1961 MOON RIVER Performed by Audrey Hepburn in the movie Breakfast at Tiffany's. Writers: Henry Mancini (music), Johnny Mercer (lyrics). UK hit singles for Danny Williams (No.1 in 1961), Greyhound (No.12 in 1972). Henry Mancini (No.44 in 1961).

1962 DAYS OF WINE AND ROSES Performed by the chorus in the movie Days of Wine and Roses. Writers: Henry Mancini (music), Johnny Mercer (lyrics).

1963 CALL ME IRRESPONSIBLE Performed by Jackie Gleason in the movie Papa's Delicate Condition. Writers: James Van Heusen (music), Sammy Cahn (lyrics).

1964 CHIM CHIM CHER-EE Performed by Dick Van Dyke in the movie Mary Poppins. Writers: Richard M and Robert B Sherman (music and lyrics).

1965 THE SHADOW OF YOUR SMILE Performed by the chorus in the movie The Sandpiper. Writers: Johnny Mandel (music), Paul Francis Webster (lyrics).

1966 BORN FREE Performed by Matt Monro in the movie Born Free. Writers: John Barry (music), Don Black (lyrics). UK hit single for Vic Reeves (No.6 in 1991).

1967 TALK TO THE ANIMALS Performed by Rex Harrison in the movie Dr Dolittle. Writers: Leslie Bricusse (music and lyrics).

1968 THE WINDMILLS OF YOUR MIND Performed by Noel Harrison in the movie The Thomas Crown Affair. Writers: Michel Legrand (music), Marilyn and Alan Bergman (lyrics). UK hit single for Noel Harrison (No.8 in 1969).

22 / 24 March 1962	29 / 31 March 1962	5 / 7 April 1962	12 / 14 April 1962
WONDERFUL LAND The Shadows	WONDERFUL LAND The Shadows	WONDERFUL LAND The Shadows	WONDERFUL LAND The Shadows
BLUE HAWAII (Soundtrack) Elvis Presley	BLUE HAWAII (Soundtrack) Elvis Presley	BLUE HAWAII (Soundtrack) Elvis Presley	BLUE HAWAII (Soundtrack) Elvis Presley

OSCAR-WINNING SONGS continued

1969 **RAINDROPS KEEP FALLIN' ON MY HEAD** Performed by B J Thomas in the movie Butch Cassidy and the Sundance Kid. Writers: Burt Bacharach (music), Hal David (lyrics). 1970 UK hit singles for Sacha Distel (No.10), B J Thomas (No.38), Bobbie Gentry (No.40).

1970 **FOR ALL WE KNOW** Performed by Larry Meredith in the movie Lovers and Other Strangers. Writers: Fred Karlin (music), James Griffin, Rob Royer (lyrics). UK hit singles for Shirley Bassey (No.6 in 1971), The Carpenters (No.18 in 1971), Nicki French (No.42 in 1995).

1971 **THEME FROM 'SHAFT'** Performed by Isaac Hayes in the movie 'Shaft'. Writers: Isaac Hayes (music and lyrics). UK hit singles for Isaac Hayes (No.4 in 1971), Eddy and The Soul Band (No.13 in 1985), Van Twist (No.52 in 1985).

1972 **THE MORNING AFTER** Performed by Maureen McGovern in the movie The Poseidon Adventure. Writers: Al Kasha, Joel Hirshhorn (music and lyrics).

1973 **THE WAY WE WERE** Performed by Barbra Streisand in the movie The Way We Were. Writers: Marvin Hamlisch (music), Marilyn and Alan Bergman (lyrics). UK hit singles for Barbra Streisand (No.31 in 1974), Gladys Knight and The Pips (No.4 in 1975).

1974 **WE MAY NEVER LOVE LIKE THIS AGAIN** Performed by Maureen McGovern in the movie The Towering Inferno. Writers: Joel Hirschhorn, Al Kasha (music and lyrics).

1975 **I'M EASY** Performed by Keith Carradine in the movie Nashville. Writer: Keith Carradine (music and lyrics).

1976 **EVERGREEN (LOVE THEME FROM A STAR IS BORN)** Performed by Barbra Streisand in the movie A Star Is Born. Writers: Barbra Streisand (music), Paul Williams (lyrics). UK hit single for Barbra Streisand (No.3 in 1977), Hazell Dean (No.63 in 1984).

1977 **YOU LIGHT UP MY LIFE** Performed by Cassie Cisyk in the movie You Light Up My Life. Writers: Joseph Brooks (music and lyrics). UK hit single for Debby Boone (No.48 in 1977).

1978 **LAST DANCE** Performed by Donna Summer in the movie Thank God it's Friday. Writer: Paul Jabara (music and lyrics). UK hit single for Donna Summer (No.58 in 1978).

1979 **IT GOES LIKE IT GOES** Performed by Jennifer Warnes in the movie Norma Rae. Writers: David Shire (music), Norman Gimbel (lyrics).

1980 **FAME** Performed by Irene Cara in the movie Fame. Writers: Michael Gore (music), Dean Pitchford (lyrics). UK hit single for Irene Cara (No.1 in 1982).

1981 **ARTHUR'S THEME (BEST THAT YOU CAN DO)** Performed by Christopher Cross in the movie Arthur. Writers: Burt Bacharach, Peter Allen, Christopher Cross, Carole Bayer Sager (music and lyrics). UK hit single for Christopher Cross (No.7 in 1982).

1982 **UP WHERE WE BELONG** Performed by Joe Cocker and Jennifer Warnes in the movie An Officer and a Gentleman. Writers: Jack Nitzsche, Buffy Sainte-Marie (music), Will Jennings (lyrics). UK hit single for Joe Cocker and Jennifer Warnes (No.7 in 1983).

1983 **FLASHDANCE ... WHAT A FEELING** Performed by Irene Cara in the movie Flashdance. Writers: Giorgio Moroder (music), Irena Cara, Keith Forsey (lyrics). UK hit singles for Irene Cara (No.2 in 1983), Björn Again (No.65 in 1993).

1984 **I JUST CALLED TO SAY I LOVE YOU** Performed by Stevie Wonder in the movie The Woman in Red. Writer: Stevie Wonder (music and lyrics). UK hit single for Stevie Wonder (No.1 in 1984).

1985 **SAY YOU, SAY ME** Performed by Lionel Richie in the movie White Nights. Writer: Lionel Richie (music and lyrics). UK hit single for Lionel Richie (No.8 in 1985).

1986 **TAKE MY BREATH AWAY** Performed by Berlin in the movie Top Gun. Writers: Giorgio Moroder (music), Tom Whitlock (lyrics). UK hit singles for Berlin (No.1 in 1986 - re-issue hit in 1988 and 1990), Soda Club featuring Hannah Alethea (No.16 in 2002).

1987 **(I'VE HAD) THE TIME OF MY LIFE** Performed by Bill Medley and Jennifer Warnes in the movie Dirty Dancing. Writers: John DeNicola, Donald Markowitz (music), Frankie Previte (lyrics), UK hit single for Bill Medley and Jennifer Warnes (No.6 in 1987 – re-issue hit in 1990).

1988 **LET THE RIVER RUN** Performed by Carly Simon in the movie Working Girl. Writer: Carly Simon (music and lyrics).

1989 **UNDER THE SEA** Performed by Samuel E Wright in the movie The Little Mermaid. Writers: Alan Menken (music), Howard Ashman (lyrics).

	19 / 21 April 1962	26 / 28 April 1962	3 / 5 May 1962	10 / 12 May 1962
UK No.1 SINGLES	**WONDERFUL LAND** The Shadows	**WONDERFUL LAND** The Shadows	**WONDERFUL LAND** The Shadows	**WONDERFUL LAND** The Shadows
UK No.1 ALBUMS	**BLUE HAWAII (Soundtrack)** Elvis Presley	**BLUE HAWAII (Soundtrack)** Elvis Presley	**BLUE HAWAII (Soundtrack)** Elvis Presley	**BLUE HAWAII (Soundtrack)** Elvis Presley

Maureen McGovern performed two Oscar-winning songs, in 1972 and 1974. Coincidentally, her only UK hit single came in 1976 with her version of 'The Continental', the song that won the first ever Best Song Oscar.

1990 **SOONER OR LATER (I ALWAYS GET MY MAN)** Performed by Madonna in the movie Dick Tracy. Writer: Stephen Sondheim (music and lyrics).

1991 **BEAUTY AND THE BEAST** Performed by Celine Dion and Peabo Bryson in the movie Beauty and the Beast. Writers: Alan Menken (music), Howard Ashman (lyrics). UK hit single for Celine Dion and Peabo Bryson (No.9 in 1992).

1992 **A WHOLE NEW WORLD** Performed by Peabo Bryson and Regina Belle in the movie Aladdin. Writers: Alan Menken (music), Tim Rice (lyrics). UK hit single for Peabo Bryson and Regina Belle (No.12 in 1993).

1993 **STREETS OF PHILADELPHIA** Performed by Bruce Springsteen in the movie Philadelphia. Writer: Bruce Springsteen (music and lyrics). UK hit single for Bruce Springsteen (No.2 in 1994).

1994 **CAN YOU FEEL THE LOVE TONIGHT** Performed by Elton John in the movie The Lion King. Writers: Elton John (music), Tim Rice (lyrics). UK hit single for Elton John (No.14 in 1994).

1995 **COLORS OF THE WIND** Performed by Vanessa Williams in the movie Pocahontas. Writers: Alan Menken (music), Stephen Schwartz (lyrics). UK hit single for Vanessa Williams (No.21 in 1995).

1996 **YOU MUST LOVE ME** Performed by Madonna in the movie Evita. Writers: Andrew Lloyd Webber (music), Tim Rice (lyrics). UK hit single for Madonna (No.10 in 1996).

1997 **MY HEART WILL GO ON** Performed by Celine Dion in the movie Titanic. Writers: James Horner (music), Will Jennings (lyrics). UK hit single for Celine Dion (No.1 in 1998).

1998 **WHEN YOU BELIEVE** Performed by Mariah Carey and Whitney Houston in the movie The Prince of Egypt. Writer: Stephen Schwartz (music and lyrics). UK hit single for Mariah Carey and Whitney Houston (No.4 in 1998).

1999 **YOU'LL BE IN MY HEART** Performed by Phil Collins and Glenn Close in the movie Tarzan. Writer: Phil Collins (music and lyrics). UK hit single for Phil Collins (No.17 in 1999).

2000 **THINGS HAVE CHANGED** Performed by Bob Dylan in the movie Wonder Boys. Writer: Bob Dylan (music and lyrics). UK hit single for Bob Dylan (No.58 in 2000).

2001 **IF I DIDN'T HAVE YOU** Performed by Billy Crystal and John Goodman in the movie Monsters, Inc. Writer: Randy Newman (music and lyrics).

2002 **LOSE YOURSELF** Performed by Eminem in the movie 8 Mile. Writers: Eminem (music and lyrics), Jeff Bass, Luis Resto (music). UK hit single for Eminem (No.1 in 2002).

2003 **INTO THE WEST** Performed by Annie Lennox in the movie The Lord of the Rings: The Return of the King. Writers: Fran Walsh, Howard Shore, Annie Lennox (music and lyrics).

2004 **AL OTRO LADO DEL RIO** Performed by Jorge Drexler in the movie The Motorcycle Diaries. Writer: Jorge Drexler (music and lyrics).

2005 **IT'S HARD OUT HERE FOR A PIMP** Performed by Three 6 Mafia in the movie Hustle & Flow. Writer: Jordon Houston, Cedric Coleman and Paul Beauregard (music and lyrics).

17 / 19 May 1962	24 / 26 May 1962	31 May / 2 June 1962	7 / 9 June 1962
NUT ROCKER B Bumble and The Stingers	**GOOD LUCK CHARM** Elvis Presley with The Jordanaires	**GOOD LUCK CHARM** Elvis Presley with The Jordanaires	**GOOD LUCK CHARM** Elvis Presley with The Jordanaires
BLUE HAWAII (Soundtrack) Elvis Presley	**BLUE HAWAII (Soundtrack)** Elvis Presley	**BLUE HAWAII (Soundtrack)** Elvis Presley	**BLUE HAWAII (Soundtrack)** Elvis Presley

KEY UK No.1 ★ UK Top 10 ● Still on chart + UK entry at No.1 ■ US No.1 ▲ UK million seller £ US million seller $
Singles re-entries are listed as (re), (2re), (3re)… which signifies that the hit re-entered the chart once, twice or three times…

Peak Position / Weeks

DAFFY DUCK featuring the GROOVE GANG
Germany, male instrumental / production group

6 Jul 91 **PARTY ZONE** *East West YZ 592* **58** 3

DAFT PUNK
France, male instrumental / production duo – Thomas Bangalter and Guy Manuel de Homem-Christo (3 Albums: 58 Weeks, 9 Singles: 40 Weeks)

1 Feb 97 ● HOMEWORK *Virgin CDV 2821* 8 17
22 Feb 97 ● **DA FUNK / MUSIQUE** *Soma / Virgin VSCDT 1625* **7** 5
26 Apr 97 ● **AROUND THE WORLD** *Virgin VSCDT 1633* **5** 5
4 Oct 97 **BURNIN'** *Virgin VSCDT 1649* **30** 2
28 Feb 98 **REVOLUTION 909** *Virgin VSCDT 1682* **47** 1
25 Nov 00 ● **ONE MORE TIME** *Virgin VSCDT 1791* **2** 12
24 Mar 01 ● DISCOVERY *Virgin CDVX 2940* 2 37
23 Jun 01 **DIGITAL LOVE** *Virgin VSCDT 1810* **14** 7
17 Nov 01 **HARDER BETTER FASTER STRONGER** *Virgin VSCDT 1822* **25** 3
26 Mar 05 ● HUMAN AFTER ALL *Virgin CDV 2996* 10 4
23 Apr 05 **ROBOT ROCK** *Virgin VSCDX 1897* **32** 3
16 Jul 05 **TECHNOLOGIC** *Virgin VSCDX 1900* **40** 2

DAISY CHAINSAW
UK, male / female vocal / instrumental group (1 Album: 1 Week, 2 Singles: 6 Weeks)

18 Jan 92 **LOVE YOUR MONEY** *Deva DEVA 001* **26** 5
28 Mar 92 **PINK FLOWER / ROOM ELEVEN** *Deva 82TP 7* **65** 1
10 Oct 92 ELEVENTEEN *Deva TPLP 100CD* 62 1

The first week on chart for 'Love Your Money' was listed under EP title 'Lovesick Pleasure'.

The DAKOTAS
(see also Billy J KRAMER and The DAKOTAS) *UK, male instrumental group*

11 Jul 63 **THE CRUEL SEA** *Parlophone R 5044* **18** 13

Jim DALE
UK, male vocalist – James Smith (4 Singles: 22 Weeks)

11 Oct 57 ● **BE MY GIRL** *Parlophone R 4343* **2** 16
10 Jan 58 **JUST BORN (TO BE MY BABY)** *Parlophone R 4376* **27** 1
17 Jan 58 **CRAZY DREAM** *Parlophone R 4376* **24** 2
7 Mar 58 **SUGARTIME** *Parlophone R 4402* **25** 3

DALE and GRACE
US, male / female vocal duo

9 Jan 64 **I'M LEAVING IT UP TO YOU** *London HL 9807* ▲ $ **42** 2

The DALE SISTERS
UK, female vocal trio (2 Singles: 7 Weeks)

17 Mar 60 **HEARTBEAT** *HMV POP 710* [1] **33** 1
23 Nov 61 **MY SUNDAY BABY** *Ember S 140* **36** 6

[1] The England Sisters

DALEK I
UK, male vocal / instrumental group

9 Aug 80 COMPASS KUMPAS *Backdoor OPEN 1* 54 2

DALI'S CAR
UK, male vocal / instrumental duo

3 Nov 84 **THE JUDGEMENT IS THE MIRROR** *Paradox DOX 1* **66** 2
1 Dec 84 THE WAKING HOUR *Paradox DOXLP 1* 84 1

DALLAS SUPERSTARS
Finland, male production duo – Heikki Liimatainen and Jaakko Slovaara

27 Sep 03 **HELIUM** *All Around the World CDGLOBE 289* **64** 1

Roger DALTREY (see also The WHO)
UK, male vocalist (5 Albums: 30 Weeks, 8 Singles: 46 Weeks)

14 Apr 73 ● **GIVING IT ALL AWAY** *Track 2094 110* **5** 11
26 May 73 ● DALTREY *Track 2406 107* 6 6
4 Aug 73 **I'M FREE** *Ode ODS 66302* [1] **13** 10
26 Jul 75 RIDE A ROCK HORSE *Polydor 2660 111* 14 10
14 May 77 **WRITTEN ON THE WIND** *Polydor 2121 319* **46** 2
4 Jun 77 ONE OF THE BOYS *Polydor 2442 146* 45 1
2 Aug 80 **FREE ME** *Polydor 2001 980* **39** 6
23 Aug 80 MCVICAR (FILM SOUNDTRACK) *Polydor POLD 5034* 39 11
11 Oct 80 **WITHOUT YOUR LOVE** *Polydor POSP 181* **55** 4
3 Mar 84 **WALKING IN MY SLEEP** *WEA U 9686* **56** 3
5 Oct 85 **AFTER THE FIRE** *10 TEN 69* **50** 5
2 Nov 85 UNDER A RAGING MOON *10 DIX 17* 52 2
8 Mar 86 **UNDER A RAGING MOON** *10 TEN 81* **43** 5

[1] With London Symphony Orchestra and English Chamber Orchestra and English Chamber Choir – conducted by David Measham

Glen DALY
UK, male vocalist

20 Nov 71 GLASGOW NIGHT OUT *Golden Guinea GGL 0479* 28 2

DAMAGE
UK, male vocal group (2 Albums: 22 Weeks, 11 Singles: 59 Weeks)

20 Jul 96 **ANYTHING** *Big Life BLRD 129* **68** 1
12 Oct 96 **LOVE II LOVE** *Big Life BLRD 131* **12** 6
14 Dec 96 ● **FOREVER** *Big Life BLRD 132* **6** 9
22 Mar 97 ● **LOVE GUARANTEED (re)** *Big Life BLRDA 133* **7** 7
19 Apr 97 FOREVER *Big Life BLRCD 31* 13 12
17 May 97 ● **WONDERFUL TONIGHT** *Big Life BLRDA 134* **3** 8
9 Aug 97 **LOVE LADY** *Big Life BLRDB 137* **33** 2
1 Jul 00 ● **GHETTO ROMANCE** *Cooltempo CDCOOL 347* **7** 7
28 Oct 00 **RUMOURS** *Cooltempo CDCOOLS 352* **22** 4
31 Mar 01 **STILL BE LOVIN' YOU (re)** *Cooltempo CDCOOLS 355* **11** 7
14 Apr 01 SINCE YOU'VE BEEN GONE *Cooltempo 5289592* 16 10
14 Jul 01 **SO WHAT IF I (re)** *Cooltempo CDCOOLS 357* **12** 6
15 Dec 01 **AFTER THE LOVE HAS GONE** *Cooltempo CDCOOL 360* **42** 2

Bobby D'AMBROSIO featuring Michelle WEEKS
US, male DJ / producer and female vocalist

2 Aug 97 **MOMENT OF MY LIFE** *Ministry of Sound MOSCDS 1* **23** 3

DAMIAN
UK, male vocalist – Damian Davis (4 Singles: 26 Weeks)

26 Dec 87 **THE TIME WARP 2** *Jive JIVE 160* **51** 6
27 Aug 88 **THE TIME WARP 2** (re-issue) *Jive JIVE 182* **64** 3
19 Aug 89 ● **THE TIME WARP** (re-mix) *Jive JIVE 209* **7** 13
16 Dec 89 **WIG WAM BAM** *Jive JIVE 236* **49** 4

The DAMNED
UK, male vocal (Dave Letts aka Dave Vanian) / instrumental group – includes Captain Sensible (Ray Burns) (8 Albums: 54 Weeks, 15 Singles: 77 Weeks)

12 Mar 77 DAMNED DAMNED DAMNED *Stiff SEEZ 1* 36 10
5 May 79 **LOVE SONG** *Chiswick CHIS 112* **20** 8
20 Oct 79 **SMASH IT UP** *Chiswick CHIS 116* **35** 5
17 Nov 79 MACHINE GUN ETIQUETTE *Chiswick CWK 3011* 31 5
1 Dec 79 **I JUST CAN'T BE HAPPY TODAY** *Chiswick CHIS 120* **46** 5
4 Oct 80 **HISTORY OF THE WORLD (PART 1)** *Chiswick CHIS 135* **51** 4
29 Nov 80 THE BLACK ALBUM *Chiswick CWK 3015* 29 3
28 Nov 81 THE BEST OF THE DAMNED *Chiswick DAM 1* 43 12
28 Nov 81 **FRIDAY 13TH (EP)** *Stale One TRY 1* **50** 4
10 Jul 82 **LOVELY MONEY** *Bronze BRO 149* **42** 4
23 Oct 82 STRAWBERRIES *Bronze BRON 542* 15 4
9 Jun 84 **THANKS FOR THE NIGHT** *Damned DAMNED 1* **43** 4
30 Mar 85 **GRIMLY FIENDISH** *MCA GRIM 1* **21** 7
22 Jun 85 **THE SHADOW OF LOVE (EDITION PREMIERE)** *MCA GRIM 2* **25** 8
27 Jul 85 PHANTASMAGORIA *MCA MCF 3275* 11 17
21 Sep 85 **IS IT A DREAM** *MCA GRIM 3* **34** 4
8 Feb 86 ● **ELOISE (re)** *MCA GRIM 4* **3** 10
22 Nov 86 **ANYTHING** *MCA GRIM 5* **32** 4

14 / 16 June 1962	21 / 23 June 1962	28 / 30 June 1962	5 / 7 July 1962
UK No.1 SINGLES			
GOOD LUCK CHARM Elvis Presley with The Jordanaires	GOOD LUCK CHARM Elvis Presley with The Jordanaires	COME OUTSIDE Mike Sarne with Wendy Richard	COME OUTSIDE Mike Sarne with Wendy Richard
UK No.1 ALBUMS			
BLUE HAWAII (Soundtrack) Elvis Presley	WEST SIDE STORY Soundtrack	WEST SIDE STORY Soundtrack	WEST SIDE STORY Soundtrack

13 Dec 86	ANYTHING *MCA MCG 6015*	40	2
7 Feb 87	**GIGOLO** *MCA GRIM 6*	**29**	3
25 Apr 87	**ALONE AGAIN OR** *MCA GRIM 7*	**27**	6
28 Nov 87	**IN DULCE DECORUM** *MCA GRIM 8*	**72**	1
12 Dec 87	LIGHT AT THE END OF THE TUNNEL *MCA MCSP 312*	87	1

Tracks on Friday 13th (EP): Disco Man / Limit Club / Billy Bad Breaks / Citadel.

Kenny DAMON *US, male vocalist*

19 May 66	**WHILE I LIVE** *Mercury MF 907*	**48**	1

Vic DAMONE
US, male vocalist – Vito Farinola (2 Albums: 8 Weeks, 3 Singles: 22 Weeks)

6 Dec 57	**AN AFFAIR TO REMEMBER (OUR LOVE AFFAIR) (re)** *Philips PB 745*	**29**	2
9 May 58 ★	**ON THE STREET WHERE YOU LIVE** *Philips PB 819*	**1**	17
1 Aug 58	**THE ONLY MAN ON THE ISLAND** *Philips PB 837*	**24**	3
25 Apr 81	NOW! *RCA INTS 5080*	28	7
2 Apr 83	VIC DAMONE SINGS THE GREAT SONGS *CBS 32261*	87	1

Richie DAN *UK, male DJ / producer – Richard Gittens*

12 Aug 00	**CALL IT FATE** *Pure Silk CDPSR 1*	**34**	3

DANA *Ireland, female vocalist – Rosemary Brown (later Scallon) (1 Album: 2 Weeks, 8 Singles: 75 Weeks)*

4 Apr 70 ★	**ALL KINDS OF EVERYTHING (re)** *Rex R 11054*	**1**	16
13 Feb 71	**WHO PUT THE LIGHTS OUT** *Rex R 11062*	**14**	11
25 Jan 75 ●	**PLEASE TELL HIM THAT I SAID HELLO** *GTO GT 6*	**8**	14
13 Dec 75 ●	**IT'S GONNA BE A COLD COLD CHRISTMAS** *GTO GT 45*	**4**	6
6 Mar 76	**NEVER GONNA FALL IN LOVE AGAIN** *GTO GT 55*	**31**	4
16 Oct 76	**FAIRYTALE** *GTO GT 66*	**13**	16
31 Mar 79	**SOMETHING'S COOKIN' IN THE KITCHEN** *GTO GT 243*	**44**	5
27 Dec 80	EVERYTHING IS BEAUTIFUL *Warwick WW 5099*	43	2
15 May 82	**I FEEL LOVE COMIN' ON** *Creole CR 32*	**66**	3

DANA INTERNATIONAL *Israel, female vocalist – Yaron Cohen*

27 Jun 98	**DIVA** *Dance Pool DANA 1CD*	**11**	4

DANCE CONSPIRACY *UK, male instrumental / production duo*

3 Oct 92	**DUB WAR** *XL Recordings XLT 34*	**72**	1

DANCE FLOOR VIRUS *Italy, male vocal / instrumental group*

21 Oct 95	**MESSAGE IN A BOTTLE** *Epic 6623742*	**49**	2

DANCE TO TIPPERARY *UK, male vocal / instrumental group*

24 May 03	**THE BHOYS ARE BACK IN TOWN** *Nede NRCD 2105*	**44**	2

DANCE 2 TRANCE
(see also JAM & SPOON featuring PLAVKA) *Germany, male instrumental / production duo – Rolf Ellmer and Dag Lerner (3 Singles: 8 Weeks)*

24 Apr 93	**P.OWER OF A.MERICAN N.ATIVES** *Logic 74321139582*	**25**	4
24 Jul 93	**TAKE A FREE FALL** *Logic 74321153602*	**36**	3
4 Feb 95	**WARRIOR** *Logic 74321257722*	**56**	1

DANCING DJS v ROXETTE NEW
UK, male producton duo and Sweden, male / female vocal duo

6 Aug 05	**FADING LIKE A FLOWER** *All Around the World CDGLOBE 426*	**18**	5

Evan DANDO (see also The LEMONHEADS)
US, male vocalist (1 Album: 1 Week, 3 Singles: 3 Weeks)

24 Jun 95	**PERFECT DAY** *Virgin VSCDT 1552* [1]	**75**	1
29 Mar 03	BABY I'M BORED *Setanta SETCD 114*	30	1
31 May 03	**STOP MY HEAD** *Setanta SETCDA 127*	**38**	1
13 Dec 03	**IT LOOKS LIKE YOU** *Setanta SETCDA 130*	**68**	1

[1] Kirsty MacColl and Evan Dando

Suzanne DANDO *UK, female exercise instructor*

17 Mar 84	SHAPE UP AND DANCE WITH SUZANNE DANDO *Lifestyle LEG 21*	87	1

The DANDY WARHOLS *US, male / female vocal (Courtney Taylor) / instrumental group (4 Albums: 21 Weeks, 12 Singles: 31 Weeks)*

28 Feb 98	**EVERY DAY SHOULD BE A HOLIDAY** *Capitol CDCL 797*	**29**	2
2 May 98	**NOT IF YOU WERE THE LAST JUNKIE ON EARTH** *Capitol CDCL 800*	**13**	4
16 May 98	COME DOWN *Capitol 8365052*	16	8
8 Aug 98	**BOYS BETTER** *Capitol CDCLS 805*	**36**	2
10 Jun 00	**GET OFF** *Capitol CDCLS 821*	**38**	2
24 Jun 00	THIRTEEN TALES FROM URBAN BOHEMIA *Capitol 8577872*	32	9
9 Sep 00	**BOHEMIAN LIKE YOU** *Capitol CDCLS 823*	**42**	1
7 Jul 01	**GODLESS** *Capitol CDCL 829*	**66**	1
10 Nov 01 ●	**BOHEMIAN LIKE YOU** (re-issue) *Parlophone / Capitol CDCLX 823*	**5**	10
16 Mar 02	**GET OFF** (re-issue) *Parlophone / Capitol CDCL 835*	**34**	2
17 May 03	**WE USED TO BE FRIENDS** *Capitol CDCL 843*	**18**	3
31 May 03	WELCOME TO THE MONKEYHOUSE *Parlophone 5901232*	20	3
9 Aug 03	**YOU WERE THE LAST HIGH** *Parlophone CDCL 845*	**34**	2
6 Dec 03	**PLAN A** *Parlophone CDCLS 851*	**66**	1
10 Sep 05	**SMOKE IT** *Parlophone CDCLS 831*	**59**	1
24 Sep 05	ODDITORIUM OR WARLORDS OF MARS *Parlophone 8745902*	67	1

The DANDYS *UK, male vocal / instrumental group (2 Singles: 2 Weeks)*

14 Mar 98	**YOU MAKE ME WANT TO SCREAM** *Artificial ATFCD 3*	**71**	1
30 May 98	**ENGLISH COUNTRY GARDEN** *Artificial ATFCD 4*	**57**	1

DANE (see also ANOTHER LEVEL)
UK, male vocalist – Dane Bowers (4 Singles: 38 Weeks)

29 Apr 00 ●	**BUGGIN** *Nulife 74321753342* [1]	**6**	8
26 Aug 00 ●	**OUT OF YOUR MIND (re)** *Nulife 74321782942* [2]	**2**	20
3 Mar 01 ●	**SHUT UP AND FORGET ABOUT IT** *Arista 74321835342*	**9**	5
7 Jul 01 ●	**ANOTHER LOVER** *Arista 74321863412*	**9**	5

[1] True Steppers featuring Dane Bowers [2] True Steppers and Dane Bowers featuring Victoria Beckham

D'ANGELO
US, male vocalist – Michael D'Angelo (2 Albums: 5 Weeks, 5 Singles: 11 Weeks)

28 Oct 95	BROWN SUGAR *Cooltempo CTCD 46*	57	2
28 Oct 95	**BROWN SUGAR** *Cooltempo CDCOOL 307*	**24**	3
2 Mar 96	**CRUISIN'** *Cooltempo CDCOOL 316*	**31**	2
2 Mar 96	**COLD WORLD** *Geffen GFSTD 22114* [1]	**40**	2
15 Jun 96	**LADY** *Cooltempo CDCOOLS 323*	**21**	2
22 May 99	**BREAK UPS 2 MAKE UPS** *Def Jam 8709272* [2]	**33**	2
26 Feb 00	VOODOO *EMI 5250712* ▲	21	3

[1] Genius / GZA featuring D'Angelo [2] Method Man featuring D'Angelo

DANGER DANGER
US, male vocal / instrumental group (3 Singles: 5 Weeks)

8 Feb 92	**MONKEY BUSINESS** *Epic 6577517*	**42**	2
28 Mar 92	**I STILL THINK ABOUT YOU** *Epic 6578387*	**46**	2
13 Jun 92	**COMIN' HOME** *Epic 6581337*	**75**	1

DAN-I *UK, male vocalist – Selmore Lewinson*

10 Nov 79	**MONKEY CHOP** *Island WIP 6520*	**30**	9

Charlie DANIELS BAND *US, male vocal / instrumental group*

22 Sep 79	**THE DEVIL WENT DOWN TO GEORGIA** *Epic EPC 7737* $	**14**	10
10 Nov 79	MILLION MILE REFLECTIONS *Epic EPC 83446*	74	1

12 / 14 July 1962	19 / 21 July 1962	26 / 28 July 1962	2 / 4 August 1962
I CAN'T STOP LOVING YOU Ray Charles	I CAN'T STOP LOVING YOU Ray Charles	I REMEMBER YOU Frank Ifield	I REMEMBER YOU Frank Ifield
WEST SIDE STORY Soundtrack	WEST SIDE STORY Soundtrack	POT LUCK Elvis Presley	POT LUCK Elvis Presley

KEY: UK No.1 ★ UK Top 10 ● Still on chart + UK entry at No.1 ■ US No.1 ▲ UK million seller £ US million seller $
Singles re-entries are listed as (re), (2re), (3re)... which signifies that the hit re-entered the chart once, twice or three times...
Peak Position / Weeks

Johnny DANKWORTH and his ORCHESTRA
UK, male orchestra – leader Johnny Dankworth – alto sax – was knighted in 2006 (2 Singles: 33 Weeks)

22 Jun 56 ● **EXPERIMENTS WITH MICE** *Parlophone R 4185* 7 12
23 Feb 61 ● **AFRICAN WALTZ** *Columbia DB 4590* 9 21

DANNY and The JUNIORS
US, male vocal (Danny Rapp, b. 10 May 1941 d. 1983) group (2 Singles: 19 Weeks)

17 Jan 58 ● **AT THE HOP** *HMV POP 436* ▲ $ 3 14
10 Jul 76 **AT THE HOP** (re-issue) *ABC 4123* 39 5

DANNY WILSON
UK, male vocal (Gary Clark) / instrumental group (3 Albums: 11 Weeks, 3 Singles: 28 Weeks)

22 Aug 87 ● **MARY'S PRAYER (re)** *Virgin VS 934* 3 18
30 Apr 88 MEET DANNY WILSON *Virgin V 2419* 65 5
17 Jun 89 **THE SECOND SUMMER OF LOVE** *Virgin VS 1186* 23 9
29 Jul 89 BEEBOP MOPTOP *Virgin V 2594* 24 5
16 Sep 89 **NEVER GONNA BE THE SAME** *Virgin VS 1203* 69 1
31 Aug 91 SWEET DANNY WILSON *Virgin V 2669* 54 1

It was not until 'Mary's Prayer' re-entered in Apr 1988 that it reached its peak position of No.3.

The DANSE SOCIETY
UK, male vocal / instrumental group (1 Album: 4 Weeks, 2 Singles: 5 Weeks)

27 Aug 83 **WAKE UP** *Society SOC 5* 61 3
5 Nov 83 **HEAVEN IS WAITING** *Society SOC 6* 60 2
11 Feb 84 HEAVEN IS WAITING *Society 205 972* 39 4

Steven DANTE
UK, male vocalist – Steven Dennis (1 Album: 1 Week, 2 Singles: 16 Weeks)

26 Sep 87 **THE REAL THING** *Chrysalis CHS 3167* [1] 13 10
9 Jul 88 **I'M TOO SCARED** *Cooltempo DANTE 1* 34 6
3 Sep 88 FIND OUT *Cooltempo CTLP 6* 87 1

[1] Jellybean featuring Steven Dante

Tonja DANTZLER
US, female vocalist

17 Dec 94 **IN AND OUT OF MY LIFE** *ffrr FCD 246* 66 1

DANZEL
Belgium, male vocalist – Johan Waem

6 Nov 04 **PUMP IT UP (re)** *Data DATA 75CDS* 11 8

DANZIG
US, male vocal / instrumental group

14 May 94 **MOTHER** *American MOMDD 1* 62 1

DAPHNE
US, female vocalist

9 Dec 95 **CHANGE** *Stress CDSTR 54* 71 1

DAPHNE & CELESTE
US, female vocal duo – Karen DeConcetto and Celeste Cruz (3 Singles: 28 Weeks)

5 Feb 00 ● **OOH STICK YOU!** *Universal MCSTD 40209* 8 12
17 Jun 00 **UGLY** *Universal MCSTD 40232* 18 12
2 Sep 00 **SCHOOL'S OUT** *Universal MCSTD 40238* 12 4

Terence Trent D'ARBY (417 Top 500)
Unpredictable US pop / soul singer / songwriter, b. 15 Mar 1962, New York, whose success came after relocating to the UK. Multi-million-selling, Grammy-winning debut album, Introducing the Hardline According to Terence Trent D'Arby, was a worldwide hit. Winner of a BRIT award in 1988 for Best International Newcomer (4 Albums: 96 Weeks, 11 Singles: 77 Weeks)

14 Mar 87 ● **IF YOU LET ME STAY** *CBS TRENT 1* 7 13
20 Jun 87 ● **WISHING WELL** *CBS TRENT 2* ▲ 4 11
25 Jul 87 ★ INTRODUCING THE HARDLINE ACCORDING TO TERENCE TRENT D'ARBY *CBS 4509111* ■ 1 67
10 Oct 87 **DANCE LITTLE SISTER (PART ONE)** *CBS TRENT 3* 20 7
9 Jan 88 ● **SIGN YOUR NAME** *CBS TRENT 4* 2 10
4 Nov 89 NEITHER FISH NOR FLESH *CBS 4658091* 12 5
20 Jan 90 **TO KNOW SOMEONE DEEPLY IS TO KNOW SOMEONE SOFTLY** *CBS TRENT 6* 55 3
17 Apr 93 **DO YOU LOVE ME LIKE YOU SAY** *Columbia 6590732* 14 6
15 May 93 ● SYMPHONY OR DAMN *Columbia 4735612* 4 19
19 Jun 93 **DELICATE** *Columbia 6593312* [1] 14 6
28 Aug 93 **SHE KISSED ME** *Columbia 6595922* 16 7
20 Nov 93 **LET HER DOWN EASY** *Columbia 6598642* 18 7
8 Apr 95 **HOLDING ON TO YOU** *Columbia 6614235* 20 6
29 Apr 95 TERENCE TRENT D'ARBY'S VIBRATOR *Columbia 4785052* 11 5
5 Aug 95 **VIBRATOR** *Columbia 6622585* 57 1

[1] Terence Trent D'Arby featuring Des'ree

Richard DARBYSHIRE (see also LIVING IN A BOX)
UK, male vocalist (3 Singles: 7 Weeks)

20 Aug 88 **COMING BACK FOR MORE** *Chrysalis JEL 4* [1] 41 3
24 Jul 93 **THIS I SWEAR** *Dome CDDOME 1003* 50 3
12 Feb 94 **WHEN ONLY LOVE WILL DO** *Dome CDDOME 1008* 54 1

[1] Jellybean featuring Richard Darbyshire

DARE
UK, male vocal / instrumental group (1 Album: 1 Week, 4 Singles: 7 Weeks)

29 Apr 89 **THE RAINDANCE** *A&M AM 483* 62 2
29 Jul 89 **ABANDON** *A&M AM 519* 71 2
10 Aug 91 **WE DON'T NEED A REASON** *A&M AM 755* 52 2
14 Sep 91 BLOOD FROM STONE *A&M 3953601* 48 1
5 Oct 91 **REAL LOVE** *A&M AM 824* 67 1

DARE
Holland, female vocal trio

13 Sep 03 **CHIHUAHUA** *All Around the World CDGLOBE 311* 45 1

Matt DAREY (see also LOST TRIBE; MDM; M3; MELT featuring LITTLE MS MARCIE; SPACE BABY; SUNBURST)
UK, male producer / instrumentalist (5 Singles: 17 Weeks)

9 Oct 99 **LIBERATION (TEMPTATION – FLY LIKE AN ANGEL** *Incentive CENT 1CDS* [1] 19 3
22 Apr 00 **FROM RUSSIA WITH LOVE** *Liquid Asset ASSETCD 003* [2] 40 2
15 Jul 00 **BEAUTIFUL** *Incentive CENT 7CDS* [3] 21 4
20 Apr 02 ● **BEAUTIFUL** (re-mix) *Incentive CENT 38CDS* [4] 10 6
14 Dec 02 **U SHINE ON** *Incentive CENT 50CDS* [5] 34 2

[1] Matt Darey presents Mash Up [2] Matt Darey presents DSP [3] Matt Darey's Mash Up presents Marcella Woods [4] Matt Darey featuring Marcella Woods [5] Matt Darey and Marcella Woods

Bobby DARIN (377 Top 500)
Singer / songwriter / actor and multi-instrumentalist who had pop, rock, R&B, country and MOR hits, b. Walden Robert Cassotto, 14 May 1936, New York, US, d. 20 Dec 1973. This Grammy winner was posthumously inducted into the Rock and Roll Hall of Fame in 1990. His 2004 bio-pic, Beyond the Sea, starred Kevin Spacey (4 Albums: 22 Weeks, 18 Singles: 162 Weeks)

1 Aug 58 **SPLISH SPLASH (re)** *London HLE 8666* $ 18 7
9 Jan 59 **QUEEN OF THE HOP** *London HLE 8737* $ 24 2
29 May 59 ★ **DREAM LOVER** *London HLE 8867* $ 1 19
25 Sep 59 ★ **MACK THE KNIFE (2re)** *London HLK 8939* ▲ $ 1 18
29 Jan 60 ● **LA MER (BEYOND THE SEA) (re)** *London HLK 9034* $ 8 13
19 Mar 60 ● THIS IS DARIN *London HA 2235* 4 8

9 / 11 August 1962	16 / 18 August 1962	23 / 25 August 1962	30 August / 1 September 1962
UK No.1 SINGLES			
I REMEMBER YOU Frank Ifield	I REMEMBER YOU Frank Ifield	I REMEMBER YOU Frank Ifield	I REMEMBER YOU Frank Ifield
UK No.1 ALBUMS			
POT LUCK Elvis Presley	POT LUCK Elvis Presley	POT LUCK Elvis Presley	WEST SIDE STORY Soundtrack

31 Mar 60 ● CLEMENTINE *London HLK 9086* 8 12
9 Apr 60 THAT'S ALL *London HAE 2172* 15 1
30 Jun 60 BILL BAILEY (re) *London HLK 9142* 34 2
16 Mar 61 ● LAZY RIVER *London HLK 9303* 2 13
6 Jul 61 NATURE BOY *London HLK 9375* 24 7
12 Oct 61 ● YOU MUST HAVE BEEN A BEAUTIFUL BABY *London HLK 9429* 10 11
26 Oct 61 THEME FROM 'COME SEPTEMBER' *London HLK 9407* [1] 50 1
21 Dec 61 ● MULTIPLICATION *London HLK 9474* 5 13
19 Jul 62 ● THINGS *London HLK 9575* 2 17
4 Oct 62 IF A MAN ANSWERS *Capitol CL 15272* 24 6
29 Nov 62 BABY FACE *London HLK 9624* 40 4
25 Jul 63 EIGHTEEN YELLOW ROSES *Capitol CL 15306* 37 4
13 Oct 66 ● IF I WERE A CARPENTER *Atlantic 584 051* 9 12
14 Apr 79 DREAM LOVER / MACK THE KNIFE (re-issue) *Lightning LIG 9017* 64 1
5 Oct 85 THE LEGEND OF BOBBY DARIN – HIS GREATEST HITS *Stylus SMR 8504* 39 6
24 Jul 04 BEYOND THE SEA – THE VERY BEST OF BOBBY DARIN *Warner.esp WSMCD 183* 26 7

[1] Bobby Darin Orchestra

DARIO G
UK, male DJ / production trio (1 Album: 4 Weeks, 7 Singles: 44 Weeks)

27 Sep 97 ● SUNCHYME *Eternal WEA 130CD* 2 18
20 Jun 98 ● CARNAVAL DE PARIS *Eternal WEA 162CD* 5 9
11 Jul 98 SUNMACHINE *Eternal 3984233782* 26 4
12 Sep 98 SUNMACHINE *Eternal WEA 173CD* 17 4
25 Mar 00 VOICES *Eternal WEA 256CD* 37 2
3 Feb 01 ● DREAM TO ME *Manifesto FESCD 79* 9 6
8 Jun 02 CARNAVAL 2002 (re-mix) *Eternal WEA 349CD* 34 3
25 Jan 03 HEAVEN IS CLOSER (FEELS LIKE HEAVEN) *Serious SER 61CD* 39 2

DARIUS
UK, male vocalist – Darius Danesh (2 Albums: 21 Weeks, 6 Singles: 52 Weeks)

10 Aug 02 ★ COLOURBLIND *Mercury 639652* ■ 1 16
7 Dec 02 ● RUSHES (re) *Mercury 0638042* 5 12
14 Dec 02 ● DIVE IN *Mercury 635922* 6 19
15 Mar 03 ● INCREDIBLE (WHAT I MEANT TO SAY) (re) *Mercury 0779772* 9 8
21 Jun 03 GIRL IN THE MOON (re) *Fontana 9808233* 21 3
30 Oct 04 ● KINDA LOVE *Mercury 9868349* 8 7
6 Nov 04 LIVE TWICE *Mercury 9868263* 36 2
22 Jan 05 ● LIVE TWICE *Mercury 9869470* 7 6

DARK GLOBE featuring Amanda GHOST
UK, male production duo and female vocalist

1 May 04 BREAK MY WORLD *Island CID 853* 52 1

DARK MONKS *UK, male production duo*

14 Sep 02 INSANE *Incentive CENT 45CDS* 62 1

DARK STAR *UK, male vocal / instrumental group (3 Singles: 6 Weeks)*

26 Jun 99 ABOUT 3AM *Harvest CDEM 545* 50 1
15 Jan 00 GRACEADELICA *Harvest CDEMS 556* 25 3
13 May 00 I AM THE SUN *Harvest CDEMS 566* 31 2

DARKMAN *UK, male rapper – Brian Mitchell (4 Singles: 7 Weeks)*

14 May 94 YABBA DABBA DOO *Wild Card CARDD 6* 49 2
20 Aug 94 WHO'S THE DARKMAN *Wild Card CARDD 8* 46 2
3 Dec 94 YABBA DABBA DOO (re-issue) *Wild Card CARDD 11* 37 2
21 Oct 95 BRAND NEW DAY *Wild Card 5771892* 74 1

The DARKNESS (see also BRITISH WHALE) *UK, male vocal (Justin Hawkins) / instrumental group (2 Albums: 50 Weeks, 6 Singles: 40 Weeks)*

8 Mar 03 GET YOUR HANDS OFF MY WOMAN *Must Destroy DUSTY 006CD* 43 2
28 Jun 03 GROWING ON ME *Must Destroy DUSTY 010CD* 11 5
19 Jul 03 ★ PERMISSION TO LAND *Must Destroy 5046674522* 1 46
4 Oct 03 ● I BELIEVE IN A THING CALLED LOVE *Must Destroy DARK 01CD* 2 11
27 Dec 03 ● CHRISTMAS TIME (DON'T LET THE BELLS END) (re) *Must Destroy DARK 02CD* 2 8
3 Apr 04 ● LOVE IS ONLY A FEELING *Must Destroy DARK 03CD* 5 8
26 Nov 05 ● ONE WAY TICKET *Atlantic DARK 04CD* 8 6+
10 Dec 05 ONE WAY TICKET TO HELL ... AND BACK *Atlantic 5101112182* 11 4+

The DARLING BUDS *UK, male / female vocal / instrumental group (1 Album: 3 Weeks, 6 Singles: 20 Weeks)*

8 Oct 88 BURST *Epic BLOND 1* 50 5
7 Jan 89 HIT THE GROUND *CBS BLOND 2* 27 5
18 Feb 89 POP SAID *Epic 462894 1* 23 3
25 Mar 89 LET'S GO ROUND THERE *CBS BLOND 3* 49 4
22 Jul 89 YOU'VE GOT TO CHOOSE *CBS BLOND 4* 45 3
2 Jun 90 TINY MACHINE *CBS BLOND 5* 60 2
12 Sep 92 SURE THING *Epic 6582157* 71 1

Guy DARRELL *UK, male vocalist*

18 Aug 73 I'VE BEEN HURT *Santa Ponsa PNS 4* 12 13

James DARREN *US, male vocalist – James Ercolani (4 Singles: 25 Weeks)*

11 Aug 60 BECAUSE THEY'RE YOUNG *Pye International 7N 25059* 29 7
14 Dec 61 GOODBYE CRUEL WORLD *Pye International 7N 25116* $ 28 9
29 Mar 62 HER ROYAL MAJESTY *Pye International 7N 25125* 36 3
21 Jun 62 CONSCIENCE *Pye International 7N 25138* 30 6

DARTS (412 Top 500)
Britain's best-known doo-wop vocal group; line-up included Den Hegarty, Griff Fender, Rita Ray and Bob Fish. The popular London-based eight-piece band had three successive No.2 hits with revivals of early US rock 'n' roll and R&B songs (4 Albums: 57 Weeks, 12 Singles: 117 Weeks)

5 Nov 77 ● DADDY COOL / THE GIRL CAN'T HELP IT *Magnet MAG 100* 6 13
3 Dec 77 ● DARTS *Magnet MAG 5020* 9 22
28 Jan 78 ● COME BACK MY LOVE *Magnet MAG 110* 2 12
6 May 78 ● THE BOY FROM NEW YORK CITY *Magnet MAG 116* 2 13
3 Jun 78 EVERYONE PLAYS DARTS *Magnet MAG 5022* 12 18
5 Aug 78 ● IT'S RAINING *Magnet MAG 126* 2 11
11 Nov 78 DON'T LET IT FADE AWAY *Magnet MAG 134* 18 11
18 Nov 78 ● AMAZING DARTS *K-Tel / Magnet DLP 7981* 8 13
10 Feb 79 ● GET IT *Magnet MAG 140* 10 9
21 Jul 79 ● DUKE OF EARL *Magnet MAG 147* 6 11
6 Oct 79 DART ATTACK *Magnet MAG 5030* 38 4
20 Oct 79 CAN'T GET ENOUGH OF YOUR LOVE *Magnet MAG 156* 43 6
1 Dec 79 REET PETITE *Magnet MAG 160* 51 7
31 May 80 LET'S HANG ON *Magnet MAG 174* 11 14
6 Sep 80 PEACHES *Magnet MAG 179* 66 3
29 Nov 80 WHITE CHRISTMAS / SH-BOOM (LIFE COULD BE A DREAM) *Magnet MAG 184* 48 7

DARUDE *Finland, male producer – Ville Virtanen (3 Singles: 29 Weeks)*

24 Jun 00 ● SANDSTORM *Neo NEOCD 033* 3 15
25 Nov 00 ● FEEL THE BEAT *Neo NEOCD 045* 5 10
15 Sep 01 OUT OF CONTROL (BACK FOR MORE) *Neo NEOCD 067* 13 4

DAS EFX *US, male production / rap duo – Andre Weston and Willie Hines (2 Singles: 5 Weeks)*

7 Aug 93 CHECK YO SELF *Fourth & Broadway BRCD 283* [1] $ 36 4
25 Apr 98 RAP SCHOLAR *East West E 3853CD* [2] 42 1

[1] Ice Cube featuring Das EFX [2] Das EFX featuring Redman

DASHBOARD CONFESSIONAL
US, male vocalist – Chris Carrabba (2 Singles: 2 Weeks)

25 Nov 03 HANDS DOWN *Vagrant 9813790* 60 1
27 Mar 04 RAPID HOPE LOSS *Vagrant 9861991* 75 1

KEY: UK No.1 ★ UK Top 10 ● Still on chart + UK entry at No.1 ■ US No.1 ▲ UK million seller £ US million seller $
Singles re-entries are listed as (re), (2re), (3re)... which signifies that the hit re-entered the chart once, twice or three times...
Peak Position / Weeks

The DATSUNS *New Zealand, male vocal / instrumental group (2 Albums: 4 Weeks, 5 Singles: 7 Weeks)*

5 Oct 02	IN LOVE *V2 VVR 5020953*	25	2
19 Oct 02	THE DATSUNS *V2 VVR 1020962*	17	3
22 Feb 03	HARMONIC GENERATOR *V2 VVR 5021223*	33	2
6 Sep 03	MF FROM HELL *V2 5021753*	55	1
12 Jun 04	BLACKEN MY THUMB *V2 VVR 5026953*	48	1
19 Jun 04	OUTTA SIGHT / OUTTA MIND *V2 VVR 1026942*	58	1
23 Oct 04	GIRLS BEST FRIEND *V2 VVR 5028893*	71	1

N'Dea DAVENPORT (see also The BRAND NEW HEAVIES) *US, female vocalist (3 Singles: 7 Weeks)*

11 Sep 93	TRUST ME *Cooltempo CDCOOL 278* [1]	34	2
20 Jun 98	BRING IT ON *Gee Street VVR 5002033*	52	1
15 Dec 01	YOU CAN'T CHANGE ME *Defected DFECT 41CDS* [2]	25	4

[1] Guru featuring N'Dea Davenport [2] Roger Sanchez featuring Armand Van Helden and N'Dea Davenport

Anne-Marie DAVID *France, female vocalist*

28 Apr 73	WONDERFUL DREAM *Epic EPC 1446*	13	9

Craig DAVID (285 Top 500)

Critically lauded singer / songwriter, b. 5 May 1981, Southampton, UK. At 18 years, 11 months and 10 days he was the youngest British male to write and sing a No.1. Won numerous awards for his songs, records and videos. Debut album Born to Do It went gold in 24 countries, with UK sales exceeding 1.5 million (3 Albums: 103 Weeks, 15 Singles: 131 Weeks)

11 Dec 99 ●	RE-REWIND THE CROWD SAY BO SELECTA *Public Demand / Relentless RELENT 1CDS* [1]	2	17
15 Apr 00 ★	FILL ME IN *Wildstar CDWILD 28* ■	1	14
15 Jul 00 ●	WOMAN TROUBLE *Public Demand / ffrr FCD 380* [2]	6	10
5 Aug 00 ★	7 DAYS (re) *Wildstar CDWILD 30* ■	1	15
26 Aug 00 ★	BORN TO DO IT *Wildstar CDWILD 32* ■	1	50
2 Dec 00 ●	WALKING AWAY *Wildstar CDWILD 35*	3	13
31 Mar 01 ●	RENDEZVOUS *Wildstar CDWILD 36*	8	10
9 Nov 02 ●	WHAT'S YOUR FLAVA? *Wildstar CDWILD 43*	8	10
23 Nov 02 ●	SLICKER THAN YOUR AVERAGE *Wildstar TWR 00252*	4	35
1 Feb 03 ●	HIDDEN AGENDA *Wildstar CDWILD 44*	10	6
10 May 03 ●	RISE & FALL *Wildstar CDWILD 45* [3]	2	10
9 Aug 03 ●	SPANISH (re) *Wildstar CDWILD 49*	8	6
25 Oct 03	WORLD FILLED WITH LOVE *Wildstar CDWILD 51*	15	4
10 Jan 04	YOU DON'T MISS YOUR WATER ('TIL THE WELL RUNS DRY) *Wildstar CDWILD 52*	43	2
20 Aug 05 ●	ALL THE WAY *Warner Bros. WEA 393CD2*	3	6
3 Sep 05 ●	THE STORY GOES ... *Warner Bros. 2564625222*	5	18+
12 Nov 05 ●	DON'T LOVE YOU NO MORE *Warner Bros. WEA 396CD2*	4	8+

[1] Artful Dodger featuring Craig David [2] Artful Dodger and Robbie Craig featuring Craig David [3] Craig David featuring Sting

FR DAVID *France, male vocalist – Robert Fitoussi (1 Album: 6 Weeks, 2 Singles: 13 Weeks)*

2 Apr 83 ●	WORDS *Carrere CAR 248*	2	12
7 May 83	WORDS *Carrere CAL 145*	46	6
18 Jun 83	MUSIC *Carrere CAR 282*	71	1

DAVID and JONATHAN (see also BLUE MINK; The PIPKINS) *UK, male vocal duo – Roger Greenaway and Roger Cook (2 Singles: 22 Weeks)*

13 Jan 66	MICHELLE *Columbia DB 7800*	11	6
7 Jul 66 ●	LOVERS OF THE WORLD UNITE *Columbia DB 7950*	7	16

Jim DAVIDSON *UK, male vocalist*

27 Dec 80	WHITE CHRISTMAS / TOO RISKY *Scratch SCR 001*	52	4

Paul DAVIDSON *Jamaica, male vocalist*

27 Dec 75 ●	MIDNIGHT RIDER *Tropical ALO 56*	10	10

Dave DAVIES (see also The KINKS) *UK, male vocalist (2 Singles: 17 Weeks)*

19 Jul 67 ●	DEATH OF A CLOWN *Pye 7N 17356*	3	10
6 Dec 67	SUZANNAH'S STILL ALIVE *Pye 7N 17429*	20	7

Billie DAVIS *UK, female vocalist – Carol Hedges (4 Singles: 33 Weeks)*

30 Aug 62	WILL I WHAT *Parlophone R 4932* [1]	18	10
7 Feb 63 ●	TELL HIM *Decca F 11572*	10	12
30 May 63	HE'S THE ONE *Decca F 11658*	40	3
9 Oct 68	I WANT YOU TO BE MY BABY *Decca F 12823*	33	8

[1] Mike Sarne with Billie Davis

Carl DAVIS and the ROYAL LIVERPOOL PHILHARMONIC ORCHESTRA *US, male conductor and orchestra*

19 Oct 91	PAUL McCARTNEY'S LIVERPOOL ORATORIO *EMI Classics PAUL 1*	36	4

Darlene DAVIS *US, female vocalist*

7 Feb 87	I FOUND LOVE *Serious 70US 1*	55	5

John DAVIS and the MONSTER ORCHESTRA *US, male vocal / instrumental group*

10 Feb 79	AIN'T THAT ENOUGH FOR YOU *Miracle M 2*	70	2

Mac DAVIS *US, male vocalist (2 Singles: 22 Weeks)*

4 Nov 72	BABY DON'T GET HOOKED ON ME *CBS 8250* ▲ $	29	6
15 Nov 80	IT'S HARD TO BE HUMBLE *Casablanca CAN 210*	27	16

Miles DAVIS *US, male trumpeter, b. 26 May 1926, d. 28 Sep 1991 (6 Albums: 9 Weeks)*

11 Jul 70	BITCHES BREW *CBS 66236*	71	1
15 Jun 85	YOU'RE UNDER ARREST *CBS 26447*	88	1
18 Oct 86	TUTU *Warner Bros. 925490 1*	74	2
3 Jun 89	AMANDLA *Warner Bros. WX 250*	49	2
5 Oct 96	THE VERY BEST OF MILES DAVIS *Columbia SONYTV 17CD*	64	1
28 Apr 01	KIND OF BLUE *Columbia CK 64935*	63	2

Roy DAVIS Jr *US, male producer (2 Singles: 5 Weeks)*

1 Nov 97	GABRIEL *XL XLS 88CD* [1]	22	4
31 Jan 04	ABOUT LOVE *Classic CMC 21*	70	1

[1] Roy Davis Jr featuring Peven Everett

Sammy DAVIS Jr (see also The RATPACK) *US, male vocalist, b. 8 Dec 1925, d. 16 May 1990 (2 Albums: 2 Weeks, 9 Singles: 37 Weeks)*

29 Jul 55	SOMETHING'S GOTTA GIVE (re) *Brunswick LAT 8296*	11	7
9 Sep 55 ●	LOVE ME OR LEAVE ME (re) *Brunswick 05428*	8	8
30 Sep 55	THAT OLD BLACK MAGIC *Brunswick 05450*	16	1
7 Oct 55	HEY THERE *Brunswick 05469*	19	1
20 Apr 56	IN A PERSIAN MARKET *Brunswick 05518*	28	1
28 Dec 56	ALL OF YOU *Brunswick 05629*	28	1
16 Jun 60	HAPPY TO MAKE YOUR ACQUAINTANCE *Brunswick 05830* [1]	46	1
22 Mar 62	WHAT KIND OF FOOL AM I? / GONNA BUILD A MOUNTAIN *Reprise R 20048*	26	8
13 Dec 62	ME AND MY SHADOW (re) *Reprise R 20128* [2]	20	9
13 Apr 63	SAMMY DAVIS JR AT THE COCONUT GROVE *Reprise R 6063/2*	19	1
6 Aug 05	THE ULTIMATE COLLECTION *WSM 8122764442*	75	1

[1] Sammy Davis Jr and Carmen McRae [2] Frank Sinatra and Sammy Davis Jr

4 / 6 October 1962	11 / 13 October 1962	18 / 20 October 1962	25 / 27 October 1962
UK No.1 SINGLES			
TELSTAR The Tornados	TELSTAR The Tornados	TELSTAR The Tornados	TELSTAR The Tornados
UK No.1 ALBUMS			
WEST SIDE STORY Soundtrack	WEST SIDE STORY Soundtrack	THE BEST OF BALL, BARBER AND BILK Kenny Ball, Chris Barber and Acker Bilk	OUT OF THE SHADOWS The Shadows

Skeeter DAVIS

US, female vocalist – Mary Penick, b. 30 Dec 1931, d. 19 Sep 2004

14 Mar 63 **THE END OF THE WORLD** *RCA 1328* $ 18 13

The Spencer DAVIS GROUP (see also Steve WINWOOD)

Big-selling Birmingham (UK) band: Spencer Davis (v/g), Peter York (d) and brothers Muff (b) and Steve Winwood (v/g/k). Both No.1s penned by reggae artist Jackie Edwards. Teenager Steve Winwood left in 1967, joining Blind Faith, then Traffic and as a soloist (3 Albums: 47 Weeks, 10 Singles: 71 Weeks)

5 Nov 64 **I CAN'T STAND IT** *Fontana TF 499* 47 3
25 Feb 65 **EVERY LITTLE BIT HURTS (re)** *Fontana TF 530* 41 3
10 Jun 65 **STRONG LOVE (re)** *Fontana TF 571* 44 4
2 Dec 65 ★ **KEEP ON RUNNING** *Fontana TF 632* 1 14
8 Jan 66 ● **THEIR 1ST LP** *Fontana TL 5242* 6 9
22 Jan 66 ● **THE 2ND LP** *Fontana TL 5295* 3 18
24 Mar 66 ★ **SOMEBODY HELP ME** *Fontana TF 679* 1 10
1 Sep 66 **WHEN I COME HOME** *Fontana TF 739* 12 9
11 Sep 66 ● **AUTUMN '66** *Fontana TL 5359* 4 20
3 Nov 66 ● **GIMME SOME LOVING** *Fontana TF 762* 2 12
26 Jan 67 ● **I'M A MAN** *Fontana TF 785* 9 7
9 Aug 67 **TIME SELLER** *Fontana TF 854* 30 5
10 Jan 68 **MR SECOND CLASS** *United Artists UP 1203* 35 4

TJ DAVIS

UK, female vocalist (2 Singles: 4 Weeks)

27 Jul 96 **BRILLIANT FEELING** *Arista 74321380902* [1] 72 1
29 Dec 01 **WONDERFUL LIFE** *Melting Pot MPRCD 20* 42 3

[1] Full Monty Allstars featuring TJ Davis

DAWN

US, male / female vocal group – leader Tony Orlando (Michael Cassavitis) (1 Album: 2 Weeks, 6 Singles: 109 Weeks)

16 Jan 71 ● **CANDIDA** *Bell 1118* 9 11
10 Apr 71 ★ **KNOCK THREE TIMES** *Bell 1146* ▲ 1 27
31 Jul 71 ● **WHAT ARE YOU DOING SUNDAY** *Bell 1169* [1] 3 12
10 Mar 73 ★ **TIE A YELLOW RIBBON ROUND THE OLE OAK TREE (re)** *Bell 1287* [1] ▲ 1 40
4 Aug 73 **SAY, HAS ANYBODY SEEN MY SWEET GYPSY ROSE** *Bell 1322* [1] 12 15
9 Mar 74 **WHO'S IN THE STRAWBERRY PATCH WITH SALLY** *Bell 1343* [2] 37 4
4 May 74 **GOLDEN RIBBONS** *Bell BELLS 236* 46 2

[1] Dawn featuring Tony Orlando [2] Tony Orlando and Dawn

DAWN OF THE REPLICANTS

UK, male vocal / instrumental group (1 Album: 1 Week, 2 Singles: 2 Weeks)

7 Feb 98 **CANDLEFIRE** *East West EW 147CD1* 52 1
28 Feb 98 **ONE HEAD TWO ARMS TWO LEGS** *East West 630196002* 62 1
4 Apr 98 **HOGWASH FARM (THE DIESEL HANDS EP)** *East West EW 157CD* 65 1

Tracks on Hogwash Farm (The Diesel Hands EP): Hogwash Farm (re-built) / Night Train to Lichtenstein / The Duchess of Surin / Crow Valley.

Dana DAWSON

US, female vocalist (4 Singles: 14 Weeks)

15 Jul 95 ● **3 IS FAMILY** *EMI CDEM 378* 9 8
28 Oct 95 **GOT TO GIVE ME LOVE** *EMI CDEM 392* 27 2
4 May 96 **SHOW ME** *EMI CDEMS 423* 28 3
20 Jul 96 **HOW I WANNA BE LOVED** *EMI CDEMS 432* 42 1

Bobby DAY

US, male vocalist – Robert Byrd, b. 1 Jul 1930, d. 27 Jul 1990

7 Nov 58 **ROCKIN' ROBIN** *London HL 8726* $ 29 2

Darren DAY

UK, male vocalist (1 Album: 1 Week, 3 Singles: 7 Weeks)

8 Oct 94 **YOUNG GIRL** *Bell 74321231082* 42 2
8 Jun 96 **SUMMER HOLIDAY MEDLEY** *RCA 74321384472* 17 4
18 Apr 98 **DARREN DAY** *Eastcoast DAYCD 01* 62 1
9 May 98 **HOW CAN I BE SURE?** *Eastcoast DDCD 001* 71 1

Doris DAY (385 Top 500)

The fifties' favourite female singer / actress, b. Doris Kappelhoff, 3 Apr 1924, Cincinnati, US. The No.1 female movie star of that era, she also had numerous British hits (not to mention 25 US best-sellers) before the UK chart first started (6 Albums: 37 Weeks, 16 Singles: 146 Weeks)

14 Nov 52 ● **SUGARBUSH (re)** *Columbia DB 3123* [1] 8 8
21 Nov 52 ● **MY LOVE AND DEVOTION** *Columbia DB 3157* 10 2
3 Apr 53 **MA SAYS, PA SAYS** *Columbia DB 3242* [2] 12 1
17 Apr 53 **FULL TIME JOB** *Columbia DB 3242* [2] 11 1
24 Jul 53 ● **LET'S WALK THAT-A-WAY** *Philips PB 157* [2] 4 14
2 Apr 54 ★ **SECRET LOVE** *Philips PB 230* ▲ 1 29
27 Aug 54 ● **THE BLACK HILLS OF DAKOTA** *Philips PB 287* 7 8
1 Oct 54 ● **IF I GIVE MY HEART TO YOU** *Philips PB 325* [3] 4 11
8 Apr 55 ● **READY, WILLING AND ABLE** *Philips PB 402* 7 9
9 Sep 55 **LOVE ME OR LEAVE ME** *Philips PB 479* 20 1
21 Oct 55 **I'LL NEVER STOP LOVING YOU (re)** *Philips PB 497* 17 3
29 Jun 56 ★ **WHATEVER WILL BE, WILL BE (QUE SERA, SERA)** *Philips PB 586* $ 1 22
13 Jun 58 **A VERY PRECIOUS LOVE** *Philips PB 799* 16 11
15 Aug 58 **EVERYBODY LOVES A LOVER (re)** *Philips PB 843* 25 4
12 Mar 64 ● **MOVE OVER DARLING** *CBS AAG 183* 8 16
6 Jan 79 **20 GOLDEN GREATS** *Warwick PR 5053* 12 11
18 Apr 87 **MOVE OVER DARLING** (re-issue) *CBS LEGS 1* 45 6
11 Nov 89 **A PORTRAIT OF DORIS DAY** *Stylus SMR 984* 32 9
6 Nov 93 **GREATEST HITS** *Telstar TCD 2659* 14 12
10 Dec 94 **THE LOVE ALBUM** *Vision VISCD2* 64 3
20 Nov 99 **THE MAGIC OF THE MOVIES** *Columbia SONYTV 79CD* 63 1
20 Apr 02 **THE BEST OF DORIS DAY – 41 HOLLYWOOD GREATS** *Columbia 5079632* 73 1

[1] Doris Day and Frankie Laine [2] Doris Day and Johnnie Ray [3] Doris Day with the Mellomen

Inaya DAY (see also Boris DLUGOSCH)

US, female vocalist – Inaya Davis (3 Singles: 11 Weeks)

22 May 99 **JUST CAN'T GET ENOUGH** *AM:PM CDAMPM 121* [1] 39 2
7 Oct 00 **FEEL IT** *Positiva CDTIV 141* 51 1
23 Jul 05 ● **NASTY GIRL** *All Around the World CDGLOBE 449* 9 8

[1] Harry 'Choo Choo' Romero presents Inaya Day

DAY ONE

UK, male vocal / instrumental duo

13 Nov 99 **I'M DOIN' FINE** *Melankolic / Virgin SADD 6* 68 1
25 Mar 00 **ORDINARY MAN** *Melankolic CDSAD 8* 70 1

Patti DAY

US, female vocalist

9 Dec 89 **RIGHT BEFORE MY EYES** *Debut DEBT 3080* 69 1

DAYEENE

Sweden, female vocal duo

17 Jul 99 **AND IT HURTS** *Pukka CDPUKKA 20* 63 1

Taylor DAYNE

US, female vocalist – Leslie Wundermann (1 Album: 17 Weeks, 11 Singles: 54 Weeks)

23 Jan 88 ● **TELL IT TO MY HEART** *Arista 109616* 3 13
5 Mar 88 **TELL IT TO MY HEART** *Arista 208898* 24 17
19 Mar 88 ● **PROVE YOUR LOVE** *Arista 109830* 8 10
11 Jun 88 **I'LL ALWAYS LOVE YOU** *Arista 111536* 41 7
18 Nov 89 **WITH EVERY BEAT OF MY HEART** *Arista 112760* 53 2
14 Apr 90 **I'LL BE YOUR SHELTER** *Arista 112996* 43 5
4 Aug 90 **LOVE WILL LEAD YOU BACK** *Arista 113277* ▲ 69 1
3 Jul 93 **CAN'T GET ENOUGH OF YOUR LOVE** *Arista 74321147852* 14 8
16 Apr 94 **I'LL WAIT** *Arista 74321203472* 29 3
4 Feb 95 **ORIGINAL SIN (THEME FROM 'THE SHADOW')** *Arista 74321223462* 63 1
18 Nov 95 **SAY A PRAYER** *Arista 74321324292* 58 1
13 Jan 96 **TELL IT TO MY HEART** (re-mix) *Arista 74321335962* 23 3

DAYTON

US, male vocal group

10 Dec 83 **THE SOUND OF MUSIC** *Capitol CL 318* 75 1

1 / 3 November 1962	8 / 10 November 1962	15 / 17 November 1962	22 / 24 November 1962
TELSTAR The Tornados	LOVESICK BLUES Frank Ifield	LOVESICK BLUES Frank Ifield	LOVESICK BLUES Frank Ifield
OUT OF THE SHADOWS The Shadows	OUT OF THE SHADOWS The Shadows	WEST SIDE STORY Soundtrack	OUT OF THE SHADOWS The Shadows

KEY
UK No.1 ★ UK Top 10 ● Still on chart + UK entry at No.1 ■ US No.1 ▲ UK million seller £ US million seller $
Singles re-entries are listed as (re), (2re), (3re)... which signifies that the hit re-entered the chart once, twice or three times...
Peak Position / Weeks

DAZZ BAND *US, male vocal / instrumental group*

3 Nov 84 **LET IT ALL BLOW** *Motown TMG 1361* 12 12

D'BORA *US, female vocalist – Deborah Walker (3 Singles: 4 Weeks)*

14 Sep 91 **DREAM ABOUT YOU** *Polydor PO 161* 75 1
1 Jul 95 **GOING ROUND** *Vibe MCSTD 2055* 40 2
30 Mar 96 **GOOD LOVE REAL LOVE** *Music Plant MCSTD 40023* 58 1

Nino DE ANGELO *Germany, male vocalist*

21 Jul 84 **GUARDIAN ANGEL** *Carrere CAR 335* 57 5

DE BOS (see also FREAKYMAN)
Holland, male DJ / producer – Andre Van Den Bosch

25 Oct 97 **ON THE RUN** *Jive JIVECD 433* 51 1

Chris DE BURGH (154 Top 500)
Irish singer / songwriter, b. Christopher Davidson, 15 Oct 1948, Buenos Aires, Argentina. The son of a diplomat, he moved to County Wexford in Ireland with his family, who can be traced back to King Richard the Lionheart, when he was 12. The balladeer has sold 45 million albums worldwide and will always be remembered for the eight million-selling No.1 he reportedly wrote for and about his wife, Diane. Daughter Rosanna was crowned Miss World in 2003 (18 Albums: 282 Weeks, 15 Singles: 71 Weeks)

12 Sep 81 BEST MOVES *A&M AMLH 68532* 65 4
9 Oct 82 THE GETAWAY *A&M AMLH 68549* 30 16
23 Oct 82 **DON'T PAY THE FERRYMAN** *A&M AMS 8256* 48 5
12 May 84 **HIGH ON EMOTION** *A&M AM 190* 44 5
19 May 84 MAN ON THE LINE *A&M AMLX 65002* 11 24
29 Dec 84 ● THE VERY BEST OF CHRIS DE BURGH *Telstar STAR 2248* 6 70
24 Aug 85 SPANISH TRAIN AND OTHER STORIES *A&M AMLH 68343* 78 3
7 Jun 86 ● INTO THE LIGHT *A&M AM 5121* 2 59
12 Jul 86 ★ **THE LADY IN RED (re)** *A&M AM 331* 1 15
20 Sep 86 **FATAL HESITATION** *A&M AM 346* 44 4
4 Oct 86 CRUSADER *A&M AMLH 64746* 72 1
13 Dec 86 **A SPACEMAN CAME TRAVELLING / THE BALLROOM OF ROMANCE** *A&M AM 365* 40 5
12 Dec 87 **THE SIMPLE TRUTH (A CHILD IS BORN) (re)** *A&M AM 427* 55 3
15 Oct 88 ★ FLYING COLOURS *A&M AMA 5224* ■ 1 30
29 Oct 88 ● **MISSING YOU** *A&M AM 474* 3 12
7 Jan 89 **TENDER HANDS** *A&M AM 486* 43 6
14 Oct 89 **THIS WAITING HEART** *A&M AM 528* 59 3
4 Nov 89 ● SPARK TO A FLAME – THE VERY BEST OF CHRIS DE BURGH *A&M CDBLP 100* 4 29
22 Sep 90 HIGH ON EMOTION – LIVE FROM DUBLIN! *A&M 3970861* 15 6
25 May 91 **THE SIMPLE TRUTH (A CHILD IS BORN)** (re-issue) *A&M RELF 1* 36 2
11 Apr 92 **SEPARATE TABLES** *A&M AM 863* 30 4
9 May 92 ● POWER OF TEN *A&M 3971882* 3 10
21 May 94 **BLONDE HAIR BLUE JEANS** *A&M 5805932* 51 1
28 May 94 ● THIS WAY UP *A&M 5402332* 5 6
18 Nov 95 BEAUTIFUL DREAMS *A&M 5404322* 33 8
9 Dec 95 **THE SNOWS OF NEW YORK** *A&M 5813132* 60 1
27 Sep 97 **SO BEAUTIFUL** *A&M 5823932* 29 4
11 Oct 97 ● THE LOVE SONGS *A&M 5407942* 8 7
18 Sep 99 **WHEN I THINK OF YOU** *A&M / Mercury 4971302* 59 1
2 Oct 99 QUIET REVOLUTION *Mercury / A&M 4904462* 23 3
31 Mar 01 THE ULTIMATE COLLECTION – NOTES FROM PLANET EARTH *Mercury / A&M 4908992* 19 4
28 Sep 02 TIMING IS EVERYTHING ... *Mercury / A&M 4934292* 41 1
27 Mar 04 THE ROAD TO FREEDOM *Ferryman FERRY 888* 75 1

DE CASTRO SISTERS *Cuba, female vocal group*

11 Feb 55 **TEACH ME TONIGHT** *London HL 8104* 20 1

Hit with Skip Martin and his Orchestra.

DE-CODE featuring Beverli SKEETE
UK, male / female vocal / instrumental group

18 May 96 **WONDERWALL / SOME MIGHT SAY** *Neoteric NRCD 2* 69 1

Etienne DE CRECY *France, male DJ / producer (2 Singles: 3 Weeks)*

28 Mar 98 **PRIX CHOC REMIXES** *Different DIF 007CD* 60 1
20 Jan 01 **AM I WRONG** *XL Recordings XLS 127CD* 44 2

DE FUNK featuring F45 *Italy / UK, male production / vocal group*

25 Sep 99 **PLEASURE LOVE** *INCredible INCS 3CD* 49 1

Lennie DE ICE *UK, male producer*

17 Apr 99 **WE ARE I. E.** *Distinctive DISNCD 50* 61 1

DE LA SOUL (493 Top 500) (see also The JUNGLE BROTHERS)
Brooklyn, New York vocal / production trio that replaced bitches and firearms with beads and flowers: Posdnous (Kelvin Mercer), Trugoy the Dove (David Jolicеur) and Mase (Vincent Mason). 3 Feet High and Rising, produced by Prince Paul, spawned four hit singles and was one of the most influential rap LPs of all time (7 Albums: 88 Weeks, 15 Singles: 63 Weeks)

25 Mar 89 3 FEET HIGH AND RISING *Big Life DLSLP 1* 13 56
8 Apr 89 **ME MYSELF AND I** *Big Life BLR 7* 22 8
8 Jul 89 **SAY NO GO** *Big Life BLR 10* 18 7
21 Oct 89 **EYE KNOW** *Big Life BLR 13* 14 7
23 Dec 89 ● **THE MAGIC NUMBER / BUDDY** *Big Life BLR 14* 7 8
24 Mar 90 **MAMA GAVE BIRTH TO THE SOUL CHILDREN** *Gee Street GEE 26* [1] 14 7
27 Apr 91 ● **RING RING RING (HA HA HEY)** *Big Life BLR 42* 10 7
25 May 91 ● DE LA SOUL IS DEAD *Big Life BLRLP 8* 7 11
3 Aug 91 **A ROLLER SKATING JAM NAMED 'SATURDAYS'** *Big Life BLR 55* 22 5
23 Nov 91 **KEEPIN' THE FAITH** *Big Life BLR 64* 50 2
18 Sep 93 **BREAKADAWN** *Big Life BLRD 103* 39 3
9 Oct 93 BUHLOONE MINDSTATE *Big Life BLRCD 25* 37 2
2 Apr 94 **FALLIN'** *Epic 6602622* [2] 59 1
29 Jun 96 **STAKES IS HIGH** *Tommy Boy TBCD 7730* 55 1
13 Jul 96 STAKES IS HIGH *Tommy Boy TBCD 1149* 42 1
8 Mar 97 **4 MORE** *Tommy Boy TBCD 7779A* [3] 52 1
9 Oct 99 3 FEET HIGH AND RISING (re-issue) *Tommy Boy TBCD 1019* 17 2
22 Jul 00 **OOOH** *Tommy Boy TBCD 2102* [4] 29 2
19 Aug 00 ART OFFICIAL INTELLIGENCE: MOSAIC THUMP *Tommy Boy TBCD 1348* 22 4
11 Nov 00 **ALL GOOD** *Tommy Boy TBCD 2154B* [5] 33 3
2 Mar 02 **BABY PHAT** *Tommy Boy TBCD 2359* 55 1
14 Jun 03 THE BEST OF *Rhino / Tommy Boy 8122736652* 17 12

[1] Queen Latifah + De La Soul [2] Teenage Fanclub and De La Soul [3] De La Soul featuring Zhané [4] De La Soul featuring Redman [5] De La Soul featuring Chaka Khan

'Buddy' listed only until 6 Jan 1990, peaking at No.8.

Donna DE LORY *US, female vocalist*

24 Jul 93 **JUST A DREAM** *MCA MCSTD 1750* 71 1

Vincent DE MOOR (see also VERACOCHA)
Holland, male producer (2 Singles: 4 Weeks)

16 Aug 97 **FLOWTATION** *XL Recordings XLS 89CD* 54 1
7 Apr 01 **FLY AWAY** *VC Recordings VCRD 87* 30 3

DE NADA *UK, male / female production / vocal group (2 Singles: 7 Weeks)*

25 Aug 01 **LOVE YOU ANYWAY** *Wildstar CDWILD 37* 15 4
9 Feb 02 **BRING IT ON TO MY LOVE** *Wildstar CDWILD 39* 24 3

29 November / 1 December 1962	6 / 8 December 1962	13 / 15 December 1962	20 / 22 December 1962
UK No.1 SINGLES			
LOVESICK BLUES Frank Ifield	LOVESICK BLUES Frank Ifield	RETURN TO SENDER Elvis Presley with The Jordanaires	RETURN TO SENDER Elvis Presley with The Jordanaires
UK No.1 ALBUMS			
ON STAGE WITH THE GEORGE MITCHELL MINSTRELS George Mitchell Minstrels	ON STAGE WITH THE GEORGE MITCHELL MINSTRELS George Mitchell Minstrels	WEST SIDE STORY Soundtrack	OUT OF THE SHADOWS The Shadows

DE NUIT *Italy, male production duo – Fabio Seveso and Francesco de Leo*

23 Nov 02 ALL THAT MATTERED (LOVE YOU DOWN) *Credence CDCRED 029* 38 2

Lynsey DE PAUL *UK, female vocalist / keyboard player – Lynsey Rubin (7 Singles: 54 Weeks)*

19 Aug 72 ● SUGAR ME *MAM 81* 5 11
2 Dec 72 GETTING A DRAG *MAM 88* 18 8
27 Oct 73 WON'T SOMEBODY DANCE WITH ME *MAM 109* 14 7
8 Jun 74 OOH I DO *Warner Bros. K 16401* 25 6
2 Nov 74 ● NO HONESTLY *Jet 747* 7 11
22 Mar 75 MY MAN AND ME *Jet 750* 40 4
26 Mar 77 ROCK BOTTOM *Polydor 2058 859* [1] 19 7

[1] Lynsey De Paul and Mike Moran

Tullio DE PISCOPO *Italy, male vocalist*

28 Feb 87 STOP BAJON ... PRIMAVERA *Greyhound GREY 9* 58 4

Manitas DE PLATA *France, male guitarist – Ricardo Baliardo*

29 Jul 67 FLAMENCO GUITAR *Philips SBL 7786* 40 1

Rebecca DE RUVO *Sweden, female vocalist*

1 Oct 94 I CAUGHT YOU OUT *Arista 74321230782* 72 1

Teri DE SARIO *US, female vocalist*

2 Sep 78 AIN'T NOTHING GONNA KEEP ME FROM YOU *Casablanca CAN 128* 52 5

Stephanie DE SYKES *UK, female vocalist – Stephanie Ryton (2 Singles: 17 Weeks)*

20 Jul 74 ● BORN WITH A SMILE ON MY FACE *Bradley's BRAD 7409* [1] 2 10
19 Apr 75 WE'LL FIND OUR DAY *Bradley's BRAD 7509* 17 7

[1] Stephanie De Sykes with Rain

Tony DE VIT *UK, male DJ / producer, b. 12 Sep 1957, d. 2 Jul 1998 (7 Singles: 13 Weeks)*

4 Mar 95 BURNING UP *Icon ICONCD 001* 25 3
12 Aug 95 HOOKED *Labello Dance LAD 18CD* [1] 28 2
9 Sep 95 TO THE LIMIT *X:Plode BANG 1CD* 44 2
30 May 96 I'LL BE THERE *Labello Dance LAD 25CD1* [1] 37 2
28 Oct 00 DAWN *Tidy Trax TIDY 140CD* 56 2
21 Dec 02 I DON'T CARE *Tidy Trax TIDY 181T* 65 1
12 Jul 03 GIVE ME A REASON *Tidy Trax TIDYTWO 123CD* [2] 53 1

[1] 99th Floor Elevators featuring Tony De Vit [2] Tony De Vit featuring Niki Mak

DEACON BLUE 168 Top 500

Scottish sextet with fervent following, led by singer / songwriter Ricky Ross (v) and featuring his wife Lorraine McIntosh (v). Named after a Steely Dan song, they achieved five Top 5 albums, including the million-selling When the World Knows Your Name (8 Albums: 217 Weeks, 20 Singles: 112 Weeks)

6 Jun 87 RAINTOWN *CBS 4505491* 14 77
23 Jan 88 DIGNITY *CBS DEAC 4* 31 8
9 Apr 88 WHEN WILL YOU MAKE MY TELEPHONE RING *CBS DEAC 5* 34 7
16 Jul 88 CHOCOLATE GIRL *CBS DEAC 6* 43 7
15 Oct 88 ● REAL GONE KID *CBS DEAC 7* 8 13
4 Mar 89 WAGES DAY *CBS DEAC 8* 18 6
15 Apr 89 ★ WHEN THE WORLD KNOWS YOUR NAME *CBS 4633211* ■ 1 54
20 May 89 FERGUS SINGS THE BLUES *CBS DEAC 9* 14 6
16 Sep 89 LOVE AND REGRET *CBS DEAC 10* 28 5
6 Jan 90 QUEEN OF THE NEW YEAR *CBS DEAC 11* 21 5
25 Aug 90 ● FOUR BACHARACH AND DAVID SONGS (EP) *CBS DEAC 12* 2 9
22 Sep 90 ● OOH LAS VEGAS *CBS 4672421* 3 8
25 May 91 YOUR SWAYING ARMS *Columbia 6568937* 23 4
15 Jun 91 ● FELLOW HOODLUMS *Columbia 4685501* 2 27
27 Jul 91 ● TWIST AND SHOUT *Columbia 6573027* 10 9
12 Oct 91 CLOSING TIME *Columbia 6575027* 42 3
14 Dec 91 COVER FROM THE SKY *Columbia 6576737* 31 4
28 Nov 92 YOUR TOWN *Columbia 6587867* 14 8
13 Feb 93 WILL WE BE LOVERS *Columbia 6589732* 31 4
13 Mar 93 ● WHATEVER YOU SAY SAY NOTHING *Columbia 4735272* 4 10
24 Apr 93 ONLY TENDER LOVE *Columbia 6591842* 22 4
17 Jul 93 HANG YOUR HEAD *Columbia 6594602* 21 3
2 Apr 94 I WAS RIGHT AND YOU WERE WRONG *Columbia 6602222* 32 3
16 Apr 94 ★ OUR TOWN – THE GREATEST HITS *Columbia 4766422* 1 38
28 May 94 DIGNITY (re-issue) *Columbia 6604485* 20 3
23 Oct 99 WALKING BACK HOME *Columbia 4963802* 39 2
28 Apr 01 EVERYTIME YOU SLEEP *Papillon BTFLY 0011* 64 1
12 May 01 HOMESICK *Papillon BTFLYCD 0014* 59 1

Tracks on Four Bacharach and David Songs (EP): I'll Never Fall in Love Again / The Look of Love / Message to Michael / Are You There (With Another Girl).

The DEAD 60S *UK, male vocal / instrumental group (1 Album: 3 Weeks, 5 Singles: 10 Weeks)*

16 Oct 04 RIOT RADIO *Deltasonic DLTCD 025* 30 2
9 Apr 05 THE LAST RESORT *Deltasonic DLTCD 2032* 24 2
25 Jun 05 LOADED GUN *Deltasonic DLTCD 2037* 28 2
24 Sep 05 RIOT RADIO (re-issue) *Deltasonic DLTCD 2041* 30 2
8 Oct 05 THE DEAD 60S *Deltasonic DLTCD 038* 23 3
3 Dec 05 GHOSTFACED KILLER *Deltasonic DLTCD 042* 25 2

DEAD CAN DANCE *Australia, male / female vocal / instrumental duo (2 Albums: 3 Weeks)*

25 Sep 93 INTO THE LABYRINTH *4AD CAD 3013CD* 47 1
29 Jun 96 SPIRITCHASER *4AD CAD 6008CD* 43 2

DEAD DRED *UK, male instrumental / production duo*

5 Nov 94 DRED BASS *Moving Shadow SHADOW 50CD* 60 2

The DEAD END KIDS *UK, male vocal / instrumental group*

26 Mar 77 ● HAVE I THE RIGHT *CBS 4972* 6 10

DEAD KENNEDYS *US, male vocal / instrumental group (2 Albums: 8 Weeks, 2 Singles: 9 Weeks)*

13 Sep 80 FRESH FRUIT FOR ROTTING VEGETABLES *Cherry Red BRED 10* 33 6
1 Nov 80 KILL THE POOR *Cherry Red CHERRY 16* 49 3
30 May 81 TOO DRUNK TO FUCK *Cherry Red CHERRY 24* 36 6
4 Jul 87 GIVE ME CONVENIENCE *Alternative Tentacles VIRUS 5* 84 2

DEAD OR ALIVE *UK, male vocal (Pete Burns) / instrumental group (3 Albums: 22 Weeks, 11 Singles: 73 Weeks)*

24 Mar 84 THAT'S THE WAY (I LIKE IT) *Epic A 4271* 22 9
28 Apr 84 SOPHISTICATED BOOM BOOM *Epic EPC 25835* 29 3
1 Dec 84 ★ YOU SPIN ME ROUND (LIKE A RECORD) *Epic A 4861* 1 23
20 Apr 85 LOVER COME BACK TO ME *Epic A 6086* 11 8
25 May 85 ● YOUTHQUAKE *Epic EPC 26420* 9 15
29 Jun 85 IN TOO DEEP *Epic A 6360* 14 8
21 Sep 85 MY HEART GOES BANG (GET ME TO THE DOCTOR) *Epic A 6571* 23 6
20 Sep 86 BRAND NEW LOVER *Epic A 650075 7* 31 4
10 Jan 87 SOMETHING IN MY HOUSE *Epic BURNS 1* 12 7
14 Feb 87 MAD BAD AND DANGEROUS TO KNOW *Epic 450 2571* 27 4
4 Apr 87 HOOKED ON LOVE *Epic BURNS 2* 69 2
3 Sep 88 TURN AROUND AND COUNT 2 TEN *Epic BURNS 4* 70 1
22 Jul 89 COME HOME WITH ME BABY *Epic BURNS 5* 62 2
17 May 03 YOU SPIN ME ROUND (re-mix) *Epic 6735782* 23 3

DEAD PREZ *US, male rap duo*

11 Mar 00 HIP HOP *Epic 6689862* 41 2

DEADLY SINS *UK / Italy, male vocal / instrumental duo*

30 Apr 94 WE ARE GOING ON DOWN *Ffrreedom TABCD 220* 45 2

27 / 29 December 1962	3 / 5 January 1963	10 / 12 January 1963	17 / 19 January 1963
RETURN TO SENDER Elvis Presley with The Jordanaires	THE NEXT TIME / BACHELOR BOY Cliff Richard and The Shadows	THE NEXT TIME / BACHELOR BOY Cliff Richard and The Shadows	THE NEXT TIME / BACHELOR BOY Cliff Richard and The Shadows
THE BLACK AND WHITE MINSTREL SHOW George Mitchell Minstrels	THE BLACK AND WHITE MINSTREL SHOW George Mitchell Minstrels	WEST SIDE STORY Soundtrack	OUT OF THE SHADOWS The Shadows

KEY: UK No.1 ★ UK Top 10 ● Still on chart + UK entry at No.1 ■ US No.1 ▲ UK million seller £ US million seller $
Singles re-entries are listed as (re), (2re), (3re)... which signifies that the hit re-entered the chart once, twice or three times...
Peak Position / Weeks

Hazell DEAN *UK, female vocalist (1 Album: 3 Weeks, 11 Singles: 71 Weeks)*

18 Feb 84	**EVERGREEN / JEALOUS LOVE** *Proto ENA 114*	63	3
21 Apr 84 ●	**SEARCHIN' (I GOTTA FIND A MAN)** *Proto ENA 109*	6	15
28 Jul 84 ●	**WHATEVER I DO (WHEREVER I GO)** *Proto ENA 119*	4	11
3 Nov 84	**BACK IN MY ARMS (ONCE AGAIN)** *Proto ENA 122*	41	4
2 Mar 85	**NO FOOL (FOR LOVE)** *Proto ENA 123*	41	5
12 Oct 85	**THEY SAY IT'S GONNA RAIN** *Parlophone R 6107*	58	4
2 Apr 88 ●	**WHO'S LEAVING WHO** *EMI EM 45*	4	11
25 Jun 88	**MAYBE (WE SHOULD CALL IT A DAY)** *EMI EM 62*	15	6
24 Sep 88	**TURN IT INTO LOVE** *EMI EM 71*	21	7
22 Oct 88	ALWAYS *EMI EMC 3546*	38	3
26 Aug 89	**LOVE PAINS** *Lisson DOLE 12*	48	4
23 Mar 91	**BETTER OFF WITHOUT YOU** *Lisson DOLE 19*	72	1

Jimmy DEAN *US, male vocalist – Seth Ward (2 Singles: 17 Weeks)*

26 Oct 61 ●	**BIG BAD JOHN** *Philips PB 1187* ▲ $	2	13
8 Nov 62	**LITTLE BLACK BOOK** *CBS AAG 122*	33	4

Letitia DEAN and Paul MEDFORD *UK, female / male vocal / actor duo*

25 Oct 86	**SOMETHING OUTA NOTHING** *BBC RESL 203*	12	7

DEAR JON *UK, female / male vocal / instrumental group*

22 Apr 95	**ONE GIFT OF LOVE** *MDMC DEVCS 2*	68	1

The DEARS
Canada, male / female vocal / instrumental group (2 Singles: 2 Weeks)

20 Nov 04	**LOST IN THE PLOT** *Bella Union BELLACD 86*	49	1
14 May 05	**22: THE DEATH OF ALL THE ROMANCE** *Bella Union BELLACD 100*	53	1

DEATH FROM ABOVE 1979 *Canada, male vocal / instrumental duo – Jesse F Keeler and Sebastien Grainger (3 Singles: 4 Weeks)*

13 Nov 04	**ROMANTIC RIGHTS** *679 Recordings 679L 090CD*	57	1
26 Feb 05	**BLOOD ON OUR HANDS** *679 Recordings 679L 078CD*	33	2
25 Jun 05	**BLACK HISTORY MONTH** *679 Recordings 679L 106CD*	48	1

DEATH IN VEGAS *UK, male instrumental / production duo – Richard Fearless and Tim Holmes (3 Albums: 16 Weeks, 6 Singles: 17 Weeks)*

29 Mar 97	DEAD ELVIS *Concrete HARD 22LPCD*	52	1
2 Aug 97	**DIRT** *Concrete HARD 27CD*	61	1
1 Nov 97	**ROCCO** *Concrete HARD 29CD*	51	1
25 Sep 99	THE CONTINO SESSIONS *Concrete HARD 41CDU*	19	12
12 Feb 00 ●	**AISHA** *Concrete HARD 43CD*	9	4
6 May 00	**DIRGE** *Concrete HARD 44CD*	24	2
21 Sep 02	**HANDS AROUND MY THROAT** *Concrete HARD 48CD*	36	1
28 Sep 02	SCORPIO RISING *Concrete / BMG HARD 53CD 2*	19	3
28 Dec 02	**SCORPIO RISING (re)** *Concrete HARD 54CD1* [1]	14	8

[1] Death in Vegas with Liam Gallagher

Uncredited vocal on 'Aisha' by Iggy Pop.

DeBARGE (see also Chico DeBARGE; El DeBARGE)
US, male / female vocal group (1 Album: 2 Weeks, 2 Singles: 17 Weeks)

6 Apr 85 ●	**RHYTHM OF THE NIGHT** *Gordy TMG 1376*	4	14
25 May 85	RHYTHM OF THE NIGHT *Gordy ZL 72340*	94	2
21 Sep 85	**YOU WEAR IT WELL** *Gordy ZB 40345* [1]	54	3

[1] El DeBarge with DeBarge

Chico DeBARGE (see also DeBARGE) *US, male vocalist*

14 Mar 98	**IGGIN' ME** *Universal UND 56170*	50	1

El DeBARGE (see also DeBARGE) *US, male vocalist (2 Singles: 3 Weeks)*

28 Jun 86	**WHO'S JOHNNY ('SHORT CIRCUIT' THEME)** *Gordy ELD 1*	60	2
31 Mar 90	**SECRET GARDEN** *Qwest W 9992* [1]	67	1

[1] Quincy Jones featuring Al B Sure!, James Ingram, El DeBarge and Barry White

Diana DECKER *US, female actor / vocalist*

23 Oct 53 ●	**POPPA PICCOLINO (re)** *Columbia DB 3325*	2	10

DECLAN *UK, male vocalist – Declan Galbraith*

5 Oct 02	DECLAN *EMI / Liberty 5416012*	44	3
21 Dec 02	**TELL ME WHY** *EMI / Liberty CDDECS 004* [1]	29	4

[1] Declan featuring Young Voices Choir

DECOY AND ROY (see also CONVERT; CUBIC 22)
Belgium, male production duo – Danny Van Wauwe and Roy Van Luffelen

1 Feb 03	**INNER LIFE** *Ministry of Sound / Data DATA 43CDS*	45	1

Dave DEE (see also Dave DEE, DOZY, BEAKY, MICK and TICH)
UK, male vocalist – David Harman

14 Mar 70	**MY WOMAN'S MAN** *Fontana TF 1074*	42	4

Dave DEE, DOZY, BEAKY, MICK and TICH 466 Top 500 (see also D, B, M and T) *Entertaining, quirkily named UK quintet who were: Dave Dee (David Harman) (v), Dozy (Trevor Davies) (b), Beaky (John Dymond) (g), Mick (Michael Wilson) (d), Tich (Ian Amey) (g). Catchy productions and ultra-commercial songs (penned by managers Howard and Blaikley) ensured a string of hits (2 Albums: 15 Weeks, 13 Singles: 141 Weeks)*

23 Dec 65	**YOU MAKE IT MOVE** *Fontana TF 630*	26	8
3 Mar 66 ●	**HOLD TIGHT!** *Fontana TF 671*	4	17
9 Jun 66 ●	**HIDEAWAY** *Fontana TF 711*	10	11
2 Jul 66	DAVE DEE DOZY BEAKY MICK AND TICH *Fontana STL 5350*	11	10
15 Sep 66 ●	**BEND IT!** *Fontana TF 746*	2	12
8 Dec 66 ●	**SAVE ME** *Fontana TF 775*	3	10
7 Jan 67	IF MUSIC BE THE FOOD OF LOVE ... PREPARE FOR INDIGESTION *Fontana STL 5388*	27	5
9 Mar 67	**TOUCH ME, TOUCH ME** *Fontana TF 798*	13	9
18 May 67 ●	**OKAY!** *Fontana TF 830*	4	11
11 Oct 67 ●	**ZABADAK!** *Fontana TF 873*	3	14
14 Feb 68 ★	**THE LEGEND OF XANADU** *Fontana TF 903*	1	12
3 Jul 68 ●	**LAST NIGHT IN SOHO** *Fontana TF 953*	8	11
2 Oct 68	**THE WRECK OF THE 'ANTOINETTE'** *Fontana TF 971*	14	9
5 Mar 69	**DON JUAN** *Fontana TF 1000*	23	9
14 May 69	**SNAKE IN THE GRASS** *Fontana TF 1020*	23	8

DEE DEE (see also IAN VAN DAHL) *Belgium, male production trio and female vocalist – Diana Trippaers (2 Singles: 9 Weeks)*

20 Jul 02	**FOREVER** *Incentive CENT 43CDS*	12	7
1 Mar 03	**THE ONE** *Incentive CENT 52CDS*	28	2

Joey DEE and The STARLITERS *US, male vocal / instrumental group*

8 Feb 62	**PEPPERMINT TWIST** *Columbia DB 4758* ▲ $	33	8

Kiki DEE *UK, female vocalist – Pauline Matthews (3 Albums: 11 Weeks, 10 Singles: 79 Weeks)*

10 Nov 73	**AMOUREUSE** *Rocket PIG 4*	13	13
7 Sep 74	**I'VE GOT THE MUSIC IN ME** *Rocket PIG 12* [1]	19	8
12 Apr 75	**(YOU DONT KNOW) HOW GLAD I AM** *Rocket PIG 16* [1]	33	4
3 Jul 76 ★	**DON'T GO BREAKING MY HEART** *Rocket ROKN 512* [2] ▲ $	1	14
11 Sep 76	**LOVING AND FREE / AMOUREUSE** (re-issue) *Rocket ROKN 515*	13	8
19 Feb 77	**FIRST THING IN THE MORNING** *Rocket ROKN 520*	32	5
26 Mar 77	KIKI DEE *Rocket ROLA 3*	24	5
11 Jun 77	**CHICAGO** *Rocket ROKN 526*	28	4
21 Feb 81	**STAR** *Ariola ARO 251*	13	10
23 May 81	**PERFECT TIMING** *Ariola ARO 257*	66	3

24 / 26 January 1963	31 January / 2 February 1963	7 / 9 February 1963	14 / 16 February 1963
UK No.1 SINGLES			
DANCE ON! The Shadows	DIAMONDS Jet Harris and Tony Meehan	DIAMONDS Jet Harris and Tony Meehan	DIAMONDS Jet Harris and Tony Meehan
UK No.1 ALBUMS			
OUT OF THE SHADOWS The Shadows	SUMMER HOLIDAY (Soundtrack) Cliff Richard and The Shadows	SUMMER HOLIDAY (Soundtrack) Cliff Richard and The Shadows	SUMMER HOLIDAY (Soundtrack) Cliff Richard and The Shadows

18 Jul 81 PERFECT TIMING *Ariola ARL 5050*....47 4
20 Nov 93 ● TRUE LOVE *Rocket EJSCX 32* [2]....2 10
9 Apr 94 THE VERY BEST OF KIKI DEE *PolyGram TV 516728*....62 2

[1] Kiki Dee Band [2] Elton John and Kiki Dee

On 18 Sep, 25 Sep and 2 Oct 1976, 'Loving and Free' was listed by itself. 'Chicago' was one side of a double-sided chart entry, the other being 'Bite Your Lip (Get Up and Dance)' by Elton John.

DEEE-LITE (see also Towa TEI featuring Kylie MINOGUE)
US / Russia / Japan, male / female vocal ("Miss Kier" Kirby) / instrumental group (2 Albums: 19 Weeks, 6 Singles: 30 Weeks)

18 Aug 90 ● GROOVE IS IN THE HEART / WHAT IS LOVE *Elektra EKR 114*....2 13
8 Sep 90 WORLD CLIQUE *Elektra EKT 77*....14 18
24 Nov 90 POWER OF LOVE / DEEE-LITE THEME *Elektra EKR 117*....25 7
23 Feb 91 HOW DO YOU SAY ... LOVE / GROOVE IS IN THE HEART (re-mix) *Elektra EKR 118*....52 2
27 Apr 91 GOOD BEAT *Elektra EKR 122*....53 3
13 Jun 92 RUNAWAY *Elektra EKR 148*....45 3
4 Jul 92 INFINITY WITHIN *Elektra 7559613132*....37 1
30 Jul 94 PICNIC IN THE SUMMERTIME *Elektra EKR 186CD1*....43 2

'What Is Love' listed only from 25 Aug 1990.

DEEJAY PUNK-ROC
US, male DJ / producer – Charles Gettis (1 Album: 1 Week, 4 Singles: 5 Weeks)

21 Mar 98 DEAD HUSBAND *Independiente ISOM 9MS*....71 1
9 May 98 MY BEATBOX *Independiente ISOM 12MS*....43 1
30 May 98 CHICKENEYE *Independiente ISOM 5CD*....47 1
8 Aug 98 FAR OUT *Independiente ISOM 17MS*....43 2
20 Feb 99 ROC-IN-IT *Independiente ISOM 21MS* [1]....59 1

[1] Deejay Punk-Roc vs Onyx

Carol DEENE
UK, female vocalist – Carole Carver (4 Singles: 25 Weeks)

26 Oct 61 SAD MOVIES (MAKE ME CRY) *HMV POP 922*....44 3
25 Jan 62 NORMAN *HMV POP 973*....24 8
5 Jul 62 JOHNNY GET ANGRY *HMV POP 1027*....32 4
23 Aug 62 SOME PEOPLE *HMV POP 1058*....25 10

Scotti DEEP *US, male producer / instrumentalist – Scott Kinchen*

15 Mar 97 BROOKLYN BEATS *Xtravaganza 0090095*....67 1

DEEP BLUE *UK, male producer – Sean O'Keefe*

16 Apr 94 HELICOPTER TUNE *Moving Shadow SHADOW 41CD*....68 2

DEEP BLUE SOMETHING *US, male vocal (Todd Pipes) / instrumental group (1 Album: 5 Weeks, 2 Singles: 17 Weeks)*

6 Jul 96 ★ BREAKFAST AT TIFFANY'S (re) *Interscope IND 80032*....1 14
5 Oct 96 HOME *Interscope IND 90002*....24 5
7 Dec 96 JOSEY *Interscope IND 95518*....27 3

DEEP C
UK, male / female vocal / instrumental group (2 Singles: 3 Weeks)

19 Jan 91 AFRICAN REIGN *M&G MAGS 4*....75 1
8 Jun 91 CHILL TO THE PANIC *M&G MAGS 10*....73 2

DEEP COVER (see also SCOTT & LEON; TRU FAITH & DUB CONSPIRACY) *UK, male production group*

11 May 02 SOUNDS OF EDEN (EVERYTIME I SEE THE GIRL) *Attitude! 0158392*....63 1

Title on the label was incorrect. Should have read 'The Sound Of Eden'.

DEEP CREED '94 *US, male producer – Armand van Helden*

7 May 94 CAN U FEEL IT *Eastern Bloc BLOCCD 005*....59 1

DEEP DISH *Iran, male instrumental / production duo – Ali 'Dubfire' Shirazinia and Sharam Tayebi (2 Albums: 3 Weeks, 5 Singles: 27 Weeks)*

26 Oct 96 STAY GOLD *Deconstruction 74321418222*....41 1
1 Nov 97 STRANDED *Deconstruction 74321512232*....60 1
18 Jul 98 JUNK SCIENCE *Deconstruction 74321580342*....37 2
3 Oct 98 THE FUTURE OF THE FUTURE (STAY GOLD) *Deconstruction 74321616252* [1]....31 2
9 Oct 04 ● FLASHDANCE *Positiva CDTIVS 211*....3 16
23 Jul 05 SAY HELLO *Positiva CDTIVS 220*....14 7
6 Aug 05 GEORGE IS ON *Positiva 3313382*....54 1

[1] Deep Dish with Everything but the Girl

DEEP FEELING *UK, male vocal / instrumental group*

25 Apr 70 DO YOU LOVE ME (re) *Page One POF 165*....34 5

DEEP FOREST *France, male instrumental duo – Eric Mouquet and Michel Sanchez (3 Albums: 17 Weeks, 4 Singles: 14 Weeks)*

5 Feb 94 ● SWEET LULLABY *Columbia 6599242*....10 6
26 Feb 94 DEEP FOREST *Columbia 4741782*....15 11
21 May 94 DEEP FOREST *Columbia 6604115*....20 4
23 Jul 94 SAVANNA DANCE *Columbia 6606355*....28 2
3 Jun 95 BOHEME *Columbia 4786232*....12 5
24 Jun 95 MARTA'S SONG *Columbia 6621402*....26 2
31 Jan 98 COMPARSA *Columbia 4887252* [1]....60 1

[1] Deep Forest III

DEEP PURPLE (142 Top 500)
Long-running legendary heavy rock group. London band's ever-changing line-up ensured many spin-off groups, among them Rainbow (founded by ex-guitarist Ritchie Blackmore), Whitesnake (featuring ex-vocalist David Coverdale) and Gillan (started by ex-vocalist Ian Gillan) (25 Albums: 280 Weeks, 15 Singles: 85 Weeks)

24 Jan 70 CONCERTO FOR GROUP AND ORCHESTRA *Harvest SHVL 767*....26 4
20 Jun 70 ● DEEP PURPLE IN ROCK *Harvest SHVL 777*....4 68
15 Aug 70 ● BLACK NIGHT *Harvest HAR 5020*....2 21
27 Feb 71 ● STRANGE KIND OF WOMAN *Harvest HAR 5033*....8 12
18 Sep 71 ★ FIREBALL *Harvest SHVL 793*....1 25
13 Nov 71 FIREBALL *Harvest HAR 5045*....15 13
1 Apr 72 NEVER BEFORE *Purple PUR 102*....35 6
15 Apr 72 ★ MACHINE HEAD *Purple TPSA 7504*....1 24
6 Jan 73 MADE IN JAPAN *Purple TPSP 351*....16 14
17 Feb 73 ● WHO DO WE THINK WE ARE *Purple TPSA 7508*....4 11
2 Mar 74 ● BURN *Purple TPA 3505*....3 21
23 Nov 74 ● STORM BRINGER *Purple TPS 3508*....6 12
5 Jul 75 24 CARAT PURPLE *Purple TPSM 2002*....14 17
22 Nov 75 COME TASTE THE BAND *Purple TPSA 7515*....19 4
27 Nov 76 MADE IN EUROPE *Purple TPSA 7517*....12 6
16 Apr 77 SMOKE ON THE WATER *Purple PUR 132* $....21 7
15 Oct 77 NEW LIVE AND RARE (EP) *Purple PUR 135*....31 4
7 Oct 78 NEW LIVE AND RARE II (EP) *Purple PUR 137*....45 3
21 Apr 79 THE MARK II PURPLE SINGLES *Purple TPS 3514*....24 6
19 Jul 80 ★ DEEPEST PURPLE *Harvest EMTV 25*....1 15
2 Aug 80 BLACK NIGHT (re-issue) *Harvest HAR 5210*....43 6
1 Nov 80 NEW LIVE AND RARE III (EP) *Harvest SHEP 101*....48 3
13 Dec 80 IN CONCERT *Harvest SHDW 4121/4122*....30 8
4 Sep 82 DEEP PURPLE LIVE IN LONDON *Harvest SHSP 4124*....23 5
10 Nov 84 ● PERFECT STRANGERS *Polydor POLH 16*....5 15
26 Jan 85 PERFECT STRANGERS *Polydor POSP 719*....48 3
15 Jun 85 KNOCKING AT YOUR BACK DOOR / PERFECT STRANGERS *Polydor POSP 749*....68 1
29 Jun 85 THE ANTHOLOGY *Harvest PUR 1*....50 3
24 Jan 87 ● THE HOUSE OF BLUE LIGHT *Polydor POLH 32*....10 9
18 Jun 88 HUSH *Polydor PO 4*....62 2
16 Jul 88 NOBODY'S PERFECT *Polydor PODV 10*....38 2
20 Oct 90 KING OF DREAMS *RCA PB 49247*....70 1
2 Nov 90 SLAVES AND MASTERS *RCA PL 90535*....45 2

21 / 23 February 1963	28 February / 2 March 1963	7 / 9 March 1963	14 / 16 March 1963
THE WAYWARD WIND Frank Ifield	THE WAYWARD WIND Frank Ifield	THE WAYWARD WIND Frank Ifield	SUMMER HOLIDAY Cliff Richard and The Shadows
SUMMER HOLIDAY (Soundtrack) Cliff Richard and The Shadows	SUMMER HOLIDAY (Soundtrack) Cliff Richard and The Shadows	SUMMER HOLIDAY (Soundtrack) Cliff Richard and The Shadows	SUMMER HOLIDAY (Soundtrack) Cliff Richard and The Shadows

KEY
UK No.1 ★ UK Top 10 ● Still on chart + UK entry at No.1 ■
US No.1 ▲ UK million seller £ US million seller $
Singles re-entries are listed as (re), (2re), (3re)… which signifies that the hit re-entered the chart once, twice or three times…
Peak Position / Weeks

2 Mar 91 **LOVE CONQUERS ALL** *RCA PB 49225* **57** 2
7 Aug 93 THE BATTLE RAGES ON … *RCA 74321154202* 21 3
24 Jun 95 **BLACK NIGHT** (re-mix) *EMI CDEM 382* **66** 1
17 Feb 96 PURPENDICULAR *RCA 74321338022* 58 1
31 Jan 98 MADE IN JAPAN (re-issue) *EMI 8578642* 73 1
24 Oct 98 30: VERY BEST OF DEEP PURPLE *EMI 4968072* 39 2
18 Jun 05 THE PLATINUM COLLECTION *EMI 5785912* 39 2

Tracks on New Live and Rare (EP): Black Night (Live) / Painted Horse / When a Blind Man Cries. Tracks on New Live and Rare II (EP): Burn (Edited Version) / Coronarias Redig / Mistreated (Interpolating Rock Me Baby). Tracks on New Live and Rare III (EP): Smoke on the Water / Bird Has Flown / Grabsplatter.

The DEEP RIVER BOYS *US, male vocal group*

7 Dec 56 **THAT'S RIGHT** *HMV POP 263* **29** 1

DEEP SENSATION *UK, male production duo*

4 Sep 04 **SOMEHOW SOMEWHERE** *In the House ITHS 07* **74** 1

DEEPEST BLUE *Israel / UK, male production / vocal duo – Matti Schwartz and Joel Edwards (1 Album: 3 Weeks, 4 Singles: 19 Weeks)*

2 Aug 03 ● **DEEPEST BLUE** *Data / MoS DATA 55CDS* **7** 8
28 Feb 04 ● **GIVE IT AWAY** *Data / MoS DATA 65CDS* **9** 8
5 Jun 04 **IS IT A SIN** *Open OPEN 3CDS* **24** 2
19 Jun 04 LATE SEPTEMBER *Open OPENCD 3* 22 3
4 Sep 04 **SHOOTING STAR** *Open OPEN 05CDS* **57** 1

Rick DEES and his CAST OF IDIOTS *US, male radio DJ / vocalist – Rigdon Dees and male / female vocal / instrumental group*

18 Sep 76 ● **DISCO DUCK (PART ONE)** *RSO 2090 204* ▲ $ **6** 9

DEETAH *Chile, female vocalist – Claudia Ogalde (2 Singles: 10 Weeks)*

26 Sep 98 **RELAX** *ffrr FCDP 345* **11** 8
1 May 99 **EL PARAISO RICO** *ffrr FCD 356* **39** 2

DEEYAH NEW *Norway, female vocalist*

12 Feb 05 **PLAN OF MY OWN** *Brainwash BRNWSHCDXS 1* **37** 2

DEF LEPPARD 183 Top 500

Mainstream UK rock stalwarts who wooed the US before their homeland: Joe Elliott (v), Phil Collen (g) (from 1983), Steve Clark (g) (d. 1991), Rick Savage (b), Rick Allen (d). In the US they achieved the feat of two consecutive albums selling more than eight million. Performed at the US Live 8 concert (11 Albums: 197 Weeks, 26 Singles: 116 Weeks)

17 Nov 79 **WASTED** *Vertigo 6059 247* **61** 3
23 Feb 80 **HELLO AMERICA** *Vertigo LEPP 1* **45** 4
22 Mar 80 ON THROUGH THE NIGHT *Vertigo 9102 040* 15 8
25 Jul 81 HIGH 'N' DRY *Vertigo 6359 045* 26 8
5 Feb 83 **PHOTOGRAPH** *Vertigo VER 5* **66** 3
12 Mar 83 PYROMANIA *Vertigo VERS 2* 18 8
27 Aug 83 **ROCK OF AGES** *Vertigo VER 6* **41** 4
1 Aug 87 ● **ANIMAL** *Bludgeon Riffola LEP 1* **6** 9
29 Aug 87 ★ HYSTERIA *Bludgeon Riffola HYSLP 1* ■ ▲ 1 101
19 Sep 87 **POUR SOME SUGAR ON ME** *Bludgeon Riffola LEP 2* **18** 6
28 Nov 87 **HYSTERIA (re)** *Bludgeon Riffola LEP 3* **26** 6
9 Apr 88 **ARMAGEDDON IT** *Bludgeon Riffola LEP 4* **20** 5
16 Jul 88 **LOVE BITES** *Bludgeon Riffola LEP 5* ▲ **11** 8
11 Feb 89 **ROCKET** *Bludgeon Riffola LEP 6* **15** 7
28 Mar 92 ● **LET'S GET ROCKED** *Bludgeon Riffola DEF 7* **2** 7
11 Apr 92 ★ ADRENALIZE *Bludgeon Riffola 5109782* ■ ▲ 1 30
27 Jun 92 **MAKE LOVE LIKE A MAN** *Bludgeon Riffola LEP 7* **12** 5
12 Sep 92 **HAVE YOU EVER NEEDED SOMEONE SO BAD** *Bludgeon Riffola LEP 8* **16** 5
30 Jan 93 **HEAVEN IS** *Bludgeon Riffola LEPCD 9* **13** 5
1 May 93 **TONIGHT** *Bludgeon Riffola LEPCD 10* **34** 3
18 Sep 93 **TWO STEPS BEHIND** *Bludgeon Riffola LEPCD 12* **32** 4
16 Oct 93 ● RETRO ACTIVE *Bludgeon Riffola 5183052* 6 5
15 Jan 94 **ACTION** *Bludgeon Riffola LEPCD 13* **14** 5
14 Oct 95 ● **WHEN LOVE AND HATE COLLIDE** *Bludgeon Riffola LEPCD 14* **2** 10
4 Nov 95 ● DEF LEPPARD GREATEST HITS 1980-1995 – VAULT *Bludgeon Riffola 5286572* 3 14
4 May 96 **SLANG** *Bludgeon Riffola LEPCD 15* **17** 5
25 May 96 ● SLANG *Bludgeon Riffola 5324932* 5 8
13 Jul 96 **WORK IT OUT** *Bludgeon Riffola LEPCD 16* **22** 3
28 Sep 96 **ALL I WANT IS EVERYTHING** *Bludgeon Riffola LEPCD 17* **38** 2
30 Nov 96 **BREATHE A SIGH** *Bludgeon Riffola LEPCD 18* **43** 1
26 Jun 99 EUPHORIA *Bludgeon Riffola 5462442* 11 5
24 Jul 99 **PROMISES** *Bludgeon Riffola 5621362* **41** 1
9 Oct 99 **GOODBYE** *Bludgeon Riffola 5622892* **54** 1
17 Aug 02 **NOW** *Bludgeon Riffola / Mercury 0639692* **23** 2
24 Aug 02 X *Bludgeon Riffola 631202* 14 3
26 Apr 03 **LONG LONG WAY TO GO** *Bludgeon Riffola 9800024* **40** 2
6 Nov 04 ● BEST OF *Bludgeon Riffola 9868512* 6 7

DEFAULT *US, male vocal / instrumental group*

8 Feb 03 **WASTING MY TIME** *TVT / Island CID 809* **73** 1

DEFINITION OF SOUND *UK, male rap duo – Donald Weekes and Kevin Clark (1 Album: 3 Weeks, 8 Singles: 25 Weeks)*

9 Mar 91 **WEAR YOUR LOVE LIKE HEAVEN** *Circa YR 61* **17** 9
1 Jun 91 **NOW IS TOMORROW** *Circa YR 66* **46** 4
29 Jun 91 LOVE AND LIFE *Circa CIRCA 14* 38 3
8 Feb 92 **MOIRA JANE'S CAFE** *Circa YR 80* **34** 4
19 Sep 92 **WHAT ARE YOU UNDER** *Circa YR 95* **68** 1
14 Nov 92 **CAN I GET OVER** *Circa YR 97* **61** 2
20 May 95 **BOOM BOOM** *Fontana DOSCD 1* **59** 1
2 Dec 95 **PASS THE VIBES** *Fontana DOSCD 2* **23** 3
24 Feb 96 **CHILD** *Fontana DOSCD 3* **48** 1

DEFTONES *US, male vocal / instrumental group (4 Albums: 8 Weeks, 5 Singles: 9 Weeks)*

8 Nov 97 AROUND THE FUR *Maverick 9362468102* 56 1
21 Mar 98 **MY OWN SUMMER (SHOVE IT)** *Maverick W 0432CD* **29** 2
11 Jul 98 **BE QUIET AND DRIVE (FAR AWAY)** *Maverick W 0445CD* **50** 1
1 Jul 00 WHITE PONY *Maverick 9362477972* 13 2
26 Aug 00 **CHANGE (IN THE HOUSE OF FLIES)** *Maverick W 531CD* **53** 1
24 Mar 01 BACK TO SCHOOL (MINI MAGGIT) *WEA 9362480822* 35 2
24 May 03 **MINERVA** *Maverick W 605CD* **15** 3
31 May 03 ● DEFTONES *Maverick 9362483912* 7 3
4 Oct 03 **HEXAGRAM** *Maverick W 623CD* **68** 2

Gavin DeGRAW NEW *US, male vocalist*

2 Jul 05 **I DON'T WANT TO BE** *J 82876702222* **38** 3

DEGREES OF MOTION featuring BITI *US, female vocal group (5 Singles: 21 Weeks)*

25 Apr 92 **DO YOU WANT IT RIGHT NOW** *ffrr F 184* **31** 5
18 Jul 92 **SHINE ON** *ffrr F 192* [1] **43** 3
7 Nov 92 **SOUL FREEDOM – FREE YOUR SOUL** *ffrr FX 201* **64** 1
19 Mar 94 ● **SHINE ON** (re-mix) *ffrr FCD 229* **8** 8
25 Jun 94 **DO YOU WANT IT RIGHT NOW** (re-mix) *ffrr FCD 236* [2] **26** 4

[1] Degrees of Motion featuring Biti with Kit West [2] Degrees of Motion

DEICIDE *US, male vocal / instrumental group*

13 May 95 ONCE UPON THE CROSS *Roadrunner RR 89492* 66 1

DEJA *US, male / female vocal duo*

29 Aug 87 **SERIOUS** *10 TEN 132* **75** 1

21 / 23 March 1963	28 / 30 March 1963	4 / 6 April 1963	11 / 13 April 1963
UK No.1 SINGLES			
SUMMER HOLIDAY Cliff Richard and The Shadows	**FOOT TAPPER** The Shadows	**SUMMER HOLIDAY** Cliff Richard and The Shadows	**HOW DO YOU DO IT?** Gerry and The Pacemakers
UK No.1 ALBUMS			
SUMMER HOLIDAY (Soundtrack) Cliff Richard and The Shadows	**SUMMER HOLIDAY (Soundtrack)** Cliff Richard and The Shadows	**SUMMER HOLIDAY (Soundtrack)** Cliff Richard and The Shadows	**SUMMER HOLIDAY (Soundtrack)** Cliff Richard and The Shadows

DEJA VU *UK, male vocal / instrumental duo*

5 Feb 94 **WHY WHY WHY** *Cowboy CDRODEO 941*....57 1

DEJURE (see also DREAM FREQUENCY; RED)
UK, male production duo – Ian Bland and Paul Fitzpatrick

23 Aug 03 **SANCTUARY** *Nebula NEBT 032*....62 1

Desmond DEKKER and The ACES *Jamaica, male vocalist – Desmond Dacres and male vocal group (1 Album: 4 Weeks, 7 Singles: 71 Weeks)*

12 Jul 67 **007 (SHANTY TOWN)** *Pyramid PYR 6004*....14 11
19 Mar 69 ★ **ISRAELITES (re)** *Pyramid PYR 6058*....1 15
25 Jun 69 ● **IT MIEK** *Pyramid PYR 6068*....7 11
5 Jul 69 THIS IS DESMOND DEKKER *Trojan TTL 4* [1]....27 4
10 Jan 70 **PICKNEY GAL** *Pyramid PYR 6078*....42 3
22 Aug 70 ● **YOU CAN GET IT IF YOU REALLY WANT** *Trojan TR 7777* [1]....2 15
10 May 75 ● **ISRAELITES** (re-recording) *Cactus CT 57* [1]....10 9
30 Aug 75 **SING A LITTLE SONG** *Cactus CT 73* [1]....16 7

[1] Desmond Dekker [1] Desmond Dekker

DEL AMITRI (401 Top 500)
Stylish soft-rock band whose name is Greek for 'from the womb'. Core members Justin Currie (v/b) and Iain Harvie (g) formed the band in Glasgow, Scotland, in 1983. 'Roll to Me' was one of the few UK records to reach the US Top 10 in the late 1990s (6 Albums: 108 Weeks, 18 Singles: 71 Weeks)

19 Aug 89 **KISS THIS THING GOODBYE** *A&M AM 515*....59 2
13 Jan 90 **NOTHING EVER HAPPENS** *A&M AM 536*....11 9
24 Feb 90 ● WAKING HOURS *A&M AMA 9006*....6 44
24 Mar 90 **KISS THIS THING GOODBYE** (re-issue) *A&M AM 551*....43 4
16 Jun 90 **MOVE AWAY JIMMY BLUE** *A&M AM 555*....36 6
3 Nov 90 **SPIT IN THE RAIN** *A&M AM 589*....21 6
9 May 92 **ALWAYS THE LAST TO KNOW** *A&M AM 870*....13 7
13 Jun 92 ● CHANGE EVERYTHING *A&M 3953852*....2 20
11 Jul 92 **BE MY DOWNFALL** *A&M AM 884*....30 4
12 Sep 92 **JUST LIKE A MAN** *A&M AM 0057*....25 4
23 Jan 93 **WHEN YOU WERE YOUNG** *A&M AMCD 0132*....20 3
18 Feb 95 **HERE AND NOW** *A&M 5809692*....21 4
11 Mar 95 ● TWISTED *A&M 5403112*....3 25
29 Apr 95 **DRIVING WITH THE BRAKES ON** *A&M 5810072*....18 4
8 Jul 95 **ROLL TO ME** *A&M 5811312*....22 4
28 Oct 95 **TELL HER THIS** *A&M 5812172*....32 2
21 Jun 97 **NOT WHERE IT'S AT** *A&M 5822532*....21 3
12 Jul 97 ● SOME OTHER SUCKER'S PARADE *A&M 5407052*....6 5
6 Dec 97 **SOME OTHER SUCKER'S PARADE** *A&M 5824352*....46 1
13 Jun 98 **DON'T COME HOME TOO SOON** *A&M 5827052*....15 4
5 Sep 98 **CRY TO BE FOUND** *A&M MERCD 513*....40 2
19 Sep 98 ● THE BEST OF DEL AMITRI – HATFUL OF RAIN *Mercury / A&M 5409402*....5 11
13 Apr 02 **JUST BEFORE YOU LEAVE** *Mercury 4976972*....37 2
20 Apr 02 CAN YOU DO ME GOOD? *Mercury / A&M 4932162*....30 3

DE'LACY *US, male / female vocal (Glen Branch) / instrumental group (1 Album: 1 Week, 3 Singles: 16 Weeks)*

1 Jul 95 HIDEAWAY *Slip 'n' Slide SLIP 023*....53 1
2 Sep 95 ● **HIDEAWAY** *Slip 'n' Slide 74321310472*....9 10
31 Aug 96 **THAT LOOK** *Slip 'n' Slide 74321398322*....19 4
14 Feb 98 **HIDEAWAY 1998** (re-mix) *Slip 'n' Slide 74321561052*....21 2

DELAGE *UK, female vocal group*

15 Dec 90 **ROCK THE BOAT** *PWL / Polydor PO 113*....63 2

DELAKOTA
UK, male vocal / instrumental duo (1 Album: 1 Week, 3 Singles: 3 Weeks)

18 Jul 98 **THE ROCK** *Go Beat GOBCD 10*....60 1
19 Sep 98 **C'MON CINCINNATI** *Go Beat GOBCD 11* [1]....55 1
3 Oct 98 ONE LOVE *Go Beat 5578612*....58 1
13 Feb 99 **555** *Go Beat GOBCD 14*....42 1

[1] Delakota featuring Rose Smith

DELANEY and BONNIE and FRIENDS *US, male / female vocal duo – Delaney and Bonnie Bramlett and instrumental group*

20 Dec 69 **COMIN' HOME** *Atlantic 584 308* [1]....16 9
6 Jun 70 ON TOUR *Atlantic 2400013*....39 3

[1] Delaney and Bonnie and Friends featuring Eric Clapton

DELAYS (see also TWISTED X) *UK, male vocal / instrumental group (1 Album: 4 Weeks, 4 Singles: 10 Weeks)*

2 Aug 03 **HEY GIRL** *Rough Trade RTRADSCD 102*....40 1
31 Jan 04 **LONG TIME COMING** *Rough Trade RTRADSCD 136*....16 4
3 Apr 04 **NEARER THAN HEAVEN** *Rough Trade RTRADSCD 175*....21 3
17 Apr 04 FADED SEASIDE GLAMOUR *Rough Trade RTRADDVCD 114*....17 4
4 Dec 04 **LOST IN A MELODY / WANDERLUST** *Rough Trade RTRADSCD 197*....28 2

DELEGATION
UK, male vocal / instrumental group (2 Singles: 7 Weeks)

23 Apr 77 **WHERE IS THE LOVE (WE USED TO KNOW)** *State STAT 40*....22 6
20 Aug 77 **YOU'VE BEEN DOING ME WRONG** *State STAT 55*....49 1

DELERIUM *Canada, male production duo – Rhys Fulber and Bill Leeb (11 Singles: 33 Weeks)*

12 Jun 99 **SILENCE** *Nettwerk 398152*....73 1
5 Feb 00 **HEAVEN'S EARTH** *Nettwerk 331032*....44 1
14 Oct 00 ● **SILENCE** (re-mix) *Nettwerk 331072* [1]....3 16
7 Jul 01 **INNOCENTE (FALLING IN LOVE)** *Nettwerk 331172* [2]....32 3
24 Nov 01 **UNDERWATER** *Nettwerk 331422* [3]....33 2
12 Jul 03 **AFTER ALL** *Nettwerk 332012* [4]....46 1
28 Feb 04 **TRULY** *Nettwerk 332202* [5]....54 2
27 Nov 04 **SILENCE 2004 (re)** *Nettwerk 332422* [1]....38 7

[1] Delerium featuring Sarah McLachlan [2] Delerium featuring Leigh Nash
[3] Delerium featuring Rani [4] Delerium featuring Jael (of Lunik)
[5] Delerium featuring Nerina Pallot

Sarah McLachlan is also the uncredited vocalist on the original version and re-mix of 'Silence'.

The DELFONICS *US, male vocal group (3 Singles: 23 Weeks)*

10 Apr 71 **DIDN'T I (BLOW YOUR MIND THIS TIME) (re)** *Bell 1099* $....22 9
10 Jul 71 **LA-LA MEANS I LOVE YOU** *Bell 1165*....19 10
16 Oct 71 **READY OR NOT HERE I COME (CAN'T HIDE FROM LOVE)** *Bell 1175*....41 4

The DELGADOS *UK, male / female vocal / instrumental group (3 Albums: 3 Weeks, 4 Singles: 4 Weeks)*

23 May 98 **PULL THE WIRES FROM THE WALL** *Chemikal CHEM 023CD*....69 1
20 Jun 98 PELOTON *Chemikal Underground CHEM 024CD*....56 1
29 Apr 00 THE GREAT EASTERN *Chemikal Underground CHEM 040CD*....72 1
3 Jun 00 **AMERICAN TRILOGY** *Chemikal Underground CHEM 039CD*....61 1
26 Oct 02 HATE *Mantra / Beggars Banquet MNTCD 1031*....57 1
1 Mar 03 **ALL YOU NEED IS HATE** *Mantra MNT 79CD*....72 1
18 Sep 04 **EVERYBODY COME DOWN** *Chemikal Underground CHEM 073CD*....67 1

DELIRIOUS? *UK, male vocal / instrumental group (3 Albums: 6 Weeks, 9 Singles: 18 Weeks)*

1 Mar 97 **WHITE RIBBON DAY** *Furious? CDFURY 1*....41 2
17 May 97 **DEEPER** *Furious? CDFURY 2*....20 3
28 Jun 97 KING OF FOOLS *Furious? FURYCD 1*....13 3
26 Jul 97 **PROMISE** *Furious? CDFURY 3*....20 2
15 Nov 97 **DEEPER (EP)** *Furious? CXFURY 4*....36 2
27 Mar 99 **SEE THE STAR** *Furious? CDFURY 5*....16 2
24 Apr 99 MEZZAMORPHIS *Furious? FURYCD 2*....25 2
4 Mar 00 **IT'S OK** *Furious? CDFURY 6*....18 2
16 Jun 01 **WAITING FOR THE SUMMER** *Furious? CDFURY 7*....26 2
18 Aug 01 AUDIO LESSONOVER? *Furious? FURYCD 4*....58 1

18 / 20 April 1963	25 / 27 April 1963	2 / 4 May 1963	9 / 11 May 1963
HOW DO YOU DO IT? Gerry and The Pacemakers	**HOW DO YOU DO IT?** Gerry and The Pacemakers	**FROM ME TO YOU** The Beatles	**FROM ME TO YOU** The Beatles
SUMMER HOLIDAY (Soundtrack) Cliff Richard and The Shadows	**SUMMER HOLIDAY (Soundtrack)** Cliff Richard and The Shadows	**SUMMER HOLIDAY (Soundtrack)** Cliff Richard and The Shadows	**PLEASE PLEASE ME** The Beatles

KEY
UK No.1 ★★ UK Top 10 ●● Still on chart ++ UK entry at No.1 ■■
US No.1 ▲▲ UK million seller £ US million seller $
Singles re-entries are listed as (re), (2re), (3re)... which signifies that the hit re-entered the chart once, twice or three times...
Peak Position / Weeks

22 Dec 01 **I COULD SING OF YOUR LOVE FOREVER** *Furious? CDFURY 9* ... 40 2
22 Oct 05 **PAINT THE TOWN RED** *Furious? CDFURY 10* ... 56 1

Tracks on Deeper (EP): Deeper / Summer of Love / Touch / Sanctify.

'DELIVERANCE' SOUNDTRACK *US, male instrumental duo – Eric Weissberg – banjo and Steve Mandell – guitar*

31 Mar 73 **DUELLING BANJOS** *Warner Bros. K 16223* $ ... 17 7

The DELLS *US, male vocal group*

16 Jul 69 **I CAN SING A RAINBOW – LOVE IS BLUE (MEDLEY)** *Chess CRS 8099* ... 15 9

DELUXE *US, female vocalist – Delores Springer*

18 Mar 89 **JUST A LITTLE MORE** *Unyque UNQ 5* ... 74 1

Tim DELUXE (see also COHEN vs DELUXE; DOUBLE 99; RIP PRODUCTIONS; SAFFRON HILL featuring Ben ONONO) *UK, male DJ / producer – Tim Liken (4 Singles: 11 Weeks)*

20 Jul 02 **IT JUST WON'T DO** *Underwater H20 016CD* [1] ... 14 7
4 Oct 03 **LESS TALK MORE ACTION** *Underwater H20 928CD* ... 45 2
7 Feb 04 **MUNDAYA (THE BOY)** *Underwater H20 040CD* [2] ... 61 1
13 Mar 04 **JUST KICK** *Intec INTEC 24XXX* [3] ... 70 1

[1] Tim Deluxe featuring Sam Obernik [2] Tim Deluxe featuring Shahin Badar [3] Cohen vs Deluxe

DEM 2 *UK, male production duo*

24 Oct 98 **DESTINY** *Locked On LOX 101CD* ... 58 2

DEMON *UK, male vocal / instrumental group (2 Albums: 5 Weeks)*

14 Aug 82 THE UNEXPECTED GUEST *Carrere CAL 139* ... 47 3
2 Jul 83 THE PLAGUE *Clay CLAYLP 6* ... 73 2

DEMON vs HEARTBREAKER *France, male production group*

19 May 01 **YOU ARE MY HIGH** *Source SOURCDSE 1032* ... 70 1

Chaka DEMUS and PLIERS *Jamaica, male vocal duo – John Taylor and Everton Bonner (1 Album: 30 Weeks, 8 Singles: 55 Weeks)*

12 Jun 93 ● **TEASE ME** *Mango CIDM 806* ... 3 15
10 Jul 93 ★ TEASE ME *Mango CIDM 1102* ... 1 30
18 Sep 93 ● **SHE DON'T LET NOBODY** *Mango CIDM 810* ... 4 10
18 Dec 93 ★ **TWIST AND SHOUT (re)** *Mango CIDM 814* [1] ... 1 14
12 Mar 94 **MURDER SHE WROTE** *Mango CIDM 812* ... 27 4
18 Jun 94 **I WANNA BE YOUR MAN** *Mango CIDM 817* ... 19 6
27 Aug 94 **GAL WINE** *Mango CIDM 818* ... 20 4
31 Aug 96 **EVERY KINDA PEOPLE** *Island Jamaica IJCD 2005* ... 47 1
30 Aug 97 **EVERY LITTLE THING SHE DOES IS MAGIC** *Virgin VSCDT 1654* ... 51 1

[1] Chaka Demus and Pliers featuring Jack Radics and Taxi Gang

Terry DENE *UK, male vocalist – Terry Williams (3 Singles: 20 Weeks)*

7 Jun 57 **A WHITE SPORT COAT (re)** *Decca F 10895* ... 18 7
19 Jul 57 **START MOVIN'** *Decca F 10914* ... 15 8
16 May 58 **STAIRWAY OF LOVE** *Decca F 11016* ... 16 5

DENISE and JOHNNY (see also THOSE 2 GIRLS; Andy WILLIAMS) *UK, male / female TV presenters / vocal duo – Denise Van Outen and Johnny Vaughan*

26 Dec 98 ● **ESPECIALLY FOR YOU (re)** *RCA 74321644722* ... 3 12

Cathy DENNIS *UK, female vocalist / songwriter (2 Albums: 35 Weeks, 13 Singles: 68 Weeks)*

21 Oct 89 **C'MON AND GET MY LOVE** *ffrr F 117* [1] ... 15 10
7 Apr 90 **THAT'S THE WAY OF THE WORLD** *ffrr F 132* [1] ... 48 3
4 May 91 ● **TOUCH ME (ALL NIGHT LONG)** *Polydor CATH 3* ... 5 10
20 Jul 91 **JUST ANOTHER DREAM** *Polydor CATH 2* ... 13 7
10 Aug 91 ● MOVE TO THIS *Polydor 8495031* ... 3 31
5 Oct 91 **TOO MANY WALLS** *Polydor CATH 4* ... 17 7
7 Dec 91 **EVERYBODY MOVE** *Polydor CATH 5* ... 25 8
29 Aug 92 **YOU LIED TO ME** *Polydor CATH 6* ... 34 4
21 Nov 92 **IRRESISTIBLE** *Polydor CATH 7* ... 24 6
23 Jan 93 ● INTO THE SKYLINE *Polydor 5139352* ... 8 4
6 Feb 93 **FALLING** *Polydor CATHD 8* ... 32 2
12 Feb 94 **WHY** *ffrr FCD 227* [1] ... 23 3
10 Aug 96 **WEST END PAD** *Polydor 5752812* ... 25 2
1 Mar 97 **WATERLOO SUNSET** *Polydor 5759612* ... 11 5
21 Jun 97 **WHEN DREAMS TURN TO DUST** *Polydor 5711852* ... 43 1

[1] D Mob with Cathy Dennis

Jackie DENNIS *UK, male vocalist (2 Singles: 10 Weeks)*

14 Mar 58 ● **LA DEE DAH** *Decca F 10992* ... 4 9
27 Jun 58 **THE PURPLE PEOPLE EATER** *Decca F 11033* ... 29 1

Stefan DENNIS *Australia, male actor / vocalist (2 Singles: 8 Weeks)*

6 May 89 **DON'T IT MAKE YOU FEEL GOOD** *Sublime LIME 105* ... 16 7
7 Oct 89 **THIS LOVE AFFAIR** *Sublime LIME 113* ... 67 1

The DENNISONS *UK, male vocal / instrumental group (2 Singles: 13 Weeks)*

15 Aug 63 **BE MY GIRL** *Decca F 11691* ... 46 6
7 May 64 **WALKING THE DOG** *Decca F 11880* ... 36 7

Sandy DENNY (see also FAIRPORT CONVENTION; FOTHERINGAY) *UK, female vocalist, b. 6 Jan 1947, d. 21 Apr 1978*

2 Oct 71 THE NORTH STAR GRASSMAN AND THE RAVENS *Island ILPS 9165* ... 31 2

Richard DENTON and Martin COOK *UK, male orchestra leaders / guitarist and keyboard player*

15 Apr 78 **THEME FROM 'HONG KONG BEAT'** *BBC RESL 52* ... 25 7

John DENVER 225 Top 500

Unmistakable light tenor singer / songwriter / guitarist with pop, country, folk and easy listening appeal, b. Henry John Deutschendorf, 31 Dec 1943, Roswell, New Mexico, US, d. 12 Oct 1997. Amassed 22 gold albums and four No.1 singles in the US (18 Albums: 256 Weeks, 2 Singles: 22 Weeks)

17 Mar 73 ROCKY MOUNTAIN HIGH *RCA SF 2308* ... 11 15
2 Jun 73 POEMS PRAYERS AND PROMISES *RCA SF 8219* ... 19 5
23 Jun 73 RHYMES AND REASONS *RCA Victor SF 8348* ... 21 5
30 Mar 74 ● THE BEST OF JOHN DENVER *RCA Victor APLI 0374* ... 7 69
17 Aug 74 ★ **ANNIE'S SONG** *RCA APBO 0295* ▲ $ ... 1 13
7 Sep 74 ● BACK HOME AGAIN *RCA Victor APLI 0548* ▲ ... 3 29
22 Mar 75 AN EVENING WITH JOHN DENVER *RCA Victor LSA 3211/12* ... 31 4
11 Oct 75 WIND SONG *RCA Victor APLI 1183* ▲ ... 14 21
15 May 76 ● LIVE IN LONDON *RCA Victor RS 1050* ... 2 29
4 Sep 76 ● SPIRIT *RCA Victor APLI 1694* ... 9 11
19 Mar 77 ● BEST OF JOHN DENVER VOLUME 2 *RCA Victor PL 42120* ... 9 9
11 Feb 78 I WANT TO LIVE *RCA PL 12561* ... 25 5
21 Apr 79 JOHN DENVER *RCA Victor PL 13075* ... 68 1
28 Nov 81 PERHAPS LOVE *CBS 73592* [1] ... 17 21
12 Dec 81 **PERHAPS LOVE** *CBS A 1905* [1] ... 46 9
22 Oct 83 IT'S ABOUT TIME *RCA RCALP 6087* ... 90 2
1 Dec 84 JOHN DENVER – THE COLLECTION *Telstar STAR 2253* ... 20 11
23 Aug 86 ONE WORLD *RCA PL 85811* ... 91 3
22 Mar 97 THE ROCKY MOUNTAIN COLLECTION *RCA 7863668372* ... 19 9
2 Oct 04 A SONG'S BEST FRIEND – THE VERY BEST OF JOHN DENVER *RCA 82876652742* ... 18 7

[1] Placido Domingo with John Denver [1] Placido Domingo and John Denver

16 / 18 May 1963	23 / 25 May 1963	30 May / 1 June 1963	6 / 8 June 1963
UK No.1 SINGLES			
FROM ME TO YOU – The Beatles	FROM ME TO YOU – The Beatles	FROM ME TO YOU – The Beatles	FROM ME TO YOU – The Beatles
UK No.1 ALBUMS			
PLEASE PLEASE ME – The Beatles	PLEASE PLEASE ME – The Beatles	PLEASE PLEASE ME – The Beatles	PLEASE PLEASE ME – The Beatles

Karl DENVER 482 Top 500

Versatile Scottish singer with multi-octave vocal range, b. Angus McKenzie, 16 Dec 1934, Glasgow, d. 21 Dec 1998. This unique artist, whose yodel-laced style added colour and contrast to the charts, reached the Top 20 with his first five singles (1 Album: 27 Weeks, 12 Singles: 127 Weeks)

22 Jun 61 ● **MARCHETA** *Decca F 11360* 8 20
19 Oct 61 ● **MEXICALI ROSE** *Decca F 11395* 8 11
23 Dec 61 ● **WIMOWEH** *Ace of Clubs ACL 1098* 7 27
25 Jan 62 ● **WIMOWEH** *Decca F 11420* 4 17
22 Feb 62 ● **NEVER GOODBYE** *Decca F 11431* 9 18
7 Jun 62 **A LITTLE LOVE A LITTLE KISS** *Decca F 11470* 19 10
20 Sep 62 **BLUE WEEK-END** *Decca F 11505* 33 5
21 Mar 63 **CAN YOU FORGIVE ME** *Decca F 11608* 32 8
13 Jun 63 **INDIAN LOVE CALL** *Decca F 11674* 32 8
22 Aug 63 **STILL** *Decca F 11720* 13 15
5 Mar 64 **MY WORLD OF BLUE** *Decca F 11828* 29 6
4 Jun 64 **LOVE ME WITH ALL YOUR HEART** *Decca F 11905* 37 6
9 Jun 90 **LAZYITIS – ONE ARMED BOXER** *Factory FAC 2227* [1] 46 3

[1] Happy Mondays and Karl Denver

DEODATO *Brazil, male multi-instrumentalist – Eumir Deodato*

5 May 73 ● **ALSO SPRACH ZARATHUSTRA (2001)** *Creed Taylor CTI 4000* 7 9

DEPARTMENT S

UK, male vocal / instrumental group (2 Singles: 13 Weeks)

4 Apr 81 **IS VIC THERE?** *RCA 1003* 22 10
11 Jul 81 **GOING LEFT RIGHT** *Stiff BUY 118* 55 3

The DEPARTURE

UK, male vocal / instrumental group (4 Singles: 5 Weeks)

14 Aug 04 **ALL MAPPED OUT** *Parlophone CDR 6642* 30 2
30 Oct 04 **BE MY ENEMY** *Parlophone CDRS 6653* 41 1
16 Apr 05 **LUMP IN MY THROAT** *Parlophone CDRS 6659* 30 1
18 Jun 05 **ALL MAPPED OUT** (re-issue) *Parlophone CDRS 6665* 33 1

DEPECHE MODE 102 Top 500

Consistently successful synth-led Essex band: Dave Gahan (v), Martin Gore (syn), Andy Fletcher (b/syn) and Vince Clarke (syn) – replaced in 1982 by Alan Wilder. One of the world's best-selling groups, who have reached the UK Top 10 with every newly recorded album over a 24 year period (16 Albums: 187 Weeks, 42 Singles: 253 Weeks)

4 Apr 81 **DREAMING OF ME** *Mute MUTE 013* 57 4
13 Jun 81 **NEW LIFE** *Mute MUTE 014* 11 15
19 Sep 81 ● **JUST CAN'T GET ENOUGH** *Mute MUTE 016* 8 10
14 Nov 81 ● **SPEAK AND SPELL** *Mute STUMM 5* 10 33
13 Feb 82 ● **SEE YOU** *Mute MUTE 018* 6 10
8 May 82 **THE MEANING OF LOVE** *Mute MUTE 022* 12 8
28 Aug 82 **LEAVE IN SILENCE** *Mute BONG 1* 18 10
9 Oct 82 ● **A BROKEN FRAME** *Mute STUMM 9* 8 11
12 Feb 83 **GET THE BALANCE RIGHT** *Mute 7BONG 2* 13 8
23 Jul 83 ● **EVERYTHING COUNTS** *Mute 7BONG 3* 6 11
3 Sep 83 ● **CONSTRUCTION TIME AGAIN** *Mute STUMM 13* 6 12
1 Oct 83 **LOVE IN ITSELF** *Mute 7BONG 4* 21 7
24 Mar 84 ● **PEOPLE ARE PEOPLE** *Mute 7BONG 5* 4 10
1 Sep 84 ● **MASTER AND SERVANT** *Mute 7BONG 6* 9 9
6 Sep 84 ● **SOME GREAT REWARD** *Mute STUMM 19* 5 12
10 Nov 84 **SOMEBODY / BLASPHEMOUS RUMOURS** *Mute 7BONG 7* 16 6
11 May 85 **SHAKE THE DISEASE** *Mute BONG 8* 18 9
28 Sep 85 **IT'S CALLED A HEART** *Mute BONG 9* 18 4
26 Oct 85 ● **THE SINGLES 81-85** *Mute MUTEL 1* 6 22
22 Feb 86 **STRIPPED** *Mute BONG 10* 15 5
29 Mar 86 ● **BLACK CELEBRATION** *Mute STUMM 26* 4 11
26 Apr 86 **A QUESTION OF LUST** *Mute BONG 11* 28 5
23 Aug 86 **A QUESTION OF TIME** *Mute BONG 12* 17 6
9 May 87 **STRANGELOVE** *Mute BONG 13* 16 5
5 Sep 87 **NEVER LET ME DOWN AGAIN** *Mute BONG 14* 22 4
10 Oct 87 ● **MUSIC FOR THE MASSES** *Mute STUMM 47* 10 4
9 Jan 88 **BEHIND THE WHEEL** *Mute BONG 15* 21 5
28 May 88 **LITTLE 15** (import) *Mute LITTLE 15* 60 2
25 Feb 89 **EVERYTHING COUNTS (LIVE)** *Mute BONG 16* 22 7
25 Mar 89 ● **101** *Mute STUMM 101* 5 8
9 Sep 89 **PERSONAL JESUS** *Mute BONG 17* 13 8
17 Feb 90 ● **ENJOY THE SILENCE** *Mute BONG 18* 6 9
31 Mar 90 ● **VIOLATOR** *Mute STUMM 64* 2 30
19 May 90 **POLICY OF TRUTH** *Mute BONG 19* 16 6
29 Sep 90 **WORLD IN MY EYES** *Mute BONG 20* 17 6
27 Feb 93 ● **I FEEL YOU** *Mute CDBONG 21* 8 7
3 Apr 93 ★ **SONGS OF FAITH AND DEVOTION** *Mute CDSTUMM 106* ■ ▲ 1 16
8 May 93 **WALKING IN MY SHOES** *Mute CDBONG 22* 14 4
25 Sep 93 ● **CONDEMNATION** *Mute CDBONG 23* 9 4
22 Jan 94 ● **IN YOUR ROOM** *Mute CDBONG 24* 8 4
15 Feb 97 ● **BARREL OF A GUN** *Mute CDBONG 25* 4 4
12 Apr 97 ● **IT'S NO GOOD** *Mute CDBONG 26* 5 5
26 Apr 97 ★ **ULTRA** *Mute CDSTUMM 148* ■ 1 11
28 Jun 97 **HOME** *Mute CDBONG 27* 23 4
1 Nov 97 **USELESS** *Mute CDBONG 28* 28 2
19 Sep 98 **ONLY WHEN I LOSE MYSELF** *Mute CDBONG 29* 17 3
10 Oct 98 ● **THE SINGLES 86-98** *Mute CDMUTEL 5* 5 6
7 Nov 98 **THE SINGLES 81-85** *Mute LCDMUTEL 1* 57 1
5 May 01 ● **DREAM ON (re)** *Mute CDBONG 30* 6 5
26 May 01 ● **EXCITER** *Mute CDSTUMM 190* 9 4
11 Aug 01 **I FEEL LOVED** *Mute CDBONG 31* 12 6
17 Nov 01 **FREELOVE** *Mute CDBONG 32* 19 3
30 Oct 04 ● **ENJOY THE SILENCE 04** *Mute LCDBONG 34* 7 5
6 Nov 04 **REMIXES 81-04** *Mute XLCDMUTEL 8* 24 2
4 Dec 04 **SOMETHING TO DO** *Mute L12BONG 34* 75 1
15 Oct 05 ● **PRECIOUS** *Mute LCDBONG 35* 4 5
29 Oct 05 ● **PLAYING THE ANGEL** *Mute LCDSTUMM 260* 6 4
24 Dec 05 **A PAIN THAT I'M USED TO** *Mute LCDBONG 36* ..... 15 2+

DEPTH CHARGE *UK, male producer – Jonathan Kane*

29 Jul 95 **LEGEND OF THE GOLDEN SNAKE** *DC DC 01CD* 75 1

DER DRITTE RAUM *Germany, male producer – Andreas Kruger*

4 Sep 99 **HALLE BOPP** *Additive 12AD 042* 75 1

Yves DERUYTER *Belgium, male DJ / producer (2 Singles: 3 Weeks)*

14 Apr 01 **BACK TO EARTH** *UK Bonzai UKBONZAICD 01* 63 1
19 Jan 02 **BACK TO EARTH** (re-mix) *UK Bonzai UKBONZAI 109CD* 56 2

DESERT *UK, male production duo*

20 Oct 01 **LETTIN' YA MIND GO** *Future Groove CDFGR 017* 74 1

DESERT EAGLE DISCS featuring Keisha WHITE

UK, male / female production / vocal group

1 Mar 03 **BIGGER BETTER DEAL** *Echo ECSCD 129* 67 1

DESERT SESSIONS *US / UK, male / female vocal / instrumental group*

15 Nov 03 **CRAWL HOME** *Island 9812964* 41 2

DESIDERIO *UK / Holland, male production duo and female vocalist*

3 Jun 00 **STARLIGHT** *Code Blue BLU 010CD* 57 1

DESIRELESS

France, female vocalist – Claudie Fritsch (2 Singles: 19 Weeks)

31 Oct 87 **VOYAGE VOYAGE** *CBS DESI 1* 53 6
14 May 88 ● **VOYAGE VOYAGE** (re-mix) *CBS DESI 2* 5 13

DESIYA featuring Melissa YIANNAKOU

UK, male / female vocal / instrumental duo

1 Feb 92 **COMIN' ON STRONG** *Black Market 12MKT 2* 74 1

DESKEE *Germany, male production duo and rapper (2 Singles: 3 Weeks)*

3 Feb 90 **LET THERE BE HOUSE** *Big One VBIG 19* 52 2
8 Sep 90 **DANCE, DANCE** *Big One VBIG 22* 74 1

13 / 15 June 1963	20 / 22 June 1963	27 / 29 June 1963	4 / 6 July 1963
FROM ME TO YOU The Beatles	I LIKE IT Gerry and The Pacemakers	I LIKE IT Gerry and The Pacemakers	I LIKE IT Gerry and The Pacemakers
PLEASE PLEASE ME The Beatles	PLEASE PLEASE ME The Beatles	PLEASE PLEASE ME The Beatles	PLEASE PLEASE ME The Beatles

KEY
UK No.1 ★ UK Top 10 ● Still on chart + UK entry at No.1 ■
US No.1 ▲ UK million seller £ US million seller $
Singles re-entries are listed as (re), (2re), (3re)... which signifies that the hit re-entered the chart once, twice or three times...

Peak Position / Weeks

DES'REE *UK, female vocalist – Desiree Weekes (3 Albums: 27 Weeks, 14 Singles: 73 Weeks)*

Date	Title / Label	Peak	Weeks
31 Aug 91	**FEEL SO HIGH** *Dusted Sound 6573667*	51	5
11 Jan 92	**FEEL SO HIGH** (re-issue) *Dusted Sound 6576897*	13	7
29 Feb 92	MIND ADVENTURES *Dusted Sound 4712632*	26	5
21 Mar 92	**MIND ADVENTURES** *Dusted Sound 6578637*	43	3
27 Jun 92	**WHY SHOULD I LOVE YOU** *Dusted Sound 6580917*	44	3
19 Jun 93	**DELICATE** *Columbia 6593312* [1]	14	6
9 Apr 94	**YOU GOTTA BE** *Dusted Sound 6601342*	20	7
21 May 94	I AIN'T MOVIN' *Dusted Sound 4758432*	13	6
18 Jun 94	**I AIN'T MOVIN'** *Dusted Sound 6604672*	44	3
3 Sep 94	**LITTLE CHILD** *Dusted Sound 6604515*	69	1
11 Mar 95	**YOU GOTTA BE** (re-mix) *Dusted Sound 6613215*	14	8
20 Jun 98 ●	**LIFE** *Sony S2 6659302*	8	15
11 Jul 98	SUPERNATURAL *Sony S2 4897192*	16	16
7 Nov 98	**WHAT'S YOUR SIGN?** *Sony S2 6665162*	19	4
3 Apr 99 ●	**YOU GOTTA BE** (2nd re-mix) *Dusted Sound / Sony S2 6668935*	10	8
16 Oct 99	**AIN'T NO SUNSHINE** *Universal Music TV 1564332* [2]	42	2
5 Apr 03	**IT'S OKAY** *Sony S2 6736492*	69	1

[1] Terence Trent D'Arby featuring Des'ree [2] Ladysmith Black Mambazo featuring Des'ree

DESTINY'S CHILD 190 Top 500

Texas-based US female R&B quartet turned trio, fronted by co-writer and co-producer Beyoncé Knowles and featuring Kelly Rowland and Michelle Williams. They have had four US No.1 singles and are the only US girl group to top the UK chart twice. Beyoncé won a BRIT and four Grammy awards in 2004 and the trio performed at the US Live 8 concert in 2005 and split later that year (6 Albums: 168 Weeks, 15 Singles: 137 Weeks)

Date	Title / Label	Peak	Weeks
14 Mar 98	DESTINY'S CHILD *Columbia 4885352*	45	4
28 Mar 98 ●	**NO, NO, NO** *Columbia 6656592* [1] $	5	8
11 Jul 98	**WITH ME** *Columbia 6661472*	19	3
7 Nov 98	**SHE'S GONE** *Columbia 6664915* [2]	24	3
23 Jan 99	**GET ON THE BUS** *East West E 3780CD* [3]	15	5
24 Jul 99 ●	**BILLS, BILLS, BILLS** *Columbia 6676902* ▲	6	9
7 Aug 99 ●	THE WRITING'S ON THE WALL *Columbia 4943942*	10	87
30 Oct 99 ●	**BUG A BOO** *Columbia 6681882*	9	7
8 Apr 00 ●	**SAY MY NAME** *Columbia 6691882* ▲	3	11
29 Jul 00 ●	**JUMPIN' JUMPIN'** *Columbia 6696292*	5	11
2 Dec 00 ★	**INDEPENDENT WOMEN PART 1** *Columbia 6705932* ■ ▲	1	15
28 Apr 01 ★	**SURVIVOR** *Columbia 6711732* ■	1	13
12 May 01 ★	SURVIVOR *Columbia 5017832* ■ ▲	1	44
4 Aug 01 ●	**BOOTYLICIOUS** *Columbia 6717382* ▲	2	11
24 Nov 01 ●	**EMOTION** *Columbia 6721112*	3	14
30 Mar 02	THIS IS THE REMIX *Columbia 5076272*	25	3
13 Nov 04 ●	**LOSE MY BREATH** *Columbia 6754912*	2	11
27 Nov 04 ●	DESTINY FULFILLED *Columbia 5179162*	5	21
19 Feb 05 ●	**SOLDIER** *Columbia 6757622* [4]	4	7
7 May 05 ●	**GIRL** *Columbia 6758952*	6	9
5 Nov 05 ●	#1'S *Columbia 82876739282* ▲	6	9+

[1] Destiny's Child featuring Wyclef Jean [2] Matthew Marsden featuring Destiny's Child [3] Destiny's Child featuring Timbaland [4] Destiny's Child featuring TI and Lil Wayne

Marcella DETROIT (see also SHAKESPEAR'S SISTER)
US, female vocalist – Marcella Levy (1 Album: 5 Weeks, 3 Singles: 16 Weeks)

Date	Title / Label	Peak	Weeks
12 Mar 94	**I BELIEVE** *London LONCD 347*	11	8
9 Apr 94	JEWEL *London 8284912*	15	5
14 May 94	**AIN'T NOTHING LIKE THE REAL THING** *London LONCD 350* [1]	24	4
16 Jul 94	**I'M NO ANGEL** *London LOCDP 351*	33	4

[1] Marcella Detroit and Elton John

DETROIT COBRAS *US, male / female vocal / instrumental group*

Date	Title / Label	Peak	Weeks
25 Sep 04	**CHA CHA TWIST** *Rough Trade RTRADSCD 189*	59	1

The DETROIT EMERALDS *US, male vocal group (4 Singles: 44 Weeks)*

Date	Title / Label	Peak	Weeks
10 Feb 73 ●	**FEEL THE NEED IN ME** *Janus 6146 020*	4	15
5 May 73	**YOU WANT IT YOU GOT IT** *Westbound 6146 103*	12	9
11 Aug 73	**I THINK OF YOU** *Westbound 6146 104*	27	9
18 Jun 77	**FEEL THE NEED** (re-recording) *Atlantic K 10945*	12	11

DETROIT GRAND PU BAHS *US, male production / vocal group*

Date	Title / Label	Peak	Weeks
8 Jul 00	**SANDWICHES** *Jive Electro 9230252*	29	3

The DETROIT SPINNERS
US, male vocal group (1 Album: 3 Weeks, 11 Singles: 93 Weeks)

Date	Title / Label	Peak	Weeks
14 Nov 70	**IT'S A SHAME** *Tamla Motown TMG 755* [1]	20	11
21 Apr 73	**COULD IT BE I'M FALLING IN LOVE** *Atlantic K 10283* $	11	11
29 Sep 73 ●	**GHETTO CHILD** *Atlantic K 10359*	7	10
19 Oct 74	**THEN CAME YOU** *Atlantic K 10495* [2] ▲ $	29	6
11 Sep 76	**THE RUBBERBAND MAN** *Atlantic K 10807* $	16	11
29 Jan 77	**WAKE UP SUSAN** *Atlantic K 10799*	29	6
7 May 77	**COULD IT BE I'M FALLING IN LOVE (EP)** *Atlantic K 10935*	32	3
14 May 77	DETROIT SPINNERS' SMASH HITS *Atlantic K 50363*	37	3
23 Feb 80 ★	**WORKING MY WAY BACK TO YOU – FORGIVE ME GIRL (MEDLEY)** *Atlantic K 11432* $	1	14
10 May 80	**BODY LANGUAGE** *Atlantic K 11392*	40	7
28 Jun 80 ●	**CUPID – I'VE LOVED YOU FOR A LONG TIME (MEDLEY)** *Atlantic K 11498*	4	10
24 Jun 95	**I'LL BE AROUND** *Cooltempo CDCOOL 306* [3]	30	4

[1] The Motown Spinners [2] Dionne Warwicke and The Detroit Spinners [3] Rappin' 4-Tay featuring The Spinners [The Detroit Spinners]

Tracks on Could It Be I'm Falling in Love (EP): Could It Be I'm Falling in Love / You're Throwing a Good Love Away / Games People Play / Lazy Susan.

In America all their releases are listed as by The Spinners.

DEUCE
UK, male / female vocal group (1 Album: 2 Weeks, 4 Singles: 23 Weeks)

Date	Title / Label	Peak	Weeks
21 Jan 95	**CALL IT LOVE** *London LONCD 355*	11	10
22 Apr 95 ●	**I NEED YOU** *London LONCD 365*	10	5
19 Aug 95	**ON THE BIBLE** *London LONCD 368*	13	6
9 Sep 95	ON THE LOOSE! *London 8286642*	18	2
29 Jun 96	**NO SURRENDER** *Love This LUVTHISCD 10*	29	2

dEUS *Belgium, male vocal / instrumental group (1 Album: 1 Week, 6 Singles: 7 Weeks)*

Date	Title / Label	Peak	Weeks
11 Feb 95	**HOTEL LOUNGE (BE THE DEATH OF ME)** *Island CID 603*	55	1
13 Jul 96	**THEME FROM TURNPIKE (EP)** *Island CID 630*	68	1
19 Oct 96	**LITTLE ARITHMETICS** *Island CID 643*	44	2
15 Mar 97	**ROSES** *Island CID 645*	56	1
3 Apr 99	THE IDEAL CRASH *Island 5246432*	64	1
24 Apr 99	**INSTANT STREET** *Island CID 742*	49	1
3 Jul 99	**SISTER DEW** *Island CID 750*	62	1

Tracks on Theme from Turnpike (EP): Theme from Turnpike / Worried About Satan / Overflow / My Little Contessa.

David DEVANT & HIS SPIRIT WIFE *UK, male vocal / instrumental group (1 Album: 1 Week, 2 Singles: 2 Weeks)*

Date	Title / Label	Peak	Weeks
5 Apr 97	**GINGER** *Rhythm King KIND 4CD*	54	1
21 Jun 97	**THIS IS FOR REAL** *Rhythm King KIND 5CD*	61	1
5 Jul 97	WORK LOVELIFE MISCELLANEOUS *Rhythm King KINDCD 1*	70	1

William DEVAUGHN *US, male vocalist (2 Singles: 10 Weeks)*

Date	Title / Label	Peak	Weeks
6 Jul 74	**BE THANKFUL FOR WHAT YOU'VE GOT** *Chelsea 2005 002*	31	5
20 Sep 80	**BE THANKFUL FOR WHAT YOU'VE GOT** (re-recording) *EMI 5101*	44	5

11 / 13 July 1963	18 / 20 July 1963	25 / 27 July 1963	1 / 3 August 1963
UK No.1 SINGLES			
I LIKE IT – Gerry and The Pacemakers	CONFESSIN' (THAT I LOVE YOU) – Frank Ifield	CONFESSIN' (THAT I LOVE YOU) – Frank Ifield	(YOU'RE THE) DEVIL IN DISGUISE – Elvis Presley with The Jordanaires
UK No.1 ALBUMS			
PLEASE PLEASE ME – The Beatles	PLEASE PLEASE ME – The Beatles	PLEASE PLEASE ME – The Beatles	PLEASE PLEASE ME – The Beatles

Sidney DEVINE *UK, male vocalist* *(2 Albums: 11 Weeks, 1 Single: 1 Week)*

Date	Title / Label	Pos	Wks
10 Apr 76	DOUBLY DEVINE *Philips 6625 019*	14	10
11 Dec 76	DEVINE TIME *Philips 6308 283*	49	1
1 Apr 78	**SCOTLAND FOREVER (EP)** *Philips SCOT 1*	48	1

Tracks on Scotland Forever (EP): Scotland Forever / Scots Wha' Hae / Flower of Scotland / Scottish Trilogy.

DEVO
US, male vocal / instrumental group (4 Albums: 22 Weeks, 5 Singles: 23 Weeks)

Date	Title / Label	Pos	Wks
22 Apr 78	**(I CAN'T ME GET NO) SATISFACTION** *Stiff BOY 1*	41	8
13 May 78	**JOCKO HOMO** *Stiff DEV 1*	62	3
12 Aug 78	**BE STIFF** *Stiff BOY 2*	71	1
2 Sep 78	**COME BACK JONEE** *Virgin VS 223*	60	4
16 Sep 78	Q: ARE WE NOT MEN? A: NO WE ARE DEVO! *Virgin V 2106*	12	7
23 Jun 79	DUTY NOW FOR THE FUTURE *Virgin V 2125*	49	6
24 May 80	FREEDOM OF CHOICE *Virgin V 2162*	47	5
22 Nov 80	**WHIP IT** *Virgin VS 383* $	51	7
5 Sep 81	NEW TRADITIONALISTS *Virgin V 2191*	50	4

Howard DEVOTO (see also The BUZZCOCKS; MAGAZINE) *UK, male vocalist*

Date	Title / Label	Pos	Wks
6 Aug 83	JERKY VERSIONS OF THE DREAM *Virgin V 2272*	57	2

DEXY'S MIDNIGHT RUNNERS (414 Top 500)
Maverick Birmingham, UK-based post-punk group who split up in 1987. Led throughout radical personnel and stylistic changes by Kevin Rowland (v/g). Transatlantic No.1 'Come on Eileen' was the top-selling UK single of 1982 (1,201,000) (6 Albums: 80 Weeks, 11 Singles: 93 Weeks)

Date	Title / Label	Pos	Wks
19 Jan 80	**DANCE STANCE** *Oddball Productions R 6028*	40	6
22 Mar 80 ★	**GENO** *Late Night Feelings R 6033*	1	14
12 Jul 80 ●	**THERE THERE MY DEAR** *Late Night Feelings R 6038*	7	9
26 Jul 80 ●	SEARCHING FOR THE YOUNG SOUL REBELS *Parlophone PCS 7213*	6	10
21 Mar 81	**PLAN B** *Parlophone R 6046*	58	2
11 Jul 81	**SHOW ME** *Mercury DEXYS 6*	16	9
20 Mar 82	**THE CELTIC SOUL BROTHERS** *Mercury DEXYS 8* [1]	45	4
3 Jul 82 ★	**COME ON EILEEN** *Mercury DEXYS 9* [1] ▲ £	1	17
7 Aug 82 ●	TOO-RYE-AY *Mercury MERS 5*	2	46
2 Oct 82 ●	**JACKIE WILSON SAID (I'M IN HEAVEN WHEN YOU SMILE)** *Mercury DEXYS 10* [2]	5	7
4 Dec 82	**LET'S GET THIS STRAIGHT (FROM THE START) / OLD** *Mercury DEXYS 11* [2]	17	9
26 Mar 83	GENO *EMI EMS 1007*	79	2
2 Apr 83	**THE CELTIC SOUL BROTHERS** *Mercury DEXYS 12* [2]	20	6
21 Sep 85	DON'T STAND ME DOWN *Mercury MERH 56*	22	6
22 Nov 86	**BECAUSE OF YOU** *Mercury BRUSH 1*	13	10
8 Jun 91	THE VERY BEST OF DEXY'S MIDNIGHT RUNNERS *Mercury 8464601*	12	15
4 Oct 03	LET'S MAKE THIS PRECIOUS – THE BEST OF DEXY'S MIDNIGHT RUNNERS *EMI 5926802*	75	1

[1] Dexy's Midnight Runners with the Emerald Express [2] Kevin Rowland and Dexy's Midnight Runners

DEXYS 8 and DEXYS 12 are different. Group was all male for first album.

Tony DI BART
UK, male vocalist – Tony Di Bartholomew (5 Singles: 19 Weeks)

Date	Title / Label	Pos	Wks
9 Apr 94 ★	**THE REAL THING** *Cleveland City Blues CCBCD 15001*	1	12
20 Aug 94	**DO IT** *Cleveland City Blues CCBCD 15003*	21	4
20 May 95	**WHY DID YA** *Cleveland City Blues CCBCD 15004*	46	1
2 Mar 96	**TURN YOUR LOVE AROUND** *Cleveland City Blues CCBCD 15006*	66	1
17 Oct 98	**THE REAL THING** (re-mix) *Cleveland City CLECD 13050*	51	1

DIAMOND HEAD
UK, male vocal / instrumental group (2 Albums: 9 Weeks, 1 Single: 2 Weeks)

Date	Title / Label	Pos	Wks
11 Sep 82	**IN THE HEAT OF THE NIGHT** *MCA DHM 102*	67	2
23 Oct 82	BORROWED TIME *MCA DH 1001*	24	5
24 Sep 83	CANTERBURY *MCA DH 1002*	32	4

WEDDING TOP 10

When it comes to life's Top 10 emotional moments, the first dance by the loving couple at their wedding reception party has to be right up there. Not surprisingly, research by The Gold Disc.com reveals a list chock full of intimate but powerful songs for this purpose.

1. **I DON'T WANT TO MISS A THING** – Aerosmith
2. **AMAZED** – Lonestar
3. **CAN'T TAKE MY EYES OFF YOU** – Andy Williams
4. **ENDLESS LOVE** – Diana Ross and Lionel Richie
5. **ANGELS** – Robbie Williams
6. **FROM THIS MOMENT ON** – Shania Twain
7. **YOU MAKE ME FEEL BRAND NEW** – Simply Red
8. **IF YOU'RE NOT THE ONE** – Daniel Bedingfield
9. **YOU TO ME ARE EVERYTHING** – The Real Thing

10=. **THREE TIMES A LADY** – The Commodores
10=. **WONDERFUL TONIGHT** – Eric Clapton

If you would like details on how to order a gold disc of a favourite hit single (or album) to mark any anniversary, birthday, wedding or other special occasion, email us at editor@bibleofpop.com or write to The Editor, British Hit Singles & Albums, Guinness World Records, 338 Euston Road, London NW1 3BD.

Jim DIAMOND (see also PhD)
UK, male vocalist (1 Album: 5 Weeks, 4 Singles: 30 Weeks)

Date	Title / Label	Pos	Wks
3 Nov 84 ★	**I SHOULD HAVE KNOWN BETTER** *A&M AM 220*	1	13
2 Feb 85	**I SLEEP ALONE AT NIGHT** *A&M AM 229*	72	1
18 May 85	**REMEMBER I LOVE YOU** *A&M AM 247*	42	5
22 Feb 86 ●	**HI HO SILVER** *A&M AM 296*	5	11
22 May 93	JIM DIAMOND *PolyGram TV 8438472*	16	5

Neil DIAMOND (38 Top 500)
World-renowned singer / guitarist / songwriter, b. 24 Jan 1941, Brooklyn, US. First found fame as the writer of 'I'm a Believer' (The Monkees) before going on to become one of the world's most popular live artists and top-selling album acts, with 120 million sales. In 2004 he received a Lifetime Achievement Award from the US Songwriters Hall of Fame (36 Albums: 606 Weeks, 13 Singles: 121 Weeks)

Date	Title / Label	Pos	Wks
7 Nov 70 ●	**CRACKLIN' ROSIE** *Uni UN 529* ▲ $	3	17
20 Feb 71 ●	**SWEET CAROLINE** *Uni UN 531* $	8	11
13 Mar 71	GOLD *Uni UNLS 116*	23	13
20 Mar 71	TAP ROOT MANUSCRIPT *Uni UNLS 117*	19	14
8 May 71 ●	**I AM ... I SAID** *Uni UN 532*	4	12
11 Dec 71	STONES *Uni UNLS 121*	18	14
13 May 72	**SONG SUNG BLUE** *Uni UN 538* ▲ $	14	13

KEY: UK No.1 ★ UK Top 10 ● Still on chart + UK entry at No.1 ■ US No.1 ▲ UK million seller £ US million seller $
Singles re-entries are listed as (re), (2re), (3re)... which signifies that the hit re-entered the chart once, twice or three times...

Peak Position / Weeks

Date		Title	Peak	Weeks
5 Aug 72	●	MOODS *Uni UNLS 128*	7	19
17 Feb 73		HOT AUGUST NIGHT *Uni ULD 1*	21	20
16 Feb 74		JONATHAN LIVINGSTON SEAGULL *CBS 69047*	35	1
9 Mar 74		RAINBOW *MCA MCF 2529*	39	5
29 Jul 74		HIS 12 GREATEST HITS *MCA MCF 2550*	13	78
9 Nov 74		SERENADE *CBS 69067*	11	14
10 Jul 76	●	BEAUTIFUL NOISE *CBS 86004*	10	26
14 Aug 76		**IF YOU KNOW WHAT I MEAN** *CBS 4398*	**35**	4
23 Oct 76		**BEAUTIFUL NOISE** *CBS 4601*	**13**	9
12 Mar 77	●	LOVE AT THE GREEK – RECORDED LIVE AT THE GREEK THEATRE *CBS 95001*	3	32
6 Aug 77		HOT AUGUST NIGHT (re-issue) *MCA MCSP 255*	60	1
17 Dec 77		I'M GLAD YOU'RE HERE WITH ME TONIGHT *CBS 86044*	16	12
24 Dec 77		**DESIREE** *CBS 5869*	**39**	6
25 Nov 78	●	20 GOLDEN GREATS *MCA EMTV 14*	2	29
25 Nov 78	●	**YOU DON'T BRING ME FLOWERS** *CBS 6803* [1] ▲ $	**5**	12
6 Jan 79		YOU DON'T BRING ME FLOWERS *CBS 86077*	15	23
3 Mar 79		**FOREVER IN BLUE JEANS** *CBS 7047*	**16**	12
19 Jan 80		SEPTEMBER MORN *CBS 86096*	14	11
15 Nov 80		**LOVE ON THE ROCKS** *Capitol CL 16173*	**17**	12
22 Nov 80	●	THE JAZZ SINGER (FILM SOUNDTRACK) *Capitol EAST 12120*	3	110
14 Feb 81		**HELLO AGAIN** *Capitol CL 16176*	**51**	4
28 Feb 81		LOVE SONGS *MCA MCF 3092*	43	6
5 Dec 81		THE WAY TO THE SKY *CBS 85343*	39	13
19 Jun 82		12 GREATEST HITS VOLUME 2 *CBS 85844*	32	8
13 Nov 82		HEARTLIGHT *CBS 25073*	43	10
20 Nov 82		**HEARTLIGHT** *CBS A 2814*	**47**	7
10 Dec 83		THE VERY BEST OF NEIL DIAMOND *K-Tel NE 1265*	33	11
28 Jul 84	●	PRIMITIVE *CBS 86306*	7	10
24 May 86		HEADED FOR THE FUTURE *CBS 26952*	36	8
28 Nov 87		HOT AUGUST NIGHT II *CBS 460 4081*	74	4
25 Feb 89		THE BEST YEARS OF OUR LIVES *CBS 463201 1*	42	6
9 Nov 91		LOVESCAPE *Columbia 4688901*	36	13
4 Jul 92	★	THE GREATEST HITS 1966-1992 *Columbia 4715022*	1	30
21 Nov 92		**MORNING HAS BROKEN** *Columbia 6588267*	**36**	2
28 Nov 92		THE CHRISTMAS ALBUM *Columbia 4724102*	50	6
9 Oct 93		UP ON THE ROOF – SONGS FROM THE BRILL BUILDING *Columbia 4743562*	28	10
17 Feb 96		TENNESSEE MOON *Columbia 4813782*	12	13
25 May 96		THE BEST OF NEIL DIAMOND *MCA MCD 11452*	68	1
31 Aug 96	●	THE ULTIMATE COLLECTION *Sony TV / Universal MOODCD 45*	5	20
14 Nov 98		THE MOVIE ALBUM – AS TIME GOES BY *Columbia 4916552*	68	2
15 Sep 01		THREE CHORD OPERA *Columbia 5024932*	49	1
16 Mar 02		THE ESSENTIAL COLLECTION *Columbia 5010662*	11	12

[1] Barbra and Neil [Barbra Streisand and Neil Diamond]

Gregg DIAMOND BIONIC BOOGIE

US, male / female vocal group – leader b. 4 May 1949, d. 14 Mar 1999

Date		Title	Peak	Weeks
20 Jan 79		**CREAM (ALWAYS RISES TO THE TOP)** *Polydor POSP 18*	**61**	3

The DIAMONDS

Canada / US, male vocal group

Date		Title	Peak	Weeks
31 May 57	●	**LITTLE DARLIN'** *Mercury MT 148* $	**3**	17

DICK and DEEDEE

US, male / female vocal duo – Dick St John (Richard Gosting), b. 1940, d. 27 Dec 2003, and Deedee Sperling

Date		Title	Peak	Weeks
26 Oct 61		**THE MOUNTAIN'S HIGH** *London HLG 9408* $	**37**	3

Charles DICKENS

UK, male vocalist – David Anthony

Date		Title	Peak	Weeks
1 Jul 65		**THAT'S THE WAY LOVE GOES** *Pye 7N 15887*	**37**	8

Gwen DICKEY (see also ROSE ROYCE)

US, female vocalist (4 Singles: 13 Weeks)

Date		Title	Peak	Weeks
27 Jan 90		**CAR WASH** *Swanyard SYR 7*	**72**	2
2 Jul 94		**AIN'T NOBODY (LOVES ME BETTER)** *X-clusive XCLU 010CD* [1]	**21**	4
14 Feb 98		**WISHING ON A STAR** *Northwestside 74321554632* [2]	**13**	4
31 Oct 98		**CAR WASH** (re-recording) *MCA MCSTD 48096* [3]	**18**	3

[1] KWS and Gwen Dickey [2] Jay-Z featuring Gwen Dickey [3] Rose Royce featuring Gwen Dickey

Neville DICKIE

UK, male pianist

Date		Title	Peak	Weeks
25 Oct 69		**ROBIN'S RETURN (re)** *Major Minor MM 644*	**33**	10

The DICKIES

US, male vocal (Leonard Graves Phillips) / instrumental group (2 Albums: 19 Weeks, 6 Singles: 28 Weeks)

Date		Title	Peak	Weeks
16 Dec 78		**SILENT NIGHT** *A&M AMS 7403*	**47**	4
17 Feb 79		THE INCREDIBLE SHRINKING DICKIES *A&M AMLE 64742*	18	17
21 Apr 79	●	**BANANA SPLITS (THE TRA LA LA SONG)** *A&M AMS 7431*	**7**	8
21 Jul 79		**PARANOID** *A&M AMS 7368*	**45**	6
15 Sep 79		**NIGHTS IN WHITE SATIN** *A&M AMS 7469*	**39**	5
24 Nov 79		DAWN OF THE DICKIES *A&M AMLE 68510*	60	2
16 Feb 80		**FAN MAIL** *A&M AMS 7504*	**57**	3
19 Jul 80		**GIGANTOR** *A&M AMS 7544*	**72**	2

Bruce DICKINSON

(see also IRON MAIDEN; SAMSON) *UK, male vocalist / aviator – Paul Dickinson (6 Albums: 16 Weeks, 8 Singles: 23 Weeks)*

Date		Title	Peak	Weeks
28 Apr 90		**TATTOOED MILLIONAIRE** *EMI EM 138*	**18**	5
19 May 90		TATTOOED MILLIONAIRE *EMI EMC 3574*	14	9
23 Jun 90		**ALL THE YOUNG DUDES** *EMI EM 142*	**23**	5
25 Aug 90		**DIVE! DIVE! DIVE!** *EMI EM 151*	**45**	2
4 Apr 92	●	**(I WANT TO BE) ELECTED** *London LON 319* [1]	**9**	5
28 May 94		**TEARS OF THE DRAGON** *EMI CDEM 322*	**28**	2
18 Jun 94		BALLS TO PICASSO *EMI CDEMX 1057*	21	3
8 Oct 94		**SHOOT ALL THE CLOWNS** *EMI CDEMS 341*	**37**	2
9 Mar 96		SKUNKWORKS *Raw Power RAWCD 106*	41	1
13 Apr 96		**BACK FROM THE EDGE** *Raw Power RAWX 1012*	**68**	1
3 May 97		**ACCIDENT OF BIRTH** *Raw Power RAWX 1042*	**54**	1
24 May 97		ACCIDENT OF BIRTH *Raw Power RAWCD 124*	53	1
26 Sep 98		THE CHEMICAL WEDDING *Air Raid AIRCD 1*	55	1
4 Jun 05		TYRANNY OF SOULS *Mayan MYNCD 035*	65	1

[1] Mr Bean and Smear Campaign featuring Bruce Dickinson

Barbara DICKSON 360 Top 500

Noted folk-inflected pop singer, b. 27 Sep 1947, Dunfermline, Scotland. A familiar face on 1970s and 1980s TV who later received acclaim for theatrical forays (notably Willy Russell's Blood Brothers) and TV acting roles (Band of Gold). Awarded an OBE in 2002 (15 Albums: 144 Weeks, 6 Singles: 49 Weeks)

Date		Title	Peak	Weeks
17 Jan 76	●	**ANSWER ME** *RSO 2090 174*	**9**	7
26 Feb 77		**ANOTHER SUITCASE IN ANOTHER HALL** *MCA 266*	**18**	7
18 Jun 77		MORNING COMES QUICKLY *RSO 2394 188*	58	1
19 Jan 80		**CARAVAN SONG** *Epic EPC 8103*	**41**	7
15 Mar 80		**JANUARY FEBRUARY** *Epic EPC 8115*	**11**	10
12 Apr 80	●	THE BARBARA DICKSON ALBUM *Epic EPC 84088*	7	12
14 Jun 80		**IN THE NIGHT** *Epic EPC 8593*	**48**	2
16 May 81		YOU KNOW IT'S ME *Epic EPC 84551*	39	6
6 Feb 82	●	ALL FOR A SONG *Epic 10030*	3	37
24 Sep 83		TELL ME IT'S NOT TRUE *Legacy LLM 101*	100	1
23 Jun 84		HEARTBEATS *Epic EPC 25706*	21	8
5 Jan 85	★	**I KNOW HIM SO WELL** *RCA CHESS 3* [1]	**1**	16
12 Jan 85	●	THE BARBARA DICKSON SONGBOOK *K-Tel NE 1287*	5	19
23 Nov 85		GOLD *K-Tel ONE 1312*	11	18
15 Nov 86		THE VERY BEST OF BARBARA DICKSON *Telstar STAR 2276*	78	8
29 Nov 86		THE RIGHT MOMENT *K-Tel ONE 1335*	39	8
6 May 89		COMING ALIVE AGAIN *Telstar STAR 2349*	30	7
15 Aug 92		DON'T THINK TWICE IT'S ALL RIGHT *Columbia MOODCD 25*	32	5

5 / 7 September 1963	12 / 14 September 1963	19 / 21 September 1963	26 / 28 September 1963
UK No.1 SINGLES			
BAD TO ME Billy J Kramer and The Dakotas	**SHE LOVES YOU** The Beatles	**SHE LOVES YOU** The Beatles	**SHE LOVES YOU** The Beatles
UK No.1 ALBUMS			
PLEASE PLEASE ME The Beatles	**PLEASE PLEASE ME** The Beatles	**PLEASE PLEASE ME** The Beatles	**PLEASE PLEASE ME** The Beatles

28 Nov 92 THE BEST OF ELAINE PAIGE AND BARBARA DICKSON *Telstar TCD 2632* [1] 22 9
5 Mar 94 PARCEL OF ROGUES *Castle Communications CTVCD 126* 30 3
20 Mar 04 THE PLATINUM COLLECTION *Sony Music TV 5161092* 35 2

[1] Elaine Paige and Barbara Dickson [1] Elaine Paige and Barbara Dickson

Tell Me it's Not True is a mini-album featuring songs from the musical Blood Brothers.

The DICTATORS *US, male vocal / instrumental group*

17 Sep 77 **SEARCH AND DESTROY (re)** *Asylum K 13091* **49** 2

Bo DIDDLEY *US, male vocalist / guitarist – Ellas McDaniel (4 Albums: 16 Weeks, 2 Singles: 10 Weeks)*

5 Oct 63 BO DIDDLEY *Pye International NPL 28026* 11 8
9 Oct 63 BO DIDDLEY IS A GUNSLINGER *Pye NJL 33* 20 1
10 Oct 63 **PRETTY THING** *Pye International 7N 25217* **34** 6
30 Nov 63 BO DIDDLEY RIDES AGAIN *Pye International NPL 28029* 19 1
15 Feb 64 BO DIDDLEY'S BEACH PARTY *Pye NPL 28032* 13 6
18 Mar 65 **HEY GOOD LOOKIN'** *Chess CRS 8000* **39** 4

DIDDY (see also BEDLAM) *UK, male producer – Richard 'Diddy' Dearlove (2 Singles: 3 Weeks)*

19 Feb 94 **GIVE ME LOVE** *Positiva CDTIV 8* **52** 1
12 Jul 97 **GIVE ME LOVE** (re-mix) *Feverpitch CDFVR 19* **23** 2

DIDO (256 Top 500) (see also FAITHLESS)

Record-breaking singer / songwriter and double BRIT award winner in 2004, b. Florian Cloud de Bounevialle Armstrong, 25 Dec 1971, London. 'No Angel' (including the Eminem sampled 'Thank You') was the world's top-selling album in 2001 (8.6 million) and is the UK's biggest-selling debut album by a female artist. Performed at four Live 8 concert venues: Hyde Park, Eden Project, Paris and Edinburgh (2 Albums: 187 Weeks, 8 Singles: 64 Weeks)

28 Oct 00 ★ NO ANGEL *Arista 74321802682* 1 133
24 Feb 01 ● **HERE WITH ME** *Cheeky / Arista 74321832732* **4** 12
2 Jun 01 ● **THANK YOU** *Cheeky / Arista 74321853042* **3** 10
22 Sep 01 **HUNTER** *Cheeky / Arista 74321885452* **17** 8
20 Apr 02 ● **ONE STEP TOO FAR** *Cheeky 74321926412* [1] **6** 3
13 Sep 03 ● **WHITE FLAG** *Cheeky / Arista 82876546022* **2** 13
11 Oct 03 ★ LIFE FOR RENT *Cheeky / Arista 82876545982* ■ 1 54
13 Dec 03 ● **LIFE FOR RENT** *Cheeky / Arista 82876579462* **8** 9
24 Apr 04 **DON'T LEAVE HOME** *Cheeky / Arista 82876611722* **25** 6
25 Sep 04 **SAND IN MY SHOES** *Cheeky / Arista 82876626922* **29** 3

[1] Faithless featuring Dido

DIESEL PARK WEST *UK, male vocal / instrumental group (2 Albums: 3 Weeks, 6 Singles: 15 Weeks)*

4 Feb 89 **ALL THE MYTHS ON SUNDAY** *Food FOOD 17* **66** 2
11 Feb 89 SHAKESPEARE ALABAMA *Food FOODLP 2* 55 2
1 Apr 89 **LIKE PRINCES DO** *Food FOOD 19* **58** 3
5 Aug 89 **WHEN THE HOODOO COMES** *Food FOOD 20* **62** 2
18 Jan 92 **FALL TO LOVE** *Food FOOD 35* **48** 3
15 Feb 92 DECENCY *Food FOODCD 7* 57 1
21 Mar 92 **BOY ON TOP OF THE NEWS** *Food FOOD 36* **58** 2
5 Sep 92 **GOD ONLY KNOWS** *Food FOOD 39* **57** 3

DIFFERENT GEAR vs POLICE *UK / Italy, male production group and UK / US, male vocal / instrumental trio*

5 Aug 00 **WHEN THE WORLD IS RUNNING DOWN** *Pagan PAGAN 039CDS* **28** 3

DIFFORD and TILBROOK (see also SQUEEZE) *UK, male vocal / instrumental duo*

30 Jun 84 **LOVE'S CRASHING WAVES** *A&M AM 193* **57** 2
14 Jul 84 DIFFORD AND TILBROOK *A&M AMLX 64985* 47 3

DIFF'RENT DARKNESS *UK, male vocal / instrumental group*

27 Dec 03 **ORCHESTRAL MANOEUVRES IN THE DARKNESS** *Guided Missile GUIDE 49CD* **66** 1

DIGABLE PLANETS *US, male / female vocal / instrumental group*

13 Feb 93 **REBIRTH OF SLICK (COOL LIKE DAT)** *Pendulum EKR 159CD* ..**67** 2

DIGITAL DREAM BABY (see also Peter AUTY and the SINFONIA OF LONDON conducted by Howard BLAKE) *UK, male producer – Steven Teear*

14 Dec 91 **WALKING IN THE AIR** *Columbia 6576067* **49** 4

Hit is a dance re-mix of 'Walking in the Air' by vocalist Peter Auty.

DIGITAL EXCITATION *Belgium, male producer – Frank de Wulf*

29 Feb 92 **PURE PLEASURE** *R&S RSUK 10* **37** 2

DIGITAL ORGASM *Belgium, male / female vocal / instrumental group (3 Singles: 14 Weeks)*

7 Dec 91 **RUNNING OUT OF TIME** *Dead Dead Good GOOD 009* **16** 9
18 Apr 92 **STARTOUCHERS** *DDG International GOOD 13* **31** 3
25 Jul 92 **MOOG ERUPTION** *DDG International GOOD 17* **62** 2

DIGITAL UNDERGROUND *US, male rap group (2 Albums: 2 Weeks, 1 Single: 4 Weeks)*

7 Apr 90 SEX PACKETS *BCM BCM 377LP* 59 1
30 Jun 90 DOOWUTCHYALIKE / PACKET MAN *BCM BCM 463X* 59 1
16 Mar 91 **SAME SONG** *Big Life BLR 40* **52** 4

DILATED PEOPLES *US, male vocal / DJ / production group (1 Album: 1 Week, 2 Singles: 6 Weeks)*

23 Feb 02 **WORST COMES TO WORST** *Capitol CDCL 834* **29** 3
2 Mar 02 EXPANSION TEAM *Capitol 5314772* 55 1
10 Apr 04 **THIS WAY** *Capitol CDCL 854* **35** 3

DILEMMA *Italy, male instrumental / production group*

6 Apr 96 **IN SPIRIT** *ffrr FCD 274* **42** 1

DILLINJA *UK, male producer – Karl Francis (8 Singles: 12 Weeks)*

9 Nov 02 **TWIST 'EM OUT** *Renegade Hardware RH 40* **50** 1
21 Dec 02 **LIVE OR DIE / SOUTH MANZ** *Valve VLV 007* **53** 1
10 May 03 **THIS IS A WARNING / SUPER DJ** *Valve VLV 008* **47** 1
28 Jun 03 **TWIST 'EM OUT** (re-mix) *Trouble on Vinyl TOV 56CD* [1] **35** 3
27 Sep 03 **FAST CAR** *Valve VLV 011* **56** 2
12 Jun 04 **ALL THE THINGS / FORSAKEN DREAMS** *Valve VLV 012* **71** 1
10 Jul 04 **IN THE GRIND / ACID TRAK** *Valve VLV 013* **71** 1
8 Jan 05 **THUGGED OUT BITCH / RAINFOREST** *Valve VLVO 14* **54** 2

[1] Dillinja featuring Skibadee

Richard DIMBLEBY *UK, male broadcaster, b. 25 May 1913, d. 22 Dec 1965*

4 Jun 66 THE VOICE OF RICHARD DIMBLEBY *MFP 1087* 14 5

DIMESTARS *UK, male / female vocal / instrumental group*

16 Jun 01 **MY SUPERSTAR** *Polydor 5870912* **72** 1

D'INFLUENCE *UK, male / female vocal / instrumental group (1 Album: 1 Week, 6 Singles: 10 Weeks)*

20 Jun 92 **GOOD LOVER** *East West A 8573* [1] **46** 2
27 Mar 93 **GOOD LOVER** (re-mix) *East West America A 8439CD* [1] **61** 1
24 Jun 95 **MIDNITE** *East West A 4418CD* [2] **58** 1
16 Aug 97 **HYPNOTIZE** *Echo ECSCD 41* **33** 2
11 Oct 97 **MAGIC** *Echo ECSCD 45* **45** 1
25 Oct 97 LONDON *Echo ECHCD 16* 56 1
5 Sep 98 **ROCK WITH YOU** *Echo ECSCD 56* **30** 3

[1] D-Influence [2] D*Influence

3 / 5 October 1963	10 / 12 October 1963	17 / 19 October 1963	24 / 26 October 1963
SHE LOVES YOU The Beatles	DO YOU LOVE ME Brian Poole and The Tremeloes	DO YOU LOVE ME Brian Poole and The Tremeloes	DO YOU LOVE ME Brian Poole and The Tremeloes
PLEASE PLEASE ME The Beatles	PLEASE PLEASE ME The Beatles	PLEASE PLEASE ME The Beatles	PLEASE PLEASE ME The Beatles

KEY UK No.1 ★ UK Top 10 ● Still on chart + UK entry at No.1 ■ US No.1 ▲ UK million seller £ US million seller $
Singles re-entries are listed as (re), (2re), (3re)… which signifies that the hit re-entered the chart once, twice or three times…
Peak Position / Weeks

Mark DINNING *US, male vocalist, b. 17 Aug 1933, d. 22 Mar 1986*

10 Mar 60 **TEEN ANGEL (re)** *MGM 1053* ▲ $ …… 37 4

DINOSAUR JR *US, male vocal (Joseph Mascis) / instrumental group (3 Albums: 7 Weeks, 7 Singles: 13 Weeks)*

2 Feb 91 **THE WAGON** *Blanco Y Negro NEG 48* …… 49 2
2 Mar 91 GREEN MIND *Blanco Y Negro BYN 24* …… 36 2
14 Nov 92 **GET ME** *Blanco Y Negro NEG 60* …… 44 1
30 Jan 93 **START CHOPPIN'** *Blanco Y Negro NEG 61CD* …… 20 3
20 Feb 93 ● WHERE YOU BEEN *Blanco Y Negro 4509916272* …… 10 3
12 Jun 93 **OUT THERE** *Blanco Y Negro NEG 63CD* …… 44 2
27 Aug 94 **FEEL THE PAIN** *Blanco Y Negro NEG 74CD* …… 25 3
10 Sep 94 WITHOUT A SOUND *Blanco Y Negro 4509969332* …… 24 2
11 Feb 95 **I DON'T THINK SO** *Blanco Y Negro NEG 77CD* …… 67 1
5 Apr 97 **TAKE A RUN AT THE SUN** *Blanco Y Negro NEG 103CD* …… 53 1

DIO *UK / US, male vocal (Ronnie James Dio) / instrumental group (6 Albums: 48 Weeks, 8 Singles: 22 Weeks)*

11 Jun 83 HOLY DIVER *Vertigo VERS 5* …… 13 15
20 Aug 83 **HOLY DIVER** *Vertigo DIO 1* …… 72 2
29 Oct 83 **RAINBOW IN THE DARK** *Vertigo DIO 2* …… 46 3
21 Jul 84 ● THE LAST IN LINE *Vertigo VERL 16* …… 4 14
11 Aug 84 **WE ROCK** *Vertigo DIO 3* …… 42 3
29 Sep 84 **MYSTERY** *Vertigo DIO 4* …… 34 4
10 Aug 85 **ROCK 'N' ROLL CHILDREN** *Vertigo DIO 5* …… 26 6
7 Sep 85 ● SACRED HEART *Vertigo VERH 30* …… 4 6
2 Nov 85 **HUNGRY FOR HEAVEN** *Vertigo DIO 6* …… 72 1
17 May 86 **HUNGRY FOR HEAVEN** (re-issue) *Vertigo DIO 7* …… 56 2
5 Jul 86 INTERMISSION *Vertigo VERB 40* …… 22 5
1 Aug 87 **I COULD HAVE BEEN A DREAMER** *Vertigo DIO 8* …… 69 1
22 Aug 87 ● DREAM EVIL *Vertigo VERH 46* …… 8 5
26 May 90 LOCK UP THE WOLVES *Vertigo 8460331* …… 28 3

DION
US, male vocalist – Dion DiMucci (1 Album: 5 Weeks, 7 Singles: 35 Weeks)

26 Jun 59 **A TEENAGER IN LOVE** *London HLU 8874* [1] $ …… 28 2
19 Jan 61 **LONELY TEENAGER** *Top Rank JAR 521* …… 47 1
2 Nov 61 **RUNAROUND SUE** *Top Rank JAR 586* ▲ $ …… 11 9
15 Feb 62 ● **THE WANDERER** *HMV POP 971* $ …… 10 12
22 May 76 **THE WANDERER** (re-issue) *Philips 6146 700* …… 16 9
12 Apr 80 20 GOLDEN GREATS *K-Tel NE 1057* [1] …… 31 5
19 Aug 89 **KING OF THE NEW YORK STREETS** *Arista 112556* …… 74 2

[1] Dion and The Belmonts [1] Dion and The Belmonts

Celine DION (53 Top 500) *French-Canadian vocalist who won the 1988 Eurovision Song Contest (for Switzerland), b. 30 Mar 1968, Quebec. She has sold a reported 155 million albums worldwide and is the only female with two UK million-selling singles as a solo artist. Best-selling single: 'My Heart Will Go On' 1,312,551 (16 Albums: 411 Weeks, 27 Singles: 250 Weeks)*

16 May 92 ● **BEAUTY AND THE BEAST** *Epic 6576607* [1] $ …… 9 7
4 Jul 92 **IF YOU ASKED ME TO (re)** *Epic 6581927* …… 57 5
14 Nov 92 **LOVE CAN MOVE MOUNTAINS** *Epic 6587787* …… 46 2
3 Apr 93 **WHERE DOES MY HEART BEAT NOW** *Epic 6563265* …… 72 1
29 Jan 94 ● **THE POWER OF LOVE** *Epic 6597992* ▲ …… 4 10
5 Mar 94 ★ THE COLOUR OF MY LOVE *Epic 4747432* …… 1 109
23 Apr 94 **MISLED** *Epic 6602922* …… 40 3
22 Oct 94 ★ **THINK TWICE** *Epic 6606422* £ …… 1 31
20 May 95 ● **ONLY ONE ROAD** *Epic 6613535* …… 8 8
9 Sep 95 ● **TU M'AIMES ENCORE (TO LOVE ME AGAIN)** *Epic 6624255* …… 7 9
16 Sep 95 UNISON *Epic 4672032* …… 55 3
7 Oct 95 ● D'EUX *Epic 4802862* …… 7 9
2 Dec 95 **MISLED** (re-issue) *Epic 6626495* …… 15 6
2 Mar 96 ● **FALLING INTO YOU** *Epic 6629795* …… 10 10
23 Mar 96 ★ FALLING INTO YOU *Epic 4837928* ■ ▲ …… 1 113
1 Jun 96 ● **BECAUSE YOU LOVED ME (THEME FROM 'UP CLOSE AND PERSONAL')** *Epic 6632382* ▲ $ …… 5 16
5 Oct 96 ● **IT'S ALL COMING BACK TO ME NOW** *Epic 6637112* $ …… 3 14
9 Nov 96 LIVE A PARIS *Epic 4866062* …… 53 1
21 Dec 96 ● **ALL BY MYSELF (re)** *Epic 6640622* …… 6 13
15 Mar 97 C'EST POUR VIVRE *Nectar Masters NTRCD 076* …… 49 3
28 Jun 97 **CALL THE MAN** *Epic 6646922* …… 11 6
15 Nov 97 ● **TELL HIM** *Epic 6653052* [2] …… 3 15
29 Nov 97 ★ LET'S TALK ABOUT LOVE *Epic 4891592* ■ ▲ …… 1 73
20 Dec 97 **THE REASON** *Epic 6653812* …… 11 8
21 Feb 98 ★ **MY HEART WILL GO ON** *Epic 6655472* ■ ▲ £ …… 1 20
18 Jul 98 ● **IMMORTALITY** *Epic 6661682* [3] …… 5 12
19 Sep 98 S'IL SUFFISAIT D'AIMER *Epic 4918592* …… 17 4
26 Sep 98 CELINE DION *Epic 4715089* …… 70 2
14 Nov 98 THESE ARE SPECIAL TIMES *Epic 4927302* …… 20 10
28 Nov 98 ● **I'M YOUR ANGEL** *Epic 6666282* [4] ▲ $ …… 3 13
10 Jul 99 **TREAT HER LIKE A LADY** *Epic 6675522* …… 29 3
27 Nov 99 ★ ALL THE WAY … A DECADE OF SONG *Epic 4960942* ■ ▲ …… 1 40
11 Dec 99 **THAT'S THE WAY IT IS** *Epic 6684622* …… 12 11
8 Apr 00 **THE FIRST TIME EVER I SAW YOUR FACE (re)** *Epic 6691942* …… 19 7
11 Nov 00 THE COLLECTOR'S SERIES – VOLUME ONE *Epic 5009952* …… 30 3
23 Mar 02 ● **A NEW DAY HAS COME** *Epic 6725032* …… 7 10
6 Apr 02 ★ A NEW DAY HAS COME *Epic 5062262* ■ ▲ …… 1 23
31 Aug 02 **I'M ALIVE** *Epic 6730652* …… 17 6
7 Dec 02 **GOODBYE'S (THE SADDEST WORD)** *Epic 6733732* …… 38 2
5 Apr 03 ● ONE HEART *Columbia 5108772* …… 4 9
20 Sep 03 **ONE HEART** *Columbia 6743482* …… 27 2
26 Jun 04 A NEW DAY – LIVE IN LAS VEGAS *Columbia 5152253* …… 22 4
23 Oct 04 ● MIRACLE – A CELEBRATION OF NEW LIFE *Columbia 5187487* [1] …… 5 5

[1] Celine Dion and Peabo Bryson [2] Barbra Streisand and Celine Dion
[3] Celine Dion with special guests The Bee Gees [4] Celine Dion and R Kelly
[1] Celine Dion & Anne Geddes

DIONNE *Canada, female vocalist*

23 Sep 89 **COME GET MY LOVIN'** *Citybeat CBC 745* …… 69 2

Wasis DIOP featuring Lena FIAGBE
Senegal, male producer and UK, female singer

10 Feb 96 **AFRICAN DREAM** *Mercury MERCD 453* …… 44 2

DIRE STRAITS (14 Top 500)
(see also David KNOPFLER; The NOTTING HILLBILLIES) *Internationally acclaimed, album-oriented rock group fronted by Mark Knopfler (g/v), b. 12 Aug 1949, Glasgow, Scotland. The London-based band was discovered after a demo tape was played on Charlie Gillett's Radio London show in 1977. Eponymous Knopfler-penned debut album (total cost just £12,500) was a transatlantic million-seller, and like their first single, 'Sultans of Swing', was even more successful in the US. By the early 1980s, they were global chart regulars, selling out shows across the USA and Europe and attracting record-breaking crowds in Australasia. In 1983, they were voted Best British Group for the first time at the BRIT Awards, and during that decade picked up countless other trophies. They released their most successful album, the Grammy and BRIT-winning Brothers in Arms, in 1985 - it topped the chart in 22 countries (as did On Every Street), sold over nine million Stateside and nearly four million in the UK. The album included the US No.1 single 'Money for Nothing' (which featured co-writer Sting), the first video seen on MTV Europe. In 1991, the group started a record-shattering world tour, which was seen by over seven million people in 25 countries and grossed around £70 million. In total, Dire Straits have sold in excess of 100 million albums around the globe (12 Albums: 1143 Weeks, 19 Singles: 119 Weeks)*

22 Jul 78 ● DIRE STRAITS *Vertigo 9102 021* …… 5 132
10 Mar 79 ● **SULTANS OF SWING** *Vertigo 6059 206* …… 8 11

31 October / 2 November 1963	7 / 9 November 1963	14 / 16 November 1963	21 / 23 November 1963
UK No.1 SINGLES			
YOU'LL NEVER WALK ALONE Gerry and The Pacemakers	**YOU'LL NEVER WALK ALONE** Gerry and The Pacemakers	**YOU'LL NEVER WALK ALONE** Gerry and The Pacemakers	**YOU'LL NEVER WALK ALONE** Gerry and The Pacemakers
UK No.1 ALBUMS			
PLEASE PLEASE ME The Beatles	**PLEASE PLEASE ME** The Beatles	**PLEASE PLEASE ME** The Beatles	**PLEASE PLEASE ME** The Beatles

23 Jun 79 ● **COMMUNIQUE** *Vertigo 9102 031* 5 32
28 Jul 79 **LADY WRITER** *Vertigo 6059 230* **51** 6
25 Oct 80 ● **MAKING MOVIES** *Vertigo 6359 034* 4 251
17 Jan 81 ● **ROMEO AND JULIET** *Vertigo MOVIE 1* **8** 11
4 Apr 81 **SKATEAWAY** *Vertigo MOVIE 2* **37** 5
10 Oct 81 **TUNNEL OF LOVE** *Vertigo MUSIC 3* **54** 3
4 Sep 82 ● **PRIVATE INVESTIGATIONS** *Vertigo DSTR 1* **2** 8
2 Oct 82 ★ **LOVE OVER GOLD** *Vertigo 6359 109* ■ 1 200
22 Jan 83 **TWISTING BY THE POOL** *Vertigo DSTR 2* **14** 7
18 Feb 84 **LOVE OVER GOLD (LIVE) / SOLID ROCK (LIVE)** *Vertigo DSTR 6* **50** 3
24 Mar 84 ● **ALCHEMY – DIRE STRAITS LIVE** *Vertigo VERY 11* 3 163
20 Apr 85 **SO FAR AWAY** *Vertigo DSTR 9* **20** 6
25 May 85 ★ **BROTHERS IN ARMS** *Vertigo VERH 25* ■ ▲ 1 228
6 Jul 85 ● **MONEY FOR NOTHING** *Vertigo DSTR 10* ▲ **4** 16
26 Oct 85 **BROTHERS IN ARMS** *Vertigo DSTR 11* **16** 13
11 Jan 86 ● **WALK OF LIFE** *Vertigo DSTR 12* **2** 11
3 May 86 **YOUR LATEST TRICK** *Vertigo DSTR 13* **26** 6
29 Oct 88 ★ **MONEY FOR NOTHING** *Vertigo VERH 64* ■ 1 64
5 Nov 88 **SULTANS OF SWING** (re-issue) *Vertigo DSTR 15* **62** 1
31 Aug 91 **CALLING ELVIS** *Vertigo DSTR 16* **21** 4
21 Sep 91 ★ **ON EVERY STREET** *Vertigo 5101601* ■ 1 35
2 Nov 91 **HEAVY FUEL** *Vertigo DSTR 17* **55** 2
29 Feb 92 **ON EVERY STREET** *Vertigo DSTR 18* **42** 2
27 Jun 92 **THE BUG** *Vertigo DSTR 19* **67** 1
22 May 93 ● **ON THE NIGHT** *Vertigo 5147662* 4 7
22 May 93 **ENCORES (EP)** *Vertigo DSCD 20* **31** 3
8 Jul 95 **LIVE AT THE BBC** *Windsong WINDCD 072X* 71 1
31 Oct 98 ● **SULTANS OF SWING – THE VERY BEST OF DIRE STRAITS** *Vertigo 5586582* 6 23
19 Nov 05 **THE BEST OF DIRE STRAITS & MARK KNOPFLER – PRIVATE INVESTIGATIONS** *Mercury 9872936* 20 7+

Tracks on Encores (EP): Your Latest Trick / The Bug / Solid Rock / Local Hero (Wild Theme).

DIRECKT (see also E-LUSTRIOUS) *UK, male instrumental / production duo – Mike 'E-Bloc' Kirwin and Danny 'Hibrid' Bennett*

13 Aug 94 **TWO FATT GUITARS (REVISITED)** *UFG UFG 7CD* **36** 2

DIRECT DRIVE

UK, male / female vocal / instrumental group (2 Singles: 3 Weeks)

26 Jan 85 **ANYTHING?** *Polydor POSP 728* **67** 2
4 May 85 **A.B.C. (FALLING IN LOVE'S NOT EASY)** *Boiling Point POSP 742* **75** 1

DIRT DEVILS (see also OCEANLAB) *UK / Finland, male production duo – Jon Grant and Paavo Siljamaki (2 Singles: 8 Weeks)*

2 Feb 02 **THE DRILL** *Nulife / Arista 74321915262* **15** 6
6 Dec 03 **MUSIC IS LIFE** *Nulife 82876571412* **53** 2

DIRTY VEGAS

UK, male production trio (1 Album: 3 Weeks, 4 Singles: 12 Weeks)

19 May 01 **DAYS GO BY** *Credence CDCRED 011* **27** 4
3 Aug 02 **GHOSTS** *Credence CDCRED 028* **31** 3
17 Aug 02 **DIRTY VEGAS** *Credence 5399852* 40 3
12 Oct 02 **DAYS GO BY** (re-issue) *Credence CDCRED 030* **16** 4
23 Oct 04 **WALK INTO THE SUN** *Parlophone CDRS 6647* **54** 1

DISCHARGE *UK, male vocal / instrumental group*

24 Oct 81 **NEVER AGAIN** *Clay CLAY 6* **64** 3
15 May 82 **HEAR NOTHING SEE NOTHING SAY NOTHING** *Clay CLAYLP 3* 40 5

DISCO ANTHEM *Holland, male producer – Lex van Coeverden*

18 Jun 94 **SCREAM** *Sweat MCSTD 1977* **47** 2

DISCO CITIZENS (see also CHICANE)

UK, male producer – Nick Bracegirdle (3 Singles: 5 Weeks)

22 Jul 95 **RIGHT HERE RIGHT NOW** *Deconstruction 74321293872* **40** 2
12 Apr 97 **FOOTPRINT** *Xtravaganza 0091115* **34** 2
4 Jul 98 **NAGASAKI BADGER** *Xtravaganza 0091595 EXT* **56** 1

Disco Citizens are Chicane under another name.

DISCO EVANGELISTS *UK, male instrumental / production group*

8 May 93 **DE NIRO** *Positiva CDTIV 2* **59** 2

DISCO TEX & the SEX-O-LETTES *US, male vocalist (Sir Monti Rock III – Joseph Montanez) and female vocal group (2 Singles: 22 Weeks)*

23 Nov 74 ● **GET DANCING** *Chelsea 2005 013* **8** 12
26 Apr 75 ● **I WANNA DANCE WIT CHOO (DOO DAT DANCE) – PART 1** *Chelsea 2005 024* [1] **6** 10

[1] Disco Tex and the Sex-O-Lettes featuring Sir Monti Rock III

DISCO TEX presents CLOUDBURST

(see also FULL INTENTION; Michael GRAY; HUSTLERS CONVENTION featuring Dave LAUDAT and Ondrea DUVERNEY; SEX-O-SONIQUE)
UK, male / female production / vocal group

24 Mar 01 **I CAN CAST A SPELL** *Absolution CDABSOL 1* **35** 2

The DISPOSABLE HEROES OF HIPHOPRISY

US, male rap / instrumental duo – Michael Franti and Rono Tse (1 Album: 3 Weeks, 2 Singles: 7 Weeks)

4 Apr 92 **TELEVISION THE DRUG OF THE NATION** (re) *Fourth & Broadway BRW 241* **44** 6
16 May 92 **HYPOCRISY IS THE GREATEST LUXURY** *Fourth & Broadway BRCD 584* 40 3
30 May 92 **LANGUAGE OF VIOLENCE** *Fourth & Broadway 12BRW 248* **68** 1

DISTANT SOUNDZ *UK, male production / vocal trio – Jack Berry, Mark Shrimpton and Rob Beaumont*

9 Mar 02 **TIME AFTER TIME** *W10 / Incentive CENT 36CDS* **20** 4

Sacha DISTEL *France, male vocalist, b. 29 Jan 1933, d. 22 Jul 2004*

10 Jan 70 ● **RAINDROPS KEEP FALLING ON MY HEAD** (4re) *Warner Bros. WB 7345* **10** 27
2 May 70 **SACHA DISTEL** *Warner Bros. WS 3003* 21 14

The DISTILLERS *Australia / US, male / female vocal / instrumental group (1 Album: 1 Week, 3 Singles: 3 Weeks)*

25 Oct 03 **CORAL FANG** *Sire 9362484202* 46 1
15 Nov 03 **DRAIN THE BLOOD** *Sire W 628CD* **51** 1
10 Apr 04 **THE HUNGER** *Sire W 636CD1* **48** 1
19 Jun 04 **BEAT YOUR HEART OUT** *Sire W 644CD* **74** 1

DISTORTED MINDS *UK, male production duo*

29 Mar 03 **T-10 / THE TENTH PLANET** (re) *Kaos KAOSCD 006* **43** 4

DISTURBED

US, male vocal / instrumental group (2 Albums: 2 Weeks, 3 Singles: 4 Weeks)

7 Apr 01 **VOICES** *Giant 74321848962* **52** 1
28 Sep 02 **PRAYER** *Reprise W 591CD1* **31** 2
5 Oct 02 **BELIEVE** *Reprise WB 483202* ▲ 41 1
14 Dec 02 **REMEMBER** *Reprise W 596CD1* **56** 1
1 Oct 05 **TEN THOUSAND FISTS** *Reprise 9362494332* ▲ 59 1

DIVA *Norway, female vocal duo (2 Singles: 2 Weeks)*

7 Oct 95 **THE SUN ALWAYS SHINES ON TV** *East West YZ 947CD* **53** 1
20 Jul 96 **EVERYBODY (MOVE YOUR BODY)** *East West EW 035CD* **44** 1

28 / 30 November 1963	5 / 7 December 1963	12 / 14 December 1963	19 / 21 December 1963
SHE LOVES YOU The Beatles	SHE LOVES YOU The Beatles	I WANT TO HOLD YOUR HAND The Beatles	I WANT TO HOLD YOUR HAND The Beatles
PLEASE PLEASE ME The Beatles	WITH THE BEATLES The Beatles	WITH THE BEATLES The Beatles	WITH THE BEATLES The Beatles

KEY UK No.1 ★★ UK Top 10 ●● Still on chart ++ UK entry at No.1 ■■ US No.1 ▲▲ UK million seller £ US million seller $
Singles re-entries are listed as (re), (2re), (3re)... which signifies that the hit re-entered the chart once, twice or three times...
Peak Position / Weeks

DIVA SURPRISE featuring Georgia JONES
(see also The ORIGINAL) *US / Spain, male production duo – Walter Taieb and Giuseppe Nuzzo and US, female vocalist*

14 Nov 98 **ON THE TOP OF THE WORLD** *Positiva CDTIV 100* ... 29 2

DIVE (see also AURORA)
UK, male production duo – Sacha Collisson and Simon Greenaway

21 Feb 98 **BOOGIE** *WEA WEA 147CD1* ... 35 1

Hit features vocalist Nasreen Shah.

DIVE DIVE NEW *UK, male vocal / instrumental group (2 Singles: 2 Weeks)*

12 Mar 05 **5-5-5 FOR FILMSTARS** *Diablo DIACD 006* ... 48 1
18 Jun 05 **THE SORRY SUITOR** *Diablo DIACD 007* ... 54 1

The DIVERSIONS *UK, male / female vocal / instrumental group*

20 Sep 75 **FATTIE BUM BUM** *Gull GULS 18* ... 34 3

DIVINE *US, male vocalist – Harris Milstead, b. 19 Oct 1945, d. 7 Mar 1988 (5 Singles: 24 Weeks)*

15 Oct 83 **LOVE REACTION** *Design Communication DES 4* ... 65 2
14 Jul 84 **YOU THINK YOU'RE A MAN** *Proto ENA 118* ... 16 10
20 Oct 84 **I'M SO BEAUTIFUL** *Proto ENA 121* ... 52 2
27 Apr 85 **WALK LIKE A MAN** *Proto ENA 125* ... 23 7
20 Jul 85 **TWISTIN' THE NIGHT AWAY** *Proto ENA 127* ... 47 3

DIVINE *US, female vocal group*

16 Oct 99 **LATELY** *Mushroom / Red Ant RA 002CDS* ▲ $ ... 52 1

The DIVINE COMEDY *UK, male vocalist / guitarist Neil Hannon (6 Albums: 46 Weeks, 15 Singles: 42 Weeks)*

11 May 96 CASANOVA *Setanta SETCD 25* ... 48 9
29 Jun 96 **SOMETHING FOR THE WEEKEND** *Setanta SETCD 26* ... 14 5
24 Aug 96 **BECOMING MORE LIKE ALFIE** *Setanta SETCD 27* ... 27 2
16 Nov 96 **THE FROG PRINCESS** *Setanta SETCD 32* ... 15 2
22 Feb 97 A SHORT ALBUM ABOUT LOVE *Setanta SETCD 036* ... 13 6
22 Mar 97 **EVERYBODY KNOWS (EXCEPT YOU)** *Setanta SETCDA 038* ... 14 4
11 Apr 98 **SOMEDAY I'LL FIND YOU / I'VE BEEN TO A MARVELLOUS PARTY** *EMI CDTCB 001* [1] ... 28 3
12 Sep 98 ● FIN DE SIECLE *Setanta SETCD 057* ... 9 14
26 Sep 98 **GENERATION SEX** *Setanta SETCDA 050* ... 19 3
28 Nov 98 **THE CERTAINTY OF CHANCE** *Setanta SETCDA 067* ... 49 1
6 Feb 99 ● **NATIONAL EXPRESS** *Setanta SETCDA 069* ... 8 7
21 Aug 99 **THE POP SINGER'S FEAR OF THE POLLEN COUNT** *Setanta SETCDA 070* ... 17 4
11 Sep 99 ● A SECRET HISTORY – THE BEST OF THE DIVINE COMEDY *Setanta SETCD 100* ... 3 11
13 Nov 99 **GIN SOAKED BOY** *Setanta SETCDA 071* ... 38 2
10 Mar 01 **LOVE WHAT YOU DO** *Parlophone CDRS 6554* ... 26 2
24 Mar 01 REGENERATION *Parlophone 5317612* ... 14 3
26 May 01 **BAD AMBASSADOR** *Parlophone CRDS 6558* ... 34 2
10 Nov 01 **PERFECT LOVESONG** *Parlophone CDR 6561* ... 42 1
3 Apr 04 **COME HOME BILLY BIRD** *Parlophone CDRS 6630* ... 25 2
10 Apr 04 ABSENT FRIENDS *Parlophone 5962802* ... 23 3
26 Jun 04 **ABSENT FRIENDS** *Parlophone CDRS 6641* ... 38 2

[1] Shola Ama and Craig Armstrong / The Divine Comedy

DIVINE INSPIRATION *UK, male / female production / vocal (Sarah-Jane Scott) group (2 Singles: 8 Weeks)*

18 Jan 03 ● **THE WAY (YOU PUT YOUR HAND IN MY HAND)** *Data / MoS DATA 42CDS* ... 5 7
15 Nov 03 **WHAT WILL BE WILL BE (DESTINY)** *Heat Recordings HEATCD 036* ... 55 1

DIVINE WORKS
(see also SACRED SPIRIT) *Germany, male producer – Claus Zundel*

16 Aug 97 DIVINE WORKS – SOUNDTRACK TO THE NEW MILLENNIUM *Virgin VTCD 119* ... 43 2

DIVINYLS
Australia, male / female vocal (Christina Amphlett) / instrumental duo

18 May 91 ● **I TOUCH MYSELF** *Virgin America VUS 36* ... 10 12
20 Jul 91 DIVINYLS *Virgin America VUSLP 30* ... 59 1

DIXIE CHICKS *US, female vocal / instrumental group (3 Albums: 20 Weeks, 3 Singles: 7 Weeks)*

3 Jul 99 WIDE OPEN SPACES *Epic 4898422* ... 26 6
3 Jul 99 **THERE'S YOUR TROUBLE** *Epic 6675162* ... 26 5
11 Sep 99 FLY *Epic 4951512* ▲ ... 38 2
6 Nov 99 **READY TO RUN** *Epic 6682472* ... 53 1
22 Mar 03 HOME *Epic 5096032* ▲ ... 33 12
19 Apr 03 **LANDSLIDE** *Columbia 6737392* ... 55 1

The DIXIE CUPS *US, female vocal group (2 Singles: 16 Weeks)*

18 Jun 64 **CHAPEL OF LOVE** *Pye International 7N 25245* ▲ $ ... 22 8
13 May 65 **IKO IKO** *Red Bird RB 10024* ... 23 8

DIZZEE RASCAL *UK, male rapper / producer – Dylan Mills (2 Albums: 26 Weeks, 7 Singles: 31 Weeks)*

7 Jun 03 **I LUV U** *XL Recordings XLS 165CD* ... 29 3
2 Aug 03 BOY IN DA CORNER *XL Recordings XLCD 170* ... 23 15
30 Aug 03 **FIX UP LOOK SHARP** *XL Recordings XLS 167CD* ... 17 5
22 Nov 03 **LUCKY STAR** *XL Recordings XLS 172CD* [1] ... 23 4
6 Dec 03 **JUS' A RASCAL** *XL Recordings XLS 175CD* ... 30 3
4 Sep 04 ● **STAND UP TALL** *XL Recordings XLS 198CD1* ... 10 6
18 Sep 04 ● SHOWTIME *XL Recordings XLCD 181* ... 8 11
20 Nov 04 **DREAM** *XL Recordings XKLS 204CD* ... 14 8
2 Apr 05 **OFF 2 WORK** *XL Recordings XLS 208CD1* ... 44 2

[1] Basement Jaxx featuring Dizzee Rascal

DIZZY HEIGHTS *UK, male rapper*

18 Dec 82 **CHRISTMAS RAPPING** *Polydor WRAP 1* ... 49 4

DJ ALIGATOR PROJECT
Denmark, male producer – Aliasghar Movasat (2 Singles: 11 Weeks)

7 Oct 00 **THE WHISTLE SONG** *EMI CDBLOW 001* ... 57 1
19 Jan 02 ● **THE WHISTLE SONG (BLOW MY WHISTLE BITCH)** (re-mix) *All Around the World CDGLOBE 247* ... 5 10

DJ AMS & KHIZA featuring Marlon BINNS & TAFARI NEW
UK, male production duo and male vocalists

12 Mar 05 **HOT LIKE FIRE** *Goldmind GM 008CD* ... 72 1

DJ BADMARSH and SHRI featuring UK APACHE
India / Yemen, male instrumental / production duo and UK, male rapper

28 Jul 01 **SIGNS** *Outcaste OUT 38CD1* ... 63 1

DJ BOBO *Switzerland, male DJ / producer / vocalist – Peter Baumann (3 Singles: 7 Weeks)*

24 Sep 94 **EVERYBODY** *PWL Continental PWCD 312* ... 47 2
17 Jun 95 **LOVE IS ALL AROUND** *Avex UK AXEXCD 7* ... 49 2
25 Oct 03 **CHIHUAHUA** *Fuelin 82876559422* ... 36 3

26 / 28 December 1963	2 / 4 January 1964	9 / 11 January 1964	16 / 18 January 1964
UK No.1 SINGLES			
I WANT TO HOLD YOUR HAND – The Beatles	I WANT TO HOLD YOUR HAND – The Beatles	I WANT TO HOLD YOUR HAND – The Beatles	GLAD ALL OVER – The Dave Clark Five
UK No.1 ALBUMS			
WITH THE BEATLES – The Beatles	WITH THE BEATLES – The Beatles	WITH THE BEATLES – The Beatles	WITH THE BEATLES – The Beatles

DJ CASPER
US, male DJ / producer / vocalist – Willie Perry (2 Singles: 24 Weeks)

13 Mar 04 ★ **CHA CHA SLIDE** *All Around the World CDGLOBE 329*....1 18
16 Oct 04 **OOPS UPSIDE YOUR HEAD** *All Around the World CDGLOBE 376* [1] 16 6

[1] DJ Casper featuring The Gap Band

DJ CHUS presents GROOVE FOUNDATION
Spain, male DJ / production duo

2 Nov 02 **THAT FEELING** *Defected DFTD 055R*....65 1

DJ DADO *Italy, male producer – Roberto Gallo (4 Singles: 9 Weeks)*

6 Apr 96 ● **X-FILES** *ZYX ZYX 8065R8*....8 6
14 Mar 98 **COMING BACK** *ffrr TABCD 247*....63 1
11 Jul 98 **GIVE ME LOVE** *VC Recordings VCRD 37* [1] 59 1
8 May 99 **READY OR NOT** *Chemistry CDKEM 006* [2] 51 1

[1] DJ Dado vs Michelle Weeks [2] DJ Dado and Simone Jay

DJ DAN presents NEEDLE DAMAGE *US, male DJ / production group*

5 May 01 **THAT ZIPPER TRACK** *Duty Free DF 026CD*....53 1

DJ DEE KLINE *UK, male DJ / producer – Nick Annand*

3 Jun 00 **I DON'T SMOKE** *East West EW 213CD*....11 6

DJ DISCIPLE *US, male DJ / producer – David Banks*

12 Nov 94 **ON THE DANCEFLOOR** *Mother MUMCD 55*....67 1

DJ DUKE *Denmark, male producer – Ken Larson (2 Singles: 7 Weeks)*

8 Jan 94 **BLOW YOUR WHISTLE** *ffrr FCD 228*....15 5
16 Jul 94 **TURN IT UP (SAY YEAH)** *ffrr FCD 235*....31 2

DJ EMPIRE presents Giorgio MORODER
Germany, male producer – Alexander Wilkie

12 Feb 00 **THE CHASE** *Logic 731482*....46 1

DJ ERIC *UK, male vocal / production trio (2 Singles: 3 Weeks)*

13 Feb 99 **WE ARE LOVE** *Distinctive DISNCD 49*....37 2
10 Jun 00 **DESIRE** *Distinctive DISNCD 56*....67 1

DJ 'FAST' EDDIE *US, male producer – Eddie Smith (4 Singles: 15 Weeks)*

11 Apr 87 **CAN U DANCE (re)** *Champion CHAMP 41*....67 4
21 Jan 89 **HIP HOUSE / I CAN DANCE** *DJ International DJIN 5*....47 4
11 Mar 89 **YO YO GET FUNKY** *DJ International DJIN 7*....54 3
28 Oct 89 **GIT ON UP** *DJ International 655366 7* [1] 49 4

[1] 'Fast' Eddie featuring Sundance

DJ FLAVOURS (see also NRG; SMOKIN BEATS featuring Lyn EDEN)
UK, male producer – Neil Rumney

11 Oct 97 **YOUR CARESS (ALL I NEED)** *All Around the World CDGLOBE 160*....19 4

DJ FORMAT *UK, male DJ / producer – Matt Ford*

22 Mar 03 **WE KNOW SOMETHING YOU DON'T KNOW** *Genuine GEN 004CDX* [1] 73 1
23 Apr 05 **IF YOU CAN'T JOIN 'EM ... BEAT 'EM** *Genuine GEN 030CD*....73 1

[1] DJ Format featuring Chali 2NA & Akil

DJ FRESH (see also BAD COMPANY; FRESH BC)
UK, male producer – Dan Stein (5 Singles: 6 Weeks)

1 Nov 03 **DALICKS / TEMPLE OF DOOM** *Breakbeat Kaos BBK 001*....60 1
31 Jul 04 **SUBMARINES** *Breakbeat Kaos BBK 004*....73 1
30 Oct 04 **WHEN THE SUN GOES DOWN** *Breakbeat Kaos BBK 005* [1] .68 1
12 Feb 05 **SUPERNATURE** *Breakbeat Kaos BBK 006* [2] 59 2
9 Jul 05 **TARANTULA / FASTEN YOUR SEATBELT** *Breakbeat Kaos BBK 009SCD* [3] 60 1

[1] DJ Fresh featuring Adam F [2] Baron & Fresh [3] Pendulum & Fresh featuring Spyda & Tenor Fly / Pendulum featuring The Freestylers

DJ GARRY *Belgium, male producer – Marino Stephano*

19 Jan 02 **DREAM UNIVERSE** *Xtravaganza XTRAV 32CDS*....36 2

DJ GERT *Belgium, male DJ / producer – Gert Rossenbacker*

26 May 01 **GIVE ME SOME MORE** *Mostika 23200253*....50 1

DJ GREGORY *France, male producer – Gregory Darsa (2 Singles: 2 Weeks)*

9 Nov 02 **TROPICAL SOUNDCLASH** *Defected DFTD 061CD*....59 1
11 Oct 03 **ELLE / TROPICAL SOUNDCLASH** *Defected DFTD 077*....73 1

DJ HYPE
UK, male producer – Kevin Ford (1 Album: 1 Week, 2 Singles: 2 Weeks)

20 Mar 93 **SHOT IN THE DARK** *Suburban Base SUBBASE 20CD*....63 1
30 Aug 97 **NEW FRONTIERS (EP)** *Parousia 74321501072* [1] 56 1
2 Jun 01 **CASINO ROYALE / DEAD A'S** *True Playaz TPRCD 004* [1] 58 1

[1] DJ Zinc / DJ Hype [1] DJ Hype presents Ganja Kru

DJ INNOCENCE featuring Alex CHARLES
UK, male producer – Gary Booker and male vocalist

6 Apr 02 **SO BEAUTIFUL** *Echo ECSCD 119*....51 1

DJ JAZZY JEFF and The FRESH PRINCE *US, male rap / DJ duo – Jeff Townes and Will Smith (5 Albums: 15 Weeks, 9 Singles: 49 Weeks)*

4 Oct 86 **GIRLS AIN'T NOTHING BUT TROUBLE** *Champion Champ 18*...21 8
28 Feb 87 **ROCK THE HOUSE** *Champion CHAMP 1004*....97 1
21 May 88 **HE'S THE DJ I'M THE RAPPER** *Jive HIP 61*....68 2
3 Aug 91 ● **SUMMERTIME (re)** *Jive JIVECD 279* $....8 12
14 Sep 91 **HOMEBASE** *Jive HIP 116*....69 1
9 Nov 91 **RING MY BELL** *Jive JIVECD 288*....53 2
11 Sep 93 ★ **BOOM! SHAKE THE ROOM** *Jive JIVECD 335* [1] 1 13
20 Nov 93 **I'M LOOKING FOR THE ONE (TO BE WITH ME)** *Jive JIVECD 345* [1] 24 4
11 Dec 93 **CODE RED** *Jive CHIP 140* [1] 50 6
19 Feb 94 **CAN'T WAIT TO BE WITH YOU** *Jive JIVECD 348* [1] 29 4
4 Jun 94 **TWINKLE TWINKLE (I'M NOT A STAR)** *Jive JIVECD 354* [1] ...62 2
2 Dec 95 **BOOM! SHAKE THE ROOM** (re-mix) *Jive JIVECD 387* [1] 40 2
16 May 98 **GREATEST HITS** *Jive 518482* [1] 20 5
11 Jul 98 **LOVELY DAZE** *Jive 0518902*....37 2

[1] Jazzy Jeff & The Fresh Prince [1] Jazzy Jeff and the Fresh Prince

'Summertime' re-entered the chart and peaked at No.29 in Aug 1994.

DJ JEAN *Holland, DJ / producer – Jan Engelaar*

11 Sep 99 ● **THE LAUNCH** *AM:PM CDAMPM 123*....2 11

DJ JURGEN presents Alice DEEJAY
Holland, male DJ / production group and female vocalist

31 Jul 99 ● **BETTER OFF ALONE** *Positiva CDTIV 113*....2 16

DJ KOOL *US, male rapper / DJ / producer – John Bowman*

22 Feb 97 ● **LET ME CLEAR MY THROAT** *American 74321452092*....8 7

DJ KRUSH
Japan, male producer – Hideaki Ishi (2 Albums: 2 Weeks, 2 Singles: 2 Weeks)

3 Sep 94 **BAD BROTHERS** *Island IMCD 8024* [1] 58 1
11 Nov 95 **MEISO** *Mo Wax MW 039CD*....64 1

KEY: UK No.1 ★ UK Top 10 ● Still on chart + UK entry at No.1 ■ US No.1 ▲ UK million seller £ US million seller $
Singles re-entries are listed as (re), (2re), (3re)... which signifies that the hit re-entered the chart once, twice or three times...

Peak Position / Weeks

16 Mar 96	**MEISO** *Mo Wax MW 042CD*	52	1
12 Oct 96	**ONLY THE STRONG SURVIVE** *Mo Wax MW 060CD*	71	1

[1] Ronny Jordan meets DJ Krush

DJ LUCK & MC NEAT *UK, male DJ / producers / rappers – Joel Samuels and Michael Rose (1 Album: 2 Weeks, 6 Singles: 44 Weeks)*

25 Dec 99 ●	**A LITTLE BIT OF LUCK** *Red Rose CDRROSLE 1*	9	15
27 May 00 ●	**MASTERBLASTER 2000** *Red Rose RROSE 002CD* [1]	5	8
7 Oct 00 ●	**AIN'T NO STOPPIN' US** *Red Rose CDRROSE 004* [1]	8	6
17 Mar 01	**PIANO LOCO** *Island CID 773*	12	8
8 Sep 01	**I'M ALL ABOUT YOU (re)** *Island CID 781* [2]	18	5
25 May 02	**IRIE** *Island CID 795* [3]	31	2
8 Jun 02	**IT'S ALL GOOD** *Island CIDD 8117* [1]	34	2

[1] DJ Luck & MC Neat featuring JJ [2] DJ Luck and MC Neat featuring Ari Gold [3] Luck & Neat [1] Luck & Neat

DJ MANTA *Holland, male / female DJ / production trio*

9 Oct 99	**HOLDING ON** *AM:PM CDAMPM 125*	47	1

DJ MARKY & XRS featuring STAMINA MC *Brazil, male DJ / production duo – Marco da Silva and Michael Nicassio (2 Singles: 8 Weeks)*

20 Jul 02	**LK 'CAROLINA CAROL BELA'** *V Recordings V 035*	17	6
16 Nov 02	**LK** (re-mix) *V Recordings V 038*	45	2

DJ MIKO *Italy, male producer – Quartobaro Manier*

13 Aug 94 ●	**WHAT'S UP** *Systematic SYSCD 2*	6	10

DJ MILANO featuring SAMANTHA FOX *Italy, male DJ / producer – Mirko Milano and UK, female vocalist (6 Singles: 2 Weeks)*

28 Mar 98	**SANTA MARIA** *All Around the World CDGLOBE 163*	31	2

DJ MISJAH and DJ TIM *Holland, male instrumental / production duo – Misjah Van Der Heiden and Tim Hoogestegger (2 Singles: 4 Weeks)*

23 Mar 96	**ACCESS** *Ffrreedom TABCD 240*	16	3
27 May 00	**ACCESS** (re-mix) *Tripoli Trax TTRAXCD 063*	45	1

DJ NATION (see also NUKLEUZ DJ'S) *UK, collection of male DJs / producers (2 Singles: 5 Weeks)*

9 Aug 03	**SUMMER EDITION** *Nukleuz 0542 FNUK*	59	2
27 Mar 04	**X-RATED** *Nukleuz 0501 FNUK*	52	3

'X-Rated' is a set of three 12" various artist singles with one common track, DJ Nation's 'X-Rated'.

DJ OTZI *Austria, male DJ / producer – Gerry Friedle (6 Singles: 48 Weeks)*

18 Aug 01	**HEY BABY** (import) *EMI 8892462*	41	5
22 Sep 01 ★	**HEY BABY (UHH, AHH) (re)** *EMI CDOTZI 001* ■	1	24
1 Dec 01 ●	**DO WAH DIDDY** *EMI CDOTZI 002*	9	9
29 Dec 01	**X-MAS TIME** *EMI CDOTZI 003*	51	2
8 Jun 02 ●	**HEY BABY (THE UNOFFICIAL WORLD CUP REMIX) (2re)** *EMI Austria / Liberty CDOTZI 004*	10	7
28 Dec 02	**LIVE IS LIFE** *EMI / Liberty CDLIVE 001* [1]	50	1

[1] Hermes House Band and DJ Otzi

DJ PIED PIPER and The MASTERS OF CEREMONIES *UK, male rap / production group*

2 Jun 01 ★	**DO YOU REALLY LIKE IT** *Relentless MOS RELMOS 1CDS* ■	1	14

DJ POWER *Italy, male producer – Steve Gambaroli*

7 Mar 92	**EVERYBODY PUMP** *Cooltempo COOL 252*	46	2

DJ PROFESSOR *Italy, male producer – Luca Lauri (4 Singles: 6 Weeks)*

10 Aug 91	**WE GOTTA DO IT** *Fourth & Broadway BRW 225* [1]	57	2
28 Mar 92	**ROCK ME STEADY** *PWL Continental PWL 219*	49	2
8 Oct 94	**ROCKIN' ME** *Citra CITRA 1CD* [2]	56	1
1 Mar 97	**WALKIN' ON UP** *Nukleuz MCSTD 40098* [3]	64	1

[1] DJ Professor featuring Francesco Zappala [2] Professor [3] DJ Prof-x-or

DJ QUICKSILVER *Turkey, male DJ / producer – Orhan Terzi (1 Album: 3 Weeks, 3 Singles: 29 Weeks)*

5 Apr 97 ●	**BELLISSIMA** *Positiva CDTIV 72*	4	17
6 Sep 97 ●	**FREE** *Positiva CDTIVS 77*	7	7
21 Feb 98	**PLANET LOVE** *Positiva CDTIV 88*	12	5
7 Mar 98	**QUICKSILVER** *Positiva 4934942*	26	3

DJ RAP *UK, female vocalist / DJ / producer – Charissa Saverio (3 Singles: 5 Weeks)*

4 Jul 98	**BAD GIRL** *Higher Ground HIGHS 8CD*	32	2
17 Oct 98	**GOOD TO BE ALIVE** *Higher Ground HIGHS 14CD*	36	2
3 Apr 99	**EVERYDAY GIRL** *Higher Ground HIGHS 19CD*	47	1

DJ ROLANDO AKA AZTEC MYSTIC *US, male DJ / producer – Rolando Rocha*

21 Oct 00	**JAGUAR** *430 West 430WUKTCD 1*	43	2

DJ SAKIN & FRIENDS *Germany, male DJ / producer – Sakin Botzkurt (2 Singles: 18 Weeks)*

20 Feb 99 ●	**PROTECT YOUR MIND (FOR THE LOVE OF A PRINCESS) (re)** *Positiva CDTIV 107*	4	11
5 Jun 99	**NOMANSLAND (DAVID'S SONG)** *Positiva CDTIV 112*	14	7

DJ SAMMY *Spain, male DJ / producer – Samuel Bouriah (1 Album: 9 Weeks, 4 Singles: 47 Weeks)*

9 Nov 02 ★	**HEAVEN** *Data / MoS DATA 45CDS* [1] ■	1	19
8 Mar 03 ●	**THE BOYS OF SUMMER** *Data / MoS DATA 49CDS*	2	13
22 Mar 03	**HEAVEN** *Ministry of Sound DATACD 01X*	14	9
21 Jun 03 ●	**SUNLIGHT** *Data / MoS DATA 54CDS*	8	9
25 Jun 05 ●	**WHY** *Data DATA 89CDS*	7	6

[1] DJ Sammy and Yanou featuring Do

DJ SANDY vs HOUSETRAP *Germany, female DJ / producer – Sande De Sutter and vocalist*

1 Jul 00	**OVERDRIVE** *Positiva CDTIV 133*	32	2

DJ SCOT PROJECT *Germany, male DJ / producer – Frank Zenker (2 Singles: 2 Weeks)*

27 Jul 96	**U (I GOT THE FEELING)** *Positiva CDTIV 55* [1]	66	1
14 Feb 98	**Y (HOW DEEP IS YOUR LOVE)** *Perfecto PERF 158CD1*	57	1

[1] Scot Project

DJ Doc SCOTT *UK, male producer – Scott McIlroy*

1 Feb 92	**NHS (EP)** *Absolute 2ABS 001DJ*	64	2

Tracks on NHS (EP): Surgery / Night Nurse.

DJ SCOTT featuring Lorna B *UK, male DJ – Scott Robertson and female vocalist (2 Singles: 5 Weeks)*

28 Jan 95	**DO YOU WANNA PARTY** *Steppin' Out SPONCD 2*	36	3
1 Apr 95	**SWEET DREAMS** *Steppin' Out SPONCD 3*	37	2

20 / 22 February 1964	27 / 29 February 1964	5 / 7 March 1964	12 / 14 March 1964
UK No.1 SINGLES			
DIANE – The Bachelors	ANYONE WHO HAD A HEART – Cilla Black	ANYONE WHO HAD A HEART – Cilla Black	ANYONE WHO HAD A HEART – Cilla Black
UK No.1 ALBUMS			
WITH THE BEATLES – The Beatles	WITH THE BEATLES – The Beatles	WITH THE BEATLES – The Beatles	WITH THE BEATLES – The Beatles

DJ SEDUCTION *UK, male producer – John Kallum (2 Singles: 8 Weeks)*

22 Feb 92	**HARDCORE HEAVEN / YOU AND ME** *Ffrreedom TAB 103*	26	5
11 Jul 92	**COME ON** *Ffrreedom TAB 111*	37	3

DJ SHADOW (see also UNKLE)
US, male producer – Josh Davis (2 Albums: 6 Weeks, 8 Singles: 11 Weeks)

25 Mar 95	**WHAT DOES YOUR SOUL LOOK LIKE** *Mo Wax MW 027CD*	59	1
14 Sep 96	**MIDNIGHT IN A PERFECT WORLD** *Mo Wax MW 057CD*	54	1
28 Sep 96	**ENDTRODUCING ...** *Mo Wax MW 059CD*	17	3
9 Nov 96	**STEM** *Mo Wax MW 058CD*	74	1
11 Oct 97	**HIGH NOON** *Mo Wax MW 063CD*	22	2
20 Dec 97	**CAMEL BOBSLED RACE** *Mo Wax MW 084CD*	62	1
24 Jan 98	**WHAT DOES YOUR SOUL LOOK LIKE (PART 1)** *Mo Wax MW 087*	54	1
1 Jun 02	**YOU CAN'T GO HOME AGAIN** *Mo Wax CID 797*	30	2
15 Jun 02 ●	**THE PRIVATE PRESS** *Island CID 8118*	8	3
2 Nov 02	**SIX DAYS** *Island CID 807*	28	2

DJ SHOG *Germany, male DJ / producer – Sven Greiner*

20 Jul 02	**THIS IS MY SOUND** *Nulife 74321942272*	40	2

DJ SNEAK featuring BEAR WHO?
Puerto Rico, male DJ / producer – Carlos Sosa and US, male DJ / producer

1 Feb 03	**FIX MY SINK** *Credence CDCREDS 033*	26	3

DJ SS *UK, male DJ / producer – Leroy Small*

20 Apr 02	**THE LIGHTER** *Formation FORM 12093*	63	1

DJ SUPREME *UK, male producer – Nick Destri (5 Singles: 11 Weeks)*

5 Oct 96	**THA WILD STYLE** *Distinctive DISNCD 19*	39	2
3 May 97	**THA WILD STYLE** (re-issue) *Distinctive DISNCD 29*	24	2
6 Dec 97	**ENTER THE SCENE** *Distinctive DISNCD 40* [1]	49	1
21 Feb 98	**THA HORNS OF JERICHO** *All Around the World CDGLOBE 164*	29	2
16 Jan 99 ●	**UP TO THE WILDSTYLE** *All Around the World CDGLOBE 170* [2]	10	4

[1] DJ Supreme vs Rhythm Masters [2] Porn Kings vs DJ Supreme

DJ TAUCHER *Germany, male DJ / producer – Ralf Armand Beck*

8 May 99	**CHILD OF THE UNIVERSE** *Additive 12AD 037*	74	1

DJ TIËSTO (see also GOURYELLA)
Holland, male producer – Tijs Verwest (1 Album: 2 Weeks, 9 Singles: 27 Weeks)

12 May 01	**FLIGHT 643** *Nebula NEBCD 016*	56	1
29 Sep 01	**URBAN TRAIN** *Nebula VCRD 95* [1]	22	3
13 Apr 02	**LETHAL INDUSTRY** *Nebula VCRD 103*	25	3
29 Jun 02	**643 (LOVE'S ON FIRE)** (re-recording) *Nebula VCRD 106* [2]	36	2
30 Nov 02	**OBSESSION** *Nebula NEBCD 029* [3]	56	1
11 Oct 03	**TRAFFIC** *Nebula NEBCD 052* [4]	48	2
15 May 04	**LOVE COMES AGAIN** *Nebula NEBCD 058* [5]	30	3
29 May 04	**JUST BE** *Nebula NEBCD 9010* [1]	54	2
23 Oct 04	**JUST BE** *Nebula NEBCD 062* [6]	43	2
23 Apr 05	**ADAGIO FOR STRINGS (re)** *Nebula NEBCD 068* [4]	37	10

[1] DJ Tiësto featuring Kirsty Hawkshaw [2] DJ Tiësto featuring Suzanne Palmer [3] Tiësto and Junkie XL [4] Tiësto [5] Tiësto featuring BT [6] Tiësto featuring Kirsty Hawkshaw [1] Tiësto

DJ TOUCHÉ (see also The WISEGUYS)
UK, male DJ / producer – Theo Keating

31 Jan 04	**THE PADDLE / THE GIRL'S A FREAK** *Southern Fried ECB 60*	65	1

DJ VISAGE featuring CLARISSA
Denmark, male DJ / producer – Martin Sig and Germany, female vocalist

10 Jun 00	**THE RETURN (TIME TO SAY GOODBYE)** *One Step Music OSMCDS 13*	58	1

DJ ZINC *UK, male DJ / producer – Benjamin Pettit (7 Singles: 9 Weeks)*

18 Nov 00	**138 TREK** *Phaze One PHAZE CDXO 3*	27	3
2 Jun 01	**CASINO ROYALE / DEAD A'S** *True Playaz TPRCD 004* [1]	58	1
13 Apr 02	**REACHOUT** *True Playaz TPR 12039*	73	1
21 Sep 02	**FAIR FIGHT / AS WE DO** *Bingo Beats BING 008*	72	1
13 Mar 04	**SKA** *True Playaz TPR 12051*	54	1
15 May 04	**STEPPIN STONES / SOUTH PACIFIC** *Bingo Beats BING 012*	62	1
8 Jan 05	**DRIVE BY CAR / INS** *Bingo Beats BINGO 023* [2]	66	1

[1] DJ Zinc / DJ Hype [2] DJ Zinc featuring Eksman

DJAIMIN *Switzerland, male producer – Dario Mancini*

19 Sep 92	**GIVE YOU** *Cooltempo COOL 262*	45	2

DJD presents HYDRAULIC DOGS *UK, male production duo*

8 Jun 02	**SHAKE IT BABY** *Direction 6721812*	56	1

DJH featuring STEFY
Italy, male instrumental / production group (3 Singles: 14 Weeks)

16 Feb 91	**THINK ABOUT ...** *RCA PB 44385*	22	6
13 Jul 91	**I LIKE IT** *RCA PB 44741*	16	7
19 Oct 91	**MOVE YOUR LOVE** *RCA PB 44965*	73	1

DJPC *Belgium, male producer – Patrick Cools (2 Singles: 5 Weeks)*

26 Oct 91	**INSSOMNIAK** *Hype 7PUM 005*	62	4
29 Feb 92	**INSSOMNIAK** (re-issue) *Hype PUMR 005*	64	1

DJ's RULE
Canada, male instrumental / production duo (2 Singles: 2 Weeks)

2 Mar 96	**GET INTO THE MUSIC** *Distinctive DISNCD 9*	72	1
5 Apr 97	**GET INTO THE MUSIC** (re-mix) *Distinctive DISNCDD 27* [1]	65	1

[1] DJ's Rule featuring Karen Brown

Boris DLUGOSCH *Germany, male producer (3 Singles: 8 Weeks)*

7 Dec 96	**KEEP PUSHIN'** *Manifesto FESCD 17* [1]	41	2
13 Sep 97	**HOLD YOUR HEAD UP HIGH** *Positiva CDTIV 79* [1]	23	2
16 Jun 01	**NEVER ENOUGH** *Positiva CDTIV 156* [2]	16	4

[1] Boris Dlugosch presents Booom!: Vocals by Inaya Davis [Inaya Day] [2] Boris Dlugosch featuring Roisin Murphy

D'LUX *UK, male / female vocal / instrumental group*

22 Jun 96	**LOVE RESURRECTION** *Logic 74321371012*	58	1

DMAC *UK, male vocalist – Derek McDonald*

27 Jul 02	**THE WORLD SHE KNOWS** *Chrysalis CDCHS 5140*	33	2

D'MENACE *UK, male production duo – Sandy Rivera and John Alvarez*

8 Aug 98	**DEEP MENACE (SPANK)** *Inferno CDFERN 8*	20	3

DO ME BAD THINGS *UK, male / female vocal / instrumental group (1 Album: 1 Week, 3 Singles: 4 Weeks)*

6 Nov 04	**TIME FOR DELIVERANCE** *Must Destroy MJDA 002CD*	57	1
9 Apr 05	**WHAT'S HIDEOUS** *Must Destroy MDA 003CD*	33	2
23 Apr 05	**YES!** *Must Destroy 5046775722*	68	1
25 Jun 05	**MOVE IN STEREO (LIV ULLMAN ON DRUMS)** *Must Destroy MDA 004CD*	49	1

Carl DOBKINS Jr *US, male vocalist*

31 Mar 60	**LUCKY DEVIL** *Brunswick 05817*	44	1

Anita DOBSON *UK, female actor / vocalist (2 Singles: 13 Weeks)*

9 Aug 86 ●	**ANYONE CAN FALL IN LOVE** *BBC RESL 191* [1]	4	9
18 Jul 87	**TALKING OF LOVE** *Parlophone R 6159*	43	4

[1] Anita Dobson featuring the Simon May Orchestra

19 / 21 March 1964	26 / 28 March 1964	2 / 4 April 1964	9 / 11 April 1964
LITTLE CHILDREN Billy J Kramer and The Dakotas	**LITTLE CHILDREN** Billy J Kramer and The Dakotas	**CAN'T BUY ME LOVE** The Beatles	**CAN'T BUY ME LOVE** The Beatles
WITH THE BEATLES The Beatles	**WITH THE BEATLES** The Beatles	**WITH THE BEATLES** The Beatles	**WITH THE BEATLES** The Beatles

KEY
UK No.1 ★ UK Top 10 ● Still on chart + UK entry at No.1 ■
US No.1 ▲ UK million seller £ US million seller $
Singles re-entries are listed as (re), (2re), (3re)... which signifies that the hit re-entered the chart once, twice or three times...
Peak Position / Weeks

Fefe DOBSON *US, female vocalist*

8 May 04 **EVERYTHING** *Mercury 9862501* 42 2

DR ALBAN *Nigeria, male vocalist – Alban Nwapa (6 Singles: 28 Weeks)*

5 Sep 92 ● **IT'S MY LIFE** *Logic 115330* 2 12
14 Nov 92 **ONE LOVE** *Logic 74321108727* 45 2
10 Apr 93 **SING HALLELUJAH!** *Logic 74321136202* 16 8
26 Mar 94 **LOOK WHO'S TALKING** *Logic 74321195342* 55 3
13 Aug 94 **AWAY FROM HOME** *Logic 74321222682* 42 2
29 Apr 95 **SWEET DREAMS** *Logic 74321251552* [1] 59 1

[1] Swing featuring Dr Alban

DOCTOR and The MEDICS (see also MEDICS) *UK, male / female vocal (Clive Jackson) / instrumental group (1 Album: 3 Weeks, 3 Singles: 25 Weeks)*

10 May 86 ★ **SPIRIT IN THE SKY** *IRS IRM 113* 1 15
21 Jun 86 **LAUGHING AT THE PIECES** *MCA MIRG 1010* 25 3
9 Aug 86 **BURN** *IRS IRM 119* 29 6
22 Nov 86 **WATERLOO** *IRS IRM 125* [1] 45 4

[1] Doctor and the Medics featuring Roy Wood

DR DRE (455 Top 500)
Controversial rapper / producer and architect of West Coast gangsta rap, b. Andre Young, 18 Feb 1965, Los Angeles, US. Former member of rap group NWA and founder of the Death Row record label whose protégés include Snoop Dogg and Eminem (2 Albums: 80 Weeks, 12 Singles: 79 Weeks)

22 Jan 94 **NUTHIN' BUT A 'G' THANG / LET ME RIDE** *Death Row A 8328CD* $ 31 3
3 Sep 94 **DRE DAY** *Death Row A 8292CD* 59 2
15 Apr 95 **NATURAL BORN KILLAZ** *Death Row A 8197CD* [1] 45 2
10 Jun 95 **KEEP THEIR HEADS RINGIN'** *Priority PTYCD 103* 25 4
13 Apr 96 ● **CALIFORNIA LOVE** *Death Row DRWCD 3* [2] 6 8
19 Oct 96 ● **NO DIGGITY** *Interscope IND 95003* [3] ▲ $ 9 7
11 Jul 98 **ZOOM** *Interscope IND 95594* [4] 15 3
14 Aug 99 ● **GUILTY CONSCIENCE** *Interscope IND 4971282* [5] 5 8
27 Nov 99 ● **2001** *Interscope 4904862* 4 76
25 Mar 00 ● **STILL D.R.E.** *Interscope 4972742* [6] 6 10
10 Jun 00 ● **FORGOT ABOUT DRE** *Interscope 4973412* [7] 7 9
9 Sep 00 **THE CHRONIC** *Interscope 7567922332* 43 4
3 Feb 01 ● **THE NEXT EPISODE (re)** *Interscope 4974762* [6] 3 12
19 Jan 02 ● **BAD INTENTIONS (re)** *Interscope 4973932* [8] 4 11

[1] Dr Dre and Ice Cube [2] 2Pac featuring Dr Dre [3] BLACKstreet featuring Dr Dre [4] Dr Dre and LL Cool J [5] Eminem featuring Dr Dre [6] Dr Dre featuring Snoop Dogg [7] Dr Dre featuring Eminem [8] Dr Dre featuring Knoc-Turn'al

DR FEELGOOD
UK, male vocal (Lee Collinson aka Lee Brilleaux, b. 10 May 1952, d. 7 Apr 1994) / instrumental group ((6 Albums: 33 Weeks) 6 Singles: 29 Weeks)

18 Oct 75 **MALPRACTICE** *United Artists UAS 29880* 17 6
2 Oct 76 ★ **STUPIDITY** *United Artists UAS 29990* 1 9
4 Jun 77 ● **SNEAKIN' SUSPICION** *United Artists UAS 30075* 10 6
11 Jun 77 **SNEAKIN' SUSPICION** *United Artists UP 36255* 47 3
24 Sep 77 **SHE'S A WIND UP** *United Artists UP 36304* 34 5
8 Oct 77 **BE SEEING YOU** *United Artists UAS 30123* 55 3
30 Sep 78 **DOWN AT THE DOCTORS** *United Artists UP 36444* 48 5
7 Oct 78 **PRIVATE PRACTICE** *United Artists UAG 30184* 41 5
20Jan 79 ● **MILK AND ALCOHOL** *United Artists UP 36468* 9 9
5 May 79 **AS LONG AS THE PRICE IS RIGHT** *United Artists YUP 36506* 40 6
2 Jun 79 **AS IT HAPPENS** *United Artists UAK 30239* 42 4
8Dec 79 **PUT HIM OUT OF YOUR MIND** *United Artists BP 306* 73 1

DR HOOK (243 Top 500) *Distinctive group fronted by vocalists Dennis Locorriere and Ray Sawyer, who had eight years of regular UK / US hits. Early recordings often featured humorous, anarchic Shel Silverstein songs, but this good-time New Jersey, US, act had greater success with later gentler material (9 Albums: 157 Weeks, 12 Singles: 104 Weeks)*

24 Jun 72 ● **SYLVIA'S MOTHER** *CBS 7929* [1] $ 2 13
25 Jun 76 ● **A LITTLE BIT MORE** *Capitol EST 23795* 5 42
26 Jun 76 ● **A LITTLE BIT MORE** *Capitol CL 15871* 2 14
30 Oct 76 ● **IF NOT YOU** *Capitol CL 15885* 5 10
29 Oct 77 **MAKING LOVE AND MUSIC** *Capitol EST 11632* 39 4
25 Mar 78 **MORE LIKE THE MOVIES** *Capitol CL 15967* 14 10
22 Sep 79 ★ **WHEN YOU'RE IN LOVE WITH A BEAUTIFUL WOMAN** *Capitol CL 16039* $ 1 17
27 Oct 79 **PLEASURE AND PAIN** *Capitol EAST 11859* 47 6
17 Nov 79 **SOMETIMES YOU WIN** *Capitol EST 12018* 14 44
5 Jan 80 ● **BETTER LOVE NEXT TIME** *Capitol CL 16112* 8 8
29 Mar 80 ● **SEXY EYES** *Capitol CL 16127* $ 4 9
23 Aug 80 **YEARS FROM NOW** *Capitol CL 16154* 47 6
8 Nov 80 **SHARING THE NIGHT TOGETHER** *Capitol CL 16171* $ 43 4
22 Nov 80 **GIRLS CAN GET IT** *Mercury MER 51* 40 5
29 Nov 80 **RISING** *Mercury 6302 076* 44 5
6 Dec 80 ● **DR HOOK GREATEST HITS** *Capitol EST 26037* 2 28
14 Nov 81 **DR HOOK LIVE IN THE UK** *Capitol EST 26706* 90 1
1 Feb 92 **WHEN YOU'RE IN LOVE WITH A BEAUTIFUL WOMAN** (re-issue) *Capitol EMCT 4* 44 4
6 Jun 92 **A LITTLE BIT MORE** (re-issue) *EMI EMCT 6* 47 4
13 Jun 92 ● **COMPLETELY HOOKED – THE BEST OF DR HOOK** *Capitol CDESTV 2* 3 19
13 Feb 99 ● **LOVE SONGS** *EMI 4979432* 8 8

[1] Dr Hook and the Medicine Show

DR JOHN *US, male vocalist / pianist – Malcolm Rebennack*

27 Jun 98 **ANUTHA ZONE** *Parlophone 4954902* 33 3

DR OCTAGON *US, male producer – Keith Thornton*

7 Sep 96 **BLUE FLOWERS** *Mo Wax MW 055CD* 66 1

DOCTOR SPIN (see also UK MIXMASTERS) *UK, male instrumental / production duo – Nigel Wright and Andrew Lloyd Webber*

3 Oct 92 ● **TETRIS** *Carpet CRPT 4* 6 8

Ken DODD (238 Top 500) *Seasoned stand-up comedian-cum-balladeer, b. 8 Nov 1929, Liverpool, UK. The tickling-stick-wielding troubadour was one of the most successful Merseyside acts in the mid-1960s, at times enjoying two Top 10 singles simultaneously. Biggest-selling single: 'Tears' 1,521,000 (4 Albums: 36 Weeks, 19 Singles: 233 Weeks)*

7 Jul 60 ● **LOVE IS LIKE A VIOLIN** *Decca F 11248* 8 18
15 Jun 61 **ONCE IN EVERY LIFETIME (2re)** *Decca F 11355* 28 18
1 Feb 62 **PIANISSIMO** *Decca F 11422* 21 15
29 Aug 63 **STILL** *Columbia DB 7094* 35 10
6 Feb 64 **EIGHT BY TEN** *Columbia DB 7191* 22 11
23 Jul 64 **HAPPINESS** *Columbia DB 7325* 31 13
26 Nov 64 **SO DEEP IS THE NIGHT** *Columbia DB 7398* 31 7
2 Sep 65 ★ **TEARS** *Columbia DB 7659* £ 1 24
18 Nov 65 ● **THE RIVER (LE COLLINE SONO IN FIORO)** *Columbia DB 7750* 3 14
25 Dec 65 ● **TEARS OF HAPPINESS** *Columbia 33SX 1793* 6 12
12 May 66 ● **PROMISES** *Columbia DB 7914* 6 14
23 Jul 66 **HITS FOR NOW AND ALWAYS** *Columbia SX 6060* 14 11
4 Aug 66 **MORE THAN LOVE** *Columbia DB 7976* 14 11
27 Oct 66 **IT'S LOVE** *Columbia DB 8031* 36 7
14 Jan 67 **FOR SOMEONE SPECIAL** *Columbia SCX 6224* 40 1
19 Jan 67 **LET ME CRY ON YOUR SHOULDER** *Columbia DB 8101* 11 10
30 Jul 69 **TEARS WON'T WASH AWAY THESE HEARTACHES** *Columbia DB 8600* 22 11
5 Dec 70 **BROKEN HEARTED (re)** *Columbia DB 8725* 15 10
10 Jul 71 **WHEN LOVE COMES ROUND AGAIN (L'ARCA DI NOE)** *Columbia DB 8796* 19 16

18 Nov 72	**JUST OUT OF REACH (OF MY TWO EMPTY ARMS)** *Columbia DB 8947*	29	11
29 Nov 75	**THINK OF ME (WHEREVER YOU ARE)** *EMI 2342*	21	8
29 Nov 80 ●	20 GOLDEN GREATS OF KEN DODD *Warwick WW 5098*	8	12
26 Dec 81	**HOLD MY HAND** *Images IMGS 0002*	44	5

DODGY *UK, male vocal (Nigel Clarke) / instrumental group (4 Albums: 54 Weeks, 12 Singles: 41 Weeks)*

8 May 93	**LOVEBIRDS** *A&M AMCD 0177*	65	2
5 Jun 93	THE DODGY ALBUM *A&M 5400822*	75	1
3 Jul 93	**I NEED ANOTHER (EP)** *A&M 5803172*	67	2
6 Aug 94	**THE MELOD-EP** *Bostin 5806772*	53	1
1 Oct 94	**STAYING OUT FOR THE SUMMER** *Bostin 5807972*	38	2
5 Nov 94	HOMEGROWN *A&M 5402822*	28	14
7 Jan 95	**SO LET ME GO FAR** *Bostin 5809032*	30	3
11 Mar 95	**MAKING THE MOST OF** *Bostin 5809892* [1]	22	3
10 Jun 95	**STAYING OUT FOR THE SUMMER** (re-mix) *Bostin 5810952*	19	5
8 Jun 96	**IN A ROOM** *A&M 5816252*	12	6
29 Jun 96 ●	FREE PEACE SWEET *A&M 5405732*	7	38
10 Aug 96 ●	**GOOD ENOUGH** *A&M 5818152*	4	8
16 Nov 96	**IF YOU'RE THINKING OF ME** *A&M 5819992*	11	4
15 Mar 97	**FOUND YOU** *A&M 5821332*	19	3
26 Sep 98	**EVERY SINGLE DAY** *A&M MERCD 512*	32	2
17 Oct 98	ACE A'S + KILLER B'S *Mercury / A&M 5410182*	55	1

[1] Dodgy with the Kick Horns

Tracks on I Need Another (EP): I Need Another / If I Fall / Hendre DDU. Tracks on The Melod-EP: Melodies Haunt You / The Snake / Don't Go / Summer Fayre.

Tim DOG *US, male rapper – Timothy Blair (2 Singles: 3 Weeks)*

29 Oct 94	**BITCH WITH A PERM** *Dis-stress DISCD 1*	49	1
11 Feb 95	**MAKE WAY FOR THE INDIAN** *Island CID 586* [1]	29	2

[1] Apache Indian and Tim Dog

DOG EAT DOG *US, male vocal (John Connor) / instrumental group (1 Album: 2 Weeks, 2 Singles: 7 Weeks)*

19 Aug 95 ●	**NO FRONTS (re)** *Roadrunner RR 23312*	9	6
13 Jul 96	**ISMS** *Roadrunner RR 23083*	43	1
27 Jul 96	PLAY GAMES *Roadrunner RR 88762*	40	2

It was not until the Apr 1996 re-entry that 'No Fronts' reached its peak position

Nate DOGG *US, male rapper – Nathan Hale (9 Singles: 54 Weeks)*

23 Jul 94 ●	**REGULATE** *Death Row A 8290CD* [1] $	5	14
3 Feb 01	**OH NO** *Rawkus RWK 302* [2]	24	4
25 Aug 01	**WHERE I WANNA BE (re)** *London LONCD 461* [3]	14	7
29 Sep 01	**AREA CODES** *Def Jam 5887722* [4]	25	3
1 Mar 03	**THE STREETS** *Def Jam 0779852* [5]	48	2
12 Jul 03 ●	**21 QUESTIONS** *Interscope 9807195* [6] ▲	6	8
1 Nov 03	**OOH WEE** *Elektra E 7490CD* [7]	15	7
14 Feb 04	**THE SET UP (YOU DON'T KNOW)** *Interscope 9815333* [8]	32	3
18 Sep 04	**I LIKE THAT** *Capitol CDCL 861* [9]	11	6

[1] Warren G and Nate Dogg [2] Mos Def and Nate Dogg featuring Pharoahe Monch [3] Shade Sheist featuring Nate Dogg and Kurupt [4] Ludacris featuring Nate Dogg [5] WC featuring Snoop Dogg and Nate Dogg [6] 50 Cent featuring Nate Dogg [7] Mark Ronson featuring Ghostface Killah and Nate Dogg [8] Obie Trice featuring Nate Dogg [9] Houston featuring Chingy, Nate Dogg & I-20

DOGS NEW *UK, male vocal / instrumental group (4 Singles: 6 Weeks)*

5 Mar 05	**SHE'S GOT A REASON** *Island CID 882*	36	1
14 May 05	**TUNED TO A DIFFERENT STATION** *Island CID 891*	29	2
30 Jul 05	**SELFISH WAYS** *Island CID 901*	45	1
10 Dec 05	**TARRED & FEATHERED** *Island CID 908*	64	1

DOGS D'AMOUR *UK, male vocal / instrumental group (6 Albums: 12 Weeks, 6 Singles: 15 Weeks)*

22 Oct 88	IN THE DYNAMITE JET SALOON *China WOL 8*	97	1
4 Feb 89	**HOW COME IT NEVER RAINS** *China CHINA 13*	44	3
25 Mar 89	A GRAVEYARD OF EMPTY BOTTLES *China 8390740*	16	4
5 Aug 89	**SATELLITE KID** *China CHINA 17*	26	3
30 Sep 89	ERROL FLYNN *China 8397001*	22	3
14 Oct 89	**TRAIL OF TEARS** *China CHINA 20*	47	3
23 Jun 90	**VICTIMS OF SUCCESS** *China CHINA 24*	36	3
15 Sep 90	**EMPTY WORLD** *China CHINA 27*	61	2
6 Oct 90	STRAIGHT *China 8437961*	32	2
7 Sep 91	DOG'S HITS AND THE BOOTLEG ALBUM *China WOL 1020*	58	1
15 May 93	... MORE UNCHARTED HEIGHTS OF DISGRACE *China WOLCD 1032*	30	1
19 Jun 93	**ALL OR NOTHING** *China WOKCD 2033*	53	1

DOGS DIE IN HOT CARS *UK, male / female vocal / instrumental group (1 Album: 2 Weeks, 3 Singles: 5 Weeks)*

8 May 04	**GODHOPPING** *V2 VVR 5025863*	24	2
17 Jul 04	**I LOVE YOU 'CAUSE I HAVE TO** *V2 VVR 5025873*	32	2
24 Jul 04	PLEASE DESCRIBE YOURSELF *V2 VVR 1027142*	44	2
16 Oct 04	**LOUNGER** *V2 VVR 5028213*	43	1

Ken DOH *UK, male producer – Michael Devlin*

30 Mar 96 ●	**NAKASAKI (EP)** *ffrr FCD 272*	7	7

Tracks on Nakasaki (EP): Nakasaki (2 mixes) / I Need a Lover Tonight (2 mixes) / Kaki Traki.

PETER DOHERTY (see also BABY SHAMBLES; The LIBERTINES) *UK, male vocalist (3 Singles: 9 Weeks)*

24 Apr 04 ●	**FOR LOVERS** *Rough Trade TRADSCD 177* [1]	7	6
22 May 04	**BABYSHAMBLES** *High Society HSCDS 003*	32	1
29 Oct 05	**THEIR WAY** *Rough Trade RTRADSCD 267* [2]	22	2

[1] Wolfman featuring Peter Doherty [2] Little'Ans featuring Peter Doherty

DOKKEN *US, male vocal / instrumental group*

21 Nov 87	BACK FOR THE ATTACK *Elektra EKT 43*	96	1

Joe DOLAN *Ireland, male vocalist (4 Singles: 40 Weeks)*

25 Jun 69 ●	**MAKE ME AN ISLAND (re)** *Pye 7N 17738*	3	19
1 Nov 69	**TERESA** *Pye 7N 17833*	20	7
28 Feb 70	**YOU'RE SUCH A GOOD LOOKING WOMAN** *Pye 7N 17891*	17	13
17 Sep 77	**I NEED YOU** *Pye 7N 45702*	43	1

Thomas DOLBY *UK, male vocalist / multi-instrumentalist – Thomas Robertson (4 Albums: 29 Weeks, 11 Singles: 51 Weeks)*

3 Oct 81	**EUROPA AND THE PIRATE TWINS** *Parlophone R 6051*	48	3
22 May 82	THE GOLDEN AGE OF WIRELESS *Venice in Peril VIP 1001*	65	10
14 Aug 82	**WINDPOWER** *Venice in Peril VIPS 103*	31	8
6 Nov 82	**SHE BLINDED ME WITH SCIENCE** *Venice in Peril VIPS 104*	49	4
16 Jul 83	**SHE BLINDED ME WITH SCIENCE** (re-issue) *Venice in Peril VIPS 105*	56	4
21 Jan 84	**HYPERACTIVE** *Parlophone Odeon R 6065*	17	9
18 Feb 84	THE FLAT EARTH *Parlophone Odeon PCS 2400341*	14	14
31 Mar 84	**I SCARE MYSELF** *Parlophone Odeon R 6067*	46	5
16 Apr 88	**AIRHEAD** *Manhattan MT 38*	53	3
7 May 88	ALIENS ATE MY BUICK *Manhattan MTL 1020*	30	3
9 May 92	**CLOSE BUT NO CIGAR** *Virgin VS 1410*	22	5
11 Jul 92	**I LOVE YOU GOODBYE** *Virgin VS 1417*	36	4
8 Aug 92	ASTRONAUTS AND HERETICS *Virgin CDV 2701*	35	2
26 Sep 92	**SILK PYJAMAS** *Virgin VS 1430*	62	2
22 Jan 94	**HYPERACTIVE!** (re-mix) *Parlophone CDEMCTS 10*	23	4

Joe DOLCE MUSIC THEATRE *US, male vocalist*

7 Feb 81 ★	**SHADDAP YOU FACE** *Epic EPC 9518*	1	10

DOLL *UK, male / female vocal / instrumental group*

13 Jan 79	**DESIRE ME** *Beggars Banquet BEG 11*	28	8

14 / 16 May 1964	21 / 23 May 1964	28 / 30 May 1964	4 / 6 June 1964
DON'T THROW YOUR LOVE AWAY The Searchers	JULIET The Four Pennies	YOU'RE MY WORLD Cilla Black	YOU'RE MY WORLD Cilla Black
THE ROLLING STONES The Rolling Stones	THE ROLLING STONES The Rolling Stones	THE ROLLING STONES The Rolling Stones	THE ROLLING STONES The Rolling Stones

KEY UK No.1 ★ UK Top 10 ● Still on chart + UK entry at No.1 ■ US No.1 ▲ UK million seller £ US million seller $
Singles re-entries are listed as (re), (2re), (3re)... which signifies that the hit re-entered the chart once, twice or three times...
Peak Position / Weeks

DOLLAR (470 Top 500)

Photogenic teen-targeted UK vocal duo who were originally one third of Guys 'n' Dolls: David Van Day and Thereze Bazar. Their Top 10 hits came from writers as diverse as John Lennon, Paul McCartney, Trevor Horn, Erasure and themselves (3 Albums: 28 Weeks, 14 Singles: 128 Weeks)

11 Nov 78 **SHOOTING STAR** *Carrere EMI 2871* 14 12
19 May 79 **WHO WERE YOU WITH IN THE MOONLIGHT** *Carrere CAR 110*..14 12
18 Aug 79 ● **LOVE'S GOTTA HOLD ON ME** *Carrere CAR 122*....4 13
15 Sep 79 SHOOTING STARS *Carrere CAL 111* 36 8
24 Nov 79 ● **I WANNA HOLD YOUR HAND** *Carrere CAR 131*....9 14
25 Oct 80 **TAKIN' A CHANCE ON YOU** *WEA K 18353*....62 3
15 Aug 81 **HAND HELD IN BLACK AND WHITE** *WEA BUCK 1*....19 12
14 Nov 81 ● **MIRROR MIRROR (MON AMOUR)** *WEA BUCK 2*....4 17
20 Mar 82 **RING RING** *Carrere CAR 225*....61 2
27 Mar 82 ● **GIVE ME BACK MY HEART** *WEA BUCK 3*....4 9
24 Apr 82 THE VERY BEST OF DOLLAR *Carrere CAL 3001* 31 9
19 Jun 82 **VIDEOTHEQUE** *WEA BUCK 4*....17 10
18 Sep 82 **GIVE ME SOME KINDA MAGIC** *WEA BUCK 5*....34 6
30 Oct 82 THE DOLLAR ALBUM *WEA DTV 1*....18 11
16 Aug 86 **WE WALKED IN LOVE** *Arista DIME 1*....61 4
26 Dec 87 ● **O L'AMOUR** *London LON 146*....7 11
16 Jul 88 **IT'S NATURE'S WAY (NO PROBLEM)** *London LON 179*....58 3

Placido DOMINGO (298 Top 500)

Perennially popular tenor, b. 21 Jan 1941, Madrid, Spain, who brought an operatic quality to the pop charts, most successfully as one of The Three Tenors, with a series of football World Cup tie-in concerts. Received an honorary knighthood in 2002 (17 Albums: 199 Weeks, 5 Singles: 28 Weeks)

28 Nov 81 PERHAPS LOVE *CBS 73592* [1] 17 21
12 Dec 81 **PERHAPS LOVE** *CBS A 1905* [1] 46 9
21 May 83 MY LIFE FOR A SONG *CBS 73683*....31 8
27 Dec 86 PLACIDO DOMINGO COLLECTION *Stylus SMR 625*....30 14
23 Apr 88 GREATEST LOVE SONGS *CBS 44701*....63 2
27 May 89 **TILL I LOVED YOU** *CBS 654843 7* [2] 24 9
17 Jun 89 GOYA ... A LIFE IN A SONG *CBS 463294 1*....36 4
17 Jun 89 THE ESSENTIAL DOMINGO *Deutsche Grammophon PDTV 1*...20 8
16 Jun 90 **NESSUN DORMA FROM 'TURANDOT'** *Epic 656005 7* [3] 59 2
1 Sep 90 ★ IN CONCERT *Decca 4304331* [2] 1 78
24 Nov 90 BE MY LOVE ... AN ALBUM OF LOVE *EMI EMTV 54* [3] 14 12
7 Dec 91 THE BROADWAY I LOVE *East West 9031755901*....45 6
13 Jun 92 DOMINGO: ARIAS AND SPANISH SONGS *Deutsche Grammophon 4371122*....47 3
8 Aug 92 FROM THE OFFICIAL BARCELONA GAMES CEREMONY *RCA Red Seal 09026612042* [4] 41 3
25 Dec 93 CHRISTMAS IN VIENNA *Sony Classical SK 53358* [5] 71 2
30 Jul 94 **LIBIAMO / LA DONNA E MOBILE** *Teldec YZ 843CD* [4] 21 4
10 Sep 94 ★ THE THREE TENORS IN CONCERT 1994 *Teldec 4509962002* [6] . 1 26
10 Dec 94 CHRISTMAS IN VIENNA II *Sony Classical SK 64304* [7] 60 2
25 Jul 98 **YOU'LL NEVER WALK ALONE** *Decca 4607982* [5] 35 4
29 Aug 98 THE THREE TENORS IN PARIS 1998 *Decca 4605002* [2] 14 6
28 Oct 00 SONGS OF LOVE *EMI CDC 5571042*....53 2
23 Dec 00 THE THREE TENORS CHRISTMAS *Sony Classical SK 89131* [8] 57 2

[1] Placido Domingo with John Denver [2] Placido Domingo and Jennifer Rush [3] Luis Cobos featuring Placido Domingo [4] José Carreras featuring Placido Domingo and Luciano Pavarotti with Mehta [5] José Carreras, Placido Domingo and Luciano Pavarotti with Mehta [1] Placido Domingo and John Denver [2] José Carreras, Placido Domingo and Luciano Pavarotti [3] Placido Domingo featuring the London Symphony Orchestra [4] Placido Domingo, José Carreras and Montserrat Caballé [5] Placido Domingo, Diana Ross and José Carreras [6] José Carreras, Placido Domingo and Luciano Pavarotti conducted by Zubin Mehta [7] Dionne Warwick and Placido Domingo [8] José Carreras, Placido Domingo and Luciano Pavarotti featuring Zubin Mehta

DOMINO *US, male rapper / vocalist – Shawn Ivy (2 Singles: 6 Weeks)*

22 Jan 94 **GETTO JAM** *Chaos 6600402*....33 4
14 May 94 **SWEET POTATOE PIE** *Chaos 6603292*....42 2

Fats DOMINO *US, male vocalist / pianist – Antoine Domino (2 Albums: 3 Weeks, 21 Singles: 111 Weeks)*

27 Jul 56 **I'M IN LOVE AGAIN (re)** *London HLU 8280* $ 12 14
30 Nov 56 ● **BLUEBERRY HILL (re)** *London HLU 8330* $ 6 15
25 Jan 57 **AIN'T THAT A SHAME** *London HLU 8173* $....23 2
1 Feb 57 **HONEY CHILE** *London HLU 8356*....29 1
29 Mar 57 **BLUE MONDAY (re)** *London HLP 8377* $ 23 2
19 Apr 57 **I'M WALKIN'** *London HLP 8407* $....19 7
19 Jul 57 **VALLEY OF TEARS** *London HLP 8449*....25 1
28 Mar 58 **THE BIG BEAT** *London HLP 8575*....20 4
4 Jul 58 **SICK AND TIRED** *London HLP 8628*....26 1
22 May 59 **MARGIE** *London HLP 8865*....18 5
16 Oct 59 **I WANT TO WALK YOU HOME** *London HLP 8942*....14 5
18 Dec 59 **BE MY GUEST (re)** *London HLP 9005*....11 13
17 Mar 60 **COUNTRY BOY** *London HLP 9073*....19 11
21 Jul 60 **WALKING TO NEW ORLEANS** *London HLP 9163*....19 10
10 Nov 60 **THREE NIGHTS A WEEK** *London HLP 9198*....45 2
5 Jan 61 **MY GIRL JOSEPHINE** *London HLP 9244*....32 4
27 Jul 61 **IT KEEPS RAININ'** *London HLP 9374*....49 1
30 Nov 61 **WHAT A PARTY** *London HLP 9456*....43 1
29 Mar 62 **JAMBALAYA** *London HLP 9520*....41 1
31 Oct 63 **RED SAILS IN THE SUNSET** *HMV POP 1219*....34 6
16 May 70 VERY BEST OF FATS DOMINO *Liberty LBS 83331*....56 1
24 Apr 76 **BLUEBERRY HILL** (re-issue) *United Artists UP 35797*....41 5
6 Mar 04 THE BEST OF FATS DOMINO *EMI 5964972*....58 2

DON PABLO'S ANIMALS *Italy, male production group*

19 May 90 ● **VENUS** *Rumour RUMA 18*....4 10

Siobhan DONAGHY

(see also SUGABABES) *UK, female vocalist (3 Singles: 5 Weeks)*

5 Jul 03 **OVERRATED** *London LONCD 476*....19 4
27 Sep 03 **TWIST OF FATE** *London LONCD 481*....52 1

DON-E *UK, male vocalist – Donald McLean (3 Singles: 8 Weeks)*

9 May 92 **LOVE MAKES THE WORLD GO ROUND** *Fourth & Broadway BRW 242*....18 6
25 Jul 92 **PEACE IN THE WORLD** *Fourth & Broadway BRW 256*....41 1
28 Feb 98 **DELICIOUS** *Mushroom MUSH 20CD* [1] 52 1

[1] Deni Hines featuring Don-E

Lonnie DONEGAN (122 Top 500)

The 'King of Skiffle', b. Anthony Donegan, 29 Apr 1931, Glasgow, Scotland, d. 3 Nov 2002. Britain's most successful and influential recording artist before The Beatles. Chalked up 24 successive Top 30 hits, and was the first UK, male to score two US Top 10s (7 Albums: 68 Weeks, 32 Singles: 326 Weeks)

6 Jan 56 ● **ROCK ISLAND LINE (2re)** *Decca F 10647* [1] 8 22
20 Apr 56 ● **LOST JOHN / STEWBALL (re)** *Pye Nixa N 15036* [1] 2 18
6 Jul 56 **SKIFFLE SESSION (EP)** *Pye Nixa NJE 1017* [1] 20 2
7 Sep 56 ● **BRING A LITTLE WATER, SYLVIE / DEAD OR ALIVE (re)** *Pye Nixa N 15071* [2] 7 13
17 Nov 56 ● LONNIE DONEGAN SHOWCASE *Pye Nixa NPT 19012*....2 21
21 Dec 56 **LONNIE DONEGAN SHOWCASE (LP)** *Pye Nixa NPT 19012* [2] 26 3
18 Jan 57 ● **DON'T YOU ROCK ME DADDY-O** *Pye Nixa N 15080* [2] 4 17
5 Apr 57 ★ **CUMBERLAND GAP** *Pye Nixa N 15087* [2] 1 12
7 Jun 57 ★ **GAMBLIN' MAN / PUTTIN' ON THE STYLE** *Pye Nixa N 15093* [2] 1 19
11 Oct 57 ● **MY DIXIE DARLING** *Pye Nixa N 15108* [2] 10 15
20 Dec 57 **JACK O' DIAMONDS** *Pye Nixa 7N 15116* [2] 14 7
11 Apr 58 ● **THE GRAND COOLIE DAM** *Pye Nixa 7N 15129* [2] 6 15
11 Jul 58 **SALLY DON'T YOU GRIEVE / BETTY, BETTY, BETTY** *Pye Nixa 7N 15148* [2] 11 7
12 Jul 58 ● LONNIE *Pye Nixa NPT 19027*....3 13

26 Sep 58 **LONESOME TRAVELLER** *Pye Nixa 7N 15158* [2] **28** 1
14 Nov 58 **LONNIE'S SKIFFLE PARTY** *Pye Nixa 7N 15165* [2] **23** 5
21 Nov 58 ● **TOM DOOLEY** *Pye Nixa 7N 15172* [2] **3** 14
6 Feb 59 ● **DOES YOUR CHEWING GUM LOSE ITS FLAVOUR (ON THE BEDPOST OVERNIGHT)** *Pye Nixa 7N 15181* [2] **3** 12
8 May 59 **FORT WORTH JAIL** *Pye Nixa 7N 15198* [2] **14** 5
26 Jun 59 ● **BATTLE OF NEW ORLEANS** *Pye 7N 15206* [2] **2** 16
11 Sep 59 **SAL'S GOT A SUGAR LIP** *Pye 7N 15223* [2] **13** 4
2 Oct 59 **HOLD BACK TOMORROW** *Pye 7N 15213* [3] **26** 2
4 Dec 59 **SAN MIGUEL** *Pye 7N 15237* [2] **19** 4
24 Mar 60 ★ **MY OLD MAN'S A DUSTMAN** *Pye 7N 15256* [4] **1** 13
26 May 60 ● **I WANNA GO HOME (THE WRECK OF THE 'JOHN B')** *Pye 7N 15267* [5] **5** 17
25 Aug 60 ● **LORELEI** *Pye 7N 15275*....................**10** 8
13 Oct 60 **ROCKIN' ALONE** *Pye 7N 15296* [6] **44** 3
24 Nov 60 **LIVELY** *Pye 7N 15312* [4] **13** 9
8 Dec 60 **VIRGIN MARY** *Pye 7N 15315*....................**27** 5
11 May 61 ● **HAVE A DRINK ON ME** *Pye 7N 15354* [4] **8** 15
31 Aug 61 ● **MICHAEL, ROW THE BOAT / LUMBERED** *Pye 7N 15371* [4] **6** 11
18 Jan 62 **THE COMANCHEROS** *Pye 7N 15410*....................**14** 10
5 Apr 62 ● **THE PARTY'S OVER** *Pye 7N 15424*....................**9** 12
16 Aug 62 **PICK A BALE OF COTTON** *Pye 7N 15455* [4] **11** 10
1 Sep 62 ● **GOLDEN AGE OF DONEGAN** *Pye Golden Guinea GGL 0135*......**3** 23
9 Feb 63 **GOLDEN AGE OF DONEGAN VOLUME 2** *Pye Golden Guinea GGL 0170*....................**15** 3
25 Feb 78 **PUTTING ON THE STYLE** *Chrysalis CHR 1158*....................**51** 3
29 Jan 00 **THE SKIFFLE SESSIONS – LIVE IN BELFAST** *Venture CDVE 945* [1] **14** 3
8 Mar 03 **PUTTIN' ON THE STYLE – THE GREATEST HITS** *Castle Music TVSAN 002*....................**45** 2

[1] Lonnie Donegan Skiffle Group [2] Lonnie Donegan and his Skiffle Group [3] Lonnie Donegan presents Miki and Griff with the Lonnie Donegan Group [4] Lonnie Donegan and his Group [5] Lonnie Donegan and Wally Stott's Orchestra [6] Miki and Griff with the Lonnie Donegan Group [4] Lonnie Donegan and his Group [1] Van Morrison / Lonnie Donegan / Chris Barber

'Stewball' had one week on the chart by itself on 20 Apr 1956. 'Lost John', the other side, replaced it on 27 Apr 1956, but 'Stewball' was given co-billing with 'Lost John' for the weeks of 11, 18 and 25 May 1956, peaking only at No.7. 'Dead or Alive' was not listed with 'Bring a Little Water Sylvie' for the week of 7 Sep 1956. 'Putting on the Style' was not listed with 'Gamblin' Man' for the weeks of 7 and 14 Jun 1956. Tracks on Skiffle Session (EP): Railroad Bill / Stockalee / Ballad of Jesse James / Ol' Riley. Tracks on Lonnie Donegan Showcase (LP): Wabash Cannonball / How Long / How Long Blues / Nobody's Child / I Shall Not Be Moved / I'm Alabammy Bound / I'm a Rambling Man / Wreck of the Old '97 / Frankie and Johnny.

Tanya DONELLY (see also BELLY)

US, female vocalist / guitarist (1 Album: 1 Week, 2 Singles: 2 Weeks)

30 Aug 97 **PRETTY DEEP** *4AD BAD 7007CD*....................**55** 1
20 Sep 97 **LOVESONGS FOR UNDERDOGS** *4AD CAD 7008CD*....................**36** 1
6 Dec 97 **THE BRIGHT LIGHT** *4AD BAD 7012CD*....................**64** 1

The DONNAS *US, female vocal / instrumental group (4 Singles: 5 Weeks)*

12 Apr 03 **TAKE IT OFF** *Atlantic AT 0148CD*....................**38** 2
5 Jul 03 **WHO INVITED YOU?** *Atlantic AT 0156CD*....................**61** 1
23 Oct 04 **FALL BEHIND ME** *Atlantic AT 0186CD*....................**55** 1
19 Mar 05 **I DON'T WANT TO KNOW (IF YOU DON'T WANT ME)** *Atlantic AT 0197CD*....................**55** 1

Ral DONNER *US, male vocalist, b. 10 Feb 1943, d. 6 Apr 1984*

21 Sep 61 **YOU DON'T KNOW WHAT YOU'VE GOT (UNTIL YOU LOSE IT)** *Parlophone R 4820*....................**25** 10

DONOVAN (418 Top 500)

Acclaimed Celtic singer / songwriter, b. Donovan Leitch, 10 May 1946, Glasgow. Initially dubbed the British version of Bob Dylan, he enjoyed massive fame on both sides of the Atlantic in the 'flower power' years of the late 1960s (7 Albums: 73 Weeks, 11 Singles: 100 Weeks)

25 Mar 65 ● **CATCH THE WIND** *Pye 7N 15801*....................**4** 13
3 Jun 65 ● **COLOURS** *Pye 7N 15866*....................**4** 12
5 Jun 65 ● **WHAT'S BIN DID AND WHAT'S BIN HID** *Pye NPL 18117*....................**3** 16
6 Nov 65 **FAIRY TALE** *Pye NPL 18128*....................**20** 2
11 Nov 65 **TURQUOISE** *Pye 7N 15984*....................**30** 6
8 Dec 66 ● **SUNSHINE SUPERMAN** *Pye 7N 17241* ▲ $....................**2** 11
9 Feb 67 ● **MELLOW YELLOW** *Pye 7N 17267* $....................**8** 8
8 Jul 67 **SUNSHINE SUPERMAN** *Pye NPL 18181*....................**25** 7
14 Oct 67 ● **UNIVERSAL SOLDIER** *Marble Arch MAL 718*....................**5** 18
25 Oct 67 ● **THERE IS A MOUNTAIN** *Pye 7N 17403*....................**8** 11
21 Feb 68 ● **JENNIFER JUNIPER** *Pye 7N 17457*....................**5** 11
11 May 68 **A GIFT FROM A FLOWER TO A GARDEN** *Pye NSPL 20000*.......**13** 14
29 May 68 ● **HURDY GURDY MAN** *Pye 7N 17537*....................**4** 10
4 Dec 68 **ATLANTIS** *Pye 7N 17660*....................**23** 8
9 Jul 69 **GOO GOO BARABAJAGAL (LOVE IS HOT)** *Pye 7N 17778* [1] ...**12** 9
12 Sep 70 **OPEN ROAD** *Dawn DNLS 3009*....................**30** 4
24 Mar 73 **COSMIC WHEELS** *Epic EPC 65450*....................**15** 12
1 Dec 90 **JENNIFER JUNIPER** *Fontana SYP 1* [2] **68** 1

[1] Donovan with the Jeff Beck Group [2] Singing Corner meets Donovan

Jason DONOVAN (283 Top 500)

The top teen idol of the late 1980s, b. 1 Jun 1968, Melbourne. The Australian actor turned singer had an impressive array of UK hits after leaving TV soap Neighbours. His debut LP, Ten Good Reasons, was the UK's top-selling album of 1989 (4 Albums: 99 Weeks, 17 Singles: 137 Weeks)

10 Sep 88 ● **NOTHING CAN DIVIDE US** *PWL PWL 17*....................**5** 12
10 Dec 88 ★ **ESPECIALLY FOR YOU** *PWL PWL 24* [1] **1** 14
4 Mar 89 ★ **TOO MANY BROKEN HEARTS** *PWL PWL 32*....................**1** 13
13 May 89 ★ **TEN GOOD REASONS** *PWL HF 7*....................**1** 54
10 Jun 89 ★ **SEALED WITH A KISS** *PWL PWL 39* ■....................**1** 10
9 Sep 89 ● **EVERY DAY (I LOVE YOU MORE)** *PWL PWL 43*....................**2** 9
9 Dec 89 ● **WHEN YOU COME BACK TO ME** *PWL PWL 46*....................**2** 11
7 Apr 90 ● **HANG ON TO YOUR LOVE** *PWL PWL 51*....................**8** 7
9 Jun 90 ● **BETWEEN THE LINES** *PWL HF 14*....................**2** 26
30 Jun 90 **ANOTHER NIGHT** *PWL PWL 58*....................**18** 5
1 Sep 90 ● **RHYTHM OF THE RAIN** *PWL PWL 60*....................**9** 6
27 Oct 90 **I'M DOING FINE** *PWL PWL 69*....................**22** 6
18 May 91 **RSVP** *PWL PWL 80*....................**17** 5
22 Jun 91 ★ **ANY DREAM WILL DO** *Really Useful RUR 7*....................**1** 12
24 Aug 91 ● **HAPPY TOGETHER** *PWL PWL 203*....................**10** 6
28 Sep 91 ● **GREATEST HITS** *PWL HF 20*....................**9** 17
7 Dec 91 **JOSEPH MEGA REMIX** *Really Useful RUR 9* [2] **13** 8
18 Jul 92 **MISSION OF LOVE** *Polydor PO 222*....................**26** 4
28 Nov 92 **AS TIME GOES BY** *Polydor PO 245*....................**26** 6
7 Aug 93 **ALL AROUND THE WORLD** *Polydor PZCD 278*....................**41** 3
11 Sep 93 **ALL AROUND THE WORLD** *Polydor 8477452*....................**27** 2

[1] Kylie Minogue and Jason Donovan [2] Jason Donovan and Original London Cast featuring Linzi Hately, David Easter and Johnny Amobi

The DOOBIE BROTHERS (see also Michael McDONALD) *US, male vocal / instrumental group (6 Albums: 33 Weeks, 8 Singles: 45 Weeks)*

9 Mar 74 **LISTEN TO THE MUSIC** *Warner Bros. K 16208*....................**29** 7
30 Mar 74 **WHAT WERE ONCE VICES ARE NOW HABITS** *Warner Bros. K 56206*....................**19** 10
17 May 75 **STAMPEDE** *Warner Bros. K 56094*....................**14** 11
7 Jun 75 **TAKE ME IN YOUR ARMS (ROCK ME A LITTLE WHILE)** *Warner Bros. K 16559*....................**29** 5
10 Apr 76 **TAKIN' IT TO THE STREETS** *Warner Bros. K 56196*....................**42** 2
19 Sep 77 **LIVING ON THE FAULT LINE** *Warner Bros. K 56383*....................**25** 5
17 Feb 79 **WHAT A FOOL BELIEVES (re)** *Warner Bros. K 17314* ▲ $......**31** 11
14 Jul 79 **MINUTE BY MINUTE** *Warner Bros. K 17411*....................**47** 4
11 Oct 80 **ONE STEP CLOSER** *Warner Bros. K 56824*....................**53** 2
24 Jan 87 **WHAT A FOOL BELIEVES** (re-issue) *Warner Bros. W 8451* [1] . **57** 3
29 Jul 89 **THE DOCTOR** *Capitol CL 536*....................**73** 2
27 Nov 93 ● **LONG TRAIN RUNNIN'** *Warner Bros. W 0217CD*....................**7** 10
14 May 94 **LISTEN TO THE MUSIC** (re-mix) *Warner Bros. W 0228CD*........**37** 3
10 Jul 04 **GREATEST HITS** *WSM 8122765112*....................**45** 3

[1] The Doobie Brothers featuring Michael McDonald

9 / 11 July 1964	16 / 18 July 1964	23 / 25 July 1964	30 July / 1 August 1964
THE HOUSE OF THE RISING SUN The Animals	IT'S ALL OVER NOW The Rolling Stones	A HARD DAY'S NIGHT The Beatles	A HARD DAY'S NIGHT The Beatles
THE ROLLING STONES The Rolling Stones	THE ROLLING STONES The Rolling Stones	A HARD DAY'S NIGHT The Beatles	A HARD DAY'S NIGHT The Beatles

KEY
UK No.1 ★ UK Top 10 ● Still on chart + UK entry at No.1 ■
US No.1 ▲ UK million seller £ US million seller $
Singles re-entries are listed as (re), (2re), (3re)... which signifies that the hit re-entered the chart once, twice or three times...
Peak Position / Weeks

DOOLALLY (see also SHANKS & BIGFOOT) *UK, male production duo – Stephen Meade and Daniel Langsman (2 Singles: 16 Weeks)*

14 Nov 98 **STRAIGHT FROM THE HEART (re)** *Locked On LOX 104CD* ... **20** 10
7 Aug 99 ● **STRAIGHT FROM THE HEART** (re-issue) *Chocolate Boy / Locked On LOX 112CD* ... **9** 6

The DOOLEYS *UK, male vocal / instrumental group (3 Albums: 27 Weeks, 10 Singles: 83 Weeks)*

13 Aug 77 **THINK I'M GONNA FALL IN LOVE WITH YOU** *GTO GT 95* ... **13** 10
12 Nov 77 ● **LOVE OF MY LIFE** *GTO GT 110* ... **9** 11
13 May 78 **DON'T TAKE IT LYIN' DOWN** *GTO GT 220* ... **60** 3
2 Sep 78 **A ROSE HAS TO DIE** *GTO GT 229* ... **11** 11
10 Feb 79 **HONEY I'M LOST** *GTO GT 242* ... **24** 9
16 Jun 79 ● **WANTED** *GTO GT 249* ... **3** 14
30 Jun 79 ● THE BEST OF THE DOOLEYS *GTO GTTV 038* ... 6 21
22 Sep 79 ● **THE CHOSEN FEW** *GTO GT 258* ... **7** 11
3 Nov 79 THE CHOSEN FEW *GTO GTLP 040* ... 56 4
8 Mar 80 **LOVE PATROL** *GTO GT 260* ... **29** 7
6 Sep 80 **BODY LANGUAGE** *GTO GT 276* ... **46** 4
25 Oct 80 FULL HOUSE *GTO GTTV 050* ... 54 2
10 Oct 81 **AND I WISH** *GTO GT 300* ... **52** 3

Val DOONICAN (184 Top 500)

Popular balladeer and TV host, b. Michael Doonican, 3 Feb 1928, Waterford, Ireland. This relaxed crooner, who was known for his rocking chair and multicoloured jumpers, had five successive Top 10 albums in the Swinging Sixties (11 Albums: 170 Weeks, 14 Singles: 143 Weeks)

15 Oct 64 ● **WALK TALL** *Decca F 11982* ... **3** 21
12 Dec 64 ● THE LUCKY 13 SHADES OF VAL DOONICAN *Decca LK 4648* ... 2 27
21 Jan 65 ● **THE SPECIAL YEARS (re)** *Decca F 12049* ... **7** 13
8 Apr 65 **I'M GONNA GET THERE SOMEHOW** *Decca F 12118* ... **25** 5
17 Mar 66 ● **ELUSIVE BUTTERFLY** *Decca F 12358* ... **5** 12
3 Nov 66 ● **WHAT WOULD I BE** *Decca F 12505* ... **2** 17
3 Dec 66 ● GENTLE SHADES OF VAL DOONICAN *Decca LK 4831* ... 5 52
23 Feb 67 **MEMORIES ARE MADE OF THIS** *Decca F 12566* ... **11** 12
25 May 67 **TWO STREETS** *Decca F 12608* ... **39** 4
18 Oct 67 ● **IF THE WHOLE WORLD STOPPED LOVIN'** *Pye 7N 17396* ... **3** 19
2 Dec 67 ★ VAL DOONICAN ROCKS BUT GENTLY *Pye NSPL 18204* ... 1 23
21 Feb 68 **YOU'RE THE ONLY ONE** *Pye 7N 17465* ... **37** 4
12 Jun 68 **NOW** *Pye 7N 17534* ... **43** 2
23 Oct 68 **IF I KNEW THEN WHAT I KNOW NOW** *Pye 7N 17616* ... **14** 13
30 Nov 68 ● VAL *Pye NSPL 18236* ... 6 11
23 Apr 69 **RING OF BRIGHT WATER** *Pye 7N 17713* ... **48** 1
14 Jun 69 ● THE WORLD OF VAL DOONICAN *Decca SPA 3* ... 2 31
13 Dec 69 SOUNDS GENTLE *Pye NSPL 18321* ... 22 9
19 Dec 70 THE MAGIC OF VAL DOONICAN *Philips 6642 003* ... 34 3
27 Nov 71 THIS IS VAL DOONICAN *Philips 6382 017* ... 40 1
4 Dec 71 **MORNING** *Philips 6006 177* ... **12** 13
10 Mar 73 **HEAVEN IS MY WOMAN'S LOVE (re)** *Philips 6028 031* ... **34** 7
22 Feb 75 I LOVE COUNTRY MUSIC *Philips 9299261* ... 37 2
21 May 77 SOME OF MY BEST FRIENDS ARE SONGS *Philips 6641 607* ... 29 5
24 Mar 90 SONGS FROM MY SKETCH BOOK *Parkfield PMLP 5014* ... 33 6

DOOP

Holland, male instrumental duo – Ferry Ridderhof and Peter Garnefski

12 Mar 94 ★ **DOOP** *Citybeat CBE 774CD* ... **1** 12

The DOORS (477 Top 500) *Controversial, uncompromising rock band. Formed 1965 in Los Angeles, 'Lizard King' Jim Morrison (v), b. 1943, d. 1971, Ray Manzarek (k), Robby Krieger (g) and John Densmore (d) were 1993 Rock and Roll Hall of Fame inductees but did not score a UK Top 10 single until 1991 and album until 2000 (13 Albums: 113 Weeks, 8 Singles: 42 Weeks)*

16 Aug 67 **LIGHT MY FIRE** *Elektra EKSN 45014* ▲ $ ... **49** 1
28 Aug 68 **HELLO, I LOVE YOU** *Elektra EKSN 45037* ▲ $ ... **15** 12
28 Sep 68 WAITING FOR THE SUN *Elektra EKS 74024* ▲ ... 16 10
11 Apr 70 MORRISON HOTEL *Elektra EKS 75007* ... 12 8
26 Sep 70 ABSOLUTELY LIVE *Elektra 2665 002* ... 69 1
31 Jul 71 L.A. WOMAN *Elektra K 42090* ... 28 4
16 Oct 71 **RIDERS ON THE STORM (re)** *Elektra K 12021* ... **22** 11
1 Apr 72 WEIRD SCENES INSIDE THE GOLD MINE *Elektra K 62009* ... 50 1
20 Mar 76 **RIDERS ON THE STORM** (re-issue) *Elektra K 12203* ... **33** 5
3 Feb 79 **HELLO I LOVE YOU** (re-issue) *Elektra K 12215* ... **71** 2
29 Oct 83 ALIVE SHE CRIED *Elektra 9602691* ... 36 5
4 Jul 87 LIVE AT THE HOLLYWOOD BOWL *Elektra EKT 40* ... 51 3
6 Apr 91 THE DOORS (FILM SOUNDTRACK) *Elektra EKT 85* ... 11 17
20 Apr 91 THE BEST OF THE DOORS *Elektra EKT 21* ... 17 18
20 Apr 91 THE DOORS *Elektra K 42012* ... 43 13
27 Apr 91 **BREAK ON THROUGH** *Elektra EKR 121* ... **64** 2
1 Jun 91 IN CONCERT *Elektra EKT 88* ... 24 5
1 Jun 91 ● **LIGHT MY FIRE** (re-issue) *Elektra EKR 125* ... **7** 8
10 Aug 91 **RIDERS ON THE STORM** (2nd re-issue) *Elektra EKR 131* ... **68** 1
21 Mar 98 THE BEST OF THE DOORS (re-issue) *Elektra K 9603452* ... 37 8
23 Sep 00 ● THE BEST OF THE DOORS *Elektra 7559624682* ... 9 20

The Best of The Doors (2000) has a different track listing to the 1991 album of the same name.

DOPE SMUGGLAZ

UK, male DJ / production trio (2 Singles: 5 Weeks)

5 Dec 98 **THE WORD** *Mushroom PERFCDS 1* ... **62** 1
7 Aug 99 **DOUBLE DOUBLE DUTCH** *Perfecto PERF 2CDS* ... **15** 4

Charlie DORE *UK, female vocalist*

17 Nov 79 **PILOT OF THE AIRWAVES** *Island WIP 6526* ... **66** 2

Andrea DORIA *Italy, male producer / instrumentalist*

26 Apr 03 **BUCCI BAG** *Southern Fried ECB 38CDS* ... **57** 1

DOROTHY (see also The CANDY GIRLS; CLERGY; HI-GATE; Paul MASTERSON presents SUSHI; SLEAZESISTERS; YOMANDA)

UK, male producer / instrumentalist – Paul Masterson

9 Dec 95 **WHAT'S THAT TUNE (DOO DOO DOO DOO DOO-DOO-DOO-DOO-DOO-DOO)** *RCA 74321330912* ... **31** 5

Lee DORSEY *US, male vocalist – Irving Dorsey, b. 24 Dec 1924, d. 1 Dec 1986 (1 Album: 3 Weeks, 4 Singles: 36 Weeks)*

3 Feb 66 **GET OUT OF MY LIFE, WOMAN** *Stateside SS 485* ... **22** 7
5 May 66 **CONFUSION** *Stateside SS 506* ... **38** 6
11 Aug 66 ● **WORKING IN THE COALMINE** *Stateside SS 528* ... **8** 11
27 Oct 66 ● **HOLY COW** *Stateside SS 552* ... **6** 12
17 Dec 66 NEW LEE DORSEY *Stateside SSL 10192* ... 34 3

Marc DORSEY *US, male vocalist*

19 Jun 99 **IF YOU REALLY WANNA KNOW** *Jive 0522592* ... **58** 1

Tommy DORSEY ORCHESTRA starring Warren COVINGTON

US, orchestra – leader Tommy Dorsey, b. 19 Nov 1905, d. 26 Nov 1956, and male trombonist

17 Oct 58 ● **TEA FOR TWO CHA CHA** *Brunswick 05757* $ ... **3** 19

DOUBLE *Switzerland, male vocal / instrumental duo – Kurt Maloo and Felix Haug (1 Album: 4 Weeks, 2 Singles: 10 Weeks)*

25 Jan 86 ● **THE CAPTAIN OF HER HEART** *Polydor POSP 779* ... **8** 9
8 Mar 86 BLUE *Polydor POLD 5187* ... 69 4
5 Dec 87 **DEVIL'S BALL** *Polydor POSP 888* ... **71** 1

DOUBLE DEE

Italy, male producer – Davide Domenella (4 Singles: 5 Weeks)

1 Dec 90 **FOUND LOVE** *Epic 6563766* 1 ... **63** 2

6 / 8 August 1964	13 / 15 August 1964	20 / 22 August 1964	27 / 29 August 1964
UK No.1 SINGLES			
A HARD DAY'S NIGHT – The Beatles	DO WAH DIDDY DIDDY – Manfred Mann	DO WAH DIDDY DIDDY – Manfred Mann	HAVE I THE RIGHT – The Honeycombs
UK No.1 ALBUMS			
A HARD DAY'S NIGHT – The Beatles	A HARD DAY'S NIGHT – The Beatles	A HARD DAY'S NIGHT – The Beatles	A HARD DAY'S NIGHT – The Beatles

25 Nov 95 **FOUND LOVE** (re-mix) *Sony S3 DANUCD 1* [1] **33** 2
27 Sep 03 **SHINING** *Positiva CDTIV 194*....**58** 1

[1] Double Dee featuring Dany

DOUBLE 99 (see also COHEN vs DELUXE; Tim DELUXE; RIP PRODUCTIONS; SAFFRON HILL featuring Ben ONONO) *UK, male instrumental / production duo – Tim Liken and Omar Adimora (2 Singles: 9 Weeks)*

31 May 97 **RIPGROOVE** *Satellite 74321485132*....**31** 3
1 Nov 97 **RIPGROOVE** (re-mix) *Satellite 74321529322*....**14** 6

DOUBLE SIX *UK, male vocal / instrumental group (2 Singles: 2 Weeks)*

19 Sep 98 **REAL GOOD** *Multiply CDMULTY 39*....**66** 1
12 Jun 99 **BREAKDOWN** *Multiply CDMULTY 50*....**59** 1

DOUBLE TROUBLE (see also AIRHEADZ) *UK, male instrumental / production duo – Leigh Guest and Michael Menson (1 Album: 1 Week, 5 Singles: 35 Weeks)*

27 May 89 **JUST KEEP ROCKIN'** *Desire WANT 9* [1] **11** 12
7 Oct 89 ● **STREET TUFF** *Desire WANT 18* [2] **3** 14
12 May 90 **TALK BACK** *Desire WANT 27* [3] **71** 1
30 Jun 90 **LOVE DON'T LIVE HERE ANYMORE** *Desire WANT 32* [4] **21** 6
4 Aug 90 **AS ONE** *Desire LULP 6*....**73** 1
15 Jun 91 **RUB-A-DUB** *Desire WANT 41*....**66** 2

[1] Double Trouble and the Rebel MC [2] Rebel MC and Double Trouble [3] With vocals by Janette Sewell [4] Double Trouble featuring Janette Sewell and Carl Brown

DOUBLE YOU? *Italy, male vocalist – Willie Morales*

2 May 92 **PLEASE DON'T GO** *ZYX ZYX 67487*....**41** 3

Rob DOUGAN (see also OUR TRIBE / ONE TRIBE; SPHINX) *Australia, male vocalist / producer (2 Singles: 4 Weeks)*

4 Apr 98 **FURIOUS ANGELS** *Cheeky CHEKCD 025*....**62** 1
6 Jul 02 **CLUBBED TO DEATH** *Cheeky / Arista 74321941702*....**24** 3

Carl DOUGLAS *Jamaica, male vocalist (4 Singles: 39 Weeks)*

17 Aug 74 ★ **KUNG FU FIGHTING** *Pye 7N 45377* ▲ $....**1** 13
30 Nov 74 **DANCE THE KUNG FU** *Pye 7N 45418*....**35** 5
3 Dec 77 **RUN BACK** *Pye 7N 46018*....**25** 10
23 May 98 ● **KUNG FU FIGHTING** (re-recording) *All Around the World CDGLOBE 173* [1] **8** 11

[1] Bus Stop featuring Carl Douglas

Carol DOUGLAS *US, female vocalist*

22 Jul 78 **NIGHT FEVER** *Gull GULS 61*....**66** 4

Craig DOUGLAS *UK, male vocalist – Terence Perkins (1 Album: 2 Weeks, 11 Singles: 113 Weeks)*

12 Jun 59 **A TEENAGER IN LOVE** *Top Rank JAR 133*....**13** 11
7 Aug 59 ★ **ONLY SIXTEEN** *Top Rank JAR 159*....**1** 15
22 Jan 60 ● **PRETTY BLUE EYES** *Top Rank JAR 268*....**4** 15
28 Apr 60 ● **THE HEART OF A TEENAGE GIRL** *Top Rank JAR 340*....**10** 9
6 Aug 60 **CRAIG DOUGLAS** *Top Rank BUY 049*....**17** 2
11 Aug 60 **OH! WHAT A DAY** *Top Rank JAR 406*....**43** 1
20 Apr 61 ● **A HUNDRED POUNDS OF CLAY** *Top Rank JAR 556*....**9** 9
29 Jun 61 ● **TIME** *Top Rank JAR 569*....**9** 14
22 Mar 62 ● **WHEN MY LITTLE GIRL IS SMILING** *Top Rank JAR 610*....**9** 13
28 Jun 62 ● **OUR FAVOURITE MELODIES** *Columbia DB 4854*....**9** 10
18 Oct 62 **OH, LONESOME ME** *Decca F 11523*....**15** 12
28 Feb 63 **TOWN CRIER** *Decca F 11575*....**36** 4

DOVE *Ireland, male / female vocal group*

11 Sep 99 **DON'T DREAM** *ZTT 135CD*....**37** 2

DOVES *UK, male vocal (Jimi Goodwin) / instrumental group (4 Albums: 54 Weeks, 10 Singles: 22 Weeks)*

14 Aug 99 **HERE IT COMES** *Casino CHIP 003CD*....**73** 1
1 Apr 00 **THE CEDAR ROOM** *Heavenly HVN 95CD*....**33** 2
15 Apr 00 **LOST SOULS** *Heavenly HVNLP 26CD*....**16** 16
10 Jun 00 **CATCH THE SUN** *Heavenly HVN 96CD*....**32** 2
11 Nov 00 **THE MAN WHO TOLD EVERYTHING** *Heavenly HVN 98CD*....**32** 2
27 Apr 02 ● **THERE GOES THE FEAR** *Heavenly HVN 111CD*....**3** 3
11 May 02 ★ **THE LAST BROADCAST** *Heavenly HVNLP 35CD* ■....**1** 23
3 Aug 02 **POUNDING** *Heavenly HVN 116CD*....**21** 3
26 Oct 02 **CAUGHT BY THE RIVER** *Heavenly HVN 126CDS*....**29** 2
11 Oct 03 **LOST SIDES** *Heavenly HVNLP 46CDX*....**50** 1
19 Feb 05 ● **BLACK AND WHITE TOWN** *Heavenly HVN 145CDS*....**6** 4
5 Mar 05 ★ **SOME CITIES** *Heavenly HVNLP 50CDX* ■....**1** 14
21 May 05 **SNOWDEN** *Heavenly HVN 150CDS*....**17** 2
24 Sep 05 **SKY STARTS FALLING** *Heavenly HVN 152CD*....**45** 1

The DOWLANDS *UK, male vocal group*

9 Jan 64 **ALL MY LOVING** *Oriole CB 1897*....**33** 7

DOWN *US, male vocal / instrumental group*

30 Sep 95 **NOLA** *Atlantic 7559618302*....**68** 1

Robert DOWNEY Jr *US, male actor / vocalist*

30 Jan 93 **SMILE** *Epic 6589052*....**68** 1
7 May 05 **THE FUTURIST** *Sony Classical SK 92654*....**56** 1

Don DOWNING *US, male vocalist*

10 Nov 73 **LONELY DAYS, LONELY NIGHTS** *People PEO 102*....**32** 10

Will DOWNING *US, male vocalist (3 Albums: 28 Weeks, 7 Singles: 35 Weeks)*

26 Mar 88 **WILL DOWNING** *Fourth & Broadway BRLP 518*....**20** 23
2 Apr 88 **A LOVE SUPREME** *Fourth & Broadway BRW 90*....**14** 10
25 Jun 88 **IN MY DREAMS** *Fourth & Broadway BRW 104*....**34** 6
1 Oct 88 **FREE** *Fourth & Broadway BRW 112*....**58** 5
21 Jan 89 **WHERE IS THE LOVE** *Fourth & Broadway BRW 122* [1] **19** 7
28 Oct 89 **TEST OF TIME** *Fourth & Broadway BRW 146*....**67** 2
18 Nov 89 **COME TOGETHER AS ONE** *Fourth & Broadway BRLP 538*....**36** 2
24 Feb 90 **COME TOGETHER AS ONE** *Fourth & Broadway BRW 159*....**48** 4
6 Apr 91 **A DREAM FULFILLED** *Fourth & Broadway BRLP 565*....**43** 3
18 Sep 93 **THERE'S NO LIVING WITHOUT YOU** *Fourth & Broadway BRCD 278*....**67** 1

[1] Mica Paris and Will Downing

Jason DOWNS featuring MILK *US, male vocalist and male rapper (1 Album: 1 Week, 2 Singles: 6 Weeks)*

12 May 01 **WHITE BOY WITH A FEATHER** *Pepper 9230412*....**19** 5
14 Jul 01 **CATS IN THE CRADLE** *Pepper 9230442*....**65** 1
28 Jul 01 **WHITE BOY WITH A FEATHER** *Pepper 9230452*....**64** 1

DRAGONHEART *UK, female vocal group*

27 Nov 04 **VIDEO KILLED THE RADIO STAR** *Lipstick 6150304*....**74** 1

Charlie DRAKE *UK, male comedian / vocalist – Charles Sprigall (5 Singles: 37 Weeks)*

8 Aug 58 ● **SPLISH SPLASH** *Parlophone R 4461*....**7** 11
24 Oct 58 **VOLARE** *Parlophone R 4478*....**28** 2
27 Oct 60 **MR CUSTER** *Parlophone R 4701*....**12** 12
5 Oct 61 **MY BOOMERANG WON'T COME BACK** *Parlophone R 4824*....**14** 11
1 Jan 72 **PUCKWUDGIE** *Columbia DB 8829*....**47** 1

Nick DRAKE *UK, male vocalist, b. 19 Jun 1948, d. 25 Nov 1974 (1 Album: 2 Weeks, 2 Singles: 3 Weeks)*

29 May 04 **MAGIC** *Island CID 854*....**32** 2

3 / 5 September 1964	10 / 12 September 1964	17 / 19 September 1964	24 / 26 September 1964
HAVE I THE RIGHT The Honeycombs	YOU REALLY GOT ME The Kinks	YOU REALLY GOT ME The Kinks	I'M INTO SOMETHING GOOD Herman's Hermits
A HARD DAY'S NIGHT The Beatles	A HARD DAY'S NIGHT The Beatles	A HARD DAY'S NIGHT The Beatles	A HARD DAY'S NIGHT The Beatles

KEY
UK No.1 ★ UK Top 10 ● Still on chart + UK entry at No.1 ■ US No.1 ▲ UK million seller £ US million seller $
Singles re-entries are listed as (re), (2re), (3re)... which signifies that the hit re-entered the chart once, twice or three times...
Peak Position / Weeks

5 Jun 04	MADE TO LOVE MAGIC *Island CID 8141*	27	2
25 Sep 04	RIVER MAN *Island CID 871*	48	1

DRAMATIS *UK, male vocal / instrumental group (2 Singles: 8 Weeks)*

5 Dec 81	LOVE NEEDS NO DISGUISE *Beggars Banquet BEG 68* [1]	33	7
13 Nov 82	I CAN SEE HER NOW *Rocket XPRES 83*	57	1

[1] Gary Numan and Dramatis

Rusty DRAPER
US, male vocalist – Farrell H Draper, b. 25 Jan 1923, d. 29 Mar 2003

11 Aug 60	MULE SKINNER BLUES *Mercury AMT 1101*	39	4

DREAD ZEPPELIN
US, male vocal / instrumental group (1 Album: 2 Weeks, 2 Singles: 3 Weeks)

11 Aug 90	UN-LED-ED *IRS EIRSA 1042*	71	2
1 Dec 90	YOUR TIME IS GONNA COME *IRS DREAD 1*	59	1
13 Jul 91	STAIRWAY TO HEAVEN *IRS DREAD 2*	62	2

DREADZONE
UK, male instrumental group (2 Albums: 5 Weeks, 7 Singles: 15 Weeks)

6 May 95	ZION YOUTH *Virgin VSCDG 1537*	49	2
10 Jun 95	SECOND LIGHT *Virgin CDV 2778*	37	4
29 Jul 95	CAPTAIN DREAD *Virgin VSCDG 1541*	49	2
23 Sep 95	MAXIMUM (EP) *Virgin VSCDT 1555*	56	2
6 Jan 96	LITTLE BRITAIN *Virgin VSCDG 1565*	20	6
30 Mar 96	LIFE LOVE AND UNITY *Virgin VSCDT 1583*	56	1
10 May 97	EARTH ANGEL *Virgin VSCDT 1593*	51	1
26 Jul 97	MOVING ON *Virgin VSCDT 1635*	58	1
9 Aug 97	BIOLOGICAL RADIO *Virgin CDV 2808*	45	1

Tracks on Maximum (EP): Maximum / Fight the Power 95 / One Way.

DREAM *US, female vocal group*

17 Mar 01	HE LOVES U NOT *Puff Daddy / Arista 74321823542*	17	7

DREAM ACADEMY *UK, male / female vocal / instrumental group (1 Album: 2 Weeks, 2 Singles: 10 Weeks)*

30 Mar 85	LIFE IN A NORTHERN TOWN *Blanco Y Negro NEG 10*	15	8
14 Sep 85	THE LOVE PARADE *Blanco Y Negro NEG 16*	68	2
12 Oct 85	THE DREAM ACADEMY *Blanco Y Negro BYN 6*	58	2

DREAM FREQUENCY (see also BEAT RENEGADES; QUAKE featuring Marcia RAE; RED) *UK, male producer – Ian Bland (5 Singles: 12 Weeks)*

12 Jan 91	LOVE PEACE AND HARMONY *Citybeat CBE 756*	71	2
25 Jan 92	FEEL SO REAL *Citybeat CBE 763* [1]	23	5
25 Apr 92	TAKE ME *Citybeat CBE 768*	39	3
21 May 94	GOOD TIMES / THE DREAM *Citybeat CBE 773CD*	67	1
10 Sep 94	YOU MAKE ME FEEL MIGHTY REAL *Citybeat CBE 775CD*	65	1

[1] Dream Frequency featuring Debbie Sharp

DREAM THEATER
US, male vocal / instrumental group (2 Albums: 2 Weeks)

15 Oct 94	AWAKE *East West 7567901262*	65	1
18 Jun 05	OCTAVARIUM *Atlantic 7567837932*	72	1

DREAM WARRIORS
Canada, male rap group (1 Album: 7 Weeks, 3 Singles: 19 Weeks)

14 Jul 90	WASH YOUR FACE IN MY SINK *Fourth & Broadway BRW 183*	16	8
24 Nov 90	MY DEFINITION OF A BOOMBASTIC JAZZ STYLE *Fourth & Broadway BRW 197*	13	8
16 Feb 91	AND NOW THE LEGACY BEGINS *Fourth & Broadway BRLP 560*	18	7
2 Mar 91	LUDI *Fourth & Broadway BRW 206*	39	3

DREAMCATCHER *UK, male / female production / vocal trio*

12 Jan 02	I DON'T WANNA LOSE MY WAY *Positiva CDTIVS 157*	14	4

DREAMHOUSE *UK, male vocal / instrumental group*

3 Jun 95	STAY *Chase CDPALACE 1*	62	2

DREAMKEEPER *UK, female vocal duo – Nines and Aleesha*

9 Aug 97	SPIRIT OF RELAXATION *Flute SPIRICD 1*	71	1

The DREAMWEAVERS *US, male / female vocal (Wade Bluff) group*

10 Feb 56 ★	IT'S ALMOST TOMORROW *Brunswick 05515*	1	18

DREEM TEEM *UK, male DJ / production trio (3 Singles: 14 Weeks)*

13 Dec 97	THE THEME *4 Liberty 74321542032*	34	4
6 Nov 99	BUDDY X 99 *4 Liberty LIBTCD 33* [1]	15	5
15 Dec 01	IT AIN'T ENOUGH *ffrr / Public Demand FCD 401* [2]	20	5

[1] Dreem Teem vs Neneh Cherry [2] Dreem Teem vs Artful Dodger featuring MZ May and MC Alistair

Eddie DRENNON and B.B.S. UNLIMITED
US, male vocal / instrumental group

28 Feb 76	LET'S DO THE LATIN HUSTLE *Pye International 7N 25702*	20	6

Alan DREW *UK, male vocalist*

26 Sep 63	ALWAYS THE LONELY ONE *Columbia DB 7090*	48	2

The DRIFTERS (216 Top 500) *Ever-changing, ever-popular US group, founded in 1953 by Clyde McPhatter (b. 1932, d. 1972) and still active today, with erstwhile members including Ben E King, Johnny Moore (b. 1934, d. 1998) and Rudy Lewis (b. 1936, d. 1964). Inducted into the Rock and Roll Hall of Fame in 1988 (9 Albums: 109 Weeks, 21 Singles: 176 Weeks)*

8 Jan 60	DANCE WITH ME (re) *London HLE 8988*	17	5
3 Nov 60 ●	SAVE THE LAST DANCE FOR ME *London HLK 9201* ▲ $	2	18
16 Mar 61	I COUNT THE TEARS *London HLK 9287*	28	6
5 Apr 62	WHEN MY LITTLE GIRL IS SMILING *London HLK 9522*	31	3
10 Oct 63	I'LL TAKE YOU HOME *London HLK 9785*	37	5
24 Sep 64	UNDER THE BOARDWALK *Atlantic AT 4001*	45	4
8 Apr 65	AT THE CLUB *Atlantic AT 4019*	35	7
29 Apr 65	COME ON OVER TO MY PLACE *Atlantic AT 4023*	40	5
2 Feb 67	BABY WHAT I MEAN *Atlantic 584 065*	49	1
18 May 68	GOLDEN HITS *Atlantic 588103*	27	7
25 Mar 72 ●	AT THE CLUB (re-issue) / SATURDAY NIGHT AT THE MOVIES (re) (re-issue) *Atlantic K 10148*	3	20
10 Jun 72	GOLDEN HITS (re-issue) *Atlantic K 40018*	26	8
26 Aug 72 ●	COME ON OVER TO MY PLACE (re-issue) *Atlantic K 10216*	9	11
4 Aug 73 ●	LIKE SISTER AND BROTHER *Bell 1313*	7	12
15 Jun 74 ●	KISSIN' IN THE BACK ROW OF THE MOVIES *Bell 1358*	2	13
12 Oct 74 ●	DOWN ON THE BEACH TONIGHT *Bell 1381*	7	9
8 Feb 75	LOVE GAMES *Bell 1396*	33	6
6 Sep 75 ●	THERE GOES MY FIRST LOVE *Bell 1433*	3	12
8 Nov 75 ●	24 ORIGINAL HITS *Atlantic K 60106*	2	34
29 Nov 75 ●	CAN I TAKE YOU HOME LITTLE GIRL *Bell 1462*	10	10
13 Dec 75	LOVE GAMES *Bell BELLS 246*	51	1
13 Mar 76	HELLO HAPPINESS *Bell 1469*	12	8
11 Sep 76	EVERY NITE'S A SATURDAY NIGHT WITH YOU *Bell 1491*	29	7
18 Dec 76 ●	YOU'RE MORE THAN A NUMBER IN MY LITTLE RED BOOK *Arista 78*	5	12
14 Apr 79	SAVE THE LAST DANCE FOR ME (re-issue) / WHEN MY LITTLE GIRL IS SMILING (re-issue) *Lightning LIG 9014*	69	2
18 Oct 86	THE VERY BEST OF THE DRIFTERS *Telstar STAR 2280*	24	15
14 Mar 87	STAND BY ME (THE ULTIMATE COLLECTION) *Atlantic WX 90* [1]	14	8

1 / 3 October 1964	8 / 10 October 1964	15 / 17 October 1964	22 / 24 October 1964
UK No.1 SINGLES			
I'M INTO SOMETHING GOOD Herman's Hermits	OH, PRETTY WOMAN Roy Orbison	OH, PRETTY WOMAN Roy Orbison	(THERE'S) ALWAYS SOMETHING THERE TO REMIND ME Sandie Shaw
UK No.1 ALBUMS			
A HARD DAY'S NIGHT The Beatles	A HARD DAY'S NIGHT The Beatles	A HARD DAY'S NIGHT The Beatles	A HARD DAY'S NIGHT The Beatles

20 Oct 90 THE VERY BEST OF BEN E. KING & THE DRIFTERS
Telstar STAR 2373 [1] 15 16
7 Nov 98 THE VERY BEST OF BEN E. KING & THE DRIFTERS
Warner.esp / Global TV RADCD 108 [1] 41 3
17 May 03 ● THE DEFINITIVE DRIFTERS Atlantic WSMCD 137....8 17

[1] Ben E King & The Drifters

'Saturday Night at the Movies' received chart credit with 'At the Club' only after the re-issue's return to the chart on 8 Apr 1972. The two albums entitled The Very Best of Ben E. King & The Drifters are different .

DRIFTWOOD *Holland, male production trio*

1 Feb 03 **FREELOADER** *Positiva CDTIV 185* **32** 2

Julie DRISCOLL, Brian AUGER and The TRINITY
UK, female vocalist and male instrumental group

17 Apr 68 ● **THIS WHEEL'S ON FIRE** *Marmalade 598 006* **5** 16
8 Jun 68 OPEN *Marmalade 608 002* 12 13

Minnie DRIVER
UK, female actor / vocalist (1 Album: 1 Week, 2 Singles: 3 Weeks)

9 Oct 04 **EVERYTHING I'VE GOT IN MY POCKET** *Liberty 8674202* **34** 2
30 Oct 04 EVERYTHING I'VE GOT IN MY POCKET *Liberty 8742702* 44 1
22 Jan 05 **INVISIBLE GIRL** *Liberty 8703422* **68** 1

DRIVER 67 *UK, male vocalist – Paul Phillips*

23 Dec 78 ● **CAR 67** *Logo GO 336* **7** 12

DRIZABONE *UK / US, male / female vocal / instrumental group (1 Album: 1 Week, 5 Singles: 18 Weeks)*

22 Jun 91 **REAL LOVE** *Fourth & Broadway BRW 223* [1] **16** 8
26 Oct 91 **CATCH THE FIRE** *Fourth & Broadway BRW 232* [1] **54** 2
23 Apr 94 **PRESSURE** *Fourth & Broadway BRCD 264* **33** 2
15 Oct 94 **BRIGHTEST STAR** *Fourth & Broadway BRCD 293* **45** 2
19 Nov 94 CONSPIRACY *Fourth & Broadway BRCD 593* 72 1
4 Mar 95 **REAL LOVE** (re-recording) *Fourth & Broadway BRCD 311* **24** 4

[1] Driza Bone

Frank D'RONE *US, male vocalist*

22 Dec 60 **STRAWBERRY BLONDE (THE BAND ROCKED ON)**
Mercury AMT 1123 ....**24** 6

DROWNING POOL
US, male vocal / instrumental group (2 Albums: 2 Weeks, 2 Singles: 3 Weeks)

16 Feb 02 SINNER *Epic 5040912* 70 1
27 Apr 02 **BODIES** *Epic 6723172* **34** 2
10 Aug 02 **TEAR AWAY** *Epic 6729832* **65** 1
1 May 04 DESENSITIZED *Epic 5154112* 66 1

DRU HILL (see also SISQO)
US, male vocal group (1 Album: 7 Weeks, 7 Singles: 42 Weeks)

15 Feb 97 **TELL ME** *Fourth & Broadway BRCD 342* **30** 3
10 May 97 **IN MY BED** *Fourth & Broadway BRCD 353* $ **16** 3
11 Oct 97 **BIG BAD MAMMA** *Def Jam 5749792* [1] **12** 3
6 Dec 97 **5 STEPS** *Island Black Music CID 675* **22** 3
24 Oct 98 ● **HOW DEEP IS YOUR LOVE (re)**
Island Black Music CID 725 [2] **9** 8
7 Nov 98 ENTER THE DRU *Island Black Music 5245422* 42 7
6 Feb 99 ● **THESE ARE THE TIMES** *Island Black Music CID 733* **4** 6
10 Jul 99 ● **WILD WILD WEST** *Columbia 6675962* [3] ▲ **2** 16

[1] Foxy Brown featuring Dru Hill [2] Dru Hill featuring Redman [3] Will Smith featuring Dru Hill – additional vocals Kool Moe Dee

DRUGSTORE *UK / US / Brazil, male / female vocal / instrumental group (2 Albums: 3 Weeks, 3 Singles: 5 Weeks)*

8 Apr 95 DRUGSTORE *Honey 8286170* 31 2
10 Jun 95 **FADER** *Honey HONCD 7* **72** 1

2 May 98 **EL PRESIDENT** *Roadrunner RR 22369* **20** 3
16 May 98 WHITE MAGIC FOR LOVERS *Roadrunner RR 87112* 45 1
4 Jul 98 **SOBER** *Roadrunner RR 22303* **68** 1

'El President' contains additional vocals by Radiohead's Thom Yorke.

DRUM CLUB *UK, male instrumental / production duo*

6 Nov 93 **SOUND SYSTEM** *Butterfly BFLD 10* **62** 1
20 Aug 94 DRUMS ARE DANGEROUS *Butterfly BFLCD 10* 53 1

DRUM THEATRE *UK, male vocal / instrumental group (2 Singles: 8 Weeks)*

15 Feb 86 **LIVING IN THE PAST** *Epic A 6798* **67** 2
17 Jan 87 **ELDORADO** *Epic EMU 1* **44** 6

DRUMSOUND & Simon 'BASSLINE' SMITH
UK, male production duo – Andy Wright and Simon Smith (2 Singles: 2 Weeks)

26 Jul 03 **JUNGLIST** *Technique TECH 021* **67** 1
12 Jun 04 **THE ODYSSEY / BODY MOVIN'** *Prototype PROUK 004* [1] **66** 1

[1] Drumsound / Simon 'Bassline' Smith

DRUNKENMUNKY (see also DA TECHNO BOHEMIAN; ITTY BITTY BOOZY WOOZY; KLUBBHEADS) *Holland, male production group*

4 Oct 03 **E** *All Around the World CDGLOBE 285* **41** 2

DRUPI *Italy, male vocalist – Giampiero Anelli*

1 Dec 73 **VADO VIA** *A&M AMS 7083* **17** 12

DTOX *UK, male / female vocal / instrumental group*

21 Nov 92 **SHATTERED GLASS** *Vitality VITal 1* **75** 1

John DU CANN *UK, male vocalist*

22 Sep 79 **DON'T BE A DUMMY** *Vertigo 6059 241* **33** 6

The DUALERS *UK, male vocal / instrumental duo – Si Christone and Tyber O'Neil (2 Singles: 3 Weeks)*

30 Oct 04 **KISS ON THE LIPS** *Galley Music GALLEY 1003* **21** 2
19 Nov 05 **TRULY MADLY DEEPLY** *Gut CDGUT 73* **23** 1

DUB PISTOLS
UK, male vocal / instrumental / production group (2 Singles: 2 Weeks)

10 Oct 98 **CYCLONE** *Concrete HARD 36CD* **63** 1
18 Oct 03 **PROBLEM IS** *Distinctive DISNCD 107* [1] **66** 1

[1] Dub Pistols featuring Terry Hall

DUB WAR *UK, male vocal / instrumental group (4 Singles: 5 Weeks)*

3 Jun 95 **STRIKE IT** *Earache MOSH 138CD* **70** 1
27 Jan 96 **ENEMY MAKER** *Earache MOSH 147CD* **41** 2
24 Aug 96 **CRY DIGNITY** *Earache MOSH 163CDD* **59** 1
29 Mar 97 **MILLION DOLLAR LOVE** *Earache MOSH 170CD1* **73** 1

The DUBLINERS *Ireland, male vocal / instrumental group (6 Albums: 91 Weeks, 5 Singles: 45 Weeks)*

30 Mar 67 ● **SEVEN DRUNKEN NIGHTS** *Major Minor MM 506* **7** 17
13 May 67 ● A DROP OF THE HARD STUFF *Major Minor MMLP 3* 5 41
30 Aug 67 **BLACK VELVET BAND** *Major Minor MM 530* **15** 15
9 Sep 67 BEST OF THE DUBLINERS *Transatlantic TRA 158* 25 11
7 Oct 67 ● MORE OF THE HARD STUFF *Major Minor MMLP 5* 8 23
20 Dec 67 **MAIDS, WHEN YOU'RE YOUNG NEVER WED AN OLD MAN**
Major Minor MM 551 ....**43** 3
2 Mar 68 DRINKIN' AND COURTIN' *Major Minor SMLP 14* 31 3
28 Mar 87 ● **THE IRISH ROVER** *Stiff BUY 258* [1] **8** 8
25 Apr 87 THE DUBLINERS 25 YEARS CELEBRATION *Stylus SMR 731* 43 10
16 Jun 90 **JACK'S HEROES / WHISKEY IN THE JAR**
Pogue Mahone YZ 500 [1] **63** 2
22 Mar 03 SPIRIT OF THE IRISH *Sanctuary TVSAN 003* 19 3

[1] The Pogues and The Dubliners

29 / 31 October 1964	5 / 7 November 1964	12 / 14 November 1964	19 / 21 November 1964
(THERE'S) ALWAYS SOMETHING THERE TO REMIND ME Sandie Shaw	**(THERE'S) ALWAYS SOMETHING THERE TO REMIND ME** Sandie Shaw	**OH, PRETTY WOMAN** Roy Orbison	**BABY LOVE** The Supremes
A HARD DAY'S NIGHT The Beatles	**A HARD DAY'S NIGHT** The Beatles	**A HARD DAY'S NIGHT** The Beatles	**A HARD DAY'S NIGHT** The Beatles

BRITISH HIT SINGLES & ALBUMS

www.bibleofpop.com

50 Years of Singles and Albums Sales

For the first time, the book of British Hit Singles & Albums presents the popularity of singles vs albums in this graph covering UK sales data from 1955 to 2005. The peaks and troughs point to some unexpected conclusions as the years unfold. We all tend to imagine that the 1960s and 70s were the golden age of record-buying. Not entirely true according to the actual sales figures presented below.

Singles (millions)	Year	Albums (millions)	
50.93	1955	8.99	Bill Haley earns the first UK million-selling single
54.41	1956	12.12	Elvis debuts in the UK chart for the first time with seven singles
64.52	1957	13.77	Skiffle at its height and the 6.5 Special TV show starts
55.84	1958	15.62	Cliff Richard enters the UK chart for the first time with 'Move It!'
51.36	1959	15.40	45s outsell 78 singles for the first time
55.61	1960	17.06	For the first time more UK acts top the chart than US acts
56.94	1961	19.39	The George Mitchell Minstrels have the first British album to sell 100,000
57.18	1962	20.36	The Beatles have their first hit single - 'Love Me Do'
61.21	1963	22.65	Merseybeat rules and Gerry and The Pacemakers score a hat-trick of No.1 singles
72.84	1964	27.83	Debut of TV's Top of the Pops and pirate radio
61.81	1965	31.47	Ken Dodd has the biggest-selling single by a solo artist so far with 'Tears'
51.20	1966	33.32	The Four Tops register the first Motown UK No.1 single, 'Reach Out I'll Be There'
51.58	1967	37.28	Sgt. Pepper is released and BBC Radio 1 begins
49.16	1968	49.18	Albums outsell singles for the first time
46.62	1969	59.57	Year of Woodstock as Led Zeppelin debut and rock LPs are all the rage
47.00	1970	65.80	Simon & Garfunkel's Bridge Over Troubled Water dominates the albums chart
48.20	1971	75.80	TV's Old Grey Whistle Test and cassette LPs make their first appearance
48.50	1972	83.83	Glam rock and teeny bopper pop boost the sales of singles

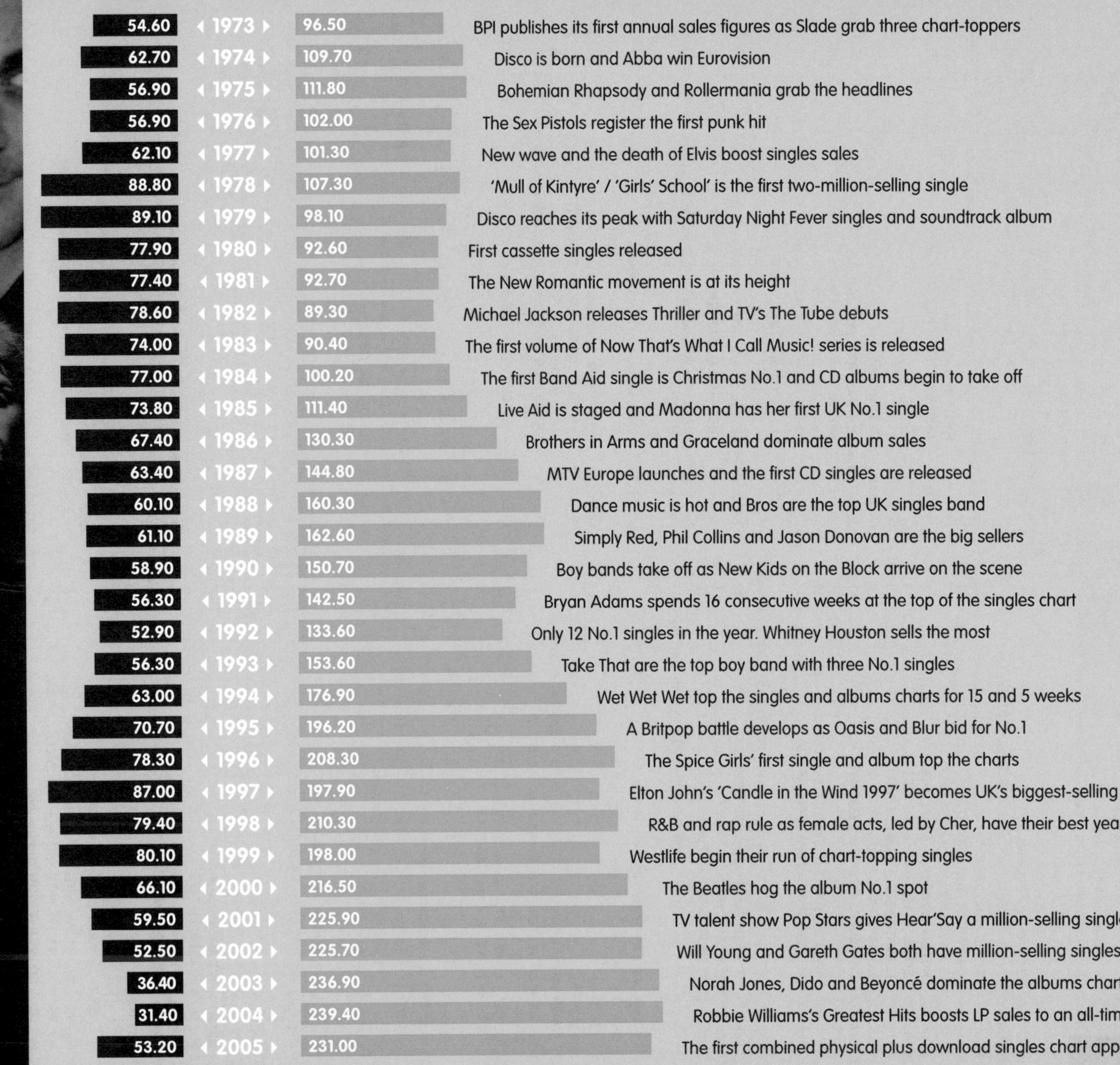

Sources for these figures are: 1955-1972 Record Retailer magazine, which this source indicates were production sales, or records pressed, Alan Smith, Dave McAleer and Chris Green.

Figures from 1973 are BPI (British Phonographic Industry) totals for trade deliveries to all retailers including all formats: eight-track, vinyl, cassette, CD, MiniDisc, download, etc.

54.60	1973	96.50	BPI publishes its first annual sales figures as Slade grab three chart-toppers
62.70	1974	109.70	Disco is born and Abba win Eurovision
56.90	1975	111.80	Bohemian Rhapsody and Rollermania grab the headlines
56.90	1976	102.00	The Sex Pistols register the first punk hit
62.10	1977	101.30	New wave and the death of Elvis boost singles sales
88.80	1978	107.30	'Mull of Kintyre' / 'Girls' School' is the first two-million-selling single
89.10	1979	98.10	Disco reaches its peak with Saturday Night Fever singles and soundtrack album
77.90	1980	92.60	First cassette singles released
77.40	1981	92.70	The New Romantic movement is at its height
78.60	1982	89.30	Michael Jackson releases Thriller and TV's The Tube debuts
74.00	1983	90.40	The first volume of Now That's What I Call Music! series is released
77.00	1984	100.20	The first Band Aid single is Christmas No.1 and CD albums begin to take off
73.80	1985	111.40	Live Aid is staged and Madonna has her first UK No.1 single
67.40	1986	130.30	Brothers in Arms and Graceland dominate album sales
63.40	1987	144.80	MTV Europe launches and the first CD singles are released
60.10	1988	160.30	Dance music is hot and Bros are the top UK singles band
61.10	1989	162.60	Simply Red, Phil Collins and Jason Donovan are the big sellers
58.90	1990	150.70	Boy bands take off as New Kids on the Block arrive on the scene
56.30	1991	142.50	Bryan Adams spends 16 consecutive weeks at the top of the singles chart
52.90	1992	133.60	Only 12 No.1 singles in the year. Whitney Houston sells the most
56.30	1993	153.60	Take That are the top boy band with three No.1 singles
63.00	1994	176.90	Wet Wet Wet top the singles and albums charts for 15 and 5 weeks
70.70	1995	196.20	A Britpop battle develops as Oasis and Blur bid for No.1
78.30	1996	208.30	The Spice Girls' first single and album top the charts
87.00	1997	197.90	Elton John's 'Candle in the Wind 1997' becomes UK's biggest-selling single
79.40	1998	210.30	R&B and rap rule as female acts, led by Cher, have their best year
80.10	1999	198.00	Westlife begin their run of chart-topping singles
66.10	2000	216.50	The Beatles hog the album No.1 spot
59.50	2001	225.90	TV talent show Pop Stars gives Hear'Say a million-selling single
52.50	2002	225.70	Will Young and Gareth Gates both have million-selling singles
36.40	2003	236.90	Norah Jones, Dido and Beyoncé dominate the albums chart
31.40	2004	239.40	Robbie Williams's Greatest Hits boosts LP sales to an all-time high
53.20	2005	231.00	The first combined physical plus download singles chart appears

KEY: UK No.1 ★ UK Top 10 ● Still on chart + UK entry at No.1 ■ US No.1 ▲ UK million seller £ US million seller $
Singles re-entries are listed as (re), (2re), (3re)... which signifies that the hit re-entered the chart once, twice or three times...
Peak Position / Weeks

DUBSTAR *UK, female / male vocal / instrumental group (2 Albums: 20 Weeks, 9 Singles: 26 Weeks)*

8 Jul 95 **STARS** *Food CDFOOD 61* 40 3
30 Sep 95 **ANYWHERE** *Food CDFOOD 67* 37 3
21 Oct 95 DISGRACEFUL *Food FOODCDX 13* 30 18
6 Jan 96 **NOT SO MANIC NOW** *Food CDFOOD 71* 18 5
30 Mar 96 **STARS** (re-issue) *Food CDFOODS 75* 15 6
3 Aug 96 **ELEVATOR SONG** *Food CDFOOD 80* 25 2
19 Jul 97 **NO MORE TALK** *Food CDFOOD 96* 20 3
20 Sep 97 **CATHEDRAL PARK** *Food CDFOOD 104* 41 1
4 Oct 97 GOODBYE *Food FOODCD 23* 18 2
7 Feb 98 **I WILL BE YOUR GIRLFRIEND** *Food CDFOODS 108* 28 2
27 May 00 **I (FRIDAY NIGHT)** *Food CDFOODS 128* 37 1

Ricardo 'Rikrok' DUCENT *Jamaica, male vocalist (3 Singles: 24 Weeks)*

17 Feb 01 **IT WASN'T ME** (import) *MCA 1558032* [1] 31 3
10 Mar 01 ★ **IT WASN'T ME** *MCA 1558022* [1] ■ ▲ £ 1 20
3 Jul 04 **YOUR EYES** *VP VPCD 6415* [2] 57 1

[1] Shaggy featuring Ricardo 'Rikrok' Ducent [2] Rik Rok featuring Shaggy

DUEL *UK, male instrumental duo – violins*

28 Feb 04 DUEL *Decca 4739992* 47 2

Hilary DUFF *US, female vocalist / actor (2 Albums: 5 Weeks, 3 Singles: 20 Weeks)*

1 Nov 03 ● **SO YESTERDAY (re)** *Hollywood HOL 003CD1* 9 8
15 Nov 03 METAMORPHOSIS *Hollywood 5046692682* ▲ 69 1
24 Apr 04 **COME CLEAN** *Hollywood HOL 005CD1* 18 4
5 Nov 05 ● **WAKE UP** *Angel ANGEDX 5* 7 8
12 Nov 05 MOST WANTED *Angel CDANGE 04* ▲ 31 4

Mary DUFF *Ireland, female vocalist (2 Albums: 9 Weeks)*

6 Apr 96 TIMELESS *Ritz RITZBCD 707* [1] 13 5
1 Oct 05 THE ULTIMATE COLLECTION *DMG TV DMGTV 019* 52 4

[1] Daniel O'Donnell and Mary Duff

DUFFO *Australia, male vocal group*

24 Mar 79 **GIVE ME BACK ME BRAIN** *Beggars Banquet BEG 15* 60 2

Stephen 'Tin Tin' DUFFY *UK, male vocalist (1 Album: 7 Weeks, 3 Singles: 24 Weeks)*

9 Jul 83 **HOLD IT** *Curve X 9763* [1] 55 4
2 Mar 85 ● **KISS ME** *10 TIN 2* 4 11
20 Apr 85 THE UPS AND DOWNS *10 DIX 5* 35 7
18 May 85 **ICING ON THE CAKE** *10 TIN 3* 14 9

[1] Tin Tin

DUKE *UK, male vocalist (3 Singles: 6 Weeks)*

25 May 96 **SO IN LOVE WITH YOU** *Encore CDCOR 009* 66 1
26 Oct 96 **SO IN LOVE WITH YOU** (re-issue) *Pukka CDPUKKA 11* 22 4
11 Nov 00 **SO IN LOVE WITH YOU** (re-mix) *48K / Perfecto SPECT 08CDS* 65 1

George DUKE *US, male vocalist / keyboard player*

12 Jul 80 **BRAZILIAN LOVE AFFAIR** *Epic EPC 8751* 36 6
26 Jul 80 BRAZILIAN LOVE AFFAIR *Epic EPC 84311* 33 4

The DUKE SPIRIT *UK, male / female vocal / instrumental group (1 Album: 1 Week, 5 Singles: 7 Weeks)*

12 Jun 04 **DARK IS LIGHT ENOUGH** *Loog 9866673* 55 1
16 Oct 04 **CUTS ACROSS THE LAND** *Loog 9868119* 45 1
19 Feb 05 **LION RIP** *Loog 9870092* 25 2
14 May 05 **LOVE IS AN UNFAMILIAR NAME** *Loog 9871175* 33 2
28 May 05 CUTS ACROSS THE LAND *Loog 9867546* 40 1
1 Oct 05 **CUTS ACROSS THE LAND** *Loog 9873986* 66 1

The DUKES (see also Steve EARLE) *UK, male vocal duo (2 Singles: 13 Weeks)*

17 Oct 81 **MYSTERY GIRL** *WEA K 18867* 47 7
1 May 82 **THANK YOU FOR THE PARTY** *WEA K 19136* 53 6

Candy DULFER *Holland, female saxophonist (2 Albums: 11 Weeks, 2 Singles: 14 Weeks)*

24 Feb 90 ● **LILY WAS HERE** *RCA ZB 43045* [1] 6 12
4 Aug 90 **SAXUALITY** *RCA PB 43769* 60 2
18 Aug 90 SAXUALITY *RCA PL 74661* 27 9
13 Mar 93 SAX-A-GO-GO *Ariola 4321111812* 56 2

[1] David A Stewart featuring Candy Dulfer

Thuli DUMAKUDE *South Africa, female vocalist*

2 Jan 88 **THE FUNERAL (SEPTEMBER 25, 1977)** *MCA MCA 1228* 75 1

The listed flip side of 'The Funeral' was 'Cry Freedom' by George Fenton and Jonas Gwangwa.

DUMDUMS *UK, male vocal / instrumental group (1 Album: 2 Weeks, 4 Singles: 15 Weeks)*

11 Mar 00 **EVERYTHING** *Good Behaviour CDGOOD 1* 21 5
8 Jul 00 **CAN'T GET YOU OUT OF MY THOUGHTS** *Good Behaviour CD GOOD 2* 18 5
23 Sep 00 **YOU DO SOMETHING TO ME** *Good Behaviour CDGOOD 3* 27 3
30 Sep 00 IT GOES WITHOUT SAYING *Good Behaviour CDGOOD 4* 27 2
17 Feb 01 **ARMY OF TWO** *Good Behaviour CDGOOD 5* 27 2

John DUMMER and Helen APRIL *UK, male / female vocal duo*

28 Aug 82 **BLUE SKIES** *Speed SPEED 8* 54 3

DUMONDE (see also JamX & DeLEON) *Germany, male production duo – Dominik De Leon and Jurgen Mutschall (2 Singles: 3 Weeks)*

27 Jan 01 **TOMORROW** *Variation VART 6* 60 1
19 May 01 **NEVER LOOK BACK** *Manifesto FESCD 83* 36 2

DUNBLANE *UK, male / female vocal / instrumental group*

21 Dec 96 ★ **KNOCKIN' ON HEAVEN'S DOOR / THROW THESE GUNS AWAY** *BMG 74321442182* ■ 1 15

Johnny DUNCAN and The BLUE GRASS BOYS *US, male vocalist, b. 7 Sep 1931, d. 15 Jul 2000, and UK, male instrumental group (3 Singles: 20 Weeks)*

26 Jul 57 ● **LAST TRAIN TO SAN FERNANDO** *Columbia DB 3959* 2 17
25 Oct 57 **BLUE, BLUE HEARTACHES** *Columbia DB 3996* 27 1
29 Nov 57 **FOOTPRINTS IN THE SNOW (re)** *Columbia DB 4029* 27 2

David DUNDAS *UK, male vocalist (2 Singles: 14 Weeks)*

24 Jul 76 ● **JEANS ON** *Air CHS 2094* 3 9
9 Apr 77 **ANOTHER FUNNY HONEYMOON** *Air CHS 2136* 29 5

Errol DUNKLEY *Jamaica, male vocalist (2 Singles: 14 Weeks)*

22 Sep 79 **OK FRED** *Scope SC 6* 11 11
2 Feb 80 **SIT DOWN AND CRY** *Scope SC 11* 52 3

Clive DUNN *UK, male actor / vocalist*

28 Nov 70 ★ **GRANDAD (re)** *Columbia DB 8726* 1 28

26 / 28 November 1964	3 / 5 December 1964	10 / 12 December 1964	17 / 19 December 1964
UK No.1 SINGLES			
BABY LOVE – The Supremes	LITTLE RED ROOSTER – The Rolling Stones	I FEEL FINE – The Beatles	I FEEL FINE – The Beatles
UK No.1 ALBUMS			
A HARD DAY'S NIGHT – The Beatles	A HARD DAY'S NIGHT – The Beatles	A HARD DAY'S NIGHT – The Beatles	BEATLES FOR SALE – The Beatles

Simon DUPREE and The BIG SOUND

UK, male vocal / instrumental group (1 Album: 1 Week, 2 Singles: 16 Weeks)

16 Aug 67 WITHOUT RESERVATIONS *Parlophone PCS 7029*....39 1
22 Nov 67 ● KITES *Parlophone R 5646*....9 13
3 Apr 68 FOR WHOM THE BELL TOLLS *Parlophone R 5670*....43 3

Jermaine DUPRI (see also Marques HOUSTON)

UK, male rapper / vocalist (2 Singles: 7 Weeks)

31 Jul 04 POP THAT BOOTY *East West E 7609CD* [1] 23 5
1 Oct 05 GOTTA GETCHA *Virgin VUSDX 309*....54 2

[1] Marques Houston featuring Jermaine "JD" Dupri

DURAN DURAN 56 Top 500 (see also ARCADIA; POWER STATION)

New Romantics turned teen idols: Simon Le Bon (v), Nick Rhodes (k), John Taylor (b), Andy Taylor (g) and Roger Taylor (d). The Birmingham band's 10 successive Top 10 hits included 'A View to a Kill', the best-selling James Bond theme ever in the UK and the US. Group received MTV Lifetime Achievement award (2003) and Outstanding Contribution to British Music award at the 2004 BRITs and returned to the Top 5 singles and albums charts in 2004 (14 Albums: 424 Weeks, 32 Singles: 229 Weeks)

21 Feb 81 PLANET EARTH *EMI 5137*....12 11
9 May 81 CARELESS MEMORIES *EMI 5168*....37 7
27 Jun 81 ● DURAN DURAN *EMI EMC 3372*....3 118
25 Jul 81 ● GIRLS ON FILM *EMI 5206*....5 11
28 Nov 81 MY OWN WAY *EMI 5254*....14 11
15 May 82 ● HUNGRY LIKE THE WOLF *EMI 5295*....5 12
22 May 82 ● RIO *EMI EMC 3411*....2 109
21 Aug 82 ● SAVE A PRAYER *EMI 5327*....2 9
13 Nov 82 ● RIO *EMI 5346*....9 11
26 Mar 83 ★ IS THERE SOMETHING I SHOULD KNOW? *EMI 5371* ■....1 9
29 Oct 83 ● UNION OF THE SNAKE (re) *EMI 5429*....3 11
3 Dec 83 ★ SEVEN AND THE RAGGED TIGER *EMI DD 1* ■....1 47
4 Feb 84 ● NEW MOON ON MONDAY *EMI DURAN 1*....9 7
28 Apr 84 ★ THE REFLEX *EMI DURAN 2* ▲....1 14
3 Nov 84 ● THE WILD BOYS *Parlophone DURAN 3*....2 14
24 Nov 84 ● ARENA *Parlophone DD 2*....6 31
18 May 85 ● A VIEW TO A KILL *Parlophone DURAN 007* ▲....2 16
1 Nov 86 ● NOTORIOUS (re) *EMI DDN 45*....7 7
6 Dec 86 NOTORIOUS *EMI DDN 331*....16 16
21 Feb 87 SKIN TRADE *EMI TRADE 1*....22 6
25 Apr 87 MEET EL PRESIDENTE *EMI TOUR 1*....24 5
1 Oct 88 I DON'T WANT YOUR LOVE *EMI YOUR 1*....14 5
29 Oct 88 BIG THING *EMI DDB 33*....15 5
7 Jan 89 ● ALL SHE WANTS IS *EMI DD 11*....9 5
22 Apr 89 DO YOU BELIEVE IN SHAME? *EMI DD 12*....30 4
25 Nov 89 ● DECADE *EMI DDX 10*....5 16
16 Dec 89 BURNING THE GROUND *EMI DD 13*....31 5
4 Aug 90 VIOLENCE OF SUMMER (LOVE'S TAKING OVER) *Parlophone DD 14*....20 4
1 Sep 90 ● LIBERTY *Parlophone PCSD 112*....8 4
17 Nov 90 SERIOUS *Parlophone DD 15*....48 3
30 Jan 93 ● ORDINARY WORLD *Parlophone CDDDS 16*....6 9
27 Feb 93 ● DURAN DURAN (THE WEDDING ALBUM) *Parlophone CDDB 34*..4 23
10 Apr 93 COME UNDONE *Parlophone CDDDS 17*....13 8
4 Sep 93 TOO MUCH INFORMATION *Parlophone CDDDS 18*....35 3
25 Mar 95 PERFECT DAY *Parlophone CDDDS 20*....28 4
8 Apr 95 THANK YOU *Parlophone CDDDB 36*....12 3
17 Jun 95 WHITE LINES (DON'T DO IT) *Parlophone CDDD 19* [1] 17 5
24 May 97 OUT OF MY MIND *Virgin VSCDT 1639*....21 2
21 Nov 98 ● GREATEST *EMI 4962392*....4 46
30 Jan 99 ELECTRIC BARBARELLA *EMI CDELEC 2000*....23 3
27 Mar 99 STRANGE BEHAVIOUR *EMI 4939722*....70 1
10 Jun 00 SOMEONE ELSE NOT ME *Hollywood / Edel 0108845 HWR*....53 1
1 Jul 00 POP TRASH *Hollywood 0107512 HWR*....53 1
16 Oct 04 ● (REACH UP FOR THE) SUNRISE *Epic 6753532*....5 4
23 Oct 04 ● ASTRONAUT *Epic 5179208*....3 4
12 Feb 05 WHAT HAPPENS TOMORROW *Epic 6756502*....11 3

[1] Duran Duran featuring Melle Mel and Grandmaster Flash and the Furious Five

Group was UK / US from 'Burning the Ground'. Group was billed as Duranduran on EMI DDB 33. Greatest peaked at No.15 on its original chart run and reached its new peak position in Feb 2004

Jimmy DURANTE

US, male vocalist / comedian, b. 10 Feb 1893, d. 29 Jan 1980

14 Dec 96 MAKE SOMEONE HAPPY *Warner Bros. W 0385CD*....69 1

Deanna DURBIN *Canada, female vocalist*

30 Jan 82 THE BEST OF DEANNA DURBIN *MCA International MCL 1634*..84 4

Judith DURHAM (see also The SEEKERS)

Australia, female vocalist (2 Albums: 16 Weeks, 1 Single: 5 Weeks)

15 Jun 67 THE OLIVE TREE *Columbia DB 8207*....33 5
23 Apr 94 ● A CARNIVAL OF HITS *EMI CDEMTV 83* [1] 7 14
30 Mar 96 MONA LISAS *EMI Premier CDJDTV 1*....46 2

[1] Judith Durham and The Seekers

Ian DURY and The BLOCKHEADS 399 Top 500

Art college lecturer-turned witty vocalist / songwriter, b. 12 May 1942, Billericay, Essex, UK, d. 27 Mar 2000. Ex-Kilburn and The High Roads member (1970-76) played his final show at the prestigious London Palladium. A 2001 tribute album included Paul McCartney and Robbie Williams (8 Albums: 123 Weeks, 9 Singles: 56 Weeks)

22 Oct 77 ● NEW BOOTS AND PANTIES!! *Stiff SEEZ 4* [1] 5 90
29 Apr 78 ● WHAT A WASTE! *Stiff BUY 27*....9 12
9 Dec 78 ★ HIT ME WITH YOUR RHYTHM STICK *Stiff BUY 38* [1] 1 15
2 Jun 79 ● DO IT YOURSELF *Stiff SEEZ 14*....2 18
4 Aug 79 ● REASONS TO BE CHEERFUL (PT.3) *Stiff BUY 50*....3 8
30 Aug 80 I WANT TO BE STRAIGHT *Stiff BUY 90*....22 7
15 Nov 80 SUPERMAN'S BIG SISTER *Stiff BUY 100*....51 3
6 Dec 80 LAUGHTER *Stiff SEEZ 30*....48 4
10 Oct 81 LORD UPMINSTER *Polydor POLD 5042*....53 4
4 Feb 84 4000 WEEKS HOLIDAY *Polydor POLD 5112* [2] 54 2
25 May 85 HIT ME WITH YOUR RHYTHM STICK (re-mix) *Stiff BUY 214*....55 4
26 Oct 85 PROFOUNDLY IN LOVE WITH PANDORA *EMI EMI 5534* [2] 45 5
27 Jul 91 HIT ME WITH YOUR RHYTHM STICK '91 (re-recording) *Flying FLYR 1*....73 1
11 Jul 98 MR. LOVE PANTS *Ronnie Harris DUR 1*....57 2
9 Oct 99 THE VERY BEST OF IAN DURY AND THE BLOCKHEADS – REASONS TO BE CHEERFUL *EMI 5228882*..40 2
11 Mar 00 DRIP FED FRED *Virgin VSCDT 1768* [3] 55 1
30 Mar 02 TEN MORE TURNIPS FROM THE TIP *Ronnie Harris DUR 2*....60 1

[1] Ian and the Blockheads [2] Ian Dury [3] Madness featuring Ian Dury
[1] Ian Dury [2] Ian Dury and the Music Students

The DUST BROTHERS *US, male production duo*

11 Dec 99 THIS IS YOUR LIFE *Restless 74321713962*....60 1

DUST JUNKYS

UK, male vocal / instrumental group (1 Album: 2 Weeks, 3 Singles: 5 Weeks)

15 Nov 97 (NONSTOPOPERATION) *Polydor 5719732*....47 2
28 Feb 98 WHAT TIME IS IT? *Polydor 5694912*....39 2
21 Mar 98 DONE AND ... DUSTED *Polydor 5570432*....35 2
16 May 98 NOTHIN' PERSONAL *Polydor 5699092*....62 1

DUSTED (see also FAITHLESS; OUR TRIBE / ONE TRIBE; ROLLO; SPHINX)

UK, male production / instrumental duo – Roland Armstrong and Mark Bates

20 Jan 01 ALWAYS REMEMBER TO RESPECT AND HONOUR YOUR MOTHER PART ONE *Go Beat / Polydor GOBCD 36*....31 2

Vocal by 12-year-old choirboy Alan Young.

Slim DUSTY

Australia, male vocalist – David Kirkpatrick, b. 13 Jun 1927, d. 19 Sep 2003

30 Jan 59 ● A PUB WITH NO BEER *Columbia DB 4212*....3 15

Hit with Dick Carr and his Bushlanders.

24 / 26 December 1964	31 December 1964 / 2 January 1965	7 / 9 January 1965	14 / 16 January 1965
I FEEL FINE The Beatles	I FEEL FINE The Beatles	I FEEL FINE The Beatles	YEH, YEH Georgie Fame and The Blue Flames
BEATLES FOR SALE The Beatles	BEATLES FOR SALE The Beatles	BEATLES FOR SALE The Beatles	BEATLES FOR SALE The Beatles

KEY UK No.1 ★ UK Top 10 ● Still on chart + UK entry at No.1 ■ US No.1 ▲ UK million seller £ US million seller $
Singles re-entries are listed as (re), (2re), (3re)... which signifies that the hit re-entered the chart once, twice or three times...
Peak Position / Weeks

DUTCH featuring CRYSTAL WATERS (see also SCUMFROG)
Holland, male producer – Jesse Houk and US, female vocalist

20 Sep 03 MY TIME *Illustrious / Epic CDILL 018* 22 4

DUTCH FORCE *Holland, male producer – Benno De Goeij*

6 May 00 DEADLINE *Inferno CDFERN 27* 35 2

DWEEB *UK, male / female vocal / instrumental trio (2 Singles: 2 Weeks)*

22 Feb 97 SCOOBY DOO *Blanco Y Negro NEG 100CD* 63 1
7 Jun 97 OH YEAH, BABY *Blanco Y Negro NEG 102CD1* 70 1

Bob DYLAN 33 Top 500 (see also TRAVELING WILBURYS)
The most influential folk / rock vocalist / composer ever, b. Robert Zimmerman, 24 May 1941, Minnesota, US. The legendary performer, who transformed and upset the 1960s folk music movement, redefined the term and, indeed, image of the singer / songwriter. He was inducted into the UK Music Hall of Fame in 2005 (47 Albums: 627 Weeks, 19 Singles: 137 Weeks)

23 May 64 ★ THE FREEWHEELIN' BOB DYLAN *CBS BPG 62193* 1 49
11 Jul 64 ● THE TIMES THEY ARE A-CHANGIN' *CBS BPG 62251* 4 20
21 Nov 64 ● ANOTHER SIDE OF BOB DYLAN *CBS BPG 62429* 8 19
25 Mar 65 ● TIMES THEY ARE A-CHANGIN' *CBS 201751* 9 11
29 Apr 65 ● SUBTERRANEAN HOMESICK BLUES *CBS 201753* 9 9
8 May 65 BOB DYLAN *CBS BPG 62022* 13 6
15 May 65 ★ BRINGING IT ALL BACK HOME *CBS BPG 62515* 1 29
17 Jun 65 MAGGIE'S FARM *CBS 201781* 22 8
19 Aug 65 ● LIKE A ROLLING STONE *CBS 201811* $ 4 12
9 Oct 65 ● HIGHWAY 61 REVISITED *CBS BPG 62572* 4 15
28 Oct 65 ● POSITIVELY 4TH STREET *CBS 201824* 8 12
27 Jan 66 CAN YOU PLEASE CRAWL OUT YOUR WINDOW *CBS 201900* 17 5
14 Apr 66 ONE OF US MUST KNOW (SOONER OR LATER) *CBS 202053* 33 5
12 May 66 ● RAINY DAY WOMEN NOS. 12 & 35 *CBS 202307* 7 8
21 Jul 66 I WANT YOU *CBS 202258* 16 9
20 Aug 66 ● BLONDE ON BLONDE *CBS DDP 66012* 3 15
14 Jan 67 ● GREATEST HITS *CBS SBPG 62847* 6 82
2 Mar 68 ★ JOHN WESLEY HARDING *CBS SBPG 63252* 1 29
14 May 69 I THREW IT ALL AWAY *CBS 4219* 30 6
17 May 69 ★ NASHVILLE SKYLINE *CBS 63601* 1 42
13 Sep 69 ● LAY LADY LAY *CBS 4434* 5 12
11 Jul 70 ★ SELF PORTRAIT *CBS 66250* ■ 1 15
28 Nov 70 ★ NEW MORNING *CBS 69001* ■ 1 11
10 Jul 71 WATCHING THE RIVER FLOW *CBS 7329* 24 9
25 Dec 71 MORE BOB DYLAN GREATEST HITS *CBS 67238/9* 12 15
29 Sep 73 PAT GARRETT & BILLY THE KID (FILM SOUNDTRACK) *CBS 69042* 29 11
6 Oct 73 KNOCKIN' ON HEAVEN'S DOOR *CBS 1762* 14 9
23 Feb 74 ● PLANET WAVES *Island ILPS 9261* ▲ 7 8
13 Jul 74 ● BEFORE THE FLOOD *Asylum IDBD 1* [1] 8 7
15 Feb 75 ● BLOOD ON THE TRACKS *CBS 69097* ▲ 4 16
26 Jul 75 ● THE BASEMENT TAPES *CBS 88147* 8 10
31 Jan 76 ● DESIRE *CBS 86003* ▲ 3 35
7 Feb 76 HURRICANE *CBS 3878* 43 4
9 Oct 76 ● HARD RAIN *CBS 86016* 3 7
1 Jul 78 ● STREET LEGAL *CBS 86067* 2 20
29 Jul 78 BABY STOP CRYING *CBS 6499* 13 11
28 Oct 78 IS YOUR LOVE IN VAIN *CBS 6718* 56 3
26 May 79 ● BOB DYLAN AT BUDOKAN *CBS 96004* 4 19
8 Sep 79 ● SLOW TRAIN COMING *CBS 86095* 2 13
28 Jun 80 ● SAVED *CBS 86113* 3 8
29 Aug 81 ● SHOT OF LOVE *CBS 85178* 6 8
12 Nov 83 ● INFIDELS *CBS 25539* 9 12
15 Dec 84 REAL LIVE *CBS 26334* 54 2
22 Jun 85 EMPIRE BURLESQUE *CBS 86313* 11 6
2 Aug 86 KNOCKED OUT LOADED *CBS 86326* 35 5
23 Apr 88 GREATEST HITS VOLUME 3 *CBS 460907 1* 47 3
25 Jun 88 DOWN IN THE GROOVE *CBS 460267 1* 32 3
18 Feb 89 DYLAN & THE DEAD *CBS 463381 1* [2] 38 3
14 Oct 89 ● OH MERCY *CBS 465800 1* 6 7
22 Sep 90 UNDER THE RED SKY *CBS 4671881* 13 3
13 Apr 91 THE BOOTLEG SERIES VOLUMES 1-3 *Columbia 4680861* 32 5
14 Nov 92 GOOD AS I BEEN TO YOU *Columbia 4727102* 18 3
20 Nov 93 WORLD GONE WRONG *Columbia 474 8572* 35 2
29 Apr 95 ● UNPLUGGED *Columbia 4783742* 10 5
20 May 95 DIGNITY *Columbia 6620762* 33 2
14 Jun 97 ● THE BEST OF BOB DYLAN *Columbia SONYTV 28CD* 6 18
11 Oct 97 ● TIME OUT OF MIND *Columbia 4869362* 10 6
11 Jul 98 LOVE SICK *Columbia 6659972* 64 1
24 Oct 98 LIVE AT THE ROYAL ALBERT HALL *Legacy 4914852* 19 2
20 May 00 THE BEST OF BOB DYLAN – VOLUME 2 *Columbia 4983612* 22 2
14 Oct 00 THINGS HAVE CHANGED *Columbia 6693792* 58 1
2 Jun 01 ● THE ESSENTIAL BOB DYLAN *Columbia STVCD 116* 9 19
22 Sep 01 ● LOVE AND THEFT *Columbia 5043642* 3 5
7 Dec 02 LIVE 1975 – THE ROLLING THUNDER REVUE *Columbia 5101403* 69 1
10 Apr 04 THE BOOTLEG SERIES VOL.6 – BOB DYLAN LIVE 1964 – CONCERT AT PHILHARMONIC HALL *Columbia 5123582* 33 1
17 Sep 05 NO DIRECTION HOME: THE SOUNDTRACK – THE BOOTLEG SERIES VOL.7 (FILM SOUNDTRACK) *Columbia 5203582* 21 5

[1] Bob Dylan / The Band [2] Bob Dylan and The Grateful Dead

DYNAMITE MC *UK, male rapper – Dominic Smith (3 Singles: 6 Weeks)*

27 Sep 03 HOTNESS *Ram RAMM 45* [1] 66 1
5 Jun 04 RIDE *Ultimate Dilemma EW 288CD* 54 1
22 Jan 05 NO MORE *V VRECSUK 003CD* [2] 26 4

[1] Dynamite MC and Origin Unknown [2] Roni Size featuring Beverley Knight & Dynamite MC

DYNAMIX II featuring TOO TOUGH TEE
US, male vocal / instrumental group and rapper

8 Aug 87 JUST GIVE THE DJ A BREAK *Cooltempo COOL 151* 50 4

DYNASTY
US, male / female vocal / instrumental group (3 Singles: 20 Weeks)

13 Oct 79 I DON'T WANT TO BE A FREAK (BUT I CAN'T HELP MYSELF) *Solar FB 1694* 20 13
9 Aug 80 I'VE JUST BEGUN TO LOVE YOU *Solar SO 10* 51 4
21 May 83 DOES THAT RING A BELL *Solar E 9911* 53 3

Ronnie DYSON *US, male vocalist, b. 5 Jun 1950, d. 10 Nov 1990*

4 Dec 71 WHEN YOU GET RIGHT DOWN TO IT *CBS 7449* 34 6

DYVERSE *UK, female vocal group*

31 Jan 04 MISGUIDED *Chilli Discs CCHIL 002* 71 1

Katherine E *US, female vocalist – Katherine Ellis (2 Singles: 7 Weeks)*

6 Apr 91 I'M ALRIGHT *Dead Dead Good GOOD 2* 41 5
18 Jan 92 THEN I FEEL GOOD *PWL Continental PWL 13* 56 2

	21 / 23 January 1965	28 / 30 January 1965	4 / 6 February 1965	11 / 13 February 1965
UK No.1 SINGLES	YEH, YEH – Georgie Fame and The Blue Flames	GO NOW – The Moody Blues	YOU'VE LOST THAT LOVIN' FEELIN' – The Righteous Brothers	YOU'VE LOST THAT LOVIN' FEELIN' – The Righteous Brothers
UK No.1 ALBUMS	BEATLES FOR SALE – The Beatles	BEATLES FOR SALE – The Beatles	THE ROLLING STONES NO.2 – The Rolling Stones	THE ROLLING STONES NO.2 – The Rolling Stones

Sheila E *US, female vocalist / percussionist – Sheila Escovedo*

Date	Title / Label	Pos	Wks
23 Feb 85	**THE BELLE OF ST MARK** *Warner Bros. W 9180*	18	9

E-LUSTRIOUS (see also DIRECKT) *UK, male instrumental / production duo – Mike Kirwin and Danny Bennett (2 Singles: 2 Weeks)*

Date	Title / Label	Pos	Wks
15 Feb 92	**DANCE NO MORE** *MOS MOS 001T* [1]	58	1
2 Jul 94	**IN YOUR DANCE** *UFG UFG 6CD*	69	1

[1] E-Lustrious featuring Deborah French

E-MALE *UK, male vocal / instrumental group*

Date	Title / Label	Pos	Wks
31 Jan 98	**WE ARE E-MALE** *East West EW 137CD*	44	1

EMF *UK, male vocal (James Atkin) / instrumental group (3 Albums: 22 Weeks, 10 Singles: 50 Weeks)*

Date	Title / Label	Pos	Wks
3 Nov 90 ●	**UNBELIEVABLE** *Parlophone R 6273* ▲	3	13
2 Feb 91 ●	**I BELIEVE** *Parlophone R 6279*	6	7
27 Apr 91	**CHILDREN** *Parlophone R 6288*	19	5
18 May 91 ●	SCHUBERT DIP *Parlophone PCS 7353*	3	19
31 Aug 91	**LIES** *Parlophone R 6295*	28	3
2 May 92	**UNEXPLAINED (EP)** *Parlophone SGE 2026*	18	4
19 Sep 92	**THEY'RE HERE** *Parlophone R 6321*	29	3
10 Oct 92	STIGMA *Parlophone CDPCSD 122*	19	2
21 Nov 92	**IT'S YOU** *Parlophone R 6327*	23	3
25 Feb 95	**PERFECT DAY** *Parlophone CDRS 6401*	27	3
18 Mar 95	CHA CHA CHA *Parlophone CDPCSD 165*	30	1
8 Jul 95 ●	**I'M A BELIEVER** *Parlophone CDR 6412* [1]	3	8
28 Oct 95	**AFRO KING** *Parlophone CDRS 6416*	51	1

[1] EMF and Reeves and Mortimer

Tracks on Unexplained (EP): Getting Through / Far From Me / The Same / Search and Destroy.

E-MOTION *UK, male vocal / instrumental duo – Alan Angus and Justin Oliver (3 Singles: 7 Weeks)*

Date	Title / Label	Pos	Wks
3 Feb 96	**THE NAUGHTY NORTH AND THE SEXY SOUTH** *Soundproof MCSTD 40017*	20	3
17 Aug 96	**I STAND ALONE** *Soundproof MCSTD 40061*	60	1
26 Oct 96	**THE NAUGHTY NORTH AND THE SEXY SOUTH** (re-mix) *Soundproof MCSTD 40076*	17	3

EPMD *US, male rap / DJ duo – Erick 'E Double E' Sermon and Parrish 'Pee MD' Smith*

Date	Title / Label	Pos	Wks
16 Feb 91	BUSINESS AS USUAL *Def Jam 4676971*	69	1
15 Aug 98	**STRICTLY BUSINESS** *Parlophone CDR 6502* [1]	43	1

[1] Kurtis Mantronik vs EPMD

E-ROTIC *Germany / US, male / female vocal / instrumental group*

Date	Title / Label	Pos	Wks
3 Jun 95	**MAX DON'T HAVE SEX WITH YOUR EX** *Stip CDSTIP 2*	45	2

E-SMOOVE featuring Latanza WATERS (see also PRAISE CATS; THICK D) *US, male producer – Eric Miller and female vocalist*

Date	Title / Label	Pos	Wks
15 Aug 98	**DEJA VU** *AM:PM 5827671*	63	1

ETA *Denmark, male instrumental group (2 Singles: 5 Weeks)*

Date	Title / Label	Pos	Wks
28 Jun 97	**CASUAL SUB (BURNING SPEAR)** *East West EW 110CD*	28	3
31 Jan 98	**CASUAL SUB (BURNING SPEAR)** (re-mix) *East West Dance EW 145CD*	28	2

E-TRAX *Germany, male production duo*

Date	Title / Label	Pos	Wks
9 Jun 01	**LET'S ROCK** *Tidy Trax TIDY 155CD*	60	1

E-TYPE *Sweden, male vocalist – Bo Eriksson (2 Singles: 2 Weeks)*

Date	Title / Label	Pos	Wks
23 Sep 95	**THIS IS THE WAY** *Ffrreedom TABCD 237*	53	1
24 Jun 00	**CAMPIONE 2000** *Polydor 1580822*	58	1

EYC *US, male vocal group (1 Album: 5 Weeks, 7 Singles: 36 Weeks)*

Date	Title / Label	Pos	Wks
11 Dec 93	**FEELIN' ALRIGHT** *MCA MCSTD 1952*	16	8
5 Mar 94	**THE WAY YOU WORK IT** *MCA MCSTD 1963*	14	7
16 Apr 94	EXPRESS YOURSELF CLEARLY *MCA MCD 11061*	14	5
14 May 94	**NUMBER ONE** *MCA MCSTD 1976*	27	5
30 Jul 94	**BLACK BOOK** *MCA MCSTD 1987*	13	6
10 Dec 94	**ONE MORE CHANCE** *MCA MCSTD 2025*	25	6
23 Sep 95	**OOH-AH-AA (I FEEL IT)** *Gasoline Alley MCSTD 2096*	33	2
2 Dec 95	**IN THE BEGINNING** *Gasoline Alley MCSTD 2107*	41	2

E-Z ROLLERS *UK, male / female vocal / instrumental group (2 Singles: 4 Weeks)*

Date	Title / Label	Pos	Wks
24 Apr 99	**WALK THIS LAND** *Moving Shadow 130CD1*	18	3
8 Feb 03	**BACK TO LOVE** *Moving Shadow 159CD*	61	1

E-ZEE POSSEE *UK, male / female vocal / instrumental group (4 Singles: 16 Weeks)*

Date	Title / Label	Pos	Wks
26 Aug 89	**EVERYTHING STARTS WITH AN 'E'** (re) *More Protein PROT 1*	15	9
20 Jan 90	**LOVE ON LOVE** *More Protein PROT 3* [1]	59	3
30 Jun 90	**THE SUN MACHINE** *More Protein PROT 4*	62	3
21 Sep 91	**BREATHING IS E-ZEE** *More Protein PROT 12* [2]	72	1

[1] E-Zee Possee with Dr Mouthquake [2] E-Zee Possee featuring Tara Newley

'Everything Starts with an 'E'' did not reach its peak position until it re-entered the chart in Mar 1990.

EAGLES (74 Top 500)

Legendary west coast rock group which includes Glenn Frey (v/g), Don Henley (v/d), Timothy B Schmit (v/b) and Joe Walsh (v/g). Also in the band since their country rock formation in 1971: Bernie Leadon, Randy Meisner and Don Felder. America's biggest-selling album group disbanded in 1982, re-united over a decade later and are one of the 21st Century's biggest earning acts on the road. No album in the US has outsold Their Greatest Hits 1971-1975 (28 million) and their total worldwide album sales are reportedly over 100 million. (12 Albums: 476 Weeks, 10 Singles: 52 Weeks)

Date	Title / Label	Pos	Wks
27 Apr 74	ON THE BORDER *Asylum SYL 9016*	28	9
12 Jul 75	DESPERADO *Asylum SYLL 9011*	39	9
12 Jul 75 ●	ONE OF THESE NIGHTS *Asylum SYLA 8759* ▲	8	41
9 Aug 75	**ONE OF THESE NIGHTS** *Asylum AYM 543* ▲	23	7
1 Nov 75	**LYIN' EYES** *Asylum AYM 548*	23	7
6 Mar 76 ●	THEIR GREATEST HITS 1971-1975 *Asylum K 53017* ▲	2	118
6 Mar 76	**TAKE IT TO THE LIMIT** *Asylum K 13029*	12	7
25 Dec 76 ●	HOTEL CALIFORNIA *Asylum K 53051* ▲	2	70
15 Jan 77	**NEW KID IN TOWN** *Asylum K 13069* ▲ $	20	7
16 Apr 77 ●	**HOTEL CALIFORNIA** *Asylum K 13079* ▲ $	8	10
16 Dec 78	**PLEASE COME HOME FOR CHRISTMAS** *Asylum K 13145*	30	5
13 Oct 79 ●	THE LONG RUN *Asylum K 52181* ▲	4	16
13 Oct 79	**HEARTACHE TONIGHT** *Asylum K 12394* ▲ $	40	5
1 Dec 79	**THE LONG RUN** *Elektra K 12404*	66	2
22 Nov 80	LIVE *Asylum K 62032*	24	13
18 May 85 ●	THE BEST OF EAGLES *Asylum EKT 5*	8	74
23 Jul 94 ●	THE VERY BEST OF THE EAGLES *Elektra 9548323752*	4	54
19 Nov 94	HELL FREEZES OVER *Geffen GED 24725* ▲	18	21
13 Jul 96	**LOVE WILL KEEP US ALIVE** *Geffen GFSTD 21980*	52	1
9 Jun 01 ●	THE VERY BEST OF THE EAGLES *Elektra 7559626802*	3	47
25 Oct 03	**HOLE IN THE WORLD** *Eagles 8122745472*	69	1
1 Nov 03	THE COMPLETE GREATEST HITS *WSM 8122737312*	27	4

'The Very Best of The Eagles' (2001) was an expanded and repackaged version of the 1994 album of the same name.

EAMON *US, male vocalist – Eamon Doyle (1 Album: 9 Weeks, 3 Singles: 26 Weeks)*

Date	Title / Label	Pos	Wks
3 Apr 04	**F**K IT (I DON'T WANT YOU BACK)** (import) *Jive 82876604852*	46	3
17 Apr 04 ●	I DON'T WANT YOU BACK *Jive 82876605892*	6	9

18 / 20 February 1965	25 / 27 February 1965	4 / 6 March 1965	11 / 13 March 1965
TIRED OF WAITING FOR YOU The Kinks	**I'LL NEVER FIND ANOTHER YOU** The Seekers	**I'LL NEVER FIND ANOTHER YOU** The Seekers	**IT'S NOT UNUSUAL** Tom Jones
THE ROLLING STONES NO.2 The Rolling Stones	**BEATLES FOR SALE** The Beatles	**THE ROLLING STONES NO.2** The Rolling Stones	**THE ROLLING STONES NO.2** The Rolling Stones

KEY: UK No.1 ★ UK Top 10 ● Still on chart + UK entry at No.1 ■ US No.1 ▲ UK million seller £ US million seller $
Singles re-entries are listed as (re), (2re), (3re)... which signifies that the hit re-entered the chart once, twice or three times...
Peak Position / Weeks

24 Apr 04 ★ F**K IT (I DON'T WANT YOU BACK) *Jive 82876608502* ■ ... 1 19
16 Oct 04 LOVE THEM *Jive 8287663912* [1] ... 27 4

[1] Eamon featuring Ghostface

Ghostface appears on a B-side re-mix of 'Love Them' and not the main version, but is credited on the sleeve. The track's full title, 'Love Them Hos', was shortened to be radio friendly. I Don't Want You Back charted initially as an import under the catalogue number Jive JIV 583702.

Robert EARL *UK, male vocalist – Monty Leigh (3 Singles: 27 Weeks)*

25 Apr 58 I MAY NEVER PASS THIS WAY AGAIN *Philips PB 805* ... 14 13
24 Oct 58 MORE THAN EVER (COME PRIMA) (re) *Philips PB 867* ... 26 4
13 Feb 59 THE WONDERFUL SECRET OF LOVE *Philips PB 891* ... 17 10

Charles EARLAND

US, male keyboard player, b. 24 May 1941, d. 11 Dec 1999

19 Aug 78 LET THE MUSIC PLAY *Mercury 6167 703* ... 46 5

Steve EARLE

US, male vocalist / guitarist (9 Albums: 22 Weeks, 2 Singles: 7 Weeks)

4 Jul 87 EXIT 0 *MCA MCF 3379* ... 77 2
15 Oct 88 COPPERHEAD ROAD *MCA MCA 1280* ... 45 6
19 Nov 88 COPPERHEAD ROAD *MCA MCF 3426* ... 42 8
31 Dec 88 JOHNNY COME LATELY *MCA MCA 1301* ... 75 1
7 Jul 90 THE HARD WAY *MCA MCG 6095* [1] ... 22 4
19 Oct 91 SHUT UP AND DIE LIKE AN AVIATOR *MCA MCA 10315* [1] ... 62 1
23 Mar 96 I FEEL ALRIGHT *Transatlantic TRACD 227* ... 44 3
18 Oct 97 EL CORAZON *Warner Bros. 9362467892* ... 59 1
6 Mar 99 THE MOUNTAIN *Grapevine GRACD 252* [2] ... 51 1
17 Jun 00 TRANSCENDENTAL BLUES *Epic 4980749* ... 32 1
4 Sep 04 THE REVOLUTION STARTS NOW *Rykodisc RCD 17023* ... 66 1

[1] Steve Earle and The Dukes [2] Steve Earle and The Del McCoury Band

The EARLIES

US / UK, male vocal / instrumental group (2 Singles: 2 Weeks)

6 Nov 04 MORNING WONDER *WEA IAMNAMES 07* ... 67 1
12 Mar 05 BRING IT BACK AGAIN *WEA IAMNAMES 09* ... 61 1

EARLY MUSIC CONSORT directed by David MUNROW

UK, male / female instrumental group

3 Apr 71 HENRY VIII SUITE (EP) *BBC RESL 1* ... 49 1

Tracks on Henry VIII Suite (EP): Fanfare, Passomezo du Roy, Gaillarde d'Escosse / Pavane, Mille Ducats / Larocque Gaillarde / Allemande / Wedding March, La Mourisque / If Love Now Reigned / Ronde, Pourquoi.

EARTH WIND AND FIRE (202 Top 500)

Colourful, mystical, Los Angeles-based group noted for flamboyant stage performances. The band featured founding member Maurice White (d/v), Philip Bailey (v), Ronnie Laws (s/fl) and Verdine White (b). Few R&B acts outsold them in the late 1970s, when they achieved eight successive US Top 10 albums (10 Albums: 167 Weeks, 18 Singles: 128 Weeks)

12 Feb 77 SATURDAY NITE *CBS 4835* ... 17 9
21 Jan 78 ALL 'N' ALL *CBS 86051* ... 13 23
11 Feb 78 FANTASY *CBS 6056* ... 14 10
13 May 78 JUPITER *CBS 6267* ... 41 5
29 Jul 78 MAGIC MIND (re) *CBS 6490* ... 54 5
7 Oct 78 GOT TO GET YOU INTO MY LIFE *CBS 6553* $ ... 33 7
9 Dec 78 ● SEPTEMBER *CBS 6922* $ ... 3 13
16 Dec 78 ● THE BEST OF EARTH WIND AND FIRE VOLUME 1 *CBS 83284* ... 6 42
12 May 79 ● BOOGIE WONDERLAND *CBS 7292* [1] $ ... 4 13
23 Jun 79 ● I AM *CBS 86084* ... 5 41
28 Jul 79 ● AFTER THE LOVE HAS GONE *CBS 7721* $ ... 4 10
6 Oct 79 STAR *CBS 7902* ... 16 8
15 Dec 79 CAN'T LET GO *CBS 8077* ... 46 7
8 Mar 80 IN THE STONE *CBS 8252* ... 53 3
11 Oct 80 LET ME TALK *CBS 8982* ... 29 5
1 Nov 80 ● FACES *CBS 88498* ... 10 6
20 Dec 80 BACK ON THE ROAD *CBS 9377* ... 63 4
7 Nov 81 ● LET'S GROOVE *CBS A 1679* $ ... 3 13
14 Nov 81 RAISE! *CBS 85272* ... 14 22
6 Feb 82 I'VE HAD ENOUGH *CBS A 1959* ... 29 6
5 Feb 83 FALL IN LOVE WITH ME *CBS A 2927* ... 47 4
19 Feb 83 POWERLIGHT *CBS 25120* ... 22 7
10 May 86 ● THE COLLECTION *K-Tel NE 1322* ... 5 13
7 Nov 87 SYSTEM OF SURVIVAL *CBS EWF 1* ... 54 3
28 Nov 92 THE VERY BEST OF EARTH WIND AND FIRE *Telstar TCD 2631* ... 40 6
28 Sep 96 BOOGIE WONDERLAND – THE VERY BEST OF EARTH WIND AND FIRE *Telstar TCD 2879* ... 29 4
31 Jul 99 SEPTEMBER (re-mix) *INCredible INCR 24CD* ... 25 3
7 Aug 99 THE ULTIMATE COLLECTION *Columbia SONYTV 66CD* ... 34 3

[1] Earth Wind and Fire with The Emotions

EARTHLING

UK, male vocal / instrumental duo (1 Album: 1 Week, 2 Singles: 2 Weeks)

3 Jun 95 RADAR *Cooltempo CTCD 44* ... 66 1
14 Oct 95 ECHO ON MY MIND PART II *Cooltempo CDCOOL 312* ... 61 1
1 Jun 96 BLOOD MUSIC (EP) *Cooltempo CDCOOL 319* ... 69 1

Tracks on Blood Music (EP): First Transmission / Because the Night / Soup or No Soup / Infinite M.

EAST 57th STREET featuring Donna ALLEN

UK, male production trio and US, female vocalist

11 Oct 97 SATURDAY *AM:PM 5823752* ... 29 3

EAST OF EDEN *UK, male instrumental group*

14 Mar 70 SNAFU *Deram SML 1050* ... 29 2
17 Apr 71 ● JIG-A-JIG *Deram DM 297* ... 7 12

EAST 17 (229 Top 500)

(see also CHILDLINERS) *Walthamstow, London-based singing, rapping and dancing lads with international teen appeal: Tony Mortimer (v/k), Brian Harvey (v), John Hendy (v), Terry Coldwell (v). Bad press and personal problems resulted in main songwriter Mortimer quitting, and a name change to E-17 for their short-lived 1998 comeback. Biggest-selling single: 'Stay Another Day' 910,000 (6 Albums: 105 Weeks, 18 Singles: 170 Weeks)*

29 Aug 92 ● HOUSE OF LOVE *London LON 325* ... 10 9
14 Nov 92 GOLD (re) *London LON 331* ... 28 8
30 Jan 93 ● DEEP *London LOCDP 334* ... 5 10
27 Feb 93 ★ WALTHAMSTOW *London 8283732* ■ ... 1 33
10 Apr 93 SLOW IT DOWN *London LONCD 339* ... 13 7
26 Jun 93 WEST END GIRLS *London LONCD 344* ... 11 7
4 Dec 93 ● IT'S ALRIGHT *London LONCD 345* ... 3 14
14 May 94 ● AROUND THE WORLD *London LONCD 349* ... 3 13
1 Oct 94 ● STEAM *London LONCD 353* ... 7 8
29 Oct 94 ● STEAM *London 8285422* ... 3 36
3 Dec 94 ★ STAY ANOTHER DAY (re) *London LONCD 354* ... 1 16
25 Mar 95 ● LET IT RAIN *London LONCD 363* ... 10 7
17 Jun 95 HOLD MY BODY TIGHT *London LONCD 367* ... 12 7
4 Nov 95 ● THUNDER *London LONCD 373* ... 4 14
25 Nov 95 ● UP ALL NIGHT *London 8286992* ... 7 15
10 Feb 96 ● DO U STILL *London LONCD 379* ... 7 7
10 Aug 96 SOMEONE TO LOVE *London LONCD 385* ... 16 8
2 Nov 96 ● IF YOU EVER *London LONCD 388* [1] ... 2 15
16 Nov 96 ● AROUND THE WORLD – HIT SINGLES – THE JOURNEY SO FAR *London 8288522* [1] ... 3 16
18 Jan 97 ● HEY CHILD *London LONCD 390* ... 3 5

18 / 20 March 1965	25 / 27 March 1965	1 / 3 April 1965	8 / 10 April 1965
UK No.1 SINGLES			
THE LAST TIME The Rolling Stones	THE LAST TIME The Rolling Stones	THE LAST TIME The Rolling Stones	CONCRETE AND CLAY Unit Four Plus Two
UK No.1 ALBUMS			
THE ROLLING STONES NO.2 The Rolling Stones	THE ROLLING STONES NO.2 The Rolling Stones	THE ROLLING STONES NO.2 The Rolling Stones	THE ROLLING STONES NO.2 The Rolling Stones

14 Nov 98 ●	**EACH TIME** *Telstar CDSTAS 3017* [2]	2	10
28 Nov 98	**RESURRECTION** *Telstar TCD 3015* [2]	43	2
13 Mar 99	**BETCHA CAN'T WAIT** *Telstar CDSTAS 3031* [2]	12	5
12 Feb 05	**THE VERY BEST OF EAST SEVENTEEN** *London WSMCD 200* [1]	34	3

[1] East 17 featuring Gabrielle [2] E-17 [1] East Seventeen [2] E-17

Walthamstow changed catalogue number to 8284262 during its chart run.

EAST SIDE BEAT *Italy, male vocal / instrumental duo – Carl Fanini and Francesco Petrocchi (3 Singles: 18 Weeks)*

30 Nov 91 ●	**RIDE LIKE THE WIND** *ffrr F 176*	3	11
19 Dec 92	**ALIVE AND KICKING** *ffrr F 206*	26	6
29 May 93	**YOU'RE MY EVERYTHING** *ffrr FCD 207*	65	1

EASTERHOUSE *UK, male vocal / instrumental group*

28 Jun 86	**CONTENDERS** *Rough Trade ROUGH 94*	91	1

EASTERN LANE *UK, male vocal / instrumental group (3 Singles: 3 Weeks)*

15 Nov 03	**FEED YOUR ADDICTION** *Rough Trade RTRADSCD 132*	72	1
13 Mar 04	**SAFFRON** *Rough Trade RTRADSCD 156*	55	1
6 Nov 04	**I SAID PIG ON FRIDAY** *Rough Trade RTRADSCD 199*	65	1

Sheena EASTON (see also PRINCE) *UK, female vocalist (5 Albums: 37 Weeks, 15 Singles: 104 Weeks)*

5 Apr 80 ●	**MODERN GIRL (re)** *EMI 5042*	8	15
19 Jul 80 ●	**9 TO 5** *EMI 5066* ▲ $	3	15
25 Oct 80	**ONE MAN WOMAN** *EMI 5114*	14	6
31 Jan 81	**TAKE MY TIME** *EMI EMC 3354*	17	19
14 Feb 81	**TAKE MY TIME** *EMI 5135*	44	5
2 May 81	**WHEN HE SHINES** *EMI 5166*	12	8
27 Jun 81 ●	**FOR YOUR EYES ONLY** *EMI 5195*	8	13
12 Sep 81	**JUST ANOTHER BROKEN HEART** *EMI 5232*	33	8
3 Oct 81	**YOU COULD HAVE BEEN WITH ME** *EMI EMC 3378*	33	6
5 Dec 81	**YOU COULD HAVE BEEN WITH ME** *EMI 5252*	54	3
31 Jul 82	**MACHINERY** *EMI 5326*	38	5
25 Sep 82	**MADNESS MONEY AND MUSIC** *EMI EMC 3414*	44	4
12 Feb 83	**WE'VE GOT TONIGHT** *Liberty UP 658* [1]	28	7
15 Oct 83	**BEST KEPT SECRET** *EMI EMC 1077951*	99	1
21 Jan 89	**THE LOVER IN ME** *MCA MCA 1289*	15	8
4 Mar 89	**THE LOVER IN ME** *MCA MCG 6036*	30	7
18 Mar 89	**DAYS LIKE THIS** *MCA MCA 1325*	43	3
15 Jul 89	**101** *MCA MCA 1348*	54	2
18 Nov 89	**THE ARMS OF ORION** *Warner Bros. W 2757* [2]	27	5
9 Dec 00	**GIVING UP GIVING IN** *Universal MCSTD 40244*	54	1

[1] Kenny Rogers and Sheena Easton [2] Prince with Sheena Easton

'Modern Girl' reached its peak position only on re-entry in Aug 1980.

EASTSIDE CONNECTION *US, disco aggregation*

8 Apr 78	**YOU'RE SO RIGHT FOR ME** *Creole CR 149*	44	3

Clint EASTWOOD *US, male actor / vocalist*

7 Feb 70	**I TALK TO THE TREES** *Paramount PARA 3004*	18	2

This is the flip side of 'Wand'rin Star' by Lee Marvin and was listed with Marvin's A-side for two weeks only.

Clint EASTWOOD and GENERAL SAINT *UK, male vocal duo (2 Albums: 3 Weeks, 2 Singles: 3 Weeks)*

6 Feb 82	**TWO BAD DJ** *Greensleeves GREL 24*	99	2
28 May 83	**STOP THAT TRAIN** *Greensleeves GREL 53*	98	1
29 Sep 84	**LAST PLANE (ONE WAY TICKET)** *MCA MCA 910*	51	3

The EASYBEATS *Australia / Holland / UK, male vocal (Steven Wright) / instrumental group (2 Singles: 24 Weeks)*

27 Oct 66 ●	**FRIDAY ON MY MIND** *United Artists UP 1157*	6	15
10 Apr 68	**HELLO, HOW ARE YOU** *United Artists UP 2209*	20	9

EASYWORLD *UK, male vocal / instrumental trio (6 Singles: 7 Weeks)*

1 Jun 02	**BLEACH** *Jive 9253552*	67	1
21 Sep 02	**YOU & ME** *Jive 9254092*	57	1
8 Feb 03	**JUNKIES** *Jive 9254522*	40	1
18 Oct 03	**2ND AMENDMENT** *Jive 82876554692*	42	1
31 Jan 04	**'TIL THE DAY** *Jive 82876585362*	27	2
11 Sep 04	**HOW DID IT EVER COME TO THIS?** *Jive 82876632102*	50	1

EAT *UK / US, male / female vocal / instrumental group*

12 Jun 93	**BLEED ME WHITE** *Fiction FICCD 48*	73	1

EAT STATIC *UK, male production duo – Marv Pepler and Joie Hinton (3 Albums: 5 Weeks, 3 Singles: 3 Weeks)*

15 May 93	**ABDUCTION** *Planet Dog BARKCD 1*	62	1
25 Jun 94	**IMPLANT** *Planet Dog BARKCD 005*	13	3
22 Feb 97	**HYBRID** *Planet Dog BARK 024CD*	41	1
27 Sep 97	**INTERCEPTOR** *Planet Dog BARK 030CD*	44	1
25 Oct 97	**SCIENCE OF THE GODS** *Planet Dog BARKCD 029*	60	1
27 Jun 98	**CONTACT ...** *Planet Dog BARK 033CD*	67	1

Cleveland EATON *US, male keyboard player*

23 Sep 78	**BAMA BOOGIE WOOGIE** *Gull GULS 63*	35	6

EAV *Austria, male vocal / instrumental group*

27 Sep 86	**BA-BA-BANKROBBERY (ENGLISH VERSION)** *Columbia DB 9139*	63	4

EAZY-E (see also NWA) *US, male rapper – Eric Wright, d. 26 Mar 1995*

6 Jan 96	**JUST TAH LET YOU KNOW** *Epic 6628162*	30	3
10 Feb 96	**STR8 OFF THA STREETZ OF MUTHAPHUKKIN COMPTON** *Ruthless 4835762*	66	1

EBONY DUBSTERS (see also SHY FX) *UK, male production duo – Andre Williams and Mark Royal (2 Singles: 3 Weeks)*

24 Jan 04	**MURDERATION** *Ebony EBR 029*	59	2
22 May 04	**NUMBER 1 / THE RITUAL** *Ebony EBR 030*	58	1

ECHELON *UK, male vocal / instrumental group*

20 Nov 04	**PLUS** *Poptones MC 5095SCD*	57	1

ECHO and The BUNNYMEN (373 Top 500)

Cult alternative rock group originally from Liverpool, UK, who named themselves after their drum machine. Ian McCulloch (v), b. 5 May 1959, front man of this moody and atmospheric group, went solo in 1988. The original line-up reformed in 1997 (10 Albums: 100 Weeks, 20 Singles: 87 Weeks)

17 May 80	**RESCUE** *Korova KOW 1*	62	1
26 Jul 80	**CROCODILES** *Korova KODE 1*	17	6
18 Apr 81	**SHINE SO HARD (EP)** *Korova ECHO 1*	37	4
6 Jun 81 ●	**HEAVEN UP HERE** *Korova KODE 3*	10	16
18 Jul 81	**A PROMISE** *Korova KOW 15*	49	4
29 May 82	**THE BACK OF LOVE** *Korova KOW 24*	19	7
22 Jan 83 ●	**THE CUTTER** *Korova KOW 26*	8	8
12 Feb 83 ●	**PORCUPINE** *Korova KODE 6*	2	17
16 Jul 83	**NEVER STOP** *Korova KOW 28*	15	7
28 Jan 84 ●	**THE KILLING MOON** *Korova KOW 32*	9	6
21 Apr 84	**SILVER** *Korova KOW 34*	30	5
12 May 84 ●	**OCEAN RAIN** *Korova KODE 8*	4	26
14 Jul 84	**SEVEN SEAS** *Korova KOW 35*	16	7
19 Oct 85	**BRING ON THE DANCING HORSES** *Korova KOW 43*	21	7
23 Nov 85 ●	**SONGS TO LEARN & SING** *Korova KODE 13*	6	15
13 Jun 87	**THE GAME** *WEA YZ 134*	28	4
18 Jul 87 ●	**ECHO AND THE BUNNYMEN** *WEA WX 108*	4	9
1 Aug 87	**LIPS LIKE SUGAR** *WEA YZ 144*	36	4
20 Feb 88	**PEOPLE ARE STRANGE** *WEA YZ 175*	29	5
2 Mar 91	**PEOPLE ARE STRANGE** (re-issue) *East West YZ 567*	34	4

15 / 17 April 1965	22 / 24 April 1965	29 April / 1 May 1965	6 / 8 May 1965
THE MINUTE YOU'RE GONE Cliff Richard	TICKET TO RIDE The Beatles	TICKET TO RIDE The Beatles	TICKET TO RIDE The Beatles
THE FREEWHEELIN' BOB DYLAN Bob Dylan	THE ROLLING STONES NO.2 The Rolling Stones	BEATLES FOR SALE The Beatles	BEATLES FOR SALE The Beatles

KEY: UK No.1 ★ UK Top 10 ● Still on chart + UK entry at No.1 ■ US No.1 ▲ UK million seller £ US million seller $
Singles re-entries are listed as (re), (2re), (3re)... which signifies that the hit re-entered the chart once, twice or three times...
Peak Position / Weeks

21 Jun 97 BALLYHOO – THE BEST OF ECHO AND THE BUNNYMEN *Korova 630191032* ... 59 1
28 Jun 97 ● NOTHING LASTS FOREVER *London LOCDP 396* ... 8 6
26 Jul 97 ● EVERGREEN *London 8289052* ... 8 7
13 Sep 97 I WANT TO BE THERE WHEN YOU COME *London LONCD 399* .. 30 2
8 Nov 97 DON'T LET IT GET YOU DOWN *London LOCDP 406* ... 50 1
27 Mar 99 RUST *London LONCD 424* ... 22 3
17 Apr 99 WHAT ARE YOU GOING TO DO WITH YOUR LIFE? *London 5560802* ... 21 2
5 May 01 IT'S ALRIGHT *Cooking Vinyl FRYCD 104* ... 41 1
26 May 01 FLOWERS *Cooking Vinyl COOKCD 208* ... 56 1
17 Sep 05 STORMY WEATHER *Cooking Vinyl FRYCD 246* ... 55 1

Tracks on Shine So Hard (EP): Crocodiles / All that Jazz / Zimbo / Over the Wall.

ECHOBASS *UK, male producer – Simon Woodgate*

14 Jul 01 YOU ARE THE WEAKEST LINK *House of Bush CDANNE 001* ... 53 1

ECHOBEATZ *UK, male DJ / production duo – Dave De Braie and Paul Moody*

25 Jul 98 ● MAS QUE NADA *Eternal WEA 176CD* ... 10 5

ECHOBELLY (see also LITHIUM and Sonya MADAN)

UK / Sweden, male / female vocal (Sonya Aurora Madan) / instrumental group (3 Albums: 28 Weeks, 8 Singles: 16 Weeks)

2 Apr 94 INSOMNIAC *Fauve FAUV 1CD* ... 47 1
2 Jul 94 I CAN'T IMAGINE THE WORLD WITHOUT ME *Fauve FAUV 2CD* ... 39 2
3 Sep 94 ● EVERYONE'S GOT ONE *Fauve FAUV 3CD* ... 8 3
5 Nov 94 CLOSE ... BUT *Fauve FAUV 4CD* ... 59 1
2 Sep 95 GREAT THINGS *Fauve FAUV 5CD* ... 13 3
30 Sep 95 ● ON *Fauve FAUV 6CD* ... 4 24
4 Nov 95 KING OF THE KERB *Fauve FAUV 7CD* ... 25 3
2 Mar 96 DARK THERAPY *Fauve FAUV 8CD* ... 20 3
23 Aug 97 THE WORLD IS FLAT *Epic 6648152* ... 31 2
8 Nov 97 HERE COMES THE BIG RUSH *Epic 6652452* ... 56 1
22 Nov 97 LUSTRA *Epic 4889672* ... 47 1

Billy ECKSTINE

US, male vocalist, b. 8 Jul 1914, d. 8 Mar 1993 (4 Singles: 48 Weeks)

12 Nov 54 ● NO ONE BUT YOU *MGM 763* ... 3 17
27 Sep 57 PASSING STRANGERS *Mercury MT 164* [1] ... 22 2
13 Feb 59 ● GIGI *Mercury AMT 1018* ... 8 14
12 Mar 69 PASSING STRANGERS (re-issue) *Mercury MF 1082* [1] ... 20 15

[1] Billy Eckstine and Sarah Vaughan

ECLIPSE (see also BINI & MARTINI; GOODFELLAS featuring Lisa MILLETT; HOUSE OF GLASS) *Italy, male producer / instrumentalist – Gianni Bini*

14 Aug 99 MAKES ME LOVE YOU *Azuli AZNYCDX 100* ... 25 4

Silvio ECOMO *Holland, male producer*

15 Jul 00 STANDING *Hooj Choons HOOJ 098CD* ... 70 1

EDDIE and The HOT RODS *UK, male vocal (Barrie Masters) / instrumental group (4 Albums: 9 Weeks, 5 Singles: 26 Weeks)*

11 Sep 76 LIVE AT THE MARQUEE (EP) *Island IEP 2* ... 43 5
13 Nov 76 TEENAGE DEPRESSION *Island WIP 6354* ... 35 4
18 Dec 76 TEENAGE DEPRESSION *Island ILPS 9457* ... 43 1
23 Apr 77 I MIGHT BE LYING *Island WIP 6388* ... 44 3
13 Aug 77 ● DO ANYTHING YOU WANNA DO *Island WIP 6401* [1] ... 9 10
3 Dec 77 LIFE ON THE LINE *Island ILPS 9509* ... 27 3
21 Jan 78 QUIT THIS TOWN *Island WIP 6411* ... 36 4
24 Mar 79 THRILLER *Island ILPS 9563* ... 50 1
24 Jul 82 WILD DOGS *Arista SPART 1196* [1] ... 75 4

[1] The Rods [1] The Rods

Tracks on Live at the Marquee (EP): 96 Tears / Get out of Denver / Medley: Gloria / Satisfaction.

EDDY *UK, female vocalist – Edith Emenike*

9 Jul 94 SOMEDAY *Positiva CDTIV 14* ... 49 2

EDDY and The SOUL BAND *US, male / female vocal / instrumental group*

23 Feb 85 THE THEME FROM 'SHAFT' *Club JAB 11* ... 13 7

Duane EDDY (210 Top 500) *Twangy guitar legend, b. 26 Apr 1938, New York, US. Early rock's No.1 solo instrumentalist assembled a long string of UK and US hit singles and was one of the first rock acts to score on the album charts (9 Albums: 88 Weeks, 23 Singles: 202 Weeks)*

5 Sep 58 REBEL-ROUSER *London HL 8669* [1] $ ... 19 10
2 Jan 59 CANNONBALL *London HL 8764* [2] ... 22 4
6 Jun 59 ● HAVE 'TWANGY' GUITAR WILL TRAVEL *London HAW 2160* ... 6 3
19 Jun 59 ● PETER GUNN (re) *London HLW 8879* ... 6 11
24 Jul 59 YEP! *London HLW B 8879* ... 17 5
4 Sep 59 FORTY MILES OF BAD ROAD *London HLW 8929* ... 11 9
31 Oct 59 ● SPECIALLY FOR YOU *London HAW 2191* ... 6 8
18 Dec 59 SOME KIND-A EARTHQUAKE *London HLW 9007* ... 12 5
19 Feb 60 BONNIE CAME BACK *London HLW 9050* ... 12 11
19 Mar 60 ● THE TWANG'S THE THANG *London HAW 2236* ... 2 25
28 Apr 60 ● SHAZAM! *London HLW 9104* ... 4 13
21 Jul 60 ● BECAUSE THEY'RE YOUNG *London HLW 9162* $ ... 2 18
10 Nov 60 KOMMOTION *London HLW 9225* ... 13 10
26 Nov 60 SONGS OF OUR HERITAGE *London HAW 2285* ... 13 5
12 Jan 61 ● PEPE *London HLW 9257* ... 2 14
1 Apr 61 ● A MILLION DOLLARS' WORTH OF TWANG *London HAW 2325* .. 5 19
20 Apr 61 ● THEME FROM DIXIE *London HLW 9324* ... 7 10
22 Jun 61 RING OF FIRE *London HLW 9370* ... 17 10
14 Sep 61 DRIVIN' HOME *London HLW 9406* ... 30 4
5 Oct 61 CARAVAN *Parlophone R 4826* ... 42 3
24 May 62 DEEP IN THE HEART OF TEXAS *RCA 1288* ... 19 8
9 Jun 62 A MILLION DOLLARS' WORTH OF TWANG VOLUME 2 *London HAW 2435* ... 18 1
21 Jul 62 ● TWISTIN' AND TWANGIN' *RCA RD 27264* ... 8 12
23 Aug 62 ● BALLAD OF PALADIN *RCA 1300* [3] ... 10 10
8 Nov 62 ● (DANCE WITH THE) GUITAR MAN *RCA 1316* [4] ... 4 16
8 Dec 62 TWANGY GUITAR – SILKY STRINGS *RCA RD 7510* ... 13 11
14 Feb 63 BOSS GUITAR *RCA 1329* [4] ... 27 8
16 Mar 63 DANCE WITH THE GUITAR MAN *RCA RD 7545* ... 14 4
30 May 63 LONELY BOY LONELY GUITAR *RCA 1344* [4] ... 35 4
29 Aug 63 YOUR BABY'S GONE SURFIN' *RCA 1357* [4] ... 49 1
8 Mar 75 ● PLAY ME LIKE YOU PLAY YOUR GUITAR *GTO GT 11* [4] ... 9 9
22 Mar 86 ● PETER GUNN (re-recording) *China WOK 6* [5] ... 8 9

[1] Duane Eddy and his Twangy Guitar [2] Duane Eddy, his Twangy Guitar & The Rebels [3] Duane Eddy – Orchestra conducted by Bob Thompson [4] Duane Eddy and The Rebelettes [5] Art of Noise featuring Duane Eddy

Randy EDELMAN *US, male vocalist / pianist (4 Singles: 18 Weeks)*

6 Mar 76 CONCRETE AND CLAY *20th Century BTC 2261* ... 11 7
18 Sep 76 UPTOWN UPTEMPO WOMAN *20th Century BTC 2225* ... 25 7
15 Jan 77 YOU *20th Century BTC 2253* ... 49 2
17 Jul 82 NOBODY MADE ME *Rocket XPRES 81* ... 60 2

EDELWEISS *Austria, male / female vocal / instrumental group*

29 Apr 89 ● BRING ME EDELWEISS *WEA YZ 353* ... 5 10

EDEN *UK / Australia, male / female vocal / instrumental group*

6 Mar 93 DO U FEEL 4 ME *Logic 74321135422* ... 51 2

13 / 15 May 1965	20 / 22 May 1965	27 / 29 May 1965	3 / 5 June 1965
UK No.1 SINGLES			
KING OF THE ROAD Roger Miller	WHERE ARE YOU NOW Jackie Trent	LONG LIVE LOVE Sandie Shaw	LONG LIVE LOVE Sandie Shaw
UK No.1 ALBUMS			
BEATLES FOR SALE The Beatles	THE FREEWHEELIN' BOB DYLAN Bob Dylan	BRINGING IT ALL BACK HOME Bob Dylan	THE SOUND OF MUSIC Soundtrack

EDISON LIGHTHOUSE

UK, male vocal (Tony Burrows) / instrumental group (2 Singles: 13 Weeks)

24 Jan 70 ★ **LOVE GROWS (WHERE MY ROSEMARY GOES)** *Bell 1091* $........1 12
30 Jan 71 **IT'S UP TO YOU PETULA** *Bell 1136*........49 1

EDITORS NEW

UK, male vocal / instrumental group (1 Album: 6 Weeks, 4 Singles: 9 Weeks)

5 Feb 05 **BULLETS** *Kitchenware SKCD 77*........54 1
30 Apr 05 **MUNICH** *Kitchenware SKCD 782*........22 3
23 Jul 05 **BLOOD** *Kitchenware SKCD 792*........18 3
6 Aug 05 THE BACK ROOM *Kitchenware KWCD 34*........13 6
8 Oct 05 **BULLETS** (re-issue) *Kitchenware SKCD 80*........27 2

Dave EDMUNDS

UK, male vocalist / guitarist (4 Albums: 21 Weeks, 12 Singles: 93 Weeks)

21 Nov 70 ★ **I HEAR YOU KNOCKING** *MAM 1* [1] 1 14
20 Jan 73 ● **BABY I LOVE YOU** *Rockfield ROC 1*........8 13
9 Jun 73 ● **BORN TO BE WITH YOU** *Rockfield ROC 2*........5 12
2 Jul 77 **I KNEW THE BRIDE** *Swansong SSK 19411*........26 8
23 Jun 79 REPEAT WHEN NECESSARY *Swansong SSK 59409*........39 12
30 Jun 79 ● **GIRLS TALK** *Swansong SSK 19418*........4 11
22 Sep 79 **QUEEN OF HEARTS** *Swansong SSK 19419*........11 9
24 Nov 79 **CRAWLING FROM THE WRECKAGE** *Swansong SSK 19420*........59 4
9 Feb 80 **SINGING THE BLUES** *Swansong SSK 19422*........28 8
28 Mar 81 **ALMOST SATURDAY NIGHT** *Swansong SSK 19424*........58 3
18 Apr 81 TWANGIN' *Swansong SSK 59411*........37 4
20 Jun 81 **THE RACE IS ON** *Swansong SSK 19425* [2] 34 6
3 Apr 82 D.E. 7TH *Arista SPART 1184*........60 3
26 Mar 83 **SLIPPING AWAY** *Arista ARIST 522*........60 4
30 Apr 83 INFORMATION *Arista 205 348*........92 2
7 Apr 90 **KING OF LOVE** *Capitol CL 568*........68 1

[1] Dave Edmunds' Rockpile [2] Dave Edmunds and The Stray Cats

Alton EDWARDS *Zimbabwe, male vocalist*

9 Jan 82 **I JUST WANNA (SPEND SOME TIME WITH YOU)** *Streetwave STRA 1897*........20 9

Dennis EDWARDS *US, male vocalist*

24 Mar 84 **DON'T LOOK ANY FURTHER (re)** *Gordy TMG 1334* [1] 45 10
14 Apr 84 DON'T LOOK ANY FURTHER *Gordy ZL 72148*........91 1

[1] Dennis Edwards featuring Siedah Garrett

The re-entry peaked at No.55 in Jun 1987.

Rupie EDWARDS *Jamaica, male vocalist (2 Singles: 16 Weeks)*

23 Nov 74 ● **IRE FEELINGS (SKANGA)** *Cactus CT 38*........9 10
8 Feb 75 **LEGO SKANGA** *Cactus CT 51*........32 6

Todd EDWARDS *US, male DJ / producer*

24 Aug 96 SAVED MY LIFE *ffrr FX 279*........69 1

Tommy EDWARDS

US, male vocalist, b. 17 Feb 1922, d. 23 Oct 1969 (2 Singles: 18 Weeks)

3 Oct 58 ★ **IT'S ALL IN THE GAME** *MGM 989* ▲ $ 1 17
7 Aug 59 **MY MELANCHOLY BABY** *MGM 1020*........29 1

EEK-A-MOUSE *Jamaica, male vocalist – Ripton Hylton*

14 Aug 82 SKIDIP *Greensleeves GREL 41*........61 3

EELS *US, male vocal (Mark Everett) / instrumental group (6 Albums: 44 Weeks, 9 Singles: 24 Weeks)*

8 Feb 97 ● BEAUTIFUL FREAK *Dreamworks DRMD 50001*........5 27
15 Feb 97 ● **NOVOCAINE FOR THE SOUL** *Dreamworks DRMCD 22174*........10 5
17 May 97 ● **SUSAN'S HOUSE** *Dreamworks DRMCD 22238*........9 5
13 Sep 97 **YOUR LUCKY DAY IN HELL** *Dreamworks DRMCD 22277*........35 2
26 Sep 98 **LAST STOP: THIS TOWN** *Dreamworks DRMCD 22346*........23 3
3 Oct 98 ELECTRO-SHOCK BLUES *Dreamworks DRD 50052*........12 4
12 Dec 98 **CANCER FOR THE CURE** *Dreamworks DRMCD 22373*........60 1
26 Feb 00 **MR E'S BEAUTIFUL BLUES** *Dreamworks DRMCD 4509762*........11 4
11 Mar 00 ● DAISIES OF THE GALAXY *Dreamworks 4502182*........8 5
24 Jun 00 **FLYSWATTER** *Dreamworks DRMCD 4509462*........55 1
22 Sep 01 **SOULJACKER PART 1** *Dreamworks DRMCD 4508922*........30 2
6 Oct 01 SOULJACKER *Dreamworks 4503462*........12 2
14 Jun 03 SHOOTENANNY *Dreamworks 4504588*........35 2
7 May 05 BLINKING LIGHTS & OTHER REVELATIONS *Dreamworks 9881785*........16 4
28 May 05 **HEY MAN (NOW YOU'RE REALLY LIVING)** *Vagrant 9881879*........45 1

EFUA *UK, female vocalist – Efua Baker*

3 Jul 93 **SOMEWHERE** *Virgin VSCDT 1463*........42 5

EGG *UK, male vocal / instrumental group*

30 Jan 99 **GETTING AWAY WITH IT** *Indochina ID 079CD*........58 1

EGGS ON LEGS *UK, male vocalist*

23 Sep 95 **COCK A DOODLE DO IT** *Avex UK AVEXCD 18*........42 1

EGYPTIAN EMPIRE *UK, male producer – Tim Taylor*

24 Oct 92 **THE HORN TRACK** *Ffrreedom TAB 115*........61 2

EIFFEL 65 *Italy, male vocal / instrumental / production trio (1 Album: 4 Weeks, 3 Singles: 36 Weeks)*

21 Aug 99 **BLUE (DA BA DEE)** (import) *Logic 74321688212*........39 5
25 Sep 99 ★ **BLUE (DA BA DEE)** *Eternal WEA 226CD1* ■ £........1 21
19 Feb 00 ● **MOVE YOUR BODY** *Eternal WEA 255CD1*........3 10
4 Mar 00 EUROPOP *Eternal 8573814552*........12 4

18 WHEELER *UK, male vocal / instrumental group*

15 Mar 97 **STAY** *Creation CRESCD 249*........59 1

EIGHTH WONDER

(see also MERRION, McCALL & KENSIT) *UK, female / male vocal (Patsy Kensit) / instrumental group (1 Album: 4 Weeks, 4 Singles: 25 Weeks)*

2 Nov 85 **STAY WITH ME** *CBS A 6594*........65 2
20 Feb 88 ● **I'M NOT SCARED** *CBS SCARE 1*........7 13
25 Jun 88 **CROSS MY HEART** *CBS 6515527*........13 8
23 Jul 88 FEARLESS *CBS 460628 1*........47 4
1 Oct 88 **BABY BABY** *CBS BABE 1*........65 2

The EIGHTIES MATCHBOX B-LINE DISASTER

UK, male vocal / instrumental group (1 Album: 1 Week, 6 Singles: 11 Weeks)

28 Sep 02 **CELEBRATE YOUR MOTHER** *No Death / Island MCSTD 40296*... 66 1
18 Jan 03 **PSYCHOSIS SAFARI** *No Death / Island MCSTD 40308*........26 2
24 May 03 **CHICKEN** *No Death / Island MCSTD 40317*........30 2
24 Jan 04 **MISTER MENTAL** *Universal MCSTD 40353*........25 2
10 Jul 04 **I COULD BE AN ANGLE** *Island MCSTD 40368*........35 2
23 Oct 04 **RISE OF THE EAGLES** *Universal MCSTD 40382*........40 2
6 Nov 04 ROYAL SOCIETY *Universal MCD 60097*........68 1

88.3 featuring Lisa MAY

UK, male production / instrumental trio and female vocalist

15 Jul 95 **WISHING ON A STAR** *Urban Guerrilla UG 3CD*........61 1

801 *UK, male vocal / instrumental group*

20 Nov 76 801 LIVE *Island ILPS 9444*........52 2

808 STATE *UK, DJ / production / instrumental group (4 Albums: 20 Weeks, 17 Singles: 70 Weeks)*

18 Nov 89 ● **PACIFIC** *ZTT ZANG 1*........10 9

10 / 12 June 1965	17 / 19 June 1965	24 / 26 June 1965	1 / 3 July 1965
LONG LIVE LOVE Sandie Shaw	CRYING IN THE CHAPEL Elvis Presley with The Jordanaires	I'M ALIVE The Hollies	CRYING IN THE CHAPEL Elvis Presley with The Jordanaires
THE SOUND OF MUSIC Soundtrack	THE SOUND OF MUSIC Soundtrack	THE SOUND OF MUSIC Soundtrack	THE SOUND OF MUSIC Soundtrack

KEY: UK No.1 ★ UK Top 10 ● Still on chart + UK entry at No.1 ■ US No.1 ▲ UK million seller £ US million seller $ Singles re-entries are listed as (re), (2re), (3re)... which signifies that the hit re-entered the chart once, twice or three times... Peak Position / Weeks

Date		Title / Label	Peak	Weeks
16 Dec 89		NINETY ZTT ZTT 2	57	5
31 Mar 90		THE EXTENDED PLEASURE OF DANCE (EP) ZTT ZANG 2T	56	1
2 Jun 90	●	THE ONLY RHYME THAT BITES ZTT ZANG 3 [1]	10	10
15 Sep 90		TUNES SPLITS THE ATOM ZTT ZANG 6 [1]	18	7
10 Nov 90	●	CUBIK / OLYMPIC ZTT ZANG 5	10	10
16 Feb 91	●	IN YER FACE ZTT ZANG 14	9	6
16 Mar 91	●	EX:EL ZTT ZTT 6	4	10
27 Apr 91		OOOPS ZTT ZANG 19 [2]	42	3
17 Aug 91		LIFT / OPEN YOUR MIND ZTT ZANG 20	38	4
29 Aug 92		TIME BOMB / NIMBUS ZTT ZANG 33	59	1
12 Dec 92		ONE IN TEN (re-mix) ZTT ZANG 39 [3]	17	8
30 Jan 93		PLAN 9 ZTT ZANG 38CD	50	2
13 Feb 93		GORGEOUS ZTT 4509911002	17	3
26 Jun 93		10 X 10 ZTT ZANG 42CD	67	1
13 Aug 94		BOMBADIN ZTT ZANG 54CD	67	1
29 Jun 96		BOND ZTT ZANG 80CD	57	1
8 Feb 97		LOPEZ ZTT ZANG 87CD	20	2
16 May 98		PACIFIC / CUBIK (re-mix) ZTT ZTT 98CD1	21	3
30 May 98		808:88:98 ZTT ZTT 100CD	40	2
6 Mar 99		THE ONLY RHYME THAT BITES 99 ZTT ZTT 125CD [1]	53	1

[1] MC Tunes versus 808 State [2] 808 State featuring Bjork [3] 808 State vs UB40

Tracks on The Extended Pleasure of Dance (EP): Cobra Bora / Ancodia / Cubik. 'Cubik' is a re-issue of one of the tracks from The Extended Pleasure of Dance (EP). 'Lopez' features the uncredited vocals of James Dean Bradfield, lead singer of Manic Street Preachers.

Ludovico EINAUDI *Italy, male pianist (2 Albums: 5 Weeks)*

Date		Title / Label	Peak	Weeks
13 Sep 03		ECHOES – THE COLLECTION BMG 82876550892	40	4
18 Sep 04		UNA MATTINA Decca 4756292	59	1

EINSTEIN (see also AMBASSADORS OF FUNK featuring MC MARIO)
UK, male rapper – Colin Case (3 Singles: 6 Weeks)

Date		Title / Label	Peak	Weeks
18 Nov 89		ANOTHER MONSTERJAM ffrr F 116 [1]	65	1
15 Dec 90		TURN IT UP Swanyard SYD 9 [2]	42	4
24 Aug 96		THE POWER 96 Arista 74321398672 [3]	42	1

[1] Simon Harris featuring Einstein [2] Technotronic featuring Melissa and Einstein [3] Snap! featuring Einstein

EL COCO *US, male vocal / instrumental group*

Date		Title / Label	Peak	Weeks
14 Jan 78		COCOMOTION Pye International 7N 25761	31	4

EL MARIACHI (see also FUNK JUNKEEZ)
US, male producer – Roger Sanchez

Date		Title / Label	Peak	Weeks
9 Nov 96		CUBA ffrr FCD 286	38	2

EL PRESIDENTE NEW *UK, male / female vocal / instrumental group (1 Album: 1 Week, 3 Singles: 5 Weeks)*

Date		Title / Label	Peak	Weeks
14 May 05		100 MPH One 82876692152	37	2
6 Aug 05		WITHOUT YOU One 82876710782	30	2
22 Oct 05		ROCKET One 82876743032	48	1
5 Nov 05		EL PRESIDENTE One 82876710712	57	1

ELASTICA *UK, female / male vocal (Justine Frischmann) / instrumental group (2 Albums: 27 Weeks, 4 Singles: 12 Weeks)*

Date		Title / Label	Peak	Weeks
12 Feb 94		LINE UP Deceptive BLUFF 004CD	20	3
22 Oct 94		CONNECTION Deceptive BLUFF 010CD	17	4
25 Feb 95		WAKING UP Deceptive BLUFF 011CD	13	4
25 Mar 95	★	ELASTICA Deceptive BLUFF 014CD ■	1	25
15 Apr 00		THE MENACE Deceptive BLUFF 075CD	24	2
24 Jun 00		MAD DOG Deceptive BLUFF 077CD	44	1

ELATE *UK, male / female vocal / instrumental trio*

Date		Title / Label	Peak	Weeks
26 Jul 97		SOMEBODY LIKE YOU VC VCRD 22	38	2

Donnie ELBERT
US, male vocalist, b. 25 May 1936, d. 26 Jan 1989 (3 Singles: 29 Weeks)

Date		Title / Label	Peak	Weeks
8 Jan 72	●	WHERE DID OUR LOVE GO? London HL 10352	8	10
26 Feb 72		I CAN'T HELP MYSELF Avco 6105 009	11	10
29 Apr 72		A LITTLE PIECE OF LEATHER London HL 10370	27	9

ELBOW *UK, male vocal (Guy Garvey) / instrumental group (3 Albums: 12 Weeks, 9 Singles: 15 Weeks)*

Date		Title / Label	Peak	Weeks
5 May 01		RED V2 VVR 5016153	36	1
19 May 01		ASLEEP IN THE BACK V2 VVR 1015882	14	5
21 Jul 01		POWDER BLUE V2 VVR 5016163	41	1
20 Oct 01		NEWBORN V2 VVR 5016173	42	1
16 Feb 02		ASLEEP IN THE BACK / COMING SECOND V2 VVR 5018703	19	3
16 Aug 03		FALLEN ANGEL V2 VVR 5021803	19	3
30 Aug 03	●	CAST OF THOUSANDS V2 VVR 1021812	7	4
8 Nov 03		FUGITIVE MOTEL V2 VVR 5021823	44	1
6 Mar 04		NOT A JOB V2 VVR 5024678	26	2
10 Sep 05		FORGET MYSELF V2 VVR 5032543	22	2
24 Sep 05		LEADERS OF THE FREE WORLD V2 VVR 1032558	12	3
19 Nov 05		LEADERS OF THE FREE WORLD V2 VVR 5035623	53	1

ELECTRA *UK, male vocal / instrumental group (2 Singles: 7 Weeks)*

Date		Title / Label	Peak	Weeks
6 Aug 88		JIBARO ffrr FFR 9	54	3
30 Dec 89		IT'S YOUR DESTINY / AUTUMN LOVE London F 121	51	4

ELECTRAFIXION
UK, male vocal / instrumental group (1 Album: 2 Weeks, 4 Singles: 6 Weeks)

Date		Title / Label	Peak	Weeks
19 Nov 94		ZEPHYR WEA YZ 865CD	47	2
9 Sep 95		LOWDOWN WEA YZ 977CD	54	2
7 Oct 95		BURNED Spacejunk 0630112482	38	2
4 Nov 95		NEVER Spacejunk WEA 022CD	58	1
16 Mar 96		SISTER PAIN Spacejunk WEA 037CD1	27	1

ELECTRASY
UK, male vocal / instrumental group (1 Album: 1 Week, 3 Singles: 7 Weeks)

Date		Title / Label	Peak	Weeks
13 Jun 98		LOST IN SPACE MCA MCSTD 40171	60	1
5 Sep 98		MORNING AFTERGLOW MCA MCSTD 40184	19	4
26 Sep 98		BEAUTIFUL INSANE MCA MCD 60051	48	1
28 Nov 98		BEST FRIEND'S GIRL MCA MCSXD 40195	41	2

ELECTRIBE 101 *UK / Germany, male / female vocal / instrumental group (1 Album: 3 Weeks, 4 Singles: 15 Weeks)*

Date		Title / Label	Peak	Weeks
28 Oct 89		TELL ME WHEN THE FEVER ENDED Mercury MER 310	32	5
24 Feb 90		TALKING WITH MYSELF Mercury MER 316	23	5
22 Sep 90		YOU'RE WALKING Mercury MER 328	50	3
20 Oct 90		ELECTRIBAL MEMORIES Mercury 8429651	26	3
10 Oct 98		TALKING WITH MYSELF (re-mix) Manifesto FESDD 49	39	2

ELECTRIC BOYS *Sweden, male vocal / instrumental group*

Date		Title / Label	Peak	Weeks
6 Jun 92		GROOVUS MAXIMUS Vertigo 5122552	61	1

ELECTRIC LIGHT ORCHESTRA 54 Top 500 *Ground-breaking and innovative UK group, fronted by multi-talented Jeff Lynne (v/g) from Birmingham, that originally included Roy Wood (The Move). Their unique sound, which featured an orchestral string section, helped them achieve numerous transatlantic hits (17 Albums: 404 Weeks, 29 Singles: 255 Weeks)*

Date		Title / Label	Peak	Weeks
29 Jul 72	●	10538 OVERTURE Harvest HAR 5053	9	8
12 Aug 72		ELECTRIC LIGHT ORCHESTRA Harvest SHVL 797	32	4
27 Jan 73	●	ROLL OVER BEETHOVEN Harvest HAR 5063	6	10
31 Mar 73		ELECTRIC LIGHT ORCHESTRA II Harvest SHVL 806	35	1
6 Oct 73		SHOWDOWN Harvest HAR 5077	12	10
9 Mar 74		MA-MA-MA-BELLE Warner Bros. K 16349	22	8

	8 / 10 July 1965	15 / 17 July 1965	22 / 24 July 1965	29 / 31 July 1965
UK No.1 SINGLES	I'M ALIVE The Hollies	I'M ALIVE The Hollies	MR TAMBOURINE MAN The Byrds	MR TAMBOURINE MAN The Byrds
UK No.1 ALBUMS	THE SOUND OF MUSIC Soundtrack	THE SOUND OF MUSIC Soundtrack	THE SOUND OF MUSIC Soundtrack	THE SOUND OF MUSIC Soundtrack

10 Jan 76 ● **EVIL WOMAN** *Jet 764* 10 8
3 Jul 76 **STRANGE MAGIC** *Jet 779* 38 3
13 Nov 76 ● **LIVIN' THING** *Jet UP 36184* 4 12
11 Dec 76 ● **A NEW WORLD RECORD** *United Artists UAG 30017* 6 100
19 Feb 77 ● **ROCKARIA!** *Jet UP 36209* 9 9
21 May 77 ● **TELEPHONE LINE** *Jet UP 36254* $ 8 10
29 Oct 77 **TURN TO STONE** *Jet UP 36313* 18 12
12 Nov 77 ● **OUT OF THE BLUE** *United Artists UAR 100* 4 108
28 Jan 78 ● **MR. BLUE SKY** *Jet UP 36342* 6 11
10 Jun 78 ● **WILD WEST HERO** *Jet JET 109* 6 14
7 Oct 78 ● **SWEET TALKIN' WOMAN** *Jet 121* 6 9
9 Dec 78 **THE ELO (EP)** *Jet ELO 1* 34 8
6 Jan 79 **THREE LIGHT YEARS** *Jet JETBX 1* 38 9
19 May 79 ● **SHINE A LITTLE LOVE** *Jet 144* 6 10
16 Jun 79 ★ **DISCOVERY** *Jet JETLX 500* ■ 1 46
21 Jul 79 ● **THE DIARY OF HORACE WIMP** *Jet 150* 8 9
1 Sep 79 ● **DON'T BRING ME DOWN** *Jet 153* $ 3 9
17 Nov 79 ● **CONFUSION / LAST TRAIN TO LONDON** *Jet 166* 8 10
1 Dec 79 ● **ELO'S GREATEST HITS** *Jet JETLX 525* 7 18
24 May 80 **I'M ALIVE** *Jet 179* $ 20 9
21 Jun 80 ★ **XANADU** *Jet 185* [1] 1 11
2 Aug 80 **ALL OVER THE WORLD** *Jet 195* 11 8
22 Nov 80 **DON'T WALK AWAY** *Jet 7004* 21 10
1 Aug 81 ● **HOLD ON TIGHT** *Jet 7011* [2] 4 12
8 Aug 81 ★ **TIME** *Jet JETLP 236* 1 32
24 Oct 81 **TWILIGHT** *Jet 7015* [2] 30 7
9 Jan 82 **TICKET TO THE MOON / HERE IS THE NEWS** *Jet 7018* [2] 24 8
18 Jun 83 **ROCK 'N' ROLL IS KING** *Jet A 3500* [2] 13 9
2 Jul 83 ● **SECRET MESSAGES** *Jet JETLX 527* 4 15
3 Sep 83 **SECRET MESSAGES** *Jet A 3720* [2] 48 3
1 Mar 86 **CALLING AMERICA** *Epic A 6844* 28 7
15 Mar 86 ● **BALANCE OF POWER** *Epic EPC 26467* 9 12
16 Dec 89 **THE GREATEST HITS** *Telstar STAR 2370* 23 21
11 May 91 **HONEST MEN PART TWO** *Telstar ELO 100* [3] 60 1
1 Jun 91 **ELECTRIC LIGHT ORCHESTRA PART II** *Telstar STAR 2503* [1] 34 4
2 Jul 94 ● **THE VERY BEST OF THE ELECTRIC LIGHT ORCHESTRA** *Dino DINCD 90* 4 11
8 Nov 97 **LIGHT YEARS – THE VERY BEST OF ELECTRIC LIGHT ORCHESTRA** *Epic 4890392* 60 4
23 Jun 01 **ZOOM** *Epic 5025002* 34 2
3 Nov 01 **THE ULTIMATE COLLECTION** *Columbia STVCD 126* 18 6
18 Jun 05 ● **THE VERY BEST OF ELECTRIC LIGHT ORCHESTRA – ALL OVER THE WORLD** *Epic 5201292* 6 11

[1] Olivia Newton-John and Electric Light Orchestra [2] ELO [3] Electric Light Orchestra Part 2 [1] ELO Part 2

'Here is the News' listed from 16 Jan 1982. Tracks on The ELO (EP): Can't Get it Out of My Head / Strange Magic / Ma-Ma-Ma-Belle / Evil Woman. A New World Record changed catalogue number to JETLP 200 and Out of the Blue to JETDP 400 during their chart runs. The Greatest Hits was also issued under the title The Very Best of Electric Light Orchestra with the same track listing and catalogue number.

The ELECTRIC PRUNES
US, male vocal / instrumental group (2 Singles: 5 Weeks)

9 Feb 67 **I HAD TOO MUCH TO DREAM (LAST NIGHT)** *Reprise RS 20532* 49 1
11 May 67 **GET ME TO THE WORLD ON TIME** *Reprise RS 20564* 42 4

ELECTRIC SIX *US, male vocal (Dick Valentine) / instrumental group (1 Album: 10 Weeks, 4 Singles: 27 Weeks)*

18 Jan 03 ● **DANGER! HIGH VOLTAGE** *XL Recordings XLS 151CD* 2 11
14 Jun 03 ● **GAY BAR** *XL Recordings XLS 158CD* 5 10
12 Jul 03 ● **FIRE** *XL Recordings XLCD 169* 7 10
25 Oct 03 **DANCE COMMANDER** *XL Recordings XLS 170CD* 40 1
25 Dec 04 **RADIO GA GA** *WEA WEA 381CD2* 21 5

The ELECTRIC SOFT PARADE *UK, male vocal / instrumental group – leaders Alex and Tom White (2 Albums: 3 Weeks, 4 Singles: 5 Weeks)*

4 Aug 01 **EMPTY AT THE END / SUMATRAN** *DB DB 006CD 7* [1] 65 1
10 Nov 01 **THERE'S A SILENCE** *DB DB 007CD 7* 52 1
16 Feb 02 **HOLES IN THE WALL** *DB DB 002CDLP* 35 2
16 Mar 02 **SILENT TO THE DARK II** *DB DB 008CD 7* 23 2
1 Jun 02 **EMPTY AT THE END / THIS GIVEN LINE** *DB DB 009CD 7* 39 1
25 Oct 03 **THE AMERICAN ADVENTURE** *BMG 82876563692* 45 1

[1] Soft Parade

ELECTRIC WIND ENSEMBLE *UK, male instrumental group*

18 Feb 84 **HAUNTING MELODIES** *Nouveau Music NML 1007* 28 9

ELECTRIQUE BOUTIQUE *UK / France, male production group*

26 Aug 00 **REVELATION** *Data DATA 14CDS* 37 2

ELECTRONIC
UK, male vocal / instrumental group (3 Albums: 24 Weeks, 8 Singles: 36 Weeks)

16 Dec 89 **GETTING AWAY WITH IT** *Factory FAC 2577* 12 9
27 Apr 91 ● **GET THE MESSAGE** *Factory FAC 2877* 8 7
8 Jun 91 ● **ELECTRONIC** *Factory FACT 290* 2 16
21 Sep 91 **FEEL EVERY BEAT** *Factory FAC 3287* 39 4
4 Jul 92 ● **DISAPPOINTED** *Parlophone R 6311* 6 5
6 Jul 96 **FORBIDDEN CITY** *Parlophone CDR 6436* 14 4
20 Jul 96 ● **RAISE THE PRESSURE** *Parlophone CDPCS 7382* 8 5
28 Sep 96 **FOR YOU** *Parlophone CDR 6445* 16 2
15 Feb 97 **SECOND NATURE** *Parlophone CDR 6455* 35 2
24 Apr 99 **VIVID** *Parlopbone CDR 6514* 17 3
8 May 99 ● **TWISTED TENDERNESS** *Parlophone 5201462* 9 3

ELECTRONICAS *Holland, male instrumental group*

19 Sep 81 **ORIGINAL BIRD DANCE** *Polydor POSP 360* 22 8

ELECTROSET
UK, male instrumental / production group (2 Singles: 4 Weeks)

21 Nov 92 **HOW DOES IT FEEL** *ffrr F 203* 27 3
15 Jul 95 **SENSATION** *Ffrreedom TABCD 231* 69 1

The ELEGANTS *US, male vocal group*

26 Sep 58 **LITTLE STAR** *HMV POP 520* ▲ $ 25 2

ELEMENTFOUR (see also OAKENFOLD; PERFECTO ALLSTARZ; VIRUS)
UK, male production duo – Paul Oakenfold and Andy Gray

9 Sep 00 ● **BIG BROTHER UK TV THEME (re)** *Channel 4 Music C4M 00072* 4 11

ELEPHANT MAN
Jamaica, male vocalist – O'Neil Bryan (2 Singles: 5 Weeks)

22 Nov 03 **PON DE RIVER, PON DE BANK** *Atlantic AT 0168CD* 29 3
4 Sep 04 **JOOK GAL** *VP VPCD 6416* 41 2

ELEVATION *UK, male instrumental / production duo*

23 May 92 **CAN U FEEL IT** *Nova Mute 12NOMU 3* 62 1

ELEVATOR SUITE *UK, male production / instrumental trio*

12 Aug 00 **BACK AROUND** *Infectious INFECT 85CDS* 71 1

ELEVATORMAN
UK, male instrumental / production group (2 Singles: 4 Weeks)

14 Jan 95 **FUNK AND DRIVE** *Wired WIRED 211* 37 3
1 Jul 95 **FIRED UP** *Wired WIRED 216* 44 1

Danny ELFMAN *US, male orchestra leader*

12 Aug 89 **BATMAN** *Warner Bros. WX 287* 45 6

The ELGINS *US, male / female vocal group (2 Singles: 20 Weeks)*

1 May 71 ● **HEAVEN MUST HAVE SENT YOU** *Tamla Motown TMG 771* 3 13
9 Oct 71 **PUT YOURSELF IN MY PLACE** *Tamla Motown TMG 787* 28 7

KEY
UK No.1 ★★ UK Top 10 ●● Still on chart ++ UK entry at No.1 ■■ US No.1 ▲▲ UK million seller £ US million seller $
Singles re-entries are listed as (re), (2re), (3re)... which signifies that the hit re-entered the chart once, twice or three times...
Peak Position / Weeks

ELIAS and his ZIG-ZAG JIVE FLUTES
South Africa, male instrumental group

25 Apr 58 ● **TOM HARK** *Columbia DB 4109* 2 14

Yvonne ELLIMAN *US, female vocalist (5 Singles: 44 Weeks)*

29 Jan 72 **I DON'T KNOW HOW TO LOVE HIM** *MCA MMKS 5077* 47 1
6 Nov 76 ● **LOVE ME** *RSO 2090 205* 6 13
7 May 77 **HELLO STRANGER** *RSO 2090 236* 26 5
13 Aug 77 **I CAN'T GET YOU OUT OF MY MIND** *RSO 2090 251* 17 13
6 May 78 ● **IF I CAN'T HAVE YOU** *RSO 2090 266* ▲ $ 4 12

'I Don't Know How to Love Him' was one of four tracks on a maxi-single, two of which were credited during the disc's one week on the chart. The other track credited was 'Superstar' by Murray Head.

Duke ELLINGTON *US, male band leader / pianist – Edward Ellington, b. 29 Apr 1899, d. 24 May 1974*

5 Mar 54 ● **SKIN DEEP** *Philips PB 243* [1] 7 4
8 Apr 61 **NUT CRACKER SUITE** *Philips BBL 7418* 11 2

[1] Duke Ellington and his Orchestra with Louis Bellson (drums)

Lance ELLINGTON *UK, male vocalist*

21 Aug 93 **LONELY (HAVE WE LOST OUR LOVE)** *RCA 74321158332* 57 1

Ray ELLINGTON
UK, male vocal / instrumental group – leader b. 17 Mar 1915, d. 27 Feb 1985

15 Nov 62 **THE MADISON (re)** *Ember S 102* 36 4

Bern ELLIOTT and The FENMEN
UK, male vocal / instrumental group (2 Singles: 22 Weeks)

21 Nov 63 **MONEY** *Decca F 11770* 14 13
19 Mar 64 **NEW ORLEANS** *Decca F 11852* 24 9

Missy 'Misdemeanor' ELLIOTT (328 Top 500)
Leading female rapper / songwriter / producer / arranger and record label (Gold Mind) boss, b. Melissa Elliott, 1 Jul 1972, Virginia, US. This multi-award-winning hip hop / R&B legend, who first surfaced in the group Sista in 1992, has recorded with countless artists and charted with 20 of them (5 Albums: 57 Weeks, 28 Singles: 154 Weeks)

30 Aug 97 **THE RAIN (SUPA DUPA FLY)** *East West E 3919CD* 16 3
29 Nov 97 **SOCKIT2ME** *East West E 3890CD* [1] 33 2
25 Apr 98 **BEEP ME 911** *East West E 3859CD* 14 3
22 Aug 98 **MAKE IT HOT** *East West E 3821CD* [2] 22 4
22 Aug 98 **HIT 'EM WIT DA HEE** *East West E 3824CD 1* [3] 25 3
26 Sep 98 ★ **I WANT YOU BACK** *Virgin VSCDT 1716* [4] ■ 1 9
21 Nov 98 **5 MINUTES** *Elektra E 3803CD* [5] 72 1
13 Mar 99 **HERE WE COME** *Virgin DINSD 179* [6] 43 1
10 Jul 99 **DA REAL WORLD** *Elektra 7559624362* 40 2
25 Sep 99 **ALL N MY GRILL** *Elektra E 3742CD* [7] 20 4
22 Jan 00 **HOT BOYZ** *Elektra E 7002CD* [8] $ 18 3
28 Apr 01 ● **GET UR FREAK ON** *East West / Elektra E 7206CD* 4 11
26 May 01 ● **MISS E ... SO ADDICTIVE** *Elektra 7559626392* 10 26
18 Aug 01 ● **ONE MINUTE MAN** *Elektra E 7245CD* [9] 10 8
13 Oct 01 **SUPERFREAKON** *East West / Elektra 7559672550* 72 1
22 Dec 01 **SON OF A GUN (I BETCHA THINK THIS SONG IS ABOUT YOU) (re)** *Virgin VUSCD 232* [10] 13 9
6 Apr 02 ● **4 MY PEOPLE** *Goldmind / Elektra E 7286CD* 5 13
16 Nov 02 ● **WORK IT** *Goldmind / Elektra E 7344CD* [11] 6 9
23 Nov 02 **UNDER CONSTRUCTION** *Elektra 7559628132* [1] 24 22
22 Mar 03 ● **GOSSIP FOLKS** *Elektra E 7380CD* [12] 9 9
22 Nov 03 ● **PASS THAT DUTCH** *East West E 7509CD* 10 11
6 Dec 03 **THIS IS NOT A TEST!** *Elektra 7559629052* [1] 49 4
13 Mar 04 **COP THAT SH*T** *Unique Corp TIMBACD 001* [13] 22 3
3 Apr 04 **I'M REALLY HOT** *Elektra E 7552CD* [11] 22 4
17 Jul 04 **PUSH** *Def Jam 9862837* [14] 34 3
13 Nov 04 ● **CAR WASH** *Dreamworks 986430* [15] 4 14
19 Mar 05 **TURN DA LIGHTS OFF** *Atlantic AT 0200CD* [16] 29 3
23 Apr 05 ● **1, 2 STEP** *LaFace 82876688192* [17] 3 11
2 Jul 05 ● **LOSE CONTROL** *Atlantic AT 0209CD* [18] 7 11
16 Jul 05 **THE COOKBOOK** *Atlantic 7567837792* [1] 33 3
8 Oct 05 **TEARY EYED** *Atlantic AT 0215CD* 47 1

[1] Missy Elliott featuring Da Brat [2] Nicole featuring Missy 'Misdemeanor' Elliott and Mocha [3] Missy 'Misdemeanor' Elliott featuring Lil' Kim [4] Melanie B featuring Missy 'Misdemeanor' Elliott [5] Lil' Mo featuring Missy 'Misdemeanor' Elliott [6] Timbaland / Missy Elliott and Magoo [7] Missy 'Misdemeanor' Elliott featuring MC Solaar [8] Missy 'Misdemeanor' Elliott featuring Nas, Eve and Q Tip [9] Missy 'Misdemeanor' Elliott featuring Ludacris [10] Janet with Carly Simon featuring Missy Elliott [11] Missy Elliott [12] Missy Elliott featuring Ludacris [13] Timbaland & Magoo featuring Missy Elliott [14] Ghostface featuring Missy Elliott [15] Christina Aguilera featuring Missy Elliott [16] Tweet Featuring Missy Elliott [17] Ciara featuring Missy Elliott [18] Missy Elliott featuring Ciara & Fat Man Scoop [1] Missy Elliott

Joey B ELLIS *US, male rapper (2 Singles: 10 Weeks)*

16 Feb 91 **GO FOR IT (HEART AND FIRE)** *Capitol CL 601* [1] 20 8
18 May 91 **THOUGHT U WERE THE ONE FOR ME** *Capitol CL 614* 58 2

[1] Rocky V featuring Joey B Ellis and Tynetta Hare

Shirley ELLIS *US, female vocalist – Shirley Elliston (2 Singles: 17 Weeks)*

6 May 65 ● **THE CLAPPING SONG** *London HLR 9961* 6 13
8 Jul 78 **THE CLAPPING SONG (EP)** *MCA MCEP 1* 59 4

Tracks on The Clapping Song (EP): The Clapping Song / Ever See a Diver Kiss His Wife While the Bubbles Bounce Above the Water / The Name Game / The Nitty Gritty. 'The Clapping Song' itself qualifies as a re-issue.

ELLIS, BEGGS and HOWARD *UK, male vocal / instrumental group*

2 Jul 88 **BIG BUBBLES, NO TROUBLES (re)** *RCA PB 42089* 41 8

Peak position reached on its re-entry in Mar 89.

Sophie ELLIS-BEXTOR (see also SPILLER; THEAUDIENCE)
UK, female vocalist (2 Albums: 46 Weeks, 7 Singles: 63 Weeks)

25 Aug 01 ● **TAKE ME HOME (A GIRL LIKE ME)** *Polydor 5872312* 2 12
15 Sep 01 ● **READ MY LIPS** *Polydor 5891742* 2 44
15 Dec 01 ● **MURDER ON THE DANCEFLOOR** *Polydor 5704942* 2 16
22 Jun 02 ● **GET OVER YOU / MOVE THIS MOUNTAIN** *Polydor 5708332* 3 13
16 Nov 02 **MUSIC GETS THE BEST OF ME** *Polydor 0659222* 14 10
25 Oct 03 ● **MIXED UP WORLD** *Polydor 9812108* 7 6
8 Nov 03 **SHOOT FROM THE HIP** *Polydor 9865834* 19 2
10 Jan 04 ● **I WON'T CHANGE YOU** *Polydor 9815124* 9 6

Jennifer ELLISON *UK, female actor / vocalist (2 Singles: 14 Weeks)*

28 Jun 03 ● **BABY I DON'T CARE** *East West EW 268CD1* 6 10
7 Aug 04 **BYE BYE BOY** *Sky-Rocket / Concept CDSKYCON 01* 13 4

Ben ELTON *UK, male comedian*

14 Nov 87 **MOTORMOUTH** *Mercury BENLP 1* 86 2

ELWOOD *US, male rapper / vocalist – Elwood Strickland*

26 Aug 00 **SUNDOWN** *Palm Pictures PPCD 70342* 72 1

EMBRACE *UK, male vocal (Danny McNamara) / instrumental group (5 Albums: 69 Weeks, 15 Singles: 58 Weeks)*

17 May 97 **FIREWORKS (EP)** *Hut HUTCD 84* 34 2
19 Jul 97 **ONE BIG FAMILY (EP)** *Hut HUTCD 86* 21 3

8 Nov 97 ● **ALL YOU GOOD GOOD PEOPLE** *Hut HUTCD 90* 8 4
6 Jun 98 ● **COME BACK TO WHAT YOU KNOW** *Hut HUTCD 93* 6 8
20 Jun 98 ★ THE GOOD WILL OUT *Hut CDHUT 46* ■ 1 21
29 Aug 98 ● **MY WEAKNESS IS NONE OF YOUR BUSINESS** *Hut HUTCD 103* 9 4
13 Nov 99 **HOOLIGAN** *Hut HUTCD 123* 18 3
25 Mar 00 **YOU'RE NOT ALONE** *Hut / Virgin HUTCD 126* 14 3
8 Apr 00 ● DRAWN FROM MEMORY *Hut CDHUT 60* 8 13
10 Jun 00 **SAVE ME (re)** *Hut / Virgin HUTCD 133* 29 3
19 Aug 00 **I WOULDN'T WANNA HAPPEN TO YOU** *Hut / Virgin HUTCD 137* 23 2
1 Sep 01 **WONDER (re)** *Hut / Virgin HUTCD 142* 14 4
15 Sep 01 ● IF YOU'VE NEVER BEEN *Hut CDHUT 68* 9 3
17 Nov 01 **MAKE IT LAST** *Hut / Virgin HUTCD 144* 35 2
6 Apr 02 FIREWORKS (SINGLES 1997-2002) *Hut CDHUT 74* 36 2
11 Sep 04 ● **GRAVITY** *Independiente ISOM 87SMS* 7 7
25 Sep 04 ★ OUT OF NOTHING *Independiente ISOM 45CD* ■ 1 30
27 Nov 04 **ASHES** *Independiente ISOM 89SMS* 11 8
26 Feb 05 **LOOKING AS YOU ARE** *Independiente ISOM 91SMS* 11 3
11 Jun 05 **A GLORIOUS DAY** *Independiente ISOM 94SMS* 28 2

Tracks on Fireworks (EP): The Last Gas / Now You're Nobody / Blind / Fireworks. Tracks on One Big Family (EP): One Big Family / Dry Kids / You've Only Got to Stop to Get Better / Butter Wouldn't Melt.

Keith EMERSON (see also EMERSON, LAKE and PALMER; EMERSON, LAKE & POWELL; The NICE) *UK, male keyboard player*

10 Apr 76 **HONKY TONK TRAIN BLUES** *Manticore K 13513* 21 5

EMERSON, LAKE and PALMER 495 Top 500

(see also ASIA; EMERSON, LAKE & POWELL) *Pioneering armour-plated progressive rock supertrio: Keith Emerson (k), ex-Nice, Greg Lake (v/b/g), ex-King Crimson, and Carl Palmer (d), ex-Atomic Rooster and Crazy World of Arthur Brown. Their classical-orientated rock helped change the face of 1970s music (10 Albums: 137 Weeks, 1 Single: 13 Weeks)*

5 Dec 70 ● EMERSON LAKE & PALMER *Island ILPS 9132* 4 28
19 Jun 71 ★ TARKUS *Island ILPS 9155* 1 17
4 Dec 71 ● PICTURES AT AN EXHIBITION *Island HELP 1* 3 5
8 Jul 72 ● TRILOGY *Island ILPS 9186* 2 29
22 Dec 73 ● BRAIN SALAD SURGERY *Manticore K 53501* 2 17
24 Aug 74 ● WELCOME BACK MY FRIENDS, TO THE SHOW THAT NEVER ENDS – LADIES AND GENTLEMEN: EMERSON LAKE & PALMER *Manticore K 63500* 5 5
9 Apr 77 ● WORKS – VOLUME 1 *Atlantic ?* 9 25
4 Jun 77 ● **FANFARE FOR THE COMMON MAN** *Atlantic K 10946* 2 13
10 Dec 77 WORKS – VOLUME 2 *Atlantic ??* 20 5
9 Dec 78 LOVE BEACH *Atlantic ???* 48 4
26 Jun 04 THE ULTIMATE COLLECTION *Sanctuary TDSAN 009X* 43 2

EMERSON, LAKE & POWELL (see also Keith EMERSON; Greg LAKE; Cozy POWELL) *UK, male vocal / instrumental group*

14 Jun 86 EMERSON LAKE & POWELL *Polydor POLD 5191* 35 5

Dick EMERY

UK, male actor / vocalist, b. 7 Feb 1917, d. 2 Jan 1983 (2 Singles: 8 Weeks)

26 Feb 69 **IF YOU LOVE HER** *Pye 7N 17644* 32 4
13 Jan 73 **YOU ARE AWFUL** *Pye 7N 45202* 43 4

EMILIA *Sweden, female vocalist – Emilia Rydberg (2 Singles: 14 Weeks)*

12 Dec 98 ● **BIG BIG WORLD** *Universal UMD 87190* 5 13
1 May 99 **GOOD SIGN** *Universal UMD 87206* 54 1

EMINEM 84 Top 500

Controversy-courting, chainsaw-wielding, multi-award-winning rap superstar, b. Marshall Mathers III, 17 Oct 1972, Detroit, US. The four time BRIT award winner and Oscar winner, also known as Slim Shady, is the most successful rap artist in UK chart history with 16 successive Top 10 hits, and announced plans to retire in 2005 (5 Albums: 297 Weeks, 17 Singles: 187 Weeks)

10 Apr 99 ● **MY NAME IS (re)** *Interscope IND 95638* 2 12
24 Apr 99 ● THE SLIM SHADY LP *Interscope IND 90321* 10 114
14 Aug 99 ● **GUILTY CONSCIENCE** *Interscope IND 4971282* [1] 5 8
3 Jun 00 ★ THE MARSHALL MATHERS LP *Interscope 4906292* ▲ 1 74
10 Jun 00 ● **FORGOT ABOUT DRE** *Interscope 4973412* [2] 7 9
8 Jul 00 ★ **THE REAL SLIM SHADY (re)** *Interscope 4973792* ■ 1 16
14 Oct 00 ● **THE WAY I AM** *Interscope 4974252* 8 9
16 Dec 00 ★ **STAN (re)** *Interscope IND 97470* ■ 1 17
1 Sep 01 **SCARY MOVIES** *Mole UK MOLEUK 045* [3] 63 1
1 Jun 02 ★ **WITHOUT ME** *Interscope 4977282* ■ 1 16
8 Jun 02 ★ THE EMINEM SHOW *Interscope 4932902* ■ ▲ 1 70
28 Sep 02 ● **CLEANIN' OUT MY CLOSET (2re)** *Interscope 4973942* 4 13
14 Dec 02 ★ **LOSE YOURSELF** *Interscope 4978282* ■ ▲ 1 21
15 Mar 03 ● **SING FOR THE MOMENT** *Interscope 4978612* 6 10
19 Jul 03 ● **BUSINESS** *Interscope 9809382* 6 9
13 Nov 04 ★ **JUST LOSE IT** *Interscope 2103183* ■ 1 12
20 Nov 04 ★ ENCORE *Interscope 9864884* ■ ▲ 1 35
12 Feb 05 ★ **LIKE TOY SOLDIERS (re)** *Interscope 2103963* ■ 1 12
14 May 05 ● **MOCKINGBIRD** *Interscope 9882073* 4 12
6 Aug 05 ● **ASS LIKE THAT** *Interscope 9883904* 4 9
10 Dec 05 ★ CURTAIN CALL – THE HITS *Interscope 9887893* ■ ▲ 1 4+
31 Dec 05 ● **WHEN I'M GONE** *Interscope 9889581* 5 1+

[1] Eminem featuring Dr Dre [2] Dr Dre featuring Eminem [3] Bad Meets Evil featuring Eminem & Royce Da 5'9"

'Stan' features uncredited vocalist Dido and samples her single 'Thank You'.

EMMA *UK, female vocalist – Emma Booth*

28 Apr 90 **GIVE A LITTLE LOVE BACK TO THE WORLD** *Big Wave BWR 33* 33 6

EMMIE (see also INDIEN)

UK, female vocalist – Emma Morton Smith (2 Singles: 9 Weeks)

23 Jan 99 ● **MORE THAN THIS** *Indirect / Manifesto FESCD 52* 5 8
16 Feb 02 **I WON'T LET YOU DOWN** *Decode / Telstar CDSTAS 3210* [1] 53 1

[1] WIP featuring Emmie

The EMOTIONS *US, female vocal group (3 Singles: 28 Weeks)*

10 Sep 77 ● **BEST OF MY LOVE** *CBS 5555* ▲ $ 4 10
24 Dec 77 **I DON'T WANNA LOSE YOUR LOVE** *CBS 5819* 40 5
12 May 79 ● **BOOGIE WONDERLAND** *CBS 7292* [1] $ 4 13

[1] Earth Wind and Fire with The Emotions

Alec EMPIRE *Germany, male producer*

13 Apr 02 **ADDICTED TO YOU** *Digital Hardcore DHRMCD 38* 64 1
4 May 02 INTELLIGENCE & SACRIFICE *Digital Hardcore DHRCD 29* 71 1

EMPIRION *UK, male instrumental / production group (2 Singles: 2 Weeks)*

6 Jul 96 **NARCOTIC INFLUENCE** *XL XLS 72CD* 64 1
21 Jun 97 **BETA** *XL XLS 77CD* 75 1

EN VOGUE

US, female vocal group (4 Albums: 52 Weeks, 14 Singles: 83 Weeks)

5 May 90 ● **HOLD ON** *East West America 7908* $ 5 11
2 Jun 90 BORN TO SING *Atlantic 7567820841* 23 13
21 Jul 90 **LIES** *East West America 7893* 44 4
4 Apr 92 ● **MY LOVIN' (re)** *East West America A 8578* 4 12
23 May 92 ● FUNKY DIVAS *East West America 7567921212* 4 29
15 Aug 92 **GIVING HIM SOMETHING HE CAN FEEL** *East West America A 8524* 44 3
7 Nov 92 **FREE YOUR MIND / GIVING HIM SOMETHING HE CAN FEEL (re-issue)** *East West America A 8468* 16 8
16 Jan 93 **GIVE IT UP TURN IT LOOSE** *East West America A 8445CD* 22 4
10 Apr 93 **LOVE DON'T LOVE YOU** *East West America A 8424CD* 64 1
9 Oct 93 **RUNAWAY LOVE** *East West America A 8359CD* 36 3
19 Mar 94 ● **WHATTA MAN** *ffrr FCD 222* [1] $ 7 10
11 Jan 97 ● **DON'T LET GO (LOVE)** *East West A 3976CD* $ 5 16
14 Jun 97 **WHATEVER** *East West E 3642CD* 14 5
28 Jun 97 ● EV3 *East West 7559620972* 9 8
6 Sep 97 **TOO GONE, TOO LONG** *East West E 3908CD* 20 3

30 September / 2 October 1965	7 / 9 October 1965	14 / 16 October 1965	21 / 23 October 1965
TEARS Ken Dodd	TEARS Ken Dodd	TEARS Ken Dodd	TEARS Ken Dodd
HELP! The Beatles	HELP! The Beatles	THE SOUND OF MUSIC Soundtrack	THE SOUND OF MUSIC Soundtrack

KEY UK No.1 ★ UK Top 10 ● Still on chart + UK entry at No.1 ■ US No.1 ▲ UK million seller £ US million seller $
Singles re-entries are listed as (re), (2re), (3re)... which signifies that the hit re-entered the chart once, twice or three times...
Peak Position / Weeks

31 Oct 98 BEST OF EN VOGUE *East West 7559623222* ... 39 2
28 Nov 98 **HOLD ON** (re-mix) *East West E 3796CD* ... 53 1
1 Jul 00 **RIDDLE** *Elektra E 7053CD* ... 33 2

[1] Salt-N-Pepa with En Vogue

EN-CORE featuring Stephen EMMANUEL & ESKA *UK, male producer – Stephen Boreland and female vocalist – Eska Mtungwazi*

9 Sep 00 **COOCHY COO** *VC Recordings VCRD 72* ... 32 2

ENCORE *France, female vocalist – Sabine Ohmes*

14 Feb 98 **LE DISC JOCKEY** *Sum CDSUM 2* ... 12 4

ENERGISE *UK, male vocal / instrumental group*

16 Feb 91 **REPORT TO THE DANCEFLOOR** *Network NWKT 16* ... 69 1

ENERGY 52 *Germany, male DJ / producer – Paul Schmitz-Moormann (3 Singles: 11 Weeks)*

8 Mar 97 **CAFE DEL MAR** *Hooj Choons HOOJCD 51* ... 51 1
25 Jul 98 **CAFE DEL MAR '98** (re-mix) *Hooj Choons HOOJ 64CD* ... 12 6
12 Oct 02 **CAFE DEL MAR** (2nd re-mix) *Lost Language LOST 019CD* ... 24 4

ENERGY ORCHARD *Ireland, male vocal / instrumental group (1 Album: 2 Weeks, 2 Singles: 6 Weeks)*

27 Jan 90 **BELFAST** *MCA MCA 1392* ... 52 4
7 Apr 90 **SAILORTOWN** *MCA MCA 1402* ... 73 2
12 May 90 ENERGY ORCHARD *MCA MCG 6083* ... 53 2

Harry ENFIELD *UK, male comedian / vocalist*

7 May 88 ● **LOADSAMONEY (DOIN' UP THE HOUSE)** *Mercury DOSH 1* ... 4 7

The ENGINEERS NEW *UK, male vocal / instrumental group*

5 Mar 05 **FORGIVENESS** *Echo ESCD 159* ... 48 1

ENGLAND BOYS *UK, male vocal group*

8 Jun 02 **GO ENGLAND** *Phonogram 5829592* ... 26 3

ENGLAND DAN and John Ford COLEY *US, male vocal duo – Dan Seals and John Ford Coley (2 Singles: 12 Weeks)*

25 Sep 76 **I'D REALLY LOVE TO SEE YOU TONIGHT** *Atlantic K 10810* $ ... 26 7
23 Jun 79 **LOVE IS THE ANSWER** *Big Tree K 11296* ... 45 5

ENGLAND FOOTBALL WORLD CUP SQUAD *UK, male football team vocalists (2 Albums: 18 Weeks)*

16 May 70 ● THE WORLD BEATERS SING THE WORLD BEATERS *Pye NSPL 18337* ... 4 8
15 May 82 THIS TIME *K-Tel NE 1169* ... 37 10

ENGLAND SUPPORTERS' BAND *UK, male instrumental group (2 Singles: 4 Weeks)*

27 Jun 98 **THE GREAT ESCAPE** *V2 VVR 5002163* ... 46 2
24 Jun 00 **THE GREAT ESCAPE 2000** (re-recording) *V2 VVR 5014293* ... 26 2

ENGLAND UNITED *UK, male / female vocal / instrumental group*

13 Jun 98 ● **(HOW DOES IT FEEL TO BE) ON TOP OF THE WORLD (re)** *London LONCD 414* ... 9 11

ENGLAND WORLD CUP SQUAD *UK, male football team vocalists (6 Singles: 48 Weeks)*

18 Apr 70 ★ **BACK HOME (re)** *Pye 7N 17920* ... 1 17
10 Apr 82 ● **THIS TIME (WE'LL GET IT RIGHT) / ENGLAND, WE'LL FLY THE FLAG** *England ER 1* ... 2 13
19 Apr 86 **WE'VE GOT THE WHOLE WORLD AT OUR FEET / WHEN WE ARE FAR FROM HOME** *Columbia DB 9128* ... 66 2
21 May 88 **ALL THE WAY** *MCA GOAL 1* [1] ... 64 2
2 Jun 90 ★ **WORLD IN MOTION ...** *Factory / MCA FAC 2937* [2] ... 1 12
15 Jun 02 **WORLD IN MOTION ...** (re-issue) *London / MCA NUDOCD 12* [2] ... 43 2

[1] England Football Team and the 'sound' of Stock, Aitken and Waterman [2] Englandneworder (New Order, Keith Allen, England footballer / rapper John Barnes and the rest of the England World Cup squad)

ENGLAND'S BARMY ARMY *UK, 5,000 male / female vocal cricket supporters*

12 Jun 99 **COME ON ENGLAND!** *Wildstar CDWILD 20* ... 45 1

Kim ENGLISH *US, female vocalist (5 Singles: 7 Weeks)*

23 Jul 94 **NITE LIFE** *Hi-Life PZCD 323* ... 35 2
4 Mar 95 **TIME FOR LOVE** *Hi-Life HICD 8* ... 48 1
9 Sep 95 **I KNOW A PLACE** *Hi-Life 5798072* ... 52 1
30 Nov 96 **NITE LIFE** (re-mix) *Hi-Life 5755332* ... 35 2
26 Apr 97 **SUPERNATURAL** *Hi-Life 5736972* ... 50 1

Scott ENGLISH *US, male vocalist*

9 Oct 71 **BRANDY** *Horse HOSS 7* ... 12 10

ENIGMA *UK, male / female vocal / instrumental group (1 Album: 3 Weeks, 2 Singles: 15 Weeks)*

23 May 81 **AIN'T NO STOPPING** *Creole CR 9* ... 11 8
8 Aug 81 **I LOVE MUSIC** *Creole CR 14* ... 25 7
5 Sep 81 AIN'T NO STOPPIN' *Creole CRX 1* ... 80 3

ENIGMA 371 Top 500

New-age, ambient and dance fusion sculpted by Michael Cretu, b. 18 May 1957, Bucharest, Romania, and initially aided by German wife Sandra Lauer and producer Frank Peterson. The title of the Gregorian chant-sampling international debut hit 'Sadeness Part 1' – referring to the Marquis de Sade – was shortened for UK release (6 Albums: 142 Weeks, 9 Singles: 45 Weeks)

15 Dec 90 ★ **SADNESS PART 1** *Virgin International DINS 101* ... 1 12
22 Dec 90 ★ MCMXC A.D. – 'THE LIMITED EDITION' *Virgin International VIR 11* ... 1 83
30 Mar 91 **MEA CULPA PART II** *Virgin International DINS 104* ... 55 3
10 Aug 91 **PRINCIPLES OF LUST** *Virgin International DINS 110* ... 59 2
11 Jan 92 **THE RIVERS OF BELIEF** *Virgin International DINS 112* ... 68 2
29 Jan 94 ● **RETURN TO INNOCENCE** *Virgin International DINSD 123* ... 3 14
19 Feb 94 ★ THE CROSS OF CHANGES *Virgin International CDVIR 20* [1] ■ ... 1 35
14 May 94 **THE EYES OF TRUTH** *Virgin International DINSD 126* ... 21 4
20 Aug 94 **AGE OF LONELINESS** *Virgin International DINSD 135* ... 21 5
7 Dec 96 LE ROI EST MORT VIVE LE ROI! *Virgin CDVIR 60* [2] ... 12 12
25 Jan 97 **BEYOND THE INVISIBLE** *Virgin International DINSD 155* [1] ... 26 2
19 Apr 97 **TNT FOR THE BRAIN** *Virgin International DINSD 161* [1] ... 60 1
29 Jan 00 ● THE SCREEN BEHIND THE MIRROR *Virgin CDVIR 100* ... 7 6
17 Nov 01 LOVE SENSUALITY DEVOTION – THE GREATEST HITS *Virgin CDVIR 150* ... 29 4
20 Sep 03 VOYAGEUR *Virgin CDVIRX 211* ... 46 2

[1] Enigma 3 [1] Enigma 2 [2] Enigma 3

Brian ENO (see also ROXY MUSIC) *UK, male producer / keyboard player (8 Albums: 17 Weeks)*

9 Mar 74 HERE COME THE WARM JETS *Island ILPS 9268* ... 26 2
21 Oct 78 MUSIC FOR FILMS *Polydor 2310 623* ... 55 1

28 / 30 October 1965	4 / 6 November 1965	11 / 13 November 1965	18 / 20 November 1965
UK No.1 SINGLES			
TEARS Ken Dodd	GET OFF OF MY CLOUD The Rolling Stones	GET OFF OF MY CLOUD The Rolling Stones	GET OFF OF MY CLOUD The Rolling Stones
UK No.1 ALBUMS			
THE SOUND OF MUSIC Soundtrack	THE SOUND OF MUSIC Soundtrack	THE SOUND OF MUSIC Soundtrack	THE SOUND OF MUSIC Soundtrack

21 Feb 81 MY LIFE IN THE BUSH OF GHOSTS *Polydor EGLP 48* [1] 29 8
8 May 82 AMBIENT 4 ON LAND *EG EGED 20*........93 1
12 Sep 92 NERVE NET *Opal 9362450332*........70 1
24 Sep 94 WAH WAH *Fontana 5228272* [2] 11 2
14 Oct 95 SPINNER *All Saints ASCD 023* [3] 71 1
25 Jun 05 ANOTHER DAY ON EARTH *Hannibal HNCD 1475*........75 1

[1] Brian Eno and David Byrne [2] James and Brian Eno [3] Brian Eno and Jah Wobble

ENTOMBED *Sweden, male vocal / instrumental group*

15 Mar 97 TO RIDE SHOOT STRAIGHT AND SPEAK THE TRUTH *Threeman Recordings CDMFN 216*........75 1

ENUFF Z'NUFF *US, male vocal / instrumental group*

13 Apr 91 STRENGTH *Atco 7567916381*........56 1

ENYA 138 Top 500

The world's top selling New Age artist, b. Eithne Ni Bhraonian 17 May 1961, County Donegal, Ireland. The multi-award-winning ex-Clannad member (1980-82), whose sales top 65 million, was the world's biggest-selling female artist in 2001 (15 million albums) (8 Albums: 279 Weeks, 17 Singles: 89 Weeks)

6 Jun 87 ENYA *BBC REB 605*........69 4
15 Oct 88 ● WATERMARK *WEA WX 199*........5 92
15 Oct 88 ★ ORINOCO FLOW *WEA YZ 312*........1 13
24 Dec 88 EVENING FALLS ... *WEA YZ 356*........20 4
10 Jun 89 STORMS IN AFRICA (PART II) *WEA YZ 368*........41 4
19 Oct 91 CARIBBEAN BLUE *WEA YZ 604*........13 7
16 Nov 91 ★ SHEPHERD MOONS *WEA WX 431* ■........1 90
7 Dec 91 HOW CAN I KEEP FROM SINGING? *WEA YZ 365*........32 5
1 Aug 92 ● BOOK OF DAYS *WEA YZ 640*........10 6
14 Nov 92 THE CELTS *WEA YZ 705*........29 4
28 Nov 92 ● THE CELTS *WEA 4509911672*........10 19
18 Nov 95 ● ANYWHERE IS *WEA WEA 023CD*........7 12
2 Dec 95 ● THE MEMORY OF TREES *WEA 0630128792*........5 24
7 Dec 96 ON MY WAY HOME *WEA WEA 047CD*........26 2
15 Nov 97 ● PAINT THE SKY WITH STARS – THE BEST OF ENYA *WEA 3984208952*........4 28
13 Dec 97 ONLY IF ... *WEA WEA 143CD*........43 2
25 Nov 00 ONLY TIME *WEA WEA 316CD*........32 3
2 Dec 00 ● A DAY WITHOUT RAIN *WEA 8573859862*........6 17
31 Mar 01 WILD CHILD *WEA WEA 324CD*........72 1
2 Feb 02 MAY IT BE *WEA W 578CD*........50 2
5 Jun 04 I DON'T WANNA KNOW (import) *Universal 9862372 PMI* [1] .71 1
12 Jun 04 ★ I DON'T WANNA KNOW *Bad Boy MCSTD 40369* [1] ■........1 14
11 Sep 04 ● YOU SHOULD REALLY KNOW *Relentless RELCD 9* [2] 8 8
3 Dec 05 ● AMARANTINE *Warner Bros. 2564627972*........8 5+
17 Dec 05 AMARANTINE *Warner Bros. WEA 397CD2*........53 1

[1] Mario Winans featuring Enya & P Diddy [2] Pirates featuring Enya, Shola Ama, Naila Boss & Ishani

'I Don't Wanna Know' and the response, 'You Should Really Know', both sample the Enya track 'Boadicea'. The Celts is a repackaged and re-issued version of Enya.

EON *UK, male producer – Ian Bela*

17 Aug 91 FEAR: THE MINDKILLER *Vinyl Solution STORM 33*........63 1

The EQUALS (see also Eddy GRANT) *UK, male vocal / instrumental group (2 Albums: 10 Weeks, 8 Singles: 69 Weeks)*

18 Nov 67 ● UNEQUALLED EQUALS *President PTL 1006*........10 9
21 Feb 68 I GET SO EXCITED *President PT 180*........44 4
9 Mar 68 EQUALS EXPLOSION *President PTLS 1015*........32 1
1 May 68 ★ BABY COME BACK (re) *President PT 135*........1 18
21 Aug 68 LAUREL AND HARDY *President PT 200*........35 5
27 Nov 68 SOFTLY SOFTLY *President PT 222*........48 3
2 Apr 69 MICHAEL AND THE SLIPPER TREE *President PT 240*........24 7
30 Jul 69 ● VIVA BOBBY JOE *President PT 260*........6 14
27 Dec 69 RUB A DUB DUB *President PT 275*........34 7
19 Dec 70 ● BLACK SKIN BLUE EYED BOYS *President PT 325*........9 11

TOP 10

ON THE DAY OF THE GREAT TRAIN ROBBERY

The Great Train Robbery on 8 August 1963 has gone down in history as a Robin Hood-style heist due to the gang's refusal to carry guns. However, this somewhat romantic view fails to acknowledge that the train driver, Jack Mills, was struck on the head with an iron bar. He never fully recovered from the attack, and never drove another train. Thirteen of the 15 'Devils in Disguise' ended up 'Confessin'', but the most infamous of the gang, Ronnie Biggs, escaped from prison to live a life of unhappy exile in Brazil.

LW	TW	
3	1	**SWEETS FOR MY SWEET** The Searchers
2	2	**CONFESSIN' (THAT I LOVE YOU)** Frank Ifield
1	3	**(YOU'RE THE) DEVIL IN DISGUISE** Elvis Presley with The Jordanaires
4	4	**TWIST AND SHOUT** Brian Poole and The Tremeloes
5	5	**DA DOO RON RON** The Crystals
8	6	**SUKIYAKI** Kyu Sakamoto
7	7	**ATLANTIS** The Shadows
19	8	**IN SUMMER** Billy Fury
6	9	**I LIKE IT** Gerry and The Pacemakers
12	10	**YOU CAN NEVER STOP ME LOVING YOU** Kenny Lynch

The scene of the crime and The Searchers

25 / 27 November 1965	2 / 4 December 1965	9 / 11 December 1965	16 / 18 December 1965
THE CARNIVAL IS OVER The Seekers	THE CARNIVAL IS OVER The Seekers	THE CARNIVAL IS OVER The Seekers	DAY TRIPPER / WE CAN WORK IT OUT The Beatles
THE SOUND OF MUSIC Soundtrack	THE SOUND OF MUSIC Soundtrack	THE SOUND OF MUSIC Soundtrack	THE SOUND OF MUSIC Soundtrack

KEY UK No.1 ★ UK Top 10 ● Still on chart + UK entry at No.1 ■ US No.1 ▲ UK million seller £ US million seller $
Singles re-entries are listed as (re), (2re), (3re)... which signifies that the hit re-entered the chart once, twice or three times...
Peak Position / Weeks

ERASURE 67 Top 500 (see also The ASSEMBLY)

Award-winning UK duo formed by Vince Clarke (k) and Andy Bell (v). After hits with Depeche Mode, Yazoo and The Assembly, this act has been Clarke's greatest success, scoring 17 Top 10 singles and having five albums enter at No.1 (13 Albums: 325 Weeks, 34 Singles: 223 Weeks)

5 Oct 85 WHO NEEDS LOVE LIKE THAT *Mute MUTE 40* 55 2
14 Jun 86 WONDERLAND *Mute STUMM 25* 71 7
25 Oct 86 ● SOMETIMES *Mute MUTE 51* 2 17
28 Feb 87 IT DOESN'T HAVE TO BE *Mute MUTE 56* 12 9
11 Apr 87 ● THE CIRCUS *Mute STUMM 35* 6 107
30 May 87 ● VICTIM OF LOVE *Mute MUTE 61* 7 9
3 Oct 87 ● THE CIRCUS *Mute MUTE 66* 6 10
5 Mar 88 ● SHIP OF FOOLS *Mute MUTE 74* 6 8
30 Apr 88 ★ THE INNOCENTS *Mute STUMM 55* ■ 1 78
11 Jun 88 CHAINS OF LOVE *Mute MUTE 83* 11 7
1 Oct 88 ● A LITTLE RESPECT *Mute MUTE 85* 4 10
10 Dec 88 ● CRACKERS INTERNATIONAL (EP) *Mute MUTE 93* 2 13
30 Sep 89 ● DRAMA! *Mute MUTE 89* 4 8
28 Oct 89 ★ WILD! *Mute STUMM 75* ■ 1 48
9 Dec 89 YOU SURROUND ME *Mute MUTE 99* 15 9
10 Mar 90 ● BLUE SAVANNAH *Mute MUTE 109* 3 10
2 Jun 90 STAR *Mute MUTE 111* 11 7
29 Jun 91 ● CHORUS *Mute MUTE 125* 3 9
21 Sep 91 ● LOVE TO HATE YOU *Mute MUTE 131* 4 9
26 Oct 91 ★ CHORUS *Mute STUMM 95* ■ 1 25
7 Dec 91 AM I RIGHT? (EP) *Mute MUTE 134* 15 6
11 Jan 92 AM I RIGHT? (EP) (re-mix) *Mute L12MUTE 134* 22 3
28 Mar 92 ● BREATH OF LIFE *Mute MUTE 142* 8 6
13 Jun 92 ★ ABBA-ESQUE (EP) *Mute MUTE 144* ■ 1 12
7 Nov 92 ● WHO NEEDS LOVE (LIKE THAT) (re-mix) *Mute MUTE 150* 10 4
28 Nov 92 ★ POP! – THE FIRST 20 HITS *Mute CDMUTEL 2* ■ 1 26
23 Apr 94 ● ALWAYS *Mute CDMUTE 152* 4 9
28 May 94 ★ I SAY I SAY I SAY *Mute LCDSTUMM 115* ■ 1 15
30 Jul 94 ● RUN TO THE SUN *Mute CDMUTE 153* 6 5
3 Dec 94 I LOVE SATURDAY *Mute CDMUTE 166* 20 6
23 Sep 95 STAY WITH ME *Mute CDMUTE 174* 15 4
4 Nov 95 ERASURE *Mute CDSTUMM 145* 14 5
9 Dec 95 FINGERS AND THUMBS (COLD SUMMER'S DAY) *Mute CDMUTE 178* 20 3
18 Jan 97 IN MY ARMS *Mute CDMUTE 190* 13 4
8 Mar 97 DON'T SAY YOUR LOVE IS KILLING ME *Mute CDMUTE 195* 23 2
12 Apr 97 ● COWBOY *Mute CDSTUMM 155* 10 4
21 Oct 00 FREEDOM *Mute CDMUTE 244* 27 2
4 Nov 00 LOVEBOAT *Mute CDSTUMM 175* 45 1
18 Jan 03 ● SOLSBURY HILL *Mute CDMUTE 275* 10 3
8 Feb 03 OTHER PEOPLE'S SONGS *Mute CDSTUMM 215* 17 2
19 Apr 03 MAKE ME SMILE (COME UP AND SEE ME) *Mute CDMUTE 292* 14 3
25 Oct 03 OH L'AMOUR *Mute CDMUTE 312* 13 3
1 Nov 03 HITS! THE VERY BEST OF ERASURE *Mute LCDMUTEL 10* 15 5
15 Jan 05 ● BREATHE *Mute CDMUTE 330* 4 6
5 Feb 05 NIGHTBIRD *Mute CDSTUMM 245* 27 2
2 Apr 05 DON'T SAY YOU LOVE ME *Mute LCDMUTE 337* 15 3
2 Jul 05 HERE I GO IMPOSSIBLE AGAIN *Mute CDMUTE 344* 25 2

Tracks on Crackers International (EP): Stop / The Hardest Part / Knocking on Your Door / She Won't Be Home. Tracks on Am I Right? (EP): Am I Right? / Carry on Clangers / Let It Flow / Waiting for Sex. Tracks on Am I Right? (re-mix EP): Am I Right? / Chorus / Love to Hate You / Perfect Stranger. Tracks on Abba-esque (EP): Lay All Your Love on Me / SOS / Take a Chance on Me / Voulez-Vous. 'Take a Chance on Me' credits MC Kinky.

ERIC and The GOOD GOOD FEELING

UK, male / female vocal / instrumental group

3 Jun 89 GOOD GOOD FEELING *Equinox EQN 1* 73 1

ERIK

UK, female vocalist (3 Singles: 5 Weeks)

10 Apr 93 LOOKS LIKE I'M IN LOVE AGAIN *PWL Sanctuary PWCD 252* [1] 46 2
29 Jan 94 GOT TO BE REAL *PWL International PWCD 278* 42 2
1 Oct 94 WE GOT THE LOVE *PWL International PWCD 305* 55 1

[1] Key West featuring Erik

ERNESTO vs BASTIAN NEW

Holland, male DJ / production duo

24 Sep 05 DARK SIDE *Nebula NEBCD 080* 48 1

EROTIC DRUM BAND

Canada, male / female vocal / instrumental group

9 Jun 79 LOVE DISCO STYLE *Scope SC 1* 47 3

ERUPTION

Jamaica, male / female vocal (Precious Wilson) / instrumental group (2 Singles: 21 Weeks)

18 Feb 78 ● I CAN'T STAND THE RAIN *Atlantic K 11068* [1] 5 11
21 Apr 79 ● ONE WAY TICKET *Atlantic / Hansa K 11266* 9 10

[1] Eruption featuring Precious Wilson

Shaun ESCOFFERY

UK, male vocalist (2 Singles: 2 Weeks)

10 Mar 01 SPACE RIDER *Oyster Music OYSCD 4* 52 1
20 Jul 02 DAYS LIKE THIS *Oyster Music OYSCDS 8* 53 1

The ESCORTS

UK, male vocal / instrumental group

2 Jul 64 THE ONE TO CRY *Fontana TF 474* 49 2

ESCRIMA (see also CAMISRA; The GRIFTERS; PARTIZAN; TALL PAUL)

UK, male producer – Paul Newman (2 Singles: 4 Weeks)

11 Feb 95 TRAIN OF THOUGHT *Ffrreedom TABCD 225* 36 2
7 Oct 95 DEEPER *Hooj Choons TABCD 236* 27 2

ESKIMOS & EGYPT

UK, male vocal / instrumental group (2 Singles: 4 Weeks)

13 Feb 93 FALL FROM GRACE *One Little Indian EEF 96CD* 51 2
29 May 93 UK-USA *One Little Indian 99TP 7CD* 52 2

ESPIRITU

UK / France, male / female vocal / instrumental duo – Vanessa Quinones and Chris Chaplin (4 Singles: 10 Weeks)

6 Mar 93 CONQUISTADOR *Heavenly HVN 28CD* 47 2
7 Aug 93 LOS AMERICANOS *Heavenly HVN 33CD* 45 2
20 Aug 94 BONITA MANANA *Columbia 6606925* 50 1
25 Mar 95 ALWAYS SOMETHING THERE TO REMIND ME *WEA YZ 911CD* [1] 14 5

[1] Tin Tin Out featuring Espiritu

ESSENCE (see also ASCENSION; CHAKRA; LUSTRAL; OXYGEN featuring Andrea BRITTON; SPACE BROTHERS)

UK, male production group – Ricky Simmonds and Stephen Jones and female vocalist

21 Mar 98 THE PROMISE *Innocent SINCD 1* 27 2

The ESSEX

US, male / female vocal group

8 Aug 63 EASIER SAID THAN DONE *Columbia DB 7077* ▲ $ 41 5

David ESSEX 134 Top 500

Actor / teeny-bop star turned popular entertainer, b. David Cook, 23 Jul 1947, London, UK. This singer / songwriter was voted No.1 British Male Vocalist (1974) and was a teen idol for more than a decade. He starred in the stage show Godspell and graduated successfully to films (20 Albums: 178 Weeks, 25 Singles: 199 Weeks)

18 Aug 73 ● ROCK ON *CBS 1693* $ 3 11
10 Nov 73 ● LAMPLIGHT *CBS 1902* 7 15
24 Nov 73 ● ROCK ON *CBS 65823* 7 22
11 May 74 AMERICA *CBS 2176* 32 5

12 Oct 74 ★ GONNA MAKE YOU A STAR *CBS 2492* 1 17
19 Oct 74 ● DAVID ESSEX *CBS 69088* 2 24
14 Dec 74 ● STARDUST *CBS 2828* 7 10
5 Jul 75 ● ROLLING STONE *CBS 3425* 5 7
13 Sep 75 ★ HOLD ME CLOSE *CBS 3572* 1 10
27 Sep 75 ● ALL THE FUN OF THE FAIR *CBS 69160* 3 20
6 Dec 75 IF I COULD *CBS 3776* 13 8
20 Mar 76 CITY LIGHTS *CBS 4050* 24 4
5 Jun 76 ON TOUR *CBS 95000* 51 1
16 Oct 76 COMING HOME *CBS 4486* 24 6
30 Oct 76 OUT ON THE STREET *CBS 86017* 31 9
17 Sep 77 COOL OUT TONIGHT *CBS 5495* 23 6
8 Oct 77 GOLD AND IVORY *CBS 86038* 29 4
11 Mar 78 STAY WITH ME BABY *CBS 6063* 45 5
19 Aug 78 ● OH WHAT A CIRCUS *Mercury 6007 185* 3 11
21 Oct 78 BRAVE NEW WORLD *CBS 6705* 55 3
6 Jan 79 THE DAVID ESSEX ALBUM *CBS 10011* 29 7
3 Mar 79 IMPERIAL WIZARD *Mercury 6007 202* 32 8
31 Mar 79 IMPERIAL WIZARD *Mercury 9109 616* 12 9
5 Apr 80 ● SILVER DREAM MACHINE (PART 1) *Mercury BIKE 1* 4 11
12 Jun 80 HOT LOVE *Mercury 6359 017* 75 1
14 Jun 80 HOT LOVE *Mercury HOT 11* 57 4
19 Jun 82 STAGE-STRUCK *Mercury MERS 4* 31 15
26 Jun 82 ME AND MY GIRL (NIGHT-CLUBBING) *Mercury MER 107* 13 10
27 Nov 82 THE VERY BEST OF DAVID ESSEX *TV TVA 4* 37 11
11 Dec 82 ● A WINTER'S TALE *Mercury MER 127* 2 10
4 Jun 83 THE SMILE *Mercury ESSEX 1* 52 4
27 Aug 83 ● TAHITI (FROM 'MUTINY ON THE BOUNTY') *Mercury BOUNT 1* 8 11
15 Oct 83 MUTINY *Mercury MERH 30* 39 4
26 Nov 83 YOU'RE IN MY HEART (re) *Mercury ESSEX 2* 59 6
17 Dec 83 THE WHISPER *Mercury MERH 34* 67 6
23 Feb 85 FALLING ANGELS RIDING *Mercury ESSEX 5* 29 7
6 Dec 86 CENTRE STAGE *K-Tel ONE 1333* 82 4
18 Apr 87 MYFANWY *Arista RIS 11* 41 7
19 Oct 91 HIS GREATEST HITS *Mercury 5103081* 13 13
10 Apr 93 ● COVER SHOT *PolyGram TV 5145632* 3 8
22 Oct 94 BACK TO BACK *PolyGram TV 5237902* 33 2
26 Nov 94 TRUE LOVE WAYS *PolyGram TV TLWCD 2* [1] 38 3
9 Dec 95 MISSING YOU *PolyGram TV 5295822* 26 9
17 May 97 A NIGHT AT THE MOVIES *PolyGram TV 5376082* 14 5
13 Jun 98 GREATEST HITS *PolyGram TV 5584842* 31 4

[1] David Essex and Catherine Zeta Jones

Mutiny is a studio recording of a musical that was not staged until 1985. Both this album and the eventual stage production starred David Essex and Frank Finlay.

Gloria ESTEFAN (105 Top 500) (see also MIAMI SOUND MACHINE)

Latin music's leading lady, b. Gloria Fajardo, 1 Sep 1957, Havana, Cuba. Successes in the dance and MOR fields have pushed her total worldwide sales to a reported 70 million, with two of her albums passing the one-million sales mark in the UK (11 Albums: 247 Weeks, 30 Singles: 182 Weeks)

16 Jul 88 ● ANYTHING FOR YOU *Epic 6516737* [1] ▲ $ 10 16
22 Oct 88 ● 1-2-3 (re) *Epic 6529587* [1] 9 10
19 Nov 88 ★ ANYTHING FOR YOU *Epic 4631251* [1] 1 54
17 Dec 88 RHYTHM IS GONNA GET YOU *Epic 6545147* [1] 16 9
11 Feb 89 ● CAN'T STAY AWAY FROM YOU *Epic 6514447* [1] 7 12
15 Jul 89 ● DON'T WANNA LOSE YOU *Epic 6550540* ▲ 6 10
5 Aug 89 ★ CUTS BOTH WAYS *Epic 4651451* ■ 1 64
16 Sep 89 OYE MI CANTO (HEAR MY VOICE) *Epic 6552877* 16 8
25 Nov 89 GET ON YOUR FEET *Epic 6554507* 23 7
3 Mar 90 HERE WE ARE *Epic 6554737* 23 6
26 May 90 CUTS BOTH WAYS *Epic 6559827* 49 5
26 Jan 91 COMING OUT OF THE DARK *Epic 6565747* ▲ 25 5
16 Feb 91 ● INTO THE LIGHT *Epic 4677821* 2 36
6 Apr 91 SEAL OUR FATE *Epic 6567737* 24 7
8 Jun 91 REMEMBER ME WITH LOVE *Epic 6569687* 22 6
21 Sep 91 LIVE FOR LOVING YOU *Epic 6573827* 33 5
24 Oct 92 ALWAYS TOMORROW *Epic 6583977* 24 4
14 Nov 92 ● GREATEST HITS *Epic 4723322* 2 47
12 Dec 92 ● MIAMI HIT MIX / CHRISTMAS THROUGH YOUR EYES *Epic 6588377* 8 9
13 Feb 93 I SEE YOUR SMILE *Epic 6589612* 48 2
3 Apr 93 GO AWAY *Epic 6590952* 13 6
3 Jul 93 MI TIERRA *Epic 6593512* 36 3
10 Jul 93 MI TIERRA *Epic 4737992* 11 11
14 Aug 93 IF WE WERE LOVERS / CON LOS AÑOS QUE ME QUEDAN *Epic 6595702* 40 3
18 Dec 93 MONTUNO *Epic 6599972* 55 2
15 Oct 94 TURN THE BEAT AROUND *Epic 6606822* 21 6
29 Oct 94 ● HOLD ME THRILL ME KISS ME *Epic 4774162* 5 19
3 Dec 94 HOLD ME THRILL ME KISS ME (re) *Epic 6610802* 11 11
18 Feb 95 EVERLASTING LOVE *Epic 6611595* 19 5
21 Oct 95 ABRIENDO PUERTAS *Epic 4809922* 70 1
25 May 96 REACH (2re) *Epic 6632642* 15 8
15 Jun 96 DESTINY *Epic 4839322* 12 9
24 Aug 96 YOU'LL BE MINE (PARTY TIME) *Epic 6636505* 18 3
14 Dec 96 I'M NOT GIVING YOU UP *Epic 6640222* 28 3
6 Jun 98 HEAVEN'S WHAT I FEEL *Epic 6660042* 17 4
13 Jun 98 GLORIA! *Epic 4898502* 16 4
10 Oct 98 OYE *Epic 6664645* 33 2
16 Jan 99 DON'T LET THIS MOMENT END *Epic 6667472* 28 2
8 Jan 00 MUSIC OF MY HEART *Epic 6685272* [2] 34 3
27 May 00 ALMA CARIBENA – CARIBBEAN SOUL *Epic 4976172* 44 1
24 Feb 01 GREATEST HITS VOL. II *Epic 5016372* 60 1

[1] Gloria Estefan & Miami Sound Machine [2] 'N Sync / Gloria Estefan
[1] Gloria Estefan & Miami Sound Machine

'Christmas Through Your Eyes' was listed only from 19 Dec 1992.

ESTELLE

UK, female rapper – Estelle Swaray (1 Album: 2 Weeks, 5 Singles: 18 Weeks)

31 Jul 04 1980 *V2 / J-Did JAD 5027813* 14 7
16 Oct 04 FREE *V2 / J-Did 5027843* 15 6
30 Oct 04 THE 18TH DAY ... *V2 JAD 1027838* 35 2
12 Feb 05 OUTSPOKEN – PART 1 *Buzzin' Fly 010 BUZZCD* [1] 74 1
9 Apr 05 GO GONE *V2 JAD 5030943* 32 3
11 Jun 05 WHY GO? *Cheeky 82876699292* [2] 49 1

[1] Ben Watt featuring Estelle [2] Faithless featuring Estelle

Don ESTELLE and Windsor DAVIES

UK, male actors / vocal duo – Don Estelle, b. 22 May 1933, d. 2 Aug 2003 (1 Album: 8 Weeks, 2 Singles: 16 Weeks)

17 May 75 ★ WHISPERING GRASS *EMI 2290* [1] 1 12
25 Oct 75 PAPER DOLL *EMI 2361* 41 4
10 Jan 76 ● SING LOFTY *EMI EMC 3102* 10 8

[1] Windsor Davies as BSM Williams and Don Estelle as Gunner Sugden (Lofty)

Deon ESTUS

US, male vocalist / bass guitarist (2 Singles: 7 Weeks)

25 Jan 86 MY GUY – MY GIRL (MEDLEY) *Sedition EDIT 3310* [1] 63 3
29 Apr 89 HEAVEN HELP ME *Mika MIKA 2* 41 4

[1] Amii Stewart and Deon Estus

ETERNAL (201 Top 500)

London-based vocal group with across-the-board appeal: sisters Easther and Vernett Bennett, Kéllé Bryan and Louise Nurding. The first all-female act to shift more than one million copies of an album in the UK. Louise left for a successful solo career in 1995, followed by Kéllé four years later. Best-selling single: 'I Wanna Be the Only One' 601,132 (4 Albums: 163 Weeks, 15 Singles: 134 Weeks)

2 Oct 93 ● STAY *EMI CDEM 283* 4 9
11 Dec 93 ● ALWAYS & FOREVER *EMI CDEMD 1053* 2 76
15 Jan 94 ● SAVE OUR LOVE *EMI CDEM 296* 8 7
30 Apr 94 ● JUST A STEP FROM HEAVEN *EMI CDEM 311* 8 10
20 Aug 94 SO GOOD *EMI CDEMS 339* 13 7
5 Nov 94 ● OH BABY I ... *EMI CDEM 353* 4 13
24 Dec 94 CRAZY *EMI CDEMX 364* 15 7
21 Oct 95 ● POWER OF A WOMAN *EMI CDEM 396* 5 8
11 Nov 95 ● POWER OF A WOMAN *EMI CDEMD 1090* 6 31
9 Dec 95 ● I AM BLESSED *EMI CDEMS 408* 7 12

20 / 22 January 1966	27 / 29 January 1966	3 / 5 February 1966	10 / 12 February 1966
KEEP ON RUNNING Spencer Davis Group	MICHELLE The Overlanders	MICHELLE The Overlanders	MICHELLE The Overlanders
RUBBER SOUL The Beatles	RUBBER SOUL The Beatles	RUBBER SOUL The Beatles	RUBBER SOUL The Beatles

KEY
UK No.1 ★ UK Top 10 ● Still on chart + UK entry at No.1 ■
US No.1 ▲ UK million seller £ US million seller $
Singles re-entries are listed as (re), (2re), (3re)... which signifies that the hit re-entered the chart once, twice or three times...

Peak Position / Weeks

9 Mar 96 ● **GOOD THING** *EMI CDEM 419* ... 8 6
17 Aug 96 ● **SOMEDAY** *EMI CDEMS 439* ... 4 9
7 Dec 96 ● **SECRETS** *EMI CDEM 459* ... 9 7
8 Mar 97 ● **DON'T YOU LOVE ME** *EMI CDEMS 465* ... 3 7
29 Mar 97 ● BEFORE THE RAIN *EMI CDEMD 1103* ... 3 29
31 May 97 ★ **I WANNA BE THE ONLY ONE** *EMI CDEM 472* [1] ■ ... 1 15
11 Oct 97 ● **ANGEL OF MINE** *EMI CDEM 493* ... 4 13
1 Nov 97 ● GREATEST HITS *EMI 8217982* ... 2 27
30 Oct 99 **WHAT 'CHA GONNA DO** *EMI CDEM 552* ... 16 4

[1] Eternal featuring BeBe Winans

ETHAN NEW (see also FUSED)
France / Sweden male production duo – Sandy Wilhelm and Sam Malm

12 Mar 05 **IN MY HEART** *Back Yard BACK 13CSC 01* ... 49 1

ETHER *UK, male vocal / instrumental group*

28 Mar 98 **WATCHING YOU** *Parlophone CDR 6491* ... 74 1

Melissa ETHERIDGE *US, female vocalist / guitarist (2 Albums: 2 Weeks)*

30 Sep 89 BRAVE AND CRAZY *Island ILPS 9939* ... 63 1
9 May 92 NEVER ENOUGH *Island CID 9990* ... 56 1

ETHICS (see also ARTEMESIA; MOVIN' MELODIES; SUBLIMINAL CUTS)
Holland, male producer – Patrick Prinz

25 Nov 95 **TO THE BEAT OF THE DRUM (LA LUNA)** *VC VCRD 5* ... 13 5

The ETHIOPIANS *Jamaica, male vocal / instrumental group*

13 Sep 67 **TRAIN TO SKAVILLE** *Rio RIO 130* ... 40 6

Tony ETORIA *UK, male vocalist*

4 Jun 77 **I CAN PROVE IT** *GTO GT 89* ... 21 8

EUROGROOVE *UK, male / female vocal group (4 Singles: 7 Weeks)*

20 May 95 **MOVE YOUR BODY** *Avex UK AVEXCD 4* ... 29 2
5 Aug 95 **DIVE TO PARADISE** *Avex UK AVEXCD 10* ... 31 2
21 Oct 95 **IT'S ON YOU (SCAN ME)** *Avex UK AVEXCD 17* ... 25 2
3 Feb 96 **MOVE YOUR BODY** (re-mix) *Avex UK AVEXCD 22* ... 44 1

EUROPE *Sweden, male vocal (Joey Tempest) / instrumental group (3 Albums: 43 Weeks, 7 Singles: 50 Weeks)*

1 Nov 86 ★ **THE FINAL COUNTDOWN** *Epic A 7127* ... 1 15
22 Nov 86 ● THE FINAL COUNTDOWN *Epic EPC 26808* ... 9 37
31 Jan 87 **ROCK THE NIGHT** *Epic EUR 1* ... 12 9
18 Apr 87 **CARRIE** *Epic EUR 2* ... 22 8
20 Aug 88 **SUPERSTITIOUS** *Epic EUR 3* ... 34 5
17 Sep 88 OUT OF THIS WORLD *Epic 4624491* ... 12 5
19 Oct 91 PRISONERS IN PARADISE *Epic 4687551* ... 61 1
1 Feb 92 **I'LL CRY FOR YOU** *Epic 6576977* ... 28 5
21 Mar 92 **HALFWAY TO HEAVEN** *Epic 6578517* ... 42 4
25 Dec 99 **THE FINAL COUNTDOWN 2000** (re-recording) *Epic 6685042* ... 36 4

EUROPEANS *UK, male vocal / instrumental group*

11 Feb 84 LIVE *A&M SCOT 1* ... 100 1

EURYTHMICS 42 Top 500 (see also VEGAS)
Innovative and internationally popular duo formed by BRIT award-winning Scottish vocalist Annie Lennox and multi-instrumentalist / songwriter / producer Dave Stewart, formerly known as The Tourists. The most charted male / female duo in the UK saw their greatest hits album sell more than two million copies in the UK and in Europe. Duo were inducted into the UK Music Hall of Fame in 2005 (12 Albums: 484 Weeks, 29 Singles: 212 Weeks)

4 Jul 81 **NEVER GONNA CRY AGAIN** *RCA 68* ... 63 3
20 Nov 82 ● **LOVE IS A STRANGER** (re) *RCA DA 1* ... 6 13
12 Feb 83 ● SWEET DREAMS (ARE MADE OF THIS) *RCA RCALP 6063* ... 3 60
12 Feb 83 ● **SWEET DREAMS (ARE MADE OF THIS)** *RCA DA 2* ▲ ... 2 14
9 Jul 83 ● **WHO'S THAT GIRL?** *RCA DA 3* ... 3 10
5 Nov 83 ● **RIGHT BY YOUR SIDE** *RCA DA 4* ... 10 11
26 Nov 83 ★ TOUCH *RCA PL 70109* ... 1 48
21 Jan 84 ● **HERE COMES THE RAIN AGAIN** *RCA DA 5* ... 8 8
9 Jun 84 TOUCH DANCE *RCA PG 70354* ... 31 5
3 Nov 84 ● **SEXCRIME (NINETEEN EIGHTY FOUR)** *Virgin VS 728* ... 4 13
24 Nov 84 1984 (FOR THE LOVE OF BIG BROTHER) *Virgin V 1984* ... 23 17
19 Jan 85 **JULIA** *Virgin VS 734* ... 44 4
20 Apr 85 **WOULD I LIE TO YOU?** *RCA PB 40101* ... 17 8
11 May 85 ● BE YOURSELF TONIGHT *RCA PL 70711* ... 3 80
6 Jul 85 ★ **THERE MUST BE AN ANGEL (PLAYING WITH MY HEART)** *RCA PB 40247* ... 1 13
2 Nov 85 ● **SISTERS ARE DOIN' IT FOR THEMSELVES** *RCA PB 40339* [1] ... 9 11
11 Jan 86 **IT'S ALRIGHT (BABY'S COMING BACK)** *RCA PB 40375* ... 12 8
14 Jun 86 **WHEN TOMORROW COMES** *RCA DA 7* ... 30 6
12 Jul 86 ● REVENGE *RCA PL 71050* ... 3 52
6 Sep 86 ● **THORN IN MY SIDE** *RCA DA 8* ... 5 11
29 Nov 86 **THE MIRACLE OF LOVE** *RCA DA 9* ... 23 9
28 Feb 87 **MISSIONARY MAN** *RCA DA 10* ... 31 4
24 Oct 87 **BEETHOVEN (I LOVE TO LISTEN TO)** *RCA DA 11* ... 25 5
21 Nov 87 ● SAVAGE *RCA PL 71555* ... 7 33
26 Dec 87 **SHAME** *RCA DA 14* ... 41 6
9 Apr 88 **I NEED A MAN** *RCA DA 15* ... 26 5
11 Jun 88 **YOU HAVE PLACED A CHILL IN MY HEART** *RCA DA 16* ... 16 8
26 Aug 89 **REVIVAL** *RCA DA 17* ... 26 6
23 Sep 89 ★ WE TOO ARE ONE *RCA PL 74251* ■ ... 1 32
4 Nov 89 **DON'T ASK ME WHY** *RCA DA 19* ... 25 6
3 Feb 90 **THE KING AND QUEEN OF AMERICA** *RCA DA 20* ... 29 5
12 May 90 **ANGEL** *RCA DA 21* ... 23 6
9 Mar 91 **LOVE IS A STRANGER** (re-issue) *RCA PB 44265* ... 46 3
30 Mar 91 ★ GREATEST HITS *RCA PL 74856* ■ ... 1 123
16 Nov 91 **SWEET DREAMS (ARE MADE OF THIS) '91** (re-recording) *RCA PB 45031* $ ... 48 2
27 Nov 93 EURYTHMICS LIVE 1983-1989 *RCA 74321171452* ... 22 7
16 Oct 99 **I SAVED THE WORLD TODAY** *RCA 74321695632* ... 11 6
30 Oct 99 ● PEACE *RCA 74321695622* ... 4 20
5 Feb 00 **17 AGAIN** *RCA 74321726262* ... 27 4
12 Nov 05 **I'VE GOT A LIFE** *RCA 82876748352* ... 14 4
19 Nov 05 ● ULTIMATE COLLECTION *RCA 82876748412* ... 5 7+

[1] Eurythmics and Aretha Franklin

'Love Is a Stranger' reached its peak position when it re-entered in Apr 1983.

EUSEBE *UK, male / female vocal group*

26 Aug 95 **SUMMERTIME HEALING** *Mama's Yard CDMAMA 4* ... 32 3

EVANESCENCE *US, female / male vocal (Amy Lee) / instrumental group (1 Album: 69 Weeks, 5 Singles: 37 Weeks)*

10 May 03 ★ FALLEN *Epic 13063* ... 1 69
31 May 03 **BRING ME TO LIFE** (import) *Epic 8734881* [1] ... 60 2
14 Jun 03 ★ **BRING ME TO LIFE** *Epic 6739762* [1] ■ ... 1 17
4 Oct 03 ● **GOING UNDER** *Epic / Wind Up 6743522* ... 8 6
20 Dec 03 ● **MY IMMORTAL** *Epic 6745422* ... 7 9
12 Jun 04 **EVERYBODY'S FOOL** *Epic 6747992* ... 24 3

[1] Evanescence featuring Paul McCoy

Faith EVANS (see also CLIPSE)
US, female vocalist (2 Albums: 5 Weeks, 11 Singles: 55 Weeks)

14 Oct 95 **YOU USED TO LOVE ME** *Puff Daddy 74321299812* ... 42 2
23 Nov 96 **STRESSED OUT** *Jive JIVECD 404* [1] ... 33 2
28 Jun 97 ★ **I'LL BE MISSING YOU** *Puff Daddy 74321499102* [2] ■ ▲ £ $ .. 1 21

17 / 19 February 1966	24 / 26 February 1966	3 / 5 March 1966	10 / 12 March 1966
◂◂ UK No.1 SINGLES ▸▸			
THESE BOOTS ARE MADE FOR WALKIN' Nancy Sinatra	THESE BOOTS ARE MADE FOR WALKIN' Nancy Sinatra	THESE BOOTS ARE MADE FOR WALKIN' Nancy Sinatra	THESE BOOTS ARE MADE FOR WALKIN' Nancy Sinatra
◂◂ UK No.1 ALBUMS ▸▸			
THE SOUND OF MUSIC Soundtrack	THE SOUND OF MUSIC Soundtrack	THE SOUND OF MUSIC Soundtrack	THE SOUND OF MUSIC Soundtrack

7 Nov 98	KEEP THE FAITH *Arista 74321614672*	69	1
14 Nov 98	**LOVE LIKE THIS** *Puff Daddy 74321625592*	**24**	4
1 May 99	**ALL NIGHT LONG** *Puff Daddy / Arista 74321665692* [3]	**23**	3
1 May 99	**GEORGY PORGY** *Warner Bros. W 478CD 2* [4]	**28**	3
30 Dec 00	**HEARTBREAK HOTEL** *Arista 74321820572* [5] $	**25**	5
24 May 03	**MA, I DON'T LOVE HER** *Arista 82876526482* [6]	**38**	3
9 Apr 05	**HOPE** *Capitol 8694660* [7]	**25**	5
14 May 05	**AGAIN** *EMI CDEMS 658*	**12**	6
28 May 05	THE FIRST LADY *EMI 4771172*	22	4
20 Aug 05	**MESMERIZED** *EMI CDEMS 665*	**48**	1

[1] A Tribe Called Quest featuring Faith Evans and Raphael Saadiq [2] Puff Daddy and Faith Evans featuring 112 [3] Faith Evans featuring Puff Daddy [4] Eric Benet featuring Faith Evans [5] Whitney Houston featuring Faith Evans and Kelly Price [6] Clipse featuring Faith Evans [7] Twista featuring Faith Evans

Maureen EVANS *UK, female vocalist (5 Singles: 37 Weeks)*

22 Jan 60	**THE BIG HURT** *Oriole CB 1533*	**26**	2
17 Mar 60	**LOVE KISSES AND HEARTACHES** *Oriole CB 1540*	**44**	1
2 Jun 60	**PAPER ROSES** *Oriole CB 1550*	**40**	5
29 Nov 62 ●	**LIKE I DO** *Oriole CB 1760*	**3**	18
27 Feb 64	**I LOVE HOW YOU LOVE ME (re)** *Oriole CB 1906*	**34**	11

Paul EVANS *US, male vocalist (3 Singles: 14 Weeks)*

27 Nov 59	**SEVEN LITTLE GIRLS SITTING IN THE BACK SEAT** *London HLL 8968* [1]	**25**	1
31 Mar 60	**MIDNITE SPECIAL** *London HLL 9045*	**41**	1
16 Dec 78 ●	**HELLO, THIS IS JOANNIE (THE TELEPHONE ANSWERING MACHINE SONG)** *Spring 2066 932*	**6**	12

[1] Paul Evans and The Curls

The EVASIONS *UK, male / female vocal / rap / instrumental group*

13 Jun 81	**WIKKA WRAP** *Groove GP 107*	**20**	8

E.V.E. *UK / US, female vocal group (2 Singles: 5 Weeks)*

1 Oct 94	**GROOVE OF LOVE** *Gasoline Alley MCSTD 2007*	**30**	3
28 Jan 95	**GOOD LIFE** *Gasoline Alley MCSTD 2038*	**39**	2

EVE (see also Missy 'Misdemeanor' ELLIOTT)
US, female rapper – Eve Jeffers (2 Albums: 13 Weeks, 8 Singles: 58 Weeks)

19 May 01 ●	**WHO'S THAT GIRL** *Interscope 4975572*	**6**	8
11 Aug 01	SCORPION *Interscope 4930212*	22	8
25 Aug 01 ●	**LET ME BLOW YA MIND** *Interscope / Polydor 4975932* [1]	**4**	12
9 Mar 02	**BROTHA PART II** *J 74321922142* [2]	**37**	2
16 Mar 02 ●	**CARAMEL** *Interscope / Polydor 4976742* [3]	**9**	10
7 Sep 02	EVE-OLUTION *Interscope / Polydor 4934722*	47	5
5 Oct 02 ●	**GANGSTA LOVIN'** *Ruff Ryders / Interscope 4978042* [4]	**6**	8
12 Apr 03	**SATISFACTION** *Ruff Ryders / Interscope 4978262*	**20**	4
6 Dec 03	**NOT TODAY** *Geffen MCSTD 40349* [5]	**40**	2
26 Mar 05 ●	**RICH GIRL** *Interscope 9880219* [6]	**4**	12

[1] Eve featuring Gwen Stefani [2] Angie Stone featuring Alicia Keys and Eve [3] City High featuring Eve [4] Eve featuring Alicia Keys [5] Mary J Blige featuring Eve [6] Gwen Stefani featuring Eve

EVERCLEAR
US, male vocal / instrumental group (3 Albums: 3 Weeks, 4 Singles: 7 Weeks)

1 Jun 96	**HEARTSPARK DOLLARSIGN** *Capitol CDCLS 773*	**48**	2
31 Aug 96	**SANTA MONICA (WATCH THE WORLD DIE)** *Capitol CDCL 775*	**40**	2
14 Mar 98	SO MUCH FOR THE AFTERGLOW *Capitol 8365032*	63	1
9 May 98	**EVERYTHING TO EVERYONE** *Capitol CDCL 799*	**41**	1
19 Aug 00	SONGS FROM AN AMERICAN MOVIE – VOL. ONE – LEARNING HOW TO SMILE *Capitol 5278642*	51	1
14 Oct 00	**WONDERFUL** *Capitol CDCLS 824*	**36**	2
28 Apr 01	SONGS FROM AN AMERICAN MOVIE – VOL. TWO – GOOD TIME FOR A BAD ATTITUDE *Capitol 5304192*	69	1

Betty EVERETT
US, female vocalist, b. 23 Nov 1939, d. 18 Aug 2001 (2 Singles: 14 Weeks)

14 Jan 65	**GETTING MIGHTY CROWDED** *Fontana TF 520*	**29**	7
30 Oct 68	**IT'S IN HIS KISS (THE SHOOP SHOOP SONG)** *President PT 215*	**34**	7

Kenny EVERETT *UK, male DJ / vocalist – Maurice Cole, b. 25 Dec 1948, d. 4 Apr 1995 (2 Singles: 12 Weeks)*

12 Nov 77	**CAPTAIN KREMMEN (RETRIBUTION)** *DJM DJS 10810* [1]	**32**	4
26 Mar 83 ●	**SNOT RAP** *RCA KEN 1*	**9**	8

[1] Kenny Everett and Mike Vickers

EVERLAST (see also HOUSE OF PAIN)
US, male vocalist – Erik Schrody (1 Album: 1 Week, 3 Singles: 5 Weeks)

27 Feb 99	**WHAT IT'S LIKE** *Tommy Boy TBCD 7470*	**34**	2
13 Mar 99	WHITEY FORD SINGS THE BLUES *Tommy Boy TBCD 1236*	65	1
3 Jul 99	**ENDS** *Tommy Boy TBCD 7346*	**47**	1
20 Jan 01	**BLACK JESUS** *Tommy Boy TBCD 2180*	**37**	2

Phil EVERLY (see also The EVERLY BROTHERS)
US, male vocalist (1 Album: 1 Week, 3 Singles: 24 Weeks)

6 Nov 82	**LOUISE** *Capitol CL 266*	**47**	6
19 Feb 83 ●	**SHE MEANS NOTHING TO ME** *Capitol CL 276* [1]	**9**	9
7 May 83	PHIL EVERLY *Capitol EST 27670*	61	1
10 Dec 94	**ALL I HAVE TO DO IS DREAM (re)** *EMI CDEMS 359* [2]	**14**	9

[1] Phil Everly and Cliff Richard [2] Cliff Richard and Phil Everly

'All I Have to Do Is Dream' was listed with its flip side, 'Miss You Nights' by Cliff Richard.

The EVERLY BROTHERS 88 Top 500
Rock 'n' roll's foremost vocal duo: Don, b. 1 Feb 1937, and Phil Everly, b. 19 Jan 1939. The Kentucky-based brothers' distinctive harmony sound has influenced scores of later groups, including The Beatles. The duo, voted the World's Top Group by NME readers in 1958, was supported by The Rolling Stones on its 1963 UK tour. They achieved a long string of transatlantic hits, many of which were self-composed, were the first duo / group inducted into the Rock and Roll Hall of Fame, and were awarded a Lifetime Grammy in 1997. In 2001 they were elected into the Country Music Hall of Fame and their home state erected statues in their honour. Total UK single sales: 4,827,957 (13 Albums: 130 Weeks, 30 Singles: 344 Weeks)

12 Jul 57 ●	**BYE BYE LOVE** *London HLA 8440* $	**6**	16
8 Nov 57 ●	**WAKE UP LITTLE SUSIE** *London HLA 8498* ▲ $	**2**	13
23 May 58 ★	**ALL I HAVE TO DO IS DREAM / CLAUDETTE** *London HLA 8618* ▲ $	**1**	21
12 Sep 58 ●	**BIRD DOG** *London HLA 8685* ▲ $	**2**	16
23 Jan 59 ●	**PROBLEMS** *London HLA 8781* $	**6**	12
22 May 59	**TAKE A MESSAGE TO MARY (2re)** *London HLA 8863*	**20**	10
29 May 59	**POOR JENNY** *London B-HLA 8863*	**14**	11
11 Sep 59 ●	**('TIL) I KISSED YOU** *London HLA 8934*	**2**	15
12 Feb 60	**LET IT BE ME (re)** *London HLA 9039*	**13**	10
14 Apr 60 ★	**CATHY'S CLOWN** *Warner Bros. WB 1* ▲	**1**	18
2 Jul 60 ●	IT'S EVERLY TIME *Warner Bros. WM 4006*	2	23
14 Jul 60 ●	**WHEN WILL I BE LOVED** *London HLA 9157*	**4**	16
22 Sep 60 ●	**LUCILLE / SO SAD (TO WATCH GOOD LOVE GO BAD)** *Warner Bros. WB 19*	**4**	15
15 Oct 60 ●	FABULOUS STYLE OF THE EVERLY BROTHERS *London HAA 2266*	4	11
15 Dec 60	**LIKE STRANGERS** *London HLA 9250*	**11**	10
9 Feb 61 ★	**WALK RIGHT BACK / EBONY EYES** *Warner Bros. WB 33*	**1**	16
4 Mar 61 ●	A DATE WITH THE EVERLY BROTHERS *Warner Bros. WM 4028*	3	14
15 Jun 61 ★	**TEMPTATION** *Warner Bros. WB 42*	**1**	15
5 Oct 61	**MUSKRAT / DON'T BLAME ME** *Warner Bros. WB 50*	**20**	6
18 Jan 62 ●	**CRYING IN THE RAIN** *Warner Bros. WB 56*	**6**	15
17 May 62	**HOW CAN I MEET HER** *Warner Bros. WB 67*	**12**	10
21 Jul 62	INSTANT PARTY *Warner Bros. WM 4061*	20	1
25 Oct 62	**NO ONE CAN MAKE MY SUNSHINE SMILE** *Warner Bros. WB 79*	**11**	11

KEY: UK No.1 ★★ UK Top 10 ●● Still on chart ++ UK entry at No.1 ■■ US No.1 ▲▲ UK million seller £ US million seller $
Singles re-entries are listed as (re), (2re), (3re)... which signifies that the hit re-entered the chart once, twice or three times...
Peak Position / Weeks

Date	Title / Label	Peak	Wks
21 Mar 63	**SO IT WILL ALWAYS BE** *Warner Bros. WB 94*	23	11
13 Jun 63	**IT'S BEEN NICE (GOODNIGHT)** *Warner Bros. WB 99*	26	5
17 Oct 63	**THE GIRL SANG THE BLUES** *Warner Bros. WB 109*	25	9
16 Jul 64	**THE FERRIS WHEEL** *Warner Bros. WB 135*	22	10
3 Dec 64	**GONE, GONE, GONE (re)** *Warner Bros. WB 146*	36	6
6 May 65	**THAT'LL BE THE DAY** *Warner Bros. WB 158*	30	4
20 May 65 ●	**THE PRICE OF LOVE** *Warner Bros. WB 161*	2	14
26 Aug 65	**I'LL NEVER GET OVER YOU** *Warner Bros. WB 5639*	35	5
21 Oct 65	**LOVE IS STRANGE** *Warner Bros. WB 5649*	11	9
8 May 68	**IT'S MY TIME** *Warner Bros. WB 7192*	39	6
12 Sep 70 ●	**ORIGINAL GREATEST HITS** *CBS 66255*	7	16
8 Jun 74	**THE VERY BEST OF THE EVERLY BROTHERS** *Warner Bros. K 46008*	43	1
29 Nov 75 ●	**WALK RIGHT BACK WITH THE EVERLYS** *Warner Bros. K 56118*	10	10
9 Apr 77	**LIVING LEGENDS** *Warwick WW 5027*	12	10
18 Dec 82	**LOVE HURTS** *K-Tel NE 1197*	22	22
7 Jan 84	**EVERLY BROTHERS REUNION CONCERT** *Impression IMDP 1*	47	6
22 Sep 84	**ON THE WINGS OF A NIGHTINGALE** *Mercury MER 170*	41	9
3 Nov 84	**THE EVERLY BROTHERS** *Mercury MERH 44*	36	4
29 May 93	**THE GOLDEN YEARS OF THE EVERLY BROTHERS – THEIR 24 GREATEST HITS** *Warner Bros. 9548319922*	26	5
1 Jun 02 ●	**THE DEFINITIVE EVERLY BROTHERS** *WSM 927473042*	10	7

'All I Have to Do Is Dream' was listed without 'Claudette' for its first week on the chart but, from 30 May 1958, both sides charted for 20 more weeks.

EVERSTRONG NEW

UK, male vocal / instrumental group

Date	Title / Label	Peak	Wks
23 Apr 05	**TAKE ME HOME (WOMBLE 'TIL I DIE)** *Cornish Blue Music CBMCD 02*	73	1

EVERTON FOOTBALL CLUB

UK, male football team vocalists (2 Singles: 8 Weeks)

Date	Title / Label	Peak	Wks
11 May 85	**HERE WE GO** *Columbia DB 9106* [1]	14	5
20 May 95	**ALL TOGETHER NOW** *MDMC DEVCS 3*	24	3

[1] Everton 1985

EVERYTHING BUT THE GIRL (296 Top 500)

Introspective pop duo, Tracey Thorn (v) and Ben Watt (k), formed in 1982, Hull, UK. They gained greatest popularity after their mid-90s conversion to low-key dance music. The re-mix of 'Missing' was the first single to spend an uninterrupted year on the US chart. Best-selling single: 'Missing' 870,000 (13 Albums: 132 Weeks, 23 Singles: 96 Weeks)

Date	Title / Label	Peak	Wks
12 May 84	**EACH AND EVERY ONE** *Blanco Y Negro NEG 1*	28	7
16 Jun 84	**EDEN** *Blanco Y Negro BYN 2*	14	22
21 Jul 84	**MINE** *Blanco Y Negro NEG 3*	58	2
6 Oct 84	**NATIVE LAND** *Blanco Y Negro NEG 6*	73	2
27 Apr 85 ●	**LOVE NOT MONEY** *Blanco Y Negro BYN 3*	10	9
2 Aug 86	**COME ON HOME** *Blanco Y Negro NEG 21*	44	7
6 Sep 86	**BABY THE STARS SHINE BRIGHT** *Blanco Y Negro BYN 9*	22	9
11 Oct 86	**DON'T LEAVE ME BEHIND** *Blanco Y Negro NEG 23*	72	2
13 Feb 88	**THESE EARLY DAYS** *Blanco Y Negro NEG 30*	75	1
12 Mar 88	**IDLEWILD** *Blanco Y Negro BYN 14*	13	9
9 Jul 88 ●	**I DON'T WANT TO TALK ABOUT IT** *Blanco Y Negro NEG 34*	3	9
6 Aug 88	**IDLEWILD** (re-issue) *Blanco Y Negro BYN 16*	21	6
27 Jan 90	**DRIVING** *Blanco Y Negro NEG 40*	54	2
17 Feb 90 ●	**THE LANGUAGE OF LIFE** *Blanco Y Negro BYN 21*	10	6
5 Oct 91	**WORLDWIDE** *Blanco Y Negro BYN 25*	29	5
22 Feb 92	**COVERS (EP)** *Blanco Y Negro NEG 54*	13	6
24 Apr 93	**THE ONLY LIVING BOY IN NEW YORK (EP)** *Blanco Y Negro NEG 62CD*	42	5
22 May 93 ●	**HOME MOVIES – THE BEST OF EVERYTHING BUT THE GIRL** *Blanco Y Negro 4509923192*	5	8
19 Jun 93	**I DIDN'T KNOW I WAS LOOKING FOR LOVE (EP)** *Blanco Y Negro NEG 64CD*	72	1
4 Jun 94	**ROLLERCOASTER (EP)** *Blanco Y Negro NEG 69CD*	65	1
25 Jun 94	**AMPLIFIED HEART** *Blanco Y Negro 4509964822*	20	15
20 Aug 94	**MISSING** *Blanco Y Negro NEG 71CD1*	69	1
28 Oct 95 ●	**MISSING** (re-mix) *Blanco Y Negro NEG 84CD*	3	22
20 Apr 96 ●	**WALKING WOUNDED** *Virgin VSCDT 1577*	6	6
18 May 96 ●	**WALKING WOUNDED** *Virgin CDV 2803*	4	27
29 Jun 96 ●	**WRONG** *Virgin VSCDT 1589*	8	7
5 Oct 96	**SINGLE** *Virgin VSCDT 1600*	20	3
9 Nov 96	**THE BEST OF EVERYTHING BUT THE GIRL** *Blanco Y Negro 630166372*	23	12
7 Dec 96	**DRIVING** (re-mix) *Blanco Y Negro NEG 99CD1*	36	2
1 Mar 97	**BEFORE TODAY** *Virgin VSCDT 1624*	25	2
3 Oct 98	**THE FUTURE OF THE FUTURE (STAY GOLD)** *Deconstruction 74321616252* [1]	31	2
25 Sep 99	**FIVE FATHOMS** *Virgin VSCDT 1742*	27	3
9 Oct 99	**TEMPERAMENTAL** *Virgin CDV 2892*	16	3
4 Mar 00	**TEMPERAMENTAL** *Virgin VSCDT 1761*	72	1
27 Jan 01	**TRACEY IN MY ROOM** *VC Recordings VCRD 78* [2]	34	2
2 Nov 02	**LIKE THE DESERTS MISS THE RAIN** *Virgin CDV 2966*	58	1

[1] Deep Dish with Everything but the Girl [2] EBTG vs Soul Vision

Tracks on Covers (EP): Love Is Strange / Tougher Than the Rest / Time After Time / Alison. Tracks on The Only Living Boy in New York (EP): The Only Living Boy in New York / Birds / Gabriel / Horses in the Room. Tracks on I Didn't Know I Was Looking for Love (EP): I Didn't Know I Was Looking for Love / My Head Is My Only House Unless It Rains / Political Science / A Piece of My Mind. Tracks on Rollercoaster (EP): Rollercoaster / Straight Back to You / Lights of Te Touan / I Didn't Know I Was Looking for Love (demo).

E'VOKE

UK, female vocal duo – Marlaine Gordon and Kerry Potter (3 Singles: 9 Weeks)

Date	Title / Label	Peak	Wks
25 Nov 95	**RUNAWAY** *Ffrreedom TABCD 238*	30	3
24 Aug 96	**ARMS OF LOREN** *Manifesto FESCD 10*	25	3
2 Feb 02	**ARMS OF LOREN** (re-mix) *Inferno CDFERN 001*	31	3

EVOLUTION

UK, male / female vocal / instrumental group (5 Singles: 12 Weeks)

Date	Title / Label	Peak	Wks
20 Mar 93	**LOVE THING** *Deconstruction 74321134272*	32	2
3 Jul 93	**EVERYBODY DANCE** *Deconstruction 74321152012*	19	5
8 Jan 94	**EVOLUTIONDANCE PART ONE (EP)** *Deconstruction 74321171912*	52	3
4 Nov 95	**LOOK UP TO THE LIGHT** *Deconstruction 74321318042*	55	1
19 Oct 96	**YOUR LOVE IS CALLING** *Deconstruction 74321422872*	60	1

Tracks on Evolutiondance Part One (EP): Escape 2 Alcatraz (re-mix) / Everybody / Don't Stop the Rain.

EX PISTOLS *UK, male vocal / instrumental group*

Date	Title / Label	Peak	Wks
2 Feb 85	**LAND OF HOPE AND GLORY** *Virginia PISTOL 76*	69	2

The EXCITERS *US, male / female vocal group (2 Singles: 7 Weeks)*

Date	Title / Label	Peak	Wks
21 Feb 63	**TELL HIM** *United Artists UP 1011*	46	1
4 Oct 75	**REACHING FOR THE BEST** *20th Century BTC 1005*	31	6

EXETER BRAMDEAN BOYS' CHOIR *UK, male choir*

Date	Title / Label	Peak	Wks
18 Dec 93	**REMEMBERING CHRISTMAS** *Golden Sounds DSCC 1*	46	3

EXILE *US, male vocal / instrumental group (3 Singles: 18 Weeks)*

Date	Title / Label	Peak	Wks
19 Aug 78 ●	**KISS YOU ALL OVER** *RAK 279* ▲ $	6	12
12 May 79	**HOW COULD THIS GO WRONG** *RAK 293*	67	2
12 Sep 81	**HEART AND SOUL** *RAK 333*	54	4

EXODUS *US, male vocal / instrumental group*

Date	Title / Label	Peak	Wks
11 Feb 89	**FABULOUS DISASTER** *Music for Nations MFN 90*	67	1

14 / 16 April 1966	21 / 23 April 1966	28 / 30 April 1966	5 / 7 May 1966
UK No.1 SINGLES			
SOMEBODY HELP ME – Spencer Davis Group	SOMEBODY HELP ME – Spencer Davis Group	YOU DON'T HAVE TO SAY YOU LOVE ME – Dusty Springfield	PRETTY FLAMINGO – Manfred Mann
UK No.1 ALBUMS			
THE SOUND OF MUSIC – Soundtrack	THE SOUND OF MUSIC – Soundtrack	AFTERMATH – The Rolling Stones	AFTERMATH – The Rolling Stones

EXOTERIX *UK, male producer – Duncan Millar (2 Singles: 2 Weeks)*

24 Apr 93 **VOID** *Positiva CDTIV 1* 58 1
5 Feb 94 **SATISFY MY LOVE** *Union UCRCD 26* 62 1

EXOTICA featuring Itsy FOSTER
UK / Italy, male / female vocal / instrumental group

16 Sep 95 **THE SUMMER IS MAGIC** *Polydor 5798392* 68 1

EXPLOITED *UK, male vocal / instrumental group (3 Albums: 26 Weeks, 4 Singles: 13 Weeks)*

18 Apr 81 **DOGS OF WAR** *Secret SHH 110* 63 4
16 May 81 PUNK'S NOT DEAD *Secret SEC 1* 20 11
17 Oct 81 **DEAD CITIES** *Secret SHH 120* 31 5
14 Nov 81 EXPLOITED LIVE *Superville EXPLP 2001* 52 3
5 Dec 81 **DON'T LET 'EM GRIND YOU DOWN** *Superville EXP 1003* [1] ..70 1
8 May 82 **ATTACK** *Secret SHH 130* 50 3
19 Jun 82 TROOPS OF TOMORROW *Secret SEC 8* 17 12

[1] Exploited and Anti-Pasti

The EXPLOSION NEW *US, male vocal / instrumental group*

26 Mar 05 **HERE I AM** *Virgin VUSDX 298* 75 1

EXPOSÉ *US, female vocal group*

28 Aug 93 **I'LL NEVER GET OVER YOU (GETTING OVER ME)** *Arista 74321158962* 75 1

EXPRESS OF SOUND *Italy, male instrumental / production group*

2 Nov 96 **REAL VIBRATION (WANT LOVE)** *Positiva CDTIV 66* 45 1

EXPRESSOS
UK, male / female vocal / instrumental group (2 Singles: 5 Weeks)

21 Jun 80 **HEY GIRL** *WEA K 18246* 60 3
14 Mar 81 **TANGO IN MONO** *WEA K 18431* 70 2

EXTREME *US, male vocal (Gary Cherone) / instrumental group (3 Albums: 75 Weeks, 9 Singles: 46 Weeks)*

1 Jun 91 EXTREME II PORNOGRAFFITTI *A&M 3953131* 12 61
8 Jun 91 **GET THE FUNK OUT** *A&M AM 737* 19 7
27 Jul 91 ● **MORE THAN WORDS** *A&M AM 792* ▲ 2 11
12 Oct 91 **DECADENCE DANCE** *A&M AM 773* 36 3
23 Nov 91 **HOLE HEARTED** *A&M AM 839* 12 7
2 May 92 **SONG FOR LOVE** *A&M AM 698* 12 6
5 Sep 92 **REST IN PEACE** *A&M AM 0055* 13 5
26 Sep 92 ● III SIDES TO EVERY STORY *A&M 5400062* 2 11
14 Nov 92 **STOP THE WORLD** *A&M AM 0096* 22 2
6 Feb 93 **TRAGIC COMIC** *A&M AMCD 0156* 15 4
11 Feb 95 ● WAITING FOR THE PUNCHLINE *A&M 5403052* 10 3
11 Mar 95 **HIP TODAY** *A&M 5809932* 44 1

EYE TO EYE featuring Taka BOOM (see also MUKKAA; UMBOZA)
UK, male producer – Stuart Crichton and US, female vocalist

9 Jun 01 **JUST CAN'T GET ENOUGH (NO NO NO NO)** *Xtravaganza XTRAV 25CD* 36 2

EYEOPENER (see also FLIP + FILL; REZONANCE Q)
UK, male / female production / vocal group

20 Nov 04 **HUNGRY EYES** *All Around the World CDGLOBE 363* 16 6

EYES CREAM *Italy, male producer – Agostino Carollo*

16 Oct 99 **FLY AWAY (BYE BYE)** *Accolade CDAC 001* 53 1

F

Adam F *UK, male producer – Adam Fenton*
(2 Albums: 3 Weeks, 10 Singles: 23 Weeks)

27 Sep 97 **CIRCLES** *Positiva CDFJ 002* 20 3
15 Nov 97 COLOURS *Positiva 8217252* 47 1
7 Mar 98 **MUSIC IN MY MIND** *Positiva CDFJ 003* 27 3
15 Sep 01 **SMASH SUMTHIN'** *Def Jam 5886932* [1] 11 7
22 Sep 01 KAOS – THE ANTI-ACOUSTIC WARFARE *Chrysalis 5342502* 44 2
1 Dec 01 **STAND CLEAR** *Chrysalis CDEM 597* [2] 43 1
6 Apr 02 **WHERE'S MY ...?** *EMI CDEMS 598* [3] 37 2
27 Apr 02 **METROSOUND** *Kaos KAOS 001P* [4] 54 1
8 Jun 02 **STAND CLEAR** (re-mix) *Kaos KAOSCD 002* [2] 50 1
31 Aug 02 **SMASH SUMTHIN'** (re-mix) *Kaos KAOSCD 003* [5] 47 2
14 Dec 02 **DIRTY HARRY'S REVENGE** *Kaos KAOS 004* [6] 50 2
30 Oct 04 **WHEN THE SUN GOES DOWN** *Breakbeat Kaos BBK 005* [7] .68 1

[1] Redman featuring Adam F [2] Adam F featuring MOP [3] Adam F featuring Lil' Mo [4] Adam F and J Majik [5] Adam F featuring Redman [6] Adam F featuring Beenie Man [7] DJ Fresh featuring Adam F

FAB *UK, male producers (1 Album: 3 Weeks, 3 Singles: 11 Weeks)*

7 Jul 90 ● **THUNDERBIRDS ARE GO** *Brothers Organisation FAB 1* [1] 5 8
20 Oct 90 **THE PRISONER** *Brothers Organisation FAB 6* [2] 56 2
10 Nov 90 POWER THEMES 90 *Telstar STAR 2430* 53 3
1 Dec 90 **THE STINGRAY MEGAMIX** *Brothers Organisation FAB 2* [3] ...66 1

[1] FAB featuring MC Parker [2] FAB featuring MC Number 6 [3] FAB featuring Aqua Marina

FC KAHUNA *UK, male production duo (3 Singles: 3 Weeks)*

6 Apr 02 **GLITTERBALL** *City Rockers ROCKERS 11CD* 64 1
20 Jul 02 **MACHINE SAYS YES** *City Rockers ROCKERS 18CD* 58 1
22 Mar 03 **HAYLING** *Skint SKINT 84CD* 49 1

FFWD *UK / Germany, male instrumental group*

13 Aug 94 FFWD *Inter INTA 001CD* 48 1

FKW *UK, male vocal / instrumental group (4 Singles: 8 Weeks)*

2 Oct 93 **NEVER GONNA (GIVE YOU UP)** *PWL International PWCD 273* .48 2
11 Dec 93 **SEIZE THE DAY** *PWL International PWCD 279* 45 2
5 Mar 94 **JINGO** *PWL International PWCD 283* 30 3
4 Jun 94 **THIS IS THE WAY** *PWL International PWCD 307* 63 1

FM
UK, male vocal / instrumental group (2 Albums: 3 Weeks, 5 Singles: 11 Weeks)

20 Sep 86 INDISCREET *Portrait PRT 26827* 76 1
31 Jan 87 **FROZEN HEART** *Portrait DIDGE 1* 64 2
20 Jun 87 **LET LOVE BE THE LEADER** *Portrait MERV 1* 71 2
5 Aug 89 **BAD LUCK** *Epic 655031 7* 54 4
7 Oct 89 **SOMEDAY (YOU'LL COME RUNNING)** *CBS DINK 1* 64 2
14 Oct 89 TOUGH IT OUT *Epic 465589 1* 34 2
10 Feb 90 **EVERYTIME I THINK OF YOU** *Epic DINK 2* 73 1

FPI PROJECT
Italy, male instrumental / production group (4 Singles: 17 Weeks)

9 Dec 89 ● **GOING BACK TO MY ROOTS / RICH IN PARADISE** *Rumour RUMAT 9* 9 12

12 / 14 May 1966	19 / 21 May 1966	26 / 28 May 1966	2 / 4 June 1966
PRETTY FLAMINGO Manfred Mann	PRETTY FLAMINGO Manfred Mann	PAINT IT BLACK The Rolling Stones	STRANGERS IN THE NIGHT Frank Sinatra
AFTERMATH The Rolling Stones	AFTERMATH The Rolling Stones	AFTERMATH The Rolling Stones	AFTERMATH The Rolling Stones

KEY: UK No.1 ★ UK Top 10 ● Still on chart + UK entry at No.1 ■ US No.1 ▲ UK million seller £ US million seller $
Singles re-entries are listed as (re), (2re), (3re)... which signifies that the hit re-entered the chart once, twice or three times...
Peak Position / Weeks

9 Mar 91 **EVERYBODY (ALL OVER THE WORLD)** *Rumour RUMA 29*........65 3
7 Aug 93 **COME ON (AND DO IT)** *Synthetic SYNTH 006CD*........59 1
13 Mar 99 **EVERYBODY (ALL OVER)** (re-mix) *99 North CDNTH 14*........67 1

'Going Back to My Roots' was a vocal track available in two formats and featured either Paolo Dini or Sharon Dee Clarke.

FAB! *Ireland, female vocal group*

1 Aug 98 **TURN AROUND** *Break Records BRCX 107*........59 1

FAB FOUR featuring Robert OWENS
Germany / Italy, male production duo and US, male vocalist

15 Feb 03 **LAST NIGHT A DJ BLEW MY MIND** *Illustrious CDILL 013*........34 1

Shelley FABARES
US, female vocalist / actor – Michelle Fabares

26 Apr 62 **JOHNNY ANGEL** *Pye International 7N 25132* ▲ $........41 4

FABIAN *US, male vocalist – Fabiano Forte*

10 Mar 60 **HOUND DOG MAN** *HMV POP 695*........46 1

Lara FABIAN *Canada (b. Belgium), female vocalist*

28 Oct 00 **I WILL LOVE AGAIN** *Columbia 6694062*........63 1

FABOLOUS
US, male rapper – John Jackson (2 Albums: 11 Weeks, 5 Singles: 27 Weeks)

2 Aug 03 SWEET DREAMS *East West 7559627912*........59 10
16 Aug 03 **CAN'T LET YOU GO** *Elektra E 7408CD* [1]........14 5
1 Nov 03 **INTO YOU** *Elektra E 7470CD* [2]........18 6
20 Mar 04 **BADABOOM** *Epic 6747512* [3]........26 5
20 Nov 04 REAL TALK *Atlantic 7567837542*........66 1
27 Nov 04 **BREATHE** *Atlantic AT 0189CD*........28 8
2 Apr 05 **BABY** *Atlantic AT 0199CDX* [4]........41 3

[1] Fabolous featuring Mike Shorey and Lil' Mo [2] Fabolous featuring Tamia [3] B2K featuring Fabolous [4] Fabolous featuring Mike Shorey

The FABULOUS BAKER BOYS *UK, male DJ / production trio*

15 Nov 97 **OH BOY** *Multiply CDMULTY 28*........34 2

The FACES *UK, male vocal / instrumental group (8 Albums: 62 Weeks, 5 Singles: 46 Weeks)*

4 Apr 70 FIRST STEP *Warner Bros. WS 3000*........45 1
8 May 71 LONG PLAYER *Warner Bros. W 3011*........31 7
18 Dec 71 ● **STAY WITH ME** *Warner Bros. K 16136*........6 14
25 Dec 71 ● A NOD IS AS GOOD AS A WINK ... TO A BLIND HORSE *Warner Bros. K 56006*........2 22
17 Feb 73 ● **CINDY INCIDENTALLY** *Warner Bros. K 16247*........2 9
21 Apr 73 ★ OOH LA LA *Warner Bros. K 56011*........1 13
8 Dec 73 ● **POOL HALL RICHARD / I WISH IT WOULD RAIN** *Warner Bros. K 16341*........8 11
26 Jan 74 ● OVERTURE AND BEGINNERS *Mercury 9100 001* [1]........3 7
7 Dec 74 **YOU CAN MAKE ME DANCE SING OR ANYTHING (EVEN TAKE THE DOG FOR A WALK, MEND A FUSE, FOLD AWAY THE IRONING BOARD, OR ANY OTHER DOMESTIC SHORT COMINGS)** *Warner Bros. K 16494* [1]........12 9
21 May 77 THE BEST OF THE FACES *Riva RVLP 3*........24 6
4 Jun 77 **THE FACES (EP)** *Riva 8*........41 3
7 Nov 92 THE BEST OF ROD STEWART AND THE FACES 1971-1975 *Mercury 5141802* [1]........58 1
1 Nov 03 CHANGING FACES – THE VERY BEST OF ROD STEWART & THE FACES – THE DEFINITIVE COLLECTION 1969-1974 *Universal TV 9812604* [1]........13 5

[1] The Faces / Rod Stewart [1] Rod Stewart and The Faces

Tracks on The Faces (EP): Memphis / You Can Make Me Dance Sing or Anything / Stay with Me / Cindy Incidentally.

FACTORY OF UNLIMITED RHYTHM
Jamaica, male / female vocal / instrumental group

1 Jun 96 **THE SWEETEST SURRENDER** *Kuff KUFFD 6*........59 1

The FADERS NEW
UK, female vocal / instrumental group (2 Singles: 9 Weeks)

2 Apr 05 **NO SLEEP TONIGHT** *Polydor 9870597*........13 6
9 Jul 05 **JUMP** *Polydor 9872017*........21 3

Donald FAGEN (see also STEELY DAN)
US, male vocalist / keyboard player (2 Albums: 25 Weeks, 1 Single: 2 Weeks)

20 Oct 82 THE NIGHTFLY *Warner Bros. 923696*........44 16
5 Jun 93 ● KAMAKIRIAD *Reprise 9362452302*........3 9
3 Jul 93 **TOMORROW'S GIRLS** *Reprise W 0180CDX*........46 2

Joe FAGIN *UK, male vocalist (2 Singles: 20 Weeks)*

7 Jan 84 ● **THAT'S LIVIN' ALRIGHT** *Towerbell TOW 46*........3 11
5 Apr 86 **BACK WITH THE BOYS AGAIN / GET IT RIGHT** *Towerbell TOW 84*........53 9

Yvonne FAIR *US, female vocalist, b. 1942, d. 6 Mar 1994*

24 Jan 76 ● **IT SHOULD HAVE BEEN ME** *Tamla Motown TMG 1013*........5 11

FAIR WEATHER (see also AMEN CORNER)
UK, male vocal (Andy Fairweather-Low) / instrumental group

18 Jul 70 ● **NATURAL SINNER** *RCA 1977*........6 12

FAIRGROUND ATTRACTION *UK, female / male vocal (Eddi Reader MBE) / instrumental group (2 Albums: 54 Weeks, 4 Singles: 27 Weeks)*

16 Apr 88 ★ **PERFECT** *RCA PB 41845*........1 13
28 May 88 ● THE FIRST OF A MILLION KISSES *RCA PL 71696*........2 52
30 Jul 88 ● **FIND MY LOVE** *RCA PB 42079*........7 10
19 Nov 88 **A SMILE IN A WHISPER** *RCA PB 42249*........75 1
28 Jan 89 **CLARE** *RCA PB 42607*........49 3
30 Jun 90 AY FOND KISS *RCA PL 74596*........55 2

Group were male only on last album.

FAIRPORT CONVENTION *UK, male / female vocal / instrumental group – includes Sandy Denny (6 Albums: 41 Weeks, 1 Single: 9 Weeks)*

23 Jul 69 **SI TU DOIS PARTIR (re)** *Island WIP 6064*........21 9
2 Aug 69 UNHALFBRICKING *Island ILPS 9102*........12 8
17 Jan 70 LIEGE & LIEF *Island ILPS 9115*........17 15
18 Jul 70 FULL HOUSE *Island ILPS 9130*........13 11
3 Jul 71 ● ANGEL DELIGHT *Island ILPS 9162*........8 5
12 Jul 75 RISING FOR THE MOON *Island ILPS 9313*........52 1
28 Jan 89 RED AND GOLD *New Routes RUE 002*........74 1

Andy FAIRWEATHER-LOW (see also AMEN CORNER; FAIR WEATHER) *UK, male vocalist (2 Singles: 18 Weeks)*

21 Sep 74 ● **REGGAE TUNE** *A&M AMS 7129*........10 8
6 Dec 75 ● **WIDE EYED AND LEGLESS** *A&M AMS 7202*........6 10

Adam FAITH 199 Top 500

Teen-idol vocalist turned top actor then financial wizard, b. Terence Nelhams-Wright, 23 Jun 1940, London, UK, d. 8 Mar 2003. One of the most charted acts of the 1960s, he became the first UK artist to lodge their initial

seven hits in the Top 5. Also one of the first UK acts to record original songs regularly (6 Albums: 46 Weeks, 24 Singles: 252 Weeks)

20 Nov 59 ★ WHAT DO YOU WANT? Parlophone R 4591 ... 1 19
22 Jan 60 ★ POOR ME Parlophone R 4623 ... 1 18
14 Apr 60 ● SOMEONE ELSE'S BABY Parlophone R 4643 ... 2 13
30 Jun 60 ● JOHNNY COMES MARCHING HOME / MADE YOU Parlophone R 4665 [1] ... 5 13
15 Sep 60 ● HOW ABOUT THAT! Parlophone R 4689 [1] ... 4 14
17 Nov 60 ● LONELY PUP (IN A CHRISTMAS SHOP) Parlophone R 4708 ... 4 11
19 Nov 60 ● ADAM Parlophone PMC 1128 ... 6 36
9 Feb 61 ● WHO AM I! / THIS IS IT! Parlophone R 4735 ... 5 14
11 Feb 61 BEAT GIRL (FILM SOUNDTRACK) Columbia 33SX 1225 ... 11 3
27 Apr 61 EASY GOING ME Parlophone R 4766 ... 12 10
20 Jul 61 DON'T YOU KNOW IT Parlophone R 4807 ... 12 10
26 Oct 61 ● THE TIME HAS COME Parlophone R 4837 ... 4 14
18 Jan 62 LONESOME Parlophone R 4864 [1] ... 12 9
24 Mar 62 ADAM FAITH Parlophone PMC 1162 ... 20 1
3 May 62 ● AS YOU LIKE IT Parlophone R 4896 [1] ... 5 15
30 Aug 62 ● DON'T THAT BEAT ALL Parlophone R 4930 [2] ... 8 11
13 Dec 62 BABY TAKE A BOW Parlophone R 4964 ... 22 6
31 Jan 63 WHAT NOW Parlophone R 4990 [2] ... 31 5
11 Jul 63 WALKIN' TALL Parlophone R 5039 ... 23 6
19 Sep 63 ● THE FIRST TIME Parlophone R 5061 [3] ... 5 13
12 Dec 63 WE ARE IN LOVE Parlophone R 5091 [3] ... 11 12
12 Mar 64 IF HE TELLS YOU Parlophone R 5109 [3] ... 25 9
28 May 64 I LOVE BEING IN LOVE WITH YOU Parlophone R 5138 [3] ... 33 6
26 Nov 64 A MESSAGE TO MARTHA (KENTUCKY BLUEBIRD) Parlophone R 5201 ... 12 11
11 Feb 65 STOP FEELING SORRY FOR YOURSELF Parlophone R 5235 ... 23 6
17 Jun 65 SOMEONE'S TAKEN MARIA AWAY Parlophone R 5289 ... 34 5
25 Sep 65 FAITH ALIVE Parlophone PMC 1249 ... 19 1
20 Oct 66 CHERYL'S GOIN' HOME Parlophone R 5516 ... 46 2
19 Dec 81 20 GOLDEN GREATS Warwick WW 5113 ... 61 3
27 Nov 93 MIDNIGHT POSTCARDS PolyGram TV 8213982 ... 43 2

[1] Adam Faith with John Barry and his Orchestra [2] Adam Faith with Johnny Keating and his Orchestra [3] Adam Faith and The Roulettes

Horace FAITH *Jamaica, male vocalist – Horace Smith*

12 Sep 70 BLACK PEARL Trojan TR 7790 ... 13 10

Percy FAITH *Canada, orchestra – leader b. 7 Apr 1908, d. 9 Feb 1976*

4 Mar 60 ● THE THEME FROM 'A SUMMER PLACE' Philips PB 989 ▲ $ ... 2 31

The FAITH BROTHERS

UK, male vocal / instrumental group (1 Album: 1 Week, 2 Singles: 6 Weeks)

13 Apr 85 THE COUNTRY OF THE BLIND Siren SIREN 2 ... 63 3
6 Jul 85 A STRANGER ON HOME GROUND Siren SIREN 4 ... 69 3
9 Nov 85 EVENTIDE Siren SIRENLP 1 ... 66 1

FAITH, HOPE AND CHARITY *US, male / female vocal group*

31 Jan 76 JUST ONE LOOK RCA 2632 ... 38 4

FAITH, HOPE AND CHARITY *UK, female vocal group*

23 Jun 90 BATTLE OF THE SEXES WEA YZ 480 ... 53 3

FAITH NO MORE *US, male vocal (Michael Patton) / instrumental group*

(6 Albums: 74 Weeks, 19 Singles: 65 Weeks)

6 Feb 88 WE CARE A LOT Slash LASH 17 ... 53 3
10 Feb 90 EPIC Slash LASH 21 ... 37 4
17 Feb 90 THE REAL THING Slash 8281541 ... 30 35
14 Apr 90 FROM OUT OF NOWHERE Slash LASH 24 ... 23 6
14 Jul 90 FALLING TO PIECES Slash LASH 25 ... 41 3
8 Sep 90 EPIC (re-issue) Slash LASH 26 ... 25 5
16 Feb 91 LIVE AT THE BRIXTON ACADEMY Slash 8282381 ... 20 4
6 Jun 92 ● MIDLIFE CRISIS Slash LASH 37 ... 10 5
20 Jun 92 ● ANGEL DUST Slash 8283212 ... 2 25
15 Aug 92 A SMALL VICTORY Slash LASH 39 ... 29 5
12 Sep 92 A SMALL VICTORY (re-mix) Slash LASHX 40 ... 55 1
21 Nov 92 EVERYTHING'S RUINED Slash LASH 43 ... 28 3
16 Jan 93 ● I'M EASY / BE AGGRESSIVE (re) Slash LACDP 44 ... 3 8
6 Nov 93 ANOTHER BODY MURDERED Epic 6597942 [1] ... 26 3
11 Mar 95 DIGGING THE GRAVE Slash LASCD 51 ... 16 4
25 Mar 95 ● KING FOR A DAY FOOL FOR A LIFETIME Slash 8285602 ... 5 6
27 May 95 RICOCHET Slash LASCD 53 ... 27 2
29 Jul 95 EVIDENCE Slash LASCD 54 ... 32 3
31 May 97 ASHES TO ASHES Slash LASCD 61 ... 15 3
21 Jun 97 ● ALBUM OF THE YEAR Slash 8289012 ... 7 3
16 Aug 97 LAST CUP OF SORROW Slash LASCD 62 ... 51 1
13 Dec 97 THIS TOWN AIN'T BIG ENOUGH FOR BOTH OF US Roadrunner RR 22513 [2] ... 40 2
17 Jan 98 ASHES TO ASHES (re-issue) Slash LACDP 63 ... 29 3
7 Nov 98 I STARTED A JOKE Slash LASCD 65 ... 49 1
21 Nov 98 WHO CARES A LOT? – THE GREATEST HITS Slash 5560572 ... 37 1

[1] Faith No More and Boo-Yaa TRIBE [2] Sparks vs Faith No More

Marianne FAITHFULL

UK, female vocalist (6 Albums: 19 Weeks, 7 Singles: 59 Weeks)

13 Aug 64 ● AS TEARS GO BY Decca F 11923 ... 9 13
18 Feb 65 ● COME AND STAY WITH ME Decca F 12075 ... 4 13
6 May 65 ● THIS LITTLE BIRD Decca F 12162 ... 6 11
5 Jun 65 COME MY WAY Decca LK 4688 ... 12 7
5 Jun 65 MARIANNE FAITHFULL Decca LK 4689 ... 15 2
22 Jul 65 ● SUMMER NIGHTS Decca F 12193 ... 10 10
4 Nov 65 YESTERDAY Decca F 12268 ... 36 4
9 Mar 67 IS THIS WHAT I GET FOR LOVING YOU? Decca F 22524 ... 43 2
24 Nov 79 BROKEN ENGLISH Island M1 ... 57 3
24 Nov 79 THE BALLAD OF LUCY JORDAN Island WIP 6491 ... 48 6
17 Oct 81 DANGEROUS ACQUAINTANCES Island ILPS 9648 ... 45 4
26 Mar 83 A CHILD'S ADVENTURE Island ILPS 9734 ... 99 1
8 Aug 87 STRANGE WEATHER Island ILPS 9874 ... 78 2

FAITHLESS 332 Top 500

(see also DIDO; DUSTED; 1 GIANT LEAP; OUR TRIBE / ONE TRIBE; ROLLO; SISTER BLISS; SPHINX)

Club favourites turned pop-house group formed in 1993. Mainstays: producers Rollo Armstrong (brother of Dido) and classically-trained Sister Bliss (b. Alayah Bentovim) plus rapper Maxi Jazz (Maxwell Frazer). Sunday 8PM was nominated for the 1999 Mercury Music Prize they uniquely issued separate remixed editions of their first three hit albums. (5 Albums: 89 Weeks, 21 Singles: 121 Weeks)

5 Aug 95 SALVA MEA (SAVE ME) Cheeky CHEKCD 008 ... 30 2
9 Dec 95 INSOMNIA Cheeky CHEKCD 010 ... 27 2
23 Mar 96 DON'T LEAVE Cheeky CHEKCD 012 ... 34 2
26 Oct 96 ● INSOMNIA (re-issue) Cheeky CHEKCD 017 ... 3 13
23 Nov 96 REVERENCE Cheeky CHEKCD 500 ... 26 14
21 Dec 96 ● SALVA MEA (re-mix) Cheeky CHEKCD 018 ... 9 7
26 Apr 97 ● REVERENCE Cheeky CHEKCD 019 ... 10 3
15 Nov 97 DON'T LEAVE (re-mix) Cheeky CHEKXCD 024 ... 21 2
5 Sep 98 ● GOD IS A DJ Cheeky CHEKCD 028 ... 6 8
3 Oct 98 ● SUNDAY 8PM Cheeky CHEKCD 503 ... 10 7
5 Dec 98 TAKE THE LONG WAY HOME Cheeky CHEKCD 031 ... 15 6
1 May 99 BRING MY FAMILY BACK Cheeky CHEKCD 035 ... 14 5
16 Jun 01 ● WE COME 1 Cheeky 74321850842 ... 3 10
30 Jun 01 ● OUTROSPECTIVE Cheeky 74321850832 ... 4 22
29 Sep 01 MUHAMMAD ALI (re) Cheeky 74321886442 ... 29 4
29 Dec 01 TARANTULA (re) Cheeky 74321903592 ... 29 5
20 Apr 02 ● ONE STEP TOO FAR Cheeky 74321926412 [1] ... 6 3
12 Jun 04 ● MASS DESTRUCTION Cheeky 82876614912 ... 7 8
19 Jun 04 ★ NO ROOTS Cheeky 82876618702 ■ ... 1 14
4 Sep 04 I WANT MORE Cheeky / BMG 82876641742 ... 22 3
30 Apr 05 INSOMNIA (re-mix) (re) Cheeky 82876690301 ... 48 19
28 May 05 ★ FOREVER FAITHLESS – THE GREATEST HITS Cheeky 82876681522 ■ ... 1 32+
11 Jun 05 WHY GO? Cheeky 82876699292 [2] ... 49 1
13 Aug 05 GOD IS A DJ (re-mix) Cheeky 82876719861 ... 66 2

7 / 9 July 1966	14 / 16 July 1966	21 / 23 July 1966	28 / 30 July 1966
SUNNY AFTERNOON The Kinks	SUNNY AFTERNOON The Kinks	GET AWAY Georgie Fame and The Blue Flames	OUT OF TIME Chris Farlowe and The Thunderbirds
THE SOUND OF MUSIC Soundtrack	THE SOUND OF MUSIC Soundtrack	THE SOUND OF MUSIC Soundtrack	THE SOUND OF MUSIC Soundtrack

KEY
UK No.1 ★ UK Top 10 ● Still on chart + UK entry at No.1 ■
US No.1 ▲ UK million seller £ US million seller $
Singles re-entries are listed as (re), (2re), (3re)... which signifies that the hit re-entered the chart once, twice or three times...
Peak Position / Weeks

13 Aug 05	**WE COME 1** (re-mix) *Cheeky 82876719871*	73	1
17 Sep 05	**INSOMNIA 2005** (2nd re-mix) **(re)** *Cheeky 82876724692*	17	15+

1 Faithless featuring Dido 2 Faithless featuring Estelle

FALCO *Austria, male vocalist – Johann Holzel, b. 19 Feb 1957, d. 6 Feb 1998 (1 Album: 15 Weeks, 4 Singles: 26 Weeks)*

22 Mar 86 ★	**ROCK ME AMADEUS** *A&M AM 278* ▲	1	15
26 Apr 86	FALCO 3 *A&M AMA 5105*	32	15
31 May 86 ●	**VIENNA CALLING** *A&M AM 318*	10	8
2 Aug 86	**JEANNY** *A&M AM 333*	68	1
27 Sep 86	**THE SOUND OF MUSIK** *WEA U 8591*	61	2

Christian FALK featuring DEMETREUS
Sweden, male producer and vocalist

26 Aug 00	**MAKE IT RIGHT** *London LONCD 452*	22	3

Thomas FALKE NEW *Germany, male producer*

13 Aug 05	**HIGH AGAIN (HIGH ON EMOTION)** *Manifesto 9871558*	55	1

The FALL *UK, male / female vocal (Mark E. Smith) / instrumental group (15 Albums: 32 Weeks, 16 Singles: 27 Weeks)*

20 Mar 82	HEX ENDUCTION HOUR *Kamera KAM 005*	71	3
20 Oct 84	THE WONDERFUL AND FRIGHTENING WORLD OF ... *Beggars Banquet BEGA 58*	62	2
5 Oct 85	THE NATION'S SAVING GRACE *Beggars Banquet BEGA 67*	54	2
13 Sep 86	**MR PHARMACIST** *Beggars Banquet BEG 168*	75	1
11 Oct 86	BEND SINISTER *Beggars Banquet BEGA 75*	36	3
20 Dec 86	**HEY! LUCIANI** *Beggars Banquet BEG 176*	59	1
9 May 87	**THERE'S A GHOST IN MY HOUSE** *Beggars Banquet BEG 187*	30	4
31 Oct 87	**HIT THE NORTH** *Beggars Banquet BEG 200*	57	5
30 Jan 88	**VICTORIA** *Beggars Banquet BEG 206*	35	3
12 Mar 88	THE FRENZ EXPERIMENT *Beggars Banquet BEGA 91*	19	4
12 Nov 88	I AM KURIOUS ORANJ *Beggars Banquet BEGA 96*	54	2
26 Nov 88	**BIG NEW PRINZ / JERUSALEM (DOUBLE SINGLE)** *Beggars Banquet FALL 2/3*	59	2
8 Jul 89	SEMINAL LIVE *Beggars Banquet BBL 102*	40	2
27 Jan 90	**TELEPHONE THING** *Cog Sinister SIN 4*	58	1
3 Mar 90	EXTRICATE *Cog Sinister 8422041*	31	3
8 Sep 90	**WHITE LIGHTNING** *Cog Sinister SIN 6*	56	2
15 Sep 90	458489 B-SIDES *Beggars Banquet BEGA 111*	44	2
4 May 91	SHIFT WORK *Cog Sinister 8485941*	17	2
14 Mar 92	**FREE RANGE** *Cog Sinister SINS 8*	40	1
28 Mar 92	CODE: SELFISH *Cog Sinister 5121622*	21	1
17 Apr 93	**WHY ARE PEOPLE GRUDGEFUL** *Permanent CDSPERM 9*	43	1
8 May 93 ●	INFOTAINMENT SCAN *Permanent PERMCD 12*	9	3
25 Dec 93	**BEHIND THE COUNTER** *Permanent CDSPERM 13*	75	1
30 Apr 94	**15 WAYS** *Permanent CDSPERM 14*	65	1
14 May 94	MIDDLE CLASS REVOLT *Permanent PERMCD 16*	48	1
11 Mar 95	CEREBRAL CAUSTIC *Permanent PERMCD 30*	67	1
17 Feb 96	**THE CHISELERS** *Jet JETSCD 500*	60	1
22 Jun 96	THE LIGHT USER SYNDROME *Jet JETCD 1012*	54	1
21 Feb 98	**MASQUERADE** *Artful CDARTFUL 1*	69	1
14 Dec 02	**THE FALL VS 2003** *Action TAKE 020CD*	64	1
10 Jul 04	**THEME FROM SPARTA FC #2** *Action TAKE 23CD*	66	1

Tracks on Big New Prinz / Jerusalem (double single): Big New Prinz / Wrong Place Right Time Number Two / Jerusalem / Acid Priest 2088. Tracks on The Fall vs 2003: Susan vs Youthclub (and re-mix) / Janey vs Johnny.

FALLACY *UK, male producer – Daniel Fahey (2 Singles: 4 Weeks)*

22 Jun 02	**THE GROUNDBREAKER** *Wordplay WORDCD 036* 1	47	2
24 May 03	**BIG N BASHY** *Virgin VSCDT 1847* 2	45	2

1 Fallacy and Fusion 2 Fallacy featuring Tubby T

FALLOUT TRUST NEW *UK, male vocal / instrumental group*

25 Jun 05	**WHEN WE ARE GONE** *At Large FUGCD 007*	73	1

Harold FALTERMEYER
Germany, male keyboard player (2 Singles: 23 Weeks)

23 Mar 85 ●	**AXEL F (re)** *MCA MCA 949*	2	22
24 Aug 85	**FLETCH THEME** *MCA MCA 991*	74	1

'Axel F' reached its peak position when it re-entered the chart in Jun 1985.

Agnetha FÄLTSKOG (see also ABBA)
Sweden, female vocalist (4 Albums: 21 Weeks, 5 Singles: 19 Weeks)

28 May 83	**THE HEAT IS ON** *Epic A 3436*	35	6
11 Jun 83	WRAP YOUR ARMS AROUND ME *Epic EPC 25505*	18	13
13 Aug 83	**WRAP YOUR ARMS AROUND ME** *Epic A 3622*	44	5
22 Oct 83	**CAN'T SHAKE LOOSE** *Epic A 3812*	63	1
4 May 85	EYES OF A WOMAN *Epic EPC 26446*	38	3
12 Mar 88	I STAND ALONE *WEA WX 150*	72	1
24 Apr 04	**IF I THOUGHT YOU'D EVER CHANGE YOUR MIND** *WEA WEA 375CD*	11	5
1 May 04	MY COLOURING BOOK *WEA 5046731222*	12	4
26 Jun 04	**WHEN YOU WALK IN THE ROOM** *WEA WEA 378CD1*	34	2

Georgie FAME (372 Top 500) *Critically-acclaimed R&B / jazz vocalist / keyboard player, b. Clive Powell, 26 Jun 1943, Lancashire, UK. The one-time rock 'n' roll tour musician, who had a string of sixties hits, is still a popular performer, often working with contemporaries such as Van Morrison and Bill Wyman (5 Albums: 72 Weeks, 13 Singles: 115 Weeks)*

17 Oct 64	FAME AT LAST *Columbia 33SX 1638*	15	8
17 Dec 64 ★	**YEH, YEH** *Columbia DB 7428* 1	1	12
4 Mar 65	**IN THE MEANTIME** *Columbia DB 7494* 1	22	8
29 Jul 65	**LIKE WE USED TO BE** *Columbia DB 7633* 1	33	7
28 Oct 65	**SOMETHING** *Columbia DB 7727* 1	23	7
14 May 66 ●	SWEET THINGS *Columbia SX 6043*	6	22
23 Jun 66 ★	**GET AWAY** *Columbia DB 7946* 1	1	11
22 Sep 66	**SUNNY** *Columbia DB 8015*	13	8
15 Oct 66 ●	SOUND VENTURE *Columbia SX 6076*	9	9
22 Dec 66	**SITTING IN THE PARK** *Columbia DB 8096* 1	12	10
11 Mar 67	HALL OF FAME *Columbia SX 6120*	12	18
23 Mar 67	**BECAUSE I LOVE YOU** *CBS 202587*	15	8
1 Jul 67	TWO FACES OF FAME *CBS SBPG 63018*	22	15
13 Sep 67	**TRY MY WORLD** *CBS 2945*	37	5
13 Dec 67 ★	**THE BALLAD OF BONNIE AND CLYDE** *CBS 3124*	1	13
9 Jul 69	**PEACEFUL** *CBS 4295*	16	9
13 Dec 69	**SEVENTH SON** *CBS 4659*	25	7
10 Apr 71	**ROSETTA** *CBS 7108* 2	11	10

1 Georgie Fame and the Blue Flames 2 Fame and Price Together

FAMILY *UK, male vocal (Roger Chapman) / instrumental group (7 Albums: 41 Weeks, 4 Singles: 44 Weeks)*

10 Aug 68	MUSIC IN A DOLL'S HOUSE *Reprise RLP 6312*	35	3
22 Mar 69 ●	FAMILY ENTERTAINMENT *Reprise RSLP 6340*	6	3
1 Nov 69	**NO MULE'S FOOL** *Reprise RS 27001*	29	7
7 Feb 70 ●	A SONG FOR ME *Reprise RSLP 9001*	4	13
22 Aug 70	**STRANGE BAND** *Reprise RS 27009*	11	12
28 Nov 70 ●	ANYWAY *Reprise RSX 9005*	7	7
17 Jul 71 ●	**IN MY OWN TIME** *Reprise K 14090*	4	13
20 Nov 71	FEARLESS *Reprise K 54003*	14	2
23 Sep 72	**BURLESQUE** *Reprise K 14196*	13	12
30 Sep 72	BANDSTAND *Reprise K 54006*	15	10
29 Sep 73	IT'S ONLY A MOVIE *Raft RA 58501*	30	3

The FAMILY CAT
UK, male vocal / instrumental group (1 Album: 1 Week, 3 Singles: 5 Weeks)

4 Jul 92	FURTHEST FROM THE SUN *Dedicated DEDCD 007*	55	1
28 Aug 93	**AIRPLANE GARDENS / ATMOSPHERIC ROAD** *Dedicated FCUK 003CD*	69	1
21 May 94	**WONDERFUL EXCUSE** *Dedicated 74321208432*	48	2
30 Jul 94	**GOLDENBOOK** *Dedicated 74321220072*	42	2

4 / 6 August 1966	11 / 13 August 1966	18 / 20 August 1966	25 / 27 August 1966
UK No.1 SINGLES			
WITH A GIRL LIKE YOU The Troggs	WITH A GIRL LIKE YOU The Troggs	YELLOW SUBMARINE / ELEANOR RIGBY The Beatles	YELLOW SUBMARINE / ELEANOR RIGBY The Beatles
UK No.1 ALBUMS			
THE SOUND OF MUSIC Soundtrack	REVOLVER The Beatles	REVOLVER The Beatles	REVOLVER The Beatles

FAMILY DOGG
UK, male / female vocal group – includes Albert Hammond

28 May 69 ● **A WAY OF LIFE** *Bell 1055* 6 14

FAMILY FOUNDATION *UK, male / female vocal / instrumental group*

13 Jun 92 **XPRESS YOURSELF** *380 PEW 1* 42 4

The FAMILY STAND *US, male / female vocal (Sandra St. Victor) / instrumental group (1 Album: 3 Weeks, 2 Singles: 13 Weeks)*

31 Mar 90 ● **GHETTO HEAVEN** *East West A 7997* 10 11
19 May 90 CHAIN *Atlantic WX 349* 52 3
17 Jan 98 **GHETTO HEAVEN** (re-mix) *Perfecto PERF 156CD1* 30 2

The FANTASTIC FOUR *US, male vocal group*

24 Feb 79 **B.Y.O.F. (BRING YOUR OWN FUNK)** *Atlantic LV 14* 62 4

The FANTASTICS *US, male vocal group*

27 Mar 71 ● **SOMETHING OLD, SOMETHING NEW** *Bell 1141* 9 12

FANTASY UFO (see also M-D-EMM)
UK, male producer – Mark Ryder (2 Singles: 6 Weeks)

29 Sep 90 **FANTASY** *XL XLT 15* 56 3
10 Aug 91 **MIND BODY SOUL** *Strictly Underground YZ 591* [1] 50 3

[1] Fantasy UFO featuring Jay Groove

FAR CORPORATION (see also TOTO) *UK / US / Germany / Switzerland, male vocal (Bobby Kimball) / instrumental group*

26 Oct 85 ● **STAIRWAY TO HEAVEN** *Arista ARIST 639* 8 11

Don FARDON *UK, male vocalist – Donald Maughn (2 Singles: 22 Weeks)*

18 Apr 70 **BELFAST BOY** *Young Blood YB 1010* 32 5
10 Oct 70 ● **INDIAN RESERVATION** *Young Blood YB 1015* 3 17

FARGETTA (see also The TAMPERER featuring MAYA)
Italy / UK, male producer – Mario Fargetta (2 Singles: 3 Weeks)

23 Jan 93 **MUSIC** *Synthetic CDR 6334* [1] 34 2
10 Aug 96 **THE MUSIC IS MOVING** *Arista 74321381572* 74 1

[1] Fargetta and Anne-Marie Smith

Chris FARLOWE
UK, male vocalist – John Deighton (2 Albums: 3 Weeks, 7 Singles: 36 Weeks)

27 Jan 66 **THINK (re)** *Immediate IM 023* 37 3
2 Apr 66 14 THINGS TO THINK ABOUT *Immediate IMLP 005* 19 1
23 Jun 66 ★ **OUT OF TIME** *Immediate IM 035* 1 13
27 Oct 66 **RIDE ON BABY** *Immediate IM 038* 31 7
10 Dec 66 THE ART OF CHRIS FARLOWE *Immediate IMLP 006* 37 2
16 Feb 67 **MY WAY OF GIVING IN** *Immediate IM 041* 48 1
29 Jun 67 **MOANIN'** *Immediate IM 056* 46 2
13 Dec 67 **HANDBAGS AND GLADRAGS** *Immediate IM 065* 33 6
27 Sep 75 **OUT OF TIME** (re-issue) *Immediate IMS 101* 44 4

The FARM *UK, male vocal (Peter Hooton) / instrumental group (1 Album: 17 Weeks, 11 Singles: 59 Weeks)*

5 May 90 **STEPPING STONE / FAMILY OF MAN** *Produce MILK 101* 58 4
1 Sep 90 ● **GROOVY TRAIN** *Produce MILK 102* 6 10
8 Dec 90 ● **ALL TOGETHER NOW** *Produce MILK 103* 4 12
16 Mar 91 ★ SPARTACUS *Produce MILKLP 1* ■ 1 17
13 Apr 91 **SINFUL! (SCARY JIGGIN' WITH DR LOVE)** *Siren SRN 138* [1] 28 5
4 May 91 **DON'T LET ME DOWN** *Produce MILK 104* 36 3
24 Aug 91 **MIND** *Produce MILK 105* 31 4
14 Dec 91 **LOVE SEE NO COLOUR** *Produce MILK 106* 58 4
4 Jul 92 **RISING SUN** *End Product 6581737* 48 3
17 Oct 92 **DON'T YOU WANT ME** *End Product 6584687* 18 5
2 Jan 93 **LOVE SEE NO COLOUR** (re-mix) *End Product 6588682* 35 4
12 Jun 04 ● **ALL TOGETHER NOW 2004** (re-recording) *DMG ENGLCD 2004* [2] 5 5

[1] Pete Wylie with The Farm [2] The Farm featuring SFX Boys' Choir, Liverpool

FARMERS BOYS
UK, male vocal / instrumental group (1 Album: 1 Week, 4 Singles: 17 Weeks)

9 Apr 83 **MUCK IT OUT!** *EMI 5380* 48 6
30 Jul 83 **FOR YOU** *EMI 5401* 66 3
29 Oct 83 GET OUT AND WALK *EMI EMC 1077991* 49 1
4 Aug 84 **IN THE COUNTRY** *EMI FAB 2* 44 5
3 Nov 84 **PHEW WOW** *EMI FAB 3* 59 3

John FARNHAM *Australia (b. UK), male vocalist*

25 Apr 87 ● **YOU'RE THE VOICE** *Wheatley PB 41093* 6 17
11 Jul 87 WHISPERING JACK *RCA PL 71224* 35 9

Joanne FARRELL *US, female vocalist*

24 Jun 95 **ALL I WANNA DO** *Big Beat A 8194CD* 40 2

Joe FARRELL *US, male saxophonist, b. 16 Dec 1937, d. 10 Jan 1986*

16 Dec 78 **NIGHT DANCING** *Warner Bros. LV 2* 57 4

Dionne FARRIS *US, female vocalist (2 Singles: 6 Weeks)*

18 Mar 95 **I KNOW (re)** *Columbia 6613542* 41 5
7 Jun 97 **HOPELESS** *Columbia 6645165* 42 1

Gene FARRIS *US, male producer*

20 Dec 03 **WELCOME TO CHICAGO** *Defected DFTD 081* 74 1

Gene FARROW with the GF BAND
UK, male vocal / instrumental group (2 Singles: 8 Weeks)

1 Apr 78 **MOVE YOUR BODY (re)** *Magnet MAG 109* 33 6
5 Aug 78 **DON'T STOP NOW (re)** *Magnet MAG 125* 71 2

The FASCINATIONS *US, female vocal group*

3 Jul 71 **GIRLS ARE OUT TO GET YOU** *Mojo 2092 004* 32 6

FASHION *UK, male vocal (Dennis Harris) / instrumental group (2 Albums: 17 Weeks, 3 Singles: 12 Weeks)*

3 Apr 82 **STREETPLAYER (MECHANIK)** *Arista ARIST 456* 46 5
3 Jul 82 ● FABRIQUE *Arista SPART 1185* 10 16
21 Aug 82 **LOVE SHADOW** *Arista ARIST 483* 51 5
18 Feb 84 **EYE TALK** *Epic A 4106* 69 2
16 Jun 84 TWILIGHT OF IDOLS *De Stijl EPC 25909* 69 1

Susan FASSBENDER *UK, female vocalist*

17 Jan 81 **TWILIGHT CAFE** *CBS 9468* 21 8

FAST FOOD ROCKERS
UK, male / female vocal group (3 Singles: 24 Weeks)

28 Jun 03 ● **FAST FOOD SONG** *Better the Devil BTD 1CD* 2 14
18 Oct 03 ● **SAY CHEESE (SMILE PLEASE)** *Better the Devil BTD 5CD* 10 7
27 Dec 03 **I LOVE CHRISTMAS** *Better the Devil BTD 6CDX* 25 3

FASTBALL *US, male vocal / instrumental trio*

3 Oct 98 **THE WAY** *Polydor 5699472* 21 5

FASTER PUSSYCAT
US, male vocal / instrumental group (2 Albums: 3 Weeks)

16 Sep 89 WAKE ME WHEN IT'S OVER *Elektra EKT 64* 35 2
22 Aug 92 WHIPPED! *Elektra 7559611242* 58 1

1 / 3 September 1966	8 / 10 September 1966	15 / 17 September 1966	22 / 24 September 1966
YELLOW SUBMARINE / ELEANOR RIGBY The Beatles	YELLOW SUBMARINE / ELEANOR RIGBY The Beatles	ALL OR NOTHING The Small Faces	DISTANT DRUMS Jim Reeves
REVOLVER The Beatles	REVOLVER The Beatles	REVOLVER The Beatles	REVOLVER The Beatles

KEY		
UK No.1 ★ UK Top 10 ● Still on chart + UK entry at No.1 ■ US No.1 ▲ UK million seller £ US million seller $	Peak Position	Weeks
Singles re-entries are listed as (re), (2re), (3re)... which signifies that the hit re-entered the chart once, twice or three times...		

FASTWAY *UK, male vocal / instrumental group*

Date		Title / Label	Peak	Weeks
2 Apr 83		**EASY LIVIN'** *CBS A 3196*	74	1
30 Apr 83		FASTWAY *CBS 25359*	43	2

FAT BOYS *US, male rap group (2 Albums: 5 Weeks, 4 Singles: 29 Weeks)*

Date		Title / Label	Peak	Weeks
4 May 85		**JAIL HOUSE RAP** *Sutra U 9123*	63	2
22 Aug 87	●	**WIPEOUT** *Urban URB 5* [1]	2	12
3 Oct 87		CRUSHIN' *Urban URBLP 3*	49	4
18 Jun 88	●	**THE TWIST (YO, TWIST)** *Urban URB 20* [2]	2	11
30 Jul 88		COMING BACK HARD AGAIN *Urban URBLP 13*	98	1
5 Nov 88		**LOUIE LOUIE** *Urban URB 26*	46	4

[1] Fat Boys and The Beach Boys [2] Fat Boys and Chubby Checker

FAT JOE
US, male rapper – Joseph Cartagena (1 Album: 10 Weeks, 7 Singles: 34 Weeks)

Date		Title / Label	Peak	Weeks
1 Apr 00		**FEELIN' SO GOOD** *Columbia 6691972* [1]	15	6
30 Mar 02		**WE THUGGIN'** *Atlantic AT 0124CD*	48	1
27 Apr 02		JEALOUS ONES STILL ENVY (J.O.S.E.) *Atlantic 7567834722*	19	10
25 May 02	●	**WHAT'S LUV?** *Atlantic AT 0128CD* [2]	4	8
14 Dec 02		**CRUSH TONIGHT** *Atlantic AT 0142CD* [3]	42	2
16 Oct 04		**LEAN BACK** *Universal MCSTD 40385* [4] ▲	24	5
28 May 05	●	**HOLD YOU DOWN** *Epic 6759342* [5]	6	9
16 Jul 05		**GET IT POPPIN'** *Atlantic AT 0210CD* [6]	34	3

[1] Jennifer Lopez featuring Big Pun and Fat Joe [2] Fat Joe featuring Ashanti [3] Fat Joe featuring Ginuwine [4] Terror Squad featuring Fat Joe & Remy [5] Jennifer Lopez featuring Fat Joe [6] Fat Joe featuring Nelly

The sleeve, not the label, of 'We Thuggin' credits: 'Fat Joe featuring R Kelly'.

FAT LADY SINGS *Ireland, male vocal / instrumental group*

Date		Title / Label	Peak	Weeks
18 May 91		TWIST *East West WX 418*	50	1
17 Jul 93		**DRUNKARD LOGIC** *East West YZ 756CD*	56	2

FAT LARRY'S BAND *US, male vocal (Larry James, d. 1987) / instrumental group (1 Album: 4 Weeks, 4 Singles: 26 Weeks)*

Date		Title / Label	Peak	Weeks
2 Jul 77		**CENTER CITY** *Atlantic K 10951*	31	5
10 Mar 79		**BOOGIE TOWN** *Fantasy FTC 168* [1]	46	4
18 Aug 79		**LOOKING FOR LOVE TONIGHT** *Fantasy FTC 179* [2]	46	6
18 Sep 82	●	**ZOOM** *Virgin VS 546*	2	11
9 Oct 82		BREAKIN' OUT *Virgin V 2229*	58	4

[1] FLB [2] Fat Larry's Band (FLB)

FAT LES (see also BLUR; ME ME ME)
UK, male / female vocal group – includes Alex James (3 Singles: 22 Weeks)

Date		Title / Label	Peak	Weeks
20 Jun 98	●	**VINDALOO** *Telstar CDSTAS 2982*	2	12
19 Dec 98		**NAUGHTY CHRISTMAS (GOBLIN IN THE OFFICE)** *Turtleneck NECKCD 001*	21	5
17 Jun 00	●	**JERUSALEM (re)** *Parlophone CDR 6540* [1]	10	5

[1] Fat Les 2000

The FATBACK BAND *US, male vocal (Bill Curtis) / instrumental group (2 Albums: 7 Weeks, 10 Singles: 67 Weeks)*

Date		Title / Label	Peak	Weeks
6 Sep 75		**YUM, YUM (GIMME SOME)** *Polydor 2066 590*	40	6
6 Dec 75		**(ARE YOU READY) DO THE BUS STOP** *Polydor 2066 637*	18	10
21 Feb 76	●	**(DO THE) SPANISH HUSTLE** *Polydor 2066 656*	10	7
6 Mar 76		RAISING HELL *Polydor 2391 203*	19	6
29 May 76		**PARTY TIME** *Polydor 2066 682*	41	4
14 Aug 76		**NIGHT FEVER** *Spring 2066 706*	38	4
12 Mar 77		**DOUBLE DUTCH** *Spring 2066 777*	31	4
9 Aug 80		**BACKSTROKIN'** *Spring POSP 149* [1]	41	9
23 Jun 84	●	**I FOUND LOVIN' (re)** *Master Mix CHE 8401*	7	16
4 May 85		**GIRLS ON MY MIND** *Atlantic / Cotillion FBACK 1* [1]	69	2
6 Sep 86		**I FOUND LOVIN'** (re-issue) *Important TAN 10*	55	5
4 Jul 87		FATBACK LIVE *Start STL 12*	80	1

[1] Fatback

The original version of 'I Found Lovin'' peaked at No.49 in 1984 and only reached its peak position on re-entry in 1987.

FATBOY SLIM (359 Top 500)
(see also FREAKPOWER; PIZZAMAN; URBAN ALL STARS)
Multi-aliased superstar DJ / producer Norman Cook, b. Quentin Cook, 31 Jul 1963, Bromley, Kent, UK. He finally achieved a solo No.1 in this guise, having already topped the chart with The Housemartins and Beats International. (4 Albums: 114 Weeks, 15 Singles: 80 Weeks)

Date		Title / Label	Peak	Weeks
28 Sep 96		BETTER LIVING THROUGH CHEMISTRY *Skint BRASSIC 2CD*	69	3
3 May 97		**GOING OUT OF MY HEAD** *Skint SKINT 19CD*	57	1
1 Nov 97		**EVERYBODY NEEDS A 303** *Skint SKINT 31CD*	34	2
20 Jun 98	●	**THE ROCKAFELLER SKANK** *Skint SKINT 35CD*	6	10
17 Oct 98	●	**GANGSTER TRIPPIN'** *Skint SKINT 39CD*	3	8
31 Oct 98	★	YOU'VE COME A LONG WAY, BABY *Skint BRASSIC 11CD*	1	86
16 Jan 99	★	**PRAISE YOU** *Skint SKINT 42CD* ■	1	12
1 May 99	●	**RIGHT HERE RIGHT NOW** *Skint SKINT 46CD*	2	10
1 May 99		**BADDER BADDER SCHWING** *Eye Q EYEUK 040CD* [1]	34	2
28 Oct 00	●	**SUNSET (BIRD OF PREY) (re)** *Skint SKINT 58CD*	9	13
18 Nov 00	●	HALFWAY BETWEEN THE GUTTER AND THE STARS *Skint BRASSIC 20CD*	8	22
20 Jan 01		**DEMONS** *Skint SKINT 60CD* [2]	16	5
5 May 01	●	**STAR 69** *Skint SKINT 64CD*	10	7
15 Sep 01		**YA MAMA / SONG FOR SHELTER** *Skint SKINT 71CD*	30	2
26 Jan 02		**RETOX** *Skint SKINT FAT 18*	73	1
2 Oct 04		**SLASHDOTDASH** *Skint SKINT 100CD*	12	3
16 Oct 04		PALOOKAVILLE *Skint BRASSIC 29CD*	14	3
11 Dec 04		**A WONDERFUL NIGHT** *Skint SKINT 104CD*	51	2
12 Mar 05		**THE JOKER** *Skint SKINT 106CD*	32	2

[1] Freddy Fresh featuring Fatboy Slim [2] Fatboy Slim featuring Macy Gray

Uncredited vocal on 'The Joker' by Bootsy Collins.

FATIMA MANSIONS *Ireland, male vocal (Cathal Coughlan) / instrumental group (1 Album: 1 Week, 4 Singles: 11 Weeks)*

Date		Title / Label	Peak	Weeks
23 May 92		**EVIL MAN** *Radioactive SKX 56*	59	1
6 Jun 92		VALHALLA AVENUE *Radioactive KWCD 18*	52	1
1 Aug 92		**1000%** *Radioactive SKX 59*	61	3
19 Sep 92	●	**(EVERYTHING I DO) I DO IT FOR YOU** *Columbia 6583827*	7	6
6 Aug 94		**THE LOYALISER** *Kitchenware SKCD 67*	58	1

'(Everything I Do) I Do It For You' was listed with 'Theme From M.A.S.H. (Suicide is Painless)' by Manic Street Preachers.

FATMAN SCOOP
US, male DJ / rapper – Isaac Freeman III (6 Singles: 33 Weeks)

Date		Title / Label	Peak	Weeks
1 Nov 03	★	**BE FAITHFUL** *Def Jam 9812716* [1] ■	1	16
21 Feb 04	●	**IT TAKES SCOOP** *Def Jam 9816983* [1]	9	6
2 Jul 05	●	**LOSE CONTROL** *Atlantic AT 0209CD* [2]	7	11

[1] Fatman Scoop featuring the Crooklyn Clan [2] Missy Elliott featuring Ciara & Fat Man Scoop

FEAR FACTORY
US, male vocal / instrumental group (5 Albums: 7 Weeks, 1 Single: 1 Week)

Date		Title / Label	Peak	Weeks
1 Jul 95		DEMANUFACTURE *Roadrunner RR 89565*	27	1
14 Jun 97		REMANUFACTURE – CLONING TECHNOLOGY *Roadrunner RR 88342*	22	1
8 Aug 98		OBSOLETE *Roadrunner RR 87522*	20	2
9 Oct 99		**CARS** *Roadrunner RR 21893*	57	1

	29 September / 1 October 1966	6 / 8 October 1966	13 / 15 October 1966	20 / 22 October 1966
UK No.1 SINGLES	DISTANT DRUMS Jim Reeves	DISTANT DRUMS Jim Reeves	DISTANT DRUMS Jim Reeves	DISTANT DRUMS Jim Reeves
UK No.1 ALBUMS	THE SOUND OF MUSIC Soundtrack	THE SOUND OF MUSIC Soundtrack	THE SOUND OF MUSIC Soundtrack	THE SOUND OF MUSIC Soundtrack

5 May 01	DIGIMORTAL *Roadrunner RR 85612*	24	2
1 May 04	ARCHETYPE *Roadrunner RR 83115*	41	1

Phil FEARON *UK, male vocalist (2 Albums: 9 Weeks, 9 Singles: 63 Weeks)*

23 Apr 83 ●	**DANCING TIGHT** *Ensign ENY 501* [1]	4	11
30 Jul 83	**WAIT UNTIL TONIGHT (MY LOVE)** *Ensign ENY 503* [1]	20	8
22 Oct 83	**FANTASY REAL** *Ensign ENY 507* [2]	41	6
10 Mar 84 ●	**WHAT DO I DO** *Ensign ENY 510* [2]	5	10
14 Jul 84 ●	**EVERYBODY'S LAUGHING** *Ensign ENY 514* [2]	10	10
25 Aug 84 ●	PHIL FEARON AND GALAXY *Ensign ENCL 2* [1]	8	8
15 Jun 85	**YOU DON'T NEED A REASON** *Ensign ENY 517* [2]	42	4
27 Jul 85	**THIS KIND OF LOVE** *Ensign ENY 521* [3]	70	3
14 Sep 85	THIS KIND OF LOVE *Ensign ENCL 4* [1]	98	1
2 Aug 86 ●	**I CAN PROVE IT** *Ensign PF 1*	8	9
15 Nov 86	**AIN'T NOTHING BUT A HOUSEPARTY** *Ensign PF 2*	60	2

[1] Galaxy featuring Phil Fearon [2] Phil Fearon and Galaxy [3] Phil Fearon and Galaxy featuring Dee Galdes [1] Phil Fearon and Galaxy

FEEDER *UK / Japan, male vocal (Grant Nicholas) / instrumental group (5 Albums: 64 Weeks, 21 Singles: 70 Weeks)*

8 Mar 97	**TANGERINE** *Echo ECSCD 32*	60	1
10 May 97	**CEMENT** *Echo ECSCX 36*	53	1
31 May 97	POLYTHENE *Echo ECHCD 15*	65	1
23 Aug 97	**CRASH** *Echo ECSCD 42*	48	1
18 Oct 97	**HIGH** *Echo ECSCD 44*	24	2
28 Feb 98	**SUFFOCATE** *Echo ECSCX 52*	37	1
3 Apr 99	**DAY IN DAY OUT** *Echo ECSCD 75*	31	2
12 Jun 99	**INSOMNIA** *Echo ECSCD 77*	22	3
21 Aug 99	**YESTERDAY WENT TOO SOON** *Echo ECSCD 79*	20	3
11 Sep 99 ●	YESTERDAY WENT TOO SOON – LIMITED EDITION *Echo ECHCD 28*	8	3
20 Nov 99	**PAPERFACES** *Echo ECSCD 85*	41	2
20 Jan 01 ●	**BUCK ROGERS** *Echo ECSCD 106*	5	6
14 Apr 01	**SEVEN DAYS IN THE SUN (re)** *Echo ECSCD 107*	14	6
5 May 01 ●	ECHO PARK *Echo ECHCD 34*	5	9
14 Jul 01	**TURN** *Echo ECSCD 116*	27	2
22 Dec 01	**JUST A DAY (EP)** *Echo ECSCD 121*	12	7
12 Oct 02	**COME BACK AROUND (re)** *Echo ECSCD 130*	14	5
2 Nov 02 ●	COMFORT IN SOUND *Echo ECHCD 43*	6	36
25 Jan 03 ●	**JUST THE WAY I'M FEELING** *Echo ECSCD 133*	10	8
17 May 03	**FORGET ABOUT TOMORROW** *Echo ECSCD 135*	12	4
4 Oct 03	**FIND THE COLOUR** *Echo ECSCD 145*	24	2
29 Jan 05 ●	**TUMBLE AND FALL** *Echo ECSCD 157*	5	5
12 Feb 05 ●	PUSHING THE SENSES *Echo ECHDV 60*	2	15
16 Apr 05	**FEELING A MOMENT** *Echo ECSCX 163*	13	4
9 Jul 05	**PUSHING THE SENSES** *Echo ECSCD 173*	30	2
22 Oct 05	**SHATTER / TENDER** *Echo ECSCX 180*	11	3

Tracks on Just a Day (EP) – CD1: Just a Day / Can't Stand Losing You / Piece By Piece (video); CD2: Just a Day (full version) / Emily / Slowburn / Just a Day (video).

Wilton FELDER (see also The CRUSADERS)
US, male tenor saxophonist (1 Album: 3 Weeks, 2 Singles: 7 Weeks)

1 Nov 80	**INHERIT THE WIND** *MCA 646*	39	5
16 Feb 85	**(NO MATTER HOW HIGH I GET) I'LL STILL BE LOOKIN' UP TO YOU** *MCA MCA 919* [1]	63	2
23 Feb 85	SECRETS *MCA MCF 3237*	77	3

[1] Wilton Felder featuring Bobby Womack and introducing Alltrina Grayson

Bobby Womack is the uncredited vocalist on 'Inherit the Wind'.

José FELICIANO
US, male vocalist / guitarist (4 Albums: 40 Weeks, 2 Singles: 23 Weeks)

18 Sep 68 ●	**LIGHT MY FIRE** *RCA 1715* $	6	16
2 Nov 68 ●	FELICIANO *RCA Victor SF 7946*	6	36
18 Oct 69	**AND THE SUN WILL SHINE** *RCA 1871*	25	7
29 Nov 69	JOSÉ FELICIANO *RCA Victor SF 8044*	29	2
14 Feb 70	10 TO 23 *RCA SF 7946*	38	1
22 Aug 70	FIREWORKS *RCA SF 8124*	65	1

FELIX
UK, male producer – Francis Wright (1 Album: 4 Weeks, 5 Singles: 29 Weeks)

8 Aug 92 ●	**DON'T YOU WANT ME** *Deconstruction 74321110507*	6	11
24 Oct 92	**IT WILL MAKE ME CRAZY** *Deconstruction 74321118137*	11	6
10 Apr 93	#1 *Deconstruction 74321137002*	26	4
22 May 93	**STARS** *Deconstruction 74321147102*	29	3
12 Aug 95 ●	**DON'T YOU WANT ME** (re-mix) *Deconstruction 74321293972*	10	5
19 Oct 96	**DON'T YOU WANT ME** (2nd re-mix) *Deconstruction 74321418142*	17	4

Julie FELIX
US, female vocalist / guitarist (1 Album: 4 Weeks, 2 Singles: 19 Weeks)

11 Sep 66	CHANGES *Fontana TL 5368*	27	4
18 Apr 70	**IF I COULD (EL CONDOR PASA)** *RAK 101*	19	11
17 Oct 70	**HEAVEN IS HERE** *RAK 105*	22	8

FELIX DA HOUSECAT
US, male producer – Felix Stallings Jr (7 Singles: 9 Weeks)

6 Sep 97	**DIRTY MOTHA** *Manifesto FESCD 29* [1]	66	1
14 Jul 01	**SILVER SCREEN SHOWER SCENE** *City Rockers ROCKERS 1CD*	55	1
2 Mar 02	**WHAT DOES IT FEEL LIKE?** *City Rockers ROCKERS 8CD*	66	1
5 Oct 02	**SILVER SCREEN SHOWER SCENE** (re-mix) *City Rockers ROCKERS 19CD*	39	2
14 Aug 04	**ROCKET RIDE** *Rykodisc ENR 522*	55	1
27 Nov 04	**WATCHING CARS GO BY** *Emperor Norton ENR 532* [2]	49	2
26 Feb 05	**READY2WEAR** *Emperor Norton ENR 562*	62	1

[1] Qwilo and Felix Da Housecat [2] Felix Da Housecat vs Sasha and Armand Van Helden

FELON *UK, female vocalist – Simone Locker*

23 Mar 02	**GET OUT** *Serious SERR 032CD*	31	2

FE-M@IL *UK, female vocal group*

5 Aug 00	**FLEE FLY FLO** *Jive 9250592*	46	2

FEMME FATALE *US, male / female vocal / instrumental group*

11 Feb 89	**FALLING IN AND OUT OF LOVE** *MCA MCA 1309*	69	2

The FENDERMEN
US, male vocalist / guitarists – Phil Humphrey and Jim Sundquist

18 Aug 60	**MULE SKINNER BLUES (2re)** *Top Rank JAR 395*	32	9

FENIX TX *US, male vocal / instrumental group*

11 May 02	**THREESOME** *MCA MCSTD 40279*	66	1

George FENTON and Jonas GWANGWA
UK / South Africa, male instrumental / production duo

2 Jan 88	**CRY FREEDOM** *MCA MCA 1228*	75	1

The listed flip side of 'Cry Freedom' was 'The Funeral' by Thuli Dumakude.

Peter FENTON *UK, male vocalist*

10 Nov 66	**MARBLE BREAKS IRON BENDS** *Fontana TF 748*	46	3

Shane FENTON and The FENTONES
(see also Alvin STARDUST) *UK, male instrumental group (6 Singles: 32 Weeks)*

26 Oct 61	**I'M A MOODY GUY** *Parlophone R 4827*	22	8
1 Feb 62	**WALK AWAY** *Parlophone R 4866*	38	5
5 Apr 62	**IT'S ALL OVER NOW** *Parlophone R 4883*	29	7
19 Apr 62	**THE MEXICAN** *Parlophone R 4899* [1]	41	3
12 Jul 62	**CINDY'S BIRTHDAY** *Parlophone R 4921*	19	8
27 Sep 62	**THE BREEZE AND I** *Parlophone R 4937* [1]	48	1

[1] The Fentones

27 / 29 October 1966	3 / 5 November 1966	10 / 12 November 1966	17 / 19 November 1966
REACH OUT I'LL BE THERE The Four Tops	REACH OUT I'LL BE THERE The Four Tops	REACH OUT I'LL BE THERE The Four Tops	GOOD VIBRATIONS The Beach Boys
THE SOUND OF MUSIC Soundtrack	THE SOUND OF MUSIC Soundtrack	THE SOUND OF MUSIC Soundtrack	THE SOUND OF MUSIC Soundtrack

KEY UK No.1 ★ UK Top 10 ● Still on chart + UK entry at No.1 ■ US No.1 ▲ UK million seller £ US million seller $
Singles re-entries are listed as (re), (2re), (3re)... which signifies that the hit re-entered the chart once, twice or three times...
Peak Position / Weeks

FERGIE *Ireland, male DJ / producer – Robert Ferguson (3 Singles: 5 Weeks)*

Date	Title	Peak	Weeks
9 Sep 00	**DECEPTION** *Duty Free DF 020CD*	47	1
25 Nov 00	**HOOVERS & HORNS** *Nukleuz NUKC 0185* [1]	57	2
10 Aug 02	**THE BASS EP** *Duty Free / Decode DFTELCX 004*	47	2

[1] Fergie & BK

Tracks on The Bass EP: Bass Generator (mixes) / Bass Has Got Me On (mixes).

Sheila FERGUSON (see also The THREE DEGREES) *US, female vocalist*

Date	Title	Peak	Weeks
5 Feb 94	**WHEN WILL I SEE YOU AGAIN** *XSrhythm CDSTAS 2711*	60	1

FERKO STRING BAND *US, male instrumental group*

Date	Title	Peak	Weeks
12 Aug 55	**ALABAMA JUBILEE** *London HL 8140*	20	2

Luisa FERNANDEZ *Spain, female vocalist*

Date	Title	Peak	Weeks
11 Nov 78	**LAY LOVE ON YOU** *Warner Bros. K 17061*	31	8

Pamela FERNANDEZ *US, female vocalist (2 Singles: 3 Weeks)*

Date	Title	Peak	Weeks
17 Sep 94	**KICKIN' IN THE BEAT** *Ore AG 5CD*	43	2
3 Jun 95	**LET'S START OVER / KICKIN' IN THE BEAT** (re-mix) *Ore AG 9CD*	59	1

FERRANTE and TEICHER
US, male pianists – Arthur Ferrante and Louis Teicher (2 Singles: 18 Weeks)

Date	Title	Peak	Weeks
18 Aug 60	**THEME FROM 'THE APARTMENT'** *London HLT 9164*	44	1
9 Mar 61 ●	**EXODUS (THEME FROM 'EXODUS')** *London HLT 9298 and HMV POP 881* $	6	17

'Exodus (Theme from 'Exodus')' was available first on London, then on HMV when the US label, United Artists, changed its UK outlet.

Ibrahim FERRER *Cuba, male vocalist / pianist*

Date	Title	Peak	Weeks
5 Jun 99	BUENA VISTA SOCIAL CLUB PRESENTS IBRAHIM FERRER *World Circuit WCD 055*	42	3

José FERRER *US, male actor / vocalist – Jose Vincente Ferrer y Centron, b. 8 Jan 1912, d. 26 Jan 1992*

Date	Title	Peak	Weeks
19 Feb 54 ●	**WOMAN (UH-HUH)** *Philips PB 220*	7	3

'Woman (Uh-Huh)' was coupled with 'Man (Uh-Huh)' by Rosemary Clooney.

Tony FERRINO *UK, male vocalist – comedian Steve Coogan*

Date	Title	Peak	Weeks
23 Nov 96	**HELP YOURSELF / BIGAMY AT CHRISTMAS** *RCA 74321430302*	42	2

Bryan FERRY (92 Top 500) *Stylish and sophisticated UK vocalist / songwriter, b. 26 Sep 1945, Tyne and Wear, who split his time between a solo career and fronting the visually stimulating Roxy Music. He was still having Top 20 albums in 2004 (16 Albums: 329 Weeks, 24 Singles: 133 Weeks)*

Date	Title	Peak	Weeks
29 Sep 73 ●	**A HARD RAIN'S A-GONNA FALL** *Island WIP 6170*	10	9
3 Nov 73 ●	THESE FOOLISH THINGS *Island ILPS 9249*	5	42
25 May 74	**THE 'IN' CROWD** *Island WIP 6196*	13	6
20 Jul 74 ●	ANOTHER TIME ANOTHER PLACE *Island ILPS 9284*	4	25
31 Aug 74	**SMOKE GETS IN YOUR EYES** *Island WIP 6205*	17	8
5 Jul 75	**YOU GO TO MY HEAD** *Island WIP 6234*	33	3
12 Jun 76 ●	**LET'S STICK TOGETHER (LET'S WORK TOGETHER)** *Island WIP 6307*	4	10
7 Aug 76 ●	**EXTENDED PLAY (EP)** *Island IEP 1*	7	9
2 Oct 76	LET'S STICK TOGETHER *Island ILPSX 1*	19	5
5 Feb 77 ●	**THIS IS TOMORROW** *Polydor 2001 704*	9	9
5 Mar 77 ●	IN YOUR MIND *Polydor 2302 055*	5	17
14 May 77	**TOKYO JOE** *Polydor 2001 711*	15	7
13 May 78	**WHAT GOES ON** *Polydor POSP 3*	67	2
5 Aug 78	**SIGN OF THE TIMES** *Polydor 2001 798*	37	8
30 Sep 78	THE BRIDE STRIPPED BARE *Polydor POLD 5003*	13	5
11 May 85 ●	**SLAVE TO LOVE** *EG FERRY 1*	10	9
15 Jun 85 ★	BOYS AND GIRLS *EG EGLP 62* ■	1	44
31 Aug 85	**DON'T STOP THE DANCE** *EG FERRY 2*	21	7
7 Dec 85	**WINDSWEPT** *EG FERRY 3*	46	3
29 Mar 86	**IS YOUR LOVE STRONG ENOUGH?** *EG FERRY 4*	22	7
26 Apr 86 ★	STREET LIFE – 20 GREAT HITS *EG EGTV 1* [1] ■	1	77
10 Oct 87	**THE RIGHT STUFF** *Virgin VS 940*	37	6
14 Nov 87 ●	BETE NOIRE *Virgin V 2474*	9	16
13 Feb 88	**KISS AND TELL** *Virgin VS 1034*	41	5
29 Oct 88	**LET'S STICK TOGETHER** (re-mix) *EG EGO 44*	12	7
19 Nov 88 ●	THE ULTIMATE COLLECTION *EG EGTV 2* [1]	6	35
11 Feb 89	**THE PRICE OF LOVE** (re-mix) *EG EGO 46*	49	3
22 Apr 89	**HE'LL HAVE TO GO** *EG EGO 48*	63	1
6 Mar 93	**I PUT A SPELL ON YOU** *Virgin VSCDG 1400*	18	5
3 Apr 93 ●	TAXI *Virgin CDV 2700*	2	14
29 May 93	**WILL YOU LOVE ME TOMORROW** *Virgin VSCDG 1455*	23	5
4 Sep 93	**GIRL OF MY BEST FRIEND** *Virgin VSCDG 1488*	57	2
17 Sep 94	MAMOUNA *Virgin CDV 2751*	11	4
29 Oct 94	**YOUR PAINTED SMILE** *Virgin VSCDG 1508*	52	1
11 Feb 95	**MAMOUNA** *Virgin VSCDG 1528*	57	1
4 Nov 95	MORE THAN THIS – THE BEST OF BRYAN FERRY AND ROXY MUSIC *Virgin CDV 2791* [1]	15	15
6 Nov 99	AS TIME GOES BY *Virgin CDVIR 89*	16	10
22 Jul 00	SLAVE TO LOVE *Virgin CDV 2921*	11	11
11 May 02 ●	FRANTIC *Virgin CDVIR 167*	6	5
19 Jun 04	THE PLATINUM COLLECTION *Virgin BFRM 1* [1]	17	4

[1] Bryan Ferry and Roxy Music

Tracks on Extended Play (EP): Price of Love / Shame Shame Shame / Heart on My Sleeve / It's Only Love.

FERRY AID *International, male / female charity ensemble*

Date	Title	Peak	Weeks
4 Apr 87 ★	**LET IT BE** *The Sun AID 1* ■	1	7

FEVER featuring Tippa IRIE
UK, male production / instrumental group and male vocalist

Date	Title	Peak	Weeks
8 Jul 95	**STAYING ALIVE 95** *Telstar CDSTAS 2776*	48	1

Lena FIAGBE *UK, female vocalist (5 Singles: 13 Weeks)*

Date	Title	Peak	Weeks
24 Jul 93	**YOU COME FROM EARTH** *Mother MUMCD 42* [1]	69	1
23 Oct 93	**GOTTA GET IT RIGHT** *Mother MUMCD 44*	20	5
16 Apr 94	**WHAT'S IT LIKE TO BE BEAUTIFUL** *Mother MUMCD 49*	52	3
25 Jun 94	**VISIONS** *Mother MUMCD 53*	48	2
10 Feb 96	**AFRICAN DREAM** *Mercury MERCD 453* [2]	44	2

[1] Lena [2] Wasis Diop featuring Lena Fiagbe

Karel FIALKA
UK, male vocalist / multi-instrumentalist (2 Singles: 12 Weeks)

Date	Title	Peak	Weeks
17 May 80	**THE EYES HAVE IT** *Blueprint BLU 2005*	52	4
5 Sep 87 ●	**HEY MATTHEW** *IRS IRM 140*	9	8

FIAT LUX *UK, male vocal / instrumental group (2 Singles: 4 Weeks)*

Date	Title	Peak	Weeks
28 Jan 84	**SECRETS** *Polydor FIAT 2*	65	3
17 Mar 84	**BLUE EMOTION** *Polydor FIAT 3*	59	1

FICTION FACTORY
UK, male vocal (Kevin Patterson) / instrumental group (2 Singles: 11 Weeks)

Date	Title	Peak	Weeks
14 Jan 84 ●	**(FEELS LIKE) HEAVEN** *CBS A 3996*	6	9
17 Mar 84	**GHOST OF LOVE** *CBS A 3819*	64	2

	24 / 26 November 1966	1 / 3 December 1966	8 / 10 December 1966	15 / 17 December 1966
UK No.1 SINGLES	GOOD VIBRATIONS – The Beach Boys	GREEN, GREEN GRASS OF HOME – Tom Jones	GREEN, GREEN GRASS OF HOME – Tom Jones	GREEN, GREEN GRASS OF HOME – Tom Jones
UK No.1 ALBUMS	THE SOUND OF MUSIC – Soundtrack	THE SOUND OF MUSIC – Soundtrack	THE SOUND OF MUSIC – Soundtrack	THE SOUND OF MUSIC – Soundtrack

FIDDLER'S DRAM *UK, male / female vocal / instrumental group*

15 Dec 79 ● **DAYTRIP TO BANGOR (DIDN'T WE HAVE A LOVELY TIME)** *Dingle's SID 211* 3 9

FIDELFATTI featuring RONNETTE
Italy, male producer – Piero Fidelfatti and female vocalist

27 Jan 90 **JUST WANNA TOUCH ME** *Urban URB 46* 65 1

Brad FIEDEL *US, male arranger*

31 Aug 91 TERMINATOR 2 (FILM SOUNDTRACK) *Vareses Sarabande VS 5335* 26 7

Billy FIELD *Australia, male vocalist*

12 Jun 82 **YOU WEREN'T IN LOVE WITH ME** *CBS A 2344* 67 3

Ernie FIELDS and his ORCHESTRA
US, orchestra – leader b. 26 Aug 1905, d. 11 May 1997

25 Dec 59 **IN THE MOOD** *London HL 8985* 13 8

Gracie FIELDS *UK, female vocalist – Grace Stansfield, b. 9 Jan 1898, d. 27 Sep 1979 (1 Album: 3 Weeks, 2 Singles: 15 Weeks)*

31 May 57 ● **AROUND THE WORLD (re)** *Columbia DB 3953* 8 9
6 Nov 59 **LITTLE DONKEY (re)** *Columbia DB 4360* 20 6
20 Dec 75 THE GOLDEN YEARS *Warwick WW 5007* 48 3

Richard 'Dimples' FIELDS *US, male vocalist, b. 1942, d. 15 Jan 2000*

20 Feb 82 **I'VE GOT TO LEARN TO SAY NO** *Epic EPC A 1918* 56 4

FIELDS OF THE NEPHILIM *UK, male vocal / instrumental group (4 Albums: 9 Weeks, 6 Singles: 10 Weeks)*

30 May 87 DAWNRAZOR *Situation 2 SITU 18* 62 2
24 Oct 87 **BLUE WATER** *Situation Two SIT 48* 75 1
4 Jun 88 **MOONCHILD** *Situation Two SIT 52* 28 3
17 Sep 88 THE NEPHILIM *Situation 2 SITU 22* 14 3
27 May 89 **PSYCHONAUT** *Situation Two SIT 57* 35 3
4 Aug 90 **FOR HER LIGHT** *Beggars Banquet BEG 244T* 54 1
6 Oct 90 ELIZIUM *Beggars Banquet BEGA 115* 22 2
24 Nov 90 **SUMERLAND (DREAMED)** *Beggars Banquet BEG 250* 37 1
6 Apr 91 EARTH INFERNO *Beggars Banquet BEGA 120* 39 2
28 Sep 02 **FROM THE FIRE** *Jungle JUNG 65CD* 62 1

FIERCE *UK, female vocal group (1 Album: 2 Weeks, 4 Singles: 23 Weeks)*

9 Jan 99 **RIGHT HERE RIGHT NOW** *Wildstar CDWILD 13* 25 5
15 May 99 **DAYZ LIKE THAT** *Wildstar CDWILD 19* 11 5
14 Aug 99 **SO LONG** *Wildstar CDWILD 27* 15 5
28 Aug 99 RIGHT HERE RIGHT NOW *Wildstar CDWILD 14* 27 2
12 Feb 00 ● **SWEET LOVE 2K** *Wildstar CDWILD 34* 3 8

FIERCE GIRL *UK, male vocal / rap duo (2 Singles: 2 Weeks)*

11 Sep 04 **DOUBLE DROP** *Red Flag RF 012CDS* 74 1
19 Feb 05 **WHAT MAKES A GIRL FIERCE** *Red Flag RF 013CDS* 52 1

The FIERY FURNACES *US, male / female production / vocal duo – Matthew and Eleanor Friedberger (2 Singles: 2 Weeks)*

6 Mar 04 **TROPICAL ICE-LAND** *Rough Trade RTRADSCD 152* 52 1
17 Jul 04 **SINGLE AGAIN** *Rough Trade RTRADSCD 190* 49 1

The 5TH DIMENSION (see also Billie DAVIS)
US, male / female vocal group (2 Singles: 21 Weeks)

16 Apr 69 **AQUARIUS – LET THE SUNSHINE IN (MEDLEY)** *Liberty LBF 15193* ▲ $ 11 12
17 Jan 70 **WEDDING BELL BLUES** *Liberty LBF 15288* ▲ $ 16 9

50 CENT 294 Top 500 (see also G-UNIT) *The hottest new rapper of the 21st Century, b. Curtis Jackson, 6 Jul 1976, Jamaica, New York. After Eminem named him his favourite rapper, 50 Cent and his crew, G-Unit, joined Eminem and Dr Dre's label. In 2005, 50 had three singles simultaneously in US Top 5 (4 Albums: 113 Weeks, 16 Singles: 116 Weeks)*

1 Mar 03 ● GET RICH OR DIE TRYIN' *Interscope ISC 4935442* ▲ 2 69
22 Mar 03 ● **IN DA CLUB** *Interscope 4978742* ▲ 3 24
12 Jul 03 ● **21 QUESTIONS** *Interscope 9807195* [1] ▲ 6 8
18 Oct 03 **P.I.M.P.** (import) *Interscope 9811812CD* 74 1
25 Oct 03 ● **P.I.M.P. (re)** *Interscope 9812333* 5 11
6 Mar 04 ● **IF I CAN'T / ... THEM THANGS** *Interscope 9815279* [2] 10 8
18 Sep 04 50 CENT IS THE FUTURE *Street Dance SDR 0166752* [1] 65 1
26 Feb 05 ● **HOW WE DO** *Interscope 9880361* [3] 5 12
19 Mar 05 ★ THE MASSACRE *Interscope 9880667* ■ ▲ 1 36
2 Apr 05 ● **CANDY SHOP** *Interscope 9881292* ▲ 4 16
21 May 05 ● **HATE IT OR LOVE IT** *Interscope 9882205* [3] 4 12
2 Jul 05 ● **JUST A LIL BIT** *Interscope 9882959* 10 9
24 Sep 05 ● **OUTTA CONTROL** *Interscope 9885269* [4] 7 10
24 Sep 05 **SO SEDUCTIVE** *Interscope 9884360* [5] 28 3
19 Nov 05 GET RICH OR DIE TRYIN' (FILM SOUNDTRACK) *Interscope 9887992* [1] 18 7+
3 Dec 05 **WINDOW SHOPPER** *Interscope 9888358* 11 5+

[1] 50 Cent featuring Nate Dogg [2] 50 Cent & G-Unit [3] The Game featuring 50 Cent [4] 50 Cent featuring Mobb Deep [5] Yayo featuring 50 Cent
[1] 50 Cent & G-Unit

'... Them Thangs' was abbreviated for the single release. The track's full title is 'Poppin' Them Thangs'.

5050 *UK, male production duo – Jason Powell and Andy Lysandrou (2 Singles: 2 Weeks)*

13 Oct 01 **WHO'S COMING ROUND** *Obsessive FIFTYCD 01* 54 1
23 Mar 02 **BAD BOYS HOLLER BOO** *Logic 74321910202* 73 1

50 GRIND featuring POKEMON ALLSTARS
UK, male vocal / instrumental group and Pokemon popsters

22 Dec 01 **GOTTA CATCH 'EM ALL** *Recognition CDREC 21* 57 1

52ND STREET *UK, male / female vocal / instrumental group (1 Album: 1 Week, 3 Singles: 13 Weeks)*

2 Nov 85 **TELL ME (HOW IT FEELS)** *10 TEN 74* 54 5
11 Jan 86 **YOU'RE MY LAST CHANCE** *10 TEN 89* 49 4
8 Mar 86 **I CAN'T LET YOU GO** *10 TEN 114* 57 4
19 Apr 86 CHILDREN OF THE NIGHT *10 DIX 25* 71 1

56K featuring BEJAY *UK, male / female production / vocal group*

19 Apr 03 **SAVE A PRAYER** *Kontor 0146495* 46 1

FIGHT CLUB featuring Laurent KONRAD
France, male producer and vocalist

7 Feb 04 **SPREAD LOVE** *Nebula NEBCD 054* 70 1

FIGHTSTAR NEW (see also BUSTED)
UK, male vocal (Charlie Simpson) / instrumental group (2 Singles: 6 Weeks)

25 Jun 05 ● **PAINT YOUR TARGET** *Island CID 897* 9 4
12 Nov 05 **GRAND UNIFICATION (PART 1)** *Island CID 916* 20 2

FILTER *US, male vocal / instrumental duo – Richard Patrick and Brian Liesgang (2 Albums: 2 Weeks, 2 Singles: 5 Weeks)*

11 Oct 97 **(CAN'T YOU) TRIP LIKE I DO** *Epic 6650862* [1] 39 2
4 Sep 99 TITLE OF RECORD *Reprise 9362473882* 75 1
18 Mar 00 **TAKE A PICTURE** *Reprise W 515CD* 25 3
10 Aug 02 THE AMALGAMUT *Reprise 9362479632* 68 1

[1] Filter and The Crystal Method

FINCH *US, male vocal / instrumental group*

5 Apr 03 **LETTERS TO YOU** *Drive-Thru / MCA MCSTD 40310* 39 2
18 Jun 05 SAY HELLO TO SUNSHINE *Geffen 9882656* 48 1

22 / 24 December 1966	29 / 31 December 1966	5 / 7 January 1967	12 / 14 January 1967
GREEN, GREEN GRASS OF HOME Tom Jones	GREEN, GREEN GRASS OF HOME Tom Jones	GREEN, GREEN GRASS OF HOME Tom Jones	GREEN, GREEN GRASS OF HOME Tom Jones
THE SOUND OF MUSIC Soundtrack	THE SOUND OF MUSIC Soundtrack	THE SOUND OF MUSIC Soundtrack	THE SOUND OF MUSIC Soundtrack

KEY
UK No.1 ★ UK Top 10 ● Still on chart + UK entry at No.1 ■
US No.1 ▲ UK million seller £ US million seller $
Singles re-entries are listed as (re), (2re), (3re)... which signifies that the hit re-entered the chart once, twice or three times...
Peak Position / Weeks

FINE YOUNG CANNIBALS (370 Top 500)

(see also TWO MEN, A DRUM MACHINE AND A TRUMPET)
Politically aware pop / soul trio from Birmingham, UK: Roland Gift (v) and ex-Beat members Andy Cox (g) and David Steele (b). Unmistakable vocalist Gift also acted in films, most notably 1989's Scandal. FYC, who were among 1989's biggest selling acts worldwide, won (and returned) two BRIT awards in 1990 (4 Albums: 107 Weeks, 12 Singles: 81 Weeks)

Date		Title / Label	Peak	Weeks
8 Jun 85	●	**JOHNNY COME HOME** *London LON 68*	8	13
9 Nov 85		**BLUE** *London LON 79*	41	6
21 Dec 85		**FINE YOUNG CANNIBALS** *London LONLP 16*	11	27
11 Jan 86	●	**SUSPICIOUS MINDS** *London LON 82*	8	9
12 Apr 86		**FUNNY HOW LOVE IS** *London LON 88*	58	4
21 Mar 87	●	**EVER FALLEN IN LOVE** *London LON 121*	9	10
7 Jan 89	●	**SHE DRIVES ME CRAZY** *London LON 199* ▲	5	11
18 Feb 89	★	**THE RAW & THE COOKED** *London 8280691* ■	1	66
15 Apr 89	●	**GOOD THING** *London LON 218* ▲	7	8
19 Aug 89		**DON'T LOOK BACK** *London LON 220*	34	4
18 Nov 89		**I'M NOT THE MAN I USED TO BE** *London LON 244*	20	8
24 Feb 90		**I'M NOT SATISFIED** *London LON 252*	46	3
15 Dec 90		**THE RAW & THE REMIX** *London 8282211* [1]	61	1
16 Nov 96		**THE FLAME** *ffrr LONCD 389*	17	3
23 Nov 96	●	**THE FINEST** *ffrr 8288542*	10	13
11 Jan 97		**SHE DRIVES ME CRAZY** (re-mix) *ffrr LONCD 391*	36	2

[1] FYC

The Raw & the Remix is a re-mix album of The Raw & the Cooked.

FINITRIBE *UK, male instrumental / production group (2 Singles: 2 Weeks)*

Date		Title / Label	Peak	Weeks
11 Jul 92		**FOREVERGREEN** *One Little Indian 74TP 12F*	51	1
19 Nov 94		**BRAND NEW** *ffrr FCD 247*	69	1

The FINK BROTHERS *UK, male vocal / instrumental duo*

Date		Title / Label	Peak	Weeks
9 Feb 85		**MUTANTS IN MEGA CITY ONE** *Zarjazz JAZZ 2*	50	4

The FINN BROTHERS (see also CROWDED HOUSE; SPLIT ENZ)

New Zealand, male vocal / instrumental duo – Neil and Tim Finn (2 Albums: 7 Weeks, 5 Singles: 10 Weeks)

Date		Title / Label	Peak	Weeks
14 Oct 95		**SUFFER NEVER** *Parlophone CDRS 6417* [1]	29	3
28 Oct 95		**FINN** *Parlophone CDFINN 1* [1]	15	3
9 Dec 95		**ANGEL'S HEAP** *Parlophone CDRS 6421* [1]	41	2
21 Aug 04		**WON'T GIVE IN** *Parlophone CDRS 6644*	26	2
4 Sep 04	●	**EVERYONE IS HERE** *Parlophone 8647762*	8	4
20 Nov 04		**NOTHING WRONG WITH YOU** *Parlophone CDRS 6655*	31	1
2 Apr 05		**EDIBLE FLOWERS** *Parlophone CDRS 6660*	32	2

[1] Finn [1] Finn

Neil FINN (see also CROWDED HOUSE; The FINN BROTHERS)

New Zealand, male vocalist / guitarist (2 Albums: 15 Weeks, 4 Singles: 6 Weeks)

Date		Title / Label	Peak	Weeks
13 Jun 98		**SHE WILL HAVE HER WAY** *Parlophone CDR 6495*	26	2
27 Jun 98	●	**TRY WHISTLING THIS** *Parlophone 4951392*	5	11
17 Oct 98		**SINNER** *Parlophone CDR 6505*	39	1
7 Apr 01		**WHEREVER YOU ARE** *Parlophone CDRS 6557*	32	2
21 Apr 01		**ONE NIL** *Parlophone 5320392*	14	4
22 Sep 01		**HOLE IN THE ICE** *Parlophone CDRS 6563*	43	1

Tim FINN (see also CROWDED HOUSE; The FINN BROTHERS)

New Zealand, male vocalist / guitarist (1 Album: 2 Weeks, 2 Singles: 6 Weeks)

Date		Title / Label	Peak	Weeks
26 Jun 93		**PERSUASION** *Capitol 6592482*	43	3
10 Jul 93		**BEFORE AND AFTER** *Capitol CDEST 2202*	29	2
18 Sep 93		**HIT THE GROUND RUNNING** *Capitol CDCLS 694*	50	3

Elisa FIORILLO *US, female vocalist (2 Singles: 14 Weeks)*

Date		Title / Label	Peak	Weeks
28 Nov 87	●	**WHO FOUND WHO** *Chrysalis CHS JEL 1* [1]	10	10
13 Feb 88		**HOW CAN I FORGET YOU** *Chrysalis ELISA 1*	50	4

[1] Jellybean featuring Elisa Fiorillo

FIRE ISLAND (see also HELLER & FARLEY PROJECT; STYLUS TROUBLE)

UK, male instrumental / production group – includes Terry Farley and Pete Heller (4 Singles: 7 Weeks)

Date		Title / Label	Peak	Weeks
8 Aug 92		**IN YOUR BONES / FIRE ISLAND** *Boy's Own BOIX 11*	66	1
12 Mar 94		**THERE BUT FOR THE GRACE OF GOD** *Junior Boy's Own JBO 18CD* [1]	32	3
4 Mar 95		**IF YOU SHOULD NEED A FRIEND** *Junior Boy's Own JBO 26CDS* [2]	51	1
11 Apr 98		**SHOUT TO THE TOP** *JBO JNR 5001573* [3]	23	2

[1] Fire Island featuring Love Nelson [2] Fire Island featuring Mark Anthoni
[3] Fire Island featuring Loleatta Holloway

The FIREBALLS

US, male vocal / instrumental group (2 Singles: 17 Weeks)

Date		Title / Label	Peak	Weeks
27 Jul 61		**QUITE A PARTY** *Pye International 7N 25092*	29	9
14 Nov 63		**SUGAR SHACK** (re) *London HLD 9789* [1] ▲ $	45	8

[1] Jimmy Gilmer and The Fireballs

FIREHOUSE *US, male vocal / instrumental group (2 Singles: 2 Weeks)*

Date		Title / Label	Peak	Weeks
13 Jul 91		**DON'T TREAT ME BAD** *Epic 6567807*	71	1
19 Dec 92		**WHEN I LOOK INTO YOUR EYES** *Epic 6588347*	65	1

The FIRM *UK, male vocal / instrumental group (2 Singles: 21 Weeks)*

Date		Title / Label	Peak	Weeks
17 Jul 82		**ARTHUR DALEY ('E'S ALRIGHT)** *Bark HID 1*	14	9
6 Jun 87	★	**STAR TREKKIN'** *Bark TREK 1*	1	12

The FIRM

(see also COVERDALE PAGE; FREE; LED ZEPPELIN) *UK, male vocal / instrumental group – Jimmy Page and Paul Rodgers (2 Albums: 8 Weeks)*

Date		Title / Label	Peak	Weeks
2 Mar 85		**THE FIRM** *Atlantic 7812391*	15	5
5 Apr 86		**MEAN BUSINESS** *Atlantic WX 35*	46	3

FIRM featuring Dawn ROBINSON

US, male rap group and female vocalist

Date		Title / Label	Peak	Weeks
29 Nov 97		**FIRM BIZ** *Columbia 6651612*	18	3

FIRST CHOICE *US, female vocal group (2 Singles: 21 Weeks)*

Date		Title / Label	Peak	Weeks
19 May 73		**ARMED AND EXTREMELY DANGEROUS** *Bell 1297*	16	10
4 Aug 73	●	**SMARTY PANTS** *Bell 1324*	9	11

FIRST CIRCLE *US, male vocal / instrumental group*

Date		Title / Label	Peak	Weeks
2 May 87		**BOYS' NIGHT OUT** *EMI America AML 3118*	70	2

FIRST CLASS *UK, male vocal group*

Date		Title / Label	Peak	Weeks
15 Jun 74		**BEACH BABY** *UK 66*	13	10

FIRST LIGHT *UK, male vocal / instrumental duo (2 Singles: 5 Weeks)*

Date		Title / Label	Peak	Weeks
21 May 83		**EXPLAIN THE REASONS** *London LON 26*	65	3
28 Jan 84		**WISH YOU WERE HERE** *London LON 43*	71	2

FIRSTBORN *Ireland, male producer – Oisin Lunny*

Date		Title / Label	Peak	Weeks
19 Jun 99		**THE MOOD CLUB** *Independiente ISOM 28MS*	69	1

FISCHER-Z

UK, male vocal / instrumental group (1 Album: 1 Week, 2 Singles: 7 Weeks)

Date		Title / Label	Peak	Weeks
26 May 79		**THE WORKER** *United Artists UP 36509*	53	5
23 Jun 79		**WORD SALAD** *United Artists UAG 30232*	66	1
3 May 80		**SO LONG** *United Artists BP 342*	72	2

	19 / 21 January 1967	26 / 28 January 1967	2 / 4 February 1967	9 / 11 February 1967
UK No.1 SINGLES	I'M A BELIEVER The Monkees	I'M A BELIEVER The Monkees	I'M A BELIEVER The Monkees	I'M A BELIEVER The Monkees
UK No.1 ALBUMS	THE SOUND OF MUSIC Soundtrack	THE SOUND OF MUSIC Soundtrack	THE MONKEES The Monkees	THE MONKEES The Monkees

FISCHERSPOONER *US, male vocal / instrumental duo – Warren Fischer and Casey Spooner (2 Singles: 4 Weeks)*

Date	Title / Label	Pos	Wks
20 Jul 02	**EMERGE** *Ministry of Sound FSMOS 1CDS*	25	3
27 Aug 05	**NEVER WIN** *EMI FSCD 3*	55	1

FISH (see also MARILLION)
UK, male vocalist – Derek Dick (8 Albums: 17 Weeks, 10 Singles: 20 Weeks)

Date	Title / Label	Pos	Wks
18 Oct 86	**SHORTCUT TO SOMEWHERE** *Charisma CB 426* [1]	75	1
28 Oct 89	**STATE OF MIND** *EMI EM 109*	32	3
6 Jan 90	**BIG WEDGE** *EMI EM 125*	25	4
10 Feb 90 ●	VIGIL IN A WILDERNESS OF MIRRORS *EMI EMD 1015*	5	6
17 Mar 90	**A GENTLEMAN'S EXCUSE ME** *EMI EM 135*	30	3
28 Sep 91	**INTERNAL EXILE** *Polydor FISHY 1*	37	2
9 Nov 91	INTERNAL EXILE *Polydor 5110491*	21	3
11 Jan 92	**CREDO** *Polydor FISHY 2*	38	2
4 Jul 92	**SOMETHING IN THE AIR** *Polydor FISHY 3*	51	2
30 Jan 93	SONGS FROM THE MIRROR *Polydor 5174992*	46	2
16 Apr 94	**LADY LET IT LIE** *Dick Bros. DDICK 3CD1*	46	1
11 Jun 94	SUITS *Dick Bros. DDICK 004CD*	18	2
1 Oct 94	**FORTUNES OF WAR** *Dick Bros. DDICK 008CD1*	67	1
26 Aug 95	**JUST GOOD FRIENDS** *Dick Bros. DDICK 014CD1* [2]	63	1
16 Sep 95	YANG *Dick Bros. DDICK 012CD*	52	1
16 Sep 95	YIN *Dick Bros. DDICK 011CD*	58	1
31 May 97	SUNSETS ON EMPIRE *Dick Bros. DDICK 25CD*	42	1
1 May 99	RAINGODS WITH ZIPPOS *Roadrunner RR 86772*	57	1

[1] Fish and Tony Banks [2] Fish featuring Sam Brown

FISHBONE
US, male vocal / instrumental group (1 Album: 1 Week, 2 Singles: 3 Weeks)

Date	Title / Label	Pos	Wks
13 Jul 91	THE REALITY OF MY SURROUNDINGS *Columbia 4676151*	75	1
1 Aug 92	**EVERYDAY SUNSHINE / FIGHT THE YOUTH** *Columbia 6581937*	60	2
28 Aug 93	**SWIM** *Columbia 6596252*	54	1

Cevin FISHER *US, male DJ / producer (5 Singles: 9 Weeks)*

Date	Title / Label	Pos	Wks
3 Oct 98	**THE FREAKS COME OUT** *Ministry of Sound MOSCDS 127* [1]	34	2
20 Feb 99	**(YOU GOT ME) BURNING UP** *Wonderboy WBOYD 013* [2]	14	4
7 Aug 99	**MUSIC SAVED MY LIFE** *Sm:)e Communications SM 90982*	67	1
20 Jan 01	**IT'S A GOOD LIFE** *Wonderboy WBOYD 022* [3]	54	1
24 Feb 01	**LOVE YOU SOME MORE** *Subversive SUB 68D* [4]	60	1

[1] Cevin Fisher's Big Break [2] Cevin Fisher / Loleatta Holloway [3] Cevin Fisher featuring Ramona Kelly [4] Cevin Fisher featuring Sheila Smith

Eddie FISHER *US, male vocalist (9 Singles: 105 Weeks)*

Date	Title / Label	Pos	Wks
2 Jan 53 ★	**OUTSIDE OF HEAVEN (re)** *HMV B 10362*	1	17
23 Jan 53 ●	**EVERYTHING I HAVE IS YOURS (re)** *HMV B 10398*	8	5
1 May 53 ●	**DOWNHEARTED** *HMV B 10450*	3	15
22 May 53 ★	**I'M WALKING BEHIND YOU** *HMV B 10489* [1] ▲	1	18
6 Nov 53 ●	**WISH YOU WERE HERE** *HMV B 10564*	8	9
22 Jan 54 ●	**OH MY PAPA (O MEIN PAPA) (3re)** *HMV B 10614* ▲	9	4
29 Oct 54	**I NEED YOU NOW (2re)** *HMV B 10755* ▲ $	13	10
18 Mar 55 ●	**(I'M ALWAYS HEARING) WEDDING BELLS** *HMV B 10839*	5	11
23 Nov 56 ●	**CINDY, OH CINDY** *HMV POP 273*	5	16

[1] Eddie Fisher with Sally Sweetland (soprano)

Mark FISHER featuring Dotty GREEN
UK, male keyboard player and female vocalist

Date	Title / Label	Pos	Wks
29 Jun 85	**LOVE SITUATION** *Total Control TOCO 3*	59	2

Toni FISHER *US, female vocalist, b. 1931, d. 12 Feb 1999*

Date	Title / Label	Pos	Wks
12 Feb 60	**THE BIG HURT** *Top Rank JAR 261*	30	1

FITS OF GLOOM *UK / Italy, male vocal duo (2 Singles: 4 Weeks)*

Date	Title / Label	Pos	Wks
4 Jun 94	**HEAVEN** *Media MCSTD 1981*	47	2
5 Nov 94	**THE POWER OF LOVE** *Media MCSTD 2016* [1]	49	2

[1] Fits of Gloom featuring Lizzy Mack

Ella FITZGERALD *US, female vocalist, b. 25 Apr 1918, d. 15 June 1996 (11 Albums: 59 Weeks, 6 Singles: 29 Weeks)*

Date	Title / Label	Pos	Wks
23 May 58	**THE SWINGIN' SHEPHERD BLUES** *HMV POP 486*	15	5
19 Jul 58 ●	ELLA FITZGERALD SINGS THE IRVING BERLIN SONG BOOK *HMV CLP 1183*	5	1
16 Oct 59	**BUT NOT FOR ME (re)** *HMV POP 657*	25	3
21 Apr 60	**MACK THE KNIFE** *HMV POP 736*	19	9
11 Jun 60	ELLA SINGS GERSHWIN *Brunswick LA 8648*	13	3
18 Jun 60	ELLA AT THE OPERA HOUSE *Columbia 33SX 10126*	16	1
23 Jul 60	ELLA SINGS GERSHWIN VOLUME 5 *HMV CLP 1353*	18	2
6 Oct 60	**HOW HIGH THE MOON** *HMV POP 782*	46	1
22 Nov 62	**DESAFINADO (re)** *Verve VS 502*	38	6
30 Apr 64	**CAN'T BUY ME LOVE** *Verve VS 519*	34	5
10 May 80	THE INCOMPARABLE ELLA *Polydor POLTV 9*	40	7
27 Feb 88	A PORTRAIT OF ELLA FITZGERALD *Stylus SMR 847*	42	10
19 Nov 94	ESSENTIAL ELLA – 21 ELLA FITZGERALD CLASSICS *PolyGram TV 5239902*	35	14
23 Mar 96	FOREVER ELLA – 21 ELLA FITZGERALD CLASSICS *Verve / PolyGram TV 5293872*	19	6
15 Feb 03	GOLD – ALL HER GREATEST HITS *Verve 654842*	15	13
18 Sep 04	ELLA AND LOUIS TOGETHER ... *UCJ 9867768* [1]	43	1
29 Oct 05	LOVE SONGS *UCJ 9831065* [2]	61	1

[1] Ella Fitzgerald and Louis Armstrong [2] Ella

Scott FITZGERALD
UK, male vocalist – William McPhail (2 Singles: 12 Weeks)

Date	Title / Label	Pos	Wks
14 Jan 78 ●	**IF I HAD WORDS** *Pepper UP 36333* [1]	3	10
7 May 88	**GO** *PRT PYS 10*	52	2

[1] Scott Fitzgerald and Yvonne Keeley with the St Thomas More School Choir

The 5.6.7.8'S
Japan, female vocal / instrumental group (2 Singles: 3 Weeks)

Date	Title / Label	Pos	Wks
17 Jul 04	**WOO HOO** *Sweet Nothing CSSN 028*	28	2
18 Sep 04	**I'M BLUE** *Sweet Nothing CSSN 029*	71	1

FIVE (292 Top 500) (see also ABS)
Superior all-boy vocal group: 'Abs' Breen, 'J' Brown, Sean Conlon, Rich Neville, Scott Robinson. Eponymous debut album sold more than four million worldwide. The first UK act to reach the Top 10 with every one of their first 11 releases split in 2001 (4 Albums: 96 Weeks, 11 Singles: 133 Weeks)

Date	Title / Label	Pos	Wks
13 Dec 97 ●	**SLAM DUNK (DA FUNK)** *RCA 74321537352*	10	9
14 Mar 98 ●	**WHEN THE LIGHTS GO OUT** *RCA 74321562312*	4	9
20 Jun 98 ●	**GOT THE FEELIN'** *RCA 74321584892*	3	13
4 Jul 98 ★	FIVE *RCA 74321589762* ■	1	36
12 Sep 98 ●	**EVERYBODY GET UP** *RCA 74321613752*	2	12
28 Nov 98 ●	**UNTIL THE TIME IS THROUGH** *RCA 74321632602*	2	12
31 Jul 99 ●	**IF YA GETTIN' DOWN** *RCA 74321689692*	2	12
6 Nov 99 ★	**KEEP ON MOVIN'** *RCA 74321709872* ■	1	17
20 Nov 99 ●	INVINCIBLE *RCA 74321713922*	4	39
18 Mar 00 ●	**DON'T WANNA LET YOU GO** *RCA 74321745292*	9	12
29 Jul 00 ★	**WE WILL ROCK YOU (re)** *RCA 74321774022* [1] ■	1	13
25 Aug 01 ★	**LET'S DANCE** *RCA 74321875962* ■	1	12
8 Sep 01 ●	KINGSIZE *RCA 74321875972*	3	11
3 Nov 01 ●	**CLOSER TO ME (re)** *RCA 74321900742*	4	12
1 Dec 01 ●	GREATEST HITS *RCA 74321913432*	9	10

[1] Five and Queen

FIVE FOR FIGHTING
US, male vocalist / guitarist – John Ondrasik

Date	Title / Label	Pos	Wks
1 Jun 02	**SUPERMAN (IT'S NOT EASY)** *Columbia 6727202*	48	1

FIVE PENNY PIECE
UK, male / female vocal / instrumental group (2 Albums: 6 Weeks)

Date	Title / Label	Pos	Wks
24 Mar 73	MAKING TRACKS *Columbia SCX 6536*	37	1
3 Jul 76 ●	KING COTTON *EMI EMC 3129*	9	5

16 / 18 February 1967	23 / 25 February 1967	2 / 4 March 1967	9 / 11 March 1967
THIS IS MY SONG Petula Clark	THIS IS MY SONG Petula Clark	RELEASE ME Engelbert Humperdinck	RELEASE ME Engelbert Humperdinck
THE MONKEES The Monkees	THE MONKEES The Monkees	THE MONKEES The Monkees	THE MONKEES The Monkees

50 YEARS AGO

Our chart consultant Dave McAleer transports you back to 1956 when rock 'n' roll made its first big impact and skiffle was the new British music craze.

In the last year that Bill Haley was king of rock 'n' roll, the heir to the throne, Elvis Presley, was exploding on to the scene for the first time. The year's first chart was headed by Haley's world-changing 'Rock Around the Clock', which was joined in the Top Five by his 'Rock-a-Beatin' Boogie'. The Top 20 also contained the ground-breaking debut hits from Pat Boone ('Aint That a Shame') and Lonnie Donegan ('Rock Island Line'). However, the fact that the year ended with a Top Five featuring Johnnie Ray, Guy Mitchell, Frankie Vaughan, Malcolm Vaughan and Bing Crosby showed that rock 'n' roll wasn't to everyone's taste in 1956 Britain.

Unlike 1955, when rock 'n' roll hits could be counted on one hand, a few dozen made the grade in 1956, with Haley's band alone clocking up nine. Among the rock 'n' roll acts making their UK chart debuts were Carl Perkins ('Blue Suede Shoes'), Gene Vincent and The Blue Caps ('Be-Bop-a-Lula'), The Platters ('The Great Pretender'/'Only You') and the first boy band, The Teenagers ('Why Do Fools Fall in Love'), led by 13-year-old Frankie Lymon.

The Elvis success story gathers pace

The year's most outstanding newcomer was the controversial and incredibly influential Elvis Presley. He amassed seven UK chart entries in his first seven months, while in the US, more than 80 per cent of TV viewers watched him on The Ed Sullivan Show. Just weeks after 'Hound Dog'/'Don't Be Cruel' had become the fastest ever US million seller (in just two weeks), 'Love Me Tender' topped that tally by racking up more than a million advance orders in America. On several occasions he held the top two places on the US pop and country charts and his debut LP was a transatlantic No.1. A total of 10 million Elvis records were sold in the US alone in 1956 and he ended the year with a record-shattering 10 tracks on the US Top 100.

NME dismisses 'Heartbreak Hotel' … as a "gimmick"

Initially Elvis was likened to 1950s teen heart-throb Johnnie Ray. His first album sleeve note said he was known as "the Hillbilly Johnnie Ray" and that there was "undoubtedly an affinity between these controversial artists, and Elvis has obviously been influenced by Johnnie". The Daily Mirror described him as having "a splash of Johnnie Ray and a sprinkling of Billy Daniels", reporting that many US impersonators were now "doing" Elvis instead of Johnnie Ray, and audiences couldn't tell the difference. However, 1956 was a very good year for the established Mr Ray, who made the front pages when his trousers were ripped off by fans in Australia, proving that he was big down under. Elvis and rock 'n' roll in general still had a lot of people to win over. Britain's NME, considered the hippest music paper, said of his debut disc, 'Heartbreak Hotel': "If you like gimmick voices Elvis Presley will slay you – if this is singing then I give up." Surprisingly, though, his supporters included Bing Crosby, who told Ed Sullivan: "He's got a darn fine voice."

It would be extremely blinkered and misleading to look at the year only through rock 'n' roll coloured glasses, as a brigade of balladeers and easy-on-the-ear bands and vocalists still dominated the hit parade in Britain. Between them, parent-preferred performers such as Tennessee Ernie Ford, Dean Martin, Kay Starr, Doris Day, Johnnie Ray and Britain's own Ronnie Hilton and Anne Shelton held the top spot for most of 1956, unlike in the US where Elvis alone was at No.1 for six months.

Lonnie Donegan reinterprets folk as the crooners still flourish

The vast majority of British record buyers still looked on rock 'n' roll as a passing fad, and considered crooners and early 1950s heart-throbs such as Frank Sinatra, Frankie Laine, Nat 'King' Cole, Eddie Fisher and Perry Como as pop music's royalty. Rock 'n' roll was still alien music to the vast majority of UK artists in 1956, when the top Brits included Jimmy Young, David Whitfield, Alma Cogan, Vera Lynn, Michael Holliday and 1955's top-selling singer Ruby Murray (although, chart-wise, she was now more korma than vindaloo). There were also numerous British orchestras hitting the heights in 1956 including those of Ted Heath, Johnny Dankworth, Humphrey Lyttelton, Frank Chacksfield and George Melachrino. George Melachrino and skiffle star Lonnie Donegan were the only UK acts to pick up US gold records in 1956. Donegan, who said of his music, "I'm merely attempting to re-create the work of authentic folk singers", is rightfully given more credit than any other British act of the era for inspiring later rock stars.

In the US, the vast majority of R&B chart singles also reached the pop Top 100 as Carl Perkins, and then Elvis, became the first acts to appear simultaneously on the pop, country and R&B charts. Bill Haley and his Comets broke box-office records coast to coast and appeared in a handful of lucrative, made-in-a-week, low-budget, rock 'n' roll films including Rock Around the Clock, (which the teen-targeted NME noted "is not for people with any degree of musical taste"), Don't Knock the Rock, which was originally intended to be called Rhythm & Blues and Mr Rock & Roll, which was about DJ Alan Freed. There were also the first releases by later hit-makers Bobby Darin, The Everly Brothers, Brenda Lee, Roy Orbison, James Brown, Johnny Burnette (whose trio backed Lonnie Donegan on his US tour), Eddie Cochran, Jerry Lee Lewis and The Coasters. To increase their sales markets, many pre-rock stars recorded rock and R&B-slanted songs or added a backbeat to their tracks. Outside of rock 'n' roll the most talked about music was calypso, whose chart attack was spearheaded by Harry Belafonte. On Broadway, the year's most successful new show was My Fair Lady starring British talents Julie Andrews and Rex Harrison.

British media craves its own Elvis

By autumn 1956, the UK media were desperate to find "Britain's answer to Elvis". When Tommy Steele appeared on the scene their prayers were answered and they gave him the kind of coverage few acts before

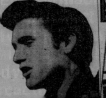

Far from being the boastful … Harry Zimmerman—"One of our

POLICE SWOOP ON ROCK-AROUND-THE-CLOCK FANS

MORE than 1,000 jazz enthusiasts flocked to the sands at Climping, near Littlehampton, last Saturday (7th), for an all-night beach jamboree organised by the Worthing New Conception Jazz Club (writes Bernard Millen).

Three Sussex bands—joined by freelancing instrumentalists from London—settled down at midnight to play a rock-around-the-clock session of traditional jazz.

All went well …

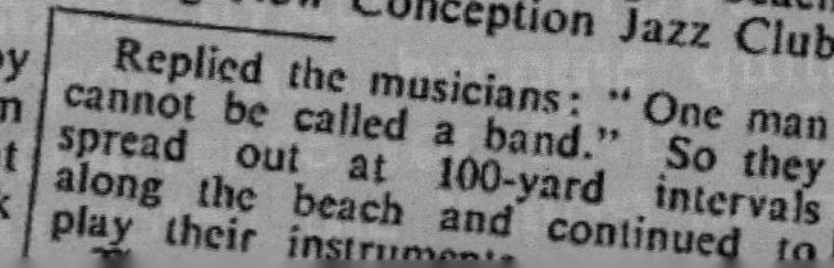

Replied the musicians: "One man cannot be called a band." So they spread out at 100-yard intervals along the beach and continued to play their instruments …

Friday, September 7, 1956 THE NEW MUSICAL EXPRESS

The world's most controversial singer writes for YOU!

HERE IT IS — THE FIRST ARTICLE EVER WRITTEN FOR A BRITISH PUBLICATION BY THAT DYNAMIC RECORDING IDOL—

ELVIS PRESLEY

STARDISCS

WEL…

RAY SONIN

'1956

or since have attracted. His shows were greeted with adulation, while his first release (the self-penned 'Rock with the Caveman') reached the Top 20. Two months later he beat Elvis to the top spot and was filming his own life story.

The NME readers' poll in November reflected the rise of rock 'n' roll when Bill Haley walked off with the award for World's Outstanding Music Personality, with Elvis in the runner-up slot. In the World's Outstanding Singer section Presley came second to Frank Sinatra – not bad for a lad who first charted just six months earlier. The Platters came second to The Four Aces in the Top Vocal Group category, and Doris Day took the trophy for Top Female. On the British front, Dickie Valentine easily won the Music Personality award with Lonnie Donegan as runner-up. Alma Cogan was voted Top Female and The Stargazers Top Vocal Group.

Teenagers pick up guitars in an attempt to emulate their idols

Other British musical happenings in 1956 included Parlophone's up-and-coming producer George Martin scoring with three simultaneous hits in the Top 20 and youthful record engineer Joe Meek adding some revolutionary sounds to several singles. It was also the year of the first Eurovision Song Contest, the first all-American UK Top 10 and the first UK albums chart (with Haley and Presley both scoring No.1s). Lonnie Donegan, who was so popular that he reached the singles chart with both an EP and an album, toured the US before performing solo in Britain. The first charity hit, 'All Star Hit Parade', reached No.2 and raised £10,000 for the National Playing Fields Association. The chart feat of the year came in September when Haley, who averaged two singles on the Top 20 every week, equalled Ruby Murray's record of having five tracks simultaneously in the Top 20. As the year ended Pat Boone became the first US rock 'n' roll star to visit the UK, and the movement's new fans and the media eagerly looked forward to the UK visit of Bill Haley and his Comets.

This remarkable year ended with the idols of three generations, Bing Crosby, Frank Sinatra and Elvis, appearing together in the US Top 10 for the only time in their long careers. The most significant change in terms of the stars of the day was that it was no longer essential for a would-be pop singer to have years of training and experience, an expensive wardrobe and even a good voice in the previously accepted sense. Thousands of teenagers, aiming to become stars, picked up guitars and tried their hand at rock 'n' roll and skiffle. The effects of this would be felt as soon as 1957.

For more in-depth information on the 1950s music scene, check out Dave McAleer's monthly articles on our website: **www.bibleofpop.com**

Lonnie Donegan, the 'King of skiffle'

KEY
UK No.1 ★★ UK Top 10 ●● Still on chart ++ UK entry at No.1 ■■
US No.1 ▲▲ UK million seller £ US million seller $
Singles re-entries are listed as (re), (2re), (3re)... which signifies that the hit re-entered the chart once, twice or three times...
Peak Position / Weeks

The FIVE SMITH BROTHERS *UK, male vocal group*

22 Jul 55 **I'M IN FAVOUR OF FRIENDSHIP** *Decca F 10527* 20 1

FIVE STAR (205 Top 500)

Britain's best known black family act: Deniece, Doris, Stedman, Lorraine and Delroy Pearson. The Essex-based group became the youngest act to top the LP chart with the UK million-seller Silk and Steel. In 1987 they were voted Top British Group in Smash Hits and at the BRIT awards. Act relocated to US and had some R&B chart success (5 Albums: 153 Weeks, 21 Singles: 140 Weeks)

4 May 85 **ALL FALL DOWN** *Tent PB 40039* 15 12
20 Jul 85 **LET ME BE THE ONE** *Tent PB 40193* 18 9
3 Aug 85 **LUXURY OF LIFE** *Tent PL 70735* 12 70
14 Sep 85 **LOVE TAKE OVER** *Tent PB 40353* 25 9
16 Nov 85 **RSVP** *Tent PB 40445* 45 5
11 Jan 86 ● **SYSTEM ADDICT** *Tent PB 40515* 3 11
12 Apr 86 ● **CAN'T WAIT ANOTHER MINUTE** *Tent PB 40697* 7 10
26 Jul 86 ● **FIND THE TIME** *Tent PB 40799* 7 10
30 Aug 86 ★ **SILK AND STEEL** *Tent PL 71100* 1 58
13 Sep 86 ● **RAIN OR SHINE** *Tent PB 40901* 2 11
22 Nov 86 **IF I SAY YES** *Tent PB 40981* 15 9
7 Feb 87 ● **STAY OUT OF MY LIFE** *Tent PB 41131* 9 8
18 Apr 87 ● **THE SLIGHTEST TOUCH** *Tent PB 41265* 4 9
22 Aug 87 **WHENEVER YOU'RE READY** *Tent PB 41477* 11 6
26 Sep 87 ● **BETWEEN THE LINES** *Tent PL 71505* 7 17
10 Oct 87 **STRONG AS STEEL** *Tent PB 41565* 16 7
5 Dec 87 **SOMEWHERE SOMEBODY** *Tent PB 41661* 23 6
4 Jun 88 **ANOTHER WEEKEND** *Tent PB 42081* 18 4
6 Aug 88 **ROCK MY WORLD** *Tent PB 42145* 28 4
27 Aug 88 **ROCK THE WORLD** *Tent PL 71747* 17 5
17 Sep 88 **THERE'S A BRAND NEW WORLD** *Tent PB 42235* 61 2
19 Nov 88 **LET ME BE YOURS** *Tent PB 42343* 51 3
8 Apr 89 **WITH EVERY HEARTBEAT** *Tent PB 42693* 49 2
21 Oct 89 **GREATEST HITS** *Tent PL 74080* 53 3
10 Mar 90 **TREAT ME LIKE A LADY** *Tent FIVE 1* 54 2
7 Jul 90 **HOT LOVE** *Tent FIVE 2* 68 1

FIVE THIRTY

UK, male vocal / instrumental group (1 Album: 1 Week, 4 Singles: 4 Weeks)

4 Aug 90 **ABSTAIN** *East West YZ 530* 75 1
25 May 91 **13TH DISCIPLE** *East West YZ 577* 67 1
3 Aug 91 **SUPERNOVA** *East West YZ 594* 75 1
31 Aug 91 **BED** *East West WX 530* 57 1
2 Nov 91 **YOU (EP)** *East West YZ 624* 72 1

Tracks on You (EP): You / Cuddly Drug / Slow Train into the Ocean.

5000 VOLTS

UK, male / female vocal / instrumental group (2 Singles: 18 Weeks)

6 Sep 75 ● **I'M ON FIRE** *Philips 6006 464* 4 9
24 Jul 76 ● **DOCTOR KISS-KISS** *Philips 6006 533* 8 9

Tina Charles is the uncredited vocalist on 'I'm on Fire'.

FIXATE *UK, male vocal group*

14 Jul 01 **24/7** *Epark EPKFIX CD1* 42 1

FIXX

UK, male vocal / instrumental group (2 Albums: 7 Weeks, 2 Singles: 8 Weeks)

24 Apr 82 **STAND OR FALL** *MCA FIXX 2* 54 4
22 May 82 **SHUTTERED ROOM** *MCA FX 1001* 54 6
17 Jul 82 **RED SKIES** *MCA FIXX 3* 57 4
21 May 83 **REACH THE BEACH** *MCA FX 1002* 91 1

Roberta FLACK

US, female vocalist (6 Albums: 50 Weeks, 9 Singles: 79 Weeks)

27 May 72 **THE FIRST TIME EVER I SAW YOUR FACE** *Atlantic K 10161* ▲ $ 14 14
15 Jul 72 **FIRST TAKE** *Atlantic K 40040* ▲ 47 2
5 Aug 72 **WHERE IS THE LOVE** *Atlantic K 10202* [1] $ 29 7
17 Feb 73 ● **KILLING ME SOFTLY WITH HIS SONG** *Atlantic K 10282* ▲ $ 6 14
13 Oct 73 **KILLING ME SOFTLY** *Atlantic K 50021* 40 2
24 Aug 74 **FEEL LIKE MAKIN' LOVE** *Atlantic K 10467* ▲ $ 34 7
6 May 78 **THE CLOSER I GET TO YOU** *Atlantic K 11099* [2] $ 42 4
17 May 80 ● **BACK TOGETHER AGAIN** *Atlantic K 11481* [1] 3 11
7 Jun 80 **ROBERTA FLACK AND DONNY HATHAWAY** *Atlantic K 50696* [1] 31 7
30 Aug 80 **DON'T MAKE ME WAIT TOO LONG** *Atlantic K 11555* 44 7
20 Aug 83 ● **TONIGHT I CELEBRATE MY LOVE** *Capitol CL 302* [3] 2 13
17 Sep 83 **BORN TO LOVE** *Capitol EST 7122841* [2] 15 10
31 Mar 84 **ROBERTA FLACK'S GREATEST HITS** *K-Tel NE 1269* 35 14
29 Jul 89 **UH-UH OOH OOH LOOK OUT (HERE IT COMES)** *Atlantic A 8941* 72 2
19 Feb 94 ● **SOFTLY WITH THESE SONGS – THE BEST OF ROBERTA FLACK** *Atlantic 7567824982* 7 15

[1] Roberta Flack and Donny Hathaway [2] Roberta Flack with Donny Hathaway
[3] Peabo Bryson and Roberta Flack [1] Roberta Flack and Donny Hathaway
[2] Peabo Bryson and Roberta Flack

The FLAMING LIPS

US, male vocal / instrumental group (2 Albums: 17 Weeks, 7 Singles: 15 Weeks)

9 Mar 96 **THIS HERE GIRAFFE** *Warner Bros. W 0335CD* 72 1
29 May 99 **THE SOFT BULLETIN** *Warner Bros. 9362473932* 39 2
26 Jun 99 **RACE FOR THE PRIZE** *Warner Bros. W 494CD 1* 39 2
20 Nov 99 **WAITIN' FOR A SUPERMAN** *Warner Bros. W 505CD 1* 73 1
27 Jul 02 **YOSHIMI BATTLES THE PINK ROBOTS** *Warner Bros. 9362481412* 13 15
31 Aug 02 **DO YOU REALIZE??** *Warner Bros. WEA W 586CD* 32 2
25 Jan 03 **YOSHIMI BATTLES THE PINK ROBOTS PT.1** *Warner Bros. W 597CD 1* 18 3
5 Jul 03 **FIGHT TEST** *Warner Bros. W 611CD 1* 28 2
27 Sep 03 **THE GOLDEN PATH** *Virgin CHEMSD 18* [1] 17 4

[1] The Chemical Brothers / The Flaming Lips

The FLAMINGOS *US, male vocal group*

4 Jun 69 **THE BOOGALOO PARTY** *Philips BF 1786* 26 5

Michael FLANDERS with the Michael SAMMES SINGERS

UK, male vocalist, b. 1 Mar 1922, d. 14 Apr 1975, and male / female vocal group – leader b. 19 Feb 1928, d. 19 May 2001

27 Feb 59 **THE LITTLE DRUMMER BOY (re)** *Parlophone R 4528* 20 3

FLASH and The PAN

Australia, male vocal (George Young) / instrumental group (1 Album: 2 Weeks, 2 Singles: 15 Weeks)

23 Sep 78 **AND THE BAND PLAYED ON (DOWN AMONG THE DEAD MEN)** *Ensign ENY 15* 54 4
21 May 83 ● **WAITING FOR A TRAIN** *Easy Beat EASY 1* 7 11
16 Jul 83 **PAN-ORAMA** *Easy Beat EASLP 100* 69 2

The FLASH BROTHERS *Israel, male production trio*

6 Nov 04 **AMEN (DON'T BE AFRAID)** *Direction 6754362* 75 1

Lester FLATT and Earl SCRUGGS

US, male banjo players – Lester Flatt, b. 28 Jun 1914, d. 11 May 1979

15 Nov 67 **FOGGY MOUNTAIN BREAKDOWN** *CBS 3038 and Mercury MF 1007* 39 6

The versions on the two labels were not the same cuts; CBS had a 1965 recording, Mercury a 1949 recording. The chart did not differentiate and listed both together.

16 / 18 March 1967	23 / 25 March 1967	30 March / 1 April 1967	6 / 8 April 1967
◂◂ UK No.1 SINGLES ▸▸			
RELEASE ME Engelbert Humperdinck	RELEASE ME Engelbert Humperdinck	RELEASE ME Engelbert Humperdinck	RELEASE ME Engelbert Humperdinck
◂◂ UK No.1 ALBUMS ▸▸			
THE MONKEES The Monkees	THE SOUND OF MUSIC Soundtrack	THE SOUND OF MUSIC Soundtrack	THE SOUND OF MUSIC Soundtrack

Fogwell FLAX and The ANKLEBITERS from FREEHOLD JUNIOR SCHOOL *UK, male vocalist and school choir*

26 Dec 81 **ONE NINE FOR SANTA** *EMI 5255*....68 2

The FLEE-REKKERS *UK, male instrumental group*

19 May 60 **GREEN JEANS** *Triumph RGM 1008*....23 13

FLEET NEW *UK, male / female vocal / instrumental group*

15 Oct 05 **GET DOWN (EP)** *Cosmos FLEET 01CD*....71 1

Tracks on Get Down (EP): Get Down / That's Why / Beautiful Body.

FLEETWOOD MAC (18 Top 500)

Record breaking, Anglo-American soft-rock superstars who started as a British blues band. Members included Mick Fleetwood (d), John McVie (b), Peter Green (Peter Greenbaum) (g), Christine (Perfect) McVie (k/v), Lindsey Buckingham (g/v) and Stevie Nicks (v). The group made its live debut at the 1967 Windsor Jazz & Blues Festival and by 1969 were one of Britain's most popular bands, thanks partly to Green's hypnotic composition 'Albatross' (which returned to the Top 3 in 1973). Green left shortly before McVie's future wife, Christine (voted Top British Female Singer in a 1969 Melody Maker poll), joined from Chicken Shack. The group's Stateside breakthrough came with its chart-topping second eponymous album, with featured new members, American singer / songwriters Buckingham and Nicks. Grammy Hall of Fame album Rumours topped the US chart for a staggering 31 weeks. It has sold 19 million in America and is ten times platinum in the UK, where it has spent longer on the chart than any album. Group members concentrated on solo projects in the 1980s, reconvening in 1987 for the hit packed Tango in the Night. They split again in 1990, reunited briefly for President Clinton's Inaugural concert in 1993 and, in 1997, Fleetwood, Buckingham, Nicks and the McVie's live recording, The Dance, topped the US chart. In 1998 they received the Outstanding Contribution to British Music Award at the BRITs and were inducted into the Rock and Roll Hall of Fame (20 Albums: 886 Weeks, 27 Singles: 223 Weeks)

2 Mar 68 ● FLEETWOOD MAC *Blue Horizon BPG 763200*....4 37
10 Apr 68 **BLACK MAGIC WOMAN** *Blue Horizon 57 3138*....37 7
17 Jul 68 **NEED YOUR LOVE SO BAD** *Blue Horizon 57 3139*....31 13
7 Sep 68 ● MR. WONDERFUL *Blue Horizon 763205*....10 11
4 Dec 68 ★ **ALBATROSS** *Blue Horizon 57 3145*....1 20
16 Apr 69 ● **MAN OF THE WORLD** *Immediate IM 080*....2 14
23 Jul 69 **NEED YOUR LOVE SO BAD (re)** (re-issue) *Blue Horizon 57 3157*....32 9
30 Aug 69 THE PIOUS BIRD OF GOOD OMEN *Blue Horizon 763215*....18 4
4 Oct 69 ● THEN PLAY ON *Reprise RSLP 9000*....6 11
4 Oct 69 ● **OH WELL** *Reprise RS 27000*....2 16
23 May 70 ● **THE GREEN MANALISHI (WITH THE TWO-PRONG CROWN)** *Reprise RS 27007*....10 12
10 Oct 70 KILN HOUSE *Reprise RSLP 9004*....39 2
19 Feb 72 GREATEST HITS *CBS 69011*....36 13
12 May 73 ● **ALBATROSS** (re-issue) *CBS 8306*....2 15
6 Nov 76 FLEETWOOD MAC *Reprise K 54043* ▲....23 19
13 Nov 76 **SAY YOU LOVE ME** *Reprise K 14447*....40 4
19 Feb 77 **GO YOUR OWN WAY** *Warner Bros. K 16872*....38 4
26 Feb 77 ★ RUMOURS *Warner Bros. K 56344* ▲....1 477
30 Apr 77 **DON'T STOP** *Warner Bros. K 16930*....32 5
9 Jul 77 **DREAMS** *Warner Bros. K 16969* ▲ $....24 9
22 Oct 77 **YOU MAKE LOVING FUN** *Warner Bros. K 17013*....45 2
11 Mar 78 **RHIANNON** *Reprise K 14430*....46 3
6 Oct 79 ● **TUSK** *Warner Bros. K 17468*....6 10
27 Oct 79 ★ TUSK *Warner Bros. K 66088*....1 26
22 Dec 79 **SARA** *Warner Bros. K 17533*....37 8
13 Dec 80 FLEETWOOD MAC LIVE *Warner Bros. K 66097*....31 9
10 Jul 82 ● MIRAGE *Warner Bros. K 56592* ▲....5 39
25 Sep 82 **GYPSY** *Warner Bros. K 17997*....46 3
18 Dec 82 ● **OH DIANE** *Warner Bros. FLEET 1*....9 15
4 Apr 87 ● **BIG LOVE** *Warner Bros. W 8398*....9 12
25 Apr 87 ★ TANGO IN THE NIGHT *Warner Bros. WX 65*....1 115
11 Jul 87 **SEVEN WONDERS** *Warner Bros. W 8317*....56 4
26 Sep 87 ● **LITTLE LIES** *Warner Bros. W 8291*....5 12
26 Dec 87 **FAMILY MAN** *Warner Bros. W 8114*....54 5
2 Apr 88 ● **EVERYWHERE** *Warner Bros. W 8143*....4 10
18 Jun 88 **ISN'T IT MIDNIGHT** *Warner Bros. W 7860*....60 2
3 Dec 88 ● GREATEST HITS *Warner Bros. WX 221*....3 53
17 Dec 88 **AS LONG AS YOU FOLLOW** *Warner Bros. W 7644*....66 3
21 Apr 90 ★ BEHIND THE MASK *Warner Bros. WX 335* ■....1 21
5 May 90 **SAVE ME** *Warner Bros. W 9866*....53 3
25 Aug 90 **IN THE BACK OF MY MIND** *Warner Bros. W 9739*....58 3
23 Sep 95 LIVE AT THE BBC *Essential EDFCD 297*....48 2
21 Oct 95 TIME *Warner Bros. 9362459202*....47 1
6 Sep 97 THE DANCE *Reprise 9362467022* ▲....15 10
26 Oct 02 ● THE VERY BEST OF FLEETWOOD MAC *WSM 8122736352*....7 27
10 May 03 ● SAY YOU WILL *WEA WB 48467*....6 8
24 Sep 05 RUMOURS (re-issue) *Warner Bros. 8122738822*....69 1

Group was UK and male only for the first six albums and Live at the BBC. All the above albums are different, although some are identically titled. Greatest Hits in 1972 changed catalogue number to 4607041 during its chart run.

The FLEETWOODS *US, male / female vocal (Gary Troxel) group*

24 Apr 59 ● **COME SOFTLY TO ME** *London HLU 8841* ▲ $....6 8

John '00' FLEMING *UK, male DJ / producer (3 Singles: 3 Weeks)*

25 Dec 99 **LOST IN EMOTION** *React CDREACT 170*....74 1
12 Aug 00 **FREE** *React CDREACT 186*....61 1
2 Feb 02 **BELFAST TRANCE** *Nebula BELFCD 001* [1]....74 1

[1] John "OO" Fleming vs Simple Minds

FLESH & BONES *Belgium, male / female production / vocal trio*

10 Aug 02 **I LOVE YOU** *Multiply CDMULTY 86*....70 1

FLICKMAN (see also A.T.G.O.C.) *Italy, male production duo – Andreas Mazzali and Giuliano Orlandi (2 Singles: 6 Weeks)*

4 Mar 00 **THE SOUND OF BAMBOO** *Inferno CDFERN 25*....11 5
28 Apr 01 **HEY! PARADISE** *Inferno CDFERN 37*....69 1

KC FLIGHTT *US, male rapper (2 Singles: 5 Weeks)*

1 Apr 89 **PLANET E** *RCA PT 49404*....48 4
12 May 01 **VOICES** *Hooj Choons HOOJ 106CD* [1]....59 1

[1] KC Flightt vs Funky Junction

Dread FLIMSTONE and The MODERN TONE AGE FAMILY *US, male vocal / instrumental group*

30 Nov 91 **FROM THE GHETTO** *Urban URB 87*....66 1

Berni FLINT *UK, male vocalist (1 Album: 6 Weeks, 2 Singles: 11 Weeks)*

19 Mar 77 ● **I DON'T WANT TO PUT A HOLD ON YOU** *EMI 2599*....3 10
2 Jul 77 I DON'T WANT TO PUT A HOLD ON YOU *EMI EMC 3184*....37 6
23 Jul 77 **SOUTHERN COMFORT** *EMI 2621*....48 1

FLINTLOCK *UK, male vocal / instrumental group*

29 May 76 **DAWN** *Pinnacle P 8419*....30 5

FLIP & FILL (see also BUS STOP; EYEOPENER) *UK, male production duo – Graham Turner and Mark Hall (1 Album: 7 Weeks, 8 Singles: 45 Weeks)*

24 Mar 01 **TRUE LOVE NEVER DIES** *All Around the World CDGLOBE 240* [1]....34 3
2 Feb 02 ● **TRUE LOVE NEVER DIES** (re-mix) *All Around the World CDGLOBE 248* [1]....7 10
27 Jul 02 ● **SHOOTING STAR** *All Around the World CDGLOBE 258*....3 10
18 Jan 03 **I WANNA DANCE WITH SOMEBODY (re)** *All Around the World CDGLOBE 275*....13 7
22 Mar 03 **SHAKE YA SHIMMY** *All Around the World CDGLOBE 213* [2]....28 2
28 Jun 03 **FIELD OF DREAMS** *All Around the World CDGLOBE 273* [3]....28 2

13 / 15 April 1967	20 / 22 April 1967	27 / 29 April 1967	4 / 6 May 1967
SOMETHIN' STUPID Nancy and Frank Sinatra	SOMETHIN' STUPID Nancy and Frank Sinatra	PUPPET ON A STRING Sandie Shaw	PUPPET ON A STRING Sandie Shaw
THE SOUND OF MUSIC Soundtrack	THE SOUND OF MUSIC Soundtrack	THE SOUND OF MUSIC Soundtrack	THE SOUND OF MUSIC Soundtrack

KEY
UK No.1 ★★ UK Top 10 ●● Still on chart ++ UK entry at No.1 ■■
US No.1 ▲▲ UK million seller £ US million seller $
Singles re-entries are listed as (re), (2re), (3re)... which signifies that the hit re-entered the chart once, twice or three times...
Peak Position / Weeks

Date	Title / Label	Peak Position	Weeks
19 Jul 03	FLOOR FILLAS *UMTV / AATW 0392192*	29	7
17 Jan 04	IRISH BLUE *All Around the World CXGLOBE 309* [4]	20	4
24 Jul 04	DISCOLAND *All Around the World CDGLOBE 346* [5]	11	7

[1] Flip & Fill featuring Kelly Llorenna [2] Porn Kings vs Flip & Fill featuring 740 Boyz [3] Flip & Fill featuring Jo James [4] Flip & Fill featuring Junior [5] Flip & Fill featuring Karen Parry

'Shooting Star' features uncredited vocalist Karen Parry.

The FLIPMODE SQUAD *US, male / female production / rap group (2 Singles: 14 Weeks)*

Date	Title / Label	Peak Position	Weeks
31 Oct 98	CHA CHA CHA *Elektra E 3810CD*	54	1
7 Jun 03 ●	I KNOW WHAT YOU WANT *J 82876528292* [1]	3	13

[1] Busta Rhymes and Mariah Carey featuring The Flipmode Squad

The FLOATERS *US, male vocal group*

Date	Title / Label	Peak Position	Weeks
23 Jul 77 ★	FLOAT ON *ABC 4187* $	1	11
20 Aug 77	FLOATERS *ABC ABCL 5229*	17	8

FLOCK *UK, male vocal / instrumental group*

Date	Title / Label	Peak Position	Weeks
2 May 70	FLOCK *CBS 63733*	59	2

A FLOCK OF SEAGULLS *UK, male vocal (Mike Score) / instrumental group (3 Albums: 59 Weeks, 7 Singles: 46 Weeks)*

Date	Title / Label	Peak Position	Weeks
27 Mar 82	I RAN *Jive JIVE 14*	43	6
17 Apr 82	A FLOCK OF SEAGULLS *Jive HOP 201*	32	44
12 Jun 82	SPACE AGE LOVE SONG *Jive JIVE 17*	34	6
6 Nov 82 ●	WISHING (IF I HAD A PHOTOGRAPH OF YOU) *Jive JIVE 25*	10	12
23 Apr 83	NIGHTMARES *Jive JIVE 33*	53	3
7 May 83	LISTEN *Jive HIP 4*	16	10
25 Jun 83	TRANSFER AFFECTION *Jive JIVE 41*	38	5
14 Jul 84	THE MORE YOU LIVE, THE MORE YOU LOVE *Jive JIVE 62*	26	11
1 Sep 84	THE STORY OF A YOUNG HEART *Jive HIP 14*	30	5
19 Oct 85	WHO'S THAT GIRL (SHE'S GOT IT) *Jive JIVE 106*	66	3

FLOETRY *UK, female vocal duo*

Date	Title / Label	Peak Position	Weeks
26 Apr 03	FLOETIC *Dreamworks 4507752*	73	1

FLOORPLAY *UK, male instrumental / production duo*

Date	Title / Label	Peak Position	Weeks
27 Jan 96	AUTOMATIC *Perfecto PERF 115CD*	50	1

FLOWERED UP *UK, male vocal / instrumental group (1 Album: 3 Weeks, 5 Singles: 17 Weeks)*

Date	Title / Label	Peak Position	Weeks
28 Jul 90	IT'S ON *Heavenly HVN 3*	54	4
24 Nov 90	PHOBIA *Heavenly HVN 7*	75	1
11 May 91	TAKE IT *London FUP 1*	34	4
17 Aug 91	IT'S ON (re-recording)/ EGG RUSH *London FUP 2*	38	3
7 Sep 91	A LIFE WITH BRIAN *London 8282441*	23	3
2 May 92	WEEKENDER *Heavenly HVN 16*	20	5

FLOWERPOT MEN *UK, male vocal group*

Date	Title / Label	Peak Position	Weeks
23 Aug 67 ●	LET'S GO TO SAN FRANCISCO *Deram DM 142*	4	12

Mike FLOWERS POPS *UK, male / female vocal / instrumental group (3 Singles: 14 Weeks)*

Date	Title / Label	Peak Position	Weeks
30 Dec 95 ●	WONDERWALL (re) *London LONCD 378*	2	9
8 Jun 96	LIGHT MY FIRE / PLEASE RELEASE ME *London LONCD 384*	39	2
28 Dec 96	DON'T CRY FOR ME ARGENTINA *Love This LUVTHIS 16*	30	3

Eddie FLOYD *US, male vocalist (1 Album: 5 Weeks, 3 Singles: 29 Weeks)*

Date	Title / Label	Peak Position	Weeks
2 Feb 67	KNOCK ON WOOD (re) *Atlantic 584 041*	19	18
16 Mar 67	RAISE YOUR HAND *Stax 601 001*	42	3
29 Apr 67	KNOCK ON WOOD *Stax 589006*	36	5
9 Aug 67	THINGS GET BETTER *Stax 601 016*	31	8

FLUFFY *UK, female vocal / instrumental group (2 Singles: 2 Weeks)*

Date	Title / Label	Peak Position	Weeks
17 Feb 96	HUSBAND *Parkway PARK 006CD*	58	1
5 Oct 96	NOTHING *Virgin VSCDT 1614*	52	1

FLUKE (see also LUCKY MONKEYS) *UK, male instrumental / production group (3 Albums: 3 Weeks, 9 Singles: 20 Weeks)*

Date	Title / Label	Peak Position	Weeks
20 Mar 93	SLID *Circa YRCD 103*	59	1
19 Jun 93	ELECTRIC GUITAR *Circa YRCD 104*	58	2
11 Sep 93	GROOVY FEELING *Circa YRCD 106*	45	3
23 Oct 93	SIX WHEELS ON MY WAGON *Circa CIRCDX 27*	41	1
23 Apr 94	BUBBLE *Circa YRCD 110*	37	2
29 Jul 95	BULLET *Circa YRCD 121*	23	3
19 Aug 95	OTO *Circa CIRCD 31*	44	1
16 Dec 95	TOSH *Circa YRCD 122*	32	3
16 Nov 96	ATOM BOMB *Circa YRCD 125*	20	3
31 May 97	ABSURD *Virgin YRCD 126*	25	2
27 Sep 97	SQUIRT *Circa YRCD 127*	46	1
11 Oct 97	RISOTTO *Virgin CIRCD 33*	45	1

A FLUX OF PINK INDIANS *UK, male vocal / instrumental group*

Date	Title / Label	Peak Position	Weeks
5 Feb 83	STRIVE TO SURVIVE CAUSING LEAST SUFFERING POSSIBLE *Spiderleg SDL 8*	79	2

The FLYING LIZARDS *UK, male / female vocal (Patti Palladin) / instrumental group (1 Album: 3 Weeks, 2 Singles: 16 Weeks)*

Date	Title / Label	Peak Position	Weeks
4 Aug 79 ●	MONEY *Virgin VS 276*	5	10
9 Feb 80	TV *Virgin VS 325*	43	6
16 Feb 80	FLYING LIZARDS *Virgin V 2150*	60	3

The FLYING PICKETS *UK, male vocal group (2 Albums: 22 Weeks, 3 Singles: 20 Weeks)*

Date	Title / Label	Peak Position	Weeks
26 Nov 83 ★	ONLY YOU *10 TEN 14*	1	11
17 Dec 83	LIVE AT THE ALBANY EMPIRE *AVM AVMLP 0001*	48	11
21 Apr 84 ●	WHEN YOU'RE YOUNG AND IN LOVE *10 TEN 20*	7	8
9 Jun 84	LOST BOYS *10 DIX 4*	11	11
8 Dec 84	WHO'S THAT GIRL *10 GIRL 1*	71	1

FOCUS *Holland, male instrumental group (5 Albums: 65 Weeks, 2 Singles: 21 Weeks)*

Date	Title / Label	Peak Position	Weeks
11 Nov 72 ●	MOVING WAVES *Polydor 2931 002*	2	34
2 Dec 72 ●	FOCUS 3 *Polydor 2383 016*	6	15
20 Jan 73	HOCUS POCUS *Polydor 2001 211*	20	10
27 Jan 73 ●	SYLVIA *Polydor 2001 422*	4	11
20 Oct 73	AT THE RAINBOW *Polydor 2442 118*	23	5
25 May 74	HAMBURGER CONCERTO *Polydor 2442 124*	20	5
9 Aug 75	FOCUS *Polydor 2384 070*	23	6

FOG (see also FUNKY GREEN DOGS) *US, male DJ / producer – Ralph Falcon (2 Singles: 4 Weeks)*

Date	Title / Label	Peak Position	Weeks
19 Feb 94	BEEN A LONG TIME *Columbia 6601212*	44	2
6 Jun 98	BEEN A LONG TIME (re-mix) *Pukka CDPUKKA 16*	27	2

Dan FOGELBERG *US, male vocalist*

Date	Title / Label	Peak Position	Weeks
15 Mar 80	LONGER *Epic EPC 8230*	59	4
29 Mar 80	PHOENIX *Epic EPC 83317*	42	3

John FOGERTY (see also CREEDENCE CLEARWATER REVIVAL) *US, male vocalist / guitarist*

Date	Title / Label	Peak Position	Weeks
16 Feb 85	CENTERFIELD *Warner Bros. 9252031* ▲	48	11

	11 / 13 May 1967	18 / 20 May 1967	25 / 27 May 1967	1 / 3 June 1967
UK No.1 SINGLES	PUPPET ON A STRING Sandie Shaw	SILENCE IS GOLDEN The Tremeloes	SILENCE IS GOLDEN The Tremeloes	SILENCE IS GOLDEN The Tremeloes
UK No.1 ALBUMS	MORE OF THE MONKEES The Monkees	THE SOUND OF MUSIC Soundtrack	MORE OF THE MONKEES The Monkees	THE SOUND OF MUSIC Soundtrack

Ben FOLDS FIVE *US, male vocal / instrumental group (5 Albums: 8 Weeks, 6 Singles: 13 Weeks)*

14 Sep 96 **UNDERGROUND** *Caroline CDCAR 008* ... **37** 2
1 Mar 97 **BATTLE OF WHO COULD CARE LESS** *Epic 6642302* ... **26** 3
15 Mar 97 WHATEVER AND EVER AMEN *Epic 4866982* ... 30 3
7 Jun 97 **KATE** *Epic 6645365* ... **39** 2
24 Jan 98 NAKED BABY PHOTOS *Caroline CAR 7554* ... 65 1
18 Apr 98 **BRICK** *Epic 6656612* ... **26** 3
24 Apr 99 **ARMY** *Epic 6672182* ... **28** 2
8 May 99 THE UNAUTHORIZED BIOGRAPHY OF REINHOLD MESSNER *Epic 4933122* ... 22 2
29 Sep 01 **ROCKIN' THE SUBURBS** *Epic 6718492* [1] ... **53** 1
6 Oct 01 ROCKIN' THE SUBURBS *Epic 5040632* [1] ... 73 1
7 May 05 SONGS FOR SILVERMAN *Epic 5170123* [1] ... 65 1

[1] Ben Folds [1] Ben Folds

Ellen FOLEY *US, female vocalist (2 Albums: 3 Weeks)*

17 Nov 79 NIGHT OUT *Epic EPC 83718* ... 68 1
4 Apr 81 SPIRIT OF ST. LOUIS *Epic EPC 84809* ... 57 2

FOLK IMPLOSION *US, male vocal / instrumental duo*

15 Jun 96 **NATURAL ONE** *London LONCD 382* ... **45** 1

Jane FONDA *US, female exercise instructor (2 Albums: 51 Weeks)*

29 Jan 83 ● JANE FONDA'S WORKOUT RECORD *CBS 88581* ... 7 47
22 Sep 84 JANE FONDA'S WORKOUT RECORD: NEW AND IMPROVED *CBS 88640* ... 60 4

Lenny FONTANA *US, male producer (2 Singles: 3 Weeks)*

4 Mar 00 **CHOCOLATE SENSATION** *ffrr FCD 375* [1] ... **39** 2
24 Mar 01 **POW POW POW** *Strictly Rhythm SRUKCD 01* [2] ... **62** 1

[1] Lenny Fontana and DJ Shorty [2] Fontana featuring Darryl D'Bonneau

Wayne FONTANA and The MINDBENDERS *UK, male vocalist – Glyn Ellis (1 Album: 1 Week, 10 Singles: 76 Weeks)*

11 Jul 63 **HELLO JOSEPHINE** *Fontana TF 404* ... **46** 2
28 May 64 **STOP LOOK AND LISTEN** *Fontana TF 451* ... **37** 4
8 Oct 64 ● **UM, UM, UM, UM, UM, UM** *Fontana TF 497* ... **5** 15
4 Feb 65 ● **GAME OF LOVE** *Fontana TF 535* ▲ $ ... **2** 11
20 Feb 65 WAYNE FONTANA AND THE MINDBENDERS *Fontana TL 5230* ... 18 1
17 Jun 65 **JUST A LITTLE BIT TOO LATE** *Fontana TF 579* ... **20** 7
30 Sep 65 **SHE NEEDS LOVE** *Fontana TF 611* ... **32** 6
9 Dec 65 **IT WAS EASIER TO HURT HER** *Fontana TF 642* [1] ... **36** 6
21 Apr 66 **COME ON HOME** *Fontana TF 684* [1] ... **16** 12
25 Aug 66 **GOODBYE BLUEBIRD** *Fontana TF 737* [1] ... **49** 1
8 Dec 66 **PAMELA, PAMELA** *Fontana TF 770* [1] ... **11** 12

[1] Wayne Fontana

FOO FIGHTERS (366 Top 500) *One man band-turned rock icons led by vocalist, multi-instrumentalist and UFOlogist Dave Grohl, b. 14 Jan 1969, Ohio, US. Debut 1995 album by act, named after World War II slang for UFOs, consisted of tracks he recorded alone while still in Kurt Cobain's band Nirvana. Group was quickly formed and every album since has reached the Top 10 (5 Albums: 120 Weeks, 18 Singles: 69 Weeks)*

1 Jul 95 ● **THIS IS A CALL** *Roswell CDCL 753* ... **5** 4
8 Jul 95 ● FOO FIGHTERS *Roswell CDSET 2266* ... 3 17
16 Sep 95 **I'LL STICK AROUND** *Roswell CDCL 757* ... **18** 3
2 Dec 95 **FOR ALL THE COWS** *Roswell CDCL 762* ... **28** 2
6 Apr 96 **BIG ME** *Roswell CDCL 768* ... **19** 3
10 May 97 **MONKEY WRENCH** *Roswell CDCLS 788* ... **12** 4
24 May 97 ● THE COLOUR AND THE SHAPE *Roswell CDEST 2295* ... 3 12
30 Aug 97 **EVERLONG** *Roswell CDCL 792* ... **18** 3
31 Jan 98 **MY HERO** *Roswell CDCL 796* ... **21** 2
29 Aug 98 **WALKING AFTER YOU: BEACON LIGHT** *Elektra E 4100CD* [1] ... **20** 3
30 Oct 99 **LEARN TO FLY** *RCA 74321706622* ... **21** 3
13 Nov 99 ● THERE IS NOTHING LEFT TO LOSE *RCA 74321716992* ... 10 16
30 Sep 00 **BREAKOUT** *RCA 74321790102* ... **29** 3
16 Dec 00 **NEXT YEAR** *RCA 74321809262* ... **42** 2
19 Oct 02 ● **ALL MY LIFE** *RCA 74321973152* ... **5** 9
2 Nov 02 ★ ONE BY ONE *RCA 74321973482* ■ ... 1 47
18 Jan 03 **TIMES LIKE THESE** *RCA 74321989552* ... **12** 5
5 Jul 03 **LOW** *RCA 82876522562* ... **21** 2
4 Oct 03 **HAVE IT ALL** *RCA 82876563702* ... **37** 2
11 Jun 05 ● **BEST OF YOU** *RCA 82876701012* ... **4** 14
25 Jun 05 ● IN YOUR HONOUR *RCA 82876701932* ... 2 28+
17 Sep 05 **DOA** *RCA 82876735392* ... **25** 3
3 Dec 05 **RESOLVE** *RCA 82876738902* ... **32** 2

[1] Foo Fighters: Ween

FOOL BOONA *UK, male DJ / producer – Colin Tevendale*

10 Apr 99 **POPPED!!** *Virgin / VC Recordings / Uber Disko VCRD 46* ... **52** 1

FOOLPROOF *US, male vocal / instrumental group*

26 Jun 04 **PAPER HOUSE** *Island CID 863* ... **53** 1

FOOL'S GARDEN *Germany, male vocal / instrumental group (2 Singles: 4 Weeks)*

25 May 96 **LEMON TREE** *Encore CDCOR 014* ... **61** 1
3 Aug 96 **LEMON TREE** (re-issue) *Encore CDCOR 018* ... **26** 3

FOR REAL *US, female vocal group (2 Singles: 2 Weeks)*

1 Jul 95 **YOU DON'T KNOW NOTHIN'** *A&M 5811232* ... **54** 1
12 Jul 97 **LIKE I DO** *Rowdy 74321486582* ... **45** 1

Steve FORBERT *US, male vocalist (2 Albums: 3 Weeks)*

9 Jun 79 ALIVE ON ARRIVAL *Epic EPC 83308* ... 56 1
24 Nov 79 JACK RABBIT SLIM *Epic EPC 83879* ... 54 2

Bill FORBES *UK, male vocalist*

15 Jan 60 **TOO YOUNG** *Columbia DB 4386* ... **29** 1

David FORBES *UK (b. Singapore), male producer*

25 Aug 01 **QUESTIONS (MUST BE ASKED)** *Serious SERR 031CD* ... **57** 1

FORCE & STYLES featuring Kelly LLORENNA (see also Darren STYLES & Mark BREEZE) *UK, male DJ duo and female vocalist*

25 Jul 98 **HEART OF GOLD** *Diverse VERSE 2CD* ... **55** 1

FORCE MD'S *US, male vocal group*

12 Apr 86 **TENDER LOVE** *Tommy Boy IS 269* ... **23** 9

Clinton FORD *UK, male vocalist – Ian Stopford Harrison (1 Album: 4 Weeks, 4 Singles: 25 Weeks)*

23 Oct 59 **OLD SHEP** *Oriole CB 1500* ... **27** 1
17 Aug 61 **TOO MANY BEAUTIFUL GIRLS** *Oriole CB 1623* ... **48** 1
8 Mar 62 **FANLIGHT FANNY** *Oriole CB 1706* ... **22** 10
26 May 62 CLINTON FORD *Oriole PS 40021* ... 16 4
5 Jan 67 **RUN TO THE DOOR** *Piccadilly 7N 35361* ... **25** 13

Emile FORD and The CHECKMATES *UK, male vocal / instrumental group – leader Emile Sweatman (8 Singles: 89 Weeks)*

30 Oct 59 ★ **WHAT DO YOU WANT TO MAKE THOSE EYES AT ME FOR?** *Pye 7N 15225* ... **1** 26
5 Feb 60 ● **ON A SLOW BOAT TO CHINA** *Pye 7N 15245* ... **3** 15
26 May 60 **YOU'LL NEVER KNOW WHAT YOU'RE MISSING ('TIL YOU TRY)** *Pye 7N 15268* ... **12** 9
1 Sep 60 **THEM THERE EYES** *Pye 7N 15282* [1] ... **18** 16

8 / 10 June 1967	15 / 17 June 1967	22 / 24 June 1967	29 June / 1 July 1967
A WHITER SHADE OF PALE Procol Harum	A WHITER SHADE OF PALE Procol Harum	A WHITER SHADE OF PALE Procol Harum	A WHITER SHADE OF PALE Procol Harum
SGT. PEPPER'S LONELY HEARTS CLUB BAND The Beatles	SGT. PEPPER'S LONELY HEARTS CLUB BAND The Beatles	SGT. PEPPER'S LONELY HEARTS CLUB BAND The Beatles	SGT. PEPPER'S LONELY HEARTS CLUB BAND The Beatles

KEY: UK No.1 ★ UK Top 10 ● Still on chart + UK entry at No.1 ■ US No.1 ▲ UK million seller £ US million seller $
Singles re-entries are listed as (re), (2re), (3re)... which signifies that the hit re-entered the chart once, twice or three times...
Peak Position / Weeks

8 Dec 60 ● **COUNTING TEARDROPS** *Pye 7N 15314*....4 12
2 Mar 61 **WHAT AM I GONNA DO** *Pye 7N 15331*....33 6
18 May 61 **HALF OF MY HEART (re)** *Piccadilly 7N 35003* [2]....42 4
8 Mar 62 **I WONDER WHO'S KISSING HER NOW** *Piccadilly 7N 35033* [2]....43 1

[1] Emile Ford: The Babs Knight Group and Johnny Keating Music [2] Emile Ford

Lita FORD *UK, female vocalist (3 Albums: 4 Weeks, 3 Singles: 7 Weeks)*

26 May 84 DANCIN' ON THE EDGE *Vertigo VERL 13*....96 1
17 Dec 88 **KISS ME DEADLY** *RCA PB 49575*....75 1
20 May 89 **CLOSE MY EYES FOREVER** *Dreamland PB 49409* [1]....47 3
23 Jun 90 STILETTO *RCA PL 82090*....66 1
11 Jan 92 **SHOT OF POISON** *RCA PB 49145*....63 3
25 Jan 92 DANGEROUS CURVES *RCA PD 90592*....51 2

[1] Lita Ford duet with Ozzy Osbourne

Martyn FORD ORCHESTRA *UK, orchestra*

14 May 77 **LET YOUR BODY GO DOWNTOWN** *Mountain TOP 26*....38 3

Penny FORD (see also SNAP!) *US, female vocalist (2 Singles: 7 Weeks)*

4 May 85 **DANGEROUS** *Total Experience FB 49975* [1]....43 5
29 May 93 **DAYDREAMING** *Columbia 6590592*....43 2

[1] Pennye Ford

Tennessee Ernie FORD
US, male vocalist, b. 13 Feb 1919, d. 17 Oct 1991 (3 Singles: 42 Weeks)

21 Jan 55 ★ **GIVE ME YOUR WORD** *Capitol CL 14005*....1 24
6 Jan 56 ★ **SIXTEEN TONS** *Capitol CL 14500* ▲ $....1 11
13 Jan 56 ● **THE BALLAD OF DAVY CROCKETT** *Capitol CL 14506*....3 7

Julia FORDHAM
UK, female vocalist (4 Albums: 36 Weeks, 7 Singles: 32 Weeks)

18 Jun 88 JULIA FORDHAM *Circa CIRCA 4*....20 22
2 Jul 88 **HAPPY EVER AFTER** *Circa YR 15*....27 9
25 Feb 89 **WHERE DOES THE TIME GO?** *Circa YR 23*....41 5
21 Oct 89 PORCELAIN *Circa CIRCA 10*....13 5
31 Aug 91 **I THOUGHT IT WAS YOU** *Circa YR 69*....64 2
2 Nov 91 SWEPT *Circa CIRCA 18*....33 6
18 Jan 92 **LOVE MOVES (IN MYSTERIOUS WAYS)** *Circa YR 73*....19 9
30 May 92 **I THOUGHT IT WAS YOU** (re-mix) *Circa YR 90*....45 3
30 Apr 94 **DIFFERENT TIME DIFFERENT PLACE** *Circa YRCD 111*....41 3
21 May 94 FALLING FORWARD *Circa CIRCD 28*....21 3
23 Jul 94 **I CAN'T HELP MYSELF** *Circa YRCD 116*....62 1

FOREIGNER (335 Top 500)

Melodic Anglo-American rock group who amassed six US Top 10 albums. Featured Londoner Mick Jones (g) and New York native Lou Gramm (v). 'Waiting for a Girl Like You' stayed at No.2 in the US for a record-setting 10 weeks (9 Albums: 129 Weeks, 13 Singles: 78 Weeks)

6 May 78 **FEELS LIKE THE FIRST TIME** *Atlantic K 11086*....39 6
15 Jul 78 **COLD AS ICE** *Atlantic K 10986*....24 10
26 Aug 78 DOUBLE VISION *Atlantic K 50476*....32 5
28 Oct 78 **HOT BLOODED** *Atlantic K 11167* $....42 3
24 Feb 79 **BLUE MORNING, BLUE DAY** *Atlantic K 11236*....45 4
25 Jul 81 ● 4 *Atlantic K 50796* ▲....5 62
29 Aug 81 **URGENT** *Atlantic K 11665*....54 4
10 Oct 81 **JUKE BOX HERO** *Atlantic K 11678*....48 4
12 Dec 81 ● **WAITING FOR A GIRL LIKE YOU** *Atlantic K 11696* $....8 13
8 May 82 **URGENT** (re-issue) *Atlantic K 11728*....45 5
18 Dec 82 RECORDS *Atlantic A 0999*....58 11
8 Dec 84 ★ **I WANT TO KNOW WHAT LOVE IS** *Atlantic A 9596* ▲ $....1 16
22 Dec 84 ★ AGENT PROVOCATEUR *Atlantic 7819991*....1 32
6 Apr 85 **THAT WAS YESTERDAY** *Atlantic A 9571*....28 6
22 Jun 85 **COLD AS ICE** (re-mix) *Atlantic A 9539*....64 2
19 Dec 87 INSIDE INFORMATION *Atlantic WX 143*....64 7
19 Dec 87 **SAY YOU WILL** *Atlantic A 9169*....71 4
6 Jul 91 UNUSUAL HEAT *Atlantic WX 424*....56 1
2 May 92 THE VERY BEST OF FOREIGNER *Atlantic 7567805112*....19 7
22 Oct 94 **WHITE LIE** *Arista 74321232862*....58 1
12 Nov 94 MR. MOONLIGHT *Arista 74321232852*....59 1
18 Jun 05 THE DEFINITIVE *Atlantic / Rhino 8122735962*....33 3

The FORMATIONS *US, male vocal group*

31 Jul 71 **AT THE TOP OF THE STAIRS (re)** *Mojo 2027 001*....28 11

George FORMBY (see also 2 IN A TENT) *UK, male vocalist / ukulele player – George Hoy Booth, b. 26 May 1904, d. 6 Mar 1961*

21 Jul 60 **HAPPY GO LUCKY ME / BANJO BOY** *Pye 7N 15269*....40 3

FORREST *US, male vocalist – Forrest M Thomas Jr (3 Singles: 20 Weeks)*

26 Feb 83 ● **ROCK THE BOAT** *CBS A 3163*....4 10
14 May 83 **FEEL THE NEED IN ME** *CBS A 3411*....17 8
17 Sep 83 **ONE LOVER (DON'T STOP THE SHOW)** *CBS A 3734*....67 2

Sharon FORRESTER *Jamaica, female vocalist*

11 Feb 95 **LOVE INSIDE** *ffrr FCD 253*....50 1

Lance FORTUNE *UK, male vocalist – Chris Morris (2 Singles: 18 Weeks)*

19 Feb 60 ● **BE MINE** *Pye 7N 15240*....4 13
5 May 60 **THIS LOVE I HAVE FOR YOU** *Pye 7N 15260*....26 5

The FORTUNES *UK, male vocal (Rod Allen / Bainbridge) / instrumental group (5 Singles: 65 Weeks)*

8 Jul 65 ● **YOU'VE GOT YOUR TROUBLES** *Decca F 12173*....2 14
7 Oct 65 ● **HERE IT COMES AGAIN** *Decca F 12243*....4 14
3 Feb 66 **THIS GOLDEN RING** *Decca F 12321*....15 9
11 Sep 71 ● **FREEDOM COME, FREEDOM GO** *Capitol CL 15693*....6 17
29 Jan 72 ● **STORM IN A TEACUP** *Capitol CL 15707*....7 11

45 KING (DJ MARK THE 45 KING) *US, male producer – Mark James*

28 Oct 89 **THE KING IS HERE / THE 900 NUMBER (re)** *Dance Trax DRX 9*....60 6

49ers (see also CAPPELLA) *Italy, male producer – Gianfranco Bortolotti (1 Album: 5 Weeks, 6 Singles: 27 Weeks)*

16 Dec 89 ● **TOUCH ME** *Fourth & Broadway BRW 157*....3 13
10 Mar 90 THE 49ERS *Fourth & Broadway BRLP 547*....51 5
17 Mar 90 **DON'T YOU LOVE ME** *Fourth & Broadway BRW 167*....12 6
9 Jun 90 **GIRL TO GIRL** *Fourth & Broadway BRW 174*....31 3
6 Jun 92 **GOT TO BE FREE** *Fourth & Broadway BRW 255*....46 2
29 Aug 92 **THE MESSAGE** *Fourth & Broadway BRW 257*....68 1
18 Mar 95 **ROCKIN' MY BODY** *Media MCSTD 2021* [1]....31 2

[1] 49ers featuring Ann-Marie Smith

FORWARD, RUSSIA! NEW
UK, male / female vocal / instrumental group

27 Aug 05 **THIRTEEN / FOURTEEN** *Drowned in Sound OPE 002CDS*....74 1

FOSTER and ALLEN (245 Top 500)

Ever-popular Irish duo formed in 1975: Mike Foster (accordian/v), Tony Allen (g/v). The folk-based performers have sold a reported 20 million albums globally, and were the only act to have at least one hit album per year between 1985-1999 (25 Albums: 213 Weeks, 6 Singles: 47 Weeks)

27 Feb 82 **A BUNCH OF THYME** *Ritz RITZ 5*....18 11
30 Oct 82 **OLD FLAMES** *Ritz RITZ 028*....51 8

5 / 8 July 1967	12 / 15 July 1967	19 / 22 July 1967	26 / 29 July 1967
UK No.1 SINGLES			
A WHITER SHADE OF PALE Procol Harum	A WHITER SHADE OF PALE Procol Harum	ALL YOU NEED IS LOVE The Beatles	ALL YOU NEED IS LOVE The Beatles
UK No.1 ALBUMS			
SGT. PEPPER'S LONELY HEARTS CLUB BAND The Beatles	SGT. PEPPER'S LONELY HEARTS CLUB BAND The Beatles	SGT. PEPPER'S LONELY HEARTS CLUB BAND The Beatles	SGT. PEPPER'S LONELY HEARTS CLUB BAND The Beatles

19 Feb 83 **MAGGIE** *Ritz RITZ 025* **27** 9
14 May 83 MAGGIE *Ritz RITZLP 0012* 72 6
29 Oct 83 **I WILL LOVE YOU ALL MY LIFE** *Ritz RITZ 056* **49** 6
5 Nov 83 I WILL LOVE YOU ALL OF MY LIFE *Ritz RITZLP 0015* 71 6
30 Jun 84 **JUST FOR OLD TIME'S SAKE** *Ritz RITZ 066* **47** 6
17 Nov 84 THE VERY BEST OF FOSTER AND ALLEN *Ritz RITZLPTV 1* 18 18
29 Mar 86 AFTER ALL THESE YEARS *Ritz RITZLP 0032* 82 2
29 Mar 86 **AFTER ALL THESE YEARS** *Ritz RITZ 106* **43** 7
25 Oct 86 REMINISCING *Stylus SMR 623* 11 15
27 Jun 87 LOVE SONGS – THE VERY BEST OF FOSTER AND ALLEN VOLUME 2 *Ritz RITZLP 0036* 92 1
10 Oct 87 REFLECTIONS *Stylus SMR 739* 16 16
30 Apr 88 REMEMBER YOU'RE MINE *Stylus SMR 853* 16 15
28 Oct 89 THE MAGIC OF FOSTER AND ALLEN – THEIR GREATEST HITS *Stylus SMR 989* 29 12
9 Dec 89 FOSTER AND ALLEN'S CHRISTMAS COLLECTION *Stylus SMR 995* 40 4
10 Nov 90 SOUVENIRS *Telstar STAR 2457* 15 12
8 Dec 90 THE CHRISTMAS COLLECTION *Telstar STAR 2459* 44 4
2 Nov 91 MEMORIES *Telstar STAR 2527* 18 11
31 Oct 92 HEART STRINGS *Telstar TCD 2608* 37 10
23 Oct 93 BY REQUEST *Telstar TCD 2670* 14 12
5 Nov 94 SONGS WE LOVE TO SING *Telstar TCD 2741* 41 9
4 Nov 95 100 GOLDEN GREATS *Telstar TCD 2791* 30 12
2 Nov 96 SOMETHING SPECIAL – 100 GOLDEN LOVE SONGS *Telstar TCD 2846* 46 10
26 Apr 97 SHADES OF GREEN *Telstar TCD 2899* 55 2
15 Nov 97 BEST FRIENDS *Telstar TV TTVCD 2935* 36 8
12 Dec 98 GREATEST HITS *Telstar TV TTVCD 3000* 52 4
25 Dec 99 ONE DAY AT A TIME *Telstar TV TTVCD 3090* 61 1
15 Nov 03 BY SPECIAL REQUEST – THE VERY BEST OF ... FOSTER & ALLEN *DMG TV DMGTV 003* 30 8
13 Nov 04 FOSTER & ALLEN SING THE SIXTIES *DMG TV DMGTV 012* 31 8
19 Nov 05 FOSTER & ALLEN SING THE NUMBER 1'S *DMG TV DMGTV 022* 30 7+

FOTHERINGAY (see also Sandy DENNY)
UK, male / female vocal / instrumental group

11 Jul 70 FOTHERINGAY *Island ILPS 9125* 18 6

The FOUNDATION featuring Natalie ROSSI
Holland, male producers and UK, female vocalist

12 Jul 03 **ALL OUT OF LOVE** *Fuelin 82876513292* **40** 2

The FOUNDATIONS *West Indies / UK / Sri Lanka, male vocal (Clem Curtis) / instrumental group (7 Singles: 57 Weeks)*

27 Sep 67 ★ **BABY NOW THAT I'VE FOUND YOU** *Pye 7N 17366* $ **1** 16
24 Jan 68 **BACK ON MY FEET AGAIN** *Pye 7N 17417* **18** 10
1 May 68 **ANY OLD TIME (YOU'RE LONELY AND SAD) (re)** *Pye 7N 17503* **48** 2
20 Nov 68 ● **BUILD ME UP BUTTERCUP** *Pye 7N 17636* **2** 15
12 Mar 69 ● **IN THE BAD BAD OLD DAYS (BEFORE YOU LOVED ME)** *Pye 7N 17702* **8** 10
13 Sep 69 **BORN TO LIVE, BORN TO DIE** *Pye 7N 17809* **46** 3
12 Dec 98 **BUILD ME UP BUTTERCUP** (re-issue) *Castle NEEX 1001* **71** 1

FOUNTAINS OF WAYNE
US, male vocal / instrumental group (1 Album: 1 Week, 7 Singles: 15 Weeks)

22 Mar 97 **RADIATION VIBE** *Atlantic 7567956262* **32** 2
10 May 97 **SINK TO THE BOTTOM** *Atlantic A 5612CD* **42** 1
7 Jun 97 FOUNTAINS OF WAYNE *Atlantic 7567927252* 67 1
26 Jul 97 **SURVIVAL CAR** *Atlantic AT 0004CD* **53** 1
27 Dec 97 **I WANT AN ALIEN FOR CHRISTMAS** *Atlantic AT 0020CD* **36** 2
20 Mar 99 **DENISE** *Atlantic AT 0053CD* **57** 1
20 Mar 04 **STACY'S MOM** *Virgin VSCDX 1860* **11** 7
18 Sep 04 **HEY JULIE** *Virgin VSCDX 1881* **57** 1

The FOUR ACES *US, male vocal (Al Alberts) group (7 Singles: 40 Weeks)*

30 Jul 54 ● **THREE COINS IN THE FOUNTAIN (re)** *Brunswick 05308* [1] **5** 6
7 Jan 55 ● **MISTER SANDMAN** *Brunswick 05355* [1] **9** 5
20 May 55 ● **STRANGER IN PARADISE** *Brunswick 05418* **6** 6
18 Nov 55 ● **LOVE IS A MANY SPLENDORED THING** *Brunswick 05480* [1] ▲ $ **2** 13
19 Oct 56 **A WOMAN IN LOVE** *Brunswick 05589* [1] **19** 3
4 Jan 57 **FRIENDLY PERSUASION (THEE I LOVE)** *Brunswick 05623* [1] **29** 1
23 Jan 59 **THE WORLD OUTSIDE** *Brunswick 05773* **18** 6

[1] The Four Aces featuring Al Alberts

The FOUR BUCKETEERS *UK, male / female vocal group*

3 May 80 **THE BUCKET OF WATER SONG** *CBS 8393* **26** 6

The FOUR ESQUIRES *US, male vocal group*

31 Jan 58 **LOVE ME FOREVER** *London HLO 8533* **23** 2

4-4-2 *UK, male vocal / instrumental group – England fans*

19 Jun 04 ● **COME ON ENGLAND** *Gut CDGUT 58* **2** 5

The single's sleeve credits 4-4-2 featuring Talksport 1089 / 1053AM Presenters.

4 HERO
UK, male instrumental duo (2 Albums: 7 Weeks, 4 Singles: 6 Weeks)

24 Nov 90 **MR KIRK'S NIGHTMARE** *Reinforced RIVET 1203* **73** 2
9 May 92 **COOKIN' UP YAH BRAIN** *Reinforced RIVET 1216* **59** 2
25 Jul 98 TWO PAGES *Talkin Loud 5584622* 38 6
15 Aug 98 **STAR CHASERS** *Talkin Loud TLCD 36* **41** 1
3 Nov 01 **LES FLEUR** *Talkin Loud TLCD 66* **53** 1
10 Nov 01 CREATING PATTERNS *Talkin Loud 5860572* 65 1

'Mr Kirk's Nightmare' was titled 'Combat Dancing (EP)' in its first week on chart.

400 BLOWS *UK, male vocal / instrumental duo*

29 Jun 85 **MOVIN'** *Illuminated ILL 61* **54** 4

The FOUR KNIGHTS
US, male vocal (Gene Alford, d. 1960) group (2 Singles: 13 Weeks)

4 Jun 54 ● **(OH BABY MINE) I GET SO LONELY (re)** *Capitol CL 14076* **5** 11
18 Oct 57 **MY PERSONAL POSSESSION** *Capitol CL 14765* [1] **21** 2

[1] Nat 'King' Cole and The Four Knights

The FOUR LADS *Canada, male vocal group (3 Singles: 23 Weeks)*

19 Dec 52 ● **FAITH CAN MOVE MOUNTAINS (re)** *Columbia DB 3154* [1] **7** 3
22 Oct 54 ● **RAIN, RAIN, RAIN** *Philips PB 311* [2] **8** 16
28 Apr 60 **STANDING ON THE CORNER** *Philips PB 1000* **34** 4

[1] Johnnie Ray and The Four Lads [2] Frankie Laine and The Four Lads

4 NON BLONDES *US, female / male vocal (Linda Perry) / instrumental group – leader Linda Perry (1 Album: 18 Weeks, 2 Singles: 19 Weeks)*

19 Jun 93 ● **WHAT'S UP** *Interscope A 8412CD* **2** 17
17 Jul 93 ● BIGGER BETTER FASTER MORE! *Interscope 7567921122* 4 18
16 Oct 93 **SPACEMAN** *Interscope A 8349CD* **53** 2

The 4 OF US *Ireland, male vocal / instrumental group (1 Album: 1 Week, 2 Singles: 6 Weeks)*

27 Feb 93 **SHE HITS ME** *Columbia 6589192* **35** 4
20 Mar 93 MAN ALIVE *Columbia 4723262* 64 1
1 May 93 **I MISS YOU** *Columbia 6591722* **62** 2

The 411 *UK, female vocal group (1 Album: 2 Weeks, 4 Singles: 26 Weeks)*

29 May 04 ● **ON MY KNEES (re)** *Sony Music 6749381* [1] **4** 11
4 Sep 04 ● **DUMB** *Sony / Streetside 6752622* **3** 10
27 Nov 04 **TEARDROPS** *Sony / Streetside 6754812* **23** 5
4 Dec 04 BETWEEN THE SHEETS *Sony Music 5190842* 46 2

[1] The 411 featuring Ghostface Killah

2 / 5 August 1967	9 / 12 August 1967	16 / 19 August 1967	23 / 26 August 1967
ALL YOU NEED IS LOVE The Beatles	**SAN FRANCISCO (BE SURE TO WEAR SOME FLOWERS IN YOUR HAIR)** Scott McKenzie	**SAN FRANCISCO (BE SURE TO WEAR SOME FLOWERS IN YOUR HAIR)** Scott McKenzie	**SAN FRANCISCO (BE SURE TO WEAR SOME FLOWERS IN YOUR HAIR)** Scott McKenzie
SGT. PEPPER'S LONELY HEARTS CLUB BAND The Beatles	**SGT. PEPPER'S LONELY HEARTS CLUB BAND** The Beatles	**SGT. PEPPER'S LONELY HEARTS CLUB BAND** The Beatles	**SGT. PEPPER'S LONELY HEARTS CLUB BAND** The Beatles

KEY
UK No.1 ★ UK Top 10 ● Still on chart + UK entry at No.1 ■
US No.1 ▲ UK million seller £ US million seller $
Singles re-entries are listed as (re), (2re), (3re)... which signifies that the hit re-entered the chart once, twice or three times...
Peak Position / Weeks

The FOUR PENNIES
UK, male vocal (Lionel Morton) / instrumental group (1 Album: 5 Weeks, 6 Singles: 56 Weeks)

Date		Title	Peak	Weeks
16 Jan 64		**DO YOU WANT ME TO (re)** *Philips BF 1296*	47	2
2 Apr 64	★	**JULIET** *Philips BF 1322*	1	15
16 Jul 64		**I FOUND OUT THE HARD WAY** *Philips BF 1349*	14	11
29 Oct 64		**BLACK GIRL** *Philips BF 1366*	20	12
7 Nov 64		TWO SIDES OF FOUR PENNIES *Philips BL 7642*	13	5
7 Oct 65		**UNTIL IT'S TIME FOR YOU TO GO** *Philips BF 1435*	19	11
17 Feb 66		**TROUBLE IS MY MIDDLE NAME** *Philips BF 1469*	32	5

The FOUR PREPS
US, male vocal group (3 Singles: 23 Weeks)

Date		Title	Peak	Weeks
13 Jun 58	●	**BIG MAN (re)** *Capitol CL 14873* $	2	14
26 May 60		**GOT A GIRL (re)** *Capitol CL 15128*	28	7
2 Nov 61		**MORE MONEY FOR YOU AND ME (MEDLEY)** *Capitol CL 15217*	39	2

Tracks on More Money for You and Me (medley): Mr Blue / Alley Oop / Smoke Gets in Your Eyes / In This Whole Wide World / A Worried Man / Tom Dooley / A Teenager in Love. All songs feature new lyrics.

The FOUR SEASONS (313 Top 500)
No.1 US group of the early 1960s: Frankie Valli (v), Bob Gaudio (k/v), Nick Massi (b/v), b. 19 Sep 1935, d. 24 Dec 2000, Tommy DeVito (g/v). Falsetto-voiced Valli's quartet were the first group to score three US No.1s in succession. In 2005, their story was turned into a successful musical, Jersey Boys (9 Albums: 68 Weeks, 18 Singles: 151 Weeks)

Date		Title	Peak	Weeks
4 Oct 62	●	**SHERRY** *Stateside SS 122* ▲ $	8	16
17 Jan 63		**BIG GIRLS DON'T CRY** *Stateside SS 145* ▲ $	13	10
28 Mar 63		**WALK LIKE A MAN** *Stateside SS 169* ▲ $	12	12
27 Jun 63		**AIN'T THAT A SHAME** *Stateside SS 194*	38	3
6 Jul 63		SHERRY *Stateside SL 10033*	20	1
27 Aug 64	●	**RAG DOLL** *Philips BF 1347* [1] ▲ $	2	13
18 Nov 65	●	**LET'S HANG ON** *Philips BF 1439* [1]	4	16
31 Mar 66		**WORKIN' MY WAY BACK TO YOU** *Philips BF 1474* [2]	50	3
2 Jun 66		**OPUS 17 (DON'T YOU WORRY 'BOUT ME)** *Philips BF 1493* [2]	20	9
29 Sep 66		**I'VE GOT YOU UNDER MY SKIN** *Philips BF 1511* [2]	12	11
12 Jan 67		**TELL IT TO THE RAIN** *Philips BF 1538* [2]	37	5
10 Apr 71		EDIZIONE D'ORO *Philips 6640002*	11	7
20 Nov 71		THE BIG ONES *Philips 6336208*	37	1
19 Apr 75	●	**THE NIGHT** *Mowest MW 3024* [3]	7	9
20 Sep 75	●	**WHO LOVES YOU** *Warner Bros. / Curb K 16602*	6	9
31 Jan 76	★	**DECEMBER, 1963 (OH, WHAT A NIGHT)** *Warner Bros. / Curb K 16688* ▲ $	1	10
6 Mar 76		THE FOUR SEASONS STORY *Private Stock DAPS 1001*	20	8
6 Mar 76		WHO LOVES YOU *Warner Bros. K 56179*	12	17
24 Apr 76	●	**SILVER STAR** *Warner Bros. / Curb K 16742*	3	9
20 Nov 76	●	GREATEST HITS *K-Tel NE 942*	4	6
27 Nov 76		**WE CAN WORK IT OUT** *Warner Bros. / Curb K 16845*	34	4
18 Jun 77		**RHAPSODY** *Warner Bros. / Curb K 16932*	37	3
20 Aug 77		**DOWN THE HALL** *Warner Bros. / Curb K 16982*	34	5
21 May 88		THE COLLECTION *Telstar STAR 2320* [1]	38	9
29 Oct 88		**DECEMBER, 1963 (OH, WHAT A NIGHT)** (re-mix) *BR 45277* [3]	49	4
7 Mar 92	●	THE VERY BEST OF FRANKIE VALLI AND THE FOUR SEASONS *PolyGram TV 5131192* [1]	7	15
13 Oct 01		THE DEFINITIVE FRANKIE VALLI AND THE FOUR SEASONS *WSM 8122735552* [1]	26	4

[1] The Four Seasons with the sound of Frankie Valli [2] The Four Seasons with Frankie Valli [3] Frankie Valli and The Four Seasons [1] Frankie Valli and The Four Seasons

The 4-SKINS
UK, male vocal / instrumental group

Date		Title	Peak	Weeks
17 Apr 82		THE GOOD THE BAD AND THE 4-SKINS *Secret SEC 4*	80	4

4 STRINGS (see also MADELYNE)
Holland, male / female production / vocal duo (5 Singles: 15 Weeks)

Date		Title	Peak	Weeks
23 Dec 00		**DAY TIME** *AM:PM 139*	48	3
11 May 02		**(TAKE ME AWAY) INTO THE NIGHT (re)** *Nebula / Virgin CDRD 107*	15	7
14 Sep 02		**DIVING** *Nebula VCRD 108*	38	2
13 Sep 03		**LET IT RAIN** *Nebula NEBCD 049*	49	1
31 Jul 04		**TURN IT AROUND** *Nebula NEBCD 059*	50	2

FOUR TET
UK, male DJ / producer – Keiran Hebden (2 Albums: 2 Weeks)

Date		Title	Peak	Weeks
17 May 03		ROUNDS *Domino WIDCD 126*	60	1
4 Jun 05		EVERYTHING ECSTATIC *Domino WIGCD 154*	59	1

4 THE CAUSE
US, male / female vocal group

Date		Title	Peak	Weeks
10 Oct 98		**STAND BY ME** *RCA 74321622442*	12	9

The FOUR TOPS (62 Top 500)
Unmistakable R&B vocal group from Detroit: Levi Stubbs, Renaldo Benson (d. 2005), Lawrence Payton (d. 1997), Abdul Fakir. The legendary Motown act performed together for a record 44 years (until Payton's death) and were inducted into the Rock and Roll Hall of Fame in 1990 (13 Albums: 256 Weeks, 33 Singles: 318 Weeks)

Date		Title	Peak	Weeks
1 Jul 65		**I CAN'T HELP MYSELF** *Tamla Motown TMG 515* ▲ $	23	9
2 Sep 65		**IT'S THE SAME OLD SONG** *Tamla Motown TMG 528*	34	8
21 Jul 66		**LOVING YOU IS SWEETER THAN EVER** *Tamla Motown TMG 568*	21	12
13 Oct 66	★	**REACH OUT I'LL BE THERE** *Tamla Motown TMG 579* ▲ $	1	16
19 Nov 66	●	FOUR TOPS ON TOP *Tamla Motown TML 11037*	9	23
12 Jan 67	●	**STANDING IN THE SHADOWS OF LOVE** *Tamla Motown TMG 589*	6	8
11 Feb 67	●	FOUR TOPS LIVE! *Tamla Motown STML 11041*	4	72
30 Mar 67	●	**BERNADETTE** *Tamla Motown TMG 601*	8	10
15 Jun 67		**SEVEN ROOMS OF GLOOM** *Tamla Motown TMG 612*	12	9
11 Oct 67		**YOU KEEP RUNNING AWAY** *Tamla Motown TMG 623*	26	7
25 Nov 67	●	REACH OUT *Tamla Motown STML 11056*	4	34
13 Dec 67	●	**WALK AWAY RENEE** *Tamla Motown TMG 634*	3	11
20 Jan 68	★	GREATEST HITS *Tamla Motown STML 11061*	1	67
13 Mar 68	●	**IF I WERE A CARPENTER** *Tamla Motown TMG 647*	7	11
21 Aug 68		**YESTERDAY'S DREAMS** *Tamla Motown TMG 665*	23	15
13 Nov 68		**I'M IN A DIFFERENT WORLD** *Tamla Motown TMG 675*	27	13
8 Feb 69		YESTERDAY'S DREAMS *Tamla Motown STML 11087*	37	1
28 May 69		**WHAT IS A MAN** *Tamla Motown TMG 698*	16	11
27 Sep 69		**DO WHAT YOU GOTTA DO** *Tamla Motown TMG 710*	11	11
21 Mar 70	●	**I CAN'T HELP MYSELF** (re-issue) *Tamla Motown TMG 732*	10	11
30 May 70	●	**IT'S ALL IN THE GAME (re)** *Tamla Motown TMG 736*	5	16
27 Jun 70		STILL WATERS RUN DEEP *Tamla Motown STML 11149*	29	8
3 Oct 70	●	**STILL WATER (LOVE) (re)** *Tamla Motown TMG 752*	10	12
1 May 71		**JUST SEVEN NUMBERS (CAN STRAIGHTEN OUT MY LIFE)** *Tamla Motown TMG 770*	36	5
29 May 71	●	MAGNIFICENT SEVEN *Tamla Motown STML 11179* [1]	6	11
26 Jun 71		**RIVER DEEP MOUNTAIN HIGH** *Tamla Motown TMG 777* [1]	11	10
25 Sep 71	●	**SIMPLE GAME** *Tamla Motown TMG 785*	3	11
20 Nov 71		**YOU GOTTA HAVE LOVE IN YOUR HEART** *Tamla Motown TMG 793* [1]	25	10
27 Nov 71		FOUR TOPS' GREATEST HITS VOLUME 2 *Tamla Motown STML 11195*	25	10
11 Mar 72		**BERNADETTE** (re-issue) *Tamla Motown TMG 803*	23	7
5 Aug 72		**WALK WITH ME TALK WITH ME DARLING** *Tamla Motown TMG 823*	32	6
18 Nov 72		**KEEPER OF THE CASTLE** *Probe PRO 575*	18	9
10 Nov 73		THE FOUR TOPS STORY 1964-72 *Tamla Motown TMSP 11241/2*	35	5
10 Nov 73		**SWEET UNDERSTANDING LOVE** *Probe PRO 604*	29	10
17 Oct 81	●	**WHEN SHE WAS MY GIRL** *Casablanca CAN 1005*	3	10
19 Dec 81		**DON'T WALK AWAY** *Casablanca CAN 1006*	16	11
13 Feb 82		THE BEST OF THE FOUR TOPS *K-Tel NE 1160*	13	13

	30 August / 2 September 1967	6 / 9 September 1967	13 / 16 September 1967	20 / 23 September 1967
UK No.1 SINGLES	SAN FRANCISCO (BE SURE TO WEAR SOME FLOWERS IN YOUR HAIR) Scott McKenzie	THE LAST WALTZ Engelbert Humperdinck	THE LAST WALTZ Engelbert Humperdinck	THE LAST WALTZ Engelbert Humperdinck
UK No.1 ALBUMS	SGT. PEPPER'S LONELY HEARTS CLUB BAND The Beatles	SGT. PEPPER'S LONELY HEARTS CLUB BAND The Beatles	SGT. PEPPER'S LONELY HEARTS CLUB BAND The Beatles	SGT. PEPPER'S LONELY HEARTS CLUB BAND The Beatles

6 Mar 82	**TONIGHT I'M GONNA LOVE YOU ALL OVER** *Casablanca CAN 1008*	43	4
26 Jun 82	**BACK TO SCHOOL AGAIN** *RSO 89*	62	2
23 Jul 88	**REACH OUT I'LL BE THERE** (re-mix) *Motown ZB 41943*	11	9
17 Sep 88	**INDESTRUCTIBLE** *Arista 111717* [2]	55	4
3 Dec 88 ●	**LOCO IN ACAPULCO** *Arista 111850*	7	13
25 Feb 89	**INDESTRUCTIBLE** (re-mix) *Arista 112074* [2]	30	7
8 Dec 90	THEIR GREATEST HITS *Telstar STAR 2437*	47	6
19 Sep 92	THE SINGLES COLLECTION *PolyGram TV 5157102*	11	5
30 Mar 02	AT THEIR VERY BEST – TEMPTATIONS / FOUR TOPS *Universal TV 5830142*	18	1

[1] The Supremes and The Four Tops [2] The Four Tops featuring Smokey Robinson [1] The Supremes and The Four Tops

The original US recording of 'Indestructible' was not issued until after the chart run of the UK-only mix. At Their Very Best – Temptations / Four Tops appeared only in the UK Compilation Chart and was not listed in the standard Top 75.

4TUNE 500 *UK, male / female production group*

16 Aug 03	**DANCING IN THE DARK** *Black Gold BLGD 04CDC 01*	75	1

4 VINI featuring Elisabeth TROY

UK, male vocal / production group and female vocalist

18 May 02	**FOREVER YOUNG** *Botchit & Scarper BOS 2CD 033*	75	1

4CLUBBERS

(see also FUTURE BREEZE) *Germany, male production group*

14 Sep 02	**CHILDREN** *Code Blue BLU 026CD*	45	1

4MANDU *UK, male vocal group (3 Singles: 6 Weeks)*

29 Jul 95	**THIS IS IT** *Final Vinyl 74321291222*	45	3
17 Feb 96	**DO IT FOR LOVE** *Arista 74321343902*	45	2
15 Jun 96	**BABY DON'T GO** *Arista 74321375914*	47	1

The FOURMOST

UK, male vocal / instrumental group (6 Singles: 64 Weeks)

12 Sep 63 ●	**HELLO LITTLE GIRL** *Parlophone R 5056*	9	17
26 Dec 63	**I'M IN LOVE** *Parlophone R 5078*	17	12
23 Apr 64 ●	**A LITTLE LOVING** *Parlophone R 5128*	6	13
13 Aug 64	**HOW CAN I TELL HER** *Parlophone R 5157*	33	4
26 Nov 64	**BABY I NEED YOUR LOVIN'** *Parlophone R 5194*	24	12
9 Dec 65	**GIRLS, GIRLS, GIRLS** *Parlophone R 5379*	33	6

14-18 (see also STOCK AITKEN WATERMAN)

UK, male vocalist – Pete Waterman

1 Nov 75	**GOODBYE-EE** *Magnet MAG 48*	33	4

FOX *UK / US, male / female vocal (Noosha Fox) / instrumental group (1 Album: 8 Weeks, 3 Singles: 29 Weeks)*

15 Feb 75 ●	**ONLY YOU CAN** *GTO GT 8*	3	11
10 May 75	**IMAGINE ME IMAGINE YOU** *GTO GT 21*	15	8
17 May 75 ●	FOX *GTO GTLP 001*	7	8
10 Apr 76 ●	**S-S-S-SINGLE BED** *GTO GT 57*	4	10

Gemma FOX featuring MC LYTE

UK, female vocalist and US, female rapper

8 May 04	**GIRLFRIEND'S STORY** *Polydor 9866362*	38	3

James FOX *UK, male vocalist*

1 May 04	**HOLD ONTO OUR LOVE** *Sony Music 6748732*	13	7

Noosha FOX (see also FOX) *UK, female vocalist*

12 Nov 77	**GEORGINA BAILEY** *GTO GT 106*	31	6

Samantha FOX (see also SOX)

UK, female vocalist (3 Albums: 18 Weeks, 17 Singles: 73 Weeks)

22 Mar 86 ●	**TOUCH ME (I WANT YOUR BODY)** *Jive FOXY 1*	3	10
28 Jun 86 ●	**DO YA DO YA (WANNA PLEASE ME)** *Jive FOXY 2*	10	7
26 Jul 86	TOUCH ME *Jive HIP 39*	17	10
6 Sep 86	**HOLD ON TIGHT** *Jive FOXY 3*	26	5
13 Dec 86	**I'M ALL YOU NEED** *Jive FOXY 4*	41	6
30 May 87 ●	**NOTHING'S GONNA STOP ME NOW** *Jive FOXY 5*	8	9
25 Jul 87	**I SURRENDER (TO THE SPIRIT OF THE NIGHT)** *Jive FOXY 6*	25	7
1 Aug 87	SAMANTHA FOX *Jive HIP 48*	22	6
17 Oct 87	**I PROMISE YOU (GET READY)** *Jive FOXY 7*	58	3
19 Dec 87	**TRUE DEVOTION** *Jive FOXY 8*	62	3
21 May 88	**NAUGHTY GIRLS (NEED LOVE TOO)** *Jive FOXY 9*	31	5
19 Nov 88	**LOVE HOUSE** *Jive FOXY 10*	32	6
28 Jan 89	**I ONLY WANNA BE WITH YOU** *Jive FOXY 11*	16	8
18 Feb 89	I WANNA HAVE SOME FUN *Jive HIP 72*	46	2
17 Jun 89	**I WANNA HAVE SOME FUN** *Jive FOXY 12*	63	2
28 Mar 98	**SANTA MARIA** *All Around the World CDGLOBE 163* [1]	31	2

[1] DJ Milano featuring Samantha Fox

Bruce FOXTON (see also The JAM)

UK, male vocalist (1 Album: 4 Weeks, 3 Singles: 9 Weeks)

30 Jul 83	**FREAK** *Arista BFOX 1*	23	5
29 Oct 83	**THIS IS THE WAY** *Arista BFOX 2*	56	3
21 Apr 84	**IT MAKES ME WONDER** *Arista BFOX 3*	74	1
12 May 84	TOUCH SENSITIVE *Arista 206 251*	68	4

Inez FOXX *US, female vocalist (2 Singles: 8 Weeks)*

23 Jul 64	**HURT BY LOVE** *Sue WI 323*	40	3
19 Feb 69	**MOCKINGBIRD (re)** *United Artists UP 2269* [1]	33	5

[1] Inez and Charlie Foxx

John FOXX

UK, male vocalist – Dennis Leigh (4 Albums: 17 Weeks, 7 Singles: 31 Weeks)

26 Jan 80	**UNDERPASS** *Virgin VS 318*	31	8
2 Feb 80	METAMATIC *Metalbeat V 2146*	18	7
29 Mar 80	**NO-ONE DRIVING (DOUBLE SINGLE)** *Virgin VS 338*	32	4
19 Jul 80	**BURNING CAR** *Virgin VS 360*	35	7
8 Nov 80	**MILES AWAY** *Virgin VS 382*	51	3
29 Aug 81	**EUROPE (AFTER THE RAIN)** *Virgin VS 393*	40	5
3 Oct 81	THE GARDEN *Virgin V 2194*	24	6
2 Jul 83	**ENDLESSLY** *Virgin VS 543*	66	3
17 Sep 83	**YOUR DRESS** *Virgin VS 615*	61	1
8 Oct 83	THE GOLDEN SECTION *Virgin V 2233*	27	3
5 Oct 85	IN MYSTERIOUS WAYS *Virgin V 2355*	85	1

Tracks on No-One Driving (double single): No-One Driving / Glimmer / This City / Mr No.

The FRAGGLES *UK / US, puppets from TV series*

18 Feb 84	**'FRAGGLE ROCK' THEME** *RCA 389*	33	8
21 Apr 84	FRAGGLE ROCK *RCA PL 70221*	38	4

FRAGMA *Germany, male production trio and female vocalists (1 Album: 12 Weeks, 5 Singles: 45 Weeks)*

25 Sep 99	**TOCA ME** *Positiva CDTIV 120*	11	6
22 Apr 00 ★	**TOCA'S MIRACLE (re)** (re-mix) *Positiva CDTIV 128* [1] ■	1	17
13 Jan 01 ●	**EVERYTIME YOU NEED ME** *Positiva CDTIV 147* [2]	3	11
27 Jan 01	TOCA *Positiva 8506770*	19	12
19 May 01 ●	**YOU ARE ALIVE** *Positiva CDTIVS 153*	4	9
8 Dec 01	**SAY THAT YOU'RE HERE** *Illustrious CDILLS 001*	25	2

[1] Vocals by Co Co [2] Fragma featuring Maria Rubia

Roddy FRAME (see also AZTEC CAMERA)

UK, male vocalist / guitarist

19 Sep 98	**REASON FOR LIVING** *Independiente ISOM 18MS*	45	2
3 Oct 98	THE NORTH STAR *Independiente ISOM 7CD*	55	1

27 / 30 September 1967	4 / 7 October 1967	11 / 14 October 1967	18 / 21 October 1967
THE LAST WALTZ Engelbert Humperdinck	**THE LAST WALTZ** Engelbert Humperdinck	**(THE NIGHT THE LIGHTS WENT OUT IN) MASSACHUSETTS** The Bee Gees	**(THE NIGHT THE LIGHTS WENT OUT IN) MASSACHUSETTS** The Bee Gees
SGT. PEPPER'S LONELY HEARTS CLUB BAND The Beatles	**SGT. PEPPER'S LONELY HEARTS CLUB BAND** The Beatles	**SGT. PEPPER'S LONELY HEARTS CLUB BAND** The Beatles	**SGT. PEPPER'S LONELY HEARTS CLUB BAND** The Beatles

KEY UK No.1 ★ UK Top 10 ● Still on chart + UK entry at No.1 ■ US No.1 ▲ UK million seller £ US million seller $
Singles re-entries are listed as (re), (2re), (3re)... which signifies that the hit re-entered the chart once, twice or three times...
Peak Position / Weeks

Peter FRAMPTON (see also The HERD; HUMBLE PIE)

UK, male vocalist (2 Albums: 49 Weeks, 4 Singles: 24 Weeks)

Date		Title	Peak	Weeks
1 May 76	●	SHOW ME THE WAY *A&M AMS 7218*	10	12
22 May 76	●	FRAMPTON COMES ALIVE! *A&M AMLM 63703* ▲	6	39
11 Sep 76		BABY I LOVE YOUR WAY *A&M AMS 7246*	43	5
6 Nov 76		DO YOU FEEL LIKE WE DO *A&M AMS 7260*	39	4
18 Jun 77		I'M IN YOU *A&M AMLK 64039*	19	10
23 Jul 77		I'M IN YOU *A&M AMS 7298*	41	3

Connie FRANCIS (228 Top 500)

The original Italian-American queen of pop, b. Concetta Franconero, 12 Dec 1938, New Jersey, US. The most successful international female vocalist of the 1950s and 1960s, the first female teenager to register a UK No.1 single and the first female solo artist to top the UK albums chart (4 Albums: 31 Weeks, 24 Singles: 244 Weeks)

Date		Title	Peak	Weeks
4 Apr 58	★	WHO'S SORRY NOW *MGM 975* $	1	25
27 Jun 58		I'M SORRY I MADE YOU CRY *MGM 982*	11	10
22 Aug 58	★	CAROLINA MOON / STUPID CUPID *MGM 985*	1	19
31 Oct 58		I'LL GET BY *MGM 993*	19	6
21 Nov 58		FALLIN' *MGM 993*	20	5
26 Dec 58		YOU ALWAYS HURT THE ONE YOU LOVE *MGM 998*	13	7
13 Feb 59	●	MY HAPPINESS (re) *MGM 1001* $	4	15
3 Jul 59	●	LIPSTICK ON YOUR COLLAR *MGM 1018* $	3	16
11 Sep 59		PLENTY GOOD LOVIN' *MGM 1036*	18	6
4 Dec 59		AMONG MY SOUVENIRS *MGM 1046* $	11	10
17 Mar 60		VALENTINO *MGM 1060*	27	8
26 Mar 60		ROCK 'N' ROLL MILLION SELLERS *MGM C 804*	12	1
19 May 60	●	MAMA / ROBOT MAN *MGM 1076* $	2	19
18 Aug 60	●	EVERYBODY'S SOMEBODY'S FOOL *MGM 1086* ▲ $	5	13
3 Nov 60	●	MY HEART HAS A MIND OF ITS OWN *MGM 1100* ▲ $	3	15
12 Jan 61		MANY TEARS AGO *MGM 1111* $	12	9
11 Feb 61		CONNIE'S GREATEST HITS *MGM C 831*	16	3
16 Mar 61	●	WHERE THE BOYS ARE / BABY ROO *MGM 1121* $	5	14
15 Jun 61		BREAKIN' IN A BRAND NEW BROKEN HEART *MGM 1136*	12	11
14 Sep 61	●	TOGETHER *MGM 1138* $	6	11
14 Dec 61		BABY'S FIRST CHRISTMAS *MGM 1145*	30	4
26 Apr 62		DON'T BREAK THE HEART THAT LOVES YOU *MGM 1157* ▲ $	39	3
2 Aug 62	●	VACATION *MGM 1165*	10	9
20 Dec 62		I'M GONNA BE WARM THIS WINTER *MGM 1185*	48	1
10 Jun 65		MY CHILD *MGM 1271*	26	6
20 Jan 66		JEALOUS HEART *MGM 1293*	44	2
18 Jun 77	★	20 ALL TIME GREATS *Polydor 2391 290*	1	22
24 Apr 93		THE SINGLES COLLECTION *PolyGram TV 5191312*	12	5

'Baby Roo' listed with 'Where the Boys Are' for first eight weeks only.

Jill FRANCIS *UK, female vocalist*

Date		Title	Peak	Weeks
3 Jul 93		MAKE LOVE TO ME *Glady Wax GW 003CD*	70	1

Claude FRANÇOIS

France (b. Egypt), male vocalist, b. 1 Feb 1939, d. 11 Mar 1978

Date		Title	Peak	Weeks
10 Jan 76		TEARS ON THE TELEPHONE *Bradley's BRAD 7528*	35	4

Kathy Barnet is the uncredited vocalist.

The FRANK AND WALTERS *Ireland, male vocal / instrumental group (1 Album: 1 Week, 4 Singles: 13 Weeks)*

Date		Title	Peak	Weeks
21 Mar 92		HAPPY BUSMAN *Setanta HOO 2*	49	2
12 Sep 92		THIS IS NOT A SONG *Setanta HOO 3*	46	3
7 Nov 92		TRAINS BOATS AND PLANES *Setanta 8283692*	36	1
9 Jan 93		AFTER ALL *Setanta HOOCD 4*	11	5
17 Apr 93		FASHION CRISIS HITS NEW YORK *Setanta HOOCD 5*	42	3

FRANKE *UK, male vocalist – Franke Pharoah (2 Singles: 3 Weeks)*

Date		Title	Peak	Weeks
7 Nov 92		UNDERSTAND THIS GROOVE *China WOK 2028*	60	2
21 May 94		LOVE COME HOME *Triangle BLUESCD 001* [1]	73	1

[1] Our Tribe with Franke Pharoah and Kristine W

FRANKEE *US, female vocalist – Nicole Francine Aiello (1 Album: 2 Weeks, 2 Singles: 19 Weeks)*

Date		Title	Peak	Weeks
1 May 04		F.U.R.B. – F U RIGHT BACK (import) *All Around the World 560342CD*	43	3
22 May 04	★	F.U.R.B. – F U RIGHT BACK *All Around the World CDGLOBE 355* ■	1	16
19 Jun 04		THE GOOD, THE BAD, THE UGLY *Universal TV 9867000*	51	2

FRANKIE GOES TO HOLLYWOOD (275 Top 500)

Fiercely marketed, controversial and regularly re-mixed Merseyside-based quintet fronted by Holly Johnson, b. 9 Feb 1960, Sudan. First act since Gerry and the Pacemakers to hit No.1 with initial three releases. During July 1984, 'Two Tribes' and 'Relax' held the top two places in the chart. Total UK single sales: 5,008,067. Best-selling single: 'Relax' 1,910,000 (4 Albums: 95 Weeks, 14 Singles: 147 Weeks)

Date		Title	Peak	Weeks
26 Nov 83	★	RELAX (re) *ZTT ZTAS 1* £	1	52
16 Jun 84	★	TWO TRIBES (re) *ZTT ZTAS 3* ■ £	1	21
10 Nov 84	★	WELCOME TO THE PLEASUREDOME *ZTT ZTTIQ 1* ■	1	66
1 Dec 84	★	THE POWER OF LOVE (re) *ZTT ZTAS 5*	1	12
30 Mar 85	●	WELCOME TO THE PLEASURE DOME *ZTT ZTAS 7*	2	11
6 Sep 86	●	RAGE HARD *ZTT ZTAS 22*	4	7
1 Nov 86	●	LIVERPOOL *ZTT ZTTIQ 8*	5	13
22 Nov 86		WARRIORS (OF THE WASTELAND) *ZTT ZTAS 25*	19	8
7 Mar 87		WATCHING THE WILDLIFE *ZTT ZTAS 26*	28	6
2 Oct 93	●	RELAX (re-issue) *ZTT FGTH 1CD*	5	7
30 Oct 93	●	BANG! – THE GREATEST HITS OF FRANKIE GOES TO HOLLYWOOD *ZTT 4509939122*	4	15
20 Nov 93		WELCOME TO THE PLEASURE DOME (re-mix) *ZTT FGTH 2CD*	18	3
18 Dec 93	●	THE POWER OF LOVE (re-issue) *ZTT FGTH 3CD*	10	7
26 Feb 94		TWO TRIBES (re-mix) *ZTT FGTH 4CD*	16	3
1 Jul 00	●	THE POWER OF LOVE (re-mix) *ZTT ZTT 150CD*	6	6
9 Sep 00		TWO TRIBES (2nd re-mix) *ZTT ZTT 154CD*	17	3
7 Oct 00		MAXIMUM JOY *ZTT ZTT 165CD*	54	1
18 Nov 00		WELCOME TO THE PLEASURE DOME (re-mix) *ZTT 166CD*	45	1

Aretha FRANKLIN (241 Top 500)

The 'Queen of Soul Music', b. 25 Mar 1942, Tennessee, US. With six decades of recording behind her, this legendary gospel-influenced vocalist has won countless awards, including induction into the UK Music Hall of Fame in 2005, and amassed more R&B hits than any other female in her homeland (11 Albums: 85 Weeks, 29 Singles: 182 Weeks)

Date		Title	Peak	Weeks
8 Jun 67	●	RESPECT *Atlantic 584 115* ▲ $	10	14
12 Aug 67		I NEVER LOVED A MAN THE WAY I LOVE YOU *Atlantic 587006*	36	2
23 Aug 67		BABY I LOVE YOU *Atlantic 584 127* $	39	4
20 Dec 67		CHAIN OF FOOLS / SATISFACTION (re) *Atlantic 584 157* $	37	7
13 Mar 68		SINCE YOU'VE BEEN GONE (SWEET SWEET BABY) *Atlantic 584 172* $	47	1
13 Apr 68		LADY SOUL *Atlantic 588099*	25	18
22 May 68		THINK *Atlantic 584 186* $	26	9
7 Aug 68	●	I SAY A LITTLE PRAYER *Atlantic 584 206* $	4	14
14 Sep 68	●	ARETHA NOW *Atlantic 588114*	6	11
22 Aug 70		DON'T PLAY THAT SONG *Atlantic 2091 027* $	13	11
2 Oct 71		SPANISH HARLEM *Atlantic 2091 138* $	14	9
8 Sep 73		ANGEL *Atlantic K 10346*	37	5
16 Feb 74		UNTIL YOU COME BACK TO ME (THAT'S WHAT I'M GONNA DO) *Atlantic K 10399* $	26	8
6 Dec 80		WHAT A FOOL BELIEVES *Arista ARIST 377*	46	7
19 Sep 81		LOVE ALL THE HURT AWAY *Arista ARIST 428* [1]	49	3
4 Sep 82		JUMP TO IT *Arista ARIST 479*	42	5
23 Jul 83		GET IT RIGHT *Arista ARIST 537*	74	2
13 Jul 85		FREEWAY OF LOVE (re) *Arista ARIST 624*	51	6
2 Nov 85	●	SISTERS ARE DOIN' IT FOR THEMSELVES *RCA PB 40339* [2]	9	11

25 / 28 October 1967	1 / 4 November 1967	8 / 11 November 1967	15 / 18 November 1967
UK No.1 SINGLES			
(THE NIGHT THE LIGHTS WENT OUT IN) MASSACHUSETTS The Bee Gees	**(THE NIGHT THE LIGHTS WENT OUT IN) MASSACHUSETTS** The Bee Gees	**BABY NOW THAT I'VE FOUND YOU** The Foundations	**BABY NOW THAT I'VE FOUND YOU** The Foundations
UK No.1 ALBUMS			
SGT. PEPPER'S LONELY HEARTS CLUB BAND The Beatles	**SGT. PEPPER'S LONELY HEARTS CLUB BAND** The Beatles	**SGT. PEPPER'S LONELY HEARTS CLUB BAND** The Beatles	**THE SOUND OF MUSIC** Soundtrack

23 Nov 85 **WHO'S ZOOMIN' WHO** *Arista ARIST 633* 11 14
18 Jan 86 WHO'S ZOOMIN' WHO? *Arista 2072 02* 49 12
22 Feb 86 **ANOTHER NIGHT** *Arista ARIST 657* 54 6
24 May 86 THE FIRST LADY OF SOUL *Stylus SMR 8506* 89 1
25 Oct 86 **JUMPIN' JACK FLASH** *Arista ARIST 678* 58 3
8 Nov 86 ARETHA *Arista 208 020* 51 13
31 Jan 87 ★ **I KNEW YOU WERE WAITING (FOR ME)** *Epic DUET 1* [3] ▲ 1 9
14 Mar 87 **JIMMY LEE** *Arista RIS 6* 46 4
6 May 89 **THROUGH THE STORM** *Arista 112185* [4] 41 3
3 Jun 89 THROUGH THE STORM *Arista 209 842* 46 1
9 Sep 89 **IT ISN'T, IT WASN'T, IT AIN'T NEVER GONNA BE** *Arista 112545* [5] 29 5
7 Apr 90 **THINK** (re-recording) *East West A 7951* 31 2
27 Jul 91 **EVERYDAY PEOPLE** *Arista 114420* 69 1
12 Feb 94 ● **A DEEPER LOVE** *Arista 74321187022* 5 7
19 Mar 94 GREATEST HITS 1980-1994 *Arista 74321162022* 27 3
25 Jun 94 **WILLING TO FORGIVE** *Arista 74321213342* 17 7
29 Oct 94 QUEEN OF SOUL – THE VERY BEST OF ARETHA FRANKLIN *Atlantic 8122713962* 20 5
9 May 98 **A ROSE IS STILL A ROSE** *Arista 74321569742* 22 4
26 Sep 98 **HERE WE GO AGAIN** *Arista 74321612742* 68 1
21 Nov 98 GREATEST HITS *Global Television RADCD 110* 38 10
15 Jun 02 RESPECT – THE VERY BEST OF ARETHA FRANKLIN *BMG TV / WSM 927470542* 15 9

[1] Aretha Franklin and George Benson [2] Eurythmics and Aretha Franklin
[3] Aretha Franklin and George Michael [4] Aretha Franklin and Elton John
[5] Aretha Franklin and Whitney Houston

'Think' (7 Apr 1990) was the flip side of 'Everybody Needs Somebody to Love' by The Blues Brothers and was listed for the first two weeks of that record's run.

Erma FRANKLIN *US, female vocalist, b. 13 Mar 1938, d. 7 Sep 2002*

10 Oct 92 ● **(TAKE A LITTLE) PIECE OF MY HEART** *Epic 6583847* 9 10

Rodney FRANKLIN *US, male pianist*

19 Apr 80 ● **THE GROOVE** *CBS 8529* 7 9
24 May 80 YOU'LL NEVER KNOW *CBS 83812* 64 2

Chevelle FRANKLYN / BEENIE MAN *Jamaica, female / male vocalists*

20 Sep 97 **DANCEHALL QUEEN** *Island Jamaica IJCD 2018* 70 1

FRANTIQUE *US, female vocal group*

11 Aug 79 ● **STRUT YOUR FUNKY STUFF** *Philadelphia Int. PIR 7728* 10 12

FRANZ FERDINAND *UK, male vocal (Alexander Kapranos) / instrumental group (2 Albums: 86 Weeks, 6 Singles: 35 Weeks)*

20 Sep 03 **DARTS OF PLEASURE** *Domino RUG 164CD* 44 1
21 Jan 04 ● **TAKE ME OUT** *Domino RUG 172CD* 3 9
21 Feb 04 ● FRANZ FERDINAND *Domino Recordings WIGCD 136X* 3 74
1 May 04 ● **MATINEE** *Domino RUG 176CD* 8 6
28 Aug 04 **MICHAEL** *Domino RUG 184CD1* 17 4
1 Oct 05 ● **DO YOU WANT TO** *Domino RUG 211CDX* 4 12
15 Oct 05 ★ YOU COULD HAVE IT SO MUCH BETTER *Domino Recordings WIGCD 161* ■ 1 12+
17 Dec 05 **WALK AWAY** *Domino RUG 215CD* 13 3+

FRASH *UK, male vocal / instrumental group*

18 Feb 95 **HERE I GO AGAIN** *PWL International FLIPCD 1* 69 1

FRAZIER CHORUS *UK, male / female vocal / instrumental group (2 Albums: 2 Weeks, 6 Singles: 14 Weeks)*

4 Feb 89 **DREAM KITCHEN** *Virgin VS 1145* 57 3
15 Apr 89 **TYPICAL!** *Virgin VS 1174* 53 2
20 May 89 SUE *Virgin V 2578* 56 1
15 Jul 89 **SLOPPY HEART** *Virgin VS 1192* 73 1
9 Jun 90 **CLOUD 8** *Virgin VS 1252* 52 3
25 Aug 90 **NOTHING** *Virgin VS 1284* 51 3
16 Feb 91 **WALKING ON AIR** *Virgin VS 1330* 60 2
16 Mar 91 RAY *Virgin VFC 2654* 66 1

FREAK OF NATURE *US / Denmark, male vocal / instrumental group*

1 Oct 94 GATHERING OF FREAKS *Music for Nations CDMFN 169* 66 1

FREAKPOWER (see also BEATS INTERNATIONAL; Norman COOK; FATBOY SLIM; The HOUSEMARTINS; MIGHTY DUB KATZ; PIZZAMAN; URBAN ALL STARS) *UK / Canada, male vocal / instrumental group (1 Album: 5 Weeks, 5 Singles: 20 Weeks)*

16 Oct 93 **TURN ON TUNE IN COP OUT** *Fourth & Broadway BRCD 284* [1] 29 5
26 Feb 94 **RUSH** *Fourth & Broadway BRCD 291* 62 2
18 Mar 95 ● **TURN ON TUNE IN COP OUT** (re-issue) *Fourth & Broadway BRCD 317* 3 9
15 Apr 95 DRIVE-THRU BOOTY *Fourth & Broadway BRCDX 606* [1] 11 5
8 Jun 96 **NEW DIRECTION** *Fourth & Broadway BRCD 331* 60 1
9 May 98 **NO WAY** *Deconstruction 74321578572* 29 3

[1] Freak Power [1] Freak Power

FREAKY REALISTIC *UK / Japan, male / female vocal / instrumental group (2 Singles: 3 Weeks)*

3 Apr 93 **KOOCHIE RYDER** *Frealism FRECD 2* 52 2
3 Jul 93 **LEONARD NIMOY** *Frealism FRECD 3* 71 1

FREAKYMAN (see also DE BOS) *Holland, male producer – Andre Van Den Bosch*

27 Sep 97 **DISCOBUG '97** *Xtravaganza 0091285 EXT* 68 1

Stan FREBERG *US, male vocalist / comedian (3 Singles: 5 Weeks)*

19 Nov 54 **SH-BOOM** *Capitol CL 14187* [1] 15 2
27 Jul 56 **ROCK ISLAND LINE / HEARTBREAK HOTEL (re)** *Capitol CL 14608* [2] 24 2
12 May 60 **THE OLD PAYOLA ROLL BLUES** *Capitol CL 15122* [3] 40 1

[1] Stan Freberg with the Toads [2] Stan Freberg and his Sniffle Group
[3] Stan Freberg with Jesse White

FRED & ROXY *UK, female vocal duo – Phaedra and Roxanna Aslami*

5 Feb 00 **SOMETHING FOR THE WEEKEND** *Echo ECSCD 81* 36 2

John FRED and The PLAYBOY BAND *US, male vocal (John Fred Gourrier, d. 2005) / instrumental group*

3 Jan 68 ● **JUDY IN DISGUISE (WITH GLASSES)** *Pye International 7N 25442* ▲ $ 3 12

FREDDIE and The DREAMERS *UK, male vocal (Freddie Garrity) / instrumental group (1 Album: 26 Weeks, 9 Singles: 85 Weeks)*

9 May 63 ● **IF YOU GOTTA MAKE A FOOL OF SOMEBODY** *Columbia DB 7032* 3 14
8 Aug 63 ● **I'M TELLING YOU NOW** *Columbia DB 7086* ▲ $ 2 11
7 Nov 63 ● **YOU WERE MADE FOR ME** *Columbia DB 7147* 3 15
9 Nov 63 ● FREDDIE AND THE DREAMERS *Columbia 33SX 1577* 4 26
20 Feb 64 **OVER YOU** *Columbia DB 7214* 13 11
14 May 64 **I LOVE YOU BABY** *Columbia DB 7286* 16 8
16 Jul 64 **JUST FOR YOU** *Columbia DB 7322* 41 3
5 Nov 64 ● **I UNDERSTAND** *Columbia DB 7381* 5 15
22 Apr 65 **A LITTLE YOU** *Columbia DB 7526* 26 5
4 Nov 65 **THOU SHALT NOT STEAL** *Columbia DB 7720* 44 3

Dee FREDRIX *UK, female vocalist (2 Singles: 5 Weeks)*

27 Feb 93 **AND SO I WILL WAIT FOR YOU** *East West YZ 725CD* 56 4
3 Jul 93 **DIRTY MONEY** *East West YZ 750CD* 74 1

22 / 25 November 1967	29 November / 2 December 1967	6 / 9 December 1967	13 / 16 December 1967
LET THE HEARTACHES BEGIN Long John Baldry	**LET THE HEARTACHES BEGIN** Long John Baldry	**HELLO, GOODBYE** The Beatles	**HELLO, GOODBYE** The Beatles
SGT. PEPPER'S LONELY HEARTS CLUB BAND The Beatles	**THE SOUND OF MUSIC** Soundtrack	**THE SOUND OF MUSIC** Soundtrack	**THE SOUND OF MUSIC** Soundtrack

KEY UK No.1 ★ UK Top 10 ● Still on chart + UK entry at No.1 ■ US No.1 ▲ UK million seller £ US million seller $
Singles re-entries are listed as (re), (2re), (3re)... which signifies that the hit re-entered the chart once, twice or three times...

Peak Position / Weeks

FREE (see also BAD COMPANY) *UK, male vocal (Paul Rodgers) / instrumental group (7 Albums: 63 Weeks, 6 Singles: 75 Weeks)*

6 Jun 70 ● **ALL RIGHT NOW (re)** *Island WIP 6082* 2 25
11 Jul 70 ● FIRE AND WATER *Island ILPS 9120* 2 18
23 Jan 71 HIGHWAY *Island ILPS 9138* 41 2
1 May 71 ● **MY BROTHER JAKE** *Island WIP 6100* 4 11
26 Jun 71 ● FREE LIVE! *Island ILPS 9160* 4 12
27 May 72 **LITTLE BIT OF LOVE** *Island WIP 6129* 13 10
17 Jun 72 ● FREE AT LAST *Island ILPS 9192* 9 9
13 Jan 73 ● **WISHING WELL** *Island WIP 6146* 7 10
3 Feb 73 ● HEARTBREAKER *Island ILPS 9217* 9 7
16 Mar 74 ● THE FREE STORY *Island ISLD 4* 2 6
18 Feb 78 **FREE (EP) (re)** *Island IEP 6* 11 10
9 Feb 91 ● **ALL RIGHT NOW** (re-mix) *Island IS 486* 8 9
2 Mar 91 ● THE BEST OF FREE – ALL RIGHT NOW *Island ILPTV 2* 9 9

'All Right Now' re-entry peaked at No.15 in Jul 1973 and the 'Free' (EP) re-entered the chart in Oct 1982, peaking at No.57. Tracks on the Free (EP): All Right Now (long version) / My Brother Jake (re-issue) / Wishing Well (re-issue).

The FREE ASSOCIATION
UK, male / female vocal / instrumental group (2 Singles: 2 Weeks)

12 Apr 03 **EVERYBODY KNOWS** *Ramp RAMP 001CDS* 74 1
13 Sep 03 **SUGARMAN** *13 Amp 9809471* 53 1

FREE SPIRIT *UK, male / female vocal duo*

13 May 95 **NO MORE RAINY DAYS** *Columbia 6612822* 68 1

FREE THE SPIRIT *UK, male instrumental duo – Nick Magnus and Rono Tse (3 Albums: 42 Weeks)*

4 Feb 95 ● PAN PIPE MOODS *PolyGram TV 5271972* 2 26
4 Nov 95 PAN PIPE MOODS TWO *PolyGram TV 5293952* 18 11
25 May 96 PAN PIPE MOODS IN PARADISE *PolyGram TV 5319612* 26 5

FREEEZ *UK, male vocal (John Rocca) / instrumental group (2 Albums: 18 Weeks, 7 Singles: 48 Weeks)*

7 Jun 80 **KEEP IN TOUCH** *Calibre CAB 103* 49 3
7 Feb 81 SOUTHERN FREEEZ *Beggars Banquet BEGA 22* 17 15
7 Feb 81 ● **SOUTHERN FREEEZ** *Beggars Banquet BEG 51* [1] 8 11
18 Apr 81 **FLYING HIGH** *Beggars Banquet BEG 55* 35 5
18 Jun 83 ● **I.O.U.** *Beggars Banquet BEG 96* 2 15
1 Oct 83 **POP GOES MY LOVE** *Beggars Banquet BEG 98* 26 6
22 Oct 83 GONNA GET YOU *Beggars Banquet BEGA 48* 46 3
17 Jan 87 **I.O.U.** (re-mix) *Citybeat CBE 709* [2] 23 6
30 May 87 **SOUTHERN FREEEZ** (re-mix) *Total Control TOCO 14* [1] 63 2

[1] Freeez featuring Ingrid Mansfield Allman [2] Freeez featuring John Rocca

FREEFALL featuring Jan JOHNSTON
UK / Australia, male DJ / production duo – Alan Bremner and Anthony Pappalardo and UK, female vocalist (3 Singles: 5 Weeks)

28 Nov 98 **SKYDIVE** *Stress CDSTR 89* [1] 75 1
22 Jul 00 **SKYDIVE** (re-mix) *Renaissance Recordings RENCDS 002* [1] 43 2
8 Sep 01 **SKYDIVE (I FEEL WONDERFUL)** (2nd re-mix) *Incentive CENT 22CDS* [1] 35 2

[1] Freefall featuring Jan Johnston

FREEFALL featuring PSYCHOTROPIC
UK / US, male instrumental / production group

27 Jul 91 **FEEL SURREAL** *ffrr FX 160* 63 1

FREEFALLER NEW
UK, male vocal (David Oliver) / instrumental group (3 Singles: 8 Weeks)

5 Feb 05 ● **DO THIS! DO THAT!** *Velocity VELOCD 2* 8 5
14 May 05 **GOOD ENOUGH FOR YOU** *Velocity VELOCD 4* 21 2
3 Dec 05 **SHE'S MY EVERYTHING / BASKET CASE** *Velocity VELOCDX 05* 36 1

FREELAND *UK / Chile, male / female production / vocal / instrumental group (2 Singles: 3 Weeks)*

13 Sep 03 **WE WANT YOUR SOUL** *Maximise Profit FREECDS 01* 35 2
7 Feb 04 **SUPERNATURAL THING** *Marine Parade MAPACDS 024* 65 1

Claire FREELAND *UK, female vocalist*

21 Jul 01 **FREE** *Statuesque CDSTATU 1* 44 1

FREELOADERS featuring The REAL THING NEW (see also N-Trance) *UK, male production duo - Dale Longworth and Kevin O'Toole*

23 Apr 05 ● **SO MUCH LOVE TO GIVE** *All Around the World CDGLOBE 412* 9 7

FREEMASONS featuring Amanda WILSON NEW
(see also PHATS & SMALL) *UK, male production duo – Russell Small and James Wiltshire and female vocalist*

3 Sep 05 **LOVE ON MY MIND** *Loaded LOAD 108CD* 11 5

FREESTYLERS
UK, male instrumental / vocal group (1 Album: 3 Weeks, 6 Singles: 11 Weeks)

7 Feb 98 **B-BOY STANCE** *Freskanova FND 7* [1] 23 3
15 Aug 98 WE ROCK HARD *Freskanova FNTCD 4* 33 3
14 Nov 98 **WARNING** *Freskanova FND 14* [2] 68 1
24 Jul 99 **HERE WE GO** *Freskanova FND 19* 45 1
20 Mar 04 **GET A LIFE** *Against the Grain ATG 008R* 66 1
26 Jun 04 **PUSH UP** *Against the Grain ATG 009CD* 22 4
12 Feb 05 **BOOM BLAST** *Against the Grain ATG 010* [3] 75 1

[1] Freestylers featuring Tenor Fly [2] Freestylers featuring Navigator
[3] Freestylers featuring Million Dan

FREHLEY'S COMET
(see also KISS) *US, male vocal / instrumental group*

18 Jun 88 SECOND SIGHTING *Atlantic 781862 1* 79 1

FREIHEIT *Germany, male vocal / instrumental group*

17 Dec 88 **KEEPING THE DREAM ALIVE** *CBS 652989 7* 14 9

Nicki FRENCH *UK, female vocalist (4 Singles: 18 Weeks)*

15 Oct 94 ● **TOTAL ECLIPSE OF THE HEART (re)** *Bags of Fun BAGSCD 1* 5 13
22 Apr 95 **FOR ALL WE KNOW** *Bags of Fun BAGSCD 4* 42 2
15 Jul 95 **DID YOU EVER REALLY LOVE ME** *Love This LUVTHISCD 2* 55 1
27 May 00 **DON'T PLAY THAT SONG AGAIN** *RCA 74321764572* 34 2

'Total Eclipse of the Heart' peaked at No.5 on re-entry in Jan 1995.

FRENCH AFFAIR *France, male production duo and female vocalist*

16 Sep 00 **MY HEART GOES BOOM** *Arista 74321780562* 44 3

Freddy FRESH
US, male producer – Frederick Schmid (2 Singles: 3 Weeks)

1 May 99 **BADDER BADDER SCHWING** *Eye Q EYEUK 040CD* [1] 34 2
31 Jul 99 **WHAT IT IS** *Eye Q EYEUK 043CD* 63 1

[1] Freddy Fresh featuring Fatboy Slim

FRESH BC (see also BAD COMPANY; DJ FRESH)
UK, male production group (4 Singles: 3 Weeks)

25 Oct 03 **SIGNAL / BIG LOVE** *Ram RAMM 46* 58 1

18 Sep 04 **COLOSSUS / HOODED** *Ram RAMM 51* 74 1
25 Dec 04 **CAPTURE THE FLAG** *Ramm RAMM 53* [1] 70 1

[1] Fresh

Doug E FRESH and The GET FRESH CREW
US, male rapper – Douglas Davis and DJ group

9 Nov 85 ● **THE SHOW** *Cooltempo COOL 116* 7 11

FRESH 4 featuring Lizz E
UK, male DJ / production group and female vocalist

7 Oct 89 ● **WISHING ON A STAR** *10 TEN 287* 10 9

The FRESHIES *UK, male vocal / instrumental group*

14 Feb 81 **I'M IN LOVE WITH THE GIRL ON A CERTAIN MANCHESTER MEGASTORE CHECKOUT DESK** *MCA 670* 54 3

Matt FRETTON *UK, male vocalist*

11 Jun 83 **IT'S SO HIGH** *Chrysalis MATT 1* 50 5

Stephen FRETWELL NEW *UK, male vocalist / guitarist*

30 Jul 05 MAGPIE *Fiction 9868907* 27 6
30 Jul 05 **EMILY** *Fiction 9871977* 42 4

FREUR *UK, male vocal / instrumental group*

23 Apr 83 **DOOT DOOT** *CBS A 3141* 59 4

Glenn FREY (see also EAGLES)
US, male vocalist (1 Album: 9 Weeks, 2 Singles: 20 Weeks)

2 Mar 85 **THE HEAT IS ON** *MCA MCA 941* 12 12
22 Jun 85 **SMUGGLER'S BLUES** *BBC RESL 170* 22 8
6 Jul 85 THE ALLNIGHTER *MCA MCF 3277* 31 9

FRIDA (see also ABBA) *Norway, female vocalist – Anni-Frid Lyngstad (2 Albums: 8 Weeks, 2 Singles: 12 Weeks)*

21 Aug 82 **I KNOW THERE'S SOMETHING GOING ON** *Epic EPC A 2603* 43 7
18 Sep 82 SOMETHING'S GOING ON *Epic EPC 85966* 18 7
17 Dec 83 **TIME** *Epic A 3983* [1] 45 5
20 Oct 84 SHINE *Epic EPC 26178* 67 1

[1] Frida and B A Robertson

FRIDAY HILL NEW (see also BLAZIN' SQUAD) *UK, male vocal / rap trio*

22 Oct 05 ● **BABY GOODBYE** *Longside LONG 1CD* 5 8

Ralph FRIDGE *Germany, male producer – Ralf Fritsch (2 Singles: 4 Weeks)*

24 Apr 99 **PARADISE** *Additive 12AD 036* 68 1
8 Apr 00 **ANGEL** *Incentive CENT 6CDS* 20 3

Dean FRIEDMAN
US, male vocalist / keyboard player (1 Album: 14 Weeks, 3 Singles: 22 Weeks)

3 Jun 78 **WOMAN OF MINE** *Lifesong LS 401* 52 5
23 Sep 78 ● **LUCKY STARS** *Lifesong LS 402* 3 10
21 Oct 78 WELL WELL SAID THE ROCKING CHAIR *Lifesong LSLP 6019* 21 14
18 Nov 78 **LYDIA** *Lifesong LS 403* 31 7

'Lucky Stars' features uncredited vocalist Denise Marsa.

FRIENDS AGAIN *UK, male vocal / instrumental group*

4 Aug 84 **THE FRIENDS AGAIN EP** *Mercury FA 1* 59 3

Tracks on The Friends Again EP: Lullaby on Board / Wand You Wave / Thank You for Being an Angel.

FRIENDS OF MATTHEW *UK, male / female vocal / instrumental group*

10 Jul 99 **OUT THERE** *Serious SERR 007CD* 61 1

FRIGID VINEGAR *UK, male rap / production duo*

21 Aug 99 **DOGMONAUT 2000 (IS THERE ANYONE OUT THERE?)** *Gut CDGUT 27* 53 1

FRIJID PINK *US, male vocal (Kelly Green) / instrumental group*

28 Mar 70 ● **THE HOUSE OF THE RISING SUN** *Deram DMR 288* $ 4 16

Robert FRIPP
(see also KING CRIMSON) *UK, male guitarist (2 Albums: 3 Weeks)*

12 May 79 EXPOSURE *Polydor EGLP 101* 71 1
17 Jul 93 THE FIRST DAY *Virgin CDVX 2712* [1] 21 2

[1] David Sylvian and Robert Fripp

Jane FROMAN
US, female vocalist – Ellen Froman, b. 10 Nov 1907, d. 22 Apr 1980

17 Jun 55 **I WONDER** *Capitol CL 14254* 14 4

FRONT 242 *Belgium / US, male vocal / instrumental group (3 Albums: 3 Weeks, 1 Single: 1 Week)*

2 Feb 91 TYRANNY FOR YOU *RRE RRE 011* 49 1
1 May 93 **RELIGION** *RRE RRE 106CD* 46 1
22 May 93 06:21:03:11 UP EVIL *RRE RRE 021CD* 44 1
4 Sep 93 05:22:09:12 OFF *RRE RRE 022CD* 46 1

FROU FROU *UK, male / female production / vocal duo*

6 Jul 02 **BREATHE IN** *Island CID 799* 44 1

John FRUSCIANTE *US, male vocalist / guitarist*

13 Mar 04 SHADOWS COLLIDE WITH PEOPLE *Warner Bros. 9362486602* 53 1

Christian FRY *UK, male vocalist (2 Singles: 3 Weeks)*

14 Nov 98 **YOU GOT ME** *Mushroom MUSH 33CDS* 45 2
3 Apr 99 **WON'T YOU SAY** *Mushroom MUSH 46CDS* 48 1

FUGAZI
US, male vocal / instrumental group (5 Albums: 7 Weeks, 1 Single: 1 Week)

21 Sep 91 STEADY DIET OF NOTHING *Dischord DISCHORD 60* 63 1
19 Jun 93 IN ON THE KILLTAKER *Dischord DIS 70CD* 24 2
13 May 95 RED MEDICINE *Dischord DIS 90CD* 18 2
25 Apr 98 END HITS *Dischord DIS 110CD* 47 1
20 Oct 01 THE ARGUMENT *Dischord DIS 130CD* 63 1
20 Oct 01 **FURNITURE** *Dischord DIS 129CD* 61 1

FUGEES *US / Haiti, male / female vocal / rap / production trio – Lauryn Hill, Wyclef Jean and Pras Michel (2 Albums: 72 Weeks, 8 Singles: 65 Weeks)*

30 Mar 96 ● THE SCORE *Columbia 4835492* ▲ 2 70
6 Apr 96 **FU-GEE-LA** *Columbia 6630662* 21 5
8 Jun 96 ★ **KILLING ME SOFTLY** *Columbia 6633435* ■ £ 1 20
14 Sep 96 ★ **READY OR NOT** *Columbia 6637215* 1 12
30 Nov 96 ● **NO WOMAN, NO CRY** *Columbia 6639925* 2 9
7 Dec 96 BOOTLEG VERSIONS *Columbia 4868242* 55 2
15 Mar 97 ● **RUMBLE IN THE JUNGLE** *Mercury 5740692* 3 8
28 Jun 97 **WE TRYING TO STAY ALIVE** *Columbia 6646815* [1] 13 5
6 Sep 97 **THE SWEETEST THING** *Columbia 6649785* [2] 18 4
27 Sep 97 **GUANTANAMERA** *Columbia 6650852* [1] 25 2

[1] Wyclef Jean and The Refugee Allstars [2] Refugee Camp Allstars featuring Lauryn Hill

Group billed as The Fugees (Refugee Camp) on The Score.

FULL CIRCLE *US, male vocal group*

7 Mar 87 **WORKIN' UP A SWEAT** *EMI America EA 229* 41 5

17 / 20 January 1968	24 / 27 January 1968	31 January / 3 February 1968	7 / 10 February 1968
HELLO, GOODBYE The Beatles	**THE BALLAD OF BONNIE AND CLYDE** Georgie Fame	**EVERLASTING LOVE** Love Affair	**EVERLASTING LOVE** Love Affair
VAL DOONICAN ROCKS BUT GENTLY Val Doonican	**THE SOUND OF MUSIC** Soundtrack	**SGT. PEPPER'S LONELY HEARTS CLUB BAND** The Beatles	**GREATEST HITS** The Four Tops

KEY: UK No.1 ★★ UK Top 10 ●● Still on chart ++ UK entry at No.1 ■■ US No.1 ▲▲ UK million seller £ US million seller $
Singles re-entries are listed as (re), (2re), (3re)… which signifies that the hit re-entered the chart once, twice or three times…
Peak Position / Weeks

FULL FORCE *US, male vocal / instrumental group (4 Singles: 37 Weeks)*

4 May 85	**I WONDER IF I TAKE YOU HOME (re)** *CBS A 6057* [1]	12	17
21 Dec 85 ●	**ALICE I WANT YOU JUST FOR ME** *CBS A 6640*	9	11
21 May 88	**NAUGHTY GIRLS (NEED LOVE TOO)** *Jive FOXY 9*	31	5
4 Jun 88	**I'M REAL** *Scotti Bros. JSB 1* [2]	31	4

[1] Lisa Lisa and Cult Jam with Full Force [2] James Brown featuring Full Force

FULL INTENTION (see also DISCO TEX presents CLOUDBURST; Michael GRAY; HUSTLERS CONVENTION featuring Dave LAUDAT and Ondrea DUVERNEY; RONALDO'S REVENGE; SEX-O-SONIQUE) *UK, male instrumental / production group (6 Singles: 8 Weeks)*

6 Apr 96	**AMERICA (I LOVE AMERICA)** *Stress CDSTR 56*	32	2
10 Aug 96	**UPTOWN DOWNTOWN** *Stress CDSTR 67*	61	1
26 Jul 97	**SHAKE YOUR BODY (DOWN TO THE GROUND)** *Sugar Daddy CDSTR 82*	34	2
22 Nov 97	**AMERICA (I LOVE AMERICA)** (re-mix) *Sugar Daddy CDSTRX 56*	56	1
6 Jun 98	**YOU ARE SOMEBODY** *Sugar Daddy CDSD 001*	75	1
1 Sep 01	**I'LL BE WAITING** *Rulin RULIN 17CDS* [1]	44	1

[1] Full Intention presents Shena

FULL MONTY ALLSTARS featuring TJ DAVIS *UK, male vocal / instrumental group and female vocalist*

27 Jul 96	**BRILLIANT FEELING** *Arista 74321380902*	72	1

Bobby FULLER FOUR *US, male vocal / instrumental group – leader b. 22 Oct 1943, d. 18 Jul 1966*

14 Apr 66	**I FOUGHT THE LAW** *London HL 10030*	33	4

FUN BOY THREE (see also The COLOURFIELD; The SPECIALS; VEGAS) *UK, male vocal (Terry Hall) / instrumental trio (2 Albums: 40 Weeks, 8 Singles: 70 Weeks)*

7 Nov 81	**THE LUNATICS (HAVE TAKEN OVER THE ASYLUM)** *Chrysalis CHS 2563*	20	12
13 Feb 82 ●	**IT AIN'T WHAT YOU DO IT'S THE WAY THAT YOU DO IT** *Chrysalis CHS 2570* [1]	4	10
20 Mar 82 ●	THE FUNBOY THREE *Chrysalis CHR 1383*	7	20
10 Apr 82 ●	**REALLY SAYING SOMETHING** *Deram NANA 1* [2]	5	10
8 May 82	**THE TELEPHONE ALWAYS RINGS** *Chrysalis CHS 2609*	17	9
31 Jul 82	**SUMMERTIME** *Chrysalis CHS 2629*	18	8
15 Jan 83	**THE MORE I SEE (THE LESS I BELIEVE)** *Chrysalis CHS 2664*	68	1
5 Feb 83 ●	**TUNNEL OF LOVE** *Chrysalis CHS 2678*	10	10
19 Feb 83	WAITING *Chrysalis CHR 1417*	14	20
30 Apr 83 ●	**OUR LIPS ARE SEALED** *Chrysalis FUNB 1*	7	10

[1] Fun Boy Three and Bananarama [2] Bananarama with Fun Boy Three

FUN DA MENTAL *UK, male rap group*

25 Jun 94	SEIZE THE TIME *Nation NATCD 33*	74	1

FUN LOVIN' CRIMINALS (488 Top 500)

Hip-hop and funk-blending trio formed in New York City in 1993: Huey Morgan (v/g), Brian 'Fast' Leiser (b/k) and Steve Borgovini (d). Act, whose catalogue includes the Pulp Fiction sampling 'Scooby Snacks' and Barry White tribute 'Love Unlimited', are more popular in the UK than in their homeland (7 Albums: 121 Weeks, 11 Singles: 32 Weeks)

8 Jun 96	**THE GRAVE AND THE CONSTANT** *Chrysalis CDCHS 5031*	72	1
13 Jul 96 ●	COME FIND YOURSELF *Chrysalis CDCHR 6113*	7	71
17 Aug 96	**SCOOBY SNACKS** *Chrysalis CDCHS 5034*	22	3
16 Nov 96	**THE FUN LOVIN' CRIMINAL** *Chrysalis CDCHS 5040*	26	3
29 Mar 97	**KING OF NEW YORK** *Chrysalis CDCHS 5049*	28	3
5 Jul 97	**I'M NOT IN LOVE / SCOOBY SNACKS** *Chrysalis CDCHS 5060*	12	5
15 Aug 98	**LOVE UNLIMITED** *Chrysalis CDCHS 5096*	18	4
5 Sep 98 ●	100% COLOMBIAN *Chrysalis 4970562*	3	26
17 Oct 98	**BIG NIGHT OUT** *Chrysalis CDCHSS 5101*	29	2
8 May 99	**KOREAN BODEGA** *Chrysalis CDCHS 5108*	15	3
11 Dec 99	MIMOSA *Chrysalis 5234592*	37	9
17 Feb 01 ●	**LOCO** *Chrysalis CDCHSS 5121*	5	6
10 Mar 01 ●	LOCO *Chrysalis 5314712*	5	6
1 Sep 01	**BUMP / RUN DADDY RUN** *Chrysalis CDCHSS 5128*	50	1
3 Aug 02	BAG OF HITS – 15 INTERGLOBAL CHARTSTOPPERS *Chrysalis 5399542*	11	6
13 Sep 03	**TOO HOT** *Sanctuary SANXD 205*	61	1
20 Sep 03	WELCOME TO POPPY'S *Sanctuary SANCD 187*	20	2
3 Sep 05	LIVIN' IN THE CITY *Sanctuary SANCD 381*	57	1

FUNERAL FOR A FRIEND *UK, male vocal / instrumental group (2 Albums: 7 Weeks, 6 Singles: 14 Weeks)*

9 Aug 03	**JUNEAU** *Infectious EW 269CD1*	19	3
18 Oct 03	**SHE DROVE ME TO DAYTIME TELEVISION** *Infectious / East West EW 274CD1*	20	2
25 Oct 03	CASUALLY DRESSED AND DEEP IN CONVERSATION *Infectious 2564609472*	12	3
14 Feb 04	**ESCAPE ARTISTS NEVER DIE** *Infectious EW 283CD*	19	3
11 Jun 05	**STREETCAR** *Atlantic ATUK 009CDX*	15	3
25 Jun 05	HOURS *Atlantic 5046784382*	12	4
10 Sep 05	**MONSTERS** *Atlantic ATUK 012CDX*	36	1
26 Nov 05	**HISTORY** *Atlantic ATUK 017CD*	21	2

FUNK D'VOID *Sweden, male producer – Lars Sandberg (2 Singles: 2 Weeks)*

20 Oct 01	**DIABLA** *Soma SOMA 112*	70	1
31 Jan 04	**EMOTIONAL CONTENT** *Soma SOMA 139*	74	1

Farley 'Jackmaster' FUNK *US, male producer – Farley Williams (3 Singles: 16 Weeks)*

23 Aug 86 ●	**LOVE CAN'T TURN AROUND** *DJ International LON 105*	10	12
11 Feb 89	**AS ALWAYS** *Champion CHAMP 90* [1]	49	2
14 Dec 96	**LOVE CAN'T TURN AROUND** (re-recording) *4 Liberty LIBTCD 27* [2]	40	2

[1] Farley 'Jackmaster' Funk presents Ricky Dillard [2] Farley 'Jackmaster' Funk with Darryl Pandy

FUNK JUNKEEZ (see also EL MARIACHI) *US, male DJ / producer – Roger Sanchez*

21 Feb 98	**GOT FUNK** *Evocative EVOKE 1CDS*	57	1

The FUNK MASTERS *UK, male / female vocal / instrumental group*

18 Jun 83 ●	**IT'S OVER** *Master Funk Records 7MP 004*	8	12

Features Gonzales on horns and uncredited vocals by Juliet Roberts.

FUNKADELIC *US, male vocal (George Clinton) / instrumental group (1 Album: 5 Weeks, 2 Singles: 13 Weeks)*

9 Dec 78 ●	**ONE NATION UNDER A GROOVE (PART 1)** *Warner Bros. K 17246*	9	12
23 Dec 78	ONE NATION UNDER A GROOVE *Warner Bros. K 56539*	56	5
21 Aug 99	**MOTHERSHIP RECONNECTION** *Virgin DINSD 185* [1]	55	1

[1] Scott Grooves featuring Parliament / Funkadelic

FUNKAPOLITAN *UK, male vocal / instrumental group*

22 Aug 81	**AS TIME GOES BY** *London LON 001*	41	7

FUNKDOOBIEST

US, male rap group (1 Album: 1 Week, 2 Singles: 6 Weeks)

Date	Title / Label	Pos	Wks
11 Dec 93	**WOPBABALUBOP** *Immortal 6597112*	37	4
5 Mar 94	**BOW WOW WOW** *Immortal 6594052*	34	2
15 Jul 95	**BROTHAS DOOBIE** *Epic 4783812*	62	1

FUNKSTAR DE LUXE

Denmark, male producer / instrumentalist – Matt Ottesen (4 Singles: 18 Weeks)

Date	Title / Label	Pos	Wks
25 Sep 99 ●	**SUN IS SHINING** *Club Tools / Edel 0066895 CLU* [1]	3	10
22 Jan 00	**RAINBOW COUNTRY** *Club Tools 0067225 CLU* [1]	11	6
13 May 00	**WALKIN IN THE NAME** *Club Tools 0067375 CLU* [2]	42	1
25 Nov 00	**PULL UP TO THE BUMPER** *Club Tools 0120375 CLU* [3]	60	1

[1] Bob Marley vs Funkstar De Luxe [2] Funkstar De Luxe vs Terry Maxx
[3] Grace Jones vs Funkstar De Luxe

FUNKY CHOAD featuring Nick SKITZ

Australia / Italy, male production duo and Australia, male vocalist

Date	Title / Label	Pos	Wks
29 Aug 98	**THE ULTIMATE** *ffrr FCD 341*	51	1

FUNKY GREEN DOGS (see also FOG)

US, male / female vocal / production trio (4 Singles: 6 Weeks)

Date	Title / Label	Pos	Wks
12 Apr 97	**FIRED UP!** *Twisted UK TWCD 10016*	17	3
28 Jun 97	**THE WAY** *Twisted UK TWCD 10026*	43	1
20 Jun 98	**UNTIL THE DAY** *Twisted UK TWCD 10034*	75	1
27 Feb 99	**BODY** *Twisted UK TWCD 110041*	46	1

FUNKY POETS

US, male vocal group

Date	Title / Label	Pos	Wks
7 May 94	**BORN IN THE GHETTO** *Epic 6603522*	72	1

FUNKY WORM

UK, male / female vocal / instrumental group (3 Singles: 14 Weeks)

Date	Title / Label	Pos	Wks
30 Jul 88	**HUSTLE! (TO THE MUSIC ...)** *Fon FON 15*	13	8
26 Nov 88	**THE SPELL!** *Fon FON 16*	61	3
20 May 89	**U + ME = LOVE** *Fon FON 19*	46	3

The FUREYS with Davey ARTHUR

Ireland, male vocal duo – Finbar and Eddie Fury and UK, male vocalist (4 Albums: 38 Weeks, 2 Singles: 14 Weeks)

Date	Title / Label	Pos	Wks
10 Oct 81	**WHEN YOU WERE SWEET SIXTEEN** *Ritz RITZ 003*	14	11
3 Apr 82	**I WILL LOVE YOU (EV'RY TIME WHEN WE ARE GONE)** *Ritz RITZ 012* [1]	54	3
8 May 82	**WHEN YOU WERE SWEET SIXTEEN** *Ritz RITZLP 0004*	99	1
10 Nov 84	**GOLDEN DAYS** *K-Tel ONE 1283*	17	19
26 Oct 85	**AT THE END OF THE DAY** *K-Tel ONE 1310*	35	11
21 Nov 87	**FUREYS FINEST** *Telstar HSTAR 2311*	65	7

[1] The Fureys

FURNITURE

UK, male / female vocal / instrumental group

Date	Title / Label	Pos	Wks
14 Jun 86	**BRILLIANT MIND** *Stiff BUY 251*	21	10

Nelly FURTADO

Canada, female vocalist (2 Albums: 61 Weeks, 6 Singles: 52 Weeks)

Date	Title / Label	Pos	Wks
10 Mar 01 ●	**I'M LIKE A BIRD** *Dreamworks 4509192*	5	16
24 Mar 01 ●	**WHOA NELLY!** *Dreamworks 4502852*	2	47
1 Sep 01 ●	**TURN OFF THE LIGHT** *Dreamworks DRMDM 50891*	4	10
19 Jan 02	**... ON THE RADIO (REMEMBER THE DAYS) (re)** *Dreamworks DRMDM 50856*	18	6
6 Dec 03	**FOLKLORE** *Dreamworks / Polydor 4505089*	11	14
20 Dec 03	**POWERLESS (SAY WHAT YOU WANT)** *Dreamworks 4504645*	13	10
27 Mar 04	**TRY** *Dreamworks 4505113*	15	7
24 Jul 04	**FORÇA** *Dreamworks 9862823*	40	3

Billy FURY (167 Top 500)

Early British rock 'n' roll (and film) star, b. Ronald Wycherley, 17 Apr 1940, Liverpool, d. 28 Jan 1983. He equalled The Beatles' record of 24 hits in the 1960s, and spent 332 weeks on the chart without a chart-topping single or album. In 2003 a bronze statue of Fury was unveiled at the National Museum of Liverpool Life (6 Albums: 51 Weeks, 29 Singles: 281 Weeks)

Date	Title / Label	Pos	Wks
27 Feb 59	**MAYBE TOMORROW (re)** *Decca F 11102*	18	9
26 Jun 59	**MARGO** *Decca F 11128*	28	1
10 Mar 60 ●	**COLETTE** *Decca F 11200*	9	10
26 May 60	**THAT'S LOVE** *Decca F 11237* [1]	19	11
4 Jun 60	**THE SOUND OF FURY** *Decca LF 1329*	18	2
22 Sep 60	**WONDROUS PLACE** *Decca F 11267*	25	9
19 Jan 61	**A THOUSAND STARS** *Decca F 11311*	14	10
27 Apr 61	**DON'T WORRY** *Decca F 11334* [2]	40	2
11 May 61 ●	**HALFWAY TO PARADISE** *Decca F 11349*	3	23
7 Sep 61 ●	**JEALOUSY** *Decca F 11384*	2	12
23 Sep 61 ●	**HALFWAY TO PARADISE** *Ace of Clubs ACL 1083*	5	9
14 Dec 61 ●	**I'D NEVER FIND ANOTHER YOU** *Decca F 11409*	5	15
15 Mar 62	**LETTER FULL OF TEARS** *Decca F 11437*	32	6
3 May 62 ●	**LAST NIGHT WAS MADE FOR LOVE** *Decca F 11458*	4	16
19 Jul 62 ●	**ONCE UPON A DREAM** *Decca F 11485*	7	13
25 Oct 62	**BECAUSE OF LOVE** *Decca F 11508*	18	14
14 Feb 63 ●	**LIKE I'VE NEVER BEEN GONE** *Decca F 11582*	3	15
11 May 63 ●	**BILLY** *Decca LK 4533*	6	21
16 May 63 ●	**WHEN WILL YOU SAY I LOVE YOU** *Decca F 11655*	3	12
25 Jul 63 ●	**IN SUMMER** *Decca F 11701*	5	11
3 Oct 63	**SOMEBODY ELSE'S GIRL** *Decca F 11744*	18	7
26 Oct 63	**WE WANT BILLY!** *Decca LK 4548* [1]	14	2
2 Jan 64	**DO YOU REALLY LOVE ME TOO? (FOOLS ERRAND)** *Decca F 11792*	13	10
30 Apr 64	**I WILL** *Decca F 11888*	14	12
23 Jul 64 ●	**IT'S ONLY MAKE BELIEVE** *Decca F 11939*	10	10
14 Jan 65	**I'M LOST WITHOUT YOU** *Decca F 12048*	16	10
22 Jul 65 ●	**IN THOUGHTS OF YOU** *Decca F 12178*	9	11
16 Sep 65	**RUN TO MY LOVIN' ARMS** *Decca F 12230*	25	7
10 Feb 66	**I'LL NEVER QUITE GET OVER YOU** *Decca F 12325*	35	5
4 Aug 66	**GIVE ME YOUR WORD** *Decca F 12459*	27	7
4 Sep 82	**LOVE OR MONEY** *Polydor POSP 488*	57	5
13 Nov 82	**DEVIL OR ANGEL** *Polydor POSP 528*	58	4
19 Feb 83	**THE BILLY FURY HIT PARADE** *Decca TAB 37*	44	15
26 Mar 83	**THE ONE AND ONLY BILLY FURY** *Polydor POLD 5069*	54	2
4 Jun 83	**FORGET HIM** *Polydor POSP 558*	59	4

[1] Billy Fury with The Four Jays [2] Billy Fury with The Four Kestrels
[1] Billy Fury and The Tornados

FUSE (see also PLASTIKMAN)

Canada, male dj / producer – Richie Hawtin

Date	Title / Label	Pos	Wks
19 Jun 93	**DIMENSION INTRUSION** *Warp WARPCD 12*	63	1

FUSED

Sweden, male instrumental / production duo and female vocalist

Date	Title / Label	Pos	Wks
20 Mar 99	**THIS PARTY SUCKS!** *Columbia 6669302*	64	1

FUTURE BREEZE (see also 4CLUBBERS)

Germany, male production duo – Markus Boehme and Martin Hensing (4 Singles: 11 Weeks)

Date	Title / Label	Pos	Wks
6 Sep 97	**WHY DON'T YOU DANCE WITH ME** *AM:PM 5823312*	50	1
20 Jan 01	**SMILE** *Nebula NEBCD 014*	67	1
13 Apr 02	**TEMPLE OF DREAMS** *Ministry of Sound / DATA 31CDS*	21	6
28 Dec 02	**OCEAN OF ETERNITY** *Ministry of Sound / DATA 44CDS*	46	3

FUTURE FORCE

UK / US, male / female vocal / instrumental duo

Date	Title / Label	Pos	Wks
17 Aug 96	**WHAT YOU WANT** *AM:PM 5816592*	47	1

FUTURE SOUND OF LONDON (see also HUMANOID; AMORPHOUS ANDROGYNOUS)

UK, male instrumental / production duo – Brian Dougans and Gary Cobain (5 Albums: 10 Weeks, 8 Singles: 25 Weeks)

Date	Title / Label	Pos	Wks
23 May 92	**PAPUA NEW GUINEA** *Jumpin' & Pumpin' TOT 17*	22	6
18 Jul 92	**ACCELERATOR** *Jumpin' & Pumpin' CDTOT 2*	75	1
6 Nov 93	**CASCADE** *Virgin VSCDT 1478*	27	3
4 Jun 94 ●	**LIFEFORMS** *Virgin CDV 2722*	6	5
30 Jul 94	**EXPANDER** *Jumpin' & Pumpin' CDSTOT 37*	72	1

13 / 16 March 1968	20 / 23 March 1968	27 / 30 March 1968	3 / 6 April 1968
CINDERELLA ROCKEFELLA Esther and Abi Ofarim	THE LEGEND OF XANADU Dave Dee, Dozy, Beaky, Mick and Tich	LADY MADONNA The Beatles	LADY MADONNA The Beatles
JOHN WESLEY HARDING Bob Dylan	JOHN WESLEY HARDING Bob Dylan	JOHN WESLEY HARDING Bob Dylan	JOHN WESLEY HARDING Bob Dylan

KEY: UK No.1 ★ UK Top 10 ● Still on chart + UK entry at No.1 ■ US No.1 ▲ UK million seller £ US million seller $
Singles re-entries are listed as (re), (2re), (3re)... which signifies that the hit re-entered the chart once, twice or three times...
Peak Position / Weeks

13 Aug 94	**LIFEFORMS** *Virgin VSCDT 1484* [1]	14	3
17 Dec 94	**ISDN** *Virgin CDV 2755*	62	1
27 May 95	**FAR-OUT SON OF LUNG AND THE RAMBLINGS OF A MADMAN** *Virgin VSCDT 1540*	22	3
17 Jun 95	**ISDN (Remix)** *Virgin CDVX 2755*	44	1
26 Oct 96	**MY KINGDOM** *Virgin VSCDT 1605*	13	3
9 Nov 96	**DEAD CITIES** *Virgin CDVX 2814*	26	2
12 Apr 97	**WE HAVE EXPLOSIVE** *Virgin VSCDX 1616*	12	3
29 Sep 01	**PAPUA NEW GUINEA 2001** (re-mix) *Jumpin' & Pumpin' CDSTOT 44*	28	3

[1] FSOL: Vocals by Elizabeth Fraser

The FUTUREHEADS *UK, male vocal (Barry Hyde) / instrumental group (1 Album: 10 Weeks, 6 Singles: 13 Weeks)*

9 Aug 03	**FIRST DAY** *Fantastic Plastic FPS 036*	58	1
7 Aug 04	**DECENT DAYS AND NIGHTS** *679 Recordings 679L 080CD*	26	2
30 Oct 04	**MEANTIME** *679 Recordings 679L 008CD 2*	49	1
5 Mar 05 ●	**HOUNDS OF LOVE** *679 Recordings 679L 099CD 2*	8	4
19 Mar 05	**THE FUTUREHEADS** *679 Recordings 5046738482*	11	10
21 May 05	**DECENT DAYS AND NIGHTS** (re-issue) *679 Recordings 679L 014CD2*	26	2
10 Dec 05	**AREA** *679 Recordings 679L 117CD2*	18	3

The Futureheads was originally released in Aug 2004 and only charted when it was repackaged with a free DVD .

FUTURESHOCK
UK, male production duo and vocalist (3 Singles: 3 Weeks)

15 Mar 03	**ON MY MIND** *Junior / Parlophone CDR 6595* [1]	51	1
16 Aug 03	**PRIDE'S PARANOIA** *Junior / Parlophone CDR 6616*	60	1
1 Nov 03	**LATE AT NIGHT** *Parlophone CDR 6617*	73	1

[1] Futureshock featuring Ben Onono

FYA *UK, female vocal trio (2 Singles: 9 Weeks)*

13 Mar 04	**MUST BE LOVE** *Def Jam 9817508* [1]	13	7
24 Jul 04	**TOO HOT** *Def Jam 9867145*	49	2

[1] Fya featuring Smujji

G

Ali G and SHAGGY *UK, male comedian / rapper – Sacha Baron Cohen and Jamaica, male vocalist – Orville Burrell*

23 Mar 02 ●	**ME JULIE** *Island CID 793*	2	14

Bobby G (see also BUCKS FIZZ) *UK, male vocalist – Robert Gubby*

1 Dec 84	**BIG DEAL (2re)** *BBC RESL 151*	46	12

Gina G *Australia, female vocalist – Gina Gardiner (1 Album: 4 Weeks, 6 Singles: 51 Weeks)*

6 Apr 96 ★	**OOH AAH ... JUST A LITTLE BIT (2re)** *Eternal WEA 041CD*	1	25
9 Nov 96 ●	**I BELONG TO YOU** *Eternal WEA 081CD*	6	11
22 Mar 97 ●	**FRESH!** *Eternal WEA 095CD*	6	7
5 Apr 97	**FRESH!** *Eternal 630178402*	12	4
7 Jun 97	**TI AMO** *Eternal WEA 107CD1*	11	5
6 Sep 97	**GIMME SOME LOVE** *Eternal WEA 101CD1*	25	2
15 Nov 97	**EVERY TIME I FALL** *Eternal WEA 134CD*	52	1

Kenny G *US, male saxophonist – Kenny Gorelick (7 Albums: 62 Weeks, 7 Singles: 26 Weeks)*

17 Mar 84	**G FORCE** *Arista 206 168*	56	5
21 Apr 84	**HI! HOW YA DOIN'?** *Arista ARIST 561*	70	3
30 Aug 86	**WHAT DOES IT TAKE (TO WIN YOUR LOVE)** *Arista ARIST 672*	64	2
4 Jul 87	**SONGBIRD** *Arista RIS 18*	22	7
8 Aug 87	**DUOTONES** *Arista 207 792*	28	5
14 Apr 90	**MONTAGE** *Arista 210621*	32	7
9 May 92	**MISSING YOU NOW** *Columbia 6579917* [1]	28	4
24 Apr 93	**FOREVER IN LOVE** *Arista 74321145552*	47	3
15 May 93 ●	**BREATHLESS** *Arista 07822186462*	4	27
17 Jul 93	**BY THE TIME THIS NIGHT IS OVER** *Arista 74321157142* [2]	56	3
19 Oct 96	**THE MOMENT** *Arista 7822189352*	19	9
8 Nov 97	**HOW COULD AN ANGEL BREAK MY HEART** *LaFace 74321531982* [3]	22	4
13 Dec 97	**GREATEST HITS** *Arista 7822189912*	38	5
14 Aug 04	**SONGBIRD – THE ULTIMATE COLLECTION** *Arista 82876625622*	24	4

[1] Michael Bolton featuring Kenny G [2] Kenny G with Peabo Bryson [3] Toni Braxton with Kenny G

Warren G
US, male rapper – Warren Griffin (2 Albums: 10 Weeks, 9 Singles: 60 Weeks)

23 Jul 94 ●	**REGULATE** *Death Row A 8290CD* [1] $	5	14
6 Aug 94	**REGULATE ... G FUNK ERA** *RAL 5233352*	25	6
12 Nov 94	**THIS DJ (re)** *RAL RALCD 1*	12	7
25 Mar 95	**DO YOU SEE** *RAL RALCD 3*	29	2
23 Nov 96 ●	**WHAT'S LOVE GOT TO DO WITH IT** *Interscope IND 97008* [2]	2	12
22 Feb 97 ●	**I SHOT THE SHERIFF** *Mercury DEFCD 31*	2	8
8 Mar 97	**TAKE A LOOK OVER YOUR SHOULDER (REALITY)** *Def Jam 5334842*	20	4
31 May 97	**SMOKIN' ME OUT** *Def Jam 5744432* [3]	14	5
10 Jan 98	**PRINCE IGOR** *Def Jam 5749652* [4]	15	7
24 Jan 98	**ALL NIGHT ALL RIGHT** *Mushroom MUSH 21CD* [5]	16	4
16 Mar 02	**LOOKIN' AT YOU** *Universal MCSTD 40275* [6]	60	1

[1] Warren G and Nate Dogg [2] Warren G featuring Adina Howard [3] Warren G featuring Ron Isley [4] Warren G featuring Sissel [5] Peter Andre featuring Warren G [6] Warren G featuring Toi

Andy G's STARSKY & HUTCH ALL STARS
UK, male producer – Andros Georgiou

3 Oct 98	**STARSKY & HUTCH – THE THEME** *Virgin VSCDT 1708*	51	1

GBH
UK, male vocal / instrumental group (1 Album: 6 Weeks, 2 Singles: 5 Weeks)

6 Feb 82	**NO SURVIVORS** *Clay CLAY 8*	63	2
14 Aug 82	**CITY BABY ATTACKED BY RATS** *Clay CLAYLP 4* [1]	17	6
20 Nov 82	**GIVE ME FIRE** *Clay CLAY 16*	69	3

[1] Charge GBH

The G-CLEFS *US, male vocal group*

30 Nov 61	**I UNDERSTAND** *London HLU 9433*	17	12

G CLUB presents BANDA SONORA *UK, male producer – Gerald Elms*

19 Oct 02	**PRESSURE COOKER** *Defected DFTD 060CDS*	46	1

10 / 13 April 1968	17 / 20 April 1968	24 / 27 April 1968	1 / 4 May 1968
◂◂ UK No.1 SINGLES ▸▸			
CONGRATULATIONS Cliff Richard	**CONGRATULATIONS** Cliff Richard	**WHAT A WONDERFUL WORLD / CABARET** Louis Armstrong Orchestra and Chorus	**WHAT A WONDERFUL WORLD / CABARET** Louis Armstrong Orchestra and Chorus
◂◂ UK No.1 ALBUMS ▸▸			
JOHN WESLEY HARDING Bob Dylan	**JOHN WESLEY HARDING** Bob Dylan	**JOHN WESLEY HARDING** Bob Dylan	**JOHN WESLEY HARDING** Bob Dylan

G4 NEW *UK, male vocal (Jonathan Ansell) group (2 Albums: 19 Weeks, 1 Single: 6 Weeks)*

12 Mar 05 ★ G4 *Sony Music 5197342* ■ 1 15
26 Mar 05 ● **BOHEMIAN RHAPSODY** *Sony Music 6758062* 9 6
10 Dec 05 ● G4 & FRIENDS *Sony Music 82876747382* ....6 4+

G NATION featuring ROSIE *UK, male production duo – Jake Moses and Mark Smith and female vocalist*

9 Aug 97 **FEEL THE NEED** *Cooltempo CDCOOL 327* 58 1

G.O.S.H. *UK, male / female charity ensemble*

28 Nov 87 **THE WISHING WELL** *MBS GOSH 1* 22 11

G.Q. *US, male vocal / instrumental group*

10 Mar 79 **DISCO NIGHTS – (ROCK FREAK)** *Arista ARIST 245* $ 42 6

GSP *UK, male instrumental / production duo – Ian Gallivan and Justin Stride*

3 Oct 92 **THE BANANA SONG** *Yoyo YOYO 1* 37 3

GTO (see also TECHNOHEAD; TRICKY DISCO) *UK, male / female instrumental / production duo – Michael Wells and Lee Newman d. 4 Aug 1995 (3 Singles: 7 Weeks)*

4 Aug 90 **PURE** *Cooltempo COOL 218* 57 3
7 Sep 91 **LISTEN TO THE RHYTHM FLOW / BULLFROG** *React REACT 7001* 72 2
2 May 92 **ELEVATION** *React REACT 4* 59 2

GTR (see also Steve HACKETT; Steve HOWE) *UK, male vocal / instrumental group*

19 Jul 86 GTR *Arista 207 716* 41 4

G-UNIT (see also Lloyd BANK$; The GAME; Tony YAYO) *US, male rap trio – leader 50 Cent (3 Albums: 19 Weeks, 4 Singles: 27 Weeks)*

29 Nov 03 BEG FOR MERCY *Interscope / Polydor 9861498* 13 11
27 Dec 03 **STUNT 101** *Interscope 9815335* 25 7
6 Mar 04 ● **IF I CAN'T / ... THEM THANGS** *Interscope 9815279* [1] 10 8
17 Apr 04 **WANNA GET TO KNOW YOU** *Interscope 9862268* 27 5
24 Apr 04 **RIDE WIT U / MORE & MORE** *Jive 82876609212* [2] 12 7
18 Sep 04 50 CENT IS THE FUTURE *Street Dance SDR 0166752* [1] 65 1
19 Nov 05 GET RICH OR DIE TRYIN' (FILM SOUNDTRACK) *Interscope 9887992* [1] ....18 7+

[1] 50 Cent & G-Unit [2] Joe featuring G-Unit [1] 50 Cent & G-Unit

'... Them Thangs' was abbreviated for the single release. The track's full title is 'Poppin' Them Thangs'.

GA GAS NEW *UK, male vocal / instrumental group*

12 Feb 05 **SEX** *Sanctuary SANXS 328* 71 1

Eric GABLE *US, male vocalist*

19 Mar 94 **PROCESS OF ELIMINATION** *Epic 6602282* 63 1

Peter GABRIEL 169 Top 500

Award-winning singer / songwriter, b. 13 Feb 1950, Surrey, UK. Fronted Genesis until 1975, when replaced by Phil Collins. He broke through internationally with 'Sledgehammer', which also made him a video innovator. He is the driving force behind the Womad festival and is a tireless Amnesty International supporter (14 Albums: 215 Weeks, 21 Singles: 114 Weeks)

12 Mar 77 ● PETER GABRIEL *Charisma CDS 4006* 7 19
9 Apr 77 **SOLSBURY HILL** *Charisma CB 301* 13 9
17 Jun 78 ● PETER GABRIEL *Charisma CDS 4013* 10 8
9 Feb 80 ● **GAMES WITHOUT FRONTIERS** *Charisma CB 354* 4 11
10 May 80 **NO SELF CONTROL** *Charisma CB 360* 33 6
7 Jun 80 ★ PETER GABRIEL *Charisma CDS 4019* 1 18
23 Aug 80 **BIKO** *Charisma CB 370* 38 3
18 Sep 82 ● PETER GABRIEL *Charisma PG 4* 6 16
25 Sep 82 **SHOCK THE MONKEY** *Charisma SHOCK 1* 58 5
18 Jun 83 ● PETER GABRIEL PLAYS LIVE *Charisma PGDL 1* 8 9
9 Jul 83 **I DON'T REMEMBER** *Charisma GAB 1* 62 3
2 Jun 84 **WALK THROUGH THE FIRE** *Virgin VS 689* 69 3
30 Apr 85 BIRDY (FILM SOUNDTRACK) *Charisma CAS 1167* 51 3
26 Apr 86 ● **SLEDGEHAMMER** *Virgin PGS 1* ▲ 4 16
31 May 86 ★ SO *Virgin PG 5* ■ 1 76
1 Nov 86 ● **DON'T GIVE UP** *Virgin PGS 2* [1] 9 11
28 Mar 87 **BIG TIME** *Charisma PGS 3* 13 7
11 Jul 87 **RED RAIN** *Charisma PGS 4* 46 3
21 Nov 87 **BIKO (LIVE)** *Charisma PGS 6* 49 6
3 Jun 89 **SHAKIN' THE TREE** *Virgin VS 1167* [2] 61 3
17 Jun 89 PASSION *Virgin RWLP 1* 29 5
1 Dec 90 SHAKING THE TREE – 16 GOLDEN GREATS *Virgin PGTV 6* 11 18
22 Dec 90 **SOLSBURY HILL** (re-issue) / **SHAKING THE TREE** (re-issue) *Virgin VS 1322* [3] 57 4
19 Sep 92 **DIGGING IN THE DIRT** *Realworld PGS 7* 24 4
10 Oct 92 ● US *Realworld PGCD 7* 2 29
16 Jan 93 ● **STEAM** *Realworld PGSDG 8* 10 7
3 Apr 93 **BLOOD OF EDEN** *Realworld PGSDG 9* 43 4
25 Sep 93 **KISS THAT FROG** *Realworld PGSDG 10* 46 3
25 Jun 94 **LOVETOWN** *Epic 6604802* 49 2
3 Sep 94 **SW LIVE (EP)** *Realworld PGSCD 11* 39 2
10 Sep 94 ● SECRET WORLD LIVE *Realworld PGDCD 8* 10 4
24 Jun 00 OVO *Realworld PGCD 9* 24 2
5 Oct 02 UP *Realworld PGCD 11* 11 4
11 Jan 03 **MORE THAN THIS** *Realworld PGSCD 14* 47 2
15 Nov 03 HIT *Realworld 5952372* 29 4

[1] Peter Gabriel and Kate Bush [2] Youssou N'Dour and Peter Gabriel
[3] Peter Gabriel / Youssou N'Dour and Peter Gabriel

Tracks available on all formats of SW Live (EP): Red Rain / San Jacinto. First four albums are different.

GABRIELLE 171 Top 500

Eyepatch-wearing soul / pop vocalist, b. Louisa Gabrielle Bobb, 16 May 1970, London, UK. She broke the record for the highest chart debut when 'Dreams' entered at No.2. Voted Best British Newcomer at the 1994 BRIT Awards and Best British Female Vocalist in 1997. Best-selling single: 'Dreams' 513,200 (5 Albums: 175 Weeks, 17 Singles: 148 Weeks)

19 Jun 93 ★ **DREAMS** *Go Beat GODCD 99* 1 15
2 Oct 93 ● **GOING NOWHERE** *Go Beat GODCD 106* 9 7
30 Oct 93 ● FIND YOUR WAY *Go Beat 8284412* 9 22
11 Dec 93 **I WISH** *Go Beat GODCD 108* 26 5
26 Feb 94 **BECAUSE OF YOU** *Go Beat GODCD 109* 24 5
24 Feb 96 ● **GIVE ME A LITTLE MORE TIME** *Go Beat GODCD 139* 5 18
8 Jun 96 GABRIELLE *Go Beat 8287242* 11 30
22 Jun 96 **FORGET ABOUT THE WORLD** *Go Beat GODCD 146* 23 5
5 Oct 96 **IF YOU REALLY CARED** *Go Beat GODCD 153* 15 5
2 Nov 96 ● **IF YOU EVER** *London LONCD 388* [1] 2 15
1 Feb 97 ● **WALK ON BY** *Go Beat GODCD 159* 7 8
9 Oct 99 ● **SUNSHINE** *Go Beat GOBCD 23* 9 8
30 Oct 99 ★ RISE *Go Beat 5477682* 1 87
5 Feb 00 ★ **RISE** *Go Beat / Polydor GOBCD 25* ■ 1 15
17 Jun 00 ● **WHEN A WOMAN** *Go Beat / Polydor GOBCD 27* 6 8
4 Nov 00 **SHOULD I STAY** *Go Beat / Polydor GOBCD 32* 13 7
21 Apr 01 ● **OUT OF REACH** *Go Beat / Polydor GOLCD 39* 4 16
3 Nov 01 ● **DON'T NEED THE SUN TO SHINE (TO MAKE ME SMILE)** *Go Beat / Polydor GOBCD 47* 9 7
24 Nov 01 ● DREAMS CAN COME TRUE – GREATEST HITS VOL.1 *Go Beat 5893742* 2 26
15 May 04 **STAY THE SAME** *Go Beat / Polydor 9866529* 20 3
29 May 04 ● PLAY TO WIN *Go Beat / Island 9866530* 10 10
14 Aug 04 **TEN YEARS TIME** *Go Beat 9867550* 43 1

[1] East 17 featuring Gabrielle

8 / 11 May 1968	15 / 18 May 1968	22 / 25 May 1968	29 May / 1 June 1968
WHAT A WONDERFUL WORLD / CABARET Louis Armstrong Orchestra and Chorus	**WHAT A WONDERFUL WORLD / CABARET** Louis Armstrong Orchestra and Chorus	**YOUNG GIRL** Union Gap featuring Gary Puckett	**YOUNG GIRL** Union Gap featuring Gary Puckett
JOHN WESLEY HARDING Bob Dylan	**SCOTT 2** Scott Walker	**JOHN WESLEY HARDING** Bob Dylan	**JOHN WESLEY HARDING** Bob Dylan

TOP 20 CHART-TOPPING ALBUMS BY WEEKS AT No.1

The South Pacific movie soundtrack LP has always dominated this particular list, but positions two to 20 make up a surprising chart that includes 10 other stage and screen releases.

POS / ALBUM / ACT / TOTAL WEEKS AT NO.1 / (SEPARATE RUNS AT NO.1)

1. SOUTH PACIFIC Soundtrack – 115 (9)
2. THE SOUND OF MUSIC Various – 70 (12)
3. THE KING AND I Soundtrack – 48 (11)
4. BRIDGE OVER TROUBLED WATER Simon and Garfunkel – 33 (8)
5. PLEASE PLEASE ME The Beatles – 30 (1)
6. SGT. PEPPER'S LONELY HEARTS CLUB BAND The Beatles – 27 (4)
7. G.I. BLUES (Film soundtrack) Elvis Presley – 22 (3)
8=. A HARD DAY'S NIGHT The Beatles – 21 (1)
8=. WITH THE BEATLES The Beatles – 21 (1)
10. MY FAIR LADY Original Broadway Cast – 19 (1)
11=. BLUE HAWAII (Film soundtrack) Elvis Presley – 18 (2)
11=. SATURDAY NIGHT FEVER Soundtrack – 18 (1)
13=. ABBEY ROAD The Beatles – 17 (2)
13=. THE SINGLES 1969-1973 The Carpenters – 17 (4)
15=. ... BUT SERIOUSLY Phil Collins – 15 (2)
15=. SPICE Spice Girls – 15 (5)
17=. BROTHERS IN ARMS Dire Straits – 14 (3)
17=. SUMMER HOLIDAY (Film soundtrack) Cliff Richard and The Shadows – 14 (1)
19=. JOHN WESLEY HARDING Bob Dylan – 13 (2)
19=. GREASE Soundtrack – 13 (1)
19=. WEST SIDE STORY Soundtrack – 13 (7)

South Pacific star Mitzi Gaynor was one of the movie's few performers to act and sing without having to be dubbed

GADJO featuring Alexandra PRINCE NEW
Germany, male production duo and female vocalist

28 May 05	**SO MANY TIMES** *All Around the World / Manifesto 9871480*	22	6

Yvonne GAGE *US, female vocalist*

16 Jun 84	**DOIN' IT IN A HAUNTED HOUSE** *Epic A 4519*	45	4

Danni'elle GAHA *Australia, female vocalist (3 Singles: 7 Weeks)*

1 Aug 92	**STUCK IN THE MIDDLE** *Epic 6581247*	68	2
27 Feb 93	**DO IT FOR LOVE** *Epic 6584612*	52	2
12 Jun 93	**SECRET LOVE** *Epic 6592212*	41	3

Dave GAHAN (see also DEPECHE MODE)
UK, male vocalist (1 Album: 2 Weeks, 3 Singles: 6 Weeks)

7 Jun 03	**DIRTY STICKY FLOORS** *Mute CDMUTE 294*	18	2
14 Jun 03	PAPER MONSTERS *Mute CDSTUMM 216*	36	2
30 Aug 03	**I NEED YOU** *Mute CDMUTE 301*	27	2
8 Nov 03	**BOTTLE LIVING** *Mute CDMUTE 310*	36	2

Billy and Sarah GAINES *US, male / female vocal duo*

14 Jun 97	**I FOUND SOMEONE** *Expansion CDEXP 27*	48	1

Rosie GAINES (see also PRINCE) *US, female vocalist (3 Singles: 15 Weeks)*

11 Nov 95	**I WANT U** *Motown 8604852*	70	1
31 May 97 ●	**CLOSER THAN CLOSE** *Big Bang CDBBANG 1*	4	12
29 Nov 97	**I SURRENDER** *Big Bang CDBBANG 2*	39	2

GALA *Italy, female vocalist – Gala Rizzatto (3 Singles: 24 Weeks)*

19 Jul 97 ●	**FREED FROM DESIRE** *Big Life BLRD 135*	2	14
6 Dec 97	**LET A BOY CRY** *Big Life BLRD 140*	11	8
22 Aug 98	**COME INTO MY LIFE** *Big Life BLRD 147*	38	2

Eve GALLAGHER *UK, female vocalist (4 Singles: 8 Weeks)*

1 Dec 90	**LOVE COME DOWN** (re) *More Protein PROT 6*	61	4
15 Apr 95	**YOU CAN HAVE IT ALL** *Cleveland City CLECD 13023*	43	2
28 Oct 95	**LOVE COME DOWN** (re-recording) *Cleveland City CLECD 13028*	57	1
6 Jul 96	**HEARTBREAK** *React CDREACT 78* [1]	44	1

[1] Mrs Wood featuring Eve Gallagher

Rory GALLAGHER (see also TASTE) *Ireland, male vocalist / guitarist, b. 2 Mar 1949, d. 14 Jun 1995 (11 Albums: 45 Weeks)*

29 May 71	RORY GALLAGHER *Polydor 2383 044*	32	2
4 Dec 71	DEUCE *Polydor 2383 076*	39	1
20 May 72 ●	LIVE! IN EUROPE *Polydor 2383 112*	9	15
24 Feb 73	BLUE PRINT *Polydor 2383 189*	12	7
17 Nov 73	TATTOO *Polydor 2383 230*	32	3
27 Jul 74	IRISH TOUR '74 *Polydor 2659 031*	36	2
30 Oct 76	CALLING CARD *Chrysalis CHR 1124*	32	1
22 Sep 79	TOP PRIORITY *Chrysalis CHR 1235*	56	4
8 Nov 80	STAGE STRUCK *Chrysalis CHR 1280*	40	3
8 May 82	JINX *Chrysalis CHR 1359*	68	5
25 Jun 05	BIG GUNS – THE VERY BEST OF RORY GALLAGHER *Capo CAPO 705*	31	2

GALLAGHER and LYLE *UK, male vocal / instrumental duo – Benny Gallagher and Graham Lyle (2 Albums: 44 Weeks, 4 Singles: 27 Weeks)*

28 Feb 76 ●	BREAKAWAY *A&M AMLH 68348*	6	35
28 Feb 76 ●	**I WANNA STAY WITH YOU** *A&M AMS 7211*	6	9
22 May 76 ●	**HEART ON MY SLEEVE** *A&M AMS 7227*	6	10
11 Sep 76	**BREAKAWAY** *A&M AMS 7245*	35	4
29 Jan 77	LOVE ON THE AIRWAYS *A&M AMLH 64620*	19	9
29 Jan 77	**EVERY LITTLE TEARDROP** *A&M AMS 7274*	32	4

5 / 8 June 1968	12 / 15 June 1968	19 / 22 June 1968	26 / 29 June 1968
UK No.1 SINGLES			
YOUNG GIRL Union Gap featuring Gary Puckett	YOUNG GIRL Union Gap featuring Gary Puckett	JUMPIN' JACK FLASH The Rolling Stones	JUMPIN' JACK FLASH The Rolling Stones
UK No.1 ALBUMS			
JOHN WESLEY HARDING Bob Dylan	LOVE ANDY Andy Williams	DOCK OF THE BAY Otis Redding	OGDENS' NUT GONE FLAKE The Small Faces

Patsy GALLANT *Canada, female vocalist*

10 Sep 77 ● **FROM NEW YORK TO L.A.** *EMI 2620* **6** 9

GALLEON *France, male vocal / production trio*

20 Apr 02 **SO I BEGIN** *Epic 6724102* **36** 2

Luke GALLIANA *UK, male vocalist*

12 May 01 **TO DIE FOR** *Jive 9201272* **42** 1

GALLIANO *UK, male / female vocal (Valerie Etienne) / instrumental group (2 Albums: 15 Weeks, 6 Singles: 14 Weeks)*

30 May 92 **SKUNK FUNK** *Talkin Loud TLK 23* **41** 2
20 Jun 92 A JOYFUL NOISE UNTO THE CREATOR *Talkin Loud 8480802* 28 3
1 Aug 92 **PRINCE OF PEACE** *Talkin Loud TLK 24* **47** 3
10 Oct 92 **JUS' REACH (RECYCLED)** *Talkin Loud TLK 29* **66** 2
28 May 94 **LONG TIME GONE** *Talkin Loud TLKCD 48* **15** 3
11 Jun 94 ● THE PLOT THICKENS *Talkin Loud 5224522* 7 12
30 Jul 94 **TWYFORD DOWN** *Talkin Loud TLKCD 49* **37** 2
27 Jul 96 **EASE YOUR MIND** *Talkin Loud TLCD 10* **45** 2

GALLON DRUNK *UK, male vocal / instrumental group*

13 Mar 93 FROM THE HEART OF TOWN *Clawfist HUNKACDL 005* 67 1

James GALWAY
UK, male flautist (12 Albums: 102 Weeks, 1 Single: 13 Weeks)

27 May 78 THE MAGIC FLUTE OF JAMES GALWAY *RCA Red Seal LRLI 5131* 43 6
27 May 78 ● **ANNIE'S SONG** *RCA Red Seal RB 5085* [1] **3** 13
1 Jul 78 THE MAN WITH THE GOLDEN FLUTE *RCA Red Seal LRLI 5127* 52 3
9 Sep 78 ● JAMES GALWAY PLAYS SONGS FOR ANNIE *RCA Red Seal RL 25163* 7 40
15 Dec 79 SONGS OF THE SEASHORE *Solar RL 25253* 39 6
31 May 80 SOMETIMES WHEN WE TOUCH *RCA PL 25296* [1] 15 14
18 Dec 82 THE JAMES GALWAY COLLECTION *Telstar STAR 2224* 41 8
8 Dec 84 IN THE PINK *RCA Red Seal RL 85315* [2] 62 6
28 Mar 87 JAMES GALWAY AND THE CHIEFTAINS IN IRELAND *RCA Red Seal RL 85798* [3] 32 5
17 Apr 93 THE ESSENTIAL FLUTE OF JAMES GALWAY *RCA Victor 74321133852* 30 5
18 Feb 95 I WILL ALWAYS LOVE YOU *RCA Victor 74321262212* 59 2
20 Jul 96 CLASSICAL MEDITATIONS *RCA Victor 74321377312* 45 5
25 Sep 04 WINGS OF SONG *Deutsche Grammophon 4775236* 45 2

[1] James Galway, flute, National Philharmonic Orchestra; Charles Gerhart, conductor [1] Cleo Laine and James Galway [2] James Galway and Henry Mancini with the National Philharmonic Orchestra [3] James Galway and The Chieftains

GAMBAFREAKS *Italy, male production duo (2 Singles: 2 Weeks)*

12 Sep 98 **INSTANT REPLAY** *Evocative EVOKE 7CDS* [1] **57** 1
13 May 00 **DOWN DOWN DOWN** *Azuli AZNYCDX 116* **57** 1

[1] Gambafreaks featuring Paco Rivaz

The GAME NEW (see also G-UNIT) *US, male rapper – Jayceon Taylor (1 Album: 33 Weeks, 6 Singles: 36 Weeks)*

5 Feb 05 ● THE DOCUMENTARY *Interscope 9864143* ▲ 7 33
26 Feb 05 ● **HOW WE DO** *Interscope 9880361* [1] **5** 12
21 May 05 ● **HATE IT OR LOVE IT** *Interscope 9882205* [1] **4** 12
13 Aug 05 ● **DREAMS** *Interscope 9883904* **8** 8
10 Sep 05 **PLAYA'S ONLY** *Jive 82876720512* [2] **33** 2
19 Nov 05 **PUT YOU ON THE GAME** *Interscope 9887827* **46** 2

[1] The Game featuring 50 Cent [2] R Kelly featuring The Game

GANG OF FOUR
UK, male vocal / instrumental group (3 Albums: 9 Weeks, 2 Singles: 5 Weeks)

16 Jun 79 **AT HOME HE'S A TOURIST** *EMI 2956* **58** 3
13 Oct 79 ENTERTAINMENT *EMI EMC 3313* 45 3
21 Mar 81 SOLID GOLD *EMI EMC 3364* 52 2
22 May 82 **I LOVE A MAN IN UNIFORM** *EMI 5299* **65** 2
29 May 82 SONGS OF THE FREE *EMI EMC 3412* 61 4

GANG STARR (see also GURU) *US, male rap duo – Christopher Martin and Keith Elam (5 Albums: 10 Weeks, 4 Singles: 8 Weeks)*

13 Oct 90 **JAZZ THING** *CBS 356377 7* **66** 2
26 Jan 91 STEP IN THE ARENA *Cooltempo ZCTLP 21* 36 3
23 Feb 91 **TAKE A REST** *Cooltempo COOL 230* **63** 1
25 May 91 **LOVESICK** *Cooltempo COOL 234* **50** 3
13 Jun 92 **2 DEEP** *Cooltempo COOL 256* **67** 2
12 Mar 94 HARD TO EARN *Cooltempo CTCD 38* 29 3
11 Apr 98 MOMENT OF TRUTH *Cooltempo 8590322* 43 1
7 Aug 99 FULL CLIP: A DECADE OF GANG STARR *Cooltempo 5211892* 47 2
5 Jul 03 THE OWNERZ *Virgin CDVUS 235* 74 1

GANT *UK, production duo – Julian Jonah and Danny Harrison*

27 Dec 97 **SOUND BWOY BURIAL / ALL NIGHT LONG** *Positiva CDTIV 85* **67** 1

The GAP BAND *US, male vocal / instrumental trio – includes Charlie Wilson (1 Album: 3 Weeks, 14 Singles: 88 Weeks)*

12 Jul 80 ● **OOPS UP SIDE YOUR HEAD** *Mercury MER 22* **6** 14
27 Sep 80 **PARTY LIGHTS** *Mercury MER 37* **30** 8
27 Dec 80 **BURN RUBBER ON ME (WHY YOU WANNA HURT ME)** *Mercury MER 52* **22** 11
11 Apr 81 **HUMPIN'** *Mercury MER 63* **36** 6
27 Jun 81 **YEARNING FOR YOUR LOVE** *Mercury MER 73* **47** 4
5 Jun 82 **EARLY IN THE MORNING** *Mercury MER 97* **55** 3
19 Feb 83 **OUTSTANDING** *Total Experience TE 001* **68** 2
31 Mar 84 **SOMEDAY** *Total Experience TE 5* **17** 8
23 Jun 84 **JAMMIN' IN AMERICA** *Total Experience TE 6* **64** 2
13 Dec 86 ● **BIG FUN** *Total Experience FB 49779* **4** 12
7 Feb 87 GAP BAND 8 *Total Experience FL 89992* 47 3
14 Mar 87 **HOW MUSIC CAME ABOUT (BOP B DA B DA DA)** *Total Experience FB 49755* **61** 2
11 Jul 87 **OOPS UP SIDE YOUR HEAD** (re-mix) *Club JAB 54* **20** 8
18 Feb 89 **I'M GONNA GIT YOU SUCKA** *Arista 112016* **63** 2
16 Oct 04 **OOPS UPSIDE YOUR HEAD** (re-recording) *All Around the World CDGLOBE 376* [1] **16** 6

[1] DJ Casper featuring The Gap Band

GARBAGE 263 Top 500 *The missing link between techno and grunge, formed Madison, Wisconsin, US, in 1993: includes Shirley Manson (v/g) (b. Edinburgh, Scotland), and Butch Vig (d), who produced Nirvana and the Smashing Pumpkins (4 Albums: 174 Weeks, 17 Singles: 74 Weeks)*

19 Aug 95 **SUBHUMAN** *Mushroom D 1138* **50** 1
30 Sep 95 **ONLY HAPPY WHEN IT RAINS** *Mushroom D 1199* **29** 3
14 Oct 95 ● GARBAGE *Mushroom D 31450* 6 100
2 Dec 95 **QUEER** *Mushroom D 1237* **13** 4
23 Mar 96 ● **STUPID GIRL** *Mushroom D 1271* **4** 7
23 Nov 96 ● **MILK (re)** *Mushroom D 1494* [1] **10** 8
9 May 98 ● **PUSH IT** *Mushroom MUSH 28CDS* **9** 5
23 May 98 ★ VERSION 2.0 *Mushroom MUSH 29CD* ■ 1 65
18 Jul 98 ● **I THINK I'M PARANOID** *Mushroom MUSH 35CDS* **9** 5
17 Oct 98 **SPECIAL** *Mushroom MUSH 39CDS* **15** 4
6 Feb 99 ● **WHEN I GROW UP** *Mushroom MUSH 43CDS* **9** 7
5 Jun 99 **YOU LOOK SO FINE** *Mushroom MUSH 49CDS* **19** 4
27 Nov 99 **THE WORLD IS NOT ENOUGH** *Radioactive RAXTD 40* **11** 9
6 Oct 01 **ANDROGYNY** *Mushroom MUSH 94CDS* **24** 2
13 Oct 01 ● BEAUTIFUL GARBAGE *Mushroom MUSH 95CD* 6 4
2 Feb 02 **CHERRY LIPS (GO BABY GO!)** *Mushroom MUSH 98CDS* **22** 4
20 Apr 02 **BREAKING UP THE GIRL** *Mushroom MUSH 101CDS* **27** 2
5 Oct 02 **SHUT YOUR MOUTH** *Mushroom MUSH 106CDS* **20** 1
16 Apr 05 ● **WHY DO YOU LOVE ME** *Mushroom WEA 385CD* **7** 6

3 / 6 July 1968	10 / 13 July 1968	17 / 20 July 1968	24 / 27 July 1968
BABY COME BACK The Equals	BABY COME BACK The Equals	BABY COME BACK The Equals	I PRETEND Des O'Connor
OGDENS' NUT GONE FLAKE The Small Faces	OGDENS' NUT GONE FLAKE The Small Faces	OGDENS' NUT GONE FLAKE The Small Faces	OGDENS' NUT GONE FLAKE The Small Faces

KEY
UK No.1 ★ UK Top 10 ● Still on chart + UK entry at No.1 ■
US No.1 ▲ UK million seller £ US million seller $
Singles re-entries are listed as (re), (2re), (3re)... which signifies that the hit re-entered the chart once, twice or three times...
Peak Position / Weeks

23 Apr 05 ● BLEED LIKE ME *Mushroom 5046776812*....4 5
25 Jun 05 SEX IS NOT THE ENEMY *A&E WEA 391CD*....24 2

[1] Garbage featuring Tricky

Jan GARBAREK *Norway, male saxophonist*

4 May 96 VISIBLE WORLD *ECM 5290862*....69 1

Adam GARCIA *Australia, male vocalist*

16 May 98 NIGHT FEVER *Polydor 5697972*....15 5

Scott GARCIA featuring MC STYLES (see also CORRUPTED CRU featuring MC NEAT) *UK, male producer and rapper – Daryl Turner*

1 Nov 97 A LONDON THING *Connected CDCONNECT 1*....29 3

Boris GARDINER *Jamaica, male vocalist / bass gutarist (4 Singles: 38 Weeks)*

17 Jan 70 ELIZABETHAN REGGAE (re) *Duke DU 39*....14 14
26 Jul 86 ★ I WANT TO WAKE UP WITH YOU *Revue REV 733*....1 15
4 Oct 86 YOU'RE EVERYTHING TO ME *Revue REV 735*....11 8
27 Dec 86 THE MEANING OF CHRISTMAS *Revue REV 740*....69 1

The first copies of 'Elizabethan Reggae', an instrumental, were printed with the label incorrectly crediting Byron Lee as the performer. The chart for the original entry, and the first four weeks of the re-entry, all reprinted this error. All charts and discs printed after 28 Feb 1970 gave Boris Gardiner the credit he deserved.

Paul GARDINER *UK, male bass gutarist*

25 Jul 81 STORMTROOPER IN DRAG *Beggars Banquet BEG 61*....49 4

Uncredited vocalist is Gary Numan.

Art GARFUNKEL (see also SIMON and GARFUNKEL) *US, male vocalist (7 Albums: 64 Weeks, 3 Singles: 37 Weeks)*

13 Oct 73 ANGEL CLARE *CBS 69021*....14 7
13 Sep 75 ★ I ONLY HAVE EYES FOR YOU *CBS 3575*....1 11
1 Nov 75 ● BREAKAWAY *CBS 86002*....7 10
18 Mar 78 WATER MARK *CBS 86054*....25 5
3 Mar 79 ★ BRIGHT EYES *CBS 6947* £....1 19
21 Apr 79 ● FATE FOR BREAKFAST *CBS 86082*....2 20
7 Jul 79 SINCE I DON'T HAVE YOU *CBS 7371*....38 7
19 Sep 81 SCISSORS CUT *CBS 85259*....51 3
17 Nov 84 THE ART GARFUNKEL ALBUM *CBS 10046*....12 13
14 Dec 96 THE VERY BEST OF ART GARFUNKEL – ACROSS AMERICA *Virgin VTCD 113*....35 6

Judy GARLAND *US, female vocalist – Frances Gumm, b. 10 Jun 1922, d. 22 Jan 1969*

10 Jun 55 THE MAN THAT GOT AWAY *Philips PB 366*....18 2
3 Mar 62 JUDY AT CARNEGIE HALL *Capitol W 1569* ▲....13 3

Jessica GARLICK *UK, female vocalist*

25 May 02 COME BACK *Columbia 6725662*....13 6

Errol GARNER *US, male pianist, b. 15 Jun 1923, d. 2 Jan 1977*

14 Jul 62 CLOSE UP IN SWING *Philips BBL 7579*....20 1

Laurent GARNIER *France, male DJ / producer (3 Singles: 4 Weeks)*

15 Feb 97 CRISPY BACON *F Communications F 055CD*....60 1
22 Apr 00 MAN WITH THE RED FACE *F Communications F 119CD*....65 1
11 Nov 00 GREED / THE MAN WITH THE RED FACE (re-issue) *F Communications F 127CDUK*....36 2

Lee GARRETT *US, male vocalist*

29 May 76 YOU'RE MY EVERYTHING *Chrysalis CHS 2087*....15 7

Leif GARRETT *US, male vocalist (2 Singles: 14 Weeks)*

20 Jan 79 ● I WAS MADE FOR DANCIN' *Scotti Brothers K 11202*....4 10
21 Apr 79 FEEL THE NEED *Scotti Brothers K 11274*....38 4

Lesley GARRETT *UK, female vocalist (8 Albums: 44 Weeks, 1 Single: 10 Weeks)*

6 Nov 93 AVE MARIA *Internal Affairs KGBD 012* [1]....16 10
12 Feb 94 THE ALBUM *Telstar TCD 2709*....25 7
18 Nov 95 SOPRANO IN RED *Silva Classics SILKTVCD 1*....59 8
19 Oct 96 SOPRANO IN HOLLYWOOD *Silva Classics SILKTVCD 2*....53 4
18 Oct 97 THE SOPRANO'S GREATEST HITS *Silva Classics SILKTVCD 3*....53 2
22 Nov 97 A SOPRANO INSPIRED *Conifer Classics 75605513292*....48 7
14 Nov 98 LESLEY GARRETT *BBC / BMG Conifer 75605513382*....34 8
27 May 00 I WILL WAIT FOR YOU *BBC / BMG Conifer 75605513542*....28 7
24 Nov 01 TRAVELLING LIGHT *EMI Classics CDC 5572512*....75 1

[1] Lesley Garrett and Amanda Thompson

David GARRICK *UK, male vocalist – Philip Core (2 Singles: 16 Weeks)*

9 Jun 66 LADY JANE *Piccadilly 7N 35317*....28 7
22 Sep 66 DEAR MRS APPLEBEE *Piccadilly 7N 35335*....22 9

GARY'S GANG *US, male vocal (Eric Matthew) / instrumental group (3 Singles: 18 Weeks)*

24 Feb 79 ● KEEP ON DANCIN' *CBS 7109*....8 10
2 Jun 79 LET'S LOVEDANCE TONIGHT *CBS 7328*....49 4
6 Nov 82 KNOCK ME OUT *Arista ARIST 499*....45 4

GAT DECOR (see also PHUNKY PHANTOM; REST ASSURED) *UK, male instrumental / production group and female vocalist (2 Singles: 10 Weeks)*

16 May 92 PASSION *Effective EFFS 1*....29 4
9 Mar 96 ● PASSION (re-mix) *Way of Life WAYDA 1*....6 6

Stephen GATELY (see also BOYZONE) *Ireland, male vocalist (1 Album: 4 Weeks, 3 Singles: 19 Weeks)*

10 Jun 00 ● NEW BEGINNING / BRIGHT EYES *A&M / Polydor 5618192*....3 11
1 Jul 00 ● NEW BEGINNING *A&M 5439102*....9 4
14 Oct 00 I BELIEVE *Polydor 5877472*....11 4
12 May 01 STAY *A&M / Mercury 5870672*....13 4

David GATES (see also BREAD) *US, male vocalist (4 Albums: 30 Weeks, 1 Single: 2 Weeks)*

31 May 75 NEVER LET HER GO *Elektra K 52012*....32 1
22 Jul 78 TOOK THE LAST TRAIN *Elektra K 12307*....50 2
29 Jul 78 GOODBYE GIRL *Elektra K 52091*....28 3
5 Jul 97 ● ESSENTIALS *Jive 9548354082* [1]....9 19
12 Oct 02 THE DAVID GATES SONGBOOK – A LIFETIME OF MUSIC *Jive 0927491402*....11 7

[1] David Gates and Bread

Gareth GATES *UK, male vocalist (2 Albums: 21 Weeks, 7 Singles: 109 Weeks)*

30 Mar 02 ★ UNCHAINED MELODY (2re) *S 74321930882* ■ £....1 30
20 Jul 02 ★ ANYONE OF US (STUPID MISTAKE) *S 74321950602* ■....1 15
5 Oct 02 ★ THE LONG AND WINDING ROAD / SUSPICIOUS MINDS *S 74321965972* [1] ■....1 18
9 Nov 02 ● WHAT MY HEART WANTS TO SAY *S 74321975172*....2 17
21 Dec 02 ● WHAT MY HEART WANTS TO SAY (re) *S 743211985592*....5 13
22 Mar 03 ★ SPIRIT IN THE SKY *S 82876511202* [2] ■....1 15
20 Sep 03 ● SUNSHINE (re) *S 82876560032*....3 10

31 July / 3 August 1968	7 / 10 August 1968	14 / 17 August 1968	21 / 24 August 1968
UK No.1 SINGLES			
MONY MONY Tommy James and The Shondells	MONY MONY Tommy James and The Shondells	FIRE The Crazy World of Arthur Brown	MONY MONY Tommy James and The Shondells
UK No.1 ALBUMS			
OGDENS' NUT GONE FLAKE The Small Faces	DELILAH Tom Jones	BOOKENDS Simon and Garfunkel	BOOKENDS Simon and Garfunkel

4 Oct 03 GO YOUR OWN WAY *S 82876557452* 11 4
13 Dec 03 ● SAY IT ISN'T SO *S 82876583412* 4 8

[1] Will Young and Gareth Gates / Gareth Gates [2] Gareth Gates featuring The Kumars

GAY DAD *UK, male / female vocal (Cliff Jones) / instrumental group (1 Album: 3 Weeks, 5 Singles: 10 Weeks)*

30 Jan 99 ● TO EARTH WITH LOVE *London LONCD 413* 10 4
5 Jun 99 JOY! *London LONCD 428* 22 3
19 Jun 99 LEISURE NOISE *London 5561032* 14 3
14 Aug 99 OH JIM *London LONCD 437* 47 1
31 Mar 01 NOW ALWAYS AND FOREVER *B-Unique BUN 004CD* 41 1
22 Sep 01 TRANSMISSION *B-Unique BUN 009CD* 58 1

GAY GORDON and The MINCE PIES *UK, male / female vocal / instrumental group*

6 Dec 86 THE ESSENTIAL WALLY PARTY MEDLEY *Lifestyle XY 2* 60 5

Marvin GAYE (124 Top 500) *One of soul's most innovative and successful singer / songwriters, b. 2 Apr 1939, Washington DC, US, d. 1 Apr 1984. He went from doo-wop group member and session drummer to superstar. Posthumously awarded a Lifetime Achievement Grammy Award in 1996 (17 Albums: 190 Weeks, 25 Singles: 202 Weeks)*

30 Jul 64 ONCE UPON A TIME *Stateside SS 316* [1] 50 1
10 Dec 64 HOW SWEET IT IS *Stateside SS 360* 49 1
29 Sep 66 LITTLE DARLIN' (I NEED YOU) *Tamla Motown TMG 574* 50 1
26 Jan 67 IT TAKES TWO *Tamla Motown TMG 590* [2] 16 11
17 Jan 68 IF I COULD BUILD MY WHOLE WORLD AROUND YOU *Tamla Motown TMG 635* [3] 41 7
16 Mar 68 GREATEST HITS *Tamla Motown STML 11065* 40 1
12 Jun 68 AIN'T NOTHIN' LIKE THE REAL THING *Tamla Motown TMG 655* [3] 34 7
2 Oct 68 YOU'RE ALL I NEED TO GET BY *Tamla Motown TMG 668* [3] 19 19
22 Jan 69 YOU AIN'T LIVIN' TILL YOU'RE LOVIN' *Tamla Motown TMG 681* [3] 21 8
12 Feb 69 ★ I HEARD IT THROUGH THE GRAPEVINE *Tamla Motown TMG 686* ▲ $ 1 15
4 Jun 69 GOOD LOVIN' AIN'T EASY TO COME BY (re) *Tamla Motown TMG 697* [3] 26 8
23 Jul 69 ● TOO BUSY THINKING 'BOUT MY BABY *Tamla Motown TMG 705* 5 16
15 Nov 69 ● ONION SONG *Tamla Motown TMG 715* [3] 9 12
9 May 70 ● ABRAHAM, MARTIN AND JOHN *Tamla Motown TMG 734* 9 14
22 Aug 70 GREATEST HITS *Tamla Motown STML 11153* [1] 60 4
19 Jan 71 ● DIANA&MARVIN *Tamla Motown STMA 8015* [2] 6 43
11 Dec 71 SAVE THE CHILDREN *Tamla Motown TMG 796* 41 6
22 Sep 73 LET'S GET IT ON *Tamla Motown TMG 868* ▲ $ 31 7
10 Nov 73 LET'S GET IT ON *Tamla Motown STMA 8013* 39 1
23 Mar 74 ● YOU ARE EVERYTHING *Tamla Motown TMG 890* [4] 5 12
20 Jul 74 STOP LOOK LISTEN (TO YOUR HEART) *Tamla Motown TMG 906* [4] 25 8
15 May 76 I WANT YOU *Tamla Motown STML 12025* 22 5
30 Oct 76 THE BEST OF MARVIN GAYE *Tamla Motown STML 12042* 56 1
7 May 77 ● GOT TO GIVE IT UP (PT.1) *Motown TMG 1069* ▲ $ 7 10
24 Feb 79 POPS, WE LOVE YOU *Motown TMG 1136* [5] 66 5
28 Feb 81 IN OUR LIFETIME *Motown STML 12149* 48 4
29 Aug 81 DIANA&MARVIN (re-issue) *Motown STMS 5001* [2] 78 2
30 Oct 82 ● (SEXUAL) HEALING *CBS A 2855* $ 4 14
20 Nov 82 ● MIDNIGHT LOVE *CBS 85977* 10 16
8 Jan 83 MY LOVE IS WAITING *CBS A 3048* 34 5
12 Nov 83 GREATEST HITS *Telstar STAR 2234* 13 61
18 May 85 SANCTIFIED LADY *CBS A 4894* 51 4
15 Jun 85 DREAM OF A LIFETIME *CBS 26239* 46 4
26 Apr 86 ● I HEARD IT THROUGH THE GRAPEVINE (re-issue) *Tamla Motown ZB 40701* 8 8
12 Nov 88 LOVE SONGS *Telstar STAR 2331* [3] 69 9
2 Nov 90 LOVE SONGS *Telstar STAR 2427* 39 5
9 Apr 94 ● THE VERY BEST OF MARVIN GAYE *Motown 5302922* 3 19
14 May 94 LUCKY LUCKY ME *Motown TMGCD 1426* 67 1
24 Jul 99 WHAT'S GOING ON *Motown 5308832* 56 4
19 Feb 00 ● THE LOVE SONGS *UMTV / Motown 5454702* 8 7
1 Sep 01 THE VERY BEST OF MARVIN GAYE *Motown 143672* 15 4
6 Oct 01 MUSIC *Polydor 4976222* [6] 36 2

[1] Marvin Gaye and Mary Wells [2] Marvin Gaye and Kim Weston [3] Marvin Gaye and Tammi Terrell [4] Diana Ross and Marvin Gaye [5] Diana Ross, Marvin Gaye, Smokey Robinson and Stevie Wonder [6] Erick Sermon featuring Marvin Gaye [1] Marvin Gaye and Tammi Terrell [2] Diana Ross and Marvin Gaye [3] Marvin Gaye and Smokey Robinson

The three Greatest Hits and the two The Very Best of Marvin Gaye albums are different.

GAYE BYKERS ON ACID *UK, male vocal / instrumental group*

31 Oct 87 GIT DOWN (SHAKE YOUR THANG) *Purple Fluid VS 1008* 54 2
14 Nov 87 DRILL YOUR OWN HOLE *Virgin V 2478* 95 1

Crystal GAYLE *US, female vocalist – Brenda Gail Webb (3 Albums: 25 Weeks, 2 Singles: 28 Weeks)*

12 Nov 77 ● DON'T IT MAKE MY BROWN EYES BLUE *United Artists UP 36307* $ 5 14
21 Jan 78 WE MUST BELIEVE IN MAGIC *United Artists UAG 30108* 15 7
26 Aug 78 TALKING IN YOUR SLEEP *United Artists UP 36422* 11 14
23 Sep 78 WHEN I DREAM *United Artists UAG 30169* 25 8
22 Mar 80 ● THE CRYSTAL GAYLE SINGLES ALBUM *United Artists UAG 30287* 7 10

Michelle GAYLE *UK, female actor / vocalist (2 Albums: 13 Weeks, 7 Singles: 52 Weeks)*

7 Aug 93 LOOKING UP *RCA 74321154532* 11 6
24 Sep 94 ● SWEETNESS *RCA 74321230192* 4 16
22 Oct 94 MICHELLE GAYLE *RCA 74321234122* 30 10
17 Dec 94 I'LL FIND YOU *RCA 74321247762* 26 7
27 May 95 FREEDOM *RCA 74321284692* 16 6
26 Aug 95 HAPPY JUST TO BE WITH YOU *RCA 74321302692* 11 7
8 Feb 97 ● DO YOU KNOW *RCA 74321419282* 6 6
26 Apr 97 SENSATIONAL *RCA 74321419302* 14 4
10 May 97 SENSATIONAL *RCA 74321419322* 17 3

GAYLE & GILLIAN *Australia, female vocal / actor duo (twins) – Gayle and Gillian Blakeney (2 Singles: 2 Weeks)*

3 Jul 93 MAD IF YA DON'T *Mushroom CDMUSH 1* 75 1
19 Mar 94 WANNA BE YOUR LOVER *Mushroom D 11598* 62 1

Gloria GAYNOR *Legendary disco diva, b. Gloria Fowles, 7 Sep 1949, New Jersey, US. Her transatlantic chart-topping feminist anthem and karaoke favourite proved it would survive by returning to the Top 5, in re-mixed form, 14 years after reaching No.1 (3 Albums: 17 Weeks, 9 Singles: 73 Weeks)*

7 Dec 74 ● NEVER CAN SAY GOODBYE *MGM 2006 463* 2 13
8 Mar 75 NEVER CAN SAY GOODBYE *MGM 2315 321* 32 8
8 Mar 75 REACH OUT, I'LL BE THERE *MGM 2006 499* 14 8
9 Aug 75 ALL I NEED IS YOUR SWEET LOVIN' *MGM 2006 531* 44 3
17 Jan 76 HOW HIGH THE MOON *MGM 2006 558* 33 4
3 Feb 79 ★ I WILL SURVIVE *Polydor 2095 017* ▲ $ 1 15
24 Mar 79 LOVE TRACKS *Polydor 2391 385* 31 7
6 Oct 79 LET ME KNOW (I HAVE A RIGHT) *Polydor STEP 5* 32 7
24 Dec 83 I AM WHAT I AM (FROM 'LA CAGE AUX FOLLES') *Chrysalis CHS 2765* 13 12
16 Aug 86 THE POWER OF GLORIA GAYNOR *Stylus SMR 618* 81 2
26 Jun 93 ● I WILL SURVIVE (re-mix) *Polydor PZCD 270* 5 10
3 Jun 00 LAST NIGHT *Logic 74321738082* 67 1

GAZ *US, male vocal / instrumental group*

24 Feb 79 SING SING *Salsoul SSOL 116* 60 4

28 / 31 August 1968	4 / 7 September 1968	11 / 14 September 1968	18 / 21 September 1968
DO IT AGAIN The Beach Boys	I'VE GOTTA GET A MESSAGE TO YOU The Bee Gees	HEY JUDE The Beatles	HEY JUDE The Beatles
BOOKENDS Simon and Garfunkel	BOOKENDS Simon and Garfunkel	BOOKENDS Simon and Garfunkel	DELILAH Tom Jones

KEY UK No.1 ★ UK Top 10 ● Still on chart + UK entry at No.1 ■ US No.1 ▲ UK million seller £ US million seller $
Singles re-entries are listed as (re), (2re), (3re)... which signifies that the hit re-entered the chart once, twice or three times...
Peak Position / Weeks

GAZZA *UK, male footballer / vocalist – Paul Gascoigne (2 Singles: 14 Weeks)*

10 Nov 90 ● **FOG ON THE TYNE (REVISITED)** *Best ZB 44083* [1] **2** 9
22 Dec 90 **GEORDIE BOYS (GAZZA RAP)** *Best ZB 44229* **31** 5

[1] Gazza and Lindisfarne

Nigel GEE *UK, male producer*

27 Jan 01 **HOOTIN'** *Neo NEOCD 040* **57** 1

J GEILS BAND *US, male vocal (Peter Wolf) / instrumental group – leader Jerome Geils (1 Albums: 15 Weeks, 4 Singles: 20 Weeks)*

9 Jun 79 **ONE LAST KISS** *EMI America AM 507* **74** 1
13 Feb 82 ● **CENTERFOLD** *EMI America EA 135* ▲ $ **3** 9
27 Feb 82 FREEZE-FRAME *EMI America AML 3020* ▲ 12 15
10 Apr 82 **FREEZE-FRAME** *EMI America EA 134* $ **27** 7
26 Jun 82 **ANGEL IN BLUE** *EMI America EA 138* **55** 3

Bob GELDOF (see also The BOOMTOWN RATS) *Ireland, male vocalist (3 Albums: 10 Weeks, 4 Singles: 15 Weeks)*

1 Nov 86 **THIS IS THE WORLD CALLING** *Mercury BOB 101* **25** 5
6 Dec 86 DEEP IN THE HEART OF NOWHERE *Mercury BOBLP 1* 79 1
21 Feb 87 **LOVE LIKE A ROCKET** *Mercury BOB 102* **61** 3
23 Jun 90 **THE GREAT SONG OF INDIFFERENCE** *Mercury BOB 104* **15** 6
4 Aug 90 THE VEGETARIANS OF LOVE *Mercury 8462501* 21 6
7 May 94 **CRAZY** *Vertigo VERCX 85* **65** 1
9 Jul 94 ● LOUDMOUTH – THE BEST OF BOB GELDOF & THE BOOMTOWN RATS *Vertigo 5222832* [1] 10 3

[1] The Boomtown Rats and Bob Geldof

GEMINI (see also CHILDLINERS) *UK, male vocal duo (twins) – Michael and David Smallwood (3 Singles: 7 Weeks)*

30 Sep 95 **EVEN THOUGH YOU BROKE MY HEART** *EMI CDEMS 391* **40** 3
10 Feb 96 **STEAL YOUR LOVE AWAY** *EMI CDEMS 407* **37** 2
29 Jun 96 **COULD IT BE FOREVER** *EMI CDEMS 426* **38** 2

GEMS FOR JEM (see also JDS) *UK, male instrumental / production duo – Steve McCutcheon and Darren Pearce*

6 May 95 **LIFTING ME HIGHER** *Box 21 CDSBOKS 3* **28** 2

GENE *UK, male vocal (Martin Rossiter) / instrumental group (4 Albums: 14 Weeks, 12 Singles: 23 Weeks)*

13 Aug 94 **BE MY LIGHT BE MY GUIDE** *Costermonger COST 002CD* **54** 1
12 Nov 94 **SLEEP WELL TONIGHT** *Costermonger COST 003CD* **36** 2
4 Mar 95 **HAUNTED BY YOU** *Costermonger COST 004CD* **32** 2
1 Apr 95 ● OLYMPIAN *Costermonger 5274462* 8 6
22 Jul 95 **OLYMPIAN** *Costermonger COST 005CD* **18** 2
13 Jan 96 **FOR THE DEAD** *Costermonger COST 006CD* **14** 3
3 Feb 96 TO SEE THE LIGHTS *Costermonger GENE 002CD* 11 3
2 Nov 96 **FIGHTING FIT** *Costermonger COST 009CD* **22** 2
1 Feb 97 **WE COULD BE KINGS** *Polydor COSCD 10* **17** 2
1 Mar 97 ● DRAWN TO THE DEEP END *Polydor GENEC 3* 8 3
10 May 97 **WHERE ARE THEY NOW?** *Polydor COSCD 11* **22** 2
9 Aug 97 **SPEAK TO ME SOMEONE** *Polydor COSCD 12* **30** 2
27 Feb 99 **AS GOOD AS IT GETS** *Polydor COSCD 14* **23** 2
13 Mar 99 REVELATIONS *Polydor GENEC 4* 25 2
24 Apr 99 **FILL HER UP** *Polydor COSCD 15* **36** 2
25 Dec 04 **LET ME MOVE ON** *Costermonger COST 10CD1* **69** 1

GENE AND JIM ARE INTO SHAKES *UK, male vocal / instrumental duo*

19 Mar 88 **SHAKE! (HOW ABOUT A SAMPLING, GENE?)** *Rough Trade RT 216* **68** 2

GENE LOVES JEZEBEL *UK, male vocal / instrumental group (2 Albums: 5 Weeks, 4 Singles: 7 Weeks)*

29 Mar 86 **SWEETEST THING** *Beggars Banquet BEG 156* **75** 1
14 Jun 86 **HEARTACHE** *Beggars Banquet BEG 161* **71** 2
19 Jul 87 DISCOVER *Beggars Banquet BEGA 73* 32 4
5 Sep 87 **THE MOTION OF LOVE** *Beggars Banquet BEG 192* **56** 3
24 Oct 87 HOUSE OF DOLLS *Beggars Banquet BEGA 87* 81 1
5 Dec 87 **GORGEOUS** *Beggars Banquet BEG 202* **68** 1

GENERAL LEVY *UK, male vocalist – Paul Levy (4 Singles: 14 Weeks)*

4 Sep 93 **MONKEY MAN** *ffrr FCD 214* **75** 1
18 Jun 94 **INCREDIBLE** *Renk RENK 42CD* [1] **39** 3
10 Sep 94 ● **INCREDIBLE** (re-mix) *Renk CD RENK 44* [1] **8** 9
13 Mar 04 **SHAKE (WHAT YA MAMA GAVE YA)** *East West EW 281CD* [2] . **51** 1

[1] M-Beat featuring General Levy [2] General Levy vs Zeus featuring Bally Jagpal

GENERAL PUBLIC (see also The BEAT) *UK, male vocal / instrumental group (2 Singles: 4 Weeks)*

10 Mar 84 **GENERAL PUBLIC** *Virgin VS 659* **60** 3
2 Jul 94 **I'LL TAKE YOU THERE** *Epic 6605532* **73** 1

GENERAL SAINT *UK, male vocalist (3 Singles: 4 Weeks)*

29 Sep 84 **LAST PLANE (ONE WAY TICKET)** *MCA MCA 910* [1] **51** 3
6 Aug 94 **SAVE THE LAST DANCE FOR ME** *Copasetic COPCD 12* [2] **75** 1

[1] Clint Eastwood and General Saint [2] General Saint featuring Don Campbell

GENERATION X (see also Billy IDOL) *UK, male vocal / instrumental group (2 Albums: 9 Weeks, 7 Singles: 31 Weeks)*

17 Sep 77 **YOUR GENERATION** *Chrysalis CHS 2165* **36** 4
11 Mar 78 **READY STEADY GO** *Chrysalis CHS 2207* **47** 3
8 Apr 78 GENERATION X *Chrysalis CHR 1169* 29 4
20 Jan 79 **KING ROCKER** *Chrysalis CHS 2261* **11** 9
17 Feb 79 VALLEY OF THE DOLLS *Chrysalis CHR 1193* 51 5
7 Apr 79 **VALLEY OF THE DOLLS** *Chrysalis CHS 2310* **23** 7
30 Jun 79 **FRIDAY'S ANGELS** *Chrysalis CHS 2330* **62** 2
18 Oct 80 **DANCING WITH MYSELF** *Chrysalis CHS 2444* [1] **62** 2
24 Jan 81 **DANCING WITH MYSELF (EP)** *Chrysalis CHS 2488* [1] **60** 4

[1] Gen X

Tracks on Dancing With Myself (EP): Dancing With Myself (re-issue) / Untouchables / Rock On / King Rocker.

GENERATOR (see also STARPARTY) *Holland, male producer – Robert Smit*

23 Oct 99 **WHERE ARE YOU NOW?** *Tidy Trax TIDY 130CD* **60** 1

GENESIS 46 Top 500 (see also MIKE and The MECHANICS)

Perennially popular UK group. Stalwart members are Tony Banks (k) and Mike Rutherford (g); others included Peter Gabriel (v), Phil Collins (v/d), Steve Hackett (g). These progressive 1970s rockers became a major act in the 1980s and had 10 consecutive newly recorded Top 3 albums (23 Albums: 500 Weeks, 29 Singles: 187 Weeks)

14 Oct 72 FOXTROT *Charisma CAS 1058* 12 7
11 Aug 73 ● GENESIS LIVE *Charisma CLASS 1* 9 10
20 Oct 73 ● SELLING ENGLAND BY THE POUND *Charisma CAS 1074* 3 21
6 Apr 74 **I KNOW WHAT I LIKE (IN YOUR WARDROBE)** *Charisma CB 224* **21** 7
11 May 74 NURSERY CRYME *Charisma CAS 1052* 39 1
7 Dec 74 ● THE LAMB LIES DOWN ON BROADWAY *Charisma CGS 101* 10 6
28 Feb 76 ● A TRICK OF THE TAIL *Charisma CDS 4001* 3 39
15 Jan 77 ● WIND & WUTHERING *Charisma CDS 4005* 7 22
26 Feb 77 **YOUR OWN SPECIAL WAY** *Charisma CB 300* **43** 3
28 May 77 **SPOT THE PIGEON (EP)** *Charisma GEN 001* **14** 7
29 Oct 77 ● SECONDS OUT *Charisma GE 2001* 4 17
11 Mar 78 ● **FOLLOW YOU FOLLOW ME** *Charisma CB 309* **7** 13
15 Apr 78 ● AND THEN THERE WERE THREE *Charisma CDS 4010* 3 32
8 Jul 78 **MANY TOO MANY** *Charisma CB 315* **43** 5

25 / 28 September 1968	2 / 5 October 1968	9 / 12 October 1968	16 / 19 October 1968
UK No.1 SINGLES			
THOSE WERE THE DAYS Mary Hopkin	THOSE WERE THE DAYS Mary Hopkin	THOSE WERE THE DAYS Mary Hopkin	THOSE WERE THE DAYS Mary Hopkin
UK No.1 ALBUMS			
BOOKENDS Simon and Garfunkel	BOOKENDS Simon and Garfunkel	THE HOLLIES' GREATEST HITS The Hollies	THE HOLLIES' GREATEST HITS The Hollies

15 Mar 80 ● **TURN IT ON AGAIN** *Charisma CB 356* 8 10
5 Apr 80 ★ **DUKE** *Charisma CBR 101* ■ 1 30
17 May 80 **DUCHESS** *Charisma CB 363* 46 5
13 Sep 80 **MISUNDERSTANDING** *Charisma CB 369* 42 5
22 Aug 81 ● **ABACAB** *Charisma CB 388* 9 8
26 Sep 81 ★ **ABACAB** *Charisma CBR 102* ■ 1 27
31 Oct 81 **KEEP IT DARK** *Charisma CB 391* 33 4
13 Mar 82 **MAN ON THE CORNER** *Charisma CB 393* 41 5
22 May 82 ● **3 X 3 (EP)** *Charisma GEN 1* 10 8
12 Jun 82 ● **THREE SIDES LIVE** *Charisma GE 2002* 2 19
3 Sep 83 ● **MAMA** *Virgin / Charisma MAMA 1* 4 10
15 Oct 83 ★ **GENESIS** *Charisma GENLP 1* ■ 1 51
12 Nov 83 **THAT'S ALL** *Charisma / Virgin TATA 1* 16 11
11 Feb 84 **ILLEGAL ALIEN (re)** *Charisma / Virgin AL 1* 46 4
31 Mar 84 **NURSERY CRYME** (re-issue) *Charisma CHC 22* 68 1
21 Apr 84 **TRESPASS** *Charisma CHC 12* 98 1
31 May 86 **INVISIBLE TOUCH** *Virgin GENS 1* ▲ 15 8
21 Jun 86 ★ **INVISIBLE TOUCH** *Charisma GENLP 2* ■ 1 96
30 Aug 86 **IN TOO DEEP** *Virgin GENS 2* 19 9
22 Nov 86 **LAND OF CONFUSION** *Virgin GENS 3* 14 12
14 Mar 87 **TONIGHT TONIGHT TONIGHT** *Virgin GENS 4* 18 6
20 Jun 87 **THROWING IT ALL AWAY** *Virgin GENS 5* 22 8
2 Nov 91 ● **NO SON OF MINE (re)** *Virgin GENS 6* 6 7
23 Nov 91 ★ **WE CAN'T DANCE** *Virgin GENLP 3* ■ 1 61
11 Jan 92 ● **I CAN'T DANCE** *Virgin GENS 7* 7 9
18 Apr 92 **HOLD ON MY HEART** *Virgin GENS 8* 16 5
25 Jul 92 **JESUS HE KNOWS ME** *Virgin GENS 9* 20 7
21 Nov 92 ● **INVISIBLE TOUCH (LIVE)** *Virgin GENS 10* 7 4
28 Nov 92 ● **LIVE – THE WAY WE WALK VOLUME ONE: THE SHORTS** *Virgin GENCD 4* 3 18
23 Jan 93 ★ **LIVE – THE WAY WE WALK VOLUME TWO: THE LONGS** *Virgin GENCD 5* ■ 1 9
20 Feb 93 **TELL ME WHY** *Virgin GENDG 11* 40 3
13 Sep 97 ● **CALLING ALL STATIONS** *Virgin GENCD 6* 2 7
27 Sep 97 **CONGO** *Virgin GENSD 12* 29 2
13 Dec 97 **SHIPWRECKED** *Virgin GENDX 14* 54 1
7 Mar 98 **NOT ABOUT US** *Virgin GENSD 15* 66 1
4 Jul 98 **ARCHIVE 1967-75** *Virgin CDBOX 6* 35 1
6 Nov 99 ● **TURN IT ON AGAIN – THE HITS** *Virgin GENCDX 8* 4 15
11 Dec 04 **PLATINUM COLLECTION** *Virgin GENCDX 9* 21 9

Tracks on Spot the Pigeon (EP): Match of the Day / Pigeons / Inside and Out.
Tracks on 3 x 3 (EP): Paperlate / You Might Recall / Me and Virgil.

GENEVA
UK, male vocal / instrumental group (1 Album: 2 Weeks, 6 Singles: 9 Weeks)

26 Oct 96 **NO ONE SPEAKS** *Nude NUD 22CD* 32 2
8 Feb 97 **INTO THE BLUE** *Nude NUD 25CD* 26 2
31 May 97 **TRANQUILIZER** *Nude NUD 28CD1* 24 2
21 Jun 97 **FURTHER** *Nude NUDE 7CD* 20 2
16 Aug 97 **BEST REGRETS** *Nude NUD 31CD1* 38 1
27 Nov 99 **DOLLARS IN THE HEAVENS** *Nude NUD 46CD1* 59 1
11 Mar 00 **IF YOU HAVE TO GO** *Nude NUD 49CD1* 69 1

GENEVIEVE *Uk, female vocalist – Susan Hunt*

5 May 66 **ONCE** *CBS 202061* 43 1

GENIUS CRU *UK, male rap / production group (2 Singles: 7 Weeks)*

3 Feb 01 **BOOM SELECTION** *Incentive CENT 17CDS* 12 5
27 Oct 01 **COURSE BRUV** *Incentive CENT 28CDS* 39 2

GENIUS / GZA (see also WU-TANG CLAN)
US, male rapper – Gary Crice (2 Albums: 2 Weeks, 1 Single: 2 Weeks)

2 Dec 95 **LIQUID SWORDS** *Geffen GED 24813* 73 1
2 Mar 96 **COLD WORLD** *Geffen GFSTD 22114* [1] 40 2
10 Jul 99 **BENEATH THE SURFACE** *MCA MCD 11969* 56 1

[1] Genius / GZA featuring D'Angelo

Jackie GENOVA *UK, female exercise instructor*

21 May 83 **WORK THAT BODY** *Island ILPS 9732* 74 2

Bobbie GENTRY *US, female vocalist – Roberta Streeter (2 Albums: 2 Weeks, 4 Singles: 48 Weeks)*

13 Sep 67 **ODE TO BILLIE JOE** *Capitol CL 15511* ▲ $ 13 11
30 Aug 69 ★ **I'LL NEVER FALL IN LOVE AGAIN** *Capitol CL 15606* 1 19
25 Oct 69 **TOUCH 'EM WITH LOVE** *Capitol EST 155* 21 1
6 Dec 69 ● **ALL I HAVE TO DO IS DREAM** *Capitol CL 15619* [1] 3 14
21 Feb 70 **RAINDROPS KEEP FALLING ON MY HEAD** *Capitol CL 15626* 40 4
28 Feb 70 **BOBBIE GENTRY AND GLEN CAMPBELL** *Capitol ST 2928* [1] 50 1

[1] Bobbie Gentry and Glen Campbell [1] Bobbie Gentry and Glen Campbell

GEORDIE (see also AC/DC)
UK, male vocal (Brian Johnson) / instrumental group (4 Singles: 35 Weeks)

2 Dec 72 **DON'T DO THAT** *Regal Zonophone RZ 3067* 32 7
17 Mar 73 ● **ALL BECAUSE OF YOU** *EMI 2008* 6 13
16 Jun 73 **CAN YOU DO IT** *EMI 2031* 13 9
25 Aug 73 **ELECTRIC LADY** *EMI 2048* 32 6

Lowell GEORGE (see also LITTLE FEAT)
US, male vocalist / guitarist, b. 13 Apr 1945, d. 29 Jun 1979

21 Apr 79 **THANKS BUT I'LL EAT IT HERE** *Warner Bros. K 56487* 71 1

Robin GEORGE *UK, male vocalist*

2 Mar 85 **DANGEROUS MUSIC** *Bronze BRON 554* 65 3
27 Apr 85 **HEARTLINE** *Bronze BRO 191* 68 2

Sophia GEORGE *Jamaica, female vocalist*

7 Dec 85 ● **GIRLIE GIRLIE** *Winner WIN 01* 7 11

The GEORGIA SATELLITES
US, male vocal / instrumental group (2 Albums: 9 Weeks, 3 Singles: 8 Weeks)

7 Feb 87 **GEORGIA SATELLITES** *Elektra 980 4961* 52 7
7 Feb 87 **KEEP YOUR HANDS TO YOURSELF** *Elektra EKR 50* 69 1
16 May 87 **BATTLESHIP CHAINS** *Elektra EKR 58* 44 4
2 Jul 88 **OPEN ALL NIGHT** *Elektra EKT 47* 39 2
21 Jan 89 **HIPPY HIPPY SHAKE** *Elektra EKR 86* 63 3

GEORGIE PORGIE *US, male producer – George Andros (3 Singles: 3 Weeks)*

12 Aug 95 **EVERYBODY MUST PARTY** *Vibe MCSTD 2068* 61 1
4 May 96 **TAKE ME HIGHER** *Music Plant MCSTD 40031* 61 1
26 Aug 00 **LIFE GOES ON** *Neo NEOCD 039* 54 1

GEORGIO *US, male vocalist – Georgio Allentin*

20 Feb 88 **LOVER'S LANE** *Motown ZB 41611* 54 3

Danyel GERARD *France, male vocalist – Gerard Daniel Kherlakian*

18 Sep 71 **BUTTERFLY** *CBS 7454* 11 12

GERIDEAU *US, male vocalist – Theo Gerideau (2 Singles: 2 Weeks)*

27 Aug 94 **BRING IT ALL BACK 2 LUV** *Fruittree FTREE 10CD* [1] 65 1
4 Jul 98 **MASQUERADE** *Inferno CDFERN 7* 63 1

[1] Project featuring Gerideau

GERRY and The PACEMAKERS (see also The CROWD) *UK, male vocal / instrumental group (2 Albums: 29 Weeks, 9 Singles: 114 Weeks)*

14 Mar 63 ★ **HOW DO YOU DO IT?** *Columbia DB 4987* 1 18
30 May 63 ★ **I LIKE IT** *Columbia DB 7041* 1 15
10 Oct 63 ★ **YOU'LL NEVER WALK ALONE** *Columbia DB 7126* 1 19

23 / 26 October 1968	30 October / 2 November 1968	6 / 9 November 1968	13 / 16 November 1968
THOSE WERE THE DAYS Mary Hopkin	**THOSE WERE THE DAYS** Mary Hopkin	**WITH A LITTLE HELP FROM MY FRIENDS** Joe Cocker	**THE GOOD, THE BAD AND THE UGLY** Hugo Montenegro, his Orchestra and Chorus
THE HOLLIES' GREATEST HITS The Hollies	**THE HOLLIES' GREATEST HITS** The Hollies	**THE HOLLIES' GREATEST HITS** The Hollies	**THE HOLLIES' GREATEST HITS** The Hollies

KEY UK No.1 ★ UK Top 10 ● Still on chart + UK entry at No.1 ■ US No.1 ▲ UK million seller £ US million seller $
Singles re-entries are listed as (re), (2re), (3re)... which signifies that the hit re-entered the chart once, twice or three times...
Peak Position / Weeks

26 Oct 63 ● HOW DO YOU LIKE IT? *Columbia 33SX 1546*.....2 28
16 Jan 64 ● I'M THE ONE *Columbia DB 7189*.....2 15
16 Apr 64 ● DON'T LET THE SUN CATCH YOU CRYING *Columbia DB 7268*...6 11
3 Sep 64 IT'S GONNA BE ALL RIGHT *Columbia DB 7353*.....24 7
17 Dec 64 ● FERRY 'CROSS THE MERSEY *Columbia DB 7437*.....8 13
6 Feb 65 FERRY 'CROSS THE MERSEY *Columbia 33SX 1676*.....19 1
25 Mar 65 I'LL BE THERE *Columbia DB 7504*.....15 9
18 Nov 65 WALK HAND IN HAND *Columbia DB 7738*.....29 7

GET READY *UK, male vocal group*

3 Jun 95 WILD WILD WEST *Mega GACXCD 2698*.....65 1

GETO BOYS featuring FLAJ *US, male rap group*

11 May 96 THE WORLD IS A GHETTO *Virgin America VUSCD 104*.....49 1

Stan GETZ *US, male saxophonist – Stanley Gayetzsky, b. 2 Feb 1927, d. 6 Jun 1991 (1 Album: 7 Weeks, 3 Singles: 29 Weeks)*

8 Nov 62 DESAFINADO *HMV POP 1061* [1] 11 13
23 Feb 63 JAZZ SAMBA *Verve SULP 9013* [1] 15 7
23 Jul 64 THE GIRL FROM IPANEMA (GAROTA DE IPANEMA) *Verve VS 520* [2] 29 10
25 Aug 84 THE GIRL FROM IPANEMA (re-issue) *Verve IPA 1* [3] 55 6

[1] Stan Getz and Charlie Byrd [2] Stan Getz and Joao Gilberto [3] Astrud Gilberto [1] Stan Getz and Charlie Byrd

The re-issue of 'The Girl from Ipanema' was credited only to Astrud Gilberto, the vocalist, even though it was exactly the same recording as the original hit.

Amanda GHOST *UK, female vocalist (2 Singles: 2 Weeks)*

8 Apr 00 IDOL *Warner Bros. W 518CD*.....63 1
1 May 04 BREAK MY WORLD *Island CID 853* [1] 52 1

[1] Dark Globe featuring Amanda Ghost

GHOST DANCE *UK, male vocal / instrumental group*

17 Jun 89 DOWN TO THE WIRE *Chrysalis CHS 3376*.....66 2

GHOSTFACE KILLAH (see also WU-TANG CLAN) *US, male rapper – Dennis Coles (1 Album: 2 Weeks, 7 Singles: 38 Weeks)*

9 Nov 96 IRONMAN *Epic 4853892*.....38 2
12 Jul 97 ALL THAT I GOT IS YOU *Epic 6646842*.....11 4
23 Jan 99 ● I WANT YOU FOR MYSELF *Northwestside 74321643632* [1] 2 8
4 Nov 00 MISS FAT BOOTY – PART II *Rawkus RWK 282CD* [2] 64 1
1 Nov 03 OOH WEE *Elektra E 7490CD* [3] 15 7
29 May 04 ● ON MY KNEES (re) *Sony Music 6749381* [4] 4 11
17 Jul 04 PUSH *Def Jam 9862837* [5] 34 3
16 Oct 04 LOVE THEM *Jive 8287663912* [6] 27 4

[1] Another Level / Ghostface Killah [2] Mos Def featuring Ghostface Killah [3] Mark Ronson featuring Ghostface Killah and Nate Dogg [4] The 411 featuring Ghostface Killah [5] Ghostface featuring Missy Elliott [6] Eamon featuring Ghostface

Andy GIBB *UK, male vocalist, b. 5 Mar 1958, d. 10 Mar 1988 (1 Album: 9 Weeks, 4 Singles: 30 Weeks)*

25 Jun 77 I JUST WANNA BE YOUR EVERYTHING *RSO 2090 237* ▲ $....26 7
13 May 78 SHADOW DANCING *RSO 001* ▲ $.....42 6
12 Aug 78 ● AN EVERLASTING LOVE *RSO 015* $.....10 10
19 Aug 78 SHADOW DANCING *RSO RSS 0001*.....15 9
27 Jan 79 (OUR LOVE) DON'T THROW IT ALL AWAY *RSO 26* $.....32 7

Barry GIBB (see also The BEE GEES) *UK, male vocalist*

6 Dec 80 GUILTY *CBS 9315* [1] $.....34 10
20 Oct 84 NOW VOYAGER *Polydor POLH 14*.....85 2

[1] Barbra Streisand and Barry Gibb

Robin GIBB (see also The BEE GEES; Alistair GRIFFIN) *UK, male vocalist (1 Album: 1 Week, 4 Singles: 25 Weeks)*

9 Jul 69 ● SAVED BY THE BELL (re) *Polydor 56337*.....2 17
7 Feb 70 AUGUST OCTOBER *Polydor 56371*.....45 3
11 Feb 84 ANOTHER LONELY NIGHT IN NEW YORK *Polydor POSP 668*..71 1
1 Feb 03 PLEASE *SPV Recordings SPV 05571463*.....23 4
15 Feb 03 MAGNET *SPV Recordings SPV 08571472*.....43 1

Beth GIBBONS & RUSTIN' MAN (see also PORTISHEAD; TALK TALK) *UK, female vocalist and male producer / instrumentalist – Paul Webb*

9 Nov 02 OUT OF SEASON *Go Beat 665742*.....28 2
15 Mar 03 TOM THE MODEL *Go Beat GOBCD 55*.....70 1

Steve GIBBONS BAND *UK, male vocal / instrumental group (1 Album: 3 Weeks, 2 Singles: 14 Weeks)*

6 Aug 77 TULANE *Polydor 2058 889*.....12 10
22 Oct 77 CAUGHT IN THE ACT *Polydor 2478 112*.....22 3
13 May 78 EDDY VORTEX *Polydor 2059 017*.....56 4

Georgia GIBBS *US, female vocalist – Freda Gibbons (2 Singles: 2 Weeks)*

22 Apr 55 TWEEDLE DEE *Mercury MB 3196* $.....20 1
13 Jul 56 KISS ME ANOTHER *Mercury MT 110*.....25 1

Debbie GIBSON *US, female vocalist / producer (3 Albums: 52 Weeks, 11 Singles: 70 Weeks)*

26 Sep 87 ONLY IN MY DREAMS (re) *Atlantic A 9322*.....11 12
23 Jan 88 ● SHAKE YOUR LOVE *Atlantic A 9187*.....7 8
30 Jan 88 OUT OF THE BLUE *Atlantic WX 139*.....26 35
7 May 88 OUT OF THE BLUE *Atlantic A 9091*.....19 7
9 Jul 88 ● FOOLISH BEAT *Atlantic A 9059* ▲.....9 9
15 Oct 88 STAYING TOGETHER *Atlantic A 9020*.....53 2
28 Jan 89 LOST IN YOUR EYES *Atlantic A 8970* ▲.....34 7
11 Feb 89 ● ELECTRIC YOUTH *Atlantic WX 231* ▲.....8 16
29 Apr 89 ELECTRIC YOUTH *Atlantic A 8919*.....14 8
19 Aug 89 WE COULD BE TOGETHER *Atlantic A 8896*.....22 8
9 Mar 91 ANYTHING IS POSSIBLE *Atlantic A 7735*.....51 2
30 Mar 91 ANYTHING IS POSSIBLE *Atlantic WX 399*.....69 1
3 Apr 93 SHOCK YOUR MAMA *Atlantic A 7386CD*.....74 1
24 Jul 93 YOU'RE THE ONE THAT I WANT *Epic 6595222* [1] 13 6

[1] Craig McLachlan and Debbie Gibson

'Only in My Dreams' made its peak position on re-entry in Mar 1988.

Don GIBSON *US, male vocalist / guitarist, b. 3 Apr 1928, d. 17 Nov 2003 (1 Album: 10 Weeks, 2 Singles: 16 Weeks)*

31 Aug 61 SEA OF HEARTBREAK *RCA 1243*.....14 13
1 Feb 62 LONESOME NUMBER ONE *RCA 1272*.....47 3
22 Mar 80 COUNTRY NUMBER ONE *Warwick WW 5079*.....13 10

Wayne GIBSON *UK, male vocalist (2 Singles: 13 Weeks)*

3 Sep 64 KELLY *Pye 7N 15680*.....48 2
23 Nov 74 UNDER MY THUMB *Pye Disco Demand DDS 2001*.....17 11

The GIBSON BROTHERS *Martinique, male vocal / instrumental group (1 Album: 3 Weeks, 6 Singles: 54 Weeks)*

10 Mar 79 CUBA *Island WIP 6483*.....41 9
21 Jul 79 ● OOH! WHAT A LIFE *Island WIP 6503*.....10 12
17 Nov 79 ● QUE SERA MI VIDA (IF YOU SHOULD GO) *Island WIP 6525*.....5 11
23 Feb 80 CUBA (re-issue) / BETTER DO IT SALSA *Island WIP 6561*.....12 9
12 Jul 80 MARIANA *Island WIP 6617*.....11 10

20 / 23 November 1968	27 / 30 November 1968	4 / 7 December 1968	11 / 14 December 1968
UK No.1 SINGLES			
THE GOOD, THE BAD AND THE UGLY Hugo Montenegro, his Orchestra and Chorus	THE GOOD, THE BAD AND THE UGLY Hugo Montenegro, his Orchestra and Chorus	THE GOOD, THE BAD AND THE UGLY Hugo Montenegro, his Orchestra and Chorus	LILY THE PINK Scaffold
UK No.1 ALBUMS			
THE SOUND OF MUSIC Soundtrack	THE HOLLIES' GREATEST HITS The Hollies	THE BEATLES (WHITE ALBUM) The Beatles	THE BEATLES (WHITE ALBUM) The Beatles

30 Aug 80	ON THE RIVIERA *Island ILPS 9620*	50	3
9 Jul 83	**MY HEART'S BEATING WILD (TIC TAC TIC TAC)** *Stiff BUY 184*	**56**	3

GIDEA PARK
UK, male vocal group – includes Adrian Baker (2 Singles: 19 Weeks)

4 Jul 81	**BEACH BOY GOLD** *Sonet SON 2162*	**11**	13
12 Sep 81	**SEASONS OF GOLD** *Polo POLO 14*	**28**	6

Johan GIELEN presents ABNEA (see also AIRSCAPE; BALEARIC BILL; BLUE BAMBOO; SVENSON and GIELEN) *Belgium, male producer*

18 Aug 01	**VELVET MOODS** *Data DATA 17T*	**74**	1

GIFTED *UK, male vocal / instrumental duo*

23 Aug 97	**DO I** *Perfecto PERF 140CD*	**60**	1

GIGOLO AUNTS *US, male vocal / instrumental group (2 Singles: 4 Weeks)*

23 Apr 94	**MRS WASHINGTON** *Fire BLAZE 68CD*	**74**	1
13 May 95	**WHERE I FIND MY HEAVEN** *Fire BLAZE 87CD*	**29**	3

Bebel GILBERTO *Brazil, female vocalist (2 Albums: 8 Weeks)*

31 Aug 02	TANTO TEMPO *East West 0927474072*	49	5
19 Jun 04	BEBEL GILBERTO *East West 5046732665*	49	3

Donna GILES *US, female vocalist (2 Singles: 4 Weeks)*

13 Aug 94	**AND I'M TELLING YOU I'M NOT GOING** *Ore AG 4CD*	**43**	2
10 Feb 96	**AND I'M TELLING YOU I'M NOT GOING** (re-mix) *Ore AGR 4CD*	**27**	2

Johnny GILL (see also NEW EDITION)
US, male vocalist (1 Album: 3 Weeks, 4 Singles: 12 Weeks)

23 Feb 91	**WRAP MY BODY TIGHT** *Motown ZB 44271*	**57**	2
28 Nov 92	**SLOW AND SEXY** *Epic 6587727* [1]	**17**	7
19 Jun 93	PROVOCATIVE *Motown 5302062*	41	3
17 Jul 93	**THE FLOOR** *Motown TMGCD 1416*	**53**	1
29 Jan 94	**A CUTE SWEET LOVE ADDICTION** *Motown TMGCD 1420*	**46**	2

[1] Shabba Ranks featuring Johnny Gill

GILLAN (see also BLACK SABBATH; DEEP PURPLE)
UK, male vocal (Ian Gillan) / instrumental group – includes Bernie Tormé (6 Albums: 53 Weeks, 8 Singles: 46 Weeks)

17 Jul 76	CHILD IN TIME *Polydor 2490 136* [1]	55	1
20 Oct 79	MR. UNIVERSE *Acrobat ACRO 3*	11	6
14 Jun 80	**SLEEPING ON THE JOB** *Virgin VS 355*	**55**	3
16 Aug 80 ●	GLORY ROAD *Virgin V 2171*	3	12
4 Oct 80	**TROUBLE** *Virgin VS 377*	**14**	6
14 Feb 81	**MUTUALLY ASSURED DESTRUCTION** *Virgin VSK 103*	**32**	5
21 Mar 81	**NEW ORLEANS** *Virgin VS 406*	**17**	10
25 Apr 81 ●	FUTURE SHOCK *Virgin VK 2196*	2	13
20 Jun 81	**NO LAUGHING IN HEAVEN** *Virgin VS 425*	**31**	6
10 Oct 81	**NIGHTMARE** *Virgin VS 441*	**36**	6
7 Nov 81	DOUBLE TROUBLE *Virgin VGD 3506*	12	15
23 Jan 82	**RESTLESS** *Virgin VS 465*	**25**	7
4 Sep 82	**LIVING FOR THE CITY** *Virgin VS 519*	**50**	3
2 Oct 82	MAGIC *Virgin V 2238*	17	6

[1] Ian Gillan Band

Ian GILLAN
(see also BLACK SABBATH; DEEP PURPLE; GILLAN) *UK, male vocalist*

28 Jul 90	NAKED THUNDER *Teldec 9031718991*	63	1

Stuart GILLIES *UK, male vocalist*

31 Mar 73	**AMANDA** *Philips 6006 293*	**13**	10

Thea GILMORE *UK, female vocalist (1 Album: 1 Week, 2 Singles: 2 Weeks)*

16 Aug 03	**JULIET (KEEP THAT IN MIND)** *Hungry Dog YRGNUHS 1*	**35**	1
23 Aug 03	AVALANCHE *Hungry Dog YRGNUHA 1*	63	1
8 Nov 03	**MAINSTREAM** *Hungry Dog YRGNUH 53*	**50**	1

David GILMOUR
(see also PINK FLOYD) *UK, male guitarist (2 Albums: 18 Weeks)*

10 Jun 78	DAVID GILMOUR *Harvest SHVL 817*	17	9
17 Mar 84	ABOUT FACE *Harvest SHSP 2400791*	21	9

James GILREATH *US, male vocalist*

2 May 63	**LITTLE BAND OF GOLD** *Pye International 7N 25190*	**29**	10

Jim GILSTRAP *US, male vocalist*

15 Mar 75 ●	**SWING YOUR DADDY** *Chelsea 2005 021*	**4**	11

Gordon GILTRAP
UK, male guitarist (1 Album: 7 Weeks, 2 Singles: 10 Weeks)

14 Jan 78	**HEARTSONG** *Electric WOT 19*	**21**	7
18 Feb 78	PERILOUS JOURNEY *Electric TRIX 4*	29	7
28 Apr 79	**FEAR OF THE DARK** *Electric WOT 29* [1]	**58**	3

[1] Gordon Giltrap Band

GIN BLOSSOMS
US, male vocal / instrumental group (2 Albums: 6 Weeks, 4 Singles: 12 Weeks)

5 Feb 94	**HEY JEALOUSY** *Fontana GINCD 3*	**24**	5
26 Feb 94	NEW MISERABLE EXPERIENCE *Fontana 3954032*	53	4
16 Apr 94	**FOUND OUT ABOUT YOU** *Fontana GINCD 4*	**40**	3
10 Feb 96	**TIL I HEAR IT FROM YOU** *A&M 5812272*	**39**	2
24 Feb 96	CONGRATULATIONS I'M SORRY *A&M 5404702*	42	2
27 Apr 96	**FOLLOW YOU DOWN** *A&M 5815512*	**30**	2

GINUWINE
US, male rapper – Elgin Lumpkin (2 Albums: 2 Weeks, 7 Singles: 27 Weeks)

25 Jan 97	**PONY** *Epic 6641282* $	**16**	6
24 May 97	**TELL ME DO U WANNA** *Epic 6645272*	**16**	3
6 Sep 97 ●	**WHEN DOVES CRY** *Epic 6649245*	**10**	5
14 Mar 98	**HOLLER** *Epic 6653372*	**13**	4
28 Mar 98	GINUWINE ... THE BACHELOR *Epic 4853912*	74	1
13 Mar 99 ●	**WHAT'S SO DIFFERENT?** *Epic 6670522*	**10**	4
27 Mar 99	100% GINUWINE *Epic 4919922*	42	1
14 Dec 02	**CRUSH TONIGHT** *Atlantic AT 0142CD* [1]	**42**	2
7 Jun 03	**HELL YEAH** *Epic 6739242*	**27**	3

[1] Fat Joe featuring Ginuwine

GIPSY KINGS *France, male vocal / instrumental group (6 Albums: 70 Weeks, 1 Single: 2 Weeks)*

15 Apr 89	GIPSY KINGS *Telstar STAR 2355*	16	29
25 Nov 89	MOSAIQUE *Telstar STAR 2398*	27	13
13 Jul 91	ESTE MUNDO *Columbia 4686481*	19	7
6 Aug 94	GREATEST HITS *Columbia 4772422*	11	11
3 Sep 94	**HITS MEDLEY** *Columbia 6606022*	**53**	2
24 Jul 99	VOLARE – THE VERY BEST OF THE GIPSY KINGS *Columbia SONYTV 69CD*	20	5
23 Jul 05	THE VERY BEST OF *Columbia 5202172*	32	5

Martine GIRAULT *UK, female vocalist (4 Singles: 7 Weeks)*

29 Aug 92	**REVIVAL** *ffrr FX 195*	**53**	2
30 Jan 93	**REVIVAL** (re-issue) *ffrr FCD 205*	**37**	3
28 Oct 95	**BEEN THINKING ABOUT YOU** *RCA 74321316142*	**63**	1
1 Feb 97	**REVIVAL** (re-mix) *RCA 74321432162*	**61**	1

GIRESSE *UK, male DJ / production duo*

14 Apr 01	**MON AMI** *Inferno CDFERN 36*	**61**	1

18 / 21 December 1968	25 / 28 December 1968	1 / 4 January 1969	8 / 11 January 1969
LILY THE PINK Scaffold	LILY THE PINK Scaffold	OB-LA-DI, OB-LA-DA Marmalade	LILY THE PINK Scaffold
THE BEATLES (WHITE ALBUM) The Beatles	THE BEATLES (WHITE ALBUM) The Beatles	THE BEATLES (WHITE ALBUM) The Beatles	THE BEATLES (WHITE ALBUM) The Beatles

KEY	
UK No.1 ★ UK Top 10 ● Still on chart + UK entry at No.1 ■ US No.1 ▲ UK million seller £ US million seller $	Peak Position / Weeks
Singles re-entries are listed as (re), (2re), (3re)... which signifies that the hit re-entered the chart once, twice or three times...	

GIRL
UK, male vocal / instrumental group (2 Albums: 6 Weeks, 1 Single: 3 Weeks)

9 Feb 80	SHEER GREED *Jet JETLP 224*	33	5
12 Apr 80	**HOLLYWOOD TEASE** *Jet 176*	50	3
23 Jan 82	WASTED YOUTH *Jet JETLP 238*	92	1

GIRL THING *UK / Holland, female vocal group (2 Singles: 13 Weeks)*

1 Jul 00 ●	**LAST ONE STANDING (re)** *RCA 74321762412*	8	10
18 Nov 00	**GIRLS ON TOP** *RCA 74321801162*	25	3

GIRLFRIEND *Australia, female vocal group (2 Singles: 5 Weeks)*

30 Jan 93	**TAKE IT FROM ME** *Arista 74321114252*	47	4
15 May 93	**GIRL'S LIFE** *Arista 74321138452*	68	1

GIRLS ALOUD (484 Top 500)
The most successful female reality TV act consists of Sarah, Nicola, Nadine, Kimberley and Cheryl. The winners of Popstars: The Rivals in 2002 have proved their impeccable pop credentials by clocking up 11 successive Top 20 singles. (3 Albums: 37 Weeks, 11 Singles: 116 Weeks)

28 Dec 02 ★	**SOUND OF THE UNDERGROUND** *Polydor 0658272* ■	1	21
24 May 03 ●	**NO GOOD ADVICE** *Polydor 9800051*	2	14
7 Jun 03 ●	SOUND OF THE UNDERGROUND *Polydor 9865315*	2	18
30 Aug 03 ●	**LIFE GOT COLD** *Polydor 9810656*	3	9
29 Nov 03 ●	**JUMP** *Polydor 9814103*	2	14
10 Jul 04 ●	**THE SHOW** *Polydor 9867040*	2	10
25 Sep 04 ●	**LOVE MACHINE** *Polydor 9867984*	2	10
27 Nov 04 ★	**I'LL STAND BY YOU** *Polydor 9869130* ■	1	14
11 Dec 04 ●	WHAT WILL THE NEIGHBOURS SAY? *Polydor 9868948*	6	16
5 Mar 05 ●	**WAKE ME UP** *Polydor 9870426*	4	9
3 Sep 05 ●	**LONG HOT SUMMER** *Polydor 9873589*	7	8
26 Nov 05 ●	**BIOLOGY** *Polydor 9875297*	4	6+
17 Dec 05	CHEMISTRY *Polydor 9875390*	11	3+
31 Dec 05 ●	**SEE THE DAY** *Polydor 9875965*	9	1+

GIRLS AT OUR BEST *UK, male / female vocal / instrumental group*

7 Nov 81	PLEASURE *Happy Birthday RVLP 1*	60	3

GIRLS @ PLAY *UK, female vocal group (2 Singles: 7 Weeks)*

24 Feb 01	**AIRHEAD** *GSM GSMCDR 1*	18	5
13 Oct 01	**RESPECTABLE** *Redbus RBMCD 101*	29	2

GIRLS OF FHM *International, female models / vocalists*

3 Jul 04 ●	**DA YA THINK I'M SEXY?** *2PSL 2PSLCD 5*	10	5

GIRLSCHOOL *UK, female vocal (Kim McAuliffe) / instrumental group (4 Albums: 23 Weeks, 5 Singles: 25 Weeks)*

5 Jul 80	DEMOLITION *Bronze BRON 525*	28	10
2 Aug 80	**RACE WITH THE DEVIL** *Bronze BRO 100*	49	6
21 Feb 81 ●	**ST VALENTINE'S DAY MASSACRE (EP)** *Bronze BRO 116* [1]	5	8
11 Apr 81	**HIT AND RUN** *Bronze BRO 118*	32	6
25 Apr 81 ●	HIT 'N' RUN *Bronze BRON 534*	5	6
11 Jul 81	**C'MON LET'S GO** *Bronze BRO 126*	42	3
3 Apr 82	**WILDLIFE (EP)** *Bronze BRO 144*	58	2
12 Jun 82	SCREAMING BLUE MURDER *Bronze BRON 541*	27	6
12 Nov 83	PLAY DIRTY *Bronze BRON 548*	66	1

[1] Motörhead and Girlschool (also known as Headgirl)

Tracks on St Valentine's Day Massacre (EP): Please Don't Touch / Emergency / Bomber. Tracks on Wildlife (EP): Don't Call It Love / Wildlife / Don't Stop.

GITTA *Denmark / Italy, male / female vocal / instrumental group*

19 Aug 00	**NO MORE TURNING BACK** *Pepper 9230302*	54	1

GLADIATOR featuring IZZY *UK, male DJ / production duo – Bobak Rembrandt and Dave Lambert and female vocalist*

29 May 04	**NOW WE ARE FREE** *Universal TV 9866813*	19	4

The GLADIATORS *UK, male / female TV gladiators vocal group*

30 Nov 96	**THE BOYS ARE BACK IN TOWN** *RCA 74321417002*	70	1

GLAM *Italy, male instrumental / production group*

1 May 93	**HELL'S PARTY** *Six6 SIXCD 001*	42	2

GLAM METAL DETECTIVES *UK, male / female vocal group*

11 Mar 95	**EVERYBODY UP!** *ZTT ZANG 62CD*	29	2

GLAMMA KID *UK, male vocalist / rapper – Lyael Constable (1 Album: 1 Week, 4 Singles: 25 Weeks)*

21 Nov 98	**FASHION '98** *WEA WEA 179CD*	49	1
17 Apr 99 ●	**TABOO** *WEA WEA 203CD* [1]	10	8
27 Nov 99 ●	**WHY** *WEA WEA 229CD 1*	10	10
2 Sep 00	**BILLS 2 PAY (re)** *WEA WEA 268CD*	17	6
16 Sep 00	KIDOLOGY *WEA 3984298572*	66	1

[1] Glamma Kid featuring Shola Ama

GLASS TIGER
Canada, male vocal / instrumental group (3 Singles: 18 Weeks)

18 Oct 86	**DON'T FORGET ME (WHEN I'M GONE)** *Manhattan MT 13*	29	9
31 Jan 87	**SOMEDAY** *Manhattan MT 17*	66	2
26 Oct 91	**MY TOWN** *EMI EM 212*	33	7

'My Town' features the uncredited vocals of Rod Stewart.

GLENN and CHRIS
UK, male footballers / vocal duo – Glenn Hoddle and Chris Waddle

18 Apr 87	**DIAMOND LIGHTS** *Record Shack KICK 1*	12	8

Gary GLITTER (236 Top 500)
Glitter rock giant, b. Paul Gadd, 8 May 1940, Oxfordshire, UK. Started recording in 1960 (as Paul Raven), and was the first act to put his first 11 hits into the Top 10. This singer / songwriter remained a popular live performer until he was jailed in 1999. Biggest-selling single: 'I Love You Love Me Love' 1,140,000 (5 Albums: 100 Weeks, 23 Singles: 170 Weeks)

10 Jun 72 ●	**ROCK AND ROLL (PARTS 1 & 2)** *Bell 1216*	2	15
23 Sep 72 ●	**I DIDN'T KNOW I LOVED YOU (TILL I SAW YOU ROCK 'N' ROLL)** *Bell 1259*	4	11
21 Oct 72 ●	GLITTER *Bell BELLS 216*	8	40
20 Jan 73 ●	**DO YOU WANNA TOUCH ME? (OH YEAH)** *Bell 1280*	2	11
7 Apr 73 ●	**HELLO! HELLO! I'M BACK AGAIN** *Bell 1299*	2	14
16 Jun 73 ●	TOUCH ME *Bell BELLS 222*	2	33
21 Jul 73 ★	**I'M THE LEADER OF THE GANG (I AM!)** *Bell 1321*	1	12
17 Nov 73 ★	**I LOVE YOU LOVE ME LOVE** *Bell 1337* ■ £	1	14
30 Mar 74 ●	**REMEMBER ME THIS WAY** *Bell 1349*	3	8
15 Jun 74 ★	**ALWAYS YOURS** *Bell 1359*	1	9
29 Jun 74 ●	REMEMBER ME THIS WAY *Bell BELLS 237*	5	14
23 Nov 74 ●	**OH YES! YOU'RE BEAUTIFUL** *Bell 1391*	2	10
3 May 75 ●	**LOVE LIKE YOU AND ME** *Bell 1423*	10	6
21 Jun 75 ●	**DOING ALRIGHT WITH THE BOYS** *Bell 1429*	6	7
8 Nov 75	**PAPA OOM MOW MOW** *Bell 1451*	38	5
13 Mar 76	**YOU BELONG TO ME** *Bell 1473*	40	5
27 Mar 76	GARY GLITTER'S GREATEST HITS *Bell BELLS 262*	33	5
22 Jan 77	**IT TAKES ALL NIGHT LONG** *Arista 85*	25	6
16 Jul 77	**A LITTLE BOOGIE WOOGIE IN THE BACK OF MY MIND** *Arista 112*	31	5
20 Sep 80	**GARY GLITTER (EP)** *GTO GT 282*	57	3

15 / 18 January 1969	22 / 25 January 1969	29 January / 1 February 1969	5 / 8 February 1969
UK No.1 SINGLES			
OB-LA-DI, OB-LA-DA Marmalade	OB-LA-DI, OB-LA-DA Marmalade	ALBATROSS Fleetwood Mac	BLACKBERRY WAY The Move
UK No.1 ALBUMS			
THE BEATLES (WHITE ALBUM) The Beatles	THE BEST OF THE SEEKERS The Seekers	THE BEATLES (WHITE ALBUM) The Beatles	THE BEST OF THE SEEKERS The Seekers

10 Oct 81	**AND THEN SHE KISSED ME** *Bell BELL 1497*	39	5
5 Dec 81	**ALL THAT GLITTERS** *Bell BELL 1498*	48	5
23 Jun 84	**DANCE ME UP** *Arista ARIST 570*	25	5
1 Dec 84 ●	**ANOTHER ROCK AND ROLL CHRISTMAS** *Arista ARIST 592*	7	7
10 Oct 92	**AND THE LEADER ROCKS ON (MEGAMIX / MEDLEY)** *EMI EM 252*	58	2
14 Nov 92	MANY HAPPY RETURNS – THE HITS *EMI CDEMTV 68*	35	8
21 Nov 92	**THROUGH THE YEARS** *EMI EM 256*	49	3
16 Dec 95	**HELLO! HELLO! I'M BACK AGAIN (AGAIN!)** (re-recording) *Carlton Sounds 3036000192*	50	2

'Rock and Roll (Part 1)' not listed with 'Part 2' for weeks of 10 and 17 Jun 1972. Tracks on Gary Glitter (EP): I'm the Leader of the Gang (I Am!) / Rock and Roll (Part 2) / Hello! Hello! I'm Back Again / Do You Wanna Touch Me? (Oh Yeah). All were re-issues. All That Glitters was a medley of re-recordings: I'm The Leader Of The Gang (I Am!) / Do You Wanna Touch Me? (Oh Yeah) / Doing Alright With the Boys / I Didn't Know I Loved You (Till I Saw You Rock 'n' Roll) / Rock and Roll (Part 2). And The Leader Rocks On was a medley of I'm The Leader Of The Gang (I Am!) / Come On, Come In, Get On / Rock On / I Didn't Know I Loved You (Till I Saw You Rock 'n' Roll) / Do You Wanna Touch Me? (Oh Yeah) / Hello! Hello! I'm Back Again.

The GLITTER BAND (see also Gary GLITTER) *UK, male vocal / instrumental group (3 Albums: 17 Weeks, 7 Singles: 60 Weeks)*

23 Mar 74 ●	**ANGEL FACE** *Bell 1348*	4	10
3 Aug 74 ●	**JUST FOR YOU** *Bell 1368*	10	8
14 Sep 74	HEY *Bell BELLS 241*	13	12
19 Oct 74 ●	**LET'S GET TOGETHER AGAIN** *Bell 1383*	8	8
18 Jan 75 ●	**GOODBYE MY LOVE** *Bell 1395*	2	9
12 Apr 75 ●	**THE TEARS I CRIED** *Bell 1416*	8	8
3 May 75	ROCK 'N' ROLL DUDES *Bell BELLS 253*	17	4
9 Aug 75	**LOVE IN THE SUN** *Bell 1437*	15	8
28 Feb 76 ●	**PEOPLE LIKE YOU AND PEOPLE LIKE ME** *Bell 1471*	5	9
19 Jun 76	GREATEST HITS *Bell BELLS 264*	52	1

The GLITTERATI NEW
UK, male vocal / instrumental group (3 Singles: 3 Weeks)

26 Mar 05	**YOU GOT NOTHING ON ME** *Atlantic ATUK 005CD*	36	1
4 Jun 05	**HEARTBREAKER** *Atlantic ATUK 008CD*	45	1
5 Nov 05	**BACK IN POWER** *Atlantic ATUK 015CD*	62	1

GLOBAL COMMUNICATION (see also COSMOS)
UK, male instrumental / production duo – Tom Middleton and Mark Pritchard

11 Jan 97	**THE WAY / THE DEEP** *Dedicated GLOBA 002CD*	51	1

GLOVE (see also The CURE; SIOUXSIE and The BANSHEES)
UK, male vocal / instrumental group

20 Aug 83	**LIKE AN ANIMAL** *Wonderland SHE 3*	52	3
17 Sep 83	BLUE SUNSHINE *Wonderland SHELP 2*	35	3

Dana GLOVER *US, female vocalist*

10 May 03	**THINKING OVER** *Dreamworks 4507762*	38	1
17 May 03	TESTIMONY *Dreamworks / Polydor 04504522*	43	2

GLOWORM *UK / US, male vocal / instrumental group (3 Singles: 17 Weeks)*

6 Feb 93	**I LIFT MY CUP** *Pulse 8 CDLOSE 37*	20	4
14 May 94 ●	**CARRY ME HOME** *Go Beat GODCD 112*	9	11
6 Aug 94	**I LIFT MY CUP** (re-issue) *Pulse 8 CDLOSE 67*	46	2

The GO-BETWEENS
Australia, male / female vocal / instrumental group (2 Albums: 2 Weeks)

13 Jun 87	TALLULAH *Beggars Banquet BEGA 81*	91	1
10 Sep 88	16 LOVERS LANE *Beggars Banquet BEGA 95*	81	1

GO GO LORENZO and The DAVIS PINCKNEY PROJECT
US, male vocal / instrumental group

6 Dec 86	**YOU CAN DANCE IF YOU WANT TO** *Boiling Point POSP 836*	46	8

GO-GO's (see also Belinda CARLISLE; Jane WIEDLIN) *US, female vocal / instrumental group (2 Albums: 4 Weeks, 3 Singles: 10 Weeks)*

15 May 82	**OUR LIPS ARE SEALED** *IRS GDN 102*	47	6
21 Aug 82	VACATION *IRS SP 70031*	75	3
26 Jan 91	**COOL JERK** *IRS AM 712*	60	1
18 Feb 95	**THE WHOLE WORLD LOST ITS HEAD** *IRS CDEIRS 190*	29	3
18 Mar 95	RETURN TO THE VALLEY OF THE GO-GO'S *IRS EIRSCD 1071*	52	1

GO WEST (344 Top 500)
Songwriting duo specialising in radio-friendly white soul sounds; Peter Cox (v) and Richard Drummie (g/k/v). Best Newcomers at the 1986 BRIT awards had a US Top 10 hit with 'The King of Wishful Thinking', from the soundtrack of Pretty Woman (4 Albums: 119 Weeks, 13 Singles: 85 Weeks)

23 Feb 85 ●	**WE CLOSE OUR EYES** *Chrysalis CHS 2850*	5	14
13 Apr 85 ●	GO WEST / BANGS AND CRASHES *Chrysalis CHR 1495*	8	83
11 May 85	**CALL ME** *Chrysalis GOW 1*	12	10
3 Aug 85	**GOODBYE GIRL** *Chrysalis GOW 2*	25	7
23 Nov 85	**DON'T LOOK DOWN – THE SEQUEL** *Chrysalis GOW 3*	13	10
29 Nov 86	**TRUE COLOURS** *Chrysalis GOW 4*	48	7
9 May 87	**I WANT TO HEAR IT FROM YOU** *Chrysalis GOW 5*	43	3
6 Jun 87	DANCING ON THE COUCH *Chrysalis CDL 1550*	19	5
12 Sep 87	**THE KING IS DEAD** *Chrysalis GOW 6*	67	2
28 Jul 90	**THE KING OF WISHFUL THINKING** *Chrysalis GOW 8*	18	10
17 Oct 92	**FAITHFUL** *Chrysalis GOW 9*	13	6
14 Nov 92	INDIAN SUMMER *Chrysalis CDCHR 1964*	13	16
16 Jan 93	**WHAT YOU WON'T DO FOR LOVE** *Chrysalis CDGOWS 10*	15	5
27 Mar 93	**STILL IN LOVE** *Chrysalis CDGOWS 11*	43	3
2 Oct 93	**TRACKS OF MY TEARS** *Chrysalis CDGOWS 12*	16	5
16 Oct 93 ●	ACES AND KINGS – THE BEST OF GO WEST *Chrysalis CDCHR 6050*	5	15
4 Dec 93	**WE CLOSE OUR EYES** (re-mix) *Chrysalis CDGOWS 13*	40	3

Bangs and Crashes is an album of re-mixed versions of Go West tracks and some new material. From 31 May 1986 both records were available together as a double album.

The GO! TEAM
UK, male / female vocal / instrumental group (2 Singles: 2 Weeks)

4 Dec 04	**LADYFLASH** *Memphis Industries MI 041CDS*	68	1
8 Oct 05	**BOTTLE ROCKET** *Memphis Industries MI 048CDS*	64	1

GOATS *US, male rap group*

29 May 93	**AAAH D YAAA / TYPICAL AMERICAN** *Ruff House 6593032*	53	2
27 Aug 94	NO GOATS NO GLORY *Columbia 4769372*	58	1

'Typical American' listed only from 5 Jun 1993, peaking at No.65.

GOD MACHINE *US, male vocal / instrumental group*

30 Jan 93	**HOME** *Fiction FICCD 47*	65	2
20 Feb 93	SCENES FROM THE SECOND STOREY *Fiction 5171562*	55	1

The GODFATHERS
UK, male vocal / instrumental group (2 Albums: 3 Weeks)

13 Feb 88	BIRTH SCHOOL WORK DEATH *Epic 460263 1*	80	2
20 May 89	MORE SONGS ABOUT LOVE AND HATE *Epic 463394 1*	49	1

GODIEGO
Japan / US, male vocal / instrumental group (2 Singles: 11 Weeks)

15 Oct 77	**THE WATER MARGIN** *BBC RESL 50*	37	4
16 Feb 80	**GANDHARA** *BBC RESL 66*	56	7

'The Water Margin' is the English version of the song, which shared chart credit with the Japanese language version by Pete Mac Jr.

GODLEY and CREME (see also HOTLEGS; 10cc)
UK, male vocal / instrumental duo – Kevin Godley and Lol Creme (4 Albums: 34 Weeks, 3 Singles: 36 Weeks)

19 Nov 77	CONSEQUENCES *Mercury CONS 017*	52	1

12 / 15 February 1969	19 / 22 February 1969	26 February / 1 March 1969	5 / 8 March 1969
(IF PARADISE IS) HALF AS NICE Amen Corner	**(IF PARADISE IS) HALF AS NICE** Amen Corner	**WHERE DO YOU GO TO (MY LOVELY)** Peter Sarstedt	**WHERE DO YOU GO TO (MY LOVELY)** Peter Sarstedt
DIANA ROSS AND THE SUPREMES JOIN THE TEMPTATIONS Diana Ross and The Supremes with The Temptations	**DIANA ROSS AND THE SUPREMES JOIN THE TEMPTATIONS** Diana Ross and The Supremes with The Temptations	**DIANA ROSS AND THE SUPREMES JOIN THE TEMPTATIONS** Diana Ross and The Supremes with The Temptations	**DIANA ROSS AND THE SUPREMES JOIN THE TEMPTATIONS** Diana Ross and The Supremes with The Temptations

KEY: UK No.1 ★★ UK Top 10 ●● Still on chart ++ UK entry at No.1 ■■ US No.1 ▲▲ UK million seller £ US million seller $
Singles re-entries are listed as (re), (2re), (3re)... which signifies that the hit re-entered the chart once, twice or three times...
Peak Position / Weeks

9 Sep 78	L *Mercury 9109 611*	47	2
12 Sep 81 ●	UNDER YOUR THUMB *Polydor POSP 322*	3	11
17 Oct 81	ISMISM *Polydor POLD 5043*	29	13
21 Nov 81 ●	WEDDING BELLS *Polydor POSP 369*	7	11
30 Mar 85	CRY (re) *Polydor POSP 732*	19	14
29 Aug 87 ●	CHANGING FACES – THE VERY BEST OF 10CC AND GODLEY AND CREME *ProTV TGCLP 1* [1]	4	18

[1] 10cc and Godley and Creme

GOD'S PROPERTY *US, male / female gospel choir*

22 Nov 97	STOMP *B-rite Music IND 95559*	60	1

GODSPEED YOU BLACK EMPEROR!
Canada, male instrumental ensemble

21 Oct 00	LIFT YOUR SKINNY FISTS LIKE ANTENNAS TO HEAVEN *Kranky KRANK 043*	66	1

Alex GOLD featuring Philip OAKEY
(see also HUMAN LEAGUE) *UK, male producer and vocalist*

26 Apr 03	L.A. TODAY *Xtravaganza XTRAV 37CDS*	68	1

Andrew GOLD (see also WAX)
US, male vocalist / pianist (1 Album: 7 Weeks, 4 Singles: 36 Weeks)

2 Apr 77	LONELY BOY *Asylum K 13076*	11	9
25 Mar 78 ●	NEVER LET HER SLIP AWAY *Asylum K 13112*	5	13
15 Apr 78	ALL THIS AND HEAVEN TOO *Asylum K 53072*	31	7
24 Jun 78	HOW CAN THIS BE LOVE *Asylum K 13126*	19	10
14 Oct 78	THANK YOU FOR BEING A FRIEND *Asylum K 13135*	42	4

GOLD BLADE *UK, male vocal / instrumental group*

22 Mar 97	STRICTLY HARDCORE *Ultimate TOPP 056CD*	64	1

GOLDBUG *UK, male / female vocal / instrumental group*

27 Jan 96 ●	WHOLE LOTTA LOVE *Acid Jazz JAZID 125CD*	3	5

GOLDEN BOY with MISS KITTIN
Germany, male producer and France, female vocalist

7 Sep 02	RIPPIN KITTEN *Illustrious CDILL 007*	67	1

GOLDEN EARRING *Holland, male vocal (Barry Hay) / instrumental group (1 Album: 4 Weeks, 2 Singles: 16 Weeks)*

8 Dec 73 ●	RADAR LOVE *Track 2094 116*	7	13
2 Feb 74	MOONTAN *Track 2406 112*	24	4
8 Oct 77	RADAR LOVE *Polydor 2121 335*	44	3

The 8 Oct 1977 version of 'Radar Love' credits Golden Earring 'Live'.

GOLDEN GIRLS
UK, male producer / instrumentalist – Mike Hazell (2 Singles: 3 Weeks)

3 Oct 98	KINETIC *Distinctive DISNCD 46*	38	2
4 Dec 99	KINETIC (re-mix) *Distinctive DISNCD 59*	56	1

GOLDENSCAN *UK, male DJ / production duo*

11 Nov 00	SUNRISE *VC Recordings VCRD 79*	52	1

GOLDFINGER *US, male vocal / instrumental group*

22 Jun 02	OPEN YOUR EYES *Jive 9270052*	75	1

GOLDFRAPP
UK, male / female vocal / instrumental duo – Alison Goldfrapp and Will Gregory (3 Albums: 46 Weeks, 9 Singles: 31 Weeks)

23 Jun 01	UTOPIA *Mute CDMUTE 264*	62	1
25 Aug 01	FELT MOUNTAIN *Mute CDSTUMM 188*	57	5
17 Nov 01	PILOTS *Mute CDMUTE 267*	68	1
26 Apr 03	TRAIN *Mute CDMUTE 291*	23	3
10 May 03	BLACK CHERRY *Mute CDSTUMM 196*	19	26
2 Aug 03	STRICT MACHINE *Mute CDMUTE 295*	25	3
15 Nov 03	TWIST *Mute CDMUTE 311*	31	2
13 Mar 04	BLACK CHERRY *Mute CDMUTE 320*	28	2
22 May 04	STRICT MACHINE (re-issue) *Mute LCDMUTE 335*	20	3
20 Aug 05 ●	OOH LA LA *Mute LCDMUTE 342*	4	12
3 Sep 05 ●	SUPERNATURE *Mute CDSTUMM 250*	2	15+
12 Nov 05 ●	NUMBER 1 *Mute LCDMUTE 351*	9	4

GOLDIE *UK, male vocal (Peter McDonald) / instrumental group*

27 May 78 ●	MAKING UP AGAIN *Bronze BRO 50*	7	11

GOLDIE
UK, male producer – Clifford Price (2 Albums: 16 Weeks, 6 Singles: 16 Weeks)

3 Dec 94	INNER CITY LIFE *ffrr FCD 251* [1]	49	2
19 Aug 95 ●	TIMELESS *ffrr 8286142*	7	12
9 Sep 95	ANGEL *ffrr FCD 266*	41	3
11 Nov 95	INNER CITY LIFE (re-mix) *ffrr FCD 267*	39	2
1 Nov 97	DIGITAL *ffrr FCD 316* [2]	13	3
24 Jan 98	TEMPERTEMPER *ffrr FCD 325* [2]	13	4
14 Feb 98	SATURNZ RETURN *ffrr 8289902*	15	4
18 Apr 98	BELIEVE *ffrr FCD 332*	36	2

[1] Goldie presents Metalheadz [2] Goldie featuring KRS One

GOLDIE and The GINGERBREADS
US, female vocal / instrumental group

25 Feb 65	CAN'T YOU HEAR MY HEART BEAT? *Decca F 12070*	25	5

GOLDIE LOOKIN CHAIN
UK, male rap / production group (2 Albums: 18 Weeks, 6 Singles: 29 Weeks)

1 May 04	HALF MAN HALF MACHINE / SELF SUICIDE *Must Destroy DUSTY 019CD*	32	4
28 Aug 04 ●	GUNS DON'T KILL PEOPLE, RAPPERS DO *Atlantic GLC 01CD*	3	9
25 Sep 04 ●	GREATEST HITS *Atlantic 5046748802*	5	15
6 Nov 04	YOUR MOTHER'S GOT A PENIS *East West GLC 02CD*	14	3
25 Dec 04	YOU KNOWS I LOVES YOU BABY *Atlantic GLC 03CD*	22	5
17 Sep 05	YOUR MISSUS IS A NUTTER *Atlantic ATUK 014CDX*	14	5
1 Oct 05	SAFE AS FUCK *Atlantic 5101103042*	16	3
3 Dec 05	R 'N' B *Atlantic ATUK 021CD*	26	3

GOLDRUSH *UK, male vocal / instrumental group (2 Singles: 2 Weeks)*

22 Jun 02	SAME PICTURE *Virgin VSCDT 1833*	64	1
7 Sep 02	WIDE OPEN SKY *Virgin VSCDT 1834*	70	1

Bobby GOLDSBORO *US, male vocalist (4 Singles: 47 Weeks)*

17 Apr 68 ●	HONEY *United Artists UP 2215* ▲ $	2	15
4 Aug 73 ●	SUMMER (THE FIRST TIME) *United Artists UP 35558*	9	10
3 Aug 74	HELLO, SUMMERTIME *United Artists UP 35705*	14	10
29 Mar 75 ●	HONEY (re-issue) *United Artists UP 35633*	2	12

Glen GOLDSMITH
UK, male vocalist (1 Album: 9 Weeks, 4 Singles: 24 Weeks)

7 Nov 87	I WON'T CRY *Reproduction PB 41493*	34	7
12 Mar 88	DREAMING *Reproduction PB 41711*	12	11
11 Jun 88	WHAT YOU SEE IS WHAT YOU GET *Reproduction PB 42075*	33	5
23 Jul 88	WHAT YOU SEE IS WHAT YOU GET *RCA PL 71750*	14	9
3 Sep 88	SAVE A LITTLE BIT *Reproduction PB 42147*	73	1

12 / 15 March 1969	19 / 22 March 1969	26 / 29 March 1969	2 / 5 April 1969
UK No.1 SINGLES			
WHERE DO YOU GO TO (MY LOVELY) Peter Sarstedt	WHERE DO YOU GO TO (MY LOVELY) Peter Sarstedt	I HEARD IT THROUGH THE GRAPEVINE Marvin Gaye	I HEARD IT THROUGH THE GRAPEVINE Marvin Gaye
UK No.1 ALBUMS			
GOODBYE Cream	GOODBYE Cream	THE BEST OF THE SEEKERS The Seekers	THE BEST OF THE SEEKERS The Seekers

GOLDTRIX presents Andrea BROWN
UK, male production / instrumental duo and US, female vocalist

19 Jan 02 ● **IT'S LOVE (TRIPPIN') (re)** *AM:PM / Serious / Evolve CDAMPM 152* 6 9

GOMEZ *UK, male vocal / instrumental group*
(5 Albums: 101 Weeks, 10 Singles: 19 Weeks)

11 Apr 98 **78 STONE WOBBLE** *Hut HUTCD 95* 44 1
25 Apr 98 BRING IT ON *Hut CDHUTX 49* 11 60
13 Jun 98 **GET MYSELF ARRESTED** *Hut HUTCD 97* 45 1
12 Sep 98 **WHIPPIN' PICCADILLY** *Hut HUTCD 105* 35 3
10 Jul 99 **BRING IT ON** *Hut HUTCD 112* 21 3
11 Sep 99 **RHYTHM & BLUES ALIBI** *Hut HUTCD 114* 18 3
25 Sep 99 ● LIQUID SKIN *Hut CDHUT 54* 2 28
27 Nov 99 **WE HAVEN'T TURNED AROUND** *Hut HUTCD 117* 38 2
7 Oct 00 ● ABANDONED SHOPPING TROLLEY HOTLINE *Hut CDHUTX 64* ..10 4
16 Mar 02 **SHOT SHOT** *Hut / Virgin HUTCD 149* 28 2
30 Mar 02 ● IN OUR GUN *Hut CDHUT 72* 8 7
15 Jun 02 **SOUND OF SOUNDS / PING ONE DOWN** *Hut / Virgin HUTCD 154* 48 1
20 Mar 04 **CATCH ME UP** *Hut / Virgin HUTDX 175* 36 2
22 May 04 **SILENCE** *Hut / Virgin HUTDX 178* 41 1
29 May 04 SPLIT THE DIFFERENCE *Hut / Virgin CDHUT 84* 35 2

GOMPIE *Holland, male vocal / instrumental group*

20 May 95 **ALICE (WHO THE X IS ALICE) (LIVING NEXT DOOR TO ALICE) (re)** *Habana HABSCD 5* 17 12

GONZALEZ *UK / US, male vocal / instrumental group*

31 Mar 79 **HAVEN'T STOPPED DANCING YET** *Sidewalk SID 102* 15 11

GOO GOO DOLLS
US, male vocal / instrumental trio (2 Albums: 2 Weeks, 3 Singles: 4 Weeks)

1 Aug 98 **IRIS** *Reprise W 0449CD* 50 1
27 Mar 99 **SLIDE** *Edel / Hollywood / Third Rail 0102035 HWR* 43 1
17 Jul 99 **IRIS** (re-issue) *Hollywood 0102485 HWR* 26 2
31 Jul 99 DIZZY UP THE GIRL *Hollywood 0102042 HWR* 47 1
4 May 02 GUTTERFLOWER *Warner Bros. 9362483112* 56 1

GOOD CHARLOTTE *US, male vocal (Joel Madden) / instrumental group (2 Albums: 44 Weeks, 7 Singles: 37 Weeks)*

25 Jan 03 THE YOUNG AND THE HOPELESS *Epic 5094889* 15 39
15 Feb 03 ● **LIFESTYLES OF THE RICH AND FAMOUS** *Epic 6735562* 8 10
17 May 03 ● **GIRLS AND BOYS** *Epic 6738772* 6 9
30 Aug 03 ● **THE ANTHEM** *Epic 6742555* 10 4
20 Dec 03 **THE YOUNG AND THE HOPELESS / HOLD ON** *Epic 6745432* 34 4
16 Oct 04 **PREDICTABLE** *Epic 6753882* 12 4
23 Oct 04 ● THE CHRONICLES OF LIFE AND DEATH *Epic 5176859* 8 5
12 Feb 05 ● **I JUST WANNA LIVE** *Epic 6756492* 9 4
18 Jun 05 **THE CHRONICLES OF LIFE AND DEATH** *Epic 6759432* 30 2

GOOD GIRLS *US, female vocal group*

24 Jul 93 **JUST CALL ME** *Motown TMGCD 1417* 75 1

Jack GOOD presents LORD ROCKINGHAM'S XI *UK, male / female instrumental group – leader Harry Robinson (3 Singles: 21 Weeks)*

24 Oct 58 ★ **HOOTS MON** *Decca F 11059* 1 17
6 Feb 59 **WEE TOM** *Decca F 11104* 16 3
25 Sep 93 **HOOTS MON** (re-issue) *Decca 8820982* [1] 60 1

[1] Lord Rockingham's XI

GOODBYE MR MACKENZIE *UK, male / female vocal / instrumental group – includes Shirley Manson (2 Albums: 4 Weeks, 5 Singles: 13 Weeks)*

20 Aug 88 **GOODBYE MR MACKENZIE** *Capitol CL 501* 62 2
11 Mar 89 **THE RATTLER** *Capitol CL 522* 37 6
22 Apr 89 GOOD DEEDS AND DIRTY RAGS *Capitol EST 2089* 26 3
29 Jul 89 **GOODWILL CITY / I'M SICK OF YOU** *Capitol CL 538* 49 2
21 Apr 90 **LOVE CHILD** *Parlophone R 6247* 52 2
23 Jun 90 **BLACKER THAN BLACK** *Parlophone R 6257* 61 1
16 Mar 91 HAMMER AND TONGS *Radioactive RAR 10227* 61 1

Roger GOODE featuring Tasha BAXTER
South Africa, male DJ / producer and female vocalist

13 Apr 02 **IN THE BEGINNING** *ffrr DFCD 004* 33 2

GOODFELLAS featuring Lisa MILLETT
(see also BINI & MARTINI; ECLIPSE; HOUSE OF GLASS) *Italy, male production duo – Paolo Martini and Gianni Bini and UK, female vocalist*

21 Jul 01 **SOUL HEAVEN** *Direction 6713852* 27 2

GOODFELLAZ *US, male vocal trio*

10 May 97 **SUGAR HONEY ICE TEA** *Wild Card 5736132* 25 2

The GOODIES
UK, male comedy / vocal group (1 Album: 11 Weeks, 5 Singles: 38 Weeks)

7 Dec 74 ● **THE INBETWEENIES / FATHER CHRISTMAS DO NOT TOUCH ME** *Bradley's BRAD 7421* 7 9
15 Mar 75 ● **FUNKY GIBBON / SICK-MAN BLUES** *Bradley's BRAD 7504* 4 10
21 Jun 75 **BLACK PUDDING BERTHA (THE QUEEN OF NORTHERN SOUL)** *Bradley's BRAD 7517* 19 7
27 Sep 75 **NAPPY LOVE / WILD THING** *Bradley's BRAD 7524* 21 6
8 Nov 75 THE NEW GOODIES LP *Bradley's BRADL 1010* 25 11
13 Dec 75 **MAKE A DAFT NOISE FOR CHRISTMAS** *Bradley's BRAD 7533* ..20 6

Cuba GOODING (see also The MAIN INGREDIENT) *US, male vocalist*

19 Nov 83 **HAPPINESS IS JUST AROUND THE BEND** *London LON 41* 72 2

Benny GOODMAN
US, male clarinet player, b. 30 May 1909, d. 13 Jun 1986

3 Apr 71 BENNY GOODMAN TODAY *Decca DDS 3* 49 1

GOODMEN (see also CHOCOLATE PUMA; JARK PRONGO; RHYTHMKILLAZ; RIVA featuring Dannii MINOGUE; TOMBA VIRA) *Holland, male instrumental / production duo – Rene Terhorst and Gaston Steenkist*

7 Aug 93 ● **GIVE IT UP (re)** *Fresh Fruit TABCD 118* 5 19

Delta GOODREM
Australia, female vocalist (2 Albums: 43 Weeks, 6 Singles: 58 Weeks)

22 Mar 03 ● **BORN TO TRY** *Epic 6736342* 3 13
28 Jun 03 ● **LOST WITHOUT YOU** *Epic 6739555* 4 11
12 Jul 03 ● INNOCENT EYES *Epic 5109512* 2 33
4 Oct 03 ● **INNOCENT EYES** *Epic 6743152* 9 9
13 Dec 03 **NOT ME, NOT I** *Epic 6745372* 18 6
20 Nov 04 ● **OUT OF THE BLUE (re)** *Epic 6754732* 9 9
4 Dec 04 MISTAKEN IDENTITY *Epic 5189159* 25 10
12 Feb 05 ● **ALMOST HERE** *Modest / Sony Music 6757352* [1] 3 10

[1] Brian McFadden & Delta Goodrem

Ron GOODWIN and his ORCHESTRA
(see also Eamonn ANDREWS) *UK, orchestra leader, b. 17 Feb 1925, d. 8 Jan 2003 (1 Album: 1 Week, 2 Singles: 24 Weeks)*

15 May 53 ● **TERRY'S THEME FROM 'LIMELIGHT'** *Parlophone R 3686* 3 23
28 Oct 55 **BLUE STAR (THE MEDIC THEME)** *Parlophone R 4074* 20 1
2 May 70 LEGEND OF THE GLASS MOUNTAIN *Studio Two TWO 220* 49 1

GOODY GOODY *US, female vocal duo*

2 Dec 78 **NUMBER ONE DEE JAY** *Atlantic LV 3* 55 5

KEY
UK No.1 ★ UK Top 10 ● Still on chart + UK entry at No.1 ■
US No.1 ▲ UK million seller £ US million seller $
Singles re-entries are listed as (re), (2re), (3re)... which signifies that the hit re-entered the chart once, twice or three times...
Peak Position / Weeks

GOOMBAY DANCE BAND *Germany / Montserrat, male / female vocal / instrumental group (1 Album: 9 Weeks, 2 Singles: 16 Weeks)*

27 Feb 82 ★ **SEVEN TEARS** *Epic EPC A 1242*....1 12
10 Apr 82 **SEVEN TEARS** *Epic EPC 85702*....16 9
15 May 82 **SUN OF JAMAICA** *Epic EPC A 2345*....50 4

The GOONS
(see also Spike MILLIGAN; Harry SECOMBE; Peter SELLERS) *UK, male comedy / vocal group (3 Albums: 31 Weeks, 3 Singles: 30 Weeks)*

29 Jun 56 ● **I'M WALKING BACKWARDS FOR CHRISTMAS / BLUEBOTTLE BLUES** *Decca F 10756*....4 10
14 Sep 56 ● **BLOODNOK'S ROCK 'N' ROLL CALL / THE YING TONG SONG** *Decca F 10780*....3 10
28 Nov 59 ● **BEST OF THE GOON SHOWS** *Parlophone PMC 1108*....8 14
17 Dec 60 **BEST OF THE GOON SHOWS VOLUME 2** *Parlophone PMC 1129*....12 6
4 Nov 72 ● **LAST GOON SHOW OF ALL** *BBC Radio Enterprise REB 142*....8 11
21 Jul 73 ● **YING TONG SONG** (re-issue) *Decca F 13414*....9 10

'Bluebottle Blues' listed only from 13 Jul 1956. It peaked at No.5.

Lonnie GORDON *US, female vocalist (6 Singles: 23 Weeks)*

24 Jun 89 **(I'VE GOT YOUR) PLEASURE CONTROL** *ffrr F 106* [1]....60 3
27 Jan 90 ● **HAPPENIN' ALL OVER AGAIN** *Supreme SUPE 159*....4 10
11 Aug 90 **BEYOND YOUR WILDEST DREAMS** *Supreme SUPE 167*....48 2
17 Nov 90 **IF I HAVE TO STAND ALONE** *Supreme SUPE 181*....68 1
4 May 91 **GONNA CATCH YOU** *Supreme SUPE 185*....32 5
7 Oct 95 **LOVE EVICTION** *X:Plode BANG 2CD* [2]....32 2

[1] Simon Harris featuring Lonnie Gordon [2] Quartz Lock featuring Lonnie Gordon

Lesley GORE *US, female vocalist – Lesley Goldstein (2 Singles: 20 Weeks)*

20 Jun 63 ● **IT'S MY PARTY** *Mercury AMT 1205* ▲ $....9 12
24 Sep 64 **MAYBE I KNOW** *Mercury MF 829*....20 8

Martin L GORE (see also DEPECHE MODE) *UK, male vocalist*

24 Jun 89 **COUNTERFEIT E.P.** *Mute STUMM 67*....51 1
26 Apr 03 **STARDUST** *Mute CDMUTE 296*....44 1

GORILLAZ 368 Top 500 (see also BLUR)
Multi-award-winning virtual cartoon character-based band who include Blur's Damon Albarn (2-D) and cult cartoonist Jamie Hewlett (Murdoc). Called 'The ultimate experiment in manufactured images', they are one of world's top selling British based acts, with Demon Days selling over 6.5 million copies worldwide (3 Albums: 93 Weeks, 8 Singles: 95 Weeks)

17 Mar 01 ● **CLINT EASTWOOD** *Parlophone CDR 6552*....4 17
7 Apr 01 ● **GORILLAZ** *Parlophone 5311380*....3 61
7 Jul 01 ● **19/2000** *Parlophone CDR 6559*....6 10
3 Nov 01 **ROCK THE HOUSE** *Parlophone CDRS 6565*....18 8
9 Mar 02 **TOMORROW COMES TODAY** (re) *Parlophone CDR 6573*....33 3
23 Mar 02 **G SIDES** *Parlophone 536942*....65 1
3 Aug 02 **LIL' DUB CHEFIN'** *Parlophone CDR 6584* [1]....73 1
23 Apr 05 ● **FEEL GOOD INC (2re)** *Parlophone R 6663*....2 34+
4 Jun 05 ★ **DEMON DAYS** *Parlophone 3116912* ■....1 31+
10 Sep 05 ★ **DARE** *Parlophone CDRS 6668* ■....1 17+
3 Dec 05 ● **DIRTY HARRY** *Parlophone CDRS 6676*....6 5+

[1] Space Monkeyz vs Gorillaz

GORKY'S ZYGOTIC MYNCI *UK, male / female vocal / instrumental group (2 Albums: 2 Weeks, 8 Singles: 8 Weeks)*

9 Nov 96 **PATIO SONG** *Fontana GZMCD 1*....41 1
29 Mar 97 **DIAMOND DEW** *Fontana GZMCD 2*....42 1
19 Apr 97 **BARAFUNDLE** *Fontana 5347692*....46 1
21 Jun 97 **YOUNG GIRLS & HAPPY ENDINGS / DARK NIGHT** *Fontana GZMCD 3*....49 1
6 Jun 98 **SWEET JOHNNY** *Fontana GZMCD 4*....60 1
29 Aug 98 **LET'S GET TOGETHER (IN OUR MINDS)** *Fontana GZMCD 5*....43 1
12 Sep 98 **GORKY 5** *Fontana 5588222*....67 1
2 Oct 99 **SPANISH DANCE TROUPE** *Mantra / Beggars Banquet MNT 47CD*....47 1
4 Mar 00 **POODLE ROCKIN'** *Mantra / Beggars Banquet MNT 52CD*....52 1
15 Sep 01 **STOOD ON GOLD** *Mantra / Beggars Banquet MNT 64CD*....65 1

Eydie GORME *US, female vocalist (4 Singles: 33 Weeks)*

24 Jan 58 **LOVE ME FOREVER** *HMV POP 432*....21 5
21 Jun 62 ● **YES MY DARLING DAUGHTER** *CBS AAG 105*....10 9
31 Jan 63 **BLAME IT ON THE BOSSA NOVA** *CBS AAG 131*....32 6
22 Aug 63 ● **I WANT TO STAY HERE** *CBS AAG 163* [1]....3 13

[1] Steve and Eydie

Matt GOSS (see also BROS) *UK, male vocalist (5 Singles: 10 Weeks)*

26 Aug 95 **THE KEY** *Atlas 5811532*....40 2
27 Apr 96 **IF YOU WERE HERE TONIGHT** *Atlas 5762932*....23 3
15 Nov 03 **I'M COMING WITH YA** *Concept CDCON 49*....22 2
31 Jul 04 **FLY** *Concept CDCON 57*....31 2
2 Oct 04 **I NEED THE KEY** (re-recording) *Inferno CDFERN 63* [1]....54 1

[1] Minimal Chic featuring Matt Goss

Luke GOSS and The BAND OF THIEVES (see also BROS) *UK, male vocal / instrumental group (2 Singles: 3 Weeks)*

12 Jun 93 **SWEETER THAN THE MIDNIGHT RAIN** *Sabre CDSAB 1*....52 2
21 Aug 93 **GIVE ME ONE MORE CHANCE** *Sabre CDSAB 2*....68 1

Irv GOTTI *US, male producer / rapper*

20 Jul 02 **IRV GOTTI PRESENTS THE INC** *Murder Inc / Mercury 630332* [1]....68 3
12 Oct 02 ● **DOWN 4 U (2re)** *Murder Inc 0639002* [1]....4 10

[1] Irv Gotti presents the Inc
[1] Irv Gotti presents Ja Rule, Ashanti, Charli Baltimore and Vita

Graham GOULDMAN (see also 10cc; WAX) *UK, male vocalist*

23 Jun 79 **SUNBURN** *Mercury SUNNY 1*....52 4

GOURYELLA (see also ALBION; MOONMAN; STARPARTY; SYSTEM F; VERACOCHA) *Holland, male production duo – Tijs Verwest and Ferry Corsten (3 Singles: 11 Weeks)*

10 Jul 99 **GOURYELLA** *Code Blue BLU 001CD*....15 7
4 Dec 99 **WALHALLA** *Code Blue BLU 006CD*....27 2
23 Dec 00 **TENSHI** *Code Blue BLU 017CD*....45 2

GRACE *UK, female vocalist – Dominique Atkins (8 Singles: 24 Weeks)*

8 Apr 95 ● **NOT OVER YET** *Perfecto PERF 104CD*....6 8
23 Sep 95 **I WANT TO LIVE** *Perfecto PERF 109CD*....30 2
24 Feb 96 **SKIN ON SKIN** *Perfecto PERF 116CD*....21 3
1 Jun 96 **DOWN TO EARTH** *Perfecto PERF 120CD*....20 2
28 Sep 96 **IF I COULD FLY** *Perfecto PERF 127CD*....29 2
3 May 97 **HAND IN HAND** *Perfecto PERF 129CD*....38 1
26 Jul 97 **DOWN TO EARTH** (re-mix) *Perfecto PERF 142CD1*....29 2
14 Aug 99 **NOT OVER YET 99** (re-recording) *Code Blue BLU 004CD1* [1]....16 4

[1] Planet Perfecto featuring Grace

GRACE BROTHERS *UK, male instrumental duo*

20 Apr 96 **ARE YOU BEING SERVED** *EMI Premier PRESCD 1*....51 1

	7 / 10 May 1969	14 / 17 May 1969	21 / 24 May 1969	28 / 31 May 1969
UK No.1 SINGLES	GET BACK The Beatles with Billy Preston	GET BACK The Beatles with Billy Preston	GET BACK The Beatles with Billy Preston	GET BACK The Beatles with Billy Preston
UK No.1 ALBUMS	ON THE THRESHOLD OF A DREAM The Moody Blues	ON THE THRESHOLD OF A DREAM The Moody Blues	NASHVILLE SKYLINE Bob Dylan	NASHVILLE SKYLINE Bob Dylan

Charlie GRACIE

US, male vocalist / guitarist – Charlie Graci (4 Singles: 41 Weeks)

19 Apr 57	**BUTTERFLY** *Parlophone R 4290* $	12	8
14 Jun 57 ●	**FABULOUS** *Parlophone R 4313*	8	16
23 Aug 57 ●	**I LOVE YOU SO MUCH IT HURTS / WANDERIN' EYES (2re)** *London HLU 8467*	6	16
10 Jan 58	**COOL BABY** *London HLU 8521*	26	1

'I Love You So Much It Hurts' and 'Wanderin' Eyes' were listed together for two weeks, then listed separately for a further two and 12 weeks respectively.

GRAFITI (see also The STREETS) *UK, male producer – Mike Skinner*

30 Aug 03	**WHAT IS THE PROBLEM?** *679 Recordings 679L 021CD*	37	2

Max GRAHAM vs YES NEW

Canada (b. UK), male DJ / producer and UK, male vocal / instrumental group

28 May 05 ●	**OWNER OF A LONELY HEART** *Data 92CDS*	9	8

Jaki GRAHAM

UK, female vocalist (2 Albums: 10 Weeks, 12 Singles: 75 Weeks)

23 Mar 85 ●	**COULD IT BE I'M FALLING IN LOVE** *Chrysalis GRAN 6* [1]	5	11
29 Jun 85 ●	**ROUND AND ROUND** *EMI JAKI 4*	9	11
31 Aug 85	**HEAVEN KNOWS** *EMI JAKI 5*	59	3
14 Sep 85	HEAVEN KNOWS *EMI JK 1*	48	5
16 Nov 85	**MATED** *EMI JAKI 6* [1]	20	10
3 May 86 ●	**SET ME FREE** *EMI JAKI 7*	7	12
9 Aug 86	**BREAKING AWAY** *EMI JAKI 8*	16	8
20 Sep 86	BREAKING AWAY *EMI EMC 3514*	25	5
15 Nov 86	**STEP RIGHT UP** *EMI JAKI 9*	15	12
9 Jul 88	**NO MORE TEARS** *EMI JAKI 12*	60	2
24 Jun 89	**FROM NOW ON** *EMI JAKI 15*	73	2
16 Jul 94	**AIN'T NOBODY** *Pulse 8 CDLOSE 64*	44	2
4 Feb 95	**YOU CAN COUNT ON ME** *Avex UK AVEXCD 1*	62	1
8 Jul 95	**ABSOLUTE E-SENSUAL** *Avex UK AVEXCD 5*	69	1

[1] David Grant and Jaki Graham

Larry GRAHAM (see also SLY and The FAMILY STONE)

US, male vocalist / bass guitarist

3 Jul 82	**SOONER OR LATER** *Warner Bros. K 17925*	54	4

Mikey GRAHAM (see also BOYZONE)

Ireland, male vocalist (2 Singles: 6 Weeks)

10 Jun 00	**YOU'RE MY ANGEL** *Public PR 001CDS*	13	5
14 Apr 01	**YOU COULD BE MY EVERYTHING** *Public PR 003CDS*	62	1

Ron GRAINER ORCHESTRA

UK, orchestra – leader b. 11 Aug 1922, d. 21 Feb 1981

9 Dec 78	**A TOUCH OF VELVET – A STING OF BRASS** *Casino Classics CC 5*	60	7

GRAND FUNK RAILROAD *US, male vocal / instrumental group*

6 Feb 71	**INSIDE LOOKING OUT** *Capitol CL 15668*	40	1
13 Feb 71	GRAND FUNK LIVE *Capitol E-STDW 1/2*	29	1

GRAND PLAZ *UK, male instrumental / production group*

8 Sep 90	**WOW WOW – NA NA** *Urban URB 60*	41	4

GRAND PRIX *UK, male vocal / instrumental group*

27 Feb 82	**KEEP ON BELIEVING** *RCA 162*	75	1
18 Jun 83	SAMURAI *Chrysalis CHR 1430*	65	2

GRAND PUBA *US, male rapper – Maxwell Dixon (2 Singles: 6 Weeks)*

13 Jan 96	**WHY YOU TREAT ME SO BAD** *Virgin VSCDT 1566* [1]	11	5
30 Mar 96	**WILL YOU BE MY BABY** *GHQ 74321339092* [2]	53	1

[1] Shaggy featuring Grand Puba [2] Infiniti featuring Grand Puba

GRAND THEFT AUDIO *UK, male vocal / instrumental group*

24 Mar 01	**WE LUV U** *Sci-Fi SCIFI 1CD*	70	1

GRANDAD ROBERTS AND HIS SON ELVIS *UK, male vocal duo*

20 Jun 98	**MEAT PIE SAUSAGE ROLL** *WEA WEA 160CD*	67	1

GRANDADDY

US, male vocal / instrumental group (2 Albums: 6 Weeks, 4 Singles: 6 Weeks)

20 May 00	THE SOPHTWARE SLUMP *V2 VVR 1012252*	36	4
2 Sep 00	**HEWLETT'S DAUGHTER** *V2 VVR 5014333*	71	1
10 Feb 01	**THE CRYSTAL LAKE** *V2 VVR 5015153*	38	2
14 Jun 03	**NOW IT'S ON** *V2 VVR 25022243*	23	2
21 Jun 03	SUMDAY *V2 VVR 1022238*	22	2
6 Sep 03	**EL CAMINOS IN THE WEST** *V2 VVR 5023663*	48	1

GRANDMASTER FLASH *US, male vocalist / rapper / DJ – Joseph Saddler (3 Albums: 20 Weeks, 10 Singles: 61 Weeks)*

28 Aug 82 ●	**THE MESSAGE** *Sugarhill SHL 117*	8	9
23 Oct 82	THE MESSAGE *Sugarhill SHLP 1007*	77	3
19 Nov 83 ●	**WHITE LINES (DON'T DON'T DO IT) (3re)** *Sugarhill SH 130* [1]	7	43
23 Jun 84	GREATEST MESSAGES *Sugarhill SHLP 5552*	41	16
16 Feb 85	**SIGN OF THE TIMES** *Elektra E 9677*	72	1
23 Feb 85	THEY SAID IT COULDN'T BE DONE *Elektra 9603891*	95	1
8 Jan 94	**WHITE LINES (DON'T DO IT)** (re-mix) *WGAF WGAFCD 103* [1]	59	3
17 Jun 95	**WHITE LINES (DON'T DO IT)** (re-recording) *Parlophone CDDD 19* [2]	17	5

[1] Grandmaster and Melle Mel [2] Duran Duran featuring Melle Mel and Grandmaster Flash and the Furious Five

'White Lines (Don't Don't Do It)' re-entered in 1984 (twice) and 1985.

GRANDMASTER MELLE MEL *US, male vocalist – Melvin Glover (1 Album: 5 Weeks, 8 Singles: 82 Weeks)*

22 Jan 83	**MESSAGE II (SURVIVAL)** *Sugarhill SH 119* [1]	74	2
19 Nov 83 ●	**WHITE LINES (DON'T DON'T DO IT) (3re)** *Sugarhill SH 130* [2]	7	43
30 Jun 84	**BEAT STREET BREAKDOWN** *Atlantic A 9659* [3]	42	7
22 Sep 84	**WE DON'T WORK FOR FREE** *Sugarhill SH 136* [3]	45	4
15 Dec 84 ●	**STEP OFF (PART 1)** *Sugarhill SHL 139* [3]	8	12
20 Oct 84	WORK PARTY *Sugarhill SHLP 5553*	45	5
16 Mar 85	**PUMP ME UP** *Sugarhill SH 141* [3]	45	6
8 Jan 94	**WHITE LINES (DON'T DO IT)** (re-mix) *WGAF WGAFCD 103* [2]	59	3
17 Jun 95	**WHITE LINES (DON'T DO IT)** (re-recording) *Parlophone CDDD 19* [4]	17	5

[1] Melle Mel and Duke Bootee [2] Grandmaster and Melle Mel [3] Grandmaster Melle Mel and the Furious Five [4] Duran Duran featuring Melle Mel and Grandmaster Flash and the Furious Five

'White Lines (Don't Don't Do It)' re-entered in 1984 (twice) and 1985.

GRANDMIXER D ST.

US, male DJ / producer - Derek Howells

24 Dec 83	**CRAZY CUTS (re)** *Island IS146*	71	3

GRANGE HILL CAST

UK, male / female vocal charity assembly / TV show cast

19 Apr 86 ●	**JUST SAY NO** *BBC RESL 183*	5	6

Gerri GRANGER *US, female vocalist*

30 Sep 78	**I GO TO PIECES (EVERYTIME)** *Casino Classics CC3*	50	3

Amy GRANT *US, female vocalist (1 Album: 15 Weeks, 8 Singles: 39 Weeks)*

11 May 91 ●	**BABY BABY** *A&M AM 727* ▲	2	13
22 Jun 91	HEART IN MOTION *A&M 3953211*	25	15
3 Aug 91	**EVERY HEARTBEAT** *A&M AM 783*	25	7

4 / 7 June 1969	11 / 14 June 1969	18 / 21 June 1969	25 / 28 June 1969
DIZZY Tommy Roe	THE BALLAD OF JOHN AND YOKO The Beatles	THE BALLAD OF JOHN AND YOKO The Beatles	THE BALLAD OF JOHN AND YOKO The Beatles
NASHVILLE SKYLINE Bob Dylan	NASHVILLE SKYLINE Bob Dylan	HIS ORCHESTRA, HIS CHORUS, HIS SINGERS, HIS SOUND Ray Conniff	HIS ORCHESTRA, HIS CHORUS, HIS SINGERS, HIS SOUND Ray Conniff

KEY: UK No.1 ★ UK Top 10 ● Still on chart + UK entry at No.1 ■ US No.1 ▲ UK million seller £ US million seller $
Singles re-entries are listed as (re), (2re), (3re)... which signifies that the hit re-entered the chart once, twice or three times...
Peak Position / Weeks

2 Nov 91	THAT'S WHAT LOVE IS FOR *A&M AM 666*	60	3
15 Feb 92	GOOD FOR ME *A&M AM 810*	60	1
13 Aug 94	LUCKY ONE *A&M 5807322*	60	1
22 Oct 94	SAY YOU'LL BE MINE *A&M 5808292*	41	2
24 Jun 95	BIG YELLOW TAXI *A&M 5809972*	20	10
14 Oct 95	HOUSE OF LOVE *A&M 5812332* [1]	46	2

[1] Amy Grant with Vince Gill

Andrea GRANT *UK, female vocalist*

14 Nov 98	REPUTATIONS (JUST BE GOOD TO ME) *WEA WEA 192CD*	75	1

David GRANT (see also LINX)
UK, male vocalist (2 Albums: 7 Weeks, 8 Singles: 59 Weeks)

30 Apr 83	STOP AND GO *Chrysalis GRAN 1*	19	9
16 Jul 83 ●	WATCHING YOU WATCHING ME *Chrysalis GRAN 2*	10	13
8 Oct 83	LOVE WILL FIND A WAY *Chrysalis GRAN 3*	24	6
5 Nov 83	DAVID GRANT *Chrysalis CHR 1448*	32	6
26 Nov 83	ROCK THE MIDNIGHT *Chrysalis GRAN 4*	46	4
23 Mar 85 ●	COULD IT BE I'M FALLING IN LOVE *Chrysalis GRAN 6* [1]	5	11
18 May 85	HOPES AND DREAMS *Chrysalis CHR 1483*	96	1
16 Nov 85	MATED *EMI JAKI 6* [1]	20	10
1 Aug 87	CHANGE *Polydor POSP 871*	55	4
12 May 90	KEEP IT TOGETHER *Fourth & Broadway BRW 169*	56	2

[1] David Grant and Jaki Graham

Eddy GRANT (427 Top 500)
Ex-lead guitarist and songwriter for The Equals, b. 5 Mar 1948, Plaisance, Guyana. Grant left the group in 1972, went into production and formed his own label, Ice. Re-mix of transatlantic No.2 'Electric Avenue' returned him to the Top 5 in 2001 (5 Albums: 62 Weeks, 14 Singles: 107 Weeks)

2 Jun 79	LIVING ON THE FRONT LINE *Ensign ENY 26*	11	11
15 Nov 80 ●	DO YOU FEEL MY LOVE? *Ensign ENY 45*	8	11
4 Apr 81	CAN'T GET ENOUGH OF YOU *Ensign ENY 207*	13	10
30 May 81	CAN'T GET ENOUGH *Ice ICELP 21*	39	6
25 Jul 81	I LOVE YOU, YES I LOVE YOU *Ensign ENY 216*	37	6
16 Oct 82 ★	I DON'T WANNA DANCE *Ice ICE 56*	1	15
27 Nov 82 ●	KILLER ON THE RAMPAGE *Ice ICELP 3023*	7	23
15 Jan 83 ●	ELECTRIC AVENUE *Ice ICE 57* $	2	9
19 Mar 83	LIVING ON THE FRONT LINE (re-issue) / DO YOU FEEL MY LOVE (re-issue) *Mercury MER 135*	47	4
23 Apr 83	WAR PARTY *Ice ICE 58*	42	4
29 Oct 83	TILL I CAN'T TAKE LOVE NO MORE *Ice ICE 60*	42	7
19 May 84	ROMANCING THE STONE *Ice ICE 61*	52	3
17 Nov 84	ALL THE HITS *K-Tel NE 1284*	23	10
23 Jan 88 ●	GIMME HOPE JO'ANNA *Ice ICE 78701*	7	12
27 May 89	WALKING ON SUNSHINE *Blue Wave R 6217*	63	2
1 Jul 89	WALKING ON SUNSHINE (THE BEST OF EDDY GRANT) *Parlophone PCSD 108*	20	8
19 May 01 ●	THE GREATEST HITS *East West 8573885972*	3	15
9 Jun 01 ●	ELECTRIC AVENUE (re) (re-mix) *Ice / East West EW 232CD*	5	12
24 Nov 01	WALKING ON SUNSHINE (re-mix) *Ice / East West EW 242CD*	57	1

Gogi GRANT *US, female vocalist – Audrey Arinsberg*

29 Jun 56 ●	THE WAYWARD WIND *London HLB 8282* ▲ $	9	11

Julie GRANT *UK, female vocalist – Vivienne Foreman (3 Singles: 17 Weeks)*

3 Jan 63	UP ON THE ROOF *Pye 7N 15483*	33	3
28 Mar 63	COUNT ON ME *Pye 7N 15508*	24	9
24 Sep 64	COME TO ME *Pye 7N 15684*	31	5

Rudy GRANT (see also The EQUALS) *Guyana, male vocalist*

14 Feb 81	LATELY *Ensign ENY 202*	58	3

GRANT LEE BUFFALO
US, male vocal / instrumental group (3 Albums: 5 Weeks)

10 Jul 93	FUZZY *Slash 8283892*	74	1
1 Oct 94	MIGHTY JOE MOON *Slash 8285412*	24	2
15 Jun 96	COPPEROPOLIS *Slash 8287602*	34	2

GRAPEFRUIT *UK, male vocal / instrumental group (2 Singles: 19 Weeks)*

14 Feb 68	DEAR DELILAH *RCA 1656*	21	9
14 Aug 68	C'MON MARIANNE *RCA 1716*	31	10

GRASS-SHOW
Sweden, male vocal / instrumental group (2 Singles: 2 Weeks)

22 Mar 97	1962 *Food CDFOOD 90*	53	1
23 Aug 97	OUT OF THE VOID *Food CDFOOD 103*	75	1

The GRATEFUL DEAD
US, male vocal / instrumental group (8 Albums: 14 Weeks)

19 Sep 70	WORKINGMAN'S DEAD *Warner Bros. WS 1869*	69	2
20 Feb 71	AMERICAN BEAUTY *Warner Bros. WS 1893*	27	2
3 Aug 74	GRATEFUL DEAD FROM THE MARS HOTEL *Atlantic K 59302*	47	1
1 Nov 75	BLUES FOR ALLAH *United Artists UAS 29895*	45	1
4 Sep 76	STEAL YOUR FACE *United Artists UAS 60131/2*	42	1
20 Aug 77	TERRAPIN STATION *Arista SPARTY 1016*	30	1
19 Sep 87	IN THE DARK *Arista 208 564*	57	3
18 Feb 89	DYLAN AND THE DEAD *CBS 4633811* [1]	38	3

[1] Bob Dylan and The Grateful Dead

GRAVEDIGGAZ (see also RZA; WU-TANG CLAN)
US, male rap group (1 Album: 1 Week, 4 Singles: 6 Weeks)

11 Mar 95	SIX FEET DEEP (EP) *Gee Street GESCD 62*	64	1
5 Aug 95	THE HELL (EP) *Fourth & Broadway BRCD 326* [1]	12	3
4 Oct 97	THE PICK THE SICKLE AND THE SHOVEL *Gee Street GEE 1000562*	24	1
24 Jan 98	THE NIGHT THE EARTH CRIED *Gee Street GEE 5001013*	44	1
25 Apr 98	UNEXPLAINED *Gee Street GEE 5001623*	48	1

[1] Tricky vs The Gravediggaz

Tracks on Six Feet Deep (EP): Bang Your Head / Mommy / Suicide. Tracks on The Hell (EP): Hell Is Round the Corner / Hell Is Round the Corner (re-mix) / Psychosis / Tonite Is a Special Nite.

David GRAY (223 Top 500) (see also ORBITAL)
Acoustic singer / songwriter sensation, b. 13 Jun 1968, Manchester, UK. Ivor Novello award-winning modern day troubadour took 66 weeks to top the UK albums chart with his two million-selling 'White Ladder'. One of the few UK acts to score Stateside in the 21st century (5 Albums: 227 Weeks, 10 Singles: 52 Weeks)

4 Dec 99	PLEASE FORGIVE ME *IHT IHTCDS 003*	72	1
13 May 00 ★	WHITE LADDER *East West 8573829832*	1	153
1 Jul 00 ●	BABYLON *IHT / East West EW 215CD1*	5	12
12 Aug 00 ●	LOST SONGS 95-98 *IHT IHTCD 002*	7	11
28 Oct 00	PLEASE FORGIVE ME (re-issue) *IHT / East West EW 219CD*	18	6
17 Mar 01	THIS YEAR'S LOVE *IHT / East West EW 228CD1*	20	5
14 Jul 01	THE EP'S 92-94 *Hut CDHUT 67*	68	1
28 Jul 01	SAIL AWAY *IHT / East West EW 234CD*	26	6
29 Dec 01	SAY HELLO WAVE GOODBYE *IHT / East West EW 244CD*	26	4
9 Nov 02 ★	A NEW DAY AT MIDNIGHT *East West 5046616582* ■	1	47
21 Dec 02	THE OTHER SIDE *IHT / East West EW 259CD*	35	3
19 Apr 03	BE MINE *IHT / East West EW 264CD*	23	3
10 Sep 05 ●	THE ONE I LOVE *IHT / Atlantic ATUK 013CDX*	8	10
24 Sep 05 ★	LIFE IN SLOW MOTION *Atlantic 5046797662* ■	1	15+
10 Dec 05	HOSPITAL FOOD *Atlantic ATUK 018UK*	34	2

2 / 5 July 1969	9 / 12 July 1969	16 / 19 July 1969	23 / 26 July 1969
UK No.1 SINGLES			
SOMETHING IN THE AIR Thunderclap Newman	SOMETHING IN THE AIR Thunderclap Newman	SOMETHING IN THE AIR Thunderclap Newman	HONKY TONK WOMEN The Rolling Stones
UK No.1 ALBUMS			
HIS ORCHESTRA, HIS CHORUS, HIS SINGERS, HIS SOUND Ray Conniff	ACCORDING TO MY HEART Jim Reeves	ACCORDING TO MY HEART Jim Reeves	ACCORDING TO MY HEART Jim Reeves

David GRAY and Tommy TYCHO
UK, male vocalist and Australia, male orchestra leader

16 Oct 76 ARMCHAIR MELODIES *K-Tel NE 927*.....21 6

Dobie GRAY *US, male vocalist – Lawrence Brown (2 Singles: 11 Weeks)*

25 Feb 65 THE 'IN' CROWD *London HL 9953*.....25 7
27 Sep 75 OUT ON THE FLOOR *Black Magic BM 107*.....42 4

Dorian GRAY *UK, male vocalist*

27 Mar 68 I'VE GOT YOU ON MY MIND *Parlophone R 5667*.....36 7

Les GRAY (see also MUD) *UK, male vocalist, b. 9 Apr 1946, d. 21 Feb 2004*

26 Feb 77 A GROOVY KIND OF LOVE *Warner Bros. K 16883*.....32 5

Macy GRAY *US, female vocalist – Natalie McIntyre (4 Albums: 82 Weeks, 10 Singles: 52 Weeks)*

3 Jul 99 DO SOMETHING *Epic 6675932*.....51 1
17 Jul 99 ● ON HOW LIFE IS *Epic 4944232*.....3 67
9 Oct 99 ● I TRY *Epic 6681832*.....6 22
25 Mar 00 STILL (re) *Epic 6689822*.....18 9
5 Aug 00 WHY DIDN'T YOU CALL ME (re) *Epic 6696682*.....38 3
20 Jan 01 DEMONS *Skint SKINT 60CD* [1].....16 5
28 Apr 01 GETO HEAVEN *MCA MCSTD 40246* [2].....48 1
12 May 01 REQUEST LINE *Interscope 4970532* [3].....31 3
15 Sep 01 SWEET BABY *Epic 6718822* [4].....23 4
29 Sep 01 ★ THE ID *Epic 5040892* ■.....1 8
8 Dec 01 SEXUAL REVOLUTION *Epic 6721462*.....45 1
3 May 03 WHEN I SEE YOU *Epic 6738402*.....26 3
10 May 03 THE TROUBLE WITH BEING MYSELF *Epic 5108102*.....17 5
11 Sep 04 THE VERY BEST OF MACY GRAY *Epic 5179132*.....36 2

[1] Fatboy Slim featuring Macy Gray [2] Common featuring Macy Gray [3] Black Eyed Peas featuring Macy Gray [4] Macy Gray featuring Erykah Badu

Michael GRAY (see also DISCO TEX presents CLOUDBURST; FULL INTENTION; HUSTLERS CONVENTION featuring Dave LAUDAT and Ondrea DUVERNEY; SEX-O-SONIQUE) *UK, male producer*

13 Nov 04 ● THE WEEKEND (re) *Eye Industries / UMTV 9828865*.....7 14

Uncredited vocal on 'The Weekend' by Sheena (McSween)

Barry GRAY ORCHESTRA *UK, orchestra (2 Singles: 8 Weeks)*

11 Jul 81 THUNDERBIRDS *PRT 7P 216*.....61 2
14 Jun 86 JOE 90 (THEME) / CAPTAIN SCARLET THEME *PRT 7PX 354* [1].....53 6

[1] Barry Gray Orchestra with Peter Beckett – keyboards

GREAT WHITE
US, male vocal / instrumental group (1 Album: 1 Week, 3 Singles: 5 Weeks)

24 Feb 90 HOUSE OF BROKEN LOVE *Capitol CL 562*.....44 2
16 Feb 91 CONGO SQUARE *Capitol CL 605*.....62 1
9 Mar 91 HOOKED *Capitol EST 2138*.....43 1
7 Sep 91 CALL IT ROCK 'N' ROLL *Capitol CL 625*.....67 2

Martin GRECH *UK, male vocalist*

3 Aug 02 OPEN HEART ZOO *Island CID 8119*.....54 2
12 Oct 02 OPEN HEART ZOO *DTOX / Island CID 811*.....68 1

Buddy GRECO *US, male vocalist – Armando Greco*

7 Jul 60 THE LADY IS A TRAMP *Fontana H 255*.....26 8

GREED featuring Ricardo DA FORCE
UK, male instrumental duo and rapper

18 Mar 95 PUMP UP THE VOLUME *Stress CDSTR 49*.....51 2

The GREEDIES *Ireland / UK / US, male vocal / instrumental group*

15 Dec 79 A MERRY JINGLE *Vertigo GREED 1*.....28 5

Adam GREEN *US, male vocalist (2 Singles: 2 Weeks)*

3 Apr 04 JESSICA / KOKOMO *Rough Trade RTRADSCD 112*.....63 1
19 Feb 05 EMILY *Rough Trade RTRADSCD 213*.....53 1

Al GREEN
US, male vocalist – Al Greene (4 Albums: 31 Weeks, 9 Singles: 68 Weeks)

9 Oct 71 ● TIRED OF BEING ALONE *London HLU 10337* $.....4 13
8 Jan 72 ● LET'S STAY TOGETHER *London HLU 10348* ▲ $.....7 12
20 May 72 LOOK WHAT YOU DONE FOR ME *London HLU 10369* $.....44 4
19 Aug 72 I'M STILL IN LOVE WITH YOU *London HLU 10382* $.....35 5
16 Nov 74 SHA-LA-LA (MAKE ME HAPPY) *London HLU 10470* $.....20 11
15 Mar 75 L.O.V.E. (LOVE) *London HLU 10482*.....24 8
26 Apr 75 AL GREEN'S GREATEST HITS *London SHU 8481*.....18 16
1 Oct 88 HI LIFE – THE BEST OF AL GREEN *K-Tel NE 1420*.....34 7
3 Dec 88 PUT A LITTLE LOVE IN YOUR HEART *A&M AM 484* [1].....28 8
21 Oct 89 THE MESSAGE IS LOVE *Breakout USA 668* [2].....38 5
24 Oct 92 AL *Beechwood AGREECD 1*.....41 2
2 Oct 93 LOVE IS A BEAUTIFUL THING *Arista 74321162692*.....56 2
16 Feb 02 L-O-V-E: THE ESSENTIAL AL GREEN *Hi ALTV 2002*.....18 6

[1] Annie Lennox and Al Green [2] Arthur Baker and The Backbeat Disciples featuring Al Green

Jesse GREEN *Jamaica, male vocalist (3 Singles: 26 Weeks)*

7 Aug 76 NICE AND SLOW *EMI 2492*.....17 12
18 Dec 76 FLIP *EMI 2564*.....26 8
11 Jun 77 COME WITH ME *EMI 2615*.....29 6

Peter GREEN (see also FLEETWOOD MAC)
UK, male vocalist / guitarist – Peter Greenbaum (4 Albums: 19 Weeks)

9 Jul 79 IN THE SKIES *Creole PULS 101*.....32 13
24 May 80 LITTLE DREAMER *PUK PULS 102*.....34 4
24 May 97 SPLINTER GROUP *Artisan SARCD 101*.....71 1
30 May 98 THE ROBERT JOHNSON SONGBOOK *Artisan SARCD 002* [1].....57 1

[1] Peter Green with Nigel Watson and The Splinter Group

Robson GREEN (see also ROBSON & JEROME) *UK, male actor / vocalist*

14 Dec 02 MOMENT IN TIME *T2 TCD 3300*.....54 4

GREEN DAY 198 Top 500
California formed US punk pop trio who are one of the world's top-selling acts of the 21st Century: Billie Joe Armstrong (v/g), Mike Dirnt (d) and Tre Cool (Frank Wright III) (b). These multi-award winners, who earned a US diamond album (10 million sales) for Dookie, were named Best Band on the Planet at the 2005 Kerrang! awards (8 Albums: 202 Weeks, 19 Singles: 99 Weeks)

20 Aug 94 BASKET CASE *Reprise W 0257CD*.....55 2
29 Oct 94 WELCOME TO PARADISE *Reprise W 0269CDX*.....20 3
5 Nov 94 DOOKIE *Reprise 9362457952*.....13 61
28 Jan 95 ● BASKET CASE (re-issue) *Reprise W 0279CD*.....7 6
18 Mar 95 LONGVIEW *Reprise W 0278CD*.....30 3
20 May 95 WHEN I COME AROUND *Reprise W 0294CD*.....27 3
7 Oct 95 GEEK STINK BREATH *Reprise W 0320CD*.....16 3
21 Oct 95 ● INSOMNIAC *Reprise 936240462*.....8 5
6 Jan 96 STUCK WITH ME *Reprise W 0327CD*.....24 3
6 Jul 96 BRAIN STEW / JADED *Reprise W 0339CD*.....28 2
11 Oct 97 HITCHIN' A RIDE *Reprise W 0424CD*.....25 2
25 Oct 97 NIMROD *Reprise 9362467942*.....11 11
31 Jan 98 TIME OF YOUR LIFE (GOOD RIDDANCE) *Reprise W 0430CD1*.....11 5
9 May 98 REDUNDANT *Reprise W 0438CD1*.....27 2
30 Sep 00 MINORITY *Reprise W 532CD*.....18 3
14 Oct 00 ● WARNING *Reprise 9362480302*.....4 14
23 Dec 00 WARNING *Reprise W 548CD1*.....27 4
10 Nov 01 WAITING *Reprise W 570CD*.....34 2
24 Nov 01 INTERNATIONAL SUPERHITS! *Reprise 9362481452*.....15 36

KEY

UK No.1 ★ UK Top 10 ● Still on chart + UK entry at No.1 ■ US No.1 ▲ UK million seller £ US million seller $

Singles re-entries are listed as (re), (2re), (3re)... which signifies that the hit re-entered the chart once, twice or three times...

Peak Position / Weeks

13 Jul 02 SHENANIGANS *Reprise 9362482082* 32 3
25 Sep 04 ● **AMERICAN IDIOT (re)** *Reprise W 652CD1* 3 8
2 Oct 04 ★ AMERICAN IDIOT *Reprise 9362488502* ■ ▲ ..... 1 66+
11 Dec 04 ● **BOULEVARD OF BROKEN DREAMS** *Reprise W 659CD* 5 21
26 Mar 05 **HOLIDAY** *Reprise W 664CD1* 11 7
25 Jun 05 ● **WAKE ME UP WHEN SEPTEMBER ENDS** *Reprise W 674CD2* 8 17
26 Nov 05 ● BULLET IN A BIBLE *Reprise 9362494662* ..... 6 6+
26 Nov 05 **JESUS OF SUBURBIA** *Reprise W 691CD* 17 3

GREEN JELLY *US, male vocal (Bill Manspeaker) / instrumental group (1 Album: 10 Weeks, 3 Singles: 15 Weeks)*

5 Jun 93 ● **THREE LITTLE PIGS** *Zoo 74321151422* 5 8
3 Jul 93 CEREAL KILLER SOUNDTRACK *Zoo 72445110382* 18 10
14 Aug 93 **ANARCHY IN THE UK** *Zoo 74321159052* 27 3
25 Dec 93 **I'M THE LEADER OF THE GANG** *Arista 74321174892* [1] 25 4

[1] Hulk Hogan with Green Jelly

GREEN ON RED *US, male vocal / instrumental group*

26 Oct 85 NO FREE LUNCH *Mercury MERM 78* 99 1

GREEN VELVET *US, male DJ / producer – Curtis Jones*

25 May 02 **LA LA LAND** *Credence CDCRED 025* 29 2

Norman GREENBAUM *US, male vocalist*

21 Mar 70 ★ **SPIRIT IN THE SKY** *Reprise RS 20885* $ 1 20

Lorne GREENE *Canada, male actor / vocalist, b. 12 Feb 1914, d. 11 Sep 1987*

17 Dec 64 **RINGO** *RCA 1428* ▲ $ 22 8

GREENSLADE *UK, male vocal / instrumental group*

14 Sep 74 SPYGLASS GUEST *Warner Bros. K 56055* 34 3

Lee GREENWOOD *US, male vocalist*

19 May 84 **THE WIND BENEATH MY WINGS** *MCA 877* 49 6

Christina GREGG *UK, female exercise instructor*

27 May 78 MUSIC 'N' MOTION *Warwick WW 5041* 51 1

Iain GREGORY *UK, male vocalist*

4 Jan 62 **CAN'T YOU HEAR THE BEAT OF A BROKEN HEART** *Pye 7N 15397* 39 2

GREYHOUND *Jamaica, male vocal / instrumental group (3 Singles: 33 Weeks)*

26 Jun 71 ● **BLACK AND WHITE** *Trojan TR 7820* 6 13
8 Jan 72 **MOON RIVER** *Trojan TR 7848* 12 11
25 Mar 72 **I AM WHAT I AM** *Trojan TR 7853* 20 9

GRID *UK, male instrumental / production duo – Richard Norris and Dave Ball (2 Albums: 4 Weeks, 10 Singles: 47 Weeks)*

7 Jul 90 **FLOATATION** *East West YZ 475* 60 2
29 Sep 90 **A BEAT CALLED LOVE** *East West YZ 498* 64 4
25 Jul 92 **FIGURE OF 8** *Virgin VSTG 1421* 50 3
3 Oct 92 **HEARTBEAT** *Virgin VST 1427* 72 2
13 Mar 93 **CRYSTAL CLEAR** *Virgin VSCDT 1442* 27 4
30 Oct 93 **TEXAS COWBOYS** *Deconstruction 74321167762* 21 3
4 Jun 94 ● **SWAMP THING** *Deconstruction 74321205842* 3 17
17 Sep 94 **ROLLERCOASTER** *Deconstruction 74321230772* 19 4
1 Oct 94 EVOLVER *Deconstruction 74321227182* 14 3
3 Dec 94 **TEXAS COWBOYS (re-issue)** *Deconstruction 74321244032* 17 6
23 Sep 95 **DIABLO** *Deconstruction 74321308402* 32 2
14 Oct 95 MUSIC FOR DANCING *Deconstruction 74321276702* 67 1

Zaine GRIFF *New Zealand, male vocalist (2 Singles: 6 Weeks)*

16 Feb 80 **TONIGHT** *Automatic K 17547* 54 3
31 May 80 **ASHES AND DIAMONDS** *Automatic K 17610* 68 3

Alistair GRIFFIN *UK, male vocalist (1 Album: 3 Weeks, 2 Singles: 9 Weeks)*

10 Jan 04 ● **BRING IT ON / MY LOVER'S PRAYER** *UMTV 9815673* 5 6
24 Jan 04 BRING IT ON *Universal TV 9816116* 12 3
27 Mar 04 **YOU AND ME (TONIGHT)** *Universal TV 981776* 18 3

'My Lover's Prayer' features Robin Gibb.

Billy GRIFFIN (see also The MIRACLES) *US, male vocalist (2 Singles: 12 Weeks)*

8 Jan 83 **HOLD ME TIGHTER IN THE RAIN** *CBS A 2935* 17 9
14 Jan 84 **SERIOUS** *CBS A 4053* 64 3

Clive GRIFFIN *UK, male vocalist (2 Singles: 5 Weeks)*

24 Jun 89 **HEAD ABOVE WATER** *Mercury STEP 4* 60 2
11 May 91 **I'LL BE WAITING** *Mercury STEP 6* 56 3

Nanci GRIFFITH *US, female vocalist / guitarist (8 Albums: 27 Weeks)*

28 Mar 88 LITTLE LOVE AFFAIRS *MCA MCF 3413* 78 1
23 Sep 89 STORMS *MCA MCG 6066* 38 3
28 Sep 91 LATE NIGHT GRANDE HOTEL *MCA MCA 10306* 40 5
20 Mar 93 OTHER VOICES / OTHER ROOMS *MCA MCD 10796* 18 6
13 Nov 93 THE BEST OF NANCI GRIFFITH *MCA MCD 10966* 27 4
1 Oct 94 FLYER *MCA MCD 11155* 20 4
5 Apr 97 BLUE ROSES FROM THE MOONS *Elektra 7559620152* 64 3
11 Aug 01 CLOCK WITHOUT HANDS *Elektra 7559626602* 61 1

Roni GRIFFITH *US, female vocalist*

30 Jun 84 **(THE BEST PART OF) BREAKING UP** *Making Waves SURF 101* 63 4

The GRIFTERS (see also CAMISRA; ESCRIMA; PARTIZAN; TALL PAUL) *UK, male production duo – Paul Newman and Brandon Block*

20 Feb 99 **FLASH** *Duty Free DF 004CD* 63 1

GRIM NORTHERN SOCIAL *UK, male vocal / instrumental group*

6 Sep 03 **URBAN PRESSURE** *One Little Indian 353TP 7CD* 60 1

GRIMETHORPE COLLIERY BAND (see also Peter SKELLERN) *UK, male brass band (2 Albums: 5 Weeks)*

6 Jun 98 BRASSED OFF (FILM SOUNDTRACK) *RCA Victor 9026687572* 36 4
11 Sep 04 THE VERY BEST OF THE GRIMETHORPE COLLIERY (UK COAL) BAND *BMG 82876637222* 59 1

Josh GROBAN *US, male vocalist*

15 Feb 03 JOSH GROBAN *Reprise 9362481542* 28 8

GROOVE ARMADA (see also WEEKEND PLAYERS) *UK, male production / instrumental duo – Andy Cato and Tom Findlay (5 Albums: 38 Weeks, 9 Singles: 32 Weeks)*

8 May 99 **IF EVERYBODY LOOKED THE SAME** *Pepper 0530292* 25 2
5 Jun 99 VERTIGO *Pepper 530332* 23 19
7 Aug 99 **AT THE RIVER** *Pepper 0530062* 19 5
27 Nov 99 **I SEE YOU BABY (re)** *Pepper 9230002* [1] 17 6

30 August 1969	6 September 1969	13 September 1969	20 September 1969
◂◂ UK No.1 SINGLES ▸▸			
IN THE YEAR 2525 (EXORDIUM AND TERMINUS) Zager and Evans	**IN THE YEAR 2525 (EXORDIUM AND TERMINUS)** Zager and Evans	**IN THE YEAR 2525 (EXORDIUM AND TERMINUS)** Zager and Evans	**BAD MOON RISING** Creedence Clearwater Revival
◂◂ UK No.1 ALBUMS ▸▸			
FROM ELVIS IN MEMPHIS Elvis Presley	**STAND UP** Jethro Tull	**STAND UP** Jethro Tull	**BLIND FAITH** Blind Faith

6 May 00 THE REMIXES *Pepper 9230102*.......68 1
25 Aug 01 **SUPERSTYLIN' (re)** *Pepper 9230472*.......**12** 7
22 Sep 01 ● GOODBYE COUNTRY (HELLO NIGHTCLUB) *Pepper 9230492*.......5 8
17 Nov 01 **MY FRIEND** *Pepper 9230532*.......**36** 2
2 Nov 02 **PURPLE HAZE** *Pepper 9230642*.......**36** 2
16 Nov 02 LOVEBOX *Pepper 9230682*.......41 2
17 May 03 **EASY** *Pepper 9230712*.......**31** 2
6 Sep 03 **BUT I FEEL GOOD** *Pepper 82876551792*.......**50** 1
2 Oct 04 **I SEE YOU BABY** *Jive 82876649982*.......**11** 5
9 Oct 04 ● THE BEST OF *Jive 82876652562*.......6 8

[1] Groove Armada featuring Gram'ma Funk

GROOVE CONNEKTION 2
UK, male producer / instrumentalist – Jeremy Sylvester

11 Apr 98 **CLUB LONELY** *XL Recordings XLT 94CD*.......**54** 1

GROOVE CORPORATION
UK / Italy, male / female vocal / instrumental group

16 Apr 94 **RAIN** *Six6 SIXCD 109*.......**71** 1

GROOVE COVERAGE NEW
Germany, male / female DJ / production / vocal group

11 Jun 05 **POISON** *All Around the World CDGLOBE 361*.......**32** 3

GROOVE CUTTERS NEW
UK, male production duo – Kev Keane and Steve Pickering

5 Mar 05 **WE CLOSE OUR EYES** *Nebula NEBCD 066*.......**33** 2

GROOVE GENERATION featuring Leo SAYER
UK, male production group

8 Aug 98 **YOU MAKE ME FEEL LIKE DANCING** *Brothers Org. CDBRUV 8*.......**32** 3

GROOVE THEORY (see also MANTRONIX)
US, male / female production / vocal duo – Bryce Wilson and Amel Larrieaux

18 Nov 95 **TELL ME** *Epic 6623882*.......**31** 3

GROOVERIDER *UK, male DJ / producer – Ray Bingham (1 Album: 1 Week, 2 Singles: 3 Weeks)*

26 Sep 98 **RAINBOWS OF COLOUR** *Higher Ground HIGHS 13CD*.......**40** 2
10 Oct 98 MYSTERIES OF FUNK *Higher Ground HIGH 6CD*.......50 1
19 Jun 99 **WHERE'S JACK THE RIPPER** *Higher Ground HIGHS 20CD*.......**61** 1

Scott GROOVES *US, male DJ / producer – Patrick Scott (3 Singles: 3 Weeks)*

16 May 98 **EXPANSIONS** *Soma Recordings SOMA 65CDS* [1].......**68** 1
28 Nov 98 **MOTHERSHIP RECONNECTION** *Soma Recordings SOMA 71CDS*.......**55** 1
21 Aug 99 **MOTHERSHIP RECONNECTION** *Virgin DINSD 185* [2].......**55** 1

[1] Scott Grooves featuring Roy Ayers [2] Scott Grooves featuring Parliament / Funkadelic

Henry GROSS *US, male vocalist*

28 Aug 76 **SHANNON** *Life Song ELS 45002* $.......**32** 4

GROUND LEVEL *Australia, male instrumental / production group*

30 Jan 93 **DREAMS OF HEAVEN** *Faze 2 CDFAZE 14*.......**54** 2

GROUNDED NEW *UK, male vocal group*

26 Feb 05 **I NEED A GIRL** *Platinum PLATGROUND 1*.......**43** 1

The GROUNDHOGS *UK, male vocal / instrumental group – leader Tony McPhee (4 Albums: 51 Weeks)*

6 Jun 70 ● THANK CHRIST FOR THE BOMB *Liberty LBS 83295*.......9 13
27 Mar 71 ● SPLIT *Liberty LBG 83401*.......5 28
18 Mar 72 ● WHO WILL SAVE THE WORLD *United Artists UAG 29237*.......8 9
13 Jul 74 SOLID *WWA WWA 004*.......31 1

GROUP THERAPY *US, male rap group*

30 Nov 96 **EAST COAST / WEST COAST KILLAS** *Interscope IND 95516*.......**51** 1

The GUESS WHO
Canada, male vocal / instrumental group (2 Singles: 14 Weeks)

16 Feb 67 **HIS GIRL** *King KG 1044*.......**45** 1
9 May 70 **AMERICAN WOMAN (re)** *RCA 1943* ▲ $.......**19** 13

David GUETTA *France, male producer (4 Singles: 8 Weeks)*

31 Aug 02 **LOVE, DON'T LET ME GO** *Virgin DINSD 243* [1].......**46** 1
12 Jul 03 **JUST FOR ONE DAY (HEROES)** *Virgin DINST 263* [2].......**73** 1
25 Oct 03 **JUST A LITTLE MORE LOVE** *Virgin DINSD 250* [1].......**19** 4
5 Mar 05 **THE WORLD IS MINE** *Virgin DINSDX 27* [3].......**49** 2

[1] David Guetta featuring Chris Willis [2] David Guetta vs Bowie [3] David Guetta featuring JD Davis

The GUILDFORD CATHEDRAL CHOIR *UK, choir*

10 Dec 66 CHRISTMAS CAROLS FROM GUILDFORD CATHEDRAL *MFP 1104*.......23 4

Record credits Barry Rose as conductor.

GUITAR CORPORATION *UK, male instrumental group*

15 Feb 92 IMAGES *Quality Television QTVCD 002*.......41 5

GUN *UK, male vocal (Adrian Curtis aka Adrian Gurvitz) / instrumental trio*

20 Nov 68 ● **RACE WITH THE DEVIL** *CBS 3734*.......**8** 11

GUN *UK, male vocal (Mark Rankin) / instrumental group (4 Albums: 23 Weeks, 14 Singles: 46 Weeks)*

1 Jul 89 **BETTER DAYS** *A&M AM 505*.......**33** 9
22 Jul 89 TAKING ON THE WORLD *A&M AMA 7007*.......44 10
16 Sep 89 **MONEY (EVERYBODY LOVES HER)** *A&M AM 520*.......**73** 2
11 Nov 89 **INSIDE OUT** *A&M AM 531*.......**57** 2
10 Feb 90 **TAKING ON THE WORLD** *A&M AM 541*.......**50** 3
14 Jul 90 **SHAME ON YOU** *A&M AM 573*.......**33** 4
14 Mar 92 **STEAL YOUR FIRE** *A&M AM 851*.......**24** 4
18 Apr 92 GALLUS *A&M 3953832*.......14 4
2 May 92 **HIGHER GROUND** *A&M AM 869*.......**48** 2
4 Jul 92 **WELCOME TO THE REAL WORLD** *A&M AM 885*.......**43** 2
9 Jul 94 ● **WORD UP** *A&M 5806672*.......**8** 7
13 Aug 94 ● SWAGGER *A&M 5402542*.......5 7
24 Sep 94 **DON'T SAY IT'S OVER** *A&M 5807572*.......**19** 3
25 Feb 95 **THE ONLY ONE** *A&M 5809552*.......**29** 3
15 Apr 95 **SOMETHING WORTHWHILE** *A&M 5810452*.......**39** 2
26 Apr 97 **CRAZY YOU** *A&M 5821932* [1].......**21** 2
24 May 97 0141 632 6326 *A&M 5407232*.......32 2
12 Jul 97 **MY SWEET JANE** *A&M 5822792* [1].......**51** 1

[1] G.U.N.

GUNS N' ROSES 76 Top 500
(see also Gilby CLARKE; Duff McKAGAN; SLASH'S SNAKEPIT)
Often controversial Los Angeles-based band. Best known line-up included Axl Rose (b. William Bailey) (v), Slash (b. Saul Hudson) (g), Izzy Stradlin (b. Jeffrey Isbell) (g). The only act to hold the top two album spots in both the UK and the US on the week of releasing both records: Use Your Illusion I and II in 1991 (7 Albums: 418 Weeks, 17 Singles: 107 Weeks)

1 Aug 87 ● APPETITE FOR DESTRUCTION *Geffen WX 125* ▲.......5 161
3 Oct 87 **WELCOME TO THE JUNGLE** *Geffen GEF 30*.......**67** 2
20 Aug 88 **SWEET CHILD O' MINE** *Geffen GEF 43* ▲.......**24** 8
29 Oct 88 **WELCOME TO THE JUNGLE** (re-issue) / **NIGHTRAIN** *Geffen GEF 47*.......**24** 5

27 September 1969	4 October 1969	11 October 1969	18 October 1969
BAD MOON RISING Creedence Clearwater Revival	**BAD MOON RISING** Creedence Clearwater Revival	**JE T'AIME ... MOI NON PLUS** Jane Birkin and Serge Gainsbourg	**I'LL NEVER FALL IN LOVE AGAIN** Bobbie Gentry
BLIND FAITH Blind Faith	**ABBEY ROAD** The Beatles	**ABBEY ROAD** The Beatles	**ABBEY ROAD** The Beatles

KEY: UK No.1 ★ UK Top 10 ● Still on chart + UK entry at No.1 ■ US No.1 ▲ UK million seller £ US million seller $
Singles re-entries are listed as (re), (2re), (3re)... which signifies that the hit re-entered the chart once, twice or three times...
Peak Position / Weeks

17 Dec 88 G N' R LIES Geffen WX 218 ... 22 41
18 Mar 89 ● PARADISE CITY Geffen GEF 50 ... 6 9
3 Jun 89 ● SWEET CHILD O' MINE (re-issue) Geffen GEF 55 ... 6 9
1 Jul 89 ● PATIENCE Geffen GEF 56 ... 10 7
2 Sep 89 NIGHTRAIN (re-issue) Geffen GEF 60 ... 17 5
13 Jul 91 ● YOU COULD BE MINE Geffen GFS 6 ... 3 10
21 Sep 91 ● DON'T CRY Geffen GFS 9 ... 8 4
28 Sep 91 ● USE YOUR ILLUSION I Geffen GEF 24415 ... 2 84
28 Sep 91 ★ USE YOUR ILLUSION II Geffen GEF 24420 ■ ▲ ... 1 84
21 Dec 91 ● LIVE AND LET DIE Geffen GFS 17 ... 5 7
7 Mar 92 ● NOVEMBER RAIN Geffen GFS 18 ... 4 5
23 May 92 ● KNOCKIN' ON HEAVEN'S DOOR Geffen GFS 21 ... 2 9
21 Nov 92 ● YESTERDAYS / NOVEMBER RAIN (re-issue) Geffen GFS 27 ... 8 9
29 May 93 THE CIVIL WAR (EP) Geffen GFSTD 43 ... 11 3
20 Nov 93 ● AIN'T IT FUN Geffen GFSTD 62 ... 9 3
4 Dec 93 ● THE SPAGHETTI INCIDENT? Geffen GED 24617 ... 2 10
4 Jun 94 ● SINCE I DON'T HAVE YOU Geffen GFSTD 70 ... 10 6
14 Jan 95 ● SYMPATHY FOR THE DEVIL Geffen GFSTD 86 ... 9 6
11 Dec 99 LIVE – ERA '87-'93 Geffen 4905142 ... 45 2
27 Mar 04 ★ GREATEST HITS Geffen / Polydor 9862108 ... 1 36

The re-issue of 'November Rain' was listed only from 28 Nov 1992. Tracks on The Civil War (EP): Civil War / Garden of Eden / Dead Horse / Interview. Appetite for Destruction changed catalogue number to Geffen / Polydor GEFD 24148 when it charted in 2004.

GUNSHOT *UK, male rap group*

19 Jun 93 PATRIOT GAMES Vinyl Solution STEAM 43CD ... 60 1

David GUNSON *UK, male after dinner speaker*

25 Dec 82 WHAT GOES UP MIGHT COME DOWN Big Ben BB 0012 ... 92 2

GUNTHER & The SUNSHINE GIRLS *Sweden, male / female vocal group*

15 May 04 DING DONG SONG WEA WEA 376CD1 ... 14 4

GURU (see also GANG STARR) *US, male rapper / producer – Keith Allam (3 Albums: 12 Weeks, 6 Singles: 12 Weeks)*

29 May 93 JAZZMATAZZ Cooltempo CTCD 34 ... 58 2
11 Sep 93 TRUST ME Cooltempo CDCOOL 278 [1] ... 34 2
13 Nov 93 NO TIME TO PLAY Cooltempo CDCOOL 282 [2] ... 25 3
15 Jul 95 JAZZMATAZZ VOLUME II – THE NEW REALITY Cooltempo CTCD 47 ... 12 9
19 Aug 95 WATCH WHAT YOU SAY Cooltempo CDCOOL 308 [3] ... 28 3
18 Nov 95 FEEL THE MUSIC Cooltempo CDCOOLS 313 ... 34 2
13 Jul 96 LIVIN' IN THIS WORLD / LIFESAVER Cooltempo CDCOOL 320 ... 61 1
14 Oct 00 STREETSOUL Virgin CDVUS 178 [1] ... 74 1
16 Dec 00 KEEP YOUR WORRIES Virgin VUSCD 177 [4] ... 57 1

[1] Guru featuring N'Dea Davenport [2] Guru featuring Dee C Lee
[3] Guru featuring Chaka Khan [4] Guru's Jazzmatazz featuring Angie Stone
[1] Guru's Jazzmatazz

GURU JOSH *UK, male producer – Paul Walden (1 Album: 2 Weeks, 2 Singles: 14 Weeks)*

24 Feb 90 ● INFINITY Deconstruction PB 43475 ... 5 10
16 Jun 90 WHOSE LAW (IS IT ANYWAY)? Deconstruction PB 43647 ... 26 4
14 Jul 90 INFINITY Deconstruction PL 74701 ... 41 2

Adrian GURVITZ *UK, male vocalist – Adrian Curtis (2 Singles: 16 Weeks)*

30 Jan 82 ● CLASSIC RAK 339 ... 8 13
12 Jun 82 YOUR DREAM RAK 343 ... 61 3

G.U.S. (FOOTWEAR) BAND & The MORRISTOWN ORPHEUS CHOIR *UK, male instrumental group and male / female vocal group*

3 Oct 70 LAND OF HOPE AND GLORY Columbia SCX 6406 ... 54 1

GUSGUS *Iceland, male / female vocal / instrumental group (6 Singles: 6 Weeks)*

21 Feb 98 POLYESTERDAY 4AD BAD 8002CD ... 55 1
13 Mar 99 LADYSHAVE 4AD BAD 9001CD ... 64 1
24 Apr 99 STARLOVERS 4AD BADD 9004CD ... 62 1
8 Feb 03 DAVID (I STILL HAVE LAST NIGHT IN MY BODY ...) Underwater H20 022CD ... 52 1
28 Jun 03 CALL OF THE WILD Underwater H20 032CD ... 75 1
10 Apr 04 DAVID (I STILL HAVE LAST NIGHT IN MY BODY ...) (Re-mix) Underwater H20 042P ... 72 1

GUSTO *US, male producer – Edward Green (2 Singles: 8 Weeks)*

2 Mar 96 ● DISCO'S REVENGE Manifesto FESCD 6 ... 9 5
7 Sep 96 LET'S ALL CHANT Manifesto FESCD 13 ... 21 3

Arlo GUTHRIE *US, male vocalist*

7 Mar 70 ALICE'S RESTAURANT Reprise RSLP 6267 ... 44 1

Gwen GUTHRIE (see also The LIMIT) *US, female vocalist, b. 9 Jul 1950, d. 3 Feb 1999 (1 Album: 14 Weeks, 4 Singles: 25 Weeks)*

19 Jul 86 ● AIN'T NOTHIN' GOIN' ON BUT THE RENT Boiling Point POSP 807 ... 5 12
23 Aug 86 GOOD TO GO LOVER Boiling Point POLD 5201 ... 42 14
11 Oct 86 (THEY LONG TO BE) CLOSE TO YOU Boiling Point POSP 822 ... 25 7
14 Feb 87 GOOD TO GO LOVER / OUTSIDE IN THE RAIN Boiling Point POSP 841 ... 37 4
4 Sep 93 AIN'T NOTHIN' GOIN' ON BUT THE RENT (re-mix) Polydor PZCD 276 ... 42 2

GUY *US, male vocal group*

4 May 91 HER MCA MCS 1575 ... 58 4
5 Feb 00 III MCA 1121702 ... 55 1

Buddy GUY *US, male vocalist / guitarist (2 Albums: 9 Weeks)*

22 Jun 91 DAMN RIGHT I'VE GOT THE BLUES Silvertone ORELP 516 ... 43 5
13 Mar 93 FEELS LIKE RAIN Silvertone ORECD 525 ... 36 4

A GUY CALLED GERALD *UK, male producer – Gerald Simpson (2 Albums: 2 Weeks, 2 Singles: 23 Weeks)*

8 Apr 89 VOODOO RAY (re) Rham! RS 804 ... 12 18
16 Dec 89 FX / EYES OF SORROW Subscape AGCG 1 ... 52 5
14 Apr 90 AUTOMANIKK Subscape 4664821 ... 68 1
1 Apr 95 BLACK SECRET TECHNOLOGY Juice Box JBCD 25 ... 64 1

GUYS 'N' DOLLS *UK, male / female vocal group (1 Album: 1 Week, 5 Singles: 33 Weeks)*

1 Mar 75 ● THERE'S A WHOLE LOT OF LOVING Magnet MAG 20 [1] ... 2 11
17 May 75 HERE I GO AGAIN Magnet MAG 30 ... 33 5
31 May 75 GUYS 'N' DOLLS Magnet MAG 5005 ... 43 1
21 Feb 76 ● YOU DON'T HAVE TO SAY YOU LOVE ME Magnet MAG 50 ... 5 8
6 Nov 76 STONEY GROUND Magnet MAG 76 ... 38 4
13 May 78 ONLY LOVING DOES IT Magnet MAG 115 ... 42 5

[1] Guys & Dolls

GUYVER *UK, male producer – Guy Mearns*

29 Mar 03 TRAPPED / DIFFERENCES Tidy Two TIDYTWO 118 ... 72 1

The GYPSYMEN (see also BLACK RIOT; ROYAL HOUSE; SWAN LAKE; *US, male producer – Todd Terry*

11 Aug 01 BABARABATIRI Sound Design SDES 09CDS ... 32 2

25 October 1969	1 November 1969	8 November 1969	15 November 1969
UK No.1 SINGLES			
SUGAR, SUGAR The Archies	SUGAR, SUGAR The Archies	SUGAR, SUGAR The Archies	SUGAR, SUGAR The Archies
UK No.1 ALBUMS			
ABBEY ROAD The Beatles	ABBEY ROAD The Beatles	ABBEY ROAD The Beatles	ABBEY ROAD The Beatles

The GYRES *UK, male vocal / instrumental group (2 Singles: 2 Weeks)*

13 Apr 96	**POP COP** *Sugar SUGA 9CD*	71	1
6 Jul 96	**ARE YOU READY** *Sugar SUGA 11CD*	71	1

H

H & CLAIRE (see also STEPS) *UK, male / female vocal duo – Ian Watkins and Claire Richards (1 Album: 1 Week, 3 Singles: 25 Weeks)*

18 May 02 ●	**DJ** *WEA WEA 347CD*	3	11
24 Aug 02 ●	**HALF A HEART (re)** *WEA WEA 359CDX*	8	6
16 Nov 02 ●	**ALL OUT OF LOVE (re)** *WEA WEA 360CD*	10	8
30 Nov 02	ANOTHER YOU ANOTHER ME *WEA 0927494622*	58	1

'All Out of Love' was a double A-side with 'Beauty and the Beast', although not listed as such on the chart.

HHC *UK, male DJ / production duo*

19 Apr 97	**WE'RE NOT ALONE** *Perfecto PERF 138CD*	44	1

H 20 *UK, male vocal / instrumental group (2 Singles: 16 Weeks)*

21 May 83	**DREAM TO SLEEP** *RCA 330*	17	10
13 Aug 83	**JUST OUTSIDE OF HEAVEN** *RCA 349*	38	6

H20 *US / Switzerland, male / female vocal / instrumental group (2 Singles: 4 Weeks)*

14 Sep 96	**NOBODY'S BUSINESS** *AM:PM 5818832* [1]	19	3
30 Aug 97	**SATISFIED (TAKE ME HIGHER)** *AM:PM 5823252*	66	1

[1] H20 featuring Billie

HWA featuring SONIC THE HEDGEHOG (see also HAYSI FANTAYZEE; Jeremy HEALY and AMOS) *UK, male producer – Jeremy Healy*

5 Dec 92	**SUPERSONIC** *Internal Affairs KGB 008*	33	6

H.I.M. *Finland, male vocal (Ville Valo) / instrumental group (3 Albums: 8 Weeks, 5 Singles: 16 Weeks)*

26 Apr 03	LOVE METAL *RCA 82876505042*	55	3
17 May 03	**BURIED ALIVE BY LOVE** *RCA 82876523162*	30	2
20 Sep 03	**MY SACRAMENT** *RCA 82876558892*	23	2
24 Jan 04	**THE FUNERAL OF HEARTS** *RCA 82876585792*	15	4
27 Mar 04	AND LOVE SAID NO ... 1997-2004 *RCA 82876606162* [1]	30	2
8 May 04 ●	**SOLITARY MAN** *RCA 82876610652*	9	4
24 Sep 05 ●	**WINGS OF A BUTTERFLY** *Sire W 686CD2* [1]	10	4
8 Oct 05	DARK LIGHT *WEA 9362494362* [1]	18	3

[1] HIM [1] HIM

HABIT *UK, male vocal / instrumental group*

30 Apr 88	**LUCY** *Virgin VS 1063*	56	2

Steve HACKETT (see also GTR; GENESIS) *UK, male vocalist / guitarist (8 Albums: 38 Weeks, 1 Single: 2 Weeks)*

1 Nov 75	VOYAGE OF THE ACOLYTE *Charisma CAS 1111*	26	4
6 May 78	PLEASE DON'T TOUCH *Charisma CDS 4012*	38	5
26 May 79	SPECTRAL MORNINGS *Charisma CDS 4017*	22	11
21 Jun 80 ●	DEFECTOR *Charisma CDS 4018*	9	7
29 Aug 81	CURED *Charisma CDS 4021*	15	5
2 Apr 83	**CELL 151** *Charisma CELL 1*	66	2
30 Apr 83	HIGHLY STRUNG *Charisma HACK 1*	16	3
19 Nov 83	BAY OF KINGS *Lamborghini LMGLP 3000*	70	1
22 Sep 84	TILL WE HAVE FACES *Lamborghini LMGLP 4000*	54	2

HADDAWAY *Trinidad and Tobago, male vocalist – Nester Haddaway (1 Album: 16 Weeks, 6 Singles: 52 Weeks)*

5 Jun 93 ●	**WHAT IS LOVE** *Logic 74321148502*	2	15
25 Sep 93 ●	**LIFE** *Logic 74321164212*	6	9
23 Oct 93 ●	HADDAWAY – THE ALBUM *Logic 74321169222*	9	16
18 Dec 93 ●	**I MISS YOU** *Logic 74321181522*	9	14
2 Apr 94 ●	**ROCK MY HEART** *Logic 74321194122*	9	9
24 Jun 95	**FLY AWAY** *Logic 74321286942*	20	3
23 Sep 95	**CATCH A FIRE** *Logic 74321306652*	39	2

Tony HADLEY (see also SPANDAU BALLET) *UK, male vocalist (2 Albums: 6 Weeks, 4 Singles: 9 Weeks)*

7 Mar 92	**LOST IN YOUR LOVE** *EMI EM 222*	42	4
29 Aug 92	**FOR YOUR BLUE EYES ONLY** *EMI EM 234*	67	2
16 Jan 93	**THE GAME OF LOVE** *EMI CDEM 254*	72	1
10 May 97	**DANCE WITH ME** *VC VCRD 17* [1]	35	2
20 Sep 97	TONY HADLEY *PolyGram TV 5393012*	45	3
10 May 03	TRUE BALLADS *Universal TV 382882*	31	3

[1] Tin Tin Out featuring Tony Hadley

Sammy HAGAR (see also HAGAR SCHON) *US, male vocalist / guitarist (5 Albums: 19 Weeks, 4 Singles: 15 Weeks)*

29 Sep 79	STREET MACHINE *Capitol EST 11983*	38	4
15 Dec 79	**THIS PLANET'S ON FIRE (BURN IN HELL) / SPACE STATION NO.5** *Capitol CL 16114*	52	5
16 Feb 80	**I'VE DONE EVERYTHING FOR YOU** *Capitol CL 16120*	36	5
22 Mar 80	LOUD AND CLEAR *Capitol EST 25330*	12	8
24 May 80	**HEARTBEAT / LOVE OR MONEY** *Capitol RED 1*	67	2
7 Jun 80	DANGER ZONE *Capitol EST 12069*	25	3
16 Jan 82	**PIECE OF MY HEART (re)** *Geffen GEFA 1884*	67	3
13 Feb 82	STANDING HAMPTON *Geffen GEF 85456*	84	2
4 Jul 87	SAMMY HAGAR *Geffen WX 114*	86	2

HAGAR SCHON AARONSON SHRIEVE (see also Sammy HAGAR) *US, male vocal / instrumental group*

19 May 84	THROUGH THE FIRE *Geffen GEF 25893*	92	1

Paul HAIG *UK, male vocalist*

28 May 83	**HEAVEN SENT** *Island IS 111*	74	3
22 Oct 83	RHYTHM OF LIFE *Crepuscule ILPS 9742*	82	2

HAIRCUT 100 *UK, male vocal (Nick Heyward) / instrumental group (1 Album: 34 Weeks, 5 Singles: 47 Weeks)*

24 Oct 81 ●	**FAVOURITE SHIRTS (BOY MEETS GIRL)** *Arista CLIP 1*	4	14
30 Jan 82 ●	**LOVE PLUS ONE** *Arista CLIP 2*	3	12
6 Mar 82 ●	PELICAN WEST *Arista HCC 100*	2	34
10 Apr 82 ●	**FANTASTIC DAY** *Arista CLIP 3*	9	9
21 Aug 82 ●	**NOBODY'S FOOL** *Arista CLIP 4*	9	7
6 Aug 83	**PRIME TIME** *Polydor HC 1*	46	5

Curtis HAIRSTON *US, male vocalist, b. 10 Oct 1961, d. 18 Jan 1996 (3 Singles: 16 Weeks)*

15 Oct 83	**I WANT YOU (ALL TONIGHT)** *RCA 368*	44	5
27 Apr 85	**I WANT YOUR LOVIN' (JUST A LITTLE BIT)** *London LON 66*	13	7
6 Dec 86	**CHILLIN' OUT** *Atlantic A 9335*	57	4

Seamus HAJI *UK, male producer*

18 Dec 04	**LAST NIGHT A DJ SAVED MY LIFE** *Big Love BL 013*	69	1

22 November 1969	29 November 1969	6 December 1969	13 December 1969
SUGAR, SUGAR The Archies	**SUGAR, SUGAR** The Archies	**SUGAR, SUGAR** The Archies	**SUGAR, SUGAR** The Archies
ABBEY ROAD The Beatles	**ABBEY ROAD** The Beatles	**ABBEY ROAD** The Beatles	**ABBEY ROAD** The Beatles

TOP 10
ON THE DAY OF THE GREAT STORM OF 1987

On 15 October 1987, the Great Storm hit the coast of Cornwall and tore across Britain, uprooting 15 million trees and causing £1.2bn worth of damage. Earlier that day, in the most notorious TV weather report of all time, Michael Fish dismissed reports of an impending hurricane: "Earlier on today, apparently a woman rang the BBC and said she heard there was a hurricane on the way ... well, if you're watching, don't worry, there isn't." In fact, Fish had been referring to a hurricane off the coast and did warn of high winds approaching England, though this was lost when the report was edited.

LW	TW	
6	1	**YOU WIN AGAIN** The Bee Gees
2	2	**FULL METAL JACKET (I WANNA BE YOUR DRILL INSTRUCTOR)** Abigail Mead and Nigel Goulding
1	3	**PUMP UP THE VOLUME / ANITINA (THE FIRST TIME I SEE SHE DANCE)** M/A/R/R/S
5	4	**CROCKETT'S THEME** Jan Hammer
12	5	**CRAZY CRAZY NIGHTS** Kiss
3	6	**BAD** Michael Jackson
15	7	**I FOUND LOVIN'** The Fatback Band
9	8	**I NEED LOVE** LL Cool J
22	9	**I FOUND LOVIN'** Steve Walsh
4	10	**NEVER GONNA GIVE YOU UP** Rick Astley

The Bee Gees

A storm damaged trunk call

HAL
Ireland, male vocal / instrumental group (1 Album: 2 Weeks, 3 Singles: 4 Weeks)

8 May 04 **WORRY ABOUT THE WIND** *Rough Trade RTRADSCD 172*..........53 1
5 Feb 05 **WHAT A LOVELY DANCE** *Rough Trade RTRADSCD 12*..........36 2
23 Apr 05 **PLAY THE HITS** *Rough Trade RTRADSCD 226*..........38 1
7 May 05 **HAL** *Rough Trade RTRADCD 160*..........31 2

HAL featuring Gillian ANDERSON
UK, male production trio and US, female actor / vocalist

24 May 97 **EXTREMIS** *Virgin VSCDT 1636*..........23 3

HALE and PACE and The STONKERS
UK, male comedy duo – Gareth Hale and Norman Pace and backing group

9 Mar 91 ★ **THE STONK** *London LON 296*..........1 7

Bill HALEY and his COMETS 290 Top 500 *Original 'King of Rock 'n' Roll', b. 6 Jul 1925, Detroit, US, d. 9 Feb 1981. The kiss-curl hairstyled front-man introduced rock to the world via a string of 1950s smashes, including 'Rock Around the Clock', the only record to return to the Top 20 on five occasions, selling 1,392,000 (4 Albums: 31 Weeks, 16 Singles: 199 Weeks)*

17 Dec 54 ● **SHAKE, RATTLE AND ROLL** *Brunswick 05338* $..........4 14
7 Jan 55 ★ **ROCK AROUND THE CLOCK (5re)** *Brunswick 05317* ▲ £ $..........1 36
15 Apr 55 **MAMBO ROCK** *Brunswick 05405*..........14 2
30 Dec 55 ● **ROCK-A-BEATIN' BOOGIE** *Brunswick 05509*..........4 9
9 Mar 56 ● **SEE YOU LATER, ALLIGATOR (re)** *Brunswick 05530* $..........7 21
25 May 56 ● **THE SAINTS ROCK 'N ROLL** *Brunswick 05565*..........5 24
4 Aug 56 ● **ROCK AROUND THE CLOCK** *Brunswick LAT 8117*..........2 17
17 Aug 56 ● **ROCKIN' THROUGH THE RYE (re)** *Brunswick 05582*..........3 23
14 Sep 56 **RAZZLE DAZZLE** *Brunswick 05453*..........13 8
20 Oct 56 ★ **ROCK 'N' ROLL STAGE SHOW** *Brunswick LAT 8139*..........1 8
9 Nov 56 ● **RIP IT UP** *Brunswick 05615*..........4 18
9 Nov 56 **ROCK 'N' ROLL STAGE SHOW (LP)** *Brunswick LAT 8139*..........30 1
23 Nov 56 **RUDY'S ROCK (re)** *Brunswick 05616*..........26 5
1 Feb 57 **ROCK THE JOINT** *London HLF 8371*..........20 4
8 Feb 57 ● **DON'T KNOCK THE ROCK** *Brunswick 05640*..........7 8
16 Feb 57 ● **ROCK THE JOINT** *London HAF 2037*..........5 1
3 Apr 68 **ROCK AROUND THE CLOCK** (re-issue) *MCA MU 1013*..........20 11
18 May 68 **ROCK AROUND THE CLOCK** (re-issue) *Ace of Hearts AH 13*....34 5
16 Mar 74 **ROCK AROUND THE CLOCK** (2nd re-issue) *MCA 128*..........12 10
25 Apr 81 **HALEY'S GOLDEN MEDLEY** *MCA 694*..........50 5

'Rock Around the Clock' peaked at No.17 on it's first visit to the chart, then re-entered peaking at No.1 in Oct 1955, No.5 in Sep 1956, No.24 in Dec 1956, No.25 in Jan 1957 and No.22 later that same month. Occasionally, some of the 'Rock Around the Clock' labels billed the song as '(We're Gonna) Rock Around the Clock'. Tracks on Rock 'n' Roll Stage Show (LP): Calling All Comets / Rockin' Through the Rye / A Rockin' Little Tune / Hide and Seek / Hey There Now / Goofin' Around / Hook Line and Sinker / Rudy's Rock / Choo Choo Ch'Boogie / Blue Comets Rock / Hot Dog Buddy Buddy / Tonight's the Night. Haley's Golden Medley comprised: Rock Around the Clock / Rock-A-Beatin' Boogie / Shake, Rattle and Roll / Choo Choo Ch'Boogie / See You Later Alligator.

HALF MAN HALF BISCUIT
UK, male vocal / instrumental group (2 Albums: 14 Weeks)

8 Feb 86 **BACK IN THE D.H.S.S.** *Probe Plus PROBE 4*..........60 9
21 Feb 87 **BACK AGAIN IN THE D.H.S.S.** *Probe Plus PROBE 8*..........59 5

Aaron HALL (see also GUY) *US, male vocalist (2 Singles: 3 Weeks)*

13 Jun 92 **DON'T BE AFRAID** *MCA MCS 1632*..........56 2
23 Oct 93 **GET A LITTLE FREAKY WITH ME** *MCA MCSTD 1936*..........66 1

Audrey HALL *Jamaica, female vocalist (2 Singles: 20 Weeks)*

25 Jan 86 **ONE DANCE WON'T DO** *Germain DG7-1985*..........20 11
5 Jul 86 **SMILE** *Germain DG 15*..........14 9

Daryl HALL (see also Daryl HALL and John OATES)
US, male vocalist – Daryl Hohl (2 Albums: 9 Weeks, 6 Singles: 26 Weeks)

2 Aug 86 **DREAMTIME** *RCA HALL 1*..........28 8

20 December 1969	27 December 1969	3 January 1970	10 January 1970
◂◂ UK No.1 SINGLES ▸▸			
TWO LITTLE BOYS Rolf Harris	**TWO LITTLE BOYS** Rolf Harris	**TWO LITTLE BOYS** Rolf Harris	**TWO LITTLE BOYS** Rolf Harris
◂◂ UK No.1 ALBUMS ▸▸			
LET IT BLEED The Rolling Stones	**ABBEY ROAD** The Beatles	**ABBEY ROAD** The Beatles	**ABBEY ROAD** The Beatles

23 Aug 86	THREE HEARTS IN THE HAPPY ENDING MACHINE *RCA PL 87196*	26	5
25 Sep 93	**I'M IN A PHILLY MOOD (re)** *Epic 6595555*	**52**	4
23 Oct 93	SOUL ALONE *Epic 4732912*	55	4
8 Jan 94	**STOP LOVING ME STOP LOVING YOU** *Epic 6599982*	**30**	6
14 May 94	**HELP ME FIND A WAY TO YOUR HEART** *Epic 6604102*	**70**	1
2 Jul 94	**GLORYLAND** *Mercury MERCD 404* [1]	**36**	4
10 Jun 95	**WHEREVER WOULD I BE** *Columbia 6620592* [2]	**44**	3

[1] Daryl Hall and Sounds of Blackness [2] Dusty Springfield and Daryl Hall

Daryl HALL and John OATES

281 Top 500 *White, soul-influenced US duo: Daryl Hall (v), b. Daryl Hohl, 11 Oct 1948, Philadelphia, and John Oates (g), b. 7 Apr 1949, New York. They met at university in 1967 and eventually became the most successful duo in US singles chart history, with 16 Top 10s and six No.1s (13 Albums: 154 Weeks, 17 Singles: 84 Weeks)*

3 Jul 76	HALL AND OATES *RCA Victor APLI 1144*	56	1
18 Sep 76	BIGGER THAN BOTH OF US *RCA Victor APLI 1467*	25	7
16 Oct 76	**SHE'S GONE** *Atlantic K 10828*	**42**	4
15 Oct 77	BEAUTY ON A BACK STREET *RCA PL 12300*	40	2
14 Jun 80	**RUNNING FROM PARADISE** *RCA RUN 1*	**41**	6
20 Sep 80	**YOU'VE LOST THAT LOVIN' FEELIN'** *RCA 1*	**55**	3
15 Nov 80	**KISS ON MY LIST** *RCA 15* ▲ $	**33**	8
23 Jan 82 ●	**I CAN'T GO FOR THAT (NO CAN DO)** *RCA 172* ▲ $	**8**	10
6 Feb 82 ●	PRIVATE EYES *RCA RCALP 6001*	8	21
10 Apr 82	**PRIVATE EYES** *RCA 134* ▲ $	**32**	7
23 Oct 82	H2O *RCA RCALP 6056*	24	35
30 Oct 82 ●	**MANEATER** *RCA 290* ▲ $	**6**	11
22 Jan 83	**ONE ON ONE** *RCA 305*	**63**	3
30 Apr 83	**FAMILY MAN** *RCA 323*	**15**	7
29 Oct 83	ROCK 'N' SOUL PART 1 *RCA PL 84858*	16	45
12 Nov 83	**SAY IT ISN'T SO** *RCA 375*	**69**	3
10 Mar 84	**ADULT EDUCATION** *RCA 396*	**63**	2
20 Oct 84	**OUT OF TOUCH** *RCA 449* ▲	**48**	5
27 Oct 84	BIG BAM BOOM *RCA PL 85309*	28	13
9 Feb 85	**METHOD OF MODERN LOVE** *RCA 472*	**21**	8
22 Jun 85	**OUT OF TOUCH** (re-mix) *RCA PB 49967*	**62**	3
21 Sep 85	**A NIGHT AT THE APOLLO LIVE!** *RCA PB 49935* [1]	**58**	2
28 Sep 85	HALL & OATES LIVE AT THE APOLLO WITH DAVID RUFFIN AND EDDIE KENDRICK *RCA PL 87035*	32	5
18 Jun 88	OOH YEAH! *RCA 208895*	52	3
29 Sep 90	**SO CLOSE** *Arista 113600* [2]	**69**	1
27 Oct 90	CHANGE OF SEASON *Arista 210548*	44	2
26 Jan 91	**EVERYWHERE I LOOK** *Arista 113980*	**74**	1
19 Oct 91 ●	THE BEST OF DARYL HALL AND JOHN OATES – LOOKING BACK *Arista PL 90388*	9	16
6 Oct 01	THE ESSENTIAL COLLECTION *RCA 74321886972*	26	2
12 Apr 03	DO IT FOR LOVE *Sanctuary SANCD 166*	37	2

[1] Daryl Hall and John Oates featuring David Ruffin and Eddie Kendrick
[2] Hall and Oates

'A Night at the Apollo Live!' is a medley of 'The Way You Do the Things You Do' and 'My Girl'.

Lynden David HALL

UK, male vocalist / guitarist, b. 7 May 1974, d. 14 Feb 2006 (2 Albums: 4 Weeks, 7 Singles: 12 Weeks)

25 Oct 97	**SEXY CINDERELLA** *Cooltempo CDCOOL 328*	**45**	2
14 Mar 98	**DO I QUALIFY?** *Cooltempo CDCOOLS 331*	**26**	2
4 Jul 98	**CRESCENT MOON** *Cooltempo CDCOOL 333*	**45**	1
31 Oct 98	**SEXY CINDERELLA** (re-issue) *Cooltempo CDCOOLS 340*	**17**	3
14 Nov 98	MEDICINE 4 MY PAIN *Cooltempo 4959952*	43	2
11 Mar 00	**FORGIVE ME** *Cooltempo CDCOOLS 346*	**30**	2
27 May 00	**SLEEPING WITH VICTOR** *Cooltempo CDCOOL 348*	**49**	1
10 Jun 00	THE OTHER SIDE *Cooltempo 5261492*	36	2
23 Sep 00	**LET'S DO IT AGAIN** *Cooltempo CDCOOL 351*	**69**	1

Pam HALL

Jamaica, female vocalist

16 Aug 86	**DEAR BOOPSIE** *Bluemountain BM 027*	**54**	4

Terry HALL

(see also FUN BOY THREE; The SPECIALS; STARVING SOULS; VEGAS) *UK, male vocalist (1 Album: 1 Week, 6 Singles: 7 Weeks)*

11 Nov 89	**MISSING** *Chrysalis CHS 3381*	**75**	1
27 Aug 94	**FOREVER J** *AnXious ANX 1024CDX*	**67**	1
12 Nov 94	**SENSE** *AnXious ANX 1027CD*	**54**	2
28 Oct 95	**RAINBOWS (EP)** *AnXious ANX 1033CD1*	**62**	1
14 Jun 97	**BALLAD OF A LANDLORD** *Southsea Bubble CDBUBBLE 1*	**50**	1
18 Oct 97	LAUGH *Southsea Bubble Co CDBUBBLE 3*	50	1
18 Oct 03	**PROBLEM IS** *Distinctive DISNCD 107* [1]	**66**	1

[1] Dub Pistols featuring Terry Hall

The sleeve, not the label, of 'Missing' credits Terry, Blair and Anouchka. Tracks on Rainbows (EP) – CD1: Chasing a Rainbow / Mistakes / See No Evil (live) / Ghost Town (live). CD2: Chasing a Rainbow / Our Lips are Sealed (live) / Thinking of You (live) / Ghost Town (live).

Geri HALLIWELL

440 Top 500 *Headline-grabbing former Ginger Spice, b. 6 Aug 1972, Watford, UK, sang on seven Spice Girls chart-toppers before achieving more solo No.1s than any other UK female. She is the only person to score as many as four consecutive No.1s both as a solo artist and as part of group (3 Albums: 59 Weeks, 9 Singles: 104 Weeks)*

22 May 99 ●	**LOOK AT ME (re)** *EMI CDEM 542*	**2**	14
19 Jun 99 ●	SCHIZOPHONIC *EMI 5210092*	4	43
28 Aug 99 ★	**MI CHICO LATINO** *EMI CDEM 548* ■	**1**	13
13 Nov 99 ★	**LIFT ME UP (re)** *EMI CDEM 554* ■	**1**	17
25 Mar 00 ★	**BAG IT UP (re)** *EMI CDEMS 560* ■	**1**	13
12 May 01 ★	**IT'S RAINING MEN** *EMI CDEMS 584* ■	**1**	15
26 May 01 ●	SCREAM IF YOU WANNA GO FASTER *EMI 5333692*	5	15
11 Aug 01 ●	**SCREAM IF YOU WANNA GO FASTER (re)** *EMI CDEMS 595*	**8**	11
8 Dec 01 ●	**CALLING** *EMI CDEMS 606*	**7**	10
4 Dec 04 ●	**RIDE IT** *Innocent SINDX 69* [1]	**4**	9
11 Jun 05	**DESIRE** *Innocent SINDX 75*	**22**	2
18 Jun 05	PASSION *Innocent CDSIN 19*	41	1

[1] Geri

HALO

UK, male vocal / instrumental group (3 Singles: 3 Weeks)

16 Feb 02	**COLD LIGHT OF DAY** *S2 6723072*	**49**	1
1 Jun 02	**SANCTIMONIOUS** *S2 6725962*	**44**	1
7 Sep 02	**NEVER ENDING** *S2 6730125*	**56**	1

HALO JAMES

UK, male vocal (Christian James) / instrumental group (1 Album: 4 Weeks, 4 Singles: 24 Weeks)

7 Oct 89	**WANTED** *Epic HALO 1*	**45**	5
23 Dec 89 ●	**COULD HAVE TOLD YOU SO** *Epic HALO 2*	**6**	12
17 Mar 90	**BABY** *Epic HALO 3*	**43**	4
14 Apr 90	WITNESS *Epic 466761*	18	4
19 May 90	**MAGIC HOUR** *Epic HALO 4*	**59**	3

The HAMBURG STUDENTS' CHOIR

Germany, male vocal group

17 Dec 60	HARK THE HERALD ANGELS SING *Pye GGL 0023*	11	6

Ashley HAMILTON

US, male vocalist

14 Jun 03	**WIMMIN' (re)** *Columbia 673902*	**27**	4

George HAMILTON IV

US, male vocalist (3 Albums: 11 Weeks, 2 Singles: 13 Weeks)

7 Mar 58	**WHY DON'T THEY UNDERSTAND** *HMV POP 429*	**22**	9
18 Jul 58	**I KNOW WHERE I'M GOIN' (re)** *HMV POP 505*	**23**	4
10 Apr 71	CANADIAN PACIFIC *RCA SF 8062*	45	1
10 Feb 79	REFLECTIONS *Lotus WH 5008*	25	9
13 Nov 82	SONGS FOR A WINTER'S NIGHT *Ronco RTL 2082*	94	1

Lynne HAMILTON

Australia (b. UK), female vocalist

29 Apr 89 ●	**ON THE INSIDE (THEME FROM 'PRISONER: CELL BLOCK H')** *A1 A1 311*	**3**	11

17 January 1970	24 January 1970	31 January 1970	7 February 1970
TWO LITTLE BOYS Rolf Harris	**TWO LITTLE BOYS** Rolf Harris	**LOVE GROWS (WHERE MY ROSEMARY GOES)** Edison Lighthouse	**LOVE GROWS (WHERE MY ROSEMARY GOES)** Edison Lighthouse
ABBEY ROAD The Beatles	**ABBEY ROAD** The Beatles	**ABBEY ROAD** The Beatles	**LED ZEPPELIN II** Led Zeppelin

KEY UK No.1 ★ UK Top 10 ● Still on chart + UK entry at No.1 ■ US No.1 ▲ UK million seller £ US million seller $
Singles re-entries are listed as (re), (2re), (3re)... which signifies that the hit re-entered the chart once, twice or three times...
Peak Position / Weeks

Russ HAMILTON *UK, male vocalist – Ronald Hulme (2 Singles: 26 Weeks)*

24 May 57 ● **WE WILL MAKE LOVE** *Oriole CB 1359* 2 20
27 Sep 57 **WEDDING RING** *Oriole CB 1388* [1] 20 6

[1] Russ Hamilton with Johnny Gregory and his Orchestra with The Tonettes

HAMILTON, Joe FRANK and REYNOLDS *US, male vocal group*

13 Sep 75 **FALLIN' IN LOVE** *Pye International 7N 25690* ▲ $ 33 6

Marvin HAMLISCH *US, male instrumentalist – piano*

30 Mar 74 **THE ENTERTAINER** *MCA 121* $ 25 13

Jan HAMMER
Czech Republic, male keyboard player (1 Album: 12 Weeks, 3 Singles: 26 Weeks)

12 Oct 85 ● **MIAMI VICE THEME** *MCA MCA 1000* ▲ 5 8
19 Sep 87 ● **CROCKETT'S THEME** *MCA MCA 1193* 2 12
14 Nov 87 **ESCAPE FROM TV** *MCA MCF 3407* 34 12
1 Jun 91 **CROCKETT'S THEME** (re-issue) / **CHANCER** *MCA MCS 1541* 47 6

Albert HAMMOND (see also FAMILY DOGG) *Gibraltar, male vocalist*

30 Jun 73 **FREE ELECTRIC BAND** *Mums 1494* 19 11

HAMPENBERG
Denmark, male / female vocal / instrumental / production trio

21 Sep 02 **DUCKTOY** *Serious SERR 49CD* 30 2

Herbie HANCOCK *US, male vocalist / keyboard player (3 Albums: 24 Weeks, 6 Singles: 41 Weeks)*

26 Aug 78 **I THOUGHT IT WAS YOU** *CBS 6530* 15 9
9 Sep 78 **SUNLIGHT** *CBS 82240* 27 6
3 Feb 79 **YOU BET YOUR LOVE** *CBS 7010* 18 10
24 Feb 79 **FEETS DON'T FAIL ME NOW** *CBS 83491* 28 8
30 Jul 83 ● **ROCKIT** *CBS A 3577* 8 12
27 Aug 83 **FUTURE SHOCK** *CBS 25540* 27 10
8 Oct 83 **AUTODRIVE** *CBS A 3802* 33 4
21 Jan 84 **FUTURE SHOCK** *CBS A 4075* 54 3
4 Aug 84 **HARDROCK** *CBS A 4616* 65 3

Tony HANCOCK
UK, male comedian, b. 12 May 1924, d. 25 Jun 1968 (4 Albums: 51 Weeks)

9 Apr 60 ● **THIS IS HANCOCK** *Pye NPL 10845* 2 22
12 Nov 60 **PIECES OF HANCOCK** *Pye NPL 18054* 17 2
3 Mar 62 **HANCOCK** *Pye NPL 18068* 12 23
14 Sep 63 **THIS IS HANCOCK** (re-issue) *Pye Golden Guinea GGL 0206* 16 4

The HANDBAGGERS *UK, male / female vocal / instrumental group*

15 Jun 96 **U FOUND OUT** *Tidy Trax TIDY 104CD* 55 1

HANDLEY FAMILY *UK, male / female vocal group*

7 Apr 73 **WAM BAM** *GL 100* 30 7

HANI *US, male DJ / producer – Hani Adnan Al-Bader*

11 Mar 00 **BABY WANTS TO RIDE** *Neo NEOCD 025* 70 1

Jayn HANNA *UK, female vocalist (2 Singles: 2 Weeks)*

13 Apr 96 **LOVELIGHT (RIDE ON A LOVE TRAIN)** *VC VCRD 10* 42 1
1 Feb 97 **LOST WITHOUT YOU** *VC VCRD 16* 44 1

HANNAH *UK, female vocalist – Hannah Waddingham*

21 Oct 00 **OUR KIND OF LOVE** *Telstar CDSTAS 3149* 41 2

Bo HANNSON *Sweden, male multi-instrumentalist*

18 Nov 72 **LORD OF THE RINGS** *Charisma CAS 1059* 32 7

HANOI ROCKS *Finland / UK, male vocal / instrumental group (2 Albums: 4 Weeks, 1 Single: 2 Weeks)*

11 Jun 83 **BACK TO MYSTERY CITY** *Lick LICLP 1* 87 1
7 Jul 84 **UP AROUND THE BEND** *CBS A 4513* 61 2
20 Oct 84 **TWO STEPS FROM THE MOVE** *CBS 26066* 28 3

HANSON *US, male vocal / instrumental group (4 Albums: 32 Weeks, 8 Singles: 54 Weeks)*

7 Jun 97 ★ **MMMBOP** *Mercury 5745012* ■ ▲ $ 1 13
21 Jun 97 ★ **MIDDLE OF NOWHERE** *Mercury 5346152* ■ 1 29
13 Sep 97 ● **WHERE'S THE LOVE** *Mercury 5749032* 4 9
22 Nov 97 ● **I WILL COME TO YOU** *Mercury 5680672* 5 9
28 Mar 98 **WEIRD** *Mercury 5685412* 19 5
13 Jun 98 **3 CAR GARAGE – INDIE RECORDINGS 95-96** *Mercury 5583992* 39 1
4 Jul 98 **THINKING OF YOU (re)** *Mercury 5688132* 23 7
29 Apr 00 **IF ONLY** *Mercury 5627502* 15 4
13 May 00 **THIS TIME AROUND** *Mercury 5427212* 33 1
5 Feb 05 ● **PENNY & ME** *Cooking Vinyl FRYCD 220* 10 5
19 Feb 05 **UNDERNEATH** *Cooking Vinyl COOKCD 326* 49 1
9 Apr 05 **LOST WITHOUT EACH OTHER** *Cooking Vinyl FRYCD 224X* 39 2

John HANSON *UK, male vocalist (3 Albums: 12 Weeks)*

23 Apr 60 **THE STUDENT PRINCE** *Pye NPL 18046* 17 1
2 Sep 61 ● **THE STUDENT PRINCE / THE VAGABOND KING** *Pye GGL 0086* .. 9 7
10 Dec 77 **JOHN HANSON SINGS 20 SHOWTIME GREATS** *K-Tel NE 1002* 16 4

The two albums The Student Prince are different, although some tracks repeat.

The HAPPENINGS *US, male vocal group (2 Singles: 14 Weeks)*

18 May 67 **I GOT RHYTHM** *Stateside SS 2013* 28 9
16 Aug 67 **MY MAMMY** *Pye International 7N 25501 and BT Puppy BTS 45530* 34 5

Pye gave the US BT Puppy label its own identification halfway through the success of 'My Mammy'.

HAPPY CLAPPERS
UK, male / female vocal / instrumental group (6 Singles: 19 Weeks)

3 Jun 95 **I BELIEVE** *Shindig SHIN 4CD* 21 3
26 Aug 95 **HOLD ON** *Shindig SHIN 7CD* 27 2
18 Nov 95 ● **I BELIEVE** (re-issue) *Shindig SHIN 9CD* 7 8
15 Jun 96 **CAN'T HELP IT** *Coliseum TOGA 004CD* 18 3
21 Dec 96 **NEVER AGAIN** *Coliseum TOGA 012CD* 49 1
22 Nov 97 **I BELIEVE** (re-mix) *Coalition COLA 027CD* 28 2

HAPPY MONDAYS (see also BLACK GRAPE) *UK, male vocal / instrumental group – leader Shaun Ryder (7 Albums: 62 Weeks, 11 Singles: 54 Weeks)*

30 Sep 89 **WFL** *Factory FAC 2327* 68 2
25 Nov 89 **MADCHESTER RAVE ON (EP)** *Factory FAC 2427* 19 14
27 Jan 90 **BUMMED** *Factory FACT 220* 59 14
7 Apr 90 ● **STEP ON** *Factory FAC 2727* 5 11
9 Jun 90 **LAZYITIS – ONE ARMED BOXER** *Factory FAC 2227* [1] 46 3
20 Oct 90 ● **KINKY AFRO** *Factory FAC 3027* 5 7
17 Nov 90 ● **PILLS 'N' THRILLS AND BELLYACHES** *Factory FACT 320* 4 29
9 Mar 91 **LOOSE FIT** *Factory FAC 3127* 17 7
12 Oct 91 **LIVE** *Factory FACT 322* 21 3
30 Nov 91 **JUDGE FUDGE** *Factory FAC 3327* 24 3
19 Sep 92 **STINKIN THINKIN** *Factory FAC 3627* 31 3
10 Oct 92 **... YES PLEASE!** *Factory FACD 420* 14 3
21 Nov 92 **SUNSHINE AND LOVE** *Factory FAC 3727* 62 1

14 February 1970	21 February 1970	28 February 1970	7 March 1970
UK No.1 SINGLES			
LOVE GROWS (WHERE MY ROSEMARY GOES) Edison Lighthouse	**LOVE GROWS (WHERE MY ROSEMARY GOES)** Edison Lighthouse	**LOVE GROWS (WHERE MY ROSEMARY GOES)** Edison Lighthouse	**WAND'RIN' STAR** Lee Marvin
UK No.1 ALBUMS			
BRITISH MOTOWN CHARTBUSTERS VOL.3 Various	**BRIDGE OVER TROUBLED WATER** Simon and Garfunkel	**BRIDGE OVER TROUBLED WATER** Simon and Garfunkel	**BRIDGE OVER TROUBLED WATER** Simon and Garfunkel

18 Nov 95 LOADS – THE BEST OF THE HAPPY MONDAYS *Factory Once 5203432* 41 2
22 May 99 **THE BOYS ARE BACK IN TOWN** *London LONCD 432* **24** 2
5 Jun 99 GREATEST HITS *London 5561052* 11 9
6 Jul 02 PILLS 'N' THRILLS AND BELLYACHES (re-issue) *London 3984282512* 47 2
29 Oct 05 **PLAYGROUND SUPERSTAR** *Big Brother RKIDSSCD 34* **51** 1

[1] Happy Mondays and Karl Denver

Tracks on Madchester Rave On (EP): Hallelujah / Holy Ghost / Clap Your Hands / Rave On.

HAPPYLIFE *UK, male vocal / instrumental group*

9 Oct 04 **SILENCE WHEN YOU'RE BURNING** *Albert Productions JASCDVUK 012* **73** 1

HAR MAR SUPERSTAR
US, male vocalist – Sean Tillman (1 Album: 1 Week, 2 Singles: 3 Weeks)

5 Jul 03 **EZ PASS** *B-Unique BUN 054CDS* **59** 1
4 Sep 04 **DUI** *Record Collection W 651CD* **46** 2
18 Sep 04 THE HANDLER *Record Collection 9362488102* 68 1

Ed HARCOURT *UK, male vocalist (2 Albums: 2 Weeks, 5 Singles: 5 Weeks)*

2 Feb 02 **APPLE OF MY EYE** *Heavenly HVN 107CDS* **61** 1
15 Feb 03 **ALL OF YOUR DAYS WILL BE BLESSED** *Heavenly HVN 127CDS* **35** 1
1 Mar 03 FROM EVERY SPHERE *Heavenly HVNLP 39CD* 39 1
11 Sep 04 **THIS ONE'S FOR YOU** *Heavenly HVN 140CD* **41** 1
25 Sep 04 STRANGERS *Heavenly HVNLP 49CD* 57 1
13 Nov 04 **BORN IN THE 70S** *Heavenly HVN 146* **61** 1
26 Feb 05 **LONELINESS** *Heavenly HVN 149CD* **59** 1

HARD-FI NEW *UK, male vocal (Richard Archer) / instrumental group (1 Album: 24 Weeks, 3 Singles: 21 Weeks)*

30 Apr 05 **TIED UP TOO TIGHT** *Necessary HARDFI 02CD* **15** 3
2 Jul 05 ● **HARD TO BEAT (2re)** *Necessary HARD 03CDX* ....**9** 12+
16 Jul 05 ● STARS OF CCTV *Atlantic / Necessary 5046786912* ....6 24+
1 Oct 05 **LIVING FOR THE WEEKEND** *Necessary HARD 04CDX* **15** 6

Paul HARDCASTLE (see also SILENT UNDERDOG) *UK, male producer / keyboard player (1 Album: 5 Weeks, 12 Singles: 66 Weeks)*

7 Apr 84 **YOU'RE THE ONE FOR ME – DAYBREAK – AM** *Total Control TOCO 1* **41** 4
28 Jul 84 **GUILTY** *Total Control TOCO 2* **55** 3
22 Sep 84 **RAIN FOREST** *Bluebird BR 8* **41** 5
17 Nov 84 **EAT YOUR HEART OUT** *Cooltempo COOL 102* **59** 4
4 May 85 ★ **19** *Chrysalis CHS 2860* **1** 16
15 Jun 85 **RAIN FOREST** (re-issue) *Bluebird / 10BR 15* **53** 4
9 Nov 85 **JUST FOR MONEY** *Chrysalis CASH 1* **19** 5
30 Nov 85 PAUL HARDCASTLE *Chrysalis CHR 1517* 53 5
1 Feb 86 ● **DON'T WASTE MY TIME** *Chrysalis PAUL 1* **8** 11
21 Jun 86 **FOOLIN' YOURSELF** *Chrysalis PAUL 2* **51** 3
11 Oct 86 **THE WIZARD** *Chrysalis PAUL 3* **15** 6
9 Apr 88 **WALK IN THE NIGHT** *Chrysalis PAUL 4* **54** 3
4 Jun 88 **40 YEARS** *Chrysalis PAUL 5* **53** 2

'Just for Money' features the voices of Laurence Olivier, Bob Hoskins, Ed O'Ross and Alan Talbot, who are credited on the sleeve only. 'Don't Waste My Time' features uncredited vocalist Carol Kenyon.

HARDCORE RHYTHM TEAM *UK, male vocal / production group*

14 Mar 92 **HARDCORE – THE FINAL CONFLICT** *Furious FRUT 001* **69** 1

HARDFLOOR *Germany, male instrumental / production duo (1 Album: 1 Week, 3 Singles: 6 Weeks)*

26 Dec 92 **HARDTRANCE ACPERIENCE** *Harthouse UK HARTUK 1* **56** 4
10 Apr 93 **TRANCESCRIPT** *Harthouse UK HARTUK 5CD* **72** 1
29 Jun 96 HOME RUN *Harthouse HHCD 019* 68 1
25 Oct 97 **ACPERIENCE** (re-mix) *Eye-q EYEUK 018CD1* **60** 1

Ronan HARDIMAN *Ireland, male composer*

2 Nov 96 MICHAEL FLATLEY'S LORD OF THE DANCE *PolyGram TV 5337572* 37 8

Tim HARDIN
US, male vocalist, b. 23 Dec 1941, d. 29 Dec 1980

5 Jan 67 **HANG ON TO A DREAM** *Verve VS 1504* **50** 1

Mike HARDING *UK, male vocalist / comedian / novelist and radio presenter (4 Albums: 24 Weeks, 1 Single: 8 Weeks)*

2 Aug 75 **ROCHDALE COWBOY** *Rubber ADUB 3* **22** 8
30 Aug 75 MRS 'ARDIN'S KID *Rubber RUB 011* 24 6
10 Jul 76 ONE MAN SHOW *Philips 6625 022* 19 10
11 Jun 77 OLD FOUR EYES IS BACK *Philips 6308 290* 31 6
24 Jun 78 CAPTAIN PARALYTIC AND THE BROWN ALE COWBOY *Philips 6641 798* 60 2

HARDSOUL featuring Ron CARROLL *Holland, male DJ / production duo – Rogier and Gregor Van Bueren and US, male vocalist*

12 Jun 04 **BACKTOGETHER** *In the House ITH 02CDS* **60** 1

Françoise HARDY *France, female vocalist (3 Singles: 27 Weeks)*

25 Jun 64 **TOUS LES GARCONS ET LES FILLES** *Pye 7N 15653* **36** 7
31 Dec 64 **ET MEME** *Pye 7N 15740* **31** 5
25 Mar 65 **ALL OVER THE WORLD** *Pye 7N 15802* **16** 15

Morten HARKET (see also A-HA) *Norway, male vocalist*

19 Aug 95 **A KIND OF CHRISTMAS CARD** *Warner Bros. W 0304CD* **53** 1

HARLEQUIN 4s / BUNKER KRU
US, male / female vocal / instrumental group and UK, male production duo

19 Mar 88 **SET IT OFF** *Champion CHAMP 64* **55** 4

Steve HARLEY and COCKNEY REBEL *UK, male vocal / instrumental group – leader Steve Nice (5 Albums: 52 Weeks, 12 Singles: 70 Weeks)*

11 May 74 ● **JUDY TEEN** *EMI 2128* [1] **5** 11
22 Jun 74 ● THE PSYCHOMODO *EMI EMC 3033* [1] 8 20
10 Aug 74 ● **MR SOFT** *EMI 2191* [1] **8** 9
8 Feb 75 ★ **MAKE ME SMILE (COME UP AND SEE ME)** *EMI 2263* **1** 9
22 Mar 75 ● THE BEST YEARS OF OUR LIVES *EMI EMC 3068* 4 19
7 Jun 75 **MR RAFFLES (MAN, IT WAS MEAN)** *EMI 2299* **13** 6
14 Feb 76 TIMELESS FLIGHT *EMI EMA 775* 18 6
31 Jul 76 ● **HERE COMES THE SUN** *EMI 2505* [2] **10** 7
6 Nov 76 **(I BELIEVE) LOVE'S A PRIMA DONNA** *EMI 2539* [2] **41** 4
27 Nov 76 LOVE'S A PRIMA DONNA *EMI EMC 3156* 28 3
30 Jul 77 FACE TO FACE – A LIVE RECORDING *EMI EMSP 320* 40 4
20 Oct 79 **FREEDOM'S PRISONER** *EMI 2994* [2] **58** 3
13 Aug 83 **BALLERINA (PRIMA DONNA)** *Stiletto STL 14* [2] **51** 5
11 Jan 86 ● **THE PHANTOM OF THE OPERA** *Polydor POSP 800* [3] **7** 10
25 Apr 92 **MAKE ME SMILE (COME UP AND SEE ME)** (re-issue) *EMI EMCT 5* [2] **46** 2
30 Dec 95 **MAKE ME SMILE (COME UP AND SEE ME)** (2nd re-issue) *EMI CDHARLEY 1* **33** 3
2 Jul 05 **MAKE ME SMILE (COME UP AND SEE ME)** (remix) *Gott Disc GOTTCD 030* [4] **55** 1

[1] Cockney Rebel [2] Steve Harley [3] Sarah Brightman and Steve Harley [4] Steve Harley + Cockney Rebel [1] Cockney Rebel

HARLEY QUINNE *UK, male vocal group*

14 Oct 72 **NEW ORLEANS** *Bell 1255* **19** 8

14 March 1970	21 March 1970	28 March 1970	4 April 1970
WAND'RIN' STAR Lee Marvin	**WAND'RIN' STAR** Lee Marvin	**BRIDGE OVER TROUBLED WATER** Simon and Garfunkel: Keyboard: Larry Knechtel	**BRIDGE OVER TROUBLED WATER** Simon and Garfunkel: Keyboard: Larry Knechtel
BRIDGE OVER TROUBLED WATER Simon and Garfunkel	**BRIDGE OVER TROUBLED WATER** Simon and Garfunkel	**BRIDGE OVER TROUBLED WATER** Simon and Garfunkel	**BRIDGE OVER TROUBLED WATER** Simon and Garfunkel

KEY UK No.1 ★ UK Top 10 ● Still on chart + UK entry at No.1 ■ US No.1 ▲ UK million seller £ US million seller $
Singles re-entries are listed as (re), (2re), (3re)... which signifies that the hit re-entered the chart once, twice or three times...
Peak Position / Weeks

HARMONIUM (see also BLOWING FREE; HYPNOSIS; IN TUNE; JAMES BOYS; RAINDANCE; SCHOOL OF EXCELLENCE)
UK, male production / instrumental duo – Stewart and Bradley Palmer

21 Mar 98 SPIRIT OF TRANQUILITY *Global Television RADCD 79* 25 4

HARMONIX *UK, male producer – Hamish Brown*

30 Mar 96 **LANDSLIDE** *Deconstruction 74321330762* **28** 2

HARMONY GRASS *UK, male vocal / instrumental group*

29 Jan 69 **MOVE IN A LITTLE CLOSER BABY** *RCA 1772* **24** 7

Ben HARPER *US, male vocalist / guitarist*

4 Apr 98 **FADED** *Virgin VUSCD 134* **54** 1

Charlie HARPER (see also UK SUBS) *UK, male vocalist – David Perez*

19 Jul 80 **BARMY LONDON ARMY** *Gem GEMS 35* **68** 1

Roy HARPER *UK, male vocalist / guitarist (4 Albums: 9 Weeks)*

9 Mar 74 VALENTINE *Harvest SHSP 4027* 27 1
21 Jun 75 H.Q. *Harvest SHSP 4046* 31 2
12 Mar 77 BULLINAMINGVASE *Harvest SHSP 4060* 25 2
16 Mar 85 WHATEVER HAPPENED TO JUGULA? *Beggars Banquet BEGA 60* [1] 44 4

[1] Roy Harper and Jimmy Page

HARPERS BIZARRE *US, male vocal group (2 Singles: 13 Weeks)*

30 Mar 67 **59TH STREET BRIDGE SONG (FEELIN' GROOVY)** *Warner Bros. WB 5890* **34** 7
4 Oct 67 **ANYTHING GOES** *Warner Bros. WB 7063* **33** 6

HARPO *Sweden, male vocalist – Jan Svensson*

17 Apr 76 **MOVIE STAR** *DJM DJS 400* **24** 6

Anita HARRIS
UK, female vocalist (1 Album: 5 Weeks, 4 Singles: 50 Weeks)

29 Jun 67 ● **JUST LOVING YOU** *CBS 2724* **6** 30
11 Oct 67 **THE PLAYGROUND** *CBS 2991* **46** 3
24 Jan 68 **ANNIVERSARY WALTZ** *CBS 3211* **21** 9
27 Jan 68 JUST LOVING YOU *CBS SBPG 63182* 29 5
14 Aug 68 **DREAM A LITTLE DREAM OF ME** *CBS 3637* **33** 8

Emmylou HARRIS
US, female vocalist / guitarist (10 Albums: 37 Weeks, 1 Single: 6 Weeks)

14 Feb 76 ELITE HOTEL *Reprise K 54060* 17 11
6 Mar 76 **HERE, THERE & EVERYWHERE** *Reprise K 14415* **30** 6
29 Jan 77 LUXURY LINER *Warner Bros. K 56344* 17 6
4 Feb 78 QUARTER MOON IN A TEN CENT TOWN *Warner Bros. K 56433* 40 5
29 Mar 80 HER BEST SONGS *K-Tel NE 1058* 36 3
14 Feb 81 EVANGELINE *Warner Bros. K 56880* 53 4
14 Mar 87 TRIO *Warner Bros. 9254911* [1] 60 4
7 Oct 95 WRECKING BALL *Grapevine GRACD 102* 46 1
29 Aug 98 SPYBOY *Grapevine GRACD 241* 57 1
30 Sep 00 RED DIRT GIRL *Grapevine GRACD 103* 45 1
4 Oct 03 STUMBLE INTO GRACE *Nonesuch 7559798052* 52 1

[1] Dolly Parton / Emmylou Harris / Linda Ronstadt

Jet HARRIS and Tony MEEHAN (see also The SHADOWS) *UK, instrumental duo – bass player Jet Harris (Terence Hawkins) and drummer Tony Meehan (Daniel Meehan), b.2 Mar 1943, d. 28 Nov 2005 (5 Singles: 57 Weeks)*

24 May 62 **BESAME MUCHO** *Decca F 11466* [1] **22** 7
16 Aug 62 **MAIN TITLE THEME (FROM 'THE MAN WITH THE GOLDEN ARM')** *Decca F 11488* [1] **12** 11
10 Jan 63 ★ **DIAMONDS** *Decca F 11563* **1** 13
25 Apr 63 ● **SCARLETT O'HARA** *Decca F 11644* **2** 13
5 Sep 63 ● **APPLEJACK** *Decca F 11710* **4** 13

[1] Jet Harris

Keith HARRIS and ORVILLE *UK, male ventriloquist vocalist and duck (1 Album: 1 Week, 3 Singles: 20 Weeks)*

18 Dec 82 ● **ORVILLE'S SONG** *BBC RESL 124* **4** 11
4 Jun 83 AT THE END OF THE RAINBOW *BBC REH 465* [1] 92 1
24 Dec 83 **COME TO MY PARTY** *BBC RESL 138* [1] **44** 4
14 Dec 85 **WHITE CHRISTMAS** *Columbia DB 9121* **40** 5

[1] Keith Harris and Orville with Dippy [1] Keith Harris, Orville and Cuddles

Major HARRIS *US, male vocalist (2 Singles: 9 Weeks)*

9 Aug 75 **LOVE WON'T LET ME WAIT** *Atlantic K 10585* $ **37** 7
5 Nov 83 **ALL MY LIFE** *London LON 37* **61** 2

Max HARRIS *UK, orchestra leader, b. 15 Sep 1918, d. 13 Mar 2004*

1 Dec 60 **GURNEY SLADE** *Fontana H 282* **11** 10

Rahni HARRIS and F.L.O. *US, male instrumental group*

16 Dec 78 **SIX MILLION STEPS (WEST RUNS SOUTH)** *Mercury 6007 198* **43** 7

Hit has credit 'vocals by T Harrington and O Rasbury'.

Richard HARRIS
Ireland, male actor / vocalist, b. 1 Oct 1930, d. 25 Oct 2002 (2 Singles: 18 Weeks)

26 Jun 68 ● **MACARTHUR PARK** *RCA 1699* $ **4** 12
8 Jul 72 **MACARTHUR PARK** (re-issue) *Probe GFF 101* **38** 6

Rolf HARRIS *Australia, male vocalist / artist / TV presenter (1 Album: 1 Week, 9 Singles: 77 Weeks)*

21 Jul 60 ● **TIE ME KANGAROO DOWN, SPORT** *Columbia DB 4483* [1] **9** 13
25 Oct 62 ● **SUN ARISE** *Columbia DB 4888* **3** 16
28 Feb 63 **JOHNNY DAY** *Columbia DB 4979* **44** 2
16 Apr 69 **BLUER THAN BLUE** *Columbia DB 8553* **30** 8
22 Nov 69 ★ **TWO LITTLE BOYS (re)** *Columbia DB 8630* **1** 25
13 Feb 93 ● **STAIRWAY TO HEAVEN** *Vertigo VERCD 73* **7** 6
1 Jun 96 **BOHEMIAN RHAPSODY** *Living Beat LBECD 41* **50** 1
25 Oct 97 **SUN ARISE** *EMI CDROO 001* **26** 3
1 Nov 97 CAN YOU TELL WHAT IT IS YET? *EMI 8218802* 70 1
14 Oct 00 **FINE DAY** *Tommy Boy TBCD 2155* **24** 3

[1] Rolf Harris with his wobble board and the Rhythm Spinners

Ronnie HARRIS *UK, male vocalist*

24 Sep 54 **THE STORY OF TINA** *Columbia DB 3499* **12** 3

Sam HARRIS *US, male vocalist*

9 Feb 85 **HEARTS ON FIRE / OVER THE RAINBOW** *Motown TMG 1370* **67** 2

Simon HARRIS (see also AMBASSADORS OF FUNK featuring MC MARIO)
UK, male / DJ producer (5 Singles: 17 Weeks)

19 Mar 88 **BASS (HOW LOW CAN YOU GO)** *ffrr FFR 4* **12** 6
29 Oct 88 **HERE COMES THAT SOUND** *ffrr FFR 12* **38** 4
24 Jun 89 **(I'VE GOT YOUR) PLEASURE CONTROL** *ffrr F 106* [1] **60** 3
18 Nov 89 **ANOTHER MONSTERJAM** *ffrr F 116* [2] **65** 1
10 Mar 90 **RAGGA HOUSE (ALL NIGHT LONG)** *Living Beat 7SMASH 9* [3] **56** 3

[1] Simon Harris featuring Lonnie Gordon [2] Simon Harris featuring Einstein
[3] Simon Harris featuring Daddy Freddy

	11 April 1970	18 April 1970	25 April 1970	2 May 1970
UK No.1 SINGLES	BRIDGE OVER TROUBLED WATER Simon and Garfunkel; Keyboard: Larry Knechtel	ALL KINDS OF EVERYTHING Dana	ALL KINDS OF EVERYTHING Dana	SPIRIT IN THE SKY Norman Greenbaum
UK No.1 ALBUMS	BRIDGE OVER TROUBLED WATER Simon and Garfunkel	BRIDGE OVER TROUBLED WATER Simon and Garfunkel	BRIDGE OVER TROUBLED WATER Simon and Garfunkel	BRIDGE OVER TROUBLED WATER Simon and Garfunkel

George HARRISON 405 Top 500 (see also TRAVELING WILBURYS)
Former Beatles guitarist, much inspired by Eastern musicians, b. 25 Feb 1943, Liverpool, UK, d. 29 Nov 2001. The first ex-Beatle to score a solo UK No.1 single and the only soloist to top the chart twice with the same single. Although not credited as a George Harrison album, the triple disc Concert for Bangladesh was instigated and performed by him and star guests such as Ravi Shankar, Bob Dylan, Eric Clapton and Ringo Starr. In 2004, he won a Grammy for Best Instrumental ('Marwa Blues'), and was added to the Rock and Roll Hall of Fame (9 Albums: 82 Weeks, 12 Singles: 94 Weeks)

26 Dec 70 ★ ALL THINGS MUST PASS *Apple STCH 639* ▲ 1 24
23 Jan 71 ★ **MY SWEET LORD** *Apple R 5884* ▲ $ 1 17
14 Aug 71 ● **BANGLA-DESH** *Apple R 5912* 10 9
2 Jun 73 ● **GIVE ME LOVE (GIVE ME PEACE ON EARTH)** *Apple R 5988* ▲ $ 8 10
7 Jul 73 ● LIVING IN THE MATERIAL WORLD *Apple PAS 10006* ▲ 2 12
21 Dec 74 **DING DONG** *Apple R 6002* 38 5
11 Oct 75 **YOU** *Apple R 6007* 38 5
18 Oct 75 EXTRA TEXTURE (READ ALL ABOUT IT) *Apple PAS 10009* 16 4
18 Dec 76 THIRTY-THREE & 1/3 *Dark Horse K 56319* 35 4
10 Mar 79 **BLOW AWAY** *Dark Horse K 17327* 51 5
17 Mar 79 GEORGE HARRISON *Dark Horse K 56562* 39 5
23 May 81 **ALL THOSE YEARS AGO** *Dark Horse K 17807* 13 7
13 Jun 81 SOMEWHERE IN ENGLAND *Dark Horse K 56870* 13 4
24 Oct 87 ● **GOT MY MIND SET ON YOU** *Dark Horse W 8178* ▲ 2 14
14 Nov 87 ● CLOUD NINE *Dark Horse WX 123* 10 23
6 Feb 88 **WHEN WE WAS FAB** *Dark Horse W 8131* 25 7
25 Jun 88 **THIS IS LOVE** *Dark Horse W 7913* 55 3
3 Feb 01 ALL THINGS MUST PASS (re-issue) *Parlophone 5304742* 68 2
26 Jan 02 ★ **MY SWEET LORD** (re-issue) *Parlophone CDR 6571* ■ 1 10
30 Nov 02 BRAINWASHED *Parlophone 5803450* 29 4
24 May 03 **ANY ROAD** *Parlophone CDRS 6601* 37 2

Jane HARRISON *UK, female vocalist*

4 Feb 89 NEW DAY *Stylus SMR 869* 70 1

Noel HARRISON *UK, male vocalist*

26 Feb 69 ● **THE WINDMILLS OF YOUR MIND** *Reprise RS 20758* 8 14

HARRY *UK, female vocalist – Victoria Harrison (2 Singles: 2 Weeks)*

2 Nov 02 **SO REAL** *Dirty Word DWRCD 003* 53 1
19 Apr 03 **UNDER THE COVERS EP** *Dirty Word DWRCD 005* 43 1

Tracks on Under the Covers EP: Imagination / Push it (Real Good) / She's in Parties.

Deborah HARRY (see also BLONDIE)
US, female vocalist (6 Albums: 53 Weeks, 10 Singles: 52 Weeks)

1 Aug 81 **BACKFIRED** *Chrysalis CHS 2526* [1] 32 6
8 Aug 81 ● KOO KOO *Chrysalis CHR 1347* [1] 6 7
15 Nov 86 ● **FRENCH KISSIN' IN THE USA** *Chrysalis CHS 3066* [1] 8 10
29 Nov 86 ROCKBIRD *Chrysalis CHR 1540* [1] 31 11
28 Feb 87 **FREE TO FALL** *Chrysalis CHS 3093* [1] 46 4
9 May 87 **IN LOVE WITH LOVE** *Chrysalis CHS 3128* [1] 45 5
17 Dec 88 ONCE MORE INTO THE BLEACH *Chrysalis CJB 2* [2] 50 4
7 Oct 89 **I WANT THAT MAN** *Chrysalis CHS 3369* 13 10
28 Oct 89 DEF DUMB AND BLONDE *Chrysalis CHR 1650* 12 7
2 Dec 89 **BRITE SIDE** *Chrysalis CHS 3452* 59 4
31 Mar 90 **SWEET AND LOW** *Chrysalis CHS 3491* 57 3
5 Jan 91 **WELL DID YOU EVAH!** *Chrysalis CHS 3646* [2] 42 4
16 Mar 91 ● THE COMPLETE PICTURE – THE VERY BEST OF DEBORAH HARRY AND BLONDIE *Chrysalis CHR 1817* [2] 3 22
3 Jul 93 **I CAN SEE CLEARLY NOW** *Chrysalis CDCHSS 4900* 23 4
31 Jul 93 DEBRAVATION *Chrysalis CDCHR 6033* 24 2
18 Sep 93 **STRIKE ME PINK** *Chrysalis CDCHSS 5000* 46 2

[1] Debbie Harry [2] Deborah Harry and Iggy Pop [1] Debbie Harry [2] Deborah Harry and Blondie

HARRY J ALL STARS *Jamaica, male instrumental group – leader Harry Johnson (2 Singles: 25 Weeks)*

25 Oct 69 ● **LIQUIDATOR** *Trojan TR 675* 9 20
29 Mar 80 **LIQUIDATOR** (re-issue) *Trojan TRO 9063* 42 5

The re-issue of 'Liquidator' was coupled with the re-issue of 'Long Shot Kick De Bucket' by The Pioneers.

Keef HARTLEY BAND *UK, male vocal / instrumental group*

5 Sep 70 THE TIME IS NEAR *Deram SML 1071* 41 3

Richard HARTLEY / Michael REED ORCHESTRA
UK, male synths player and orchestra

25 Feb 84 ● **THE MUSIC OF TORVILL AND DEAN (EP)** *Safari SKATE 1* 9 10

Tracks on EP: Bolero / Capriccio Espagnole Opus 34 (Nos. 4 and 5) – Richard Hartley, Barnum on Ice / Discoskate – Michael Reed Orchestra.

Dan HARTMAN
US, male vocalist, b. 8 Dec 1950, d. 22 Mar 1994 (5 Singles: 34 Weeks)

21 Oct 78 ● **INSTANT REPLAY** *Blue Sky SKY 6706* 8 15
13 Jan 79 **THIS IS IT** *Blue Sky SKY 6999* 17 8
18 May 85 **SECOND NATURE** *MCA MCA 957* 66 2
24 Aug 85 **I CAN DREAM ABOUT YOU** *MCA MCA 988* 12 8
1 Apr 95 **KEEP THE FIRE BURNIN'** *Columbia 6611552* [1] 49 1

[1] Dan Hartman starring Loleatta Holloway

HARVEY (see also SO SOLID CREW) *UK, male rapper – Michael Harvey*

7 Sep 02 **GET UP AND MOVE** *Go Beat GOBCD 52* 24 2

Brian HARVEY (see also EAST 17; TRUE STEPPERS)
UK, male vocalist (2 Singles: 5 Weeks)

28 Apr 01 **STRAIGHT UP NO BENDS** *Edel 0126605 ERE* 26 2
27 Oct 01 **LOVING YOU (OLE OLE OLE)** *Blacklist 0132325 ERE* [1] 20 3

[1] Brian Harvey and The Refugee Crew

PJ HARVEY *UK, female vocalist – Polly Jean Harvey (8 Albums: 36 Weeks, 16 Singles: 27 Weeks)*

29 Feb 92 **SHEELA-NA-GIG** *Too Pure PURE 008* 69 1
11 Apr 92 DRY *Too Pure PURECD 10* 11 5
1 May 93 **50 FT QUEENIE** *Island CID 538* 27 2
8 May 93 ● RID OF ME *Island CID 8002* 3 4
17 Jul 93 **MAN-SIZE** *Island CID 569* 42 2
30 Oct 93 4-TRACK DEMOS *Island IMCD 170* 19 2
18 Feb 95 **DOWN BY THE WATER** *Island CID 607* 38 2
11 Mar 95 TO BRING YOU MY LOVE *Island CID 8035* 12 6
22 Jul 95 **C'MON BILLY** *Island CID 614* 29 2
28 Oct 95 **SEND HIS LOVE TO ME** *Island CID 610* 34 2
9 Mar 96 **HENRY LEE** *Mute CDMUTE 189* [1] 36 1
5 Oct 96 DANCE HALL AT LOUSE POINT *Island CID 8051* [1] 46 1
23 Nov 96 **THAT WAS MY VEIL** *Island CID 648* [2] 75 1
26 Sep 98 **A PERFECT DAY ELISE** *Island CID 718* 25 2
10 Oct 98 IS THIS DESIRE? *Island CID 8076* 17 2
23 Jan 99 **THE WIND** *Island CID 730* 29 2
4 Nov 00 STORIES FROM THE CITY STORIES FROM THE SEA *Island CID 8099* 23 13
25 Nov 00 **GOOD FORTUNE** *Island CID 769* 41 2
10 Mar 01 **A PLACE CALLED HOME** *Island CID 771* 43 2
20 Oct 01 **THIS IS LOVE** *Island CID 785* 41 1
29 May 04 **THE LETTER** *Island CIDX 861* 28 2
12 Jun 04 UH HUH HER *Island CIDX 8143* 12 3
31 Jul 04 **YOU COME THROUGH** *Island CIDX 869* 41 2
2 Oct 04 **SHAME** *Island CID 873* 45 1

[1] Nick Cave and the Bad Seeds and PJ Harvey [2] John Parish and Polly Jean Harvey [1] John Parish / Polly Jean Harvey

For the first three singles and albums, PJ Harvey was the name of the entire group, not just the lead singer.

9 May 1970	16 May 1970	23 May 1970	30 May 1970
SPIRIT IN THE SKY Norman Greenbaum	**BACK HOME** England World Cup Squad	**BACK HOME** England World Cup Squad	**BACK HOME** England World Cup Squad
BRIDGE OVER TROUBLED WATER Simon and Garfunkel	**BRIDGE OVER TROUBLED WATER** Simon and Garfunkel	**LET IT BE** The Beatles	**LET IT BE** The Beatles

KEY: UK No.1 ★ UK Top 10 ● Still on chart + UK entry at No.1 ■ US No.1 ▲ UK million seller £ US million seller $
Singles re-entries are listed as (re), (2re), (3re)... which signifies that the hit re-entered the chart once, twice or three times...
Peak Position / Weeks

Steve HARVEY *UK, male vocalist (2 Singles: 6 Weeks)*

28 May 83	**SOMETHING SPECIAL** *London LON 25*	46	4
29 Oct 83	**TONIGHT** *London LON 36*	63	2

Richard HARVEY and FRIENDS *UK, male instrumental group*

6 May 89	**EVENING FALLS** *Telstar STAR 2350*	72	1

HARVEY DANGER *US, male vocal / instrumental group*

1 Aug 98	**FLAGPOLE SITTA** *Slash LASCD 64*	57	1

Gordon HASKELL
UK, male vocalist (2 Albums: 11 Weeks, 1 Single: 6 Weeks)

29 Dec 01 ●	**HOW WONDERFUL YOU ARE** *Flying Sparks TDBCDS 04*	2	6
19 Jan 02 ●	**HARRY'S BAR** *East West 927439762*	2	10
26 Oct 02	**SHADOWS ON THE WALL** *Flying Sparks TDBCD 068*	44	1

Lee HASLAM *UK, male DJ / producer*

14 Aug 04	**LIBERATE / HERE COMES THE PAIN** *Tidy Trax TIDTRWO 135*	71	1

David HASSELHOFF *US, male vocalist / actor*

13 Nov 93	**IF I COULD ONLY SAY GOODBYE** *Arista 74321172262*	35	2

Tony HATCH *UK, orchestra*

4 Oct 62	**OUT OF THIS WORLD** *Pye 7N 15460*	50	1

Juliana HATFIELD
US, female vocalist / guitarist (2 Albums: 3 Weeks, 2 Singles: 2 Weeks)

14 Aug 93	**BECOME WHAT YOU ARE** *Mammoth 4509935292* [1]	44	2
11 Sep 93	**MY SISTER** *Mammoth YZ 767CD* [1]	71	1
18 Mar 95	**UNIVERSAL HEART-BEAT** *East West YZ 916CD*	65	1
8 Apr 95	**ONLY EVERYTHING** *East West 4509998862*	59	1

[1] Juliana Hatfield Three [1] Juliana Hatfield Three

HATFIELD AND THE NORTH (see also Dave STEWART)
UK, male / female vocal / instrumental group

29 Mar 75	**ROTTERS CLUB** *Virgin V 2030*	43	1

Lalah HATHAWAY *US, female vocalist (3 Singles: 10 Weeks)*

1 Sep 90	**HEAVEN KNOWS** *Virgin America VUS 28*	66	2
2 Feb 91	**BABY DON'T CRY** *Virgin America VUS 35*	54	3
27 Jul 91	**FAMILY AFFAIR** *Ten TEN 369*	37	5

Charlotte HATHERLEY (see also ASH)
UK, female vocalist / guitarist (1 Album: 1 Week, 2 Singles: 4 Weeks)

21 Aug 04	**SUMMER** *Double Dragon DD 2014CD*	31	2
28 Aug 04	**GREY WILL FADE** *Double Dragon DD 2015CD*	51	1
5 Mar 05	**BASTARDO** *Double Dragon DD 2019CD*	31	2

HATIRAS featuring SLARTA JOHN
Canada, male producer – George Hatiris and UK, male rapper – Mark James

27 Jan 01	**SPACED INVADER** *Defected DFECT 25CDS*	14	5

HAVANA *UK, male instrumental / production group*

6 Mar 93	**ETHNIC PRAYER** *Limbo LIMBO 007CD*	71	1

HAVEN
UK, male vocal / instrumental group (1 Album: 3 Weeks, 4 Singles: 7 Weeks)

22 Sep 01	**LET IT LIVE** *Radiate RDT 3*	72	1
2 Feb 02	**SAY SOMETHING** *Radiate RDT 4*	24	3
16 Feb 02	**BETWEEN THE SENSES** *Radiate RDTCD 1*	26	3
4 May 02	**TIL THE END** *Radiate RDT 6*	28	2
27 Mar 04	**WOULDN'T CHANGE A THING** *Radiate RDTCD 14*	57	1

Nic HAVERSON *UK, male vocalist*

30 Jan 93	**HEAD OVER HEELS** *Telstar CDHOH 1*	48	3

Chesney HAWKES
UK, male vocalist (1 Album: 8 Weeks, 6 Singles: 27 Weeks)

23 Feb 91 ★	**THE ONE AND ONLY** *Chrysalis CHS 3627*	1	16
13 Apr 91	**BUDDY'S SONG (FILM SOUNDTRACK)** *Chrysalis CHR 1812*	18	8
22 Jun 91	**I'M A MAN NOT A BOY** *Chrysalis CHS 3708*	27	5
28 Sep 91	**SECRETS OF THE HEART** *Chrysalis CHS 3681*	57	3
29 May 93	**WHAT'S WRONG WITH THIS PICTURE** *Chrysalis CDCHS 3969*	63	1
12 Jan 02	**STAY AWAY BABY JANE** *Arc DSART 13*	74	1
4 Jun 05	**ANOTHER FINE MESS** *Right Track CHESCD 001*	48	1

Screamin' Jay HAWKINS
US, male vocalist – Jalacy Hawkins, b. 18 Jul 1929, d. 12 Feb 2000

3 Apr 93	**HEART ATTACK AND VINE** *Columbia 6591092*	42	3

Sophie B HAWKINS
US, female vocalist (2 Albums: 6 Weeks, 6 Singles: 37 Weeks)

4 Jul 92	**DAMN I WISH I WAS YOUR LOVER** *Columbia 6581077*	14	9
1 Aug 92	**TONGUES AND TAILS** *Columbia 4688232*	46	2
12 Sep 92	**CALIFORNIA HERE I COME** *Columbia 6583177*	53	3
6 Feb 93	**I WANT YOU** *Columbia 6587772*	49	2
13 Aug 94	**RIGHT BESIDE YOU** *Columbia 6606915*	13	12
3 Sep 94	**WHALER** *Columbia 4765122*	46	4
26 Nov 94	**DON'T DON'T TELL ME NO** *Columbia 6610152*	36	5
11 Mar 95	**AS I LAY ME DOWN** *Columbia 6612125*	24	6

Ted HAWKINS *US, male vocalist / guitarist, b. 28 Oct 1936, d. 1 Jan 1995*

18 Apr 87	**HAPPY HOUR** *Windows on the World WOLP 2*	82	1

Edwin HAWKINS SINGERS *US, male / female vocal group*

21 May 69 ●	**OH HAPPY DAY (re)** *Buddah 201 048* $	2	13

Kirsty HAWKSHAW
(see also OPUS III) *UK, female vocalist (5 Singles: 9 Weeks)*

24 Jun 00	**DREAMING** *Headspace HEDSCD 002* [1]	38	2
29 Sep 01	**URBAN TRAIN** *Nebula VCRD 95* [2]	22	3
21 Sep 02	**STEALTH** *Distinctive Breaks DISNCD 90* [3]	67	1
23 Nov 02	**FINE DAY** *Mainline CDMAIN 002*	62	1
23 Oct 04	**JUST BE** *Nebula NEBCD 062* [4]	43	2

[1] BT featuring Kirsty Hawkshaw [2] DJ Tiësto featuring Kirsty Hawkshaw [3] Way Out West featuring Kirsty Hawkshaw [4] Tiësto featuring Kirsty Hawkshaw

HAWKWIND *UK, male vocal (Dave Brock) / instrumental group and female dancer (22 Albums: 101 Weeks, 3 Singles: 28 Weeks)*

6 Nov 71	**IN SEARCH OF SPACE** *United Artists UAS 29202*	18	19
1 Jul 72 ●	**SILVER MACHINE (2re)** *United Artists UP 35381*	3	22
23 Dec 72	**DOREMI FASOL LATIDO** *United Artists UAS 29364*	14	5
2 Jun 73 ●	**SPACE RITUAL ALIVE** *United Artists UAD 60037/8*	9	5
11 Aug 73	**URBAN GUERRILLA** *United Artists UP 35566*	39	3
21 Sep 74	**HALL OF THE MOUNTAIN GRILL** *United Artists UAG 29672*	16	5
31 May 75	**WARRIOR ON THE EDGE OF TIME** *United Artists UAG 29766*	13	7
24 Apr 76	**ROAD HAWKS** *United Artists UAK 29919*	34	4
18 Sep 76	**ASTONISHING SOUNDS AMAZING MUSIC** *Charisma CDS 4004*	33	5
9 Jul 77	**QUARK STRANGENESS AND CHARM** *Charisma CDS 4008*	30	6
21 Oct 78	**25 YEARS ON** *Charisma CD 4014* [1]	48	3

6 June 1970	13 June 1970	20 June 1970	27 June 1970
UK No.1 SINGLES			
YELLOW RIVER Christie	IN THE SUMMERTIME Mungo Jerry	IN THE SUMMERTIME Mungo Jerry	IN THE SUMMERTIME Mungo Jerry
UK No.1 ALBUMS			
LET IT BE The Beatles	BRIDGE OVER TROUBLED WATER Simon and Garfunkel	BRIDGE OVER TROUBLED WATER Simon and Garfunkel	BRIDGE OVER TROUBLED WATER Simon and Garfunkel

30 Jun 79 PXR 5 *Charisma CDS 4016* 59 5
19 Jul 80 **SHOT DOWN IN THE NIGHT** *Bronze BRO 98* 59 3
9 Aug 80 LIVE 1979 *Bronze BRON 527* 15 7
8 Nov 80 LEVITATION *Bronze BRON 530* 21 4
24 Oct 81 SONIC ATTACK *RCA RCALP 5004* 19 5
22 May 82 CHURCH OF HAWKWIND *RCA RCALP 9004* 26 6
23 Oct 82 CHOOSE YOUR MASQUES *RCA RCALP 6055* 29 5
5 Nov 83 ZONES *Flicknife SHARP 014* 57 2
25 Feb 84 HAWKWIND *Liberty SLS 1972921* 75 1
16 Nov 85 CHRONICLE OF THE BLACK SWORD *Flicknife SHARP 033* 65 2
14 May 88 THE XENON CODEX *GWR GWLP 26* 79 2
6 Oct 90 SPACE BANDITS *GWR GWLP 103* 70 1
23 May 92 ELECTRIC TEPEE *Essential ESSCD 181* 53 1
6 Nov 93 IT IS THE BUSINESS OF THE FUTURE TO BE DANGEROUS *Essential ESCDCD 196* 75 1

[1] Hawklords

'Silver Machine' re-entries were in 1978 and 1983.

Richard HAWLEY NEW
(see also LONGPIGS) *UK, male vocalist / guitarist*

17 Sep 05 COLES CORNER *Mute CDSTUMM 251* 55 1

Bill HAYES with Archie BLEYER'S ORCHESTRA *US, male vocalist*

6 Jan 56 ● **THE BALLAD OF DAVY CROCKETT** *London HLA 8220* ▲ $ 2 9

Darren HAYES (see also SAVAGE GARDEN)
Australia, male vocalist (2 Albums: 30 Weeks, 6 Singles: 38 Weeks)

30 Mar 02 ● **INSATIABLE** *Columbia 6723995* 8 14
13 Apr 02 ● SPIN *Columbia 5053192* 2 28
20 Jul 02 **STRANGE RELATIONSHIP** *Columbia 6728685* 15 8
16 Nov 02 **I MISS YOU (re)** *Columbia 6733312* 20 5
1 Feb 03 **CRUSH (1980 ME)** *Columbia 6734902* 19 3
11 Sep 04 **POP!ULAR** *Columbia 6751112* 12 5
25 Sep 04 THE TENSION AND THE SPARK *Columbia 5154312* 13 2
12 Nov 05 **SO BEAUTIFUL** *Columbia 82876739402* 15 3

Gemma HAYES
Ireland, female vocalist (1 Album: 1 Week, 2 Singles: 2 Weeks)

25 May 02 **HANGING AROUND** *Source SOURCD 046* 62 1
8 Jun 02 NIGHT ON MY SIDE *Source CDSOUR 049* 52 1
10 Aug 02 **LET A GOOD THING GO** *Source SOURCD 051* 54 1

Isaac HAYES *US, male vocalist / multi-instrumentalist (2 Albums: 14 Weeks, 4 Singles: 35 Weeks)*

4 Dec 71 ● **THEME FROM 'SHAFT'** *Stax 2025 069* ▲ $ 4 12
18 Dec 71 SHAFT (FILM SOUNDTRACK) *Polydor 2659 007* ▲ 17 13
12 Feb 72 BLACK MOSES *Stax 2628 004* 38 1
3 Apr 76 ● **DISCO CONNECTION** *ABC 4100* [1] 10 9
26 Dec 98 ★ **CHOCOLATE SALTY BALLS (PS I LOVE YOU)** *Columbia 6667985* [2] 1 13
30 Sep 00 **THEME FROM 'SHAFT'** (re-recording) *LaFace / Arista 74321792582* 53 1

[1] Isaac Hayes Movement [2] Chef

HAYSI FANTAYZEE *UK, male / female production / vocal duo – Jeremy Healy and Kate Garner (1 Album: 5 Weeks, 4 Singles: 25 Weeks)*

24 Jul 82 **JOHN WAYNE IS BIG LEGGY** *Regard RG 100* 11 10
13 Nov 82 **HOLY JOE** *Regard RG 104* 51 3
22 Jan 83 **SHINY SHINY** *Regard RG 106* 16 10
26 Feb 83 BATTLE HYMNS FOR CHILDREN SINGING *Regard RGLP 6000* 53 5
25 Jun 83 **SISTER FRICTION** *Regard RG 108* 62 2

Justin HAYWARD (see also The MOODY BLUES)
UK, male vocalist – David Hayward (5 Albums: 35 Weeks, 2 Singles: 20 Weeks)

29 Mar 75 ● BLUE JAYS *Threshold THS 12* [1] 4 18
25 Oct 75 ● **BLUE GUITAR** *Threshold TH 21* [1] 8 7
5 Mar 77 SONGWRITER *Deram SDL 15* 28 5
8 Jul 78 ● **FOREVER AUTUMN** *CBS 6368* [2] 5 13
19 Jul 80 NIGHT FLIGHT *Decca TXS 138* 41 4
19 Oct 85 MOVING MOUNTAINS *Towerbell TOWLP 15* 78 1
28 Oct 89 CLASSIC BLUE *Trax MODEM 1040* [2] 47 7

[1] Justin Hayward and John Lodge [2] From Jeff Wayne's 'War of the Worlds' featuring Justin Hayward [1] Justin Hayward and John Lodge [2] Justin Hayward, Mike Batt and the London Philharmonic Orchestra

Leon HAYWOOD *US, male vocalist*

15 Mar 80 **DON'T PUSH IT DON'T FORCE IT** *20th Century Fox TC 2443* 12 11

HAYWOODE *UK, female vocalist – Sharon Haywoode (6 Singles: 31 Weeks)*

17 Sep 83 **A TIME LIKE THIS** *CBS A 3651* 48 7
29 Sep 84 **I CAN'T LET YOU GO** *CBS A 4664* 63 4
13 Apr 85 **ROSES** *CBS A 6069* 65 3
5 Oct 85 **GETTING CLOSER** *CBS A 6582* 67 2
21 Jun 86 **ROSES** (re-issue) *CBS A 7224* 11 11
13 Sep 86 **I CAN'T LET YOU GO** (re-issue) *CBS 650076 7* 50 4

Ofra HAZA
Israel, female vocalist, b. 19 Nov 1959, d. 23 Feb 2000 (3 Singles: 12 Weeks)

30 Apr 88 **IM NIN'ALU** *WEA YZ 190* 15 8
17 Jun 95 **MY LOVE IS FOR REAL** *Virgin America VUSCD 91* [1] 28 3
3 Apr 99 **BABYLON** *Warner.esp WESP 006CD1* [2] 65 1

[1] Paula Abdul featuring Ofra Haza [2] Black Dog featuring Ofra Haza

HAZIZA *Sweden, male production duo*

28 Apr 01 **ONE MORE** *Tidy Trax TIDY 152T* 75 1

The HAZZARDS *US, female vocal duo – Sydney Maresca and Anne Harris*

22 Nov 03 **GAY BOYFRIEND** *Better the Devil BTD 3CD* 67 1

HEAD AUTOMATICA NEW *US, male vocal / instrumental group*

12 Feb 05 **BEATING HEART BABY** *WEA W 663CD* 44 2

Murray HEAD *UK, male vocalist (2 Singles: 15 Weeks)*

29 Jan 72 **SUPERSTAR** *MCA MMKS 5077* [1] 47 1
10 Nov 84 **ONE NIGHT IN BANGKOK (re)** *RCA CHESS 1* 12 14

[1] Murray Head with the Trinidad Singers

'Superstar' was one of four tracks on a maxi single, two of which were credited during the disc's one week on the chart. The other track credited was 'I Don't Know How to Love Him' by Yvonne Elliman.

Roy HEAD *US, male vocalist*

4 Nov 65 **TREAT HER RIGHT** *Vocalion V-P 9248* 30 5

The HEADBANGERS *UK, male vocal / instrumental group*

10 Oct 81 **STATUS ROCK** *Magnet MAG 206* 60 3

The HEADBOYS *UK, male vocal / instrumental group*

22 Sep 79 **THE SHAPE OF THINGS TO COME** *RSO 40* 45 8

HEADS *UK, male instrumental group*

21 Jun 86 **AZTEC LIGHTNING (THEME FROM BBC WORLD CUP GRANDSTAND)** *BBC RESL 184* 45 4

HEADS with Shaun RYDER
US / UK, male / female vocal / instrumental group

9 Nov 96 **DON'T TAKE MY KINDNESS FOR WEAKNESS** *Radioactive MCSTD 48024* 60 1

Heads are Talking Heads minus lead singer David Byrne.

4 July 1970	11 July 1970	18 July 1970	25 July 1970
IN THE SUMMERTIME Mungo Jerry	IN THE SUMMERTIME Mungo Jerry	IN THE SUMMERTIME Mungo Jerry	IN THE SUMMERTIME Mungo Jerry
BRIDGE OVER TROUBLED WATER	SELF PORTRAIT	BRIDGE OVER TROUBLED WATER	BRIDGE OVER TROUBLED WATER

KEY: UK No.1 ★★ UK Top 10 ●● Still on chart ++ UK entry at No.1 ■■ US No.1 ▲▲ UK million seller £ US million seller $
Singles re-entries are listed as (re), (2re), (3re)... which signifies that the hit re-entered the chart once, twice or three times...
Peak Position / Weeks

HEADSWIM
UK, male vocal / instrumental group (1 Album: 2 Weeks, 3 Singles: 5 Weeks)

25 Feb 95 **CRAWL** *Epic 6612252* 64 1
14 Feb 98 **TOURNIQUET** *Epic 6650442* 30 3
16 May 98 **BETTER MADE** *Epic 6658402* 42 1
30 May 98 DESPITE YOURSELF *Epic 4877262* 24 2

Jeff HEALEY BAND
Canada, male vocal / instrumental group (4 Albums: 16 Weeks)

14 Jan 89 SEE THE LIGHT *Arista 209441* 58 7
9 Jun 90 HELL TO PAY *Arista 210815* 18 6
28 Nov 92 FEEL THIS *Arista 74321120872* 72 1
18 Mar 95 COVER TO COVER *Arista 74321238882* 50 2

Jeremy HEALY and AMOS (see also HWA featuring SONIC THE HEDGEHOG; HAYSI FANTAYZEE)
UK, male production / vocal duo – Jeremy Healy and Amos Pizzey (2 Singles: 7 Weeks)

12 Oct 96 **STAMP!** *Positiva CDTIV 65* 11 5
31 May 97 **ARGENTINA** *Positiva CDTIV 74* 30 2

HEAR 'N' AID
International, male / female vocal / instrumental charity assembly

19 Apr 86 **STARS** *Vertigo HEAR 1* 26 6

HEAR'SAY (see also Myleene KLASS; Kym MARSH)
UK, female / male vocal group (2 Albums: 32 Weeks, 4 Singles: 60 Weeks)

24 Mar 01 ★ **PURE AND SIMPLE** *Polydor 5870069* ■ £ 1 25
7 Apr 01 ★ POPSTARS *Polydor 5498212* ■ 1 27
7 Jul 01 ★ **THE WAY TO YOUR LOVE (re)** *Polydor 5871482* ■ 1 17
8 Dec 01 ● **EVERYBODY** *Polydor 5705122* 4 11
15 Dec 01 EVERYBODY *Polydor 5895412* 24 5
24 Aug 02 ● **LOVIN' IS EASY (re)** *Polydor 5708542* 6 7

HEART (314 Top 500)
Giants of Stateside AOR who first tasted success in Canada and are regarded as key players on the Seattle music scene. Fronted by Californian-born Wilson sisters Ann (v/g/f), b. 19 Jun 1951, and Nancy (g/v), b. 16 Mar 1954. UK chart career began a full decade after their US debut (9 Albums: 143 Weeks, 12 Singles: 76 Weeks)

22 Jan 77 DREAMBOAT ANNIE *Arista ARTY 139* 36 8
23 Jul 77 LITTLE QUEEN *Portrait PRT 82075* 34 4
19 Jun 82 PRIVATE AUDITION *Epic EPC 85792* 77 2
26 Oct 85 HEART *Capitol EJ 2403721* ▲ 19 43
29 Mar 86 **THESE DREAMS** *Capitol CL 394* ▲ 62 4
6 Jun 87 ● BAD ANIMALS *Capitol ESTU 2032* 7 56
13 Jun 87 ● **ALONE** *Capitol CL 448* ▲ 3 16
19 Sep 87 **WHO WILL YOU RUN TO** *Capitol CL 457* 30 7
12 Dec 87 **THERE'S THE GIRL** *Capitol CL 473* 34 7
5 Mar 88 ● **NEVER / THESE DREAMS** (re-issue) *Capitol CL 482* 8 9
14 May 88 **WHAT ABOUT LOVE** *Capitol CL 487* 14 6
22 Oct 88 **NOTHIN' AT ALL** *Capitol CL 507* 38 3
24 Mar 90 ● **ALL I WANNA DO IS MAKE LOVE TO YOU** *Capitol CL 569* 8 13
14 Apr 90 ● BRIGADE *Capitol ESTU 2121* 3 20
28 Jul 90 **I DIDN'T WANT TO NEED YOU** *Capitol CL 580* 47 3
17 Nov 90 **STRANDED** *Capitol CL 595* 60 2
14 Sep 91 **YOU'RE THE VOICE** *Capitol CLS 624* 56 2
28 Sep 91 ROCK THE HOUSE 'LIVE' *Capitol ESTU 2154* 45 2
20 Nov 93 **WILL YOU BE THERE (IN THE MORNING)** *Capitol CDCLS 700* 19 4
11 Dec 93 DESIRE WALKS ON *Capitol CDEST 2216* 32 2
19 Apr 97 THESE DREAMS – GREATEST HITS *Capitol CDEMC 3765* 33 6

Heart changed label number during its chart run to Capitol LOVE 1.

HEARTBEAT
UK, male / female vocal / instrumental group (2 Singles: 5 Weeks)

24 Oct 87 **TEARS FROM HEAVEN** *Priority P 17* 32 4
23 Apr 88 **THE WINNER** *Priority P 19* 70 1

HEARTBEAT COUNTRY *UK, male vocalist / actor – Bill Maynard*

31 Dec 94 **HEARTBEAT** *MMM MMM 01CD* 75 1

The HEARTBREAKERS (see also TELEVISION)
US, male vocal / instrumental group

5 Nov 77 L.A.M.F. *Track 2409 218* 55 1

The HEARTISTS *Italy, male DJ / production trio (2 Singles: 5 Weeks)*

9 Aug 97 **BELO HORIZONTI** *VC VCRD 23* 42 3
31 Jan 98 **BELO HORIZONTI** (re-mix) *VC VCRD 28* 40 2

HEARTLESS CREW
UK, male DJ / production trio (1 Album: 2 Weeks, 2 Singles: 4 Weeks)

18 May 02 ● HEARTLESS CREW PRESENTS CRISP BISCUIT VOL.1 *East West 927460172* 10 2
25 May 02 **THE HEARTLESS THEME AKA 'THE SUPERGLUE RIDDIM'** *East West HEART 02CD* 21 3
28 Jun 03 **WHY (LOOKING BACK)** *East West HEART 03CD* 50 1

Album appeared on the Compilations Chart only

Ted HEATH and his MUSIC *UK, orchestra – leader b. 30 Mar 1900, d. 18 Nov 1969 (1 Album: 5 Weeks, 9 Singles: 56 Weeks)*

16 Jan 53 **VANESSA** *Decca F 9983* 11 1
3 Jul 53 ● **HOT TODDY** *Decca F 10093* 6 11
23 Oct 53 ● **DRAGNET (4re)** *Decca F 10176* 9 5
12 Feb 54 ● **SKIN DEEP** *Decca F 10246* 9 3
6 Jul 56 **THE FAITHFUL HUSSAR** *Decca F 10746* 18 9
14 Mar 58 ● **SWINGIN' SHEPHERD BLUES** *Decca F 11000* 3 14
11 Apr 58 **TEQUILA** *Decca F 11003* 21 6
4 Jul 58 **TOM HARK** *Decca F 11025* 24 2
5 Oct 61 **SUCU SUCU (re)** *Decca F 11392* 36 5
21 Apr 62 BIG BAND PERCUSSION *Decca PFM 24004* 17 5

HEATWAVE *UK / US, male vocal (Johnnie Wilder) / instrumental group (4 Albums: 27 Weeks, 9 Singles: 80 Weeks)*

22 Jan 77 ● **BOOGIE NIGHTS** *GTO GT 77* $ 2 14
7 May 77 **TOO HOT TO HANDLE / SLIP YOUR DISC TO THIS** *GTO GT 91* 15 11
11 Jun 77 TOO HOT TO HANDLE *GTO GTLP 013* 46 2
14 Jan 78 **THE GROOVE LINE** *GTO GT 115* $ 12 8
6 May 78 CENTRAL HEATING *GTO GTLP 027* 26 15
3 Jun 78 **MIND BLOWING DECISIONS** *GTO GT 226* 12 11
4 Nov 78 ● **ALWAYS AND FOREVER / MIND BLOWING DECISIONS** (re-mix) *GTO GT 236* $ 9 14
26 May 79 **RAZZLE DAZZLE** *GTO GT 248* 43 5
17 Jan 81 **GANGSTERS OF THE GROOVE** *GTO GT 285* 19 8
14 Feb 81 CANDLES *GTO GTLP 047* 29 9
21 Mar 81 **JITTERBUGGIN'** *GTO GT 290* 34 7
1 Sep 90 **MIND BLOWING DECISIONS** (re-recording) *Brothers Organisation HW 1* 65 2
23 Feb 91 GANGSTERS OF THE GROOVE – 90'S MIX *Telstar STAR 2434* 56 1

HEAVEN 17 (320 Top 500) (see also HONEYROOT)
Politically astute electronic pop trio from Sheffield, UK: Martyn Ware (k), Ian Craig Marsh (k) (both previously in Human League) and Glenn Gregory (v). Act, named after a fictional band in cult film A Clockwork Orange, reunited and played their first ever gigs in 1997 (6 Albums: 128 Weeks, 14 Singles: 87 Weeks)

21 Mar 81 **(WE DON'T NEED THIS) FASCIST GROOVE THANG** *Virgin VS 400* 45 5
5 Sep 81 **PLAY TO WIN** *Virgin VS 433* 46 7
26 Sep 81 PENTHOUSE AND PAVEMENT *Virgin V 2208* 14 76

1 August 1970	8 August 1970	15 August 1970	22 August 1970
UK No.1 SINGLES			
THE WONDER OF YOU Elvis Presley	THE WONDER OF YOU Elvis Presley	THE WONDER OF YOU Elvis Presley	THE WONDER OF YOU Elvis Presley
UK No.1 ALBUMS			
BRIDGE OVER TROUBLED WATER Simon and Garfunkel	BRIDGE OVER TROUBLED WATER Simon and Garfunkel	BRIDGE OVER TROUBLED WATER Simon and Garfunkel	A QUESTION OF BALANCE The Moody Blues

14 Nov 81 **PENTHOUSE AND PAVEMENT** *Virgin VS 455* 57 3
30 Oct 82 **LET ME GO** *Virgin VS 532* 41 6
16 Apr 83 ● **TEMPTATION** *Virgin VS 570* 2 13
7 May 83 ● THE LUXURY GAP *Virgin V 2253* 4 36
25 Jun 83 ● **COME LIVE WITH ME** *Virgin VS 607* 5 11
10 Sep 83 **CRUSHED BY THE WHEELS OF INDUSTRY** *Virgin VS 628* 17 7
1 Sep 84 **SUNSET NOW** *Virgin VS 708* 24 6
6 Oct 84 HOW MEN ARE *B.E.F. V 2326* 12 11
27 Oct 84 **THIS IS MINE** *Virgin VS 722* 23 7
19 Jan 85 **... (AND THAT'S NO LIE)** *Virgin VS 740* 52 5
12 Jul 86 ENDLESS *Virgin TCVB / CDV 2383* 70 2
29 Nov 86 PLEASURE ONE *Virgin V 2400* 78 1
17 Jan 87 **TROUBLE** *Virgin VS 920* 51 3
21 Nov 92 ● **TEMPTATION** (re-mix) *Virgin VS 1446* 4 11
27 Feb 93 **(WE DON'T NEED THIS) FASCIST GROOVE THANG** (re-mix) *Virgin VSCDT 1451* 40 2
20 Mar 93 HIGHER AND HIGHER – THE BEST OF HEAVEN 17 *Virgin CDV 2717* 31 2
10 Apr 93 **PENTHOUSE AND PAVEMENT** (re-mix) *Virgin VSCDT 1457* 54 1

Carol Kenyon is the uncredited vocalist on 'Temptation'.

HEAVENS CRY *Holland, male production duo*

6 Oct 01 **TILL TEARS DO US PART (re)** *Tidy Trax 158CD* 68 2

HEAVY D and The BOYZ
Jamaica / US, male rap / vocal group (1 Album: 3 Weeks, 5 Singles: 28 Weeks)

6 Dec 86 **MR BIG STUFF** *MCA MCA 1106* 61 8
15 Jul 89 **WE GOT OUR OWN THANG** *MCA MCA 23942* 69 2
6 Jul 91 ● **NOW THAT WE FOUND LOVE** *MCA MCS 1550* 2 12
10 Aug 91 PEACEFUL JOURNEY *MCA MCA 10289* 40 3
28 Sep 91 **IS IT GOOD TO YOU** *MCA MCS 1564* 46 3
8 Oct 94 **THIS IS YOUR NIGHT** *MCA MCSTD 2010* 30 3

HEAVY PETTIN'
UK, male vocal / instrumental group (2 Albums: 4 Weeks, 1 Single: 2 Weeks)

29 Oct 83 LETTIN' LOOSE *Polydor HEPLP 1* 55 2
17 Mar 84 **LOVE TIMES LOVE** *Polydor HEP 3* 69 2
13 Jul 85 ROCK AIN'T DEAD *Polydor HEPLP 2* 81 2

HEAVY STEREO *UK, male vocal / instrumental group (4 Singles: 4 Weeks)*

22 Jul 95 **SLEEP FREAK** *Creation CRESCD 203* 46 1
28 Oct 95 **SMILER** *Creation CRESCD 213* 46 1
10 Feb 96 **CHINESE BURN** *Creation CRESCD 218* 45 1
24 Aug 96 **MOUSE IN A HOLE** *Creation CRESCD 230* 53 1

HEAVY WEATHER *US, male vocalist – Peter Lee*

29 Jun 96 **LOVE CAN'T TURN AROUND** *Pukka CDPUKKA 6* 56 1

Bobby HEBB *US, male vocalist (2 Singles: 15 Weeks)*

8 Sep 66 **SUNNY** *Philips BF 1503* $ 12 9
19 Aug 72 **LOVE LOVE LOVE** *Philips 6051 023* 32 6

Sharlene HECTOR with the NEW INSPIRATIONAL CHOIR
UK, female vocalist and choir

17 Apr 04 **I WISH I KNEW HOW IT WOULD FEEL TO BE FREE** *Radar RAD 006CD* 28 4

HED BOYS (see also AKABU featuring Linda CLIFFORD; BAMBOO; IL PADRINOS featuring Jocelyn BROWN; JAKATTA; Li KWAN; Joey NEGRO; PHASE II; RAVEN MAIZE; Z FACTOR) *UK, male instrumental / production duo – Dave Lee and Andrew Livingstone (2 Singles: 6 Weeks)*

6 Aug 94 **GIRLS + BOYS** *Deconstruction 74321223322* 21 4
4 Nov 95 **GIRLS + BOYS** (re-mix) *Deconstruction 74321322032* 36 2

(HED) PLANET EARTH *US, male rap / vocal / instrumental group*

2 Sep 00 BROKE *Music for Nations CDMFN 262* 73 1

HEDGEHOPPERS ANONYMOUS *UK, male vocal / instrumental group*

30 Sep 65 ● **IT'S GOOD NEWS WEEK** *Decca F 12241* 5 12

HEFNER *UK, male vocal / instrumental group (3 Singles: 3 Weeks)*

26 Aug 00 **GOOD FRUIT** *Too Pure PURE 108CDS* 50 1
14 Oct 00 **THE GREEDY UGLY PEOPLE** *Too Pure PURE 111CDS* 64 1
8 Sep 01 **ALAN BEAN** *Too Pure PURE 118CDS* 58 1

Neal HEFTI *US, male orchestra*

9 Apr 88 **BATMAN THEME** *RCA PB 49571* 55 4

Den HEGARTY (see also The DARTS) *UK, male vocalist*

31 Mar 79 **VOODOO VOODOO** *Magnet MAG 143* 73 2

HEINZ (see also The TORNADOS) *UK (b. Germany), male vocalist – Heinz Burt, b. 24 Jul 1942, d. 7 Apr 2000 (5 Singles: 35 Weeks)*

8 Aug 63 ● **JUST LIKE EDDIE** *Decca F 11693* 5 15
28 Nov 63 **COUNTRY BOY** *Decca F 11768* 26 9
27 Feb 64 **YOU WERE THERE** *Decca F 11831* 26 8
15 Oct 64 **QUESTIONS I CAN'T ANSWER** *Columbia DB 7374* 39 2
18 Mar 65 **DIGGIN' MY POTATOES** *Columbia DB 7482* [1] 49 1

[1] Heinz and The Wild Boys

HELICOPTER (see also MUTINY UK) *UK, male instrumental / production duo – Dylan Barnes and Rob Davy (2 Singles: 4 Weeks)*

27 Aug 94 **ON YA WAY** *Helicopter TIG 007CD* 32 2
22 Jun 96 **ON YA WAY** (re-mix) *Systematic SYSCD 27* 37 2

HELIOCENTRIC WORLD *UK, male / female vocal / instrumental group*

14 Jan 95 **WHERE'S YOUR LOVE BEEN** *Talkin Loud TLKCD 51* 71 2

HELIOTROPIC featuring Verna V
UK, male production duo – Nick Hale and Gez Dewar and female vocalist

16 Oct 99 **ALIVE** *Multiply CDMULTY 52* 33 2

HELL IS FOR HEROES (see also SYMPOSIUM)
UK, male vocal / instrumental group (1 Album: 2 Weeks, 8 Singles: 10 Weeks)

9 Feb 02 **YOU DROVE ME TO IT** *Wishakismo CDWISH 003* 63 1
17 Aug 02 **I CAN CLIMB MOUNTAINS** *Chrysalis CDCHS 5143* 41 2
2 Nov 02 **NIGHT VISION** *Chrysalis CDCHSS 5147* 38 1
1 Feb 03 **YOU DROVE ME TO IT** (re-issue) *EMI CDCHSS 5149* 28 2
15 Feb 03 THE NEON HANDSHAKE *EMI 5409232* 16 2
17 May 03 **RETREAT** *EMI CDEMS 619* 39 1
28 Aug 04 **ONE OF US** *Captains of Industry CAPT 008* 71 1
27 Nov 04 **KAMICHI** *Factotum TUM 001CD* 72 1
12 Mar 05 **MODELS FOR THE PROGRAMME** *Factotum TUM 002CD2* 56 1

Pete HELLER
(see also HELLER & FARLEY PROJECT) *UK, male DJ / producer*

15 May 99 **BIG LOVE** *Essential Recordings ESCD 4* 12 7

HELLER & FARLEY PROJECT
(see also FIRE ISLAND; STYLUS TROUBLE) *UK, male instrumental / production duo – Pete Heller and Terry Farley (2 Singles: 7 Weeks)*

24 Feb 96 **ULTRA FLAVA** *AM:PM 5814372* 22 3
28 Dec 96 **ULTRA FLAVA** (re-mix) *AM:PM 5820552* 32 4

HELLO
UK, male vocal (Bob Bradbury) / instrumental group (2 Singles: 21 Weeks)

9 Nov 74 ● **TELL HIM** *Bell 1377* 6 12
18 Oct 75 ● **NEW YORK GROOVE** *Bell 1438* 9 9

29 August 1970	5 September 1970	12 September 1970	19 September 1970
THE WONDER OF YOU Elvis Presley	**THE WONDER OF YOU** Elvis Presley	**THE TEARS OF A CLOWN** Smokey Robinson and The Miracles	**BAND OF GOLD** Freda Payne
A QUESTION OF BALANCE The Moody Blues	**A QUESTION OF BALANCE** The Moody Blues	**COSMO'S FACTORY** Creedence Clearwater Revival	**GET YER YA-YA'S OUT!** The Rolling Stones

KEY
UK No.1 ★ UK Top 10 ● Still on chart + UK entry at No.1 ■
US No.1 ▲ UK million seller £ US million seller $
Singles re-entries are listed as (re), (2re), (3re)... which signifies that the hit re-entered the chart once, twice or three times...
Peak Position / Weeks

HELLOWEEN
US, male vocal / instrumental group (3 Albums: 9 Weeks, 3 Singles: 7 Weeks)

27 Aug 88 **DR STEIN** *Noise International 7HELLO 1* 57 3
17 Sep 88 KEEPER OF THE SEVEN KEYS PART 2 *Noise International NUK 117* 24 5
12 Nov 88 **I WANT OUT** *Noise International 7HELLO 2* 69 2
15 Apr 89 LIVE IN THE UK *EMI EMC 3558* 26 2
2 Mar 91 **KIDS OF THE CENTURY** *EMI EM 178* 56 2
23 Mar 91 PINK BUBBLES GO APE *EMI EMC 3588* 41 2

HELMET *US, male vocal / instrumental group*

2 Jul 94 BETTY *Interscope 6544924042* 38 1

Bobby HELMS
US, male vocalist, b. 15 Aug 1935, d. 19 Jul 1997 (3 Singles: 7 Weeks)

29 Nov 57 **MY SPECIAL ANGEL** *Brunswick 05721* [1] $ 22 3
21 Feb 58 **NO OTHER BABY** *Brunswick 05730* 30 1
1 Aug 58 **JACQUELINE** *Brunswick 05748* [1] 20 3

[1] Bobby Helms with the Anita Kerr Singers

Jimmy HELMS (see also LONDONBEAT) *US, male vocalist*

24 Feb 73 ● **GONNA MAKE YOU AN OFFER YOU CAN'T REFUSE** *Cube BUG 27* 8 10

HELTAH SKELTAH and ORIGINOO GUNN CLAPPAZ as the FABULOUS FIVE *US, male rap / vocal / production group*

1 Jun 96 **BLAH** *Priority PTYCD 117* 60 1

Ainslie HENDERSON *UK, male vocalist*

8 Mar 03 ● **KEEP ME A SECRET** (re) *Mercury 0779812* 5 7

Eddie HENDERSON *US, male trumpet player*

28 Oct 78 **PRANCE ON** *Capitol CL 16015* 44 6

Joe 'Mr Piano' HENDERSON
UK, male pianist, b. 2 May 1920, d. 4 May 1980 (5 Singles: 23 Weeks)

3 Jun 55 **SING IT WITH JOE** *Polygon P 1167* 14 4
2 Sep 55 **SING IT AGAIN WITH JOE** *Polygon P 1184* 18 3
25 Jul 58 **TRUDIE** (re) *Pye Nixa N 15147* 14 14
23 Oct 59 **TREBLE CHANCE** *Pye 7N 15224* 28 1
24 Mar 60 **OOH! LA! LA!** *Pye 7N 15257* 44 1

First two hits are medleys as follows: Sing It with Joe: Margie / I'm Nobody's Sweetheart / Somebody Stole My Gal / Moonlight Bay / By the Light of the Silvery Moon / Cuddle Up a Little Closer. Sing It Again with Joe: Put Your Arms Around Me Honey / Ain't She Sweet / When You're Smiling / Shine on Harvest Moon / My Blue Heaven / Show Me the Way to Go Home.

Billy HENDRIX
(see also THREE 'N ONE) *Germany, male producer – Sharam Khososi*

12 Sep 98 **THE BODY SHINE (EP)** *Hooj Choons HOOJ 65CD* 55 2

Tracks on The Body Shine (EP): The Body Shine / Funky Shine / Colour Systems (Inc's Amber Dub) / Timewriter (re-mix).

The Jimi HENDRIX EXPERIENCE 145 Top 500
Guitar ace and hugely influential 20th-century icon, b. Johnny Allen Hendrix (renamed James Marshall Hendrix), 27 Nov 1942, Seattle, US, d. 18 Sep 1970, London. After being 'discovered' and then managed by Animals' bassist Chas Chandler, the left-handed guitarist and vocalist formed The Jimi Hendrix Experience, featuring Mitch Mitchell (d) and Noel Redding (b). His timeless appeal consistently generates annual global sales of about three million albums. He was added to the UK Music Hall of Fame in 2005 (29 Albums: 275 Weeks, 11 Singles: 88 Weeks)

29 Dec 66 ● **HEY JOE** *Polydor 56 139* 6 11
23 Mar 67 ● **PURPLE HAZE** *Track 604 001* 3 14
11 May 67 ● **THE WIND CRIES MARY** *Track 604 004* 6 11
27 May 67 ● ARE YOU EXPERIENCED *Track 612001* [1] 2 33
30 Aug 67 **BURNING OF THE MIDNIGHT LAMP** *Track 604 007* 18 9
16 Dec 67 ● AXIS: BOLD AS LOVE *Track 613003* [1] 5 16
27 Apr 68 ● SMASH HITS *Track 613004* [1] 4 25
18 May 68 GET THAT FEELING *London HA 8349* [2] 39 2
23 Oct 68 ● **ALL ALONG THE WATCHTOWER** *Track 604 025* 5 11
16 Nov 68 ● ELECTRIC LADYLAND *Track 613008/9* [1] ▲ 6 12
16 Apr 69 **CROSSTOWN TRAFFIC** *Track 604 029* 37 3
4 Jul 70 ● BAND OF GYPSIES *Track 2406001* 6 22
7 Nov 70 ★ **VOODOO CHILE** *Track 2095 001* 1 13
3 Apr 71 ● THE CRY OF LOVE *Track 2408101* 2 14
28 Aug 71 ● EXPERIENCE *Ember NR 5057* 9 6
30 Oct 71 **GYPSY EYES / REMEMBER** *Track 2094 010* 35 5
20 Nov 71 JIMI HENDRIX AT THE ISLE OF WIGHT *Track 2302 016* 17 2
4 Dec 71 RAINBOW BRIDGE *Reprise K 44159* 16 8
5 Feb 72 ● HENDRIX IN THE WEST *Polydor 2302 018* 7 14
12 Feb 72 **JOHNNY B GOODE** *Polydor 2001 277* [1] 35 5
11 Nov 72 WAR HEROES *Polydor 2302 020* 23 3
21 Jul 73 SOUNDTRACK RECORDINGS FROM THE FILM 'JIMI HENDRIX' *Warner Bros. K 64017* 37 1
29 Mar 75 JIMI HENDRIX *Polydor 2343 080* 35 4
30 Aug 75 CRASH LANDING *Polydor 2310 398* 35 3
29 Nov 75 MIDNIGHT LIGHTNING *Polydor 2310 415* 46 1
14 Aug 82 THE JIMI HENDRIX CONCERTS *CBS 88592* 16 11
19 Feb 83 THE SINGLES ALBUM *Polydor PODV 6* 77 4
11 Mar 89 RADIO ONE *Castle Collectors CCSLP 212* 30 6
21 Apr 90 **CROSSTOWN TRAFFIC** (re-issue) *Polydor PO 71* [1] 61 3
20 Oct 90 **ALL ALONG THE WATCHTOWER (EP)** *Polydor PO 100* [1] 52 3
3 Nov 90 ● CORNERSTONES 1967-1970 *Polydor 8472311* 5 16
14 Nov 92 THE ULTIMATE EXPERIENCE *PolyGram TV 5172352* 25 26
30 Apr 94 ● BLUES *Polydor 5210372* 10 3
13 Aug 94 WOODSTOCK *Polydor 5233842* 32 3
10 May 97 FIRST RAYS OF THE NEW RISING SUN *MCA MCD 11599* 37 2
2 Aug 97 ELECTRIC LADYLAND (re-issue) *MCA MCD 11600* 47 1
13 Sep 97 EXPERIENCE HENDRIX – THE BEST OF JIMI HENDRIX *Telstar TV TTVCD 2930* 18 15
13 Jun 98 BBC SESSIONS *MCA MCD 11742* [1] 42 2
23 Sep 00 ● EXPERIENCE HENDRIX – THE BEST OF JIMI HENDRIX *Universal TV 1123832* 10 7
20 Jul 02 ● VOODOO CHILD – THE JIMI HENDRIX COLLECTION *UMTV 1703222* 10 13

[1] Jimi Hendrix [1] The Jimi Hendrix Experience [2] Jimi Hendrix and Curtis Knight

Tracks on All Along the Watchtower (EP): All Along the Watchtower / Voodoo Chile / Hey Joe (re-issues). Experience Hendrix – The Best of Jimi Hendrix (2000) had a different track listing to the 1997 album of the same name and was repackaged with a bonus disc.

Nona HENDRYX (see also LaBELLE) *US, female vocalist*

16 May 87 **WHY SHOULD I CRY** *EMI America EA 234* 60 2

Don HENLEY (see also EAGLES)
US, male vocalist / drummer (3 Albums: 30 Weeks, 5 Singles: 30 Weeks)

12 Feb 83 **DIRTY LAUNDRY** *Asylum E 9894* $ 59 3
9 Feb 85 **THE BOYS OF SUMMER** *Geffen A 4945* 12 10
9 Mar 85 BUILDING THE PERFECT BEAST *Geffen GEF 25939* 14 11
8 Jul 89 THE END OF THE INNOCENCE *Geffen WX 253* 17 16
29 Jul 89 **THE END OF THE INNOCENCE** *Geffen GEF 57* 48 5
3 Oct 92 **SOMETIMES LOVE JUST AIN'T ENOUGH** *MCA MCS 1692* [1] 22 6
18 Jul 98 **BOYS OF SUMMER** (re-issue) *Geffen GFSTD 22350* 12 6
3 Jun 00 INSIDE JOB *Warner Bros. 9362470832* 25 3

[1] Patty Smyth with Don Henley

	26 September 1970	3 October 1970	10 October 1970	17 October 1970
UK No.1 SINGLES	BAND OF GOLD Freda Payne	BAND OF GOLD Freda Payne	BAND OF GOLD Freda Payne	BAND OF GOLD Freda Payne
UK No.1 ALBUMS	GET YER YA-YA'S OUT! The Rolling Stones	BRIDGE OVER TROUBLED WATER Simon and Garfunkel	PARANOID Black Sabbath	BRIDGE OVER TROUBLED WATER Simon and Garfunkel

Cassius HENRY *UK, male vocalist (2 Singles: 3 Weeks)*

30 Mar 02 **BROKE** *Blacklist 0130265 ERE*....31 2
3 Jul 04 **THE ONE** *Universal MCSTD 40334* [1] 56 1

[1] Cassius Henry featuring Freeway

Clarence 'Frogman' HENRY
US, male vocalist / keyboard player (4 Singles: 35 Weeks)

4 May 61 ● **BUT I DO** *Pye International 7N 25078*....3 19
13 Jul 61 ● **YOU ALWAYS HURT THE ONE YOU LOVE** *Pye International 7N 25089*....6 12
21 Sep 61 **LONELY STREET / WHY CAN'T YOU** *Pye International 7N 25108*....42 2
17 Jul 93 **(I DON'T KNOW WHY) BUT I DO** (re-issue) *MCA MCSTD 1797*....65 2

Pauline HENRY (see also The CHIMES)
UK, female vocalist (1 Album: 1 Week, 8 Singles: 21 Weeks)

18 Sep 93 **TOO MANY PEOPLE** *Sony S2 6595942*....38 2
6 Nov 93 **FEEL LIKE MAKING LOVE** *Sony S2 6597972*....12 7
29 Jan 94 **CAN'T TAKE YOUR LOVE** *Sony S2 6599902*....30 3
19 Feb 94 **PAULINE** *Sony S2 4747442*....45 1
21 May 94 **WATCH THE MIRACLE START** *Sony S2 6602772*....54 1
30 Sep 95 **SUGAR FREE** *Sony S2 6624362*....57 2
23 Dec 95 **LOVE HANGOVER** *Sony S2 6626132*....37 3
24 Feb 96 **NEVER KNEW LOVE LIKE THIS** *Sony S2 6629382* [1] 40 2
1 Jun 96 **HAPPY** *Sony S2 6630692*....46 1

[1] Pauline Henry featuring Wayne Marshall

Pierre HENRY *France, male composer / instrumentalist*

4 Oct 97 **PSYCHE ROCK** *Hi-Life 4620312*....58 1

Paul HENRY and the Mayson GLEN ORCHESTRA
UK, male actor / vocalist and orchestra

14 Jan 78 **BENNY'S THEME** *Pye 7N 46027*....39 2

HEPBURN *UK, female vocal (Jamie Benson) / instrumental group (1 Album: 2 Weeks, 3 Singles: 15 Weeks)*

29 May 99 ● **I QUIT** *Columbia 6674012*....8 7
28 Aug 99 **BUGS** *Columbia 6677382*....14 5
11 Sep 99 **HEPBURN** *Columbia 4948352*....28 2
19 Feb 00 **DEEP DEEP DOWN** *Columbia 6683382*....16 3

Band and Chorus of HER MAJESTY'S GUARDS DIVISION
UK, military band

22 Nov 75 **30 SMASH HITS OF THE WAR YEARS** *Warwick WW 5006*....38 4

HERBALISER
UK, male DJ / production duo – Jake Wherry and Ollie 'Teeba' Trattles

30 Mar 02 **SOMETHING WICKED THIS WAY COMES** *Ninja Tune ZENCD 64*....71 1

The HERD *UK, male vocal (Peter Frampton) / instrumental group (1 Album: 1 Week, 3 Singles: 35 Weeks)*

13 Sep 67 ● **FROM THE UNDERWORLD** *Fontana TF 856*....6 13
20 Dec 67 **PARADISE LOST** *Fontana TF 887*....15 9
24 Feb 68 **PARADISE LOST** *Fontana STL 5458*....38 1
10 Apr 68 ● **I DON'T WANT OUR LOVING TO DIE** *Fontana TF 925*....5 13

HERD & FITZ featuring Abigail BAILEY NEW
UK, male production duo – Jason Herd and Jon Fitz and female vocalist

17 Dec 05 **I JUST CAN'T GET ENOUGH** *All Around the World CDGLOBE 473*....11 3+

HERMAN'S HERMITS 308 Top 500
Manchester quintet fronted by teenage vocalist Peter Noone, b. 5 Nov 1947, whose US popularity in the mid-1960s rivalled The Beatles. This band sold more than 40 million records and at times had three singles simultaneously in the US Top 20. Peter was the youngest UK vocalist to top the US singles chart (3 Albums: 11 Weeks, 20 Singles: 211 Weeks)

20 Aug 64 ★ **I'M INTO SOMETHING GOOD** *Columbia DB 7338*....1 15
19 Nov 64 **SHOW ME GIRL** *Columbia DB 7408*....19 9
18 Feb 65 ● **SILHOUETTES** *Columbia DB 7475*....3 12
29 Apr 65 ● **WONDERFUL WORLD** *Columbia DB 7546*....7 9
2 Sep 65 **JUST A LITTLE BIT BETTER** *Columbia DB 7670*....15 9
18 Sep 65 **HERMAN'S HERMITS** *Columbia 33SX 1727*....16 2
23 Dec 65 ● **A MUST TO AVOID** *Columbia DB 7791*....6 11
24 Mar 66 **YOU WON'T BE LEAVING** *Columbia DB 7861*....20 7
23 Jun 66 **THIS DOOR SWINGS BOTH WAYS** *Columbia DB 7947*....18 7
6 Oct 66 ● **NO MILK TODAY** *Columbia DB 8012*....7 11
1 Dec 66 **EAST WEST** *Columbia DB 8076*....33 7
9 Feb 67 ● **THERE'S A KIND OF HUSH** *Columbia DB 8123* $....7 11
17 Jan 68 **I CAN TAKE OR LEAVE YOUR LOVING** *Columbia DB 8327*....11 9
1 May 68 **SLEEPY JOE** *Columbia DB 8404*....12 10
17 Jul 68 ● **SUNSHINE GIRL** *Columbia DB 8446*....8 14
18 Dec 68 ● **SOMETHING'S HAPPENING** *Columbia DB 8504*....6 15
23 Apr 69 ● **MY SENTIMENTAL FRIEND** *Columbia DB 8563*....2 12
8 Nov 69 **HERE COMES THE STAR** *Columbia DB 8626*....33 9
7 Feb 70 ● **YEARS MAY COME, YEARS MAY GO (re)** *Columbia DB 8656*....7 12
23 May 70 **BET YER LIFE I DO** *RAK 102*....22 10
14 Nov 70 **LADY BARBARA** *RAK 106* [1] 13 12
25 Sep 71 **THE MOST OF HERMAN'S HERMITS** *MFP 5216*....14 5
8 Oct 77 **GREATEST HITS** *K-Tel NE 1001*....37 4

[1] Peter Noone and Herman's Hermits

HERMES HOUSE BAND
Holland, male / female vocal / instrumental group (3 Singles: 14 Weeks)

15 Dec 01 ● **COUNTRY ROADS** *EMI / Liberty CDHHB 001*....7 12
13 Apr 02 **QUE SERA SERA** *EMI / Liberty CDHHB 002*....53 1
28 Dec 02 **LIVE IS LIFE** *EMI / Liberty CDLIVE 001* [1] 50 1

[1] Hermes House Band and DJ Otzi

HERNANDEZ *UK, male vocalist*

15 Apr 89 **ALL MY LOVE** *Epic HER 1*....58 3

Patrick HERNANDEZ *Guadeloupe, male vocalist*

16 Jun 79 ● **BORN TO BE ALIVE** *Gem GEM 4* $....10 14

The HERREYS *Sweden, male vocal group*

26 May 84 **DIGGI LOO-DIGGI LEY** *Panther PAN 5*....46 3

Kristin HERSH (see also THROWING MUSES)
US, female vocalist (2 Albums: 5 Weeks, 2 Singles: 3 Weeks)

22 Jan 94 **YOUR GHOST** *4AD BAD 4001CD*....45 2
5 Feb 94 ● **HIPS AND MAKERS** *4AD CAD 4002CD*....7 4
16 Apr 94 **STRINGS** *4AD BAD 4006CD*....60 1
14 Feb 98 **STRANGE ANGELS** *4AD CAD 8003CD*....64 1

Nick HEYWARD (see also HAIRCUT 100)
UK, male vocalist (1 Album: 13 Weeks, 13 Singles: 65 Weeks)

19 Mar 83 **WHISTLE DOWN THE WIND** *Arista HEY 1*....13 8
4 Jun 83 **TAKE THAT SITUATION** *Arista HEY 2*....11 10
24 Sep 83 **BLUE HAT FOR A BLUE DAY** *Arista HEY 3*....14 8
29 Oct 83 ● **NORTH OF A MIRACLE** *Arista NORTH 1*....10 13
3 Dec 83 **ON A SUNDAY** *Arista HEY 4*....52 5
2 Jun 84 **LOVE ALL DAY** *Arista HEY 5*....31 6
3 Nov 84 **WARNING SIGN (re)** *Arista HEY 6*....25 9
8 Jun 85 **LAURA** *Arista HEY 8*....45 4
10 May 86 **OVER THE WEEKEND** *Arista HEY 9*....43 5

24 October 1970	31 October 1970	7 November 1970	14 November 1970
BAND OF GOLD Freda Payne	**WOODSTOCK** Matthews' Southern Comfort	**WOODSTOCK** Matthews' Southern Comfort	**WOODSTOCK** Matthews' Southern Comfort
ATOM HEART MOTHER Pink Floyd	**MOTOWN CHARTBUSTERS VOL.4** Various	**LED ZEPPELIN III** Led Zeppelin	**LED ZEPPELIN III** Led Zeppelin

KEY UK No.1 ★ UK Top 10 ● Still on chart + UK entry at No.1 ■ US No.1 ▲ UK million seller £ US million seller $ Singles re-entries are listed as (re), (2re), (3re)... which signifies that the hit re-entered the chart once, twice or three times... — Peak Position / Weeks

10 Sep 88	**YOU'RE MY WORLD** *Warner Bros. W 7758*	67	2
21 Aug 93	**KITE** *Epic 6594882*	44	2
16 Oct 93	**HE DOESN'T LOVE YOU LIKE I DO** *Epic 6597282*	58	2
30 Sep 95	**THE WORLD** *Epic 6623845*	47	2
13 Jan 96	**ROLLERBLADE** *Epic 6627912*	37	2

HI-FIVE *US, male vocal group (2 Singles: 8 Weeks)*

1 Jun 91	**I LIKE THE WAY (THE KISSING GAME)** *Jive JIVE 271* ▲	43	6
24 Oct 92	**SHE'S PLAYING HARD TO GET** *Jive JIVE 316*	55	2

HI-GATE
(see also The CANDY GIRLS; CLERGY; DOROTHY; Paul MASTERSON presents SUSHI; PRECOCIOUS BRATS featuring KEVIN and PERRY; SLEAZESISTERS; STIX 'N' STONED; YOMANDA) *UK, male production duo – Julius (Judge Jules) O'Riordan and Paul Masterson (3 Singles: 14 Weeks)*

29 Jan 00 ●	**PITCHIN' (IN EVERY DIRECTION)** *Incentive CENT 3CD*	6	6
26 Aug 00	**I CAN HEAR VOICES / CANED AND UNABLE** *Incentive CENT 9CDS*	12	5
7 Apr 01	**GONNA WORK IT OUT** *Incentive CENT 20CDS*	25	3

HI GLOSS *US, disco aggregation*

8 Aug 81	**YOU'LL NEVER KNOW** *Epic EPC A 1387*	12	13

HI JACK *US, male vocal group*

19 Oct 91	**THE HORNS OF JERICHO** *Warner Bros. 7599263861*	54	1

HI-LUX *UK, male instrumental / production duo (2 Singles: 3 Weeks)*

18 Feb 95	**FEEL IT** *Cheeky CHEKCD 006*	41	2
2 Sep 95	**NEVER FELT THIS WAY / FEEL IT** (re-issue) *Champion CHAMPCD 319*	58	1

HI POWER *Germany, male rap group*

1 Sep 90	**CULT OF SNAP / SIMBA GROOVE** *Rumour RUMAT 24*	73	1

HI-TEK featuring JONELL *US, male producer – Tony Cottrell*

20 Oct 01	**ROUND & ROUND** *Rawkus RWK 3432*	73	1

HI-TEK 3 featuring YA KID K (see also TECHNOTRONIC)
Belgium, male / female vocal / instrumental group (2 Singles: 10 Weeks)

3 Feb 90	**SPIN THAT WHEEL** *Brothers Organisation BORG 1*	69	3
29 Sep 90	**SPIN THAT WHEEL (TURTLES GET REAL)** (re-issue) *Brothers Organisation BORG 16*	15	7

HI TENSION *UK, male vocal (David Joseph) / instrumental group (1 Album: 4 Weeks, 2 Singles: 23 Weeks)*

6 May 78	**HI TENSION** *Island WIP 6422*	13	12
12 Aug 78 ●	**BRITISH HUSTLE / PEACE ON EARTH** *Island WIP 6446*	8	11
6 Jan 79	HI TENSION *Island ILPS 9564*	74	4

'Peace on Earth' credited with 'British Hustle' from 2 Sep 1978 to the end of its chart run.

John HIATT *US, male vocalist (3 Albums: 3 Weeks)*

7 Jul 90	STOLEN MOMENTS *A&M 3953101*	72	1
11 Sep 93	PERFECTLY GOOD GUITAR *A&M 5401302*	67	1
11 Nov 95	WALK ON *Capitol CDP 8334162*	74	1

Al HIBBLER *US, male vocalist, b. 16 Aug 1915, d. 24 Apr 2001*

13 May 55 ●	**UNCHAINED MELODY** *Brunswick 05420* $	2	17

Hinda HICKS *UK, female vocalist (1 Album: 4 Weeks, 5 Singles: 15 Weeks)*

7 Mar 98	**IF YOU WANT ME** *Island CID 689*	25	3
16 May 98	**YOU THINK YOU OWN ME** *Island CID 700*	19	4
15 Aug 98	**I WANNA BE YOUR LADY** *Island CID 709*	14	5
29 Aug 98	HINDA *Island CID 8068*	20	4
24 Oct 98	**TRULY** *Island CID 721*	31	2
14 Oct 00	**MY REMEDY** *Island CID 765*	61	1

The HIDDEN CAMERAS *Canada, male vocal collective*

14 Jun 03	**A MIRACLE** *Rough Trade RTRADSCD 105*	70	1

Bertie HIGGINS *US, male vocalist*

5 Jun 82	**KEY LARGO** *Epic EPC A 2168*	60	4

HIGH *UK, male vocal group (1 Album: 2 Weeks, 4 Singles: 11 Weeks)*

25 Aug 90	**UP AND DOWN** *London LON 272*	53	4
27 Oct 90	**TAKE YOUR TIME** *London LON 280*	56	2
17 Nov 90	SOMEWHERE SOON *London 8282241*	59	2
12 Jan 91	**BOX SET GO** *London LONG 286*	28	3
6 Apr 91	**MORE ...** *London LON 297*	67	2

HIGH CONTRAST
UK, male producer – Lincoln Barrett (4 Singles: 4 Weeks)

1 Jun 02	**GLOBAL LOVE** *Hospital NHS 44CD*	68	1
9 Aug 03	**BASEMENT TRACK** *Hospital NHS 60*	65	1
26 Jun 04	**TWILIGHTS LAST GLEAMING / MADE IT LAST** *Hospital NHS 73*	74	1
18 Sep 04	**RACING GREEN** *Hospital CSSN 029*	73	1

HIGH FIDELITY *UK, male vocal / instrumental group*

25 Jul 98	**LUV DUP** *Plastique FAKE 03CDS*	70	1

The HIGH LLAMAS *UK, male vocal / instrumental group*

6 Apr 96	HAWAII *Alpaca CDWOOL 2*	62	1

The HIGH NUMBERS *UK, male vocal / instrumental group*

5 Apr 80	**I'M THE FACE** *Back Door DOOR 4*	49	4

The High Numbers were an early version of The Who.

HIGH SOCIETY *UK, male vocal / instrumental group*

15 Nov 80	**I NEVER GO OUT IN THE RAIN** *Eagle ERS 002*	53	4

HIGHLY LIKELY *UK, male vocal / instrumental group*

21 Apr 73	**WHATEVER HAPPENED TO YOU ('LIKELY LADS' THEME)** *BBC RESL 10*	35	4

The HIGHWAYMEN *US, male vocal group (2 Singles: 18 Weeks)*

7 Sep 61 ★	**MICHAEL** *HMV POP 910* ▲ $	1	14
7 Dec 61	**THE GYPSY ROVER (re)** *HMV POP 948*	41	4

HIJACK *UK, male rap group*

6 Jan 90	**THE BADMAN IS ROBBIN'** *Rhyme Syndicate 655517 7*	56	3

Benny HILL *UK, male comedian / vocalist – Alfred Hill, b. 21 Jan 1924, d. 20 Apr 1992 (1 Album: 8 Weeks, 5 Singles: 43 Weeks)*

16 Feb 61	**GATHER IN THE MUSHROOMS** *Pye 7N 15327*	12	8
1 Jun 61	**TRANSISTOR RADIO** *Pye 7N 15359*	24	6
16 May 63	**HARVEST OF LOVE** *Pye 7N 15520*	20	8
13 Nov 71 ★	**ERNIE (THE FASTEST MILKMAN IN THE WEST)** *Columbia DB 8833*	1	17
11 Dec 71 ●	WORDS AND MUSIC *Columbia SCX 6479*	9	8
30 May 92	**ERNIE (THE FASTEST MILKMAN IN THE WEST)** (re-issue) *EMI ERN 1*	29	4

	21 November 1970	28 November 1970	5 December 1970	12 December 1970
UK No.1 SINGLES	VOODOO CHILE – The Jimi Hendrix Experience	I HEAR YOU KNOCKING – Dave Edmunds' Rockpile	I HEAR YOU KNOCKING – Dave Edmunds' Rockpile	I HEAR YOU KNOCKING – Dave Edmunds' Rockpile
UK No.1 ALBUMS	LED ZEPPELIN III – Led Zeppelin	NEW MORNING – Bob Dylan	GREATEST HITS – Andy Williams	LED ZEPPELIN III – Led Zeppelin

Chris HILL *UK, male vocalist / DJ / producer (2 Singles: 14 Weeks)*

6 Dec 75 ● **RENTA SANTA** *Philips 6006 491* **10** 7
4 Dec 76 ● **BIONIC SANTA** *Philips 6006 551* **10** 7

Dan HILL *Canada, male vocalist*

18 Feb 78 **SOMETIMES WHEN WE TOUCH (re)** *20th Century BTC 2355* $ .. **13** 13

Faith HILL
US, female vocalist – Audrey Hill (3 Albums: 29 Weeks, 7 Singles: 34 Weeks)

14 Nov 98 **THIS KISS** *Warner Bros. W 463CD* $ **13** 11
17 Apr 99 **LET ME LET GO** *Warner Bros. W 473CD* **72** 1
20 May 00 **BREATHE** *WEA WEA 520CD* **33** 2
3 Jun 00 **BREATHE** *Warner Bros. 9362473732* ▲ 19 16
21 Apr 01 **THE WAY YOU LOVE ME** *Warner Bros. W 51CD* **15** 5
30 Jun 01 ● **THERE YOU'LL BE** *Warner Bros. W 563CD* **3** 11
13 Oct 01 **BREATHE** (re-mix) *Warner Bros. W 572CD* **36** 2
27 Oct 01 ● **THERE YOU'LL BE** *Warner Bros. 9362482402* 6 11
26 Oct 02 **CRY** *Warner Bros. W 593CD* **25** 2
9 Nov 02 **CRY** *Warner Bros. 9362483682* ▲ 29 2

Lauryn HILL (see also FUGEES)
US, female vocalist (2 Albums: 74 Weeks, 6 Singles: 35 Weeks)

6 Sep 97 **THE SWEETEST THING** *Columbia 6649785* [1] **18** 4
27 Dec 97 **ALL MY TIME** *World Entertainment OWECD 2* [2] **57** 1
3 Oct 98 ● **DOO WOP (THAT THING)** *Ruffhouse 6665152* ▲ **3** 7
10 Oct 98 ● **THE MISEDUCATION OF LAURYN HILL** *Columbia 4898432* ▲ .. 2 72
27 Feb 99 ● **EX-FACTOR (re)** *Columbia / Ruffhouse 6669452* **4** 10
10 Jul 99 **EVERYTHING IS EVERYTHING**
Columbia / Ruffhouse 6675742 ..... **19** 6
11 Dec 99 **TURN YOUR LIGHTS DOWN LOW** *Columbia 6684362* [3] **15** 7
18 May 02 **MTV UNPLUGGED 2.0** *Columbia 5080032* 40 2

[1] Refugee Camp Allstars featuring Lauryn Hill [2] Paid & Live featuring Lauryn Hill [3] Bob Marley featuring Lauryn Hill

Lonnie HILL *US, male vocalist*

22 Mar 86 **GALVESTON BAY** *10 TEN 111* **51** 4

Roni HILL *US, female vocalist*

7 May 77 **YOU KEEP ME HANGIN' ON – STOP IN THE NAME OF LOVE (MEDLEY)** *Creole CR 138* **36** 4

Vince HILL *UK, male vocalist (2 Albums: 10 Weeks, 11 Singles: 91 Weeks)*

7 Jun 62 **THE RIVER'S RUN DRY (re)** *Piccadilly 7N 35043* **41** 2
6 Jan 66 **TAKE ME TO YOUR HEART AGAIN** *Columbia DB 7781* **13** 11
17 Mar 66 **HEARTACHES** *Columbia DB 7852* **28** 5
2 Jun 66 **MERCI CHERI** *Columbia DB 7924* **36** 6
9 Feb 67 ● **EDELWEISS** *Columbia DB 8127* **2** 17
11 May 67 **ROSES OF PICARDY** *Columbia DB 8185* **13** 11
20 May 67 **EDELWEISS** *Columbia SCX 6141* 23 9
27 Sep 67 **LOVE LETTERS IN THE SAND** *Columbia DB 8268* **23** 9
26 Jun 68 **THE IMPORTANCE OF YOUR LOVE** *Columbia DB 8414* **32** 12
12 Feb 69 **DOESN'T ANYBODY KNOW MY NAME?** *Columbia DB 8515* **50** 1
25 Oct 69 **LITTLE BLUE BIRD** *Columbia DB 8616* **42** 1
25 Sep 71 **LOOK AROUND (AND YOU'LL FIND ME THERE)**
Columbia DB 8804 ..... **12** 16
29 Apr 78 **THAT LOVING FEELING** *K-Tel NE 1017* 51 1

Steve HILLAGE *UK, male vocalist / guitarist (8 Albums: 40 Weeks)*

3 May 75 **FISH RISING** *Virgin V 2031* 33 3
16 Oct 76 ● **L** *Virgin V 2066* 10 12
22 Oct 77 **MOTIVATION RADIO** *Virgin V 2777* 28 5
29 Apr 78 **GREEN VIRGIN** *Virgin 2098* 30 8
17 Feb 79 **LIVE HERALD** *Virgin VGD 3502* 54 5
5 May 79 **RAINBOW DOME MUSIC** *Virgin VR 1* 48 4
27 Oct 79 **OPEN** *Virgin V 2135* 71 1
5 Mar 83 **FOR TO NEXT** *Virgin V 2244* 48 2

HILLMAN MINX *UK / France, male / female vocal / instrumental group*

5 Sep 98 **I'VE HAD ENOUGH** *Mercury MERCD 509* **72** 1

The HILLTOPPERS *US, male vocal group (3 Singles: 30 Weeks)*

27 Jan 56 ● **ONLY YOU (AND YOU ALONE) (re)** *London HLD 8221* **3** 23
14 Sep 56 **TRYIN'** *London HLD 8298* **30** 1
5 Apr 57 **MARIANNE (re)** *London HLD 8381* **20** 6

Ronnie HILTON *UK, male vocalist – Adrian Hill, b. 26 Jan 1926, d. 21 Feb 2001 (18 Singles: 136 Weeks)*

26 Nov 54 ● **I STILL BELIEVE** *HMV B 10785* **3** 14
10 Dec 54 **VENI VIDI VICI** *HMV B 10785* **12** 8
11 Mar 55 ● **A BLOSSOM FELL** *HMV B 10808* **10** 5
26 Aug 55 **STARS SHINE IN YOUR EYES** *HMV B 10901* **13** 7
11 Nov 55 **THE YELLOW ROSE OF TEXAS** *HMV B 10924* **15** 2
10 Feb 56 **YOUNG AND FOOLISH (2re)** *HMV POP 154* **17** 3
20 Apr 56 ★ **NO OTHER LOVE** *HMV POP 198* **1** 14
29 Jun 56 ● **WHO ARE WE** *HMV POP 221* **6** 12
21 Sep 56 **A WOMAN IN LOVE** *HMV POP 248* **30** 1
9 Nov 56 **TWO DIFFERENT WORLDS** *HMV POP 274* **13** 13
24 May 57 ● **AROUND THE WORLD** *HMV POP 338* **4** 18
2 Aug 57 **WONDERFUL! WONDERFUL!** *HMV POP 364* **27** 2
21 Feb 58 **MAGIC MOMENTS** *HMV POP 446* **22** 2
18 Apr 58 **I MAY NEVER PASS THIS WAY AGAIN (2re)** *HMV POP 468* [1] **27** 3
9 Jan 59 **THE WORLD OUTSIDE** *HMV POP 559* [1] **18** 6
21 Aug 59 **THE WONDER OF YOU** *HMV POP 638* **22** 3
21 May 64 **DON'T LET THE RAIN COME DOWN** *HMV POP 1291* **21** 10
11 Feb 65 **A WINDMILL IN OLD AMSTERDAM** *HMV POP 1378* **23** 13

[1] Ronnie Hilton with The Michael Sammes Singers

HINDSIGHT *UK, male vocal / instrumental group*

5 Sep 87 **LOWDOWN** *Circa YR 5* **62** 3

Deni HINES *Australia, female vocalist (4 Singles: 6 Weeks)*

14 Jun 97 **IT'S ALRIGHT** *Mushroom D 1593* **35** 2
20 Sep 97 **I LIKE THE WAY** *Mushroom MUSH 7CDX* **37** 2
28 Feb 98 **DELICIOUS** *Mushroom MUSH 20CD* [1] **52** 1
23 May 98 **JOY** *Mushroom MUSH 30CDS* **47** 1

[1] Deni Hines featuring Don-E

HIPSWAY
UK, male vocal / instrumental group (1 Album: 23 Weeks, 6 Singles: 21 Weeks)

13 Jul 85 **THE BROKEN YEARS** *Mercury MER 193* **72** 3
14 Sep 85 **ASK THE LORD** *Mercury MER 195* **72** 1
22 Feb 86 **THE HONEYTHIEF** *Mercury MER 212* **17** 9
19 Apr 86 **HIPSWAY** *Mercury MERH 85* 42 23
10 May 86 **ASK THE LORD** (re-recording) *Mercury LORD 1* **50** 5
20 Sep 86 **LONG WHITE CAR** *Mercury MER 230* **55** 2
1 Apr 89 **YOUR LOVE** *Mercury MER 279* **66** 1

David HIRSCHFELDER *Australia, male composer*

8 Feb 97 **SHINE (FILM SOUNDTRACK)** *Philips 4547102* 46 9

The HISS *US, male vocal / instrumental group (3 Singles: 3 Weeks)*

1 Mar 03 **TRIUMPH** *Loog / Polydor 0657782* **53** 1
9 Aug 03 **CLEVER KICKS** *Polydor 9809465* **49** 1
15 Nov 03 **BACK ON THE RADIO** *Polydor 9813415* **65** 1

HISTORY featuring Q-TEE *UK, male production duo and female rapper*

21 Apr 90 **AFRIKA** *SBK SBK 7008* **42** 5

Carol HITCHCOCK *Australia, female vocalist*

30 May 87 **GET READY** *A&M AM 391* **56** 5

19 December 1970	26 December 1970	2 January 1971	9 January 1971
I HEAR YOU KNOCKING Dave Edmunds' Rockpile	I HEAR YOU KNOCKING Dave Edmunds' Rockpile	I HEAR YOU KNOCKING Dave Edmunds' Rockpile	GRANDAD Clive Dunn
GREATEST HITS Andy Williams	GREATEST HITS Andy Williams	GREATEST HITS Andy Williams	GREATEST HITS Andy Williams

KEY: UK No.1 ★ UK Top 10 ● Still on chart + UK entry at No.1 ■ US No.1 ▲ UK million seller £ US million seller $
Singles re-entries are listed as (re), (2re), (3re)... which signifies that the hit re-entered the chart once, twice or three times...
Peak Position / Weeks

HITHOUSE *Holland, male producer – Peter Slaghuis, b. 21 Aug 1961, d. 5 Sep 1991 (2 Singles: 13 Weeks)*

5 Nov 88 JACK TO THE SOUND OF THE UNDERGROUND *Supreme SUPE 137* 14 12
19 Aug 89 MOVE YOUR FEET TO THE RHYTHM OF THE BEAT *Supreme SUPE 149* 69 1

The HIVES *Sweden, male vocal / instrumental group (2 Albums: 37 Weeks, 4 Singles: 15 Weeks)*

12 Jan 02 ● YOUR NEW FAVOURITE BAND *Poptones MC 5055CD* 7 30
23 Feb 02 HATE TO SAY I TOLD YOU SO *Burning Heart BHR 1059* 23 3
18 May 02 MAIN OFFENDER *Poptones MC 5076SCD* 24 2
17 Jul 04 WALK IDIOT WALK *Polydor 9867038* 13 9
31 Jul 04 ● TYRANNOSAURUS HIVES *Polydor 9866991* 7 7
30 Oct 04 TWO-TIMING TOUCH AND BROKEN BONES *Polydor 9868351* 44 1

Edmund HOCKRIDGE *Canada, male vocalist (3 Singles: 18 Weeks)*

17 Feb 56 ● YOUNG AND FOOLISH (2re) *Nixa N 15039* 10 9
11 May 56 NO OTHER LOVE (2re) *Nixa N 15048* 24 4
31 Aug 56 BY THE FOUNTAINS OF ROME *Pye Nixa N 15063* 17 5

Eddie HODGES *US, male vocalist (2 Singles: 10 Weeks)*

28 Sep 61 I'M GONNA KNOCK ON YOUR DOOR *London HLA 9369* 37 6
9 Aug 62 (GIRLS GIRLS GIRLS) MADE TO LOVE *London HLA 9576* 37 4

Roger HODGSON (see also SUPERTRAMP) *UK, male vocalist / bassist*

20 Oct 84 IN THE EYE OF THE STORM *A&M AMA 5004* 70 4

Gerard HOFFNUNG *UK (b. Germany), male comedian / musician, b. 1925, d. 28 Sep 1959*

3 Sep 60 ● AT THE OXFORD UNION *Decca LF 1330* 4 20

Susanna HOFFS (see also The BANGLES) *US, female vocalist (1 Album: 2 Weeks, 3 Singles: 8 Weeks)*

2 Mar 91 MY SIDE OF THE BED *Columbia 6565547* 44 4
6 Apr 91 WHEN YOU'RE A BOY *Columbia 4672021* 56 2
11 May 91 UNCONDITIONAL LOVE *Columbia 6567827* 65 2
19 Oct 96 ALL I WANT *London LONCD 387* 32 2

Hulk HOGAN with GREEN JELLY *US, male wrestler / vocalist – Terry Bollea and vocal / instrumental group*

25 Dec 93 I'M THE LEADER OF THE GANG *Arista 74321174892* 25 4

HOGGBOY *UK, male vocal / instrumental group*

27 Apr 02 SHOULDN'T LET THE SIDE DOWN *Sobriety SOB 4CDA* 74 1

Demi HOLBORN *UK, female vocalist*

27 Jul 02 I'D LIKE TO TEACH THE WORLD TO SING *Universal Classics & Jazz 0190982* 27 2

HOLDEN & THOMPSON *UK, male producer – James Holden and female vocalist – Julie Thompson*

17 May 03 NOTHING *Loaded LOAD 98CD* 51 1

HOLE *US / Canada, female / male vocal / instrumental group – leader Courtney Love (3 Albums: 10 Weeks, 7 Singles: 15 Weeks)*

12 Oct 91 PRETTY ON THE INSIDE *City Slang E 04071* 59 1
17 Apr 93 BEAUTIFUL SON *City Slang EFA 0491603* 54 1
9 Apr 94 MISS WORLD *City Slang EFA 049362* 64 1
23 Apr 94 LIVE THROUGH THIS *City Slang EFA 049352* 13 5
15 Apr 95 DOLL PARTS *Geffen GFSTD 91* 16 3
29 Jul 95 VIOLET *Geffen GFSTD 94* 17 2
12 Sep 98 CELEBRITY SKIN *Geffen GFSTD 22345* 19 4
19 Sep 98 CELEBRITY SKIN *Geffen GED 25164* 11 4
30 Jan 99 MALIBU *Geffen GFSTD 22369* 22 2
10 Jul 99 AWFUL *Geffen INTDE 97098* 42 2

HOLE IN ONE *Holland, male DJ / producer – Marcel Hol*

15 Feb 97 LIFE'S TOO SHORT *Manifesto FESCD 21* 36 2

Billie HOLIDAY *US, female vocalist – Eleanor Fagan Gough, b. 7 Apr 1915, d. 17 Jul 1959 (2 Albums: 11 Weeks)*

16 Nov 85 THE LEGEND OF BILLIE HOLIDAY *MCA BHTV 1* 60 10
6 Sep 97 LADY DAY – THE VERY BEST OF BILLIE HOLIDAY *Sony TV / Universal MOODCD 52* 63 1

HOLIDAY PLAN *UK, male vocal / instrumental group*

26 Jun 04 STORIES / SUNSHINE *Island CID 858* 58 1

Jools HOLLAND and his RHYTHM & BLUES ORCHESTRA (see also SQUEEZE) *UK, male vocalist / pianist and orchestra (8 Albums: 84 Weeks, 1 Single: 3 Weeks)*

5 May 90 WORLD OF HIS OWN *IRS EIRSA 1018* [1] 71 1
26 Oct 96 SEX & JAZZ & ROCK & ROLL *Coliseum HF 51CD* 38 2
25 Oct 97 LIFT THE LID *Coalition 3984205252* 50 1
24 Feb 01 I'M IN THE MOOD FOR LOVE *Warner.esp WSMS 001CD* [1] 29 3
1 Dec 01 ● SMALL WORLD BIG BAND *WSM 927426562* [2] 8 37
30 Nov 02 SMALL WORLD BIG BAND 2 – MORE FRIENDS *WSM 0927494192* 17 14
29 Nov 03 SMALL WORLD BIG BAND FRIENDS 3 – JACK O THE GREEN *Radar RADAR 001CD* 39 9
9 Oct 04 ● TOM JONES & JOOLS HOLLAND *Radar 004CD* [3] 5 13
19 Nov 05 SWINGING THE BLUES DANCING THE SKA *Radar RADAR 006CD* 36 7+

[1] Jools Holland and Jamiroquai [1] Jools Holland [2] Jools Holland and his Rhythm & Blues Orchestra and Friends [3] Tom Jones & Jools Holland

HOLLAND-DOZIER featuring Lamont DOZIER *US, male vocal duo*

28 Oct 72 WHY CAN'T WE BE LOVERS *Invictus INV 525* 29 5

Jennifer HOLLIDAY *US, female vocalist*

4 Sep 82 AND I'M TELLING YOU I'M NOT GOING *Geffen GEF A 2644* 32 6

Michael HOLLIDAY *UK, male vocalist – Norman Milne, b. 26 Nov 1925, d. 29 Oct 1963 (10 Singles: 66 Weeks)*

30 Mar 56 NOTHIN' TO DO (re) *Columbia DB 3746* 20 3
15 Jun 56 HOT DIGGITY (DOG ZIGGITY BOOM) / THE GAL WITH THE YALLER SHOES (2re) *Columbia DB 3783* 13 11
5 Oct 56 TEN THOUSAND MILES *Columbia DB 3813* 24 3
17 Jan 58 ★ THE STORY OF MY LIFE *Columbia DB 4058* 1 15
14 Mar 58 IN LOVE *Columbia DB 4087* 26 3
16 May 58 ● STAIRWAY OF LOVE *Columbia DB 4121* 3 13
11 Jul 58 I'LL ALWAYS BE IN LOVE WITH YOU *Columbia DB 4155* 27 1
1 Jan 60 ★ STARRY EYED *Columbia DB 4378* 1 13
14 Apr 60 SKYLARK *Columbia DB 4437* 39 3
1 Sep 60 LITTLE BOY LOST *Columbia DB 4475* 50 1

When 'Hot Diggity (Dog Ziggity Boom)' / 'The Gal with the Yaller Shoes' re-entered the chart on 3 Aug 1956, 'Hot Diggity (Dog Ziggity Boom)' was listed by itself on 3 Aug and 10 Aug. Both sides were listed on 17 Aug – 'The Gal with the Yaller Shoes' peaking at No.25. 'Starry Eyed' is with the Michael Sammes Singers.

16 January 1971	23 January 1971	30 January 1971	6 February 1971
UK No.1 SINGLES			
GRANDAD Clive Dunn	GRANDAD Clive Dunn	MY SWEET LORD George Harrison	MY SWEET LORD George Harrison
UK No.1 ALBUMS			
BRIDGE OVER TROUBLED WATER Simon and Garfunkel	BRIDGE OVER TROUBLED WATER Simon and Garfunkel	BRIDGE OVER TROUBLED WATER Simon and Garfunkel	ALL THINGS MUST PASS George Harrison

The HOLLIES 89 Top 500

(see also CROSBY, STILLS, NASH and YOUNG) *Distinctive, influential and well-respected Manchester group: Allan Clarke (v), Graham Nash (g), Tony Hicks (g), Eric Haydock (b), Bobby Elliott (d). They were among the most regular chart visitors of the 1960s, and their No.1s span 23 years. Total single sales: 4,597,450 (14 Albums: 154 Weeks, 32 Singles: 318 Weeks)*

30 May 63 **(AIN'T THAT) JUST LIKE ME** *Parlophone R 5030* **25** 10
29 Aug 63 **SEARCHIN'** *Parlophone R 5052* **12** 14
21 Nov 63 ● **STAY** *Parlophone R 5077* **8** 16
15 Feb 64 ● STAY WITH THE HOLLIES *Parlophone PMC 1220* 2 25
27 Feb 64 ● **JUST ONE LOOK** *Parlophone R 5104* **2** 13
21 May 64 ● **HERE I GO AGAIN** *Parlophone R 5137* **4** 12
17 Sep 64 ● **WE'RE THROUGH** *Parlophone R 5178* **7** 11
28 Jan 65 ● **YES I WILL** *Parlophone R 5232* **9** 13
27 May 65 ★ **I'M ALIVE** *Parlophone R 5287* **1** 14
2 Sep 65 ● **LOOK THROUGH ANY WINDOW** *Parlophone R 5322* **4** 11
2 Oct 65 ● HOLLIES *Parlophone PMC 1261* 8 14
9 Dec 65 **IF I NEEDED SOMEONE** *Parlophone R 5392* **20** 9
24 Feb 66 ● **I CAN'T LET GO** *Parlophone R 5409* **2** 10
23 Jun 66 ● **BUS STOP** *Parlophone R 5469* **5** 9
16 Jul 66 WOULD YOU BELIEVE? *Parlophone PMC 7008* 16 8
13 Oct 66 ● **STOP STOP STOP** *Parlophone R 5508* **2** 12
17 Dec 66 FOR CERTAIN BECAUSE *Parlophone PCS 17011* 12 7
16 Feb 67 ● **ON A CAROUSEL** *Parlophone R 5562* **4** 11
1 Jun 67 ● **CARRIE-ANNE** *Parlophone R 5602* **3** 11
17 Jun 67 EVOLUTION *Parlophone PCS 7022* 13 10
27 Sep 67 **KING MIDAS IN REVERSE** *Parlophone R 5637* **18** 8
27 Mar 68 ● **JENNIFER ECCLES** *Parlophone R 5680* **7** 11
17 Aug 68 ★ THE HOLLIES' GREATEST HITS *Parlophone PCS 7057* 1 27
2 Oct 68 **LISTEN TO ME** *Parlophone R 5733* **11** 11
5 Mar 69 ● **SORRY SUZANNE** *Parlophone R 5765* **3** 12
17 May 69 ● HOLLIES SING DYLAN *Parlophone PCS 7078* 3 7
4 Oct 69 ● **HE AIN'T HEAVY, HE'S MY BROTHER** *Parlophone R 5806* **3** 15
18 Apr 70 ● **I CAN'T TELL THE BOTTOM FROM THE TOP** *Parlophone R 5837* **7** 10
3 Oct 70 **GASOLINE ALLEY BRED** *Parlophone R 5862* **14** 7
28 Nov 70 CONFESSIONS OF THE MIND *Parlophone PCS 7117* 30 5
22 May 71 **HEY WILLY** *Parlophone R 5905* **22** 7
26 Feb 72 **THE BABY** *Polydor 2058 199* **26** 6
2 Sep 72 **LONG COOL WOMAN IN A BLACK DRESS** *Parlophone R 5939* **$** **32** 8
13 Oct 73 **THE DAY THAT CURLY BILLY SHOT DOWN CRAZY SAM MCGHEE** *Polydor 2058 403* **24** 6
9 Feb 74 ● **THE AIR THAT I BREATHE** *Polydor 2058 435* **$** **2** 13
16 Mar 74 HOLLIES *Polydor 2383 262* 38 3
19 Mar 77 ● HOLLIES LIVE HITS *Polydor 2383 428* 4 12
22 Jul 78 ● 20 GOLDEN GREATS *EMI EMTV 11* 2 20
14 Jun 80 **SOLDIER'S SONG** *Polydor 2059 246* **58** 3
29 Aug 81 **HOLLIEDAZE (A MEDLEY)** *EMI 5229* **28** 7
3 Sep 88 ★ **HE AIN'T HEAVY, HE'S MY BROTHER** (re-issue) *EMI EM 74* **1** 11
1 Oct 88 ALL THE HITS AND MORE *EMI EM 1301* 51 5
3 Dec 88 **THE AIR THAT I BREATHE** (re-issue) *EMI EM 80* **60** 5
20 Mar 93 **THE WOMAN I LOVE** *EMI CDEM 264* **42** 2
3 Apr 93 THE AIR THAT I BREATHE – THE BEST OF THE HOLLIES *EMI CDEMTV 74* 15 7
5 Apr 03 GREATEST HITS *EMI 5820122* 21 4

The 1972 hit 'The Baby' featured Swedish lead vocalist Mikael Rickfors. 'Holliedaze (A Medley)' comprised: Just One Look / Here I Go Again / I'm Alive / I Can't Let Go / Long Cool Woman In A Black Dress / Bus Stop / Carrie-Anne. The two Hollies albums are different.

Mark HOLLIS *UK, male vocalist / instrumentalist*

14 Feb 98 MARK HOLLIS *Polydor 5376882* 53 1

Loleatta HOLLOWAY *US, female vocalist (7 Singles: 21 Weeks)*

31 Aug 91 **GOOD VIBRATIONS** *Interscope A 8764* [1] ▲ **14** 7
18 Jan 92 **TAKE ME AWAY** *PWL Continental PWL 210* [2] **25** 5
26 Mar 94 **STAND UP** *Six6 SIXCD 111* **68** 1
1 Apr 95 **KEEP THE FIRE BURNIN'** *Columbia 6611552* [3] **49** 1
11 Apr 98 **SHOUT TO THE TOP** *JBO JNR 5001573* [4] **23** 2
20 Feb 99 **(YOU GOT ME) BURNING UP** *Wonderboy WBOYD 013* [5] **14** 4
25 Nov 00 **DREAMIN'** *Defected DFECT 22CDS* **59** 1

[1] Marky Mark and the Funky Bunch featuring Loleatta Holloway [2] Cappella featuring Loleatta Holloway [3] Dan Hartman starring Loleatta Holloway [4] Fire Island featuring Loleatta Holloway [5] Cevin Fisher / Loleatta Holloway

HOLLOWAY & CO *UK, male producer – Nicky Holloway*

21 Aug 99 **I'LL DO ANYTHING – TO MAKE YOU MINE** *INCredible INCS 2CD* **58** 1

Buddy HOLLY 73 Top 500

Highly respected and exceptionally influential singer / songwriter, b. Charles Hardin Holley, 7 Sep 1936, Texas, US, d. 3 Feb 1959 (aka 'the day the music died'). Despite a relatively brief career, his records and songs are still frequently heard around the globe (16 Albums: 339 Weeks, 23 Singles: 190 Weeks)

6 Dec 57 ● **PEGGY SUE** *Coral Q 72293* **$** **6** 17
14 Mar 58 **LISTEN TO ME** *Coral Q 72288* **16** 2
20 Jun 58 ● **RAVE ON** *Coral Q 72325* **5** 14
29 Aug 58 **EARLY IN THE MORNING** *Coral Q 72333* **17** 4
16 Jan 59 **HEARTBEAT** *Coral Q 72346* **30** 1
27 Feb 59 ★ **IT DOESN'T MATTER ANYMORE** *Coral Q 72360* **1** 21
2 May 59 ● THE BUDDY HOLLY STORY *Coral LVA 9105* 2 156
31 Jul 59 **MIDNIGHT SHIFT** *Brunswick 05800* **26** 3
11 Sep 59 **PEGGY SUE GOT MARRIED** *Coral Q 72376* **13** 10
28 Apr 60 **HEARTBEAT** (re-issue) *Coral Q 72392* **30** 3
26 May 60 **TRUE LOVE WAYS** *Coral Q 72397* **25** 7
15 Oct 60 ● THE BUDDY HOLLY STORY VOLUME 2 *Coral LVA 9127* 7 14
20 Oct 60 **LEARNING THE GAME** *Coral Q 72411* **36** 3
26 Jan 61 **WHAT TO DO** *Coral Q 72419* **34** 6
6 Jul 61 **BABY I DON'T CARE / VALLEY OF TEARS** *Coral Q 72432* **12** 14
21 Oct 61 ● THAT'LL BE THE DAY *Ace of Hearts AH 3* 5 14
15 Mar 62 **LISTEN TO ME** (re-issue) *Coral Q 72449* **48** 1
13 Sep 62 **REMINISCING** *Coral Q 72455* **17** 11
14 Mar 63 ● **BROWN-EYED HANDSOME MAN** *Coral Q 72459* **3** 17
6 Apr 63 ● REMINISCING *Coral LVA 9212* 2 31
6 Jun 63 ● **BO DIDDLEY** *Coral Q 72463* **4** 12
5 Sep 63 ● **WISHING** *Coral Q 72466* **10** 11
19 Dec 63 **WHAT TO DO** (re-recording) *Coral Q 72469* **27** 8
14 May 64 **YOU'VE GOT LOVE** *Coral Q 72472* [1] **40** 6
13 Jun 64 ● BUDDY HOLLY SHOWCASE *Coral LVA 9222* 3 16
10 Sep 64 **LOVE'S MADE A FOOL OF YOU** *Coral Q 72475* **39** 6
26 Jun 65 HOLLY IN THE HILLS *Coral LVA 9227* 13 6
15 Jul 67 ● BUDDY HOLLY'S GREATEST HITS *Ace of Hearts AH 148* 9 40
3 Apr 68 **PEGGY SUE** (re-issue) **/ RAVE ON** *MCA MU 1012* **32** 9
12 Apr 69 GIANT *MCA MUPS 371* 13 1
21 Aug 71 BUDDY HOLLY'S GREATEST HITS (re-issue) *Coral CP 8* 32 6
12 Jul 75 BUDDY HOLLY'S GREATEST HITS (2nd re-issue) *Coral CDLM 8007* 42 3
11 Mar 78 ★ 20 GOLDEN GREATS *MCA EMTV 8* [1] 1 20
8 Sep 84 BUDDY HOLLY'S GREATEST HITS (3rd re-issue) *MCA MCL 1618* 100 1
10 Dec 88 **TRUE LOVE WAYS** (re-issue) *MCA MCA 1302* **65** 4
18 Feb 89 ● TRUE LOVE WAYS *Telstar STAR 2339* 8 11
20 Feb 93 ★ WORDS OF LOVE *PolyGram TV 5144872* [1] ■ 1 9
7 Dec 96 THE VERY BEST OF BUDDY HOLLY *Dino DINCD 133* 24 8
28 Aug 99 THE VERY BEST OF BUDDY HOLLY AND THE CRICKETS *Universal Music TV 1120462* [1] 25 3

[1] Buddy Holly and The Crickets [1] Buddy Holly and The Crickets

Buddy Holly's version of 'Love's Made a Fool of You' is not the same version as The Crickets' hit of 1959, on which Holly did not appear. 'Valley of Tears' was not listed together with 'Baby I Don't Care' until 13 Jul 1961.

HOLLY and The IVYS *UK, male / female vocal / instrumental group*

19 Dec 81 **CHRISTMAS ON 45** *Decca SANTA 1* **40** 4

The HOLLYWOOD ARGYLES *US, male vocal group*

21 Jul 60 **ALLEY-OOP** *London HLU 9146* ▲ **$** **24** 10

13 February 1971	20 February 1971	27 February 1971	6 March 1971
MY SWEET LORD George Harrison	**MY SWEET LORD** George Harrison	**MY SWEET LORD** George Harrison	**BABY JUMP** Mungo Jerry
ALL THINGS MUST PASS George Harrison	**ALL THINGS MUST PASS** George Harrison	**ALL THINGS MUST PASS** George Harrison	**ALL THINGS MUST PASS** George Harrison

ANNIVERSARY OF

December 2006 marks the 30th anniversary of the first punk hit single, 'Anarchy in the UK' by the Sex Pistols. Forgetting the fact that "punk" and "hit singles" might be contradictory terms, the story behind the arrival of this controversial chart entry and the subsequent firing of the band by EMI makes for a fascinating rollercoaster read. The Pistols signed to EMI Limited's Records Division in October 1976 when Brian Southall was head of the EMI Records' domestic Group Repertoire Division (GRD) press office. Here he recounts what went on during the three months when the establishment and the anti-establishment met head on … and how it all ended in a flurry of corporate outrage over the antics – both true and false – of Johnny Rotten and his cohorts.

In April 1976 the music press first alerted us to the Sex Pistols. NME dubbed them "a quartet of spiky teenage misfits from the wrong end of various London streets" and, as the coverage increased, so record companies began to take notice of the phenomenon that was dubbed punk. In the months leading up to a deal, EMIR's A&R people enthusiastically trailed the Pistols and even offered an early demo record to interested parties around the company – me included. I recall it was a version of 'Pretty Vacant' and, to my mind, it wasn't very good. But long-haired, vaguely professional 30-years-olds brought up on The Beatles, Stones and Motown weren't exactly the target audience. It never really registered that it would be good for the company. I was reminded of the fact by the person who told me it was all about the kids and not boring old farts like me. After all, in the mid 1970s, EMIR was famous for still having The Beatles and Cliff alongside the likes of Queen, Pink Floyd and Paul McCartney. New talent was pretty thin on the ground – it said something when The Wurzels were among the company's newest chart acts.

EMI PAYS A 'BARGAIN' £40,000 FOR THE PISTOLS

The fact that we could get the Pistols for just £40,000 (spread over two years and for two albums) meant that we could perhaps achieve both credibility and commerciality at a bargain price. Beating off competition from Polydor, Chrysalis and RAK, the deal committing the Pistols to EMI – home to brain scanners, electronics, bingo halls and cinemas – was completed on 8 October 1976. Having secured the Pistols – and astounded the media who assumed that EMI would be too stuffy and too establishment for the likes of manager Malcolm McLaren, Johnny Rotten, Glen Matlock, Steve Jones and Paul Cook – the next question was what to do with them. We used a variety of labels for our acts and we had to decide whether the Pistols should go on EMI (Cliff and Queen), Parlophone (Beatles and McCartney) or Harvest (Floyd and Roy Harper). We plumped for Harvest. It was already home to a bunch of oddball acts but the band announced they weren't going on a label which was full of "hippie shit". They were happy to be part of Harvest, but the Pistols wanted their records to have the same EMI label as releases by the likes of Cilla and Cliff.

At this early stage dealings were confined to those directly involved in the release of the first Pistols single but debates over which track, and which version of which track, delayed things for weeks. 'Pretty Vacant' and 'Anarchy in the UK' were the contenders and the band got their way with 'Anarchy'. But which version to use? Recordings by Dave Goodman, Mike Thorne or Chris Thomas? Again, McLaren and the band won the day with Thomas's recording of 'Anarchy in the UK' set for release on the EMI label (EMI 2566) on 26 November. However, our plans to make 'Anarchy' the country's first punk single had gone out of the window when it was beaten by The Damned's 'New Rose', but we comforted ourselves with the thought that we could still have the first punk hit. Meanwhile, EMI Limited's corporate officers (and the MD of EMI Records who did not have to approve mere £40,000 signings) remained blissfully unaware of the Pistols. But the release of 'Anarchy' alerted the corporation to its latest acquisition.

Initial concerns about the song's lyrics were overcome, but McLaren's poster for the single – a torn Union Jack held together with paper clips and safety pins – got attention. The company's PR chiefs were annoyed at this treatment of the national flag and we won the day only by pointing out that, as it wasn't our poster and EMI wasn't mentioned anywhere, there wasn't much we could do. On the back of the release of their single, the Pistols planned their 19-date Anarchy in the UK tour. Opening night was set for 3 December at Norwich's University of East Anglia but, two days before, the band made an unforgettable and genuinely life-changing appearance on television.

"DO SOMETHING OUTRAGEOUS"

They were invited on to Thames TV's early evening London programme Today when the Musicians' Union failed to clear the new video for Queen's latest single 'Somebody to Love'. Initially both the band and manager McLaren were against the idea of being interviewed on a local magazine show but eventually agreed, and we sent a limo (complete with champagne) to collect them. Host, veteran journalist/broadcaster Bill Grundy, was assigned to interview the last-minute add-ons. He urged them to say something outrageous and the assembled punks duly responded with a stream of profanities. What followed was absolute pandemonium. The band were headline news; outraged viewers complained in their thousands and Thames TV, which was actually half-owned by EMI, issued a public apology while its controller suspended Grundy for his part in the debacle.

News of the band's behaviour made it up to the sixth floor at EMI's Manchester Square HQ and now the Pistols really were on the

THE FIRST PUNK HIT

corporate agenda. EMI's chairman Sir John Read deputed the MD of EMI Records, Leslie Hill, to go tell manager McLaren and his band exactly how the company expected their acts to behave. The band still had their contract but revolution was in the air. Fellow workers in EMI's defence electronics wrote to the house newspaper deploring the record division's decision to sign the band, while packers at the record factory went on strike and the company's senior executives were fearful of the reaction from politicians, shareholders, investors and the media.

Although within the record business we were championed by rival companies for our bravery in signing and releasing 'Anarchy', radio and TV stations started to ban the single while retailers refused to stock the record and halls and hotels turned the band away. The Pistols' tour was now in disarray as venue after venue was cancelled, and when they finally got to play at Leeds, on 6 December, there was more trouble. Encouraged by reporters desperate for a story to "do something outrageous", the band threw potted plants across a hotel foyer and the Daily Mirror had its story: "Four man punk rock group wreck hotel lobby."

Adding fuel to the fire, the band chose Leeds to perform 'God Save the Queen' and, according to reports, shouted "**** the Queen" during the show. EMI's Read was outraged and summoned Hill to his office. The head of EMIR, sensing further trouble, was quick to reassure his boss that in fact the band had shouted "**** Queen", a reference to their fellow EMI artists.

The corporation's December AGM brought more media attention with coverage of Read's speech condemning the Pistols' behaviour as "disgraceful" and assuring shareholders that the company would "do everything to restrain their public behaviour".

The various relationships between McLaren, EMI Records, EMI Limited and the Sex Pistols were now strained to the limit. McLaren was using the press to question the company's commitment; shareholders and directors wanted the band sacked; we in records – who in mid-December achieved our aim of having the country's first punk hit single – were concerned about being told what to do about one of our acts by our corporate masters.

"AND NOW THE END IS NEAR"

But, as 1977 arrived, it all finally fell apart. The Pistols flew to Amsterdam on 4 January and out of nowhere reports appeared in the UK press that the band had vomited and sworn while at a KLM airline check-in desk. Despite assurances by EMI's man on the spot that absolutely nothing had happened, it was all too much for Read. Having read the reports, and supposedly had the story confirmed by airport execs, he instructed Hill to fly to Amsterdam, meet McLaren and arrange for the band's departure from the company. My own enquiries amongst the press suggested that airport and airline staff had been "persuaded" to agree to a story about the Pistols vomiting and swearing.

Fit up or not, it was good enough to seal the band's fate with the ultra-conservative executives of EMI, who within two days announced a mutual termination of the band's contract. It was formally signed on 17 January and McLaren and the Sex Pistols left EMI with the £20,000 balance of their advance (plus a reported £10,000 from their cancelled EMI Music Publishing contract) and the company's best wishes: "EMI Records wish the Sex Pistols every success with their next recording contract."

For their part the Pistols sacked bass player Matlock, replacing him with Sid Vicious, and signed a deal with A&M Records. The deal concluded in March lasted less than a week when, after damage to the company's offices and an assault in a London club, the Pistols were given anywhere between £40,000 and £75,000 to go away.

By May the band had signed to Virgin Records and Richard Branson – who claimed he had offered to take them off EMI's hands way back in December. There they stayed until, just before Vicious's arrest for murder and his subsequent death, the band went their separate ways after a January 1978 gig in San Francisco.

A book by Brian Southall detailing the full story of EMI and the Sex Pistols is due to be published in late 2006.

KEY: UK No.1 ★ UK Top 10 ● Still on chart + UK entry at No.1 ■ US No.1 ▲ UK million seller £ US million seller $
Singles re-entries are listed as (re), (2re), (3re)... which signifies that the hit re-entered the chart once, twice or three times...
Peak Position / Weeks

HOLLYWOOD BEYOND
UK, male vocal (Mark Rogers) group (2 Singles: 14 Weeks)

12 Jul 86 ● **WHAT'S THE COLOUR OF MONEY?** *WEA YZ 76* **7** 10
20 Sep 86 **NO MORE TEARS** *WEA YZ 81* **47** 4

Eddie HOLMAN *US, male vocalist*

19 Oct 74 ● **(HEY THERE) LONELY GIRL** *ABC 4012* $ **4** 13

Dave HOLMES *UK, male producer*

26 May 01 **DEVOTION** *Tidy Trax TIDY 154CD* **66** 1

David HOLMES *UK, male producer (3 Albums: 5 Weeks, 5 Singles: 8 Weeks)*

22 Jul 95 **THIS FILM'S CRAP LET'S SLASH THE SEATS** *Go Discs 8286312* **51** 1
6 Apr 96 **GONE** *Go Discs GODCD 140* **75** 1
23 Aug 97 **GRITTY SHAKER** *Go Beat GOBCD 2* **53** 1
13 Sep 97 **LET'S GET KILLED** *Go Beat 5391002* **34** 2
10 Jan 98 **DON'T DIE JUST YET** *Go Beat GOLCD 6* **33** 3
4 Apr 98 **MY MATE PAUL** *Go Beat GOBCD 8* **39** 2
24 Jun 00 **BOW DOWN TO THE EXIT SIGN** *Go Beat 5438662* **22** 2
19 Aug 00 **69 POLICE** *Go Beat / Polydor GOBCD 30* **53** 1

Rupert HOLMES *US (b. UK), male vocalist (2 Singles: 14 Weeks)*

12 Jan 80 **ESCAPE (THE PINA COLADA SONG)** *Infinity INF 120* ▲ $ **23** 7
22 Mar 80 **HIM** *MCA 565* **31** 7

John HOLT *Jamaica, male vocalist*

14 Dec 74 ● **HELP ME MAKE IT THROUGH THE NIGHT** *Trojan TR 7909* **6** 14
1 Feb 75 **ONE THOUSAND VOLTS OF HOLT** *Trojan TRLS 75* **42** 2

Nichola HOLT *UK, female vocalist*

21 Oct 00 **THE GAME** *RCA 74321798992* **72** 1

Paul HOLT *UK, male vocalist*

18 Dec 04 **FIFTY GRAND FOR CHRISTMAS** *Sanctuary SANXS 348* **35** 3

HOME *UK, male vocal / instrumental group*

11 Nov 72 **HOME** *CBS 67522* **41** 1

A HOMEBOY, a HIPPIE and a FUNKI DREDD
UK, male vocal / instrumental group (3 Singles: 9 Weeks)

13 Oct 90 **TOTAL CONFUSION** *Tam Tam 7TTT 031* **56** 3
29 Dec 90 **FREEDOM** *Tam Tam 7TTT 039* **68** 4
8 Jan 94 **HERE WE GO AGAIN** *Polydor PZCD 302* **57** 2

HONDY *Italy, male / female production / vocal group*

12 Apr 97 **HONDY (NO ACCESS)** *Manifesto FESCD 20* **26** 2

HONEYBUS *UK, male vocal (Peter Blumson) / instrumental group*

20 Mar 68 ● **I CAN'T LET MAGGIE GO** *Deram DM 182* **8** 12

The HONEYCOMBS *UK, male / female vocal (Dennis Dalziel, d. 2005) / instrumental group (4 Singles: 39 Weeks)*

23 Jul 64 ★ **HAVE I THE RIGHT** *Pye 7N 15664* **1** 15
22 Oct 64 **IS IT BECAUSE** *Pye 7N 15705* **38** 6
29 Apr 65 **SOMETHING BETTER BEGINNING** *Pye 7N 15827* **39** 4
5 Aug 65 **THAT'S THE WAY** *Pye 7N 15890* **12** 14

HONEYCRACK
UK, male vocal / instrumental group (1 Album: 1 Week, 5 Singles: 9 Weeks)

4 Nov 95 **SITTING AT HOME** *Epic 6625382* **42** 2
24 Feb 96 **GO AWAY** *Epic 6628642* **41** 2
11 May 96 **KING OF MISERY** *Epic 6631472* **32** 2
1 Jun 96 **PROZAIC** *Epic 4842302* **34** 1
20 Jul 96 **SITTING AT HOME** (re-issue) *Epic 6635032* **32** 2
16 Nov 96 **ANYWAY** *EG EGO 52A* **67** 1

The HONEYDRIPPERS
(see also Robert PLANT) *UK / US, male vocal / instrumental group*

1 Dec 84 **THE HONEYDRIPPERS VOLUME ONE** *Es Paranza 790220* **56** 10
2 Feb 85 **SEA OF LOVE** *Es Paranza YZ 33* **56** 3

The HONEYMOON MACHINE NEW
UK, male vocal / instrumental group (2 Singles: 2 Weeks)

21 May 05 **INTO YOUR HEAD** *Easy Street EASYST 009CD* **66** 1
22 Oct 05 **FAITH IN PEOPLE** *Easy Street EASYST 011CD* **64** 1

HONEYROOT NEW
(see also HEAVEN 17) *UK, male vocal / instrumental / production duo – Glenn Gregory and Keith Lowndes*

7 May 05 **LOVE WILL TEAR US APART** *Just Music TAOS 003* **70** 1

HONEYZ (see also ANOTHERSIDE)
UK / France, female vocal trio (1 Album: 22 Weeks, 7 Singles: 57 Weeks)

5 Sep 98 ● **FINALLY FOUND** *1st Avenue / Mercury HNZCD 1* **4** 12
5 Dec 98 **WONDER NO.8** *Mercury 5588142* **33** 22
19 Dec 98 ● **END OF THE LINE (re)** *1st Avenue / Mercury HNZCD 2* **5** 14
24 Apr 99 ● **LOVE OF A LIFETIME** *1st Avenue / Mercury HNZCD 3* **9** 9
23 Oct 99 ● **NEVER LET YOU DOWN** *1st Avenue / Mercury HNZCD 4* **7** 6
11 Mar 00 ● **WON'T TAKE IT LYING DOWN (re)** *1st Avenue / Mercury HNZCD 5* **7** 8
28 Oct 00 **NOT EVEN GONNA TRIP (2re)** *1st Avenue / Mercury HNZCD 7* **24** 5
18 Aug 01 **I DON'T KNOW** *1st Avenue / Mercury HNZCD 8* **28** 3

HONKY *UK, male vocal / instrumental group*

28 May 77 **JOIN THE PARTY** *Creole CR 137* **28** 5

HONKY *UK, male vocal / instrumental group (4 Singles: 5 Weeks)*

30 Oct 93 **THE HONKY DOODLE DAY EP** *ZTT ZANG 45CD* **61** 1
19 Feb 94 **THE WHISTLER** *ZTT ZANG 48CD* **41** 2
20 Apr 96 **HIP HOP DON'T YA DROP** *Higher Ground HIGHS 1CD* **70** 1
10 Aug 96 **WHAT'S GOIN DOWN** *Higher Ground HIGHS 2CD* **49** 1

Tracks on The Honky Doodle Day EP: KKK (Boom Boom Tra La La La) / Honky Doodle Dub / Chains.

HOOBASTANK
US, male vocal / instrumental group (1 Album: 5 Weeks, 2 Singles: 9 Weeks)

13 Apr 02 **CRAWLING IN THE DARK** *Mercury 5828622* **47** 2
5 Jun 04 **THE REASON** *Mercury 9862261* **41** 5
12 Jun 04 **THE REASON** *Mercury 9862567* **12** 7

Frank HOOKER and POSITIVE PEOPLE
US, male / female vocal / instrumental group

5 Jul 80 **THIS FEELIN'** *DJM DJS 10947* **48** 4

John Lee HOOKER *US, male vocalist / guitarist, b. 22 Aug 1917, d. 21 Jun 2001 (6 Albums: 31 Weeks, 6 Singles: 23 Weeks)*

11 Jun 64 **DIMPLES** *Stateside SS 297* **23** 10
4 Feb 67 **HOUSE OF THE BLUES** *Marble Arch MAL 663* **34** 2
11 Nov 89 **THE HEALER** *Silvertone ORELP 508* **63** 8
21 Sep 91 ● **MR. LUCKY** *Silvertone ORELP 519* **3** 10
24 Oct 92 **BOOM BOOM** *Pointblank POB 3* **16** 5
7 Nov 92 **BOOM BOOM** *Pointblank VPBCD 12* **15** 4
16 Jan 93 **BOOGIE AT RUSSIAN HILL** *Pointblank POBDX 4* **53** 2

	13 March 1971	20 March 1971	27 March 1971	3 April 1971
UK No.1 SINGLES	BABY JUMP – Mungo Jerry	HOT LOVE – T. Rex	HOT LOVE – T. Rex	HOT LOVE – T. Rex
UK No.1 ALBUMS	ALL THINGS MUST PASS – George Harrison	ALL THINGS MUST PASS – George Harrison	ALL THINGS MUST PASS – George Harrison	HOME LOVIN' MAN – Andy Williams

15 May 93 **GLORIA** *Exile VANCD 11* [1] 31 3
11 Feb 95 **CHILL OUT (THINGS GONNA CHANGE)** *Pointblank POBD 10*....45 2
4 Mar 95 CHILL OUT *Pointblank VPBCD 22*....23 5
20 Apr 96 **BABY LEE** *Silvertone ORECD 81* [2] 65 1
22 Mar 97 DON'T LOOK BACK *Pointblank VPBCD 39*....63 2

[1] Van Morrison and John Lee Hooker [2] John Lee Hooker with Robert Cray

The HOOTERS *US, male vocal / instrumental group*

21 Nov 87 **SATELLITE** *CBS 651168 7*....22 9

HOOTIE & THE BLOWFISH *US, male vocal (Darius Rucker) / instrumental group (3 Albums: 30 Weeks, 4 Singles: 6 Weeks)*

25 Feb 95 **HOLD MY HAND** *Atlantic A 7230CD*....50 3
18 Mar 95 CRACKED REAR VIEW *Atlantic 7826132* ▲ 12 11
27 May 95 **LET HER CRY** *Atlantic A 7188CD*....75 1
4 May 96 ● FAIRWEATHER JOHNSON *Atlantic 7567828862* ▲ 9 16
4 May 96 **OLD MAN AND ME (WHEN I GET TO HEAVEN)** *Atlantic A 5513CD*....57 1
26 Sep 98 MUSICAL CHAIRS *Atlantic 7567831362*....15 3
7 Nov 98 **I WILL WAIT** *Atlantic AT 0048CD*....57 1

HOPE A.D. (see also MIND OF KANE) *UK, male producer – David Hope*

4 Jun 94 **TREE FROG** *Sun-Up SUN 003CD*....73 1

HOPE OF THE STATES *UK, male vocal / instrumental group (1 Album: 2 Weeks, 3 Singles: 7 Weeks)*

11 Oct 03 **ENEMIES / FRIENDS** *Sony Music 6742572*....25 2
5 Jun 04 **THE RED THE WHITE THE BLACK THE BLUE** *Sony Music 6749922*....15 3
19 Jun 04 THE LOST RIOTS *Sony Music 5172649*....21 2
28 Aug 04 **NEHEMIAH** *Sony Music 6752472*....30 2

Mary HOPKIN (see also OASIS) *UK, female vocalist / guitarist (1 Album: 9 Weeks, 7 Singles: 74 Weeks)*

4 Sep 68 ★ **THOSE WERE THE DAYS** *Apple 2* $ 1 21
1 Mar 69 ● POSTCARD *Apple SAPCOR 5*....3 9
2 Apr 69 ● **GOODBYE** *Apple 10*....2 14
31 Jan 70 ● **TEMMA HARBOUR** *Apple 22*....6 11
28 Mar 70 ● **KNOCK KNOCK WHO'S THERE** *Apple 26*....2 14
31 Oct 70 **THINK ABOUT YOUR CHILDREN (re)** *Apple 30*....19 9
31 Jul 71 **LET MY NAME BE SORROW** *Apple 34*....46 1
20 Mar 76 **IF YOU LOVE ME (I WON'T CARE)** *Good Earth GD 2*....32 4

Anthony HOPKINS *UK, male actor / vocalist*

27 Dec 86 **DISTANT STAR** *Juice AA 5*....75 1

James HORNER *US, male composer (3 Albums: 82 Weeks)*

23 Sep 95 BRAVEHEART (FILM SOUNDTRACK) *Decca 4482952* [1] 27 9
31 Jan 98 ★ TITANIC (FILM SOUNDTRACK) *Sony Classical SK 63213*....1 55
12 Sep 98 ● BACK TO TITANIC *Sony Classical SK 60691*....10 18

[1] London Symphony Orchestra, music composed and conducted by James Horner

Bruce HORNSBY and The RANGE *US, male vocal / instrumental group (4 Albums: 54 Weeks, 3 Singles: 15 Weeks)*

2 Aug 86 **THE WAY IT IS** *RCA PB 49805* ▲ 15 10
13 Sep 86 THE WAY IT IS *RCA PL 89901*....16 26
25 Apr 87 **MANDOLIN RAIN** *RCA PB 49769*....70 1
14 May 88 SCENES FROM THE SOUTHSIDE *RCA PL 86686*....18 18
28 May 88 **THE VALLEY ROAD** *RCA PB 49561*....44 4
30 Jun 90 A NIGHT ON THE TOWN *RCA PL 82041*....23 7
8 May 93 HARBOR LIGHTS *RCA 07863661142*....32 3

Jane HORROCKS *UK, female actor / vocalist*

21 Oct 00 THE FURTHER ADVENTURES OF LITTLE VOICE *Liberty 5287542*....63 1

HORSE *UK, female / male vocal / instrumental group (2 Albums: 4 Weeks, 5 Singles: 10 Weeks)*

23 Jun 90 THE SAME SKY *Echo Chamber EST 2123*....44 2
24 Nov 90 **CAREFUL** *Capitol CL 587*....52 3
21 Aug 93 **SHAKE THIS MOUNTAIN** *Oxygen GASPD 7*....52 2
23 Oct 93 **GOD'S HOME MOVIE** *Oxygen GASXD 10*....56 1
13 Nov 93 GOD'S HOME MOVIE *Oxygen MCD 10935*....42 2
15 Jan 94 **CELEBRATE** *Oxygen GASPD 11*....49 2
5 Apr 97 **CAREFUL** (re-mix) *Stress CDSTRX 79*....44 2

HORSLIPS *Ireland, male vocal / instrumental group*

30 Apr 77 THE BOOK OF INVASIONS – A CELTIC SYMPHONY *DJM DJF 20498*....39 3

Johnny HORTON *US, male vocalist, b. 30 Apr 1925, d. 5 Nov 1960 (2 Singles: 15 Weeks)*

26 Jun 59 **THE BATTLE OF NEW ORLEANS** *Philips PB 932* ▲ $ 16 4
19 Jan 61 **NORTH TO ALASKA** *Philips PB 1062*....23 11

HOT ACTION COP *US, male vocal / instrumental group*

14 Jun 03 **FEVER FOR THE FLAVA** *Lava AT 0152CD*....41 1

HOT BLOOD *France, male instrumental group*

9 Oct 76 **SOUL DRACULA** *Creole CR 132*....32 5

HOT BUTTER *US, production duo – Bill and Steve Jerome featuring Stan Free*

22 Jul 72 ● **POPCORN (re)** *Pye International 7N 25583*....5 19

HOT CHOCOLATE 103 Top 500 *London-based band who were chart regulars throughout the 1970s and 1980s. Group founders were West Indian-born Errol Brown (v) and Tony Wilson (b/v). The act had at least one hit every year between 1970 and 1984 and 'You Sexy Thing' made the Top 10 in three decades: 70s, 80s and 90s (8 Albums: 153 Weeks, 35 Singles: 283 Weeks)*

15 Aug 70 ● **LOVE IS LIFE** *RAK 103*....6 12
6 Mar 71 **YOU COULD HAVE BEEN A LADY** *RAK 110*....22 9
28 Aug 71 ● **I BELIEVE (IN LOVE)** *RAK 118*....8 11
28 Oct 72 **YOU'LL ALWAYS BE A FRIEND** *RAK 139*....23 8
14 Apr 73 ● **BROTHER LOUIE** *RAK 149*....7 10
18 Aug 73 **RUMOURS** *RAK 157*....44 3
16 Mar 74 ● **EMMA** *RAK 168*....3 10
30 Nov 74 **CHERI BABE** *RAK 188*....31 9
24 May 75 **DISCO QUEEN** *RAK 202*....11 7
9 Aug 75 ● **A CHILD'S PRAYER** *RAK 212*....7 10
8 Nov 75 ● **YOU SEXY THING** *RAK 221* $ 2 12
15 Nov 75 HOT CHOCOLATE *RAK SRAK 516*....34 7
20 Mar 76 **DON'T STOP IT NOW** *RAK 230*....11 8
26 Jun 76 **MAN TO MAN** *RAK 238*....14 8
7 Aug 76 MAN TO MAN *RAK SRAK 522*....32 7
21 Aug 76 **HEAVEN IS IN THE BACK SEAT OF MY CADILLAC** *RAK 240*....25 8
20 Nov 76 ● GREATEST HITS *RAK SRAK 524*....6 35
18 Jun 77 ★ **SO YOU WIN AGAIN** *RAK 259*....1 11
26 Nov 77 ● **PUT YOUR LOVE IN ME** *RAK 266*....10 9
4 Mar 78 **EVERY 1'S A WINNER** *RAK 270* $ 12 11
8 Apr 78 EVERY 1'S A WINNER *RAK SRAK 531*....30 8
2 Dec 78 **I'LL PUT YOU TOGETHER AGAIN (FROM DEAR ANYONE)** *RAK 286*....13 11
19 May 79 **MINDLESS BOOGIE** *RAK 292*....46 5
28 Jul 79 **GOING THROUGH THE MOTIONS** *RAK 296*....53 4
15 Dec 79 ● 20 HOTTEST HITS *RAK EMTV 22*....3 19
3 May 80 ● **NO DOUBT ABOUT IT** *RAK 310*....2 11
19 Jul 80 **ARE YOU GETTING ENOUGH OF WHAT MAKES YOU HAPPY** *RAK 318*....17 7
13 Dec 80 **LOVE ME TO SLEEP** *RAK 324*....50 5
30 May 81 **YOU'LL NEVER BE SO WRONG** *RAK 331*....52 4
17 Apr 82 ● **GIRL CRAZY** *RAK 341*....7 11
10 Jul 82 ● **IT STARTED WITH A KISS** *RAK 344*....5 12

10 April 1971	17 April 1971	24 April 1971	1 May 1971
HOT LOVE T. Rex	HOT LOVE T. Rex	HOT LOVE T. Rex	DOUBLE BARREL Dave and Ansil Collins
HOME LOVIN' MAN Andy Williams	MOTOWN CHARTBUSTERS VOL.5 Various	MOTOWN CHARTBUSTERS VOL.5 Various	MOTOWN CHARTBUSTERS VOL.5 Various

KEY UK No.1 ★ UK Top 10 ● Still on chart + UK entry at No.1 ■ US No.1 ▲ UK million seller £ US million seller $
Singles re-entries are listed as (re), (2re), (3re)... which signifies that the hit re-entered the chart once, twice or three times...
Peak Position / Weeks

Date		Title	Peak	Weeks
25 Sep 82		MYSTERY *RAK SRAK 549*	24	7
25 Sep 82		CHANCES *RAK 350*	32	5
7 May 83	●	WHAT KINDA BOY YOU LOOKING FOR (GIRL) *RAK 357*	10	9
17 Sep 83		TEARS ON THE TELEPHONE *RAK 363*	37	5
4 Feb 84		I GAVE YOU MY HEART (DIDN'T I) *RAK 369*	13	10
17 Jan 87	●	YOU SEXY THING (re-mix) *EMI 5592*	10	10
21 Feb 87	★	THE VERY BEST OF HOT CHOCOLATE *RAK EMTV 42*	1	28
4 Apr 87		EVERY 1'S A WINNER (re-mix) *EMI 5607*	69	2
6 Mar 93		IT STARTED WITH A KISS (re-issue) *EMI CDEMCTS 7*	31	5
20 Mar 93	★	THEIR GREATEST HITS *EMI CDEMTV 73*	1	42
22 Nov 97	●	YOU SEXY THING (re-issue) *EMI CDHOT 100*	6	8
14 Feb 98		IT STARTED WITH A KISS (2nd re-issue) *EMI CDHOT 101* [1]	18	3

[1] Hot Chocolate featuring Errol Brown

HOT HOT HEAT *Canada, male vocal / instrumental group (2 Albums: 4 Weeks, 4 Singles: 7 Weeks)*

Date		Title	Peak	Weeks
5 Apr 03		BANDAGES *B-Unique BUN 045CDS*	25	3
12 Apr 03		MAKE UP THE BREAKDOWN *WEA 5046646202*	35	2
9 Aug 03		NO, NOT NOW *Sub Pop W 615CD*	38	1
7 May 05		ELEVATOR *Sire 9362489882*	34	2
28 May 05		GOODNIGHT GOODNIGHT *Sire W 670CD2*	36	2
30 Jul 05		MIDDLE OF NOWHERE *Sire W 677CD2*	47	1

HOT HOUSE *UK, male / female vocal / instrumental group (2 Singles: 3 Weeks)*

Date		Title	Peak	Weeks
14 Feb 87		DON'T COME TO STAY *Deconstruction CHEZ 1*	74	1
24 Sep 88		DON'T COME TO STAY (re-issue) *Deconstruction PB 42233*	70	2

HOT PANTZ *UK, female vocal duo*

Date		Title	Peak	Weeks
25 Dec 04		GIVE U ONE 4 CHRISTMAS *Tug CDSNOG 13*	64	1

HOT STREAK *US, male vocal / instrumental group*

Date		Title	Peak	Weeks
10 Sep 83		BODY WORK *Polydor POSP 642*	19	8

HOTHOUSE FLOWERS *Ireland, male vocal (Liam O'Maonlai) / instrumental group (3 Albums: 51 Weeks, 10 Singles: 36 Weeks)*

Date		Title	Peak	Weeks
14 May 88		DON'T GO *London LON 174*	11	8
18 Jun 88	●	PEOPLE *London LONLP 58*	2	19
23 Jul 88		I'M SORRY *London LON 187*	53	3
12 May 90		GIVE IT UP *London LON 258*	30	5
16 Jun 90	●	HOME *London 8281971*	5	21
28 Jul 90		I CAN SEE CLEARLY NOW *London LON 269*	23	7
20 Oct 90		MOVIES *London LON 276*	68	2
13 Feb 93		EMOTIONAL TIME *London LONCD 335*	38	4
20 Mar 93	●	SONGS FROM THE RAIN *London 8283502*	7	11
8 May 93		ONE TONGUE *London LOCDP 340*	45	3
19 Jun 93		ISN'T IT AMAZING *London LOCDP 343*	46	2
27 Nov 93		THIS IS IT (YOUR SOUL) *London LONCD 346*	67	1
16 May 98		YOU CAN LOVE ME NOW *London LONCD 410*	65	1

HOTLEGS
(see also GODLEY and CREME; 10cc) *UK, male vocal / instrumental group*

Date		Title	Peak	Weeks
4 Jul 70	●	NEANDERTHAL MAN *Fontana 6007 019*	2	14

The HOTSHOTS *UK, male vocal group*

Date		Title	Peak	Weeks
2 Jun 73	●	SNOOPY VS THE RED BARON *Mooncrest MOON 5*	4	15

Steven HOUGHTON
UK, male actor / vocalist (1 Album: 7 Weeks, 2 Singles: 22 Weeks)

Date		Title	Peak	Weeks
29 Nov 97		STEVEN HOUGHTON *RCA 74321542592*	21	7
29 Nov 97	●	WIND BENEATH MY WINGS *RCA 74321529272*	3	15
7 Mar 98		TRULY (re) *RCA 74321558552*	23	7

HOUND DOGS NEW *UK / Italy, male production / vocal group*

Date		Title	Peak	Weeks
31 Dec 05		I LIKE GIRLS *Direction 82876777022*	26	1+

A HOUSE *Ireland, male vocal / instrumental group (4 Singles: 8 Weeks)*

Date		Title	Peak	Weeks
13 Jun 92		ENDLESS ART *Setanta AHOU 1*	46	3
8 Aug 92		TAKE IT EASY ON ME *Setanta AHOU 2*	55	2
25 Jun 94		WHY ME *Setanta CDAHOU 4*	52	1
1 Oct 94		HERE COME THE GOOD TIMES *Setanta CDAHOUS 5*	37	2

HOUSE ENGINEERS *UK, male vocal / instrumental duo*

Date		Title	Peak	Weeks
5 Dec 87		GHOST HOUSE *Syncopate SY 8*	69	2

HOUSE OF GLASS
(see also BINI & MARTINI; ECLIPSE; GOODFELLAS featuring Lisa MILLETT) *Italy, male production duo – Gianni Bini and Paolo Martini*

Date		Title	Peak	Weeks
14 Apr 01		DISCO DOWN *Azuli AZNY 138*	72	1

HOUSE OF LOVE *UK, male vocal (Guy Chadwick) / instrumental group (4 Albums: 14 Weeks, 9 Singles: 22 Weeks)*

Date		Title	Peak	Weeks
22 Apr 89		NEVER *Fontana HOL 1*	41	2
18 Nov 89		I DON'T KNOW WHY I LOVE YOU *Fontana HOL 2*	41	3
3 Feb 90		SHINE ON *Fontana HOL 3*	20	4
10 Mar 90	●	THE HOUSE OF LOVE *Fontana 8422931*	8	10
7 Apr 90		BEATLES AND THE STONES *Fontana HOL 4*	36	4
10 Nov 90		THE HOUSE OF LOVE *Fontana 8469781*	49	1
26 Oct 91		THE GIRL WITH THE LONELIEST EYES *Fontana HOL 5*	58	1
2 May 92		FEEL *Fontana HOL 6*	45	3
27 Jun 92		YOU DON'T UNDERSTAND *Fontana HOL 7*	46	3
18 Jul 92		BABE RAINBOW *Fontana 5125492*	34	2
5 Dec 92		CRUSH ME *Fontana HOL 810*	67	1
3 Jul 93		AUDIENCE WITH THE MIND *Fontana 5148802*	38	1
26 Feb 05		LOVE YOU TOO MUCH *Art & Industry 2 ARTCD*	73	1

The two identically titled albums are different.

HOUSE OF PAIN
US, male rap group (2 Albums: 7 Weeks, 8 Singles: 35 Weeks)

Date		Title	Peak	Weeks
10 Oct 92		JUMP AROUND *Ruffness XLS 32* $	32	4
21 Nov 92		HOUSE OF PAIN *XL XLCD 111*	73	1
22 May 93	●	JUMP AROUND (re-issue) / TOP O' THE MORNING TO YA *Ruffness XL 43CD*	8	7
23 Oct 93		SHAMROCKS AND SHENANIGANS / WHO'S THE MAN *Ruffness XLS 46CD*	23	4
16 Jul 94		ON POINT *Ruffness XLS 52CD*	19	3
30 Jul 94	●	SAME AS IT EVER WAS *XL XLCD 115*	8	6
12 Nov 94		IT AIN'T A CRIME *Ruffness XLS 55CD1*	37	2
1 Jul 95		OVER THERE (I DON'T CARE) *Ruffness XLS 61CD1*	20	3
5 Oct 96		FED UP *Tommy Boy TBCD 7744*	68	1
20 Nov 04		JUMP AROUND (3re) *Tommy Boy 5046960110*	44	11

HOUSE OF VIRGINISM (see also APOLLO presents HOUSE OF VIRGINISM) *Sweden, male vocal / instrumental group (3 Singles: 6 Weeks)*

Date		Title	Peak	Weeks
20 Nov 93		I'LL BE THERE FOR YOU (DOYA DODODO DOYA) *ffrr FCD 221*	29	3
30 Jul 94		REACHIN *ffrr FCD 238*	35	2
17 Feb 96		EXCLUSIVE *Logic 74321324102*	67	1

HOUSE TRAFFIC *Italy / UK, male / female vocal / production group*

Date		Title	Peak	Weeks
4 Oct 97		EVERY DAY OF MY LIFE *Logic 74321249442*	24	3

	8 May 1971	15 May 1971	22 May 1971	29 May 1971
UK No.1 SINGLES	DOUBLE BARREL Dave and Ansil Collins	KNOCK THREE TIMES Dawn	KNOCK THREE TIMES Dawn	KNOCK THREE TIMES Dawn
UK No.1 ALBUMS	STICKY FINGERS The Rolling Stones	STICKY FINGERS The Rolling Stones	STICKY FINGERS The Rolling Stones	STICKY FINGERS The Rolling Stones

The HOUSEMARTINS (see also The BEAUTIFUL SOUTH; BISCUIT BOY)

UK, male vocal / instrumental group – leaders Norman Cook and Paul Heaton (5 Albums: 74 Weeks, 9 Singles: 60 Weeks)

8 Mar 86 **SHEEP (re)** *Go Discs GOD 9* **54** 4
7 Jun 86 ● **HAPPY HOUR** *Go Discs GOD 11* **3** 13
5 Jul 86 ● LONDON 0 HULL 4 *Go Discs AGOLP 7* 3 41
4 Oct 86 **THINK FOR A MINUTE** *Go Discs GOD 13* **18** 8
6 Dec 86 ★ **CARAVAN OF LOVE** *Go Discs GOD 16* **1** 11
27 Dec 86 THE HOUSEMARTINS' CHRISTMAS SINGLES BOX *Go Discs GOD 816* 84 1
23 May 87 **FIVE GET OVER EXCITED** *Go Discs GOD 18* **11** 6
5 Sep 87 **ME AND THE FARMER** *Go Discs GOD 19* **15** 5
3 Oct 87 ● THE PEOPLE WHO GRINNED THEMSELVES TO DEATH *Go Discs AGOLP 9* 9 18
21 Nov 87 **BUILD** *Go Discs GOD 21* **15** 8
23 Apr 88 **THERE IS ALWAYS SOMETHING THERE TO REMIND ME** *Go Discs GOD 22* **35** 4
21 May 88 ● NOW THAT'S WHAT I CALL QUITE GOOD *Go Discs AGOLP 11* ... 8 11
10 May 03 **CHANGE THE WORLD** *Free 2 Air 0146685 F2A* [1] **51** 1
10 Apr 04 THE BEST OF THE HOUSEMARTINS *Go Discs 9818214* 29 3

[1] Dino Lenny vs The Housemartins

HOUSEMASTER BOYZ and The RUDE BOY OF HOUSE

US, male vocal / instrumental group

9 May 87 ● **HOUSE NATION (re)** *Magnetic Dance MAGD 1* **8** 14

HOUSTON *US, male rapper – Houston Summers (2 Singles: 9 Weeks)*

18 Sep 04 **I LIKE THAT** *Capitol CDCL 861* [1] **11** 6
5 Feb 05 **AIN'T NOTHING WRONG** *Capitol CDCL 866* **33** 3

[1] Houston featuring Chingy, Nate Dogg & I-20

Marques HOUSTON

US, male vocalist (1 Album: 1 Week, 4 Singles: 12 Weeks)

14 Feb 04 MH *Elektra 7559629352* 73 1
20 Mar 04 **CLUBBIN'** *Elektra E 7544CD* [1] **15** 6
31 Jul 04 **POP THAT BOOTY** *East West E 7609CD* [2] **23** 5
27 Nov 04 **BECAUSE OF YOU** *Atlantic AT 0188CD* **51** 1

[1] Marques Houston featuring Joe Budden and Pied Piper [2] Marques Houston featuring Jermaine "JD" Dupri

Thelma HOUSTON *US, female vocalist (4 Singles: 22 Weeks)*

5 Feb 77 **DON'T LEAVE ME THIS WAY** *Motown TMG 1060* ▲ $ **13** 8
27 Jun 81 **IF YOU FEEL IT** *RCA 77* **48** 4
1 Dec 84 **YOU USED TO HOLD ME SO TIGHT** *MCA MCA 932* **49** 8
21 Jan 95 **DON'T LEAVE ME THIS WAY** (re-recording) *Dynamo DYND 001* **35** 2

Whitney HOUSTON (41 Top 500)

Multi-award-winning, record-shattering vocalist, b. 9 Aug 1963, New Jersey, US. Mrs Bobby Brown scored a record seven successive No.1s in the US and, in 2001, with sales exceeding 150 million behind her, she signed a record-breaking $100m recording deal. Best-selling single: 'I Will Always Love You' 1,355,055 (7 Albums: 383 Weeks, 33 Singles: 315 Weeks)

16 Nov 85 ★ **SAVING ALL MY LOVE FOR YOU** *Arista ARIST 640* ▲ $ **1** 16
14 Dec 85 ● WHITNEY HOUSTON *Arista 206978* ▲ 2 119
25 Jan 86 ● **HOW WILL I KNOW** *Arista ARIST 656* ▲ $ **5** 12
25 Jan 86 **HOLD ME** *Asylum EKR 32* [1] **44** 5
12 Apr 86 ● **GREATEST LOVE OF ALL** *Arista ARIST 658* ▲ $ **8** 11
23 May 87 ★ **I WANNA DANCE WITH SOMEBODY (WHO LOVES ME)** *Arista RIS 1* ▲ $ **1** 16
13 Jun 87 ★ WHITNEY *Arista 208141* ■ ▲ 1 101
22 Aug 87 **DIDN'T WE ALMOST HAVE IT ALL** *Arista RIS 31* ▲ **14** 8
14 Nov 87 ● **SO EMOTIONAL** *Arista RIS 43* ▲ $ **5** 11
12 Mar 88 **WHERE DO BROKEN HEARTS GO** *Arista 109793* ▲ **14** 8
28 May 88 ● **LOVE WILL SAVE THE DAY** *Arista 111516* **10** 7
24 Sep 88 ★ **ONE MOMENT IN TIME** *Arista 111613* **1** 12
9 Sep 89 **IT ISN'T, IT WASN'T, IT AIN'T NEVER GONNA BE** *Arista 112545* [2] **29** 5
20 Oct 90 ● **I'M YOUR BABY TONIGHT (re)** *Arista 113594* ▲ **5** 10
17 Nov 90 ● I'M YOUR BABY TONIGHT *Arista 211039* 4 29
22 Dec 90 **ALL THE MAN THAT I NEED** *Arista 114000* ▲ **13** 10
6 Jul 91 **MY NAME IS NOT SUSAN** *Arista 114510* **29** 5
28 Sep 91 **I BELONG TO YOU** *Arista 114727* **54** 2
14 Nov 92 ★ **I WILL ALWAYS LOVE YOU (re)** *Arista 74321120657* ▲ £ $ **1** 29
20 Feb 93 ● **I'M EVERY WOMAN** *Arista 74321131502* **4** 11
24 Apr 93 ● **I HAVE NOTHING** *Arista 74321146142* **3** 10
31 Jul 93 **RUN TO YOU** *Arista 74321153332* **15** 6
6 Nov 93 **QUEEN OF THE NIGHT** *Arista 74321169302* **14** 5
22 Jan 94 **SOMETHING IN COMMON** *MCA MCSTD 1957* [3] **16** 5
18 Nov 95 **EXHALE (SHOOP SHOOP)** *Arista 74321332472* ▲ $ **11** 9
24 Feb 96 **COUNT ON ME** *Arista 74321345842* [4] **12** 6
21 Dec 96 **STEP BY STEP** *Arista 74321449332* **13** 13
4 Jan 97 THE PREACHER'S WIFE (FILM SOUNDTRACK) *Arista 74321441252* 35 7
29 Mar 97 **I BELIEVE IN YOU AND ME** *Arista 74321468602* $ **16** 5
28 Nov 98 ● MY LOVE IS YOUR LOVE *Arista 7822190372* 4 68
19 Dec 98 ● **WHEN YOU BELIEVE (re)** *Columbia 6667522* [5] **4** 13
6 Mar 99 ● **IT'S NOT RIGHT (BUT IT'S OK)** *Arista 74321652402* **3** 15
3 Jul 99 ● **MY LOVE IS YOUR LOVE** *Arista 74321672862* $ **2** 12
11 Dec 99 **I LEARNED FROM THE BEST** *Arista 74321723992* **19** 11
27 May 00 ★ THE GREATEST HITS *Arista 74321757392* ■ 1 56
17 Jun 00 ● **IF I TOLD YOU THAT (re)** *Arista 74321766282* [6] **9** 11
14 Oct 00 ● **COULD I HAVE THIS KISS FOREVER** *Arista 74321795992* [7] ... **7** 8
30 Dec 00 **HEARTBREAK HOTEL** *Arista 74321820572* [8] $ **25** 5
16 Feb 02 LOVE WHITNEY *Arista 74321910272* 22 3
9 Nov 02 **WHATCHULOOKINAT** *Arista 74321973062* **13** 3

[1] Teddy Pendergrass with Whitney Houston [2] Aretha Franklin and Whitney Houston [3] Bobby Brown and Whitney Houston [4] Whitney Houston and CeCe Winans [5] Mariah Carey & Whitney Houston [6] Whitney Houston / George Michael [7] Whitney Houston and Enrique Iglesias [8] Whitney Houston featuring Faith Evans and Kelly Price

'I Will Always Love You' re-entered the chart in Dec 1993 and peaked at No.25.

Adina HOWARD *US, female vocalist (2 Singles: 16 Weeks)*

4 Mar 95 **FREAK LIKE ME (re)** *East West A 4473CD* $ **33** 4
23 Nov 96 ● **WHAT'S LOVE GOT TO DO WITH IT** *Interscope IND 97008* [1] .. **2** 12

[1] Warren G featuring Adina Howard

Billy HOWARD *UK, male comedian / vocalist*

13 Dec 75 ● **KING OF THE COPS** *Penny Farthing PEN 892* **6** 12

Miki HOWARD *US, female vocalist*

26 May 90 **UNTIL YOU COME BACK (THAT'S WHAT I'M GONNA DO)** *East West 7935* **67** 2

Nick HOWARD *Australia, male vocalist*

21 Jan 95 **EVERYBODY NEEDS SOMEBODY** *Bell 74321220942* **64** 1

Robert HOWARD (see also BLOW MONKEYS) *US, male vocalist*

14 Jan 89 ● **WAIT** *RCA PB 42595* **7** 10

Steve HOWE (see also ANDERSON BRUFORD WAKEMAN HOWE; ASIA; GTR; YES) *UK, male vocalist / guitarist (2 Albums: 6 Weeks)*

15 Nov 75 BEGINNINGS *Atlantic K 50151* 22 4
24 Nov 79 THE STEVE HOWE ALBUM *Atlantic K 50621* 68 2

Danny HOWELLS & Dick TREVOR featuring ERIRE

(see also SCIENCE DEPARTMENT featuring ERIRE)
UK, male production duo and female vocalist

9 Oct 04 **DUSK TIL DAWN** *C2 CDC 2004* **37** 2

5 June 1971	12 June 1971	19 June 1971	26 June 1971
KNOCK THREE TIMES Dawn	KNOCK THREE TIMES Dawn	CHIRPY CHIRPY CHEEP CHEEP Middle of the Road	CHIRPY CHIRPY CHEEP CHEEP Middle of the Road
RAM Paul and Linda McCartney	RAM Paul and Linda McCartney	STICKY FINGERS The Rolling Stones	TARKUS Emerson, Lake and Palmer

KEY
UK No.1 ★ UK Top 10 ● Still on chart + UK entry at No.1 ■ US No.1 ▲ UK million seller £ US million seller $
Singles re-entries are listed as (re), (2re), (3re)... which signifies that the hit re-entered the chart once, twice or three times...
Peak Position / Weeks

HOWLIN' WOLF
US, male vocalist – Chester Burnette, b. 10 Jun 1910, d. 10 Jan 1976

Date		Title	Peak	Weeks
4 Jun 64		**SMOKESTACK LIGHTNIN'** *Pye International 7N 25244*	42	5

The HUDDERSFIELD CHORAL SOCIETY
UK, male / female choir (2 Albums: 14 Weeks)

Date		Title	Peak	Weeks
15 Mar 86	●	**THE HYMNS ALBUM** *EMI EMTV 40*	8	10
13 Dec 86		**THE CAROLS ALBUM** *EMI EMTV 43*	29	4

Al HUDSON
US, male vocalist (3 Singles: 20 Weeks)

Date		Title	Peak	Weeks
9 Sep 78		**DANCE, GET DOWN (FEEL THE GROOVE) / HOW DO YOU DO** *ABC 4229*	57	4
15 Sep 79		**YOU CAN DO IT** *MCA 511* [1]	15	10
8 Dec 79		**MUSIC** *MCA 542* [2]	56	6

[1] Al Hudson and The Partners [2] One Way featuring Al Hudson

Lavine HUDSON
UK, female vocalist

Date		Title	Peak	Weeks
21 May 88		**INTERVENTION** *Virgin VS 1067*	57	3

HUDSON-FORD
(see also The MONKS; The STRAWBS) *UK, male vocal / instrumental duo – Richard Hudson and John Ford (3 Singles: 20 Weeks)*

Date		Title	Peak	Weeks
18 Aug 73	●	**PICK UP THE PIECES** *A&M AMS 7078*	8	9
16 Feb 74		**BURN BABY BURN** *A&M AMS 7096*	15	9
29 Jun 74		**FLOATING IN THE WIND** *A&M AMS 7116*	35	2

HUE AND CRY
UK, male vocal / instrumental duo – Pat and Greg Kane (5 Albums: 74 Weeks, 11 Singles: 59 Weeks)

Date		Title	Peak	Weeks
13 Jun 87	●	**LABOUR OF LOVE** *Circa YR 4*	6	16
19 Sep 87		**STRENGTH TO STRENGTH** *Circa YR 6*	46	5
7 Nov 87		**SEDUCED AND ABANDONED** *Circa CIRCA 2*	22	11
30 Jan 88		**I REFUSE** *Circa YR 8*	47	3
22 Oct 88		**ORDINARY ANGEL** *Circa YR 18*	42	6
10 Dec 88	●	**REMOTE / THE BITTER SUITE** *Circa CIRCA 6*	10	48
28 Jan 89		**LOOKING FOR LINDA** *Circa YR 24*	15	9
6 May 89		**VIOLENTLY (EP)** *Circa YR 29*	21	6
30 Sep 89		**SWEET INVISIBILITY** *Circa YR 37*	55	3
25 May 91		**MY SALT HEART** *Circa YR 64*	47	3
29 Jun 91	●	**STARS CRASH DOWN** *Circa CIRCA 15*	10	9
3 Aug 91		**LONG TERM LOVERS OF PAIN (EP)** *Circa YR 71*	48	3
11 Jul 92		**PROFOUNDLY YOURS** *Fidelity FIDEL 1*	74	1
29 Aug 92		**TRUTH AND LOVE** *Fidelity FIDELCD 1*	33	2
13 Mar 93		**LABOUR OF LOVE** (re-mix) *Circa HUESCD 1*	25	4
10 Apr 93		**LABOURS OF LOVE – THE BEST OF HUE AND CRY** *Circa HACCD 1*	27	4

Tracks on Violently (EP): Violently / The Man with the Child in his Eyes / Calamity John. Tracks on Long Term Lovers of Pain (EP): Long Term Lovers of Pain / Heart of Saturday Night / Remembrance and Gold / Stars Crash Down.
Remote re-entered the chart on 16 Dec 89 when it was made available with the free album 'The Bitter Suite'.

The HUES CORPORATION
US, male / female vocal group (2 Singles: 16 Weeks)

Date		Title	Peak	Weeks
27 Jul 74	●	**ROCK THE BOAT** *RCA APBO 0232* ▲ $	6	10
19 Oct 74		**ROCKIN' SOUL** *RCA PB 10066*	24	6

HUFF & HERB
(see also HUFF & PUFF) *UK, male DJ / production duo – Ben Langmaid and Jeff Patterson (2 Singles: 4 Weeks)*

Date		Title	Peak	Weeks
6 Dec 97		**FEELING GOOD** *Planet 3 GXY 2018CD*	31	3
7 Nov 98		**FEELING GOOD '98** (re-mix) *Planet 3 GXY 2020CD*	69	1

HUFF & PUFF
(see also DUSTED; FAITHLESS; HUFF & HERB; OUR TRIBE / ONE TRIBE; ROLLO) *UK, male instrumental / production duo – Ben Langmaid and Roland Armstrong (2 Singles: 4 Weeks)*

Date		Title	Peak	Weeks
2 Nov 96		**HELP ME MAKE IT** *Skyway SKYWCD 4*	31	2
21 Jun 97		**HELP ME MAKE IT** (re-mix) *Skyway SKYWCD 8*	37	2

David HUGHES
UK, male vocalist – Geoffrey Paddison, b. 11 Oct 1929, d. 19 Oct 1972

Date		Title	Peak	Weeks
21 Sep 56		**BY THE FOUNTAINS OF ROME** *Philips PB 606*	27	1

HUGO and LUIGI
US, orchestra and chorus – leaders Hugo Peretti, b. 6 Dec 1916, d. 1 May 1986, and Luigi Creatore

Date		Title	Peak	Weeks
24 Jul 59		**LA PLUME DE MA TANTE** *RCA 1127*	29	2

Alan HULL
(see also LINDISFARNE) *UK, male vocalist, b. 20 Feb 1945, d. 17 Nov 1995*

Date		Title	Peak	Weeks
28 Jul 73		**PIPEDREAM** *Charisma CAS 1069*	29	3

HUMAN LEAGUE
111 Top 500

Early 1980s UK pop sensation, fronted by Philip Oakey, b. 2 Oct 1955, Sheffield (v/syn) and joined in 1980 by vocalists Joanne Catherall and Susanne Sulley. The group, which also topped the US chart, won Best Newcomers at the 1982 BRIT awards. Best-selling single: 'Don't You Want Me' 1,430,000 (12 Albums: 263 Weeks, 23 Singles: 156 Weeks)

Date		Title	Peak	Weeks
3 May 80		**HOLIDAY 80 (DOUBLE SINGLE) (re)** *Virgin VS 105*	46	10
31 May 80		**TRAVELOGUE** *Virgin V 2160*	16	42
21 Jun 80		**EMPIRE STATE HUMAN** *Virgin VS 351*	62	2
28 Feb 81		**BOYS AND GIRLS** *Virgin VS 395*	48	4
2 May 81		**THE SOUND OF THE CROWD** *Virgin VS 416*	12	10
8 Aug 81	●	**LOVE ACTION (I BELIEVE IN LOVE)** *Virgin VS 435*	3	13
22 Aug 81		**REPRODUCTION** *Virgin V 2133*	34	23
10 Oct 81	●	**OPEN YOUR HEART** *Virgin VS 453*	6	9
24 Oct 81	★	**DARE** *Virgin V 2192*	1	72
5 Dec 81	★	**DON'T YOU WANT ME** *Virgin VS 466* ▲ £ $	1	13
9 Jan 82	●	**BEING BOILED** *EMI FAST 4*	6	9
17 Jul 82	●	**LOVE AND DANCING** *Virgin OVED 6* [1]	3	52
20 Nov 82	●	**MIRROR MAN** *Virgin VS 522*	2	10
23 Apr 83	●	**(KEEP FEELING) FASCINATION** *Virgin VS 569*	2	9
5 May 84		**THE LEBANON (re)** *Virgin VS 672*	11	7
19 May 84	●	**HYSTERIA** *Virgin V 2315*	3	18
30 Jun 84		**LIFE ON YOUR OWN** *Virgin VS 688*	16	6
17 Nov 84		**LOUISE** *Virgin VS 723*	13	10
23 Aug 86	●	**HUMAN** *Virgin VS 880* ▲	8	8
20 Sep 86	●	**CRASH** *Virgin V 2391*	7	6
22 Nov 86		**I NEED YOUR LOVING** *Virgin VS 900*	72	1
15 Oct 88		**LOVE IS ALL THAT MATTERS** *Virgin VS 1025*	41	5
12 Nov 88	●	**GREATEST HITS** *Virgin HLTV 1*	3	24
18 Aug 90		**HEART LIKE A WHEEL** *Virgin VS 1262*	29	5
22 Sep 90		**ROMANTIC?** *Virgin V 2624*	24	2
7 Jan 95	●	**TELL ME WHEN** *East West YZ 882CD1*	6	9
4 Feb 95	●	**OCTOPUS** *East West 4509987502*	6	12
18 Mar 95		**ONE MAN IN MY HEART** *East West YZ 904CD1*	13	8
17 Jun 95		**FILLING UP WITH HEAVEN** *East West YZ 944CD1*	36	2
28 Oct 95		**DON'T YOU WANT ME** (re-mix) *Virgin VSCDT 1557*	16	3
11 Nov 95		**GREATEST HITS** *Virgin CDV 2792*	28	8
20 Jan 96		**STAY WITH ME TONIGHT** *East West EW 020CD*	40	2
11 Aug 01		**ALL I EVER WANTED** *Papillon BTFLYS 0012*	47	1
18 Aug 01		**SECRETS** *Papillon BTFLYCD 0019*	44	1
27 Sep 03		**THE VERY BEST OF THE HUMAN LEAGUE** *Virgin HLCDX 2*	24	3

[1] League Unlimited Orchestra

'Holiday 80 (Double Single)' only reached its peak position on re-entry in 1982. Tracks on Holiday 80 (Double Single): Being Boiled / Marianne / Rock and Roll – Nightclubbing / Dancevision.

HUMAN MOVEMENT featuring Sophie MOLETA
UK, male production duo and Australia, female vocalist

Date		Title	Peak	Weeks
3 Feb 01		**LOVE HAS COME AGAIN** *Renaissance Recordings RENCDS 005*	53	1

3 July 1971	10 July 1971	17 July 1971	24 July 1971
UK No.1 SINGLES			
CHIRPY CHIRPY CHEEP CHEEP Middle of the Road	CHIRPY CHIRPY CHEEP CHEEP Middle of the Road	CHIRPY CHIRPY CHEEP CHEEP Middle of the Road	GET IT ON T. Rex
UK No.1 ALBUMS			
BRIDGE OVER TROUBLED WATER Simon and Garfunkel	BRIDGE OVER TROUBLED WATER Simon and Garfunkel	BRIDGE OVER TROUBLED WATER Simon and Garfunkel	BRIDGE OVER TROUBLED WATER Simon and Garfunkel

HUMAN NATURE *Australia, male vocal group (4 Singles: 7 Weeks)*

10 May 97 **WISHES** *Epic 6644485* 44 1
30 Aug 97 **WHISPER YOUR NAME** *Epic 6649465* 53 1
10 Mar 01 **HE DON'T LOVE YOU** *Epic 6708922* 18 4
30 Jun 01 **WHEN WE WERE YOUNG** *Epic 6713792* 43 1

HUMAN RESOURCE
Holland / US, male production / rap / instrumental group (2 Singles: 14 Weeks)

14 Sep 91 **DOMINATOR** *R&S RSUK 4* 36 7
21 Dec 91 **THE COMPLETE DOMINATOR** (re-mix) *R&S RSUK 4X* 18 7

HUMANOID (see also AMORPHOUS ANDROGYNOUS; FUTURE SOUND OF LONDON) *UK, male producer – Brian Dougans (4 Singles: 14 Weeks)*

26 Nov 88 **STAKKER HUMANOID** *Westside WSR 12* 17 8
22 Apr 89 **SLAM** *Westside WSR 14* 54 2
8 Aug 92 **STAKKER HUMANOID** (re-issue) *Jumpin' + Pumpin' TOT 27* 40 3
3 Mar 01 **STAKKER HUMANOID** (re-mix) *Jumpin' + Pumpin' CDSTOT 43* 65 1

HUMATE *Germany, male production trio*

30 Jan 99 **LOVE STIMULATION** *Deviant DVNT 22CDS* 18 4

HUMBLE PIE *UK, male vocal / instrumental group – includes Steve Marriott and Peter Frampton (4 Albums: 10 Weeks, 1 Single: 10 Weeks)*

23 Aug 69 ● **NATURAL BORN BUGIE** *Immediate IM 082* 4 10
6 Sep 69 AS SAFE AS YESTERDAY IS *Immediate IMSP 025* 32 1
22 Jan 72 PERFORMANCE ROCKIN' THE FILLMORE *A&M AMLH 63506* 32 2
15 Apr 72 SMOKIN' *A&M AMLS 64342* 28 5
7 Apr 73 EAT IT *A&M AMLS 6004* 34 2

Engelbert HUMPERDINCK (77 Top 500) *Internationally popular cabaret entertainer and easy-on-the-ear vocalist, b. Arnold Dorsey, 2 May 1936, Madras, India. After a slow career start, an unlikely name change helped him to become one of the biggest-earning performers of the 1960s. This Vegas veteran was the UK's biggest-selling artist of 1967 and has reportedly amassed a personal fortune of £100m. Best-selling single: 'Release Me' 1,365,000 (16 Albums: 268 Weeks, 17 Singles: 240 Weeks)*

26 Jan 67 ★ **RELEASE ME** *Decca F 12541* £ 1 56
20 May 67 ● RELEASE ME *Decca SKL 4868* 6 58
25 May 67 ● **THERE GOES MY EVERYTHING** *Decca F 12610* 2 29
23 Aug 67 ★ **THE LAST WALTZ** *Decca F 12655* £ 1 27
25 Nov 67 ● THE LAST WALTZ *Decca SKL 4901* 3 33
10 Jan 68 ● **AM I THAT EASY TO FORGET** *Decca F 12722* 3 13
24 Apr 68 ● **A MAN WITHOUT LOVE** *Decca F 12770* 2 15
3 Aug 68 ● A MAN WITHOUT LOVE *Decca SKL 4939* 3 45
25 Sep 68 ● **LES BICYCLETTES DE BELSIZE** *Decca F 12834* 5 15
5 Feb 69 ● **THE WAY IT USED TO BE** *Decca F 12879* 3 14
1 Mar 69 ● ENGELBERT *Decca SKL 4985* 3 8
9 Aug 69 **I'M A BETTER MAN (FOR HAVING LOVED YOU)** *Decca F 12957* 15 13
15 Nov 69 ● **WINTER WORLD OF LOVE** *Decca F 12980* 7 13
6 Dec 69 ● ENGELBERT HUMPERDINCK *Decca SKL 5030* 5 23
30 May 70 **MY MARIE** *Decca F 13032* 31 7
11 Jul 70 WE MADE IT HAPPEN *Decca SKL 5054* 17 11
12 Sep 70 **SWEETHEART** (re) *Decca F 13068* 22 7
11 Sep 71 **ANOTHER TIME, ANOTHER PLACE** *Decca F 13212* 13 12
18 Sep 71 ANOTHER TIME, ANOTHER PLACE *Decca SKL 5097* 48 1
26 Feb 72 LIVE AT THE RIVIERA LAS VEGAS *Decca TXS 105* 45 1
4 Mar 72 **TOO BEAUTIFUL TO LAST** *Decca F 13281* 14 10
20 Oct 73 **LOVE IS ALL** (re) *Decca F 13443* 44 4
21 Dec 74 ★ ENGELBERT HUMPERDINCK – HIS GREATEST HITS *Decca SKL 5198* 1 34
4 May 85 GETTING SENTIMENTAL *Telstar STAR 2254* 35 10
4 Apr 87 THE ENGELBERT HUMPERDINCK COLLECTION *Telstar STAR 2294* 35 9
10 Jun 95 LOVE UNCHAINED *EMI CDEMTV 94* 16 6
30 Jan 99 **QUANDO QUANDO QUANDO** *The Hit Label HLC 15* 40 3
8 Apr 00 ● AT HIS VERY BEST *Universal Music TV 8449742* 5 14
6 May 00 **HOW TO WIN YOUR LOVE** *Universal TV 8822682* 59 1
20 Oct 01 I WANT TO WAKE UP WITH YOU *Universal Music TV 149462* 42 2
20 Mar 04 ● HIS GREATEST LOVE SONGS *Universal TV 9817857* 4 12
12 Jun 04 **RELEASE ME** (re-issue) *Universal TV 9819567* 51 1
26 Feb 05 LET THERE BE LOVE *Decca 4756606* [1] 67 1

[1] Engelbert

HUNDRED REASONS *UK, male vocal (Colin Doran) / instrumental group (2 Albums: 9 Weeks, 8 Singles: 15 Weeks)*

18 Aug 01 **EP TWO** *Columbia 6713922* 47 1
15 Dec 01 **EP THREE** *Columbia 6720782* 37 2
16 Mar 02 **IF I COULD** *Columbia 6724402* 19 3
18 May 02 **SILVER** *Columbia 6726642* 15 3
1 Jun 02 ● IDEAS ABOVE OUR STATION *Columbia 5081482* 6 7
28 Sep 02 **FALTER** *Columbia 6731452* 38 1
15 Nov 03 **THE GREAT TEST** *Columbia 6743762* 29 2
28 Feb 04 **WHAT YOU GET** *Columbia 6745492* 30 2
13 Mar 04 SHATTERPROOF IS NOT A CHALLENGE *Columbia 5136932* 20 2
16 Oct 04 **HOW SOON IS NOW?** *Sore Point SORE 029CDS* 47 1

Tracks on EP Two: Remmus / Soapbox / Shine. Tracks on EP Three: I'll Find You / Sunny / Slow Motion.

Geraldine HUNT *Canada, female vocalist*

25 Oct 80 **CAN'T FAKE THE FEELING** *Champagne FIZZ 501* 44 5

Marsha HUNT *US, female vocalist (2 Singles: 3 Weeks)*

21 May 69 **WALK ON GILDED SPLINTERS** *Track 604 030* 46 2
2 May 70 **KEEP THE CUSTOMER SATISFIED** *Track 604 037* 41 1

Tommy HUNT *US, male vocalist – Charles Hunt (3 Singles: 17 Weeks)*

11 Oct 75 **CRACKIN' UP** *Spark SRL 1132* 39 5
21 Aug 76 **LOVING ON THE LOSING SIDE** *Spark SRL 1146* 28 9
4 Dec 76 **ONE FINE MORNING** *Spark SRL 1148* 44 3

Alfonzo HUNTER *US, male rapper / instrumentalist*

22 Feb 97 **JUST THE WAY** *Cooltempo CDCOOL 326* 38 2

Ian HUNTER (see also MOTT THE HOOPLE) *UK, male vocalist (5 Albums: 26 Weeks, 1 Single: 10 Weeks)*

12 Apr 75 IAN HUNTER *CBS 80710* 21 15
3 May 75 **ONCE BITTEN TWICE SHY** *CBS 3194* 14 10
29 May 76 ALL AMERICAN ALIEN BOY *CBS 81310* 29 4
5 May 79 YOU'RE NEVER ALONE WITH A SCHIZOPHRENIC *Chrysalis CHR 1214* 49 3
26 Apr 80 WELCOME TO THE CLUB *Chrysalis CJT 6* 61 2
29 Aug 81 SHORT BACK 'N' SIDES *Chrysalis CHR 1326* 79 2

Tab HUNTER
US, male actor / vocalist – Andrew Arthur Kelm (2 Singles: 30 Weeks)

8 Feb 57 ★ **YOUNG LOVE** *London HLD 8380* ▲ $ 1 18
12 Apr 57 ● **NINETY-NINE WAYS** (re) *London HLD 8410* 5 12

Terry HUNTER *US, male DJ / producer*

26 Jul 97 **HARVEST FOR THE WORLD** *Delirious DELICD 4* 48 1

HUNTER featuring Ruby TURNER
UK, male TV gladiator / vocalist and female vocalist

9 Dec 95 **SHAKABOOM!** *Telstar HUNTCD 1* 64 1

Steve 'Silk' HURLEY
(see also JM SILK; VOICES OF LIFE) *US, male producer*

10 Jan 87 ★ **JACK YOUR BODY** *DJ International LON 117* 1 9

31 July 1971	7 August 1971	14 August 1971	21 August 1971
GET IT ON T. Rex	GET IT ON T. Rex	GET IT ON T. Rex	I'M STILL WAITING Diana Ross
BRIDGE OVER TROUBLED WATER Simon and Garfunkel	HOT HITS 6 Various	EVERY GOOD BOY DESERVES FAVOUR The Moody Blues	TOP OF THE POPS VOL.18 Various

KEY: UK No.1 ★ UK Top 10 ● Still on chart + UK entry at No.1 ■ US No.1 ▲ UK million seller £ US million seller $
Singles re-entries are listed as (re), (2re), (3re)... which signifies that the hit re-entered the chart once, twice or three times...
Peak Position / Weeks

HURLEY & TODD
UK / South Africa, male production duo – Ross Hurley and Drew Todd

29 Apr 00 **SUNSTORM** *Multiply CDMULTY 58* 38 2

HURRAH! *UK, male vocal / instrumental group*

28 Feb 87 **TELL GOD I'M HERE** *Kitchenware 208 201* 71 1

HURRICANE #1
UK, male vocal / instrumental group (2 Albums: 3 Weeks, 7 Singles: 17 Weeks)

10 May 97 **STEP INTO MY WORLD** *Creation CRESCD 253* 29 2
5 Jul 97 **JUST ANOTHER ILLUSION** *Creation CRESCD 264* 35 2
6 Sep 97 **CHAIN REACTION** *Creation CRESCD 271* 30 2
27 Sep 97 **HURRICANE #1** *Creation CRECD 206* 11 2
1 Nov 97 **STEP INTO MY WORLD** (re-mix) *Creation CRESCD 276* 19 3
21 Feb 98 **ONLY THE STRONGEST WILL SURVIVE** *Creation CRESCD 285* ... 19 6
24 Oct 98 **RISING SIGN** *Creation CRESCD 303* 47 1
3 Apr 99 **THE GREATEST HIGH** *Creation CRESCD 309* 43 1
1 May 99 **ONLY THE STRONG WILL SURVIVE** *Creation CRECD 237* 55 1

Phil HURTT *US, male vocalist*

11 Nov 78 **GIVING IT BACK** *Fantasy FTC 161* 36 5

HÜSKER DÜ
(see also Bob MOULD; SUGAR) *US, male vocal / instrumental group*

14 Feb 87 **WAREHOUSE: SONGS AND STORIES** *Warner Bros. 925 5441* .. 72 1

HUSTLERS CONVENTION featuring Dave LAUDAT and Ondrea DUVERNEY
(see also DISCO TEX presents CLOUDBURST; FULL INTENTION; Michael GRAY; SEX-O-SONIQUE)
UK, male production duo and male vocalist and US, female vocalist

20 May 95 **DANCE TO THE MUSIC** *Stress CDSTR 53* 71 1

Willie HUTCH *US, male vocalist – Willie Hutchinson (2 Singles: 8 Weeks)*

4 Dec 82 **IN AND OUT** *Motown TMG 1285* 51 7
6 Jul 85 **KEEP ON JAMMIN'** *Motown ZB 40173* 73 1

June HUTTON and Axel STORDAHL
US, female vocalist, b. 11 Aug 1921, d. 2 May 1973, and male orchestra leader

7 Aug 53 ● **SAY YOU'RE MINE AGAIN (re)** *Capitol CL 13918* 6 7

Act were joined by 'The Boys Next Door' on this hit.

HYBRID *UK, male production trio (1 Album: 1 Week, 4 Singles: 5 Weeks)*

10 Jul 99 **FINISHED SYMPHONY** *Distinctive DISNCD 52* 58 1
11 Sep 99 **IF I SURVIVE** *Distinctive DISNCD 55* [1] 52 1
25 Sep 99 **WIDE ANGLE** *Distinctive DISNCD 54* 45 1
3 Jun 00 **KID 2000** *Virgin / EMI VTS CD2* [2] 32 2
20 Sep 03 **TRUE TO FORM** *Distinctive DISNCD 111* [3] 59 1

[1] Hybrid featuring Julee Cruise [2] Hybrid featuring Chrissie Hynde [3] Hybrid featuring Peter Cook

Brian HYLAND *US, male vocalist (7 Singles: 72 Weeks)*

7 Jul 60 ● **ITSY BITSY TEENIE WEENIE YELLOW POLKADOT BIKINI** *London HLR 9161* ▲ $ 8 13
20 Oct 60 **FOUR LITTLE HEELS** *London HLR 9203* 29 6
10 May 62 ● **GINNY COME LATELY** *HMV POP 1013* 5 15
2 Aug 62 ● **SEALED WITH A KISS** *HMV POP 1051* $ 3 15
8 Nov 62 **WARMED OVER KISSES** *HMV POP 1079* 28 6
27 Mar 71 **GYPSY WOMAN (re)** *Uni UN 530* $ 42 6
28 Jun 75 ● **SEALED WITH A KISS** (re-issue) *ABC 4059* 7 11

Sheila HYLTON *Jamaica, female vocalist (2 Singles: 12 Weeks)*

15 Sep 79 **BREAKFAST IN BED** *United Artists BP 304* 57 5
17 Jan 81 **THE BED'S TOO BIG WITHOUT YOU** *Island WIP 6671* 35 7

Phyllis HYMAN *US, female vocalist, b. 6 Jul 1950, d. 30 Jun 1995 (1 Album: 1 Week, 2 Singles: 9 Weeks)*

16 Feb 80 **YOU KNOW HOW TO LOVE ME** *Arista ARIST 323* 47 6
12 Sep 81 **YOU SURE LOOK GOOD TO ME** *Arista ARIST 424* 56 3
20 Sep 86 **LIVING ALL ALONE** *Philadelphia International PHIL 4001* 97 1

Dick HYMAN TRIO
US, male instrumental trio, leader Dick Hyman – keyboard player

16 Mar 56 ● **THEME FROM 'THE THREEPENNY OPERA'** *MGM 890* 9 10

Chrissie HYNDE (see also The PRETENDERS)
US, female vocalist / guitarist (7 Singles: 41 Weeks)

3 Aug 85 ★ **I GOT YOU BABE** *DEP International DEP 20* [1] 1 13
18 Jun 88 ● **BREAKFAST IN BED** *DEP International DEP 29* [1] 6 11
12 Oct 91 **SPIRITUAL HIGH (STATE OF INDEPENDENCE)** *Arista 114528* [2] 66 2
23 Jan 93 **SPIRITUAL HIGH (STATE OF INDEPENDENCE)** (re-mix) *Arista 74321127712* [2] 47 2
18 Mar 95 ★ **LOVE CAN BUILD A BRIDGE** *London CO CD1* [3] 1 8
3 Jun 00 **KID 2000** *Virgin / EMI VTS CD2* [4] 32 2
7 Feb 04 **STRAIGHT AHEAD** *Direction 6746222* [5] 29 3

[1] UB40 featuring Chrissie Hynde [2] Moodswings featuring Chrissie Hynde [3] Cher, Chrissie Hynde and Neneh Cherry with Eric Clapton [4] Hybrid featuring Chrissie Hynde [5] Tube & Berger featuring Chrissie Hynde

HYPER GO GO *UK, male instrumental / production duo – Jamie Diplock and Alex Bell (7 Singles: 15 Weeks)*

22 Aug 92 **HIGH** *Deconstruction 74321110497* 30 5
31 Jul 93 **NEVER LET GO** *Positiva CDTIV 3* 45 3
5 Feb 94 **RAISE** *Positiva CDTIV 9* 36 2
26 Nov 94 **IT'S ALRIGHT** *Positiva CDTIV 20* 49 1
6 Apr 96 **DO WATCHA DO** *Avex UK AVEXCD 24* [1] 54 1
12 Oct 96 **HIGH** (re-mix) *Distinctive DISNCD 24* 32 2
12 Apr 97 **DO WATCHA DO** (re-mix) *Distinctive DISNCD 28* [1] 60 1

[1] Hyper Go Go and Adeva

HYPERLOGIC *UK, male instrumental / production trio (2 Singles: 3 Weeks)*

29 Jul 95 **ONLY ME** *Systematic SYSCD 15* 35 2
9 May 98 **ONLY ME** (re-mix) *Tidy Trax TIDY 113CD1* 48 1

HYPERSTATE *UK, male / female vocal / instrumental duo*

6 Feb 93 **TIME AFTER TIME** *M&G MAGCD 34* 71 1

HYPNOSIS (see also BLOWING FREE; HARMONIUM; IN TUNE; The JAMES BOYS; RAINDANCE; SCHOOL OF EXCELLENCE) *UK, male production / instrumental duo – Stewart and Bradley Palmer (2 Albums: 16 Weeks)*

17 Aug 96 **VOICES OF TRANQUILITY** *Dino DINCD 123* 16 12
15 Mar 97 **VOICES OF TRANQUILITY – VOLUME 2** *Dino DINCD 135* 32 4

HYPNOTIST (see also R.H.C.)
UK, male producer – Caspar Pound (2 Singles: 5 Weeks)

28 Sep 91 **THE HOUSE IS MINE** *Rising High RSN 4* 65 2
21 Dec 91 **THE HARDCORE EP** *Rising High RSN 13* 68 3

Tracks on The Hardcore EP: Hardcore U Know the Score / The Ride / Night of the Livin' E Heads / God of the Universe.

	28 August 1971	4 September 1971	11 September 1971	18 September 1971
UK No.1 SINGLES	I'M STILL WAITING Diana Ross	I'M STILL WAITING Diana Ross	I'M STILL WAITING Diana Ross	HEY GIRL DON'T BOTHER ME The Tams
UK No.1 ALBUMS	TOP OF THE POPS VOL.18 Various	TOP OF THE POPS VOL.18 Various	BRIDGE OVER TROUBLED WATER Simon and Garfunkel	WHO'S NEXT The Who

HYPO PSYCHO *UK / US, male vocal / instrumental group*

24 Jul 04 **PUBLIC ENEMY NO:1** *Believe / Snapper SMASCD 059*..............**53** 1

HYSTERIC EGO *UK, male producer – Rob White (4 Singles: 8 Weeks)*

31 Aug 96 **WANT LOVE** *WEA WEA 070CD*..............**28** 4
21 Jun 97 **MINISTRY OF LOVE** *WEA WEA 094CD*..............**39** 2
28 Feb 98 **WANT LOVE – THE REMIXES** *WEA WEA 150CD*..............**46** 1
13 Feb 99 **TIME TO GET BACK** *WEA WEA 198CD*..............**50** 1

The HYSTERICS *UK, male vocal / instrumental group*

12 Dec 81 **JINGLE BELLS LAUGHING ALL THE WAY** *Record Delivery KA 5*..............**44** 5

HYSTERIX *UK, male / female vocal / instrumental group (2 Singles: 4 Weeks)*

7 May 94 **MUST BE THE MUSIC** *Deconstruction 74321207362*..............**40** 3
18 Feb 95 **EVERYTHING** *Deconstruction 74321236882*..............**65** 1

I

I AM KLOOT *UK, male vocal / instrumental group (2 Albums: 2 Weeks, 3 Singles: 3 Weeks)*

21 Jun 03 **LIFE IN A DAY** *Echo ECSCD 140*..............**43** 1
20 Sep 03 **3 FEET TALL** *Echo ECDCD 143*..............**46** 1
27 Sep 03 I AM KLOOT *Echo ECHCD 46*..............68 1
2 Apr 05 **OVER MY SHOULDER** *Echo ECSD 160*..............**38** 1
23 Apr 05 GODS AND MONSTERS *Echo ECHCD 62*..............74 1

I DREAM featuring FRANKIE & CALVIN

(see also S CLUB JUNIORS) *UK, male / female actors / vocal group*

27 Nov 04 **DREAMING** *19 9868872*..............**19** 7

I KAMANCHI *UK, male production duo*

14 Jun 03 **NEVER CAN TELL / SOUL BEAT CALLING** *Full Cycle FCY 052*..............**69** 1

I-LEVEL

UK, male vocal / instrumental group (1 Album: 4 Weeks, 2 Singles: 9 Weeks)

16 Apr 83 **MINEFIELD** *Virgin VS 563*..............**52** 6
18 Jun 83 **TEACHER** *Virgin VS 595*..............**56** 3
9 Jul 83 I-LEVEL *Virgin V 2270*..............50 4

I MONSTER

UK, male production / vocal duo – Dean Honer and Jarrod Gosling

16 Jun 01 **DAYDREAM IN BLUE** *Instant Karma KARMA 7CD*..............**20** 6

IQ *UK, male vocal / instrumental group*

22 Jun 85 THE WAKE *Sahara SAH 136*..............72 1

Janis IAN *US, female vocalist – Janis Fink (2 Singles: 10 Weeks)*

17 Nov 79 **FLY TOO HIGH** *CBS 7936*..............**44** 7
28 Jun 80 **THE OTHER SIDE OF THE SUN** *CBS 8611*..............**44** 3

IAN VAN DAHL (see also DEE DEE) *Belgium, male / female production / vocal group – leader AnneMie Coenen (1 Album: 7 Weeks, 6 Singles: 49 Weeks)*

21 Jul 01 ● **CASTLES IN THE SKY** *Nulife 74321867142*..............**3** 16
22 Dec 01 ● **WILL I** *Nulife 74321903402*..............**5** 13
1 Jun 02 ● **REASON** *Nulife 74321938722*..............**8** 8
8 Jun 02 ● ACE *Nulife 74321934812*..............7 7
12 Oct 02 **TRY** *Nulife 74321967942*..............**15** 5
1 Nov 03 **I CAN'T LET YOU GO** *Nulife 82876570712*..............**20** 4
17 Jul 04 **BELIEVE** *Nulife 82876626532*..............**27** 3

ICE CUBE

US, male rapper – O'Shea Jackson (5 Albums: 11 Weeks, 11 Singles: 39 Weeks)

28 Jul 90 AMERIKKKA'S MOST WANTED *Fourth & Broadway BRLP 551*..............48 5
9 Mar 91 KILL AT WILL *Fourth & Broadway BRLM 572*..............66 3
5 Dec 92 THE PREDATOR *Fourth & Broadway BRCD 592* ▲..............73 1
27 Mar 93 **IT WAS A GOOD DAY** *Fourth & Broadway BRCD 270*..............**27** 4
7 Aug 93 **CHECK YO SELF** *Fourth & Broadway BRCD 283* [1] $..............**36** 4
11 Sep 93 **WICKED** *Fourth & Broadway BRCD 282*..............**62** 1
18 Dec 93 LETHAL INJECTION *Fourth & Broadway BRCD 609*..............52 1
18 Dec 93 **REALLY DOE** *Fourth & Broadway BRCD 302*..............**66** 1
26 Mar 94 **YOU KNOW HOW WE DO IT (re)** *Fourth & Broadway BRCD 303*..............**41** 5
27 Aug 94 **BOP GUN (ONE NATION)** *Fourth & Broadway BRCD 308* [2]..............**22** 3
11 Mar 95 **HAND OF THE DEAD BODY** *Virgin America VUSCD 88* [3]..............**41** 2
15 Apr 95 **NATURAL BORN KILLAZ** *Death Row A 8197CD* [4]..............**45** 2
22 Mar 97 **THE WORLD IS MINE** *Jive JIVECD 419*..............**60** 1
1 Apr 00 WAR & PEACE – VOL. II (THE PEACE DISC) *Priority CDPTY 183*..............56 1
11 Dec 04 ● **YOU CAN DO IT** *All Around the World CDGLOBE 396* [5]..............**2** 13
12 Feb 05 **ROLL CALL / WHAT U GON' DO** *TVT TVTUKCDX 2* [6]..............**38** 3

[1] Ice Cube featuring Das EFX [2] Ice Cube featuring George Clinton [3] Scarface featuring Ice Cube [4] Dr Dre and Ice Cube [5] Ice Cube featuring Mack 10 + Ms Toi [6] Lil Jon & The East Side Boyz featuring Ice Cube / featuring Lil' Scrappy

ICE MC *UK, male rapper – Ian Campbell (3 Singles: 5 Weeks)*

6 Aug 94 **THINK ABOUT THE WAY (BOM DIGI DIGI BOM ...)** *WEA YZ 829CD*..............**42** 2
8 Apr 95 **IT'S A RAINY DAY** *Eternal YZ 902CD*..............**73** 1
14 Sep 96 **BOM DIGI BOM (THINK ABOUT THE WAY)** (re-issue) *Eternal WEA 073CD*..............**38** 2

ICE-T

US, male rapper – Tracy Morrow (4 Albums: 15 Weeks, 9 Singles: 29 Weeks)

18 Mar 89 **HIGH ROLLERS** *Sire W 7574*..............**63** 2
21 Oct 89 THE ICEBERG / FREEDOM OF SPEECH *Warner Bros. WX 316*...42 2
17 Feb 90 **YOU PLAYED YOURSELF** *Sire W 9994*..............**64** 2
29 Sep 90 **SUPERFLY 1990** *Capitol CL 586* [1]..............**48** 3
25 May 91 OG – ORIGINAL GANGSTER *Sire WX 412*..............38 4
3 Apr 93 HOME INVASION *Rhyme Syndicate RSYND 1*..............15 7
8 May 93 **I AIN'T NEW TA THIS** *Rhyme Syndicate SYNDD 1*..............**62** 2
18 Dec 93 **THAT'S HOW I'M LIVIN'** *Rhyme Syndicate SYNDD 2*..............**21** 6
9 Apr 94 **GOTTA LOTTA LOVE** *Rhyme Syndicate SYNDD 3*..............**24** 4
10 Dec 94 **BORN TO RAISE HELL** *Fox 74321230152* [2]..............**47** 2
1 Jun 96 **I MUST STAND** *Rhyme Syndicate SYNDD 5*..............**23** 3
8 Jun 96 VI: RETURN OF THE REAL *Virgin RSYND 3*..............26 2
7 Dec 96 **THE LANE** *Rhyme Syndicate SYNDD 6*..............**18** 5

[1] Curtis Mayfield and Ice-T [2] Motörhead / Ice-T / Whitfield Crane

ICEBERG SLIMM *UK, male rapper – Duane Dyer (2 Singles: 3 Weeks)*

7 Oct 00 **NURSERY RHYMES** *Polydor 5877632*..............**37** 2
6 Nov 04 **STARSHIP** *V2 ARV 5029063* [1]..............**73** 1

[1] Iceberg Slimm featuring Coree

25 September 1971	2 October 1971	9 October 1971	16 October 1971
HEY GIRL DON'T BOTHER ME The Tams	HEY GIRL DON'T BOTHER ME The Tams	MAGGIE MAY Rod Stewart	MAGGIE MAY Rod Stewart
FIREBALL Deep Purple	EVERY PICTURE TELLS A STORY Rod Stewart	EVERY PICTURE TELLS A STORY Rod Stewart	EVERY PICTURE TELLS A STORY Rod Stewart

KEY UK No.1 ★ UK Top 10 ● Still on chart + UK entry at No.1 ■ US No.1 ▲ UK million seller £ US million seller $
Singles re-entries are listed as (re), (2re), (3re)... which signifies that the hit re-entered the chart once, twice or three times...
Peak Position / Weeks

ICEHOUSE *Australia, male vocal / instrumental group (2 Albums: 7 Weeks, 5 Singles: 28 Weeks)*

Date	Title	Label	Peak Position	Weeks
5 Feb 83	**HEY LITTLE GIRL**	*Chrysalis CHS 2670*	17	10
5 Mar 83	LOVE IN MOTION	*Chrysalis CHR 1390*	64	6
23 Apr 83	**STREET CAFE**	*Chrysalis COOL 1*	62	4
3 May 86	**NO PROMISES**	*Chrysalis CHS 2978*	72	1
29 Aug 87	**CRAZY (re)**	*Chrysalis CHS 3156*	38	9
2 Apr 88	MAN OF COLOURS	*Chrysalis CHR 1592*	93	1
14 May 88	**ELECTRIC BLUE**	*Chrysalis CHS 3239*	53	4

The ICICLE WORKS *UK, male vocal / instrumental group – leader Ian McNabb (6 Albums: 19 Weeks, 7 Singles: 28 Weeks)*

Date	Title	Label	Peak Position	Weeks
24 Dec 83	**LOVE IS A WONDERFUL COLOUR**	*Beggars Banquet BEG 99*	15	8
10 Mar 84	**BIRDS FLY (WHISPER TO A SCREAM) / IN THE CAULDRON OF LOVE**	*Beggars Banquet BEG 108*	53	4
31 Mar 84	THE ICICLE WORKS	*Beggars Banquet BEGA 50*	24	6
28 Sep 85	THE SMALL PRICE OF A BICYCLE	*Beggars Banquet BEGA 61*	55	3
1 Mar 86	SEVEN SINGLES DEEP	*Beggars Banquet BEGA 71*	52	2
26 Jul 86	**UNDERSTANDING JANE**	*Beggars Banquet BEG 160*	52	3
4 Oct 86	**WHO DO YOU WANT FOR YOUR LOVE?**	*Beggars Banquet BEG 172*	54	4
14 Feb 87	**EVANGELINE**	*Beggars Banquet BEG 181*	53	4
21 Mar 87	IF YOU WANT TO DEFEAT YOUR ENEMY SING HIS SONG	*Beggars Banquet BEGA 78*	28	4
30 Apr 88	**LITTLE GIRL LOST**	*Beggars Banquet BEG 215*	59	4
14 May 88	BLIND	*Beggars Banquet IWA 2*	40	3
17 Mar 90	**MOTORCYCLE RIDER**	*Epic WORKS 100*	73	1
5 Sep 92	THE BEST OF THE ICICLE WORKS	*Beggars Banquet BEGA 124CD*	60	1

ICON *UK, male / female vocal / instrumental duo*

Date	Title	Label	Peak Position	Weeks
15 Jun 96	**TAINTED LOVE**	*Eternal WEA 057CD*	51	1

IDEAL *UK, male producer – Jon Da Silva*

Date	Title	Label	Peak Position	Weeks
6 Aug 94	**HOT**	*Cleveland City CLECD 13019*	49	2

IDEAL U.S. featuring LIL' MO *US, male vocal group and female vocalist*

Date	Title	Label	Peak Position	Weeks
23 Sep 00	**WHATEVER**	*Virgin VUSCD 172*	31	3

The IDES OF MARCH *US, male vocal / instrumental group*

Date	Title	Label	Peak Position	Weeks
6 Jun 70	**VEHICLE**	*Warner Bros. WB 7378*	31	9

Eric IDLE featuring Richard WILSON
(see also MONTY PYTHON'S FLYING CIRCUS) *UK, male actors / vocalists*

Date	Title	Label	Peak Position	Weeks
17 Dec 94	**ONE FOOT IN THE GRAVE**	*Victa CDVICTA 1*	50	3

IDLEWILD *UK, male vocal (Roddy Woomble) / instrumental group (4 Albums: 16 Weeks, 15 Singles: 36 Weeks)*

Date	Title	Label	Peak Position	Weeks
9 May 98	**A FILM FOR THE FUTURE**	*Food CDFOOD 111*	53	1
25 Jul 98	**EVERYONE SAYS YOU'RE SO FRAGILE**	*Food CDFOOD 113*	47	1
24 Oct 98	**I'M A MESSAGE**	*Food CDFOOD 114*	41	1
7 Nov 98	HOPE IS IMPORTANT	*Food FOODCD 28*	53	1
13 Feb 99	**WHEN I ARGUE I SEE SHAPES**	*Food CDFOOD 116*	19	2
2 Oct 99	**LITTLE DISCOURAGE**	*Food CDFOOD 124*	24	2
8 Apr 00	**ACTUALLY IT'S DARKNESS**	*Food CDFOOD 127*	23	3
22 Apr 00	100 BROKEN WINDOWS	*Food FOODCD 32*	15	4
24 Jun 00	**THESE WOODEN IDEAS**	*Food CDFOOD 132*	32	3
28 Oct 00	**ROSEABILITY**	*Food CDFOODS 134*	38	2
4 May 02 ●	**YOU HELD THE WORLD IN YOUR ARMS**	*Parlophone CDRS 6575*	9	4
13 Jul 02	**AMERICAN ENGLISH**	*Parlophone CDRS 6582*	15	7
27 Jul 02 ●	THE REMOTE PART	*Parlophone 5402430*	3	8
2 Nov 02	**LIVE IN A HIDING PLACE**	*Parlophone CDRS 6587*	26	2
22 Feb 03	**A MODERN WAY OF LETTING GO**	*Parlophone CDR 6598*	28	2
5 Mar 05	**LOVE STEALS US FROM LONELINESS**	*Parlophone CDRS 6658*	16	3
19 Mar 05 ●	WARNINGS / PROMISES	*Parlophone 5607752*	9	3
14 May 05	**I UNDERSTAND IT**	*Parlophone CDRS 6662*	32	2
23 Jul 05	**EL CAPITAN**	*Parlophone CDRS 6667*	39	1

Billy IDOL (340 Top 500)

Snarling rock 'n' roll rebel of the 1980s. Former vocalist of punk group Generation X, b. William Broad, 30 Nov 1955, Middlesex, UK. He had his greatest success in the US, where four singles reached the Top 10 and 'Mony Mony' reached No.1 (6 Albums: 100 Weeks, 17 Singles: 106 Weeks)

Date	Title	Label	Peak Position	Weeks
11 Sep 82	**HOT IN THE CITY**	*Chrysalis CHS 2625*	58	4
24 Mar 84	**REBEL YELL**	*Chrysalis IDOL 2*	62	2
30 Jun 84	**EYES WITHOUT A FACE**	*Chrysalis IDOL 3*	18	11
29 Sep 84	**FLESH FOR FANTASY**	*Chrysalis IDOL 4*	54	3
8 Jun 85 ●	VITAL IDOL	*Chrysalis CUX 1502*	7	34
13 Jul 85 ●	**WHITE WEDDING**	*Chrysalis IDOL 5*	6	15
14 Sep 85 ●	**REBEL YELL** (re-issue)	*Chrysalis IDOL 6*	6	12
28 Sep 85	REBEL YELL	*Chrysalis CHR 1450*	36	11
4 Oct 86	**TO BE A LOVER**	*Chrysalis IDOL 8*	22	8
1 Nov 86 ●	WHIPLASH SMILE	*Chrysalis CDL 1514*	8	20
7 Mar 87	**DON'T NEED A GUN**	*Chrysalis IDOL 9*	26	5
13 Jun 87	**SWEET SIXTEEN**	*Chrysalis IDOL 10*	17	9
3 Oct 87 ●	**MONY MONY**	*Chrysalis IDOL 11* ▲	7	10
16 Jan 88	**HOT IN THE CITY** (re-mix)	*Chrysalis IDOL 12*	13	9
2 Jul 88 ●	IDOL SONGS: 11 OF THE BEST	*Chrysalis BILTVD 1*	2	25
13 Aug 88	**CATCH MY FALL**	*Chrysalis IDOL 13*	63	3
28 Apr 90	**CRADLE OF LOVE**	*Chrysalis IDOL 14*	34	4
12 May 90	CHARMED LIFE	*Chrysalis CHR 1735*	15	8
11 Aug 90	**L.A. WOMAN**	*Chrysalis IDOL 15*	70	2
22 Dec 90	**PRODIGAL BLUES**	*Chrysalis IDOL 16*	47	4
26 Jun 93	**SHOCK TO THE SYSTEM**	*Chrysalis CDCHS 3994*	30	3
10 Jul 93	CYBERPUNK	*Chrysalis CDCHR 6000*	20	2
10 Sep 94	**SPEED**	*Fox 74321223472*	47	2

The IDOLS *UK, male / female vocal group*

Date	Title	Label	Peak Position	Weeks
27 Dec 03 ●	**HAPPY XMAS (WAR IS OVER)**	*S 82876583822*	5	5

Frank IFIELD (264 Top 500)

Early 60s superstar, b. 30 Nov 1937, Coventry, UK, and raised in Australia. This pop vocalist / yodeller had four No.1s in 12 months with revivals of US standards. Unlike many of his early 1960s UK contemporaries, his records also did well internationally. Best-selling single: 'I Remember You' 1,096,000 (4 Albums: 83 Weeks, 16 Singles: 163 Weeks)

Date	Title	Label	Peak Position	Weeks
19 Feb 60	**LUCKY DEVIL (re)**	*Columbia DB 4399*	22	8
29 Sep 60	**GOTTA GET A DATE**	*Columbia DB 4496*	49	1
5 Jul 62 ★	**I REMEMBER YOU**	*Columbia DB 4856* £	1	28
25 Oct 62 ★	**LOVESICK BLUES**	*Columbia DB 4913*	1	17
24 Jan 63 ★	**THE WAYWARD WIND**	*Columbia DB 4960*	1	13
16 Feb 63 ●	I'LL REMEMBER YOU	*Columbia 33SX 1467*	3	36
11 Apr 63 ●	**NOBODY'S DARLIN' BUT MINE**	*Columbia DB 7007*	4	16
27 Jun 63 ★	**CONFESSIN' (THAT I LOVE YOU)**	*Columbia DB 7062*	1	16
21 Sep 63 ●	BORN FREE	*Columbia 33SX 1462*	3	32
17 Oct 63	**MULE TRAIN**	*Columbia DB 7131*	22	6
9 Jan 64 ●	**DON'T BLAME ME**	*Columbia DB 7184*	8	13
28 Mar 64 ●	BLUE SKIES	*Columbia 55SX 1588*	10	12
23 Apr 64	**ANGRY AT THE BIG OAK TREE**	*Columbia DB 7263*	25	8
23 Jul 64	**I SHOULD CARE**	*Columbia DB 7319*	33	3
1 Oct 64	**SUMMER IS OVER**	*Columbia DB 7355*	25	6
19 Dec 64 ●	GREATEST HITS	*Columbia 33SX 1633*	9	3
19 Aug 65	**PARADISE**	*Columbia DB 7655*	26	9
23 Jun 66	**NO ONE WILL EVER KNOW**	*Columbia DB 7940*	25	4
8 Dec 66	**CALL HER YOUR SWEETHEART**	*Columbia DB 8078*	24	11
7 Dec 91	**SHE TAUGHT ME HOW TO YODEL**	*EMI 7YODEL 1* [1]	40	4

[1] Frank Ifield featuring The Backroom Boys

	23 October 1971	30 October 1971	6 November 1971	13 November 1971
UK No.1 SINGLES	**MAGGIE MAY** Rod Stewart	**MAGGIE MAY** Rod Stewart	**MAGGIE MAY** Rod Stewart	**COZ I LUV YOU** Slade
UK No.1 ALBUMS	**EVERY PICTURE TELLS A STORY** Rod Stewart	**IMAGINE** John Lennon and The Plastic Ono Band with The Flux Fiddlers	**IMAGINE** John Lennon and The Plastic Ono Band with The Flux Fiddlers	**EVERY PICTURE TELLS A STORY** Rod Stewart

Enrique IGLESIAS (415 Top 500)

Multi-award-winning Latin superstar, b. 8 May 1975, Madrid, Spain. The son of Julio Iglesias (they are the only father / son to both top the UK singles chart). This top-selling Spanish language artist has sold over 40 million albums across the globe (2 Albums: 84 Weeks, 11 Singles: 89 Weeks)

11 Sep 99	●	**BAILAMOS** *Interscope IND 97131* ▲	4	9
18 Dec 99		**RHYTHM DIVINE** *Interscope 4972242*	45	2
14 Oct 00	●	**COULD I HAVE THIS KISS FOREVER** *Arista 74321795992* [1]	7	8
26 Jan 02	★	**ESCAPE** *Interscope 4931822*	1	71
2 Feb 02	★	**HERO** *Interscope IND 97671* [2] ■	1	19
27 Apr 02		**ESCAPE** (import) *Interscope 4976922* [2]	71	2
25 May 02	●	**ESCAPE** *Interscope 4977062* [2]	3	14
7 Sep 02		**LOVE TO SEE YOU CRY** *Interscope IND 97760*	12	7
7 Dec 02		**MAYBE** *Interscope 4978222* [2]	12	9
26 Apr 03		**TO LOVE A WOMAN** *Mercury 0779082* [3]	19	4
29 Nov 03		**ADDICTED** *Interscope 9814327*	11	6
6 Dec 03		**7** *Interscope / Polydor 9861477*	13	13
20 Mar 04	●	**NOT IN LOVE** *Interscope 9862022* [4]	5	9

[1] Whitney Houston and Enrique Iglesias [2] Enrique [3] Lionel Richie featuring Enrique Iglesias [4] Enrique featuring Kelis

Julio IGLESIAS (258 Top 500)

Spain's most successful vocalist of all time with reported world sales of more than 225 million albums, b. 23 Sep 1943, Madrid. Suave singer was still adding to his hits and awards in the 21st century, and his son Enrique is also a top-selling Latin artists (14 Albums: 175 Weeks, 9 Singles: 75 Weeks)

24 Oct 81	★	**BEGIN THE BEGUINE (VOLVER A EMPEZAR)** *CBS A 1612*	1	14
7 Nov 81		**DE NINA A MUJER** *CBS 85063*	43	5
28 Nov 81	●	**BEGIN THE BEGUINE** *CBS 85462*	5	28
6 Mar 82	●	**QUIEREME MUCHO (YOURS)** *CBS A 1939*	3	9
9 Oct 82		**AMOR** *CBS A 2801*	32	7
16 Oct 82		**AMOR** *CBS 25103*	14	14
9 Apr 83		**HEY!** *CBS JULIO 1*	31	7
2 Jul 83	●	**JULIO** *CBS 10038*	5	17
7 Apr 84		**TO ALL THE GIRLS I'VE LOVED BEFORE** *CBS A 4252* [1] $	17	10
7 Jul 84		**ALL OF YOU** *CBS A 4522* [2]	43	8
1 Sep 84		**1100 BEL AIR PLACE** *CBS 86308*	14	14
19 Oct 85		**LIBRA** *CBS 26623*	61	4
6 Aug 88	●	**MY LOVE** *CBS JULIO 2* [3]	5	11
3 Sep 88		**NON STOP** *CBS 460990 1*	33	14
1 Dec 90		**STARRY NIGHT** *CBS 4672841*	27	20
28 May 94	●	**CRAZY** *Columbia 4747382*	6	37
4 Jun 94		**CRAZY (re)** *Columbia 6603695*	43	5
26 Nov 94		**FRAGILE (re)** *Columbia 6610192*	53	4
12 Aug 95	●	**LA CARRETERA** *Columbia 4807042*	6	6
30 Nov 96		**TANGO** *Columbia 4866752*	56	3
7 Nov 98		**MY LIFE – THE GREATEST HITS** *Columbia 4910902*	18	9
22 Jul 00		**NOCHE DE CUATRO LUNAS** *Columbia 4974222*	32	3
19 Jul 03		**LOVE SONGS** *Columbia 5126042*	64	1

[1] Julio Iglesias and Willie Nelson [2] Julio Iglesias and Diana Ross [3] Julio Iglesias featuring Stevie Wonder

The IGNORANTS *UK, male vocal duo*

25 Dec 93		**PHAT GIRLS** *Spaghetti CIOCD 8*	59	3

IIO *US, male / female production duo – Marcus Moser and Nadia Ali (2 Singles: 15 Weeks)*

10 Nov 01	●	**RAPTURE** *Made / Data / MoS DATA 27CDS*	2	12
14 Jun 03		**AT THE END** *Free 2 Air 0148065 F2A*	20	3

IKARA COLT

UK, male / female vocal / instrumental group (4 Singles: 4 Weeks)

2 Mar 02		**RUDD** *Fantastic Plastic FPS 029*	72	1
28 Feb 04		**WANNA BE THAT WAY** *Fantastic Plastic FPS 038*	49	1
5 Jun 04		**WAKE IN THE CITY** *Fantastic Plastic FPS 040*	55	1
23 Oct 04		**MODERN FEELING** *Fantastic Plastic FPS 042*	61	1

IL DIVO

France / Spain / Switzerland / US, male vocal group (2 Albums: 38 Weeks)

13 Nov 04	★	**IL DIVO** *Syco Music 82876651952* ■	1	31
19 Nov 05	★	**ANCORA** *Syco Music 82876731062* ■	1	7+

IL PADRINOS featuring Jocelyn BROWN

(see also AKABU featuring Linda CLIFFORD; HED BOYS; JAKATTA; Li KWAN; Joey NEGRO; PHASE II; RAVEN MAIZE; Z FACTOR) *UK, male production duo – Dave Lee and Danny Rampling and US, female vocalist*

7 Sep 02		**THAT'S HOW GOOD YOUR LOVE IS** *Defected DFTD 057CDS*	54	1

ILLEGAL MOTION featuring Simone CHAPMAN

UK, male / female vocal / instrumental duo

9 Oct 93		**SATURDAY LOVE** *Arista 74321163032*	67	1

ILLICIT featuring GRAM'MA FUNK

UK, male production duo and US, female vocalist

2 Sep 00		**CHEEKY ARMADA** *Yola YOLACDX 01*	72	1

ILS *UK, male producer*

23 Feb 02		**NEXT LEVEL** *Marine Parade MAPA 012*	75	1

IMAANI (see also TRU FAITH & DUB CONSPIRACY)

UK, female vocalist – Imaani Saleem (Melanie Crosdale)

9 May 98		**WHERE ARE YOU** *EMI CDEM 510*	15	7

IMAGINATION (300 Top 500)

Distinctive London-based trio, who created a unique blend of soul and dance music: Leee John (v), Ashley Ingram (v/k) and Errol Kennedy (d). One of the most original British acts of the early 1980s, they were fronted by a charismatic and flamboyant lead singer (5 Albums: 122 Weeks, 12 Singles: 105 Weeks)

16 May 81	●	**BODY TALK** *R&B RBS 201*	4	18
5 Sep 81		**IN AND OUT OF LOVE** *R&B RBS 202*	16	9
24 Oct 81		**BODY TALK** *R&B RBLP 1001*	20	53
14 Nov 81		**FLASHBACK** *R&B RBS 206*	16	13
6 Mar 82	●	**JUST AN ILLUSION** *R&B RBS 208*	2	11
26 Jun 82	●	**MUSIC AND LIGHTS** *R&B RBS 210*	5	9
11 Sep 82	●	**IN THE HEAT OF THE NIGHT** *R&B RBLP 1002*	7	29
25 Sep 82		**IN THE HEAT OF THE NIGHT** *R&B RBS 211*	22	8
11 Dec 82		**CHANGES** *R&B RBS 213*	31	8
14 May 83	●	**NIGHT DUBBING** *R&B RBDUB 1*	9	20
4 Jun 83		**LOOKING AT MIDNIGHT** *R&B RBS 214*	29	7
5 Nov 83		**NEW DIMENSIONS** *R&B RBS 216*	56	3
12 Nov 83		**SCANDALOUS** *R&B RBLP 1004*	25	8
26 May 84		**STATE OF LOVE** *R&B RBS 218*	67	2
24 Nov 84		**THANK YOU MY LOVE** *R&B RBS 219*	22	15
16 Jan 88		**INSTINCTUAL** *RCA PB 41697*	62	2
12 Aug 89	●	**IMAGINATION – ALL THE HITS** *Stylus SMR 985*	4	12

IMAJIN *US, male vocal group (4 Singles: 7 Weeks)*

27 Jun 98		**SHORTY (YOU KEEP PLAYING WITH MY MIND)** *Jive 0521212* [1]	22	3
20 Feb 99		**NO DOUBT** *Jive 0521772*	42	2
24 Apr 99		**BOUNCE, ROCK, SKATE, ROLL** *Jive 0522142* [2]	45	1
12 Feb 00		**FLAVA** *Jive 9250012*	64	1

[1] Imajin featuring Keith Murray [2] Baby D featuring Imajin

Natalie IMBRUGLIA (369 Top 500)

Australian actor turned sultry pop singer, b. 4 Feb 1975, Sydney. The star of long-running soap Neighbours (1991-94) won six ARIAs (Australian music awards) in 1998 and two BRITs in 1999. Although only a No.2 hit, the Grammy-nominated 'Torn' is among the UK's all-time Top 100 best-sellers (3 Albums: 118 Weeks, 9 Singles: 70 Weeks)

8 Nov 97	●	**TORN** *RCA 74321527982*	2	17
6 Dec 97	●	**LEFT OF THE MIDDLE** *RCA 74321544412*	5	87

20 November 1971	27 November 1971	4 December 1971	11 December 1971
COZ I LUV YOU Slade	**COZ I LUV YOU** Slade	**COZ I LUV YOU** Slade	**ERNIE (THE FASTEST MILKMAN IN THE WEST)** Benny Hill
EVERY PICTURE TELLS A STORY Rod Stewart	**TOP OF THE POPS VOL.20** Various	**FOUR SYMBOLS (LED ZEPPELIN IV)** Led Zeppelin	**FOUR SYMBOLS (LED ZEPPELIN IV)** Led Zeppelin

KEY
UK No.1 ★ UK Top 10 ● Still on chart + UK entry at No.1 ■
US No.1 ▲ UK million seller £ US million seller $
Singles re-entries are listed as (re), (2re), (3re)… which signifies that the hit re-entered the chart once, twice or three times…

Peak Position / Weeks

14 Mar 98 ● **BIG MISTAKE** *RCA 74321566782* 2 10
6 Jun 98 **WISHING I WAS THERE** *RCA 74321585062* 19 5
17 Oct 98 ● **SMOKE** *RCA 74321621942* 5 7
10 Nov 01 **THAT DAY (re)** *RCA 74321896792* 11 5
17 Nov 01 WHITE LILIES ISLAND *RCA 74321891212* 15 15
23 Mar 02 ● **WRONG IMPRESSION** *RCA 74321928352* 10 7
3 Aug 02 **BEAUTY ON THE FIRE** *RCA 74321947022* 26 2
2 Apr 05 ● **SHIVER** *Brightside 82876686872* 8 12
16 Apr 05 ★ COUNTING DOWN THE DAYS *BMG 82876683712* ■ 1 16
6 Aug 05 **COUNTING DOWN THE DAYS** *Brightside 82876715592* 23 5

IMMACULATE FOOLS *UK, male vocal / instrumental group*

26 Jan 85 **IMMACULATE FOOLS** *A&M AM 227* 51 4
11 May 85 HEARTS OF FORTUNE *A&M AMA 5030* 65 2

IMMATURE featuring SMOOTH
US, male vocal group and female vocalist

16 Mar 96 **WE GOT IT** *MCA MCSTD 48009* 26 2

The IMPALAS *US, male vocal group*

21 Aug 59 **SORRY (I RAN ALL THE WAY HOME)** *MGM 1015* $ 28 1

IMPEDANCE *UK, male producer – Daniel Haydon*

11 Nov 89 **TAINTED LOVE** *Jumpin' & Pumpin' TOT 4* 54 4

IMPERIAL DRAG *UK, male vocal / instrumental group*

12 Oct 96 **BOY OR A GIRL** *Columbia 6632992* 54 1

IMPERIAL TEEN *US, male / female vocal / instrumental group*

7 Sep 96 **YOU'RE ONE** *Slash LASCD 57* 69 1

The IMPERIALS *US, male vocal group*

24 Dec 77 **WHO'S GONNA LOVE ME** *Power Exchange PX 266* 17 9

The IMPRESSIONS *US, male vocal group*

22 Nov 75 **FIRST IMPRESSIONS** *Curtom K 16638* 16 10

The IN CROWD *UK, male vocal / instrumental group*

20 May 65 **THAT'S HOW STRONG MY LOVE IS** *Parlophone R 5276* 48 1

IN TUA NUA *Ireland, male / female vocal / instrumental group*

14 May 88 **ALL I WANTED** *Virgin VS 1072* 69 2

IN TUNE (see also BLOWING FREE; HYPNOSIS; The JAMES BOYS; RAINDANCE; SCHOOL OF EXCELLENCE)
UK, male instrumental duo – Bradley and Stewart Palmer

17 Jun 95 ACOUSTIC MOODS *Global Television RADCD 13* 21 3

INAURA *UK, male vocal / instrumental group*

18 May 96 **COMA AROMA** *EMI CDEM 421* 57 1

INCANTATION
UK, male instrumental group (3 Albums: 52 Weeks, 1 Single: 12 Weeks)

4 Dec 82 **CACHARPAYA (ANDES PUMPSA DAESI)** *Beggars Banquet BEG 84* 12 12
11 Dec 82 ● CACHARPAYA (PANPIPES OF THE ANDES) *Beggars Banquet BEGA 39* 9 26
17 Dec 83 DANCE OF THE FLAMES *Beggars Banquet BEGA 49* 61 7
28 Dec 85 BEST OF INCANTATION – MUSIC FROM THE ANDES *West Five CODA 19* 28 19

INCOGNITO *UK, male / female vocal / instrumental group (6 Albums: 19 Weeks, 13 Singles: 38 Weeks)*

15 Nov 80 **PARISIENNE GIRL** *Ensign ENY 44* 73 2
18 Apr 81 JAZZ FUNK *Ensign ENVY 504* 28 8
29 Jun 91 ● **ALWAYS THERE** *Talkin Loud TLK 10* [1] 6 9
27 Jul 91 INSIDE LIFE *Talkin Loud 8485461* 44 2
14 Sep 91 **CRAZY FOR YOU** *Talkin Loud TLK 14* [2] 59 2
6 Jun 92 **DON'T YOU WORRY 'BOUT A THING** *Talkin Loud TLK 21* 19 6
4 Jul 92 TRIBES VIBES AND SCRIBES *Talkin Loud 5123632* 41 2
15 Aug 92 **CHANGE** *Talkin Loud TLK 26* 52 2
21 Aug 93 **STILL A FRIEND OF MINE** *Talkin Loud TLKCD 42* 47 2
6 Nov 93 POSITIVITY *Talkin Loud 5182602* 55 2
20 Nov 93 **GIVIN' IT UP** *Talkin Loud TLKCD 44* 43 2
12 Mar 94 **PIECES OF A DREAM** *Talkin Loud TLKCD 46* 35 2
27 May 95 **EVERYDAY** *Talkin Loud TLKCD 55* 23 3
17 Jun 95 100 DEGREES AND RISING *Talkin Loud 5280002* 11 4
5 Aug 95 **I HEAR YOUR NAME** *Talkin Loud TLKCD 56* 42 3
11 May 96 **JUMP TO MY LOVE / ALWAYS THERE** (re-recording) *Talkin Loud TLCD 7* 29 3
1 Jun 96 REMIXED *Talkin Loud 5323092* 56 1
26 Oct 96 **OUT OF THE STORM** *Talkin Loud TLCD 14* 57 1
10 Apr 99 **NIGHTS OVER EGYPT** *Talkin Loud TLCD 40* 56 1

[1] Incognito featuring Jocelyn Brown [2] Incognito featuring Chyna

The INCREDIBLE STRING BAND
UK, male / female vocal / instrumental group (7 Albums: 37 Weeks)

21 Oct 67 5000 SPIRITS OR THE LAYERS OF THE ONION *Elektra EUKS 257* 25 5
6 Apr 68 ● THE HANGMAN'S BEAUTIFUL DAUGHTER *Elektra EVKS 7258* 5 21
20 Jul 68 THE INCREDIBLE STRING BAND *Elektra EKL 254* 34 3
24 Jan 70 CHANGING HORSES *Elektra EKS 74057* 30 1
9 May 70 I LOOKED UP *Elektra 2469002* 30 4
31 Oct 70 U *Elektra 2665001* 34 2
30 Oct 71 LIQUID ACROBAT AS REGARDS THE AIR *Island ILPS 9172* 46 1

INCUBUS *US, male vocal (Brandon Boyd) / instrumental group (2 Albums: 8 Weeks, 6 Singles: 12 Weeks)*

20 May 00 **PARDON ME** *Epic 6693462* 61 1
23 Jun 01 **DRIVE** *Epic 6713782* 40 2
3 Nov 01 MORNING VIEW *Epic 5040612* 15 4
2 Feb 02 **WISH YOU WERE HERE** *Epic 6722552* 27 3
14 Sep 02 **ARE YOU IN?** *Epic 6728482* 34 2
7 Feb 04 **MEGALOMANIAC** *Epic 6746462* 23 3
14 Feb 04 ● A CROW LEFT OF THE MURDER … *Epic 5150473* 6 4
19 Jun 04 **TALK SHOWS ON MUTE** *Epic 6749022* 43 1

INDEEP *US, male / female vocal / rap group (2 Singles: 11 Weeks)*

22 Jan 83 **LAST NIGHT A DJ SAVED MY LIFE** *Sound of New York SNY 1* 13 9
14 May 83 **WHEN BOYS TALK** *Sound of New York SNY 3* 67 2

INDIA *US, female vocalist – Linda Caballero (7 Singles: 15 Weeks)*

26 Feb 94 **LOVE AND HAPPINESS (YEMAYA Y OCHUN)** *Cooltempo CDCOOL 287* [1] 50 2
5 Aug 95 **I CAN'T GET NO SLEEP** *A&M 5811412* [2] 44 2
16 Mar 96 **OYE COMO VA** *Media MCSTD 40013* [3] 36 2
8 Feb 97 **RUNAWAY** *Talkin Loud TLCD 20* [4] 24 4
19 Jul 97 **OYE COMO VA** (re-issue) *Nukleuz MCSTD 40120* [3] 56 1
31 Jul 99 **TO BE IN LOVE** *Defected DEFECT 5CDS* [5] 23 3
6 Jul 02 **BACKFIRED** *SuSu CDSUSU 4* [6] 62 1

[1] River Ocean featuring India [2] Masters at Work presents India [3] Tito Puente Jr and the Latin Rhythm featuring Tito Puente, India and Cali Aleman [4] Nuyorican Soul featuring India [5] MAW presents India [6] Masters at Work featuring India

18 December 1971	25 December 1971	1 January 1972	8 January 1972
UK No.1 SINGLES			
ERNIE (THE FASTEST MILKMAN IN THE WEST) Benny Hill	**ERNIE (THE FASTEST MILKMAN IN THE WEST)** Benny Hill	**ERNIE (THE FASTEST MILKMAN IN THE WEST)** Benny Hill	**I'D LIKE TO TEACH THE WORLD TO SING (IN PERFECT HARMONY)** The New Seekers
UK No.1 ALBUMS			
ELECTRIC WARRIOR T. Rex	**ELECTRIC WARRIOR** T. Rex	**ELECTRIC WARRIOR** T. Rex	**ELECTRIC WARRIOR** T. Rex

INDIAN VIBES *UK, male vocal / instrumental group (2 Singles: 2 Weeks)*

24 Sep 94 **MATHAR** *Virgin International DINSD 136* 68 1
2 May 98 **MATHAR** (re-mix) *VC Recordings VCRD 32* 52 1

INDIEN (see also EMMIE) *UK, male / female production / vocal duo – Mark Hadfield and Emma Morton-Smith*

9 Aug 03 **SHOW ME LOVE** *Concept CDCON 40* 69 1

INDIGO GIRLS *US, female vocal / instrumental duo – Amy Ray and Emily Saliers (2 Albums: 3 Weeks)*

11 Jun 94 **SWAMP OPHELIA** *Epic 4759312* 66 1
15 Jul 95 **4.5** *Epic 4804392* 43 2

INDO *US, female vocal duo*

18 Apr 98 **R U SLEEPING** *Satellite 74321568212* 31 3

INDUSTRY STANDARD
UK, male DJ / production duo – Clayton Mitchell and Dave Dellar

10 Jan 98 **VOLUME 1 (WHAT YOU WANT WHAT YOU NEED)** *Satellite 74321543742* 34 3

INFA RIOT *UK, male vocal / instrumental group*

7 Aug 82 **STILL OUT OF ORDER** *Secret SEC 7* 42 4

INFRARED vs Gil FELIX
UK / Switzerland, male production duo and Brazil, male vocalist / guitarist

4 Oct 03 **CAPOEIRA** *Infrared INFRA 24CD* 67 1

INGRAM *US, male vocal / instrumental group*

11 Jun 83 **SMOOTHIN' GROOVIN'** *Streetwave WAVE 3* 56 2

James INGRAM
US, male vocalist (2 Albums: 19 Weeks, 5 Singles: 42 Weeks)

12 Feb 83 **BABY COME TO ME** *Qwest K 15005* [1] ▲ $ 11 10
18 Feb 84 **YAH MO B THERE (2re)** *Qwest 9394* [2] 12 16
31 Mar 84 **IT'S YOUR NIGHT** *Qwest 9239701* 25 17
30 Aug 86 **NEVER FELT SO GOOD** *Qwest WX 44* 72 2
11 Jul 87 ● **SOMEWHERE OUT THERE** *MCA MCA 1132* [3] 8 13
31 Mar 90 **SECRET GARDEN** *Qwest W 9992* [4] 67 1
16 Apr 94 **THE DAY I FALL IN LOVE** *Columbia 6600282* [5] 64 2

[1] Patti Austin and James Ingram [2] James Ingram with Michael McDonald [3] Linda Ronstadt and James Ingram [4] Quincy Jones featuring Al B Sure!, James Ingram, El DeBarge and Barry White [5] Dolly Parton and James Ingram

The INK SPOTS *US, male vocal (Charlie Fuqua, d. 1970) group*

29 Apr 55 ● **MELODY OF LOVE** *Parlophone R 3977* 10 4

John INMAN *UK, male actor / vocalist*

25 Oct 75 **ARE YOU BEING SERVED SIR?** *DJM DJS 602* 39 6

INMATES *UK, male vocal / instrumental group*

8 Dec 79 **THE WALK** *Radar ADA 47* 36 9

INME *UK, male vocal / instrumental group (2 Albums: 3 Weeks, 7 Singles: 10 Weeks)*

27 Jul 02 **UNDERDOSE** *Music for Nations CDKUT 195* 66 1
28 Sep 02 **FIREFLY** *Music for Nations CDKUT 197* 43 1
18 Jan 03 **CRUSHED LIKE FRUIT** *Music for Nations CDKUT 200* 25 2
8 Feb 03 **OVERGROWN EDEN** *Music for Nations CDMFNX 275* 15 2
26 Apr 03 **NEPTUNE** *Music for Nations CDKUT 201* 46 1
5 Jun 04 **FASTER THE CHASE** *Music for Nations CDKUT 210* 31 2
2 Jul 05 **WHITE BUTTERFLY** *V2 PBCD 001NME* 56 1
30 Jul 05 **7 WEEKS** *V2 / Pandora's Box PB 002NMECD* 36 2
22 Oct 05 **SO YOU KNOW** *Pandora's Box PB 003NMECD* 33 1

INNER CIRCLE *Jamaica, male vocal / instrumental group (1 Album: 2 Weeks, 5 Singles: 35 Weeks)*

24 Feb 79 **EVERYTHING IS GREAT** *Island WIP 6472* 37 8
12 May 79 **STOP BREAKING MY HEART** *Island WIP 6488* 50 3
31 Oct 92 ● **SWEAT (A LA LA LA LA LONG) (re)** *Magnet 9031776802* 3 19
29 May 93 **BAD TO THE BONE** *Magnet 9031776772* 44 2
31 Jul 93 **BAD BOYS** *Magnet MAG 1017CD* 52 3
10 Sep 94 **GAMES PEOPLE PLAY** *Magnet MAG 1026CD* 67 2

'Sweat (A La La La La Long)' peaked on re-entry in May 1993.

INNER CITY
(see also REESE PROJECT; TRONIKHOUSE) *US, male / female vocal (Paris Grey) / production group (4 Albums: 39 Weeks, 18 Singles: 81 Weeks)*

3 Sep 88 ● **BIG FUN** *10 TEN 240* [1] 8 14
10 Dec 88 ● **GOOD LIFE** *10 TEN 249* 4 12
22 Apr 89 ● **AIN'T NOBODY BETTER** *10 TEN 252* 10 7
20 May 89 ● **PARADISE** *10 DIX 81* 3 30
29 Jul 89 **DO YOU LOVE WHAT YOU FEEL** *10 TEN 273* 16 7
18 Nov 89 **WATCHA GONNA DO WITH MY LOVIN'** *10 TEN 290* 12 9
10 Feb 90 **PARADISE REMIXED** *10 XID 81* 17 6
13 Oct 90 **THAT MAN (HE'S ALL MINE)** *10 TEN 334* 42 4
23 Feb 91 **TILL WE MEET AGAIN** *Ten TEN 337* 47 2
7 Dec 91 **LET IT REIGN** *Ten TEN 392* 51 2
4 Apr 92 **HALLELUJAH '92** *Ten TEN 398* 22 4
13 Jun 92 **PENNIES FROM HEAVEN** *Ten TEN 405* 24 4
11 Jul 92 **PRAISE** *Ten 4718862* 52 1
12 Sep 92 **PRAISE** *Ten TENX 408* 59 2
27 Feb 93 **TILL WE MEET AGAIN** (re-mix) *Ten TENCD 414* 55 1
15 May 93 **TESTAMENT 93** *Ten CDOVD 438* 33 2
14 Aug 93 **BACK TOGETHER AGAIN** *Six6 SIXCD 104* 49 1
5 Feb 94 **DO YA** *Six6 SIXCD 107* 44 2
9 Jul 94 **SHARE MY LIFE** *Six6 SIXCD 114* 62 1
10 Feb 96 **YOUR LOVE** *Six6 SIXCD 127* 28 2
5 Oct 96 **DO ME RIGHT** *Six6 SIXXCD 2* 47 1
6 Feb 99 ● **GOOD LIFE (BUENA VIDA)** (re-recording) *Pias Recordings PIASX 002CD* 10 6

[1] Inner City featuring Kevin Saunderson

INNER SANCTUM *Canada, male producer – Steve Bolton*

23 May 98 **HOW SOON IS NOW** *Malarky MLKD 6* 75 1

INNERZONE ORCHESTRA *US, male producer – Carl Craig*

28 Sep 96 **BUG IN THE BASSBIN** *Mo Wax MW 049CD* 68 1

INNOCENCE *UK, male / female vocal / instrumental group (2 Albums: 20 Weeks, 8 Singles: 33 Weeks)*

3 Mar 90 **NATURAL THING** *Cooltempo COOL 201* 16 7
21 Jul 90 **SILENT VOICE** *Cooltempo COOL 212* 37 5
13 Oct 90 **LET'S PUSH IT** *Cooltempo COOL 220* 25 6
10 Nov 90 **BELIEF** *Cooltempo CTLP 20* 24 19
8 Dec 90 **A MATTER OF FACT** *Cooltempo COOL 223* 37 7
30 Mar 91 **REMEMBER THE DAY** *Cooltempo COOL 226* 56 2
20 Jun 92 **I'LL BE THERE** *Cooltempo COOL 255* 26 3
3 Oct 92 **ONE LOVE IN MY LIFETIME** *Cooltempo COOL 263* 40 2
31 Oct 92 **BUILD** *Cooltempo CTCD 26* 66 1
21 Nov 92 **BUILD** *Cooltempo COOL 267* 72 1

INSANE CLOWN POSSE *US, male rap duo (2 Singles: 2 Weeks)*

17 Jan 98 **HALLS OF ILLUSION** *Island CID 685* 56 1
6 Jun 98 **HOKUS POKUS** *Island CIDX 705* 53 1

INSPIRAL CARPETS *UK, male vocal / instrumental group (6 Albums: 37 Weeks, 16 Singles: 51 Weeks)*

18 Nov 89 **MOVE** *Cow DUNG 6* 49 2

15 January 1972	22 January 1972	29 January 1972	5 February 1972
I'D LIKE TO TEACH THE WORLD TO SING (IN PERFECT HARMONY) The New Seekers	**I'D LIKE TO TEACH THE WORLD TO SING (IN PERFECT HARMONY)** The New Seekers	**I'D LIKE TO TEACH THE WORLD TO SING (IN PERFECT HARMONY)** The New Seekers	**TELEGRAM SAM** T. Rex
ELECTRIC WARRIOR T. Rex	**ELECTRIC WARRIOR** T. Rex	**CONCERT FOR BANGLADESH** Various	**ELECTRIC WARRIOR** T. Rex

KEY UK No.1 ★ UK Top 10 ● Still on chart + UK entry at No.1 ■ US No.1 ▲ UK million seller £ US million seller $
Singles re-entries are listed as (re), (2re), (3re)... which signifies that the hit re-entered the chart once, twice or three times...

Peak Position / Weeks

17 Mar 90 THIS IS HOW IT FEELS *Cow DUNG 7* 14 8
5 May 90 ● LIFE *Cow DUNG 8* 2 21
30 Jun 90 SHE COMES IN THE FALL *Cow DUNG 10* 27 6
17 Nov 90 ISLAND HEAD (EP) *Cow DUNG 11* 21 4
30 Mar 91 CARAVAN *Cow DUNG 13* 30 5
4 May 91 ● THE BEAST INSIDE *Cow DUNG 14* 5 6
22 Jun 91 PLEASE BE CRUEL *Cow DUNG 15* 50 2
29 Feb 92 DRAGGING ME DOWN *Cow DUNG 16* 12 5
30 May 92 TWO WORLDS COLLIDE *Cow DUNG 17* 32 2
19 Sep 92 GENERATIONS *Cow DUNG 18T* 28 3
17 Oct 92 REVENGE OF THE GOLDFISH *Cow DUNG 19* 17 3
14 Nov 92 BITCHES BREW *Cow DUNG 20T* 36 2
5 Jun 93 HOW IT SHOULD BE *Cow DUNG 22CD* 49 1
22 Jan 94 SATURN 5 *Cow DUNG 23CD* 20 4
5 Mar 94 I WANT YOU *Cow DUNG 24CD* [1] 18 3
19 Mar 94 ● DEVIL HOPPING *Cow LDUNG 25CD* 10 3
7 May 94 UNIFORM *Cow DUNG 26CD* 51 1
16 Sep 95 JOE *Cow DUNG 27CD* 37 2
30 Sep 95 THE SINGLES *Cow CDMOOTEL 3* 17 3
31 May 03 COOL AS *Mute DUNG 30CD* 65 1
26 Jul 03 COME BACK TOMORROW *Mute DUNG 31CD* 43 1

[1] Inspiral Carpets featuring Mark E Smith

Tracks on Island Head (EP): Biggest Mountain / Gold Top / Weakness / I'll Keep it in Mind.

INSPIRATIONAL CHOIR
US, male / female choir (1 Album: 4 Weeks, 2 Singles: 11 Weeks)

22 Dec 84 ABIDE WITH ME *Epic A 4997* 44 5
14 Dec 85 ABIDE WITH ME (re-issue) *Portrait A 4997* 36 6
18 Jan 86 SWEET INSPIRATION *Portrait PRT 10048* 59 4

Label credits the Royal Choral Society.

INSPIRATIONS
UK, male keyboard player – Neil Palmer (5 Albums: 35 Weeks)

29 Apr 95 ● PAN PIPE INSPIRATIONS *Pure Music PMCD 7011* 10 10
23 Sep 95 ● PAN PIPE DREAMS *Pure Music PMCD 7016* 10 8
11 Nov 95 PURE EMOTIONS *Pure Music PMCD 7023* 37 4
6 Apr 96 PAN PIPE IMAGES *Telstar TCD 2819* 23 6
12 Oct 96 THE VERY BEST OF THE PAN PIPES *Telstar TCD 2845* 37 7

INSTANT FUNK *US, male vocal / instrumental group*

20 Jan 79 GOT MY MIND MADE UP *Salsoul SSOL 114* $ 46 5

INTASTELLA
UK, male / female vocal / instrumental group (4 Singles: 6 Weeks)

25 May 91 DREAM SOME PARADISE *MCA MCS 1520* 69 1
24 Aug 91 PEOPLE *MCA MCS 1559* 74 2
16 Nov 91 CENTURY *MCA MCS 1585* 70 2
23 Sep 95 THE NIGHT *Planet 3 GXY 2005CD* 60 1

INTELLIGENT HOODLUM *US, male rapper – Percy Chapman*

6 Oct 90 BACK TO REALITY *A&M AM 598* 55 3

INTENSO PROJECT *UK, male production / vocal group (3 Singles: 7 Weeks)*

17 Aug 02 LUV DA SUNSHINE *Inferno CDFERN 47* 22 2
26 Jul 03 YOUR MUSIC *Concept CDCON 43* [1] 32 2
4 Dec 04 GET IT ON *Inspired INSPMOS 1CDS* [2] 23 3

[1] Intenso Project featuring Laura Jaye [2] Intenso Project featuring Lisa Scott-Lee

INTERACTIVE
Germany, male instrumental / production group (2 Singles: 6 Weeks)

13 Apr 96 FOREVER YOUNG *Ffrreedom TABCD 235* 28 4
8 Mar 03 FOREVER YOUNG (re-mix) *All Around the World CDGLOBE 253* 37 2

INTERNATIONAL AIRPORT / TEENAGE FANCLUB
UK, male vocal / instrumental groups

4 Sep 04 ASSOCIATION *Geographic GEOG 29CD* 75 1

INTERPOL
US, male vocal / instrumental group (1 Album: 3 Weeks, 7 Singles: 11 Weeks)

23 Nov 02 OBSTACLE 1 *Matador OLE 5702* 72 1
26 Apr 03 SAY HELLO TO THE ANGELS / NYC *Matador OLE 5822* 65 1
27 Sep 03 OBSTACLE 1 *Matador OLE 5942* 41 1
25 Sep 04 SLOW HANDS *Matador OLE 6362* 36 2
9 Oct 04 ANTICS *Matador OLE 6162* 21 3
15 Jan 05 EVIL *Matador OLE 6376* 18 3
23 Apr 05 C'MERE *Matador OLE 6642* 19 2
9 Jul 05 SLOW HANDS (re-issue) *Matador OLE 6692* 44 1

INTI ILLIMANI-GUAMARY
Chile, male vocal / instrumental group – panpipes

17 Dec 83 THE FLIGHT OF THE CONDOR – ORIGINAL TV SOUNDTRACK *BBC REB 440* 62 7

The INTRUDERS *US, male vocal group (3 Singles: 21 Weeks)*

13 Apr 74 I'LL ALWAYS LOVE MY MAMA *Philadelphia International PIR 2159* 32 7
6 Jul 74 WIN, PLACE OR SHOW (SHE'S A WINNER) *Philadelphia International PIR 2212* 14 9
22 Dec 84 WHO DO YOU LOVE? *Streetwave KHAN 34* 65 5

INVISIBLE MAN *UK, male producer – Graham Mew*

17 Apr 99 GIVE A LITTLE LOVE *Serious SERR 006CD* 48 1

INXS
136 Top 500 (see also MAX Q) *Stadium-packing rock sextet led by Australian Michael Hutchence, b. 22 Jan 1960, Sydney, d. 22 Nov 1997. Both Hutchence and his group won BRIT awards in 1991 and the video for their US chart-topper 'Need You Tonight' won five MTV awards in 1988. In 2005, the group recruited a new lead singer, JD Fortune, via TV reality show Rock Star (9 Albums: 240 Weeks, 26 Singles: 132 Weeks)*

8 Feb 86 LISTEN LIKE THIEVES *Mercury MERH 82* 48 15
19 Apr 86 WHAT YOU NEED *Mercury INXS 5* 51 6
28 Jun 86 LISTEN LIKE THIEVES *Mercury INXS 6* 46 7
30 Aug 86 KISS THE DIRT (FALLING DOWN THE MOUNTAIN) *Mercury INXS 7* 54 3
24 Oct 87 NEED YOU TONIGHT *Mercury INXS 8* ▲ 58 3
28 Nov 87 ● KICK *Mercury MERH 114* 9 103
9 Jan 88 NEW SENSATION *Mercury INXS 9* 25 6
12 Mar 88 DEVIL INSIDE *Mercury INXS 10* 47 5
25 Jun 88 NEVER TEAR US APART *Mercury INXS 11* 24 7
12 Nov 88 ● NEED YOU TONIGHT (re-issue) *Mercury INXS 12* 2 11
8 Apr 89 MYSTIFY *Mercury INXS 13* 14 7
15 Sep 90 SUICIDE BLONDE *Mercury INXS 14* 11 6
6 Oct 90 ● X *Mercury 8466681* 2 44
8 Dec 90 DISAPPEAR *Mercury INXS 15* 21 8
26 Jan 91 GOOD TIMES *Atlantic A 7751* [1] 18 8
30 Mar 91 BY MY SIDE *Mercury INXS 16* 42 4
13 Jul 91 BITTER TEARS *Mercury INXS 17* 30 3
2 Nov 91 SHINING STAR (EP) *Mercury INXS 18* 27 3
16 Nov 91 ● LIVE BABY LIVE *Mercury 5105801* 8 9
18 Jul 92 HEAVEN SENT *Mercury INXS 19* 31 3
15 Aug 92 ★ WELCOME TO WHEREVER YOU ARE *Mercury 5125072* ■ 1 33
5 Sep 92 BABY DON'T CRY *Mercury INXS 20* 20 5
14 Nov 92 TASTE IT *Mercury INXS 23* 21 4

12 February 1972	19 February 1972	26 February 1972	4 March 1972
UK No.1 SINGLES			
TELEGRAM SAM T. Rex	SON OF MY FATHER Chicory Tip	SON OF MY FATHER Chicory Tip	SON OF MY FATHER Chicory Tip
UK No.1 ALBUMS			
ELECTRIC WARRIOR T. Rex	NEIL REID Neil Reid	NEIL REID Neil Reid	NEIL REID Neil Reid

Date	Title / Label	Pos	Wks
13 Feb 93	BEAUTIFUL GIRL *Mercury INXCD 24*	23	5
23 Oct 93	THE GIFT *Mercury INXCD 25*	11	4
13 Nov 93 ●	FULL MOON DIRTY HEARTS *Mercury 5186372*	3	8
11 Dec 93	PLEASE (YOU GOT THAT ...) *Mercury INXCD 26*	50	3
22 Oct 94	THE STRANGEST PARTY (THESE ARE THE TIMES) *Mercury INXCD 27*	15	5
12 Nov 94 ●	THE GREATEST HITS *Mercury 5262302*	3	22
22 Mar 97	ELEGANTLY WASTED *Mercury INXCD 28*	20	4
19 Apr 97	ELEGANTLY WASTED *Mercury 5346132*	16	3
7 Jun 97	EVERYTHING *Mercury INXDD 29*	71	1
18 Aug 01	PRECIOUS HEART (re) *Duty Free / Decode DFTELCD 001* [2]	14	5
3 Nov 01	I'M SO CRAZY (re) *Credence CDCRED 016* [3]	19	6
26 Oct 02	DEFINITIVE INXS *Mercury 0633562*	15	3

[1] Jimmy Barnes and Inxs [2] Tall Paul vs Inxs [3] Par-T-One vs Inxs

Tracks on Shining Star (EP): Shining Star / Send a Message (Live) / Faith in Each Other (Live) / Bitter Tears (Live). Although uncredited, 'Please (You Got That ...)' is a duet with Ray Charles.

Tippa IRIE *UK, male vocalist – Anthony Henry (4 Singles: 14 Weeks)*

Date	Title / Label	Pos	Wks
22 Mar 86	HELLO DARLING *Greensleeves / UK Bubblers TIPPA 4*	22	7
19 Jul 86	HEARTBEAT *Greensleeves / UK Bubblers TIPPA 5*	59	3
15 May 93	SHOUTING FOR THE GUNNERS *London LONCD 342* [1]	34	3
8 Jul 95	STAYING ALIVE 95 *Telstar CDSTAS 2776* [2]	48	1

[1] Arsenal FA Cup Squad featuring Tippa Irie and Peter Hunnigale

[2] Fever featuring Tippa Irie

IRON MAIDEN (129 Top 500) *Legendary London-based group named after a medieval torture device. Lead vocalists have included Paul Di'Anno and Blaze Bayley, but it was with frontman Bruce Dickinson that they became one of the world's top metal bands. Act inducted into the Kerrang! Hall of Fame in 2005 (33 Albums: 209 Weeks, 36 Singles: 178 Weeks)*

Date	Title / Label	Pos	Wks
23 Feb 80	RUNNING FREE *EMI 5032*	34	5
26 Apr 80 ●	IRON MAIDEN *EMI EMC 3330*	4	15
7 Jun 80	SANCTUARY *EMI 5065*	29	5
8 Nov 80	WOMEN IN UNIFORM *EMI 5105*	35	4
28 Feb 81	KILLERS *EMI EMC 3357*	12	8
14 Mar 81	TWILIGHT ZONE / WRATH CHILD *EMI 5145*	31	5
27 Jun 81	PURGATORY *EMI 5184*	52	3
26 Sep 81	MAIDEN JAPAN (EP) *EMI 5219*	43	4
20 Feb 82 ●	RUN TO THE HILLS *EMI 5263*	7	10
10 Apr 82 ★	THE NUMBER OF THE BEAST *EMI EMC 3400* ■	1	31
15 May 82	THE NUMBER OF THE BEAST *EMI 5287*	18	8
23 Apr 83	FLIGHT OF ICARUS *EMI 5378*	11	6
28 May 83 ●	PIECE OF MIND *EMI EMA 800*	3	18
2 Jul 83	THE TROOPER *EMI 5397*	12	7
18 Aug 84	2 MINUTES TO MIDNIGHT *EMI 5849*	11	6
15 Sep 84 ●	POWERSLAVE *EMI POWER 1*	2	13
3 Nov 84	ACES HIGH *EMI 5502*	20	5
15 Jun 85	IRON MAIDEN (re-issue) *Fame FA 4131211*	71	2
5 Oct 85	RUNNING FREE (LIVE) *EMI 5532*	19	5
26 Oct 85 ●	LIVE AFTER DEATH *EMI RIP 1*	2	14
14 Dec 85	RUN TO THE HILLS (LIVE) *EMI 5542*	26	6
6 Sep 86	WASTED YEARS *EMI 5583*	18	4
11 Oct 86 ●	SOMEWHERE IN TIME *EMI EMC 3512*	3	11
22 Nov 86	STRANGER IN A STRANGE LAND (re) *EMI 5589*	22	6
20 Jun 87	THE NUMBER OF THE BEAST (re-issue) *Fame FA 3178*	98	1
26 Mar 88 ●	CAN I PLAY WITH MADNESS *EMI EM 49*	3	6
23 Apr 88 ★	SEVENTH SON OF A SEVENTH SON *EMI EMD 1006* ■	1	18
13 Aug 88 ●	THE EVIL THAT MEN DO *EMI EM 64*	5	6
19 Nov 88 ●	THE CLAIRVOYANT *EMI EM 79*	6	8
18 Nov 89 ●	INFINITE DREAMS (re) *EMI EM 117*	6	6
24 Feb 90 ●	RUNNING FREE / SANCTUARY *EMI IRN 1*	10	4
3 Mar 90 ●	WOMEN IN UNIFORM / TWILIGHT ZONE *EMI IRN 2*	10	3
10 Mar 90 ●	PURGATORY / MAIDEN JAPAN *EMI IRN 3*	5	3
17 Mar 90 ●	RUN TO THE HILLS / THE NUMBER OF THE BEAST *EMI IRN 4*	3	2
24 Mar 90 ●	FLIGHT OF ICARUS / THE TROOPER *EMI IRN 5*	7	2
31 Mar 90	2 MINUTES TO MIDNIGHT / ACES HIGH *EMI IRN 6*	11	2
7 Apr 90 ●	RUNNING FREE (LIVE) / RUN TO THE HILLS (LIVE) *EMI IRN 7*	9	2
14 Apr 90 ●	WASTED YEARS / STRANGER IN A STRANGE LAND *EMI IRN 8*	9	2
21 Apr 90 ●	CAN I PLAY WITH MADNESS / THE EVIL THAT MEN DO *EMI IRN 9*	10	3
28 Apr 90	THE CLAIRVOYANT / INFINITE DREAMS (LIVE) *EMI IRN 10*	11	2
22 Sep 90 ●	HOLY SMOKE *EMI EM 153*	3	4
13 Oct 90 ●	NO PRAYER FOR THE DYING *EMI EMD 1017*	2	14
5 Jan 91 ★	BRING YOUR DAUGHTER ... TO THE SLAUGHTER *EMI EMPD 171* ■	1	5
25 Apr 92 ●	BE QUICK OR BE DEAD *EMI EM 229*	2	4
23 May 92 ★	FEAR OF THE DARK *EMI CDEMD 1032* ■	1	5
11 Jul 92	FROM HERE TO ETERNITY *EMI EMS 240*	21	4
13 Mar 93 ●	FEAR OF THE DARK (LIVE) *EMI CDEMS 263*	8	3
3 Apr 93 ●	A REAL LIVE ONE *EMI CDEMD 1042*	3	4
16 Oct 93 ●	HALLOWED BE THY NAME (LIVE) *EMI CDEM 288*	9	3
30 Oct 93	A REAL DEAD ONE *EMI CDEMD 1048*	12	3
20 Nov 93	LIVE AT DONNINGTON *EMI CDDON 1*	23	1
7 Oct 95 ●	MAN ON THE EDGE *EMI CDEMS 398*	10	3
14 Oct 95 ●	THE X FACTOR *EMI CDEMD 1087*	8	4
21 Sep 96	VIRUS *EMI CDEM 443*	16	3
5 Oct 96	BEST OF THE BEAST *EMI CDEMD 1097*	16	5
21 Mar 98	THE ANGEL AND THE GAMBLER *EMI CDEM 507*	18	3
4 Apr 98	VIRTUAL XI *EMI 4939152*	16	2
20 May 00 ●	THE WICKER MAN *EMI CDEMS 568*	9	4
10 Jun 00 ●	BRAVE NEW WORLD *EMI 5266052*	7	4
4 Nov 00	OUT OF THE SILENT PLANET *EMI CDEM 576*	20	3
23 Mar 02 ●	RUN TO THE HILLS (re-recording) *EMI CDEM 612*	9	4
6 Apr 02	ROCK IN RIO *EMI 5386430*	15	3
16 Nov 02	EDWARD THE GREAT – THE GREATEST HITS *EMI 05431032*	57	1
13 Sep 03 ●	WILDEST DREAMS *EMI CDEM 627*	6	6
20 Sep 03 ●	DANCE OF DEATH *EMI 5923402*	2	5
6 Dec 03	RAINMAKER *EMI CDEM 633*	13	5
15 Jan 05 ●	THE NUMBER OF THE BEAST (re-issue) *EMI CDEMS 666*	3	6
27 Aug 05 ●	THE TROOPER (re-recording) *EMI CDEM 662*	5	3
10 Sep 05	DEATH ON THE ROAD *EMI 3364372*	22	2

'Run to the Hills' (2002) is a re-recorded live version of the 1985 release. Tracks on Maiden Japan (EP): Remember Tomorrow (live) / Killers (live) / Running Free (live) / Innocent Exile (live). Entries from Feb to Apr 1990 are double 12-inch singles ineligible for the singles chart due to their retail price.

IRONHORSE (see also Randy BACHMAN) *Canada, male vocal / instrumental group*

Date	Title / Label	Pos	Wks
5 May 79	SWEET LUI-LOUISE *Scotti Brothers K 11271*	60	3

Big Dee IRWIN *US, male vocalist – Difosco Erwin, b. 4 Aug 1939, d. 27 Aug 1995*

Date	Title / Label	Pos	Wks
21 Nov 63 ●	SWINGING ON A STAR *Colpix PX 11010*	7	17

Single was a vocal duet by Big Dee Irwin and Little Eva (uncredited).

Gregory ISAACS *Jamaica, male vocalist (2 Albums: 6 Weeks)*

Date	Title / Label	Pos	Wks
12 Sep 81	MORE GREGORY *Charisma PREX 9*	93	1
4 Sep 82	NIGHT NURSE *Island ILPS 9721*	32	5

Chris ISAAK *US, male vocalist (3 Albums: 38 Weeks, 5 Singles: 22 Weeks)*

Date	Title / Label	Pos	Wks
24 Nov 90 ●	WICKED GAME *London LON 279*	10	10
26 Jan 91 ●	WICKED GAME *Reprise WX 406*	3	30
2 Feb 91	BLUE HOTEL *Reprise W 0005*	17	7
3 Apr 93	CAN'T DO A THING (TO STOP ME) *Reprise W 0161CD*	36	3
24 Apr 93	SAN FRANCISCO DAYS *Reprise 9362451162*	12	5
10 Jul 93	SAN FRANCISCO DAYS *Reprise W 0182CD*	62	1
3 Jun 95	FOREVER BLUE *Reprise 9362458452*	27	3
2 Oct 99	BABY DID A BAD BAD THING *Reprise W 503CD*	44	1

ISHA-D *UK, male / female vocal / instrumental duo – Phil Coxon and Beverley Reppion (2 Singles: 4 Weeks)*

Date	Title / Label	Pos	Wks
22 Jul 95	STAY (TONIGHT) *Cleveland City Blues CCBCD 15005*	28	3
5 Jul 97	STAY (re-issue) *Satellite 74321498212*	58	1

11 March 1972	18 March 1972	25 March 1972	1 April 1972
WITHOUT YOU Nilsson	WITHOUT YOU Nilsson	WITHOUT YOU Nilsson	WITHOUT YOU Nilsson
HARVEST Neil Young	PAUL SIMON Paul Simon	FOG ON THE TYNE Lindisfarne	FOG ON THE TYNE Lindisfarne

KEY	
UK No.1 ★★ UK Top 10 ●● Still on chart ++ UK entry at No.1 ■■	Peak Position
US No.1 ▲▲ UK million seller £ US million seller $	Weeks
Singles re-entries are listed as (re), (2re), (3re)… which signifies that the hit re-entered the chart once, twice or three times…	

The ISLEY BROTHERS *US, male vocal / instrumental group (6 Albums: 25 Weeks, 14 Singles: 108 Weeks)*

25 Jul 63 **TWIST AND SHOUT** *Stateside SS 112*..........42 1
28 Apr 66 ● **THIS OLD HEART OF MINE (IS WEAK FOR YOU) (re)** *Tamla Motown TMG 555*..........3 17
1 Sep 66 **I GUESS I'LL ALWAYS LOVE YOU** *Tamla Motown TMG 572*.....45 2
14 Dec 68 THIS OLD HEART OF MINE *Tamla Motown STML 11034*..........23 6
15 Jan 69 **I GUESS I'LL ALWAYS LOVE YOU** (re-issue) *Tamla Motown TMG 683*..........11 9
16 Apr 69 ● **BEHIND A PAINTED SMILE** *Tamla Motown TMG 693*..........5 12
25 Jun 69 **IT'S YOUR THING** *Major Minor MM 621* **$**..........30 5
30 Aug 69 **PUT YOURSELF IN MY PLACE** *Tamla Motown TMG 708*..........13 11
22 Sep 73 **THAT LADY** *Epic EPC 1704* **$**..........14 9
19 Jan 74 **HIGHWAYS OF MY LIFE** *Epic EPC 1980*..........25 8
25 May 74 **SUMMER BREEZE** *Epic EPC 2244*..........16 8
10 Jul 76 ● **HARVEST FOR THE WORLD** *Epic EPC 4369*..........10 8
14 Aug 76 HARVEST FOR THE WORLD *Epic EPC 81268*..........50 5
14 May 77 GO FOR YOUR GUNS *Epic EPC 86027*..........46 2
13 May 78 **TAKE ME TO THE NEXT PHASE** *Epic EPC 6292*..........50 4
24 Jun 78 SHOWDOWN *Epic EPC 86039*..........50 1
3 Nov 79 **IT'S A DISCO NIGHT (ROCK DON'T STOP)** *Epic EPC 7911*..........14 11
16 Jul 83 **BETWEEN THE SHEETS** *Epic A 3513*..........52 3
5 Mar 88 GREATEST HITS *Telstar STAR 2306*..........41 10
30 Jul 05 SUMMER BREEZE – GREATEST HITS *Epic 5204612*..........69 1

'This Old Heart of Mine (Is Weak for You)' originally peaked at No.47 before making No.3 in Nov 1968.

ISLEY JASPER ISLEY *US, male vocal / instrumental group*

23 Nov 85 **CARAVAN OF LOVE** *Epic A 6612*..........52 5

ISOTONIK *UK, male producer – Chris Paul (2 Singles: 9 Weeks)*

11 Jan 92 **DIFFERENT STROKES** *Ffrreedom TAB 101*..........12 5
2 May 92 **EVERYWHERE I GO / LET'S GET DOWN** *Ffrreedom TAB 108*...25 4

'Let's Get Down' listed only from 9 May 1992.

IT BITES *UK, male vocal (Francis Dunnery) / instrumental group (4 Albums: 12 Weeks, 5 Singles: 21 Weeks)*

12 Jul 86 ● **CALLING ALL THE HEROES** *Virgin VS 872*..........6 12
6 Sep 86 THE BIG LAD IN THE WINDMILL *Virgin V 2378*..........35 5
18 Oct 86 **WHOLE NEW WORLD** *Virgin VS 896*..........54 3
23 May 87 **THE OLD MAN AND THE ANGEL** *Virgin VS 941*..........72 1
2 Apr 88 ONCE AROUND THE WORLD *Virgin V 2456*..........43 3
13 May 89 **STILL TOO YOUNG TO REMEMBER** *Virgin VS 1184*..........66 3
24 Jun 89 EAT ME IN ST. LOUIS *Virgin V 2591*..........40 3
24 Feb 90 **STILL TOO YOUNG TO REMEMBER** (re-issue) *Virgin VS 1238*..60 2
31 Aug 91 THANK YOU AND GOODNIGHT *Virgin VGD 24233*..........59 1

IT'S A BEAUTIFUL DAY *US, male / female vocal / instrumental group (2 Albums: 3 Weeks)*

23 May 70 IT'S A BEAUTIFUL DAY *CBS 63722*..........58 1
18 Jul 70 MARRYING MAIDEN *CBS 66236*..........45 2

IT'S IMMATERIAL *UK, male vocal / instrumental group (1 Album: 3 Weeks, 2 Singles: 10 Weeks)*

12 Apr 86 **DRIVING AWAY FROM HOME (JIM'S TUNE)** *Siren SIREN 15*....18 7
2 Aug 86 **ED'S FUNKY DINER (FRIDAY NIGHT, SATURDAY MORNING)** *Siren SIREN 24*..........65 3
27 Sep 86 LIFE'S HARD AND THEN YOU DIE *Siren SIRENLP 4*..........62 3

ITTY BITTY BOOZY WOOZY (see also DA TECHNO BOHEMIAN; KLUBBHEADS) *Holland, male instrumental / production duo – Addy Van Der Zwan and Koen Groeneveld*

25 Nov 95 **TEMPO FIESTA (PARTY TIME)** *Systematic SYSCD 23*..........34 2

Burl IVES *US, male vocalist, b. 14 Jun 1909, d. 14 Apr 1995 (2 Singles: 25 Weeks)*

25 Jan 62 ● **A LITTLE BITTY TEAR** *Brunswick 05863*..........9 15
17 May 62 **FUNNY WAY OF LAUGHIN'** *Brunswick 05868*..........29 10

The IVY LEAGUE *UK, male vocal trio (4 Singles: 31 Weeks)*

4 Feb 65 ● **FUNNY HOW LOVE CAN BE** *Piccadilly 7N 35222*..........8 9
6 May 65 **THAT'S WHY I'M CRYING** *Piccadilly 7N 35228*..........22 8
24 Jun 65 ● **TOSSING AND TURNING** *Piccadilly 7N 35251*..........3 13
14 Jul 66 **WILLOW TREE** *Piccadilly 7N 35326*..........50 1

IZIT *UK, male / female vocal / instrumental group*

2 Dec 89 **STORIES** *ffrr F 122*..........52 3

Ray J *US, male vocalist – Willie Ray Norwood Jr (4 Singles: 14 Weeks)*

17 Oct 98 **THAT'S WHY I LIE** *Atlantic AT 0049CD*..........71 1
16 Jun 01 ● **ANOTHER DAY IN PARADISE** *WEA WEA 327CD1* [1]..........5 10
11 Aug 01 **WAIT A MINUTE** *Atlantic AT 0106CD* [2]..........54 1
12 Nov 05 **ONE WISH** *Sanctuary Urban SANXD 397*..........26 2

[1] Brandy and Ray J [2] Ray J featuring Lil' Kim

J.A.L.N. BAND *UK / Jamaica, male vocal / instrumental group (3 Singles: 17 Weeks)*

11 Sep 76 **DISCO MUSIC / I LIKE IT** *Magnet MAG 73*..........21 9
27 Aug 77 **I GOT TO SING** *Magnet MAG 97*..........40 4
1 Jul 78 **GET UP (AND LET YOURSELF GO)** *Magnet MAG 118*..........53 4

JB's ALL STARS *UK, male / female vocal / instrumental group*

11 Feb 84 **BACKFIELD IN MOTION** *RCA Victor RCA 384*..........48 4

JC *UK, male producer*

7 Feb 98 **SO HOT** *East West EW 146CD*..........74 1

JC-001 *UK, male rapper – Jonathan Chandra (2 Singles: 4 Weeks)*

24 Apr 93 **NEVER AGAIN** *AnXious ANX 1012CD*..........67 2
26 Jun 93 **CUPID** *AnXious ANX 1014CD*..........56 2

JD aka 'DREADY' *UK, male vocalist – Karl Jairzhino Daniel*

2 Aug 03 **SIGNAL** *Independiente SSB 2MS*..........64 1

JDS (see also GEMS FOR JEM) *Italy / UK, male DJ / production duo – Julian Napolitano and Darren Pearce (3 Singles: 3 Weeks)*

27 Sep 97 **NINE WAYS** *ffrr FCD 310*..........61 1
23 May 98 **LONDON TOWN** *Jive 0530042*..........49 1
3 Mar 01 **NINE WAYS** (re-mix) *ffrr FCD 391*..........47 1

	8 April 1972	15 April 1972	22 April 1972	29 April 1972
UK No.1 SINGLES	**WITHOUT YOU** Nilsson	**AMAZING GRACE** Pipes and Drums and Military Band of the Royal Scots Dragoon Guards	**AMAZING GRACE** Pipes and Drums and Military Band of the Royal Scots Dragoon Guards	**AMAZING GRACE** Pipes and Drums and Military Band of the Royal Scots Dragoon Guards
UK No.1 ALBUMS	**FOG ON THE TYNE** Lindisfarne	**FOG ON THE TYNE** Lindisfarne	**MACHINE HEAD** Deep Purple	**MACHINE HEAD** Deep Purple

JFK *UK, male producer – J.F. Kinch (3 Singles: 3 Weeks)*

15 Sep 01 **GOOD GOD** *Y2K Y2K 025CD* 71 1
26 Jan 02 **WHIPLASH** *Y2K Y2K 027CD* 47 1
4 May 02 **THE SOUND OF BLUE** *Y2K Y2K 030CD* 55 1

Frankie J featuring BABY BASH NEW
Mexico, male vocalist – Francis Bautista and US, male rapper – Ronald Bryant

20 Aug 05 **OBSESSION (NO ES AMOR)** *Columbia 6760212* 38 2

JJ *UK, male / female vocal / instrumental duo*

9 Feb 91 **IF THIS IS LOVE** *Columbia 6566097* 55 3

JJ72 *Ireland, male / female vocal / instrumental group (2 Albums: 22 Weeks, 7 Singles: 14 Weeks)*

3 Jun 00 **LONG WAY SOUTH** *Lakota LAK 0015CD* 68 1
26 Aug 00 **OXYGEN** *Lakota LAK 0016CD* 23 3
9 Sep 00 JJ72 *Lakota LAKCD 0017* 16 20
4 Nov 00 **OCTOBER SWIMMER** *Lakota LAK 0018CD* 29 3
10 Feb 01 **SNOW** *Lakota LAK 0019CD* 21 3
12 Oct 02 **FORMULAE** *Lakota / Columbia 6731592* 28 2
26 Oct 02 I TO SKY *Lakota 5095292* 20 2
22 Feb 03 **ALWAYS AND FOREVER** *Columbia 6734322* 43 1
10 Sep 05 **COMING HOME** *Lakota LAK 0035* 52 1

JKD BAND *UK, male vocal / instrumental group*

1 Jul 78 **DRAGON POWER** *Satril SAT 132* 58 4

JM SILK (see also VOICES OF LIFE) *US, male vocal / instrumental duo – Steve 'Silk' Hurley and Keith Nunnally (2 Singles: 6 Weeks)*

25 Oct 86 **I CAN'T TURN AROUND** *RCA PB 49793* 62 3
7 Mar 87 **LET THE MUSIC TAKE CONTROL** *RCA PB 49767* 47 3

J PAC *UK, male vocal / instrumental duo*

22 Jul 95 **ROCK 'N' ROLL (DOLE)** *East West YZ 953CD* 51 2

JT and The BIG FAMILY *Italy, male production trio*

3 Mar 90 ● **MOMENTS IN SOUL** *Champion CHAMP 237* 7 8

JT PLAYAZ *UK, male production trio (2 Singles: 4 Weeks)*

5 Apr 97 **JUST PLAYIN'** *Pukka CDJTP 1* 30 3
2 May 98 **LET'S GET DOWN** *MCA MCSTD 40161* 64 1

JTQ
UK, male vocal / instrumental group (3 Albums: 5 Weeks, 3 Singles: 6 Weeks)

3 Apr 93 **LOVE THE LIFE** *Big Life BLRD 93* [1] 34 3
1 May 93 SUPERNATURAL FEELING *Big Life BLRCD 21* [1] 36 3
3 Jul 93 **SEE A BRIGHTER DAY** *Big Life BLRDA 97* [1] 49 2
29 Oct 94 EXTENDED PLAY *Acid Jazz JAZID 110CD* [2] 70 1
25 Feb 95 **LOVE WILL KEEP US TOGETHER** *Acid Jazz JAZID 112CD* [2] 63 1
11 Mar 95 IN THE HAND OF THE INEVITABLE *Acid Jazz JAZIDCD 115* [2] 63 1

[1] JTQ with Noel McKoy [2] JTQ featuring Alison Limerick [1] JTQ with Noel McKoy [2] James Taylor Quartet

JX *UK, male producer – Jake Williams (6 Singles: 36 Weeks)*

2 Apr 94 **SON OF A GUN** *Internal Dance IDC 5* 13 6
1 Apr 95 **YOU BELONG TO ME** *Ffrreedom TABCD 227* 17 5
19 Aug 95 ● **SON OF A GUN** (re-mix) *Ffrreedom TABCD 233* 6 6
18 May 96 ● **THERE'S NOTHING I WON'T DO** *Ffrreedom TABCD 241* 4 13
8 Mar 97 **CLOSE TO YOUR HEART** *Ffrreedom TABCD 245* 18 3
6 Mar 04 **RESTLESS** *Tidy Two TIDYTWOJX 1C* 22 3

J-KWON *US, male rapper – Jerrell Jones*

24 Jul 04 ● **TIPSY (re)** *LaFace 82876624362* 4 12

JA RULE 396 Top 500 *Mobo winner Jeffrey Atkins (hence JA), b. New York, US, 29 Feb 1976. One of this millennium's most regular transatlantic chart entrants, and one of very few acts to replace themselves at the top of the US chart (4 Albums: 67 Weeks, 14 Singles: 113 Weeks)*

13 Mar 99 **CAN I GET A ...** *Def Jam 5668472* [1] 24 3
3 Mar 01 **BETWEEN ME AND YOU** *Def Jam 5727402* [2] 26 3
27 Oct 01 ● PAIN IS LOVE *Def Jam 5864372* ▲ 3 50
10 Nov 01 **LIVIN' IT UP** *Def Jam 5888142* [3] 27 4
10 Nov 01 ● **I'M REAL** *Epic 6720322* [4] ▲ 4 15
2 Feb 02 ● **ALWAYS ON TIME** *Def Jam 5889462* [5] ▲ 6 13
23 Mar 02 ● **AIN'T IT FUNNY** *Epic 6724922* [6] ▲ 4 13
3 Aug 02 ● **LIVIN' IT UP** (re-issue) *Def Jam 0639782* [3] 5 8
24 Aug 02 **RAINY DAYZ** *MCA MCSTD 40288* [7] 17 5
12 Oct 02 ● **DOWN 4 U (2re)** *Murder Inc 0639002* [8] 4 10
30 Nov 02 THE LAST TEMPTATION *Def Jam / Mercury 0635432* 14 13
21 Dec 02 **THUG LOVIN'** *Def Jam 0637872* [9] 15 8
29 Mar 03 **MESMERIZE** *Murder Inc / Mercury 0779582* [5] 12 8
15 Nov 03 BLOOD IN MY EYE *Def Jam / Mercury 9861329* 51 2
6 Dec 03 ● **CLAP BACK / REIGNS** *Def Jam / Mercury 9814618* 9 9
6 Nov 04 ★ **WONDERFUL** *Def Jam 9864605* [10] ■ 1 10
20 Nov 04 R.U.L.E. *Def Jam 9862918* 33 2
30 Apr 05 **CAUGHT UP** *The Inc 9881232* [11] 20 4

[1] Jay-Z featuring Amil & Ja Rule [2] Ja Rule featuring Christina Milian [3] Ja Rule featuring Case [4] Jennifer Lopez featuring Ja Rule [5] Ja Rule featuring Ashanti [6] Jennifer Lopez featuring Ja Rule & Caddillac Tah [7] Mary J Blige featuring Ja Rule [8] Irv Gotti presents Ja Rule, Ashanti, Charli Baltimore and Vita [9] Ja Rule featuring Bobby Brown [10] Ja Rule featuring R Kelly & Ashanti [11] Ja Rule featuring Lloyd

JACK 'N' CHILL *UK, male instrumental group (2 Singles: 21 Weeks)*

6 Jun 87 ● **THE JACK THAT HOUSE BUILT (re)** *Oval / 10 / Virgin TEN 174* 6 16
9 Jul 88 **BEATIN' THE HEAT** *10 TEN 234* 42 5

'The Jack that House Built' reached its peak position only on re-entry in Jan 1988.

Terry JACKS
(see also The POPPY FAMILY) *Canada, male vocalist (2 Singles: 21 Weeks)*

23 Mar 74 ★ **SEASONS IN THE SUN** *Bell 1344* ▲ $ 1 12
29 Jun 74 ● **IF YOU GO AWAY** *Bell 1362* 8 9

Alan JACKSON *US, male vocalist / guitarist*

3 Jul 04 THE VERY BEST OF ALAN JACKSON *Arista Nashville 82876601122* 47 2

Chad JACKSON *UK, male DJ / producer – Mark Chadwick*

2 Jun 90 ● **HEAR THE DRUMMER (GET WICKED)** *Big Wave BWR 36* 3 10

Dee D JACKSON *UK, female vocalist – Deirdre Cozier (2 Singles: 14 Weeks)*

22 Apr 78 ● **AUTOMATIC LOVER** *Mercury 6007 171* 4 9
2 Sep 78 **METEOR MAN** *Mercury 6007 182* 48 5

Freddie JACKSON
US, male vocalist (4 Albums: 48 Weeks, 8 Singles: 31 Weeks)

18 May 85 ROCK ME TONIGHT *Capitol EJ 24403161* 27 22
23 Nov 85 **YOU ARE MY LADY** *Capitol CL 379* 49 4
22 Feb 86 **ROCK ME TONIGHT (FOR OLD TIME'S SAKE)** *Capitol CL 358* 18 9
11 Oct 86 **TASTY LOVE** *Capitol CL 428* 73 1
8 Nov 86 JUST LIKE THE FIRST TIME *Capitol EST 2023* 30 15
7 Feb 87 **HAVE YOU EVER LOVED SOMEBODY** *Capitol CL 437* 33 6
9 Jul 88 **NICE 'N' SLOW** *Capitol CL 502* 56 2
30 Jul 88 DON'T LET LOVE SLIP AWAY *Capitol EST 2067* 24 9
15 Oct 88 **CRAZY (FOR ME)** *Capitol CL 510* 41 3
17 Nov 90 DO ME AGAIN *Capitol EST 2134E* 48 2
5 Sep 92 **ME AND MRS JONES** *Capitol CL 668* 32 5
15 Jan 94 **MAKE LOVE EASY** *RCA 74321179162* 70 1

6 May 1972	13 May 1972	20 May 1972	27 May 1972
AMAZING GRACE Pipes and Drums and Military Band of the Royal Scots Dragoon Guards	**AMAZING GRACE** Pipes and Drums and Military Band of the Royal Scots Dragoon Guards	**METAL GURU** T. Rex	**METAL GURU** T. Rex
PROPHETS SEERS AND SAGES ... / MY PEOPLE WERE FAIR ... T. Rex	**MACHINE HEAD** Deep Purple	**BOLAN BOOGIE** T. Rex	**BOLAN BOOGIE** T. Rex

KEY		
UK No.1 ★ UK Top 10 ● Still on chart + UK entry at No.1 ■ US No.1 ▲ UK million seller £ US million seller $ Singles re-entries are listed as (re), (2re), (3re)... which signifies that the hit re-entered the chart once, twice or three times...	Peak Position	Weeks

Gisele JACKSON *US, female vocalist*

30 Aug 97 LOVE COMMANDMENTS *Manifesto FESCD 28* 54 1

Janet JACKSON (63 Top 500)

(see also Herb ALPERT and The TIJUANA BRASS) *Multi-award-winning, record-breaking vocalist / performer, b. 16 May 1966, Indiana, US. Although not an overnight sensation, the youngest of the talented Jackson family has amassed a staggering collection of gold albums and singles. Best-selling single: 'Together Again' 747,238 (8 Albums: 270 Weeks, 41 Singles: 297 Weeks)*

22 Mar 86 ● WHAT HAVE YOU DONE FOR ME LATELY *A&M AM 308* 3 14
5 Apr 86 ● CONTROL *A&M AMA 5016* ▲ 8 72
31 May 86 NASTY *A&M AM 316* 19 9
9 Aug 86 ● WHEN I THINK OF YOU *A&M AM 337* ▲ 10 10
1 Nov 86 CONTROL *A&M AM 359* 42 5
21 Mar 87 ● LET'S WAIT AWHILE *Breakout USA 601* 3 10
13 Jun 87 PLEASURE PRINCIPLE *Breakout USA 604* 24 5
14 Nov 87 CONTROL – THE REMIXES *Breakout MIXLP 1* 20 14
14 Nov 87 FUNNY HOW TIME FLIES (WHEN YOU'RE HAVING FUN) *A&M Breakout USA 613* 59 2
2 Sep 89 MISS YOU MUCH *Breakout USA 663* ▲ $ 22 7
30 Sep 89 ● JANET JACKSON'S RHYTHM NATION 1814 *A&M AMA 3920* ▲ 4 43
4 Nov 89 RHYTHM NATION *Breakout USA 673* 23 5
27 Jan 90 COME BACK TO ME *Breakout USA 681* 20 7
31 Mar 90 ESCAPADE *Breakout USA 684* ▲ 17 7
7 Jul 90 ALRIGHT *A&M USA 693* 20 5
8 Sep 90 BLACK CAT *A&M AM 587* ▲ 15 6
27 Oct 90 LOVE WILL NEVER DO (WITHOUT YOU) *A&M AM 700* ▲ 34 4
15 Aug 92 ● THE BEST THINGS IN LIFE ARE FREE *Perspective PERSS 7400* [1] 2 13
8 May 93 ● THAT'S THE WAY LOVE GOES *Virgin VSCDG 1460* ▲ $ 2 10
29 May 93 ★ JANET / JANET. REMIXED *Virgin CDV 2720* ■ ▲ 1 57
31 Jul 93 IF *Virgin VSCDT 1474* 14 7
20 Nov 93 ● AGAIN *Virgin VSCDG 1481* ▲ $ 6 11
12 Mar 94 BECAUSE OF LOVE *Virgin VSCDG 1488* 19 4
18 Jun 94 ANY TIME ANY PLACE *Virgin VSCDT 1501* 13 5
26 Nov 94 YOU WANT THIS *Virgin VSCDT 1519* 14 3
18 Mar 95 ● WHOOPS NOW / WHAT'LL I DO *Virgin VSCDT 1533* 9 8
10 Jun 95 ● SCREAM (re) *Epic 6620222* [2] $ 3 13
24 Jun 95 SCREAM (re-mix) *Epic 6621277* [2] 43 2
23 Sep 95 ● RUNAWAY *A&M 5811972* 6 7
14 Oct 95 ● DESIGN OF A DECADE 1986-1996 *A&M 5404222* 2 21
16 Dec 95 ● THE BEST THINGS IN LIFE ARE FREE (re-mix) *A&M 5813092* [3] 7 7
6 Apr 96 TWENTY FOREPLAY *A&M 5815112* 22 4
4 Oct 97 ● GOT 'TIL IT'S GONE *Virgin VSCDG 1666* [4] 6 9
18 Oct 97 ● THE VELVET ROPE *Virgin CDV 2860* [1] ▲ 6 43
13 Dec 97 ● TOGETHER AGAIN *Virgin VSCDG 1670* [5] ▲ 4 19
4 Apr 98 ● I GET LONELY *Virgin VSCDT 1683* [6] 5 7
27 Jun 98 GO DEEP *Virgin VSCDT 1680* [5] 13 5
19 Dec 98 EVERY TIME *Virgin VSCDT 1720* [5] 46 1
17 Apr 99 GIRLFRIEND / BOYFRIEND *Interscope IND 95640* [7] 11 7
1 May 99 ● WHAT'S IT GONNA BE?! *Elektra E 3762CD 1* [8] 6 7
19 Aug 00 ● DOESN'T REALLY MATTER *Def Soul 5629152* ▲ 5 11
21 Apr 01 ● ALL FOR YOU *Virgin VSCDT 1801* ▲ 3 11
5 May 01 ● ALL FOR YOU *Virgin CDV 2950* [1] ▲ 2 18
11 Aug 01 SOMEONE TO CALL MY LOVER *Virgin VSCDT 1813* 11 5
22 Dec 01 SON OF A GUN (I BETCHA THINK THIS SONG IS ABOUT YOU) (re) *Virgin VUSCD 232* [9] 13 9
28 Sep 02 ● FEEL IT BOY (re) *Virgin VUSCD 258* [10] 9 7
10 Apr 04 DAMITA JO *Virgin CDVUS 251* [1] 32 2
24 Apr 04 JUST A LITTLE WHILE *Virgin VUSCD 285* [5] 15 5
19 Jun 04 ALL NITE (DON'T STOP) / I WANT YOU *Virgin VUSDX 292* [5] 19 4

[1] Luther Vandross and Janet Jackson with special guests BBD and Ralph Tresvant [2] Michael Jackson and Janet Jackson [3] Luther Vandross and Janet Jackson [4] Janet featuring Q-Tip and Joni Mitchell [5] Janet [6] Janet featuring BLACKstreet [7] BLACKstreet with Janet [8] Busta Rhymes featuring Janet [9] Janet with Carly Simon featuring Missy Elliott [10] Beenie Man featuring Janet [1] Janet

From 25 Mar 95 Janet was listed with the re-mix album Janet. Remixed.

Jermaine JACKSON (see also The JACKSONS)

US, male vocalist (2 Albums: 12 Weeks, 7 Singles: 43 Weeks)

10 May 80 ● LET'S GET SERIOUS *Motown TMG 1183* 8 11
31 May 80 LET'S GET SERIOUS *Motown STML 12127* 22 6
26 Jul 80 BURNIN' HOT *Motown TMG 1194* 32 6
30 May 81 YOU LIKE ME DON'T YOU *Motown TMG 1222* 41 5
12 May 84 DYNAMITE *Arista 206 317* 57 6
12 May 84 SWEETEST SWEETEST *Arista JJK 1* 52 4
27 Oct 84 WHEN THE RAIN BEGINS TO FALL *Arista ARIST 584* [1] 68 2
16 Feb 85 ● DO WHAT YOU DO *Arista ARIST 609* 6 13
21 Oct 89 DON'T TAKE IT PERSONAL *Arista 112634* 69 2

[1] Jermaine Jackson and Pia Zadora

'Let's Get Serious' features uncredited vocalist Stevie Wonder.

Joe JACKSON (475 Top 500)

Many faceted singer / songwriter and pianist, b. 11 Aug 1955, Staffordshire, UK. A unique and critically acclaimed recording artist whose five Grammy nominations span 1979 to 2001 (when Symphony No.1 became his first winner). His original 1980s band re-united in 2003 (11 Albums: 106 Weeks, 8 Singles: 49 Weeks)

17 Mar 79 LOOK SHARP! *A&M AMLH 64743* 40 11
4 Aug 79 IS SHE REALLY GOING OUT WITH HIM? *A&M AMS 7459* 13 9
13 Oct 79 I'M THE MAN *A&M AMLH 64794* 12 16
12 Jan 80 ● IT'S DIFFERENT FOR GIRLS *A&M AMS 7493* 5 9
18 Oct 80 BEAT CRAZY *A&M AMLH 64837* 42 3
4 Jul 81 JUMPIN' LIVE *A&M AMLH 68530* [1] 14 14
4 Jul 81 JUMPIN' JIVE *A&M AMS 8145* [1] 43 5
3 Jul 82 ● NIGHT AND DAY *A&M AMLH 64906* 3 27
8 Jan 83 ● STEPPIN' OUT *A&M AMS 8262* 6 8
12 Mar 83 BREAKING US IN TWO *A&M AM 101* 59 4
7 Apr 84 BODY AND SOUL *A&M AMLX 65000* 14 14
28 Apr 84 HAPPY ENDING *A&M AM 186* 58 3
7 Jul 84 BE MY NUMBER TWO *A&M AM 200* 70 2
5 Apr 86 BIG WORLD *A&M JWA 3* 41 5
7 Jun 86 LEFT OF CENTER *A&M AM 320* [2] 32 9
7 May 88 LIVE 1980/86 *A&M AMA 6706* 66 2
29 Apr 89 BLAZE OF GLORY *A&M AMA 5249* 36 3
15 Sep 90 ● STEPPING OUT – THE VERY BEST OF JOE JACKSON *A&M 3970521* 7 9
11 May 91 LAUGHTER AND LUST *Virgin America VUSLP 34* 41 2

[1] Joe Jackson's Jumpin' Jive [2] Suzanne Vega featuring Joe Jackson [1] Joe Jackson's Jumpin' Jive

Michael JACKSON (8 Top 500) (see also The JACKSONS)

The self-proclaimed "King of Pop", b. 29 Aug 1958, Indiana, US, is arguably the best-known living musical entertainer. The youngest vocalist (age 11, fronting The Jackson Five) to top the US singles chart, he was also the first artist to enter that chart at No.1, with 'You Are Not Alone'. In 1991, he became the first US act to enter the UK chart at No.1 since Elvis Presley in 1960 (whose daughter, Lisa Marie, he married in 1994). This outstanding, innovative singer / songwriter and performer has broken countless other records for his singles, albums, videos and tours. Thriller is the world's biggest-selling record, with global sales estimates varying between 47 and 51.2 million, including 27 million in the US alone. It topped the US albums chart for an unprecedented 37 weeks and had a record 12 Grammy nominations. Also on the album front, HIStory – Past Present and Future Book 1 sold more copies in its first week than any previous double album. Dangerous sold a staggering 10 million worldwide in its first month and Number Ones returned him to the top in 2003. Both Thriller and Bad have sold more than three million copies in the UK. Jackson, whose private life,

	3 June 1972	10 June 1972	17 June 1972	24 June 1972
UK No.1 SINGLES	METAL GURU T. Rex	METAL GURU T. Rex	VINCENT Don McLean	VINCENT Don McLean
UK No.1 ALBUMS	BOLAN BOOGIE T. Rex	EXILE ON MAIN ST The Rolling Stones	20 DYNAMIC HITS Various	20 DYNAMIC HITS Various

court cases and physical appearance have attracted much media attention, was the first entertainer to earn more than $100 million in a year and the first to receive an award for selling at least 100 million albums outside the US. Jacko was inducted into the UK Music Hall of Fame in 2004. Total UK single sales: 11,310,958. Best-selling single: 'Earth Song' 1,038,821 (26 Albums: 976 Weeks, 55 Singles: 515 Weeks)

12 Feb 72 ● GOT TO BE THERE *Tamla Motown TMG 797*..........5 11
20 May 72 ● ROCKIN' ROBIN *Tamla Motown TMG 816* $..........3 14
3 Jun 72 GOT TO BE THERE *Tamla Motown STML 11205*..........37 5
19 Aug 72 ● AIN'T NO SUNSHINE *Tamla Motown TMG 826*..........8 11
25 Nov 72 ● BEN *Tamla Motown TMG 834* ▲ $..........7 14
13 Jan 73 BEN *Tamla Motown STML 11220*..........17 7
18 Nov 78 EASE ON DOWN THE ROAD *MCA 396* [1]..........45 4
15 Sep 79 ● DON'T STOP 'TIL YOU GET ENOUGH *Epic EPC 7763* ▲ $..........3 12
29 Sep 79 ● OFF THE WALL *Epic EPC 83468*..........5 189
24 Nov 79 ● OFF THE WALL *Epic EPC 8045* $..........7 10
9 Feb 80 ● ROCK WITH YOU *Epic EPC 8206* ▲ $..........7 9
3 May 80 ● SHE'S OUT OF MY LIFE *Epic EPC 8384* $..........3 9
26 Jul 80 GIRLFRIEND *Epic EPC 8782*..........41 5
23 May 81 ★ ONE DAY IN YOUR LIFE *Motown TMG 976*..........1 14
4 Jul 81 THE BEST OF MICHAEL JACKSON *Motown STMR 9009*..........11 18
18 Jul 81 ONE DAY IN YOUR LIFE *Motown STML 12158*..........29 8
1 Aug 81 WE'RE ALMOST THERE *Motown TMG 977*..........46 4
6 Nov 82 ● THE GIRL IS MINE (re) *Epic EPC A 2729* [2] $..........8 10
11 Dec 82 ★ THRILLER *Epic EPC 85930* ▲..........1 201
29 Jan 83 ★ BILLIE JEAN *Epic EPC A 3084* ▲ $..........1 15
12 Feb 83 E.T. – THE EXTRA TERRESTRIAL *MCA 7000*..........82 2
9 Apr 83 ● BEAT IT *Epic EPC A 3258* ▲ $..........3 12
11 Jun 83 ● WANNA BE STARTIN' SOMETHIN' *Epic A 3427*..........8 9
9 Jul 83 ★ 18 GREATEST HITS *Telstar STAR 2232* [1]..........1 58
23 Jul 83 HAPPY (LOVE THEME FROM 'LADY SINGS THE BLUES') *Tamla Motown TMG 986*..........52 3
15 Oct 83 ● SAY SAY SAY *Parlophone R 6062* [3] ▲ $..........2 15
19 Nov 83 ● THRILLER *Epic A 3643* $..........10 18
3 Dec 83 MICHAEL JACKSON 9 SINGLE PACK *Epic MJ 1*..........66 3
31 Mar 84 P.Y.T. (PRETTY YOUNG THING) *Epic A 4136*..........11 8
2 Jun 84 ● FAREWELL MY SUMMER LOVE *Motown TMG 1342*..........7 12
9 Jun 84 ● FAREWELL MY SUMMER LOVE *Motown ZL 72227*..........9 14
11 Aug 84 GIRL YOU'RE SO TOGETHER *Motown TMG 1355*..........33 8
15 Nov 86 DIANA ROSS. MICHAEL JACKSON. GLADYS KNIGHT. STEVIE WONDER. THEIR VERY BEST BACK TO BACK *PrioriTyV PTVR 2* [2]..........21 10
8 Aug 87 ★ I JUST CAN'T STOP LOVING YOU *Epic 650202 7* ▲ $..........1 9
12 Sep 87 ★ BAD *Epic EPC 4502901* ■ ▲..........1 125
26 Sep 87 ● BAD *Epic 651155 7* ▲..........3 11
31 Oct 87 LOVE SONGS *Telstar STAR 2298* [3]..........12 24
5 Dec 87 ● THE WAY YOU MAKE ME FEEL *Epic 651275 7* ▲..........3 10
26 Dec 87 THE MICHAEL JACKSON MIX *Stylus SMR 745*..........27 25
20 Feb 88 MAN IN THE MIRROR *Epic 651388 7* ▲..........21 5
16 Apr 88 ● I WANT YOU BACK *Motown ZB 41919* [4]..........8 9
28 May 88 GET IT *Motown ZB 41883* [5]..........37 4
16 Jul 88 ● DIRTY DIANA *Epic 651546 7* ▲..........4 8
30 Jul 88 SOUVENIR SINGLES PACK *Epic MJ 5*..........91 1
10 Sep 88 ANOTHER PART OF ME *Epic 652844 7*..........15 6
26 Nov 88 ● SMOOTH CRIMINAL *Epic 653026 7*..........8 10
25 Feb 89 ● LEAVE ME ALONE *Epic 654672 7*..........2 9
15 Jul 89 LIBERIAN GIRL *Epic 654947 0*..........13 6
23 Nov 91 ★ BLACK OR WHITE *Epic 6575987* ■ ▲ $..........1 10
30 Nov 91 ★ DANGEROUS *Epic 4658021* ■ ▲..........1 96
18 Jan 92 BLACK OR WHITE (re-mix) *Epic 6577316*..........14 4
15 Feb 92 ● REMEMBER THE TIME / COME TOGETHER *Epic 6577747*..........3 8
29 Feb 92 MOTOWN'S GREATEST HITS *Motown 5300142*..........53 2
2 May 92 ● IN THE CLOSET *Epic 6580187*..........8 6
25 Jul 92 ● WHO IS IT *Epic 6581797*..........10 7
15 Aug 92 TOUR SOUVENIR PACK *Epic MJ 4*..........32 3
12 Sep 92 JAM *Epic 6583607*..........13 5
5 Dec 92 ● HEAL THE WORLD *Epic 6584887*..........2 15
27 Feb 93 ● GIVE IN TO ME *Epic 6590692*..........2 9
10 Jul 93 ● WILL YOU BE THERE *Epic 6592222*..........9 8
18 Dec 93 GONE TOO SOON *Epic 6599762*..........33 5

TOP 10
ON THE DAY OF THE QUEEN'S CORONATION

The coronation of Queen Elizabeth II took place in front of 8,000 guests at Westminster Abbey on 2 June 1953. The event inspired three hits that were in the Top 10 at the time – "In a Golden Coach (There's a Heart of Gold)" by both Billy Cotton and his Band and Dickie Valentine and Winifred Atwell's "Coronation Rag".

LW	TW	
1	1	**I BELIEVE** Frankie Laine
3	2	**TERRY'S THEME FROM 'LIMELIGHT'** Frank Chacksfield and his Orchestra
8	3	**IN A GOLDEN COACH (THERE'S A HEART OF GOLD)** Billy Cotton and his Band
4	3	**DOWNHEARTED** Eddie Fisher
2	4	**PRETEND** Nat 'King' Cole
6	4	**HOLD ME, THRILL ME, KISS ME** Muriel Smith
12	5	**CORONATION RAG** Winifred Atwell
7	6	**I'M WALKING BEHIND YOU** Eddie Fisher with Sally Sweetland
-	7	**IN A GOLDEN COACH (THERE'S A HEART OF GOLD)** Dickie Valentine
10	8	**THE SONG FROM THE MOULIN ROUGE** Mantovani
5	9	**PRETTY LITTLE BLACK-EYED SUSIE** Guy Mitchell
11	10	**TERRY'S THEME FROM 'LIMELIGHT'** Ron Goodwin and his Orchestra

* Two songs were tied for Nos.3 and 4, so the chart is a Top 12

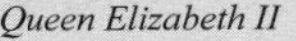
Queen Elizabeth II

Frankie Laine

1 July 1972	8 July 1972	15 July 1972	22 July 1972
TAKE ME BAK 'OME Slade	**PUPPY LOVE** Donny Osmond	**PUPPY LOVE** Donny Osmond	**PUPPY LOVE** Donny Osmond
20 DYNAMIC HITS Various	**20 DYNAMIC HITS** Various	**20 DYNAMIC HITS** Various	**20 DYNAMIC HITS** Various

KEY
UK No.1 ★★ UK Top 10 ●● Still on chart ++ UK entry at No.1 ■■
US No.1 ▲▲ UK million seller £ US million seller $
Singles re-entries are listed as (re), (2re), (3re)... which signifies that the hit re-entered the chart once, twice or three times...

Peak Position / Weeks

10Jun 95 ● **SCREAM** (re) *Epic 6620222* [6] $ 3 13
24 Jun 95 ★ HISTORY – PAST PRESENT AND FUTURE BOOK 1 *Epic 4747092* ■ ▲ 1 78
24 Jun 95 **SCREAM** (re-mix) *Epic 6621277* [6] 43 2
2 Sep 95 ★ **YOU ARE NOT ALONE** *Epic 6623102* ▲ $ 1 15
9 Dec 95 ★ **EARTH SONG** *Epic 6626955* ■ £ 1 17
20 Apr 96 ● **THEY DON'T CARE ABOUT US** (2re) *Epic 6629502* 4 14
24 Aug 96 ● **WHY** *Epic 6629502* [7] 2 9
16 Nov 96 ● **STRANGER IN MOSCOW** (re) *Epic 6637872* 4 11
3 May 97 ★ **BLOOD ON THE DANCE FLOOR** *Epic 6644625* ■ 1 9
24 May 97 ★ BLOOD ON THE DANCE FLOOR – HISTORY IN THE MIX *Epic 4875002* ■ 1 16
19 Jul 97 ● THE BEST OF MICHAEL JACKSON AND THE JACKSON 5IVE – THE MOTOWN YEARS *PolyGram TV 5308042* [4] 5 12
19 Jul 97 ● **HISTORY / GHOSTS** *Epic 6647962* 5 8
20 Oct 01 ● **YOU ROCK MY WORLD** *Epic 6720292* 2 15
10 Nov 01 ★ INVINCIBLE *Epic 4951742* ■ ▲ 1 12
24 Nov 01 GREATEST HITS – HISTORY VOLUME 1 *Epic 5018692* 15 16
22 Dec 01 **CRY** *Epic 6721822* 25 4
29 Nov 03 ★ NUMBER ONES *Epic 5138002* ■ 1 40
6 Dec 03 ● **ONE MORE CHANCE** *Epic 6744802* 5 7
4 Dec 04 THE ULTIMATE COLLECTION *Epic 5177433* 75 1
30 Jul 05 ● THE ESSENTIAL MICHAEL JACKSON *Epic 5204222* 2 10

[1] Diana Ross and Michael Jackson [2] Michael Jackson and Paul McCartney [3] Paul McCartney and Michael Jackson [4] Michael Jackson with The Jackson Five [5] Stevie Wonder and Michael Jackson [6] Michael Jackson and Janet Jackson [7] 3T featuring Michael Jackson [1] Michael Jackson plus The Jackson Five [2] Diana Ross / Michael Jackson / Gladys Knight / Stevie Wonder [3] Diana Ross and Michael Jackson [4] Michael Jackson and The Jackson Five

The sleeve of 'I Just Can't Stop Loving You' credits Siedah Garrett but the label does not. 'Come Together' was listed only from 7 Mar 1992. It peaked at No.10. Chart rules allow for a maximum of three formats; the additional three formats of 'Scream' – which each included re-mixed versions – were therefore listed separately (see 24 Jun 1995). Off the Wall changed its catalogue number to 4500861 during its chart run. From 14 Jan 89, when multi-artist albums were excluded from the main chart, Love Songs was listed in the compilation albums chart.

Mick JACKSON *UK, male vocalist (2 Singles: 16 Weeks)*

30 Sep 78 **BLAME IT ON THE BOOGIE** *Atlantic K 11102* 15 8
3 Feb 79 **WEEKEND** *Atlantic K 11224* 38 8

Millie JACKSON

US, female vocalist (2 Albums: 7 Weeks, 3 Singles: 8 Weeks)

18 Nov 72 **MY MAN, A SWEET MAN** *Mojo 2093 022* 50 1
18 Feb 84 E.S.P. *Sire 250382* 59 5
10 Mar 84 **I FEEL LIKE WALKIN' IN THE RAIN** *Sire W 9348* 55 2
6 Apr 85 LIVE & UNCENSORED *Important TADLP 001* 81 2
15 Jun 85 **ACT OF WAR** *Rocket EJS 8* [1] 32 5

[1] Elton John and Millie Jackson

Paul JACKSON / Steve SMITH *UK, male producer and vocalist*

24 Jan 04 **THE PUSH (FAR FROM HERE)** *Underwater H20 041CD* 51 2

Stonewall JACKSON *US, male vocalist*

17 Jul 59 **WATERLOO** *Philips PB 941* $ 24 2

Wanda JACKSON *US, female vocalist (2 Singles: 11 Weeks)*

1 Sep 60 **LET'S HAVE A PARTY** *Capitol CL 15147* 32 8
26 Jan 61 **MEAN MEAN MAN** (re) *Capitol CL 15176* 40 3

Tony JACKSON and The VIBRATIONS (see also The SEARCHERS)

UK, male vocal / instrumental group – leader b. 16 Jul 1940, d. 18 Aug 2003

8 Oct 64 **BYE BYE BABY** *Pye 7N 15685* 38 3

JACKSON SISTERS *US, female vocal group*

20 Jun 87 **I BELIEVE IN MIRACLES** *Urban URB 4* 72 2

The JACKSONS (119 Top 500)

One of the world's biggest-selling and most popular groups: brothers Jackie, Tito, Jermaine, Marlon and solo superstar Michael Jackson, with Randy joining in 1977. The Indiana quintet topped the US chart with their first four hits and have reportedly sold more than 100 million records (14 Albums: 162 Weeks, 27 Singles: 235 Weeks)

31 Jan 70 ● **I WANT YOU BACK** *Tamla Motown TMG 724* [1] ▲ $ 2 13
21 Mar 70 DIANA ROSS PRESENTS THE JACKSON 5 *Tamla Motown STML 11142* [1] 16 4
16 May 70 ● **ABC** *Tamla Motown TMG 738* [1] ▲ $ 8 11
1 Aug 70 ● **THE LOVE YOU SAVE** *Tamla Motown TMG 746* [1] ▲ $ 7 9
15 Aug 70 ABC *Tamla Motown STML 11153* [1] 22 6
21 Nov 70 ● **I'LL BE THERE** *Tamla Motown TMG 758* [1] ▲ $ 4 16
10 Apr 71 **MAMA'S PEARL** *Tamla Motown TMG 769* [1] $ 25 7
17 Jul 71 **NEVER CAN SAY GOODBYE** *Tamla Motown TMG 778* [1] $ 33 7
7 Oct 72 GREATEST HITS *Tamla Motown STML 11212* [1] 26 14
11 Nov 72 ● **LOOKIN' THROUGH THE WINDOWS** *Tamla Motown TMG 833* [1] 9 11
18 Nov 72 LOOKIN' THROUGH THE WINDOWS *Tamla Motown STML 11214* [1] 16 8
23 Dec 72 **SANTA CLAUS IS COMING TO TOWN** *Tamla Motown TMG 837* [1] 43 3
17 Feb 73 ● **DOCTOR MY EYES** *Tamla Motown TMG 842* [1] 9 10
9 Jun 73 **HALLELUJAH DAY** *Tamla Motown TMG 856* [1] 20 9
8 Sep 73 **SKYWRITER** *Tamla Motown TMG 865* [1] 25 8
9 Apr 77 **ENJOY YOURSELF** *Epic EPC 5063* $ 42 4
4 Jun 77 ★ **SHOW YOU THE WAY TO GO** *Epic EPC 5266* 1 10
16 Jul 77 THE JACKSONS *Epic EPC 86009* 54 1
13 Aug 77 **DREAMER** *Epic EPC 5458* 22 9
5 Nov 77 **GOIN' PLACES** *Epic EPC 5732* 26 7
3 Dec 77 GOIN' PLACES *Epic EPC 86035* 45 1
11 Feb 78 **EVEN THOUGH YOU'VE GONE** *Epic EPC 5919* 31 4
23 Sep 78 ● **BLAME IT ON THE BOOGIE** *Epic EPC 6683* 8 12
3 Feb 79 **DESTINY** *Epic EPC 6983* 39 6
24 Mar 79 ● **SHAKE YOUR BODY (DOWN TO THE GROUND)** *Epic EPC 7181* $ 4 12
5 May 79 DESTINY *Epic EPC 83200* 33 7
11 Oct 80 TRIUMPH *Epic EPC 86112* 13 16
25 Oct 80 **LOVELY ONE** *Epic EPC 9302* 29 6
13 Dec 80 **HEARTBREAK HOTEL** *Epic EPC 9391* 44 6
28 Feb 81 ● **CAN YOU FEEL IT** *Epic EPC 9554* 6 15
4 Jul 81 ● **WALK RIGHT NOW** *Epic EPC A 1294* 7 11
12 Dec 81 LIVE *Epic EPC 88562* 53 9
9 Jul 83 ★ 18 GREATEST HITS *Telstar STAR 2232* [2] 1 58
7 Jul 84 **STATE OF SHOCK** *Epic A 4431* [2] $ 14 8
21 Jul 84 ● VICTORY *Epic EPC 86303* 3 13
8 Sep 84 **TORTURE** *Epic A 4675* 26 6
16 Apr 88 ● **I WANT YOU BACK** (re-mix) *Motown ZB 41913* [3] 8 9
13 May 89 **NOTHIN' (THAT COMPARES 2 U)** *Epic 654808 7* 33 6
1 Jul 89 2300 JACKSON ST *Epic 463352 1* 39 3
19 Jul 97 ● THE BEST OF MICHAEL JACKSON AND THE JACKSON 5IVE – THE MOTOWN YEARS *PolyGram TV 5308042* [3] 5 12
10 Jul 04 ● THE VERY BEST OF THE JACKSONS *Sony TV / Universal TV 5163669* 7 10

[1] The Jackson Five [2] The Jacksons, lead vocals Mick Jagger and Michael Jackson [3] Michael Jackson with The Jackson Five [1] The Jackson Five [2] Michael Jackson plus The Jackson Five [3] Michael Jackson and The Jackson Five

JADAKISS *US, male rapper – Jason Phillips*

3 Jul 04 KISS OF DEATH *Interscope 9862661* ▲ 65 1

29 July 1972	5 August 1972	12 August 1972	19 August 1972
UK No.1 SINGLES			
PUPPY LOVE Donny Osmond	PUPPY LOVE Donny Osmond	SCHOOL'S OUT Alice Cooper	SCHOOL'S OUT Alice Cooper
UK No.1 ALBUMS			
20 DYNAMIC HITS Various	20 DYNAMIC HITS Various	20 FANTASTIC HITS Various	20 FANTASTIC HITS Various

JADE *US, female vocal group (1 Album: 3 Weeks, 5 Singles: 28 Weeks)*

20 Mar 93 ● **DON'T WALK AWAY** *Giant W 0160CD* ... **7** 8
29 May 93 JADE TO THE MAX *Giant 74321148002* ... 43 3
3 Jul 93 **I WANNA LOVE YOU** *Giant 74321151662* ... 13 7
18 Sep 93 **ONE WOMAN** *Giant 74321165122* ... 22 5
5 Feb 94 **ALL THRU THE NITE** *Giant 74321187552* [1] ... 32 3
11 Feb 95 **EVERY DAY OF THE WEEK** *Giant 74321260242* ... 19 5

[1] POV featuring Jade

JAGGED EDGE *UK, male vocal / instrumental group*

15 Sep 90 **YOU DON'T LOVE ME** *Polydor PO 97* ... **66** 2

JAGGED EDGE (see also NIVEA)
US, male vocal group and rapper (2 Singles: 8 Weeks)

27 Oct 01 **WHERE THE PARTY AT?** *Columbia 6719012* [1] ... 25 3
21 Feb 04 **WALKED OUTTA HEAVEN** *Columbia 6745452* ... 21 5

[1] Jagged Edge featuring Nelly

Mick JAGGER (see also The ROLLING STONES)
UK, male vocalist (4 Albums: 24 Weeks, 8 Singles: 45 Weeks)

14 Nov 70 **MEMO FROM TURNER** *Decca F 13067* ... 32 5
7 Jul 84 **STATE OF SHOCK** *Epic A 4431* [1] $ ... 14 8
16 Feb 85 **JUST ANOTHER NIGHT** *CBS A 4722* ... 32 6
16 Mar 85 ● SHE'S THE BOSS *CBS 86310* ... 6 11
7 Sep 85 ★ **DANCING IN THE STREET** *EMI America EA 204* [2] ■ ... 1 12
12 Sep 87 **LET'S WORK** *CBS 651028 7* ... 31 7
26 Sep 87 PRIMITIVE COOL *CBS 460 1231* ... 26 5
6 Feb 93 **SWEET THING** *Atlantic A 7410CD* ... **24** 4
20 Feb 93 WANDERING SPIRIT *Atlantic 7567824362* ... 12 4
1 Dec 01 GODDESS IN THE DOORWAY *Virgin CDVUS 214* ... 44 4
23 Mar 02 **VISIONS OF PARADISE** *Virgin VUSCD 240* ... 43 1
6 Nov 04 **OLD HABITS DIE HARD** *Virgin VSCDX 1887* [3] ... **45** 2

[1] The Jacksons, lead vocals Mick Jagger and Michael Jackson [2] David Bowie and Mick Jagger [3] Mick Jagger and Dave Stewart

The JAGS *UK, male vocal / instrumental group (2 Singles: 11 Weeks)*

8 Sep 79 **BACK OF MY HAND** *Island WIP 6501* ... **17** 10
2 Feb 80 **WOMAN'S WORLD** *Island WIP 6531* ... **75** 1

JAHEIM
US, male rapper – Jaheim Hoagland (1 Album: 1 Week, 4 Singles: 10 Weeks)

24 Mar 01 **COULD IT BE** *Warner Bros. W 551CD* ... 33 3
7 Apr 01 GHETTO LOVE *Warner Bros. 9362474522* ... 50 1
11 Aug 01 **JUST IN CASE** *Warner Bros. W 564CD* ... 34 2
29 Jun 02 **JUST IN CASE** (re-mix) *Warner Bros. WEA W 581CD* ... 38 3
8 Mar 03 **FABULOUS** *Warner Bros. WEA W 598CD* ... **41** 2

JAIMESON *UK, male producer –*
Jamie Williams (1 Album: 2 Weeks, 4 Singles: 24 Weeks)

14 Sep 02 **SELECTA (URBAN HEROES)**
Universal Soundproof SPR 1CD [1] ... **51** 1
25 Jan 03 ● **TRUE** *V2 / J-Did JAD 5021363* [2] ... 4 10
23 Aug 03 ● **COMPLETE** *V2 / J-Did JAD 5021713* ... 4 8
7 Feb 04 **TAKE CONTROL** *V2 / J-Did JAD 5021738* [3] ... 16 5
21 Feb 04 THINK ON YOUR FEET *V2 / J-Did JAD 1021722* ... 42 2

[1] Jameson and Viper [2] Jaimeson featuring Angel Blu [3] Jaimeson featuring Angel Blu and CK

Jaimeson released 'Selecta (Urban Heroes)' under the name Jameson.

JAKATTA (see also Li KWAN; Joey NEGRO; PHASE II; SEAL)
UK, male producer – Dave Lee (1 Album: 4 Weeks, 5 Singles: 30 Weeks)

24 Feb 01 ● **AMERICAN DREAM** (re) *Rulin RULIN 15CDS* ... 3 14
11 Aug 01 **AMERICAN DREAM** (re-mix) *Rulin RULIN 20CDS* ... 63 1
16 Feb 02 ● **SO LONELY** *Rulin RULIN 25CDS* ... **8** 5
12 Oct 02 ● **MY VISION** *Rulin RULIN 26CDS* [1] ... **6** 8
26 Oct 02 VISIONS *Rulin RULINCD 01* ... 12 4
1 Mar 03 **ONE FINE DAY** *MoS / RULIN 29CDS* ... **39** 2

[1] Jakatta featuring Seal

The JAM (114 Top 500) *Influential and extremely popular punk-based mod trio from Surrey: Paul Weller (v/g), Bruce Foxton (b), Rick Buckler (d). They hold the record for the most simultaneous Top 75 singles with 13 (all reactivated by their 1982 dissolution). Mass waves of re-entries dominated the charts on 26 Apr 1980 and 22 Jan 1983. Total UK single sales: 5,094,055 (18 Albums: 203 Weeks, 22 Singles: 206 Weeks)*

7 May 77 **IN THE CITY** (2re) *Polydor 2058 866* ... **40** 14
28 May 77 IN THE CITY *Polydor 2383 447* ... 20 18
23 Jul 77 **ALL AROUND THE WORLD** (2re) *Polydor 2058 903* ... 13 15
5 Nov 77 **THE MODERN WORLD** (2re) *Polydor 2058 945* ... 36 11
26 Nov 77 THIS IS THE MODERN WORLD *Polydor 2383 475* ... 22 5
11 Mar 78 **NEWS OF THE WORLD** (2re) *Polydor 2058 995* ... **27** 12
26 Aug 78 **DAVID WATTS / 'A' BOMB IN WARDOUR STREET** (2re)
Polydor 2059 054 ... **25** 15
21 Oct 78 **DOWN IN THE TUBE STATION AT MIDNIGHT** (re)
Polydor POSP 8 ... **15** 13
11 Nov 78 ● ALL MOD CONS *Polydor POLD 5008* ... 6 17
17 Mar 79 **STRANGE TOWN** (2re) *Polydor POSP 34* ... **15** 18
25 Aug 79 **WHEN YOU'RE YOUNG** (re) *Polydor POSP 69* ... **17** 11
3 Nov 79 ● **THE ETON RIFLES** (re) *Polydor POSP 83* ... 3 15
24 Nov 79 ● SETTING SONS *Polydor POLD 5028* ... 4 19
22 Mar 80 ★ **GOING UNDERGROUND / DREAMS OF CHILDREN** (re)
Polydor POSP 113 ■ ... 1 15
23 Aug 80 ★ **START** (re) *Polydor 2059 266* ... 1 10
6 Dec 80 ● SOUND AFFECTS *Polydor POLD 5035* ... 2 19
7 Feb 81 **THAT'S ENTERTAINMENT** (import) *Metronome 0030 364* ... 21 7
6 Jun 81 ● **FUNERAL PYRE** *Polydor POSP 257* ... 4 6
24 Oct 81 ● **ABSOLUTE BEGINNERS** *Polydor POSP 350* ... 4 6
13 Feb 82 ★ **TOWN CALLED MALICE / PRECIOUS** (re) *Polydor POSP 400* ■ .. 1 9
20 Mar 82 ★ THE GIFT *Polydor POLD 5055* ■ ... 1 24
3 Jul 82 ● **JUST WHO IS THE FIVE O'CLOCK HERO** *Polydor 2059 504* ... 8 5
18 Sep 82 ● **THE BITTEREST PILL (I EVER HAD TO SWALLOW)**
Polydor POSP 505 ... 2 7
4 Dec 82 ★ **BEAT SURRENDER** *Polydor POSP 540* ■ ... 1 9
18 Dec 82 ● DIG THE NEW BREED *Polydor POLD 5075* ... 2 15
29 Jan 83 **THAT'S ENTERTAINMENT** *Polydor POSP 482* ... **60** 3
27 Aug 83 IN THE CITY (re-issue) *Polydor SPELP 27* ... 100 1
22 Oct 83 ● SNAP! *Polydor SNAP 1* ... 2 30
29 Jun 91 **THAT'S ENTERTAINMENT** (re-issue) *Polydor PO 155* ... **57** 2
13 Jul 91 ● GREATEST HITS *Polydor 8495541* ... 2 21
18 Apr 92 EXTRAS *Polydor 5131772* ... 15 4
6 Nov 93 LIVE JAM *Polydor 5196672* ... 28 2
27 Jul 96 THE JAM COLLECTION *Polydor 5314932* ... 58 1
7 Jun 97 ● DIRECTION REACTION CREATION *Polydor 5371432* ... 8 4
11 Oct 97 **THE BITTEREST PILL (I EVER HAD TO SWALLOW)** (re-issue) *Polydor 5715992* ... **30** 2
25 Oct 97 ● THE VERY BEST OF THE JAM
Polydor / PolyGram TV 5374232 ... 9 10
11 May 02 **IN THE CITY** (re-issue) *Polydor 5876117* ... **36** 1
18 May 02 ● THE SOUND OF THE JAM *Polydor 5897812* ... 3 7
15 Jun 02 THE JAM AT THE BBC *Polydor 5896902* ... 33 2
2 Jul 05 COMPACT SNAP! (re-issue) *Polydor 8217122* ... 39 4

Snap! and Compact Snap! are greatest hits sets featuring singles from 1977-1982

JAM & SPOON featuring PLAVKA (see also DANCE 2 TRANCE; STORM; TOKYO GHETTO PUSSY) *Germany, male production duo – Rolf Ellmer and Markus Löeffel, b. 27 Nov 1966, d. 11 Jan 2006, and US, female vocalist – Plavka Lonich (1 Album: 1 Week, 9 Singles: 26 Weeks)*

2 May 92 **TALES FROM A DANCEOGRAPHIC OCEAN (EP)**
R&S RSUK 14 [1] ... **49** 1
6 Jun 92 **THE COMPLETE STELLA** (re-mix) *R&S RSUK 14X* [1] ... **66** 2
19 Feb 94 TRIPTOMATIC FAIRYTALES 2001 *Epic 4749282* [1] ... 71 1

26 August 1972	2 September 1972	9 September 1972	16 September 1972
SCHOOL'S OUT Alice Cooper	YOU WEAR IT WELL Rod Stewart	MAMA WEER ALL CRAZEE NOW Slade	MAMA WEER ALL CRAZEE NOW Slade
20 FANTASTIC HITS Various	20 FANTASTIC HITS Various	20 FANTASTIC HITS Various	NEVER A DULL MOMENT Rod Stewart

KEY UK No.1 ★ UK Top 10 ● Still on chart + UK entry at No.1 ■ US No.1 ▲ UK million seller £ US million seller $
Singles re-entries are listed as (re), (2re), (3re)... which signifies that the hit re-entered the chart once, twice or three times...

Peak Position | Weeks

26 Feb 94 **RIGHT IN THE NIGHT (FALL IN LOVE WITH MUSIC)** *Epic 6600822* 31 4
24 Sep 94 **FIND ME (ODYSSEY TO ANYOONA)** *Epic 6608082* 37 3
10 Jun 95 ● **RIGHT IN THE NIGHT (FALL IN LOVE WITH MUSIC)** (re-issue) *Epic 6620182* 10 8
16 Sep 95 **FIND ME (ODYSSEY TO ANYOONA)** (re-issue) *Epic 6623242* 22 3
25 Nov 95 **ANGEL (LADADI O-HEYO)** *Epic 6626382* 26 2
30 Aug 97 **KALEIDOSCOPE SKIES** *Epic 6647614* 48 1
2 Mar 02 **BE ANGELED** *Nulife / Arista 74321878992* [2] 31 2

[1] Jam and Spoon [2] Jam & Spoon featuring Rea [1] Jam & Spoon

Tracks on Tales From a Danceographic Ocean (EP): Stella / Keep on Movin' / My First Fantastic FF. 'The Complete Stella' is a re-mix of a track from the EP.

JAM MACHINE *Italy / US, male vocal / instrumental group*

23 Dec 89 **EVERYDAY** *Deconstruction PB 43299* 68 1

JAM ON THE MUTHA *UK, male vocal / instrumental group*

11 Aug 90 **HOTEL CALIFORNIA** *M&G MAGS 3* 62 2

JAM TRONIK *Germany, male / female vocal / instrumental group*

24 Mar 90 **ANOTHER DAY IN PARADISE** *Debut DEBT 3093* 19 7

JAMAICA UNITED *Jamaica, male vocal ensemble*

4 Jul 98 **RISE UP** *Columbia 6660522* 54 1

JAMELIA

UK, female vocalist – Jamelia Davis (2 Albums: 45 Weeks, 9 Singles: 77 Weeks)

31 Jul 99 **I DO** *Parlophone Rhythm Series CDRHYTHM 21* 36 2
4 Mar 00 ● **MONEY** *Parlophone Rhythm Series CDRHYTHM 27* [1] 5 9
24 Jun 00 **CALL ME** *Parlophone Rhythm Series CDRHYTHM 28* 11 5
8 Jul 00 DRAMA *Parlophone Rhythm 5272272* 39 2
21 Oct 00 **BOY NEXT DOOR** *Parlophone Rhythm Series CDRHYTHM 29* 42 2
21 Jun 03 **BOUT** *Parlophone CDRS 6597* [2] 37 2
27 Sep 03 ● **SUPERSTAR** *Parlophone CDR 6615* 3 20
11 Oct 03 ● THANK YOU *Parlophone 5837772* 4 43
6 Mar 04 ● **THANK YOU** *Parlophone CDR 6621* 2 14
24 Jul 04 ● **SEE IT IN A BOY'S EYES** *Parlophone CDRS 6635* 5 11
13 Nov 04 ● **DJ / STOP** *Parlophone CDR 6646* 9 12

[1] Jamelia featuring Beenie Man [2] Jamelia featuring Rah Digga

JAMES (268 Top 500)

(see also BOOTH and The BAD ANGEL) *Anthemic indie pop band formed in 1982 in Manchester, UK, by mainstays Tim Booth (v) (left in 2001) and Larry Gott (g). After several hit-less years, critically-acclaimed releases and record company changes, they became one of the most consistently successful acts of the 1990s (10 Albums: 155 Weeks, 21 Singles: 89 Weeks)*

2 Aug 86 STUTTER *Blanco Y Negro JIMLP 1* 68 2
8 Oct 88 STRIP MINE *Sire JIMLP 2* 90 1
12 May 90 **HOW WAS IT FOR YOU?** *Fontana JIM 5* 32 3
16 Jun 90 ● GOLD MOTHER *Fontana 8485951* 2 34
7 Jul 90 **COME HOME** *Fontana JIM 6* 32 4
8 Dec 90 **LOSE CONTROL** *Fontana JIM 7* 38 5
30 Mar 91 ● **SIT DOWN** *Fontana JIM 8* 2 10
30 Nov 91 ● **SOUND** *Fontana JIM 9* 9 7
1 Feb 92 **BORN OF FRUSTRATION** *Fontana JIM 10* 13 6
29 Feb 92 ● SEVEN *Fontana 5109322* 2 14
4 Apr 92 **RING THE BELLS** *Fontana JIM 11* 37 2
18 Jul 92 **SEVEN (EP)** *Fontana JIM 12* 46 2
11 Sep 93 **SOMETIMES** *Fontana JIMCD 13* 18 4
9 Oct 93 ● LAID *Fontana 5149432* 3 16
13 Nov 93 **LAID** *Fontana JIMCD 14* 25 4
2 Apr 94 **JAM J / SAY SOMETHING** *Fontana JIMCD 15* 24 4
24 Sep 94 WAH WAH *Fontana 5228272* [1] 11 2
22 Feb 97 ● **SHE'S A STAR** *Fontana JIMCD 16* 9 5
8 Mar 97 ● WHIPLASH *Fontana 5343542* 9 19
3 May 97 **TOMORROW** *Fontana JIMCD 17* 12 3
5 Jul 97 **WALTZING ALONG** *Fontana JIMCD 18* 23 4
21 Mar 98 **DESTINY CALLING** *Fontana JIMCD 19* 17 4
4 Apr 98 ★ THE BEST OF *Fontana 5368982* ■ 1 53
6 Jun 98 **RUNAGROUND** *Fontana JIMCD 20* 29 2
21 Nov 98 ● **SIT DOWN** (re-mix) *Fontana JIMCD 21* 7 7
31 Jul 99 **I KNOW WHAT I'M HERE FOR** *Mercury JIMCD 22* 22 5
16 Oct 99 **JUST LIKE FRED ASTAIRE** *Mercury JIMCD 23* 17 3
23 Oct 99 ● MILLIONAIRES *Mercury 5467892* 2 11
25 Dec 99 **WE'RE GOING TO MISS YOU** *Mercury JIMCD 24* 48 2
7 Jul 01 **GETTING AWAY WITH IT (ALL MESSED UP)** *Mercury JIMCD 25* 22 3
14 Jul 01 PLEASED TO MEET YOU *Mercury 5861462* 11 3

[1] James and Brian Eno

Tracks on Seven (EP): Seven / Goalie's Ball / William Burroughs / Still Alive. 'Say Something' listed with 'Jam J' only for first two weeks of record's run.

David JAMES *UK, male DJ / producer*

11 Aug 01 **ALWAYS A PERMANENT STATE** *Hooj Choons HOOJ 108CD* 60 1

Dick JAMES *UK, male vocalist – Isaac Vapnic, b. 12 Dec 1920, d. 1 Feb 1986 (2 Singles: 13 Weeks)*

20 Jan 56 **ROBIN HOOD / THE BALLAD OF DAVY CROCKETT** (re) *Parlophone R 4117* 14 9
11 Jan 57 **GARDEN OF EDEN** *Parlophone R 4255* 18 4

'Robin Hood' is with Stephen James and his Chums. 'The Ballad of Davy Crockett' listed only from 18 May 1956.

Duncan JAMES & KEEDIE (see also BLUE) *UK, male and female vocalists*

23 Oct 04 ● **I BELIEVE MY HEART** *Innocent 8677122* 2 7

Etta JAMES *US, female vocalist – Jamesetta Hawkins*

10 Feb 96 ● **I JUST WANT TO MAKE LOVE TO YOU** *MCA MCSTD 48003* 5 7

Freddie JAMES *Canada, male vocalist*

24 Nov 79 **GET UP AND BOOGIE** *Warner Bros. K 17478* 54 3

Joni JAMES *US, female vocalist – Joan Babbo (2 Singles: 2 Weeks)*

6 Mar 53 **WHY DON'T YOU BELIEVE ME?** *MGM 582* ▲ 11 1
30 Jan 59 **THERE MUST BE A WAY** *MGM 1002* 24 1

Nate JAMES NEW *UK, male vocalist (3 Singles: 3 Weeks)*

19 Mar 05 **SET THE TONE** *Morethan4 / Onetwo ONETCDS 001* 69 1
25 Jun 05 **LOVIN' YOU** *Positiva CDTIVS 218* [1] 43 1
30 Jul 05 **UNIVERSAL** *Morethan4 / Onetwo ONET CDX02* 72 1

[1] Poker Pets featuring Nate James

Rick JAMES *US, male vocalist – James Johnson, b. 1 Jan 1948, d. 6 Aug 2004 (1 Album: 2 Weeks, 6 Singles: 30 Weeks)*

8 Jul 78 **YOU AND I** *Motown TMG 1110* 46 7
7 Jul 79 **I'M A SUCKER FOR YOUR LOVE** *Motown TMG 1146* [1] 43 8
6 Sep 80 **BIG TIME** *Motown TMG 1198* 41 6
4 Jul 81 **GIVE IT TO ME BABY** *Motown TMG 1229* 47 3
12 Jun 82 **STANDING ON THE TOP (PART 1)** *Motown TMG 1263* [2] 53 3
3 Jul 82 **DANCE WIT' ME** *Motown TMG 1266* 53 3
24 Jul 82 THROWIN' DOWN *Motown STML 12167* 93 2

[1] Teena Marie, co-lead vocals Rick James [2] The Temptations featuring Rick James

	23 September 1972	30 September 1972	7 October 1972	14 October 1972
UK No.1 SINGLES	MAMA WEER ALL CRAZEE NOW Slade	HOW CAN I BE SURE David Cassidy	HOW CAN I BE SURE David Cassidy	MOULDY OLD DOUGH Lieutenant Pigeon
UK No.1 ALBUMS	NEVER A DULL MOMENT Rod Stewart	FANTASTIC HITS Various	20 ALL TIME HITS OF THE FIFTIES Various	20 ALL TIME HITS OF THE FIFTIES Various

Sonny JAMES *US, male vocalist – James Loden (2 Singles: 8 Weeks)*

30 Nov 56 **THE CAT CAME BACK** *Capitol CL 14635*......30 1
8 Feb 57 **YOUNG LOVE** *Capitol CL 14683* $......11 7

Tyler JAMES *UK, male vocalist (3 Singles: 9 Weeks)*

13 Nov 04 **WHY DO I DO?** *Island CID 872*......25 4
19 Mar 05 **FOOLISH** *Island CID 884*......16 4
3 Sep 05 **YOUR WOMAN** *Island CIDX 900*......60 1

Wendy JAMES (see also TRANSVISION VAMP)
UK, female vocalist (1 Album: 1 Week, 2 Singles: 4 Weeks)

20 Feb 93 **THE NAMELESS ONE** *MCA MCSTD 1732*......34 3
20 Mar 93 NOW AIN'T THE TIME FOR YOUR TEARS *MCA MCD 10800*......43 1
17 Apr 93 **LONDON'S BRILLIANT** *MCA MCSTD 1763*......62 1

Jimmy JAMES and The VAGABONDS
UK, male vocal / instrumental group (3 Singles: 25 Weeks)

11 Sep 68 **RED RED WINE** *Pye 7N 17579*......36 8
24 Apr 76 **I'LL GO WHERE YOUR MUSIC TAKES ME** *Pye 7N 45585*......23 8
17 Jul 76 ● **NOW IS THE TIME** *Pye 7N 45606*......5 9

Tommy JAMES and The SHONDELLS *US, male vocal / instrumental group – leader Thomas Jackson (2 Singles: 25 Weeks)*

21 Jul 66 **HANKY PANKY** *Roulette RK 7000* ▲ $......38 7
5 Jun 68 ★ **MONY MONY** *Major Minor MM 567* $......1 18

The JAMES BOYS
(see also BLOWING FREE; HYPNOSIS; IN TUNE; RAINDANCE; SCHOOL OF EXCELLENCE) *UK, male vocal duo – Bradley and Stewart Palmer*

19 May 73 **OVER AND OVER** *Penny Farthing PEN 806*......39 6

JAMESTOWN *US, male instrumentalist / producer – Kent Brainerd and US, female vocalist (2 Singles: 4 Weeks)*

14 Sep 91 **SHE GOT SOUL** *A&M AM 819*......57 3
27 Mar 99 **I BELIEVE** *Playola 0091705 PLA* [1] 62 1

[1] Jamestown featuring Jocelyn Brown

JAMESY P NEW *St. Vincent, male vocalist – James Morgan*

24 Sep 05 **NOOKIE** *Smoove SMOOVE 04CDS*......14 5

JAMIROQUAI 125 Top 500
One of the world's biggest-selling acts of the late 1990s features hat-wearing vocalist Jay Kay, b. 30 Dec 1969, Manchester, UK. The group, whose videos have also earned numerous accolades, sold seven million copies of 1996 album Travelling Without Moving and 1999 album Synkronized topped many European charts (6 Albums: 232 Weeks, 26 Singles: 158 Weeks)

31 Oct 92 **WHEN YOU GONNA LEARN** (re) *Acid Jazz JAZID 46*......52 3
13 Mar 93 ● **TOO YOUNG TO DIE** *Sony S2 6590112*......10 7
5 Jun 93 **BLOW YOUR MIND** *Sony S2 6592972*......12 6
26 Jun 93 ★ EMERGENCY ON PLANET EARTH *Sony S2 4740692* ■......1 32
14 Aug 93 **EMERGENCY ON PLANET EARTH** *Sony S2 6595782*......32 3
25 Sep 93 **WHEN YOU GONNA LEARN** (re-issue) *Sony S2 6596952*......28 3
8 Oct 94 **SPACE COWBOY** *Sony S2 6608512*......17 5
29 Oct 94 ● THE RETURN OF THE SPACE COWBOY *Sony S2 4778132*......2 29
19 Nov 94 **HALF THE MAN** *Sony S2 6610032*......15 8
1 Jul 95 ● **STILLNESS IN TIME** *Sony S2 6620255*......9 5
1 Jun 96 **DO U KNOW WHERE YOU'RE COMING FROM** *Renk CDRENK 63* [1] 12 5
31 Aug 96 ● **VIRTUAL INSANITY** *Sony S2 6636132*......3 11
21 Sep 96 ● TRAVELLING WITHOUT MOVING *Sony S2 4839999*......2 74
7 Dec 96 ● **COSMIC GIRL** *Sony S2 6638292*......6 10
10 May 97 ● **ALRIGHT** *Sony S2 6643252*......6 5
13 Dec 97 **HIGH TIMES** *Sony S2 6653702*......20 6
25 Jul 98 ★ **DEEPER UNDERGROUND** *Sony S2 6662182* ■......1 11
5 Jun 99 ● **CANNED HEAT** *Sony S2 6673022*......4 10
26 Jun 99 ★ SYNKRONIZED *Sony S2 4945172* ■......1 29
25 Sep 99 **SUPERSONIC** *Sony S2 6678392*......22 4
11 Dec 99 **KING FOR A DAY** *Sony S2 6679732*......20 7
24 Feb 01 **I'M IN THE MOOD FOR LOVE** *Warner.esp WSMS 001CD* [2] ...29 3
25 Aug 01 ● **LITTLE L** *Sony S2 6717182*......5 11
15 Sep 01 ★ A FUNK ODYSSEY *Sony S2 5040692* ■......1 51
1 Dec 01 **YOU GIVE ME SOMETHING** *Sony S2 6720072*......16 9
9 Mar 02 **LOVE FOOLOSOPHY** (re) *Sony S2 6723252*......14 6
20 Jul 02 **CORNER OF THE EARTH** *Sony S2 6727882*......31 3
18 Jun 05 ● **FEELS JUST LIKE IT SHOULD** *Sony S2 6759682*......8 9
2 Jul 05 ● DYNAMITE *Sony Music 5201112*......3 17
27 Aug 05 **SEVEN DAYS IN SUNNY JUNE** *Sony Music 6760642*......14 5
19 Nov 05 **(DON'T) GIVE HATE A CHANCE** *Sony Music 82876750652*......27 3

[1] M-Beat featuring Jamiroquai [2] Jools Holland and Jamiroquai

The JAMMERS *US, male vocal / instrumental group*

29 Jan 83 **BE MINE TONIGHT** *Salsoul Sal 101*......65 2

JamX & DeLEON (see also DUMONDE)
Germany, male production duo – Jurgen Mutschall and Dominik DeLeon

7 Sep 02 **CAN U DIG IT?** *Serious SERR 052CD*......40 2

JAN and DEAN *US, male vocal duo – Jan Berry, b. 3 Apr 1941, d. 27 Mar 2004, and Dean Torrence (1 Album: 2 Weeks, 2 Singles: 18 Weeks)*

24 Aug 61 **HEART AND SOUL** *London HLH 9395*......24 8
15 Aug 63 **SURF CITY** *Liberty LIB 55580* ▲ $......26 10
12 Jul 80 THE JAN AND DEAN STORY *K-Tel NE 1084*......67 2

JAN and KJELD *Denmark, male vocal duo – Jan and Kjeld Wennick*

21 Jul 60 **BANJO BOY** *Ember S 101*......36 4

JANE'S ADDICTION
US, male vocal / instrumental group (2 Albums: 5 Weeks, 4 Singles: 10 Weeks)

8 Sep 90 RITUAL DE LO HABITUAL *Warner Bros. WX 306*......37 2
23 Mar 91 **BEEN CAUGHT STEALING** *Warner Bros. W 0011*......34 3
1 Jun 91 **CLASSIC GIRL** *Warner Bros. W 0031*......60 1
26 Jul 03 **JUST BECAUSE** *Capitol CDCL 847*......14 4
2 Aug 03 STRAYS *Parlophone 5921980*......14 3
8 Nov 03 **TRUE NATURE** *Parlophone CDCL 850*......41 2

Horst JANKOWSKI, his Orchestra and Chorus *Germany, male pianist*

29 Jul 65 ● **A WALK IN THE BLACK FOREST** *Mercury MF 861*......3 18

Samantha JANUS *UK, female vocalist*

11 May 91 **A MESSAGE TO YOUR HEART** *Hollywood HWD 104*......30 3

Philip JAP *UK, male vocalist (2 Singles: 8 Weeks)*

31 Jul 82 **SAVE US** *A&M AMS 8217*......53 4
25 Sep 82 **TOTAL ERASURE** *A&M JAP 1*......41 4

JAPAN 318 Top 500 *Rock quintet who subsequently became New Romantic figureheads fronted by David Sylvian (v), b. David Batt, 23 Feb 1958, London, UK, who later recorded critically acclaimed solo work. Group folded in 1982, but full line-up briefly reconvened as Rain Tree Crow in 1991 (6 Albums: 135 Weeks, 12 Singles: 81 Weeks)*

9 Feb 80 QUIET LIFE *Ariola Hansa AHAL 8011*......53 8
18 Oct 80 **GENTLEMEN TAKE POLAROIDS** *Virgin VS 379*......60 2
15 Nov 80 GENTLEMEN TAKE POLAROIDS *Virgin V 2180*......45 10
9 May 81 **THE ART OF PARTIES** *Virgin VS 409*......48 5
19 Sep 81 **QUIET LIFE** *Hansa HANSA 6*......19 9
26 Sep 81 ASSEMBLAGE *Hansa HANLP 1*......26 46
7 Nov 81 **VISIONS OF CHINA** *Virgin VS 436*......32 12
28 Nov 81 TIN DRUM *Virgin V 2209*......12 50

21 October 1972	28 October 1972	4 November 1972	11 November 1972
MOULDY OLD DOUGH Lieutenant Pigeon	**MOULDY OLD DOUGH** Lieutenant Pigeon	**MOULDY OLD DOUGH** Lieutenant Pigeon	**CLAIR** Gilbert O'Sullivan
20 ALL TIME HITS OF THE FIFTIES Various	**20 ALL TIME HITS OF THE FIFTIES** Various	**20 ALL TIME HITS OF THE FIFTIES** Various	**20 ALL TIME HITS OF THE FIFTIES** Various

KEY
UK No.1 ★★ UK Top 10 ●● Still on chart ++ UK entry at No.1 ■■
US No.1 ▲▲ UK million seller £ US million seller $
Singles re-entries are listed as (re), (2re), (3re)… which signifies that the hit re-entered the chart once, twice or three times…
Peak Position / Weeks

23 Jan 82 **EUROPEAN SON** *Hansa HANSA 10* 31 6
20 Mar 82 ● **GHOSTS** *Virgin VS 472* 5 8
22 May 82 **CANTONESE BOY** *Virgin VS 502* 24 6
3 Jul 82 ● **I SECOND THAT EMOTION** *Hansa HANSA 12* 9 11
9 Oct 82 **LIFE IN TOKYO** *Hansa HANSA 17* 28 6
20 Nov 82 **NIGHT PORTER** *Virgin VS 554* 29 9
12 Mar 83 **ALL TOMORROW'S PARTIES** *Hansa HANSA 18* 38 4
21 May 83 **CANTON (LIVE)** *Virgin VS 581* 42 3
18 Jun 83 ● OIL ON CANVAS *Virgin VD 2513* 5 14
8 Dec 84 EXORCISING GHOSTS *Virgin VGD 3510* 45 7

JARK PRONGO (see also CHOCOLATE PUMA; GOODMEN; RHYTHMKILLAZ; RIVA featuring Dannii MINOGUE; TOMBA VIRA)
Holland, male production duo – Rene Ter Horst and Gaston Steenkist

3 Apr 99 **MOVIN' THRU YOUR SYSTEM** *Hooj Choons HOOJ 72CD* 58 1

Jeff JARRATT and Don REEDMAN
(see also Pierre BELMONDE) *UK, male producers*

22 Nov 80 MASTERWORKS *K-Tel ONE 1093* 39 8

Jean-Michel JARRE (218 Top 500)
Distinctive synthesizer wizard, b. 24 Aug 1948, Lyon, France. The son of composer / conductor Maurice has sold over 60 million albums worldwide and his spectacular, futuristic, live sound and light extravaganzas have frequently helped break attendance records (18 Albums: 243 Weeks, 12 Singles: 40 Weeks)

20 Aug 77 ● OXYGENE *Polydor 2310 555* 2 24
27 Aug 77 ● **OXYGENE PART IV** *Polydor 2001 721* 4 9
16 Dec 78 EQUINOXE *Polydor POLD 5007* 11 26
20 Jan 79 **EQUINOXE PART 5** *Polydor POSP 20* 45 5
6 Jun 81 ● MAGNETIC FIELDS *Polydor POLS 1033* 6 17
15 May 82 ● THE CONCERTS IN CHINA *Polydor PODV 3* 6 17
12 Nov 83 THE ESSENTIAL JEAN-MICHEL JARRE *Polystar PROLP 3* 14 29
24 Nov 84 ZOOLOOK *Polydor POLH 15* 47 14
12 Apr 86 ● RENDEZ-VOUS *Polydor POLH 27* 9 38
23 Aug 86 **FOURTH RENDEZ-VOUS** *Polydor POSP 788* 65 4
18 Jul 87 EN CONCERT HOUSTON / LYON *Polydor POLH 36* 18 15
8 Oct 88 ● REVOLUTIONS *Polydor POLH 45* 2 13
5 Nov 88 **REVOLUTIONS** *Polydor PO 25* 52 2
7 Jan 89 **LONDON KID** *Polydor PO 32* [1] 52 3
7 Oct 89 **OXYGENE PART IV** (re-mix) *Polydor PO 55* 65 2
14 Oct 89 JARRE LIVE *Polydor 841258 1* 16 4
23 Jun 90 WAITING FOR COUSTEAU *Dreyfus 8436141* 14 10
26 Oct 91 IMAGES – THE BEST OF JEAN-MICHEL JARRE *Dreyfus 5113061* 14 12
5 Jun 93 CHRONOLOGIE *Polydor 5193732* 11 8
26 Jun 93 **CHRONOLOGIE PART 4** *Polydor POCS 274* 55 2
30 Oct 93 **CHRONOLOGIE PART 4** (re-mix) *Polydor POCS 274* 56 1
28 May 94 CHRONOLOGIE PART 6 *Polydor 5195792* 60 1
1 Mar 97 OXYGENE 7-13 *Epic 4869849* 11 5
22 Mar 97 **OXYGENE 8** *Epic 6643232* 17 3
5 Jul 97 **OXYGENE 10** *Epic 6647152* 21 2
23 May 98 ODYSSEY THROUGH O2 *Epic 4897646* 50 2
11 Jul 98 **RENDEZ-VOUS 98** *Epic 6661102* [2] 12 6
12 Feb 00 METAMORPHOSES *Epic 4960222* 37 1
26 Feb 00 **C'EST LA VIE** *Epic 6689302* [3] 40 1
2 Oct 04 AERO *WSM 256461852* 14 7

[1] Jean-Michel Jarre featuring Hank Marvin [2] Jean-Michel Jarre and Apollo 440 [3] Jean-Michel Jarre featuring Natacha Atlas

Al JARREAU
US, male vocalist (4 Albums: 37 Weeks, 7 Singles: 30 Weeks)

5 Sep 81 BREAKIN' AWAY *Warner Bros. K 56917* 60 8
26 Sep 81 **WE'RE IN THIS LOVE TOGETHER** *Warner Bros. K 17849* 55 4
30 Apr 83 JARREAU *WEA International U 0070* 39 18
14 May 83 **MORNIN'** *WEA U9929* 28 6
16 Jul 83 **TROUBLE IN PARADISE** *WEA Int. U9871* 36 5
24 Sep 83 **BOOGIE DOWN** *WEA U9814* 63 3
17 Nov 84 HIGH CRIME *WEA 250807* 81 1
16 Nov 85 **DAY BY DAY** *Polydor POSP 770* [1] 53 3
5 Apr 86 **THE MUSIC OF GOODBYE (LOVE THEME FROM 'OUT OF AFRICA')** *MCA MCA 1038* [2] 75 1
13 Sep 86 L IS FOR LOVER *WEA International 253 0801* 45 10
7 Mar 87 ● **'MOONLIGHTING' THEME** *WEA U8407* 8 8

[1] Shakatak featuring Al Jarreau [2] Melissa Manchester and Al Jarreau

Kenny 'Jammin' JASON and 'Fast' Eddie SMITH
US, male DJ / production duo

11 Apr 87 **CAN U DANCE** (re) *Champion CHAMP 41* 67 4

The JAVELLS featuring Nosmo KING
(see also The TRUTH) *UK, male vocalist – Stephen Gold*

9 Nov 74 **GOODBYE NOTHING TO SAY** *Pye Disco Demand DDS 2003* 26 8

JAVINE
UK, female vocalist – Javine Hylton (1 Album: 1 Week, 5 Singles: 26 Weeks)

19 Jul 03 ● **REAL THINGS** *Innocent SINCD 46* 4 9
22 Nov 03 **SURRENDER (YOUR LOVE)** *Innocent SINCD 52* 15 5
26 Jun 04 **BEST OF MY LOVE** *Innocent SINDX 63* 18 4
10 Jul 04 SURRENDER *Innocent CDSIN 15* 73 1
21 Aug 04 **DON'T WALK AWAY** *Innocent SINDX 65* 16 4
28 May 05 **TOUCH MY FIRE** *Shalit Productions 9871694* 18 4

Peter JAY and The JAYWALKERS
UK, male instrumental group – leader Peter Jay – drums

8 Nov 62 **CAN CAN '62** *Decca F 11531* 31 11

Candee JAY
Holland, female vocalist (2 Singles: 8 Weeks)

19 Jun 04 **IF I WERE YOU** *Incentive CENT 58CDX* 14 6
13 Nov 04 **BACK FOR ME** *Incentive CENT 67CDS* 23 2

Oris JAY presents DELSENA (see also PERAN)
Holland, male producer – Peran van Dijk and UK, female vocalist

23 Mar 02 **TRIPPIN'** *Gusto CDGUS 3* 42 2

JAYDEE
Holland, male DJ / producer – Robin Albers (2 Singles: 7 Weeks)

20 Sep 97 **PLASTIC DREAMS** *R&S RS 97117CD* 18 3
10 Jan 04 **PLASTIC DREAMS 2003** (re-recording) *Positiva CDTIVS 198* 35 4

The JAYHAWKS
US, male / female vocal / instrumental group (4 Albums: 4 Weeks, 1 Single: 1 Week)

25 Feb 95 TOMORROW THE GREEN GRASS *American 74321236802* 41 1
15 Jul 95 **BAD TIME** *American 74321291632* 70 1
3 May 97 SOUND OF LIES *American Recordings 74321464062* 61 1
20 May 00 SMILE *Columbia 4979712* 60 1
19 Apr 03 RAINY DAY MUSIC *American 0771362* 70 1

JAY-Z (354 Top 500)
Foremost East Coast rapper, b. Shawn Carter, 4 Dec 1969, New York, US, whose original rap name was "Jazzy". The owner of Rock-A-Fella Records has had 16 Top 20 singles and eight No.1 albums in the US. He took over as president of Def Jam Records in Jan 2005 and performed at the US Live 8 concert in Philadelphia (7 Albums: 38 Weeks, 29 Singles: 159 Weeks)

1 Mar 97 **CAN'T KNOCK THE HUSTLE** *Northwestside 74321447192* [1] 30 2
10 May 97 **AIN'T NO PLAYA** *Northwestside 74321474842* [2] 31 2
21 Jun 97 ● **I'LL BE** *Def Jam 75710432* [3] 9 5
23 Aug 97 **WHO YOU WIT** *Qwest W 0411CD* 65 1
25 Oct 97 **SUNSHINE** *Northwestside 74321528702* [4] 25 2

18 November 1972	25 November 1972	2 December 1972	9 December 1972
UK No.1 SINGLES			
CLAIR Gilbert O'Sullivan	MY DING-A-LING Chuck Berry	MY DING-A-LING Chuck Berry	MY DING-A-LING Chuck Berry
UK No.1 ALBUMS			
20 ALL TIME HITS OF THE FIFTIES Various	20 ALL TIME HITS OF THE FIFTIES Various	25 ROCKIN' AND ROLLIN' GREATS Various	25 ROCKIN' AND ROLLIN' GREATS Various

14 Feb 98 **WISHING ON A STAR** *Northwestside 74321554632* [5] 13 4
27 Jun 98 **THE CITY IS MINE** *Northwestside 74321588012* [6] 38 2
12 Dec 98 ● **HARD KNOCK LIFE (GHETTO ANTHEM)** *Northwestside 74321635332* 2 11
13 Mar 99 **CAN I GET A ...** *Def Jam 5668472* [7] 24 3
10 Apr 99 **BE ALONE NO MORE** *Northwestside 74321658472* [8] 11 9
19 Jun 99 **LOBSTER & SCRIMP** *Virgin DINSD 186* [9] 48 1
6 Nov 99 ● **HEARTBREAKER** *Columbia 6683012* [10] ▲....5 13
4 Dec 99 **WHAT YOU THINK OF THAT** *Def Jam 8708292* [11] 58 1
26 Feb 00 **ANYTHING** *Def Jam 5626502*....18 4
24 Jun 00 **BIG PIMPIN'** *Def Jam 5627742*....29 3
16 Dec 00 **I JUST WANNA LOVE U (GIVE IT 2 ME)** *Def Jam 5727462*....17 8
23 Jun 01 **FIESTA** *Jive 9252142* [12] 23 3
29 Sep 01 THE BLUEPRINT *Roc-A-Fella 5863962*....30 4
27 Oct 01 **IZZO (H.O.V.A.)** *Roc-A-Fella / Def Jam 5888152*....21 4
19 Jan 02 **GIRLS, GIRLS, GIRLS** (re) *Roc-A-Fella / Def Jam 5889062*....11 7
30 Mar 02 CHAPTER ONE *Roc-A-Fella 74321920462*....65 1
30 Mar 02 THE BEST OF BOTH WORLDS *Jive 9223512* [1] 37 2
25 May 02 **HONEY** *Jive 9253662* [13] 35 2
30 Nov 02 THE BLUEPRINT 2 – THE GIFT & THE CURSE *Def Jam / Mercury 0633812* ▲....23 7
1 Feb 03 ● **'03 BONNIE & CLYDE** *Roc-A-Fella 0770102* [14] 2 12
26 Apr 03 **EXCUSE ME MISS** *Roc-A-Fella 0779122*....17 7
5 Jul 03 **JOGI / BEWARE OF THE BOYS** *Showbiz / Dharma DHARMA ICDS* [15] 25 3
16 Aug 03 ● **FRONTIN'** *Arista 8267655332* [16] 6 10
29 Nov 03 THE BLACK ALBUM *Roc-A-Fella / Mercury 9861121* ▲....34 7
20 Dec 03 **CHANGE CLOTHES** *Roc-A-Fella 9815225*....32 7
22 May 04 **99 PROBLEMS / DIRT OFF YOUR SHOULDER** (re) *Roc-A-Fella 9862391*....12 10
6 Nov 04 2004 UNFINISHED BUSINESS *Jive 82876658682* [1] ▲....61 1
4 Dec 04 **NUMB** (re-recording) **/ ENCORE** *WEA W 660CD* [17] 14 23
11 Dec 04 COLLISION COURSE *WEA 9362489662* [2] ▲....15 16

[1] Jay-Z featuring Mary J Blige [2] Jay-Z featuring Foxy Brown [3] Foxy Brown featuring Jay-Z [4] Jay-Z featuring Babyface and Foxy Brown [5] Jay-Z featuring Gwen Dickey [6] Jay-Z featuring BLACKstreet [7] Jay-Z featuring Amil & Ja Rule [8] Another Level featuring Jay-Z [9] Timbaland featuring Jay-Z [10] Mariah Carey featuring Jay-Z [11] Memphis Bleek featuring Jay-Z [12] R Kelly featuring Jay-Z [13] R Kelly & Jay-Z [14] Jay-Z featuring Beyoncé Knowles [15] Panjabi MC featuring Jay-Z (Jay-Z appears on 'Beware Of The Boys' only) [16] Pharrell Williams featuring Jay-Z [17] Jay-Z / Linkin Park [1] R Kelly and Jay-Z [2] Jay-Z / Linkin Park

'Numb / Encore' is one song that combines Linkin Park's 'Numb' and Jay-Z's 'Encore'.

JAZZ and The BROTHERS GRIMM *UK, male vocal / instrumental group*

9 Jul 88 **(LET'S ALL GO BACK) DISCO NIGHTS** *Ensign ENY 616*....57 2

JAZZY DEE *US, male rapper / instrumentalist – Darren Williams*

5 Mar 83 **GET ON UP** *Laurie LRS 101*....53 5

JAZZY M *UK, male DJ / producer – Michael Connelly*

21 Oct 00 **JAZZIN' THE WAY YOU KNOW** *Perfecto PERF 08CDS*....47 2

Wyclef JEAN (see also FUGEES) *Haiti, male rapper / vocalist / producer (3 Albums: 23 Weeks, 11 Singles: 75 Weeks)*

28 Jun 97 **WE TRYING TO STAY ALIVE** *Columbia 6646815* [1] 13 5
5 Jul 97 THE CARNIVAL *Columbia 4874422* [1] 40 6
27 Sep 97 **GUANTANAMERA** *Columbia 6650852* [1] 25 2
28 Mar 98 ● **NO, NO, NO** *Columbia 6656592* [2] $....5 8
16 May 98 ● **GONE TILL NOVEMBER** *Columbia 6658712*....3 9
14 Nov 98 ● **ANOTHER ONE BITES THE DUST** *Dreamworks DRMCD 22364* [3] 5 6
23 Oct 99 **NEW DAY** *Columbia 6682122* [4] 23 2
2 Sep 00 ● THE ECLEFTIC – 2 SIDES II A BOOK *Columbia 4979792*....5 15
16 Sep 00 ● **IT DOESN'T MATTER** *Columbia 6697782* [5] 3 8
16 Dec 00 ● **911** *Columbia 6706122* [6] 9 10
21 Jul 01 ● **PERFECT GENTLEMEN** *Columbia 6710522*....4 14
8 Dec 01 **WISH YOU WERE HERE** (re) *Columbia 6721562*....28 5
6 Jul 02 **TWO WRONGS** *Columbia 6728902* [7] 14 6
20 Jul 02 MASQUERADE *Columbia 5078542*....30 2

[1] Wyclef Jean and The Refugee Allstars [2] Destiny's Child featuring Wyclef Jean [3] Queen with Wyclef Jean featuring Pras and Free [4] Wyclef Jean featuring Bono [5] Wyclef Jean featuring The Rock and Melky Sedeck [6] Wyclef Jean featuring Mary J Blige [7] Wyclef Jean featuring Claudette Ortiz [1] Wyclef Jean and The Refugee Allstars

The JEEVAS *UK, male vocal / instrumental group (2 Singles: 2 Weeks)*

22 Mar 03 **ONCE UPON A TIME IN AMERICA** *Cowboy Music COWCDA 005*....61 1
28 Feb 04 **HAVE YOU EVER SEEN THE RAIN** *Cowboy Music COWCDB 008*....70 1

JEFFERSON *UK, male vocalist – Geoff Turton*

9 Apr 69 **COLOUR OF MY LOVE** *Pye 7N 17706*....22 8

JEFFERSON AIRPLANE (see also Grace SLICK; STARSHIP) *US / UK, female / male vocal / instrumental group (7 Albums: 29 Weeks)*

28 Jun 69 BLESS ITS POINTED LITTLE HEAD *RCA SF 8019*....38 1
7 Mar 70 VOLUNTEERS *RCA SF 8076*....34 7
13 Feb 71 BLOWS AGAINST THE EMPIRE *RCA SF 8163* [1] 12 6
2 Oct 71 BARK *Grunt FTR 1001*....42 1
2 Sep 72 LONG JOHN SILVER *Grunt FTR 1007*....30 1
31 Jul 76 SPITFIRE *Grunt RFL 1557* [2] 30 2
9 Feb 80 FREEDOM AT POINT ZERO *Grunt FL 13452* [2] 22 11

[1] Paul Kantner and Jefferson Airplane [2] Jefferson Starship

Garland JEFFREYS *US, male vocalist*

8 Feb 92 **HAIL HAIL ROCK 'N' ROLL** *RCA PB 49171*....72 1

JELLYBEAN *US, male producer – John Benitez (2 Albums: 35 Weeks, 6 Singles: 47 Weeks)*

1 Feb 86 **SIDEWALK TALK** *EMI America EA 210* [1] 47 4
26 Sep 87 **THE REAL THING** *Chrysalis CHS 3167* [2] 13 10
31 Oct 87 JUST VISITING THIS PLANET *Chrysalis CHR 1569*....15 28
28 Nov 87 ● **WHO FOUND WHO** *Chrysalis CHS JEL 1* [3] 10 10
12 Dec 87 **JINGO** *Chrysalis JEL 2*....12 10
12 Mar 88 **JUST A MIRAGE** *Chrysalis JEL 3* [4] 13 10
20 Aug 88 **COMING BACK FOR MORE** *Chrysalis JEL 4* [5] 41 3
3 Sep 88 ROCKS THE HOUSE! *Chrysalis CJB 1*....16 7

[1] Jellybean featuring Catherine Buchanan [2] Jellybean featuring Steven Dante [3] Jellybean featuring Elisa Fiorillo [4] Jellybean featuring Adele Bertei [5] Jellybean featuring Richard Darbyshire

JELLYFISH *US, male vocal / instrumental group (1 Album: 2 Weeks, 6 Singles: 20 Weeks)*

26 Jan 91 **THE KING IS HALF UNDRESSED** *Charisma CUSS 1*....39 6
27 Apr 91 **BABY'S COMING BACK** *Charisma CUSS 2*....51 4
3 Aug 91 **THE SCARY-GO-ROUND EP** *Charisma CUSS 3*....49 3
26 Oct 91 **I WANNA STAY HOME** *Charisma CUSS 4*....59 2
1 May 93 **THE GHOST AT NUMBER ONE** *Charisma CUSDG 10*....43 3
22 May 93 SPILT MILK *Charisma CDCUS 20*....21 2
17 Jul 93 **NEW MISTAKE** *Charisma CUSDG 11*....55 2

Tracks on The Scary-Go-Round EP: Now She Knows She's Wrong / Bedspring Kiss / She Still Loves Him (Live) / Baby's Coming Back (Live).

JEM NEW *UK, female vocalist – Jem Griffiths (1 Album: 32 Weeks, 3 Singles: 26 Weeks)*

5 Mar 05 ● FINALLY WOKEN *Ato 82876655682*....6 32
26 Mar 05 ● **THEY** (re) *Ato 82876685182*....6 15
25 Jun 05 **JUST A RIDE** *Ato 82876705862*....16 8
24 Sep 05 **WISH I** *Ato 82876727722*....24 3

16 December 1972	23 December 1972	30 December 1972	6 January 1973
MY DING-A-LING Chuck Berry	**LONG HAIRED LOVER FROM LIVERPOOL** Little Jimmy Osmond with The Mike Curb Congregation	**LONG HAIRED LOVER FROM LIVERPOOL** Little Jimmy Osmond with The Mike Curb Congregation	**LONG HAIRED LOVER FROM LIVERPOOL** Little Jimmy Osmond with The Mike Curb Congregation
25 ROCKIN' AND ROLLIN' GREATS Various	**20 ALL TIME HITS OF THE FIFTIES** Various	**20 ALL TIME HITS OF THE FIFTIES** Various	**20 ALL TIME HITS OF THE FIFTIES** Various

KEY
UK No.1 ★ UK Top 10 ● Still on chart + UK entry at No.1 ■
US No.1 ▲ UK million seller £ US million seller $
Singles re-entries are listed as (re), (2re), (3re)... which signifies that the hit re-entered the chart once, twice or three times...
Peak Position / Weeks

JEMINI *UK, male / female vocal duo – Jemma Abbey and Chris Crosby*

7 Jun 03 **CRY BABY** *Integral INTEG 001CD* 15 3

Katherine JENKINS *UK, female vocalist (3 Albums: 40 Weeks)*

17 Apr 04 PREMIERE *UCJ 9866064* 31 4
30 Oct 04 SECOND NATURE *UCJ 9868047* 16 28
12 Nov 05 ● LIVING A DREAM *UCJ 4763067* 4 8+

JENTINA *UK, female vocalist – Jentina Chapman (2 Singles: 6 Weeks)*

3 Jul 04 **BAD ASS STRIPPA** *Virgin VSCDX 1873* 22 3
9 Oct 04 **FRENCH KISSES** *Virgin VSCDX 1877* 20 3

JERU THE DAMAJA *US, male rapper – Kendrick Davis*

7 Dec 96 **YA PLAYIN YASELF** *ffrr FCD 289* 67 1

JESSICA *Sweden, female vocalist – Jessica Folker*

20 Mar 99 **HOW WILL I KNOW (WHO YOU ARE)** *Jive 0522412* 47 1

JESSY *Belgium, female vocalist – Jessy de Smet*

12 Apr 03 **LOOK AT ME NOW** *Data / Ministry of Sound DATA 46CDS* 29 3

JESUS AND MARY CHAIN *UK, male vocal / instrumental group (8 Albums: 40 Weeks, 20 Singles: 59 Weeks)*

2 Mar 85 **NEVER UNDERSTAND** *Blanco Y Negro NEG 8* 47 4
8 Jun 85 **YOU TRIP ME UP** *Blanco Y Negro NEG 13* 55 3
12 Oct 85 **JUST LIKE HONEY** *Blanco Y Negro NEG 17* 45 3
30 Nov 85 PSYCHOCANDY *Blanco Y Negro BYN 7* 31 10
26 Jul 86 **SOME CANDY TALKING** *Blanco Y Negro NEG 19* 13 5
2 May 87 ● **APRIL SKIES** *Blanco Y Negro NEG 24* 8 6
15 Aug 87 **HAPPY WHEN IT RAINS** *Blanco Y Negro NEG 25* 25 5
12 Sep 87 ● DARKLANDS *Blanco Y Negro BYN 11* 5 7
7 Nov 87 **DARKLANDS** *Blanco Y Negro NEG 29* 33 4
9 Apr 88 **SIDEWALKING** *Blanco Y Negro NEG 32* 30 3
30 Apr 88 ● BARBED WIRE KISSES *Blanco Y Negro BYN 15* 9 7
23 Sep 89 **BLUES FROM A GUN** *Blanco Y Negro NEG 41* 32 2
21 Oct 89 AUTOMATIC *Blanco Y Negro BYN 20* 11 4
18 Nov 89 **HEAD ON** *Blanco Y Negro NEG 42* 57 2
8 Sep 90 **ROLLERCOASTER (EP)** *Blanco Y Negro NEG 45* 46 2
15 Feb 92 ● **REVERENCE** *Blanco Y Negro NEG 55* 10 4
14 Mar 92 **FAR GONE AND OUT** *Blanco Y Negro NEG 56* 23 3
4 Apr 92 HONEY'S DEAD *Blanco Y Negro 9031765542* 14 5
4 Jul 92 **ALMOST GOLD** *Blanco Y Negro NEG 57* 41 2
10 Jul 93 **SOUND OF SPEED (EP)** *Blanco Y Negro NEG 66CD* 30 2
24 Jul 93 THE SOUND OF SPEED *Blanco Y Negro 4509931052* 15 3
30 Jul 94 **SOMETIMES ALWAYS** *Blanco Y Negro NEG 70CD* 22 3
27 Aug 94 STONED AND DETHRONED *Blanco Y Negro 4509967172* 13 3
22 Oct 94 **COME ON** *Blanco Y Negro NEG 73CD1* 52 2
17 Jun 95 **I HATE ROCK 'N' ROLL** *Blanco Y Negro NEG 81CD* 61 1
18 Apr 98 **CRACKING UP** *Creation CRESCD 292* 35 2
30 May 98 **ILOVEROCKNROLL** *Creation CRESCD 296* 38 1
13 Jun 98 MUNKI *Creation CRECD 232* 47 1

Tracks on Rollercoaster (EP): Rollercoaster / Silverblade / Lowlife / Tower of Song. Tracks on Sound of Speed (EP): Snakedriver / Something I Can't Have / Write Record Release Blues / Little Red Rooster.

JESUS JONES *UK, male vocal (Mike Edwards) / instrumental group (3 Albums: 31 Weeks, 13 Singles: 52 Weeks)*

25 Feb 89 **INFO-FREAKO** *Food FOOD 18* 42 3
8 Jul 89 **NEVER ENOUGH** *Food FOOD 21* 42 3
23 Sep 89 **BRING IT ON DOWN** *Food FOOD 22* 46 3
14 Oct 89 LIQUIDIZER *Food FOODLP 3* 32 3
7 Apr 90 **REAL REAL REAL** *Food FOOD 24* 19 8
6 Oct 90 **RIGHT HERE RIGHT NOW** *Food FOOD 25* 31 4
12 Jan 91 ● **INTERNATIONAL BRIGHT YOUNG THING** *Food FOOD 27* 7 7
9 Feb 91 ★ DOUBT *Food FOODLP 5* ■ 1 24
2 Mar 91 **WHO? WHERE? WHY?** *Food FOOD 28* 21 7
20 Jul 91 **RIGHT HERE RIGHT NOW** (re-issue) *Food FOOD 30* 31 4
9 Jan 93 ● **THE DEVIL YOU KNOW** *Food CDPERV 1* 10 5
6 Feb 93 ● PERVERSE *Food FOODCD 8* 6 4
10 Apr 93 **THE RIGHT DECISION** *Food CDPERV 2* 36 3
10 Jul 93 **ZEROES & ONES** *Food CDFOODS 44* 30 3
14 Jun 97 **THE NEXT BIG THING** *Food CDFOOD 95* 49 1
16 Aug 97 **CHEMICAL #1** *Food CDFOOD 102* 71 1

JESUS LIZARD *US, male vocal / instrumental group*

6 Mar 93 **PUSS** *Touch and Go TG 83CD* 12 2
10 Sep 94 DOWN *Touch and Go TG 131CD* 64 1

The listed flip side of 'Puss' was 'Oh, the Guilt' by Nirvana.

JESUS LOVES YOU (see also CULTURE CLUB) *UK, male vocalist – Boy George (George O'Dowd) (1 Album: 1 Week, 4 Singles: 18 Weeks)*

11 Nov 89 **AFTER THE LOVE** *More Protein PROT 2* 68 1
23 Feb 91 **BOW DOWN MISTER** *More Protein PROT 8* 27 8
13 Apr 91 THE MARTYR MANTRAS *More Protein CUMLP 1* 60 1
8 Jun 91 **GENERATIONS OF LOVE** *More Protein PROT 10* 35 8
12 Dec 92 **SWEET TOXIC LOVE** *Virgin VS 1449* 65 1

JET *Australia, male vocal / instrumental group (1 Album: 38 Weeks, 6 Singles: 16 Weeks)*

6 Sep 03 **ARE YOU GONNA BE MY GIRL** *Elektra E 7456CD1* 23 2
27 Sep 03 GET BORN *Elektra 7559628922* 14 38
15 Nov 03 **ROLLOVER DJ** *Elektra E 748CCD1* 34 2
20 Mar 04 **LOOK WHAT YOU'VE DONE** *Elektra E 75257CD* 28 3
5 Jun 04 **ARE YOU GONNA BE MY GIRL** (re-issue) *Elektra E 7599CD* 16 5
18 Sep 04 **COLD HARD BITCH** *Elektra E 7607CD* 34 2
8 Jan 05 **GET ME OUTTA HERE** *Elektra E 7625* 37 2

JETHRO TULL (193 Top 500)
Unique folk / rock outfit, fronted by the unmistakable, eccentrically dressed Ian Anderson (fl/v), who ranked among the world's top album sellers of the progressive rock era. Surprisingly, picked up the first ever Grammy for hard rock / heavy metal in 1989 (27 Albums: 236 Weeks, 10 Singles: 68 Weeks)

2 Nov 68 ● THIS WAS *Island ILPS 9085* 10 22
1 Jan 69 **LOVE STORY** *Island WIP 6048* 29 8
14 May 69 ● **LIVING IN THE PAST** *Island WIP 6056* 3 14
9 Aug 69 ★ STAND UP *Island ILPS 9103* ■ 1 29
1 Nov 69 ● **SWEET DREAM** *Chrysalis WIP 6070* 7 11
24 Jan 70 ● **TEACHER / THE WITCH'S PROMISE** *Chrysalis WIP 6077* 4 9
9 May 70 ● BENEFIT *Island ILPS 9123* 3 13
3 Apr 71 ● AQUALUNG *Island ILPS 9145* 4 21
18 Sep 71 **LIFE IS A LONG SONG / UP THE POOL** *Chrysalis WIP 6106* 11 8
18 Mar 72 ● THICK AS A BRICK *Chrysalis CHR 1003* ▲ 5 14
15 Jul 72 ● LIVING IN THE PAST *Chrysalis CJT 1* 8 11
28 Jul 73 A PASSION PLAY *Chrysalis CHR 1040* ▲ 13 8
2 Nov 74 WAR CHILD *Chrysalis CHR 1067* 14 4
27 Sep 75 MINSTREL IN THE GALLERY *Chrysalis CHR 1082* 20 6
31 Jan 76 M.U. THE BEST OF JETHRO TULL *Chrysalis CHR 1078* 44 5
15 May 76 TOO OLD TO ROCK 'N' ROLL: TOO YOUNG TO DIE! *Chrysalis CHR 1111* 25 10
11 Dec 76 **RING OUT SOLSTICE BELLS (EP)** *Chrysalis CXP 2* 28 6
19 Feb 77 SONGS FROM THE WOOD *Chrysalis CHR 1132* 13 12
29 Apr 78 HEAVY HORSES *Chrysalis CHR 1175* 20 10
14 Oct 78 LIVE BURSTING OUT *Chrysalis CJT 4* 17 8
6 Oct 79 STORMWATCH *Chrysalis CDL 1238* 27 4
6 Sep 80 A *Chrysalis CDL 1301* 25 5
17 Apr 82 BROADSWORD AND THE BEAST *Chrysalis CDL 1380* 27 19
15 Sep 84 UNDER WRAPS *Chrysalis CDL 1461* 18 5

13 January 1973	20 January 1973	27 January 1973	3 February 1973
UK No.1 SINGLES			
LONG HAIRED LOVER FROM LIVERPOOL Little Jimmy Osmond with The Mike Curb Congregation	**LONG HAIRED LOVER FROM LIVERPOOL** Little Jimmy Osmond with The Mike Curb Congregation	**BLOCKBUSTER!** The Sweet	**BLOCKBUSTER!** The Sweet
UK No.1 ALBUMS			
SLAYED? Slade	**BACK TO FRONT** Gilbert O'Sullivan	**SLAYED?** Slade	**SLAYED?** Slade

15 Sep 84 **LAP OF LUXURY** *Chrysalis TULL 1* 70 2
2 Nov 85 **ORIGINAL MASTERS** *Chrysalis JTTV 1* 63 3
19 Sep 87 **CREST OF A KNAVE** *Chrysalis CDL 1590* 19 10
16 Jan 88 **SAID SHE WAS A DANCER** *Chrysalis TULL 4* 55 4
9 Jul 88 **20 YEARS OF JETHRO TULL** *Chrysalis TBOX 1* 78 1
2 Sep 89 **ROCK ISLAND** *Chrysalis CHR 1708* 18 6
14 Sep 91 **CATFISH RISING** *Chrysalis CHR 1886* 27 3
21 Mar 92 **ROCKS ON THE ROAD** *Chrysalis TULLX 7* 47 3
26 Sep 92 **A LITTLE LIGHT MUSIC** *Chrysalis CCD 1954* 34 2
22 May 93 **LIVING IN THE (SLIGHTLY MORE RECENT) PAST** *Chrysalis CDCHSS 3970* 32 3
16 Sep 95 **ROOTS TO BRANCHES** *Chrysalis CDCHR 6109* 20 3
29 Jun 96 **AQUALUNG** *Chrysalis CD25 AQUA 1* 53 1
4 Sep 99 **J-TULL DOT COM** *Papillon BTFLYCD 0001* 44 1

Tracks on Ring Out Solstice Bells (EP): Ring Out Solstice Bells / March the Mad Scientist / The Christmas Song / Pan Dance. 'Living in the (Slightly More Recent) Past' is a live version of 'Living in the Past'.

The JETS
UK, male vocal / instrumental group (1 Album: 6 Weeks, 8 Singles: 38 Weeks)

22 Aug 81 **SUGAR DOLL** *EMI 5211* 55 3
31 Oct 81 **YES TONIGHT JOSEPHINE** *EMI 5247* 25 11
6 Feb 82 **LOVE MAKES THE WORLD GO ROUND** *EMI 5262* 21 9
10 Apr 82 **100 PERCENT COTTON** *EMI EMC 3399* 30 6
24 Apr 82 **THE HONEYDRIPPER** *EMI 5289* 58 3
9 Oct 82 **SOMEBODY TO LOVE** *EMI 5342* 56 3
6 Aug 83 **BLUE SKIES** *EMI 5405* 53 3
17 Dec 83 **ROCKIN' AROUND THE CHRISTMAS TREE** *PRT 7P 297* 62 4
13 Oct 84 **PARTY DOLL** *PRT JETS 2* 72 2

The JETS *US, male / female vocal / instrumental group (1 Album: 4 Weeks, 3 Singles: 19 Weeks)*

31 Jan 87 ● **CRUSH ON YOU** *MCA MCA 1048* 5 13
11 Apr 87 **CRUSH ON YOU** *MCA MCF 3312* 57 4
25 Apr 87 **CURIOSITY** *MCA MCA 1119* 41 4
28 May 88 **ROCKET 2 U** *MCA MCA 1226* 69 2

Joan JETT and The BLACKHEARTS
US, female vocalist – leader Jean Larkin and male vocal / instrumental group (1 Album: 7 Weeks, 5 Singles: 21 Weeks)

24 Apr 82 ● **I LOVE ROCK 'N' ROLL** *Epic EPC A 2152* ▲ $ 4 10
8 May 82 **I LOVE ROCK-N-ROLL** *Epic EPC 85686* 25 7
10 Jul 82 **CRIMSON AND CLOVER** *Epic EPC A 2485* 60 3
20 Aug 88 **I HATE MYSELF FOR LOVING YOU** *London LON 195* 46 6
31 Mar 90 **DIRTY DEEDS** *Chrysalis CHS 3518* [1] 69 1
19 Feb 94 **I LOVE ROCK & ROLL** (re-issue) *Reprise W 0232CD* 75 1

[1] Joan Jett

JEWEL *US, female vocalist / guitarist – Jewel Kilcher (2 Albums: 4 Weeks, 5 Singles: 9 Weeks)*

14 Jun 97 **WHO WILL SAVE YOUR SOUL** *Atlantic A 8514CD* 52 1
9 Aug 97 **YOU WERE MEANT FOR ME** (re) *Atlantic A 5463CD* $ 32 3
21 Nov 98 **HANDS** *Atlantic AT 0055CD* 41 2
28 Nov 98 **SPIRIT** *Atlantic 7567829502* 54 1
26 Jun 99 **DOWN SO LONG** *Atlantic AT 0069CD* 38 2
9 Mar 02 **THIS WAY** *Atlantic 7567835192* 34 3
30 Aug 03 **INTUITION** *Atlantic W 619CD* 52 1

JEZ & CHOOPIE
UK / Israel, male DJ / production duo – Jeremy Ansell and David Geyra

21 Mar 98 **YIM** *Multiply CDMULTY 31* 36 2

JHELISA *US, female vocalist – Jhelisa Anderson*

1 Jul 95 **FRIENDLY PRESSURE** *Dorado DOR 040CD* 75 1

JIGSAW
UK, male vocal (Des Dyer) / instrumental group (2 Singles: 16 Weeks)

1 Nov 75 ● **SKY HIGH** *Splash CPI 1* 9 11
6 Aug 77 **IF I HAVE TO GO AWAY** *Splash CP 11* 36 5

JILTED JOHN *UK, male vocalist – Graham Fellows*

12 Aug 78 ● **JILTED JOHN** *EMI International INT 567* 4 12

JIMMY EAT WORLD
US, male vocal / instrumental group (2 Albums: 6 Weeks, 5 Singles: 10 Weeks)

17 Nov 01 **SALT SWEAT SUGAR** *Dreamworks 4508782* 60 1
9 Feb 02 **JIMMY EAT WORLD** *Dreamworks 4503482* 62 4
9 Feb 02 **THE MIDDLE** *Dreamworks 4508482* 26 3
15 Jun 02 **SWEETNESS** *Dreamworks 4508342* 38 2
16 Oct 04 **PAIN** *Interscope 9864179* 38 2
23 Oct 04 **FUTURES** *Interscope 9864241* 22 2
9 Apr 05 **WORK** *Interscope 9880673* 49 2

JIMMY THE HOOVER *UK, male / female vocal / instrumental group*

25 Jun 83 **TANTALISE (WO WO EE YEH YEH)** *Innervision A 3406* 18 8

JIN NEW *US, male rapper – Jin Au-Yeung*

19 Mar 05 **LEARN CHINESE** *Virgin VUSDX 300* 59 1

JINGLE BELLES *US / UK, female vocal group*

17 Dec 83 **CHRISTMAS SPECTRE** *Passion PASH 14* 37 4

JINNY *Italy, female vocalist – Janine Brown (4 Singles: 16 Weeks)*

29 Jun 91 **KEEP WARM** *Virgin VS 1356* 68 3
22 May 93 **FEEL THE RHYTHM** *Logic 401633001022* 74 1
15 Jul 95 **KEEP WARM** (re-mix) *Multiply CDMULTY 5* 11 8
16 Dec 95 **WANNA BE WITH YOU** *Multiply CDMULTY 8* 30 4

JIVE BUNNY and The MASTERMIXERS *UK, male DJ / production group (2 Albums: 29 Weeks, 11 Singles: 70 Weeks)*

15 Jul 89 ★ **SWING THE MOOD** *Music Factory Dance MFD 001* 1 19
14 Oct 89 ★ **THAT'S WHAT I LIKE** *Music Factory Dance MFD 002* 1 12
2 Dec 89 **IT TAKES TWO BABY** *Spartan CIN 101* [1] 53 2
9 Dec 89 ● **JIVE BUNNY – THE ALBUM** *Telstar STAR 2390* 2 22
16 Dec 89 ★ **LET'S PARTY** *Music Factory Dance MFD 003* ■ 1 6
17 Mar 90 ● **THAT SOUNDS GOOD TO ME** *Music Factory Dance MFD 004* 4 6
25 Aug 90 ● **CAN CAN YOU PARTY** *Music Factory Dance MFD 007* 8 6
17 Nov 90 **LET'S SWING AGAIN** *Music Factory Dance MFD 009* 19 5
8 Dec 90 **IT'S PARTY TIME** *Telstar STAR 2449* 23 7
22 Dec 90 **THE CRAZY PARTY MIXES** *Music Factory Dance MFD 010* 13 5
23 Mar 91 **OVER TO YOU JOHN (HERE WE GO AGAIN)** *Music Factory Dance MFD 012* 28 5
20 Jul 91 **HOT SUMMER SALSA** *Music Factory Dance MFD 013* 43 2
23 Nov 91 **ROCK 'N' ROLL DANCE PARTY** *Music Factory Dance MFD 015* 48 2

[1] Liz Kershaw, Bruno Brookes, Jive Bunny and Londonbeat

JO JINGLES *UK, male / female vocal group (2 Singles: 6 Weeks)*

13 Nov 04 **WIND THE BOBBIN UP!** *Jo Jingles JJ 21CD* 21 3
12 Nov 05 **D.I.S.C.O.** *Jo Jingles JJ 27* 44 3

JO JO GUNNE *US, male vocal (Jay Ferguson) / instrumental group*

25 Mar 72 ● **RUN RUN RUN** *Asylum AYM 501* 6 12

JOAN COLLINS FAN CLUB *UK, male comedian / vocalist – Julian Clary*

18 Jun 88 **LEADER OF THE PACK** *10 TEN 227* 60 3

John Paul JOANS *UK, male vocalist*

19 Dec 70 **THE MAN FROM NAZARETH** (re) *RAK 107* 25 7

10 February 1973	17 February 1973	24 February 1973	3 March 1973
BLOCKBUSTER! The Sweet	**BLOCKBUSTER!** The Sweet	**BLOCKBUSTER!** The Sweet	**CUM ON FEEL THE NOIZE** Slade
DON'T SHOOT ME I'M ONLY THE PIANO PLAYER Elton John	**DON'T SHOOT ME I'M ONLY THE PIANO PLAYER** Elton John	**DON'T SHOOT ME I'M ONLY THE PIANO PLAYER** Elton John	**DON'T SHOOT ME I'M ONLY THE PIANO PLAYER** Elton John

KEY
UK No.1 ★ UK Top 10 ● Still on chart + UK entry at No.1 ■
US No.1 ▲ UK million seller £ US million seller $
Singles re-entries are listed as (re), (2re), (3re)... which signifies that the hit re-entered the chart once, twice or three times...
Peak Position / Weeks

JOBOXERS *UK / US, male vocal (Dig Wayne) / instrumental group (1 Album: 5 Weeks, 4 Singles: 33 Weeks)*

19 Feb 83 ●	**BOXERBEAT** *RCA BOX 1*	3	15
21 May 83 ●	**JUST GOT LUCKY** *RCA BOXX 2*	7	9
13 Aug 83	**JOHNNY FRIENDLY** *RCA BOXX 3*	31	8
24 Sep 83	LIKE GANGBUSTERS *RCA BOXXLP 1*	18	5
12 Nov 83	**JEALOUS LOVE** *RCA BOXX 4*	72	1

JOCASTA *UK, male vocal / instrumental group (2 Singles: 2 Weeks)*

15 Feb 97	**GO** *Epic 6641415*	50	1
3 May 97	**CHANGE ME** *Epic 6643902*	60	1

JOCKO
US, male DJ / rapper – Doug "Jocko" Henderson, b. 8 Mar 1918, d. 15 Jul 2000

23 Feb 80	**RHYTHM TALK** *Philadelphia International PIR 8222*	56	3

JODE featuring YO-HANS *UK, male / female vocal duo*

19 Dec 98	**WALK ... (THE DOG) LIKE AN EGYPTIAN** *Logic 74321640332*	48	2

JODECI (see also K-CI & JOJO)
US, male vocal group (1 Album: 8 Weeks, 7 Singles: 19 Weeks)

16 Jan 93	**CHERISH** *Uptown MCSTD 1726*	56	2
11 Dec 93	**CRY FOR YOU** *Uptown MCSTD 1951*	56	1
16 Jul 94	**FEENIN'** *Uptown MCSTD 1984*	18	3
28 Jan 95	**CRY FOR YOU** (re-issue) *Uptown MCSTD 2039*	20	3
24 Jun 95	**FREEK 'N YOU** *Uptown MCSTD 2072*	17	5
29 Jul 95 ●	THE SHOW THE AFTER-PARTY THE HOTEL *Uptown MCD 11258*	4	8
9 Dec 95	**LOVE U 4 LIFE** *Uptown MCSTD 2105*	23	3
25 May 96	**GET ON UP** *MCA MCSTD 48010*	20	2

JODIE *Australia, female vocalist – Jodie Wilson*

25 Feb 95	**ANYTHING YOU WANT** *Mercury MERCD 423*	47	1

JOE
US, male vocalist – Joseph Thomas (4 Albums: 12 Weeks, 16 Singles: 52 Weeks)

22 Jan 94	**I'M IN LUV** *Mercury JOECD 1*	22	4
12 Feb 94	EVERYTHING *Vertigo 5188072*	53	1
25 Jun 94	**THE ONE FOR ME** *Mercury JOECD 2*	34	2
22 Oct 94	**ALL OR NOTHING** *Mercury JOECD 3*	56	1
27 Apr 96	**ALL THE THINGS (YOUR MAN WON'T DO)** *Island CID 634*	34	3
14 Jun 97	**DON'T WANNA BE A PLAYER** *Jive JIVECD 410*	16	3
9 Aug 97	ALL THAT I AM *Jive CHIP 183*	26	4
27 Sep 97	**THE LOVE SCENE** *Jive JIVECD 430*	22	2
10 Jan 98	**GOOD GIRLS** *Jive JIVECD 442*	29	3
22 Aug 98	**NO ONE ELSE COMES CLOSE** *Jive 0521682*	41	2
31 Oct 98	**ALL THAT I AM** *Jive 0518532*	52	1
11 Mar 00 ●	**THANK GOD I FOUND YOU** (re) *Columbia 6690582* [1] ▲	10	10
29 Apr 00	MY NAME IS JOE *Jive 9220352*	46	4
15 Jul 00	**TREAT HER LIKE A LADY** *Jive 9250772*	60	1
17 Feb 01 ●	**STUTTER** *Jive 9251632* [2] ▲	7	8
5 May 01	**I WANNA KNOW** *Jive 9252102*	37	2
16 Feb 02	**LET'S STAY HOME TONIGHT** *Jive 9253222*	29	2
14 Sep 02	**WHAT IF A WOMAN** *Jive 9253962*	53	1
24 Apr 04	**RIDE WIT U / MORE & MORE** *Jive 82876609212* [3]	12	7
8 May 04	AND THEN ... *Jive 82876586402*	73	3

[1] Mariah Carey featuring Joe and 98 Degrees [2] Joe featuring Mystikal
[3] Joe featuring G-Unit

JOE PUBLIC *US, male rap group (2 Singles: 5 Weeks)*

11 Jul 92	**LIVE AND LEARN** *Columbia 6575267*	43	4
28 Nov 92	**I'VE BEEN WATCHIN'** *Columbia 6587657*	75	1

Billy JOEL (80 Top 500)
Platinum-plated singer / songwriter / pianist, b. 9 May 1949, Long Island, US. This relatively youthful Grammy Living Legend Award recipient was the first artist to have five albums pass the seven-million mark Stateside. Best-selling single: 'Uptown Girl' 974,000 (18 Albums: 355 Weeks, 20 Singles: 146 Weeks)

11 Feb 78	**JUST THE WAY YOU ARE** *CBS 5872* $	19	9
25 Mar 78	THE STRANGER *CBS 82311*	25	40
24 Jun 78	**MOVIN' OUT (ANTHONY'S SONG)** *CBS 6412*	35	6
25 Nov 78 ●	52ND STREET *CBS 83181* ▲	10	43
2 Dec 78	**MY LIFE** *CBS 6821* $	12	15
28 Apr 79	**UNTIL THE NIGHT** *CBS 7242*	50	3
22 Mar 80 ●	GLASS HOUSES *CBS 86108* ▲	9	24
12 Apr 80	**ALL FOR LEYNA** *CBS 8325*	40	4
9 Aug 80	**IT'S STILL ROCK AND ROLL TO ME** *CBS 8753* ▲ $	14	11
10 Oct 81	SONGS IN THE ATTIC *CBS 85273*	57	3
2 Oct 82	THE NYLON CURTAIN *CBS 85959*	27	8
10 Sep 83 ●	AN INNOCENT MAN *CBS 25554*	2	95
15 Oct 83 ★	**UPTOWN GIRL** *CBS A 3775* $	1	17
10 Dec 83 ●	**TELL HER ABOUT IT** *CBS A 3655* ▲	4	10
4 Feb 84	COLD SPRING HARBOUR *CBS 32400*	95	1
18 Feb 84 ●	**AN INNOCENT MAN** *CBS A 4142*	8	10
28 Apr 84	**THE LONGEST TIME** *CBS A 4280*	25	8
23 Jun 84	PIANO MAN *CBS 32002*	98	1
23 Jun 84	**LEAVE A TENDER MOMENT ALONE / GOODNIGHT SAIGON** *CBS A 4521*	29	7
20 Jul 85 ●	GREATEST HITS – VOLUME I & VOLUME II *CBS 88666*	7	39
22 Feb 86	**SHE'S ALWAYS A WOMAN / JUST THE WAY YOU ARE** (re-issue) *CBS A 6862*	53	1
16 Aug 86	THE BRIDGE *CBS 86323*	38	10
20 Sep 86	**A MATTER OF TRUST** *CBS 650057 7*	52	4
28 Nov 87	KOHYEPT – LIVE IN LENINGRAD *CBS 460 4071*	92	1
30 Sep 89 ●	**WE DIDN'T START THE FIRE** *CBS JOEL 1* ▲	7	10
4 Nov 89 ●	STORM FRONT *CBS 4656581* ▲	5	25
16 Dec 89	**LENINGRAD** *CBS JOEL 3*	53	4
10 Mar 90	**I GO TO EXTREMES** *CBS JOEL 2*	70	2
29 Aug 92	**ALL SHOOK UP** *Columbia 6583437*	27	4
31 Jul 93 ●	**THE RIVER OF DREAMS** *Columbia 6595432*	3	14
14 Aug 93 ●	RIVER OF DREAMS *Columbia 4738722* ▲	3	26
23 Oct 93	**ALL ABOUT SOUL** *Columbia 6597362*	32	4
26 Feb 94	**NO MAN'S LAND** *Columbia 6599202*	50	3
1 Nov 97	GREATEST HITS – VOLUME III *Columbia 4882362*	23	4
13 Jun 98	GREATEST HITS – VOLUMES I II & III *Columbia 4912742*	33	4
27 May 00	2000 YEARS – THE MILLENNIUM CONCERT *Columbia 4979812*	68	1
31 Mar 01 ●	THE ULTIMATE COLLECTION *Columbia SONYTV 98CD*	4	24
27 Nov 04	PIANO MAN – THE VERY BEST OF BILLY JOEL *Columbia 5190182*	40	6

'Goodnight Saigon' listed only from 30 Jun 1984.

JOHANN *Germany, male producer – Johann Bley*

16 Mar 96	**NEW KICKS** *Perfecto PERF 118CD*	54	1

Elton JOHN (6 Top 500) *Flamboyant singer / songwriter / pianist, b. Reginald Dwight, 25 Mar 1947, Pinner, Middlesex, UK. Almost as famous for his outrageous wardrobe as his music, Elton was the biggest-selling pop act of the 1970s and has sold more albums in the UK and US than any British male singer, with total worldwide sales exceeding 150 million. He is the only British act to enter the US singles chart at No.1, recorded the first two albums to enter the US chart at No.1 and holds the record for headlining appearances at New York's Madison Square Garden. Elton, twice chairman of Watford Football Club, is the only act to chart every year from 1971 to 1999 in the UK and US. His Greatest Hits album has sold more than 16 million in the US and he has topped the US adult contemporary chart a record 16 times. 'Candle*

10 March 1973	17 March 1973	24 March 1973	31 March 1973
◂◂ UK No.1 SINGLES ▸▸			
CUM ON FEEL THE NOIZE Slade	CUM ON FEEL THE NOIZE Slade	CUM ON FEEL THE NOIZE Slade	THE TWELFTH OF NEVER Donny Osmond
◂◂ UK No.1 ALBUMS ▸▸			
DON'T SHOOT ME I'M ONLY THE PIANO PLAYER Elton John	DON'T SHOOT ME I'M ONLY THE PIANO PLAYER Elton John	BILLION DOLLAR BABIES Alice Cooper	FLASHBACK GREAT HITS OF THE SIXTIES Various

in the Wind 1997' (which he performed at the funeral of Diana, Princess of Wales) topped the chart in almost every country. In the UK it sold nearly five million copies in six weeks and in the US had record advance orders of 8.7 million (and total sales in excess of 11 million). It also spent a staggering three years in the Canadian Top 20, which included 45 weeks at No.1. It is the world's best-selling single, with sales of 33 million (4,864,611 in the UK). His lyric-writing partners have included, most influentially, Bernie Taupin and, more recently, Sir Tim Rice. He became Sir Elton John in 1998 and has the distinction of having performed at both Live Aid and Live 8 London concerts *(41 Albums: 991 Weeks,* ***86 Singles: 652 Weeks****)*

23 May 70 ● ELTON JOHN *DJM DJLPS 406* 5 22
16 Jan 71 ● TUMBLEWEED CONNECTION *DJM DJLPS 410* 2 20
23 Jan 71 ● **YOUR SONG** *DJM DJS 233* **7** 12
1 May 71 THE ELTON JOHN LIVE ALBUM 17-11-70 *DJM DJLPS 414* 20 2
22 Apr 72 ● **ROCKET MAN (I THINK IT'S GOING TO BE A LONG LONG TIME)** *DJM DJX 501* 2 13
20 May 72 MADMAN ACROSS THE WATER *DJM DJLPH 420* 41 2
3 Jun 72 ● HONKY CHÂTEAU *DJM DJLPH 423* ▲ 2 23
9 Sep 72 **HONKY CAT** *DJM DJS 269* 31 6
4 Nov 72 ● **CROCODILE ROCK** *DJM DJS 271* ▲ $ 5 14
20 Jan 73 ● **DANIEL** *DJM DJS 275* $ 4 10
10 Feb 73 ★ DON'T SHOOT ME I'M ONLY THE PIANO PLAYER *DJM DJLPH 427* ■ ▲ 1 42
7 Jul 73 ● **SATURDAY NIGHT'S ALRIGHT FOR FIGHTING** *DJM DJX 502* **7** 9
29 Sep 73 ● **GOODBYE YELLOW BRICK ROAD** *DJM DJS 285* $ 6 16
3 Nov 73 ★ GOODBYE YELLOW BRICK ROAD *DJM DJLPO 1001* ▲ 1 84
8 Dec 73 **STEP INTO CHRISTMAS** *DJM DJS 290* 24 7
2 Mar 74 **CANDLE IN THE WIND** *DJM DJS 297* 11 9
1 Jun 74 **DON'T LET THE SUN GO DOWN ON ME** *DJM DJS 302* 16 8
13 Jul 74 ★ CARIBOU *DJM DJLPH 439* ■ ▲ 1 18
14 Sep 74 **THE BITCH IS BACK** *DJM DJS 322* 15 7
23 Nov 74 ★ GREATEST HITS *DJM DJLPH 442* ■ ▲ 1 84
23 Nov 74 ● **LUCY IN THE SKY WITH DIAMONDS** *DJM DJS 340* ▲ $ 10 10
8 Mar 75 **PHILADELPHIA FREEDOM** *DJM DJS 354* [1] ▲ $ 12 9
7 Jun 75 ● CAPTAIN FANTASTIC AND THE BROWN DIRT COWBOY *DJM DJLPX 1* ▲ 2 24
28 Jun 75 **SOMEONE SAVED MY LIFE TONIGHT** *DJM DJS 385* $ 22 5
4 Oct 75 **ISLAND GIRL** *DJM DJS 610* ▲ $ 14 8
8 Nov 75 ● ROCK OF THE WESTIES *DJM DJLPH 464* ▲ 5 12
20 Mar 76 ● **PINBALL WIZARD** *DJM DJS 652* **7** 7
15 May 76 ● HERE AND THERE *DJM DJLPH 473* 6 9
3 Jul 76 ★ **DON'T GO BREAKING MY HEART** *Rocket ROKN 512* [2] ▲ $ 1 14
25 Sep 76 **BENNIE AND THE JETS** *DJM DJS 10705* ▲ $ 37 5
6 Nov 76 ● BLUE MOVES *Rocket ROSP 1* 3 15
13 Nov 76 **SORRY SEEMS TO BE THE HARDEST WORD** *Rocket ROKN 517* $ 11 10
26 Feb 77 **CRAZY WATER** *Rocket ROKN 521* 27 6
11 Jun 77 **BITE YOUR LIP (GET UP AND DANCE)** *Rocket ROKN 526* 28 4
15 Oct 77 ● ELTON JOHN'S GREATEST HITS VOLUME II *DJM DJH 20520* 6 24
15 Apr 78 **EGO** *Rocket ROKN 538* 34 6
21 Oct 78 **PART TIME LOVE** *Rocket XPRES 1* 15 13
4 Nov 78 ● A SINGLE MAN *Rocket TRAIN 1* 8 26
16 Dec 78 ● **SONG FOR GUY** *Rocket XPRES 5* 4 10
12 May 79 **ARE YOU READY FOR LOVE** *Rocket XPRES 13* 42 6
20 Oct 79 VICTIM OF LOVE *Rocket HISPD 125* 41 3
8 Mar 80 LADY SAMANTHA *DJM 22085* 56 2
24 May 80 **LITTLE JEANNIE** *Rocket XPRES 32* $ 33 7
31 May 80 21 AT 33 *Rocket HISPD 126* 12 13
23 Aug 80 **SARTORIAL ELOQUENCE** *Rocket XPRES 41* **44** 5
25 Oct 80 THE VERY BEST OF ELTON JOHN *K-Tel NE 1094* 24 13
21 Mar 81 **I SAW HER STANDING THERE** *DJM DJS 10965* [3] **40** 4
23 May 81 **NOBODY WINS** *Rocket XPRES 54* 42 5
30 May 81 THE FOX *Rocket TRAIN 16* 12 12
27 Mar 82 ● **BLUE EYES** *Rocket XPRES 71* 8 10
17 Apr 82 JUMP UP! *Rocket HISPD 127* 13 12
12 Jun 82 **EMPTY GARDEN** *Rocket XPRES 77* **51** 4
6 Nov 82 LOVE SONGS *TV TVA 3* 39 13
30 Apr 83 ● **I GUESS THAT'S WHY THEY CALL IT THE BLUES** *Rocket XPRES 91* 5 15
11 Jun 83 ● TOO LOW FOR ZERO *Rocket HISPD 24* 7 73
30 Jul 83 ● **I'M STILL STANDING** *Rocket EJS 1* 4 11
15 Oct 83 **KISS THE BRIDE** *Rocket EJS 2* 20 7
10 Dec 83 **COLD AS CHRISTMAS (IN THE MIDDLE OF THE YEAR)** *Rocket EJS 3* 33 6
26 May 84 ● **SAD SONGS (SAY SO MUCH)** *Rocket PH 7* **7** 12
30 Jun 84 ● BREAKING HEARTS *Rocket HISPD 25* 2 23
11 Aug 84 ● **PASSENGERS** *Rocket EJS 5* **5** 11
20 Oct 84 **WHO WEARS THESE SHOES** *Rocket EJS 6* **50** 3
2 Mar 85 **BREAKING HEARTS (AIN'T WHAT IT USED TO BE)** *Rocket EJS 7* **59** 3
15 Jun 85 **ACT OF WAR** *Rocket EJS 8* [4] 32 5
12 Oct 85 ● **NIKITA** *Rocket EJS 9* 3 13
9 Nov 85 **THAT'S WHAT FRIENDS ARE FOR** *Arista ARIST 638* [5] ▲ $ 16 9
16 Nov 85 ● ICE ON FIRE *Rocket HISPD 26* 3 23
7 Dec 85 **WRAP HER UP** *Rocket EJS 10* 12 10
1 Mar 86 **CRY TO HEAVEN** *Rocket EJS 11* **47** 4
4 Oct 86 **HEARTACHE ALL OVER THE WORLD** *Rocket EJS 12* **45** 4
15 Nov 86 LEATHER JACKETS *Rocket EJLP 1* 24 9
29 Nov 86 **SLOW RIVERS** *Rocket EJS 13* [6] **44** 8
20 Jun 87 **FLAMES OF PARADISE** *CBS 6508657* [7] **59** 3
12 Sep 87 LIVE IN AUSTRALIA WITH THE MELBOURNE SYMPHONY ORCHESTRA *Rocket EJBXL 1* [1] 43 7
16 Jan 88 ● **CANDLE IN THE WIND** *Rocket EJS 15* **5** 11
4 Jun 88 **I DON'T WANNA GO ON WITH YOU LIKE THAT** *Rocket EJS 16* 30 8
16 Jul 88 REG STRIKES BACK *Rocket EJLP 3* 18 6
3 Sep 88 **TOWN OF PLENTY** *Rocket EJS 17* **74** 1
6 May 89 **THROUGH THE STORM** *Arista 112185* [8] **41** 3
26 Aug 89 **HEALING HANDS** *Rocket EJS 19* **45** 5
23 Sep 89 ★ SLEEPING WITH THE PAST *Rocket 8388391* 1 42
4 Nov 89 **SACRIFICE** *Rocket EJS 20* **55** 3
9 Jun 90 ★ **SACRIFICE / HEALING HANDS** (re-issues) *Rocket EJS 22* 1 15
18 Aug 90 **CLUB AT THE END OF THE STREET / WHISPERS** *Rocket EJS 23* **47** 3
20 Oct 90 **YOU GOTTA LOVE SOMEONE** *Rocket EJS 24* 33 4
10 Nov 90 ★ THE VERY BEST OF ELTON JOHN *Rocket 8469471* ■ 1 97
15 Dec 90 **EASIER TO WALK AWAY** (re) *Rocket EJS 25* 63 2
7 Dec 91 ★ **DON'T LET THE SUN GO DOWN ON ME** *Epic 6576467* [9] ■ ▲ 1 10
6 Jun 92 ● **THE ONE** *Rocket EJS 28* 10 8
27 Jun 92 ● THE ONE *Rocket 5123602* 2 18
1 Aug 92 **RUNAWAY TRAIN** *Rocket EJS 29* [10] 31 4
7 Nov 92 **THE LAST SONG** *Rocket EJS 30* 21 4
22 May 93 **SIMPLE LIFE** *Rocket EJSCD 31* **44** 2
20 Nov 93 ● **TRUE LOVE** *Rocket EJSCX 32* [2] 2 10
4 Dec 93 ● DUETS *Rocket 5184782* 5 18
26 Feb 94 ● **DON'T GO BREAKING MY HEART** (re-recording) *Rocket EJRCD 33* [11] 7 7
14 May 94 **AIN'T NOTHING LIKE THE REAL THING** *London LONCD 350* [12] 24 4
9 Jul 94 **CAN YOU FEEL THE LOVE TONIGHT** *Mercury EJCD 34* 14 9
8 Oct 94 **CIRCLE OF LIFE** *Rocket EJSCD 35* 11 12
4 Mar 95 **BELIEVE** *Rocket EJSCD 36* 15 7
1 Apr 95 ● MADE IN ENGLAND *Rocket 5261852* 3 14
20 May 95 **MADE IN ENGLAND** *Rocket EJSCD 37* 18 5
18 Nov 95 ● LOVE SONGS *Rocket 5287882* 4 48
3 Feb 96 **PLEASE** *Rocket EJSCD 40* 33 3
14 Dec 96 ● **LIVE LIKE HORSES** *Rocket LLHDD 1* [13] 9 6
20 Sep 97 ★ **CANDLE IN THE WIND 1997 / SOMETHING ABOUT THE WAY YOU LOOK TONIGHT** *Rocket PTCD 1* ■ ▲ £ $ 1 24
11 Oct 97 ● THE BIG PICTURE *Rocket 5362662* 3 23
14 Feb 98 **RECOVER YOUR SOUL** *Rocket EJSCD 42* 16 3
13 Jun 98 **IF THE RIVER CAN BEND** *Rocket EJSDD 43* 32 2
6 Mar 99 ● **WRITTEN IN THE STARS** (re) *Mercury EJSCD 45* [14] 10 8
3 Apr 99 ELTON JOHN AND TIM RICE'S AIDA *Mercury 5246512* [2] 29 2
25 Nov 00 ● ONE NIGHT ONLY – THE GREATEST HITS *Mercury 5483342* 7 13
6 Oct 01 ● **I WANT LOVE** *Rocket / Mercury 5887062* 9 10
13 Oct 01 ● SONGS FROM THE WEST COAST *Mercury 5863302* 2 34
20 Oct 01 GOODBYE YELLOW BRICK ROAD (re-issue) *Rocket 5281592* 41 4
26 Jan 02 **THIS TRAIN DON'T STOP THERE ANYMORE** *Rocket / Mercury 588962* 24 4
13 Apr 02 **ORIGINAL SIN** *Rocket / Mercury 5889992* 39 2
27 Jul 02 ● **YOUR SONG** (re) (re-recording) *Mercury 639972* [15] 4 10

7 April 1973	14 April 1973	21 April 1973	28 April 1973
GET DOWN Gilbert O'Sullivan	**GET DOWN** Gilbert O'Sullivan	**TIE A YELLOW RIBBON ROUND THE OLE OAK TREE** Dawn	**TIE A YELLOW RIBBON ROUND THE OLE OAK TREE** Dawn
FLASHBACK GREAT HITS OF THE SIXTIES Various	**HOUSES OF THE HOLY** Led Zeppelin	**HOUSES OF THE HOLY** Led Zeppelin	**OOH LA LA** The Faces

KEY UK No.1 ★ UK Top 10 ● Still on chart + UK entry at No.1 ■ US No.1 ▲ UK million seller £ US million seller $
Singles re-entries are listed as (re), (2re), (3re)… which signifies that the hit re-entered the chart once, twice or three times…
Peak Position / Weeks

23 Nov 02 ● GREATEST HITS 1970-2002 *Mercury 634992* ... 3 54
21 Dec 02 ★ SORRY SEEMS TO BE THE HARDEST WORD (re-recording) *Innocent SINDX 43* 16 ■ ... 1 17
19 Jul 03 ARE YOU READY FOR LOVE 12" (re-mix) *Southern Fried ECB 50LOVE* ... 66 1
6 Sep 03 ★ ARE YOU READY FOR LOVE (re-mix) *Southern Fried ECB 50CDS* ... 1 13
13 Nov 04 ALL THAT I'M ALLOWED (I'M THANKFUL) *Rocket / Mercury 9868257* ... 20 5
20 Nov 04 PEACHTREE ROAD *Rocket 9868762* ... 21 8
16 Apr 05 TURN THE LIGHTS OUT WHEN YOU LEAVE *Rocket / Mercury 9870663* ... 32 2
2 Jul 05 ★ GHETTO GOSPEL *Interscope 9883248* 17 ■ ... 1 18
23 Jul 05 ● ELECTRICITY *Rocket 9872183* ... 4 4

1 Elton John Band 2 Elton John and Kiki Dee 3 Elton John Band featuring John Lennon and the Muscle Shoals Horns 4 Elton John and Millie Jackson 5 Dionne Warwick and Friends featuring Elton John, Stevie Wonder and Gladys Knight 6 Elton John and Cliff Richard 7 Jennifer Rush and Elton John 8 Aretha Franklin and Elton John 9 George Michael and Elton John 10 Elton John and Eric Clapton 11 Elton John with RuPaul 12 Marcella Detroit and Elton John 13 Elton John & Luciano Pavarotti 14 Elton John and LeAnn Rimes 15 Elton John & Alessandro Safina 16 Blue featuring Elton John 17 2Pac (featuring Elton John) 1 Elton John with the Melbourne Symphony Orchestra 2 Elton John and Friends

'Bite Your Lip (Get Up and Dance)' was one side of a double-sided chart entry, the other being 'Chicago' by Kiki Dee. 'Wrap Her Up' and 'Nikita' feature George Michael as uncredited co-vocalist. 'Candle in the Wind' 1988 was a live recording. Live in Australia with the Melbourne Symphony Orchestra re-appeared in 1988 with the catalogue number EJLP 2; EJBXL 1 was the original 'de luxe' version. The two The Very Best of Elton John and Love Songs albums are different.

Robert JOHN
US, male vocalist – Robert John Pedrick (2 Singles: 13 Weeks)

17 Jul 68 IF YOU DON'T WANT MY LOVE *CBS 3436* ... 42 5
20 Oct 79 SAD EYES *EMI American EA 101* ▲ $ ... 31 8

JOHNNA *US, female vocalist – Johnna Cummings (2 Singles: 3 Weeks)*

10 Feb 96 DO WHAT YOU FEEL *PWL International PWL 323CD* ... 43 2
11 May 96 IN MY DREAMS *PWL International PWL 325CD* ... 66 1

JOHNNY and CHARLEY *Spain, male vocal duo*

14 Oct 65 LA YENKA *Pye International 7N 25326* ... 49 1

JOHNNY and The HURRICANES *US, male instrumental group – leader Johnny Pocisk (2 Albums: 5 Weeks, 7 Singles: 88 Weeks)*

9 Oct 59 ● RED RIVER ROCK *London HL 8948* ... 3 16
25 Dec 59 REVEILLE ROCK *London HL 9017* ... 14 5
17 Mar 60 ● BEATNIK FLY *London HLI 9072* ... 8 19
16 Jun 60 ● DOWN YONDER *London HLX 9134* ... 8 11
29 Sep 60 ● ROCKING GOOSE *London HLX 9190* ... 3 20
3 Dec 60 STORMSVILLE *London HAI 2269* ... 18 1
2 Mar 61 JA-DA *London HLX 9289* ... 14 9
1 Apr 61 BIG SOUND OF JOHNNY AND THE HURRICANES *London HAK 2322* ... 14 4
6 Jul 61 OLD SMOKIE / HIGH VOLTAGE *London HLX 9378* ... 24 8

JOHNNY BOY *UK, male / female production / vocal duo*

14 Aug 04 YOU ARE THE GENERATION THAT BOUGHT MORE SHOES AND YOU GET WHAT YOU DESERVE *Mercury 9866935* ... 50 2

JOHNNY CORPORATE *US, male production duo*

28 Oct 00 SUNDAY SHOUTIN' *Defected DFECT 21CDS* ... 45 2

JOHNNY HATES JAZZ *UK, male vocal (Clark Datchler) / instrumental group (1 Album: 39 Weeks, 5 Singles: 45 Weeks)*

11 Apr 87 ● SHATTERED DREAMS *Virgin VS 948* ... 5 14
29 Aug 87 I DON'T WANT TO BE A HERO *Virgin VS 1000* ... 11 10
21 Nov 87 TURN BACK THE CLOCK *Virgin VS 1017* ... 12 11
23 Jan 88 ★ TURN BACK THE CLOCK *Virgin V 2475* ■ ... 1 39
27 Feb 88 HEART OF GOLD *Virgin VS 1045* ... 19 7
9 Jul 88 DON'T SAY IT'S LOVE *Virgin VS 1081* ... 48 3

JOHNNY PANIC *UK, male vocal / instrumental group (2 Singles: 2 Weeks)*

18 Sep 04 BURN YOUR MOUTH *Concept CDCON 59* ... 69 1
14 May 05 MINORITY OF ONE *Concept CDCON 63* ... 60 1

JOHNSON *UK, male / female vocal / instrumental duo*

27 Mar 99 SAY YOU LOVE ME *Higher Ground HIGHS 18CD* ... 56 1

Andreas JOHNSON
Sweden, male vocalist (1 Album: 2 Weeks, 2 Singles: 12 Weeks)

5 Feb 00 ● GLORIOUS *WEA WEA 254CD* ... 4 11
19 Feb 00 LIEBLING *WEA 3984269142* ... 46 2
27 May 00 THE GAMES WE PLAY *WEA WEA 264* ... 41 1

Bryan JOHNSON *UK, male vocalist, b. 18 Jul 1926, d. 18 Oct 1995*

10 Mar 60 LOOKING HIGH, HIGH, HIGH *Decca F 11213* ... 20 11

Carey JOHNSON *Australia, male vocalist – Reginald Johnson*

25 Apr 87 REAL FASHION REGGAE STYLE *Oval TEN 170* ... 19 8

Denise JOHNSON *UK, female vocalist (2 Singles: 4 Weeks)*

24 Aug 91 DON'T FIGHT IT FEEL IT *Creation CRE 110* 1 ... 41 2
14 May 94 RAYS OF THE RISING SUN *Magnet MAG 1022CD* ... 45 2

1 Primal Scream featuring Denise Johnson

Don JOHNSON *US, male vocalist / actor (2 Singles: 12 Weeks)*

18 Oct 86 HEARTBEAT *Epic 650064 7* ... 46 5
5 Nov 88 TILL I LOVED YOU (LOVE THEME FROM 'GOYA') *CBS BARB 2* 1 ... 16 7

1 Barbra Streisand and Don Johnson

Holly JOHNSON (see also FRANKIE GOES TO HOLLYWOOD) *UK, male vocalist – William Johnson (1 Album: 17 Weeks, 7 Singles: 38 Weeks)*

14 Jan 89 ● LOVE TRAIN *MCA MCA 1306* ... 4 11
1 Apr 89 ● AMERICANOS *MCA MCA 1323* ... 4 11
6 May 89 ★ BLAST *MCA MCG 6042* ■ ... 1 17
20 May 89 ★ FERRY 'CROSS THE MERSEY *PWL PWL 41* 1 ■ ... 1 7
24 Jun 89 ATOMIC CITY *MCA MCA 1342* ... 18 4
30 Sep 89 HEAVEN'S HERE *MCA MCA 1365* ... 62 2
1 Dec 90 WHERE HAS LOVE GONE? *MCA MCA 1460* ... 73 1
25 Dec 99 THE POWER OF LOVE *Pleasure Dome PLDCD 1005* ... 56 2

1 The Christians, Holly Johnson, Paul McCartney, Gerry Marsden and Stock Aitken Waterman

Howard JOHNSON *US, male vocalist*

4 Sep 82 KEEPIN' LOVE NEW / SO FINE *A&M USA 1221* ... 45 6

'Keepin' Love New' listed on 4 Sep 1982 only.

Jack JOHNSON NEW
US, male vocalist / guitarist (1 Album: 35 Weeks, 2 Singles: 5 Weeks)

12 Mar 05 ● IN BETWEEN DREAMS *Island 9880252* ... 10 35+
25 Jun 05 GOOD PEOPLE *Island MCSTD 40417* ... 50 3
17 Sep 05 BREAKDOWN *Island MCSTD 40430* ... 73 2

5 May 1973	12 May 1973	19 May 1973	26 May 1973
UK No.1 SINGLES			
TIE A YELLOW RIBBON ROUND THE OLE OAK TREE Dawn	TIE A YELLOW RIBBON ROUND THE OLE OAK TREE Dawn	SEE MY BABY JIVE Wizzard: Vocal backing by The Suedettes	SEE MY BABY JIVE Wizzard: Vocal backing by The Suedettes
UK No.1 ALBUMS			
ALADDIN SANE David Bowie	ALADDIN SANE David Bowie	ALADDIN SANE David Bowie	ALADDIN SANE David Bowie

Johnny JOHNSON and The BANDWAGON
US, male vocal group (5 Singles: 50 Weeks)

16 Oct 68 ●	**BREAKIN' DOWN THE WALLS OF HEARTACHE** *Direction 58-3670* [1]	4	15
5 Feb 69	**YOU** *Direction 58-3923*	34	4
28 May 69	**LET'S HANG ON** *Direction 58-4180*	36	6
25 Jul 70 ●	**SWEET INSPIRATION** (re) *Bell 1111*	10	13
28 Nov 70 ●	**(BLAME IT) ON THE PONY EXPRESS** *Bell 1128*	7	12

[1] Bandwagon

Kevin JOHNSON *Australia, male vocalist*

11 Jan 75	**ROCK 'N ROLL (I GAVE YOU THE BEST YEARS OF MY LIFE)** *UK UKR 84*	23	6

Laurie JOHNSON ORCHESTRA *UK, orchestra (2 Singles: 14 Weeks)*

28 Sep 61 ●	**SUCU SUCU** *Pye 7N 15383*	9	12
17 May 97	**THEME FROM 'THE PROFESSIONALS'** *Virgin VSCDT 1643* [1]	36	2

[1] Laurie Johnson's London Big Band

Linton Kwesi JOHNSON *Jamaica, male poet (3 Albums: 8 Weeks)*

30 Jun 79	**FORCES OF VICTORY** *Island ILPS 9566*	66	1
31 Oct 80	**BASS CULTURE** *Island ILPS 9605*	46	5
10 Mar 84	**MAKING HISTORY** *Island ILPS 9770*	73	2

LJ JOHNSON *US, male vocalist – Louis Johnson*

7 Feb 76	**YOUR MAGIC PUT A SPELL ON ME** *Philips 6006 492*	27	6

Lou JOHNSON *US, male vocalist*

26 Nov 64	**A MESSAGE TO MARTHA (KENTUCKY BLUEBIRD)** *London HL 9929*	36	2

Marv JOHNSON
US, male vocalist, b. 15 Oct 1938, d. 16 May 1993 (5 Singles: 40 Weeks)

12 Feb 60 ●	**YOU GOT WHAT IT TAKES** *London HLT 9013*	7	17
5 May 60	**I LOVE THE WAY YOU LOVE** *London HLT 9109*	35	3
11 Aug 60	**AIN'T GONNA BE THAT WAY** *London HLT 9165*	50	1
22 Jan 69 ●	**I'LL PICK A ROSE FOR MY ROSE** *Tamla Motown TMG 680*	10	11
25 Oct 69	**I MISS YOU BABY** *Tamla Motown TMG 713*	25	8

Paul JOHNSON
UK, male vocalist (2 Albums: 3 Weeks, 2 Singles: 7 Weeks)

21 Feb 87	**WHEN LOVE COMES CALLING** *CBS PJOHN 1*	52	5
4 Jul 87	**PAUL JOHNSON** *CBS 450640 1*	63	2
25 Feb 89	**NO MORE TOMORROWS** *CBS PJOHN 7*	67	2
16 Sep 89	**PERSONAL** *CBS 463284 1*	70	1

Paul JOHNSON
US, male producer / instrumentalist (2 Albums: 3 Weeks, 2 Singles: 9 Weeks)

25 Sep 99 ●	**GET GET DOWN** *Defected DEFECT 7CDS*	5	8
27 Aug 05	**SHE GOT ME ON** *Data DATA 86CDS*	70	1

Puff JOHNSON *US, female vocalist (2 Singles: 6 Weeks)*

18 Jan 97	**OVER AND OVER** *Columbia 6640345*	20	4
12 Apr 97	**FOREVER MORE** *Work 644075*	29	2

Romina JOHNSON *Italy, female vocalist (2 Singles: 13 Weeks)*

4 Mar 00 ●	**MOVIN TOO FAST** (re) *Locked On XL LOX 117CD* [1]	2	12
17 Jun 00	**MY FORBIDDEN LOVER** *51 Lexington CDLEX 1* [2]	59	1

[1] Artful Dodger and Romina Johnson [2] Romina Johnson featuring Luci Martin and Norma Jean

Syleena JOHNSON *US, female vocalist (2 Singles: 10 Weeks)*

26 Oct 02	**TONIGHT I'M GONNA LET GO** *Jive 9254252*	38	2
19 Jun 04 ●	**ALL FALLS DOWN** *Roc-A-Fella 9862670* [1]	10	8

[1] Kanye West featuring Syleena Johnson

Sleeve of 'Tonight I'm Gonna Let Go' credits Syleena Johnson featuring Busta Rhymes, Rampage, Sham & Spliff Star (of Flipmode Squad).

Ana JOHNSSON *Sweden, female vocalist*

14 Aug 04 ●	**WE ARE** *Epic 6751622*	8	6

Brian JOHNSTON *UK, male broadcaster, d. 5 Jan 1994*

5 Mar 94	**AN EVENING WITH JOHNNERS** *Listen for Pleasure LFP 7742*	46	3

Bruce JOHNSTON (see also The BEACH BOYS) *US, male keyboard player*

27 Aug 77	**PIPELINE** *CBS 5514*	33	4

James A JOHNSTON *US, male composer, aka Jim Johnston (III) (2 Albums: 17 Weeks)*

13 Nov 99	**WORLD WRESTLING FEDERATION – THE MUSIC – VOLUME 4** *Koch International 333612*	44	9
10 Mar 01	**WORLD WRESTLING FEDERATION – THE MUSIC – VOLUME 5** *Koch KOCCD 8830*	11	8

Jan JOHNSTON *UK, female vocalist (7 Singles: 12 Weeks)*

8 Feb 97	**TAKE ME BY THE HAND** *AM:PM 5821012* [1]	28	2
28 Nov 98	**SKYDIVE** *Stress CDSTR 89* [2]	75	1
12 Feb 00	**LOVE WILL COME** *Xtravaganza XTRAV 6CDS* [3]	31	2
22 Jul 00	**SKYDIVE** (re-mix) *Renaissance Recordings RENCDS 002* [2]	43	2
21 Apr 01	**FLESH** *Perfecto PERF 05CDS*	36	2
28 Jul 01	**SILENT WORDS** *Perfecto PERF 16CDS*	57	1
8 Sep 01	**SKYDIVE (I FEEL WONDERFUL)** (2nd re-mix) *Incentive CENT 22CDS* [2]	35	2

[1] Submerge featuring Jan Johnston [2] Freefall featuring Jan Johnston [3] Tomski featuring Jan Johnston

Sabrina JOHNSTON *US, female vocalist (5 Singles: 19 Weeks)*

7 Sep 91 ●	**PEACE** *East West YZ 616*	8	10
7 Dec 91	**FRIENDSHIP** *East West YZ 637*	58	4
11 Jul 92	**I WANNA SING** *East West YZ 661*	46	2
3 Oct 92	**PEACE** (re-mix) *Epic 6584377*	35	2
13 Aug 94	**SATISFY MY LOVE** *Champion CHAMPCD 311*	62	1

The listed flipside of 'Peace' (re-mix) was 'Gypsy Woman' (re-mix) by Crystal Waters.

The JOHNSTON BROTHERS *UK, male vocal group – leader Johnny Johnston (Johnny Reine), d. Jun 1998 (10 Singles: 33 Weeks)*

3 Apr 53 ●	**OH, HAPPY DAY** *Decca F 10071*	4	8
5 Nov 54	**WAIT FOR ME, DARLING** *Decca F 10362* [1]	18	1
21 Jan 55	**HAPPY DAYS AND LONELY NIGHTS** *Decca F 10389* [2]	14	2
7 Oct 55 ★	**HERNANDO'S HIDEAWAY** *Decca F 10608*	1	13
30 Dec 55 ●	**JOIN IN AND SING AGAIN** *Decca F 10636* [3]	9	1
13 Apr 56	**NO OTHER LOVE** *Decca F 10721*	22	1
30 Nov 56	**IN THE MIDDLE OF THE HOUSE** *Decca F 10781*	27	1
7 Dec 56	**JOIN IN AND SING NO.3** (re) *Decca F 10814*	24	2
8 Feb 57	**GIVE HER MY LOVE** *Decca F 10828*	27	1
19 Apr 57	**HEART** *Decca F 10860*	23	3

[1] Joan Regan with The Johnston Brothers [2] Suzi Miller and The Johnston Brothers [3] The Johnston Brothers and the George Chisholm Sour-Note Six

The following two hits were medleys: Join In and Sing Again: Sheik of Araby / Yes Sir That's My Baby / California Here I Come / Some of These Days / Charleston / Margie. Join In and Sing No.3: Coal Black Morning / When You're Smiling / Alexander's Ragtime Band / Sweet Sue Just You / When You Wore a Tulip / If You Were the Only Girl in the World.

KEY
UK No.1 ★ UK Top 10 ● Still on chart + UK entry at No.1 ■
US No.1 ▲ UK million seller £ US million seller $
Singles re-entries are listed as (re), (2re), (3re)... which signifies that the hit re-entered the chart once, twice or three times...
Peak Position / Weeks

JOJO *US, female vocalist – Joanne Levesque (1 Album: 17 Weeks, 2 Singles: 17 Weeks)*

11 Sep 04 ● LEAVE (GET OUT) *Mercury 9867841* ... 2 8
18 Sep 04 JOJO *Mercury 9867855* ... 22 17
27 Nov 04 ● BABY IT'S YOU *Mercury 9869056* [1] ... 8 9

[1] JoJo featuring Bow Wow

JOLLY BROTHERS *Jamaica, male vocal / instrumental group*

28 Jul 79 CONSCIOUS MAN *United Artists UP 36415* ... 46 7

JOLLY ROGER *UK, male instrumentalist / producer – Eddie Richards*

10 Sep 88 ACID MAN *10 TEN 236* ... 23 12

Al JOLSON *US, male vocalist – Asa Yoelson, b. 26 Mar 1886, d. 23 Oct 1950 (2 Albums: 11 Weeks)*

14 Mar 81 20 GOLDEN GREATS *MCA MCTV 4* ... 18 7
17 Dec 83 THE AL JOLSON COLLECTION *Ronco RON LP 5* ... 67 4

JOMANDA *US, female vocal group (4 Singles: 10 Weeks)*

22 Apr 89 MAKE MY BODY ROCK *RCA PB 42749* ... 44 3
29 Jun 91 GOT A LOVE FOR YOU *Giant W 0040* ... 43 4
11 Sep 93 I LIKE IT *Big Beat A 8377CD* ... 67 1
13 Nov 93 NEVER *Big Beat A 8347CD* ... 40 2

JON and VANGELIS
UK, male vocalist and Greece, male multi-instrumentalist – Jon Anderson and Evangelos Papathanassiou (5 Albums: 53 Weeks, 4 Singles: 28 Weeks)

5 Jan 80 ● I HEAR YOU NOW *Polydor POSP 96* ... 8 11
26 Jan 80 ● SHORT STORIES *Polydor POLD 5030* ... 4 11
11 Jul 81 THE FRIENDS OF MR. CAIRO *Polydor POLD 5039* ... 17 8
12 Dec 81 ● I'LL FIND MY WAY HOME *Polydor JV 1* ... 6 13
23 Jan 82 ● THE FRIENDS OF MR. CAIRO (re-issue) *Polydor POLD 5053* ... 6 15
2 Jul 83 PRIVATE COLLECTION *Polydor POLH 4* ... 22 10
30 Jul 83 HE IS SAILING *Polydor JV 4* ... 61 2
11 Aug 84 THE BEST OF JON AND VANGELIS *Polydor POLH 6* ... 42 9
18 Aug 84 STATE OF INDEPENDENCE *Polydor JV 5* ... 67 2

JON OF THE PLEASED WIMMIN
UK, male DJ / producer – Jonathan Cooper (2 Singles: 5 Weeks)

18 Feb 95 PASSION *Perfecto YZ 884CD* ... 27 3
6 Apr 96 GIVE ME STRENGTH *Perfecto PERF 119CD* ... 30 2

JON THE DENTIST vs Ollie JAYE *UK, male DJs / producers – John Vaughan and Ollie Jaye (2 Singles: 2 Weeks)*

24 Jul 99 IMAGINATION *Tidy Trax TIDY 126CD* ... 72 1
10 Jun 00 FEEL SO GOOD *Tidy Trax TIDY 135CD* ... 72 1

JONAH *Holland, male production group*

22 Jul 00 SSSST (LISTEN) *VC Recordings VCRD 69* ... 25 4

Aled JONES (361 Top 500)
Welsh boy soprano, b. 29 Dec 1970, Llandegfan, Anglesey, who matured into a baritone, performed in classical, traditional, religious and pop styles and appeared as a TV presenter, most notably on Songs of Praise. In Jul 1985, he became the youngest soloist to feature on simultaneous Top 10 albums (12 Albums: 169 Weeks, 4 Singles: 24 Weeks)

27 Apr 85 ● VOICES FROM THE HOLY LAND *BBC REC 564* [1] ... 6 43
29 Jun 85 ● ALL THROUGH THE NIGHT *BBC REH 569* [1] ... 2 44
20 Jul 85 MEMORY: THEME FROM THE MUSICAL 'CATS' *BBC RESL 175* ... 42 4
23 Nov 85 ALED JONES WITH THE BBC WELSH CHORUS *10 / BBC AJ 1* [1] ... 11 10
30 Nov 85 ● WALKING IN THE AIR *HMV ALED 1* ... 5 11
14 Dec 85 PICTURES IN THE DARK *Virgin VS 836* [1] ... 50 6
22 Feb 86 WHERE E'ER YOU WALK *10 DIX 21* ... 36 6
12 Jul 86 PIE JESU *10 AJ 2* ... 25 16
29 Nov 86 AN ALBUM OF HYMNS *Telstar STAR 2272* ... 18 11
20 Dec 86 A WINTER STORY *HMV ALED 2* ... 51 3
14 Mar 87 ALED (MUSIC FROM THE TV SERIES) *10 AJ 3* ... 52 6
5 Dec 87 THE BEST OF ALED JONES *10 AJ 5* ... 59 5
26 Oct 02 ALED *UCJ 0644792* ... 27 12
11 Oct 03 HIGHER *UCJ 9865579* ... 21 7
4 Dec 04 THE CHRISTMAS ALBUM *UCJ 9868649* ... 28 5
29 Oct 05 NEW HORIZONS *UCJ 4763062* [2] ... 21 4

[1] Mike Oldfield featuring Aled Jones, Anita Hegerland and Barry Palmer
[1] Aled Jones with the BBC Welsh Chorus [2] Aled

In Mar 2005 a repackaged version of Aled, featuring three new tracks and previously unavailable material from Aled as a boy, charted under the catalogue number UCJ 9827998. It peaked at No.33.

Barbara JONES *Jamaica, female vocalist – Barbara Nation*

31 Jan 81 JUST WHEN I NEEDED YOU MOST *Sonet SON 2221* ... 31 7

Catherine Zeta JONES *UK, female actor / vocalist (3 Singles: 9 Weeks)*

19 Sep 92 FOR ALL TIME *Columbia 6583547* ... 36 5
26 Nov 94 TRUE LOVE WAYS *PolyGram TV TLWCD 2* [1] ... 38 3
1 Apr 95 IN THE ARMS OF LOVE *Wow! WOWCD 7101* ... 72 1

[1] David Essex and Catherine Zeta Jones

Donell JONES *US, male vocalist (2 Albums: 5 Weeks, 5 Singles: 20 Weeks)*

15 Feb 97 KNOCKS ME OFF MY FEET *LaFace 74321458502* ... 58 1
22 Jan 00 ● U KNOW WHAT'S UP *LaFace 74321722752* ... 2 11
29 Jan 00 WHERE I WANNA BE *LaFace 73008260602* ... 47 3
20 May 00 SHORTY (GOT HER EYES ON ME) *LaFace 74321748902* ... 19 3
2 Dec 00 TRUE STEP TONIGHT *Nulife 74321811312* [1] ... 25 3
22 Jun 02 LIFE GOES ON *Arista 74321941552* ... 62 2
24 Aug 02 YOU KNOW THAT I LOVE YOU *Arista 74321956962* ... 41 2

[1] True Steppers featuring Brian Harvey and Donell Jones

Glenn JONES *US, male vocalist*

31 Oct 87 GLENN JONES *Jive HIP 51* ... 62 1

Grace JONES *Jamaica, female vocalist – Grace Mendoza (6 Albums: 80 Weeks, 10 Singles: 46 Weeks)*

26 Jul 80 PRIVATE LIFE *Island WIP 6629* ... 17 8
30 Aug 80 WARM LEATHERETTE *Island ILPS 9592* ... 45 2
23 May 81 NIGHTCLUBBING *Island ILPS 9624* ... 35 16
20 Jun 81 PULL UP TO THE BUMPER *Island WIP 6696* ... 53 4
30 Oct 82 THE APPLE STRETCHING / NIPPLE TO THE BOTTLE *Island WIP 6779* ... 50 4
20 Nov 82 LIVING MY LIFE *Island ILPS 9722* ... 15 22
9 Apr 83 MY JAMAICAN GUY *Island IS 103* ... 56 3
12 Oct 85 SLAVE TO THE RHYTHM *ZTT IS 206* ... 12 8
9 Nov 85 SLAVE TO THE RHYTHM *ZTT GRACE 1* ... 12 8
14 Dec 85 ● ISLAND LIFE *Island GJ 1* ... 4 30
18 Jan 86 PULL UP TO THE BUMPER / LA VIE EN ROSE (re-issue) *Island IS 240* ... 12 9
1 Mar 86 LOVE IS THE DRUG *Island IS 266* ... 35 4
15 Nov 86 I'M NOT PERFECT (BUT I'M PERFECT FOR YOU) *Manhattan MT 15* ... 56 3
29 Nov 86 INSIDE STORY *Manhattan MTL 1007* ... 61 2
7 May 94 SLAVE TO THE RHYTHM (re-mix) *Zance ZANG 50CD1* ... 28 2
25 Nov 00 PULL UP TO THE BUMPER (re-recording) *Club Tools 0120375 CLU* [1] ... 60 1

[1] Grace Jones vs Funkstar De Luxe

'La Vie En Rose' was listed only from 1 Feb 1986.

30 June 1973	7 July 1973	14 July 1973	21 July 1973
UK No.1 SINGLES			
SKWEEZE ME PLEEZE ME Slade	SKWEEZE ME PLEEZE ME Slade	SKWEEZE ME PLEEZE ME Slade	WELCOME HOME Peters and Lee
UK No.1 ALBUMS			
THAT'LL BE THE DAY Various	THAT'LL BE THE DAY Various	THAT'LL BE THE DAY Various	THAT'LL BE THE DAY Various

Hannah JONES *US, female vocalist (2 Singles: 9 Weeks)*

14 Sep 91 **BRIDGE OVER TROUBLED WATER** *Dance Pool 6565467*..........21 8
30 Jan 93 **KEEP IT ON** *TMRC CDTMRC 7*..........67 1

Howard JONES (301 Top 500)

Accomplished singer / songwriter, b. John Howard Jones, 23 Feb 1955, Southampton, UK, who was a regular chart visitor in the mid-1980s with his brand of synth-based pop. Jones, who was equally popular in the US, appeared at Live Aid (6 Albums: 122 Weeks, 14 Singles: 103 Weeks)

17 Sep 83 ● **NEW SONG** (re) *WEA HOW 1*..........3 15
26 Nov 83 ● **WHAT IS LOVE** *WEA HOW 2*..........2 15
18 Feb 84 **HIDE AND SEEK** *WEA HOW 3*..........12 9
17 Mar 84 ★ HUMAN'S LIB *WEA WX 1* ■..........1 57
26 May 84 ● **PEARL IN THE SHELL** *WEA HOW 4*..........7 10
11 Aug 84 ● **LIKE TO GET TO KNOW YOU WELL** *WEA HOW 5*..........4 12
8 Dec 84 THE 12" ALBUM *WEA WX 14*..........15 33
9 Feb 85 ● **THINGS CAN ONLY GET BETTER** *WEA HOW 6*..........6 8
23 Mar 85 ● DREAM INTO ACTION *WEA WX 15*..........2 25
20 Apr 85 ● **LOOK MAMA** *WEA HOW 7*..........10 6
29 Jun 85 **LIFE IN ONE DAY** *WEA HOW 8*..........14 7
15 Mar 86 **NO ONE IS TO BLAME** *WEA HOW 9*..........16 7
4 Oct 86 **ALL I WANT** *WEA HOW 10*..........35 4
25 Oct 86 ● ONE TO ONE *WEA WX 68*..........10 4
29 Nov 86 **YOU KNOW I LOVE YOU ... DON'T YOU?** *WEA HOW 11*..........43 3
21 Mar 87 **LITTLE BIT OF SNOW** *WEA HOW 12*..........70 1
4 Mar 89 **EVERLASTING LOVE** *WEA HOW 13*..........62 3
1 Apr 89 CROSS THAT LINE *WEA WX 225*..........64 1
11 Apr 92 **LIFT ME UP** *East West HOW 15*..........52 3
5 Jun 93 THE BEST OF HOWARD JONES *East West 4509927012*..........36 2

Jack JONES *US, male vocalist (6 Albums: 70 Weeks)*

29 Apr 72 ● A SONG FOR YOU *RCA Victor SF 8228*..........9 6
3 Jun 72 ● BREAD WINNERS *RCA Victor SF 8280*..........7 36
7 Apr 73 ● TOGETHER *RCA Victor SF 8342*..........8 10
23 Feb 74 ● HARBOUR *RCA Victor APLI 0408*..........10 5
19 Feb 77 THE FULL LIFE *RCA Victor PL 12067*..........41 5
21 May 77 ● ALL TO YOURSELF *RCA TVL 2*..........10 8

Janie JONES *UK, female vocalist – Marion Mitchell*

27 Jan 66 **WITCHES BREW** *HMV POP 1495*..........46 3

Jimmy JONES *US, male vocalist (5 Singles: 47 Weeks)*

17 Mar 60 ● **HANDY MAN** (re) *MGM 1051* $..........3 24
16 Jun 60 ★ **GOOD TIMIN'** *MGM 1078* $..........1 15
8 Sep 60 **I JUST GO FOR YOU** *MGM 1091*..........35 4
17 Nov 60 **READY FOR LOVE** *MGM 1103*..........46 1
30 Mar 61 **I TOLD YOU SO** *MGM 1123*..........33 3

Juggy JONES *US, male multi-instrumentalist – Henry Murray*

7 Feb 76 **INSIDE AMERICA** *Contempo CS 2080*..........39 4

Lavinia JONES *South Africa, female vocalist*

18 Feb 95 **SING IT TO YOU (DEE-DOOB-DEE-DOO)** *Virgin International DINDG 142*..........45 2

Norah JONES (423 Top 500)

The most successful new jazz artist in the rock era, b. 30 Mar 1979, New York, US, is the daughter of Ravi Shankar. In 2003, the vocalist / pianist received a record-equalling five Grammy awards and the International Breakthrough Artist award at the BRITs and was a World Music Award-winner in 2004 (2 Albums: 164 Weeks, 4 Singles: 6 Weeks)

11 May 02 ★ COME AWAY WITH ME *Parlophone 5386092* ▲..........1 128
25 May 02 **DON'T KNOW WHY** *Parlophone CDCL 836*..........59 1
17 Aug 02 **FEELIN' THE SAME WAY** *Parlophone CDCL 838*..........72 1
23 Aug 03 **DON'T KNOW WHY** (re-issue) / **I'LL BE YOUR BABY TONIGHT** *Parlophone CDCL 848*..........67 1
21 Feb 04 ★ FEELS LIKE HOME *Blue Note 5983660* ■ ▲..........1 36
10 Apr 04 **SUNRISE** *Blue Note CDCL 853*..........30 3

Oran 'Juice' JONES *US, male vocalist*

15 Nov 86 ● **THE RAIN** *Def Jam A 7303*..........4 14

Paul JONES (see also The BLUES BAND; MANFRED MANN)

UK, male vocalist – Paul Pond (4 Singles: 34 Weeks)

6 Oct 66 ● **HIGH TIME** *HMV POP 1554*..........4 15
19 Jan 67 ● **I'VE BEEN A BAD, BAD BOY** *HMV POP 1576*..........5 9
23 Aug 67 **THINKIN' AIN'T FOR ME** (re) *HMV POP 1602*..........32 8
5 Feb 69 **AQUARIUS** *Columbia DB 8514*..........45 2

Quincy JONES *US, male producer / keyboard player (3 Albums: 41 Weeks, 8 Singles: 42 Weeks)*

29 Jul 78 **STUFF LIKE THAT** *A&M AMS 7367*..........34 9
11 Apr 81 **AI NO CORRIDA (I-NO-KO-REE-DA)** *A&M AMS 8109* [1]..........14 10
18 Apr 81 THE DUDE *A&M AMLK 63721*..........19 25
20 Jun 81 **RAZZAMATAZZ** *A&M AMS 8140*..........11 9
5 Sep 81 **BETCHA' WOULDN'T HURT ME** *A&M AMS 8157*..........52 3
20 Mar 82 THE BEST *A&M AMLH 68542*..........41 4
13 Jan 90 **I'LL BE GOOD TO YOU** *Qwest W 2697* [2]..........21 7
20 Jan 90 BACK ON THE BLOCK *Qwest WX 313*..........26 12
31 Mar 90 **SECRET GARDEN** *Qwest W 9992* [3]..........67 1
14 Sep 96 **STOMP** *Qwest W 0372CD* [4]..........28 2
1 Aug 98 **SOUL BOSSA NOVA** *Manifesto FESCD 48* [5]..........47 1

[1] Quincy Jones featuring Dune [2] Quincy Jones featuring Ray Charles and Chaka Khan [3] Quincy Jones featuring Al B Sure!, James Ingram, El DeBarge and Barry White [4] Quincy Jones featuring Melle Mel, Coolio, Yo-Yo, Shaquille O'Neal, The Luniz [5] Cool, the Fab and the Groovy present Quincy Jones

Uncredited vocals on 'Stuff Like That' were by Ashford and Simpson and Chaka Khan, and on 'Razzamatazz' and 'Betcha' Wouldn't Hurt Me' by Patti Austin.

Rickie Lee JONES

US, female vocalist / guitarist (5 Albums: 39 Weeks, 1 Single: 9 Weeks)

16 Jun 79 RICKIE LEE JONES *Warner Bros. K 56628*..........18 19
23 Jun 79 **CHUCK E'S IN LOVE** *Warner Bros. K 17390*..........18 9
8 Aug 81 PIRATES *Warner Bros. K 56816*..........37 11
2 Jul 83 GIRL AT HER VOLCANO *Warner Bros. 9238051*..........51 3
13 Oct 84 THE MAGAZINE *Warner Bros. 925117*..........40 4
7 Oct 89 FLYING COWBOYS *Geffen WX 309*..........50 2

Sonny JONES featuring Tara CHASE

Germany, male vocalist and Canada, female rapper

7 Oct 00 **FOLLOW YOU FOLLOW ME** *Logic 74321772892*..........42 2

Tammy JONES *UK, female vocalist*

26 Apr 75 ● **LET ME TRY AGAIN** *Epic EPC 3211*..........5 10
12 Jul 75 LET ME TRY AGAIN *Epic EPC 80853*..........38 5

Tom JONES (25 Top 500)

Unmistakable entertainer who has been an international headliner for five decades, b. Thomas Woodward, 7 Jun 1940, South Wales. Despite the failure of his first two Joe Meek-produced singles, the Welsh wonder, re-named after the popular 1963 film, became one of world's most popular singers, with hits in the pop, country, R&B and easy listening fields. The Vegas veteran, who hosted his own very successful late-1960s TV series, has had hits on 10 labels. This 60-something sex symbol, who was the top British solo singer of the 1960s on both sides of Atlantic, had his best-selling album in 1999 with 'Reload' and received an Outstanding Contribution to British Music BRIT Award in 2003. He was knighted in 2006. Best-selling single: 'Green, Green Grass of Home' 1,205,000 (29 Albums: 522 Weeks, 43 Singles: 394 Weeks)

11 Feb 65 ★ **IT'S NOT UNUSUAL** *Decca F 12062*..........1 14
6 May 65 **ONCE UPON A TIME** *Decca F 12121*..........32 4
5 Jun 65 ALONG CAME JONES *Decca LK 6693*..........11 5

28 July 1973	4 August 1973	11 August 1973	18 August 1973
I'M THE LEADER OF THE GANG (I AM!) Gary Glitter	I'M THE LEADER OF THE GANG (I AM!) Gary Glitter	I'M THE LEADER OF THE GANG (I AM!) Gary Glitter	I'M THE LEADER OF THE GANG (I AM!) Gary Glitter
THAT'LL BE THE DAY Various	THAT'LL BE THE DAY Various	THAT'LL BE THE DAY Various	WE CAN MAKE IT Peters and Lee

KEY UK No.1 ★ UK Top 10 ● Still on chart + UK entry at No.1 ■ US No.1 ▲ UK million seller £ US million seller $
Singles re-entries are listed as (re), (2re), (3re)… which signifies that the hit re-entered the chart once, twice or three times…
Peak Position / Weeks

8 Jul 65 **WITH THESE HANDS** *Decca F 12191* 13 11
12 Aug 65 **WHAT'S NEW PUSSYCAT?** *Decca F 12203* 11 10
13 Jan 66 **THUNDERBALL** *Decca F 12292* 35 4
19 May 66 **ONCE THERE WAS A TIME / NOT RESPONSIBLE** *Decca F 12390* 18 9
18 Aug 66 **THIS AND THAT** *Decca F 12461* 44 3
8 Oct 66 FROM THE HEART *Decca LK 4814* 23 8
10 Nov 66 ★ **GREEN, GREEN GRASS OF HOME** *Decca F 22511* £ 1 22
16 Feb 67 ● **DETROIT CITY** *Decca F 22555* 8 10
8 Apr 67 ● GREEN GREEN GRASS OF HOME *Decca SKL 4855* 3 49
13 Apr 67 ● **FUNNY FAMILIAR FORGOTTEN FEELINGS** *Decca F 12599* 7 15
24 Jun 67 ● LIVE AT THE TALK OF THE TOWN *Decca SKL 4874* 6 90
26 Jul 67 ● **I'LL NEVER FALL IN LOVE AGAIN** *Decca F 12639* $ 2 25
22 Nov 67 ● **I'M COMING HOME** *Decca F 12693* 2 16
30 Dec 67 ● 13 SMASH HITS *Decca SKL 4909* 5 49
28 Feb 68 ● **DELILAH** *Decca F 12747* 2 17
17 Jul 68 ● **HELP YOURSELF** *Decca F 12812* 5 26
27 Jul 68 ★ DELILAH *Decca SKL 4946* 1 29
27 Nov 68 **A MINUTE OF YOUR TIME** *Decca F 12854* 14 15
21 Dec 68 ● HELP YOURSELF *Decca SKL 4982* 4 9
14 May 69 ● **LOVE ME TONIGHT** *Decca F 12924* 9 12
28 Jun 69 ● THIS IS TOM JONES *Decca SKL 5007* 2 20
15 Nov 69 ● TOM JONES LIVE IN LAS VEGAS *Decca SKL 5032* 2 45
13 Dec 69 ● **WITHOUT LOVE** (re) *Decca F 12990* $ 10 12
18 Apr 70 ● **DAUGHTER OF DARKNESS** *Decca F 13013* 5 15
25 Apr 70 ● TOM *Decca SKL 5045* 4 18
15 Aug 70 **I (WHO HAVE NOTHING)** (re) *Decca F 13061* 16 11
14 Nov 70 ● I WHO HAVE NOTHING *Decca SKL 5072* 10 10
16 Jan 71 **SHE'S A LADY** (re) *Decca F 13113* $ 13 10
29 May 71 ● SHE'S A LADY *Decca SKL 5089* 9 7
5 Jun 71 **PUPPET MAN** (re) *Decca F 13183* 49 2
23 Oct 71 ● **TILL** *Decca F 13236* 2 15
27 Nov 71 LIVE AT CAESAR'S PALACE *Decca 1/11/2* 27 5
1 Apr 72 ● **THE YOUNG NEW MEXICAN PUPPETEER** *Decca F 13298* 6 12
24 Jun 72 CLOSE UP *Decca SKL 5132* 17 4
14 Apr 73 **LETTER TO LUCILLE** *Decca F 13393* 31 8
23 Jun 73 THE BODY AND SOUL OF TOM JONES *Decca SKL 5162* 31 1
5 Jan 74 GREATEST HITS *Decca SKL 5176* 15 13
7 Sep 74 **SOMETHING 'BOUT YOU BABY I LIKE** *Decca F 13550* 36 5
22 Mar 75 ★ 20 GREATEST HITS *Decca TJD 1/11/2* ■ 1 21
16 Apr 77 **SAY YOU'LL STAY UNTIL TOMORROW** *EMI 2583* 40 3
7 Oct 78 I'M COMING HOME *Lotus WH 5001* 12 9
18 Apr 87 ● **A BOY FROM NOWHERE** *Epic OLE 1* 2 12
16 May 87 THE GREATEST HITS *Telstar STAR 2296* 16 12
30 May 87 **IT'S NOT UNUSUAL** (re-issue) *Decca F 103* 17 8
2 Jan 88 **I WAS BORN TO BE ME** *Epic OLE 4* 61 1
29 Oct 88 ● **KISS** *China CHINA 11* [1] 5 7
29 Apr 89 **MOVE CLOSER** *Jive JIVE 203* 49 3
13 May 89 AT THIS MOMENT *Jive TOMTV 1* 34 3
8 Jul 89 AFTER DARK *Stylus SMR 978* 46 4
26 Jan 91 **COULDN'T SAY GOODBYE** *Dover ROJ 10* 51 2
16 Mar 91 **CARRYING A TORCH** *Dover ROJ 12* 57 2
6 Apr 91 CARRYING A TORCH *Dover ADD 20* 44 4
27 Jun 92 ● THE COMPLETE TOM JONES *The Hit Label 8442862* 8 6
4 Jul 92 **DELILAH** (re-issue) *The Hit Label TOM 10* 68 2
6 Feb 93 **ALL YOU NEED IS LOVE** *Childline CHILDCD 93* 19 4
5 Nov 94 **IF I ONLY KNEW** *ZTT ZANG 59CD* 11 9
26 Nov 94 THE LEAD AND HOW TO SWING IT *ZTT 6544924982* 55 1
14 Nov 98 THE ULTIMATE HITS COLLECTION *PolyGram TV 8449012* 26 6
25 Sep 99 ● **BURNING DOWN THE HOUSE** *Gut CDGUT 26* [2] 7 7
9 Oct 99 ★ RELOAD *Gut GUTCD 009* ■ 1 65
18 Dec 99 **BABY, IT'S COLD OUTSIDE** *Gut CDGUT 29* [3] 17 7
18 Mar 00 ● **MAMA TOLD ME NOT TO COME** *Gut CDGUT 031* [4] 4 7
20 May 00 ● **SEX BOMB** *Gut CDGUT 33* [5] 3 10
18 Nov 00 **YOU NEED LOVE LIKE I DO** *GUT CDGUT 36* [6] 24 3
9 Nov 02 **TOM JONES INTERNATIONAL** *V2 VVR 5021083* 31 2
16 Nov 02 MR. JONES *V2 VVR 1021072* 36 2
1 Mar 03 ● GREATEST HITS *Universal TV 8828632* 2 14
8 Mar 03 **BLACK BETTY / I WHO HAVE NOTHING** (re-issue) *V2 VVR 5021763* 50 2
9 Oct 04 ● TOM JONES & JOOLS HOLLAND *Radar 004CD* [1] 5 13

[1] Art of Noise featuring Tom Jones [2] Tom Jones and The Cardigans [3] Tom Jones and Cerys Matthews [4] Tom Jones and Stereophonics [5] Tom Jones and Mousse T [6] Tom Jones and Heather Small [1] Tom Jones & Jools Holland

The two Greatest Hits albums, and the album entitled The Greatest Hits, are all different.

JONESTOWN *US, male vocal duo*

13 Jun 98 **SWEET THANG** *Universal UMD 70376* 49 1

Janis JOPLIN
US, female vocalist, b. 19 Jan 1943, d. 4 Oct 1970 (3 Albums: 14 Weeks)

13 Mar 71 PEARL *CBS 64188* ▲ 20 4
22 Jul 72 JANIS JOPLIN IN CONCERT *CBS 67241* 30 6
29 Aug 98 THE ULTIMATE COLLECTION *Columbia SONYTV 52CD* 26 4

Alison JORDAN *UK, female vocalist*

9 May 92 **BOY FROM NEW YORK CITY** *Arista 74321100427* 23 4

Dick JORDAN *UK, male vocalist (2 Singles: 4 Weeks)*

17 Mar 60 **HALLELUJAH, I LOVE HER SO** *Oriole CB 1534* 47 1
9 Jun 60 **LITTLE CHRISTINE** *Oriole CB 1548* 39 3

Montell JORDAN
US, male vocalist (2 Albums: 3 Weeks, 5 Singles: 21 Weeks)

13 May 95 **THIS IS HOW WE DO IT** *Def Jam DEFCD 07* ▲ $ 11 8
24 Jun 95 THIS IS HOW WE DO IT *RAL 5271792* 53 2
2 Sep 95 **SOMETHIN' 4 DA HONEYZ** *Def Jam DEFCD 10* 15 4
14 Sep 96 MORE … *Def Jam 5331912* 66 1
19 Oct 96 **I LIKE** *Def Jam DEFCD 19* [1] 24 3
23 May 98 **LET'S RIDE** *Def Jam 5686912* [2] $ 25 2
8 Apr 00 **GET IT ON TONITE** *Def Soul 5627222* 15 4

[1] Montell Jordan featuring Slick Rick [2] Montell Jordan featuring Master P and Silkk the Shocker

Ronny JORDAN
UK, male guitarist – Ronnie Simpson (3 Albums: 7 Weeks, 4 Singles: 7 Weeks)

1 Feb 92 **SO WHAT!** *Antilles ANN 14* 32 4
7 Mar 92 THE ANTIDOTE *Island CID 9988* 52 4
25 Sep 93 **UNDER YOUR SPELL** *Island CID 565* 72 1
9 Oct 93 THE QUIET REVOLUTION *Island CID 8009* 49 2
15 Jan 94 **TINSEL TOWN** *Island CID 566* 64 1
28 May 94 **COME WITH ME** *Island CID 584* 63 1
3 Sep 94 BAD BROTHERS *Island IMCD 8024* [1] 58 1

[1] Ronny Jordan meets DJ Krush

JORIO *US, male producer – Fred Jorio*

24 Feb 01 **REMEMBER ME** *Wonderboy WBOYD 021* 54 1

David JOSEPH *UK, male vocalist (4 Singles: 21 Weeks)*

26 Feb 83 **YOU CAN'T HIDE (YOUR LOVE FROM ME)** *Island IS 101* 13 9
28 May 83 **LET'S LIVE IT UP (NITE PEOPLE)** *Island IS 116* 26 5
18 Feb 84 **JOYS OF LIFE** *Island IS 153* 61 2
31 May 86 **EXPANSIONS '86 (EXPAND YOUR MIND)** *Fourth & Broadway BRW 48* [1] 58 5

[1] Chris Paul featuring David Joseph

	25 August 1973	1 September 1973	8 September 1973	15 September 1973
UK No.1 SINGLES	YOUNG LOVE Donny Osmond	YOUNG LOVE Donny Osmond	YOUNG LOVE Donny Osmond	YOUNG LOVE Donny Osmond
UK No.1 ALBUMS	WE CAN MAKE IT Peters and Lee	SING IT AGAIN ROD Rod Stewart	SING IT AGAIN ROD Rod Stewart	SING IT AGAIN ROD Rod Stewart

Mark JOSEPH

UK, male vocalist – Mark Joseph Muzsnyai (4 Singles: 5 Weeks)

1 Mar 03 **GET THROUGH** *Mark Joseph MJR 003* 38 1
30 Aug 03 **FLY** *14th Floor MJM 010* 28 1
27 Mar 04 **BRINGING BACK THOSE MEMORIES** *14th Floor MJM 02CD* 34 1
26 Feb 05 **LADY LADY** *14th Floor MJM 05CD2* 36 2

Martyn JOSEPH *UK, male vocalist (4 Singles: 10 Weeks)*

20 Jun 92 **DOLPHINS MAKE ME CRY** *Epic 6581347* 34 4
12 Sep 92 **WORKING MOTHER** *Epic 6582937* 65 1
9 Jan 93 **PLEASE SIR** *Epic 6588552* 45 3
3 Jun 95 **TALK ABOUT IT IN THE MORNING** *Epic 6613342* 43 2

JOURNEY *US, male vocal (Steve Perry) / instrumental group (4 Albums: 30 Weeks, 2 Singles: 9 Weeks)*

27 Feb 82 **DON'T STOP BELIEVIN'** *CBS A 1728* 62 4
20 Mar 82 ESCAPE *CBS 85138* ▲ 32 16
11 Sep 82 **WHO'S CRYING NOW** *CBS A 2725* 46 5
19 Feb 83 ● FRONTIERS *CBS 25261* 6 8
6 Aug 83 EVOLUTION *CBS 32342* 100 1
24 May 86 RAISED ON RADIO *CBS 26902* 22 5

JOY DIVISION (see also NEW ORDER)

UK, male vocal (Ian Curtis, b. 15 Jul 1956, d. 18 May 1980) / instrumental group (6 Albums: 33 Weeks, 3 Singles: 24 Weeks)

28 Jun 80 **LOVE WILL TEAR US APART** (re) *Factory FAC 23* 13 16
26 Jul 80 ● CLOSER *Factory FACT 25* 6 8
30 Aug 80 UNKNOWN PLEASURES *Factory FACT 10* 71 1
17 Oct 81 ● STILL *Factory FACT 40* 5 12
18 Jun 88 **ATMOSPHERE** *Factory FAC 2137* 34 5
23 Jul 88 ● 1977-1980 SUBSTANCE *Factory FAC 250* 7 8
17 Jun 95 **LOVE WILL TEAR US APART** (re-mix) *London YOJCD 1* 19 3
1 Jul 95 PERMANENT – 1995 *London 8286242* 16 3
7 Feb 98 HEART AND SOUL *London 8289682* 70 1

'Love Will Tear Us Apart' re-entered and peaked at No.19 in Oct 1983.

Ruth JOY *UK, female vocalist – Ann Saunderson (3 Singles: 4 Weeks)*

26 Aug 89 **DON'T PUSH IT** *MCA RJOY 1* 66 2
22 Feb 92 **FEEL** *MCA MCS 1574* 67 1
14 Nov 92 **WALKING ON SUNSHINE** *Network NWK 55* [1] 71 1

[1] Krush featuring Ruth Joy

The JOY STRINGS

UK, male / female vocal / instrumental group (2 Singles: 11 Weeks)

27 Feb 64 **IT'S AN OPEN SECRET** *Regal-Zonophone RZ 501* 32 7
17 Dec 64 **A STARRY NIGHT** *Regal-Zonophone RZ 504* 34 4

JOY ZIPPER

US, male / female vocal / instrumental duo (2 Singles: 2 Weeks)

24 Apr 04 **BABY YOU SHOULD KNOW** *13 Amp / Vertigo 9866235* 59 1
20 Aug 05 **1** *Vertigo 9872947* 73 1

JOYRIDER *UK, male vocal / instrumental group (2 Singles: 4 Weeks)*

27 Jul 96 **RUSH HOUR** *Paradox PDOXD 012* 22 3
28 Sep 96 **ALL GONE AWAY** *A&M 5819552* 54 1

JUDAS PRIEST *UK, male vocal (Rob Halford) / instrumental group (14 Albums: 80 Weeks, 13 Singles: 51 Weeks)*

14 May 77 SIN AFTER SIN *CBS 82008* 23 6
25 Feb 78 STAINED CLASS *CBS 82430* 27 5
11 Nov 78 KILLING MACHINE *CBS 83135* 32 9
20 Jan 79 **TAKE ON THE WORLD** *CBS 6915* 14 10
12 May 79 **EVENING STAR** *CBS 7312* 53 4
6 Oct 79 ● UNLEASHED IN THE EAST *CBS 83852* 10 8
29 Mar 80 **LIVING AFTER MIDNIGHT** *CBS 8379* 12 7
19 Apr 80 ● BRITISH STEEL *CBS 84160* 4 17
7 Jun 80 **BREAKING THE LAW** *CBS 8644* 12 6
23 Aug 80 **UNITED** *CBS 8897* 26 8
21 Feb 81 **DON'T GO** *CBS 9520* 51 3
7 Mar 81 POINT OF ENTRY *CBS 84834* 14 5
25 Apr 81 **HOT ROCKIN'** *CBS A 1153* 60 3
17 Jul 82 SCREAMING FOR VENGEANCE *CBS 85941* 11 9
21 Aug 82 **YOU'VE GOT ANOTHER THING COMIN'** *CBS A 2611* 66 2
21 Jan 84 **FREEWHEEL BURNIN'** *CBS A 4054* 42 3
28 Jan 84 DEFENDERS OF THE FAITH *CBS 25713* 19 5
19 Apr 86 TURBO *CBS 26641* 33 4
13 Jun 87 PRIEST LIVE *CBS 450 6391* 47 2
23 Apr 88 **JOHNNY B GOODE** *Atlantic A 9114* 64 2
28 May 88 RAM IT DOWN *CBS 461108 1* 24 5
15 Sep 90 **PAINKILLER** *CBS 656273 7* 74 1
22 Sep 90 PAINKILLER *CBS 4672901* 26 2
23 Mar 91 **A TOUCH OF EVIL** *Columbia 6565897* 58 1
24 Apr 93 **NIGHT CRAWLER** *Columbia 6590972* 63 1
8 May 93 METAL WORKS 73-93 *Columbia 4730502* 37 1
12 Mar 05 ANGEL OF RETRIBUTION *Sony Music 5193003* 39 2

JUDGE DREAD *UK, male vocalist – Alex Hughes, b. 1945, d. 13 Mar 1998 (2 Albums: 14 Weeks, 11 Singles: 95 Weeks)*

26 Aug 72 **BIG SIX** *Big Shot BI 608* 11 27
9 Dec 72 ● **BIG SEVEN** *Big Shot BI 613* 8 18
21 Apr 73 **BIG EIGHT** *Big Shot BI 619* 14 10
5 Jul 75 ● **JE T'AIME (MOI NON PLUS)** *Cactus CT 65* 9 9
27 Sep 75 **BIG TEN** *Cactus CT 77* 14 7
6 Dec 75 BEDTIME STORIES *Cactus CTLP 113* 26 12
6 Dec 75 **CHRISTMAS IN DREADLAND / COME OUTSIDE** *Cactus CT 80* ..14 7
8 May 76 **THE WINKLE MAN** *Cactus CT 90* 35 4
28 Aug 76 **Y VIVA SUSPENDERS** *Cactus CT 99* 27 4
2 Apr 77 **5TH ANNIVERSARY (EP)** *Cactus CT 98* 31 4
14 Jan 78 **UP WITH THE COCK / BIG PUNK** *Cactus CT 110* 49 1
16 Dec 78 **HOKEY COKEY / JINGLE BELLS** *EMI 2881* 59 4
7 Mar 81 40 BIG ONES *Creole BIG 1* 51 2

'Y Viva Suspenders' was listed, additionally, with 'Confessions of a Bouncer' in its second week on the chart. Tracks on 5th Anniversary (EP): Jamaica Jerk (Off) / Bring Back the Skins / End of the World / Big Everything.

JUICE *Denmark, female vocal trio (2 Singles: 3 Weeks)*

18 Apr 98 **BEST DAYS** *Chrysalis CDCHS 5081* 28 2
22 Aug 98 **I'LL COME RUNNIN'** *Chrysalis CDCHS 5090* 48 1

JUICY *US, male / female vocal duo*

22 Feb 86 **SUGAR FREE** *Epic A 6917* 45 5

JUICY LUCY

UK, male vocal / instrumental group (2 Albums: 5 Weeks, 2 Singles: 17 Weeks)

7 Mar 70 **WHO DO YOU LOVE** *Vertigo V 1* 14 12
18 Apr 70 JUICY LUCY *Vertigo VO 2* 41 4
10 Oct 70 **PRETTY WOMAN** (re) *Vertigo 6059 015* 44 5
21 Nov 70 LIE BACK AND ENJOY IT *Vertigo 6360 014* 53 1

Gary JULES *US, male vocalist*

27 Dec 03 ★ **MAD WORLD**
Adventures in Music / Sanctuary SANXD 250 [1] ■ 1 15
31 Jan 04 TRADING SNAKEOIL FOR WOLFTICKETS
Adventures in Music / Sanctuary SANDP 252 ......12 3

[1] Michael Andrews featuring Gary Jules

Thomas JULES-STOCK *UK, male vocalist (2 Singles: 4 Weeks)*

15 Aug 98 **DIDN'T I TELL YOU TRUE** *Mercury MERCD 501* 59 1
4 Dec 04 **CARELESS WHISPER** *Inferno 2PSLCD 06* [1] 29 3

[1] 2Play featuring Thomas Jules & Jucxi D

22 September 1973	29 September 1973	6 October 1973	13 October 1973
ANGEL FINGERS (A TEEN BALLAD) Wizzard: Vocal backing: The Suedettes and The Bleach Boys	**EYE LEVEL (THEME FROM THE TV SERIES 'VAN DER VALK')** The Simon Park Orchestra	**EYE LEVEL (THEME FROM THE TV SERIES 'VAN DER VALK')** The Simon Park Orchestra	**EYE LEVEL (THEME FROM THE TV SERIES 'VAN DER VALK')** The Simon Park Orchestra
GOAT'S HEAD SOUP The Rolling Stones	**GOAT'S HEAD SOUP** The Rolling Stones	**SLADEST** Slade	**SLADEST** Slade

TOP 20 ALBUMS BY FEMALE ACTS

Based on the total number of weeks on the UK chart, here are the 20 best performing albums.

POS / ALBUM / ACT / WEEKS ON ALBUMS CHART

1. THE IMMACULATE COLLECTION Madonna – 213
2. TRACY CHAPMAN Tracy Chapman – 189
3. JAGGED LITTLE PILL Alanis Morissette – 172
4. LIKE A VIRGIN Madonna – 152
5. PRIVATE DANCER Tina Turner – 147
6. SIMPLY THE BEST Tina Turner – 141
7. COME ON OVER Shania Twain – 138
8. NO ANGEL Dido – 133
9. LOVE SONGS Barbra Streisand – 129
10. COME AWAY WITH ME Norah Jones – 128
11. MADONNA / THE FIRST ALBUM Madonna – 123
12. WHITNEY HOUSTON Whitney Houston – 119
13. RAY OF LIGHT Madonna – 116
14. FALLING INTO YOU Celine Dion – 113
15. THE COLOUR OF MY LOVE Celine Dion – 109

16=. SONGBIRD Eva Cassidy – 101
16=. WHITNEY Whitney Houston – 101
18. DIAMOND LIFE Sade – 99
19. OVER AND OVER Nana Mouskouri – 97
20. WATERMARK Enya – 92

Mariah Carey was a four-time winner at the 2005 Billboard Music Awards and also spent more weeks on the UK albums chart in 2005 than any other female performer, which contributed to her seventh position on the all-time list

TOP 20 FEMALE ACTS ON THE ALBUMS CHART

With all their albums taken into account, here are the top 20 females in the history of the charts.

POS / ACT / WEEKS ON ALBUMS CHART / (POSITION IN TOP 500 ALBUMS ACTS)

1. MADONNA – 1,038 (7)
2. DIANA ROSS – 743 (21)
3. BARBRA STREISAND – 537 (34)
4. TINA TURNER – 533 (36)
5. CELINE DION – 411 (54)
6. WHITNEY HOUSTON – 383 (61)
7. MARIAH CAREY – 355 (72)
8. KYLIE MINOGUE – 319 (80)
9. CHER – 310 (82)
10. SHIRLEY BASSEY – 294 (90)
11. KATE BUSH – 290 (94)
12. ENYA – 279 (102)
13. JANET JACKSON – 270 (108)
14. GLORIA ESTEFAN – 247 (119)
15. BRITNEY SPEARS – 234 (131)

16=. THE SUPREMES – 229 (136)
16=. TRACY CHAPMAN – 229 (137)
18. SHANIA TWAIN – 227 (142)
19. ELKIE BROOKS – 223 (148)
20. ALANIS MORISSETTE – 220 (151)

Madonna tops both our female albums lists, which is not surprising for a woman who has never had an album hit a peak position lower than No.6

THE OFFICIAL UK ALBUM CHART 50 YEARS

JULIA and COMPANY
US, male / female vocal group – leader Julia McGirt (2 Singles: 10 Weeks)

3 Mar 84	**BREAKIN' DOWN (SUGAR SAMBA)** *London LON 46*	15	8
23 Feb 85	**I'M SO HAPPY** *Next Plateau LON 61*	56	2

JULIET NEW *US, female vocalist*

23 Apr 05	**AVALON** *Virgin VUSDX 299*	24	3

JULIETTE & THE LICKS NEW *US, female actor / vocalist –*
Juliette Lewis and male vocal / instrumental group (2 Singles: 3 Weeks)

21 May 05	**YOU'RE SPEAKING MY LANGUAGE** *Hassle HOFF 003CDS*	35	2
1 Oct 05	**GOT LOVE TO KILL** *Hassle HOFF 005CDS*	56	1

JULUKA (see also Johnny CLEGG and SAVUKA)
UK / South Africa, male / female vocal / instrumental group

12 Feb 83	**SCATTERLINGS OF AFRICA** *Safari ZULU 1*	44	4
23 Jul 83	SCATTERLINGS *Safari SHAKA 1*	50	3

JUMP *UK, male instrumental group*

1 Mar 97	**FUNKATARIUM** *Heat Recordings HEATCD 005*	56	1

Wally JUMP Jr and The CRIMINAL ELEMENT
(see also Jack E MAKOSSA) *US, male producer / multi-instrumentalist – Arthur Baker (5 Singles: 19 Weeks)*

28 Feb 87	**TURN ME LOOSE** *London LON 126*	60	2
5 Sep 87	**PUT THE NEEDLE TO THE RECORD** *Cooltempo COOL 150* [1]	63	3
12 Dec 87	**TIGHTEN UP / I JUST CAN'T STOP DANCIN'** *Breakout USA 621*	24	7
19 Mar 88	**PRIVATE PARTY** *Breakout USA 624*	57	3
6 Oct 90	**EVERYBODY (RAP)** *Deconstruction PB 44701* [2]	30	4

[1] Criminal Element Orchestra [2] Criminal Element Orchestra and Wendell Williams

Rosemary JUNE *US, female vocalist*

23 Jan 59	**(I'LL BE WITH YOU) IN APPLE BLOSSOM TIME** *Pye International 7N 25005*	14	9

JUNGLE BOOK *US, male / female vocal group*

8 May 93	**THE JUNGLE BOOK GROOVE** *Hollywood HWCD 128*	14	8

The JUNGLE BOYS *UK, male celebrity vocal trio (2 Singles: 6 Weeks)*

20 Mar 04	**JUNGLE ROCK** *Bushtucker JUNGLE 001CD*	30	5
31 Jul 04	**IN THE SUMMERTIME** *MCS JUNGLE 002CD*	72	1

The JUNGLE BROTHERS *US, male rap duo – Nathaniel Hall*
and Michael Small (1 Album: 3 Weeks, 12 Singles: 40 Weeks)

22 Oct 88	**I'LL HOUSE YOU** *Gee Street GEE 003* [1]	22	5
18 Mar 89	**BLACK IS BLACK / STRAIGHT OUT OF THE JUNGLE** *Gee Street GEE 15*	72	1
3 Feb 90	DONE BY THE FORCES OF NATURE *Eternal WX 332*	41	3
31 Mar 90	**WHAT 'U' WAITIN' '4'** *Eternal W 9865*	35	5
21 Jul 90	**DOIN' OUR OWN DANG** *Eternal W 9754*	33	6
19 Jul 97	**BRAIN** *Gee Street GEE 5000388*	52	1
29 Nov 97	**JUNGLE BROTHER** (re) *Gee Street GEE 5000493*	18	5
11 Jul 98	**I'LL HOUSE YOU '98** (re-mix) *Gee Street FCD 338*	26	5
28 Nov 98	**BECAUSE I GOT IT LIKE THAT** *Gee Street GEE 5003593*	32	2
10 Jul 99	**V.I.P.** *Gee Street / V2 GEE 5007953*	33	3
6 Nov 99	**GET DOWN** *Gee Street / V2 GEE 5010153*	52	1
25 Mar 00	**FREAKIN' YOU** *Gee Street GEE 5008808*	70	1
7 Feb 04	**BREATHE, DON'T STOP** *Positiva / Incentive CDTIVS 201* [2]	21	5

[1] Richie Rich meets The Jungle Brothers [2] Mr On vs The Jungle Brothers

'Doin' Our Own Dang' features the uncredited De La Soul and Monie Love. 'Jungle Brother' reached its peak position on re-entering the chart in May 1998.

JUNGLE HIGH with BLUE PEARL *UK / Germany, male production / instrumental duo and UK / US, male / female vocal / instrumental group*

27 Nov 93	**FIRE OF LOVE** *Logic 74321170292*	71	1

JUNIOR *UK, male vocalist –*
Norman Giscombe (1 Album: 14 Weeks, 11 Singles: 57 Weeks)

24 Apr 82 ●	**MAMA USED TO SAY** *Mercury MER 98*	7	13
5 Jun 82	JI *Mercury MERS 3*	28	14
10 Jul 82	**TOO LATE** *Mercury MER 112*	20	9
25 Sep 82	**LET ME KNOW / I CAN'T HELP IT** *Mercury MER 116*	53	3
23 Apr 83	**COMMUNICATION BREAKDOWN** *Mercury MER 134*	57	3
8 Sep 84	**SOMEBODY** *London LON 50*	64	2
9 Feb 85	**DO YOU REALLY (WANT MY LOVE)** *London LON 60*	47	4
30 Nov 85	**OH LOUISE** *London LON 75*	74	3
4 Apr 87 ●	**ANOTHER STEP (CLOSER TO YOU)** *MCA KIM 5* [1]	6	11
25 Aug 90	**STEP OFF** *MCA MCA 1432* [2]	63	3
15 Aug 92	**THEN CAME YOU** *MCA MCS 1676* [2]	32	5
31 Oct 92	**ALL OVER THE WORLD** *MCA MCS 1691* [2]	74	1

[1] Kim Wilde and Junior [2] Junior Giscombe

JUNIOR JACK (see also ROOM 5 featuring Oliver CHEATHAM)
Italy, male producer – Vito Lucente (5 Singles: 20 Weeks)

16 Dec 00	**MY FEELING** *Defected DFECT 24CDS*	31	4
2 Mar 02	**THRILL ME** *VC Recordings VCRD 102*	29	3
27 Sep 03	**E SAMBA** *Defected DFTDO 76CDS*	34	3
14 Feb 04	**DA HYPE** *Defected DFTD 083CDS* [1]	25	4
3 Jul 04	**STUPIDISCO** *Defected DFTD 089CDS*	26	6

[1] Junior Jack featuring Robert Smith

JUNIOR M.A.F.I.A. *US, male / female rap ensemble (2 Singles: 2 Weeks)*

3 Feb 96	**I NEED YOU TONIGHT** *Big Beat A 8130CD* [1]	66	1
19 Oct 96	**GETTIN' MONEY** *Big Beat A 5674CD*	63	1

[1] Junior M.A.F.I.A. featuring Aaliyah

JUNIOR SENIOR *Denmark, male vocal / instrumental duo – Jesper Mortensen and Jeppe Laursen (1 Album: 3 Weeks, 2 Singles: 20 Weeks)*

8 Mar 03 ●	**MOVE YOU FEET** *Mercury 0198192*	3	17
22 Mar 03	D D DON'T STOP THE BEAT *Mercury FROG 0262CD*	29	3
9 Aug 03	**RHYTHM BANDITS** *Mercury 9810210*	22	3

JUNKIE XL
Holland, male producer – Tom Holkenborg (5 Singles: 19 Weeks)

22 Jul 00	**ZEROTONINE** *Manifesto FESCD 71*	63	1
22 Jun 02 ★	**A LITTLE LESS CONVERSATION** *RCA 74321943572* [1] ■	1	12
30 Nov 02	**OBSESSION** *Nebula NEBCD 029* [2]	56	1
7 Jun 03	**CATCH UP TO MY STEP** *Roadrunner RR 20209* [3]	63	1
7 May 05 ●	**A LITTLE LESS CONVERSATION** (re-issue) *RCA 82876666832* [1]	3	4

[1] Elvis vs JXL [2] Tiësto and Junkie XL [3] Junkie XL featuring Solomon Burke

JUNO REACTOR *UK / Germany, male production duo*

8 Feb 97	**JUNGLE HIGH** *Perfecto PERF 133CD*	45	1

JUPITER ACE featuring SHEENA NEW
UK, male producer and female vocalist

23 Jul 05	**1000 YEARS (JUST LEAVE ME NOW)** *Manifesto 9871706*	51	2

JURASSIC 5 *US, male rap group (3 Albums: 6 Weeks, 2 Singles: 4 Weeks)*

13 Jun 98	JURASSIC 5 *Pan PAN 015CD*	70	1
25 Jul 98	**JAYOU** *Pan PAN 018CD*	56	1
24 Oct 98	**CONCRETE SCHOOLYARD** *Pan PAN 020CD*	35	3
1 Jul 00	QUALITY CONTROL *Interscope 4907102*	23	3
19 Oct 02	POWER IN NUMBERS *Interscope 4934372*	46	2

20 October 1973	27 October 1973	3 November 1973	10 November 1973
EYE LEVEL (THEME FROM THE TV SERIES 'VAN DER VALK') The Simon Park Orchestra	DAYDREAMER / THE PUPPY SONG David Cassidy	DAYDREAMER / THE PUPPY SONG David Cassidy	DAYDREAMER / THE PUPPY SONG David Cassidy
SLADEST Slade	HELLO Status Quo	PINUPS David Bowie	PINUPS David Bowie

KEY
UK No.1 ★★ UK Top 10 ●● Still on chart ++ UK entry at No.1 ■■
US No.1 ▲▲ UK million seller £ US million seller $
Singles re-entries are listed as (re), (2re), (3re)... which signifies that the hit re-entered the chart once, twice or three times...
Peak Position / Weeks

Christopher JUST *Austria, male producer (2 Singles: 2 Weeks)*

13 Dec 97 **I'M A DISCO DANCER** *Slut Trax SLUT 001CD* ...72 1
6 Feb 99 **I'M A DISCO DANCER** (re-mix) *XL Recordings XLS 105CD* ...69 1

JUST 4 JOKES featuring MC RB
UK, male production duo and rapper

28 Sep 02 **JUMP UP** *Serious SERR 050CD* ...67 1

JUST LUIS *Spain, male vocalist – Luis Sierra Pizarro*

14 Oct 95 **AMERICAN PIE** (re) *Pro-Activ CDPTV 1* ...31 3

Jimmy JUSTICE *UK, male vocalist – James Little (3 Singles: 35 Weeks)*

29 Mar 62 ● **WHEN MY LITTLE GIRL IS SMILING** *Pye 7N 15421* ...9 13
14 Jun 62 ● **AIN'T THAT FUNNY** *Pye 7N 15443* ...8 11
23 Aug 62 **SPANISH HARLEM** *Pye 7N 15457* ...20 11

JUSTIFIED ANCIENTS OF MU MU
(see also The KLF; The TIMELORDS; 2K) *UK, male production duo*

9 Nov 91 ● **IT'S GRIM UP NORTH** (re) *KLF Communications JAMS 028* ...10 6

JUSTIN *UK, male vocalist – Justin Osuji (4 Singles: 13 Weeks)*

22 Aug 98 **THIS BOY** *Virgin STCDT 1* ...34 2
16 Jan 99 **OVER YOU** *Virgin STCDT 2* ...11 4
17 Jul 99 **IT'S ALL ABOUT YOU** *Innocent STCDT 3* ...34 3
22 Jan 00 **LET IT BE ME** *Innocent STCDTX 4* ...15 4

Bill JUSTIS *US, male alto saxophonist, b. 14 Oct 1926, d. 15 Jul 1982*

10 Jan 58 **RAUNCHY** (re) *London HLS 8517* ...11 8

Patrick JUVET *Switzerland, male vocalist (2 Singles: 19 Weeks)*

2 Sep 78 **GOT A FEELING** *Casablanca CAN 127* ...34 7
4 Nov 78 **I LOVE AMERICA** *Casablanca CAN 132* ...12 12

K

Frank K featuring Wiston OFFICE
Italy / US, male vocal / instrumental duo

26 Jan 91 **EVERYBODY LET'S SOMEBODY LOVE** *Urban URB 66* ...61 1

Leila K *Sweden, female rapper – Leila El Khalifi (4 Singles: 22 Weeks)*

25 Nov 89 ● **GOT TO GET** *Arista 112696* ...8 14
17 Mar 90 **ROK THE NATION** *Arista 112971* ...41 3
23 Jan 93 **OPEN SESAME** *Polydor PQCD 1* ...23 4
3 Jul 93 **CA PLANE POUR MOI** *Polydor PQCD 3* ...69 1

KC and The SUNSHINE BAND *US, male vocal (Harry Wayne Casey) / instrumental group (3 Albums: 17 Weeks, 14 Singles: 104 Weeks)*

17 Aug 74 ● **QUEEN OF CLUBS** *Jayboy BOY 88* ...7 12
23 Nov 74 **SOUND YOUR FUNKY HORN** *Jayboy BOY 83* ...17 9
29 Mar 75 **GET DOWN TONIGHT** *Jayboy BOY 93* ▲ $ ...21 9
2 Aug 75 ● **THAT'S THE WAY (I LIKE IT)** *Jayboy BOY 99* ▲ $ ...4 10
30 Aug 75 KC AND THE SUNSHINE BAND *Jayboy JSL 9* ...26 7
22 Nov 75 **I'M SO CRAZY ('BOUT YOU)** *Jayboy BOY 101* ...34 3
17 Jul 76 **(SHAKE, SHAKE, SHAKE) SHAKE YOUR BOOTY** *Jayboy BOY 110* ▲ $ ...22 8
11 Dec 76 **KEEP IT COMIN' LOVE** *Jayboy BOY 112* ...31 8
30 Apr 77 **I'M YOUR BOOGIE MAN** *TK XB 2167* ▲ $ ...41 4
6 May 78 **BOOGIE SHOES** *TK TKR 6025* ...34 5
22 Jul 78 **IT'S THE SAME OLD SONG** *TK TKR 6037* ...47 5
8 Dec 79 ● **PLEASE DON'T GO** *TK TKR 7558* ▲ ...3 12
1 Mar 80 ● GREATEST HITS *TK TKR 83385* ...10 6
16 Jul 83 ★ **GIVE IT UP** *Epic EPC A 3017* ...1 14
27 Aug 83 ALL IN A NIGHT'S WORK *Epic EPC 85847* ...46 4
24 Sep 83 **(YOU SAID) YOU'D GIMME SOME MORE** *Epic A 2760* ...41 3
11 May 91 **THAT'S THE WAY I LIKE IT** (re-mix) *Music Factory Dance M7FAC 2* ...59 2

K-CI & JOJO *US, male vocal duo – Cedric and Joel Hailey (2 Albums: 3 Weeks, 7 Singles: 29 Weeks)*

27 Jul 96 **HOW DO YOU WANT IT** *Death Row DRWCD 4* [1] ▲ $ ...17 4
28 Jun 97 LOVE ALWAYS *MCA MCD 11613* ...51 2
23 Aug 97 **YOU BRING ME UP** *MCA MCSTD 48057* ...21 2
18 Apr 98 ● **ALL MY LIFE** *MCA MCSTD 48076* ▲ ...8 11
19 Sep 98 **DON'T RUSH (TAKE LOVE SLOWLY)** *MCA MCSTD 48090* ...16 3
3 Jul 99 IT'S REAL *MCA MCD 11975* ...56 1
2 Oct 99 **TELL ME IT'S REAL** *MCA MCSTD 40211* ...40 2
23 Sep 00 **TELL ME IT'S REAL** (re-mix) *AM:PM CDAMPM 135* ...16 5
12 May 01 **CRAZY** *MCA MCSTD 40253* ...35 2

[1] 2Pac featuring K-Ci and JoJo

K CREATIVE *UK, male vocal / instrumental group*

7 Mar 92 **THREE TIMES A MAYBE** *Talkin Loud TLK 17* ...58 2

The listed flipside of 'Three Times a Maybe' was 'Feed the Feeling' by Perception.

Ernie K-DOE
US, male vocalist – Ernest Kador, b. 22 Feb 1936, d. 5 Jul 2001

11 May 61 **MOTHER-IN-LAW** *London HLU 9330* ▲ $ ...29 7

K-GEE *UK, male producer – Karl Gordon*

4 Nov 00 **I DON'T REALLY CARE** *Instant Karma KARMA 3CD* ...22 3

K.I.D. *Antilles, male / female vocal / instrumental group*

28 Feb 81 **DON'T STOP** *EMI 5143* ...49 4

K-KLASS *UK, male / female vocal (Bobbi Depasois) / instrumental group (1 Album: 1 Week, 7 Singles: 31 Weeks)*

4 May 91 **RHYTHM IS A MYSTERY** *Deconstruction CREED 11* [1] ...61 2
9 Nov 91 ● **RHYTHM IS A MYSTERY** (re-issue) *Deconstruction R 6302* [2] ...3 10
25 Apr 92 **SO RIGHT** *Deconstruction R 6309* ...20 5
7 Nov 92 **DON'T STOP** *Deconstruction R 6325* ...32 3
27 Nov 93 **LET ME SHOW YOU** *Deconstruction CDR 6367* ...13 7
28 May 94 **WHAT YOU'RE MISSING** *Deconstruction CDRS 6380* ...24 3
4 Jun 94 UNIVERSAL *Deconstruction CDPCSDX 149* ...73 1
1 Aug 98 **BURNIN'** *Parlophone CDK 2001* ...45 1

[1] K-Klass featuring Bobbie Depasois [2] K-Klass with vocals by Bobbie Depasois

The KLF (see also JUSTIFIED ANCIENTS OF MU MU; The TIMELORDS; 2K) *UK, male vocal / instrumental duo – Bill Drummond and Jimmy Cauty (1 Album: 46 Weeks, 5 Singles: 51 Weeks)*

11 Aug 90 ● **WHAT TIME IS LOVE? (LIVE AT TRANCENTRAL)** *KLF Communications KLF 004* [1] ...5 12

17 November 1973	24 November 1973	1 December 1973	8 December 1973
UK No.1 SINGLES			
I LOVE YOU LOVE ME LOVE Gary Glitter	I LOVE YOU LOVE ME LOVE Gary Glitter	I LOVE YOU LOVE ME LOVE Gary Glitter	I LOVE YOU LOVE ME LOVE Gary Glitter
UK No.1 ALBUMS			
PINUPS David Bowie	PINUPS David Bowie	PINUPS David Bowie	STRANDED Roxy Music

19 Jan 91 ★ 3:A.M. ETERNAL *KLF Communications KLF 005* [1] 1 11
16 Mar 91 ● THE WHITE ROOM *KLF Communications JAMSLP 6*..........3 46
4 May 91 ● LAST TRAIN TO TRANCENTRAL *KLF Communications KLF 008*..........2 9
7 Dec 91 ● JUSTIFIED AND ANCIENT *KLF Communications KLF 099* [2] ..2 12
7 Mar 92 ● AMERICA: WHAT TIME IS LOVE? (re-mix) *KLF Communications KLFUSA 004*..........4 7

[1] The KLF featuring the Children of the Revolution [2] The KLF – guest vocals: Tammy Wynette

KMC featuring DHANY *Italy, male production duo and female vocalist*

25 May 02 I FEEL SO FINE *Incentive CENT 39CDS*..........33 2

KP & ENVYI *US, female vocal / rap duo – Kia Philips and Susan Hedgepath*

13 Jun 98 SWING MY WAY *East West E 3849CD*..........14 4

KRS ONE
US, male rapper – Lawrence Parker (1 Album: 1 Week, 5 Singles: 8 Weeks)

18 May 96 RAPPAZ R N DAINJA *Jive JIVECD 396*..........47 1
8 Feb 97 WORD PERFECT *Jive JIVECD 418*..........70 1
26 Apr 97 STEP INTO A WORLD (RAPTURE'S DELIGHT) *Jive JIVECD 411*..........24 2
31 May 97 I GOT NEXT *Jive CHIP 179*..........58 1
20 Sep 97 HEARTBEAT / A FRIEND *Jive JIVECD 431*..........66 1
1 Nov 97 DIGITAL *ffrr FCD 316* [1] 13 3

[1] Goldie featuring KRS One

K7 *US, male vocal / rap group (1 Album: 3 Weeks, 3 Singles: 22 Weeks)*

11 Dec 93 ● COME BABY COME *Big Life BLRD 105*..........3 16
5 Feb 94 SWING BATTA SWING *Big Life BLRCD 27*..........27 3
2 Apr 94 HI DE HO *Big Life BLRD 108* [1] 17 5
25 Jun 94 ZUNGA ZENG *Big Life BLRD 111* [1] 63 1

[1] K7 and The Swing Kids

K3M *Italy, male / female vocal / instrumental duo*

21 Mar 92 LISTEN TO THE RHYTHM *PWL Continental PWL 214*..........71 1

K2 FAMILY *UK, male production / rap / vocal group*

27 Oct 01 BOUNCING FLOW *Relentless RELENT 22CD*..........27 3

K-WARREN featuring LEE-O *UK, male producer – Kevin Warren Williams and UK, vocalist – Leo Ihenacho*

5 May 01 COMING HOME *Go Beat GOBCD 41*..........32 2

KWS *UK, male vocal / instrumental group (7 Singles: 36 Weeks)*

25 Apr 92 ★ PLEASE DON'T GO / GAME BOY *Network NWK 46*..........1 16
22 Aug 92 ● ROCK YOUR BABY *Network NWK 54*..........8 7
12 Dec 92 HOLD BACK THE NIGHT *Network NWK 65* [1] 30 5
5 Jun 93 CAN'T GET ENOUGH OF YOUR LOVE *Network NWKCD 72*..........71 1
9 Apr 94 IT SEEMS TO HANG ON *X-clusive XCLU 006CD*..........58 1
2 Jul 94 AIN'T NOBODY (LOVES ME BETTER) *X-clusive XCLU 010CD* [2] 21 4
19 Nov 94 THE MORE I GET THE MORE I WANT *X-clusive XCLU 011CD* [3] 35 2

[1] KWS features guest vocal from The Trammps [2] KWS and Gwen Dickey [3] KWS featuring Teddy Pendergrass

'Game Boy' was listed only from 9 May 1992.

KACI
US, female vocalist – Kaci Battaglia (1 Album: 2 Weeks, 4 Singles: 23 Weeks)

10 Mar 01 PARADISE *Curb / London CUBC 61*..........11 9
28 Jul 01 TU AMOR *Curb / London CUBC 71*..........24 3
2 Feb 02 ● I THINK I LOVE YOU *Curb / London CUBC 076*..........10 10
16 Feb 02 PARADISE *Curb / London 927402192*..........47 2
9 Aug 03 I'M NOT ANYBODY'S GIRL *Curb / London CUBC 091*..........55 1

Joshua KADISON
US, male vocalist (1 Album: 4 Weeks, 4 Singles: 19 Weeks)

26 Feb 94 JESSIE (re) *SBK CDSBK 43*..........48 5
12 Nov 94 BEAUTIFUL IN MY EYES *SBK CDSBK 50*..........65 1
29 Apr 95 JESSIE (re-issue) *SBK CDSBK 53*..........15 10
27 May 95 PAINTED DESERT SERENADE *SBK SBKCD 22*..........45 4
12 Aug 95 BEAUTIFUL IN MY EYES (re-issue) *SBK CDSBK 55*..........37 3

KADOC *UK / Spain, male vocal / instrumental group (3 Singles: 11 Weeks)*

6 Apr 96 THE NIGHTTRAIN *Positiva CDTIV 26*..........14 8
17 Aug 96 YOU GOT TO BE THERE *Positiva CDTIV 58*..........45 1
23 Aug 97 ROCK THE BELLS *Manifesto FESCD 30*..........34 2

Bert KAEMPFERT and his Orchestra *Germany, orchestra – leader b. 16 Oct 1923, d. 21 Jun 1980 (10 Albums: 104 Weeks, 1 Single: 10 Weeks)*

23 Dec 65 BYE BYE BLUES *Polydor BM 56 504*..........24 10
5 Mar 66 ● BYE BYE BLUES *Polydor BM 84086*..........4 22
16 Apr 66 BEST OF BERT KAEMPFERT *Polydor 84012*..........27 1
28 May 66 SWINGING SAFARI *Polydor LPHM 46384*..........20 15
30 Jul 66 STRANGERS IN THE NIGHT *Polydor LPHM 84053*..........13 26
4 Feb 67 RELAXING SOUND OF BERT KAEMPFERT *Polydor 583501*..........33 3
18 Feb 67 BERT KAEMPFERT – BEST SELLER *Polydor 583551*..........25 18
29 Apr 67 HOLD ME *Polydor 184072*..........36 5
26 Aug 67 KAEMPFERT SPECIAL *Polydor 236207*..........24 5
19 Jun 71 ORANGE COLOURED SKY *Polydor 2310091*..........49 1
5 Jul 80 SOUNDS SENSATIONAL *Polydor POLTB 10*..........17 8

KAISER CHIEFS *UK, male vocal (Ricky Wilson) / instrumental group (1 Album: 42 Weeks, 6 Singles: 60 Weeks)*

29 May 04 OH MY GOD *Drowned in Sound DIS 03*..........66 1
13 Nov 04 I PREDICT A RIOT (re) *B-Unique BUN 088CD*..........22 6
5 Mar 05 ● OH MY GOD (2re) (re-issue) *B-Unique BUN 092CDX*..........6 12
19 Mar 05 ● EMPLOYMENT *B-Unique / Polydor BUN 093CDX*..........3 42+
28 May 05 ● EVERYDAY I LOVE YOU LESS AND LESS *B-Unique BUN 094CDX*..........10 18
3 Sep 05 ● I PREDICT A RIOT (re-issue) / SINK THAT SHIP *B-Unique BUN 96CDX*..........9 18+
19 Nov 05 MODERN WAY *B-Unique BUN 100CDX*..........11 5

KAJAGOOGOO *UK, male vocal (Chris Hamill aka Limahl) / instrumental group (2 Albums: 23 Weeks, 7 Singles: 50 Weeks)*

22 Jan 83 ★ TOO SHY *EMI 5359*..........1 13
2 Apr 83 ● OOH TO BE AH *EMI 5383*..........7 8
30 Apr 83 ● WHITE FEATHERS *EMI EMC 3433*..........5 20
4 Jun 83 HANG ON NOW *EMI 5394*..........13 7
17 Sep 83 ● BIG APPLE *EMI 5423*..........8 8
3 Mar 84 THE LION'S MOUTH *EMI 5449*..........25 7
5 May 84 TURN YOUR BACK ON ME *EMI 5646*..........47 4
26 May 84 ISLANDS *EMI KAJA 1*..........35 3
21 Sep 85 SHOULDN'T DO THAT *Parlophone R 6106* [1] 63 3

[1] Kaja

KALEEF *UK, male rap / vocal group (5 Singles: 12 Weeks)*

30 Mar 96 WALK LIKE A CHAMPION *Payday KACD 5* [1] 23 3
7 Dec 96 GOLDEN BROWN *Unity UNITY 010CD*..........22 4
14 Jun 97 TRIALS OF LIFE *Unity UNITY 012CD*..........75 1
11 Oct 97 I LIKE THE WAY (THE KISSING GAME) *Unity UNITY 015CD1*..........58 1
24 Jan 98 SANDS OF TIME *Unity UNITY 016CD*..........26 3

[1] Kaliphz featuring Prince Naseem

Preeya KALIDAS *UK, female vocalist*

13 Jul 02 SHAKALAKA BABY *Sony Classical 6726322*..........38 2

15 December 1973	22 December 1973	29 December 1973	5 January 1974
MERRY XMAS EVERYBODY Slade	MERRY XMAS EVERYBODY Slade	MERRY XMAS EVERYBODY Slade	MERRY XMAS EVERYBODY Slade
DREAMS ARE NOTHIN' MORE THAN WISHES David Cassidy	GOODBYE YELLOW BRICK ROAD Elton John	GOODBYE YELLOW BRICK ROAD Elton John	TALES FROM TOPOGRAPHIC OCEANS Yes

KEY UK No.1 ★ UK Top 10 ● Still on chart + UK entry at No.1 ■ US No.1 ▲ UK million seller £ US million seller $
Singles re-entries are listed as (re), (2re), (3re)... which signifies that the hit re-entered the chart once, twice or three times...
Peak Position / Weeks

The KALIN TWINS
US, male vocal duo – Herb and Hal Kalin, b. 16 Feb 1934, d. 24 Aug 2005

18 Jul 58 ★ **WHEN** *Brunswick 05751* $ ... 1 18

Kitty KALLEN *US, female vocalist*

2 Jul 54 ★ **LITTLE THINGS MEAN A LOT** *Brunswick 05287* ▲ ... 1 23

Gunter KALLMAN CHOIR *Germany, male / female vocal group*

24 Dec 64 **ELISABETH SERENADE** *Polydor NH 24678* ... 39 3

KAMASUTRA featuring Jocelyn BROWN
Italy, male DJ / production duo and US, female vocalist

22 Nov 97 **HAPPINESS** *Sony S2 KAMCD 2* ... 45 1

Nick KAMEN *UK, male vocalist (1 Album: 7 Weeks, 5 Singles: 33 Weeks)*

8 Nov 86 ● **EACH TIME YOU BREAK MY HEART** *WEA YZ 90* ... 5 12
28 Feb 87 **LOVING YOU IS SWEETER THAN EVER** *WEA YZ 106* ... 16 9
18 Apr 87 NICK KAMEN *WEA WX 84* ... 34 7
16 May 87 **NOBODY ELSE** *WEA YZ 122* ... 47 3
28 May 88 **TELL ME** *WEA YZ 184* ... 40 5
28 Apr 90 **I PROMISED MYSELF** *WEA YZ 454* ... 50 4

Ini KAMOZE *Jamaica, male vocalist*

7 Jan 95 ● **HERE COMES THE HOTSTEPPER** *Columbia 6610472* ▲ $ ... 4 15

KANDI *US, female vocalist – Kandi Burruss*

11 Nov 00 ● **DON'T THINK I'M NOT** *Columbia 6705102* ... 9 10

KANDIDATE *UK, male vocal / instrumental group (4 Singles: 28 Weeks)*

19 Aug 78 **DON'T WANNA SAY GOODNIGHT** *RAK 280* ... 47 6
17 Mar 79 **I DON'T WANNA LOSE YOU** *RAK 289* ... 11 12
4 Aug 79 **GIRLS GIRLS GIRLS** *RAK 295* ... 34 7
22 Mar 80 **LET ME ROCK YOU** *RAK 306* ... 58 3

KANE *Holland, male vocal / instrumental group*

4 Sep 04 **RAIN DOWN ON ME** *BMG 82876627232* ... 38 2

Eden KANE
UK (b. India), male vocalist – Richard Sarstedt (5 Singles: 73 Weeks)

1 Jun 61 ★ **WELL I ASK YOU** *Decca F 11353* ... 1 21
14 Sep 61 ● **GET LOST** *Decca F 11381* ... 10 11
18 Jan 62 ● **FORGET ME NOT** *Decca F 11418* ... 3 14
10 May 62 ● **I DON'T KNOW WHY** *Decca F 11460* ... 7 13
30 Jan 64 ● **BOYS CRY** *Fontana TF 438* ... 8 14

KANE GANG
UK, male vocal / instrumental group (2 Albums: 12 Weeks, 6 Singles: 37 Weeks)

19 May 84 **SMALLTOWN CREED** *Kitchenware SK 11* ... 60 2
7 Jul 84 **CLOSEST THING TO HEAVEN** *Kitchenware SK 15* ... 12 11
10 Nov 84 **RESPECT YOURSELF** (re) *Kitchenware SK 16* ... 21 11
23 Feb 85 THE BAD AND LOWDOWN WORLD OF THE KANE GANG *Kitchenware KWLP 2* ... 21 8
9 Mar 85 **GUN LAW** *Kitchenware SK 20* ... 53 4
27 Jun 87 **MOTORTOWN** *Kitchenware SK 30* ... 45 5
8 Aug 87 MIRACLE *Kitchenware KWLP 7* ... 41 4
16 Apr 88 **DON'T LOOK ANY FURTHER** *Kitchenware SK 33* ... 52 4

KANO NEW
US, male rapper – Kane Robinson (1 Album: 8 Weeks, 4 Singles: 12 Weeks)

12 Mar 05 **TYPICAL ME** *679 Recordings 679L 096CD2* ... 22 3
19 Mar 05 **ROUTINE CHECK** *The Beats BEATS 8* [1] ... 42 2
25 Jun 05 **REMEMBER ME** *679 Recordings 679L 101CD2* ... 71 1
9 Jul 05 HOME SWEET HOME *679 Recordings 679L 097CD* ... 36 8
24 Sep 05 **NITE NITE** (re) *679 Recordings 679L 108CD2* ... 25 6

[1] The Mitchell Brothers featuring Kano and The Streets

'Typical Me' features an uncredited Ghetto.

KANSAS *US, male vocal / instrumental group*

1 Jul 78 **CARRY ON WAYWARD SON** *Kirshner KIR 4932* ... 51 7

Mory KANTE *Guinea, male vocalist (3 Singles: 14 Weeks)*

23 Jul 88 **YEKE YEKE** *London LON 171* ... 29 9
11 Mar 95 **YEKE YEKE** (re-issue) *Ffrreedom TABCD 226* ... 25 3
30 Nov 96 **YEKE YEKE** (re-mix) *ffrr FCD 288* ... 28 2

KAOMA *France, male / female vocal (Loalwa Braz) / instrumental group (2 Singles: 20 Weeks)*

21 Oct 89 ● **LAMBADA** *CBS 655011 7* ... 4 18
27 Jan 90 **DANCANDO LAMBADA** *CBS 655235 7* ... 62 2

KAOTIC CHEMISTRY *UK, male instrumental / production group*

31 Oct 92 **LSD (EP)** *Moving Shadow SHADOW 20* ... 68 1

Tracks on LSD (EP): Space Cakes / LSD / Illegal Substances / Drumtrip II.

KARAJA *Germany, female vocalist*

19 Oct 02 **SHE MOVES (LA LA LA)** *Ministry of Sound / Substance SUBS 14CDS* ... 42 1

KARIYA *US, female vocalist*

8 Jul 89 **LET ME LOVE YOU FOR TONIGHT** (re) *Sleeping Bag SBUK 4* ... 44 9

Mick KARN (see also JAPAN) *UK, male bassist – Anthony Michaelides (2 Albums: 4 Weeks, 2 Singles: 6 Weeks)*

20 Nov 82 TITLES *Virgin V 2249* ... 74 3
9 Jul 83 **AFTER A FASHION** *Musicfest FEST 1* [1] ... 39 4
17 Jan 87 **BUOY** *Virgin VS 910* [2] ... 63 2
28 Feb 87 DREAMS OF REASON PRODUCE MONSTERS *Virgin V 2389* ... 89 1

[1] Midge Ure and Mick Karn [2] Mick Karn featuring David Sylvian

KARTOON KREW *US, rap / instrumental group*

7 Dec 85 **INSPECTOR GADGET** *Champion CHAMP 6* ... 58 6

KASABIAN *UK, male vocal (Tom Meighan) / instrumental group (1 Album: 56 Weeks, 5 Singles: 25 Weeks)*

22 May 04 **CLUB FOOT** *BMG PARADISE 08* ... 19 3
21 Aug 04 ● **L.S.F.** *RCA PARADISE 14* ... 10 7
18 Sep 04 ● KASABIAN *RCA PARADISE 16* ... 4 56
23 Oct 04 **PROCESSED BEATS** *RCA PARADISE 21* ... 17 3
15 Jan 05 ● **CUTT OFF** *RCA PARADISE 26* ... 8 7
2 Apr 05 **CLUB FOOT** (re-issue) *RCA PARADISE 30* ... 21 5

The KASENETZ-KATZ SINGING ORCHESTRAL CIRCUS
US, male vocal / instrumental group

20 Nov 68 **QUICK JOEY SMALL (RUN JOEY RUN)** *Buddah 201 022* ... 19 15

KATCHA *UK, male DJ / producer – Jerry Dickens*

21 Aug 99 **TOUCHED BY GOD** *Hooj Choons HOOJ 77CD* ... 57 1

	12 January 1974	19 January 1974	26 January 1974	2 February 1974
UK No.1 SINGLES	MERRY XMAS EVERYBODY Slade	YOU WON'T FIND ANOTHER FOOL LIKE ME The New Seekers featuring Lyn Paul	TIGER FEET Mud	TIGER FEET Mud
UK No.1 ALBUMS	TALES FROM TOPOGRAPHIC OCEANS Yes	SLADEST Slade	AND I LOVE YOU SO Perry Como	THE SINGLES 1969-1973 The Carpenters

KATOI *Thailand, female DJ / producer – Kat Henderson*

29 Mar 03 **TOUCH YOU** *Arista Dance 743219644*..........70 1

KATRINA and The WAVES *US / UK, female / male vocal (Katrina Leskanich) / instrumental group (2 Albums: 7 Weeks, 4 Singles: 34 Weeks)*

4 May 85 ● **WALKING ON SUNSHINE** *Capitol CL 354*..........8 12
8 Jun 85 KATRINA AND THE WAVES *Capitol KTW 1*..........28 6
10 May 86 WAVES *Capitol EST 2010*..........70 1
5 Jul 86 **SUN STREET** *Capitol CL 407*..........22 9
8 Jun 96 **WALKING ON SUNSHINE** (re-issue) *EMI Premier PRESCD 2*..53 1
10 May 97 ● **LOVE SHINE A LIGHT** *Eternal WEA 106CD1*..........3 12

KAVANA
UK, male vocalist – Anthony Kavanagh (1 Album: 2 Weeks, 8 Singles: 26 Weeks)

11 May 96 **CRAZY CHANCE** *Nemesis NMSD 1*..........35 3
24 Aug 96 **WHERE ARE YOU** *Nemesis NMSD 2*..........26 2
11 Jan 97 ● **I CAN MAKE YOU FEEL GOOD** *Nemesis NMSDX 3*..........8 5
19 Apr 97 ● **MFEO** *Nemesis NMSD 4*..........8 4
10 May 97 KAVANA *Nemesis CDNMS 1*..........29 2
13 Sep 97 **CRAZY CHANCE 97** (re-recording) *Nemesis NMSD 5*..........16 3
29 Aug 98 **SPECIAL KIND OF SOMETHING** *Virgin VSCDT 1704*..........13 4
12 Dec 98 **FUNKY LOVE** (re) *Virgin VSCDT 1711*..........32 3
20 Mar 99 **WILL YOU WAIT FOR ME** *Virgin VSCDT 1726*..........29 2

Niamh KAVANAGH *Ireland, female vocalist*

12 Jun 93 **IN YOUR EYES** *Arista 74321154152*..........24 5

KAWALA *UK, male vocal / instrumental / production group*

26 Feb 00 **HUMANISTIC** *Pepper 9230022*..........68 1

Janet KAY *UK, female vocalist – Janet Bogle (3 Singles: 24 Weeks)*

9 Jun 79 ● **SILLY GAMES** *Scope SC 2*..........2 14
11 Aug 90 **SILLY GAMES** (re-recording) *Arista 113452* [1]..........22 7
11 Aug 90 **SILLY GAMES** (re-mix) *Music Factory Dance MFD 006*..........62 3

[1] Lindy Layton featuring Janet Kay

Peter KAY NEW *UK, male comedian / vocalist*

26 Mar 05 ★ **(IS THIS THE WAY TO) AMARILLO** (re) (re-issue) *Universal TV 9828606* [1] ■ £..........1 26+
3 Dec 05 THE BEST OF PETER KAY ... SO FAR *EMI Virgin VTCD 768*......62 1

[1] Tony Christie featuring Peter Kay

Danny KAYE
US, male actor / vocalist – David Kaminsky, b. 18 Jan 1913, d. 3 Mar 1987

27 Feb 53 ● **WONDERFUL COPENHAGEN** *Brunswick 05023*..........5 10

With Gordon Jenkins and his Orchestra and Chorus.

The KAYE SISTERS *UK, female vocal group (5 Singles: 45 Weeks)*

25 May 56 **IVORY TOWER** *HMV POP 209* [1]..........20 5
1 Nov 57 ● **GOT-TA HAVE SOMETHING IN THE BANK, FRANK** *Philips PB 751* [2]..........8 11
3 Jan 58 **SHAKE ME I RATTLE / ALONE** *Philips PB 752*..........27 1
1 May 59 ● **COME SOFTLY TO ME** *Philips PB 913* [2]..........9 9
7 Jul 60 ● **PAPER ROSES** *Philips PB 1024*..........7 19

[1] The Three Kayes [2] Frankie Vaughan and The Kaye Sisters

KAYESTONE *UK, male DJ / production duo*

29 Jul 00 **ATMOSPHERE** *Distinctive DISNCD 62*..........55 1

KÉ *US, male vocalist – Kevin Griudis*

13 Apr 96 **STRANGE WORLD** *Venture 74321349412*..........73 1

KEANE *UK, male vocal (Tom Chaplin) / instrumental group (1 Album: 72 Weeks, 4 Singles: 35 Weeks)*

28 Feb 04 ● **SOMEWHERE ONLY WE KNOW** (re) *Island CID 849*..........3 13
15 May 04 ● **EVERYBODY'S CHANGING** (re) *Island CID 855*..........4 9
22 May 04 ★ HOPES AND FEARS *Island CID 8145* ■..........1 72
28 Aug 04 ● **BEDSHAPED** *Island CID 870*..........10 7
4 Dec 04 **THIS IS THE LAST TIME** *Island CID 880*..........18 6

Johnny KEATING *UK, orchestra*

1 Mar 62 ● **THEME FROM 'Z CARS' (JOHNNY TODD)** *Piccadilly 7N 35032*..........8 14

Ronan KEATING (222 Top 500) *Record-setting Irish vocalist, b. 3 Mar 1977, Dublin, who is still adding to his unprecedented chart start of 29 Top 10 singles (27 of them making the Top 5), including those as a member of Boyzone. In addition, seven of his nine albums (including three solo) entered at No.1. He formerly co-managed Westlife. Best-selling single: 'When You Say Nothing at All' 528,600 (4 Albums: 135 Weeks, 13 Singles: 144 Weeks)*

7 Aug 99 ★ **WHEN YOU SAY NOTHING AT ALL** (2re) *Polydor 5612902* ■.....1 17
22 Jul 00 ★ **LIFE IS A ROLLERCOASTER** *Polydor 5619362* ■..........1 14
12 Aug 00 ★ RONAN *Polydor 5491032* ■..........1 56
2 Dec 00 ● **THE WAY YOU MAKE ME FEEL** (re) *Polydor 5878852*..........6 12
28 Apr 01 ● **LOVIN' EACH DAY** *Polydor 5876872*..........2 14
18 May 02 ★ **IF TOMORROW NEVER COMES** *Polydor 5707182* ■..........1 15
1 Jun 02 ★ DESTINATION *Polydor 5897892* ■..........1 40
21 Sep 02 ● **I LOVE IT WHEN WE DO** (2re) *Polydor 5709032*..........5 11
7 Dec 02 ● **WE'VE GOT TONIGHT** *Polydor 0658612* [1]..........4 13
10 May 03 ● **THE LONG GOODBYE** *Polydor 0657372*..........3 10
22 Nov 03 ● **LOST FOR WORDS** *Polydor 9813304*..........9 4
29 Nov 03 TURN IT ON *Polydor 9865882*..........21 17
21 Feb 04 ● **SHE BELIEVES (IN ME)** *Polydor 9816652*..........2 7
15 May 04 ● **LAST THING ON MY MIND** *Polydor / Curb 9866595* [2]..........5 9
9 Oct 04 ● **I HOPE YOU DANCE** *Polydor / Curb 9868261*..........2 7
23 Oct 04 ★ 10 YEARS OF HITS *Polydor 9868455* ■..........1 22
25 Dec 04 ● **FATHER AND SON** *Polydor 9869406* [3]..........2 11

[1] Ronan Keating featuring Lulu [2] Ronan Keating & LeAnn Rimes [3] Ronan Keating featuring Yusuf

KEEDIE *UK, female vocalist (2 Singles: 9 Weeks)*

23 Oct 04 ● **I BELIEVE MY HEART** *Innocent 8677122* [1]..........2 7
24 Dec 05 **JERUSALEM** *Hyperactive CXSTUMP 1* [2]..........19 2+

[1] Duncan James & Keedie [2] Keedie & The England Cricket Team

Kevin KEEGAN *UK, male footballer / vocalist*

9 Jun 79 **HEAD OVER HEELS IN LOVE** *EMI 2965*..........31 6

KEEL *US, male vocal / instrumental group*

17 May 86 THE FINAL FRONTIER *Vertigo VERH 33*..........83 2

Howard KEEL *US, male vocalist – Harold Leek (3 Albums: 36 Weeks)*

14 Apr 84 ● AND I LOVE YOU SO *Warwick WW 5137*..........6 19
9 Nov 85 REMINISCING – THE HOWARD KEEL COLLECTION *Telstar STAR 2259*..........20 12
28 Mar 88 JUST FOR YOU *Telstar STAR 2318*..........51 5

Nelson KEENE *UK, male vocalist – Malcolm Holland*

25 Aug 60 **IMAGE OF A GIRL** (re) *HMV POP 771*..........37 5

KEITH *US, male vocalist – James Keefer (2 Singles: 8 Weeks)*

26 Jan 67 **98.6** *Mercury MF 955*..........24 7
16 Mar 67 **TELL ME TO MY FACE** *Mercury MF 968*..........50 1

KEITH 'N' SHANE (see also BOYZONE)
Ireland, male vocal duo – Keith Duffy and Shane Lynch

23 Dec 00 **GIRL YOU KNOW IT'S TRUE** *Polydor 5879462*..........36 3

9 February 1974	16 February 1974	23 February 1974	2 March 1974
TIGER FEET Mud	TIGER FEET Mud	DEVIL GATE DRIVE Suzi Quatro	DEVIL GATE DRIVE Suzi Quatro
THE SINGLES 1969-1973 The Carpenters	THE SINGLES 1969-1973 The Carpenters	THE SINGLES 1969-1973 The Carpenters	OLD NEW BORROWED AND BLUE Slade

KEY

UK No.1 ★ UK Top 10 ● Still on chart + UK entry at No.1 ■ US No.1 ▲ UK million seller £ US million seller $

Singles re-entries are listed as (re), (2re), (3re)... which signifies that the hit re-entered the chart once, twice or three times...

Peak Position / Weeks

KELIS

US, female vocalist – Kelis Rogers (2 Albums: 53 Weeks, 14 Singles: 94 Weeks)

Date		Title / Label	Peak	Weeks
26 Feb 00		**CAUGHT OUT THERE** (import) *Virgin 8965102CD*	52	1
4 Mar 00	●	**CAUGHT OUT THERE** (re) *Virgin VUSCD 158*	4	12
11 Mar 00		KALEIDOSCOPE *Virgin CDVUS 167*	43	13
17 Jun 00		**GOOD STUFF** *Virgin VUSCD 164*	19	5
8 Jul 00		**GOT YOUR MONEY** *Elektra E 7077CD* [1]	11	8
21 Oct 00		**GET ALONG WITH YOU** *Virgin VUSCD 174*	51	1
3 Nov 01		**YOUNG FRESH N' NEW** *Virgin VUSCD 212*	32	2
5 Oct 02		**HELP ME** *Perfecto PERF 42CDS* [2]	65	1
23 Aug 03	●	**FINEST DREAMS** *Virgin RXCD 2* [3]	8	5
23 Aug 03		**LET'S GET ILL** *Bad Boy / Meanwhile MCSTD 40331* [4]	25	3
17 Jan 04		TASTY *Virgin CDV 2978*	11	40
17 Jan 04	●	**MILKSHAKE** *Virgin VSCDX 1863*	2	15
20 Mar 04	●	**NOT IN LOVE** *Interscope 9862022* [5]	5	9
5 Jun 04	●	**TRICK ME** *Virgin VSCDX 1872*	2	14
30 Oct 04	●	**MILLIONAIRE** *Virgin VSCDX 1885* [6]	3	12
16 Apr 05		**IN PUBLIC** *Virgin VSCDT 1893* [7]	17	6

[1] Ol' Dirty Bastard featuring Kelis [2] Timo Maas featuring Kelis [3] Richard X featuring Kelis [4] P Diddy featuring Kelis [5] Enrique featuring Kelis [6] Kelis featuring André 3000 [7] Kelis featuring Nas

Jerry KELLER *US, male vocalist*

Date		Title / Label	Peak	Weeks
28 Aug 59	★	**HERE COMES SUMMER** *London HLR 8890*	1	14

Frank KELLY *Ireland, male actor / vocalist – Francis O'Kelly*

Date		Title / Label	Peak	Weeks
24 Dec 83		**CHRISTMAS COUNTDOWN** (re) *Ritz RITZ 062*	26	5

Re-entry peaked at No.54 in Dec 1984.

Frankie KELLY *US, male vocalist / instrumentalist*

Date		Title / Label	Peak	Weeks
2 Nov 85		**AIN'T THAT THE TRUTH** *10 TEN 87*	65	2

Keith KELLY *UK, male vocalist – Michael Pailthorpe (2 Singles: 5 Weeks)*

Date		Title / Label	Peak	Weeks
5 May 60		**TEASE ME (MUST YOU ALWAYS)** (re) *Parlophone R 4640*	27	4
18 Aug 60		**LISTEN LITTLE GIRL** *Parlophone R 4676*	47	1

R KELLY (118 Top 500)

Phenomenally successful R&B vocalist, b. Robert Kelly, 8 Jan 1971, Chicago, US, whose writing and production skills are constantly in demand by other top artists. Amazingly, 1998 album R yielded seven Top 20 hits but never reached the Top 20 itself. Best-selling single: 'I Believe I Can Fly' 677,060 (11 Albums: 155 Weeks, 37 Singles: 242 Weeks)

Date		Title / Label	Peak	Weeks
29 Feb 92		BORN INTO THE 90'S *Jive CHIP 123* [1]	67	1
9 May 92		**SHE'S GOT THAT VIBE** *Jive JIVET 292* [1]	57	2
20 Nov 93		**SEX ME** *Jive JIVECD 346* [1]	75	1
27 Nov 93		12 PLAY *Jive CHIP 144*	20	44
14 May 94		**YOUR BODY'S CALLIN'** *Jive JIVECD 353*	19	4
3 Sep 94		**SUMMER BUNNIES** *Jive JIVECD 358*	23	3
22 Oct 94	●	**SHE'S GOT THAT VIBE** (re-issue) *Jive JIVECD 364*	3	13
21 Jan 95	●	**BUMP 'N' GRIND** *Jive JIVECD 368* ▲ $	8	9
6 May 95		**THE 4 PLAY EPS** *Jive JIVECD 376*	23	3
11 Nov 95		**YOU REMIND ME OF SOMETHING** *Jive JIVECD 388* $	24	3
25 Nov 95		R KELLY *Jive CHIP 166* ▲	18	10
2 Mar 96		**DOWN LOW (NOBODY HAS TO KNOW)** *Jive JIVECD 392* [2] $	23	3
22 Jun 96		**THANK GOD IT'S FRIDAY** *Jive JIVECD 395*	14	4
29 Mar 97	★	**I BELIEVE I CAN FLY** *Jive JIVECD 415* $	1	17
19 Jul 97	●	**GOTHAM CITY** *Jive JIVECD 428*	9	8
18 Jul 98	●	**BE CAREFUL** (re) *Jive 0521452* [3]	7	7
26 Sep 98		**HALF ON A BABY** *Jive 0521802*	16	4
14 Nov 98		**HOME ALONE** *Jive 0522392* [4]	17	5
21 Nov 98		R *Jive 517932*	27	26
28 Nov 98	●	**I'M YOUR ANGEL** *Epic 6666282* [5] ▲ $	3	13
31 Jul 99		**DID YOU EVER THINK** *Jive 0523612*	20	5
16 Oct 99		**IF I COULD TURN BACK THE HANDS OF TIME** (import) *Jive 550642*	57	2
30 Oct 99	●	**IF I COULD TURN BACK THE HANDS OF TIME** *Jive 0523182*	2	19
19 Feb 00		**SATISFY YOU** (re) (import) *Bad Boy / Arista 792832* [6]	73	2
11 Mar 00	●	**SATISFY YOU** *Bad Boy / Arista 74321745592* [6]	8	8
22 Apr 00		**ONLY THE LOOT CAN MAKE ME HAPPY / WHEN A WOMAN'S FED UP / I CAN'T SLEEP BABY (IF I)** *Jive 9250282* $	24	3
21 Oct 00		**I WISH** *Jive 9251262*	12	6
18 Nov 00		TP-2.COM *Jive 9220262* ▲	21	3
31 Mar 01		**THE STORM IS OVER NOW** *Jive 9251782*	18	6
23 Jun 01		**FIESTA** *Jive 9252142* [7]	23	3
2 Mar 02	●	**THE WORLD'S GREATEST** *Jive 9253242*	4	12
30 Mar 02		THE BEST OF BOTH WORLDS *Jive 9223512* [2]	37	2
25 May 02		**HONEY** *Jive 9253662* [8]	35	2
1 Mar 03	●	CHOCOLATE FACTORY *Jive 9225082* ▲	10	22
17 May 03	★	**IGNITION** *Jive 9254972* ■	1	20
23 Aug 03	●	**SNAKE** *Jive 82876547232* [9]	10	5
4 Oct 03	●	THE R IN R & B – GREATEST HITS COLLECTION – VOL.1 *Jive 82876561792*	4	34
15 Nov 03		**STEP IN THE NAME OF LOVE / THOIA THOING** *Jive 82876573912*	14	4
20 Mar 04		**CLUBBIN'** *Elektra E 7544CD* [10]	15	6
29 May 04	●	**HOTEL** *J 82876618532* [11]	3	14
4 Sep 04		HAPPY PEOPLE / U SAVED ME *BMG 82876615082*	11	8
30 Oct 04	●	**HAPPY PEOPLE / U SAVED ME** (re) *Jive 82876656182*	6	11
6 Nov 04		2004 UNFINISHED BUSINESS *Jive 82876658682* [2] ▲	61	1
6 Nov 04	★	**WONDERFUL** *Def Jam 9864605* [12] ■	1	10
20 Nov 04		**SO SEXY** *Atlantic AT 0187CD* [13]	28	3
16 Jul 05		TP.3 RELOADED *Jive 82876710062* ▲	23	4
10 Sep 05		**PLAYA'S ONLY** *Jive 82876720512* [14]	33	2

[1] R Kelly and Public Announcement [2] R Kelly featuring Ronald Isley [3] Sparkle featuring R Kelly [4] R Kelly featuring Keith Murray [5] Celine Dion and R Kelly [6] Puff Daddy featuring R Kelly [7] R Kelly featuring Jay-Z [8] R Kelly & Jay-Z [9] R Kelly featuring Big Tigger [10] Marques Houston featuring Joe Budden and Pied Piper [11] Cassidy featuring R Kelly [12] Ja Rule featuring R Kelly & Ashanti [13] Twista featuring R Kelly [14] R. Kelly featuring The Game [1] R Kelly and Public Announcement [2] R Kelly and Jay-Z

Tracks on 4 Play EPs: Your Body's Callin' / Homie Lover Friend / Honey Love / Slow Dance (Hey Mr. DJ). R Kelly appeared on 'Clubbin'' under the name Pied Piper.

Roberta KELLY *US, female vocalist*

Date		Title / Label	Peak	Weeks
21 Jan 78		**ZODIACS** (re) *Oasis / Hansa 3*	44	3

KELLY FAMILY *Ireland, male / female vocal / instrumental group*

Date		Title / Label	Peak	Weeks
21 Oct 95		**AN ANGEL** *EMI CDEM 390*	69	1

Johnny KEMP *Barbados, male vocalist*

Date		Title / Label	Peak	Weeks
27 Aug 88		**JUST GOT PAID** *CBS 651470 7*	68	1

Tara KEMP *US, female vocalist*

Date		Title / Label	Peak	Weeks
20 Apr 91		**HOLD YOU TIGHT** *Giant W 0020*	69	2

Felicity KENDAL *UK, female exercise instructor / actor*

Date		Title / Label	Peak	Weeks
19 Jun 82		SHAPE UP AND DANCE (VOLUME 1) *Lifestyle LEG 1*	29	47

Graham KENDRICK *UK, male vocalist*

Date		Title / Label	Peak	Weeks
9 Sep 89		**LET THE FLAME BURN BRIGHTER** *Power P 30*	55	4

Eddie KENDRICKS (see also The TEMPTATIONS)

US, male vocalist, b. 17 Dec 1939, d. 5 Oct 1992 (3 Singles: 20 Weeks)

Date		Title / Label	Peak	Weeks
3 Nov 73		**KEEP ON TRUCKIN'** *Tamla Motown TMG 873* ▲ $	18	14

	9 March 1974	16 March 1974	23 March 1974	30 March 1974
UK No.1 SINGLES	JEALOUS MIND – Alvin Stardust	BILLY DON'T BE A HERO – Paper Lace	BILLY DON'T BE A HERO – Paper Lace	BILLY DON'T BE A HERO – Paper Lace
UK No.1 ALBUMS	THE SINGLES 1969-1973 – The Carpenters	THE SINGLES 1969-1973 – The Carpenters	THE SINGLES 1969-1973 – The Carpenters	THE SINGLES 1969-1973 – The Carpenters

16 Mar 74 **BOOGIE DOWN** *Tamla Motown TMG 888* $ 39 4
21 Sep 85 **A NIGHT AT THE APOLLO LIVE!** *RCA PB 49935* [1] 58 2

[1] Daryl Hall and John Oates featuring David Ruffin and Eddie Kendrick

'A Night at the Apollo Live!' is a medley of 'The Way You Do the Things You Do' and 'My Girl'. Kendricks dropped the 's' from his name for this release.

KENICKIE *UK, female / male vocal (Lauren Laverne) / instrumental group (2 Albums: 5 Weeks, 7 Singles: 13 Weeks)*

14 Sep 96 **PUNKA** *Emidisc CDDISC 001* 43 2
16 Nov 96 **MILLIONAIRE SWEEPER** *Emidisc CDDISC 002* 60 1
11 Jan 97 **IN YOUR CAR** *Emidisc CDDISC 005* 24 3
3 May 97 **NIGHTLIFE** *Emidisc CDDISC 006* 27 2
24 May 97 ● AT THE CLUB *Emidisc ADISCCD 002* 9 3
5 Jul 97 **PUNKA** (re-issue) *Emidisc CDDISC 007* 38 2
6 Jun 98 **I WOULD FIX YOU** *EMI CDEM 513* 36 2
22 Aug 98 **STAY IN THE SUN** *EMI CDEMS 520* 43 1
12 Sep 98 GET IN *EMI 4958512* 32 2

Jane KENNAWAY and STRANGE BEHAVIOUR *UK, female vocalist and male instrumental group*

24 Jan 81 **I.O.U.** *Deram DM 436* 65 3

Brian KENNEDY *Ireland, male vocalist (2 Albums: 4 Weeks, 4 Singles: 9 Weeks)*

31 Mar 90 THE GREAT WAR OF WORDS *RCA PL 74475* 64 1
22 Jun 96 **A BETTER MAN** *RCA 74321382642* 28 3
21 Sep 96 **LIFE, LOVE AND HAPPINESS** *RCA 74321409921* 27 3
19 Oct 96 A BETTER MAN *RCA 74321409132* 19 3
5 Apr 97 **PUT THE MESSAGE IN THE BOX** *RCA 74321462272* 37 2
31 Dec 05 **GEORGE BEST – A TRIBUTE** *Curb CUBC 116* [1] ....21 1+

[1] Brian Kennedy and Peter Corry

Tracks on 'George Best – A Tribute': 'You Raise Me Up' – Brian Kennedy / 'The Long And Winding Road' – Peter Corry / 'Bring Him Home' / Vincent medley featuring Peter Corry & Brian Kennedy

Kevin KENNEDY *UK, male actor / vocalist – Kevin Williams*

24 Jun 00 **BULLDOG NATION** *D2M 74321759742* 70 1

Nigel KENNEDY *UK, male violinist (9 Albums: 124 Weeks)*

1 Mar 86 ELGAR: VIOLIN CONCERTO *EMI EMX 4120581* [1] 97 1
7 Oct 89 ● VIVALDI: THE FOUR SEASONS *EMI NIGE 2* [2] 3 81
5 May 90 MENDELSSOHN / BRUCH / SCHUBERT *HMV 7496631* [3] 28 15
6 Apr 91 BRAHMS: VIOLIN CONCERTO *EMI NIGE 3* 16 12
22 Feb 92 JUST LISTEN ... *EMI Classics CDNIGE 4* 56 1
21 Nov 92 BEETHOVEN: VIOLIN CONCERTO *EMI Classics CDC 7545742* [4] 40 6
29 Jun 96 KAFKA *EMI CDEMD 1095* 67 1
6 Nov 99 CLASSIC KENNEDY *EMI Classics CDC 5568902* [2] 51 6
2 Nov 02 NIGEL KENNEDY'S GREATEST HITS *EMI Classics 5574112* 71 1

[1] Nigel Kennedy with the London Philharmonic Orchestra conducted by Vernon Handley [2] Nigel Kennedy with the English Chamber Orchestra [3] Nigel Kennedy with Jeffrey Tate and the English Chamber Orchestra [4] Nigel Kennedy with Klaus Tennstedt and the North German Radio Symphony Orchestra

KENNY *Ireland, male vocalist – Tony Kenny (2 Singles: 16 Weeks)*

3 Mar 73 **HEART OF STONE** *RAK 144* 11 13
30 Jun 73 **GIVE IT TO ME NOW** *RAK 153* 38 3

KENNY *UK, male vocal (Richard Driscoll) / instrumental group (1 Album: 1 Week, 4 Singles: 39 Weeks)*

7 Dec 74 ● **THE BUMP** *RAK 186* 3 15
8 Mar 75 ● **FANCY PANTS** *RAK 196* 4 9
7 Jun 75 **BABY I LOVE YOU, OK!** *RAK 207* 12 7
16 Aug 75 ● **JULIE ANNE** *RAK 214* 10 8
17 Jan 76 THE SOUND OF SUPER K *RAK SRAK 518* 56 1

Although uncredited, all lead and background vocals on 'The Bump' were performed by Barry Palmer.

Gerard KENNY *US, male vocalist (1 Album: 4 Weeks, 4 Singles: 21 Weeks)*

9 Dec 78 **NEW YORK, NEW YOR4mK** *RCA PB 5117* 43 8
21 Jul 79 MADE IT THROUGH THE RAIN *RCA Victor PL 25218* 19 4
21 Jun 80 **FANTASY** (re) *RCA PB 5256* 34 6
18 Feb 84 **THE OTHER WOMAN, THE OTHER MAN** *Impression IMS 3* 69 4
4 May 85 **NO MAN'S LAND** *WEA YZ 38* 56 3

KENT *Sweden, male vocal / instrumental group*

13 Mar 99 **747** *RCA 74321645912* 61 1

Klark KENT (see also The POLICE) *US, male vocalist / multi-instrumentalist – Stewart Copeland*

26 Aug 78 **DON'T CARE** *A&M AMS 7376* 48 4

KERBDOG *Ireland, male vocal / instrumental group (1 Album: 1 Week, 4 Singles: 5 Weeks)*

12 Mar 94 **DRY RISER** *Vertigo VERCC 83* 60 1
6 Aug 94 **DUMMY CRUSHER** *Vertigo VERCD 86* 37 2
12 Oct 96 **SALLY** *Fontana KERCD 2* 69 1
29 Mar 97 **MEXICAN WAVE** *Fontana KERCD 3* 49 1
12 Apr 97 ON THE TURN *Fontana 5329992* 64 1

KERRI and MICK *Australia, female / male vocal duo*

28 Apr 84 **'SONS AND DAUGHTERS' THEME** *A1 A1 286* 68 3

KERRI-ANN *Ireland, female vocalist*

8 Aug 98 **DO YOU LOVE ME BOY?** *Raglan Road 5671012* 58 1

Liz KERSHAW and Bruno BROOKES *UK, female / male DJ / vocal duo (2 Singles: 3 Weeks)*

2 Dec 89 **IT TAKES TWO BABY** *Spartan CIN 101* [1] 53 2
1 Dec 90 **LET'S DANCE** *Jive BRUNO 1* [2] 54 1

[1] Liz Kershaw, Bruno Brookes, Jive Bunny and Londonbeat [2] Bruno and Liz and the Radio 1 DJ Posse

Nik KERSHAW (367 Top 500) *One time jazz-funk guitarist whose melodic pop repertoire made him a mid-1980s teen idol, b. 1 Mar 1958, Bristol, UK. His 50 weeks on the singles chart in 1984 beat all other soloists. He appeared at Live Aid, and penned hits for Let Loose, The Hollies and a No.1 for Chesney Hawkes (3 Albums: 100 Weeks, 14 Singles: 89 Weeks)*

19 Nov 83 **I WON'T LET THE SUN GO DOWN ON ME** *MCA MCA 816* 47 5
28 Jan 84 ● **WOULDN'T IT BE GOOD** *MCA NIK 2* 4 14
10 Mar 84 ● HUMAN RACING *MCA MCF 3197* 5 61
14 Apr 84 **DANCING GIRLS** *MCA NIK 3* 13 9
16 Jun 84 ● **I WON'T LET THE SUN GO DOWN ON ME** (re-issue) *MCA NIK 4* 2 13
15 Sep 84 **HUMAN RACING** *MCA NIK 5* 19 7
17 Nov 84 ● **THE RIDDLE** *MCA NIK 6* 3 11
1 Dec 84 ● THE RIDDLE *MCA MCF 3245* 8 36
16 Mar 85 ● **WIDE BOY** *MCA NIK 7* 9 8
3 Aug 85 ● **DON QUIXOTE** *MCA NIK 8* 10 7
30 Nov 85 **WHEN A HEART BEATS** *MCA NIK 9* 27 7
11 Oct 86 **NOBODY KNOWS** *MCA NIK 10* 44 3
8 Nov 86 RADIO MUSICOLA *MCA MCG 6016* 47 3
13 Dec 86 **RADIO MUSICOLA** *MCA NIK 11* 43 2
4 Feb 89 **ONE STEP AHEAD** *MCA NIK 12* 55 1
27 Feb 99 **SOMEBODY LOVES YOU** *Eagle EAGXA 023* 70 1
7 Aug 99 **SOMETIMES** *Wall of Sound WALLD 054* [1] 56 1

[1] Les Rythmes Digitales featuring Nik Kershaw

6 April 1974	13 April 1974	20 April 1974	27 April 1974
SEASONS IN THE SUN Terry Jacks	SEASONS IN THE SUN Terry Jacks	SEASONS IN THE SUN Terry Jacks	SEASONS IN THE SUN Terry Jacks
THE SINGLES 1969-1973 The Carpenters	THE SINGLES 1969-1973 The Carpenters	THE SINGLES 1969-1973 The Carpenters	THE SINGLES 1969-1973 The Carpenters

KEY
UK No.1 ★ UK Top 10 ● Still on chart + UK entry at No.1 ■
US No.1 ▲ UK million seller £ US million seller $
Singles re-entries are listed as (re), (2re), (3re)… which signifies that the hit re-entered the chart once, twice or three times…
Peak Position / Weeks

KEVIN THE GERBIL *UK, male gerbil vocalist*

4 Aug 84 **SUMMER HOLIDAY** *Magnet RAT 3* **50** 6

KEY SESSIONS QUARTET *UK, male instrumental group*

20 Mar 04 THE PIANO SESSIONS *T2 / Telstar TCD 3387* 54 2

KEY WEST featuring ERIK (see also The RAH BAND) *UK, male producer – Richard Hewson and female vocalist*

10 Apr 93 **LOOKS LIKE I'M IN LOVE AGAIN** *PWL Sanctuary PWCD 252* **46** 2

Alicia KEYS (402 Top 500) *Multi-award-winning R&B singer / songwriter and pianist, b. Alicia Cook, 25 Jan 1981, New York, US. Her three albums entered at No.1 in the US and the first sold over 10 million copies worldwide. She picked up a record-equalling five Grammy awards in 2002 and performed at the US Live 8 concert (3 Albums: 116 Weeks, 9 Singles: 63 Weeks)*

22 Sep 01 ● SONGS IN A MINOR *J 80813200022* ▲ 6 79
10 Nov 01 ● **FALLIN'** *J 74321903692* ▲ 3 10
9 Mar 02 **BROTHA PART II** *J 74321922142* [1] 37 2
30 Mar 02 **A WOMAN'S WORTH** *J 74321928692* 18 8
20 Jul 02 **HOW COME YOU DON'T CALL ME** *J 74321943122* 26 3
5 Oct 02 ● **GANGSTA LOVIN'** *Ruff Ryders / Interscope 4978042* [2] 6 8
7 Dec 02 **GIRLFRIEND** *J 74321974972* 24 5
13 Dec 03 THE DIARY OF ALICIA KEYS *J 82876586202* ▲ 13 36
20 Dec 03 **YOU DON'T KNOW MY NAME** *J 82876581612* 19 9
10 Apr 04 **IF I AIN'T GOT YOU** *J 82876608172* 18 5
13 Nov 04 ● **MY BOO** *LaFace / Arista 82876655292* [3] ▲ 5 13
22 Oct 05 UNPLUGGED *J 82876718082* ▲ 52 1

[1] Angie Stone featuring Alicia Keys and Eve [2] Eve featuring Alicia Keys [3] Usher featuring Alicia Keys

Chaka KHAN (see also RUFUS) *US, female vocalist – Yvette Stevens (5 Albums: 45 Weeks, 16 Singles: 97 Weeks)*

2 Dec 78 **I'M EVERY WOMAN** *Warner Bros. K 17269* 11 13
31 Mar 84 ● **AIN'T NOBODY** *Warner Bros. RCK 1* [1] 8 12
21 Apr 84 STOMPIN' AT THE SAVOY *Warner Bros. 923679* [1] 64 5
20 Oct 84 I FEEL FOR YOU *Warner Bros. 925 162* 15 22
20 Oct 84 ★ **I FEEL FOR YOU** *Warner Bros. W 9209* $ 1 16
19 Jan 85 **THIS IS MY NIGHT** *Warner Bros. W 9097* 14 6
20 Apr 85 **EYE TO EYE** *Warner Bros. W 9009* 16 7
12 Jul 86 **LOVE OF A LIFETIME** *Warner Bros. W 8671* 52 4
9 Aug 86 DESTINY *Warner Bros. WX 45* 77 2
21 Jan 89 **IT'S MY PARTY** *Warner Bros. W 7678* 71 2
6 May 89 ● **I'M EVERY WOMAN** (re-mix) *Warner Bros. W 2963* 8 8
3 Jun 89 LIFE IS A DANCE – THE REMIX PROJECT *Warner Bros. WX 268* 14 15
8 Jul 89 ● **AIN'T NOBODY** (re-mix) *Warner Bros. W 2880* [1] 6 9
7 Oct 89 **I FEEL FOR YOU** (re-mix) *Warner Bros. W 2764* 45 2
13 Jan 90 **I'LL BE GOOD TO YOU** *Qwest W 2697* [2] 21 7
28 Mar 92 **LOVE YOU ALL MY LIFETIME** *Warner Bros. W 0087* 49 3
17 Jul 93 **DON'T LOOK AT ME THAT WAY** *Warner Bros. W 0192CD* 73 1
19 Aug 95 **WATCH WHAT YOU SAY** *Cooltempo CDCOOL 308* [3] 28 3
1 Mar 97 **NEVER MISS THE WATER** *Reprise W 1393CD* [4] 59 1
4 Sep 99 BEST OF CHAKA KHAN – I'M EVERY WOMAN *Warner.esp 9362475072* 62 1
11 Nov 00 **ALL GOOD** *Tommy Boy TBCD 2154B* [5] 33 3

[1] Rufus and Chaka Khan [2] Quincy Jones featuring Ray Charles and Chaka Khan [3] Guru featuring Chaka Khan [4] Chaka Khan featuring Me'Shell Ndegeocello [5] De La Soul featuring Chaka Khan [1] Rufus and Chaka Khan

Nusrat Fateh Ali KHAN / Michael BROOK *Pakistan, male vocalist and Canada, male producer / guitarist*

6 Apr 96 NIGHT SONG *Realworld CDRW 50* 65 1

Praga KHAN *Belgium, male producer – Maurice Engelen (3 Singles: 9 Weeks)*

4 Apr 92 **FREE YOUR BODY / INJECTED WITH A POISON** *Profile PROFT 347* [1] 16 6
11 Jul 92 **RAVE ALERT** *Profile PROF 369* 39 2
24 Nov 01 **INJECTED WITH A POISON** (re-mix) *Nukleuz NUKC 0238* 52 1

[1] Praga Khan featuring Jade 4 U

Aram KHATCHATURIAN / VIENNA PHILHARMONIC ORCHESTRA *Armenia, male conductor and Austria, orchestra*

22 Jan 72 SPARTACUS *Decca SXL 6000* 16 15

KHIA *US, female vocalist – Khia Finch*

16 Oct 04 ● **MY NECK, MY BACK (LICK IT)** *Direction 6753802* 4 14

Mary KIANI (see also The TIME FREQUENCY) *UK, female vocalist (5 Singles: 15 Weeks)*

12 Aug 95 **WHEN I CALL YOUR NAME** *Mercury MERCD 440* 18 4
23 Dec 95 **I GIVE IT ALL TO YOU / I IMAGINE** *Mercury MERCD 449* 35 4
27 Apr 96 **LET THE MUSIC PLAY** *Mercury MERCD 456* 19 3
18 Jan 97 **100%** *Mercury MERCD 469* 23 3
21 Jun 97 **WITH OR WITHOUT YOU** *Mercury MERCD 487* 46 1

KICK SQUAD *UK / Germany, male vocal / instrumental group*

10 Nov 90 **SOUND CLASH (CHAMPION SOUND)** *Kickin KICK 2* 59 2

KICKING BACK with TAXMAN *UK, male / female vocal / instrumental duo and male rapper (2 Singles: 8 Weeks)*

17 Mar 90 **DEVOTION** *10 TEN 297* 47 4
7 Jul 90 **EVERYTHING** *10 TEN 307* 54 4

KICKS LIKE A MULE *UK, male instrumental / production duo – Nick Halkes and Richard Russell*

1 Feb 92 ● **THE BOUNCER** *Tribal Bass TRIBE 3S* 7 6

KID CREME *Belgium, male producer – Nicolas Skaravilli (2 Singles: 3 Weeks)*

22 Mar 03 **DOWN AND UNDER (TOGETHER)** *Ink NIBNE 13CD* [1] 55 1
10 May 03 **HYPNOTISING** *Positiva CDTIV 189* [2] 31 2

[1] Kid Creme featuring Shurakano [2] Kid Creme featuring Charlise

KID 'N' PLAY *US, male rap duo (3 Singles: 7 Weeks)*

18 Jul 87 **LAST NIGHT** *Cooltempo COOL 148* 71 1
26 Mar 88 **DO THIS MY WAY** *Cooltempo COOL 164* 48 3
17 Sep 88 **GITTIN' FUNKY** *Cooltempo COOL 168* 55 3

KID ROCK *US, male vocalist / rapper – Robert Ritchie (1 Album: 1 Week, 3 Singles: 8 Weeks)*

23 Oct 99 **COWBOY** *Atlantic AT 0076CD* 36 2
10 Jun 00 THE HISTORY OF ROCK *Atlantic 7567833142* 73 1
9 Sep 00 **AMERICAN BAD ASS** *Atlantic AT 0085CD* 25 4
12 May 01 **BAWITDABA** *Atlantic AT 0098CD* 41 2

KID UNKNOWN *UK, male producer – Paul Fitzpatrick*

2 May 92 **NIGHTMARE** *Warp WAP 20CD* 64 1

Carol KIDD featuring Terry WAITE *UK, female vocalist / male vocalist – humanitarian*

17 Oct 92 **WHEN I DREAM** *The Hit Label HLS 1* 58 3

	4 May 1974	11 May 1974	18 May 1974	25 May 1974
UK No.1 SINGLES	WATERLOO Abba	WATERLOO Abba	SUGAR BABY LOVE The Rubettes	SUGAR BABY LOVE The Rubettes
UK No.1 ALBUMS	THE SINGLES 1969-1973 The Carpenters	THE SINGLES 1969-1973 The Carpenters	THE SINGLES 1969-1973 The Carpenters	JOURNEY TO THE CENTRE OF THE EARTH Rick Wakeman

Johnny KIDD and The PIRATES *UK, male vocal / instrumental group – leader b. Frederick Heath, 23 Dec 1939, d. 7 Oct 1966 (9 Singles: 62 Weeks)*

Date		Title / Label	Pos	Wks
12 Jun 59		**PLEASE DON'T TOUCH** (re) *HMV POP 615*	25	5
12 Feb 60		**YOU GOT WHAT IT TAKES** *HMV POP 698*	25	3
16 Jun 60	★	**SHAKIN' ALL OVER** *HMV POP 753*	1	19
6 Oct 60		**RESTLESS** *HMV POP 790*	22	7
13 Apr 61		**LINDA LU** *HMV POP 853*	47	1
10 Jan 63		**A SHOT OF RHYTHM AND BLUES** *HMV POP 1088*	48	1
25 Jul 63	●	**I'LL NEVER GET OVER YOU** *HMV POP 1173*	4	15
28 Nov 63		**HUNGRY FOR LOVE** *HMV POP 1228*	20	10
30 Apr 64		**ALWAYS AND EVER** *HMV POP 1269*	46	1

Nicole KIDMAN *Australia, female actor / vocalist (2 Singles: 17 Weeks)*

Date		Title / Label	Pos	Wks
6 Oct 01		**COME WHAT MAY** *Interscope / Polydor 4976302* [1]	27	5
22 Dec 01	★	**SOMETHIN' STUPID** *Chrysalis CDCHS 5132* [2] ■	1	12

[1] Nicole Kidman and Ewan McGregor [2] Robbie Williams and Nicole Kidman

The KIDS FROM 'FAME' (486 Top 500)

TV's original 'Fame' academy students along with singing dance teacher Debbie Allen. These US actor / singers (backed by session musicians), who spent 12 weeks at No.1 with their debut album, oddly failed to crack the Top 40 in their homeland (5 Albums: 117 Weeks, 4 Singles: 36 Weeks)

Date		Title / Label	Pos	Wks
24 Jul 82	★	THE KIDS FROM 'FAME' *BBC REP 447*	1	45
14 Aug 82	●	**HI-FIDELITY** *RCA 254* [1]	5	10
2 Oct 82	●	**STARMAKER** *RCA 280*	3	10
16 Oct 82	●	THE KIDS FROM 'FAME' AGAIN *RCA RCALP 6057*	2	21
11 Dec 82		**MANNEQUIN** *RCA 299* [2]	50	6
26 Feb 83	●	THE KIDS FROM 'FAME' LIVE *BBC KIDLP 003*	8	28
9 Apr 83		**FRIDAY NIGHT (LIVE VERSION)** *RCA 320*	13	10
14 May 83		THE KIDS FROM 'FAME' SONGS *BBC KIDLP 004*	14	16
20 Aug 83		THE KIDS FROM 'FAME' SING FOR YOU *BBC KIDLP 005*	28	7

[1] The Kids from 'Fame' featuring Valerie Landsberg [2] The Kids from 'Fame' featuring Gene Anthony Ray

Greg KIHN BAND *US, male vocal / instrumental group*

Date		Title / Label	Pos	Wks
23 Apr 83		**JEOPARDY** *Beserkley E 9847*	63	2

KILL CITY *UK, female / male vocal / instrumental group*

Date		Title / Label	Pos	Wks
14 Aug 04		**JUST LIKE BRUCE LEE** *Poptones MC 5091SCD*	63	1

KILLAH PRIEST *US, male rapper – Walter Reed*

Date		Title / Label	Pos	Wks
7 Feb 98		**ONE STEP** *Geffen GFSTD 22318*	45	1

KILLER MIKE (see also OUTKAST) *US, male rapper – Michael Render*

Date		Title / Label	Pos	Wks
10 May 03		**A.D.I.D.A.S.** *Columbia 6738652*	22	3

The KILLERS *US, male vocal (Brandon Flowers) / instrumental group (1 Album: 77 Weeks, 5 Singles: 31 Weeks)*

Date		Title / Label	Pos	Wks
27 Mar 04		**SOMEBODY TOLD ME** *Lizard King LIZARD 009*	28	2
5 Jun 04	●	**MR BRIGHTSIDE** *Lizard King LIZARD 010CD2*	10	4
19 Jun 04	★	HOT FUSS *Lizard King LIZARD 011*	1	77+
11 Sep 04		**ALL THESE THINGS THAT I'VE DONE** *Lizard King LIZARD 012*	18	4
22 Jan 05	●	**SOMEBODY TOLD ME** (re) (re-issue) *Lizard King LIZARD 014CD2*	3	15
14 May 05		**SMILE LIKE YOU MEAN IT** (re) *Lizard King LIZARD 015*	11	6

KILLING JOKE *UK, male vocal / instrumental group (11 Albums: 35 Weeks, 16 Singles: 50 Weeks)*

Date		Title / Label	Pos	Wks
25 Oct 80		KILLING JOKE *Polydor EGMD 545*	39	4
23 May 81		**FOLLOW THE LEADERS** *Malicious Damage EGMDS 101*	55	5
20 Jun 81		WHAT'S THIS FOR *Malicious Damage EGMD 550*	42	4
20 Mar 82		**EMPIRE SONG** *Malicious Damage EGO 4*	43	4
8 May 82		REVELATIONS *Malicious Damage EGMD 3*	12	6
30 Oct 82		**BIRDS OF A FEATHER** *EG EGO 10*	64	2
27 Nov 82		'HA' – KILLING JOKE LIVE *EG EGMDT 4*	66	2
25 Jun 83		**LET'S ALL (GO TO THE FIRE DANCES)** *EG EGO 11*	51	3
23 Jul 83		FIRE DANCES *EG EGMD 5*	29	3
15 Oct 83		**ME OR YOU?** *EG EGO 14*	57	1
7 Apr 84		**EIGHTIES** *EG EGO 16*	60	5
21 Jul 84		**A NEW DAY** *EG EGO 17*	56	2
2 Feb 85		**LOVE LIKE BLOOD** *EG EGO 20*	16	9
9 Mar 85		NIGHT TIME *EG EGLP 61*	11	9
30 Mar 85		**KINGS AND QUEENS** *EG EGO 21*	58	3
16 Aug 86		**ADORATIONS** *EG EGO 27*	42	6
18 Oct 86		**SANITY** *EG EGO 30*	70	1
22 Nov 86		BRIGHTER THAN A THOUSAND SUNS *EG EGLP 66*	54	1
9 Jul 88		OUTSIDE THE GATE *EG EGLP 73*	92	1
7 May 94		**MILLENNIUM** *Butterfly BFLD 12*	34	2
16 Jul 94		**THE PANDEMONIUM SINGLE** *Butterfly BFLD 17*	28	3
6 Aug 94		PANDEMONIUM *Butterfly BFLCD 9*	16	3
4 Feb 95		**JANA** *Butterfly BFLDA 21*	54	1
23 Mar 96		**DEMOCRACY** *Butterfly BFLDA 33*	39	1
13 Apr 96		DEMOCRACY *Butterfly BFLCD 17*	71	1
26 Jul 03		**LOOSE CANNON** *Zuma ZUMAD 004*	25	2
9 Aug 03		KILLING JOKE *Zuma ZUMACD 002*	43	1

The KILLS *UK, male / female vocal / instrumental duo – Jamie 'Hotel' Hince and Alison 'VV' Mosshart (2 Albums: 2 Weeks, 4 Singles: 5 Weeks)*

Date		Title / Label	Pos	Wks
22 Mar 03		KEEP ON YOUR MEAN SIDE *Domino WIGCD 124*	47	1
26 Apr 03		**FRIED MY LITTLE BRAINS** *Domino RUG 154CD*	55	1
19 Feb 05		**THE GOOD ONES** *Domino RUG 190CD*	23	2
5 Mar 05		NO WOW *Domino WIGCD 149X*	56	1
11 Jun 05		**LOVE IS A DESERTER** *Domino RUG 198CD*	44	1
12 Nov 05		**NO WOW** *Domino RUG 207CD*	53	1

KILLSWITCH ENGAGE *US, male vocal / instrumental group*

Date		Title / Label	Pos	Wks
22 May 04		THE END OF HEARTACHE *Roadrunner RR 83732*	40	1

Andy KIM *Canada, male vocalist – Andrew Joachim*

Date		Title / Label	Pos	Wks
24 Aug 74	●	**ROCK ME GENTLY** *Capitol CL 15787* ▲ $	2	12

KIMERA with the LONDON SYMPHONY ORCHESTRA *Korea, female vocalist and UK, orchestra*

Date		Title / Label	Pos	Wks
26 Oct 85		HITS ON OPERA *Stylus SMR 8505*	38	4

KINANE *Ireland, female vocalist – Bianca Kinane (4 Singles: 4 Weeks)*

Date		Title / Label	Pos	Wks
18 May 96		**ALL THE LOVER I NEED** *Coliseum TOGA 003CD* [1]	59	1
21 Sep 96		**THE WOMAN IN ME** *Coliseum TOGA 007CD* [1]	73	1
16 May 98		**HEAVEN** *Coalition COLA 047CD*	49	1
22 Aug 98		**SO FINE** *Coalition COLA 055CD1*	63	1

[1] Bianca Kinane

KINESIS *UK, male vocal / instrumental group (3 Singles: 3 Weeks)*

Date		Title / Label	Pos	Wks
22 Mar 03		**... AND THEY OBEY** *Independiente ISOM 68MS*	63	1
28 Jun 03		**FOREVER REELING** *Independiente ISOM 74MS*	65	1
27 Sep 03		**ONE WAY MIRROR** *Independiente ISOM 77MS*	71	1

KING *UK / Ireland, male vocal (Paul King) / instrumental group (2 Albums: 32 Weeks, 5 Singles: 44 Weeks)*

Date		Title / Label	Pos	Wks
12 Jan 85	●	**LOVE AND PRIDE** *CBS A 4988*	2	14
9 Feb 85	●	STEPS IN TIME *CBS 26095*	6	21
23 Mar 85		**WON'T YOU HOLD MY HAND NOW** *CBS A 6094*	24	8
17 Aug 85	●	**ALONE WITHOUT YOU** *CBS A 6308*	8	9
19 Oct 85		**THE TASTE OF YOUR TEARS** *CBS A 6618*	11	9
23 Nov 85		BITTER SWEET *CBS 86320*	16	11
11 Jan 86		**TORTURE** *CBS A 6761*	23	4

1 June 1974	8 June 1974	15 June 1974	22 June 1974
SUGAR BABY LOVE The Rubettes	**SUGAR BABY LOVE** The Rubettes	**THE STREAK** Ray Stevens	**ALWAYS YOURS** Gary Glitter
THE SINGLES 1969-1973 The Carpenters	**DIAMOND DOGS** David Bowie	**DIAMOND DOGS** David Bowie	**DIAMOND DOGS** David Bowie

KEY UK No.1 ★★ UK Top 10 ●● Still on chart ++ UK entry at No.1 ■■ US No.1 ▲▲ UK million seller £ US million seller $
Singles re-entries are listed as (re), (2re), (3re)... which signifies that the hit re-entered the chart once, twice or three times...

Peak Position / Weeks

B.B. KING
US, male vocalist / guitarist – Riley King (3 Albums: 24 Weeks, 2 Singles: 10 Weeks)

Date		Title / Label	Pos	Wks
25 Aug 79		TAKE IT HOME *MCA MCF 3010*	60	5
15 Apr 89	●	WHEN LOVE COMES TO TOWN *Island IS 411* [1]	6	7
18 Jul 92		SINCE I MET YOU BABY *Virgin VS 1423* [2]	59	3
1 May 99		HIS DEFINITIVE GREATEST HITS *Universal Music TV 5473402*	24	4
24 Jun 00		RIDING WITH THE KING *Reprise 9362476122* [1]	15	15

[1] U2 with BB King [2] Gary Moore and BB King [1] BB King and Eric Clapton

Ben E KING
(see also The DRIFTERS) *US, male vocalist – Benjamin Nelson (4 Albums: 30 Weeks, 5 Singles: 35 Weeks)*

Date		Title / Label	Pos	Wks
2 Feb 61		FIRST TASTE OF LOVE *London HLK 9258*	27	11
22 Jun 61		STAND BY ME (re) *London HLK 9358*	27	7
5 Oct 61		AMOR, AMOR *London HLK 9416*	38	4
1 Jul 67		SPANISH HARLEM *Atlantic 590001*	30	3
14 Feb 87	★	STAND BY ME (re-issue) *Atlantic A 9361*	1	11
14 Mar 87		STAND BY ME (THE ULTIMATE COLLECTION) *Atlantic WX 90* [1]	14	8
4 Jul 87		SAVE THE LAST DANCE FOR ME *Manhattan MT 25*	69	2
20 Oct 90		THE VERY BEST OF BEN E. KING & THE DRIFTERS *Telstar STAR 2373* [1]	15	16
7 Nov 98		THE VERY BEST OF BEN E. KING & THE DRIFTERS *Warner.esp / Global TV RADCD 108* [1]	41	3

[1] Ben E King & The Drifters

KING BISCUIT TIME NEW
(see also The BETA BAND) *UK, male vocalist / guitarist – Stephen Mason*

Date		Title / Label	Pos	Wks
8 Oct 05		C I AM 15 *No Style MC 5103SCD*	67	1

Carole KING
US, female vocalist / pianist – Carole Klein (5 Albums: 108 Weeks, 3 Singles: 29 Weeks)

Date		Title / Label	Pos	Wks
20 Sep 62	●	IT MIGHT AS WELL RAIN UNTIL SEPTEMBER *London HLU 9591*	3	13
24 Jul 71	●	TAPESTRY *A&M AMLS 2025* ▲	4	90
7 Aug 71	●	IT'S TOO LATE *A&M AMS 849* ▲ $	6	12
15 Jan 72		MUSIC *A&M AMLH 67013* ▲	18	10
28 Oct 72		IT MIGHT AS WELL RAIN UNTIL SEPTEMBER (re-issue) *London HL 10391*	43	4
2 Dec 72		RHYMES AND REASONS *Ode 77016*	40	2
7 Feb 98		TAPESTRY (re-issue) *Epic CD 32110*	24	3
30 Sep 00		NATURAL WOMAN – THE VERY BEST OF CAROLE KING *Columbia SONYTV 93CD*	31	3

Dave KING
UK, male vocalist, b. 23 Jun 1929, d. 17 Apr 2002 (4 Singles: 29 Weeks)

Date		Title / Label	Pos	Wks
17 Feb 56	●	MEMORIES ARE MADE OF THIS *Decca F 10684* [1]	5	15
13 Apr 56		YOU CAN'T BE TRUE TO TWO *Decca F 10720* [1]	11	9
21 Dec 56		CHRISTMAS AND YOU *Decca F 10791*	23	2
24 Jan 58		THE STORY OF MY LIFE *Decca F 10973*	20	3

[1] Dave King featuring The Keynotes

Diana KING
Jamaica, female vocalist (1 Album: 2 Weeks, 3 Singles: 22 Weeks)

Date		Title / Label	Pos	Wks
8 Jul 95	●	SHY GUY *Columbia 6621682*	2	13
12 Aug 95		TOUGHER THAN LOVE *Columbia 4777562*	50	2
28 Oct 95		AIN'T NOBODY *Columbia 6625495*	13	5
1 Nov 97		I SAY A LITTLE PRAYER *Columbia 6651472*	17	4

Evelyn 'Champagne' KING
US, female vocalist (1 Album: 9 Weeks, 11 Singles: 76 Weeks)

Date		Title / Label	Pos	Wks
13 May 78		SHAME *RCA PC 1122* $	39	23
3 Feb 79		I DON'T KNOW IF IT'S RIGHT *RCA PB 1386* $	67	2
27 Jun 81		I'M IN LOVE *RCA 95* [1]	27	11
26 Sep 81		IF YOU WANT MY LOVIN' *RCA 131* [1]	43	6
28 Aug 82	●	LOVE COME DOWN *RCA 249* [1]	7	13
11 Sep 82		GET LOOSE *RCA RCALP 3093*	35	9
20 Nov 82		BACK TO LOVE *RCA 287* [1]	40	4
19 Feb 83		GET LOOSE *RCA 315* [1]	45	5
9 Nov 85		YOUR PERSONAL TOUCH *RCA PB 49915*	37	5
29 Mar 86		HIGH HORSE *RCA PB 49891*	55	3
23 Jul 88		HOLD ON TO WHAT YOU'VE GOT *Manhattan MT 49*	47	3
10 Oct 92		SHAME (re-mix) *Network NWKTEN 56* [2]	74	1

[1] Evelyn King [2] Altern 8 vs Evelyn King

Jonathan KING
UK, male producer / vocalist – Kenneth King (17 Singles: 128 Weeks)

Date		Title / Label	Pos	Wks
29 Jul 65	●	EVERYONE'S GONE TO THE MOON *Decca F 12187*	4	11
10 Jan 70		LET IT ALL HANG OUT *Decca F 12988*	26	7
16 Jan 71		IT'S THE SAME OLD SONG *B&C CB 139* [1]	19	9
3 Apr 71		SUGAR SUGAR *RCA 2064* [2]	12	14
29 May 71		LAZY BONES *Decca F 13177*	23	8
20 Nov 71		HOOKED ON A FEELING *Decca F 13241*	23	10
5 Feb 72		FLIRT! *Decca F 13276*	22	9
14 Oct 72	●	LOOP DI LOVE *UK 7* [3]	4	13
26 Jan 74		(I CAN'T GET NO) SATISFACTION *UK 53* [4]	29	5
6 Sep 75	●	UNA PALOMA BLANCA (WHITE DOVE) *UK 105*	5	11
20 Sep 75		CHICK-A-BOOM (DON'T YA JES LOVE IT) *UK 2012 002* [5]	36	4
7 Feb 76		IN THE MOOD *UK 121* [6]	46	3
26 Jun 76	●	IT ONLY TAKES A MINUTE *UK 135* [7]	9	9
7 Oct 78		ONE FOR YOU, ONE FOR ME *GTO GT 237*	29	6
16 Dec 78		LICK A SMURP FOR CHRISTMAS (ALL FALL DOWN) *Petrol GAS 1 / Magnet MAG 139* [8]	58	4
16 Jun 79		YOU'RE THE GREATEST LOVER *UK International INT 586*	67	2
3 Nov 79		GLORIA *Ariola ARO 198*	65	3

[1] Weathermen [2] Sakkarin [3] Shag [4] Bubblerock [5] 53rd and 3rd featuring the Sound of Shag [6] Sound 9418 [7] One Hundred Ton and a Feather [8] Father Abraphart and The Smurps

Mark KING
(see also LEVEL 42) *UK, male vocalist / bass guitarist*

Date		Title / Label	Pos	Wks
21 Jul 84		INFLUENCES *Polydor MKLP 1*	77	2

Paul KING
(see also KING) *UK, male vocalist*

Date		Title / Label	Pos	Wks
2 May 87		I KNOW *CBS PKING 1*	59	3

Solomon KING
US, male vocalist – Allen Levy, b. 13 Aug 1930, d. 20 Jan 2005 (1 Album: 1 Week, 2 Singles: 28 Weeks)

Date		Title / Label	Pos	Wks
3 Jan 68	●	SHE WEARS MY RING *Columbia DB 8325*	3	18
1 May 68		WHEN WE WERE YOUNG *Columbia DB 8402*	21	10
22 Jun 68		SHE WEARS MY RING *Columbia SCX 6250*	40	1

KING ADORA
UK, male vocal / instrumental group (1 Album: 1 Week, 4 Singles: 6 Weeks)

Date		Title / Label	Pos	Wks
4 Nov 00		SMOULDER *Superior Quality / A&M RQSD 010CD*	62	1
3 Mar 01		SUFFOCATE *Superior Quality / A&M RQS 11DD*	39	2
26 May 01		BIONIC *Superior Quality / A&M RQS 012CD*	30	2
2 Jun 01		VIBRATE YOU *Superior Quality RQS 13CD*	30	1
31 May 03		BORN TO LOSE / KAMIKAZE *MHR MHRCD 001*	68	1

KING BEE
Holland, male rapper (2 Singles: 6 Weeks)

Date		Title / Label	Pos	Wks
26 Jan 91		MUST BEE THE MUSIC *Columbia 6565827* [1]	44	4
23 Mar 91		BACK BY DOPE DEMAND *First Bass 7RUFF 6X*	61	2

[1] King Bee featuring Michele

	29 June 1974	6 July 1974	13 July 1974	20 July 1974
UK No.1 SINGLES	SHE Charles Aznavour	SHE Charles Aznavour	SHE Charles Aznavour	SHE Charles Aznavour
UK No.1 ALBUMS	DIAMOND DOGS David Bowie	THE SINGLES 1969-1973 The Carpenters	CARIBOU Elton John	CARIBOU Elton John

The KING BROTHERS *UK, male vocal trio (8 Singles: 74 Weeks)*

31 May 57 ● **A WHITE SPORT COAT (AND A PINK CARNATION)** *Parlophone R 4310*....6 14
9 Aug 57 **IN THE MIDDLE OF AN ISLAND** *Parlophone R 4338*....19 13
6 Dec 57 **WAKE UP LITTLE SUSIE** *Parlophone R 4367*....22 3
31 Jan 58 **PUT A LIGHT IN THE WINDOW** (2re) *Parlophone R 4389*....25 4
14 Apr 60 ● **STANDING ON THE CORNER** *Parlophone R 4639*....4 11
28 Jul 60 **MAIS OUI** *Parlophone R 4672*....16 10
12 Jan 61 **DOLL HOUSE** *Parlophone R 4715*....21 8
2 Mar 61 **76 TROMBONES** *Parlophone R 4737*....19 11

KING CRIMSON

(see also ANDERSON BRUFORD WAKEMAN HOWE; Robert FRIPP; Greg LAKE) *UK / US, male vocal / instrumental group (11 Albums: 55 Weeks)*

1 Nov 69 ● IN THE COURT OF THE CRIMSON KING *Island ILPS 9111*....5 18
30 May 70 ● IN THE WAKE OF POSEIDON *Island ILPS 9127*....4 13
16 Jan 71 LIZARD *Island ILPS 9141*....29 2
8 Jan 72 ISLANDS *Island ILPS 9175*....30 1
7 Apr 73 LARKS' TONGUES IN ASPIC *Island ILPS 9230*....20 4
13 Apr 74 STARLESS AND BIBLE BLACK *Island ILPS 9275*....28 2
26 Oct 74 RED *Island ILPS 9308*....45 1
10 Oct 81 DISCIPLINE *EG EGLP 49*....41 4
26 Jun 82 BEAT *EG EGLP 51*....39 5
31 Mar 84 THREE OF A PERFECT PAIR *EG EGLP 55*....30 4
15 Apr 95 THRAK *Virgin KCCDY 1*....58 1

KING KURT *UK, male vocal / instrumental group (2 Albums: 5 Weeks, 5 Singles: 16 Weeks)*

15 Oct 83 **DESTINATION ZULULAND** *Stiff BUY 189*....36 6
10 Dec 83 OOH WALLAH WALLAH *Stiff SEEZ 52*....99 1
28 Apr 84 **MACK THE KNIFE** *Stiff BUY 199*....55 4
4 Aug 84 **BANANA BANANA** *Stiff BUY 206*....54 4
8 Mar 86 BIG COCK *Stiff SEEZ 62*....50 4
15 Nov 86 **AMERICA** *Polydor KURT 1*....73 1
2 May 87 **THE LAND OF RING DANG DO** *Polydor KURT 2*....67 1

KING SUN-D'MOET *US, male rap / DJ duo*

11 Jul 87 **HEY LOVE** *Flame MELT 5*....66 3

KING TRIGGER *UK, male / female vocal / instrumental group*

14 Aug 82 **THE RIVER** *Chrysalis CHS 2623*....57 4

KINGDOM COME *US, male vocal / instrumental group (2 Albums: 10 Weeks, 2 Singles: 2 Weeks)*

28 Mar 88 KINGDOM COME *Polydor KCLP 1*....43 6
16 Apr 88 **GET IT ON** *Polydor KCS 1*....75 1
6 May 89 **DO YOU LIKE IT** *Polydor KCS 3*....73 1
13 May 89 IN YOUR FACE *Polydor 839192 1*....25 4

KINGMAKER

UK, male vocal / instrumental group (2 Albums: 10 Weeks, 8 Singles: 22 Weeks)

19 Oct 91 EAT YOURSELF WHOLE *Scorch CHR 1878*....29 3
18 Jan 92 **IDIOTS AT THE WHEEL (EP)** *Scorch SCORCH 3*....30 3
23 May 92 **EAT YOURSELF WHOLE** *Scorch SCORCHG 5*....15 3
31 Oct 92 **ARMCHAIR ANARCHIST** *Scorch SCORCHG 6*....47 2
8 May 93 **10 YEARS ASLEEP** *Scorch CDSCORCHS 8*....15 4
29 May 93 SLEEPWALKING *Scorch CDCHR 6014*....15 7
19 Jun 93 **QUEEN JANE** *Scorch CDSCORS 9*....29 4
30 Oct 93 **SATURDAY'S NOT WHAT IT USED TO BE** *Scorch CDSCORCH 10*....63 1
15 Apr 95 **YOU AND I WILL NEVER SEE THINGS EYE TO EYE** *Scorch CDSCORCHS 11*....33 3
3 Jun 95 **IN THE BEST POSSIBLE TASTE (PART 2)** *Scorch CDSCORCHS 12*....41 2

Tracks on Idiots at the Wheel (EP): Really Scrape the Sky / Revelation / Every Teenage Suicide / Strip Away.

The Choir of KING'S COLLEGE CAMBRIDGE *UK, choir*

11 Dec 71 THE WORLD OF CHRISTMAS *Argo SPAA 104*....38 3

KINGS OF CONVENIENCE *Norway, male vocal / instrumental duo (2 Albums: 2 Weeks, 3 Singles: 3 Weeks)*

10 Feb 01 QUIET IS THE NEW LOUD *Source SOURCD 019*....72 1
21 Apr 01 **TOXIC GIRL** *Source SOURCDSE 1025*....44 1
14 Jul 01 **FAILURE** *Source SOURCD 036*....63 1
3 Jul 04 RIOT ON AN EMPTY STREET *Source CDSOUR 099*....49 1
4 Sep 04 **I'D RATHER DANCE WITH YOU** *Source SOURCDX 102*....60 1

KINGS OF LEON *US, male vocal (Caleb Followill) / instrumental group (2 Albums: 42 Weeks, 8 Singles: 18 Weeks)*

8 Mar 03 **HOLY ROLLER NOVOCAINE** *Hand Me Down / RCA HMD 21*....53 1
14 Jun 03 **WHAT I SAW** *Hand Me Down HMD 23*....22 3
19 Jul 03 ● YOUTH & YOUNG MANHOOD *Hand Me Down HMD 27*....3 26
23 Aug 03 **MOLLY'S CHAMBERS** *Hand Me Down HMD 29*....23 3
1 Nov 03 **WASTED TIME** *Hand Me Down HMD 32*....51 2
28 Feb 04 **CALIFORNIA WAITING** *Hand Me Down HMD 36*....61 1
6 Nov 04 **THE BUCKET** *Hand Me Down HMD 41*....16 3
13 Nov 04 ● AHA SHAKE HEARTBREAK *Hand Me Down HMD 39*....3 16
22 Jan 05 **FOUR KICKS** *Hand Me Down HMD 45*....24 3
23 Apr 05 **KING OF THE RODEO** *Hand Me Down HMD 49*....41 2

KINGS OF SWING ORCHESTRA *Australia, orchestra*

1 May 82 **SWITCHED ON SWING** *Philips Swing 1*....48 5
29 May 82 SWITCHED ON SWING *K-Tel ONE 1166*....28 11

KINGS OF TOMORROW

(see also LAYO & BUSHWACKA!) *US, male production / instrumental duo – Sandy Rivera and Jason Sealee (6 Singles: 9 Weeks)*

14 Apr 01 **FINALLY** *Distance DI 2029* [1]....54 1
29 Sep 01 **FINALLY** (re-mix) *Defected DFECT 37CDS* [1]....24 3
13 Apr 02 **YOUNG HEARTS** *Defected DFECT 46CDS*....45 2
25 Oct 03 **DREAMS / THROUGH** *Defected DFTD 079*....74 1
31 Jul 04 **DREAMS** *Defected DFTD 090CDS* [2]....69 1
26 Feb 05 **THRU** *Defected DFTD 099* [2]....55 1

[1] Kings of Tomorrow featuring Julie McKnight
[2] Kings of Tomorrow featuring Haze

KING'S X *US, male vocal / instrumental group (4 Albums: 4 Weeks)*

1 Jul 89 GRETCHEN GOES TO NEBRASKA *Atlantic WX 279*....52 1
10 Nov 90 FAITH HOPE LOVE *Megaforce 756821451*....70 1
28 Mar 92 KING'S X *Atlantic 7567805062*....46 1
12 Feb 94 DOGMAN *Atlantic 7567825582*....49 1

The KINGSMEN *US, male vocal / instrumental group*

30 Jan 64 **LOUIE, LOUIE** *Pye International 7N 25231* $....26 7

The KINGSTON TRIO

US, male vocal / instrumental group (2 Singles: 15 Weeks)

21 Nov 58 ● **TOM DOOLEY** *Capitol CL 14951* ▲ $....5 14
4 Dec 59 **SAN MIGUEL** *Capitol CL 15073*....29 1

The KINKS 150 Top 500

Well-respected, influential and innovative London band who had few equals in the 1960s: Ray Davies (v/g), Dave Davies (g), Pete Quaife (b) and Mick Avory (d). Ray Davies, regarded as one of rock's premier songwriters, remains active over 40 years after the group's first hit. They were added to the UK Music Hall of Fame in 2005 (14 Albums: 140 Weeks, 25 Singles: 217 Weeks)

13 Aug 64 ★ **YOU REALLY GOT ME** *Pye 7N 15673*....1 12
17 Oct 64 ● KINKS *Pye NPL 18096*....3 25
29 Oct 64 ● **ALL DAY AND ALL OF THE NIGHT** *Pye 7N 15714*....2 14
21 Jan 65 ★ **TIRED OF WAITING FOR YOU** *Pye 7N 15759*....1 10

27 July 1974	3 August 1974	10 August 1974	17 August 1974
ROCK YOUR BABY George McCrae	ROCK YOUR BABY George McCrae	ROCK YOUR BABY George McCrae	WHEN WILL I SEE YOU AGAIN The Three Degrees
BAND ON THE RUN Paul McCartney and Wings	BAND ON THE RUN Paul McCartney and Wings	BAND ON THE RUN Paul McCartney and Wings	BAND ON THE RUN Paul McCartney and Wings

KEY		Peak Position	Weeks
UK No.1 ★ UK Top 10 ● Still on chart + UK entry at No.1 ■ US No.1 ▲ UK million seller £ US million seller $ Singles re-entries are listed as (re), (2re), (3re)... which signifies that the hit re-entered the chart once, twice or three times...			

13 Mar 65 ● KINDA KINKS *Pye NPL 18112* 3 15
25 Mar 65 EVERYBODY'S GONNA BE HAPPY *Pye 7N 15813* 17 8
27 May 65 ● SET ME FREE *Pye 7N 15854* 9 11
5 Aug 65 ● SEE MY FRIEND *Pye 7N 15919* 10 9
2 Dec 65 ● TILL THE END OF THE DAY *Pye 7N 15981* 8 12
4 Dec 65 ● THE KINK KONTROVERSY *Pye NPL 18131* 9 12
3 Mar 66 ● DEDICATED FOLLOWER OF FASHION *Pye 7N 17064* 4 11
9 Jun 66 ★ SUNNY AFTERNOON *Pye 7N 17125* 1 13
11 Sep 66 ● WELL RESPECTED KINKS *Marble Arch MAL 612* 5 31
5 Nov 66 FACE TO FACE *Pye NPL 18149* 12 11
24 Nov 66 ● DEAD END STREET *Pye 7N 17222* 5 11
11 May 67 ● WATERLOO SUNSET *Pye 7N 17321* 2 11
14 Oct 67 SOMETHING ELSE *Pye NSPL 18193* 35 2
18 Oct 67 ● AUTUMN ALMANAC *Pye 7N 17400* 3 11
2 Dec 67 ● SUNNY AFTERNOON *Marble Arch MAL 716* 9 11
17 Apr 68 WONDERBOY *Pye 7N 17468* 36 5
17 Jul 68 DAYS *Pye 7N 17573* 12 10
16 Apr 69 PLASTIC MAN *Pye 7N 17724* 31 4
10 Jan 70 VICTORIA *Pye 7N 17865* 33 4
4 Jul 70 ● LOLA *Pye 7N 17961* 2 14
12 Dec 70 ● APEMAN *Pye 7N 45016* 5 14
23 Oct 71 GOLDEN HOUR OF THE KINKS *Golden Hour GH 501* 21 4
27 May 72 SUPERSONIC ROCKET SHIP *RCA 2211* 16 8
14 Oct 78 20 GOLDEN GREATS *Ronco RPL 2031* 19 6
27 Jun 81 BETTER THINGS *Arista ARIST 415* 46 5
6 Aug 83 COME DANCING *Arista ARIST 502* 12 9
15 Oct 83 DON'T FORGET TO DANCE *Arista ARIST 524* 58 3
15 Oct 83 YOU REALLY GOT ME (re-issue) *PRT KD1* 47 4
5 Nov 83 KINKS GREATEST HITS – DEAD END STREET *PRT KINK 1* 96 1
16 Sep 89 THE ULTIMATE COLLECTION *Castle Communications CTVLP 001* 35 7
18 Sep 93 THE DEFINITIVE COLLECTION *PolyGram TV 5164652* 18 7
18 Jan 97 THE DAYS EP *When! WENX 1016* 35 2
12 Apr 97 THE VERY BEST OF THE KINKS *PolyGram TV 5375542* 42 3
8 Jun 02 THE ULTIMATE COLLECTION *Sanctuary SANDD 109* 32 5
18 Sep 04 YOU REALLY GOT ME (2nd re-issue) *Sanctuary SANXD 317* 42 2

Tracks on The Days EP: Days / You Really Got Me / Dead End Street / Lola.

KINKY (see also ERASURE) *UK, female rapper – Caron Geary*

24 Aug 96 EVERYBODY *Feverpitch CDFVR 1009* 71 1

KINKY MACHINE
UK, male vocal / instrumental group (4 Singles: 4 Weeks)

6 Mar 93 SUPERNATURAL GIVER *Lemon LEMON 006CD* 70 1
29 May 93 SHOCKAHOLIC *Oxygen GASPD 5* 70 1
14 Aug 93 GOING OUT WITH GOD *Oxygen GASPD 9* 74 1
2 Jul 94 10 SECOND BIONIC MAN *Oxygen GASPD 14* 66 1

Fern KINNEY *US, female vocalist – Fern Kinney-Lewis*

16 Feb 80 ★ TOGETHER WE ARE BEAUTIFUL *WEA K 79111* 1 11

KIOKI *Japan, male vocalist*

17 Aug 02 DO & DON'T FOR LOVE *V2 VVR 5020803* 66 1

KIRA *Belgium, female vocalist – Natasja De Witte*

1 Mar 03 ● I'LL BE YOUR ANGEL *Nulife 74321970362* 9 5

Kathy KIRBY *UK, female vocalist – Kathleen O'Rourke (1 Album: 8 Weeks, 5 Singles: 54 Weeks)*

15 Aug 63 DANCE ON *Decca F 11682* 11 13
7 Nov 63 ● SECRET LOVE *Decca F 11759* 4 18
4 Jan 64 16 HITS FROM STARS AND GARTERS *Decca LK 5475* 11 8
20 Feb 64 ● LET ME GO LOVER! *Decca F 11832* 10 11
7 May 64 YOU'RE THE ONE *Decca F 11892* 17 9
4 Mar 65 I BELONG *Decca F 12087* 36 3

Bo KIRKLAND and Ruth DAVIS *US, male / female vocal duo*

4 Jun 77 YOU'RE GONNA GET NEXT TO ME *EMI International INT 532* 12 9

Dominic KIRWAN *Ireland, male vocalist*

1 Nov 97 THE MUSIC'S BACK *Ritz RITZCD 0084* 54 1

KISS (see also FREHLEY'S COMET; Gene SIMMONS; Vinnie VINCENT)
US / Israel, male vocal / instrumental group (19 Albums: 71 Weeks, 13 Singles: 57 Weeks)

29 May 76 DESTROYER *Casablanca CBSP 4008* 22 5
25 Jun 76 ALIVE! *Casablanca CBSP 401* 49 2
17 Dec 77 ALIVE *Casablanca CALD 5004* 60 1
30 Jun 79 I WAS MADE FOR LOVIN' YOU *Casablanca CAN 152* $ 50 7
7 Jul 79 DYNASTY *Casablanca CALH 2051* 50 6
28 Jun 80 UNMASKED *Mercury 6302 032* 48 3
5 Dec 81 THE ELDER *Casablanca 6302 163* 51 3
20 Feb 82 A WORLD WITHOUT HEROES *Casablanca KISS 002* 55 3
26 Jun 82 KILLERS *Casablanca CANL 1* 42 6
6 Nov 82 CREATURES OF THE NIGHT *Casablanca CANL 4* 22 4
30 Apr 83 CREATURES OF THE NIGHT *Casablanca KISS 4* 34 4
8 Oct 83 ● LICK IT UP *Vertigo VERL 9* 7 7
29 Oct 83 LICK IT UP *Vertigo KISS 5* 31 5
8 Sep 84 HEAVEN'S ON FIRE *Vertigo VER 12* 43 3
6 Oct 84 ANIMALIZE *Vertigo VERL 18* 11 4
5 Oct 85 ASYLUM *Vertigo VERH 32* 12 3
9 Nov 85 TEARS ARE FALLING *Vertigo KISS 6* 57 2
3 Oct 87 ● CRAZY CRAZY NIGHTS *Vertigo KISS 7* 4 9
7 Nov 87 ● CRAZY NIGHTS *Vertigo VERH 49* 4 14
5 Dec 87 REASON TO LIVE *Vertigo KISS 8* 33 7
10 Sep 88 TURN ON THE NIGHT *Vertigo KISS 9* 41 3
10 Dec 88 SMASHES THRASHES AND HITS *Vertigo 836759 1* 62 2
4 Nov 89 HOT IN THE SHADE *Fontana 838913 1* 35 2
18 Nov 89 HIDE YOUR HEART *Vertigo KISS 10* 59 2
31 Mar 90 FOREVER *Vertigo KISS 11* 65 2
11 Jan 92 ● GOD GAVE ROCK AND ROLL TO YOU II *Interscope A 8696* 4 8
9 May 92 UNHOLY *Mercury KISS 12* 26 2
23 May 92 ● REVENGE *Mercury 8480372* 10 3
29 May 93 ALIVE III *Mercury 5148272* 24 2
23 Mar 96 MTV UNPLUGGED *Mercury 5289502* 74 1
12 Jul 97 GREATEST HITS *PolyGram TV 5361592* 58 2
3 Oct 98 PSYCHO-CIRCUS *Mercury 5589922* 47 1

KISS AMC *UK, female rap duo (2 Singles: 5 Weeks)*

1 Jul 89 A BIT OF U2 (re) *Syncopate SY 29* 58 4
3 Feb 90 MY DOCS *Syncopate XAMC 1* 66 1

Before its re-entry in Aug '89, due to copyright problems, 'A Bit of U2' was unable to be given its full title.

KISSING THE PINK *UK, male / female vocal / instrumental group*

5 Mar 83 LAST FILM *Magnet KTP 3* 19 14
4 Jun 83 NAKED *Magnet KTPL 1001* 54 5

Mac and Katie KISSOON
Trinidad / UK, male / female vocal duo (5 Singles: 33 Weeks)

19 Jun 71 CHIRPY CHIRPY CHEEP CHEEP *Young Blood YB 1026* 41 1
18 Jan 75 ● SUGAR CANDY KISSES *Polydor 2058 531* 3 10
3 May 75 ● DON'T DO IT BABY *State STAT 4* 9 8
30 Aug 75 LIKE A BUTTERFLY *State STAT 9* 18 9
15 May 76 THE TWO OF US *State STAT 21* 46 5

	24 August 1974	31 August 1974	7 September 1974	14 September 1974
UK No.1 SINGLES	WHEN WILL I SEE YOU AGAIN The Three Degrees	LOVE ME FOR A REASON The Osmonds	LOVE ME FOR A REASON The Osmonds	LOVE ME FOR A REASON The Osmonds
UK No.1 ALBUMS	BAND ON THE RUN Paul McCartney and Wings	BAND ON THE RUN Paul McCartney and Wings	BAND ON THE RUN Paul McCartney and Wings	HERGEST RIDGE Mike Oldfield

Kevin KITCHEN *UK, male vocalist*

20 Apr 85 **PUT MY ARMS AROUND YOU** *China WOK 1*....64 3

KITCHENS OF DISTINCTION

UK, male vocal / instrumental group (2 Albums: 2 Weeks)

30 Mar 91 **STRANGE FREE WORLD** *One Little Indian TPLP 19*....45 1
15 Aug 92 **THE DEATH OF COOL** *One Little Indian TPLP 39CD*....72 1

Joy KITIKONTI *Italy, male producer – Massimo Chiticonti*

17 Nov 01 **JOYENERGIZER** *BXR BXRC 0347*....57 2

Eartha KITT *US, female vocalist (1 Album: 1 Week, 6 Singles: 34 Weeks)*

1 Apr 55 ● **UNDER THE BRIDGES OF PARIS** (re) *HMV B 10647*....7 10
11 Feb 61 **REVISITED** *London HA 2296*....17 1
3 Dec 83 **WHERE IS MY MAN** *Record Shack SOHO 11*....36 11
7 Jul 84 **I LOVE MEN** *Record Shack SOHO 21*....50 3
12 Apr 86 **THIS IS MY LIFE** *Record Shack SOHO 61*....73 1
1 Jul 89 **CHA CHA HEELS** *Arista 112331* [1]....32 7
5 Mar 94 **IF I LOVE YA THEN I NEED YA IF I NEED YA THEN I WANT YOU AROUND** *RCA 74321190342*....43 2

[1] Eartha Kitt and Bronski Beat

KITTIE *Canada, female vocal / instrumental group (2 Singles: 2 Weeks)*

25 Mar 00 **BRACKISH** *Epic 6691292*....46 1
22 Jul 00 **CHARLOTTE** *Epic 6696222*....60 1

Myleene KLASS (see also HEAR'SAY) *UK, female vocalist / pianist*

1 Nov 03 **MOVING ON** *UCJ 9865632*....32 3

The KLAXONS *Belgium, male vocal / instrumental group*

10 Dec 83 **THE CLAP CLAP SOUND** *PRT 7P 290*....45 6

KLEA *UK, male / female production / vocal / rap trio*

7 Sep 02 **TIC TOC** *Incentive CENT 41CDS*....61 1

KLEEER *US, male / female vocal / instrumental group (1 Album: 1 Week, 2 Singles: 10 Weeks)*

17 Mar 79 **KEEEP YOUR BODY WORKIN'** *Atlantic LV 21*....51 6
14 Mar 81 **GET TOUGH** *Atlantic 11560*....49 4
6 Jul 85 **SEEEKRET** *Atlantic 7812541*....96 1

KLESHAY *UK, female vocal trio (2 Singles: 5 Weeks)*

19 Sep 98 **REASONS** *Epic KLE 1CD*....33 2
20 Feb 99 **RUSH** *Epic KLE 2CD*....19 3

KLUBBHEADS (see also DA TECHNO BOHEMIAN; DRUNKENMUNKY; ITTY BITTY BOOZY WOOZY) *Holland, male instrumental / production group (3 Singles: 10 Weeks)*

11 May 96 ● **KLUBBHOPPING** *AM:PM 5815572*....10 6
16 Aug 97 **DISCOHOPPING** *AM:PM 5823032*....35 2
15 Aug 98 **KICKIN' HARD** *Wonderboy WBOYD 011*....36 2

KLUSTER featuring Ron CARROLL

France, male DJ / production duo

28 Apr 01 **MY LOVE** *Scorpio Music 1928112*....73 1

The KNACK *US, male vocal (Doug Fieger) / instrumental group (1 Album: 2 Weeks, 2 Singles: 12 Weeks)*

30 Jun 79 ● **MY SHARONA** *Capitol CL 16087* ▲ $....6 10
4 Aug 79 **GET THE KNACK** *Capitol EST 11948* ▲....65 2
13 Oct 79 **GOOD GIRLS DON'T** *Capitol CL 16097*....66 2

Beverley KNIGHT *UK, female vocalist – Beverley Smith (3 Albums: 47 Weeks, 16 Singles: 62 Weeks)*

8 Apr 95 **FLAVOUR OF THE OLD SCHOOL** *Dome CDDOME 101*....50 2
2 Sep 95 **DOWN FOR THE ONE** *Dome CDDOME 102*....55 1
21 Oct 95 **FLAVOUR OF THE OLD SCHOOL** (re-mix) *Dome CDDOME 105*....33 2
23 Mar 96 **MOVING ON UP (ON THE RIGHT SIDE)** *Dome CDDOME 107*....42 1
30 May 98 **MADE IT BACK** *Parlophone Rhythm CDRHYTHM 11* [1]....21 3
22 Aug 98 **REWIND (FIND A WAY)** *Parlophone Rhythm CDRHYTHS 13*....40 2
5 Sep 98 **PRODIGAL SISTA** *Parlophone Rhythm 4962962*....42 14
10 Apr 99 **MADE IT BACK 99** (re-mix) *Parlophone Rhythm CDRHYTHM 18*....19 5
17 Jul 99 **GREATEST DAY** *Parlophone Rhythm CDRHYTHS 22*....14 5
4 Dec 99 **SISTA SISTA** *Parlophone Rhythm CDRHYTHM 26*....31 2
17 Nov 01 **GET UP** *Parlophone CDRS 6564*....17 4
9 Mar 02 ● **SHOULDA WOULDA COULDA** *Parlophone CDRS 6570*....10 9
23 Mar 02 ● **WHO I AM** *Parlophone 5360320*....7 24
6 Jul 02 **GOLD** *Parlophone CDRS 6580*....27 4
3 Jul 04 ● **COME AS YOU ARE** *Parlophone CDRS 6636*....9 10
10 Jul 04 **AFFIRMATION** *Parlophone 4733102*....11 9
9 Oct 04 **NOT TOO LATE FOR LOVE** *Parlophone CDRS 6645*....31 2
22 Jan 05 **NO MORE** *V VRECSUK 003CD* [2]....26 4
26 Mar 05 **KEEP THIS FIRE BURNING** *Parlophone CDRS 6657*....16 6

[1] Beverley Knight featuring Redman [2] Roni Size featuring Beverley Knight & Dynamite MC

Frederick KNIGHT *US, male vocalist*

10 Jun 72 **I'VE BEEN LONELY SO LONG** *Stax 2025 098*....22 10

Gladys KNIGHT and The PIPS

195 Top 500 *One of soul music's foremost female singers for almost 40 years, b. 28 May 1944, Georgia, US. The celebrated vocalist (who first appeared on US TV aged eight) and her family quartet The Pips (they split in 1989) were inducted into the Rock and Roll Hall of Fame in 1996 (10 Albums: 117 Weeks, 24 Singles: 187 Weeks)*

8 Jun 67 **TAKE ME IN YOUR ARMS AND LOVE ME** *Tamla Motown TMG 604*....13 15
27 Dec 67 **I HEARD IT THROUGH THE GRAPEVINE** *Tamla Motown TMG 629*....47 1
17 Jun 72 **JUST WALK IN MY SHOES** *Tamla Motown TMG 813*....35 8
25 Nov 72 **HELP ME MAKE IT THROUGH THE NIGHT** *Tamla Motown TMG 830*....11 17
3 Mar 73 **THE LOOK OF LOVE** *Tamla Motown TMG 844*....21 9
26 May 73 **NEITHER ONE OF US (WANTS TO BE THE FIRST TO SAY GOODBYE)** *Tamla Motown TMG 855*....31 7
5 Apr 75 ● **THE WAY WE WERE – TRY TO REMEMBER** *Buddah BDS 428*....4 15
31 May 75 **I FEEL A SONG** *Buddah BDLP 4030*....20 15
2 Aug 75 ● **BEST THING THAT EVER HAPPENED TO ME** *Buddah BDS 432* $....7 10
15 Nov 75 **PART TIME LOVE** *Buddah BDS 438*....30 5
28 Feb 76 ● **THE BEST OF GLADYS KNIGHT & THE PIPS** *Buddah BDLH 5013*....6 43
8 May 76 ● **MIDNIGHT TRAIN TO GEORGIA** *Buddah BDS 444* ▲ $....10 9
21 Aug 76 **MAKE YOURS A HAPPY HOME** *Buddah BDS 447*....35 4
6 Nov 76 **SO SAD THE SONG** *Buddah BDS 448*....20 9
15 Jan 77 **NOBODY BUT YOU** *Buddah BDS 451*....34 2
28 May 77 ● **BABY DON'T CHANGE YOUR MIND** *Buddah BDS 458*....4 12
16 Jul 77 **STILL TOGETHER** *Buddah BDLH 5014*....42 3
24 Sep 77 **HOME IS WHERE THE HEART IS** *Buddah BDS 460*....35 4
12 Nov 77 ● **30 GREATEST** *K-Tel NE 1004*....3 22
8 Apr 78 **THE ONE AND ONLY** (re) *Buddah BDS 470*....32 5
24 Jun 78 **COME BACK AND FINISH WHAT YOU STARTED** *Buddah BDS 473*....15 13
30 Sep 78 **IT'S A BETTER THAN GOOD TIME** *Buddah BDS 478*....59 4
30 Aug 80 **TASTE OF BITTER LOVE** *CBS 8890*....35 6
4 Oct 80 **A TOUCH OF LOVE** *K-Tel NE 1090*....16 6
8 Nov 80 **BOURGIE, BOURGIE** *CBS 9081*....32 6
26 Dec 81 **WHEN A CHILD IS BORN** *CBS S 1758* [1]....74 2
4 Feb 84 **THE COLLECTION – 20 GREATEST HITS** *Starblend NITE 1*....43 5

21 September 1974	28 September 1974	5 October 1974	12 October 1974
KUNG FU FIGHTING Carl Douglas	KUNG FU FIGHTING Carl Douglas	KUNG FU FIGHTING Carl Douglas	ANNIE'S SONG John Denver
HERGEST RIDGE Mike Oldfield	HERGEST RIDGE Mike Oldfield	TUBULAR BELLS Mike Oldfield	ROLLIN' Bay City Rollers

KEY UK No.1 ★ UK Top 10 ● Still on chart + UK entry at No.1 ■ US No.1 ▲ UK million seller £ US million seller $
Singles re-entries are listed as (re), (2re), (3re)... which signifies that the hit re-entered the chart once, twice or three times...
Peak Position / Weeks

9 Nov 85 **THAT'S WHAT FRIENDS ARE FOR** *Arista ARIST 638* [2] ▲ $ ... 16 9
15 Nov 86 **DIANA ROSS, MICHAEL JACKSON, GLADYS KNIGHT, STEVIE WONDER. THEIR VERY BEST BACK TO BACK** *Priority TV PTVR 2* [1] ... 21 10
16 Jan 88 **LOVE OVERBOARD** *MCA MCA 1223* ... 42 4
27 Feb 88 **ALL OUR LOVE** *MCA MCF 3409* ... 80 1
10 Jun 89 ● **LICENCE TO KILL** *MCA MCA 1339* [3] ... 6 11
28 Oct 89 **THE SINGLES ALBUM** *PolyGram GKTV 1* ... 13 10
29 Mar 97 **THE SINGLES ALBUM** (re-issue) *PolyGram TV 8420032* ... 69 2

[1] Johnny Mathis and Gladys Knight [2] Dionne Warwick and Friends featuring Elton John, Stevie Wonder and Gladys Knight [3] Gladys Knight [1] Diana Ross / Michael Jackson / Gladys Knight / Stevie Wonder

Jordan KNIGHT (see also NEW KIDS ON THE BLOCK) *US, male vocalist*

16 Oct 99 ● **GIVE IT TO YOU** (re) *Interscope 4971672* ... 5 9

Robert KNIGHT *US, male vocalist (3 Singles: 26 Weeks)*

17 Jan 68 **EVERLASTING LOVE** *Monument MON 1008* ... 40 2
24 Nov 73 ● **LOVE ON A MOUNTAIN TOP** *Monument MNT 1875* ... 10 16
9 Mar 74 **EVERLASTING LOVE** (re-issue) *Monument MNT 2106* ... 19 8

The KNIGHTSBRIDGE STRINGS *UK, male orchestra*

25 Jun 60 **STRING SWAY** *Top Rank BUY 017* ... 20 1

David KNOPFLER (see also DIRE STRAITS) *UK, male vocalist / guitarist*

19 Nov 83 **RELEASE** *Peach River DAVID 1* ... 82 1

Mark KNOPFLER (see also DIRE STRAITS; The NOTTING HILLBILLIES) *UK, male vocalist / guitarist (8 Albums: 71 Weeks, 4 Singles: 9 Weeks)*

12 Mar 83 **GOING HOME (THEME OF 'LOCAL HERO')** *Vertigo DSTR 4* ... 56 3
16 Apr 83 **LOCAL HERO (FILM SOUNDTRACK)** *Vertigo VERL 4* ... 14 11
20 Oct 84 **CAL (FILM SOUNDTRACK)** *Vertigo VERH 17* ... 65 3
24 Nov 90 **NECK AND NECK** *CBS 4674351* [1] ... 41 11
16 Mar 96 **DARLING PRETTY** *Vertigo VERCD 88* ... 33 2
6 Apr 96 ● **GOLDEN HEART** *Vertigo 5147322* ... 9 17
25 May 96 **CANNIBALS** *Vertigo VERCD 89* ... 42 2
7 Oct 00 ● **SAILING TO PHILADELPHIA** *Mercury 5429812* ... 4 13
12 Oct 02 ● **THE RAGPICKER'S DREAM** *Mercury 0632932* ... 7 5
2 Oct 04 **BOOM, LIKE THAT** *Mercury 9867839* ... 34 2
9 Oct 04 **SHANGRI-LA** *Mercury 9867715* ... 11 4
19 Nov 05 **THE BEST OF DIRE STRAITS & MARK KNOPFLER - PRIVATE INVESTIGATIONS** *Mercury 9872936* ... 20 7+

[1] Chet Atkins and Mark Knopfler

KNOWLEDGE *Italy, male production duo*

8 Nov 97 **AS (UNTIL THE DAY)** *ffrr FCD 312* ... 70 1

Buddy KNOX *US, male vocalist, b. 20 Jul 1933, d. 14 Feb 1999 (2 Singles: 5 Weeks)*

10 May 57 **PARTY DOLL** *Columbia DB 3914* ▲ $ ... 29 3
16 Aug 62 **SHE'S GONE** *Liberty LIB 55473* ... 45 2

Frankie KNUCKLES *US, male producer (1 Album: 2 Weeks, 7 Singles: 19 Weeks)*

17 Jun 89 **TEARS** *ffrr F 108* [1] ... 50 3
21 Oct 89 **YOUR LOVE** *Trax TRAXT 3* ... 59 4
27 Jul 91 **THE WHISTLE SONG** *Virgin America VUS 47* ... 17 5
17 Aug 91 **BEYOND THE MIX** *Virgin America VUSLP 6* ... 59 2
23 Nov 91 **IT'S HARD SOMETIMES** *Virgin America VUS 52* ... 67 1
6 Jun 92 **RAIN FALLS** *Virgin America VUST 60* [2] ... 48 2
27 May 95 **TOO MANY FISH** *Virgin America VUSCD 89* [3] ... 34 2
18 Nov 95 **WHADDA U WANT (FROM ME)** *Virgin America VUSCD 98* [3] 36 2

[1] Frankie Knuckles presents Satoshi Tomiie [2] Frankie Knuckles featuring Lisa Michaelis [3] Frankie Knuckles featuring Adeva

Moe KOFFMAN QUARTETTE *Canada, male instrumental group – leader Moe Koffman – flute, b. 28 Dec 1928, d. 28 Mar 2001*

28 Mar 58 **SWINGIN' SHEPHERD BLUES** *London HLJ 8549* ... 23 2

Mike KOGLIN *Germany, male producer (2 Singles: 4 Weeks)*

28 Nov 98 **THE SILENCE** *Multiply CDMULTY 44* ... 20 2
29 May 99 **ON MY WAY** *Multiply CDMULTY 51* [1] ... 28 2

[1] Mike Koglin featuring Beatrice

KOKOMO *US, male pianist – Jimmy Wisner*

13 Apr 61 **ASIA MINOR** *London HLU 9305* ... 35 7

KOKOMO *UK, male / female vocal / instrumental group*

29 May 82 **A LITTLE BIT FURTHER AWAY** *CBS A 2064* ... 45 3

KON KAN *Canada, male vocal / instrumental duo – Barry Harris and Kevin Wynne*

4 Mar 89 ● **I BEG YOUR PARDON** *Atlantic A 8969* ... 5 13

John KONGOS *South Africa, male vocalist / multi-instrumentalist (1 Album: 2 Weeks, 2 Singles: 25 Weeks)*

22 May 71 ● **HE'S GONNA STEP ON YOU AGAIN** *Fly BUG 8* ... 4 14
20 Nov 71 ● **TOKOLOSHE MAN** *Fly BUG 14* ... 4 11
15 Jan 72 **KONGOS** *Fly HIFLY 7* ... 29 2

KONKRETE *UK, female production duo*

22 Sep 01 **LAW UNTO MYSELF** *Perfecto PERF 23CDS* ... 60 1

KONTAKT (see also VINYLGROOVER and The RED HED) *UK, male production duo – Scott Attrill and Jim Sullivan*

20 Sep 03 **SHOW ME A SIGN** *Nulife 82876557432* ... 19 4

The KOOKS NEW *UK, male vocal / instrumental group (2 Singles: 3 Weeks)*

23 Jul 05 **EDDIE'S GUN** *Virgin VSCDT 2000* ... 35 1
29 Oct 05 **SOFA SONG** *Virgin VSCDT 1904* ... 28 2

KOOL and The GANG 165 Top 500

One of the most consistently successful R&B acts, hailing from New Jersey and including Robert 'Kool' Bell (b) and James 'JT' Taylor (v). The band spent 10 years as top US R&B stars before starting an impressive run of international hits (8 Albums: 116 Weeks, 24 Singles: 218 Weeks)

27 Oct 79 ● **LADIES NIGHT** *Mercury KOOL 7* $ ... 9 12
19 Jan 80 **TOO HOT** *Mercury KOOL 8* ... 23 8
12 Jul 80 **HANGIN' OUT** *De-Lite KOOL 9* ... 52 4
1 Nov 80 ● **CELEBRATION** *De-Lite KOOL 10* ▲ $ ... 7 13
21 Feb 81 **JONES VS JONES / SUMMER MADNESS** *De-Lite KOOL 11* ... 17 11
30 May 81 **TAKE IT TO THE TOP** *De-Lite DE 2* ... 15 9
31 Oct 81 **STEPPIN' OUT** *De-Lite DE 4* ... 12 13
21 Nov 81 ● **SOMETHING SPECIAL** *De-Lite DSR 001* ... 10 20
19 Dec 81 ● **GET DOWN ON IT** *De-Lite DE 5* ... 3 12
6 Mar 82 **TAKE MY HEART (YOU CAN HAVE IT IF YOU WANT IT)** *De-Lite DE 6* ... 29 7
7 Aug 82 **BIG FUN** *De-Lite DE 7* ... 14 8
2 Oct 82 **AS ONE** *De-Lite DSR 3* ... 49 10
16 Oct 82 ● **OOH LA LA LA (LET'S GO DANCIN')** *De-Lite DE 9* ... 6 9

19 October 1974	26 October 1974	2 November 1974	9 November 1974
UK No.1 SINGLES			
SAD SWEET DREAMER Sweet Sensation	EVERYTHING I OWN Ken Boothe	EVERYTHING I OWN Ken Boothe	EVERYTHING I OWN Ken Boothe
UK No.1 ALBUMS			
SMILER Rod Stewart	ROLLIN' Bay City Rollers	SMILER Rod Stewart	ROLLIN' Bay City Rollers

Date		Title / Label	Pos	Wks
4 Dec 82		**HI DE HI, HI DE HO** *De-Lite DE 14*	29	8
7 May 83	●	TWICE AS KOOL *De-Lite PROLP 2*	4	23
10 Dec 83		**STRAIGHT AHEAD** *De-Lite DE 15*	15	10
14 Jan 84		IN THE HEART *De-Lite DSR 4*	18	23
11 Feb 84	●	**JOANNA / TONIGHT** *De-Lite DE 16*	2	11
14 Apr 84	●	**(WHEN YOU SAY YOU LOVE SOMEBODY) IN THE HEART** *De-Lite DE 17*	7	8
24 Nov 84		**FRESH** *De-Lite DE 18*	11	12
15 Dec 84		EMERGENCY *De-Lite DSR 6*	47	25
9 Feb 85		**MISLED** *De-Lite DE 19*	28	5
11 May 85	●	**CHERISH** *De-Lite DE 20*	4	22
2 Nov 85		**EMERGENCY** *De-Lite DE 21*	50	3
22 Nov 86		**VICTORY** (re) *Club JAB 44*	30	12
21 Mar 87		**STONE LOVE** *Club JAB 47*	45	4
12 Nov 88		THE SINGLES COLLECTION *De-Lite KGTV 1*	28	13
31 Dec 88		**CELEBRATION** (re-mix) *Club JAB 78*	56	5
27 Oct 90		KOOL LOVE *Telstar STAR 2435*	50	1
6 Jul 91		**GET DOWN ON IT** (re-mix) *Mercury MER 346*	69	1
27 Dec 03	●	**LADIES NIGHT** (re-recording) *Innocent SINCD 53* [1]	8	11
26 Jun 04		THE HITS: RELOADED *Unique Corp / Virgin / EMI VTDCD 618*	56	1

[1] Atomic Kitten featuring Kool and The Gang

'Jones vs Jones' and 'Summer Madness' were labelled as A and B sides with 'Funky Stuff' and 'Hollywood Swinging' as the C and D sides of a two-disc release.

KOOPA NEW *UK, male vocal / instrumental trio*

Date		Title / Label	Pos	Wks
3 Dec 05		**NO TREND** *Mad Cow MCR 741*	71	1

The KORGIS *UK, male vocal (James Warren) / instrumental group (1 Album: 4 Weeks, 3 Singles: 27 Weeks)*

Date		Title / Label	Pos	Wks
23 Jun 79		**IF I HAD YOU** *Rialto TREB 103*	13	12
24 May 80	●	**EVERYBODY'S GOT TO LEARN SOMETIME** *Rialto TREB 115*	5	12
26 Jul 80		DUMB WAITERS *Rialto TENOR 104*	40	4
30 Aug 80		**IF IT'S ALRIGHT WITH YOU BABY** *Rialto TREB 118*	56	3

KORN *US, male vocal (Jonathan Davis) / instrumental group (7 Albums: 21 Weeks, 11 Singles: 27 Weeks)*

Date		Title / Label	Pos	Wks
19 Oct 96		**NO PLACE TO HIDE** *Epic 6638452*	26	2
26 Oct 96		LIFE IS PEACHY *Epic 4853692*	32	2
15 Feb 97		**A.D.I.D.A.S.** *Epic 6642042*	22	2
7 Jun 97		**GOOD GOD** *Epic 6646585*	25	2
22 Aug 98		**GOT THE LIFE** *Epic 6663912*	23	2
29 Aug 98	●	FOLLOW THE LEADER *Epic 4912212* ▲	5	4
8 May 99		**FREAK ON A LEASH** *Epic 6672522*	24	2
27 Nov 99		ISSUES *Epic 4963592* ▲	37	1
12 Feb 00		**FALLING AWAY FROM ME** *Epic 6688692*	24	2
3 Jun 00		**MAKE ME BAD** *Epic 6694332*	25	2
1 Jun 02		**HERE TO STAY** *Epic 6727425*	12	5
22 Jun 02	●	UNTOUCHABLES *Epic 5017700*	4	9
21 Sep 02		**THOUGHTLESS** *Epic 6731572*	37	2
23 Aug 03		**DID MY TIME** *Epic 6741422*	15	4
6 Dec 03		TAKE A LOOK IN THE MIRROR *Epic 05133253*	53	1
16 Oct 04		GREATEST HITS VOL.1 *Epic 5187923*	22	3
3 Dec 05		**TWISTED TRANSISTOR** *Virgin VUSCD 316*	27	2
17 Dec 05		SEE YOU ON THE OTHER SIDE *Virgin CDVUS 274*	71	1

KOSHEEN *UK, male / female production / vocal (Sian Evans) trio (2 Albums: 29 Weeks, 8 Singles: 31 Weeks)*

Date		Title / Label	Pos	Wks
17 Jun 00		**EMPTY SKIES / HIDE U** *Moksha Recordings MOKSHA 05CD*	73	1
14 Apr 01		**(SLIP & SLIDE) SUICIDE** *Moksha Recordings MOKSHA 07CD*	50	2
1 Sep 01	●	**HIDE U** (re) (re-mix) *Arista 74321879412*	6	7
29 Sep 01	●	RESIST *Arista 74321880812*	8	23
22 Dec 01		**CATCH** *Moksha / Arista 74321913722*	15	8
4 May 02		**HUNGRY** *Moksha / Arista 74321934382*	13	4
31 Aug 02		**HARDER** *Moksha / Arista 74321954452*	53	1
9 Aug 03	●	**ALL IN MY HEAD** (re) *Moksha / Arista 82876527242*	7	7
23 Aug 03	●	KOKOPELLI *Moksha / Arista 82876527232*	7	6
1 Nov 03		**WASTING MY TIME** *Moksha / Arista 82876570022*	49	1

KRAFTWERK 480 Top 500 *German electronic robot 'n' roll pioneers: Ralf Hutter (k/v), Florian Schneider (prc/v), Karl Bartos (prc) and Wolfgang Flur (prc). The first German act to top the UK singles chart, they influenced disco and synth pop movements and helped to lay the foundation stones for hip hop (9 Albums: 75 Weeks, 12 Singles: 79 Weeks)*

Date		Title / Label	Pos	Wks
10 May 75		**AUTOBAHN** *Vertigo 6147 012*	11	9
17 May 75	●	AUTOBAHN *Vertigo 6360 620*	4	18
20 May 78	●	THE MAN-MACHINE *Capitol EST 11728*	9	13
28 Oct 78		**NEON LIGHTS** *Capitol CL 15998*	53	3
9 May 81		**POCKET CALCULATOR** *EMI 5175*	39	6
23 May 81		COMPUTER WORLD *EMI EMC 3370*	15	22
11 Jul 81	★	**COMPUTER LOVE / THE MODEL** (re) *EMI 5207*	1	21
6 Feb 82		TRANS-EUROPE EXPRESS *Capitol EST 11603*	49	7
20 Feb 82		**SHOWROOM DUMMIES** *EMI 5272*	25	5
6 Aug 83		**TOUR DE FRANCE** (re) *EMI 5413*	22	19
22 Jun 85		AUTOBAHN (re-issue) *Parlophone AUTO 1*	61	3
15 Nov 86		ELECTRIC CAFÉ *EMI EMD 1001*	58	2
1 Jun 91		**THE ROBOTS** *EMI EM 192*	20	4
22 Jun 91		THE MIX *EMI EM 1408*	15	6
2 Nov 91		**RADIOACTIVITY** (re-mix) *EMI EM 201*	43	2
23 Oct 99		**TOUR DE FRANCE** (re-issue) *EMI 8874210*	61	1
18 Mar 00		**EXPO 2000** *EMI CDEM 562*	27	2
19 Jul 03		**TOUR DE FRANCE 2003** (re-mix) *EMI CDEM 626*	20	4
16 Aug 03		TOUR DE FRANCE SOUNDTRACKS *EMI 5917082*	21	2
27 Mar 04		**AERODYNAMIK** *EMI CDEM 637*	33	3
18 Jun 05		MINIMUM – MAXIMUM *EMI 5606112*	29	2

'Computer Love / The Model' did not make No.1 until re-entry in Dec 1981. 'Tour de France' peaked at No.24 after re-entry in Aug 1984.

Diana KRALL *Canada, female vocalist / pianist (4 Albums: 22 Weeks)*

Date		Title / Label	Pos	Wks
12 Jun 99		WHEN I LOOK IN YOUR EYES *Verve 503042*	72	1
29 Sep 01		THE LOOK OF LOVE *Verve 5498462*	23	7
23 Nov 02		LIVE IN PARIS *Verve 0653692*	30	6
24 Apr 04	●	THE GIRL IN THE OTHER ROOM *Verve 9862063*	4	8

Billy J KRAMER and The DAKOTAS *UK, male vocal / instrumental group (1 Album: 17 Weeks, 6 Singles: 71 Weeks)*

Date		Title / Label	Pos	Wks
2 May 63	●	**DO YOU WANT TO KNOW A SECRET?** *Parlophone R 5023*	2	15
1 Aug 63	★	**BAD TO ME** *Parlophone R 5049*	1	14
7 Nov 63	●	**I'LL KEEP YOU SATISFIED** *Parlophone R 5073*	4	13
16 Nov 63		LISTEN TO BILLY J. KRAMER *Parlophone PMC 1209*	11	17
27 Feb 64	★	**LITTLE CHILDREN** *Parlophone R 5105*	1	13
23 Jul 64	●	**FROM A WINDOW** *Parlophone R 5156*	10	8
20 May 65		**TRAINS AND BOATS AND PLANES** *Parlophone R 5285*	12	8

The KRANKIES *UK, male / female vocal duo*

Date		Title / Label	Pos	Wks
7 Feb 81		**FAN'DABI'DOZI** (re) *Monarch MON 21*	46	6

Alison KRAUSS and UNION STATION *US, female vocalist / violinist and male instrumental group*

Date		Title / Label	Pos	Wks
25 Aug 01		NEW FAVORITE *Rounder RRCD 0495*	72	1

Lenny KRAVITZ 374 Top 500 *Grammy and BRIT-winning soulful rock vocalist and multi-instrumentalist who has worked with Madonna, Mick Jagger, David Bowie and Stevie Wonder, b. 26 May 1964, New York, US. His Greatest Hits album reached the Top 10 in 25 countries and sold more than eight million worldwide (8 Albums: 114 Weeks, 19 Singles: 72 Weeks)*

Date		Title / Label	Pos	Wks
26 May 90		LET LOVE RULE *Virgin America VUSLP 10*	56	4
2 Jun 90		**MR CABDRIVER** *Virgin America VUS 20*	58	2
4 Aug 90		**LET LOVE RULE** *Virgin America VUS 26*	39	4
30 Mar 91		**ALWAYS ON THE RUN** *Virgin America VUS 34*	41	3
13 Apr 91	●	MAMA SAID *Virgin America VUSLP 31*	8	27
15 Jun 91		**IT AIN'T OVER TIL IT'S OVER** *Virgin America VUS 43*	11	8
14 Sep 91		**STAND BY MY WOMAN** *Virgin America VUS 45*	55	3
20 Feb 93	●	**ARE YOU GONNA GO MY WAY** *Virgin America VUSDG 65*	4	11
13 Mar 93	★	ARE YOU GONNA GO MY WAY *Virgin America CDVUS 60* ■	1	47

16 November 1974	23 November 1974	30 November 1974	7 December 1974
GONNA MAKE YOU A STAR David Essex	GONNA MAKE YOU A STAR David Essex	GONNA MAKE YOU A STAR David Essex	YOU'RE THE FIRST, THE LAST, MY EVERYTHING Barry White
ROLLIN' Bay City Rollers	GREATEST HITS Elton John	GREATEST HITS Elton John	GREATEST HITS Elton John

KEY UK No.1 ★ UK Top 10 ● Still on chart + UK entry at No.1 ■ US No.1 ▲ UK million seller £ US million seller $
Singles re-entries are listed as (re), (2re), (3re)... which signifies that the hit re-entered the chart once, twice or three times...

Peak Position / Weeks

22 May 93 **BELIEVE** *Virgin America VUSCD 72* 30 5
28 Aug 93 **HEAVEN HELP** *Virgin America VUSDG 73* 20 7
4 Dec 93 **BUDDHA OF SUBURBIA** *Arista 74321177052* [1] 35 3
4 Dec 93 **IS THERE ANY LOVE IN YOUR HEART** *Virgin America VUSDG 76* 52 2
9 Sep 95 **ROCK AND ROLL IS DEAD** *Virgin America VUSCD 93* 22 3
23 Sep 95 ● CIRCUS *Virgin America CDVUS 86* 5 4
23 Dec 95 **CIRCUS** *Virgin America VUSCD 96* 54 2
2 Mar 96 **CAN'T GET YOU OFF MY MIND** *Virgin America VUSCD 100* 54 2
16 May 98 **IF YOU CAN'T SAY NO** *Virgin VUSCD 130* 48 2
23 May 98 5 *Virgin CDVUS 140* 18 13
10 Oct 98 **I BELONG TO YOU** *Virgin VUSCD 138* 75 1
20 Feb 99 ★ **FLY AWAY** *Virgin VUSCD 141* ■ 1 10
4 Nov 00 GREATEST HITS *Virgin CDVUSX 183* 12 17
10 Nov 01 LENNY *Virgin CDVUS 213* 55 1
6 Apr 02 **STILLNESS OF HEART** *Virgin VUSCD 236* 44 1
7 Feb 04 **SHOW ME YOUR SOUL** *Puff Daddy / Island MCSTD 40350* [2] 35 2
29 May 04 BAPTISM *Virgin CDVUS 252* 74 1
24 Jul 04 **CALIFORNIA** *Virgin VUSCD 294* 62 1

[1] David Bowie featuring Lenny Kravitz [2] Lenny Kravitz / P Diddy / Loon / Pharrell Williams

KRAY TWINZ featuring TWISTA, LETHAL B & Gappy RANKS NEW
(see also LETHAL BIZZLE) *UK, male production duo and US / UK, male rappers*

12 Nov 05 **WHAT WE DO** *Gana / W10 01CDS* 23 3

KRAZE *US, male / female vocal / instrumental group (2 Singles: 6 Weeks)*

22 Oct 88 **THE PARTY** *MCA MCA 1288* 29 5
17 Jun 89 **LET'S PLAY HOUSE** *MCA MCA 1337* 71 1

KREUZ *UK, male vocal group*

18 Mar 95 KREUZ KONTROL *Diesel DESCD 01* 48 2
8 Jul 95 **PARTY ALL NIGHT** *Diesel DES 004C* 75 1

Chantal KREVIAZUK *Canada, female vocalist*

6 Mar 99 **LEAVING ON A JET PLANE** *Epic 6666272* 59 1

The KREW-KATS *UK, male instrumental group*

9 Mar 61 **TRAMBONE** (re) *HMV POP 840* 33 10

KRISS KROSS *US, male rap duo – Chris Kelly and Chris Smith (1 Album: 8 Weeks, 5 Singles: 22 Weeks)*

30 May 92 ● **JUMP** *Ruff House 6578547* ▲ $ 2 8
27 Jun 92 TOTALLY KROSSED OUT *Columbia 4714342* ▲ 31 8
25 Jul 92 **WARM IT UP** *Ruff House 6582187* 16 6
17 Oct 92 **I MISSED THE BUS** *Ruff House 6583927* 57 1
19 Dec 92 **IT'S A SHAME** *Ruff House 6588587* 31 5
11 Sep 93 **ALRIGHT** *Ruff House 6595652* 47 2

Chad KROEGER featuring Josey SCOTT
(see also NICKELBACK; SALIVA) *Canada / US, male vocal / instrumental duo*

22 Jun 02 ● **HERO** *Roadrunner RR 20463* 4 14

KROKUS *Switzerland / Malta, male vocal / instrumental group (3 Albums: 11 Weeks, 1 Single: 2 Weeks)*

21 Feb 81 HARDWARE *Ariola ARL 5064* 44 4
16 May 81 **INDUSTRIAL STRENGTH (EP)** *Ariola ARO 258* 62 2
20 Feb 82 ONE VICE AT A TIME *Arista SPART 1189* 28 5
16 Apr 83 HEADHUNTER *Arista 205 255* 74 2

Tracks on Industrial Strength (EP): Bedside Radio / Easy Rocker / Celebration / Bye Bye Baby.

KRUSH *UK, male / female vocal / instrumental group (2 Singles: 16 Weeks)*

5 Dec 87 ● **HOUSE ARREST** *Club JAB 63* 3 15
14 Nov 92 **WALKING ON SUNSHINE** *Network NWK 55* [1] 71 1

[1] Krush featuring Ruth Joy

KRUSH PERSPECTIVE *US, female vocal group*

16 Jan 93 **LET'S GET TOGETHER (SO GROOVY NOW)** *Perspective PERD 7416* 61 2

KRUST
UK, male producer / instrumentalist – Keith Thompson (2 Singles: 2 Weeks)

23 Oct 99 **CODED LANGUAGE** *Talkin Loud TLCD 51* [1] 66 1
26 Jan 02 **SNAPPED IT** *Full Cycle FCY 034* 58 1

[1] Krust featuring Saul Williams

KUBB NEW
UK, male vocal / instrumental group (1 Album: 1 Week, 2 Singles: 4 Weeks)

3 Sep 05 **REMAIN** *Mercury 9873116* 45 1
19 Nov 05 **WICKED SOUL** *Mercury 9874772* 25 3
26 Nov 05 MOTHER *Mercury 9870767* 66 1

KUJAY DADA *UK, male production group*

17 Jan 04 **YOUNG HEARTS** *Nebula NEBCD 057* 41 3

KULA SHAKER *UK, male vocal (Crispian Mills) / instrumental group (2 Albums: 54 Weeks, 8 Singles: 48 Weeks)*

4 May 96 **GRATEFUL WHEN YOU'RE DEAD – JERRY WAS THERE** *Columbia KULACD 2* 35 3
6 Jul 96 ● **TATTVA** *Columbia KULACD 3* 4 8
7 Sep 96 ● **HEY DUDE** *Columbia KULACD 4* 2 7
28 Sep 96 ★ K *Columbia SHAKER 1CDK* ■ 1 44
23 Nov 96 ● **GOVINDA** *Columbia KULACD 5* 7 8
8 Mar 97 ● **HUSH** (re) *Columbia KULACD 6* 2 9
2 May 98 ● **SOUND OF DRUMS** *Columbia KULA 21CD* 3 6
6 Mar 99 **MYSTICAL MACHINE GUN** *Columbia KULA 22CD* 14 3
20 Mar 99 ● PEASANTS, PIGS & ASTRONAUTS *Columbia SHAKER 2CD* 9 10
15 May 99 **SHOWER YOUR LOVE** *Columbia KULA 23CD* 14 4

KULAY *Philippines, male / female vocal group*

12 Sep 98 **DELICIOUS** *INCredible INCRL 4CD* 73 1

KUMARA *Holland, male production duo*

7 Oct 00 **SNAP YOUR FINGAZ** *Y2K Y2K 018CD* 70 1

Charlie KUNZ *US, male pianist, b. 18 Aug 1896, d. 16 Mar 1958*

17 Dec 54 **PIANO MEDLEY NO.114** (re) *Decca F 10419* 16 4
14 Jun 69 ● THE WORLD OF CHARLIE KUNZ *Decca SPA 15* 9 11

Medley titles: There Must Be a Reason / Hold My Hand / If I Give My Heart to You / Little Things Mean a Lot / Make Her Mine / My Son My Son.

KURSAAL FLYERS *UK, male vocal / instrumental group*

20 Nov 76 **LITTLE DOES SHE KNOW** *CBS 4689* 14 10

KURUPT (see also THA DOGG POUND)
US, male rapper – Ricardo Brown (2 Singles: 10 Weeks)

25 Aug 01 **WHERE I WANNA BE** (re) *London LONCD 461* [1] 14 7
13 Oct 01 **IT'S OVER** *Pias Recordings PIASB 024CD* 21 3

[1] Shade Sheist featuring Nate Dogg and Kurupt

14 December 1974	21 December 1974	28 December 1974	4 January 1975
UK No.1 SINGLES			
YOU'RE THE FIRST, THE LAST, MY EVERYTHING Barry White	LONELY THIS CHRISTMAS Mud	LONELY THIS CHRISTMAS Mud	LONELY THIS CHRISTMAS Mud
UK No.1 ALBUMS			
GREATEST HITS Elton John	GREATEST HITS Elton John	GREATEST HITS Elton John	GREATEST HITS Elton John

KUT KLOSE *US, female vocal group*

29 Apr 95 **I LIKE** *Elektra EKR 200CD*......72 1

Li KWAN (see also AKABU featuring Linda CLIFFORD; HED BOYS; IL PADRINOS featuring Jocelyn BROWN; JAKATTA; Joey NEGRO; PHASE II; RAVEN MAIZE; Z FACTOR) *UK, male producer – Dave Lee*

17 Dec 94 **I NEED A MAN** *Deconstruction 74321252192*......51 2

Talib KWELI featuring Mary J BLIGE
US, male rapper and female vocalist

18 Dec 04 **I TRY** *Island MCSTD 40390*......59 1

L

Jonny L (see also TRUE STEPPERS) *UK, male vocalist / instrumentalist / producer – Johny Lisners (2 Singles: 2 Weeks)*

28 Aug 93 **OOH I LIKE IT** *XL Recordings XLS 44CD*......73 1
31 Oct 98 **20 DEGREES** *XL Recordings XLS 103CD* [1]......66 1

[1] Jonny L featuring Silvah Bullet

LA GANZ *US, male vocal / instrumental group*

9 Nov 96 **LIKE A PLAYA** *Jive JIVECD 405*......75 1

L.A. GUNS *US, male / female vocal / instrumental group (3 Albums: 4 Weeks, 2 Singles: 4 Weeks)*

5 Mar 88 L.A. GUNS *Vertigo VERH 55*......73 1
30 Sep 89 COCKED AND LOADED *Vertigo 8385921*......45 2
13 Jul 91 HOLLYWOOD VAMPIRES *Mercury 8496041*......44 1
30 Nov 91 **SOME LIE 4 LOVE** *Mercury MER 358*......61 1
21 Dec 91 **THE BALLAD OF JAYNE** *Mercury MER 361*......53 3

L.A. MIX
UK, male / female vocal / instrumental / production trio (7 Singles: 25 Weeks)

10 Oct 87 **DON'T STOP (JAMMIN')** *Breakout USA 615*......47 4
21 May 88 ● **CHECK THIS OUT** *Breakout USA 629*......6 7
8 Jul 89 **GET LOOSE** *Breakout USA 659* [1]......25 6
16 Sep 89 **LOVE TOGETHER** *Breakout USA 662* [2]......66 2
15 Sep 90 **COMING BACK FOR MORE** *A&M AM 579*......50 3
19 Jan 91 **MYSTERIES OF LOVE** *A&M AM 707*......46 2
23 Mar 91 **WE SHOULDN'T HOLD HANDS IN THE DARK** *A&M AM 755*......69 1

[1] LA Mix featuring Jazzi P [2] LA Mix featuring Kevin Henry

LCD *UK, male production group (2 Singles: 9 Weeks)*

27 Jun 98 **ZORBA'S DANCE** *Virgin VSCDT 1693*......20 5
9 Oct 99 **ZORBA'S DANCE** (re-issue) *Virgin VSCDT 1757*......22 4

LCD SOUNDSYSTEM *US, male production duo – James Murphy and Tim Goldsworthy (1 Album: 4 Weeks, 4 Singles: 6 Weeks)*

20 Nov 04 **MOVEMENT** *EMI DFAEMI 2141CD*......52 1
5 Feb 05 LCD SOUNDSYSTEM *DFA / EMI DFAEMI 2138CD*......20 4
12 Mar 05 **DAFT PUNK IS PLAYING AT MY HOUSE** *DFA / EMI DFAEMI 2143CD*......29 3
18 Jun 05 **DISCO INFILTRATOR** *DFA / EMI DFAEMI 2145CD*......49 1
8 Oct 05 **TRIBULATIONS** *DFA / EMI DFAEMI 2151CD*......59 1

LFO *UK, male instrumental group (2 Albums: 3 Weeks, 3 Singles: 15 Weeks)*

14 Jul 90 **LFO** *Warp WAP 5*......12 10
6 Jul 91 **WE ARE BACK / NURTURE** *Warp 7WAP 14*......47 3
3 Aug 91 FREQUENCIES *Warp WARPLP 3*......42 2
1 Feb 92 **WHAT IS HOUSE (EP)** *Warp WAP 17*......62 2
10 Feb 96 ADVANCE *Warp WARPCD 39*......44 1

Tracks on What Is House (EP): Tan Ta Ra / Mashed Potato / What Is House / Syndrome.

LL COOL J 453 Top 500 *With a moniker abbreviated from Ladies Love Cool James, this most durable rap star, b. James Todd Smith, 18 Jun 1968, New York, US, was the first solo rap act to score a UK Top 10 hit with 'I Need Love', which was also the first successful rap 'ballad'. He has amassed a record eight US No.1 rap hits (10 Albums: 44 Weeks, 22 Singles: 115 Weeks)*

15 Feb 86 RADIO *Def Jam DEF 26745*......71 1
13 Jun 87 BIGGER AND DEFFER *Def Jam 450 5151*......54 19
4 Jul 87 **I'M BAD** *Def Jam 650856 7*......71 1
12 Sep 87 ● **I NEED LOVE** *Def Jam 651101 7*......8 10
21 Nov 87 **GO CUT CREATOR GO** *Def Jam LLCJ 1*......66 2
13 Feb 88 **GOING BACK TO CALI / JACK THE RIPPER** *Def Jam LLCJ 2*......37 4
10 Jun 89 **I'M THAT TYPE OF GUY** *Def Jam LLCJ 3*......43 5
8 Jul 89 WALKING WITH A PANTHER *Def Jam 465112 1*......43 3
13 Oct 90 MAMA SAID KNOCK YOU OUT *Def Jam 4673151*......49 2
1 Dec 90 **AROUND THE WAY GIRL / MAMA SAID KNOCK YOU OUT** *Def Jam 6564470*......41 4
9 Mar 91 **AROUND THE WAY GIRL** (re-mix) *Columbia 6564470*......36 4
10 Apr 93 **HOW I'M COMIN'** *Def Jam 6591692*......37 2
17 Apr 93 14 SHOTS TO THE DOME *Def Jam 4736782*......74 1
20 Jan 96 **HEY LOVER** *Def Jam DEFCD 14* [1] $......17 4
1 Jun 96 **DOIN' IT** *Def Jam DEFCD 15* [2]......15 3
5 Oct 96 ● **LOUNGIN'** *Def Jam DEFCD 30* $......7 8
16 Nov 96 ALL WORLD *Def Jam 5341252*......23 8
8 Feb 97 ★ **AIN'T NOBODY** *Geffen GFSTD 22195* ■......1 9
5 Apr 97 ● **HIT EM HIGH (THE MONSTARS' ANTHEM)** *Atlantic A 5449CD* [3]......8 6
25 Oct 97 PHENOMENON *Def Jam 5391862*......37 4
1 Nov 97 ● **PHENOMENON** *Def Jam 5681172*......9 5
28 Mar 98 ● **FATHER** *Def Jam 5685292*......10 5
11 Jul 98 **ZOOM** *Interscope IND 95594* [4]......15 3
5 Dec 98 **INCREDIBLE** *Jive 0522102* [5]......52 1
23 Sep 00 G.O.A.T. FEATURING JAMES T. SMITH – THE GREATEST OF ALL TIME *Def Jam 5429972* ▲......29 2
26 Oct 02 ● **LUV U BETTER** *Def Jam 0638722*......7 7
2 Nov 02 10 *Def Jam 0632192*......26 3
22 Feb 03 **PARADISE** *Def Jam 0637032* [6]......18 5
22 Mar 03 ● **ALL I HAVE** *Epic 6736782* [7] ▲......2 13
28 Aug 04 **HEADSPRUNG** *Def Jam 9863759*......25 4
11 Sep 04 THE DEFINITION *Def Jam 9863650*......66 1
26 Feb 05 ● **HUSH** *Def Jam 2103773* [8]......3 10

[1] LL Cool J featuring Boyz II Men [2] LL Cool J, guest vocals by LeShaun [3] B Real / Busta Rhymes / Coolio / LL Cool J / Method Man [4] Dr Dre and LL Cool J [5] Keith Murray featuring LL Cool J [6] LL Cool J featuring Amerie [7] Jennifer Lopez featuring LL Cool J [8] LL Cool J featuring 7 Aurelius

'Jack the Ripper' listed only from 20 Feb 1988.

LMC vs U2
UK, male production trio and Ireland, male vocal / instrumental group

7 Feb 04 ★ **TAKE ME TO THE CLOUDS ABOVE** *All Around the World CDGLOBE 313* ■......1 12

LNM PROJEKT featuring Bonnie BAILEY NEW
UK, male production trio and female vocalist

19 Mar 05 **EVERYWHERE** *Hed Kandi HEDKCDS 012*......38 2

11 January 1975	18 January 1975	25 January 1975	1 February 1975
LONELY THIS CHRISTMAS Mud	**DOWN DOWN** Status Quo	**MS GRACE** The Tymes	**JANUARY** Pilot
GREATEST HITS Elton John	**GREATEST HITS** Elton John	**GREATEST HITS** Elton John	**GREATEST HITS** Elton John

KEY: UK No.1 ★ UK Top 10 ● Still on chart + UK entry at No.1 ■ US No.1 ▲ UK million seller £ US million seller $
Singles re-entries are listed as (re), (2re), (3re)... which signifies that the hit re-entered the chart once, twice or three times...
Peak Position / Weeks

LNR *US, male vocal / instrumental duo*

3 Jun 89 **WORK IT TO THE BONE** *Kool Kat KOOL 501* 64 2

L.O.C. NEW *Jamaica / UK, male vocal / rap / production group*

9 Jul 05 **RING DING DING** *Street Tuff STRCD 3539* 58 1

LSG (see also Oliver LIEB presents SMOKED)
Germany, male DJ / producer – Oliver Lieb

10 May 97 **NETHERWORLD** *Hooj Choons HOOJCD 52* 63 1

L7 *US, female vocal / instrumental group*
(2 Albums: 8 Weeks, 5 Singles: 18 Weeks)

4 Apr 92 **PRETEND WE'RE DEAD** *Slash LASH 34* 21 7
2 May 92 **BRICKS ARE HEAVY** *Slash 8283072* 24 6
30 May 92 **EVERGLADE** *Slash LASH 36* 27 3
12 Sep 92 **MONSTER** *Slash LASH 38* 33 3
28 Nov 92 **PRETEND WE'RE DEAD** (re-issue) *Slash LASH 42* 50 3
9 Jul 94 **ANDRES** *Slash LASCD 48* 34 2
23 Jul 94 **HUNGRY FOR STINK** *Slash 8285312* 26 2

L.T.D. (see also Jeffrey OSBORNE) *US, male vocal / instrumental group*

9 Sep 78 **HOLDING ON (WHEN LOVE IS GONE)** *A&M AMS 7378* 70 3

LV *US, male vocalist – Larry Sanders (3 Singles: 25 Weeks)*

28 Oct 95 ★ **GANGSTA'S PARADISE** *Tommy Boy MCSTD 2104* [1] ■ ▲ £ $ 1 20
23 Dec 95 **THROW YOUR HANDS UP / GANGSTA'S PARADISE** (re-recording) *Tommy Boy TBCD 699* 24 4
4 May 96 **I AM LV** *Tommy Boy TBCD 7724* 64 1

[1] Coolio featuring LV

Coolio does not appear on the re-recorded version of 'Gangsta's Paradise'.

LWS *Italy, male instrumental group*

29 Oct 94 **GOSP** *Transworld TRANNY 4CD* 65 1

L'ORCHESTRE ELECTRONIQUE *UK, male synthesized orchestra*

29 Oct 83 **SOUND WAVES** *Nouveau Musique NML 1005* 75 1

LA BELLE EPOQUE *France, female vocal trio*

27 Aug 77 ● **BLACK IS BLACK** (re) *Harvest HAR 5133* 2 14

LA BOUCHE *US, male / female rap / vocal duo – Lane McCray and Melanie Thornton, b. 13 May 1967, d. 21 Nov 2001 (5 Singles: 12 Weeks)*

24 Sep 94 **SWEET DREAMS** *Bell 74321223912* 63 1
15 Jul 95 **BE MY LOVER** *Arista 74321265402* 27 4
30 Sep 95 **FALLING IN LOVE** *Arista 74321305102* 43 2
2 Mar 96 **BE MY LOVER** (re-mix) *Arista 74321339822* 25 4
7 Sep 96 **SWEET DREAMS** (re-issue) *Arista 74321398542* 44 1

LA FLEUR *Holland, male / female vocal / instrumental group*

30 Jul 83 **BOOGIE NIGHTS** *Proto ENA 111* 51 4

Sam LA MORE *Australia, male producer – Sam Littlemore*

5 Apr 03 **TAKIN' HOLD** *Underwater H20 023X* 70 1

Danny LA RUE *Ireland, male vocalist – Daniel Carroll*

18 Dec 68 **ON MOTHER KELLY'S DOORSTEP** *Page One POF 108* 33 9

LaBELLE (see also Nona HENDRYX)
US, female vocal group – lead vocal Patti LaBelle

22 Mar 75 **LADY MARMALADE (VOULEZ-VOUS COUCHER AVEC MOI CE SOIR?)** *Epic EPC 2852* ▲ $ 17 9

Patti LaBELLE (see also LaBELLE)
US, female vocalist – Patricia Holt (1 Album: 17 Weeks, 3 Singles: 21 Weeks)

3 May 86 ● **ON MY OWN** *MCA MCA 1045* [1] ▲ $ 2 13
24 May 86 **WINNER IN YOU** *MCA MCF 3319* ▲ 30 17
2 Aug 86 **OH, PEOPLE** *MCA MCA 1075* 26 6
3 Sep 94 **THE RIGHT KINDA LOVER** *MCA MCSTD 1995* 50 2

[1] Patti LaBelle and Michael McDonald

LADIES CHOICE *UK, male vocal / instrumental group*

25 Jan 86 **FUNKY SENSATION** *Sure Delight SD 01* 41 4

LADIES FIRST *UK, female vocal trio (2 Singles: 8 Weeks)*

24 Nov 01 **MESSIN'** *Polydor 5873422* 30 2
13 Apr 02 **I CAN'T WAIT** *Polydor 5706912* 19 6

Act were a duo by second hit.

LADY OF RAGE *US, female rapper – Robin Allen*

8 Oct 94 **AFRO PUFFS** *Interscope A 8288CD* 72 1

LADY SAW *Jamaica, female vocalist – Marion Hall (2 Singles: 3 Weeks)*

16 Dec 00 **BUMP N GRIND (I AM FEELING HOT TONIGHT)** *Telstar CDSTAS 3129* [1] 59 1
20 Oct 01 **SINCE I MET YOU LADY / SPARKLE OF MY EYES** *DEP International DEPD 55* [2] 40 2

[1] M Dubs featuring Lady Saw [2] UB40 featuring Lady Saw

LADY SOVEREIGN NEW *UK, female rapper (3 Singles: 5 Weeks)*

26 Mar 05 **RANDOM** *Casual CDLOUPE 15* 73 1
20 Aug 05 **9 TO 5** *Island CIDX 898* 33 2
3 Dec 05 **HOODIE** *Island CIDX 914* 44 2

LADYSMITH BLACK MAMBAZO
South Africa, male vocal group (5 Albums: 69 Weeks, 6 Singles: 26 Weeks)

11 Apr 87 **SHAKA ZULU** *Warner Bros. WX 94* 34 11
3 Jun 95 **SWING LOW SWEET CHARIOT** *PolyGram TV SWLOW 2* [1] 15 6
3 Jun 95 **WORLD IN UNION '95** *PolyGram TV RUGBY 2* [2] 47 5
15 Nov 97 **INKANYEZI NEZAZI (THE STAR AND THE WISEMAN)** *A&M 5823892* 33 3
22 Nov 97 **HEAVENLY** *A&M 5407902* 53 16
11 Jul 98 **THE STAR AND THE WISEMAN** (re-issue) *AM:PM 5825692* 63 1
3 Oct 98 ● **THE BEST OF LADYSMITH BLACK MAMBAZO – THE STAR AND THE WISEMAN** *PolyGram TV 5652982* 2 34
16 Oct 99 **IN HARMONY** *Universal Music TV 1537392* 15 5
16 Oct 99 **AIN'T NO SUNSHINE** *Universal Music TV 1564332* [3] 42 2
18 Dec 99 **I SHALL BE THERE** *Glow Worm / Epic 6683332* [4] 13 9
12 May 01 **THE ULTIMATE COLLECTION** *Universal Music TV 5566822* 37 3

[1] Ladysmith Black Mambazo featuring China Black [2] Ladysmith Black Mambazo featuring PJ Powers [3] Ladysmith Black Mambazo featuring Des'ree [4] B*Witched featuring Ladysmith Black Mambazo

The Best of Ladysmith Black Mambazo – The Star and the Wiseman changed label to Universal Music TV from 13 Mar 1999.

LADYTRON
UK / Bulgaria, male / female vocal production group (5 Singles: 5 Weeks)

7 Dec 02 **SEVENTEEN** *Telstar / Invicta Hi-Fi CDSTAS 3284* 68 1
22 Mar 03 **BLUE JEANS** *Invicta Hi-Fi / Telstar CDSTAS 3311* 43 1
12 Jul 03 **EVIL** *Invicta Hi-Fi / Telstar CDSTAS 3331* 44 1
2 Jul 05 **SUGAR** *Island CID 896* 45 1
1 Oct 05 **DESTROY EVERYTHING YOU TOUCH** *Island CIDX 905* 42 1

	8 February 1975	15 February 1975	22 February 1975	1 March 1975
UK No.1 SINGLES	JANUARY Pilot	JANUARY Pilot	MAKE ME SMILE (COME UP AND SEE ME) Steve Harley and Cockney Rebel	MAKE ME SMILE (COME UP AND SEE ME) Steve Harley and Cockney Rebel
UK No.1 ALBUMS	HIS GREATEST HITS Engelbert Humperdinck	HIS GREATEST HITS Engelbert Humperdinck	HIS GREATEST HITS Engelbert Humperdinck	ON THE LEVEL Status Quo

LAGUNA (see also SPILLER)
Italy, male DJ / production duo – Cristiano Spiller and Tommy Vee

1 Nov 97		**SPILLER FROM RIO (DO IT EASY)** *Positiva CDTIV 83*	40	2

LAID BACK *Denmark, male vocal / instrumental duo*

5 May 90		**BAKERMAN** *Arista 112356*	44	4

Cleo LAINE *UK, female vocalist – Clementina Campbell (3 Albums: 37 Weeks, 2 Singles: 14 Weeks)*

29 Dec 60		**LET'S SLIP AWAY** *Fontana H 269*	42	1
14 Sep 61	●	**YOU'LL ANSWER TO ME** *Fontana H 326*	5	13
7 Jan 78		**BEST OF FRIENDS** *RCA RS 1094* [1]	18	22
2 Dec 78		**CLEO** *Arcade ADEP 37*	68	1
31 May 80		**SOMETIMES WHEN WE TOUCH** *RCA PL 25296* [2]	15	14

[1] Cleo Laine and John Williams [2] Cleo Laine and James Galway

Frankie LAINE (185 Top 500)
Powerfully-voiced No.1 hitmaker of the pre-rock years, b. Frank Lovecchio, 30 Mar 1913, Chicago, US. He spent an unequalled 27 weeks at the top of the UK chart in 1953, including a record 18 with 'I Believe', and at one time had three singles in the Top 5 (2 Albums: 29 Weeks, 27 Singles: 282 Weeks)

14 Nov 52	●	**SUGARBUSH** (re) *Columbia DB 3123* [1]	8	8
14 Nov 52	●	**HIGH NOON (DO NOT FORSAKE ME)** *Columbia DB 3113*	7	7
20 Mar 53		**THE GIRL IN THE WOOD** *Columbia DB 2907*	11	1
3 Apr 53	★	**I BELIEVE** *Philips PB 117*	1	36
8 May 53	●	**TELL ME A STORY** (re) *Philips PB 126* [2]	5	16
4 Sep 53	●	**WHERE THE WINDS BLOW** *Philips PB 167*	2	12
16 Oct 53	★	**HEY JOE!** *Philips PB 172*	1	8
30 Oct 53	★	**ANSWER ME** *Philips PB 196*	1	17
8 Jan 54	●	**BLOWING WILD** *Philips PB 207*	2	12
26 Mar 54	●	**GRANADA** (re) *Philips PB 242*	9	2
16 Apr 54	●	**THE KID'S LAST FIGHT** *Philips PB 258*	3	10
13 Aug 54	●	**MY FRIEND** *Philips PB 316*	3	15
8 Oct 54	●	**THERE MUST BE A REASON** *Philips PB 306*	9	9
22 Oct 54	●	**RAIN, RAIN, RAIN** *Philips PB 311* [3]	8	16
11 Mar 55		**IN THE BEGINNING** *Philips PB 404*	20	1
24 Jun 55	●	**COOL WATER** *Philips PB 465* [4]	2	22
15 Jul 55	●	**STRANGE LADY IN TOWN** *Philips PB 478*	6	13
11 Nov 55		**HUMMING BIRD** *Philips PB 498*	16	1
25 Nov 55	●	**HAWK-EYE** *Philips PB 519*	7	8
20 Jan 56	●	**SIXTEEN TONS** *Philips PB 539* [4]	10	3
4 May 56		**HELL HATH NO FURY** *Philips PB 585*	28	1
7 Sep 56	★	**A WOMAN IN LOVE** *Philips PB 617*	1	21
28 Dec 56		**MOONLIGHT GAMBLER** (re) *Philips PB 638* $	13	13
26 Apr 57		**LOVE IS A GOLDEN RING** *Philips PB 676* [5]	19	5
4 Oct 57		**GOOD EVENING FRIENDS / UP ABOVE MY HEAD, I HEAR MUSIC IN THE AIR** *Philips PB 708* [6]	25	4
13 Nov 59	●	**RAWHIDE** (re) *Philips PB 965*	6	20
11 May 61		**GUNSLINGER** *Philips PB 1135*	50	1
24 Jun 61	●	**HELL BENT FOR LEATHER** *Philips BBL 7468*	7	23
24 Sep 77	●	**THE VERY BEST OF FRANKIE LAINE** *Warwick PR 5032*	7	6

[1] Doris Day and Frankie Laine [2] Jimmy Boyd – Frankie Laine [3] Frankie Laine and The Four Lads [4] Frankie Laine with the Mellomen [5] Frankie Laine and the Easy Riders [6] Frankie Laine and Johnnie Ray

Greg LAKE (see also EMERSON, LAKE and PALMER; EMERSON, LAKE & POWELL; KING CRIMSON) *UK, male vocalist*

6 Dec 75	●	**I BELIEVE IN FATHER CHRISTMAS** (2re) *Manticore K 13511*	2	12
17 Oct 81		**GREG LAKE** *Chrysalis CHR 1357*	62	3

Re-entries occurred in Dec '82 and Dec '83.

LAMB *UK, male / female vocal / production duo – Andy Barlow and Louise Rhodes (2 Albums: 2 Weeks, 3 Singles: 4 Weeks)*

29 Mar 97		**GORECKI** *Fontana LAMCD 4*	30	2
3 Apr 99		**B LINE** *Fontana LAMCD 5*	52	1
22 May 99		**ALL IN YOUR HANDS** *Fontana LAMCD 6*	71	1
29 May 99		**FEAR OF FOURS** *Fontana 5588212*	37	1
20 Oct 01		**WHAT SOUND** *Mercury 5865382*	54	1

TOP 10
ON THE DAY PRINCESS DIANA DIED

In the early hours of Sunday, 31 August 1997, news broke that Diana, Princess of Wales, had died in a Paris car crash. You might remember where you were when the shocking news reached you that morning in late summer, but no one is expected to recall what was No.1 in the singles chart that day. It was, in fact, the almost prophetic 'Men in Black' by Will Smith. Little did the record buying public realise just how appropriate this and some of their other contributions to the Top 10 would be that Sunday.

LW	TW	
1	1	**MEN IN BLACK** Will Smith
2	2	**TUBTHUMPING** Chumbawamba
-	3	**HONEY** Mariah Carey
-	4	**I KNOW WHERE IT'S AT** All Saints
-	5	**TRAVELLERS TUNE** Ocean Colour Scene
4	6	**I'LL BE MISSING YOU** Puff Daddy & Faith Evans featuring 112
-	7	**FREE** DJ Quicksilver
-	8	**KARMA POLICE** Radiohead
5	9	**FREED FROM DESIRE** Gala
-	10	**WHEN DOVES CRY** Ginuwine

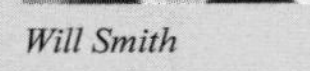

Will Smith

Diana, Princess of Wales

8 March 1975	15 March 1975	22 March 1975	29 March 1975
IF Telly Savalas	**IF** Telly Savalas	**BYE BYE BABY** Bay City Rollers	**BYE BYE BABY** Bay City Rollers
ON THE LEVEL Status Quo	**PHYSICAL GRAFFITI** Led Zeppelin	**20 GREATEST HITS** Tom Jones	**20 GREATEST HITS** Tom Jones

KEY
UK No.1 ★ UK Top 10 ● Still on chart + UK entry at No.1 ■
US No.1 ▲ UK million seller £ US million seller $
Singles re-entries are listed as (re), (2re), (3re)... which signifies that the hit re-entered the chart once, twice or three times...
Peak Position / Weeks

Annabel LAMB *UK, female vocalist*

Date	Title	Peak Position	Weeks
27 Aug 83	**RIDERS ON THE STORM** *A&M AM 131*	27	7
28 Apr 84	THE FLAME *A&M AMLX 68564*	84	1

LAMBCHOP *US, male / female vocal / instrumental group (3 Albums: 5 Weeks, 1 Single: 1 Week)*

Date	Title	Peak Position	Weeks
19 Feb 00	NIXON *City Slang 201522*	60	1
20 May 00	**UP WITH PEOPLE** *City Slang 201592*	66	1
2 Mar 02	IS A WOMAN *City Slang 201902*	38	2
21 Feb 04	AW CMON / NO YOU CMON *City Slang 5958900*	45	2

The LAMBRETTAS *UK, male vocal / instrumental group (1 Album: 8 Weeks, 3 Singles: 24 Weeks)*

Date	Title	Peak Position	Weeks
1 Mar 80 ●	**POISON IVY** *Rocket XPRESS 25*	7	12
24 May 80	**D-A-A-ANCE** *Rocket XPRESS 33*	12	8
5 Jul 80	BEAT BOYS IN THE JET AGE *Rocket TRAIN 10*	28	8
23 Aug 80	**ANOTHER DAY (ANOTHER GIRL)** *Rocket XPRESS 36*	49	4

The LAMPIES *US, male / female / canine cartoon vocal group*

Date	Title	Peak Position	Weeks
22 Dec 01	**LIGHT UP THE WORLD FOR CHRISTMAS** *Bluecrest LAMPCD 001*	48	3

The LANCASTRIANS *UK, male vocal / instrumental group*

Date	Title	Peak Position	Weeks
24 Dec 64	**WE'LL SING IN THE SUNSHINE** *Pye 7N 15732*	44	2

Major LANCE *US, male vocalist, b. 4 Apr 1942, d. 3 Sep 1994*

Date	Title	Peak Position	Weeks
13 Feb 64	**UM, UM, UM, UM, UM, UM** *Columbia DB 7205*	40	2

Charlie LANDSBOROUGH *UK, male vocalist / guitarist (7 Albums: 26 Weeks)*

Date	Title	Peak Position	Weeks
12 Oct 96	WITH YOU IN MIND *Ritz RITZCD 0078*	49	6
8 Nov 97	FURTHER DOWN THE ROAD *Ritz RITZCD 0085*	42	3
10 Oct 98	THE VERY BEST OF CHARLIE LANDSBOROUGH *Ritz RZCD 0087*	41	2
2 Oct 99	STILL CAN'T SAY GOODBYE *Ritz RZCD 0092*	39	2
16 Aug 03	SMILE *Telstar Premiere TPECD 5516*	37	6
26 Feb 05	A PORTRAIT OF CHARLIE LANDSBOROUGH – THE ULTIMATE COLLECTION *DMG TV DMGTV 014*	23	5
22 Oct 05	MY HEART WOULD KNOW *Rosette ROSCD 2056*	60	2

LANDSCAPE *UK, male vocal / instrumental group (1 Album: 12 Weeks, 2 Singles: 20 Weeks)*

Date	Title	Peak Position	Weeks
28 Feb 81 ●	**EINSTEIN A GO-GO** *RCA 22*	5	13
21 Mar 81	FROM THE TEAROOMS OF MARS TO THE HELLHOLES OF URANUS *RCA RCALP 5003*	13	12
23 May 81	**NORMAN BATES** *RCA 60*	40	7

Ronnie LANE (see also The SMALL FACES) *UK, male vocalist, b. 1 Apr 1946, d. 4 Jun 1997 (2 Albums: 4 Weeks, 2 Singles: 12 Weeks)*

Date	Title	Peak Position	Weeks
12 Jan 74	**HOW COME?** *GM GMS 011* [1]	11	8
15 Jun 74	**THE POACHER** *GM GMS 024*	36	4
17 Aug 74	ANYMORE FOR ANYMORE .. *GM GML 1013* [1]	48	1
15 Oct 77	ROUGH MIX *Polydor 2442147* [2]	44	3

[1] Ronnie Lane accompanied by the band Slim Chance [1] Ronnie Lane with the band Slim Chance [2] Pete Townshend and Ronnie Lane

Mark LANEGAN BAND *US, male vocal / instrumental group*

Date	Title	Peak Position	Weeks
14 Aug 04	BUBBLEGUM *Beggars Banquet BBQCD 237*	43	1

Don LANG *UK, male vocalist / trombone player – Gordon Langhorn, b. 19 Jan 1925, d. 3 Aug 1992 (4 Singles: 18 Weeks)*

Date	Title	Peak Position	Weeks
4 Nov 55	**CLOUDBURST** (2re) *HMV POP 115*	16	4
5 Jul 57	**SCHOOL DAY (RING! RING! GOES THE BELL)** *HMV POP 350* [1]	26	2
23 May 58 ●	**WITCH DOCTOR** *HMV POP 488* [1]	5	11
10 Mar 60	**SINK THE BISMARCK** *HMV POP 714*	43	1

[1] Don Lang and his Frantic Five

kd lang *Canada, female vocalist – Katherine Dawn Lang (6 Albums: 71 Weeks, 8 Singles: 25 Weeks)*

Date	Title	Peak Position	Weeks
28 Mar 92 ●	INGENUE *Sire 7599268402*	3	52
16 May 92	**CONSTANT CRAVING** *Sire W 0100*	52	4
22 Aug 92	**CRYING** *Virgin America VUS 63* [1]	13	6
27 Feb 93	**CONSTANT CRAVING** (re-issue) *Sire W 0157CD*	15	8
1 May 93	**THE MIND OF LOVE (WHERE IS YOUR HEAD, KATHRYN?)** *Sire W 0170CD1*	72	1
26 Jun 93	**MISS CHATELAINE** *Sire W 0181CDX*	68	2
13 Nov 93	EVEN COWGIRLS GET THE BLUES *Sire 9362454332*	36	2
11 Dec 93	**JUST KEEP ME MOVING** *Sire W 0227CD*	59	1
30 Sep 95	**IF I WERE YOU** *Sire W 0319CD*	53	1
14 Oct 95 ●	ALL YOU CAN EAT *Warner Bros. 9362460342*	7	5
18 May 96	**YOU'RE OK** *Warner Bros. W 0332CD*	44	2
12 Jul 97	DRAG *Warner Bros. 9362466232*	19	3
15 Jul 00	INVINCIBLE SUMMER *Warner Bros. 9362476052*	17	6
5 Jul 03	A WONDERFUL WORLD *Columbia 5098702* [1]	33	3

[1] Roy Orbison (duet with kd lang) [1] Tony Bennett & kd lang

Thomas LANG *UK, male vocalist*

Date	Title	Peak Position	Weeks
30 Jan 88	**THE HAPPY MAN** *Epic VOW 4*	67	3
20 Feb 88	SCALLYWAG JAZ *Epic 450996 1*	92	1

LANGE *UK, male producer – Stuart Langelaan (3 Singles: 8 Weeks)*

Date	Title	Peak Position	Weeks
19 Jun 99	**I BELIEVE** *Additive 12AD 039* [1]	68	1
19 Jan 02 ●	**DRIFTING AWAY** *VC Recordings VCRD 101* [2]	9	6
22 Feb 03	**DON'T THINK IT (FEEL IT)** *Nebula NEBCD 037* [3]	59	1

[1] Lange featuring Sarah Dwyer [2] Lange featuring Skye [3] Lange featuring Leah

The LANTERNS *UK, male / female vocal / instrumental trio*

Date	Title	Peak Position	Weeks
6 Feb 99	**HIGHRISE TOWN** *Columbia 6665712*	50	1

Mario LANZA *US, male vocalist – Alfredo Cocozza, b. 31 Jan 1921, d. 7 Oct 1959 (8 Albums: 68 Weeks, 5 Singles: 32 Weeks)*

Date	Title	Peak Position	Weeks
14 Nov 52 ●	**BECAUSE YOU'RE MINE** *HMV DA 2017*	3	24
4 Feb 55	**DRINKING SONG** *HMV DA 2065*	13	1
18 Feb 55	**I'LL WALK WITH GOD** (re) *HMV DA 2062*	18	2
22 Apr 55	**SERENADE** (re) *HMV DA 2065*	15	3
11 Aug 56 ●	THE STUDENT PRINCE *HMV ALP 1186* ▲	5	1
14 Sep 56	**SERENADE** (re) *HMV DA 2085*	25	2
6 Dec 58 ●	THE STUDENT PRINCE / THE GREAT CARUSO *RCA RB 16113*	4	21
23 Jul 60 ●	THE GREAT CARUSO *RCA RB 16112*	3	15
9 Jan 71	HIS GREATEST HITS VOLUME 1 *RCA LSB 4000*	39	1
5 Sep 81	THE LEGEND OF MARIO LANZA *K-Tel NE 1110*	29	11
14 Nov 87	A PORTRAIT OF MARIO LANZA *Stylus SMR 741*	49	8
12 Mar 94	MARIO LANZA – THE ULTIMATE COLLECTION *RCA Victor 74321185742*	13	7
12 Jun 04	THE DEFINITIVE COLLECTION *BMG 82876614032*	41	4

DA 2065 and DA 2085 are two different songs. The two The Great Caruso albums are different, the first being a film soundtrack.

LAPTOP *US, male vocalist / instrumentalist – Jesse Hartman*

Date	Title	Peak Position	Weeks
12 Jun 99	**NOTHING TO DECLARE** *Island CID 744*	74	1

LARD *UK, male vocal / instrumental group*

Date	Title	Peak Position	Weeks
6 Oct 90	THE LAST TEMPTATION OF REID *Alternative Tentacles VIRUS 84*	69	1

	5 April 1975	12 April 1975	19 April 1975	26 April 1975
UK No.1 SINGLES	BYE BYE BABY – Bay City Rollers	BYE BYE BABY – Bay City Rollers	BYE BYE BABY – Bay City Rollers	BYE BYE BABY – Bay City Rollers
UK No.1 ALBUMS	20 GREATEST HITS – Tom Jones	20 GREATEST HITS – Tom Jones	THE BEST OF THE STYLISTICS – The Stylistics	THE BEST OF THE STYLISTICS – The Stylistics

Julius LAROSA *US, male vocalist*

4 Jul 58	**TORERO** *RCA 1063*	15	9

The LA's *UK, male vocal / instrumental group (1 Album: 22 Weeks, 6 Singles: 20 Weeks)*

14 Jan 89	**THERE SHE GOES** *Go Discs GOLASEP 2*	59	4
15 Sep 90	**TIMELESS MELODY** *Go Discs GOLAS 4*	57	2
13 Oct 90	THE LA'S *Go Discs 8282021*	30	22
3 Nov 90	**THERE SHE GOES** (re-issue) *Go Discs GOLAS 5*	13	9
16 Feb 91	**FEELIN'** *Go Discs GOLAS 6*	43	3
10 May 97	**FEVER PITCH THE EP** *Blanco Y Negro NEG 104CD* [1]	65	1
2 Oct 99	**THERE SHE GOES** (2nd re-issue) *Polydor 5614032*	65	1

[1] The Pretenders, The La's, Orlando, Neil MacColl, Nick Hornby

Tracks on Fever Pitch the EP: Goin' Back – The Pretenders / There She Goes – The La's / How Can We Hang on to a Dream – Orlando / Football – Neil MacColl, Boo Hewerdine and Nick Hornby.

LAS KETCHUP *Spain, female vocal trio (2 Singles: 26 Weeks)*

21 Sep 02	**THE KETCHUP SONG (ASEREJE)** (import) *Columbia 6729602CD*	49	4
19 Oct 02 ★	**THE KETCHUP SONG (ASEREJE)** *Columbia 6731932* ■	1	22

Denise LASALLE *US, female vocalist – Denise Craig*

15 Jun 85 ●	**MY TOOT TOOT** *Epic A 6334*	6	13

LASGO *Belgium, male / female production / vocal (Evi Goffin) / instrumental trio (1 Album: 3 Weeks, 4 Singles: 34 Weeks)*

9 Mar 02 ●	**SOMETHING** *Positiva CDTIV 169*	4	15
24 Aug 02 ●	**ALONE** *Positiva CDTIVS 176*	7	8
7 Sep 02	SOME THINGS *Positiva 5419362*	30	3
30 Nov 02	**PRAY** *Positiva CDTIVS 182*	17	7
1 May 04	**SURRENDER** *Positiva CDTIVS 205*	24	4

Lisa LASHES *UK, female DJ / producer – Lisa Rose-Wyatt (2 Singles: 3 Weeks)*

8 Jul 00	**UNBELIEVABLE** *Tidy Trax TIDY 138CD*	63	1
25 Oct 03	**WHAT CAN YOU DO 4 ME?** *Tidy Trax TIDY 194CD*	52	2

James LAST 98 Top 500

The most charted big band formed in 1964 and was fronted by a German producer / arranger / conductor / composer, b. Hans Last, 17 Apr 1929. Known for his non-stop dance party records, he has reportedly sold in excess of 70 million albums worldwide (64 Albums: 446 Weeks, 1 Single: 4 Weeks)

15 Apr 67 ●	THIS IS JAMES LAST *Polydor 104678* [1]	6	48
22 Jul 67	HAMMOND A-GO-GO *Polydor 249043*	27	10
26 Aug 67	LOVE THIS IS MY SONG *Polydor 583553*	32	2
26 Aug 67	NON-STOP DANCING *Polydor 236203*	35	1
22 Jun 68	JAMES LAST GOES POP *Polydor 249160*	32	3
8 Feb 69	DANCING '68 VOLUME 1 *Polydor 249216*	40	1
31 May 69	TRUMPET A-GO-GO *Polydor 249239*	13	1
9 Aug 69	NON-STOP DANCING '69 *Polydor 249294*	26	1
24 Jan 70	NON-STOP DANCING '69/2 *Polydor 249354*	27	3
23 May 70	NON-STOP EVERGREENS *Polydor 249370*	26	1
11 Jul 70	CLASSICS UP TO DATE *Polydor 249371*	67	1
11 Jul 70	NON-STOP DANCING '70 *Polydor 237104*	44	1
24 Oct 70	VERY BEST OF JAMES LAST *Polydor 2371054*	45	4
8 May 71	NON-STOP DANCING '71 *Polydor 2371111*	21	4
26 Jun 71	SUMMER HAPPENING *Polydor 2371133*	38	1
18 Sep 71	BEACH PARTY 2 *Polydor 2371211*	47	1
2 Oct 71	YESTERDAY'S MEMORIES *Contour 2870117*	17	14
16 Oct 71	NON-STOP DANCING 12 *Polydor 2371141*	30	3
19 Feb 72	NON-STOP DANCING 13 *Polydor 2371189*	32	2
4 Mar 72	POLKA PARTY *Polydor 2371190*	22	3
29 Apr 72	JAMES LAST IN CONCERT *Polydor 2371191*	13	6
24 Jun 72	VOODOO PARTY *Polydor 2371235*	45	1
16 Sep 72	CLASSICS UP TO DATE VOLUME 2 *Polydor 184061*	49	1
30 Sep 72	LOVE MUST BE THE REASON *Polydor 2371281*	32	2
27 Jan 73	THE MUSIC OF JAMES LAST *Polydor 2683010*	19	12
24 Feb 73	JAMES LAST IN RUSSIA *Polydor 2371293*	12	9
24 Feb 73	NON-STOP DANCING VOLUME 14 *Polydor 2371319*	27	3
28 Jul 73	OLE *Polydor 2371384*	24	5
1 Sep 73	NON-STOP DANCING VOLUME 15 *Polydor 2371376*	34	2
20 Apr 74	NON-STOP DANCING VOLUME 16 *Polydor 2371444*	43	2
29 Jun 74	IN CONCERT VOLUME 2 *Polydor 2371320*	49	1
23 Nov 74	GOLDEN MEMORIES *Polydor 2371472*	39	2
26 Jul 75 ●	TEN YEARS NON-STOP JUBILEE *Polydor 2660111*	5	16
2 Aug 75	VIOLINS IN LOVE *K-Tel 1*	60	1
22 Nov 75 ●	MAKE THE PARTY LAST *Polydor 2371612*	3	19
8 May 76	CLASSICS UP TO DATE VOLUME 3 *Polydor 2371538*	54	1
6 May 78	EAST TO WEST *Polydor 2630092*	49	4
14 Apr 79 ●	LAST THE WHOLE NIGHT LONG *Polydor PTD 001*	2	45
3 May 80	**THE SEDUCTION (LOVE THEME)** *Polydor PD 2071* [1]	48	4
23 Aug 80	THE BEST FROM 150 GOLD RECORDS *Polydor 2681 211*	56	3
1 Nov 80	CLASSICS FOR DREAMING *Polydor POLTV 11*	12	18
14 Feb 81	ROSES FROM THE SOUTH *Polydor 2372 051*	41	5
21 Nov 81	HANSIMANIA *Polydor POLTV 14*	18	13
28 Nov 81	LAST FOREVER *Polydor 2630 135*	88	2
5 Mar 83	BLUEBIRD *Polydor POLD 5072*	57	3
30 Apr 83	NON-STOP DANCING '83 – PARTY POWER *Polydor POLD 5094*	56	2
30 Apr 83	THE BEST OF MY GOLD RECORDS *Polydor PODV 7*	42	5
3 Dec 83	THE GREATEST SONGS OF THE BEATLES *Polydor POLD 5119*	52	8
24 Mar 84	THE ROSE OF TRALEE AND OTHER IRISH FAVOURITES *Polydor POLD 5131*	21	11
13 Oct 84	PARADISE *Polydor POLD 5163*	74	2
8 Dec 84	JAMES LAST IN SCOTLAND *Polydor POLD 5166*	68	9
14 Sep 85	LEAVE THE BEST TO LAST *Polydor PROLP 7*	11	27
18 Apr 87	BY REQUEST *Polydor POLH 34*	22	11
26 Nov 88	DANCE DANCE DANCE *Polydor JLTV 1*	38	8
14 Apr 90	CLASSICS BY MOONLIGHT *Polydor 8432181*	12	12
15 Jun 91 ●	POP SYMPHONIES *Polydor 8494291*	10	11
9 Nov 91	TOGETHER AT LAST *Delphine / Polydor 5115251* [2]	14	15
12 Sep 92	VIVA ESPANA *PolyGram TV 5172202*	23	5
20 Nov 93	JAMES LAST PLAYS ANDREW LLOYD WEBBER *Polydor 5199102*	12	10
19 Nov 94	IN HARMONY *Polydor 5238242* [2]	28	7
18 Nov 95	THE VERY BEST OF JAMES LAST & HIS ORCHESTRA *Polydor 5295562*	36	7
28 Mar 98	POP SYMPHONIES 2 *Polydor 5396242* [3]	32	3
24 Apr 99	COUNTRY ROADS *Polydor / Universal TV 5474022*	18	5
3 Nov 01	JAMES LAST AND HIS ORCHESTRA PLAYS ABBA *Polydor 5891982* [3]	29	4
6 Sep 03	THE CLASSICAL COLLECTION *UCJ 9810457*	44	3

[1] James Last Band [1] James Last Band [2] Richard Clayderman and James Last [3] James Last and his Orchestra

LAST RHYTHM *Italy, male instrumental / production group*

14 Sep 96	**LAST RHYTHM** *Stress CDSTR 76*	62	1

The LATE SHOW *UK, male vocal / instrumental group*

3 Mar 79	**BRISTOL STOMP** *Decca F 13822*	40	6

LATIN QUARTER *UK, male / female vocal / instrumental group (2 Albums: 3 Weeks, 2 Singles: 10 Weeks)*

18 Jan 86	**RADIO AFRICA** *Rockin' Horse RH 102*	19	9
1 Mar 86	MODERN TIMES *Rockin' Horse RHLP 1*	91	2
18 Apr 87	**NOMZAMO (ONE PEOPLE ONE CAUSE)** *Rockin' Horse RH 113*	73	1
6 Jun 87	MICK AND CAROLINE *Rockin' Horse 208 142*	96	1

LATIN THING *Canada / Spain, male / female vocal / instrumental group*

13 Jul 96	**LATIN THING** *Faze 2 CDFAZE 33*	41	1

Gino LATINO *Italy, male producer – Giacomo Maiolini (aka Lorenzo Cherubini)*

20 Jan 90	**WELCOME** *ffrr F 126*	17	7

3 May 1975	10 May 1975	17 May 1975	24 May 1975
OH BOY Mud	**OH BOY** Mud	**STAND BY YOUR MAN** Tammy Wynette	**STAND BY YOUR MAN** Tammy Wynette
ONCE UPON A STAR Bay City Rollers	**ONCE UPON A STAR** Bay City Rollers	**ONCE UPON A STAR** Bay City Rollers	**THE BEST OF THE STYLISTICS** The Stylistics

KEY UK No.1 ★ UK Top 10 ● Still on chart + UK entry at No.1 ■ US No.1 ▲ UK million seller £ US million seller $
Singles re-entries are listed as (re), (2re), (3re)... which signifies that the hit re-entered the chart once, twice or three times...
Peak Position / Weeks

LATOUR *US, male vocalist / producer – William LaTour*

8 Jun 91 **PEOPLE ARE STILL HAVING SEX** *Polydor PO 147* 15 7

Stacy LATTISAW *US, female vocalist (2 Singles: 14 Weeks)*

14 Jun 80 ● **JUMP TO THE BEAT** *Atlantic / Cotillion K 11496* 3 11
30 Aug 80 **DYNAMITE** *Atlantic K 11554* 51 3

Cyndi LAUPER (358 Top 500)

Flamboyant and versatile singer / songwriter, b. 20 Jun 1953, New York, US. Her debut album, She's So Unusual, spawned four Top 5 US singles, and she won a Grammy for Best New Artist of 1984 easily outpacing her major female rival, Madonna (6 Albums: 92 Weeks, 17 Singles: 103 Weeks)

14 Jan 84 ● **GIRLS JUST WANT TO HAVE FUN** *Portrait A 3943* $ 2 12
18 Feb 84 SHE'S SO UNUSUAL *Portrait PRT 25792* 16 32
24 Mar 84 ● **TIME AFTER TIME** (re) *Portrait A 4290* ▲ 3 17
1 Sep 84 **SHE BOP** *Portrait A 4620* 46 5
17 Nov 84 **ALL THROUGH THE NIGHT** *Portrait A 4849* 64 2
20 Sep 86 **TRUE COLOURS** *Portrait 650026 7* ▲ 12 11
11 Oct 86 TRUE COLORS *Portrait PRT 26948* 25 12
27 Dec 86 **CHANGE OF HEART** (re) *Portrait CYNDI 1* 67 2
28 Mar 87 **WHAT'S GOING ON** *Portrait CYN 1* 57 3
20 May 89 ● **I DROVE ALL NIGHT** *Epic CYN 4* 7 12
1 Jul 89 ● A NIGHT TO REMEMBER *Epic 462499 1* 9 12
5 Aug 89 **MY FIRST NIGHT WITHOUT YOU** *Epic CYN 5* 53 4
30 Dec 89 **HEADING WEST** *Epic CYN 6* 68 1
6 Jun 92 **THE WORLD IS STONE** *Epic 6579707* 15 7
13 Nov 93 **THAT'S WHAT I THINK** *Epic 6598782* 31 4
27 Nov 93 HAT FULL OF STARS *Epic 4730542* 56 1
8 Jan 94 **WHO LET IN THE RAIN** *Epic 6590392* 32 4
3 Sep 94 ● TWELVE DEADLY CYNS ... AND THEN SOME *Epic 4773632* 2 34
17 Sep 94 ● **HEY NOW (GIRLS JUST WANT TO HAVE FUN)** (re-recording) *Epic 6608072* 4 13
11 Feb 95 **I'M GONNA BE STRONG** *Epic 6611962* 37 2
26 Aug 95 **COME ON HOME** *Epic 6614255* 39 2
1 Feb 97 **YOU DON'T KNOW** *Epic 6641845* 27 2
22 Feb 97 SISTERS OF AVALON *Epic 4853702* 59 1

LAUREL and HARDY *UK / US, male comedians / actors / vocal / instrumental duo – Stan Laurel, b. Arthur Jefferson, 16 Jun 1890, d. 23 Feb 1965, and Oliver Hardy, b. 18 Jan 1892, d. 7 Aug 1957*

22 Nov 75 ● **THE TRAIL OF THE LONESOME PINE** *United Artists UP 36026* [1] 2 10
6 Dec 75 THE GOLDEN AGE OF HOLLYWOOD COMEDY *United Artists UAG 29676* 55 4

[1] Laurel and Hardy with The Avalon Boys featuring Chill Wills

LAUREL and HARDY *UK, male vocal / instrumental duo*

2 Apr 83 **CLUNK CLINK** *CBS A 3213* 65 2

LAURNEA *US, female vocalist – Laurnea Wilkinson*

12 Jul 97 **DAYS OF YOUTH** *Epic 6646932* 36 2

Avril LAVIGNE (456 Top 500)

Internationally successful pop punk princess who was the first female soloist under the age of 20 to top the albums chart, b. 30 Sep 1984, Ontario, Canada. Let Go sold over 14 million worldwide and she won Best Female Pop / Rock Artist at the 2004 World Music Awards (2 Albums: 97 Weeks, 9 Singles: 61 Weeks)

7 Sep 02 **COMPLICATED** (re) (import) *RCA 74321955782* 64 2
14 Sep 02 ★ LET GO *Arista 74321949312* 1 66
5 Oct 02 ● **COMPLICATED** *Arista 74321965962* 3 9
28 Dec 02 ● **SK8ER BOI** *Arista 74321979782* 8 9
12 Apr 03 ● **I'M WITH YOU** *Arista 82876506712* 7 10
19 Jul 03 **LOSING GRIP** (re) *Arista 82876534542* 22 6
22 May 04 ● **DON'T TELL ME** *Arista 82876617422* 5 9
5 Jun 04 ★ UNDER MY SKIN *Arista 82876617872* ■ ▲ 1 31
14 Aug 04 ● **MY HAPPY ENDING** *Arista 82876636492* 5 9
27 Nov 04 **NOBODY'S HOME** *Arista 82876663652* 24 4
9 Apr 05 **HE WASN'T** *Arista 82876683052* 23 3

Joanna LAW *UK, female vocalist (2 Singles: 8 Weeks)*

7 Jul 90 **FIRST TIME EVER** *Citybeat CBE 752* 67 3
14 Sep 96 **THE GIFT** *Deconstruction 74321401912* [1] 15 5

[1] Way Out West featuring Miss Joanna Law

Law's contribution to 'The Gift' is a sample from 'First Time Ever'.

The LAW

UK, male vocal / instrumental duo – Paul Rodgers and Kenny Jones

6 Apr 91 THE LAW *Atlantic 7567821951* 61 1

Steve LAWLER *UK, male DJ / producer*

11 Nov 00 **RISE 'IN** *Bedrock BEDRCDS 008* 50 1

Belle LAWRENCE *UK, female vocalist*

30 Mar 02 **EVERGREEN** *Euphoric CDUPH 024* 73 1

Joey LAWRENCE

US, male vocalist (1 Album: 3 Weeks, 4 Singles: 15 Weeks)

26 Jun 93 **NOTHIN' MY LOVE CAN'T FIX** *EMI CDEM 271* 13 7
31 Jul 93 JOEY LAWRENCE *EMI CDEMC 3657* 39 3
28 Aug 93 **I CAN'T HELP MYSELF** *EMI CDEM 277* 27 4
30 Oct 93 **STAY FOREVER** *EMI CDEM 289* 41 3
19 Sep 98 **NEVER GONNA CHANGE MY MIND** *Curb CUBC 34* 49 1

Lee LAWRENCE

UK, male vocalist – Leon Siroto, b. 1921, d. Feb 1961 (2 Singles: 10 Weeks)

20 Nov 53 ● **CRYING IN THE CHAPEL** (re) *Decca F 10177* 7 6
2 Dec 55 **SUDDENLY THERE'S A VALLEY** (re) *Columbia DB 3681* 14 4

With Ray Martin and his Orchestra.

Sophie LAWRENCE *UK, female actor / vocalist*

3 Aug 91 **LOVE'S UNKIND** *IQ ZB 44821* 21 7

Steve LAWRENCE

US, male vocalist – Sidney Leibowitz (3 Singles: 27 Weeks)

21 Apr 60 ● **FOOTSTEPS** *HMV POP 726* 4 13
18 Aug 60 **GIRLS, GIRLS, GIRLS** *London HLT 9166* 49 1
22 Aug 63 ● **I WANT TO STAY HERE** *CBS AAG 163* [1] 3 13

[1] Steve and Eydie

Syd LAWRENCE

UK, orchestra – leader b. 26 Jun 1924, d. 5 May 1998 (4 Albums: 9 Weeks)

8 Aug 70 MORE MILLER AND OTHER BIG BAND MAGIC *Philips 6642 001* 14 4
25 Dec 71 MUSIC OF GLENN MILLER IN SUPER STEREO *Philips 6641017* 43 2
25 Dec 71 SYD LAWRENCE WITH THE GLENN MILLER SOUND *Fontana SFL 13178* 31 2
26 Feb 72 SOMETHING OLD SOMETHING NEW *Philips 6308 090* 34 1

Ronnie LAWS *US, male vocalist / saxophonist*

17 Oct 81 SOLID GROUND *Liberty LBG 30336* 100 1

	31 May 1975	7 June 1975	14 June 1975	21 June 1975
UK No.1 SINGLES	**STAND BY YOUR MAN** Tammy Wynette	**WHISPERING GRASS** Windsor Davies as BSM Williams and Don Estelle as Gunner Sugden (Lofty)	**WHISPERING GRASS** Windsor Davies as BSM Williams and Don Estelle as Gunner Sugden (Lofty)	**WHISPERING GRASS** Windsor Davies as BSM Williams and Don Estelle as Gunner Sugden (Lofty)
UK No.1 ALBUMS	**THE BEST OF THE STYLISTICS** The Stylistics	**THE BEST OF THE STYLISTICS** The Stylistics	**THE BEST OF THE STYLISTICS** The Stylistics	**THE BEST OF THE STYLISTICS** The Stylistics

LAYO & BUSHWACKA! *UK, male DJ / production duo – Layo Paskin and Matthew Benjamin (1 Album: 1 Week, 3 Singles: 12 Weeks)*

22 Jun 02 **LOVE STORY** *XL Recordings XLS 144CD*....30 2
13 Jul 02 **NIGHT WORKS** *XL Recordings XLCD 154*....61 1
25 Jan 03 ● **LOVE STORY (VS FINALLY)** *XL Recordings XLS 154CD*....8 7
16 Aug 03 **IT'S UP TO YOU (SHINING THROUGH)** *XL Recordings XLS 163CD*....25 3

Lindy LAYTON *UK, female vocalist – Belinda Layton (6 Singles: 28 Weeks)*

10 Feb 90 ★ **DUB BE GOOD TO ME** *Go Beat GOD 39* [1]....1 13
11 Aug 90 **SILLY GAMES** (re-recording) *Arista 113452* [2]....22 7
26 Jan 91 **ECHO MY HEART** *Arista 113845*....42 2
31 Aug 91 **WITHOUT YOU (ONE AND ONE)** *Arista 114636*....71 2
24 Apr 93 **WE GOT THE LOVE** *PWL International PWCD 250*....38 3
30 Oct 93 **SHOW ME** *PWL International PWCD 275*....47 1

[1] Beats International featuring Lindy Layton [2] Lindy Layton featuring Janet Kay

Peter LAZONBY *UK, male DJ / producer*

10 Jun 00 **SACRED CYCLES** *Hooj Choons HOOJ 93CD*....49 1

Doug LAZY
US, male rapper – Gene Finley (1 Album: 1 Week, 3 Singles: 9 Weeks)

15 Jul 89 **LET IT ROLL** *Atlantic A 8866* [1]....27 5
4 Nov 89 **LET THE RHYTHM PUMP** *Atlantic A 8784*....45 3
10 Mar 90 **DOUG LAZY GETTIN' CRAZY** *Atlantic 7567820661*....65 1
26 May 90 **LET THE RHYTHM PUMP** (re-mix) *East West A 7919*....63 1

[1] Raze presents Doug Lazy

LE CLICK
Sweden / US, male / female vocal duo – Kayo Shekoni and Robert Haynes

30 Aug 97 **CALL ME** *Logic 74321509672*....38 2

Kele LE ROC *UK, female vocalist – Kelly Biggs (1 Album: 2 Weeks, 4 Singles: 17 Weeks)*

31 Oct 98 ● **LITTLE BIT OF LOVIN'** *1st Avenue / Wild Card / Polydor 5672812*....8 7
27 Mar 99 ● **MY LOVE** *1st Avenue / Wild Card / Polydor 5636112*....8 7
10 Apr 99 **EVERYBODY'S SOMEBODY** *Wild Card 5596662*....44 2
30 Sep 00 **THINKING OF YOU** *Telstar CDSTAS 3136* [1]....70 1
7 Jun 03 **FEELIN' U** *London FCD 409* [2]....34 2

[1] Curtis Lynch Jr featuring Kele Le Roc and Red Rat [2] Shy FX and T-Power featuring Kele Le Roc

LE TIGRE NEW *US, female vocal group (2 Singles: 3 Weeks)*

15 Jan 05 **TKO** *Universal MCSTD 40398*....50 2
7 May 05 **AFTER DARK** *Universal MCSTD 40411*....63 1

Vicky LEANDROS
Greece, female vocalist – Vassiliki Papathanassiou (3 Singles: 29 Weeks)

8 Apr 72 ● **COME WHAT MAY** *Philips 6000 049*....2 16
23 Dec 72 **THE LOVE IN YOUR EYES** (2re) *Philips 6000 081*....40 8
7 Jul 73 **WHEN BOUZOUKIS PLAYED** (re) *Philips 6000 111*....44 5

Denis LEARY *US, male vocalist / comedian*

13 Jan 96 **ASSHOLE** *A&M 5813352*....58 2

The LEAVES *Iceland, male vocal / instrumental group*

18 May 02 **RACE** *B-Unique BUN 020CDS*....66 1
31 Aug 02 **BREATHE** *B-Unique 0927487392*....71 1

LED ZEPPELIN 79 Top 500 (see also COVERDALE PAGE)
Hard rock's most successful album act: Robert Plant (v), Jimmy Page (MBE) (g), John Paul Jones (b/k) and John Bonham (d), d. 1980. This innovative, pioneering quartet have sold an estimated 200 million albums including over 100 million in the US, where they scored seven No.1s from 1969-2003 (18 Albums: 499 Weeks, 1 Single: 2 Weeks)

12 Apr 69 ● **LED ZEPPELIN** *Atlantic 588171*....6 71
8 Nov 69 ★ **LED ZEPPELIN II** *Atlantic 588198* ▲....1 136
7 Nov 70 ★ **LED ZEPPELIN III** *Atlantic 2401002* ■ ▲....1 40
27 Nov 71 ★ **FOUR SYMBOLS (LED ZEPPELIN IV)** *Atlantic K 2401012*....1 69
14 Apr 73 ★ **HOUSES OF THE HOLY** *Atlantic K 50014* ■ ▲....1 13
15 Mar 75 ★ **PHYSICAL GRAFFITI** *Swan Song SSK 89400* ■ ▲....1 31
24 Apr 76 ★ **PRESENCE** *Swan Song SSK 59402* ■ ▲....1 14
6 Nov 76 ★ **THE SONG REMAINS THE SAME** *Swan Song SSK 89402*....1 15
8 Sep 79 ★ **IN THROUGH THE OUT DOOR** *Swan Song SSK 59410* ■ ▲....1 16
4 Dec 82 ● **CODA** *Swan Song A 0051*....4 7
27 Oct 90 ● **REMASTERS** *Atlantic ZEP 1*....10 45
10 Nov 90 **LED ZEPPELIN** *Atlantic 7567821441*....48 2
9 Oct 93 **LED ZEPPELIN BOXED SET II** *Atlantic 7567824772*....56 1
13 Sep 97 **WHOLE LOTTA LOVE** *Atlantic ATT 0013CD* $....21 2
29 Nov 97 **BBC SESSIONS** *Atlantic 7567830612*....23 7
1 Apr 00 **EARLY DAYS – THE BEST OF LED ZEPPELIN VOLUME ONE** *Atlantic 7567832682*....55 1
1 Apr 00 **LATTER DAYS – THE BEST OF LED ZEPPELIN VOLUME TWO** *Atlantic 7567832782*....40 1
8 Mar 03 **VERY BEST OF – EARLY DAYS & LATTER DAYS** *Atlantic 7567836195*....11 23
7 Jun 03 ● **HOW THE WEST WAS WON** *Atlantic 7567835872* ▲....5 7

Led Zeppelin II changed label and catalogue number to Atlantic K 40037 and Four Symbols (Led Zeppelin IV) changed to Atlantic K 50008 during their chart runs. The fourth Led Zeppelin album appeared on the chart under various guises: The Fourth Led Zeppelin Album, Runes, The New Led Zeppelin Album, Led Zeppelin IV and Four Symbols. The two Led Zeppelin albums are different (the 1990 entry is a boxed CD set of old and previously unreleased material).

Angel LEE *UK, female vocalist – Angelique Beckford*

3 Jun 00 **WHAT'S YOUR NAME?** *WEA WEA 258CD*....39 1

Ann LEE *UK, female vocalist – Annerley Gordon (3 Singles: 21 Weeks)*

11 Sep 99 **2 TIMES** (import) *ZYX ZYX 90188*....57 2
16 Oct 99 ● **2 TIMES** *Systematic SYSCD 31*....2 16
4 Mar 00 **VOICES** *Systematic SYSCD 32*....27 3

Brenda LEE 233 Top 500 *The biggest-selling teenage female vocalist of the early rock years, b. Brenda Tarpley, 11 Dec 1944, Georgia, US. She first recorded aged 11, had back-to-back UK / US hits in the early 1960s, was inducted into the Country Music Hall of Fame in 1997 and the Rock and Roll Hall of Fame in 2002 (8 Albums: 64 Weeks, 22 Singles: 210 Weeks)*

17 Mar 60 ● **SWEET NUTHIN'S** (re) *Brunswick 05819* $....4 19
30 Jun 60 **I'M SORRY** *Brunswick 05833* ▲ $....12 16
20 Oct 60 **I WANT TO BE WANTED** *Brunswick 05839* ▲....31 6
19 Jan 61 **LET'S JUMP THE BROOMSTICK** *Brunswick 05823*....12 15
6 Apr 61 **EMOTIONS** *Brunswick 05847*....45 1
20 Jul 61 **DUM DUM** *Brunswick 05854*....22 8
16 Nov 61 **FOOL NUMBER ONE** *Brunswick 05860*....38 3
8 Feb 62 **BREAK IT TO ME GENTLY** *Brunswick 05864*....46 2
5 Apr 62 ● **SPEAK TO ME PRETTY** *Brunswick 05867*....3 12
21 Jun 62 ● **HERE COMES THAT FEELING** *Brunswick 05871*....5 12
13 Sep 62 **IT STARTED ALL OVER AGAIN** *Brunswick 05876*....15 11
24 Nov 62 **ALL THE WAY** *Brunswick LAT 8383*....20 2
29 Nov 62 ● **ROCKIN' AROUND THE CHRISTMAS TREE** *Brunswick 05880*....6 7
17 Jan 63 ● **ALL ALONE AM I** *Brunswick 05882* $....7 17
16 Feb 63 **BRENDA – THAT'S ALL** *Brunswick LAT 8516*....13 9
28 Mar 63 ● **LOSING YOU** *Brunswick 05886*....10 16
13 Apr 63 ● **ALL ALONE AM I** *Brunswick LAT 8530*....8 20
18 Jul 63 **I WONDER** *Brunswick 05891*....14 9
31 Oct 63 **SWEET IMPOSSIBLE YOU** *Brunswick 05896*....28 6
9 Jan 64 ● **AS USUAL** *Brunswick 05899*....5 15
9 Apr 64 **THINK** *Brunswick 05903*....26 8
10 Sep 64 **IS IT TRUE** *Brunswick 05915*....17 8
10 Dec 64 **CHRISTMAS WILL BE JUST ANOTHER LONELY DAY** *Brunswick 05921*....25 5

28 June 1975	5 July 1975	12 July 1975	19 July 1975
I'M NOT IN LOVE 10cc	I'M NOT IN LOVE 10cc	TEARS ON MY PILLOW Johnny Nash	GIVE A LITTLE LOVE Bay City Rollers
VENUS AND MARS Wings	HORIZON The Carpenters	HORIZON The Carpenters	VENUS AND MARS Wings

KEY
UK No.1 ★★ UK Top 10 ●● Still on chart ++ UK entry at No.1 ■■
US No.1 ▲▲ UK million seller £ US million seller $
Singles re-entries are listed as (re), (2re), (3re)... which signifies that the hit re-entered the chart once, twice or three times...
Peak Position / Weeks

4 Feb 65 **THANKS A LOT** *Brunswick 05927* 41 2
29 Jul 65 **TOO MANY RIVERS** *Brunswick 05936* 22 12
16 Jul 66 **BYE BYE BLUES** *Brunswick LAT 8649* 21 2
1 Nov 80 **LITTLE MISS DYNAMITE** *Warwick WW 5083* 15 11
7 Jan 84 **25TH ANNIVERSARY** *MCA MCLD 609* 65 4
30 Mar 85 **THE VERY BEST OF BRENDA LEE** *MCA LETV 1* 16 9
15 Oct 94 **THE VERY BEST OF BRENDA LEE ... WITH LOVE** *Telstar TCD 2738* 20 7

Curtis LEE *US, male vocalist*

31 Aug 61 **PRETTY LITTLE ANGEL EYES** (re) *London HLX 9397* 47 2

Dee C LEE (see also The STYLE COUNCIL)
UK, female vocalist – Diane Sealey (3 Singles: 20 Weeks)

9 Nov 85 ● **SEE THE DAY** *CBS A 6570* 3 12
8 Mar 86 **COME HELL OR WATERS HIGH** *CBS A 6869* 46 5
13 Nov 93 **NO TIME TO PLAY** *Cooltempo CDCOOL 282* [1] 25 3

[1] Guru featuring Dee C Lee

Garry LEE and SHOWDOWN *Canada, male vocal / instrumental group*

31 Jul 93 **THE RODEO SONG** *Party Dish VCD 101* 44 3

Jackie LEE *UK, female vocalist – Jackie Flood (2 Singles: 31 Weeks)*

10 Apr 68 ● **WHITE HORSES** *Philips BF 1647* [1] 10 14
2 Jan 71 **RUPERT** *Pye 7N 45003* 14 17

[1] Jacky

Leapy LEE *UK, male vocalist – Lee Graham (2 Singles: 28 Weeks)*

21 Aug 68 ● **LITTLE ARROWS** *MCA MU 1028* 2 21
20 Dec 69 **GOOD MORNING** (re) *MCA MK 5021* 29 7

Peggy LEE *US, female vocalist – Norma Jean Egstrom, b. 26 May 1920, d. 22 Jan 2002 (4 Albums: 23 Weeks, 4 Singles: 29 Weeks)*

24 May 57 ● **MR WONDERFUL** *Brunswick 05671* 5 13
15 Aug 58 ● **FEVER** *Capitol CL 14902* 5 11
4 Jun 60 ● **LATIN A LA LEE** *Capitol T 1290* 8 15
11 Jun 60 **BEAUTY AND THE BEAT** *Capitol T 1219* [1] 16 6
23 Mar 61 **TILL THERE WAS YOU** (re) *Capitol CL 15184* 30 4
20 May 61 **BEST OF PEGGY LEE VOLUME 2** *Brunswick LAT 8355* 18 1
21 Oct 61 **BLACK COFFEE** *Ace of Hearts AH 5* 20 1
22 Aug 92 **FEVER** (re-issue) *Capitol PEG 1* 75 1

[1] Peggy Lee and George Shearing

Toney LEE *US, male vocalist*

29 Jan 83 **REACH UP** *TMT TMT 2* 64 4

Tracey LEE *US, male vocalist*

19 Jul 97 **THE THEME** *Universal UND 56133* 51 1

LEE-CABRERA *US, male production duo – Steve Lee and Albert Cabrera (4 Singles: 10 Weeks)*

12 Apr 03 **SHAKE IT (NO TE MUEVAS TANTO)** *Credence 12CDRED 035* 58 1
6 Sep 03 **SHAKE IT (MOVE A LITTLE CLOSER)** *Credence CDCRED 039* [1] 16 6
15 Nov 03 **SPECIAL 2003** *Credence CDCRED 040* 45 2
10 Jul 04 **VOODOO LOVE** *C2 CDC 2001* [2] 58 1

[1] Lee-Cabrera featuring Alex Cartaña [2] Lee-Cabrera presents Phase 2

'Shake it (Move a Little Closer)' is an English language version of the first hit.

LEEDS UNITED FC *UK, male football team vocalists (2 Singles: 13 Weeks)*

29 Apr 72 ● **LEEDS UNITED** *Chapter One SCH 168* 10 10
25 Apr 92 **LEEDS, LEEDS, LEEDS** (re) *Q Music LUFC 2* 54 3

Raymond LEFEVRE
France, male orchestra leader (2 Albums: 9 Weeks, 1 Single: 2 Weeks)

7 Oct 67 ● **RAYMOND LEFEVRE** *Major Minor MMLP 4* 10 7
17 Feb 68 **RAYMOND LEFEVRE VOLUME 2** *Major Minor SMLP 13* 37 2
15 May 68 **SOUL COAXING** *Major Minor MM 559* 46 2

LEFTFIELD *UK, male instrumental / production duo – Neil Barnes and Paul Daley (3 Albums: 117 Weeks, 7 Singles: 23 Weeks)*

12 Dec 92 **SONG OF LIFE** *Hard Hands HAND 002T* 59 1
13 Nov 93 **OPEN UP** *Hard Hands HAND 009CD* [1] 13 5
11 Feb 95 ● **LEFTISM** *Hard Hands HANDCD 2* 3 94
25 Mar 95 **ORIGINAL** *Hard Hands HAND 18CD* [2] 18 3
5 Aug 95 **THE AFRO-LEFT EP** *Hard Hands HAND 23CD* [3] 22 3
20 Jan 96 **RELEASE THE PRESSURE** *Hard Hands HAND 29CD* 13 3
18 Sep 99 ● **AFRIKA SHOX** *Hard Hands HAND 057CD1* [4] 7 5
2 Oct 99 ★ **RHYTHM AND STEALTH** *Higher Ground / Hard Hands HANDCD 4* ■ 1 20
11 Dec 99 **DUSTED** (re) *Hard Hands HAND 058CD1* [5] 28 3
15 Oct 05 **A FINAL HIT – GREATEST HITS** *Hard Hands 82876726072* 32 3

[1] Leftfield Lydon [2] Leftfield Halliday [3] Leftfield featuring Djum Djum [4] Leftfield / Bambaataa [5] Leftfield / Roots Manuva

Tracks on The Afro-Left EP: Afro-Left / Afro Ride / Afro Central / Afro Sol.

LEGEND B *Germany, male production duo*

22 Feb 97 **LOST IN LOVE** *Perfecto PERF 132CD* 45 1

John LEGEND NEW *US, male vocalist / pianist – John Stephens (1 Album: 34 Weeks, 3 Singles: 12 Weeks)*

22 Jan 05 **GET LIFTED** *Columbia 5185772* 12 34
26 Mar 05 **USED TO LOVE U** *Columbia 6758021* 29 3
18 Jun 05 **ORDINARY PEOPLE** *Columbia 6759642* 27 8
3 Sep 05 **NUMBER ONE** *Columbia 82876724532* 62 1

Tom LEHRER *US, male comedian / vocalist (2 Albums: 26 Weeks)*

8 Nov 58 ● **SONGS BY TOM LEHRER** *Decca LF 1311* 7 19
25 Jun 60 ● **AN EVENING WASTED WITH TOM LEHRER** *Decca LK 4332* 7 7

Jody LEI *South Africa, female vocalist*

22 Feb 03 **SHOWDOWN** *Independiente ISOM 66MS* 34 2

Denise LEIGH & Jane GILCHRIST *UK, female vocalists*

8 Nov 03 **OPERATUNITY WINNERS** *EMI Classics 05575942* 60 2

LEILANI *UK, female vocalist – Leilani Sen (3 Singles: 7 Weeks)*

6 Feb 99 **MADNESS THING** *ZTT ZTT 124CD* 19 4
12 Jun 99 **DO YOU WANT ME?** *ZTT ZTT 134CD* 40 2
3 Jun 00 **FLYING ELVIS** *ZTT ZTT 145CD* 73 1

Paul LEKAKIS *US, male vocalist*

30 May 87 **BOOM BOOM (LET'S GO BACK TO MY ROOM)** *Champion CHAMP 43* 60 4

LEMAR
UK, male vocalist – Lemar Obika (2 Albums: 50 Weeks, 6 Singles: 58 Weeks)

30 Aug 03 ● **DANCE (WITH U)** *Sony Music 6741325* 2 11
29 Nov 03 ● **50/50 / LULLABY** *Sony Music 6744182* 5 11
6 Dec 03 **DEDICATED** *Sony Music 5137912* 16 23
6 Mar 04 ● **ANOTHER DAY** *Sony Music 6746592* 9 6
27 Nov 04 ● **IF THERE'S ANY JUSTICE** *Sony Music 6756072* 3 16
11 Dec 04 ● **TIME TO GROW** *Sony Music 5190822* 8 27

26 July 1975	2 August 1975	9 August 1975	16 August 1975
UK No.1 SINGLES			
GIVE A LITTLE LOVE Bay City Rollers	**GIVE A LITTLE LOVE** Bay City Rollers	**BARBADOS** Typically Tropical	**CAN'T GIVE YOU ANYTHING (BUT MY LOVE)** The Stylistics
UK No.1 ALBUMS			
HORIZON The Carpenters	**HORIZON** The Carpenters	**HORIZON** The Carpenters	**THE BEST OF THE STYLISTICS** The Stylistics

9 Apr 05 ● TIME TO GROW *Sony Music 6758122* ... 9 10
13 Aug 05 DON'T GIVE IT UP *Sony Music 6760452* ... 21 4

LEMON JELLY *UK, male production duo – Fred Deakin and Nick Franglan (2 Albums: 9 Weeks, 5 Singles: 11 Weeks)*

19 Oct 02 SPACE WALK *Impotent Fury / XL Recordings IFXLS 150CD* ... 36 2
2 Nov 02 LOST HORIZONS *Impotent Fury / XL Recordings IFXLCD 160* ... 20 6
1 Feb 03 NICE WEATHER FOR DUCKS *Impotent Fury / XL Recordings IFXLS 156CD* ... 16 3
4 Dec 04 STAY WITH YOU *Impotent Fury / XL Recordings IFXL 201CD* ... 31 3
5 Feb 05 THE SHOUTY TRACK *Impotent Fury / XL Recordings IFXLS 205CD1* ... 21 2
12 Feb 05 '64-'95 *XL Recordings IFXLCD 182X* ... 17 3
23 Jul 05 MAKE THINGS RIGHT *Impotent Fury / XL Recordings IFXLS 211CD* ... 33 1

The LEMON PIPERS *US, male vocal (Ivan Browne) / instrumental group (2 Singles: 16 Weeks)*

7 Feb 68 ● GREEN TAMBOURINE *Pye International 7N 25444* ▲ $ ... 7 11
1 May 68 RICE IS NICE *Pye International 7N 25454* ... 41 5

The LEMON TREES *UK, male vocal / instrumental group – includes Guy Chambers (5 Singles: 9 Weeks)*

26 Sep 92 LOVE IS IN YOUR EYES *Oxygen GASP 1* ... 75 1
7 Nov 92 THE WAY I FEEL *Oxygen GASP 2* ... 62 2
13 Feb 93 LET IT LOOSE *Oxygen GASPD 3* ... 55 2
17 Apr 93 CHILD OF LOVE *Oxygen GASPD 4* ... 55 3
3 Jul 93 I CAN'T FACE THE WORLD *Oxygen GASPD 6* ... 52 1

LEMONESCENT *UK, female vocal group (5 Singles: 5 Weeks)*

29 Jun 02 BEAUTIFUL *Supertone SUPTCD 1* ... 70 1
9 Nov 02 SWING MY HIPS (SEX DANCE) *Supertone SUPTCD 2* ... 48 1
5 Apr 03 HELP ME MAMA *Supertone SUPTCD 4* ... 36 1
21 Jun 03 CINDERELLA *Supertone SUPTCD 8* ... 31 1
3 Jul 04 ALL RIGHT NOW *Supertone SUPTCD 11* ... 37 1

The LEMONHEADS *US / Australia, male vocal (Evan Dando) / instrumental group (3 Albums: 32 Weeks, 9 Singles: 26 Weeks)*

1 Aug 92 IT'S A SHAME ABOUT RAY *Atlantic 7567824602* ... 33 16
17 Oct 92 IT'S A SHAME ABOUT RAY *Atlantic A 7423* ... 70 1
5 Dec 92 MRS ROBINSON / BEIN' AROUND *Atlantic A 7401* ... 19 9
6 Feb 93 CONFETTI / MY DRUG BUDDY *Atlantic A 7430CD* ... 44 2
10 Apr 93 IT'S A SHAME ABOUT RAY (re-issue) *Atlantic A 5764CD* ... 31 3
16 Oct 93 INTO YOUR ARMS *Atlantic A 7302CD* ... 14 4
23 Oct 93 ● COME ON FEEL THE LEMONHEADS *Atlantic 7567825372* ... 5 14
27 Nov 93 IT'S ABOUT TIME *Atlantic A 7296CD* ... 57 2
14 May 94 BIG GAY HEART *Atlantic A 7259CD* ... 55 2
28 Sep 96 IF I COULD TALK I'D TELL YOU *Atlantic A 5561CD* ... 39 2
12 Oct 96 CAR BUTTON CLOTH *Atlantic 7567927262* ... 28 2
14 Dec 96 IT'S ALL TRUE *Atlantic A 5635CD* ... 61 1

Group was a male / female vocal / instrumental group on their first album.

LEN *Canada, male / female DJ / vocal group (2 Singles: 15 Weeks)*

18 Dec 99 ● STEAL MY SUNSHINE *Columbia 6685062* ... 8 13
10 Jun 00 CRYPTIK SOULS CREW *Columbia 6693832* ... 28 2

John LENNON (65 Top 500)

One of the century's greatest musical talents, b. 9 Oct 1940, Liverpool, UK, d. 8 Dec 1980. World-famous singer / songwriter who, together with Paul McCartney, fronted The Beatles and penned their hits. Three of his singles topped the UK chart in the two months after his murder in New York. In 2002 he was included in the BBC's Top 10 Great Britons of all time. Best-selling single: 'Imagine' 1,486,581 (16 Albums: 354 Weeks, 21 Singles: 200 Weeks)

9 Jul 69 ● GIVE PEACE A CHANCE (re) *Apple 13* [1] ... 2 18
1 Nov 69 COLD TURKEY *Apple APPLES 1001* [1] ... 14 8
21 Feb 70 ● INSTANT KARMA *Apple APPLES 1003* [2] $ ... 5 9
16 Jan 71 ● JOHN LENNON / PLASTIC ONO BAND *Apple PCS 7124* [1] ... 8 11
20 Mar 71 ● POWER TO THE PEOPLE *Apple R 5892* [3] ... 7 9
30 Oct 71 ★ IMAGINE *Apple PAS 10004* [2] ■ ▲ ... 1 101
14 Oct 72 SOMETIME IN NEW YORK CITY *Apple PCSP 716* [3] ... 11 6
9 Dec 72 ● HAPPY XMAS (WAR IS OVER) (4re) *Apple R 5970* [4] ... 2 26
24 Nov 73 MIND GAMES *Apple R 5994* ... 26 9
8 Dec 73 MIND GAMES *Apple PCS 7165* ... 13 12
19 Oct 74 ● WALLS AND BRIDGES *Apple PCTC 253* ▲ ... 6 10
19 Oct 74 WHATEVER GETS YOU THRU' THE NIGHT *Apple R 5998* [5] ▲ ... 36 4
8 Feb 75 #9 DREAM *Apple R 6003* ... 23 8
8 Mar 75 ● ROCK 'N' ROLL *Apple PCS 7169* ... 6 28
3 May 75 STAND BY ME *Apple R 6005* ... 30 7
1 Nov 75 ★ IMAGINE (re) *Apple R 6009* £ ... 1 24
8 Nov 75 ● SHAVED FISH *Apple PCS 7173* ... 8 29
8 Nov 80 ★ (JUST LIKE) STARTING OVER *Geffen K 79186* ▲ $ ... 1 15
22 Nov 80 ★ DOUBLE FANTASY *Geffen K 99131* [4] ▲ ... 1 36
24 Jan 81 ★ WOMAN *Geffen K 79195* $ ... 1 11
21 Mar 81 I SAW HER STANDING THERE *DJM DJS 10965* [6] ... 40 4
4 Apr 81 WATCHING THE WHEELS *Geffen K 79207* ... 30 6
20 Nov 82 ★ THE JOHN LENNON COLLECTION *Parlophone EMTV 37* ... 1 43
20 Nov 82 LOVE *Parlophone R 6059* ... 41 7
21 Jan 84 ● NOBODY TOLD ME *Ono Music / Polydor POSP 700* ... 6 6
4 Feb 84 ● MILK AND HONEY *Polydor POLH 5* [4] ... 3 13
17 Mar 84 BORROWED TIME *Polydor POSP 701* ... 32 6
30 Nov 85 JEALOUS GUY *Parlophone R 6117* ... 65 2
8 Mar 86 LIVE IN NEW YORK CITY *Parlophone PCS 7031* ... 55 3
22 Oct 88 IMAGINE (FILM SOUNDTRACK) *Parlophone PCSP 722* ... 64 6
10 Dec 88 IMAGINE / JEALOUS GUY / HAPPY XMAS (WAR IS OVER) (re-issues) *Parlophone R 6199* ... 45 5
8 Nov 97 ● LENNON LEGEND – THE VERY BEST OF JOHN LENNON *Parlophone 8219542* ... 4 44
14 Nov 98 ANTHOLOGY *Capitol 8306142* ... 62 1
25 Dec 99 ● IMAGINE (re) (2nd re-issue) *Parlophone CDR 6534* ... 3 13
26 Feb 00 IMAGINE (re-issue) *Parlophone 5248582* ... 51 1
20 Dec 03 HAPPY XMAS (WAR IS OVER) (2nd re-issue) *Parlophone CDR 6627* [7] ... 33 3
15 Oct 05 WORKING CLASS HERO – THE DEFINITIVE LENNON *Parlophone 3400802* ... 11 10+

[1] Plastic Ono Band [2] Lennon, Ono and the Plastic Ono Band [3] John Lennon / Plastic Ono Band [4] John and Yoko and the Plastic Ono Band with the Harlem Community Choir [5] John Lennon with the Plastic Ono Nuclear Band [6] Elton John Band featuring John Lennon and the Muscle Shoals Horns [7] John and Yoko and the Plastic Ono Band [1] John Lennon and the Plastic Ono Band [2] John Lennon and the Plastic Ono Band with the Flux Fiddlers [3] John and Yoko Lennon with the Plastic Ono Band and Elephant's Memory [4] John Lennon and Yoko Ono

'Give Peace a Chance' re-entry made No.33 in Jan 1981. 'Happy Xmas (War Is Over)' peaked at No.4 in Dec 1972, No.48 in Jan 1975, and No.2 in Dec 1980, and the re-entry made No.28 in Dec 1981 and peaked at No.56 in Dec 1982. 'Imagine' peaked at No.6 in 1975, and topped the chart on re-entry in Dec 1980.
Imagine changed its label credit to Parlophone PAS 10004 between its initial chart run and later runs. Imagine (film soundtrack) includes tracks by The Beatles.

Julian LENNON *UK, male vocalist (3 Albums: 20 Weeks, 9 Singles: 47 Weeks)*

6 Oct 84 ● TOO LATE FOR GOODBYES *Charisma JL 1* ... 6 11
3 Nov 84 VALOTTE *Charisma JLLP 1* ... 20 15
15 Dec 84 VALOTTE *Charisma JL 2* ... 55 6
9 Mar 85 SAY YOU'RE WRONG *Charisma JL 3* ... 75 1
7 Dec 85 BECAUSE *EMI 5538* ... 40 7
5 Apr 86 THE SECRET VALUE OF DAYDREAMING *Charisma CAS 1171* ... 93 1
11 Mar 89 NOW YOU'RE IN HEAVEN *Virgin VS 1154* ... 59 3
24 Aug 91 ● SALTWATER *Virgin VS 1361* ... 6 13
5 Oct 91 HELP YOURSELF *Virgin V 2668* ... 42 4
30 Nov 91 HELP YOURSELF *Virgin VS 1379* ... 53 2
25 Apr 92 GET A LIFE *Virgin VS 1398* ... 56 3
23 May 98 DAY AFTER DAY *Music from Another JULIAN 4CD* ... 66 1

23 August 1975	30 August 1975	6 September 1975	13 September 1975
CAN'T GIVE YOU ANYTHING (BUT MY LOVE) The Stylistics	CAN'T GIVE YOU ANYTHING (BUT MY LOVE) The Stylistics	SAILING Rod Stewart	SAILING Rod Stewart
THE BEST OF THE STYLISTICS The Stylistics	ATLANTIC CROSSING Rod Stewart	ATLANTIC CROSSING Rod Stewart	ATLANTIC CROSSING Rod Stewart

KEY: UK No.1 ★ UK Top 10 ● Still on chart + UK entry at No.1 ■ US No.1 ▲ UK million seller £ US million seller $
Singles re-entries are listed as (re), (2re), (3re)... which signifies that the hit re-entered the chart once, twice or three times...
Peak Position / Weeks

Annie LENNOX 326 Top 500 *Innovative, respected singer / songwriter who performed at the Hyde Park and Edinburgh Live 8 concerts in 2005, b. 25 Dec 1954, Aberdeen, Scotland. The former focal point of The Tourists and Eurythmics has won more BRIT awards than any other female performer and won a Best Song Oscar in 2004 for 'Into the West' from The Lord of The Rings: The Return of the King (3 Albums: 143 Weeks, 10 Singles: 68 Weeks)*

3 Dec 88 **PUT A LITTLE LOVE IN YOUR HEART** *A&M AM 484* [1] 28 8
28 Mar 92 ● **WHY** *RCA PB 45317*....5 8
18 Apr 92 ★ DIVA *RCA PD 75326* ■....1 80
6 Jun 92 **PRECIOUS** *RCA 74321100257*....23 5
22 Aug 92 ● **WALKING ON BROKEN GLASS** *RCA 74321107227*....8 8
31 Oct 92 **COLD** *RCA 74321116902*....26 4
13 Feb 93 ● **LITTLE BIRD / LOVE SONG FOR A VAMPIRE** *RCA 74321133832*....3 12
18 Feb 95 ● **NO MORE "I LOVE YOU'S"** *RCA 74321257162*....2 12
18 Mar 95 ★ MEDUSA *RCA 74321257172* ■....1 49
10 Jun 95 **A WHITER SHADE OF PALE** *RCA 74321284822*....16 6
30 Sep 95 **WAITING IN VAIN** *RCA 74321316132*....31 3
9 Dec 95 **SOMETHING SO RIGHT** *RCA 74321332392* [2] 44 2
21 Jun 03 ● BARE *RCA 82876524052*....3 14

[1] Annie Lennox and Al Green [2] Annie Lennox featuring Paul Simon

Dino LENNY *Italy, male producer (2 Singles: 2 Weeks)*

4 May 02 **I FEEL STEREO** *Incentive CENT 40CDS*....60 1
10 May 03 **CHANGE THE WORLD** *Free 2 Air 0146685 F2A* [1] 51 1

[1] Dino Lenny vs The Housemartins

Phillip LEO *UK, male vocalist (2 Singles: 3 Weeks)*

23 Jul 94 **SECOND CHANCE** *EMI CDEM 327*....57 2
25 Mar 95 **THINKING ABOUT YOUR LOVE** *EMI CDEM 358*....64 1

Deke LEONARD *UK, male vocalist / guitarist*

13 Apr 74 KAMIKAZE *United Artists UAG 29544*....50 1

Paul LEONI *UK, male pan flute player*

24 Sep 83 FLIGHTS OF FANCY *Nouveau Music NML 1002*....17 19

Kristian LEONTIOU
UK, male vocalist (1 Album: 11 Weeks, 3 Singles: 14 Weeks)

5 Jun 04 ● **STORY OF MY LIFE** *Polydor 9866632*....9 7
12 Jun 04 SOME DAY SOON *Polydor 9866206*....14 11
28 Aug 04 **SHINING** *Polydor 9867640*....13 6
4 Dec 04 **SOME SAY** *Polydor 9868820*....54 1

LES RYTHMES DIGITALES *UK, male DJ / producer – Jacques Lu Cont (Stuart Price) (1 Album: 1 Week, 4 Singles: 9 Weeks)*

25 Apr 98 **MUSIC MAKES YOU LOSE CONTROL** *Wall of Sound WALLD 037*....69 1
5 Jun 99 DARKDANCER *Wall of Sound WALLCD 021*....53 1
7 Aug 99 **SOMETIMES** *Wall of Sound WALLD 054* [1] 56 1
30 Oct 99 **JACQUES YOUR BODY (MAKE ME SWEAT)** *Wall of Sound WALLD 060*....60 1
10 Sep 05 ● **JACQUES YOUR BODY (MAKE ME SWEAT)** *Data DATA 93CDS*....9 6

[1] Les Rythmes Digitales featuring Nik Kershaw

LESS THAN JAKE *US, male vocal / instrumental group (1 Album: 2 Weeks, 3 Singles: 3 Weeks)*

5 Aug 00 **ALL MY BEST FRIENDS ARE METALHEADS** *Golf CDSHOLE 027*....51 1
8 Sep 01 **GAINESVILLE ROCK CITY** *Golf CDSHOLE 48*....57 1
24 May 03 **SHE'S GONNA BREAK SOON** *Sire W 606CD*....39 1
31 May 03 ANTHEM *Sire 9362484852*....37 2

Ketty LESTER
US, female vocalist – Revoyda Frierson (2 Singles: 16 Weeks)

19 Apr 62 ● **LOVE LETTERS** *London HLN 9527* $....4 12
19 Jul 62 **BUT NOT FOR ME** *London HLN 9574*....45 4

LET LOOSE *UK, male vocal (Richard Wermerling) / instrumental group (2 Albums: 15 Weeks, 10 Singles: 62 Weeks)*

24 Apr 93 **CRAZY FOR YOU** *Vertigo VERCD 74*....44 3
9 Apr 94 **SEVENTEEN** *Mercury MERCD 400*....44 2
25 Jun 94 ● **CRAZY FOR YOU** (re) (re-issue) *Mercury MERCD 402*....2 24
22 Oct 94 **SEVENTEEN** (re) (re-mix) *Mercury MERCD 406*....11 9
19 Nov 94 LET LOOSE *Mercury 5260182*....20 14
28 Jan 95 **ONE NIGHT STAND** *Mercury MERCD 419*....12 6
29 Apr 95 ● **BEST IN ME** *Mercury MERCD 428*....8 5
4 Nov 95 **EVERYBODY SAY EVERYBODY DO** (re) *Mercury MERCD 446*....29 4
22 Jun 96 ● **MAKE IT WITH YOU** *Mercury MERCD 464*....7 6
7 Sep 96 **TAKE IT EASY** *Mercury MERCD 472*....25 2
5 Oct 96 ROLLERCOASTER *Mercury 5329552*....42 1
16 Nov 96 **DARLING BE HOME SOON** *Mercury MERCD 475*....65 1

LETHAL BIZZLE NEW (see also MORE FIRE CREW)
UK, male rapper – Maxwell Ansah (4 Singles: 15 Weeks)

1 Jan 05 **POW! (FORWARD)** *Relentless RELDX 15*....11 7
6 Aug 05 **UH OH! (I'M BACK)** *J-Did / V2 JAD 5033613*....47 2
29 Oct 05 **FIRE** *J-Did / V2 JAD 5035653*....34 3
12 Nov 05 **WHAT WE DO** *Gana / W10 01CDS* [1] 23 3

[1] Kray Twinz featuring Twista, Lethal B & Gappy Ranks

The LETTERMEN *US, male vocal group*

23 Nov 61 **THE WAY YOU LOOK TONIGHT** *Capitol CL 15222*....36 3

LEVEL 42 116 Top 500 *Critically-acclaimed London based band: Mark King (v/b), Boon Gould (g), Mike Lindup (k/v), Phil Gould (d). Boasting a world-class bass player in King, they went from Brit-funk cult heroes to international stardom (13 Albums: 228 Weeks, 29 Singles: 177 Weeks)*

30 Aug 80 **LOVE MEETING LOVE** *Polydor POSP 170*....61 4
18 Apr 81 **LOVE GAMES** *Polydor POSP 234*....38 6
8 Aug 81 **TURN IT ON** *Polydor POSP 286*....57 6
29 Aug 81 LEVEL 42 *Polydor POLS 1036*....20 18
14 Nov 81 **STARCHILD** *Polydor POSP 343*....47 4
10 Apr 82 THE EARLY TAPES JULY-AUGUST 1980 *Polydor POLS 1064*....46 6
8 May 82 **ARE YOU HEARING (WHAT I HEAR)?** *Polydor POSP 396*....49 5
18 Sep 82 THE PURSUIT OF ACCIDENTS *Polydor POLD 5067*....17 16
2 Oct 82 **WEAVE YOUR SPELL** *Polydor POSP 500*....43 4
15 Jan 83 **THE CHINESE WAY** *Polydor POSP 538*....24 8
16 Apr 83 **OUT OF SIGHT, OUT OF MIND** *Polydor POSP 570*....41 4
30 Jul 83 ● **THE SUN GOES DOWN (LIVING IT UP)** *Polydor POSP 622*....10 12
3 Sep 83 ● STANDING IN THE LIGHT *Polydor POLD 5110*....9 13
22 Oct 83 **MICRO KID** *Polydor POSP 643*....37 5
1 Sep 84 **HOT WATER** *Polydor POSP 697*....18 9
13 Oct 84 TRUE COLOURS *Polydor POLH 10*....14 8
3 Nov 84 **THE CHANT HAS BEGUN** *Polydor POSP 710*....41 5
6 Jul 85 A PHYSICAL PRESENCE *Polydor POLH 23*....28 5
21 Sep 85 ● **SOMETHING ABOUT YOU** *Polydor POSP 759*....6 17
26 Oct 85 ● WORLD MACHINE *Polydor POLH 25*....3 72
7 Dec 85 **LEAVING ME NOW** *Polydor POSP 776*....15 11
26 Apr 86 ● **LESSONS IN LOVE** *Polydor POSP 790*....3 13
14 Feb 87 ● **RUNNING IN THE FAMILY** *Polydor POSP 842*....6 10
28 Mar 87 ● RUNNING IN THE FAMILY *Polydor POLH 42*....2 54
25 Apr 87 ● **TO BE WITH YOU AGAIN** *Polydor POSP 855*....10 7
12 Sep 87 ● **IT'S OVER** *Polydor POSP 900*....10 8
12 Dec 87 **CHILDREN SAY** *Polydor POSP 911*....22 6
3 Sep 88 **HEAVEN IN MY HANDS** *Polydor PO 14*....12 5

	20 September 1975	27 September 1975	4 October 1975	11 October 1975
UK No.1 SINGLES	SAILING – Rod Stewart	SAILING – Rod Stewart	HOLD ME CLOSE – David Essex	HOLD ME CLOSE – David Essex
UK No.1 ALBUMS	ATLANTIC CROSSING – Rod Stewart	ATLANTIC CROSSING – Rod Stewart	WISH YOU WERE HERE – Pink Floyd	ATLANTIC CROSSING – Rod Stewart

1 Oct 88 ● STARING AT THE SUN *Polydor POLH 50* 2 11
29 Oct 88 **TAKE A LOOK** *Polydor PO 24* 32 4
21 Jan 89 **TRACIE** *Polydor PO 34* **25** 5
28 Oct 89 **TAKE CARE OF YOURSELF** *Polydor PO 58* **39** 3
18 Nov 89 ● LEVEL BEST *Polydor LEVTV 1* 5 15
17 Aug 91 **GUARANTEED** *RCA PB 44745* **17** 4
14 Sep 91 ● GUARANTEED *RCA PL 75005* 3 5
19 Oct 91 **OVERTIME** *RCA PB 44997* **62** 2
18 Apr 92 **MY FATHER'S SHOES** *RCA PB 45271* **55** 1
26 Feb 94 **FOREVER NOW** *RCA 74321190272* **19** 4
26 Mar 94 ● FOREVER NOW *RCA 74321189962* 8 3
30 Apr 94 **ALL OVER YOU** *RCA 74321205662* **26** 2
6 Aug 94 **LOVE IN A PEACEFUL WORLD** *RCA 74321220332* 31 3
7 Nov 98 THE VERY BEST OF LEVEL 42 *Polydor 5593732* 41 2

LEVELLERS *UK, male vocal (Mark Chadwick) / instrumental group (7 Albums: 81 Weeks, 20 Singles: 60 Weeks)*

21 Sep 91 **ONE WAY** *China WOK 2008* **51** 2
19 Oct 91 LEVELLING THE LAND *China WOL 1022* 14 30
7 Dec 91 **FAR FROM HOME** *China WOK 2010* **71** 1
23 May 92 **15 YEARS (EP)** *China WOKX 2020* 11 5
10 Jul 93 **BELARUSE** *China WOKCD 2034* 12 5
4 Sep 93 ● LEVELLERS *China WOLCD 1034* 2 14
30 Oct 93 **THIS GARDEN** *China WOKCD 2039* 12 4
14 May 94 **JULIE (EP)** *China WOKCD 2042* **17** 3
12 Aug 95 **HOPE ST** *China WOKCD 2059* 12 5
9 Sep 95 ★ ZEITGEIST *China WOLCD 1064* 1 14
14 Oct 95 **FANTASY** *China WOKCD 2067* **16** 3
23 Dec 95 **JUST THE ONE** *China WOKCD 2076* [1] 12 8
20 Jul 96 **EXODUS – LIVE** *China WOKCD 2082* **24** 2
31 Aug 96 BEST LIVE – HEADLIGHTS WHITE LINES BLACK TAR RIVERS *China WOLCDX 1074* 13 4
9 Aug 97 **WHAT A BEAUTIFUL DAY** *China WOKCD 2088* 13 5
6 Sep 97 ● MOUTH TO MOUTH *China WOLCD 1084* 5 6
18 Oct 97 **CELEBRATE** *China WOKCD 2089* **28** 2
20 Dec 97 **DOG TRAIN** *China WOKCD 2090* 24 5
14 Mar 98 **TOO REAL** *China WOKCD 2091* **46** 1
24 Oct 98 **BOZOS** *China WOKCD 2096* **44** 2
7 Nov 98 ONE WAY OF LIFE – BEST OF THE LEVELLERS *China / Jive 521732* 15 11
6 Feb 99 **ONE WAY** (re-recording) *China WOKCD 2102* 33 2
9 Sep 00 **HAPPY BIRTHDAY REVOLUTION** *China EW 218CD* **57** 1
16 Sep 00 HELLO PIG *China 8573843392* 28 2
21 Sep 02 **COME ON** *Eagle / Hag EHAGXS 001* **44** 1
18 Jan 03 **WILD AS ANGELS EP** *Eagle / Hag EHAGXS 003* 34 2
30 Apr 05 **MAKE U HAPPY** *Eagle EOTFXS 303* 38 1

[1] Levellers, special guest Joe Strummer

Tracks on 15 Years (EP): 15 Years / Dance Before the Storm / The River Flow (Live) / Plastic Jeezus. Tracks on Julie (EP): Julie / English Civil War / Lowlands of Holland / 100 Years of Solitude.

LEVERT *US, male vocal group*

22 Aug 87 ● **CASANOVA** *Atlantic A 9217* **9** 10
29 Aug 87 THE BIG THROWDOWN *Atlantic 7817731* 86 1

LEVERT SWEAT GILL (see also Johnny GILL; Keith SWEAT) *US, male vocal group (3 Singles: 7 Weeks)*

14 Mar 98 **MY BODY** *East West E 3857CD* 21 3
6 Jun 98 **CURIOUS** *East West E 3842CD* 23 2
12 Sep 98 **DOOR #1** *East West E 3817CD* **45** 2

Hank LEVINE *US, orchestra*

21 Dec 61 **IMAGE** *HMV POP 947* **45** 4

LEVITATION *UK, male vocal / instrumental group*

16 May 92 NEED FOR NOT *Rough Trade R 2862* 45 1

LEVITICUS *UK, male producer – J.J. Frost*

25 Mar 95 **BURIAL** *ffrr FCD 255* **66** 1

Barrington LEVY *Jamaica, male vocalist (4 Singles: 13 Weeks)*

2 Feb 85 **HERE I COME** *London LON 62* **41** 4
15 Jun 91 **TRIBAL BASE** *Desire WANT 44* [1] **20** 6
24 Sep 94 **WORK** *MCA MCSTD 2003* **65** 1
13 Oct 01 **HERE I COME (SING DJ)** (re-recording) *Nulife / Arista 74321895622* [2] **37** 2

[1] Rebel MC featuring Tenor Fly and Barrington Levy [2] Talisman P featuring Barrington Levy

Jona LEWIE (see also Terry DACTYL and The DINOSAURS) *UK, male vocalist – John Lewis (2 Singles: 20 Weeks)*

10 May 80 **YOU'LL ALWAYS FIND ME IN THE KITCHEN AT PARTIES** *Stiff BUY 73* **16** 9
29 Nov 80 ● **STOP THE CAVALRY** *Stiff BUY 104* 3 11

On some copies first title was simply 'Kitchen at Parties'.

CJ LEWIS *UK, male vocalist – Steven James Lewis (1 Album: 2 Weeks, 5 Singles: 32 Weeks)*

23 Apr 94 ● **SWEETS FOR MY SWEET** *Black Market BMITD 017* 3 13
23 Jul 94 ● **EVERYTHING IS ALRIGHT (UPTIGHT)** *Black Market BMITD 019* **10** 7
3 Sep 94 DOLLARS *Black Market MCD 11131* 44 2
8 Oct 94 **BEST OF MY LOVE** *Black Market BMITD 021* 13 6
17 Dec 94 **DOLLARS** *Black Market BMITD 023* **34** 4
9 Sep 95 **R TO THE A** *Black Market BMITD 030* **34** 2

Danny J LEWIS *UK, male producer*

20 Jun 98 **SPEND THE NIGHT** *Locked On LOX 98CD* **29** 2

Darlene LEWIS *US, female vocalist*

16 Apr 94 **LET THE MUSIC (LIFT YOU UP)** *KMS / Eastern Bloc KMSCD 10* **16** 4

All formats of 'Let the Music (Lift You Up)' featured versions by Loveland featuring Rachel McFarlane and also by Darlene Lewis.

Dee LEWIS *UK, female vocalist*

18 Jun 88 **BEST OF MY LOVE** *Mercury DEE 3* **47** 5

Donna LEWIS *UK, female vocalist (1 Album: 1 Week, 2 Singles: 16 Weeks)*

7 Sep 96 ● **I LOVE YOU ALWAYS FOREVER** *Atlantic A 5495CD* **5** 14
12 Oct 96 NOW IN A MINUTE *Atlantic 7567827622* 52 1
8 Feb 97 **WITHOUT LOVE** *Atlantic A 5468CD* **39** 2

Gary LEWIS and The PLAYBOYS *US, male vocal / instrumental group – leader Gary Levitch*

8 Feb 75 **MY HEART'S SYMPHONY** *United Artists UP 35780* **36** 7

Huey LEWIS and The NEWS 450 Top 500

One of the most popular 1980s US acts formed in San Francisco in 1980. The Grammy and BRIT-winning band fronted by Lewis, b. Hugh Cregg III, 5 Jul 1950, New York, took 'The Power of Love' into the Top 20 twice within six months (5 Albums: 94 Weeks, 9 Singles: 66 Weeks)

27 Oct 84 **IF THIS IS IT** *Chrysalis CHS 2803* **39** 6
31 Aug 85 **THE POWER OF LOVE** *Chrysalis HUEY 1* ▲ 11 10
14 Sep 85 SPORTS *Chrysalis CHR 1412* ▲ 23 24
23 Nov 85 **HEART AND SOUL (EP)** *Chrysalis HUEY 2* **61** 4
8 Feb 86 ● **THE POWER OF LOVE** (re-issue) / **DO YOU BELIEVE IN LOVE** *Chrysalis HUEY 3* 9 12
10 May 86 **THE HEART OF ROCK AND ROLL** *Chrysalis HUEY 4* **49** 3
23 Aug 86 **STUCK WITH YOU** *Chrysalis HUEY 5* ▲ 12 12

18 October 1975	25 October 1975	1 November 1975	8 November 1975
HOLD ME CLOSE David Essex	**I ONLY HAVE EYES FOR YOU** Art Garfunkel	**I ONLY HAVE EYES FOR YOU** Art Garfunkel	**SPACE ODDITY** David Bowie
ATLANTIC CROSSING Rod Stewart	**40 GOLDEN GREATS** Jim Reeves	**40 GOLDEN GREATS** Jim Reeves	**40 GOLDEN GREATS** Jim Reeves

KEY UK No.1 ★ UK Top 10 ● Still on chart + UK entry at No.1 ■ US No.1 ▲ UK million seller £ US million seller $
Singles re-entries are listed as (re), (2re), (3re)... which signifies that the hit re-entered the chart once, twice or three times...

Peak Position / Weeks

20 Sep 86 ● FORE! *Chrysalis CDL 1534* ▲ 8 52
6 Dec 86 HIP TO BE SQUARE *Chrysalis HUEY 6* 41 8
21 Mar 87 SIMPLE AS THAT *Chrysalis HUEY 7* 47 5
16 Jul 88 PERFECT WORLD *Chrysalis HUEY 10* 48 6
6 Aug 88 SMALL WORLD *Chrysalis CDL 1622* 12 8
18 May 91 HARD AT PLAY *Chrysalis CHR 1847* 39 2
21 Nov 92 THE HEART OF ROCK & ROLL – THE BEST OF HUEY LEWIS AND THE NEWS *Chrysalis CDCHR 1934* 23 8

Tracks on Heart and Soul (EP): Heart and Soul / Hope You Love Me Like You Say You Do / Heart of Rock and Roll / Buzz Buzz Buzz. 'Do You Believe in Love' listed only from 15 Feb 1986.

Jerry LEWIS *US, male actor / vocalist – Joseph Levitch*

8 Feb 57 ROCK-A-BYE YOUR BABY WITH A DIXIE MELODY (re) *Brunswick 05636* $ 12 8

Jerry Lee LEWIS
US, male vocalist / pianist (1 Album: 6 Weeks, 10 Singles: 68 Weeks)

27 Sep 57 ● WHOLE LOTTA SHAKIN' GOIN' ON (re) *London HLS 8457* $ 8 11
20 Dec 57 ★ GREAT BALLS OF FIRE *London HLS 8529* $ 1 12
11 Apr 58 ● BREATHLESS *London HLS 8592* 8 7
23 Jan 59 HIGH SCHOOL CONFIDENTIAL *London HLS 8780* 12 6
1 May 59 LOVIN' UP A STORM *London HLS 8840* 28 1
9 Jun 60 BABY, BABY, BYE BYE *London HLS 9131* 47 1
4 May 61 ● WHAT'D I SAY (re) *London HLS 9335* 10 14
2 Jun 62 JERRY LEE LEWIS VOLUME 2 *London HA 2440* 14 6
6 Sep 62 SWEET LITTLE SIXTEEN *London HLS 9584* 38 5
14 Mar 63 GOOD GOLLY MISS MOLLY *London HLS 9688* 31 6
6 May 72 CHANTILLY LACE *Mercury 6052 141* 33 5

Linda LEWIS *UK, female vocalist (1 Album: 4 Weeks, 5 Singles: 31 Weeks)*

2 Jun 73 ROCK-A-DOODLE-DOO *Raft RA 18502* 15 11
12 Jul 75 ● IT'S IN HIS KISS *Arista 17* 6 8
9 Aug 75 NOT A LITTLE GIRL ANYMORE *Arista ARTY 109* 40 4
17 Apr 76 BABY I'M YOURS *Arista 43* 33 6
2 Jun 79 I'D BE SURPRISINGLY GOOD FOR YOU *Ariola ARO 166* 40 5
19 Aug 00 REACH OUT *Skint SKINT 54CD* [1] 61 1

[1] Midfield General featuring Linda Lewis

Ramsey LEWIS *US, male pianist*

21 May 66 HANG ON RAMSEY *Chess CRL 4520* [1] 20 4
15 Apr 72 WADE IN THE WATER *Chess 6145 004* 31 8

[1] Ramsey Lewis Trio

Shaznay LEWIS (see also ALL SAINTS)
UK, female vocalist (1 Album: 3 Weeks, 2 Singles: 11 Weeks)

17 Jul 04 ● NEVER FELT LIKE THIS BEFORE *London LONCD 484* 8 10
31 Jul 04 OPEN *London 2564617602* 22 3
30 Oct 04 YOU *London LONCD 486* 56 1

John LEYTON *UK, male vocalist / actor (9 Singles: 70 Weeks)*

3 Aug 61 ★ JOHNNY REMEMBER ME *Top Rank JAR 577* 1 15
5 Oct 61 ● WILD WIND *Top Rank JAR 585* 2 10
28 Dec 61 SON THIS IS SHE *HMV POP 956* 15 10
15 Mar 62 LONE RIDER *HMV POP 992* 40 5
3 May 62 LONELY CITY *HMV POP 1014* 14 11
23 Aug 62 DOWN THE RIVER NILE *HMV POP 1054* 42 3
21 Feb 63 CUPBOARD LOVE *HMV POP 1122* 22 12
18 Jul 63 I'LL CUT YOUR TAIL OFF (re) *HMV POP 1175* 36 3
20 Feb 64 MAKE LOVE TO ME *HMV POP 1264* [1] 49 1

[1] John Leyton and The LeRoys

The LEYTON BUZZARDS *UK, male vocal / instrumental group*

3 Mar 79 SATURDAY NIGHT (BENEATH THE PLASTIC PALM TREES) *Chrysalis CHS 2288* 53 5

The LIARS *US, male vocal / instrumental group*

21 Feb 04 THERE'S ALWAYS ROOM ON THE BROOM *Mute CDMUTE 317* ..74 1

LIBERACE *US, male pianist / vocalist – Wladziu Valentino Liberace, b. 16 May 1919, d. 4 Feb 1987 (2 Singles: 2 Weeks)*

17 Jun 55 UNCHAINED MELODY *Philips PB 430* 20 1
19 Oct 56 I DON'T CARE (AS LONG AS YOU CARE FOR ME) *Columbia DB 3834* 28 1

LIBERATION
UK, male instrumental / production duo – William Linch and David Cooper

24 Oct 92 LIBERATION *ZYX ZYX 68657* 28 3

The LIBERTINES (see also BABY SHAMBLES; LITTLE'ANS featuring Peter DOHERTY) *UK, male vocal (Peter Doherty) / instrumental group (2 Albums: 28 Weeks, 6 Singles: 20 Weeks)*

15 Jun 02 WHAT A WASTER *Rough Trade RTRADSCD 054* 37 2
12 Oct 02 UP THE BRACKET *Rough Trade RTRADSCD 064* 29 2
2 Nov 02 UP THE BRACKET *Rough Trade RTRADCD 065* 35 7
25 Jan 03 TIME FOR HEROES *Rough Trade RTRADSCD 074* 20 2
30 Aug 03 DON'T LOOK BACK INTO THE SUN *Rough Trade RTRADSCD 199* 11 4
21 Aug 04 ● CAN'T STAND ME NOW *Rough Trade RTRADSCD 163* 2 6
11 Sep 04 ★ THE LIBERTINES *Rough Trade RTRADCD 166* ■ 1 21
6 Nov 04 ● WHAT BECAME OF THE LIKELY LADS *Rough Trade RTRADSCD 215* 9 4

LIBERTY X (472 Top 500) *Reality TV show rejects-turned true pop stars. This BRIT and Ivor Novello-winning female / male vocal quintet comprises Jessica, Kelli, Kevin and Michelle from the UK and Tony from Ireland. Despite a forced name change the act have had ten successive Top 20 singles (3 Albums: 64 Weeks, 10 Singles: 91 Weeks)*

6 Oct 01 ● THINKING IT OVER *V2 VVR 5017773* [1] 5 8
15 Dec 01 DOIN' IT *V2 VVR 5017793* [1] 14 6
25 May 02 ★ JUST A LITTLE *V2 VVR 5018963* ■ 1 16
8 Jun 02 ● THINKING IT OVER *V2 VVR 1017782* 3 58
21 Sep 02 ● GOT TO HAVE YOUR LOVE *V2 VVR 5020503* 2 12
14 Dec 02 ● HOLDING ON FOR YOU *V2 VVR 5020763* 5 11
29 Mar 03 ● BEING NOBODY *Virgin RXCD 1* [2] 3 11
1 Nov 03 ● JUMPIN' (re) *V2 VVR 5023543* 6 7
15 Nov 03 BEING SOMEBODY *V2 VVR 1023562* 12 4
24 Jan 04 EVERYBODY CRIES *V2 VVR 5023558* 13 5
8 Oct 05 ● SONG 4 LOVERS *EMI Virgin / Unique VTSCDX 8* [3] 5 9
22 Oct 05 X *EMI Virgin / Unique CDVCM 1* 27 2
26 Nov 05 ● A NIGHT TO REMEMBER *EMI Virgin / Unique VTSCDX 9* ....6 6+

[1] Liberty [2] Richard X vs Liberty X [3] Liberty X featuring Rev Run from Run DMC

LIBIDO *Norway, male vocal / instrumental group*

31 Jan 98 OVERTHROWN *Fire BLAZE 119CD* 53 1

LIBRA *US, male / female production / vocal trio (2 Singles: 3 Weeks)*

26 Oct 96 ANOMALY – CALLING YOUR NAME *Platipus PLATCD 24* 71 1
18 Mar 00 ANOMALY – CALLING YOUR NAME (re-mix) *Platipus PLATCD 56* [1] 43 2

[1] Libra Presents Taylor

LICK THE TINS *UK, male / female vocal / instrumental group*

29 Mar 86 CAN'T HELP FALLING IN LOVE *Sedition EDIT 3308* 42 8

Oliver LIEB presents SMOKED (see also LSG) *Germany, male producer*

30 Sep 00 METROPOLIS *Duty Free DF 019CD* 72 1

15 November 1975	22 November 1975	29 November 1975	6 December 1975
UK No.1 SINGLES			
SPACE ODDITY David Bowie	D.I.V.O.R.C.E. Billy Connolly	BOHEMIAN RHAPSODY Queen	BOHEMIAN RHAPSODY Queen
UK No.1 ALBUMS			
WE ALL HAD DOCTORS' PAPERS Max Boyce	WE ALL HAD DOCTORS' PAPERS Max Boyce	WE ALL HAD DOCTORS' PAPERS Max Boyce	WE ALL HAD DOCTORS' PAPERS Max Boyce

Ben LIEBRAND *Holland, male DJ / producer*

9 Jun 90 **PULS(T)AR** *Epic LIEB 1* 68 2

LIEUTENANT PIGEON

UK, male / female instrumental group (2 Singles: 29 Weeks)

16 Sep 72 ★ **MOULDY OLD DOUGH** *Decca F 13278* 1 19
16 Dec 72 **DESPERATE DAN** *Decca F 13365* 17 10

LIFEHOUSE *US, male vocal / instrumental group*

8 Sep 01 **HANGING BY A MOMENT** *Dreamworks / Polydor 4975612* 25 4

LIGHT OF THE WORLD

UK, male vocal / instrumental group (1 Album: 1 Week, 6 Singles: 25 Weeks)

14 Apr 79 **SWINGIN'** *Ensign ENY 22* 45 5
14 Jul 79 **MIDNIGHT GROOVIN'** *Ensign ENY 29* 72 1
18 Oct 80 **LONDON TOWN** *Ensign ENY 43* 41 5
17 Jan 81 **I SHOT THE SHERIFF** *Ensign ENY 46* 40 5
24 Jan 81 ROUND TRIP *Ensign ENVY 14* 73 1
28 Mar 81 **I'M SO HAPPY / TIME** *Ensign MER 64* 35 6
21 Nov 81 **RIDE THE LOVE TRAIN** *EMI 5242* 49 3

LIGHTER SHADE OF BROWN *US, male vocal duo*

9 Jul 94 **HEY DJ** *Mercury MERCD 401* 33 3

Gordon LIGHTFOOT

Canada, male vocalist / guitarist (2 Albums: 2 Weeks, 4 Singles: 26 Weeks)

19 Jun 71 **IF YOU COULD READ MY MIND** *Reprise RS 20974* 30 9
20 May 72 DON QUIXOTE *Reprise K 44166* 44 1
3 Aug 74 **SUNDOWN** *Reprise K 14327* ▲ $ 33 7
17 Aug 74 SUNDOWN *Reprise K 54020* ▲ 45 1
15 Jan 77 **THE WRECK OF THE EDMUND FITZGERALD** *Reprise K 14451* 40 4
16 Sep 78 **DAYLIGHT KATY** *Warner Bros. K 17214* 41 6

Terry LIGHTFOOT'S NEW ORLEANS JAZZMEN

UK, male vocalist / clarinet player and band (3 Singles: 17 Weeks)

7 Sep 61 **TRUE LOVE** *Columbia DB 4696* 33 4
23 Nov 61 **KING KONG** *Columbia SCD 2165* 29 12
3 May 62 **TAVERN IN THE TOWN** *Columbia DB 4822* 49 1

LIGHTFORCE *Germany, male production duo*

28 Oct 00 **JOIN ME** *Slinky Music SLINKY 004CD* 53 1

LIGHTHOUSE FAMILY (158 Top 500)

Smooth, easy-on-the-ear pop / soul duo formed in Newcastle-upon-Tyne, UK: Nigerian-born Tunde Baiyewu (v) and Londoner Paul Tucker (k). After a slow start, their debut album sold more than 1.6 million copies in the UK. Tunde had solo success in 2004 (5 Albums: 263 Weeks, 14 Singles: 89 Weeks)

27 May 95 **LIFTED** *Wild Card CARDW 17* 61 2
14 Oct 95 **OCEAN DRIVE** *Wild Card 5797072* 34 3
18 Nov 95 ● OCEAN DRIVE *Wild Card 5237872* 3 154
10 Feb 96 ● **LIFTED** (re-issue) *Wild Card 5779432* 4 10
1 Jun 96 **OCEAN DRIVE** (re-issue) *Wild Card 5766192* 11 8
21 Sep 96 **GOODBYE HEARTBREAK** *Wild Card 5753492* 14 6
21 Dec 96 **LOVING EVERY MINUTE** *Wild Card 5731012* 20 7
11 Oct 97 ● **RAINCLOUD** *Wild Card 5717932* 6 7
1 Nov 97 ● POSTCARDS FROM HEAVEN *Wild Card 5395162* 2 73
10 Jan 98 ● **HIGH** *Polydor 5691492* 4 14
27 Jun 98 ● **LOST IN SPACE** *Polydor 5670592* 6 8
10 Oct 98 **QUESTION OF FAITH** *Wild Card 5673932* 21 5
9 Jan 99 **POSTCARD FROM HEAVEN** *Wild Card 5633952* 24 6
24 Nov 01 ● **(I WISH I KNEW HOW IT WOULD FEEL TO BE) FREE / ONE** *Wild Card / Polydor 5873812* 6 9
1 Dec 01 ● WHATEVER GETS YOU THROUGH THE DAY *Wild Card 5894122* 7 18
9 Mar 02 **RUN** *Wild Card / Polydor 5705702* 30 3
6 Jul 02 **HAPPY** *Wild Card / Polydor 5707902* 51 1
30 Nov 02 GREATEST HITS *Wild Card / Polydor 0654482* 23 6
19 Apr 03 ● THE VERY BEST OF LIGHTHOUSE FAMILY *Wild Card / Polydor 0761662* 9 12

The LIGHTNING SEEDS (273 Top 500)

Conceived as a 'perfect pop' studio project by producer and group veteran Ian Broudie (v/g), b. 4 Aug 1958, Liverpool, UK. England's most popular football anthem, 'Three Lions', became the first song to top the charts twice with different lyrics (7 Albums: 139 Weeks, 18 Singles: 104 Weeks)

22 Jul 89 **PURE** *Ghetto GTG 4* 16 8
10 Feb 90 CLOUDCUCKOOLAND *Ghetto GHETT 3* 50 2
14 Mar 92 **THE LIFE OF RILEY** *Virgin VS 1402* 28 6
18 Apr 92 SENSE *Virgin CDV 2690* 53 1
30 May 92 **SENSE** *Virgin VS 1414* 31 5
20 Aug 94 **LUCKY YOU** *Epic 6606282* 43 2
17 Sep 94 JOLLIFICATION *Epic 4772379* 12 58
14 Jan 95 **CHANGE** *Epic 6609865* 13 6
15 Apr 95 **MARVELLOUS** *Epic 6614265* 24 5
22 Jul 95 **PERFECT** *Epic 6621792* 18 5
21 Oct 95 **LUCKY YOU** (re-issue) *Epic 6625182* 15 6
9 Mar 96 **READY OR NOT** *Epic 6629672* 20 4
18 May 96 PURE LIGHTNING SEEDS *Virgin CDV 2805* 27 9
1 Jun 96 ★ **THREE LIONS (THE OFFICIAL SONG OF THE ENGLAND FOOTBALL TEAM)** *Epic 6632732* [1] ■ 1 15
2 Nov 96 **WHAT IF ...** (re) *Epic 6638635* 14 4
23 Nov 96 DIZZY HEIGHTS *Epic 4866402* 11 26
18 Jan 97 **SUGAR COATED ICEBERG** *Epic 6640432* 12 4
26 Apr 97 ● **YOU SHOWED ME** *Epic 6643282* 8 5
22 Nov 97 ● LIKE YOU DO ... BEST OF THE LIGHTNING SEEDS *Epic 4890342* 5 41
13 Dec 97 **WHAT YOU SAY** *Epic 6653572* 41 5
20 Jun 98 ★ **THREE LIONS '98** (re-recording) *Epic 6660982* [1] ■ 1 13
27 Nov 99 **LIFE'S TOO SHORT** (re) *Epic 6681502* 27 4
4 Dec 99 TILT *Epic 4962632* 46 2
18 Mar 00 **SWEETEST SOUL SENSATIONS** *Epic 6689422* 67 1
15 Jun 02 **THREE LIONS '98** (re) (re-issue) *Epic 6728152* [2] 16 6

[1] Baddiel and Skinner and The Lightning Seeds [2] Baddiel, Skinner and The Lightning Seeds

LIL' DEVIOUS (see also PERCY FILTH)

UK, male production duo – Mark Baker and Gary Little

15 Sep 01 **COME HOME** *Rulin RULIN 16CDS* 55 1

LIL' FLIP *US, male rapper (2 Singles: 6 Weeks)*

11 Sep 04 **NEVER REALLY WAS** *Bad Boy MCSTD 40372* [1] 44 2
30 Oct 04 **SUNSHINE** *Columbia 6751842* 14 4

[1] Mario Winans featuring Lil' Flip

LIL JON & The EAST SIDE BOYZ

US, male rap group (1 Album: 2 Weeks, 5 Singles: 28 Weeks)

27 Mar 04 ★ **YEAH!** *Arista 82876606002* [1] ■ ▲ 1 14
12 Feb 05 **ROLL CALL / WHAT U GON' DO** *TVT TVTUKCDX 2* [2] 38 3
26 Feb 05 **LET'S GO** *Atlantic AT 0193CD* [3] 26 2
14 May 05 ● **GET LOW / LOVERS & FRIENDS** *TVT TVTUKCD 9* [4] 10 7
28 May 05 CRUNK JUICE *TVT TVTCD 1* 52 2
16 Jul 05 **GIRLFIGHT** *Virgin VUSDX 301* [5] 35 2

[1] Usher featuring Lil' Jon & Ludacris [2] Lil Jon & The East Side Boyz featuring Ice Cube / featuring Lil' Scrappy [3] Trick Daddy featuring Twista and Lil' Jon [4] Lil Jon & The East Side Boyz featuring Ying Yang Twins / featuring Usher and Ludacris [5] Brooke Valentine featuring Big Boi & Lil Jon

LIL' KIM *US, female vocalist – Kimberly Jones (1 Album: 1 Week, 13 Singles: 64 Weeks)*

26 Apr 97 **NO TIME** *Atlantic A 5594CD* [1] 45 1
5 Jul 97 **CRUSH ON YOU** (re) *Atlantic AT 0002CD* 23 5
16 Aug 97 **NOT TONIGHT** *Atlantic AT 0007CD* 11 5

13 December 1975	20 December 1975	27 December 1975	3 January 1976
BOHEMIAN RHAPSODY Queen	BOHEMIAN RHAPSODY Queen	BOHEMIAN RHAPSODY Queen	BOHEMIAN RHAPSODY Queen
WE ALL HAD DOCTORS' PAPERS Max Boyce	WE ALL HAD DOCTORS' PAPERS Max Boyce	A NIGHT AT THE OPERA Queen	A NIGHT AT THE OPERA Queen

KEY UK No.1 ★ UK Top 10 ● Still on chart + UK entry at No.1 ■ US No.1 ▲ UK million seller £ US million seller $
Singles re-entries are listed as (re), (2re), (3re)... which signifies that the hit re-entered the chart once, twice or three times...

Peak Position / Weeks

22 Aug 98 **HIT 'EM WIT DA HEE** *East West E 3824CD 1* [2] 25 3
5 Feb 00 **NOTORIOUS B.I.G.** *Puff Daddy / Arista 74321737312* [3] 16 5
8 Jul 00 THE NOTORIOUS K.I.M. *Atlantic 7567928402*............................67 1
2 Sep 00 **NO MATTER WHAT THEY SAY** *Atlantic 7567846972*...................35 2
30 Jun 01 ★ **LADY MARMALADE** *Interscope / Polydor 4975612* [4] ■ ▲....1 16
11 Aug 01 **WAIT A MINUTE** *Atlantic AT 0106CD* [5] 54 1
22 Sep 01 **IN THE AIR TONITE** *WEA WEA 331CD* [6] 26 2
10 May 03 **THE JUMP OFF** *Atlantic AT 0151CD* [7] 16 7
20 Sep 03 ● **CAN'T HOLD US DOWN** *RCA 87876556332* [8] 6 9
28 May 05 **SUGAR (GIMME SOME)** *Atlantic AT 0202CDX* [9] 61 1
19 Nov 05 **LIGHTERS UP** *Atlantic AT 0226CD*..12 7+

[1] Lil' Kim featuring Puff Daddy [2] Missy 'Misdemeanor' Elliott featuring Lil' Kim [3] Notorious BIG featuring Puff Daddy and Lil' Kim [4] Christina Aguilera, Lil' Kim, Mya and Pink [5] Ray J featuring Lil' Kim [6] Lil' Kim featuring Phil Collins [7] Lil' Kim featuring Mr Cheeks [8] Christina Aguilera featuring Lil' Kim [9] Trick Daddy featuring Ludacris, Lil' Kim & Cee-Lo

'Crush on You' peaked at No.23 when it re-entered in Oct 97.

LIL' LOUIS (see also BLACK MAGIC)

US, male producer – Marvin Burns (1 Album: 5 Weeks, 4 Singles: 21 Weeks)

29 Jul 89 ● **FRENCH KISS** *ffrr FX 115*...2 11
26 Aug 89 FRENCH KISSES *ffrr 828170 1*..35 5
13 Jan 90 **I CALLED U** *ffrr F 123*..16 6
26 Sep 92 **SAVED MY LIFE** *ffrr FX 197* [1] 74 1
12 Aug 00 **HOW'S YOUR EVENING SO FAR** *ffrr FCD 384* [2] 23 3

[1] Lil' Louis and the World [2] Josh Wink and Lil' Louis

LIL' LOVE NEW *Italy, male / female production / vocal trio*

27 Aug 05 **LITTLE LOVE** *Positiva CDTIVS 222*..34 2

LIL' MO *US, female vocalist – Cynthia Long (5 Singles: 12 Weeks)*

21 Nov 98 **5 MINUTES** *Elektra E 3803CD* [1] 72 1
23 Sep 00 **WHATEVER** *Virgin VUSCD 172* [2] 31 3
6 Apr 02 **WHERE'S MY ...?** *EMI CDEMS 598* [3] 37 2
15 Feb 03 **IF I COULD GO!** *Elektra E 7331CD* [4] 61 1
16 Aug 03 **CAN'T LET YOU GO** *Elektra E 7408CD* [5] 14 5

[1] Lil' Mo featuring Missy 'Misdemeanor' Elliott [2] Ideal US featuring Lil' Mo [3] Adam F featuring Lil' Mo [4] Angie Martinez featuring Lil' Mo and Sacario [5] Fabolous featuring Mike Shorey and Lil' Mo

LIL MO' YIN YANG

(see also PIANOHEADZ; REEL 2 REAL featuring The MAD STUNTMAN) *US, male instrumental / production duo – Erick 'More' Morillo and 'Lil' Louis Vega*

9 Mar 96 **REACH** *Multiply CDMULTY 9*..28 2

LIL' ROMEO *US, male rapper – Percy Miller*

22 Sep 01 **MY BABY** *Priority PTYCD 136*...67 1

LILYS *US, male vocal / instrumental group*

21 Feb 98 **A NANNY IN MANHATTAN** *Che CHE 77CD*...................................16 4

LIMAHL (see also KAJAGOOGOO)

UK, male vocalist – Chris Hamill (1 Album: 3 Weeks, 3 Singles: 25 Weeks)

5 Nov 83 **ONLY FOR LOVE** (re) *EMI LML 1*..16 8
2 Jun 84 **TOO MUCH TROUBLE** *EMI LML 2*...64 3
13 Oct 84 ● **NEVER ENDING STORY** *EMI LML 3*..4 14
1 Dec 84 DON'T SUPPOSE *EMI PLML 1*..63 3

Alison LIMERICK

UK, female vocalist (1 Album: 2 Weeks, 13 Singles: 41 Weeks)

30 Mar 91 **WHERE LOVE LIVES** *Arista 144208*...27 8
12 Oct 91 **COME BACK (FOR REAL LOVE)** *Arista 114530*.............................53 2
21 Dec 91 **MAGIC'S BACK (THEME FROM 'THE GHOSTS OF OXFORD STREET')** *RCA PB 45223* [1] 42 4
29 Feb 92 **MAKE IT ON MY OWN** *Arista 114996*...16 6
4 Apr 92 AND STILL I RISE *Arista 262365*...53 2
18 Jul 92 **GETTIN' IT RIGHT** *Arista 74321102867*......................................57 2
28 Nov 92 **HEAR MY CALL** *Arista 115337*..73 1
8 Jan 94 **TIME OF OUR LIVES** *Arista 74321180332*...................................36 4
19 Mar 94 **LOVE COME DOWN** *Arista 74321191952*.....................................36 2
25 Feb 95 **LOVE WILL KEEP US TOGETHER** *Acid Jazz JAZID 112CD* [2] 63 1
6 Jul 96 ● **WHERE LOVE LIVES** (re-mix) *Arista 74321381592*.......................9 6
14 Sep 96 **MAKE IT ON MY OWN** (re-mix) *Arista 74321407812*....................30 2
23 Aug 97 **PUT YOUR FAITH IN ME** *MBA XES 9001*......................................42 1
15 Mar 03 **WHERE LOVE LIVES** (2nd re-mix) *Arista Dance 74321981442*...44 2

[1] Malcolm McLaren featuring Alison Limerick [2] JTQ featuring Alison Limerick

The LIMIT

Holland, male vocal / instrumental duo – Bernard Oates and Rob van Schaik

5 Jan 85 **SAY YEAH** *Portrait A 4808*..17 8

Gwen Guthrie is the uncredited vocalist on 'Say Yeah'.

LIMMIE and The FAMILY COOKIN'

US, male / female vocal (Limmie Snell) group (3 Singles: 28 Weeks)

21 Jul 73 ● **YOU CAN DO MAGIC** *Avco 6105 019*..3 13
20 Oct 73 **DREAMBOAT** *Avco 6105 025*..31 5
6 Apr 74 ● **A WALKIN' MIRACLE** *Avco 6105 027*...6 10

LIMP BIZKIT 457 Top 500

Masters of the metal, punk and hip hop mixing 'rapcore' genre, formed in 1995, Florida, US, include Fred Durst (v) and Wes Borland (g), who was replaced in 2003 by Mike Smith (ex-Snot). The award-winning quintet have sold 30 million albums worldwide (5 Albums: 96 Weeks, 7 Singles: 62 Weeks)

3 Jul 99 ● SIGNIFICANT OTHER *Interscope IND 90335* ▲.........................10 37
15 Jul 00 ● **TAKE A LOOK AROUND (THEME FROM 'MI:2')** *Interscope 4973682*..3 13
9 Sep 00 THREE DOLLAR BILL Y'ALL$ *Interscope IND 90124*....................50 5
28 Oct 00 ★ CHOCOLATE STARFISH AND THE HOT DOG FLAVORED WATER *Interscope 4907932* ▲...1 48
11 Nov 00 **MY GENERATION** (re) *Interscope IND 97448*...............................15 8
27 Jan 01 ★ **ROLLIN'** *Interscope IND 97474* ■ 1 13
23 Jun 01 ● **MY WAY** *Interscope 4975732*..6 10
10 Nov 01 **BOILER** *Interscope 4976362*...18 5
27 Sep 03 ● **EAT YOU ALIVE** *Interscope 9811757*...10 7
4 Oct 03 ● RESULTS MAY VARY *Interscope 9860971*.....................................7 5
6 Dec 03 **BEHIND BLUE EYES** *Interscope 9814744*....................................18 6
14 May 05 THE UNQUESTIONABLE TRUTH – PT.1 *Geffen 9882180*...........71 1

The Unquestionable Truth – Pt.1 is a seven-track mini album.

LINA *US, female vocalist*

3 Mar 01 **PLAYA NO MO'** *Atlantic AT 0094CD*..46 1

LINCOLN CITY FC featuring Michael COURTNEY

UK, male football team and vocalist

4 May 02 **CHIRPY CHIRPY CHEEP CHEEP / JAGGED END** *Nap Music SLCPD 0001*..64 1

Bob LIND *US, male vocalist (2 Singles: 10 Weeks)*

10 Mar 66 ● **ELUSIVE BUTTERFLY** *Fontana TF 670*..5 9
26 May 66 **REMEMBER THE RAIN** *Fontana TF 702*...46 1

LINDISFARNE 416 Top 500

Perennial folk-rock hybrid who blend wistful sensitivity, social sentiments and boozy revelry. They formed in 1969 in Newcastle-upon-Tyne and included Alan Hull (v/g/p), b. 1945, d. 1996, and

10 January 1976	17 January 1976	24 January 1976	31 January 1976
◂◂ UK No.1 SINGLES ▸▸			
BOHEMIAN RHAPSODY Queen	BOHEMIAN RHAPSODY Queen	BOHEMIAN RHAPSODY Queen	MAMMA MIA Abba
◂◂ UK No.1 ALBUMS ▸▸			
40 GREATEST HITS Perry Como	A NIGHT AT THE OPERA Queen	A NIGHT AT THE OPERA Queen	THE BEST OF ROY ORBISON Roy Orbison

Ray Jackson (g). Fog on the Tyne was the top selling album by a UK act in 1971 (8 Albums: 118 Weeks, 6 Singles: 55 Weeks)

30 Oct 71	★	**FOG ON THE TYNE** *Charisma CAS 1050*	1	56
15 Jan 72	●	**NICELY OUT OF TUNE** *Charisma CAS 1025*	8	30
26 Feb 72	●	**MEET ME ON THE CORNER** *Charisma CB 173*	**5**	11
13 May 72	●	**LADY ELEANOR** *Charisma CB 153*	3	11
23 Sep 72		**ALL FALL DOWN** *Charisma CB 191*	**34**	5
30 Sep 72	●	**DINGLY DELL** *Charisma CAS 1057*	5	10
11 Aug 73		**LINDISFARNE LIVE** *Charisma CLASS 2*	25	6
18 Oct 75		**FINEST HOUR** *Charisma CAS 1108*	55	1
3 Jun 78	●	**RUN FOR HOME** *Mercury 6007 177*	**10**	15
24 Jun 78		**BACK AND FOURTH** *Mercury 9109 609*	22	11
7 Oct 78		**JUKE BOX GYPSY** *Mercury 6007 187*	**56**	4
9 Dec 78		**MAGIC IN THE AIR** *Mercury 6641 877*	71	1
23 Oct 82		**SLEEPLESS NIGHTS** *LMP GET 1*	59	3
10 Nov 90	●	**FOG ON THE TYNE (REVISITED)** *Best ZB 44083* [1]	2	9

[1] Gazza and Lindisfarne

LINDSAY *UK, female vocalist – Lindsay Dracas*

12 May 01		**NO DREAM IMPOSSIBLE** *Universal TV 1589562*	32	4

LINER *UK, male vocal / instrumental group (2 Singles: 6 Weeks)*

10 Mar 79		**KEEP REACHING OUT FOR LOVE** *Atlantic K 11235*	**49**	3
26 May 79		**YOU AND ME** *Atlantic K 11285*	**44**	3

Andy LING *UK, male producer*

13 May 00		**FIXATION** *Hooj Choons HOOJ 094CD*	**55**	1

Laurie LINGO and The DIPSTICKS
UK, male DJ / vocal duo – Dave Lee Travis and Paul Burnett

17 Apr 76	●	**CONVOY GB** *State STAT 23*	**4**	7

LINK *US, male rapper – Lincoln Browder*

7 Nov 98		**WHATCHA GONE DO?** *Relativity 6666055*	**48**	1

LINKIN PARK 315 Top 500 (see also X-ECUTIONERS featuring Mike SHINODA and Mr HAHN of LINKIN PARK)
Pioneering metal / rap-rock sextet formed in Los Angeles, US. Members include Chester Bennington (v), Mike Shinoda (rap/v) and Joseph Hahn (DJ). The Grammy-winning 'Hybrid Theory' was the top selling US album of 2001 with 4.8 million (world total now more than 17 million). The band performed at the US Live 8 concert (5 Albums: 137 Weeks, 10 Singles: 80 Weeks)

20 Jan 01	●	**(HYBRID THEORY)** *Warner Bros. 9362477552*	4	77
27 Jan 01		**ONE STEP CLOSER** *Warner Bros. W 550CD*	24	4
21 Apr 01		**CRAWLING** *Warner Bros. W 556CD*	16	8
30 Jun 01		**PAPERCUT** *Warner Bros. W 562CD*	14	6
20 Oct 01	●	**IN THE END** *Warner Bros. W 569CD*	8	9
3 Aug 02	●	**H! VLTG3 / PTS.OF.ATHRTY** *Warner Bros. W 588CD*	9	6
10 Aug 02	●	**REANIMATION** *Warner Bros. 9362483542*	3	8
29 Mar 03	●	**SOMEWHERE I BELONG** *Warner Bros. W 602CD*	10	8
5 Apr 03	★	**METEORA** *Warner Bros. 9362484612* ■ ▲	1	33
21 Jun 03		**FAINT** *Warner Bros. W 610CD1*	15	8
20 Sep 03		**NUMB** *Warner Bros. W 622CD1*	14	6
6 Dec 03		**LIVE IN TEXAS** *Warner Bros. WB 485632*	47	3
19 Jun 04		**BREAKING THE HABIT** *Warner Bros. W 645CD*	39	2
4 Dec 04		**NUMB** (re-recording) **/ ENCORE** *WEA W 660CD* [1]	14	23
11 Dec 04		**COLLISION COURSE** *WEA 9362489662* [1] ▲	15	16

[1] Jay-Z / Linkin Park [1] Jay-Z / Linkin Park

'Numb / Encore' is one song that combines Linkin Park's 'Numb' and Jay-Z's 'Encore'. Reanimation is a re-mix album of songs from (Hybrid Theory).

LINOLEUM *UK, male / female vocal / instrumental group*

12 Jul 97		**MARQUIS** *Lino Vinyl LINO 004CD1*	**73**	1

LINUS LOVES featuring Sam OBERNIK
UK, male producer – Linus O'Brien and female vocalist

22 Nov 03		**STAND BACK** *Data / MoS DATA 62CD*	**31**	3

LINX *UK, male vocal / instrumental duo – David Grant and Peter Martin (2 Albums: 23 Weeks, 6 Singles: 45 Weeks)*

20 Sep 80		**YOU'RE LYING** *Chrysalis CHS 2461*	**15**	10
7 Mar 81	●	**INTUITION** *Chrysalis CHS 2500*	**7**	11
28 Mar 81	●	**INTUITION** *Chrysalis CHR 1332*	8	19
13 Jun 81		**THROW AWAY THE KEY** *Chrysalis CHS 2519*	21	9
5 Sep 81		**SO THIS IS ROMANCE** *Chrysalis CHS 2546*	**15**	9
31 Oct 81		**GO AHEAD** *Chrysalis CHR 1358*	35	4
21 Nov 81		**CAN'T HELP MYSELF** *Chrysalis CHS 2565*	**55**	3
10 Jul 82		**PLAYTHING** *Chrysalis CHS 2621*	**48**	3

LIONROCK
UK, male producer – Justin Robertson (2 Albums: 3 Weeks, 8 Singles: 14 Weeks)

5 Dec 92		**LIONROCK** *Deconstruction 74321124381*	**63**	1
8 May 93		**PACKET OF PEACE** *Deconstruction 74321144372*	32	3
23 Oct 93		**CARNIVAL** *Deconstruction 74321164862*	34	2
27 Aug 94		**TRIPWIRE** *Deconstruction 74321204702*	**44**	1
6 Apr 96		**STRAIGHT AT YER HEAD** *Deconstruction 74321342972*	33	2
20 Apr 96		**AN INSTINCT FOR DETECTION** *Deconstruction 74321342812*	30	2
27 Jul 96		**FIRE UP THE SHOESAW** *Deconstruction 74321382652*	**43**	1
14 Mar 98		**RUDE BOY ROCK** *Concrete HARD 31CD*	20	3
28 Mar 98		**CITY DELIRIOUS** *Concrete HARD 32LPCD*	73	1
30 May 98		**SCATTER & SWING** *Concrete HARD 35CD*	**54**	1

LIPPS INC *US, male / female vocal (Cynthia Johnson) / instrumental group*

17 May 80	●	**FUNKYTOWN** *Casablanca CAN 194* ▲ $	2	13

LIQUID *UK, male producer – Eamon Downes (7 Singles: 20 Weeks)*

21 Mar 92		**SWEET HARMONY** *XL Recordings XLS 28*	**15**	6
5 Sep 92		**THE FUTURE MUSIC (EP)** *XL Recordings XLT 33*	**59**	2
20 Mar 93		**TIME TO GET UP** *XL Recordings XLS 40CD*	**46**	2
8 Jul 95		**SWEET HARMONY** (re-mix) **/ ONE LOVE FAMILY** *XL Recordings XLS 65CD*	**14**	6
21 Oct 95		**CLOSER** *XL Recordings XLS 66CD*	**47**	2
25 Jul 98		**STRONG** *Higher Ground HIGHS 7CD*	**59**	1
21 Oct 00		**ORLANDO DAWN** *Xtravaganza XTRAV 16CDS*	**53**	1

Tracks on The Future Music (EP): Liquid Is Liquid / Music / House (Is a Feeling) / The Year 3000. On the first two hits act also included Shane Heneghan.

LIQUID CHILD
Germany, male production duo – Tobias Menguser and Jurgen Herbarth

23 Oct 99		**DIVING FACES** *Essential Recordings ESCD 9*	**25**	2

LIQUID GOLD *UK, male / female vocal (Ellie Hope) / instrumental group (1 Album: 3 Weeks, 6 Singles: 46 Weeks)*

2 Dec 78		**ANYWAY YOU DO IT** *Creole CR 159*	**41**	7
23 Feb 80	●	**DANCE YOURSELF DIZZY** *Polo POLO 1*	2	14
31 May 80	●	**SUBSTITUTE** *Polo POLO 4*	**8**	9
16 Aug 80		**LIQUID GOLD** *Polo POLP 101*	34	3
1 Nov 80		**THE NIGHT THE WINE AND THE ROSES** *POLO 6*	32	7
28 Mar 81		**DON'T PANIC** *Polo POLO 8*	**42**	5
21 Aug 82		**WHERE DID WE GO WRONG** *Polo POLO 23*	**56**	4

LIQUID OXYGEN *US, male producer – Frankie Bones*

28 Apr 90		**THE PLANET DANCE (MOVE YA BODY)** *Champion CHAMP 242*	**56**	2

LIQUID PEOPLE *UK, male production duo (2 Singles: 2 Weeks)*

20 Jul 02		**MONSTER** *Defected DFECT 49* [1]	**67**	1
21 Jun 03		**IT'S MY LIFE** (re-mix) *Nebula NEBCD 045* [2]	**64**	1

[1] Liquid People vs Simple Minds [2] Liquid People vs Talk Talk

7 February 1976	14 February 1976	21 February 1976	28 February 1976
MAMMA MIA Abba	**FOREVER AND EVER** Slik	**DECEMBER, 1963 (OH, WHAT A NIGHT)** The Four Seasons	**DECEMBER, 1963 (OH, WHAT A NIGHT)** The Four Seasons
THE VERY BEST OF SLIM WHITMAN Slim Whitman	**THE VERY BEST OF SLIM WHITMAN** Slim Whitman	**THE VERY BEST OF SLIM WHITMAN** Slim Whitman	**THE VERY BEST OF SLIM WHITMAN** Slim Whitman

KEY UK No.1 ★ UK Top 10 ● Still on chart + UK entry at No.1 ■ US No.1 ▲ UK million seller £ US million seller $ Singles re-entries are listed as (re), (2re), (3re)... which signifies that the hit re-entered the chart once, twice or three times... — Peak Position / Weeks

LIQUID STATE featuring Marcella WOODS (see also SOLAR STONE; Z2)
UK, male production duo – Rich Mowat and Andy Bury and female vocalist

30 Mar 02 **FALLING** *Perfecto PERF 29CDS* 60 1

LISA LISA
US, female vocalist – Lisa Velez (1 Album: 1 Week, 5 Singles: 32 Weeks)

4 May 85 **I WONDER IF I TAKE YOU HOME** (re) *CBS A 6057* [1] 12 17
21 Sep 85 LISA LISA AND CULT JAM WITH FULL FORCE *CBS 26593* [1] 96 1
31 Oct 87 **LOST IN EMOTION** *CBS 651036 7* [2] ▲ 58 4
13 Jul 91 **LET THE BEAT HIT 'EM** *Columbia 6572867* [2] 17 6
24 Aug 91 **LET THE BEAT HIT 'EM PART 2** *Columbia 6573747* [2] 49 2
26 Mar 94 **SKIP TO MY LU** *Chrysalis CDCHS 5006* 34 3

[1] Lisa Lisa and Cult Jam with Full Force [2] Lisa Lisa and Cult Jam
[1] Lisa Lisa and Cult Jam with Full Force

LISA MARIE EXPERIENCE *UK, male instrumental / production duo – Dean Marriot and Neil Hynde (2 Singles: 15 Weeks)*

27 Apr 96 ● **KEEP ON JUMPIN'** (re) *ffrr FCD 271* 7 13
10 Aug 96 **DO THAT TO ME** *Positiva CDTIV 57* 33 2

LISBON LIONS featuring Martin O'NEILL & CELTIC CHORUS
UK, male football supporters vocal group

11 May 02 **THE BEST DAY OF OUR LIVES** *Concept CDCON 32* 17 4

LIT
US, male vocal / instrumental group (1 Album: 1 Week, 3 Singles: 7 Weeks)

26 Jun 99 **MY OWN WORST ENEMY** *RCA 74321669992* 16 4
10 Jul 99 A PLACE IN THE SUN *RCA 7863677752* 55 1
25 Sep 99 **ZIP – LOCK** *RCA 74321701852* 60 1
19 Aug 00 **OVER MY HEAD** *Capitol 8889532* 37 2

LITHIUM and Sonya MADAN
(see also ALCATRAZ; ECHOBELLY; SUBMERGE featuring Jan JOHNSTON)
US, male producer – Victor Imbres and UK, female vocalist

1 Mar 97 **RIDE A ROCKET** *ffrr FCD 293* 40 2

De Etta LITTLE and Nelson PIGFORD *US, female / male vocal duo*

13 Aug 77 **YOU TAKE MY HEART AWAY** *United Artists UP 36257* 35 5

LITTLE ANGELS *UK, male vocal (Toby Jepson) / instrumental group (4 Albums: 15 Weeks, 13 Singles: 41 Weeks)*

4 Mar 89 **BIG BAD EP** *Polydor LTLEP 2* 74 1
24 Feb 90 **KICKING UP DUST** *Polydor LTL 5* 46 4
12 May 90 **RADICAL YOUR LOVER** *Polydor LTL 6* [1] 34 4
4 Aug 90 **SHE'S A LITTLE ANGEL** *Polydor LTL 7* 21 3
2 Feb 91 **BONEYARD** *Polydor LTL 8* 33 4
2 Mar 91 YOUNG GODS *Polydor 8478461* 17 6
30 Mar 91 **PRODUCT OF THE WORKING CLASS** *Polydor LTL 9* 40 2
1 Jun 91 **YOUNG GODS** *Polydor LTL 10* 34 2
20 Jul 91 **I AIN'T GONNA CRY** *Polydor LTL 11* 26 3
7 Nov 92 **TOO MUCH TOO YOUNG** *Polydor LTL 12* 22 3
9 Jan 93 **WOMANKIND** *Polydor LTLCD 13* 12 5
6 Feb 93 ★ JAM *Polydor 5176422* ■ 1 5
24 Apr 93 **SOAPBOX** *Polydor LTLCD 14* 33 4
25 Sep 93 **SAIL AWAY** *Polydor LTLCD 15* 45 3
9 Apr 94 **TEN MILES HIGH** *Polydor LTLCD 16* 18 3
23 Apr 94 LITTLE OF THE PAST *Polydor 5219362* 20 2
2 Jul 94 TOO POSH TO MOSH TOO GOOD TO LAST! *Essential ESSCD 213* 18 2

[1] Little Angels featuring the Big Bad Horns

Tracks on Big Bad EP: She's a Little Angel / Don't Waste My Time / Better Than the Rest / Sex in Cars.

LITTLE'ANS featuring Peter DOHERTY NEW (see also BABY SHAMBLES; The LIBERTINES) *UK, male vocalist / guitarist and vocalist*

29 Oct 05 **THEIR WAY** *Rough Trade RTRADS CD 267* 22 2

LITTLE ANTHONY and The IMPERIALS
US, male vocal group – leader Anthony Geordine

31 Jul 76 **BETTER USE YOUR HEAD** *United Artists UP 36141* 42 4

LITTLE BARRIE NEW *UK, male vocal / instrumental trio*

5 Feb 05 **FREE SALUTE** *Genuine GEN 032CD* 73 1

LITTLE BENNY and The MASTERS *US, male rapper / trumpet player – Benjamin Harris and instrumental group*

2 Feb 85 **WHO COMES TO BOOGIE** *Bluebird 10 BR 13* 33 7

LITTLE CAESAR *UK, male vocalist*

9 Jun 90 **THE WHOLE OF THE MOON** *A1 EAU 1* 68 3

LITTLE EVA (see also Big Dee IRWIN) *US, female vocalist – Eva Boyd, b. 29 Jun 1945, d. 10 Apr 2003 (3 Singles: 45 Weeks)*

6 Sep 62 ● **THE LOCO-MOTION** (re) *London HL 9581* ▲ $ 2 28
3 Jan 63 **KEEP YOUR HANDS OFF MY BABY** *London HLU 9633* 30 5
7 Mar 63 **LET'S TURKEY TROT** *London HLU 9687* 13 12

'The Loco-motion' peaked at No.11 on re-entry in Jul 1972.

LITTLE FEAT
US, male vocal (Lowell George) / instrumental group (5 Albums: 19 Weeks)

6 Dec 75 THE LAST RECORD ALBUM *Warner Bros. K 56156* 36 3
21 May 77 ● TIME LOVES A HERO *Warner Bros. K 56349* 8 11
11 Mar 78 WAITING FOR COLUMBUS *Warner Bros. K 66075* 43 1
1 Dec 79 DOWN ON THE FARM *Warner Bros. K 56667* 46 3
8 Aug 81 HOY-HOY! *Warner Bros. K 666100* 76 1

LITTLE RICHARD
US, male vocalist / pianist – Richard Penniman (18 Singles: 116 Weeks)

14 Dec 56 **RIP IT UP** *London HLO 8336* 30 1
8 Feb 57 ● **LONG TALL SALLY** *London HLO 8366* $ 3 16
22 Feb 57 **TUTTI FRUTTI** *London HLO 8366* 29 1
8 Mar 57 **SHE'S GOT IT** (re) *London HLO 8382* 15 9
15 Mar 57 ● **THE GIRL CAN'T HELP IT** *London HLO 8382* 9 11
28 Jun 57 ● **LUCILLE** *London HLO 8446* 10 9
13 Sep 57 **JENNY JENNY** *London HLO 8470* 11 5
29 Nov 57 **KEEP A KNOCKIN'** *London HLO 8509* 21 7
28 Feb 58 ● **GOOD GOLLY MISS MOLLY** *London HLU 8560* 8 9
11 Jul 58 **OOH! MY SOUL** (re) *London HLO 8647* 22 4
2 Jan 59 ● **BABY FACE** *London HLU 8770* 2 15
3 Apr 59 **BY THE LIGHT OF THE SILVERY MOON** *London HLU 8831* 17 5
5 Jun 59 **KANSAS CITY** *London HLU 8868* 26 5
11 Oct 62 **HE GOT WHAT HE WANTED (BUT HE LOST WHAT HE HAD)** *Mercury AMT 1189* 38 4
4 Jun 64 **BAMA LAMA BAMA LOO** *London HL 9896* 20 7
2 Jul 77 **GOOD GOLLY MISS MOLLY / RIP IT UP** (re-recordings) *Creole CR 140* 37 4
14 Jun 86 **GREAT GOSH A'MIGHTY! (IT'S A MATTER OF TIME)** *MCA MCA 1049* 62 2
25 Oct 86 **OPERATOR** *WEA YZ 89* 67 2

LITTLE STEVEN *US, male vocalist / guitarist – Steven Van Zandt (2 Albums: 4 Weeks, 1 Single: 3 Weeks)*

6 Nov 82 MEN WITHOUT WOMEN *EMI America 3027* [1] 73 2

6 March 1976	13 March 1976	20 March 1976	27 March 1976
UK No.1 SINGLES			
I LOVE TO LOVE (BUT MY BABY LOVES TO DANCE) Tina Charles	I LOVE TO LOVE (BUT MY BABY LOVES TO DANCE) Tina Charles	I LOVE TO LOVE (BUT MY BABY LOVES TO DANCE) Tina Charles	SAVE YOUR KISSES FOR ME Brotherhood of Man
UK No.1 ALBUMS			
THE VERY BEST OF SLIM WHITMAN Slim Whitman	THE VERY BEST OF SLIM WHITMAN Slim Whitman	BLUE FOR YOU Status Quo	BLUE FOR YOU Status Quo

23 May 87 **BITTER FRUIT** *Manhattan MT 21* 66 3
6 Jun 87 FREEDOM NO COMPROMISE *Manhattan MTL 1010* 52 2

[1] Little Steven and The Disciples of Soul

LITTLE TONY and his BROTHERS
Italy, male vocal group – leader Anthony Ciacci

15 Jan 60 **TOO GOOD** *Decca F 11190* 19 3

LITTLE TREES *Denmark, female vocal group*

1 Sep 01 **HELP! I'M A FISH** *RCA 74321874652* 11 7

LITTLE VILLAGE *UK / US, male vocal / instrumental group*

29 Feb 92 LITTLE VILLAGE *Reprise 7599267132* 23 4

LIVE
US, male vocal / instrumental group (3 Albums: 9 Weeks, 7 Singles: 13 Weeks)

18 Feb 95 **I ALONE** *Radioactive RAXTD 13* 48 4
1 Jul 95 **SELLING THE DRAMA** *Radioactive RAXTD 17* 30 2
15 Jul 95 THROWING COPPER *Radioactive RAD 10997* ▲ 37 6
7 Oct 95 **ALL OVER YOU** *Radioactive RAXTD 20* 48 1
13 Jan 96 **LIGHTNING CRASHES** *Radioactive RAXTD 23* 33 2
15 Mar 97 **LAKINI'S JUICE** *Radioactive RAD 49023* 29 2
29 Mar 97 SECRET SAMADHI *Radioactive RAD 11590* ▲ 31 2
12 Jul 97 **FREAKS** *Radioactive RAXTD 29* 60 1
16 Oct 99 THE DISTANCE TO HERE *Radioactive RAD 11966* 56 1
5 Feb 00 **THE DOLPHIN'S CRY** *Radioactive RAXTD 39* 62 1

LIVE ELEMENT
US, male production duo – Greg Bahary and Chris Malinchak

26 Jan 02 **BE FREE** *Strictly Rhythm SRUKCD 11* 26 2

LIVE REPORT *UK, male vocal / instrumental group*

20 May 89 **WHY DO I ALWAYS GET IT WRONG** *Brouhaha CUE 7* 73 1

LIVERPOOL EXPRESS
UK, male vocal / instrumental group (4 Singles: 26 Weeks)

26 Jun 76 **YOU ARE MY LOVE** *Warner Bros. K 16743* 11 9
16 Oct 76 **HOLD TIGHT** *Warner Bros. K 16799* 46 2
18 Dec 76 **EVERY MAN MUST HAVE A DREAM** *Warner Bros. K 16854* 17 11
4 Jun 77 **DREAMIN'** *Warner Bros. K 16933* 40 4

LIVERPOOL FC *UK, male football team vocalists (5 Singles: 21 Weeks)*

28 May 77 **WE CAN DO IT (EP)** *State STAT 50* 15 4
23 Apr 83 **LIVERPOOL (WE'RE NEVER GONNA …) / LIVERPOOL (ANTHEM)** *Mean MEAN 102* 54 4
17 May 86 **SITTING ON THE TOP OF THE WORLD** *Columbia DB 9116* 50 2
14 May 88 ● **ANFIELD RAP (RED MACHINE IN FULL EFFECT)** *Virgin LFC 1* 3 6
18 May 96 ● **PASS AND MOVE (IT'S THE LIVERPOOL GROOVE)** *Telstar LFCCD 96* [1] 4 5

[1] Liverpool FC and The Boot Room Boyz

Tracks on We Can Do It (EP): We Can Do It / Liverpool Lou / We Shall Not Be Moved / You'll Never Walk Alone.

LIVIN' JOY (see also ALEX PARTY) *US / Italy, male / female vocal / instrumental group – leader Paolo Visnadi (1 Album: 2 Weeks, 6 Singles: 44 Weeks)*

3 Sep 94 **DREAMER** *Undiscovered MCSTD 1993* 18 6
13 May 95 ★ **DREAMER** (re-mix) *Undiscovered MCSTD 2056* ■ 1 11
15 Jun 96 ● **DON'T STOP MOVIN'** *Undiscovered MCSTD 40041* 5 14
2 Nov 96 ● **FOLLOW THE RULES** *Undiscovered MCSTD 40081* 9 5
16 Nov 96 DON'T STOP MOVIN' *Undiscovered MCD 60023* 41 2
5 Apr 97 **WHERE CAN I FIND LOVE** *Undiscovered MCSTD 40108* 12 4
23 Aug 97 **DEEP IN YOU** *Universal MCSTD 40136* 17 4

LIVING COLOUR
US, male vocal / instrumental group (2 Albums: 22 Weeks, 6 Singles: 22 Weeks)

15 Sep 90 TIME'S UP *Epic 4669201* 20 19
27 Oct 90 **TYPE** *Epic LCL 7* 75 1
2 Feb 91 **LOVE REARS ITS UGLY HEAD** *Epic 6565937* 12 11
1 Jun 91 **SOLACE OF YOU** *Epic 6569087* 33 5
26 Oct 91 **CULT OF PERSONALITY** *Epic 6575357* 67 2
20 Feb 93 **LEAVE IT ALONE** *Epic 6589762* 34 2
6 Mar 93 STAIN *Epic 4728562* 19 3
17 Apr 93 **AUSLANDER** *Epic 6591732* 53 1

LIVING IN A BOX *UK, male vocal (Richard Darbyshire) / instrumental group (2 Albums: 35 Weeks, 8 Singles: 62 Weeks)*

4 Apr 87 ● **LIVING IN A BOX** *Chrysalis LIB 1* 5 13
9 May 87 LIVING IN A BOX *Chrysalis CDL 1547* 25 19
13 Jun 87 **SCALES OF JUSTICE** *Chrysalis LIB 2* 30 6
26 Sep 87 **SO THE STORY GOES** *Chrysalis LIB 3* [1] 34 8
30 Jan 88 **LOVE IS THE ART** *Chrysalis LIB 4* 45 4
18 Feb 89 ● **BLOW THE HOUSE DOWN** *Chrysalis LIB 5* 10 9
10 Jun 89 **GATECRASHING** *Chrysalis LIB 6* 36 6
8 Jul 89 GATECRASHING *Chrysalis CDl 1676* 21 16
23 Sep 89 ● **ROOM IN YOUR HEART** *Chrysalis LIB 7* 5 13
30 Dec 89 **DIFFERENT AIR** (re) *Chrysalis LIB 8* 57 3

[1] Living in a Box featuring Bobby Womack

Dandy LIVINGSTONE *Jamaica, male vocalist – Robert Livingstone Thompson (2 Singles: 19 Weeks)*

2 Sep 72 **SUZANNE BEWARE OF THE DEVIL** *Horse HOSS 16* 14 11
13 Jan 73 **BIG CITY / THINK ABOUT THAT** *Horse HOSS 25* 26 8

LLAMA FARMERS
UK, male / female vocal / instrumental group (2 Singles: 2 Weeks)

6 Feb 99 **BIG WHEELS** *Beggars Banquet BBQ 333CD* 67 1
15 May 99 **GET THE KEYS AND GO** *Beggars Banquet BBQ 335CD* 74 1

Kelly LLORENNA (see also N-TRANCE)
UK, female vocalist (1 Album: 2 Weeks, 8 Singles: 36 Weeks)

7 May 94 **SET YOU FREE** *All Around the World CDGLOBE 124* [1] 39 4
24 Feb 96 **BRIGHTER DAY** *Pukka CDPUKKA 5* 43 2
25 Jul 98 **HEART OF GOLD** *Diverse VERSE 2CD* [2] 55 1
24 Mar 01 **TRUE LOVE NEVER DIES** *All Around the World CDGLOBE 240* [3] 34 3
2 Feb 02 ● **TRUE LOVE NEVER DIES** (re-mix) *All Around the World CDGLOBE 248* [3] 7 10
6 Jul 02 ● **TELL IT TO MY HEART** *All Around the World CDGLOBE 256* 9 8
30 Nov 02 **HEART OF GOLD** (re-recording) *All Around the World CDGLOBE 271* 19 4
7 Dec 02 ALL CLUBBED UP – THE BEST OF KELLY LLORENNA *Universal TV 0666082* 62 2
6 Mar 04 **THIS TIME I KNOW IT'S FOR REAL** *All Around the World CXGLOBE 295* 14 4

[1] N-Trance featuring Kelly Llorenna [2] Force & Styles featuring Kelly Llorenna
[3] Flip & Fill featuring Kelly Llorenna

Andrew LLOYD WEBBER
UK, male composer / producer (3 Albums: 44 Weeks)

11 Feb 78 ● VARIATIONS *MCA MCF 2824* 2 19
23 Mar 85 ● REQUIEM *HMV ALW 1* 4 18
25 Dec 04 ANDREW LLOYD WEBBER'S THE PHANTOM OF THE OPERA (FILM SOUNDTRACK) – SPECIAL EDITION *Sony Classical SK 93521* 40 7

Variations features cellist Julian Lloyd Webber. Requiem credits Placido Domingo, Sarah Brightman, Paul Miles-Kingston, the Winchester Cathedral Choir and the English Chamber Orchestra conducted by Lorin Maazel. Andrew Lloyd Webber's The Phantom of the Opera features the London Boys Choir.

3 April 1976	10 April 1976	17 April 1976	24 April 1976
SAVE YOUR KISSES FOR ME Brotherhood of Man	**SAVE YOUR KISSES FOR ME** Brotherhood of Man	**SAVE YOUR KISSES FOR ME** Brotherhood of Man	**SAVE YOUR KISSES FOR ME** Brotherhood of Man
BLUE FOR YOU Status Quo	**ROCK FOLLIES (TV Soundtrack)** Various	**ROCK FOLLIES (TV Soundtrack)** Various	**PRESENCE** Led Zeppelin

KEY
UK No.1 ★ UK Top 10 ● Still on chart + UK entry at No.1 ■
US No.1 ▲ UK million seller £ US million seller $
Singles re-entries are listed as (re), (2re), (3re)… which signifies that the hit re-entered the chart once, twice or three times…
Peak Position / Weeks

Julian LLOYD WEBBER
(see also Andrew LLOYD WEBBER) *UK, male cellist (3 Albums: 19 Weeks)*

14 Sep 85 **PIECES** *Polydor PROLP 6*....59 5
21 Feb 87 **ELGAR CELLO CONCERTO** *Philips 416 3541*....94 1
27 Oct 90 **LLOYD WEBBER PLAYS LLOYD WEBBER** *Philips 4322911*....15 13

The first two albums credit the London Symphony Orchestra and the third credits the Royal Philharmonic Orchestra.

LO FIDELITY ALLSTARS
UK, male vocal / instrumental group (1 Album: 4 Weeks, 3 Singles: 5 Weeks)

11 Oct 97 **DISCO MACHINE GUN** *Skint SKINT 30CD*....50 1
2 May 98 **VISION INCISION** *Skint SKINT 33CD*....30 2
6 Jun 98 **HOW TO OPERATE WITH A BLOWN MIND** *Skint BRASSIC 8CD* 15 4
28 Nov 98 **BATTLEFLAG** *Skint SKINT 38CD* [1] 36 2

[1] Lo Fidelity Allstars featuring Pigeonhed

LOBO *US, male vocalist – Kent LaVoie (2 Singles: 25 Weeks)*

19 Jun 71 ● **ME AND YOU AND A DOG NAMED BOO** *Philips 6073 801*....4 14
8 Jun 74 ● **I'D LOVE YOU TO WANT ME** *UK 68* $ 5 11

LOBO *Holland, male vocalist – Imrich Lobo*

25 Jul 81 ● **THE CARIBBEAN DISCO SHOW** *Polydor POSP 302*....8 11

LOCK 'N' LOAD *Holland, male DJ / production duo – Francis Rooijen and Nilz Pijpers (2 Singles: 13 Weeks)*

15 Apr 00 ● **BLOW YA MIND** (re) *Pepper 9230162*....6 11
3 Mar 01 **HOUSE SOME MORE** *Pepper 9230422*....45 2

Josef LOCKE *Ireland, male vocalist – Joseph McLaughlin, b. 23 Mar 1917, d. 15 Oct 1999 (3 Albums: 20 Weeks)*

28 Jun 69 **THE WORLD OF JOSEF LOCKE TODAY** *Decca SPA 21*....29 1
21 Mar 92 ● **HEAR MY SONG (THE BEST OF JOSEF LOCKE)** *EMI CDGO 2034*....7 17
27 Jun 92 **TAKE A PAIR OF SPARKLING EYES** *EMI CDGO 2038*....41 2

Kimberley LOCKE *US, female vocalist*

31 Jul 04 **8TH WORLD WONDER** *Curb / London CUBC 097*....49 2

Hank LOCKLIN
US, male vocalist – Lawrence Locklin (4 Singles: 41 Weeks)

11 Aug 60 ● **PLEASE HELP ME, I'M FALLING** *RCA 1188*....9 19
15 Feb 62 **FROM HERE TO THERE TO YOU** *RCA 1273*....44 3
15 Nov 62 **WE'RE GONNA GO FISHIN'** *RCA 1305*....18 11
5 May 66 **I FEEL A CRY COMING ON** *RCA 1510*....29 8

LOCKSMITH *US, male vocal / instrumental group*

23 Aug 80 **UNLOCK THE FUNK** *Arista ARIST 364*....42 6

LOCOMOTIVE *UK, male vocal / instrumental group*

16 Oct 68 **RUDI'S IN LOVE** *Parlophone R 5718*....25 8

John LODGE (see also The MOODY BLUES)
UK, male vocalist / guitarist (2 Albums: 20 Weeks, 1 Single: 7 Weeks)

29 Mar 75 ● **BLUE JAYS** *Threshold THS 12* [1] 4 18
25 Oct 75 ● **BLUE GUITAR** *Threshold TH 21* [1] 8 7
19 Feb 77 **NATURAL AVENUE** *Decca TXS 120*....38 2

[1] Justin Hayward and John Lodge [1] Justin Hayward and John Lodge

LODGER *UK, male / female vocal / instrumental group*

2 May 98 **I'M LEAVING** *Island CID 693*....40 2

Lisa LOEB and NINE STORIES *US, female / male vocal / instrumental group (1 Album: 2 Weeks, 2 Singles: 17 Weeks)*

3 Sep 94 ● **STAY (I MISSED YOU)** *RCA 74321212522* ▲....6 15
16 Sep 95 **DO YOU SLEEP?** *Geffen GFSTD 96*....45 2
7 Oct 95 **TAILS** *Geffen GED 24734*....39 2

Nils LOFGREN
US, male vocalist / guitarist (8 Albums: 30 Weeks, 1 Single: 3 Weeks)

17 Apr 76 ● **CRY TOUGH** *A&M AMLH 64573*....8 11
26 Mar 77 **I CAME TO DANCE** *A&M AMLH 64628*....30 4
5 Nov 77 **NIGHT AFTER NIGHT** *A&M AMLH 68439*....38 2
26 Sep 81 **NIGHT FADES AWAY** *Backstreet MCF 3121*....50 3
1 May 82 **A RHYTHM ROMANCE** *A&M AMLH 68543*....100 1
8 Jun 85 **SECRETS IN THE STREET** *Towerbell TOW 68*....53 3
6 Jul 85 **FLIP** *Towerbell TOWLP 11*....36 7
5 Apr 86 **CODE OF THE ROAD** *Towerbell TOWDLP 17*....86 1
27 Apr 91 **SILVER LINING** *Essential ESSLP 145*....61 1

Johnny LOGAN *Ireland, male vocalist – Sean Sherrard (1 Album: 1 Week, 3 Singles: 24 Weeks)*

3 May 80 ★ **WHAT'S ANOTHER YEAR** *Epic EPC 8572*....1 8
23 May 87 ● **HOLD ME NOW** *Epic LOG 1*....2 11
22 Aug 87 **HOLD ME NOW** *CBS 451 0731*....83 1
22 Aug 87 **I'M NOT IN LOVE** *Epic LOG 2*....51 5

Kenny LOGGINS *US, male vocalist / instrumentalist (2 Singles: 21 Weeks)*

28 Apr 84 ● **FOOTLOOSE** *CBS A 4101* ▲ $ 6 10
1 Nov 86 **DANGER ZONE** *CBS A 7188*....45 11

LOGO featuring Dawn JOSEPH
UK, male production duo and female vocalist

8 Dec 01 **DON'T PANIC** *Manifesto FESCD 89*....42 1

Lindsay LOHAN NEW *US, female actor / vocalist*

7 May 05 **OVER** *Universal MCSTD 40412*....27 3

LOLA *US, female vocalist – Lola Blank*

28 Mar 87 **WAX THE VAN** *Syncopate SY 1*....65 1

LOLLY
UK, female vocalist – Anna Kumble (1 Album: 12 Weeks, 5 Singles: 44 Weeks)

10 Jul 99 ● **VIVA LA RADIO** *Polydor 5639492*....6 9
18 Sep 99 ● **MICKEY** *Polydor 5613682*....4 10
2 Oct 99 **MY FIRST ALBUM** *Polydor 5479622*....21 12
4 Dec 99 ● **BIG BOYS DON'T CRY / ROCKIN' ROBIN** *Polydor 5615552*....10 9
6 May 00 **PER SEMPRE AMORE (FOREVER IN LOVE)** (re) *Polydor 5617882*....11 10
9 Sep 00 **GIRLS JUST WANNA HAVE FUN** *Polydor 5619762*....14 6

Julie LONDON
US, female vocalist – Julie Peck, b. 26 Sep 1926, d. 18 Oct 2000

5 Apr 57 **CRY ME A RIVER** *London HLU 8240*....22 3

Laurie LONDON *UK, male vocalist*

8 Nov 57 **HE'S GOT THE WHOLE WORLD IN HIS HANDS** *Parlophone R 4359* $ 12 12

Hit with Geoff Love, his Orchestra and Chorus.

LONDON BOYS *UK, male vocal duo – Edem Ephraim, b. 1959, and Dennis Fuller, b. 1960, both d. 21 Sep 1996 (1 Album: 29 Weeks, 6 Singles: 46 Weeks)*

10 Dec 88 ● **REQUIEM** (re) *WEA YZ 345*....4 21
1 Jul 89 ● **LONDON NIGHTS** *WEA YZ 393*....2 9
29 Jul 89 ● **THE TWELVE COMMANDMENTS OF DANCE** *WEA WX 278*....2 29

	1 May 1976	8 May 1976	15 May 1976	22 May 1976
UK No.1 SINGLES	SAVE YOUR KISSES FOR ME Brotherhood of Man	FERNANDO Abba	FERNANDO Abba	FERNANDO Abba
UK No.1 ALBUMS	ROCK FOLLIES (TV Soundtrack) Various	GREATEST HITS Abba	GREATEST HITS Abba	GREATEST HITS Abba

16 Sep 89	**HARLEM DESIRE** *WEA YZ 415*	**17**	7
2 Dec 89	**MY LOVE** *WEA YZ 433*	**46**	6
16 Jun 90	**CHAPEL OF LOVE** *East West YZ 458*	**75**	1
19 Jan 91	**FREEDOM** *East West YZ 554*	**54**	2

'Requiem' peaked at No.4 after re-entering in April 1989.

LONDON PHILHARMONIC CHOIR
(see also ADIEMUS) *UK, choir (3 Albums: 20 Weeks)*

3 Dec 60 ●	**THE MESSIAH** *Pye Golden Guinea GGL 0062* [1]	**10**	7
13 Nov 76 ●	**SOUND OF GLORY** *Arcade ADEP 25* [2]	**10**	10
13 Apr 91	**PRAISE – 18 CHORAL MASTERPIECES** *Pop & Arts PATLP 301* [3]	**54**	3

[1] London Philharmonic Choir with the London Orchestra conducted by Peter Susskind [2] London Philharmonic Choir with the National Philharmonic Orchestra conducted by John Aldiss [3] London Philharmonic Choir with the National Philharmonic Orchestra

LONDON PHILHARMONIC ORCHESTRA
UK, orchestra (3 Albums: 22 Weeks)

23 Apr 60	**RAVEL'S BOLERO** *London HAV 2189*	**15**	4
8 Apr 61	**VICTORY AT SEA** *Pye GGL 0073*	**12**	1
21 May 83 ●	**DRESSED FOR THE OCCASION** *EMI EMC 3432* [1]	**7**	17

[1] Cliff Richard and the London Philharmonic Orchestra

LONDON STRING CHORALE *UK, orchestra / choir*

15 Dec 73	**GALLOPING HOME** (re) *Polydor 2058 280*	**31**	13

LONDON SYMPHONY ORCHESTRA (288 Top 500)
(see also Andrea BOCELLI) *One of the chart's largest acts was formed in 1904. Principal conductors have included Andre Previn, Sir Colin Davis and John Williams. Famous for global tours and soundtrack recordings, the orchestra achieved its greatest chart success with symphonic arrangements of rock classics (21 Albums: 221 Weeks, 3 Singles: 10 Weeks)*

18 Mar 72	**TOP TV THEMES** *Studio Two STWO 372*	**13**	7
16 Dec 72 ●	**THE STRAUSS FAMILY** *Polydor 2659 014* [1]	**2**	21
5 Jul 75	**MUSIC FROM 'EDWARD VII'** *Polydor 2659 041*	**52**	1
18 Dec 76	**THE SNOW GOOSE** *RCA RS 1088* [2]	**49**	1
21 Jan 78	**STAR WARS (FILM SOUNDTRACK)** *20th Century BTD 541*	**21**	12
8 Jul 78 ●	**CLASSIC ROCK** *K-Tel ONE 1009*	**3**	39
6 Jan 79	**THEME FROM 'SUPERMAN' (MAIN TITLE)** *Warner Bros. K 17292*	**32**	5
10 Feb 79	**CLASSIC ROCK – THE SECOND MOVEMENT** *K-Tel NE 1039*	**26**	8
5 Jan 80	**RHAPSODY IN BLACK** *K-Tel ONE 1063*	**34**	5
1 Aug 81 ●	**CLASSIC ROCK – ROCK CLASSICS** *K-Tel ONE 1123*	**5**	23
27 Nov 82	**THE BEST OF CLASSIC ROCK** *K-Tel ONE 1080*	**35**	11
27 Aug 83	**CLASSIC ROCK – ROCK SYMPHONIES** *K-Tel ONE 1243*	**40**	9
26 Oct 85	**HITS ON OPERA** *Stylus SMR 8505* [3]	**38**	4
16 Nov 85	**THE POWER OF CLASSIC ROCK** *Portrait PRT 10049*	**13**	15
14 Nov 87	**CLASSIC ROCK COUNTDOWN** *CBS MOOD 3*	**32**	16
18 Nov 89	**CLASSIC ROCK – THE LIVING YEARS** *CBS MOOD 9*	**51**	6
18 Jan 92	**WIND OF CHANGE – CLASSIC ROCK** *Columbia MOODCD 19* [4]	**24**	8
19 Nov 94	**THE WORKS OF RICE AND LLOYD WEBBER** *Vision VISCD 4*	**55**	2
23 Sep 95	**BRAVEHEART (FILM SOUNDTRACK)** *Decca 4482952* [5]	**27**	9
25 Oct 97	**PAUL McCARTNEY'S STANDING STONE** *EMI Classics CDC 5564842* [6]	**34**	2
6 Dec 97	**JUST SHOW ME HOW TO LOVE YOU** *Coalition COLA 035CD* [1]	**54**	2
15 May 99 ●	**STAR WARS – THE PHANTOM MENACE (FILM SOUNDTRACK)** *Sony Classical SK 61816*	**8**	17
11 May 02	**STAR WARS EPISODE II – ATTACK OF THE CLONES (FILM SOUNDTRACK)** *Sony Classical SK 89932*	**15**	5
4 Jun 05	**BATTLE OF THE HEROES – FROM STAR WARS REVENGE OF THE SITH** *Sony Classical 6759562* [2]	**25**	3

[1] Sarah Brightman and the LSO featuring Jose Cura [2] John Williams / London Symphony Orchestra [1] London Symphony Orchestra conducted by Cyril Ornadel [2] Spike Milligan with the London Symphony Orchestra [3] Kimera with the London Symphony Orchestra [4] London Symphony Orchestra and the Royal Choral Society [5] London Symphony Orchestra, music composed and conducted by James Horner [6] London Symphony Orchestra conducted by Lawrence Foster

Orchestra conducted by John Williams. Star Wars – The Phantom Menace and Star Wars Episode II – Attack of the Clones are conducted by John Williams.

LONDON WELSH MALE VOICE CHOIR *UK, male choir*

5 Sep 81	**SONGS OF THE VALLEYS** *K-Tel NE 1117*	**61**	10

LONDONBEAT *UK / US, male vocal group – includes Jimmy Helms (1 Album: 6 Weeks, 11 Singles: 47 Weeks)*

26 Nov 88	**9 AM (THE COMFORT ZONE)** *AnXious ANX 008*	**19**	10
18 Feb 89	**FAILING IN LOVE AGAIN** *AnXious ANX 007*	**60**	2
2 Dec 89	**IT TAKES TWO BABY** *Spartan CIN 101* [1]	**53**	2
1 Sep 90 ●	**I'VE BEEN THINKING ABOUT YOU** *AnXious ANX 14* ▲	**2**	13
13 Oct 90	**IN THE BLOOD** *AnXious ZL 74810*	**34**	6
24 Nov 90	**A BETTER LOVE** *AnXious ANX 21*	**52**	5
2 Mar 91	**NO WOMAN NO CRY** *AnXious ANX 25*	**64**	2
20 Jul 91	**A BETTER LOVE** (re-issue) *AnXious ANX 32*	**23**	6
27 Jun 92	**YOU BRING ON THE SUN** *AnXious ANX 37*	**32**	4
24 Oct 92	**THAT'S HOW I FEEL ABOUT YOU** *AnXious ANX 40*	**69**	1
8 Apr 95	**I'M JUST YOUR PUPPET ON A ... (STRING)** *AnXious 74321270982*	**55**	1
20 May 95	**COME BACK** *AnXious 74321226682*	**69**	1

[1] Liz Kershaw, Bruno Brookes, Jive Bunny and Londonbeat

LONE JUSTICE *US, female / male vocal / instrumental group (2 Albums: 5 Weeks, 1 Single: 4 Weeks)*

6 Jul 85	**LONE JUSTICE** *Geffen GEF 26288*	**49**	2
8 Nov 86	**SHELTER** *Geffen WX 73*	**84**	3
7 Mar 87	**I FOUND LOVE** *Geffen GEF 18*	**45**	4

LONE STAR *UK, male vocal / instrumental group (2 Albums: 7 Weeks)*

2 Oct 76	**LONE STAR** *Epic EPC 81545*	**47**	1
17 Sep 77	**FIRING ON ALL SIX** *CBS 82213*	**36**	6

LONESTAR *US, male vocal / instrumental group (2 Singles: 24 Weeks)*

15 Apr 00	**AMAZED** *BMG / Grapevine 74321742582* ▲	**21**	22
7 Oct 00	**SMILE** *BMG / Grapevine 74321786132*	**55**	2

Shorty LONG
US, male vocalist – Frederick Long, b. 20 May 1940, d. 29 Jun 1969

17 Jul 68	**HERE COMES THE JUDGE** *Tamla Motown TMG 663*	**30**	7

The LONG AND THE SHORT
UK, male vocal / instrumental group (2 Singles: 8 Weeks)

10 Sep 64	**THE LETTER** *Decca F 11964*	**35**	5
24 Dec 64	**CHOC ICE** *Decca F 12043*	**40**	3

LONG RYDERS *US, male vocal / instrumental group*

5 Oct 85	**LOOKING FOR LEWIS AND CLARKE** *Island IS 237*	**59**	4
16 Nov 85	**STATE OF OUR UNION** *Island ILPS 9802*	**66**	1

LONGPIGS **(see also Richard HAWLEY)** *UK, male vocal / instrumental group (2 Albums: 10 Weeks, 8 Singles: 17 Weeks)*

22 Jul 95	**SHE SAID** *Mother MUMCD 66*	**67**	1
28 Oct 95	**JESUS CHRIST** *Mother MUMCD 68*	**61**	1
17 Feb 96	**FAR** *Mother MUMCD 71*	**37**	2
13 Apr 96	**ON AND ON** *Mother MUMCD 74*	**16**	3
11 May 96	**THE SUN IS OFTEN OUT** *Mother MUMCD 9602*	**26**	9
22 Jun 96	**SHE SAID** (re-issue) *Mother MUMCD 77*	**16**	4
5 Oct 96	**LOST MYSELF** *Mother MUMCD 82*	**22**	3
9 Oct 99	**BLUE SKIES** *Mother MUMCD 113*	**21**	2
23 Oct 99	**MOBILE HOME** *Mother MUMCD 9901*	**33**	1
18 Dec 99	**THE FRANK SONATA** *Mother MUMCD 114*	**57**	1

29 May 1976	5 June 1976	12 June 1976	19 June 1976
FERNANDO Abba	**NO CHARGE** JJ Barrie	**THE COMBINE HARVESTER (BRAND NEW KEY)** The Wurzels	**THE COMBINE HARVESTER (BRAND NEW KEY)** The Wurzels
GREATEST HITS Abba	**GREATEST HITS** Abba	**GREATEST HITS** Abba	**GREATEST HITS** Abba

KEY UK No.1 ★ UK Top 10 ● Still on chart + UK entry at No.1 ■ US No.1 ▲ UK million seller £ US million seller $
Singles re-entries are listed as (re), (2re), (3re)… which signifies that the hit re-entered the chart once, twice or three times…

Peak Position / Weeks

Joe LONGTHORNE
UK, male vocalist (5 Albums: 32 Weeks, 2 Singles: 6 Weeks)

3 Dec 88 THE JOE LONGTHORNE SONGBOOK *Telstar STAR 2353* 16 12
29 Jul 89 ESPECIALLY FOR YOU *Telstar STAR 2365* 22 10
9 Dec 89 THE JOE LONGTHORNE CHRISTMAS ALBUM *Telstar STAR 2385* 44 4
13 Nov 93 I WISH YOU LOVE *EMI CDEMC 3662* 47 4
30 Apr 94 **YOUNG GIRL** *EMI CDEM 310* 61 2
8 Oct 94 LIVE AT THE ROYAL ALBERT HALL *Premier CDDPR 126* 57 2
10 Dec 94 **PASSING STRANGERS** *EMI CDEM 362* [1] 34 4

[1] Joe Longthorne and Liz Dawn

LONGVIEW
UK, male vocal / instrumental group (1 Album: 6 Weeks, 7 Singles: 11 Weeks)

26 Oct 02 **WHEN YOU SLEEP** *4:45 Recordings LVIEW 02CD* 74 1
8 Feb 03 **NOWHERE** *4:45 Recordings LVIEW 03CD* 72 1
19 Jul 03 **FURTHER** *14th Floor 14FLR 01CD 1* 27 2
2 Aug 03 MERCURY *14th Floor 5046668862* [1] 29 6
11 Oct 03 **CAN'T EXPLAIN** *14th Floor 14FLR 02CD 1* 51 1
10 Jul 04 **IN A DREAM** *14th Floor 14FLR 06CD* 38 1
22 Jan 05 **COMING DOWN / WHEN YOU SLEEP** (re-mix) *14th Floor 14FLR 09CD* [1] 32 2
20 Aug 05 **FURTHER** (re-mix) *14th Floor 14FLR 12CD* [1] 24 3

[1] Long-View [1] Long-View

Mercury stalled at No.45 in 2003 and only reached its peak position in 2005.

LONYO (see also BON GARÇON)
UK, male vocalist / producer – Lonyo Engele (2 Singles: 9 Weeks)

8 Jul 00 ● **SUMMER OF LOVE** *Riverhorse RIVHCD 3* [1] 8 7
7 Apr 01 **GARAGE GIRLS** *Riverhorse RIVHCD 12* [2] 39 2

[1] Lonyo – Comme Ci Comme Ça [2] Lonyo featuring MC Onyx Stone

The LOOK *UK, male vocal (Johnny Whetstone) / instrumental group (2 Singles: 15 Weeks)*

20 Dec 80 ● **I AM THE BEAT** *MCA 647* 6 12
29 Aug 81 **FEEDING TIME** *MCA 736* 50 3

LOOP *UK, male vocal / instrumental group (2 Albums: 2 Weeks)*

4 Feb 89 FADE OUT *Chapter 22 CHAPLP 34* 51 1
3 Feb 90 A GILDED ETERNITY *Situation Two SITU 27* 39 1

LOOP DA LOOP *UK, male producer – Nick Dresti (2 Singles: 4 Weeks)*

7 Jun 97 **GO WITH THE FLOW** *Manifesto FESCD 24* 47 1
20 Feb 99 **HAZEL** *Manifesto FESCD 53* 20 3

LOOSE ENDS *UK, male vocal / instrumental trio (6 Albums: 41 Weeks, 14 Singles: 76 Weeks)*

25 Feb 84 **TELL ME WHAT YOU WANT** *Virgin VS 658* 74 1
21 Apr 84 A LITTLE SPICE *Virgin V 2301* 46 9
28 Apr 84 **EMERGENCY (DIAL 999)** *Virgin VS 677* 41 6
21 Jul 84 **CHOOSE ME (RESCUE ME)** *Virgin VS 697* 59 3
23 Feb 85 **HANGIN' ON A STRING (CONTEMPLATING)** *Virgin VS 748* 13 13
20 Apr 85 SO WHERE ARE YOU? *Virgin V 2340* 13 13
11 May 85 **MAGIC TOUCH** *Virgin VS 761* 16 7
27 Jul 85 **GOLDEN YEARS** *Virgin VS 795* 59 4
14 Jun 86 **STAY A LITTLE WHILE, CHILD** *Virgin VS 819* 52 5
20 Sep 86 **SLOW DOWN** *Virgin VS 884* 27 7
18 Oct 86 ZAGORA *Virgin V 2384* 15 8
29 Nov 86 **NIGHTS OF PLEASURE** *Virgin VS 919* 42 7
4 Jun 88 **MR BACHELOR** *Virgin VS 1080* 50 4
2 Jul 88 THE REAL CHUCKEEBOO *Virgin V 2528* 52 4
25 Aug 90 **DON'T BE A FOOL** *10 TEN 312* 13 9
22 Sep 90 LOOK HOW LONG *Ten DIX 94* 19 5
17 Nov 90 **LOVE'S GOT ME** *10 TEN 330* 40 4
20 Jun 92 **HANGIN' ON A STRING** (re-mix) *Ten TEN 406* 25 5
5 Sep 92 **MAGIC TOUCH** (re-mix) *Ten TEN 409* 75 1
19 Sep 92 TIGHTEN UP VOLUME 1 *Ten DIXCD 112* 40 2

Lisa 'Left Eye' LOPES (see also TLC)
US, female rapper, b. 27 May 1971, d. 25 Apr 2002 (2 Singles: 20 Weeks)

1 Apr 00 ★ **NEVER BE THE SAME AGAIN** (re) *Virgin VSCDT 1762* [1] ■ 1 16
27 Oct 01 **THE BLOCK PARTY** *LaFace / Arista 74321895912* 16 4

[1] Melanie C / Lisa 'Left Eye' Lopes

Jennifer LOPEZ 176 Top 500
Globally successful, photogenic singer / actress. J. Lo, b. 24 Jul 1970, The Bronx, New York, US, has starred in many movies including The Wedding Planner, The Cell, Monster-in-Law and Selena, the life story of the late Latin superstar (5 Albums: 148 Weeks, 15 Singles: 169 Weeks)

3 Jul 99 ● **IF YOU HAD MY LOVE** *Columbia 6675772* ▲ $ 4 13
17 Jul 99 ON THE 6 *Columbia 4949302* 14 30
13 Nov 99 ● **WAITING FOR TONIGHT** *Columbia 6683072* 5 12
1 Apr 00 **FEELIN' SO GOOD** *Columbia 6691972* [1] 15 6
20 Jan 01 ★ **LOVE DON'T COST A THING** (re) *Epic 6707282* ■ 1 11
3 Feb 01 ● J.LO *Epic 5005502* ▲ 2 48
12 May 01 ● **PLAY** (re) *Epic 6712272* 3 12
18 Aug 01 ● **AIN'T IT FUNNY** (re) *Epic 6717592* 3 9
10 Nov 01 ● **I'M REAL** *Epic 6720322* [2] ▲ 4 15
23 Mar 02 ● **AIN'T IT FUNNY** *Epic 6724922* [3] ▲ 4 13
30 Mar 02 ● J TO THA L-O – THE REMIXES *Epic 5060242* ▲ 4 27
13 Jul 02 ● **I'M GONNA BE ALRIGHT** *Epic 6728442* [4] 3 10
30 Nov 02 ● **JENNY FROM THE BLOCK** *Epic 6733572* 3 13
7 Dec 02 THIS IS ME … THEN *Epic 5101282* 13 34
22 Mar 03 ● **ALL I HAVE** *Epic 6736782* [5] ▲ 2 13
21 Jun 03 **I'M GLAD** *Epic 6740152* 11 9
20 Mar 04 ● **BABY I LOVE U** *Epic 6747902* 3 10
26 Feb 05 ★ **GET RIGHT** *Epic 6757562* ■ 1 14
12 Mar 05 ● REBIRTH *Epic 5193912* 8 9
28 May 05 ● **HOLD YOU DOWN** *Epic 6759342* [6] 6 9

[1] Jennifer Lopez featuring Big Pun and Fat Joe [2] Jennifer Lopez featuring Ja Rule [3] Jennifer Lopez featuring Ja Rule & Caddillac Tah [4] Jennifer Lopez featuring Nas [5] Jennifer Lopez featuring LL Cool J [6] Jennifer Lopez featuring Fat Joe

The two singles titled 'Ain't it Funny' are different songs.

Trini LOPEZ
US, male vocalist – Trinidad Lopez (2 Albums: 42 Weeks, 5 Singles: 37 Weeks)

12 Sep 63 ● **IF I HAD A HAMMER** *Reprise R 20198* $ 4 17
26 Oct 63 ● TRINI LOPEZ AT P.J.'S *Reprise R 6093* 7 25
12 Dec 63 **KANSAS CITY** *Reprise R 20236* 35 5
12 May 66 **I'M COMING HOME CINDY** *Reprise R 20455* 28 5
25 Mar 67 ● TRINI LOPEZ IN LONDON *Reprise RSLP 6238* 6 17
6 Apr 67 **GONNA GET ALONG WITHOUT YA NOW** *Reprise R 20547* 41 5
19 Dec 81 **TRINI TRAX** *RCA 154* 59 5

Jeff LORBER *US, male vocalist / keyboard player*

18 May 85 STEP BY STEP *Club JABH 9* 97 2

LORD TANAMO *Trinidad and Tobago, male vocalist – Joseph Gordon*

1 Dec 90 **I'M IN THE MOOD FOR LOVE** *Mooncrest MOON 1009* 58 2

LORD TARIQ and Peter GUNZ
US, male vocal / rap duo – Sean Hamilton and Peter Panky

2 May 98 **DEJA VU (UPTOWN BABY)** *Columbia 6658722* $ 21 3

	26 June 1976	3 July 1976	10 July 1976	17 July 1976
UK No.1 SINGLES	YOU TO ME ARE EVERYTHING – The Real Thing	YOU TO ME ARE EVERYTHING – The Real Thing	YOU TO ME ARE EVERYTHING – The Real Thing	THE ROUSSOS PHENOMENON (EP) – Demis Roussos
UK No.1 ALBUMS	GREATEST HITS – Abba	GREATEST HITS – Abba	A NIGHT ON THE TOWN – Rod Stewart	A NIGHT ON THE TOWN – Rod Stewart

Jerry LORDAN
UK, male vocalist, b. 30 Apr 1934, d. 24 Jul 1995 (3 Singles: 16 Weeks)

8 Jan 60	**I'LL STAY SINGLE** (re) *Parlophone R 4588*	26	3
26 Feb 60	**WHO COULD BE BLUER** (re) *Parlophone R 4627*	16	11
2 Jun 60	**SING LIKE AN ANGEL** *Parlophone R 4653*	36	2

LORDS OF THE UNDERGROUND *US, male rap group*

12 Nov 94	KEEPERS OF THE FUNK *Pendulum CDCHR 6088*	68	1

Traci LORDS *US, female vocalist – Nora Kuzma*

7 Oct 95	**FALLEN ANGEL** *Radioactive RAXTD 18*	72	1

Trey LORENZ (see also Mariah CAREY)
US, male vocalist – Lloyd Lorenz Smith (2 Singles: 5 Weeks)

21 Nov 92	**SOMEONE TO HOLD** *Epic 6587857*	65	2
30 Jan 93	**PHOTOGRAPH OF MARY** *Epic 6589542*	38	3

LORI and The CHAMELEONS
UK, female / male vocal / instrumental group

8 Dec 79	**TOUCH** *Sire SIR 4025*	70	1

LOS BRAVOS *Spain / Germany, male vocal (Mike Kogel) / instrumental group (1 Album: 1 Week, 2 Singles: 24 Weeks)*

8 Oct 64	BLACK IS BLACK *Decca LK 4822*	29	1
30 Jun 66 ●	**BLACK IS BLACK** *Decca F 22419*	2	13
8 Sep 66	**I DON'T CARE** *Decca F 22484*	16	11

LOS DEL MAR featuring Wil VELOZ
Cuba / Canada, male vocal / instrumental group

8 Jun 96	**MACARENA** (re) *Pulse 8 CDLOSE 101*	43	7

LOS DEL RIO
Spain, male vocal / instrumental duo – Antonio Monge and Rafael Perdigones

1 Jun 96 ●	**MACARENA** (re) *RCA 74321345372* ▲ $	2	19

LOS INDIOS TABAJARAS
Brazil, male guitarists – Natalicio and Antenor Lima – guitars

31 Oct 63 ●	**MARIA ELENA** *RCA 1365*	5	17

LOS LOBOS *US, male vocal (David Hildago) / instrumental group (2 Albums: 9 Weeks, 3 Singles: 24 Weeks)*

6 Apr 85	HOW WILL THE WOLF SURVIVE? *Slash SLMP 3*	77	6
6 Apr 85	**DON'T WORRY BABY / WILL THE WOLF SURVIVE** *London LASH 4*	57	4
7 Feb 87	BY THE LIGHT OF THE MOON *Slash SLAP 13*	77	3
18 Jul 87 ★	**LA BAMBA** *Slash LASH 13* ▲	1	11
26 Sep 87	**COME ON LET'S GO** *Slash LASH 14*	18	9

LOS NIÑOS *UK, male instrumental group*

22 Jul 95	FRAGILE – MYSTICAL SOUNDS OF THE PANPIPE *Pearls DPWKF 4253*	74	1

LOS POP TOPS *Spain, male vocal group*

9 Oct 71	**MAMY BLUE** *A&M AMS 859*	35	6

LOS UMBRELLOS *Denmark, male / female vocal trio*

3 Oct 98	**NO TENGO DINERO** *Virgin VUSCD 139*	33	2

Joe LOSS and his ORCHESTRA *UK, orchestra – leader b. 22 Jun 1909, d. 6 Jun 1990 (2 Albums: 20 Weeks, 5 Singles: 52 Weeks)*

29 Jun 61	**WHEELS CHA CHA** *HMV POP 880*	21	21
19 Oct 61	**SUCU SUCU** *HMV POP 937*	48	1
29 Mar 62	**THE MAIGRET THEME** *HMV POP 995*	20	10

MOST WEEKS ON THE ALBUMS CHART BY ACT

Although Elvis overtook The Beatles during 2005, Queen are the album chart heavyweight champions of all time owing to the repetitive presence of their back catalogue, not to mention a new release featuring lead vocalist Paul Rodgers.

POSITION / ACT / TOTAL WEEKS ON CHART

1. QUEEN – 1,332
2. ELVIS PRESLEY – 1,299
3. THE BEATLES – 1,293
4. U2 – 1,165
5. DIRE STRAITS – 1,143
6. SIMON AND GARFUNKEL – 1,114
7. MADONNA – 1,038
8. DAVID BOWIE – 1,006
9. ELTON JOHN – 991
10. MICHAEL JACKSON – 976
11. ROD STEWART – 927
12. PINK FLOYD – 923
13. FRANK SINATRA – 892
14. ABBA – 891
15. FLEETWOOD MAC – 886
16. PHIL COLLINS – 846
17. CLIFF RICHARD – 819
18. THE SHADOWS – 812
19. THE ROLLING STONES – 805
20. MEAT LOAF – 789

Queen have spent more weeks on the albums chart than any other act, including 30 weeks during 2005. Brian May and Roger Taylor show off their British Hit Singles & Albums awards to mark this achievement on stage at the Dominion Theatre, London, after a special presentation by We Will Rock You writer Ben Elton

24 July 1976	31 July 1976	7 August 1976	14 August 1976
DON'T GO BREAKING MY HEART Elton John and Kiki Dee	**DON'T GO BREAKING MY HEART** Elton John and Kiki Dee	**DON'T GO BREAKING MY HEART** Elton John and Kiki Dee	**DON'T GO BREAKING MY HEART** Elton John and Kiki Dee
20 GOLDEN GREATS The Beach Boys	**20 GOLDEN GREATS** The Beach Boys	**20 GOLDEN GREATS** The Beach Boys	**20 GOLDEN GREATS** The Beach Boys

KEY: UK No.1 ★ UK Top 10 ● Still on chart + UK entry at No.1 ■ US No.1 ▲ UK million seller £ US million seller $
Singles re-entries are listed as (re), (2re), (3re)... which signifies that the hit re-entered the chart once, twice or three times...

Peak Position / Weeks

1 Nov 62 **MUST BE MADISON** *HMV POP 1075* ... 20 13
5 Nov 64 **MARCH OF THE MODS** (2re) *HMV POP 1351* ... 31 7
30 Oct 71 ALL-TIME PARTY HITS *MFP 5227* ... 24 10
19 Nov 77 ● 30 GOLDEN GREATS *EMI EMTV 7* [1] ... 10 10

[1] George Mitchell Minstrels with the Joe Loss Orchestra

LOST *UK, male / instrumental / production duo*

22 Jun 91 **TECHNO FUNK** *Perfecto PT 44560* ... 75 1

LOST BOYZ *US, male rap group (1 Album: 1 Week, 2 Singles: 2 Weeks)*

6 Jul 96 LEGAL DRUG MONEY *Universal UND 53010* ... 64 1
2 Nov 96 **MUSIC MAKES ME HIGH** *Universal MCSTD 48015* ... 42 1
12 Jul 97 **LOVE, PEACE & NAPPINESS** *Universal UND 56131* ... 57 1

LOST BROTHERS featuring G Tom MAC
UK, male production group and vocalist

20 Dec 03 **CRY LITTLE SISTER (I NEED U NOW)** *Incentive CENT 60CDS* ... 21 9

LOST IT.COM *UK, male vocal / production duo*

7 Apr 01 **ANIMAL** *Perfecto PERF 13CDS* ... 70 1

LOST TRIBE
(see also MDM; MELT featuring LITTLE MS MARCIE; SUNBURST)
UK, male production duo – Matt Darey and Red Jerry (2 Singles: 4 Weeks)

11 Sep 99 **GAMEMASTER** *Hooj Choons HOOJ 81CD* ... 24 3
6 Dec 03 **GAMEMASTER (re-mix)** *Liquid Asset ASSETCD 12015* ... 61 1

LOST WITNESS
UK, male production duo and female vocalist (4 Singles: 13 Weeks)

29 May 99 **HAPPINESS HAPPENING** *Ministry of Sound MOSCDS 129* ... 18 4
18 Sep 99 **RED SUN RISING** *Ministry of Sound MOSCDS 133* ... 22 3
16 Dec 00 **7 COLOURS** *Data DATA 15CDS* ... 28 3
18 May 02 **DID I DREAM (SONG TO THE SIREN)** *Ministry of Sound / Data DATA 28CDS* ... 28 3

LOSTPROPHETS *UK, male vocal (Ian Watkins) / instrumental group (2 Albums: 36 Weeks, 7 Singles: 26 Weeks)*

8 Dec 01 **SHINOBI VS DRAGON NINJA** *Visible Noise TORMENT 16* ... 41 2
2 Mar 02 THEFAKESOUNDOFPROGRESS *Visible Noise TORMENT 10CD* ... 44 8
23 Mar 02 **THE FAKE SOUND OF PROGRESS** *Visible Noise TORMENT 19* ... 21 3
15 Nov 03 **BURN BURN** *Visible Noise TORMENT 29CD* ... 17 3
7 Feb 04 ● **LAST TRAIN HOME** *Visible Noise TORMENT 36CD* ... 8 7
14 Feb 04 ● START SOMETHING *Visible Noise TORMENT 32* ... 4 28
15 May 04 **WAKE UP (MAKE A MOVE)** *Visible Noise TORMENT 40CD* ... 18 4
4 Sep 04 **LAST SUMMER** *Visible Noise TORMENT 43CD* ... 13 5
4 Dec 04 **GOODBYE TONIGHT** *Visible Noise TORMENT 47CD* ... 42 2

The LOTUS EATERS *UK, male vocal / instrumental duo – Peter Coyle and Jerry Kelley (1 Album: 1 Week, 2 Singles: 16 Weeks)*

2 Jul 83 **FIRST PICTURE OF YOU** *Sylvan SYL 1* ... 15 12
8 Oct 83 **YOU DON'T NEED SOMEONE NEW** *Sylvan SYL 2* ... 53 4
16 Jun 84 NO SENSE OF SIN *Sylvan 206 263* ... 96 1

Bonnie LOU *US, female vocalist – Bonnie Lou Kath*

5 Feb 54 ● **TENNESSEE WIG WALK** *Parlophone R 3730* ... 4 10

Lippy LOU *UK, female rapper*

22 Apr 95 **LIBERATION** *More Protein PROCD 105* ... 57 2

Louchie LOU and Michie ONE (see also Olav BASOSKI) *UK, female rap duo – Louise Gold and Michelle Charles (6 Singles: 36 Weeks)*

29 May 93 ● **SHOUT** *ffrr FCD 211* ... 7 8
14 Aug 93 **SOMEBODY ELSE'S GUY** *ffrr FCD 216* ... 54 2
26 Aug 95 **GET DOWN ON IT** *China WOKCD 2054* ... 58 1
13 Apr 96 ● **CECILIA** (2re) *WEA WEA 042CD1* [1] ... 4 19
15 Jun 96 **GOOD SWEET LOVIN'** *Indochina ID 050CD* ... 34 2
21 Sep 96 **NO MORE ALCOHOL** *WEA WEA 065CD1* [1] ... 24 4

[1] Suggs featuring Louchie Lou and Michie One

LOUD *UK, male vocal / instrumental group*

28 Mar 92 **EASY** *China WOK 2016* ... 67 2

John D LOUDERMILK *US, male vocalist*

4 Jan 62 **THE LANGUAGE OF LOVE** *RCA 1269* ... 13 10

Louie LOUIE *US, male vocalist – Louie Cordero*

19 Dec 92 **THE THOUGHT OF IT** *Hardback YZ 724* ... 34 5

LOUIS XIV NEW *US, male vocal / instrumental group (2 Singles: 2 Weeks)*

30 Jul 05 **GOD KILLED THE QUEEN** *Atlantic AT 0211CD* ... 68 1
22 Oct 05 **FINDING OUT TRUE LOVE IS BLIND** *Atlantic AT 0214CD* ... 57 1

LOUISE (see also ETERNAL) *UK, female vocalist – Louise Redknapp (4 Albums: 59 Weeks, 12 Singles: 83 Weeks)*

7 Oct 95 ● **LIGHT OF MY LIFE** *EMI CDEMS 397* ... 8 8
16 Mar 96 **IN WALKED LOVE** *EMI CDEMS 413* ... 17 6
8 Jun 96 ● **NAKED** *EMI CDEM 431* ... 5 8
6 Jul 96 ● NAKED *EMI CDEMC 3748* ... 7 31
31 Aug 96 ● **UNDIVIDED LOVE** *EMI CDEM 441* ... 5 6
30 Nov 96 ● **ONE KISS FROM HEAVEN** *EMI CDEM 454* ... 9 7
4 Oct 97 ● **ARMS AROUND THE WORLD** *EMI CDEM 490* ... 4 7
18 Oct 97 ● WOMAN IN ME *EMI 8219032* ... 5 19
29 Nov 97 ● **LET'S GO ROUND AGAIN** *EMI CDEM 500* ... 10 9
4 Apr 98 **ALL THAT MATTERS** (re) *1st Avenue CDEM 506* ... 11 6
29 Jul 00 ● **2 FACED** *1st Avenue / EMI CDEMS 570* ... 3 8
12 Aug 00 ELBOW BEACH *EMI 5276142* ... 12 4
11 Nov 00 **BEAUTIFUL INSIDE** *1st Avenue / EMI CDEMS 575* ... 13 4
8 Sep 01 ● **STUCK IN THE MIDDLE WITH YOU** *1st Avenue / EMI CDEM 600* ... 4 9
22 Sep 01 ● CHANGING FACES – THE BEST OF LOUISE *EMI 5349672* ... 9 5
27 Sep 03 ● **PANDORA'S KISS / DON'T GIVE UP** *Positive POSCDS 001* ... 5 5

'Don't Give Up' joined 'Pandora's Kiss' on the chart from 4 Oct 2003.

Jacques LOUSSIER *France, male pianist*

30 Mar 85 THE BEST OF PLAY BACH *Start STL 1* ... 58 3

LOVE *US, male vocal / instrumental group (2 Albums: 9 Weeks)*

24 Feb 68 FOREVER CHANGES *Elektra EKS 74013* ... 24 7
16 May 70 OUT HERE *Harvest Show 3/4* ... 29 2

Courtney LOVE *US, female vocalist / guitarist – Love Michelle Harrison*

21 Feb 04 AMERICA'S SWEETHEART *Virgin CDVUS 249* ... 56 1
27 Mar 04 **MONO** *Virgin VUSDX 283* ... 41 2

Darlene LOVE (see also The CRYSTALS)
US, female vocalist – Darlene Wright

19 Dec 92 **ALL ALONE ON CHRISTMAS** (re) *Arista 74321124767* ... 31 5

Re-entry made No.72 in Jan 1994.

Geoff LOVE
(see also Laurie LONDON; MANUEL and The MUSIC OF THE MOUNTAINS)
UK, male orchestra leader, b. 4 Sep 1917, d. 8 Jul 1991 (3 Albums: 28 Weeks)

7 Aug 71 BIG WAR MOVIE THEMES *MFP 5171* ... 11 20

	21 August 1976	28 August 1976	4 September 1976	11 September 1976
UK No.1 SINGLES	DON'T GO BREAKING MY HEART Elton John and Kiki Dee	DON'T GO BREAKING MY HEART Elton John and Kiki Dee	DANCING QUEEN Abba	DANCING QUEEN Abba
UK No.1 ALBUMS	20 GOLDEN GREATS The Beach Boys	20 GOLDEN GREATS The Beach Boys	20 GOLDEN GREATS The Beach Boys	20 GOLDEN GREATS The Beach Boys

21 Aug 71 BIG WESTERN MOVIE THEMES *MFP 5204*......38 3
30 Oct 71 BIG LOVE MOVIE THEMES *MFP 5221*......28 5

Helen LOVE
UK, male / female vocal / instrumental group (2 Singles: 2 Weeks)

20 Sep 97 **DOES YOUR HEART GO BOOM** *Che CHE 72CD*......**71** 1
19 Sep 98 **LONG LIVE THE UK MUSIC SCENE** *Che CHE 82CD*......**65** 1

Monie LOVE *UK, female rapper – Simone Johnson (1 Album: 3 Weeks, 11 Singles: 51 Weeks)*

4 Feb 89 **I CAN DO THIS** *Cooltempo COOL 177*......**37** 4
24 Jun 89 **GRANDPA'S PARTY** *Cooltempo COOL 184*......**16** 9
14 Jul 90 **MONIE IN THE MIDDLE** *Cooltempo COOL 210*......**46** 3
22 Sep 90 **IT'S A SHAME (MY SISTER)** *Cooltempo COOL 219* [1] 12 8
20 Oct 90 DOWN TO EARTH *Cooltempo CTLP 14*......30 3
1 Dec 90 **DOWN TO EARTH** *Cooltempo COOL 222*......31 6
6 Apr 91 **RING MY BELL** *Cooltempo COOL 224* [2] 20 5
25 Jul 92 **FULL TERM LOVE** *Cooltempo COOL 258*......34 4
13 Mar 93 **BORN 2 B.R.E.E.D.** *Cooltempo CDCOOL 269*......18 5
12 Jun 93 **IN A WORD OR 2 / THE POWER** *Cooltempo CDCOOL 273*......33 3
21 Aug 93 **NEVER GIVE UP** *Cooltempo CDCOOL 276*......41 2
22 Apr 00 **SLICE OF DA PIE** *Relentless RELENT 2CDS*......29 2

[1] Monie Love featuring True Image [2] Monie Love vs Adeva

LOVE AFFAIR
UK, male vocal (Steve Ellis) / instrumental group (5 Singles: 56 Weeks)

3 Jan 68 ★ **EVERLASTING LOVE** *CBS 3125*......1 12
17 Apr 68 ● **RAINBOW VALLEY** *CBS 3366*......5 13
11 Sep 68 ● **A DAY WITHOUT LOVE** *CBS 3674*......6 12
19 Feb 69 **ONE ROAD** *CBS 3994*......16 9
16 Jul 69 ● **BRINGING ON BACK THE GOOD TIMES** *CBS 4300*......9 10

LOVE AND MONEY *UK, male vocal / instrumental group (2 Albums: 2 Weeks, 6 Singles: 23 Weeks)*

24 May 86 **CANDYBAR EXPRESS** *Mercury MONEY 1*......**56** 4
25 Apr 87 **LOVE AND MONEY** *Mercury MONEY 4*......**68** 4
17 Sep 88 **HALLELUIAH MAN** *Fontana MONEY 5*......63 4
29 Oct 88 STRANGE KIND OF LOVE *Fontana SFLP 7*......71 1
14 Jan 89 **STRANGE KIND OF LOVE** *Fontana MONEY 6*......45 5
25 Mar 89 **JOCELYN SQUARE** *Fontana MONEY 7*......51 4
3 Aug 91 DOGS IN THE TRAFFIC *Fontana 8489931*......41 1
16 Nov 91 **WINTER** *Fontana MONEY 9*......52 2

LOVE BITE *Italy, male / female production / vocal group*

7 Oct 00 **TAKE YOUR TIME** *AM:PM CDAMPM 134*......**56** 1

LOVE BITES NEW *UK, female vocal / instrumental group*

29 Oct 05 **YOU BROKE MY HEART** *Island MCSXD 40427*......13 3

LOVE CITY GROOVE *UK, male / female vocal / rap / instrumental group*

8 Apr 95 ● **LOVE CITY GROOVE** *Planet 3 GXY 2003CD*......7 11

LOVE CONNECTION
Italy / Germany, male / female vocal / production group

2 Dec 00 **THE BOMB** *Multiply CDMULTY 63*......53 1

LOVE DECADE
UK, male / female vocal / instrumental group (5 Singles: 14 Weeks)

6 Jul 91 **DREAM ON (IS THIS A DREAM)** *All Around the World GLOBE 100*......52 2
23 Nov 91 **SO REAL** *All Around the World GLOBE 106*......14 7
11 Apr 92 **I FEEL YOU** *All Around the World GLOBE 107*......34 3
6 Feb 93 **WHEN THE MORNING COMES** *All Around the World CDGLOBE 114*......69 1
17 Feb 96 **IS THIS A DREAM** (re-recording) *All Around the World CDGLOBE 132*......39 1

LOVE DECREE *UK, male vocal / instrumental group*

16 Sep 89 **SOMETHING SO REAL (CHINHEADS THEME)** *Ariola 112642*......**61** 4

LOVE / HATE
US, male vocal / instrumental group (2 Albums: 5 Weeks, 2 Singles: 4 Weeks)

30 Nov 91 **EVIL TWIN** *Columbia 6575967*......**59** 1
7 Mar 92 WASTED IN AMERICA *Columbia 4694532*......20 4
4 Apr 92 **WASTED IN AMERICA** *Columbia 6578897*......38 3
24 Jul 93 LET'S RUMBLE *RCA 74321153112*......24 1

LOVE INC. *Jamaica / Canada, male / female production / vocal duo – Chris Sheppard and Simone Denny (3 Singles: 22 Weeks)*

28 Dec 02 ● **YOU'RE A SUPERSTAR** *Nulife / Arista 74321973842*......7 13
31 May 03 ● **BROKEN BONES** *Nulife / Arista 82876523172*......8 7
6 Mar 04 **INTO THE NIGHT** *Nulife 82876585782*......39 2

LOVE INCORPORATED featuring MC NOISE
UK, male vocal / production duo

9 Feb 91 **LOVE IS THE MESSAGE** *Love EVOL 1*......**59** 3

LOVE SCULPTURE
(see also Dave EDMUNDS) *UK, male vocal / instrumental group*

27 Nov 68 ● **SABRE DANCE** *Parlophone R 5744*......**5** 14

A LOVE SUPREME *UK, male vocal / instrumental group*

17 Apr 99 **NIALL QUINN'S DISCO PANTS** *A Love Supreme / Cherry Red CDVINNIE 3*......**59** 2

[LOVE] TATTOO *Australia, male producer – Stephen Allkins*

6 Oct 01 **DROP SOME DRUMS** *Positiva CDTIV 162*......**58** 1

LOVE TO INFINITY (see also SODA CLUB) *UK, male production duo – Andy and Pete Lee and female vocalist – Louise Bailey (3 Singles: 4 Weeks)*

24 Jun 95 **KEEP LOVE TOGETHER** *Mushroom D 00467*......38 2
18 Nov 95 **SOMEDAY** *Mushroom D 1143*......**75** 1
3 Aug 96 **PRAY FOR LOVE** *Mushroom D 1213*......**69** 1

LOVE TRIBE *US, male / female vocal / instrumental duo – Tanya Walters and Dewey Bullock*

29 Jun 96 **STAND UP** *AM:PM 5816272*......23 3

LOVE UNLIMITED *US, female vocal group (2 Singles: 19 Weeks)*

17 Jun 72 **WALKIN' IN THE RAIN WITH THE ONE I LOVE** *Uni UN 539* $..**14** 10
25 Jan 75 **IT MAY BE WINTER OUTSIDE (BUT IN MY HEART IT'S SPRING)** *20th Century BTC 2149*......**11** 9

LOVE UNLIMITED ORCHESTRA *US, orchestra – leader Barry White*

2 Feb 74 ● **LOVE'S THEME** *Pye International 7N 25635* ▲ $......**10** 10

LOVEBUG *UK, male / female production / vocal trio*

18 Oct 03 **WHO'S THE DADDY** *Sony Music 6742702*......35 2

LOVEBUG STARSKI *US, male rapper – Kevin Smith*

31 May 86 **AMITYVILLE (THE HOUSE ON THE HILL)** *Epic A 7182*......12 9

The LOVEFREEKZ NEW (see also LOVELAND featuring the voice of Rachel McFARLANE; LUCID) *UK, male producer – Mark Hadfield*

5 Feb 05 ● **SHINE** *Positiva CDTIVS 214*......6 6

LOVEHAPPY
US / UK, male / female vocal / instrumental group (2 Singles: 3 Weeks)

18 Feb 95 **MESSAGE OF LOVE** *MCA MCSTD 2040*......37 2
20 Jul 96 **MESSAGE OF LOVE** (re-mix) *MCA MCSTD 40052*......**70** 1

18 September 1976	25 September 1976	2 October 1976	9 October 1976
DANCING QUEEN Abba	DANCING QUEEN Abba	DANCING QUEEN Abba	DANCING QUEEN Abba
20 GOLDEN GREATS The Beach Boys	20 GOLDEN GREATS The Beach Boys	BEST OF THE STYLISTICS VOLUME 2 The Stylistics	STUPIDITY Dr Feelgood

KEY UK No.1 ★ UK Top 10 ● Still on chart + UK entry at No.1 ■ US No.1 ▲ UK million seller £ US million seller $
Singles re-entries are listed as (re), (2re), (3re)... which signifies that the hit re-entered the chart once, twice or three times...

Peak Position / Weeks

Bill LOVELADY *UK, male vocalist*

18 Aug 79 REGGAE FOR IT NOW *Charisma CB 337* 12 10

LOVELAND featuring the voice of Rachel McFARLANE (see also The LOVEFREEKZ) *UK, male / female vocal / instrumental group (7 Singles: 17 Weeks)*

16 Apr 94 LET THE MUSIC (LIFT YOU UP) *KMS / Eastern Bloc KMSCD 10* 16 4
5 Nov 94 (KEEP ON) SHINING / HOPE (NEVER GIVE UP) *Eastern Bloc BLOCCD 016* 37 2
14 Jan 95 I NEED SOMEBODY *Eastern Bloc BLOCCD 019* 21 3
10 Jun 95 DON'T MAKE ME WAIT *Eastern Bloc BLOC 20CD* 22 3
2 Sep 95 THE WONDER OF LOVE *Eastern Bloc BLOC 22CD* 53 1
11 Nov 95 I NEED SOMEBODY (re-mix) *Eastern Bloc BLOC 23CD* 38 2
1 Aug 98 LOVER *Multiply CDMULTY 37* [1] 38 2

[1] Rachel McFarlane

All formats of 'Let the Music (Lift You Up)' feature versions by Loveland featuring Rachel McFarlane and also by Darlene Lewis.

The LOVER SPEAKS *UK, male vocal / instrumental duo*

16 Aug 86 NO MORE "I LOVE YOU'S" *A&M AM 326* 58 5

Michael LOVESMITH *US, male vocalist*

5 Oct 85 AIN'T NOTHIN' LIKE IT *Motown ZB 40369* 75 1

LOVESTATION *UK, male / female vocal / instrumental group (6 Singles: 21 Weeks)*

13 Mar 93 SHINE ON ME *RCA 743211337912* [1] 71 1
13 Nov 93 BEST OF MY LOVE *Fresh FRSHD 1* 73 1
18 Mar 95 LOVE COME RESCUE ME *Fresh FRSHD 22* 42 2
1 Aug 98 TEARDROPS *Fresh FRSHD 65* 14 6
5 Dec 98 SENSUALITY *Fresh FRSHD 71* 16 7
5 Feb 00 TEARDROPS (re-mix) *Fresh FRSHD 79* 24 4

[1] Lovestation featuring Lisa Hunt

Lyle LOVETT *US, male vocalist (2 Albums: 2 Weeks)*

8 Oct 94 I LOVE EVERYBODY *MCA MCD 10808* 54 1
29 Jun 96 THE ROAD TO ENSENADA *MCA MCD 11409* 62 1

Lene LOVICH *US, female vocalist – Lili Premilovich (2 Albums: 17 Weeks, 6 Singles: 38 Weeks)*

17 Feb 79 ● LUCKY NUMBER *Stiff BUY 42* 3 11
17 Mar 79 STATELESS *Stiff SEEZ 7* 35 11
12 May 79 SAY WHEN *Stiff BUY 46* 19 10
20 Oct 79 BIRD SONG *Stiff BUY 53* 39 7
2 Feb 80 FLEX *Stiff SEEZ 19* 19 6
29 Mar 80 WHAT WILL I DO WITHOUT YOU *Stiff BUY 69* 58 3
14 Mar 81 NEW TOY *Stiff BUY 97* 53 5
27 Nov 82 IT'S YOU ONLY YOU (MEIN SCHMERZ) *Stiff BUY 164* 68 2

The LOVIN' SPOONFUL *US / Canada, male vocal (John Sebastian) / instrumental group (1 Album: 11 Weeks, 4 Singles: 33 Weeks)*

14 Apr 66 ● DAYDREAM *Pye International 7N 25361* $ 2 13
7 May 66 ● DAYDREAM *Pye NPL 28078* 8 11
14 Jul 66 ● SUMMER IN THE CITY *Kama Sutra KAS 200* ▲ $ 8 11
5 Jan 67 NASHVILLE CATS *Kama Sutra KAS 204* 26 7
9 Mar 67 DARLING BE HOME SOON *Kama Sutra KAS 207* 44 2

LOVINDEER *Jamaica, male vocalist*

27 Sep 86 MAN SHORTAGE *TSOJ TS 1* 69 3

LOW NEW *US, male / female vocal / instrumental group*

5 Feb 05 THE GREAT DESTROYER *Rough Trade RTRADSCD 206* 72 1
5 Mar 05 CALIFORNIA *Rough Trade RTRADSCD 221* 57 1

Gary LOW *Italy, male vocalist*

8 Oct 83 I WANT YOU *Savoir Faire FAIS 004* 52 3

Jim LOWE and The HIGH FIVES *US, male vocalist*

26 Oct 56 ● THE GREEN DOOR *London HLD 8317* $ 8 9

Nick LOWE (see also ROCKPILE) *UK, male vocalist (3 Albums: 17 Weeks, 4 Singles: 27 Weeks)*

11 Mar 78 THE JESUS OF COOL *Radar RAD 1* 22 9
11 Mar 78 ● I LOVE THE SOUND OF BREAKING GLASS *Radar ADA 1* 7 8
9 Jun 79 CRACKING UP *Radar ADA 34* 34 5
23 Jun 79 LABOUR OF LUST *Radar RAD 21* 43 6
25 Aug 79 CRUEL TO BE KIND *Radar ADA 43* 12 11
20 Feb 82 NICK THE KNIFE *F-Beat XXLP 14* 99 2
26 May 84 HALF A BOY AND HALF A MAN *F-Beat XX 34* 53 3

LOWGOLD *UK, male vocal / instrumental group (1 Album: 2 Weeks, 4 Singles: 4 Weeks)*

30 Sep 00 BEAUTY DIES YOUNG *Nude NUD 52CD* 67 1
10 Feb 01 MERCURY *Nude NUD 53CD* 48 1
24 Feb 01 JUST BACKWARD OF SQUARE *Nude NUDE 17CD* 33 2
12 May 01 COUNTERFEIT *Nude NUD 55CD* 52 1
8 Sep 01 BEAUTY DIES YOUNG (re-issue) (re-mix) *Nude NUD 59CD1* 40 1

LOWRELL *US, male vocalist – Lowrell Simon*

24 Nov 79 MELLOW MELLOW RIGHT ON *AVI AVIS 108* 37 9

LUCAS *Denmark, male vocalist – Lucas Secon*

6 Aug 94 LUCAS WITH THE LID OFF *WEA YZ 832CD* 37 4

Carrie LUCAS *US, female vocalist*

16 Jun 79 DANCE WITH YOU *Solar FB 1482* 40 6

LUCIANA *UK, female vocalist – Luciana Caporaso (3 Singles: 5 Weeks)*

23 Apr 94 GET IT UP FOR LOVE *Chrysalis CDCHS 5008* 55 2
6 Aug 94 IF YOU WANT *Chrysalis CDCHS 5009* 47 2
5 Nov 94 WHAT GOES AROUND / ONE MORE RIVER *Chrysalis CDCHS 5015* 67 1

LUCID (see also The LOVEFREEKZ) *UK, male / female vocal (Clare Canty) / instrumental group (3 Singles: 15 Weeks)*

8 Aug 98 ● I CAN'T HELP MYSELF *ffrr FCD 339* 7 8
27 Feb 99 CRAZY *ffrr / Delirious / Indirect FCD 355* 14 5
16 Oct 99 STAY WITH ME TILL DAWN *ffrr FCD 368* 25 2

LUCKY MONKEYS (see also FLUKE) *UK, male instrumental group*

9 Nov 96 BJANGO *Hi-Life 5757132* 50 1

LUCY PEARL *US, male / female vocal / rap / instrumental / production trio (3 Singles: 7 Weeks)*

29 Jul 00 DANCE TONIGHT *Virgin VSCDT 1775* 36 2
25 Nov 00 DON'T MESS WITH MY MAN *Virgin VSCDT 1778* 20 4
28 Jul 01 WITHOUT YOU *Virgin VSCDT 1805* 51 1

LUDACRIS *US, male rapper – Christopher Bridges (2 Albums: 6 Weeks, 16 Singles: 79 Weeks)*

9 Jun 01 WHAT'S YOUR FANTASY *Def Jam 5729842* 19 5

	16 October 1976	23 October 1976	30 October 1976	6 November 1976
UK No.1 SINGLES	MISSISSIPPI Pussycat	MISSISSIPPI Pussycat	MISSISSIPPI Pussycat	MISSISSIPPI Pussycat
UK No.1 ALBUMS	GREATEST HITS Abba	GREATEST HITS Abba	SOUL MOTION Various	SOUL MOTION Various

18 Aug 01 ●	**ONE MINUTE MAN** *Elektra E 7245CD* [1]	10	8
29 Sep 01	**AREA CODES** *Def Jam 5887722* [2]	25	3
22 Jun 02	**ROLLOUT (MY BUSINESS)** *Def Jam 5829632*	20	7
29 Jun 02	**WORD OF MOUF** *Def Jam 5864462*	57	2
5 Oct 02	**SATURDAY (OOOH OOOH)** *Def Jam 0639142*	31	2
9 Nov 02	**WHY DON'T WE FALL IN LOVE** *Columbia 6732212* [3]	40	2
22 Mar 03 ●	**GOSSIP FOLKS** *Elektra E 7389CD* [4]	9	9
18 Oct 03	**CHICKEN 'N' BEER** *Def Jam / Mercury 9861137* ▲	44	4
22 Nov 03	**STAND UP** *Def Jam / Mercury 9814001* [5] ▲	14	7
21 Feb 04	**HOLIDAE IN** *Capitol CDCL 852* [6]	35	3
27 Mar 04 ★	**YEAH!** *Arista 82876606002* [7] ■ ▲	1	14
14 May 05 ●	**GET LOW / LOVERS & FRIENDS** *TVT TVTUKCD 9* [8]	10	7
21 May 05	**NUMBER ONE SPOT** *Def Jam 9881665*	30	2
28 May 05	**SUGAR (GIMME SOME)** *Atlantic AT 0202CDX* [9]	61	1
13 Aug 05 ●	**OH** *LaFace 82876711372* [10]	4	9

[1] Missy 'Misdemeanor' Elliott featuring Ludacris [2] Ludacris featuring Nate Dogg [3] Amerie featuring Ludacris [4] Missy Elliott featuring Ludacris [5] Ludacris featuring Shawnna [6] Chingy featuring Ludacris & Snoop Dogg [7] Usher featuring Lil' Jon & Ludacris [8] Lil Jon & The East Side Boyz featuring Ying Yang Twins / featuring Usher and Ludacris [9] Trick Daddy featuring Ludacris, Lil' Kim & Cee-Lo [10] Ciara featuring Ludacris

LUDES *Canada, male vocal / instrumental group*

18 Dec 04	**RADIO** *Double Dragon DD 2018CD*	68	1

Baz LUHRMANN
Australia, male film producer / director – Bazmark Luhrmann

12 Jun 99 ★	**EVERYBODY'S FREE (TO WEAR SUNSCREEN) – THE SUNSCREEN SONG (CLASS OF '99)** *EMI CDBAZ 001* ■	1	16

Uncredited vocals by actor Lee Perry.

Robin LUKE *US, male vocalist*

17 Oct 58	**SUSIE DARLIN'** (2re) *London HLD 8676* $	23	6

LUKK featuring Felicia COLLINS
US, male / female vocal / instrumental group

28 Sep 85	**ON THE ONE** *Important TAN 6*	72	1

LULU (333 Top 500)
One of Scotland's best-known vocalists, b. Marie Lawrie, 3 Nov 1948, Strathclyde. She scored her first hit aged 15, had a US chart-topper ('To Sir with Love') aged 18, won the Eurovision Song Contest aged 20, and finally reached No.1 aged 44 (6 Albums: 22 Weeks, 27 Singles: 188 Weeks)

14 May 64 ●	**SHOUT** *Decca F 11884* [1]	7	13
12 Nov 64	**HERE COMES THE NIGHT** *Decca F 12017*	50	1
17 Jun 65 ●	**LEAVE A LITTLE LOVE** *Decca F 12169*	8	11
2 Sep 65	**TRY TO UNDERSTAND** *Decca F 12214*	25	8
13 Apr 67 ●	**THE BOAT THAT I ROW** *Columbia DB 8169*	6	11
29 Jun 67	**LET'S PRETEND** *Columbia DB 8221*	11	11
8 Nov 67	**LOVE LOVES TO LOVE LOVE** *Columbia DB 8295*	32	6
28 Feb 68 ●	**ME, THE PEACEFUL HEART** *Columbia DB 8358*	9	9
5 Jun 68	**BOY** *Columbia DB 8425*	15	7
6 Nov 68 ●	**I'M A TIGER** *Columbia DB 8500*	9	13
12 Mar 69 ●	**BOOM BANG-A-BANG** *Columbia DB 8550*	2	13
22 Nov 69	**OH ME OH MY (I'M A FOOL FOR YOU BABY)** *Atco 226008*	47	2
25 Sep 71	**THE MOST OF LULU** *MFP 5215*	15	6
26 Jan 74 ●	**THE MAN WHO SOLD THE WORLD** *Polydor 2001 490*	3	9
19 Apr 75	**TAKE YOUR MAMA FOR A RIDE** *Chelsea 2005 022*	37	4
12 Dec 81	**I COULD NEVER MISS YOU (MORE THAN I DO)** (re) *Alfa ALFA 1700*	62	5
19 Jul 86 ●	**SHOUT** (re-recording) *Jive LULU 1 / Decca SHOUT 1*	8	11
30 Jan 93	**INDEPENDENCE** *Dome CDDOME 1001*	11	5
6 Mar 93	**INDEPENDENCE** *Dome DOMECD 1*	67	1
3 Apr 93	**I'M BACK FOR MORE** *Dome CDDOME 1002* [2]	27	5
4 Sep 93	**LET ME WAKE UP IN YOUR ARMS** *Dome CDDOME 1005*	51	2
9 Oct 93 ★	**RELIGHT MY FIRE** *RCA 74321167722* [3] ■	1	14
27 Nov 93	**HOW 'BOUT US** *Dome CDDOME 1007*	46	3
27 Aug 94	**GOODBYE BABY AND AMEN** *Dome CDDOME 1011*	40	2
26 Nov 94	**EVERY WOMAN KNOWS** *Dome CDDOME 1013*	44	2
29 May 99	**HURT ME SO BAD** *Rocket / Mercury 5726132*	42	2
8 Jan 00	**BETTER GET READY** *Mercury 5625852*	59	1
18 Mar 00	**WHERE THE POOR BOYS DANCE** *Mercury 1568452*	24	5
1 Jun 02 ●	**TOGETHER** *Mercury 630212*	4	9
7 Dec 02 ●	**WE'VE GOT TONIGHT** *Polydor 0658612* [4]	4	13
22 Nov 03	**THE GREATEST HITS** *Mercury / Universal TV 9865879*	35	2
27 Mar 04	**BACK ON TRACK** *Mercury 9866136*	68	1
20 Aug 05	**A LITTLE SOUL IN YOUR HEART** *Globe Records 9872859*	29	3

[1] Lulu and The Luvvers [2] Lulu and Bobby Womack [3] Take That featuring Lulu [4] Ronan Keating featuring Lulu

The newly recorded 'Shout' entered the chart on 19 Jul 1986, and the next week the original Decca version by Lulu and The Luvvers also charted. For all subsequent weeks Gallup amalgamated both versions under one entry and we have added an extra week on chart for the 'double week' to take account of this.

Bob LUMAN *US, male vocalist, b. 15 Apr 1937, d. 27 Dec 1978 (1 Album: 1 Week, 3 Singles: 21 Weeks)*

8 Sep 60 ●	**LET'S THINK ABOUT LIVING** *Warner Bros. WB 18*	6	18
15 Dec 60	**WHY, WHY, BYE, BYE** *Warner Bros. WB 28*	46	1
14 Jan 61	**LET'S THINK ABOUT LIVING** *Warner Bros. WM 4025*	18	1
4 May 61	**THE GREAT SNOWMAN** *Warner Bros. WB 37*	49	2

LUMIDEE *US, female vocalist – Lumidee Cadino (1 Album: 3 Weeks, 2 Singles: 14 Weeks)*

9 Aug 03 ●	**NEVER LEAVE YOU – UH OOH, UH OOOH!** *Universal MCSTD 40328*	2	13
16 Aug 03	**ALMOST FAMOUS** *Universal 9860622*	73	3
29 Nov 03	**CRASHIN' A PARTY** *Universal MCSTD 40341* [1]	55	1

[1] Lumidee featuring NORE

LUNIZ *US, male rap duo – Jerrold 'Yukmouth' Ellis Jr and Garrick 'Knumbskull' Husbands (1 Album: 3 Weeks, 3 Singles: 18 Weeks)*

17 Feb 96 ●	**I GOT 5 ON IT** *Virgin America VUSCD 101* $	3	13
16 Mar 96	**OPERATION STACKOLA** *Virgin VUSMC 94*	41	3
11 May 96	**PLAYA HATA** *Virgin America VUSCD 103*	20	3
31 Oct 98	**I GOT 5 ON IT** (re-mix) *Virgin VCRD 41*	28	2

LUPINE HOWL *UK, male vocal / instrumental group*

22 Jan 00	**VAPORIZER** *Vinyl Hiss VHISSCD 001*	68	1

The LURKERS
UK, male vocal / instrumental group (1 Album: 1 Week, 5 Singles: 11 Weeks)

3 Jun 78	**AIN'T GOT A CLUE** *Beggars Banquet BEG 6*	45	3
1 Jul 78	**FULHAM FALLOUT** *Beggars Banquet BEGA 2*	57	1
5 Aug 78	**I DON'T NEED TO TELL HER** *Beggars Banquet BEG 9*	49	4
3 Feb 79	**JUST THIRTEEN** *Beggars Banquet BEG 14*	66	2
9 Jun 79	**OUT IN THE DARK / CYANIDE** *Beggars Banquet BEG 19*	72	1
17 Nov 79	**NEW GUITAR IN TOWN** *Beggars Banquet BEG 28*	72	1

LUSCIOUS JACKSON
US, female vocal / instrumental group (1 Album: 1 Week, 4 Singles: 5 Weeks)

18 Mar 95	**DEEP SHAG / CITYSONG** *Capitol CDCL 739*	69	1
21 Oct 95	**HERE** *Capitol CDCL 758*	59	1
12 Apr 97	**NAKED EYE** *Capitol CDCL 786*	25	2
26 Apr 97	**FEVER IN FEVER OUT** *Capitol CDEST 2290*	55	1
3 Jul 99	**LADYFINGERS** *Grand Royal / Parlophone CDCL 813*	43	1

LUSH *UK, female / male vocal (Miki Berenyi) / instrumental group (3 Albums: 10 Weeks, 9 Singles: 19 Weeks)*

10 Mar 90	**MAD LOVE (EP)** *4AD BAD 003*	55	1
27 Oct 90	**SWEETNESS AND LIGHT** *4AD BAD 0013*	47	2
19 Oct 91	**NOTHING NATURAL** *4AD AD 1016*	43	2

13 November 1976	20 November 1976	27 November 1976	4 December 1976
IF YOU LEAVE ME NOW Chicago	**IF YOU LEAVE ME NOW** Chicago	**IF YOU LEAVE ME NOW** Chicago	**UNDER THE MOON OF LOVE** Showaddywaddy
THE SONG REMAINS THE SAME Led Zeppelin	**22 GOLDEN GUITAR GREATS** Bert Weedon	**GLEN CAMPBELL'S TWENTY GOLDEN GREATS** Glen Campbell	**GLEN CAMPBELL'S TWENTY GOLDEN GREATS** Glen Campbell

KEY UK No.1 ★ UK Top 10 ● Still on chart + UK entry at No.1 ■ US No.1 ▲ UK million seller £ US million seller $
Singles re-entries are listed as (re), (2re), (3re)... which signifies that the hit re-entered the chart once, twice or three times...

Peak Position / Weeks

11 Jan 92 **FOR LOVE (EP)** *4AD BAD 2001* ... 35 2
8 Feb 92 ● **SPOOKY** *4AD CAD 2002CD* ... 7 3
11 Jun 94 **HYPOCRITE** *4AD BAD 4008CD* ... 52 2
11 Jun 94 **DESIRE LINES** *4AD BAD 4010CD* ... 60 1
25 Jun 94 **SPLIT** *4AD CAD 4011CD* ... 19 2
20 Jan 96 **SINGLE GIRL** *4AD BAD 6001CD* ... 21 3
9 Mar 96 **LADYKILLERS** *4AD BAD 6002CD* ... 22 3
30 Mar 96 ● **LOVELIFE** *4AD CAD 6004CD* ... 8 5
27 Jul 96 **500 (SHAKE BABY SHAKE)** *4AD BAD 6009CD* ... 21 3

Tracks on Mad Love (EP): De-Luxe / Leaves Me Cold / Downer / Thoughtforms. Tracks on For Love (EP): For Love / Starlust / Outdoor Miner / Astronaut.

LUSTRAL (see also ASCENSION; CHAKRA; OXYGEN featuring Andrea BRITTON; SPACE BROTHERS) *UK, male DJ / production duo – Ricky Simmons and Steve Jones (2 Singles: 3 Weeks)*

18 Oct 97 **EVERYTIME** *Hooj Choons HOOJCD 55* ... 60 1
4 Dec 99 **EVERYTIME** (re-mix) *Hooj Choons HOOJ 83CD* ... 30 2

LUZON *US, male producer – Stacy Burket*

14 Jul 01 **THE BAGUIO TRACK** *Renaissance RENCDS 006* ... 67 1

Annabella LWIN *Myanmar, female vocalist – Myant Myant Aye*

28 Jan 95 **DO WHAT YOU DO** *Sony S2 6611235* ... 61 1

John LYDON (see also PUBLIC IMAGE LTD (PIL); SEX PISTOLS) *UK, male vocalist (2 Singles: 6 Weeks)*

13 Nov 93 **OPEN UP** *Hard Hands HAND 009CD* [1] ... 13 5
2 Aug 97 **SUN** *Virgin VUSCD 122* ... 42 1

[1] Leftfield Lydon

Frankie LYMON and The TEENAGERS *US, male vocal group – leader b. 30 Sep 1942, d. 28 Feb 1968 (4 Singles: 38 Weeks)*

29 Jun 56 ★ **WHY DO FOOLS FALL IN LOVE** *Columbia DB 3772* [1] $ ... 1 16
29 Mar 57 **I'M NOT A JUVENILE DELINQUENT** *Columbia 33DB 3878* ... 12 7
12 Apr 57 ● **BABY, BABY** *Columbia DB 3878* ... 4 12
20 Sep 57 **GOODY GOODY** *Columbia DB 3983* ... 24 3

[1] The Teenagers featuring Frankie Lymon

Des LYNAM featuring WIMBLEDON CHORAL SOCIETY *UK, male vocalist / TV presenter and choir*

12 Dec 98 **IF – READ TO FAURE'S 'PAVANE'** *BBC Worldwide WMSS 60062* ... 45 3

Curtis LYNCH Jr featuring Kele LE ROC and RED RAT *UK, male producer and female vocalist and Jamaica, male vocalist*

30 Sep 00 **THINKING OF YOU** *Telstar CDSTAS 3136* ... 70 1

Kenny LYNCH *UK, male vocalist (8 Singles: 59 Weeks)*

30 Jun 60 **MOUNTAIN OF LOVE** *HMV POP 751* ... 33 3
13 Sep 62 **PUFF** (re) *HMV POP 1057* ... 33 6
6 Dec 62 ● **UP ON THE ROOF** *HMV POP 1090* ... 10 12
20 Jun 63 ● **YOU CAN NEVER STOP ME LOVING YOU** *HMV POP 1165* ... 10 14
16 Apr 64 **STAND BY ME** *HMV POP 1280* ... 39 7
27 Aug 64 **WHAT AM I TO YOU** (re) *HMV POP 1321* ... 37 6
17 Jun 65 **I'LL STAY BY YOU** *HMV POP 1430* ... 29 7
20 Aug 83 **HALF THE DAY'S GONE AND WE HAVEN'T EARNED A PENNY** *Satril SAT 510* ... 50 4

Liam LYNCH *US, male vocalist*

7 Dec 02 ● **UNITED STATES OF WHATEVER** *Global Warming WARMCD 17* ... 10 9

Cheryl LYNN *US, female vocalist*

8 Sep 84 **ENCORE** *Streetwave KHAN 23* ... 68 2

Patti LYNN *UK, female vocalist*

10 May 62 **JOHNNY ANGEL** *Fontana H 391* ... 37 5

Tami LYNN *US, female vocalist (2 Singles: 20 Weeks)*

22 May 71 ● **I'M GONNA RUN AWAY FROM YOU** *Mojo 2092 001* ... 4 14
3 May 75 **I'M GONNA RUN AWAY FROM YOU** (re-issue) *Contempo Raries CS 9026* ... 36 6

Vera LYNN *UK, female vocalist – Vera Welch (2 Albums: 15 Weeks, 9 Singles: 46 Weeks)*

14 Nov 52 ● **AUF WIEDERSEH'N SWEETHEART** *Decca F 9927* ▲ ... 10 1
14 Nov 52 ● **FORGET-ME-NOT** (re) *Decca F 9985* ... 5 6
14 Nov 52 ● **THE HOMING WALTZ** *Decca F 9959* ... 9 3
5 Jun 53 **THE WINDSOR WALTZ** *Decca F 10092* ... 11 1
15 Oct 54 ★ **MY SON, MY SON** *Decca F 10372* [1] ... 1 14
8 Jun 56 **WHO ARE WE** *Decca F 10715* ... 30 1
26 Oct 56 **A HOUSE WITH LOVE IN IT** *Decca F 10799* ... 17 13
15 Mar 57 **THE FAITHFUL HUSSAR (DON'T CRY MY LOVE)** *Decca F 10846* ... 29 2
21 Jun 57 **TRAVELLIN' HOME** *Decca F 10903* ... 20 5
21 Nov 81 **20 FAMILY FAVOURITES** *EMI EMTV 28* ... 25 12
9 Sep 89 **WE'LL MEET AGAIN** *Telstar STAR 2369* ... 44 3

[1] Vera Lynn with Frank Weir, his Saxophone, his Orchestra and Chorus

Jeff LYNNE (see also ELECTRIC LIGHT ORCHESTRA; TRAVELING WILBURYS) *UK, male vocalist*

30 Jun 90 **EVERY LITTLE THING** *Reprise W 9799* ... 59 4
4 Aug 90 **ARMCHAIR THEATRE** *Reprise WX 347* ... 24 4

Shelby LYNNE *US, female vocalist*

29 Apr 00 **LEAVIN'** *Mercury 5627372* ... 73 1

Philip LYNOTT (see also THIN LIZZY; Midge URE) *Ireland, male vocalist / guitarist, b. 20 Aug 1949, d. 4 Jan 1986 (2 Albums: 16 Weeks, 5 Singles: 36 Weeks)*

5 Apr 80 **DEAR MISS LONELY HEARTS** *Vertigo SOLO 1* ... 32 6
26 Apr 80 **SOLO IN SOHO** *Vertigo 9102 038* ... 28 6
21 Jun 80 **KING'S CALL** *Vertigo SOLO 2* ... 35 6
21 Mar 81 **YELLOW PEARL** (re) *Vertigo SOLO 3* ... 14 12
18 May 85 ● **OUT IN THE FIELDS** *10 TEN 49* [1] ... 5 10
24 Jan 87 **KING'S CALL** (re-mix) *Vertigo LYN 1* ... 68 2
14 Nov 87 **SOLDIER OF FORTUNE – THE BEST OF PHIL LYNOTT AND THIN LIZZY** *Telstar STAR 2300* [1] ... 55 10

[1] Gary Moore and Phil Lynott [1] Phil Lynott and Thin Lizzy

'Yellow Pearl' made its peak position on re-entry in Dec 1981.

LYNYRD SKYNYRD *US, male vocal / instrumental group (7 Albums: 21 Weeks, 1 Single: 21 Weeks)*

3 May 75 **NUTHIN' FANCY** *MCA MCF 2700* ... 43 1
28 Feb 76 **GIMME BACK MY BULLETS** *MCA MCF 2744* ... 34 5
11 Sep 76 **SWEET HOME ALABAMA / DOUBLE TROUBLE** (2re) *MCA 251* ... 21 21
6 Nov 76 **ONE MORE FROM THE ROAD** *MCA MCPS 279* ... 17 4
12 Nov 77 **STREET SURVIVORS** *MCA MCG 3525* ... 13 4
4 Nov 78 **SKYNYRD'S FIRST AND LAST** *MCA MCG 3529* ... 50 1

11 December 1976	18 December 1976	25 December 1976	1 January 1977
UK No.1 SINGLES			
UNDER THE MOON OF LOVE Showaddywaddy	UNDER THE MOON OF LOVE Showaddywaddy	WHEN A CHILD IS BORN (SOLEADO) Johnny Mathis	WHEN A CHILD IS BORN (SOLEADO) Johnny Mathis
UK No.1 ALBUMS			
GLEN CAMPBELL'S TWENTY GOLDEN GREATS Glen Campbell	GLEN CAMPBELL'S TWENTY GOLDEN GREATS Glen Campbell	GLEN CAMPBELL'S TWENTY GOLDEN GREATS Glen Campbell	GLEN CAMPBELL'S TWENTY GOLDEN GREATS Glen Campbell

9 Feb 80 THE VERY BEST OF LYNYRD SKYNYRD – GOLD & PLATINUM *MCA MCSP 308*......49 4
18 Jun 05 GREATEST HITS *UMTV 9830565*......47 2

'Sweet Home Alabama' / 'Double Trouble' was alternatively listed as the 'Freebird EP' for the two re-entries, which peaked at No.43 in Dec 1979 and No.21 in Jun 1982. The tracks peaked at No.31 in Sep 1976.

Barbara LYON
US, female vocalist, b. 9 Sep 1931, d. 10 Jul 1985 (2 Singles: 12 Weeks)

24 Jun 55 **STOWAWAY** *Columbia DB 3619*......12 8
21 Dec 56 **LETTER TO A SOLDIER** *Columbia DB 3865*......27 4

LYTE FUNKIE ONES
US, male vocal / rap group (1 Album: 1 Week, 4 Singles: 20 Weeks)

22 May 99 **CAN'T HAVE YOU** *Logic 74321649152*......54 1
18 Sep 99 **SUMMER GIRLS** *Logic 74321701152*......16 7
5 Feb 00 ● **GIRL ON TV** *Logic 74321717582*......6 9
26 Feb 00 LYTE FUNKIE ONES *Logic 74321706832*......62 1
27 Apr 02 **EVERY OTHER TIME** *Logic 74321925502*......24 3

Humphrey LYTTELTON BAND *UK, male jazz band*

13 Jul 56 **BAD PENNY BLUES** *Parlophone R 4184*......19 6

Kevin LYTTLE
St Vincent, male vocalist - Lescott Coombs (2 Singles: 23 Weeks)

25 Oct 03 ● **TURN ME ON** *Atlantic AT 0167CD*......2 19
29 May 04 **LAST DROP** *Atlantic AT 0176CD*......22 4

m

M
UK, male vocalist / multi-instrumentalist – Robin Scott (5 Singles: 39 Weeks)

7 Apr 79 ● **POP MUZIK** *MCA 413* ▲ $......2 14
8 Dec 79 **MOONLIGHT AND MUZAK** *MCA 541*......33 9
15 Mar 80 **THAT'S THE WAY THE MONEY GOES** *MCA 570*......45 5
22 Nov 80 **OFFICIAL SECRETS** *MCA 650*......64 2
10 Jun 89 **POP MUZIK** (re-mix) *Freestyle FRS 1*......15 9

Bobby M featuring Jean CARN
US, male / female vocal / instrumental duo

29 Jan 83 **LET'S STAY TOGETHER** *Gordy TMG 1288*......53 3

M and O BAND
UK, male vocal / instrumental duo – Muff Murfin and Colin Owen

28 Feb 76 **LET'S DO THE LATIN HUSTLE** *Creole CR 120*......16 6

M&S presents GIRL NEXT DOOR
UK, male production duo and female vocalist – Natasha Bryce

7 Apr 01 ● **SALSOUL NUGGET (IF U WANNA)** *ffrr FCD 393*......6 13

M-BEAT *UK, male producer – Marlon Hart (4 Singles: 24 Weeks)*

18 Jun 94 **INCREDIBLE** *Renk RENK 42CD* [1]......39 3
10 Sep 94 ● **INCREDIBLE** (re-mix) *Renk CDRENK 44* [1]......8 9
17 Dec 94 **SWEET LOVE** *Renk CDRENK 49* [2]......18 7
1 Jun 96 **DO U KNOW WHERE YOU'RE COMING FROM** *Renk CDRENK 63* [3]......12 5

[1] M-Beat featuring General Levy [2] M-Beat featuring Nazlyn
[3] M-Beat featuring Jamiroquai

M-D-EMM (see also FANTASY UFO)
UK, male producer – Mark Ryder (2 Singles: 3 Weeks)

22 Feb 92 **GET DOWN** *Strictly Underground 7STUR 13*......55 2
30 May 92 **MOVE YOUR FEET** *Strictly Underground STUR 15*......67 1

MDM (see also LOST TRIBE; MELT featuring LITTLE MS MARCIE; SUNBURST) *UK, male producer – Matt Darey*

27 Oct 01 **MASH IT UP** *Nulife / Arista 74321870472*......66 1

M DUBS featuring LADY SAW
UK, male producer and Jamaica, female vocalist

16 Dec 00 **BUMP N GRIND (I AM FEELING HOT TONIGHT)** *Telstar CDSTAS 3129*......59 1

MFSB *US, orchestra (3 Singles: 18 Weeks)*

27 Apr 74 **TSOP (THE SOUND OF PHILADELPHIA)** *Philadelphia International PIR 2289* [1] ▲ $......22 9
26 Jul 75 **SEXY** *Philadelphia International PIR 3381*......37 5
31 Jan 81 **MYSTERIES OF THE WORLD** *Sound of Philadelphia PIR 9501*......41 4

[1] MFSB featuring The Three Degrees

M FACTOR (see also NU-BIRTH; NUSH; 187 LOCKDOWN) *UK, male DJ / production duo – Danny Harrison and Julian Jonah (2 Singles: 4 Weeks)*

6 Jul 02 **MOTHER** *Serious SERR 042CD*......18 3
26 Jul 03 **COME TOGETHER** *Credence CDCRED 037*......46 1

MK *US, male producer – Mark Kinchen (2 Singles: 3 Weeks)*

4 Feb 95 **ALWAYS** *Activ CDTV 3* [1]......69 1
27 May 95 **BURNING '95** *Activ CDTVR 6*......44 2

[1] MK featuring Alana

Alana appears on both hits, although she is credited only on the first.

M + M
(see also MARTHA and The MUFFINS) *Canada, male / female vocal duo*

28 Jul 84 **BLACK STATIONS WHITE STATIONS** *RCA 426*......46 4

M + M are Martha and a Muffin.

MN8
UK / Trinidad, male vocal group (1 Album: 4 Weeks, 7 Singles: 38 Weeks)

4 Feb 95 ● **I'VE GOT A LITTLE SOMETHING FOR YOU** *Columbia 6608802*....2 13
29 Apr 95 ● **IF YOU ONLY LET ME IN** *Columbia 6613252*......6 7
27 May 95 TO THE NEXT LEVEL *Columbia 4802802*......13 4
15 Jul 95 ● **HAPPY** *Columbia 6622192*......8 7
4 Nov 95 **BABY IT'S YOU** (re) *Columbia 6624522*......22 3
24 Feb 96 **PATHWAY TO THE MOON** *Columbia 6629212*......25 2
31 Aug 96 **TUFF ACT TO FOLLOW** *Columbia 6635345*......15 3
26 Oct 96 **DREAMING** *Columbia 6638302*......21 3

MNO *Belgium, male instrumental / production group*

28 Sep 91 **GOD OF ABRAHAM** *A&M AM 820*......66 2

M.O.P. *US, male rap duo – Jamal Grinnage and Eric Murry (1 Album: 3 Weeks, 4 Singles: 20 Weeks)*

12 May 01 ● **COLD AS ICE** *Epic 6711762*......4 10
18 Aug 01 ● **ANTE UP** (re) *Epic 6717882* [1]......7 8

8 January 1977	15 January 1977	22 January 1977	29 January 1977
WHEN A CHILD IS BORN (SOLEADO) Johnny Mathis	**DON'T GIVE UP ON US** David Soul	**DON'T GIVE UP ON US** David Soul	**DON'T GIVE UP ON US** David Soul
A DAY AT THE RACES Queen	**ARRIVAL** Abba	**RED RIVER VALLEY** Slim Whitman	**RED RIVER VALLEY** Slim Whitman

KEY UK No.1 ★ UK Top 10 ● Still on chart + UK entry at No.1 ■ US No.1 ▲ UK million seller £ US million seller $
Singles re-entries are listed as (re), (2re), (3re)... which signifies that the hit re-entered the chart once, twice or three times...
Peak Position / Weeks

25 Aug 01	WARRIORZ *Epic 4982779*	40	3
1 Dec 01	**STAND CLEAR** *Chrysalis CDEM 597* [2]	43	1
8 Jun 02	**STAND CLEAR** (re-mix) *Kaos KAOSCD 002* [2]	50	1

[1] MOP featuring Busta Rhymes [2] Adam F featuring MOP

M1 *UK, male producer – Michael Woods*

22 Feb 03	**HEAVEN SENT** *Inferno CDFERN 51*	72	1

M PEOPLE 109 Top 500
Club favourites turned pop soul sophisticates: Heather Small (v), Paul Heard, Mike Pickering (both k/prog) and Shovell (prc). In 1994 and 1995, this Manchester act was voted Best British Dance Act at the BRITs and won the 1994 Mercury Music Prize for Elegant Slumming. Small has had success as a solo artist (7 Albums: 283 Weeks, 20 Singles: 137 Weeks)

26 Oct 91	**HOW CAN I LOVE YOU MORE?** *Deconstruction PB 44855*	29	9
7 Mar 92	**COLOUR MY LIFE** *Deconstruction PB 45241*	35	4
18 Apr 92	**SOMEDAY** *Deconstruction PB 45369* [1]	38	3
10 Oct 92	**EXCITED** *Deconstruction 74321116337*	29	5
6 Feb 93 ●	**HOW CAN I LOVE YOU MORE?** (re-mix) *Deconstruction 74321130232*	8	8
6 Mar 93	NORTHERN SOUL *Deconstruction 74321117772*	53	2
26 Jun 93 ●	**ONE NIGHT IN HEAVEN** *Deconstruction 74321151852*	6	11
25 Sep 93 ●	**MOVING ON UP** *Deconstruction 74321166162*	2	11
16 Oct 93 ●	ELEGANT SLUMMING *Deconstruction 74321166782*	2	87
4 Dec 93 ●	**DON'T LOOK ANY FURTHER** *Deconstruction 74321177112*	9	10
12 Mar 94 ●	**RENAISSANCE** *Deconstruction 74321194132*	5	7
17 Sep 94	**ELEGANTLY AMERICAN: ONE NIGHT IN HEAVEN / MOVING ON UP (EP)** (re-mix) *Deconstruction 74321231882*	31	2
19 Nov 94 ●	**SIGHT FOR SORE EYES** *Deconstruction 74321245472*	6	9
26 Nov 94 ●	BIZARRE FRUIT / BIZARRE FRUIT II *Deconstruction 74321240812*	3	115
4 Feb 95 ●	**OPEN YOUR HEART** *Deconstruction 74321261532*	9	7
24 Jun 95 ●	**SEARCH FOR THE HERO** *Deconstruction 74321287962*	9	7
16 Sep 95	NORTHERN SOUL (re-issue) *RCA PD 75157*	26	3
14 Oct 95	**LOVE RENDEZVOUS** *Deconstruction 74321319282*	32	4
25 Nov 95	**ITCHYCOO PARK** *Deconstruction 74321330732*	11	8
4 Oct 97 ●	**JUST FOR YOU** *BMG 74321523002*	8	7
25 Oct 97 ●	FRESCO *M People 74321524902*	2	40
6 Dec 97	**FANTASY ISLAND** (re) *BMG 74321542932*	33	9
28 Mar 98 ●	**ANGEL STREET** *M People 74321564182*	8	6
7 Nov 98	**TESTIFY** *M People 74321621742*	12	6
14 Nov 98 ●	THE BEST OF M PEOPLE *M People 74321613872*	2	31
13 Feb 99	**DREAMING** *M People 74321645352*	13	4
5 Mar 05	ULTIMATE COLLECTION *Sony BMG 82876669192* [1]	17	5

[1] M People with Heather Small [1] M People featuring Heather Small

From 9 Dec 1995 Bizarre Fruit was listed with the re-mix album Bizarre Fruit II.

M3 *UK, male / female production / vocal trio*

30 Oct 99	**BAILAMOS** *Inferno CDFERN 21*	40	2

M2M
Norway, female vocal / instrumental duo – Marit Larsen and Marion Raven

1 Apr 00	**DON'T SAY YOU LOVE ME** *Atlantic AT 0081CD*	16	6

M.V.P. NEW *US, male production / rap / vocal group*

2 Jul 05 ●	**ROC YA BODY 'MIC CHECK 1,2'** *Positiva CDTIVS 219*	5	14

MXM *Italy, male / female vocal / instrumental group*

2 Jun 90	**NOTHING COMPARES 2 U** *London LON 267*	68	1

Timo MAAS
Germany, male DJ / producer (1 Album: 3 Weeks, 6 Singles: 11 Weeks)

1 Apr 00	**DER SCHIEBER** *48k / Perfecto SPECT 07CDS*	50	1
30 Sep 00	**UBIK** *Perfecto PERF 10CDS* [1]	33	2
23 Feb 02	**TO GET DOWN** *Perfecto PERF 30CDS*	14	4
16 Mar 02	LOUD *Perfecto PERFALB 08CD*	41	3
11 May 02	**SHIFTER** *Perfecto PERF 31CDS* [2]	38	2
5 Oct 02	**HELP ME** *Perfecto PERF 42CDS* [3]	65	1
11 Jun 05	**FIRST DAY** *A&E WEA 387CD2*	51	1

[1] Timo Mass featuring Martin Bettinghaus [2] Timo Maas featuring MC Chickaboo [3] Timo Maas featuring Kelis

Pete MAC Jr *US, male vocalist*

15 Oct 77	**THE WATER MARGIN** *BBC RESL 50*	37	4

This is the Japanese version of the song which shared chart credit with the English language version by Godiego.

MAC BAND featuring the McCAMPBELL BROTHERS
US, male vocal group (1 Album: 3 Weeks, 2 Singles: 17 Weeks)

18 Jun 88 ●	**ROSES ARE RED** *MCA MCA 1264*	8	13
20 Aug 88	THE MAC BAND *MCA MCC 6032*	61	3
10 Sep 88	**STALEMATE** *MCA MCA 1271*	40	4

'Stalemate' credits the McCampbell Brothers on the sleeve only, not on the label.

Keith MAC PROJECT *UK, male / female vocal / instrumental group*

25 Jun 94	**DE DAH DAH (SPICE OF LIFE)** *Public Demand PPDCD 3*	66	1

Steve MAC vs MOSQUITO featuring Steve SMITH NEW
UK, male producer, rapper and vocalist

22 Oct 05	**LOVIN' YOU MORE (THAT BIG TRACK)** *CR2 C2MOS 01CDS*	73	1

David McALMONT
(see also McALMONT & BUTLER) *UK, male vocalist (3 Singles: 5 Weeks)*

27 Apr 96	**HYMN** *Blanco Y Negro NEG 87CD* [1]	65	1
9 Aug 97	**LOOK AT YOURSELF** *Hut HUTCD 87*	40	2
22 Nov 97	**DIAMONDS ARE FOREVER** *East West EW 141CD* [2]	39	2

[1] Ultramarine featuring David McAlmont [2] David McAlmont / David Arnold

McALMONT & BUTLER (see also SUEDE; The TEARS)
UK, male vocal / instrumental duo – David McAlmont and Bernard Butler (2 Albums: 10 Weeks, 4 Singles: 17 Weeks)

27 May 95 ●	**YES** *Hut HUTCD 53*	8	8
4 Nov 95	**YOU DO** *Hut HUTCD 57*	17	4
9 Dec 95	THE SOUND OF MCALMONT AND BUTLER *Hut CDHUT 32*	33	8
10 Aug 02	**FALLING** *Chrysalis CDCHS 5141*	23	3
24 Aug 02	BRING IT BACK *Chrysalis 5399772*	18	2
9 Nov 02	**BRING IT BACK** *Chrysalis CDCHSS 5145*	36	2

Neil MacARTHUR
(see also The ZOMBIES) *UK, male vocalist – Colin Blunstone*

5 Feb 69	**SHE'S NOT THERE** *Deram DM 225*	34	5

David MacBETH *UK, male vocalist*

30 Oct 59	**MR BLUE** *Pye 7N 15231*	18	4

Nicko McBRAIN (see also IRON MAIDEN) *UK, male vocalist / drums*

13 Jul 91	**RHYTHM OF THE BEAST** *EMI NICK 01*	72	1

Frankie McBRIDE *Ireland, male vocalist*

9 Aug 67	**FIVE LITTLE FINGERS** *Emerald MD 1081*	19	15
17 Feb 68	FRANKIE MCBRIDE *Emerald SLD 28*	29	3

The MACC LADS *UK, male vocal / instrumental group*

7 Oct 89	FROM BEER TO ETERNITY *Hectic House HHLP 12*	72	1

	5 February 1977	12 February 1977	19 February 1977	26 February 1977
UK No.1 SINGLES	DON'T GIVE UP ON US David Soul	DON'T CRY FOR ME ARGENTINA Julie Covington	WHEN I NEED YOU Leo Sayer	WHEN I NEED YOU Leo Sayer
UK No.1 ALBUMS	RED RIVER VALLEY Slim Whitman	RED RIVER VALLEY Slim Whitman	20 GOLDEN GREATS The Shadows	20 GOLDEN GREATS The Shadows

Dan McCAFFERTY (see also NAZARETH) *UK, male vocalist*

13 Sep 75 **OUT OF TIME** *Mountain TOP 1* ... **41** 3

CW McCALL *US, male vocalist – William Fries*

14 Feb 76 ● **CONVOY** *MGM 2006 560* ▲ $ ... 2 10

David McCALLUM *UK, male actor / vocalist*

14 Apr 66 **COMMUNICATION** *Capitol CL 15439* ... 32 4

Linda McCARTNEY *US, female vocalist – Linda Eastman, b. 24 Sep 1942, d. 17 Apr 1998 (1 Album: 24 Weeks, 3 Singles: 7 Weeks)*

5 Jun 71 ★ RAM *Apple PAS 10003* [1] ■ ... 1 24
28 Aug 71 **BACK SEAT OF MY CAR** *Apple R 5914* [1] ... 39 5
21 Nov 98 **WIDE PRAIRIE** *Parlophone CDR 6510* ... **74** 1
6 Feb 99 **THE LIGHT COMES FROM WITHIN** *Parlophone CDR 6513* ... **56** 1

[1] Paul and Linda McCartney [1] Paul and Linda McCartney

Paul McCARTNEY (20 Top 500)

Pop's most successful singer / songwriter and the richest man in British music, b. James McCartney, 18 Jun 1942, Liverpool. His composition 'Yesterday' is the world's most recorded song and has had more than eight million plays on US radio alone. This ex-Beatle performed at both Live Aid and Live 8 (London), broke attendance records when his 50-date 2002 US tour grossed a record $100m and his 1999 internet show attracted at least 50 million hits. The winner of a record number of Ivor Novello awards, he was also awarded the only Rhodium record (from Guinness World Records) to honour outstanding sales and received a Lifetime Achievement Grammy (1990) and a knighthood (1997). He has reportedly amassed a personal fortune of £500m. Sir Paul is the only artist to have No.1s as a solo artist, part of a duo, trio, quartet, quintet and charity group. Total UK single sales over 10 million. Best-selling single: 'Mull of Kintyre' / 'Girls' School' 2,050,000 (31 Albums: 573 Weeks, 55 Singles: 417 Weeks)

2 May 70 ● McCARTNEY *Apple PCS 7102* ▲ ... 2 32
27 Feb 71 ● **ANOTHER DAY** *Apple R 5889* ... 2 12
5 Jun 71 ★ RAM *Apple PAS 10003* [1] ■ ... 1 24
28 Aug 71 **BACK SEAT OF MY CAR** *Apple R 5914* [1] ... 39 5
18 Dec 71 WILD LIFE *Apple PCS 7142* [2] ... 11 9
26 Feb 72 **GIVE IRELAND BACK TO THE IRISH** *Apple R 5936* [2] ... 16 8
27 May 72 ● **MARY HAD A LITTLE LAMB** *Apple R 5949* [2] ... 9 11
9 Dec 72 ● **HI, HI, HI / C MOON** *Apple R 5973* [2] ... 5 13
7 Apr 73 ● **MY LOVE** *Apple R 5985* [3] ▲ $ ... 9 11
19 May 73 ● RED ROSE SPEEDWAY *Apple PCTC 251* [3] ▲ ... 5 16
9 Jun 73 ● **LIVE AND LET DIE** (re) *Apple R 5987* [2] $ ... 9 14
3 Nov 73 **HELEN WHEELS** *Apple R 5993* [3] ... 12 12
15 Dec 73 ★ BAND ON THE RUN *Apple PAS 10007* [3] ▲ ... 1 124
2 Mar 74 ● **JET** *Apple R 5996* [3] ... 7 9
6 Jul 74 ● **BAND ON THE RUN** *Apple R 5997* [3] ▲ $ ... 3 11
9 Nov 74 **JUNIOR'S FARM** *Apple R 5999* [3] ... 16 10
31 May 75 ● **LISTEN TO WHAT THE MAN SAID** *Capitol R 6006* [2] ▲ $ ... 6 8
21 Jun 75 ★ VENUS AND MARS *Apple PCTC 254* [2] ▲ ... 1 29
18 Oct 75 **LETTING GO** *Capitol R 6008* [2] ... 41 3
17 Apr 76 ● WINGS AT THE SPEED OF SOUND *Apple PAS 10010* [2] ▲ ... 2 35
15 May 76 ● **SILLY LOVE SONGS** *Parlophone R 6014* [2] ▲ $ ... 2 11
7 Aug 76 ● **LET 'EM IN** *Parlophone R 6015* [2] $ ... 2 10
15 Jan 77 ● WINGS OVER AMERICA *Parlophone PAS 720* [2] ▲ ... 8 22
19 Feb 77 **MAYBE I'M AMAZED** *Parlophone R 6017* [2] ... 28 5
19 Nov 77 ★ **MULL OF KINTYRE / GIRLS' SCHOOL** *Capitol R 6018* [2] £ ... 1 17
1 Apr 78 ● **WITH A LITTLE LUCK** *Parlophone R 6019* [2] ▲ ... 5 9
15 Apr 78 ● LONDON TOWN *Parlophone PAS 10012* [2] ... 4 23
1 Jul 78 **I'VE HAD ENOUGH** *Parlophone R 6020* [2] ... 42 7
9 Sep 78 **LONDON TOWN** *Parlophone R 6021* [2] ... 60 4
16 Dec 78 ● WINGS GREATEST HITS *Parlophone PCTC 256* [2] ... 5 32
7 Apr 79 ● **GOODNIGHT TONIGHT** *Parlophone R 6023* [2] $ ... 5 10
16 Jun 79 **OLD SIAM SIR** *Parlophone R 6026* [2] ... 35 6
23 Jun 79 ● BACK TO THE EGG *Parlophone PCTC 257* [2] ... 6 15
1 Sep 79 **GETTING CLOSER / BABY'S REQUEST** *R 6027* [2] ... 60 3
1 Dec 79 ● **WONDERFUL CHRISTMASTIME** *Parlophone R 6029* ... 6 8
19 Apr 80 ● **COMING UP** *Parlophone R 6035* ▲ $ ... 2 9
31 May 80 ★ McCARTNEY II *Parlophone PCTC 258* ■ ... 1 18
21 Jun 80 ● **WATERFALLS** *Parlophone R 6037* ... 9 8
7 Mar 81 THE McCARTNEY INTERVIEW *EMI CHAT 1* ... 34 4
10 Apr 82 ★ **EBONY AND IVORY** *Parlophone R 6054* [4] ▲ $ ... 1 10
8 May 82 ★ TUG OF WAR *Parlophone PCTC 259* ■ ▲ ... 1 27
3 Jul 82 **TAKE IT AWAY** *Parlophone R 6056* ... **15** 10
9 Oct 82 **TUG OF WAR** *Parlophone R 6057* ... **53** 3
6 Nov 82 ● **THE GIRL IS MINE** (re) *Epic EPC A 2729* [5] $ ... **8** 10
15 Oct 83 ● **SAY SAY SAY** *Parlophone R 6062* [6] ▲ $ ... 2 15
12 Nov 83 ● PIPES OF PEACE *Parlophone PCTC 1652301* ... 4 23
17 Dec 83 ★ **PIPES OF PEACE** *Parlophone R 6064* ... 1 12
6 Oct 84 ● **NO MORE LONELY NIGHTS (BALLAD)** *Parlophone R 6080* ... 2 15
3 Nov 84 ★ GIVE MY REGARDS TO BROAD STREET *Parlophone PCTC 2* ■ ... 1 21
24 Nov 84 ● **WE ALL STAND TOGETHER** (re) *Parlophone R 6086* [7] ... 3 18
30 Nov 85 **SPIES LIKE US** *Parlophone R 6118* ... 13 10
26 Jul 86 **PRESS** *Parlophone R 6133* ... 25 8
13 Sep 86 ● PRESS TO PLAY *Parlophone PCSD 103* ... 8 6
13 Dec 86 **ONLY LOVE REMAINS** *Parlophone R 6148* ... 34 5
14 Nov 87 ● ALL THE BEST! *Parlophone PMTV 1* ... 2 21
28 Nov 87 ● **ONCE UPON A LONG AGO** *Parlophone R 6170* ... 10 7
20 May 89 ★ **FERRY 'CROSS THE MERSEY** *PWL PWL 41* [8] ■ ... 1 7
20 May 89 **MY BRAVE FACE** *Parlophone R 6213* ... 18 5
17 Jun 89 ★ FLOWERS IN THE DIRT *Parlophone PCSD 106* ... 1 20
29 Jul 89 **THIS ONE** *Parlophone R 6223* ... 18 6
25 Nov 89 **FIGURE OF EIGHT** *Parlophone R 6235* ... 42 3
17 Feb 90 **PUT IT THERE** *Parlophone R 6246* ... 32 2
20 Oct 90 **BIRTHDAY** *Parlophone R 6271* ... 29 3
17 Nov 90 TRIPPING THE LIVE FANTASTIC – HIGHLIGHTS! *Parlophone PCST 7346* ... 17 11
8 Dec 90 **ALL MY TRIALS** *Parlophone CDR 6278* ... 35 5
1 Jun 91 ● UNPLUGGED – THE OFFICIAL BOOTLEG *Parlophone PCSD 116* ... 7 3
12 Oct 91 CHOBA B CCCP (THE RUSSIAN ALBUM) *Parlophone CDPCSD 117* ... 63 1
9 Jan 93 **HOPE OF DELIVERANCE** *Parlophone CDR 6330* ... 18 6
13 Feb 93 ● OFF THE GROUND *Parlophone CDPCSD 125* ... 5 4
6 Mar 93 **C'MON PEOPLE** *Parlophone CDRS 6338* ... 41 3
20 Nov 93 PAUL IS LIVE *Parlophone PDPCSD 147* ... 34 2
10 May 97 **YOUNG BOY** *Parlophone CDRS 6462* ... 19 3
17 May 97 ● FLAMING PIE *Parlophone CDPCSD 171* ... 2 15
19 Jul 97 **THE WORLD TONIGHT** *Parlophone CDR 6472* ... 23 2
27 Dec 97 **BEAUTIFUL NIGHT** *Parlophone CDR 6489* ... 25 4
27 Mar 99 BAND ON THE RUN (re-issue) *Parlophone 4991762* [3] ... 69 1
16 Oct 99 RUN DEVIL RUN *Parlophone 5223512* ... 12 11
6 Nov 99 **NO OTHER BABY / BROWN EYED HANDSOME MAN** *Parlophone CDR 6527* ... 42 2
19 May 01 ● WINGSPAN – HITS AND HISTORY *Parlophone 5328502* ... 5 7
10 Nov 01 **FROM A LOVER TO A FRIEND** *Parlophone CDR 6567* ... 45 2
24 Nov 01 DRIVING RAIN *Parlophone 5355102* ... 46 1
29 Mar 03 ● BACK IN THE WORLD *Parlophone 5830052* ... 5 13
2 Oct 04 **TROPIC ISLAND HUM / WE ALL STAND TOGETHER** (re-issue) *Parlophone CDR 6649* ... 21 3
10 Sep 05 **FINE LINE** *Parlophone CDR 6673* ... 20 2
24 Sep 05 ● CHAOS AND CREATION IN THE BACKYARD *Parlophone 3379582* ... 10 3
3 Dec 05 **JENNY WREN** *Parlophone CDRS 6678* ... 22 2

[1] Paul and Linda McCartney [2] Wings [3] Paul McCartney and Wings [4] Paul McCartney with Stevie Wonder [5] Michael Jackson and Paul McCartney [6] Paul McCartney and Michael Jackson [7] Paul McCartney and the Frog Chorus [8] The Christians, Holly Johnson, Paul McCartney, Gerry Marsden and Stock Aitken Waterman [1] Paul and Linda McCartney [2] Wings [3] Paul McCartney and Wings

R 6027 (1 Sep 79) credits no label at all, although the number is a Parlophone one.

Kirsty MacCOLL *UK, female vocalist, b. 10 Oct 1959, d. 18 Dec 2000 (6 Albums: 65 Weeks, 13 Singles: 66 Weeks)*

13 Jun 81 **THERE'S A GUY WORKS DOWN THE CHIPSHOP SWEARS HE'S ELVIS** *Polydor POSP 250* ... **14** 9

5 March 1977	12 March 1977	19 March 1977	26 March 1977
WHEN I NEED YOU Leo Sayer	CHANSON D'AMOUR Manhattan Transfer	CHANSON D'AMOUR Manhattan Transfer	CHANSON D'AMOUR Manhattan Transfer
20 GOLDEN GREATS The Shadows	20 GOLDEN GREATS The Shadows	20 GOLDEN GREATS The Shadows	20 GOLDEN GREATS The Shadows

KEY
UK No.1 ★ UK Top 10 ● Still on chart + UK entry at No.1 ■ US No.1 ▲ UK million seller £ US million seller $
Singles re-entries are listed as (re), (2re), (3re)… which signifies that the hit re-entered the chart once, twice or three times…
Peak Position / Weeks

19 Jan 85 ● **A NEW ENGLAND** *Stiff BUY 216* 7 10
15 Nov 86 **GREETINGS TO THE NEW BRUNETTE** *Go Discs GOD 15* [1] 58 2
5 Dec 87 ● **FAIRYTALE OF NEW YORK** *Pogue Mahone NY 7* [2] 2 9
8 Apr 89 **FREE WORLD** *Virgin KMA 1* 43 6
20 May 89 KITE *Virgin KMLP 1* 34 12
1 Jul 89 **DAYS** *Virgin KMA 2* 12 9
25 May 91 **WALKING DOWN MADISON** *Virgin VS 1348* 23 7
6 Jul 91 ELECTRIC LANDLADY *Virgin V 2663* 17 8
17 Aug 91 **MY AFFAIR** *Virgin VS 1354* 56 2
14 Dec 91 **FAIRYTALE OF NEW YORK** (re-issue) *PM YZ 628* [2] 36 5
12 Mar 94 TITANIC DAYS *ZTT 4509947112* 46 2
4 Mar 95 **CAROLINE** *Virgin VSCDX 1517* 58 2
18 Mar 95 ● GALORE – THE BEST OF KIRSTY MACCOLL *Virgin CDV 2763* 6 27
24 Jun 95 **PERFECT DAY** *Virgin VSCDT 1552* [3] 75 1
29 Jul 95 **DAYS** (re-issue) *Virgin VSCDT 1558* 42 3
1 Apr 00 TROPICAL BRAINSTORM *V2 VVR 1009872* 39 9
13 Aug 05 THE BEST OF KIRSTY MACCOLL *Virgin CDV 3008* 12 7
31 Dec 05 ● **FAIRYTALE OF NEW YORK** (2nd re-issue) *Warner Bros. WEA 400CD* [2] .... 3 1+

[1] Billy Bragg with Johnny Marr and Kirsty MacColl [2] The Pogues featuring Kirsty MacColl [3] Kirsty MacColl and Evan Dando

Marilyn McCOO and Billy DAVIS Jr
(see also The 5TH DIMENSION) *US, female / male vocal duo*

19 Mar 77 ● **YOU DON'T HAVE TO BE A STAR (TO BE IN MY SHOW)** *ABC 4147* ▲ $ 7 9

Van McCOY *US, orchestra – leader b. 6 Jan 1940, d. 6 Jul 1979 (1 Album: 11 Weeks, 4 Singles: 36 Weeks)*

31 May 75 ● **THE HUSTLE** *Avco 6105 038* [1] ▲ $ 3 12
5 Jul 75 DISCO BABY *Avco 9109 004* [1] 32 11
1 Nov 75 **CHANGE WITH THE TIMES** *Avco 6105 042* 36 4
12 Feb 77 **SOUL CHA CHA** *H&L 6105 065* 34 6
9 Apr 77 ● **THE SHUFFLE** *H&L 6105 076* 4 14

[1] Van McCoy with the Soul City Symphony [1] Van McCoy and the Soul City Symphony

The McCOYS *US, male vocal (Rick Zehringer aka Rick Derringer) / instrumental group (2 Singles: 18 Weeks)*

2 Sep 65 ● **HANG ON SLOOPY** *Immediate IM 001* ▲ $ 5 14
16 Dec 65 **FEVER** *Immediate IM 021* 44 4

George McCRAE
US, male vocalist (2 Albums: 29 Weeks, 8 Singles: 62 Weeks)

29 Jun 74 ★ **ROCK YOUR BABY** *Jayboy BOY 85* ▲ $ 1 14
3 Aug 74 ROCK YOUR BABY *Jayboy JSL 3* 13 28
5 Oct 74 ● **I CAN'T LEAVE YOU ALONE** *Jayboy BOY 90* 9 9
14 Dec 74 **YOU CAN HAVE IT ALL** *Jayboy BOY 92* 23 9
22 Mar 75 **SING A HAPPY SONG** *Jayboy BOY 95* 38 4
19 Jul 75 ● **IT'S BEEN SO LONG** *Jayboy BOY 100* 4 11
13 Sep 75 GEORGE MCCRAE *Jayboy JSL 10* 54 1
18 Oct 75 **I AIN'T LYIN'** *Jayboy BOY 105* 12 7
24 Jan 76 **HONEY I** *Jayboy BOY 107* 33 4
25 Feb 84 **ONE STEP CLOSER (TO LOVE)** *President PT 522* 57 4

Gwen McCRAE *US, female vocalist – Gwen Mosley (2 Singles: 5 Weeks)*

30 Apr 88 **ALL THIS LOVE THAT I'M GIVING** *Flame MELT 7* 63 2
13 Feb 93 **ALL THIS LOVE I'M GIVING** (re-recording) *KTDA CDKTDA 2* [1] 36 3

[1] Music and Mystery featuring Gwen McCrae

The McCRARYS *US, male / female vocal group*

31 Jul 82 **LOVE ON A SUMMER NIGHT** *Capitol CL 251* 52 4

Mindy McCREADY *US, female vocalist*

1 Aug 98 **OH ROMEO** *BNA 74321597242* 41 3

Dave McCULLEN NEW
(see also LASGO) *Belgium, male producer – David Veervoort*

24 Dec 05 **B*TCH** *Nebula NEBCD 078* .... 54 2+

Ian McCULLOCH (see also ECHO and The BUNNYMEN)
UK, male vocalist (2 Albums: 4 Weeks, 5 Singles: 15 Weeks)

15 Dec 84 **SEPTEMBER SONG** *Korova KOW 40* 51 5
2 Sep 89 **PROUD TO FALL** *WEA YZ 417* 51 4
7 Oct 89 CANDLELAND *WEA WX 303* 18 3
12 May 90 **CANDLELAND (THE SECOND COMING)** *East West YZ 452* [1] 75 1
22 Feb 92 **LOVER LOVER LOVER** *East West YZ 643* 47 4
21 Mar 92 MYSTERIO *East West 9031762642* 46 1
26 Apr 03 **SLIDING** *Cooking Vinyl FRYCD 146* 61 1

[1] Ian McCulloch featuring Elizabeth Fraser

Martine McCUTCHEON *UK, female actor / vocalist – Martine Ponting (3 Albums: 36 Weeks, 6 Singles: 65 Weeks)*

18 Nov 95 **ARE YOU MAN ENOUGH** *Avex UK AVEXCD 14* [1] 62 1
17 Apr 99 ★ **PERFECT MOMENT** (re) *Innocent SINCD 7* ■ 1 20
11 Sep 99 ● **I'VE GOT YOU** *Innocent SINCD 12* 6 10
18 Sep 99 ● YOU ME & US *Innocent CDSIN 4* 2 20
4 Dec 99 ● **TALKING IN YOUR SLEEP / LOVE ME** *Innocent SINCD 14* 6 16
4 Nov 00 ● **I'M OVER YOU** *Innocent SINCD 20* 2 10
25 Nov 00 WISHING *Innocent CDSIN 7* 25 14
3 Feb 01 ● **ON THE RADIO** *Innocent SINCD 21* 7 8
14 Dec 02 MUSICALITY *EMI / Liberty 5805492* 55 2

[1] Uno Clio featuring Martine McCutcheon

Gene McDANIELS *US, male vocalist*

16 Nov 61 **TOWER OF STRENGTH** (re) *London HLG 9448* 49 2

Charles McDEVITT SKIFFLE GROUP featuring Nancy WHISKEY
UK, male / female vocal / instrumental group – Nancy Whiskey, b. 4 Mar 1935, d. 1 Feb 2003 (2 Singles: 20 Weeks)

12 Apr 57 ● **FREIGHT TRAIN** (re) *Oriole CB 1352* 5 18
14 Jun 57 **GREENBACK DOLLAR** (re) *Oriole CB 1371* 28 2

Jane McDONALD
UK, female vocalist (4 Albums: 43 Weeks, 1 Single: 7 Weeks)

25 Jul 98 ★ JANE MCDONALD *Focus Music International FMCD 1* ■ 1 27
26 Dec 98 ● **CRUISE INTO CHRISTMAS MEDLEY** *Focus Music Int CDFM 2* 10 7
17 Jun 00 ● INSPIRATION *Universal Music TV 1578612* 6 9
27 Oct 01 LOVE AT THE MOVIES *Universal Music TV 149472* 24 3
5 Feb 05 YOU BELONG TO ME *DMG TV DMGTV 013* 21 4

Michael McDONALD (see also The DOOBIE BROTHERS)
US, male vocalist / instrumentalist (5 Albums: 52 Weeks, 6 Singles: 49 Weeks)

18 Feb 84 **YAH MO B THERE** (2re) *Qwest 9394* [1] 12 16
3 May 86 ● **ON MY OWN** *MCA MCA 1045* [2] ▲ $ 2 13
26 Jul 86 **I KEEP FORGETTIN'** *Warner Bros. K 17992* 43 6
6 Sep 86 **SWEET FREEDOM** *MCA MCA 1073* 12 10
22 Nov 86 ● SWEET FREEDOM: BEST OF MICHAEL MCDONALD *Warner Bros. WX 67* 6 35
24 Jan 87 **WHAT A FOOL BELIEVES** (re-issue) *Warner Bros. W 8451* [3] 57 3
26 May 90 TAKE IT TO HEART *Reprise WX 285* 35 4
17 Mar 01 THE VERY BEST OF MICHAEL MCDONALD *Rhino 8122735302* 21 6
5 Oct 02 **SWEET FREEDOM** (re-recording) *Serious SERR 55CD* [4] 54 1

2 April 1977	9 April 1977	16 April 1977	23 April 1977
UK No.1 SINGLES			
KNOWING ME, KNOWING YOU Abba	KNOWING ME, KNOWING YOU Abba	KNOWING ME, KNOWING YOU Abba	KNOWING ME, KNOWING YOU Abba
UK No.1 ALBUMS			
PORTRAIT OF SINATRA Frank Sinatra	PORTRAIT OF SINATRA Frank Sinatra	ARRIVAL Abba	ARRIVAL Abba

17 May 03 MOTOWN – A COLLECTION OF MOTOWN CLASSICS *Universal TV 9800233*....29 4
19 Feb 05 MOTOWN TWO *Mercury 9869523*....29 3

[1] James Ingram with Michael McDonald [2] Patti LaBelle and Michael McDonald [3] The Doobie Brothers featuring Michael McDonald [4] Safri Duo featuring Michael McDonald

'Yah Mo B There' peaked at No.44 in Feb 1984 and No.69 on re-entry in Apr 1984. The track returned to the chart for a third time in Jan 1985 as a re-mix of the original hit but with the same catalogue number. It peaked at No.12. Motown Two was released as a double CD set with Motown – A Collection of Motown Classics.

Carrie McDOWELL *US, female vocalist*

26 Sep 87 **UH UH NO NO CASUAL SEX** *Motown ZV 41501*....68 3

John McENROE and Pat CASH with the FULL METAL RACKETS *US / Australia, male tennis players / vocal / instrumental duo and UK, backing group*

13 Jul 91 **ROCK 'N' ROLL** *Music for Nations KUT 141*....66 1

Reba McENTIRE *US, female vocalist*

19 Jun 99 **DOES HE LOVE YOU** *MCA Nashville MCSTD 55569*....62 1

Brian McFADDEN (see also WESTLIFE) *Ireland, male vocalist (1 Album: 13 Weeks, 4 Singles: 35 Weeks)*

18 Sep 04 ★ **REAL TO ME** *Modest! / Sony Music 6753032* ■....1 12
4 Dec 04 ● **IRISH SON** *Modest! / Sony Music 6745871*....6 11
11 Dec 04 IRISH SON *Modest! / Sony Music 5190022*....24 13
12 Feb 05 ● **ALMOST HERE** *Modest! / Sony Music 6757352* [1]....3 10
4 Jun 05 **DEMONS** *Modest! / Sony Music 6759102*....28 2

[1] Brian McFadden & Delta Goodrem

McFADDEN and WHITEHEAD *US, male vocal duo – Gene McFadden b.1949, d.17 Jan 2006 and John Whitehead, b. 2 Jul 1948, d. 11 May 2004*

19 May 79 ● **AIN'T NO STOPPIN' US NOW** *Philadelphia International PIR 7365* $....5 10

Rachel McFARLANE (see also LOVELAND featuring the voice of Rachel McFARLANE) *UK, female vocalist (2 Singles: 4 Weeks)*

1 Aug 98 **LOVER** *Multiply CDMULTY 37*....38 2
29 Jan 05 **LOVER** (re-recording) *All Around the World CDGLOBE 250*....36 2

Bobby McFERRIN *US, male vocalist (1 Album: 1 Week, 2 Singles: 15 Weeks)*

24 Sep 88 ● **DON'T WORRY BE HAPPY** *Manhattan MT 56* ▲....2 11
29 Oct 88 SIMPLE PLEASURES *Manhattan MTL 1018*....92 1
17 Dec 88 **THINKIN' ABOUT YOUR BODY** *Manhattan BLUE 6*....46 4

McFLY *UK, male vocal / instrumental group (2 Albums: 55 Weeks, 8 Singles: 71 Weeks)*

10 Apr 04 ★ **5 COLOURS IN HER HAIR** *Universal MCSTD 40357* ■....1 12
3 Jul 04 ★ **OBVIOUSLY** *Universal MCSTD 40364* ■....1 13
17 Jul 04 ★ ROOM ON THE 3RD FLOOR *Universal MCD 60094* ■....1 38
18 Sep 04 ● **THAT GIRL** (re) *Universal MCSXD 40378*....3 9
27 Nov 04 ● **ROOM ON THE 3RD FLOOR** *Island MCSXD 40389*....5 9
19 Mar 05 ★ **ALL ABOUT YOU / YOU'VE GOT A FRIEND** *Island MCSTD 40409* ■....1 13
27 Aug 05 ★ **I'LL BE OK** *Island MCSXD 40428* ■....1 9
10 Sep 05 ★ WONDERLAND *Island MCD 60099* ■....1 17+
29 Oct 05 ● **I WANNA HOLD YOU** *Island MCSXD 40436*....3 4
24 Dec 05 ● **ULTRAVIOLET / THE BALLAD OF PAUL K** *Island MCSXD 40442*....9 2+

The McGANNS *UK, male actors / vocal trio (2 Singles: 4 Weeks)*

14 Nov 98 **JUST MY IMAGINATION** *Coalition COLA 062CD*....59 1
6 Feb 99 **A HEARTBEAT AWAY** *Coalition COLA 069CD*....42 3

Kate and Anna McGARRIGLE *Canada, female vocal duo*

26 Feb 77 DANCER WITH BRUISED KNEES *Warner Bros. K 56356*....35 4

Mike McGEAR (see also The SCAFFOLD) *UK, male vocalist – Peter McCartney*

5 Oct 74 **LEAVE IT** *Warner Bros. K 16446*....36 4

Maureen McGOVERN *US, female vocalist*

5 Jun 76 **THE CONTINENTAL** *20th Century BTC 2222*....16 8

Shane MacGOWAN (see also The POGUES) *UK, male vocalist (2 Albums: 3 Weeks, 5 Singles: 9 Weeks)*

12 Dec 92 **WHAT A WONDERFUL WORLD** *Mute MUTE 151* [1]....72 1
3 Sep 94 **THE CHURCH OF THE HOLY SPOOK** *ZTT ZANG 57CD* [2]....74 1
15 Oct 94 **THAT WOMAN'S GOT ME DRINKING** *ZTT ZANG 56CD* [2]....34 3
29 Oct 94 THE SNAKE *ZTT 4509981042* [1]....37 2
29 Apr 95 **HAUNTED** *ZTT ZANG 65CD* [3]....30 2
20 Apr 96 **MY WAY** *ZTT ZANG 79CD*....29 2
8 Nov 97 THE CROCK OF GOLD *ZTT MACG 002CD* [1]....59 1

[1] Nick Cave and Shane MacGowan [2] Shane MacGowan and The Popes [3] Shane MacGowan and Sinead O'Connor [1] Shane MacGowan and The Popes

Freddie McGREGOR *Jamaica, male vocalist (2 Singles: 16 Weeks)*

27 Jun 87 ● **JUST DON'T WANT TO BE LONELY** *Germain DG 24*....9 11
19 Sep 87 **THAT GIRL (GROOVY SITUATION)** *Polydor POSP 884*....47 5

Mary MacGREGOR *US, female vocalist*

19 Feb 77 ● **TORN BETWEEN TWO LOVERS** *Ariola America AA 111* ▲ $....4 10
23 Apr 77 TORN BETWEEN TWO LOVERS *Ariola America AAS 1504*....59 1

McGUINNESS FLINT (see also MANFRED MANN) *UK, male vocal / instrumental group (1 Album: 2 Weeks, 2 Singles: 26 Weeks)*

21 Nov 70 ● **WHEN I'M DEAD AND GONE** *Capitol CL 15662*....2 14
23 Jan 71 ● MCGUINNESS FLINT *Capitol EAST 22625*....9 2
1 May 71 ● **MALT AND BARLEY BLUES** *Capitol CL 15682*....5 12

Barry McGUIRE *US, male vocalist*

9 Sep 65 ● **EVE OF DESTRUCTION** *RCA 1469* ▲ $....3 13

The McGUIRE SISTERS *US, female vocal group (5 Singles: 24 Weeks)*

1 Apr 55 **NO MORE** *Vogue Coral Q 72050*....20 1
15 Jul 55 **SINCERELY** *Vogue Coral Q 72050* ▲ $....14 4
1 Jun 56 **DELILAH JONES** *Vogue Coral Q 72161*....24 2
14 Feb 58 **SUGARTIME** *Coral Q 72305* $....14 6
1 May 59 **MAY YOU ALWAYS** (re) *Coral Q 72356* $....15 11

Duff McKAGAN (see also GUNS N' ROSES) *US, male vocalist / bass guitarist*

9 Oct 93 BELIEVE IN ME *Geffen GED 24605*....27 2

McKAY *US, female vocalist – Stephanie McKay*

23 Aug 03 **TAKE ME OVER** *Go Beat GOBCD 57*....65 1

Maria McKEE *US, female vocalist (2 Albums: 6 Weeks, 5 Singles: 23 Weeks)*

24 Jun 89 MARIA MCKEE *Geffen WX 270*....49 3
15 Sep 90 ★ **SHOW ME HEAVEN** *Epic 656303 7*....1 14
26 Jan 91 **BREATHE** *Geffen GFS 1*....59 1
1 Aug 92 **SWEETEST CHILD** *Geffen GFS 23*....45 4
22 May 93 **I'M GONNA SOOTHE YOU** *Geffen GFSTD 39*....35 3
12 Jun 93 YOU GOTTA SIN TO GET SAVED *Geffen GED 24508*....26 3
18 Sep 93 **I CAN'T MAKE IT ALONE** *Geffen GFSTD 53*....74 1

30 April 1977	7 May 1977	14 May 1977	21 May 1977
KNOWING ME, KNOWING YOU Abba	FREE Deniece Williams	FREE Deniece Williams	I DON'T WANT TO TALK ABOUT IT / FIRST CUT IS THE DEEPEST Rod Stewart
ARRIVAL Abba	ARRIVAL Abba	ARRIVAL Abba	ARRIVAL Abba

KEY		Peak Position	Weeks
UK No.1 ★ UK Top 10 ● Still on chart + UK entry at No.1 ■ US No.1 ▲ UK million seller £ US million seller $ Singles re-entries are listed as (re), (2re), (3re)... which signifies that the hit re-entered the chart once, twice or three times...			

Kenneth McKELLAR
UK, male vocalist (2 Albums: 10 Weeks, 1 Single: 4 Weeks)

10 Mar 66	**A MAN WITHOUT LOVE** *Decca F 12341*	30	4
28 Jun 69	THE WORLD OF KENNETH MCKELLAR *Decca SPA 11*	27	7
31 Jan 70	ECCO DI NAPOLI *Decca SKL 5018*	45	3

Billy MacKENZIE (see also ASSOCIATES)
UK, male vocalist, b. 27 Mar 1957, d. 22 Jan 1997

18 Oct 97	BEYOND THE SUN *Nude NUDE 8CD*	64	1

Gisele MacKENZIE
Canada, female vocalist – Gisele LeFleche, b. 10 Jan 1927, d. 5 Sep 2003

17 Jul 53 ●	**SEVEN LONELY DAYS** (2re) *Capitol CL 13920*	6	6

Scott McKENZIE *US, male vocalist – Philip Blondheim (2 Singles: 18 Weeks)*

12 Jul 67 ★	**SAN FRANCISCO (BE SURE TO WEAR SOME FLOWERS IN YOUR HAIR)** *CBS 2816*	1	17
1 Nov 67	**LIKE AN OLD TIME MOVIE** *CBS 3009* [1]	50	1

[1] The Voice of Scott McKenzie

Ken MACKINTOSH, his Saxophone and his Orchestra
UK, orchestra – leader b. 4 Aug 1919, d. 22 Nov 2005 (3 Singles: 9 Weeks)

15 Jan 54 ●	**THE CREEP** (re) *HMV BD 1295*	10	2
7 Feb 58	**RAUNCHY** *HMV POP 426*	19	6
10 Mar 60	**NO HIDING PLACE** *HMV POP 713*	45	1

Brian McKNIGHT *US, male vocalist (2 Singles: 4 Weeks)*

6 Jun 98	**ANYTIME** *Motown 8607752*	48	2
3 Oct 98	**YOU SHOULD BE MINE** *Motown 8608412*	36	2

Julie McKNIGHT
(see also LAYO & BUSHWACKA!) *US, female vocalist (4 Singles: 6 Weeks)*

14 Apr 01	**FINALLY** *Distance DI 2029* [1]	54	1
29 Sep 01	**FINALLY** (re-mix) *Defected DFECT 37CDS* [1]	24	3
15 Jun 02	**HOME** *Defected DFECT 51CDS*	61	1
23 Nov 02	**DIAMOND LIFE** *Distance DI 2409* [2]	52	1

[1] Kings of Tomorrow featuring Julie McKnight [2] Louie Vega and Jay 'Sinister' Sealee starring Julie McKnight

Vivienne McKONE *UK, female vocalist (2 Singles: 5 Weeks)*

25 Jul 92	**SING (OOH-EE-OOH)** *ffrr F 183*	47	4
31 Oct 92	**BEWARE** *ffrr F 202*	69	1

McKOY *UK, male / female vocal group*

6 Mar 93	**FIGHT** *Rightrack CDTUM 1*	54	2

Craig McLACHLAN *Australia, male actor / vocalist (8 Singles: 40 Weeks)*

16 Jun 90 ●	**MONA** *Epic 655784 7* [1]	2	11
21 Jul 90 ●	CRAIG MCLACHLAN AND CHECK 1-2 *Epic 4663471* [1]	10	11
4 Aug 90	**AMANDA** *Epic 656170 7* [1]	19	6
10 Nov 90	**I ALMOST FELT LIKE CRYING** *Epic 656310 7* [1]	50	3
23 May 92	**ONE REASON WHY** *Epic 6580677*	29	6
14 Nov 92	**ON MY OWN** *Epic 6584677*	59	2
24 Jul 93	**YOU'RE THE ONE THAT I WANT** *Epic 6595222* [2]	13	6
25 Dec 93	**GREASE** *Epic 6600242*	44	4
8 Jul 95	**EVERYDAY** *MDMC DEVCS 6* [3]	65	2

[1] Craig McLachlan and Check 1-2 [2] Craig McLachlan and Debbie Gibson [3] Craig McLachlan and The Culprits [1] Craig McLachlan and Check 1-2

Sarah McLACHLAN *Canada, female vocalist / guitarist (2 Albums: 15 Weeks, 9 Singles: 17 Weeks)*

3 Oct 98	**ADIA** *Arista 74321613902*	18	5
17 Oct 98	SURFACING *Arista 189702*	47	2
2 Feb 02	**ANGEL** (re-mix) *Nettwerk 331482*	36	3
14 Feb 04	AFTERGLOW *Arista 82876596712*	33	13
20 Mar 04	**FALLEN** *Arista 82876590652*	50	1
26 Jun 04	**WORLD ON FIRE** *Arista 8287662832*	72	1
27 Nov 04	**SILENCE 2004** (re) *Nettwerk 332422* [1]	38	7

[1] Delerium featuring Sarah McLachlan

Tommy McLAIN *US, male vocalist*

8 Sep 66	**SWEET DREAMS** *London HL 10065*	49	1

Malcolm McLAREN
UK, male vocalist (5 Albums: 41 Weeks, 10 Singles: 65 Weeks)

4 Dec 82 ●	**BUFFALO GALS** *Charisma MALC 1* [1]	9	12
26 Feb 83	**SOWETO** *Charisma MALC 2* [2]	32	5
4 Jun 83	DUCK ROCK *Charisma MMLP 1*	18	17
2 Jul 83 ●	**DOUBLE DUTCH** *Charisma MALC 3*	3	13
17 Dec 83	**DUCK FOR THE OYSTER** *Charisma MALC 4*	54	5
26 May 84	WOULD YA LIKE MORE SCRATCHIN' *Charisma CLAM 1* [1]	44	4
1 Sep 84	**MADAM BUTTERFLY (UN BEL DI VEDREMO)** *Charisma MALC 5*	13	9
29 Dec 84	FANS *Charisma MMDL 2*	47	8
27 May 89	**WALTZ DARLING** *Epic WALTZ 2* [3]	31	8
15 Jul 89	WALTZ DARLING *Epic 460736 1* [2]	30	11
19 Aug 89	**SOMETHING'S JUMPIN' IN YOUR SHIRT** *Epic WALTZ 3* [4]	29	7
25 Nov 89	**HOUSE OF THE BLUE DANUBE** *Epic WALTZ 4* [3]	73	1
21 Dec 91	**MAGIC'S BACK (THEME FROM 'THE GHOSTS OF OXFORD STREET')** *RCA PB 45223* [5]	42	4
20 Aug 94	PARIS *No! NOCD 101*	44	1
3 Oct 98	**BUFFALO GALS STAMPEDE** (re-mix) *Virgin VSCDT 1717* [6]	65	1

[1] Malcolm McLaren and the World's Famous Supreme Team [2] Malcolm McLaren and The McLarenettes [3] Malcolm McLaren and the Bootzilla Orchestra [4] Malcolm McLaren and the Bootzilla Orchestra featuring Lisa Marie [5] Malcolm McLaren featuring Alison Limerick [6] Malcolm McLaren and the World's Famous Supreme Team plus Rakim and Roger Sanchez [1] Malcolm McLaren and the World's Famous Supreme Team [2] Malcolm McLaren and the Bootzilla Orchestra

Bitty McLEAN *UK, male vocalist (1 Album: 11 Weeks, 10 Singles: 50 Weeks)*

31 Jul 93 ●	**IT KEEPS RAININ' (TEARS FROM MY EYES)** *Brilliant CDBRIL 1*	2	15
30 Oct 93	**PASS IT ON** *Brilliant CDBRIL 2*	35	3
15 Jan 94 ●	**HERE I STAND** *Brilliant CDBRIL 3*	10	6
19 Feb 94	JUST TO LET YOU KNOW *Brilliant BRILCD 1*	19	11
9 Apr 94 ●	**DEDICATED TO THE ONE I LOVE** *Brilliant CDBRIL 4*	6	10
6 Aug 94	**WHAT GOES AROUND** *Brilliant CDBRIL 5*	36	3
8 Apr 95	**OVER THE RIVER** *Brilliant CDBRIL 9*	27	4
17 Jun 95	**WE'VE ONLY JUST BEGUN** *Brilliant CDBRIL 10*	23	5
30 Sep 95	**NOTHING CAN CHANGE THIS LOVE** *Brilliant CDBRIL 11*	55	2
27 Jan 96	**NATURAL HIGH** *Brilliant CDBRIL 12*	63	1
5 Oct 96	**SHE'S ALRIGHT** *Kuff KUFFD 9*	53	1

Don McLEAN (446 Top 500)
Celebrated singer / songwriter / guitarist, b. 2 Oct 1945, New York, US. The 8.5 minute 'American Pie', which was America's top single of 1972, is regarded as one of the all time great rock era records. No.1 song 'Killing Me Softly' was written about him (6 Albums: 92 Weeks, 6 Singles: 68 Weeks)

22 Jan 72 ●	**AMERICAN PIE** *United Artists UP 35325* ▲ $	2	16
11 Mar 72 ●	AMERICAN PIE *United Artists UAS 29285* ▲	3	54

	28 May 1977	4 June 1977	11 June 1977	18 June 1977
UK No.1 SINGLES	I DON'T WANT TO TALK ABOUT IT / FIRST CUT IS THE DEEPEST Rod Stewart	I DON'T WANT TO TALK ABOUT IT / FIRST CUT IS THE DEEPEST Rod Stewart	I DON'T WANT TO TALK ABOUT IT / FIRST CUT IS THE DEEPEST Rod Stewart	LUCILLE Kenny Rogers
UK No.1 ALBUMS	ARRIVAL Abba	ARRIVAL Abba	ARRIVAL Abba	THE BEATLES AT THE HOLLYWOOD BOWL The Beatles

13 May 72 ★	VINCENT United Artists UP 35359	1	15
17 Jun 72	TAPESTRY United Artists UAS 29350	16	12
14 Apr 73	EVERYDAY United Artists UP 35519	38	5
24 Nov 73	PLAYIN' FAVOURITES United Artists UAG 29528	42	2
10 May 80 ★	CRYING EMI 5051	1	14
14 Jun 80	CHAIN LIGHTNING EMI International INS 3025	19	9
27 Sep 80 ●	THE VERY BEST OF DON MCLEAN United Artists UAG 30314	4	12
17 Apr 82	CASTLES IN THE AIR EMI 5258	47	8
5 Oct 91	AMERICAN PIE (re-issue) Liberty EMCT 3	12	10
15 Apr 00	AMERICAN PIE – THE GREATEST HITS Capitol 5258472	30	3

Jackie McLEAN *US, male alto saxophone player*

7 Jul 79	DOCTOR JACKYLL AND MISTER FUNK RCA PB 1575	53	4

Phil McLEAN *US, male vocalist*

18 Jan 62	SMALL SAD SAM Top Rank JAR 597	34	4

McLUSKEY *UK, male vocal / instrumental group*

8 May 04	THAT MAN WILL NOT HANG Too Pure PURE 153CDS	71	1

Andy McNAB *UK, male author*

21 May 94	BRAVO TWO ZERO PolyGram TV 5222002	45	2

Ian McNABB (see also The ICICLE WORKS)
UK, male vocalist (3 Albums: 5 Weeks, 6 Singles: 7 Weeks)

23 Jan 93	IF LOVE WAS LIKE GUITARS This Way Up WAY 233	67	1
30 Jan 93	TRUTH AND BEAUTY This Way Up 5143782	51	1
2 Jul 94	YOU MUST BE PREPARED TO DREAM This Way Up WAY 3199 [1]	54	1
16 Jul 94	HEAD LIKE A ROCK This Way Up 5222982	29	2
17 Sep 94	GO INTO THE LIGHT This Way Up WAY 3699	66	2
27 Apr 96	DON'T PUT YOUR SPELL ON ME This Way Up WAY 5033	72	1
18 May 96	MERSEYBEAST This Way Up 5242152	30	2
6 Jul 96	MERSEYBEAST This Way Up WAY 5266	74	1
28 May 05	LET THE YOUNG GIRL DO WHAT SHE WANTS TO Fairfield FAIR CD5	38	1

[1] Ian McNabb featuring Ralph Molina and Billy Talbot

Lutricia McNEAL
US, female vocalist (1 Album: 16 Weeks, 4 Singles: 43 Weeks)

29 Nov 97 ●	AIN'T THAT JUST THE WAY Wildstar CXSTAS 2907	6	18
23 May 98 ●	STRANDED Wildstar CXSTAS 2973	3	12
25 Jul 98	LUTRICIA MCNEAL Wildstar CDWILD 5	16	16
26 Sep 98 ●	SOMEONE LOVES YOU HONEY Wildstar CDWILD 9	9	7
19 Dec 98	THE GREATEST LOVE YOU'LL NEVER KNOW Wildstar CDWILD 11	17	6

Patrick MacNEE and Honor BLACKMAN
UK, male / female actors / vocal duo

1 Dec 90 ●	KINKY BOOTS Deram KINKY 1	5	7

Rita MacNEIL *Canada, female vocalist*

6 Oct 90	WORKING MAN Polydor PO 98	11	10
24 Nov 90	REASON TO BELIEVE Polydor 8471061	32	4

Clyde McPHATTER *US, male vocalist, b. 15 Nov 1932, d. 13 Jun 1972*

24 Aug 56	TREASURE OF LOVE London HLE 8293	27	1

Tom McRAE
UK, male vocalist / guitarist (2 Albums: 3 Weeks, 1 Single: 1 Week)

15 Feb 03	JUST LIKE BLOOD DB DB 006CDLP	26	2
24 May 03	KARAOKE SOUL DB DB 016CD	48	1
14 May 05	ALL MAPS WELCOME BMG 82876689502	47	1

Ian McSHANE *UK, male vocalist*

21 Nov 92	FROM BOTH SIDES NOW PolyGram TV 5176192	40	7

Ralph McTELL *UK, male vocalist / guitarist – Ralph May (3 Albums: 17 Weeks, 2 Singles: 18 Weeks)*

18 Nov 72	NOT TILL TOMORROW Reprise K 44210	36	1
2 Mar 74	EASY Reprise K 54013	31	4
7 Dec 74 ●	STREETS OF LONDON Reprise K 14380	2	12
15 Feb 75	STREETS Warner Bros. K 56105	13	12
20 Dec 75	DREAMS OF YOU Warner Bros. K 16648	36	6

Christine McVIE (see also CHICKEN SHACK; FLEETWOOD MAC)
UK, female vocalist – Christine Perfect

11 Feb 84	CHRISTINE MCVIE Warner Bros. 925059	58	4

David McWILLIAMS
UK, male vocalist, b. 4 Jul 1945, d. 9 Jan 2002 (3 Albums: 9 Weeks)

10 Jun 67	DAVID MCWILLIAMS SINGS Major Minor MMLP 2	38	2
4 Nov 67	DAVID MCWILLIAMS VOLUME 2 Major Minor MMLP 10	23	6
9 Mar 68	DAVID MCWILLIAMS VOLUME 3 Major Minor MMLP 11	39	1

MACEO & THE MACKS *US, male vocal / instrumental group*

16 May 87	CROSS THE TRACK (WE BETTER GO BACK) Urban URBX 1	54	5

MACHEL *Trinidad and Tobago, male vocalist – Machel Montano*

14 Sep 96	COME DIG IT London LONCD 386	56	2

MACHINE HEAD
UK, male vocal / instrumental group (4 Albums: 9 Weeks, 3 Singles: 4 Weeks)

20 Aug 94	BURN MY EYES Roadrunner RR 90169	25	3
27 May 95	OLD Roadrunner RR 23403	43	2
5 Apr 97	THE MORE THINGS CHANGE ... Roadrunner RR 88602	16	3
6 Dec 97	TAKE MY SCARS Roadrunner RR 22573	73	1
21 Aug 99	THE BURNING RED Roadrunner RR 86512	13	2
18 Dec 99	FROM THIS DAY Roadrunner RR 21383	74	1
13 Oct 01	SUPERCHARGER Roadrunner 12085002	34	1

Billy MACK *UK, male actor / vocalist – Bill Nighy*

27 Dec 03	CHRISTMAS IS ALL AROUND Island CID 841	26	3

Craig MACK *US, male rapper (3 Singles: 5 Weeks)*

12 Nov 94	FLAVA IN YA EAR Bad Boy 74321242582 $	57	2
1 Apr 95	GET DOWN Puff Daddy 74321263402	54	1
7 Jun 97	SPIRIT Perspective 5822312 [1]	35	2

Lizzy MACK *UK, female vocalist (2 Singles: 3 Weeks)*

5 Nov 94	THE POWER OF LOVE Media MCSTD 2016 [1]	49	2
4 Nov 95	DON'T GO Power Station MCSTD 40004	52	1

[1] Fits of Gloom featuring Lizzy Mack

Lonnie MACK *US, male guitarist – Lonnie McIntosh*

14 Apr 79	MEMPHIS Lightning LIG 9011	47	3

'Memphis' was coupled with 'Let's Dance' by Chris Montez.

The MACK VIBE featuring JACQUELINE
US, male / female vocal / instrumental duo

4 Feb 95	I CAN'T LET YOU GO MCA MCSTD 20020	53	1

MAD COBRA featuring Richie STEPHENS *Jamaica / UK, male vocal duo*

15 May 93	LEGACY Columbia 6592852	64	1

25 June 1977	2 July 1977	9 July 1977	16 July 1977
SHOW YOU THE WAY TO GO The Jacksons	SO YOU WIN AGAIN Hot Chocolate	SO YOU WIN AGAIN Hot Chocolate	SO YOU WIN AGAIN Hot Chocolate
THE MUPPET SHOW The Muppets	A STAR IS BORN (Soundtrack) Barbra Streisand / Kris Kristofferson	A STAR IS BORN (Soundtrack) Barbra Streisand / Kris Kristofferson	THE JOHNNY MATHIS COLLECTION Johnny Mathis

KEY
UK No.1 ★ UK Top 10 ● Still on chart + UK entry at No.1 ■
US No.1 ▲ UK million seller £ US million seller $
Singles re-entries are listed as (re), (2re), (3re)... which signifies that the hit re-entered the chart once, twice or three times...

Peak Position / Weeks

MAD DONNA *US, female vocalist*

Date	Title	Peak	Weeks
4 May 02	THE WHEELS ON THE BUS *Star Harbour / All Around the World DISCO 0202R*	17	4

MAD JOCKS featuring JOCKMASTER B.A.
UK, male vocal / instrumental group (2 Singles: 9 Weeks)

Date	Title	Peak	Weeks
19 Dec 87	JOCK MIX 1 *Debut DEBT 3037*	46	5
18 Dec 93	PARTY FOUR (EP) *SMP CDSSKM 24*	57	4

Tracks on Party Four (EP): No Lager / Here We Go Again / Jock Party Mix / Jock Jak Mix.

MAD MOSES *US, male DJ / producer – 'Mad' Mitch Moses*

Date	Title	Peak	Weeks
16 Aug 97	PANTHER PARTY *Hi-Life 5744932*	50	1

MAD SEASON *UK, male vocal / instrumental group*

Date	Title	Peak	Weeks
25 Mar 95	ABOVE *Columbia 4785072*	41	1

MADASUN *UK, female vocal group (3 Singles: 13 Weeks)*

Date	Title	Peak	Weeks
11 Mar 00	DON'T YOU WORRY *V2 VVR 5011523*	14	6
27 May 00	WALKING ON WATER *V2 VVR 5012418*	14	4
2 Sep 00	FEEL GOOD *V2 VVR 5012983*	29	3

Danny MADDEN *US, male vocalist*

Date	Title	Peak	Weeks
14 Jul 90	THE FACTS OF LIFE *Eternal YZ 473*	72	2

MADDER ROSE *US, male / female vocal / instrumental group (1 Album: 2 Weeks, 2 Singles: 2 Weeks)*

Date	Title	Peak	Weeks
26 Mar 94	PANIC ON *Atlantic A 8301CD*	65	1
9 Apr 94	PANIC ON *Atlantic 7567825812*	52	2
16 Jul 94	CAR SONG *Seed A 7256CD*	68	1

MADE IN LONDON *UK / Norway, female vocal group (2 Singles: 6 Weeks)*

Date	Title	Peak	Weeks
13 May 00	DIRTY WATER *RCA 74321746192*	15	5
9 Sep 00	SHUT YOUR MOUTH *RCA 74321772602*	74	1

MADELYNE (see also 4 STRINGS) *Holland, male producer – Carlo Resoort*

Date	Title	Peak	Weeks
7 Sep 02	BEAUTIFUL CHILD (A DEEPER LOVE) *Xtravaganza XTRAV 36CDS*	63	1

MADEMOISELLE *France, male production / instrumental duo*

Date	Title	Peak	Weeks
8 Sep 01	DO YOU LOVE ME *RCA 74321878952*	56	1

MAD'HOUSE *France / Holland, male / female production / vocal (Buse Unlu) trio (1 Album: 1 Week, 2 Singles: 14 Weeks)*

Date	Title	Peak	Weeks
17 Aug 02 ●	LIKE A PRAYER *Serious SERR 046CD*	3	11
31 Aug 02	ABSOLUTELY MAD *Serious / Mercury SERRCD 001*	57	1
9 Nov 02	HOLIDAY *Serious SER 058CD*	24	3

MADISON AVENUE *Australia, male producer – Andy Van Dorsselaer and female vocalist – Cheyne Coates (1 Album: 1 Week, 4 Singles: 25 Weeks)*

Date	Title	Peak	Weeks
13 Nov 99	DON'T CALL ME BABY (2re) *VC Recordings VCRD 56*	30	6
20 May 00 ★	DON'T CALL ME BABY (re-issue) *VC Recordings VCRD 64* ■	1	12
21 Oct 00 ●	WHO THE HELL ARE YOU *VC Recordings VCRD 70*	10	5
4 Nov 00	THE POLYESTER EMBASSY *VC Recordings CDVCR 7*	74	1
27 Jan 01	EVERYTHING YOU NEED *VC Recordings VCRD 82*	33	2

MADNESS (45 Top 500) (see also SUGGS)
London-based band whose ska-rooted 'nutty' sound earned them a huge haul of hits. The 2002 Madness-based production, Our House, won an Olivier Award for Best New Musical. This good-time septet, fronted by Graham 'Suggs' McPherson, spent more weeks on the chart in the 1980s than any other group (15 Albums: 418 Weeks, 33 Singles: 270 Weeks)

Date	Title	Peak	Weeks
1 Sep 79	THE PRINCE *2 Tone TT 3*	16	11
3 Nov 79 ●	ONE STEP BEYOND ... *Stiff SEEZ 17*	2	78
10 Nov 79 ●	ONE STEP BEYOND ... *Stiff BUY 56*	7	14
5 Jan 80 ●	MY GIRL *Stiff BUY 62*	3	10
5 Apr 80 ●	WORK REST AND PLAY (EP) *Stiff BUY 71*	6	8
13 Sep 80 ●	BAGGY TROUSERS *Stiff BUY 84*	3	20
4 Oct 80 ●	ABSOLUTELY *Stiff SEEZ 29*	2	46
22 Nov 80 ●	EMBARRASSMENT *Stiff BUY 102*	4	12
24 Jan 81 ●	THE RETURN OF THE LOS PALMAS SEVEN *Stiff BUY 108*	7	11
25 Apr 81 ●	GREY DAY *Stiff BUY 112*	4	10
26 Sep 81 ●	SHUT UP *Stiff BUY 126*	7	9
10 Oct 81 ●	MADNESS 7 *Stiff SEEZ 39*	5	29
5 Dec 81 ●	IT MUST BE LOVE *Stiff BUY 134*	4	12
20 Feb 82	CARDIAC ARREST *Stiff BUY 140*	14	10
1 May 82 ★	COMPLETE MADNESS *Stiff HIT-TV 1*	1	88
22 May 82 ★	HOUSE OF FUN *Stiff BUY 146*	1	9
24 Jul 82 ●	DRIVING IN MY CAR *Stiff BUY 153*	4	8
13 Nov 82 ●	MADNESS PRESENTS THE RISE AND FALL *Stiff SEEZ 46*	10	22
27 Nov 82 ●	OUR HOUSE *Stiff BUY 163*	5	13
19 Feb 83 ●	TOMORROW'S (JUST ANOTHER DAY) / MADNESS (IS ALL IN THE MIND) *Stiff BUY 169*	8	9
20 Aug 83 ●	WINGS OF A DOVE *Stiff BUY 181*	2	10
5 Nov 83 ●	THE SUN AND THE RAIN *Stiff BUY 192*	5	10
11 Feb 84	MICHAEL CAINE *Stiff BUY 196*	11	8
3 Mar 84 ●	KEEP MOVING *Stiff SEEZ 53*	6	19
2 Jun 84	ONE BETTER DAY *Stiff BUY 201*	17	7
31 Aug 85	YESTERDAY'S MEN *Zarjazz JAZZ 5*	18	7
12 Oct 85	MAD NOT MAD *Zarjazz JZLP 1*	16	9
26 Oct 85	UNCLE SAM *Zarjazz JAZZ 7*	21	11
1 Feb 86	SWEETEST GIRL *Zarjazz JAZZ 8*	35	6
8 Nov 86	(WAITING FOR) THE GHOST TRAIN (re) *Zarjazz JAZZ 9*	18	8
6 Dec 86	UTTER MADNESS *Zarjazz JZLP 2*	29	8
19 Mar 88	I PRONOUNCE YOU *Virgin VS 1054* [1]	44	4
7 May 88	THE MADNESS *Virgin V 2507*	65	1
15 Feb 92 ●	IT MUST BE LOVE (re-issue) *Virgin VS 1405*	6	9
7 Mar 92 ★	DIVINE MADNESS *Virgin CDV 2692*	1	96
25 Apr 92	HOUSE OF FUN (re-issue) *Virgin VS 1413*	40	3
8 Aug 92	MY GIRL (re-issue) *Virgin VS 1425*	27	4
14 Nov 92	MADSTOCK *Go Discs 8283672*	22	9
28 Nov 92	THE HARDER THEY COME *Go Discs GOD 93*	44	3
27 Feb 93	NIGHT BOAT TO CAIRO *Virgin VSCDT 1447*	56	2
13 Jun 98	THE HEAVY HEAVY HITS *Virgin CDV 2862*	19	5
31 Jul 99 ●	LOVESTRUCK *Virgin VSCDT 1737*	10	7
6 Nov 99	JOHNNY THE HORSE *Virgin VSCDT 1740*	44	2
13 Nov 99	WONDERFUL *Virgin CDV 2889*	17	2
11 Mar 00	DRIP FED FRED *Virgin VSCDT 1768* [2]	55	1
2 Nov 02	OUR HOUSE – THE ORIGINAL SONGS *Virgin CDV 2965*	45	2
6 Aug 05	SHAME & SCANDAL *V2 VVR 5033243*	38	2
13 Aug 05	THE DANGERMEN SESSIONS – VOLUME ONE *V2 VVR 1033232*	11	4

[1] The Madness [2] Madness featuring Ian Dury

Tracks on Work Rest and Play (EP): Night Boat to Cairo / Deceives the Eye / The Young and the Old / Don't Quote Me on That. 'Night Boat to Cairo' in 1993 is a re-issue of a track from the Work Rest and Play EP.

MADONNA (5 Top 500)
The most successful female chart act of all time in the UK and US, with her label claiming worldwide sales of 200 million albums, b. Madonna Ciccone, 16 Aug 1958, Michigan, US. Ground-breaking and trend-setting, this often controversial artist performed at Live Aid (JFK) and Live 8 (London) and amassed an unequalled 34 consecutive UK Top 10 singles (including two re-entries, a re-mix and a re-issue) and an unbeatable tally of Top 5 entries.

	23 July 1977	30 July 1977	6 August 1977	13 August 1977
UK No.1 SINGLES	I FEEL LOVE Donna Summer	I FEEL LOVE Donna Summer	I FEEL LOVE Donna Summer	I FEEL LOVE Donna Summer
UK No.1 ALBUMS	THE JOHNNY MATHIS COLLECTION Johnny Mathis	THE JOHNNY MATHIS COLLECTION Johnny Mathis	THE JOHNNY MATHIS COLLECTION Johnny Mathis	GOING FOR THE ONE Yes

She has also had more UK No.1 singles and albums than any other female soloist and at one time held the top two slots on the singles chart (1985). Her accumulated UK Top 10 entries are more than The Beatles and The Rolling Stones combined and her album The Immaculate Collection has sold more than 3.6 million copies in the UK alone. In the US, the multi-award-winning singer holds the female record for 27 consecutive Top 20 entries and 16 successive Top 5s, plus a dozen No.1s – 10 of which she wrote. Madonna, who is a founder member of the UK Music Hall of Fame and the most imitated performer on Stars in their Eyes, has produced more No.1s than any female, played to packed stadiums around the globe and starred in several successful films. She was again voted Best International Female Singer at the 2001 BRITs and grossed £40m for the 28 US dates of her Drowned World Tour – the highest figure for a female performer in 2001. Her 2000 album Music topped charts in 26 countries, while 2005's Confessions on a Dance Floor, which topped the UK and US albums charts simultaneously, was No.1 in 25 countries and shipped four million copies (16 Albums: 1038 Weeks, 62 Singles: 628 Weeks)

14 Jan 84 ● **HOLIDAY** (re) *Sire W 9405*....2 21
11 Feb 84 ● **MADONNA / THE FIRST ALBUM** *Sire 923867*....6 123
17 Mar 84 **LUCKY STAR** *Sire W 9522*....**14** 9
2 Jun 84 ● **BORDERLINE** (re) *Sire W 9260*....2 13
17 Nov 84 ● **LIKE A VIRGIN** *Sire W 9210* ▲ $....3 18
24 Nov 84 ★ **LIKE A VIRGIN** *Sire 925157* ▲....1 152
2 Mar 85 ● **MATERIAL GIRL** *Sire W 9083*....3 10
8 Jun 85 ● **CRAZY FOR YOU** *Geffen A 6323* ▲ $....2 15
27 Jul 85 ★ **INTO THE GROOVE** *Sire W 8934*....1 14
21 Sep 85 ● **ANGEL** *Sire W 8881* $....5 9
12 Oct 85 ● **GAMBLER** (re) *Geffen A 6585*....4 12
7 Dec 85 ● **DRESS YOU UP** *Sire W 8848*....5 11
26 Apr 86 ● **LIVE TO TELL** *Sire W 8717* ▲....2 12
28 Jun 86 ★ **PAPA DON'T PREACH** *Sire W 8636* ▲....1 14
12 Jul 86 ★ **TRUE BLUE** *Sire WX 54* ■ ▲....1 85
4 Oct 86 ★ **TRUE BLUE** *Sire W 8550*....1 15
13 Dec 86 ● **OPEN YOUR HEART** *Sire W 8480* ▲....4 9
4 Apr 87 ★ **LA ISLA BONITA** *Sire W 8378*....1 11
18 Jul 87 ★ **WHO'S THAT GIRL** *Sire W 8341* ▲....1 10
19 Sep 87 ● **CAUSING A COMMOTION** *Sire W 8224*....4 9
28 Nov 87 ● **YOU CAN DANCE** *Sire WX 76*....5 16
12 Dec 87 ● **THE LOOK OF LOVE** *Sire W 8115*....9 7
18 Mar 89 ★ **LIKE A PRAYER** *Sire W 7539* ▲ $....1 12
1 Apr 89 ★ **LIKE A PRAYER** *Sire WX 239* ■ ▲....1 70
3 Jun 89 ● **EXPRESS YOURSELF** *Sire W 2948*....5 10
16 Sep 89 ● **CHERISH** *Sire W 2883*....3 8
16 Dec 89 ● **DEAR JESSIE** *Sire W 2668*....5 9
7 Apr 90 ★ **VOGUE** *Sire W 9851* ▲ $....1 14
2 Jun 90 ● **I'M BREATHLESS** *Sire WX 351*....2 20
21 Jul 90 ● **HANKY PANKY** *Sire W 9789*....2 9
24 Nov 90 ★ **THE IMMACULATE COLLECTION** *Sire WX 370* ■....1 213
8 Dec 90 ● **JUSTIFY MY LOVE** *Sire W 9000* ▲ $....2 10
2 Mar 91 ● **CRAZY FOR YOU** (re-mix) *Sire W 0008*....2 8
13 Apr 91 ● **RESCUE ME** *Sire W 0024*....3 8
8 Jun 91 ● **HOLIDAY** (re-issue) *Sire W 0037*....5 7
25 Jul 92 ● **THIS USED TO BE MY PLAYGROUND** *Sire W 0122* ▲....3 9
17 Oct 92 ● **EROTICA** (re) *Maverick W 0138*....3 9
24 Oct 92 ● **EROTICA** *Maverick 9362450312*....2 38
12 Dec 92 ● **DEEPER AND DEEPER** *Maverick W 0146*....6 9
6 Mar 93 ● **BAD GIRL** *Maverick W 0154CD*....10 7
3 Apr 93 ● **FEVER** *Maverick W 0168CD*....6 6
31 Jul 93 ● **RAIN** *Maverick W 0190CD*....7 8
2 Apr 94 ● **I'LL REMEMBER** *Maverick W 0240CD*....7 8
8 Oct 94 ● **SECRET** *Maverick W 0268CD*....5 9
5 Nov 94 ● **BEDTIME STORIES** *Maverick 9362457672*....2 27
17 Dec 94 **TAKE A BOW** *Maverick W 0278CD* ▲....**16** 9
25 Feb 95 ● **BEDTIME STORY** (re) *Maverick W 0285CD*....4 9
26 Aug 95 ● **HUMAN NATURE** *Maverick W 0300CD*....8 5
4 Nov 95 ● **YOU'LL SEE** *Maverick W 0324CD*....5 13
18 Nov 95 ● **SOMETHING TO REMEMBER** *Maverick 9362461002*....3 29
6 Jan 96 **OH FATHER** *Maverick W 0326CD*....**16** 6
23 Mar 96 **ONE MORE CHANCE** *Maverick W 0337CD*....**11** 4
2 Nov 96 ● **YOU MUST LOVE ME** (2re) *Warner Bros. W 0378CD*....**10** 6
9 Nov 96 ★ **EVITA (FILM SOUNDTRACK)** *Warner Bros. 9362464322* [1]....1 36
28 Dec 96 ● **DON'T CRY FOR ME ARGENTINA** *Warner Bros. W 0384CD*....3 12
29 Mar 97 ● **ANOTHER SUITCASE IN ANOTHER HALL** *Warner Bros. W 0388CD*....**7** 5
7 Mar 98 ★ **FROZEN** *Maverick W 0433CD* ■....1 13
14 Mar 98 ★ **RAY OF LIGHT** *Maverick 9362468472* ■....1 116
9 May 98 ● **RAY OF LIGHT** (re) *Maverick W 0444CD*....2 10
5 Sep 98 ● **DROWNED WORLD (SUBSTITUTE FOR LOVE)** *Maverick W 0453CD1*....**10** 5
5 Dec 98 ● **THE POWER OF GOODBYE / LITTLE STAR** *Maverick W 459CD*....6 9
13 Mar 99 ● **NOTHING REALLY MATTERS** (re) *Maverick W 471CD*....**7** 9
19 Jun 99 ● **BEAUTIFUL STRANGER** *Maverick W 495CD*....2 16
11 Mar 00 ★ **AMERICAN PIE** (re) *Maverick W 519CD* ■....1 14
2 Sep 00 ★ **MUSIC** *Maverick W 537CD1* ■ ▲ $....1 23
30 Sep 00 ★ **MUSIC** *Maverick 9362478652* ■ ▲....1 64
9 Dec 00 ● **DON'T TELL ME** *Maverick W 547CD1*....4 10
28 Apr 01 ● **WHAT IT FEELS LIKE FOR A GIRL** (re) *Maverick W 533CD*....7 11
24 Nov 01 ● **GHV2: GREATEST HITS VOLUME 2** *Maverick 9362480002*....2 24
9 Nov 02 ● **DIE ANOTHER DAY** *Warner W 595CD*....3 16
19 Apr 03 **AMERICAN LIFE** (import) *Maverick 166582*....**57** 1
26 Apr 03 ● **AMERICAN LIFE** *Maverick W 603CD1*....2 11
3 May 03 ★ **AMERICAN LIFE** *Maverick / Warner Bros. 9362484542* ■ ▲....1 19
19 Jul 03 ● **HOLLYWOOD** *Maverick W 614CD1*....2 7
22 Nov 03 ● **ME AGAINST THE MUSIC** *Jive 82876576432* [1]....2 12
20 Dec 03 **LOVE PROFUSION** *Maverick W 634CD1*....**11** 6
19 Nov 05 ★ **HUNG UP** *Warner Bros. W 695CD2* ■....1 7+
26 Nov 05 ★ **CONFESSIONS ON A DANCE FLOOR** *Warner Bros. 9362494602* ■ ▲....1 6+

[1] Britney Spears featuring Madonna [1] Madonna / Various

'Holiday' peaked at No.6 in 1984, making No.2 only on re-entry in Aug 1985. 'Borderline' peaked at No.56 in 1984, making No.2 only on re-entry in Jan 1986. From 22 Aug 85 Madonna was repackaged as The First Album with the catalogue number Sire WX 22. Like a Virgin changed catalogue number to Sire WX 20 during its chart run. The Immaculate Collection changed catalogue number to Sire 7599264402 for its 2004 chart run.

Lisa MAFFIA (see also SO SOLID CREW)

UK, female vocalist (1 Album: 1 Week, 2 Singles: 15 Weeks)

3 May 03 ● **ALL OVER** *Independiente ISOM 69MS*....2 11
9 Aug 03 **IN LOVE** *Independiente ISOM 75MS*....**13** 4
23 Aug 03 **FIRST LADY** *Independiente ISOM 39CD*....44 1

MAGAZINE

UK, male vocal / instrumental group – lead vocal Howard Devoto (5 Albums: 24 Weeks, 2 Singles: 7 Weeks)

11 Feb 78 **SHOT BY BOTH SIDES** *Virgin VS 200*....**41** 4
24 Jun 78 **REAL LIFE** *Virgin V 2100*....29 8
14 Apr 79 **SECONDHAND DAYLIGHT** *Virgin V 2121*....38 8
10 May 80 **CORRECT USE OF SOAP** *Virgin V 2156*....28 4
26 Jul 80 **SWEET HEART CONTRACT** *Virgin VS 368*....**54** 3
13 Dec 80 **PLAY** *Virgin V 2184*....69 1
27 Jun 81 **MAGIC MURDER AND THE WEATHER** *Virgin V 2200*....39 3

MAGIC AFFAIR

US / Germany, male / female vocal / instrumental group (3 Singles: 8 Weeks)

4 Jun 94 **OMEN III** *EMI CDEM 317*....**17** 4
27 Aug 94 **GIVE ME ALL YOUR LOVE** *EMI CDEM 340*....**30** 2
5 Nov 94 **IN THE MIDDLE OF THE NIGHT** *EMI CDEM 349*....**38** 2

MAGIC LADY

US, female vocal duo

14 May 88 **BETCHA CAN'T LOSE (WITH MY LOVE)** *Motown ZB 42003*....**58** 3

The MAGIC LANTERNS

UK, male vocal / instrumental group

7 Jul 66 **EXCUSE ME BABY** (2re) *CBS 202094*....**44** 3

The MAGIC NUMBERS NEW

Trinidad / UK, male / female vocal / instrumental group (1 Album: 28 Weeks, 3 Singles: 16 Weeks)

4 Jun 05 **FOREVER LOST** *Heavenly HVN 151CD*....**15** 6

20 August 1977	27 August 1977	3 September 1977	10 September 1977
ANGELO Brotherhood of Man	**FLOAT ON** The Floaters	**WAY DOWN** Elvis Presley: Vocal acc. JD Sumner & The Stamps Qt., K Westmoreland, S Neilson and M Smith	**WAY DOWN** Elvis Presley: Vocal acc. JD Sumner & The Stamps Qt., K Westmoreland, S Neilson and M Smith
GOING FOR THE ONE Yes	**20 ALL TIME GREATS** Connie Francis	**20 ALL TIME GREATS** Connie Francis	**40 GREATEST HITS** Elvis Presley

KEY: UK No.1 ★ UK Top 10 ● Still on chart + UK entry at No.1 ■ US No.1 ▲ UK million seller £ US million seller $
Singles re-entries are listed as (re), (2re), (3re)... which signifies that the hit re-entered the chart once, twice or three times...
Peak Position / Weeks

25 Jun 05 ● THE MAGIC NUMBERS *Heavenly HVNLP 53CD* ... 7 28+
20 Aug 05 LOVE ME LIKE YOU *Heavenly HVN 153CDS* ... 12 7
5 Nov 05 LOVE'S A GAME *Heavenly HVN 154CD* ... 24 3

MAGNA CARTA
UK, male vocal / instrumental group

8 Aug 70 SEASONS *Vertigo 6360 003* ... 55 2

MAGNOLIA *Italy, male producer and UK, female vocalist*

24 Jul 04 IT'S ALL VAIN *Data DATA 69CDS* ... 55 1

MAGNUM *UK, male vocal (Bob Catley) / instrumental group (11 Albums: 47 Weeks, 7 Singles: 26 Weeks)*

16 Sep 78 KINGDOM OF MADNESS *Jet JETLP 210* ... 58 1
22 Mar 80 MAGNUM (DOUBLE SINGLE) *Jet 175* ... 47 6
19 Apr 80 MARAUDER *Jet JETLP 230* ... 34 5
6 Mar 82 CHASE THE DRAGON *Jet JETLP 235* ... 17 7
21 May 83 THE ELEVENTH HOUR *Jet JETLP 240* ... 38 4
25 May 85 ON A STORYTELLER'S NIGHT *FM WKFMLP 34* ... 24 7
12 Jul 86 LONELY NIGHT *Polydor POSP 798* ... 70 2
4 Oct 86 VIGILANTE *Polydor POLD 5198* ... 24 5
19 Mar 88 DAYS OF NO TRUST *Polydor POSP 910* ... 32 4
9 Apr 88 ● WINGS OF HEAVEN *Polydor POLD 5221* ... 5 9
7 May 88 START TALKING LOVE *Polydor POSP 920* ... 22 4
2 Jul 88 IT MUST HAVE BEEN LOVE *Polydor POSP 930* ... 33 4
23 Jun 90 ROCKIN' CHAIR *Polydor PO 88* ... 27 4
21 Jul 90 ● GOODNIGHT L.A. *Polydor 8435681* ... 9 5
25 Aug 90 HEARTBROKE AND BUSTED *Polydor PO 94* ... 49 2
14 Sep 91 THE SPIRIT *Polydor 5111691* ... 50 1
24 Oct 92 SLEEPWALKING *Music for Nations CDMFN 143* ... 27 2
18 Jun 94 ROCK ART *EMI CDEMD 1066* ... 57 1

Tracks on Magnum (double single): Invasion / Kingdom of Madness / All of My Life / Great Adventure.

MAGOO (see also Missy 'Misdemeanor' ELLIOTT; TIMBALAND)
US, male rapper – Melvin Barcliff (3 Singles: 4 Weeks)

13 Mar 99 HERE WE COME *Virgin DINSD 179* [1] ... 43 1
13 Mar 04 COP THAT SH*T *Unique Corp TIMBACD 001* [2] ... 22 3

[1] Timbaland / Missy Elliott and Magoo [2] Timbaland & Magoo featuring Missy Elliott

MAGOO; MOGWAI
UK, male vocal / instrumental group

4 Apr 98 BLACK SABBATH / SWEET LEAF *Fierce Panda NING 47CD* ... 60 1

Sean MAGUIRE (see also CHILDLINERS)
UK, male vocalist / actor (2 Albums: 3 Weeks, 8 Singles: 34 Weeks)

20 Aug 94 SOMEONE TO LOVE *Parlophone CDR 6390* ... 14 7
5 Nov 94 TAKE THIS TIME (re) *Parlophone CDR 6395* ... 27 5
26 Nov 94 SEAN MAGUIRE *Parlophone CDPCSDX 164* ... 75 1
25 Mar 95 SUDDENLY *Parlophone CDR 6403* ... 18 5
24 Jun 95 NOW I'VE FOUND YOU *Parlophone CDLEEPYS 1* ... 22 3
18 Nov 95 YOU TO ME ARE EVERYTHING *Parlophone CDR 6420* ... 16 3
25 May 96 GOOD DAY *Parlophone CDR 6432* ... 12 4
15 Jun 96 SPIRIT *Parlophone CDPCSD 169* ... 43 2
3 Aug 96 DON'T PULL YOUR LOVE *Parlophone CDR 6440* ... 14 4
29 Mar 97 TODAY'S THE DAY *Parlophone CDR 6459* ... 27 3

MAHAVISHNU ORCHESTRA
UK / US, male instrumental group (2 Albums: 14 Weeks)

31 Mar 73 BIRDS OF FIRE *CBS 65321* ... 20 5
28 Jul 73 ● LOVE DEVOTION SURRENDER *CBS 69037* [1] ... 7 9

[1] Carlos Santana and Mahavishnu John McLaughlin

MAI TAI *Guyana, female vocal group (1 Album: 1 Week, 3 Singles: 30 Weeks)*

25 May 85 ● HISTORY *Virgin VS 773* ... 8 13
6 Jul 85 HISTORY *Virgin V 2359* ... 91 1
3 Aug 85 ● BODY AND SOUL *Virgin VS 801* ... 9 13
15 Feb 86 FEMALE INTUITION *Virgin VS 844* ... 54 4

The MAIN INGREDIENT *US, male vocal group – includes Cuba Gooding*

29 Jun 74 JUST DON'T WANT TO BE LONELY *RCA APBO 0205* $ ... 27 7

The MAISONETTES *UK, male / female vocal group*

11 Dec 82 ● HEARTACHE AVENUE *Ready Steady Go! RSG 1* ... 7 12

The MAJESTICS *UK, male / female vocal group*

4 Apr 87 TUTTI FRUTTI *BBC REN 629* ... 64 4

J MAJIK *UK, male producer – Jamie Spratling (3 Singles: 4 Weeks)*

5 May 01 LOVE IS NOT A GAME *Defected DFECT 31CDS* [1] ... 34 2
27 Apr 02 METROSOUND *Kaos KAOS 001P* [2] ... 54 1
22 May 04 SCOOBY DOO / SPYCATCHER *Infrared INFRA 28* [3] ... 67 1

[1] J Majik featuring Kathy Brown [2] Adam F and J Majik [3] J Majik and Wickaman

MAKADOPOULOS and his GREEK SERENADERS
Greece, male vocal / instrumental group

20 Oct 60 NEVER ON SUNDAY *Palette PG 9005* ... 36 14

Jack E MAKOSSA (see also Wally JUMP Jr and The CRIMINAL ELEMENT) *US, male producer / multi-instrumentalist – Arthur Baker*

12 Sep 87 THE OPERA HOUSE *Champion CHAMP 50* ... 48 5

MALACHI *UK, male vocalist – Malachi Cush*

5 Apr 03 MALACHI *Mercury / Universal TV 0772802* ... 17 4
19 Apr 03 JUST SAY YOU LOVE ME *Mercury / Universal TV 0779072* ... 49 1

MALAIKA *US, female vocalist*

31 Jul 93 GOTTA KNOW (YOUR NAME) *A&M 5802732* ... 68 1

Carl MALCOLM *Jamaica, male vocalist*

13 Sep 75 ● FATTIE BUM BUM *UK 108* ... 8 8

Stephen MALKMUS (see also PAVEMENT)
US, male vocalist (2 Albums: 2 Weeks, 1 Single: 1 Week)

24 Feb 01 STEPHEN MALKMUS *Domino Recordings WIGCD 90* ... 49 1
28 Apr 01 DISCRETION GROVE *Domino RUG 123CD* ... 60 1
29 Mar 03 PIG LIB *Domino Recordings WIGCD 122X* ... 63 1

Yngwie J. MALMSTEEN *Sweden, male guitarist (4 Albums: 11 Weeks)*

21 May 88 ODYSSEY *Polydor POLD 5224* ... 27 7
4 Nov 89 TRIAL BY FIRE – LIVE IN LENINGRAD *Polydor 839726 1* ... 65 1
28 Apr 90 ECLIPSE *Polydor 8434611* ... 43 2
29 Feb 92 FIRE AND ICE *Elektra 7559611372* ... 57 1

Raul MALO (see also The MAVERICKS) *US, male vocalist*

18 May 02 I SAID I LOVE YOU *Gravity 74321923082* ... 57 1

17 September 1977	24 September 1977	1 October 1977	8 October 1977
UK No.1 SINGLES			
WAY DOWN Elvis Presley: Vocal acc. JD Sumner & The Stamps Qt., K Westmoreland, S Neilson and M Smith	**WAY DOWN** Elvis Presley: Vocal acc. JD Sumner & The Stamps Qt., K Westmoreland, S Neilson and M Smith	**WAY DOWN** Elvis Presley: Vocal acc. JD Sumner & The Stamps Qt., K Westmoreland, S Neilson and M Smith	**SILVER LADY** David Soul
UK No.1 ALBUMS			
20 GOLDEN GREATS Diana Ross and The Supremes	**20 GOLDEN GREATS** Diana Ross and The Supremes	**20 GOLDEN GREATS** Diana Ross and The Supremes	**20 GOLDEN GREATS** Diana Ross and The Supremes

MAMA CASS (see also The MAMAS and The PAPAS) *US, female vocalist – Ellen Cohen, b. 19 Sep 1941, d. 29 Jul 1974 (2 Singles: 27 Weeks)*

14 Aug 68 DREAM A LITTLE DREAM OF ME *RCA 1726*....11 12
16 Aug 69 ● IT'S GETTING BETTER *Stateside SS 8021*....8 15

MAMA'S BOYS *Ireland, male vocal / instrumental group*

6 Apr 85 POWER AND PASSION *Jive HIP 24*....55 4

The MAMAS and The PAPAS (see also MAMA CASS) *US, male / female vocal / instrumental group (7 Albums: 71 Weeks, 7 Singles: 71 Weeks)*

28 Apr 66 CALIFORNIA DREAMIN' *RCA 1503* $....23 9
12 May 66 ● MONDAY MONDAY *RCA 1516* ▲ $....3 13
25 Jun 66 ● THE MAMAS AND PAPAS *RCA Victor RD 7803* ▲....3 18
28 Jul 66 I SAW HER AGAIN *RCA 1533*....11 11
28 Jan 67 CASS JOHN MICHELLE DENNY *RCA Victor SF 7639*....24 6
9 Feb 67 WORDS OF LOVE *RCA 1564*....47 3
6 Apr 67 ● DEDICATED TO THE ONE I LOVE *RCA 1576*....2 17
24 Jun 67 ● MAMAS AND PAPAS DELIVER *RCA Victor SF 7880*....4 22
26 Jul 67 ● CREEQUE ALLEY *RCA 1613*....9 11
26 Apr 69 ● HITS OF GOLD *Stateside S 5007*....7 2
18 Jun 77 ● THE BEST OF THE MAMAS AND PAPAS *Arcade ADEP 30*....6 13
28 Jan 95 CALIFORNIA DREAMIN' – THE VERY BEST OF THE MAMAS AND THE PAPAS *PolyGram TV 5239732*....14 6
2 Aug 97 ● CALIFORNIA DREAMIN' (re-issue) *MCA MCSTD 48058*....9 7
6 Sep 97 CALIFORNIA DREAMIN' – GREATEST HITS OF THE MAMAS AND THE PAPAS *Telstar TV TTVCD 2931*....30 4

MAN *UK, male vocal / instrumental group (4 Albums: 11 Weeks)*

20 Oct 73 BACK INTO THE FUTURE *United Artists UAD 60053/4*....23 3
25 May 74 RHINOS WINOS AND LUNATICS *United Artists UAG 29631*....24 4
11 Oct 75 MAXIMUM DARKNESS *United Artists UAG 29872*....25 2
17 Apr 76 WELSH CONNECTION *MCA MCF 2753*....40 2

A MAN CALLED ADAM *UK, male / female vocal / instrumental group*

29 Sep 90 BAREFOOT IN THE HEAD (re) *Big Life BLR 28*....60 4

MAN TO MAN
US, male vocal / instrumental group (2 Singles: 19 Weeks)

13 Sep 86 ● MALE STRIPPER (2re) *Bolts BOLTS 4* [1] 4 16
4 Jul 87 I NEED A MAN / ENERGY'S EUROBEAT *Bolts BOLTS 5*....43 3

[1] Man 2 Man meet Man Parrish

'Male Stripper' reached its peak position on its second re-entry in Feb 1987.

MAN WITH NO NAME
UK, male producer – Martin Freeland (5 Singles: 6 Weeks)

30 Sep 95 FLOOR-ESSENCE *Perfecto PERF 108CD*....68 1
20 Jan 96 PAINT A PICTURE *Perfecto PERF 114CD* [1] 42 2
12 Oct 96 TELEPORT / SUGAR RUSH *Perfecto PERF 126CD*....55 1
2 May 98 VAVOOM! *Perfecto PERF 159CD1*....43 1
18 Jul 98 THE FIRST DAY (HORIZON) *Perfecto PERF 164CD*....72 1

[1] Man with No Name featuring Hannah

MANCHESTER BOYS CHOIR *UK, male choir*

21 Dec 85 THE NEW SOUND OF CHRISTMAS *K-Tel ONE 1314*....80 2

MANCHESTER UNITED FOOTBALL CLUB
UK, male football team vocalists (8 Singles: 56 Weeks)

8 May 76 MANCHESTER UNITED *Decca F 13633*....50 1
21 May 83 GLORY GLORY MAN UNITED *EMI 5390*....13 5
18 May 85 ● WE ALL FOLLOW MAN UNITED *Columbia DB 9107*....10 5
19 Jun 93 UNITED (WE LOVE YOU) *Living Beat LBECD 026* [1] 37 2
30 Apr 94 ★ COME ON YOU REDS *PolyGram TV MANU 2*....1 15
13 May 95 ● WE'RE GONNA DO IT AGAIN *PolyGram TV MANU 952* [2] 6 6
4 May 96 ● MOVE MOVE MOVE (THE RED TRIBE) (re) *Music Collection MANUCD 1* [3] 6 15
29 May 99 LIFT IT HIGH (ALL ABOUT BELIEF) (re) *Music Collection MANUCD 4* [4] 11 7

[1] Manchester United and the Champions [2] Manchester United Football Squad featuring Stryker [3] 1996 Manchester United FA Cup Squad [4] 1999 Manchester United Squad

MANCHILD (see also STEREOPHONICS)
UK, male production duo – Max Odell and Brett Parker (2 Singles: 2 Weeks)

16 Sep 00 THE CLICHES ARE TRUE *One Little Indian 176TP 7CD* [1] 60 1
25 Aug 01 NOTHING WITHOUT ME *One Little Indian 183TP 7CD*....40 1

[1] Manchild featuring Kelly Jones

Henry MANCINI & his ORCHESTRA *US, orchestra / chorus – leader b. 16 Apr 1924, d. 14 Jun 1994 (4 Albums: 23 Weeks, 4 Singles: 23 Weeks)*

7 Dec 61 MOON RIVER (re) *RCA 1256*....44 3
24 Sep 64 ● HOW SOON *RCA 1414*....10 12
25 Mar 72 THEME FROM 'CADE'S COUNTY' *RCA 2182*....42 1
16 Oct 76 HENRY MANCINI *Arcade ADEP 24*....26 8
11 Feb 84 MAIN THEME FROM 'THE THORN BIRDS' *Warner Bros. 9677*... 23 7
30 Jun 84 MAMMA *Decca 411959* [1] 96 1
8 Dec 84 IN THE PINK *RCA Red Seal RL 85315* [2] 62 6
13 Dec 86 THE HOLLYWOOD MUSICALS *CBS 4502581* [3] 46 8

[1] Luciano Pavarotti with the Henry Mancini Orchestra [2] James Galway and Henry Mancini and the National Philharmonic Orchestra [3] Johnny Mathis and Henry Mancini

MANDO DIAO NEW
Sweden, male vocal / instrumental group (2 Singles: 2 Weeks)

5 Mar 05 YOU CAN'T STEAL MY LOVE *Majesty 8708962*....73 1
18 Jun 05 GOD KNOWS *Majesty 8726022*....64 1

MANFRED MANN (175 Top 500) (see also McGUINNESS FLINT)
One of the most regular chart entrants of the 1960s: Manfred Mann, b. S. Africa (k), Mike Vickers (g), Tom McGuinness (b), Mike Hugg (d) and Paul Jones (v) (replaced by Mike D'Abo in 1966). They were the first south of England-based group to top the US charts during 1964's so-called 'British Invasion' (12 Albums: 100 Weeks, 22 Singles: 217 Weeks)

23 Jan 64 ● 5-4-3-2-1 *HMV POP 1252*....5 13
16 Apr 64 HUBBLE BUBBLE (TOIL AND TROUBLE) *HMV POP 1282*....11 8
16 Jul 64 ★ DO WAH DIDDY DIDDY *HMV POP 1320* ▲ $....1 14
19 Sep 64 ● FIVE FACES OF MANFRED MANN *HMV CLP 1731*....3 24
15 Oct 64 ● SHA LA LA *HMV POP 1346*....3 12
14 Jan 65 ● COME TOMORROW *HMV POP 1381*....4 9
15 Apr 65 OH NO, NOT MY BABY *HMV POP 1413*....11 10
16 Sep 65 ● IF YOU GOTTA GO, GO NOW *HMV POP 1466*....2 12
23 Oct 65 ● MANN MADE *HMV CLP 1911*....7 11
21 Apr 66 ★ PRETTY FLAMINGO *HMV POP 1523*....1 12
7 Jul 66 YOU GAVE ME SOMEBODY TO LOVE *HMV POP 1541*....36 4
4 Aug 66 ● JUST LIKE A WOMAN *Fontana TF 730*....10 10
17 Sep 66 MANN MADE HITS *HMV CLP 3559*....11 17
27 Oct 66 ● SEMI-DETACHED SUBURBAN MR JAMES *Fontana TF 757*....2 12
29 Oct 66 AS IS *Fontana TL 5377*....22 4
21 Jan 67 SOUL OF MANN *HMV CSD 3594*....40 1
30 Mar 67 ● HA! HA! SAID THE CLOWN *Fontana TF 812*....4 11
25 May 67 SWEET PEA *Fontana TF 828*....36 4
24 Jan 68 ★ MIGHTY QUINN *Fontana TF 897*....1 11
12 Jun 68 ● MY NAME IS JACK *Fontana TF 943*....8 11
18 Dec 68 ● FOX ON THE RUN *Fontana TF 985*....5 12
30 Apr 69 ● RAGAMUFFIN MAN *Fontana TF 1013*....8 11
8 Sep 73 ● JOYBRINGER *Vertigo 6059 083* [1] 9 10
28 Aug 76 ● BLINDED BY THE LIGHT *Bronze BRO 29* [1] ▲ $....6 10
18 Sep 76 ● THE ROARING SILENCE *Bronze ILPS 9357* [1] 10 9
20 May 78 ● DAVY'S ON THE ROAD AGAIN *Bronze BRO 52* [1] 6 12
17 Jun 78 WATCH *Bronze BRON 507* [1] 33 6

15 October 1977	22 October 1977	29 October 1977	5 November 1977
SILVER LADY David Soul	SILVER LADY David Soul	YES SIR, I CAN BOOGIE Baccara	THE NAME OF THE GAME Abba
20 GOLDEN GREATS Diana Ross and The Supremes	20 GOLDEN GREATS Diana Ross and The Supremes	20 GOLDEN GREATS Diana Ross and The Supremes	40 GOLDEN GREATS Cliff Richard

TOP 10

ON THE DAY IN 1963 PRESIDENT KENNEDY WAS ASSASSINATED

On 22 November 1963, John F Kennedy, the 35th President of the United States, was shot dead in Dallas, Texas. The Warren report, commissioned to investigate the President's death, concluded that Lee Harvey Oswald had gunned down Kennedy from a window in the School Book Depository building as the presidential convoy made its way from Dallas airport to the city centre. Oswald was charged with the assassination of President Kennedy but was shot dead two days later by nightclub owner Jack Ruby. The incident inspired the band name Dead Kennedys and The Wedding Present's 'Kennedy'. Marilyn Manson dedicated their Mechanical Animals album to JFK.

LW	TW	
1	1	**YOU'LL NEVER WALK ALONE** Gerry and The Pacemakers
3	2	**SHE LOVES YOU** The Beatles
2	3	**SUGAR AND SPICE** The Searchers
5	4	**BE MY BABY** The Ronettes
7	5	**DON'T TALK TO HIM** Cliff Richard and The Shadows
12	6	**SECRET LOVE** Kathy Kirby
4	7	**BLUE BAYOU / MEAN WOMAN BLUES** Roy Orbison
9	8	**I (WHO HAVE NOTHING)** Shirley Bassey
11	9	**I'LL KEEP YOU SATISFIED** Billy J Kramer and The Dakotas
6	10	**LET IT ROCK / MEMPHIS TENNESSEE** Chuck Berry

JFK

Gerry and The Pacemakers

17Mar 79 **YOU ANGEL YOU** *Bronze BRO 68* [1] **54** 5
24 Mar 79 ANGEL STATION *Bronze BRON 516* [1] 30 8
7 Jul 79 **DON'T KILL IT CAROL** *Bronze BRO 77* [1] **45** 4
15 Sep 79 ● SEMI-DETACHED SUBURBAN *EMI EMTV 19* 9 14
26 Feb 83 **SOMEWHERE IN AFRIKA** *Bronze BRON 543* [1] **87** 1
23 Jan 93 AGES OF MANN *PolyGram TV 5143622* 23 4
10 Sep 94 THE VERY BEST OF MANFRED MANN'S EARTH BAND *Arcade ARC 3100162* [1] 69 1

[1] Manfred Mann's Earth Band [1] Manfred Mann's Earth Band

MANHATTAN TRANSFER (465 Top 500)

Multi-faceted four-part harmony vocal group formed in New York, US, in 1969, whose recordings include songs from the 1930s-80s. Their nostalgic sound earned them 10 Grammy awards, although, oddly, their No.1 single did not chart in the US (6 Albums: 85 Weeks, 9 Singles: 72 Weeks)

7 Feb 76 **TUXEDO JUNCTION** *Atlantic K 10670* **24** 6
5 Feb 77 ★ **CHANSON D'AMOUR** *Atlantic K 10886* **1** 13
12 Mar 77 COMING OUT *Atlantic K 50291* 12 20
19 Mar 77 MANHATTAN TRANSFER *Atlantic K 50138* 49 7
28 May 77 **DON'T LET GO** *Atlantic K 10930* **32** 6
18 Feb 78 **WALK IN LOVE** (re) *Atlantic K 11075* **12** 12
25 Feb 78 ● PASTICHE *Atlantic K 50444* 10 34
20 May 78 **ON A LITTLE STREET IN SINGAPORE** *Atlantic K 11136* **20** 9
16 Sep 78 **WHERE DID OUR LOVE GO / JE VOULAIS (TE DIRE QUE JE T'ATTENDS)** *Atlantic K 11182* **40** 4
11 Nov 78 ● LIVE *Atlantic K 50540* 4 17
23 Dec 78 **WHO, WHAT, WHEN, WHERE, WHY** *Atlantic K 11233* **49** 6
17 Nov 79 EXTENSIONS *Atlantic K 50674* 63 3
17 May 80 **TWILIGHT ZONE – TWILIGHT TONE (MEDLEY)** *Atlantic K 11476* **25** 8
21 Jan 84 **SPICE OF LIFE** *Atlantic A 9728* **19** 8
18 Feb 84 BODIES AND SOULS *Atlantic 780104* 53 4

The MANHATTANS

US, male vocal (George Smith) group (1 Album: 3 Weeks, 5 Singles: 31 Weeks)

19 Jun 76 ● **KISS AND SAY GOODBYE** *CBS 4317* ▲ $ **4** 11
14 Aug 76 MANHATTANS *CBS 81513* 37 3
2 Oct 76 ● **HURT** *CBS 4562* **4** 11
23 Apr 77 **IT'S YOU** *CBS 5093* **43** 3
26 Jul 80 **SHINING STAR** *CBS 8624* $ **45** 4
6 Aug 83 **CRAZY** *CBS A 3578* **63** 2

MANIA *UK, female vocal duo – Niara Scarlett and Giselle Sommerville*

7 Aug 04 **LOOKING FOR A PLACE** *RCA 82876617852* **29** 2

M.A.N.I.C. *UK, male vocal / production duo*

18 Apr 92 **I'M COMIN' HARDCORE** *Union City UCRT 2* **60** 1

MANIC MCs featuring Sara CARLSON

UK, male production duo and female vocalist

12 Aug 89 **MENTAL** *RCA PB 43037* **30** 5

MANIC STREET PREACHERS (144 Top 500)

Best-selling Welsh act of the 1990s: James Dean Bradfield (v/g), Nicky Wire (b), Sean Moore (d) and Richey Edwards (v/g – missing since 1995 and officially declared dead in 2002). Won trophies for the Best British Group and Best Album at the 1997 and 1999 BRIT Awards (9 Albums: 205 Weeks, 37 Singles: 158 Weeks)

25 May 91 **YOU LOVE US** *Heavenly HVN 10* **62** 2
10 Aug 91 **STAY BEAUTIFUL** *Columbia 6573377* **40** 3
9 Nov 91 **LOVE'S SWEET EXILE / REPEAT** *Columbia 6575827* **26** 3
1 Feb 92 **YOU LOVE US** (re-issue) *Columbia 6577247* **16** 4
22 Feb 92 GENERATION TERRORISTS *Columbia 4710602* 13 17
28 Mar 92 **SLASH 'N' BURN** *Columbia 6578737* **20** 4
13 Jun 92 **MOTORCYCLE EMPTINESS** *Columbia 6580837* **17** 6
19 Sep 92 ● **THEME FROM M.A.S.H. (SUICIDE IS PAINLESS)** *Columbia 6583827* **7** 6

	12 November 1977	19 November 1977	26 November 1977	3 December 1977
UK No.1 SINGLES	THE NAME OF THE GAME Abba	THE NAME OF THE GAME Abba	THE NAME OF THE GAME Abba	MULL OF KINTYRE / GIRLS' SCHOOL Wings
UK No.1 ALBUMS	NEVER MIND THE BOLLOCKS HERE'S THE SEX PISTOLS Sex Pistols	NEVER MIND THE BOLLOCKS HERE'S THE SEX PISTOLS Sex Pistols	THE SOUND OF BREAD Bread	THE SOUND OF BREAD Bread

21 Nov 92 **LITTLE BABY NOTHING** *Columbia 6587967*....29 3
12 Jun 93 **FROM DESPAIR TO WHERE** *Columbia 6593372*....25 4
3 Jul 93 ● GOLD AGAINST THE SOUL *Columbia 4640642*....8 11
31 Jul 93 **LA TRISTESSE DURERA (SCREAM TO A SIGH)** *Columbia 6594772*....22 5
2 Oct 93 **ROSES IN THE HOSPITAL** *Columbia 6597272*....15 3
12 Feb 94 **LIFE BECOMING A LANDSLIDE** *Columbia 6600702*....36 2
11 Jun 94 **FASTER / PCP** *Epic 6604472*....16 3
13 Aug 94 **REVOL** *Epic 6606862*....22 3
10 Sep 94 ● THE HOLY BIBLE *Epic 4774219*....6 4
15 Oct 94 **SHE IS SUFFERING** *Epic 6608952*....25 3
27 Apr 96 ● **A DESIGN FOR LIFE** (re) *Epic 6630705*....2 11
1 Jun 96 ● EVERYTHING MUST GO *Epic 4839302*....2 82
3 Aug 96 ● **EVERYTHING MUST GO** *Epic 6634685*....5 6
12 Oct 96 ● **KEVIN CARTER** *Epic 6637752*....9 4
14 Dec 96 ● **AUSTRALIA** *Epic 6640442*....7 7
13 Sep 97 **MOTORCYCLE EMPTINESS** (re-issue) *Epic MANIC 5CD*....41 2
13 Sep 97 **YOU LOVE US** (2nd re-issue) *Epic MANIC 3CD*....49 1
13 Sep 97 **LITTLE BABY NOTHING** (re-issue) *Epic MANIC 6CD*....50 1
13 Sep 97 **STAY BEAUTIFUL** (re-issue) *Epic MANIC 1CD*....52 1
13 Sep 97 **SLASH 'N' BURN** (re-issue) *Epic MANIC 4CD*....54 1
13 Sep 97 **LOVE'S SWEET EXILE** (re-issue) *Epic MANIC 2CD*....55 1
5 Sep 98 ★ **IF YOU TOLERATE THIS YOUR CHILDREN WILL BE NEXT** (re) *Epic 6663452* ■....1 11
26 Sep 98 ★ THIS IS MY TRUTH TELL ME YOURS *Epic 4917039* ■....1 60
12 Dec 98 **THE EVERLASTING** *Epic 6666862*....11 8
20 Mar 99 ● **YOU STOLE THE SUN FROM MY HEART** *Epic 6669532*....5 8
17 Jul 99 **TSUNAMI** *Epic 6674112*....11 5
22 Jan 00 ★ **THE MASSES AGAINST THE CLASSES** (re) *Epic 6685302* ■....1 7
10 Mar 01 ● **FOUND THAT SOUL** (re) *Epic 6708332*....9 4
10 Mar 01 ● **SO WHY SO SAD** *Epic 6708322*....8 7
31 Mar 01 ● KNOW YOUR ENEMY *Epic 5018802*....2 14
16 Jun 01 **OCEAN SPRAY** *Epic 6712532*....15 4
22 Sep 01 **LET ROBESON SING** *Epic 6717732*....19 2
26 Oct 02 ● **THERE BY THE GRACE OF GOD** (re) *Epic 6731662*....6 5
9 Nov 02 ● FOREVER DELAYED – THE GREATEST HITS *Epic 5095519*....4 12
26 Jul 03 LIPSTICK TRACES – A SECRET HISTORY OF MANIC STREET PREACHERS *Sony Music 5123862*....11 3
30 Oct 04 ● **THE LOVE OF RICHARD NIXON** *Sony Music 6753422*....2 4
13 Nov 04 LIFEBLOOD *Sony Music 5188852*....13 2
22 Jan 05 ● **EMPTY SOULS** *Columbia 6756102*....2 4

The listed flipside of 'Theme From M.A.S.H. (Suicide Is Painless)' was '(Everything I Do) I Do It for You' by Fatima Mansions.

MANIJAMA featuring MUKUPA & L'IL T
UK, male / female production / vocal group

8 Feb 03 **NO NO NO** *Defected DFTD 058CDS*....66 1

Barry MANILOW (83 Top 500)
Middle-of-the-road superstar, b. Barry Pincus, 17 Jun 1946, Brooklyn, US. This crowd-pulling singer / songwriter / pianist with a vast and loyal following on both sides of the Atlantic has sold in excess of 60 million albums (24 Albums: 356 Weeks, 20 Singles: 136 Weeks)

22 Feb 75 **MANDY** *Arista 1* ▲ $....11 9
6 May 78 **CAN'T SMILE WITHOUT YOU** *Arista 176* $....43 7
29 Jul 78 **SOMEWHERE IN THE NIGHT / COPACABANA (AT THE COPA)** *Arista 196* $....42 10
23 Sep 78 EVEN NOW *Arista SPART 1047*....12 28
23 Dec 78 **COULD IT BE MAGIC** *Arista ARIST 229*....25 10
3 Mar 79 ● MANILOW MAGIC – THE BEST OF BARRY MANILOW *Arista ARTV 2*....3 151
20 Oct 79 ONE VOICE *Arista SPART 1106*....18 7
8 Nov 80 **LONELY TOGETHER** *Arista ARIST 373*....21 13
29 Nov 80 ● BARRY *Arista DLART 2*....5 34
7 Feb 81 **I MADE IT THROUGH THE RAIN** *Arista ARIST 384*....37 6
11 Apr 81 **BERMUDA TRIANGLE** *Arista ARIST 406*....15 9
25 Apr 81 GIFT SET *Arista BOX 1*....62 1
26 Sep 81 **LET'S HANG ON** *Arista ARIST 429*....12 11
3 Oct 81 ● IF I SHOULD LOVE AGAIN *Arista BMAN 1*....5 26
12 Dec 81 **THE OLD SONGS** *Arista ARIST 443*....48 8
20 Feb 82 **IF I SHOULD LOVE AGAIN** *Arista ARIST 453*....66 2
17 Apr 82 **STAY** *Arista ARIST 464* [1]....23 8
1 May 82 ★ BARRY LIVE IN BRITAIN *Arista ARTV 4* ■....1 23
16 Oct 82 ● **I WANNA DO IT WITH YOU** *Arista ARIST 495*....8 8
27 Nov 82 ● I WANNA DO IT WITH YOU *Arista BMAN 2*....7 9
4 Dec 82 **I'M GONNA SIT RIGHT DOWN AND WRITE MYSELF A LETTER** *Arista ARIST 503*....36 7
25 Jun 83 **SOME KIND OF FRIEND** *Arista ARIST 516*....48 2
27 Aug 83 **YOU'RE LOOKING HOT TONIGHT** *Arista ARIST 542*....47 6
8 Oct 83 ● A TOUCH MORE MAGIC *Arista BMAN 3*....10 12
10 Dec 83 **READ 'EM AND WEEP** *Arista ARIST 551*....17 7
1 Dec 84 2:00 AM PARADISE CAFÉ *Arista 206 496*....28 6
16 Nov 85 MANILOW *RCA PL 87044*....40 6
20 Feb 88 SWING STREET *Arista 208860*....81 1
8 Apr 89 **PLEASE DON'T BE SCARED** *Arista 112186*....35 5
20 May 89 SONGS TO MAKE THE WHOLE WORLD SING *Arista 209927*....20 4
17 Mar 90 LIVE ON BROADWAY *Arista 303785*....19 3
30 Jun 90 THE SONGS 1975-1990 *Arista 303868*....13 7
2 Nov 91 SHOWSTOPPERS *Arista 212091*....53 3
3 Apr 93 HIDDEN TREASURES *Arista 74321135682*....36 7
10 Apr 93 **COPACABANA (AT THE COPA)** (re-mix) *Arista 74321136912*....22 4
20 Nov 93 **COULD IT BE MAGIC 1993** *Arista 74321174882*....36 3
27 Nov 93 GREATEST HITS – THE PLATINUM COLLECTION *Arista 74321175452*....37 6
6 Aug 94 **LET ME BE YOUR WINGS** *EMI CDEM 336* [2]....73 1
5 Nov 94 SINGIN' WITH THE BIG BANDS *Arista 07822187712*....54 2
30 Nov 96 SUMMER OF '78 *Arista 7822188092*....66 2
21 Nov 98 MANILOW SINGS SINATRA *Arista 7822190332*....72 2
25 May 02 HERE AT THE MAYFLOWER *Columbia 5077342*....18 3
20 Mar 04 ● ULTIMATE MANILOW *Arista 82876604552*....8 12
3 Sep 05 ULTIMATE LIVE *Sony BMG 82876719142*....51 1

[1] Barry Manilow featuring Kevin Desimone and James Jolis [2] Barry Manilow and Debra Byrd

'Stay' was available as both a live and studio recording.

MANIX *UK, male producer (3 Singles: 6 Weeks)*

23 Nov 91 **MANIC MINDS** *Reinforced RIVET 1209*....63 2
7 Mar 92 **OBLIVION (HEAD IN THE CLOUDS) (EP)** *Reinforced RIVET 1212*....43 3
8 Aug 92 **RAINBOW PEOPLE** *Reinforced RIVET 1221*....57 1

Tracks on Oblivion (Head in the Clouds) (EP): Oblivion (Head in the Clouds) / Never Been to Belgium (Gotta Rush) / I Can't Stand It / You Held My Hand.

MANKEY *UK, male producer – Andy Manston*

16 Nov 96 **BELIEVE IN ME** *Frisky DISKY 3*....74 1

MANKIND *UK, male instrumental group*

25 Nov 78 **DR WHO** *Pinnacle PIN 71*....25 12

Aimee MANN *US, female vocalist (3 Albums: 3 Weeks, 4 Singles: 9 Weeks)*

31 Oct 87 **TIME STAND STILL** *Vertigo RUSH 13* [1]....42 3
28 Aug 93 **I SHOULD'VE KNOWN** *Imago 72787250437*....55 2
18 Sep 93 WHATEVER *Imago 72787210172*....39 1
20 Nov 93 **STUPID THING** *Imago 72787250527*....47 2
5 Mar 94 **I SHOULD'VE KNOWN** (re-issue) *Imago 72787250602*....45 2
11 Nov 95 I'M WITH STUPID *Geffen GED 24951*....51 1
14 Sep 02 LOST IN SPACE *V2 VVR 1020882*....72 1

[1] Rush with Aimee Mann

Roberto MANN *UK, male orchestra leader*

9 Dec 67 GREAT WALTZES *Deram SML 1010*....19 9

Johnny MANN SINGERS *US, male / female vocal group*

12 Jul 67 ● **UP-UP AND AWAY** *Liberty LIB 55972*....6 13

Shelly MANNE *US, male percussionist, b. 11 Jun 1920, d. 29 Sep 1984*

18 Jun 60 MY FAIR LADY *Vogue LAC 12100*....20 1

10 December 1977	17 December 1977	24 December 1977	31 December 1977
MULL OF KINTYRE / GIRLS' SCHOOL Wings	MULL OF KINTYRE / GIRLS' SCHOOL Wings	MULL OF KINTYRE / GIRLS' SCHOOL Wings	MULL OF KINTYRE / GIRLS' SCHOOL Wings
DISCO FEVER Various	DISCO FEVER Various	DISCO FEVER Various	DISCO FEVER Various

KEY: UK No.1 ★ UK Top 10 ● Still on chart + UK entry at No.1 ■ US No.1 ▲ UK million seller £ US million seller $
Singles re-entries are listed as (re), (2re), (3re)... which signifies that the hit re-entered the chart once, twice or three times...
Peak Position / Weeks

MANOWAR *US, male vocal / instrumental group (2 Albums: 3 Weeks)*

18 Feb 84	HAIL TO ENGLAND *Music for Nations MFN 19*	83	2
6 Oct 84	SIGN OF THE HAMMER *10 DIX 10*	73	1

MANSUN *UK, male vocal (Paul Draper) / instrumental group (3 Albums: 27 Weeks, 15 Singles: 45 Weeks)*

6 Apr 96	ONE (EP) *Parlophone CDR 6430*	37	2
15 Jun 96	TWO (EP) *Parlophone CDR 6437*	32	2
21 Sep 96	THREE (EP) *Parlophone CDR 6447*	19	3
17 Dec 96	WIDE OPEN SPACE *Parlophone CDR 6453*	15	4
15 Feb 97 ●	SHE MAKES MY NOSE BLEED *Parlophone CDR 6453*	9	5
1 Mar 97 ★	ATTACK OF THE GREY LANTERN *Parlophone CDPCS 7387* ■	1	19
10 May 97	TAXLOSS *Parlophone CDRS 6465*	15	3
18 Oct 97 ●	CLOSED FOR BUSINESS *Parlophone CDRS 6482*	10	3
11 Jul 98 ●	LEGACY (EP) *Parlophone CDRS 6497*	7	4
5 Sep 98	BEING A GIRL (PART ONE) (EP) *Parlophone CDR 6503*	13	3
19 Sep 98 ●	SIX *Parlophone 4967232*	6	4
7 Nov 98	NEGATIVE *Parlophone CDR 6508*	27	2
13 Feb 99	SIX *Parlophone CDR 6511*	16	3
12 Aug 00 ●	I CAN ONLY DISAPPOINT U *Parlophone CDR 6544*	8	6
26 Aug 00	LITTLE KIX *Parlophone 5277822*	12	4
18 Nov 00	ELECTRIC MAN *Parlophone CDR 6550*	23	2
10 Feb 01	FOOL *Parlophone CDRS 6553*	28	2
2 Oct 04	SLIPPING AWAY *Parlophone R 6650*	55	1

Tracks on One (EP): Egg Shaped Fred / Ski Jump Nose / Lemonade Secret Drinker / Thief. Tracks on Two (EP): Take It Easy Chicken / Drastic Sturgeon / The Greatest Pain / Moronica. Tracks on Three (EP): Stripper Vicar / An Open Letter to the Lyrical Trainspotter / No One Knows Us / Things Keep Falling Off Buildings. Tracks on Legacy (EP) – CD1: Legacy (Extended version) / Can't Afford to Die / Spasm of Identity / Check Under the Bed. CD2: Legacy / Wide Open Space (The Perfecto Remix) / GSOH / Face in the Crowd. Tracks on Being a Girl (Part One) (EP): Being a Girl / I Care / Been Here Before / Hideout / Railings.

MANTOVANI (357 Top 500) (see also David WHITFIELD)

Britain's most successful album act before The Beatles: leader b. Annunzio Paulo Mantovani, 15 Nov 1905, Venice, Italy, d. 29 Mar 1980. They were the first act to sell one million stereo albums and had six albums simultaneously in the US Top 30 in 1959 (12 Albums: 143 Weeks, 5 Singles: 52 Weeks)

19 Dec 52 ●	WHITE CHRISTMAS *Decca F 10017*	6	3
29 May 53 ★	THE SONG FROM THE MOULIN ROUGE (2re) *Decca F 10094*	1	23
23 Oct 53 ●	SWEDISH RHAPSODY (re) *Decca F 10168*	2	18
11 Feb 55	LONELY BALLERINA (re) *Decca F 10395*	16	4
31 May 57	AROUND THE WORLD *Decca F 10888*	20	4
21 Feb 59 ●	CONTINENTAL ENCORES *Decca LK 4298*	4	12
18 Feb 61	CONCERT SPECTACULAR *Decca LK 4377*	16	2
16 Apr 66 ●	MANTOVANI MAGIC *Decca LK 7949*	3	15
15 Oct 66	MR MUSIC – MANTOVANI *Decca LK 4809*	24	3
14 Jan 67 ●	MANTOVANI'S GOLDEN HITS *Decca SKL 4818*	10	35
30 Sep 67	HOLLYWOOD *Decca SKL 4887*	37	1
14 Jun 69 ●	THE WORLD OF MANTOVANI *Decca SPA 1*	6	31
4 Oct 69 ●	THE WORLD OF MANTOVANI VOLUME 2 *Decca SPA 36*	4	19
16 May 70	MANTOVANI TODAY *Decca SKL 5003*	16	8
26 Feb 72	TO LOVERS EVERYWHERE *Decca SKL 5112*	44	1
3 Nov 79 ●	20 GOLDEN GREATS *Warwick WW 5067*	9	13
16 Mar 85	MANTOVANI MAGIC *Telstar STAR 2237* [1]	52	3

[1] Mantovani Orchestra conducted by Roland Shaw

Kurtis MANTRONIK (see also MANTRONIX) *US, male vocalist / instrumentalist / producer – Kurtis Kahleel (3 Singles: 6 Weeks)*

15 Aug 98	STRICTLY BUSINESS *Parlophone CDR 6502* [1]	43	1
9 Nov 02	77 STRINGS *Southern Fried ECB 35* [2]	71	1
28 Jun 03	HOW DID YOU KNOW *Southern Fried ECB 43CDS* [2]	16	4

[1] Kurtis Mantronik vs EPMD [2] Kurtis Mantronik presents Chamonix

MANTRONIX (see also Kurtis MANTRONIK) *US / Jamaica, male vocal / instrumental duo – Kurtis Kahleel and MC Tee (Toure Embden) (replaced Bryce Wilson in 1989) (5 Albums: 17 Weeks, 10 Singles: 48 Weeks)*

22 Feb 86	LADIES *10 TEN 116*	55	4
29 Mar 86	THE ALBUM *10 DIX 37*	45	3
17 May 86	BASSLINE *10 TEN 118*	34	6
13 Dec 86	MUSICAL MADNESS *10 DIX 50*	66	3
7 Feb 87	WHO IS IT? *10 TEN 137*	40	6
4 Jul 87	SCREAM (PRIMAL SCREAM) *10 TEN 169*	46	4
30 Jan 88	SING A SONG (BREAK IT DOWN) *10 TEN 206*	61	2
12 Mar 88	SIMPLE SIMON (YOU GOTTA REGARD) *10 TEN 217*	72	2
2 Apr 88	IN FULL EFFECT *10 DIX 74*	39	3
6 Jan 90 ●	GOT TO HAVE YOUR LOVE *Capitol CL 559* [1]	4	11
17 Feb 90	THIS SHOULD MOVE YA *Capitol EST 2117*	18	6
12 May 90 ●	TAKE YOUR TIME *Capitol CL 573* [1]	10	7
2 Mar 91	DON'T GO MESSIN' WITH MY HEART *Capitol CL 608*	22	5
30 Mar 91	THE INCREDIBLE SOUND MACHINE *Capitol EST 2139*	36	2
22 Jun 91	STEP TO ME (DO ME) *Capitol CL 613*	59	1

[1] Mantronix featuring Wondress

MANUEL and The MUSIC OF THE MOUNTAINS

UK, orchestra – leader Geoff Love, b. 4 Sep 1917, d. 8 Jul 1991 (3 Albums: 38 Weeks, 4 Singles: 31 Weeks)

28 Aug 59	THE HONEYMOON SONG (2re) *Columbia DB 4323*	22	9
10 Sep 60	MUSIC OF THE MOUNTAINS *Columbia 33SX 1212*	17	1
13 Oct 60	NEVER ON SUNDAY *Columbia DB 4515*	29	10
13 Oct 66	SOMEWHERE MY LOVE *Columbia DB 7969*	42	2
7 Aug 71	THIS IS MANUEL *Studio Two STWO 5*	18	19
31 Jan 76 ●	CARNIVAL *Studio Two TWO 337*	3	18
31 Jan 76 ●	RODRIGO'S GUITAR CONCERTO DE ARANJUEZ (THEME FROM 2ND MOVEMENT) *EMI 2383*	3	10

Roots MANUVA *UK, male rapper – Rodney Hylton Smith (3 Albums: 7 Weeks, 6 Singles: 12 Weeks)*

11 Dec 99	DUSTED (re) *Hard Hands HAND 058CD1* [1]	28	3
4 Aug 01	WITNESS (1 HOPE) *Big Dada BDCDS 022*	45	2
25 Aug 01	RUN COME SAVE ME *Big Dada BDCD 032*	33	3
20 Oct 01	DREAMY DAYS *Big Dada BDCDS 033*	53	1
20 Jul 02	DUB COME SAVE ME *Big Dada BDCD 040*	75	1
8 May 04	OH U WANT MORE? *Big Dada BDCDS 066* [2]	65	1
29 Jan 05	COLOSSAL INSIGHT *Big Dada BDCDM 073*	33	2
12 Feb 05	AWFULLY DEEP *Big Dada BDCD 072X*	24	3
2 Apr 05	TOO COLD *Big Dada BDCDS 078*	39	3

[1] Leftfield / Roots Manuva [2] Ty featuring Roots Manuva

Phil MANZANERA (see also ROXY MUSIC) *UK, male vocalist / guitarist – Philip Targett-Adams*

24 May 75	DIAMOND HEAD *Island ILPS 9315*	40	1

MARATHON *Germany / UK, male vocal / instrumental group*

25 Jan 92	MOVIN' *Ten TEN 395*	36	3

The MARAUDERS *UK, male vocal / instrumental group*

8 Aug 63	THAT'S WHAT I WANT (re) *Decca F 11695*	43	4

The MARBLES

UK, male vocal duo – Graham Bonnet and Trevor Gordon (2 Singles: 18 Weeks)

25 Sep 68 ●	ONLY ONE WOMAN *Polydor 56 272*	5	12
26 Mar 69	THE WALLS FELL DOWN *Polydor 56 310*	28	6

MARC et CLAUDE *Germany, male DJ / production duo – Marc Romboy and Klaus Derichs (4 Singles: 15 Weeks)*

21 Nov 98	LA *Positiva CDTIV 104*	28	3
22 Jul 00	I NEED YOUR LOVIN' (LIKE THE SUNSHINE) *Positiva CDTIV 136*	12	7
6 Apr 02	TREMBLE *Positiva CDTIVS 170*	29	3
19 Apr 03	LOVING YOU '03 *Positiva CDTIV 190*	37	2

7 January 1978	14 January 1978	21 January 1978	28 January 1978
UK No.1 SINGLES			
MULL OF KINTYRE / GIRLS' SCHOOL – Wings	MULL OF KINTYRE / GIRLS' SCHOOL – Wings	MULL OF KINTYRE / GIRLS' SCHOOL – Wings	MULL OF KINTYRE / GIRLS' SCHOOL – Wings
UK No.1 ALBUMS			
DISCO FEVER – Various	DISCO FEVER – Various	THE SOUND OF BREAD – Bread	RUMOURS – Fleetwood Mac

The MARCELS
US, male vocal (Cornelius Harp) group (2 Singles: 17 Weeks)

13 Apr 61 ★ BLUE MOON *Pye International 7N 25073* ▲ $ 1 13
8 Jun 61 SUMMERTIME *Pye International 7N 25083* 46 4

Little Peggy MARCH *US, female vocalist – Margaret Battavio*

12 Sep 63 HELLO HEARTACHE, GOODBYE LOVE *RCA 1362* 29 7

MARCO POLO *Italy, male instrumental / production duo*

8 Apr 95 A PRAYER TO THE MUSIC *Hi-Life HICD 7* 65 1

MARCY PLAYGROUND *US, male vocal / instrumental trio*

18 Apr 98 SEX AND CANDY *EMI CDEM 508* 29 3
9 May 98 MARCY PLAYGROUND *EMI 8535692* 61 1

MARDI GRAS *UK, male vocal / instrumental group*

5 Aug 72 TOO BUSY THINKING ABOUT MY BABY *Bell 1226* 19 9

The MARDOUS NEW *UK, male vocal / instrumental trio*

20 Aug 05 REVOLUTION OVER THE PHONE *Poptones MC 5102SCD* 74 1

Kelly MARIE
UK, female vocalist – Jacqueline McKinnon (4 Singles: 36 Weeks)

2 Aug 80 ★ FEELS LIKE I'M IN LOVE *Calibre PLUS 1* 1 16
18 Oct 80 LOVING JUST FOR FUN *Calibre PLUS 4* 21 7
7 Feb 81 HOT LOVE *Calibre PLUS 5* 22 10
30 May 81 LOVE TRIAL *Calibre PLUS 7* 51 3

Rose MARIE
Ireland, female vocalist (5 Albums: 35 Weeks, 1 Single: 5 Weeks)

19 Nov 83 WHEN I LEAVE THE WORLD BEHIND (2re) *A1 284* 63 5
13 Apr 85 ROSE MARIE SINGS JUST FOR YOU *A1 RMTV 1* 30 13
24 May 86 SO LUCKY *A1-Spartan RMLP 2* 62 3
14 Nov 87 SENTIMENTALLY YOURS *Telstar STAR 2302* 22 11
19 Nov 88 TOGETHER AGAIN *Telstar STAR 2333* 52 7
23 Mar 96 MEMORIES OF HOME *Telstar TCD 2788* 51 1

Teena MARIE *US, female vocalist – Mary Brockert (5 Singles: 28 Weeks)*

7 Jul 79 I'M A SUCKER FOR YOUR LOVE *Motown TMG 1146* [1] 43 8
31 May 80 ● BEHIND THE GROOVE *Motown TMG 1185* 6 10
11 Oct 80 I NEED YOUR LOVIN' *Motown TMG 1203* 28 6
26 Mar 88 OOO LA LA LA *Epic 651423 7* 74 2
10 Nov 90 SINCE DAY ONE *Epic 656429 7* 69 2

[1] Teena Marie, co-lead vocals Rick James

MARILLION 234 Top 500 *Progressive rock group formed in Buckinghamshire and originally named after Tolkien's novel Silmarillion. They reached their peak of popularity in the 80s when fronted by Scottish vocalist / songwriter Fish (b. Derek Dick). When Fish left in 1989 the band continued to make regular visits to the charts with Steve Hogarth in the role of vocalist / songwriter (16 Albums: 165 Weeks, 25 Singles: 108 Weeks)*

20 Nov 82 MARKET SQUARE HEROES (re) *EMI 5351* 53 8
12 Feb 83 HE KNOWS YOU KNOW *EMI 5362* 35 4
26 Mar 83 ● SCRIPT FOR A JESTER'S TEAR *EMI EMC 3429* 7 31
18 Jun 83 GARDEN PARTY *EMI 5393* 16 5
11 Feb 84 PUNCH AND JUDY *EMI MARIL 1* 29 4
24 Mar 84 ● FUGAZI *EMI EMC 2400851* 5 20
12 May 84 ASSASSING *EMI MARIL 2* 22 5
17 Nov 84 ● REAL TO REEL *EMI JEST 1* 8 22
18 May 85 ● KAYLEIGH *EMI MARIL 3* 2 14
29 Jun 85 ★ MISPLACED CHILDHOOD *EMI MRL 2* ■ 1 41
7 Sep 85 ● LAVENDER *EMI MARIL 4* 5 9
30 Nov 85 HEART OF LOTHIAN *EMI MARIL 5* 29 6
23 May 87 ● INCOMMUNICADO *EMI MARIL 6* 6 5
4 Jul 87 ● CLUTCHING AT STRAWS *EMI EMD 1002* 2 15
25 Jul 87 SUGAR MICE *EMI MARIL 7* 22 5
7 Nov 87 WARM WET CIRCLES *EMI MARIL 8* 22 4
23 Jul 88 B SIDES THEMSELVES *EMI EMS 1295* 64 6
26 Nov 88 FREAKS (LIVE) *EMI MARIL 9* 24 3
10 Dec 88 THE THIEVING MAGPIE *EMI MARIL 1* 25 6
9 Sep 89 HOOKS IN YOU *Capitol MARIL 10* 30 3
7 Oct 89 ● SEASON'S END *EMI EMD 1011 22* 7 4
9 Dec 89 UNINVITED GUEST *EMI MARIL 11* 53 2
14 Apr 90 EASTER *EMI MARIL 12* 34 2
8 Jun 91 COVER MY EYES (PAIN AND HEAVEN) *EMI MARIL 13* 34 4
6 Jul 91 ● HOLIDAYS IN EDEN *EMI EMD 1022* 7 7
3 Aug 91 NO ONE CAN *EMI MARIL 14* 33 4
5 Oct 91 DRY LAND *EMI MARIL 15* 34 2
23 May 92 SYMPATHY *EMI MARIL 16* 17 3
20 Jun 92 A SINGLES COLLECTION 1982-1992 *EMI CDEMD 1033* 27 3
1 Aug 92 NO ONE CAN (re-issue) *EMI MARIL 17* 26 4
19 Feb 94 ● BRAVE *EMI CDEMC 1054* 10 4
26 Mar 94 THE HOLLOW MAN *EMI CDEMS 307* 30 2
7 May 94 ALONE AGAIN IN THE LAP OF LUXURY *EMI CDEMS 318* 53 3
10 Jun 95 BEAUTIFUL *EMI CDMARILS 18* 29 2
8 Jul 95 AFRAID OF SUNLIGHT *EMI CDEMD 1079* 16 2
6 Apr 96 MADE AGAIN *EMI CDEMD 1094* 37 1
3 May 97 THIS STRANGE ENGINE *Raw Power RAWCD 121* 27 2
3 Oct 98 RADIATION *Raw Power RAWCD 126* 35 1
30 Oct 99 MARILLION.COM *Intact / Raw Power RAWCD 144* 53 1
1 May 04 ● YOU'RE GONE *Intact CDINTACT 1* 7 3
24 Jul 04 DON'T HURT YOURSELF *Intact CDINTACT 2* 16 2

MARILYN *UK, male vocalist – Peter Robinson (4 Singles: 26 Weeks)*

5 Nov 83 ● CALLING YOUR NAME *Mercury MAZ 1* 4 12
11 Feb 84 CRY AND BE FREE *Mercury MAZ 2* 31 6
21 Apr 84 YOU DON'T LOVE ME *Mercury MAZ 3* 40 7
13 Apr 85 BABY U LEFT ME (IN THE COLD) *Mercury MAZ 4* 70 1

MARILYN MANSON *US, male vocal (Brian Warner aka Marilyn Manson) / instrumental group (6 Albums: 21 Weeks, 11 Singles: 42 Weeks)*

26 Oct 96 ANTICHRIST SUPERSTAR *Interscope IND 90086* 73 1
7 Jun 97 THE BEAUTIFUL PEOPLE *Nothing 95541* 18 3
20 Sep 97 TOURNIQUET *Nothing 95552* 28 2
26 Sep 98 ● MECHANICAL ANIMALS *Interscope IND 90273* ▲ 8 4
21 Nov 98 THE DOPE SHOW *Nothing 95610* 12 3
26 Jun 99 ROCK IS DEAD *Maverick W 486CD* 23 2
27 Nov 99 THE LAST TOUR ON EARTH *Interscope 4905242* 61 1
18 Nov 00 DISPOSABLE TEENS *Nothing 4974372* 12 3
25 Nov 00 HOLY WOOD *Nothing 4908292* 23 2
3 Mar 01 THE FIGHT SONG *Nothing / Interscope 4974902* 24 3
15 Sep 01 THE NOBODIES *Nothing IND 97604* 34 2
30 Mar 02 ● TAINTED LOVE *Maverick / Warner Bros. W 579CD* 5 11
24 May 03 ● THE GOLDEN AGE OF THE GROTESQUE *Interscope / Polydor 9800093* ▲ 4 7
14 Jun 03 MOBSCENE *Interscope / Polydor 9807726* 13 6
13 Sep 03 THIS IS THE NEW *HIT *Interscope / Polydor 9810793* 29 2
9 Oct 04 ● LEST WE FORGET – THE BEST OF *Interscope 9863975* 4 6
16 Oct 04 PERSONAL JESUS *Interscope 9864166* 13 5

Marino MARINI and his QUARTET
Italy, male vocalist and instrumental group (3 Singles: 23 Weeks)

3 Oct 58 VOLARE (NEL BLU DIPINTO DI BLU) *Durium DC 16632* 13 7
10 Oct 58 ● COME PRIMA *Durium DC 16632* 2 14
20 Mar 59 CIAO CIAO BAMBINA (PIOVE) (re) *Durium DC 16636* 24 2

MARIO
US, male vocalist – Mario Barrett (1 Album: 22 Weeks, 5 Singles: 30 Weeks)

12 Apr 03 JUST A FRIEND *J 82876508082* 18 4
12 Jul 03 C'MON *J 82876528282* 28 2
12 Feb 05 ● TURNING POINT *J 82876618852* 8 22
19 Mar 05 LET ME LOVE YOU (import) *J 82876679752* 53 1
2 Apr 05 ● LET ME LOVE YOU *J 82876682852* ▲ 2 15
9 Jul 05 HERE I GO AGAIN *J 82876705592* 11 8

4 February 1978	11 February 1978	18 February 1978	25 February 1978
UPTOWN TOP RANKING Althia and Donna	FIGARO Brotherhood of Man	TAKE A CHANCE ON ME Abba	TAKE A CHANCE ON ME Abba
THE ALBUM Abba	THE ALBUM Abba	THE ALBUM Abba	THE ALBUM Abba

KEY UK No.1 ★ UK Top 10 ● Still on chart + UK entry at No.1 ■ US No.1 ▲ UK million seller £ US million seller $
Singles re-entries are listed as (re), (2re), (3re)… which signifies that the hit re-entered the chart once, twice or three times…

Peak Position / Weeks

MARION *UK, male vocal (Jamie Harding) / instrumental group (1 Album: 2 Weeks, 6 Singles: 9 Weeks)*

25 Feb 95 **SLEEP** *London LONCD 360* **53** 1
13 May 95 **TOYS FOR BOYS** *London LONCD 366* **57** 1
21 Oct 95 **LET'S ALL GO TOGETHER** *London LONCD 371* **37** 2
3 Feb 96 **TIME** *London LONCD 377* **29** 2
17 Feb 96 ● THIS WORLD AND BODY *London 8286952* 10 2
30 Mar 96 **SLEEP** (re-mix) *London LONCD 381* **17** 2
7 Mar 98 **MIYAKO HIDEAWAY** *London LONCD 403* **45** 1

MARK 'OH *Germany, male producer – Marko Albrecht*

6 May 95 **TEARS DON'T LIE** *Systematic SYSCD 9* **24** 3

Pigmeat MARKHAM *US, male vocalist / comedian, b. 18 Apr 1904, d. 13 Dec 1981*

17 Jul 68 **HERE COMES THE JUDGE** *Chess CRS 8077* **19** 8

Biz MARKIE *US, male rapper – Marcel Hall*

26 May 90 **JUST A FRIEND** *Cold Chillin' W 9823* $ **55** 2

Yannis MARKOPOULOS *Greece, orchestra*

17 Dec 77 **WHO PAYS THE FERRYMAN?** *BBC RESL 51* **11** 8
26 Aug 78 WHO PAYS THE FERRYMAN *BBC REB 315* 22 8

Guy MARKS *US, male vocalist – Mario Scarpo, b. 1923, d. 28 Nov 1987*

13 May 78 **LOVING YOU HAS MADE ME BANANAS** *ABC 4211* **25** 8

MARKY MARK and The FUNKY BUNCH *US, male / female vocal / rap / instrumental group (1 Album: 1 Week, 3 Singles: 14 Weeks)*

31 Aug 91 **GOOD VIBRATIONS** *Interscope A 8764* [1] ▲ **14** 7
5 Oct 91 MUSIC FOR THE PEOPLE *Interscope 7567917371* 61 1
2 Nov 91 **WILDSIDE** *Interscope A 8674* **42** 3
12 Dec 92 **YOU GOTTA BELIEVE** *Interscope A 8480* **54** 4

[1] Marky Mark and the Funky Bunch featuring Loleatta Holloway

Bob MARLEY & The WAILERS (39 Top 500)

Legendary, globally successful Jamaican group fronted by Bob Marley (v/g), nicknamed 'Tuff Gong', b. Robert Marley, 6 Feb 1945, Nine Miles, Saint Ann, Jamaica, d. 11 May 1981, Miami, US. Varying line-up included Peter Tosh (v/g), b. 19 Oct 1944, d. 11 Sep 1987, and Bunny Wailer (v/prc). Their compilation Legend – The Best of Bob Marley and The Wailers is the biggest-selling reggae album in the world with sales of more than 17 million (10 million in the US alone). Marley became a founder member of the UK Music Hall of Fame in 2004, and in 2005 had a series of singles re-issued in successive weeks (19 Albums: 550 Weeks, 28 Singles: 173 Weeks)

27 Sep 75 ● **NO WOMAN NO CRY** (re) *Island WIP 6244* **8** 18
4 Oct 75 NATTY DREAD *Island ILPS 9281* 43 5
20 Dec 75 LIVE! *Island ILPS 9376* 38 11
8 May 76 RASTAMAN VIBRATION *Island ILPS 9383* 15 13
11 Jun 77 ● EXODUS *Island ILPS 9498* 8 56
25 Jun 77 **EXODUS** *Island WIP 6390* **14** 9
10 Sep 77 **WAITING IN VAIN** *Island WIP 6402* **27** 6
10 Dec 77 ● **JAMMING / PUNKY REGGAE PARTY** *Island WIP 6410* **9** 12
25 Feb 78 ● **IS THIS LOVE** *Island WIP 6420* **9** 9
1 Apr 78 ● KAYA *Island ILPS 9517* 4 24
10 Jun 78 **SATISFY MY SOUL** *Island WIP 6440* **21** 10
16 Dec 78 BABYLON BY BUS *Island ISLD 11* 40 11
13 Oct 79 SURVIVAL *Island ILPS 9542* 20 6
20 Oct 79 **SO MUCH TROUBLE IN THE WORLD** *Island WIP 6510* **56** 4
21 Jun 80 ● **COULD YOU BE LOVED** *Island WIP 6610* **5** 12
28 Jun 80 ● UPRISING *Island ILPS 9596* 6 17
13 Sep 80 **THREE LITTLE BIRDS** *Island WIP 6641* **17** 9
7 May 83 ● **BUFFALO SOLDIER** *Island / Tuff Gong IS 108* **4** 12
28 May 83 ● CONFRONTATION *Island ILPS 9760* 5 19
21 Apr 84 ● **ONE LOVE – PEOPLE GET READY** *Island IS 169* **5** 11
19 May 84 ★ LEGEND – THE BEST OF BOB MARLEY AND THE WAILERS *Tuff Gong BMWX 1* ■ 1 339
23 Jun 84 **WAITING IN VAIN** (re-issue) *Island IS 180* **31** 7
8 Dec 84 **COULD YOU BE LOVED** (re-issue) *Island IS 210* **71** 2
28 Jul 86 REBEL MUSIC *Island ILPS 9843* 54 3
18 May 91 **ONE LOVE – PEOPLE GET READY** (re-issue) *Tuff Gong TGX 1* **42** 3
19 Sep 92 ● **IRON LION ZION** *Tuff Gong TGX 2* **5** 9
3 Oct 92 ● SONGS OF FREEDOM *Tuff Gong TGCBX 1* [1] 10 5
28 Nov 92 **WHY SHOULD I / EXODUS** (re) *Tuff Gong TGX 3* **42** 4
20 May 95 **KEEP ON MOVING** *Tuff Gong TGXCD 4* **17** 4
3 Jun 95 ● NATURAL MYSTIC *Tuff Gong BMWCD 2* 5 8
8 Jun 96 **WHAT GOES AROUND COMES AROUND** *Anansi ANACS 002* **42** 1
4 Sep 99 THE SUN IS SHINING *Club Tools CLU 66730* [2] 40 3
25 Sep 99 ● **SUN IS SHINING** *Club Tools / Edel 0066895 CLU* [1] **3** 10
11 Dec 99 **TURN YOUR LIGHTS DOWN LOW** *Columbia 6684362* [2] **15** 7
22 Jan 00 **RAINBOW COUNTRY** *Club Tools 0067225 CLU* [1] **11** 6
24 Jun 00 **JAMMIN'** *Tuff Gong TGXCD 9* [3] **42** 2
2 Jun 01 ● ONE LOVE – THE VERY BEST OF BOB MARLEY & THE WAILERS *Tuff Gong BMWCD 3* 5 15
7 Jul 01 LIVELY UP YOURSELF *Music Collection 12691* [1] 75 1
10 Nov 01 ONE LOVE – THE VERY BEST OF BOB MARLEY & THE WAILERS *Tuff Gong 5865512* 24 8
5 Jun 04 ROOTS OF A LEGEND *Trojan TJODX 176* 51 2
12 Nov 05 **NO WOMAN, NO CRY** *Tuff Gong TGXCD 13* **58** 1
19 Nov 05 AFRICA UNITE: THE SINGLES COLLECTION *Tuff Gong BMWCD 4* 26 4
19 Nov 05 **I SHOT THE SHERIFF** *Tuff Gong TGXCD 14* **67** 1
26 Nov 05 **SUN IS SHINING** (re-issue) *Tuff Gong TGXCD 15* **54** 1
3 Dec 05 **SLOGANS** *Tuff Gong TGXCDS 11* **45** 1
10 Dec 05 **AFRICA UNITE** *Tuff Gong TGXCD 16* **49** 1
17 Dec 05 **STAND UP JAMROCK** *Tuff Gong TGXCD 17* **56** 1

[1] Bob Marley vs Funkstar De Luxe [2] Bob Marley featuring Lauryn Hill [3] Bob Marley featuring MC Lyte [1] Bob Marley [2] Bob Marley vs Funkstar De Luxe

'No Woman No Cry' reached No.22 on its first chart visit before its peaking at No.8 on re-entry in Jun 1981. 'Exodus' on Tuff Gong TGX 3 listed with 'Why Should I' only from 5 Dec 1992, and is a different version from the Island hit. It peaked at No.53. The version of 'No Woman, No Cry' in 2005 is a live recording.
Live! returned to the chart in 1981 under the title Live at the Lyceum. The Sun is Shining is an import single that was too long to be eligible for the singles chart. One Love – The Very Best of Bob Marley & The Wailers (10 Nov 2001) is a repackaged version of the 2 Jun 2001 album and includes a bonus CD of rare tracks.

Damian 'Jr. Gong' MARLEY NEW
Jamaica, male vocalist (1 Album: 7 Weeks, 2 Singles: 7 Weeks)

24 Sep 05 WELCOME TO JAMROCK *Island 9885698* 34 7
1 Oct 05 **WELCOME TO JAMROCK** *Island MCSTD 40432* **13** 6
24 Dec 05 **THE MASTER HAS COME BACK** *Tuff Gong MCSTD 40443* **74** 1

Ziggy MARLEY and The MELODY MAKERS
Jamaica, male / female vocal / instrumental group (2 Singles: 11 Weeks)

11 Jun 88 **TOMORROW PEOPLE** *Virgin VS 1049* **22** 10
23 Sep 89 **LOOK WHO'S DANCING** *Virgin America VUS 5* **65** 1

Lene MARLIN *Norway, female vocalist – Lene Marlin Pederson (1 Album: 34 Weeks, 4 Singles: 20 Weeks)*

11 Mar 00 ● **SITTING DOWN HERE** *Virgin DINSD 183* **5** 11
25 Mar 00 PLAYING MY GAME *Virgin CDVIR 83* 18 34
16 Sep 00 **UNFORGIVABLE SINNER** *Virgin DINSD 202* **13** 6
13 Jan 01 **WHERE I'M HEADED** *Virgin DINSD 196* **31** 2
4 Oct 03 **YOU WEREN'T THERE** *Virgin DINSD 262* **59** 1

MARLO *UK, male vocal / instrumental group*

24 Jul 99 **HOW DO I KNOW?** *Polydor 5611362* **56** 1

4 March 1978	11 March 1978	18 March 1978	25 March 1978
UK No.1 SINGLES			
TAKE A CHANCE ON ME Abba	WUTHERING HEIGHTS Kate Bush	WUTHERING HEIGHTS Kate Bush	WUTHERING HEIGHTS Kate Bush
UK No.1 ALBUMS			
THE ALBUM Abba	THE ALBUM Abba	THE ALBUM Abba	20 GOLDEN GREATS Buddy Holly and The Crickets

MARLY *Denmark, female vocalist – Ditte-Marie Lyfeldt*

28 Aug 04 **YOU NEVER KNOW** *All Around the World CDGLOBE 363*..........23 2

MARMALADE *UK, male vocal / instrumental group – includes Junior Campbell (11 Singles: 130 Weeks)*

22 May 68 ● **LOVIN' THINGS** *CBS 3412*..........6 13
23 Oct 68 **WAIT FOR ME MARY-ANNE** *CBS 3708*..........30 5
4 Dec 68 ★ **OB-LA-DI, OB-LA-DA** *CBS 3892*..........1 20
11 Jun 69 ● **BABY MAKE IT SOON** *CBS 4287*..........9 13
20 Dec 69 ● **REFLECTIONS OF MY LIFE** *Decca F 12982*..........3 12
18 Jul 70 ● **RAINBOW** *Decca F 13035*..........3 14
27 Mar 71 **MY LITTLE ONE** *Decca F 13135*..........15 11
4 Sep 71 ● **COUSIN NORMAN** *Decca F 13214*..........6 11
27 Nov 71 **BACK ON THE ROAD** (re) *Decca F 13251*..........35 8
1 Apr 72 ● **RADANCER** *Decca F 13297*..........6 12
21 Feb 76 ● **FALLING APART AT THE SEAMS** *Target TGT 105*..........9 11

MARMION
Spain / Holland, male instrumental / production duo (2 Singles: 2 Weeks)

18 May 96 **SCHONEBERG** *Hooj Choons HOOJCD 43*..........53 1
14 Feb 98 **SCHONEBERG** (re-mix) *ffrr FCD 324*..........56 1

MAROON5 *US, male vocal (Adam Levine) / instrumental group (2 Albums: 74 Weeks, 5 Singles: 40 Weeks)*

31 Jan 04 ★ SONGS ABOUT JANE *J 82876584302*..........1 73
31 Jan 04 **HARDER TO BREATHE** *J 82876566922*..........13 7
1 May 04 ● **THIS LOVE** *J 82876608452*..........3 14
4 Sep 04 ● **SHE WILL BE LOVED** *J 82876643632*..........4 10
18 Dec 04 **SUNDAY MORNING** *J 82876668042*..........27 7
5 Mar 05 1.22.03.ACOUSTIC *J OCTN 624682*..........58 1
23 Apr 05 **MUST GET OUT** *J 82876689062*..........39 2

1.22.03.Acoustic is a seven-track live CD featuring two new songs.

MARRADONA *UK, male DJ / production group (2 Singles: 5 Weeks)*

26 Feb 94 **OUT OF MY HEAD** *Peach PWCD 282*..........38 3
26 Jul 97 **OUT OF MY HEAD 97** (re-mix) *Soopa SPCD 1*..........39 2

Neville MARRINER and The ACADEMY OF ST MARTIN IN THE FIELDS *UK, male conductor and chamber orchestra*

6 Apr 85 AMADEUS (FILM SOUNDTRACK) *London LONDP 6*..........64 6

M/A/R/R/S *UK, male instrumental / production group*

5 Sep 87 ★ **PUMP UP THE VOLUME / ANITINA (THE FIRST TIME I SEE SHE DANCE)** *4AD AD 70* $..........1 14

The MARS VOLTA
US, male vocal / instrumental group (2 Albums: 3 Weeks, 4 Singles: 8 Weeks)

5 Jul 03 DE-LOUSED IN THE COMATORIUM *Universal 9860460*..........43 1
11 Oct 03 **INERTIATIC ESP** *Universal MCSTD 40332*..........42 2
13 Mar 04 **TELEVATORS** *Universal MCSTD 40352*..........41 1
5 Mar 05 FRANCES THE MUTE *Universal 2103977*..........23 2
26 Mar 05 **THE WIDOW** *Universal MCSTD 40408*..........20 4
23 Jul 05 **L'VIA L'VIAQUEZ** *Universal MCSTD 40420*..........53 1

Bernie MARSDEN (see also WHITESNAKE) *UK, male vocalist / guitarist*

5 Sep 81 LOOK AT ME NOW *Parlophone PCF 7217*..........71 2

Matthew MARSDEN *UK, male actor / vocalist (2 Singles: 10 Weeks)*

11 Jul 98 **THE HEART'S LONE DESIRE** *Columbia 6661152*..........13 7
7 Nov 98 **SHE'S GONE** *Columbia 6664915* [1]..........24 3

[1] Matthew Marsden featuring Destiny's Child

Kym MARSH (see also HEAR'SAY)
UK, female vocalist (1 Album: 3 Weeks, 3 Singles: 21 Weeks)

19 Apr 03 ● **CRY** *Island MCSTD 40314*..........2 12
19 Jul 03 ● **COME ON OVER** *Universal MCSTD 40323*..........10 7
2 Aug 03 ● STANDING TALL *Universal 9800035*..........9 3
8 Nov 03 **SENTIMENTAL** *Universal MCSTD 40340*..........35 2

Stevie MARSH *UK, female vocalist*

4 Dec 59 **IF YOU WERE THE ONLY BOY IN THE WORLD** (re) *Decca F 11181*..........24 4

Amanda MARSHALL *Canada, female vocalist*

3 Aug 96 AMANDA MARSHALL *Epic 4837912*..........47 2

Joy MARSHALL *UK, female vocalist*

23 Jun 66 **THE MORE I SEE YOU** *Decca F 12422*..........34 2

Keith MARSHALL *UK, male vocalist*

4 Apr 81 **ONLY CRYING** *Arrival PIK 2*..........12 10

Wayne MARSHALL *UK, male vocalist (4 Singles: 7 Weeks)*

1 Oct 94 **OOH AAH (G-SPOT)** *Soultown SOULCDS 322*..........29 3
3 Jun 95 **SPIRIT** *Soultown SOULCDS 00352*..........58 1
24 Feb 96 **NEVER KNEW LOVE LIKE THIS** *Sony S2 6629382* [1]..........40 2
7 Dec 96 **G SPOT** (re-mix) *MBA INTER 9006*..........50 1

[1] Pauline Henry featuring Wayne Marshall

MARSHALL HAIN *UK, male / female vocal / instrumental duo – Julian Marshall and Kit Hain (2 Singles: 19 Weeks)*

3 Jun 78 ● **DANCING IN THE CITY** *Harvest HAR 5157*..........3 15
14 Oct 78 **COMING HOME** *Harvest HAR 5168*..........39 4

MARTAY featuring ZZ TOP
UK, female rapper – Melone McKenzy and US, male vocal / instrumental trio

16 Oct 99 **GIMME ALL YOUR LOVIN' 2000** *Riverhorse RIVHCD 2*..........28 2

Lena MARTELL *UK, female vocalist – Helen Thomson (6 Albums: 71 Weeks, 1 Single: 18 Weeks)*

25 May 74 THAT WONDERFUL SOUND OF LENA MARTELL *Pye SPL 18427*..........35 2
8 Jan 77 THE BEST OF LENA MARTELL *Pye NSPL 18506*..........13 16
27 May 78 THE LENA MARTELL COLLECTION *Ronco RTL 2028*..........12 19
29 Sep 79 ★ **ONE DAY AT A TIME** *Pye 7N 46021*..........1 18
20 Oct 79 ● LENA'S MUSIC ALBUM *Pye N 123*..........4 18
19 Apr 80 ● BY REQUEST *Ronco RTL 2046*..........9 9
29 Nov 80 BEAUTIFUL SUNDAY *Ronco RTL 2052*..........23 7

MARTHA and The MUFFINS (see also M + M)
Canada, female / male vocal (Martha Johnson) / instrumental group

1 Mar 80 ● **ECHO BEACH** *Dindisc DIN 9*..........10 10
15 Mar 80 METRO MUSIC *Dindisc DID 1*..........34 6

MARTIKA
US, female vocalist – Marta Marrera (2 Albums: 52 Weeks, 7 Singles: 57 Weeks)

29 Jul 89 ● **TOY SOLDIERS** *CBS 655049 7* ▲..........5 11
16 Sep 89 MARTIKA *CBS 463355 1*..........11 37
14 Oct 89 ● **I FEEL THE EARTH MOVE** *CBS 655294 7*..........7 14
13 Jan 90 **MORE THAN YOU KNOW** *CBS 655526 7*..........15 7
17 Mar 90 **WATER** *CBS 655731 7*..........59 3
17 Aug 91 ● **LOVE ... THY WILL BE DONE** *Columbia 6573137*..........9 9
7 Sep 91 MARTIKA'S KITCHEN *Columbia 4671891*..........15 15
30 Nov 91 **MARTIKA'S KITCHEN** *Columbia 6575687*..........17 10
22 Feb 92 **COLOURED KISSES** *Columbia 6577097*..........41 3

Billie Ray MARTIN *Germany, female vocalist – Birgit Dieckmann (1 Album: 2 Weeks, 6 Singles: 20 Weeks)*

19 Nov 94 **YOUR LOVING ARMS** *Magnet MAG 1028CD*..........38 3
20 May 95 ● **YOUR LOVING ARMS** (re-mix) *Magnet MAG 1031CD*..........6 10

1 April 1978	8 April 1978	15 April 1978	22 April 1978
WUTHERING HEIGHTS Kate Bush	**MATCHSTALK MEN AND MATCHSTALK CATS AND DOGS (LOWRY'S SONG)** Brian and Michael	**MATCHSTALK MEN AND MATCHSTALK CATS AND DOGS (LOWRY'S SONG)** Brian and Michael	**MATCHSTALK MEN AND MATCHSTALK CATS AND DOGS (LOWRY'S SONG)** Brian and Michael
20 GOLDEN GREATS Buddy Holly and The Crickets	**20 GOLDEN GREATS** Buddy Holly and The Crickets	**20 GOLDEN GREATS** Nat 'King' Cole	**20 GOLDEN GREATS** Nat 'King' Cole

KEY
UK No.1 ★ UK Top 10 ● Still on chart + UK entry at No.1 ■
US No.1 ▲ UK million seller £ US million seller $
Singles re-entries are listed as (re), (2re), (3re)... which signifies that the hit re-entered the chart once, twice or three times...
Peak Position / Weeks

2 Sep 95 **RUNNING AROUND TOWN** *Magnet MAG 1035CD* 29 2
6 Jan 96 **IMITATION OF LIFE** *Magnet MAG 1040CD* 29 3
3 Feb 96 DEADLINE FOR MY MEMORIES *Magnet 630121802* 47 2
6 Apr 96 **SPACE OASIS** *Magnet MAG 1042CD* 66 1
21 Aug 99 **HONEY** *React CDREACT 129* 54 1

Dean MARTIN 299 Top 500 (see also The RATPACK)

Acclaimed vocalist / entertainer / film actor and cabaret performer, b. Dino Crocetti, 7 Jun 1917, Ohio, US, d. 25 Dec 1995. He first found fame partnering Jerry Lewis (1946-56), and had a long and successful solo career. He was a member of Frank Sinatra's 'Rat Pack' and has an impressive 51-year chart span (13 Albums: 64 Weeks, 19 Singles: 163 Weeks)

18 Sep 53 ● **KISS** (re) *Capitol CL 13893* 5 8
22 Jan 54 ● **THAT'S AMORE** *Capitol CL 14008* 2 11
1 Oct 54 ● **SWAY** *Capitol CL 14138* 6 7
22 Oct 54 **HOW DO YOU SPEAK TO AN ANGEL** (re) *Capitol CL 14150* 15 6
28 Jan 55 ● **THE NAUGHTY LADY OF SHADY LANE** *Capitol CL 14226* 5 10
4 Feb 55 **MAMBO ITALIANO** *Capitol CL 14227* 14 2
25 Feb 55 ● **LET ME GO, LOVER** *Capitol CL 14226* 3 9
1 Apr 55 ● **UNDER THE BRIDGES OF PARIS** *Capitol CL 14255* 6 8
10 Feb 56 ★ **MEMORIES ARE MADE OF THIS** *Capitol CL 14523* ▲ $ 1 16
2 Mar 56 **YOUNG AND FOOLISH** *Capitol CL 14519* 20 1
27 Apr 56 **INNAMORATA** *Capitol CL 14507* 21 3
22 Mar 57 **THE MAN WHO PLAYS THE MANDOLINO** *Capitol CL 14690* 21 2
13 Jun 58 ● **RETURN TO ME** *Capitol CL 14844* 2 22
29 Aug 58 ● **VOLARE (NEL BLU DIPINTO DI BLU)** *Capitol CL 14910* 2 14
13 May 61 THIS TIME I'M SWINGIN'! *Capitol T 1442* 18 1
27 Aug 64 **EVERYBODY LOVES SOMEBODY** *Reprise R 20281* ▲ $ 11 13
12 Nov 64 **THE DOOR IS STILL OPEN TO MY HEART** *Reprise R 20307* 42 4
25 Feb 67 AT EASE WITH DEAN *Reprise RSLP 6322* 35 1
4 Nov 67 WELCOME TO MY WORLD *Philips DBL 001* 39 1
12 Oct 68 DEAN MARTIN'S GREATEST HITS VOLUME 1 *Reprise RSLP 6301* 40 1
5 Feb 69 ● **GENTLE ON MY MIND** (re) *Reprise RS 23343* 2 24
22 Feb 69 ● GENTLE ON MY MIND *Reprise RSLP 6330* 9 8
22 Feb 69 ● THE BEST OF DEAN MARTIN *Capitol ST 21194* 9 1
27 Nov 71 WHITE CHRISTMAS *MFP 524* [1] 45 1
13 Nov 76 ● 20 ORIGINAL DEAN MARTIN HITS *Reprise K 54066* 7 11
22 Jun 96 **THAT'S AMORE** (re-issue) *EMI Premier PRESCD 3* 43 2
5 Jun 99 ● THE VERY BEST OF DEAN MARTIN – THE CAPITOL & REPRISE YEARS *EMI 4967212* 5 29
21 Aug 99 **SWAY** (re-issue) *Capitol CDSWAY 001* 66 1
26 Aug 00 THE VERY BEST OF DEAN MARTIN VOLUME 2 – THE CAPITOL & REPRISE YEARS *Capitol 5277712* 40 2
16 Feb 02 LOVE SONGS *Capitol 5377482* 24 3
10 Jan 04 VERY BEST OF DEAN MARTIN *EMI 5920802* 59 2
18 Sep 04 DINO – THE ESSENTIAL DEAN MARTIN *EMI 8665272* 25 3

[1] Nat 'King' Cole and Dean Martin

George MARTIN *UK, male producer*

4 Apr 98 ● IN MY LIFE *Echo ECHCD 20* 5 13

Juan MARTIN *Spain, male guitarist (1 Album: 9 Weeks, 2 Singles: 7 Weeks)*

28 Jan 84 ● **LOVE THEME FROM 'THE THORN BIRDS'** *WEA X 9518* 10 7
11 Feb 84 SERENADE *K-Tel NE 1267* [1] 21 9

[1] Juan Martin and the Royal Philharmonic Orchestra

Linda MARTIN *Ireland, female vocalist*

30 May 92 **WHY ME** *Columbia 6581317* 59 2

Ray MARTIN and his CHORUS and ORCHESTRA

(see also Lee LAWRENCE) *UK, orchestra – leader b. 11 Oct 1918, d. 7 Feb 1988 (3 Singles: 11 Weeks)*

14 Nov 52 ● **BLUE TANGO** (re) *Columbia DB 3051* 8 4
4 Dec 53 ● **SWEDISH RHAPSODY** (re) *Columbia DB 3346* 4 4
15 Jun 56 **THE CAROUSEL WALTZ** (re) *Columbia DB 3771* 24 3

Ricky MARTIN 467 Top 500

Ex-boy band singer and soap star who put the Latin into platinum, b. Enrique Martin Morales, 24 Dec 1971, Puerto Rico. The energetic entertainer has sold over 40 million albums, recorded the world's biggest-selling football single ('The Cup of Life') and had the world's top-selling Spanish language album (Vuelve). Biggest-selling UK single: 'Livin' La Vida Loca' 775,700 (4 Albums: 76 Weeks, 9 Singles: 80 Weeks)

20 Sep 97 ● **(UN, DOS, TRES) MARIA** *Columbia 6649595* 6 6
11 Jul 98 **THE CUP OF LIFE** *Columbia 6661502* 29 3
12 Jun 99 ● RICKY MARTIN *Columbia 4944060* ▲ 2 48
17 Jul 99 ★ **LIVIN' LA VIDA LOCA** *Columbia 6676402* ■ ▲ $ 1 17
20 Nov 99 **SHAKE YOUR BON-BON** *Columbia 6683412* 12 9
29 Apr 00 ● **PRIVATE EMOTION** *Columbia 6692692* [1] 9 9
4 Nov 00 ● **SHE BANGS** *Columbia 6705422* 3 15
18 Nov 00 SOUND LOADED *Columbia 4977692* 14 21
10 Mar 01 ● **NOBODY WANTS TO BE LONELY** *Columbia 6709462* [2] 4 12
28 Jul 01 **LOADED** *Columbia 6714642* 19 4
1 Dec 01 THE BEST OF RICKY MARTIN *Columbia 5050192* 42 6
15 Oct 05 **I DON'T CARE** *Sony BMG 6760662* 11 5
22 Oct 05 LIFE *Columbia 5205492* 40 1

[1] Ricky Martin featuring Meja [2] Ricky Martin and Christina Aguilera

Tony MARTIN *US, male vocalist – Alvin Morris Jr. (2 Singles: 28 Weeks)*

22 Apr 55 ● **STRANGER IN PARADISE** *HMV B 10849* 6 13
13 Jul 56 ● **WALK HAND IN HAND** *HMV POP 222* 2 15

Both hits with Hugo Winterhalter's Orchestra and Chorus.

Wink MARTINDALE

US, male vocalist – Winston Martindale (2 Singles: 41 Weeks)

4 Dec 59 ● **DECK OF CARDS** (3re) *London HLD 8962* $ 5 29
20 Oct 73 **DECK OF CARDS** (re-issue) *Dot DOT 109* 22 12

'Deck of Cards' on the London label made No.18 in 1959, re-entered at No.28 in Jan 1960 and again at No.45 in Mar 1960 before making No.5 with the third re-entry in Apr 1963.

Alice MARTINEAU *UK, female vocalist, b. 8 Jun 1972, d. 6 Mar 2003*

23 Nov 02 **IF I FALL** *Epic 6732332* 45 1

Angie MARTINEZ featuring LIL' MO & SACARIO *US, female vocal / rap trio*

15 Feb 03 **IF I COULD GO!** *Elektra E 7331CD* 61 1

Al MARTINO *US, male vocalist – Alfred Cini (10 Singles: 87 Weeks)*

14 Nov 52 ★ **HERE IN MY HEART** *Capitol CL 13779* ▲ 1 18
21 Nov 52 ● **TAKE MY HEART** *Capitol CL 13769* 9 1
30 Jan 53 ● **NOW** *Capitol CL 13835* 3 12
10 Jul 53 ● **RACHEL** (re) *Capitol CL 13879* 10 5
4 Jun 54 ● **WANTED** (2re) *Capitol CL 14128* 4 16
1 Oct 54 ● **THE STORY OF TINA** *Capitol CL 14163* 10 8
23 Sep 55 **THE MAN FROM LARAMIE** (re) *Capitol CL 14343* 19 3
31 Mar 60 **SUMMERTIME** *Top Rank JAR 312* 49 1
29 Aug 63 **I LOVE YOU BECAUSE** *Capitol CL 15300* 48 1
22 Aug 70 ● **SPANISH EYES** (re) *Capitol CL 15430* 5 22

'Spanish Eyes' peaked at No.49 in 1970 before re-entering in Jul 1973 when it reached No.5.

John MARTYN (see also SISTER BLISS)

UK, male vocalist / guitarist (10 Albums: 30 Weeks)

4 Feb 78 ONE WORLD *Island ILPS 9492* 54 1

29 April 1978	6 May 1978	13 May 1978	20 May 1978
UK No.1 SINGLES			
NIGHT FEVER The Bee Gees	**NIGHT FEVER** The Bee Gees	**RIVERS OF BABYLON / BROWN GIRL IN THE RING** Boney M	**RIVERS OF BABYLON / BROWN GIRL IN THE RING** Boney M
UK No.1 ALBUMS			
20 GOLDEN GREATS Nat 'King' Cole	**SATURDAY NIGHT FEVER** Soundtrack	**SATURDAY NIGHT FEVER** Soundtrack	**SATURDAY NIGHT FEVER** Soundtrack

1 Nov 80	GRACE AND DANGER *Island ILPS 9560*	54 2
26 Sep 81	GLORIOUS FOOL *Geffen K 99178*	25 7
4 Sep 82	WELL KEPT SECRET *WEA K 99255*	20 7
17 Nov 84	SAPPHIRE *Island ILPS 9779*	57 2
8 Mar 86	PIECE BY PIECE *Island ILPS 9807*	28 4
10 Oct 92	COULDN'T LOVE YOU MORE *Permanent PERMCD 9*	65 2
10 Aug 96	AND *Go Discs 8287982*	32 3
4 Apr 98	THE CHURCH WITH ONE BELL *Independiente ISOM 3CD*	51 1
3 Jun 00	GLASGOW WALKER *Independiente ISOM 15CD*	66 1

The MARVELETTES *US, female vocal group*

15 Jun 67 **WHEN YOU'RE YOUNG AND IN LOVE** *Tamla Motown TMG 609* .. 13 10

MARVIN and TAMARA *UK, male / female vocal duo – Marvin Simmonds and Tamara Nicole (2 Singles: 9 Weeks)*

7 Aug 99 **GROOVE MACHINE** *Epic 6675582* 11 5
25 Dec 99 **NORTH, SOUTH, EAST, WEST** *Epic 6684902* 38 4

Hank MARVIN (see also The SHADOWS) *UK, male vocalist / guitarist – Brian Rankin (12 Albums: 72 Weeks, 6 Singles: 36 Weeks)*

13 Sep 69 ● **THROW DOWN A LINE** *Columbia DB 8615* [1] 7 9
22 Nov 69 HANK MARVIN *Columbia SCX 6352* 14 2
21 Feb 70 **THE JOY OF LIVING** *Columbia DB 8657* [1] 25 8
6 Mar 82 **DON'T TALK** *Polydor POSP 420* 49 4
20 Mar 82 WORDS AND MUSIC *Polydor POLD 5054* 66 3
22 Mar 86 ★ **LIVING DOLL** *WEA YZ 65* [2] 1 11
7 Jan 89 **LONDON KID** *Polydor PO 32* [3] 52 3
17 Oct 92 **WE ARE THE CHAMPIONS** *PolyGram TV PO 229* [4] 66 1
31 Oct 92 INTO THE LIGHT *Polydor 5171482* 18 10
20 Nov 93 HEARTBEAT *PolyGram TV 52132222* 17 9
22 Oct 94 THE BEST OF HANK MARVIN AND THE SHADOWS *PolyGram TV 5238212* [1] 19 11
18 Nov 95 HANK PLAYS CLIFF *PolyGram TV 5294262* 33 7
23 Nov 96 HANK PLAYS HOLLY *PolyGram TV 5337132* 34 7
5 Apr 97 HANK PLAYS LIVE *PolyGram TV 5374282* 71 1
22 Nov 97 PLAY ANDREW LLOYD WEBBER AND TIM RICE *PolyGram TV 5394792* [1] 41 6
14 Nov 98 VERY BEST OF HANK MARVIN AND THE SHADOWS - THE FIRST 40 YEARS *PolyGram TV 5592112* [1] 56 5
15 Apr 00 MARVIN AT THE MOVIES *Universal Music TV 1570572* 17 5
20 Apr 02 ● GUITAR PLAYER *UMTV 171242* 10 6

[1] Cliff and Hank [2] Cliff Richard and The Young Ones featuring Hank B Marvin [3] Jean-Michel Jarre featuring Hank Marvin [4] Hank Marvin featuring Brian May [1] Hank Marvin and The Shadows

Lee MARVIN *US, male actor / vocalist, b. 19 Feb 1924, d. 28 Aug 1987*

7 Feb 70 ★ **WAND'RIN' STAR** (2re) *Paramount PARA 3004* 1 23

'I Talk to the Trees' by Clint Eastwood, the flip side of 'Wand'rin' Star', was listed for 7 Feb and 14 Feb 1970 only.

MARVIN THE PARANOID ANDROID *UK, male robot*

16 May 81 **MARVIN** *Polydor POSP 261* 53 4

MARVIN, WELCH and FARRAR (see also Hank MARVIN; The SHADOWS) *UK, male vocal / instrumental group*

3 Apr 71 MARVIN, WELCH AND FARRAR *Regal Zonophone SRZA 8502* 30 4

Richard MARX *US, male vocalist (5 Albums: 42 Weeks, 15 Singles: 75 Weeks)*

27 Feb 88 **SHOULD'VE KNOWN BETTER** *Manhattan MT 32* 50 5
9 Apr 88 RICHARD MARX *Manhattan MTL 1017* 68 2
14 May 88 **ENDLESS SUMMER NIGHTS** *Manhattan MT 39* 50 3
20 May 89 ● REPEAT OFFENDER *EMI-USA MTL 1043* ▲ 8 12
17 Jun 89 **SATISFIED** *EMI-USA MT 64* ▲ 52 4
2 Sep 89 ● **RIGHT HERE WAITING** *EMI-USA MT 72* ▲ $ 2 10
11 Nov 89 **ANGELIA** *EMI-USA MT 74* 45 4
24 Mar 90 **TOO LATE TO SAY GOODBYE** *EMI-USA MT 80* 38 3
7 Jul 90 **CHILDREN OF THE NIGHT** *EMI-USA MT 84* 54 2
1 Sep 90 **ENDLESS SUMMER NIGHTS** (re-issue) / **HOLD ON TO THE NIGHTS** *EMI-USA MT 89* ▲ 60 2
19 Oct 91 **KEEP COMING BACK** *Capitol CL 634* 55 2
16 Nov 91 ● RUSH STREET *Capitol ESTU 2158* 7 20
9 May 92 ● **HAZARD** *Capitol CL 654* 3 15
29 Aug 92 **TAKE THIS HEART** *Capitol CL 667* 13 6
28 Nov 92 **CHAINS AROUND MY HEART** *Capitol CL 676* 29 6
29 Jan 94 **NOW AND FOREVER** *Capitol CDCLS 703* 13 6
19 Feb 94 PAID VACATION *Capitol CDESTU 2208* 11 5
30 Apr 94 **SILENT SCREAM** *Capitol CDCLS 714* 32 4
13 Aug 94 **THE WAY SHE LOVES ME** *Capitol CDCL 721* 38 3
21 Feb 98 GREATEST HITS *Capitol 8219142* 34 3

MARXMAN *UK / Ireland, male rap / instrumental group (1 Album: 1 Week, 2 Singles: 5 Weeks)*

6 Mar 93 **ALL ABOUT EVE** *Talkin Loud TLKCD 35* 28 4
3 Apr 93 33 REVOLUTIONS PER MINUTE *Talkin Loud 5145382* 69 1
1 May 93 **SHIP AHOY** *Talkin Loud TLKCD 39* 64 1

Sinead O'Connor provides uncredited vocals on 'Ship Ahoy'.

MARY JANE GIRLS *US, female vocal group (1 Album: 9 Weeks, 4 Singles: 15 Weeks)*

21 May 83 **CANDY MAN** *Motown TMG 1301* 60 4
28 May 83 MARY JANE GIRLS *Gordy STML 12189* 51 9
25 Jun 83 **ALL NIGHT LONG** *Gordy TMG 1309* 13 9
8 Oct 83 **BOYS** *Gordy TMG 1315* 74 1
18 Feb 95 **ALL NIGHT LONG** (re-mix) *Motown TMGCD 1436* 51 1

MARY MARY *US, female vocal duo – Erica and Tina Atkins (2 Singles: 14 Weeks)*

10 Jun 00 ● **SHACKLES (PRAISE YOU)** *Columbia 6694202* 5 12
18 Nov 00 **I SINGS** *Columbia 6699742* 32 2

Carolyne MAS *US, female vocalist*

2 Feb 80 **QUOTE GOODBYE QUOTE** *Mercury 6167 873* 71 2

MASAI *UK, female vocal duo – Sharon Amos and Anna Crane*

1 Mar 03 **DO THAT THING** *Concept CDCON 36* 42 1

MA$E *US, male rapper – Mason Betha (3 Albums: 10 Weeks, 9 Singles: 55 Weeks)*

29 Mar 97 **CAN'T NOBODY HOLD ME DOWN** *Arista 74321464552* [1] ▲ $ 19 4
9 Aug 97 ● **MO MONEY MO PROBLEMS** *Puff Daddy 74321492492* [2] ▲ $ 6 10
27 Dec 97 ● **FEEL SO GOOD** *Puff Daddy 74321526442* $ 10 8
24 Jan 98 HARLEM WORLD *Puff Daddy 78612730172* ▲ 53 7
18 Apr 98 **WHAT YOU WANT** *Puff Daddy 74321578772* [3] 15 5
19 Sep 98 **HORSE AND CARRIAGE** *Epic 6662612* [4] 12 4
10 Oct 98 ● **TOP OF THE WORLD** (re) *Atlantic AT 0046CD* [5] 2 9
12 Dec 98 ● **TAKE ME THERE** *Interscope IND 95620* [6] 7 9
10 Jul 99 **GET READY** *Puff Daddy / Arista 74321682602* [7] 32 4
24 Jul 99 DOUBLE UP *Puff Daddy 74321674332* 47 2
4 Sep 04 WELCOME BACK *Bad Boy 9863122* 68 1
20 Nov 04 **WELCOME BACK / BREATHE, STRETCH, SHAKE** *Bad Boy MCSTD 40392* 29 2

[1] Puff Daddy featuring Ma$e [2] Notorious BIG featuring Puff Daddy and Ma$e [3] Ma$e featuring Total [4] Cam'ron featuring Ma$e [5] Brandy featuring Ma$e [6] BLACKstreet and Mya featuring Ma$e and Blinky Blink [7] Ma$e featuring BLACKstreet

MASH *US, male vocal / instrumental group*

10 May 80 ★ **THEME FROM M*A*S*H (SUICIDE IS PAINLESS)** *CBS 8536* 1 12

KEY: UK No.1 ★ UK Top 10 ● Still on chart + UK entry at No.1 ■ US No.1 ▲ UK million seller £ US million seller $
Singles re-entries are listed as (re), (2re), (3re)... which signifies that the hit re-entered the chart once, twice or three times...
Peak Position / Weeks

MASH! UK / US, male / female vocal group (2 Singles: 3 Weeks)

21 May 94 U DON'T HAVE TO SAY U LOVE ME *React CDREACT 37* 37 2
4 Feb 95 LET'S SPEND THE NIGHT TOGETHER *Playa CDXPLAYA 2* 66 1

Barbara MASON US, female vocalist

21 Jan 84 ANOTHER MAN *Streetwave KHAN 3* 45 5

Glen MASON UK, male vocalist – Tommy Lennon (2 Singles: 7 Weeks)

28 Sep 56 GLENDORA *Parlophone R 4203* 28 2
16 Nov 56 THE GREEN DOOR *Parlophone R 4244* 24 5

John MASON UK, male instrumentalist

27 Dec 75 STRINGS OF SCOTLAND *Philips 6382 108* 50 1

Mary MASON UK, female vocalist

8 Oct 77 ANGEL OF THE MORNING – ANY WAY THAT YOU WANT ME (MEDLEY) *Epic EPC 5552* 27 6

Willy MASON NEW

US, male vocalist / guitarist (1 Album: 6 Weeks, 2 Singles: 5 Weeks)

19 Feb 05 WHERE THE HUMANS EAT *Virgin CDV 2993* 38 6
26 Feb 05 OXYGEN *Virgin VSCDX 1892* 23 3
14 May 05 SO LONG *Virgin VSCDX 1898* 45 2

MASQUERADE UK, male / female vocal group (2 Singles: 10 Weeks)

11 Jan 86 ONE NATION *Streetwave KHAN 59* 54 6
5 Jul 86 (SOLUTION TO) THE PROBLEM (re) *Streetwave KHAN 67* 64 4

MASS ORDER US, male vocal / instrumental duo – Eugene Hanes and Marc Valentine (2 Singles: 5 Weeks)

14 Mar 92 LIFT EVERY VOICE (TAKE ME AWAY) *Columbia 6577487* 35 3
23 May 92 LET'S GET HAPPY *Columbia 6580737* 45 2

MASS PRODUCTION

US, male vocal / instrumental group (2 Singles: 7 Weeks)

12 Mar 77 WELCOME TO OUR WORLD (OF MERRY MUSIC) *Atlantic K 10898* 44 3
17 May 80 SHANTE *Atlantic K 11475* 59 4

MASS SYNDICATE featuring Su Su BOBIEN

US, male producer and female vocalist

24 Oct 98 YOU DON'T KNOW *ffrr FCD 347* 71 1

MASSED WELSH CHOIRS UK, male choir

9 Aug 69 ● CYMANSA GANN *BBC REC 53M* 5 7

Zeitia MASSIAH UK, female vocalist (2 Singles: 2 Weeks)

12 Mar 94 I SPECIALIZE IN LOVE *Union City UCRCD 27* [1] 74 1
24 Sep 94 THIS IS THE PLACE *Virgin VSCDT 1511* 62 1

[1] Arizona featuring Zeitia

MASSIEL Spain, female vocalist – Maria Espinosa

24 Apr 68 LA LA LA *Philips BF 1667* 35 4

MASSIVE ATTACK 235 Top 500

(see also Shara NELSON; NICOLETTE) *Trip hop titans who emerged from Bristol's legendary Wild Bunch: mainstays Robert '3D' Del Naja (v), Grant 'Daddy-G' Marshall (v) and Andrew 'Mushroom' Vowles (k). BRIT-nominated band entered the European chart at No.1 in 2003 with 100th Window (which featured Del Naja only) (5 Albums: 227 Weeks, 10 Singles: 44 Weeks)*

23 Feb 91 UNFINISHED SYMPATHY *Wild Bunch WBRS 2* [1] 13 9
20 Apr 91 BLUE LINES *Wild Bunch WBRLP 1* 13 88
8 Jun 91 SAFE FROM HARM *Wild Bunch WBRS 3* 25 6
22 Feb 92 MASSIVE ATTACK (EP) *Wild Bunch WBRS 4* 27 4
8 Oct 94 ● PROTECTION / NO PROTECTION *Wild Bunch WBRCD 2* 4 78
29 Oct 94 SLY *Wild Bunch WBRDX 5* 24 4
21 Jan 95 PROTECTION *Wild Bunch WBRX 6* [2] 14 4
1 Apr 95 KARMACOMA *Wild Bunch WBRX 7* 28 4
19 Jul 97 RISINGSON *Circa WBRX 8* 11 3
2 May 98 ★ MEZZANINE *Virgin WBRCD 4* ■ 1 54
9 May 98 ● TEARDROP *Virgin WBRX 9* 10 6
25 Jul 98 ANGEL *Virgin WBRX 10* 30 2
22 Feb 03 ★ 100TH WINDOW *Virgin CDV 2967* ■ 1 6
8 Mar 03 SPECIAL CASES *Virgin VSCDT 1839* 15 2
23 Oct 04 DANNY THE DOG – ORIGINAL MOTION PICTURE SOUNDTRACK *Virgin CDV 2988* 70 1

[1] Massive [2] Massive Attack featuring Tracey Thorn

Shara Nelson is the vocalist on the first three releases. Tracks on Massive Attack (EP): Hymn of the Big Wheel / Home of the Whale / Be Thankful / Any Love. 'Teardrop' features Elizabeth Fraser (Cocteau Twins) and 'Special Cases' features Sinead O'Connor, both as uncredited vocalists. From 4 Mar 95 Protection was listed with the re-mix album No Protection.

MASSIVO featuring TRACY

UK, male / female vocal / instrumental group

26 May 90 LOVING YOU *Debut DEBT 3097* 25 11

MASTER BLASTER Germany, male production trio

7 Aug 04 HYPNOTIC TANGO *Mondo Pop 9867100* 64 1

The MASTER SINGERS UK, male vocal group (2 Singles: 8 Weeks)

14 Apr 66 HIGHWAY CODE *Parlophone R 5428* 25 6
17 Nov 66 WEATHER FORECAST (re) *Parlophone R 5523* 45 2

Sammy MASTERS US, male vocalist – Samuel Lawmaster

9 Jun 60 ROCKIN' RED WING *Warner Bros. WB 10* 36 5

MASTERS AT WORK

(see also NUYORICAN SOUL) *US, male production / instrumental duo – 'Lil' Louis Vega and Kenny 'Dope' Gonzales (3 Singles: 6 Weeks)*

5 Aug 95 I CAN'T GET NO SLEEP *A&M 5811412* [1] 44 2
31 Jul 99 TO BE IN LOVE *Defected DEFECT 5CDS* [2] 23 3
6 Jul 02 BACKFIRED *SuSu CDSUSU 4* [3] 62 1

[1] Masters at Work presents India [2] MAW presents India [3] Masters at Work featuring India

Paul MASTERSON presents SUSHI (see also The CANDY GIRLS; CLERGY; DOROTHY; HI-GATE; SLEAZESISTERS; YOMANDA) UK, male producer

2 Nov 02 THE EARTHSHAKER *Nulife 74321970372* 35 2

MATCH UK, male vocal / instrumental group

16 Jun 79 BOOGIE MAN *Flamingo FM 2* 48 3

MATCHBOX UK, male vocal (Graham Fenton) / instrumental group (2 Albums: 14 Weeks, 8 Singles: 66 Weeks)

3 Nov 79 ROCKABILLY REBEL *Magnet MAG 155* 18 12
19 Jan 80 BUZZ BUZZ A DIDDLE IT *Magnet MAG 157* 22 8
2 Feb 80 MATCHBOX *Magnet MAG 5031* 44 5
10 May 80 MIDNITE DYNAMOS *Magnet MAG 169* 14 12
27 Sep 80 ● WHEN YOU ASK ABOUT LOVE *Magnet MAG 191* 4 12
11 Oct 80 MIDNITE DYNAMOS *Magnet MAG 5036* 23 9
29 Nov 80 OVER THE RAINBOW – YOU BELONG TO ME (MEDLEY) *Magnet MAG 192* 15 11

	24 June 1978	1 July 1978	8 July 1978	15 July 1978
UK No.1 SINGLES	YOU'RE THE ONE THAT I WANT John Travolta and Olivia Newton-John	YOU'RE THE ONE THAT I WANT John Travolta and Olivia Newton-John	YOU'RE THE ONE THAT I WANT John Travolta and Olivia Newton-John	YOU'RE THE ONE THAT I WANT John Travolta and Olivia Newton-John
UK No.1 ALBUMS	SATURDAY NIGHT FEVER Soundtrack	SATURDAY NIGHT FEVER Soundtrack	SATURDAY NIGHT FEVER Soundtrack	SATURDAY NIGHT FEVER Soundtrack

4 Apr 81 **BABES IN THE WOOD** *Magnet MAG 193* 46 6
1 Aug 81 **LOVE'S MADE A FOOL OF YOU** *Magnet MAG 194* 63 3
29 May 82 **ONE MORE SATURDAY NIGHT** *Magnet MAG 223* 63 2

MATCHBOX TWENTY *US, male vocal / instrumental group – leader Rob Thomas (3 Albums: 5 Weeks, 4 Singles: 5 Weeks)*

11 Apr 98 **PUSH** *Atlantic AT 0021CD* [1] 38 2
25 Apr 98 YOURSELF OR SOMEONE LIKE YOU *Atlantic 7567927212* [1] 50 1
4 Jul 98 **3 AM** *Atlantic AT 0034CD* [1] 64 1
3 Jun 00 MAD SEASON *Atlantic 7567833392* 31 2
17 Feb 01 **IF YOU'RE GONE** *Atlantic AT 0090CD* 50 1
22 Feb 03 **DISEASE** *Atlantic AT 0145CD* 50 1
8 Mar 03 MORE THAN YOU THINK YOU ARE *Atlantic ATL 836122* 31 2

[1] Matchbox 20 [1] Matchbox 20

Mireille MATHIEU *France, female vocalist*

13 Dec 67 **LA DERNIERE VALSE** *Columbia DB 8323* 26 7
2 Mar 68 MIREILLE MATHIEU *Columbia SCX 6210* 39 1

Johnny MATHIS (140 Top 500)

Legendary MOR vocal superstar, b. 30 Sep 1935, San Francisco, US. Frank Sinatra and Elvis Presley are the only males with more hit albums in the US, where his greatest hits album charted for almost 10 years – a record for a solo performer (27 Albums: 228 Weeks, 16 Singles: 138 Weeks)

23 May 58 **TEACHER, TEACHER** *Fontana H 130* 27 5
26 Sep 58 ● **A CERTAIN SMILE** *Fontana H 142* 4 16
8 Nov 58 ● WARM *Fontana TBA TFL 5015* 6 2
19 Dec 58 **WINTER WONDERLAND** *Fontana H 165* 17 3
24 Jan 59 ● SWING SOFTLY *Fontana TBA TFL 5039* 10 1
7 Aug 59 ● **SOMEONE** *Fontana H 199* 6 15
27 Nov 59 **THE BEST OF EVERYTHING** *Fontana H 218* 30 1
29 Jan 60 **MISTY** (re) *Fontana H 219* 12 12
13 Feb 60 ● RIDE ON A RAINBOW *Fontana TFL 5061* 10 2
24 Mar 60 **YOU ARE BEAUTIFUL** (re) *Fontana H 234* 38 9
28 Jul 60 **STARBRIGHT** *Fontana H 254* 47 2
6 Oct 60 ● **MY LOVE FOR YOU** *Fontana H 267* 9 18
10 Dec 60 ● RHYTHMS AND BALLADS OF BROADWAY *Fontana SET 101* 6 10
17 Jun 61 I'LL BUY YOU A STAR *Fontana TFL 5143* 18 1
4 Apr 63 **WHAT WILL MARY SAY** *CBS AAG 135* 49 1
16 May 70 RAINDROPS KEEP FALLING ON MY HEAD *CBS 63587* 23 10
3 Apr 71 LOVE STORY *CBS 64334* 27 5
9 Sep 72 FIRST TIME EVER I SAW YOUR FACE *CBS 64930* 40 3
16 Dec 72 MAKE IT EASY ON YOURSELF *CBS 65161* 49 1
25 Jan 75 ● **I'M STONE IN LOVE WITH YOU** *CBS 2653* 10 12
8 Mar 75 I'M COMING HOME *CBS 65690* 18 11
5 Apr 75 THE HEART OF A WOMAN *CBS 80533* 39 2
26 Jul 75 WHEN WILL I SEE YOU AGAIN *CBS 80738* 13 10
3 Jul 76 I ONLY HAVE EYES FOR YOU *CBS 81329* 14 12
13 Nov 76 ★ **WHEN A CHILD IS BORN (SOLEADO)** *CBS 4599* 1 12
19 Feb 77 GREATEST HITS VOLUME IV *CBS 86022* 31 5
18 Jun 77 ★ THE JOHNNY MATHIS COLLECTION *CBS 10003* 1 40
17 Dec 77 SWEET SURRENDER *CBS 86036* 55 1
25 Mar 78 ● **TOO MUCH, TOO LITTLE, TOO LATE** *CBS 6164* [1] ▲ $ 3 14
29 Apr 78 ● YOU LIGHT UP MY LIFE *CBS 86055* 3 19
29 Jul 78 **YOU'RE ALL I NEED TO GET BY** *CBS 6483* [1] 45 6
26 Aug 78 THAT'S WHAT FRIENDS ARE FOR *CBS 86068* [1] 16 11
7 Apr 79 THE BEST DAYS OF MY LIFE *CBS 86080* 38 5
11 Aug 79 **GONE, GONE, GONE** *CBS 7730* 15 10
3 Nov 79 MATHIS MAGIC *CBS 86103* 59 4
8 Mar 80 ★ TEARS AND LAUGHTER *CBS 10019* 1 15
12 Jul 80 ALL FOR YOU *CBS 86115* 20 8
19 Sep 81 ● CELEBRATION *CBS 10028* 9 16
26 Dec 81 **WHEN A CHILD IS BORN** (re-recording) *CBS S 1758* [2] 74 2
15 May 82 FRIENDS IN LOVE *CBS 85652* 34 7
17 Sep 83 ● UNFORGETTABLE: A MUSICAL TRIBUTE TO NAT 'KING' COLE *CBS 10042* [2] 5 16
15 Sep 84 A SPECIAL PART OF ME *CBS 25475* 45 3
13 Dec 86 THE HOLLYWOOD MUSICALS *CBS 4502581* [3] 46 8

[1] Johnny Mathis and Deniece Williams [2] Johnny Mathis and Gladys Knight
[1] Johnny Mathis and Deniece Williams [2] Johnny Mathis and Natalie Cole
[3] Johnny Mathis and Henry Mancini

Ivan MATIAS *US, male vocalist*

6 Apr 96 **SO GOOD (TO COME HOME TO) / I'VE HAD ENOUGH** *Arista 74321345072* 69 1

MATT BIANCO *UK, male / female vocal / instrumental duo (4 Albums: 67 Weeks, 10 Singles: 65 Weeks)*

11 Feb 84 **GET OUT OF YOUR LAZY BED** *WEA BIANCO 1* 15 8
14 Apr 84 **SNEAKING OUT THE BACK DOOR / MATT'S MOOD** *WEA YZ 3* ...44 7
8 Sep 84 WHOSE SIDE ARE YOU ON *WEA WX 7* 35 39
10 Nov 84 **HALF A MINUTE** *WEA YZ 26* 23 10
2 Mar 85 **MORE THAN I CAN BEAR** *WEA YZ 34* 50 7
5 Oct 85 **YEH YEH** *WEA YZ 46* 13 10
1 Mar 86 **JUST CAN'T STAND IT** *WEA YZ 62* 66 2
22 Mar 86 MATT BIANCO *WEA WX 35* 26 13
14 Jun 86 **DANCING IN THE STREET** *WEA YZ 72* 64 3
4 Jun 88 **DON'T BLAME IT ON THAT GIRL / WAP-BAM-BOOGIE** *WEA YZ 188* 11 13
9 Jul 88 INDIGO *WEA WX 181* 23 13
27 Aug 88 **GOOD TIMES** *WEA YZ 302* 55 3
4 Feb 89 **NERVOUS / WAP-BAM-BOOGIE** (re-mix) *WEA YZ 328* 59 2
2 Nov 90 THE BEST OF MATT BIANCO *East West WX 376* 49 2

'Matt's Mood' credited only from 5 May 1984. Act was a UK / Poland, male / female vocal / instrumental group on first five singles and first album.

MATTAFIX NEW *UK / St Vincent, male vocal / instrumental / production duo – Preetesh Hirji and Marlon Roudette*

20 Aug 05 **BIG CITY LIFE** *Buddhist Punk ANGEDX 1* 15 7

Kathy MATTEA *US, female vocalist (2 Albums: 2 Weeks)*

15 Apr 95 READY FOR THE STORM (FAVOURITE CUTS) *Mercury 5280062* . 61 1
8 Feb 97 LOVE TRAVELS *Mercury 5328992* 65 1

Al MATTHEWS *US, male vocalist*

23 Aug 75 **FOOL** *CBS 3429* 16 8

Cerys MATTHEWS (see also CATATONIA)

UK, female vocalist (1 Album: 5 Weeks, 3 Singles: 16 Weeks)

7 Mar 98 ● **THE BALLAD OF TOM JONES** *Gut CDGUT 018* [1] 4 8
18 Dec 99 **BABY, IT'S COLD OUTSIDE** *Gut CDGUT 29* [2] 17 7
31 May 03 COCKAHOOP *Blanco Y Negro 2564603062* 30 5
2 Aug 03 **CAUGHT IN THE MIDDLE** *Blano Y Negro NEG 147CD1* 47 1

[1] Space with Cerys of Catatonia [2] Tom Jones & Cerys Matthews

Summer MATTHEWS *UK, female actor / vocalist – Holly Wilkinson*

28 Feb 04 **LITTLE MISS PERFECT** *Sony Music 6744732* 32 2

Dave MATTHEWS BAND *US, male vocal / instrumental group*

1 Dec 01 **THE SPACE BETWEEN** *RCA 74321883192* 35 2

MATTHEWS' SOUTHERN COMFORT

UK, male vocal (Ian Matthews) / instrumental group

25 Jul 70 SECOND SPRING *Uni UNLS 112* 52 4
26 Sep 70 ★ **WOODSTOCK** *Uni UNS 526* 1 18

MATUMBI *UK, male vocal / instrumental group*

29 Sep 79 **POINT OF VIEW (SQUEEZE A LITTLE LOVIN)** *Matumbi RIC 101* 35 7

Susan MAUGHAN *UK, female vocalist (3 Singles: 25 Weeks)*

11 Oct 62 ● **BOBBY'S GIRL** *Philips 326544 BF* 3 19
14 Feb 63 **HAND A HANDKERCHIEF TO HELEN** *Philips 326562 BF* 41 3
9 May 63 **SHE'S NEW TO YOU** *Philips 326586 BF* 45 3

22 July 1978	29 July 1978	5 August 1978	12 August 1978
YOU'RE THE ONE THAT I WANT John Travolta and Olivia Newton-John	YOU'RE THE ONE THAT I WANT John Travolta and Olivia Newton-John	YOU'RE THE ONE THAT I WANT John Travolta and Olivia Newton-John	YOU'RE THE ONE THAT I WANT John Travolta and Olivia Newton-John
SATURDAY NIGHT FEVER Soundtrack	SATURDAY NIGHT FEVER Soundtrack	SATURDAY NIGHT FEVER Soundtrack	SATURDAY NIGHT FEVER Soundtrack

KEY: UK No.1 ★ UK Top 10 ● Still on chart + UK entry at No.1 ■ US No.1 ▲ UK million seller £ US million seller $
Singles re-entries are listed as (re), (2re), (3re)... which signifies that the hit re-entered the chart once, twice or three times...
Peak Position / Weeks

MAUREEN *UK, female vocalist – Maureen Walsh (3 Singles: 22 Weeks)*

26 Nov 88 ● **SAY A LITTLE PRAYER** *Rhythm King DOOD 3* [1] 10 10
16 Jun 90 **THINKING OF YOU** *Urban URB 55* [2] 11 9
12 Jan 91 **WHERE HAS ALL THE LOVE GONE** *Urban URB 65*....51 3

[1] Bomb the Bass featuring Maureen [2] Maureen Walsh

Paul MAURIAT and his ORCHESTRA *France, orchestra*

21 Feb 68 **LOVE IS BLUE (L'AMOUR EST BLEU)** *Philips BF 1637* ▲ $....12 14

The MAVERICKS *US, male vocal (Raul Malo) / instrumental group (4 Albums: 60 Weeks, 3 Singles: 23 Weeks)*

11 May 96 MUSIC FOR ALL OCCASIONS *MCA MCD 11344*....56 1
14 Mar 98 ● TRAMPOLINE *MCA Nashville UMD 80456*....10 48
2 May 98 ● **DANCE THE NIGHT AWAY** *MCA Nashville MCSTD 48081*....4 18
26 Sep 98 **I'VE GOT THIS FEELING** *MCA Nashville MCSTD 48095*....27 4
5 Jun 99 **SOMEONE SHOULD TELL HER** *MCA Nashville MCSTD 55567*..45 1
4 Dec 99 THE BEST OF THE MAVERICKS *Mercury / Universal TV 1701202*....40 9
4 Oct 03 MAVERICKS *Sanctuary SANCD 192*....65 2

MAX LINEN *UK, male production duo*

17 Nov 01 **THE SOULSHAKER** *Global Cuts GC 73CD*....55 1

MAX Q (see also INXS) *Australia, male vocal / instrumental duo*

4 Nov 89 MAX Q *Mercury 838942 1*....69 1
17 Feb 90 **SOMETIMES** *Mercury MXQ 2*....53 3

MAX WEBSTER *Canada, male vocal / instrumental group*

19 May 79 **PARADISE SKIES** *Capitol CL 16079*....43 3

MAXEE *US, female vocalist*

17 Mar 01 **WHEN I LOOK INTO YOUR EYES** *Mercury 5628702*....55 1

MAXIM (see also The PRODIGY) *UK, male producer / vocalist – Keith Palmer (2 Singles: 3 Weeks)*

10 Jun 00 **CARMEN QUEASY** *XL Recordings XLS 119CD* [1] 33 2
23 Sep 00 **SCHEMING** *XL Recordings XLS 121CD*....53 1

[1] Maxim: vocal by Skin

MAXIMA featuring LILY *UK / Spain, male / female vocal / instrumental duo*

14 Aug 93 **IBIZA** *Yo! Yo! CDLILY 1*....55 2

MAXÏMO PARK NEW *UK, male vocal / instrumental group (1 Album: 12 Weeks, 4 Singles: 11 Weeks)*

5 Mar 05 **APPLY SOME PRESSURE** *Warp WAP 185CD*....20 2
14 May 05 **GRAFFITI** *Warp WAP 187CDR*....15 3
28 May 05 A CERTAIN TRIGGER *Warp WARPCD 130*....15 12
30 Jul 05 **GOING MISSING** *Warp WAP 190CD*....20 3
5 Nov 05 **APPLY SOME PRESSURE** (re-issue) *Warp WAP 198CD*....17 3

MAXTREME *Holland, male production group*

9 Mar 02 **MY HOUSE IS YOUR HOUSE** *Y2K Y2K 028CD*....66 1

MAXWELL *US, male vocalist – Maxwell Menard (4 Albums: 20 Weeks, 4 Singles: 10 Weeks)*

13 Apr 96 URBAN HANG SUITE *Columbia 4836992*....39 10
11 May 96 **... TIL THE COPS COME KNOCKIN'** *Columbia 6631792*....63 1
24 Aug 96 **ASCENSION NO ONE'S GONNA LOVE YOU SO DON'T EVER WONDER** *Columbia 6636265*....39 3
1 Mar 97 **SUMTHIN' SUMTHIN' THE MANTRA** *Columbia 6638642*....27 3
24 May 97 **ASCENSION DON'T EVER WONDER** (re-issue) *Columbia 6645952*....28 3
26 Jul 97 MTV UNPLUGGED (EP) *Columbia 4882922*....45 2
4 Jul 98 EMBRYA *Columbia 4894202*....11 6
22 Sep 01 NOW *Columbia 4974542* ▲....46 2

MAXX *UK / Sweden / Germany, male / female vocal / instrumental group (1 Album: 1 Week, 4 Singles: 24 Weeks)*

21 May 94 ● **GET-A-WAY** *Pulse 8 CDLOSE 59*....4 12
23 Jul 94 TO THE MAXXIMUM *Pulse 8 PULSE 15CD*....66 1
6 Aug 94 ● **NO MORE (I CAN'T STAND IT)** *Pulse 8 CDLOSE 66*....8 8
29 Oct 94 **YOU CAN GET IT** *Pulse 8 CDLOSE 75*....21 3
22 Jul 95 **I CAN MAKE YOU FEEL LIKE** *Pulse 8 CDLOSE 88*....56 1

Billy MAY and his Orchestra *US, orchestra – leader b. 10 Nov 1916, d. 22 Jan 2004*

27 Apr 56 ● **MAIN TITLE THEME FROM 'MAN WITH THE GOLDEN ARM'** *Capitol CL 14551*....9 10

Brian MAY (see also QUEEN) *UK, male vocalist / guitarist, awarded CBE in 2005 (4 Albums: 23 Weeks, 9 Singles: 33 Weeks)*

5 Nov 83 **STAR FLEET** *EMI 5436* [1] 65 3
12 Nov 83 STAR FLEET PROJECT *EMI SFLT 1078061* [1] 35 4
7 Dec 91 ● **DRIVEN BY YOU** *Parlophone R 6304*....6 9
5 Sep 92 ● **TOO MUCH LOVE WILL KILL YOU** *Parlophone R 6320*....5 9
10 Oct 92 ● BACK TO THE LIGHT *Parlophone CDPCSD 123*....6 14
17 Oct 92 **WE ARE THE CHAMPIONS** *PolyGram TV PO 229* [2] 66 1
21 Nov 92 **BACK TO THE LIGHT** *Parlophone R 6329*....19 4
19 Jun 93 **RESURRECTION** *Parlophone CDRS 6351* [3] 23 3
18 Dec 93 **LAST HORIZON** *Parlophone CDR 6371*....51 2
19 Feb 94 LIVE AT THE BRIXTON ACADEMY *Parlophone CDPCSD 150* [2] 20 3
6 Jun 98 **THE BUSINESS** *Parlophone CDR 6498*....51 1
13 Jun 98 ANOTHER WORLD *Parlophone 4949732*....23 2
12 Sep 98 **WHY DON'T WE TRY AGAIN** *Parlophone CDR 6504*....44 1

[1] Brian May and Friends [2] Hank Marvin featuring Brian May [3] Brian May with Cozy Powell [1] Brian May and Friends [2] Brian May Band

Lisa MAY *UK, female vocalist (2 Singles: 2 Weeks)*

15 Jul 95 **WISHING ON A STAR** *Urban Gorilla UG 3CD* [1] 61 1
14 Sep 96 **THE CURSE OF VOODOO RAY** *Fontana VOOCD 1*....64 1

[1] 883 featuring Lisa May

Mary MAY *UK, female vocalist*

27 Feb 64 **ANYONE WHO HAD A HEART** *Fontana TF 440*....49 1

Simon MAY ORCHESTRA *UK, orchestra (1 Album: 7 Weeks, 5 Singles: 42 Weeks)*

9 Oct 76 ● **THE SUMMER OF MY LIFE** *Pye 7N 45627* [1] 7 8
21 May 77 **WE'LL GATHER LILACS – ALL MY LOVING (MEDLEY)** (re) *Pye 7N 45688* [1] 49 2
26 Oct 85 **HOWARD'S WAY** *BBC RESL 174*....21 11
9 Aug 86 ● **ANYONE CAN FALL IN LOVE** *BBC RESL 191* [2] 4 9
20 Sep 86 **ALWAYS THERE** *BBC RESL 190* [3] 13 12
27 Sep 86 SIMON'S WAY *BBC REB 594*....59 7

[1] Simon May [2] Anita Dobson featuring the Simon May Orchestra
[3] Marti Webb and the Simon May Orchestra

Shernette MAY *UK, female vocalist*

6 Jun 98 **ALL THE MAN THAT I NEED** *Virgin VSCDT 1691*....50 1

	19 August 1978	26 August 1978	2 September 1978	9 September 1978
UK No.1 SINGLES	THREE TIMES A LADY The Commodores	THREE TIMES A LADY The Commodores	THREE TIMES A LADY The Commodores	THREE TIMES A LADY The Commodores
UK No.1 ALBUMS	SATURDAY NIGHT FEVER Soundtrack	SATURDAY NIGHT FEVER Soundtrack	SATURDAY NIGHT FEVER Soundtrack	NIGHT FLIGHT TO VENUS Boney M

John MAYALL

UK, male vocalist, awarded OBE in 2005 (14 Albums: 115 Weeks)

30 Jul 66 ●	BLUES BREAKERS *Decca LK 4804* [1]	6	17
4 Mar 67 ●	A HARD ROAD *Decca SKL 4853*	10	19
23 Sep 67 ●	CRUSADE *Decca SKL 4890*	8	14
25 Nov 67	THE BLUES ALONE *Ace of Clubs SCL 1243*	24	5
16 Mar 68	DIARY OF A BAND VOLUME 1 *Decca SKL 4918*	27	9
16 Mar 68	DIARY OF A BAND VOLUME 2 *Decca SKL 4919*	28	5
20 Jul 68 ●	BARE WIRES *Decca SKL 4945*	3	17
18 Jan 69	BLUES FROM LAUREL CANYON *Decca SKL 4972*	33	3
23 Aug 69	LOOKING BACK *Decca SKL 5010*	14	7
15 Nov 69	THE TURNING POINT *Polydor 583571*	11	7
11 Apr 70 ●	EMPTY ROOMS *Polydor 583580*	9	8
12 Dec 70	U.S.A. UNION *Polydor 2425020*	50	1
26 Jun 71	BACK TO THE ROOTS *Polydor 2657005*	31	2
17 Apr 93	WAKE UP CALL *Silvertone ORECD 527*	61	1

[1] John Mayall and Eric Clapton

John MAYER

US, male vocalist / guitarist (1 Album: 1 Week, 2 Singles: 2 Weeks)

23 Aug 03	**NO SUCH THING** *Columbia 6732322*	42	1
25 Oct 03	HEAVIER THINGS *Columbia 5134722* ▲	74	1
28 Feb 04	**BIGGER THAN MY BODY** *Columbia 6744392*	72	1

Curtis MAYFIELD

US, male vocalist / guitarist, b. 6 Jun 1942, d. 26 Dec 1999 (3 Albums: 5 Weeks, 5 Singles: 20 Weeks)

20 Mar 71	CURTIS *Buddah 2318 015*	30	1
31 Jul 71	**MOVE ON UP** *Buddah 2011 080*	12	10
31 Mar 73	SUPERFLY *Buddah 2318 065* ▲	26	2
2 Dec 78	**NO GOODBYES** *Atlantic LV 1*	65	3
30 May 87	**(CELEBRATE) THE DAY AFTER YOU** *RCA MONK 6* [1]	52	2
29 Sep 90	**SUPERFLY 1990** *Capitol CL 586* [2]	48	3
15 Feb 97	NEW WORLD ORDER *Warner Bros. 9362463482*	44	2
16 Jun 01	**ASTOUNDED** *Virgin VUSCD 194* [3]	40	2

[1] The Blow Monkeys with Curtis Mayfield [2] Curtis Mayfield and Ice-T
[3] Bran Van 3000 featuring Curtis Mayfield

The MAYTALS

Jamaica, male vocal / instrumental group

25 Apr 70	**MONKEY MAN** (re) *Trojan TR 7711*	47	4

MAYTE

US, female vocalist – Mayte Garcia

18 Nov 95	**IF EYE LOVE U 2 NIGHT** *NPG 0061635*	67	1

MAZE featuring Frankie BEVERLY

US, male vocal / instrumental group (4 Albums: 25 Weeks, 3 Singles: 14 Weeks)

7 May 83	WE ARE ONE *Capitol EST 12262*	38	6
9 Mar 85	CAN'T STOP THE LOVE *Capitol MAZE 1*	41	12
20 Jul 85	**TOO MANY GAMES** *Capitol CL 363*	36	7
23 Aug 86	**I WANNA BE WITH YOU** *Capitol CL 421*	55	3
27 Sep 86	LIVE IN LOS ANGELES *Capitol ESTSP 24*	70	2
27 May 89	**JOY AND PAIN** *Capitol CL 531* [1]	57	4
16 Sep 89	SILKY SOUL *Warner Bros. WX 301*	43	5

[1] Maze

Kym MAZELLE

US, female vocalist – Kimberley Grigsby (15 Singles: 66 Weeks)

12 Nov 88	**USELESS (I DON'T NEED YOU NOW)** *Syncopate SY 18*	53	3
14 Jan 89 ●	**WAIT** *RCA PB 42595* [1]	7	10
25 Mar 89	**GOT TO GET YOU BACK** *Syncopate SY 25*	29	4
7 Oct 89	**LOVE STRAIN** *Syncopate SY 30*	52	3
20 Jan 90	**WAS THAT ALL IT WAS** *Syncopate SY 32*	33	6
26 May 90	**USELESS (I DON'T NEED YOU NOW)** (re-mix) *Syncopate SY 36*	48	2
24 Nov 90	**MISSING YOU** *Ten TEN 345* [2]	22	7
25 May 91	**NO ONE CAN LOVE YOU MORE THAN ME** *Parlophone R 6287*	62	2
26 Dec 92	**LOVE ME THE RIGHT WAY** *Arista 74321128097* [3]	22	10
11 Jun 94	**NO MORE TEARS (ENOUGH IS ENOUGH)** *Bell 74321209032* [4]	13	7
8 Oct 94	**GIMME ALL YOUR LOVIN'** *Bell 74321231322* [5]	22	3
23 Dec 95	**SEARCHING FOR THE GOLDEN EYE** *Eternal WEA 027CD* [6]	40	3
28 Sep 96	**LOVE ME THE RIGHT WAY** (re-mix) *Logic 74321404442* [3]	55	1
16 Aug 97	**YOUNG HEARTS RUN FREE** *EMI CDEM 488*	20	4
19 Feb 00	**TRULY** *Island Blue PFACD 4* [7]	55	1

[1] Robert Howard and Kym Mazelle [2] Soul II Soul featuring Kym Mazelle
[3] Rapination and Kym Mazelle [4] Kym Mazelle and Jocelyn Brown
[5] Jocelyn Brown and Kym Mazelle [6] Motiv 8 and Kym Mazelle
[7] Peshay featuring Kym Mazelle

MAZZY STAR

US, male / female vocal / instrumental group (2 Albums: 2 Weeks, 2 Singles: 3 Weeks)

9 Oct 93	SO TONIGHT THAT I MIGHT SEE *Capitol CDEST 2206*	68	1
27 Aug 94	**FADE INTO YOU** *Capitol CDCL 720*	48	1
2 Nov 96	**FLOWERS IN DECEMBER** *Capitol CDCL 781*	40	2
16 Nov 96	AMONG MY SWAN *Capitol CDEST 2288*	57	1

MC DALE & The BAR-CODES featuring Alison BROWN

UK, male / female vocal group – includes Dale Winton

17 Dec 94	**SUPERMARKET SWEEP (WILL YOU DANCE WITH ME)** *Blanca Casa BC 101CD*	72	1

MC DUKE

UK, male rapper – Anthony Hilaire

11 Mar 89	**I'M RIFFIN (ENGLISH RASTA)** *Music of Life 7NOTE 25*	75	1

MC HAMMER

US, male rapper – Stanley Burrell (3 Albums: 67 Weeks, 12 Singles: 68 Weeks)

9 Jun 90 ●	**U CAN'T TOUCH THIS** *Capitol CL 578*	3	16
28 Jul 90 ●	PLEASE HAMMER DON'T HURT 'EM *Capitol EST 2120* ▲	8	59
6 Oct 90 ●	**HAVE YOU SEEN HER** *Capitol CL 590*	8	7
8 Dec 90 ●	**PRAY** *Capitol CL 599*	8	10
23 Feb 91	**HERE COMES THE HAMMER** *Capitol CL 610*	15	5
6 Apr 91	LET'S GET IT STARTED *Capitol EST 2140*	46	2
1 Jun 91	**YO!! SWEETNESS** *Capitol CL 616*	16	5
20 Jul 91	**(HAMMER HAMMER) THEY PUT ME IN THE MIX** *Capitol CL 607*	20	4
26 Oct 91	**2 LEGIT 2 QUIT** *Capitol CL 636* [1] $	60	2
2 Nov 91	TOO LEGIT TO QUIT *Capitol ESTP 26* [1]	41	6
21 Dec 91 ●	**ADDAMS GROOVE** *Capitol CL 642* [1]	4	9
21 Mar 92	**DO NOT PASS ME BY** *Capitol CL 650* [1]	14	6
12 Mar 94	**IT'S ALL GOOD** *RCA 74321188612* [1]	52	2
13 Aug 94	**DON'T STOP** *RCA 74321220012* [1]	72	1
3 Jun 95	**STRAIGHT TO MY FEET** *Priority PTYCD 102* [2]	57	1

[1] Hammer [2] Hammer featuring Deion Saunders [1] Hammer

MC JIG

Germany, male DJ / producer (2 Singles: 7 Weeks)

21 Feb 04	**CHA-CHA SLIDE** (import) *ZYX ZYX 95838*	37	3
13 Mar 04	**CHA-CHA SLIDE** *NM Music SLIDE 001*	33	4

MC LETHAL

UK, male producer – Lee Whitney

14 Nov 92	**THE RAVE DIGGER** *Network NWKT 60*	66	1

MC LYTE

US, female rapper – Lana Moorer (8 Singles: 19 Weeks)

15 Jan 94	**RUFFNECK** *Atlantic A 8336CD*	67	1
29 Jun 96	**KEEP ON KEEPIN' ON** *East West A 4287CD* [1]	39	2
18 Jan 97	**COLD ROCK A PARTY** *East West A 3975CD*	15	4
19 Apr 97	**KEEP ON KEEPIN' ON** (re-issue) *East West A 3950CD 1* [1]	27	2
5 Sep 98	**I CAN'T MAKE A MISTAKE** *Elektra E 3813CD*	46	1
19 Dec 98	**IT'S ALL YOURS** *East West E 3789CD* [2]	36	4
24 Jun 00	**JAMMIN'** *Tuff Gong TGXCD 9* [3]	42	2
8 May 04	**GIRLFRIEND'S STORY** *Polydor 9866362* [4]	38	3

[1] MC Lyte featuring Xscape [2] MC Lyte featuring Gina Thompson
[3] Bob Marley featuring MC Lyte [4] Gemma Fox featuring MC Lyte

16 September 1978	23 September 1978	30 September 1978	7 October 1978
THREE TIMES A LADY The Commodores	**DREADLOCK HOLIDAY** 10cc	**SUMMER NIGHTS** John Travolta, Olivia Newton-John and cast	**SUMMER NIGHTS** John Travolta, Olivia Newton-John and cast
NIGHT FLIGHT TO VENUS Boney M	**NIGHT FLIGHT TO VENUS** Boney M	**NIGHT FLIGHT TO VENUS** Boney M	**GREASE** Soundtrack

KEY UK No.1 ★ UK Top 10 ● Still on chart + UK entry at No.1 ■ US No.1 ▲ UK million seller £ US million seller $
Singles re-entries are listed as (re), (2re), (3re)... which signifies that the hit re-entered the chart once, twice or three times...
Peak Position / Weeks

MC MIKER 'G' and Deejay SVEN *Holland, male vocal / instrumental / rap duo – Lucien Witteveen and Sven Van Veen*

6 Sep 86 ● **HOLIDAY RAP** *Debut DEBT 3008* ... 6 7

MC SKAT KAT and The STRAY MOB *US, male cartoon feline rap / vocal group*

9 Nov 91 **SKAT STRUT** *Virgin America VUS 51* ... 64 2

MC SPY-D + FRIENDS *UK, male / female vocal / instrumental group*

11 Mar 95 **THE AMAZING SPIDER-MAN** *Parlophone CDR 6404* ... 37 2

MC TUNES
UK, male rapper – Nicholas Lockett (1 Album: 3 Weeks, 4 Singles: 19 Weeks)

2 Jun 90 ● **THE ONLY RHYME THAT BITES** *ZTT ZANG 3* [1] ... 10 10
15 Sep 90 **TUNES SPLITS THE ATOM** *ZTT ZANG 6* [1] ... 18 7
13 Oct 90 THE NORTH AT ITS HEIGHTS *ZTT ZTT 3* ... 26 3
1 Dec 90 **PRIMARY RHYMING** *ZTT ZANG 10* ... 67 1
6 Mar 99 **THE ONLY RHYME THAT BITES 99** (re-recording) *ZTT ZTT 125CD* [1] ... 53 1

[1] MC Tunes versus 808 State

MC WILDSKI *UK, male rapper (2 Singles: 10 Weeks)*

8 Jul 89 **BLAME IT ON THE BASSLINE** *Go Beat GOD 33* [1] ... 29 6
3 Mar 90 **WARRIOR** *Arista 112956* ... 49 4

[1] Norman Cook featuring MC Wildski

'Blame It on the Bassline' was listed with 'Won't Talk About It' by Norman Cook featuring Billy Bragg.

ME AND YOU featuring WE THE PEOPLE BAND
Jamaica / UK, male / female vocal / instrumental group

28 Jul 79 **YOU NEVER KNOW WHAT YOU'VE GOT** *Laser LAS 8* ... 31 9

ME ME ME (see also FAT LES) *UK, male vocal / instrumental group*

17 Aug 96 **HANGING AROUND** *Indolent DUFF 005CD* ... 19 4

Abigail MEAD and Nigel GOULDING
UK / US, female / male producers / actors – Vivian Kubrick and Nigel Goulding

26 Sep 87 ● **FULL METAL JACKET (I WANNA BE YOUR DRILL INSTRUCTOR)** *Warner Bros. W 8187* ... 2 10

Vaughn MEADER
US, male comedian, b. 20 Mar 1936, d. 29 Oct 2004

29 Dec 62 THE FIRST FAMILY *London HAA 8048* ▲ ... 12 8

Robert MEADMORE NEW *UK, male vocalist*

12 Mar 05 AFTER A DREAM *Dramatico DRAMCD 0003* ... 49 3

MEAT BEAT MANIFESTO *UK, male production duo*

20 Feb 93 **MINDSTREAM** *Play It Again Sam BIAS 232CD* ... 55 1

MEAT LOAF (23 Top 500)

Larger-than-life vocalist / actor, b. Marvin Lee Aday, 27 Sep 1948, Dallas, US. His collaborations with producer / songwriter Jim Steinman resulted in some of rock's finest recordings. Bat Out of Hell sold more than 30 million copies worldwide and spent almost 10 years in total in the UK chart.

Best-selling single: 'I'd Do Anything for Love (But I Won't Do That)' 761,200
(13 Albums: 789 Weeks, 24 Singles: 152 Weeks)

11 Mar 78 ● BAT OUT OF HELL *Cleveland International EPC 82419* ... 9 474
20 May 78 **YOU TOOK THE WORDS RIGHT OUT OF MY MOUTH** *Epic EPC 5980* ... 33 8
19 Aug 78 **TWO OUT OF THREE AIN'T BAD** *Epic EPC 6281* $ ... 32 8
10 Feb 79 **BAT OUT OF HELL** *Epic EPC 7018* ... 15 7
12 Sep 81 ★ DEAD RINGER *Epic EPC 83645* ■ ... 1 46
26 Sep 81 **I'M GONNA LOVE HER FOR BOTH OF US** *Epic EPCA 1580* ... 62 3
28 Nov 81 ● **DEAD RINGER FOR LOVE** *Epic EPCA 1697* ... 5 17
7 May 83 ● MIDNIGHT AT THE LOST AND FOUND *Epic EPC 25243* ... 7 23
28 May 83 **IF YOU REALLY WANT TO** *Epic A 3357* ... 59 2
24 Sep 83 **MIDNIGHT AT THE LOST AND FOUND** *Epic A 3748* ... 17 8
14 Jan 84 **RAZOR'S EDGE** *Epic A 4080* ... 41 3
6 Oct 84 **MODERN GIRL** *Arista ARIST 585* ... 17 9
10 Nov 84 ● BAD ATTITUDE *Arista 206 619* ... 8 16
22 Dec 84 **NOWHERE FAST** *Arista ARIST 600* ... 67 4
26 Jan 85 ● HITS OUT OF HELL *Epic EPC 26156* ... 2 80
23 Mar 85 **PIECE OF THE ACTION** *Arista ARIST 603* ... 47 5
30 Aug 86 **ROCK 'N' ROLL MERCENARIES** *Arista ARIST 666* [1] ... 31 6
11 Oct 86 BLIND BEFORE I STOP *Arista 207 741* ... 28 6
7 Nov 87 LIVE AT WEMBLEY *RCA 208599* ... 60 2
22 Jun 91 **DEAD RINGER FOR LOVE** (re-issue) *Epic 6569827* ... 53 2
27 Jun 92 **TWO OUT OF THREE AIN'T BAD** (re-issue) *Epic 6574917* ... 69 1
18 Sep 93 ★ BAT OUT OF HELL II – BACK INTO HELL *Virgin CDV 2710* ■ ▲ ... 1 59
9 Oct 93 ★ **I'D DO ANYTHING FOR LOVE (BUT I WON'T DO THAT)** *Virgin VSCDT 1443* ▲ $ ... 1 19
18 Dec 93 ● **BAT OUT OF HELL** (re-issue) *Epic 6600062* ... 8 9
19 Feb 94 **ROCK AND ROLL DREAMS COME THROUGH** *Virgin VSCDT 1479* ... 11 7
7 May 94 **OBJECTS IN THE REAR VIEW MIRROR MAY APPEAR CLOSER THAN THEY ARE** *Virgin VSCDT 1492* ... 26 4
22 Oct 94 ALIVE IN HELL *Pure Music PMCD 7002* ... 33 4
28 Oct 95 ● **I'D LIE FOR YOU (AND THAT'S THE TRUTH)** *Virgin VSCDT 1563* ... 2 11
11 Nov 95 ● WELCOME TO THE NEIGHBOURHOOD *Virgin CDV 2799* ... 3 27
27 Jan 96 ● **NOT A DRY EYE IN THE HOUSE** *Virgin VSCDT 1567* ... 7 6
27 Apr 96 **RUNNIN' FOR THE RED LIGHT (I GOTTA LIFE)** *Virgin VSCDX 1582* ... 21 3
14 Nov 98 THE VERY BEST OF MEAT LOAF *Virgin / Sony TV CDV 2868* ... 14 34
17 Apr 99 **IS NOTHING SACRED** *Virgin VSCDT 1734* [2] ... 15 4
3 May 02 ● COULDN'T HAVE SAID IT BETTER *Mercury 0761192* ... 4 14
26 Apr 03 **COULDN'T HAVE SAID IT BETTER** *Mercury 0656842* ... 31 2
6 Dec 03 **MAN OF STEEL** *Mercury 9815114* ... 21 4
30 Oct 04 BAT OUT OF HELL LIVE WITH THE MELBOURNE SYMPHONY ORCHESTRA *Mercury 9868074* ... 14 4

[1] Meat Loaf featuring John Parr [2] Meat Loaf featuring Patti Russo

'Dead Ringer for Love' features Cher as uncredited co-vocalist. 'I'd Do Anything For Love (But I Won't Do That)' features uncredited vocals by Lorraine Crosby (aka Mrs Loud). Hits Out of Hell changed catalogue number to 4504471 during its chart run.

MECO *US, orchestra – leader Meco Monardo*

1 Oct 77 ● **STAR WARS THEME – CANTINA BAND** *RCA XB 1028* ▲ $ ... 7 9

Glenn MEDEIROS
US, male vocalist (1 Album: 2 Weeks, 3 Singles: 26 Weeks)

18 Jun 88 ★ **NOTHING'S GONNA CHANGE MY LOVE FOR YOU** *London LON 184* ... 1 13
3 Sep 88 **LONG AND LASTING LOVE (ONCE IN A LIFETIME)** *London LON 202* ... 42 4
8 Oct 88 NOT ME *London LONLP 68* ... 63 2
30 Jun 90 **SHE AIN'T WORTH IT** *London LON 265* [1] ▲ ... 12 9

[1] Glenn Medeiros featuring Bobby Brown

MEDIAEVAL BAEBES *UK, female vocal collective (2 Albums: 7 Weeks)*

29 Nov 97 SALVA NOS *Venture CDVE 935* ... 62 6
31 Oct 98 WORLDES BLYSSE *Venture CDVE 941* ... 73 1

14 October 1978	21 October 1978	28 October 1978	4 November 1978
UK No.1 SINGLES			
SUMMER NIGHTS John Travolta, Olivia Newton-John and cast	**SUMMER NIGHTS**J ohn Travolta, Olivia Newton-John and cast	**SUMMER NIGHTS** John Travolta, Olivia Newton-John and cast	**SUMMER NIGHTS** John Travolta, Olivia Newton-John and cast
UK No.1 ALBUMS			
GREASE Soundtrack	**GREASE** Soundtrack	**GREASE** Soundtrack	**GREASE** Soundtrack

MEDICINE HEAD *UK, male vocal / instrumental duo – John Fiddler and Peter Hope Evans (4 Singles: 37 Weeks)*

26 Jun 71 **(AND THE) PICTURES IN THE SKY** *Dandelion DAN 7003*..........22 8
5 May 73 ● **ONE AND ONE IS ONE** *Polydor 2001 432*..........3 13
4 Aug 73 **RISING SUN** *Polydor 2058 389*..........11 9
9 Feb 74 **SLIP AND SLIDE** *Polydor 2058 436*..........22 7

Bill MEDLEY
(see also The RIGHTEOUS BROTHERS) *US, male vocalist (2 Singles: 29 Weeks)*

31 Oct 87 ● **(I'VE HAD) THE TIME OF MY LIFE** (re) *RCA PB 49625* [1] ▲ $..6 23
27 Aug 88 **HE AIN'T HEAVY, HE'S MY BROTHER** *Scotti Brothers PO 10*....25 6

[1] Bill Medley and Jennifer Warnes

'(I've Had) The Time of My Life' re-entered the chart in Dec 1990, peaking at No.8.

MEDWAY *US, male producer – Jesse Skeens (2 Singles: 2 Weeks)*

29 Apr 00 **FAT BASTARD (EP)** *Hooj Choons HOOJ 92CD*..........69 1
10 Mar 01 **RELEASE** *Hooj Choons HOOJ 105*..........67 1

Tracks on Fat Bastard (EP): Release / Flanker / Faith.

Michael MEDWIN, Bernard BRESSLAW, Alfie BASS and Leslie FYSON *UK, male actors / vocalists*

30 May 58 ● **THE SIGNATURE TUNE OF 'THE ARMY GAME'** *HMV POP 490*....5 9

MEECHIE *US, female vocalist*

2 Sep 95 **YOU BRING ME JOY** *Vibe MCSTD 2069*..........74 1

Tony MEEHAN (see also Jet HARRIS and Tony MEEHAN; The SHADOWS) *UK, male drummer – Daniel Meehan*

16 Jan 64 **SONG OF MEXICO** *Decca F 11801*..........39 4

MEEKER *UK, female vocal / production duo*

26 Feb 00 **SAVE ME** *Underwater H20 009CD*..........60 1

MEGA CITY FOUR
UK, male vocal / instrumental group (3 Albums: 3 Weeks, 5 Singles: 7 Weeks)

17 Jun 89 TRANZOPHOBIA *Decoy DYL 3*..........67 1
19 Oct 91 **WORDS THAT SAY** *Big Life MEGA 2*..........66 1
8 Feb 92 **STOP (EP)** *Big Life MEGA 3*..........36 2
7 Mar 92 SEBASTOPOL ROAD *Big Life MEGCD 1*..........41 1
16 May 92 **SHIVERING SAND** *Big Life MEGA 4*..........35 2
1 May 93 **IRON SKY** *Big Life MEGAD 5*..........48 1
22 May 93 MAGIC BULLETS *Big Life MEGCD 3*..........57 1
17 Jul 93 **WALLFLOWER** *Big Life MEGAD 6*..........69 1

Tracks on Stop (EP): Stop / Desert Song / Back to Zero / Overlap.

MEGADETH *US, male vocal (Dave Mustaine) / instrumental group (8 Albums: 27 Weeks, 10 Singles: 32 Weeks)*

19 Dec 87 **WAKE UP DEAD** *Capitol CL 476*..........65 2
27 Feb 88 **ANARCHY IN THE UK** *Capitol CL 480*..........45 3
26 Mar 88 SO FAR, SO GOOD ... SO WHAT *Capitol EST 2053*..........18 5
21 May 88 **MARY JANE** *Capitol CL 489*..........46 2
13 Jan 90 **NO MORE MR NICE GUY** *SBK SBK 4*..........13 6
29 Sep 90 **HOLY WARS ... THE PUNISHMENT DUE** *Capitol CLP 588*..........24 3
6 Oct 90 ● RUST IN PEACE *Capitol EST 2132*..........8 4
16 Mar 91 **HANGAR 18** *Capitol CLS 604*..........26 4
27 Jun 92 **SYMPHONY OF DESTRUCTION** *Capitol CLS 662*..........15 3
18 Jul 92 ● COUNTDOWN TO EXTINCTION *Capitol CDESTU 2175*..........5 8
24 Oct 92 **SKIN O' MY TEETH** *Capitol CLP 669*..........13 3
29 May 93 **SWEATING BULLETS** *Capitol CDCL 682*..........26 3
5 Nov 94 ● YOUTHANASIA / HIDDEN TREASURE *Capitol CDEST 2244*..........6 5
7 Jan 95 **TRAIN OF CONSEQUENCES** *Capitol CDCL 730*..........22 3
19 Jul 97 CRYPTIC WRITINGS *Capitol CDEST 2297*..........38 1
18 Sep 99 RISK *Capitol 4991340*..........29 2
26 May 01 THE WORLD NEEDS A HERO *Metal Is MISCD 006*..........45 1
25 Sep 04 THE SYSTEM HAS FAILED *Sanctuary SANCD 297*..........60 1

From 25 Mar 95 Youthanasia was listed with bonus album Hidden Treasure.

MEJA *Sweden, female vocalist – Meja Beckman (2 Singles: 14 Weeks)*

24 Oct 98 **ALL 'BOUT THE MONEY** *Columbia 6665662*..........12 5
29 Apr 00 ● **PRIVATE EMOTION** *Columbia 6692692* [1]..........9 9

[1] Ricky Martin featuring Meja

MEKKA *UK, male producer – Jake Williams*

24 Mar 01 **DIAMOND BACK** *Perfecto PERF 12CDS*..........67 1

MEKON *UK, male producer – John Gosling (2 Singles: 2 Weeks)*

23 Sep 00 **WHAT'S GOING ON** *Wall of Sound WALD 064* [1]..........43 1
13 Mar 04 **D-FUNKTIONAL** *Wall of Sound WALLD 092* [2]..........72 1

[1] Mekon featuring Roxanne Shante [2] Mekon featuring Afrika Bambaataa

MEL and KIM *UK, female vocal duo (sisters) – Mel, b. 11 Jul 1966, d. 18 Jan 1990, and Kim Appleby (1 Album: 25 Weeks, 4 Singles: 51 Weeks)*

20 Sep 86 ● **SHOWING OUT (GET FRESH AT THE WEEKEND)** *Supreme SUPE 107*..........3 19
7 Mar 87 ★ **RESPECTABLE** *Supreme SUPE 111*..........1 15
25 Apr 87 ● F.L.M. *Supreme SU 2*..........3 25
11 Jul 87 ● **F.L.M.** *Supreme SUPE 113*..........7 10
27 Feb 88 ● **THAT'S THE WAY IT IS** *Supreme SUPE 117*..........10 7

George MELACHRINO ORCHESTRA
UK, orchestra – leader b. 1 May 1909, d. 18 Jun 1965

12 Oct 56 **AUTUMN CONCERTO** *HMV B 10958*..........18 9

MELANIE *US, female vocalist / guitarist – Melanie Safka (6 Albums: 66 Weeks, 5 Singles: 35 Weeks)*

19 Sep 70 ● CANDLES IN THE RAIN *Buddah 2318 009*..........5 31
26 Sep 70 ● **RUBY TUESDAY** (re) *Buddah 2011 038*..........9 15
16 Jan 71 LEFTOVER WINE *Buddah 2318 011*..........22 4
16 Jan 71 **WHAT HAVE THEY DONE TO MY SONG MA** *Buddah 2011 038*..39 1
29 May 71 ● THE GOOD BOOK *Buddah 2322 001*..........9 9
1 Jan 72 ● **BRAND NEW KEY** *Buddah 2011 105* ▲ $..........4 12
8 Jan 72 GATHER ME *Buddah 2322 002*..........14 14
1 Apr 72 GARDEN IN THE CITY *Buddah 2318 054*..........19 6
7 Oct 72 THE FOUR SIDES OF MELANIE *Buddah 2659 013*..........23 2
16 Feb 74 **WILL YOU LOVE ME TOMORROW** *Neighbourhood NBH 9*..........37 5
24 Sep 83 **EVERY BREATH OF THE WAY** *Neighbourhood HOOD NB1*..........70 2

MELKY SEDECK *US, male / female vocal / instrumental duo – Melky and Sedeck Jean (2 Singles: 9 Weeks)*

8 May 99 **RAW** *MCA MCSTD 48107*..........50 1
16 Sep 00 ● **IT DOESN'T MATTER** *Columbia 6697782* [1]..........3 8

[1] Wyclef Jean featuring The Rock and Melky Sedeck

John Cougar MELLENCAMP
US, male vocalist / guitarist (7 Albums: 31 Weeks, 4 Singles: 18 Weeks)

23 Oct 82 **JACK AND DIANE** *Riva RIVA 37* [1] ▲ $..........25 8
6 Nov 82 AMERICAN FOOL *Riva RVLP 16* [1] ▲..........37 6
3 Mar 84 UH-HUH *Riva RIVL 1*..........92 1
1 Feb 86 **SMALL TOWN** *Riva JCM 5*..........53 4
10 May 86 **R.O.C.K. IN THE USA** *Riva JCM 6*..........67 3
3 Oct 87 THE LONESOME JUBILEE *Mercury MERH 109*..........31 12
27 May 89 BIG DADDY *Mercury MERH 838220 1*..........25 4
19 Oct 91 WHENEVER WE WANTED *Mercury 5101511*..........39 2
18 Sep 93 HUMAN WHEELS *Mercury 5180882*..........37 2
3 Sep 94 **WILD NIGHT** *Mercury MERCD 409* [2]..........34 3
17 Jan 98 THE BEST THAT I COULD DO *PolyGram TV 5367382* [2]..........25 4

[1] John Cougar [2] John Mellencamp featuring Me'Shell Ndegeocello
[1] John Cougar [2] John Mellencamp

11 November 1978	18 November 1978	25 November 1978	2 December 1978
SUMMER NIGHTS John Travolta, Olivia Newton-John and cast	**RAT TRAP** The Boomtown Rats	**RAT TRAP** The Boomtown Rats	**DA YA THINK I'M SEXY?** Rod Stewart
GREASE Soundtrack	**GREASE** Soundtrack	**GREASE** Soundtrack	**GREASE** Soundtrack

KEY UK No.1 ★ UK Top 10 ● Still on chart + UK entry at No.1 ■ US No.1 ▲ UK million seller £ US million seller $
Singles re-entries are listed as (re), (2re), (3re)... which signifies that the hit re-entered the chart once, twice or three times...
Peak Position / Weeks

Will MELLOR *UK, male actor / vocalist (2 Singles: 9 Weeks)*

28 Feb 98 ● **WHEN I NEED YOU** *Unity UNITY 017RCD*....................5 6
27 Jun 98 **NO MATTER WHAT I DO** *Jive 0540012*....................23 3

MELLOW TRAX *Germany, male producer – Christian Schwarnweber*

14 Oct 00 **OUTTA SPACE** *Substance SUBS 3CDS*....................41 2

The MELODIANS *Jamaica, male vocal / instrumental group*

10 Jan 70 **SWEET SENSATION** *Trojan TR 695*....................41 1

MELT featuring LITTLE MS MARCIE (see also LOST TRIBE; MDM; SUNBURST) *UK, male producer – Matt Darey and female vocalist*

8 Apr 00 **HARD HOUSE MUSIC** *WEA WEA 257CD*....................59 1

MELTDOWN *UK / US, male instrumental / production duo*

27 Apr 96 **MY LIFE IS IN YOUR HANDS** *Sony S3 DANU 7CD*....................44 1

Katie MELUA *UK (b. Georgia), female vocalist / guitarist – Ketevan Melua (2 Albums: 85 Weeks, 5 Singles: 43 Weeks)*

15 Nov 03 ★ CALL OFF THE SEARCH *Dramatico DRAMCD 0002*....................1 72
13 Dec 03 ● **THE CLOSEST THING TO CRAZY** *Dramatico DRAMCDS 003*....................10 20
27 Mar 04 **CALL OFF THE SEARCH** *Dramatico DRAMCDS 0004*....................19 4
31 Jul 04 **CRAWLING UP A HILL** *Dramatico DRAMCDS 0007*....................46 2
1 Oct 05 ● **NINE MILLION BICYCLES** *Dramatico DRAMCDS 0012*....................5 14+
8 Oct 05 ★ PIECE BY PIECE *Dramatico DRAMCD 0007* ■....................1 13+
17 Dec 05 **I CRIED FOR YOU / JUST LIKE HEAVEN** *Dramatico DRAMCDS 0013*....................35 3+

Harold MELVIN and The BLUENOTES *US, male vocal group – leader b. 25 Jun 1939, d. 24 Mar 1997 (9 Singles: 52 Weeks)*

13 Jan 73 ● **IF YOU DON'T KNOW ME BY NOW** *CBS 8496* $....................9 9
12 Jan 74 **THE LOVE I LOST (PART 1)** *Philadelphia International PIR 1879* $....................21 8
13 Apr 74 **SATISFACTION GUARANTEED (OR TAKE YOUR LOVE BACK)** *Philadelphia International PIR 2187*....................32 6
31 May 75 **GET OUT (AND LET ME CRY)** *Route RT 06* [1]....................35 5
28 Feb 76 **WAKE UP EVERYBODY (PART 1)** *Philadelphia International PIR 3866*....................23 7
22 Jan 77 ● **DON'T LEAVE ME THIS WAY** *Philadelphia International PIR 4909* [2]....................5 10
2 Apr 77 **REACHING FOR THE WORLD** *ABC 4161* [1]....................48 1
28 Apr 84 **DON'T GIVE ME UP** *London LON 47* [1]....................59 4
4 Aug 84 **TODAY'S YOUR LUCKY DAY** *London LON 52* [3]....................66 2

[1] Harold Melvin and the Blue Notes [2] Harold Melvin and the Bluenotes featuring Theodore Pendergrass [3] Harold Melvin and the Blue Notes featuring Nikko

The MEMBERS *UK, male vocal / instrumental group (1 Album: 5 Weeks, 2 Singles: 14 Weeks)*

3 Feb 79 **THE SOUND OF THE SUBURBS** *Virgin VS 242*....................12 9
7 Apr 79 **OFFSHORE BANKING BUSINESS** *Virgin VS 248*....................31 5
28 Apr 79 AT THE CHELSEA NIGHTCLUB *Virgin V 2120*....................45 5

MEMBERS OF MAYDAY *Germany, male production duo – Klaus Jankuhn and Maximilian Lenz (2 Singles: 4 Weeks)*

23 Jun 01 **10 IN 01** *Deviant DVNT 42CDS*....................31 3
13 Apr 02 **SONIC EMPIRE** *Low Spirit DVNT 49CDS*....................59 1

MEMPHIS BLEEK featuring JAY-Z *US, male rappers – Malik Cox and Shawn Carter*

4 Dec 99 **WHAT YOU THINK OF THAT** *Def Jam 8708292*....................58 1

MEN AT WORK *Australia / UK, male vocal (Colin James Hay) / instrumental group (2 Albums: 71 Weeks, 5 Singles: 39 Weeks)*

30 Oct 82 **WHO CAN IT BE NOW?** *Epic EPC A 2392* ▲....................45 5
8 Jan 83 ★ **DOWN UNDER** *Epic EPC A 1980* ▲ $....................1 12
15 Jan 83 ★ BUSINESS AS USUAL *Epic EPC 85669* ▲....................1 44
9 Apr 83 **OVERKILL** *Epic EPC A 3220*....................21 10
30 Apr 83 ● CARGO *Epic EPC 25372*....................8 27
2 Jul 83 **IT'S A MISTAKE** *Epic EPC A 3475*....................33 6
10 Sep 83 **DR HECKYLL AND MR JIVE** *Epic EPC A 3668*....................31 6

MEN OF VIZION *US, male vocal group*

27 Mar 99 **DO YOU FEEL ME? (... FREAK YOU)** *MJJ / Epic 6670912*....................36 2

The MEN THEY COULDN'T HANG *UK, male vocal / instrumental group (5 Albums: 9 Weeks, 1 Single: 4 Weeks)*

27 Jul 85 NIGHT OF A THOUSAND CANDLES *Imp FIEND 50*....................91 2
8 Nov 86 HOW GREEN IS THE VALLEY *MCA MCF 3337*....................68 2
2 Apr 88 **THE COLOURS** *Magnet SELL 6*....................61 4
23 Apr 88 WAITING FOR BONAPARTE *Magnet MAGL 5075*....................41 2
6 May 89 SILVER TOWN *Silvertone ORELP 503*....................39 2
1 Sep 90 THE DOMINO CLUB *Silvertone ORELP 512*....................53 1

MEN WITHOUT HATS *Canada, male vocal (Ivan Dodoschuk) / instrumental group*

8 Oct 83 ● **THE SAFETY DANCE** *Statik TAK 1*....................6 11
12 Nov 83 RHYTHM OF YOUTH *Statik STATLP 10*....................96 1

Sergio MENDES *Brazil, male conductor*

9 Jul 83 **NEVER GONNA LET YOU GO** *A&M AM 118*....................45 5

Uncredited vocals by Joe Pizzulo and Leza Miller.

Andrea MENDEZ *UK, female vocalist*

3 Aug 96 **BRING ME LOVE** *AM:PM 5817872*....................44 1

MENSWEAR *UK, male vocal (Johnny Dean) / instrumental group (1 Album: 6 Weeks, 6 Singles: 18 Weeks)*

15 Apr 95 **I'LL MANAGE SOMEHOW** *Laurel LAUCD 4*....................49 1
1 Jul 95 **DAYDREAMER** *Laurel LAUCD 5*....................14 4
30 Sep 95 **STARDUST** *Laurel LAUCD 6*....................16 3
21 Oct 95 NUISANCE *Laurel 8286792*....................11 6
16 Dec 95 **SLEEPING IN** *Laurel LAUCD 7*....................24 3
23 Mar 96 ● **BEING BRAVE** *Laurel LAUCD 8*....................10 4
7 Sep 96 **WE LOVE YOU** *Laurel LAUCD 11*....................22 3

MENTAL AS ANYTHING *Australia, male vocal (Chris O'Doherty) / instrumental group*

7 Feb 87 ● **LIVE IT UP** *Epic ANY 1*....................3 13

Natalie MERCHANT (see also 10,000 MANIACS) *US, female vocalist (2 Albums: 3 Weeks)*

1 Jul 95 TIGERLILY *Elektra 7559617452*....................39 2
13 Jun 98 OPHELIA *Elektra 7559621962*....................52 1

Freddie MERCURY (see also QUEEN) *UK (b. Zanzibar), male vocalist – Farrokh Bulsara (4 Albums: 65 Weeks, 11 Singles: 79 Weeks)*

22 Sep 84 ● **LOVE KILLS** *CBS A 4735*....................10 8
20 Apr 85 **I WAS BORN TO LOVE YOU** *CBS A 6019*....................11 10
11 May 85 ● MR BAD GUY *CBS 86312*....................6 23
13 Jul 85 **MADE IN HEAVEN** *CBS A 6413*....................57 4

9 December 1978	16 December 1978	23 December 1978	30 December 1978
◂◂ UK No.1 SINGLES ▸▸			
MARY'S BOY CHILD - OH MY LORD Boney M	MARY'S BOY CHILD - OH MY LORD Boney M	MARY'S BOY CHILD - OH MY LORD Boney M	MARY'S BOY CHILD - OH MY LORD Boney M
◂◂ UK No.1 ALBUMS ▸▸			
GREASE Soundtrack	GREASE Soundtrack	GREASE Soundtrack	GREASE Soundtrack

21 Sep 85 **LIVING ON MY OWN** *CBS A 6555* ... **50** 3
24 May 86 **TIME** *EMI EMI 5559* ... 32 5
7 Mar 87 ● **THE GREAT PRETENDER** *Parlophone R 6151* ... **4** 9
7 Nov 87 ● **BARCELONA** *Polydor POSP 887* [1] ... **8** 9
22 Oct 88 BARCELONA *Polydor POLH 44* [1] ... 15 8
8 Aug 92 ● **BARCELONA** (re-issue) *Polydor PO 221* [1] ... 2 8
28 Nov 92 ● THE FREDDIE MERCURY ALBUM *Parlophone CDPCSD 124* ... 4 25
12 Dec 92 ● **IN MY DEFENCE** *Parlophone R 6331* ... 8 7
6 Feb 93 **THE GREAT PRETENDER** (re-issue) *Parlophone CDR 6336* ... 29 3
31 Jul 93 ★ **LIVING ON MY OWN** (re-mix) *Parlophone CDR 6355* ... 1 13
4 Nov 00 SOLO *Parlophone 5280472* ... 13 9

[1] Freddie Mercury and Montserrat Caballé [1] Freddie Mercury and Montserrat Caballé

MERCURY REV
US, male vocal / instrumental group (4 Albums: 19 Weeks, 9 Singles: 15 Weeks)

12 Jun 93 BOCES *Beggars Banquet BBQCD 140* ... 43 1
17 Oct 98 DESERTER'S SONGS *V2 VVR 1002772* ... 27 12
14 Nov 98 **GODDESS ON A HIWAY** *V2 VVR 5003323* ... **51** 1
6 Feb 99 **DELTA SUN BOTTLENECK STOMP** *V2 VVR 5005413* ... 26 2
22 May 99 **OPUS 40** *V2 VVR 5006963* ... 31 2
28 Aug 99 **GODDESS ON A HIWAY** (re-issue) *V2 VVR 5008493* ... 26 2
8 Sep 01 ALL IS DREAM *V2 VVR 1017528* ... 11 4
6 Oct 01 **NITE AND FOG** *V2 VVR 5017723* ... **47** 1
26 Jan 02 **THE DARK IS RISING** *V2 VVR 5018713* ... 16 3
27 Jul 02 **LITTLE RHYMES** *V2 VVR 5019783* ... **51** 1
29 Jan 05 **IN A FUNNY WAY** *V2 VVR 509223* ... 28 2
5 Feb 05 THE SECRET MIGRATION *V2 VVR 1029238* ... 16 2
2 Apr 05 **ACROSS YER OCEAN** *V2 VVR 5031033* ... **54** 1

MERCY MERCY *UK, male vocal / instrumental group*

21 Sep 85 **WHAT ARE WE GONNA DO ABOUT IT?** *Ensign ENY 522* ... **59** 2

MERLE and ROY *UK, female / male vocal / instrumental duo*

26 Sep 87 REQUESTS *Mynod Mawr RMBR 8713* ... **74** 5

MERO *UK, male vocal duo – Tommy Clark and Derek McDonald*

25 Mar 00 **IT MUST BE LOVE** *RCA 74321664772* ... 33 2

Tony MERRICK *UK, male vocalist*

2 Jun 66 **LADY JANE** *Columbia DB 7913* ... **49** 1

MERRION, McCALL & KENSIT (see also BO SELECTA; EIGHTH WONDER) *UK, male comedian / vocalist – Leigh Francis and female TV celebrities / vocalists – Davina McCall and Patsy Kensit*

25 Dec 04 ● **I GOT YOU BABE / SODA POP** *BMG 82876669872* ... 5 5

The MERSEYBEATS
UK, male vocal / instrumental group (1 Album: 9 Weeks, 7 Singles: 64 Weeks)

12 Sep 63 **IT'S LOVE THAT REALLY COUNTS** *Fontana TF 412* ... 24 12
16 Jan 64 ● **I THINK OF YOU** *Fontana TF 431* ... 5 17
16 Apr 64 **DON'T TURN AROUND** *Fontana TF 459* ... 13 11
20 Jun 64 THE MERSEYBEATS *Fontana TL 5210* ... 12 9
9 Jul 64 **WISHIN' AND HOPIN'** *Fontana TF 482* ... 13 10
5 Nov 64 **LAST NIGHT** *Fontana TF 504* ... 40 3
14 Oct 65 **I LOVE YOU, YES I DO** *Fontana TF 607* ... 22 8
20 Jan 66 **I STAND ACCUSED** *Fontana TF 645* ... 38 3

The MERSEYS *UK, male vocal duo*

28 Apr 66 ● **SORROW** *Fontana TF 694* ... 4 13

The MERTON PARKAS *UK, male vocal / instrumental group*

4 Aug 79 **YOU NEED WHEELS** *Beggars Banquet BEG 22* ... 40 6

MERZ
UK, male vocalist / instrumentalist – Conrad Lambert (2 Singles: 2 Weeks)

17 Jul 99 **MANY WEATHERS APART** *Epic 6674972* ... **48** 1
16 Oct 99 **LOVELY DAUGHTER** *Epic 6679132* ... **60** 1

Mady MESPLE and Danielle MILLET with the PARIS OPERA-COMIQUE ORCHESTRA conducted by Alain LOMBARD
France, female vocal duo and orchestra

6 Apr 85 **FLOWER DUET (FROM 'LAKME')** *EMI 5481* ... **47** 4

MESSIAH *UK, male instrumental / production group (3 Singles: 13 Weeks)*

20 Jun 92 **TEMPLE OF DREAMS** *Kickin KICK 12S* ... 20 5
26 Sep 92 **I FEEL LOVE** *Kickin KICK 22S* [1] ... 19 5
27 Nov 93 **THUNDERDOME** *WEA YZ 790CD1* ... 29 3

[1] Messiah featuring Precious Wilson

METAL GURUS *UK, male vocal / instrumental group*

8 Dec 90 **MERRY XMAS EVERYBODY** *Mercury GURU 1* ... **55** 2

METALLICA 347 Top 500
Perennially popular hard rock group formed in 1981 in Los Angeles by Denmark-born Lars Ulrich (d) and fronted by James Hetfield (v/g). The festival favourites and multi-award-winners have sold more than 60 million albums in the US alone and St Anger topped charts in 13 countries (12 Albums: 129 Weeks, 19 Singles: 72 Weeks)

11 Aug 84 RIDE THE LIGHTNING *Music for Nations MFN 27* ... 87 2
15 Mar 86 MASTER OF PUPPETS *Music for Nations MFN 60* ... 41 4
22 Aug 87 **THE $5.98 EP – GARAGE DAYS RE-REVISITED** *Vertigo METAL 112* ... 27 4
3 Sep 88 **HARVESTER OF SORROW** *Vertigo METAL 212* ... 20 3
17 Sep 88 ● ... AND JUSTICE FOR ALL *Vertigo VERH 61* ... 4 6
22 Apr 89 **ONE** *Vertigo METAL 5* ... 13 7
19 May 90 THE GOOD THE BAD AND THE LIVE *Vertigo 8754871* ... 56 1
10 Aug 91 ● **ENTER SANDMAN** *Vertigo METAL 7* ... 5 4
24 Aug 91 ★ METALLICA *Vertigo 5100221* ■ ▲ ... 1 72
9 Nov 91 **THE UNFORGIVEN** *Vertigo METAL 8* ... 15 4
2 May 92 ● **NOTHING ELSE MATTERS** *Vertigo METAL 10* ... 6 6
31 Oct 92 **WHEREVER I MAY ROAM** *Vertigo METAL 9* ... 25 4
20 Feb 93 **SAD BUT TRUE** *Vertigo METCD 11* ... 20 3
11 Dec 93 LIVE SHIT – BINGE AND PURGE *Vertigo 5187250* ... 54 1
1 Jun 96 ● **UNTIL IT SLEEPS** *Vertigo METCD 12* ... 5 4
15 Jun 96 ★ LOAD *Vertigo 5326182* ■ ▲ ... 1 18
28 Sep 96 **HERO OF THE DAY** *Vertigo METCD 13* ... 17 4
5 Oct 96 HERO OF THE DAY *Vertigo METCY 13* ... 47 1
7 Dec 96 **MAMA SAID** *Vertigo METCD 14* ... 19 2
22 Nov 97 **THE MEMORY REMAINS** *Vertigo METCD 15* ... 13 3
29 Nov 97 ● RELOAD *Vertigo 5364092* ▲ ... 4 9
7 Mar 98 **THE UNFORGIVEN II** *Vertigo METDD 17* ... 15 4
4 Jul 98 **FUEL** *Vertigo METCD 16* ... 31 2
5 Dec 98 GARAGE INC. *Vertigo 5383512* ... 29 2
27 Feb 99 **WHISKEY IN THE JAR** *Vertigo METCD 19* ... 29 2
4 Dec 99 S&M *Vertigo 5467972* ... 33 2
12 Aug 00 **I DISAPPEAR** *Hollywood 0113875 HWR* ... 35 3
14 Jun 03 ● ST ANGER *Vertigo 9865338* ▲ ... 3 11
5 Jul 03 ● **ST ANGER** *Vertigo 9865412* ... 9 8
4 Oct 03 **FRANTIC** *Vertigo 9811513* ... 16 3
24 Jan 04 **THE UNNAMED FEELING** *Vertigo 9815661* ... 42 2

Tracks on The $5.98 EP – Garage Days Re-Revisited: Helpless / Crash Course in Brain Surgery / The Small Hours / Last Caress / Green Hell. Live Shit – Binge and Purge is a boxed set containing two CDs, three video cassettes and a book.

METEOR SEVEN *Germany, male producer – Jans Ebert*

18 May 02 **UNIVERSAL MUSIC** *Bulletproof PROOF 16CD* ... 71 1

The METEORS *UK, male vocal / instrumental group*

26 Feb 83 WRECKIN' CREW *ID NOSE 1* ... 53 3
26 Feb 83 **JOHNNY REMEMBER ME** *ID EYE 1* ... 66 2

6 January 1979	13 January 1979	20 January 1979	27 January 1979
Y.M.C.A. Village People	**Y.M.C.A.** Village People	**Y.M.C.A.** Village People	**HIT ME WITH YOUR RHYTHM STICK** Ian and The Blockheads
GREATEST HITS (1976-1978) Showaddywaddy	**GREATEST HITS (1976-1978)** Showaddywaddy	**DON'T WALK - BOOGIE** Various	**DON'T WALK - BOOGIE** Various

KEY
UK No.1 ★ UK Top 10 ● Still on chart + UK entry at No.1 ■
US No.1 ▲ UK million seller £ US million seller $
Singles re-entries are listed as (re), (2re), (3re)... which signifies that the hit re-entered the chart once, twice or three times...
Peak Position / Weeks

METHOD MAN (see also WU-TANG CLAN)

US, male rapper – Clifford Smith (3 Albums: 7 Weeks, 6 Singles: 24 Weeks)

29 Apr 95 **RELEASE YO' SELF** *Def Jam DEFCD 6* ... 46 1
29 Jul 95 ● **I'LL BE THERE FOR YOU – YOU'RE ALL I NEED TO GET BY** *Def Jam DEFCD 11* [1] $ ... 10 5
5 Apr 97 ● **HIT EM HIGH (THE MONSTARS' ANTHEM)** *Atlantic A 5449CD* [2] ... 8 6
28 Nov 98 **TICAL 2000: JUDGEMENT DAY** *Def Jam 5589202* ... 49 1
22 May 99 **BREAK UPS 2 MAKE UPS** *Def Jam 8709272* [3] ... 33 2
9 Oct 99 **BLACKOUT!** *Def Jam 5466092* [1] ... 45 3
27 Sep 03 **LOVE @ 1ST SIGHT** *MCA MCSTD 40338* [4] ... 18 5
22 May 04 **WHAT'S HAPPENIN'** *Def Jam 9862517* [5] ... 17 5
29 May 04 **TICAL 0: THE PREQUEL** *Def Jam / Mercury 9862641* ... 29 3

[1] Method Man featuring Mary J Blige [2] B Real / Busta Rhymes / Coolio / LL Cool J / Method Man [3] Method Man featuring D'Angelo [4] Mary J Blige featuring Method Man [5] Method Man featuring Busta Rhymes
[1] Method Man and Redman

MEW *Denmark, male vocal / instrumental group (5 Singles: 5 Weeks)*

5 Apr 03 **COMFORTING SOUNDS** *Epic 6736432* ... 48 1
28 Jun 03 **AM I WRY? NO** *Epic 6739395* ... 47 1
27 Dec 03 **SHE CAME HOME FOR CHRISTMAS** *Epic 6744942* ... 55 1
30 Jul 05 **APOCALYPSO** *Evil Office EVIL 02* ... 75 1
1 Oct 05 **SPECIAL** *Evil Office 6760621* ... 46 1

MEZZOFORTE

Iceland, male instrumental group (2 Albums: 10 Weeks, 2 Singles: 10 Weeks)

5 Mar 83 **SURPRISE SURPRISE** *Steinar STELP 02* ... 23 9
5 Mar 83 **GARDEN PARTY** *Steinar STE 705* ... 17 9
11 Jun 83 **ROCKALL** *Steinar STE 710* ... 75 1
2 Jul 83 **CATCHING UP WITH MEZZOFORTE** *Steinar STELP 03* ... 95 1

MIAMI SOUND MACHINE (see also Gloria ESTEFAN)

Cuba, male / female vocal / instrumental group (8 Singles: 88 Weeks)

11 Aug 84 ● **DR BEAT** *Epic A 4614* ... 6 14
17 May 86 **BAD BOY** *Epic A 6537* ... 16 11
16 Jul 88 ● **ANYTHING FOR YOU** *Epic 6516737* [1] ▲ $ ... 10 16
22 Oct 88 ● **1-2-3** (re) *Epic 6529587* [1] ... 9 10
17 Dec 88 **RHYTHM IS GONNA GET YOU** *Epic 6545147* [1] ... 16 9
11Feb 89 ● **CAN'T STAY AWAY FROM YOU** *Epic 6514447* [1] ... 7 12
17 Sep 05 ● **DOCTOR PRESSURE** *Breastfed BFD 017CD2* [2] ... 3 16+

[1] Gloria Estefan & Miami Sound Machine [2] Mylo vs Miami Sound Machine

George MICHAEL (57 Top 500) (see also Elton JOHN; Lisa MOORISH)

Previously half of internationally celebrated duo Wham!, b. Georgios Panayiotou, 25 Jun 1963, London, UK. This multi-talented, award-winning singer / songwriter / producer / arranger and instrumentalist successfully made the difficult transition from teeny-bopper hero to world-renowned solo star. In 2004, after returning to Sony, the label he fell out with earlier in his career, he announced he was retiring from the music business. Best-selling single: 'Careless Whisper' 1,365,995 (6 Albums: 344 Weeks, 32 Singles: 287 Weeks)

4 Aug 84 ★ **CARELESS WHISPER** *Epic A 4603* ▲ £ $ ... 1 17
5 Apr 86 ★ **A DIFFERENT CORNER** *Epic A 7033* ... 1 10
31 Jan 87 ★ **I KNEW YOU WERE WAITING (FOR ME)** *Epic DUET 2* [1] ▲ ... 1 9
13 Jun 87 ● **I WANT YOUR SEX** *Epic LUST 1* $ ... 3 10
24 Oct 87 ● **FAITH** *Epic EMU 3* ▲ ... 2 12
14 Nov 87 ★ **FAITH** *Epic 4600001* ■ ▲ ... 1 77
9 Jan 88 **FATHER FIGURE** *Epic EMU 4* ▲ ... 11 6
23 Apr 88 ● **ONE MORE TRY** *Epic EMU 5* ▲ ... 8 7
16 Jul 88 **MONKEY** *Epic EMU 6* ▲ ... 13 6
3 Dec 88 **KISSING A FOOL** *Epic EMU 7* ... 18 6
25 Aug 90 ● **PRAYING FOR TIME** *Epic GEO 1* ▲ ... 6 7
15 Sep 90 ★ **LISTEN WITHOUT PREJUDICE VOLUME 1** *Epic 4672951* ■ ... 1 57
27 Oct 90 **WAITING FOR THAT DAY** *Epic GEO 2* ... 23 5
15 Dec 90 **FREEDOM!** *Epic GEO 3* ... 28 6
16 Feb 91 **HEAL THE PAIN** *Epic 6566477* ... 31 4
30 Mar 91 **COWBOYS AND ANGELS** *Epic 6567747* ... 45 3
7 Dec 91 ★ **DON'T LET THE SUN GO DOWN ON ME** *Epic 6576467* [2] ■ ▲ ... 1 10
13 Jun 92 ● **TOO FUNKY** *Epic 6580587* ... 4 9
1 May 93 ★ **FIVE LIVE (EP)** (re) *Parlophone CDRS 6340* [3] ■ ... 1 12
20 Jan 96 ★ **JESUS TO A CHILD** (2re) *Virgin VSCDG 1571* ■ ... 1 13
4 May 96 ★ **FASTLOVE** *Virgin VSCDG 1579* ■ ... 1 14
25 May 96 ★ **OLDER** *Virgin CDV 2802* ■ ... 1 99
31 Aug 96 ● **SPINNING THE WHEEL** *Virgin VSCDG 1595* ... 2 12
1 Feb 97 ● **OLDER / I CAN'T MAKE YOU LOVE ME** (re) *Virgin VSCDG 1626* ... 3 9
10 May 97 ● **STAR PEOPLE '97** (re) *Virgin VSCDG 1641* ... 2 13
7 Jun 97 ● **WALTZ AWAY DREAMING** *Aegean AECD 01* [4] ... 10 4
20 Sep 97 ● **YOU HAVE BEEN LOVED / THE STRANGEST THING '97** *Virgin VSCD 1663* ... 2 8
31 Oct 98 ● **OUTSIDE** (re) *Epic 6665625* ... 2 16
21 Nov 98 ★ **LADIES & GENTLEMEN – THE BEST OF GEORGE MICHAEL** *Epic 4917052* ■ ... 1 71
13 Mar 99 ● **AS** *Epic 6670122* [5] ... 4 10
18 Dec 99 ● **SONGS FROM THE LAST CENTURY** *Virgin CDVX 2920* ... 2 17
17 Jun 00 ● **IF I TOLD YOU THAT** (re) *Arista 74321766282* [6] ... 9 11
30 Mar 02 ● **FREEEK!** *Polydor 5706812* ... 7 10
10 Aug 02 **SHOOT THE DOG** (re) *Polydor 5709242* ... 12 5
13 Mar 04 ● **AMAZING** *Aegean / Sony 6747262* ... 4 11
27 Mar 04 ★ **PATIENCE** *Aegean / Sony 5154022* ■ ... 1 23
10 Jul 04 ● **FLAWLESS (GO TO THE CITY)** *Aegean / Sony 6750682* ... 8 10
13 Nov 04 **ROUND HERE** *Aegean / Sony 6754702* ... 32 2

[1] Aretha Franklin and George Michael [2] George Michael and Elton John [3] George Michael and Queen with Lisa Stansfield [4] Toby Bourke with George Michael [5] George Michael and Mary J Blige [6] Whitney Houston / George Michael

Tracks on Five Live (EP): Somebody to Love / These Are the Days of Our Lives / Calling You / Papa Was a Rolling Stone – Killer (medley). Track one features Queen, the second Queen and Lisa Stansfield, and the last track Queen.

MICHAELA *UK, female vocalist – Michaela Strachan (2 Singles: 6 Weeks)*

2 Sep 89 **H-A-P-P-Y RADIO** *London H 1* ... 62 4
28 Apr 90 **TAKE GOOD CARE OF MY HEART** *London WAC 90* ... 66 2

Pras MICHEL (see also FUGEES) *US, male rapper / producer – Prakazrel Michael (1 Album: 3 Weeks, 4 Singles: 36 Weeks)*

27 Jun 98 ● **GHETTO SUPASTAR (THAT IS WHAT YOU ARE)** *Interscope IND 95593* [1] ... 2 17
7 Nov 98 ● **BLUE ANGELS** *Ruffhouse 6666215* [2] ... 6 10
14 Nov 98 **GHETTO SUPASTAR** *Columbia 4914892* [1] ... 44 3
14 Nov 98 ● **ANOTHER ONE BITES THE DUST** *Dreamworks DRMCD 22364* [3] ... 5 6
1 Sep 01 **MISS CALIFORNIA** *Elektra E 7192CD* [4] ... 25 3

[1] Pras Michel featuring ODB & introducing Mya [2] Pras [3] Queen with Wyclef Jean featuring Pras and Free [4] Dante Thomas featuring Pras [1] Pras

Keith MICHELL

Australia, male actor / vocalist (1 Album: 12 Weeks, 3 Singles: 25 Weeks)

27 Mar 71 **I'LL GIVE YOU THE EARTH (TOUS LES BATEAUX, TOUS LES OISEAUX)** (re) *Spark SRL 1046* ... 30 11
26 Jan 80 ● **CAPTAIN BEAKY / WILFRED THE WEASEL** *Polydor POSP 106* .. 5 10
9 Feb 80 **CAPTAIN BEAKY AND HIS BAND** *Polydor 238 3462* ... 28 12
29 Mar 80 **THE TRIAL OF HISSING SID** *Polydor HISS 1* [1] ... 53 4

[1] Keith Michell, Captain Beaky and his Band

MICHELLE *Trinidad, female vocalist*

8 Jun 96 **STANDING HERE ALL ALONE** *Positiva CDTIV 54* ... 69 1

	3 February 1979	10 February 1979	17 February 1979	24 February 1979
UK No.1 SINGLES	HEART OF GLASS Blondie	HEART OF GLASS Blondie	HEART OF GLASS Blondie	HEART OF GLASS Blondie
UK No.1 ALBUMS	DON'T WALK - BOOGIE Various	ACTION REPLAY Various	PARALLEL LINES Blondie	PARALLEL LINES Blondie

MICHELLE *UK, female vocalist – Michelle McManus (1 Album: 7 Weeks, 2 Singles: 15 Weeks)*

17 Jan 04 ★ **ALL THIS TIME** *S 82876590652* ■ 1 11
28 Feb 04 ● THE MEANING OF LOVE *S 82876590662* 3 7
17 Apr 04 **THE MEANING OF LOVE** *S 82876604032* 16 4

Yvette MICHELLE *US, female vocalist – Michele Bryant*

5 Apr 97 **I'M NOT FEELING YOU** *Loud 74321465222* 36 3

MICROBE *UK, male vocalist – Ian Doody, the youngest solo male chart entrant, aged three*

14 May 69 **GROOVY BABY** *CBS 4158* 29 7

MICRODISNEY *Ireland, male vocal / instrumental group*

21 Feb 87 **TOWN TO TOWN** *Virgin VS 927* 55 3

MIDDLE OF THE ROAD *UK, male / female vocal (Sally Carr) / instrumental group (5 Singles: 76 Weeks)*

5 Jun 71 ★ **CHIRPY CHIRPY CHEEP CHEEP** *RCA 2047* 1 34
4 Sep 71 ● **TWEEDLE DEE, TWEEDLE DUM** *RCA 2110* 2 17
11 Dec 71 ● **SOLEY SOLEY** *RCA 2151* 5 12
25 Mar 72 **SACRAMENTO (A WONDERFUL TOWN)** (re) *RCA 2184* 23 7
29 Jul 72 **SAMSON AND DELILAH** *RCA 2237* 26 6

MIDDLESBROUGH FC featuring Bob MORTIMER and Chris REA *UK, male football team, comedian / vocalist and vocalist / guitarist*

24 May 97 **LET'S DANCE** *Magnet EW 112CD* 44 1

MIDFIELD GENERAL featuring LINDA LEWIS *UK, male producer – Damian Harris and female vocalist*

19 Aug 00 **REACH OUT** *Skint / SKINT 54CD* 61 1

MIDGET *UK, male vocal / instrumental group (2 Singles: 2 Weeks)*

31 Jan 98 **ALL FALL DOWN** *Radarscope TINYCDS 6X* 57 1
18 Apr 98 **INVISIBLE BALLOON** *Radarscope TINYCDS 7* 66 1

MIDI XPRESS *UK, male vocal / instrumental duo*

11 May 96 **CHASE** *Labello Dance LAD 26CD* 73 1

Bette MIDLER *US, female vocalist (5 Albums: 40 Weeks, 3 Singles: 27 Weeks)*

17 Jun 89 ● **WIND BENEATH MY WINGS** *Atlantic A 8972* ▲ $ 5 12
15 Jul 89 BEACHES (FILM SOUNDTRACK) *Atlantic 7819931* 21 9
13 Oct 90 ● **FROM A DISTANCE** (re) *Atlantic A 7820* $ 6 14
13 Jul 91 ● SOME PEOPLE'S LIVES *Atlantic 7567821291* 5 11
15 Feb 92 FOR THE BOYS (FILM SOUNDTRACK) *Atlantic 7567823292* 75 1
30 Oct 93 ● EXPERIENCE THE DIVINE – GREATEST HITS *Atlantic 7567824972* 3 15
25 Nov 95 BETTE OF ROSES *Atlantic 7567828232* 55 4
5 Dec 98 **MY ONE TRUE FRIEND** *Warner Bros. W 460CD* 58 1

'From A Distance' peaked at No.6 on re-entry in Jun 1991.

MIDNIGHT COWBOY SOUNDTRACK *US, orchestra*

8 Nov 80 **MIDNIGHT COWBOY** *United Artists UP 634* 47 4

MIDNIGHT OIL *Australia, male vocal (Peter Garrett) / instrumental group (3 Albums: 21 Weeks, 8 Singles: 32 Weeks)*

23 Apr 88 **BEDS ARE BURNING** *Sprint OIL 1* 48 5
25 Jun 88 DIESEL AND DUST *CBS 4600051* 19 16
2 Jul 88 **THE DEAD HEART** *Sprint OIL 2* 68 2
25 Mar 89 ● **BEDS ARE BURNING** (re-issue) *Sprint OIL 3* 6 13
1 Jul 89 **THE DEAD HEART** (re-issue) *Sprint OIL 4* 62 4
10 Feb 90 **BLUE SKY MINE** *CBS OIL 5* 66 2
10 Mar 90 BLUE SKY MINING *CBS 4656531* 28 3
17 Apr 93 **TRUGANINI** *Columbia 6590492* 29 4
1 May 93 EARTH AND SUN AND MOON *Columbia 4736052* 27 2
3 Jul 93 **MY COUNTRY** *Columbia 6593702* 66 1
6 Nov 93 **IN THE VALLEY** *Columbia 6598492* 60 1

MIDNIGHT STAR *US, male / female vocal (Belinda Lipscomb) / instrumental group (2 Albums: 6 Weeks, 5 Singles: 26 Weeks)*

2 Feb 85 PLANETARY INVASION *Solar MCF 3251* 85 2
23 Feb 85 **OPERATOR** *Solar MCA 942* 66 2
28 Jun 86 **HEADLINES** *Solar MCA 1065* 16 8
5 Jul 86 HEADLINES *Solar MCF 3322* 42 4
4 Oct 86 ● **MIDAS TOUCH** *Solar MCA 1096* 8 10
7 Feb 87 **ENGINE NO.9** *Solar MCA 1117* 64 3
2 May 87 **WET MY WHISTLE** *Solar MCA 1127* 60 3

The MIGHTY AVENGERS *UK, male vocal / instrumental group*

26 Nov 64 **SO MUCH IN LOVE** *Decca F 11962* 46 2

MIGHTY DUB KATZ (see also BEATS INTERNATIONAL; Norman COOK; FATBOY SLIM; FREAKPOWER; The HOUSEMARTINS; PIZZAMAN; URBAN ALL STARS) *UK, male producer – Norman Cook (3 Singles: 6 Weeks)*

7 Dec 96 **JUST ANOTHER GROOVE** *ffrr FCD 287* 43 1
2 Aug 97 **MAGIC CARPET RIDE** *ffrr FCD 306* 24 4
7 Dec 02 **LET THE DRUMS SPEAK** *Southern Fried ECB 31X* 73 1

MIGHTY LEMON DROPS *UK, male vocal / instrumental group (2 Albums: 5 Weeks, 3 Singles: 6 Weeks)*

13 Sep 86 **THE OTHER SIDE OF YOU** *Blue Guitar AZUR 1* 67 1
4 Oct 86 HAPPY HEAD *Blue Guitar AZLP 1* 58 2
18 Apr 87 **OUT OF HAND** *Blue Guitar AZUR 4* 66 3
23 Jan 88 **INSIDE OUT** *Blue Guitar AZUR 6* 74 2
27 Feb 88 THE WORLD WITHOUT END *Blue Guitar AZLP 4* 34 3

The MIGHTY MIGHTY BOSSTONES *US, male vocal / instrumental group (1 Album: 2 Weeks, 2 Singles: 6 Weeks)*

25 Apr 98 **THE IMPRESSION THAT I GET** *Mercury 5748432* 12 5
16 May 98 LET'S FACE IT *Mercury 5344722* 40 2
27 Jun 98 **THE RASCAL KING** *Mercury 5661092* 63 1

MIGHTY MORPH'N POWER RANGERS *US, male / female vocal group*

17 Dec 94 ● **POWER RANGERS** (3re) *RCA 74321253022* 3 13
24 Dec 94 POWER RANGERS – THE ALBUM *RCA 74321252982* 50 3

The MIGIL FIVE *UK, male vocal / instrumental group (2 Singles: 20 Weeks)*

19 Mar 64 ● **MOCKINGBIRD HILL** *Pye 7N 15597* 10 13
4 Jun 64 **NEAR YOU** *Pye 7N 15645* 31 7

MIG29 *Italy, male instrumental / production group*

22 Feb 92 **MIG29** *Champion CHAMP 292* 62 2

MIKE *UK, male producer – Mark Jolley*

19 Nov 94 **TWANGLING THREE FINGERS IN A BOX** *Pukka CDMIKE 100* ..40 2

MIKE and The MECHANICS 432 Top 500 *Adult-orientated, radio-friendly pop act formed by Genesis guitarist Mike Rutherford. Vocalists included former Ace frontman Paul Carrack and ex-Sad Café singer Paul Young (d. 2000). 'The Living Years' has been heard more than four million times on US radio (9 Albums: 101 Weeks, 13 Singles: 67 Weeks)*

15 Feb 86 **SILENT RUNNING (ON DANGEROUS GROUND)** *WEA U 8908* ..21 9
15 Mar 86 MIKE AND THE MECHANICS *WEA WX 49* 78 3
31 May 86 **ALL I NEED IS A MIRACLE** *WEA U 8765* 53 4
26 Nov 88 ● THE LIVING YEARS *WEA WX 203* 2 19
14 Jan 89 ● **THE LIVING YEARS** *WEA U 7717* ▲ 2 11

3 March 1979	10 March 1979	17 March 1979	24 March 1979
TRAGEDY The Bee Gees	TRAGEDY The Bee Gees	I WILL SURVIVE Gloria Gaynor	I WILL SURVIVE Gloria Gaynor
PARALLEL LINES Blondie	PARALLEL LINES Blondie	SPIRITS HAVING FLOWN The Bee Gees	SPIRITS HAVING FLOWN The Bee Gees

THE TOP 100

It has taken pop researcher Stuart Devoy seven years to complete the task of creating a chart of the most successful songwriters in chart history.

He has searched all the songwriting credits on every one of the 27,295 hit songs from 1952 until the last chart of 2005. His resulting list is based on the total number of weeks each songwriter has enjoyed seeing his or her creative writing make the official UK singles chart. So, for the first time in the pages of this book – or for any other book for that matter – here are the 100 most successful songwriters in pop.

POS	SONGWRITER	WEEKS
1	PAUL McCARTNEY	1,633
2	JOHN LENNON	1,388
3	PETE WATERMAN	898
4	MIKE STOCK	895
5	BARRY GIBB	880
6	ROBIN GIBB	804
7	MATT AITKEN	787
8	MAURICE GIBB	734
9	LAMONT DOZIER	699
10	STEVIE WONDER	685
11=	JAMES HARRIS	677
11=	TERRY LEWIS	677
13	GERRY GOFFIN	663
14	MIKE CHAPMAN	653
15	EDDIE HOLLAND	645
16	ELTON JOHN	644
17	BURT BACHARACH	643
18	HAL DAVID	632
19	MICK JAGGER	620
20	BRIAN HOLLAND	606
21	NICKY CHINN	601
22	KEITH RICHARDS	599
23	BERNIE TAUPIN	596
24=	ROGER GREENAWAY	562
24=	CAROLE KING	562
26	MADONNA	530
27	NILE RODGERS	528
28	BERNARD EDWARDS	512
29	ROGER COOK	501
30=	PRINCE	498
30=	DIANE WARREN	498
32	DAVID BOWIE	493
33	KENNY GAMBLE	488
34	MICHAEL JACKSON	481
35	BARRY MANN	477
36	LEON HUFF	473
37	GEORGE MICHAEL	456
38	HOWARD GREENFIELD	452

SONGWRITERS

www.bibleofpop.com

39 ROBERT JOHN LANGE 451
40 JERRY LEIBER 446
41= NORMAN WHITFIELD 445
41= BOB DYLAN 445
43 PAUL WELLER 431
44 PHIL COLLINS 421
45 MIKE STOLLER 418
46= KENNY EDMONDS (BABYFACE) 409
46= JEFF BARRY 409
46= NOEL GALLAGHER 409
49= BENNY ANDERSSON 406
49= BJORN ULVAEUS 406
51 PAUL HEWSON (BONO) 400
52 NEIL SEDAKA 399
53= DAVID EVANS (THE EDGE) 390
53= TONY MACAULEY 390
55 PHARRELL WILLIAMS 385
56 GIORGIO MORODER 384
57 RONALD BELL 381
58 FREDDIE MERCURY 368
59= PAUL ANKA 378
59= LIONEL RICHIE 378
61= ROBERT BELL 377
61= CLAYDES SMITH 377
61= GEORGE BROWN 377
64= ADAM CLAYTON 376
64= LARRY MULLEN 376
64= LES REED 376
67 CARL SIGMAN 375
68 CYNTHIA WEIL 374
69 RICHARD STANNARD 370
70 GORDON SUMNER (STING) 369
71 BOB CREWE 366
72 R KELLY 359
73 GEOFF STEPHENS 357
74 BARRY MASON 356
75 JEFF LYNNE 353
76 RICK NOWELS 352
77 ROY ORBISON 344
78 MORT SHUMAN 343
79 PHIL SPECTOR 342
80 MAX MARTIN 340
81= GEORGE DAVID WEISS 337
81= BERRY GORDY 337
83 DESMOND CHILD 333
84 VINCE CLARKE 330
85 DAVE A STEWART 326
86= BRYAN ADAMS 312
86= ANDREW LLOYD WEBBER 312
88 CHAD HUGO 310
89 ALBERT HAMMOND 308
90 GUY CHAMBERS 304
91= PAUL FRANCIS WEBSTER 303
91= ERROL BROWN 303
93= DOC POMUS 302
93= MARSHALL MATHERS (EMINEM) 302
95 RAY DAVIES 301
96 ELLIE GREENWICH 300
97 PETE TOWNSHEND 299
98= ANNIE LENNOX 295
98= ROD STEWART 295
100= WILLIAM (SMOKEY) ROBINSON 294
100= CHUCK BERRY 294
100= LES VAN DYKE (JOHNNY WORTH) 294

Top songwriter Paul McCartney (left), whose 1,633 weeks in the chart are made up of credits as all four Beatles, Lennon and McCartney, McCartney and Lennon, solo, with Denny Laine, Linda McCartney, Michael Jackson, Elvis Costello, Alison Clarkson, John Coxon, David Clayton, Sinead O'Connor, John Reynolds, Tim Simenon and Thelonious Monk.

Pictured on this page: Top female songwriter Carole King who wrote solo, as one half of Goffin and King and with Howard Greenfield, Mark Hudson and William Wells, Jerry Wexler, David Foster and Carole Bayer Sager.

KEY
UK No.1 ★★ UK Top 10 ●● Still on chart ++ UK entry at No.1 ■■
US No.1 ▲▲ UK million seller £ US million seller $
Singles re-entries are listed as (re), (2re), (3re)... which signifies that the hit re-entered the chart once, twice or three times...

Peak Position / Weeks

16Mar 91 **WORD OF MOUTH** *Virgin VS 1345* ... **13** 10
27 Apr 91 WORD OF MOUTH *Virgin V 2662* ... 11 7
15 Jun 91 **A TIME AND PLACE** *Virgin VS 1351* ... **58** 3
8 Feb 92 **EVERYBODY GETS A SECOND CHANCE** *Virgin VS 1396* ... **56** 4
25 Feb 95 **OVER MY SHOULDER** *Virgin VSCDT 1526* ... **12** 9
18 Mar 95 ● BEGGAR ON A BEACH OF GOLD *Virgin CDV 2772* ... 9 33
17 Jun 95 **A BEGGAR ON A BEACH OF GOLD** *Virgin VSCDT 1535* ... **33** 5
2 Sep 95 **ANOTHER CUP OF COFFEE** *Virgin VSCDT 1554* ... **51** 4
17 Feb 96 **ALL I NEED IS A MIRACLE** (re-mix) *Virgin VSCDT 1576* ... **27** 4
2 Mar 96 THE LIVING YEARS (re-issue) *Atlantic K 2560042* ... 67 2
16 Mar 96 ● HITS *Virgin CDV 2797* ... 3 31
1 Jun 96 **SILENT RUNNING** (re-issue) *Virgin VSCDT 1585* ... **61** 1
5 Jun 99 **NOW THAT YOU'VE GONE** *Virgin VSCDT 1732* ... **35** 2
12 Jun 99 MIKE AND THE MECHANICS *Virgin CDV 2885* ... 14 4
28 Aug 99 **WHENEVER I STOP** *Virgin VSCDT 1743* ... **73** 1
19 Jun 04 REWIRED *Virgin CDVX 2984* [1] ... 61 1
18 Sep 04 REWIRED + THE HITS – THE LATEST + GREATEST *Virgin CDVX 2990* ... 42 1

[1] Mike and The Mechanics & Paul Carrack

The two Mike and The Mechanics albums are different. Rewired (19 Jun 2004) was released with a video DVD and was then re-issued in Sep 2004 as a two-CD set containing a greatest hits CD in place of the DVD.

MIKI and GRIFF

UK, female / male vocal duo – Barbara Salisbury, b. 20 Jun 1920, d. 20 Apr 1989, and Emyr Griffith, b. 9 May 1923, d. 24 Sep 1995 (4 Singles: 25 Weeks)

2 Oct 59 **HOLD BACK TOMORROW** *Pye 7N 15213* [1] ... **26** 2
13 Oct 60 **ROCKIN' ALONE** *Pye 7N 15296* [2] ... **44** 3
1 Feb 62 **A LITTLE BITTY TEAR** *Pye 7N 15412* ... **16** 13
22 Aug 63 **I WANT TO STAY HERE** *Pye 7N 15555* ... **23** 7

[1] Lonnie Donegan presents Miki and Griff with the Lonnie Donegan Group
[2] Miki and Griff with the Lonnie Donegan Group

John MILES

UK, male vocalist / multi-instrumentalist (5 Albums: 25 Weeks, 4 Singles: 30 Weeks)

18 Oct 75 **HIGHFLY** *Decca F 13595* ... **17** 6
20 Mar 76 ● **MUSIC** *Decca F 13627* ... **3** 9
27 Mar 76 ● REBEL *Decca SKL 5231* ... 9 10
16 Oct 76 **REMEMBER YESTERDAY** *Decca F 13667* ... **32** 5
26 Feb 77 STRANGER IN THE CITY *Decca TXS 118* ... 37 3
18 Jun 77 ● **SLOW DOWN** *Decca F 13709* ... **10** 10
1 Apr 78 ZARAGON *Decca TXS 126* ... 43 5
21 Apr 79 MORE MILES PER HOUR *Decca TXS 135* ... 46 5
29 Aug 81 MILES HIGH *EMI EMC 3374* ... 96 2

Robert MILES

Italy, male keyboard player – Roberto Concina (2 Albums: 51 Weeks, 5 Singles: 49 Weeks)

24 Feb 96 ● **CHILDREN** *Deconstruction 74321348322* ... **2** 18
8 Jun 96 ● **FABLE** (2re) *Deconstruction 74321382622* ... **7** 9
22 Jun 96 ● DREAMLAND *Deconstruction 74321391262* ... 7 48
16 Nov 96 ● **ONE & ONE** *Deconstruction 74321427692* [1] ... **3** 17
29 Nov 97 **FREEDOM** *Deconstruction 74321536952* [2] ... **15** 4
6 Dec 97 23AM *Deconstruction 74321541132* ... 42 3
28 Jul 01 **PATHS** *Salt SALT 002CD* [3] ... **74** 1

[1] Robert Miles featuring Maria Nayler [2] Robert Miles featuring Kathy Sledge
[3] Robert Miles featuring Nina Miranda

Christina MILIAN (see also JA RULE)

US, female vocalist (2 Albums: 15 Weeks, 6 Singles: 50 Weeks)

3 Mar 01 **BETWEEN ME AND YOU** *Def Jam 5727402* [1] ... **26** 3
26 Jan 02 ● **AM TO PM** *Def Soul 5889332* ... **3** 11
2 Feb 02 CHRISTINA MILIAN *Def Soul 5867392* ... 23 11
29 Jun 02 ● **WHEN YOU LOOK AT ME** *Def Soul 5829802* ... **3** 10
9 Nov 02 ● **IT'S ALL GRAVY** *Relentless RELENT 32CD* [2] ... **9** 6
15 May 04 ● **DIP IT LOW** *Def Jam 9862395* ... **2** 13
12 Jun 04 IT'S ABOUT TIME *Def Jam UK / Mercury 9862835* ... 21 4
16 Oct 04 ● **WHATEVER U WANT** *Def Jam 9864266* [3] ... **9** 7

[1] Ja Rule featuring Christina Milian [2] Romeo featuring Christina Milian
[3] Christina Milian featuring Joe Budden

MILK AND HONEY featuring Gali ATARI

Israel, male / female vocal / instrumental group

14 Apr 79 ● **HALLELUJAH** *Polydor 2001 870* ... **5** 8

MILK & SUGAR

Germany, male production duo – Michael Kronenberger and Steffan Harning (2 Singles: 7 Weeks)

12 Jan 02 **LOVE IS IN THE AIR** (re-recording) *Positiva CDTIV 166* [1] ... **25** 3
11 Oct 03 **LET THE SUNSHINE IN** *Data / MoS DATA 64CDS* [2] ... **18** 4

[1] Milk and Sugar vs John Paul Young [2] Milk and Sugar featuring Lizzy Pattinson

MILK INC.

Belgium, male / female production / vocal duo – Regi Penxten and An Vervoort (1 Album: 1 Week, 4 Singles: 21 Weeks)

28 Feb 98 **GOOD ENOUGH (LA VACHE)** *Malarky MLKD 5* [1] ... **23** 3
25 May 02 ● **IN MY EYES** *All Around the World CDGLOBE 252* ... **9** 8
21 Sep 02 ● **WALK ON WATER** *Positiva CDTIV 179* ... **10** 6
5 Oct 02 MILK INC. *Positiva 5419532* ... 47 1
11 Jan 03 **LAND OF THE LIVING** *Positiva CDTIVS 184* ... **18** 4

[1] Milk Incorporated

MILKY

Italy, male production duo and Egypt, female vocalist – Sabrina Kassel (2 Singles: 7 Weeks)

31 Aug 02 ● **JUST THE WAY YOU ARE** *Multiply CDMULTY 87* ... **8** 6
7 Dec 02 **IN MY MIND** *Multiply CDMULTY 92* ... **48** 1

MILLA

US, female actor / vocalist – Milla Jovovich

18 Jun 94 **GENTLEMAN WHO FELL** *SBK CDSBK 49* ... **65** 1

Dominic MILLER

Argentina, male instrumentalist

14 Jun 03 SHAPES *BBC Music WMSF 60702* ... 38 3

Frankie MILLER

UK, male vocalist (1 Album: 1 Week, 4 Singles: 32 Weeks)

4 Jun 77 **BE GOOD TO YOURSELF** *Chrysalis CHS 2147* ... **27** 6
14 Oct 78 ● **DARLIN'** *Chrysalis CHS 2255* ... **6** 15
20 Jan 79 **WHEN I'M AWAY FROM YOU** *Chrysalis CHS 2276* ... **42** 5
14 Apr 79 FALLING IN LOVE *Chrysalis CHR 1220* ... 54 1
21 Mar 92 **CALEDONIA** *MCS MCS 2001* ... **45** 6

Gary MILLER

UK, male vocalist – Neville Williams, b. 1924, d. 15 Jun 1968 (6 Singles: 35 Weeks)

21 Oct 55 **THE YELLOW ROSE OF TEXAS** *Nixa N 15004* ... **13** 5
13 Jan 56 ● **ROBIN HOOD** *Nixa N 15020* ... **10** 6
11 Jan 57 **GARDEN OF EDEN** (re) *Pye Nixa N 15070* ... **14** 7
19 Jul 57 **WONDERFUL, WONDERFUL** *Pye Nixa N 15094* ... **29** 1
17 Jan 58 **THE STORY OF MY LIFE** *Pye Nixa N 15120* ... **14** 6
21 Dec 61 **THERE GOES THAT SONG AGAIN / THE NIGHT IS YOUNG (AND YOU'RE SO BEAUTIFUL)** (re) *Pye 7N 15404* ... **29** 10

'The Night is Young (And You're So Beautiful)' listed with 'There Goes That Song Again' for 21 and 28 Dec 1961 and 4 Jan 1962 only. It peaked at No.32.

Glenn MILLER

US, orchestra leader / trombone player, b. 1 Mar 1904, d. 15 Dec 1944 (11 Albums: 82 Weeks, 2 Singles: 9 Weeks)

12 Mar 54 **MOONLIGHT SERENADE** *HMV BD 5942* ... **12** 1
28 Jan 61 ● GLENN MILLER PLAYS SELECTIONS FROM 'THE GLENN MILLER STORY' AND OTHER HITS *RCA 27068 0023* .. 10 18

31 March 1979	7 April 1979	14 April 1979	21 April 1979
◂◂ UK No.1 SINGLES ▸▸			
I WILL SURVIVE Gloria Gaynor	**I WILL SURVIVE** Gloria Gaynor	**BRIGHT EYES** Art Garfunkel	**BRIGHT EYES** Art Garfunkel
◂◂ UK No.1 ALBUMS ▸▸			
BARBRA STREISAND'S GREATEST HITS VOLUME 2 Barbra Streisand	**BARBRA STREISAND'S GREATEST HITS VOLUME 2** Barbra Streisand	**BARBRA STREISAND'S GREATEST HITS VOLUME 2** Barbra Streisand	**BARBRA STREISAND'S GREATEST HITS VOLUME 2** Barbra Streisand

5 Jul 69 ●	THE BEST OF GLENN MILLER *RCA International 1002*	5 14
6 Sep 69	NEARNESS OF YOU *RCA International INTS 1019*	30 2
25 Apr 70	A MEMORIAL 1944-1969 *RCA GM 1*	18 17
25 Dec 71	THE REAL GLENN MILLER AND HIS ORCHESTRA PLAY THE ORIGINAL MUSIC OF THE FILM 'THE GLENN MILLER STORY' AND OTHER HITS (re-issue) *RCA International NTS 1157*	28 2
24 Jan 76	**MOONLIGHT SERENADE / LITTLE BROWN JUG / IN THE MOOD** *RCA 2644* ▲	13 8
14 Feb 76	A LEGENDARY PERFORMER *RCA Victor DPM 2065*	41 5
14 Feb 76	A LEGENDARY PERFORMER VOLUME 2 *RCA Victor CPL 11349*	53 2
9 Apr 77 ●	THE UNFORGETTABLE GLENN MILLER *RCA Victor TVL 1*	4 8
20 Mar 93	THE ULTIMATE GLENN MILLER *Bluebird 74321131372*	11 6
25 Feb 95	THE LOST RECORDINGS *Happy Days CDHD 4012*	22 6
18 Oct 03	IN THE MOOD – THE DEFINITIVE GLENN MILLER *BMG 82876560302*	43 2

US No.1 symbol refers only to 'In the Mood', which hit the top spot in 1939. The Real Glenn Miller and his Orchestra Play ... is a re-titled re-issue of the first album.

Jody MILLER *US, female vocalist*

21 Oct 65	**HOME OF THE BRAVE** *Capitol CL 15415*	**49** 1

Mitch MILLER, his Orchestra and Chorus *US, orchestra and chorus*

7 Oct 55 ●	**THE YELLOW ROSE OF TEXAS** *Philips PB 505* ▲ $	2 13

Ned MILLER *US, male vocalist (2 Singles: 22 Weeks)*

14 Feb 63 ●	**FROM A JACK TO A KING** *London HL 9658*	2 21
18 Feb 65	**DO WHAT YOU DO DO WELL** *London HL 9937*	**48** 1

Roger MILLER *US, male vocalist / guitarist, b. 2 Jan 1936, d. 25 Oct 1992 (5 Singles: 42 Weeks)*

18 Mar 65 ★	**KING OF THE ROAD** *Philips BF 1397* $	1 15
3 Jun 65	**ENGINE ENGINE NO.9** *Philips BF 1416*	33 5
21 Oct 65	**KANSAS CITY STAR** *Philips BF 1437*	**48** 1
16 Dec 65	**ENGLAND SWINGS** (re) *Philips BF 1456*	13 8
27 Mar 68	**LITTLE GREEN APPLES** (2re) *Mercury MF 1021*	**19** 13

Steve MILLER BAND *US, male vocal / instrumental group (6 Albums: 51 Weeks, 4 Singles: 36 Weeks)*

12 Jun 76	FLY LIKE AN EAGLE *Mercury 9286 177*	11 17
23 Oct 76	**ROCK 'N ME** *Mercury 6078 804* ▲	**11** 9
4 Jun 77	BOOK OF DREAMS *Mercury 9286 456*	12 12
19 Jun 82 ●	ABRACADABRA *Mercury 6302 204*	10 16
19 Jun 82 ●	**ABRACADABRA** *Mercury STEVE 3* ▲ $	2 11
4 Sep 82	**KEEPS ME WONDERING WHY** *Mercury STEVE 4*	**52** 3
7 May 83	STEVE MILLER BAND LIVE! *Mercury MERL 18*	79 2
11 Aug 90 ★	**THE JOKER** *Capitol CL 583* ▲ $	1 13
6 Oct 90	THE BEST OF 1968-1973 *Capitol EST 2133*	34 3
10 Oct 98	GREATEST HITS *PolyGram TV 5592402*	58 1

Suzi MILLER and The JOHNSTON BROTHERS *UK, female vocalist – Renee Lester and male vocal group*

21 Jan 55	**HAPPY DAYS AND LONELY NIGHTS** *Decca F 10389*	**14** 2

MILLI VANILLI *Germany / France, male vocal duo – Rob Pilatus, b. 8 Jun 1965, d. 2 Apr 1998, and Fabrice Morvan (1 Album: 25 Weeks, 5 Singles: 50 Weeks)*

1 Oct 88 ●	**GIRL YOU KNOW IT'S TRUE** *Cooltempo COOL 170* $	3 13
17 Dec 88	**BABY DON'T FORGET MY NUMBER** *Cooltempo COOL 178* ▲	16 11
21 Jan 89 ●	ALL OR NOTHING / 2X2 *Cooltempo CTLP 11*	6 25
22 Jul 89	**BLAME IT ON THE RAIN** (re) *Cooltempo COOL 180* ▲ $	52 10
30 Sep 89 ●	**GIRL I'M GONNA MISS YOU** *Cooltempo COOL 191* ▲	2 15
10 Mar 90	**ALL OR NOTHING** *Cooltempo COOL 199*	**74** 1

All or Nothing was repackaged and available with free re-mix album 2x2 from 16 Oct 1989 onwards.

MILLICAN and NESBIT *UK, male vocal duo – Alan Millican and Tim Nesbit (2 Albums: 24 Weeks, 2 Singles: 14 Weeks)*

1 Dec 73	**VAYA CON DIOS (MAY GOD BE WITH YOU)** *Pye 7N 45310*	**20** 11
23 Mar 74 ●	MILLICAN AND NESBIT *Pye NSPL 18428*	3 21
18 May 74	**FOR OLD TIME'S SAKE** *Pye 7N 45357*	**38** 3
4 Jan 75	EVERYBODY KNOWS MILLICAN AND NESBIT *Pye NSPL 18446*	23 3

MILLIE *Jamaica, female vocalist – Millie Small (4 Singles: 33 Weeks)*

12 Mar 64 ●	**MY BOY LOLLIPOP** *Fontana TF 449* $	2 18
25 Jun 64	**SWEET WILLIAM** *Fontana TF 479*	30 9
11 Nov 65	**BLOODSHOT EYES** *Fontana TF 617*	**48** 1
25 Jul 87	**MY BOY LOLLIPOP** (re-issue) *Island WIP 6574*	**46** 5

Spike MILLIGAN (see also The GOONS) *UK, male comedian, b. 16 Apr 1918, d. 27 Feb 2002 (3 Albums: 6 Weeks)*

25 Nov 61	MILLIGAN PRESERVED *Parlophone PMC 1152*	11 4
18 Apr 64	HOW TO WIN AN ELECTION *Philips AL 3464* [1]	20 1
18 Dec 76	THE SNOW GOOSE *RCA RS 1088* [2]	49 1

[1] Harry Secombe, Peter Sellers and Spike Milligan [2] Spike Milligan with the London Symphony Orchestra

MILLION DAN *UK, male rapper – Michael Dunn (2 Singles: 2 Weeks)*

27 Sep 03	**DOGZ N SLEDGEZ** *Gut CDGUT 52*	**66** 1
12 Feb 05	**BOOM BLAST** *Against the Grain ATG 010* [1]	**75** 1

[1] Freestylers featuring Million Dan

MILLION DEAD *UK / Australia, male vocal / instrumental group (2 Singles: 2 Weeks)*

29 May 04	**I GAVE MY EYES TO STEVIE WONDER** *Xtra Mile XMR 101*	72 1
2 Apr 05	**LIVING THE DREAM** *Xtra Mile XRM 105*	**60** 1

MILLIONAIRE HIPPIES *UK, male producer – Danny Rampling (2 Singles: 4 Weeks)*

18 Dec 93	**I AM THE MUSIC HEAR ME!** *Deconstruction 74321175432*	52 3
10 Sep 94	**C'MON** *Deconstruction 74321229372*	**59** 1

The MILLS BROTHERS *US, male vocal group*

9 Jan 53 ●	**THE GLOW WORM** *Brunswick 05007*	**10** 1

With Hal McIntyre and his Orchestra.

Garry MILLS *UK, male vocalist (3 Singles: 31 Weeks)*

7 Jul 60 ●	**LOOK FOR A STAR** *Top Rank JAR 336*	**7** 14
20 Oct 60	**TOP TEEN BABY** *Top Rank JAR 500*	24 12
22 Jun 61	**I'LL STEP DOWN** *Decca F 11358*	39 5

Hayley MILLS *UK, female actor / vocalist*

19 Oct 61	**LET'S GET TOGETHER** *Decca F 21396*	**17** 11

Stephanie MILLS *US, female vocalist (6 Singles: 33 Weeks)*

18 Oct 80 ●	**NEVER KNEW LOVE LIKE THIS BEFORE** *20th Century TC 2460* $	4 14
23 May 81	**TWO HEARTS** *20th Century TC 2492* [1]	**49** 5
15 Sep 84	**THE MEDICINE SONG** *Club JAB 8*	29 9
5 Sep 87	**(YOU'RE PUTTIN') A RUSH ON ME** *MCA MCA 1187*	62 2
1 May 93	**NEVER DO YOU WRONG** *MCA MCSTD 1767*	**57** 2
10 Jul 93	**ALL DAY ALL NIGHT** *MCA MCSTD 1778*	**68** 1

[1] Stephanie Mills featuring Teddy Pendergrass

Warren MILLS *Zambia, male vocalist*

28 Sep 85	**SUNSHINE** *Jive JIVE 99*	**74** 1

28 April 1979	5 May 1979	12 May 1979	19 May 1979
BRIGHT EYES Art Garfunkel	BRIGHT EYES Art Garfunkel	BRIGHT EYES Art Garfunkel	BRIGHT EYES Art Garfunkel
THE VERY BEST OF LEO SAYER Leo Sayer	THE VERY BEST OF LEO SAYER Leo Sayer	THE VERY BEST OF LEO SAYER Leo Sayer	VOULEZ-VOUS Abba

KEY: UK No.1 ★★ UK Top 10 ●● Still on chart ++ UK entry at No.1 ■■ US No.1 ▲▲ UK million seller £ US million seller $
Singles re-entries are listed as (re), (2re), (3re)… which signifies that the hit re-entered the chart once, twice or three times…
Peak Position / Weeks

The MILLTOWN BROTHERS *UK, male vocal / instrumental group (1 Album: 5 Weeks, 5 Singles: 16 Weeks)*

2 Feb 91	**WHICH WAY SHOULD I JUMP?** *A&M AM 711*	38	5
23 Mar 91	**SLINKY** *A&M 3953461*	27	5
13 Apr 91	**HERE I STAND** *A&M AM 758*	41	4
6 Jul 91	**APPLE GREEN** *A&M AM 787*	43	4
22 May 93	**TURN OFF** *A&M 5802692*	55	1
17 Jul 93	**IT'S ALL OVER NOW BABY BLUE** *A&M 5803332*	48	2

MILLWALL FC *UK, male football team vocal group*

29 May 04	**OH MILLWALL** *Absolute CDAME 4*	41	1

CB MILTON *Holland, male vocalist (3 Singles: 5 Weeks)*

21 May 94	**IT'S A LOVING THING** *Logic 74321208062*	49	2
25 Mar 95	**IT'S A LOVING THING** (re-mix) *Logic 74321267212*	34	2
19 Aug 95	**HOLD ON** *Logic 74321292112*	62	1

Garnet MIMMS and TRUCKIN' CO *US, male vocalist and instrumental group*

25 Jun 77	**WHAT IT IS** *Arista 109*	44	1

MIND OF KANE (see also HOPE A.D.) *UK, male producer – David Hope*

27 Jul 91	**STABBED IN THE BACK** *Deja Vu DJV 007*	64	1

The MINDBENDERS *UK, male vocal / instrumental group (2 Albums: 5 Weeks, 10 Singles: 79 Weeks)*

11 Jul 63	**HELLO JOSEPHINE** *Fontana TF 404* [1]	46	2
28 May 64	**STOP LOOK AND LISTEN** *Fontana TF 451* [1]	37	4
8 Oct 64 ●	**UM, UM, UM, UM, UM, UM** *Fontana TF 497* [1]	5	15
4 Feb 65 ●	**GAME OF LOVE** *Fontana TF 535* [1] ▲ $	2	11
20 Feb 65	**WAYNE FONTANA AND THE MINDBENDERS** *Fontana TL 5230*	18	1
17 Jun 65	**JUST A LITTLE BIT TOO LATE** *Fontana TF 579* [1]	20	7
30 Sep 65	**SHE NEEDS LOVE** *Fontana TF 611* [1]	32	6
13 Jan 66 ●	**A GROOVY KIND OF LOVE** *Fontana TF 644* $	2	14
5 May 66	**CAN'T LIVE WITH YOU CAN'T LIVE WITHOUT YOU** *Fontana TF 697*	28	7
25 Jun 66	**THE MINDBENDERS** *Fontana TL 5324*	28	4
25 Aug 66	**ASHES TO ASHES** *Fontana TF 731*	14	9
20 Sep 67	**THE LETTER** *Fontana TF 869*	42	4

[1] Wayne Fontana and The Mindbenders

MINDFUNK *US, male vocal / instrumental group*

15 May 93	**DROPPED** *Megaforce CDZAZ 3*	60	1

MINDS OF MEN *UK, male / female vocal / instrumental group*

22 Jun 96	**BRAND NEW DAY** *Perfecto PERF 121CD*	41	1

Sal MINEO *US, male vocalist / actor, b. 10 Jan 1939, d. 12 Feb 1976*

12 Jul 57	**START MOVIN' (IN MY DIRECTION)** *Philips PB 707*	16	11

Marcello MINERBI *Italy, orchestra*

22 Jul 65 ●	**ZORBA'S DANCE** *Durium DRS 54001*	6	16

MINIMAL CHIC featuring Matt GOSS (see also BROS) *Italy, male production duo and UK, male vocalist*

2 Oct 04	**I NEED THE KEY** *Inferno CDFERN 63*	54	1

MINIMAL FUNK 2 *Italy, male production duo (2 Singles: 2 Weeks)*

18 Jul 98	**THE GROOVY THANG** *Cleveland City CLECD 13046*	65	1
18 May 02	**DEFINITION OF HOUSE** *Junior BRG 033* [1]	63	1

[1] Minimal Funk

MINIMALISTIX *Belgium, male production duo – Andy Vandierendonck and Peter Bellaert (2 Singles: 7 Weeks)*

16 Mar 02	**CLOSE COVER** *Data DATA 32CDS*	12	5
19 Jul 03	**MAGIC FLY** *Data / MoS DATA 48CDS*	36	2

MINI*POPS *UK, male / female vocal group (2 Albums: 12 Weeks, 1 Single: 2 Weeks)*

26 Dec 81	**MINIPOPS** *K-Tel NE 1102*	63	7
19 Feb 83	**WE'RE THE MINIPOPS** *K-Tel ONE 1187*	54	5
26 Dec 87	**SONGS FOR CHRISTMAS '87 (EP)** *Bright BULB 9*	39	2

Tracks on Songs for Christmas '87 (EP): Thanks for Giving Us Christmas / The Man in Red / Christmas Time Around the World / Shine On.

MINISTERS DE LA FUNK *US, male production trio (2 Singles: 4 Weeks)*

11 Mar 00	**BELIEVE** *Defected DFECT 14CDS*	45	2
27 Jan 01	**BELIEVE** (re-mix) *Defected DFECT 26CDS* [1]	42	2

[1] Ministers De La Funk featuring Jocelyn Brown

MINISTRY (see also REVOLTING COCKS) *US, male vocal / instrumental group (2 Albums: 6 Weeks, 2 Singles: 3 Weeks)*

25 Jul 92	**PSALM 69** *Sire 7599267272*	33	5
8 Aug 92	**NWO** *Sire W 0125TE*	49	1
6 Jan 96	**THE FALL** *Warner Bros. W 0328CD*	53	2
10 Feb 96	**FILTH PIG** *Warner Bros. 9362458382*	43	1

MINK DeVILLE *US, male vocal / instrumental group*

6 Aug 77	**SPANISH STROLL** *Capitol CLX 103*	20	9

MINKY *UK, male producer – Gary Dedman*

30 Oct 99	**THE WEEKEND HAS LANDED** *Offbeat OFFCD 1001*	70	1

Liza MINNELLI *US, female vocalist (4 Albums: 27 Weeks, 4 Singles: 15 Weeks)*

7 Apr 73 ●	**LIZA WITH A 'Z'** *CBS 65212*	9	15
16 Jun 73	**THE SINGER** *CBS 65555*	45	1
12 Aug 89 ●	**LOSING MY MIND** *Epic ZEE 1*	6	7
7 Oct 89	**DON'T DROP BOMBS** *Epic ZEE 2*	46	3
21 Oct 89 ●	**RESULTS** *Epic 465511 1*	6	10
25 Nov 89	**SO SORRY I SAID** *Epic ZEE 3*	62	2
3 Mar 90	**LOVE PAINS** *Epic ZEE 4*	41	3
6 Jul 96	**GENTLY** *Angel CDQ 8354702*	58	1

Dannii MINOGUE 497 Top 500 (see also CHILDLINERS) *Australian singer / actor, b. 20 Oct 1971, Melbourne, who, like older sister Kylie, rose to fame in a TV soap (Home and Away) and had a successful chart comeback. The Minogues have had more singles success than any other sisters (4 Albums: 29 Weeks, 19 Singles: 121 Weeks)*

30 Mar 91 ●	**LOVE AND KISSES** *MCA MCS 1529*	8	8
18 May 91	**$UCCE$$** *MCA MCS 1538*	11	7
15 Jun 91 ●	**LOVE AND KISSES** *MCA MCA 10340*	8	20
27 Jul 91 ●	**JUMP TO THE BEAT** *MCA MCS 1556*	8	6
19 Oct 91	**BABY LOVE** *MCA MCS 1580*	14	6
14 Dec 91	**I DON'T WANNA TAKE THIS PAIN** *MCA MCS 1600*	40	5
1 Aug 92	**SHOW YOU THE WAY TO GO** *MCA MCS 1671*	30	3
12 Dec 92	**LOVE'S ON EVERY CORNER** *MCA MCSR 1723*	44	4
17 Jul 93 ●	**THIS IS IT** *MCA MCSTD 1790*	10	8
2 Oct 93	**THIS IS THE WAY** *MCA MCSTD 1935*	27	3
16 Oct 93	**GET INTO YOU** *MCA MCD 10909*	52	1

26 May 1979	2 June 1979	9 June 1979	16 June 1979
UK No.1 SINGLES			
SUNDAY GIRL Blondie	SUNDAY GIRL Blondie	SUNDAY GIRL Blondie	RING MY BELL Anita Ward
UK No.1 ALBUMS			
VOULEZ-VOUS Abba	VOULEZ-VOUS Abba	VOULEZ-VOUS Abba	DISCOVERY Electric Light Orchestra

11 Jun 94 GET INTO YOU *Mushroom D 11751* 36 2
23 Aug 97 ● ALL I WANNA DO *Eternal WEA 119CD* [1] 4 8
20 Sep 97 GIRL *Eternal 3984205482* [1] 57 1
1 Nov 97 EVERYTHING I WANTED *Eternal WEA 137CD* [1] 15 4
28 Mar 98 DISREMEMBRANCE *Eternal WEA 153CD* [1] 21 3
1 Dec 01 ● WHO DO YOU LOVE NOW (STRINGER) *ffrr DFCD 002* [2] 3 15
16 Nov 02 ● PUT THE NEEDLE ON IT *London LONCD 470* 7 11
15 Mar 03 ● I BEGIN TO WONDER *London LONCD 473* 2 11
29 Mar 03 ● NEON NIGHTS *London 2564600032* 8 7
21 Jun 03 ● DON'T WANNA LOSE THIS FEELING (re) *London LONCD 478* 5 9
6 Nov 04 ● YOU WON'T FORGET ABOUT ME
All Around the World CXGLOBE 379 [3] 7 5
29 Oct 05 PERFECTION *All Around the World CDGLOBE 483* [4] 11 3

[1] Dannii [2] Riva featuring Dannii Minogue [3] Dannii Minogue vs Flower Power [4] Dannii Minogue & The Soul Seekerz [1] Dannii

Kylie MINOGUE (43 Top 500)

Aussie soap teen star turned sex siren and the mistress of reinvention, b. 28 May 1968, Melbourne. She had the best ever chart start for a female soloist with 13 successive Top 10 entries and has the longest span of UK No.1 singles of any female solo artist – 15 years and 9 months. 'Come Into My World' won a Grammy in 2004. Best-selling single: 'Can't Get You Out of My Head' 1,037,235 (14 Albums: 319 Weeks, 41 Singles: 373 Weeks)

23 Jan 88 ★ I SHOULD BE SO LUCKY *PWL PWL 8* 1 16
14 May 88 ● GOT TO BE CERTAIN *PWL PWL 12* 2 12
16 Jul 88 ★ KYLIE *PWL HF 3* 1 67
6 Aug 88 ● THE LOCO-MOTION *PWL PWL 14* 2 11
22 Oct 88 ● JE NE SAIS PAS POURQUOI *PWL PWL 21* 2 13
10 Dec 88 ★ ESPECIALLY FOR YOU *PWL PWL 24* [1] 1 14
6 May 89 ★ HAND ON YOUR HEART *PWL PWL 35* 1 11
5 Aug 89 ● WOULDN'T CHANGE A THING *PWL PWL 42* 2 9
21 Oct 89 ★ ENJOY YOURSELF *PWL HF 9* ■ 1 33
4 Nov 89 ● NEVER TOO LATE *PWL PWL 45* 4 10
20 Jan 90 ★ TEARS ON MY PILLOW *PWL PWL 47* 1 8
12 May 90 ● BETTER THE DEVIL YOU KNOW *PWL PWL 56* 2 10
3 Nov 90 ● STEP BACK IN TIME *PWL PWL 64* 4 8
24 Nov 90 ● RHYTHM OF LOVE *PWL HF 18* [1] 9 22
2 Feb 91 ● WHAT DO I HAVE TO DO *PWL PWL 72* 6 8
1 Jun 91 ● SHOCKED *PWL PWL 81* [2] 6 7
7 Sep 91 WORD IS OUT *PWL PWL 204* 16 5
26 Oct 91 LET'S GET TO IT *PWL HF 21* [1] 15 12
2 Nov 91 ● IF YOU WERE WITH ME NOW *PWL PWL 208* [3] 4 7
30 Nov 91 KEEP ON PUMPIN' IT *PWL PWL 207* [4] 49 1
25 Jan 92 ● GIVE ME JUST A LITTLE MORE TIME *PWL PWL 212* 2 8
25 Apr 92 FINER FEELINGS *PWL International PWL 227* [5] 11 6
22 Aug 92 WHAT KIND OF FOOL (HEARD ALL THAT BEFORE)
PWL International PWL 241 14 5
5 Sep 92 ★ GREATEST HITS *PWL International HFCD 25* [1] ■ 1 10
28 Nov 92 CELEBRATION *PWL International PWL 257* 20 7
10 Sep 94 ● CONFIDE IN ME *Deconstruction 74321227482* 2 10
1 Oct 94 ● KYLIE MINOGUE *Deconstruction 74321227492* 4 15
26 Nov 94 PUT YOURSELF IN MY PLACE *Deconstruction 74321246572* 11 9
22 Jul 95 WHERE IS THE FEELING *Deconstruction 74321293612* 16 3
14 Oct 95 WHERE THE WILD ROSES GROW *Mute CDMUTE 185* [6] 11 4
20 Sep 97 SOME KIND OF BLISS *Deconstruction 74321517252* 22 5
6 Dec 97 DID IT AGAIN *Deconstruction 74321535702* 14 6
21 Mar 98 BREATHE *Deconstruction 74321570132* 14 4
4 Apr 98 ● KYLIE MINOGUE *Deconstruction 74321517272* 10 4
15 Aug 98 MIXES *Deconstruction 74321587152* 63 1
31 Oct 98 GBI *Arthrob ART 021CD* [7] 63 1
1 Jul 00 ★ SPINNING AROUND *Parlophone CDRS 6542* ■ 1 11
23 Sep 00 ● ON A NIGHT LIKE THIS (re) *Parlophone CDRS 6546* [5] 2 8
7 Oct 00 ● LIGHT YEARS *Parlophone 5284002* 2 28
21 Oct 00 ● KIDS (2re) *Chrysalis CDCHS 5119* [8] 2 19
28 Oct 00 HITS + *Deconstruction 74321785342* 41 1
23 Dec 00 ● PLEASE STAY *Parlophone CDRS 6551* [5] 10 7
29 Sep 01 ★ CAN'T GET YOU OUT OF MY HEAD
Parlophone CDRS 6562 ■ £ 1 25
13 Oct 01 ★ FEVER *Parlophone 5358042* [1] ■ 1 70
2 Mar 02 ● IN YOUR EYES *Parlophone CDRS 6569* 3 17
22 Jun 02 ● LOVE AT FIRST SIGHT *Parlophone CDRS 6577* 2 12
23 Nov 02 ● COME INTO MY WORLD *Parlophone CDR 6590* [5] 8 10
30 Nov 02 GREATEST HITS 87-92 *PWL 9224682* [1] 20 11
15 Nov 03 ★ SLOW *Parlophone CDR 6625* [5] ■ 1 10
29 Nov 03 ● BODY LANGUAGE *Parlophone 5957582* 6 18
13 Mar 04 ● RED BLOODED WOMAN *Parlophone CDRS 6633* 5 9
10 Jul 04 ● CHOCOLATE *Parlophone CDRS 6639* [5] 6 7
4 Dec 04 ● ULTIMATE KYLIE *Parlophone 8753652* [1] 4 27
18 Dec 04 ● I BELIEVE IN YOU *Parlophone CDRS 6656* [5] 2 12
9 Apr 05 ● GIVING YOU UP *Parlophone CDRS 6661* [5] 6 8

[1] Kylie Minogue and Jason Donovan [2] Kylie Minogue / rap by Jazzie P [3] Kylie Minogue and Keith Washington [4] Visionmasters with Tony King and Kylie Minogue [5] Kylie [6] Nick Cave and the Bad Seeds + Kylie Minogue [7] Towa Tei featuring Kylie Minogue [8] Robbie Williams / Kylie Minogue [1] Kylie

The single 'GBI' is an abbreviation of German Bold Italic. Both eponymously titled albums are different. The second Kylie Minogue was changed from its original title, Impossible Princess, following the death of Diana, Princess of Wales. The 2002 Greatest Hits album has a slightly different tracklisting to the 1992 album of the same name and includes an additional CD of re-mixes.

Morris MINOR and The MAJORS

UK, male vocal (Tony Hawks) / rap group

19 Dec 87 ● STUTTER RAP (NO SLEEP 'TIL BEDTIME) *10 TEN 203* 4 11

Sugar MINOTT *Jamaica, male vocalist (2 Singles: 16 Weeks)*

28 Mar 81 ● GOOD THING GOING (WE'VE GOT A GOOD THING GOING)
RCA 58 4 12
17 Oct 81 NEVER MY LOVE *RCA 138* 52 4

MINT CONDITION *US, male vocal group (2 Singles: 3 Weeks)*

21 Jun 97 WHAT KIND OF MAN WOULD I BE *Wild Card 5710492* 38 2
4 Oct 97 LET ME BE THE ONE *Wild Card 5717132* 63 1

The MINT JULEPS *UK, female vocal group (2 Singles: 7 Weeks)*

22 Mar 86 ONLY LOVE CAN BREAK YOUR HEART *Stiff BUY 241* 62 2
30 May 87 EVERY KINDA PEOPLE *Stiff BUY 257* 58 5

MINT ROYALE

UK, male production duo – Neil Claxton and Chris Baker (5 Singles: 14 Weeks)

5 Feb 00 DON'T FALTER *Faith & Hope FHCD 014* [1] 15 4
6 May 00 TAKE IT EASY *Faith & Hope FHCD 016* 66 1
7 Sep 02 SEXIEST MAN IN JAMAICA *Faith & Hope FHCD 025* 20 3
8 Feb 03 BLUE SONG *Faith & Hope FHCD 030* 35 2
3 Sep 05 SINGIN' IN THE RAIN *Direction 82876720492* 20 4

[1] Mint Royale featuring Lauren Laverne

MINTY *Australia, female vocalist – Angela Kelly*

23 Jan 99 I WANNA BE FREE *Virgin VSCDT 1728* 67 1

MINUTEMAN *UK, male vocal / instrumental group (3 Singles: 3 Weeks)*

20 Jul 02 BIG BOY *Ignition IGNSCD 225* 69 1
21 Sep 02 5000 MINUTES OF PAIN *Ignition IGNSCD 27* 75 1
15 Feb 03 BIG BOY (re-issue) / MOTHER FIXATION
Ignition IGNSCD 28 45 1

The MIRACLES (see also Smokey ROBINSON)

US, male vocal group (10 Singles: 81 Weeks)

24 Feb 66 GOING TO A GO-GO *Tamla Motown TMG 547* 44 5
22 Dec 66 (COME 'ROUND HERE) I'M THE ONE YOU NEED
Tamla Motown TMG 584 37 2
27 Dec 67 I SECOND THAT EMOTION *Tamla Motown TMG 631* [1] $ 27 11
3 Apr 68 IF YOU CAN WAIT *Tamla Motown TMG 648* [1] 50 1

23 June 1979	30 June 1979	7 July 1979	14 July 1979
RING MY BELL Anita Ward	ARE 'FRIENDS' ELECTRIC? Tubeway Army	ARE 'FRIENDS' ELECTRIC? Tubeway Army	ARE 'FRIENDS' ELECTRIC? Tubeway Army
DISCOVERY Electric Light Orchestra	DISCOVERY Electric Light Orchestra	DISCOVERY Electric Light Orchestra	DISCOVERY Electric Light Orchestra

KEY: UK No.1 ★ UK Top 10 ● Still on chart + UK entry at No.1 ■ US No.1 ▲ UK million seller £ US million seller $
Singles re-entries are listed as (re), (2re), (3re)… which signifies that the hit re-entered the chart once, twice or three times…
Peak Position / Weeks

7 May 69 ● **TRACKS OF MY TEARS** *Tamla Motown TMG 696* [1] 9 13
1 Aug 70 ★ **THE TEARS OF A CLOWN** *Tamla Motown TMG 745* [1] ▲ $...1 14
30 Jan 71 **(COME 'ROUND HERE) I'M THE ONE YOU NEED** (re-issue) *Tamla Motown TMG 761* [1] 13 9
5 Jun 71 **I DON'T BLAME YOU AT ALL** *Tamla Motown TMG 774* [1] 11 10
10 Jan 76 ● **LOVE MACHINE** *Tamla Motown TMG 1015* ▲ $....3 10
2 Oct 76 **THE TEARS OF A CLOWN** (re-issue) *Tamla Motown TMG 1048* [1] 34 6

[1] Smokey Robinson and The Miracles

MIRAGE
UK, male production group (3 Albums: 33 Weeks, 7 Singles: 35 Weeks)

14 Jan 84 **GIVE ME THE NIGHT (MEDLEY)** *Passion PASH 15* [1] 49 4
9 May 87 ● **JACK MIX II / III** *Debut DEBT 3022*....4 11
25 Jul 87 **SERIOUS MIX** *Debut DEBT 3028*....42 4
7 Nov 87 ● **JACK MIX IV** *Debut DEBT 3035*....8 10
26 Dec 87 ● **THE BEST OF MIRAGE – JACK MIX '88** *Stylus SMR 746*....7 15
27 Feb 88 **JACK MIX VII** *Debut DEBT 3042*....50 3
25 Jun 88 ● **JACK MIX IN FULL EFFECT** *Stylus SMR 856*....7 12
2 Jul 88 **PUSH THE BEAT** *Debut DEBT 3050*....67 2
7 Jan 89 **ROYAL MIX '89** *Stylus SMR 871*....34 6
11 Nov 89 **LATINO HOUSE** *Debut DEBT 3085*....70 1

[1] Mirage featuring Roy Gayle

'Jack Mix III' listed with 'Jack Mix II' only from 6 Jun 1987.

MIRAGE *UK, male instrumental trio*

23 Sep 95 **CLASSIC GUITAR MOODS** *PolyGram TV 5290562*....25 3

Danny MIRROR *Holland, male vocalist – Eddy Ouwens*

17 Sep 77 ● **I REMEMBER ELVIS PRESLEY (THE KING IS DEAD)** *Sonet SON 2121*....4 9

MIRRORBALL (see also PF PROJECT featuring Ewan McGREGOR; TZANT)
UK, male production duo – Jamie White and Jamie Ford and female vocalist (2 Singles: 5 Weeks)

13 Feb 99 **GIVEN UP** *Multiply CDMULTY 46*....12 4
24 Jun 00 **BURNIN'** *Multiply CDMULTY 56*....47 1

MIRWAIS *France, male producer – Mirwais Ahmadzai (2 Singles: 3 Weeks)*

20 May 00 **DISCO SCIENCE** *Epic 6693102*....68 1
23 Dec 00 **NAIVE SONG** *Epic 6706922*....50 2

MISHKA *Bermuda, male vocalist – Alexander Mishka Frith*

15 May 99 **GIVE YOU ALL THE LOVE** *Creation CRESCD 311*....34 2

MISS BEHAVIN' *UK, female DJ / producer – Nichola Potterton*

18 Jan 03 **SUCH A GOOD FEELIN'** *Tidy Two TIDYTWO 115CD*....62 1

MS DYNAMITE *UK, female rapper / vocalist – Niomi McLean-Daley (2 Albums: 44 Weeks, 5 Singles: 35 Weeks)*

23 Jun 01 **BOOO!** *ffrr / Public Demand / Social Circles FCD 399* [1] 12 6
1 Jun 02 ● **IT TAKES MORE** *Polydor 5707982*....7 10
22 Jun 02 ● **A LITTLE DEEPER** *Polydor 5899552*....10 42
7 Sep 02 ● **DY-NA-MI-TEE** *Polydor 5709782*....5 10
14 Dec 02 **PUT HIM OUT** *Polydor 0658942*....19 6
8 Oct 05 **JUDGEMENT DAY** *Polydor 9873970*....25 3
15 Oct 05 **JUDGEMENT DAYS** *Polydor 9873594*....43 2

[1] Sticky featuring Ms Dynamite

MISS JANE *Italy, male production duo and UK, female vocalist*

30 Oct 99 **IT'S A FINE DAY** *G1 Recordings G 1001CD*....62 1

MISS SHIVA *Germany, female DJ / producer – Khadra Bungardt*

10 Nov 01 **DREAMS** *VC Recordings VCRD 99*....30 2

MISS X *UK, female vocalist – Joyce Blair*

1 Aug 63 **CHRISTINE** *Ember S 175*....37 6

The MISSION *UK, male vocal (Wayne Hussey) / instrumental group (9 Albums: 48 Weeks, 17 Singles: 58 Weeks)*

14 Jun 86 **SERPENTS KISS** *Chapter 22 CHAP 6*....70 3
26 Jul 86 **GARDEN OF DELIGHT / LIKE A HURRICANE** *Chapter 22 CHAP 7*....49 4
18 Oct 86 **STAY WITH ME** *Mercury MYTH 1*....30 4
22 Nov 86 **GOD'S OWN MEDICINE** *Mercury MERH 102*....14 20
17 Jan 87 **WASTELAND** *Mercury MYTH 2*....11 6
14 Mar 87 **SEVERINA** *Mercury MYTH 3*....25 5
4 Jul 87 **THE FIRST CHAPTER** *Mercury MISH 1*....35 4
13 Feb 88 **TOWER OF STRENGTH** *Mercury MYTH 4*....12 7
12 Mar 88 ● **CHILDREN** *Mercury MISH 2*....2 9
23 Apr 88 **BEYOND THE PALE** *Mercury MYTH 6*....32 4
13 Jan 90 **BUTTERFLY ON A WHEEL** *Mercury MYTH 8*....12 4
17 Feb 90 ● **CARVED IN SAND** *Mercury 8422511*....7 8
10 Mar 90 **DELIVERANCE** *Mercury MYTH 9*....27 4
2 Jun 90 **INTO THE BLUE** *Mercury MYTH 10*....32 3
2 Nov 90 **GRAINS OF SAND** *Mercury 8469371*....28 2
17 Nov 90 **HANDS ACROSS THE OCEAN** *Mercury MYTH 11*....28 2
25 Apr 92 **NEVER AGAIN** *Mercury MYTH 12*....34 3
20 Jun 92 **LIKE A CHILD AGAIN** *Mercury MYTH 13*....30 2
4 Jul 92 **MASQUE** *Vertigo 5121212*....23 2
17 Oct 92 **SHADES OF GREEN** *Vertigo MYTH 14*....49 2
8 Jan 94 **TOWER OF STRENGTH** (re-mix) *Vertigo MYTCD 15*....33 3
19 Feb 94 **SUM AND SUBSTANCE** *Vertigo 5184472*....49 1
26 Mar 94 **AFTERGLOW** *Vertigo MYTCD 16*....53 1
4 Feb 95 **SWOON** *Neverland HOOKCD 002*....73 1
25 Feb 95 **NEVERLAND** *Neverland SMEECD 001*....58 1
15 Jun 96 **BLUE** *Equator SMEECD 002*....73 1

MISSJONES *US, female vocalist – Tarsha Jones*

10 Oct 98 **2 WAY STREET** *Motown 8608572*....49 1

MISTA E (see also NOMAD) *UK, male producer – Damon Rochefort*

10 Dec 88 **DON'T BELIEVE THE HYPE** *Urban URB 28*....41 5

MIS-TEEQ *UK, female vocal trio (3 Albums: 54 Weeks, 8 Singles: 70 Weeks)*

20 Jan 01 ● **WHY** *Inferno / Telstar CDFERN 35*....8 7
23 Jun 01 ● **ALL I WANT** *Inferno / Telstar CDSTAS 3184*....2 11
27 Oct 01 ● **ONE NIGHT STAND** *Inferno / Telstar CDSTAS 3208*....5 12
10 Nov 01 ● **LICKIN' ON BOTH SIDES** *Inferno / Telstar TCD 3212*....3 31
2 Mar 02 ● **B WITH ME** *Inferno / Telstar CDSTAS 3243*....5 8
29 Jun 02 ● **ROLL ON / THIS IS HOW WE DO IT** *Inferno / Telstar CDSTAS 3255*....7 7
29 Mar 03 ● **SCANDALOUS** *Telstar CDSTAS 3319*....2 11
12 Apr 03 ● **EYE CANDY** *Telstar TCD 3304*....6 21
12 Jul 03 ● **CAN'T GET IT BACK** *Telstar CDSTAS 3337*....8 9
29 Nov 03 **STYLE** (re) *Telstar CDSTAS 3369*....13 5
7 May 05 **GREATEST HITS** *Universal TV 9871410*....28 2

MR and MRS SMITH *UK, male / female instrumental / production group*

12 Oct 96 **GOTTA GET LOOSE** *Hooj Choons HOOJCD 46*....70 1

MR BEAN and SMEAR CAMPAIGN featuring Bruce DICKINSON
UK, male comedian – Rowan Atkinson and vocalist

4 Apr 92 ● **(I WANT TO BE) ELECTED** *London LON 319*....9 5

	21 July 1979	28 July 1979	4 August 1979	11 August 1979
UK No.1 SINGLES	ARE 'FRIENDS' ELECTRIC? Tubeway Army	I DON'T LIKE MONDAYS The Boomtown Rats	I DON'T LIKE MONDAYS The Boomtown Rats	I DON'T LIKE MONDAYS The Boomtown Rats
UK No.1 ALBUMS	REPLICAS Tubeway Army	THE BEST DISCO ALBUM IN THE WORLD Various	THE BEST DISCO ALBUM IN THE WORLD Various	THE BEST DISCO ALBUM IN THE WORLD Various

MR BIG

UK, male vocal (Jeff Dicken) / instrumental group (2 Singles: 14 Weeks)

12 Feb 77 ● **ROMEO** *EMI 2567*....4 10
21 May 77 **FEEL LIKE CALLING HOME** *EMI 2610*....35 4

MR BIG *US, male vocal (Eric Martin) / instrumental group (3 Albums: 14 Weeks, 4 Singles: 17 Weeks)*

22 Jul 89 **MR. BIG** *Atlantic 781990 1*....60 1
13 Apr 91 **LEAN INTO IT** *Atlantic 7567822091*....28 12
7 Mar 92 ● **TO BE WITH YOU** *Atlantic A 7514* ▲....3 11
23 May 92 **JUST TAKE MY HEART** *Atlantic A 7490*....26 4
8 Aug 92 **GREEN TINTED SIXTIES MIND** *Atlantic A 7468*....72 1
2 Oct 93 **BUMP AHEAD** *Atlantic 7567824952*....61 1
20 Nov 93 **WILD WORLD** *Atlantic A 7310CD*....59 1

MR BLOBBY

UK, male pink and yellow spotted blob vocalist (2 Singles: 16 Weeks)

4 Dec 93 ★ **MR BLOBBY** *Destiny Music CDDMUS 104*....1 12
16 Dec 95 **CHRISTMAS IN BLOBBYLAND** *Destiny DMUSCD 108*....36 4

MR BLOE *UK, male instrumental group*

9 May 70 ● **GROOVIN' WITH MR BLOE** *DJM DJS 216*....2 18

MR. BUNGLE *US, male vocal / instrumental group*

21 Sep 91 **MR BUNGLE** *London 8282671*....57 1

MR FINGERS *US, male producer – Larry Heard (3 Singles: 5 Weeks)*

17 Mar 90 **WHAT ABOUT THIS LOVE** *ffrr F 131*....74 1
7 Mar 92 **CLOSER** *MCA MCS 1601*....50 3
23 May 92 **ON MY WAY** *MCA MCS 1630*....71 1

MR FOOD *UK, male vocalist*

9 Jun 90 **... AND THAT'S BEFORE ME TEA!** *Tangible TGB 005*....62 3

MR HANKEY *US, male Xmas excrement vocalist*

25 Dec 99 ● **MR HANKEY THE CHRISTMAS POO** *Columbia 6685582*....4 6

MR JACK *Belgium, male producer – Lucente Vito*

25 Jan 97 **WIGGLY WORLD** *Extravaganza 0090965*....32 2

MR LEE *US, male producer – Leroy Haggard (2 Singles: 6 Weeks)*

6 Aug 88 **PUMP UP LONDON** *Breakout USA 639*....64 2
11 Nov 89 **GET BUSY** (re) *Jive JIVE 231*....41 4

MR MISTER *US, male vocal (Richard Page) / instrumental group (1 Album: 24 Weeks, 2 Singles: 22 Weeks)*

21 Dec 85 ● **BROKEN WINGS** *RCA PB 49945* ▲....4 13
15 Feb 86 ● **WELCOME TO THE REAL WORLD** *RCA PL 89647* ▲....6 24
1 Mar 86 **KYRIE** *RCA PB 49927* ▲....11 9

MR OIZO *France, male producer – Quentin Dupieux*

3 Apr 99 ★ **FLAT BEAT** (re) *F Communications / Pias Recordings F 104CDUK* ■....1 15

MR ON vs The JUNGLE BROTHERS

UK, male producer and US, male rap duo

7 Feb 04 **BREATHE, DON'T STOP** *Positiva / Incentive CDTIVS 201*....21 5

MR PINK presents The PROGRAM *UK, male producer – Leiam Sullivan*

19 Jan 02 **LOVE AND AFFECTION** *Manifesto FESCD 90*....22 4

MR PRESIDENT *Germany, male / female vocal group (3 Singles: 13 Weeks)*

14 Jun 97 ● **COCO JAMBOO** *WEA WEA 110CD*....8 11
20 Sep 97 **I GIVE YOU MY HEART** *WEA WEA 126CD*....52 1
25 Apr 98 **JOJO ACTION** *WEA WEA 156CD*....73 1

MR REDS vs DJ SKRIBBLE

UK, male producers – Reduan Nabbach and Scott Ialachi

24 May 03 **EVERYBODY COME ON (CAN U FEEL IT)** *ffrr FCD 410*....13 6

MR ROY *UK, male instrumental / production group (3 Singles: 6 Weeks)*

7 May 94 **SOMETHING ABOUT YOU** *Fresh FRSHD 11*....74 1
21 Jan 95 **SAVED** *Fresh FRSHD 21*....24 4
16 Dec 95 **SOMETHING ABOUT U (CAN'T BE BEAT)** (re-mix) *Fresh FRSHCD 33*....49 1

MR SCRUFF *UK, male DJ / producer – Andy Carthy*

21 Sep 02 **TROUSER JAZZ** *Ninja Tune ZENCD 65*....29 2
14 Dec 02 **SWEETSMOKE** *Ninja Tune ZENCDS 12124*....75 1

MR SMASH & FRIENDS featuring the ENGLAND SUPPORTER'S BAND (see also MADNESS) *UK, male vocal football supporters group*

8 Jun 02 **WE'RE COMING OVER** *RGR RGRCD 2*....67 1

MR V *UK, male producer – Rob Villiers*

6 Aug 94 **GIVE ME LIFE** *Cheeky CHEKCD 005*....40 2

MR VEGAS *Jamaica, male vocalist – Clifford Smith (2 Singles: 7 Weeks)*

22 Aug 98 **HEADS HIGH** *Greensleeves GRECD 650*....71 1
13 Nov 99 **HEADS HIGH** (re-issue) *Greensleeves GRECD 785*....16 6

MRS MILLS *UK, female pianist – Gladys Mills, b. 1921, d. 25 Feb 1978 (4 Albums: 13 Weeks, 2 Singles: 6 Weeks)*

14 Dec 61 **MRS MILLS MEDLEY** *Parlophone R 4856*....18 5
31 Dec 64 **MRS MILLS PARTY MEDLEY** *Parlophone R 5214*....50 1
10 Dec 66 **COME TO MY PARTY** *Parlophone PMC 7010*....17 7
28 Dec 68 **MRS. MILLS' PARTY PIECES** *Parlophone PCS 7066*....32 3
13 Dec 69 **LET'S HAVE ANOTHER PARTY** *Parlophone PCS 7035*....23 2
6 Nov 71 **I'M MIGHTY GLAD** *MFP 5225*....49 1

Mrs Mills Medley: I Want to Be Happy / Sheik of Araby / Baby Face / Somebody Stole My Gal / Ma (He's Making Eyes at Me) / Swanee / Ain't She Sweet / California Here I Come. Mrs Mills Party Medley: You Made Me Love You (I Didn't Want to Do it) / Shine on Harvest Moon / I Don't Want to Set the World on Fire / Around the World / Ramona / Charmaine.

MRS WOOD *UK, female producer – Jane Rolink (4 Singles: 6 Weeks)*

16 Sep 95 **JOANNA** *React CDREACT 066*....40 2
6 Jul 96 **HEARTBREAK** *React CDREACT 78* [1]....44 1
4 Oct 97 **JOANNA** (re-mix) *React CDREACT 107*....34 2
15 Aug 98 **1234** *React CDREACT 121*....54 1

[1] Mrs Wood featuring Eve Gallagher

MISTURA featuring Lloyd MICHELS

US, male instrumental group – Lloyd Michels – trumpet

15 May 76 **THE FLASHER** *Route RT 30*....23 10

Des MITCHELL *UK, male DJ / producer*

29 Jan 00 ● **(WELCOME) TO THE DANCE** *Code Blue BLUE 0087CD1*....5 5

Guy MITCHELL (436 Top 500) *Extremely popular pre-rock vocalist, b. Al Cernik, 27 Feb 1927, Detroit, US, d. 1 Jul 1999. He appeared on the first and last charts of the 1950s, and was one of most consistently successful singers and performers of that decade (15 Singles: 165 Weeks)*

14 Nov 52 ● **FEET UP!** *Columbia DB 3151*....2 10
13 Feb 53 ★ **SHE WEARS RED FEATHERS** (re) *Columbia DB 3238*....1 16
24 Apr 53 ● **PRETTY LITTLE BLACK-EYED SUSIE** *Columbia DB 3255*....2 11
28 Aug 53 ★ **LOOK AT THAT GIRL** *Philips PB 162*....1 14

18 August 1979	25 August 1979	1 September 1979	8 September 1979
I DON'T LIKE MONDAYS The Boomtown Rats	WE DON'T TALK ANY MORE Cliff Richard	WE DON'T TALK ANY MORE Cliff Richard	WE DON'T TALK ANY MORE Cliff Richard
THE BEST DISCO ALBUM IN THE WORLD Various	THE BEST DISCO ALBUM IN THE WORLD Various	THE BEST DISCO ALBUM IN THE WORLD Various	IN THROUGH THE OUT DOOR Led Zeppelin

KEY

UK No.1 ★ UK Top 10 ● Still on chart + UK entry at No.1 ■ US No.1 ▲ UK million seller £ US million seller $

Singles re-entries are listed as (re), (2re), (3re)... which signifies that the hit re-entered the chart once, twice or three times...

Peak Position / Weeks

6 Nov 53 ● **CHICKA BOOM** (re) *Philips PB 178*....4 15
18 Dec 53 ● **CLOUD LUCKY SEVEN** *Philips PB 210A*....2 16
19 Feb 54 ● **THE CUFF OF MY SHIRT** (2re) *Philips PB 225*....9 3
26 Feb 54 **SIPPIN' SODA** *Philips PB 210B*....11 1
30 Apr 54 ● **A DIME AND A DOLLAR** (re) *Philips PB 248*....8 5
7 Dec 56 ★ **SINGING THE BLUES** *Philips PB 650* ▲ $....1 22
15 Feb 57 ● **KNEE DEEP IN THE BLUES** *Philips PB 669*....3 12
26 Apr 57 ★ **ROCK-A-BILLY** *Philips PB 685*....1 14
26 Jul 57 **IN THE MIDDLE OF A DARK, DARK NIGHT / SWEET STUFF** (re) *Philips PB 712*....25 4
11 Oct 57 **CALL ROSIE ON THE PHONE** *Philips PB 743*....17 6
27 Nov 59 ● **HEARTACHES BY THE NUMBER** (re) *Philips PB 964* ▲ $....5 16

Joni MITCHELL *Canada, female vocalist / guitarist – Roberta Anderson (17 Albums: 120 Weeks, 2 Singles: 24 Weeks)*

6 Jun 70 ● LADIES OF THE CANYON *Reprise RSLP 6376*....8 25
13 Jun 70 **BIG YELLOW TAXI** *Reprise RS 20906*....11 15
24 Jul 71 ● BLUE *Reprise K 44128*....3 18
16 Mar 74 COURT AND SPARK *Asylum SYLA 8756*....14 11
1 Feb 75 MILES OF AILES *Asylum SYSP 902*....34 4
27 Dec 75 THE HISSING OF SUMMER LAWNS *Asylum SYLA 8763*....14 10
11 Dec 76 HEJIRA *Asylum K 53053*....11 5
21 Jan 78 DON JUAN'S RECKLESS DAUGHTER *Asylum K 63003*....20 7
14 Jul 79 MINGUS *Asylum K 53091*....24 7
4 Oct 80 SHADOWS AND LIGHT *Elektra K 62030*....63 3
4 Dec 82 WILD THINGS RUN FAST *Geffen GEF 25102*....32 8
30 Nov 85 DOG EAT DOG *Geffen GEF 26455*....57 3
2 Apr 88 CHALK MARK IN A RAIN STORM *Geffen WX 141*....26 7
9 Mar 91 NIGHT RIDE HOME *Geffen GEF 24302*....25 5
5 Nov 94 TURBULENT INDIGO *Reprise 9362457862*....53 2
4 Oct 97 ● **GOT 'TIL IT'S GONE** *Virgin VSCDG 1666* [1]....6 9
10 Oct 98 TAMING THE TIGER *Reprise 9362464512*....57 1
11 Mar 00 BOTH SIDES NOW *Reprise 9362476202*....50 2
25 Sep 04 DREAMLAND *WSM 8122765202*....43 2

[1] Janet featuring Q-Tip and Joni Mitchell

'Got 'Til It's Gone' uses samples from 'Big Yellow Taxi'.

The MITCHELL BROTHERS NEW *UK, male rap duo – Tony and Teddy Mitchell (1 Album: 1 Week, 3 Singles: 4 Weeks)*

19 Mar 05 **ROUTINE CHECK** *The Beats BEATS 8* [1]....42 2
4 Jun 05 **HARVEY NICKS** *The Beats BEATS 15* [2]....62 1
20 Aug 05 **EXCUSE MY BROTHER** *The Beats BEATS 19*....58 1
3 Sep 05 A BREATH OF FRESH ATTIRE *Beats Recordings 2564625892*..56 1

[1] The Mitchell Brothers featuring Kano and The Streets [2] The Mitchell Brothers featuring Sway

George MITCHELL MINSTRELS (206 Top 500)

Last and biggest-selling British minstrel band – leader b. 27 Feb 1917, Falkirk, Scotland, d. 27 Aug 2002. Non-PC now, this ensemble, which featured Tony Mercer, Dai Francis and John Boulter, were the stars of a popular BBC TV series, The Black and White Minstrel Show, which ran for two decades from 1958 (11 Albums: 292 Weeks)

26 Nov 60 ★ THE BLACK AND WHITE MINSTREL SHOW *HMV CLP 1399*....1 142
21 Oct 61 ★ ANOTHER BLACK AND WHITE MINSTREL SHOW *HMV CLP 1460*....1 64
20 Oct 62 ★ ON STAGE WITH THE GEORGE MITCHELL MINSTRELS *HMV CLP 1599*....1 26
2 Nov 63 ● ON TOUR WITH THE GEORGE MITCHELL MINSTRELS *HMV CLP 1667*....6 18
12 Dec 64 ● SPOTLIGHT ON THE GEORGE MITCHELL MINSTRELS *HMV CLP 1803*....6 7
4 Dec 65 ● MAGIC OF THE MINSTRELS *HMV CLP 1917*....9 7
26 Nov 66 HERE COME THE MINSTRELS *HMV CLP 3579*....11 11
16 Dec 67 SHOWTIME *HMV CSD 3642*....26 2
14 Dec 68 SING THE IRVING BERLIN SONGBOOK *Columbia SCX 6267*....33 1
19 Dec 70 THE MAGIC OF CHRISTMAS *Columbia SCX 6431*....32 4
19 Nov 77 ● 30 GOLDEN GREATS *EMI EMTV 7* [1]....10 10

[1] George Mitchell Minstrels with the Joe Loss Orchestra

Willie MITCHELL *US, male guitarist (2 Singles: 3 Weeks)*

24 Apr 68 **SOUL SERENADE** *London HLU 10186*....43 1
11 Dec 76 **THE CHAMPION** *London HL 10545*....47 2

MIX FACTORY *UK, male / female vocal / instrumental group*

30 Jan 93 **TAKE ME AWAY (PARADISE)** *All Around the World CDGLOBE 120*....51 2

MIXMASTER (see also BLACK BOX) *Italy, male producer – Daniele Davoli*

4 Nov 89 ● **GRAND PIANO** *BCM BCM 344*....9 10

The MIXTURES *Australia, male vocal (Mick Flinn) / instrumental group*

16 Jan 71 ● **THE PUSHBIKE SONG** *Polydor 2058 083*....2 21

Hank MIZELL *US, male vocalist, b. 1924, d. Dec 1992*

20 Mar 76 ● **JUNGLE ROCK** *Charly CS 1005*....3 13

MOBB DEEP *US, male rap group (2 Albums: 2 Weeks, 1 Single: 10 Weeks)*

23 Nov 96 HELL ON EARTH *Loud 74321425582*....67 1
21 Aug 04 AMERIKAZ NIGHTMARE *Jive 82876571312*....68 1
24 Sep 05 ● **OUTTA CONTROL** *Interscope 9885269* [1]....7 10

[1] 50 Cent featuring Mobb Deep

The MOBILES

UK, male / female vocal (Anna Marie) / instrumental group (2 Singles: 14 Weeks)

9 Jan 82 ● **DROWNING IN BERLIN** *Rialto RIA 3*....9 10
27 Mar 82 **AMOUR AMOUR** *Rialto RIA 5*....45 4

MOBO ALLSTARS *UK / US, male / female vocal / instrumental group*

26 Dec 98 **AIN'T NO STOPPING US NOW** *PolyGram TV 5632302*....47 3

Artists featured include: Another Level, Shola Ama, Kéllé Bryan, Celetia, Cleopatra, Damage, Des'ree, D'Influence, E17, Michelle Gayle, Glamma Kid, Lynden David Hall, Hinda Hicks, Honeyz, Kle'Shay, Beverley Knight, Kele Le Roc, Tony Momrelle, Nine Yards, Mica Paris, Karen Ramirez, Connor Reeves, Roachford, 7th Son, Byron Stingily, Truce, Soundproof, Ultimate Kaos.

MOBY (327 Top 500)

Genre-bending, maverick producer / vocalist, b. Richard Hall, 11 Sep 1965, New York, US, who is a descendant of 'Moby Dick' author Herman Melville. The BRIT and Grammy-nominated Play was the UK's biggest-selling independent album of 2000 and went platinum in more than 20 countries (7 Albums: 136 Weeks, 21 Singles: 75 Weeks)

27 Jul 91 ● **GO** (re) *Outer Rhythm FOOT 15*....10 10
3 Jul 93 **I FEEL IT** *Equinox AXISCD 001*....38 3
11 Sep 93 **MOVE** *Mute CDMUTE 158*....21 5
28 May 94 **HYMN** *Mute CDMUTE 161*....31 2
29 Oct 94 **FEELING SO REAL** *Mute CDMUTE 173*....30 2
25 Feb 95 **EVERY TIME YOU TOUCH ME** *Mute CDMUTE 176*....28 3
25 Mar 95 EVERYTHING IS WRONG / MIXED & REMIXED *Mute LCDSTUMM 130*....21 7
1 Jul 95 **INTO THE BLUE** *Mute CDMUTE 179A*....34 2
7 Sep 96 **THAT'S WHEN I REACH FOR MY REVOLVER** *Mute CDMUTE 184*....50 1
5 Oct 96 ANIMAL RIGHTS *Mute LCDSTUMM 150*....38 1
15 Nov 97 ● **JAMES BOND THEME** (re) *Mute CDMUTE 210*....8 8
5 Sep 98 **HONEY** *Mute CDMUTE 218*....33 2

	15 September 1979	22 September 1979	29 September 1979	6 October 1979
UK No.1 SINGLES	WE DON'T TALK ANY MORE Cliff Richard	CARS Gary Numan	MESSAGE IN A BOTTLE The Police	MESSAGE IN A BOTTLE The Police
UK No.1 ALBUMS	IN THROUGH THE OUT DOOR Led Zeppelin	THE PLEASURE PRINCIPLE Gary Numan	OCEANS OF FANTASY Boney M	THE PLEASURE PRINCIPLE Gary Numan

Date	Title / Label	Pos	Wks
8 May 99	**RUN ON** *Mute CDMUTE 221*	33	2
29 May 99 ★	PLAY *Mute CDSTUMM 172*	1	83
24 Jul 99	**BODYROCK** *Mute CDMUTE 225*	38	2
23 Oct 99	**WHY DOES MY HEART FEEL SO BAD** *Mute CDMUTE 230*	16	4
18 Mar 00	**NATURAL BLUES** *Mute CDMUTE 251*	11	6
24 Jun 00 ●	**PORCELAIN** *Mute CDMUTE 252*	5	6
1 Jul 00	I LIKE TO SCORE *Mute CDSTUMM 168*	54	2
28 Oct 00	**WHY DOES MY HEART FEEL SO BAD** (re-issue) *Mute CDMUTE 255*	17	5
4 Nov 00	PLAY: THE B SIDES *Mute LCDSTUMM 172*	24	3
11 May 02	**WE ARE ALL MADE OF STARS** *Mute CDMUTE 268*	11	4
25 May 02 ★	18 *Mute CDSTUMM 202* ■	1	34
31 Aug 02	**EXTREME WAYS** *Mute CDMUTE 270*	39	1
16 Nov 02	**IN THIS WORLD** *Mute CDMUTE 276*	35	2
12 Mar 05	**LIFT ME UP** *Mute CDMUTE 340*	18	4
26 Mar 05 ●	HOTEL *Mute LCDSTUMM 240*	8	6
11 Jun 05	**SPIDERS** *Mute LCDMUTE 350*	50	1

The MOCK TURTLES *UK, male / female vocal / instrumental group (2 Albums: 4 Weeks, 3 Singles: 18 Weeks)*

Date	Title / Label	Pos	Wks
9 Mar 91	**CAN YOU DIG IT?** *Siren SRN 136*	18	11
25 May 91	TURTLE SOUP *Imaginary ILLUSION 012*	54	1
29 Jun 91	**AND THEN SHE SMILES** *Siren SRN 139*	44	4
27 Jul 91	TWO SIDES *Siren SRNLP 31*	33	3
15 Mar 03	**CAN YOU DIG IT?** (re-mix) *Virgin CDMOCK 001*	19	3

MODERN EON *UK, male vocal / instrumental group*

Date	Title / Label	Pos	Wks
13 Jun 81	FICTION TALES *DinDisc DID 11*	65	1

MODERN ROMANCE *UK, male vocal / instrumental group (2 Albums: 13 Weeks, 8 Singles: 77 Weeks)*

Date	Title / Label	Pos	Wks
15 Aug 81	**EVERYBODY SALSA** *WEA K 18815*	12	10
7 Nov 81 ●	**AY AY AY AY MOOSEY** *WEA K 18883*	10	12
30 Jan 82	**QUEEN OF THE RAPPING SCENE (NOTHING EVER GOES THE WAY YOU PLAN)** *WEA K 18928*	37	8
14 Aug 82	**CHERRY PINK AND APPLE BLOSSOM WHITE** *WEA K 19245* [1]	15	8
13 Nov 82 ●	**BEST YEARS OF OUR LIVES** *WEA ROM 1*	4	13
26 Feb 83 ●	**HIGH LIFE** *WEA ROM 2*	8	8
16 Apr 83	TRICK OF THE LIGHT *WEA X 0127*	53	7
7 May 83	**DON'T STOP THAT CRAZY RHYTHM** *WEA ROM 3*	14	6
6 Aug 83 ●	**WALKING IN THE RAIN** *WEA X 9733*	7	12
3 Dec 83	PARTY TONIGHT *Ronco RONLP 3*	45	6

[1] Modern Romance featuring John du Prez

MODERN TALKING *Germany, male vocal / instrumental duo – Thomas Anders and Dieter Bohlen (1 Album: 3 Weeks, 4 Singles: 22 Weeks)*

Date	Title / Label	Pos	Wks
15 Jun 85	**YOU'RE MY HEART, YOU'RE MY SOUL** (re) *Magnet MAG 277*	56	7
12 Oct 85	**YOU CAN WIN IF YOU WANT** *Magnet MAG 282*	70	2
16 Aug 86 ●	**BROTHER LOUIE** *RCA PB 40875*	4	10
4 Oct 86	**ATLANTIS IS CALLING (S.O.S. FOR LOVE)** *RCA PB 40969*	55	3
11 Oct 86	READY FOR ROMANCE *RCA PL 71133*	76	3

The MODERN NEW *UK, male / female vocal / instrumental group*

Date	Title / Label	Pos	Wks
26 Nov 05	**JANE FALLS DOWN** *Mercury 9874798*	35	1

MODEST MOUSE *US, male vocal / instrumental group*

Date	Title / Label	Pos	Wks
24 Jul 04	**FLOAT ON** *Epic 6750692*	46	1
31 Jul 04	GOOD NEWS FOR PEOPLE WHO LOVE BAD NEWS *Epic 5162722*	40	2

The MODETTES *UK, female vocal / instrumental group (2 Singles: 6 Weeks)*

Date	Title / Label	Pos	Wks
12 Jul 80	**PAINT IT BLACK** *Deram DET-R 1*	42	5
18 Jul 81	**TONIGHT** *Deram DET 3*	68	1

MODEY LEMON *US, male vocal / instrumental group (2 Singles: 2 Weeks)*

Date	Title / Label	Pos	Wks
22 May 04	**CROWS** *Mute CDMUTE 328*	75	1
28 May 05	**SLEEPWALKERS** *Mute CDMUTE 331*	71	1

MODJO *France, male production / vocal duo – Yann Destangol and Romain Tranchart (3 Singles: 29 Weeks)*

Date	Title / Label	Pos	Wks
16 Sep 00 ★	**LADY (HEAR ME TONIGHT)** *Polydor 5877582* ■	1	20
14 Apr 01	**CHILLIN'** *Polydor 5870092*	12	8
6 Oct 01	**WHAT I MEAN** *Polydor 5873462*	59	1

Domenico MODUGNO *Italy, male vocalist, b. 9 Jan 1928, d. 6 Aug 1994 (2 Singles: 13 Weeks)*

Date	Title / Label	Pos	Wks
5 Sep 58 ●	**VOLARE (NEL BLU DIPINTO DI BLU)** *Oriole ICB 5000* ▲ $	10	12
27 Mar 59	**CIAO CIAO BAMBINA (PIOVE)** *Oriole CB 1489*	29	1

The MOFFATTS *Canada, male vocal / instrumental group (1 Album: 1 Week, 3 Singles: 6 Weeks)*

Date	Title / Label	Pos	Wks
20 Feb 99	**CRAZY** *Chrysalis CDEM 533*	16	3
6 Mar 99	CHAPTER 1: A NEW BEGINNING *Chrysalis 4992072*	62	1
26 Jun 99	**UNTIL YOU LOVED ME** *Chrysalis CDEM 541*	36	2
23 Oct 99	**MISERY** *EMI CDEM 551*	47	1

MOGUAI *Germany, male producer – Andre Tegeler*

Date	Title / Label	Pos	Wks
8 Feb 03	**U KNOW Y** *Hope HOPECDS 038*	62	1

MOGWAI *UK, male vocal / instrumental group (4 Albums: 7 Weeks, 3 Singles: 3 Weeks)*

Date	Title / Label	Pos	Wks
8 Nov 97	YOUNG TEAM *Chemikal Underground CHEM 018CD*	75	1
4 Apr 98	**SWEET LEAF / BLACK SABBATH** *Fierce Panda NING 47CD* [1]	60	1
11 Apr 98	**FEAR SATAN** (re-mix) *Eye-Q EYEUK 032CD*	57	1
11 Jul 98	**NO EDUCATION NO FUTURE (F**K THE CURFEW)** *Chemikal CHEM 026CD*	68	1
10 Apr 99	COME ON DIE YOUNG *Chemikal Underground CHEM 033CD*	29	2
12 May 01	ROCK ACTION *Southpaw PAWCD 1*	23	2
21 Jun 03	HAPPY SONGS FOR HAPPY PEOPLE *PIAS PIASX 035CD*	47	2

[1] Mogwai: Magoo

MOHAIR NEW *UK, male vocal / instrumental group*

Date	Title / Label	Pos	Wks
17 Dec 05	**END OF THE LINE** *Ear Candy ECYCD 025*	52	1

The MOHAWKS *Jamaica, male vocal / instrumental group*

Date	Title / Label	Pos	Wks
24 Jan 87	**THE CHAMP** *Pama PM 1*	58	2

Frank'o MOIRAGHI featuring AMNESIA *Italy, male / female vocal / instrumental duo (2 Singles: 4 Weeks)*

Date	Title / Label	Pos	Wks
1 Jun 96	**FEEL MY BODY** *Multiply CDMULTY 10*	39	2
26 Oct 96	**FEEL MY BODY** (re-mix) *Multiply CDMULTY 15*	40	2

MOIST *Canada, male vocal / instrumental group (1 Album: 3 Weeks, 4 Singles: 10 Weeks)*

Date	Title / Label	Pos	Wks
12 Nov 94	**PUSH** *Chrysalis CDCHS 5016*	35	3
25 Feb 95	**SILVER** *Chrysalis CDCHS 5019*	50	2
29 Apr 95	**FREAKY BE BEAUTIFUL** *Chrysalis CDCHS 5022*	47	2
19 Aug 95	**PUSH** (re-issue) *Chrysalis CDCHS 5024*	20	3
26 Aug 95	SILVER *Chrysalis CDCHR 6080*	49	3

MOJO *UK, male instrumental group*

Date	Title / Label	Pos	Wks
22 Aug 81	**DANCE ON** *Creole CR 17*	70	3

MOJOLATORS featuring CAMILLA *US, male production duo and female vocalist*

Date	Title / Label	Pos	Wks
6 Oct 01	**DRIFTING** *Multiply CDMULTY 81*	52	1

13 October 1979	20 October 1979	27 October 1979	3 November 1979
MESSAGE IN A BOTTLE The Police	**VIDEO KILLED THE RADIO STAR** The Buggles	**ONE DAY AT A TIME** Lena Martell	**ONE DAY AT A TIME** Lena Martell
EAT TO THE BEAT Blondie / **REGGATTA DE BLANC** The Police (two charts published)	**REGGATTA DE BLANC** The Police	**REGGATTA DE BLANC** The Police	**REGGATTA DE BLANC** The Police

KEY UK No.1 ★ UK Top 10 ● Still on chart + UK entry at No.1 ■ US No.1 ▲ UK million seller £ US million seller $
Singles re-entries are listed as (re), (2re), (3re)… which signifies that the hit re-entered the chart once, twice or three times…
Peak Position / Weeks

The MOJOS
UK, male vocal (Stuart Slater) / instrumental group (3 Singles: 26 Weeks)

26 Mar 64 ● **EVERYTHING'S ALRIGHT** *Decca F 11853* 9 11
11 Jun 64 **WHY NOT TONIGHT** *Decca F 11918* 25 10
10 Sep 64 **SEVEN DAFFODILS** *Decca F 11959* 30 5

MOKENSTEF *US, female vocal group*

23 Sep 95 **HE'S MINE** *Def Jam DEFCD 13* 70 1

MOLELLA featuring The OUTHERE BROTHERS
Italy, male producer – Maurizio Molella and US, male rap / vocal duo – Lamar Mahone and Craig Simpkins

16 Dec 95 ● **IF YOU WANNA PARTY** *Eternal WEA 030CD* 9 10

MOLLY HALF HEAD *UK, male vocal / instrumental group*

3 Jun 95 **SHINE** *Columbia 6620732* 73 1

MOLLY HATCHET *US, male vocal / instrumental group*

25 Jan 86 DOUBLE TROUBLE – LIVE *Epic EPC 88670* 94 1

MOLOKO (see also PSYCHEDELIC WALTONS)
Ireland / UK, male / female vocal / instrumental duo – Roisin Murphy and Mark Brydon (3 Albums: 30 Weeks, 10 Singles: 39 Weeks)

24 Feb 96 **DOMINOID** *Echo ECSCD 016* 65 1
25 May 96 **FUN FOR ME** *Echo ECSCD 20* 36 2
20 Jun 98 **THE FLIPSIDE** *Echo ECSCD 54* 53 1
5 Sep 98 I AM NOT A DOCTOR *Echo ECHCD 21* 64 1
27 Mar 99 **SING IT BACK** *Echo ECSCD 71* 45 2
4 Sep 99 ● **SING IT BACK** (re-mix) *Echo ECSCD 82* 4 9
1 Apr 00 ● **THE TIME IS NOW** *Echo ECSCD 88* 2 10
22 Apr 00 ● THINGS TO MAKE AND DO *Echo ECHCD 31* 3 26
5 Aug 00 **PURE PLEASURE SEEKER** *Echo ECSCD 99* 21 5
25 Nov 00 **INDIGO** *Echo ECSCD 104* 51 1
1 Mar 03 ● **FAMILIAR FEELING** *Echo ECSCD 131* 10 4
15 Mar 03 STATUES *Echo ECHCD 44* 18 3
5 Jul 03 **FOREVER MORE** *Echo ECSCD 136* 17 4

MOMBASSA *UK, male production duo*

8 Mar 97 **CRY FREEDOM** *Soundproof SPCD 021* 63 1

The MOMENTS *US, male vocal group (4 Singles: 32 Weeks)*

8 Mar 75 ● **GIRLS** *All Platinum 6146 302* [1] 3 10
19 Jul 75 ● **DOLLY MY LOVE** *All Platinum 6146 306* 10 9
25 Oct 75 **LOOK AT ME (I'M IN LOVE)** *All Platinum 6146 309* 42 4
22 Jan 77 ● **JACK IN THE BOX** *All Platinum 6146 318* 7 9

[1] The Moments and The Whatnauts

Tony MOMRELLE *UK, male vocalist*

15 Aug 98 **LET ME SHOW YOU** *Art & Soul ART 1CDS* 67 1

MONACO (see also JOY DIVISION; NEW ORDER)
UK, male vocal / instrumental duo – Peter Hook and David Potts (1 Album: 3 Weeks, 3 Singles: 11 Weeks)

15 Mar 97 **WHAT DO YOU WANT FROM ME?** *Polydor 5731912* 11 6
31 May 97 **SWEET LIPS** *Polydor 5710552* 18 4
21 Jun 97 MUSIC FOR PLEASURE *Polydor 5372422* 11 3
20 Sep 97 **SHINE (SOMEONE WHO NEEDS ME)** *Polydor 5714182* 55 1

Pharoahe MONCH
US, male rapper – Troy Jamerson (5 Singles: 11 Weeks)

19 Feb 00 **SIMON SAYS** *Rawkus RWK 205CD* 24 2
19 Aug 00 **LIGHT** *Rawkus RWK 259CD* 72 1
3 Feb 01 **OH NO** *Rawkus RWK 302* [1] 24 4
1 Dec 01 **GOT YOU** *Priority PTYCD 145* 27 3
14 Sep 02 **THE LIFE** *MCA MCSTD 402292* [2] 50 1

[1] Mos Def and Nate Dogg featuring Pharoahe Monch [2] Styles and Pharoahe Monch

Jay MONDI and The LIVING BASS
US, male / female vocal / instrumental group

24 Mar 90 **ALL NIGHT LONG** *10 TEN 304* 63 3

MONDO KANE *UK, male vocal / instrumental group*

16 Aug 86 **NEW YORK AFTERNOON** *Lisson DOLE 2* 70 3

MONE *US, female vocalist (2 Singles: 2 Weeks)*

12 Aug 95 **WE CAN MAKE IT** *A&M 5811592* 64 1
16 Mar 96 **MOVIN'** *AM:PM 5814392* 48 1

MONEY MARK *US, male vocalist / instrumentalist / producer –*
Mark Ramos-Nishita (2 Albums: 6 Weeks, 2 Singles: 3 Weeks)

9 Sep 95 MARK'S KEYBOARD REPAIR *Mo Wax MW 034CD* 35 2
28 Feb 98 **HAND IN YOUR HEAD** *Mo Wax MW 066CD* 40 2
16 May 98 PUSH THE BUTTON *Mo Wax MW 090CD* 17 4
6 Jun 98 **MAYBE I'M DEAD** *Mo Wax MW 089CD1* 45 1

Zoot MONEY and The BIG ROLL BAND
UK, male vocal / instrumental group – leader George Bruno Money

18 Aug 66 **BIG TIME OPERATOR** *Columbia DB 7975* 25 8
15 Oct 66 ZOOT *Columbia SX 6075* 23 3

MONICA *US, female vocalist –*
Monica Arnold (1 Album: 10 Weeks, 7 Singles: 37 Weeks)

29 Jul 95 **DON'T TAKE IT PERSONAL (JUST ONE OF DEM DAYS)** *Arista 74321301452* $ 32 3
17 Feb 96 **LIKE THIS AND LIKE THAT** *Rowdy 74321344222* 33 2
8 Jun 96 **BEFORE YOU WALK OUT OF MY LIFE** *Rowdy 74321374042* $ 22 3
24 May 97 **FOR YOU I WILL** *Atlantic A 5437CD* $ 27 2
6 Jun 98 ● **THE BOY IS MINE** *Atlantic AT 0036CD* [1] ▲ $ 2 20
25 Jul 98 THE BOY IS MINE *Arista 7822190112* 52 10
17 Oct 98 ● **THE FIRST NIGHT** *Rowdy 74321619342* ▲ $ 6 6
4 Sep 99 **ANGEL OF MINE** *Arista 74321692892* ▲ $ 55 1

[1] Brandy and Monica

MONIFAH *US, female vocalist – Monifah Carter*

30 Jan 99 **TOUCH IT** *Universal UND 56218* 29 2

TS MONK *US, male / female vocal / instrumental group (2 Singles: 6 Weeks)*

7 Mar 81 **BON BON VIE** *Mirage K 11653* 63 2
25 Apr 81 **CANDIDATE FOR LOVE** *Mirage K 11648* 58 4

The MONKEES 312 Top 500
The world's top act of 1967: Davy Jones (v/g), Mike Nesmith (v/g), Peter Tork (v/k), Mickey Dolenz (v/d). This Anglo-American quartet was hand-picked for a Beatles-style TV series, which helped to rocket them, albeit briefly, to the very top (8 Albums: 118 Weeks, 13 Singles: 101 Weeks)

5 Jan 67 ★ **I'M A BELIEVER** *RCA 1560* ▲ $ 1 17
26 Jan 67 **LAST TRAIN TO CLARKSVILLE** *RCA 1547* ▲ $ 23 7
28 Jan 67 ★ THE MONKEES *RCA Victor SF 7844* ▲ 1 36
6 Apr 67 ● **A LITTLE BIT ME, A LITTLE BIT YOU** *RCA 1580* $ 3 12
15 Apr 67 ★ MORE OF THE MONKEES *RCA Victor SF 7868* ▲ 1 25
22 Jun 67 ● **ALTERNATE TITLE** *RCA 1604* 2 12

10 November 1979	17 November 1979	24 November 1979	1 December 1979
UK No.1 SINGLES			
ONE DAY AT A TIME Lena Martell	WHEN YOU'RE IN LOVE WITH A BEAUTIFUL WOMAN Dr Hook	WHEN YOU'RE IN LOVE WITH A BEAUTIFUL WOMAN Dr Hook	WHEN YOU'RE IN LOVE WITH A BEAUTIFUL WOMAN Dr Hook
UK No.1 ALBUMS			
TUSK Fleetwood Mac	GREATEST HITS VOLUME 2 Abba	GREATEST HITS VOLUME 2 Abba	GREATEST HITS VOLUME 2 Abba

8 Jul 67 ●	HEADQUARTERS *RCA Victor SF 7886* ▲	2	19
16 Aug 67	**PLEASANT VALLEY SUNDAY** *RC 1620* $	**11**	8
15 Nov 67 ●	**DAYDREAM BELIEVER** *RCA 1645* ▲ $	**5**	17
13 Jan 68 ●	PISCES AQUARIUS CAPRICORN & JONES LTD. *RCA Victor SF 7912* ▲	5	11
27 Mar 68	**VALLERI** *RCA 1673* $	**12**	8
26 Jun 68	**DW WASHBURN** *RCA 1706*	**17**	6
26 Mar 69	**TEAR DROP CITY** *RCA 1802*	**46**	1
25 Jun 69	**SOMEDAY MAN** *RCA 1824*	**47**	1
15 Mar 80	**THE MONKEES EP** *Arista ARIST 326*	33	9
28 Nov 81	THE MONKEES *Arista DARTY 12*	99	1
18 Oct 86	**THAT WAS THEN, THIS IS NOW** *Arista ARIST 673*	**68**	1
1 Apr 89	**THE MONKEES EP** *Arista 112157*	62	2
15 Apr 89	HEY HEY IT'S THE MONKEES – GREATEST HITS *K-Tel NE 1432*	12	9
22 Mar 97	HERE THEY COME ... THE GREATEST HITS OF THE MONKEES *Warner.esp / Telstar 9548352182*	15	10
10 Mar 01	THE DEFINITIVE MONKEES *WSM 8573866922*	15	7

Tracks on Arista 326 EP: I'm a Believer / Daydream Believer / Last Train to Clarksville / A Little Bit Me, a Little Bit You. Tracks on Arista 112157 EP: Daydream Believer / Monkees Theme / Last Train to Clarksville. The two albums titled The Monkees are different.

MONKEY BARS featuring Gabrielle WIDMAN
UK, male production / instrumental duo and female vocalist

8 May 04	**SHUGGIE LOVE** *Subliminal SUB 117CD*	**61**	1

MONKEY HANGERZ NEW
UK, male / female Hartlepool FC vocal supporters

19 Nov 05	**2 LITTLE BOYS / NEVER SAY DIE** *Poolie Pride 1908*	**24**	1

MONKEY MAFIA *UK, male vocal / instrumental / DJ / production group (1 Album: 1 Week, 3 Singles: 3 Weeks)*

10 Aug 96	**WORK MI BODY** *Heavenly HVN 53CD* [1]	**75**	1
7 Jun 97	**15 STEPS (EP)** *Heavenly HVN 67CD*	**67**	1
2 May 98	**LONG AS I CAN SEE THE LIGHT** *Heavenly HVN 84CD*	**51**	1
16 May 98	SHOOT THE BOSS *Heavenly HVNLP 21CD*	69	1

[1] Monkey Mafia featuring Patra

Tracks on 15 Steps (EP): Lion in the Hall / Krash the Decks: Slaughter the Vinyl / Metro Love / Beats in the Hall.

The MONKS (see also HUDSON-FORD; The STRAWBS)
UK, male vocal / instrumental duo – Richard Hudson and John Ford

21 Apr 79	**NICE LEGS SHAME ABOUT HER FACE** *Carrere CAR 104*	**19**	9

The Monks were Hudson-Ford under a different name.

MONKS AND CHOIRBOYS OF DOWNSIDE ABBEY
UK, male monastic choir (2 Albums: 6 Weeks)

2 Nov 96	THE ABBEY *Virgin VTCD 99*	54	5
3 Jan 98	GREGORIAN MOODS *Virgin / EMI VTCD 171*	59	1

MONKS OF AMPLEFORTH ABBEY *UK, male monastic choir*

17 Jun 95	VISION OF PEACE *Classic FM CFMCD 1783*	73	2

MONO *UK, male / female vocal / instrumental duo*

2 May 98	**LIFE IN MONO** *Echo ECSCD 64*	**60**	1
8 Aug 98	FORMICA BLUES *Echo ECHCD 17*	71	1

MONOBOY featuring DELORES
Ireland, male producer – Ian Masterson and female vocalist

7 Jul 01	**THE MUSIC IN YOU** *Perfecto PERF 18CDS*	**50**	1

The MONOCHROME SET *UK, male vocal / instrumental group*

3 May 80	STRANGE BOUTIQUE *DinDisc DID 4*	62	4

Tony MONOPOLY *Australia, male vocalist*

12 Jun 76	TONY MONOPOLY *BUK BULP 2000*	25	4

Matt MONRO 492 Top 500
UK, male vocalist – Terence Parsons, b. 1 Dec 1932, d. 7 Feb 1985. This former bus conductor was the UK's answer to many of the early 60s American crooners who featured as much on television as they did on record (5 Albums: 25 Weeks, 13 Singles: 127 Weeks)

15 Dec 60 ●	**PORTRAIT OF MY LOVE** *Parlophone R 4714*	3	16
9 Mar 61 ●	**MY KIND OF GIRL** *Parlophone R 4755*	**5**	12
18 May 61	**WHY NOT NOW / CAN THIS BE LOVE** *Parlophone R 4775*	**24**	9
28 Sep 61	**GONNA BUILD A MOUNTAIN** *Parlophone R 4819*	**44**	3
8 Feb 62 ●	**SOFTLY AS I LEAVE YOU** *Parlophone R 4868*	**10**	18
14 Jun 62	**WHEN LOVE COMES ALONG** *Parlophone R 4911*	**46**	3
8 Nov 62	**MY LOVE AND DEVOTION** *Parlophone R 4954*	**29**	5
14 Nov 63	**FROM RUSSIA WITH LOVE** *Parlophone R 5068*	**20**	13
17 Sep 64 ●	**WALK AWAY** *Parlophone R 5171*	**4**	20
24 Dec 64	**FOR MAMA** *Parlophone R 5215*	23	4
25 Mar 65	**WITHOUT YOU** *Parlophone R 5251*	**37**	4
7 Aug 65	I HAVE DREAMED *Parlophone PMC 1250*	20	1
21 Oct 65 ●	**YESTERDAY** *Parlophone R 5348*	**8**	12
17 Sep 66	THIS IS THE LIFE *Capitol T 2540*	25	2
26 Aug 67	INVITATION TO THE MOVIES *Capitol ST 2730*	30	1
24 Nov 73	**AND YOU SMILED** *EMI 2091*	**28**	8
15 Mar 80 ●	HEARTBREAKERS *EMI EMTV 23*	5	11
12 Feb 05 ●	THE ULTIMATE MATT MONRO *EMI 5609392*	7	10

MONROE *UK / Jamaica / Nigeria / Sri Lanka / Morocco, female vocal group*

31 Jul 04	**SMILE** *Zu ZUDB 001*	**60**	1

Gerry MONROE *UK, male vocalist (6 Singles: 57 Weeks)*

23 May 70 ●	**SALLY** *Chapter One CH 122*	**4**	20
19 Sep 70	**CRY** *Chapter One CH 128*	**38**	5
14 Nov 70 ●	**MY PRAYER** *Chapter One CH 132*	**9**	12
17 Apr 71	**IT'S A SIN TO TELL A LIE** *Chapter One CH 144*	**13**	12
21 Aug 71	**LITTLE DROPS OF SILVER** *Chapter One CH 152*	**37**	6
12 Feb 72	**GIRL OF MY DREAMS** *Chapter One CH 159*	**43**	2

Hollis P MONROE *Canada, male producer*

24 Apr 99	**I'M LONELY** *City Beat CBE 778CD*	**51**	1

MONSOON
UK, male / female vocal / instrumental group (2 Singles: 12 Weeks)

3 Apr 82	**EVER SO LONELY** *Mobile Suit Corp CORP 2*	12	9
5 Jun 82	**SHAKTI (THE MEANING OF WITHIN)** *Mobile Suit Corp CORP 4*	**41**	3

MONSTA BOY featuring DENZIE
UK, male production / vocal / instrumental duo

7 Oct 00	**SORRY (I DIDN'T KNOW)** *Locked On LOX 125CD*	**25**	3

MONSTER MAGNET
US, male vocal / instrumental group (2 Albums: 2 Weeks, 5 Singles: 6 Weeks)

29 May 93	**TWIN EARTH** *A&M 5802812*	**67**	1
18 Mar 95	**NEGASONIC TEENAGE WARHEAD** *A&M 5809812*	**49**	1
1 Apr 95	DOPES TO INFINITY *A&M 5403152*	51	1
6 May 95	**DOPES TO INFINITY** *A&M 5810332*	**58**	1
13 Jun 98	POWERTRIP *A&M 5409082*	65	1
23 Jan 99	**POWERTRIP** *A&M 5828232*	39	2
6 Mar 99	**SPACE LORD** *A&M 5632752*	**45**	1

MONTAGE *UK, female vocal trio*

15 Feb 97	**THERE AIN'T NOTHIN' LIKE THE LOVE** *Wildcard 5733172*	**64**	1

MONTANA SEXTET *US, male instrumental group*

15 Jan 83	**HEAVY VIBES** *Virgin VS 560*	**59**	1

8 December 1979	15 December 1979	22 December 1979	29 December 1979
WALKING ON THE MOON The Police	**ANOTHER BRICK IN THE WALL (PART 2)** Pink Floyd	**ANOTHER BRICK IN THE WALL (PART 2)** Pink Floyd	**ANOTHER BRICK IN THE WALL (PART 2)** Pink Floyd
GREATEST HITS Rod Stewart	GREATEST HITS Rod Stewart	GREATEST HITS Rod Stewart	GREATEST HITS Rod Stewart

KEY
UK No.1 ★★ UK Top 10 ●● Still on chart ++ UK entry at No.1 ■■
US No.1 ▲▲ UK million seller £ US million seller $
Singles re-entries are listed as (re), (2re), (3re)… which signifies that the hit re-entered the chart once, twice or three times…
Peak Position / Weeks

MONTANO vs The TRUMPET MAN
UK, male production / instrumental duo

18 Sep 99 **ITZA TRUMPET THING** *Serious SERR 010CD*............ **46** 1

Hugo MONTENEGRO, his Orchestra and Chorus
US, orchestra – leader b. 1 Jan 1925, d. 6 Feb 1981 (2 Singles: 26 Weeks)

11 Sep 68 ★ **THE GOOD, THE BAD AND THE UGLY** (re) *RCA 1727*............ **1** 25
8 Jan 69 **HANG 'EM HIGH** *RCA 1771*............ **50** 1

Chris MONTEZ *US, male vocalist – Ezekiel Montanez (6 Singles: 61 Weeks)*

4 Oct 62 ● **LET'S DANCE** *London HLU 9596* $............ **2** 18
17 Jan 63 ● **SOME KINDA FUN** *London HLU 9650*............ **10** 9
30 Jun 66 ● **THE MORE I SEE YOU** *Pye International 7N 25369*............ **3** 13
22 Sep 66 **THERE WILL NEVER BE ANOTHER YOU** *Pye International 7N 25381*............ **37** 4
14 Oct 72 ● **LET'S DANCE** (re-issue) *London HLU 10205*............ **9** 14
14 Apr 79 **LET'S DANCE** (2nd re-issue) *Lightning LIG 9011*............ **47** 3

The second re-issue of 'Let's Dance' on Lightning was coupled with 'Memphis' by Lonnie Mack as a double A-side.

MONTROSE *US, male vocal / instrumental group*

15 Jun 74 MONTROSE *Warner Bros. K 46276*............ 43 1
28 Jun 80 **SPACE STATION NUMBER 5 / GOOD ROCKIN' TONIGHT** *Warner Bros. WBHM 9*............ **71** 2

MONTROSE AVENUE
UK, male vocal / instrumental group (3 Singles: 4 Weeks)

28 Mar 98 **WHERE DO I STAND?** *Columbia 6656072*............ **38** 2
20 Jun 98 **SHINE** *Columbia 6660012*............ **58** 1
17 Oct 98 **START AGAIN** *Columbia 6664255*............ **59** 1

MONTY PYTHON'S FLYING CIRCUS
(see also Eric IDLE featuring Richard WILSON)
UK, male vocal comedy group (8 Albums: 33 Weeks, 1 Single: 9 Weeks)

30 Oct 71 ANOTHER MONTY PYTHON RECORD *Charisma CAS 1049*............ 26 3
27 Jan 73 MONTY PYTHON'S PREVIOUS ALBUM *Charisma CAS 1063*............ 39 3
23 Feb 74 MATCHING TIE & HANDKERCHIEF *Charisma CAS 1080*............ 49 2
27 Jul 74 MONTY PYTHON LIVE AT DRURY LANE *Charisma CLASS 4*............ 19 8
9 Aug 75 THE ALBUM OF THE SOUNDTRACK OF THE TRAILER OF THE FILM OF MONTY PYTHON AND THE HOLY GRAIL *Charisma CAS 1003*............ 45 4
24 Nov 79 LIFE OF BRIAN *Warner Bros. K 56751*............ 63 3
18 Oct 80 MONTY PYTHON'S CONTRACTUAL OBLIGATION ALBUM *Charisma CAS 1152*............ 13 8
5 Oct 91 ● **ALWAYS LOOK ON THE BRIGHT SIDE OF LIFE** *Virgin PYTH 1* [1]............ **3** 9
16 Nov 91 MONTY PYTHON SINGS *Virgin MONT 1*............ 62 2

[1] Monty Python

MONYAKA *US / Jamaica, male vocal / instrumental group*

10 Sep 83 **GO DEH YAKA (GO TO THE TOP)** *Polydor POSP 641*............ **14** 8

MOOD *UK, male vocal / instrumental group (3 Singles: 10 Weeks)*

6 Feb 82 **DON'T STOP** *RCA 171*............ **59** 4
22 May 82 **PARIS IS ONE DAY AWAY** *RCA 211*............ **42** 5
30 Oct 82 **PASSION IN DARK ROOMS** *RCA 276*............ **74** 1

MOOD II SWING
US, male production / vocal duo – Jon Ciafone and Lem Springsteen

31 Jan 04 **CAN'T GET AWAY** *Defected DFTD 078CDS*............ **45** 2

MOODSWINGS / CHRISSIE HYNDE
(see also The PRETENDERS) *UK, male instrumental group and US, female vocalist / guitarist (2 Singles: 4 Weeks)*

12 Oct 91 **SPIRITUAL HIGH (STATE OF INDEPENDENCE)** *Arista 114528*............ **66** 2
23 Jan 93 **SPIRITUAL HIGH (STATE OF INDEPENDENCE)** (re-mix) *Arista 74321127712*............ **47** 2

The MOODY BLUES (99 Top 500)
Long-lived and internationally popular cosmic rock quintet from Birmingham, UK. Line-up has included Denny Laine (v/g), Ray Thomas (fl/v), Mike Pinder (k/v), Graeme Edge (d), Justin Hayward (v/g) and John Lodge (b/v). This album-orientated act has sold more than 55 million records worldwide (19 Albums: 335 Weeks, 12 Singles: 114 Weeks)

10 Dec 64 ★ **GO NOW** *Decca F 12022*............ **1** 14
4 Mar 65 **I DON'T WANT TO GO ON WITHOUT YOU** *Decca F 12095*............ **33** 9
10 Jun 65 **FROM THE BOTTOM OF MY HEART** *Decca F 12166*............ **22** 9
18 Nov 65 **EVERYDAY** *Decca F 12266*............ **44** 2
27 Dec 67 ● **NIGHTS IN WHITE SATIN** (2re) *Deram DM 161* $............ **9** 34
27 Jan 68 DAYS OF FUTURE PASSED *Deram SML 707*............ 27 16
3 Aug 68 ● IN SEARCH OF THE LOST CHORD *Deram SML 711*............ 5 32
7 Aug 68 **VOICES IN THE SKY** *Deram DM 196*............ **27** 10
4 Dec 68 **RIDE MY SEE-SAW** *Deram DM 213*............ **42** 1
3 May 69 ★ ON THE THRESHOLD OF A DREAM *Deram SML 1035*............ 1 73
6 Dec 69 ● TO OUR CHILDREN'S CHILDREN'S CHILDREN *Threshold THS 1*............ 2 44
2 May 70 ● **QUESTION** *Threshold TH 4*............ **2** 12
15 Aug 70 ★ A QUESTION OF BALANCE *Threshold THS 3*............ 1 19
7 Aug 71 ★ EVERY GOOD BOY DESERVES FAVOUR *Threshold THS 5*............ 1 21
6 May 72 **ISN'T LIFE STRANGE** *Threshold TH 9*............ **13** 10
2 Dec 72 ● SEVENTH SOJOURN *Threshold THS 7* ▲............ 5 18
10 Feb 73 **I'M JUST A SINGER (IN A ROCK & ROLL BAND)** *Threshold TH 13*............ **36** 4
16 Nov 74 THIS IS THE MOODY BLUES *Threshold MB 1/2*............ 14 18
24 Jun 78 ● OCTAVE *Decca TXS 129*............ 6 18
10 Nov 79 OUT OF THIS WORLD *K-Tel NE 1051*............ 15 10
23 May 81 ● LONG DISTANCE VOYAGER *Threshold TXS 139* ▲............ 7 19
20 Aug 83 **BLUE WORLD** *Threshold TH 30*............ **35** 5
10 Sep 83 THE PRESENT *Threshold TXS 140*............ 15 8
10 May 86 THE OTHER SIDE OF LIFE *Threshold POLD 5190*............ 24 6
25 Jun 88 SUR LA MER *Polydor POLH 43*............ 21 5
25 Jun 88 **I KNOW YOU'RE OUT THERE SOMEWHERE** *Polydor POSP 921*............ **52** 4
20 Jan 90 GREATEST HITS *Threshold 8406591*............ 71 1
13 Jul 91 KEYS OF THE KINGDOM *Threshold 8494331*............ 54 2
5 Oct 96 THE VERY BEST OF THE MOODY BLUES *PolyGram TV 5358002*............ 13 15
22 Apr 00 THE VERY BEST OF THE MOODY BLUES (re-issue) / STRANGE TIMES *Universal Music TV 5414242*............ 19 6
11 May 02 THE VERY BEST OF THE MOODY BLUES (2nd re-issue) *UMTV 5833442*............ 27 4

'Nights in White Satin' peaked at No.19 on its original chart visit, No.9 in Dec 1972 and No.14 in Nov 1979. The Very Best of The Moody Blues *(2002) is an expanded version of the 1996 album of the same name.*

Michael MOOG *US, male producer – Shivaun Gaines (2 Singles: 3 Weeks)*

11 Dec 99 **THAT SOUND** *ffrr FCD 374*............ **32** 2
25 Aug 01 **YOU BELONG TO ME** *Strictly Rhythm SRUKECD 04*............ **62** 1

MOOGWAI
Switzerland, male producer - Francois Chabloz (2 Singles: 2 Weeks)

6 May 00 **VIOLA** *Platipus PLATCD 71*............ **55** 1
26 May 01 **THE LABYRINTH** *Platipus PLATCD 83*............ **68** 1

The MOONEY SUZUKI NEW *US, male vocal / instrumental group*

29 Jan 05 **ALIVE & AMPLIFIED** *Columbia SAMMY 138CD*............ **38** 2

MOONMAN (see also ALBION; Ferry CORSTEN; GOURYELLA; STARPARTY; SYSTEM F; VERACOCHA)
Holland, male DJ / producer – Ferry Corsten (3 Singles: 4 Weeks)

9 Aug 97 **DON'T BE AFRAID** *Heat Recordings HEATCD 009*............ **60** 1

5 January 1980	12 January 1980	19 January 1980	26 January 1980
UK No.1 SINGLES			
ANOTHER BRICK IN THE WALL (PART 2) Pink Floyd	ANOTHER BRICK IN THE WALL (PART 2) Pink Floyd	BRASS IN POCKET The Pretenders	BRASS IN POCKET The Pretenders
UK No.1 ALBUMS			
GREATEST HITS Rod Stewart	GREATEST HITS VOLUME 2 Abba	PRETENDERS The Pretenders	PRETENDERS The Pretenders

27 Nov 99 **DON'T BE AFRAID '99** (re-mix) *Heat Recordings HEATCD 022*.....41 2
7 Oct 00 **GALAXIA** *Heat Recordings HEATCD 025* [1] 50 1

[1] Moonman featuring Chantal

The MOONTREKKERS *UK, male instrumental group*

2 Nov 61 **NIGHT OF THE VAMPIRE** *Parlophone R 4814*.....50 1

MOONY (see also DB BOULEVARD)
Italy, female vocalist – Monica Bragato (2 Singles: 9 Weeks)

15 Jun 02 ● **DOVE (I'LL BE LOVING YOU)** *Positiva / Cream CDMNY 1*.....9 8
1 Mar 03 **ACROBATS (LOOKING FOR BALANCE)** *WEA WEA 363CD*.....64 1

Ian MOOR *US, male vocalist / instrumentalist*

7 Oct 00 NATURALLY *BMG TV Projects 74321783862*.....38 2

Chanté MOORE *US, female vocalist (3 Singles: 11 Weeks)*

20 Mar 93 **LOVE'S TAKEN OVER** *MCA MCSTD 1744*.....54 3
4 Mar 95 **FREE / SAIL ON** *MCA MCSTD 2042*.....69 1
7 Apr 01 **STRAIGHT UP** (re) *MCA MCSTD 40250*.....11 7

Christy MOORE *Ireland, male vocalist (4 Albums: 8 Weeks)*

4 May 91 SMOKE AND STRONG WHISKEY *Newberry CM 21*.....49 3
21 Sep 91 THE CHRISTY MOORE COLLECTION *East West WX 434*.....69 1
6 Nov 93 KING PUCK *Equator ATLASCD 003*.....66 2
14 Sep 96 GRAFFITI TONGUE *Grapevine GRACD 215*.....35 2

Dorothy MOORE *US, female vocalist (3 Singles: 24 Weeks)*

19 Jun 76 ● **MISTY BLUE** *Contempo CS 2087*.....5 12
16 Oct 76 **FUNNY HOW TIME SLIPS AWAY** *Contempo CS 2092*.....38 3
15 Oct 77 **I BELIEVE YOU** *Epic EPC 5573*.....20 9

Dudley MOORE
(see also Peter COOK and Dudley MOORE) *UK, male comedian / vocalist / pianist, b. 19 Apr 1935, d. 27 Mar 2002 (3 Albums: 24 Weeks)*

4 Dec 65 THE OTHER SIDE OF DUDLEY MOORE *Decca LK 4732*.....11 9
11 Jun 66 GENUINE DUD *Decca LK 4788*.....13 10
26 Jan 91 ORCHESTRA! *Decca 4308361* [1] 38 5

[1] Sir George Solti and Dudley Moore

Gary MOORE 338 Top 500
(see also BBM) *Noted blues guitarist, b. 4 Apr 1952, Belfast, Northern Ireland. Played in early 1970s Irish band Skid Row (with Phil Lynott), as well as Thin Lizzy and Colosseum II, before successfully launching his solo career (16 Albums: 104 Weeks, 22 Singles: 103 Weeks)*

3 Feb 79 BACK ON THE STREETS *MCA MCF 2853*.....70 1
21 Apr 79 ● **PARISIENNE WALKWAYS** *MCA 419*.....8 11
16 Oct 82 CORRIDORS OF POWER *Virgin V 2245*.....30 6
21 Jan 84 **HOLD ON TO LOVE** *10 TEN 13*.....65 3
18 Feb 84 VICTIMS OF THE FUTURE *10 DIX 2*.....12 7
11 Aug 84 **EMPTY ROOMS** *10 TEN 25*.....51 5
13 Oct 84 WE WANT MOORE! *10 GMDL 1*.....32 3
18 May 85 ● **OUT IN THE FIELDS** *10 TEN 49* [1] 5 10
27 Jul 85 **EMPTY ROOMS** (re-issue) *10 TEN 58*.....23 8
14 Sep 85 RUN FOR COVER *10 DIX 16*.....12 8
12 Jul 86 ROCKIN' EVERY NIGHT *10 XID 1*.....99 1
20 Dec 86 **OVER THE HILLS AND FAR AWAY** *10 TEN 134*.....20 8
28 Feb 87 **WILD FRONTIER** *10 TEN 159*.....35 5
14 Mar 87 ● WILD FRONTIER *10 DIX 56*.....8 14
9 May 87 **FRIDAY ON MY MIND** *10 TEN 164*.....26 6
29 Aug 87 **THE LONER** *10 TEN 178*.....53 5
5 Dec 87 **TAKE A LITTLE TIME (DOUBLE SINGLE)** *10 TEN 190*.....75 1
14 Jan 89 **AFTER THE WAR** *Virgin GMS 1*.....37 4
11 Feb 89 AFTER THE WAR *Virgin V 2575*.....23 5
18 Mar 89 **READY FOR LOVE** *Virgin GMS 2*.....56 2
24 Mar 90 **OH PRETTY WOMAN** *Virgin VS 1233* [2] 48 3
7 Apr 90 STILL GOT THE BLUES *Virgin V 2612*.....13 26
12 May 90 **STILL GOT THE BLUES (FOR YOU)** *Virgin VS 1267*.....31 7
18 Aug 90 **WALKING BY MYSELF** *Virgin VS 1281*.....48 5
15 Dec 90 **TOO TIRED** *Virgin VS 1306*.....71 1
22 Feb 92 **COLD DAY IN HELL** *Virgin VS 1393*.....24 5
21 Mar 92 ● AFTER HOURS *Virgin CDV 2684*.....4 13
9 May 92 **STORY OF THE BLUES** *Virgin VS 1412*.....40 4
18 Jul 92 **SINCE I MET YOU BABY** *Virgin VS 1423* [3] 59 3
24 Oct 92 **SEPARATE WAYS** *Virgin VS 1437*.....59 1
8 May 93 **PARISIENNE WALKWAYS** (re-recording) *Virgin VSCDX 1456*..32 4
22 May 93 ● BLUES ALIVE *Virgin CDVX 2716*.....8 5
26 Nov 94 BALLADS AND BLUES 1982-1994 *Virgin CDV 2768*.....33 6
10 Jun 95 BLUES FOR GREENEY *Virgin CDV 2784*.....14 5
17 Jun 95 **NEED YOUR LOVE SO BAD** *Virgin VSCDG 1546*.....48 2
7 Jun 97 DARK DAYS IN PARADISE *Virgin CDV 2826*.....43 2
31 Oct 98 OUT IN THE FIELDS – THE VERY BEST OF GARY MOORE *Virgin CDVX 2871*.....54 1
24 Mar 01 BACK TO THE BLUES *Sanctuary SANCD 072*.....53 1

[1] Gary Moore and Phil Lynott [2] Gary Moore featuring Albert King
[3] Gary Moore and BB King

'Parisienne Walkways' features uncredited vocals by Phil Lynott. Tracks on Take a Little Time (double single): Take a Little Time / Out in the Fields / All Messed Up / Thunder Rising.

Jackie MOORE *US, female vocalist*

15 Sep 79 **THIS TIME BABY** *CBS 7722*.....49 5

Mandy MOORE *US, female vocalist (1 Album: 1 Week, 2 Singles: 18 Weeks)*

6 May 00 ● **CANDY** *Epic 6693452*.....6 13
20 May 00 I WANNA BE WITH YOU *Epic 4982769*.....52 1
19 Aug 00 **I WANNA BE WITH YOU** *Epic 6695922*.....21 5

Melba MOORE *US, female vocalist – Melba Hill (5 Singles: 29 Weeks)*

15 May 76 ● **THIS IS IT** *Buddah BDS 443*.....9 8
26 May 79 **PICK ME UP, I'LL DANCE** *Epic EPC 7234*.....48 5
9 Oct 82 **LOVE'S COMIN' AT YA** *EMI America EA 146*.....15 8
15 Jan 83 **MIND UP TONIGHT** *Capitol CL 272*.....22 6
5 Mar 83 **UNDERLOVE** *Capitol CL 281*.....60 2

Ray MOORE
UK, male radio DJ / vocalist, b. 1942, d. Jan 1989 (2 Singles: 9 Weeks)

29 Nov 86 **O' MY FATHER HAD A RABBIT** *Play PLAY 213*.....24 7
5 Dec 87 **BOG EYED JOG** *Play PLAY 224*.....61 2

Sam MOORE and LOU REED (see also SAM and DAVE; The VELVET UNDERGROUND) *US, male duo – Sam Moore and Lou Firbank*

17 Jan 87 **SOUL MAN** *A&M AM 364*.....30 10

Tina MOORE *US, female vocalist (2 Singles: 18 Weeks)*

30 Aug 97 ● **NEVER GONNA LET YOU GO** *Delirious 74321511052*.....7 15
25 Apr 98 **NOBODY BETTER** *RCA 74321571612*.....20 3

Lisa MOORISH *UK, female vocalist – Lisa Morrish (4 Singles: 11 Weeks)*

7 Jan 95 **JUST THE WAY IT IS** *Go Beat GODCD 123*.....42 3
19 Aug 95 **I'M YOUR MAN** *Go Beat GODCD 128*.....24 3
3 Feb 96 **MR FRIDAY NIGHT** *Go Beat GODCD 137*.....24 3
18 May 96 **LOVE FOR LIFE** *Go Beat GODCD 145*.....37 2

'I'm Your Man' features the uncredited vocals of George Michael.

Angel MORAES *US, male producer (2 Singles: 2 Weeks)*

16 Nov 96 **HEAVEN KNOWS – DEEP DEEP DOWN** *ffrr FCD 282*.....72 1
17 May 97 **I LIKE IT** *AM:PM 5871792*.....70 1

David MORALES (see also BOSS; PULSE featuring Antoinette ROBERSON) *US, male DJ / producer (7 Singles: 22 Weeks)*

10 Jul 93 **GIMME LUV (EENIE MEENIE MINY MO)** *Mercury MERCD 390* [1] 37 3

2 February 1980	9 February 1980	16 February 1980	23 February 1980
THE SPECIAL A.K.A. LIVE! EP The Specials	THE SPECIAL A.K.A. LIVE! EP The Specials	COWARD OF THE COUNTY Kenny Rogers	COWARD OF THE COUNTY Kenny Rogers
PRETENDERS The Pretenders	PRETENDERS The Pretenders	THE LAST DANCE Various	THE LAST DANCE Various

KEY: UK No.1 ★ UK Top 10 ● Still on chart + UK entry at No.1 ■ US No.1 ▲ UK million seller £ US million seller $ Singles re-entries are listed as (re), (2re), (3re)… which signifies that the hit re-entered the chart once, twice or three times… | Peak Position | Weeks

20 Nov 93 **THE PROGRAM** *Mercury MERCD 396* [1] 66 1
24 Aug 96 **IN DE GHETTO** *Manifesto FESCD 12* [2] 35 2
15 Aug 98 ● **NEEDIN' U** *Manifesto FESCD 46* [3] 8 8
24 Jun 00 **HIGHER** *Azuli AZNYCDX 120* [4] 41 2
20 Jan 01 **NEEDIN' U II** *Manifesto FESCD 78* [5] 11 5
2 Oct 04 **HOW WOULD U FEEL** *DMI DMI 01* [6] 71 1

[1] David Morales and The Bad Yard Club [2] David Morales and The Bad Yard Club featuring Crystal Waters and Delta [3] David Morales presents The Face [4] David Morales and Albert Cabrera present Moca featuring Deanna [5] David Morales presents The Face featuring Juliet Roberts [6] David Morales featuring Lea Lorien

Patrick MORAZ (see also YES)
Switzerland, male keyboard player (2 Albums: 8 Weeks)

10 Apr 76 PATRICK MORAZ *Charisma CDS 4002* 28 7
23 Jul 77 OUT IN THE SUN *Charisma CDS 4007* 44 1

MORCHEEBA *UK, male / female vocal (Skye Edwards) / instrumental group (6 Albums: 112 Weeks, 10 Singles: 14 Weeks)*

13 Jul 96 **TAPE LOOP** *Indochina ID 045CD* 42 1
5 Oct 96 **TRIGGER HIPPIE** *Indochina ID 052CD* 40 2
15 Feb 97 **THE MUSIC THAT WE HEAR (MOOG ISLAND)** *Indochina ID 054CD* 47 1
12 Apr 97 WHO CAN YOU TRUST? *Indochina ZEN 009CD* 57 3
11 Oct 97 **SHOULDER HOLSTER** *Indochina ID 064CD* 53 1
28 Mar 98 BIG CALM *Indochina ZEN 017CD* 18 71
11 Apr 98 **BLINDFOLD** *Indochina ID 070CD* 56 1
20 Jun 98 **LET ME SEE** *Indochina ID 076CD* 46 1
29 Aug 98 **PART OF THE PROCESS** *China WOKCD 2097* 38 2
22 Jul 00 ● FRAGMENTS OF FREEDOM *East West 8573836022* 6 14
5 Aug 00 **ROME WASN'T BUILT IN A DAY** *East West EW 214CD* 34 3
31 Mar 01 **WORLD LOOKING IN** *East West EW 225CD* 48 1
6 Jul 02 **OTHERWISE** *East West EW 247CD* 64 1
13 Jul 02 ● CHARANGO *East West 927469632* 7 8
12 Jul 03 ● PARTS OF THE PROCESS *East West 5046658702* 6 12
21 May 05 THE ANTIDOTE *Echo ECHCD 65* 17 4

MORDRED *UK, male vocal / instrumental group*

16 Feb 91 IN THIS LIFE *Noise International NO 1591* 70 1

MORE *UK, male vocal / instrumental group*

14 Mar 81 **WE ARE THE BAND** *Atlantic K 11561* 59 2

MORE FIRE CREW (see also LETHAL BIZZLE)
UK, male vocal / rap / production trio – includes Lethal B (2 Singles: 10 Weeks)

16 Mar 02 ● **OI!** *Go Beat GOBCD 48* [1] 8 8
25 Jan 03 **BACK THEN** *Go Beat GOBCD 54* 45 2

[1] Platinum 45 featuring More Fire Crew

MOREL *US, male vocalist / producer – Richard Morel*

12 Aug 00 **TRUE (THE FAGGOT IS YOU)** *Hooj Choons HOOJ 097CD* 64 1

George MOREL featuring Heather WILDMAN
US, male / female vocal / instrumental duo

26 Oct 96 **LET'S GROOVE** *Positiva CDTIV 62* 42 2

MORGAN *UK, male vocal / instrumental duo*

27 Nov 99 **MISS PARKER** *Source CDSOUR 002* 74 1

Debelah MORGAN *US, female vocalist*

24 Feb 01 ● **DANCE WITH ME** *Atlantic AT 0087CD* 10 9

Derrick MORGAN *Jamaica, male vocalist*

17 Jan 70 **MOON HOP** *Crab 32* 49 1

Jamie J MORGAN *US, male vocalist*

10 Feb 90 **WALK ON THE WILD SIDE** *Tabu 655596 7* 27 6

Jane MORGAN *US, female vocalist – Jane Currier (3 Singles: 22 Weeks)*

5 Dec 58 ★ **THE DAY THE RAINS CAME** *London HLR 8751* 1 16
22 May 59 **IF ONLY I COULD LIVE MY LIFE AGAIN** *London HLR 8810* 27 1
21 Jul 60 **ROMANTICA** *London HLR 9120* 39 5

Meli'sa MORGAN *US, female vocalist (2 Singles: 7 Weeks)*

9 Aug 86 **FOOL'S PARADISE** *Capitol CL 415* 41 5
25 Jun 88 **GOOD LOVE** *Capitol CL 483* 59 2

Ray MORGAN *UK, male vocalist*

25 Jul 70 **THE LONG AND WINDING ROAD** *B&C CB 128* 32 6

Erick MORILLO (see also LIL MO' YIN YANG; PIANOHEADZ; REAL TO REEL) *US, male DJ / producer / instrumentalist (3 Singles: 4 Weeks)*

4 Feb 95 **HIGHER (FEEL IT)** *A&M 5809412* [1] 74 1
26 Jun 04 **BREAK DOWN THE DOORS** *Subliminal SUB 124CD* [2] 44 2
12 Feb 05 **WHAT DO YOU WANT** *Subliminal SUB 138CD* [3] 61 1

[1] Erick 'More' Morillo presents RAW [2] Morillo featuring Audio Bullys [3] Morillo featuring Terra Deva

Alanis MORISSETTE (224 Top 500) *Internationally successful, frank and rebellious Canadian singer / songwriter, b. 1 Jun 1974, Ottawa. The child prodigy's BRIT and Grammy-winning, 30 million-selling Jagged Little Pill became the first album by a female to simultaneously top the US and UK charts (7 Albums: 220 Weeks, 14 Singles: 58 Weeks)*

5 Aug 95 **YOU OUGHTA KNOW** *Maverick W 0307CD* 22 7
26 Aug 95 ★ JAGGED LITTLE PILL *Maverick 9362459012* ▲ 1 172
28 Oct 95 **HAND IN MY POCKET** *Maverick W 0312CD* 26 3
24 Feb 96 **YOU LEARN** *Maverick W 0334CD* 24 4
20 Apr 96 **IRONIC** *Maverick W 0343CD* 11 9
3 Aug 96 ● **HEAD OVER FEET** *Maverick W 0355CD* 7 7
7 Dec 96 **ALL I REALLY WANT** *Maverick W 0382CD* 59 1
31 Oct 98 ● **THANK U** *Maverick W 0458CD* 5 10
14 Nov 98 ● SUPPOSED FORMER INFATUATION JUNKIE *Maverick 9362470942* ▲ 3 21
13 Mar 99 **JOINING YOU** *Maverick W 472CD1* 28 2
31 Jul 99 **SO PURE** *Maverick W 492CD1* 38 2
4 Dec 99 MTV UNPLUGGED *Maverick 9362475892* 56 5
2 Mar 02 **HANDS CLEAN** *Maverick W 574CD* 12 7
16 Mar 02 ● UNDER RUG SWEPT *Maverick 9362482722* ▲ 2 10
17 Aug 02 **PRECIOUS ILLUSIONS** *Maverick W 582CD* 53 1
22 May 04 **EVERYTHING** *Maverick W 641CD1* 22 3
29 May 04 ● SO-CALLED CHAOS *Maverick / Warner Bros. 9362487732* 8 4
31 Jul 04 **OUT IS THROUGH** *Maverick W 647CD1* 56 1
6 Aug 05 JAGGED LITTLE PILL ACOUSTIC *Maverick 9362493452* 12 6
12 Nov 05 **CRAZY** *Maverick W 694CD2* 65 1
26 Nov 05 THE COLLECTION *Maverick 9362494902* 44 2

MORJAC featuring Raz CONWAY
Denmark, male production duo and vocalist

11 Oct 03 **STARS** *Credence CDCRED 036* 38 2

MORNING RUNNER NEW
UK, male vocal / instrumental group (3 Singles: 4 Weeks)

4 Jun 05 **DRAWING SHAPES (EP)** *Parlophone CDR 6666* 70 1

13 Aug 05 **GONE UP IN FLAMES** *Parlophone CDRS 6669*..........39 2
5 Nov 05 **BE ALL YOU WANT ME TO BE** *Parlophone CDR 6674*..........44 1

Tracks on Drawing Shapes (EP): Work / Hold Your Breath / It's Not Like Everyone's My Friend.

Giorgio MORODER

Italy, male producer / synths player** (1 Album: 5 Weeks,* ***6 Singles: 36 Weeks)

24 Sep 77 **FROM HERE TO ETERNITY** *Oasis 1* [1]..........16 10
17 Mar 79 **CHASE** *Casablanca CAN 144*..........48 6
22 Sep 84 ● **TOGETHER IN ELECTRIC DREAMS** *Virgin VS 713* [2]..........3 13
29 Jun 85 **GOOD-BYE BAD TIMES** *Virgin VS 772* [3]..........44 5
10 Aug 85 PHILIP OAKEY AND GIORGIO MORODER *Virgin V 2351* [1]..........52 5
11 Jul 98 **CARRY ON** *Almighty CDALMY 120* [4]..........65 1
12 Feb 00 **THE CHASE** (re-recording) *Logic 74321732112* [5]..........46 1

[1] Giorgio [2] Giorgio Moroder and Phil Oakey [3] Philip Oakey and Giorgio Moroder [4] Donna Summer and Giorgio Moroder [5] DJ Empire presents Giorgio Moroder [1] Philip Oakey and Giorgio Moroder

Ennio MORRICONE

Italy, orchestra** (5 Albums: 17 Weeks,* ***1 Single: 12 Weeks)

11 Apr 81 ● **CHI MAI (THEME FROM THE TV SERIES 'THE LIFE AND TIMES OF DAVID LLOYD GEORGE')** *BBC RESL 92*..........2 12
2 May 81 THIS IS ENNIO MORRICONE *EMI THIS 33*..........23 5
9 May 81 CHI MAI *BBC REH 414*..........29 6
7 Mar 87 THE MISSION (FILM SOUNDTRACK) *Virgin V 2402* [1]..........73 4
30 Sep 00 THE VERY BEST OF ENNIO MORRICONE *Virgin CDV 2929*..........48 1
10 Apr 04 MOVIE MASTERPIECES *BMG 82876596932*..........69 1

[1] Ennio Morricone and the London Philharmonic Orchestra

Mark MORRISON *UK, male vocalist – Abdul Rahman*

(2 Albums: 39 Weeks, ***10 Singles: 69 Weeks)***

22 Apr 95 **CRAZY** *WEA YZ 907CD*..........19 4
16 Sep 95 **LET'S GET DOWN** *WEA WEA 001CD*..........39 2
16 Mar 96 ★ **RETURN OF THE MACK** (re) *WEA WEA 040CD* $..........1 24
4 May 96 ● RETURN OF THE MACK *WEA 630145862*..........4 38
27 Jul 96 ● **CRAZY** (re) (re-mix) *WEA WEA 054CD1*..........6 9
19 Oct 96 ● **TRIPPIN'** *WEA WEA 079CD1*..........8 6
21 Dec 96 ● **HORNY** *WEA WEA 090CD1*..........5 9
15 Mar 97 ● **MOAN & GROAN** *WEA WEA 096CD1*..........7 6
20 Sep 97 **WHO'S THE MACK!** *WEA WEA 128CD1*..........13 5
27 Sep 97 ONLY GOD CAN JUDGE ME *WEA 630195392*..........50 1
4 Sep 99 **BEST FRIEND** *WEA WEA 221CD1* [1]..........23 3
14 Aug 04 **JUST A MAN / BACKSTABBERS** *2 Wikid WKDCD 007*..........48 1

[1] Mark Morrison and Conner Reeves

Van MORRISON (194 Top 500)

(see also Linda Gail LEWIS; THEM) ***Critically acclaimed singer / songwriter who has amassed many international hits over five decades, b. 31 Aug 1945, Belfast, Northern Ireland. Received an Outstanding Contribution BRIT award (1994) and OBE (1996) and 'Brown Eyed Girl' achieved more than seven million radio plays Stateside but never charted in the UK. Similarly, Astral Weeks is regarded as one of the greatest ever albums by critics but failed to chart here*** *(31 Albums: 283 Weeks,* ***11 Singles: 21 Weeks)***

18 Apr 70 MOONDANCE *Warner Bros. WS 1835*..........32 2
13 Feb 71 VAN MORRISON, HIS BAND AND THE STREET CHOIR *Warner Bros. WS 1884*..........18 6
11 Aug 73 HARD NOSE THE HIGHWAY *Warner Bros. K 46242*..........22 3
16 Nov 74 VEEDON FLEECE *Warner Bros. K 56068*..........41 1
7 May 77 A PERIOD OF TRANSITION *Warner Bros. K 56322*..........23 5
21 Oct 78 WAVELENGTH *Warner Bros. K 56526*..........27 6
8 Sep 79 INTO THE MUSIC *Vertigo 9120 852*..........21 9
20 Oct 79 **BRIGHT SIDE OF THE ROAD** *Mercury 6001 121*..........63 3
20 Sep 80 THE COMMON ONE *Mercury 6302 021*..........53 3
27 Feb 82 BEAUTIFUL VISION *Mercury 6302 122*..........31 14
26 Mar 83 INARTICULATE SPEECH OF THE HEART *Mercury MERL 16*..........14 8
3 Mar 84 LIVE AT THE GRAND OPERA HOUSE BELFAST *Mercury MERL 36*..........47 4
9 Feb 85 A SENSE OF WONDER *Mercury MERH 54*..........25 5
2 Aug 86 NO GURU NO METHOD NO TEACHER *Mercury MERH 94*..........27 5
19 Sep 87 POETIC CHAMPIONS COMPOSE *Mercury MERH 110*..........26 6
2 Jul 88 IRISH HEARTBEAT *Mercury MERH 124* [1]..........18 7
10 Jun 89 AVALON SUNSET *Polydor 839262 1*..........13 14
1 Jul 89 **HAVE I TOLD YOU LATELY** *Polydor VANS 1*..........74 1
9 Dec 89 **WHENEVER GOD SHINES HIS LIGHT** *Polydor VANS 2* [1]..........20 6
7 Apr 90 ● THE BEST OF VAN MORRISON *Polydor 8419701*..........4 87
20 Oct 90 ● ENLIGHTENMENT *Polydor 8471001*..........5 14
21 Sep 91 ● HYMNS TO THE SILENCE *Polydor 8490261*..........5 6
27 Feb 93 THE BEST OF VAN MORRISON VOLUME 2 *Polydor 5177602*..........31 3
15 May 93 **GLORIA** *Exile VANCD 11* [2]..........31 3
12 Jun 93 ● TOO LONG IN EXILE *Exile 5192192*..........4 9
30 Apr 94 ● A NIGHT IN SAN FRANCISCO *Polydor 5212902*..........8 5
18 Mar 95 **HAVE I TOLD YOU LATELY THAT I LOVE YOU** (re-recording) *RCA 74321271702* [3]..........71 1
10 Jun 95 **DAYS LIKE THIS** *Exile VANCD 12*..........65 1
24 Jun 95 ● DAYS LIKE THIS *Exile 5273072*..........5 15
2 Dec 95 **NO RELIGION** *Exile 5775792*..........54 1
1 Mar 97 **THE HEALING GAME** *Exile 5733912*..........46 1
15 Mar 97 ● THE HEALING GAME *Exile 5371012*..........10 7
27 Jun 98 THE PHILOSOPHER'S STONE *Exile 5317892*..........20 3
6 Mar 99 **PRECIOUS TIME** *Pointblank / Virgin POBD 14*..........36 2
20 Mar 99 BACK ON TOP *Pointblank VPBCD 50*..........11 16
22 May 99 **BACK ON TOP** *Exile / Pointblank / Virgin POBD 15*..........69 1
29 Jan 00 THE SKIFFLE SESSIONS – LIVE IN BELFAST *Venture CDVE 945* [2]..........14 3
7 Oct 00 YOU WIN AGAIN *Pointblank VPBCD 54* [3]..........34 2
18 May 02 **HEY MR DJ** *Polydor / Exile 5705962*..........58 1
25 May 02 ● DOWN THE ROAD *Exile 5891772*..........6 6
1 Nov 03 WHAT'S WRONG WITH THIS PICTURE *Blue Note 5901672*..........43 2
28 May 05 ● MAGIC TIME *Exile 9870945*..........3 7

[1] Van Morrison with Cliff Richard [2] Van Morrison and John Lee Hooker [3] The Chieftains with Van Morrison [1] Van Morrison and The Chieftains [2] Van Morrison / Lonnie Donegan / Chris Barber [3] Van Morrison and Linda Gail Lewis

MORRISSEY (407 Top 500)

Witty, often provocative vocalist / lyricist, b. Steven Morrissey, 22 May 1959, Manchester, UK, who has now had more Top 20 singles and albums as a solo artist than as leader of the legendary Smiths. He was awarded the prestigious Nordoff-Robbins Silver Clef Award in 2004 for "his amazing contribution to music" *(12 Albums: 77 Weeks,* ***29 Singles: 98 Weeks)***

27 Feb 88 ● **SUEDEHEAD** *HMV POP 1618*..........5 6
26 Mar 88 ★ VIVA HATE *HMV CSD 3787* ■..........1 20
11 Jun 88 ● **EVERYDAY IS LIKE SUNDAY** *HMV POP 1619*..........9 6
11 Feb 89 ● **LAST OF THE FAMOUS INTERNATIONAL PLAYBOYS** *HMV POP 1620*..........6 5
29 Apr 89 ● **INTERESTING DRUG** *HMV POP 1621*..........9 4
25 Nov 89 **OUIJA BOARD OUIJA BOARD** *HMV POP 1622*..........18 4
5 May 90 **NOVEMBER SPAWNED A MONSTER** *HMV POP 1623*..........12 4
20 Oct 90 **PICCADILLY PALARE** *HMV POP 1624*..........18 2
27 Oct 90 ● BONA DRAG *HMV CLP 3788*..........9 4
23 Feb 91 **OUR FRANK** *HMV POP 1625*..........26 3
16 Mar 91 ● KILL UNCLE *HMV CSD 3789*..........8 4
13 Apr 91 **SING YOUR LIFE** *HMV POP 1626*..........33 2
27 Jul 91 **PREGNANT FOR THE LAST TIME** *HMV POP 1627*..........25 4
12 Oct 91 **MY LOVE LIFE** *HMV POP 1628*..........29 2
9 May 92 **WE HATE IT WHEN OUR FRIENDS BECOME SUCCESSFUL** *HMV POP 1629*..........17 3
18 Jul 92 **YOU'RE THE ONE FOR ME, FATTY** *HMV POP 1630*..........19 3
8 Aug 92 ● YOUR ARSENAL *HMV CDCSD 3790*..........4 5
19 Dec 92 **CERTAIN PEOPLE I KNOW** *HMV POP 1631*..........35 4
22 May 93 BEETHOVEN WAS DEAF *HMV CDCSD 3791*..........13 2
12 Mar 94 ● **THE MORE YOU IGNORE ME THE CLOSER I GET** *Parlophone CDR 6372*..........8 3
26 Mar 94 ★ VAUXHALL AND I *Parlophone CDPCSD 148* ■..........1 5
11 Jun 94 **HOLD ON TO YOUR FRIENDS** *Parlophone CDR 6383*..........47 2
20 Aug 94 **INTERLUDE** *Parlophone CDR 6365* [1]..........25 2

29 March 1980	5 April 1980	12 April 1980	19 April 1980
GOING UNDERGROUND / DREAMS OF CHILDREN The Jam	**GOING UNDERGROUND / DREAMS OF CHILDREN** The Jam	**WORKING MY WAY BACK TO YOU - FORGIVE ME GIRL (MEDLEY)** The Detroit Spinners	**WORKING MY WAY BACK TO YOU - FORGIVE ME GIRL (MEDLEY)** The Detroit Spinners
TEARS AND LAUGHTER Johnny Mathis	**DUKE** Genesis	**DUKE** Genesis	**GREATEST HITS** Rose Royce

KEY UK No.1 ★ UK Top 10 ● Still on chart + UK entry at No.1 ■ US No.1 ▲ UK million seller £ US million seller $
Singles re-entries are listed as (re), (2re), (3re)… which signifies that the hit re-entered the chart once, twice or three times… Peak Position Weeks

28 Jan 95	**BOXERS** *Parlophone CDR 6400*	23	3
18 Feb 95	WORLD OF MORRISSEY *Parlophone CDPCSD 163*	15	2
2 Sep 95	**DAGENHAM DAVE** *RCA Victor 74321299802*	26	2
9 Sep 95 ●	SOUTHPAW GRAMMAR *RCA Victor 74321299532*	4	3
9 Dec 95	**THE BOY RACER** *RCA Victor 74321332952*	36	2
23 Dec 95	**SUNNY** *Parlophone CDR 6243*	42	2
2 Aug 97	**ALMA MATTERS** *Island CID 667*	16	3
23 Aug 97 ●	MALADJUSTED *Island CID 8059*	8	3
20 Sep 97	THE BEST OF MORRISSEY – 'SUEDEHEAD' *EMI CDEMC 3771*	25	9
18 Oct 97	**ROY'S KEEN** *Island CID 671*	42	1
10 Jan 98	**SATAN REJECTED MY SOUL** *Island CID 686*	39	2
22 May 04 ●	**IRISH BLOOD, ENGLISH HEART** *Attack ATKXS 002*	3	5
29 May 04 ●	YOU ARE THE QUARRY *Attack ATKDX 001*	2	18
24 Jul 04 ●	**FIRST OF THE GANG TO DIE** *Attack ATKXS 003*	6	7
23 Oct 04 ●	**LET ME KISS YOU** *Attack ATKXD 008*	8	3
25 Dec 04 ●	**I HAVE FORGIVEN JESUS** *Attack ATKXD 011*	10	5
9 Apr 05	**REDONDO BEACH / THERE IS A LIGHT THAT NEVER GOES OUT** *Attack ATKXD 015*	11	4
16 Apr 05	LIVE AT EARLS COURT *Attack ATKCD 014*	18	2

[1] Morrissey and Siouxsie

The Best of Morrissey – 'Suedehead' reached its peak position in 2004.

MORRISSEY MULLEN
UK, male vocal / instrumental duo (3 Albums: 11 Weeks)

18 Jul 81	BADNESS *Beggars Banquet BEGA 27*	43	5
3 Apr 82	LIFE ON THE WIRE *Beggars Banquet BEGA 33*	47	5
23 Apr 83	IT'S ABOUT TIME *Beggars Banquet BEGA 44*	95	1

Buddy MORROW *US, orchestra – leader Muni Zudecoff*

20 Mar 53	**NIGHT TRAIN** *HMV B 10347*	12	1

MORTIIS *Norway, male vocal / instrumental group (2 Singles: 2 Weeks)*

28 Aug 04	**THE GRUDGE** *Earache MOSH 284CD*	51	1
7 May 05	**DECADENT & DESPERATE** *Earache MOSH 306CD*	49	1

MOS DEF
US, male rapper – Dante Smith (1 Album: 1 Week, 3 Singles: 6 Weeks)

24 Jun 00	**UMI SAYS** *Rawkus RWK 232CD*	60	1
4 Nov 00	**MISS FAT BOOTY – PART II** *Rawkus RWK 282CD* [1]	64	1
3 Feb 01	**OH NO** *Rawkus RWK 302* [2]	24	4
30 Oct 04	THE NEW DANGER *Geffen 9864634*	56	1

[1] Mos Def featuring Ghostface Killah [2] Mos Def and Nate Dogg featuring Pharoahe Monch

Mickie MOST *UK, male vocalist, b. 20 Jun 1938, d. 30 May 2003*

25 Jul 63	**MR PORTER** *Decca F 11664*	45	1

The MOTELS
US / UK, male / female vocal / instrumental group (2 Singles: 7 Weeks)

11 Oct 80	**WHOSE PROBLEM?** *Capitol CL 16162*	42	4
10 Jan 81	**DAYS ARE O.K.** *Capitol CL 16149*	41	3

Wendy MOTEN
US, female vocalist (1 Album: 2 Weeks, 2 Singles: 13 Weeks)

5 Feb 94 ●	**COME IN OUT OF THE RAIN** *EMI-USA CDMT 105*	8	9
19 Mar 94	WENDY MOTEN *EMI CDMTL 1073*	42	2
14 May 94	**SO CLOSE TO LOVE** *EMI-USA CDMTS 106*	35	4

MOTHER *UK, male instrumental / production duo – Jools Brettle and Lee Fisher (3 Singles: 4 Weeks)*

12 Jun 93	**ALL FUNKED UP** *Bosting BYSNCD 101*	34	2
1 Oct 94	**GET BACK** *Six6 SIXT 119*	73	1
31 Aug 96	**ALL FUNKED UP** (re-mix) *Six6 SIXXCD 1*	66	1

MOTHER EARTH *UK, male vocal / instrumental group*

5 Mar 94	THE PEOPLE TREE *Acid Jazz JAZIDCD 083*	45	2

The MOTHERS OF INVENTION (see also Frank ZAPPA)
US, male vocal / instrumental group (3 Albums: 12 Weeks)

29 Jun 68	WE'RE ONLY IN IT FOR THE MONEY *Verve SVLP 9199*	32	5
28 Mar 70	BURNT WEENY SANDWICH *Reprise RSLP 6370*	17	3
3 Oct 70	WEASELS RIPPED MY FLESH *Reprise RSLP 2028*	28	4

MOTHER'S PRIDE *UK, male DJ / production duo (2 Singles: 2 Weeks)*

21 Mar 98	**FLORIBUNDA** *Heat Recordings HEATCD 013*	42	1
6 Nov 99	**LEARNING TO FLY** *Devolution DEVR 001CDS*	54	1

MOTIV 8 *UK, male producer – Steve Rodway (5 Singles: 11 Weeks)*

17 Jul 93	**ROCKIN' FOR MYSELF** *Nuff Respect NUFF 002CD* [1]	67	1
7 May 94	**ROCKIN' FOR MYSELF** (re-mix) *WEA YZ 814CD*	18	4
21 Oct 95	**BREAK THE CHAIN** *Eternal WEA 010CD*	31	2
23 Dec 95	**SEARCHING FOR THE GOLDEN EYE** *Eternal WEA 027CD* [2]	40	3
19 Feb 05	**RIDING ON THE WINGS** *Concept CDCON 52X*	44	1

[1] Motiv 8 featuring Angie Brown [2] Motiv 8 and Kym Mazelle

Jocelyn Brown is uncredited vocalist on 'Riding on the Wings'.

MOTIVATION *Holland, male producer – Francis Louwers*

17 Nov 01	**PARA MI** *Definitive CDDEF 1*	71	1

MÖTLEY CRÜE (see also Vince NEIL) *US, male vocal / instrumental group (6 Albums: 28 Weeks, 11 Singles: 29 Weeks)*

13 Jul 85	THEATRE OF PAIN *Elektra EKT 8*	36	3
24 Aug 85	**SMOKIN' IN THE BOYS ROOM** *Elektra EKR 16*	71	2
8 Feb 86	**HOME SWEET HOME / SMOKIN' IN THE BOYS ROOM** (re-issue) *Elektra EKR 33*	51	3
30 May 87	GIRLS GIRLS GIRLS *Elektra EKT 39*	14	11
1 Aug 87	**GIRLS, GIRLS, GIRLS** *Elektra EKR 59*	26	6
16 Jan 88	**YOU'RE ALL I NEED / WILD SIDE** *Elektra EKR 65*	23	4
16 Sep 89 ●	DR. FEELGOOD *Elektra EKT 59* ▲	4	7
4 Nov 89	**DR FEELGOOD** *Elektra EKR 97*	50	3
12 May 90	**WITHOUT YOU** *Elektra EKR 109*	39	3
7 Sep 91	**PRIMAL SCREAM** *Elektra EKR 133*	32	2
19 Oct 91	DECADE OF DECADENCE '81-'91 *Elektra EKT 95*	20	3
11 Jan 92	**HOME SWEET HOME** (re-mix) *Elektra EKR 136*	37	2
5 Mar 94	**HOOLIGAN'S HOLIDAY** *Elektra EKR 180CDX*	36	2
26 Mar 94	MÖTLEY CRÜE *Elektra 7559615342*	17	2
19 Jul 97	**AFRAID** *Elektra E 3936CD 1*	58	1
4 Jun 05	**IF I DIE TOMORROW** *Mercury 9871754*	63	1
11 Jun 05	RED, WHITE & CRUE *Universal 9871160*	67	2

'Wild Side' listed with 'You're All I Need' only from 30 Jan 1988. It peaked at No.26.

MOTORCYCLE *US, male / female production / vocal trio*

17 Jan 04	**AS THE RUSH COMES** *Positiva CDTIVS 203*	11	9

MOTÖRHEAD (379 Top 500)
Unashamedly loud mainstays of UK heavy rock who formed in 1975 after Lemmy (v/b), b. Ian Willis (later changed to Ian Kilmister), 24 Dec 1945, Stoke-on-Trent, left Hawkwind. Much admired in punk circles, they helped to pave the way for 1980s heavy metal bands such as Metallica. The track 'Whiplash' won them a Grammy in 2005 (16 Albums: 103 Weeks, 18 Singles: 81 Weeks)

24 Sep 77	MOTÖRHEAD *Chiswick WIK 2*	43	5
16 Sep 78	**LOUIE LOUIE** (re) *Bronze BRO 60*	68	2

26 April 1980	3 May 1980	10 May 1980	17 May 1980
◂◂ UK No.1 SINGLES ▸▸			
CALL ME Blondie	**GENO** Dexy's Midnight Runners	**GENO** Dexy's Midnight Runners	**WHAT'S ANOTHER YEAR** Johnny Logan
◂◂ UK No.1 ALBUMS ▸▸			
GREATEST HITS Rose Royce	**SKY 2** Sky	**SKY 2** Sky	**THE MAGIC OF BONEY M - 20 GOLDEN HITS** Boney M

10 Mar 79 **OVERKILL** (re) *Bronze BRO 67* 39 7
24 Mar 79 OVERKILL *Bronze BRON 515* 24 11
30 Jun 79 **NO CLASS** *Bronze BRO 78* 61 4
27 Oct 79 BOMBER *Bronze BRON 523* 12 13
1 Dec 79 **BOMBER** *Bronze BRO 85* 34 7
8 Dec 79 ON PAROLE *United Artists LBR 1004* 65 2
3 May 80 ● **THE GOLDEN YEARS (EP)** *Bronze BRO 92* 8 7
1 Nov 80 **ACE OF SPADES** *Bronze BRO 106* 15 12
8 Nov 80 ● ACE OF SPADES *Bronze BRON 531* 4 16
22 Nov 80 **BEER DRINKERS AND HELL RAISERS** *Big Beat SWT 61* 43 4
21 Feb 81 ● **ST VALENTINE'S DAY MASSACRE (EP)** *Bronze BRO 116* [1] 5 8
27 Jun 81 ★ NO SLEEP 'TIL HAMMERSMITH *Bronze BRON 535* ■ 1 21
11 Jul 81 ● **MOTÖRHEAD (LIVE)** *Bronze BRO 124* 6 7
3 Apr 82 **IRON FIST** *Bronze BRO 146* 29 5
17 Apr 82 ● IRON FIST *Bronze BRNA 539* 6 9
26 Feb 83 WHAT'S WORDS WORTH *Big Beat NED 2* 71 2
21 May 83 **I GOT MINE** *Bronze BRO 165* 46 2
4 Jun 83 ANOTHER PERFECT DAY *Bronze BRON 546* 20 4
30 Jul 83 **SHINE** *Bronze BRO 167* 59 2
1 Sep 84 **KILLED BY DEATH** *Bronze BRO 185* 51 2
15 Sep 84 NO REMORSE *Bronze PROTV MOTOR 1* 14 6
5 Jul 86 **DEAF FOREVER** *GWR GWR 2* 67 1
9 Aug 86 ORGASMATRON *GWR GWLP 1* 21 4
5 Sep 87 ROCK 'N' ROLL *GWR GWLP 14* 34 3
15 Oct 88 NO SLEEP AT ALL *GWR GWR 31* 79 1
5 Jan 91 **THE ONE TO SING THE BLUES** *Epic 6565787* 45 3
2 Feb 91 1916 *Epic 4674811* 24 4
8 Aug 92 MARCH OR DIE *Epic 4717232* 60 1
14 Nov 92 **'92 TOUR (EP)** *Epic 6588096* 63 1
11 Sep 93 **ACE OF SPADES** *WGAF CDWGAF 101* 23 5
10 Dec 94 **BORN TO RAISE HELL** *Fox 74321230152* [2] 47 2
9 Sep 00 THE BEST OF MOTÖRHEAD *Metal Is MISDD 002* 52 1

[1] Motörhead and Girlschool (also known as Headgirl) [2] Motörhead / Ice-T / Whitfield Crane

Tracks on The Golden Years (EP): Dead Men Tell No Tales / Too Late Too Late / Leaving Here / Stone Dead Forever. Tracks on St Valentine's Day Massacre (EP): Please Don't Touch / Emergency / Bomber. Tracks on '92 Tour (EP): Hellraiser / You Better Run / Going to Brazil / Ramones.

The MOTORS

UK, male vocal / instrumental group (2 Albums: 6 Weeks, 4 Singles: 29 Weeks)

24 Sep 77 **DANCING THE NIGHT AWAY** *Virgin VS 186* 42 4
15 Oct 77 THE MOTORS *Virgin V 2089* 46 5
3 Jun 78 APPROVED BY THE MOTORS *Virgin V 2101* 60 1
10 Jun 78 ● **AIRPORT** *Virgin VS 219* 4 13
19 Aug 78 **FORGET ABOUT YOU** *Virgin VS 222* 13 9
12 Apr 80 **LOVE AND LONELINESS** *Virgin VS 263* 58 3

MOTT THE HOOPLE *UK, male vocal (Ian Hunter) / instrumental group (8 Albums: 32 Weeks, 7 Singles: 55 Weeks)*

2 May 70 MOTT THE HOOPLE *Island ILPS 9108* 66 1
17 Oct 70 MAD SHADOWS *Island ILPS 9119* 48 2
17 Apr 71 WILD LIFE *Island ILPS 9144* 44 2
12 Aug 72 ● **ALL THE YOUNG DUDES** *CBS 8271* 3 11
23 Sep 72 ALL THE YOUNG DUDES *CBS 65184* 21 4
16 Jun 73 **HONALOOCHIE BOOGIE** *CBS 1530* 12 9
11 Aug 73 ● MOTT *CBS 69038* 7 15
8 Sep 73 ● **ALL THE WAY FROM MEMPHIS** *CBS 1764* 10 8
24 Nov 73 ● **ROLL AWAY THE STONE** *CBS 1895* 8 12
30 Mar 74 **THE GOLDEN AGE OF ROCK 'N' ROLL** *CBS 2177* 16 7
13 Apr 74 THE HOOPLE *CBS 69062* 11 5
22 Jun 74 **FOXY, FOXY** *CBS 2439* 33 5
2 Nov 74 **SATURDAY GIG** *CBS 2754* 41 3
23 Nov 74 LIVE *CBS 69093* 32 2
4 Oct 75 DRIVE ON *CBS 69154* 45 1

Bob MOULD (see also HÜSKER DÜ; SUGAR)

US, male vocalist / guitarist (2 Albums: 2 Weeks)

11 May 96 BOB MOULD *Creation CRECD 188* 52 1
5 Sep 98 THE LAST DOG AND PONY SHOW *Creation CRECD 215* 58 1

MOUNT RUSHMORE presents The KNACK

UK, male production duo and female vocalist

3 Apr 99 **YOU BETTER** *Universal MCSTD 40192* 53 1

MOUNTAIN

US / Canada, male vocal / instrumental group (2 Albums: 4 Weeks)

5 Jun 71 NANTUCKET SLEIGHRIDE *Island ILPS 9148* 43 1
8 Jul 72 THE ROAD GOES EVER ON *Island ILPS 9199* 21 3

Nana MOUSKOURI (317 Top 500)

Greece's No.1 musical export, b. 15 Oct 1934, Athens. This distinctive, bespectacled, folk-based singer and guitarist, who collected the first of her numerous worldwide gold and platinum records in 1961, became a Member of the European Parliament in 1994 (11 Albums: 205 Weeks, 1 Single: 11 Weeks)

7 Jun 69 ● OVER AND OVER *Fontana S 5511* 10 97
4 Apr 70 ● THE EXQUISITE NANA MOUSKOURI *Fontana STL 5536* 10 25
10 Oct 70 RECITAL '70 *Fontana 6312 003* 68 1
3 Apr 71 TURN ON THE SUN *Fontana 6312 008* 16 15
29 Jul 72 BRITISH CONCERT *Fontana 6651 003* 29 11
28 Apr 73 SONGS FROM HER TV SERIES *Fontana 6312 036* 29 11
28 Sep 74 SPOTLIGHT ON NANA MOUSKOURI *Fontana 6641 197* 38 6
10 Jul 76 ● PASSPORT *Philips 9101 061* 3 16
11 Jan 86 ● **ONLY LOVE** *Philips PH 38* 2 11
22 Feb 86 ALONE *Philips PHH 3* 19 10
8 Oct 88 THE MAGIC OF NANA MOUSKOURI *Philips NMTV 1* 44 8
3 Mar 01 AT HER VERY BEST *Philips 5485492* 39 5

MOUSSE T

Germany, male producer – Mustafa Gundogdu (5 Singles: 44 Weeks)

6 Jun 98 ● **HORNY** *AM:PM 5826712* [1] 2 17
20 May 00 ● **SEX BOMB** *Gut CDGUT 33* [2] 3 10
10 Aug 02 **FIRE** *Serious SERR 44CD* [3] 58 1
4 Sep 04 ● **IS IT COS I'M COOL?** (re) *Fre2air F2A 1CDX* [3] 9 11
18 Dec 04 **RIGHT ABOUT NOW** *Fre2air F2A CDX* [3] 28 5

[1] Mousse T vs Hot 'N' Juicy [2] Tom Jones and Mousse T [3] Mousse T featuring Emma Lanford

MOUTH and MACNEAL

Holland, male / female vocal duo – Willem Duyn and Sjoukje Van't Spijker

4 May 74 ● **I SEE A STAR** *Decca F 13504* 8 10

The MOVE

UK, male vocal / instrumental group – included Carl Wayne, b. 18 Aug 1943, d. 31 Aug 2004, and Roy Wood (1 Album: 9 Weeks, 10 Singles: 110 Weeks)

5 Jan 67 ● **NIGHT OF FEAR** *Deram DM 109* 2 10
6 Apr 67 ● **I CAN HEAR THE GRASS GROW** *Deram DM 117* 5 10
6 Sep 67 ● **FLOWERS IN THE RAIN** *Regal Zonophone RZ 3001* 2 13
7 Feb 68 ● **FIRE BRIGADE** *Regal Zonophone RZ 3005* 3 11
13 Apr 68 MOVE *Regal Zonophone SLPZ 1002* 15 9
25 Dec 68 ★ **BLACKBERRY WAY** *Regal Zonophone RZ 3015* 1 12
23 Jul 69 **CURLY** *Regal Zonophone RZ 3021* 12 12
25 Apr 70 ● **BRONTOSAURUS** *Regal Zonophone RZ 3026* 7 10
3 Jul 71 **TONIGHT** *Harvest HAR 5038* 11 10
23 Oct 71 **CHINATOWN** *Harvest HAR 5043* 23 8
13 May 72 ● **CALIFORNIA MAN** *Harvest HAR 5050* 7 14

MOVEMENT *US, male vocal / instrumental group*

24 Oct 92 **JUMP!** *Arista 74321116677* 57 2

MOVEMENT 98 featuring Carroll THOMPSON

UK, male / female vocal / instrumental group (2 Singles: 8 Weeks)

19 May 90 **JOY AND HEARTBREAK** *Circa YR 45* 27 5
15 Sep 90 **SUNRISE** *Circa YR 51* 58 3

24 May 1980	31 May 1980	7 June 1980	14 June 1980
WHAT'S ANOTHER YEAR Johnny Logan	**THEME FROM M*A*S*H (SUICIDE IS PAINLESS)** Mash	**THEME FROM M*A*S*H (SUICIDE IS PAINLESS)** Mash	**THEME FROM M*A*S*H (SUICIDE IS PAINLESS)** Mash
THE MAGIC OF BONEY M - 20 GOLDEN HITS Boney M	**McCARTNEY II** Paul McCartney	**McCARTNEY II** Paul McCartney	**PETER GABRIEL** Peter Gabriel

KEY UK No.1 ★ UK Top 10 ● Still on chart + UK entry at No.1 ■ US No.1 ▲ UK million seller £ US million seller $ Singles re-entries are listed as (re), (2re), (3re)... which signifies that the hit re-entered the chart once, twice or three times... Peak Position / Weeks

MOVIN' MELODIES (see also ARTEMESIA; ETHICS; SUBLIMINAL CUTS)
Holland, male producer – Patrick Prinz (3 Singles: 3 Weeks)

22 Oct 94 **LA LUNA** *Effective EFFS 017CD* [1] 64 1
29 Jun 96 **INDICA** *Hooj Choons HOOJCD 44* 62 1
26 Jul 97 **ROLLERBLADE** *Movin' Melodies 5822352* 71 1

[1] Movin' Melodies Production

Alison MOYET (186 Top 500)
After five Top 20 hits with Yazoo, the distinctive, bluesy-voiced vocalist, nicknamed Alf, b. 18 Jun 1961, Essex, UK, enjoyed a string of solo successes. Her biggest hits included revivals of songs made popular by Billie Holiday and Ketty Lester (8 Albums: 202 Weeks, 16 Singles: 107 Weeks)

23 Jun 84 ● **LOVE RESURRECTION** *CBS A 4497* 10 11
13 Oct 84 ● **ALL CRIED OUT** *CBS A 4757* 8 11
17 Nov 84 ★ ALF *CBS 26229* 1 84
1 Dec 84 **INVISIBLE** *CBS A 4930* 21 10
16 Mar 85 ● **THAT OLE DEVIL CALLED LOVE** *CBS A 6044* 2 10
29 Nov 86 ● **IS THIS LOVE?** *CBS MOYET 1* 3 16
7 Mar 87 ● **WEAK IN THE PRESENCE OF BEAUTY** *CBS MOYET 2* 6 10
18 Apr 87 ● RAINDANCING *CBS 450 1521* 2 52
30 May 87 **ORDINARY GIRL** *CBS MOYET 3* 43 4
28 Nov 87 ● **LOVE LETTERS** *CBS MOYET 5* 4 10
6 Apr 91 **IT WON'T BE LONG** *Columbia 6567577* 50 4
4 May 91 HOODOO *Columbia 4682721* 11 6
1 Jun 91 **WISHING YOU WERE HERE** *Columbia 6569397* 72 1
12 Oct 91 **THIS HOUSE** *Columbia 6575157* 40 5
16 Oct 93 **FALLING** *Columbia 6595962* 42 3
12 Mar 94 **WHISPERING YOUR NAME** *Columbia 6601622* 18 7
2 Apr 94 ESSEX *Columbia 4759552* 24 4
28 May 94 **GETTING INTO SOMETHING** *Columbia 6603565* 51 2
22 Oct 94 **ODE TO BOY** *Columbia 6607952* 59 1
3 Jun 95 ★ SINGLES *Columbia 4806632* ■ 1 35
26 Aug 95 **SOLID WOOD** *Columbia 6623265* 44 2
22 Sep 01 THE ESSENTIAL ALISON MOYET *Columbia STVCD 123* 16 4
31 Aug 02 HOMETIME *Sanctuary SANCD 128* 18 9
18 Sep 04 ● VOICE *Sanctuary SANCD 270* 7 8

MOZAIC *UK, female vocal group (3 Singles: 7 Weeks)*

5 Aug 95 **SING IT (THE HALLELUJAH SONG)** *Perfecto PERF 106CD* 14 4
10 Aug 96 **RAYS OF THE RISING SUN** *Perfecto PERF 123CD* 32 2
30 Nov 96 **MOVING UP MOVING ON** *Perfecto PERF 131CD* 62 1

MTUME *US, male / female vocal / instrumental group (1 Album: 1 Week, 2 Singles: 12 Weeks)*

14 May 83 **JUICY FRUIT** *Epic A 3424* 34 9
22 Sep 84 **PRIME TIME** *Epic A 4720* 57 3
6 Oct 84 YOU ME AND HE *Epic EPC 26077* 85 1

MUD (352 Top 500)
Rock 'n' roll-influenced '70s stars: Les Gray (v), b. 7 Apr 1946, d. 21 Feb 2004, Rob Davis (g/v), Ray Stiles (b/v) and Dave Mount (d/v). After joining RAK Records and teaming with writers / producers Nicky Chinn and Mike Chapman, this good-time British band had a noteworthy run of hits, including three No.1s. Davis was one of the UK's most successful songwriters in the early 21st century, penning No.1 hits for Kylie Minogue and Spiller (4 Albums: 58 Weeks, 15 Singles: 139 Weeks)

10 Mar 73 **CRAZY** *RAK 146* 12 12
23 Jun 73 **HYPNOSIS** *RAK 152* 16 13
27 Oct 73 ● **DYNA-MITE** *RAK 159* 4 12
19 Jan 74 ★ **TIGER FEET** *RAK 166* 1 11
13 Apr 74 ● **THE CAT CREPT IN** *RAK 170* 2 9
27 Jul 74 ● **ROCKET** *RAK 178* 6 9
28 Sep 74 ● MUD ROCK *RAK SRAK 508* 8 35
30 Nov 74 ★ **LONELY THIS CHRISTMAS** (re) *RAK 187* 1 13
15 Feb 75 ● **THE SECRETS THAT YOU KEEP** *RAK 194* 3 9
26 Apr 75 ★ **OH BOY** *RAK 201* 1 9
21 Jun 75 ● **MOONSHINE SALLY** *RAK 208* 10 7
26 Jul 75 ● MUD ROCK VOLUME 2 *RAK SRAK 513* 6 12
2 Aug 75 **ONE NIGHT** *RAK 213* 32 4
4 Oct 75 ● **L'L'LUCY** *Private Stock PVT 41* 10 6
1 Nov 75 MUD'S GREATEST HITS *RAK SRAK 6755* 25 6
29 Nov 75 ● **SHOW ME YOU'RE A WOMAN** *Private Stock PVT 45* 8 8
27 Dec 75 USE YOUR IMAGINATION *Private Stock PVLP 1003* 33 5
15 May 76 **SHAKE IT DOWN** *Private Stock PVT 65* 12 8
27 Nov 76 ● **LEAN ON ME** *Private Stock PVT 85* 7 9

'Lonely This Christmas' peaked at No.61 when it re-entered the chart in Dec 1985.

MUDHONEY
US, male vocal / instrumental group (3 Albums: 5 Weeks, 2 Singles: 2 Weeks)

17 Aug 91 **LET IT SLIDE** *Subpop SP 15154* 60 1
31 Aug 91 EVERY GOOD BOY DESERVES FUDGE *Subpop SP 18160* 34 2
17 Oct 92 PIECE OF CAKE *Reprise 9362450902* 39 2
24 Oct 92 **SUCK YOU DRY** *Reprise W 0137* 65 1
8 Apr 95 MY BROTHER THE COW *Reprise 9362458402* 70 1

The MUDLARKS
UK, male / female vocal (Mary Mudd) group (3 Singles: 19 Weeks)

2 May 58 ● **LOLLIPOP** *Columbia DB 4099* 2 9
6 Jun 58 ● **BOOK OF LOVE** *Columbia DB 4133* 8 9
27 Feb 59 **THE LOVE GAME** *Columbia DB 4250* 30 1

Idris MUHAMMAD *US, male percussionist*

17 Sep 77 **COULD HEAVEN EVER BE LIKE THIS** *Kudu 935* 42 3

Vocal by Frank Floyd.

MUKKAA (see also EYE TO EYE featuring Taka BOOM; UMBOZA)
UK, male instrumental / production duo – Stuart Crichton and Billy Kiltie

27 Feb 93 **BURUCHACCA** *Limbo LIMBO 008* 74 1

Maria MULDAUR *US, female vocalist – Maria D'Amato*

29 Jun 74 **MIDNIGHT AT THE OASIS** *Reprise K 14331* 21 8

MULL HISTORICAL SOCIETY
UK, male vocal / instrumental group (3 Albums: 5 Weeks, 5 Singles: 7 Weeks)

21 Jul 01 **ANIMAL CANNABUS** *Rough Trade RTRADSCD 021* 53 1
27 Oct 01 LOSS *Blanco Y Negro 927413072* 43 1
9 Feb 02 **WATCHING XANADU** *Blanco Y Negro NEG 138CD* 36 2
1 Mar 03 **THE FINAL ARREARS** *Blanco Y Negro NEG 144CD* 32 2
15 Mar 03 US *Blanco Y Negro 09276499562* 19 3
14 Jun 03 **AM I WRONG** *Blanco Y Negro NEG 146CD* 51 1
24 Jul 04 **HOW 'BOUT I LOVE YOU MORE** *B-Unique BUN 080CDS* 37 1
31 Jul 04 THIS IS HOPE *B-Unique BUN 082* 58 1

Gerry MULLIGAN and Ben WEBSTER
US, male instrumental duo – baritone and tenor sax – Gerry Mulligan, b. 6 Apr 1927, d. 20 Jan 1996, and Ben Webster, b. 27 Mar 1909, d. 20 Sep 1973

24 Sep 60 GERRY MULLIGAN MEETS BEN WEBSTER *HMV CLP 1373* 15 1

Shawn MULLINS
US, male vocalist (1 Album: 1 Week, 2 Singles: 11 Weeks)

6 Mar 99 ● **LULLABY** *Columbia 6669592* 9 10
20 Mar 99 SOUL'S CORE *Columbia 4930372* 60 1
2 Oct 99 **WHAT IS LIFE** *Columbia 6678212* 62 1

	21 June 1980	28 June 1980	5 July 1980	12 July 1980
UK No.1 SINGLES	CRYING Don McLean	CRYING Don McLean	CRYING Don McLean	XANADU Olivia Newton-John and Electric Light Orchestra
UK No.1 ALBUMS	PETER GABRIEL Peter Gabriel	FLESH AND BLOOD Roxy Music	EMOTIONAL RESCUE The Rolling Stones	EMOTIONAL RESCUE The Rolling Stones

MULU *UK, male / female vocal / instrumental duo*

2 Aug 97		**PUSSYCAT** *Dedicated MULU 003CD1*	**50**	1

Omero MUMBA *Ireland, male vocalist*

20 Jul 02		**LIL' BIG MAN** *Polydor 5708852*	42	2

Samantha MUMBA
Ireland, female vocalist (1 Album: 16 Weeks, 6 Singles: 69 Weeks)

8 Jul 00	●	**GOTTA TELL YOU** *Wild Card / Polydor 5618832*	2	12
28 Oct 00	●	**BODY II BODY** *Wild Card / Polydor 5877742*	**5**	12
11 Nov 00	●	GOTTA TELL YOU *Wild Card 5492262*	9	16
3 Mar 01	●	**ALWAYS COME BACK TO YOUR LOVE** *Wild Card / Polydor 5879252*	3	15
22 Sep 01	●	**BABY COME ON OVER** *Wild Card / Polydor 5872352*	**5**	10
22 Dec 01	●	**LATELY** *Wild Card / Polydor 5705232*	**6**	12
26 Oct 02	●	**I'M RIGHT HERE** (re) *Wild Card / Polydor 0659372*	**5**	8

MUNDY *Ireland, male vocalist – Edmund Enright (2 Singles: 2 Weeks)*

3 Aug 96		**TO YOU I BESTOW** *Epic MUNDY 1CD*	**60**	1
5 Oct 96		**LIFE'S A CINCH** *Epic MUNDY 2CD*	**75**	1

MUNGO JERRY *UK, male vocal (Ray Dorset) / instrumental group (2 Albums: 14 Weeks, 9 Singles: 88 Weeks)*

6 Jun 70	★	**IN THE SUMMERTIME** *Dawn DNX 2502* **$**	1	20
8 Aug 70		MUNGO JERRY *Dawn DNLS 3008*	13	6
6 Feb 71	★	**BABY JUMP** (re) *Dawn DNX 2505*	1	13
10 Apr 71		ELECTRONICALLY TESTED *Dawn DNLS 3020*	14	8
29 May 71	●	**LADY ROSE** *Dawn DNX 2510*	**5**	12
18 Sep 71		**YOU DON'T HAVE TO BE IN THE ARMY TO FIGHT IN THE WAR** *Dawn DNX 2513*	13	8
22 Apr 72		**OPEN UP** *Dawn DNX 2514*	21	8
7 Jul 73	●	**ALRIGHT, ALRIGHT, ALRIGHT** *Dawn DNS 1037*	3	12
10 Nov 73		**WILD LOVE** *Dawn DNS 1051*	32	5
6 Apr 74		**LONG LEGGED WOMAN DRESSED IN BLACK** *Dawn DNS 1061*	13	9
29 May 99		**SUPPORT THE TOON – IT'S YOUR DUTY (EP)** *Saraja TOONCD 001* [1]	**57**	1

[1] Mungo Jerry and Toon Travellers

Tracks on Support the Toon – It's Your Duty (EP): Blaydon Races / Going to Wembley / Bottle of Beer.

MUNICH MACHINE
Germany, male instrumental group (2 Singles: 8 Weeks)

10 Dec 77		**GET ON THE FUNK TRAIN** *Oasis OASIS 2*	41	4
4 Nov 78		**A WHITER SHADE OF PALE** *Oasis OASIS 5* [1]	42	4

[1] Munich Machine introducing Chris Bennett

The MUNROS featuring David METHREN *UK, male pipe band*

27 Jun 98		THE LONE PIPER *Virgin VTCD 185*	46	3

The MUPPETS
US, frog-fronted puppet ensemble (2 Albums: 45 Weeks, 2 Singles: 15 Weeks)

28 May 77	●	**HALFWAY DOWN THE STAIRS** *Pye 7N 45698*	7	8
11 Jun 77	★	THE MUPPET SHOW *Pye NSPH 19*	1	35
17 Dec 77		**THE MUPPET SHOW MUSIC HALL EP** *Pye 7NX 8004*	19	7
25 Feb 78		THE MUPPET SHOW VOLUME 2 *Pye NSPH 21*	16	10

'Halfway Down the Stairs' is sung by Jerry Nelson as Kermit the Frog's nephew, Robin. Tracks on The Muppet Show Music Hall EP: Don't Dilly Dally on the Way / Waiting at the Church / The Boy in the Gallery / Wotcher (Knocked 'Em in the Old Kent Road).

The MURDERDOLLS
US, male vocal / instrumental group (1 Album: 1 Week, 2 Singles: 4 Weeks)

31 Aug 02		BEYOND THE VALLEY OF THE MURDERDOLLS *Roadrunner RR 84262*	40	1
16 Nov 02		**DEAD IN HOLLYWOOD** *Roadrunner RR 20223*	**54**	1
26 Jul 03		**WHITE WEDDING** *Roadrunner RR 20155*	24	3

TOP 10
ON THE DAY MARGARET THATCHER BECAME PRIME MINISTER

The "Iron Maiden" moved in to 10 Downing Street on 4 May 1979, and stayed there for a record-breaking 11 years and 209 days. She was the UK's first female prime minister and the longest-serving leader for more than 150 years. Despite this auspicious start to her career, she failed to do a Take That and leave on a high. A leadership challenge by Michael Heseltine (Gary Barlow to her Robbie Williams) saw her ousted from the hot seat, to be replaced by John Major (er, Howard Donald?).

LW	TW	
1	1	**BRIGHT EYES** Art Garfunkel
2	2	**SOME GIRLS** Racey
5	3	**POP MUZIK** M
19	4	**HOORAY HOORAY, IT'S A HOLI-HOLIDAY** Boney M
9	5	**GOODNIGHT TONIGHT** Wings
4	6	**SHAKE YOUR BODY (DOWN TO THE GROUND)** The Jacksons
6	7	**HALLELUJAH** Milk and Honey featuring Gali Atari
3	8	**COOL FOR CATS** Squeeze
7	9	**THE LOGICAL SONG** Supertramp
20	10	**KNOCK ON WOOD** Amii Stewart

Art Garfunkel

Margaret Thatcher

19 July 1980	26 July 1980	2 August 1980	9 August 1980
XANADU Olivia Newton-John and Electric Light Orchestra	**USE IT UP AND WEAR IT OUT** Odyssey	**USE IT UP AND WEAR IT OUT** Odyssey	**THE WINNER TAKES IT ALL** Abba
THE GAME Queen	**THE GAME** Queen	**DEEPEST PURPLE** Deep Purple	**BACK IN BLACK** AC/DC

KEY
UK No.1 ★ UK Top 10 ● Still on chart + UK entry at No.1 ■ US No.1 ▲ UK million seller £ US million seller $
Singles re-entries are listed as (re), (2re), (3re)... which signifies that the hit re-entered the chart once, twice or three times...
Peak Position / Weeks

Lydia MURDOCK *US, female vocalist*

24 Sep 83 **SUPERSTAR** *Korova KOW 30* **14** 9

Shirley MURDOCK *US, female vocalist*

12 Apr 86 **TRUTH OR DARE** *Elektra EKR 36* **60** 2

Eddie MURPHY featuring Shabba Ranks

US, male actor / singer and Jamaican male vocalist

6 Mar 93 **I WAS A KING** *Motown TMGCD 1414* **64** 1

Noel MURPHY *Ireland, male vocalist*

27 Jun 87 **MURPHY AND THE BRICKS** *Murphy's STACK 1* **57** 4

Peter MURPHY (see also BAUHAUS) *UK, male vocalist*

26 Jul 86 SHOULD THE WORLD FAIL TO FALL APART *Beggars Banquet BEGA 69* 82 1

Walter MURPHY and The BIG APPLE BAND *US, orchestra*

10 Jul 76 **A FIFTH OF BEETHOVEN** *Private Stock PVT 59* ▲ $ 28 9

Anne MURRAY

Canada, female vocalist (1 Album: 10 Weeks, 5 Singles: 40 Weeks)

24 Oct 70 **SNOWBIRD** *Capitol CL 15654* $ 23 17
21 Oct 72 **DESTINY** *Capitol CL 15734* **41** 4
9 Dec 78 **YOU NEEDED ME** *Capitol CL 16011* ▲ $ 22 14
21 Apr 79 **I JUST FALL IN LOVE AGAIN** *Capitol CL 16069* **58** 2
19 Apr 80 **DAYDREAM BELIEVER** *Capitol CL 16123* **61** 3
3 Oct 81 THE VERY BEST OF ANNE MURRAY *Capitol EMTV 31* 14 10

Keith MURRAY *US, male rapper (4 Singles: 10 Weeks)*

2 Nov 96 **THE RHYME** *Jive JIVECD 407* **59** 1
27 Jun 98 **SHORTY (YOU KEEP PLAYING WITH MY MIND)** *Jive 0521212* [1] 22 3
14 Nov 98 **HOME ALONE** *Jive 0522392* [2] **17** 5
5 Dec 98 **INCREDIBLE** *Jive 0522102* [3] **52** 1

[1] Imajin featuring Keith Murray [2] R Kelly featuring Keith Murray [3] Keith Murray featuring LL Cool J

Ruby MURRAY *UK, female vocalist, b. 29 Mar 1935, d. 17 Dec 1996 (10 Singles: 114 Weeks)*

3 Dec 54 ● **HEARTBEAT** *Columbia DB 3542* 3 16
28 Jan 55 ★ **SOFTLY, SOFTLY** (re) *Columbia DB 3558* 1 23
4 Feb 55 ● **HAPPY DAYS AND LONELY NIGHTS** *Columbia DB 3577* 6 8
4 Mar 55 ● **LET ME GO LOVER** *Columbia DB 3577* 5 7
18 Mar 55 ● **IF ANYONE FINDS THIS, I LOVE YOU** *Columbia DB 3580* [1] 4 11
1 Jul 55 ● **EVERMORE** *Columbia DB 3617* 3 17
14 Oct 55 ● **I'LL COME WHEN YOU CALL** *Columbia DB 3643* 6 7
31 Aug 56 **YOU ARE MY FIRST LOVE** (re) *Columbia DB 3770* **16** 5
12 Dec 58 **REAL LOVE** *Columbia DB 4192* **18** 6
5 Jun 59 ● **GOODBYE JIMMY, GOODBYE** (re) *Columbia DB 4305* 10 14

[1] Ruby Murray with Anne Warren

Pauline MURRAY and The INVISIBLE GIRLS

(see also PENETRATION) *UK, female vocalist and male (really) vocal / instrumental group*

2 Aug 80 **DREAM SEQUENCE (ONE)** *Illusive IVE 1* **67** 2
11 Oct 80 PAULINE MURRAY AND THE INVISIBLE GIRLS *Illusive 2394 227* 25 4

Junior MURVIN *Jamaica, male vocalist – Mervin Smith*

3 May 80 **POLICE AND THIEVES** *Island WIP 6539* 23 9

MUSE 496 Top 500

Innovative British rock band formed in 1999 in Teignmouth, Devon, by Matt Bellamy (v/g), Chris Wolstenhole (b) and Dominic Howard (d). The winners of the BRIT Award for Best Live Act in 2005, which saw Absolution reach the Top 10 in 10 countries (4 Albums: 99 Weeks, 15 Singles: 51 Weeks)

26 Jun 99 **UNO** *Mushroom / Taste Media MUSH 50CDS* **73** 1
18 Sep 99 **CAVE** *Mushroom / Taste Media MUSH 58CDS* **52** 1
16 Oct 99 SHOWBIZ *Mushroom MUSH 59CD* 29 16
4 Dec 99 **MUSCLE MUSEUM** *Mushroom / Taste Media MUSH 66CDS* **43** 2
4 Mar 00 **SUNBURN** *Mushroom / Taste Media MUSH 68CDS* 22 2
17 Jun 00 **UNINTENDED** *Mushroom / Taste Media MUSH 72CDS* 20 4
21 Oct 00 **MUSCLE MUSEUM** (re-issue) *Mushroom / Taste Media MUSH 84CDS* **25** 3
24 Mar 01 **PLUG IN BABY** *Mushroom / Taste Media MUSH 89CDS* 11 5
16 Jun 01 **NEW BORN** *Mushroom / Taste Media MUSH 92CDS* 12 4
30 Jun 01 ● ORIGIN OF SYMMETRY *Mushroom MUSH 93CDX* 3 24
1 Sep 01 **BLISS** *Mushroom / Taste Media MUSH 96CDS* 22 2
1 Dec 01 **HYPER MUSIC / FEELING GOOD** *Mushroom MUSH 97CDS* 24 3
29 Jun 02 **DEAD STAR / IN YOUR WORLD** *Mushroom MUSH 104CDS* 13 3
13 Jul 02 ● HULLABALOO SOUNDTRACK *Mushroom MUSH 105CD* 10 4
20 Sep 03 ● **TIME IS RUNNING OUT** *East West EW 272CD* 8 8
4 Oct 03 ★ ABSOLUTION *East West 5046685872* ■ 1 55
13 Dec 03 **HYSTERIA** *East West EW 278CD* **17** 6
29 May 04 **SING FOR ABSOLUTION** *East West EW 285CD* **16** 4
2 Oct 04 **BUTTERFLIES & HURRICANES** *Atlantic ATUK 003CD* **14** 3

The MUSIC

UK, male vocal (Robert Harvey) / instrumental group (2 Albums: 10 Weeks, 5 Singles: 14 Weeks)

31 Aug 02 **TAKE THE LONG ROAD AND WALK IT** *Hut / Virgin HUTCD 158* **14** 3
14 Sep 02 ● THE MUSIC *Hut / Virgin CDHUTX 76* 4 5
30 Nov 02 **GETAWAY** *Hut / Virgin HUTCD 162* 26 2
1 Mar 03 **THE TRUTH IS NO WORDS** *Hut / Virgin VSCDT 1845* **18** 2
18 Sep 04 **FREEDOM FIGHTERS** *Virgin VSCDX 1883* **15** 4
2 Oct 04 ● WELCOME TO THE NORTH *Virgin CDV 2989* 8 5
22 Jan 05 **BREAKIN'** *Virgin VSCDX 1894* 20 3

MUSIC and MYSTERY featuring Gwen McCRAE

UK, male production group and US, female vocalist

13 Feb 93 **ALL THIS LOVE I'M GIVING** (re-recording) *KTDA CDKTDA 2* 36 3

MUSIC RELIEF '94

UK, male / female vocal / instrumental group

5 Nov 94 **WHAT'S GOING ON** *Jive RWANDACD 1* **70** 1

MUSICAL YOUTH

(see also Donna SUMMER) *UK, male vocal (Dennis Seaton) / instrumental group (1 Album: 22 Weeks, 7 Singles: 55 Weeks)*

25 Sep 82 ★ **PASS THE DUTCHIE** (re) *MCA YOU 1* 1 13
20 Nov 82 **YOUTH OF TODAY** *MCA YOU 2* 13 9
4 Dec 82 THE YOUTH OF TODAY *MCA YOULP 1* 24 22
12 Feb 83 ● **NEVER GONNA GIVE YOU UP** *MCA YOU 3* 6 10
16 Apr 83 **HEARTBREAKER** *MCA YOU 4* **44** 3
9 Jul 83 **TELL ME WHY** *MCA YOU 5* 33 6
22 Oct 83 **007** *MCA YOU 6* 26 6
14 Jan 84 **SIXTEEN** *MCA YOU 7* 23 8

MUSIQUE *US, female vocal group*

18 Nov 78 **IN THE BUSH** *CBS 6791* **16** 12

16 August 1980	23 August 1980	30 August 1980	6 September 1980
UK No.1 SINGLES			
THE WINNER TAKES IT ALL Abba	ASHES TO ASHES David Bowie	ASHES TO ASHES David Bowie	START The Jam
UK No.1 ALBUMS			
BACK IN BLACK AC/DC	FLESH AND BLOOD Roxy Music	FLESH AND BLOOD Roxy Music	FLESH AND BLOOD Roxy Music

MUSIQUE vs U2

(see also PF PROJECT featuring Ewan McGREGOR) *UK, male production duo – Nick Hanson and Moussa Clarke and Ireland, male vocal / instrumental group*

2 Jun 01 **NEW YEAR'S DUB** (re) *Serious SERR 030CD* **15** 5

MUTINY UK (see also HELICOPTER)

UK, male production duo – Dylan Barnes and Rob Davy (2 Singles: 3 Weeks)

19 May 01 **SECRETS** *Sunflower VCRD 86* [1] **47** 1
25 Aug 01 **VIRUS** *VC Recordings VCRD 91* **42** 2

[1] Vocals by Lorraine Cato

The MUTTON BIRDS *New Zealand, male vocal / instrumental group*

12 Jul 97 ENVY OF ANGELS *Virgin CDVIR 55* 64 1

MY BLOODY VALENTINE *UK, male / female vocal / instrumental group (1 Album: 2 Weeks, 2 Singles: 5 Weeks)*

5 May 90 **SOON** *Creation CRE 073* **41** 3
16 Feb 91 **TO HERE KNOWS WHEN** *Creation CRE 085* **29** 2
23 Nov 91 LOVELESS *Creation CRELP 060* 24 2

MY CHEMICAL ROMANCE *US, male vocal / instrumental group (1 Album: 15 Weeks, 5 Singles: 14 Weeks)*

25 Dec 04 **THANK YOU FOR THE VENOM** *Reprise W 661* **71** 1
19 Mar 05 **I'M NOT OKAY (I PROMISE)** *Reprise W 666CD1* **19** 3
26 Mar 05 THREE CHEERS FOR SWEET REVENGE *WEA WB 486152* 34 15
4 Jun 05 **HELENA** *Reprise W 671CD* **20** 4
10 Sep 05 **THE GHOST OF YOU** *Reprise W 683CD2* **27** 2
19 Nov 05 **I'M NOT OKAY (I PROMISE)** (re-issue) *Reprise W 692CD2* **28** 4

MY LIFE STORY *UK, male / female vocal / instrumental group (1 Album: 1 Week, 8 Singles: 12 Weeks)*

17 Aug 96 **12 REASONS WHY I LOVE HER** *Parlophone CDR 6442* **32** 2
9 Nov 96 **SPARKLE** *Parlophone CDR 6450* **34** 2
1 Mar 97 **THE KING OF KISSINGDOM** *Parlophone CDRS 6457* **35** 1
22 Mar 97 THE GOLDEN MILE *Parlophone CDPCS 7386* 36 1
17 May 97 **STRUMPET** *Parlophone CDR 6464* **27** 2
23 Aug 97 **DUCHESS** *Parlophone CDR 6474* **39** 1
19 Jun 99 **IT'S A GIRL THING** *IT ITR 001* **37** 2
30 Oct 99 **EMPIRE LINE** *IT ITR 003* **58** 1
19 Feb 00 **WALK / DON'T WALK** *IT ITR 007* **48** 1

MY MORNING JACKET

US, male vocal / instrumental group (2 Albums: 2 Weeks)

20 Sep 03 IT STILL MOVES *RCA 82876559252* 62 1
29 Oct 05 Z *RCA 82876716942* 74 1

MY RED CELL *UK, male vocal / instrumental group*

12 Jun 04 **IN A CAGE (ON PROZAC)** *V2 VVR 5027133* **61** 1

MY VITRIOL *UK, male / female vocal / instrumental group (1 Album: 2 Weeks, 5 Singles: 7 Weeks)*

22 Jul 00 **CEMENTED SHOES** *Infectious INFECT 89CDS* **65** 1
11 Nov 00 **PIECES** *Infectious INFECT 94CDS* **56** 1
24 Feb 01 **ALWAYS: YOUR WAY** *Infectious INFECT 95CDS* **31** 2
17 Mar 01 FINELINES *Infectious INFECT 96CD* 24 2
19 May 01 **GROUNDED** *Infectious INFECT 97CD* **29** 2
27 Jul 02 **MOODSWINGS / THE GENTLE ART OF CHOKING** *Infectious INFECT 107CDSX* **39** 1

MYA *US, female vocalist – Mya Harrison (7 Singles: 66 Weeks)*

27 Jun 98 ● **GHETTO SUPASTAR (THAT IS WHAT YOU ARE)** *Interscope IND 95593* [1] **2** 17
12 Dec 98 ● **TAKE ME THERE** *Interscope IND 95620* [2] **7** 9
10 Feb 01 ● **CASE OF THE EX** *Interscope 4974772* **3** 11
24 Mar 01 **GIRLS DEM SUGAR** *Virgin VUSCD 173* [3] **13** 5
9 Jun 01 **FREE** *Interscope 4975002* **11** 6
30 Jun 01 ★ **LADY MARMALADE** *Interscope / Polydor 4975612* [4] ■ ▲ **1** 16
20 Sep 03 **MY LOVE IS LIKE ... WO** *Interscope / Polydor 9810305* **33** 2

[1] Pras Michel featuring ODB & introducing Mya [2] BLACKstreet and Mya featuring Ma$e and Blinky Blink [3] Beenie Man featuring Mya [4] Christina Aguilera, Lil' Kim, Mya and Pink

Alicia MYERS *US, female vocalist*

1 Sep 84 **YOU GET THE BEST FROM ME (SAY, SAY, SAY)** *MCA MCA 914* **58** 3

Billie MYERS

UK, female vocalist (1 Album: 9 Weeks, 2 Singles: 12 Weeks)

11 Apr 98 ● **KISS THE RAIN** *Universal UND 56182* **4** 9
2 May 98 GROWING PAINS *Universal UND 53100* 19 9
25 Jul 98 **TELL ME** *Universal UND 56201* **28** 3

Richard MYHILL *UK, male vocalist*

1 Apr 78 **IT TAKES TWO TO TANGO** *Mercury 6007 167* **17** 9

Alannah MYLES

Canada, female vocalist (1 Album: 21 Weeks, 2 Singles: 17 Weeks)

17 Mar 90 ● **BLACK VELVET** *East West A 8742* ▲ **2** 15
28 Apr 90 ● ALANNAH MYLES *Atlantic 7819561* 3 21
16 Jun 90 **LOVE IS** *East West A 8918* **61** 2

MYLO

UK, male producer – Myles MacInnes (1 Album: 17 Weeks, 4 Singles: 34 Weeks)

30 Oct 04 **DROP THE PRESSURE** (re) *Breastfed BFD 009CD* **19** 7
15 Jan 05 DESTROY ROCK & ROLL *Breastfed BFD 007CD* 26 17
5 Feb 05 **DESTROY ROCK & ROLL** *Breastfed BFD 014CD* **15** 4
28 May 05 **IN MY ARMS** *Breastfed BFD 016CD* **13** 7
17 Sep 05 ● **DOCTOR PRESSURE** *Breastfed BFD 017CD2* [1] .... **3** 16+

[1] Mylo vs Miami Sound Machine

Marie MYRIAM *France, female vocalist*

28 May 77 **L'OISEAU ET L'ENFANT** *Polydor 2056 634* **42** 4

MYRON *US, male vocalist – Myron Davis*

22 Nov 97 **WE CAN GET DOWN** *Island Black Music CID 677* **74** 1

MYSTERY (see also Ron VAN DEN BEUKEN)

Holland, male production duo (2 Singles: 2 Weeks)

6 Oct 01 **MYSTERY** *Inferno CDFERN 42* **56** 1
10 Aug 02 **ALL I EVER WANTED (DEVOTION)** *Xtravaganza XTRAV 33CDS* **57** 1

MYSTERY JETS NEW

UK, male vocal / instrumental group (2 Singles: 3 Weeks)

24 Sep 05 **YOU CAN'T FOOL ME DENNIS** *679 Recordings 679L 109CD* **44** 2
17 Dec 05 **ALAS AGNES** *679 Recordings 679L 115CD* **34** 1

MYSTIC MERLIN *US, male vocal / instrumental group*

26 Apr 80 **JUST CAN'T GIVE YOU UP** *Capitol CL 16133* **20** 9

MYSTIC 3 *UK / Italy, male production group (aka Blockster)*

24 Jun 00 **SOMETHING'S GOIN' ON** *Rulin RULIN 2CDS* **63** 1

MYSTICA *Israel, male production trio (2 Singles: 2 Weeks)*

24 Jan 98 **EVER REST** *Perfecto PERF 152CD* **62** 1
9 May 98 **AFRICAN HORIZON** *Perfecto PERF 161CD* **59** 1

13 September 1980	20 September 1980	27 September 1980	4 October 1980
FEELS LIKE I'M IN LOVE Kelly Marie	**FEELS LIKE I'M IN LOVE** Kelly Marie	**DON'T STAND SO CLOSE TO ME** The Police	**DON'T STAND SO CLOSE TO ME** The Police
TELEKON Gary Numan	**NEVER FOR EVER** Kate Bush	**SCARY MONSTERS AND SUPER CREEPS** David Bowie	**SCARY MONSTERS AND SUPER CREEPS** David Bowie

KEY
UK No.1 ★ UK Top 10 ● Still on chart + UK entry at No.1 ■
US No.1 ▲ UK million seller £ US million seller $
Singles re-entries are listed as (re), (2re), (3re)... which signifies that the hit re-entered the chart once, twice or three times...

Peak Position / Weeks

MYSTIKAL
US, male rapper – Michael Tyler (6 Singles: 23 Weeks)

Date	Title / Label	Peak	Weeks
9 Dec 00	**SHAKE YA ASS** *Jive 9251552*	**30**	5
17 Feb 01 ●	**STUTTER** *Jive 9251632* [1] ▲	**7**	8
3 Mar 01	**DANGER (BEEN SO LONG)** *Jive 9251722* [2]	**28**	3
29 Dec 01	**NEVER TOO FAR / DON'T STOP (FUNKIN' 4 JAMAICA)** *Virgin VUSCD 228* [3]	32	4
23 Feb 02	**BOUNCIN' BACK (BUMPIN' ME AGAINST THE WALL)** *Jive 9253272*	**45**	1
10 May 03	**LAUNDROMAT / DON'T MESS WITH MY MAN** *Jive 9254822* [4]	33	2

[1] Joe featuring Mystikal [2] Mystikal featuring Nivea [3] Mariah Carey / Mariah Carey featuring Mystikal [4] Nivea featuring Brian and Brandon Casey of Jagged Edge and Mystikal

MYTOWN *Ireland, male vocal group*

Date	Title / Label	Peak	Weeks
13 Mar 99	**PARTY ALL NIGHT** *Universal UND 56231*	22	2

N

N-JOI *UK, male instrumental / production group (7 Singles: 28 Weeks)*

Date	Title / Label	Peak	Weeks
27 Oct 90	**ANTHEM** *Deconstruction PB 44041*	**45**	5
2 Mar 91	**ADRENALIN (EP)** *Deconstruction PT 44344*	23	5
6 Apr 91 ●	**ANTHEM** (re-issue) *Deconstruction PB 44445*	8	8
22 Feb 92	**LIVE IN MANCHESTER (PARTS 1 + 2)** *Deconstruction PT 45252*	12	5
24 Jul 93	**THE DRUMSTRUCK EP** *Deconstruction 74321154832*	33	3
17 Dec 94	**PAPILLON** *Deconstruction 74321252132*	**70**	1
8 Jul 95	**BAD THINGS** *Deconstruction 74321277292* [1]	**57**	1

[1] NJOI

Tracks on Adrenalin (EP): Adrenalin / The Kraken / Rhythm Zone / Phoenix. Tracks on The Drumstruck EP: The Void / Boom Bass / Drumstruck.

N'n'G featuring KALLAGHAN
UK, male / female production / vocal group

Date	Title / Label	Peak	Weeks
1 Apr 00	**RIGHT BEFORE MY EYES** *Urban Heat UHTCD 003*	12	6

N.O.R.E.
US, male rapper – Victor Santiago (1 Album: 1 Week, 2 Singles: 9 Weeks)

Date	Title / Label	Peak	Weeks
25 Jul 98	N.O.R.E. *Penalty Recordings PENCD 3077* [1]	72	1
21 Sep 02	**NOTHIN'** (re) *Def Jam 639262*	11	8
29 Nov 03	**CRASHIN' A PARTY** *Def Jam MCSTD 40341* [1]	**55**	1

[1] Lumidee featuring NORE [1] Noreaga

'Nothin' peaked at No.72 when it re-entered the chart in May 2004.

NRG (see also DJ FLAVOURS; SMOKIN BEATS featuring Lyn EDEN)
UK, male DJ / producer – Neil Rumney (3 Singles: 3 Weeks)

Date	Title / Label	Peak	Weeks
29 Mar 97	**NEVER LOST HIS HARDCORE** *Top Banana TOPCD 04*	**71**	1
12 Dec 98	**NEVER LOST HIS HARDCORE '98** (re-mix) *Top Banana TOPCD 010*	**61**	1
20 Mar 04	**NEVER LEFT HIS HARDCORE** *Tidy Trax TIDY 200T*	**59**	1

'N SYNC *US, male vocal group (3 Albums: 32 Weeks, 12 Singles: 79 Weeks)*

Date	Title / Label	Peak	Weeks
13 Sep 97	**TEARIN' UP MY HEART** *Arista 74321505152*	**40**	2
22 Nov 97	**I WANT YOU BACK** *Arista 74321541122*	**62**	1
27 Feb 99 ●	**I WANT YOU BACK** (re) (re-issue) *Transcontinental / Northwestside 74321646972*	5	10
26 Jun 99 ●	**TEARIN' UP MY HEART** (re) (re-issue) *Northwestside / Arista 74321675832*	9	10
17 Jul 99	*N SYNC *Northwestside 74321681902*	30	2
8 Jan 00	**MUSIC OF MY HEART** *Epic 6685272* [1]	**34**	3
11 Mar 00 ●	**BYE BYE BYE** *Jive 9250202*	3	8
1 Apr 00	NO STRINGS ATTACHED *Jive 9220272* ▲	14	22
22 Jul 00	**I'LL NEVER STOP** *Jive 9250762*	13	6
16 Sep 00 ●	**IT'S GONNA BE ME** *Jive 9251082* ▲	9	8
2 Dec 00	**THIS I PROMISE YOU** *Jive 9251302*	21	7
21 Jul 01 ●	**POP** *Jive 9252422*	9	8
4 Aug 01	CELEBRITY *Jive 9222032* ▲	12	8
8 Dec 01	**GONE** (re) *Jive 9252772*	24	4
27 Apr 02 ●	**GIRLFRIEND** *Jive 9253312* [2]	2	12

[1] 'N Sync / Gloria Estefan [2] 'N Sync featuring Nelly

NT GANG *Germany, male vocal / instrumental group*

Date	Title / Label	Peak	Weeks
2 Apr 88	**WAM BAM** *Cooltempo COOL 163*	**71**	1

N-TRANCE (see also FREELOADERS) *UK, male production duo – Dale Longworth and Kevin O'Toole (15 Singles: 86 Weeks)*

Date	Title / Label	Peak	Weeks
7 May 94	**SET YOU FREE** *All Around the World CDGLOBE 124* [1]	39	4
22 Oct 94	**TURN UP THE POWER** *All Around the World CDGLOBE 125*	23	3
14 Jan 95 ●	**SET YOU FREE** (re-mix) *All Around the World CDGLOBE 126*	2	15
16 Sep 95 ●	**STAYIN' ALIVE** *All Around the World CDGLOBE 131* [2]	2	11
24 Feb 96	**ELECTRONIC PLEASURE** *All Around the World CDGLOBE 135*	11	4
5 Apr 97	**D.I.S.C.O.** *All Around the World CDGLOBE 153*	11	6
23 Aug 97	**THE MIND OF THE MACHINE** *All Around the World CDGLOBE 159*	15	4
1 Nov 97 ●	**DA YA THINK I'M SEXY** *All Around the World CDGLOBE 150* [3]	7	10
12 Sep 98	**PARADISE CITY** *All Around the World CDGLOBE 140*	28	3
19 Dec 98	**TEARS IN THE RAIN** *All Around the Globe CDGLOBE 185*	**53**	1
20 May 00	**SHAKE YA BODY** *All Around the World CDGLOBE 204*	37	1
22 Sep 01 ●	**SET YOU FREE** (re) (2nd re-mix) *All Around the World CDGLOBE 242*	4	12
14 Sep 02 ●	**FOREVER** (re) *All Around the World CDGLOBE 257*	6	8
19 Jul 03	**DESTINY** *All Around the World CDGLOBE 282*	37	2
4 Dec 04	**I'M IN HEAVEN** *All Around the World CDGLOBE 343*	**46**	2

[1] N-Trance featuring Kelly Llorenna [2] N-Trance featuring Ricardo Da Force [3] N-Trance featuring Rod Stewart

Although she is vocalist on all versions of 'Set You Free', Kelly Llorenna is given label credit only on the first entry. Similarly, Ricardo da Force appears on several tracks but receives label credit only for 'Stayin' Alive'.

N-TYCE *UK, female vocal group (1 Album: 1 Week, 4 Singles: 15 Weeks)*

Date	Title / Label	Peak	Weeks
5 Jul 97	**HEY DJ! (PLAY THAT SONG)** *Telstar CDSTAS 2885*	20	2
13 Sep 97	**WE COME TO PARTY** *Telstar CDSTAS 2915*	12	4
28 Feb 98	**TELEFUNKIN'** *Telstar CDSTAS 2944*	16	5
6 Jun 98	**BOOM BOOM** *Telstar CDSTAS 2971*	18	4
20 Jun 98	ALL DAY EVERY DAY *Telstar TCD 2945*	44	1

N.W.A. (see also DR DRE; EAZY-E; ICE CUBE)
US, male rap group (4 Albums: 14 Weeks, 4 Singles: 15 Weeks)

Date	Title / Label	Peak	Weeks
9 Sep 89	**EXPRESS YOURSELF** (re) *Fourth & Broadway BRW 144*	26	9
30 Sep 89	STRAIGHT OUTTA COMPTON *Fourth & Broadway BRLP 534*	41	6
1 Sep 90	**GANGSTA, GANGSTA** *Fourth & Broadway BRW 191*	**70**	1

11 October 1980	18 October 1980	25 October 1980	1 November 1980

◂◂ UK No.1 SINGLES ▸▸

DON'T STAND SO CLOSE TO ME The Police	DON'T STAND SO CLOSE TO ME The Police	WOMAN IN LOVE Barbra Streisand	WOMAN IN LOVE Barbra Streisand

◂◂ UK No.1 ALBUMS ▸▸

ZENYATTA MONDATTA The Police	ZENYATTA MONDATTA The Police	ZENYATTA MONDATTA The Police	ZENYATTA MONDATTA The Police

10 Nov 90	**100 MILES AND RUNNIN'** *Fourth & Broadway BRW 200*	38 3
15 Jun 91	EFIL4ZAGGIN *Fourth & Broadway BRLP 562* ▲	25 2
23 Nov 91	**ALWAYZ INTO SOMETHIN'** *Fourth & Broadway BRW 238*	60 2
31 Aug 96	GREATEST HITS *Priority CDPTY 126*	56 1
4 Oct 03	STRAIGHT OUTTA COMPTON (re-issue) *Priority 5379362*	35 5

'Express Yourself' made No.50 on its first visit and peaked at No.26 on re-entry in May 1990.

NYCC *Germany, male rap trio (2 Singles: 6 Weeks)*

30 May 98	**FIGHT FOR YOUR RIGHT (TO PARTY)** *Control 0042645 CON*	14 5
19 Sep 98	**CAN YOU FEEL IT (ROCK DA HOUSE)** *Control 0042785 CON*	68 1

NADA SURF *US, male vocal / instrumental group*

24 May 03	**INSIDE OF LOVE** *Heavenly HVN 133CD*	73 1

NADIA *Portugal, transgender vocalist – Nadia Almada*

11 Dec 04	**A LITTLE BIT OF ACTION** *Virgin / EMI VISCDX 6*	27 5

Jimmy NAIL (459 Top 500) *UK singer / songwriter, b. James Michael Aloysius Bradford, b. 1954, Newcastle, whose R&B mixed with a Geordie take on country provided a flip side to an acting career which included key characters in both Auf Wiedersehen Pet and Spender. His longest stay on the charts was courtesy of another TV series, Crocodile Shoes, in which he combined acting and singing (5 Albums: 85 Weeks, 11 Singles: 73 Weeks)*

27 Apr 85 ●	**LOVE DON'T LIVE HERE ANYMORE** *Virgin VS 764*	3 11
11 Jul 92 ★	**AIN'T NO DOUBT** *East West YZ 686*	1 12
8 Aug 92 ●	GROWING UP IN PUBLIC *East West 4509901442*	2 12
3 Oct 92	**LAURA** *East West YZ 702*	58 2
26 Nov 94 ●	**CROCODILE SHOES** (2re) *East West YZ 867CD*	4 20
3 Dec 94 ●	CROCODILE SHOES *East West 4509985562*	2 31
11 Feb 95	**COWBOY DREAMS** *East West YZ 878CD*	13 7
6 May 95	**CALLING OUT YOUR NAME** *East West YZ 935CD*	65 1
28 Oct 95	**BIG RIVER** *East West EW 008CD*	18 5
18 Nov 95 ●	BIG RIVER *East West 0630128232*	8 15
23 Dec 95	**LOVE** *East West EW 018CD*	33 4
3 Feb 96	**BIG RIVER** (re-mix) *East West EW 024CD*	72 2
16 Nov 96	**COUNTRY BOY** *East West EW 070CD*	25 8
30 Nov 96 ●	CROCODILE SHOES II *East West 630169352*	10 13
18 Oct 97 ●	THE NAIL FILE – THE BEST OF JIMMY NAIL *East West 3984207392*	8 14
21 Nov 98	**THE FLAME STILL BURNS** *London LONCD 420* [1]	47 1

[1] Jimmy Nail with Strange Fruit

NAILBOMB *Brazil / UK, male vocal / instrumental duo*

2 Apr 94	POINT BLANK *Roadrunner RR 90552*	62 1

NAKATOMI *UK, male / female production group (2 Singles: 4 Weeks)*

7 Feb 98	**CHILDREN OF THE NIGHT** *Peach PCHCD 006*	47 2
26 Oct 02	**CHILDREN OF THE NIGHT** (re-mix) *Jive 9254212*	31 2

NAKED EYES (see also CLIMIE FISHER) *UK, male vocal / instrumental duo – Pete Byrne and Rob Fisher, b. 5 Nov 1959, d. 25 Aug 1999*

23 Jul 83	**ALWAYS SOMETHING THERE TO REMIND ME** *RCA 348*	59 3

NALIN & KANE *Germany, male DJ / production duo – Andreas Bialek and Ralf Beck (3 Singles: 7 Weeks)*

1 Nov 97	**BEACHBALL** *ffrr FCD 318*	48 1
28 Mar 98	**PLANET VIOLET** *Logic 74321565702* [1]	51 1
3 Oct 98	**BEACHBALL** (re-mix) *LONDON FCD 349*	17 5

[1] Nalin INC

NAPALM DEATH *UK, male vocal / instrumental group (3 Albums: 3 Weeks)*

15 Sep 90	HARMONY OF CORRUPTION *Earache MOSH 19*	67 1
30 May 92	UTOPIA BANISHED *Earache MOSH 53CD*	58 1
3 Feb 96	DIATRIBES *Earache MOSH 141CDD*	74 1

NAPOLEON XIV *US, male vocalist – Jerry Samuels*

4 Aug 66 ●	**THEY'RE COMING TO TAKE ME AWAY, HA-HAAA!** *Warner Bros. WB 5831*	4 10

NARCOTIC THRUST *UK, male DJ / production duo – Stuart Crichton and Andy Morris (3 Singles: 11 Weeks)*

10 Aug 02	**SAFE FROM HARM** *ffrr FCD 406*	24 3
17 Apr 04 ●	**I LIKE IT** *Fre2Air 0153656 F2A*	9 6
22 Jan 05	**WHEN THE DAWN BREAKS** *Fre2Air F2A 3CDX*	28 2

NAS *US, male rapper – Nasir Jones (4 Albums: 18 Weeks, 14 Singles: 65 Weeks)*

28 May 94	**IT AIN'T HARD TO TELL** *Columbia 6604702*	64 1
13 Jul 96	IT WAS WRITTEN *Columbia 4841962* ▲	38 6
17 Aug 96	**IF I RULED THE WORLD** *Columbia 6634022*	12 7
25 Jan 97	**STREET DREAMS** *Columbia 6641302*	12 4
14 Jun 97	**HEAD OVER HEELS** *Epic 6645942* [1]	18 3
17 Apr 99	I AM ... *Columbia 4894192* ▲	31 4
29 May 99	**HATE ME NOW** *Columbia 6672562* [2]	14 6
15 Jan 00	**NASTRADAMUS** *Columbia 6685572*	24 3
22 Jan 00	**HOT BOYZ** *Elektra E 7002CD* [3] $	18 3
21 Apr 01	**OOCHIE WALLY** *Columbia 67010852* [4]	30 3
2 Feb 02	**GOT UR SELF A ...** (re) *Columbia 6723022*	30 5
13 Jul 02 ●	**I'M GONNA BE ALRIGHT** *Epic 6728442* [5]	3 10
25 Jan 03	GOD'S SON *Columbia 5098115* [1]	57 6
25 Jan 03	**MADE YOU LOOK** *Columbia 6734792*	27 3
5 Apr 03	**I CAN** *Columbia 6737382*	19 7
20 Nov 04	**BRIDGING THE GAP** *Columbia 6754682* [6]	18 4
11 Dec 04	STREET'S DISCIPLE *Columbia 5177249* [1]	45 2
16 Apr 05	**IN PUBLIC** *Virgin VSCDT 1893* [7]	17 6

[1] Allure featuring Nas [2] Nas featuring Puff Daddy [3] Missy 'Misdemeanor' Elliott featuring Nas, Eve and Q Tip [4] QB Finest featuring Nas & Bravehearts [5] Jennifer Lopez featuring Nas [6] Nas / Olu Dara [7] Kelis featuring Nas
[1] Nasir Jones

Graham NASH (see also CROSBY, STILLS, NASH and YOUNG; The HOLLIES) *UK, male vocalist (2 Albums: 13 Weeks)*

26 Jun 71	SONGS FOR BEGINNERS *Atlantic 2401011*	13 8
13 May 72	GRAHAM NASH DAVID CROSBY *Atlantic K 50011* [1]	13 5

[1] Graham Nash David Crosby

Johnny NASH *US, male vocalist / actor (2 Albums: 17 Weeks, 11 Singles: 106 Weeks)*

7 Aug 68 ●	**HOLD ME TIGHT** *Regal Zonophone RZ 3010*	5 16
8 Jan 69 ●	**YOU GOT SOUL** *Major Minor MM 586*	6 12
2 Apr 69 ●	**CUPID** (re) *Major Minor MM 603*	6 12
1 Apr 72	**STIR IT UP** *CBS 7800*	13 12
24 Jun 72 ●	**I CAN SEE CLEARLY NOW** *CBS 8113* ▲ $	5 15
5 Aug 72	I CAN SEE CLEARLY NOW *CBS 64860*	39 6
7 Oct 72 ●	**THERE ARE MORE QUESTIONS THAN ANSWERS** *CBS 8351*	9 9
14 Jun 75 ★	**TEARS ON MY PILLOW** *CBS 3220*	1 11
11 Oct 75	**LET'S BE FRIENDS** *CBS 3597*	42 3
12 Jun 76	**(WHAT A) WONDERFUL WORLD** *Epic EPC 4294*	25 7
10 Dec 77	JOHNNY NASH COLLECTION *Epic EPC 10008*	18 11
9 Nov 85	**ROCK ME BABY** *2000 ADFED 19*	47 4
15 Apr 89	**I CAN SEE CLEARLY NOW** (re-mix) *Epic JN 1*	54 5

NASH THE SLASH *Canada, male vocalist / multi-instrumentalist – Jeff Plewman*

21 Feb 81	CHILDREN OF THE NIGHT *DinDisc DID 9*	61 1

The NASHVILLE TEENS *UK, male vocal / instrumental group (5 Singles: 36 Weeks)*

9 Jul 64 ●	**TOBACCO ROAD** *Decca F 11930*	6 13
22 Oct 64 ●	**GOOGLE EYE** *Decca F 12000*	10 10

8 November 1980	15 November 1980	22 November 1980	29 November 1980
WOMAN IN LOVE Barbra Streisand	THE TIDE IS HIGH Blondie	THE TIDE IS HIGH Blondie	SUPER TROUPER Abba
GUILTY	GUILTY	SUPER TROUPER	SUPER TROUPER

KEY UK No.1 ★★ UK Top 10 ●● Still on chart ++ UK entry at No.1 ■■ US No.1 ▲▲ UK million seller £ US million seller $
Singles re-entries are listed as (re), (2re), (3re)... which signifies that the hit re-entered the chart once, twice or three times...
Peak Position / Weeks

4 Mar 65 FIND MY WAY BACK HOME *Decca F 12089* 34 6
20 May 65 THIS LITTLE BIRD *Decca F 12143* 38 4
3 Feb 66 THE HARD WAY (re) *Decca F 12316* 45 3

NATASHA
UK, female vocalist – Natasha England (1 Album: 3 Weeks, 2 Singles: 16 Weeks)

5 Jun 82 ● IKO IKO *Towerbell TOW 22* 10 11
4 Sep 82 THE BOOM BOOM ROOM *Towerbell TOW 25* 44 5
9 Oct 82 CAPTURED *Towerbell TOWLP 2* 53 3

Ultra NATÉ
US, female vocalist – Ultra Naté Wyche (1 Album: 4 Weeks, 10 Singles: 41 Weeks)

9 Dec 89 IT'S OVER NOW *Eternal YZ 440* 62 3
23 Feb 91 IS IT LOVE? *Eternal YZ 509* [1] 71 1
29 Jan 94 SHOW ME *Warner Bros. W 0219CD* 62 1
14 Jun 97 ● FREE *AM:PM 5822432* 4 17
24 Jan 98 FREE (re-mix) *AM:PM 5825012* 33 2
18 Apr 98 ● FOUND A CURE *AM:PM 5826452* 6 7
9 May 98 SITUATION: CRITICAL *AM:PM 5408242* 17 4
25 Jul 98 NEW KIND OF MEDICINE *AM:PM 5827492* 14 5
22 Jul 00 DESIRE *AM:PM CDAMPM 133* 40 2
9 Jun 01 GET IT UP (THE FEELING) *AM:PM CDAMPM 140* 51 1
28 May 05 FREAK ON (re) *Hed Kandi HEDKCDX 10* [2] 37 2

[1] Basement Boys present Ultra Naté [2] Stonebridge vs Ultra Naté

NATHAN NEW
UK, male vocalist – Nathan Fagan-Gayle

12 Mar 05 COME INTO MY ROOM *V2 JAD 5029593* 37 2

NATIONAL BRASS BAND
UK, orchestra

10 May 80 GOLDEN MELODIES *K-Tel ONE 1075* 15 10

NATIVE
(see also BEAT RENEGADES; DREAM FREQUENCY; QUAKE featuring Marcia RAE; RED) *UK, male production duo*

10 Feb 01 FEEL THE DRUMS *Slinky Music SLINKY 009CD* 46 2

NATURAL
US, male vocal group

10 Aug 02 PUT YOUR ARMS AROUND ME *Ariola 74321947892* 32 2

NATURAL BORN CHILLERS
UK, male production duo – Arif Salih and Lee Parker

1 Nov 97 ROCK THE FUNKY BEAT *East West EW 138CD1* 30 3

NATURAL BORN GROOVES
Belgium, male DJ / production duo – Burn Boon and Jaco van Rijsvijck (2 Singles: 3 Weeks)

2 Nov 96 FORERUNNER *XL XLS 76CD* 64 1
19 Apr 97 GROOVEBIRD *Positiva CDTIV 75* 21 2

NATURAL LIFE
UK, male / female vocal / instrumental group

7 Mar 92 NATURAL LIFE *Tribe NLIFE 3* 47 3

NATURAL SELECTION
US, male vocal / instrumental duo

9 Nov 91 DO ANYTHING *East West A 8724* 69 2

The NATURALS
UK, male vocal / instrumental group

20 Aug 64 I SHOULD HAVE KNOWN BETTER *Parlophone R 5165* 24 9

David NAUGHTON
US, male actor / vocalist

25 Aug 79 MAKIN' IT *RSO 32* $ 44 6

NAUGHTY BY NATURE
US, male rap group (2 Albums: 5 Weeks, 9 Singles: 19 Weeks)

9 Nov 91 O.P.P. *Big Life BLR 62* $ 73 1
20 Jun 92 O.P.P. (re-issue) *Big Life BLR 74* 35 3
30 Jan 93 HIP HOP HOORAY *Big Life BLRD 89* $ 22 3
6 Mar 93 19 NAUGHTY III *Big Life BLRCD 23* 40 2
19 Jun 93 IT'S ON *Big Life BLRD 99* 48 2
27 Nov 93 HIP HOP HOORAY (re-mix) *Big Life BLRDA 104* 20 4
29 Apr 95 FEEL ME FLOW *Big Life BLRD 115* 23 3
27 May 95 POVERTY'S PARADISE *Big Life BLRCD 28* 20 3
11 Sep 99 JAMBOREE *Arista 74321692882* [1] 51 1
19 Oct 02 FEELS GOOD (DON'T WORRY BOUT A THING) *Island CID 806* [2] 44 1
8 Jan 05 O.P.P. (2nd re-issue) *Tommy Boy 5046759840* 71 1

[1] Naughty By Nature featuring Zhané [2] Naughty By Nature featuring 3LW

Maria NAYLER
UK, female vocalist (5 Singles: 26 Weeks)

9 Mar 96 BE AS ONE *Deconstruction 74321342962* [1] 17 4
16 Nov 96 ● ONE & ONE *Deconstruction 74321427692* [2] 3 17
7 Mar 98 NAKED AND SACRED *Deconstruction 74321534242* 32 3
5 Sep 98 WILL YOU BE WITH ME / LOVE IS THE GOD *Deconstruction 74321591772* 65 1
27 May 00 ANGRY SKIES *Deconstruction 74321759492* 42 1

[1] Sasha and Maria [2] Robert Miles featuring Maria Nayler

NAZARETH
(see also Dan McCAFFERTY) *UK, male vocal / instrumental group (7 Albums: 51 Weeks, 11 Singles: 75 Weeks)*

5 May 73 ● BROKEN DOWN ANGEL *Mooncrest MOON 1* 9 11
26 May 73 RAZAMANAZ *Mooncrest CREST 1* 11 25
21 Jul 73 ● BAD BAD BOY *Mooncrest MOON 9* 10 9
13 Oct 73 THIS FLIGHT TONIGHT *Mooncrest MOON 14* 11 13
24 Nov 73 ● LOUD 'N' PROUD *Mooncrest CREST 4* 10 7
23 Mar 74 SHANGHAI'D IN SHANGHAI *Mooncrest MOON 22* 41 4
18 May 74 RAMPANT *Mooncrest CREST 15* 13 3
14 Jun 75 MY WHITE BICYCLE *Mooncrest MOON 47* 14 8
15 Nov 75 HOLY ROLLER *Mountain TOP 3* 36 4
13 Dec 75 GREATEST HITS *Mountain TOPS 108* 54 1
24 Sep 77 HOT TRACKS (EP) *Mountain NAZ 1* 15 11
18 Feb 78 GONE DEAD TRAIN *Mountain NAZ 002* 49 2
13 May 78 PLACE IN YOUR HEART (re) *Mountain TOP 37* 70 2
27 Jan 79 MAY THE SUNSHINE *Mountain NAZ 003* 22 8
3 Feb 79 NO MEAN CITY *Mountain TOPS 123* 34 9
28 Jul 79 STAR *Mountain TOP 45* 54 3
28 Feb 81 THE FOOL CIRCLE *NEMS NEL 6019* 60 3
3 Oct 81 NAZARETH LIVE *NEMS NELD 102* 78 3

Tracks on Hot Tracks (EP): Love Hurts / This Flight Tonight / Broken Down Angel / Hair of the Dog.

Me'Shell NDEGEOCELLO
US, female vocalist / bass guitarist (3 Singles: 5 Weeks)

12 Feb 94 IF THAT'S YOUR BOYFRIEND (HE WASN'T LAST NIGHT) *Maverick W 0223CD1* 74 1
3 Sep 94 WILD NIGHT *Mercury MERCD 409* [1] 34 3
1 Mar 97 NEVER MISS THE WATER *Reprise W 0393CD* [2] 59 1

[1] John Mellencamp featuring Me'Shell Ndegeocello [2] Chaka Khan featuring Me'Shell Ndegeocello

Youssou N'DOUR
Senegal, male vocalist (5 Singles: 35 Weeks)

3 Jun 89 SHAKIN' THE TREE *Virgin VS 1167* [1] 61 3
22 Dec 90 SHAKIN' THE TREE (re-issue) *Virgin VS 1322* [1] 57 4
25 Jun 94 ● 7 SECONDS (re) *Columbia 6605082* [2] 3 25
14 Jan 95 UNDECIDED *Columbia 6609712* 53 2
10 Oct 98 HOW COME *Interscope IND 95598* [3] 52 1

[1] Youssou N'Dour and Peter Gabriel [2] Youssou N'Dour (featuring Neneh Cherry) [3] Youssou N'Dour and Canibus

The re-issue of 'Shaking the Tree' was listed with its flip side, 'Solsbury Hill' by Peter Gabriel.

	6 December 1980	13 December 1980	20 December 1980	27 December 1980
UK No.1 SINGLES	SUPER TROUPER Abba	SUPER TROUPER Abba	(JUST LIKE) STARTING OVER John Lennon	THERE'S NO ONE QUITE LIKE GRANDMA St Winifred's School Choir
UK No.1 ALBUMS	SUPER TROUPER Abba	SUPER TROUPER Abba	SUPER TROUPER Abba	SUPER TROUPER Abba

NEARLY GOD (see also TRICKY)
UK, male / female vocal / instrumental group

20 Apr 96 **POEMS** *Durban Poison DPCD 3* ... 28 2
4 May 96 ● **NEARLY GOD** *Fourth & Broadway DPCD 1001* ... 10 4

Terry NEASON *UK, female vocalist*

25 Jun 94 **LIFEBOAT** *WEA YZ 830* ... 72 1

NEBULA II *UK, male instrumental / production group (2 Singles: 3 Weeks)*

1 Feb 92 **SEANCE / ATHEAMA** *Reinforced RIVET 1211* ... 55 2
16 May 92 **FLATLINERS** *J4M 12NEBULA 2* ... 54 1

NED'S ATOMIC DUSTBIN *UK, male vocal (Jonn Penney) / instrumental group (3 Albums: 8 Weeks, 8 Singles: 24 Weeks)*

14 Jul 90 **KILL YOUR TELEVISION** *Chapter 22 CHAP 48* ... 53 2
27 Oct 90 **UNTIL YOU FIND OUT** *Chapter 22 CHAP 52* ... 51 2
9 Feb 91 **BITE** (import) *Rough Trade Germany RTD 14011831* ... 72 1
9 Mar 91 **HAPPY** *Columbia 6566807* ... 16 4
13 Apr 91 ● **GOD FODDER** *Furtive 4681121* ... 4 5
21 Sep 91 **TRUST** *Furtive 6574627* ... 21 4
10 Oct 92 **NOT SLEEPING AROUND** *Furtive 6583866* ... 19 3
31 Oct 92 **ARE YOU NORMAL?** *Furtive 4726332* ... 13 2
5 Dec 92 **INTACT** *Furtive 6588166* ... 36 6
25 Mar 95 **ALL I ASK OF MYSELF IS THAT I HOLD TOGETHER** *Furtive 6613565* ... 33 2
15 Jul 95 **STUCK** *Furtive 6620562* ... 64 1

Raja NEE *US, female vocalist*

4 Mar 95 **TURN IT UP** *Perspective 5874872* ... 42 2

Joey NEGRO
(see also AKABU featuring Linda CLIFFORD; HED BOYS; IL PADRINOS featuring Jocelyn BROWN; JAKATTA; Li KWAN; PHASE II; RAVEN MAIZE; Z FACTOR) *UK, male producer – Dave Lee (6 Singles: 15 Weeks)*

16 Nov 91 **DO WHAT YOU FEEL** *Ten TEN 391* [1] ... 36 3
21 Dec 91 **REACHIN'** *Republic LIC 160* [1] ... 70 1
18 Jul 92 **ENTER YOUR FANTASY (EP)** *Ten TEN 397* ... 35 3
25 Sep 93 **WHAT HAPPENED TO THE MUSIC** *Virgin VSCD 1466* ... 51 2
19 Feb 00 ● **MUST BE THE MUSIC** *Incentive CENT 4CDS* [2] ... 8 5
16 Sep 00 **SATURDAY** *Yola YOLA CDX 03* [2] ... 41 1

[1] Joey Negro presents Phase II [2] Joey Negro featuring Taka Boom

Tracks on Enter Your Fantasy (EP): Love Fantasy / Get Up / Enter Your Mind / Everybody.

neil *UK, male actor / vocalist – Nigel Planer*

14 Jul 84 ● **HOLE IN MY SHOE** *WEA YZ 10* ... 2 10

Vince NEIL (see also MÖTLEY CRÜE) *US, male vocalist – Vince Wharton*

3 Oct 92 **YOU'RE INVITED (BUT YOUR FRIEND CAN'T COME)** *Hollywood HWD 123* ... 63 1
8 May 93 **EXPOSED** *Warner Bros. 9362452602* ... 44 1

NEILS CHILDREN NEW *UK, male vocal / instrumental trio*

18 Jun 05 **ALWAYS THE SAME** *Poptones MC 5100SCD* ... 56 1

NEJA *Italy, female vocalist – Agnese Cacciola*

26 Sep 98 **RESTLESS (I KNOW YOU KNOW)** *Panorama CDPAN 1* ... 47 1

NEK *Italy, male vocalist*

29 Aug 98 **LAURA** *Coalition COLA 054CD* ... 59 1

NELLY (262 Top 500)
Southern rap superstar, b. Cornell Haynes, 2 Nov 1974, Travis, Texas, US. Leader of the St Louis rap pack, St Lunatics. He was the first act since The Beatles to have his initial two US No.1 hits replace each other at the top (5 Albums: 101 Weeks, 16 Singles: 147 Weeks)

11 Nov 00 ● **(HOT S**T) COUNTRY GRAMMAR** *Universal MCSTD 40242* ... 7 9
3 Feb 01 **COUNTRY GRAMMAR** *Universal 1577432* ▲ ... 14 31
24 Feb 01 **EI** *Universal MCSTD 40249* ... 11 5
19 May 01 ● **RIDE WIT ME** *Universal MCSTD 40252* [1] ... 3 12
15 Sep 01 **BATTER UP** *Universal MCSTD 40261* [2] ... 28 3
27 Oct 01 **WHERE THE PARTY AT?** *Columbia MCSTD 6719012* [3] ... 25 3
27 Apr 02 ● **GIRLFRIEND** *Jive 9253312* [4] ... 2 12
29 Jun 02 ● **HOT IN HERRE** *Universal MCSTD 40289* ▲ ... 4 15
13 Jul 02 ● **NELLYVILLE** *Universal 186902* ▲ ... 2 38
26 Oct 02 ★ **DILEMMA** *Universal MCSTD 40299* [5] ■ ▲ ... 1 21
15 Mar 03 ● **WORK IT** *Universal MCSCD 40312* [6] ... 7 11
20 Sep 03 ● **SHAKE YA TAILFEATHER** *Bad Boy MCSTD 40337* [7] ▲ ... 10 7
13 Dec 03 **IZ U** *Universal MCSTD 40346* ... 36 4
11 Sep 04 ★ **MY PLACE / FLAP YOUR WINGS** *Universal MCSTD 40379* ■ ... 1 11
25 Sep 04 ● **SUIT** *Universal 9863936* ▲ ... 8 21
25 Sep 04 **SWEAT** *Universal 9863935* ... 11 4
4 Dec 04 ● **TILT YA HEAD BACK** *Universal MCSTD 40396* [8] ... 5 12
5 Mar 05 ★ **OVER AND OVER** *Curb / Derrty / Island MCSTD 40402* [9] ■ ... 1 12
28 May 05 **SWEAT SUIT** *Universal 9882176* ... 41 7
25 Jun 05 ● **N DEY SAY** *Universal MCSTD 40414* ... 6 7
16 Jul 05 **GET IT POPPIN'** *Atlantic AT 0210CD* [10] ... 34 3

[1] Nelly featuring City Spud [2] Nelly and St Lunatics [3] Jagged Edge featuring Nelly [4] 'N Sync featuring Nelly [5] Nelly featuring Kelly Rowland [6] Nelly featuring Justin Timberlake [7] Nelly, P Diddy and Murphy Lee [8] Nelly & Christina Aguilera [9] Nelly featuring Tim McGraw [10] Fat Joe featuring Nelly

'My Place' features uncredited vocalist Jaheim. Sweat Suit features tracks from the simultaneously-released albums Sweat and Suit.

NELSON *US, male vocal duo*

27 Oct 90 **(CAN'T LIVE WITHOUT YOUR) LOVE AND AFFECTION** *DGC GEF 82* ▲ ... 54 3

Bill NELSON (see also BE BOP DELUXE; RED NOISE) *UK, male vocalist / guitarist / synths player (5 Albums: 21 Weeks, 4 Singles: 12 Weeks)*

24 Feb 79 **SOUND ON SOUND** *Harvest SHSP 4095* [1] ... 33 5
24 Feb 79 **FURNITURE MUSIC** *Harvest HAR 5176* [1] ... 59 3
5 May 79 **REVOLT INTO STYLE** *Harvest HAR 5183* [1] ... 69 2
5 Jul 80 **DO YOU DREAM IN COLOUR?** *Cocteau COQ 1* ... 52 4
23 May 81 ● **QUIT DREAMING AND GET ON THE BEAM** *Mercury 6359 055* ... 7 6
13 Jun 81 **YOUTH OF NATION ON FIRE** *Mercury WILL 2* ... 73 3
3 Jul 82 **THE LOVE THAT WHIRLS (DIARY OF A THINKING HEART)** *Mercury WHIRL 3* ... 28 4
14 May 83 **CHIMERA** *Mercury MERB 19* ... 30 5
3 May 86 **GETTING THE HOLY GHOST ACROSS** *Portrait PRT 26602* ... 91 1

[1] Bill Nelson's Red Noise [1] Bill Nelson's Red Noise

Phyllis NELSON *US, female vocalist, b. 3 Oct 1950, d. 12 Jan 1998 (1 Album: 10 Weeks, 2 Singles: 24 Weeks)*

23 Feb 85 ★ **MOVE CLOSER** *Carrere CAR 337* ... 1 21
20 Apr 85 **MOVE CLOSER** *Carrere CAL 203* ... 29 10
21 May 94 **MOVE CLOSER** (re-issue) *EMI CDEMCT 9* ... 34 3

Ricky NELSON (498 Top 500)
TV star turned teen idol and later singer / songwriter, b. 8 May 1940, New Jersey, US, d. 31 Dec 1985. He was virtually raised on a US radio / TV f amily show. In the 1950s, he enjoyed sales on a par with Elvis Presley and Pat Boone. Both his father, Ozzie, and his two sons (who recorded as Nelson), also topped the US chart (1935 and 1990) (19 Singles: 150 Weeks)

21 Feb 58 **STOOD UP** (re) *London HLP 8542* $ ... 27 2
22 Aug 58 ● **POOR LITTLE FOOL** (re) *London HLP 8670* ▲ $ ... 4 14
7 Nov 58 ● **SOMEDAY** *London HLP 8732* ... 9 13
21 Nov 58 **I GOT A FEELING** *London HLP 8732* ... 27 1
17 Apr 59 ● **IT'S LATE** *London HLP 8817* $ ... 3 20
15 May 59 **NEVER BE ANYONE ELSE BUT YOU** (re) *London HLP 8817* ... 14 10

3 January 1981	10 January 1981	17 January 1981	24 January 1981
THERE'S NO ONE QUITE LIKE GRANDMA St Winifred's School Choir	**IMAGINE** John Lennon	**IMAGINE** John Lennon	**IMAGINE** John Lennon
SUPER TROUPER Abba	**SUPER TROUPER** Abba	**SUPER TROUPER** Abba	**KINGS OF THE WILD FRONTIER** Adam and The Ants

KEY
UK No.1 ★ UK Top 10 ● Still on chart + UK entry at No.1 ■
US No.1 ▲ UK million seller £ US million seller $
Singles re-entries are listed as (re), (2re), (3re)... which signifies that the hit re-entered the chart once, twice or three times...

Peak Position / Weeks

4 Sep 59 **SWEETER THAN YOU** *London HLP 8927* 19 3
11 Sep 59 **JUST A LITTLE TOO MUCH** *London HLP 8927* 11 8
15 Jan 60 **I WANNA BE LOVED** *London HLP 9021* 30 1
7 Jul 60 **YOUNG EMOTIONS** *London HLP 9121* 48 1
1 Jun 61 ● **HELLO MARY LOU / TRAVELLIN' MAN** *London HLP 9347* ▲ $ 2 18
16 Nov 61 **EVERLOVIN'** *London HLP 9440* [1] 23 5
29 Mar 62 **YOUNG WORLD** *London HLP 9524* 19 13
30 Aug 62 **TEENAGE IDOL** *London HLP 9583* [1] 39 4
17 Jan 63 **IT'S UP TO YOU** *London HLP 9648* [1] 22 9
17 Oct 63 **FOOLS RUSH IN** *Brunswick 05895* [1] 12 9
30 Jan 64 **FOR YOU** *Brunswick 05900* [1] 14 10
21 Oct 72 **GARDEN PARTY** *MCA MU 1165* [1] $ 41 4
24 Aug 91 **HELLO MARY LOU (GOODBYE HEART)** (re-issue) *Liberty EMCT 2* 45 5

[1] Rick Nelson

Sandy NELSON

US, male drummer – Sander Nelson (4 Singles: 42 Weeks)

6 Nov 59 ● **TEEN BEAT** (re) *Top Rank JAR 197* $ 9 12
14 Dec 61 ● **LET THERE BE DRUMS** *London HLP 9466* 3 16
22 Mar 62 **DRUMS ARE MY BEAT** *London HLP 9521* 30 6
7 Jun 62 **DRUMMIN' UP A STORM** *London HLP 9558* 39 8

Shara NELSON (see also MASSIVE ATTACK)

UK, female vocalist (2 Albums: 11 Weeks, 7 Singles: 23 Weeks)

24 Jul 93 **DOWN THAT ROAD** *Cooltempo CDCOOL 275* 19 6
18 Sep 93 **ONE GOODBYE IN TEN** *Cooltempo CDCOOL 279* 21 5
2 Oct 93 **WHAT SILENCE KNOWS** *Cooltempo CTCD 35* 22 9
12 Feb 94 **UPTIGHT** *Cooltempo CDCOOL 286* 19 5
4 Jun 94 **NOBODY** *Cooltempo CDCOOL 290* 49 1
10 Sep 94 **INSIDE OUT / DOWN THAT ROAD** (re-mix) *Cooltempo CDCOOLX 295* 34 3
16 Sep 95 **ROUGH WITH THE SMOOTH** *Cooltempo CDCOOL 311* 30 2
7 Oct 95 **FRIENDLY FIRE** *Cooltempo CTCD 48* 44 2
5 Dec 98 **SENSE OF DANGER** *Pagan PAGAN 024CDS* [1] 61 1

[1] Presence featuring Shara Nelson

Willie NELSON

US, male vocalist / guitarist (2 Singles: 13 Weeks)

31 Jul 82 **ALWAYS ON MY MIND** *CBS A 2511* $ 49 3
7 Apr 84 **TO ALL THE GIRLS I'VE LOVED BEFORE** *CBS A 4252* [1] $ ... 17 10

[1] Julio Iglesias and Willie Nelson

NENA

Germany, female / male vocal (Gabriele Kerner) / instrumental group (1 Album: 5 Weeks, 2 Singles: 14 Weeks)

4 Feb 84 ★ **99 RED BALLOONS** *Epic A 4074* $ 1 12
24 Mar 84 **NENA** *Epic EPC 25925* 31 5
5 May 84 **JUST A DREAM** *Epic H 3249* 70 2

NEO CORTEX

Italy, male production trio

23 Oct 04 **ELEMENTS** *All Around the World CDGLOBE 332* 67 1

The NEPTUNES (see also N*E*R*D; P DIDDY)

US, male production / vocal / rap duo – Pharrell Williams and Chad Hugo

30 Aug 03 ● **THE NEPTUNES PRESENT ... CLONES** *Arista 82876533852* ▲ 2 8

The Neptunes Present ... Clones appeared on the Compilations Chart only.

N*E*R*D (see also The NEPTUNES)

US, male vocal / production trio (2 Albums: 34 Weeks, 5 Singles: 27 Weeks)

9 Jun 01 **LAPDANCE** *Virgin VUSCD 196* [1] 33 2
10 Aug 02 **ROCK STAR** *Virgin VUSCD 253* 15 4
17 Aug 02 **IN SEARCH OF ...** *Virgin CDVUSX 216* 28 18
29 Mar 03 **PROVIDER / LAPDANCE** *Virgin VUSCD 262* [1] 20 4
27 Mar 04 ● **SHE WANTS TO MOVE** *Virgin VUSCD 284* 5 12
3 Apr 04 ● **FLY OR DIE** *Virgin CDVUS 250* 4 16
26 Jun 04 **MAYBE** *Virgin VUSDX 291* 25 5

[1] N*E*R*D featuring Lee Harvey and Vita

Frances NERO

US, female vocalist

13 Apr 91 **FOOTSTEPS FOLLOWING ME** *Debut DEBT 3109* 17 9

NERO and The GLADIATORS

UK, male instrumental group (2 Singles: 6 Weeks)

23 Mar 61 **ENTRY OF THE GLADIATORS** (re) *Decca F 11329* 37 5
27 Jul 61 **IN THE HALL OF THE MOUNTAIN KING** *Decca F 11367* 48 1

Ann NESBY

US, female vocalist (2 Singles: 3 Weeks)

21 Dec 96 **WITNESS (EP)** *AM:PM 5875612* 42 2
17 May 97 **HOLD ON (EP)** *AM:PM 5822332* 75 1

Tracks on Witness (EP): Can I Get a Witness / In the Spirit / I'm Still Wearing Your Name. Tracks on Hold On (EP): Hold On (Mousse T's Uplifting Garage Edit) / Hold On (Mousse T's Hard Soul Remix) / Hold On (Klub Head Mix) / This Weekend (Laidback Mix).

Michael NESMITH (see also The MONKEES)

US, male vocalist / guitarist – Robert Nesmith

26 Mar 77 **RIO** *Island WIP 6373* 28 6

NETWORK

UK, male vocal / instrumental group

12 Dec 92 **BROKEN WINGS** *Chrysalis CHS 3923* 46 4

NEVADA

UK, male / female vocal / instrumental group

8 Jan 83 **IN THE BLEAK MID WINTER** *Polydor POSP 203* 71 1

Robbie NEVIL

US, male vocalist (1 Album: 1 Week, 3 Singles: 24 Weeks)

20 Dec 86 ● **C'EST LA VIE** *Manhattan MT 14* 3 11
2 May 87 **DOMINOES** *Manhattan MT 19* 26 6
13 Jun 87 **C'EST LA VIE** *Manhattan MTL 1006* 93 1
11 Jul 87 **WOT'S IT TO YA** *Manhattan MT 24* 43 7

Tom NEVILLE

UK, male DJ / producer

6 Mar 04 **JUST FUCK** *Nukleuz 0555PNUK* 60 1

The NEVILLE BROTHERS

US, male vocal / instrumental group (1 Album: 3 Weeks, 2 Singles: 7 Weeks)

25 Nov 89 **WITH GOD ON OUR SIDE** *A&M AM 545* 47 6
7 Jul 90 **BIRD ON A WIRE** *A&M AM 568* 72 1
18 Aug 90 **BROTHER'S KEEPER** *A&M 3953121* 35 3

Jason NEVINS

US, male DJ / producer (6 Singles: 29 Weeks)

21 Feb 98 **IT'S LIKE THAT (GERMAN IMPORT)** (import) *Columbia 6652932* [1] 63 3
14 Mar 98 **IT'S LIKE THAT (US IMPORT)** (import) *Columbia 6652932* [1] . 65 1
21 Mar 98 ★ **IT'S LIKE THAT** *Sm:)e Communications SM 90652* [1] ■ £ 1 16
18 Apr 98 **IT'S TRICKY** (import) *Epidrome EPD 6656982* [1] 74 1
26 Jun 99 **INSANE IN THE BRAIN** *INCredible INCRL 17CD* [2] 19 3
16 Aug 03 ● **I'M IN HEAVEN** *Fre2Air / Incentive 0148665 F2A* [3] 9 5

[1] Run-DMC vs Jason Nevins [2] Jason Nevins vs Cypress Hill [3] Jason Nevins featuring UKNY / Holly James

NEW ATLANTIC

UK, male instrumental / production duo – Richard Lloyd and Cameron Saunders (4 Singles: 15 Weeks)

29 Feb 92 **I KNOW** *3 Beat 3BT 1* 12 7
3 Oct 92 **INTO THE FUTURE** *3 Beat 3BT 2* [1] 70 1

31 January 1981	7 February 1981	14 February 1981	21 February 1981
◂◂ UK No.1 SINGLES ▸▸			
IMAGINE John Lennon	**WOMAN** John Lennon	**WOMAN** John Lennon	**SHADDAP YOU FACE** Joe Dolce Music Theatre
◂◂ UK No.1 ALBUMS ▸▸			
KINGS OF THE WILD FRONTIER Adam and The Ants	**DOUBLE FANTASY** John Lennon and Yoko Ono	**DOUBLE FANTASY** John Lennon and Yoko Ono	**FACE VALUE** Phil Collins

13 Feb 93 **TAKE OFF SOME TIME** *3 Beat 3BTCD 14* 64 1
26 Nov 94 **THE SUNSHINE AFTER THE RAIN** *Ffrreedom TABCD 223* [2] 26 6

[1] New Atlantic featuring Linda Wright [2] New Atlantic / U4EA featuring Berri

A re-mix of 'The Sunshine After the Rain' in 1995 was credited simply to the vocalist Berri.

Choir of NEW COLLEGE OXFORD / Edward HIGGINBOTTOM

UK, choir / male conductor (2 Albums: 7 Weeks)

12 Oct 96 AGNUS DEI *Erato 630146342* 49 5
18 Apr 98 AGNUS DEI II *Erato 3984216592* 57 2

NEW EDITION (see also BELL BIV DEVOE)

US, male vocal group (1 Album: 3 Weeks, 6 Singles: 36 Weeks)

16 Apr 83 ★ **CANDY GIRL** *London LON 21* 1 13
13 Aug 83 **POPCORN LOVE** *London LON 31* 43 5
23 Feb 85 **MR TELEPHONE MAN** *MCA MCA 938* 19 9
15 Apr 89 **CRUCIAL** *MCA MCA 23934* 70 1
10 Aug 96 **HIT ME OFF** *MCA MCSTD 48014* 20 4
14 Sep 96 HOME AGAIN *MCA MCD 11480* ▲ 22 3
7 Jun 97 **SOMETHING ABOUT YOU** *MCA MCSTD 48032* 16 4

NEW FAST AUTOMATIC DAFFODILS

UK, male vocal / instrumental group (2 Albums: 2 Weeks)

17 Nov 90 PIGEON HOLE *Play It Again Sam BIAS 185* 49 1
24 Oct 92 BODY EXIT MIND *Play It Again Sam BIAS 205CD* 57 1

NEW FOUND GLORY *US, male vocal (Jordan Pundik) / instrumental group*

(2 Albums: 10 Weeks, 6 Singles: 8 Weeks)

16 Jun 01 **HIT OR MISS (WAITED TOO LONG)** *MCA 1558232* 58 1
29 Jun 02 ● STICKS AND STONES *MCA 1129452* 10 8
3 Aug 02 **MY FRIENDS OVER YOU** *MCA MCSTD 40286* 30 3
19 Oct 02 **HEAD ON COLLISION** *MCA MCSTD 40298* 64 1
29 May 04 CATALYST *Geffen / Polydor 9862440* 27 2
12 Jun 04 **ALL DOWNHILL FROM HERE** *Geffen 9862523* 58 1
11 Sep 04 **FAILURE'S NOT FLATTERING** *Geffen MCSTD 40380* 67 1
26 Feb 05 **I DON'T WANNA KNOW** *Geffen 2103972* 48 1

NEW GENERATION *UK, male vocal / instrumental group*

26 Jun 68 **SMOKEY BLUES AWAY** *Spark SRL 1007* 38 5

NEW KIDS ON THE BLOCK (355 Top 500)

Vocal group that kick-started the 1990's boy band boom: Jordan and Jon Knight, Donnie Wahlberg, Danny Wood and Joey McIntyre. Formed in Boston, US, by producer / manager Maurice Starr as a pop version of his act New Edition. In 1990, they grossed a reported $861 million and became the first group to score eight UK Top 10 entries in a year (7 Albums: 106 Weeks, 14 Singles: 90 Weeks)

16 Sep 89 **HANGIN' TOUGH** *CBS BLOCK 1* $ 52 4
11 Nov 89 ★ **YOU GOT IT (THE RIGHT STUFF)** *CBS BLOCK 2* 1 13
9 Dec 89 ● HANGIN' TOUGH *CBS 4608741* ▲ 2 41
6 Jan 90 ★ **HANGIN' TOUGH** (re-issue) *CBS BLOCK 3* ▲ 1 9
17 Mar 90 ● **I'LL BE LOVING YOU (FOREVER)** *CBS BLOCK 4* ▲ 5 8
12 May 90 ● **COVER GIRL** *CBS BLOCK 5* 4 8
16 Jun 90 ● **STEP BY STEP** *CBS BLOCK 6* ▲ $ 2 7
30 Jun 90 ★ STEP BY STEP *CBS 4666861* ■ ▲ 1 31
4 Aug 90 ● **TONIGHT** *CBS BLOCK 7* 3 10
13 Oct 90 ● **LET'S TRY AGAIN / DIDN'T I BLOW YOUR MIND** *CBS BLOCK 8* 8 5
2 Nov 90 ● NEW KIDS ON THE BLOCK *CBS 4675041* 6 13
8 Dec 90 ● **THIS ONE'S FOR THE CHILDREN** *CBS BLOCK 9* 9 7
15 Dec 90 MERRY MERRY CHRISTMAS *CBS 4659071* 13 5
9 Feb 91 **GAMES** *CBS 6566267* 14 4
2 Mar 91 NO MORE GAMES – THE REMIX ALBUM *Columbia 4674941* 15 11
18 May 91 **CALL IT WHAT YOU WANT** *Columbia 6567857* 12 5
14 Dec 91 ● **IF YOU GO AWAY** *Columbia 6576667* 9 5
21 Dec 91 H.I.T.S. *Columbia 4694381* 50 4

19 Feb 94 **DIRTY DAWG** *Columbia 6600362* [1] 27 3
12 Mar 94 FACE THE MUSIC *Columbia 4743592* [1] 36 1
26 Mar 94 **NEVER LET YOU GO** *Columbia 6602072* [1] 42 2

[1] NKOTB [1] NKOTB

NEW MODEL ARMY

UK, male vocal / instrumental group (8 Albums: 21 Weeks, 14 Singles: 33 Weeks)

12 May 84 VENGEANCE *Abstract ABT 008* 73 5
27 Apr 85 **NO REST** *EMI NMA 1* 28 5
25 May 85 NO REST FOR THE WICKED *EMI NMAL 1* 22 3
3 Aug 85 **BETTER THAN THEM / NO SENSE** *EMI NMA 2* 49 2
30 Nov 85 **BRAVE NEW WORLD** *EMI NMA 3* 57 1
11 Oct 86 THE GHOST OF CAIN *EMI EMC 3516* 45 3
8 Nov 86 **51ST STATE** *EMI NMA 4* 71 2
28 Feb 87 **POISON STREET** *EMI NMA 5* 64 1
26 Sep 87 **WHITE COATS (EP)** *EMI NMA 6* 50 3
21 Jan 89 **STUPID QUESTIONS** *EMI NMA 7* 31 3
18 Feb 89 THUNDER AND CONSOLATION *EMI EMC 3552* 20 3
11 Mar 89 **VAGABONDS** *EMI NMA 8* 37 3
10 Jun 89 **GREEN AND GREY** *EMI NMA 9* 37 3
8 Sep 90 **GET ME OUT** *EMI NMA 10* 34 3
6 Oct 90 IMPURITY *EMI EMC 3581* 23 2
3 Nov 90 **PURITY** *EMI NMA 11* 61 2
8 Jun 91 **SPACE** *EMI NMA 12* 39 2
22 Jun 91 RAW MELODY MEN *EMI EMC 3595* 43 2
20 Feb 93 **HERE COMES THE WAR** *Epic 6589352* 25 2
10 Apr 93 THE LOVE OF HOPELESS CAUSES *Epic 4735622* 22 2
24 Jul 93 **LIVING IN THE ROSE (THE BALLADS EP)** *Epic 6592492* 51 1
25 Apr 98 STRANGE BROTHERHOOD *Eagle EAGCD 021* 72 1

'Better Than Them' / 'No Sense' are the lead tracks from 'The Acoustic EP', which also included the tracks 'Adrenalin' and 'Trust'. Tracks on White Coats (EP): White Coats / The Charge / Chinese Whispers / My Country. Tracks on Living in the Rose (The Ballads EP): Living in the Rose / Drummy B / Marry the Sea / Sleepwalking.

NEW MUSIK *UK, male vocal / instrumental group*

(2 Albums: 11 Weeks, 4 Singles: 27 Weeks)

6 Oct 79 **STRAIGHT LINES** *GTO GT 255* 53 5
19 Jan 80 **LIVING BY NUMBERS** *GTO GT 261* 13 8
26 Apr 80 **THIS WORLD OF WATER** *GTO GT 268* 31 7
17 May 80 FROM A TO B *GTO GTLP 041* 35 9
12 Jul 80 **SANCTUARY** *GTO GT 275* 31 7
14 Mar 81 ANYWHERE *GTO GTLP 044* 68 2

NEW ORDER (152 Top 500) (see also ELECTRONIC; MONACO; The OTHER TWO)

Innovative Mancunian group featuring three former members of the critically acclaimed Joy Division: Bernard Sumner (v/g), Peter Hook (b) and Stephen Morris (d), plus Gillian Gilbert (k) (left 2001). The group were inducted into the UK Music Hall of Fame in 2005. 'Blue Monday' remains the UK's biggest-selling 12-inch single and is their best-selling single (all formats totalling 1,001,400) (13 Albums: 158 Weeks, 34 Singles: 199 Weeks)

14 Mar 81 **CEREMONY** *Factory FAC 33* 34 5
3 Oct 81 **PROCESSION / EVERYTHING'S GONE GREEN** *Factory FAC 53* ..38 5
28 Nov 81 MOVEMENT *Factory FACT 50* 30 10
22 May 82 **TEMPTATION** *Factory FAC 63* 29 7
19 Mar 83 ● **BLUE MONDAY** (2re) *Factory FAC 73* £ 9 38
14 May 83 ● POWER, CORRUPTION AND LIES *Factory FACT 75* 4 29
3 Sep 83 **CONFUSION** *Factory FAC 93* 12 7
28 Apr 84 **THIEVES LIKE US** *Factory FAC 103* 18 5
25 May 85 ● LOW-LIFE *Factory FACT 100* 7 10
25 May 85 **THE PERFECT KISS** *Factory FAC 123* 46 4
9 Nov 85 **SUB-CULTURE** *Factory FAC 133* 63 4
29 Mar 86 **SHELLSHOCK** *Factory FAC 143* 28 5
27 Sep 86 **STATE OF THE NATION** *Factory FAC 153* 30 3
27 Sep 86 **THE PEEL SESSIONS (1ST JUNE 1982) EP** *Strange Fruit SFPS 001* 54 1
11 Oct 86 ● BROTHERHOOD *Factory FACT 150* 9 5
15 Nov 86 **BIZARRE LOVE TRIANGLE** *Factory FAC 163* 56 2
1 Aug 87 ● **TRUE FAITH** *Factory FAC 183/7* 4 10
29 Aug 87 ● SUBSTANCE 1987 *Factory FACT 200* 3 37

28 February 1981	7 March 1981	14 March 1981	21 March 1981
SHADDAP YOU FACE Joe Dolce Music Theatre	SHADDAP YOU FACE Joe Dolce Music Theatre	JEALOUS GUY Roxy Music	JEALOUS GUY Roxy Music
FACE VALUE Phil Collins	FACE VALUE Phil Collins	KINGS OF THE WILD FRONTIER Adam and The Ants	KINGS OF THE WILD FRONTIER Adam and The Ants

KEY
UK No.1 ★ UK Top 10 ● Still on chart + UK entry at No.1 ■ US No.1 ▲ UK million seller £ US million seller $
Singles re-entries are listed as (re), (2re), (3re)... which signifies that the hit re-entered the chart once, twice or three times...
Peak Position / Weeks

19 Dec 87 **TOUCHED BY THE HAND OF GOD** *Factory FAC 1937*....20 7
7 May 88 ● **BLUE MONDAY** (re-mix) *Factory FAC 737*....3 11
10 Dec 88 **FINE TIME** *Factory FAC 2237*....11 8
11 Feb 89 ★ **TECHNIQUE** *Factory FACT 275* ■....1 14
11 Mar 89 **ROUND AND ROUND** *Factory FAC 2637*....21 7
9 Sep 89 **RUN 2** *Factory FAC 273*....49 2
2 Jun 90 ★ **WORLD IN MOTION ...** *Factory / MCA FAC 2937* [1]....1 12
22 Feb 92 **BBC RADIO 1 LIVE IN CONCERT** *Windsong International WINCD 011*....33 2
17 Apr 93 ● **REGRET** *Centredate Co. NUOCD 1*....4 7
15 May 93 ★ **REPUBLIC** *London 8284132* ■....1 19
3 Jul 93 **RUINED IN A DAY** *Centredate Co. NUOCD 2*....22 4
17 Jul 93 **SUBSTANCE 1987** (re-issue) *London 5200082*....32 2
4 Sep 93 **WORLD (THE PRICE OF LOVE)** *Centredate Co. NUOCD 3*....13 5
18 Dec 93 **SPOOKY** *Centredate Co. NUOCD 4*....22 4
19 Nov 94 ● **TRUE FAITH** (re-mix) *Centredate Co. NUOCD 5*....9 8
3 Dec 94 ● **? (THE BEST OF) NEW ORDER / ? (THE REST OF) NEW ORDER** *Centredate Co. 8285802*....4 17
21 Jan 95 **NINETEEN63** *London NUOCD 6*....21 4
5 Aug 95 **BLUE MONDAY** (2nd re-mix) *London NUOCD 7*....17 4
25 Aug 01 ● **CRYSTAL** *London NUOCD 8*....8 4
8 Sep 01 ● **GET READY** *London 8573896212*....6 4
1 Dec 01 **60 MILES AN HOUR** *London NUOCD 9*....29 2
27 Apr 02 **HERE TO STAY** *London NUOCD 11*....15 3
15 Jun 02 **WORLD IN MOTION ...** (re-issue) *London / MCA NUDOCD 12* [1]....43 2
30 Nov 02 **CONFUSION** *Whacked WACKT 002CD* [2]....64 1
19 Mar 05 ● **KRAFTY** *London NUOCD 13*....8 4
9 Apr 05 ● **WAITING FOR THE SIRENS' CALL** *London 2564622022*....5 4
28 May 05 **JETSTREAM** *London NUCDP 19* [3]....20 2
8 Oct 05 **WAITING FOR THE SIRENS' CALL** *London NUO 15V1*....21 2
15 Oct 05 **SINGLES** *London 2564626902*....14 5

[1] Englandneworder (New Order, Keith Allen, England footballer / rapper John Barnes and the rest of the England World Cup squad) [2] Arthur Baker vs New Order [3] New Order featuring Ana Matronic

Group was male only on first hit. 'Blue Monday''s first visit to the chart peaked at No.12, with the first re-entry making No.9 in Oct 1983 and the second re-entry peaking at No.52 in Jan 1984. 'Blue Monday' (1983) was made available on seven-inch for the first time, hence the slightly different catalogue number. Sales for the re-mix and the original were combined from 7 May 1988 onwards when calculating its chart position. Tracks on The Peel Sessions (1st June 1982) EP: Turn the Heater On / We All Stand / Too Late / 5-8-6. From 2 Sep 95 ? (The Best of) New Order was listed with the re-mix album ? (The Rest of) New Order.

NEW POWER GENERATION (see also PRINCE) *US, male / female vocal / instrumental group (1 Album: 3 Weeks, 13 Singles: 64 Weeks)*

31 Aug 91 ● **GETT OFF** *Paisley Park W 0056* [1]....4 8
21 Sep 91 **CREAM** *Paisley Park W 0061* [1] ▲....15 7
7 Dec 91 **DIAMONDS AND PEARLS** *Paisley Park W 0075* [1]....25 6
28 Mar 92 **MONEY DON'T MATTER 2 NIGHT** *Paisley Park W 0091* [1]....19 5
27 Jun 92 **THUNDER** *Paisley Park W 0113* [1]....28 3
18 Jul 92 ● **SEXY MF / STROLLIN'** *Paisley Park W 0123* [1]....4 7
10 Oct 92 ● **MY NAME IS PRINCE** *Paisley Park W 0132* [1]....7 5
14 Nov 92 **MY NAME IS PRINCE** (re-mix) *Paisley Park W 0142T* [1]....51 1
5 Dec 92 **7** *Paisley Park W 0147* [1]....27 6
13 Mar 93 **THE MORNING PAPERS** *Paisley Park W 0162CD* [1]....52 3
1 Apr 95 **GET WILD** *NPG 0061045*....19 4
8 Apr 95 **EXODUS** *NPG 0061032*....11 3
19 Aug 95 **THE GOOD LIFE** (re) *NPG 0061515*....15 8
21 Nov 98 **COME ON** *RCA 74321634722*....65 1

[1] Prince and the New Power Generation

'The Good Life' peaked at No.29 on its first visit before re-entering at its peak position in Jul 1997.

NEW RADICALS *US, male vocalist – Gregg Alexander (1 Album: 14 Weeks, 2 Singles: 18 Weeks)*

3 Apr 99 ● **YOU GET WHAT YOU GIVE** *MCA MCSTD 48111*....5 17
17 Apr 99 ● **MAYBE YOU'VE BEEN BRAINWASHED TOO** *MCA MCD 11858*....10 14
25 Sep 99 **SOMEDAY WE'LL KNOW** *MCA MCSTD 40217*....48 1

NEW RHODES *UK, male vocal / instrumental group (3 Singles: 3 Weeks)*

7 Aug 04 **I WISH I WAS YOU** *Moshi Moshi MOSH 11CD*....63 1
26 Feb 05 **YOU'VE GIVEN ME SOMETHING THAT I CAN'T GIVE BACK** *Moshi Moshi MOSHI 15CD*....38 1
27 Aug 05 **FROM THE BEGINNING** *Moshi Moshi MOSHI 24CD*....64 1

The NEW SEEKERS (362 Top 500)

UK / Australia, male / female vocal / instrumental group: Keith Potger, Eve Graham, Lyn Paul, Peter Doyle (d.2001), Paul Layton and Marty Kristian. Hits included a Coca-Cola advertisement and a Eurovision entry. The group sold more than 25 million records worldwide and equalled the eight Top 20 entries by The Seekers. Biggest-selling single: 'I'd Like to Teach the World to Sing' 990,000 (6 Albums: 49 Weeks, 14 Singles: 143 Weeks)

17 Oct 70 **WHAT HAVE THEY DONE TO MY SONG MA** (re) *Philips 6006 027*....44 2
10 Jul 71 ● **NEVER ENDING SONG OF LOVE** *Philips 6006 125*....2 19
18 Dec 71 ★ **I'D LIKE TO TEACH THE WORLD TO SING (IN PERFECT HARMONY)** *Polydor 2058 184* $....1 21
5 Feb 72 **NEW COLOURS** *Polydor 2383 066*....40 4
4 Mar 72 ● **BEG, STEAL OR BORROW** *Polydor 2058 201*....2 13
1 Apr 72 ● **WE'D LIKE TO TEACH THE WORLD TO SING** *Polydor 2883 103*....2 25
10 Jun 72 ● **CIRCLES** *Polydor 2058 242*....4 16
12 Aug 72 **NEVER ENDING SONG OF LOVE** *Polydor 2383 126*....35 4
14 Oct 72 **CIRCLES** *Polydor 2442 102*....23 5
2 Dec 72 **COME SOFTLY TO ME** *Polydor 2058 315* [1]....20 11
24 Feb 73 **PINBALL WIZARD – SEE ME, FEEL ME (MEDLEY)** *Polydor 2058 338*....16 8
7 Apr 73 **NEVERTHELESS (I'M IN LOVE WITH YOU)** *Polydor 2068 340* [2]....34 5
21 Apr 73 **NOW** *Polydor 2383 195*....47 2
16 Jun 73 **GOODBYE IS JUST ANOTHER WORD** *Polydor 2058 368*....36 5
24 Nov 73 ★ **YOU WON'T FIND ANOTHER FOOL LIKE ME** *Polydor 2058 421* [3]....1 16
9 Mar 74 ● **I GET A LITTLE SENTIMENTAL OVER YOU** *Polydor 2058 439* [3]....5 9
30 Mar 74 **TOGETHER** *Polydor 2383 264*....12 9
14 Aug 76 **IT'S SO NICE (TO HAVE YOU HOME)** *CBS 4391*....44 4
29 Jan 77 **I WANNA GO BACK** *CBS 4786*....25 4
15 Jul 78 **ANTHEM (ONE DAY IN EVERY WEEK)** *CBS 6413*....21 10

[1] The New Seekers featuring Marty Kristian [2] Eve Graham and The New Seekers [3] The New Seekers featuring Lyn Paul

The NEW VAUDEVILLE BAND *UK, male vocal / instrumental group (4 Singles: 43 Weeks)*

8 Sep 66 ● **WINCHESTER CATHEDRAL** *Fontana TF 741* ▲ $....4 19
26 Jan 67 ● **PEEK-A-BOO** *Fontana TF 784* [1]....7 11
11 May 67 **FINCHLEY CENTRAL** *Fontana TF 824*....11 9
2 Aug 67 **GREEN STREET GREEN** *Fontana TF 853*....37 4

[1] The New Vaudeville Band featuring Tristram

NEW VISION (see also LEE-CABRERA; David MORALES) *US, male vocal / instrumental duo – Samuel Morales and Albert Cabrera*

29 Jan 00 **(JUST) YOU AND ME** *AM:PM CDAMPM 128*....23 2

NEW WORLD *Australia, male vocal / instrumental group (5 Singles: 53 Weeks)*

27 Feb 71 **ROSE GARDEN** *RAK 111*....15 11
3 Jul 71 ● **TOM-TOM TURNAROUND** *RAK 117*....6 15
4 Dec 71 **KARA, KARA** *RAK 123*....17 13
13 May 72 ● **SISTER JANE** *RAK 130*....9 13
12 May 73 **ROOFTOP SINGING** *RAK 148*....50 1

NEW WORLD THEATRE ORCHESTRA *UK, orchestra*

24 Dec 60 LET'S DANCE TO THE HITS OF THE 30'S AND 40'S *Pye Golden Guinea GGL 0026* 20 1

NEW YORK CITY *US, male vocal group*

21 Jul 73 **I'M DOIN' FINE NOW** *RCA 2351* 20 11

NEW YORK SKYY *US, male / female vocal / instrumental group*

16 Jan 82 **LET'S CELEBRATE** (re) *Epic EPC A 1898* **67** 2

The NEWBEATS

US, male vocal (Larry Henley) group (2 Singles: 22 Weeks)

10 Sep 64 **BREAD AND BUTTER** *Hickory 1269* $ 15 9
23 Oct 71 ● **RUN, BABY, RUN** *London HLE 10341* 10 13

Booker NEWBERRY III *US, male vocalist (2 Singles: 11 Weeks)*

28 May 83 ● **LOVE TOWN** *Polydor POSP 613* 6 8
8 Oct 83 **TEDDY BEAR** *Polydor POSP 637* **44** 3

Mickey NEWBURY

US, male vocalist / guitarist – Milton Newbury, b. 19 May 1940, d. 29 Sep 2002

1 Jul 72 **AMERICAN TRILOGY** *Elektra K 12047* 42 5

NEWCLEUS *US, male rap / instrumental group*

3 Sep 83 **JAM ON REVENGE (THE WIKKI WIKKI SONG)** *Beckett BKS 8* **44** 6
25 Aug 84 JAM ON REVENGE *Sunnyview SVLP 6600* 84 2

Bob NEWHART *US, male comedian*

1 Oct 60 ● BUTTON-DOWN MIND OF BOB NEWHART *Warner Bros. WM 4010* ▲ 2 37

Anthony NEWLEY (478 Top 500)

Acclaimed actor / vocalist and composer, b. 24 Sep 1931, London, UK, d. 14 Apr 1999. He appeared in more than 20 films before his singing career started. He was among the most innovative UK acts of the early rock years before moving into musicals and cabaret (3 Albums: 24 Weeks, 12 Singles: 130 Weeks)

1 May 59 ● **I'VE WAITED SO LONG** *Decca F 11127* 3 15
8 May 59 **IDLE ON PARADE (EP)** *Decca DFE 6566* 13 4
12 Jun 59 ● **PERSONALITY** *Decca F 11142* 6 12
15 Jan 60 ★ **WHY** *Decca F 11194* 1 18
24 Mar 60 ★ **DO YOU MIND** *Decca F 11220* 1 15
14 May 60 LOVE IS A NOW AND THEN THING *Decca LK 4343* 19 2
14 Jul 60 ● **IF SHE SHOULD COME TO YOU** *Decca F 11254* 4 15
24 Nov 60 ● **STRAWBERRY FAIR** *Decca F 11295* 3 11
16 Mar 61 ● **AND THE HEAVENS CRIED** *Decca F 11331* 6 12
15 Jun 61 **POP GOES THE WEASEL / BEE BOM** *Decca F 11362* 12 9
8 Jul 61 ● TONY *Decca LK 4406* 5 12
3 Aug 61 **WHAT KIND OF FOOL AM I?** *Decca F 11376* 36 8
25 Jan 62 **D-DARLING** *Decca F 11419* 25 6
26 Jul 62 **THAT NOISE** *Decca F 11486* 34 5
28 Sep 63 ● FOOL BRITANNIA *Ember CEL 902* [1] 10 10

[1] Anthony Newley, Peter Sellers, Joan Collins

'Bee Bom' listed with 'Pop Goes the Weasel' only for weeks of 15 and 22 Jun 1961. It peaked at No.15. Tracks on Idle on Parade (EP): I've Waited So Long / Idle Rock-a-Boogie / Idle on Parade / Saturday Night Rock-a-Boogie.

Anthony NEWLEY, Peter SELLERS, Joan COLLINS

UK, male / female actors – Anthony Newley, b. 24 Sep 1931, d. 14 Apr 1999, Peter Sellers, b. Richard Sellers, 8 Sep 1925, d. 24 Jul 1980, and Joan Collins

28 Sep 63 ● FOOL BRITANNIA *Ember CEL 902* 10 10

Brad NEWMAN

UK, male vocalist – Charles Thomas, b. 1938, d. 18 Jan 1999

22 Feb 62 **SOMEBODY TO LOVE** *Fontana H 357* **47** 1

Dave NEWMAN *UK, male vocalist*

15 Apr 72 **THE LION SLEEPS TONIGHT (WIMOWEH)** (re) *Pye 7N 45134* 34 6

The NEWS *UK, male vocal / instrumental group*

29 Aug 81 **AUDIO VIDEO** *George GEORGE 1* **52** 3

NEWTON *UK, male vocalist – William Myers (3 Singles: 6 Weeks)*

15 Jul 95 **SKY HIGH** *Bags of Fun BAGSCD 6* **56** 2
15 Feb 97 **SOMETIMES WHEN WE TOUCH** *Dominion CDDMIN 202* 32 3
16 Aug 97 **DON'T WORRY** *Dominion CDDMIN 206* **61** 1

Juice NEWTON *US, female vocalist – Judy Newton*

2 May 81 **ANGEL OF THE MORNING** *Capitol CL 16189* $ **43** 6

Olivia NEWTON-JOHN (159 Top 500)

Top female vocalist in the US in the 1970s, b. 26 Sep 1948, Cambridge, UK. This photogenic Australian-raised singer / actress has won numerous pop and country awards and was the first solo female to score a dozen US Top 5 singles (14 Albums: 116 Weeks, 26 Singles: 234 Weeks)

20 Mar 71 ● **IF NOT FOR YOU** *Pye International 7N 25543* 7 11
23 Oct 71 ● **BANKS OF THE OHIO** *Pye International 7N 25568* 6 17
11 Mar 72 **WHAT IS LIFE** *Pye International 7N 25575* **16** 8
13 Jan 73 **TAKE ME HOME COUNTRY ROADS** *Pye International 7N 25599* **15** 13
2 Mar 74 MUSIC MAKES MY DAY *Pye NSPL 28186* 37 3
16 Mar 74 **LONG LIVE LOVE** *Pye International 7N 25638* 11 8
29 Jun 74 LONG LIVE LOVE *EMI EMC 3028* 40 2
12 Oct 74 **I HONESTLY LOVE YOU** *EMI 2216* ▲ $ 22 6
26 Apr 75 HAVE YOU NEVER BEEN MELLOW *EMI EMC 3069* ▲ 37 2
29 May 76 COME ON OVER *EMI EMC 3124* 49 4
11 Jun 77 ● **SAM** *EMI 2616* 6 11
27 Aug 77 MAKING A GOOD THING BETTER *EMI EMC 3192* 60 1
21 Jan 78 GREATEST HITS *EMI EMA 785* 19 9
20 May 78 ★ **YOU'RE THE ONE THAT I WANT** *RSO 006* [1] ▲ £ $ 1 26
16 Sep 78 ★ **SUMMER NIGHTS** *RSO 18* [2] £ $ 1 19
4 Nov 78 ● **HOPELESSLY DEVOTED TO YOU** *RSO 17* $ 2 11
9 Dec 78 TOTALLY HOT *EMI EMA 789* 30 9
16 Dec 78 ● **A LITTLE MORE LOVE** *EMI 2879* $ 4 12
30 Jun 79 **DEEPER THAN THE NIGHT** *EMI 2954* **64** 3
21 Jun 80 ★ **XANADU** *Jet 185* [3] 1 11
23 Aug 80 **MAGIC** *Jet 196* ▲ $ 32 7
25 Oct 80 **SUDDENLY** *Jet 7002* [4] **15** 7
10 Oct 81 ● **PHYSICAL** *EMI 5234* ▲ $ 7 16
31 Oct 81 PHYSICAL *EMI EMC 3386* 11 22
16 Jan 82 **LANDSLIDE** *EMI 5257* **18** 9
17 Apr 82 **MAKE A MOVE ON ME** *EMI 5291* **43** 3
23 Oct 82 ● GREATEST HITS *EMI EMTV 36* 8 38
23 Oct 82 **HEART ATTACK** *EMI 5347* **46** 4
15 Jan 83 **I HONESTLY LOVE YOU** (re-issue) *EMI 5360* **52** 4
12 Nov 83 **TWIST OF FATE** *EMI 5438* **57** 2
8 Mar 86 SOUL KISS *Mercury MERH 77* 66 3
22 Dec 90 ● **THE GREASE MEGAMIX** *Polydor PO 114* [1] 3 10
23 Mar 91 **GREASE – THE DREAM MIX** *PWL / Polydor PO 136* [5] **47** 2
4 Jul 92 **I NEED LOVE** *Mercury MER 370* **75** 1
25 Jul 92 BACK TO BASICS – THE ESSENTIAL COLLECTION 1971-1992 *Mercury 5126412* 12 6
4 Feb 95 GAIA (ONE WOMAN'S JOURNEY) *D-Sharp DSHLCD 7017* 33 4
9 Dec 95 **HAD TO BE** *EMI CDEMS 410* [6] 22 4
25 Jul 98 ● **YOU'RE THE ONE THAT I WANT** (re-issue) *Polydor 0441332* [1] 4 9
30 Oct 04 THE DEFINITIVE COLLECTION *Universal TV 5842792* 11 11
23 Apr 05 INDIGO – WOMEN OF SONG *UMTV 9870906* 27 2

[1] John Travolta and Olivia Newton-John [2] John Travolta, Olivia Newton-John and Cast [3] Olivia Newton-John and Electric Light Orchestra [4] Olivia Newton-John and Cliff Richard [5] Frankie Valli, John Travolta and Olivia Newton-John [6] Cliff Richard and Olivia Newton-John

25 April 1981	2 May 1981	9 May 1981	16 May 1981
MAKING YOUR MIND UP Bucks Fizz	MAKING YOUR MIND UP Bucks Fizz	STAND AND DELIVER Adam and The Ants	STAND AND DELIVER Adam and The Ants
KINGS OF THE WILD FRONTIER Adam and The Ants	KINGS OF THE WILD FRONTIER Adam and The Ants	KINGS OF THE WILD FRONTIER Adam and The Ants	KINGS OF THE WILD FRONTIER Adam and The Ants

KEY: UK No.1 ★ UK Top 10 ● Still on chart + UK entry at No.1 ■ US No.1 ▲ UK million seller £ US million seller $
Singles re-entries are listed as (re), (2re), (3re)... which signifies that the hit re-entered the chart once, twice or three times...
Peak Position / Weeks

NEXT US, male vocal trio (2 Singles: 8 Weeks)

6 Jun 98 TOO CLOSE Arista 74321580672 ▲ $ 24 3
16 Sep 00 WIFEY Arista 74321790912 19 5

NEXT OF KIN UK, male vocal / instrumental group (2 Singles: 6 Weeks)

20 Feb 99 24 HOURS FROM YOU Universal MCSTD 40201 13 4
19 Jun 99 MORE LOVE Universal MCSTD 40207 33 2

NIAGRA UK, male / female vocal / DJ / production duo

27 Sep 97 CLOUDBURST Freeflow FLOWCD 2 65 1

The NICE (see also Keith EMERSON) UK, male instrumental / vocal group (3 Albums: 38 Weeks, 1 Single: 15 Weeks)

10 Jul 68 AMERICA Immediate IM 068 21 15
13 Sep 69 ● NICE Immediate IMSP 026 3 6
27 Jun 70 ● FIVE BRIDGES Charisma CAS 1014 2 21
17 Apr 71 ● ELEGY Charisma CAS 1030 5 11

Hector NICHOL UK, male comedian

28 Apr 84 BRAVO JULIET! Klub KLP 42 92 1

Paul NICHOLAS UK, male actor / vocalist – Paul Beuselinck (1 Album: 8 Weeks, 4 Singles: 31 Weeks)

17 Apr 76 REGGAE LIKE IT USED TO BE RSO 2090 185 17 8
9 Oct 76 ● DANCING WITH THE CAPTAIN RSO 2090 206 8 9
4 Dec 76 ● GRANDMA'S PARTY RSO 2090 216 9 11
9 Jul 77 HEAVEN ON THE 7TH FLOOR RSO 2090 249 $ 40 3
29 Nov 86 JUST GOOD FRIENDS K-Tel ONE 1334 30 8

Grandma's Party was an EP featuring Grandma's Party / Flat Foot Floyd / Mr. Sax and the Girl / Shufflin' Shoes.

Sue NICHOLLS UK, female actor / vocalist

3 Jul 68 WHERE WILL YOU BE Pye 7N 17565 17 8

NICKELBACK Canada, male vocal (Chad Kroeger) / instrumental group (3 Albums: 83 Weeks, 7 Singles: 48 Weeks)

19 Jan 02 ★ SILVER SIDE UP Roadrunner 12084852 1 67
23 Feb 02 HOW YOU REMIND ME (import) Roadrunner 23203323CD 65 2
9 Mar 02 ● HOW YOU REMIND ME Roadrunner 23203320 ▲ 4 21
7 Sep 02 ● TOO BAD (re) Roadrunner 20373 9 9
7 Dec 02 NEVER AGAIN Roadrunner RR 20253 30 2
27 Sep 03 ● SOMEDAY Roadrunner RR 20088 6 9
4 Oct 03 ● THE LONG ROAD Roadrunner RR 84002 5 12
27 Mar 04 FEELIN' WAY TOO DAMN GOOD Roadrunner RR 39983 39 2
8 Oct 05 PHOTOGRAPH Roadrunner RR 39553 29 3
15 Oct 05 ALL THE RIGHT REASONS Roadrunner RR 83002 ▲ 13 4

Stevie NICKS (see also FLEETWOOD MAC) US, female vocalist (7 Albums: 82 Weeks, 9 Singles: 30 Weeks)

8 Aug 81 BELLA DONNA WEA K 99169 ▲ 11 16
15 Aug 81 STOP DRAGGIN' MY HEART AROUND WEA K 79231 [1] 50 4
2 Jul 83 THE WILD HEART WEA 2500711 28 19
14 Dec 85 ROCK A LITTLE Modern PCS 7300 30 22
25 Jan 86 I CAN'T WAIT Parlophone R 6110 54 4
29 Mar 86 TALK TO ME Parlophone R 6124 68 2
6 May 89 ROOMS ON FIRE EMI EM 90 16 7
10 Jun 89 ● THE OTHER SIDE OF THE MIRROR EMI EMD 1008 3 14
12 Aug 89 LONG WAY TO GO EMI EM 97 60 2
11 Nov 89 WHOLE LOTTA TROUBLE EMI EM 114 62 2
24 Aug 91 SOMETIMES IT'S A BITCH EMI EM 203 40 4
14 Sep 91 TIMESPACE – THE BEST OF STEVIE NICKS EMI EMD 3595 15 6
9 Nov 91 I CAN'T WAIT (re-issue) EMI EM 214 47 2
4 Jun 94 STREET ANGEL EMI CDEMC 3671 16 3
2 Jul 94 MAYBE LOVE EMI CDEMS 328 42 3
12 May 01 TROUBLE IN SHANGRI-LA Reprise 9362473722 43 2

[1] Stevie Nicks with Tom Petty and the Heartbreakers

NICOLE Germany, female vocalist – Nicole Hohloch (1 Album: 2 Weeks, 2 Singles: 10 Weeks)

8 May 82 ★ A LITTLE PEACE CBS A 2365 1 9
21 Aug 82 GIVE ME MORE TIME CBS A 2467 75 1
2 Oct 82 A LITTLE PEACE CBS 85011 85 2

NICOLE US, female vocalist – Nicole McLeod (3 Singles: 9 Weeks)

28 Dec 85 NEW YORK EYES Portrait A 6805 [1] 41 7
26 Dec 92 ROCK THE HOUSE React 12REACT 12 [2] 63 1
6 Jul 96 RUNNIN' AWAY Ore AG 18CD 69 1

[1] Nicole with Timmy Thomas [2] Source featuring Nicole

NICOLETTE (see also MASSIVE ATTACK) UK, female vocalist – Nicolette Suwoton

23 Dec 95 NO GOVERNMENT Talkin Loud TLCD 1 67 1
10 Aug 96 LET NO-ONE LIVE RENT FREE IN YOUR HEAD Talkin Loud 5328142 36 2

NIGEL & MARVIN Trinidad, male vocal duo – Nigel and Marvin Lewis

18 May 02 ● FOLLOW DA LEADER Relentless RELENT 19CD 5 10

NIGHTBREED (see also ANGEL CITY) Holland, male production duo – Aldwin Oomen and Hugo Zentveld

9 Oct 04 PACK OF WOLVES Ram RAMM 52CD 45 1

NIGHTCRAWLERS featuring John REID UK, male / female vocal / production group (1 Album: 5 Weeks, 8 Singles: 36 Weeks)

15 Oct 94 PUSH THE FEELING ON ffrr FCD 245 [1] 22 5
4 Mar 95 ● PUSH THE FEELING ON (re-mix) ffrr FCD 257 3 11
27 May 95 ● SURRENDER YOUR LOVE Final Vinyl 74321283982 7 7
9 Sep 95 DON'T LET THE FEELING GO Final Vinyl 7432129882 13 4
30 Sep 95 LET'S PUSH IT Final Vinyl 74321309702 14 5
20 Jan 96 LET'S PUSH IT Final Vinyl 74321328142 23 4
20 Apr 96 SHOULD I EVER (FALL IN LOVE) Arista 74321358072 34 2
27 Jul 96 KEEP ON PUSHING OUR LOVE Arista 74321390422 [2] 30 2
3 Jul 99 NEVER KNEW LOVE Riverhorse RIVHCD 1 [1] 59 1

[1] Nightcrawlers [2] Nightcrawlers featuring John Reid and Alysha Warren

Maxine NIGHTINGALE UK, female vocalist (2 Singles: 16 Weeks)

1 Nov 75 ● RIGHT BACK WHERE WE STARTED FROM United Artists UP 36015 $ 8 8
12 Mar 77 LOVE HIT ME United Artists UP 36215 11 8

NIGHTMARES ON WAX UK, male producer / vocalist / instrumentalist – George Evelyn (2 Albums: 4 Weeks, 2 Singles: 6 Weeks)

27 Oct 90 AFTERMATH / I'M FOR REAL Warp WAP 6 38 5
24 Apr 99 CAR BOOT SOUL Warp WARPCD 61 71 2
26 Jun 99 FINER Warp WAP 123CD 63 1
14 Sep 02 MIND ELEVATION Warp WARPCD 95 47 2

NIGHTWISH Finland, male / female vocal / instrumental group

9 Oct 04 WISH I HAD AN ANGEL Nuclear Blast NB 1336CD 60 1

NIGHTWRITERS US, male vocal / instrumental duo

23 May 92 LET THE MUSIC USE YOU Ffrreedom TABX 112 51 2

	23 May 1981	30 May 1981	6 June 1981	13 June 1981
UK No.1 SINGLES	STAND AND DELIVER Adam and The Ants	STAND AND DELIVER Adam and The Ants	STAND AND DELIVER Adam and The Ants	BEING WITH YOU Smokey Robinson
UK No.1 ALBUMS	STARS ON 45 Starsound	STARS ON 45 Starsound	STARS ON 45 Starsound	STARS ON 45 Starsound

NIKKE? NICOLE! *US, female rapper – Nicole Miller*

1 Jun 91 **NIKKE DOES IT BETTER** *Love EVOL 5* 73 1

Markus NIKOLAI *Germany, male producer*

6 Oct 01 **BUSHES** *Southern Fried ECB 24CD* 74 1

Kurt NILSEN *Norway, male vocalist*

29 May 04 **SHE'S SO HIGH** *RCA 82876610882* 25 3

NILSSON *US, male vocalist – Harry Nilsson, b. 15 Jun 1941, d. 15 Jan 1994 (4 Albums: 43 Weeks, 6 Singles: 55 Weeks)*

27 Sep 69 **EVERYBODY'S TALKIN'** (2re) *RCA 1876* 23 15
29 Jan 72 THE POINT *RCA Victor SF 8166* 46 1
5 Feb 72 ● NILSSON SCHMILSSON *RCA Victor SF 8242* 4 22
5 Feb 72 ★ **WITHOUT YOU** *RCA 2165* ▲ $ 1 20
3 Jun 72 **COCONUT** *RCA 2214* 42 5
19 Aug 72 SON OF SCHMILSSON *RCA Victor SF 8297* 41 1
28 Jul 73 A LITTLE TOUCH OF SCHMILSSON IN THE NIGHT *RCA Victor SF 8371* 20 19
16 Oct 76 **WITHOUT YOU** (re-issue) *RCA 2733* 22 8
20 Aug 77 **ALL I THINK ABOUT IS YOU** *RCA PB 9104* 43 3
19 Feb 94 **WITHOUT YOU** (2nd re-issue) *RCA 74321193092* 47 4

'Everybody's Talkin'' made No.50 on its first chart visit, followed by No.23 on first re-entry in Oct 1969 and No.39 on second re-entry in Mar 1970.

Charlotte NILSSON *Sweden, female vocalist*

3 Jul 99 **TAKE ME TO YOUR HEAVEN** *Arista 74321686952* 20 4

NINA and FREDERIK *Denmark, female / male vocal duo – Baroness Nina and Baron Frederik von Pallandt, b. 14 May 1934, d. 15 May 1994 (2 Albums: 6 Weeks, 5 Singles: 29 Weeks)*

18 Dec 59 **MARY'S BOY CHILD** *Columbia DB 4375* 26 1
13 Feb 60 ● NINA AND FREDERIK *Pye NPT 19023* 9 2
10 Mar 60 **LISTEN TO THE OCEAN** (re) *Columbia DB 4332* 46 2
17 Nov 60 ● **LITTLE DONKEY** *Columbia DB 4536* 3 10
29 Apr 61 NINA AND FREDERIK *Columbia COL 1314* 11 4
28 Sep 61 **LONGTIME BOY** *Columbia DB 4703* 43 3
5 Oct 61 **SUCU-SUCU** *Columbia DB 4632* 23 13

The two eponymous albums are different.

NINA SKY *US, female vocal duo – Natalie and Nicole Albino*

17 Jul 04 ● **MOVE YA BODY** *Universal MCSTD 40373* 6 11

'Move Ya Body' features the uncredited vocals of Jabba.

9 BELOW ZERO
UK, male vocal / instrumental group (2 Albums: 12 Weeks)

14 Mar 81 DON'T POINT YOUR FINGER *A&M AMLH 68521* 56 6
20 Mar 82 THIRD DEGREE *A&M AMLH 68537* 38 6

NINE BLACK ALPS NEW *UK, male vocal / instrumental group (1 Album: 3 Weeks, 4 Singles: 7 Weeks)*

19 Mar 05 **SHOT DOWN** *Island CID 885* 25 2
4 Jun 05 **NOT EVERYONE** *Island CID 892* 31 2
25 Jun 05 EVERYTHING IS *Island CID 8158* 51 3
20 Aug 05 **UNSATISFIED** *Island CID 899* 30 2
12 Nov 05 **JUST FRIENDS** *Island CID 915* 52 1

NINE INCH NAILS *US, male vocal (Trent Reznor) / instrumental group (6 Albums: 17 Weeks, 8 Singles: 21 Weeks)*

14 Sep 91 **HEAD LIKE A HOLE** *TVT IS 484* 45 4
12 Oct 91 PRETTY HATE MACHINE *TVT ILPS 9973* 67 1
16 Nov 91 **SIN** *TVT IS 508* 35 2
17 Oct 92 BROKEN *Island IMCD 8004* 18 3
19 Mar 94 ● THE DOWNWARD SPIRAL *Island CID 8012* 9 4
9 Apr 94 **MARCH OF THE PIGS** *TVT CID 592* 45 3
18 Jun 94 **CLOSER** *TVT CIDX 596* 25 3
13 Sep 97 **THE PERFECT DRUG** *Interscope IND 95542* 43 1
9 Oct 99 ● THE FRAGILE *Island CIDD 8091* ▲ 10 4
18 Dec 99 **WE'RE IN THIS TOGETHER** *Island 4971402* 39 2
16 Mar 02 AND ALL THAT COULD HAVE BEEN – LIVE *Nothing CID 8113* ..54 1
30 Apr 05 ● **THE HAND THAT FEEDS** *Island CID 888* 7 3
14 May 05 ● WITH TEETH *Island CID 8155* ▲ 3 4
6 Aug 05 **ONLY** *Island CID 903* 20 3

999
UK, male vocal / instrumental group (1 Album: 1 Week, 5 Singles: 13 Weeks)

25 Mar 78 999 *United Artists UAG 30199* 53 1
25 Nov 78 **HOMICIDE** *United Artists UP 36467* 40 3
27 Oct 79 **FOUND OUT TOO LATE** *Radar ADA 46* 69 2
16 May 81 **OBSESSED** *Albion ION 1011* 71 1
18 Jul 81 **LIL RED RIDING HOOD** *Albion ION 1017* 59 3
14 Nov 81 **INDIAN RESERVATION** *Albion ION 1023* 51 4

911
UK, male vocal trio (4 Albums: 26 Weeks, 13 Singles: 94 Weeks)

11 May 96 **NIGHT TO REMEMBER** *Ginga CDGINGA 1* 38 2
10 Aug 96 **LOVE SENSATION** *Ginga CDGINGA 2* 21 4
9 Nov 96 ● **DON'T MAKE ME WAIT** (re) *Ginga VSCDT 1618* 10 8
22 Feb 97 ● **THE DAY WE FIND LOVE** *Virgin VSCDT 1619* 4 8
8 Mar 97 THE JOURNEY *Virgin CDV 2820* 13 17
3 May 97 ● **BODYSHAKIN'** *Virgin VSCDT 1634* 3 7
12 Jul 97 ● **THE JOURNEY** *Virgin VSCDT 1645* 3 7
1 Nov 97 ● **PARTY PEOPLE ... FRIDAY NIGHT** (re) *Ginga / Virgin VSCDT 1658* 5 10
4 Apr 98 ● **ALL I WANT IS YOU** (re) *Virgin VSCDT 1681* 4 7
4 Jul 98 ● **HOW DO YOU WANT ME TO LOVE YOU?** (re) *Ginga VSCDT 1686* 10 9
18 Jul 98 ● MOVING ON *Virgin CDV 2852* 10 4
24 Oct 98 ● **MORE THAN A WOMAN** (re) *Virgin VSCDT 1707* 2 13
23 Jan 99 ★ **A LITTLE BIT MORE** *Virgin VSCDT 1719* ■ 1 9
6 Feb 99 ● THERE IT IS *Virgin CDV 2873* 8 4
15 May 99 ● **PRIVATE NUMBER** *Virgin VSCDT 1730* 3 7
23 Oct 99 **WONDERLAND** *Virgin VSCDT 1755* 13 3
6 Nov 99 THE GREATEST HITS AND A LITTLE BIT MORE ... *Virgin CDV 2899* 40 1

9.9 *US, female vocal group*

6 Jul 85 **ALL OF ME FOR ALL OF YOU** *RCA PB 49951* 53 3

NINE YARDS *UK, male vocal group (3 Singles: 3 Weeks)*

21 Nov 98 **LONELINESS IS GONE** *Virgin VSCDT 1696* 70 1
10 Apr 99 **MATTER OF TIME** *Virgin VSCDT 1723* 59 1
28 Aug 99 **ALWAYS FIND A WAY** *Virgin VSCDT 1746* 50 1

1910 FRUITGUM CO.
US, male vocal (Mark Gutkowski) / instrumental group

20 Mar 68 ● **SIMON SAYS** *Pye International 7N 25447* $ 2 16

1927 *Australia, male vocal / instrumental group*

22 Apr 89 **THAT'S WHEN I THINK OF YOU** *WEA YZ 351* 46 6

98° *US, male vocal group (6 Singles: 17 Weeks)*

29 Nov 97 **INVISIBLE MAN** *Motown 8607092* 66 1
31 Oct 98 **TRUE TO YOUR HEART** *Motown 8608832* [1] 51 1
13 Mar 99 **BECAUSE OF YOU** *Motown 8609012* $ 36 2
11 Mar 00 ● **THANK GOD I FOUND YOU** (re) *Columbia 6690582* [2] ▲ 10 10
11 Mar 00 **THE HARDEST THING** *Universal MCSTD 40228* 29 2
2 Dec 00 **GIVE ME JUST ONE MORE NIGHT (UNA NOCHE)** *Universal MCSTD 40243* 61 1

[1] 98° featuring Stevie Wonder [2] Mariah Carey featuring Joe and 98°

20 June 1981	27 June 1981	4 July 1981	11 July 1981
BEING WITH YOU Smokey Robinson	**ONE DAY IN YOUR LIFE** Michael Jackson	**ONE DAY IN YOUR LIFE** Michael Jackson	**GHOST TOWN** The Specials
STARS ON 45 Starsound	**NO SLEEP 'TIL HAMMERSMITH** Motörhead	**DISCO DAZE AND DISCO NITES** Various	**LOVE SONGS** Cliff Richard

KEY
UK No.1 ★ UK Top 10 ● Still on chart + UK entry at No.1 ■
US No.1 ▲ UK million seller £ US million seller $
Singles re-entries are listed as (re), (2re), (3re)... which signifies that the hit re-entered the chart once, twice or three times...
Peak Position / Weeks

99TH FLOOR ELEVATORS *UK, male DJ / production duo – Adrian Fusiarski and Clive Latham (3 Singles: 5 Weeks)*

12 Aug 95 **HOOKED** *Labello Dance LAD 18CD* [1] 28 2
30 May 96 **I'LL BE THERE** *Labello Dance LAD 25CD1* [1] 37 2
8 Apr 00 **HOOKED** (re-mix) *Tripoli Trax TTRAX 061CD*....66 1

[1] 99th Floor Elevators featuring Tony De Vit

NIO *UK, male vocalist / rapper / producer – Robert Medcalf*

23 Aug 03 **DO YOU THINK YOU'RE SPECIAL** *Echo ECSD 132*....52 1

NIRVANA *UK / Ireland, male vocal / instrumental duo*

15 May 68 **RAINBOW CHASER** *Island WIP 6029*....34 6

NIRVANA 143 Top 500
Legendary grunge pioneers: Kurt Cobain (g/v), d. 1994, Krist Novoselic (b) and Dave Grohl (d) (founder of Foo Fighters). These notorious Seattle superstars topped the US albums chart twice before and twice after Cobain's suicide. XFM listeners voted 'Smells Like Teen Spirit' the Greatest Record of All Time (9 Albums: 328 Weeks, 7 Singles: 36 Weeks)

5 Oct 91 ● NEVERMIND *DGC DGC 24425* ▲....7 196
30 Nov 91 ● **SMELLS LIKE TEEN SPIRIT** *DGC DGCS 5* $....7 6
7 Mar 92 BLEACH *Tupelo TUPCD 6*....33 7
14 Mar 92 ● **COME AS YOU ARE** *DGC DGCS 7*....9 5
25 Jul 92 **LITHIUM** *DGC DGCS 9*....11 6
12 Dec 92 **IN BLOOM** *Geffen GFS 34*....28 7
26 Dec 92 INCESTICIDE *Geffen GED 24504*....14 11
6 Mar 93 **OH, THE GUILT** *Touch and Go TG 83CD*....12 2
11 Sep 93 ● **HEART-SHAPED BOX** *Geffen GFSTD 54*....5 5
25 Sep 93 ★ IN UTERO *Geffen GED 24536* ■ ▲....1 43
18 Dec 93 **ALL APOLOGIES / RAPE ME** *Geffen GFSTD 66*....32 5
12 Nov 94 ★ MTV UNPLUGGED IN NEW YORK *Geffen GED 24727* ■ ▲....1 40
12 Oct 96 ● FROM THE MUDDY BANKS OF THE WISHKAH *Geffen GED 25105* ▲....4 6
9 Nov 02 ● NIRVANA *Geffen / Polydor 4935232*....3 23
4 Dec 04 WITH THE LIGHTS OUT *Geffen 9864838*....56 1
12 Nov 05 SLIVER – THE BEST OF THE BOX *Geffen 9886718*....56 1

The listed flip side of 'Oh, the Guilt' was 'Puss' by Jesus Lizard. Nevermind re-entered the chart in 2004 and 2005 with the catalogue number Geffen / Polydor DGCD 24425.

NITRO DELUXE
US, male multi-instrumentalist – Lee Junior (2 Singles: 16 Weeks)

14 Feb 87 **THIS BRUTAL HOUSE** (re) *Cooltempo COOL 142*....47 11
6 Feb 88 **LET'S GET BRUTAL** (re-mix) *Cooltempo COOLX 142*....24 5

'Let's Get Brutal' is a re-mixed version of 'This Brutal House'.

NITZER EBB *UK, male vocal / instrumental group (3 Singles: 3 Weeks)*

11 Jan 92 **GODHEAD** *Mute 1MUTE 135T*....56 1
11 Apr 92 **ASCEND** *Mute 110MUTE 145*....52 1
4 Mar 95 **KICK IT** *Mute LCDMUTE 155*....75 1

NIVEA *US, female vocalist – Nivea Hamilton (4 Singles: 8 Weeks)*

3 Mar 01 **DANGER (BEEN SO LONG)** *Jive 9251722* [1] 28 3
4 May 02 **RUN AWAY (I WANNA BE WITH U) / DON'T MESS WITH THE RADIO** *Jive 9253362*....48 1
21 Sep 02 **DON'T MESS WITH MY MAN** *Jive 9254082* [2] 41 2
10 May 03 **LAUNDROMAT / DON'T MESS WITH MY MAN** (re-mix) *Jive 9254822* [3] 33 2

[1] Mystikal featuring Nivea [2] Nivea featuring Brian and Brandon Casey
[3] Nivea featuring Brian and Brandon Casey of Jagged Edge and Mystikal

NIZLOPI NEW
UK, male vocal / instrumental duo – Luke Concannon and John Parker

24 Dec 05 ★ **JCB SONG** *FDM FDMNIZ 008* ■....1 2+

NO AUTHORITY *US, male vocal group*

14 Mar 98 **DON'T STOP** *Epic 6655592*....54 1

NO DICE *UK, male vocal / instrumental group*

5 May 79 **COME DANCING** *EMI 2927*....65 2

NO DOUBT 473 Top 500 *Critically-acclaimed Grammy and World Music Award-winning Californian new wave rock band formed in 1986 and fronted by Gwen Stefani, b. 3 Oct 1969. They won Grammys for 'Hey Baby' and 'Underneath It All', and Tragic Kingdom sold over 15 million worldwide. Stefani, who is married to Gavin Rossdale of Bush, was one of the world's top selling female artists in 2005. Best-selling single: 'Don't Speak' 834,000 (4 Albums: 81 Weeks, 13 Singles: 74 Weeks)*

26 Oct 96 **JUST A GIRL** *Interscope IND 80034*....38 2
18 Jan 97 ● TRAGIC KINGDOM *Interscope IND 90003* ▲....3 44
22 Feb 97 ★ **DON'T SPEAK** *Interscope IND 95515* ■....1 18
5 Jul 97 ● **JUST A GIRL** (re-issue) *Interscope IND 95539*....3 7
4 Oct 97 **SPIDERWEBS** *Interscope IND 95551*....16 3
20 Dec 97 **SUNDAY MORNING** *Interscope IND 95566*....50 3
12 Jun 99 **NEW** *Higher Ground HIGHS 22CD*....30 2
25 Mar 00 **EX-GIRLFRIEND** *Interscope 4972992*....23 3
22 Apr 00 RETURN OF SATURN *Interscope 4906382*....31 2
7 Oct 00 **SIMPLE KIND OF LIFE** *Interscope 4974162*....69 1
16 Feb 02 ROCK STEADY *Interscope 4931582*....43 6
16 Feb 02 ● **HEY BABY** *Interscope 4976682*....2 9
15 Jun 02 **HELLA GOOD** *Interscope 4977362*....12 7
12 Oct 02 **UNDERNEATH IT ALL** *Interscope 4977792*....18 5
6 Dec 03 **IT'S MY LIFE** *Interscope 9813724*....20 7
13 Dec 03 ● THE SINGLES 1992-2003 *Interscope / Polydor 9861382*....5 29
13 Mar 04 **IT'S MY LIFE (re-issue) / BATHWATER** *Interscope 9861993*....17 7

Bounty Killer supplied uncredited vocals on 'Hey Baby'.

NO MERCY
US, male vocal / instrumental group (1 Album: 4 Weeks, 3 Singles: 26 Weeks)

18 Jan 97 ● **WHERE DO YOU GO** *Arista 74321401502*....2 15
24 May 97 ● **PLEASE DON'T GO** *Arista 74321481372*....4 7
7 Jun 97 MY PROMISE *Arista 74321466902*....17 4
6 Sep 97 **KISS YOU ALL OVER** *Arista 7432151452*....16 4

NO REASON *UK, male vocal group*

11 Sep 04 **MAN LIKE ME** *Mad as Toast TOAST 002*....53 1

NO SWEAT *Ireland, male vocal / instrumental group (2 Singles: 5 Weeks)*

13 Oct 90 **HEART AND SOUL** *London LON 274*....64 4
2 Feb 91 **TEAR DOWN THE WALLS** *London LON 257*....61 1

NO WAY JOSÉ *US, male instrumental group*

3 Aug 85 **TEQUILA** *Fourth & Broadway BRW 28*....47 6

NO WAY SIS *UK, male vocal / instrumental group*

21 Dec 96 **I'D LIKE TO TEACH THE WORLD TO SING** *EMI CDEM 461*....27 4

NODDY
Toytown / UK, male animated character / vocalist and female vocal trio

20 Dec 03 **MAKE WAY FOR NODDY** *BMG 82876582142*....29 4

NODESHA *US, female vocalist – Nodesha Felix (2 Singles: 8 Weeks)*

6 Sep 03 ● **MISS PERFECT** *BMG 82876556742* [1] 5 7
1 Nov 03 **GET IT WHILE IT'S HOT** *Arista 82876559592*....55 1

[1] Abs featuring Nodesha

	18 July 1981	25 July 1981	1 August 1981	8 August 1981
UK No.1 SINGLES	GHOST TOWN The Specials	GHOST TOWN The Specials	GREEN DOOR Shakin' Stevens	GREEN DOOR Shakin' Stevens
UK No.1 ALBUMS	LOVE SONGS Cliff Richard	LOVE SONGS Cliff Richard	LOVE SONGS Cliff Richard	LOVE SONGS Cliff Richard

NOFX *US, male vocal / instrumental group (4 Albums: 4 Weeks)*

10 Feb 96 HEAVY PETTING ZOO *Epitaph 864572* 60 1
10 Jun 00 PUMP UP THE VALUUM *Epitaph 65842* 50 1
23 Mar 02 SPLIT SERIES – VOL.3 *BYO BYO 079CD* [1] 75 1
17 May 03 WAR ON ERRORISM *Fat Wreck FAT 657CD* 48 1

[1] Rancid / NOFX

The NOISE NEXT DOOR
UK, male vocal / instrumental trio (3 Singles: 10 Weeks)

6 Nov 04 **LOCK UP YA DAUGHTERS / MINISTRY OF MAYHEM** *Us & Them USTHEMS 10* **12** 4
19 Feb 05 **CALENDAR GIRL** *Us & Them USTHEMS 12* **11** 4
11 Jun 05 **SHE MIGHT** *Us & Them WEA 386CD2* **27** 2

Bernie NOLAN (see also The NOLANS) *Ireland, female actor / vocalist*

6 Mar 04 **MACUSHLA** *Laurel Bank 4KATECD 1* **38** 3

The NOLANS 413 Top 500 (see also Bernie NOLAN)
Ireland, female vocal group (6 Albums: 84 Weeks, 9 Singles: 90 Weeks)

20 Jul 78 ● 20 GIANT HITS *Target TGS 502* [1] 3 12
6 Oct 79 **SPIRIT BODY AND SOUL** *Epic EPC 7796* [1] **34** 6
22 Dec 79 ● **I'M IN THE MOOD FOR DANCING** *Epic EPC 8068* **3** 15
19 Jan 80 NOLANS *Epic EPC 83892* 15 13
12 Apr 80 **DON'T MAKE WAVES** *Epic EPC 8349* **12** 11
13 Sep 80 ● **GOTTA PULL MYSELF TOGETHER** *Epic EPC 8878* **9** 13
25 Oct 80 MAKING WAVES *Epic EPC 10023* 11 33
6 Dec 80 **WHO'S GONNA ROCK YOU** *Epic EPC 9325* **12** 11
14 Mar 81 ● **ATTENTION TO ME** *Epic EPC 9571* **9** 13
15 Aug 81 **CHEMISTRY** *Epic EPC A 1485* **15** 8
20 Feb 82 **DON'T LOVE ME TOO HARD** *Epic EPC A 1927* **14** 12
27 Mar 82 ● PORTRAIT *Epic EPC 10033* 7 10
20 Nov 82 ALTOGETHER *Epic EPC 10037* 52 8
17 Nov 84 GIRLS JUST WANNA HAVE FUN *Towerbell TOWLP 10* 39 8
1 Apr 95 **I'M IN THE MOOD FOR DANCING** (re-recording) *Living Beat LBECD 31* **51** 1

[1] The Nolan Sisters [1] The Nolan Sisters

NOMAD *UK, male / female vocal / instrumental duo – Damon Rochefort and Sharon Dee Clarke (1 Album: 2 Weeks, 6 Singles: 22 Weeks)*

2 Feb 91 ● **(I WANNA GIVE YOU) DEVOTION** *Rumour RUMA 25* [1] **2** 10
4 May 91 **JUST A GROOVE** *Rumour RUMA 33* **16** 6
22 Jun 91 CHANGING CABINS *Rumour RULP 100* 48 2
28 Sep 91 **SOMETHING SPECIAL** *Rumour RUMA 35* **73** 1
25 Apr 92 **YOUR LOVE IS LIFTING ME** *Rumour RUMA 48* **60** 2
7 Nov 92 **24 HOURS A DAY** *Rumour RUMA 60* **61** 1
25 Nov 95 **(I WANNA GIVE YOU) DEVOTION** (re-mix) *Rumour RUMACD 75* **42** 2

[1] Nomad featuring MC Mikee Freedom

NONCHALANT *US, female vocalist – Tanya Pointer*

29 Jun 96 **5 O'CLOCK** *MCA MCSTD 48011* **44** 1

Peter NOONE (see also HERMAN'S HERMITS) *UK, male vocalist*

22 May 71 **OH YOU PRETTY THING** *RAK 114* **12** 9

NOOTROPIC *UK, male instrumental / production duo*

16 Mar 96 **I SEE ONLY YOU** *Hi-Life 5779832* **42** 1

NORTH AND SOUTH
UK, male vocal (Lee Otter) / instrumental group (4 Singles: 16 Weeks)

17 May 97 ● **I'M A MAN NOT A BOY** *RCA 74321461142* **7** 5
9 Aug 97 **TARANTINO'S NEW STAR** *RCA 74321501242* **18** 5
8 Nov 97 **BREATHING** *RCA 74321528422* **27** 2
4 Apr 98 **NO SWEAT '98** *RCA 74321562212* **29** 4

NORTHERN HEIGHTZ *UK, male / female DJ / production / vocal group*

20 Mar 04 **LOOK AT US** *Iconic CDXIC 002* **29** 3

NORTHERN LINE *UK / South Africa, male vocal group (3 Singles: 12 Weeks)*

9 Oct 99 **RUN FOR YOUR LIFE** *Global Talent GTR 002CDS1* **18** 4
11 Mar 00 **LOVE ON THE NORTHERN LINE** *Global Talent GTR 003CDS1* **15** 5
17 Jun 00 **ALL AROUND THE WORLD** *Global Talent GTR 004CDS1* **27** 3

NORTHERN UPROAR
UK, male vocal / instrumental group (1 Album: 2 Weeks, 6 Singles: 11 Weeks)

21 Oct 95 **ROLLERCOASTER / ROUGH BOYS** *Heavenly HVN 047CD* **41** 2
3 Feb 96 **FROM A WINDOW / THIS MORNING** *Heavenly HVN 051CD* **17** 3
20 Apr 96 **LIVIN' IT UP** *Heavenly HVN 52CD* **24** 2
11 May 96 NORTHERN UPROAR *Heavenly HVNLP 12CD* 22 2
22 Jun 96 **TOWN** *Heavenly HVN 54CD* **48** 1
7 Jun 97 **ANY WAY YOU LOOK** *Heavenly HVN 70CD* **36** 2
23 Aug 97 **A GIRL I ONCE KNEW** *Heavenly HVN 73CD* **63** 1

NORTHSIDE
UK, male vocal / instrumental group (1 Album: 3 Weeks, 3 Singles: 12 Weeks)

9 Jun 90 **SHALL WE TAKE A TRIP / MOODY PLACES** *Factory FAC 268* **50** 5
3 Nov 90 **MY RISING STAR** *Factory FAC 2987* **32** 3
1 Jun 91 **TAKE 5** *Factory FAC 3087* **40** 4
29 Jun 91 CHICKEN RHYTHMS *Factory FACT 310* 19 3

NOT THE 9 O'CLOCK NEWS CAST (see also MR BEAN and SMEAR CAMPAIGN featuring Bruce DICKINSON; SMITH and JONES; Mel SMITH)
UK / New Zealand, male / female comedians (3 Albums: 51 Weeks)

8 Nov 80 ● NOT THE 9 O'CLOCK NEWS *BBC REB 400* 5 23
17 Oct 81 ● HEDGEHOG SANDWICH *BBC REB 421* 5 24
23 Oct 82 THE MEMORY KINDA LINGERS *BBC REF 453* 63 4

Freddie NOTES and The RUDIES *Jamaica, male vocal / instrumental group*

10 Oct 70 **MONTEGO BAY** *Trojan TR 7791* **45** 2

NOTORIOUS B.I.G. *US, male rapper – Christopher Wallace, b. 21 May 1972, d. 9 Mar 1997 (2 Albums: 17 Weeks, 10 Singles: 36 Weeks)*

29 Oct 94 **JUICY** *Bad Boy 74321240102* **72** 1
1 Apr 95 **BIG POPPA** *Puff Daddy 74321263412* $ **63** 1
15 Jul 95 **CAN'T YOU SEE** *Tommy Boy TBCD 700* [1] **43** 2
19 Aug 95 **ONE MORE CHANCE / STAY WITH ME** *Puff Daddy 74321300782* $ **34** 2
5 Apr 97 LIFE AFTER DEATH *Puff Daddy 78612730112* ▲ 23 16
3 May 97 ● **HYPNOTIZE** *Arista 74321466412* ▲ $ **10** 4
9 Aug 97 ● **MO MONEY MO PROBLEMS** *Puff Daddy 74321492492* [2] ▲ $ **6** 10
14 Feb 98 **SKY'S THE LIMIT** *Puff Daddy 74321561992* [3] **35** 2
18 Jul 98 **RUNNIN'** *Black Jam BJAM 9005* [4] **15** 3
18 Dec 99 BORN AGAIN *Puff Daddy 74321717182* ▲ 70 1
5 Feb 00 **NOTORIOUS B.I.G** *Puff Daddy / Arista 74321737312* [5] **16** 5
31 Jan 04 **RUNNIN' (DYING TO LIVE)** *Interscope / Polydor 9815329* [6] **17** 6

[1] Total featuring Notorious BIG [2] Notorious BIG featuring Puff Daddy and Ma$e [3] Notorious BIG featuring 112 [4] 2Pac and Notorious BIG [5] Notorious BIG featuring Puff Daddy and Lil' Kim [6] Tupac featuring Notorious BIG

The NOTTING HILLBILLIES (see also DIRE STRAITS)
UK, male vocal / instrumental group – leader Mark Knopfler

17 Mar 90 ● MISSING ... PRESUMED HAVING A GOOD TIME *Vertigo 8426711* 2 14

NOTTINGHAM FOREST with PAPER LACE
UK, male football team and vocal / instrumental group

4 Mar 78 **WE GOT THE WHOLE WORLD IN OUR HANDS** *Warner Bros. K 17110* **24** 6

15 August 1981	22 August 1981	29 August 1981	5 September 1981
GREEN DOOR Shakin' Stevens	GREEN DOOR Shakin' Stevens	JAPANESE BOY Aneka	TAINTED LOVE Soft Cell
THE OFFICIAL BBC ALBUM OF THE ROYAL WEDDING	THE OFFICIAL BBC ALBUM OF THE ROYAL WEDDING	TIME Electric Light Orchestra	TIME Electric Light Orchestra

KEY: UK No.1 ★ UK Top 10 ● Still on chart + UK entry at No.1 ■ US No.1 ▲ UK million seller £ US million seller $
Singles re-entries are listed as (re), (2re), (3re)... which signifies that the hit re-entered the chart once, twice or three times...
Peak Position / Weeks

Heather NOVA

Bermuda, female vocalist (2 Albums: 2 Weeks, 1 Single: 1 Week)

25 Feb 95 WALK THIS WORLD *Butterfly BFLD 19*....69 1
8 Apr 95 OYSTER *Butterfly BFLCD 12*....72 1
20 Jun 98 SIREN *V2 VVR 1001872*....55 1

Nancy NOVA *UK, female vocalist*

4 Sep 82 NO, NO, NO *EMI 5328*....63 2

NOVACANE vs NO ONE DRIVING *UK, male production group*

15 Jun 02 LOVE BE MY LOVER (PLAYA SOL) *Direction 6727792*....69 1

NOVASPACE

Germany, male / female production / vocal duo – Felix Gauder and Jessica Bohrs

22 Feb 03 TIME AFTER TIME *MoS / Substance SUBS 15CDS*....29 3

Tom NOVY

Germany, male producer – Thomas Reichold (6 Singles: 14 Weeks)

2 May 98 SUPERSTAR *D:disco 74321569352* [1] 32 3
3 Jun 00 PUMPIN *Positiva CDTIV 132* [1] 19 3
2 Sep 00 I ROCK *Rulin RULIN 3CDS* [2] 55 1
4 Aug 01 NOW OR NEVER *Rulin RULIN 14CDS* [3] 64 1
19 Nov 05 UNITED NATIONS OF HOUSE VOL.1 *CR2 12C 2014* [4] 71 1
3 Dec 05 ● YOUR BODY *Data DATA 102CDS* [5] ....10 5+

[1] Novy vs Eniac [2] Tom Novy featuring Virginia [3] Tom Novy featuring Lima [4] Tom Novy / United People of Zion featuring Regina / Tiefschwarz [5] Tom Novy featuring Michael Marshall

Tracks on United Nations of House Vol.1: Your Body – Tom Novy; Moment With You – United People of Zion featuring Regina; Music – Tiefschwarz

NU-BIRTH (see also M FACTOR; NUSH; 187 LOCKDOWN) *UK, male production duo – Danny Harrison and Julian Jonah (2 Singles: 2 Weeks)*

6 Sep 97 ANYTIME *XL Recordings XLS 85CD*....48 1
6 Jun 98 ANYTIME (re-issue) *Locked On LOX 97CD*....41 1

NU CIRCLES featuring Emma B

UK, male producer – Andy Lysandrou and female vocalist – Emma Blocksage

8 Feb 03 WHAT YOU NEED (TONIGHT) *East West EW 258CD*....46 1

NU COLOURS

UK, male / female vocal / instrumental group (6 Singles: 11 Weeks)

6 Jun 92 TEARS *Wild Card CARD 1*....55 2
10 Oct 92 POWER *Wild Card CARD 3*....64 1
5 Jun 93 WHAT IN THE WORLD *Wild Card CARDD 4*....57 2
27 Nov 93 POWER (re-mix) *Wild Card CARDD 5*....40 2
25 May 96 DESIRE *Wild Card 5763652*....31 2
24 Aug 96 SPECIAL KIND OF LOVER *Wild Card 5752012*....38 2

NU GENERATION

UK, male producer – Aston Harvey (2 Singles: 9 Weeks)

29 Jan 00 ● IN YOUR ARMS (RESCUE ME) *Concept CDCON 7*....8 8
21 Oct 00 NOWHERE TO RUN 2000 *Concept CDCON 16*....66 1

NU-MATIC *UK, male instrumental / production duo*

8 Aug 92 SPRING IN MY STEP *XL Recordings XLS 31*....58 1

NU SHOOZ *US, male / female vocal duo – John Smith and Valerie Day (1 Album: 8 Weeks, 2 Singles: 17 Weeks)*

24 May 86 ● I CAN'T WAIT *Atlantic A 9446*....2 14
14 Jun 86 POOLSIDE *Atlantic WX 60*....32 8
26 Jul 86 POINT OF NO RETURN *Atlantic A 9392*....48 3

NU SOUL featuring Kelli RICH *US, male / female vocal / instrumental duo – Carnell Newbill and Kelli Richardson*

13 Jan 96 HIDE-A-WAY *ffrr FCD 269*....27 2

NUANCE featuring Vikki LOVE

US, male / female vocal / instrumental group

19 Jan 85 LOVERIDE *Fourth & Broadway BRW 20*....59 3

NUCLEAR ASSAULT *US, male vocal / instrumental group*

7 Oct 89 HANDLE WITH CARE *Under One Flag FLAG 35*....60 1

NUCLEUS *UK, male instrumental group*

11 Jul 70 ELASTIC ROCK *Vertigo 6360 006*....46 1

Ted NUGENT *US, male vocalist / guitarist (6 Albums: 14 Weeks)*

4 Sep 76 TED NUGENT *Epic EPC 81268*....56 1
30 Oct 76 FREE FOR ALL *Epic EPC 81397*....33 2
2 Jul 77 CAT SCRATCH FEVER *Epic EPC 82010*....28 5
11 Mar 78 DOUBLE LIVE GONZO! *Epic EPC 88282*....47 2
14 Jun 80 SCREAM DREAM *Epic EPC 86111*....37 3
25 Apr 81 INTENSITIES IN 10 CITIES *Epic EPC 84917*....75 1

NUKLEUZ DJ'S (see also DJ NATION)

UK, collection of male DJs / producers (3 Singles: 9 Weeks)

24 Aug 02 DJ NATION *Nukleuz NUKF 0440*....40 2
8 Feb 03 DJ NATION – BOOTLEG EDITION (re) *Nukleuz 0468 FNUK*....33 4
15 Nov 03 DJ NATION – HARDER EDITION *Nukleuz 0572 FNUK* [1] 48 3

[1] Various

All releases contain tracks by various DJs / producers spread across three chart-eligible 12-inch singles, each including the track 'DJ Nation'.

Gary NUMAN (180 Top 500) (see also Paul GARDINER)

The moody, synthesized sound of Gary Webb, b. 8 Mar 1958, London, first hit the charts in 1979 under the group name Tubeway Army. Five-times chart hit 'Cars' was also the basis of Armand Van Helden's Top 20 hit 'Koochy' in 2000 (27 Albums: 145 Weeks, 38 Singles: 169 Weeks)

19 May 79 ★ ARE 'FRIENDS' ELECTRIC? *Beggars Banquet BEG 18* [1] 1 16
9 Jun 79 ★ REPLICAS *Beggars Banquet BEGA 7* [1] 1 31
25 Aug 79 TUBEWAY ARMY *Beggars Banquet BEGA 4* [1] 14 10
1 Sep 79 ★ CARS *Beggars Banquet BEG 23*....1 11
22 Sep 79 ★ THE PLEASURE PRINCIPLE *Beggars Banquet BEGA 10* ■ 1 21
24 Nov 79 ● COMPLEX *Beggars Banquet BEG 29*....6 9
24 May 80 ● WE ARE GLASS *Beggars Banquet BEG 35*....5 7
30 Aug 80 ● I DIE: YOU DIE *Beggars Banquet BEG 46*....6 7
13 Sep 80 ★ TELEKON *Beggars Banquet BEGA 19* ■ 1 11
20 Dec 80 THIS WRECKAGE *Beggars Banquet BEG 50*....20 7
2 May 81 LIVING ORNAMENTS 1979 *Beggars Banquet BEGA 24*....47 3
2 May 81 ● LIVING ORNAMENTS 1979-1980 *Beggars Banquet BOX 1*....2 4
2 May 81 LIVING ORNAMENTS 1980 *Beggars Banquet BEGA 25*....39 3
29 Aug 81 ● SHE'S GOT CLAWS *Beggars Banquet BEG 62*....6 6
12 Sep 81 ● DANCE *Beggars Banquet BEGA 28*....3 8
5 Dec 81 LOVE NEEDS NO DISGUISE *Beggars Banquet BEG 68* [2] 33 7
6 Mar 82 MUSIC FOR CHAMELEONS *Beggars Banquet BEG 70*....19 7
19 Jun 82 ● WE TAKE MYSTERY (TO BED) *Beggars Banquet BEG 77*....9 4
28 Aug 82 WHITE BOYS AND HEROES *Beggars Banquet BEG 81*....20 4
18 Sep 82 ● I ASSASSIN *Beggars Banquet BEGA 40*....8 6
27 Nov 82 NEW MAN NUMAN – THE BEST OF GARY NUMAN *TV TVA 7*..45 7
3 Sep 83 WARRIORS *Beggars Banquet BEG 95*....20 5
24 Sep 83 WARRIORS *Beggars Banquet BEGA 47*....12 6

12 September 1981	19 September 1981	26 September 1981	3 October 1981
UK No.1 SINGLES			
TAINTED LOVE Soft Cell	PRINCE CHARMING Adam and The Ants	PRINCE CHARMING Adam and The Ants	PRINCE CHARMING Adam and The Ants
UK No.1 ALBUMS			
DEAD RINGER Meat Loaf	DEAD RINGER Meat Loaf	ABACAB Genesis	ABACAB Genesis

22 Oct 83	**SISTER SURPRISE** *Beggars Banquet BEG 101*	32	3
6 Oct 84	**THE PLAN 1978** *Beggars Banquet BEGA 55*	29	4
3 Nov 84	**BERSERKER** *Numa NU 4*	32	5
24 Nov 84	**BERSERKER** *Numa NUMA 1001*	45	3
22 Dec 84	**MY DYING MACHINE** *Numa NU 6*	66	1
9 Feb 85	**CHANGE YOUR MIND** *Polydor POSP 722* [3]	17	8
13 Apr 85	**WHITE NOISE – LIVE** *Numa NUMAD 1002*	29	5
25 May 85	**THE LIVE EP** *Numa NUM 7*	27	4
10 Aug 85	**YOUR FASCINATION** *Numa NU 9*	46	5
21 Sep 85	**CALL OUT THE DOGS** *Numa NU 11*	49	2
28 Sep 85	**THE FURY** *Numa NUMA 1003*	24	5
16 Nov 85	**MIRACLES** *Numa NU 13*	49	3
19 Apr 86	**THIS IS LOVE** *Numa NU 16*	28	3
28 Jun 86	**I CAN'T STOP** *Numa NU 17*	27	4
4 Oct 86	**NEW THING FROM LONDON TOWN** *Numa NU 19* [3]	52	3
8 Nov 86	**STRANGE CHARM** *Numa NUMA 1005*	59	2
6 Dec 86	**I STILL REMEMBER** *Numa NU 21*	74	1
28 Mar 87	**RADIO HEART** *GFM GFM 109*	35	6
13 Jun 87	**LONDON TIMES** *GFM GFM 112*	48	2
19 Sep 87	**CARS (E REG MODEL) / ARE 'FRIENDS' ELECTRIC?** (re-mixes) *Beggars Banquet BEG 199*	16	7
3 Oct 87	**EXHIBITION** *Beggars Banquet BEGA 88*	43	3
30 Jan 88	**NO MORE LIES** *Polydor POSP 894* [3]	34	3
1 Oct 88	**NEW ANGER** *Illegal ILS 1003*	46	2
8 Oct 88	**METAL RHYTHM** *Illegal ILP 035*	48	2
3 Dec 88	**AMERICA** *Illegal ILS 1004*	49	1
3 Jun 89	**I'M ON AUTOMATIC** *Polydor PO 43* [3]	44	2
8 Jul 89	**AUTOMATIC** *Polydor 8395201* [2]	59	1
28 Oct 89	**SKIN MECHANIC** *IRS EIRSA 1019*	55	1
16 Mar 91	**HEART** *IRS NUMAN 1*	43	2
30 Mar 91	**OUTLAND** *IRS EIRSA 1039*	39	1
21 Mar 92	**THE SKIN GAME** *Numa NU 23*	68	1
1 Aug 92	**MACHINE + SOUL** *Numa NUM 124*	72	1
22 Aug 92	**MACHINE AND SOUL** *Numa NUMACD 1009*	42	1
4 Sep 93	**CARS** (2nd re-mix) *Beggars Banquet BEG 264CD*	53	1
2 Oct 93	**BEST OF GARY NUMAN 1978-83** *Beggars Banquet BEGA 150CD*	70	1
16 Mar 96	**CARS** (re-issue of re-mix) *PolyGram TV PRMCD 1*	17	4
30 Mar 96	**THE PREMIER HITS** *PolyGram TV 5311492* [3]	21	3
1 Nov 97	**EXILE** *Eagle EAGCD 008*	48	1
21 Oct 00	**PURE** *Eagle EAGCD 078*	58	1
1 Jun 02	**EXPOSURE – THE BEST OF GARY NUMAN 1977-2002** *Jagged Halo JHCD 2*	44	1
13 Jul 02	**RIP** *Jagged Halo JHCD 5*	29	2
5 Jul 03	**CRAZIER** *Jagged Halo JHCDV 6* [4]	13	3

[1] Tubeway Army [2] Gary Numan and Dramatis [3] Sharpe and Numan [4] Gary Numan vs Rico [1] Tubeway Army [2] Sharpe and Numan [3] Gary Numan / Tubeway Army

Tracks on The Live EP: Are 'Friends' Electric? / Berserker / Cars / We Are Glass. Living Ornaments 1979-1980 is a boxed set of Living Ornaments 1979 and Living Ornaments 1980.

NUMBER ONE CUP *US, male vocal / instrumental group*

2 Mar 96	**DIVEBOMB** *Blue Rose BRRC 10032*	61	1

Jose NUNEZ featuring OCTAHVIA (see also CHOO CHOO PROJECT)
US, male DJ / producer (2 Singles: 2 Weeks)

5 Sep 98	**IN MY LIFE** *Ministry of Sound MOSCDS 126*	56	1
5 Jun 99	**HOLD ON** *Ministry of Sound MOSCDS 130*	44	1

Bobby NUNN *US, male vocalist / multi-instrumentalist – Ulysses Nunn, b. 20 Sep 1925, d. 5 Nov 1986*

4 Feb 84	**DON'T KNOCK IT (UNTIL YOU TRY IT)** *Motown TMG 1323*	65	3

NUSH (see also M FACTOR; NU-BIRTH; 187 LOCKDOWN)
UK, male instrumental / production duo – Danny Matlock and Danny Harrison (3 Singles: 7 Weeks)

23 Jul 94	**U GIRLS** *Blunted Vinyl BLNCDX 006*	58	1
22 Apr 95	**MOVE THAT BODY** *Blunted Vinyl BLNCD 012*	46	2
16 Sep 95	**U GIRLS (LOOK SO SEXY)** (re-mix) *Blunted Vinyl BLNCD 13*	15	4

NUT *UK, female vocalist (3 Singles: 4 Weeks)*

8 Jun 96	**BRAINS** *Epic NUTCD 2*	64	1
21 Sep 96	**CRAZY** *Epic NUTCD 5*	56	1
11 Jan 97	**SCREAM** *Epic NUTCD 6*	43	2

NUTTIN' NYCE *US, female vocal group (2 Singles: 2 Weeks)*

10 Jun 95	**DOWN 4 WHATEVA** *Jive JIVECD 365*	62	1
12 Aug 95	**FROGGY STYLE** *Jive JIVECD 381*	68	1

NUYORICAN SOUL (see also MASTERS AT WORK)
US, male DJ / production group (1 Album: 2 Weeks, 3 Singles: 8 Weeks)

8 Feb 97	**RUNAWAY** *Talkin Loud TLCD 20* [1]	24	4
1 Mar 97	**NUYORICAN SOUL** *Talkin Loud 5344602*	25	2
10 May 97	**IT'S ALRIGHT, I FEEL IT!** *Talkin Loud TLCD 22* [2]	26	2
25 Oct 97	**I AM THE BLACK GOLD OF THE SUN** *Talkin Loud TLCD 26* [2]	31	2

[1] Nuyorican Soul featuring India [2] Nuyorican Soul featuring Jocelyn Brown

NYLON MOON *Italy, male instrumental duo*

13 Apr 96	**SKY PLUS** *Positiva CDTIV 50*	43	2

Michael NYMAN *UK, male pianist*

12 Feb 94	**THE PIANO (FILM SOUNDTRACK)** *Venture CDVE 919*	31	15
19 Mar 94	**THE HEART ASKS PLEASURE FIRST / THE PROMISE** *Virgin VEND 3*	60	2

O

OMC *New Zealand, male vocalist – Paul Fuemana Lawrence (2 Singles: 17 Weeks)*

20 Jul 96 ●	**HOW BIZARRE** *Polydor 5776202*	5	16
18 Jan 97	**ON THE RUN** *Polydor 5732452*	56	1

OPM *US, male vocal (Matthew Lo) / instrumental group (1 Album: 8 Weeks, 2 Singles: 18 Weeks)*

14 Jul 01 ●	**HEAVEN IS A HALFPIPE** *Atlantic AT 0107CD*	4	14
21 Jul 01	**MENACE TO SOBRIETY** *Atlantic 7567929772*	31	8
12 Jan 02	**EL CAPITAN** (re) *Atlantic AT 0118CD*	20	4

O.R.G.A.N. *Spain, male DJ / producer – Vidana Crespo*

16 May 98	**TO THE WORLD** *Multiply CDMULTY 34*	33	2

O-TOWN *US, male vocal group (1 Album: 5 Weeks, 5 Singles: 27 Weeks)*

28 Apr 01 ●	**LIQUID DREAMS** *J 74321853202*	3	10
4 Aug 01 ●	**ALL OR NOTHING** *J 74321875822*	4	10
18 Aug 01 ●	**O-TOWN** *RCA / J Records 74321882992*	7	5
3 Nov 01	**WE FIT TOGETHER** (re) *J 74321893692*	20	4
23 Feb 02	**LOVE SHOULD BE A CRIME** *J 74321920232*	38	2
15 Feb 03	**THESE ARE THE DAYS** *J 82876503052*	36	1

10 October 1981	17 October 1981	24 October 1981	31 October 1981
PRINCE CHARMING Adam and The Ants	**IT'S MY PARTY** Dave Stewart and Barbara Gaskin	**IT'S MY PARTY** Dave Stewart and Barbara Gaskin	**IT'S MY PARTY** Dave Stewart and Barbara Gaskin
GHOST IN THE MACHINE The Police	**GHOST IN THE MACHINE** The Police	**GHOST IN THE MACHINE** The Police	**DARE** Human League

READERS' TOP

In May 2005 we invited readers of the 18th edition of British Hit Singles & Albums to vote for their favourite albums. Members of nme.com came on board shortly after, and all this resulted in the most comprehensive and authoritative poll yet undertaken to mark the 50th anniversary of the UK albums chart. How can we back up these claims? Three main reasons: the sheer size of the mountain of votes, absolutely no voting restrictions with more than 3,000 different albums receiving your votes and a resulting chart compiled from the opinions of what we believe are the most knowledgeable music fans in the UK.

1. **DEFINITELY MAYBE** Oasis
2. **SGT. PEPPER'S LONELY HEARTS CLUB BAND** The Beatles
3. **REVOLVER** The Beatles
4. **OK COMPUTER** Radiohead
5. **(WHAT'S THE STORY) MORNING GLORY?** Oasis
6. **NEVERMIND** Nirvana
7. **STONE ROSES** The Stone Roses
8. **DARK SIDE OF THE MOON** Pink Floyd
9. **THE QUEEN IS DEAD** The Smiths
10. **THE BENDS** Radiohead
11. **THE JOSHUA TREE** U2
12. **LONDON CALLING** The Clash
13. **THE BEATLES (WHITE ALBUM)** The Beatles
14. **ABBEY ROAD** The Beatles
15. **UP THE BRACKET** The Libertines
16. **NEVER MIND THE BOLLOCKS HERE'S THE SEX PISTOLS** Sex Pistols
17. **FOUR SYMBOLS (LED ZEPPELIN IV)** Led Zeppelin
18. **THE RISE AND FALL OF ZIGGY STARDUST AND THE SPIDERS FROM MARS** David Bowie
19. **A NIGHT AT THE OPERA** Queen
20. **IS THIS IT** The Strokes
21. **HOT FUSS** The Killers
22. **PET SOUNDS** The Beach Boys
23. **GRACE** Jeff Buckley
24. **THE HOLY BIBLE** Manic Street Preachers
25. **BAT OUT OF HELL** Meat Loaf
26. **APPETITE FOR DESTRUCTION** Guns N' Roses
27. **EMPLOYMENT** Kaiser Chiefs
28. **RUBBER SOUL** The Beatles
29. **RUMOURS** Fleetwood Mac
30. **THE LIBERTINES** The Libertines
31. **URBAN HYMNS** The Verve
32. **AMERICAN IDIOT** Green Day
33. **A RUSH OF BLOOD TO THE HEAD** Coldplay
34. **PARKLIFE** Blur
35. **THRILLER** Michael Jackson
36. **THE WALL** Pink Floyd
37. **AUTOMATIC FOR THE PEOPLE** R.E.M.
38. **FRANZ FERDINAND** Franz Ferdinand
39. **TUBULAR BELLS** Mike Oldfield
40. **ACHTUNG BABY** U2
41. **WISH YOU WERE HERE** Pink Floyd
42. **EXILE ON MAIN ST** The Rolling Stones
43. **BRIDGE OVER TROUBLED WATER** Simon & Garfunkel

Illustrated here is the front cover image of what turned out to be the narrow winner in our poll. Definitely Maybe was written by Noel Gallagher, produced by Oasis and Mark Coyle with additional production and mixing by Owen Morris plus Dave Batchelor (who produced 'Slide Away' only). The cover photography and design, featuring the band surrounded by pictures of their heroes,

100 ALBUMS

www.bibleofpop.com

NME.COM

44. **LED ZEPPELIN II** Led Zeppelin
45. **PARALLEL LINES** Blondie
46. **BROTHERS IN ARMS** Dire Straits
47. **BLOOD ON THE TRACKS** Bob Dylan
48. **HUNKY DORY** David Bowie
49. **X&Y** Coldplay
50. **WHO'S NEXT** The Who
51. **HOPES AND FEARS** Keane
52. **PARACHUTES** Coldplay
53. **ARRIVAL** Abba
54. **DIFFERENT CLASS** Pulp
55. **THE VELVET UNDERGROUND & NICO** The Velvet Underground & Nico
56. **FOREVER CHANGES** Love
57. **WHAT'S GOING ON** Marvin Gaye
58. **LET IT BLEED** The Rolling Stones
59. **ELEPHANT** The White Stripes
60. **DOOLITTLE** Pixies
61. **ABSOLUTION** Muse
62. **GOODBYE YELLOW BRICK ROAD** Elton John
63. **SHEER HEART ATTACK** Queen
64. **COME ON OVER** Shania Twain
65. **SIGN 'O' THE TIMES** Prince
66. **10** Pearl Jam
67. **KASABIAN** Kasabian
68. **DOOKIE** Green Day
69. **ORIGIN OF SYMMETRY** Muse
70. **THE HOUNDS OF LOVE** Kate Bush
71. **BLONDE ON BLONDE** Bob Dylan
72. **ALL MOD CONS** The Jam
73. **BLUE** Joni Mitchell
74. **WHITE BLOOD CELLS** The White Stripes
75. **DOG MAN STAR** Suede
76. **METALLICA (THE BLACK ALBUM)** Metallica
77. **DARE!** Human League
78. **CLOSER** Joy Division
79. **IN UTERO** Nirvana
80. **BACK IN BLACK** AC/DC
81. **FUNERAL** Arcade Fire
82. **UP ALL NIGHT** Razorlight
83. **RAY OF LIGHT** Madonna
84. **BORN TO RUN** Bruce Springsteen
85. **PHYSICAL GRAFFITI** Led Zeppelin
86. **WHATEVER PEOPLE SAY I AM, THAT'S WHAT I'M NOT** Arctic Monkeys
87. **A DAY AT THE RACES** Queen
88. **THE LEXICON OF LOVE** ABC
89. **SPICE** Spice Girls
90. **VIOLATOR** Depeche Mode
91. **FINAL STRAW** Snow Patrol
92. **ELECTRIC WARRIOR** T. Rex
93. **JAGGED LITTLE PILL** Alanis Morissette
94. **UNKNOWN PLEASURES** Joy Division
95. **KID A** Radiohead
96. **OUT OF THE BLUE** Electric Light Orchestra
97. **THE SMITHS** The Smiths
98. **ELECTRIC LADYLAND** Jimi Hendrix
99. **RAGE AGAINST THE MACHINE** Rage Against The Machine
100. **HOTEL CALIFORNIA** Eagles

Burt Bacharach, Rodney Marsh and George Best, was by Michael Spencer Jones and Brian Cannon. Definitely Maybe tracklisting: Rock 'n' Roll Star / Shakermaker / Live Forever / Up in the Sky / Columbia / Supersonic / Bring it on Down / Cigarettes & Alcohol / Digsy's Dinner / Slide Away / Married with Children / Sad Song

KEY
UK No.1 ★ UK Top 10 ● Still on chart + UK entry at No.1 ■ US No.1 ▲ UK million seller £ US million seller $
Singles re-entries are listed as (re), (2re), (3re)... which signifies that the hit re-entered the chart once, twice or three times...
Peak Position / Weeks

OTT *Ireland, male vocal group (4 Singles: 18 Weeks)*

15 Feb 97 LET ME IN *Epic 6642052* 12 5
17 May 97 FOREVER GIRL *Epic 6645082* 24 3
23 Aug 97 ALL OUT OF LOVE *Epic 6649152* 11 4
24 Jan 98 THE STORY OF LOVE *Epic OTT 1CD* 11 6

O-ZONE *Moldova, male vocal trio*

19 Jun 04 ● DRAGOSTEA DIN TEI *Jive 82876618412* 3 17

OAKENFOLD (see also ELEMENTFOUR; PERFECTO ALLSTARZ; VIRUS) *UK, male DJ / producer – Paul Oakenfold (1 Album: 12 Weeks, 5 Singles: 16 Weeks)*

25 Aug 01 PLANET ROCK *Tommy Boy TBCD 2266* [1] 47 1
22 Jun 02 SOUTHERN SUN / READY STEADY GO *Perfecto PERF 17CDS* 16 4
6 Jul 02 BUNKKA *Perfecto PERFALB 09CD* 25 12
31 Aug 02 ● STARRY EYED SURPRISE *Perfecto PERF 27CDS* 6 8
22 Feb 03 THE HARDER THEY COME *Perfecto PERF 49CDS* 38 2
27 Sep 03 HYPNOTISED *East West EW 271CD* 57 1

[1] Paul Oakenfold presents Afrika Bambaataa and the Soulsonic Force

Philip OAKEY (see also HUMAN LEAGUE) *UK, male vocalist / keyboard player (1 Album: 5 Weeks, 3 Singles: 19 Weeks)*

22 Sep 84 ● TOGETHER IN ELECTRIC DREAMS *Virgin VS 713* [1] 3 13
29 Jun 85 GOOD-BYE BAD TIMES *Virgin VS 772* [2] 44 5
10 Aug 85 PHILIP OAKEY AND GIORGIO MORODER *Virgin V 2351* [1] 52 5
26 Apr 03 L.A. TODAY *Xtravaganza XTRAV 37CDS* [3] 68 1

[1] Giorgio Moroder and Phil Oakey [2] Philip Oakey and Giorgio Moroder [3] Alex Gold featuring Philip Oakey [1] Philip Oakey and Giorgio Moroder

OASIS *UK, male / female vocal / instrumental group – includes Mary Hopkin and Peter Skellern*

28 Apr 84 OASIS *WEA WX 3* 23 15

OASIS (24 Top 500) (see also BUFFALO TOM)
Peerless Manchester-based, Beatles-influenced band featuring brothers Liam (v) and Noel (g/v) Gallagher. Current line-up includes Gem Archer (g), Andy Bell (b) and, since 1994, Zak Starkey (d), son of Ringo Starr. The often controversial Britpop group smashed the record for most weeks on the chart in one year (134 in 1996), and sold 356,000 copies of Be Here Now in one day and a million in a record 17 days in the UK. Their first five albums all sold over a million in the UK. Best-selling single: 'Wonderwall' 966,940 (11 Albums: 541 Weeks, 24 Singles: 381 Weeks)

23 Apr 94 SUPERSONIC (5re) *Creation CRESCD 176* 31 14
2 Jul 94 SHAKERMAKER (5re) *Creation CRESCD 182* 11 15
20 Aug 94 ● LIVE FOREVER (6re) *Creation CRESCD 185* 10 18
10 Sep 94 ★ DEFINITELY MAYBE *Creation CRECD 169* ■ 1 187
22 Oct 94 ● CIGARETTES & ALCOHOL (9re) *Creation CRESCD 190* 7 35
31 Dec 94 ● WHATEVER (8re) *Creation CRESCD 195* 3 50
6 May 95 ★ SOME MIGHT SAY (6re) *Creation CRESCD 204* ■ 1 27
13 May 95 SOME MIGHT SAY *Creation CRE 204T* 71 1
26 Aug 95 ● ROLL WITH IT (3re) *Creation CRESCD 212* 2 18
14 Oct 95 ★ (WHAT'S THE STORY) MORNING GLORY? *Creation CRECD 189* ■ 1 145
11 Nov 95 ● WONDERWALL (2re) *Creation CRESCD 215* 2 34
25 Nov 95 WIBBLING RIVALRY (INTERVIEWS WITH NOEL AND LIAM GALLAGHER) *Fierce Panda NING 12CD* [1] 52 2
2 Mar 96 ★ DON'T LOOK BACK IN ANGER (2re) *Creation CRESCD 221* ■ 1 24
16 Nov 96 DEFINITELY MAYBE SINGLES BOX – SILVER *Creation CREDM 002* 23 3
16 Nov 96 (WHAT'S THE STORY) MORNING GLORY? SINGLES BOX – GOLD *Creation CREMG 002* 24 3
19 Jul 97 ★ D'YOU KNOW WHAT I MEAN? *Creation CRESCD 256* ■ 1 18
30 Aug 97 ★ BE HERE NOW *Creation CRECD 219* ■ 1 36
4 Oct 97 ● STAND BY ME *Creation CRESCD 278* 2 18
24 Jan 98 ★ ALL AROUND THE WORLD (re) *Creation CRESCD 282* ■ 1 9
14 Nov 98 ● THE MASTERPLAN *Creation CRECD 241* 2 28
19 Feb 00 ★ GO LET IT OUT (re) *Big Brother RKIDSCD 001* ■ 1 12
11 Mar 00 ★ STANDING ON THE SHOULDER OF GIANTS *Big Brother RKIDCD 002* ■ 1 29
29 Apr 00 ● WHO FEELS LOVE? (re) *Big Brother RKIDSCD 003* 4 8
17 Jun 00 (WHAT'S THE STORY) MORNING GLORY? (re-issue) *Big Brother RKIDCD 008* 27 26
15 Jul 00 ● SUNDAY MORNING CALL *Big Brother RKIDSCD 004* 4 6
25 Nov 00 ● FAMILIAR TO MILLIONS *Big Brother RKIDCD 005* 5 10
27 Apr 02 ★ THE HINDU TIMES *Big Brother RKIDSCD 23* ■ 1 11
29 Jun 02 ● STOP CRYING YOUR HEART OUT *Big Brother RKIDSCD 24* 2 10
13 Jul 02 ★ HEATHEN CHEMISTRY *Big Brother RKIDCD 25* ■ 1 44
5 Oct 02 ● LITTLE BY LITTLE / SHE IS LOVE *Big Brother RKIDSCD 26* 2 8
15 Feb 03 ● SONGBIRD *Big Brother RKIDSCD 27* 3 10
28 May 05 ★ LYLA *Big Brother RKIDSCD 29* ■ 1 13
11 Jun 05 ★ DON'T BELIEVE THE TRUTH *Big Brother RKIDCD 30* ■ 1 30+
3 Sep 05 ★ THE IMPORTANCE OF BEING IDLE (re) *Big Brother RKIDSCD 31* ■ 1 16
10 Dec 05 ● LET THERE BE LOVE *Big Brother RKIDSCD 32* 2 4+

[1] Oas*s

Chart rules allow for a maximum of three formats. The 12-inch of 'Some Might Say' – already available on CD, seven-inch and cassette – was therefore listed separately. Oasis had a record number of re-entries between 1995 and 1997 as new releases were accompanied by the regular return of singles from their back catalogue. The re-issued (What's the Story) Morning Glory? (17 Jun 2000) reached its peak position in 2005.

OBERNKIRCHEN CHILDREN'S CHOIR *Germany, children's choir*

22 Jan 54 ● THE HAPPY WANDERER (re) *Parlophone R 3799* 2 26

OBI PROJECT featuring HARRY, ASHER D and DJ WHAT? *UK, male vocal / rap / production group (2 Singles: 1 Week)*

4 Aug 01 BABY, CAN I GET YOUR NUMBER *East West EW 235CD* 75 1

OBITUARY *US, male vocal / instrumental group (2 Albums: 2 Weeks)*

18 Apr 92 THE END COMPLETE *Roadrunner RC 92012* 52 1
17 Sep 94 WORLD DEMISE *Roadrunner RR 89955* 65 1

Dermot O'BRIEN and his CLUBMEN *Ireland, male vocal / instrumental group*

20 Oct 66 THE MERRY PLOUGHBOY (re) *Envoy ENV 016* 46 2

Billy OCEAN (200 Top 500) *Top British-based R&B singer / songwriter of the 1980s, b. Leslie Charles, 21 Jan 1950, Trinidad and Tobago. He waited seven years after scoring his first four UK Top 20 hits before accumulating an impressive run of transatlantic successes, including three US No.1s (7 Albums: 145 Weeks, 19 Singles: 153 Weeks)*

21 Feb 76 ● LOVE REALLY HURTS WITHOUT YOU *GTO GT 52* 2 10
10 Jul 76 L.O.D. (LOVE ON DELIVERY) *GTO GT 62* 19 8
13 Nov 76 STOP ME (IF YOU'VE HEARD IT ALL BEFORE) *GTO GT 72* 12 11
19 Mar 77 ● RED LIGHT SPELLS DANGER *GTO GT 85* 2 10
1 Sep 79 AMERICAN HEARTS *GTO GT 244* 54 5
19 Jan 80 ARE YOU READY *GTO GT 259* 42 7
13 Oct 84 ● CARIBBEAN QUEEN (NO MORE LOVE ON THE RUN) *Jive JIVE 77* ▲ 6 14
24 Nov 84 ● SUDDENLY *Jive JIP 12* 9 59
19 Jan 85 LOVERBOY *Jive JIVE 80* 15 10
11 May 85 ● SUDDENLY *Jive JIVE 90* 4 14
17 Aug 85 MYSTERY LADY *Jive JIVE 98* 49 4

	7 November 1981	14 November 1981	21 November 1981	28 November 1981
UK No.1 SINGLES	IT'S MY PARTY Dave Stewart and Barbara Gaskin	EVERY LITTLE THING SHE DOES IS MAGIC The Police	UNDER PRESSURE Queen and David Bowie	UNDER PRESSURE Queen and David Bowie
UK No.1 ALBUMS	SHAKY Shakin' Stevens	GREATEST HITS Queen	GREATEST HITS Queen	GREATEST HITS Queen

25 Jan 86 ★ WHEN THE GOING GETS TOUGH, THE TOUGH GET GOING *Jive JIVE 114*....1 13
12 Apr 86 THERE'LL BE SAD SONGS (TO MAKE YOU CRY) *Jive JIVE 117* ▲....12 13
17 May 86 ● LOVE ZONE *Jive HIP 35*....2 32
9 Aug 86 LOVE ZONE *Jive JIVE 124*....49 3
11 Oct 86 BITTERSWEET *Jive JIVE 133*....44 4
10 Jan 87 LOVE IS FOREVER *Jive JIVE 134*....34 7
6 Feb 88 ● GET OUTTA MY DREAMS GET INTO MY CAR *Jive BOS 1* ▲....3 11
19 Mar 88 ● TEAR DOWN THESE WALLS *Jive HIP 57*....3 13
7 May 88 CALYPSO CRAZY *Jive BOS 2*....35 4
6 Aug 88 THE COLOUR OF LOVE *Jive BOS 3*....65 3
28 Oct 89 ● GREATEST HITS *Jive BOTV 1*....4 15
6 Feb 93 PRESSURE *Jive BOSCD 6*....55 2
16 Aug 97 ● LOVE IS FOR EVER *Jive BOCD 2*....7 21
15 Feb 03 LET'S GET BACK TOGETHER *Jive 9225232*....69 1
19 Jun 04 THE ULTIMATE COLLECTION *Jive 82876614022*....28 4

OCEAN COLOUR SCENE (302 Top 500) (see also BUFFALO TOM)

Birmingham-based retro-rockers formed in 1990 include Simon Fowler (v) and Steve Cradock (g). The band has been publicly championed by Paul Weller and Noel Gallagher, whose brother Liam partnered Cradock on Top 10 hit 'Carnation' (see Buffalo Tom). They ended the 1990s with nine successive Top 20 singles (10 Albums: 152 Weeks, 20 Singles: 73 Weeks)

23 Mar 91 YESTERDAY TODAY *!Phfft FIT 2*....49 1
17 Feb 96 THE RIVERBOAT SONG *MCA MCSTD 40021*....15 5
6 Apr 96 ● YOU'VE GOT IT BAD *MCA MCSTD 40036*....7 4
20 Apr 96 ● MOSELEY SHOALS *MCA MCD 60008*....2 73
15 Jun 96 ● THE DAY WE CAUGHT THE TRAIN *MCA MCSTD 40046*....4 11
21 Sep 96 OCEAN COLOUR SCENE *Fontana 5122692*....54 2
28 Sep 96 ● THE CIRCLE *MCA MCSTD 40077*....6 6
15 Mar 97 ● B-SIDES SEASIDES & FREERIDES *MCA MCD 60034*....4 14
28 Jun 97 ● HUNDRED MILE HIGH CITY *MCA MCSTD 40133*....4 7
6 Sep 97 ● TRAVELLERS TUNE *MCA MCSTD 40144*....5 5
27 Sep 97 ★ MARCHIN' ALREADY *MCA MCD 60048* ■....1 37
22 Nov 97 ● BETTER DAY *MCA MCSTD 40151*....9 5
28 Feb 98 IT'S A BEAUTIFUL THING *MCA MCSTD 40157*....12 4
4 Sep 99 PROFIT IN PEACE *Island CID 757*....13 5
25 Sep 99 ● ONE FROM THE MODERN *Island CID 8090*....4 11
27 Nov 99 SO LOW *Island CID 759*....34 2
8 Jul 00 JULY / I AM THE NEWS *Island CID 763*....31 2
7 Apr 01 UP ON THE DOWN SIDE *Island CID 774*....19 3
21 Apr 01 ● MECHANICAL WONDER *Island CID 8104*....7 4
14 Jul 01 MECHANICAL WONDER *Island CID 779*....49 1
17 Nov 01 SONGS FOR THE FRONT ROW – THE BEST OF OCEAN COLOUR SCENE *Island CID 8111*....16 4
22 Dec 01 CRAZY LOWDOWN WAYS *Island CID 787*....64 1
12 Jul 03 I JUST NEED MYSELF *Sanctuary SANXD 159*....13 3
19 Jul 03 NORTH ATLANTIC DRIFT *Sanctuary SANDP 160*....14 3
6 Sep 03 MAKE THE DEAL *Sanctuary SANXD 219*....35 2
13 Sep 03 ANTHOLOGY *Island 9807210*....75 1
10 Jan 04 GOLDEN GATE BRIDGE *Sanctuary SANXD 244*....40 3
19 Mar 05 FREE MY NAME *Sanctuary SANXD 344*....23 2
2 Apr 05 A HYPERACTIVE WORKOUT FOR THE FLYING SQUAD *Sanctuary SANCD 332*....30 3
2 Jul 05 THIS DAY SHOULD LAST FOREVER *Sanctuary SANXS 380*....53 1

OCEANIA *New Zealand / UK, male / female vocal / instrumental group*

23 Oct 99 OCEANIA *Universal TV / Point Music 5367752*....70 1

OCEANIC *UK, male / female vocal / instrumental group (1 Album: 2 Weeks, 4 Singles: 26 Weeks)*

24 Aug 91 ● INSANITY *Dead Dead Good GOOD 4*....3 15
30 Nov 91 WICKED LOVE (re) *Dead Dead Good GOOD 5*....25 5
13 Jun 92 CONTROLLING ME *Dead Dead Good GOOD 14*....14 5
4 Jul 92 THAT ALBUM BY OCEANIC *Dead Dead Good 4509900832*....49 2
14 Nov 92 IGNORANCE *Dead Dead Good GOOD 22* [1]....72 1

[1] Oceanic featuring Siobhan Maher

Only copies of the album on vinyl and cassette were called That Album By Oceanic; the CD version was entitled That Compact Disc By Oceanic.

OCEANLAB (see also DIRT DEVILS)

UK / Finland, male production trio (2 Singles: 5 Weeks)

27 Apr 02 CLEAR BLUE WATER *Code Blue BLU 024CD* [1]....48 1
1 May 04 SATELLITE *Nulife 82876614002*....19 4

[1] Oceanlab featuring Justine Suissa

OCEANSIZE *UK, male vocal / instrumental group*

14 Feb 04 CATALYST *Beggars Banquet BBQ 375CD*....73 1

Des O'CONNOR (439 Top 500)

Entertainer, comedian and MOR vocalist, b. 12 Jan 1932. This London-based all-rounder toured with Buddy Holly and Lonnie Donegan in the 1950s, had a series of hits in the 1960s and has been a top-rated TV star for over 40 years (7 Albums: 47 Weeks, 8 Singles: 117 Weeks)

1 Nov 67 ● CARELESS HANDS *Columbia DB 8275*....6 17
8 May 68 ★ I PRETEND *Columbia DB 8397*....1 36
20 Nov 68 ● ONE, TWO THREE O'LEARY *Columbia DB 8492*....4 11
7 Dec 68 ● I PRETEND *Columbia SCX 6295*....8 10
7 May 69 DICK-A-DUM-DUM (KING'S ROAD) *Columbia DB 8566*....14 10
29 Nov 69 LONELINESS *Columbia DB 8632*....18 11
14 Mar 70 I'LL GO ON HOPING *Columbia DB 8661*....30 7
26 Sep 70 THE TIP OF MY FINGERS *Columbia DB 8713*....15 15
5 Dec 70 WITH LOVE *Columbia SCX 6417*....40 4
2 Dec 72 SING A FAVOURITE SONG *Pye NSPL 18390*....25 6
2 Feb 80 JUST FOR YOU *Warwick WW 5071*....17 7
13 Oct 84 DES O'CONNOR NOW *Telstar STAR 2245*....24 14
8 Nov 86 ● THE SKYE BOAT SONG *Tembo TML 119* [1]....10 10
5 Dec 92 PORTRAIT *Columbia 4727302*....63 4
17 Nov 01 A TRIBUTE TO THE CROONERS *UMTV / Decca 4704702*....51 2

[1] Roger Whittaker and Des O'Connor

'Careless Hands' is with the Michael Sammes Singers.

Hazel O'CONNOR

UK, female vocalist (2 Albums: 45 Weeks, 7 Singles: 46 Weeks)

9 Aug 80 ● BREAKING GLASS (FILM SOUNDTRACK) *A&M AMLH 64820*....5 38
16 Aug 80 ● EIGHTH DAY *A&M AMS 7553*....5 11
25 Oct 80 GIVE ME AN INCH *A&M AMS 7569*....41 4
21 Mar 81 ● D-DAYS *Albion ION 1009*....10 9
23 May 81 ● WILL YOU *A&M AMS 8131*....8 10
1 Aug 81 (COVER PLUS) WE'RE ALL GROWN UP *Albion ION 1018*....41 6
12 Sep 81 COVER PLUS *Albion ALB 108*....32 7
3 Oct 81 HANGING AROUND *Albion ION 1022*....45 3
23 Jan 82 CALLS THE TUNE *A&M AMS 8203*....60 3

Sinead O'CONNOR (471 Top 500)

Distinctive singer / songwriter who never ducked controversy, b. 12 Dec 1966, Glenageary, Ireland. The one time In Tua Nua vocalist, who has also provided vocals on hits for Jah Wobble, Conjure One and Marxman, will always be remembered for her chart-topping rendition of the Prince-penned ballad. She was the first Irish woman to top both the UK and US albums charts and the first person to refuse to collect BRIT or Grammy awards (1991) (7 Albums: 90 Weeks, 15 Singles: 65 Weeks)

16 Jan 88 MANDINKA *Ensign ENY 611*....17 9
23 Jan 88 THE LION AND THE COBRA *Ensign CHEN 7*....27 20
20 Jan 90 ★ NOTHING COMPARES 2 U *Ensign ENY 630* ▲....1 14
24 Mar 90 ★ I DO NOT WANT WHAT I HAVEN'T GOT *Ensign CHEN 14* ■ ▲....1 51
21 Jul 90 THE EMPEROR'S NEW CLOTHES *Ensign ENY 633*....31 5
20 Oct 90 THREE BABIES *Ensign ENY 635*....42 4
8 Jun 91 MY SPECIAL CHILD *Ensign ENY 646*....42 3
14 Dec 91 SILENT NIGHT *Ensign ENY 652*....60 4
12 Sep 92 SUCCESS HAS MADE A FAILURE OF OUR HOME *Ensign ENY 656*....18 4
26 Sep 92 ● AM I NOT YOUR GIRL? *Ensign CCD 1952*....6 6
12 Dec 92 DON'T CRY FOR ME ARGENTINA *Ensign ENY 657*....53 4
19 Feb 94 YOU MADE ME THE THIEF OF YOUR HEART *Island CID 588*....42 3
24 Sep 94 UNIVERSAL MOTHER *Ensign CDCHEN 34*....19 8

5 December 1981	12 December 1981	19 December 1981	26 December 1981
BEGIN THE BEGUINE (VOLVER A EMPEZAR) Julio Iglesias	DON'T YOU WANT ME Human League	DON'T YOU WANT ME Human League	DON'T YOU WANT ME Human League
GREATEST HITS Queen	CHART HITS '81 Various	THE VISITORS Abba	THE VISITORS Abba

KEY UK No.1 ★ UK Top 10 ● Still on chart + UK entry at No.1 ■ US No.1 ▲ UK million seller £ US million seller $
Singles re-entries are listed as (re), (2re), (3re)... which signifies that the hit re-entered the chart once, twice or three times...
Peak Position / Weeks

26 Nov 94 **THANK YOU FOR HEARING ME** *Ensign CDENYS 662* 13 7
29 Apr 95 **HAUNTED** *ZTT ZANG 65CD* [1] 30 2
26 Aug 95 **FAMINE** *Ensign CDENY 663* 51 1
17 May 97 **GOSPEL OAK (EP)** *Chrysalis CDCHS 5051* 28 3
22 Nov 97 SO FAR ... THE BEST OF SINEAD O'CONNOR *Chrysalis 8215812* 28 3
6 Dec 97 **THIS IS A REBEL SONG** *Columbia 6652992* 60 1
24 Jun 00 FAITH AND COURAGE *Atlantic 7567833372* 61 1
24 Aug 02 **TROY (THE PHOENIX FROM THE FLAME)** *Devolution DEVR 003CDS* 48 1
19 Oct 02 SEAN NOS NUA *R&M Entertainment RAMCD 001* 52 1

[1] Shane MacGowan and Sinead O'Connor

Tracks on Gospel Oak (EP): This Is to Mother You / I Am Enough for Myself / Petit Poulet / 4 My Love.

OCTAVE ONE featuring Ann SAUNDERSON
US, male production trio and female vocalist (2 Singles: 2 Weeks)

16 Feb 02 **BLACKWATER** *Concept / 430 West CDCON 26* 47 1
28 Sep 02 **BLACKWATER** (re-mix) *Concept / 430 CDCON 34* 69 1

OCTOPUS
UK / France, male vocal / instrumental group (3 Singles: 5 Weeks)

22 Jun 96 **YOUR SMILE** *Food CDFOOD 78* 42 2
14 Sep 96 **SAVED** *Food CDFOODS 84* 40 2
23 Nov 96 **JEALOUSY** *Food CDFOODS 87* 59 1

Alan O'DAY *US, male vocalist*

2 Jul 77 **UNDERCOVER ANGEL** *Atlantic K 10926* ▲ 43 3

Daniel O'DONNELL (239 Top 500)
Britain's top MOR vocalist, b. 12 Dec 1961, County Donegal, Ireland. This hugely popular live performer, who received an MBE in 2002, held six of the top seven places on the UK country chart in 1991 and is the only act with at least one hit album every year since 1988 (24 Albums: 201 Weeks, 18 Singles: 68 Weeks)

15 Oct 88 FROM THE HEART *Telstar STAR 2327* 56 12
28 Oct 89 THOUGHTS OF HOME *Telstar STAR 2372* 43 10
21 Apr 90 FAVOURITES *Ritz RITZLP 052* 61 3
17 Nov 90 THE LAST WALTZ *Ritz RITZALP 058* 46 7
9 Nov 91 THE VERY BEST OF DANIEL O'DONNELL *Ritz RITZBLD 700* 34 14
12 Sep 92 **I JUST WANT TO DANCE WITH YOU** *Ritz RITZ 250P* 20 7
21 Nov 92 FOLLOW YOUR DREAM *Ritz RITZBCD 701* 17 9
2 Jan 93 **THE THREE BELLS** *Ritz RITZCD 239* 71 1
8 May 93 **THE LOVE IN YOUR EYES** *Ritz RITZCD 257* 47 3
7 Aug 93 **WHAT EVER HAPPENED TO OLD FASHIONED LOVE** *Ritz RITZCD 262* 21 5
6 Nov 93 A DATE WITH DANIEL O'DONNELL LIVE *Ritz RITZBCD 702* 21 10
16 Apr 94 **SINGING THE BLUES** *Ritz RITZCD 270* 23 3
22 Oct 94 ESPECIALLY FOR YOU *Ritz RITZBCD 703* 14 11
26 Nov 94 **THE GIFT** *Ritz RITZCD 275* 46 3
3 Dec 94 CHRISTMAS WITH DANIEL *Ritz RITZBCD 704* 34 5
10 Jun 95 **SECRET LOVE** *Ritz RITZCD 285* [1] 28 3
11 Nov 95 THE CLASSIC COLLECTION *Ritz RITZBCD 705* 34 9
9 Mar 96 **TIMELESS** *Ritz RITZCD 293* [1] 32 3
6 Apr 96 TIMELESS *Ritz RITZBCD 707* [1] 13 5
20 Jul 96 IRISH COLLECTION *Ritz RITZCD 0080* 35 3
28 Sep 96 **FOOTSTEPS** *Ritz RITZCD 300* 25 5
26 Oct 96 SONGS OF INSPIRATION *Ritz RITZBCD 709* 11 16
7 Jun 97 **THE LOVE SONGS EP** *Ritz RITZCD 306* 27 4
8 Nov 97 I BELIEVE *Ritz RITZBCD 710* 11 11
11 Apr 98 ● **GIVE A LITTLE LOVE** *Ritz RITZCD 315* 7 5
17 Oct 98 **THE MAGIC IS THERE** *Ritz RZCD 320* 16 4
31 Oct 98 ● LOVE SONGS *Ritz RZBCD 715* 9 10
20 Mar 99 **THE WAY DREAMS ARE** *Ritz RZCD 325* 18 3
24 Jul 99 **UNO MAS** *Ritz RZCD 326* 25 3
2 Oct 99 ● GREATEST HITS *Ritz RZBCD 716* 10 8
18 Dec 99 **A CHRISTMAS KISS** *Ritz RZCD 330* 20 4
15 Apr 00 **LIGHT A CANDLE** *Ritz RZCD 335* 23 4
28 Oct 00 ● FAITH & INSPIRATION *Ritz RZBCD 717* 4 10
16 Dec 00 **MORNING HAS BROKEN** *Ritz RZCD 341* 32 4
1 Dec 01 LIVE, LAUGH, LOVE *Rosette ROSCD 2002* 27 5
2 Nov 02 YESTERDAY'S MEMORIES *Rosette ROSCD 2020* 19 3
22 Mar 03 ● DANIEL IN BLUE JEANS – 20 GREAT ROCK 'N' ROLL LOVE SONGS *DMG DMGTV 001* 3 10
25 Oct 03 AT THE END OF THE DAY *Rosette ROSCD 2040* 11 6
13 Dec 03 **YOU RAISE ME UP** *Rosette ROSCD 310* 22 4
20 Mar 04 ● THE JUKEBOX YEARS – 20 MORE BLUE JEANS CLASSICS *DMG TV DMGTV 005* 3 8
23 Oct 04 ● WELCOME TO MY WORLD – 20 CLASSICS FROM THE JIM REEVES SONGBOOK *Rosette ROSCD 2050* 6 10
1 Oct 05 ● TEENAGE DREAMS – 20 GREAT ROCK 'N' ROLL MEMORIES *Rosette ROSCD 2060* 10 6

[1] Daniel O'Donnell and Mary Duff [1] Daniel O'Donnell and Mary Duff

Tracks on The Love Songs EP: Save the Last Dance for Me / I Can't Stop Loving You / You're the Only Good Thing / Limerick You're a Lady.

Ryan & Rachel O'DONNELL
Ireland, male / female vocal / instrumental duo (2 Albums: 13 Weeks)

16 Mar 02 THE CELTIC CHILLOUT ALBUM *Decadance DECTV 001* 17 10
22 Mar 03 THE CELTIC CHILLOUT ALBUM 2 *Decadance DECTV 009* 37 3

ODYSSEY *US, male / female vocal / instrumental group (5 Albums: 32 Weeks, 9 Singles: 82 Weeks)*

24 Dec 77 ● **NATIVE NEW YORKER** *RCA PC 1129* 5 11
21 Jun 80 ★ **USE IT UP AND WEAR IT OUT** *RCA PB 1962* 1 12
16 Aug 80 HANG TOGETHER *RCA PL 13526* 38 3
13 Sep 80 ● **IF YOU'RE LOOKIN' FOR A WAY OUT** *RCA 5* 6 15
17 Jan 81 **HANG TOGETHER** *RCA 23* 36 7
30 May 81 ● **GOING BACK TO MY ROOTS** *RCA 85* 4 12
4 Jul 81 I'VE GOT THE MELODY *RCA RCALP 5028* 29 7
19 Sep 81 **IT WILL BE ALRIGHT** *RCA 128* 43 5
12 Jun 82 ● **INSIDE OUT** *RCA 226* 3 11
3 Jul 82 HAPPY TOGETHER *RCA RCALP 6036* 21 9
11 Sep 82 **MAGIC TOUCH** *RCA 275* 41 5
20 Nov 82 THE MAGIC TOUCH OF ODYSSEY *Telstar STAR 2223* 69 5
17 Aug 85 **(JOY) I KNOW IT** *Mirror BUTCH 12* 51 4
26 Sep 87 THE GREATEST HITS *Stylus SMR 735* 26 8

Esther and Abi OFARIM *Israel, female / male vocal duo – Esther Zaled and Abraham Reichstadt (2 Albums: 24 Weeks, 2 Singles: 22 Weeks)*

14 Feb 68 ★ **CINDERELLA ROCKEFELLA** *Philips BF 1640* 1 13
24 Feb 68 ● 2 IN 3 *Philips SBL 7825* 6 20
19 Jun 68 **ONE MORE DANCE** *Philips BF 1678* 13 9
12 Jul 69 OFARIM CONCERT – LIVE '69 *Philips XL 4* 29 4

OFF-SHORE *Germany, male instrumental / production duo – Jens Lissat and Peter Harder (2 Singles: 12 Weeks)*

22 Dec 90 ● **I CAN'T TAKE THE POWER** *CBS 6565707* 7 11
17 Aug 91 **I GOT A LITTLE SONG** *Dance Pool 6568257* 64 1

The OFFSPRING (404 Top 500)
Celebrated California-based punk pop band formed in 1984 and fronted by 'Dexter' Holland (v), b. 29 Dec 1966. Smash sold more than 11 million worldwide and their No.1 single reportedly had a record 22 million downloads – pretty fly for a white group (6 Albums: 113 Weeks, 13 Singles: 64 Weeks)

25 Feb 95 **SELF ESTEEM** *Golf CDSHOLE 001* 37 3
4 Mar 95 SMASH *Epitaph E 864322* 21 34
19 Aug 95 **GOTTA GET AWAY** *Out of Step WOOS 2CDS* 43 2
1 Feb 97 **ALL I WANT** *Epitaph 64912* 31 2

	2 January 1982	9 January 1982	16 January 1982	23 January 1982
UK No.1 SINGLES	DON'T YOU WANT ME Human League	DON'T YOU WANT ME Human League	THE LAND OF MAKE BELIEVE Bucks Fizz	THE LAND OF MAKE BELIEVE Bucks Fizz
UK No.1 ALBUMS	THE VISITORS Abba	DARE Human League	DARE Human League	DARE Human League

15 Feb 97	IXNAY ON THE HOMBRE *Epitaph 64872*	17	3
26 Apr 97	**GONE AWAY** *Epitaph 64982*	42	1
28 Nov 98 ●	AMERICANA *Columbia 4916562*	10	44
30 Jan 99 ★	**PRETTY FLY (FOR A WHITE GUY)** *Columbia 666802* ■	1	11
8 May 99 ●	**WHY DON'T YOU GET A JOB?** *Columbia 6673542*	2	8
11 Sep 99	**THE KIDS AREN'T ALRIGHT** *Columbia 6677632*	11	6
4 Dec 99	**SHE'S GOT ISSUES** *Columbia 6683772*	41	2
18 Nov 00 ●	**ORIGINAL PRANKSTER** *Columbia 6699972*	6	8
25 Nov 00	CONSPIRACY OF ONE *Columbia 4984819*	12	18
31 Mar 01	**WANT YOU BAD** (re) *Columbia 6709292*	15	9
7 Jul 01	**MILLION MILES AWAY** *Columbia 6714082*	21	4
13 Dec 03	SPLINTER *Columbia 5122013*	35	7
31 Jan 04	**HIT THAT** *Columbia 6745475*	11	7
5 Jun 04	**(CAN'T GET MY) HEAD AROUND YOU** *Columbia 6748262*	48	1
16 Jul 05	GREATEST HITS *Columbia 5187462*	14	7

OH WELL *Germany, male producer – Ackim Faulker (2 Singles: 7 Weeks)*

14 Oct 89	**OH WELL** *Parlophone R 6236*	28	6
3 Mar 90	**RADAR LOVE** *Parlophone R 6244*	65	1

Mary O'HARA *UK, female vocalist / harp (2 Albums: 12 Weeks)*

8 Apr 78	MARY O'HARA AT THE ROYAL FESTIVAL HALL *Chrysalis CHR 1159*	37	3
1 Dec 79	TRANQUILLITY *Warwick WW 5072*	12	9

The OHIO EXPRESS *US, male vocal (Joey Levine) / instrumental group*

5 Jun 68 ●	**YUMMY YUMMY YUMMY** *Pye International 7N 25459*	5	15

The OHIO PLAYERS *US, male vocal / instrumental group*

10 Jul 76	**WHO'D SHE COO?** *Mercury PLAY 001*	43	4

The O'JAYS *US, male vocal group (9 Singles: 72 Weeks)*

23 Sep 72	**BACK STABBERS** *CBS 8270*	14	9
3 Mar 73 ●	**LOVE TRAIN** *CBS 1181* ▲	9	13
31 Jan 76	**I LOVE MUSIC** *Philadelphia International PIR 3879*	13	9
12 Feb 77	**DARLIN' DARLIN' BABY (SWEET, TENDER, LOVE)** *Philadelphia International PIR 4834*	24	6
8 Apr 78	**I LOVE MUSIC** (re-issue) *Philadelphia International PIR 6093*	36	3
17 Jun 78	**USED TA BE MY GIRL** *Philadelphia International PIR 6332*	12	12
30 Sep 78	**BRANDY** *Philadelphia International PIR 6658*	21	9
29 Sep 79	**SING A HAPPY SONG** *Philadelphia International PIR 7825*	39	6
30 Jul 83	**PUT OUR HEADS TOGETHER** *Philadelphia International A 3642*	45	5

OK GO *US, male vocal / instrumental group*

22 Mar 03	**GET OVER IT** *Capitol CDR 6603*	21	3

John O'KANE *UK, male vocalist*

9 May 92	**STAY WITH ME** *Circa YR 88*	41	4

OL' DIRTY BASTARD (see also WU-TANG CLAN) *US, male rapper – Russell Jones, b. 15 Nov 1968, d. 13 Nov 2004 (2 Singles: 25 Weeks)*

27 Jun 98 ●	**GHETTO SUPASTAR (THAT IS WHAT YOU ARE)** *Interscope IND 95593* [1]	2	17
8 Jul 00	**GOT YOUR MONEY** *Elektra E 7077CD* [2]	11	8

[1] Pras Michel featuring ODB & introducing Mya [2] Ol' Dirty Bastard featuring Kelis

OLD SKOOL ORCHESTRA (see also STRETCH 'N' VERN present "MADDOG") *UK, male DJ / production duo*

23 Jan 99	**B-BOY HUMP** *East West EW 186CD1*	55	1

Mike OLDFIELD (51 Top 500)

Composer / producer / multi-instrumentalist, b. 15 May 1953, Reading, UK. His chart-topping 1973 debut album, Tubular Bells, spent five years on the chart and, 19 years later, the eagerly-anticipated Tubular Bells II also reached No.1 (25 Albums: 551 Weeks, 20 Singles: 113 Weeks)

14 Jul 73 ★	TUBULAR BELLS *Virgin V 2001*	1	279
13 Jul 74	**MIKE OLDFIELD'S SINGLE (THEME FROM TUBULAR BELLS)** *Virgin VS 101*	31	6
14 Sep 74 ★	HERGEST RIDGE *Virgin V 2013* ■	1	17
8 Feb 75	THE ORCHESTRAL TUBULAR BELLS *Virgin V 2026* [1]	17	7
15 Nov 75 ●	OMMADAWN *Virgin V 2043*	4	23
20 Dec 75 ●	**IN DULCE JUBILO / ON HORSEBACK** *Virgin VS 131*	4	10
20 Nov 76	BOXED *Virgin V BOX 1*	22	13
27 Nov 76 ●	**PORTSMOUTH** *Virgin VS 163*	3	12
9 Dec 78	INCANTATIONS *Virgin VDT 101*	14	17
23 Dec 78	**TAKE 4 (EP)** *Virgin VS 238*	72	3
21 Apr 79	**GUILTY** *Virgin VS 245*	22	8
11 Aug 79	EXPOSED *Virgin VD 2511*	16	9
8 Dec 79	PLATINUM *Virgin V 2141*	24	9
8 Dec 79	**BLUE PETER** *Virgin VS 317*	19	9
8 Nov 80	QE 2 *Virgin V 2181*	27	12
20 Mar 82	**FIVE MILES OUT** *Virgin VS 464* [1]	43	5
27 Mar 82 ●	FIVE MILES OUT *Virgin V 2222*	7	27
12 Jun 82	**FAMILY MAN** *Virgin VS 489* [1]	45	6
28 May 83 ●	**MOONLIGHT SHADOW** *Virgin VS 586* [2]	4	17
4 Jun 83 ●	CRISES *Virgin V 2262*	6	29
14 Jan 84	**CRIME OF PASSION** *Virgin VS 648*	61	3
30 Jun 84	**TO FRANCE** *Virgin VS 686* [1]	48	7
7 Jul 84	DISCOVERY *Virgin V 2308*	15	16
15 Dec 84	THE KILLING FIELDS *Virgin V 2328*	97	1
2 Nov 85	THE COMPLETE MIKE OLDFIELD *Virgin MOC 1*	36	17
14 Dec 85	**PICTURES IN THE DARK** *Virgin VS 836* [3]	50	6
10 Oct 87	ISLANDS *Virgin V 2466*	29	5
22 Jul 89	EARTH MOVING *Virgin V 2610*	30	5
9 Jun 90	AMAROK *Virgin V 2640*	49	2
12 Sep 92 ★	TUBULAR BELLS II *WEA 4509906182* ■	1	30
3 Oct 92 ●	**SENTINEL** *WEA YZ 698*	10	6
19 Dec 92	**TATTOO** *WEA YZ 708*	33	5
17 Apr 93	**THE BELL** *WEA YZ 737CD*	50	2
25 Sep 93 ●	ELEMENTS – THE BEST OF MIKE OLDFIELD *Virgin VTCD 18*	5	10
9 Oct 93	**MOONLIGHT SHADOW** (re-issue) *Virgin VSCDT 1477*	52	2
3 Dec 94	THE SONGS OF DISTANT EARTH *WEA 4509985812*	24	6
17 Dec 94	**HIBERNACULUM** *WEA YZ 871CD*	47	3
2 Sep 95	**LET THERE BE LIGHT** *WEA YZ 880CD*	51	1
7 Sep 96	VOYAGER *WEA 630158962*	12	5
22 Nov 97	**WOMEN OF IRELAND** *WEA WEA 093CD*	70	1
12 Sep 98 ●	TUBULAR BELLS III *WEA 3984243492*	4	7
24 Apr 99	**FAR ABOVE THE CLOUDS** *WEA WEA 206CD1*	53	1
5 Jun 99	GUITARS *WEA 3984274012*	40	2
16 Jun 01	THE BEST OF TUBULAR BELLS *Virgin CDV 2936*	60	2
7 Jun 03	TUBULAR BELLS 2003 *WEA 2564602042*	51	1

[1] Mike Oldfield featuring Maggie Reilly [2] Mike Oldfield with vocals by Maggie Reilly [3] Mike Oldfield featuring Aled Jones, Anita Hegerland and Barry Palmer [1] Mike Oldfield with the Royal Philharmonic Orchestra

Tracks on Take 4 (EP): Portsmouth / In Dulce Jubilo / Wrekorder Wrondo / Sailors Hornpipe. Barry Palmer supplied uncredited vocals on 'Crime of Passion'. MC on 'The Bell' is Viv Stanshall.

Sally OLDFIELD *UK, female vocalist*

9 Dec 78	**MIRRORS** *Bronze BRO 66*	19	13

Misty OLDLAND *UK, female vocalist (3 Singles: 7 Weeks)*

16 Oct 93	**GOT ME A FEELING** *Columbia 6597872*	59	2
12 Mar 94	**A FAIR AFFAIR (JE T'AIME)** *Columbia 6601612*	49	4
9 Jul 94	**I WROTE YOU A SONG** *Columbia 6603732*	73	1

OLGA *Italy, female vocalist*

1 Oct 94	**I'M A BITCH** *UMM UMM 144UKCD*	68	1

30 January 1982	6 February 1982	13 February 1982	20 February 1982
OH JULIE Shakin' Stevens	COMPUTER LOVE / THE MODEL Kraftwerk	TOWN CALLED MALICE / PRECIOUS The Jam	TOWN CALLED MALICE / PRECIOUS The Jam
LOVE SONGS Barbra Streisand	LOVE SONGS Barbra Streisand	LOVE SONGS Barbra Streisand	LOVE SONGS Barbra Streisand

KEY
UK No.1 ★ UK Top 10 ● Still on chart + UK entry at No.1 ■
US No.1 ▲ UK million seller £ US million seller $
Singles re-entries are listed as (re), (2re), (3re)... which signifies that the hit re-entered the chart once, twice or three times...
Peak Position / Weeks

OLIVE *UK, male / female vocal (Ruth Ann Boyle) / instrumental group (1 Album: 3 Weeks, 5 Singles: 24 Weeks)*

7 Sep 96 **YOU'RE NOT ALONE** *RCA 74321406272* ... 42 4
15 Mar 97 **MIRACLE** *RCA 74321461242* ... 41 2
17 May 97 ★ **YOU'RE NOT ALONE** (re-issue) *RCA 74321473232* ■ ... 1 13
31 May 97 **EXTRA VIRGIN** *RCA 74321392302* ... 15 3
16 Aug 97 **OUTLAW** *RCA 74321508372* ... 14 4
8 Nov 97 **MIRACLE** (re-mix) *RCA 74321530842* ... 41 1

OLIVER
US, male vocalist – William Swofford, b. 22 Feb 1945, d. 12 Feb 2000

9 Aug 69 ● **GOOD MORNING STARSHINE** (re) *CBS 4435* ... 6 18

Frankie OLIVER *UK, male vocalist*

7 Jun 97 **GIVE HER WHAT SHE WANTS** *Island Jamaica IJCD 2011* ... 58 1

OLLIE and JERRY
US, male vocal duo – Ollie Brown and Jerry Knight (2 Singles: 14 Weeks)

23 Jun 84 ● **BREAKIN' ... THERE'S NO STOPPING US** *Polydor POSP 690* ... 5 11
9 Mar 85 **ELECTRIC BOOGALOO** *Polydor POSP 730* ... 57 3

OLYMPIC ORCHESTRA *UK, orchestra*

1 Oct 83 **REILLY** *Red Bus RBUS 82* ... 26 15

The OLYMPIC RUNNERS
UK, male vocal / instrumental group (4 Singles: 21 Weeks)

13 May 78 **WHATEVER IT TAKES** *RCA PC 5078* ... 61 2
14 Oct 78 **GET IT WHILE YOU CAN** *Polydor RUN 7* ... 35 6
20 Jan 79 **SIR DANCEALOT** *Polydor POSP 17* ... 35 6
28 Jul 79 **THE BITCH** *Polydor POSP 63* ... 37 7

The OLYMPICS *US, male vocal group (2 Singles: 9 Weeks)*

3 Oct 58 **WESTERN MOVIES** *HMV POP 528* ... 12 8
19 Jan 61 **I WISH I COULD SHIMMY LIKE MY SISTER KATE** *Vogue V 9174* ... 40 1

OMAR
UK, male vocalist – Omar Hammer (5 Albums: 14 Weeks, 7 Singles: 18 Weeks)

14 Jul 90 **THERE'S NOTHING LIKE THIS** *Kongo Dance KDLP 2* ... 54 4
22 Jun 91 **THERE'S NOTHING LIKE THIS** *Talkin Loud TLK 9* ... 14 7
27 Jul 91 **THERE'S NOTHING LIKE THIS** (re-issue) *Talkin Loud 5100211* .. 19 6
23 May 92 **YOUR LOSS MY GAIN** *Talkin Loud TLK 22* ... 47 2
26 Sep 92 **MUSIC** *Talkin Loud TLK 28* ... 53 2
24 Oct 92 **MUSIC** *Talkin Loud 5124012* ... 37 2
2 Jul 94 **FOR PLEASURE** *RCA 74321208532* ... 50 1
23 Jul 94 **OUTSIDE / SATURDAY** *RCA 74321213982* ... 43 2
15 Oct 94 **KEEP STEPPIN'** *RCA 74321233682* ... 57 1
2 Aug 97 **SAY NOTHIN'** *RCA 74321502872* ... 29 2
16 Aug 97 **THIS IS NOT A LOVE SONG** *RCA 74321496262* ... 50 1
18 Oct 97 **GOLDEN BROWN** *RCA 74321525422* ... 37 2

OMARION NEW
US, male vocalist – Omarion Grandberry (4 Singles: 10 Weeks)

23 Jul 05 **O** *Epic 6759862* ... 47 2
8 Oct 05 **LET ME HOLD YOU** (import) *Sony BMG 6760602* [1] ... 64 2
22 Oct 05 **LET ME HOLD YOU** *Columbia 6760601* [1] ... 27 6

[1] Bow Wow featuring Omarion

Jo O'MEARA NEW (see also S CLUB 7) *UK, female vocalist*

8 Oct 05 **WHAT HURTS THE MOST** *Sanctuary SANXD 403* ... 13 5
15 Oct 05 **RELENTLESS** *Sanctuary SANCD 402* ... 48 2

OMNI TRIO
UK, male producer – Rob Haigh (2 Albums: 2 Weeks, 2 Singles: 4 Weeks)

11 Feb 95 **THE DEEPEST CUT VOL.1** *Moving Shadow ASHADOW 1CD* ... 60 1
24 Aug 96 **THE HAUNTED SCIENCE** *Moving Shadow ASHADOW 6CD* ... 43 1
7 Jul 01 **THE ANGELS & SHADOWS PROJECT** *Moving Shadow SHADOW 150CD* ... 44 3
26 Jul 03 **RENEGADE SNARES** *Moving Shadow SHADOW 166* ... 61 1

The ONE *UK, male vocal group*

11 Jan 97 **ONE MORE CHANCE** *Mercury MERDD 478* ... 31 2

ONE DOVE (see also Dot ALLISON) *UK, male / female vocal / instrumental group (1 Album: 2 Weeks, 3 Singles: 9 Weeks)*

7 Aug 93 **WHITE LOVE** *Boy's Own BOICD 14* ... 43 3
25 Sep 93 **MORNING DOVE WHITE** *London 8283522* ... 30 2
16 Oct 93 **BREAKDOWN** *Boy's Own BOICD 15* ... 24 3
15 Jan 94 **WHY DON'T YOU TAKE ME** *Boy's Own BOICD 16* ... 30 3

187 LOCKDOWN
(see also M FACTOR; NU-BIRTH; NUSH; REFLEX featuring MC VIPER) *UK, male production duo – Danny Harrison and Julian Jonah (5 Singles: 16 Weeks)*

15 Nov 97 **GUNMAN** *East West EW 140CD* ... 16 4
25 Apr 98 ● **KUNG-FU** *East West EW 155CD* ... 9 5
25 Jul 98 **GUNMAN** (re-mix) *East West EW 176CD* ... 17 4
3 Oct 98 **THE DON** *East West EW 180CD* ... 29 2
13 Feb 99 **ALL 'N' ALL** *East West EW 194CD* [1] ... 43 1

[1] 187 Lockdown (featuring D'Empress)

1 GIANT LEAP
UK, male production duo – Jamie Catto and Duncan Bridgeman

20 Apr 02 ● **MY CULTURE** *Palm Pictures PPCD 70732* ... 9 6
27 Apr 02 **ONE GIANT LEAP** *Palm Pictures PALMCD 2077* ... 51 3

'My Culture' features vocals by Robbie Williams and Maxi Jazz (Faithless).

101 STRINGS *Germany, orchestra (5 Albums: 35 Weeks)*

26 Sep 59 ● **GYPSY CAMPFIRES** *Pye GGL 0009* ... 9 7
26 Mar 60 **THE SOUL OF SPAIN** *Pye GGL 0017* ... 17 1
16 Apr 60 ● **GRAND CANYON SUITE** *Pye GGL 0048* ... 10 1
27 Aug 60 ★ **DOWN DRURY LANE TO MEMORY LANE** *Pye GGL 0061* ... 1 21
15 Oct 83 **MORNING NOON AND NIGHT** *Ronco RTL 2094* ... 32 5

The orchestra was American based for last album.

ONEHUNDREDPERCENT featuring Jennifer JOHN
UK, male production duo and female vocalist

25 Dec 04 **JUST CAN'T WAIT (SATURDAY)** *CR2 CDC2X 005* ... 28 6

ONE MINUTE SILENCE *UK, male vocal / rap / instrumental group (1 Album: 1 Week, 2 Singles: 2 Weeks)*

22 Apr 00 **BUY NOW ... SAVED LATER** *V2 VVR 1012362* ... 61 1
20 Jan 01 **FISH OUT OF WATER** *V2 VVR 5013213* ... 56 1
5 Jul 03 **I WEAR MY SKIN** *Taste Media TMCDS 5005* ... 44 1

112 *US, male vocal / instrumental group (5 Singles: 34 Weeks)*

28 Jun 97 ★ **I'LL BE MISSING YOU** *Puff Daddy 74321499102* [1] ■ ▲ £ $ .. 1 21
10 Jan 98 **ALL CRIED OUT** *Epic 6652715* [2] ... 12 5
14 Feb 98 **SKY'S THE LIMIT** *Puff Daddy 74321561992* [3] ... 35 2
30 Jun 01 **IT'S OVER NOW** *Puff Daddy / Arista 74321849912* ... 22 3
8 Sep 01 **PEACHES & CREAM** *Arista 74321882632* ... 32 3

[1] Puff Daddy and Faith Evans featuring 112 [2] Allure featuring 112
[3] Notorious BIG featuring 112

	27 February 1982	6 March 1982	13 March 1982	20 March 1982
UK No.1 SINGLES	TOWN CALLED MALICE / PRECIOUS The Jam	THE LION SLEEPS TONIGHT Tight Fit	THE LION SLEEPS TONIGHT Tight Fit	THE LION SLEEPS TONIGHT Tight Fit
UK No.1 ALBUMS	LOVE SONGS Barbra Streisand	LOVE SONGS Barbra Streisand	LOVE SONGS Barbra Streisand	THE GIFT The Jam

ONE THE JUGGLER *UK, male vocal / instrumental group*

19 Feb 83	**PASSION KILLER** *Regard RG 107*	**71**	1

1000 CLOWNS *US, male / female vocal / rap group*

22 May 99	**(NOT THE) GREATEST RAPPER** *Elektra E 3759CD*	23	4

ONE TRUE VOICE *UK, male vocal group (2 Singles: 14 Weeks)*

28 Dec 02 ●	**SACRED TRUST / AFTER YOU'RE GONE (I'LL STILL BE LOVING YOU)** *Ebul / Jive 9201532*	2	9
14 Jun 03 ●	**SHAKESPEARE'S (WAY WITH) WORDS** (re) *Ebul / Jive 9201572*	**10**	5

ONE 2 MANY

Norway, male / female vocal / instrumental group (2 Singles: 11 Weeks)

12 Nov 88	**DOWNTOWN** *A&M AM 476*	**65**	4
3 Jun 89	**DOWNTOWN** (re-issue) *A&M AM 456*	**43**	7

ONE WAY *US, male vocal / instrumental group (2 Singles: 8 Weeks)*

8 Dec 79	**MUSIC** *MCA 542* [1]	**56**	6
29 Jun 85	**LET'S TALK ABOUT SHHH** *MCA 972*	**64**	2

[1] One Way featuring Al Hudson

ONE WORLD *UK, male vocal / instrumental group*

9 Jun 90	ONE WORLD ONE VOICE *Virgin V 2632*	27	3

ONE WORLD PROJECT NEW

UK / US, male / female vocal / instrumental ensemble

5 Feb 05 ●	**GRIEF NEVER GROWS OLD** *One World OWR 1*	**4**	4

Artists involved: Cliff Richard, Boy George, Brian Wilson, Russell Watson, Robin and Barry Gibb, Steve Winwood, Rick Wakeman, Kenny Jones, Gary Moore, Bill Wyman, Hank Linderman, Jon Anderson, Celina Cherry, Dewey Bunnell, Gerry Beckley and Mike Read.

Alexander O'NEAL 230 Top 500 *Soulful ex-vocalist with Minneapolis-based Flyte Time (line-up featured star producers Jimmy Jam and Terry Lewis, who worked on most of his hits), b. 15 Nov 1953, Mississippi, US. Co-wrote his biggest hit and clocked up impressive five Top 20 albums between 1985 and 1993 (7 Albums: 168 Weeks, 24 Singles: 107 Weeks)*

1 Jun 85	ALEXANDER O'NEAL *Tabu TBU 26485*	19	18
28 Dec 85 ●	**SATURDAY LOVE** *Tabu A 6829* [1]	**6**	11
15 Feb 86	**IF YOU WERE HERE TONIGHT** *Tabu A 6391*	**13**	10
5 Apr 86	**A BROKEN HEART CAN MEND** *Tabu A 6244*	**53**	4
6 Jun 87	**FAKE** *Tabu 650891 7*	33	6
8 Aug 87 ●	HEARSAY / ALL MIXED UP *Tabu 4509361*	4	103
31 Oct 87 ●	**CRITICIZE** *Tabu 651211 7*	**4**	14
6 Feb 88	**NEVER KNEW LOVE LIKE THIS** *Tabu 651382 7* [2]	26	7
28 May 88	**THE LOVERS** *Tabu 651595 7*	28	4
23 Jul 88	**(WHAT CAN I SAY) TO MAKE YOU LOVE ME** *Tabu 652852 7*	27	5
24 Sep 88	**FAKE '88** (re-mix) *Tabu 652949 7*	**16**	7
10 Dec 88	**CHRISTMAS SONG (CHESTNUTS ROASTING ON AN OPEN FIRE) / THANK YOU FOR A GOOD YEAR** *Tabu 653182 7*	30	5
17 Dec 88	MY GIFT TO YOU *Tabu 463152 1*	53	3
25 Feb 89	**HEARSAY '89** *Tabu 654667 7*	**56**	2
2 Sep 89	**SUNSHINE** *Tabu 655191 7*	**72**	1
9 Dec 89	**HITMIX (OFFICIAL BOOTLEG MEGA-MIX)** *Tabu 655504 7*	**19**	7
24 Mar 90	**SATURDAY LOVE** (re-mix) *Tabu 655680 7* [1]	**55**	2
12 Jan 91	**ALL TRUE MAN** *Tabu 6565717*	**18**	6
2 Feb 91 ●	ALL TRUE MAN *Tabu 4658821*	2	16
23 Mar 91	**WHAT IS THIS THING CALLED LOVE?** *Tabu 6567317*	**53**	2
11 May 91	**SHAME ON ME** *Tabu 6568737*	**71**	1
9 May 92	**SENTIMENTAL** *Tabu 6580147*	**53**	2
30 May 92 ●	THIS THING CALLED LOVE – THE GREATEST HITS OF ALEXANDER O'NEAL *Tabu 4717142*	4	18
30 Jan 93	**LOVE MAKES NO SENSE** *Tabu AMCD 7708*	26	3
20 Feb 93	LOVE MAKES NO SENSE *Tabu 5495022*	14	4
3 Jul 93	**IN THE MIDDLE** *Tabu 5877152*	32	3
25 Sep 93	**ALL THAT MATTERS TO ME** *Tabu 6577232*	**67**	1
2 Nov 96	**LET'S GET TOGETHER** *EMI Premier PRESCD 11*	**38**	2
2 Aug 97	**BABY COME TO ME** *One World OWECD 1* [2]	**56**	1
12 Dec 98	**CRITICIZE '98 MIX** (re-recording) *One World OWECD 3*	**51**	1
4 Sep 04	GREATEST HITS *EMI 5785022*	12	6

[1] Cherrelle with Alexander O'Neal [2] Alexander O'Neal featuring Cherrelle

All Mixed Up, a re-mixed album of Hearsay, was listed with Hearsay from 15 Jul 1989.

Shaquille O'NEAL *US, male rapper (3 Singles: 4 Weeks)*

26 Mar 94	**I'M OUTSTANDING** *Jive JIVECD 349*	**70**	1
1 Feb 97	**YOU CAN'T STOP THE REIGN** *Interscope IND 95522*	**40**	2
17 Oct 98	**THE WAY IT'S GOIN' DOWN (T.W.I.S.M. FOR LIFE)** *A&M 5827932*	**62**	1

The ONES *US, male production trio (2 Singles: 13 Weeks)*

20 Oct 01 ●	**FLAWLESS** (re) *Positiva CDTIV 164*	**7**	12
1 Mar 03	**SUPERSTAR** *Positiva CDTIVS 186*	**45**	1

The ONLY ONES

UK, male vocal / instrumental group (3 Albums: 8 Weeks, 1 Single: 2 Weeks)

3 Jun 78	THE ONLY ONES *CBS 82830*	56	1
31 Mar 79	EVEN SERPENTS SHINE *CBS 83451*	42	2
3 May 80	BABY'S GOT A GUN *CBS 84089*	37	5
1 Feb 92	**ANOTHER GIRL – ANOTHER PLANET** *Columbia 6577507*	**57**	2

Yoko ONO

Japan, female vocalist (4 Albums: 57 Weeks, 5 Singles: 45 Weeks)

21 Feb 70 ●	**INSTANT KARMA** *Apple APPLES 1003* [1] **$**	**5**	9
14 Oct 72	SOMETIME IN NEW YORK CITY *Apple PCSP 716* [1]	11	6
9 Dec 72 ●	**HAPPY XMAS (WAR IS OVER)** (4re) *Apple R 5970* [2]	2	26
22 Nov 80 ★	DOUBLE FANTASY *Geffen K 99131* [2] ▲	1	36
28 Feb 81	**WALKING ON THIN ICE** *Geffen K 79202*	**35**	5
20 Jun 81	SEASON OF GLASS *Geffen K 99164*	47	2
4 Feb 84 ●	MILK AND HONEY *Polydor POLH 5* [2]	3	13
14 Jun 03	**WALKING ON THIN ICE** (re-mix) *Parlophone CDMINDS 002* [3]	**35**	2
20 Dec 03	**HAPPY XMAS (WAR IS OVER)** (re-issue) *Parlophone CDR 6627* [4]	33	3

[1] Lennon, Ono and the Plastic Ono Band [2] John and Yoko and the Plastic Ono Band with the Harlem Community Choir [3] Ono [4] John and Yoko and the Plastic Ono Band [1] John and Yoko Lennon with the Plastic Ono Band and Elephant's Memory [2] John Lennon and Yoko Ono

ONSLAUGHT *UK, male vocal / instrumental group*

6 May 89	**LET THERE BE ROCK** *London LON 224*	**50**	3
20 May 89	IN SEARCH OF SANITY *London 828142 1*	46	2

ONYX *US, male rap group (1 Album: 3 Weeks, 3 Singles: 8 Weeks)*

28 Aug 93	**SLAM** *Columbia 6596302*	31	4
4 Sep 93	BACDAFUCUP *Columbia 4729802*	59	3
27 Nov 93	**THROW YA GUNZ** *Columbia 6598312*	34	3
20 Feb 99	**ROC-IN-IT** *Independiente ISOM 21MS* [1]	**59**	1

[1] Deejay Punk-Roc vs Onyx

ONYX featuring Gemma J *UK, male production duo and female vocalist*

11 Dec 04	**EVERY LITTLE TIME** *Data DATA 78CDS*	**66**	1

OO LA LA *UK, male vocal / instrumental group*

5 Sep 92	**OO ... AH ... CANTONA** *North Speed OOAH 1*	**64**	2

OOBERMAN

UK, male / female vocal / instrumental group (4 Singles: 5 Weeks)

8 May 99	**BLOSSOMS FALLING** *Independiente ISOM 26MS*	39	2

27 March 1982	3 April 1982	10 April 1982	17 April 1982
SEVEN TEARS Goombay Dance Band	**SEVEN TEARS** Goombay Dance Band	**SEVEN TEARS** Goombay Dance Band	**MY CAMERA NEVER LIES** Bucks Fizz
LOVE SONGS Barbra Streisand	**LOVE SONGS** Barbra Streisand	**THE NUMBER OF THE BEAST** Iron Maiden	**THE NUMBER OF THE BEAST** Iron Maiden

KEY: UK No.1 ★ UK Top 10 ● Still on chart + UK entry at No.1 ■ US No.1 ▲ UK million seller £ US million seller $
Singles re-entries are listed as (re), (2re), (3re)... which signifies that the hit re-entered the chart once, twice or three times...
Peak Position / Weeks

17 Jul 99 **MILLION SUNS** *Independiente ISOM 30MS* 43 1
23 Oct 99 **TEARS FROM A WILLOW** *Independiente ISOM 37MS* 63 1
8 Apr 00 **SHORLEY WALL** *Independiente ISOM 41MS* **47** 1

The OPEN *UK, male vocal / instrumental group (1 Album: 1 Week, 4 Singles: 4 Weeks)*

13 Mar 04 **CLOSE MY EYES** *Logic / Polydor 9817294* **46** 1
3 Jul 04 **JUST WANT TO LIVE** *Loog / Polydor 9866489* 52 1
17 Jul 04 THE SILENT HOURS *Loog / Polydor 9866160* 72 1
11 Sep 04 **ELEVATION** *Loog / Polydor 9867495* **54** 1
13 Nov 04 **NEVER ENOUGH** *Loog / Polydor 9868779* 53 1

OPEN ARMS featuring ROWETTA
UK, male / female vocal / instrumental group

15 Jun 96 **HEY MR DJ** *All Around the World CDGLOBE 136* 62 1

OPERABABES *UK, female vocal duo – Karen England and Rebecca Knight*

8 Jun 02 BEYOND IMAGINATION *Sony Classical SK 89916* 24 6
6 Jul 02 **ONE FINE DAY** *Sony Classical 6727062* **54** 1

OPETH NEW *Sweden, male vocal / instrumental group*

10 Sep 05 GHOST REVERIES *Roadrunner RR 81232* 62 1

OPTIMYSTIC *UK, male / female vocal group (3 Singles: 6 Weeks)*

17 Sep 94 **CAUGHT UP IN MY HEART** *WEA YZ 841CD* **49** 3
10 Dec 94 **NOTHING BUT LOVE** *WEA 864CD1* 37 2
13 May 95 **BEST THING IN THE WORLD** *WEA YZ 920CD* **70** 1

OPUS *Austria, male vocal (Herwig Rudisser) / instrumental group*

15 Jun 85 ● **LIVE IS LIFE** *Polydor POSP 743* 6 15

OPUS III *UK, male / female vocal (Kirsty Hawkshaw) / instrumental group (3 Singles: 10 Weeks)*

22 Feb 92 ● **IT'S A FINE DAY** *PWL International PWL 215* 5 8
27 Jun 92 **I TALK TO THE WIND** *PWL International PWL 235* 52 1
11 Jun 94 **WHEN YOU MADE THE MOUNTAIN** *PWL International PWCD 302* **71** 1

ORANGE *UK, male vocal / instrumental group*

8 Oct 94 **JUDY OVER THE RAINBOW** *Chrysalis CDCHS 5012* 73 1

ORANGE JUICE (see also Edwyn COLLINS)
UK, male vocal / instrumental group (3 Albums: 18 Weeks, 9 Singles: 34 Weeks)

7 Nov 81 **L.O.V.E. ... LOVE** *Polydor POSP 357* **65** 2
30 Jan 82 **FELICITY** *Polydor POSP 386* 63 3
6 Mar 82 YOU CAN'T HIDE YOUR LOVE FOREVER *Polydor POLS 1057* 21 6
21 Aug 82 **TWO HEARTS TOGETHER / HOKOYO** *Polydor POSP 470* **60** 2
23 Oct 82 **I CAN'T HELP MYSELF** *Polydor POSP 522* 42 3
20 Nov 82 RIP IT UP *Holden Caulfield Universal POLS 1076* 39 8
19 Feb 83 ● **RIP IT UP** *Polydor POSP 547* 8 11
4 Jun 83 **FLESH OF MY FLESH** *Polydor OJ 4* 41 6
25 Feb 84 **BRIDGE** *Polydor OJ 5* **67** 2
10 Mar 84 TEXAS FEVER *Polydor OJMLP 1* 34 4
12 May 84 **WHAT PRESENCE?** *Polydor OJ 6* **47** 4
27 Oct 84 **LEAN PERIOD** *Polydor OJ 7* **74** 1

The ORB *UK, male instrumental / production duo – Dr Alex Paterson and Kris Weston (7 Albums: 28 Weeks, 8 Singles: 32 Weeks)*

27 Apr 91 ORB'S ADVENTURES BEYOND THE ULTRAWORLD *Big Life BLRDLP 5* 29 5
15 Jun 91 **PERPETUAL DAWN** (re) *Big Life BLRD 46* **18** 6
20 Jun 92 ● **BLUE ROOM** *Big Life BLRT 75* 8 6
18 Jul 92 ★ U.F. ORB *Big Life BLRCD 18* ■ 1 9
17 Oct 92 **ASSASSIN** *Big Life BLRT 81* 12 5
13 Nov 93 ● **LITTLE FLUFFY CLOUDS** *Big Life BLRD 98* 10 5
4 Dec 93 LIVE 93 *Island CIDD 8022* 23 2
25 Jun 94 ● POMME FRITZ *Inter-Modo ORBCD 1* 6 4
1 Apr 95 ORBVS TERRARVM *Island CIDX 8037* 20 3
27 May 95 **OXBOW LAKES** *Island CID 609* **38** 2
8 Feb 97 ● **TOXYGENE** *Island CID 652* 4 4
8 Mar 97 ORBLIVION *Island CID 8055* 19 3
24 May 97 **ASYLUM** *Island CID 657* **20** 2
17 Oct 98 U.F. OFF – THE BEST OF THE ORB *Island CID 8078* 38 2
24 Feb 01 **ONCE MORE** *Island CID 767* 38 2

'Perpetual Dawn' made No.61 on its original visit to the chart before re-entering in Feb 1994 and making its peak position.

Roy ORBISON 60 Top 500 (see also TRAVELING WILBURYS)
Unmistakable vocalist, b. 23 Apr 1936, Texas, US, d. 6 Dec 1988. The "Big O" recorded for the legendary Sun label in the mid-1950s and was the most popular US singer in Britain during the Beat Boom era (1963-65), when The Beatles supported him on tour. The performer, whose trademark was his dark glasses, had a hit span of 44 years and was enjoying a successful comeback, both as a soloist and as a member of supergroup The Traveling Wilburys, when he died of a heart attack. This multi-award-winner is in the Grammy Hall of Fame, as well as the Songwriters' and Rock and Roll Halls of Fame (22 Albums: 248 Weeks, 34 Singles: 345 Weeks)

28 Jul 60 ★ **ONLY THE LONELY (KNOW HOW I FEEL)** (re) *London HLU 9149* 1 24
27 Oct 60 **BLUE ANGEL** *London HLU 9207* **11** 16
25 May 61 ● **RUNNING SCARED** *London HLU 9342* ▲ 9 15
21 Sep 61 **CRYIN'** *London HLU 9405* **25** 9
8 Mar 62 ● **DREAM BABY** *London HLU 9511* 2 14
28 Jun 62 **THE CROWD** *London HLU 9561* **40** 4
8 Nov 62 **WORKIN' FOR THE MAN** *London HLU 9607* **50** 1
28 Feb 63 ● **IN DREAMS** *London HLU 9676* 6 23
30 May 63 ● **FALLING** *London HLU 9727* 9 11
8 Jun 63 LONELY AND BLUE *London HAU 2342* 15 8
29 Jun 63 CRYING *London HAU 2437* 17 3
19 Sep 63 ● **BLUE BAYOU / MEAN WOMAN BLUES** *London HLU 9777* 3 19
30 Nov 63 ● IN DREAMS *London HAU 8108* 6 57
20 Feb 64 **BORNE ON THE WIND** *London HLU 9845* **15** 10
30 Apr 64 ★ **IT'S OVER** *London HLU 9882* 1 18
25 Jul 64 THE EXCITING SOUNDS OF ROY ORBISON *Ember NR 5013* 17 2
10 Sep 64 ★ **OH, PRETTY WOMAN** *London HLU 9919* ▲ 1 18
19 Nov 64 ● **PRETTY PAPER** *London HLU 9930* 6 11
5 Dec 64 ● OH PRETTY WOMAN *London HAU 8207* 4 16
11 Feb 65 **GOODNIGHT** *London HLU 9951* **14** 9
22 Jul 65 **(SAY) YOU'RE MY GIRL** *London HLU 9978* 23 8
9 Sep 65 **RIDE AWAY** *London HLU 9986* 34 6
25 Sep 65 ● THERE IS ONLY ONE ROY ORBISON *London HAU 8252* 10 12
4 Nov 65 **CRAWLING BACK** *London HLU 10000* **19** 9
27 Jan 66 **BREAKIN' UP IS BREAKIN' MY HEART** *London HLU 10015* 22 6
26 Feb 66 THE ORBISON WAY *London HAU 8279* 11 10
7 Apr 66 **TWINKLE TOES** *London HLU 10034* **29** 5
16 Jun 66 **LANA** *London HLU 10051* **15** 9
18 Aug 66 ● **TOO SOON TO KNOW** *London HLU 10067* 3 17
24 Sep 66 THE CLASSIC ROY ORBISON *London HAU 8297* 12 8
1 Dec 66 **THERE WON'T BE MANY COMING HOME** *London HLU 10096* 12 9
23 Feb 67 **SO GOOD** *London HLU 10113* 32 6
22 Jul 67 ORBISONGS *Monument SMO 5004* 40 1
30 Sep 67 ROY ORBISON'S GREATEST HITS *Monument SMO 5007* 40 1
24 Jul 68 **WALK ON** *London HLU 10206* 39 10
25 Sep 68 **HEARTACHE** *London HLU 10222* **44** 4
30 Apr 69 **MY FRIEND** *London HLU 10261* 35 4
13 Sep 69 **PENNY ARCADE** (re) *London HLU 10285* **27** 14
27 Jan 73 ALL-TIME GREATEST HITS *Monument MNT 67290* 39 3
29 Nov 75 ★ THE BEST OF ROY ORBISON *Arcade ADEP 19* 1 20
18 Jul 81 GOLDEN DAYS *CBS 10026* 63 1
4 Jul 87 IN DREAMS: THE GREATEST HITS *Virgin VGD 3514* 86 2

	24 April 1982	1 May 1982	8 May 1982	15 May 1982
UK No.1 SINGLES	**EBONY AND IVORY** Paul McCartney with Stevie Wonder	**EBONY AND IVORY** Paul McCartney with Stevie Wonder	**EBONY AND IVORY** Paul McCartney with Stevie Wonder	**A LITTLE PEACE** Nicole
UK No.1 ALBUMS	**1982** Status Quo	**BARRY LIVE IN BRITAIN** Barry Manilow	**TUG OF WAR** Paul McCartney	**TUG OF WAR** Paul McCartney

29 Oct 88	★	THE LEGENDARY ROY ORBISON *Telstar STAR 2330*	1	38
14 Jan 89	●	**YOU GOT IT** *Virgin VS 1166*	3	10
11 Feb 89	●	MYSTERY GIRL *Virgin V 2576*	2	23
1 Apr 89		**SHE'S A MYSTERY TO ME** *Virgin VS 1173*	27	5
25 Nov 89		A BLACK AND WHITE NIGHT *Virgin V 2601*	51	3
2 Nov 90		BALLADS – 22 CLASSIC LOVE SONGS *Telstar STAR 2441*	38	10
4 Jul 92	●	**I DROVE ALL NIGHT** *MCA MCS 1652*	7	10
22 Aug 92		**CRYING** *Virgin America VUS 63* [1]	13	6
7 Nov 92		**HEARTBREAK RADIO** *Virgin America VUS 68*	36	3
28 Nov 92		KING OF HEARTS *Virgin America CDVUS 58*	23	4
13 Nov 93		**I DROVE ALL NIGHT** (re-issue) *Virgin America VUSCD 79*	47	2
16 Nov 96		THE VERY BEST OF ROY ORBISON *Virgin CDV 2804*	18	11
10 Feb 01	●	LOVE SONGS *Virgin VTDCD 360*	4	10
14 Aug 04		THE PLATINUM COLLECTION *Virgin / EMI VTDCDX 632*	16	5

[1] Roy Orbison (duet with kd lang)

William ORBIT (see also BASS-O-MATIC) *UK, male producer – William Wainwright (1 Album: 14 Weeks, 4 Singles: 29 Weeks)*

26 Jun 93		**WATER FROM A VINE LEAF** *Guerilla VSCDT 1465*	59	1
18 Dec 99	●	**BARBER'S ADAGIO FOR STRINGS** (re) *WEA WEA 247CD*	4	15
29 Jan 00	●	PIECES IN A MODERN STYLE *WEA 3984289572*	2	14
6 May 00		**RAVEL'S PAVANE POUR UNE INFANTE DEFUNTE** *WEA WEA 269CD*	31	2
19 Jul 03	●	**FEEL GOOD TIME** *Columbia 6741062* [1]	3	11

[1] Pink featuring William Orbit

ORBITAL *UK, male instrumental duo – Paul and Phil Hartnoll (10 Albums: 37 Weeks, 17 Singles: 58 Weeks)*

24 Mar 90		**CHIME** *ffrr F B5*	17	7
22 Sep 90		**OMEN** *ffrr F 145*	46	3
19 Jan 91		**SATAN** *ffrr FX 149*	31	4
12 Oct 91		ORBITAL *ffrr 8282481*	71	1
15 Feb 92		**MUTATIONS (EP)** *ffrr FCD 181*	24	3
26 Sep 92		**RADICCIO (EP)** *Internal LIARX 1*	37	2
5 Jun 93		ORBITAL *Internal TRUCD 2*	28	2
21 Aug 93		**LUSH** *Internal LIECD 7*	43	2
19 Mar 94		PEEL SESSIONS *Internal LIECD 12*	32	2
20 Aug 94	●	SNIVILISATION *Internal TRUCD 5*	4	4
24 Sep 94		**ARE WE HERE?** *Internal LIECD 15*	33	2
27 May 95		**BELFAST** *Volume VOLCD 1*	53	1
27 Apr 96		**THE BOX** *Internal LIECD 30*	11	4
11 May 96	●	IN SIDES *Internal TRUCD 10*	5	12
11 Jan 97	●	**SATAN** (re-recording) *Internal LIECD 37*	3	6
25 Jan 97		SATAN LIVE *Internal LIARX 37*	48	1
19 Apr 97	●	**THE SAINT** *ffrr FCD 296*	3	7
20 Mar 99		**STYLE** *ffrr FCD 358*	13	4
17 Apr 99	●	THE MIDDLE OF NOWHERE *ffrr 5560762*	4	7
17 Jul 99		**NOTHING LEFT** *ffrr FCD 365*	32	2
11 Mar 00		**BEACHED** *ffrr FCD 377* [1]	36	3
28 Apr 01		**FUNNY BREAK (ONE IS ENOUGH)** *ffrr FCD 395*	21	3
12 May 01		THE ALTOGETHER *ffrr 8573877822*	11	4
8 Jun 02		**REST & PLAY (EP)** *ffrr FCD 407*	33	3
15 Jun 02		WORK 1989-2002 *London 927461902*	36	3
3 Jul 04		BLUE ALBUM *Orbital Music ORBITALCD 001*	44	1
17 Jul 04		**ONE PERFECT SUNRISE** *Orbital Music ORBITALCD 03X*	29	2

[1] Orbital and Angelo Badalamenti

Tracks on Mutations (EP): Chime Crime / Oolaa / Farenheit 3D 3 / Speed Freak. Tracks on Radiccio (EP): Halcyon / The Naked and the Dead / Sunday. Tracks on Rest & Play (EP): Frenetic / Illuminate (featuring David Gray) / Chime. The listed flip side of 'Belfast' was 'Innocent X' by Therapy?. The first two albums are different.

ORCHESTRA ON THE HALF SHELL *US, male vocal / instrumental group*

15 Dec 90		**TURTLE RHAPSODY** *SBK SBK 17*	36	6

ORCHESTRAL MANOEUVRES IN THE DARK (106 Top 500)

***One of the most regular chart visitors of the 1980s had a nucleus of Andy McCluskey (v/syn/b) and Paul Humphries (syn), who left in 1989. This Liverpool-based synthesizer band, often abbreviated to OMD, had numerous international hits including 'Maid of Orleans (The Waltz Joan of Arc)', which was Germany's biggest seller in 1982** (12 Albums: 226 Weeks, **30 Singles: 201 Weeks**)*

9 Feb 80		**RED FRAME WHITE LIGHT** *DinDisc DIN 6*	67	2
1 Mar 80		ORCHESTRAL MANOEUVRES IN THE DARK *DinDisc DID 2*	27	29
10 May 80		**MESSAGES** *DinDisc DIN 15*	13	11
4 Oct 80	●	**ENOLA GAY** *DinDisc DIN 22*	8	15
1 Nov 80	●	ORGANISATION *DinDisc DID 6*	6	25
29 Aug 81	●	**SOUVENIR** *DinDisc DIN 24*	3	12
24 Oct 81	●	**JOAN OF ARC** *DinDisc DIN 36*	5	14
14 Nov 81	●	ARCHITECTURE & MORALITY *DinDisc DID 12*	3	39
23 Jan 82	●	**MAID OF ORLEANS (THE WALTZ JOAN OF ARC)** *DinDisc DIN 40*	4	10
19 Feb 83		**GENETIC ENGINEERING** *Virgin VS 527*	20	8
12 Mar 83	●	DAZZLE SHIPS *Telegraph V 2261*	5	13
9 Apr 83		**TELEGRAPH** *Virgin VS 580*	42	4
14 Apr 84	●	**LOCOMOTION** *Virgin VS 660*	5	11
12 May 84	●	JUNK CULTURE *Virgin V 2310*	9	27
16 Jun 84		**TALKING LOUD AND CLEAR** *Virgin VS 685*	11	10
8 Sep 84		**TESLA GIRLS** *Virgin VS 705*	21	8
10 Nov 84		**NEVER TURN AWAY** *Virgin VS 727*	70	2
25 May 85		**SO IN LOVE** *Virgin VS 766*	27	7
29 Jun 85		CRUSH *Virgin V 2349*	13	12
20 Jul 85		**SECRET** *Virgin VS 796*	34	7
26 Oct 85		**LA FEMME ACCIDENT** *Virgin VS 811*	42	4
3 May 86		**IF YOU LEAVE** *Virgin VS 843*	48	4
6 Sep 86		**(FOREVER) LIVE AND DIE** *Virgin VS 888*	11	10
11 Oct 86		THE PACIFIC AGE *Virgin V 2398*	15	7
15 Nov 86		**WE LOVE YOU** *Virgin VS 911*	54	5
2 May 87		**SHAME** *Virgin VS 938*	52	3
6 Feb 88		**DREAMING** (re) *Virgin VS 987*	50	6
12 Mar 88	●	THE BEST OF O.M.D. *Virgin OMD 1*	2	33
30 Mar 91	●	**SAILING ON THE SEVEN SEAS** *Virgin VS 1310*	3	13
18 May 91	●	SUGAR TAX *Virgin V 2648*	3	29
6 Jul 91	●	**PANDORA'S BOX** *Virgin VS 1331*	7	10
14 Sep 91		**THEN YOU TURN AWAY** *Virgin VS 1368*	50	4
7 Dec 91		**CALL MY NAME** *Virgin VS 1380*	50	2
15 May 93		**STAND ABOVE ME** *Virgin VSCDG 1444*	21	4
26 Jun 93		LIBERATOR *Virgin CDV 2715*	14	6
17 Jul 93		**DREAM OF ME (BASED ON LOVE'S THEME)** *Virgin VSCDT 1461*	24	5
18 Sep 93		**EVERYDAY** *Virgin VSCDT 1471*	59	2
17 Aug 96		**WALKING ON THE MILKY WAY** *Virgin VSCDT 1599*	17	5
14 Sep 96		UNIVERSAL *Virgin CDV 2807*	24	2
2 Nov 96		**UNIVERSAL** *Virgin VSCDT 1606*	55	1
26 Sep 98		**THE OMD REMIXES (EP)** *Virgin VSCDT 1694*	35	2
10 Oct 98		THE O.M.D. SINGLES *Virgin CDV 2859*	16	4

Tracks on The OMD Remixes (EP): Enola Gay / Souvenir / Electricity.

The ORDINARY BOYS *UK, male vocal / instrumental group (2 Albums: 6 Weeks, 5 Singles: 12 Weeks)*

17 Apr 04		**WEEK IN WEEK OUT** *B-Unique WEA 372CD*	36	3
10 Jul 04		**TALK TALK TALK** *B-Unique WEA 377CD2*	17	3
17 Jul 04		OVER THE COUNTER CULTURE *B-Unique 5046745432*	19	4
2 Oct 04		**SEASIDE** *B-Unique WEA 379CD2*	27	2
18 Jun 05		**BOYS WILL BE BOYS** *B-Unique WEA 389CD2*	16	3
2 Jul 05		BRASSBOUND *B-Unique 5046791822*	31	2
10 Sep 05		**LIFE WILL BE THE DEATH OF ME** *B-Unique WEA 394CD2*	50	1

Raul ORELLANA *Spain, male producer*

30 Sep 89		**THE REAL WILD HOUSE** *RCA BCM 322*	29	8

ORIGIN *UK, male production duo*

12 Aug 00		**WIDE EYED ANGEL** *Lost Language LOST 001CD*	73	1

ORIGIN UNKNOWN *UK, male instrumental / production duo (3 Singles: 3 Weeks)*

13 Jul 96		**VALLEY OF THE SHADOWS** *Ram RAMM 16CD*	60	1

22 May 1982	29 May 1982	5 June 1982	12 June 1982
A LITTLE PEACE Nicole	HOUSE OF FUN Madness	HOUSE OF FUN Madness	GOODY TWO SHOES Adam Ant
COMPLETE MADNESS Madness	COMPLETE MADNESS Madness	AVALON Roxy Music	COMPLETE MADNESS Madness

KEY UK No.1 ★★ UK Top 10 ●● Still on chart ++ UK entry at No.1 ■■ US No.1 ▲▲ UK million seller £ US million seller $ Singles re-entries are listed as (re), (2re), (3re)... which signifies that the hit re-entered the chart once, twice or three times... — Peak Position / Weeks

11 May 02 **TRULY ONE** *Ram RAMM 38CD* 53 1
27 Sep 03 **HOTNESS** *Ram RAMM 45* [1] 66 1

[1] Dynamite MC and Origin Unknown

The ORIGINAL
(see also DIVA SURPRISE featuring Georgia JONES) *US, male vocal / instrumental duo – Everett Bradley and Walter Taieb (3 Singles: 14 Weeks)*

14 Jan 95 **I LUV U BABY** *Ore AG 8CD* 31 3
19 Aug 95 ● **I LUV U BABY** (re-mix) *Ore AGR 8CD* 2 9
11 Nov 95 **B 2 GETHER** *Ore AG 12CD* 29 2

ORION
(see also ANGELIC; CITIZEN CANED; DT8 PROJECT; Jurgen VRIES) *UK, male / female production / vocal / instrumental duo – Darren Tate and Sarah J*

7 Oct 00 **ETERNITY** *Incentive CENT 11CDS* 38 2

ORION TOO *Belgium, male producer and female vocalist*

9 Nov 02 **HOPE AND WAIT** *Data DATA 40CDS* 46 1

Tony ORLANDO (see also DAWN) *US, male vocalist – Michael Anthony Orlando Cassavitis (5 Singles: 82 Weeks)*

5 Oct 61 ● **BLESS YOU** *Fontana H 330* 5 11
31 Jul 71 ● **WHAT ARE YOU DOING SUNDAY** *Bell 1169* [1] 3 12
10 Mar 73 ★ **TIE A YELLOW RIBBON ROUND THE OLE OAK TREE** (re) *Bell 1287* [1] ▲ 1 40
4 Aug 73 **SAY, HAS ANYBODY SEEN MY SWEET GYPSY ROSE** *Bell 1322* [1] 12 15
9 Mar 74 **WHO'S IN THE STRAWBERRY PATCH WITH SALLY** *Bell 1343* [2] 37 4

[1] Dawn featuring Tony Orlando [2] Tony Orlando and Dawn

The ORLONS *US, female / male vocal group*

27 Dec 62 **DON'T HANG UP** (re) *Cameo Parkway C 231* 39 3

ORN *UK, male DJ / producer – Omio Nourizadeh*

1 Mar 97 **SNOW** *Deconstruction 74321447612* 61 1

Stacie ORRICO
US, female vocalist (1 Album: 19 Weeks, 4 Singles: 22 Weeks)

23 Aug 03 ● **STUCK** *Virgin VUSCD 269* 9 8
4 Oct 03 **STACIE ORRICO** *Virgin CDVUS 238* 37 19
1 Nov 03 **(THERE'S GOTTA BE) MORE TO LIFE** *Virgin VUSCD 275* 12 8
24 Jan 04 **I PROMISE** *Virgin VUSCD 280* 22 4
12 Jun 04 **I COULD BE THE ONE** *Virgin VUSDX 289* 34 2

Beth ORTON
UK, female vocalist (4 Albums: 18 Weeks, 8 Singles: 13 Weeks)

26 Oct 96 **TRAILER PARK** *Heavenly HVNLP 17CD* 68 3
1 Feb 97 **TOUCH ME WITH YOUR LOVE** *Heavenly HVN 64CD* 60 1
5 Apr 97 **SOMEONE'S DAUGHTER** *Heavenly HVN 65CD* 49 1
14 Jun 97 **SHE CRIES YOUR NAME** *Heavenly HVN 68CD* 40 2
13 Dec 97 **BEST BIT (EP)** *Heavenly HVN 72CD* [1] 36 3
13 Mar 99 **STOLEN CAR** *Heavenly HVN 89CD* 34 2
27 Mar 99 **CENTRAL RESERVATION** *Heavenly HVNLP 22CD* 17 8
25 Sep 99 **CENTRAL RESERVATION** *Heavenly HVN 92CD* 37 2
10 Aug 02 ● **DAYBREAKER** *Heavenly HVNLP 37CD* 8 5
16 Nov 02 **ANYWHERE** *Heavenly HVN 125CDS* 55 1
12 Apr 03 **THINKING ABOUT TOMORROW** *Heavenly HVN 129CD* 57 1
4 Oct 03 **PASS IN TIME – THE DEFINITIVE COLLECTION** *Heavenly HVNLP 45CD* 45 2

[1] Beth Orton featuring Terry Callier

Tracks on Best Bit (EP): Best Bit / Skimming Stone / Dolphins / Lean on Me.

Jeffrey OSBORNE (see also L.T.D.)
US, male vocalist (2 Albums: 10 Weeks, 6 Singles: 38 Weeks)

17 Sep 83 **DON'T YOU GET SO MAD** *A&M AM 140* 54 2
14 Apr 84 **STAY WITH ME TONIGHT** *A&M AM 188* 18 11
5 May 84 **STAY WITH ME TONIGHT** *A&M AMLX 64940* 56 7
23 Jun 84 **ON THE WINGS OF LOVE** *A&M AM 198* 11 14
13 Oct 84 **DON'T STOP** *A&M AMA 5017* 59 3
20 Oct 84 **DON'T STOP** *A&M AM 222* 61 2
26 Jul 86 **SOWETO** (re) *A&M AM 334* 44 6
15 Aug 87 **LOVE POWER** *Arista RIS 27* [1] 63 3

[1] Dionne Warwick and Jeffrey Osborne

Joan OSBORNE
US, female vocalist (1 Album: 18 Weeks, 2 Singles: 13 Weeks)

10 Feb 96 ● **ONE OF US** *Blue Gorilla JOACD 1* 6 10
9 Mar 96 ● **RELISH** *Blue Gorilla 5266992* 5 18
8 Jun 96 **ST TERESA** *Blue Gorilla JOACD 3* 33 3

Tony OSBORNE SOUND *UK, orchestra (2 Singles: 3 Weeks)*

23 Feb 61 **THE MAN FROM MADRID** *HMV POP 827* [1] 50 1
3 Feb 73 **THE SHEPHERD'S SONG** *Philips 6006 266* 46 2

[1] Tony Osborne Sound featuring Joanne Brown

Kelly OSBOURNE
UK, female vocalist (2 Albums: 3 Weeks, 5 Singles: 41 Weeks)

24 Aug 02 **PAPA DON'T PREACH** (import) *Epic 6729152* 65 3
21 Sep 02 ● **PAPA DON'T PREACH** (re) *Epic 6731602* 3 10
8 Feb 03 **SHUT UP** *Epic 6735552* 12 6
22 Feb 03 **SHUT UP** *Epic 5094782* 31 2
20 Dec 03 ★ **CHANGES** *Sanctuary SANXD 234* [1] ■ 1 16
21 May 05 ● **ONE WORD** *Sanctuary SANXD 349* 9 6
4 Jun 05 **SLEEPING IN THE NOTHING** *Sanctuary SANCD 338* 57 1

[1] Kelly and Ozzy Osbourne

Ozzy OSBOURNE (see also BLACK SABBATH)
UK, male vocalist – John Osbourne (14 Albums: 68 Weeks, 14 Singles: 65 Weeks)

13 Sep 80 **CRAZY TRAIN** *Jet 197* [1] 49 4
20 Sep 80 ● **BLIZZARD OF OZZ** *Jet JETLP 234* [1] 7 8
15 Nov 80 **MR CROWLEY** *Jet 7003* [1] 46 3
7 Nov 81 **DIARY OF A MADMAN** *Jet JETLP 237* 14 12
27 Nov 82 **TALK OF THE DEVIL** *Jet JETDP 401* 21 6
26 Nov 83 **BARK AT THE MOON** *Epic A 3915* 21 8
10 Dec 83 **BARK AT THE MOON** *Epic EPC 25739* 24 7
2 Jun 84 **SO TIRED** *Epic A 4452* 20 9
1 Feb 86 **SHOT IN THE DARK** *Epic A 6859* 20 6
22 Feb 86 ● **THE ULTIMATE SIN** *Epic EPC 26404* 8 10
9 Aug 86 **THE ULTIMATE SIN / LIGHTNING STRIKES** *Epic A 7311* 72 1
23 May 87 **TRIBUTE** *Epic 450 4751* 13 6
22 Oct 88 **NO REST FOR THE WICKED** *Epic 462581 1* 23 4
20 May 89 **CLOSE MY EYES FOREVER** *Dreamland PB 49409* [2] 47 3
17 Mar 90 **JUST SAY OZZY** *Epic 4659401* 69 1
28 Sep 91 **NO MORE TEARS** *Epic 6574407* 32 3
19 Oct 91 **NO MORE TEARS** *Epic 4678591* 17 3
30 Nov 91 **MAMA I'M COMING HOME** *Epic 6576177* 46 2
4 Nov 95 **OZZMOSIS** *Epic 4810222* 22 3
25 Nov 95 **PERRY MASON** *Epic 6626395* 23 2
31 Aug 96 **I JUST WANT YOU** *Epic 6635702* 43 1
15 Nov 97 **THE OZZMAN COMETH – THE BEST OF OZZY OSBOURNE** *Epic 4872602* 68 1
27 Oct 01 **DOWN TO EARTH** *Epic 4984742* 19 3

	19 June 1982	26 June 1982	3 July 1982	10 July 1982
UK No.1 SINGLES	GOODY TWO SHOES Adam Ant	I'VE NEVER BEEN TO ME Charlene	HAPPY TALK Captain Sensible	HAPPY TALK Captain Sensible
UK No.1 ALBUMS	AVALON Roxy Music	AVALON Roxy Music	THE LEXICON OF LOVE ABC	THE LEXICON OF LOVE ABC

8 Jun 02	**DREAMER / GETS ME THROUGH** *Epic 6724122*	18	6
15 Mar 03	**THE ESSENTIAL OZZY OSBOURNE** *Epic 5108402*	21	3
20 Dec 03 ★	**CHANGES** *Sanctuary SANXD 234* [3] ■	1	16
10 Dec 05	**UNDER COVER** *Epic 82876743142*	67	1
24 Dec 05	**IN MY LIFE** *Epic 82876743122* [4]	63	1

[1] Ozzy Osbourne's Blizzard of Ozz [2] Lita Ford duet with Ozzy Osbourne [3] Kelly and Ozzy Osbourne [4] Ozzy [1] Ozzy Osbourne's Blizzard of Ozz

OSIBISA

Ghana / Nigeria, male vocal / instrumental group (2 Albums: 17 Weeks, 2 Singles: 12 Weeks)

22 May 71	**OSIBISA** *MCA MDKS 8001*	11	10
5 Feb 72	**WOYAYA** *MCA MDKS 8005*	11	7
17 Jan 76	**SUNSHINE DAY** *Bronze BRO 20*	17	6
5 Jun 76	**DANCE THE BODY MUSIC** *Bronze BRO 26*	31	6

Donny OSMOND (272 Top 500) (see also Donny and Marie OSMOND)

Teenage teen-idol vocalist, b. 9 Dec 1957, Utah, US. The main focal point of the hit-making family act The Osmonds, he was one of the most popular pin-ups of the 1970s, had three solo No.1s before his 16th birthday and was still having chart success in the 21st century (9 Albums: 120 Weeks, 12 Singles: 123 Weeks)

17 Jun 72 ★	**PUPPY LOVE** (3re) *MGM 2006 104*	1	23
16 Sep 72 ●	**TOO YOUNG** (re) *MGM 2006 113*	5	15
23 Sep 72 ●	**PORTRAIT OF DONNY** *MGM 2315 108*	5	43
11 Nov 72 ●	**WHY** *MGM 2006 119*	3	20
16 Dec 72 ●	**TOO YOUNG** *MGM 2315 113*	7	24
10 Mar 73 ★	**THE TWELFTH OF NEVER** *MGM 2006 199*	1	14
26 May 73 ●	**ALONE TOGETHER** *MGM 2315 210*	6	19
18 Aug 73 ★	**YOUNG LOVE** *MGM 2006 300*	1	10
10 Nov 73 ●	**WHEN I FALL IN LOVE** *MGM 2006 365*	4	13
15 Dec 73 ●	**A TIME FOR US** *MGM 2315 273*	4	13
9 Nov 74	**WHERE DID ALL THE GOOD TIMES GO** *MGM 2006 468*	18	10
8 Feb 75	**DONNY** *MGM 2315 314*	16	4
2 Oct 76	**DISCOTRAIN** *Polydor 2391 226*	59	1
26 Sep 87	**I'M IN IT FOR LOVE** *Virgin VS 994*	70	1
6 Aug 88	**SOLDIER OF LOVE** *Virgin VS 1094*	29	8
12 Nov 88	**IF IT'S LOVE THAT YOU WANT** *Virgin VS 1140*	70	2
9 Feb 91	**MY LOVE IS A FIRE** *Capitol CL 600*	64	2
21 Apr 01 ●	**THIS IS THE MOMENT** *Decca 1587772*	10	3
7 Dec 02	**SOMEWHERE IN TIME** *Decca 0665302*	12	10
2 Oct 04 ●	**BREEZE ON BY** *Decca 9863140*	8	5
27 Nov 04	**WHAT I MEANT TO SAY** *Decca 9863139*	26	3

Donny and Marie OSMOND

US, male / female vocal duo (3 Albums: 19 Weeks, 4 Singles: 37 Weeks)

3 Aug 74 ●	**I'M LEAVING IT (ALL) UP TO YOU** *MGM 2006 446*	2	12
2 Nov 74	**I'M LEAVING IT ALL UP TO YOU** *MGM 2315 307*	13	15
14 Dec 74 ●	**MORNING SIDE OF THE MOUNTAIN** *MGM 2006 474*	5	12
21 Jun 75	**MAKE THE WORLD GO AWAY** *MGM 2006 523*	18	6
26 Jul 75	**MAKE THE WORLD GO AWAY** *MGM 2315 343*	30	3
17 Jan 76	**DEEP PURPLE** *MGM 2006 561*	25	7
5 Jun 76	**DEEP PURPLE** *Polydor 2391 220*	48	1

Little Jimmy OSMOND

US, male vocalist (1 Album: 12 Weeks, 3 Singles: 50 Weeks)

25 Nov 72 ★	**LONG HAIRED LOVER FROM LIVERPOOL** (re) *MGM 2006 109* [1]	1	27
17 Feb 73	**KILLER JOE** *MGM 2315 157*	20	12
31 Mar 73 ●	**TWEEDLEE DEE** *MGM 2006 175*	4	13
23 Mar 74	**I'M GONNA KNOCK ON YOUR DOOR** *MGM 2006 389* [2]	11	10

[1] Little Jimmy Osmond with the Mike Curb Congregation [2] Jimmy Osmond

Marie OSMOND

(see also Donny and Marie OSMOND) *US, female vocalist – Olive Osmond*

17 Nov 73 ●	**PAPER ROSES** *MGM 2006 315*	2	15
9 Feb 74	**PAPER ROSES** *MGM 2315 262*	46	1

The OSMOND BOYS

US, male vocal group (2 Singles: 6 Weeks)

9 Nov 91	**BOYS WILL BE BOYS** *Curb 6573847*	65	2
11 Jan 92	**SHOW ME THE WAY** *Curb 6577227*	60	4

The OSMONDS (321 Top 500)

Top teeny-bop act of the '70s: brothers Donny, Alan, Wayne, Merrill and Jay Osmond from Utah, US. This polished pop quintet created hysteria wherever they appeared. The Osmond family (including Marie and Little Jimmy) had a record 13 UK hits in 1973 (9 Albums: 119 Weeks, 12 Singles: 94 Weeks)

25 Mar 72	**DOWN BY THE LAZY RIVER** *MGM 2006 096*	40	5
11 Nov 72 ●	**CRAZY HORSES** *MGM 2006 142*	2	18
18 Nov 72	**OSMONDS LIVE** *MGM 2315 117*	13	22
16 Dec 72 ●	**CRAZY HORSES** *MGM 2315 123*	9	19
14 Jul 73 ●	**GOIN' HOME** *MGM 2006 288*	4	10
25 Aug 73 ●	**THE PLAN** *MGM 2315 251*	6	25
27 Oct 73 ●	**LET ME IN** *MGM 2006 321*	2	14
20 Apr 74	**I CAN'T STOP** *MCA 129*	12	10
17 Aug 74 ●	**OUR BEST TO YOU** *MGM 2315 300*	5	20
24 Aug 74 ★	**LOVE ME FOR A REASON** *MGM 2006 458*	1	9
7 Dec 74	**LOVE ME FOR A REASON** *MGM 2315 312*	13	9
1 Mar 75	**HAVING A PARTY** *MGM 2006 492*	28	8
24 May 75 ●	**THE PROUD ONE** *MGM 2006 520*	5	8
14 Jun 75	**I'M STILL GONNA NEED YOU** *MGM 2315 342*	19	7
15 Nov 75	**I'M STILL GONNA NEED YOU** *MGM 2006 551*	32	4
10 Jan 76	**AROUND THE WORLD – LIVE IN CONCERT** *MGM 2659 044*	41	1
30 Oct 76	**I CAN'T LIVE A DREAM** *Polydor 2066 726*	37	5
23 Sep 95	**CRAZY HORSES** (re-mix) *Polydor 5793212*	50	1
20 Apr 96	**THE VERY BEST OF THE OSMONDS** *Polydor 5270722*	17	5
12 Jun 99	**CRAZY HORSES** (re-issue of re-mix) *Polydor 5611372*	34	2
12 Jul 03 ●	**ULTIMATE COLLECTION** *Polydor / Universal TV 9808355*	4	11

Gilbert O'SULLIVAN (162 Top 500)

Distinctive singer / songwriter / pianist, b. Raymond O'Sullivan, 1 Dec 1946, Waterford. His unusual image – short trousers, flat cap and pudding-basin haircut – helped to launch the successful international career of the performer Record Mirror voted No.1 UK Male Singer of 1972 (8 Albums: 201 Weeks, 16 Singles: 145 Weeks)

28 Nov 70 ●	**NOTHING RHYMED** *MAM 3*	8	11
3 Apr 71	**UNDERNEATH THE BLANKET GO** (re) *MAM 13*	40	4
24 Jul 71	**WE WILL** *MAM 30*	16	11
25 Sep 71 ●	**HIMSELF** *MAM 501*	5	82
27 Nov 71 ●	**NO MATTER HOW I TRY** *MAM 53*	5	15
4 Mar 72 ●	**ALONE AGAIN (NATURALLY)** *MAM 66* ▲	3	12
17 Jun 72 ●	**OOH-WAKKA-DOO-WAKKA-DAY** *MAM 78*	8	11
21 Oct 72 ★	**CLAIR** *MAM 84*	1	14
18 Nov 72 ★	**BACK TO FRONT** *MAM 502*	1	65
17 Mar 73 ★	**GET DOWN** *MAM 96*	1	13
15 Sep 73	**OOH BABY** *MAM 107*	18	7
6 Oct 73 ●	**I'M A WRITER, NOT A FIGHTER** *MAMS 505*	2	25
10 Nov 73 ●	**WHY, OH WHY, OH WHY** *MAM 111*	6	14
9 Feb 74	**HAPPINESS IS ME AND YOU** *MAM 114*	19	7
24 Aug 74	**A WOMAN'S PLACE** *MAM 122*	42	3
26 Oct 74 ●	**A STRANGER IN MY OWN BACK YARD** *MAM MAMS 506*	9	8
14 Dec 74	**CHRISTMAS SONG** *MAM 124*	12	6
14 Jun 75	**I DON'T LOVE YOU BUT I THINK I LIKE YOU** *MAM 130*	14	6
18 Dec 76	**GREATEST HITS** *MAM MAMA 2003*	13	11
27 Sep 80	**WHAT'S IN A KISS** *CBS 8929*	19	9
12 Sep 81	**20 GOLDEN GREATS** *K-Tel NE 1133*	98	1
24 Feb 90	**SO WHAT** *Dover ROJ 3*	70	2
11 May 91	**NOTHING BUT THE BEST** *Castle Communications CTVLP 107*	50	4
27 Mar 04	**THE BERRY VEST OF** *EMI 5986722*	20	5

The OTHER TWO (see also NEW ORDER)

UK, male / female vocal / instrumental duo – Stephen Morris and Gillian Gilbert (2 Singles: 5 Weeks)

9 Nov 91	**TASTY FISH** *Factory FAC 3297*	41	3
6 Nov 93	**SELFISH** *London TWOCD 1*	46	2

The OTHERS

UK, male vocal / instrumental group (1 Album: 1 Week, 4 Singles: 7 Weeks)

29 May 04	**THIS IS FOR THE POOR** *Poptones MC 5090SCD*	42	1

17 July 1982	24 July 1982	31 July 1982	7 August 1982
FAME Irene Cara	**FAME** Irene Cara	**FAME** Irene Cara	**COME ON EILEEN** Dexy's Midnight Runners with The Emerald Express
THE LEXICON OF LOVE ABC	**THE LEXICON OF LOVE** ABC / **FAME** Soundtrack (equal top)	**FAME** Soundtrack	**THE KIDS FROM 'FAME'** Kids From 'Fame'

KEY: UK No.1 ★ UK Top 10 ● Still on chart + UK entry at No.1 ■ US No.1 ▲ UK million seller £ US million seller $
Singles re-entries are listed as (re), (2re), (3re)... which signifies that the hit re-entered the chart once, twice or three times...
Peak Position / Weeks

6 Nov 04 **STAN BOWLES** *Vertigo 9868521* 36 2
29 Jan 05 **LACKEY** *Vertigo 9869350* 21 3
12 Feb 05 **THE OTHERS** *Mercury / Poptones 2103607* 51 1
16 Apr 05 **WILLIAM** *Poptones 9870861* 29 1

Johnny OTIS SHOW
US, band – leader John Veliotes (2 Singles: 22 Weeks)

22 Nov 57 ● **MA (HE'S MAKING EYES AT ME)** *Capitol CL 14794* [1] 2 15
10 Jan 58 **BYE BYE BABY** *Capitol CL 14817* [2] 20 7

[1] Johnny Otis and his Orchestra with Marie Adams and The Three Tons of Joy [2] Johnny Otis Show, vocals by Marie Adams and Johnny Otis

OTTAWAN *France, male / female vocal duo – Jean Patrick and Annette (4 Singles: 45 Weeks)*

13 Sep 80 ● **D.I.S.C.O.** *Carrere CAR 161* 2 18
13 Dec 80 **YOU'RE OK** *Carrere CAR 168* 56 6
29 Aug 81 ● **HANDS UP (GIVE ME YOUR HEART)** *Carrere CAR 183* 3 15
5 Dec 81 **HELP, GET ME SOME HELP!** *Carrere CAR 215* 49 6

John OTWAY and Wild Willy BARRETT
UK, male vocal / instrumental duo (1 Album: 1 Week, 3 Singles: 15 Weeks)

3 Dec 77 **REALLY FREE** *Polydor 2058 951* 27 8
1 Jul 78 **DEEP AND MEANINGLESS** *Polydor 2382 501* 44 1
5 Jul 80 **DK 50-80** *Polydor 2059 250* [1] 45 4
12 Oct 02 ● **BUNSEN BURNER** *U-Vibe OTWAY 02X* [2] 9 3

[1] Otway and Barrett [2] John Otway

OUI 3 *UK / US / Switzerland, male / female rap / instrumental group (1 Album: 3 Weeks, 6 Singles: 21 Weeks)*

20 Feb 93 **FOR WHAT IT'S WORTH** *MCA MCSTD 1736* 28 6
24 Apr 93 **ARMS OF SOLITUDE** *MCA MCSTD 1759* 54 2
17 Jul 93 **BREAK FROM THE OLD ROUTINE** *MCA MCSTD 1793* 17 6
7 Aug 93 **OUI LOVE YOU** *MCA MCD 10833* 39 3
23 Oct 93 **FOR WHAT IT'S WORTH** (re-mix) *MCA MCSTD 1941* 26 3
29 Jan 94 **FACT OF LIFE** *MCA MCSTD 1939* 38 2
27 May 95 **JOY OF LIVING** *MCA MCSTD 2057* 55 2

OUR DAUGHTER'S WEDDING *US, male vocal / instrumental group*

1 Aug 81 **LAWNCHAIRS** *EMI America EA 124* 49 6

OUR HOUSE *Australia, male instrumental / production duo*

31 Aug 96 **FLOOR SPACE** *Perfecto PERF 125CD* 52 1

OUR KID *UK, male vocal (Kevin Rown) group*

29 May 76 ● **YOU JUST MIGHT SEE ME CRY** *Polydor 2058 729* 2 11

OUR LADY PEACE *Canada, male vocal / instrumental group*

15 Jan 00 **ONE MAN ARMY** *Epic 6688662* 70 1

OUR TRIBE / ONE TRIBE
(see also DUSTED; FAITHLESS; ROLLO; SPHINX)
UK / US, male / female vocal / instrumental group (7 Singles: 13 Weeks)

20 Jun 92 **WHAT HAVE YOU DONE (IS THIS ALL)** *Inner Rhythm HEART 03* [1] 52 2
27 Mar 93 **I BELIEVE IN YOU** *Ffrreedom TABCD 117* [2] 42 2
30 Apr 94 **HOLD THAT SUCKER DOWN** *Cheeky CHEKCD 004* [3] 24 3
21 May 94 **LOVE COME HOME** *Triangle BLUESCD 001* [4] 73 1
13 May 95 **HIGH AS A KITE** *ffrr FCD 259* [5] 55 1
30 Sep 95 **HOLD THAT SUCKER DOWN** (re-mix) *Cheeky CHEKCD 009* [3] 26 3
9 Dec 00 **HOLD THAT SUCKER DOWN** (re-issue) *Champion CHAMPCD 786* [3] 45 1

[1] One Tribe featuring Gem [2] Our Tribe [3] OT Quartet [4] Our Tribe with Franke Pharoah and Kristine W [5] One Tribe featuring Roger

OUT OF MY HAIR *UK, male vocal / instrumental group*

1 Jul 95 **MISTER JONES** *RCA 74321267812* 73 1

The OUTHERE BROTHERS *US, male rap / vocal duo – Lamar Mahone and Craig Simpkins (2 Albums: 9 Weeks, 5 Singles: 50 Weeks)*

18 Mar 95 ★ **DON'T STOP (WIGGLE WIGGLE)** *Eternal YZ 917CD* 1 15
27 May 95 **1 POLISH 2 BISCUITS AND A FISH SANDWICH** *Eternal 0630105852* 56 5
17 Jun 95 ★ **BOOM BOOM BOOM** *Eternal YZ 938CD* 1 15
23 Sep 95 ● **LA LA LA HEY HEY** *Eternal YZ 974CD* 7 7
16 Dec 95 ● **IF YOU WANNA PARTY** [1] *Eternal WEA 030CD* 9 10
30 Dec 95 **THE PARTY ALBUM** *Eternal 0630127812* 41 4
25 Jan 97 **LET ME HEAR YOU SAY 'OLE OLE'** *WEA 089CD* 18 3

[1] Molella featuring the Outhere Brothers

The Party Album is a sanitized version of 1 Polish 2 Biscuits And A Fish Sandwich.

OUTKAST *US, male rap / vocal duo – "André 3000" Benjamin and Antwan "Big Boi" Patton (2 Albums: 71 Weeks, 10 Singles: 68 Weeks)*

23 Dec 00 **B.O.B (BOMBS OVER BAGHDAD)** *LaFace / Arista 74321822942* 61 1
20 Jan 01 ● **STANKONIA** *LaFace 73008260722* 10 15
3 Feb 01 **MS JACKSON** (import) *LaFace 73008245252* 48 4
3 Mar 01 ● **MS JACKSON** *LaFace / Arista 74321836822* ▲ 2 10
9 Jun 01 **SO FRESH, SO CLEAN** *LaFace / Arista 74321863402* 16 8
6 Apr 02 **THE WHOLE WORLD** *LaFace 74321917592* [1] 19 5
27 Jul 02 **LAND OF A MILLION DRUMS** *Atlantic AT 0134CD* [2] 46 1
4 Oct 03 **GHETTO MUSIK** *Arista 82876567232* 55 1
11 Oct 03 ● **SPEAKERBOXXX / THE LOVE BELOW** *Arista 82876529052* ▲ 8 56
22 Nov 03 ● **HEY YA!** *Arista 82876579532* ▲ 3 21
3 Apr 04 ● **THE WAY YOU MOVE** *Arista 82876605602* [3] ▲ 7 10
3 Jul 04 ● **ROSES** *Arista 82876624392* 4 7

[1] Outkast featuring Killer Mike [2] Outkast featuring Killer Mike and Sleepy Brown [3] Outkast featuring Sleepy Brown

Speakerboxxx / The Love Below equalled its original peak position of No.8 when it re-entered the chart in Jan 2005.

OUTLANDER *Belgium, male producer – Marcos Salon (2 Singles: 3 Weeks)*

31 Aug 91 **VAMP** *R&S RSUK 1* 51 2
7 Feb 98 **THE VAMP (REVAMPED)** *R&S RS 97113CDX* 62 1

OUTLANDISH *Morocco / Pakistan / Honduras, male rap / production trio*

31 May 03 **GUANTANAMO** *RCA 82876517702* 31 2

The OUTLAWS *UK, male instrumental group (5 Singles: 29 Weeks)*

13 Apr 61 **SWINGIN' LOW** *HMV POP 844* 46 2
8 Jun 61 **AMBUSH** *HMV POP 877* 43 2
12 Oct 61 **TRIBUTE TO BUDDY HOLLY** *HMV POP 912* [1] 24 6
3 Jan 63 ● **DON'T YOU THINK IT'S TIME** *HMV POP 1105* [1] 6 12
11 Apr 63 **MY LITTLE BABY** *HMV POP 1142* [1] 34 7

[1] Mike Berry and The Outlaws

OUTRAGE *US, male vocalist (2 Singles: 2 Weeks)*

11 Mar 95 **TALL 'N' HANDSOME** *Effective ECFL 001CD* 57 1
23 Nov 96 **TALL 'N' HANDSOME** (re-mix) *Positiva CDTIV 64* 51 1

OUTSIDAZ featuring Rah DIGGA and Melanie BLATT
US, male rap group and female rapper and UK, female vocalist

2 Mar 02 **I'M LEAVIN'** *Rufflife RLCDM 03* 41 2

	14 August 1982	21 August 1982	28 August 1982	4 September 1982
UK No.1 SINGLES	**COME ON EILEEN** Dexy's Midnight Runners with The Emerald Express	**COME ON EILEEN** Dexy's Midnight Runners with The Emerald Express	**COME ON EILEEN** Dexy's Midnight Runners with The Emerald Express	**EYE OF THE TIGER** Survivor
UK No.1 ALBUMS	**THE KIDS FROM 'FAME'** Kids From 'Fame'	**THE KIDS FROM 'FAME'** Kids From 'Fame'	**THE KIDS FROM 'FAME'** Kids From 'Fame'	**THE KIDS FROM 'FAME'** Kids From 'Fame'

The OVERLANDERS *UK, male vocal (Laurie Mason) / instrumental group*

13 Jan 66 ★ **MICHELLE** *Pye 7N 17034*..........1 10

OVERLORD X *UK, male rapper – Benjamin Balogun*

4 Feb 89 **WEAPON IS MY LYRIC** *Mango Street ILPS 9924*..........68 1

OVERWEIGHT POOCH featuring Ce Ce PENISTON
US, female rapper and female vocalist

18 Jan 92 **I LIKE IT** *A&M AM 847*..........58 2

Mark OWEN (see also TAKE THAT)
UK, male vocalist (2 Albums: 12 Weeks, 7 Singles: 37 Weeks)

30 Nov 96 ● **CHILD** (re) *RCA 74321424422*..........3 15
14 Dec 96 **GREEN MAN** *RCA 74321435142*..........33 11
15 Feb 97 ● **CLEMENTINE** *RCA 74321454982*..........3 6
23 Aug 97 **I AM WHAT I AM** *RCA 74321501222*..........29 3
16 Aug 03 ● **FOUR MINUTE WARNING** *Universal MCSTD 40329*..........4 9
8 Nov 03 **ALONE WITHOUT YOU** *Universal MCSTD 40342*..........26 2
15 Nov 03 **IN YOUR OWN TIME** *Universal MCD 60092*..........59 1
19 Jun 04 **MAKIN' OUT** *Sedna CDSEDNA 1*..........30 1
3 Sep 05 **BELIEVE IN THE BOOGIE** *Sedna SEDNACS 1*..........57 1

Reg OWEN and his ORCHESTRA
UK, orchestra – leader b. 3 Feb 1921, d. 1978 (2 Singles: 10 Weeks)

27 Feb 59 **MANHATTAN SPIRITUAL** *Pye International 7N 25009*..........20 8
27 Oct 60 **OBSESSION** *Palette PG 9004*..........43 2

Sid OWEN *UK, male actor / vocalist – David Sutton (2 Singles: 6 Weeks)*

16 Dec 95 **BETTER BELIEVE IT (CHILDREN IN NEED)** *Trinity TDM 001CD* [1]..........60 1
8 Jul 00 **GOOD THING GOING** *Mushroom MUSH 74CDS*..........14 5

[1] Sid Owen and Patsy Palmer

Robert OWENS *US, male vocalist (4 Singles: 6 Weeks)*

7 Dec 91 **I'LL BE YOUR FRIEND** *Perfecto PB 45161*..........75 2
26 Apr 97 **I'LL BE YOUR FRIEND** (re-mix) *Perfecto PERF 137CD1*..........25 2
24 Feb 01 **MINE TO GIVE** *Science QEDCD 10* [1]..........44 1
15 Feb 03 **LAST NIGHT A DJ BLEW MY MIND** *Illustrious CDILL 013* [2] .34 1

[1] Photek featuring Robert Owens [2] Fab Four featuring Robert Owens

OXIDE & NEUTRINO
(see also SO SOLID CREW) *UK, male production / rap duo – Alex Rivers and Mark Oseitutu (3 Albums: 22 Weeks, 6 Singles: 45 Weeks)*

6 May 00 **BOUND 4 DA RELOAD (CASUALTY)** *East West OXIDE 01T*..........71 1
6 May 00 ★ **BOUND 4 DA RELOAD (CASUALTY)** *East West OXIDE 01CD1* ■ .1 11
30 Dec 00 ● **NO GOOD 4 ME** *East West OXIDE 02CD* [1]..........6 8
26 May 01 ● **UP MIDDLE FINGER** *East West OXIDE 03CD*..........7 7
9 Jun 01 **EXECUTE** *East West 8573885592*..........11 19
28 Jul 01 **DEVIL'S NIGHTMARE** *East West OXIDE 07CD1*..........16 5
8 Dec 01 **RAP DIS (U CAN'T STOP DIS S**T) / ONLY WANNA KNOW U COS URE FAMOUS** *East West OXIDE 08CD*..........12 8
28 Sep 02 ● **DEM GIRLZ (I DON'T KNOW WHY)** (re) *East West OXIDE 09CD1* [2]..........10 6
12 Oct 02 **2 STEPZ AHEAD** *East West 5046607562*..........28 2

[1] Oxide & Neutrino featuring Megaman, Romeo and Lisa Maffia [2] Oxide & Neutrino featuring Kowdean

The double 12-inch vinyl format of the act's No.1 single was ineligible for the singles chart but sales were sufficient to qualify for a place on the albums chart.

OXYGEN featuring Andrea BRITTON
(see also ASCENSION; CHAKRA; ESSENCE; LUSTRAL; SPACE BROTHERS)
UK, male production duo and female vocalist

11 Jan 03 **AM I ON YOUR MIND** *Innocent SINCD 40*..........30 3

OZOMATLI *US, male vocal / instrumental group (2 Singles: 2 Weeks)*

20 Mar 99 **CUT CHEMIST SUITE** *Almo Sounds CDALM 62*..........58 1
22 May 99 **SUPER BOWL SUNDAE** *Almo Sounds CDALM 63*..........68 1

OZRIC TENTACLES
UK, male instrumental / vocal group (3 Albums: 7 Weeks)

31 Aug 91 **STRANGEITUDE** *Dovetail DOVELP 3*..........70 1
1 May 93 **JURASSIC SHIFT** *Dovetail DOVECD 6*..........11 4
9 Jul 94 **ARBORESCENCE** *Dovetail DOVECD 7*..........18 2

P

Jazzi P *UK, female rapper – Pauline Bennett (3 Singles: 12 Weeks)*

8 Jul 89 **GET LOOSE** *Breakout USA 659* [1]..........25 6
9 Jun 90 **FEEL THE RHYTHM** *A&M USA 691*..........51 2
3 Aug 91 **REBEL WOMAN** *DNA 7DNA 001* [2]..........42 4

[1] LA Mix featuring Jazzi P [2] DNA featuring Jazzi P

P DIDDY (383 Top 500) *World Music Award-winning rapper / songwriter / producer and record label owner, formerly known as Puff Daddy, and now plain Diddy, b. Sean Combs 1970, New York, US. The only producer to score three successive No.1 singles in the 1990s, 'I'll Be Missing You', a tribute to his discovery Notorious B.I.G., is the most successful rap single of all time and sold 1,409,688 copies in the UK (3 Albums: 31 Weeks, 28 Singles: 154 Weeks)*

29 Mar 97 **CAN'T NOBODY HOLD ME DOWN** *Arista 74321464552* [1] ▲ $..........19 4
26 Apr 97 **NO TIME** *Atlantic A 5594CD* [2]..........45 1
28 Jun 97 ★ **I'LL BE MISSING YOU** *Puff Daddy 74321499102* [3] ■ ▲ £ $...1 21
2 Aug 97 ● **NO WAY OUT** *Puff Daddy 78612730122* [1] ▲..........8 13
9 Aug 97 ● **MO MONEY MO PROBLEMS** *Puff Daddy 74321492492* [4] ▲ $..6 10
13 Sep 97 **SOMEONE** *RCA 74321513942* [5]..........34 2
1 Nov 97 **BEEN AROUND THE WORLD** (re) *Puff Daddy 74321539442* [6] $..........20 6
7 Feb 98 **IT'S ALL ABOUT THE BENJAMINS** *Puff Daddy 74321561972* [6] $..........18 3
1 Aug 98 **COME WITH ME** (import) *Epic 34K 78954* [7]..........75 1
8 Aug 98 ● **COME WITH ME** *Epic 6662842* [7] $..........2 10
1 May 99 **ALL NIGHT LONG** *Puff Daddy / Arista 74321665692* [8]..........23 3
29 May 99 **HATE ME NOW** *Columbia 6672562* [9]..........14 6
21 Aug 99 **P.E. 2000** *Puff Daddy / Arista 74321694972* [10]..........13 4
4 Sep 99 ● **FOREVER** *Puff Daddy 74321689052*..........9 6
20 Nov 99 **BEST FRIEND** *Puff Daddy / Arista 74321712312* [11]..........24 4
5 Feb 00 **NOTORIOUS B.I.G.** *Puff Daddy / Arista 74321737312* [12]..........16 5
19 Feb 00 **SATISFY YOU** (re) (import) *Bad Boy / Arista 7928322* [13]..........73 2
11 Mar 00 ● **SATISFY YOU** (import) *Puff Daddy / Arista 74321745592* [13]...8 8
6 Oct 01 **BAD BOY FOR LIFE** *Bad Boy / Arista 74321889982* [14]..........13 6
26 Jan 02 **DIDDY** *Puff Daddy / Arista 74321911652* [15]..........19 4
8 Jun 02 **WE INVENTED THE REMIX** *Puff Daddy 74321945402* [2]..........17 12
8 Jun 02 **PASS THE COURVOISIER – PART II** (re) *J 74321937902* [16]...16 8
10 Aug 02 ● **I NEED A GIRL (PART ONE)** *Puff Daddy / Arista 74321947242* [17]..........4 11
29 Mar 03 **BUMP, BUMP, BUMP** *Epic 6736452* [18]..........11 8
23 Aug 03 **LET'S GET ILL** *Bad Boy / Meanwhile MCSTD 40331* [19]..........25 3
20 Sep 03 ● **SHAKE YA TAILFEATHER** *Bad Boy MCSTD 40337* [20]..........10 7
7 Feb 04 **SHOW ME YOUR SOUL** *Puff Daddy / Island MCSTD 40350* [21] 35 2

11 September 1982	18 September 1982	25 September 1982	2 October 1982
EYE OF THE TIGER Survivor	**EYE OF THE TIGER** Survivor	**EYE OF THE TIGER** Survivor	**PASS THE DUTCHIE** Musical Youth
THE KIDS FROM 'FAME' Kids From 'Fame'	**THE KIDS FROM 'FAME'** Kids From 'Fame'	**THE KIDS FROM 'FAME'** Kids From 'Fame'	**LOVE OVER GOLD** Dire Straits

KEY: UK No.1 ★ UK Top 10 ● Still on chart + UK entry at No.1 ■ US No.1 ▲ UK million seller £ US million seller $ Singles re-entries are listed as (re), (2re), (3re)... which signifies that the hit re-entered the chart once, twice or three times...

Peak Position / Weeks

5 Jun 04 I DON'T WANNA KNOW (import) *Universal 9862372 PMI* [22] 71 1
12 Jun 04 ★ I DON'T WANNA KNOW *Bad Boy MCSTD 40369* [22] ■ 1 14

[1] Puff Daddy featuring Ma$e [2] Lil' Kim featuring Puff Daddy [3] Puff Daddy and Faith Evans featuring 112 [4] Notorious BIG featuring Puff Daddy and Ma$e [5] SWV featuring Puff Daddy [6] Puff Daddy and The Family [7] Puff Daddy featuring Jimmy Page [8] Faith Evans featuring Puff Daddy [9] Nas featuring Puff Daddy [10] Puff Daddy featuring Hurricane G [11] Puff Daddy featuring Mario Winans [12] Notorious BIG featuring Puff Daddy and Lil' Kim [13] Puff Daddy featuring R Kelly [14] P Diddy, Black Rob and Mark Curry [15] P Diddy featuring The Neptunes [16] Busta Rhymes featuring P Diddy and Pharrell [17] P Diddy featuring Usher and Loon [18] B2K featuring P Diddy [19] P Diddy featuring Kelis [20] Nelly, P Diddy and Murphy Lee [21] Lenny Kravitz / P Diddy / Loon / Pharrell Williams [22] Mario Winans featuring Enya & P Diddy
[1] Puff Daddy and The Family [2] P Diddy & The Bad Boy Family

PF PROJECT featuring Ewan McGREGOR
(see also MIRRORBALL; MUSIQUE vs U2; TZANT)
UK, male production duo – Jamie White and Moussa Clarke and actor

15 Nov 97 ● CHOOSE LIFE *Positiva CDTIV 84* 6 11

PhD *UK, male vocal (Jim Diamond) / instrumental trio*

3 Apr 82 ● I WON'T LET YOU DOWN *WEA K 79209* 3 14
1 May 82 PHD *WEA K 99150* 33 8

PJ *Canada, male producer – Paul Jacobs (2 Singles: 2 Weeks)*

20 Sep 97 HAPPY DAYS *Deconstruction 74321511822* 72 1
4 Sep 99 HAPPY DAYS (re-mix) *Defected DEFECT 6CDS* 57 1

PJB featuring HANNAH and her SISTERS (see also Hannah JONES)
Germany, male production group and US, female vocalists

14 Sep 91 BRIDGE OVER TROUBLED WATER *Dance Pool 6565467* 21 8

PKA *UK, male producer – Phil Kelsey (2 Singles: 2 Weeks)*

20 Apr 91 TEMPERATURE RISING *Stress SS 4* 68 1
7 Mar 92 POWERGEN (ONLY YOUR LOVE) *Stress PKA 1* 70 1

PM DAWN *US, male vocal / instrumental / rap duo – Attrell and Jarrett Cordes (2 Albums: 17 Weeks, 10 Singles: 39 Weeks)*

8 Jun 91 A WATCHER'S POINT OF VIEW (DON'T CHA THINK) *Gee Street GEE 32* 36 5
17 Aug 91 ● SET ADRIFT ON MEMORY BLISS *Gee Street GEE 33* ▲ 3 8
14 Sep 91 ● OF THE HEART OF THE SOUL AND OF THE CROSS *Gee Street GEEA 7* 8 12
19 Oct 91 PAPER DOLL *Gee Street GEE 35* 49 3
22 Feb 92 REALITY USED TO BE A FRIEND OF MINE *Gee Street GEE 37* 29 4
7 Nov 92 I'D DIE WITHOUT YOU *Gee Street GEE 39* 30 5
13 Mar 93 LOOKING THROUGH PATIENT EYES *Gee Street GESCD 47* 11 7
3 Apr 93 ● THE BLISS ALBUM ...? *Gee Street GEED 9* 9 5
12 Jun 93 MORE THAN LIKELY *Gee Street GESCD 49* [1] 40 3
30 Sep 95 DOWNTOWN VENUS *Gee Street GESCD 63* 58 2
6 Apr 96 SOMETIMES I MISS YOU SO MUCH *Gee Street GESCD 65* 58 1
31 Oct 98 GOTTA BE ... MOVIN' ON UP *Gee Street GEE 5003933* [2] 68 1

[1] PM Dawn featuring Boy George [2] PM Dawn featuring Ky-Mani

POB featuring DJ Patrick REID
UK, male producer – Paul Brogden and DJ

11 Dec 99 BLUEBOTTLE / FLY *Platipus PLAT 63CD* 74 1

P.O.D.
US, male vocal / instrumental group (1 Album: 6 Weeks, 4 Singles: 10 Weeks)

19 Jan 02 SATELLITE *Atlantic 7567834752* 16 6
2 Feb 02 ALIVE *Atlantic AT 0119CD* 19 6
18 May 02 YOUTH OF THE NATION *Atlantic AT 0127CD* 36 2
7 Jun 03 SLEEPING AWAKE *Maverick W 608CD* 42 1
24 Jan 04 WILL YOU *Atlantic AT 0169CD* 68 1

P.O.V. featuring JADE *US, male / female vocal groups*

5 Feb 94 ALL THRU THE NITE *Giant 74321187552* 32 3

PPK *Russia, male production / instrumental duo – Sergey Pimenov and Alexander Polyakov (2 Singles: 17 Weeks)*

8 Dec 01 ● RESURECTION *Perfecto PERF 32CDS* 3 15
26 Oct 02 RELOAD *Perfecto PERF 41CDS* 39 2

PQM featuring CICA *US, male producer and female vocalist*

9 Dec 00 THE FLYING SONG *Renaissance / Yoshitoshi RENCDS 004* 68 1

Petey PABLO *US, male rapper – Moses Barrett (3 Singles: 11 Weeks)*

9 Feb 02 I *Jive 9253092* 51 1
15 Jan 05 GOODIES (import) *Jive 82876648252* [1] ▲ 68 1
29 Jan 05 ★ GOODIES *LaFace 8287665882* [1] ■ ▲ 1 9

[1] Ciara featuring Petey Pablo

Thom PACE *US, male vocalist*

19 May 79 MAYBE *RSO 34* 14 15

PACIFICA *UK, male production duo*

31 Jul 99 LOST IN THE TRANSLATION *Wildstar CDWILD 25* 54 1

PACK featuring Nigel BENN
UK, male vocal / instrumental group and boxer / rapper

8 Dec 90 STAND AND FIGHT *IQ ZB 44237* 61 2

The PACKABEATS *UK, male instrumental group*

23 Feb 61 GYPSY BEAT *Parlophone R 4729* 49 1

The PADDINGTONS
UK, male vocal / instrumental group (1 Album: 1 Week, 4 Singles: 6 Weeks)

23 Oct 04 21 / SOME OLD GIRL *Poptones MC 5093SCD* 47 1
7 May 05 PANIC ATTACK *Poptones 9870603* 25 2
23 Jul 05 50 TO A £ *Poptones 9872739* 32 2
29 Oct 05 SORRY *Poptones 9873961* 41 1
12 Nov 05 FIRST COMES FIRST *Mercury 9873476* 65 1

José PADILLA featuring Angela JOHN
Spain, male DJ and UK, female vocalist

8 Aug 98 WHO DO YOU LOVE *Manifesto FESCD 45* 59 1

PAFFENDORF *Germany, male production duo – Gottfried Engels and Ramon Zenker (2 Singles: 8 Weeks)*

15 Jun 02 ● BE COOL *Data DATA 29CDS* 7 7
26 Apr 03 CRAZY SEXY MARVELLOUS *Data / MoS DATA 51CDS* 52 1

PAGANINI TRAXX *Italy, male DJ / producer – Sam Paganini*

1 Feb 97 ZOE *Sony S3 DANUCD 18X* 47 1

Jimmy PAGE (see also COVERDALE PAGE; LED ZEPPELIN) *UK, male guitarist – awarded an MBE in 2005 (6 Albums: 37 Weeks, 4 Singles: 16 Weeks)*

27 Feb 82 DEATHWISH II (FILM SOUNDTRACK) *Swansong SSK 59415* 40 4
16 Mar 85 WHATEVER HAPPENED TO JUGULA? *Beggars Banquet BEGA 60* [1] 44 4

	9 October 1982	16 October 1982	23 October 1982	30 October 1982
UK No.1 SINGLES	PASS THE DUTCHIE – Musical Youth	PASS THE DUTCHIE – Musical Youth	DO YOU REALLY WANT TO HURT ME – Culture Club	DO YOU REALLY WANT TO HURT ME – Culture Club
UK No.1 ALBUMS	LOVE OVER GOLD – Dire Straits	LOVE OVER GOLD – Dire Straits	LOVE OVER GOLD – Dire Straits	THE KIDS FROM 'FAME' – Kids From 'Fame'

2 Jul 88	OUTRIDER *Geffen WX 155*	27	6
19 Nov 94 ●	NO QUARTER *Fontana 5263622* [2]	7	13
17 Dec 94	**GALLOWS POLE** *Fontana PPCD 2* [1]	35	3
11 Apr 98	**MOST HIGH** *Mercury 5687512* [2]	26	2
2 May 98 ●	WALKING INTO CLARKSDALE *Mercury 5580252* [2]	3	6
1 Aug 98	**COME WITH ME** (import) *Epic 34K 78954* [3]	75	1
8 Aug 98 ●	**COME WITH ME** *Epic 6662842* [3] $	2	10
22 Jul 00	LIVE AT THE GREEK *SPV Recordings SPV 09172022* [3]	39	4

[1] Jimmy Page and Robert Plant [2] Page and Plant [3] Puff Daddy featuring Jimmy Page [1] Roy Harper with Jimmy Page [2] Jimmy Page and Robert Plant [3] Jimmy Page and The Black Crowes

Patti PAGE *US, female vocalist – Clara Ann Fowler*

27 Mar 53 ●	**(HOW MUCH IS) THAT DOGGIE IN THE WINDOW** *Oriole CB 1156* ▲	9	5

Tommy PAGE *US, male vocalist*

26 May 90	**I'LL BE YOUR EVERYTHING** *Sire W 9959* ▲	53	3

PAGLIARO *Canada, male vocalist – Michel Pagliaro*

19 Feb 72	**LOVING YOU AIN'T EASY** *Pye 7N 45111*	31	6

PAID & LIVE featuring Lauryn HILL

US, male production duo and female rapper / vocalist

27 Dec 97	**ALL MY TIME** *World Entertainment OWECD 2*	57	1

Elaine PAIGE (350 Top 500)

Revered UK actor / vocalist who has been a West End stage regular for 40 years, b. Elaine Bickerstaff, 5 Mar 1948, London. An entertainer who will forever be associated with Andrew Lloyd Webber / Tim Rice musicals. Of the 600 recordings of 'Memory', hers was the biggest hit (14 Albums: 159 Weeks, 7 Singles: 41 Weeks)

21 Oct 78	**DON'T WALK AWAY TILL I TOUCH YOU** *EMI 2862*	46	5
6 Jun 81 ●	**MEMORY** (re) *Polydor POSP 279*	6	15
1 May 82	ELAINE PAIGE *WEA K 58385*	56	6
5 Nov 83 ●	STAGES *K-Tel NE 1262*	2	48
14 Apr 84	**SOMETIMES (THEME FROM 'CHAMPIONS')** *Island IS 174*	72	1
20 Oct 84	CINEMA *K-Tel NE 1282*	12	25
5 Jan 85 ★	**I KNOW HIM SO WELL** *RCA CHESS 3* [1]	1	16
16 Nov 85 ●	LOVE HURTS *WEA WX 28*	8	20
29 Nov 86	CHRISTMAS *WEA WX 80*	27	6
21 Nov 87	**THE SECOND TIME (THEME FROM 'BILITIS')** *WEA YZ 163*	69	1
5 Dec 87	MEMORIES – THE BEST OF ELAINE PAIGE *Telstar STAR 2313*	14	15
19 Nov 88	THE QUEEN ALBUM *Siren SRNLP 22*	51	8
27 Apr 91	LOVE CAN DO THAT *RCA PL 74932*	36	4
28 Nov 92	THE BEST OF ELAINE PAIGE AND BARBARA DICKSON *Telstar TCD 2632* [1]	22	9
10 Apr 93	ROMANCE AND THE STAGE *RCA 74321136152*	71	1
19 Nov 94	PIAF *WEA 4509946412*	46	3
21 Jan 95	**HYMNE A L'AMOUR (IF YOU LOVE ME)** *WEA YZ 899CD*	68	1
1 Jul 95	ENCORE *WEA 0630104762*	20	6
24 Oct 98	**MEMORY** (re-recording) *WEA WEA 197CD*	36	2
28 Nov 98	ON REFLECTION – THE VERY BEST OF ELAINE PAIGE *Telstar TV / WEA TTVCD 2999*	60	4
5 Jun 04	CENTRE STAGE – THE VERY BEST OF ELAINE PAIGE *WSM WSMCD 171*	35	4

[1] Elaine Paige and Barbara Dickson [1] Elaine Paige and Barbara Dickson

Hal PAIGE and The WHALERS *US, male vocal / instrumental group*

25 Aug 60	**GOING BACK TO MY HOME TOWN** *Melodisc MEL 1553*	50	1

Jennifer PAIGE *US, female vocalist (1 Album: 1 Week, 2 Singles: 13 Weeks)*

12 Sep 98 ●	**CRUSH** *EAR 0039425*	4	12
31 Oct 98	JENNIFER PAIGE *EAR 0039842 ERE*	67	1
20 Mar 99	**SOBER** *EAR / Edel 0044185 ERE*	68	1

Orchestre de Chambre Jean-Francois PAILLARD

France, male conductor and orchestra

20 Aug 88	**THEME FROM 'VIETNAM' (CANON IN D)** *Debut DEBT 3053*	61	3

PALE *Ireland, male vocal / instrumental group*

13 Jun 92	**DOGS WITH NO TAILS** *A&M AM 866*	51	2

PALE FOUNTAINS

UK, male vocal / instrumental group (2 Albums: 3 Weeks, 1 Single: 6 Weeks)

27 Nov 82	**THANK YOU** *Virgin VS 557*	48	6
10 Mar 84	PACIFIC STREET *Virgin V 2274*	85	2
16 Feb 85	FROM ACROSS THE KITCHEN TABLE *Virgin V 2333*	94	1

PALE SAINTS *UK, male / female vocal / instrumental group (2 Albums: 3 Weeks, 1 Single: 1 Week)*

24 Feb 90	THE COMFORTS OF MADNESS *4AD CAD 0002*	40	2
6 Jul 91	**KINKY LOVE** *4AD AD 1009*	72	1
4 Apr 92	IN RIBBONS *4AD CAD 2004CD*	61	1

PALE X *Holland, male producer – Michael Pollen*

3 Feb 01	**NITRO** *Nukleuz NUKP 0280*	74	1

PALLAS *UK, male vocal / instrumental group (2 Albums: 4 Weeks)*

25 Feb 84	SENTINEL *Harvest SHSP 2400121*	41	3
22 Feb 86	THE WEDGE *Harvest SHVL 850*	70	1

Nerina PALLOT *UK, female vocalist (2 Singles: 3 Weeks)*

18 Aug 01	**PATIENCE** *Polydor 5872122*	61	1
28 Feb 04	**TRULY** *Nettwerk 332202* [1]	54	2

[1] Delerium featuring Nerina Pallot

Jhay PALMER featuring MC IMAGE

UK, male producer / vocalist and UK, male rapper

27 Apr 02	**HELLO** *Bagatrix CDBTX 002*	69	1

Robert PALMER (203 Top 500)

Grammy-winning UK rock group veteran and former member of Vinegar Joe, b. Alan Palmer, 19 Jan 1949, Yorkshire, d. 26 Sep 2003. This vocalist's hottest run of transatlantic hits came after he fronted short-lived Anglo-American supergroup Power Station in 1985. He benefited from some striking, award-winning videos featuring an all-female backing band (parodied in the video for Shania Twain's 'Man! I Feel Like a Woman!') (14 Albums: 166 Weeks, 25 Singles: 129 Weeks)

6 Nov 76	SOME PEOPLE CAN DO WHAT THEY LIKE *Island ILPS 9420*	46	1
20 May 78	**EVERY KINDA PEOPLE** *Island WIP 6425*	53	4
7 Jul 79	**BAD CASE OF LOVIN' YOU (DOCTOR DOCTOR)** *Island WIP 6481*	61	2
14 Jul 79	SECRETS *Island ILPS 9544*	54	4
6 Sep 80	CLUES *Island ILPS 9595*	31	8
6 Sep 80	**JOHNNY AND MARY** *Island WIP 6638*	44	8
22 Nov 80	**LOOKING FOR CLUES** *Island WIP 6651*	33	9
13 Feb 82	**SOME GUYS HAVE ALL THE LUCK** *Island WIP 6754*	16	8
3 Apr 82	MAYBE IT'S LIVE *Island ILPS 9665*	32	6
2 Apr 83	**YOU ARE IN MY SYSTEM** *Island IS 104*	53	4
23 Apr 83	PRIDE *Island ILPS 9720*	37	9
18 Jun 83	**YOU CAN HAVE IT (TAKE MY HEART)** *Island IS 121*	66	2
16 Nov 85 ●	RIPTIDE *Island ILPS 9801*	5	37
10 May 86 ●	**ADDICTED TO LOVE** *Island IS 270* ▲	5	15
19 Jul 86 ●	**I DIDN'T MEAN TO TURN YOU ON** *Island IS 283*	9	9
1 Nov 86	**DISCIPLINE OF LOVE** *Island IS 242*	68	1
26 Mar 88	**SWEET LIES** *Island IS 352*	58	3
11 Jun 88	**SIMPLY IRRESISTABLE** *EMI EM 61*	44	4
9 Jul 88	HEAVY NOVA *EMI EMD 1007*	17	25
15 Oct 88 ●	**SHE MAKES MY DAY** *EMI EM 65*	6	12
13 May 89	**CHANGE HIS WAYS** *EMI EM 85*	28	7
26 Aug 89	**IT COULD HAPPEN TO YOU** *EMI EM 99*	71	1

6 November 1982	13 November 1982	20 November 1982	27 November 1982
DO YOU REALLY WANT TO HURT ME Culture Club	I DON'T WANNA DANCE Eddy Grant	I DON'T WANNA DANCE Eddy Grant	I DON'T WANNA DANCE Eddy Grant
THE KIDS FROM 'FAME' Kids From 'Fame'	THE KIDS FROM 'FAME' Kids From 'Fame'	THE KIDS FROM 'FAME' Kids From 'Fame'	THE SINGLES - THE FIRST TEN YEARS Abba

KEY UK No.1 ★ UK Top 10 ● Still on chart + UK entry at No.1 ■ US No.1 ▲ UK million seller £ US million seller $
Singles re-entries are listed as (re), (2re), (3re)... which signifies that the hit re-entered the chart once, twice or three times...

Peak Position / Weeks

11 Nov 89 ● ADDICTIONS VOLUME 1 *Island ILPS 9944* 7 17
3 Nov 90 ● **I'LL BE YOUR BABY TONIGHT** *EMI EM 167* [1] 6 10
17 Nov 90 ● DON'T EXPLAIN *EMI EMDX 1018* 9 20
5 Jan 91 ● **MERCY MERCY ME – I WANT YOU** *EMI EM 173* 9 9
15 Jun 91 **DREAMS TO REMEMBER** *EMI EM 193* 68 1
7 Mar 92 **EVERY KINDA PEOPLE** (re-mix) *Island IS 498* 43 3
4 Apr 92 ADDICTIONS VOLUME 2 *Island CIDTV 4* 12 7
17 Oct 92 **WITCHCRAFT** *EMI EM 251* 50 3
31 Oct 92 RIDIN' HIGH *EMI CDEMD 1038* 32 3
9 Jul 94 **GIRL U WANT** *EMI CDEMS 331* 57 2
3 Sep 94 **KNOW BY NOW** *EMI CDEMS 343* 25 5
24 Sep 94 HONEY *EMI CDEMD 1069* 25 4
24 Dec 94 **YOU BLOW ME AWAY** *EMI CDEMS 350* 38 4
14 Oct 95 **RESPECT YOURSELF** *EMI CDEMS 399* 45 2
28 Oct 95 ● THE VERY BEST OF ROBERT PALMER *EMI CDEMD 1088* 4 21
16 Nov 02 AT HIS VERY BEST *Universal TV 697812* 38 4
18 Jan 03 **ADDICTED TO LOVE** *Serious SER 060CD* [2] 42 1

[1] Robert Palmer and UB40 [2] Shake B4 Use vs Robert Palmer

PAN POSITION *Italy / Venezuela, male instrumental / production group*

18 Jun 94 **ELEPHANT PAW (GET DOWN TO THE FUNK)** *Positiva CDTIV 13* 55 1

PANDORA'S BOX *US, male / female vocal / instrumental group*

21 Oct 89 **IT'S ALL COMING BACK TO ME NOW** *Virgin VS 1216* 51 3

Darryl PANDY *US, male vocalist (3 Singles: 5 Weeks)*

14 Dec 96 **LOVE CAN'T TURN AROUND** *4 Liberty LIBTCD 27* [1] 40 2
20 Feb 99 **RAISE YOUR HANDS** *VC Recordings VCRD 44* [2] 40 2
2 Oct 99 **SUNSHINE & HAPPINESS** *Azuli AZNYCD 103* [3] 68 1

[1] Farley 'Jackmaster' Funk with Darryl Pandy [2] Big Room Girl featuring Darryl Pandy [3] Darryl Pandy / Nerio's Dubwork

Johnny PANIC and The BIBLE OF DREAMS (see also TEARS FOR FEARS) *UK, male / female vocal / instrumental group (2 Singles: 2 Weeks)*

2 Feb 91 **JOHNNY PANIC AND THE BIBLE OF DREAMS** *Fontana PANIC 1* 70 2

PANJABI MC *UK, male DJ / producer – Rajinder Singh (3 Singles: 19 Weeks)*

4 Jan 03 **MUNDIAN TO BACH KE** (import) *Big Star BIGCDMO 76* 59 3
25 Jan 03 ● **MUNDIAN TO BACH KE** *Showbiz / Instant Karma KARMA 28CD* 5 13
5 Jul 03 **JOGI / BEWARE OF THE BOYS** *Showbiz / Dharma DHARMA ICDS* [1] 25 3

[1] Panjabi MC featuring Jay-Z (Jay-Z appears on 'Beware Of The Boys' only)

PANTERA *US, male vocal (Philip Anselmo) / instrumental group (5 Albums: 10 Weeks, 4 Singles: 8 Weeks)*

7 Mar 92 VULGAR DISPLAY OF POWER *Atco 7567917582* 64 1
10 Oct 92 **MOUTH FOR WAR** *Atco A 5845T* 73 1
27 Feb 93 **WALK** *Atco B 6076CD* 35 2
19 Mar 94 **I'M BROKEN** *Atco B 5932CD1* 19 2
2 Apr 94 ● FAR BEYOND DRIVEN *Atco 7567923752* ▲ 3 4
22 Oct 94 **PLANET CARAVAN** *East West A 5836CD1* 26 3
18 May 96 THE GREAT SOUTHERN TRENDKILL *East West 7559619082* 17 3
30 Aug 97 OFFICIAL LIVE – 101 PROOF *East West 7559620682* 54 1
8 Apr 00 REINVENTING THE STEEL *Elektra 7559624512* 33 1

PAPA ROACH *US, male vocal (Coby Dick) / instrumental group (3 Albums: 45 Weeks, 5 Singles: 27 Weeks)*

13 Jan 01 ● INFEST *Dreamworks 4502232* 9 36
17 Feb 01 ● **LAST RESORT** *Dreamworks / Polydor 4509212* 3 10
5 May 01 **BETWEEN ANGELS & INSECTS** *Dreamworks / Polydor 4509082* 17 6
22 Jun 02 **SHE LOVES ME NOT** *Dreamworks / Polydor 4508182* 14 8
29 Jun 02 ● LOVEHATETRAGEDY *Dreamworks 4503672* 4 7
2 Nov 02 **TIME AND TIME AGAIN** *Dreamworks / Polydor 4508052* 54 1
11 Sep 04 GETTING AWAY WITH MURDER *Geffen 9863643* 30 2
18 Sep 04 **GETTING AWAY WITH MURDER** *Geffen 9863647* 45 2

The PAPER DOLLS *UK, female vocal group*

13 Mar 68 **SOMETHING HERE IN MY HEART (KEEPS A-TELLIN' ME NO)** *Pye 7N 17456* 11 13

PAPER LACE *UK, male vocal (Phil Wright) / instrumental group (4 Singles: 41 Weeks)*

23 Feb 74 ★ **BILLY DON'T BE A HERO** *Bus Stop BUS 1014* 1 14
4 May 74 ● **THE NIGHT CHICAGO DIED** *Bus Stop BUS 1016* ▲ 3 11
24 Aug 74 **THE BLACK EYED BOYS** *Bus Stop BUS 1019* 11 10
4 Mar 78 **WE GOT THE WHOLE WORLD IN OUR HANDS** *Warner Bros. K 17110* [1] 24 6

[1] Nottingham Forest with Paper Lace

PAPERDOLLS *UK, female vocal group*

12 Sep 98 **GONNA MAKE YOU BLUSH** *MCA MCSTD 40175* 65 1

PAPPA BEAR featuring VAN DER TOORN *US, male rapper – June Rollocks and Holland, male vocalist – Jan Van Der Toorn*

16 May 98 **CHERISH** *Universal UMD 70316* 47 1

PAR-T-ONE vs INXS *Italy, male production trio and Australia, male vocal / instrumental group*

3 Nov 01 **I'M SO CRAZY** (re) *Credence CDCRED 016* 19 6

PARA BEATS featuring Carmen REECE NEW *UK, male producer and female vocalist*

27 Aug 05 **U GOT ME** *Onetwo ONETCDS 003* 59 1

Vanessa PARADIS *France, female vocalist (1 Album: 2 Weeks, 4 Singles: 30 Weeks)*

13 Feb 88 ● **JOE LE TAXI** *FA Productions POSP 902* 3 10
10 Oct 92 ● **BE MY BABY** *Remark PO 235* 6 15
7 Nov 92 VANESSA PARADIS *Remark 5139542* 45 2
27 Feb 93 **SUNDAY MONDAYS** *Remark PZCD 251* 49 4
24 Jul 93 **JUST AS LONG AS YOU ARE THERE** *Remark PZCD 272* 57 1

PARADISE *UK, male vocal / instrumental group*

10 Sep 83 **ONE MIND, TWO HEARTS** *Priority P 1* 42 4

PARADISE NEW *UK, male production trio and female vocalist*

9 Jul 05 **SEE THE LIGHT** *Turbulence CDTURB 1* 73 1

PARADISE LOST *UK, male vocal / instrumental group (3 Albums: 6 Weeks, 3 Singles: 3 Weeks)*

20 May 95 **THE LAST TIME** *Music for Nations CDKUT 165* 60 1
24 Jun 95 DRACONIAN TIMES *Music for Nations CDMFNX 184* 16 3
7 Oct 95 **FOREVER FAILURE** *Music for Nations CDKUT 169* 66 1
28 Jun 97 **SAY JUST WORDS** *Music for Nations CDKUT 174* 53 1
26 Jul 97 ONE SECOND *Music for Nations CDMFNX 222* 31 2
19 Jun 99 HOST *EMI 5205672* 61 1

PARADISE ORGANISATION *UK, male instrumental / production group*

23 Jan 93 **PRAYER TOWER** *Cowboy RODEO 13* 70 1

PARADOX *UK, male instrumental duo*

24 Feb 90 **JAILBREAK** *Ronin 7R2* 66 2

	4 December 1982	11 December 1982	18 December 1982	25 December 1982
UK No.1 SINGLES	BEAT SURRENDER The Jam	BEAT SURRENDER The Jam	SAVE YOUR LOVE Renée and Renato	SAVE YOUR LOVE Renée and Renato
UK No.1 ALBUMS	THE JOHN LENNON COLLECTION John Lennon	THE JOHN LENNON COLLECTION John Lennon	THE JOHN LENNON COLLECTION John Lennon	THE JOHN LENNON COLLECTION John Lennon

Norrie PARAMOR (see also BIG BEN BANJO BAND) *UK, orchestra – leader b. 1913, d. 9 Sep 1979 (1 Album: 16 Weeks, 3 Singles: 25 Weeks)*

17 Mar 60 **THEME FROM 'A SUMMER PLACE'** *Columbia DB 4419*.....36 2
21 Oct 61 ★ **21 TODAY** *Columbia 33SX 1368* [1].....1 16
22 Mar 62 **THEME FROM 'Z CARS'** *Columbia DB 4789*.....33 6
10 May 62 ● **I'M LOOKING OUT THE WINDOW** *Columbia DB 4828* [1].....2 17

[1] Cliff Richard with the Norrie Paramor Orchestra
[1] Cliff Richard, The Shadows and Norrie Paramor and his Orchestra

The PARAMOUNTS *UK, male vocal / instrumental group*

16 Jan 64 **POISON IVY** *Parlophone R 5093*.....35 7

PARCHMENT *UK, male / female vocal / instrumental group*

16 Sep 72 **LIGHT UP THE FIRE** *Pye 7N 45178*.....31 5

PARIS *UK, male / female vocal group*

19 Jun 82 **NO GETTING OVER YOU** *RCA 222*.....49 4

PARIS *US, male vocalist – Oscar Jackson*

21 Jan 95 **GUERRILLA FUNK** *Priority PTYCD 100*.....38 2

PARIS RED
US / Germany, male / female vocal / instrumental duo (2 Singles: 2 Weeks)

29 Feb 92 **GOOD FRIEND** *Columbia 6569417*.....61 1
15 May 93 **PROMISES** *Columbia 6592342*.....59 1

PARIS ANGELS *UK, male / female vocal / instrumental group (1 Album: 2 Weeks, 3 Singles: 5 Weeks)*

3 Nov 90 **SCOPE** *Sheer Joy SHEER 0047*.....75 1
20 Jul 91 **PERFUME** *Virgin VS 1360*.....55 3
17 Aug 91 **SUNDEW** *Virgin V 2667*.....37 2
21 Sep 91 **FADE** *Virgin VS 1365*.....70 1

Mica PARIS *UK, female vocalist – Michelle Wallen (4 Albums: 40 Weeks, 15 Singles: 63 Weeks)*

7 May 88 ● **MY ONE TEMPTATION** *Fourth & Broadway BRW 85*.....7 11
30 Jul 88 **LIKE DREAMERS DO** *Fourth & Broadway BRW 108* [1].....26 5
3 Sep 88 ● **SO GOOD** *Fourth & Broadway BRLP 525*.....6 32
22 Oct 88 **BREATHE LIFE INTO ME** *Fourth & Broadway BRW 115*.....26 10
21 Jan 89 **WHERE IS THE LOVE** *Fourth & Broadway BRW 122* [2].....19 7
6 Oct 90 **CONTRIBUTION** *Fourth & Broadway BRW 188*.....33 4
27 Oct 90 **CONTRIBUTION** *Fourth & Broadway BRLP 558*.....26 3
1 Dec 90 **SOUTH OF THE RIVER** *Fourth & Broadway BRW 199*.....50 2
23 Feb 91 **IF I LOVE U 2 NITE** *Fourth & Broadway BRW 207*.....43 3
31 Aug 91 **YOUNG SOUL REBELS** *Big Life BLR 57*.....61 3
3 Apr 93 **I NEVER FELT LIKE THIS BEFORE** *Fourth & Broadway BRCD 263*.....15 5
5 Jun 93 **I WANNA HOLD ON TO YOU** *Fourth & Broadway BRCD 275*.....27 3
26 Jun 93 **WHISPER A PRAYER** *Fourth & Broadway BRCD 591*.....20 4
7 Aug 93 **TWO IN A MILLION** *Fourth & Broadway BRCD 285*.....51 2
4 Dec 93 **WHISPER A PRAYER** *Fourth & Broadway BRCD 287*.....65 1
8 Apr 95 **ONE** *Cooltempo CDCOOL 304*.....29 4
16 May 98 **STAY** *Cooltempo CDCOOL 334*.....40 2
22 Aug 98 **BLACK ANGEL** *Cooltempo 4958132*.....59 1
14 Nov 98 **BLACK ANGEL** *Cooltempo CDCOOL 341*.....72 1

[1] Mica Paris featuring Courtney Pine [2] Mica Paris and Will Downing

Ryan PARIS *France, male vocalist – Fabio Roscioli*

3 Sep 83 ● **DOLCE VITA** *Carrere CAR 289*.....5 10

PARIS & SHARP *UK, male production duo*

1 Dec 01 **APHRODITE** *Cream / Parlophone CREAM 16CD*.....61 1

John PARISH and Polly Jean HARVEY (see also PJ HARVEY) *US, male producer / multi-instrumentalist and UK, female vocalist*

23 Nov 96 **THAT WAS MY VEIL** *Island CID 648*.....75 1

The Simon PARK ORCHESTRA *UK, orchestra*

25 Nov 72 ★ **EYE LEVEL (THEME FROM THE TV SERIES 'VAN DER VALK')** (re) *Columbia DB 8946* £.....1 24

'Eye Level' made No.41 on its original visit to the chart before re-entering and peaking at No.1 in Sep 1973.

Graham PARKER and The RUMOUR *UK, male vocal / instrumental group (6 Albums: 35 Weeks, 3 Singles: 16 Weeks)*

27 Nov 76 **HEAT TREATMENT** *Vertigo 6360 137*.....52 2
19 Mar 77 **THE PINK PARKER EP** *Vertigo PARK 001*.....24 5
12 Nov 77 **STICK TO ME** *Vertigo 9102 017*.....19 4
22 Apr 78 **HEY LORD, DON'T ASK ME QUESTIONS** *Vertigo PARK 002*.....32 7
27 May 78 **PARKERILLA** *Vertigo 6641 797*.....14 5
7 Apr 79 **SQUEEZING OUT SPARKS** *Vertigo 9102 030*.....18 8
7 Jun 80 **THE UP ESCALATOR** *Stiff SEEZ 23*.....11 10
20 Mar 82 **TEMPORARY BEAUTY** *RCA PARK 100* [1].....50 4
27 Mar 82 **ANOTHER GREY AREA** *RCA RCALP 6029* [1].....40 6

[1] Graham Parker [1] Graham Parker

Tracks on The Pink Parker EP: Hold Back the Night / (Let Me Get) Sweet on You / White Honey / Soul Shoes.

Ray PARKER Jr (see also RAYDIO) *US, male vocalist / guitarist (1 Album: 7 Weeks, 4 Singles: 47 Weeks)*

25 Aug 84 ● **GHOSTBUSTERS** *Arista ARIST 580* ▲.....2 31
18 Jan 86 **GIRLS ARE MORE FUN** *Arista ARIST 641*.....46 4
3 Oct 87 **I DON'T THINK THAT MAN SHOULD SLEEP ALONE** *Geffen GEF 27*.....13 10
10 Oct 87 **AFTER DARK** *WEA WX 122*.....40 7
30 Jan 88 **OVER YOU** *Geffen GEF 33*.....65 2

Robert PARKER *US, male vocalist / saxophone*

4 Aug 66 **BAREFOOTIN'** *Island WI 286*.....24 8

Sara PARKER *US, female vocalist*

12 Apr 97 **MY LOVE IS DEEP** *Manifesto FESCD 22*.....22 2

Jimmy PARKINSON *Australia, male vocalist (3 Singles: 19 Weeks)*

2 Mar 56 ● **THE GREAT PRETENDER** *Columbia DB 3729*.....9 13
17 Aug 56 **WALK HAND IN HAND** (re) *Columbia DB 3775*.....26 2
9 Nov 56 **IN THE MIDDLE OF THE HOUSE** (re) *Columbia DB 3833*.....20 4

Alex PARKS *UK, female vocalist (2 Albums: 17 Weeks, 2 Singles: 13 Weeks)*

29 Nov 03 ● **MAYBE THAT'S WHAT IT TAKES** *Polydor 9814581*.....3 9
6 Dec 03 ● **INTRODUCTION** *Polydor 9866005*.....5 15
28 Feb 04 **CRY** *Polydor 9816985*.....13 4
5 Nov 05 **HONESTY** *Polydor 9873924*.....24 2

PARKS & WILSON
UK, male production duo – Michael Parks and Michael Wilson

9 Sep 00 **FEEL THE DRUM (EP)** *Hooj Choons HOOJ 099*.....71 1

Tracks on Feel the Drum (EP): My Orbit / The Dragon / My Orbit (re-mix) / Drum Parade (No UFOs).

John PARR *UK, male vocalist (1 Album: 2 Weeks, 3 Singles: 22 Weeks)*

14 Sep 85 ● **ST ELMO'S FIRE (MAN IN MOTION)** *London LON 73* ▲.....6 13
2 Nov 85 **JOHN PARR** *London LONLP 12*.....60 2
18 Jan 86 **NAUGHTY NAUGHTY** *London LON 80*.....58 3
30 Aug 86 **ROCK 'N' ROLL MERCENARIES** *Arista ARIST 666* [1].....31 6

[1] Meat Loaf featuring John Parr

1 January 1983	8 January 1983	15 January 1983	22 January 1983
SAVE YOUR LOVE Renée and Renato	**SAVE YOUR LOVE** Renée and Renato	**YOU CAN'T HURRY LOVE** Phil Collins	**YOU CAN'T HURRY LOVE** Phil Collins
THE JOHN LENNON COLLECTION John Lennon	**THE JOHN LENNON COLLECTION** John Lennon	**RAIDERS OF THE POP CHARTS** Various	**RAIDERS OF THE POP CHARTS** Various

THE FIRST ALBUM CHART

Until very recently the first albums chart was thought to have appeared in November 1958. However, some dogged excavation by chartologists Alan Smith, Keith Badman and Dave McAleer brought to light a Top Five heralded by Record Mirror in 1956. In the summer of that year, the paper promised something ground-breaking. "A new feature, the first of its kind in Britain. We shall be building the TOP FIVE charts for LPs. It is a feature which reflects a definite trend in the industry - an important feature which, to quote ourselves, is one to watch."

So was born, in the week ending 28 July 1956, a rival to the singles chart, the best-selling long-players chart. This interview with one of the men responsible for tracking down the earliest LP chart shows just how the discovery came about.

What made you first question the date of the earliest album chart?

ALAN SMITH It was always a feeling that I had, that November 1958 seemed a little late for the first ever LP chart. I always suspected that there might be an earlier listing.

Where did your research first take you?

ALAN SMITH I was actually researching the early history of singles charts, and Dave McAleer, who is Guinness Hit Singles/Albums researcher, kindly sent me photocopies from a May 1958 edition of Record Mirror. On viewing these, I saw a reference to the Top Five LP chart, which, as this was May 1958, meant it was at least a good six months older than the earliest Melody Maker LP chart.

When you investigated further back to a 1956 LP chart, what did you do next?

ALAN SMITH I then contacted Keith Badman, who is a well-known author and music researcher. Keith had far easier access to the music library at Colindale in London and was able to trace the origin of the Record Mirror LP chart, via the bound volumes of Record Mirror held at the library, back to 28 July 1956, the commencing date of the Record Mirror LP chart. We contacted David Roberts, the editor of the book of British Hit Singles & Albums, who was very interested on hearing this news. We also contacted Ajax Scott at Music Week and the Official UK Chart Company, who expressed surprise at this development. All parties agreed that a new milestone in chart history should be established and the first albums chart date would from that moment on be 28 July 1956.

What or who was the driving force or reason behind an LP chart in the 1950s?

ALAN SMITH As Record Mirror itself stated in its 28 July 1956 edition, sales of 10-inch and the new 12-inch format of long-playing records had reached a level where the paper felt a Top Five listing of the best-sellers could be accomplished and published. Additionally a chart was seen as a good way of advertising and plugging new product.

Have you any idea how the first Top Fives were calculated?

ALAN SMITH It would have been on the same basis as the singles chart. Record Mirror from 1955 to 1961 actually published the top 10 selling singles from each shop providing returns on its chart pages. Though the shops did tally exact sales figures, they would simplify things by sending a Top 10 list of titles without the precise sales figures. Record Mirror would then calculate 10 points for a No.1, nine points for No.2 and so on. Whether the same number of shops which provided singles lists also provided LP data is unknown, but it is likely that LP lists were tallied using the same method.

Why do you think the early Top Five album charts are worthy of inclusion in the book of British Hit Singles & Albums?

ALAN SMITH Well, now the book has carried this extra information, it is proven to be of historical interest! The very first LP charts coincided with the first ever manufacture and sale of the new 12-inch format of long-playing records. Record Mirror prided itself on giving a professional chart guide to singles and long-playing records. Also, it had never been certain that the 8 November 1958 Melody Maker LP chart had been heralded as the very first LP chart. Record Mirror made it quite clear that its Top Five LP chart of 28 July 1956 was the country's inaugural chart.

Finally, what first got you interested in the history of the UK's pop charts?

ALAN SMITH From when I was about 10 years old (1965) I had always studied the charts in my cousin's collection of music papers, and became fascinated in the varying positions in each week. However, it was my purchase of a book called The Pop Industry Inside Out by journalist Michael Cable that really intrigued me. Michael Cable was the first person to describe how charts were compiled and regulated. This book whetted my appetite to find out for myself all about the early years of chart compiling.

The front cover of the first Record Mirror to carry an albums chart and the inaugural Top Five.

Best Selling Long-Players

FIRST FIVE

1. SONGS FOR SWINGIN' LOVERS — Frank Sinatra (Capitol)
2. "CAROUSEL" — Film Sound Track (Capitol)
3. MEL TORME AT "THE CRESCENDO" — Mel Torme (Vogue-Coral)
4. AT "THE CRESCENDO" — Louis Armstrong (Brunswick)
5. "OKLAHOMA!" — Film Sound Track (Capitol)

Dean PARRISH *US, male vocalist – Phil Anastasi*

8 Feb 75	**I'M ON MY WAY** *UK USA 2*	**38**	5

Man PARRISH
US, male DJ / producer – Manny Parrish (3 Singles: 26 Weeks)

26 Mar 83	**HIP HOP, BE BOP (DON'T STOP)** *Polydor POSP 575*	**41**	6
23 Mar 85	**BOOGIE DOWN (BRONX)** *Boiling Point POSP 731*	**56**	4
13 Sep 86 ●	**MALE STRIPPER** (2re) *Bolts BOLTS 4* [1]	**4**	16

[1] Man 2 Man meet Man Parrish

'Male Stripper' made No.64 on its first chart visit followed by No.63 in Jan 1987 and No.4 on its second re-entry in Feb 1987.

Bill PARSONS *US, male vocalist*

10 Apr 59	**THE ALL AMERICAN BOY** *London HL 8798*	22	2

Record erroneously credited to Bill Parsons; actual vocalist is Bobby Bare.

The Alan PARSONS PROJECT *UK, male vocal / instrumental group (10 Albums: 38 Weeks, 2 Singles: 4 Weeks)*

28 Aug 76	TALES OF MYSTERY AND IMAGINATION *Charisma CDS 4003*	56	1
13 Aug 77	I ROBOT *Arista SPARTY 1016*	30	1
10 Jun 78	PYRAMID *Arista SPART 1054*	49	4
29 Sep 79	EVE *Arista SPARTY 1100*	74	1
15 Nov 80	THE TURN OF A FRIENDLY CARD *Arista DLART 1*	38	4
29 May 82	EYE IN THE SKY *Arista 204 666*	27	11
15 Jan 83	**OLD AND WISE** *Arista ARIST 494* [1]	**74**	1
26 Nov 83	THE BEST OF THE ALAN PARSONS PROJECT *Arista APP 1*	99	1
3 Mar 84	AMMONIA AVENUE *Arista 206 100*	24	8
10 Mar 84	**DON'T ANSWER ME** *Arista ARIST 553*	**58**	3
23 Feb 85	VULTURE CULTURE *Arista 206 577*	40	5
14 Feb 87	GAUDI *Arista 208 084*	66	2

[1] The Alan Parsons Project: lead vocals by Colin Blunstone

The PARTISANS *UK, male vocal / instrumental group*

19 Feb 83	THE PARTISANS *No Future PUNK 4*	94	1

PARTIZAN (see also CAMISRA; ESCRIMA; The GRIFTERS; TALL PAUL) *UK, male DJ / production duo – 'Tall Paul' Newman and Craig Daniel-Yefet (2 Singles: 3 Weeks)*

8 Feb 97	**DRIVE ME CRAZY** *Multiply CDMULTY 17*	36	2
6 Dec 97	**KEEP YOUR LOVE** *Multiply CDMULTY 29* [1]	53	1

[1] Partizan featuring Natalie Robb

PARTNERS IN KRYME
US, male rap duo – James Alpern and Richard Usher

21 Jul 90 ★	**TURTLE POWER** *SBK TURTLE 1*	**1**	10

David PARTON *UK, male vocalist*

15 Jan 77 ●	**ISN'T SHE LOVELY** *Pye 7N 45663*	**4**	9

Dolly PARTON
US, female vocalist / guitarist (10 Albums: 46 Weeks, 6 Singles: 34 Weeks)

15 May 76 ●	**JOLENE** *RCA 2675*	**7**	10
25 Nov 78	BOTH SIDES *Lotus WH 5006*	45	12
21 Feb 81	**9 TO 5** *RCA 25* ▲ $	**47**	5
12 Nov 83 ●	**ISLANDS IN THE STREAM** *RCA 378* [1] ▲ $	**7**	15
7 Apr 84	**HERE YOU COME AGAIN** *RCA 395* $	**75**	1
7 Sep 85	GREATEST HITS *RCA PL 84422*	74	1
14 Mar 87	TRIO *Warner Bros. 9254911* [1]	60	4
16 Apr 94	**THE DAY I FALL IN LOVE** *Columbia 6600282* [2]	**64**	2
22 Oct 94	THE GREATEST HITS *Telstar TCD 2739*	65	2
8 Nov 97	A LIFE IN MUSIC – ULTIMATE COLLECTION *RCA 74321443632*	38	3
26 Sep 98	HUNGRY AGAIN *MCA Nashville UMD 80522*	41	3
24 Feb 01	LITTLE SPARROW *Sanctuary SANCD 074*	30	6
3 Mar 01	GOLD – GREATEST HITS *RCA 74321840202*	23	5
20 Jul 02	HALOS & HORNS *Sanctuary SANCD 126*	37	4
19 Oct 02	**IF** *Sanctuary SANX 139*	**73**	1
2 Aug 03	ULTIMATE DOLLY PARTON *RCA 82876542012*	17	6

[1] Kenny Rogers and Dolly Parton [2] Dolly Parton and James Ingram
[1] Dolly Parton / Emmylou Harris / Linda Ronstadt

Stella PARTON *US, female vocalist*

22 Oct 77	**THE DANGER OF A STRANGER** *Elektra K 12272*	35	4

Alan PARTRIDGE *UK, male comedian – Steve Coogan*

18 Mar 95	KNOWING ME KNOWING YOU 3 *BBC Canned Laughter ZBBC 1671CD*	41	3

Don PARTRIDGE
UK, male vocalist / instrumentalist – one-man band (3 Singles: 32 Weeks)

7 Feb 68 ●	**ROSIE** *Columbia DB 8330*	**4**	12
29 May 68 ●	**BLUE EYES** *Columbia DB 8416*	3	13
19 Feb 69	**BREAKFAST ON PLUTO** *Columbia DB 8538*	26	7

The PARTRIDGE FAMILY (see also David CASSIDY) *US, male / female actor / vocal group (4 Albums: 13 Weeks, 5 Singles: 53 Weeks)*

13 Feb 71	**I THINK I LOVE YOU** *Bell 1130* [1] ▲ $	**18**	9
8 Jan 72	UP TO DATE *Bell SBLL 143*	46	2
26 Feb 72	**IT'S ONE OF THOSE NIGHTS (YES LOVE)** *Bell 1203* [1]	**11**	11
22 Apr 72	THE PARTRIDGE FAMILY SOUND MAGAZINE *Bell BELLS 206*	14	7
8 Jul 72 ●	**BREAKING UP IS HARD TO DO** *Bell MABEL 1* [1]	3	13
30 Sep 72	SHOPPING BAG *Bell BELLS 212*	28	3
9 Dec 72	CHRISTMAS CARD *Bell BELLS 214*	45	1
3 Feb 73 ●	**LOOKING THRU THE EYES OF LOVE** *Bell 1278* [2]	**9**	9
19 May 73 ●	**WALKING IN THE RAIN** *Bell 1293* [2]	**10**	11

[1] The Partridge Family starring Shirley Jones featuring David Cassidy
[2] The Partridge Family starring David Cassidy

PARTY ANIMALS *Holland, male instrumental / production duo and rappers (2 Singles: 3 Weeks)*

1 Jun 96	**HAVE YOU EVER BEEN MELLOW** *Mokum DB 17553*	56	1
19 Oct 96	**HAVE YOU EVER BEEN MELLOW (EP)** *Mokum DB 17413*	43	2

Tracks on Have You Ever Been Mellow (EP): Have You Ever Been Mellow / Hava Naquilla / Aquarius. The title track qualifies as a re-issue.

PARTY BOYS *Holland, male production group*

10 Jan 04	**BUILD ME UP BUTTERCUP 2003** *Liberty CDUP 001*	44	2

PARTY FAITHFUL *UK, male / female vocal / instrumental group*

22 Jul 95	**BRASS: LET THERE BE HOUSE** *Ore AG 10CD*	54	1

The PASADENAS
UK, male vocal group (2 Albums: 32 Weeks, 10 Singles: 57 Weeks)

28 May 88 ●	**TRIBUTE (RIGHT ON)** *CBS PASA 1*	**5**	14
17 Sep 88	**RIDING ON A TRAIN** *CBS PASA 2*	13	9
22 Oct 88 ●	TO WHOM IT MAY CONCERN *CBS 462877 1*	3	21
26 Nov 88	**ENCHANTED LADY** *CBS PASA 3*	31	6
12 May 90	**LOVE THING** *CBS PASA 4*	22	5
14 Jul 90	**REELING** *CBS PASA 5*	**75**	1
1 Feb 92 ●	**I'M DOING FINE NOW** *Columbia 6577187*	**4**	10
7 Mar 92 ●	YOURS SINCERELY *Columbia 4712642*	6	11
4 Apr 92	**MAKE IT WITH YOU** *Columbia 6579257*	20	4
6 Jun 92	**I BELIEVE IN MIRACLES** *Columbia 6580567*	34	3
29 Aug 92	**MOVING IN THE RIGHT DIRECTION** *Columbia 6583417*	49	2
21 Nov 92	**LET'S STAY TOGETHER** *Columbia 6587747*	22	3

29 January 1983	5 February 1983	12 February 1983	19 February 1983
DOWN UNDER Men at Work	DOWN UNDER Men at Work	DOWN UNDER Men at Work	TOO SHY Kajagoogoo
BUSINESS AS USUAL Men at Work	BUSINESS AS USUAL Men at Work	BUSINESS AS USUAL Men at Work	BUSINESS AS USUAL Men at Work

KEY UK No.1 ★ UK Top 10 ● Still on chart + UK entry at No.1 ■ US No.1 ▲ UK million seller £ US million seller $ Singles re-entries are listed as (re), (2re), (3re)… which signifies that the hit re-entered the chart once, twice or three times… — Peak Position / Weeks

PASCAL featuring Karen PARRY
(see also FLIP & FILL) *UK, male producer and female vocalist*

28 Dec 02 **I THINK WE'RE ALONE NOW** *All Around the World CDGLOBE 267* 23 5

PASSENGERS *Ireland / UK / Italy, male vocal / instrumental group*

18 Nov 95 **ORIGINAL SOUNDTRACKS 1** *Island CID 8043* 12 5
2 Dec 95 ● **MISS SARAJEVO** *Island CID 625* 6 9

Single features Bono and Luciano Pavarotti.

PASSION *UK, male vocal / rap group*

25 Jan 97 **SHARE YOUR LOVE (NO DIGGITY)** *Charm CRTCDS 269* 62 1

The PASSIONS *UK, male / female vocal / instrumental group*

31 Jan 81 **I'M IN LOVE WITH A GERMAN FILM STAR** *Polydor POSP 222* 25 8
3 Oct 81 **THIRTY THOUSAND FEET OVER CHINA** *Polydor POLS 1041* 92 1

PAT and MICK
UK, male DJ / vocal duo – Pat Sharp and Mick Brown (5 Singles: 27 Weeks)

9 Apr 88 **LET'S ALL CHANT / ON THE NIGHT** *PWL PWL 10* [1] 11 9
25 Mar 89 ● **I HAVEN'T STOPPED DANCING YET** *PWL PWL 33* 9 8
14 Apr 90 **USE IT UP AND WEAR IT OUT** *PWL PWL 55* 22 6
23 Mar 91 **GIMME SOME** *PWL PWL 75* 53 2
15 May 93 **HOT HOT HOT** *PWL International PARKCD 1* 47 2

[1] Mick and Pat

'On the Night' listed only from 4 Jun 1988. It peaked at No.70.

PATIENCE and PRUDENCE
US, female vocal duo – Patience and Prudence McIntyre (2 Singles: 8 Weeks)

2 Nov 56 **TONIGHT YOU BELONG TO ME** *London HLU 8321* $ 28 3
1 Mar 57 **GONNA GET ALONG WITHOUT YA NOW** (re) *London HLU 8369* 22 5

PATRA *Jamaica, female vocalist (3 Singles: 11 Weeks)*

25 Dec 93 **FAMILY AFFAIR** *Polydor PZCD 304* [1] 18 8
30 Sep 95 **PULL UP TO THE BUMPER** *Epic 6623942* 50 2
10 Aug 96 **WORK MI BODY** *Heavenly HVN 53CD* [2] 75 1

[1] Shabba Ranks featuring Patra and Terri & Monica [2] Monkey Mafia featuring Patra

PATRIC (see also WORLDS APART) *UK, male vocalist – Patric Osborne*

9 Jul 94 **LOVE ME** *Bell 7432125352* 54 2

Dee PATTEN *UK, male DJ / producer*

30 Jan 99 **WHO'S THE BAD MAN?** *Higher Ground HIGHS 15CD* 42 1

Kellee PATTERSON *US, female vocalist*

18 Feb 78 **IF IT DON'T FIT DON'T FORCE IT** *EMI International INT 544* 44 7

Rahsaan PATTERSON *US, male vocalist (2 Singles: 2 Weeks)*

26 Jul 97 **STOP BY** *MCA MCSTD 48055* 50 1
21 Mar 98 **WHERE YOU ARE** *MCA MCSTD 48073* 55 1

Billy PAUL *US, male vocalist – Paul Williams (7 Singles: 44 Weeks)*

13 Jan 73 **ME AND MRS JONES** *Epic EPC 1055* ▲ $ 12 9
12 Jan 74 **THANKS FOR SAVING MY LIFE** *Philadelphia International PIR 1928* 33 6
22 May 76 **LET'S MAKE A BABY** *Philadelphia International PIR 4144* 30 5
30 Apr 77 **LET 'EM IN** *Philadelphia International PIR 5143* 26 5
16 Jul 77 **YOUR SONG** *Philadelphia International PIR 5391* 37 7
19 Nov 77 **ONLY THE STRONG SURVIVE** *Philadelphia International PIR 5699* 33 7
14 Jul 79 **BRING THE FAMILY BACK** *Philadelphia International PIR 7456* 51 5

Chris PAUL
(see also ISOTONIK) *UK, male producer / guitarist (3 Singles: 8 Weeks)*

31 May 86 **EXPANSIONS '86 (EXPAND YOUR MIND)** *Fourth & Broadway BRW 48* [1] 58 5
21 Nov 87 **BACK IN MY ARMS** *Syncopate SY 5* 74 2
13 Aug 88 **TURN THE MUSIC UP** *Syncopate SY 13* 73 1

[1] Chris Paul featuring David Joseph

Les PAUL and Mary FORD *US, male guitarist – Les Polsfuss and female vocalist – Colleen Summers, b. 7 Jul 1924, d. 30 Sep 1977*

20 Nov 53 ● **VAYA CON DIOS (MAY GOD BE WITH YOU)** *Capitol CL 13943* ▲ 7 4

Lyn PAUL
(see also The NEW SEEKERS) *UK, female vocalist – Lynda Belcher*

28 Jun 75 **IT OUGHTA SELL A MILLION** *Polydor 2058 602* 37 6

Owen PAUL *UK, male vocalist – Owen McGee*

31 May 86 ● **MY FAVOURITE WASTE OF TIME** *Epic A 7125* 3 14

Sean PAUL (489 Top 500)
Dancehall reggae rap superstar, b. Sean Paul Henriques, 8 Jan 1975, Kingston, Jamaica, who scored his first local hit in 1996. In 2003, he had his first five UK Top 10 hits in just eight months, and at times had two singles in the Top 3 simultaneously (2 Albums: 54 Weeks, 10 Singles: 98 Weeks)

21 Sep 02 **GIMME THE LIGHT** (re) *VP VPCD 6400* 32 7
15 Feb 03 ● **GIMME THE LIGHT** (re-issue) *VP / Atlantic AT 0146CD* 5 10
10 May 03 ● **DUTTY ROCK** *Atlantic 7567836202* 2 45
24 May 03 ● **GET BUSY** *VP / Atlantic AT 0155CD* ▲ 4 7
19 Jul 03 **BREATHE** (import) *Arista 8786509842* [1] 59 3
9 Aug 03 ★ **BREATHE** *Arista 82876545722* [1] ■ 1 18
6 Sep 03 ● **LIKE GLUE** *VP / Atlantic AT 0162CD* 3 10
18 Oct 03 ● **BABY BOY** (re) *Columbia 6744082* [2] ▲ 2 11
17 Jan 04 ● **I'M STILL IN LOVE WITH YOU** *VP / Atlantic AT 0170CD* [3] 6 14
24 Sep 05 ● **WE BE BURNIN'** *VP / Atlantic AT 0218CDX* 2 14+
8 Oct 05 **THE TRINITY** *Atlantic / VP 7567837882* 11 9
10 Dec 05 **EVER BLAZIN'** *Atlantic / VP AT 0227CDX* 12 4+

[1] Blu Cantrell featuring Sean Paul [2] Beyoncé featuring Sean Paul [3] Sean Paul featuring Sasha

PAUL and PAULA *US, male / female vocal duo – Ray Hildebrand and Jill Jackson (2 Singles: 31 Weeks)*

14 Feb 63 ● **HEY PAULA** (re) *Philips 304012 BF* ▲ $ 8 17
18 Apr 63 ● **YOUNG LOVERS** *Philips 304016 BF* 9 14

Luciano PAVAROTTI (170 Top 500)
(see also PASSENGERS) *The world's best known opera singer, b. 12 Oct 1935, Modena, Italy. The tenor, who first took opera to the top of the pop charts and onto the world's football terraces, was also the first Italian to score a No.1 album (19 Albums: 298 Weeks, 5 Singles: 30 Weeks)*

15 May 82 **PAVAROTTI'S GREATEST HITS** *Decca D 2362* 95 1
30 Jun 84 **MAMMA** *Decca 411959* [1] 96 1
9 Aug 86 **THE PAVAROTTI COLLECTION** *Stylus SMR 8617* 12 34
16 Jul 88 **THE NEW PAVAROTTI COLLECTION LIVE!** *Stylus SMR 857* 63 8
17 Mar 90 ★ **THE ESSENTIAL PAVAROTTI** *Decca 4302101* 1 72

	26 February 1983	5 March 1983	12 March 1983	19 March 1983
UK No.1 SINGLES	TOO SHY Kajagoogoo	BILLIE JEAN Michael Jackson	TOTAL ECLIPSE OF THE HEART Bonnie Tyler	TOTAL ECLIPSE OF THE HEART Bonnie Tyler
UK No.1 ALBUMS	BUSINESS AS USUAL Men at Work	THRILLER Michael Jackson	WAR U2	THRILLER Michael Jackson

16 Jun 90 ● **NESSUN DORMA** *Decca PAV 03*..........2 11
1 Sep 90 ★ IN CONCERT *Decca 4304331* [2]..........1 78
20 Jul 91 ★ ESSENTIAL PAVAROTTI II *Decca 4304701*..........1 28
15 Feb 92 PAVAROTTI IN HYDE PARK *Decca 4363202*..........19 7
24 Oct 92 **MISERERE** *London LON 329* [1]..........**15** 5
4 Sep 93 TI AMO – PUCCINI'S GREATEST LOVE SONGS *Decca 4250992*..........23 4
12 Feb 94 MY HEART'S DELIGHT *Decca 4432602*..........44 4
30 Jul 94 **LIBIAMO / LA DONNA E MOBILE** *Teldec YZ 843CD* [2]..........21 4
10 Sep 94 ★ THE THREE TENORS IN CONCERT 1994 *Teldec 4509962002* [3] 1 26
30 Mar 96 TOGETHER FOR THE CHILDREN OF BOSNIA *Decca 4521002* [4]..........11 6
14 Dec 96 FOR WAR CHILD *Decca 4529002* [4]..........45 4
14 Dec 96 ● **LIVE LIKE HORSES** *Rocket LLHDD 1* [3]..........**9** 6
25 Oct 97 THE ULTIMATE COLLECTION *Decca 4580002*..........39 5
25 Jul 98 **YOU'LL NEVER WALK ALONE** *Decca 4607982* [4]..........**35** 4
29 Aug 98 THE THREE TENORS IN PARIS 1998 *Decca 4605002* [2]..........14 6
19 Jun 99 LOVE SONGS *Decca 4664002*..........26 6
23 Dec 00 THE THREE TENORS CHRISTMAS *Sony Classical SK 89131* [5]..........57 2
21 Jul 01 AMORE – THE LOVE ALBUM *Decca 4701302*..........41 2
15 Nov 03 TI ADORO *Decca 4754602*..........21 4

[1] Zucchero with Luciano Pavarotti [2] José Carreras featuring Placido Domingo and Luciano Pavarotti with Mehta [3] Elton John & Luciano Pavarotti [4] José Carreras, Placido Domingo and Luciano Pavarotti with Mehta [1] Luciano Pavarotti with the Henry Mancini Orchestra [2] José Carreras, Placido Domingo and Luciano Pavarotti [3] José Carreras, Placido Domingo and Luciano Pavarotti conducted by Zubin Mehta [4] Pavarotti and Friends [5] José Carreras, Placido Domingo and Luciano Pavarotti featuring Zubin Mehta

PAVEMENT (see also Stephen MALKMUS)

US, male vocal / instrumental group (6 Albums: 13 Weeks, 5 Singles: 6 Weeks)

25 Apr 92 SLANTED AND ENCHANTED *Big Cat ABB 34CD*..........72 1
28 Nov 92 **WATERY, DOMESTIC (EP)** *Big Cat ABB 38T*..........**58** 1
3 Apr 93 WESTING (BY MUSKET AND SEXTANT) *Big Cat ABBCD 40*..........30 2
12 Feb 94 **CUT YOUR HAIR** *Big Cat ABB 55SCD*..........**52** 1
26 Feb 94 CROOKED RAIN CROOKED RAIN *Big Cat ABB 56CD*..........15 3
22 Apr 95 WOWEE ZOWEE *Big Cat ABB 84CD*..........18 2
8 Feb 97 **STEREO** *Domino RUG 51CD*..........**48** 1
22 Feb 97 BRIGHTEN THE CORNERS *Domino Recordings WIGCD 31*..........27 2
3 May 97 **SHADY LANE** *Domino RUG 53CD*..........**40** 1
22 May 99 **CARROT ROPE** *Domino RUG 90CD1*..........**27** 2
19 Jun 99 TERROR TWILIGHT *Domino Recordings WIGCD 66*..........19 3

Tracks on Watery, Domestic (EP): Texas Never Whispers / Frontwards / Feed 'Em / The Linden Lions / Shoot the Singer (1 Sick Verse).

Rita PAVONE *Italy, female vocalist (2 Singles: 19 Weeks)*

1 Dec 66 **HEART** *RCA 1553*..........**27** 12
19 Jan 67 **YOU ONLY YOU** *RCA 1561*..........21 7

Tom PAXTON *US, male vocalist (3 Albums: 11 Weeks)*

13 Jun 70 NO.6 *Elektra 2469003*..........23 5
27 Mar 71 THE COMPLEAT TOM PAXTON *Elektra EKD 2003*..........18 5
1 Jul 72 PEACE WILL COME *Reprise K 44182*..........47 1

PAY AS U GO *UK, male rap / production group*

27 Apr 02 **CHAMPAGNE DANCE** *So Urban 6721362*..........13 4

Freda PAYNE *US, female vocalist (3 Singles: 30 Weeks)*

5 Sep 70 ★ **BAND OF GOLD** *Invictus INV 502* $..........1 19
21 Nov 70 **DEEPER AND DEEPER** *Invictus INV 505*..........33 9
27 Mar 71 **CHERISH WHAT IS DEAR TO YOU (WHILE IT'S NEAR TO YOU)** *Invictus INV 509*..........**46** 2

Tammy PAYNE *UK, female vocalist*

20 Jul 91 **TAKE ME NOW** *Talkin Loud TLK 12*..........**55** 2

PEACE BY PIECE *UK, male vocal group (2 Singles: 2 Weeks)*

21 Sep 96 **SWEET SISTER** *Blanco Y Negro NEG 94CD*..........**46** 1
25 Apr 98 **NOBODY'S BUSINESS** *Blanco Y Negro NEG 110CD1*..........**50** 1

Heather PEACE *UK, female vocalist*

13 May 00 **THE ROSE** *RCA 74321742892*..........**56** 1

PEACH *UK / Belgium, female / male vocal / production group*

17 Jan 98 **ON MY OWN** *Mute CDMUTE 215*..........**69** 1

PEACHES

Canada, female producer / vocalist – Merrill Nisker (2 Singles: 5 Weeks)

15 Jun 02 **SET IT OFF** *Epic 6726862*..........36 2
17 Jan 04 **KICK IT** *XL Recordings XLS 176CD* [1]..........39 3

[1] Peaches featuring Iggy Pop

PEACHES and HERB *US, female / male vocal duo – Linda Green and Herbert Feemster (2 Singles: 23 Weeks)*

20 Jan 79 **SHAKE YOUR GROOVE THING** *Polydor 2066 992* $..........26 10
21 Apr 79 ● **REUNITED** *Polydor POSP 43* ▲ $..........**4** 13

PEARL JAM (441 Top 500)

Stadium-packing Seattle rock band fronted by Eddie Vedder, b. Edward Mueller, 23 Dec 1966, Illinois, US. The quintet that evolved from revered pioneers Mother Love Bone have released over 50 live albums, with a record 18 of them charting Stateside (9 Albums: 120 Weeks, 15 Singles: 43 Weeks)

15 Feb 92 **ALIVE** *Epic 6575727*..........**16** 6
7 Mar 92 TEN *Epic 4688842*..........18 65
18 Apr 92 **EVEN FLOW** *Epic 6578577*..........27 3
26 Sep 92 **JEREMY** *Epic 6582587*..........15 4
23 Oct 93 ● VS *Epic 4745492* ▲..........2 24
1 Jan 94 **DAUGHTER** *Epic 6600202*..........**18** 5
28 May 94 **DISSIDENT** *Epic 6604415*..........**14** 4
26 Nov 94 ● **SPIN THE BLACK CIRCLE** *Epic 6610362*..........**10** 3
3 Dec 94 ● VITALOGY *Epic 4778611* ▲..........4 11
25 Feb 95 **NOT FOR YOU** *Epic 6612032*..........**34** 2
16 Dec 95 **MERKINBALL** *Epic 6627162*..........**25** 3
17 Aug 96 **WHO YOU ARE** *Epic 6635392*..........**18** 2
7 Sep 96 ● NO CODE *Epic 4844482* ▲..........3 5
31 Jan 98 **GIVEN TO FLY** *Epic 6653942*..........12 3
14 Feb 98 ● YIELD *Epic 4893652*..........7 7
23 May 98 **WISHLIST** *Epic 6657902*..........30 2
5 Dec 98 LIVE – ON TWO LEGS *Epic 4928592*..........68 1
14 Aug 99 **LAST KISS** *Epic 6674791*..........**42** 1
13 May 00 **NOTHING AS IT SEEMS** *Epic 6693742*..........22 2
27 May 00 ● BINAURAL *Epic 4945902*..........5 4
22 Jul 00 **LIGHT YEARS** *Epic 6696282*..........**52** 1
9 Nov 02 **I AM MINE** *Epic 6733082*..........26 2
23 Nov 02 RIOT ACT *Epic 5100002*..........34 2
11 Dec 04 REARVIEWMIRROR (GREATEST HITS '91-'03) *Epic 5191132*..........58 1

'Merkinball' is the title of the single featuring 'I Got Id' and 'Long Road'.

The PEARLS

UK, female vocal duo – Lyn Cornell and Ann Simmons (4 Singles: 24 Weeks)

27 May 72 **THIRD FINGER, LEFT HAND** *Bell 1217*..........31 6
23 Sep 72 **YOU CAME, YOU SAW, YOU CONQUERED** *Bell 1254*..........32 5
24 Mar 73 **YOU ARE EVERYTHING** *Bell 1284*..........**41** 3
1 Jun 74 ● **GUILTY** *Bell 1352*..........**10** 10

Johnny PEARSON Orchestra

UK, orchestra – leader Johnny Pearson – piano

18 Dec 71 ● **SLEEPY SHORES** *Penny Farthing PEN 778*..........**8** 15

David PEASTON *UK, male vocalist*

26 Aug 89 INTRODUCING ... DAVID PEASTON *Geffen 924228 1*..........66 1

26 March 1983	2 April 1983	9 April 1983	16 April 1983
IS THERE SOMETHING I SHOULD KNOW? Duran Duran	**IS THERE SOMETHING I SHOULD KNOW?** Duran Duran	**LET'S DANCE** David Bowie	**LET'S DANCE** David Bowie
THE HURTING Tears for Fears	**THE FINAL CUT** Pink Floyd	**THE FINAL CUT** Pink Floyd	**FASTER THAN THE SPEED OF NIGHT** Bonnie Tyler

KEY UK No.1 ★ UK Top 10 ● Still on chart + UK entry at No.1 ■ US No.1 ▲ UK million seller £ US million seller $
Singles re-entries are listed as (re), (2re), (3re)… which signifies that the hit re-entered the chart once, twice or three times…
Peak Position / Weeks

PEBBLES
US, female vocalist – Perri McKissack (1 Album: 4 Weeks, 3 Singles: 17 Weeks)

19 Mar 88 ● **GIRLFRIEND** *MCA MCA 1233* 8 11
14 May 88 **PEBBLES** *MCA MCF 3418* 56 4
28 May 88 **MERCEDES BOY** *MCA MCA 1248* 42 4
27 Oct 90 **GIVING YOU THE BENEFIT** *MCA MCA 1448* 73 2

The PEDDLERS
UK, male vocal / instrumental group (2 Albums: 16 Weeks, 3 Singles: 14 Weeks)

7 Jan 65 **LET THE SUNSHINE IN** *Philips BF 1375* 50 1
16 Mar 68 **FREE WHEELERS** *CBS SBPG 63183* 27 13
23 Aug 69 **BIRTH** *CBS 4449* 17 9
31 Jan 70 **GIRLIE** *CBS 4720* 34 4
7 Feb 70 **BIRTHDAY** *CBS 63682* 16 3

PEE BEE SQUAD
UK, male vocalist – Paul Burnett

5 Oct 85 **RUGGED AND MEAN, BUTCH AND ON SCREEN** *Project PRO 3* 52 3

Ann PEEBLES
US, female vocalist

20 Apr 74 **I CAN'T STAND THE RAIN** (re) *London HLU 10428* 41 3

The PEECH BOYS
US, male vocal / instrumental group

30 Oct 82 **DON'T MAKE ME WAIT** *TMT TMT 7001* 49 3

Kevin PEEK
(see also SKY) *UK, male guitarist (2 Albums: 8 Weeks)*

21 Mar 81 **AWAKENING** *Ariola ARL 5065* 52 2
13 Oct 84 **BEYOND THE PLANETS** *Telstar STAR 2244* [1] 64 6

[1] Kevin Peek and Rick Wakeman

Beyond the Planets also features Jeff Wayne, with narration by Patrick Allen.

Donald PEERS
UK, male vocalist, b. 10 Jul 1908, d. 9 Aug 1973 (3 Singles: 28 Weeks)

29 Dec 66 **GAMES THAT LOVERS PLAY** *Columbia DB 8079* 46 1
18 Dec 68 ● **PLEASE DON'T GO** (re) *Columbia DB 8502* 3 21
24 Jun 72 **GIVE ME ONE MORE CHANCE** *Decca F 13302* 36 6

PELE
UK, male / female vocal / instrumental group (3 Singles: 3 Weeks)

15 Feb 92 **MEGALOMANIA** *M&G MAGS 20* 73 1
13 Jun 92 **FAIR BLOWS THE WIND FOR FRANCE** *M&G MAGS 24* 62 1
31 Jul 93 **FAT BLACK HEART** *M&G MAGCD 43* 75 1

Marti PELLOW
(see also WET WET WET) *UK, male vocalist – Mark McLoughlin (3 Albums: 16 Weeks, 3 Singles: 9 Weeks)*

16 Jun 01 ● **CLOSE TO YOU** *Mercury MERCD 532* 9 6
7 Jul 01 ● **SMILE** *Mercury 5860032* 7 7
1 Dec 01 **I'VE BEEN AROUND THE WORLD** *Mercury 5887772* 28 2
30 Nov 02 **MARTI PELLOW SINGS THE HITS OF WET WET WET & SMILE** *UMTV TV 0632902* 36 8
22 Nov 03 **A LOT OF LOVE** *Universal TV 9813763* 59 1
29 Nov 03 **BETWEEN THE COVERS** *Universal TV 9812067* 66 1

Debbie PENDER
US, female vocalist

30 May 98 **MOVIN' ON** *AM:PM 5826492* 41 1

Teddy PENDERGRASS
(see also Harold MELVIN and The BLUENOTES) *US, male vocalist – Theodore Pendergrass (2 Albums: 11 Weeks, 6 Singles: 24 Weeks)*

21 May 77 **THE WHOLE TOWN'S LAUGHING AT ME** *Philadelphia International PIR 5116* 44 3
28 Oct 78 **ONLY YOU / CLOSE THE DOOR** *Philadelphia International PIR 6713* 41 6
23 May 81 **TWO HEARTS** *20th Century TC 2492* [1] 49 5
25 Jan 86 **HOLD ME** *Asylum EKR 32* [2] 44 5
21 May 88 **JOY** *Elektra 960775 1* 45 8
28 May 88 **JOY** *Elektra EKR 75* 58 3
19 Nov 94 **THE MORE I GET THE MORE I WANT** *X-clusive XCLU 011CD* [3] 35 2
20 Mar 04 **SATISFACTION GUARANTEED – THE VERY BEST OF TEDDY PENDERGRASS** *WSM WSMCD 166* 26 3

[1] Stephanie Mills featuring Teddy Pendergrass [2] Teddy Pendergrass with Whitney Houston [3] KWS featuring Teddy Pendergrass

PENDULUM
Australia, male DJ / production trio (1 Album: 1 Week, 4 Singles: 6 Weeks)

6 Mar 04 **ANOTHER PLANET / VOYAGER** *Breakbeat Kaos BBK 003* 46 2
30 Apr 05 **GUNS AT DAWN** *Breakbeat Kaos BBK 008* [1] 71 1
9 Jul 05 **TARANTULA / FASTEN YOUR SEATBELT** *Breakbeat Kaos BBK 009SCD* [2] 60 1
6 Aug 05 **HOLD YOUR COLOUR** *Breakbeat Kaos BBK 002CD* 68 1
1 Oct 05 **SLAM / OUT HERE** *Breakbeat Kaos BBK 011SCD* 34 2

[1] DJ Baron featuring Pendulum [2] Pendulum & Fresh featuring Spyda & Tenor Fly / Pendulum featuring The Freestylers

PENETRATION
UK, male / female vocal / instrumental group (2 Albums: 8 Weeks)

28 Oct 78 **MOVING TARGETS** *Virgin V 2109* 22 4
6 Oct 79 **COMING UP FOR AIR** *Virgin V 2131* 36 4

PENGUIN CAFE ORCHESTRA
UK, male instrumental group

4 Apr 87 **SIGNS OF LIFE** *Edition EG EGED 50* 49 5

Ce Ce PENISTON
US, female vocalist – Cecelia Peniston (2 Albums: 21 Weeks, 12 Singles: 53 Weeks)

12 Oct 91 **FINALLY** *A&M AM 822* 29 7
11 Jan 92 ● **WE GOT A LOVE THANG** *A&M AM 846* 6 8
18 Jan 92 **I LIKE IT** *A&M AM 847* [1] 58 2
8 Feb 92 ● **FINALLY** *A&M 3971822* 10 19
21 Mar 92 ● **FINALLY** (re-issue) *A&M AM 858* 2 8
23 May 92 ● **KEEP ON WALKIN'** *A&M AM 878* 10 6
5 Sep 92 **CRAZY LOVE** *A&M AM 0060* 44 3
12 Dec 92 **INSIDE THAT I CRIED** *A&M AM 0121* 42 2
15 Jan 94 **I'M IN THE MOOD** *A&M 5804552* 16 4
5 Feb 94 **THOUGHT 'YA KNEW** *A&M 5402012* 31 2
2 Apr 94 **KEEP GIVIN' ME YOUR LOVE** *A&M 5805492* 36 2
6 Aug 94 **HIT BY LOVE** *A&M 5806932* 33 2
13 Sep 97 **FINALLY** (re-mix) *AM:PM 5823432* 26 5
7 Feb 98 **SOMEBODY ELSE'S GUY** *AM:PM 5825112* 13 4

[1] Overweight Pooch featuring Ce Ce Peniston

Dawn PENN
Jamaica, female vocalist – Dawn Pickering

11 Jun 94 ● **YOU DON'T LOVE ME (NO, NO, NO)** *Big Beat A 8295CD* 3 12
9 Jul 94 **NO NO NO** *Big Beat 7567923652* 51 2

Barbara PENNINGTON
US, female vocalist (2 Singles: 8 Weeks)

27 Apr 85 **FAN THE FLAME** *Record Shack SOHO 37* 62 3
27 Jul 85 **ON A CROWDED STREET** *Record Shack SOHO 49* 57 5

Tricia PENROSE
UK, female actor / vocalist (2 Singles: 2 Weeks)

7 Dec 96 **WHERE DID OUR LOVE GO** *RCA 74321428152* 71 1
4 Mar 00 **DON'T WANNA BE ALONE** *Doop DP 2001CD* 44 1

PENTANGLE
UK, male / female vocal (Jacqui McShee) / instrumental group (3 Albums: 39 Weeks, 2 Singles: 4 Weeks)

15 Jun 68 **THE PENTANGLE** *Transatlantic TRA 162* 21 9

	23 April 1983	30 April 1983	7 May 1983	14 May 1983
UK No.1 SINGLES	LET'S DANCE David Bowie	TRUE Spandau Ballet	TRUE Spandau Ballet	TRUE Spandau Ballet
UK No.1 ALBUMS	LET'S DANCE David Bowie	LET'S DANCE David Bowie	LET'S DANCE David Bowie	TRUE Spandau Ballet

28 May 69 **ONCE I HAD A SWEETHEART** *Big T BIG 124* **46** 1
1 Nov 69 ● BASKET OF LIGHT *Transatlantic TRA 205* 5 28
14 Feb 70 **LIGHT FLIGHT** (re) *Big T BIG 128* **43** 3
12 Dec 70 CRUEL SISTER *Transatlantic TRA 228* 51 2

PENTHOUSE 4 *UK, male vocal / instrumental duo*

23 Apr 88 **BUST THIS HOUSE DOWN** *Syncopate SY 10* **56** 3

PEOPLES CHOICE

US, male vocal / instrumental group (2 Singles: 9 Weeks)

20 Sep 75 **DO IT ANY WAY YOU WANNA** *Philadelphia International PIR 3500* **$** 36 5
21 Jan 78 **JAM, JAM, JAM (ALL NIGHT LONG)** *Philadelphia International PIR 5891* [1] **40** 4

[1] People's Choice

PEPE DELUXE *Finland, male DJ / production group*

26 May 01 **BEFORE YOU LEAVE** *Catskills / INCredible 6712392* 20 3

Danny PEPPERMINT and The JUMPING JACKS

US, male vocal / instrumental group – leader Danny Lamego

18 Jan 62 **THE PEPPERMINT TWIST** *London HLL 9478* 26 8

The PEPPERS *France, male instrumental group*

26 Oct 74 ● **PEPPER BOX** *Spark SRL 1100* 6 12

PEPSI and SHIRLIE *UK, female vocal duo – Helen DeMacque and Shirley Holliman (1 Album: 2 Weeks, 4 Singles: 24 Weeks)*

17 Jan 87 ● **HEARTACHE** *Polydor POSP 837* 2 12
30 May 87 ● **GOODBYE STRANGER** *Polydor POSP 865* 9 7
26 Sep 87 **CAN'T GIVE ME LOVE** *Polydor POSP 885* **58** 3
7 Nov 87 ALL RIGHT NOW *Polydor POLH 38* 69 2
12 Dec 87 **ALL RIGHT NOW** *Polydor POSP 896* **50** 2

PERAN (see also Oris JAY presents DELSENA)

Holland, male producer – Peran van Dijk

23 Mar 02 **GOOD TIME** *Incentive CENT 37CDS* 37 2

PERCEPTION *UK, male vocal group*

7 Mar 92 **FEED THE FEELING** *Talkin Loud TLK 17* **58** 2

The listed flip side of 'Feed the Feeling' was 'Three Times a Maybe' by K Creative.

Lance PERCIVAL *UK, male vocalist / comedian*

28 Oct 65 **SHAME AND SCANDAL IN THE FAMILY** *Parlophone R 5335* 37 3

PERCY FILTH (see also LIL' DEVIOUS)

UK, male production duo – Mark Baker and Gary Little

9 Aug 03 **SHOW ME YOUR MONKEY** *Southern Fried ECB 53CDS* **72** 1

A PERFECT CIRCLE *US, male vocal / instrumental group (2 Albums: 2 Weeks, 2 Singles: 2 Weeks)*

3 Jun 00 MER DE NOMS *Virgin CDVUS 173* 55 1
18 Nov 00 **THE HOLLOW** *Virgin VUSCD 181* **72** 1
13 Jan 01 **3 LIBRAS** *Virgin VUSCD 184* **49** 1
27 Sep 03 THIRTEENTH STEP *Virgin CDVUS 247* 37 1

PERFECT DAY *UK, male vocal / instrumental group (2 Singles: 4 Weeks)*

21 Jan 89 **LIBERTY TOWN** *London LON 214* **58** 3
1 Apr 89 **JANE** *London LON 188* **68** 1

PERFECT PHASE *Holland, male production duo – Freek Fontein and Willem Faber (2 Singles: 8 Weeks)*

25 Dec 99 **HORNY HORNS** *Positiva CDTIV 123* 21 7
12 Jun 04 **BLOW YOUR HORNY HORNS** *Feverpitch 12FEV 3* **75** 1

PERFECTLY ORDINARY PEOPLE *UK, male vocal / instrumental group*

22 Oct 88 **THEME FROM P.O.P.** *Urban URB 25* **61** 3

PERFECTO ALLSTARZ (see also OAKENFOLD; RISE; VIRUS)

UK, male instrumental / production duo – Paul Oakenfold and Steve Osborne

4 Feb 95 ● **REACH UP (PAPA'S GOT A BRAND NEW PIG BAG)** *Perfecto YZ 892CD* 6 11

PERFUME *UK, male vocal / instrumental group*

10 Feb 96 **HAVEN'T SEEN YOU** *Aromasound AROMA 005CDS* **71** 1

Emilio PERICOLI *Italy, male vocalist*

28 Jun 62 **AL DI LA** *Warner Bros. WB 69* 30 14

Carl PERKINS *US, male vocalist, b. 9 Apr 1932, d. 19 Jan 1998*

18 May 56 ● **BLUE SUEDE SHOES** *London HLU 8271* **$** 10 8
15 Apr 78 OL' BLUE SUEDES IS BACK *Jet UATV 30146* 38 3

PERPETUAL MOTION *UK, male instrumental / production group*

2 May 98 **KEEP ON DANCIN' (LET'S GO)** *Positiva CDTIV 90* 12 5

Lee 'Scratch' PERRY

(see also The UPSETTERS) *Jamaica, male producer / vocalist*

26 Jul 97 ARKOLOGY *Island Jamaica CRNCD 6* 49 1

Steve PERRY *UK, male vocalist*

4 Aug 60 **STEP BY STEP** *HMV POP 745* **41** 1

Steve PERRY (see also JOURNEY) *US, male vocalist (2 Albums: 3 Weeks)*

14 Jul 84 STREET TALK *CBS 25967* 59 2
27 Aug 94 FOR THE LOVE OF STRANGE MEDICINE *Columbia 4771962* 64 1

Nina PERSSON and David ARNOLD (see also The CARDIGANS)

Sweden, female vocalist and UK, male multi-instrumentalist / producer

29 Apr 00 **THEME FROM 'RANDALL & HOPKIRK (DECEASED)'** *Island CID 762* **49** 1

Jon PERTWEE *UK, male actor / vocalist, b. 7 Jul 1919, d. 20 May 1996*

1 Mar 80 **WORZEL'S SONG** *Decca F 13885* 33 7

PESHAY

UK, male DJ / producer – Paul Pesce (1 Album: 1 Week, 5 Singles: 6 Weeks)

9 May 98 **MILES FROM HOME** *Mo Wax MW 092* **75** 1
17 Jul 99 **SWITCH** *Island Blue PFACD 1* **59** 1
31 Jul 99 MILES FROM HOME *Island Blue PFA 1CD* 63 1
19 Feb 00 **TRULY** *Island Blue PFACD 4* [1] **55** 1
4 May 02 **YOU GOT ME BURNING / FUZION** *Cubik Music CUBIKSAMPCD 001CD* [2] **41** 2
24 Aug 02 **SATISFY MY LOVE** *Cubik Music CUBIK 002CD* [3] **67** 1

[1] Peshay featuring Kym Mazelle [2] Peshay featuring Co-ordinate
[3] Peshay vs Flytronix

PESTALOZZI CHILDREN'S CHOIR

International, male / female vocal group

26 Dec 81 SONGS OF JOY *K-Tel NE 1140* 65 2

PET SHOP BOYS 59 Top 500

Critically-acclaimed and quintessentially English duo: former assistant editor of Smash Hits, Neil Tennant (v), and Chris Lowe (k). No duo has amassed more chart entries than this act, whose first hit was voted Best British Single at the 1987 BRIT Awards (14 Albums: 352 Weeks, 38 Singles: 244 Weeks)

23 Nov 85 ★ **WEST END GIRLS** *Parlophone R 6115* ▲ 1 15
8 Mar 86 **LOVE COMES QUICKLY** *Parlophone R 6116* 19 9

21 May 1983	28 May 1983	4 June 1983	11 June 1983
TRUE Spandau Ballet	CANDY GIRL New Edition	EVERY BREATH YOU TAKE The Police	EVERY BREATH YOU TAKE The Police
THRILLER Michael Jackson	THRILLER Michael Jackson	THRILLER Michael Jackson	THRILLER Michael Jackson

KEY: UK No.1 ★ UK Top 10 ● Still on chart + UK entry at No.1 ■ US No.1 ▲ UK million seller £ US million seller $
Singles re-entries are listed as (re), (2re), (3re)… which signifies that the hit re-entered the chart once, twice or three times…
Peak Position / Weeks

5 Apr 86 ● PLEASE *Parlophone PSB 1* 3 82
31 May 86 OPPORTUNITIES (LET'S MAKE LOTS OF MONEY) *Parlophone R 6129* 11 8
4 Oct 86 ● SUBURBIA *Parlophone R 6140* 8 9
29 Nov 86 DISCO *EMI PRG 1001* 15 72
27 Jun 87 ★ IT'S A SIN *Parlophone R 6158* 1 11
22 Aug 87 ● WHAT HAVE I DONE TO DESERVE THIS? *Parlophone R 6163* [1] 2 9
19 Sep 87 ● ACTUALLY *Parlophone PCSD 104* 2 59
24 Oct 87 ● RENT *Parlophone R 6168* 8 7
12 Dec 87 ★ ALWAYS ON MY MIND *Parlophone R 6171* 1 11
2 Apr 88 ★ HEART *Parlophone R 6177* 1 10
24 Sep 88 ● DOMINO DANCING *Parlophone R 6190* 7 8
22 Oct 88 ● INTROSPECTIVE *Parlophone PCS 7325* 2 39
26 Nov 88 ● LEFT TO MY OWN DEVICES *Parlophone R 6198* 4 8
8 Jul 89 ● IT'S ALRIGHT *Parlophone R 6220* 5 8
6 Oct 90 ● SO HARD *Parlophone R 6269* 4 6
3 Nov 90 ● BEHAVIOUR *Parlophone PCSD 113* 2 14
24 Nov 90 BEING BORING *Parlophone R 6275* 20 8
23 Mar 91 ● WHERE THE STREETS HAVE NO NAME – CAN'T TAKE MY EYES OFF YOU / HOW CAN YOU EXPECT TO BE TAKEN SERIOUSLY *Parlophone R 6285* 4 8
8 Jun 91 JEALOUSY *Parlophone R 6283* 12 5
26 Oct 91 DJ CULTURE *Parlophone R 6301* 13 3
16 Nov 91 ● DISCOGRAPHY – THE COMPLETE SINGLES COLLECTION *Parlophone PMTV 3* 3 30
23 Nov 91 DJ CULTURE (re-mix) *Parlophone 12RX 6301* 40 2
21 Dec 91 WAS IT WORTH IT? *Parlophone R 6306* 24 4
12 Jun 93 ● CAN YOU FORGIVE HER *Parlophone CDR 6348* 7 7
18 Sep 93 ● GO WEST *Parlophone CDR 6356* 2 9
9 Oct 93 ★ VERY *Parlophone CDPCSD 143* ■ 1 22
11 Dec 93 I WOULDN'T NORMALLY DO THIS KIND OF THING *Parlophone CDR 6370* 13 7
16 Apr 94 LIBERATION *Parlophone CDR 6377* 14 5
11 Jun 94 ● ABSOLUTELY FABULOUS *Spaghetti CDR 6382* [2] 6 7
10 Sep 94 YESTERDAY WHEN I WAS MAD *Parlophone CDR 6386* 13 4
24 Sep 94 ● DISCO 2 *Parlophone CDPCSD 159* 6 4
5 Aug 95 PANINARO *Parlophone CDR 6414* 15 4
19 Aug 95 ● ALTERNATIVE *Parlophone CDPCSD 166* 2 5
4 May 96 ● BEFORE *Parlophone CDR 6431* 7 5
24 Aug 96 ● SE A VIDA É (THAT'S THE WAY LIFE IS) *Parlophone CDR 6443* 8 8
14 Sep 96 ● BILINGUAL *Parlophone CDPCSD 170* 4 8
23 Nov 96 SINGLE *Parlophone CDR 6452* 14 3
29 Mar 97 ● A RED LETTER DAY *Parlophone CDR 6460* 9 3
5 Jul 97 ● SOMEWHERE *Parlophone CDR 6470* 9 5
31 Jul 99 I DON'T KNOW WHAT YOU WANT BUT I CAN'T GIVE IT ANYMORE *Parlophone CDR 6523* 15 3
9 Oct 99 NEW YORK CITY BOY *Parlophone CDR 6525* 14 4
23 Oct 99 ● NIGHTLIFE *Parlophone 5218572* 7 3
15 Jan 00 ● YOU ONLY TELL ME YOU LOVE ME WHEN YOU'RE DRUNK *Parlophone CDR 6533* 8 4
30 Mar 02 HOME AND DRY *Parlophone CDRS 6572* 14 6
13 Apr 02 ● RELEASE *Parlophone 5381502* 7 4
27 Jul 02 I GET ALONG *Parlophone CDRS 6581* 18 3
15 Feb 03 DISCO 3 *Parlophone 5821402* 36 1
29 Nov 03 ● MIRACLES *Parlophone CDR 6620* 10 4
6 Dec 03 THE HITS – POPART *Parlophone 5950932* 30 9
10 Apr 04 FLAMBOYANT *Parlophone CDRS 6629* 12 4

[1] Pet Shop Boys and Dusty Springfield [2] Absolutely Fabulous

PETER and GORDON
UK, male vocal duo – Peter Asher and Gordon Waller (1 Album: 1 Week, 7 Singles: 77 Weeks)

12 Mar 64 ★ A WORLD WITHOUT LOVE *Columbia DB 7225* ▲ $ 1 14
4 Jun 64 ● NOBODY I KNOW *Columbia DB 7292* 10 11
20 Jun 64 PETER AND GORDON *Columbia 33SX 1630* 18 1
8 Apr 65 ● TRUE LOVE WAYS *Columbia DB 7524* 2 15
24 Jun 65 ● TO KNOW YOU IS TO LOVE YOU *Columbia DB 7617* 5 10
21 Oct 65 BABY I'M YOURS *Columbia DB 7729* 19 9
24 Feb 66 WOMAN *Columbia DB 7834* 28 7
22 Sep 66 LADY GODIVA *Columbia DB 8003* 16 11

PETER, PAUL and MARY
US, male / female vocal / instrumental group (4 Albums: 26 Weeks, 4 Singles: 38 Weeks)

10 Oct 63 BLOWING IN THE WIND *Warner Bros. WB 104* $ 13 16
4 Jan 64 PETER PAUL AND MARY *Warner Bros. WM 4064* ▲ 18 1
21 Mar 64 IN THE WIND *Warner Bros. WM 8142* ▲ 11 19
16 Apr 64 TELL IT ON THE MOUNTAIN *Warner Bros. WB 127* 33 4
15 Oct 64 THE TIMES THEY ARE A-CHANGIN' *Warner Bros. WB 142* 44 2
13 Feb 65 IN CONCERT VOLUME 1 *Warner Bros. WM 8158* 20 2
17 Jan 70 ● LEAVING ON A JET PLANE *Warner Bros. WB 7340* ▲ $ 2 16
5 Sep 70 TEN YEARS TOGETHER *Warner Bros. WS 2552* 60 4

PETERS and LEE
307 Top 500 (see also LEE)

London-based Opportunity Knocks-winning MOR duo: Lennie Peters (p/v), b. 1939, d. 10 Oct 1992, and Diane Lee (v). Peters, Rolling Stone Charlie Watts' uncle and blind since 16, first recorded in 1962 backed by The Migil Five. Lee married Wizzard's Rick Price (5 Albums: 166 Weeks, 5 Singles: 57 Weeks)

26 May 73 ★ WELCOME HOME *Philips 6006 307* 1 24
30 Jun 73 ★ WE CAN MAKE IT *Philips 6308 165* 1 55
3 Nov 73 BY YOUR SIDE *Philips 6006 339* 39 4
22 Dec 73 ● BY YOUR SIDE *Philips 6308 192* 9 48
20 Apr 74 ● DON'T STAY AWAY TOO LONG *Philips 6006 388* 3 15
17 Aug 74 RAINBOW *Philips 6006 406* 17 7
21 Sep 74 ● RAINBOW *Philips 6308 208* 6 27
4 Oct 75 ● FAVOURITES *Philips 9109 205* 2 32
6 Mar 76 HEY MR MUSIC MAN *Philips 6006 502* 16 7
18 Dec 76 INVITATION *Philips 9101 027* 44 4

Jonathan PETERS presents LUMINAIRE
US, male DJ / producer

24 Jul 99 FLOWER DUET *Pelican PELID 001* 75 1

Ray PETERSON
US, male vocalist, b. 23 Apr 1939, d. 25 Jan 2005 (3 Singles: 9 Weeks)

4 Sep 59 THE WONDER OF YOU *RCA 1131* 23 1
24 Mar 60 ANSWER ME *RCA 1175* 47 1
19 Jan 61 CORINNA, CORINNA (re) *London HLX 9246* 41 7

Tom PETTY and The HEARTBREAKERS
(see also TRAVELING WILBURYS) *US, male vocal / instrumental group (14 Albums: 104 Weeks, 11 Singles: 43 Weeks)*

4 Jun 77 TOM PETTY AND THE HEARTBREAKERS *Shelter ISA 5014* 24 12
25 Jun 77 ANYTHING THAT'S ROCK 'N' ROLL *Shelter WIP 6396* 36 3
13 Aug 77 AMERICAN GIRL *Shelter WIP 6403* 40 5
1 Jul 78 YOU'RE GONNA GET IT *Island ISA 5017* 34 5
17 Nov 79 DAMN THE TORPEDOES *MCA MCF 3044* 57 4
23 May 81 HARD PROMISES *MCA MCF 3098* 32 5
15 Aug 81 STOP DRAGGIN' MY HEART AROUND *WEA K 79231* [1] 50 4
20 Nov 82 LONG AFTER DARK *MCA MCF 3155* 45 4
13 Apr 85 DON'T COME AROUND HERE NO MORE *MCA MCA 926* 50 4
20 Apr 85 SOUTHERN ACCENTS *MCA MCF 3260* 23 6
2 May 87 LET ME UP (I'VE HAD ENOUGH) *MCA MCG 6014* 59 2
13 May 89 I WON'T BACK DOWN *MCA MCA 1334* [2] 28 10
8 Jul 89 ● FULL MOON FEVER *MCA MCG 6034* [1] 8 16
12 Aug 89 RUNNIN' DOWN A DREAM *MCA MCA 1359* [2] 55 4
25 Nov 89 FREE FALLIN' *MCA MCA 1381* [2] 64 2
29 Jun 91 LEARNING TO FLY *MCA MCS 1555* 46 4
20 Jul 91 ● INTO THE GREAT WIDE OPEN *MCA MCA 10317* 3 18
4 Apr 92 TOO GOOD TO BE TRUE *MCA MCS 1616* 34 3
30 Oct 93 SOMETHING IN THE AIR *MCA MCSTD 1945* [2] 53 2
13 Nov 93 ● GREATEST HITS *MCA MCD 10964* 10 20
12 Mar 94 MARY JANE'S LAST DANCE *MCA MCSTD 1966* 52 2
12 Nov 94 WILDFLOWERS *Warner Bros. 9362457592* [1] 36 2

	18 June 1983	25 June 1983	2 July 1983	9 July 1983
UK No.1 SINGLES	EVERY BREATH YOU TAKE The Police	EVERY BREATH YOU TAKE The Police	BABY JANE Rod Stewart	BABY JANE Rod Stewart
UK No.1 ALBUMS	THRILLER Michael Jackson	SYNCHRONICITY The Police	SYNCHRONICITY The Police	FANTASTIC Wham!

24 Aug 96	SHE'S THE ONE (FILM SOUNDTRACK) *Warner Bros. 9362462852*	37	2
1 May 99	ECHO *Warner Bros. 9362472942*	43	2
16 Jun 01	ANTHOLOGY – THROUGH THE YEARS *MCA 1701772*	14	6

[1] Stevie Nicks with Tom Petty and the Heartbreakers [2] Tom Petty [1] Tom Petty

Madeleine PEYROUX NEW *US, female vocalist*

19 Mar 05 ●	CARELESS LOVE *Rounder 9823583*	7	18

PEYTON *UK, male production group*

22 May 04	A HIGHER PLACE *Hed Kandi HEDK 12006*	**68**	1

PHANTOM PLANET NEW
US, male vocal (Alexander Greenwald) / instrumental group

19 Mar 05 ●	CALIFORNIA *Epic 6726672*	9	14

PHARAO *Germany, male / female vocal / instrumental group*

4 Mar 95	THERE IS A STAR *Epic 6611832*	43	2

The PHARCYDE
US, male rap group (2 Albums: 2 Weeks, 3 Singles: 6 Weeks)

31 Jul 93	PASSIN' ME BY *Atlantic A 8360CD*	**55**	3
21 Aug 93	BIZARRE RIDE II THE PHARCYDE *Atlantic 756792222*	58	1
6 Apr 96	RUNNIN' *Go Beat GODCD 142*	36	2
13 Apr 96	LABCABINCALIFORNIA *Go Beat 8287332*	46	1
10 Aug 96	SHE SAID *Go Beat GODCD 144*	**51**	1

PHARRELL (see also N*E*R*D; The NEPTUNES)
US, male producer / vocalist – Pharrell Williams (13 Singles: 74 Weeks)

8 Jun 02	PASS THE COURVOISIER – PART II (re) *J 74321937902* [1]	16	8
10 Aug 02 ●	BOYS *Jive 9253912* [2]	7	8
5 Apr 03	BEAUTIFUL *Priority CDCL 842* [3]	23	20
16 Aug 03 ●	FRONTIN' *Arista 8267655332* [4]	6	10
29 Nov 03	LIGHT YOUR ASS ON FIRE *Arista 82876572512* [5]	62	1
7 Feb 04	SHOW ME YOUR SOUL *Puff Daddy / Island MCSTD 40350* [6]	35	2
11 Dec 04 ●	DROP IT LIKE IT'S HOT *Geffen 2103461* [7] ▲	10	11
5 Mar 05	LET'S GET BLOWN (re) *Geffen 9880425* [7]	13	6
12 Nov 05 ●	CAN I HAVE IT LIKE THAT *Virgin VUSCD 315* [8]	3	8+

[1] Busta Rhymes featuring P Diddy and Pharrell [2] Britney Spears featuring Pharrell Williams [3] Snoop Dogg featuring Pharrell, Uncle Charlie Wilson [4] Pharrell Williams featuring Jay-Z [5] Busta Rhymes featuring Pharrell [6] Lenny Kravitz / P Diddy / Loon / Pharrell Williams [7] Snoop Dogg featuring Pharrell [8] Pharrell featuring Gwen Stefani

PHASE II (see also Li KWAN; Joey NEGRO)
UK, male producer – Dave Lee (2 Singles: 2 Weeks)

18 Mar 89	REACHIN' *Republic LICT 006*	**70**	1
21 Dec 91	REACHIN' (re-mix) *Republic LIC 160* [1]	**70**	1

[1] Joey Negro presents Phase II

PHAT 'N' PHUNKY *UK, male production duo*

14 Jun 97	LET'S GROOVE *Chase CDCHASE 8*	61	1

PHATS & SMALL *UK, male DJ / production duo – Jason Hayward and Russell Small (5 Singles: 36 Weeks)*

10 Apr 99 ●	TURN AROUND *Multiply CDMULTY 49*	2	16
14 Aug 99 ●	FEEL GOOD *Multiply CDMULTY 54*	7	8
4 Dec 99	TONITE *Multiply CDMULTY 57*	11	6
30 Jun 01	THIS TIME AROUND *Multiply CDMULTY 75*	15	5
24 Nov 01	CHANGE *Multiply CDMULTY 80*	45	1

PHATT B *Holland, male DJ / producer – Bernsquil Verndoom*

11 Nov 00	AND DA DRUM MACHINE *Nulife / Arista 74321801902*	**58**	1

Barrington PHELOUNG
Australia, male conductor (4 Albums: 55 Weeks, 1 Single: 2 Weeks)

2 Mar 91 ●	INSPECTOR MORSE MUSIC FROM THE TV SERIES *Virgin Television VTLP 2*	4	30
7 Mar 92	INSPECTOR MORSE VOLUME 2 *Virgin Television VTCD 14*	18	12
16 Jan 93	INSPECTOR MORSE VOLUME 3 *Virgin Television VTCD 16*	20	11
13 Mar 93	'INSPECTOR MORSE' THEME *Virgin VSCDT 1458*	**61**	2
25 Nov 00	THE MAGIC OF INSPECTOR MORSE *Virgin VTDCD 353*	62	2

PHENOMENA *UK, male vocal / instrumental group*

6 Jul 85	PHENOMENA *Bronze PM 1*	63	2

PHILADELPHIA INTERNATIONAL ALL-STARS
US, male / female vocal / instrumental group

13 Aug 77	LET'S CLEAN UP THE GHETTO *Philadelphia International PIR 5451*	**34**	8

PHILHARMONIA ORCHESTRA, conductor Lorin MAAZEL
UK, orchestra and US, male conductor

30 Jul 69	THUS SPAKE ZARATHUSTRA *Columbia DB 8607*	33	7

Arlene PHILLIPS (see also FUNK FEDERATION)
UK, female exercise instructor (2 Albums: 24 Weeks)

28 Aug 82	KEEP IN SHAPE SYSTEM *Supershape SUP 01*	41	23
18 Feb 84	KEEP IN SHAPE SYSTEM VOLUME 2 *Supershape SUP 2*	100	1

Keep in Shape System features music by Funk Federation.

Chynna PHILLIPS (see also WILSON PHILLIPS) *US, female vocalist*

3 Feb 96	NAKED AND SACRED *EMI CDEM 409*	**62**	1

Esther PHILLIPS
US, female vocalist – Esther Mae Jones, b. 23 Dec 1935, d. 7 Aug 1984

4 Oct 75 ●	WHAT A DIFFERENCE A DAY MADE *Kudu 925*	6	8

PHIXX *UK, male vocal group (4 Singles: 15 Weeks)*

8 Nov 03 ●	HOLD ON ME *Concept CDCON 51*	10	4
20 Mar 04	LOVE REVOLUTION *Concept CDCON 55*	13	5
3 Jul 04	WILD BOYS *Concept CON 56X*	12	3
5 Feb 05	STRANGE LOVE *Concept CDCON 60*	19	3

PHOEBE ONE *UK, female rapper – Phoebe Espirit (2 Singles: 3 Weeks)*

12 Dec 98	DOIN' OUR THING / ONE MAN'S BITCH *Mecca Recordings MECX 1020*	**59**	1
15 May 99	GET ON IT *Mecca Recordings MECX 1026*	38	2

PHOENIX *France, male vocal / instrumental group (3 Singles: 3 Weeks)*

3 Feb 01	IF I EVER FEEL BETTER *Source DINSD 210*	**65**	1
1 May 04	RUN RUN RUN *Source SOURCD 094*	**66**	1
24 Jul 04	EVERYTHING IS EVERYTHING *Source SOURCDX 097*	**74**	1

Paul PHOENIX *UK, male vocalist*

3 Nov 79	NUNC DIMITTIS *Different HAVE 20*	**56**	4

Full artist credit on hit as follows: Paul Phoenix (treble) with instrumental ensemble – James Watson (trumpet), John Scott (organ), conducted by Barry Rose.

PHOTEK
UK, male producer – Rupert Parkes (3 Albums: 4 Weeks, 3 Singles: 4 Weeks)

15 Jun 96	THE HIDDEN CAMERA *Science QEDCD 1*	39	1
22 Mar 97	NI-TEN-ICHI-RYU (TWO SWORDS TECHNIQUE) *Science QEDCD 2*	37	2
27 Sep 97	MODUS OPERANDI *Science CDQED 1*	30	2
28 Feb 98	MODUS OPERANDI *Virgin QEDCD 6*	**66**	1

16 July 1983	23 July 1983	30 July 1983	6 August 1983
BABY JANE Rod Stewart	WHEREVER I LAY MY HAT (THAT'S MY HOME) Paul Young	WHEREVER I LAY MY HAT (THAT'S MY HOME) Paul Young	WHEREVER I LAY MY HAT (THAT'S MY HOME) Paul Young
FANTASTIC Wham!	YOU AND ME BOTH Yazoo	YOU AND ME BOTH Yazoo	THE VERY BEST OF THE BEACH BOYS The Beach Boys

KEY: UK No.1 ★ UK Top 10 ● Still on chart + UK entry at No.1 ■ US No.1 ▲ UK million seller £ US million seller $
Singles re-entries are listed as (re), (2re), (3re)... which signifies that the hit re-entered the chart once, twice or three times...
Peak Position / Weeks

26 Sep 98 FORM & FUNCTION *Science CDQED 2* ... 61 1
24 Feb 01 MINE TO GIVE *Science QEDCD 10* [1] ... 44 1

[1] Photek featuring Robert Owens

The PHOTOS *UK, male / female vocal (Wendy Wu) / instrumental group*

17 May 80 IRENE *Epic EPC 8517* ... 56 4
21 Jun 80 ● THE PHOTOS *CBS PHOTO 5* ... 4 9

PHUNKY PHANTOM (see also GAT DECOR; REST ASSURED)
UK, male producer – Lawrence Nelson

16 May 98 GET UP STAND UP *Club for Life DISNCD 44* ... 27 3

PHUTURE ASSASSINS *UK, male instrumental / production group*

6 Jun 92 FUTURE SOUND (EP) *Suburban Base SUBBASE 010* ... 64 1

Tracks on Future Sound (EP): Future Sound / African Sanctus / Rydim Come Forward / Freedom Sound.

Edith PIAF
France, female vocalist – Edith Gassion, b. 19 Dec 1915, d. 11 Oct 1963

12 May 60 MILORD (re) *Columbia DC 754* ... 24 15
26 Sep 87 HEART AND SOUL *Stylus SMR 736* ... 58 5

PIANOHEADZ (see also LIL MO' YIN YANG; REAL TO REEL)
US, male DJ / production duo – Erick Morillo and Jose Nunez

11 Jul 98 IT'S OVER (DISTORTION) *INCredible Music INCRL 3CD* ... 39 2

PIANOMAN (see also BASS BOYZ)
UK, male producer – James Sammon (2 Singles: 8 Weeks)

15 Jun 96 ● BLURRED *Ffrreedom TABCD 243* ... 6 7
26 Apr 97 PARTY PEOPLE (LIVE YOUR LIFE BE FREE) *3 Beat 3BTCD 1* ... 43 1

Mark PICCHIOTTI presents BASSTOY featuring DANA
(see also ABSOLUTE; SANDSTORM) *US, male / female production / vocal duo*

19 Jan 02 RUNNIN' (re-mix) *Black & White NEOCD 073* ... 13 5

Wilson PICKETT
US, male vocalist, b. 18 Mar 1941, d. 19 Jan 2006 (9 Singles: 61 Weeks)

23 Sep 65 IN THE MIDNIGHT HOUR *Atlantic AT 4036* ... 12 11
25 Nov 65 DON'T FIGHT IT *Atlantic AT 4052* ... 29 8
10 Mar 66 634-5789 *Atlantic AT 4072* ... 36 5
1 Sep 66 LAND OF 1000 DANCES *Atlantic 584 039* ... 22 9
15 Dec 66 MUSTANG SALLY *Atlantic 584 066* ... 28 7
27 Sep 67 FUNKY BROADWAY *Atlantic 584 130* ... 43 3
11 Sep 68 I'M A MIDNIGHT MOVER *Atlantic 584 203* ... 38 6
8 Jan 69 HEY JUDE *Atlantic 584 236* ... 16 9
21 Nov 87 IN THE MIDNIGHT HOUR (re-recording) *Motown ZB 41583* ... 62 3

Bobby 'Boris' PICKETT and The CRYPT-KICKERS
US, male vocal / instrumental group

1 Sep 73 ● MONSTER MASH *London HLU 10320* ▲ $ ... 3 13

PICKETTYWITCH *UK, male / female vocal (Polly Brown) / instrumental group (3 Singles: 34 Weeks)*

28 Feb 70 ● THAT SAME OLD FEELING *Pye 7N 17887* ... 5 14
4 Jul 70 (IT'S LIKE A) SAD OLD KINDA MOVIE *Pye 7N 17951* ... 16 10
7 Nov 70 BABY I WON'T LET YOU DOWN *Pye 7N 45002* ... 27 10

Mauro PICOTTO (see also CRW; R.A.F.)
Italy, male producer (8 Singles: 23 Weeks)

12 Jun 99 LIZARD (GONNA GET YOU) *VC Recordings VCRD 50* ... 27 3
20 Nov 99 LIZARD (GONNA GET YA) (re-mix) *VC Recordings VCRD 57* ... 33 2
15 Jul 00 IGUANA *VC Recordings VCRD 68* ... 33 3
13 Jan 01 KOMODO (SAVE A SOUL) *VC Recordings VCRD 85* ... 13 5
11 Aug 01 LIKE THIS LIKE THAT *VC Recordings VCRD 92* ... 21 4
25 Aug 01 VERDI *BXR BXRP 0318* ... 74 1
16 Mar 02 PULSAR 2002 *BXR BXRC 0162* ... 35 3
3 Aug 02 BACK TO CALI *BXR BXRC 0433* ... 42 2

PIGBAG
UK, male instrumental group (1 Album: 14 Weeks, 4 Singles: 20 Weeks)

7 Nov 81 SUNNY DAY *Y Records Y 12* ... 53 3
27 Feb 82 GETTING UP *Y Records Y 16* ... 61 3
13 Mar 82 DR HECKLE AND MR JIVE *Y Records Y 17* ... 18 14
3 Apr 82 ● PAPA'S GOT A BRAND NEW PIGBAG *Y Records Y 10* ... 3 11
10 Jul 82 THE BIG BEAN *Y Records Y 24* ... 40 3

The PIGLETS *UK, female vocal (Barbara Kay) group*

6 Nov 71 ● JOHNNY REGGAE *Bell 1180* ... 3 12

PILOT *UK, male vocal (David Paton) / instrumental group (1 Album: 1 Week, 4 Singles: 29 Weeks)*

2 Nov 74 MAGIC *EMI 2217* $ ... 11 11
18 Jan 75 ★ JANUARY *EMI 2255* ... 1 10
19 Apr 75 CALL ME ROUND *EMI 2287* ... 34 4
31 May 75 SECOND FLIGHT *EMI EMC 3075* ... 48 1
27 Sep 75 JUST A SMILE *EMI 2338* ... 31 4

The PILTDOWN MEN *US, male instrumental group (3 Singles: 36 Weeks)*

8 Sep 60 MCDONALD'S CAVE *Capitol CL 15149* ... 14 18
12 Jan 61 PILTDOWN RIDES AGAIN *Capitol CL 15175* ... 14 10
9 Mar 61 GOODNIGHT MRS. FLINTSTONE *Capitol CL 15186* ... 18 8

Courtney PINE
UK, male saxophonist (2 Albums: 13 Weeks, 2 Singles: 6 Weeks)

25 Oct 86 JOURNEY TO THE URGE WITHIN *Island ILPS 9846* ... 39 11
6 Feb 88 DESTINY'S SONGS *Antilles AN 8275* ... 54 2
30 Jul 88 LIKE DREAMERS DO *Fourth & Broadway BRW 108* [1] ... 26 5
7 Jul 90 I'M STILL WAITING *Mango MNG 749* [2] ... 66 1

[1] Mica Paris featuring Courtney Pine [2] Courtney Pine featuring Carroll Thompson

'PING PING' and AL VERLAINE *Belgium, male vocal duo*

28 Sep 61 SUCU SUCU *Oriole CB 1589* ... 41 4

PINK (247 Top 500) *BRIT-winning diva whose hair colour often matches her name, b. Alecia Moore, 8 Sep 1979, Pennsylvania, US. Rock-influenced UK million-selling M!ssundaztood was 2002's top-selling album by a female artist in both the US and UK. She won a Best Female Rock Performance Grammy in 2004 for 'Trouble' (3 Albums: 138 Weeks, 13 Singles: 119 Weeks)*

27 May 00 CAN'T TAKE ME HOME *Arista 73008260622* ... 13 41
10 Jun 00 ● THERE YOU GO *LaFace / Arista 74321757602* ... 6 9
30 Sep 00 ● MOST GIRLS *LaFace / Arista 74321792012* ... 5 8
27 Jan 01 ● YOU MAKE ME SICK *LaFace / Arista 74321828702* ... 9 6
30 Jun 01 ★ LADY MARMALADE *Interscope / Polydor 4975612* [1] ■ ▲ ... 1 16
26 Jan 02 ● GET THE PARTY STARTED *LaFace / Arista 74321913372* ... 2 15
9 Feb 02 ● M!SSUNDAZTOOD *Arista 7822147182* ... 3 73
25 May 02 ● DON'T LET ME GET ME *Arista 74321939212* ... 6 11
28 Sep 02 ★ JUST LIKE A PILL *Arista 74321959652* ■ ... 1 11
14 Dec 02 FAMILY PORTRAIT (import) *Arista 74321982102* ... 66 1
21 Dec 02 FAMILY PORTRAIT *Arista 74321982052* ... 11 9
19 Jul 03 ● FEEL GOOD TIME *Columbia 6741062 XXX* [2] ... 3 11
8 Nov 03 ● TROUBLE *Arista 82876572172* ... 7 12

13 August 1983	20 August 1983	27 August 1983	3 September 1983
UK No.1 SINGLES			
GIVE IT UP KC and The Sunshine Band	GIVE IT UP KC and The Sunshine Band	GIVE IT UP KC and The Sunshine Band	RED RED WINE UB40
UK No.1 ALBUMS			
THE VERY BEST OF THE BEACH BOYS The Beach Boys	18 GREATEST HITS Michael Jackson plus The Jackson Five	18 GREATEST HITS Michael Jackson plus The Jackson Five	18 GREATEST HITS Michael Jackson plus The Jackson Five

22 Nov 03 ● TRY THIS *Arista 82876571852* [1] 3 24
7 Feb 04 GOD IS A DJ *Arista 829876589352*....11 6
1 May 04 LAST TO KNOW *Arista 82876611732*....21 4

[1] Christina Aguilera, Lil' Kim, Mya and Pink [2] Pink featuring William Orbit
[1] P!nk

The PINK FAIRIES *UK, male vocal / instrumental group*

29 Jul 72 WHAT A BUNCH OF SWEETIES *Polydor 2383 132*....48 1

PINK FLOYD 21 Top 500

One of the world's most respected rock groups, formed in London in 1965: David Gilmour (g), Roger Waters (b), Rick Wright (k) and Nick Mason (d). In the US, Dark Side of the Moon has spent a record 28 years on the albums chart and The Wall has sold over 23 million. In 2005 they were added to the UK Music Hall of Fame, and reformed for one performance at the 2005 Live 8 concert in Hyde Park. The group's legendary songwriting member Syd Barrett is one of the most written about characters in rock, even though he left the band in 1968 (23 Albums: 923 Weeks, 9 Singles: 55 Weeks)

30 Mar 67 ARNOLD LAYNE *Columbia DB 8156*....20 8
22 Jun 67 ● SEE EMILY PLAY *Columbia DB 8214*....6 12
19 Aug 67 ● THE PIPER AT THE GATES OF DAWN *Columbia SCX 6157*....6 14
13 Jul 68 ● A SAUCERFUL OF SECRETS *Columbia SCX 6258*....9 11
28 Jun 69 ● MORE (FILM SOUNDTRACK) *Columbia SCX 6346*....9 5
15 Nov 69 ● UMMAGUMMA *Harvest SHDW 1/2*....5 21
24 Oct 70 ★ ATOM HEART MOTHER *Harvest SHVL 781* ■....1 18
7 Aug 71 RELICS *Starline SRS 5071*....32 6
20 Nov 71 ● MEDDLE *Harvest SHVL 795*....3 82
17 Jun 72 ● OBSCURED BY CLOUDS (FILM SOUNDTRACK) *Harvest SHSP 4020*....6 14
31 Mar 73 ● THE DARK SIDE OF THE MOON *Harvest SHVL 804* ▲....2 367
19 Jan 74 A NICE PAIR (re-issue) *Harvest SHDW 403*....21 20
27 Sep 75 ★ WISH YOU WERE HERE *Harvest SHVL 814* ▲....1 90
19 Feb 77 ● ANIMALS *Harvest SHVL 815*....2 33
1 Dec 79 ★ ANOTHER BRICK IN THE WALL (PART 2) *Harvest HAR 5194* ▲ 1 12
8 Dec 79 ● THE WALL *Harvest SHDW 411* ▲....3 57
5 Dec 81 A COLLECTION OF GREAT DANCE SONGS *Harvest SHVL 822*..37 10
7 Aug 82 WHEN THE TIGERS BROKE FREE *Harvest HAR 5222*....39 5
2 Apr 83 ★ THE FINAL CUT *Harvest SHPF 1983* ■....1 25
7 May 83 NOT NOW JOHN *Harvest HAR 5224*....30 4
19 Sep 87 ● A MOMENTARY LAPSE OF REASON *EMI EMD 1003*....3 34
19 Dec 87 ON THE TURNING AWAY *EMI EM 34*....55 4
25 Jun 88 ONE SLIP *EMI EM 52*....50 3
3 Dec 88 DELICATE SOUND OF THUNDER *EMI EQ 5009*....11 12
9 Apr 94 ★ THE DIVISION BELL *EMI CDEMD 1055* ■ ▲....1 51
4 Jun 94 TAKE IT BACK *EMI CDEMS 309*....23 4
29 Oct 94 HIGH HOPES / KEEP TALKING *EMI CDEMS 342*....26 3
10 Jun 95 ★ PULSE *EMI CDEMD 1078* ■ ▲....1 21
9 Mar 96 RELICS (re-issue) *EMI CDEMD 1082*....48 2
16 Aug 97 THE PIPER AT THE GATES OF DAWN (re-issue) *EMI CDEMD 1110*....44 2
8 Apr 00 IS THERE ANYBODY OUT THERE? – THE WALL LIVE 1980-81 *EMI 5235622*....15 5
17 Nov 01 ● ECHOES – THE BEST OF PINK FLOYD *EMI 5361112*....2 23

A Nice Pair is a double re-issue of the first two albums.

PINK GREASE *UK, male vocal / instrumental group (3 Singles: 5 Weeks)*

26 Jun 04 THE PINK G.R.EASE *Mute CDMUTE 316*....75 1
22 Jan 05 STRIP *Mute CDMUTE 325*....36 2
9 Apr 05 PEACHES *Mute CDMUTE 343*....44 2

The PINKEES *UK, male vocal / instrumental group*

18 Sep 82 ● DANGER GAMES *Creole CR 39*....8 9

PINKERTON'S ASSORTED COLOURS

UK, male vocal (Samuel Kemp) / instrumental group (2 Singles: 12 Weeks)

13 Jan 66 ● MIRROR MIRROR *Decca F 12307*....9 11
21 Apr 66 DON'T STOP LOVING ME BABY *Decca F 12377*....50 1

PINKY and PERKY *UK, pig puppet duo*

29 May 93 REET PETITE *Telstar CDPIGGY 1*....47 3

Lisa PIN-UP *UK, female DJ / producer – Lisa Chilcott (2 Singles: 4 Weeks)*

25 May 02 TURN UP THE SOUND *Nukleuz NUKC 0406*....60 1
21 Dec 02 BLOW YOUR MIND (I AM THE WOMAN) *Nukleuz 0450 FNUK*..60 3

The PIONEERS

Jamaica, male vocal / instrumental group (4 Singles: 34 Weeks)

18 Oct 69 LONG SHOT KICK DE BUCKET (re) *Trojan TR 672*....21 11
31 Jul 71 ● LET YOUR YEAH BE YEAH *Trojan TR 7825*....5 12
15 Jan 72 GIVE AND TAKE *Trojan TR 7846*....35 6
29 Mar 80 LONG SHOT KICK DE BUCKET (re-issue) *Trojan TRO 9063*....42 5

The re-issue of 'Long Shot Kick De Bucket' was coupled with the re-issue of 'Liquidator' by the Harry J All Stars.

Billie PIPER *UK, female vocalist (2 Albums: 27 Weeks, 8 Singles: 87 Weeks)*

11 Jul 98 ★ BECAUSE WE WANT TO *Innocent SINCD 2* [1] ■....1 12
17 Oct 98 ★ GIRLFRIEND (re) *Innocent SINCD 3* [1] ■....1 12
31 Oct 98 HONEY TO THE B *Innocent CDSIN 1* [1]....14 23
19 Dec 98 ● SHE WANTS YOU (re) *Innocent SINDXX 6* [1]....3 13
3 Apr 99 ● HONEY TO THE BEE (re) *Innocent SINCD 8* [1]....3 11
10 Apr 99 ● THANK ABBA FOR THE MUSIC *Epic ABCD 1* [2]....4 13
27 May 00 ★ DAY & NIGHT (re) *Innocent SINCD 11* ■....1 12
30 Sep 00 ● SOMETHING DEEP INSIDE (re) *Innocent SINCD 19*....4 9
14 Oct 00 WALK OF LIFE *Innocent CDSINX 3*....14 4
23 Dec 00 WALK OF LIFE *Innocent SINCD 23*....25 5

[1] Billie [2] Steps, Tina Cousins, Cleopatra, B*Witched, Billie [1] Billie

The PIPETTES NEW *UK, female vocal trio*

26 Nov 05 DIRTY MIND *Memphis Industries MI 053CDS*....63 1

The PIPKINS (see also BLUE MINK; BROTHERHOOD OF MAN; DAVID and JONATHAN; EDISON LIGHTHOUSE; WHITE PLAINS)

UK, male vocal duo – Roger Greenaway and Tony Burrows

28 Mar 70 ● GIMME DAT DING *Columbia DB 8662*....6 10

The PIRANHAS *UK, male vocal (Bob Grover) / instrumental group (1 Album: 3 Weeks, 2 Singles: 21 Weeks)*

2 Aug 80 ● TOM HARK *Sire SIR 4044*....6 12
20 Sep 80 PIRANHAS *Sire SRK 6098*....69 3
16 Oct 82 ZAMBESI *Dakota DAK 6* [1]....17 9

[1] The Piranhas featuring Boring Bob Grover

The PIRATES

UK, male vocal / instrumental group (1 Album: 3 Weeks, 8 Singles: 57 Weeks)

12 Feb 60 YOU GOT WHAT IT TAKES *HMV POP 698* [1]....25 3
16 Jun 60 ★ SHAKIN' ALL OVER *HMV POP 753* [1]....1 19
6 Oct 60 RESTLESS *HMV POP 790* [1]....22 7
13 Apr 61 LINDA LU *HMV POP 853* [1]....47 1
10 Jan 63 A SHOT OF RHYTHM AND BLUES *HMV POP 1088* [1]....48 1
25 Jul 63 ● I'LL NEVER GET OVER YOU *HMV POP 1173* [1]....4 15
28 Nov 63 HUNGRY FOR LOVE *HMV POP 1228* [1]....20 10
30 Apr 64 ALWAYS AND EVER *HMV POP 1269* [1]....46 1
19 Nov 77 OUT OF THEIR SKULLS *Warner Bros. K 56411*....57 3

[1] Johnny Kidd and The Pirates

PIRATES featuring ENYA, SHOLA AMA, NAILA BOSS & ISHANI

UK, male production duo – Mohammed Nabulsi and Ryan Perera and Ireland / UK, female vocalists

11 Sep 04 ● YOU SHOULD REALLY KNOW *Relentless RELCD 9*....8 8

'You Should Really Know' is a response to 'I Don't Wanna Know' by Mario Winans featuring Enya & P Diddy.

10 September 1983	17 September 1983	24 September 1983	1 October 1983
RED RED WINE UB40	RED RED WINE UB40	KARMA CHAMELEON Culture Club	KARMA CHAMELEON Culture Club
THE VERY BEST OF THE BEACH BOYS The Beach Boys	NO PARLEZ Paul Young	LABOUR OF LOVE UB40	NO PARLEZ Paul Young

KEY UK No.1 ★ UK Top 10 ● Still on chart + UK entry at No.1 ■ US No.1 ▲ UK million seller £ US million seller $
Singles re-entries are listed as (re), (2re), (3re)... which signifies that the hit re-entered the chart once, twice or three times...
Peak Position / Weeks

PITCHSHIFTER
UK, male vocal / instrumental group (2 Albums: 2 Weeks, 4 Singles: 4 Weeks)

28 Feb 98	**GENIUS** *Geffen GFSTD 22324*	71	1
26 Sep 98	**MICROWAVED** *Geffen GFSTD 22348*	54	1
3 Jun 00	DEVIANT *MCA 1122542*	35	1
21 Oct 00	**DEAD BATTERY** *MCA MCSTD 40241*	71	1
11 May 02	P.S.I *Mayan MYNCD 004*	54	1
29 Jun 02	**SHUTDOWN** *Mayan MYNX 008*	66	1

Gene PITNEY (214 Top 500)
Leading US performer in the 1960s, b. 17 Feb 1941, Connecticut. This unmistakable vocalist and songwriter had a longer and more impressive track record in the UK than in his homeland. Nonetheless, it took him 28 years to reach No.1 (11 Albums: 75 Weeks, 22 Singles: 212 Weeks)

23 Mar 61	**(I WANNA) LOVE MY LIFE AWAY** *London HL 9270*	26	11
8 Mar 62	**TOWN WITHOUT PITY** *HMV POP 952*	32	6
5 Dec 63 ●	**TWENTY FOUR HOURS FROM TULSA** *United Artists UP 1035*	5	19
5 Mar 64 ●	**THAT GIRL BELONGS TO YESTERDAY** *United Artists UP 1045*	7	12
11 Apr 64 ●	BLUE GENE *United Artists ULP 1061*	7	11
15 Oct 64	**IT HURTS TO BE IN LOVE** *United Artists UP 1063*	36	4
12 Nov 64 ●	**I'M GONNA BE STRONG** *Stateside SS 358*	2	14
6 Feb 65	GENE PITNEY'S BIG 16 *Stateside SL 10118*	12	6
18 Feb 65 ●	**I MUST BE SEEING THINGS** *Stateside SS 390*	6	10
20 Mar 65	I'M GONNA BE STRONG *Stateside SL 10120*	15	2
10 Jun 65 ●	**LOOKING THRU THE EYES OF LOVE** *Stateside SS 420*	3	12
4 Nov 65 ●	**PRINCESS IN RAGS** *Stateside SS 471*	9	12
20 Nov 65	LOOKIN' THRU THE EYES OF LOVE *Stateside SL 10148*	15	5
17 Feb 66 ●	**BACKSTAGE** *Stateside SS 490*	4	10
9 Jun 66 ●	**NOBODY NEEDS YOUR LOVE** *Stateside SS 518*	2	13
17 Sep 66	NOBODY NEEDS YOUR LOVE *Stateside SL 10183*	13	17
10 Nov 66 ●	**JUST ONE SMILE** *Stateside SS 558*	8	12
23 Feb 67	**(IN THE) COLD LIGHT OF DAY** *Stateside SS 597*	38	6
4 Mar 67	YOUNG WARM AND WONDERFUL *Stateside SSL 10194*	39	1
22 Apr 67	GENE PITNEY'S BIG SIXTEEN *Stateside SSL 10199*	40	1
15 Nov 67 ●	**SOMETHING'S GOTTEN HOLD OF MY HEART** *Stateside SS 2060*	5	13
3 Apr 68	**SOMEWHERE IN THE COUNTRY** *Stateside SS 2103*	19	9
27 Nov 68	**YOURS UNTIL TOMORROW** *Stateside SS 2131*	34	7
5 Mar 69	**MARIA ELENA** *Stateside SS 2142*	25	6
20 Sep 69 ●	BEST OF GENE PITNEY *Stateside SSL 10286*	8	9
14 Mar 70	**A STREET CALLED HOPE** *Stateside SS 2164*	37	5
3 Oct 70	**SHADY LADY** *Stateside SS 2177*	29	8
28 Apr 73	**24 SYCAMORE** *Pye International 7N 25606*	34	7
2 Nov 74	**BLUE ANGEL** (re) *Bronze BRO 11*	39	4
2 Oct 76 ●	HIS 20 GREATEST HITS *Arcade ADEP 22*	6	14
14 Jan 89 ★	**SOMETHING'S GOTTEN HOLD OF MY HEART** *Parlophone R 6201* [1]	1	12
20 Oct 90	BACKSTAGE – THE GREATEST HITS AND MORE *Polydor 8471191*	17	7
22 Sep 01	LOOKING THROUGH – THE ULTIMATE COLLECTION *Sequel NEECD 380*	40	2

[1] Marc Almond featuring special guest star Gene Pitney

Mario PIU
Italy, male DJ / producer (2 Singles: 14 Weeks)

11 Dec 99 ●	**COMMUNICATION (SOMEBODY ANSWER THE PHONE)** *Incentive CENT 2CDS*	5	9
10 Mar 01	**THE VISION** (re) *BXR BXRC 0253* [1]	16	5

[1] Mario Piu presents DJ Arabesque

PIXIES
US, male / female vocal (Frank Black aka Black Francis – Charles Thompson IV) / instrumental group (8 Albums: 34 Weeks, 6 Singles: 13 Weeks)

1 Apr 89	**MONKEY GONE TO HEAVEN** *4AD AD 904*	60	3
29 Apr 89 ●	DOOLITTLE *4AD CAD 905*	8	9
1 Jul 89	**HERE COMES YOUR MAN** *4AD AD 909*	54	1
28 Jul 90	**VELOURIA** *4AD AD 0009*	28	3
25 Aug 90 ●	BOSSANOVA *4AD CAD 0010*	3	8
10 Nov 90	**DIG FOR FIRE** *4AD AD 0014*	62	1
8 Jun 91	**PLANET OF SOUND** *4AD AD 1008*	27	3
5 Oct 91 ●	TROMPE LE MONDE *4AD CAD 1014*	7	5
4 Oct 97	**DEBASER** *4AD BAD 7010CD*	23	2
18 Oct 97	DEATH TO THE PIXIES *4AD DAD 7011CD*	28	3
18 Oct 97	DEATH TO THE PIXIES – DELUXE EDITION *4AD DADD 7011CD*	20	2
18 Jul 98	AT THE BBC *4AD GAD 8013CD*	45	1
17 Mar 01	COMPLETE 'B' SIDES *4AD GAD 2103CD*	53	1
15 May 04	BEST OF PIXIES – WAVE OF MUTILATION *4AD CAD 2406CD*	16	5

PIZZAMAN (see also BEATS INTERNATIONAL; FREAKPOWER; The HOUSEMARTINS; MIGHTY DUB KATZ; URBAN ALL STARS)
UK, male producer – Norman Cook (5 Singles: 18 Weeks)

27 Aug 94	**TRIPPIN' ON SUNSHINE** *Cowboy Records CDLOAD 16*	33	2
10 Jun 95	**SEX ON THE STREETS** (re) *Cowboy Records CDLOAD 24*	23	8
18 Nov 95	**HAPPINESS** *Cowboy Records CDLOAD 29*	19	4
1 Jun 96	**TRIPPIN' ON SUNSHINE** (re-issue) *Cowboy Records CDLOAD 32*	18	3
14 Sep 96	**HELLO HONKY TONKS (ROCK YOUR BODY)** *Cowboy Records CDLOAD 39*	41	1

PIZZICATO FIVE
Japan, male / female vocal / instrumental group

1 Nov 97	**MON AMOUR TOKYO** *Matador OLE 2902*	72	1

PLACEBO
Belgium / Sweden / UK, male vocal (Brian Molko) / instrumental group (5 Albums: 51 Weeks, 13 Singles: 51 Weeks)

29 Jun 96 ●	PLACEBO *Elevator Music CDFLOORX 2*	5	13
28 Sep 96	**TEENAGE ANGST** *Elevator Music FLOORCD 3*	30	3
1 Feb 97 ●	**NANCY BOY** *Elevator Music FLOORCD 4*	4	6
24 May 97	**BRUISE PRISTINE** *Elevator Music FLOORCD 5*	14	3
15 Aug 98 ●	**PURE MORNING** *Hut FLOORCD 6*	4	6
10 Oct 98 ●	**YOU DON'T CARE ABOUT US** *Hut FLOORCD 7*	5	5
24 Oct 98 ●	WITHOUT YOU I'M NOTHING *Hut CDFLOOR 8*	7	17
6 Feb 99	**EVERY YOU EVERY ME** *Hut / Virgin FLOORCD 9*	11	5
29 Jul 00	**TASTE IN MEN** *Hut / Virgin FLOORCD 11*	16	6
7 Oct 00	**SLAVE TO THE WAGE** *Hut / Virgin FLOORCD 12*	19	3
21 Oct 00 ●	BLACK MARKET MUSIC *Hut CDFLOORX 13*	6	5
22 Mar 03	**THE BITTER END** *Hut / Virgin FLOORCD 16*	12	5
5 Apr 03	SLEEPING WITH GHOSTS *Hut / Virgin CDFLOORX 17*	11	11
28 Jun 03	**THIS PICTURE** *Hut / Virgin FLOORCD 18*	23	2
27 Sep 03	**SPECIAL NEEDS** *Hut / Virgin FLOORCD 19*	27	2
6 Mar 04	**ENGLISH SUMMER RAIN** *Hut / Virgin FLOORDX 21*	23	2
30 Oct 04	**TWENTY YEARS** *Virgin FLOORDX 24*	18	3
6 Nov 04 ●	ONCE MORE WITH FEELING – SINGLES 1996-2004 *Virgin CDFLOORX 23*	8	5

PLANET FUNK
Italy / UK / Finland, male / female vocal / production group (4 Singles: 13 Weeks)

10 Feb 01 ●	**CHASE THE SUN** (re) *Virgin VSCDT 1794*	5	9
26 Apr 03	**WHO SAID (STUCK IN THE UK)** *Illustrious / Bustin' Loose CDILL 015*	36	2
16 Aug 03	**THE SWITCH** *Illustrious / Bustin' Loose CDILL 017*	52	1
19 Mar 05	**THE SWITCH** (re-mix) *Direction 6757882*	66	1

PLANET PATROL
US, male vocal / instrumental group

17 Sep 83	**CHEAP THRILLS** *Polydor POSP 639*	64	3

PLANET PERFECTO
UK, male production group (4 Singles: 15 Weeks)

14 Aug 99	**NOT OVER YET 99** *Code Blue BLU 004CD1* [1]	16	4
13 Nov 99	**BULLET IN THE GUN** *Perfecto PERF 3CDS*	15	4

	8 October 1983	15 October 1983	22 October 1983	29 October 1983
UK No.1 SINGLES	KARMA CHAMELEON Culture Club	KARMA CHAMELEON Culture Club	KARMA CHAMELEON Culture Club	KARMA CHAMELEON Culture Club
UK No.1 ALBUMS	NO PARLEZ Paul Young	GENESIS Genesis	COLOUR BY NUMBERS Culture Club	COLOUR BY NUMBERS Culture Club

16 Sep 00 ● **BULLET IN THE GUN 2000** (re-mix) *Perfecto PERF 03CDSX*......**7** 6
29 Sep 01 **BITES DA DUST** *Perfecto PERF 19CDS*..........**52** 1

[1] Planet Perfecto featuring Grace

The PLANETS *UK, male vocal / instrumental group (2 Singles: 8 Weeks)*

18 Aug 79 **LINES** *Rialto TREB 104*..........**36** 6
25 Oct 80 **DON'T LOOK DOWN** *Rialto TREB 116*..........**66** 2

The PLANETS *UK, male / female instrumental group*

2 Mar 02 CLASSICAL GRAFFITI *EMI / Dramatico CDC 5573162*..........34 13

PLANK 15 *UK, male producer – Andrew Holt*

2 Feb 02 **STRINGS OF LIFE** *Multiply CDMULTY 82*..........**60** 1

Robert PLANT (see also The HONEYDRIPPERS; LED ZEPPELIN)

UK, male vocalist (11 Albums: 89 Weeks, 10 Singles: 35 Weeks)

10 Jul 82 ● PICTURES AT ELEVEN *Swansong SSK 59418*..........2 15
9 Oct 82 **BURNING DOWN ONE SIDE** *Swansong SSK 19429*..........**73** 1
16 Jul 83 **BIG LOG** *WEA B 9848*..........**11** 10
23 Jul 83 ● THE PRINCIPLES OF MOMENTS *WEA 7901011*..........7 14
1 Jun 85 SHAKEN 'N' STIRRED *Es Paranza 7902651*..........19 4
30 Jan 88 **HEAVEN KNOWS** *Es Paranza A 9373*..........33 5
12 Feb 88 ● NOW AND ZEN *Es Paranza WX 149*..........10 7
31 Mar 90 MANIC NIRVANA *Es Paranza WX 339*..........15 9
28 Apr 90 **HURTING KIND (I'VE GOT MY EYES ON YOU)** *Es Paranza A 8985*..........**45** 3
8 May 93 **29 PALMS** *Fontana FATEX 1*..........21 5
5 Jun 93 ● FATE OF NATIONS *Es Paranza 5148672*..........6 8
3 Jul 93 **I BELIEVE** *Fontana FATEX 2*..........**64** 2
25 Dec 93 **IF I WERE A CARPENTER** *Fontana FATEX 4*..........63 2
19 Nov 94 ● NO QUARTER *Fontana 5263622* [1]..........7 13
17 Dec 94 **GALLOWS POLE** *Fontana PPCD 2* [1]..........35 3
11 Apr 98 **MOST HIGH** *Mercury 5687512* [2]..........26 2
2 May 98 ● WALKING INTO CLARKSDALE *Mercury 5580252* [1]..........3 6
6 Jul 02 DREAMLAND *Mercury 630252*..........20 3
15 Nov 03 SIXTY SIX TO TIMBUKTU *Mercury 9813199*..........27 3
7 May 05 **SHINE IT ALL AROUND** *Sanctuary SANXS 369* [3]..........32 2
14 May 05 ● MIGHTY REARRANGER *Sanctuary SANCD 356* [2]..........4 7

[1] Jimmy Page and Robert Plant [2] Page and Plant [3] Robert Plant & The Strange Sensation [1] Jimmy Page and Robert Plant [2] Robert Plant & The Strange Sensation

The PLASMATICS *US, female / male vocal / instrumental group*

26 Jul 80 **BUTCHER BABY** *Stiff BUY 76*..........**55** 4
11 Oct 80 NEW HOPE FOR THE WRETCHED *Stiff SEEZ 24*..........55 3

PLASTIC BERTRAND

Belgium, male vocalist – Roger Jouret (2 Singles: 17 Weeks)

13 May 78 ● **ÇA PLANE POUR MOI** *Sire 6078 616*..........8 12
5 Aug 78 **SHA LA LA LA LEE** *Vertigo 6059 209*..........39 5

PLASTIC BOY featuring ROZALLA

Belgium, male producer – Mike Dierickx and Zimbabwe, female vocalist

22 Nov 03 **LIVE ANOTHER LIFE** *Inferno CDFERN 59*..........**55** 1

PLASTIC PENNY (see also CONGREGATION)

UK, male vocal (Brian Keith) / instrumental group

3 Jan 68 ● **EVERYTHING I AM** *Page One POF 051*..........6 10

PLASTIK MAN (see also FUSE)

Canada, male DJ / producer – Richie Hawtin

19 Nov 94 MUSIK *Novamute NOMU 37CD*..........58 1

PLATINUM 45 featuring MORE FIRE CREW

UK, male producer and vocal / rap / production trio

16 Mar 02 ● **OI!** *Go Beat GOBCD 48*..........8 8

PLATINUM HOOK *US, male vocal / instrumental group*

2 Sep 78 **STANDING ON THE VERGE (OF GETTING IT ON)** *Motown TMG 1115*..........**72** 1

The PLATTERS *US, male / female vocal (Tony Williams, b. 16 Apr 1928, d. 14 Aug 1992) group (1 Album: 13 Weeks, 9 Singles: 92 Weeks)*

7 Sep 56 ● **THE GREAT PRETENDER / ONLY YOU** (re) *Mercury MT 117* $...**5** 13
2 Nov 56 ● **MY PRAYER** (2re) *Mercury MT 120* ▲ $..........4 13
25 Jan 57 **YOU'LL NEVER NEVER KNOW / IT ISN'T RIGHT** (2re) *Mercury MT 130*..........23 3
29 Mar 57 **ONLY YOU (AND YOU ALONE)** (2re) *Mercury MT 117*..........**18** 3
17 May 57 **I'M SORRY** (2re) *Mercury MT 145*..........**18** 8
16 May 58 ● **TWILIGHT TIME** *Mercury MT 214* ▲ $..........3 18
16 Jan 59 ★ **SMOKE GETS IN YOUR EYES** *Mercury AMT 1016* ▲ $..........1 20
28 Aug 59 **REMEMBER WHEN** *Mercury AMT 1053*..........**25** 2
29 Jan 60 **HARBOUR LIGHTS** *Mercury AMT 1081*..........**11** 12
8 Apr 78 ● 20 CLASSIC HITS *Mercury 9100 049*..........8 13

PLAYER *US / UK, male vocal / instrumental group*

25 Feb 78 **BABY COME BACK** *RSO 2090 254* ▲ $..........32 7

The PLAYERS ASSOCIATION

US, male vocal / instrumental group (1 Album: 4 Weeks, 3 Singles: 17 Weeks)

10 Mar 79 ● **TURN THE MUSIC UP!** *Vanguard VS 5011*..........8 9
17 Mar 79 TURN THE MUSIC UP *Vanguard VSD 79421*..........54 4
5 May 79 **RIDE THE GROOVE** *Vanguard VS 5012*..........**42** 5
9 Feb 80 **WE GOT THE GROOVE** *Vanguard VS 5016*..........**61** 3

PLAYGROUP *UK, male producer – Trevor Jackson*

24 Nov 01 **NUMBER ONE** *Source SOURCD 026*..........**66** 1

PLAYN JAYN *UK, male vocal / instrumental group*

1 Sep 84 FRIDAY THE 13TH (AT THE MARQUEE CLUB) *A&M JAYN 13*...93 1

PLAYTHING (see also TRIPLE X) *Italy, male production duo – Luca Moretti and Riccardo Romanini (2 Singles: 6 Weeks)*

5 May 01 **INTO SPACE** *Manifesto FESCD 81*..........**48** 1
24 Aug 02 **DO YOU SEE THE LIGHT?** (re-mix) *Data MoS DATA 33CDS* [1] **14** 5

[1] Snap! vs Plaything

PLUMB *US, female vocalist – Tiffany Arbuckle-Lee*

14 Feb 04 **REAL** *Curb / London CUBC 095*..........**41** 2

PLUMMET *US, male producer – Eric B Muniz and female vocalist – Cheramy Burgess (2 Singles: 12 Weeks)*

26 Apr 03 **DAMAGED** *Serious SER 68CD*..........12 10
8 May 04 **CHERISH THE DAY** *Manifesto 9866389*..........**35** 2

PLUS ONE featuring SIRRON

UK, male / female vocal / instrumental group

19 May 90 **IT'S HAPPENIN'** *MCA MCA 1405*..........**40** 4

PLUX featuring Georgia JONES

US, male / female vocal / instrumental group

4 May 96 **OVER AND OVER** *ffrr FCD 277*..........33 2

The POETS *UK, male vocal / instrumental group*

29 Oct 64 **NOW WE'RE THRU** *Decca F 11995*..........31 5

The POGUES 448 Top 500

Irish band originally named Pogue Mahone who presented an aggressive, compelling collision of folk, punk and rock, led by Shane McGowan (v/g).

5 November 1983	12 November 1983	19 November 1983	26 November 1983
UPTOWN GIRL Billy Joel	UPTOWN GIRL Billy Joel	UPTOWN GIRL Billy Joel	UPTOWN GIRL Billy Joel
COLOUR BY NUMBERS Culture Club	CAN'T SLOW DOWN Lionel Richie	COLOUR BY NUMBERS Culture Club	COLOUR BY NUMBERS Culture Club

KEY: UK No.1 ★ UK Top 10 ● Still on chart + UK entry at No.1 ■ US No.1 ▲ UK million seller £ US million seller $
Singles re-entries are listed as (re), (2re), (3re)... which signifies that the hit re-entered the chart once, twice or three times...

Peak Position / Weeks

b. 25 Dec 1957. 'The Irish Rover' was the final Top 20 hit released by the legendary Stiff label (9 Albums: 89 Weeks, 19 Singles: 71 Weeks)

3 Nov 84	RED ROSES FOR ME *Stiff SEEZ 55*	89	1
6 Apr 85	**A PAIR OF BROWN EYES** *Stiff BUY 220*	72	2
22 Jun 85	**SALLY MACLENNANE** *Stiff BUY 224*	51	4
17 Aug 85	RUM SODOMY & THE LASH *Stiff SEEZ 58*	13	14
14 Sep 85	**DIRTY OLD TOWN** *Stiff BUY 229*	62	3
8 Mar 86	**POGUETRY IN MOTION (EP)** *Stiff BUY 243*	29	6
30 Aug 86	**HAUNTED** *MCA MCA 1084*	42	4
28 Mar 87 ●	**THE IRISH ROVER** *Stiff BUY 258* [1]	8	8
5 Dec 87 ●	**FAIRYTALE OF NEW YORK** *Pogue Mahone NY 7* [2]	2	9
30 Jan 88 ●	IF I SHOULD FALL FROM GRACE WITH GOD *Stiff NYR 1*	3	16
5 Mar 88	**IF I SHOULD FALL FROM GRACE WITH GOD** *Pogue Mahone PG 1*	58	3
16 Jul 88	**FIESTA** *Pogue Mahone PG 2*	24	5
17 Dec 88	**YEAH, YEAH, YEAH, YEAH, YEAH** *Pogue Mahone YZ 355*	43	4
8 Jul 89	**MISTY MORNING, ALBERT BRIDGE** *PM YZ 407*	41	3
29 Jul 89 ●	PEACE AND LOVE *WEA WX 247*	5	8
16 Jun 90	**JACK'S HEROES / WHISKEY IN THE JAR** *PM YZ 500* [1]	63	2
15 Sep 90	**SUMMER IN SIAM** *PM YZ 519*	64	2
13 Oct 90	HELL'S DITCH *Pogue Mahone WX 366*	12	5
21 Sep 91	**A RAINY NIGHT IN SOHO** *PM YZ 603*	67	1
12 Oct 91	THE BEST OF THE POGUES *PM WX 430*	11	17
14 Dec 91	**FAIRYTALE OF NEW YORK** (re-issue) *PM YZ 628* [2]	36	5
30 May 92	**HONKY TONK WOMEN** *PM YZ 673*	56	2
21 Aug 93	**TUESDAY MORNING** *PM YZ 758CD*	18	5
11 Sep 93	WAITING FOR HERB *PM 4509934632*	20	3
22 Jan 94	**ONCE UPON A TIME** *PM YZ 771CD*	66	2
17 Mar 01	THE VERY BEST OF THE POGUES *WSM 8573874592*	18	19
19 Mar 05	THE ULTIMATE COLLECTION *WSM 2564622542*	15	6
31 Dec 05 ●	**FAIRYTALE OF NEW YORK** (2nd re-issue) *Warner Bros. WEA 400CD* [2]	3	1+

[1] The Pogues and The Dubliners [2] The Pogues featuring Kirsty MacColl

Tracks on Poguetry in Motion (EP): London Girl / The Body of an American / A Rainy Night in Soho / Planxty Noel Hill. The Pogues were male / female for their first two albums.

POINT BREAK

UK, male vocal group (1 Album: 3 Weeks, 5 Singles: 21 Weeks)

9 Oct 99	**DO WE ROCK** *Eternal WEA 216CD1*	29	2
22 Jan 00 ●	**STAND TOUGH** *Eternal WEA 248CD1*	7	5
22 Apr 00	**FREAKYTIME** *Eternal WEA 265CD1*	13	6
5 Aug 00	**YOU** *Eternal WEA 290CD1*	14	5
19 Aug 00	APOCADELIC *Eternal 8573828882*	21	3
2 Dec 00	**WHAT ABOUT US** *Eternal WEA 314CD1*	24	3

The POINTER SISTERS (410 Top 500)

Talented sibling vocal quartet formed in 1971, Oakland, California, US, whose recordings touched many musical bases. Reduced to a trio – June, Anita and Ruth – when Bonnie left in 1978. Soulful sisters surprisingly won a country music Grammy for 'Fairytale' in 1974 (4 Albums: 88 Weeks, 10 Singles: 87 Weeks)

3 Feb 79	**EVERYBODY IS A STAR** *Planet K 12324*	61	3
17 Mar 79	**FIRE** *Planet K 12339* $	34	8
22 Aug 81 ●	**SLOWHAND** *Planet K 12530* $	10	11
29 Aug 81	BLACK AND WHITE *Planet K 52300*	21	13
5 Dec 81	**SHOULD I DO IT?** *Planet K 12578*	50	5
14 Apr 84 ●	**AUTOMATIC** *Planet RPS 105*	2	15
5 May 84 ●	BREAK OUT *Planet PL 84705*	9	58
23 Jun 84 ●	**JUMP (FOR MY LOVE)** *Planet RPS 106*	6	10
11 Aug 84	**I NEED YOU** *Planet RPS 107*	25	9
27 Oct 84	**I'M SO EXCITED** *Planet RPS 108*	11	11
12 Jan 85	**NEUTRON DANCE** *Planet RPS 109*	31	7
20 Jul 85	**DARE ME** *RCA PB 49957*	17	8
27 Jul 85	CONTACT *Planet PL 85457*	34	7
29 Jul 89	JUMP – THE BEST OF THE POINTER SISTERS *RCA PL 90319*	11	10

POISON

US, male vocal (Bret Michaels) / instrumental group (4 Albums: 37 Weeks, 11 Singles: 43 Weeks)

23 May 87	**TALK DIRTY TO ME** *Music for Nations KUT 125*	67	1
7 May 88	**NOTHIN' BUT A GOOD TIME** *Capitol CL 486*	35	3
21 May 88	OPEN UP AND SAY ... AAH! *Capitol EST 2059*	18	21
5 Nov 88	**FALLEN ANGEL** *Capitol CL 500*	59	1
11 Feb 89	**EVERY ROSE HAS ITS THORN** *Capitol CL 520* ▲	13	9
29 Apr 89	**YOUR MAMA DON'T DANCE** *Capitol CL 523*	13	7
23 Sep 89	**NOTHIN' BUT A GOOD TIME** (re-issue) *Capitol CL 539*	48	3
30 Jun 90	**UNSKINNY BOP** *Capitol CL 582*	15	7
21 Jul 90 ●	FLESH AND BLOOD *Enigma EST 2126*	3	11
27 Oct 90	**SOMETHING TO BELIEVE IN** *Enigma CL 594*	35	4
23 Nov 91	**SO TELL ME WHY** *Capitol CL 640*	25	2
14 Dec 91	SWALLOW THIS LIVE *Capitol ESTU 2159*	52	2
13 Feb 93	**STAND** *Capitol CDCL 679*	25	3
6 Mar 93	NATIVE TONGUE *Capitol CDSETU 2190*	20	3
24 Apr 93	**UNTIL YOU SUFFER SOME (FIRE AND ICE)** *Capitol CDCL 685*	32	3

POKER PETS featuring Nate JAMES NEW

Sweden, male production duo and UK, male vocalist

25 Jun 05	**LOVIN' YOU** *Positiva CDTIVS 218*	43	1

The POLECATS

UK, male vocal / instrumental group (1 Album: 2 Weeks, 3 Singles: 18 Weeks)

7 Mar 81	**JOHN I'M ONLY DANCING / BIG GREEN CAR** *Mercury POLE 1*	35	8
16 May 81	**ROCKABILLY GUY** *Mercury POLE 2*	35	6
4 Jul 81	POLECATS *Vertigo 6359 057*	28	2
22 Aug 81	**JEEPSTER / MARIE CELESTE** *Mercury POLE 3*	53	4

The POLICE (64 Top 500)

(see also Klark KENT) *World-famous Anglo-American rock trio: Sting (v/b) (b. Gordon Sumner), Andy Summers (g/v) and Stewart Copeland (d/v). These BRIT and Grammy award-winners and Rock and Roll Hall of Fame members were one of the 1980s' most popular acts. 'Every Breath You Take' has had over eight million US radio plays. They had five successive albums enter the UK chart at No.1. Total UK single sales: 5,617,175 (9 Albums: 405 Weeks, 20 Singles: 153 Weeks)*

7 Oct 78 ●	**CAN'T STAND LOSING YOU (re)** *A&M AMS 7381*	2	16
21 Apr 79 ●	OUTLANDOS D'AMOUR *A&M AMLH 68502*	6	96
28 Apr 79	**ROXANNE** *A&M AMS 7348*	12	9
22 Sep 79 ★	**MESSAGE IN A BOTTLE** *A&M AMS 7474*	1	11
13 Oct 79 ★	REGGATTA DE BLANC *A&M AMLH 64792* ■	1	74
17 Nov 79	**FALL OUT** *Illegal IL 001*	47	4
1 Dec 79 ★	**WALKING ON THE MOON** *A&M AMS 7494*	1	10
16 Feb 80 ●	**SO LONELY** *A&M AMS 7402*	6	10
14 Jun 80	**SIX PACK** *A&M AMPP 6001*	17	4
27 Sep 80 ★	**DON'T STAND SO CLOSE TO ME** *A&M AMS 7564* ■	1	10
11 Oct 80 ★	ZENYATTA MONDATTA *A&M AMLH 64831* ■	1	31
13 Dec 80 ●	**DE DO DO DO, DE DA DA DA** *A&M AMS 7578*	5	8
26 Sep 81 ●	**INVISIBLE SUN** *A&M AMS 8164*	2	8
10 Oct 81 ★	GHOST IN THE MACHINE *A&M AMLK 63730* ■	1	27
24 Oct 81 ★	**EVERY LITTLE THING SHE DOES IS MAGIC** *A&M AMS 8174*	1	13
12 Dec 81	**SPIRITS IN THE MATERIAL WORLD** *A&M AMS 8194*	12	8
28 May 83 ★	**EVERY BREATH YOU TAKE** *A&M AM 117* ▲ $	1	11
25 Jun 83 ★	SYNCHRONICITY *A&M AMLX 63735* ■ ▲	1	48
23 Jul 83 ●	**WRAPPED AROUND YOUR FINGER** *A&M AM 127*	7	7
5 Nov 83	**SYNCHRONICITY II** *A&M AM 153*	17	4
14 Jan 84	**KING OF PAIN** *A&M AM 176*	17	5
11 Oct 86	**DON'T STAND SO CLOSE TO ME '86** (re-mix) *A&M AM 354*	24	4
8 Nov 86 ★	EVERY BREATH YOU TAKE – THE SINGLES *A&M EVERY 1* ■	1	55
10 Oct 92 ●	GREATEST HITS *A&M 5400302*	10	21
13 May 95	**CAN'T STAND LOSING YOU (LIVE)** *A&M 5810372*	27	2
10 Jun 95	LIVE! *A&M 540222*	25	3

	3 December 1983	10 December 1983	17 December 1983	24 December 1983
UK No.1 SINGLES	UPTOWN GIRL Billy Joel	ONLY YOU The Flying Pickets	ONLY YOU The Flying Pickets	ONLY YOU The Flying Pickets
UK No.1 ALBUMS	SEVEN AND THE RAGGED TIGER Duran Duran	NO PARLEZ Paul Young	NOW THAT'S WHAT I CALL MUSIC! Various	NOW THAT'S WHAT I CALL MUSIC! Various

22 Nov 97 ★	THE VERY BEST OF STING AND THE POLICE *A&M 5404282* [1] ■	1	50
20 Dec 97	ROXANNE '97 (re-mix) *A&M 5824552* [1]	17	6
5 Aug 00	WHEN THE WORLD IS RUNNING DOWN *Pagan PAGAN 039CDS* [2]	28	3

[1] Sting and The Police [2] Different Gear vs The Police [1] Sting and The Police

'Can't Stand Losing You' made No.42 on its first chart visit and peaked at No.2 only on re-entry in Jul 1979. 'Six Pack' consists of six separate Police singles as follows: The Bed's Too Big Without You / Roxanne / Message in a Bottle / Walking on the Moon / So Lonely / Can't Stand Losing You. The Very Best of Sting and The Police originally peaked at No.11. On 2 Mar 2002, an updated version containing three new tracks re-entered the chart and sales were combined with the original album.

Su POLLARD
UK, female actor / vocalist (1 Album: 3 Weeks, 2 Singles: 11 Weeks)

5 Oct 85	COME TO ME (I AM WOMAN) *Rainbow RBR 1*	71	1
1 Feb 86 ●	STARTING TOGETHER *Rainbow RBR 4*	2	10
22 Nov 86	SU *K-Tel NE 1327*	86	3

Jimi POLO *US, male vocalist (3 Singles: 5 Weeks)*

9 Nov 91	NEVER GOIN' DOWN *MCA MCS 1578* [1]	51	2
1 Aug 92	EXPRESS YOURSELF *Perfecto 74321101827*	59	2
9 Aug 97	EXPRESS YOURSELF *Perfecto PERF 146CD1*	62	1

[1] Adamski featuring Jimi Polo

The listed flip side of 'Never Goin' Down' was 'Born to Be Alive' by Adamski featuring Soho.

POLOROID *UK, male / female production / vocal trio*

11 Oct 03	SO DAMN BEAUTIFUL *Decode / Telstar CDSTAS 3351*	28	2

POLTERGEIST (see also ART OF TRANCE; VICIOUS CIRCLES)
UK, male producer – Simon Berry

6 Jul 96	VICIOUS CIRCLES *Manifesto FESCD 8*	32	2

Peter POLYCARPOU *UK, male actor / vocalist*

20 Feb 93	LOVE HURTS *Soundtrack Music CDEM 259*	26	4

POLYGON WINDOW (see also AFX; APHEX TWIN; POWERPILL)
UK, male producer – Richard James

3 Apr 93	QUOTH *Warp WAP 33CD*	49	1

The POLYPHONIC SPREE *US, male / female vocal / instrumental ensemble (2 Albums: 2 Weeks, 4 Singles: 5 Weeks)*

2 Nov 02	HANGING AROUND *679 Recordings 679L 012CD*	39	1
22 Feb 03	LIGHT AND DAY *679 Recordings 679L 015CD 1*	40	1
12 Jul 03	THE BEGINNING STAGES OF ... THE POLYPHONIC SPREE *679 Recordings 5046609182*	70	1
26 Jul 03	SOLDIER GIRL *679 Recordings 679L 014CD*	26	2
24 Jul 04	TOGETHER WE'RE HEAVY *Good POLYCD 1*	61	1
7 Aug 04	HOLD ME NOW *Good CDPOLY 1*	72	1

PONDLIFE NEW *UK, male production group*

18 Jun 05	RING DING DING *Gut CDSBOG 14*	11	8

The PONI-TAILS *US, female vocal group (2 Singles: 14 Weeks)*

19 Sep 58 ●	BORN TOO LATE *HMV POP 516*	5	11
10 Apr 59	EARLY TO BED *HMV POP 596*	26	3

Glyn POOLE *UK, male vocalist*

20 Oct 73	MILLY MOLLY MANDY *York SYK 565*	35	8

Ian POOLEY *Germany, male DJ / producer (3 Singles: 3 Weeks)*

10 Mar 01	900 DEGREES *V2 VVR 5015143*	57	1
11 Aug 01	BALMES *V2 VVR 5016613* [1]	65	1
23 Nov 02	PIHA *Honchos Music HONMO 019CD* [2]	53	1

[1] Ian Pooley featuring Esthero [2] Ian Pooley and Magik J

POP! *UK, male / female vocal group (3 Singles: 8 Weeks)*

12 Jun 04	HEAVEN AND EARTH *Jive 82876619582*	14	2
11 Sep 04	CAN'T SAY GOODBYE *Jive 82876639492*	26	3
22 Jan 05	SERIOUS *Ebul / Jive 82876668682*	16	3

Sales for the CD single of 'Heaven and Earth' excluded from chart statistics after one week, because it contained a combined track length longer than that permitted for the format.

Iggy POP *US, male vocalist – James Jewel Osterburg (9 Albums: 27 Weeks, 9 Singles: 31 Weeks)*

9 Apr 77	THE IDIOT *RCA Victor PL 12275*	30	3
4 Jun 77	RAW POWER *Embassy 31464* [1]	44	2
1 Oct 77	LUST FOR LIFE *RCA PL 12488*	28	5
19 May 79	NEW VALUES *Arista SPART 1092*	60	4
16 Feb 80	SOLDIER *Arista SPART 1117*	62	2
11 Oct 86	BLAH-BLAH-BLAH *A&M AMA 5145*	43	7
13 Dec 86 ●	REAL WILD CHILD (WILD ONE) *A&M AM 368*	10	11
2 Jul 88	INSTINCT *A&M AMA 5198*	61	1
10 Feb 90	LIVIN' ON THE EDGE OF THE NIGHT *Virgin America VUS 18*	51	4
21 Jul 90	BRICK BY BRICK *Virgin America VUSLP 19*	50	2
13 Oct 90	CANDY *Virgin America VUS 29*	67	1
5 Jan 91	WELL DID YOU EVAH! *Chrysalis CHS 3646* [1]	42	4
4 Sep 93	WILD AMERICA (EP) *Virgin America VUSCD 74*	63	1
25 Sep 93	AMERICAN CAESAR *Virgin CDVUS 64*	43	1
21 May 94	BESIDE YOU *Virgin America VUSCD 77*	47	2
23 Nov 96	LUST FOR LIFE *Virgin America VUSCD 116*	26	2
7 Mar 98	THE PASSENGER *Virgin VSCDT 1689*	22	3
17 Jan 04	KICK IT *XL Recordings XLS 176CD* [2]	39	3

[1] Deborah Harry and Iggy Pop [2] Peaches featuring Iggy Pop [1] Iggy and The Stooges

Tracks on Wild America (EP): Wild America / Credit Card / Come Back Tomorrow / My Angel.

POP WILL EAT ITSELF *UK, male vocal (Clint Mansell) / instrumental group (7 Albums: 14 Weeks, 15 Singles: 43 Weeks)*

30 Jan 88	THERE IS NO LOVE BETWEEN US ANYMORE *Chapter 22 CHAP 20*	66	1
23 Jul 88	DEF CON ONE *Chapter 22 PWEI 001*	63	4
11 Feb 89	CAN U DIG IT? *RCA PB 42621*	38	4
22 Apr 89	WISE UP! SUCKER *RCA PB 42761*	41	3
13 May 89	THIS IS THE DAY ... THIS IS THE HOUR ... THIS IS THIS! *RCA PL 74141*	24	2
2 Sep 89	VERY METAL NOISE POLLUTION (EP) *RCA PB 42883*	45	3
9 Jun 90	TOUCHED BY THE HAND OF CICCIOLINA *RCA PB 43735*	28	4
13 Oct 90	DANCE OF THE MAD *RCA PB 44023*	32	2
2 Nov 90	CURE FOR SANITY *RCA PL 74828*	33	3
12 Jan 91	X Y & ZEE *RCA PB 44243*	15	4
1 Jun 91	92°F *RCA PB 44555*	23	3
6 Jun 92	KARMADROME / EAT ME DRINK ME LOVE ME *RCA PB 45467*	17	2
29 Aug 92	BULLETPROOF! *RCA 74321110137*	24	3
19 Sep 92	THE LOOKS OR THE LIFESTYLE *RCA 74321102652*	15	3
16 Jan 93 ●	GET THE GIRL! KILL THE BADDIES! *RCA 74321128802*	9	4
6 Mar 93	WEIRD'S BAR AND GRILL *RCA 74321133432*	44	1
16 Oct 93	RSVP / FAMILIUS HORRIBILUS *Infectious INFECT 1CD*	27	2
6 Nov 93	16 DIFFERENT FLAVOURS OF HELL *RCA 74321153172*	73	1
12 Mar 94	ICH BIN EIN AUSLANDER *Infectious INFECT 4CD*	28	2
10 Sep 94	EVERYTHING'S COOL? *Infectious INFECT 9CD*	23	2
1 Oct 94	DOS DEDOS MIS AMIGOS *Infectious INFECT 10CDX*	11	2
18 Mar 95	TWO FINGERS MY FRIENDS *Infectious INFECT 10CDRX*	25	2

Tracks on Very Metal Noise Pollution (EP): Def Con 1989 AD Including the Twilight Zone / Preaching to the Perverted / PWEI-zation / 92°F. Two Fingers My Friends is a re-mixed version of Dos Dedos Mis Amigos.

31 December 1983	7 January 1984	14 January 1984	21 January 1984
ONLY YOU The Flying Pickets	ONLY YOU The Flying Pickets	PIPES OF PEACE Paul McCartney	PIPES OF PEACE Paul McCartney
NOW THAT'S WHAT I CALL MUSIC! Various	NOW THAT'S WHAT I CALL MUSIC! Various	NO PARLEZ Paul Young	NOW THAT'S WHAT I CALL MUSIC! Various

KEY: UK No.1 ★★ UK Top 10 ●● Still on chart ++ UK entry at No.1 ■■ US No.1 ▲▲ UK million seller £ US million seller $ Singles re-entries are listed as (re), (2re), (3re)... which signifies that the hit re-entered the chart once, twice or three times... Peak Position / Weeks

POPE JOHN PAUL II *Poland, male pontiff – Karol J Wojtyla, b. 18 May 1920, d. 2 Apr 2005 (2 Albums: 8 Weeks)*

3 Jul 82 JOHN PAUL II – THE PILGRIM POPE *BBC REB 445* 71 4
10 Dec 94 THE ROSARY *Pure Music PMCD 7009* 50 4

The Rosary is a double CD or cassette, one with the Rosary in Latin by the Pope, the other featuring its English reading by Father Kilcoyne.

POPPERS presents AURA *UK, male production trio and female vocalist*

25 Oct 97 **EVERY LITTLE TIME** *VC VCRD 26* **44** 1

The POPPY FAMILY *Canada, male / female vocal / instrumental duo – Terry Jacks and Susan Peklevits*

15 Aug 70 ● **WHICH WAY YOU GOIN' BILLY?** *Decca F 22976* $ **7** 14

The POPPY FIELDS (see also The ALARM) *UK, male vocal / instrumental group*

21 Feb 04 **45 R.P.M.** *Snapper Music SMASCD 054* **28** 2

The Poppy Fields is The Alarm under a different name.

PORN KINGS *UK, male instrumental / production group (5 Singles: 12 Weeks)*

28 Sep 96 **UP TO NO GOOD** *All Around the World CDGLOBE 145* **28** 2
21 Jun 97 **AMOUR (C'MON)** *All Around the World CDGLOBE 152* **17** 3
16 Jan 99 ● **UP TO THE WILDSTYLE** *All Around the World CDGLOBE 170* [1] **10** 4
10 Feb 01 **SLEDGER** *All Around the World CDGLOBE 229* **71** 1
22 Mar 03 **SHAKE YA SHIMMY** *All Around the World CDGLOBE 213* [2] **28** 2

[1] Porn Kings vs DJ Supreme [2] Porn Kings vs Flip & Fill featuring 740 Boyz

PORNO FOR PYROS *US, male vocal / instrumental group (2 Albums: 5 Weeks, 1 Single: 2 Weeks)*

8 May 93 PORNO FOR PYROS *Warner Bros. 9362452282* 13 3
5 Jun 93 **PETS** *Warner Bros. W 0177CD* **53** 2
8 Jun 96 GOOD GOD'S URGE *Warner Bros. 9362461262* 40 2

PORTISHEAD *UK, male / female vocal (Beth Gibbons) / instrumental group (3 Albums: 95 Weeks, 5 Singles: 20 Weeks)*

13 Aug 94 **SOUR TIMES (re)** *Go Beat GODCD 116* **13** 5
3 Sep 94 ● DUMMY *Go Beat 8285222* 2 71
14 Jan 95 **GLORY BOX** *Go Beat GODCD 120* **13** 7
20 Sep 97 ● **ALL MINE** *Go Beat 5715972* **8** 4
11 Oct 97 ● PORTISHEAD *Go Beat 5391892* 2 22
22 Nov 97 **OVER** *Go Beat 5719932* **25** 2
14 Mar 98 **ONLY YOU** *Go Beat 5694752* **35** 2
14 Nov 98 PNYC *Go Beat 5594242* 40 2

'Sour Times' made No.57 on its first chart visit and peaked at No.13 in Apr 1995.

Gary PORTNOY *US, male vocalist*

25 Feb 84 **THEME FROM 'CHEERS'** *Starblend CHEER 1* **58** 3

PORTOBELLA *UK, male / female vocal / instrumental group*

26 Jun 04 **COVERED IN PUNK** *Island CID 962* **54** 1

PORTRAIT *US, male vocal group (3 Singles: 6 Weeks)*

27 Mar 93 **HERE WE GO AGAIN** *Capitol CDCL 683* **37** 3
8 Apr 95 **I CAN CALL YOU** *Capitol CDCL 740* **61** 1
8 Jul 95 **HOW DEEP IS YOUR LOVE** *Capitol CDCL 751* **41** 2

PORTSMOUTH SINFONIA *UK, orchestra*

12 Sep 81 **CLASSICAL MUDDLY** *Island WIP 6736* **38** 4

Sandy POSEY *US, female vocalist (1 Album: 1 Week, 4 Singles: 32 Weeks)*

15 Sep 66 **BORN A WOMAN** *MGM 1321* **24** 11
5 Jan 67 **SINGLE GIRL** *MGM 1330* **15** 13
11 Mar 67 BORN A WOMAN *MGM MGMCS 8035* 39 1
13 Apr 67 **WHAT A WOMAN IN LOVE WON'T DO** *MGM 1335* **48** 3
6 Sep 75 **SINGLE GIRL** (re-issue) *MGM 2006 533* **35** 5

The POSIES *US, male vocal / instrumental group*

19 Mar 94 **DEFINITE DOOR** *Geffen GFSTD 68* **67** 1

POSITIVE FORCE *US, female vocal duo – Brenda Reynolds and Vicki Drayton*

22 Dec 79 **WE GOT THE FUNK** *Sugarhill SHL 102* **18** 9

POSITIVE GANG *UK, male / female vocal / instrumental group (2 Singles: 5 Weeks)*

17 Apr 93 **SWEET FREEDOM** *PWL Continental PWCD 261* **34** 4
31 Jul 93 **SWEET FREEDOM PART 2** *PWL Continental PWCD 264* **67** 1

POSITIVE K *US, male rapper – Darryl Gibson*

15 May 93 **I GOT A MAN** *Fourth & Broadway BRCD 280* **43** 2

Mike POST *US, orchestra (3 Singles: 18 Weeks)*

9 Aug 75 **AFTERNOON OF THE RHINO (re)** *Warner Bros. K 16588* [1] **47** 2
16 Jan 82 **THEME FROM 'HILL STREET BLUES'** *Elektra K 12576* [2] **25** 11
29 Sep 84 **THE A TEAM** *RCA 443* **45** 5

[1] Mike Post Coalition [2] Mike Post featuring Larry Carlton

Robert POST NEW *Norway, male vocalist*

3 Sep 05 **GOT NONE** *Mercury 9872370* **42** 2

The POTTERS *UK, male Stoke City football supporters vocal group*

1 Apr 72 **WE'LL BE WITH YOU** *Pye JT 100* **34** 2

Frank POURCEL *France, male orchestra – leader b. 1 Jan 1915, d. 12 Dec 2000*

20 Nov 71 ● THIS IS POURCEL *Studio Two STWO 7* 8 7

POWDER *UK, male / female vocal / instrumental group*

24 Jun 95 **AFRODISIAC** *Parkway PARK 002CD* **72** 1

Bryan POWELL *UK, male vocalist (3 Singles: 3 Weeks)*

13 Mar 93 **IT'S ALRIGHT** *Talkin Loud TLKCD 34* **73** 1
15 May 93 **I THINK OF YOU** *Talkin Loud TLKCD 38* **61** 1
7 Aug 93 **NATURAL** *Talkin Loud TLKCD 41* **73** 1

Cozy POWELL (see also BLACK SABBATH; Graham BONNET; EMERSON, LAKE & POWELL; Bernie MARSDEN; Gary MOORE; RAINBOW; Michael SCHENKER GROUP; WHITESNAKE) *UK, male drummer – Colin Flooks, b. 29 Dec 1947, d. 5 Apr 1998 (3 Albums: 8 Weeks, 5 Singles: 38 Weeks)*

8 Dec 73 ● **DANCE WITH THE DEVIL** *RAK 164* **3** 15
25 May 74 **THE MAN IN BLACK** *RAK 173* **18** 8
10 Aug 74 ● **NA NA NA** *RAK 180* **10** 10
10 Nov 79 **THEME ONE** *Ariola ARO 189* **62** 2
26 Jan 80 OVER THE TOP *Ariola ARL 5038* 34 3
19 Sep 81 TILT *Polydor POLD 5047* 58 4
28 May 83 OCTOPUSS *Polydor POLD 5093* 86 1
19 Jun 93 **RESURRECTION** *Parlophone CDRS 6351* [1] **23** 3

[1] Brian May with Cozy Powell

28 January 1984	4 February 1984	11 February 1984	18 February 1984
UK No.1 SINGLES			
RELAX Frankie Goes to Hollywood	RELAX Frankie Goes to Hollywood	RELAX Frankie Goes to Hollywood	RELAX Frankie Goes to Hollywood
UK No.1 ALBUMS			
THRILLER Michael Jackson	TOUCH Eurythmics	TOUCH Eurythmics	SPARKLE IN THE RAIN Simple Minds

Peter POWELL *UK, male exercise instructor*

20 Mar 82 ● KEEP FIT AND DANCE *K-Tel NE 1167*.....9 13

POWER OF DREAMS
Ireland, male vocal / instrumental group (2 Singles: 2 Weeks)

19 Jan 91 **AMERICAN DREAM** *Polydor PO 117*.....**74** 1
11 Apr 92 **THERE I GO AGAIN** *Polydor PO 200*.....**65** 1

POWER STATION (see also CHIC; DURAN DURAN; Robert PALMER) *UK / US, male vocal / instrumental group (1 Album: 23 Weeks, 4 Singles: 17 Weeks)*

16 Mar 85 **SOME LIKE IT HOT** *Parlophone R 6091*.....**14** 8
6 Apr 85 THE POWER STATION *Parlophone POST 1*.....12 23
11 May 85 **GET IT ON** *Parlophone R 6096*.....**22** 7
9 Nov 85 **COMMUNICATION** *Parlophone R 6114*.....**75** 1
12 Oct 96 **SHE CAN ROCK IT** *Chrysalis CDCHS 5039*.....**63** 1

POWERCUT featuring NUBIAN PRINZ
US, male vocal / instrumental group

22 Jun 91 **GIRLS** *Eternal YZ 570*.....**50** 4

POWERHOUSE
UK, male production duo – Hamilton Dean and Julian Slatter

20 Dec 97 **RHYTHM OF THE NIGHT** *Satellite 74321522592*.....**38** 4

POWERHOUSE featuring Duane HARDEN (see also Armand VAN HELDEN) *US, male producer – Lenny Fontana and vocalist*

22 May 99 **WHAT YOU NEED** *Defected DEFECT 3CDS*.....**13** 5

POWERPILL (see also AFX; APHEX TWIN; POLYGON WINDOW)
UK, male instrumentalist / producer – Richard James

6 Jun 92 **PAC-MAN** *Ffrreedom TABX 110*.....**43** 3

POWERS THAT BE
UK / Sweden, male production duo – Giles Goodman and Pierre Jerksten

26 Jul 03 **PLANET ROCK / FUNKY PLANET** *Defected DFTD 074*.....**63** 1

Will POWERS *US, female vocalist – Lyn Goldsmith*

1 Oct 83 **KISSING WITH CONFIDENCE** *Island IS 134*.....**17** 9

Hit features uncredited vocals by Carly Simon.

Daniel POWTER NEW *Canada, male vocalist / keyboard player*

6 Aug 05 ● **BAD DAY** *Warner Bros. W 682CD2*.....**2** 22+
20 Aug 05 ● DANIEL POWTER *Warner Bros. 9362493322*.....5 20+

Perez PRADO and his Orchestra *Cuba, orchestra – leader Damas Prado, b. 11 Dec 1916, d. 14 Sep 1989 (3 Singles: 57 Weeks)*

25 Mar 55 ★ **CHERRY PINK AND APPLE BLOSSOM WHITE** *HMV B 10833* [1] ▲ $.....**1** 17
25 Jul 58 ● **PATRICIA** *RCA 1067* $.....**8** 16
10 Dec 94 ● **GUAGLIONE (2re)** *RCA 74321250192* [2].....**2** 24

[1] Perez 'Prez' Prado and his Orchestra, the King of the Mambo [2] Perez 'Prez' Prado and his Orchestra

'Guaglione' did not made its peak position until its second re-entry in May 1995 after first making No.41 in 1994 and No.58 on its first re-entry.

PRAISE *UK, male / female vocal / instrumental group*

2 Feb 91 ● **ONLY YOU** *Epic 6566117*.....**4** 7

Uncredited vocals by Miriam Stockley.

PRAISE CATS (see also E-SMOOVE featuring Latanza WATERS; THICK D)
US, male producer – Eric 'E-Smoove' Miller (2 Singles: 5 Weeks)

26 Oct 02 **SHINED ON ME** *Pias PIAS 028CD*.....**56** 1
21 May 05 **SHINED ON ME** (re-mix) *All Around the World CDGLOBE 380* [1].....**24** 4

[1] Praise Cats featuring Andrea Love

PRATT and McCLAIN with BROTHERLOVE
US, male vocal duo – Truett Pratt and Jerry McClain and instrumental group

1 Oct 77 **HAPPY DAYS** *Reprise K 14435*.....**31** 6

PRAXIS featuring KATHY BROWN *UK, male producer – David Shaw and US, female vocalist (2 Singles: 5 Weeks)*

25 Nov 95 **TURN ME OUT** *Stress CDSTR 40*.....**44** 2
20 Sep 97 **TURN ME OUT (TURN TO SUGAR)** (re-mix) *ffrr FCD 314*.....**35** 3

PRAYING MANTIS *UK, male vocal / instrumental group*

31 Jan 81 **CHEATED** *Arista ARIST 378*.....**69** 2
11 Apr 81 TIME TELLS NO LIES *Arista SPART 1153*.....60 2

PRECIOUS *UK, female vocal group (4 Singles: 20 Weeks)*

29 May 99 ● **SAY IT AGAIN (re)** *EMI CDEM 544*.....**6** 11
1 Apr 00 **REWIND** *EMI CDEM 557*.....**11** 5
15 Jul 00 **IT'S GONNA BE MY WAY** *EMI CDEM 569*.....**27** 3
25 Nov 00 **NEW BEGINNING** *EMI CDEM 573*.....**50** 1

PRECOCIOUS BRATS featuring KEVIN and PERRY
(see also CLERGY; HI-GATE) *UK, male production duo – Julius O'Riordan (Judge Jules) and Matt Smith and male / female vocal / comedy duo – Harry Enfield and Kathy Burke*

6 May 00 **BIG GIRL** *Virgin / EMI VTSCD 1*.....**16** 4

PREFAB SPROUT (435 Top 500)
Critically-acclaimed, intelligent, fragile pop band, formed in 1978 in Newcastle, UK. Named after a phrase from the Frank Sinatra / Lee Hazlewood song 'Jackson' misheard by group leader / songwriter Paddy McAloon (v/g). Stevie Wonder and Pete Townshend guested on From Langley Park to Memphis (8 Albums: 106 Weeks, 16 Singles: 60 Weeks)

28 Jan 84 **DON'T SING** *Kitchenware SK 9*.....**62** 2
17 Mar 84 SWOON *Kitchenware KWLP 1*.....22 7
22 Jun 85 STEVE MCQUEEN *Kitchenware KWLP 3*.....21 35
20 Jul 85 **FARON YOUNG** *Kitchenware SK 22*.....**74** 1
9 Nov 85 **WHEN LOVE BREAKS DOWN** *Kitchenware SK 21*.....**25** 10
8 Feb 86 **JOHNNY JOHNNY** *Kitchenware SK 24*.....**64** 2
13 Feb 88 **CARS AND GIRLS** *Kitchenware SK 35*.....**44** 5
26 Mar 88 ● FROM LANGLEY PARK TO MEMPHIS *Kitchenware KWLP 9*.....5 24
30 Apr 88 ● **THE KING OF ROCK 'N' ROLL** *Kitchenware SK 37*.....**7** 10
23 Jul 88 **HEY MANHATTAN!** *Kitchenware SK 38*.....**72** 2
1 Jul 89 PROTEST SONGS *Kitchenware KWLP 4*.....18 4
18 Aug 90 **LOOKING FOR ATLANTIS** *Kitchenware SK 47*.....**51** 3
8 Sep 90 ● JORDAN: THE COMEBACK *Kitchenware KWLP 14*.....7 17
20 Oct 90 **WE LET THE STARS GO** *Kitchenware SK 48*.....**50** 3
5 Jan 91 **JORDAN: THE EP** *Kitchenware SK 49*.....**35** 4
13 Jun 92 **THE SOUND OF CRYING** *Kitchenware SK 58*.....**23** 5
11 Jul 92 ● A LIFE OF SURPRISES – THE BEST OF PREFAB SPROUT *Kitchenware 4718862*.....3 13
8 Aug 92 **IF YOU DON'T LOVE ME** *Kitchenware SK 60*.....**33** 4
3 Oct 92 **ALL THE WORLD LOVES LOVERS** *Kitchenware SK 62*.....**61** 2
9 Jan 93 **LIFE OF SURPRISES** *Kitchenware SKCD 63*.....**24** 4
10 May 97 **A PRISONER OF THE PAST** *Columbia SKZD 70*.....**30** 2
17 May 97 ● ANDROMEDA HEIGHTS *Columbia KWCD 30*.....7 5
2 Aug 97 **ELECTRIC GUITARS** *Columbia SKZD 71*.....**53** 1
30 Jun 01 THE GUNMAN AND OTHER STORIES *Liberty 5326132*.....60 1

Tracks on Jordan: The EP: Carnival 2000 / The Ice Maiden / One of the Broken / Jordan: The Comeback.

25 February 1984	3 March 1984	10 March 1984	17 March 1984
RELAX Frankie Goes to Hollywood	99 RED BALLOONS Nena	99 RED BALLOONS Nena	99 RED BALLOONS Nena
INTO THE GAP Thompson Twins	INTO THE GAP Thompson Twins	INTO THE GAP Thompson Twins	HUMAN'S LIB Howard Jones

KEY
UK No.1 ★ UK Top 10 ● Still on chart + UK entry at No.1 ■ US No.1 ▲ UK million seller £ US million seller $
Singles re-entries are listed as (re), (2re), (3re)... which signifies that the hit re-entered the chart once, twice or three times...
Peak Position / Weeks

PRESENCE UK, male / female vocal / production group (2 Singles: 2 Weeks)

PRELUDE UK, male / female vocal group (4 Singles: 26 Weeks)

26 Jan 74 **AFTER THE GOLDRUSH** *Dawn DNS 1052* 21 9
26 Apr 80 **PLATINUM BLONDE** *EMI 5046* 45 7
22 May 82 **AFTER THE GOLDRUSH** (re-recording) *After Hours AFT 02* 28 7
31 Jul 82 **ONLY THE LONELY** *After Hours AFT 06* 55 3

PRESENCE UK, male / female vocal / production group (2 Singles: 2 Weeks)

5 Dec 98 **SENSE OF DANGER** *Pagan PAGAN 024CDS* [1] 61 1
19 Jun 99 **FUTURE LOVE** *Pagan PAGAN 028CDS* 66 1

[1] Presence featuring Shara Nelson

The PRESIDENTS OF THE UNITED STATES OF AMERICA

US, male vocal (Chris Ballew) / instrumental trio (2 Albums: 31 Weeks, 5 Singles: 21 Weeks)

6 Jan 96 **LUMP** *Columbia 6624962* 15 7
13 Jan 96 THE PRESIDENTS OF THE UNITED STATES OF AMERICA *Columbia 4810392* 14 29
20 Apr 96 ● **PEACHES** *Columbia 6631072* 8 7
20 Jul 96 **DUNE BUGGY** *Columbia 6634892* 15 4
2 Nov 96 **MACH 5** *Columbia 6638812* 29 2
16 Nov 96 II *Columbia 4850922* 36 2
1 Aug 98 **VIDEO KILLED THE RADIO STAR** *Maverick W 0450CD* 52 1

Elvis PRESLEY (1 Top 500)

Elvis Aron Presley is the most influential and impersonated artist of the last 50 years, b. 8 Jan 1935, Mississippi, US, d. 16 Aug 1977. The singer, whose first five US singles failed to reach the pop charts, went from rock 'n' roll rebel to Las Vegas veteran and on the way sold more records than any other performer in history. He holds perhaps the most important UK chart-related record: more No.1s (21) than any act in chart history. No other solo artist of the rock era can match his number of singles (if you include re-issues) and album chart entries in the UK or US, nor his collection of platinum and gold records. The "King of Rock 'n' Roll" was the first artist to enter the UK chart at No.1 and the first to amass US advance orders in excess of one million copies for a single. In the UK, Elvis has a 46-year span of No.1 albums, holds the record for most simultaneous album chart entries (27 in the Top 100) and held the record for the most entries on the UK singles chart (nine) – yet he only ever spent two hours in Britain – at Prestick Airport, Scotland, on 3 March 1960, on his way back from Germany after serving in the US Army. The most documented entertainer ever has won hundreds of awards, starred in dozens of successful films, broken numerous box office records in North America (the only continent he ever performed in), made Memphis a major tourist attraction and was the first artist credited with sales of one billion records (20 million of which were reportedly sold the day after his death). In 2002, after a 25-year gap, he returned to top the UK singles chart and his album 'ELV1S' entered at No.1 in 17 countries. In 2004, he became a founder member of the UK Music Hall of Fame, and in 2005 a record-shattering 17 of his previous No.1 hits returned to the Top 5 in consecutive weeks. UK singles sales over 20 million. Best-selling single: 'It's Now or Never' 1,210,000 (120 Albums: 1299 Weeks, 154 Singles: 1279 Weeks)

11 May 56 ● **HEARTBREAK HOTEL** (re) *HMV POP 182* ▲ $ 2 22
25 May 56 ● **BLUE SUEDE SHOES** (re) *HMV POP 213* 9 10
13 Jul 56 **I WANT YOU, I NEED YOU, I LOVE YOU** (re) *HMV POP 235* ▲ $ 14 11
21 Sep 56 ● **HOUND DOG** *HMV POP 249* ▲ $ 2 23
3 Nov 56 ★ ROCK 'N ROLL *HMV CLP 1093* 1 16
16 Nov 56 ● **BLUE MOON** *HMV POP 272* 9 11
23 Nov 56 **I DON'T CARE IF THE SUN DON'T SHINE** (re) *HMV POP 272* 23 4
7 Dec 56 **LOVE ME TENDER** *HMV POP 253* ▲ $ 11 9
15 Feb 57 **MYSTERY TRAIN** *HMV POP 295* 25 5
8 Mar 57 **RIP IT UP** *HMV POP 305* 27 1
4 May 57 ● ROCK 'N ROLL (NO.2) *HMV CLP 1105* 3 3
10 May 57 ● **TOO MUCH** (re) *HMV POP 330* [1] ▲ $ 6 9
14 Jun 57 ★ **ALL SHOOK UP** (re) *HMV POP 359* [1] ▲ $ 1 21
12 Jul 57 ● **(LET ME BE YOUR) TEDDY BEAR** *RCA 1013* [1] ▲ $ 3 19
30 Aug 57 ● **PARALYZED** *HMV POP 378* 8 10
31 Aug 57 ★ LOVING YOU (SOUNDTRACK) *RCA RC 24001* ▲ 1 25
4 Oct 57 ● **PARTY** *RCA 1020* [1] 2 15
18 Oct 57 **GOT A LOT O' LIVIN' TO DO** *RCA 1020* [1] 17 4
26 Oct 57 ● THE BEST OF ELVIS *RCA DLP 1159* 3 7
1 Nov 57 **LOVING YOU** *RCA 1013* [1] 24 2
1 Nov 57 **TRYING TO GET TO YOU** *HMV POP 408* 16 4
8 Nov 57 **LAWDY MISS CLAWDY** *HMV POP 408* 15 5
15 Nov 57 ● **SANTA BRING MY BABY BACK (TO ME)** *RCA 1025* 7 8
30 Nov 57 ● ELVIS' CHRISTMAS ALBUM *RCA RD 27052* ▲ 2 6
17 Jan 58 **I'M LEFT, YOU'RE RIGHT, SHE'S GONE** (re) *HMV POP 428* 21 3
24 Jan 58 ★ **JAILHOUSE ROCK** (re) *RCA 1028* ■ ▲ $ 1 20
31 Jan 58 **JAILHOUSE ROCK (EP)** *RCA RCX 106* [1] 18 5
28 Feb 58 ● **DON'T** *RCA 1043* [1] ▲ $ 2 11
2 May 58 ● **WEAR MY RING AROUND YOUR NECK** *RCA 1058* [1] $ 3 10
25 Jul 58 ● **HARD HEADED WOMAN** *RCA 1070* [1] ▲ $ 2 11
13 Sep 58 ★ KING CREOLE (FILM SOUNDTRACK) *RCA RD 27086* 1 22
3 Oct 58 ● **KING CREOLE** *RCA 1081* [1] 2 15
11 Oct 58 ● ELVIS' GOLDEN RECORDS *RCA RB 16069* 2 48
23 Jan 59 ★ **ONE NIGHT / I GOT STUNG** *RCA 1100* $ 1 12
24 Apr 59 ★ **A FOOL SUCH AS I / I NEED YOUR LOVE TONIGHT** *RCA 1113* [1] $ 1 15
24 Jul 59 ● **A BIG HUNK O' LOVE** *RCA 1136* [1] ▲ $ 4 9
8 Aug 59 ● A DATE WITH ELVIS *RCA RD 27128* 4 15
12 Feb 60 **STRICTLY ELVIS (EP)** *RCA RCX 175* 26 1
7 Apr 60 ● **STUCK ON YOU** *RCA 1187* [1] ▲ $ 3 14
18 Jun 60 ● ELVIS' GOLDEN RECORDS VOLUME 2 *RCA RD 27159* 4 20
18 Jun 60 ★ ELVIS IS BACK! *RCA RD 27171* 1 27
28 Jul 60 ● **A MESS OF BLUES** *RCA 1194* [1] 2 18
3 Nov 60 ★ **IT'S NOW OR NEVER** *RCA 1207* [1] ■ ▲ £ $ 1 19
10 Dec 60 ★ G.I. BLUES (FILM SOUNDTRACK) *RCA RD 27192* ▲ 1 55
19 Jan 61 ★ **ARE YOU LONESOME TO-NIGHT?** *RCA 1216* [1] ▲ $ 1 15
9 Mar 61 ★ **WOODEN HEART** *RCA 1226* 1 27
20 May 61 ● HIS HAND IN MINE *RCA RD 27211* 3 25
25 May 61 ★ **SURRENDER** *RCA 1227* [1] ▲ $ 1 15
7 Sep 61 ● **WILD IN THE COUNTRY / I FEEL SO BAD** *RCA 1244* [1] 4 12
2 Nov 61 ★ **(MARIE'S THE NAME) HIS LATEST FLAME / LITTLE SISTER** *RCA 1258* 1 13
4 Nov 61 ● SOMETHING FOR EVERYBODY *RCA RD 27224* ▲ 2 18
9 Dec 61 ★ BLUE HAWAII (FILM SOUNDTRACK) *RCA RD 27238* ▲ 1 65
1 Feb 62 ★ **ROCK-A-HULA BABY / CAN'T HELP FALLING IN LOVE** *RCA 1270* [1] $ 1 20
10 May 62 ★ **GOOD LUCK CHARM** *RCA 1280* [1] ▲ $ 1 17
21 Jun 62 **FOLLOW THAT DREAM (EP)** *RCA RCX 211* 34 2
7 Jul 62 ★ POT LUCK *RCA RD 27265* 1 25
30 Aug 62 ★ **SHE'S NOT YOU** *RCA 1303* [1] 1 14
29 Nov 62 ★ **RETURN TO SENDER** *RCA 1320* [1] $ 1 14
8 Dec 62 ● ROCK 'N' ROLL NO.2 (re-issue) *RCA RD 7528* 3 17
26 Jan 63 ● GIRLS! GIRLS! GIRLS! (FILM SOUNDTRACK) *RCA RD 7534* 2 21
28 Feb 63 **ONE BROKEN HEART FOR SALE** *RCA 1337* [2] 12 9
11 May 63 ● IT HAPPENED AT THE WORLD'S FAIR (FILM SOUNDTRACK) *RCA RD 7565* 4 21
4 Jul 63 ★ **(YOU'RE THE) DEVIL IN DISGUISE** *RCA 1355* [1] $ 1 12
24 Oct 63 **BOSSA NOVA BABY** *RCA 1374* [1] 13 8
19 Dec 63 **KISS ME QUICK** *RCA 1375* [1] 14 10
28 Dec 63 ● FUN IN ACAPULCO (FILM SOUNDTRACK) *RCA RD 7609* 9 14
12 Mar 64 **VIVA LAS VEGAS** *RCA 1390* [1] 17 12
11 Apr 64 ● ELVIS' GOLDEN RECORDS VOLUME 3 *RCA RD 7630* 6 13
25 Jun 64 ● **KISSIN' COUSINS** *RCA 1404* [1] 10 11
4 Jul 64 ● KISSIN' COUSINS (FILM SOUNDTRACK) *RCA RD 7645* 5 17
20 Aug 64 **SUCH A NIGHT** *RCA 1411* [1] 13 10
29 Oct 64 **AIN'T THAT LOVING YOU BABY** *RCA 1422* 15 8
3 Dec 64 **BLUE CHRISTMAS** *RCA 1430* [1] 11 7
9 Jan 65 ROUSTABOUT (FILM SOUNDTRACK) *RCA RD 7678* ▲ 12 4
11 Mar 65 **DO THE CLAM** *RCA 1443* [3] 19 8
1 May 65 ● GIRL HAPPY (FILM SOUNDTRACK) *RCA RD 7714* 8 18

24 March 1984	31 March 1984	7 April 1984	14 April 1984
UK No.1 SINGLES			
HELLO Lionel Richie	HELLO Lionel Richie	HELLO Lionel Richie	HELLO Lionel Richie
UK No.1 ALBUMS			
HUMAN'S LIB Howard Jones	CAN'T SLOW DOWN Lionel Richie	CAN'T SLOW DOWN Lionel Richie	NOW THAT'S WHAT I CALL MUSIC! 2 Various

27 May 65 ★ **CRYING IN THE CHAPEL** *RCA 1455* [1] $ 1 15
25 Sep 65 FLAMING STAR AND SUMMER KISSES *RCA RD 7723* 11 4
11 Nov 65 **TELL ME WHY** *RCA 1489* [1] 15 10
4 Dec 65 ● ELVIS FOR EVERYONE *RCA RD 7782* 8 8
15 Jan 66 HAREM HOLIDAY (FILM SOUNDTRACK) *RCA RD 7767* 11 5
24 Feb 66 **BLUE RIVER** *RCA 1504* 22 7
7 Apr 66 **FRANKIE AND JOHNNY** *RCA 1509* 21 9
30 Apr 66 FRANKIE AND JOHNNY (FILM SOUNDTRACK) *RCA RD 7793* 11 5
7 Jul 66 ● **LOVE LETTERS** *RCA 1526* 6 10
6 Aug 66 ● PARADISE HAWAIIAN STYLE (FILM SOUNDTRACK) *RCA Victor RD 7810* 7 9
13 Oct 66 **ALL THAT I AM** *RCA 1545* [1] 18 8
26 Nov 66 CALIFORNIA HOLIDAY (FILM SOUNDTRACK) *RCA Victor RD 7820* 17 5
1 Dec 66 ● **IF EVERY DAY WAS LIKE CHRISTMAS** *RCA 1557* [4] 9 7
9 Feb 67 **INDESCRIBABLY BLUE** *RCA 1565* [4] 21 5
8 Apr 67 HOW GREAT THOU ART *RCA Victor SF 7867* 11 14
11 May 67 **YOU GOTTA STOP / THE LOVE MACHINE** *RCA 1593* 38 5
16 Aug 67 **LONG LEGGED GIRL (WITH THE SHORT DRESS ON)** *RCA RCA 1616* [1] 49 2
2 Sep 67 DOUBLE TROUBLE (FILM SOUNDTRACK) *RCA Victor SF 7892* 34 1
21 Feb 68 **GUITAR MAN** *RCA 1663* 19 9
20 Apr 68 CLAMBAKE (FILM SOUNDTRACK) *RCA Victor SD 7917* 39 1
15 May 68 **U.S. MALE** *RCA 1688* [1] 15 8
17 Jul 68 **YOUR TIME HASN'T COME YET BABY** *RCA 1714* [1] 22 11
16 Oct 68 **YOU'LL NEVER WALK ALONE** *RCA 1747* [1] 44 3
26 Feb 69 **IF I CAN DREAM** *RCA 1795* 11 10
3 May 69 ● ELVIS – NBC TV SPECIAL *RCA RD 8011* 2 26
11 Jun 69 ● **IN THE GHETTO** (re) *RCA 1831* $ 2 17
5 Jul 69 ● ELVIS SINGS FLAMING STAR *RCA International INTS 1012* 2 14
23 Aug 69 ★ FROM ELVIS IN MEMPHIS *RCA SF 8029* 1 13
6 Sep 69 **CLEAN UP YOUR OWN BACK YARD** *RCA 1869* 21 7
29 Nov 69 ● **SUSPICIOUS MINDS** *RCA 1900* ▲ $ 2 14
28 Feb 70 PORTRAIT IN MUSIC (import) *RCA 558* 36 1
28 Feb 70 ● **DON'T CRY DADDY** *RCA 1916* $ 8 11
14 Mar 70 ● FROM MEMPHIS TO VEGAS – FROM VEGAS TO MEMPHIS *RCA SF 8080/1* 3 16
16 May 70 **KENTUCKY RAIN** (re) *RCA 1949* 21 12
11 Jul 70 ★ **THE WONDER OF YOU** (re) *RCA 1974* $ 1 21
1 Aug 70 ● ON STAGE – FEBRUARY 1970 *RCA SF 8128* 2 18
14 Nov 70 ● **I'VE LOST YOU** *RCA 1999* 9 12
5 Dec 70 ELVIS' GOLDEN RECORDS VOLUME 1 (re-issue) *RCA SF 8129* 21 11
12 Dec 70 WORLDWIDE 50 GOLD AWARD HITS VOLUME 1 *RCA LPM 6401* 49 2
9 Jan 71 ● **YOU DON'T HAVE TO SAY YOU LOVE ME** (re) *RCA 2046* 9 10
30 Jan 71 THAT'S THE WAY IT IS *RCA SF 8162* 12 35
20 Mar 71 ● **THERE GOES MY EVERYTHING** *RCA 2060* [5] 6 11
10 Apr 71 ● I'M 10000 YEARS OLD – ELVIS COUNTRY *RCA SF 8172* 6 9
15 May 71 ● **RAGS TO RICHES** *RCA 2084* [5] 9 11
17 Jul 71 ● **HEARTBREAK HOTEL / HOUND DOG** (re-issues) *RCA Maximillion 2104* 10 12
24 Jul 71 ● LOVE LETTERS FROM ELVIS *RCA SF 8202* 7 5
7 Aug 71 ● C'MON EVERYBODY *RCA International INTS 1286* 5 21
7 Aug 71 YOU'LL NEVER WALK ALONE *RCA Camden CDM 1088* 20 4
25 Sep 71 ALMOST IN LOVE *RCA International INTS 1206* 38 2
2 Oct 71 **I'M LEAVIN'** *RCA 2125* [5] 23 9
4 Dec 71 ● ELVIS' CHRISTMAS ALBUM (re-issue) *RCA International INTS 1126* 7 5
4 Dec 71 ● **I JUST CAN'T HELP BELIEVING** *RCA 2158* [6] 6 16
11 Dec 71 **JAILHOUSE ROCK** (re-issue) *RCA Maximillion 2153* 42 5
18 Dec 71 I GOT LUCKY *RCA International INTS 1322* 26 3
1 Apr 72 ● **UNTIL IT'S TIME FOR YOU TO GO** *RCA 2188* [5] 5 9
27 May 72 ELVIS NOW *RCA Victor SF 8266* 12 8
3 Jun 72 ELVIS FOR EVERYONE (re-issue) *RCA Victor SF 8232* 48 1
3 Jun 72 ROCK AND ROLL (re-issue) *RCA Victor SF 8233* 34 4
17 Jun 72 ● **AN AMERICAN TRILOGY** *RCA 2229* 8 11
15 Jul 72 ● ELVIS AS RECORDED AT MADISON SQUARE GARDEN *RCA Victor SF 8296* 3 20
12 Aug 72 HE TOUCHED ME *RCA Victor SF 8275* 38 3
30 Sep 72 ● **BURNING LOVE** *RCA 2267* [7] $ 7 9
16 Dec 72 ● **ALWAYS ON MY MIND** *RCA 2304* [7] 9 13
24 Feb 73 ALOHA FROM HAWAII VIA SATELLITE *RCA Victor DPS 2040* ▲ 11 10
26 May 73 **POLK SALAD ANNIE** *RCA 2359* 23 7
11 Aug 73 **FOOL** *RCA 2393* [7] 15 10
15 Sep 73 ELVIS *RCA Victor SF 8378* 16 4
24 Nov 73 **RAISED ON ROCK** *RCA 2435* 36 7
2 Mar 74 ELVIS – A LEGENDARY PERFORMER VOL.1 *RCA Victor CPLI 0341* 20 3
16 Mar 74 **I'VE GOT A THING ABOUT YOU BABY** *RCA APBO 0196* [7] 33 5
25 May 74 GOOD TIMES *RCA Victor APLI 0475* 42 1
13 Jul 74 **IF YOU TALK IN YOUR SLEEP** *RCA APBO 0280* 40 3
7 Sep 74 ELVIS RECORDED LIVE ON STAGE IN MEMPHIS *RCA Victor APLI 0606* 44 1
16 Nov 74 ● **MY BOY** *RCA 2458* 5 13
18 Jan 75 ● **PROMISED LAND** *RCA PB 10074* 9 8
22 Feb 75 PROMISED LAND *RCA Victor APLI 0873* 21 4
24 May 75 **T.R.O.U.B.L.E.** *RCA 2562* 31 4
14 Jun 75 TODAY *RCA Victor RS 1011* 48 3
5 Jul 75 ★ 40 GREATEST HITS *Arcade ADEP 12* 1 38
6 Sep 75 THE ELVIS PRESLEY SUN COLLECTION *RCA Starcall HY 1001* 16 13
29 Nov 75 **GREEN GREEN GRASS OF HOME** *RCA 2635* 29 7
1 May 76 **HURT** *RCA 2674* 37 5
19 Jun 76 FROM ELVIS PRESLEY BOULEVARD MEMPHIS TENNESSEE *RCA Victor RS 1060* 29 5
4 Sep 76 ● **THE GIRL OF MY BEST FRIEND** *RCA 2729* 9 12
25 Dec 76 ● **SUSPICION** *RCA 2768* 9 12
19 Feb 77 ELVIS IN DEMAND *RCA Victor PL 42003* 12 11
5 Mar 77 ● **MOODY BLUE** *RCA PB 0857* [8] 6 9
13 Aug 77 ★ **WAY DOWN** *RCA PB 0998* [9] $ 1 13
27 Aug 77 ● MOODY BLUE *RCA PL 12428* 3 15
3 Sep 77 G.I. BLUES (FILM SOUNDTRACK) (re-issue) *RCA SF 5078* 14 10
3 Sep 77 ● WELCOME TO MY WORLD *RCA PL 12274* 7 9
3 Sep 77 **ALL SHOOK UP** (re-issue) *RCA PB 2694* [1] 41 2
3 Sep 77 **ARE YOU LONESOME TONIGHT?** (re-issue) *RCA PB 2699* [1] 46 1
3 Sep 77 **CRYING IN THE CHAPEL** (re-issue) *RCA PB 2708* [1] 43 2
3 Sep 77 **IT'S NOW OR NEVER** (re-issue) *RCA PB 2698* [1] 39 2
3 Sep 77 **JAILHOUSE ROCK** (2nd re-issue) *RCA PB 2695* [1] 44 2
3 Sep 77 **RETURN TO SENDER** (re-issue) *RCA PB 2706* [1] 42 3
3 Sep 77 **THE WONDER OF YOU** (re-issue) *RCA PB 2709* 48 1
3 Sep 77 **WOODEN HEART** (re-issue) *RCA PB 2700* 49 1
10 Sep 77 BLUE HAWAII (FILM SOUNDTRACK) (re-issue) *RCA SF 8145* 49 2
10 Sep 77 ELVIS' GOLDEN RECORDS VOLUME 2 (re-issue) *RCA SF 8151* 27 4
10 Sep 77 ELVIS' GOLDEN RECORDS VOLUME 3 (re-issue) *RCA SF 7630* 26 6
10 Sep 77 HITS OF THE 70'S *RCA LPLI 7527* 30 4
10 Sep 77 PICTURES OF ELVIS *RCA Starcall HY 1023* 52 1
8 Oct 77 THE SUN YEARS *Charly SUN 1001* 31 2
15 Oct 77 LOVING YOU (SOUNDTRACK) (re-issue) *RCA PL 42358* 24 3
19 Nov 77 ELVIS IN CONCERT *RCA PL 02578* 13 11
10 Dec 77 ● **MY WAY** *RCA PB 1165* [10] 9 8
22 Apr 78 HE WALKS BESIDE ME *RCA PL 12772* 37 1
3 Jun 78 THE '56 SESSIONS VOLUME 1 *RCA PL 42101* 47 4
24 Jun 78 **DON'T BE CRUEL** *RCA PB 9265* 24 12
2 Sep 78 TV SPECIAL *RCA PL 42370* 50 2
11 Nov 78 40 GREATEST HITS (re-issue) *RCA PL 42691* 40 14
3 Feb 79 A LEGENDARY PERFORMER VOLUME 3 *RCA PL 13082* 43 3
5 May 79 OUR MEMORIES OF ELVIS *RCA PL 13279* 72 1
24 Nov 79 ● LOVE SONGS *K-Tel NE 1062* 4 13
15 Dec 79 **IT WON'T SEEM LIKE CHRISTMAS (WITHOUT YOU)** *RCA PB 9464* 13 6
21 Jun 80 ELVIS PRESLEY SINGS LEIBER AND STOLLER *RCA International INTS 5031* 32 5
23 Aug 80 ELVIS ARON PRESLEY *RCA ELVIS 25* 21 4
23 Aug 80 PARADISE HAWAIIAN STYLE (FILM SOUNDTRACK) (re-issue) *RCA International INTS 5037* 53 2
30 Aug 80 ● **IT'S ONLY LOVE / BEYOND THE REEF** *RCA 4* 3 10
29 Nov 80 ● INSPIRATION *K-Tel NE 1101* 6 8
6 Dec 80 **SANTA CLAUS IS BACK IN TOWN** *RCA 16* 41 6

21 April 1984	28 April 1984	5 May 1984	12 May 1984
HELLO Lionel Richie	HELLO Lionel Richie	THE REFLEX Duran Duran	THE REFLEX Duran Duran
NOW THAT'S WHAT I CALL MUSIC! 2 Various	NOW THAT'S WHAT I CALL MUSIC! 2 Various	NOW THAT'S WHAT I CALL MUSIC! 2 Various	NOW THAT'S WHAT I CALL MUSIC! 2 Various

KEY
UK No.1 ★ UK Top 10 ● Still on chart + UK entry at No.1 ■ US No.1 ▲ UK million seller £ US million seller $
Singles re-entries are listed as (re), (2re), (3re)… which signifies that the hit re-entered the chart once, twice or three times…

Peak Position / Weeks

14 Feb 81 **GUITAR MAN** (re-recording) *RCA 43*....43 4
14 Mar 81 GUITAR MAN *RCA RCALP 5010*....33 5
18 Apr 81 **LOVING ARMS** *RCA 48*....47 6
9 May 81 THIS IS ELVIS PRESLEY *RCA RCALP 5029*....47 4
28 Nov 81 THE ULTIMATE PERFORMANCE *K-Tel NE 1141*....45 6
13 Feb 82 THE SOUND OF YOUR CRY *RCA RCALP 3060*....31 12
6 Mar 82 ELVIS PRESLEY EP PACK *RCA EP1*....97 1
13 Mar 82 **ARE YOU LONESOME TO-NIGHT? (LIVE)** *RCA 196* [10]....25 7
26 Jun 82 **THE SOUND OF YOUR CRY** *RCA 232* [5]....59 2
21 Aug 82 ROMANTIC ELVIS / ROCKIN' ELVIS *RCA RCALP 1000/1*....62 5
18 Dec 82 IT WON'T SEEM LIKE CHRISTMAS WITHOUT YOU *RCA INTS 5235*....80 1
30 Apr 83 JAILHOUSE ROCK / LOVE IN LAS VEGAS *RCA RCALP 9020*....40 2
7 May 83 **BABY I DON'T CARE** *RCA 332*....61 3
20 Aug 83 I WAS THE ONE *RCA RCALP 3105*....83 1
3 Dec 83 A LEGENDARY PERFORMER VOLUME 4 *RCA PL 84848*....91 1
3 Dec 83 **I CAN HELP** *RCA 369* [11]....30 9
7 Apr 84 I CAN HELP *RCA PL 89287*....71 3
21 Jul 84 THE FIRST LIVE RECORDINGS *RCA International PG 89387*....69 2
10 Nov 84 **THE LAST FAREWELL** *RCA 459* [8]....48 6
19 Jan 85 **THE ELVIS MEDLEY** *RCA 476* [1]....51 3
26 Jan 85 20 GREATEST HITS VOLUME 2 *RCA International NL 89168*....98 1
25 May 85 RECONSIDER BABY *RCA PL 85418*....92 1
10 Aug 85 **ALWAYS ON MY MIND** (re-mix) *RCA PB 49943*....59 4
12 Oct 85 BALLADS *Telstar STAR 2264*....23 17
11 Apr 87 **AIN'T THAT LOVIN' YOU BABY / BOSSA NOVA BABY** (re-recordings) *RCA ARON 1*....47 5
22 Aug 87 **LOVE ME TENDER / IF I CAN DREAM** (re-issues) *RCA ARON 2*....56 3
29 Aug 87 ● PRESLEY – THE ALL TIME GREATEST HITS *RCA PL 90100*....4 34
16 Jan 88 **STUCK ON YOU** (re-issue) *RCA PB 49595* [1]....58 2
28 Jan 89 STEREO '57 (ESSENTIAL ELVIS VOLUME 2) *RCA PL 90250*....60 2
21 Jul 90 HITS LIKE NEVER BEFORE (VOL.3) *RCA PL 90486*....71 1
1 Sep 90 THE GREAT PERFORMANCES *RCA PL 82227*....62 1
17 Aug 91 **ARE YOU LONESOME TONIGHT (LIVE)** (re-issue) *RCA PB 49177*....68 2
24 Aug 91 COLLECTORS GOLD *RCA PL 90574*....57 1
22 Feb 92 ● FROM THE HEART – HIS GREATEST LOVE SONGS *RCA PD 90642*....4 18
29 Aug 92 **DON'T BE CRUEL** (re-issue) *RCA 74321110777* [1]....42 2
10 Sep 94 ● THE ESSENTIAL COLLECTION *RCA 74321228712*....6 25
11 Nov 95 **THE TWELFTH OF NEVER** *RCA 74321320122* [11]....21 3
11 May 96 ELVIS 56 *RCA 7863668562*....42 3
18 May 96 **HEARTBREAK HOTEL** (2nd re-issue) **/ I WAS THE ONE** *RCA 74321336862*....45 1
24 May 97 **ALWAYS ON MY MIND** (re-issue) (re-mix) *RCA 74321485412*....13 6
7 Jun 97 ● ALWAYS ON MY MIND – ULTIMATE LOVE SONGS *RCA 74321489842*....3 33
28 Feb 98 BLUE SUEDE SHOES *RCA 74321556282*....39 4
2 Dec 00 ● THE 50 GREATEST HITS *RCA 74321811022*....8 25
31 Mar 01 THE LIVE GREATEST HITS *RCA 74321847082*....50 3
14 Apr 01 **SUSPICIOUS MINDS (LIVE)** *RCA 74321855822*....15 4
10 Nov 01 **AMERICA THE BEAUTIFUL** *RCA 74321904022*....69 1
24 Nov 01 THE 50 GREATEST LOVE SONGS *RCA 74321900752*....21 9
22 Jun 02 ★ **A LITTLE LESS CONVERSATION** *RCA 74321943572* [12] ■....1 12
5 Oct 02 ★ ELV1S – 30 #1 HITS *RCA 7863680792* ■ ▲....1 45
4 Oct 03 ● **RUBBERNECKIN' (re)** *RCA 82876543412*....5 8
18 Oct 03 ● 2ND TO NONE *RCA 82876570852*....4 12
6 Dec 03 CHRISTMAS PEACE *RCA 82876574892*....41 10
17 Jul 04 ● **THAT'S ALL RIGHT (re)** *RCA 82876619212*....3 7
15 Jan 05 ★ **JAILHOUSE ROCK** (3rd re-issue) *RCA 82876667152* ■....1 7
22 Jan 05 ★ **ONE NIGHT / I GOT STUNG** (re-issue) *RCA 82876666682* ■....1 6
29 Jan 05 ● **A FOOL SUCH AS I / I NEED YOUR LOVE TONIGHT** (re-issues) *RCA 82876666582*....2 5
5 Feb 05 ★ **IT'S NOW OR NEVER** (2nd re-issue) *RCA 82876666592* ■....1 4
12 Feb 05 ● LOVE, ELVIS *RCA 82876674482*....8 7
12 Feb 05 ● **ARE YOU LONESOME TO-NIGHT?** (2nd re-issue) *RCA 82876666602*....2 6
19 Feb 05 ● **WOODEN HEART** (2nd re-issue) *RCA 82876666612*....2 5
26 Feb 05 ● **SURRENDER** (re-issue) *RCA 82876666692*....2 5
5 Mar 05 ● **HIS LATEST FLAME** (re-issue) *RCA 82876666702*....3 4
12 Mar 05 ● **ROCK-A-HULA BABY** (re-issue) *RCA 82876666732*....3 4
19 Mar 05 ● **GOOD LUCK CHARM** (re-issue) *RCA 82876666752*....2 4
26 Mar 05 ● **SHE'S NOT YOU** (re-issue) *RCA 82876666762*....3 4
2 Apr 05 ● **RETURN TO SENDER** (2nd re-issue) *RCA 82876666772*....5 4
9 Apr 05 ● **(YOU'RE THE) DEVIL IN DISGUISE** (re-issue) *RCA 82876666782*....2 5
16 Apr 05 ● **CRYING IN THE CHAPEL** (2nd re-issue) *RCA 82876666802*....2 4
23 Apr 05 ● **THE WONDER OF YOU** (2nd re-issue) *RCA 82876666812*....4 4
30 Apr 05 ● **WAY DOWN** (re-issue) *RCA 82876666822*....2 4
7 May 05 ● **A LITTLE LESS CONVERSATION** (re-issue) *RCA 82876666832* [12]....3 4
28 May 05 ELVIS BY THE PRESLEYS *Sony BMG TV 82876678832*....13 5
19 Nov 05 HITSTORY *RCA 82876739352*....31 7+

[1] With the Jordanaires [2] With the Mellomen [3] With the Jordanaires Jubilee Four & Carol Lombard Trio [4] With the Jordanaires and Imperials Quartet [5] Vocal accompaniment: the Imperials Quartet [6] Vocal acc the Imperials Quartet & the Sweet Inspirations [7] Vocal acc JD Sumner & the Stamps [8] Vocal acc JD Sumner & the Stamps Qt Kathy Westmoreland, Myrna Smith [9] Vocal acc JD Sumner & the Stamps Qt K Westmoreland, S Neilson & M Smith [10] Vocal acc JD Sumner & the Stamps, the Sweet Inspirations and Kathy Westmoreland [11] Vocal accompaniment the Voice [12] Elvis vs JXL

'Jailhouse Rock' (24 Jan 58) re-entry was in Feb 1983, peaking at No.27. Tracks on Jailhouse Rock (EP) (31 Jan 58): Jailhouse Rock / Young and Beautiful / I Want to Be Free / Don't Leave Me Now / Baby I Don't Care. Tracks on Strictly Elvis (EP) (12 Feb 60): Old Shep / Any Place is Paradise / Paralyzed / Is it So Strange. Tracks on Follow That Dream (EP) (21 Jun 62): Follow That Dream / Angel / What a Wonderful Life / I'm Not the Marrying Kind. On 5 Jul 1962, a note on the Top 50 for that week stated: "Due to difficulties in assessing returns of Follow That Dream EP, it has been decided not to include it in Britain's Top 50. It is of course No.1 in the EP charts." Therefore this EP had only a two-week run on the chart when its sales would certainly have justified a much longer one. 'Beyond the Reef' listed only from 30 Aug to 13 Sep 1980. It peaked at No.7. 'Can't Help Falling in Love' credited from 1 Mar 1962. Tracks on The Elvis Medley (1 Jan 85): Jailhouse Rock / Teddy Bear / Hound Dog / Don't Be Cruel / Burning Love / Suspicious Minds. 'Guitar Man' on 14 Feb 1981 is an overdubbed release.

Sharp-eyed readers will have counted 17 US No.1 hits listed for 'The King'. However, he actually scored 18 chart-toppers – 'Don't Be Cruel' gets an individual top placing in the US in addition to a joint listing with 'Hound Dog'. Rock and Roll (3 Jun 1972) is a re-issue of the first album. 40 Greatest Hits (5 Jul 1975) peaked at No.16 on 1 Jan 1976 on its first chart run and only reached No.1 on 10 Sep 1977 following Elvis' death.

Lisa Marie PRESLEY *US, female vocalist*

12 Jul 03 **LIGHTS OUT (re)** *Capitol CDCL 844*....16 5
26 Jul 03 TO WHOM IT MAY CONCERN *Capitol 5905220*....52 1

PRESSURE DROP *UK, male vocal / instrumental duo (2 Singles: 2 Weeks)*

21 Mar 98 **SILENTLY BAD MINDED** *Higher Ground HIGHS 6CD*....53 1
17 Mar 01 **WARRIOR SOUND** *Higher Ground 6697192*....72 1

Billy PRESTON *US, male vocalist / keyboard player (5 Singles: 51 Weeks)*

23 Apr 69 ★ **GET BACK (2re)** *Apple R 5777* [1] ■ ▲ $....1 23
2 Jul 69 **THAT'S THE WAY GOD PLANNED IT** *Apple 12*....11 10
16 Sep 72 **OUTA SPACE** *A&M AMS 7007* $....44 3
15 Dec 79 ● **WITH YOU I'M BORN AGAIN** *Motown TMG 1159* [2]....2 11
8 Mar 80 **IT WILL COME IN TIME** *Motown TMG 1175* [2]....47 4

[1] The Beatles with Billy Preston [2] Billy Preston and Syreeta

	19 May 1984	26 May 1984	2 June 1984	9 June 1984
UK No.1 SINGLES	THE REFLEX – Duran Duran	THE REFLEX – Duran Duran	WAKE ME UP BEFORE YOU GO GO – Wham!	WAKE ME UP BEFORE YOU GO GO – Wham!
UK No.1 ALBUMS	LEGEND - THE BEST OF BOB MARLEY AND THE WAILERS – Bob Marley & The Wailers	LEGEND - THE BEST OF BOB MARLEY AND THE WAILERS – Bob Marley & The Wailers	LEGEND - THE BEST OF BOB MARLEY AND THE WAILERS – Bob Marley & The Wailers	LEGEND - THE BEST OF BOB MARLEY AND THE WAILERS – Bob Marley & The Wailers

Johnny PRESTON *US, male vocalist – Johnny Courville (5 Singles: 46 Weeks)*

12 Feb 60 ★	**RUNNING BEAR (re)** *Mercury AMT 1079* ▲ $	1	16
21 Apr 60 ●	**CRADLE OF LOVE** *Mercury AMT 1092*	2	16
28 Jul 60	**I'M STARTING TO GO STEADY** *Mercury AMT 1104*	49	1
11 Aug 60	**FEEL SO FINE** *Mercury AMT 1104*	18	10
8 Dec 60	**CHARMING BILLY (re)** *Mercury AMT 1114*	34	3

Mike PRESTON *UK, male vocalist – Jack Davis (4 Singles: 33 Weeks)*

30 Oct 59	**MR BLUE** *Decca F 11167*	12	8
25 Aug 60	**I'D DO ANYTHING** *Decca F 11255*	23	10
22 Dec 60	**TOGETHERNESS** *Decca F 11287*	41	5
9 Mar 61	**MARRY ME** *Decca F 11335*	14	10

The PRETENDERS 196 Top 500

Internationally successful, British-based post-punk group with an ever-changing line-up, but with ex-NME journalist Chrissie Hynde (v/g), b. 7 Sep 1951, Ohio, US, as a common factor. Hynde was briefly married to the lead singer of Simple Minds, Jim Kerr, and had a child with Ray Davies of The Kinks (11 Albums: 171 Weeks, 19 Singles: 132 Weeks)

10 Feb 79	**STOP YOUR SOBBING** *Real ARE 6*	34	9
14 Jul 79	**KID** *Real ARE 9*	33	7
17 Nov 79 ★	**BRASS IN POCKET** *Real ARE 11*	1	17
19 Jan 80 ★	PRETENDERS *Real RAL 3* ■	1	35
5 Apr 80 ●	**TALK OF THE TOWN** *Real ARE 12*	8	8
14 Feb 81	**MESSAGE OF LOVE** *Real ARE 15*	11	7
15 Aug 81 ●	PRETENDERS II *Real SRK 3572*	7	27
12 Sep 81	**DAY AFTER DAY** *Real ARE 17*	45	4
14 Nov 81 ●	**I GO TO SLEEP** *Real ARE 18*	7	10
2 Oct 82	**BACK ON THE CHAIN GANG** *Real ARE 19*	17	9
26 Nov 83	**2000 MILES** *Real ARE 20*	15	9
21 Jan 84	LEARNING TO CRAWL *Real WX 2*	11	16
9 Jun 84	**THIN LINE BETWEEN LOVE AND HATE** *Real ARE 22*	49	3
11 Oct 86 ●	**DON'T GET ME WRONG** *Real YZ 85*	10	9
1 Nov 86 ●	GET CLOSE *WEA WX 64*	6	28
13 Dec 86 ●	**HYMN TO HER** *Real YZ 93*	8	12
15 Aug 87	**IF THERE WAS A MAN** *Real YZ 149* [1]	49	6
7 Nov 87 ●	THE SINGLES *WEA WX 135*	6	32
26 May 90	PACKED! *WEA WX 346*	19	5
23 Apr 94 ●	**I'LL STAND BY YOU** *WEA YZ 815CD*	10	10
21 May 94 ●	LAST OF THE INDEPENDENTS *WEA 4509958222*	8	13
2 Jul 94	**NIGHT IN MY VEINS** *WEA YZ 825CD*	25	5
15 Oct 94	**977** *WEA YZ 848CD1*	66	2
14 Oct 95	**KID** (re-recording) *WEA 014CD*	73	1
28 Oct 95	THE ISLE OF VIEW *WEA 0630120592*	23	4
10 May 97	**FEVER PITCH THE EP** *Blanco Y Negro NEG 104CD* [2]	65	1
15 May 99	**HUMAN** *WEA WEA 207CD*	33	3
29 May 99	VIVA EL AMOR *WEA 3984271522*	32	2
30 Sep 00	GREATEST HITS *Warner.esp 8573846072*	21	8
31 May 03	LOOSE SCREW *Eagle EAGCD 256*	55	1

[1] The Pretenders for 007 [2] The Pretenders, The La's, Orlando, Neil MacColl, Nick Hornby

Tracks on Fever Pitch the EP: Goin' Back – The Pretenders; There She Goes – The La's; How Can We Hang on to a Dream – Orlando; Football – Neil MacColl; Boo Hewerdine – Nick Hornby.

PRETTY BOY FLOYD *US, male vocal / instrumental group*

10 Mar 90	**ROCK AND ROLL (IS GONNA SET THE NIGHT ON FIRE)** *MCA MCA 1393*	75	1

PRETTY RICKY NEW *US, male rap / vocal group*

24 Sep 05	**GRIND WITH ME** *Atlantic AT 0212CDX*	26	6

The PRETTY THINGS *UK, male vocal (Phil May) / instrumental group (2 Albums: 13 Weeks, 7 Singles: 41 Weeks)*

18 Jun 64	**ROSALYN** *Fontana TF 469*	41	5
22 Oct 64 ●	**DON'T BRING ME DOWN** *Fontana TF 503*	10	11

TOP 10

ON THE DAY ENGLAND WON THE WORLD CUP

On 30 July 1966, Chris Farlowe was No.1 with 'Out of Time' as the German football team ran out of time in extra time in the World Cup final at Wembley Stadium. England ran out 4-2 winners and Chris Farlowe celebrated his only chart-topper with a raucous rendering of a Jagger – Richards composition.

LW	TW	
3	1	**OUT OF TIME** Chris Farlowe
6	2	**BLACK IS BLACK** Los Bravos
10	3	**WITH A GIRL LIKE YOU** The Troggs
1	4	**GET AWAY** Georgie Fame and The Blue Flames
2	5	**SUNNY AFTERNOON** The Kinks
7	6	**I COULDN'T LIVE WITHOUT YOUR LOVE** Petula Clark
13	7	**THE MORE I SEE YOU** Chris Montez
9	8	**LOVE LETTERS** Elvis Presley
4	9	**RIVER DEEP – MOUNTAIN HIGH** Ike and Tina Turner
12	10	**GOIN' BACK** Dusty Springfield

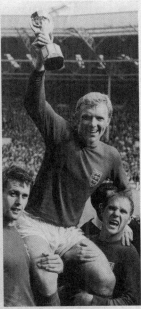

Chris Farlowe

Hurst, Moore and Wilson

16 June 1984	23 June 1984	30 June 1984	7 July 1984
TWO TRIBES Frankie Goes to Hollywood	**TWO TRIBES** Frankie Goes to Hollywood	**TWO TRIBES** Frankie Goes to Hollywood	**TWO TRIBES** Frankie Goes to Hollywood
LEGEND - THE BEST OF BOB MARLEY AND THE WAILERS Bob Marley & The Wailers	**LEGEND - THE BEST OF BOB MARLEY AND THE WAILERS** Bob Marley & The Wailers	**LEGEND - THE BEST OF BOB MARLEY AND THE WAILERS** Bob Marley & The Wailers	**LEGEND - THE BEST OF BOB MARLEY AND THE WAILERS** Bob Marley & The Wailers

KEY
UK No.1 ★ UK Top 10 ● Still on chart + UK entry at No.1 ■
US No.1 ▲ UK million seller £ US million seller $
Singles re-entries are listed as (re), (2re), (3re)... which signifies that the hit re-entered the chart once, twice or three times...

Peak Position / Weeks

25Feb 65 **HONEY I NEED** *Fontana TF 537* 13 10
27 Mar 65 ● **PRETTY THINGS** *Fontana TL 5239* 6 10
15 Jul 65 **CRY TO ME** *Fontana TF 585* 28 7
20 Jan 66 **MIDNIGHT TO SIX MAN** *Fontana TF 647* 46 1
5 May 66 **COME SEE ME** *Fontana TF 688* 43 5
21 Jul 66 **A HOUSE IN THE COUNTRY** (re) *Fontana TF 722* 50 2
27 Jun 70 **PARACHUTE** *Harvest SHVL 774* 43 3

Alan PRICE (see also The ANIMALS)

UK, male vocalist / pianist (1 Album: 10 Weeks, 11 Singles: 87 Weeks)

31 Mar 66 ● **I PUT A SPELL ON YOU** *Decca F 12367* [1] 9 10
14 Jul 66 **HI LILI, HI LO** *Decca F 12442* [1] 11 12
2 Mar 67 ● **SIMON SMITH AND HIS AMAZING DANCING BEAR** *Decca F 12570* [1] 4 12
2 Aug 67 ● **THE HOUSE THAT JACK BUILT** *Decca F 12641* [1] 4 10
15 Nov 67 **SHAME** *Decca F 12691* [1] 45 2
31 Jan 68 **DON'T STOP THE CARNIVAL** *Decca F 12731* [1] 13 8
10 Apr 71 **ROSETTA** *CBS 7108* [2] 11 10
25 May 74 ● **JARROW SONG** *Warner Bros. K 16372* 6 9
8 Jun 74 ● **BETWEEN TODAY AND YESTERDAY** *Warner Bros. K 56032* 9 10
29 Apr 78 **JUST FOR YOU** *Jet UP 36358* 43 7
17 Feb 79 **BABY OF MINE / JUST FOR YOU** (re-issue) *Jet 135* 32 3
30 Apr 88 **CHANGES** *Ariola 109911* 54 4

[1] Alan Price Set [2] Fame and Price Together

Kelly PRICE *US, female vocalist (3 Singles: 10 Weeks)*

7 Nov 98 **FRIEND OF MINE** *Island Black Music CID 723* 25 3
8 May 99 **SECRET LOVE** *Island Black Music CID 739* 26 2
30 Dec 00 **HEARTBREAK HOTEL** *Arista 74321820572* [1] $ 25 5

[1] Whitney Houston featuring Faith Evans and Kelly Price

Lloyd PRICE *US, male vocalist (5 Singles: 36 Weeks)*

13 Feb 59 ● **STAGGER LEE** *HMV POP 580* ▲ $ 7 14
15 May 59 **WHERE WERE YOU (ON OUR WEDDING DAY)?** *HMV POP 598* 15 6
12 Jun 59 ● **PERSONALITY** (re) *HMV POP 626* $ 9 10
11 Sep 59 **I'M GONNA GET MARRIED** *HMV POP 650* $ 23 5
21 Apr 60 **LADY LUCK** *HMV POP 712* 45 1

PRICKLY HEAT *UK, male producer*

26 Dec 98 **OOOIE, OOOIE, OOOIE** *Virgin VSCDT 1727* 57 1

Charley PRIDE *US, male vocalist (4 Albums: 17 Weeks)*

10 Apr 71 **CHARLEY PRIDE SPECIAL** *RCA SF 8171* 29 1
28 May 77 **SHE'S JUST AN OLD LOVE TURNED MEMORY** *RCA Victor PL 12261* 34 2
3 Jun 78 **SOMEONE LOVES YOU HONEY** *RCA PL 12478* 48 2
26 Jan 80 ● **GOLDEN COLLECTION** *K-Tel NE 1056* 6 12

Dickie PRIDE

UK, male vocalist – Richard Kneller, b. 21 Oct 1941, d. May 1969

30 Oct 59 **PRIMROSE LANE** *Columbia DB 4340* 28 1

Maxi PRIEST

UK, male vocalist – Max Elliott (5 Albums: 35 Weeks, 20 Singles: 106 Weeks)

29 Mar 86 **STROLLIN' ON** *10 TEN 84* 32 9
12 Jul 86 **IN THE SPRINGTIME** *10 TEN 127* 54 3
8 Nov 86 **CRAZY LOVE** *10 TEN 135* 67 5
6 Dec 86 **INTENTIONS** *10 DIX 32* 96 1
4 Apr 87 **LET ME KNOW** *10 TEN 156* 49 4
24 Oct 87 **SOME GUYS HAVE ALL THE LUCK** *10 TEN 198* 12 12
5 Dec 87 **MAXI** *10 DIX 64* 25 15
20 Feb 88 **HOW CAN WE EASE THE PAIN** *10 TEN 207* 41 6
4 Jun 88 ● **WILD WORLD** *10 TEN 221* 5 9
27 Aug 88 **GOODBYE TO LOVE AGAIN** *10 TEN 238* 57 3
9 Jun 90 ● **CLOSE TO YOU** *10 TEN 294* ▲ 7 10
15 Jul 90 **BONAFIDE** *10 DIX 92* 11 13
1 Sep 90 **PEACE THROUGHOUT THE WORLD** *10 TEN 317* [1] 41 4
1 Dec 90 **HUMAN WORK OF ART** (re) *10 TEN 328* 71 4
24 Aug 91 **HOUSECALL** *Epic 6573477* [2] 31 7
5 Oct 91 **THE MAXI PRIEST EP** *Ten TEN 343* 62 3
9 Nov 91 **BEST OF ME** *10 DIX 111* 23 5
26 Sep 92 **GROOVIN' IN THE MIDNIGHT** *Ten TEN 412* 50 2
14 Nov 92 **FE REAL** *10 DIXCD 113* 60 1
28 Nov 92 **JUST WANNA KNOW / FE' REAL** *Ten TEN 416* [3] 33 3
20 Mar 93 **ONE MORE CHANCE** *Ten TENCD 420* 40 3
8 May 93 ● **HOUSECALL** (re-mix) *Epic 6592842* [2] 8 8
31 Jul 93 **WAITING IN VAIN** *GRP MCSTD 1921* [4] 65 2
22 Jun 96 **THAT GIRL** *Virgin America VUSCD 106* [5] 15 7
21 Sep 96 **WATCHING THE WORLD GO BY** *Virgin America VUSCD 108* 36 2

[1] Maxi Priest featuring Jazzie B [2] Shabba Ranks featuring Maxi Priest [3] Maxi Priest / Maxi Priest featuring Apache Indian [4] Lee Ritenour and Maxi Priest [5] Maxi Priest featuring Shaggy

Tracks on The Maxi Priest EP: Just a Little Bit Longer / Best of Me / Searching / Fever.

Louis PRIMA *US, male vocalist, b. 7 Dec 1911, d. 24 Aug 1978*

21 Feb 58 **BUONA SERA** *Capitol CL 14821* 25 1

PRIMA DONNA *UK, male / female vocal group*

26 Apr 80 **LOVE ENOUGH FOR TWO** *Ariola ARO 221* 48 4

PRIMAL SCREAM *UK, male vocal (Bobby Gillespie) / instrumental group (8 Albums: 76 Weeks, 18 Singles: 54 Weeks)*

17 Oct 87 **SONIC FLOWER GROOVE** *Elevation ELV 2* 62 1
3 Mar 90 **LOADED** *Creation CRE 070* 16 9
18 Aug 90 **COME TOGETHER** *Creation CRE 078* 26 6
22 Jun 91 **HIGHER THAN THE SUN** *Creation CRE 096* 40 2
24 Aug 91 **DON'T FIGHT IT FEEL IT** *Creation CRE 110* [1] 41 2
5 Oct 91 ● **SCREAMADELICA** *Creation CRELP 076* 8 30
8 Feb 92 **DIXIE-NARCO (EP)** *Creation CRE 117* 11 6
12 Mar 94 ● **ROCKS / FUNKY JAM** *Creation CRESCD 129* 7 5
9 Apr 94 ● **GIVE OUT BUT DON'T GIVE UP** *Creation CRECD 146* 2 18
18 Jun 94 **JAILBIRD** *Creation CRESCD 145* 29 2
10 Dec 94 **(I'M GONNA) CRY MYSELF BLIND** *Creation CRESCD 183* 49 2
15 Jun 96 **THE BIG MAN AND THE SCREAM TEAM MEET THE BARMY ARMY UPTOWN** *Creation CRESCD 194* [2] 17 2
17 May 97 ● **KOWALSKI** *Creation CRESCD 245* 8 3
28 Jun 97 **STAR** *Creation CRESCD 263* 16 3
19 Jul 97 ● **VANISHING POINT** *Creation CRECD 178* 2 10
25 Oct 97 **BURNING WHEEL** *Creation CRESCD 272* 17 2
8 Nov 97 **ECHO DEK** *Creation CRECD 224* 43 1
20 Nov 99 **SWASTIKA EYES** *Creation CRESCD 326* 22 2
12 Feb 00 ● **EXTERMINATOR** *Creation CRECD 239* 3 10
1 Apr 00 **KILL ALL HIPPIES** *Creation CRESCD 332* 24 2
23 Sep 00 **ACCELERATOR** *Creation CRESCD 333* 34 1
3 Aug 02 **MISS LUCIFER** *Columbia 6728252* 25 2
17 Aug 02 ● **EVIL HEAT** *Columbia 5089232* 9 3
9 Nov 02 **AUTOBAHN 66** *Columbia 6733122* 44 1
15 Nov 03 **DIRTY HITS** *Columbia 5136039* 25 3
29 Nov 03 **SOME VELVET MORNING** *Columbia 6744022* [3] 44 2

[1] Primal Scream featuring Denise Johnson [2] Primal Scream, Irvine Welsh and On-U Sound [3] Primal Scream featuring Kate Moss

Tracks on Dixie-Narco (EP): Movin' On Up / Stone My Soul / Carry Me Home / Screamadelica.

PRIME MOVERS *US, male vocal / instrumental group*

8 Feb 86 **ON THE TRAIL** *Island IS 263* 74 1

14 July 1984	21 July 1984	28 July 1984	4 August 1984
UK No.1 SINGLES			
TWO TRIBES Frankie Goes to Hollywood	**TWO TRIBES** Frankie Goes to Hollywood	**TWO TRIBES** Frankie Goes to Hollywood	**TWO TRIBES** Frankie Goes to Hollywood
UK No.1 ALBUMS			
LEGEND - THE BEST OF BOB MARLEY AND THE WAILERS Bob Marley & The Wailers	**LEGEND - THE BEST OF BOB MARLEY AND THE WAILERS** Bob Marley & The Wailers	**LEGEND - THE BEST OF BOB MARLEY AND THE WAILERS** Bob Marley & The Wailers	**LEGEND - THE BEST OF BOB MARLEY AND THE WAILERS** Bob Marley & The Wailers

PRIMITIVE RADIO GODS *US, male vocalist – Chris O'Connor*

30 Mar 96 **STANDING OUTSIDE A BROKEN PHONE BOOTH WITH MONEY IN MY HAND** *Columbia 6627692* **74** 1

The PRIMITIVES *UK / Australia, male / female vocal (Tracy Cattell) / instrumental group (3 Albums: 13 Weeks, 6 Singles: 27 Weeks)*

27 Feb 88 ● **CRASH** *Lazy PB 41761* **5** 10
9 Apr 88 ● LOVELY *RCA PL 71688* 6 10
30 Apr 88 **OUT OF REACH** *Lazy PB 42011* **25** 4
3 Sep 88 **WAY BEHIND ME** *Lazy PB 42209* **36** 4
29 Jul 89 **SICK OF IT** *Lazy PB 42947* **24** 4
2 Sep 89 LAZY 86-88 *Lazy 15* 73 1
30 Sep 89 **SECRETS** *Lazy PB 43173* **49** 3
28 Oct 89 PURE *RCA PL 74252* 33 2
3 Aug 91 **YOU ARE THE WAY** *RCA PB 44481* **58** 2

PRIMUS *US, male vocal / instrumental group*

8 May 93 PORK SODA *Interscope 75679922572* 56 1

PRINCE (35 Top 500) (see also NEW POWER GENERATION)

Prolific singer / songwriter / producer / multi-instrumentalist / actor / label and studio owner, b. Prince Rogers Nelson, 7 Jun 1958, Minneapolis, US. This often controversial entertainer, who has packed stadiums and collected awards worldwide, has recorded under a variety of monikers, including a symbol and "The Artist Formerly Known as Prince". He was seen by over 1.4 million people on his 2004 tour (23 Albums: 450 Weeks, 52 Singles: 306 Weeks)

19 Jan 80 **I WANNA BE YOUR LOVER** *Warner Bros. K 17537* $ **41** 3
29 Jan 83 **1999** *Warner Bros. W 9896* **25** 7
30 Apr 83 **LITTLE RED CORVETTE** *Warner Bros. W 9688* **54** 6
26 Nov 83 **LITTLE RED CORVETTE** (re-issue) *Warner Bros. W 9436* **66** 2
30 Jun 84 ● **WHEN DOVES CRY** *Warner Bros. W 9286* ▲ $ **4** 15
21 Jul 84 ● PURPLE RAIN (FILM SOUNDTRACK) *Warner Bros. 9251101* [1] ▲ 7 91
8 Sep 84 1999 *Warner Bros. 923720* 30 21
22 Sep 84 ● **PURPLE RAIN** *Warner Bros. W 9174* [1] $ **8** 9
8 Dec 84 **I WOULD DIE 4 U** *Warner Bros. W 9121* [1] **58** 6
19 Jan 85 ● **1999** (re-issue) **/ LITTLE RED CORVETTE** (2nd re-issue) *Warner Bros. W 1999* **2** 10
23 Feb 85 ● **LET'S GO CRAZY / TAKE ME WITH U** *Warner Bros. W 2000* [1] ▲ $ **7** 9
4 May 85 ● AROUND THE WORLD IN A DAY *Warner Bros. 92-5286-1* [1] ▲ 5 20
25 May 85 **PAISLEY PARK** *WEA W 9052* [1] **18** 10
27 Jul 85 **RASPBERRY BERET** *WEA W 8929* [1] **25** 8
26 Oct 85 **POP LIFE** *Paisley Park W 8858* [1] **60** 2
8 Mar 86 ● **KISS** *Paisley Park W 8751* [1] ▲ $ **6** 9
12 Apr 86 ● PARADE – MUSIC FROM 'UNDER THE CHERRY MOON' (FILM SOUNDTRACK) *Warner Bros. WX 39* [1] 4 26
14 Jun 86 **MOUNTAINS** *Paisley Park W 8711* [1] **45** 4
16 Aug 86 **GIRLS AND BOYS** *Paisley Park W 8586* [1] **11** 8
1 Nov 86 **ANOTHERLOVERHOLENYOHEAD** *Paisley Park W 8521* [1] **36** 3
14 Mar 87 ● **SIGN 'O' THE TIMES** *Paisley Park W 8399* **10** 9
11 Apr 87 ● SIGN 'O' THE TIMES *Paisley Park WX 88* 4 32
20 Jun 87 **IF I WAS YOUR GIRLFRIEND** *Paisley Park W 8334* **20** 6
15 Aug 87 **U GOT THE LOOK** *Paisley Park W 8289* **11** 9
28 Nov 87 **I COULD NEVER TAKE THE PLACE OF YOUR MAN** *Paisley Park W 8288* **29** 6
7 May 88 ● **ALPHABET STREET** *Paisley Park W 7900* **9** 6
21 May 88 ★ LOVESEXY *Paisley Park WX 164* ■ 1 32
23 Jul 88 **GLAM SLAM** *Paisley Park W 7806* **29** 4
5 Nov 88 **I WISH U HEAVEN** *Paisley Park W 7745* **24** 5
24 Jun 89 ● **BATDANCE** *Warner Bros. W 2924* ▲ $ **2** 12
1 Jul 89 ★ BATMAN (FILM SOUNDTRACK) *Warner Bros. WX 281* ■ ▲ 1 20
9 Sep 89 **PARTYMAN** *Warner Bros. W 2814* **14** 6
18 Nov 89 **THE ARMS OF ORION** *Warner Bros. W 2757* [2] **27** 5
4 Aug 90 ● **THIEVES IN THE TEMPLE** *Paisley Park W 9751* **7** 6
1 Sep 90 ★ GRAFFITI BRIDGE *Paisley Park WX 361* ■ 1 8
10 Nov 90 **NEW POWER GENERATION** *Paisley Park W 9525* **26** 4
24 Aug 91 GETT OFF (import) *Paisley Park 9401382* 33 3
31 Aug 91 ● **GETT OFF** *Paisley Park W 0056* [3] **4** 8
21 Sep 91 **CREAM** *Paisley Park W 0061* [3] ▲ **15** 7
12 Oct 91 ● DIAMONDS AND PEARLS *Paisley Park WX 432* [2] 2 57
7 Dec 91 **DIAMONDS AND PEARLS** *Paisley Park W 0075* [3] **25** 6
28 Mar 92 **MONEY DON'T MATTER 2 NIGHT** *Paisley Park W 0091* [3] **19** 5
27 Jun 92 **THUNDER** *Paisley Park W 0113* [3] **28** 3
18 Jul 92 ● **SEXY MF / STROLLIN'** *Paisley Park W 0123* [3] **4** 7
10 Oct 92 ● **MY NAME IS PRINCE** *Paisley Park W 0132* [3] **7** 5
17 Oct 92 ★ SYMBOL *Paisley Park 9362450372* [2] ■ 1 21
14 Nov 92 **MY NAME IS PRINCE** (re-mix) *Paisley Park W 0142T* [3] **51** 1
5 Dec 92 **7** *Paisley Park W 0147* [3] **27** 6
13 Mar 93 **THE MORNING PAPERS** *Paisley Park W 0162CD* [3] **52** 3
25 Sep 93 ● THE HITS 1 *Paisley Park 9362454312* 5 27
25 Sep 93 ● THE HITS 2 *Paisley Park 9362454352* 5 28
25 Sep 93 ● THE HITS / THE B-SIDES *Paisley Park 9362454402* 4 14
16 Oct 93 **PEACH** *Paisley Park W 0210CD* **14** 5
11 Dec 93 ● **CONTROVERSY** *Paisley Park W 0215CD1* **5** 5
9 Apr 94 ★ **THE MOST BEAUTIFUL GIRL IN THE WORLD** *NPG NPG 60155* [4] **1** 12
4 Jun 94 **THE BEAUTIFUL EXPERIENCE** (re-mix) *NPG NPG 60212* [4] **18** 3
27 Aug 94 ★ COME *Warner Bros. 9362457002* ■ 1 8
10 Sep 94 **LETITGO** *Warner Bros. W 0260CD* **30** 4
3 Dec 94 THE BLACK ALBUM *Warner Bros. 9362457932* 36 3
18 Mar 95 **PURPLE MEDLEY** *Warner Bros. W 0289CD* **33** 2
23 Sep 95 **EYE HATE U** *Warner Bros. W 0315CD* **20** 3
7 Oct 95 ● THE GOLD EXPERIENCE *Warner Bros. 9362459992* [3] 4 5
9 Dec 95 ● **GOLD** *Warner Bros. W 0325CD* **10** 9
20 Jul 96 CHAOS AND DISORDER *Warner Bros. 9362463172* [4] 14 4
3 Aug 96 **DINNER WITH DELORES** *Warner Bros. 9362437422* **36** 2
30 Nov 96 EMANCIPATION *NPG CDEMD 1102* [5] 18 6
14 Dec 96 **BETCHA BY GOLLY WOW** *NPG CDEM 463* [5] **11** 7
8 Mar 97 **THE HOLY RIVER** *EMI CDEM 467* [5] **19** 3
11 Jul 98 NEWPOWER SOUL *RCA 74321605982* [5] 38 2
9 Jan 99 ● **1999 (re)** (2nd re-issue) *Warner Bros. W 467CD* **10** 9
4 Sep 99 THE VAULT ... OLD FRIENDS 4 SALE *Warner Bros. 9362475222* 47 1
26 Feb 00 **THE GREATEST ROMANCE EVER SOLD** *NPG / Arista 74321745002* [5] **65** 1
11 Aug 01 ● THE VERY BEST OF PRINCE *Warner Bros. 8122742722* 2 15
1 May 04 ● MUSICOLOGY *Columbia / NPG 5171659* 3 6
20 Nov 04 **CINNAMON GIRL** *Columbia 6751422* **43** 1

[1] Prince and the Revolution [2] Prince with Sheena Easton [3] Prince and the New Power Generation [4] (Symbol) [5] The Artist [1] Prince and the Revolution [2] Prince and the New Power Generation [3] (Symbol) [4] TAFKAP [5] The Artist

Although uncredited, Sheena Easton also sings on 'U Got the Look'. 'Let's Go Crazy' was the track from the double A-side single that topped the US chart. 'The Beautiful Experience' was a seven-track CD featuring 'The Most Beautiful Girl in the World' and six further mixes of the track. Re-recorded tracks on 'Purple Medley': Batdance / When Doves Cry / Kiss / Erotic City / Darling Nikki / 1999 / Baby I'm a Star / Diamonds and Pearls / Purple Rain / Let's Go Crazy. The Hits / The B-Sides, a three-disc boxed set, returned to the Top 20 in Mar 2005 with the same catalogue number. It peaked at No.20.

PRINCE BUSTER

Jamaica, male vocalist – Cecil Campbell (2 Singles: 16 Weeks)

23 Feb 67 **AL CAPONE** *Blue Beat BB 324* **18** 13
4 Apr 98 **WHINE AND GRINE** *Island CID 691* **21** 3

PRINCE CHARLES and The CITY BEAT BAND

US, male vocal / instrumental group

30 Apr 83 STONE KILLERS *Virgin V 2271* 84 1
22 Feb 86 **WE CAN MAKE IT HAPPEN** *PRT 7P 348* **56** 2

PRINCESS

UK, female vocalist – Desiree Heslop (1 Album: 14 Weeks, 6 Singles: 44 Weeks)

3 Aug 85 ● **SAY I'M YOUR NUMBER ONE** *Supreme SUPE 101* **7** 12
9 Nov 85 **AFTER THE LOVE HAS GONE** *Supreme SUPE 103* **28** 13
19 Apr 86 **I'LL KEEP ON LOVING YOU** *Supreme SUPE 105* **16** 8

11 August 1984	18 August 1984	25 August 1984	1 September 1984
TWO TRIBES Frankie Goes to Hollywood	CARELESS WHISPER George Michael	CARELESS WHISPER George Michael	CARELESS WHISPER George Michael
NOW THAT'S WHAT I CALL MUSIC! 3 Various	NOW THAT'S WHAT I CALL MUSIC! 3 Various	NOW THAT'S WHAT I CALL MUSIC! 3 Various	NOW THAT'S WHAT I CALL MUSIC! 3 Various

KEY: UK No.1 ★★ UK Top 10 ●● Still on chart ++ UK entry at No.1 ■■ US No.1 ▲▲ UK million seller £ US million seller $
Singles re-entries are listed as (re), (2re), (3re)... which signifies that the hit re-entered the chart once, twice or three times...

Peak Position / Weeks

Date	Title / Label	Peak	Weeks
17 May 86	PRINCESS *Supreme SU 1*	15	14
5 Jul 86	TELL ME TOMORROW *Supreme SUPE 106*	34	5
25 Oct 86	IN THE HEAT OF A PASSIONATE MOMENT *Supreme SUPE 109*	74	1
13 Jun 87	RED HOT *Polydor POSP 868*	58	5

PRINCESS IVORI *US, female rapper*

Date	Title / Label	Peak	Weeks
17 Mar 90	WANTED *Supreme SUPE 163*	69	2

PRINCESS SUPERSTAR *US, female vocalist – Concetta Kirschner*

Date	Title / Label	Peak	Weeks
2 Mar 02	BAD BABYSITTER *Rapster RR 007CDM*	11	7

PRIORY OF THE RESURRECTION *UK, choir*

Date	Title / Label	Peak	Weeks
31 Mar 01	ETERNAL LIGHT – MUSIC OF INNER PEACE *Deutsche Grammophon 4710902*	68	1

PRIVATE LIVES *UK, male vocal / instrumental duo*

Date	Title / Label	Peak	Weeks
11 Feb 84	LIVING IN A WORLD (TURNED UPSIDE DOWN) *EMI PRIV 2*	53	4

PRIZNA featuring DEMOLITION MAN *UK, male vocal / instrumental group*

Date	Title / Label	Peak	Weeks
29 Apr 95	FIRE *Labello Blanco NLBCDX 18*	33	2

PROBOT *US, male vocal / instrumental group*

Date	Title / Label	Peak	Weeks
28 Feb 04	PROBOT *Southern Lord STHL 302*	34	2

PJ PROBY *US, male vocalist – James Marcus Smith (1 Album: 3 Weeks, 12 Singles: 91 Weeks)*

Date	Title / Label	Peak	Weeks
28 May 64 ●	HOLD ME *Decca F 11904*	3	15
3 Sep 64 ●	TOGETHER *Decca F 11967*	8	11
10 Dec 64 ●	SOMEWHERE *Liberty LIB 10182*	6	12
25 Feb 65	I APOLOGISE *Liberty LIB 10188*	11	8
27 Feb 65	I'M PJ PROBY *Liberty LBY 1235*	16	3
8 Jul 65	LET THE WATER RUN DOWN *Liberty LIB 10206*	19	8
30 Sep 65	THAT MEANS A LOT *Liberty LIB 10215*	30	6
25 Nov 65 ●	MARIA *Liberty LIB 10218*	8	9
10 Feb 66	YOU'VE COME BACK *Liberty LIB 10223*	25	7
16 Jun 66	TO MAKE A BIG MAN CRY *Liberty LIB 10236*	34	3
27 Oct 66	I CAN'T MAKE IT ALONE *Liberty LIB 10250*	37	5
6 Mar 68	IT'S YOUR DAY TODAY *Liberty LBF 15046*	32	5
28 Dec 96	YESTERDAY HAS GONE (re) *EMI Premier CDPRESX 13* [1]	58	2

[1] PJ Proby and Marc Almond featuring the My Life Story Orchestra

The PROCLAIMERS *UK, male vocal / instrumental duo – Charlie and Craig Reid (twins) (7 Albums: 63 Weeks, 9 Singles: 50 Weeks)*

Date	Title / Label	Peak	Weeks
9 May 87	THIS IS THE STORY *Chrysalis CHR 1602*	43	21
14 Nov 87 ●	LETTER FROM AMERICA *Chrysalis CHS 3178*	3	10
5 Mar 88	MAKE MY HEART FLY *Chrysalis CLAIM 1*	63	3
27 Aug 88	I'M GONNA BE (500 MILES) *Chrysalis CLAIM 2*	11	11
24 Sep 88 ●	SUNSHINE ON LEITH *Chrysalis CHR 1668*	6	27
12 Nov 88	SUNSHINE ON LEITH *Chrysalis CLAIM 3*	41	5
11 Feb 89	I'M ON MY WAY *Chrysalis CLAIM 4*	43	4
24 Nov 90 ●	KING OF THE ROAD (EP) *Chrysalis CLAIM 5*	9	8
19 Feb 94	LET'S GET MARRIED *Chrysalis CDCLAIMS 6*	21	4
19 Mar 94 ●	HIT THE HIGHWAY *Chrysalis CDCHR 6066*	8	6
16 Apr 94	WHAT MAKES YOU CRY *Chrysalis CDCLAIMS 7*	38	3
22 Oct 94	THESE ARMS OF MINE *Chrysalis CDCLAIM 8*	51	2
9 Jun 01	PERSEVERE *Persevere PERSRECCD 04*	61	1
25 May 02	THE BEST OF THE PROCLAIMERS *Chrysalis 5386822*	30	6
27 Sep 03	BORN INNOCENT *Persevere PERSRECCD 09*	70	1
20 Aug 05	RESTLESS SOUL *Persevere PERSRECCD 10*	74	1

Tracks on King of the Road (EP): King of the Road / Long Black Veil / Lulu Selling Tea / Not Ever.

PROCOL HARUM *UK, male vocal (Gary Brooker) / instrumental group (6 Albums: 11 Weeks, 7 Singles: 56 Weeks)*

Date	Title / Label	Peak	Weeks
25 May 67 ★	A WHITER SHADE OF PALE *Deram DM 126*	1	15
4 Oct 67 ●	HOMBURG *Regal Zonophone RZ 3003*	6	10
24 Apr 68	QUITE RIGHTLY SO *Regal Zonophone RZ 3007*	50	1
18 Jun 69	A SALTY DOG (2re) *Regal Zonophone RZ 3019*	44	3
19 Jul 69	A SALTY DOG *Regal Zonophone SLRZ 1009*	27	2
27 Jun 70	HOME *Regal Zonophone SLRZ 1014*	49	1
3 Jul 71	BROKEN BARRICADES *Island ILPS 9158*	42	1
22 Apr 72	A WHITER SHADE OF PALE (re-issue) *Fly Magnifly ECHO 101*	13	13
6 May 72	A WHITER SHADE OF PALE / A SALTY DOG (re-issue) *Fly Double Back TOOFA 7/8*	26	4
6 May 72	PROCOL HARUM IN CONCERT WITH THE EDMONTON SYMPHONY ORCHESTRA *Chrysalis CHR 1004*	48	1
5 Aug 72	CONQUISTADOR *Chrysalis CHS 2003*	22	7
23 Aug 75	PANDORA'S BOX *Chrysalis CHS 2073*	16	7
30 Aug 75	PROCOL'S NINTH *Chrysalis CHR 1080*	41	2

A Whiter Shade of Pale / A Salty Dog is a double re-issue, even though A Whiter Shade of Pale was not previously a hit album.

The PRODIGY (148 Top 500) *Confrontational dance-rock collision masterminded by Liam Howlett (k/prog) and featuring charismatic Keith Flint (v). This act achieved a run of 14 successive Top 20 singles, and their 1997 album, Fat of the Land, debuted at No.1 in more than 20 countries, including the UK and the US. MC / dancer Maxim went solo in 2000. Best-selling single: 'Breathe' 722,554 (5 Albums: 205 Weeks, 16 Singles: 154 Weeks)*

Date	Title / Label	Peak	Weeks
24 Aug 91 ●	CHARLY (re) *XL XL Recordings 21CD*	3	11
4 Jan 92 ●	EVERYBODY IN THE PLACE (EP) (re) *XL XL Recordings 26CD1*	2	10
26 Sep 92	FIRE / JERICHO (re) *XL XL Recordings 30CD*	11	5
10 Oct 92	EXPERIENCE *XL Recordings XLCD 110*	12	31
21 Nov 92 ●	OUT OF SPACE / RUFF IN THE JUNGLE BIZNESS (re) *XL XL Recordings 35CD*	5	14
17 Apr 93	WIND IT UP (REWOUND) (re) *XL XL Recordings 39CD*	11	8
16 Oct 93 ●	ONE LOVE *XL XL Recordings 47CD*	8	6
28 May 94 ●	NO GOOD (START THE DANCE) (re) *XL XL Recordings 51CD*	4	14
16 Jul 94 ★	MUSIC FOR THE JILTED GENERATION *XL Recordings XLCD 114* ■	1	98
24 Sep 94	VOODOO PEOPLE (re) *XL XL Recordings 54CD*	13	6
18 Mar 95	POISON (re) *XL XL Recordings 58CD*	15	7
30 Mar 96 ★	FIRESTARTER (2re) *XL XL Recordings 70CD* ■	1	30
23 Nov 96 ★	BREATHE (re) *XL XL Recordings 80CD* ■	1	18
12 Jul 97 ★	THE FAT OF THE LAND *XL Recordings XLCD 121* ■ ▲	1	60
29 Nov 97 ●	SMACK MY BITCH UP *XL XL Recordings 90CD*	8	10
13 Jul 02 ●	BABY'S GOT A TEMPER *XL Recordings XLS 145CD*	5	6
4 Sep 04 ★	ALWAYS OUTNUMBERED, NEVER OUTGUNNED *XL Recordings XLCD 183* ■	1	6
11 Sep 04	GIRLS *XL Recordings XLS 195CD*	19	4
4 Dec 04	CHARLY (re-mix) *XL Recordings XLXV 1506*	73	1
15 Oct 05	VOODOO PEOPLE / OUT OF SPACE (re-mixes) *XL Recordings XLS 219CD*	20	4
29 Oct 05 ★	THEIR LAW – THE SINGLES 1990-2005 *XL Recordings XLCD 190X* ■	1	10+

Tracks on Everybody in the Place (EP): Everybody in the Place / Crazy Man / G-Force (Energy Flow) / Rip Up the Sound System. Eight of their singles re-entered the chart in Apr 1996.

The PROFESSIONALS *UK, male vocal / instrumental group*

Date	Title / Label	Peak	Weeks
11 Oct 80	1-2-3 *Virgin VS 376*	43	4

PROGRESS FUNK *Italy, male production trio*

Date	Title / Label	Peak	Weeks
11 Oct 97	AROUND MY BRAIN *Deconstruction 74321518182*	73	1

	8 September 1984	15 September 1984	22 September 1984	29 September 1984
UK No.1 SINGLES	I JUST CALLED TO SAY I LOVE YOU Stevie Wonder	I JUST CALLED TO SAY I LOVE YOU Stevie Wonder	I JUST CALLED TO SAY I LOVE YOU Stevie Wonder	I JUST CALLED TO SAY I LOVE YOU Stevie Wonder
UK No.1 ALBUMS	NOW THAT'S WHAT I CALL MUSIC! 3 Various	NOW THAT'S WHAT I CALL MUSIC! 3 Various	NOW THAT'S WHAT I CALL MUSIC! 3 Various	NOW THAT'S WHAT I CALL MUSIC! 3 Various

PROGRESS presents the BOY WUNDA
UK, male DJ / producer – Robert Webster

18 Dec 99 ● **EVERYBODY** *Manifesto FESCD 65* **7** 10

PROJECT D (see also SYMPHONIQUE) *UK, male instrumental duo – Chris Cozens and Nick Magnus (2 Albums: 18 Weeks)*

17 Feb 90 THE SYNTHESIZER ALBUM *Telstar STAR 2371* 13 11
29 Sep 90 SYNTHESIZED VOL.2 *Telstar STAR 2428* 25 7

PROJECT featuring GERIDEAU *US, male vocal / instrumental / production duo – Jose Burgos and Theo Gerideau*

27 Aug 94 **BRING IT BACK 2 LUV** *Fruittree FTREE 10CD* **65** 1

PROJECT ONE *UK, male producer – Mark Williams (2 Singles: 3 Weeks)*

16 May 92 **ROUGHNECK (EP)** *Rising High RSN 22* **49** 2
29 Aug 92 **DON GARGON COMIN'** *Rising High RSN 35* **64** 1

Tracks on Roughneck (EP): Come My Selector / Can't Take the Heartbreak / Live Vibe 4 (Summer Vibes).

PRONG *US, male vocal / instrumental group*

25 Apr 92 **WHOSE FIST IS THIS ANYWAY (EP)** *Epic 6580026* **58** 1
12 Feb 94 CLEANSING *Epic 4747962* 71 1

Tracks on Whose Fist Is This Anyway (EP): Prove You Wrong / Hell If I Could / (Get a) Grip (On Yourself) / Prove You Wrong (re-mix).

PROPAGANDA *Germany, male / female vocal / instrumental group (3 Albums: 16 Weeks, 5 Singles: 35 Weeks)*

17 Mar 84 **DR MABUSE** *ZTT ZTAS 2* **27** 9
4 May 85 **DUEL** *ZTT ZTAS 8* **21** 12
13 Jul 85 A SECRET WISH *ZTT ZTTIQ 3* 16 12
10 Aug 85 **P MACHINERY** *ZTT ZTAS 12* **50** 5
23 Nov 85 WISHFUL THINKING *ZTT ZTTIQ 20* 82 2
28 Apr 90 **HEAVEN GIVE ME WORDS** *Virgin VS 1245* **36** 5
9 Jun 90 1234 *Virgin V 2625* 46 2
8 Sep 90 **ONLY ONE WORD** *Virgin VS 1271* **71** 4

PROPELLERHEADS *UK, male instrumental / production duo – Alex Gifford and Will White (1 Album: 13 Weeks, 5 Singles: 15 Weeks)*

7 Dec 96 **TAKE CALIFORNIA** *Wall of Sound WALLD 024* **69** 1
17 May 97 **SPYBREAK!** *Wall of Sound WALLD 029X* **40** 1
18 Oct 97 ● **ON HER MAJESTY'S SECRET SERVICE** *East West EW 136CD* [1] **7** 5
20 Dec 97 **HISTORY REPEATING** *Wall of Sound WALLD 036* [2] **19** 7
7 Feb 98 ● DECKSANDRUMSANDROCKANDROLL *Wall of Sound WALLCD 015* 6 13
27 Jun 98 **BANG ON!** *Wall of Sound WALLD 039* **53** 1

[1] Propellerheads / David Arnold [2] Propellerheads featuring Miss Shirley Bassey

PROPHETS OF SOUND
UK, male instrumental / production duo (2 Singles: 2 Weeks)

14 Nov 98 **HIGH** *Distinctive DISNCD 47* **73** 1
23 Feb 02 **NEW DAWN** *Ink NIBNE 10CD* **51** 1

PROSPECT PARK / Carolyn HARDING
UK, male / female vocal / production duo

8 Aug 98 **MOVIN' ON** *AM:PM 5827312* **55** 1

Brian PROTHEROE *UK, male vocalist*

7 Sep 74 **PINBALL** *Chrysalis CHS 2043* **22** 6

PROTOCOL NEW *UK, male vocal / instrumental group*

22 Oct 05 **SHE WAITS FOR ME** *Polydor 9871400* **65** 1

PROUD MARY *UK, male vocal / instrumental group*

25 Aug 01 **VERY BEST FRIEND** *Sour Mash JDNCSCD 004* **75** 1

Dorothy PROVINE
US, female actor / vocalist (2 Albums: 49 Weeks, 2 Singles: 15 Weeks)

2 Dec 61 ● THE ROARING TWENTIES – SONGS FROM THE TV SERIES *Warner Bros. WM 4035* 3 42
7 Dec 61 **DON'T BRING LULU** *Warner Bros. WB 53* **17** 12
10 Feb 62 ● VAMP OF THE ROARING TWENTIES *Warner Bros. WM 4053* 9 7
28 Jun 62 **CRAZY WORDS, CRAZY TUNE** *Warner Bros. WB 70* **45** 3

Eric PRYDZ *Sweden, male producer (2 Singles: 26 Weeks)*

21 Aug 04 **WOZ NOT WOZ** *C2 CDC 2002* [1] **55** 1
25 Sep 04 ★ **CALL ON ME (re)** *Data DATA 68CDS* ■ **1** 25

[1] Eric Prydz & Steve Angello

PSEUDO ECHO *Australia, male vocal (Brian Canham) / instrumental group*

18 Jul 87 ● **FUNKY TOWN** *RCA PB 49705* **8** 12

The PSYCHEDELIC FURS *UK, male vocal / instrumental group (8 Albums: 39 Weeks, 7 Singles: 31 Weeks)*

15 Mar 80 PSYCHEDELIC FURS *CBS 84084* 18 6
2 May 81 **DUMB WAITERS** *CBS A 1166* **59** 2
23 May 81 TALK TALK TALK *CBS 84892* 30 9
27 Jun 81 **PRETTY IN PINK** *CBS A 1327* **43** 5
31 Jul 82 **LOVE MY WAY** *CBS A 2549* **42** 6
2 Oct 82 FOREVER NOW *CBS 85909* 20 6
31 Mar 84 **HEAVEN** *CBS A 4300* **29** 6
19 May 84 MIRROR MOVES *CBS 25950* 15 9
16 Jun 84 **GHOST IN YOU** *CBS A 4470* **68** 2
23 Aug 86 **PRETTY IN PINK** (re-recording) *CBS A 7242* **18** 9
14 Feb 87 MIDNIGHT TO MIDNIGHT *CBS 450 2561* 12 5
9 Jul 88 **ALL THAT MONEY WANTS** *CBS FURS 4* **75** 1
13 Aug 88 ALL OF THIS AND NOTHING *CBS 461101* 67 2
18 Nov 89 BOOK OF DAYS *CBS 465982 1* 74 1
13 Jul 91 WORLD OUTSIDE *East West WX 422* 68 1

PSYCHEDELIC WALTONS (see also MOLOKO; SOUL II SOUL) *UK, male production duo – Nellee Hooper and Fabien Waltmann (2 Singles: 3 Weeks)*

19 Jan 02 **WONDERLAND** *Echo ECSCD 120* [1] **37** 2
12 Apr 03 **PAYBACK TIME** *Sony Music 6737622* [2] **48** 1

[1] Psychedelic Waltons featuring Roisin Murphy
[2] Dysfunctional Psychedelic Waltons

PSYCHIC TV
UK, male / female vocal / instrumental group (2 Singles: 4 Weeks)

26 Apr 86 **GODSTAR** *Temple TOPY 009* [1] **67** 2
20 Sep 86 **GOOD VIBRATIONS / ROMAN P** *Temple TOPY 23* **65** 2

[1] Psychic TV and The Angels of Light

PUBLIC ANNOUNCEMENT
US, male vocal / instrumental group (3 Singles: 5 Weeks)

9 May 92 **SHE'S GOT THAT VIBE** *Jive JIVET 292* [1] **57** 2
20 Nov 93 **SEX ME** *Jive JIVECD 346* [1] **75** 1
4 Jul 98 **BODY BUMPIN' (YIPPEE-YI-YO)** *A&M 5826972* $ **38** 2

[1] R Kelly and Public Announcement

PUBLIC DEMAND *UK, male vocal group*

15 Feb 97 **INVISIBLE** *ZTT ZANG 85CD* **41** 2

PUBLIC DOMAIN *UK, male production / vocal group (3 Singles: 18 Weeks)*

2 Dec 00 ● **OPERATION BLADE (BASS IN THE PLACE)** *Xtrahard / Xtravaganza X2H 1CDS* **5** 13

6 October 1984	13 October 1984	20 October 1984	27 October 1984
I JUST CALLED TO SAY I LOVE YOU Stevie Wonder	I JUST CALLED TO SAY I LOVE YOU Stevie Wonder	FREEDOM Wham!	FREEDOM Wham!
TONIGHT David Bowie	THE UNFORGETTABLE FIRE U2	THE UNFORGETTABLE FIRE U2	STEELTOWN Big Country

KEY
UK No.1 ★ UK Top 10 ● Still on chart + UK entry at No.1 ■
US No.1 ▲ UK million seller £ US million seller $
Singles re-entries are listed as (re), (2re), (3re)... which signifies that the hit re-entered the chart once, twice or three times...
Peak Position / Weeks

23 Jun 01 **ROCK DA FUNKY BEATS** *Xtrahard / Xtravaganza X2H 3CDS* [1] 19 3
12 Jan 02 **TOO MANY MC'S / LET ME CLEAR MY THROAT** *Xtrahard / Xtravaganza X2H 8CDS*....34 2

[1] Public Domain featuring Chuck D

PUBLIC ENEMY *US, male rap group – leader Chuck D (8 Albums: 40 Weeks, 16 Singles: 53 Weeks)*

21 Nov 87 **REBEL WITHOUT A PAUSE (re)** *Def Jam 651245 7*....37 7
9 Jan 88 **BRING THE NOISE** *Def Jam 651335 7*....32 5
2 Jul 88 **DON'T BELIEVE THE HYPE** *Def Jam 652833 7*....18 5
30 Jul 88 ● IT TAKES A NATION OF MILLIONS TO HOLD US BACK *Def Jam 4624151*....8 9
15 Oct 88 **NIGHT OF THE LIVING BASEHEADS** *Def Jam 6530460*....63 2
24 Jun 89 **FIGHT THE POWER** *Motown ZB 42877*....29 5
20 Jan 90 **WELCOME TO THE TERRORDOME** *Def Jam 655476 0*....18 4
7 Apr 90 **911 IS A JOKE** *Def Jam 655830 7*....41 3
28 Apr 90 ● FEAR OF A BLACK PLANET *Def Jam 4662811*....4 10
23 Jun 90 **BROTHERS GONNA WORK IT OUT** *Def Jam 656018 1*....46 2
3 Nov 90 **CAN'T DO NUTTIN' FOR YA MAN** *Def Jam 656385 7*....53 2
12 Oct 91 **CAN'T TRUSS IT** *Def Jam 6575307*....22 4
19 Oct 91 ● APOCALYPSE 91 – THE ENEMY STRIKES BLACK *Def Jam 4687511*....8 7
25 Jan 92 **SHUT 'EM DOWN** *Def Jam 6577617*....21 3
11 Apr 92 **NIGHTTRAIN** *Def Jam 6578647*....55 2
3 Oct 92 GREATEST MISSES *Def Jam 4720312*....14 3
13 Aug 94 **GIVE IT UP** *Def Jam DEFCD 1*....18 3
3 Sep 94 MUSE SICK-N-HOUR MESS AGE *Def Jam 5233622*....12 3
29 Jul 95 **SO WATCHA GONNA DO NOW** *Def Jam DEFCD 5*....50 1
16 May 98 HE GOT GAME (FILM SOUNDTRACK) *Def Jam 5581302*....50 4
6 Jun 98 **HE GOT GAME** *Def Jam 5689852* [1] 16 4
31 Jul 99 THERE'S A POISON GOIN ON ... *Pias Recordings PIASXCD 004*....55 1
25 Sep 99 **DO YOU WANNA GO OUR WAY???** *Pias Recordings PIASX 005CDX*....66 1
13 Aug 05 POWER TO THE PEOPLE AND THE BEATS – PUBLIC ENEMY'S GREATEST HITS *Def Jam / UMTV 9861661*....39 3

[1] Public Enemy featuring Stephen Stills

PUBLIC IMAGE LTD (PIL) (see also John LYDON) *UK, male vocal / instrumental group (12 Albums: 51 Weeks, 12 Singles: 61 Weeks)*

21 Oct 78 ● **PUBLIC IMAGE** *Virgin VS 228*....9 8
23 Dec 78 PUBLIC IMAGE *Virgin V 2114*....22 11
7 Jul 79 **DEATH DISCO** *Virgin VS 274*....20 7
20 Oct 79 **MEMORIES** *Virgin VS 299*....60 2
8 Dec 79 METAL BOX *Virgin METAL 1*....18 8
8 Mar 80 SECOND EDITION OF PIL *Virgin VD 2512*....46 2
22 Nov 80 PARIS AU PRINTEMPS (PARIS IN THE SPRING) *Virgin V 2183*....61 2
4 Apr 81 **FLOWERS OF ROMANCE** *Virgin VS 397*....24 7
18 Apr 81 FLOWERS OF ROMANCE *Virgin V 2189*....11 5
17 Sep 83 ● **THIS IS NOT A LOVE SONG** *Virgin VS 529*....5 10
8 Oct 83 LIVE IN TOKYO *Virgin VGD 3508*....28 6
19 May 84 **BAD LIFE** *Virgin VS 675*....71 2
21 Jul 84 THIS IS WHAT YOU WANT ... THIS IS WHAT YOU GET *Virgin V 2309*....56 2
1 Feb 86 **RISE** *Virgin VS 841*....11 8
15 Feb 86 ALBUM / CASSETTE / COMPACT DISC *Virgin V 2366*....14 6
3 May 86 **HOME** *Virgin VS 855*....75 1
22 Aug 87 **SEATTLE** *Virgin VS 988*....47 4
26 Sep 87 HAPPY? *Virgin V 2455*....40 2
6 May 89 **DISAPPOINTED** *Virgin VS 1181*....38 5
10 Jun 89 9 *Virgin V 2588*....36 2
20 Oct 90 **DON'T ASK ME** *Virgin VS 1231*....22 5
10 Nov 90 THE GREATEST HITS, SO FAR *Virgin V 2644*....20 3
22 Feb 92 **CRUEL** *Virgin VS 1390*....49 2
7 Mar 92 THAT WHAT IS NOT *Virgin CDV 2681*....46 2

Gary PUCKETT and The UNION GAP *US, male vocal / instrumental group (1 Album: 4 Weeks, 4 Singles: 47 Weeks)*

17 Apr 68 ★ **YOUNG GIRL** *CBS 3365* [1] $....1 17
29 Jun 68 UNION GAP *CBS 63342*....24 4
7 Aug 68 ● **LADY WILLPOWER** *CBS 3551* [1] $....5 16
28 Aug 68 **WOMAN, WOMAN** *CBS 3110* $....48 1
15 Jun 74 ● **YOUNG GIRL** (re-issue) *CBS 8202*....6 13

[1] Union Gap featuring Gary Puckett

PUDDLE OF MUDD *US, male vocal (Wes Scantlin) / instrumental group (1 Album: 36 Weeks, 4 Singles: 22 Weeks)*

2 Feb 02 COME CLEAN *Interscope 4930742*....12 36
23 Feb 02 **CONTROL (re)** *Flawless / Geffen 4976822*....15 5
15 Jun 02 ● **BLURRY** *Flawless / Geffen 4977342*....8 9
28 Sep 02 **SHE HATES ME** *Flawless / Geffen 4977982*....14 7
13 Dec 03 **AWAY FROM ME** *Flawless / Geffen 9814810*....55 1

Tito PUENTE Jr and The LATIN RHYTHM featuring Tito PUENTE, INDIA and Cali ALEMAN *US, male / female vocal / instrumental group (2 Singles: 3 Weeks)*

16 Mar 96 **OYE COMO VA** *Media MCSTD 40013*....36 2
19 Jul 97 **OYE COMA VA** (re-mix) *Nukleuz MCSTD 40120*....56 1

PULP (325 Top 500)

Jarvis Cocker, b. 19 Sep 1963, Sheffield, UK, is frontman of Pulp, or Arabacus Pulp as his band was called in 1978. After countless line-up changes and modest commercial success, 17 years passed before No.1 album Different Class and a string of Top 10 singles troubled the charts. Cocker's unique brand of wit and wisdom was then exposed to the wider world, culminating in the legendary bottom-wiggling "protest" at Michael Jackson's 1996 BRIT Awards performance (6 Albums: 138 Weeks, 13 Singles: 74 Weeks)

27 Nov 93 **LIP GLOSS** *Island CID 567*....50 2
2 Apr 94 **DO YOU REMEMBER THE FIRST TIME (re)** *Island CID 574*....33 5
30 Apr 94 ● HIS 'N' HERS *Island CID 8025*....9 43
4 Jun 94 **THE SISTERS (EP)** *Island CID 595*....19 4
3 Jun 95 ● **COMMON PEOPLE** *Island CID 613*....2 13
7 Oct 95 ● **MIS-SHAPES / SORTED FOR E'S AND WIZZ (re)** *Island CID 620*....2 11
11 Nov 95 ★ DIFFERENT CLASS *Island CID 8041* ■....1 64
9 Dec 95 ● **DISCO 2000** *Island CID 623*....7 11
23 Mar 96 ● COUNTDOWN 1992-1983 *Nectar Masters NTMCDD 521*....10 6
6 Apr 96 ● **SOMETHING CHANGED (2re)** *Island CID 632*....10 7
22 Nov 97 ● **HELP THE AGED (re)** *Island CID 679*....8 9
28 Mar 98 **THIS IS HARDCORE** *Island CID 695*....12 4
11 Apr 98 ★ THIS IS HARDCORE *Island CID 8066* ■....1 21
20 Jun 98 **A LITTLE SOUL** *Island CID 708*....22 2
19 Sep 98 **PARTY HARD** *Island CID 719*....29 2
20 Oct 01 **SUNRISE / THE TREES** *Island CID 786*....23 2
3 Nov 01 ● WE LOVE LIFE *Island CID 8110*....6 3
27 Apr 02 **BAD COVER VERSION** *Island CID 794*....27 2
30 Nov 02 HITS *Island / Uni-Island CID 8126*....71 1

Tracks on The Sisters (EP): Babies / Your Sister's Clothes / Seconds / His 'n' Hers.

PULSE featuring Antoinette ROBERSON (see also BOSS) *US, male / female vocal / production duo – David Morales and Antoinette Roberson*

25 May 96 **THE LOVER THAT YOU ARE** *ffrr FCD 278*....22 3

PUNK CHIC *Sweden, male producer – Johan Strandkvist*

6 Oct 01 **DJ SPINNIN'** *WEA WEA 333CD*....69 1

	3 November 1984	10 November 1984	17 November 1984	24 November 1984
UK No.1 SINGLES	FREEDOM Wham!	I FEEL FOR YOU Chaka Khan	I FEEL FOR YOU Chaka Khan	I FEEL FOR YOU Chaka Khan
UK No.1 ALBUMS	GIVE MY REGARDS TO BROAD STREET Paul McCartney	WELCOME TO THE PLEASUREDOME Frankie Goes to Hollywood	MAKE IT BIG Wham!	MAKE IT BIG Wham!

PUNX *Germany, male production trio*

16 Nov 02 **THE ROCK** *Data / Ministry of Sound DATA 38CDS* **59** 1

PURE REASON REVOLUTION

UK, male vocal / instrumental group (2 Singles: 2 Weeks)

1 May 04 **APPRENTICE OF THE UNIVERSE** *Poptones MC 5089SCD* **74** 1
23 Apr 05 **THE BRIGHT AMBASSADORS OF MORNING** *Sony Music 6758072* **68** 1

PURE SUGAR *UK, male / female vocal / instrumental trio*

24 Oct 98 **DELICIOUS** *Geffen GFSTD 22355* **70** 1

PURESSENCE

UK, male vocal / instrumental group (1 Album: 2 Weeks, 4 Singles: 6 Weeks)

23 May 98 **THIS FEELING** *Island CID 688* **33** 2
8 Aug 98 **IT DOESN'T MATTER ANYMORE** *Island CID 703* **47** 1
29 Aug 98 ONLY FOREVER *Island CID 8064* 36 2
21 Nov 98 **ALL I WANT** *Island CID 722* **39** 2
5 Oct 02 **WALKING DEAD** *Island CID 803* **40** 1

PURETONE *Australia, male producer – Josh Abrahams (2 Singles: 17 Weeks)*

12 Jan 02 ● **ADDICTED TO BASS** *Gusto CDGUS 6* **2** 15
10 May 03 **STUCK IN A GROOVE** *Illustrious CDILL 014* **26** 2

James and Bobby PURIFY *US, male vocal duo – James Purify and Robert Dickey (2 Singles: 16 Weeks)*

24 Apr 76 **I'M YOUR PUPPET** *Mercury 6167 324* **12** 10
7 Aug 76 **MORNING GLORY** *Mercury 6167 380* **27** 6

The PURPLE HEARTS

UK, male vocal / instrumental group (2 Singles: 5 Weeks)

22 Sep 79 **MILLIONS LIKE US** *Fiction FICS 003* **57** 3
8 Mar 80 **JIMMY** *Fiction FICS 9* **60** 2

PURPLE KINGS

UK, male vocal / instrumental duo – Rob Tillen and Glen Williamson

15 Oct 94 **THAT'S THE WAY YOU DO IT** *Positiva CDTIV 21* **26** 3

PUSH *Belgium, male producer – Dirk Dierickx (9 Singles: 19 Weeks)*

15 May 99 **UNIVERSAL NATION** *Bonzai / Inferno CDFERN 16* **36** 2
9 Oct 99 **UNIVERSAL NATION '99** (re-mix) *Inferno CDFERN 20* **35** 2
23 Sep 00 **TILL WE MEET AGAIN** *Inferno CDFERN 29* **46** 1
12 May 01 **STRANGE WORLD** *Inferno CDFERN 38* **21** 4
20 Oct 01 **PLEASE SAVE ME** *Inferno / Five AM FAMFERN 1CD* [1] **36** 2
3 Nov 01 **THE LEGACY** *Inferno CDFERN 43* **22** 4
4 May 02 **TRANZY STATE OF MIND** *Inferno CDFERN 45* **31** 2
5 Oct 02 **STRANGE WORLD / THE LEGACY** (re-issues) *Inferno CDFERN 49* **55** 1
15 Mar 03 **UNIVERSAL NATION** (2nd re-mix) *Inferno CDFERN 53* **54** 1

[1] Sunscreem vs Push

PUSSY 2000 *UK, male production duo*

3 Nov 01 **IT'S GONNA BE ALRIGHT** *Ink NIBNE 9CD* **70** 1

PUSSYCAT

Holland, male / female vocal / instrumental group (2 Singles: 30 Weeks)

28 Aug 76 ★ **MISSISSIPPI** *Sonet SON 2077* **1** 22
25 Dec 76 **SMILE** *Sonet SON 2096* **24** 8

The PUSSYCAT DOLLS NEW

US, female vocal group (1 Album: 15 Weeks, 3 Singles: 21 Weeks)

10 Sep 05 **DON'T CHA** (import) *A&M AMB 000468322* [1] **44** 1
17 Sep 05 ★ **DON'T CHA** *A&M 9885051* [1] ■ .... **1** 16+
24 Sep 05 ● PCD *A&M 9885657* .... 8 15+
10 Dec 05 ★ **STICKWITU** *A&M 9888582* ■ .... **1** 4+

[1] Pussycat Dolls featuring Busta Rhymes

The PYRAMIDS (see also SYMARIP) *Jamaica, male vocal / instrumental group*

22 Nov 67 **TRAIN TOUR TO RAINBOW CITY** *President PT 161* **35** 4

PYTHON LEE JACKSON *Australia, male vocal / instrumental group*

30 Sep 72 ● **IN A BROKEN DREAM** *Youngblood YB 1002* **3** 12

Uncredited lead vocals by Rod Stewart.

Q

Q *UK, male instrumental / production duo – Mark Taylor and Terry Adams (2 Singles: 6 Weeks)*

5 Jun 93 **GET HERE** *Arista 74321145972* [1] **37** 4
12 Mar 94 **(EVERYTHING I DO) I DO IT FOR YOU** *Bell 74321193062* [2] **47** 2

[1] Q featuring Tracy Ackerman [2] Q featuring Tony Jackson

QB FINEST featuring NAS & BRAVEHEARTS *US, male rappers*

21 Apr 01 **OOCHIE WALLY** *Columbia 6710852* **30** 3

Q-BASS *UK, male production / instrumental duo*

8 Feb 92 **HARDCORE WILL NEVER DIE** *Suburban Base SUBBASE 007* **64** 1

Q-CLUB *Italy, male / female vocal / instrumental group*

6 Jan 96 **TELL IT TO MY HEART** *Manifesto FESCD 5* **28** 3

QFX *UK, male / female vocal / instrumental group (1 Album: 1 Week, 6 Singles: 18 Weeks)*

6 May 95 **FREEDOM (EP)** *Epidemic EPICD 004* **41** 3
3 Feb 96 **EVERYTIME YOU TOUCH ME** *Epidemic EPICD 006* **22** 4
3 Aug 96 **YOU GOT THE POWER** *Epidemic EPICD 007* **33** 3
18 Jan 97 **FREEDOM 2** (re-mix) *Epidemic EPICD 008* **21** 4
8 Mar 97 ALIEN CHILD *Epidemic EPICD 009* 62 1
20 Mar 99 **SAY YOU'LL BE MINE** *Quality Recordings QUAL 005CD* **34** 2
23 Aug 03 **FREEDOM** *Data / MoS DATA 57CDS* **36** 2

Tracks on Freedom (EP): Freedom / Metropolis / Sianora Baby / The Machine.

Q-TEE *UK, female rapper – Tatiana Mais (2 Singles: 7 Weeks)*

21 Apr 90 **AFRIKA** *SBK SBK 7008* [1] **42** 5
10 Feb 96 **GIMME THAT BODY** *Heavenly HVN 48CD* **40** 2

[1] History featuring Q-Tee

Q-TEX *UK, male / female vocal / instrumental group (5 Singles: 7 Weeks)*

9 Apr 94 **THE POWER OF LOVE** *Stoatin' STOAT 002CD* **65** 1
26 Nov 94 **BELIEVE** *23rd Precinct THIRD 2CD* **41** 2
15 Jun 96 **LET THE LOVE** *23rd Precinct THIRD 4CD* **30** 2
30 Nov 96 **DO YOU WANT ME** *23rd Precinct THIRD 5CD* **48** 1
28 Jun 97 **POWER OF LOVE '97** (re-mix) *23rd Precinct THIRD 7CD* **49** 1

1 December 1984	8 December 1984	15 December 1984	22 December 1984
I SHOULD HAVE KNOWN BETTER Jim Diamond	**THE POWER OF LOVE** Frankie Goes to Hollywood	**DO THEY KNOW IT'S CHRISTMAS?** Band Aid	**DO THEY KNOW IT'S CHRISTMAS?** Band Aid
THE HITS ALBUM / THE HITS TAPE Various	**THE HITS ALBUM / THE HITS TAPE** Various	**THE HITS ALBUM / THE HITS TAPE** Various	**THE HITS ALBUM / THE HITS TAPE** Various

KEY
UK No.1 ★ UK Top 10 ● Still on chart + UK entry at No.1 ■ US No.1 ▲ UK million seller £ US million seller $
Singles re-entries are listed as (re), (2re), (3re)... which signifies that the hit re-entered the chart once, twice or three times...
Peak Position / Weeks

Q-TIP (see also DEEE-LITE; A TRIBE CALLED QUEST)
US, male rapper – John Davis (5 Singles: 23 Weeks)

4 Oct 97 ● **GOT 'TIL IT'S GONE** *Virgin VSCDG 1666* [1] ...6 9
19 Jun 99 **GET INVOLVED** *Hollywood 0101185 HWR* [2] ...36 2
22 Jan 00 **HOT BOYZ** *Elektra E 7002CD* [3] ...18 3
12 Feb 00 **BREATHE AND STOP** *Arista 74321727062*...12 7
6 May 00 **VIVRANT THING** *Arista 74321751302*...39 2

[1] Janet featuring Q-Tip and Joni Mitchell [2] Raphael Saadiq and Q-Tip
[3] Missy 'Misdemeanor' Elliott featuring Nas, Eve and Q-Tip

Q-TIPS (see also Paul YOUNG) *UK, male vocal / instrumental group*

30 Aug 80 **Q-TIPS** *Chrysalis CHR 1255*...50 1

QATTARA (see also Alex WHITCOMBE & BIG C)
UK, male production duo – Andy Cato and Alex Whitcombe

15 Mar 97 **COME WITH ME** *Positiva CDTIV 71*...31 2

QUAD CITY DJs *US, male rap duo*

15 Nov 97 **SPACE JAM** *Atlantic EW 773*...57 1

QUADROPHONIA
Belgium, male instrumental / production group (3 Singles: 15 Weeks)

13 Apr 91 **QUADROPHONIA** *ARS 6567687*...14 9
6 Jul 91 **THE WAVE OF THE FUTURE** *ARS 6569937*...40 3
21 Dec 91 **FIND THE TIME (PART ONE)** *ARS 6576260*...41 3

The QUADS *UK, male vocal / instrumental group*

22 Sep 79 **THERE MUST BE THOUSANDS** *Big Bear BB 23*...66 2

QUAKE featuring Marcia RAE
(see also BEAT RENEGADES; DREAM FREQUENCY; NATIVE; RED)
UK, male producers – Rob Tissera and Ian Bland and female vocalist

29 Aug 98 **THE DAY WILL COME** *ffrr FCD 344*...53 1

QUANTUM JUMP *UK, male vocal (Rupert Hine) / instrumental group*

2 Jun 79 ● **THE LONE RANGER** *Electric WOT 33*...5 10

QUARTERFLASH *US, male / female vocal / instrumental group*

27 Feb 82 **HARDEN MY HEART** *Geffen GEF A 1838*...49 5

QUARTZ *UK, male instrumental group (3 Singles: 19 Weeks)*

17 Mar 90 **WE'RE COMIN' AT YA** *Mercury ITMR 2* [1] ...65 2
2 Feb 91 ● **IT'S TOO LATE** *Mercury ITM 3* [2] ...8 14
15 Jun 91 **NAKED LOVE (JUST SAY YOU WANT ME)** *Mercury ITM 4* [3] .39 3

[1] Quartz featuring Stepz [2] Quartz introducing Dina Carroll
[3] Quartz and Dina Carroll

Jakie QUARTZ *France, female vocalist*

11 Mar 89 **A LA VIE, A L'AMOUR** *PWL PWL 30*...55 3

QUARTZ LOCK featuring Lonnie GORDON *UK, male production / instrumental duo – Mark Andrews and Donald Lynch and US, female vocalist*

7 Oct 95 **LOVE EVICTION** *X:Plode BANG 2CD* ...32 2

Suzi QUATRO *US, female vocalist / guitarist – Suzi Quatrocchio (2 Albums: 13 Weeks, 16 Singles: 122 Weeks)*

19 May 73 ★ **CAN THE CAN** *RAK 150*...1 14
28 Jul 73 ● **48 CRASH** *RAK 158*...3 9
13 Oct 73 **SUZI QUATRO** *RAK SRAK 505*...32 4
27 Oct 73 **DAYTONA DEMON** *RAK 161*...14 13
9 Feb 74 ★ **DEVIL GATE DRIVE** *RAK 167*...1 11
29 Jun 74 **TOO BIG** *RAK 175*...14 6
9 Nov 74 ● **THE WILD ONE** *RAK 185*...7 10
8 Feb 75 **YOUR MAMMA WON'T LIKE ME** *RAK 191*...31 5
5 Mar 77 **TEAR ME APART** *RAK 248*...27 6
18 Mar 78 ● **IF YOU CAN'T GIVE ME LOVE** *RAK 271*...4 13
22 Jul 78 **THE RACE IS ON** *RAK 278*...43 5
11 Nov 78 **STUMBLIN' IN** *RAK 285* [1] $...41 8
20 Oct 79 **SHE'S IN LOVE WITH YOU** *RAK 299*...11 9
19 Jan 80 **MAMA'S BOY** *RAK 303*...34 5
5 Apr 80 **I'VE NEVER BEEN IN LOVE** *RAK 307*...56 3
26 Apr 80 ● **SUZI QUATRO'S GREATEST HITS** *RAK EMTV 24*...4 9
25 Oct 80 **ROCK HARD** *Dreamland DLSP 6*...68 2
13 Nov 82 **HEART OF STONE** *Polydor POSP 477*...60 3

[1] Suzi Quatro and Chris Norman

Finley QUAYE
UK, male vocalist / guitarist (3 Albums: 59 Weeks, 6 Singles: 23 Weeks)

21 Jun 97 **SUNDAY SHINING** *Epic 6644552*...16 6
13 Sep 97 ● **EVEN AFTER ALL** *Epic 6649712*...10 5
4 Oct 97 ● **MAVERICK A STRIKE** *Epic 4887582*...3 56
29 Nov 97 **IT'S GREAT WHEN WE'RE TOGETHER** *Epic 6653382*...29 3
7 Mar 98 **YOUR LOVE GETS SWEETER** *Epic 6656065*...16 5
15 Aug 98 **ULTRA STIMULATION** *Epic 6660792*...51 1
23 Sep 00 **SPIRITUALIZED** *Epic 6698032*...26 3
14 Oct 00 **VANGUARD** *Epic 4997102*...35 2
11 Oct 03 **MUCH MORE THAN LOVE** *Sony Music 5125492*...56 1

QUEEN (3 Top 500)

World-renowned British quartet who have spent longer on the albums chart than any other act: Freddie Mercury (v), b. 5 Sep 1946, d. 24 Nov 1991, Brian May CBE (g/v), John Deacon (b/v) and Roger Taylor (d/v). 'Bohemian Rhapsody', which in places has 180 vocal overdubs, was voted 'No.1 Single of All-Time' by the readers of this book. It was the first recording to top the UK singles chart on two occasions, selling over a million each time, and was No.1 in a record four calendar years. They were also the first act to have chart-topping singles in the 1970s, 1980s, 1990s and the 21st century. Frontman Mercury is rightfully regarded as one of the greatest entertainers in rock and the group, who stole the show at Live Aid, have attracted millions to their concerts around the globe. Queen have sold over 25 million Greatest Hits albums and are the only act to sell in excess of two million copies of two Greatest Hits albums in the UK. Additionally, they have held the top four places on the UK video chart (1992) and 'We Are the Champions' has become the most popular song chanted by the world's sporting crowds. The group, which has contributed enormously to AIDS awareness, won a BRIT award for Outstanding Contribution to British Music (1992) and were inducted into the Rock and Roll Hall of Fame in 2000. The Queen musical We Will Rock You, penned by Ben Elton and backed by Robert De Niro, has been running successfully since 2002. The band were inducted into the UK Music Hall of Fame in 2004, and in 2005 successfully toured with new vocalist Paul Rodgers. Total UK single sales: 10,334,713. Best-selling single: 'Bohemian Rhapsody' 2,130,000 (28 Albums: 1332 Weeks, 52 Singles: 423 Weeks)

9 Mar 74 ● **SEVEN SEAS OF RHYE** *EMI 2121*...10 10
23 Mar 74 ● **QUEEN 2** *EMI EMA 767*...5 29
30 Mar 74 **QUEEN** *EMI EMC 3006*...24 18
26 Oct 74 ● **KILLER QUEEN** *EMI 2229*...2 12
23 Nov 74 ● **SHEER HEART ATTACK** *EMI EMC 3061*...2 42
25 Jan 75 **NOW I'M HERE** *EMI 2256*...11 7
8 Nov 75 ★ **BOHEMIAN RHAPSODY** *EMI 2375* £ $...1 17
13 Dec 75 ★ **A NIGHT AT THE OPERA** *EMI EMTC 103*...1 50
3 Jul 76 ● **YOU'RE MY BEST FRIEND** *EMI 2494*...7 8
27 Nov 76 ● **SOMEBODY TO LOVE** *EMI 2565*...2 9
25 Dec 76 ★ **A DAY AT THE RACES** *EMI EMTC 104*...1 24
19 Mar 77 **TIE YOUR MOTHER DOWN** *EMI 2593*...31 4
4 Jun 77 **QUEEN'S FIRST EP** *EMI 2623*...17 10

	29 December 1984	5 January 1985	12 January 1985	19 January 1985
UK No.1 SINGLES	DO THEY KNOW IT'S CHRISTMAS? Band Aid	DO THEY KNOW IT'S CHRISTMAS? Band Aid	DO THEY KNOW IT'S CHRISTMAS? Band Aid	I WANT TO KNOW WHAT LOVE IS Foreigner
UK No.1 ALBUMS	THE HITS ALBUM / THE HITS TAPE Various	THE HITS ALBUM / THE HITS TAPE Various	THE HITS ALBUM / THE HITS TAPE Various	ALF Alison Moyet

22 Oct 77 ● WE ARE THE CHAMPIONS *EMI 2708* $ ... 2 11
12 Nov 77 ● NEWS OF THE WORLD *EMI EMA 784* ... 4 20
25 Feb 78 SPREAD YOUR WINGS *EMI 2757* ... 34 4
28 Oct 78 BICYCLE RACE / FAT BOTTOMED GIRLS *EMI 2870* ... 11 12
25 Nov 78 ● JAZZ *EMI EMA 788* ... 2 27
10 Feb 79 ● DON'T STOP ME NOW *EMI 2910* ... 9 12
7 Jul 79 ● LIVE KILLERS *EMI EMSP 330* ... 3 29
14 Jul 79 LOVE OF MY LIFE *EMI 2959* ... 63 2
20 Oct 79 ● CRAZY LITTLE THING CALLED LOVE *EMI 5001* ▲ $ ... 2 14
2 Feb 80 SAVE ME *EMI 5022* ... 11 6
14 Jun 80 PLAY THE GAME *EMI 5076* ... 14 8
12 Jul 80 ★ THE GAME *EMI EMA 795* ▲ ... 1 18
6 Sep 80 ● ANOTHER ONE BITES THE DUST *EMI 5102* ▲ $ ... 7 9
6 Dec 80 ● FLASH *EMI 5126* ... 10 13
20 Dec 80 ● FLASH GORDON (FILM SOUNDTRACK) *EMI EMC 3351* ... 10 15
7 Nov 81 ★ GREATEST HITS *Parlophone EMYV 30* ... 1 450
14 Nov 81 ★ UNDER PRESSURE *EMI 5250* [1] ... 1 11
1 May 82 BODY LANGUAGE *EMI 5293* ... 25 6
15 May 82 ● HOT SPACE *EMI EMA 797* ... 4 19
12 Jun 82 LAS PALABRAS DE AMOR *EMI 5316* ... 17 8
21 Aug 82 BACKCHAT *EMI 5325* ... 40 4
4 Feb 84 ● RADIO GAGA *EMI QUEEN 1* ... 2 9
10 Mar 84 ● THE WORKS *EMI EMC 240014* ... 2 93
14 Apr 84 ● I WANT TO BREAK FREE *EMI QUEEN 2* ... 3 15
28 Jul 84 ● IT'S A HARD LIFE *EMI QUEEN 3* ... 6 9
22 Sep 84 HAMMER TO FALL *EMI QUEEN 4* ... 13 7
8 Dec 84 THANK GOD IT'S CHRISTMAS *EMI QUEEN 5* ... 21 6
16 Nov 85 ● ONE VISION *EMI QUEEN 6* ... 7 10
29 Mar 86 ● A KIND OF MAGIC *EMI QUEEN 7* ... 3 11
14 Jun 86 ★ A KIND OF MAGIC *EMI EU 3509* ■ ... 1 63
21 Jun 86 FRIENDS WILL BE FRIENDS *EMI QUEEN 8* ... 14 8
27 Sep 86 WHO WANTS TO LIVE FOREVER *EMI QUEEN 9* ... 24 5
13 Dec 86 ● LIVE MAGIC *EMI EMC 3519* ... 3 43
13 May 89 ● I WANT IT ALL *Parlophone QUEEN 10* ... 3 7
3 Jun 89 ★ THE MIRACLE *Parlophone PCSD 107* ■ ... 1 32
1 Jul 89 ● BREAKTHRU' *Parlophone QUEEN 11* ... 7 7
19 Aug 89 THE INVISIBLE MAN *Parlophone QUEEN 12* ... 12 6
21 Oct 89 SCANDAL *Parlophone QUEEN 14* ... 25 4
9 Dec 89 THE MIRACLE *Parlophone QUEEN 15* ... 21 5
16 Dec 89 QUEEN AT THE BEEB *Band of Joy BOJLP 001* ... 67 1
26 Jan 91 ★ INNUENDO *Parlophone QUEEN 16* ■ ... 1 6
16 Feb 91 ★ INNUENDO *Parlophone PCSD 115* ■ ... 1 37
25 May 91 I'M GOING SLIGHTLY MAD *Parlophone QUEEN 17* ... 22 5
25 May 91 HEADLONG *Parlophone QUEEN 18* ... 14 4
26 Oct 91 THE SHOW MUST GO ON (re) *Parlophone QUEEN 19* ... 16 10
9 Nov 91 ★ GREATEST HITS II *Parlophone PMTV 2* ■ ... 1 106
21 Dec 91 ★ BOHEMIAN RHAPSODY (re-issue) / THESE ARE THE DAYS OF OUR LIVES *Parlophone QUEEN 20* ■ £ ... 1 14
6 Jun 92 ● LIVE AT WEMBLEY '86 *Parlophone CDPCSP 725* ... 2 15
1 May 93 ★ FIVE LIVE (EP) (re) *Parlophone CDRS 6340* [2] ■ ... 1 12
19 Nov 94 GREATEST HITS I AND II *Parlophone CDPCSD 161* ... 37 7
4 Nov 95 ● HEAVEN FOR EVERYONE *Parlophone CDQUEEN 21* ... 2 12
18 Nov 95 ★ MADE IN HEAVEN *Parlophone CDPCSD 167* ■ ... 1 28
23 Dec 95 ● A WINTER'S TALE *Parlophone CDQUEEN 22* ... 6 6
9 Mar 96 TOO MUCH LOVE WILL KILL YOU *Parlophone CDQUEEN 23* ... 15 6
29 Jun 96 ● LET ME LIVE *Parlophone CDQUEEN 24* ... 9 4
30 Nov 96 YOU DON'T FOOL ME *Parlophone CDQUEEN 25* ... 17 4
15 Nov 97 ● QUEEN ROCKS *Parlophone 8230912* ... 7 12
17 Jan 98 NO-ONE BUT YOU / TIE YOUR MOTHER DOWN (re-issue) *Parlophone CDQUEEN 27* ... 13 4
14 Nov 98 ● ANOTHER ONE BITES THE DUST (re-recording) *Dreamworks DRMCD 22364* [3] ... 5 6
20 Nov 99 ● GREATEST HITS III *Parlophone 5238942* [1] ... 5 19
18 Dec 99 UNDER PRESSURE (re-mix) *Parlophone CDQUEEN 28* [1] ... 14 7
29 Jul 00 ★ WE WILL ROCK YOU (re) *RCA 74321774022* [4] ■ ... 1 13
25 Nov 00 ● GREATEST HITS I II & III – THE PLATINUM COLLECTION *Parlophone 5298832* ... 2 116
29 Mar 03 FLASH *Nebula NEBCD 041* [5] ... 15 4
21 Jun 03 LIVE AT WEMBLEY '86 (re-issue) *Parlophone 5904402* ... 30 11
6 Nov 04 QUEEN ON FIRE – LIVE AT THE BOWL *Parlophone 8632112* ... 20 4
1 Oct 05 RETURN OF THE CHAMPIONS *Parlophone 3369792* [2] ... 12 4

[1] Queen and David Bowie [2] George Michael and Queen with Lisa Stansfield [3] Queen with Wyclef Jean featuring Pras and Free [4] Five and Queen [5] Queen & Vanguard [1] Queen+ [2] Queen + Paul Rodgers

Tracks on Queen's First EP: Good Old Fashioned Lover Boy / Death on Two Legs (Dedicated to ...) / Tenement Funster / White Queen (As it Began). Tracks on Five Live (EP): Somebody to Love / These Are the Days of Our Lives / Calling You / Papa Was a Rolling Stone – Killer (medley). Queen appear only on the first two tracks. The first credits George Michael and Queen and the second George Michael with Lisa Stansfield. The Works changed label number to EMI WORK 1 during its chart run. Greatest Hits III features band members' solo tracks and collaborations in addition to the hits of Queen. The re-issued Live at Wembley '86 (2003) reached its peak position in 2005. Return of the Champions, a live album, features hits made famous by Paul Rodgers' previous bands, Free and Bad Company, as well as Queen

QUEEN LATIFAH *US, female rapper – Dana Owens (6 Singles: 17 Weeks)*

24 Mar 90 MAMA GAVE BIRTH TO THE SOUL CHILDREN *Gee Street GEE 26* [1] ... 14 7
26 May 90 FIND A WAY *Ahead of Our Time CCUT 8* [2] ... 52 2
31 Aug 91 FLY GIRL *Gee Street GEE 34* ... 67 1
26 Jun 93 WHAT'CHA GONNA DO *Epic 6593072* [3] ... 21 4
26 Mar 94 U.N.I.T.Y. *Motown TMGCD 1422* ... 74 1
12 Apr 97 MR BIG STUFF *Motown 5736572* [4] ... 31 2

[1] Queen Latifah + De La Soul [2] Coldcut featuring Queen Latifah [3] Shabba Ranks featuring Queen Latifah [4] Queen Latifah, Shades and Free

QUEEN PEN *US, female rapper – Lynise Walters (3 Singles: 10 Weeks)*

7 Mar 98 MAN BEHIND THE MUSIC *Interscope IND 95562* ... 38 2
9 May 98 ALL MY LOVE *Interscope IND 95584* [1] ... 11 5
5 Sep 98 IT'S TRUE *Interscope IND 95597* ... 24 3

[1] Queen Pen featuring Eric Williams

QUEENS OF THE STONE AGE *US, male vocal (Josh Homme) / instrumental group (3 Albums: 33 Weeks, 6 Singles: 20 Weeks)*

26 Aug 00 THE LOST ART OF KEEPING A SECRET *Interscope 4973912* ... 31 2
2 Sep 00 R *Interscope 4906832* ... 54 3
7 Sep 02 ● SONGS FOR THE DEAF *Interscope / Polydor 4934440* ... 4 22
16 Nov 02 NO ONE KNOWS *Interscope / Polydor 4978122* ... 15 7
19 Apr 03 GO WITH THE FLOW *Interscope / Polydor 4978702* ... 21 3
30 Aug 03 FIRST IT GIVETH *Interscope / Polydor 9810505* ... 33 2
26 Mar 05 LITTLE SISTER *Interscope / Polydor 98890670* ... 18 5
2 Apr 05 ● LULLABIES TO PARALYZE *Interscope 9880313* ... 4 8
23 Jul 05 IN MY HEAD *Interscope / Polydor 9883541* ... 44 1

QUEENSRŸCHE
US, male vocal / instrumental group (6 Albums: 12 Weeks, 8 Singles: 21 Weeks)

29 Sep 84 THE WARNING *EMI America EJ 2402201* ... 100 1
26 Jul 86 RAGE FOR ORDER *EMI America AML 3105* ... 66 1
4 Jun 88 OPERATION MINDCRIME *Manhattan MTL 1023* ... 58 3
13 May 89 EYES OF A STRANGER *EMI USA MT 65* ... 59 1
22 Sep 90 EMPIRE *EMI-USA MTL 1058* ... 13 3
10 Nov 90 EMPIRE *EMI USA MT 90* ... 61 1
20 Apr 91 SILENT LUCIDITY *EMI USA MT 94* ... 34 5
6 Jul 91 BEST I CAN *EMI USA MT 97* ... 36 3
7 Sep 91 JET CITY WOMAN *EMI USA MT 98* ... 39 2
8 Aug 92 SILENT LUCIDITY (re-issue) *EMI USA MT 104* ... 18 4
22 Oct 94 PROMISED LAND *EMI CDMTL 1081* ... 13 3
28 Jan 95 I AM I *EMI CDMT 109* ... 40 2
25 Mar 95 BRIDGE *EMI CDMT 111* ... 40 3
29 Mar 97 HEAR IN THE NOW FRONTIER *EMI CDEMC 3764* ... 46 1

QUENCH *Australia, male instrumental / production duo*

17 Feb 96 DREAMS *Infectious INFECT 3CD* ... 75 1

QUENTIN and ASH
UK, female actor / vocal duo – Caroline Quentin and Leslie Ash

6 Jul 96 TELL HIM *East West EW 049CD* ... 25 3

26 January 1985	2 February 1985	9 February 1985	16 February 1985
I WANT TO KNOW WHAT LOVE IS Foreigner	I WANT TO KNOW WHAT LOVE IS Foreigner	I KNOW HIM SO WELL Elaine Paige and Barbara Dickson	I KNOW HIM SO WELL Elaine Paige and Barbara Dickson
AGENT PROVOCATEUR Foreigner	AGENT PROVOCATEUR Foreigner	AGENT PROVOCATEUR Foreigner	BORN IN THE U.S.A. Bruce Springsteen

KEY
UK No.1 ★ UK Top 10 ● Still on chart + UK entry at No.1 ■
US No.1 ▲ UK million seller £ US million seller $
Singles re-entries are listed as (re), (2re), (3re)… which signifies that the hit re-entered the chart once, twice or three times…
Peak Position / Weeks

? (QUESTION MARK) and The MYSTERIANS
US, male vocal / instrumental group

17 Nov 66 **96 TEARS** *Cameo Parkway C 428* ▲ $ **37** 4

The QUESTIONS
UK, male vocal / instrumental group (3 Singles: 8 Weeks)

23 Apr 83 **PRICE YOU PAY** *Respond KOB 702* **56** 3
17 Sep 83 **TEAR SOUP** *Respond KOB 705* **66** 1
10 Mar 84 **TUESDAY SUNSHINE** *Respond KOB 707* **46** 4

QUICK *UK, male vocal / instrumental group*

15 May 82 **RHYTHM OF THE JUNGLE** *Epic EPC A 2013* **41** 7

Tommy QUICKLY and The REMO FOUR
UK, male vocalist and vocal / instrumental group

22 Oct 64 **WILD SIDE OF LIFE** *Pye 7N 15708* **33** 8

The QUIET FIVE *UK, male vocal / instrumental group (2 Singles: 3 Weeks)*

13 May 65 **WHEN THE MORNING SUN DRIES THE DEW** *Parlophone R 5273* **45** 1
21 Apr 66 **HOMEWARD BOUND** *Parlophone R 5421* **44** 2

QUIET RIOT *US, male vocal / instrumental group*

3 Dec 83 **METAL HEALTH / CUM ON FEEL THE NOIZE** *Epic A 3968* $ **45** 5
4 Aug 84 CONDITION CRITICAL *Epic EPC 26075* 71 1

'Cum on Feel the Noize' credited only from 10 Dec 1983.

Eimear QUINN *Ireland, female vocalist*

15 Jun 96 **THE VOICE** *Polydor 5768842* **40** 2

Paul QUINN and EDWYN COLLINS
UK, male vocalists / instrumentalists (2 Singles: 2 Weeks)

11 Aug 84 **PALE BLUE EYES** *Swamplands SWP 1* **72** 2

Sinead QUINN
UK, female vocalist (1 Album: 2 Weeks, 2 Singles: 15 Weeks)

22 Feb 03 ● **I CAN'T BREAK DOWN** *Mercury 0637282* **2** 12
12 Jul 03 **WHAT YOU NEED IS ... (re)** *Fontana 980971* **19** 3
26 Jul 03 READY TO RUN *Fontana 9865367* 48 2

QUINTESSENCE
UK / Australia, male vocal / instrumental group (3 Albums: 6 Weeks)

27 Jun 70 QUINTESSENCE *Island ILPS 9128* 22 4
3 Apr 71 DIVE DEEP *Island ILPS 9143* 43 1
27 May 72 SELF *RCA Victor SF 8273* 50 1

The QUIREBOYS *UK, male vocal (Spike Grey) / instrumental group (2 Albums: 17 Weeks, 6 Singles: 27 Weeks)*

4 Nov 89 **7 O'CLOCK** *Parlophone R 6230* **36** 4
6 Jan 90 **HEY YOU** *Parlophone R 6241* **14** 7
10 Feb 90 ● A BIT OF WHAT YOU FANCY *Parlophone PCS 7335* 2 15
7 Apr 90 **I DON'T LOVE YOU ANYMORE** *Parlophone R 6248* **24** 6
8 Sep 90 **THERE SHE GOES AGAIN / MISLED** *Parlophone R 6267* **37** 4
10 Oct 92 **TRAMPS AND THIEVES** *Parlophone RS 6323* **41** 3
20 Feb 93 **BROTHER LOUIE** *Parlophone CDR 6335* **31** 3
27 Mar 93 BITTER SWEET AND TWISTED *Parlophone CDPCSD 120* 31 2

QUIVVER *UK, male instrumental / production duo (2 Singles: 3 Weeks)*

5 Mar 94 **SAXY LADY** *A&M 5805152* **56** 2
18 Nov 95 **BELIEVE IN ME** *Perfecto PERF 111CD* **56** 1

QUO VADIS *UK, male production trio*

16 Dec 00 **SONIC BOOM (LIFE'S TOO SHORT)** *Serious SERR 028CD* **49** 1

R

R.A.F.
(see also CRW) *Italy, male producer – Mauro Picotto (4 Singles: 6 Weeks)*

14 Mar 92 **WE'VE GOT TO LIVE TOGETHER** *PWL Continental PWL 218* **34** 3
5 Mar 94 **TAKE ME HIGHER** *Media MRLCD 0012* **71** 1
23 Mar 96 **TAKE ME HIGHER** (re-mix) *Media MCSTD 40026* **59** 1
27 Jul 96 **ANGEL'S SYMPHONY** *Media MCSTD 40051* **73** 1

R.E.M. 31 Top 500
"America's Best Rock Band", according to Rolling Stone: Michael Stipe (v), Peter Buck (g), Mike Mills (b), Bill Berry (d). This Georgia group went from the US college circuit to packing stadiums worldwide and performed at the Live 8 London concert. In 1996, the award-winning, platinum-album-earning quartet signed an $80 million record deal. (17 Albums: 594 Weeks, 38 Singles: 184 Weeks)

28 Apr 84 RECKONING *IRS A 7045* 91 2
29 Jun 85 FABLES OF THE RECONSTRUCTION *IRS MIRF 1003* 35 4
6 Sep 86 LIFE'S RICH PAGEANT *IRS MIRG 1014* 43 4
16 May 87 DEAD LETTER OFFICE *IRS SP 70054* 60 2
26 Sep 87 DOCUMENT *IRS MIRG 1025* 28 5
28 Nov 87 **THE ONE I LOVE** *IRS IRM 46* **51** 8
30 Apr 88 **FINEST WORKSONG** *IRS IRM 161* **50** 2
29 Oct 88 EPONYMOUS *IRS MIRG 1038* 69 3
19 Nov 88 GREEN *Warner Bros. WX 234* 27 22
4 Feb 89 **STAND** *Warner Bros. W 7577* **51** 3
3 Jun 89 **ORANGE CRUSH** *Warner Bros. W 2960* **28** 5
12 Aug 89 **STAND** (re-issue) *Warner Bros. W 2833* **48** 2
9 Mar 91 **LOSING MY RELIGION** *Warner Bros. W 0015* **19** 9
23 Mar 91 ★ OUT OF TIME *Warner Bros. WX 404* ■ ▲ 1 183
18 May 91 ● **SHINY HAPPY PEOPLE** *Warner Bros. W 0027* **6** 11
17 Aug 91 **NEAR WILD HEAVEN** *Warner Bros. W 0055* **27** 4
21 Sep 91 **THE ONE I LOVE** (re-issue) *IRS IRM 178* **16** 6
12 Oct 91 ● THE BEST OF R.E.M. *IRS MIRH 1* 7 28
16 Nov 91 **RADIO SONG** *Warner Bros. W 0072* **28** 3
14 Dec 91 **IT'S THE END OF THE WORLD AS WE KNOW IT** *IRS IRM 180* **39** 4
3 Oct 92 **DRIVE** *Warner Bros. W 0136* **11** 5
10 Oct 92 ★ AUTOMATIC FOR THE PEOPLE *Warner Bros. 9362450552* ■ 1 179
28 Nov 92 **MAN ON THE MOON** *Warner Bros. W 0143* **18** 8
20 Feb 93 **THE SIDEWINDER SLEEPS TONITE** *Warner Bros. W 0152CD1* **17** 6
17 Apr 93 ● **EVERYBODY HURTS** *Warner Bros. W 0169CD1* **7** 12
24 Jul 93 **NIGHTSWIMMING** *Warner Bros. W 0184CD* **27** 5
11 Dec 93 **FIND THE RIVER** *Warner Bros. W 0211CD* **54** 1
17 Sep 94 ● **WHAT'S THE FREQUENCY, KENNETH** *Warner Bros. W 0265CD* **9** 7
8 Oct 94 ★ MONSTER *Warner Bros. 9362457632* ■ ▲ 1 56
12 Nov 94 **BANG AND BLAME** *Warner Bros. W 0275CD* **15** 4
4 Feb 95 **CRUSH WITH EYELINER** *Warner Bros. W 0281CD* **23** 3
15 Apr 95 ● **STRANGE CURRENCIES** *Warner Bros. W 0290CD* **9** 4
29 Jul 95 **TONGUE** *Warner Bros. W 0308CD* **13** 5
31 Aug 96 ● **E-BOW THE LETTER** *Warner Bros. W 0369CD* **4** 5
21 Sep 96 ★ NEW ADVENTURES IN HI-FI *Warner Bros. 9362463202* ■ 1 20

23 February 1985	2 March 1985	9 March 1985	16 March 1985
UK No.1 SINGLES			
I KNOW HIM SO WELL Elaine Paige and Barbara Dickson	I KNOW HIM SO WELL Elaine Paige and Barbara Dickson	YOU SPIN ME ROUND (LIKE A RECORD) Dead or Alive	YOU SPIN ME ROUND (LIKE A RECORD) Dead or Alive
UK No.1 ALBUMS			
MEAT IS MURDER The Smiths	NO JACKET REQUIRED Phil Collins	NO JACKET REQUIRED Phil Collins	NO JACKET REQUIRED Phil Collins

2 Nov 96 **BITTERSWEET ME** *Warner Bros. W 0377CD* 19 2
14 Dec 96 **ELECTROLITE** *Warner Bros. W 0383CD* 29 2
24 Oct 98 ● **DAYSLEEPER** *Warner Bros. W 0455CD* 6 6
7 Nov 98 ● UP *Warner Bros. 9362471122* 2 29
19 Dec 98 **LOTUS** *Warner Bros. W 466CD* 26 5
20 Mar 99 ● **AT MY MOST BEAUTIFUL** *Warner Bros. W 477CD* 10 4
5 Feb 00 ● **THE GREAT BEYOND** *Warner Bros. W 516CD* 3 10
12 May 01 ● **IMITATION OF LIFE** *Warner Bros. W 559CD* 6 9
26 May 01 ★ REVEAL *Warner Bros. 9362479462* ■ 1 15
4 Aug 01 **ALL THE WAY TO RENO** *Warner Bros. W 568CD* 24 3
1 Dec 01 **I'LL TAKE THE RAIN** *Warner Bros. W 573CD* 44 1
25 Oct 03 ● **BAD DAY** *Warner Bros. W 624CD1* 8 7
8 Nov 03 ★ THE BEST OF R.E.M. – IN TIME – 1988-2003 *Warner Bros. 9362483812* ■ 1 34
8 Nov 03 THE BEST OF R.E.M. – IN TIME – 1988-2003 *Warner Bros. 9362486022* 36 1
17 Jan 04 **ANIMAL** *Warner Bros. W 633CD* 33 2
9 Oct 04 ● **LEAVING NEW YORK** *Warner Bros. W 654CD1* 5 5
16 Oct 04 ★ AROUND THE SUN *Warner Bros. 9362489112* ■ 1 7
11 Dec 04 **AFTERMATH** *Warner Bros. W 658CD* 41 2
12 Mar 05 **ELECTRON BLUE** *Warner Bros. W 665CD2* 26 2
23 Jul 05 **WANDERLUST** *Warner Bros. W 676CD2* 27 2

The two albums titled The Best of R.E.M. – In Time – 1988-2003 are different. Warner Bros. 9362486022 is a limited edition set containing an additional CD of B-sides, live and acoustic tracks and demos.

REO SPEEDWAGON *US, male vocal (Kevin Cronin) / instrumental group (2 Albums: 36 Weeks, 3 Singles: 38 Weeks)*

11 Apr 81 ● **KEEP ON LOVING YOU** *Epic EPC 9544* ▲ $ 7 14
25 Apr 81 ● HI INFIDELITY *Epic EPC 84700* ▲ 6 29
27 Jun 81 **TAKE IT ON THE RUN** *Epic EPC A 1207* $ 19 14
17 Jul 82 GOOD TROUBLE *Epic EPC 85789* 29 7
16 Mar 85 **CAN'T FIGHT THIS FEELING** *Epic A 4880* ▲ $ 16 10

R.H.C. (see also HYPNOTIST) *UK / US, male / female vocal / instrumental / production trio*

11 Jan 92 **FEVER CALLED LOVE** *R&S RSUK 9* 65 1

RIP PRODUCTIONS (see also CARNIVAL featuring RIP vs RED RAT; COHEN vs DELUXE; Tim DELUXE; DOUBLE 99; SAFFRON HILL featuring Ben ONONO) *UK, male production duo*

29 Nov 97 **THE CHANT (WE R) / RIP PRODUCTIONS** *Satellite 74321534022* 58 1

RM PROJECT *UK, male production group*

3 Jul 99 **GET IT UP** *Inferno CDFERN 15* 49 1

RMXCRW featuring EBON-E plus AMBUSH *Holland, male production group*

17 Jan 04 **TURN ME ON** *Digi Dance 871486697203* 52 2

Eddie RABBITT *US, male vocalist, b. 27 Nov 1941, d. 7 May 1998 (2 Singles: 14 Weeks)*

27 Jan 79 **EVERY WHICH WAY BUT LOOSE** *Elektra K 12331* 41 9
28 Feb 81 **I LOVE A RAINY NIGHT** *Elektra K 12498* ▲ $ 53 5

Steve RACE *UK, male pianist*

28 Feb 63 **PIED PIPER (THE BEEJE)** *Parlophone R 4981* 29 9

RACEY *UK, male vocal / instrumental group (4 Singles: 44 Weeks)*

25 Nov 78 ● **LAY YOUR LOVE ON ME** *RAK 284* 3 14
31 Mar 79 ● **SOME GIRLS** *RAK 291* 2 11
18 Aug 79 **BOY OH BOY** *RAK 297* 22 9
20 Dec 80 **RUNAROUND SUE** *RAK 325* 13 10

The RACING CARS *UK, male vocal / instrumental group*

12 Feb 77 **THEY SHOOT HORSES DON'T THEY?** *Chrysalis CHS 2129* 14 7
19 Feb 77 DOWNTOWN TONIGHT *Chrysalis CHR 1099* 39 6

Jimmy RADCLIFFE *US, male vocalist, b. 18 Nov 1936, d. 27 Jul 1973*

4 Feb 65 **LONG AFTER TONIGHT IS ALL OVER** *Stateside SS 374* 40 2

RADHA KRISHNA TEMPLE *UK, male / female vocal / instrumental group (2 Singles: 17 Weeks)*

13 Sep 69 **HARE KRISHNA MANTRA** *Apple 15* 12 9
28 Mar 70 **GOVINDA** *Apple 25* 23 8

RADICAL ROB *UK, male producer – Rob McLuan*

11 Jan 92 **MONKEY WAH** *R&S RSUK 8* 67 1

RADIO 4 *US, male vocal / instrumental group (2 Singles: 2 Weeks)*

24 Jul 04 **PARTY CRASHERS** *City Slang 5494920* 75 1
18 Sep 04 **ABSOLUTE AFFIRMATION** *Labels 5498030* 61 1

RADIO HEART featuring Gary NUMAN *UK, male instrumental group and vocalist / keyboard player (2 Singles: 8 Weeks)*

28 Mar 87 **RADIO HEART** *GFM GFM 109* 35 6
13 Jun 87 **LONDON TIMES** *GFM GFM 112* 48 2

The RADIO STARS *UK, male vocal / instrumental group*

4 Feb 78 **NERVOUS WRECK** *Chiswick NS 23* 39 3

RADIOHEAD 107 Top 500

Innovative, boundary-bending group famous for their tortured tales of angst and alienation who are regular Top 10 album fixtures around the globe. This Grammy-winning band, formed in Oxford in 1991, consists of Thom Yorke (v/g), Jonny Greenwood (g), Ed O'Brien (g/v), Colin Greenwood (b) and Phil Selway (d). They became the first contemporary UK act to top the US chart in the 21st century (8 Albums: 362 Weeks, 16 Singles: 63 Weeks)

13 Feb 93 **ANYONE CAN PLAY GUITAR** *Parlophone CDR 6333* 32 2
6 Mar 93 PABLO HONEY *Parlophone CDPCS 7360* 22 82
22 May 93 **POP IS DEAD** *Parlophone CDR 6345* 42 2
18 Sep 93 ● **CREEP** *Parlophone CDR 6359* 7 6
8 Oct 94 **MY IRON LUNG** *Parlophone CDR 6394* 24 2
11 Mar 95 **HIGH AND DRY / PLANET TELEX** *Parlophone CDR 6405* 17 4
25 Mar 95 ● THE BENDS *Parlophone CDPCS 7372* 4 160
27 May 95 **FAKE PLASTIC TREES** *Parlophone CDR 6411* 20 4
2 Sep 95 **JUST** *Parlophone CDR 6415* 19 3
3 Feb 96 ● **STREET SPIRIT (FADE OUT)** *Parlophone CDR 6419* 5 4
7 Jun 97 ● **PARANOID ANDROID** *Parlophone CDODATAS 01* 3 5
28 Jun 97 ★ OK COMPUTER *Parlophone CDNODATA 02* ■ 1 76
6 Sep 97 ● **KARMA POLICE** *Parlophone CDODATAS 03* 8 4
24 Jan 98 ● **NO SURPRISES (re)** *Parlophone CDODATAS 04* 4 7
14 Oct 00 ★ KID A *Parlophone CDKIDA 1* ■ ▲ 1 15
2 Jun 01 ● **PYRAMID SONG** *Parlophone CDSFHEIT 45102* 5 5
16 Jun 01 ★ AMNESIAC *Parlophone CDFHEIT 45101* ■ 1 12
18 Aug 01 **KNIVES OUT** *Parlophone CDFHEIT 45103* 13 4
24 Nov 01 I MIGHT BE WRONG – LIVE RECORDINGS *Parlophone CDFHEIT 45104* 23 2
7 Jun 03 ● **THERE THERE** *Parlophone CDR 6608* 4 4
21 Jun 03 ★ HAIL TO THE THIEF *Parlophone 5848082* ■ 1 14
30 Aug 03 **GO TO SLEEP** *Parlophone CDR 6613* 12 4
29 Nov 03 **2+2=5** *Parlophone CDR 6623* 15 3
22 May 04 COM LAG – 2+2=5 *Parlophone TOCP 66280* 37 1

RADISH *US, male vocal / instrumental group (2 Singles: 3 Weeks)*

30 Aug 97 **LITTLE PINK STARS** *Mercury MERCD 494* 32 2
15 Nov 97 **SIMPLE SINCERITY** *Mercury MERCD 498* 50 1

23 March 1985	30 March 1985	6 April 1985	13 April 1985
EASY LOVER Philip Bailey (duet with Phil Collins)	**EASY LOVER** Philip Bailey (duet with Phil Collins)	**EASY LOVER** Philip Bailey (duet with Phil Collins)	**EASY LOVER** Philip Bailey (duet with Phil Collins)
NO JACKET REQUIRED Phil Collins	**NO JACKET REQUIRED** Phil Collins	**THE SECRET OF ASSOCIATION** Paul Young	**HITS 2** Various

KEY

UK No.1 ★★ UK Top 10 ●● Still on chart ++ UK entry at No.1 ■■ US No.1 ▲▲ UK million seller £ US million seller $

Singles re-entries are listed as (re), (2re), (3re)... which signifies that the hit re-entered the chart once, twice or three times...

Peak Position / Weeks

Fonda RAE *US, female vocalist*

6 Oct 84 **TUCH ME** *Streetwave KHAN 28* ... **49** 4

Jesse RAE *UK, male vocalist*

11 May 85 **OVER THE SEA** *Scotland-Video YZ 36* ... **65** 2

RAE & CHRISTIAN *UK, male production duo*

6 Mar 99 **ALL I ASK** *Grand Central GCCD 120* [1] ... **67** 1
10 Mar 01 SLEEPWALKING *K7 K 7096CD* ... 57 1

[1] Rae and Christian featuring Veba

Gerry RAFFERTY (see also STEALERS WHEEL)
UK, male vocalist (7 Albums: 99 Weeks, 6 Singles: 47 Weeks)

18 Feb 78 ● **BAKER STREET** *United Artists UP 36346* $ ... **3** 15
25 Feb 78 ● CITY TO CITY *United Artists UAS 30104* ▲ ... 6 37
26 May 79 ● **NIGHT OWL** *United Artists UP 36512* ... **5** 13
2 Jun 79 ● NIGHT OWL *United Artists UAK 30238* ... 9 24
18 Aug 79 **GET IT RIGHT NEXT TIME** *United Artists BP 301* ... **30** 9
22 Mar 80 **BRING IT ALL HOME** *United Artists BP 340* ... **54** 4
26 Apr 80 SNAKES AND LADDERS *United Artists UAK 30298* ... 15 9
21 Jun 80 **ROYAL MILE** *United Artists BP 354* ... **67** 2
25 Sep 82 SLEEPWALKING *Liberty LBG 30352* ... 39 4
21 May 88 NORTH AND SOUTH *London LONLP 55* ... 43 4
10 Mar 90 **BAKER STREET** (re-mix) *EMI EM 132* ... **53** 4
13 Feb 93 ON A WING & A PRAYER *A&M 5174952* ... 73 1
28 Oct 95 ONE MORE DREAM – THE VERY BEST OF GERRY RAFFERTY *PolyGram TV 5292792* ... 17 20

RAGE (see also SWEET DREAMS)
UK, male vocal (Tony Jackson) / instrumental group (3 Singles: 15 Weeks)

31 Oct 92 ● **RUN TO YOU** *Pulse 8 LOSE 33* ... **3** 11
27 Feb 93 **WHY DON'T YOU** *Pulse 8 CDLOSE 39* ... **44** 2
15 May 93 **HOUSE OF THE RISING SUN** *Pulse 8 CDLOSE 43* ... **41** 2

RAGE AGAINST THE MACHINE *US, male vocal (Zack DeLa Rocha) / instrumental group (4 Albums: 53 Weeks, 7 Singles: 19 Weeks)*

13 Feb 93 RAGE AGAINST THE MACHINE *Epic 4722242* ... 17 43
27 Feb 93 **KILLING IN THE NAME** *Epic 6584922* ... **25** 4
8 May 93 **BULLET IN THE HEAD** *Epic 6592582* ... **16** 4
4 Sep 93 **BOMBTRACK** *Epic 6594712* ... **37** 2
13 Apr 96 ● **BULLS ON PARADE** *Epic 6631522* ... **8** 3
27 Apr 96 ● EVIL EMPIRE *Epic 4810262* ▲ ... 4 7
7 Sep 96 **PEOPLE OF THE SUN** *Epic 6636282* ... **26** 2
6 Nov 99 **GUERRILLA RADIO** *Epic 6683142* ... **32** 2
13 Nov 99 THE BATTLE OF LOS ANGELES *Epic 4919932* ▲ ... 23 2
15 Apr 00 **SLEEP NOW IN THE FIRE** *Epic 6691362* ... **43** 2
9 Dec 00 RENEGADES *Epic 4999210* ... 71 1

RAGGA TWINS *UK, male vocal duo – Flinty Badman and Deman Rocker (1 Album: 5 Weeks, 5 Singles: 10 Weeks)*

10 Nov 90 **ILLEGAL GUNSHOT / SPLIFFHEAD** *Shut Up and Dance SUAD 7* ... **51** 2
6 Apr 91 **WIPE THE NEEDLE / JUGGLING** *Shut Up and Dance SUAD 12S* ... **71** 2
1 Jun 91 REGGAE OWES ME MONEY *Shut Up and Dance SUADLP 2* ... 26 5
6 Jul 91 **HOOLIGAN 69** *Shut Up and Dance SUAD 16S* ... **56** 2
7 Mar 92 **MIXED TRUTH / BRING UP THE MIC SOME MORE** *Shut Up and Dance SUAD 27S* ... **65** 2
11 Jul 92 **SHINE EYE** *Shut Up and Dance SUAD 32S* [1] ... **63** 2

[1] Ragga Twins featuring Junior Reid

RAGHAV
Canada, male vocalist – Raghav Mathur (1 Album: 2 Weeks, 5 Singles: 37 Weeks)

24 Jan 04 ● **SO CONFUSED** *2PSL 2PSLCD 002* [1] ... **6** 13
28 Feb 04 ● **CAN'T GET ENOUGH** *A&R ANR 1CDS* ... **10** 8
22 May 04 ● **IT CAN'T BE RIGHT** *2PSL / Inferno 2PSLCD 04* [2] ... **8** 7
4 Sep 04 **LET'S WORK IT OUT** *V2 ARV 5028628* [3] ... **15** 3
18 Sep 04 STORYTELLER *V2 ARV 1028642* ... 36 2
19 Feb 05 ● **ANGEL EYES** *A&R / V2 ARV 5028638* ... **7** 6

[1] 2Play featuring Raghav & Jucxi [2] 2Play featuring Raghav & Naila Boss
[3] Raghav featuring Jahaziel

RAGING SPEEDHORN
UK, male vocal / instrumental group (1 Album: 1 Week, 2 Singles: 2 Weeks)

16 Jun 01 **THE GUSH** *ZTT GIR 004CD* ... **47** 1
6 Jul 02 **THE HATE SONG** *ZTT RSH 001CD* ... **69** 1
17 Aug 02 WE WILL BE DEAD TOMORROW *ZTT RSH 002CD* ... 63 1

The RAGTIMERS *UK, male instrumental group*

16 Mar 74 **THE STING (re)** *Pye 7N 45323* ... **31** 8

The RAH BAND (see also KEY WEST featuring ERIK)
UK, male / female vocal / instrumental group – leaders Richard A and Liz Hewson (1 Album: 6 Weeks, 7 Singles: 50 Weeks)

9 Jul 77 ● **THE CRUNCH** *Good Earth GD 7* ... **6** 12
1 Nov 80 **FALCON** *DJM DJS 10954* ... **35** 7
7 Feb 81 **SLIDE** *DJM DJS 10964* ... **50** 7
1 May 82 **PERFUMED GARDEN** *KR KR 5* ... **45** 7
9 Jul 83 **MESSAGES FROM THE STARS** *TMT TMT 5* ... **42** 5
19 Jan 85 **ARE YOU SATISFIED? (FUNKA NOVA)** *RCA RCA 470* ... **70** 2
30 Mar 85 ● **CLOUDS ACROSS THE MOON** *RCA PB 40025* ... **6** 10
6 Apr 85 MYSTERY *RCA PL 70640* ... 60 6

The RAILWAY CHILDREN
UK, male vocal / instrumental group (2 Albums: 3 Weeks, 4 Singles: 13 Weeks)

21 May 88 RECURRENCE *Virgin V 2525* ... 96 1
24 Mar 90 **EVERY BEAT OF THE HEART (re)** *Virgin VS 1237* ... **24** 8
2 Jun 90 **MUSIC STOP** *Virgin VS 1255* ... **66** 2
20 Oct 90 **SO RIGHT** *Virgin VS 1289* ... **68** 1
16 Mar 91 NATIVE PLACE *Virgin V 2627* ... 59 2
20 Apr 91 **SOMETHING SO GOOD** *Virgin VS 1318* ... **57** 2

'Every Beat of the Heart' debuted on the chart at No.68 before making its peak position after re-entry in Feb 1991.

The RAIN BAND *UK, male vocal / instrumental group (2 Singles: 2 Weeks)*

1 Mar 03 **EASY RIDER** *Temptation TEMPCD 003* ... **63** 1
19 Jul 03 **KNEE DEEP AND DOWN** *Temptation TEMPTCD 007* ... **56** 1

RAIN PARADE *US, male vocal / instrumental group*

29 Jun 85 BEYOND THE SUNSET *Island IMA 17* ... 78 1

RAIN TREE CROW (see also JAPAN) *UK, male vocal / instrumental group*

30 Mar 91 **BLACKWATER** *Virgin VS 1340* ... **62** 1
20 Apr 91 RAIN TREE CROW *Virgin V 2659* ... 24 3

Group is Japan under an assumed name.

RAINBOW 303 Top 500

Melodic Anglo-American hard rock band with ever-changing personnel, formed in the UK in 1975 by ex-Deep Purple guitarist Ritchie Blackmore. Original vocalist Ronnie James Dio replaced by Graham Bonnet (1979), then Joe Lynn Turner (1980). After the band split in 1984, Blackmore rejoined Deep Purple (11 Albums: 163 Weeks, 11 Singles: 62 Weeks)

13 Sep 75 RITCHIE BLACKMORE'S RAINBOW *Oyster OYA 2001* [1] ... 11 6
5 Jun 76 RAINBOW RISING *Polydor 2490 137* [1] ... 11 33
30 Jul 77 ● ON STAGE *Polydor 2657 016* ... 7 10

20 April 1985	27 April 1985	4 May 1985	11 May 1985
UK No.1 SINGLES			
WE ARE THE WORLD USA for Africa	WE ARE THE WORLD USA for Africa	MOVE CLOSER Phyllis Nelson	19 Paul Hardcastle
UK No.1 ALBUMS			
HITS 2 Various	HITS 2 Various	HITS 2 Various	HITS 2 Various

17 Sep 77	**KILL THE KING** *Polydor 2066 845*	44	3
8 Apr 78	**LONG LIVE ROCK 'N' ROLL** *Polydor 2066 913*	33	3
6 May 78 ●	LONG LIVE ROCK 'N' ROLL *Polydor POLD 5002*	7	12
30 Sep 78	**L.A. CONNECTION** *Polydor 2066 968*	40	4
18 Aug 79 ●	DOWN TO EARTH *Polydor POLD 5023*	6	37
15 Sep 79 ●	**SINCE YOU'VE BEEN GONE** *Polydor POSP 70*	6	10
16 Feb 80 ●	**ALL NIGHT LONG** *Polydor POSP 104*	5	11
31 Jan 81 ●	**I SURRENDER** *Polydor POSP 221*	3	10
21 Feb 81 ●	DIFFICULT TO CURE *Polydor POLD 5036*	3	22
20 Jun 81	**CAN'T HAPPEN HERE** *Polydor POSP 251*	20	8
11 Jul 81	**KILL THE KING** (re-issue) *Polydor POSP 274*	41	4
8 Aug 81	RITCHIE BLACKMORE'S RAINBOW (re-issue) *Polydor 2940141* [1]	91	2
21 Nov 81	THE BEST OF RAINBOW *Polydor POLDV 2*	14	17
3 Apr 82	**STONE COLD** *Polydor POSP 421*	34	4
24 Apr 82 ●	STRAIGHT BETWEEN THE EYES *Polydor POLD 5056*	5	14
27 Aug 83	**STREET OF DREAMS** *Polydor POSP 631*	52	3
17 Sep 83	BENT OUT OF SHAPE *Polydor POLD 5116*	11	6
5 Nov 83	**CAN'T LET YOU GO** *Polydor POSP 654*	43	2
8 Mar 86	FINYL VINYL *Polydor PODV 8*	31	4

[1] Ritchie Blackmore's Rainbow

RAINBOW
UK, male puppet rappers – DJ George and MC Zippy (Roy Skelton)

14 Dec 02	**IT'S A RAINBOW** *BBC Music ZIPPCD 1*	15	6

RAINBOW COTTAGE *UK, male vocal / instrumental group*

6 Mar 76	**SEAGULL** *Penny Farthing PEN 906*	33	4

RAINDANCE (see also BLOWING FREE; HYPNOSIS; IN TUNE; The JAMES BOYS; SCHOOL OF EXCELLENCE)
UK, male production / instrumental duo – Stewart and Bradley Palmer

27 Apr 96	RAINDANCE *PolyGram TV 5298622*	15	7

RAINMAKERS *US, male vocal / instrumental group*

7 Mar 87	**LET MY PEOPLE GO-GO** *Mercury MER 238*	18	11

Marvin RAINWATER *US, male vocalist – Marvin Percy (2 Singles: 22 Weeks)*

7 Mar 58 ★	**WHOLE LOTTA WOMAN** *MGM 974*	1	15
6 Jun 58	**I DIG YOU BABY** *MGM 980*	19	7

RAISSA *UK, female vocalist – Raissa Khan-Panni*

12 Feb 00	**HOW LONG DO I GET** *Polydor 5616282*	47	1

Bonnie RAITT
US, female vocalist / guitarist (6 Albums: 17 Weeks, 4 Singles: 9 Weeks)

28 Apr 90	NICK OF TIME *Capitol EST 2095* ▲	51	5
6 Jul 91	LUCK OF THE DRAW *Capitol EST 2145*	38	3
14 Dec 91	**I CAN'T MAKE YOU LOVE ME** *Capitol CL 639*	50	4
9 Apr 94	**LOVE SNEAKIN' UP ON YOU** *Capitol CDCL 713*	69	1
16 Apr 94	LONGING IN THEIR HEARTS *Capitol CDEST 2227* ▲	26	5
18 Jun 94	**YOU** *Capitol CDCLS 718*	31	2
11 Nov 95	**ROCK STEADY** *Capitol CDCL 763* [1]	50	2
25 Nov 95	ROAD TESTED *Capitol CDEST 2274*	69	1
18 Apr 98	FUNDAMENTAL *Capitol 8563972*	52	1
24 May 03	BEST OF *Capitol 5821132*	37	2

[1] Bonnie Raitt and Bryan Adams

Dionne RAKEEM *UK, female vocalist*

4 Aug 01	**SWEETER THAN WINE** *Virgin VSCDT 1809*	46	2

The RAKES
UK, male vocal / instrumental group (1 Album: 2 Weeks, 4 Singles: 6 Weeks)

9 Oct 04	**STRASBOURG** *City Rockers ROCKERS 28CD*	57	1
30 Apr 05	**RETREAT** *Moshi Moshi MOSHI 18CD*	24	2
13 Aug 05	**WORK, WORK, WORK (PUB, CLUB, SLEEP)** *V2 VVR 5032773*	28	2
27 Aug 05	CAPTURE / RELEASE *V2 VVR 1032762*	32	2
12 Nov 05	**22 GRAND JOB** *V2 VVR 5034613*	39	1

RAKIM (see also Eric B and RAKIM)
US, male rapper – William Griffin Jr (1 Album: 1 Week, 4 Singles: 17 Weeks)

22 Nov 97	18TH LETTER *Universal U 253113*	72	1
27 Dec 97	**GUESS WHO'S BACK** *Universal UND 56151*	32	3
22 Aug 98	**STAY A WHILE** *Universal UND 56203*	53	1
3 Oct 98	**BUFFALO GIRLS STAMPEDE** (re-mix) *Virgin VSCDT 1717* [1]	65	1
31 Aug 02 ●	**ADDICTIVE** *Aftermath / Interscope 4977782* [2]	3	12

[1] Malcolm McLaren and the World's Famous Supreme Team plus Rakim and Roger Sanchez [2] Truth Hurts featuring Rakim

Tony RALLO and The MIDNITE BAND
France / US, male vocal / instrumental group

23 Feb 80	**HOLDIN' ON** *Calibre CAB 150*	34	8

Sheryl Lee RALPH *US, female vocalist*

26 Jan 85	**IN THE EVENING** *Arista ARIST 595*	64	2

RAM JAM
US, male vocal (Myke Scavone) / instrumental group (2 Singles: 20 Weeks)

10 Sep 77 ●	**BLACK BETTY** *Epic EPC 5492*	7	12
17 Feb 90	**BLACK BETTY** (re-mix) *Epic 655430 7*	13	8

RAM TRILOGY *UK, male production trio (3 Singles: 3 Weeks)*

6 Jul 02	**CHAPTER FOUR** *Ram RAMM 39*	71	1
20 Jul 02	**CHAPTER 5** *Ram RAMM 40*	62	1
3 Aug 02	**CHAPTER 6** *Ram RAMM 41*	60	1

The RAMBLERS (from the Abbey Hey Junior School) *UK, children's choir*

13 Oct 79	**THE SPARROW** *Decca F 13860*	11	15

Karen RAMIREZ
UK, female vocalist – Karen Ramelize (1 Album: 2 Weeks, 3 Singles: 15 Weeks)

28 Mar 98	**TROUBLED GIRL** *Manifesto FESCD 31*	50	1
27 Jun 98 ●	**LOOKING FOR LOVE** *Manifesto FESCD 44*	8	11
1 Aug 98	DISTANT DREAMS *Manifesto 5586742*	45	2
21 Nov 98	**IF WE TRY** *Manifesto FESCD 50*	23	3

RAMMSTEIN *Germany, male vocal / instrumental group (2 Albums: 2 Weeks, 6 Singles: 11 Weeks)*

25 May 02	**ICH WILL** *Motor / Universal MCSTD 40280*	30	2
23 Nov 02	**FEUER FREI** *Universal MCSTD 40302*	35	2
14 Aug 04	**MEIN TEIL** (import) *Universal 9866978*	61	2
9 Oct 04	REISE, REISE *Universal 9868150*	37	1
30 Oct 04	**AMERIKA** *Universal MCSTD 40394*	38	2
12 Mar 05	**KEINE LUST** *Universal MCSTD 40405*	35	2
29 Oct 05	**BENZIN** *Universal 9874302*	58	1
12 Nov 05	ROSENROT *Universal 9874588*	29	1

The RAMONES
US, male vocal (Jeffrey Hyman aka Joey Ramone, b. 19 May 1951, d. 15 April 2001) / instrumental group (11 Albums: 30 Weeks, 8 Singles: 32 Weeks)

23 Apr 77	LEAVE HOME *Philips 9103 254*	45	1
21 May 77	**SHEENA IS A PUNK ROCKER** *Sire RAM 001*	22	7
6 Aug 77	**SWALLOW MY PRIDE** *Sire 6078 607*	36	3
24 Dec 77	ROCKET TO RUSSIA *Sire 9103 255*	60	2
30 Sep 78	**DON'T COME CLOSE** *Sire SRE 1031*	39	5
7 Oct 78	ROAD TO RUIN *Sire SRK 6063*	32	2
16 Jun 79	IT'S ALIVE *Sire SRK 26074*	27	8
8 Sep 79	**ROCK 'N' ROLL HIGH SCHOOL** *Sire SIR 4021*	67	2
19 Jan 80	END OF THE CENTURY *Sire SRK 6077*	14	8

18 May 1985	25 May 1985	1 June 1985	8 June 1985
19 Paul Hardcastle	19 Paul Hardcastle	19 Paul Hardcastle	19 Paul Hardcastle
HITS 2 Various	BROTHERS IN ARMS Dire Straits	BROTHERS IN ARMS Dire Straits	OUR FAVOURITE SHOP The Style Council

KEY: UK No.1 ★★ UK Top 10 ●● Still on chart ++ UK entry at No.1 ■■ US No.1 ▲▲ UK million seller £ US million seller $
Singles re-entries are listed as (re), (2re), (3re)… which signifies that the hit re-entered the chart once, twice or three times…
Peak Position / Weeks

26 Jan 80 ● **BABY, I LOVE YOU** *Sire SIR 4031* 8 9
19 Apr 80 **DO YOU REMEMBER ROCK 'N' ROLL RADIO?** *Sire SIR 4037* 54 3
26 Jan 85 **TOO TOUGH TO DIE** *Beggars Banquet BEGA 59* 63 3
10 May 86 **SOMEBODY PUT SOMETHING IN MY DRINK / SOMETHING TO BELIEVE IN** *Beggars Banquet BEG 157* 69 1
31 May 86 **ANIMAL BOY** *Beggars Banquet BEGA 70* 38 2
10 Oct 87 **HALFWAY TO SANITY** *Beggars Banquet BEGA 89* 78 1
19 Aug 89 **BRAIN DRAIN** *Chrysalis CHR 1725* 75 1
19 Dec 92 **POISON HEART** *Chrysalis CHS 3917* 69 2
8 Jul 95 **¡ADIOS AMIGOS!** *Chrysalis CDCHR 6104* 62 1
9 Jun 01 **ANTHOLOGY – HEY HO LET'S GO!** *Warner Bros. 8122735572* .. 74 1

RAMP (see also SLACKER)
UK, male instrumental / production duo – Shem McCauley and Simon Rogers

8 Jun 96 **ROCK THE DISCOTEK** *Loaded LOADCD 30* 49 1

RAMPAGE *UK, male DJ / production group*

25 Nov 95 **THE MONKEES** *Almo Sounds CDALMOS 017* 51 1

RAMPAGE featuring Billy LAWRENCE
US, male rapper – Roger McNair and US, male vocalist

18 Oct 97 **TAKE IT TO THE STREETS** *Elektra E 3914CD* 58 1

The RAMRODS *US, male / female instrumental group*

23 Feb 61 ● **RIDERS IN THE SKY** *London HLU 9282* 8 12

RAMSEY and FEN featuring Lynsey MOORE
UK, male production duo and female vocalist

10 Jun 00 **LOVE BUG** *Nebula VCNEBD 4* 75 1

RANCID
US, male vocal / instrumental group (5 Albums: 7 Weeks, 2 Singles: 3 Weeks)

2 Sep 95 **... AND OUT COME THE WOLVES** *Epitaph 864442* 55 1
7 Oct 95 **TIME BOMB** *Out of Step WOOS 8CDS* 56 1
4 Jul 98 **LIFE WON'T WAIT** *Epitaph 864972* 32 2
5 Aug 00 **RANCID** *Hellcat 4272* 68 1
23 Mar 02 **SPLIT SERIES – VOL.3** *BYO BYO 079CD* [1] 75 1
6 Sep 03 **INDESTRUCTIBLE** *WEA 9362485392* 29 2
27 Sep 03 **FALL BACK DOWN** *Hellcat / WEA W 618CD* 42 2

[1] Rancid / NOFX

RANGERS FC *UK, male football team vocalists*

4 Oct 97 **GLASGOW RANGERS (NINE IN A ROW)** *Gers GERSCD 1* 54 2

RANK 1 *Holland, male production duo – Piet Bervoets and Benno de Goeij*

15 Apr 00 ● **AIRWAVE** *Manifesto FESCD 69* 10 5

Shabba RANKS *Jamaica, male vocalist – Rexton Rawlston Fernando Gordon (3 Albums: 10 Weeks, 12 Singles: 67 Weeks)*

16 Mar 91 **SHE'S A WOMAN** *Virgin VS 1333* [1] 20 7
18 May 91 **TRAILER LOAD A GIRLS** *Epic 6568747* 63 2
22 Jun 91 **AS RAW AS EVER** *Epic 4681021* 51 2
24 Aug 91 **HOUSECALL** *Epic 6573477* [2] 31 7
8 Aug 92 **MR LOVERMAN** *Epic 6582517* 23 7
22 Aug 92 **ROUGH AND READY VOLUME 1** *Epic 4714422* 71 2
28 Nov 92 **SLOW AND SEXY** *Epic 6587727* [3] 17 7
6 Mar 93 **I WAS A KING** *Motown TMGCD 1414* [4] 64 1
13 Mar 93 ● **MR LOVERMAN** (re-issue) *Epic 6590782* 3 11
24 Apr 93 **X-TRA NAKED** *Epic 4723332* 38 6
8 May 93 ● **HOUSECALL** (re-mix) *Epic 6592842* [2] 8 8
26 Jun 93 **WHAT'CHA GONNA DO** *Epic 6593072* [5] 21 4
25 Dec 93 **FAMILY AFFAIR** *Polydor PZCD 304* [6] 18 8
29 Apr 95 **LET'S GET IT ON** *Epic 6614122* 22 3
5 Aug 95 **SHINE EYE GAL** *Epic 6622332* [7] 46 2

[1] Scritti Politti featuring Shabba Ranks [2] Shabba Ranks featuring Maxi Priest [3] Shabba Ranks featuring Johnny Gill [4] Eddie Murphy featuring Shabba Ranks [5] Shabba Ranks featuring Queen Latifah [6] Shabba Ranks featuring Patra and Terri & Monica [7] Shabba Ranks (featuring Mykal Rose)

RAPINATION *Italy, male instrumental / production duo – Marco Sabiu and Charlie Mallozzi (3 Singles: 12 Weeks)*

26 Dec 92 **LOVE ME THE RIGHT WAY** *Logic 74321128097* [1] 22 10
10 Jul 93 **HERE'S MY A** *Logic 74321153092* [2] 69 1
28 Sep 96 **LOVE ME THE RIGHT WAY** (re-mix) *Logic 7432140442* [1] 55 1

[1] Rapination featuring Kym Mazelle [2] Rapination featuring Carol Kenyon

RAPPIN' 4-TAY *US, male rapper – Anthony Forte (2 Singles: 5 Weeks)*

24 Jun 95 **I'LL BE AROUND** *Cooltempo CDCOOL 306* [1] 30 4
30 Sep 95 **PLAYAZ CLUB** *Cooltempo CDCOOL 310* 63 1

[1] Rappin' 4-Tay featuring The Spinners [The Detroit Spinners]

The RAPTURE
US, male vocal / instrumental group (1 Album: 2 Weeks, 3 Singles: 4 Weeks)

6 Sep 03 **HOUSE OF JEALOUS LOVERS** *Vertigo 9810767* 27 2
20 Sep 03 **ECHOES** *DFA / Output / Vertigo 9865447* 32 2
13 Dec 03 **SISTER SAVIOUR** *DFA / Output / Vertigo 9814181* 51 1
21 Feb 04 **LOVE IS ALL** *DFA / Output / Vertigo 9816808* 38 1

RARE *UK, male / female vocal / instrumental group*

17 Feb 96 **SOMETHING WILD** *Equator AXISCD 011* 57 1

RARE BIRD *UK, male vocal / instrumental group*

14 Feb 70 **SYMPATHY** *Charisma CB 120* 27 8

The RASMUS *Finland, male vocal (Lauri Ylonen) / instrumental group (2 Albums: 24 Weeks, 4 Singles: 24 Weeks)*

3 Apr 04 ● **DEAD LETTERS** *Motor 9806934* 10 23
17 Apr 04 ● **IN THE SHADOWS** *Universal MCSXD 40351* 3 16
21 Aug 04 **GUILTY** *Universal MCSTD 40376* 15 6
13 Nov 04 **FIRST DAY OF MY LIFE** *Universal MCSTD 40391* 50 1
17 Sep 05 **NO FEAR** *Universal MCSXD 40429* 43 1
24 Sep 05 **HIDE FROM THE SUN** *Universal 9873612* 65 1

Roland RAT SUPERSTAR
UK, male rodent vocalist / rapper (1 Album: 3 Weeks, 3 Singles: 20 Weeks)

19 Nov 83 **RAT RAPPING** *Rodent RAT 1* 14 12
28 Apr 84 **LOVE ME TENDER** *Rodent RAT 2* 32 7
15 Dec 84 **THE CASSETTE OF THE ALBUM** *Rodent RATL 1001* 67 3
2 Mar 85 **NO.1 RAT FAN** *Rodent RAT 4* 72 1

The RATPACK *US, male vocalists – Sammy Davis Jr, b. 6 Dec 1925, d. 16 May 1990, Dean Martin, b. 7 Jun 1917, d. 25 Dec 1995, and Frank Sinatra, b. 12 Dec 1915, d. 14 May 1998*

27 Nov 04 **BOYS NIGHT OUT** *Capitol 5708902* 70 1

RATPACK *UK, male instrumental / production duo*

6 Jun 92 **SEARCHIN' FOR MY RIZLA** *Big Giant BIGT 02* 58 3

RATT *US, male vocal / instrumental group (4 Albums: 5 Weeks)*

13 Jul 85 **INVASION OF YOUR PRIVACY** *Atlantic 7812571* 50 2
25 Oct 86 **DANCING UNDERCOVER** *Atlantic 7816831* 51 1

15 June 1985	22 June 1985	29 June 1985	6 July 1985
UK No.1 SINGLES			
YOU'LL NEVER WALK ALONE The Crowd	YOU'LL NEVER WALK ALONE The Crowd	FRANKIE Sister Sledge	FRANKIE Sister Sledge
UK No.1 ALBUMS			
BOYS AND GIRLS Bryan Ferry	BOYS AND GIRLS Bryan Ferry	MISPLACED CHILDHOOD Marillion	BORN IN THE U.S.A. Bruce Springsteen

12 Nov 88	REACH FOR THE SKY *Atlantic 781929*	82	1
8 Sep 90	DETONATOR *Atlantic 7567821271*	55	1

The RATTLES *Germany, male vocal (Achim Reichel) / instrumental group*

3 Oct 70 ●	THE WITCH *Decca F 23058*	8	15

Mark RATTRAY *UK, male vocalist (2 Albums: 8 Weeks)*

8 Dec 90	SONGS OF THE MUSICALS *Telstar STAR 2458*	46	7
10 Oct 92	THE MAGIC OF THE MUSICALS *Quality Television QTV 013* [1]	55	1

[1] Marti Webb and Mark Rattray

RATTY *Germany, male production group*

24 Mar 01	SUNRISE (HERE I AM) *Neo NEOCD 051*	51	1

RAVEN *UK, male vocal / instrumental group*

17 Oct 81	ROCK UNTIL YOU DROP *Neat NEAT 1001*	63	3

RAVEN MAIZE (see also AKABU featuring Linda CLIFFORD; HED BOYS; IL PADRINOS featuring Jocelyn BROWN; JAKATTA; Li KWAN; Joey NEGRO; PHASE II; Z FACTOR) *UK, male producer – Dave Lee (3 Singles: 9 Weeks)*

5 Aug 89	FOREVER TOGETHER *Republic LIC 014*	67	1
18 Aug 01	THE REAL LIFE (re) *Rulin / MoS / Credence RULIN 18CDS*	12	6
17 Aug 02	FASCINATED *Ministry of Sound / Rulin RULIN 27CDS*	37	2

The RAVEONETTES *Denmark, male / female vocal / instrumental group (2 Albums: 2 Weeks, 5 Singles: 7 Weeks)*

21 Dec 02	ATTACK OF THE GHOSTRIDERS *Columbia 6733892*	73	1
30 Aug 03	THAT GREAT LOVE SOUND *Columbia RAVEON 005*	34	2
6 Sep 03	CHAIN GANG OF LOVE *Columbia 5123782*	43	1
20 Dec 03	HEARTBREAK STROLL *Columbia RAVEON 008*	49	1
22 May 04	THAT GREAT LOVE SOUND *Columbia RAVEON 010*	52	1
23 Jul 05	LOVE IN A TRASHCAN *Columbia RAVEON 017*	26	2
6 Aug 05	PRETTY IN BLACK *Columbia 5194269*	71	1

RAVESIGNAL III (see also CJ BOLLAND; SONIC SOLUTION) *Belgium, male producer – Christian Bolland*

14 Dec 91	HORSEPOWER *R&S RSUK 6*	61	2

RAW SILK *US, female vocal group (2 Singles: 12 Weeks)*

16 Oct 82	DO IT TO THE MUSIC *KR KR 14*	18	9
10 Sep 83	JUST IN TIME *West End WEND 2*	49	3

RAW STYLUS *UK, male / female vocal / instrumental duo*

26 Oct 96	BELIEVE IN ME *Wired WIRED 234*	66	1

Lou RAWLS *US, male vocalist, b. 1 Dec 1935, d. 6 Jan 2006*

31 Jul 76 ●	YOU'LL NEVER FIND ANOTHER LOVE LIKE MINE *Philadelphia International PIR 4372* $	10	10

Jimmy RAY *UK, male vocalist – James Edwards (2 Singles: 6 Weeks)*

25 Oct 97	ARE YOU JIMMY RAY? *Sony S2 6650125*	13	5
14 Feb 98	GOIN' TO VEGAS *Sony S2 6654652*	49	1

Johnnie RAY 429 Top 500 *A sensation in the 1950s, the heart-wrenching vocal delivery of the 'Cry Guy', b. 10 Jan 1927, Oregon, US, d. 25 Feb 1990, influenced many acts including Elvis and was the prime target for teen hysteria in the pre-Presley days (21 Singles: 168 Weeks)*

14 Nov 52	WALKIN' MY BABY BACK HOME *Columbia DB 3060*	12	1
19 Dec 52 ●	FAITH CAN MOVE MOUNTAINS (re) *Columbia DB 3154* [1]	7	3
3 Apr 53	MA SAYS, PA SAYS *Columbia DB 3242* [2]	12	1
10 Apr 53 ●	SOMEBODY STOLE MY GAL (3re) *Philips PB 123*	6	7
17 Apr 53	FULL TIME JOB *Columbia DB 3242* [2]	11	1
24 Jul 53 ●	LET'S WALK THAT-A-WAY *Philips PB 157* [2]	4	14
9 Apr 54 ★	SUCH A NIGHT *Philips PB 244*	1	18
8 Apr 55 ●	IF YOU BELIEVE (re) *Philips PB 379*	7	11
20 May 55	PATHS OF PARADISE *Philips PB 441*	20	1
7 Oct 55	HERNANDO'S HIDEAWAY *Philips PB 495*	11	5
14 Oct 55 ●	HEY THERE *Philips PB 495*	5	9
28 Oct 55 ●	SONG OF THE DREAMER *Philips PB 516*	10	5
17 Feb 56	WHO'S SORRY NOW *Philips PB 546*	17	2
20 Apr 56	AIN'T MISBEHAVIN' (re) *Philips PB 580*	17	7
12 Oct 56 ★	JUST WALKING IN THE RAIN *Philips PB 624* $	1	19
18 Jan 57	YOU DON'T OWE ME A THING *Philips PB 655*	12	15
8 Feb 57 ●	LOOK HOMEWARD ANGEL *Philips PB 655*	7	16
10 May 57 ★	YES TONIGHT JOSEPHINE *Philips PB 686*	1	16
6 Sep 57	BUILD YOUR LOVE (ON A STRONG FOUNDATION) *Philips PB 721*	17	7
4 Oct 57	GOOD EVENING FRIENDS / UP ABOVE MY HEAD, I HEAR MUSIC IN THE AIR *Philips PB 708* [3]	25	4
4 Dec 59	I'LL NEVER FALL IN LOVE AGAIN (2re) *Philips PB 952*	26	6

[1] Johnnie Ray and The Four Lads [2] Doris Day and Johnnie Ray [3] Frankie Laine and Johnnie Ray

The chart history of 'You Don't Owe Me a Thing' and 'Look Homeward Angel' is complicated and is as follows: 'You Don't Owe Me a Thing' entered the chart by itself on 18 Jan 1957. On 8 and 15 Feb 1957, 'Look Homeward Angel' was coupled with 'You Don't Owe Me a Thing', but from 22 Feb 1957 the two sides went their individual ways on the chart and were listed separately: 'You Don't Owe Me a Thing' for a further 10 weeks and 'Look Homeward Angel' for a further 14 weeks.

Nicole RAY *US, female vocalist – Nicole Wray (2 Singles: 5 Weeks)*

22 Aug 98	MAKE IT HOT *East West E 3821CD* [1]	22	4
5 Dec 98	I CAN'T SEE *East West E 3801CD*	55	1

[1] Nicole featuring Missy 'Misdemeanor' Elliott and Mocha

RAYDIO (see also Ray PARKER Jr) *US, male vocal / instrumental group (2 Singles: 21 Weeks)*

8 Apr 78	JACK AND JILL *Arista 161*	11	12
8 Jul 78	IS THIS A LOVE THING *Arista 193*	27	9

Dana RAYNE NEW *US, female vocalist*

15 Jan 05 ●	OBJECT OF MY DESIRE *Incentive CENTMOS 1CDS*	7	8

RAYVON *Barbados, male rapper / vocalist – Bruce Brewster (3 Singles: 26 Weeks)*

8 Jul 95 ●	IN THE SUMMERTIME *Virgin VSCDT 1542* [1]	5	9
9 Jun 01 ★	ANGEL *MCA MCSTD 40257* [1] ■ ▲	1	16
3 Aug 02	2-WAY *MCA MCSTD 40287*	67	1

[1] Shaggy featuring Rayvon

RAZE *US, male / female vocal / instrumental group (8 Singles: 48 Weeks)*

1 Nov 86	JACK THE GROOVE (re) *Champion CHAMP 23*	20	15
28 Feb 87	LET THE MUSIC MOVE U *Champion CHAMP 27*	57	3
31 Dec 88	BREAK 4 LOVE (re) *Champion CHAMP 67*	28	16
15 Jul 89	LET IT ROLL *Atlantic A 8866* [1]	27	5
27 Jan 90	ALL 4 LOVE (BREAK 4 LOVE 1990) *Champion CHAMP 228* [2]	30	5
10 Feb 90	CAN YOU FEEL IT / CAN YOU FEEL IT *Champion CHAMP 227* [3]	62	1
24 Sep 94	BREAK 4 LOVE (re-mix) *Champion CHAMPCD 314*	44	2
29 Mar 03	BREAK 4 LOVE (2nd re-mix) *Champion CHAMPCD 784*	64	1

[1] Raze presents Doug Lazy [2] Raze featuring Lady J and Secretary of Entertainment [3] Raze / Championship Legend

'Can You Feel It' by Championship Legend is a montage of six Raze tracks.

RAZORLIGHT *UK, male vocal (Johnny Borrell) / instrumental group (1 Album: 63 Weeks, 7 Singles: 42 Weeks)*

30 Aug 03	ROCK 'N' ROLL LIES *Vertigo 9800413*	56	1
22 Nov 03	RIP IT UP *Vertigo 9814045*	42	1

13 July 1985	20 July 1985	27 July 1985	3 August 1985
FRANKIE Sister Sledge	**FRANKIE** Sister Sledge	**THERE MUST BE AN ANGEL (PLAYING WITH MY HEART)** Eurythmics	**INTO THE GROOVE** Madonna
BORN IN THE U.S.A. Bruce Springsteen	**BORN IN THE U.S.A.** Bruce Springsteen	**BORN IN THE U.S.A.** Bruce Springsteen	**BROTHERS IN ARMS** Dire Straits

KEY UK No.1 ★ UK Top 10 ● Still on chart + UK entry at No.1 ■ US No.1 ▲ UK million seller £ US million seller $ Singles re-entries are listed as (re), (2re), (3re)... which signifies that the hit re-entered the chart once, twice or three times... Peak Position Weeks

7 Feb 04 **STUMBLE & FALL** *Vertigo 9816396* 27 3
26 Jun 04 ● **GOLDEN TOUCH** *Vertigo 9866836* 9 7
10 Jul 04 ● UP ALL NIGHT *Vertigo 9866944* 3 63
25 Sep 04 **VICE** *Vertigo 9867759* 18 4
11 Dec 04 **RIP IT UP (re)** (re-recording) *Vertigo 9869076* 20 5
23 Apr 05 ● **SOMEWHERE ELSE** *Vertigo 9869893* 2 21

RE-FLEX *UK, male vocal / instrumental group*

28 Jan 84 **THE POLITICS OF DANCING** *EMI FLEX 2* 28 9

Chris REA (85 Top 500)

One of the most popular UK singer / songwriters of the late 1980s, b. 4 Mar 1951, Middlesbrough. He was already a major European star by the time he finally cracked the UK Top 10 with his 18th chart entry, 'The Road to Hell (Part 2)' (23 Albums: 362 Weeks, 33 Singles: 120 Weeks)

7 Oct 78 **FOOL (IF YOU THINK IT'S OVER)** *Magnet MAG 111* 30 7
21 Apr 79 **DIAMONDS** *Magnet MAG 144* 44 3
28 Apr 79 DELTICS *Magnet MAG 5028* 54 3
12 Apr 80 TENNIS *Magnet MAG 5032* 60 1
27 Mar 82 **LOVING YOU** *Magnet MAG 215* 65 3
3 Apr 82 CHRIS REA *Magnet MAGL 5040* 52 4
18 Jun 83 WATER SIGN *Magnet MAGL 5048* 64 2
1 Oct 83 **I CAN HEAR YOUR HEARTBEAT** *Magnet MAG 244* 60 2
17 Mar 84 **I DON'T KNOW WHAT IT IS BUT I LOVE IT** *Magnet MAG 255* 65 2
21 Apr 84 WIRED TO THE MOON *Magnet MAGL 5057* 35 7
30 Mar 85 **STAINSBY GIRLS** *Magnet MAG 276* 26 10
25 May 85 SHAMROCK DIARIES *Magnet MAGL 5062* 15 14
29 Jun 85 **JOSEPHINE** *Magnet MAG 280* 67 2
29 Mar 86 **IT'S ALL GONE** *Magnet MAG 283* 69 1
26 Apr 86 ON THE BEACH *Magnet MAGL 5069* 11 37
31 May 86 **ON THE BEACH (2re)** *Magnet MAG 294* 57 8
6 Jun 87 **LET'S DANCE** *Magnet MAG 299* 12 10
29 Aug 87 **LOVING YOU AGAIN** *Magnet MAG 300* 47 4
26 Sep 87 ● DANCING WITH STRANGERS *Magnet MAGL 5071* 2 46
5 Dec 87 **JOYS OF CHRISTMAS** *Magnet MAG 314* 67 1
13 Feb 88 **QUE SERA** *Magnet MAG 318* 73 2
13 Aug 88 ON THE BEACH (re-issue) *WEA WX 191* 37 10
13 Aug 88 **ON THE BEACH SUMMER '88** (re-recording) *WEA YZ 195* 12 6
22 Oct 88 **I CAN HEAR YOUR HEARTBEAT** (re-recording) *WEA YZ 320* 74 2
29 Oct 88 ● NEW LIGHT THROUGH OLD WINDOWS *WEA WX 200* 5 51
17 Dec 88 **THE CHRISTMAS EP** *WEA YZ 325* 53 3
18 Feb 89 **WORKING ON IT** *WEA YZ 350* 53 3
14 Oct 89 ● **THE ROAD TO HELL (PART 2)** *WEA YZ 431* 10 9
11 Nov 89 ★ THE ROAD TO HELL *WEA WX 317* ■ 1 76
10 Feb 90 **TELL ME THERE'S A HEAVEN** *East West YZ 455* 24 6
5 May 90 **TEXAS** *East West YZ 468* 69 1
16 Feb 91 **AUBERGE** *East West YZ 555* 16 6
9 Mar 91 ★ AUBERGE *East West 9031735801* ■ 1 37
6 Apr 91 **HEAVEN** *East West YZ 566* 57 2
29 Jun 91 **LOOKING FOR THE SUMMER** *East West YZ 584* 49 3
9 Nov 91 **WINTER SONG** *East West YZ 629* 27 4
24 Oct 92 **NOTHING TO FEAR** *East West YZ 699* 16 4
14 Nov 92 ● GOD'S GREAT BANANA SKIN *East West 4509909952* 4 15
28 Nov 92 **GOD'S GREAT BANANA SKIN** *East West YZ 706* 31 3
30 Jan 93 **SOFT TOP HARD SHOULDER** *East West YZ 710CD* 53 2
23 Oct 93 **JULIA** *East West YZ 772CD* 18 5
13 Nov 93 ● ESPRESSO LOGIC *East West 4509943112* 8 10
5 Nov 94 ● THE BEST OF CHRIS REA *East West 4509980402* 3 18
12 Nov 94 **YOU CAN GO YOUR OWN WAY** *East West YZ 835CD* 28 3
24 Dec 94 **TELL ME THERE'S A HEAVEN** (re-issue) *East West YZ 885CD* 70 1
16 Nov 96 **'DISCO' LA PASSIONE** *East West EW 072CD* [1] 41 1
23 Nov 96 LA PASSIONE (FILM SOUNDTRACK) *East West 630166952* 43 4
24 May 97 **LET'S DANCE** (re-recording) *Magnet EW 112CD* [2] 44 1
31 Jan 98 ● THE BLUE CAFÉ *East West 3984216882* 10 7
20 Nov 99 THE ROAD TO HELL – PART 2 *East West 8573803992* 54 1
14 Oct 00 KING OF THE BEACH *East West 8573850172* 26 3
1 Dec 01 THE VERY BEST OF CHRIS REA *East West 927421282* 69 1
28 Sep 02 DANCING DOWN THE STONY ROAD *Jazzee Blue JBLUECD 01X* 14 7
3 Apr 04 THE BLUE JUKEBOX *Jazzee Blue JBLUECD 08X* 27 3
13 Aug 05 HEARTBEATS – GREATEST HITS *WSM 5046754542* 24 5

[1] Chris Rea and Shirley Bassey [2] Middlesbrough FC featuring Bob Mortimer and Chris Rea

Tracks on The Christmas EP: Driving Home for Christmas / Footsteps in the Snow / Joys of Christmas / Smile.

REACT 2 RHYTHM *UK, male production group*

28 Jun 97 **INTOXICATION** *Jackpot WIN 014CD* 73 1

REACTOR *UK, male vocal / instrumental group*

10 Apr 04 **FEELING THE LOVE** *Liberty CDREACT 001* 56 1

Eddi READER (see also FAIRGROUND ATTRACTION)

UK, female vocalist (4 Albums: 21 Weeks, 5 Singles: 14 Weeks)

7 Mar 92 MIRMAMA *RCA PD 75156* 34 2
4 Jun 94 **PATIENCE OF ANGELS** *Blanco Y Negro NEG 68CD* 33 5
2 Jul 94 ● EDDI READER *Blanco Y Negro 4509961772* 4 12
13 Aug 94 **JOKE (I'M LAUGHING)** *Blanco Y Negro NEG 72CD* 42 3
5 Nov 94 **DEAR JOHN** *Blanco Y Negro NEG 75CD1* 48 2
22 Jun 96 **TOWN WITHOUT PITY** *Blanco Y Negro NEG 90CD1* 26 3
20 Jul 96 CANDYFLOSS AND MEDICINE *Blanco Y Negro 630151202* 24 5
23 May 98 ANGELS & ELECTRICITY *Blanco Y Negro 3984228162* 49 2
21 Aug 99 **FRAGILE THING** *Track TRACK 0004A* [1] 69 1

[1] Big Country featuring Eddi Reader

READY FOR THE WORLD

US, male vocal / instrumental group (2 Singles: 8 Weeks)

26 Oct 85 **OH SHEILA** *MCA MCA 1005* ▲ 50 5
14 Mar 87 **LOVE YOU DOWN** *MCA MCA 1110* 60 3

REAL & RICHARDSON featuring JOBABE

UK, male production duo and female vocalist

10 May 03 **SUNSHINE ON A RAINY DAY** *Nukleuz 0489 CNUK* 69 1

REAL EMOTION *UK, male / female vocal / instrumental group*

1 Jul 95 **BACK FOR GOOD** *Living Beat LBECD 34* 67 1

REAL McCOY *Germany / US, male / female vocal / instrumental trio (1 Album: 5 Weeks, 6 Singles: 36 Weeks)*

6 Nov 93 **ANOTHER NIGHT** *Logic 74321173732* [1] $ 61 1
5 Nov 94 ● **ANOTHER NIGHT** (re-issue) *Logic 74321236992* [1] 2 12
28 Jan 95 ● **RUN AWAY** *Logic 74321258822* [1] 6 10
22 Apr 95 **LOVE AND DEVOTION** *Logic 74321272702* [1] 11 8
20 May 95 ● ANOTHER NIGHT – U.S. ALBUM *Logic 74321280972* 6 5
26 Aug 95 **COME AND GET YOUR LOVE** *Logic 74321301272* 19 4
11 Nov 95 **AUTOMATIC LOVER (CALL FOR LOVE)** *Logic 74321325042* 58 1

[1] (MC Sar &) Real McCoy

Trio were a duo for first three hits.

REAL PEOPLE

UK, male vocal / instrumental group (1 Album: 1 Week, 5 Singles: 8 Weeks)

16 Feb 91 **OPEN UP YOUR MIND (LET ME IN)** *CBS 6566127* 70 1
20 Apr 91 **THE TRUTH** *Columbia 6567877* 73 1
18 May 91 THE REAL PEOPLE *Columbia 4680841* 59 1
6 Jul 91 **WINDOW PANE (EP)** *Columbia 6569327* 60 1

	10 August 1985	17 August 1985	24 August 1985	31 August 1985
UK No.1 SINGLES	INTO THE GROOVE Madonna	INTO THE GROOVE Madonna	INTO THE GROOVE Madonna	I GOT YOU BABE UB40 featuring Chrissie Hynde
UK No.1 ALBUMS	BROTHERS IN ARMS Dire Straits	NOW THAT'S WHAT I CALL MUSIC! 5 Various	NOW THAT'S WHAT I CALL MUSIC! 5 Various	NOW THAT'S WHAT I CALL MUSIC! 5 Various

11 Jan 92	**THE TRUTH** (re-issue) *Columbia 6576987*	**41**	3
23 May 92	**BELIEVER** *Columbia 6580067*	**38**	2

Tracks on Window Pane (EP): Window Pane / See Through You / Everything Must Change.

REAL ROXANNE
US, female rapper – Joanne Martinez (2 Singles: 10 Weeks)

28 Jun 86	**(BANG ZOOM) LET'S GO-GO** *Cooltempo COOL 124* [1]	**11**	9
12 Nov 88	**RESPECT** *Cooltempo COOL 176*	**71**	1

[1] Real Roxanne with Hitman Howie Tee

The REAL THING
UK, male vocal group (4 Albums: 17 Weeks, 15 Singles: 121 Weeks)

5 Jun 76 ★	**YOU TO ME ARE EVERYTHING** *Pye International 7N 25709*	**1**	11
4 Sep 76 ●	**CAN'T GET BY WITHOUT YOU** *Pye 7N 45618*	**2**	10
6 Nov 76	REAL THING *Pye NSPL 18507*	34	3
12 Feb 77	**YOU'LL NEVER KNOW WHAT YOU'RE MISSING** *Pye 7N 45662*	**16**	9
30 Jul 77	**LOVE'S SUCH A WONDERFUL THING** *Pye 7N 45701*	**33**	5
4 Mar 78	**WHENEVER YOU WANT MY LOVE** *Pye 7N 46045*	**18**	9
3 Jun 78	**LET'S GO DISCO** *Pye 7N 46078*	**39**	7
12 Aug 78	**RAININ' THROUGH MY SUNSHINE** *Pye 7N 46113*	**40**	8
17 Feb 79 ●	**CAN YOU FEEL THE FORCE?** *Pye 7N 46147*	**5**	11
7 Apr 79	CAN YOU FEEL THE FORCE *Pye NSPH 18601*	73	1
21 Jul 79	**BOOGIE DOWN (GET FUNKY NOW)** *Pye 7P 109*	**33**	6
10 May 80	20 GREATEST HITS *K-Tel NE 1073*	56	2
22 Nov 80	**SHE'S A GROOVY FREAK** *Calibre CAB 105*	**52**	4
8 Mar 86 ●	**YOU TO ME ARE EVERYTHING (THE DECADE REMIX 76-86) (re)** *PRT 7P 349*	**5**	13
24 May 86 ●	**CAN'T GET BY WITHOUT YOU (THE SECOND DECADE REMIX)** *PRT 7P 352*	**6**	13
12 Jul 86	BEST OF THE REAL THING *West Five NRT 1*	24	11
2 Aug 86	**CAN YOU FEEL THE FORCE? ('86 REMIX)** *PRT 7P 358*	**24**	6
25 Oct 86	**STRAIGHT TO THE HEART** *Jive JIVE 129*	**71**	2
23 Apr 05 ●	**SO MUCH LOVE TO GIVE** *All Around the World CDGLOBE 412* [1]	**9**	7

[1] Freeloaders featuring The Real Thing

REAL TO REEL (see also LIL MO' YIN YANG; Erick MORILLO)
US, male vocal / instrumental group

21 Apr 84	**LOVE ME LIKE THIS** *Arista ARIST 565*	**68**	2

REBEL MC
UK, male rapper – Mike West (2 Albums: 11 Weeks, 9 Singles: 52 Weeks)

27 May 89	**JUST KEEP ROCKIN'** *Desire WANT 9* [1]	**11**	12
7 Oct 89 ●	**STREET TUFF** *Desire WANT 18* [2]	**3**	14
31 Mar 90	**BETTER WORLD** *Desire WANT 25*	**20**	6
28 Apr 90	REBEL MUSIC *Desire LUVLP 5*	18	7
2 Jun 90	**REBEL MUSIC** *Desire WANT 31*	**53**	2
6 Apr 91	**WICKEDEST SOUND** *Desire WANT 40* [3]	**43**	6
15 Jun 91	**TRIBAL BASE** *Desire WANT 44* [4]	**20**	6
13 Jul 91	BLACK MEANING GOOD *Desire LUVLP 12*	23	4
31 Aug 91	**BLACK MEANING GOOD** *Desire WANT 47*	**73**	1
21 Mar 92	**RICH AH GETTING RICHER** *Big Life BLR 70* [5]	**48**	4
8 Aug 92	**HUMANITY** *Big Life BLR 78* [6]	**62**	1

[1] Double Trouble and the Rebel MC [2] Rebel MC and Double Trouble [3] Rebel MC featuring Tenor Fly [4] Rebel MC featuring Tenor Fly and Barrington Levy [5] Rebel MC introducing Little T [6] Rebel MC featuring Lincoln Thompson

Ivan REBROFF *Germany, male vocalist – Hans Rippert*

16 Jun 90	THE VERY BEST OF IVAN REBROFF *BBC REB 778*	57	4

Ezz RECO and The LAUNCHERS with Boysie GRANT
Jamaica, male vocal / instrumental group

5 Mar 64	**KING OF KINGS** *Columbia DB 7217*	**44**	4

RECOIL *UK, male vocal / instrumental group*

21 Mar 92	**FAITH HEALER** *Mute MUTE 110*	**60**	1

RED (see also BEAT RENEGADES; DREAM FREQUENCY; QUAKE featuring Marcia RAE) *UK, male production duo – Ian Bland and Paul Fitzpatrick*

20 Jan 01	**HEAVEN & EARTH** *Slinky Music SLINKY 008CD*	**41**	1

RED 'N' WHITE MACHINES
UK, Southampton Football Club supporters vocal group

24 May 03	**SOUTHAMPTON BOYS** *Centric CEN 008*	**16**	1

RED BOX *UK, male vocal / instrumental duo – Julian Close and Simon Toulson (1 Album: 4 Weeks, 3 Singles: 28 Weeks)*

24 Aug 85 ●	**LEAN ON ME (AH-LI-AYO)** *Sire W 8926*	**3**	14
25 Oct 86 ●	**FOR AMERICA** *Sire YZ 84*	**10**	12
6 Dec 86	THE CIRCLE AND THE SQUARE *Sire WX 79*	73	4
31 Jan 87	**HEART OF THE SUN** *Sire YZ 100*	**71**	2

RED CAR AND THE BLUE CAR *UK, male vocal / instrumental group*

14 Dec 91	**HOME FOR CHRISTMAS DAY** *Virgin VS 1394*	**44**	4

RED CARPET *Belgium, male production duo and female vocalist*

11 Dec 04	**ALRIGHT** *Positiva CDTIVS 212*	**58**	2

RED DRAGON with Brian and Tony GOLD *Jamaica, male vocal group*

30 Jul 94 ●	**COMPLIMENTS ON YOUR KISS (re)** *Mango CIDM 820*	**2**	15

RED EYE *UK, male instrumental / production duo*

3 Dec 94	**KUT IT** *Champion CHAMPCD 315*	**62**	1

RED 5 *Germany, male producer – Thomas Kukula (2 Singles: 10 Weeks)*

10 May 97	**I LOVE YOU ... STOP!** *Multiply CDMULTY 20*	**11**	5
20 Dec 97	**LIFT ME UP** *Multiply CDMULTY 30*	**26**	5

RED HILL CHILDREN *UK, male / female children's choir*

30 Nov 96	**WHEN CHILDREN RULE THE WORLD** *Really Useful 5797262*	**40**	2

RED HOT CHILI PEPPERS 93 Top 500

Los Angeles-based funk rock quartet formed by high school pals Anthony Kiedis (v) and Michael "Flea" Balzary (b) in 1983 and now featuring John Frusciante (g) and Chad Smith (d). By the Way sold more than a million copies in both the UK and US in 2002, taking their worldwide album sales close to 35 million. Their three Hyde Park concerts in London were seen by over 250,000 people and grossed £9.7 million – a 2004 record (9 Albums: 364 Weeks, 21 Singles: 91 Weeks)

10 Feb 90	**HIGHER GROUND** *EMI-USA MT 75*	**55**	3
23 Jun 90	**TASTE THE PAIN** *EMI-USA MT 85*	**29**	3
8 Sep 90	**HIGHER GROUND** (re-issue) *EMI-USA MT 88*	**54**	3
12 Oct 91	BLOOD SUGAR SEX MAGIK *Warner Bros. WX 441*	25	86
14 Mar 92	**UNDER THE BRIDGE** *Warner Bros. W 0084*	**26**	4
15 Aug 92	**BREAKING THE GIRL** *Warner Bros. W 0126*	**41**	3
17 Oct 92	WHAT HITS!? *EMI-USA CDMTL 1071*	23	6
5 Feb 94 ●	**GIVE IT AWAY** *Warner Bros. W 0225CD1*	**9**	4
30 Apr 94	**UNDER THE BRIDGE** (re-issue) *Warner Bros. W 0237CD*	**13**	6
19 Nov 94	OUT IN L.A. *EMI CDMTL 1082*	61	1
2 Sep 95	**WARPED** *Warner Bros. W 0316CD*	**31**	2
23 Sep 95 ●	ONE HOT MINUTE *Warner Bros. 9362457332*	2	11
21 Oct 95	**MY FRIENDS** *Warner Bros. W 0317CD*	**29**	2
17 Feb 96	**AEROPLANE** *Warner Bros. W 0331CD*	**11**	3
14 Jun 97 ●	**LOVE ROLLERCOASTER** *Geffen GFSTD 22188*	**7**	8
12 Jun 99	**SCAR TISSUE** *Warner Bros. W 490CD*	**15**	6
19 Jun 99 ●	CALIFORNICATION *Warner Bros. 9362473862*	5	130
4 Sep 99	**AROUND THE WORLD** *Warner Bros. W 500CD1*	**35**	2
12 Feb 00	**OTHERSIDE** *Warner Bros. W 510CD1*	**33**	2

7 September 1985	14 September 1985	21 September 1985	28 September 1985
DANCING IN THE STREET David Bowie and Mick Jagger	**DANCING IN THE STREET** David Bowie and Mick Jagger	**DANCING IN THE STREET** David Bowie and Mick Jagger	**DANCING IN THE STREET** David Bowie and Mick Jagger
NOW THAT'S WHAT I CALL MUSIC! 5 Various	**NOW THAT'S WHAT I CALL MUSIC! 5** Various	**LIKE A VIRGIN** Madonna	**HOUNDS OF LOVE** Kate Bush

KEY: UK No.1 ★ UK Top 10 ● Still on chart + UK entry at No.1 ■ US No.1 ▲ UK million seller £ US million seller $
Singles re-entries are listed as (re), (2re), (3re)… which signifies that the hit re-entered the chart once, twice or three times…
Peak Position / Weeks

19 Aug 00 CALIFORNICATION *Warner Bros. W 534CD* 16 5
13 Jan 01 ROAD TRIPPIN' *Warner Bros. W 546CD1* 30 2
13 Jul 02 ● BY THE WAY *Warner Bros. W 580CD* 2 10
20 Jul 02 ★ BY THE WAY *Warner Bros. 9362481402* ■ 1 77
2 Nov 02 THE ZEPHYR SONG *Warner Bros. W 592CD* 11 10
22 Feb 03 CAN'T STOP *Warner Bros. W 599CD1* 22 6
5 Apr 03 WHAT HITS!? (re-issue) *EMI CDP 7947622* 44 5
28 Jun 03 UNIVERSALLY SPEAKING *Warner Bros. W 609CD1* 27 2
22 Nov 03 FORTUNE FADED *Warner Bros. W 630CD1* 11 5
29 Nov 03 ● GREATEST HITS *Warner Bros. 9362485962* 4 39
7 Aug 04 ★ LIVE IN HYDE PARK *Warner Bros. 9362488632* ■ 1 9

Blood Sugar Sex Magik had a new catalogue number, Warner Bros. 7599266812, when it returned to the chart in 2004.

RED HOUSE PAINTERS
US, male vocal / instrumental group (2 Albums: 2 Weeks)

5 Jun 93 RED HOUSE PAINTERS *4AD DAD 3008CD* 63 1
30 Oct 93 RED HOUSE PAINTERS *4AD CAD 3016CD* 68 1

These identically titled albums are different.

RED RAW featuring 007 (see also CLOCK)
UK, male vocal / instrumental duo – Stuart Allen and Peter Pritchard

28 Oct 95 OOH LA LA LA *Media MCSTD 2065* 59 1

RED SNAPPER *UK, male vocal / instrumental / production group (2 Albums: 2 Weeks, 1 Single: 1 Week)*

21 Sep 96 PRINCE BLIMEY *Warp WARPCD 45* 60 1
10 Oct 98 MAKING BONES *Warp WARPCD 56* 59 1
21 Nov 98 IMAGE OF YOU *Warp WAP 111CD* 60 1

REDBONE *US, male vocal / instrumental group*

25 Sep 71 ● THE WITCH QUEEN OF NEW ORLEANS *Epic EPC 7351* 2 12

Sharon REDD *US, female vocalist, b. 19 Oct 1945, d. 1 May 1992 (1 Album: 5 Weeks, 5 Singles: 32 Weeks)*

28 Feb 81 CAN YOU HANDLE IT *Epic EPC 9572* 31 8
2 Oct 82 NEVER GIVE YOU UP *Prelude PRL A 2755* 20 9
23 Oct 82 REDD HOTT *Prelude PRL 25056* 59 5
15 Jan 83 IN THE NAME OF LOVE *Prelude PRL A 2905* 31 5
22 Oct 83 LOVE HOW YOU FEEL *Prelude A 3868* 39 5
1 Feb 92 CAN YOU HANDLE IT (re-recording) *EMI EM 219* [1] 17 5

[1] DNA featuring Sharon Redd

REDD KROSS
US, male vocal / instrumental group (3 Singles: 4 Weeks)

5 Feb 94 VISIONARY *This Way Up WAY 2733* 75 1
10 Sep 94 YESTERDAY ONCE MORE *A&M 5807932* 45 2
1 Feb 97 GET OUT OF MYSELF *This Way Up WAY 5466* 63 1

The listed flip side of 'Yesterday Once More' was 'Superstar' by Sonic Youth.

REDD SQUARE featuring Tiff LACEY
UK, male production group and female vocalist

26 Oct 02 IN YOUR HANDS *Inferno CDFERN 50* 64 1

Otis REDDING (149 Top 500)
Peerless singer / songwriter, b. 9 Sep 1941, Georgia, US, d. 10 Dec 1967. He was one of the first and most influential Sixties soul stars. He replaced Elvis as the World's Top Male Singer in a Melody Maker poll shortly before his death in a plane crash (13 Albums: 235 Weeks, 16 Singles: 124 Weeks)

25 Nov 65 MY GIRL *Atlantic AT 4050* 11 16
19 Feb 66 ● OTIS BLUE / OTIS REDDING SINGS SOUL *Atlantic ATL 5041* 6 21
7 Apr 66 (I CAN'T GET NO) SATISFACTION *Atlantic AT 4080* 33 4
23 Apr 66 SOUL BALLADS *Atlantic ATL 5029* 30 1
14 Jul 66 MY LOVER'S PRAYER *Atlantic 584 019* 37 6
23 Jul 66 THE SOUL ALBUM *Atlantic 587011* 22 9
25 Aug 66 I CAN'T TURN YOU LOOSE *Atlantic 584 030* 29 8
24 Nov 66 FA FA FA FA FA (SAD SONG) *Atlantic 584 049* 23 9
21 Jan 67 OTIS BLUE (re-issue) *Atlantic 587036* 23 16
21 Jan 67 ● COMPLETE & UNBELIEVABLE – THE OTIS REDDING DICTIONARY OF SOUL *Atlantic 588050* 7 54
26 Jan 67 TRY A LITTLE TENDERNESS *Atlantic 584 070* 46 4
23 Mar 67 DAY TRIPPER *Stax 601 005* 43 6
29 Apr 67 PAIN IN MY HEART *Atlantic 587042* 28 9
4 May 67 LET ME COME ON HOME *Stax 601 007* 48 1
15 Jun 67 SHAKE *Stax 601 011* 28 10
1 Jul 67 KING & QUEEN *Atlantic 589007* [1] 18 17
19 Jul 67 TRAMP *Stax 601 012* [1] 18 11
11 Oct 67 KNOCK ON WOOD *Stax 601 021* [1] 35 5
10 Feb 68 ● HISTORY OF OTIS REDDING *Volt S 418* 2 43
14 Feb 68 MY GIRL (re-issue) *Atlantic 584 092* 36 9
21 Feb 68 ● (SITTIN' ON) THE DOCK OF THE BAY *Stax 601 031* ▲ $ 3 15
30 Mar 68 OTIS REDDING IN EUROPE *Stax 589016* 14 16
29 May 68 THE HAPPY SONG (DUM-DUM) *Stax 601 040* 24 5
1 Jun 68 ★ DOCK OF THE BAY *Stax 231001* 1 15
31 Jul 68 HARD TO HANDLE *Atlantic 584 199* 15 12
12 Oct 68 THE IMMORTAL OTIS REDDING *Atlantic 588113* 19 8
9 Jul 69 LOVE MAN *Atco 226 001* 43 3
11 Sep 93 DOCK OF THE BAY – THE DEFINITIVE COLLECTION *Atlantic 9548317092* 44 18
11 Nov 00 THE VERY BEST OF OTIS REDDING *Atco 9548380872* 26 8

[1] Otis Redding and Carla Thomas [1] Otis Redding and Carla Thomas

Helen REDDY
Australia, female vocalist (2 Albums: 27 Weeks, 2 Singles: 18 Weeks)

18 Jan 75 ● ANGIE BABY *Capitol CL 15799* ▲ $ 5 10
8 Feb 75 FREE AND EASY *Capitol EST 11348* 17 9
14 Feb 76 ● THE BEST OF HELEN REDDY *Capitol EST 11467* 5 18
28 Nov 81 I CAN'T SAY GOODBYE TO YOU *MCA 744* 43 8

REDHEAD KINGPIN and The FBI *US, male rapper – David Guppy and rap group (1 Album: 3 Weeks, 2 Singles: 11 Weeks)*

22 Jul 89 DO THE RIGHT THING *10 TEN 271* 13 10
9 Sep 89 A SHADE OF RED *10 DIX 85* 35 3
2 Dec 89 SUPERBAD SUPERSLICK *10 TEN 286* 68 1

REDMAN
US, male rapper – Reggie Noble (2 Albums: 7 Weeks, 9 Singles: 38 Weeks)

25 Apr 98 RAP SCHOLAR *East West E 3853CD* [1] 42 1
30 May 98 MADE IT BACK *Parlophone Rhythm CDRHYTHM 11* [2] 21 3
24 Oct 98 ● HOW DEEP IS YOUR LOVE (re) *Island Black Music CID 725* [3] 9 8
12 Jun 99 DA GOODNESS *Def Jam 8709232* 52 1
9 Oct 99 BLACKOUT! *Def Jam 5466092* [1] 45 3
22 Jul 00 OOOH *Tommy Boy TBCD 2102* [4] 29 2
9 Jun 01 MALPRACTICE *Def Jam 5483812* 57 4
15 Sep 01 SMASH SUMTHIN' *Def Jam 5886932* [5] 11 7
31 Aug 02 SMASH SUMTHIN' (re-mix) *Kaos KAOSCD 003* [6] 47 2
23 Nov 02 ★ DIRRTY *RCA 74321962722* [7] ■ 1 9
11 Jan 03 REACT *J 74321988492* [8] 14 5

[1] Das EFX featuring Redman [2] Beverley Knight featuring Redman [3] Dru Hill featuring Redman [4] De La Soul featuring Redman [5] Redman featuring Adam F [6] Adam F featuring Redman [7] Christina Aguilera featuring Redman [8] Erick Sermon featuring Redman [1] Method Man and Redman

	5 October 1985	12 October 1985	19 October 1985	26 October 1985
UK No.1 SINGLES	IF I WAS Midge Ure	THE POWER OF LOVE Jennifer Rush	THE POWER OF LOVE Jennifer Rush	THE POWER OF LOVE Jennifer Rush
UK No.1 ALBUMS	HOUNDS OF LOVE Kate Bush	LIKE A VIRGIN Madonna	HOUNDS OF LOVE Kate Bush	THE LOVE SONGS George Benson

REDNEX
Sweden, male / female vocal / instrumental group (3 Singles: 23 Weeks)

17 Dec 94 ★ **COTTON EYE JOE** *Internal Affairs KGBCD 016*......**1** 16
25 Mar 95 **OLD POP IN AN OAK** *Internal Affairs KGBD 019*......**12** 6
21 Oct 95 **WILD 'N FREE** *Internal Affairs KGBD 024*......**55** 1

REDS UNITED
UK, male vocal group – 40 Manchester United FC fans (2 Singles: 13 Weeks)

6 Dec 97 **SING UP FOR THE CHAMPIONS** *Music Collection MANUCDP 2*..**12** 9
9 May 98 **UNITED CALYPSO '98** *Music Collection MANUCDP 3*......**33** 4

REDSKINS
UK, male vocal / instrumental trio (1 Album: 4 Weeks, 3 Singles: 12 Weeks)

10 Nov 84 **KEEP ON KEEPIN' ON** *Decca F 1*......**43** 5
22 Jun 85 **BRING IT DOWN (THIS INSANE THING)** *Decca F 2*......**33** 5
22 Feb 86 **THE POWER IS YOURS** *Decca F 3*......**59** 2
22 Mar 86 NEITHER WASHINGTON NOR MOSCOW ... *Decca FLP 1*......31 4

Alex REECE *UK, male producer (1 Album: 5 Weeks, 4 Singles: 7 Weeks)*

16 Dec 95 **FEEL THE SUNSHINE** *Blunted Vinyl BLNCD 016*......**69** 1
11 May 96 **FEEL THE SUNSHINE** (re-mix) *Fourth & Broadway BRCD 332*......**26** 3
27 Jul 96 **CANDLES** *Fourth & Broadway BRCD 333*......**33** 2
17 Aug 96 SO FAR *Fourth & Broadway BRCD 621*......19 5
18 Nov 96 **ACID LAB** *Fourth & Broadway BRCD 344*......**64** 1

Jimmy REED *US, male vocalist / guitarist / harmonica – Mathis Reed, b. 6 Sep 1925, d. 29 Aug 1976*

10 Sep 64 **SHAME, SHAME, SHAME** *Stateside SS 330*......**45** 2

Lou REED (see also The VELVET UNDERGROUND)
US, male vocalist – Lou Firbank (18 Albums: 98 Weeks, 3 Singles: 26 Weeks)

21 Apr 73 TRANSFORMER *RCA Victor LSP 4807*......13 26
12 May 73 ● **WALK ON THE WILD SIDE** *RCA 2303*......**10** 9
20 Oct 73 ● BERLIN *RCA Victor RS 1002*......7 5
16 Mar 74 ROCK 'N' ROLL ANIMAL *RCA Victor APLI 0472*......26 1
14 Feb 76 CONEY ISLAND BABY *RCA Victor RS 1035*......52 1
3 Jul 82 TRANSFORMER (re-issue) *RCA INTS 5061*......91 2
9 Jun 84 NEW SENSATIONS *RCA PL 84998*......92 1
24 May 86 MISTRIAL *RCA PL 87190*......69 1
17 Jan 87 **SOUL MAN** *A&M AM 364* [1] **30** 10
28 Jan 89 NEW YORK *Sire WX 246*......14 22
7 Oct 89 RETRO *RCA PL 90389*......29 5
5 May 90 SONGS FOR DRELLA *Sire WX 345* [1] 22 5
25 Jan 92 ● MAGIC AND LOSS *Sire 7599266622*......6 6
28 Oct 95 THE BEST OF LOU REED & THE VELVET UNDERGROUND *Global Television RADCD 21* [2] 56 4
2 Mar 96 SET THE TWILIGHT REELING *Warner Bros. 9362461592*......26 2
7 Feb 98 TRANSFORMER (2nd re-issue) *RCA ND 83806*......16 10
15 Apr 00 ECSTASY *Reprise 9362474252*......54 1
24 May 03 NYC MAN *BMG 74321984012*......31 3
31 Jul 04 ● **SATELLITE OF LOVE '04** *Nulife 82876636472*......**10** 7
7 Aug 04 NYC MAN – GREATEST HITS *BMG 82876631122*......43 2
9 Oct 04 TRANSFORMER (3rd re-issue) *RCA 74321601812*......45 1

[1] Sam Moore and Lou Reed [1] Lou Reed and John Cale [2] Lou Reed and The Velvet Underground

NYC Man – Greatest Hits is a slimmed-down version of the double-disc retrospective NYC Man but contains additional re-mixes.

Dan REED NETWORK
US, male vocal / instrumental group (2 Albums: 6 Weeks, 6 Singles: 16 Weeks)

4 Nov 89 SLAM *Mercury 8388681*......66 2
20 Jan 90 **COME BACK BABY** *Mercury DRN 2*......**51** 3
17 Mar 90 **RAINBOW CHILD** *Mercury DRN 3*......**60** 3
21 Jul 90 **STARDATE 1990 / RAINBOW CHILD** (re-issue) *Mercury DRN 4*......**39** 4
8 Sep 90 **LOVER / MONEY** *Mercury DRN 5*......**45** 3
13 Jul 91 **MIX IT UP** *Mercury MER 345*......**49** 2
27 Jul 91 THE HEAT *Mercury 8488551*......15 4
21 Sep 91 **BABY NOW I** *Mercury MER 352*......**65** 1

REEF *UK, male vocal (Gary Stringer) / instrumental group (5 Albums: 55 Weeks, 15 Singles: 48 Weeks)*

15 Apr 95 **GOOD FEELING** *Sony S2 6613602*......**24** 4
3 Jun 95 **NAKED** *Sony S2 6620622*......**11** 5
1 Jul 95 ● REPLENISH *Sony S2 4806982*......9 11
5 Aug 95 **WEIRD** *Sony S2 6622772*......**19** 3
2 Nov 96 ● **PLACE YOUR HANDS** *Sony S2 6635712*......**6** 7
25 Jan 97 ● **COME BACK BRIGHTER** *Sony S2 6640972*......**8** 5
8 Feb 97 ★ GLOW *Sony S2 4869402* ■......1 32
5 Apr 97 **CONSIDERATION** *Sony S2 6643125*......**13** 4
2 Aug 97 **YER OLD** *Sony S2 6647032*......**21** 3
10 Apr 99 **I'VE GOT SOMETHING TO SAY** *Sony S2 6669542*......**15** 6
1 May 99 ● RIDES *Sony S2 4928822*......3 7
5 Jun 99 **SWEETY** *Sony S2 6673732*......**46** 1
11 Sep 99 **NEW BIRD** *Sony S2 6678512*......**73** 1
12 Aug 00 **SET THE RECORD STRAIGHT** *Sony S2 6695952*......**19** 5
2 Sep 00 GETAWAY *Sony S2 4988912*......15 4
16 Dec 00 **SUPERHERO** *Sony S2 66999382*......**55** 1
19 May 01 **ALL I WANT** *Sony S2 6708222*......**51** 1
25 Jan 03 **GIVE ME YOUR LOVE** *Sony S2 6731645*......**44** 1
8 Feb 03 TOGETHER – THE BEST OF *Sony S2 5094352*......52 1
28 Jun 03 **WASTER** *Snapper / Reef SMASCD 051*......**56** 1

REEL *Ireland, male vocal group (2 Singles: 3 Weeks)*

24 Nov 01 **LIFT ME UP** *Universal TV 0154632*......**39** 1
8 Jun 02 **YOU TAKE ME AWAY** *Universal TV 0190172*......**31** 2

REEL BIG FISH *US, male vocal / instrumental group*

6 Apr 02 **SOLD OUT (EP)** *Jive 9270002*......**62** 1

Tracks on Sold Out (EP): Sell Out / Take on Me / Hungry Like the Wolf.

REEL 2 REAL featuring The MAD STUNTMAN (see also LIL MO' YIN YANG; PIANOHEADZ) *US, male vocal / production duo – Erick Morillo and Mark 'The Mad Stuntman' Quashie (1 Album: 8 Weeks, 7 Singles: 53 Weeks)*

12 Feb 94 ● **I LIKE TO MOVE IT** *Positiva CDTIV 10*......**5** 20
2 Jul 94 ● **GO ON MOVE** *Positiva CDTIV 15*......**7** 9
1 Oct 94 **CAN YOU FEEL IT?** *Positiva CDTIV 22*......**13** 5
22 Oct 94 ● MOVE IT! *Positiva CDTIVA 1003*......8 8
3 Dec 94 **RAISE YOUR HANDS** *Positiva CDTIV 27*......**14** 6
1 Apr 95 **CONWAY** *Positiva CDTIVS 30*......**27** 4
6 Jul 96 ● **JAZZ IT UP** *Positiva CDTIV 59* [1] **7** 7
5 Oct 96 **ARE YOU READY FOR SOME MORE** *Positiva CDTIV 56* [1] **24** 2

[1] Reel 2 Real

The REELISTS *UK, male vocal / production duo – Kaywan Qazzaz and Saif Naqui (2 Singles: 13 Weeks)*

19 Jan 02 ● **HATERS** *Relentless RELENT 23CD* [1] **8** 7
25 May 02 **FREAK MODE (re)** *Go Beat GOBCD 45*......**16** 6

[1] So Solid Crew presents Mr Shabz featuring MBD and The Reelists

Maureen REES *UK, female TV learner driver / vocalist*

20 Dec 97 **DRIVING IN MY CAR** *Eagle EAGXS 014*......**49** 4

Tony REES and The COTTAGERS
UK, male vocal group – Fulham FC supporters

10 May 75 **VIVA EL FULHAM** *Sonet SON 2059*......**46** 1

REESE PROJECT (see also INNER CITY; TRONIKHOUSE)
US, male producer – Kevin Saunderson (5 Singles: 7 Weeks)

8 Aug 92 **THE COLOUR OF LOVE** *Network NWK 51*......**52** 2
12 Dec 92 **I BELIEVE** *Network NWKT 63*......**74** 1

2 November 1985	9 November 1985	16 November 1985	23 November 1985
THE POWER OF LOVE Jennifer Rush	THE POWER OF LOVE Jennifer Rush	A GOOD HEART Feargal Sharkey	A GOOD HEART Feargal Sharkey
ONCE UPON A TIME Simple Minds	THE LOVE SONGS George Benson	PROMISE Sade	PROMISE Sade

THE ULTIMATE CHART-TOPPERS

We define an 'ultimate' in this case as an act that has done these four things at the same time: the same UK No.1 single and US No.1 single and the same UK No.1 album and US No.1 album all in the same week. Not surprisingly, only six acts have achieved this feat. If there were such a thing as an ultimate of ultimates act, then that description would be best applied to Rod Stewart, who managed to be top in all four charts for three weeks running with the same single and album.

The Beatles, who are the only act to have managed to be transatlantic double-toppers on two separate occasions, have also simultaneously topped all four charts on four other weeks but with different records. That's a feat that both Phil Collins and The Monkees also managed. However, in chronological order, the ultimate toppers look like this:

Date	Act	UK and US No.1 single / UK and US No.1 album
1 Aug / 30 Jul 1964*	**THE BEATLES**	A Hard Day's Night / A Hard Day's Night
8 Aug / 6 Aug 1964*	**THE BEATLES**	A Hard Day's Night / A Hard Day's Night
8 Jan / 6 Jan 1966*	**THE BEATLES**	We Can Work It Out / Rubber Soul
15 Jan / 13 Jan 1966*	**THE BEATLES**	We Can Work It Out / Rubber Soul
4 Feb / 2 Feb 1967*	**THE MONKEES**	I'm a Believer / The Monkees
28 Mar 1970	**SIMON AND GARFUNKEL**	Bridge Over Troubled Water / Bridge over Troubled Water
4 Apr 1970	**SIMON AND GARFUNKEL**	Bridge Over Troubled Water / Bridge over Troubled Water
9 Oct 1971	**ROD STEWART**	Maggie May / Every Picture Tells a Story
16 Oct 1971	**ROD STEWART**	Maggie May / Every Picture Tells a Story
23 Oct 1971	**ROD STEWART**	Maggie May / Every Picture Tells a Story
29 Jan 1983	**MEN AT WORK**	Down Under / Business as Usual
12 Feb 1983	**MEN AT WORK**	Down Under / Business as Usual
5 Mar 1983	**MICHAEL JACKSON**	Billie Jean / Thriller

* Singles/albums chart dates were on different days of the week

Transatlantic double-topper Rod Stewart is the ultimate of our ultimates list. His 'Maggie May' single and album, Every Picture Tells a Story, were top in all four charts for three consecutive weeks

	30 November 1985	7 December 1985	14 December 1985	21 December 1985
UK No.1 SINGLES	**I'M YOUR MAN** Wham!	**I'M YOUR MAN** Wham!	**SAVING ALL MY LOVE FOR YOU** Whitney Houston	**SAVING ALL MY LOVE FOR YOU** Whitney Houston
UK No.1 ALBUMS	**THE GREATEST HITS OF 1985** Various	**NOW THAT'S WHAT I CALL MUSIC! 6** Various	**NOW THAT'S WHAT I CALL MUSIC! 6** Various	**NOW! - THE CHRISTMAS ALBUM** Various

13Mar 93 **SO DEEP** *Network NWKCD 68* **54** 2
24 Sep 94 **THE COLOUR OF LOVE** (re-mix) *Network NWKCD 81* **55** 1
6 May 95 **DIRECT-ME** *Network NWKCD 87* **44** 1

Conner REEVES *UK, male vocalist (1 Album: 8 Weeks, 5 Singles: 18 Weeks)*

30 Aug 97 **MY FATHER'S SON** *Wildstar CDWILD 1* **12** 5
22 Nov 97 **EARTHBOUND** *Wildstar CDWILD 2* **14** 4
6 Dec 97 EARTHBOUND *Wildstar CDWILD 3* 25 8
11 Apr 98 **READ MY MIND** *Wildstar CXWILD 4* **19** 4
3 Oct 98 **SEARCHING FOR A SOUL** *Wildstar CDWILD 6* **28** 2
4 Sep 99 **BEST FRIEND** *WEA WEA 221CD1* [1] **23** 3

[1] Mark Morrison and Conner Reeves

Jim REEVES (37 Top 500) *Internationally acclaimed velvet-voiced vocalist, b. 20 Aug 1924, Texas, US, d. 31 Jul 1964. 'Gentleman Jim', who only managed two hit LPs in his lifetime then 31 posthumously, had a record-breaking eight albums simultaneously on the UK chart three months after his death in a plane crash (33 Albums: 408 Weeks, 26 Singles: 322 Weeks)*

24 Mar 60 **HE'LL HAVE TO GO (re)** *RCA 1168* $ **12** 31
16 Mar 61 **WHISPERING HOPE** *RCA 1223* **50** 1
23 Nov 61 **YOU'RE THE ONLY GOOD THING (THAT HAPPENED TO ME)** *RCA 1261* **17** 19
28 Jun 62 **ADIOS AMIGO** *RCA 1293* **23** 21
22 Nov 62 **I'M GONNA CHANGE EVERYTHING** *RCA 1317* **42** 2
13 Jun 63 ● **WELCOME TO MY WORLD** *RCA 1342* **6** 15
17 Oct 63 **GUILTY** *RCA 1364* **29** 7
20 Feb 64 ● **I LOVE YOU BECAUSE** *RCA 1385* **5** 39
28 Mar 64 ● GOOD 'N' COUNTRY *RCA Camden CDN 5114* 10 34
9 May 64 ● GENTLEMAN JIM *RCA RD 7541* 3 23
18 Jun 64 ● **I WON'T FORGET YOU (re)** *RCA 1400* **3** 26
15 Aug 64 ● A TOUCH OF VELVET *RCA RD 7521* 8 9
15 Aug 64 INTERNATIONAL JIM REEVES *RCA RD 7577* 11 15
22 Aug 64 HE'LL HAVE TO GO *RCA RD 27176* 16 4
29 Aug 64 ● GOD BE WITH YOU *RCA RD 7636* 10 10
29 Aug 64 THE INTIMATE JIM REEVES *RCA RD 27193* 12 4
5 Sep 64 ● MOONLIGHT AND ROSES *RCA RD 7639* 2 51
19 Sep 64 COUNTRY SIDE OF JIM REEVES *RCA Camden CDN 5100* 12 5
26 Sep 64 WE THANK THEE *RCA RD 7637* 17 3
5 Nov 64 ● **THERE'S A HEARTACHE FOLLOWING ME** *RCA 1423* **6** 13
28 Nov 64 ● TWELVE SONGS OF CHRISTMAS *RCA RD 7663* 3 17
30 Jan 65 ● THE BEST OF JIM REEVES *RCA RD 7666* 3 47
4 Feb 65 ● **IT HURTS SO MUCH (TO SEE YOU GO)** *RCA 1437* **8** 10
10 Apr 65 HAVE I TOLD YOU LATELY THAT I LOVE YOU *RCA Camden CDN 5122* 12 5
15 Apr 65 **NOT UNTIL THE NEXT TIME** *RCA 1446* **13** 12
6 May 65 **HOW LONG HAS IT BEEN** *RCA 1445* **45** 5
22 May 65 THE JIM REEVES WAY *RCA RD 7694* 16 4
15 Jul 65 **THIS WORLD IS NOT MY HOME** *RCA 1412* **22** 9
11 Nov 65 **IS IT REALLY OVER** *RCA 1488* **17** 9
18 Aug 66 ★ **DISTANT DRUMS** *RCA 1537* **1** 25
5 Nov 66 ● DISTANT DRUMS *RCA Victor RD 7814* 2 34
2 Feb 67 **I WON'T COME IN WHILE HE'S THERE** *RCA 1563* **12** 11
26 Jul 67 **TRYING TO FORGET** *RCA 1611* **33** 5
22 Nov 67 **I HEARD A HEART BREAK LAST NIGHT** *RCA 1643* **38** 6
27 Mar 68 **PRETTY BROWN EYES** *RCA 1672* **33** 5
18 Jan 69 A TOUCH OF SADNESS *RCA SF 7978* 15 5
25 Jun 69 **WHEN TWO WORLDS COLLIDE** *RCA 1830* **17** 17
5 Jul 69 ★ ACCORDING TO MY HEART *RCA International INTS 1013* 1 14
23 Aug 69 JIM REEVES AND SOME FRIENDS *RCA SF 8022* 24 4
29 Nov 69 ON STAGE *RCA SF 8047* 13 4
6 Dec 69 **BUT YOU LOVE ME DADDY** *RCA 1899* **15** 16
21 Mar 70 **NOBODY'S FOOL** *RCA 1915* **32** 5
12 Sep 70 **ANGELS DON'T LIE (re)** *RCA 1997* **32** 3
26 Dec 70 MY CATHEDRAL *RCA SF 8146* 48 2
26 Jun 71 **I LOVE YOU BECAUSE** (re-issue) / **HE'LL HAVE TO GO** (re-issue) / **MOONLIGHT & ROSES** *RCA Maximillion 2092* **34** 8
3 Jul 71 JIM REEVES WRITES YOU A RECORD *RCA SF 8176* 47 2
7 Aug 71 ● JIM REEVES' GOLDEN RECORDS *RCA International INTS 1070* 9 21
14 Aug 71 ● THE INTIMATE JIM REEVES (re-issue) *RCA International INTS 1256* 8 15
21 Aug 71 GIRLS I HAVE KNOWN *RCA International INTS 1140* 35 5
27 Nov 71 A TOUCH OF VELVET (re-issue) *RCA International INTS 1089* 49 2
27 Nov 71 ● TWELVE SONGS OF CHRISTMAS (re-issue) *RCA International INTS 1188* 3 6
19 Feb 72 **YOU'RE FREE TO GO** *RCA 2174* **48** 2
15 Apr 72 MY FRIEND *RCA SF 8258* 32 5
20 Sep 75 ★ 40 GOLDEN GREATS *Arcade ADEP 16* 1 25
6 Sep 80 COUNTRY GENTLEMAN *K-Tel NE 1088* 53 4
8 Aug 92 ● THE DEFINITIVE JIM REEVES *Arcade ARC 94982* 9 10
28 Sep 96 THE ULTIMATE COLLECTION *RCA Victor 74321410872* 17 6
5 Jul 03 GENTLEMAN JIM – DEFINITIVE COLLECTION *RCA 82876530372* 21 10
3 Jul 04 GENTLEMAN JIM – MEMORIES ARE MADE OF THIS *RCA 82876627842* 35 3

Martha REEVES and The VANDELLAS
US, female vocal trio (10 Singles: 85 Weeks)

29 Oct 64 **DANCING IN THE STREET** *Stateside SS 345* [1] $ **28** 8
1 Apr 65 **NOWHERE TO RUN** *Tamla Motown TMG 502* [1] **26** 8
1 Dec 66 **I'M READY FOR LOVE** *Tamla Motown TMG 582* [1] **22** 8
30 Mar 67 **JIMMY MACK (re)** *Tamla Motown TMG 599* [1] **21** 21
17 Jan 68 **HONEY CHILE** *Tamla Motown TMG 636* **30** 9
15 Jan 69 ● **DANCING IN THE STREET** (re-issue) *Tamla Motown TMG 684* **4** 12
16 Apr 69 **NOWHERE TO RUN** (re-issue) *Tamla Motown TMG 694* **42** 3
13 Feb 71 **FORGET ME NOT** *Tamla Motown TMG 762* **11** 8
8 Jan 72 **BLESS YOU** *Tamla Motown TMG 794* **33** 5
23 Jul 88 **NOWHERE TO RUN** (2nd re-issue) *A&M AM 444* **52** 3

[1] Martha and the Vandellas

The listed flip side of 'Nowhere to Run' in 1988 was 'I Got You (I Feel Good)' by James Brown. 'Jimmy Mack' re-entry peaked at No.21 in 1970.

Vic REEVES *UK, male comedian / vocalist – Jim Moir (1 Album: 9 Weeks, 4 Singles: 29 Weeks)*

27 Apr 91 ● **BORN FREE** *Sense SIGH 710* [1] **6** 6
26 Oct 91 ★ **DIZZY** *Sense SIGH 712* [2] **1** 12
16 Nov 91 I WILL CURE YOU *Sense SIGH 111* 16 9
14 Dec 91 **ABIDE WITH ME** *Sense SIGH 713* **47** 3
8 Jul 95 ● **I'M A BELIEVER** *Parlophone CDR 6412* [3] **3** 8

[1] Vic Reeves and The Roman Numerals [2] Vic Reeves and The Wonder Stuff [3] EMF and Reeves and Mortimer

REFLEKT featuring Delline BASS NEW
UK, male production duo – Julian Peake and Seb Fontaine, and female vocalist

5 Mar 05 **NEED TO FEEL LOVED** *Positiva CDTIVS 213* **14** 5

REFLEX featuring MC VIPER (see also 187 LOCKDOWN)
UK, male production duo – Danny Harrison and Julian Jonah and rapper

19 May 01 **PUT YOUR HANDS UP** *Gusto CDGUS 2* **72** 1

Joan REGAN *UK, female vocalist (11 Singles: 62 Weeks)*

11 Dec 53 ● **RICOCHET (re)** *Decca F 10193* [1] **8** 5
14 May 54 ● **SOMEONE ELSE'S ROSES** *Decca F 10257* **5** 8
1 Oct 54 ● **IF I GIVE MY HEART TO YOU (re)** *Decca F 10373* **3** 11
5 Nov 54 **WAIT FOR ME, DARLING** *Decca F 10362* [2] **18** 1
25 Mar 55 ● **PRIZE OF GOLD** *Decca F 10432* **6** 8
6 May 55 **OPEN UP YOUR HEART** *Decca F 10474* [3] **19** 1
1 May 59 ● **MAY YOU ALWAYS** *HMV POP 593* **9** 16
5 Feb 60 **HAPPY ANNIVERSARY (re)** *Pye 7N 15238* **29** 2
28 Jul 60 **PAPA LOVES MAMA** *Pye 7N 15278* **29** 8
24 Nov 60 **ONE OF THE LUCKY ONES** *Pye 7N 15310* **47** 1
5 Jan 61 **IT MUST BE SANTA** *Pye 7N 15303* **42** 1

[1] Joan Regan with The Squadronaires [2] Joan Regan with The Johnston Brothers [3] Joan and Rusty Regan

28 December 1985	4 January 1986	11 January 1986	18 January 1986
MERRY CHRISTMAS EVERYONE Shakin' Stevens	MERRY CHRISTMAS EVERYONE Shakin' Stevens	WEST END GIRLS Pet Shop Boys	WEST END GIRLS Pet Shop Boys
NOW! - THE CHRISTMAS ALBUM Various	NOW THAT'S WHAT I CALL MUSIC! 6 Various	NOW THAT'S WHAT I CALL MUSIC! 6 Various	BROTHERS IN ARMS Dire Straits

KEY: UK No.1 ★ UK Top 10 ● Still on chart + UK entry at No.1 ■ US No.1 ▲ UK million seller £ US million seller $
Singles re-entries are listed as (re), (2re), (3re)... which signifies that the hit re-entered the chart once, twice or three times...
Peak Position / Weeks

The REGENTS
UK, male / female vocal / instrumental group (2 Singles: 14 Weeks)

22 Dec 79 **7 TEEN** *Rialto TREB 111* ... **11** 12
7 Jun 80 **SEE YOU LATER** *Arista ARIST 350* ... **55** 2

REGGAE BOYZ
Jamaica, male vocal / instrumental group

27 Jun 98 **KICK IT** *Universal MCSTD 40167* ... **59** 1

REGGAE PHILHARMONIC ORCHESTRA
UK, male / female vocal / instrumental group (2 Singles: 11 Weeks)

19 Nov 88 **MINNIE THE MOOCHER** *Mango IS 378* ... **35** 9
28 Jul 90 **LOVELY THING** *Mango MNG 742* [1] ... **71** 2

[1] Featuring Jazzy Joyce

REGINA
US, female vocalist – Regina Richards

1 Feb 86 **BABY LOVE** *Funkin' Marvellous MARV 01* ... **50** 3

REID
UK, male vocal group (4 Singles: 12 Weeks)

8 Oct 88 **ONE WAY OUT** *Syncopate SY 16* ... **66** 2
11 Feb 89 **REAL EMOTION** *Syncopate SY 24* ... **65** 2
15 Apr 89 **GOOD TIMES** *Syncopate SY 27* ... **55** 6
21 Oct 89 **LOVIN' ON THE SIDE** *Syncopate REID 1* ... **71** 2

Mike REID
UK, male actor / comedian (2 Singles: 10 Weeks)

22 Mar 75 ● **THE UGLY DUCKLING** *Pye 7N 45434* ... **10** 8
24 Apr 99 **THE MORE I SEE YOU** *Telstar TV CDSTAS 3049* [1] ... **46** 2

[1] Barbara Windsor and Mike Reid

Neil REID
UK, male vocalist (2 Albums: 18 Weeks, 2 Singles: 26 Weeks)

1 Jan 72 ● **MOTHER OF MINE** *Decca F 13264* ... **2** 20
5 Feb 72 ★ NEIL REID *Decca SKL 5122* ... 1 16
8 Apr 72 **THAT'S WHAT I WANT TO BE (re)** *Decca F 13300* ... **45** 6
2 Sep 72 SMILE *Decca SKL 5136* ... 47 2

Keith RELF (see also The YARDBIRDS)
UK, male vocalist, b. 22 Mar 1943, d. 14 May 1976

26 May 66 **MR ZERO** *Columbia DB 7920* ... **50** 1

The REMBRANDTS
US, male vocal / instrumental duo – Danny Wilde and Phil Solem (1 Album: 5 Weeks, 2 Singles: 28 Weeks)

2 Sep 95 ● **I'LL BE THERE FOR YOU (THEME FROM 'FRIENDS') (re)** *East West A 4390CD* ... **3** 27
23 Sep 95 LP *East West 7559617522* ... 14 5
20 Jan 96 **THIS HOUSE IS NOT A HOME** *East West A 4336CD* ... **58** 1

The re-entry of 'I'll Be There For You' made No.5 in May 1997.

REMY ZERO
US, male vocal / instrumental group

27 Apr 02 **SAVE ME** *Elektra E 7297CD* ... **55** 1

RENAISSANCE
UK, male / female vocal (Annie Haslam) / instrumental group (3 Albums: 10 Weeks, 1 Single: 11 Weeks)

21 Feb 70 RENAISSANCE *Island ILPS 9114* ... 60 1
15 Jul 78 ● **NORTHERN LIGHTS** *Warner Bros. K 17177* ... **10** 11
19 Aug 78 A SONG FOR ALL SEASONS *Warner Bros. K 56460* ... 35 8
2 Jun 79 AZUR D'OR *Warner Bros. K 56633* ... 73 1

RENÉ and ANGELA
US, male / female vocal duo – René Moore and Angela Winbush (3 Singles: 15 Weeks)

15 Jun 85 **SAVE YOUR LOVE (FOR #1)** *Club JAB 14* [1] ... **66** 2
7 Sep 85 **I'LL BE GOOD** *Club JAB 18* ... **22** 10
2 Nov 85 **SECRET RENDEZVOUS** *Champion CHAMP 5* ... **54** 3

[1] René and Angela featuring Kurtis Blow

RENÉ and YVETTE
UK, male / female TV characters / vocal duo

22 Nov 86 **JE T'AIME ('ALLO 'ALLO) / RENÉ DMC (DEVASTATING MACHO CHARISMA)** *Sedition EDIT 3319* ... **57** 4

Nicole RENÉE
US, female vocalist

12 Dec 98 **STRAWBERRY** *Atlantic AT 0050CD* ... **55** 1

RENÉE and RENATO
UK / Italy, female / male vocal duo – Hilary Lester and Renato Pagliari (1 Album: 14 Weeks, 2 Singles: 22 Weeks)

30 Oct 82 ★ **SAVE YOUR LOVE** *Hollywood HWD 003* ... **1** 16
25 Dec 82 SAVE YOUR LOVE *Lifestyle LEG 9* [1] ... 26 14
12 Feb 83 **JUST ONE MORE KISS** *Hollywood HWD 006* ... **48** 6

[1] Renato

RENEGADE SOUNDWAVE
UK, male vocal / instrumental group (1 Album: 1 Week, 2 Singles: 7 Weeks)

3 Feb 90 **PROBABLY A ROBBERY** *Mute MUTE 102* ... **38** 6
24 Mar 90 SOUNDCLASH *Mute STUMM 63* ... 74 1
5 Feb 94 **RENEGADE SOUNDWAVE** *Mute CDMUTE 146* ... **64** 1

REPARATA and The DELRONS
US, female vocal group (2 Singles: 12 Weeks)

20 Mar 68 **CAPTAIN OF YOUR SHIP** *Bell 1002* ... **13** 10
18 Oct 75 **SHOES** *Dart 2066 562* [1] ... **43** 2

[1] Reparata

REPUBLICA
UK / Nigeria, female / male vocal (Samantha Sprackling aka Saffron) / instrumental group (2 Albums: 38 Weeks, 4 Singles: 18 Weeks)

27 Apr 96 **READY TO GO** *Deconstruction 74321326132* ... **43** 2
1 Mar 97 **READY TO GO** (re-issue) *Deconstruction 74321421332* ... **13** 6
15 Mar 97 ● REPUBLICA *Deconstruction 74321410522* ... 4 36
3 May 97 ● **DROP DEAD GORGEOUS** *Deconstruction 74321408442* ... **7** 7
3 Oct 98 **FROM RUSH HOUR WITH LOVE** *Deconstruction 74321610472* ... **20** 3
17 Oct 98 SPEED BALLADS *Deconstruction 74321610462* ... 37 2

The RESEARCH
UK, male vocal / instrumental group (3 Singles: 3 Weeks)

27 Nov 04 **SHE'S NOT LEAVING** *At Large FUGCD 005* ... **73** 1
3 Sep 05 **C'MON CHAMELEON / I LOVE YOU, BUT** *At Large FUGCD 008* ... **63** 1
29 Oct 05 **THE WAY YOU USED TO SMILE** *At Large FUGCD 010* ... **66** 1

RESONANCE featuring The BURRELLS
US, male producer and vocal duo

26 May 01 **DJ** *Strictly Rhythm SRUKCD 02* ... **67** 1

RESOURCE
Germany, male production / vocal group

31 May 03 **(I JUST) DIED IN YOUR ARMS** *Substance SUBS 17CDS* ... **42** 2

REST ASSURED
(see also GAT DECOR; PHUNKY PHANTOM) *UK, male production trio*

28 Feb 98 **TREAT INFAMY** *ffrr FCD 333* ... **14** 7

REUBEN
UK, male vocal / instrumental trio (4 Singles: 4 Weeks)

19 Jun 04 **FREDDY KREUGER** *Xtra Mile XMR 102* ... **53** 1
28 Aug 04 **MOVING TO BLACKWATER** *Xtra Mile XMR 104* ... **59** 1
25 Jun 05 **A KICK IN THE MOUTH** *Xtra Mile XMR 108* ... **58** 1
17 Sep 05 **KEEP IT TO YOURSELF** *Xtra Mile XMR 109* ... **62** 1

	25 January 1986	1 February 1986	8 February 1986	15 February 1986
UK No.1 SINGLES	THE SUN ALWAYS SHINES ON TV A-ha	THE SUN ALWAYS SHINES ON TV A-ha	WHEN THE GOING GETS TOUGH, THE TOUGH GET GOING Billy Ocean	WHEN THE GOING GETS TOUGH, THE TOUGH GET GOING Billy Ocean
UK No.1 ALBUMS	BROTHERS IN ARMS Dire Straits	BROTHERS IN ARMS Dire Straits	BROTHERS IN ARMS Dire Straits	BROTHERS IN ARMS Dire Straits

REUNION *US, male vocal group*

21 Sep 74 **LIFE IS A ROCK (BUT THE RADIO ROLLED ME)** *RCA PB 10056* 33 4

REVELATION *UK, male / female production / vocal group*

10 May 03 **JUST BE DUB TO ME** *Multiply CDMULTY 99* 36 2

REVIVAL 3000 *UK, male DJ / production trio*

1 Nov 97 **THE MIGHTY HIGH** *Hi-Life 5718092* 47 1

REVOLTING COCKS

(see also MINISTRY) *US, male vocal / instrumental group*

18 Sep 93 **DA YA THINK I'M SEXY** *Devotion CDDVN 111* 61 1
2 Oct 93 LINGER FICKEN' GOOD *Devotion CDDVN 22* 39 1

Debbie REYNOLDS *US, female actor / vocalist – Mary Reynolds*

30 Aug 57 ● **TAMMY** *Vogue-Coral Q 72274* ▲ $ 2 17

Jody REYNOLDS *US, male vocalist*

14 Apr 79 **ENDLESS SLEEP** *Lightning LIG 9015* 66 1

'Endless Sleep' was coupled with 'To Know Him Is to Love Him' by The Teddy Bears as a double A-side.

LJ REYNOLDS *US, male vocalist – Larry Reynolds*

30 Jun 84 **DON'T LET NOBODY HOLD YOU DOWN** *Club JAB 5* 53 3

The REYNOLDS GIRLS *UK, female vocal duo – Linda and Aisling Reynolds*

25 Feb 89 ● **I'D RATHER JACK** *PWL PWL 25* 8 12

The REZILLOS *UK, male / female vocal / instrumental group (2 Albums: 15 Weeks, 4 Singles: 21 Weeks)*

5 Aug 78 CAN'T STAND THE REZILLOS *Sire WEA K 56530* 16 10
12 Aug 78 **TOP OF THE POPS** *Sire SIR 4001* 17 9
25 Nov 78 **DESTINATION VENUS** *Sire SIR 4008* 43 4
28 Apr 79 MISSION ACCOMPLISHED BUT THE BEAT GOES ON *Sire SRK 6069* 30 5
18 Aug 79 **I WANNA BE YOUR MAN / I CAN'T STAND MY BABY (re)** *Sensible SAB 1* 71 2
26 Jan 80 **MOTORBIKE BEAT** *DinDisc DIN 5* [1] 45 6

[1] The Revillos

REZONANCE Q (see also EYEOPENER)

UK, male / female production / vocal duo – Mike Di Scala and Nanzene

1 Mar 03 **SOMEDAY** *All Around the World CDGLOBE 266* 29 2

RHIANNA *UK, female vocalist – Rhianna Kelly (2 Singles: 6 Weeks)*

1 Jun 02 **OH BABY** *S2 6726232* 18 5
14 Sep 02 **WORD LOVE** *S2 6730112* 41 1

RHODA with the SPECIAL AKA (see also The SPECIALS)

UK, female vocalist and male vocal / instrumental group

23 Jan 82 **THE BOILER** *2 Tone CHSTT 18* 35 5

Busta RHYMES (see also Syleena JOHNSON)

US, male rapper – Trevor Smith (6 Albums: 21 Weeks, 22 Singles: 113 Weeks)

30 Mar 96 THE COMING *Elektra 7559617422* 48 4
11 May 96 ● **WOO-HAH!! GOT YOU ALL IN CHECK** *Elektra EKR 220CD* $ 8 7
21 Sep 96 **IT'S A PARTY** *Elektra EKR 226CD* [1] 23 2
5 Apr 97 ● **HIT EM HIGH (THE MONSTARS' ANTHEM)** *Atlantic A 5449CD* [2] 8 6
3 May 97 **DO MY THING** *Elektra EKR 235CD* 39 1
4 Oct 97 WHEN DISASTER STRIKES ... *Elektra 7559621542* 34 5
18 Oct 97 **PUT YOUR HANDS WHERE MY EYES COULD SEE** *Elektra E 3900CD* 16 3
20 Dec 97 **DANGEROUS** *Elektra E 3877CD* 32 4
18 Apr 98 ● **TURN IT UP / FIRE IT UP** *Elektra E 3847CD* 2 10
11 Jul 98 **ONE** *Elektra E 3833CD 1* [3] 23 3
16 Jan 99 EXTINCTION LEVEL EVENT / FINAL WORLD FRONT *Elektra 7559622112* 54 7
30 Jan 99 ● **GIMME SOME MORE** *Elektra E 3782CD* 5 6
1 May 99 ● **WHAT'S IT GONNA BE?!** *Elektra E 3762CD 1* [4] 6 7
1 Jul 00 ANARCHY *Elektra 7559625172* 38 1
22 Jul 00 **GET OUT** *Elektra E 7075CD* 57 1
16 Dec 00 **FIRE** *East West E 7136* 60 1
18 Aug 01 ● **ANTE UP (re)** *Epic 6717882* [5] 7 8
29 Sep 01 TURN IT UP! – THE VERY BEST *Elektra 8122735802* 44 3
16 Mar 02 **BREAK YA NECK** *J 74321922332* 11 6
23 Mar 02 GENESIS *J 80813200092* 58 1
8 Jun 02 **PASS THE COURVOISIER – PART II (re)** *J 74321937902* [6] 16 8
8 Feb 03 **MAKE IT CLAP** *J 82876502062* [7] 16 4
7 Jun 03 ● **I KNOW WHAT YOU WANT** *J 82876528292* [8] 3 13
29 Nov 03 **LIGHT YOUR ASS ON FIRE** *Arista 82876572512* [9] 62 1
22 May 04 **WHAT'S HAPPENIN'** *Def Jam 9862517* [10] 17 5
10 Sep 05 **DON'T CHA** (import) *A&M AMB 000468322* [11] 44 1
17 Sep 05 ★ **DON'T CHA** *A&M 9885051* [11] ■ ....1 16+

[1] Busta Rhymes featuring Zhané [2] B Real / Busta Rhymes / Coolio / LL Cool J / Method Man [3] Busta Rhymes featuring Erykah Badu [4] Busta Rhymes featuring Janet [5] MOP featuring Busta Rhymes [6] Busta Rhymes featuring P Diddy and Pharrell [7] Busta Rhymes featuring Spliff Star [8] Busta Rhymes and Mariah Carey featuring The Flipmode Squad [9] Busta Rhymes featuring Pharrell [10] Method Man featuring Busta Rhymes [11] Pussycat Dolls featuring Busta Rhymes

Dylan RHYMES featuring K. ELLIS NEW (see also RUFF DRIVERZ)

UK, male producer and female vocalist – Marvin Beaver and Katherine Ellis

29 Jan 05 **SALTY** *Kingsize KS 93* 70 1

RHYTHIM IS RHYTHIM *US, male producer – Derrick May*

11 Nov 89 **STRINGS OF LIFE** *Kool Kat KOOL 509* 74 1

RHYTHM ETERNITY *UK, male / female vocal / instrumental group*

23 May 92 **PINK CHAMPAGNE** *Dead Dead Good GOOD 15T* 72 1

RHYTHM FACTOR *US, male / female vocal / instrumental group*

29 Apr 95 **YOU BRING ME JOY** *Multiply CDMULTY 4* 53 2

RHYTHM MASTERS

(see also BIG ROOM GIRL featuring Darryl PANDY; RHYTHMATIC JUNKIES) *UK / Malta, male DJ / production duo (4 Singles: 4 Weeks)*

16 Aug 97 **COME ON Y'ALL** *Faze 2 CDFAZE 37* 49 1
6 Dec 97 **ENTER THE SCENE** *Distinctive DISNCD 40* [1] 49 1
18 Aug 01 **UNDERGROUND** *Black & Blue NEOCD 056* 50 1
30 Mar 02 **GHETTO** *Black & Blue NEOCD 074* [2] 71 1

[1] DJ Supreme vs Rhythm Masters [2] Rhythm Masters featuring Joe Watson

RHYTHM-N-BASS *UK, male vocal group (2 Singles: 4 Weeks)*

19 Sep 92 **ROSES** *Epic 6582907* 56 2
3 Jul 93 **CAN'T STOP THIS FEELING** *Epic 6592002* 59 2

RHYTHM OF LIFE *UK, male DJ / producer – Steve Burgess*

13 May 00 **YOU PUT ME IN HEAVEN WITH YOUR TOUCH** *Xtravaganza XTRAV 4CDS* 24 2

RHYTHM ON THE LOOSE *UK, male producer – Geoff Hibbert*

19 Aug 95 **BREAK OF DAWN** *Six6 SIXCD 126* 36 2

RHYTHM QUEST *UK, male producer – Mark Hadfield*

20 Jun 92 **CLOSER TO ALL YOUR DREAMS** *Network NWK 40* 45 2

RHYTHM SECTION *UK, male vocal / instrumental group*

18 Jul 92 **MIDSUMMER MADNESS (EP)** *Rhythm Section RSEC 006* 66 1

22 February 1986	1 March 1986	8 March 1986	15 March 1986
WHEN THE GOING GETS TOUGH, THE TOUGH GET GOING Billy Ocean	**WHEN THE GOING GETS TOUGH, THE TOUGH GET GOING** Billy Ocean	**CHAIN REACTION** Diana Ross	**CHAIN REACTION** Diana Ross
BROTHERS IN ARMS Dire Straits	**BROTHERS IN ARMS** Dire Straits	**BROTHERS IN ARMS** Dire Straits	**BROTHERS IN ARMS** Dire Straits

KEY UK No.1 ★ UK Top 10 ● Still on chart + UK entry at No.1 ■ US No.1 ▲ UK million seller £ US million seller $ Singles re-entries are listed as (re), (2re), (3re)... which signifies that the hit re-entered the chart once, twice or three times... Peak Position / Weeks

RHYTHM SOURCE *UK, male / female vocal / instrumental group*

17 Jun 95 **LOVE SHINE** *A&M 5810672*......74 1

RHYTHMATIC *UK, male instrumental / production duo (2 Singles: 3 Weeks)*

12 May 90 **TAKE ME BACK (re)** *Network NWK 8*......71 2
3 Nov 90 **FREQUENCY** *Network NWK 13*......62 1

RHYTHMATIC JUNKIES *UK, male vocal / production group*

15 May 99 **THE FEELIN (CLAP YOUR HANDS)** *Sound of Ministry RIDE 2CDS*......67 1

RHYTHMKILLAZ (see also CHOCOLATE PUMA; GOODMEN; JARK PRONGO; RIVA featuring Dannii MINOGUE; TOMBA VIRA)

Holland, male production duo – Rene ter Horst and Gaston Steenkist

31 Mar 01 **WACK ASS MF** *Incentive CENT 18CDS*......32 2

RIALTO

UK, male vocal / instrumental group (1 Album: 3 Weeks, 4 Singles: 8 Weeks)

8 Nov 97 **MONDAY MORNING 5:19** *East West EW 116CD*......37 2
17 Jan 98 **UNTOUCHABLE** *East West EW 107CD 1*......20 3
28 Mar 98 **DREAM ANOTHER DREAM** *East West EW 156CD 1*......39 2
25 Jul 98 RIALTO *China WOLCD 1086*......21 3
17 Oct 98 **SUMMER'S OVER** *China WOKCDR 2099*......60 1

Rosie RIBBONS *UK, female vocalist (2 Singles: 7 Weeks)*

2 Nov 02 **BLINK** *T2 / Telstar CDSTAS 3288*......12 4
25 Jan 03 **A LITTLE BIT** *T2 / Telstar CDSTAS 3312*......19 3

Reva RICE and Greg ELLIS *UK, male / female vocal duo*

27 Mar 93 **NEXT TIME YOU FALL IN LOVE** *Really Useful RURCD 12*......59 2

Damien RICE

Ireland, male vocalist / guitarist (1 Album: 97 Weeks, 5 Singles: 20 Weeks)

2 Aug 03 ● O *DRM / 14th Floor DRM 002CD*......8 97
1 Nov 03 **CANNONBALL** *DRM / 14th Floor DR 03CD1*......32 2
17 Jul 04 **CANNONBALL** (re-mix) **(re)** *DRM / 14th Floor DR 03CD2*......19 7
25 Dec 04 **THE BLOWERS DAUGHTER** *14th Floor DR 06CD*......27 5
2 Apr 05 **VOLCANO** *DRM / 14th Floor DR 07CD2*......29 3
2 Jul 05 **UNPLAYED PIANO** *DRM / 14th Floor DR 08CD* [1]......24 3

[1] Damien Rice & Lisa Hannigan

The re-mix of 'Cannonball' was released on two CDs, the first featuring a 'radio mix' and the second a live version. O returned to its peak position in Jan 2005.

Charlie RICH *US, male vocalist / keyboard player, b. 14 Dec 1932, d. 25 July 1995 (2 Albums: 28 Weeks, 3 Singles: 29 Weeks)*

16 Feb 74 ● **THE MOST BEAUTIFUL GIRL** *Epic EPC 1897* ▲ $......2 14
23 Mar 74 ● BEHIND CLOSED DOORS *Epic 65716*......4 26
13 Apr 74 **BEHIND CLOSED DOORS** *Epic EPC 1539* $......16 10
13 Jul 74 VERY SPECIAL LOVE SONGS *Epic 80031*......34 2
1 Feb 75 **WE LOVE EACH OTHER** *Epic EPC 2868*......37 5

The RICH KIDS *UK, male vocal / instrumental group*

28 Jan 78 **RICH KIDS** *EMI 2738*......24 5
7 Oct 78 GHOSTS OF PRINCES IN TOWERS *EMI EMC 3263*......51 1

Richie RICH *UK, male DJ / producer – Richard Morgan (1 Album: 1 Week, 6 Singles: 16 Weeks)*

16 Jul 88 **TURN IT UP** *Club JAB 68*......48 3
22 Oct 88 **I'LL HOUSE YOU** *Gee Street GEE 003* [1]......22 5
10 Dec 88 **MY DJ (PUMP IT UP SOME)** *Gee Street GEE 7*......74 1
22 Jul 89 I CAN MAKE YOU DANCE *Gee Street GEEA 3*......65 1
2 Sep 89 **SALSA HOUSE** *ffrr F 113*......50 3
9 Mar 91 **YOU USED TO SALSA** *ffrr F 156* [2]......52 3
29 Mar 97 **STAY WITH ME** *Castle CATX 1001* [3]......58 1

[1] Richie Rich meets The Jungle Brothers [2] Richie Rich featuring Ralphi Rosario [3] Richie Rich and Esera Tuaolo

'You Used to Salsa' is a re-mix of 'Salsa House'.

Tony RICH PROJECT

US, male vocalist – Antonio Jeffries (1 Album: 10 Weeks, 3 Singles: 22 Weeks)

4 May 96 ● **NOBODY KNOWS** *LaFace 74321356422* $......4 17
25 May 96 WORDS *LaFace 73008260222*......27 10
31 Aug 96 **LIKE A WOMAN** *LaFace 74321401612*......27 4
14 Dec 96 **LEAVIN'** *LaFace 74321438382*......52 1

Cliff RICHARD (2 Top 500)

'The Peter Pan of Pop' – Britain's most successful solo vocalist, b. Harry Webb, 14 Oct 1940, Lucknow, India. Ex-member of The Dick Teague Skiffle Group was instantly successful and almost overnight became the UK's No.1 rock 'n' roll star, despite bad press due to "too sexy" live performances. He has had more different chart singles than any other artist, more than 760 hit singles worldwide and was the first UK act named World's No.1 Artist by Billboard (1963): Elvis was second and The Shadows third. Between 1959 and 2005, Cliff had a staggering 37 Top 10 albums, including seven No.1s, and had more Top 10 albums in the 1980s than any other artist. He was brought to a wider audience by a successful series of films, including Summer Holiday, was seen on the first Top of the Pops and has appeared on the TV show more than any other solo artist. He is one of the few performers to top the chart with two different recordings of the same song ('Living Doll'). This seemingly ageless entertainer's record number of 66 Top 10 singles entries spans 46 years, and at times he held the record for being the youngest (1959) and oldest (1999) British singer to top the chart. Cliff, who has sold more than 260 million records (singles, albums, EPs) worldwide, was awarded the Outstanding Contribution to British Music trophy at the 1989 BRITs, was made an OBE in 1980, was knighted in 1995, and holds the unique achievement of a UK No.1 single in five different decades. Cliff was inducted into the UK Music Hall of Fame in 2004. Best-selling single: 'The Young Ones' 1,052,000 (58 Albums: 819 Weeks, 130 Singles: 1166 Weeks)

12 Sep 58 ● **MOVE IT!** *Columbia DB 4178* [1]......2 17
21 Nov 58 ● **HIGH CLASS BABY** *Columbia DB 4203* [1]......7 10
30 Jan 59 **LIVIN' LOVIN' DOLL** *Columbia DB 4249* [1]......20 6
18 Apr 59 ● CLIFF *Columbia 33SX 1147* [1]......4 31
8 May 59 ● **MEAN STREAK** *Columbia DB 4290 A* [1]......10 9
15 May 59 **NEVER MIND** *Columbia DB 4290 B* [1]......21 2
10 Jul 59 ★ **LIVING DOLL (2re)** *Columbia DB 4306* [1]......1 23
9 Oct 59 ★ **TRAVELLIN' LIGHT** *Columbia DB 4351 B* [2]......1 17
9 Oct 59 **DYNAMITE (re)** *Columbia DB 4351 A* [2]......16 4
14 Nov 59 ● CLIFF SINGS *Columbia 33SX 1192* [2]......2 36
15 Jan 60 **EXPRESSO BONGO (EP)** *Columbia SEG 7971* [2]......14 7
22 Jan 60 ● **A VOICE IN THE WILDERNESS (re)** *Columbia DB 4398* [2]......2 16
24 Mar 60 ● **FALL IN LOVE WITH YOU** *Columbia DB 4431* [2]......2 15
30 Jun 60 ★ **PLEASE DON'T TEASE** *Columbia DB 4479* [2]......1 18
22 Sep 60 ● **NINE TIMES OUT OF TEN** *Columbia DB 4506* [2]......3 12
15 Oct 60 ● ME AND MY SHADOWS *Columbia 33SX 1261* [2]......2 33
1 Dec 60 ★ **I LOVE YOU** *Columbia DB 4547* [2]......1 16
2 Mar 61 ● **THEME FOR A DREAM** *Columbia DB 4593* [2]......3 14
30 Mar 61 ● **GEE WHIZ IT'S YOU** *Columbia DC 756* [2]......4 14
22 Apr 61 ● LISTEN TO CLIFF *Columbia 33SX 1320*......2 28
22 Jun 61 ● **A GIRL LIKE YOU** *Columbia DB 4667* [2]......3 14
19 Oct 61 ● **WHEN THE GIRL IN YOUR ARMS IS THE GIRL IN YOUR HEART** *Columbia DB 4716*......3 15
21 Oct 61 ★ 21 TODAY *Columbia 33SX 1368* [3]......1 16
23 Dec 61 ★ THE YOUNG ONES (FILM SOUNDTRACK) *Columbia 33SX 1384* [4]......1 42
11 Jan 62 ★ **THE YOUNG ONES** *Columbia DB 4761* [2] ■ £......1 21

10 May 62 ● I'M LOOKING OUT THE WINDOW / DO YOU WANT TO DANCE *Columbia DB 4828* 3 .... 2 17
6 Sep 62 ● IT'LL BE ME *Columbia DB 4886* 2 .... 2 12
29 Sep 62 ● 32 MINUTES AND 17 SECONDS *Columbia 33SX 1431* 2 .... 3 21
6 Dec 62 ★ THE NEXT TIME / BACHELOR BOY *Columbia DB 4950* 2 .... 1 18
26 Jan 63 ★ SUMMER HOLIDAY (FILM SOUNDTRACK) *Columbia 33SX 1472* 2 .... 1 36
21 Feb 63 ★ SUMMER HOLIDAY *Columbia DB 4977* 2 .... 1 18
9 May 63 ● LUCKY LIPS *Columbia DB 7034* 2 .... 4 15
13 Jul 63 ● CLIFF'S HIT ALBUM *Columbia 33SX 1512* 2 .... 2 19
22 Aug 63 ● IT'S ALL IN THE GAME *Columbia DB 7089* 2 13
28 Sep 63 ● WHEN IN SPAIN *Columbia 33SX 1541* 2 .... 8 10
7 Nov 63 ● DON'T TALK TO HIM (re) *Columbia DB 7150* 2 .... 2 14
6 Feb 64 ● I'M THE LONELY ONE *Columbia DB 7203* 2 .... 8 10
30 Apr 64 ● CONSTANTLY *Columbia DB 7272* 4 13
2 Jul 64 ● ON THE BEACH *Columbia DB 7305* 2 .... 7 13
11 Jul 64 ● WONDERFUL LIFE (FILM SOUNDTRACK) *Columbia 33SX 1628* 2 .... 2 23
8 Oct 64 ● THE TWELFTH OF NEVER *Columbia DB 7372* 8 11
10 Dec 64 ● I COULD EASILY FALL *Columbia DB 7420* 2 .... 6 11
9 Jan 65 HITS FROM ALADDIN AND HIS WONDERFUL LAMP (PANTOMIME) *Columbia 33SX 1676* 2 .... 13 5
11 Mar 65 ★ THE MINUTE YOU'RE GONE *Columbia DB 7496* 1 14
17 Apr 65 ● CLIFF RICHARD *Columbia 33SX 1709* 5 .... 9 5
10 Jun 65 ON MY WORD *Columbia DB 7596* 12 10
14 Aug 65 MORE HITS BY CLIFF *Columbia 33SX 1737* 20 1
19 Aug 65 THE TIME IN BETWEEN *Columbia DB 7660* 2 .... 22 8
4 Nov 65 ● WIND ME UP (LET ME GO) *Columbia DB 7745* 2 16
8 Jan 66 LOVE IS FOREVER *Columbia 33SX 1769* 19 1
24 Mar 66 BLUE TURNS TO GREY *Columbia DB 7866* 2 .... 15 9
21 May 66 ● KINDA LATIN *Columbia SX 6039* 9 12
21 Jul 66 ● VISIONS *Columbia DB 7968* 7 12
13 Oct 66 ● TIME DRAGS BY *Columbia DB 8017* 2 .... 10 11
15 Dec 66 ● IN THE COUNTRY *Columbia DB 8094* 2 .... 6 10
17 Dec 66 ● FINDERS KEEPERS (FILM SOUNDTRACK) *Columbia SX 6079* 2 .... 6 18
7 Jan 67 CINDERELLA (PANTOMIME) *Columbia 33SX 6103* 2 .... 30 6
16 Mar 67 ● IT'S ALL OVER *Columbia DB 8150* 9 10
15 Apr 67 DON'T STOP ME NOW! *Columbia SCX 6133* 23 9
8 Jun 67 I'LL COME RUNNIN' *Columbia DB 8210* 26 8
16 Aug 67 ● THE DAY I MET MARIE *Columbia DB 8245* 10 14
11 Nov 67 GOOD NEWS *Columbia SCX 6167* 37 1
15 Nov 67 ● ALL MY LOVE *Columbia DB 8293* 6 12
20 Mar 68 ★ CONGRATULATIONS *Columbia DB 8376* 1 13
1 Jun 68 CLIFF IN JAPAN *Columbia SCX 6244* 29 2
26 Jun 68 I'LL LOVE YOU FOREVER TODAY *Columbia DB 8437* 27 6
25 Sep 68 MARIANNE *Columbia DB 8476* 22 8
16 Nov 68 ESTABLISHED 1958 *Columbia SCX 6282* 2 .... 30 4
27 Nov 68 DON'T FORGET TO CATCH ME *Columbia DB 8503* 2 .... 21 10
26 Feb 69 GOOD TIMES (BETTER TIMES) *Columbia DB 8548* 12 11
28 May 69 ● BIG SHIP *Columbia DB 8581* 8 10
12 Jul 69 ● THE BEST OF CLIFF *Columbia SCX 6343* 5 17
13 Sep 69 ● THROW DOWN A LINE *Columbia DB 8615* 4 .... 7 9
27 Sep 69 SINCERELY *Columbia SCX 6357* 24 3
6 Dec 69 WITH THE EYES OF A CHILD *Columbia DB 8641* 20 11
21 Feb 70 THE JOY OF LIVING *Columbia DB 8657* 4 .... 25 8
6 Jun 70 ● GOODBYE SAM, HELLO SAMANTHA *Columbia DB 8685* 6 15
5 Sep 70 I AIN'T GOT TIME ANYMORE *Columbia DB 8708* 21 7
12 Dec 70 TRACKS 'N' GROOVES *Columbia SCX 6435* 37 2
23 Jan 71 SUNNY HONEY GIRL *Columbia DB 8747* 19 8
10 Apr 71 SILVERY RAIN *Columbia DB 8774* 27 6
17 Jul 71 FLYING MACHINE *Columbia DB 8797* 37 7
13 Nov 71 SING A SONG OF FREEDOM *Columbia DB 8836* 13 12
11 Mar 72 JESUS *Columbia DB 8864* 35 3
26 Aug 72 LIVING IN HARMONY *Columbia DB 8917* 12 10
23 Dec 72 THE BEST OF CLIFF VOLUME 2 *Columbia SCX 6519* 49 2
17 Mar 73 ● POWER TO ALL OUR FRIENDS *EMI 2012* 4 12
12 May 73 HELP IT ALONG / TOMORROW RISING *EMI 2022* 29 6
1 Dec 73 TAKE ME HIGH *EMI 2088* 27 12
19 Jan 74 TAKE ME HIGH (FILM SOUNDTRACK) *EMI EMC 3016* 41 4
18 May 74 (YOU KEEP ME) HANGIN' ON *EMI 2150* 13 8
7 Feb 76 MISS YOU NIGHTS *EMI 2376* 15 10
8 May 76 ● DEVIL WOMAN *EMI 2458* $ 9 8
29 May 76 ● I'M NEARLY FAMOUS *EMI EMC 3122* 5 21
21 Aug 76 I CAN'T ASK FOR ANYTHING MORE THAN YOU *EMI 2499* 17 8
4 Dec 76 HEY MR DREAM MAKER *EMI 2559* 31 5
5 Mar 77 MY KINDA LIFE *EMI 2584* 15 8
26 Mar 77 ● EVERY FACE TELLS A STORY *EMI EMC 3172* 8 10
16 Jul 77 WHEN TWO WORLDS DRIFT APART *EMI 2633* 46 3
22 Oct 77 ★ 40 GOLDEN GREATS *EMI EMTV 6* 1 19
4 Mar 78 SMALL CORNERS *EMI EMC 3219* 33 5
21 Oct 78 GREEN LIGHT *EMI EMC 3231* 25 3
17 Feb 79 ● THANK YOU VERY MUCH – REUNION CONCERT AT THE LONDON PALLADIUM *EMI EMTV 15* 2 .... 5 12
31 Mar 79 GREEN LIGHT *EMI 2920* 57 3
21 Jul 79 ★ WE DON'T TALK ANYMORE *EMI 2975* 1 14
15 Sep 79 ● ROCK 'N' ROLL JUVENILE *EMI EMC 3307* 3 22
3 Nov 79 HOT SHOT *EMI 5003* 46 5
2 Feb 80 ● CARRIE *EMI 5006* 4 10
16 Aug 80 ● DREAMIN' *EMI 5095* 8 10
13 Sep 80 ● I'M NO HERO *EMI EMA 796* 4 12
25 Oct 80 SUDDENLY *Jet 7002* 5 .... 15 7
24 Jan 81 A LITTLE IN LOVE *EMI 5123* 15 8
4 Jul 81 ★ LOVE SONGS *EMI EMTV 27* 1 43
29 Aug 81 ● WIRED FOR SOUND *EMI 5221* 4 9
26 Sep 81 ● WIRED FOR SOUND *EMI EMC 3377* 4 25
21 Nov 81 ● DADDY'S HOME *EMI 5251* 2 12
17 Jul 82 ● THE ONLY WAY OUT *EMI 5318* 10 9
4 Sep 82 ● NOW YOU SEE ME ... NOW YOU DON'T *EMI EMC 3415* 4 14
25 Sep 82 WHERE DO WE GO FROM HERE *EMI 5341* 60 3
4 Dec 82 LITTLE TOWN *EMI 5348* 11 7
19 Feb 83 ● SHE MEANS NOTHING TO ME *Capitol CL 276* 6 .... 9 9
16 Apr 83 ● TRUE LOVE WAYS *EMI 5385* 7 .... 8 8
21 May 83 ● DRESSED FOR THE OCCASION *EMI EMC 3432* 6 .... 7 17
4 Jun 83 DRIFTING *DJM SHEIL 1* 8 .... 64 2
3 Sep 83 NEVER SAY DIE (GIVE A LITTLE BIT MORE) *EMI 5415* 15 7
15 Oct 83 ● SILVER *EMI EMC 1077871* 7 24
26 Nov 83 ● PLEASE DON'T FALL IN LOVE *EMI 5437* 7 9
31 Mar 84 BABY YOU'RE DYNAMITE / OCEAN DEEP (re) *EMI 5457* 27 7
14 Jul 84 20 ORIGINAL GREATS *EMI CRS 1* 2 .... 43 6
3 Nov 84 SHOOTING FROM THE HEART *EMI RICH 1* 51 4
1 Dec 84 THE ROCK CONNECTION *EMI CLIF 2* 43 5
9 Feb 85 HEART USER *EMI RICH 2* 46 3
14 Sep 85 SHE'S SO BEAUTIFUL *EMI 5531* 17 9
7 Dec 85 IT'S IN EVERY ONE OF US *EMI 5537* 45 6
22 Mar 86 ★ LIVING DOLL *WEA YZ 65* 9 .... 1 11
4 Oct 86 ● ALL I ASK OF YOU *Polydor POSP 802* 10 .... 3 16
29 Nov 86 SLOW RIVERS *Rocket EJS 13* 11 .... 44 8
20 Jun 87 ● MY PRETTY ONE *EMI EM 4* 6 10
29 Aug 87 ● SOME PEOPLE *EMI EM 18* 3 10
26 Sep 87 ● ALWAYS GUARANTEED *EMI EMD 1004* 5 25
31 Oct 87 REMEMBER ME *EMI EM 31* 35 4
13 Feb 88 TWO HEARTS *EMI EM 42* 34 3
19 Nov 88 ★ PRIVATE COLLECTION 1979-1988 *EMI CRTV 30* 1 26
3 Dec 88 ★ MISTLETOE AND WINE *EMI EM 78* 1 8
10 Jun 89 ● THE BEST OF ME *EMI EM 92* 2 7
26 Aug 89 ● I JUST DON'T HAVE THE HEART *EMI EM 101* 3 8
14 Oct 89 LEAN ON YOU *EMI EM 105* 17 6
11 Nov 89 ● STRONGER *EMI EMD 1012* 7 21
9 Dec 89 WHENEVER GOD SHINES HIS LIGHT *Polydor VANS 2* 12 .... 20 6
24 Feb 90 STRONGER THAN THAT *EMI EM 129* 14 5
25 Aug 90 ● SILHOUETTES *EMI EM 152* 10 7
13 Oct 90 FROM A DISTANCE *EMI EM 155* 11 6
17 Nov 90 ● FROM A DISTANCE ... THE EVENT *EMI CRTV 31* 3 15
8 Dec 90 ★ SAVIOUR'S DAY *EMI XMAS 90* 1 7
14 Sep 91 MORE TO LIFE *EMI EM 205* 23 5
30 Nov 91 ● TOGETHER WITH CLIFF RICHARD *EMI EMD 1028* 10 7
7 Dec 91 ● WE SHOULD BE TOGETHER *EMI XMAS 91* 10 6
11 Jan 92 THIS NEW YEAR *EMI EMS 218* 30 2
5 Dec 92 ● I STILL BELIEVE IN YOU *EMI EM 255* 7 6
27 Mar 93 ● PEACE IN OUR TIME *EMI CDEM 265* 8 5
1 May 93 ★ THE ALBUM *EMI CDEMD 1043* ■ 1 15

19 April 1986	26 April 1986	3 May 1986	10 May 1986
A DIFFERENT CORNER George Michael	A DIFFERENT CORNER George Michael	A DIFFERENT CORNER George Michael	ROCK ME AMADEUS Falco
HITS 4 Various	STREET LIFE - 20 GREAT HITS Bryan Ferry and Roxy Music	STREET LIFE - 20 GREAT HITS Bryan Ferry and Roxy Music	STREET LIFE - 20 GREAT HITS Bryan Ferry and Roxy Music

KEY UK No.1 ★ UK Top 10 ● Still on chart + UK entry at No.1 ■ US No.1 ▲ UK million seller £ US million seller $
Singles re-entries are listed as (re), (2re), (3re)... which signifies that the hit re-entered the chart once, twice or three times...
Peak Position / Weeks

12 Jun 93 **HUMAN WORK OF ART** *EMI CDEM 267* ... 24 4
2 Oct 93 **NEVER LET GO** *EMI CDEM 281* ... 32 3
18 Dec 93 **HEALING LOVE** *EMI CDEM 294* ... 19 5
15 Oct 94 ● THE HIT LIST *EMI CDEMTV 84* ... 3 21
10 Dec 94 **ALL I HAVE TO DO IS DREAM / MISS YOU NIGHTS (re)** (re-issue) *EMI CDEM 359* 13 ... 14 9
2 Oct 95 **MISUNDERSTOOD MAN** *EMI CDEM 394* ... 19 3
11 Nov 95 SONGS FROM 'HEATHCLIFF' *EMI CDEMD 1091* ... 15 9
9 Dec 95 **HAD TO BE** *EMI CDEM 410* 14 ... 22 4
30 Mar 96 **THE WEDDING** *EMI CDEM 422* 15 ... 40 1
24 Aug 96 AT THE MOVIES – 1959-1974 *EMI CDEMD 1096* ... 17 3
25 Jan 97 **BE WITH ME ALWAYS** *EMI CDEM 453* ... 52 1
2 Aug 97 THE ROCK 'N' ROLL YEARS *EMI CDEMD 1109* ... 32 3
24 Oct 98 ● **CAN'T KEEP THIS FEELING IN** *EMI CDEM 526* ... 10 4
31 Oct 98 ● REAL AS I WANNA BE *EMI 4974062* ... 10 9
7 Aug 99 **THE MIRACLE** *EMI / Blacknight CDEM 546* ... 23 2
27 Nov 99 ★ **THE MILLENNIUM PRAYER** *Papillon PROMISECD 01* ... 1 16
21 Oct 00 ● THE WHOLE STORY – HIS GREATEST HITS *EMI 5293222* ... 6 13
17 Nov 01 WANTED *Papillon WANTED 1* ... 11 8
15 Dec 01 **SOMEWHERE OVER THE RAINBOW / WHAT A WONDERFUL WORLD** *Papillon CLIFF CD1* ... 11 6
13 Apr 02 **LET ME BE THE ONE** *Papillon CLIFF CD2* ... 29 3
29 Nov 03 ● CLIFF AT CHRISTMAS *EMI 5934982* ... 9 8
20 Dec 03 ● **SANTA'S LIST** *EMI SANTA 01* ... 5 5
23 Oct 04 ● **SOMETHIN' IS GOIN' ON** *Decca / UCJ 4756419* ... 9 3
6 Nov 04 ● SOMETHING'S GOIN' ON *Decca / UCJ 4756408* ... 7 5
25 Dec 04 **I CANNOT GIVE YOU MY LOVE** *Decca / UCJ 4756611* ... 13 4
21 May 05 **WHAT CAR** *Decca 4756943* ... 12 3
26 Nov 05 PLATINUM COLLECTION *EMI 3338032* ... 51 6+

1 Cliff Richard and The Drifters 2 Cliff Richard and the Shadows 3 Cliff Richard with the Norrie Paramor Orchestra / Cliff Richard / The Shadows 4 Cliff and Hank 5 Olivia Newton-John and Cliff Richard 6 Phil Everly and Cliff Richard 7 Cliff Richard with the London Philharmonic Orchestra 8 Sheila Walsh and Cliff Richard 9 Cliff Richard and The Young Ones featuring Hank B Marvin 10 Cliff Richard and Sarah Brightman 11 Elton John and Cliff Richard 12 Van Morrison with Cliff Richard 13 Cliff Richard with Phil Everly / Cliff Richard 14 Cliff Richard and Olivia Newton-John 15 Cliff Richard featuring Helen Hobson
1 Cliff Richard and The Drifters 2 Cliff Richard and The Shadows 3 Cliff Richard, The Shadows and Norrie Paramor and his Orchestra 4 Cliff Richard – The Shadows with Grazina Frame 5 Cliff Richard with The Shadows 6 Cliff Richard and the London Philharmonic Orchestra

Tracks on Expresso Bongo (EP): Love / A Voice in the Wilderness / The Shrine on the Second Floor / Bongo Blues. 'Bongo Blues' features only The Shadows. 'Gee Whiz it's You' is an 'export' single. 'Bachelor Boy' was listed with 'The Next Time' from 10 Jan 1963. 'Ocean Deep' listed from 28 Apr 1984 onwards. It peaked at No.41. 'I Cannot Give You My Love' features uncredited vocalist Barry Gibb.

Keith RICHARDS (see also The ROLLING STONES)
UK, male vocalist / guitarist (2 Albums: 4 Weeks)

15 Oct 88 TALK IS CHEAP *Virgin V 2554* ... 37 3
31 Oct 92 MAIN OFFENDER *Virgin America CDVUS 59* ... 45 1

Calvin RICHARDSON *US, male vocalist*

27 Mar 04 **I'VE GOT TO MOVE** *Hollywood HOL 004CD* ... 74 1

Lionel RICHIE (52 Top 500)
Singer / composer / producer, b. 20 Jun 1949, Alabama, US. Launched a solo career in 1982 after 12 years fronting The Commodores. Arguably the most successful US songwriter of the 1980s, who composed at least one US chart-topper per year for a record nine successive years (11 Albums: 473 Weeks, 26 Singles: 190 Weeks)

12 Sep 81 ● **ENDLESS LOVE** *Motown TMG 1240* 1 ▲ $ ... 7 12
20 Nov 82 ● **TRULY** *Motown TMG 1284* ▲ $ ... 6 11
27 Nov 82 ● LIONEL RICHIE *Motown STMA 8037* ... 9 86
29 Jan 83 **YOU ARE** *Motown TMG 1290* ... 43 7
7 May 83 **MY LOVE** *Motown TMG 1300* ... 70 3
1 Oct 83 ● **ALL NIGHT LONG (ALL NIGHT)** *Motown TMG 1319* ▲ $ ... 2 16
29 Oct 83 ★ CAN'T SLOW DOWN *Motown STMA 8041* ▲ ... 1 154
3 Dec 83 ● **RUNNING WITH THE NIGHT** *Motown TMG 1324* ... 9 12
10 Mar 84 ★ **HELLO** *Motown TMG 1330* ▲ $ ... 1 15
23 Jun 84 **STUCK ON YOU** *Motown TMG 1341* ... 12 12
20 Oct 84 **PENNY LOVER** *Motown TMG 1356* ... 18 7
16 Nov 85 ● **SAY YOU, SAY ME** *Motown ZB 40421* ▲ $ ... 8 11
26 Jul 86 ● **DANCING ON THE CEILING** *Motown LIO 1* ... 7 11
23 Aug 86 ● DANCING ON THE CEILING *Motown ZL 72412* ▲ ... 2 53
11 Oct 86 **LOVE WILL CONQUER ALL** *Motown LIO 2* ... 45 5
20 Dec 86 **BALLERINA GIRL / DEEP RIVER WOMAN** *Motown LIO 3* ... 17 8
28 Mar 87 **SELA** *Motown LIO 4* ... 43 6
9 May 92 **DO IT TO ME** *Motown TMG 1407* ... 33 6
6 Jun 92 ★ BACK TO FRONT *Motown 5300182* ■ ... 1 81
22 Aug 92 ● **MY DESTINY** *Motown TMG 1408* ... 7 13
28 Nov 92 **LOVE OH LOVE (re)** *Motown TMG 1413* ... 52 4
6 Apr 96 **DON'T WANNA LOSE YOU** *Mercury MERCD 461* ... 17 5
20 Apr 96 LOUDER THAN WORDS *Mercury 5322412* ... 11 5
23 Nov 96 **STILL IN LOVE** *Mercury MERCD 477* ... 66 1
31 Jan 98 ● TRULY – THE LOVE SONGS *Motown / PolyGram TV 5308432* ... 5 21
27 Jun 98 **CLOSEST THING TO HEAVEN** *Mercury 5661312* ... 26 2
11 Jul 98 TIME *Mercury 5585182* ... 31 3
21 Oct 00 **ANGEL** *Mercury 5726702* ... 18 5
28 Oct 00 ● RENAISSANCE *Island 5482222* ... 6 24
23 Dec 00 **DON'T STOP THE MUSIC** *Mercury 5688992* ... 34 5
17 Mar 01 **TENDER HEART** *Mercury 5728462* ... 29 3
23 Jun 01 **I FORGOT** *Mercury 5729922* ... 34 2
7 Dec 02 ● ENCORE *Mercury 0633482* ... 8 10
26 Apr 03 **TO LOVE A WOMAN** *Mercury 0779082* 2 ... 19 4
22 Nov 03 ● THE DEFINITIVE COLLECTION *Universal TV 9861394* 1 ... 10 28
20 Mar 04 ● JUST FOR YOU *Mercury 9861710* ... 5 8
20 Mar 04 **JUST FOR YOU** *Mercury 9862071* ... 20 4

1 Diana Ross and Lionel Richie 2 Lionel Richie featuring Enrique Iglesias
1 Lionel Richie & The Commodores

'Deep River Woman' was listed only from 17 Jan 1987. It has the credit: 'background vocal Alabama'.

Shane RICHIE *UK, male actor / vocalist*

6 Dec 03 ● **I'M YOUR MAN** *BMG 82876578582* ... 2 14

Jonathan RICHMAN and The MODERN LOVERS *US, male vocal / instrumental group (1 Album: 3 Weeks, 3 Singles: 27 Weeks)*

16 Jul 77 **ROADRUNNER** *Beserkley BZZ 1* ... 11 9
27 Aug 77 ROCK 'N' ROLL WITH THE MODERN LOVERS *Beserkley BSERK 9* ... 50 3
29 Oct 77 ● **EGYPTIAN REGGAE** *Beserkley BZZ 2* ... 5 14
21 Jan 78 **THE MORNING OF OUR LIVES** *Beserkley BZZ 7* 1 ... 29 4

1 The Modern Lovers

RICHMOND STRINGS / Michael SAMMES SINGERS *UK, orchestra and male / female vocal group – leader b. 19 Feb 1928, d. 19 May 2001*

19 Jan 76 MUSIC OF AMERICA *Ronco TRD 2016* ... 18 7

Adam RICKITT
UK, male actor / vocalist (1 Album: 1 Week, 3 Singles: 19 Weeks)

26 Jun 99 ● **I BREATHE AGAIN** *Polydor 5611862* ... 5 10
16 Oct 99 **EVERYTHING MY HEART DESIRES** *Polydor 5614392* ... 15 6
30 Oct 99 GOOD TIMES *Polydor 5431422* ... 41 1
5 Feb 00 **BEST THING** *Polydor 5616132* ... 25 3

RICKY *UK, male vocal / instrumental group (2 Singles: 2 Weeks)*

18 Sep 04 **THAT EXTRA MILE** *Garcia GARCIA 004CD* ... 50 1
5 Feb 05 **THE JOURNEY / STOP KNOCKING THE WALLS DOWN** *Beat Crazy BEAT 001CD* 1 ... 32 1

1 Amsterdam / Ricky

17 May 1986	24 May 1986	31 May 1986	7 June 1986
UK No.1 SINGLES			
THE CHICKEN SONG Spitting Image	THE CHICKEN SONG Spitting Image	THE CHICKEN SONG Spitting Image	SPIRIT IN THE SKY Doctor and The Medics
UK No.1 ALBUMS			
STREET LIFE - 20 GREAT HITS Bryan Ferry and Roxy Music	STREET LIFE - 20 GREAT HITS Bryan Ferry and Roxy Music	SO Peter Gabriel	SO Peter Gabriel

Frank RICOTTI ALL STARS *UK, male instrumental group*

26 Jun 93 THE BEIDERBECKE COLLECTION *Dormouse DM 20CD* ... 73 1

The Beiderbecke Collection first entered the chart on 24 Dec 88 as a compilation.

RIDE *UK, male vocal / instrumental group*
(4 Albums: 16 Weeks, 10 Singles: 22 Weeks)

27 Jan 90 **RIDE (EP)** *Creation CRE 072T* ... 71 2
14 Apr 90 **PLAY (EP)** *Creation CRE 075T* ... 32 3
29 Sep 90 **FALL (EP)** *Creation CRE 087T* ... 34 3
27 Oct 90 NOWHERE *Creation CRELP 074* ... 11 5
16 Mar 91 **TODAY FOREVER (EP)** *Creation CRE 100T* ... 14 4
15 Feb 92 ● **LEAVE THEM ALL BEHIND** *Creation CRE 123T* ... 9 3
21 Mar 92 ● GOING BLANK AGAIN *Creation CRECD 124* ... 5 5
25 Apr 92 **TWISTERELLA** *Creation CRE 150T* ... 36 2
30 Apr 94 **BIRDMAN** *Creation CRESCD 155* ... 38 2
25 Jun 94 **HOW DOES IT FEEL TO FEEL** *Creation CRESCD 184* ... 58 1
2 Jul 94 ● CARNIVAL OF LIGHT *Creation CRECD 147* ... 5 4
8 Oct 94 **I DON'T KNOW WHERE IT COMES FROM** *Creation CRESCD 189R* ... 46 1
24 Feb 96 **BLACK NITE CRASH** *Creation CRESCD 199* ... 67 1
23 Mar 96 TARANTULA *Creation CRECD 180* ... 21 2

Tracks on Ride (EP): Chelsea Girl / Drive Blind / All I Can See / Close My Eyes. Tracks on Play (EP): Like a Daydream / Silver / Furthest Sense / Perfect Time. Tracks on Fall (EP): Dreams Burn Down / Taste / Hear and Now / Nowhere. Tracks on Today Forever (EP): Unfamiliar / Sennen / Beneath / Today.

RIDER & Terry VENABLES
UK, male vocal / instrumental group and football pundit / vocalist

1 Jun 02 **ENGLAND CRAZY** *East West EW 248CD* ... 46 2

Andrew RIDGELEY (see also WHAM!) *UK, male vocalist*

31 Mar 90 **SHAKE** *Epic AJR 1* ... 58 3

Stan RIDGWAY *US, male vocalist*

5 Jul 86 ● **CAMOUFLAGE** *IRS IRM 114* ... 4 12

André RIEU *Holland, male orchestra leader and producer*

22 Apr 00 CELEBRATION! *Philips 5430692* ... 51 2

The RIFLES NEW
UK, male vocal / instrumental group (2 Singles: 3 Weeks)

11 Jun 05 **WHEN I'M ALONE** *Xtra Mile XMR 007CD* ... 64 1
5 Nov 05 **LOCAL BOY** *Right Hook RHK 001CD* ... 36 2

RIGHEIRA *Italy, male vocal duo*

24 Sep 83 **VAMOS A LA PLAYA** *A&M AM 137* ... 53 3

RIGHT SAID FRED *UK, male vocal (Richard Fairbrass) / instrumental group (2 Albums: 53 Weeks, 9 Singles: 66 Weeks)*

27 Jul 91 ● **I'M TOO SEXY** *Tug SNOG 1* ▲ $ ... 2 16
7 Dec 91 ● **DON'T TALK JUST KISS** *Tug SNOG 2* [1] ... 3 11
21 Mar 92 ★ **DEEPLY DIPPY** *Tug SNOG 3* ... 1 14
28 Mar 92 ★ UP *Tug SNOGCD 1* ... 1 49
1 Aug 92 **THOSE SIMPLE THINGS / DAYDREAM** *Tug SNOG 4* ... 29 5
27 Feb 93 ● **STICK IT OUT** *Tug CDCOMIC 1* [2] ... 4 7
23 Oct 93 **BUMPED** *Tug CDSNOG 7* ... 32 4
13 Nov 93 SEX AND TRAVEL *Tug SNOGCD 2* ... 35 4
18 Dec 93 **HANDS UP (4 LOVERS)** *Tug CDSNOG 8* ... 60 3
19 Mar 94 **WONDERMAN** *Tug CDSNOG 9* ... 55 1
13 Oct 01 **YOU'RE MY MATE** *Kingsize 74321895632* ... 18 5

[1] Right Said Fred Guest vocals: Jocelyn Brown [2] Right Said Fred and Friends

The RIGHTEOUS BROTHERS
US, male vocal duo – Bill Medley and Bobby Hatfield, b. 10 Aug 1940, d. 5 Nov 2003 (1 Album: 17 Weeks, 10 Singles: 86 Weeks)

14 Jan 65 ★ **YOU'VE LOST THAT LOVIN' FEELIN'** *London HLU 9943* ▲ $ ... 1 10
12 Aug 65 **UNCHAINED MELODY** *London HL 9975* $ ... 14 12
13 Jan 66 **EBB TIDE** *London HL 10011* ... 48 2
14 Apr 66 **(YOU'RE MY) SOUL AND INSPIRATION** *Verve VS 535* ▲ $ ... 15 10
10 Nov 66 **THE WHITE CLIFFS OF DOVER** *London HL 10086* ... 21 9
22 Dec 66 **ISLAND IN THE SUN** *Verve VS 547* ... 24 5
12 Feb 69 ● **YOU'VE LOST THAT LOVIN' FEELIN'** (re-issue) *London HL 10241* ... 10 11
19 Nov 77 **YOU'VE LOST THAT LOVIN' FEELIN'** (2nd re-issue) *Phil Spector International 2010 022* ... 42 4
27 Oct 90 ★ **UNCHAINED MELODY** (re-issue) *Verve / Polydor PO 101* ... 1 14
1 Dec 90 THE VERY BEST OF THE RIGHTEOUS BROTHERS *Verve 8472481* ... 11 17
15 Dec 90 ● **YOU'VE LOST THAT LOVIN' FEELIN'** (3rd re-issue) / **EBB TIDE** (re-issue) *Verve / Polydor PO 116* ... 3 9

RIHANNA NEW *Barbados, female vocalist – Robyn Rihanna Fenty (1 Album: 3 Weeks, 2 Singles: 18 Weeks)*

3 Sep 05 ● **PON DE REPLAY (re)** *Def Jam 984575* ... 2 14
10 Sep 05 MUSIC OF THE SUN *Def Jam 9885146* ... 35 3
10 Dec 05 **IF IT'S LOVIN' THAT YOU WANT** *Def Jam 9888412* ... 11 4+

RIK ROK *Jamaica, male rapper – Ricardo Ducent (3 Singles: 24 Weeks)*

17 Feb 01 **IT WASN'T ME** (import) *MCA 1558032* [1] ... 31 3
10 Mar 01 ★ **IT WASN'T ME** *MCA 1558022* [1] ■ ▲ £ ... 1 20
3 Jul 04 **YOUR EYES** *VP VPCD 6415* [2] ... 57 1

[1] Shaggy featuring Ricardo "Rikrok" Ducent [2] Rik Rok featuring Shaggy

RIKKI and DAZ featuring Glen CAMPBELL *UK, male production duo – John Matthews and Darren Sampson and US, male vocalist*

30 Nov 02 **RHINESTONE COWBOY (GIDDY UP GIDDY UP)** *Serious SER 059CD* ... 12 8

Cheryl Pepsii RILEY *US, female vocalist*

28 Jan 89 **THANKS FOR MY CHILD** *CBS 653153 7* ... 75 1

Jeannie C RILEY *US, female vocalist – Jeanne C Stephenson*

16 Oct 68 **HARPER VALLEY P.T.A.** *Polydor 56748* ▲ $ ... 12 15

Teddy RILEY
(see also BLACKSTREET) *US, male producer (2 Singles: 5 Weeks)*

21 Mar 92 **IS IT GOOD TO YOU** *MCA MCS 1611* [1] ... 53 2
19 Jun 93 **BABY BE MINE** *MCA MCSTD 1772* [2] ... 37 3

[1] Teddy Riley featuring Tammy Lucas [2] BLACKstreet featuring Teddy Riley

RIMES featuring Shaila PROSPERE *UK, male rapper – Julian Johnson*

22 May 99 **IT'S OVER** *Universal MCSTD 40199* ... 51 1

LeAnn RIMES 444 Top 500

Country child prodigy turned pop idol, b. Margaret LeAnn Rimes, 28 Aug 1982, Jackson, Mississippi, US, who first recorded at 11 and, at 13, became the youngest artist to top the US country albums chart. She won two Grammys at the age of 14 and twice topped the US pop albums chart before she was 15. Her best-selling single, 'How Do I Live' (713,900), spent a record four years on the US country sales Top 20 (4 Albums: 60 Weeks, 13 Singles: 102 Weeks)

7 Mar 98 ● **HOW DO I LIVE (re)** *Curb CUBCX 30* $ ... 7 34
6 Jun 98 SITTIN' ON TOP OF THE WORLD *Curb / The Hit Label 5560202* ... 11 22
12 Sep 98 **LOOKING THROUGH YOUR EYES / COMMITMENT** *Curb CUBC 32* ... 38 2
12 Dec 98 **BLUE** *Curb CUBC 39* ... 23 6
6 Mar 99 ● **WRITTEN IN THE STARS (re)** *Mercury EJSCD 45* [1] ... 10 8
18 Dec 99 **CRAZY** *Curb CUBC 52* ... 36 3
25 Nov 00 ★ **CAN'T FIGHT THE MOONLIGHT** *Curb CUBC 58* ■ ... 1 17
31 Mar 01 **I NEED YOU (re)** *Curb CUBC 60* ... 13 7
14 Apr 01 ● I NEED YOU *Curb / London 8573876382* ... 7 15

14 June 1986	21 June 1986	28 June 1986	5 July 1986
SPIRIT IN THE SKY Doctor and The Medics	**SPIRIT IN THE SKY** Doctor and The Medics	**THE EDGE OF HEAVEN / WHERE DID YOUR HEART GO** Wham!	**THE EDGE OF HEAVEN / WHERE DID YOUR HEART GO** Wham!
A KIND OF MAGIC Queen	**INVISIBLE TOUCH** Genesis	**INVISIBLE TOUCH** Genesis	**INVISIBLE TOUCH** Genesis

KEY
UK No.1 ★★ UK Top 10 ●● Still on chart ++ UK entry at No.1 ■■
US No.1 ▲▲ UK million seller £ US million seller $
Singles re-entries are listed as (re), (2re), (3re)... which signifies that the hit re-entered the chart once, twice or three times...

Peak Position / Weeks

23 Feb 02 **BUT I DO LOVE YOU** *London / Curb CUBC 075* **20** 4
12 Oct 02 **LIFE GOES ON** *Curb CUBC 085* **11** 8
26 Oct 02 **TWISTED ANGEL** *Curb / London 5046611562* 14 3
8 Mar 03 **SUDDENLY** *Curb / London CUBC 088* **47** 1
23 Aug 03 **WE CAN** *Curb / London CUBC 092* **27** 2
14 Feb 04 ● **THE BEST OF** *Curb / London 5046714812* 2 20
14 Feb 04 **THIS LOVE** *Curb / London CUBC 096* **54** 1
15 May 04 ● **LAST THING ON MY MIND** *Polydor / Curb 9866595* [2] **5** 9

[1] Elton John and LeAnn Rimes [2] Ronan Keating & LeAnn Rimes

The RIMSHOTS *US, male / female vocal / instrumental group*

19 Jul 75 **7-6-5-4-3-2-1 (BLOW YOUR WHISTLE)** *All Platinum 6146 304* **26** 5

RIO and MARS
France / UK, male / female vocal / instrumental duo (2 Singles: 3 Weeks)

28 Jan 95 **BOY I GOTTA HAVE YOU** *Dome CDDOME 1014* **43** 2
13 Apr 96 **BOY I GOTTA HAVE YOU** (re-issue) *Feverpitch CDFVR 1007* **46** 1

Miguel RIOS *Spain, male vocalist*

11 Jul 70 **SONG OF JOY** *A&M AMS 790* **16** 12

Waldo de los RIOS
Argentina, orchestra – leader Osvaldo Ferraro Guiterrez

10 Apr 71 ● **MOZART SYMPHONY NO.40 IN G MINOR K550 1ST MOVEMENT (ALLEGRO MOLTO)** *A&M AMS 836* **5** 16
1 May 71 ● **SYMPHONIES FOR THE SEVENTIES** *A&M AMLS 2014* 6 26

RIOT ACT NEW *US / Canada, male / female production / vocal trio*

4 Jun 05 **CALIFORNIA SOUL** *Nebula NEBCD 070* **59** 1

RIP RIG AND PANIC *UK / US, male / female vocal / instrumental group*

26 Jun 82 **I AM COLD** *Virgin V 2228* 67 3

Minnie RIPERTON *US, female vocalist, b. 8 Nov 1947, d. 12 Jul 1979*

12 Apr 75 ● **LOVIN' YOU** *Epic EPC 3121* ▲ $ **2** 10
17 May 75 **PERFECT ANGEL** *Epic EPC 80426* 33 3

Angela RIPPON *UK, female broadcaster / exercise instructor*

17 Apr 82 ● **SHAPE UP AND DANCE (VOLUME II)** *Lifestyle LEG 2* 8 26

RISE (see also OAKENFOLD; PERFECTO ALLSTARZ; VIRUS)
UK, male production duo – Paul Oakenfold and Steve Osborne

3 Sep 94 **THE SINGLE** *East West YZ 839CD* **70** 1

The RISHI RICH PROJECT *UK, male production / vocal / rap group – leader Rishpal Rekhi (2 Singles: 15 Weeks)*

20 Sep 03 **DANCE WITH YOU (NACHNA TERE NAAL)** *Relentless RELCD 1* [1] **12** 5
3 Jul 04 ● **EYES ON YOU** *Relentless RELCD 5* [2] **6** 10

[1] The Rishi Rich Project featuring Jay Sean & Juggy D [2] Jay Sean featuring The Rishi Rich Project

The RITCHIE FAMILY *US, female vocal group (3 Singles: 19 Weeks)*

23 Aug 75 **BRAZIL** *Polydor 2058 625* **41** 4
18 Sep 76 ● **THE BEST DISCO IN TOWN** *Polydor 2058 777* **10** 9
17 Feb 79 **AMERICAN GENERATION** *Mercury 6007 199* **49** 6

Lee RITENOUR and Maxi PRIEST
US, male guitarist and UK, male vocalist

31 Jul 93 **WAITING IN VAIN** *GRP MCSTD 1921* **65** 2

RITMO-DYNAMIC *France, male producer – Laurent Debuire*

15 Nov 03 **CALINDA** *Xtravaganza XTRAV 42CDS* **68** 1

Tex RITTER *US, male vocalist – Maurice Ritter, b. 12 Jan 1905, d. 3 Jan 1974*

22 Jun 56 ● **THE WAYWARD WIND** *Capitol CL 14581* **8** 14

RIVA featuring Dannii MINOGUE (see also CHOCOLATE PUMA; GOODMEN; JARK PRONGO; RHYTHMKILLAZ; TOMBA VIRA)
Holland, male production duo – Rene ter Horst and Gaston Steenkist and Australia, female vocalist

1 Dec 01 ● **WHO DO YOU LOVE NOW (STRINGER)** *ffrr DFCD 002* **3** 15

RIVAL SCHOOLS
US, male vocal / instrumental group (2 Singles: 2 Weeks)

30 Mar 02 **USED FOR GLUE** *Mercury 5889652* **42** 1
20 Jul 02 **GOOD THINGS** *Mercury 5829662* **74** 1

RIVER CITY PEOPLE *UK, male / female vocal / instrumental group (2 Albums: 10 Weeks, 7 Singles: 27 Weeks)*

12 Aug 89 **(WHAT'S WRONG WITH) DREAMING?** *EMI EM 95* **70** 3
3 Mar 90 **WALKING ON ICE** *EMI EM 130* **62** 2
30 Jun 90 **CARRY THE BLAME / CALIFORNIA DREAMIN'** *EMI EM 145* **13** 10
25 Aug 90 **SAY SOMETHING GOOD** *EMI EMCX 3561* 23 9
22 Sep 90 **(WHAT'S WRONG WITH) DREAMING?** (re-issue) *EMI EM 156* **40** 3
2 Mar 91 **WHEN I WAS YOUNG** *EMI EM 176* **62** 2
28 Sep 91 **SPECIAL WAY** *EMI EM 207* **44** 3
2 Nov 91 **THIS IS THE WORLD** *EMI EMC 3611* 56 1
22 Feb 92 **STANDING IN THE NEED OF LOVE** *EMI EM 216* **36** 4

RIVER DETECTIVES *UK, male vocal / instrumental duo*

29 Jul 89 **CHAINS** *WEA YZ 383* **51** 4
23 Sep 89 **SATURDAY NIGHT SUNDAY MORNING** *WEA WX 2955* 51 1

RIVER OCEAN featuring INDIA
US, male producer – Louie Vega and female vocalist

26 Feb 94 **LOVE AND HAPPINESS (YEMAYA Y OCHUN)** *Cooltempo CDCOOL 287* **50** 2

Robbie RIVERA *Puerto Rico, male producer (2 Singles: 8 Weeks)*

2 Sep 00 **BANG** *Multiply CDMULTY 64* [1] **13** 7
12 Oct 02 **SEX** *352 Recordings 352CD 001* [2] **55** 1

[1] Robbie Rivera presents Rhythm Bangers [2] Robbie Rivera vs Billy Paul W

Sandy RIVERA (see also KINGS OF TOMORROW)
US, male producer (2 Singles: 3 Weeks)

18 Jan 03 **CHANGES** *Defected DFTD 059* [1] **48** 2
5 Apr 03 **I CAN'T STOP** *Defected DFTD 063* **58** 1

[1] Sandy Rivera featuring Haze

Danny RIVERS *UK, male vocalist – David Baker*

12 Jan 61 **CAN'T YOU HEAR MY HEART** *Decca F 11294* **36** 3

David ROACH *UK, male vocalist / saxophonist*

14 Apr 84 **I LOVE SAX** *Nouveau Music NML 1006* 73 1

ROACH MOTEL
UK, male instrumental / production group (2 Singles: 2 Weeks)

21 Aug 93 **AFRO SLEEZE / TRANSATLANTIC** *Junior Boy's Own JBO 1412* **73** 1
10 Dec 94 **HAPPY BIZZNESS / WILD LUV** *Junior Boy's Own JBO 24* **75** 1

12 July 1986	19 July 1986	26 July 1986	2 August 1986
UK No.1 SINGLES			
PAPA DON'T PREACH Madonna	PAPA DON'T PREACH Madonna	PAPA DON'T PREACH Madonna	THE LADY IN RED Chris De Burgh
UK No.1 ALBUMS			
TRUE BLUE Madonna	TRUE BLUE Madonna	TRUE BLUE Madonna	TRUE BLUE Madonna

ROACHFORD *UK, male / female vocal / instrumental group – leader Andrew Roachford (4 Albums: 56 Weeks, 13 Singles: 61 Weeks)*

18 Jun 88 CUDDLY TOY *CBS ROA 2* 61 4
23 Jul 88 ROACHFORD *CBS 460630 1* 11 27
14 Jan 89 ● CUDDLY TOY (re-issue) *CBS ROA 4* 4 9
18 Mar 89 FAMILY MAN *CBS ROA 5* 25 6
1 Jul 89 KATHLEEN *CBS ROA 6* 43 5
13 Apr 91 GET READY! *Columbia 6567057* 22 8
18 May 91 GET READY! *Columbia 4681361* 20 5
19 Mar 94 ONLY TO BE WITH YOU *Columbia 6601562* 21 7
16 Apr 94 PERMANENT SHADE OF BLUE *Columbia 4758429* 25 21
18 Jun 94 LAY YOUR LOVE ON ME *Columbia 6603722* 36 5
20 Aug 94 THIS GENERATION *Columbia 6607452* 38 4
3 Dec 94 CRY FOR ME *Columbia 6610742* 46 2
1 Apr 95 I KNOW YOU DON'T LOVE ME *Columbia 6612525* 42 2
11 Oct 97 THE WAY I FEEL *Columbia 6651042* 20 4
25 Oct 97 FEEL *Columbia 4885262* 19 3
14 Feb 98 HOW COULD I? (INSECURITY) *Columbia 6653462* 34 3
11 Jul 98 NAKED WITHOUT YOU *Columbia 6659362* 53 2

ROADRUNNER UNITED
International, male vocalists / guitarists / drummers

22 Oct 05 THE ALL-STAR SESSIONS *Roadrunner RR 81578* 45 2

The All-Star Sessions celebrates the 25th anniversary of Roadrunner Records and features 55 artists from 42 bands from the label's roster, past and present, collaborating under the leadership of Joey Jordison (Slipknot), Dino Cazares (ex-Fear Factory), Robert Flynn (Machine Head) and Matthew Heafy (Trivium).

ROB 'N' RAZ featuring Leila K
Sweden, male production duo – Robert Watz and Rasmus Lindwall and female rapper – Leila El Kahalifi (2 Singles: 17 Weeks)

25 Nov 89 ● GOT TO GET *Arista 112696* 8 14
17 Mar 90 ROK THE NATION *Arista 112971* 41 3

Kate ROBBINS and BEYOND
UK, female / male vocal / instrumental group

30 May 81 ● MORE THAN IN LOVE *RCA 69* 2 10

Marty ROBBINS *US, male vocalist / guitarist – Marty Robinson, b. 26 Sep 1925, d. 8 Dec 1982 (2 Albums: 15 Weeks, 4 Singles: 33 Weeks)*

29 Jan 60 EL PASO (re) *Fontana H 233* ▲ $ 19 9
26 May 60 BIG IRON *Fontana H 229* 48 1
13 Aug 60 GUNFIGHTER BALLADS AND TRAIL SONGS *Fontana TFL 5063* 20 1
27 Sep 62 ● DEVIL WOMAN *CBS AAG 114* 5 17
17 Jan 63 RUBY ANN *CBS AAG 128* 24 6
10 Feb 79 ● MARTY ROBBINS COLLECTION *Lotus WH 5009* 5 14

Robert POST *Norway, male vocalist*

3 Sep 05 GOT NONE *Mercury 9872370* 42 2

Austin ROBERTS *US, male vocalist*

25 Oct 75 ROCKY *Private Stock PVT 33* 22 7

Joe ROBERTS *UK, male vocalist (6 Singles: 17 Weeks)*

28 Aug 93 BACK IN MY LIFE *ffrr FCD 215* 59 1
29 Jan 94 LOVER *ffrr FCD 220* 22 5
14 May 94 BACK IN MY LIFE (re-issue) *ffrr FCD 230* 39 3
6 Aug 94 ADORE *ffrr FCD 240* 45 3
18 Feb 95 YOU ARE EVERYTHING *Columbia 6611755* [1] 28 4
24 Feb 96 HAPPY DAYS *Grass Green GRASS 10CD* [2] 63 1

[1] Melanie Williams and Joe Roberts [2] Sweet Mercy featuring Joe Roberts

Juliet ROBERTS *UK, female vocalist (1 Album: 1 Week, 8 Singles: 34 Weeks)*

31 Jul 93 CAUGHT IN THE MIDDLE *Cooltempo CDCOOL 272* 24 6
6 Nov 93 FREE LOVE *Cooltempo CDCOOL 281* 25 3
19 Mar 94 AGAIN / I WANT YOU *Cooltempo CDCOOL 285* 33 3
2 Apr 94 NATURAL THING *Cooltempo CTCD 39* 65 1
2 Jul 94 CAUGHT IN THE MIDDLE (re-mix) *Cooltempo CDCOOL 291* 14 5
15 Oct 94 I WANT YOU (re-issue) *Cooltempo CDCOOL 297* 28 3
31 Jan 98 SO GOOD / FREE LOVE 98 (re-mix) *Delirious 74321554002* 15 4
23 Jan 99 BAD GIRLS / I LIKE *Delirious DELICD 11* 17 5
20 Jan 01 NEEDIN' U II *Manifesto FESCD 78* [1] 11 5

[1] David Morales presents The Face featuring Juliet Roberts

Malcolm ROBERTS
UK, male vocalist, b. 31 Mar 1944, d. 7 Feb 2003 (3 Singles: 29 Weeks)

11 May 67 TIME ALONE WILL TELL *RCA 1578* 45 2
30 Oct 68 ● MAY I HAVE THE NEXT DREAM WITH YOU (re) *Major Minor MM 581* 8 15
22 Nov 69 LOVE IS ALL *Major Minor MM 637* 12 12

Paddy ROBERTS
South Africa, male vocalist, b. 1910, d. Sep 1975 (2 Albums: 6 Weeks)

26 Sep 59 ● STRICTLY FOR GROWN-UPS *Decca LF 1322* 8 5
17 Sep 60 PADDY ROBERTS TRIES AGAIN *Decca LK 4358* 16 1

B A ROBERTSON *UK, male vocalist – Brian Alexander Robertson (2 Albums: 10 Weeks, 6 Singles: 60 Weeks)*

28 Jul 79 ● BANG BANG *Asylum K 13152* 2 12
27 Oct 79 ● KNOCKED IT OFF *Asylum K 12396* 8 12
1 Mar 80 KOOL IN THE KAFTAN *Asylum K 12427* 17 12
29 Mar 80 INITIAL SUCCESS *Asylum K 52216* 32 8
31 May 80 ● TO BE OR NOT TO BE *Asylum K 12449* 9 11
4 Apr 81 BULLY FOR YOU *Asylum K 52275* 61 2
17 Oct 81 HOLD ME *Swansong BAM 1* [1] 11 8
17 Dec 83 TIME *Epic A 3983* [2] 45 5

[1] B A Robertson and Maggie Bell [2] Frida and B A Robertson

Don ROBERTSON *US, male pianist / whistler*

11 May 56 ● THE HAPPY WHISTLER *Capitol CL 14575* 8 9

Robbie ROBERTSON (see also The BAND)
Canada, male vocalist / guitarist (2 Albums: 16 Weeks, 2 Singles: 11 Weeks)

14 Nov 87 ROBBIE ROBERTSON *Geffen WX 133* 23 14
23 Jul 88 SOMEWHERE DOWN THE CRAZY RIVER *Geffen GEF 40* 15 10
12 Oct 91 STORYVILLE *Geffen GEF 24303* 30 2
11 Apr 98 TAKE YOUR PARTNER BY THE HAND *Polydor 5693272* [1] 74 1

[1] Howie B featuring Robbie Robertson

Ivo ROBIC *Croatia, male vocalist, b. 28 Jan 1923, d. 9 Mar 2000*

6 Nov 59 MORGEN *Polydor 23923* 23 1

Floyd ROBINSON *US, male vocalist*

16 Oct 59 ● MAKIN' LOVE *RCA 1146* 9 9

Smokey ROBINSON (see also The MIRACLES) *US, male vocalist – William Robinson (2 Albums: 19 Weeks, 14 Singles: 109 Weeks)*

27 Dec 67 I SECOND THAT EMOTION *Tamla Motown TMG 631* [1] $ 27 11
3 Apr 68 IF YOU CAN WANT *Tamla Motown TMG 648* [1] 50 1
7 May 69 ● TRACKS OF MY TEARS *Tamla Motown TMG 696* [1] 9 13
1 Aug 70 ★ THE TEARS OF A CLOWN *Tamla Motown TMG 745* [1] ▲ $ 1 14
30 Jan 71 (COME 'ROUND HERE) I'M THE ONE YOU NEED (re-issue) *Tamla Motown TMG 761* [1] 13 9
5 Jun 71 I DON'T BLAME YOU AT ALL *Tamla Motown TMG 774* [1] 11 10
23 Feb 74 JUST MY SOUL RESPONDING *Tamla Motown TMG 883* 35 6
2 Oct 76 THE TEARS OF A CLOWN (re-issue) *Tamla Motown TMG 1048* [1] 34 6
24 Feb 79 POPS, WE LOVE YOU *Motown TMG 1136* [2] 66 5
9 May 81 ★ BEING WITH YOU *Motown TMG 1223* $ 1 13
20 Jun 81 BEING WITH YOU *Motown STML 12151* 17 10

9 August 1986	16 August 1986	23 August 1986	30 August 1986
THE LADY IN RED Chris De Burgh	THE LADY IN RED Chris De Burgh	I WANT TO WAKE UP WITH YOU Boris Gardiner	I WANT TO WAKE UP WITH YOU Boris Gardiner
TRUE BLUE Madonna	TRUE BLUE Madonna	NOW THAT'S WHAT I CALL MUSIC! 7 Various	NOW THAT'S WHAT I CALL MUSIC! 7 Various

KEY
UK No.1 ★ UK Top 10 ● Still on chart + UK entry at No.1 ■ US No.1 ▲ UK million seller £ US million seller $
Singles re-entries are listed as (re), (2re), (3re)... which signifies that the hit re-entered the chart once, twice or three times...
Peak Position / Weeks

13 Mar 82 TELL ME TOMORROW *Motown TMG 1255* 51 4
28 Mar 87 JUST TO SEE HER *Motown ZB 41147* 52 6
17 Sep 88 INDESTRUCTIBLE *Arista 111717* [3] 55 4
12 Nov 88 LOVE SONGS *Telstar STAR 2331* [1] 69 9
25 Feb 89 INDESTRUCTIBLE *Arista 112074* [3] 30 7

[1] Smokey Robinson and The Miracles [2] Diana Ross, Marvin Gaye, Smokey Robinson and Stevie Wonder [3] The Four Tops featuring Smokey Robinson [1] Marvin Gaye and Smokey Robinson

The 1976 re-issue of 'The Tears of a Clown' was a double A-side Motown release with 'Tracks of My Tears'. The original US recording of 'Indestructible' was not issued until after the chart run of the UK-only mix.

Smokey ROBINSON and The MIRACLES (see also The MIRACLES)
US, male vocal group (1 Album: 2 Weeks, 7 Singles: 64 Weeks)

27 Dec 67 I SECOND THAT EMOTION *Tamla Motown TMG 631* [1] $....27 11
3 Apr 68 IF YOU CAN WANT *Tamla Motown TMG 648* [1] 50 1
7 May 69 ● TRACKS OF MY TEARS *Tamla Motown TMG 696* [1] 9 13
1 Aug 70 ★ THE TEARS OF A CLOWN *Tamla Motown TMG 745* [1] ▲ $...1 14
30 Jan 71 (COME 'ROUND HERE) I'M THE ONE YOU NEED (re-issue) *Tamla Motown TMG 761* [1] 13 9
5 Jun 71 I DON'T BLAME YOU AT ALL *Tamla Motown TMG 774* [1] 11 10
2 Oct 76 THE TEARS OF A CLOWN (re-issue) *Tamla Motown TMG 1048* [1] 34 6
14 Nov 92 THE GREATEST HITS *PolyGram TV 5301212* 65 2

1976 re-issue of 'The Tears of a Clown' was a double A-side Motown release with 'Tracks of My Tears'.

Tom ROBINSON BAND
UK, male vocal (Tom Robinson) / instrumental group (3 Albums: 23 Weeks, 7 Singles: 41 Weeks)

22 Oct 77 ● 2-4-6-8 MOTORWAY *EMI 2715* 5 9
18 Feb 78 RISING FREE (EP) *EMI 2749* 18 6
13 May 78 UP AGAINST THE WALL *EMI 2787* 33 6
3 Jun 78 ● POWER IN THE DARKNESS *EMI EMC 3226* 4 12
17 Mar 79 BULLY FOR YOU *EMI 2916* 68 2
24 Mar 79 TRB TWO *EMI EMC 3296* 18 6
25 Jun 83 ● WAR BABY *Panic NIC 2* [1] 6 9
12 Nov 83 LISTEN TO THE RADIO: ATMOSPHERICS *Panic NIC 3* [1] 39 6
15 Sep 84 RIKKI DON'T LOSE THAT NUMBER *Castaway TR 2* [1] 58 3
29 Sep 84 HOPE AND GLORY *Castaway ZL 70483* [1] 21 5

[1] Tom Robinson [1] Tom Robinson

Tracks on Rising Free (EP): Don't Take No for an Answer / Sing if You're Glad to Be Gay / Martin / Right on Sister.

Vicki Sue ROBINSON
US, female vocalist, b. 31 May 1954, d. 27 Apr 2000

27 Sep 97 HOUSE OF JOY *Logic 74321511492* 48 1

ROBSON & JEROME
UK, male actors / vocal duo – Robson Green and Jerome Flynn (3 Albums: 53 Weeks, 3 Singles: 45 Weeks)

20 May 95 ★ UNCHAINED MELODY / (THERE'LL BE BLUEBIRDS OVER) THE WHITE CLIFFS OF DOVER (re) *RCA 74321284362* [1] ■ £....1 17
11 Nov 95 ★ I BELIEVE / UP ON THE ROOF *RCA 74321326882* ■ £....1 14
25 Nov 95 ★ ROBSON & JEROME *RCA 74321323902* ■ 1 31
9 Nov 96 ★ WHAT BECOMES OF THE BROKENHEARTED / SATURDAY NIGHT AT THE MOVIES / YOU'LL NEVER WALK ALONE *RCA 74321424732* ■ 1 14
23 Nov 96 ★ TAKE TWO *RCA 74321426252* ■ 1 16
29 Nov 97 HAPPY DAYS – THE BEST OF ROBSON & JEROME *RCA 74321542602* 20 6

[1] Robson Green & Jerome Flynn

ROBYN
Sweden, female vocalist – Robyn Carlsson (4 Singles: 14 Weeks)

20 Jul 96 YOU'VE GOT THAT SOMETHIN' *RCA 74321393462* 54 1
16 Aug 97 DO YOU KNOW (WHAT IT TAKES) *RCA 74321509932* 26 3
7 Mar 98 ● SHOW ME LOVE *RCA 74321555032* 8 6
30 May 98 DO YOU REALLY WANT ME *RCA 74321582982* 20 4

ROC PROJECT featuring Tina ARENA
US, male producer – Ray Checo and Australia, female vocalist

12 Apr 03 NEVER (PAST TENSE) *Illustrious CDILL 010* 42 1

Erin ROCHA
UK, female vocalist

27 Dec 03 CAN'T DO RIGHT FOR DOING WRONG *Flying Sparks TDBCDS 76* 36 5

ROCHELLE
US, female vocalist

1 Feb 86 MY MAGIC MAN *Warner Bros. W 8838* 27 6

Chubb ROCK
US, male rapper – Richard Simpson

19 Jan 91 TREAT 'EM RIGHT *Champion CHAMP 272* 67 1

Pete ROCK and CL SMOOTH
US, male DJ / rap duo – Peter Phillips and Corey Penn

19 Nov 94 THE MAIN INGREDIENT *Elektra 7559616612* 69 1

ROCK AID ARMENIA
UK, male vocal / instrumental charity ensemble

16 Dec 89 SMOKE ON THE WATER *Life Aid Armenia ARMEN 001* 39 5

ROCK CANDY
UK, male vocal / instrumental group

11 Sep 71 REMEMBER *MCA MK 5069* 32 6

ROCK GODDESS
UK, female vocal / instrumental group (2 Albums: 3 Weeks, 2 Singles: 5 Weeks)

5 Mar 83 MY ANGEL *A&M AMS 8311* 64 2
12 Mar 83 ROCK GODDESS *A&M AMLH 68554* 65 2
29 Oct 83 HELL HATH NO FURY *A&M AMLX 68560* 84 1
24 Mar 84 I DIDN'T KNOW I LOVED YOU (TILL I SAW YOU ROCK 'N' ROLL) *A&M AMS 185* 57 3

ROCKER'S REVENGE featuring Donnie CALVIN
US, male / female vocal / instrumental group (2 Singles: 20 Weeks)

14 Aug 82 ● WALKING ON SUNSHINE *London LON 11* 4 13
29 Jan 83 THE HARDER THEY COME *London LON 18* 30 7

ROCKET FROM THE CRYPT
US, male vocal / instrumental group (2 Albums: 4 Weeks, 4 Singles: 7 Weeks)

27 Jan 96 BORN IN 69 *Elemental ELM 32CD* 68 1
3 Feb 96 SCREAM DRACULA SCREAM! *Elemental ELM 34CD* 41 3
13 Apr 96 YOUNG LIVERS *Elemental ELM 33CDS* 67 1
14 Sep 96 ON A ROPE *Elemental ELM 38CDS 1* 12 4
18 Jul 98 RFTC *Elemental ELM 50CD* 63 1
29 Aug 98 LIPSTICK *Elemental ELM 48CDS 1* 64 1

ROCKFORD FILES
UK, male instrumental / production duo – Ben McColl and Matthew Brooks (2 Singles: 4 Weeks)

11 Mar 95 YOU SEXY DANCER *Escapade CDJAPE 7* 34 3
6 Apr 96 YOU SEXY DANCER (re-issue) *Escapade CDJAPE 14* 59 1

The ROCKIN' BERRIES
UK, male vocal / instrumental group – includes Geoff 'Jefferson' Turton (1 Album: 1 Week, 6 Singles: 41 Weeks)

1 Oct 64 I DIDN'T MEAN TO HURT YOU *Piccadilly 7N 35197* 43 1
15 Oct 64 ● HE'S IN TOWN *Piccadilly 7N 35203* 3 13
21 Jan 65 WHAT IN THE WORLD'S COME OVER YOU *Piccadilly 7N 35217* 23 7

	6 September 1986	13 September 1986	20 September 1986	27 September 1986
UK No.1 SINGLES	I WANT TO WAKE UP WITH YOU – Boris Gardiner	DON'T LEAVE ME THIS WAY – Communards with Sarah Jane Morris	DON'T LEAVE ME THIS WAY – Communards with Sarah Jane Morris	DON'T LEAVE ME THIS WAY – Communards with Sarah Jane Morris
UK No.1 ALBUMS	NOW THAT'S WHAT I CALL MUSIC! 7 – Various	NOW THAT'S WHAT I CALL MUSIC! 7 – Various	NOW THAT'S WHAT I CALL MUSIC! 7 – Various	SILK AND STEEL – Five Star

13 May 65	●	**POOR MAN'S SON** *Piccadilly 7N 35236*	5	11
19 Jun 65		THEY'RE IN TOWN *Pye NPL 38013*	15	1
26 Aug 65		**YOU'RE MY GIRL** *Piccadilly 7N 35254*	40	7
6 Jan 66		**THE WATER IS OVER MY HEAD (re)** *Piccadilly 7N 35270*	43	2

ROCKPILE

(see also Dave EDMUNDS; Nick LOWE) *UK, male vocal / instrumental group*

21 Nov 70	★	**I HEAR YOU KNOCKING** *MAM 1* [1]	1	14
18 Oct 80		SECONDS OF PLEASURE *F-Beat XXLP 7*	34	5

[1] Dave Edmunds' Rockpile

The ROCKSTEADY CREW

US, male / female vocal group (1 Album: 1 Week, 2 Singles: 16 Weeks)

1 Oct 83	●	**(HEY YOU) THE ROCKSTEADY CREW** *Charisma / Virgin RSC 1*	6	12
5 May 84		**UPROCK** *Charisma / Virgin RSC 2*	64	4
16 Jun 84		READY FOR BATTLE *Charisma RSC LP1*	73	1

ROCKWELL *US, male vocalist – Kennedy Gordy*

4 Feb 84	●	**SOMEBODY'S WATCHING ME** *Motown TMG 1331* $	6	11
25 Feb 84		SOMEBODY'S WATCHING ME *Motown ZL 72147*	52	5

'Somebody's Watching Me' features uncredited vocal by Michael Jackson.

ROCOCO *UK / Italy, male / female vocal / instrumental group*

16 Dec 89		**ITALO HOUSE MIX** *Mercury MER 314*	54	5

RODEO JONES

UK / Grenada, male / female vocal / instrumental group (2 Singles: 2 Weeks)

30 Jan 93		**NATURAL WORLD** *A&M AMCD 0165*	75	1
3 Apr 93		**SHADES OF SUMMER** *A&M AMCD 212*	59	1

Clodagh RODGERS

Ireland, female vocalist (1 Album: 1 Week, 6 Singles: 59 Weeks)

26 Mar 69	●	**COME BACK AND SHAKE ME** *RCA 1792*	3	14
9 Jul 69	●	**GOODNIGHT MIDNIGHT (re)** *RCA 1852*	4	12
13 Sep 69		CLODAGH RODGERS *RCA SF 8033*	27	1
8 Nov 69		**BILJO** *RCA 1891*	22	9
4 Apr 70		**EVERYBODY GO HOME THE PARTY'S OVER** *RCA 1930*	47	2
20 Mar 71	●	**JACK IN THE BOX** *RCA 2066*	4	10
9 Oct 71		**LADY LOVE BUG** *RCA 2117*	28	12

Jimmie RODGERS *US, male vocalist (5 Singles: 37 Weeks)*

1 Nov 57		**HONEYCOMB** *Columbia DB 3986* ▲ $	30	1
20 Dec 57	●	**KISSES SWEETER THAN WINE** *Columbia DB 4052* $	7	11
28 Mar 58		**OH-OH, I'M FALLING IN LOVE AGAIN** *Columbia DB 4078*	18	6
19 Dec 58		**WOMAN FROM LIBERIA** *Columbia DB 4206*	18	6
14 Jun 62	●	**ENGLISH COUNTRY GARDEN** *Columbia DB 4847*	5	13

Paul RODGERS (see also BAD COMPANY; The FIRM; FREE; The LAW)

UK, male vocalist (3 Albums: 15 Weeks, 1 Single: 2 Weeks)

3 Jul 93	●	MUDDY WATER BLUES *London 8284242*	9	7
12 Feb 94		**MUDDY WATER BLUES** *Victory ROGCD 1*	45	2
15 Feb 97		NOW *SPV Recordings SPV 08544662*	30	4
1 Oct 05		RETURN OF THE CHAMPIONS *Parlophone 3369792* [1]	12	4

[1] Queen + Paul Rodgers

Return of the Champions, a live album, features hits made famous by Free and Bad Company as well as Queen

Tommy ROE *US, male vocalist (6 Singles: 74 Weeks)*

6 Sep 62	●	**SHEILA** *HMV POP 1060* ▲ $	3	14
6 Dec 62		**SUSIE DARLIN'** *HMV POP 1092*	37	5
21 Mar 63	●	**THE FOLK SINGER** *HMV POP 1138*	4	13
26 Sep 63	●	**EVERYBODY (re)** *HMV POP 1207*	9	14
16 Apr 69	★	**DIZZY** *Stateside SS 2143* ▲ $	1	19
23 Jul 69		**HEATHER HONEY** *Stateside SS 2152*	24	9

ROFO *UK, male instrumental / production duo*

1 Aug 92		**ROFO'S THEME** *PWL Continental PWLT 236*	44	3

ROGER (see also ZAPP) *US, male vocalist – Roger Troutman, b. 29 Nov 1951, d. 24 Apr 1999 (3 Singles: 8 Weeks)*

17 Oct 87		**I WANT TO BE YOUR MAN** *Reprise W 8229*	61	4
12 Nov 88		**BOOM! THERE SHE WAS** *Virgin VS 1143*	55	3
13 May 95		**HIGH AS A KITE** *ffrr FCD 259* [1]	55	1

[1] One Tribe featuring Roger

Julie ROGERS *UK, female vocalist – Julie Rolls (3 Singles: 38 Weeks)*

13 Aug 64	●	**THE WEDDING** *Mercury MF 820* [1]	3	23
10 Dec 64		**LIKE A CHILD** *Mercury MF 838*	20	9
25 Mar 65		**HAWAIIAN WEDDING SONG** *Mercury MF 849*	31	6

[1] Julie Rogers with Johnny Arthey and his Orchestra and Chorus

Kenny ROGERS (310 Top 500)

Celebrated crossover country vocalist / actor, b. 21 Aug 1938, Houston, US, who was one of the top-selling artists of the US past 35 years. This Grammy-winning ex-New Christy Minstrel has collected more than 20 US gold albums and is a household name in many countries (10 Albums: 111 Weeks, 10 Singles: 109 Weeks)

18 Oct 69	●	**RUBY, DON'T TAKE YOUR LOVE TO TOWN** *Reprise RS 20829* [1]	2	23
7 Feb 70	●	**SOMETHING'S BURNING** *Reprise RS 20888* [1]	8	14
30 Apr 77	★	**LUCILLE** *United Artists UP 36242* $	1	14
18 Jun 77		KENNY ROGERS *United Artists UAS 30046*	14	7
17 Sep 77		**DAYTIME FRIENDS** *United Artists UP 36289*	39	4
2 Jun 79		**SHE BELIEVES IN ME** *United Artists UP 36533* $	42	7
6 Oct 79		THE KENNY ROGERS SINGLES ALBUM *United Artists UAK 30263*	12	22
26 Jan 80	★	**COWARD OF THE COUNTY** *United Artists UP 614* $	1	12
9 Feb 80	●	KENNY ROGERS *United Artists UAG 30273*	7	10
15 Nov 80		**LADY** *United Artists UP 635* ▲ $	12	12
31 Jan 81		LADY *Liberty LBG 30334*	40	5
12 Feb 83		**WE'VE GOT TONIGHT** *Liberty UP 658* [2]	28	7
1 Oct 83		EYES THAT SEE IN THE DARK *RCA RCALP 6088*	53	19
22 Oct 83		**EYES THAT SEE IN THE DARK** *RCA 358*	61	1
12 Nov 83	●	**ISLANDS IN THE STREAM** *RCA 378* [3] ▲ $	7	15
27 Oct 84		WHAT ABOUT ME? *RCA PL 85043*	97	1
27 Jul 85	●	THE KENNY ROGERS STORY *Liberty EMTV 39*	4	29
25 Sep 93		DAYTIME FRIENDS – THE VERY BEST OF KENNY ROGERS *EMI CDEMTV 79*	16	5
22 Nov 97		LOVE SONGS *Virgin KENNYCD 1*	27	7
29 May 99		ALL THE HITS & ALL NEW LOVE SONGS *EMI 5207782*	14	6

[1] Kenny Rogers and the First Edition [2] Kenny Rogers and Sheena Easton [3] Kenny Rogers and Dolly Parton

ROKOTTO *UK, male vocal / instrumental group (2 Singles: 10 Weeks)*

22 Oct 77		**BOOGIE ON UP** *State STAT 62*	40	4
10 Jun 78		**FUNK THEORY** *State STAT 80*	49	6

ROLL DEEP NEW

UK, male rap collective (1 Album: 4 Weeks, 2 Singles: 12 Weeks)

18 Jun 05		IN AT THE DEEP END *Relentless CDRELX 07*	50	4
30 Jul 05		**THE AVENUE** *Relentless RELDX 19*	11	7
22 Oct 05		**SHAKE A LEG** *Relentless RELDX 22*	24	5

ROLLERGIRL *Germany, female vocalist – Nicci Saft*

16 Sep 00		**DEAR JESSIE** *Neo NEOCD 038*	22	3

The ROLLING STONES (16 Top 500)

'World's No.1 rock group': Sir Mick Jagger (v), Keith Richards (g), Brian Jones (g), d. 1969, Bill Wyman (b) (left 1991) and Charlie Watts (d). Ron Wood (g) joined in 1975, replacing Mick Taylor. No group has accumulated more UK or US Top 10 albums, more gold and platinum albums and grossed more

4 October 1986	11 October 1986	18 October 1986	25 October 1986
DON'T LEAVE ME THIS WAY Communards with Sarah Jane Morris	TRUE BLUE Madonna	EVERY LOSER WINS Nick Berry	EVERY LOSER WINS Nick Berry
GRACELAND Paul Simon	GRACELAND Paul Simon	GRACELAND Paul Simon	GRACELAND Paul Simon

KEY UK No.1 ★ UK Top 10 ● Still on chart + UK entry at No.1 ■ US No.1 ▲ UK million seller £ US million seller $ Singles re-entries are listed as (re), (2re), (3re)... which signifies that the hit re-entered the chart once, twice or three times... Peak Position Weeks

income from touring than this legendary British band, who have broken box office records on every continent and are still the world's highest earning live band. Transportation of the 300 person entourage and 350 tons of stage set during the 2003 40 Licks tour required 10 buses, 53 trucks and a tour jet. 'Satisfaction' has received over six million US radio plays. They played in front of a world record-paying crowd of 489,176 when they topped the bill at a 2003 Toronto gig. Jagger and Richards, nicknamed The Glimmer Twins, were inducted into the Songwriters' Hall of Fame and the group, who were early members of the Rock and Roll Hall of Fame, received a Grammy Lifetime Achievement award in 1986. Jagger was awarded a knighthood in 2002 and the band were inducted into the UK Music Hall of Fame in 2004 (46 Albums: 805 Weeks, 52 Singles: 380 Weeks)

25 Jul 63 **COME ON** *Decca F 11675* 21 14
14 Nov 63 **I WANNA BE YOUR MAN** *Decca F 11764* 12 16
27 Feb 64 ● **NOT FADE AWAY** *Decca F 11845* 3 15
25 Apr 64 ★ THE ROLLING STONES *Decca LK 4605* 1 51
2 Jul 64 ★ **IT'S ALL OVER NOW** *Decca F 11934* 1 15
19 Nov 64 ★ **LITTLE RED ROOSTER** *Decca F 12014* 1 12
23 Jan 65 ★ THE ROLLING STONES NO.2 *Decca LK 4661* 1 37
4 Mar 65 ★ **THE LAST TIME** *Decca F 12104* 1 13
26 Aug 65 ★ **(I CAN'T GET NO) SATISFACTION** *Decca F 12220* ▲ $ 1 12
2 Oct 65 ● OUT OF OUR HEADS *Decca LK 4733* ▲ 2 24
28 Oct 65 ★ **GET OFF OF MY CLOUD** *Decca F 12263* ▲ 1 12
10 Feb 66 ● **NINETEENTH NERVOUS BREAKDOWN** *Decca F 12331* $ 2 8
23 Apr 66 ★ AFTERMATH *Decca LK 4786* 1 28
19 May 66 ★ **PAINT IT BLACK** *Decca F 12395* ▲ $ 1 10
29 Sep 66 ● **HAVE YOU SEEN YOUR MOTHER BABY STANDING IN THE SHADOW** *Decca F 12497* 5 8
12 Nov 66 ● BIG HITS (HIGH TIDE AND GREEN GRASS) *Decca TXS 101* 3 43
19 Jan 67 ● **LET'S SPEND THE NIGHT TOGETHER / RUBY TUESDAY** *Decca F 12546* ▲ $ 3 10
28 Jan 67 ● BETWEEN THE BUTTONS *Decca SKL 4852* 3 22
23 Aug 67 ● **WE LOVE YOU / DANDELION** *Decca F 12654* 8 8
23 Dec 67 ● THEIR SATANIC MAJESTIES REQUEST *Decca TXS 103* 3 13
29 May 68 ★ **JUMPIN' JACK FLASH** *Decca F 12782* $ 1 11
21 Dec 68 ● BEGGARS BANQUET *Decca SKL 4955* 3 12
9 Jul 69 ★ **HONKY TONK WOMEN** *Decca F 12952* ▲ $ 1 17
27 Sep 69 ● THROUGH THE PAST DARKLY (BIG HITS VOL.2) *Decca SKL 5019* 2 37
20 Dec 69 ★ LET IT BLEED *Decca SKL 5025* ■ 1 29
19 Sep 70 ★ GET YER YA-YA'S OUT! *Decca SKL 5065* ■ 1 15
27 Mar 71 ● STONE AGE *Decca SKL 5084* 4 8
24 Apr 71 ● **BROWN SUGAR / BITCH / LET IT ROCK** *Rolling Stones RS 19100* ▲ $ 2 13
8 May 71 ★ STICKY FINGERS *Rolling Stones COC 59100* ■ ▲ 1 25
3 Jul 71 **STREET FIGHTING MAN** *Decca F 13195* 21 8
18 Sep 71 GIMME SHELTER *Decca SKL 5101* 19 5
11 Mar 72 MILESTONES *Decca SKL 5098* 14 8
29 Apr 72 ● **TUMBLING DICE** *Rolling Stones RS 19103* 5 8
10 Jun 72 ★ EXILE ON MAIN ST *Rolling Stones COC 69100* ■ ▲ 1 16
11 Nov 72 ROCK 'N' ROLLING STONES *Decca SKL 5149* 41 1
1 Sep 73 ● **ANGIE** *Rolling Stones RS 19105* ▲ $ 5 10
22 Sep 73 ★ GOAT'S HEAD SOUP *Rolling Stones COC 59101* ■ ▲ 1 14
3 Aug 74 ● **IT'S ONLY ROCK AND ROLL** *Rolling Stones RS 19114* 10 7
2 Nov 74 ● IT'S ONLY ROCK 'N' ROLL *Rolling Stones COC 59103* ▲ 2 9
28 Jun 75 MADE IN THE SHADE *Rolling Stones COC 59104* 14 12
28 Jun 75 METAMORPHOSIS *Decca SKL 5212* 45 1
20 Sep 75 **OUT OF TIME** *Decca F 13597* 45 2
29 Nov 75 ● ROLLED GOLD – THE VERY BEST OF THE ROLLING STONES *Decca ROST 1/2* 7 50
1 May 76 ● **FOOL TO CRY** *Rolling Stones RS 19121* 6 10
8 May 76 ● BLACK AND BLUE *Rolling Stones COC 59106* ▲ 2 14
8 Oct 77 ● LOVE YOU LIVE *Rolling Stones COC 89101* 3 8
5 Nov 77 ● GET STONED *Arcade ADEP 32* 8 15
3 Jun 78 ● **MISS YOU / FARAWAY EYES** *Rolling Stones EMI 2802* ▲ $ 3 13
24 Jun 78 ● SOME GIRLS *Rolling Stones CUN 39108* ▲ 2 25
30 Sep 78 **RESPECTABLE** *Rolling Stones EMI 2861* 23 9
5 Jul 80 ★ EMOTIONAL RESCUE *Rolling Stones CUN 39111* ■ ▲ 1 18
5 Jul 80 ● **EMOTIONAL RESCUE** *Rolling Stones RSR 105* 9 8
4 Oct 80 **SHE'S SO COLD** *Rolling Stones RSR 106* 33 6
29 Aug 81 ● **START ME UP** *Rolling Stones RSR 108* 7 9
12 Sep 81 ● TATTOO YOU *Rolling Stones CUNS 39114* ▲ 2 29
12 Dec 81 **WAITING ON A FRIEND** *Rolling Stones RSR 109* 50 6
12 Jun 82 ● STILL LIFE (AMERICAN CONCERTS 1981) *Rolling Stones CUN 39115* 4 18
12 Jun 82 **GOING TO A GO GO** *Rolling Stones RSR 110* 26 6
31 Jul 82 IN CONCERT (import) *Decca (Holland) 6640 037* 94 3
2 Oct 82 **TIME IS ON MY SIDE** *Rolling Stones RSR 111* 62 2
11 Dec 82 STORY OF THE STONES *K-Tel NE 1201* 24 12
12 Nov 83 **UNDERCOVER OF THE NIGHT** *Rolling Stones RSR 113* 11 9
19 Nov 83 ● UNDERCOVER *Rolling Stones CUN 1654361* 3 18
11 Feb 84 **SHE WAS HOT** *Rolling Stones RSR 114* 42 4
7 Jul 84 REWIND 1971-1984 (THE BEST OF THE ROLLING STONES) *Rolling Stones 4501991* 23 18
21 Jul 84 **BROWN SUGAR** (re-issue) *Rolling Stones SUGAR 1* 58 2
15 Mar 86 **HARLEM SHUFFLE** *Rolling Stones A 6864* 13 7
5 Apr 86 ● DIRTY WORK *Rolling Stones CUN 86321* 4 10
2 Sep 89 **MIXED EMOTIONS** *Rolling Stones 655193 7* 36 5
23 Sep 89 ● STEEL WHEELS *CBS 4657521* 2 18
2 Dec 89 **ROCK AND A HARD PLACE** *Rolling Stones 655422 7* 63 1
23 Jun 90 **PAINT IT BLACK** (re-issue) *London LON 264* 61 3
30 Jun 90 **ALMOST HEAR YOU SIGH** *Rolling Stones 656065 7* 31 5
7 Jul 90 ● HOT ROCKS 1964-1971 *London 8201401* 3 24
30 Mar 91 **HIGHWIRE** *Rolling Stones 6567567* 29 4
20 Apr 91 ● FLASHPOINT *Rolling Stones 4681351* 6 7
1 Jun 91 **RUBY TUESDAY (LIVE)** *Rolling Stones 6568927* 59 2
4 Dec 93 THE BEST OF THE ROLLING STONES – JUMP BACK – '71-'93 *Virgin CDV 2726* 16 28
2 Jul 94 STICKY FINGERS (re-issue) *Virgin CDVX 2730* 74 1
16 Jul 94 **LOVE IS STRONG** *Virgin VSCDT 1503* 14 5
23 Jul 94 ★ VOODOO LOUNGE *Virgin CDV 2750* ■ 1 24
8 Oct 94 **YOU GOT ME ROCKING** *Virgin VSCDG 1518* 23 3
10 Dec 94 **OUT OF TEARS** *Virgin VSCDT 1524* 36 4
15 Jul 95 **I GO WILD** *Virgin VSCDX 1539* 29 3
11 Nov 95 **LIKE A ROLLING STONE** *Virgin VSCDT 1562* 12 5
25 Nov 95 ● STRIPPED *Virgin CDV 2801* 9 11
4 Oct 97 **ANYBODY SEEN MY BABY?** *Virgin VSCDT 1653* 22 3
11 Oct 97 ● BRIDGES TO BABYLON *Virgin CDV 2840* 6 6
7 Feb 98 **SAINT OF ME** *Virgin VSCDT 1667* 26 2
22 Aug 98 **OUT OF CONTROL** *Virgin VSCDT 1700* 51 1
14 Nov 98 NO SECURITY *Virgin CDV 2880* 67 1
12 Oct 02 ● FORTY LICKS *Virgin / Decca CDVDX 2964* 2 29
28 Dec 02 **DON'T STOP** *Virgin VCSDT 1838* 36 2
13 Sep 03 **SYMPATHY FOR THE DEVIL** *Mercury 9810612* 14 6
13 Nov 04 LIVE LICKS *Virgin CDVDX 3000* 38 4
3 Sep 05 **STREETS OF LOVE / ROUGH JUSTICE** *Virgin VSCDT 1905* 15 4
17 Sep 05 ● A BIGGER BANG *Virgin CDV 3012* 2 4
17 Dec 05 **RAIN FALL DOWN** *Virgin VSCDX 1907* 33 2

'Faraway Eyes' was listed from 15 July 1978, with a peak position of No.10. US No.1 symbol referring to 'Let's Spend The Night Together / Ruby Tuesday' applies only to Ruby Tuesday, which hit the top spot in 1967.

ROLLINS BAND

US, male vocal / instrumental group (1 Album: 2 Weeks, 2 Singles: 4 Weeks)

12 Sep 92 **TEARING** *Imago 72787250187* 54 2
23 Apr 94 WEIGHT *Imago 72787210342* 22 2
10 Sep 94 **LIAR / DISCONNECT** *Imago 74321213052* 27 2

ROLLO (see also DUSTED; FAITHLESS; OUR TRIBE / ONE TRIBE; SPHINX)

UK, male producer – Roland Armstrong (3 Singles: 8 Weeks)

29 Jan 94 **GET OFF YOUR HIGH HORSE (re)** *Cheeky CHEKCD 003* [1] 43 4
10 Jun 95 **LOVE LOVE LOVE – HERE I COME** *Cheeky CHEKCD 007* [2] 32 2
8 Jun 96 **LET THIS BE A PRAYER** *Cheeky CHEKCD 013* [3] 26 2

[1] Rollo Goes Camping [2] Rollo Goes Mystic [3] Rollo Goes Spiritual with Pauline Taylor

1 November 1986	8 November 1986	15 November 1986	22 November 1986
UK No.1 SINGLES			
EVERY LOSER WINS Nick Berry	TAKE MY BREATH AWAY (LOVE THEME FROM 'TOP GUN') Berlin	TAKE MY BREATH AWAY (LOVE THEME FROM 'TOP GUN') Berlin	TAKE MY BREATH AWAY (LOVE THEME FROM 'TOP GUN') Berlin
UK No.1 ALBUMS			
GRACELAND Paul Simon	EVERY BREATH YOU TAKE - THE SINGLES The Police	EVERY BREATH YOU TAKE - THE SINGLES The Police	HITS 5 Various

ROMAN HOLLIDAY
UK, male vocal / instrumental group (1 Album: 3 Weeks, 3 Singles: 19 Weeks)

2 Apr 83 **STAND BY** *Jive JIVE 31* 61 3
2 Jul 83 **DON'T TRY TO STOP IT** *Jive JIVE 39* 14 9
24 Sep 83 **MOTORMANIA** *Jive JIVE 49* 40 7
22 Oct 83 COOKIN' ON THE ROOF *Jive HIP 9* 31 3

ROMEO (see also SO SOLID CREW) *UK, male rapper – Marvin Dawkins (1 Album: 2 Weeks, 4 Singles: 24 Weeks)*

30 Dec 00 ● **NO GOOD 4 ME** *East West OXIDE 02CD* [1] 6 8
24 Aug 02 ● **ROMEO DUNN** *Relentless RELENT 29CD* 3 9
9 Nov 02 ● **IT'S ALL GRAVY** *Relentless RELENT 32CD* [2] 9 6
23 Nov 02 SOLID LOVE *Relentless RELEN 006CD* 46 2
6 Dec 03 **I SEE GIRLS (CRAZY)** *Multiply CDMULTY 109* [3] 52 1

[1] Oxide & Neutrino featuring Megaman, Romeo and Lisa Maffia [2] Romeo featuring Christina Milian [3] Studio B / Romeo and Harry Brooks

Max ROMEO *Jamaica, male vocalist – Maxie Smith*

28 May 69 ● **WET DREAM (re)** *Unity UN 503* 10 25

Harry 'Choo-Choo' ROMERO
(see also CHOO CHOO PROJECT) *US, male producer (2 Singles: 3 Weeks)*

22 May 99 **JUST CAN'T GET ENOUGH** *AM:PM CDAMPM 121* [1] 39 2
1 Sep 01 **I WANT OUT (I CAN'T BELIEVE)** *Perfecto PERF 22CDS* 51 1

[1] Harry 'Choo Choo' Romero presents Inaya Day

RONALDO'S REVENGE
(see also DISCO TEX presents CLOUDBURST; FULL INTENTION; HUSTLERS CONVENTION featuring Dave LAUDAT and Ondrea DUVERNEY; SEX-O-SONIQUE; SHÉNA) *UK, male production duo – Mike Gray and Jean Pearn*

1 Aug 98 **MAS QUE MANCADA** *AM:PM 5827532* 37 2

RONDO VENEZIANO
Italy, orchestra (3 Albums: 33 Weeks, 1 Single: 3 Weeks)

22 Oct 83 **LA SERENISSIMA (THEME FROM 'VENICE IN PERIL')** *Ferroway 7 RON 1* 58 3
5 Nov 83 VENICE IN PERIL *Ferroway RON 1* 39 13
10 Nov 84 THE GENIUS OF VENICE *Ferroway RON 2* 60 13
9 Jul 88 VENICE IN PERIL (re-issue) *Fanfare RON 1* 34 7

The RONETTES
US, female vocal (Veronica Bennett) group (4 Singles: 34 Weeks)

17 Oct 63 ● **BE MY BABY** *London HLU 9793* $ 4 13
9 Jan 64 **BABY, I LOVE YOU** *London HLU 9826* 11 14
27 Aug 64 **(THE BEST PART OF) BREAKIN' UP** *London HLU 9905* 43 3
8 Oct 64 **DO I LOVE YOU** *London HLU 9922* 35 4

Mark RONSON featuring GHOSTFACE KILLAH & Nate DOGG
UK, male DJ / producer and US, male rapper and vocalist

1 Nov 03 **OOH WEE** *Elektra E 7490CD* 15 7

Mick RONSON (see also MOTT THE HOOPLE) *UK, male vocalist / guitarist, b. 26 May 1946, d. 29 Apr 1993 (2 Albums: 10 Weeks, 2 Singles: 1 Week)*

16 Mar 74 ● SLAUGHTER ON TENTH AVENUE *RCA Victor APLI 0353* 9 7
8 Mar 75 PLAY DON'T WORRY *RCA Victor APLI 0681* 29 3
7 May 94 **DON'T LOOK DOWN** *Epic 6603582* [1] 55 1

[1] Mick Ronson with Joe Elliott

Linda RONSTADT
US, female vocalist (10 Albums: 46 Weeks, 5 Singles: 34 Weeks)

8 May 76 **TRACKS OF MY TEARS** *Asylum K 13034* 42 3
4 Sep 76 HASTEN DOWN THE WIND *Asylum K 53045* 32 8
25 Dec 76 GREATEST HITS *Asylum K 53055* 37 9
1 Oct 77 SIMPLE DREAMS *Asylum K 53065* ▲ 15 5
28 Jan 78 **BLUE BAYOU** *Asylum K 13106* $ 35 4
14 Oct 78 LIVING IN THE USA *Asylum K 53085* ▲ 39 2
26 May 79 **ALISON** *Asylum K 13149* 66 2
8 Mar 80 MAD LOVE *Asylum K 52210* 65 1
28 Jan 84 WHAT'S NEW *Asylum 96 0260* [1] 31 5
19 Jan 85 LUSH LIFE *Asylum 9603871* [1] 100 1
14 Mar 87 TRIO *Warner Bros. 9254911* [2] 60 4
11 Jul 87 ● **SOMEWHERE OUT THERE** *MCA MCA 1132* [1] 8 13
11 Nov 89 CRY LIKE A RAINSTORM – HOWL LIKE THE WIND *Elektra EKT 76* 43 8
11 Nov 89 ● **DON'T KNOW MUCH** *Elektra EKR 101* [2] 2 12
11 Oct 03 THE VERY BEST OF LINDA RONSTADT *Elektra 8122736052* 46 3

[1] Linda Ronstadt and James Ingram [2] Linda Ronstadt featuring Aaron Neville
[1] Linda Ronstadt with the Nelson Riddle Orchestra [2] Dolly Parton / Emmylou Harris / Linda Ronstadt

The ROOFTOP SINGERS *US, male / female vocal group*

31 Jan 63 ● **WALK RIGHT IN** *Fontana 271700 TF* ▲ $ 10 12

ROOM 5 featuring Oliver CHEATHAM (see also JUNIOR JACK) *Italy, male producer – Vito Lucente and US, male vocalist (2 Singles: 17 Weeks)*

5 Apr 03 ★ **MAKE LUV** *Positiva CDTIV 187* [1] ■ 1 15
6 Dec 03 **MUSIC & YOU** *Positiva CDTIV 197* [1] 38 2

[1] Room 5 featuring Oliver Cheatham

ROONEY *US, male vocal / instrumental group*

26 Jun 04 **I'M SHAKIN'** *Geffen 9862557* 73 1

ROOSTER *UK, male vocal (Nick Atkinson) / instrumental group (1 Album: 15 Weeks, 4 Singles: 20 Weeks)*

23 Oct 04 ● **COME GET SOME** *Brightside 82876652382* 7 6
22 Jan 05 ● **STARING AT THE SUN** *Brightside 82876672372* 5 8
5 Feb 05 ● ROOSTER *Brightside 82876676352* 3 15
7 May 05 **YOU'RE SO RIGHT FOR ME** *Brightside 82876689582* 14 4
23 Jul 05 **DEEP AND MEANINGLESS** *Brightside 82876708392* 29 2

ROOTJOOSE
UK, male vocal / instrumental group (1 Album: 1 Week, 3 Singles: 3 Weeks)

17 May 97 **CAN'T KEEP LIVING THIS WAY** *Rage RAGECD 2* 73 1
2 Aug 97 **MR FIXIT** *Rage RAGECDX 3* 54 1
4 Oct 97 **LONG WAY** *Rage RAGECD 5* 68 1
18 Oct 97 RHUBARB *Rage RAGECD 6* 58 1

ROOTS
US, male rap / production group (1 Album: 1 Week, 4 Singles: 6 Weeks)

3 May 97 **WHAT THEY DO** *Geffen GFSTD 22240* 49 1
6 Mar 99 **YOU GOT ME** *MCA MCSTD 48110* [1] 31 2
12 Apr 03 **THE SEED (2.0)** *MCA MCSTD 40316* [2] 33 2
16 Aug 03 **BREAK YOU OFF** *MCA MCSTD 40330* [3] 59 1
24 Jul 04 THE TIPPING POINT *Geffen 9863067* 71 1

[1] Roots featuring Erykah Badu [2] Roots featuring Cody ChestnuTT [3] Roots featuring Musiq

ROSE OF ROMANCE ORCHESTRA *UK, orchestra*

9 Jan 82 **TARA'S THEME FROM 'GONE WITH THE WIND'** *BBC RESL 108* 71 1

ROSE ROYCE (409 Top 500)
The best-selling nine-piece soul / dance combo from Los Angeles, US, whose biggest hits featured vocalist Gwen Dickey, started as a backing band for Motown acts and topped the UK albums chart with their Greatest Hits collection in 1980 (5 Albums: 62 Weeks, 15 Singles: 113 Weeks)

25 Dec 76 ● **CAR WASH** *MCA 267* ▲ $ 9 12
22 Jan 77 **PUT YOUR MONEY WHERE YOUR MOUTH IS** *MCA 259* 44 5

29 November 1986	6 December 1986	13 December 1986	20 December 1986
TAKE MY BREATH AWAY (LOVE THEME FROM 'TOP GUN') Berlin	THE FINAL COUNTDOWN Europe	THE FINAL COUNTDOWN Europe	CARAVAN OF LOVE The Housemartins
HITS 5 Various	NOW THAT'S WHAT I CALL MUSIC! 8 Various	NOW THAT'S WHAT I CALL MUSIC! 8 Various	NOW THAT'S WHAT I CALL MUSIC! 8 Various

KEY: UK No.1 ★ UK Top 10 ● Still on chart + UK entry at No.1 ■ US No.1 ▲ UK million seller £ US million seller $
Singles re-entries are listed as (re), (2re), (3re)… which signifies that the hit re-entered the chart once, twice or three times…
Peak Position / Weeks

2 Apr 77 **I WANNA GET NEXT TO YOU** *MCA 278*......14 8
24 Sep 77 **DO YOUR DANCE** *Whitfield K 17006*......30 6
22 Oct 77 IN FULL BLOOM *Warner Bros. K 56394*......18 13
14 Jan 78 ● **WISHING ON A STAR** *Whitfield K 17060*......3 14
6 May 78 **IT MAKES YOU FEEL LIKE DANCIN'** *Whitfield K 17148*......16 10
16 Sep 78 ● **LOVE DON'T LIVE HERE ANYMORE** *Whitfield K 17236*......2 10
30 Sep 78 ● STRIKES AGAIN *Whitfield 56257*......7 11
3 Feb 79 **I'M IN LOVE (AND I LOVE THE FEELING)** *Whitfield K 17291*......51 4
22 Sep 79 RAINBOW CONNECTION IV *Atlantic K 56714*......72 2
17 Nov 79 **IS IT LOVE YOU'RE AFTER** *Whitfield K 17456*......13 13
1 Mar 80 ★ GREATEST HITS *Whitfield K RRTV 1*......1 34
8 Mar 80 **OOH BOY** *Whitfield K 17575*......46 7
21 Nov 81 **R.R. EXPRESS** *Whitfield K 17875*......52 3
1 Sep 84 **MAGIC TOUCH** *Streetwave KHAN 21*......43 8
13 Oct 84 MUSIC MAGIC *Streetwave MKL 2*......69 2
6 Apr 85 **LOVE ME RIGHT NOW** *Streetwave KHAN 39*......60 3
11 Jun 88 **CAR WASH / IS IT LOVE YOU'RE AFTER** (re-issues) *MCA MCA 1253*......20 7
31 Oct 98 **CAR WASH** (re-recording) *MCA MCSTD 48096* [1]......18 3

[1] Rose Royce featuring Gwen Dickey

ROSE TATTOO *Australia, male vocal / instrumental group*

11 Jul 81 **ROCK 'N' ROLL OUTLAW** *Carrere CAR 200*......60 4
26 Sep 81 ASSAULT AND BATTERY *Carrere CAL 127*......40 4

Jimmy ROSELLI *US, male vocalist (2 Singles: 8 Weeks)*

5 Mar 83 **WHEN YOUR OLD WEDDING RING WAS NEW** *A1 282*......51 5
20 Jun 87 **WHEN YOUR OLD WEDDING RING WAS NEW** (re-issue) *First Night SCORE 9*......52 3

ROSETTA LIFE featuring Billy BRAGG NEW

UK, male / female vocal / instrumental group and male guitarist

12 Nov 05 **WE LAUGHED** *Cooking Vinyl FRYCD 252*......11 5

Diana ROSS 13 Top 500

Perennially popular ex-leader of The Supremes, the most successful girl group of all time, b. Diane Earle, 26 Mar 1944, Detroit, US. Ross continued to clock up worldwide hits after leaving the trio in 1970 and sang lead on at least one hit every year for a record 33 years (1964-1996). She has a UK chart span of 41 years. The classy vocalist has also had more albums on the UK chart than any other American female artist. Diana, who starred in the movies Lady Sings the Blues (1972), Mahogany (1976) and The Wiz (1978), moved from Motown to RCA in 1981 for a (female) record $20 million. In 1994, she was the star of the opening ceremony of football's World Cup and in 1998 was sampled on US chart-topping singles by Puff Daddy and Monica. In her homeland, this supreme song stylist has collected a staggering 22 Top 5 entries during her career, even though she has not had a major hit there since 1984. She has been inducted into the Soul Train and Songwriters' Hall of Fame and was the recipient of a Lifetime Achievement trophy at the World Music Awards in 1996 (53 Albums: 743 Weeks, 78 Singles: 562 Weeks)

30 Aug 67 ● **REFLECTIONS** *Tamla Motown TMG 616* [1] $......5 14
29 Nov 67 **IN AND OUT OF LOVE** *Tamla Motown TMG 632* [1]......13 13
20 Jan 68 ★ GREATEST HITS *Tamla Motown STML 11063* [1] ▲......1 60
30 Mar 68 ● LIVE AT THE TALK OF THE TOWN *Tamla Motown STML 11070* [1]......6 18
10 Apr 68 **FOREVER CAME TODAY** *Tamla Motown TMG 650* [1]......28 8
3 Jul 68 **SOME THINGS YOU NEVER GET USED TO** *Tamla Motown TMG 662* [1]......34 6
20 Jul 68 REFLECTIONS *Tamla Motown STML 11073* [1]......30 2
20 Nov 68 **LOVE CHILD** *Tamla Motown TMG 677* [1] ▲ $......15 14
25 Jan 69 ★ DIANA ROSS AND THE SUPREMES JOIN THE TEMPTATIONS *Tamla Motown STML 11096* [2] ▲......1 15
29 Jan 69 ● **I'M GONNA MAKE YOU LOVE ME (re)** *Tamla Motown TMG 685* [2] $......3 12
1 Feb 69 ● LOVE CHILD *Tamla Motown STML 11095* [1]......8 6
23 Apr 69 **I'M LIVIN' IN SHAME (re)** *Tamla Motown TMG 695* [1]......14 10
28 Jun 69 TCB *Tamla Motown STML 11110* [2]......11 12
16 Jul 69 **NO MATTER WHAT SIGN YOU ARE** *Tamla Motown TMG 704* [1]......37 7
20 Sep 69 **I SECOND THAT EMOTION** *Tamla Motown TMG 709* [2]......18 8
13 Dec 69 **SOMEDAY WE'LL BE TOGETHER** *Tamla Motown TMG 721* [1] ▲ $......13 13
14 Feb 70 TOGETHER *Tamla Motown STML 11122* [2]......28 4
21 Mar 70 **WHY (MUST WE FALL IN LOVE)** *Tamla Motown TMG 730* [2]......31 7
18 Jul 70 **REACH OUT AND TOUCH** *Tamla Motown TMG 743*......33 5
12 Sep 70 ● **AIN'T NO MOUNTAIN HIGH ENOUGH** *Tamla Motown TMG 751* ▲ $......6 12
24 Oct 70 DIANA ROSS *Tamla Motown SFTML 11159*......14 5
3 Apr 71 ● **REMEMBER ME** *Tamla Motown TMG 768*......7 12
19 Jun 71 EVERYTHING IS EVERYTHING *Tamla Motown STML 11178*......31 3
31 Jul 71 ★ **I'M STILL WAITING** *Tamla Motown TMG 781*......1 14
9 Oct 71 ● DIANA *Tamla Motown STMA 8001*......10 11
9 Oct 71 I'M STILL WAITING *Tamla Motown STML 11193*......43 1
30 Oct 71 ● **SURRENDER** *Tamla Motown TMG 792*......10 11
13 May 72 **DOOBEDOOD'NDOOBE DOOBEDOOD'NDOOBE** *Tamla Motown TMG 812*......12 9
11 Nov 72 GREATEST HITS *Tamla Motown STMA 8006*......34 10
14 Jul 73 ● **TOUCH ME IN THE MORNING (re)** *Tamla Motown TMG 861* ▲ $......9 13
1 Sep 73 ● TOUCH ME IN THE MORNING *Tamla Motown STML 11239*......7 35
27 Oct 73 LADY SINGS THE BLUES *Tamla Motown TMSP 1131* ▲......50 1
5 Jan 74 ● **ALL OF MY LIFE** *Tamla Motown TMG 880*......9 13
19 Jan 74 ● DIANA & MARVIN *Tamla Motown STMA 8015* [3]......6 43
2 Mar 74 LAST TIME I SAW HIM *Tamla Motown STML 11255*......41 1
23 Mar 74 ● **YOU ARE EVERYTHING** *Tamla Motown TMG 890* [3]......5 12
4 May 74 **LAST TIME I SAW HIM** *Tamla Motown TMG 893*......35 4
8 Jun 74 LIVE *Tamla Motown STML 11248*......21 8
20 Jul 74 **STOP LOOK LISTEN (TO YOUR HEART)** *Tamla Motown TMG 906* [3]......25 8
24 Aug 74 **BABY LOVE** (re-issue) *Tamla Motown TMG 915* [1]......12 10
28 Sep 74 **LOVE ME** *Tamla Motown TMG 917*......38 5
29 Mar 75 **SORRY DOESN'T ALWAYS MAKE IT RIGHT** *Tamla Motown TMG 941*......23 9
27 Mar 76 ● DIANA ROSS *Tamla Motown STML 12022*......4 26
3 Apr 76 ● **THEME FROM 'MAHOGANY' (DO YOU KNOW WHERE YOU'RE GOING TO)** *Tamla Motown TMG 1010* ▲ $......5 8
24 Apr 76 ● **LOVE HANGOVER** *Tamla Motown TMG 1024* ▲ $......10 10
10 Jul 76 **I THOUGHT IT TOOK A LITTLE TIME (BUT TODAY I FELL IN LOVE)** *Tamla Motown TMG 1032*......32 5
7 Aug 76 ● GREATEST HITS 2 *Tamla Motown STML 12036*......2 29
16 Oct 76 **I'M STILL WAITING** (re-issue) *Tamla Motown TMG 1041*......41 4
19 Mar 77 AN EVENING WITH DIANA ROSS *Motown TMSP 6005*......52 1
17 Sep 77 ★ 20 GOLDEN GREATS *Motown EMTV 5* [1] ■......1 34
19 Nov 77 **GETTIN' READY FOR LOVE** *Motown TMG 1090*......23 7
22 Jul 78 **LOVIN' LIVIN' AND GIVIN'** *Motown TMG 1112*......54 6
18 Nov 78 **EASE ON DOWN THE ROAD** *MCA 396* [4]......45 4
24 Feb 79 **POPS, WE LOVE YOU** *Motown TMG 1136* [5]......66 5
21 Jul 79 **THE BOSS** *Motown TMG 1150*......40 7
4 Aug 79 THE BOSS *Motown STML 12118*......52 2
6 Oct 79 **NO ONE GETS THE PRIZE** *Motown TMG 1160*......59 3
17 Nov 79 ● 20 GOLDEN GREATS *Motown EMTV 21*......2 29
24 Nov 79 **IT'S MY HOUSE** *Motown TMG 1169*......32 10
21 Jun 80 DIANA *Motown STMA 8033*......12 32
19 Jul 80 ● **UPSIDE DOWN** *Motown TMG 1195* ▲ $......2 12
20 Sep 80 ● **MY OLD PIANO** *Motown TMG 1202*......5 9
15 Nov 80 **I'M COMING OUT** *Motown TMG 1210*......13 10
17 Jan 81 **IT'S MY TURN** *Motown TMG 1217*......16 8
28 Mar 81 TO LOVE AGAIN *Motown STML 12152*......26 10
28 Mar 81 **ONE MORE CHANCE** *Motown TMG 1227*......49 5
13 Jun 81 **CRYIN' MY HEART OUT FOR YOU** *Motown TMG 1233*......58 3

	27 December 1986	3 January 1987	10 January 1987	17 January 1987
UK No.1 SINGLES	REET PETITE (THE SWEETEST GIRL IN TOWN) Jackie Wilson	REET PETITE (THE SWEETEST GIRL IN TOWN) Jackie Wilson	REET PETITE (THE SWEETEST GIRL IN TOWN) Jackie Wilson	REET PETITE (THE SWEETEST GIRL IN TOWN) Jackie Wilson
UK No.1 ALBUMS	NOW THAT'S WHAT I CALL MUSIC! 8 Various	NOW THAT'S WHAT I CALL MUSIC! 8 Various	NOW THAT'S WHAT I CALL MUSIC! 8 Various	THE WHOLE STORY Kate Bush

29 Aug 81 DIANA AND MARVIN (re-issue) *Motown STMS 5001* [3] 78 2
12 Sep 81 ● **ENDLESS LOVE** *Motown TMG 1240* [6] ▲ $..........7 12
7 Nov 81 WHY DO FOOLS FALL IN LOVE *Capitol EST 26733*..........17 24
7 Nov 81 ● **WHY DO FOOLS FALL IN LOVE** *Capitol CL 226*..........4 12
21 Nov 81 ALL THE GREAT HITS *Motown STMA 8036*..........21 31
23 Jan 82 **TENDERNESS (re)** *Motown TMG 1248*..........73 2
30 Jan 82 **MIRROR MIRROR** *Capitol CL 234*..........36 5
13 Feb 82 DIANA'S DUETS *Motown STML 12163*..........43 6
29 May 82 ● **WORK THAT BODY** *Capitol CL 241*..........7 11
7 Aug 82 **IT'S NEVER TOO LATE** *Capitol CL 256*..........41 4
23 Oct 82 SILK ELECTRIC *Capitol EAST 27313*..........33 12
23 Oct 82 **MUSCLES** *Capitol CL 268*..........15 9
4 Dec 82 ● LOVE SONGS *K-Tel NE 1200*..........5 17
15 Jan 83 **SO CLOSE** *Capitol CL 277*..........43 4
19 Jul 83 ROSS *Capitol EST 1867051*..........44 5
23 Jul 83 **PIECES OF ICE** *Capitol CL 298*..........46 3
24 Dec 83 ● PORTRAIT *Telstar STAR 2238*..........8 31
7 Jul 84 **ALL OF YOU** *CBS A 4522* [7] 43 8
15 Sep 84 **TOUCH BY TOUCH** *Capitol CL 337*..........47 6
6 Oct 84 SWEPT AWAY *Capitol ROSS 1*..........40 5
28 Sep 85 EATEN ALIVE *Capitol ROSS 2*..........11 19
28 Sep 85 **EATEN ALIVE** *Capitol CL 372*..........71 1
25 Jan 86 ★ **CHAIN REACTION** *Capitol CL 386*..........1 17
3 May 86 **EXPERIENCE** *Capitol CL 400*..........47 3
15 Nov 86 DIANA ROSS. MICHAEL JACKSON. GLADYS KNIGHT. STEVIE WONDER. THEIR VERY BEST BACK TO BACK *PrioriTyV PTVR 2* [4] 21 10
30 May 87 RED HOT RHYTHM 'N' BLUES *EMI EMC 3532*..........47 4
13 Jun 87 **DIRTY LOOKS** *EMI EM 2*..........49 3
31 Oct 87 LOVE SONGS *Telstar STAR 2298* [5] 12 24
8 Oct 88 **MR LEE** *EMI EM 73*..........58 2
26 Nov 88 **LOVE HANGOVER** (re-mix) *Motown ZB 42307*..........75 1
18 Feb 89 **STOP! IN THE NAME OF LOVE** (re-issue) *Motown ZB 41963* [1] 62 1
6 May 89 **WORKIN' OVERTIME** *EMI EM 91*..........32 5
27 May 89 WORKIN' OVERTIME *EMI EMD 1009*..........23 4
29 Jul 89 **PARADISE** *EMI EM 94*..........61 2
25 Nov 89 GREATEST HITS LIVE *EMI EMDC 1001*..........34 6
7 Jul 90 **I'M STILL WAITING** (re-mix) *Motown ZB 43781*..........21 6
30 Nov 91 ● **WHEN YOU TELL ME THAT YOU LOVE ME** *EMI EM 217*..........2 11
14 Dec 91 THE FORCE BEHIND THE POWER *EMI EMD 1023*..........11 31
15 Feb 92 **THE FORCE BEHIND THE POWER** *EMI EM 221*..........27 3
29 Feb 92 MOTOWN'S GREATEST HITS *Motown 5300132*..........20 11
20 Jun 92 ● **ONE SHINING MOMENT** *EMI EM 239*..........10 8
28 Nov 92 **IF WE HOLD ON TOGETHER** *EMI EM 257*..........11 10
13 Mar 93 **HEART (DON'T CHANGE MY MIND)** *EMI CDEM 261*..........31 3
24 Apr 93 LIVE STOLEN MOMENTS *EMI CDEMD 1044*..........45 2
9 Oct 93 **CHAIN REACTION** (re-issue) *EMI CDEM 290*..........20 5
30 Oct 93 ★ ONE WOMAN – THE ULTIMATE COLLECTION *EMI CDONE 1*..........1 67
11 Dec 93 **YOUR LOVE** *EMI CDEM 299*..........14 8
25 Dec 93 CHRISTMAS IN VIENNA *Sony Classical SK 53358* [6] 71 2
2 Apr 94 **THE BEST YEARS OF MY LIFE** *EMI CDEM 305*..........28 4
23 Apr 94 DIANA EXTENDED – THE REMIXES *EMI CDDREX 1*..........58 1
9 Jul 94 **WHY DO FOOLS FALL IN LOVE / I'M COMING OUT** (re-issue) (re-mix) *EMI CDEM 332*..........36 4
26 Nov 94 A VERY SPECIAL SEASON *EMI CDEMD 1075*..........37 6
2 Sep 95 **TAKE ME HIGHER** *EMI CDEM 388*..........32 4
16 Sep 95 ● TAKE ME HIGHER *EMI CDEMD 1085*..........10 3
25 Nov 95 **I'M GONE** *EMI CDEM 402*..........36 3
17 Feb 96 **I WILL SURVIVE** *EMI CDEM 415* [8] 14 4
23 Nov 96 VOICE OF LOVE *EMI CDEMD 1100*..........42 7
21 Dec 96 **IN THE ONES YOU LOVE** *EMI CDEM 457*..........34 4
31 Oct 98 40 GOLDEN MOTOWN GREATS *Motown / PolyGram TV 5309612* [1] 35 4
6 Nov 99 ● **NOT OVER YOU YET (re)** *EMI CDEMS 553*..........9 7
20 Nov 99 EVERY DAY IS A NEW DAY *EMI 5214762*..........71 1
17 Nov 01 LOVE & LIFE – THE VERY BEST OF DIANA ROSS *EMI / Universal TV 5358622*..........28 7
29 May 04 THE NO 1'S *Motown 9818019* [1] 26 3
24 Dec 05 ● **WHEN YOU TELL ME THAT YOU LOVE ME** (re-recording) *S 82876767382* [9] ....2 2+

[1] Diana Ross and The Supremes [2] Diana Ross and The Supremes and The Temptations [3] Diana Ross and Marvin Gaye [4] Diana Ross and Michael Jackson [5] Diana Ross, Marvin Gaye, Smokey Robinson and Stevie Wonder [6] Diana Ross and Lionel Richie [7] Julio Iglesias and Diana Ross [8] Diana [9] Westlife with Diana Ross [1] Diana Ross and The Supremes [2] Diana Ross and The Supremes with The Temptations [3] Diana Ross and Marvin Gaye [4] Diana Ross / Michael Jackson / Gladys Knight / Stevie Wonder [5] Diana Ross and Michael Jackson [6] Placido Domingo, Diana Ross and José Carreras

The two Diana albums and the three Diana Ross titles are all different. From 14 Jan 89, when multi-artist albums were excluded from the main chart, Love Songs by Diana Ross and Michael Jackson was listed in the Compilation Albums chart.

Ricky ROSS (see also DEACON BLUE)

UK, male vocalist (1 Album: 1 Week, 2 Singles: 3 Weeks)

18 May 96 **RADIO ON** *Epic 6631352*..........35 2
15 Jun 96 WHAT YOU ARE *Epic 4839982*..........36 1
10 Aug 96 **GOOD EVENING PHILADELPHIA** *Epic 6635335*..........58 1

Francis ROSSI (see also STATUS QUO)

UK, male vocalist (2 Singles: 6 Weeks)

11 May 85 **MODERN ROMANCE (I WANT TO FALL IN LOVE AGAIN)** *Vertigo FROS 1* [1] 54 4
3 Aug 96 **GIVE MYSELF TO LOVE** *Virgin VSCDT 1594* [2] 42 2

[1] Francis Rossi and Bernard Frost [2] Francis Rossi of Status Quo

Nini ROSSO *Italy, male trumpeter – Celeste Rosso*

26 Aug 65 ● **IL SILENZIO** *Durium DRS 54000*..........8 14

ROSTAL and SCHAEFER *UK, male instrumental duo*

14 Jul 79 BEATLES CONCERTO *Parlophone PAS 10014*..........61 2

David Lee ROTH (see also VAN HALEN)

US, male vocalist (5 Albums: 32 Weeks, 6 Singles: 15 Weeks)

23 Feb 85 **CALIFORNIA GIRLS** *Warner Bros. W 9102*..........68 2
2 Mar 85 CRAZY FROM THE HEAT *Warner Bros. 9252221*..........91 2
19 Jul 86 EAT 'EM AND SMILE *Warner Bros. WX 56*..........28 9
6 Feb 88 SKYSCRAPER *Warner Bros. 925671 1*..........11 12
5 Mar 88 **JUST LIKE PARADISE** *Warner Bros. W 8119*..........27 7
3 Sep 88 **DAMN GOOD / STAND UP** *Warner Bros. W 7753*..........72 1
12 Jan 91 **A LIL' AIN'T ENOUGH** *Warner Bros. W 0002*..........32 3
26 Jan 91 ● A LITTLE AIN'T ENOUGH *Warner Bros. WX 403*..........4 7
19 Feb 94 **SHE'S MY MACHINE** *Reprise W 0229CD*..........64 1
19 Mar 94 YOUR FILTHY LITTLE MOUTH *Reprise 9362453912*..........28 2
28 May 94 **NIGHT LIFE** *Reprise W 0249CD*..........72 1

Uli Jon ROTH and ELECTRIC SUN

Germany, male vocal / instrumental group

23 Feb 85 BEYOND THE ASTRAL SKIES *EMI ROTH 1*..........64 2

ROTTERDAM TERMINATION SOURCE

Holland, male instrumental / production duo – Maurice Steenbergen and Danny Scholte (2 Singles: 6 Weeks)

7 Nov 92 **POING** *SEP EDGE 74*..........27 4
25 Dec 93 **MERRY X-MESS** *React CDREACT 33*..........73 2

ROUND SOUND presents ONYX STONE & MC MALIBU *UK, male production trio and rappers*

16 Mar 02 **WHADDA WE LIKE?** *Cooltempo CDCOOL 358*..........69 1

Josh ROUSE NEW *US, male vocalist / guitarist*

26 Feb 05 NASHVILLE *Rykodisc RCD 10679*..........66 1

24 January 1987	31 January 1987	7 February 1987	14 February 1987
JACK YOUR BODY Steve 'Silk' Hurley	JACK YOUR BODY Steve 'Silk' Hurley	I KNEW YOU WERE WAITING (FOR ME) Aretha Franklin and George Michael	I KNEW YOU WERE WAITING (FOR ME) Aretha Franklin and George Michael
THE WHOLE STORY Kate Bush	GRACELAND Paul Simon	GRACELAND Paul Simon	GRACELAND Paul Simon

KEY
UK No.1 ★ UK Top 10 ● Still on chart + UK entry at No.1 ■
US No.1 ▲ UK million seller £ US million seller $
Singles re-entries are listed as (re), (2re), (3re)... which signifies that the hit re-entered the chart once, twice or three times...
Peak Position / Weeks

Demis ROUSSOS 363 Top 500 *Unmistakable Greek MOR vocalist / multi-instrumentalist and entertainer, b. 15 Jun 1947, Egypt. He was in Aphrodite's Child (with Vangelis) before embarking on a successful solo career. 'The Roussos Phenomenon' was the first four track EP to top the singles chart (7 Albums: 147 Weeks, 6 Singles: 44 Weeks)*

22 Jun 74 ● FOREVER AND EVER *Philips 6325 021* 2 68
19 Apr 75 SOUVENIRS *Philips 6325 201* 25 18
22 Nov 75 ● HAPPY TO BE ON AN ISLAND IN THE SUN *Philips 6042 033* 5 10
28 Feb 76 CAN'T SAY HOW MUCH I LOVE YOU *Philips 6042 114* 35 5
24 Apr 76 ● HAPPY TO BE *Philips 9101 027* 4 34
26 Jun 76 ★ THE ROUSSOS PHENOMENON (EP) *Philips DEMIS 001* 1 12
3 Jul 76 MY ONLY FASCINATION *Philips 6325 094* 39 6
2 Oct 76 ● WHEN FOREVER HAS GONE *Philips 6042 186* 2 10
19 Mar 77 BECAUSE *Philips 6042 245* 39 4
16 Apr 77 THE MAGIC OF DEMIS ROUSSOS *Philips 9101 131* 29 6
18 Jun 77 KYRILA (EP) *Philips DEMIS 002* 33 3
28 Oct 78 LIFE AND LOVE *Philips 9199 873* 29 11
16 Mar 02 FOREVER AND EVER – THE DEFINITIVE COLLECTION *Philips 5867702* 17 4

Tracks on The Roussos Phenomenon (EP): Forever and Ever / Sing an Ode to Love / So Dreamy / My Friend the Wind. Tracks on Kyrila (EP): Kyrila / I'm Gonna Fall in Love / I Dig You / Sister Emilyne.

ROUTE-1 featuring Jenny FROST NEW (see also ATOMIC KITTEN) *UK, male / female production trio and female vocalist*

22 Oct 05 CRASH LANDING *All Aroud The World CDGLOBE 446* 47 1

The ROUTERS *US, male instrumental group*

27 Dec 62 LET'S GO *Warner Bros. WB 77* 32 7

Maria ROWE *UK, female vocalist*

20 May 95 SEXUAL *ffrr FCD 248* 67 2

Kelly ROWLAND (see also DESTINY'S CHILD) *US, female vocalist – Kelendria Rowland (1 Album: 26 Weeks, 5 Singles: 54 Weeks)*

26 Oct 02 ★ DILEMMA *Universal MCSTD 40299* [1] ■ ▲ 1 21
28 Dec 02 STOLE (import) *Columbia 6732122* 57 5
8 Feb 03 ● STOLE (re) *Columbia 6735182* 2 14
15 Feb 03 ★ SIMPLY DEEP *Columbia 5096042* ■ 1 26
10 May 03 ● CAN'T NOBODY *Columbia 6738142* 5 10
16 Aug 03 TRAIN ON A TRACK *Columbia 6742155* 20 4

[1] Nelly featuring Kelly Rowland

John ROWLES *New Zealand, male vocalist (2 Singles: 28 Weeks)*

13 Mar 68 ● IF I ONLY HAD TIME *MCA MU 1000* 3 18
19 Jun 68 HUSH ... NOT A WORD TO MARY *MCA MU 1023* 12 10

Lisa ROXANNE *UK, female vocalist – Lisa Roxanne Naraine*

9 Jun 01 NO FLOW *Palm Pictures PPCD 70542* 18 2

ROXETTE 187 Top 500 *The most successful Scandinavian act in the US singles chart: Marie Fredriksson (v) and Per Gessle (v/g). The duo, who have even appeared on postage stamps in their homeland, can claim total worldwide sales in excess of 40 million. In Sweden, Gessle scored a solo No.1 album in 2003 and Fredriksson followed suit in 2004 (7 Albums: 161 Weeks, 26 Singles: 148 Weeks)*

22 Apr 89 ● THE LOOK *EMI EM 87* ▲ 7 10
17 Jun 89 ● LOOK SHARP! *EMI EMC 3557* 4 53
15 Jul 89 DRESSED FOR SUCCESS *EMI EM 96* 48 5
28 Oct 89 LISTEN TO YOUR HEART *EMI EM 108* ▲ 62 3
2 Jun 90 ● IT MUST HAVE BEEN LOVE *EMI EM 141* ▲ 3 14
11 Aug 90 ● LISTEN TO YOUR HEART (re-issue) / DANGEROUS *EMI EM 149* 6 9
27 Oct 90 DRESSED FOR SUCCESS (re-issue) *EMI EM 162* 18 7
9 Mar 91 ● JOYRIDE *EMI EM 177* ▲ 4 10
13 Apr 91 ● JOYRIDE *EMI EMD 1019* 2 48
11 May 91 FADING LIKE A FLOWER (EVERY TIME YOU LEAVE) *EMI EM 190* 12 6
7 Sep 91 THE BIG L *EMI EM 204* 21 6
23 Nov 91 SPENDING MY TIME *EMI EM 215* 22 4
28 Mar 92 CHURCH OF YOUR HEART *EMI EM 227* 21 4
1 Aug 92 HOW DO YOU DO! *EMI EM 241* 13 7
12 Sep 92 ● TOURISM *EMI CDEMD 1036* 2 17
7 Nov 92 QUEEN OF RAIN *EMI EM 253* 28 4
24 Jul 93 ● ALMOST UNREAL *EMI CDEM 268* 7 9
18 Sep 93 ● IT MUST HAVE BEEN LOVE (re-issue) *EMI CDEM 285* 10 8
26 Mar 94 SLEEPING IN MY CAR *EMI CDEM 314* 14 6
23 Apr 94 ● CRASH BOOM BANG *EMI CDEMD 1056* 3 16
4 Jun 94 CRASH! BOOM! BANG! *EMI CDEM 324* 26 5
17 Sep 94 FIREWORKS *EMI CDEM 345* 30 4
3 Dec 94 RUN TO YOU *EMI CDEM 360* 27 6
8 Apr 95 VULNERABLE *EMI CDEM 369* 44 2
4 Nov 95 ● DON'T BORE US – GET TO THE CHORUS! – ROXETTE'S GREATEST HITS *EMI CDXEMTV 98* 5 20
25 Nov 95 THE LOOK (re-mix) *EMI CDEM 406* 28 3
30 Mar 96 YOU DON'T UNDERSTAND ME *EMI CDEM 418* 42 2
20 Jul 96 JUNE AFTERNOON *EMI CDEM 437* 52 1
20 Mar 99 WISH I COULD FLY *EMI CDEM 537* 11 7
10 Apr 99 HAVE A NICE DAY *EMI 4994612* 28 3
9 Oct 99 STARS *EMI CDEM 550* 56 1
15 Feb 03 THE BALLAD HITS *Capitol 5427982* 11 4
6 Aug 05 FADING LIKE A FLOWER *All Around the World CDGLOBE 426* [1] 18 5

[1] Dancing DJs v Roxette

ROXY MUSIC 61 Top 500 *Stylish art-rock group regarded as highly influential pioneers. Nucleus of oft-changing group line-up: Bryan Ferry (v), Andy Mackay (sax), Phil Manzanera (g). A major act of its time, this group amassed 11 Top 10 albums (17 Albums: 430 Weeks, 18 Singles: 155 Weeks)*

29 Jul 72 ● ROXY MUSIC *Island ILPS 9200* 10 16
19 Aug 72 ● VIRGINIA PLAIN *Island WIP 6144* 4 12
10 Mar 73 ● PYJAMARAMA *Island WIP 6159* 10 12
7 Apr 73 ● FOR YOUR PLEASURE *Island ILPS 9232* 4 27
17 Nov 73 ● STREET LIFE *Island WIP 6173* 9 12
1 Dec 73 ★ STRANDED *Island ILPS 9252* 1 17
12 Oct 74 ALL I WANT IS YOU *Island WIP 6208* 12 8
30 Nov 74 ● COUNTRY LIFE *Island ILPS 9303* 3 10
11 Oct 75 ● LOVE IS THE DRUG *Island WIP 6248* 2 10
8 Nov 75 ● SIREN *Island ILPS 9344* 4 17
27 Dec 75 BOTH ENDS BURNING *Island WIP 6262* 25 7
31 Jul 76 ● VIVA! ROXY MUSIC *Island ILPS 9400* 6 12
22 Oct 77 VIRGINIA PLAIN (re-issue) *Polydor 2001 739* 11 6
19 Nov 77 GREATEST HITS *Polydor 2302 073* 20 11
3 Mar 79 TRASH *Polydor POSP 32* 40 6
24 Mar 79 ● MANIFESTO *Polydor POLH 001* 7 34
28 Apr 79 ● DANCE AWAY *Polydor POSP 44* 2 14
11 Aug 79 ● ANGEL EYES *Polydor POSP 67* 4 11
17 May 80 ● OVER YOU *Polydor POSP 93* 5 9
31 May 80 ★ FLESH AND BLOOD *Polydor POLH 002* 1 60
2 Aug 80 ● OH YEAH (ON THE RADIO) *Polydor 2001 972* 5 8
8 Nov 80 THE SAME OLD SCENE *Polydor ROXY 1* 12 7
21 Feb 81 ★ JEALOUS GUY *EG ROXY 2* 1 11
3 Apr 82 ● MORE THAN THIS *EG ROXY 3* 6 8
5 Jun 82 ★ AVALON *EG EGLP 50* ■ 1 57
19 Jun 82 AVALON *EG ROXY 4* 13 6
25 Sep 82 TAKE A CHANCE WITH ME *EG ROXY 5* 26 6
19 Mar 83 THE HIGH ROAD (import) *EG EGMLP 1* 26 7
12 Nov 83 ATLANTIC YEARS 1973-1980 *EG EGLP 54* 23 25

	21 February 1987	28 February 1987	7 March 1987	14 March 1987
UK No.1 SINGLES	STAND BY ME – Ben E King	STAND BY ME – Ben E King	STAND BY ME – Ben E King	EVERYTHING I OWN – Boy George
UK No.1 ALBUMS	THE PHANTOM OF THE OPERA – Original London Cast	THE PHANTOM OF THE OPERA – Original London Cast	THE PHANTOM OF THE OPERA – Original London Cast	THE VERY BEST OF HOT CHOCOLATE – Hot Chocolate

26 Apr 86 ★ STREET LIFE – 20 GREAT HITS *EG EGTV 1* [1] ■ 1 77
19 Nov 88 ● THE ULTIMATE COLLECTION *EG EGTV 2* [1] 6 35
4 Nov 95 MORE THAN THIS – THE BEST OF BRYAN FERRY AND ROXY MUSIC *Virgin CDV 2791* [1] 15 15
27 Apr 96 LOVE IS THE DRUG (re-mix) *EG VSCDT 1580*....33 2
23 Jun 01 THE BEST OF ROXY MUSIC *Virgin CDV 2939*....12 6
19 Jun 04 THE PLATINUM COLLECTION *Virgin BFRM 1* [1] 17 4

[1] Bryan Ferry and Roxy Music

Central Band of the ROYAL AIR FORCE, Conductor W/Cdr AE SIMS OBE *UK, military band*

21 Oct 55 THE DAM BUSTERS MARCH *HMV B 10877*....18 1

Billy Joe ROYAL *US, male vocalist*

7 Oct 65 DOWN IN THE BOONDOCKS *CBS 201802*....38 4

ROYAL GIGOLOS *Germany / UK, male production / vocal group*

31 Jul 04 CALIFORNIA DREAMIN' *Manifesto 9866931*....44 3

The ROYAL GUARDSMEN

US, male vocal (Barry Winslow) / instrumental group (2 Singles: 17 Weeks)

19 Jan 67 ● SNOOPY VS THE RED BARON *Stateside SS 574* $....8 13
6 Apr 67 RETURN OF THE RED BARON *Stateside SS 2010*....37 4

ROYAL HOUSE (see also BLACK RIOT; The GYPSYMEN; SWAN LAKE)

US, male DJ / producer – Todd Terry (2 Singles: 18 Weeks)

10 Sep 88 CAN YOU PARTY *Champion CHAMP 79*....14 14
7 Jan 89 YEAH! BUDDY *Champion CHAMP 91*....35 4

ROYAL PHILHARMONIC ORCHESTRA 398 Top 500

(see also Julian LLOYD WEBBER) *Formed in 1946 by Sir Thomas Beecham, who wanted a first rate ensemble that would attract the countries top musicians. Since his death (1961), it has come under various maestros including Andre Previn and Louis Clark (who was behind its biggest sellers) (17 Albums: 158 Weeks, 5 Singles: 22 Weeks)*

8 Jan 77 CLASSICAL GOLD *Ronco RTD 42020*....24 13
23 Dec 78 CLASSIC GOLD VOLUME 2 *Ronco RTD 42032*....31 4
25 Jul 81 ● HOOKED ON CLASSICS *RCA 109* [1] 2 11
19 Sep 81 ● HOOKED ON CLASSICS *K-Tel ONE 1146*....4 43
24 Oct 81 HOOKED ON CAN-CAN *RCA 151* [1] 47 3
10 Apr 82 I'M YOUR TOY *F Beat XX 21* [2] 51 3
10 Jul 82 BBC WORLD CUP GRANDSTAND *BBC RESL 116*....61 3
31 Jul 82 CAN'T STOP THE CLASSICS – HOOKED ON CLASSICS 2 *K-Tel ONE 1173*....13 26
7 Aug 82 IF YOU KNEW SOUSA (AND FRIENDS) *RCA 256* [1] 71 2
9 Apr 83 JOURNEY THROUGH THE CLASSICS – HOOKED ON CLASSICS 3 *K-Tel ONE 1266*....19 15
8 Oct 83 LOVE CLASSICS *Nouveau Music NML 1003* [1] 30 9
10 Dec 83 THE BEST OF HOOKED ON CLASSICS *K-Tel ONE 1266*....51 6
11 Feb 84 SERENADE *K-Tel ONE 1267* [2] 21 9
26 May 84 AS TIME GOES BY *Telstar STAR 2240* [3] 95 2
27 Oct 84 GREATEST LOVE CLASSICS *EMI ANDY 1* [4] 22 10
26 Nov 88 RHYTHM AND CLASSICS *Telstar STAR 2344*....96 1
22 Sep 90 MUSIC FOR THE LAST NIGHT OF THE PROMS *Cirrus TVLP 501* [5] 39 4
5 Oct 91 SERIOUSLY ORCHESTRAL *Virgin RPOLP 1*....31 6
14 Nov 92 THE VERY BEST OF RICHARD CLAYDERMAN *Decca Delphine 8283362* [6] 47 5
30 Jul 94 BIG SCREEN CLASSICS *Quality Television GIGSCD 1*....49 2
13 Apr 96 AMAZING *Carlton Premiere 3036000282* [7] 49 2
26 Jun 04 SYMPHONIC ROCK *Virgin / EMI VTDCD 620*....42 1

[1] Royal Philharmonic Orchestra, arranged and conducted by Louis Clark
[2] Elvis Costello and The Attractions with the Royal Philharmonic Orchestra
[1] Royal Philharmonic Orchestra conducted by Nick Portlock [2] Juan Martin and the Royal Philharmonic Orchestra [3] Royal Philharmonic Orchestra conducted by Harry Rabinowitz [4] Andy Williams and the Royal Philharmonic Orchestra [5] Sir Charles Groves and the Royal Philharmonic Orchestra and Chorus with Sarah Walker [6] Richard Clayderman with the Royal Philharmonic Orchestra [7] Elkie Brooks with the Royal Philharmonic Orchestra

Pipes and Drums and Military Band of the ROYAL SCOTS DRAGOON GUARDS *UK, military band (3 Singles: 43 Weeks)*

1 Apr 72 ★ AMAZING GRACE (re) *RCA 2191*....1 27
19 Aug 72 HEYKENS SERENADE (STANDCHEN) / THE DAY IS ENDED (THE DAY THOU GAVE US LORD, IS ENDED) *RCA 2251*....30 7
2 Dec 72 LITTLE DRUMMER BOY *RCA 2301*....13 9

ROYALLE DELITE *US, female vocal group*

14 Sep 85 (I'LL BE A) FREAK FOR YOU *Streetwave KHAN 51*....45 6

RÖYKSOPP *Norway, male production duo – Svein Berge and Torbjorn Brundtland (2 Albums: 48 Weeks, 8 Singles: 16 Weeks)*

15 Dec 01 POOR LENO *Wall of Sound WALLD 073*....59 1
17 Aug 02 REMIND ME / SO EASY *Wall of Sound WALLD 074X*....21 3
24 Aug 02 ● MELODY AM *Wall of Sound WALLCD 027*....9 41
30 Nov 02 POOR LENO (re-issue) *Wall of Sound WALLD 079CD*....38 2
8 Mar 03 EPLE *Wall of Sound WALLD 080*....16 3
28 Jun 03 SPARKS *Wall of Sound WALLD 084*....41 1
9 Jul 05 ONLY THIS MOMENT *Wall of Sound WALLD 014*....33 2
16 Jul 05 THE UNDERSTANDING *Wall of Sound WALLCD 035*....13 7
8 Oct 05 49 PERCENT *Wall of Sound WALLD 107X*....55 1
17 Dec 05 WHAT ELSE IS THERE? *Wall of Sound WALLD 111*....32 3+

Lita ROZA *UK, female vocalist (3 Singles: 18 Weeks)*

13 Mar 53 ★ (HOW MUCH IS) THAT DOGGIE IN THE WINDOW *Decca F 10070*....1 11
7 Oct 55 HEY THERE *Decca F 10611*....17 2
23 Mar 56 JIMMY UNKNOWN *Decca F 10679*....15 5

ROZALLA *Zimbabwe, female vocalist – Rozalla Miller (1 Album: 4 Weeks, 13 Singles: 49 Weeks)*

27 Apr 91 FAITH (IN THE POWER OF LOVE) *Pulse 8 LOSE 7*....65 2
7 Sep 91 ● EVERYBODY'S FREE (TO FEEL GOOD) *Pulse 8 LOSE 13*....6 11
16 Nov 91 FAITH (IN THE POWER OF LOVE) (re-issue) *Pulse 8 LOSE 15*....11 6
22 Feb 92 ARE YOU READY TO FLY *Pulse 8 LOSE 21*....14 6
4 Apr 92 EVERYBODY'S FREE *Pulse 8 PULSECD 3*....20 4
9 May 92 LOVE BREAKDOWN *Pulse 8 LOSE 25*....65 2
15 Aug 92 IN 4 CHOONS LATER *Pulse 8 LOSE 29*....50 2
30 Oct 93 DON'T PLAY WITH ME *Pulse 8 CDLOSE 52*....50 1
5 Feb 94 I LOVE MUSIC *Epic 6598932*....18 5
6 Aug 94 THIS TIME I FOUND LOVE *Epic 6603742*....33 3
29 Oct 94 YOU NEVER LOVE THE SAME WAY TWICE *Epic 6609052*....16 5
4 Mar 95 BABY *Epic 6611955*....26 3
31 Aug 96 EVERYBODY'S FREE (re-mix) *Pulse 8 CDLOSE 110*....30 2
22 Nov 03 LIVE ANOTHER LIFE *Inferno CDFERN 59* [1] 55 1

[1] Plastic Boy featuring Rozalla

RUBBADUBB *UK, male / female vocal / instrumental group*

18 Jul 98 TRIBUTE TO OUR ANCESTORS *Perfecto PERF 165CD*....56 1

The RUBETTES

UK, male vocal / instrumental group (1 Album: 1 Week, 9 Singles: 68 Weeks)

4 May 74 ★ SUGAR BABY LOVE *Polydor 2058 442*....1 10
13 Jul 74 TONIGHT *Polydor 2058 499*....12 9
16 Nov 74 ● JUKE BOX JIVE *Polydor 2058 529*....3 12
8 Mar 75 ● I CAN DO IT *State STAT 1*....7 9
10 May 75 WE CAN DO IT *State ETAT 001*....41 1
21 Jun 75 FOE-DEE-O-DEE *State STAT 7*....15 6
22 Nov 75 LITTLE DARLING *State STAT 13*....30 5
1 May 76 YOU'RE THE REASON WHY *State STAT 20*....28 4

21 March 1987	28 March 1987	4 April 1987	11 April 1987
EVERYTHING I OWN Boy George	RESPECTABLE Mel and Kim	LET IT BE Ferry Aid	LET IT BE Ferry Aid
THE JOSHUA TREE U2	THE JOSHUA TREE U2	NOW THAT'S WHAT I CALL MUSIC! 9 Various	NOW THAT'S WHAT I CALL MUSIC! 9 Various

KEY UK No.1 ★★ UK Top 10 ●● Still on chart ++ UK entry at No.1 ■■ US No.1 ▲▲ UK million seller £ US million seller $
Singles re-entries are listed as (re), (2re), (3re)... which signifies that the hit re-entered the chart once, twice or three times...

Peak Position / Weeks

25 Sep 76 UNDER ONE ROOF *State STAT 27* 40 3
12 Feb 77 ● BABY I KNOW *State STAT 37* 10 10

Maria RUBIA (see also FRAGMA) *UK, female vocalist (2 Singles: 13 Weeks)*

13 Jan 01 ● EVERYTIME YOU NEED ME *Positiva CDTIV 147* [1] 3 11
19 May 01 SAY IT *Neo NEOCD 055* 40 2

[1] Fragma featuring Maria Rubia

Paulina RUBIO *Mexico, female vocalist – Paulina Dosamantes*

28 Sep 02 DON'T SAY GOODBYE *Universal MCSTD 40291* 68 1

RUBY and The ROMANTICS *US, female / male vocal group*

28 Mar 63 OUR DAY WILL COME *London HLR 9679* ▲ $ 38 6

RUFF DRIVERZ

(see also Brad CARTER; Dylan RHYMES featuring K. ELLIS) *UK, male / female vocal (Katherine Ellis) / production trio (6 Singles: 21 Weeks)*

7 Feb 98 DON'T STOP *Inferno CDFERN 003* 30 2
23 May 98 DEEPER LOVE *Inferno CDFERN 006* 19 3
24 Oct 98 SHAME *Inferno CXFERN 9* 51 2
28 Nov 98 ● DREAMING *Inferno CXFERN 11* [1] 10 8
24 Apr 99 LA MUSICA *Inferno CDFERN 14* [1] 14 4
2 Oct 99 WAITING FOR THE SUN *Inferno CDFERN 19* 37 2

[1] Ruff Driverz presents Arrola

RUFF ENDZ *US, male vocal duo – David Chance and Dante Jordan*

19 Aug 00 NO MORE *Epic 6696202* 11 5

Frances RUFFELLE *UK, female vocalist*

16 Apr 94 LONELY SYMPHONY *Virgin VSCDT 1499* 25 6

Bruce RUFFIN

Jamaica, male vocalist – Bernardo Balderamus (2 Singles: 23 Weeks)

1 May 71 RAIN *Trojan TR 7814* 19 11
24 Jun 72 ● MAD ABOUT YOU *Rhino RNO 101* 9 12

David RUFFIN (see also The TEMPTATIONS)

US, male vocalist, b. 18 Jan 1941, d. 1 Jun 1991 (2 Singles: 10 Weeks)

17 Jan 76 ● WALK AWAY FROM LOVE *Tamla Motown TMG 1017* 10 8
21 Sep 85 A NIGHT AT THE APOLLO LIVE! *RCA PB 49935* [1] 58 2

[1] Daryl Hall and John Oates featuring David Ruffin and Eddie Kendrick

Jimmy RUFFIN

US, male vocalist (2 Albums: 10 Weeks, 12 Singles: 106 Weeks)

27 Oct 66 ● WHAT BECOMES OF THE BROKENHEARTED *Tamla Motown TMG 577* 8 15
9 Feb 67 I'VE PASSED THIS WAY BEFORE *Tamla Motown TMG 593* 29 7
20 Apr 67 GONNA GIVE HER ALL THE LOVE I'VE GOT *Tamla Motown TMG 603* 26 6
13 May 67 THE JIMMY RUFFIN WAY *Tamla Motown STML 11048* 32 6
9 Aug 69 I'VE PASSED THIS WAY BEFORE (re-issue) *Tamla Motown TMG 703* 33 6
28 Feb 70 ● FAREWELL IS A LONELY SOUND *Tamla Motown TMG 726* 8 16
4 Jul 70 ● I'LL SAY FOREVER MY LOVE *Tamla Motown TMG 740* 7 12
17 Oct 70 ● IT'S WONDERFUL (TO BE LOVED BY YOU) *Tamla Motown TMG 753* 6 14
1 Jun 74 GREATEST HITS *Tamla Motown STML 11259* 41 4
27 Jul 74 ● WHAT BECOMES OF THE BROKENHEARTED (re-issue) *Tamla Motown TMG 911* 4 12
2 Nov 74 FAREWELL IS A LONELY SOUND (re-issue) *Tamla Motown TMG 922* 30 5
16 Nov 74 TELL ME WHAT YOU WANT *Polydor 2058 433* 39 4
3 May 80 ● HOLD ON TO MY LOVE *RSO 57* 7 8
26 Jan 85 THERE WILL NEVER BE ANOTHER YOU *EMI 5541* 68 1

RUFFNECK featuring YAVAHN

US, male production group and female vocalist (3 Singles: 6 Weeks)

11 Nov 95 EVERYBODY BE SOMEBODY *Positiva CDTIV 46* 13 4
7 Sep 96 MOVE YOUR BODY *Positiva CDTIV 61* 60 1
1 Dec 01 EVERYBODY BE SOMEBODY (re-mix) *Strictly Rhythm SRUKCD 08* 66 1

RUFUS *US, male / female vocal (Chaka Khan) / instrumental group (2 Albums: 7 Weeks, 1 Single: 12 Weeks)*

12 Apr 75 RUFUSIZED *ABC ABCL 5063* 48 2
31 Mar 84 ● AIN'T NOBODY *Warner Bros. RCK 1* [1] 8 12
21 Apr 84 STOMPIN' AT THE SAVOY *Warner Bros. 923679* [1] 64 5

[1] Rufus and Chaka Khan [1] Rufus and Chaka Khan

RUMPLE-STILTS-SKIN *US, male / female vocal / instrumental group*

24 Sep 83 I THINK I WANT TO DANCE WITH YOU *Polydor POSP 649* 51 4

RUN-DMC (see also LIBERTY X) *US, male rap group (5 Albums: 44 Weeks, 14 Singles: 62 Weeks)*

19 Jul 86 MY ADIDAS / PETER PIPER *London LON 101* 62 2
26 Jul 86 RAISING HELL *Profile LONLP 21* 41 26
6 Sep 86 ● WALK THIS WAY *London LON 104* 8 10
7 Feb 87 YOU BE ILLIN' *Profile LON 118* 42 4
30 May 87 IT'S TRICKY *Profile LON 130* 16 7
12 Dec 87 CHRISTMAS IN HOLLIS *Profile LON 163* 56 4
21 May 88 RUN'S HOUSE *London LON 177* 37 4
4 Jun 88 TOUGHER THAN LEATHER *Profile LONLP 38* 13 5
2 Sep 89 GHOSTBUSTERS *MCA 1360* 65 2
1 Dec 90 WHAT'S IT ALL ABOUT *Profile PROF 315* 48 3
27 Mar 93 DOWN WITH THE KING *Profile PROFCD 39* 69 2
15 May 93 DOWN WITH THE KING *Profile FILECD 440* 44 2
21 Feb 98 IT'S LIKE THAT (GERMAN IMPORT) (import) *Columbia 6652932* [1] 63 3
14 Mar 98 IT'S LIKE THAT (US IMPORT) (import) *Columbia 6652932* [1] 65 1
21 Mar 98 ★ IT'S LIKE THAT *Sm:)e Communications SM 90652* [1] ■ £ 1 16
18 Apr 98 IT'S TRICKY (import) *Epidrome EPD 6656982* [1] 74 1
6 Jun 98 TOGETHER FOREVER – GREATEST HITS 1983-1998 *Profile FILECD 474* 31 3
19 Apr 03 IT'S TRICKY 2003 (re-mix) *Arista 82876513712* [2] 20 3
26 Apr 03 GREATEST HITS *Arista 74321980602* 15 8

[1] Run-DMC vs Jason Nevins [2] Run-DMC featuring Jacknife Lee

'Walk This Way' features Steve Tyler and Joe Perry of Aerosmith.

RUN TINGS *UK, male instrumental / production duo*

16 May 92 FIRES BURNING *Suburban Base SUBBASE 009* 58 1

Todd RUNDGREN (see also UTOPIA)

US, male vocalist / guitarist (2 Albums: 9 Weeks, 2 Singles: 8 Weeks)

30 Jun 73 I SAW THE LIGHT *Bearsville K 15506* 36 6
29 Jan 77 RA *Bearsville K 55514* 27 6
6 May 78 HERMIT OF MINK HOLLOW *Bearsville K 55521* 42 3
14 Dec 85 LOVING YOU'S A DIRTY JOB BUT SOMEBODY'S GOTTA DO IT *CBS A 6662* [1] 73 2

[1] Bonnie Tyler, guest vocals Todd Rundgren

Bic RUNGA *New Zealand, female vocalist*

3 Apr 04 BEAUTIFUL COLLISION *Epic 5127279* 55 2

	18 April 1987	25 April 1987	2 May 1987	9 May 1987
UK No.1 SINGLES	LET IT BE Ferry Aid	LA ISLA BONITA Madonna	LA ISLA BONITA Madonna	NOTHING'S GONNA STOP US NOW Starship
UK No.1 ALBUMS	NOW THAT'S WHAT I CALL MUSIC! 9 Various	NOW THAT'S WHAT I CALL MUSIC! 9 Various	NOW THAT'S WHAT I CALL MUSIC! 9 Various	KEEP YOUR DISTANCE Curiosity Killed the Cat

RUNRIG *UK, male vocal (Donnie Munro) / instrumental group (11 Albums: 50 Weeks, 10 Singles: 28 Weeks)*

26 Nov 88	ONCE IN A LIFETIME *Chrysalis CHR 1695*	61	2
7 Oct 89	SEARCHLIGHT *Chrysalis CHR 1713*	11	4
29 Sep 90	**CAPTURE THE HEART (EP)** *Chrysalis CHS 3594*	49	2
22 Jun 91 ●	THE BIG WHEEL *Chrysalis CHR 1858*	4	15
7 Sep 91	**HEARTHAMMER (EP)** *Chrysalis CHS 3754*	25	4
9 Nov 91	**FLOWER OF THE WEST** *Chrysalis CHS 3805*	43	2
6 Mar 93	**WONDERFUL** *Chrysalis CDCHS 3952*	29	3
27 Mar 93 ●	AMAZING THINGS *Chrysalis CDCHR 2000*	2	6
15 May 93	**THE GREATEST FLAME** *Chrysalis CDCHS 3975*	36	3
26 Nov 94	TRANSMITTING LIVE *Chrysalis CDCHR 6090*	41	3
7 Jan 95	**THIS TIME OF YEAR** *Chrysalis CDCHS 5018*	38	2
6 May 95	**AN UBHAL AS AIRDE (THE HIGHEST APPLE)** *Chrysalis CDCHS 5021*	18	5
20 May 95	THE CUTTER AND THE CLAN *Chrysalis CCD 1669*	45	2
4 Nov 95	**THINGS THAT ARE** *Chrysalis CDCHS 5029*	40	2
18 Nov 95	MARA *Chrysalis CDCHR 6111*	24	4
12 Oct 96	**RHYTHM OF MY HEART** *Chrysalis CDCHS 5035*	24	2
19 Oct 96	LONG DISTANCE – THE BEST OF RUNRIG *Chrysalis CDCHRS 6116*	13	10
11 Jan 97	**THE GREATEST FLAME** (re-issue) *Chrysalis CDCHSS 5045*	30	3
23 May 98	THE GAELIC COLLECTION 1973-1995 *Ridge RR 009*	71	1
13 Mar 99	IN SEARCH OF ANGELS *Ridge RR 010*	29	2
26 May 01	THE STAMPING GROUND *Ridge RR 016*	64	1

Tracks on Capture the Heart (EP): Stepping Down the Glory Road / Satellite Flood / Harvest Moon / The Apple Came Down. Tracks on Hearthammer (EP): Hearthammer / Pride of the Summer (Live) / Loch Lomond (Live) / Solus Na Madain.

RuPAUL
US, male female impersonator vocalist – Rupaul Charles (6 Singles: 19 Weeks)

26 Jun 93	**SUPERMODEL (YOU BETTER WORK)** *Union City UCRD 21*	39	4
18 Sep 93	**HOUSE OF LOVE / BACK TO MY ROOTS** *Union City UCRD 23*	40	2
22 Jan 94	**SUPERMODEL** (re-mix) **/ LITTLE DRUMMER BOY** *Union City UCRD 25*	61	2
26 Feb 94 ●	**DON'T GO BREAKING MY HEART** *Rocket EJCD 33* [1]	7	7
21 May 94	**HOUSE OF LOVE** *Union City UCRDG 29*	68	1
28 Feb 98	**IT'S RAINING MEN ... THE SEQUEL** *Logic 74321555412* [2]	21	3

[1] Elton John with RuPaul [2] Martha Wash featuring RuPaul

RUPEE *Barbados (b. Germany), male vocalist*

23 Oct 04	**TEMPTED TO TOUCH** *Atlantic AT 0185CD*	44	2

Kate RUSBY *UK, female vocalist / guitarist (2 Albums: 2 Weeks)*

9 Jun 01	LITTLE LIGHTS *Pure PRCD 07*	75	1
17 Sep 05	THE GIRL WHO COULDN'T FLY *Pure PRCD 017*	45	1

RUSH *Canada, male vocal (Geddy Lee) / instrumental group (17 Albums: 101 Weeks, 12 Singles: 43 Weeks)*

8 Oct 77	FAREWELL TO KINGS *Mercury 9100 042*	22	4
11 Feb 78	**CLOSER TO THE HEART** *Mercury RUSH 7*	36	3
25 Nov 78	HEMISPHERES *Mercury 9100 059*	14	6
26 Jan 80 ●	PERMANENT WAVES *Mercury 9100 071*	3	16
15 Mar 80	**THE SPIRIT OF RADIO** *Mercury RADIO 7*	13	7
21 Feb 81 ●	MOVING PICTURES *Mercury 6337 160*	3	11
28 Mar 81	**VITAL SIGNS / A PASSAGE TO BANGKOK** *Mercury VITAL 7*	41	4
31 Oct 81	**TOM SAWYER** *Mercury EXIT 7*	25	6
7 Nov 81 ●	EXIT ... STAGE LEFT *Mercury 6619 053*	6	14
4 Sep 82	**NEW WORLD MAN** *Mercury RUSH 8*	42	3
18 Sep 82 ●	SIGNALS *Mercury 6337 243*	3	9
30 Oct 82	**SUBDIVISIONS** *Mercury RUSH 9*	53	2
7 May 83	**COUNTDOWN / NEW WORLD MAN (LIVE)** *Mercury RUSH 10*	36	5
28 Apr 84 ●	GRACE UNDER PRESSURE *Vertigo VERH 12*	5	12
26 May 84	**THE BODY ELECTRIC** *Vertigo RUSH 11*	56	3
12 Oct 85	**THE BIG MONEY** *Vertigo RUSH 12*	46	3
9 Nov 85 ●	POWER WINDOWS *Vertigo VERH 31*	9	4
31 Oct 87	**TIME STAND STILL** *Vertigo RUSH 13* [1]	42	3

TOP 10

ON THE DAY BRITAIN WENT DECIMAL

On 15 February 1971, shopkeepers of the world united in horror at the idea of adopting decimal currency, a feat our French neighbours achieved in 1799. Despite disgruntled butchers, grocers and stationers all bemoaning the loss of their precious shillings, half crowns and sixpences, the handover went smoothly. In the week that Perry Como sang 'It's Impossible' and Clive Dunn's 'Grandad' was firmly lodged in the Top 10, pop pickers paid about 37.5 "new pence" for their George Harrison single, which had cost them seven shillings and sixpence the week before.

LW	TW	
1	1	**MY SWEET LORD** George Harrison
2	2	**THE PUSHBIKE SONG** The Mixtures
4	3	**THE RESURRECTION SHUFFLE** Ashton, Gardner and Dyke
3	4	**STONED LOVE** The Supremes
5	5	**AMAZING GRACE** Judy Collins
6	6	**NO MATTER WHAT** Badfinger
13	7	**IT'S IMPOSSIBLE** Perry Como
7	8	**YOUR SONG** Elton John
9	9	**GRANDAD** Clive Dunn
10	10	**CANDIDA** Dawn

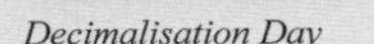

Decimalisation Day

George Harrison

16 May 1987	23 May 1987	30 May 1987	6 June 1987
NOTHING'S GONNA STOP US NOW Starship	**NOTHING'S GONNA STOP US NOW** Starship	**NOTHING'S GONNA STOP US NOW** Starship	**I WANNA DANCE WITH SOMEBODY (WHO LOVES ME)** Whitney Houston
KEEP YOUR DISTANCE Curiosity Killed the Cat	**BETTER TO TRAVEL** Swing Out Sister	**BETTER TO TRAVEL** Swing Out Sister	**LIVE IN THE CITY OF LIGHT** Simple Minds

KEY
UK No.1 ★ UK Top 10 ● Still on chart + UK entry at No.1 ■ US No.1 ▲ UK million seller £ US million seller $
Singles re-entries are listed as (re), (2re), (3re)... which signifies that the hit re-entered the chart once, twice or three times...
Peak Position / Weeks

21 Nov 87 ● HOLD YOUR FIRE *Vertigo VERH 47* ... 10 4
23 Apr 88 **PRIME MOVER** *Vertigo RUSH 14* ... 43 3
28 Jan 89 A SHOW OF HANDS *Vertigo 836346* ... 12 4
9 Dec 89 PRESTO *Atlantic WX 327* ... 27 2
13 Oct 90 CHRONICLES *Vertigo CBTV 1* ... 42 2
14 Sep 91 ● ROLL THE BONES *Atlantic WX 436* ... 10 4
7 Mar 92 **ROLL THE BONES** *Atlantic A 7524* ... 49 1
30 Oct 93 COUNTERPARTS *Atlantic 7567825282* ... 14 3
21 Sep 96 TEST FOR ECHO *Atlantic 7567829252* ... 25 3
25 May 02 VAPOR TRAILS *Atlantic 7567835312* ... 38 2
17 Jul 04 FEEDBACK (EP) *Atlantic 7567837282* ... 68 1

[1] Rush with Aimee Mann

Tracks on Feedback (EP): Summertime Blues / Heart Full of Soul / The Seeker / For What it's Worth / Shapes of Things / Mr Soul / Crossroads / Seven and Seven is.

Donell RUSH *US, male vocalist*

5 Dec 92 **SYMPHONY** *ID 6587977* ... 66 1

Ed RUSH & OPTICAL / UNIVERSAL PROJECT
UK, male production duo and production group (2 Singles: 2 Weeks)

1 Jun 02 **VESSEL** *Virus VRS 010* ... 61 1
20 Nov 04 **REMIXES – VOL.2** *Virus VRS 0146* [1] ... 69 1

[1] Ed Rush & Optical

Jennifer RUSH
US, female vocalist – Heidi Stern (3 Albums: 43 Weeks, 4 Singles: 58 Weeks)

29 Jun 85 ★ **THE POWER OF LOVE (re)** *CBS A 5003* £ ... 1 36
16 Nov 85 ● JENNIFER RUSH *CBS 26488* ... 7 35
14 Dec 85 **RING OF ICE** *CBS A 4745* ... 14 10
3 May 86 MOVIN' *CBS 26710* ... 32 5
18 Apr 87 HEART OVER MIND *CBS 450 4701* ... 48 3
20 Jun 87 **FLAMES OF PARADISE** *CBS 650865 7* [1] ... 59 3
27 May 89 **TILL I LOVED YOU** *CBS 654843 7* [2] ... 24 9

[1] Jennifer Rush and Elton John [2] Placido Domingo and Jennifer Rush

'The Power of Love' peaked at No.55 as a re-entry in Dec 1986.

Patrice RUSHEN
US, female vocalist (2 Albums: 17 Weeks, 5 Singles: 25 Weeks)

1 Mar 80 **HAVEN'T YOU HEARD** *Elektra K 12414* ... 62 3
24 Jan 81 **NEVER GONNA GIVE YOU UP (WON'T LET YOU BE)** *Elektra K 12494* ... 66 3
24 Apr 82 ● **FORGET ME NOTS** *Elektra K 13173* ... 8 11
1 May 82 STRAIGHT FROM THE HEART *Elektra K 52352* ... 24 14
10 Jul 82 **I WAS TIRED OF BEING ALONE** *Elektra K 13184* ... 39 5
9 Jun 84 **FEELS SO REAL (WON'T LET GO)** *Elektra E 9742* ... 51 3
16 Jun 84 NOW *Elektra 960360* ... 73 3

RUSLANA *Ukraine, female vocalist*

19 Jun 04 **WILD DANCES** *Liberty 5490542* ... 47 1

RUSSELL *US, male vocalist – Russell Taylor*

27 May 00 **FOOL FOR LOVE** *Rulin RULIN 1CDS* ... 52 1

Brenda RUSSELL *US, female vocalist / keyboard player – Brenda Gordon (1 Album: 4 Weeks, 2 Singles: 17 Weeks)*

19 Apr 80 **SO GOOD SO RIGHT / IN THE THICK OF IT** *A&M AM 7515* ... 51 5
12 Mar 88 **PIANO IN THE DARK** *Breakout USA 623* ... 23 12
23 Apr 88 GET HERE *A&M AMA 5178* ... 77 4

Leon RUSSELL *US, male vocalist*

3 Jul 71 LEON RUSSELL AND THE SHELTER PEOPLE *A&M AMLS 65003* ... 29 1

RUTH *UK, male vocal / instrumental group*

12 Apr 97 **I DON'T KNOW** *Arc 5737812* ... 66 1

Mike RUTHERFORD (see also GENESIS; MIKE and The MECHANICS)
UK, male vocalist / guitarist (2 Albums: 11 Weeks)

23 Feb 80 SMALLCREEP'S DAY *Charisma CAS 1149* ... 13 7
18 Sep 82 ACTING VERY STRANGE *WEA K 99249* ... 23 4

Paul RUTHERFORD (see also FRANKIE GOES TO HOLLYWOOD)
UK, male vocalist (2 Singles: 6 Weeks)

8 Oct 88 **GET REAL** *Fourth & Broadway BRW 113* ... 47 3
19 Aug 89 **OH WORLD** *Fourth & Broadway BRW 136* ... 61 3

RUTHLESS RAP ASSASSINS *UK, male rap group (2 Singles: 2 Weeks)*

9 Jun 90 **JUST MELLOW** *Syncopate SY 35* ... 75 1
1 Sep 90 **AND IT WASN'T A DREAM** *Syncopate SY 38* [1] ... 75 1

[1] Ruthless Rap Assassins featuring Tracey Carmen

The RUTLES
UK, male vocal group (1 Album: 11 Weeks, 2 Singles: 5 Weeks)

15 Apr 78 THE RUTLES *Warner Bros. K 56459* ... 12 11
15 Apr 78 **I MUST BE IN LOVE (re)** *Warner Bros. K 17125* ... 39 4
16 Nov 96 **SHANGRI-LA** *Virgin America VUSCD 117* ... 68 1

The RUTS *UK, male vocal (Malcolm Owen) / instrumental group (2 Albums: 10 Weeks, 4 Singles: 28 Weeks)*

16 Jun 79 ● **BABYLON'S BURNING** *Virgin VS 271* ... 7 11
8 Sep 79 **SOMETHING THAT I SAID** *Virgin VS 285* ... 29 5
13 Oct 79 THE CRACK *Virgin V 2132* ... 16 6
19 Apr 80 **STARING AT THE RUDE BOYS** *Virgin VS 327* ... 22 8
30 Aug 80 **WEST ONE (SHINE ON ME)** *Virgin VS 370* ... 43 4
18 Oct 80 GRIN AND BEAR IT *Virgin V 2188* ... 28 4

John RUTTER *UK, male composer*

2 Nov 02 THE JOHN RUTTER COLLECTION *UCJ 4726222* ... 75 1

The John Rutter Collection features the Cambridge Singers and the City of London Sinfonia.

Barry RYAN (see also Paul and Barry RYAN)
UK, male vocalist – Barry Sapherson (6 Singles: 33 Weeks)

23 Oct 68 ● **ELOISE** *MGM 1442* ... 2 12
19 Feb 69 **LOVE IS LOVE** *MGM 1464* ... 25 4
4 Oct 69 **THE HUNT** *Polydor 56 348* ... 34 5
21 Feb 70 **MAGICAL SPIEL** *Polydor 56 370* ... 49 1
16 May 70 **KITSCH** *Polydor 2001 035* [1] ... 37 6
15 Jan 72 **CAN'T LET YOU GO** *Polydor 2001 256* ... 32 5

[1] Barry Ryan with the Paul Ryan Orchestra

Joshua RYAN *US, male producer*

27 Jan 01 **PISTOL WHIP** *Nulife / Arista 74321825482* ... 29 3

Lee RYAN NEW (see also BLUE)
UK, male vocalist (1 Album: 4 Weeks, 2 Singles: 15 Weeks)

30 Jul 05 ● **ARMY OF LOVERS** *Brightside 82876713182* ... 3 9
13 Aug 05 ● LEE RYAN *Brightside 82876719152* ... 6 4
22 Oct 05 **TURN YOUR CAR AROUND** *Brightside 82876743372* ... 12 6

Marion RYAN
UK, female vocalist – Marion Sapherson, b. 4 Feb 1931, d. 15 Jan 1999

24 Jan 58 ● **LOVE ME FOREVER** *Pye Nixa N 15121* ... 5 11

With the Peter Knight Orchestra and the Beryl Stott Chorus.

	13 June 1987	20 June 1987	27 June 1987	4 July 1987
UK No.1 SINGLES	I WANNA DANCE WITH SOMEBODY (WHO LOVES ME) Whitney Houston	STAR TREKKIN' The Firm	STAR TREKKIN' The Firm	IT'S A SIN Pet Shop Boys
UK No.1 ALBUMS	WHITNEY Whitney Houston	WHITNEY Whitney Houston	WHITNEY Whitney Houston	WHITNEY Whitney Houston

Paul and Barry RYAN
UK, male vocal duo – Paul, b. 24 Oct 1948, d. 28 Nov 1992, and Barry Sapherson (8 Singles: 43 Weeks)

11 Nov 65 **DON'T BRING ME YOUR HEARTACHES** *Decca F 12260* **13** 9
3 Feb 66 **HAVE PITY ON THE BOY** *Decca F 12319* **18** 6
12 May 66 **I LOVE HER** *Decca F 12391* **17** 8
14 Jul 66 **I LOVE HOW YOU LOVE ME** *Decca F 12445* **21** 7
29 Sep 66 **HAVE YOU EVER LOVED SOMEBODY** *Decca F 12494* **49** 1
8 Dec 66 **MISSY MISSY** *Decca F 12520* **43** 4
2 Mar 67 **KEEP IT OUT OF SIGHT** *Decca F 12567* **30** 6
29 Jun 67 **CLAIRE** *Decca F 12633* **47** 2

Rebekah RYAN
UK, female vocalist (3 Singles: 5 Weeks)

18 May 96 **YOU LIFT ME UP** *MCA MCSTD 40022* **26** 3
7 Sep 96 **JUST A LITTLE BIT OF LOVE** *MCA MCSTD 40063* **51** 1
17 May 97 **WOMAN IN LOVE** *MCA MCSTD 40109* **64** 1

Bobby RYDELL
US, male vocalist – Robert Ridarelli (8 Singles: 60 Weeks)

10 Mar 60 ● **WILD ONE (re)** *Columbia DB 4429* $ **7** 15
30 Jun 60 **SWINGIN' SCHOOL** *Columbia DB 4471* **44** 1
1 Sep 60 **VOLARE (re)** *Columbia DB 4495* $ **22** 6
15 Dec 60 **SWAY** *Columbia DB 4545* **12** 13
23 Mar 61 **GOOD TIME BABY** *Columbia DB 4600* **42** 7
19 Apr 62 **TEACH ME TO TWIST** *Columbia DB 4802* [1] **45** 1
20 Dec 62 **JINGLE BELL ROCK** *Cameo Parkway C 205* [1] **40** 3
23 May 63 **FORGET HIM** *Cameo Parkway C 108* **13** 14

[1] Chubby Checker and Bobby Rydell

Mitch RYDER and The DETROIT WHEELS
US, male vocal / instrumental group

10 Feb 66 **JENNY TAKE A RIDE (re)** *Stateside SS 481* **33** 5

Mark RYDER (see also FANTASY UFO; M-D-EMM)
UK, male producer – Mark Rydquist

31 Mar 01 **JOY** *Relentless Public Demand RELENT 9CDS* **34** 2

RYTHM SYNDICATE *US, male vocal / instrumental group*

27 Jul 91 **P.A.S.S.I.O.N.** *Impact American EM 197* **58** 5

RYZE *UK, male vocal trio*

2 Nov 02 **IN MY LIFE** *Inferno Cool CDFERN 48* **46** 1

RZA (see also GRAVEDIGGAZ; WU-TANG CLAN)
US, male producer / rapper – Robert Diggs

28 Nov 98 **BOBBY DIGITAL IN STEREO** *Gee Street GEE 1003802* **70** 1

S

Robin S
US, female vocalist – Robin Stone (1 Album: 3 Weeks, 9 Singles: 37 Weeks)

16 Jan 93 ● **SHOW ME LOVE (re)** *Champion CHAMPCD 300* **6** 16
31 Jul 93 **LUV 4 LUV** *Champion CHAMPCD 301* **11** 7
4 Sep 93 **SHOW ME LOVE** *Champion CHAMPCD 1028* **34** 3
4 Dec 93 **WHAT I DO BEST** *Champion CHAMPCD 307* **43** 2
19 Mar 94 **I WANT TO THANK YOU** *Champion CHAMPCD 310* **48** 1
5 Nov 94 **BACK IT UP** *Champion CHAMPCD 312* **43** 2
8 Mar 97 ● **SHOW ME LOVE** (re-mix) *Champion CHAMPCD 326* **9** 5
12 Jul 97 **IT MUST BE LOVE** *Atlantic A 5596CD* **37** 2
4 Oct 97 **YOU GOT THE LOVE** *Champion CHAMPCD 330* **62** 1
7 Dec 02 **SHOW ME LOVE** (2nd re-mix) *Champion CHAMPCD 796* **61** 1

S CLUB JUNIORS (see also I DREAM featuring FRANKIE & CALVIN)
UK, male / female vocal group (2 Albums: 17 Weeks, 7 Singles: 78 Weeks)

4 May 02 ● **ONE STEP CLOSER** *Polydor 5707322* **2** 16
3 Aug 02 ● **AUTOMATIC HIGH** *Polydor 5708922* **2** 13
19 Oct 02 ● **NEW DIRECTION** *Polydor 0659692* **2** 13
2 Nov 02 ● **TOGETHER** *Polydor 0652502* **5** 13
21 Dec 02 ● **PUPPY LOVE / SLEIGH RIDE (re)** *Polydor 0658442* **6** 10
12 Jul 03 ● **FOOL NO MORE** *Polydor 9808753* [1] **4** 8
11 Oct 03 ● **SUNDOWN** *Polydor 9865703* [1] **4** 10
25 Oct 03 **SUNDOWN** *Polydor 9865703* [1] **13** 4
10 Jan 04 **DON'T TELL ME YOU'RE SORRY** *Polydor 9815342* [1] **11** 8

[1] S Club 8 [1] S Club 8

S CLUB 7 (177 Top 500)
Made-for-TV act (hit series Miami 7 was seen in more than 100 countries) who had the best start to a career of any mixed vocal group with nine Top 3 hits from their first nine releases, including four No.1s. The award-winning septet: Jo O'Meara, Tina Barrett, Hannah Spearritt, Rachel Stevens, Paul Cattermole, Bradley McIntosh and Jon Lee are the largest vocal group ever to top the chart. When Cattermole left in 2002, the six remaining members became S Club before they disbanded in 2003. Pop pin-up Stevens has since launched a successful solo career. Best-selling single: 'Don't Stop Movin'' – 709,198 (5 Albums: 149 Weeks, 13 Singles: 166 Weeks)

19 Jun 99 ★ **BRING IT ALL BACK** *Polydor 5610852* ■ **1** 15
2 Oct 99 ● **S CLUB PARTY (re)** *Polydor 5614172* **2** 14
16 Oct 99 ● **S CLUB** *Polydor 5431032* **2** 46
25 Dec 99 ● **TWO IN A MILLION / YOU'RE MY NUMBER ONE** *Polydor 5615962* **2** 11
3 Jun 00 ● **REACH** *Polydor 5618302* **2** 17
24 Jun 00 ★ **7** *Polydor 5438572* ■ **1** 61
23 Sep 00 ● **NATURAL (re)** *Polydor 5877602* **3** 16
9 Dec 00 ★ **NEVER HAD A DREAM COME TRUE (re)** *Polydor 5879032* ■ **1** 18
5 May 01 ★ **DON'T STOP MOVIN'** *Polydor 5870832* ■ **1** 19
1 Dec 01 ★ **HAVE YOU EVER** *Polydor 5705002* ■ **1** 14
8 Dec 01 ● **SUNSHINE** *Polydor 5894092* **3** 24
23 Feb 02 ● **YOU** *Polydor 5705812* **2** 14
30 Nov 02 ● **ALIVE (2re)** *Polydor 0658912* [1] **5** 16
7 Dec 02 **SEEING DOUBLE** *Polydor 0654962* [1] **17** 5
7 Jun 03 ● **SAY GOODBYE / LOVE AIN'T GONNA WAIT FOR YOU** *Polydor 9807139* [1] **2** 12
14 Jun 03 ● **BEST – THE GREATEST HITS OF S CLUB 7** *Polydor 9807374* **2** 13

[1] S Club [1] S Club

S-EXPRESS *UK, male / female vocal / instrumental group – leader Mark Moore (1 Album: 9 Weeks, 7 Singles: 50 Weeks)*

16 Apr 88 ★ **THEME FROM S-EXPRESS** *Rhythm King LEFT 21* **1** 13
23 Jul 88 ● **SUPERFLY GUY** *Rhythm King LEFT 28* **5** 9
18 Feb 89 ● **HEY MUSIC LOVER** *Rhythm King LEFT 30* **6** 10
1 Apr 89 ● **ORIGINAL SOUNDTRACK** *Rhythm King LEFTLP 8* **5** 9
16 Sep 89 **MANTRA FOR A STATE OF MIND** *Rhythm King LEFT 35* **21** 8
15 Sep 90 **NOTHING TO LOSE** *Rhythm King SEXY 01* **32** 4
30 May 92 **FIND 'EM, FOOL 'EM, FORGET 'EM** *Rhythm King 6580137* **43** 2
11 May 96 **THEME FROM S-EXPRESS** (re-mix) *Rhythm King SEXY 9CD* [1] **14** 4

[1] Mark Moore presents S Express

SFX *UK, male instrumental / production duo*

15 May 93 **LEMMINGS** *Parlophone CDR 6343* **51** 3

11 July 1987	18 July 1987	25 July 1987	1 August 1987
IT'S A SIN Pet Shop Boys	IT'S A SIN Pet Shop Boys	WHO'S THAT GIRL Madonna	LA BAMBA Los Lobos
WHITNEY Whitney Houston	WHITNEY Whitney Houston	INTRODUCING THE HARDLINE ACCORDING TO TERENCE TRENT D'ARBY Terence Trent D'Arby	HITS 6 Various

KEY
UK No.1 ★★ UK Top 10 ●● Still on chart ++ UK entry at No.1 ■■
US No.1 ▲▲ UK million seller £ US million seller $
Singles re-entries are listed as (re), (2re), (3re)... which signifies that the hit re-entered the chart once, twice or three times...
Peak Position / Weeks

S-J *UK, female vocalist – Sarah James Jiminez-Heany (3 Singles: 4 Weeks)*

11 Jan 97	**FEVER** *React CDREACT 93*	**46**	1
24 Jan 98	**I FEEL DIVINE** *React CDREACT 113*	**30**	2
7 Nov 98	**SHIVER** *React CDREACT 138*	**59**	1

SL2 (see also SLIPMATT) *UK, male DJ / production duo – Matt 'Slipmatt' Nelson and John 'Lime' Fernandez (4 Singles: 25 Weeks)*

2 Nov 91	**DJS TAKE CONTROL / WAY IN MY BRAIN (re)** *XL Recordings XLS 24*	**11**	6
18 Apr 92 ●	**ON A RAGGA TIP** *XL Recordings XLS 29*	**2**	11
19 Dec 92	**WAY IN MY BRAIN** (re-mix) **/ DRUMBEATS** *XL Recordings XLS 36*	**26**	6
15 Feb 97	**ON A RAGGA TIP '97** (re-mix) *XL Recordings XLSR 29CD*	**31**	2

The S.O.S. BAND *US, male / female vocal / instrumental group (2 Albums: 19 Weeks, 8 Singles: 46 Weeks)*

19 Jul 80	**TAKE YOUR TIME (DO IT RIGHT) PART 1** *Tabu TBU 8564* $	**51**	4
26 Feb 83	**GROOVIN' (THAT'S WHAT WE'RE DOIN')** *Tabu TBU A 3120*	**72**	1
7 Apr 84	**JUST BE GOOD TO ME** *Tabu A 3626*	**13**	11
4 Aug 84	**JUST THE WAY YOU LIKE IT** *Tabu A 4621*	**32**	7
1 Sep 84	JUST THE WAY YOU LIKE IT *Tabu TBU 26058*	29	10
13 Oct 84	**WEEKEND GIRL** *Tabu A 4785*	**51**	5
29 Mar 86	**THE FINEST** *Tabu A 6997*	**17**	10
17 May 86	SANDS OF TIME *Tabu TBU 26863*	15	9
5 Jul 86	**BORROWED LOVE** *Tabu A 7241*	**50**	5
2 May 87	**NO LIES** *Tabu 650444 7*	**64**	3

SWV *US, female vocal group (3 Albums: 27 Weeks, 9 Singles: 43 Weeks)*

1 May 93	**I'M SO INTO YOU** *RCA 74321144972*	**17**	6
26 Jun 93	**WEAK** *RCA 74321153352* ▲ $	**33**	3
17 Jul 93	IT'S ABOUT TIME *RCA 7863660742*	17	17
28 Aug 93 ●	**RIGHT HERE** *RCA 74321160482*	**3**	12
26 Feb 94	**DOWNTOWN** *RCA 74321189012*	**19**	5
11 Jun 94	**ANYTHING** *RCA 74321212212*	**24**	3
4 May 96	NEW BEGINNING *RCA 7863664872*	26	5
25 May 96	**YOU'RE THE ONE** *RCA 74321383312*	**13**	3
21 Dec 96	**IT'S ALL ABOUT U** *RCA 74321442152*	**36**	5
12 Apr 97	**CAN WE** *Jive JIVECD 423*	**18**	4
16 Aug 97	RELEASE SOME TENSION *RCA 74321493162*	19	5
13 Sep 97	**SOMEONE** *RCA 74321513942* [1]	**34**	2

[1] SWV featuring Puff Daddy

Raphael SAADIQ (see also LUCY PEARL; TONY TONI TONÉ) *US, male vocalist – Raphael Wiggins (2 Singles: 4 Weeks)*

23 Nov 96	**STRESSED OUT** *Jive JIVECD 404* [1]	**33**	2
19 Jun 99	**GET INVOLVED** *Hollywood 0101185 HWR* [2]	**36**	2

[1] A Tribe Called Quest featuring Faith Evans and Raphael Saadiq [2] Raphael Saadiq and Q-Tip

SABRE featuring PRESIDENT BROWN *Jamaica, male vocal duo*

19 Aug 95	**WRONG OR RIGHT** *Greensleeves GRECD 485*	**71**	1

SABRES OF PARADISE *UK, male production group (2 Albums: 3 Weeks, 3 Singles: 8 Weeks)*

2 Oct 93	**SMOKEBELCH II** *Sabres of Paradise PT 009CD*	**55**	3
23 Oct 93	SABRESONIC *Warp WARPCD 16*	29	2
9 Apr 94	**THEME** *Sabres of Paradise PT 014CD*	**56**	3
17 Sep 94	**WILMOT** *Warp WAP 50CD*	**36**	2
10 Dec 94	HAUNTED DANCEHALL *Warp WARPCD 26*	57	1

SABRINA *Italy, female vocalist – Sabrina Salerno (3 Singles: 22 Weeks)*

6 Feb 88 ●	**BOYS (SUMMERTIME LOVE) (re)** *IBIZA IBIZ 1*	**3**	14
1 Oct 88	**ALL OF ME** *PWL PWL 19*	**25**	7
1 Jul 89	**LIKE A YO-YO** *Videogram DCUP 1*	**72**	1

'Boys (Summertime Love)' peaked during re-entry in Jun 1988.

SACRED SPIRIT (see also DIVINE WORKS) *Germany, male production trio utilising Native American chants (2 Albums: 30 Weeks, 3 Singles: 5 Weeks)*

1 Apr 95 ●	CHANTS AND DANCES OF THE NATIVE AMERICANS *Virgin CDV 2753*	9	27
15 Apr 95	**YEHA-NOHA (WISHES OF HAPPINESS AND PROSPERITY)** *Virgin VSCDT 1514*	**71**	1
18 Nov 95	**WISHES OF HAPPINESS AND PROSPERITY (YEHA-NOHA)** (re-issue) *Virgin VSC 1568*	**37**	2
16 Mar 96	**WINTER CEREMONY (TOR-CHENEY-NAHANA)** *Virgin VSCDT 1574*	**45**	2
26 Apr 97	SACRED SPIRIT VOLUME 2 – CULTURE CLASH *Virgin CDV 2827*	24	3

SAD CAFÉ *UK, male vocal (Paul Young, d. 2000) / instrumental group (6 Albums: 36 Weeks, 6 Singles: 44 Weeks)*

1 Oct 77	FANX TA RA *RCA PL 25101*	56	1
29 Apr 78	MISPLACED IDEALS *RCA PL 25133*	50	1
22 Sep 79 ●	**EVERY DAY HURTS** *RCA PB 5180*	**3**	12
29 Sep 79 ●	FACADES *RCA PL 25249*	8	23
19 Jan 80	**STRANGE LITTLE GIRL** *RCA PB 5202*	**32**	5
15 Mar 80	**MY OH MY** *RCA SAD 3*	**14**	11
21 Jun 80	**NOTHING LEFT TOULOUSE** *RCA SAD 4*	**62**	4
27 Sep 80	**LA-DI-DA** *RCA SAD 5*	**41**	6
25 Oct 80	SAD CAFÉ *RCA SADLP 4*	46	5
20 Dec 80	**I'M IN LOVE AGAIN** *RCA SAD 6*	**40**	6
21 Mar 81	LIVE *RCA SADLP 5*	37	4
24 Oct 81	OLE *Polydor POLD 5045*	72	2

SADE (220 Top 500) *Ever popular jazz-styled vocalist, b. Helen Folasade Adu, 16 Jan 1959, Nigeria. This UK-based BRIT and Grammy winner, who received an OBE in 2002, is the only African artist to top the albums chart in the UK or US (where all her albums have reached the Top 10) (7 Albums: 213 Weeks, 13 Singles: 69 Weeks)*

25 Feb 84 ●	**YOUR LOVE IS KING (re)** *Epic A 4137*	**6**	12
26 May 84	**WHEN AM I GONNA MAKE A LIVING** *Epic A 4437*	**36**	5
28 Jul 84 ●	DIAMOND LIFE *Epic EPC 26044*	2	99
15 Sep 84	**SMOOTH OPERATOR** *Epic A 4655*	**19**	10
12 Oct 85	**THE SWEETEST TABOO** *Epic A 6609*	**31**	5
16 Nov 85 ★	PROMISE *Epic EPC 86318* ■ ▲	1	31
11 Jan 86	**IS IT A CRIME** *Epic A 6742*	**49**	3
2 Apr 88	**LOVE IS STRONGER THAN PRIDE** *Epic SADE 1*	**44**	3
14 May 88 ●	STRONGER THAN PRIDE *Epic 460497 1*	3	17
4 Jun 88	**PARADISE** *Epic SADE 2*	**29**	7
10 Oct 92	**NO ORDINARY LOVE (re)** *Epic 6583562*	**14**	11
7 Nov 92 ●	LOVE DELUXE *Epic 4726262*	10	27
28 Nov 92	**FEEL NO PAIN** *Epic 6588297*	**56**	2
8 May 93	**KISS OF LIFE** *Epic 6591162*	**44**	3
31 Jul 93	**CHERISH THE DAY** *Epic 6594812*	**53**	2
12 Nov 94 ●	THE BEST OF SADE *Epic 4777932*	6	16
18 Nov 00	**BY YOUR SIDE** *Epic 6699992*	**17**	5
25 Nov 00	LOVERS ROCK *Epic 5007662*	18	21
24 Mar 01	**KING OF SORROW** *Epic 6708672*	**59**	1
2 Mar 02	LOVERS LIVE *Epic 5061252*	51	2

'No Ordinary Love' first peaked at No.26 and did not reach its peak position until re-entering in Jun 1993.

Staff Sergeant Barry SADLER *US, male vocalist, b. 1 Nov 1940, d. 5 Nov 1989*

24 Mar 66	**THE BALLAD OF THE GREEN BERETS** *RCA 1506* ▲ $	**24**	8

SAFFRON (see also REPUBLICA) *UK, female vocalist – Samantha Sprackling*

16 Jan 93	**CIRCLES** *WEA SAFF 9CD*	**60**	2

	8 August 1987	15 August 1987	22 August 1987	29 August 1987
UK No.1 SINGLES	LA BAMBA Los Lobos	I JUST CAN'T STOP LOVING YOU Michael Jackson	I JUST CAN'T STOP LOVING YOU Michael Jackson	NEVER GONNA GIVE YOU UP Rick Astley
UK No.1 ALBUMS	HITS 6 Various	HITS 6 Various	HITS 6 Various	HYSTERIA Def Leppard

SAFFRON HILL featuring Ben ONONO
(see also COHEN vs DELUXE; Tim DELUXE; DOUBLE 99; RIP PRODUCTIONS)
UK, male DJ / producer – Tim Liken and vocalist

17 May 03 **MY LOVE IS ALWAYS** *Illustrious CDILL 016* ... 28 3

Alessandro SAFINA
Italy, male vocalist (1 Album: 2 Weeks, 2 Singles: 10 Weeks)

30 Mar 02 **SAFINA** *Mercury 167432* ... 27 2
27 Jul 02 ● **YOUR SONG (re)** *Mercury 639972* [1] ... 4 10

[1] Elton John & Alessandro Safina

SAFRI DUO *Denmark, male instrumental / production duo – Uffe Savery and Morten Friis (2 Singles: 10 Weeks)*

3 Feb 01 ● **PLAYED-A-LIVE (THE BONGO SONG)** *AM:PM CDAMPM 141* ... 6 9
5 Oct 02 **SWEET FREEDOM** *Serious SERR 55CD* [1] ... 54 1

[1] Safri Duo featuring Michael McDonald

Mike SAGAR and The CRESTERS *UK, male vocalist*

8 Dec 60 **DEEP FEELING** *HMV POP 819* ... 44 5

SAGAT *US, male rapper – Faustin Lenon (2 Singles: 6 Weeks)*

4 Dec 93 **FUNK DAT** *ffrr FCD 224* ... 25 5
3 Dec 94 **LUVSTUFF** *ffrr FCD 250* ... 71 1

Carole Bayer SAGER *US, female vocalist*

28 May 77 ● **YOU'RE MOVING OUT TODAY** *Elektra K 12257* ... 6 9

Bally SAGOO *UK (b. India), male producer / instrumentalist (1 Album: 1 Week, 4 Singles: 8 Weeks)*

3 Sep 94 **CHURA LIYA** *Columbia 6607092* ... 64 1
22 Apr 95 **CHOLI KE PEECHE** *Columbia 6613352* ... 45 1
19 Oct 96 **DIL CHEEZ (MY HEART ...)** *Higher Ground 6634882* ... 12 3
9 Nov 96 **RISING FROM THE EAST** *Higher Ground 4850162* ... 63 1
1 Feb 97 **TUM BIN JIYA** *Higher Ground 6641372* ... 21 3

SAILOR *UK, male vocal (Georg Hultgreen aka Georg Kajanus) / instrumental group (1 Album: 8 Weeks, 3 Singles: 24 Weeks)*

6 Dec 75 ● **GLASS OF CHAMPAGNE** *Epic EPC 3770* ... 2 12
7 Feb 76 **TROUBLE** *Epic EPC 69192* ... 45 8
27 Mar 76 ● **GIRLS GIRLS GIRLS** *Epic EPC 3858* ... 7 8
19 Feb 77 **ONE DRINK TOO MANY** *Epic EPC 4804* ... 35 4

SAINT featuring Suzanna DEE
UK, male production duo – Mark Smith and Dave Pickard and female vocalist

12 Apr 03 **SHOW ME HEAVEN** *Inferno CDFERN 52* ... 36 2

ST ANDREWS CHORALE *UK, church choir*

14 Feb 76 **CLOUD 99** *Decca F 13617* ... 31 5

ST CECILIA *UK, male vocal / instrumental group*

19 Jun 71 **LEAP UP AND DOWN (WAVE YOUR KNICKERS IN THE AIR)** *Polydor 2058 104* ... 12 17

SAINT ETIENNE *UK, female / male vocal (Sarah Cracknell) / instrumental group (10 Albums: 32 Weeks, 20 Singles: 56 Weeks)*

18 May 91 **NOTHING CAN STOP US / SPEEDWELL** *Heavenly HVN 009* ... 54 3
7 Sep 91 **ONLY LOVE CAN BREAK YOUR HEART / FILTHY** *Heavenly HVN 12* ... 39 4
26 Oct 91 **FOXBASE ALPHA** *Heavenly HVNLP 1* ... 34 3
16 May 92 **JOIN OUR CLUB / PEOPLE GET REAL** *Heavenly HVN 15* ... 21 3
17 Oct 92 **AVENUE** *Heavenly HVN 2312* ... 40 2
13 Feb 93 **YOU'RE IN A BAD WAY** *Heavenly HVN 25CD* ... 12 5
6 Mar 93 ● **SO TOUGH** *Heavenly HVNLP 6CD* ... 7 7
22 May 93 **HOBART PAVING / WHO DO YOU THINK YOU ARE** *Heavenly HVN 29CD* ... 23 5
18 Dec 93 **I WAS BORN ON CHRISTMAS DAY** *Heavenly HVN 36CD* [1] ... 37 5
19 Feb 94 **PALE MOVIE** *Heavenly HVN 37CD* ... 28 3
12 Mar 94 ● **TIGER BAY** *Heavenly HVNLP 8CD* ... 8 4
28 May 94 **LIKE A MOTORWAY** *Heavenly HVN 40CD* ... 47 2
1 Oct 94 **HUG MY SOUL** *Heavenly HVN 42CD* ... 32 2
11 Nov 95 **HE'S ON THE PHONE** *Heavenly HVN 50CDR* [2] ... 11 5
25 Nov 95 **TOO YOUNG TO DIE – THE SINGLES** *Heavenly HVNLP 10CD* ... 17 9
27 Jan 96 **RESERECTION** *Virgin DINSD 150* [1] ... 50 1
19 Oct 96 **CASINO CLASSICS** *Heavenly HVNLP 16CD* ... 34 2
7 Feb 98 **SYLVIE** *Creation CRESCD 279* ... 12 3
2 May 98 **THE BAD PHOTOGRAPHER** *Creation CRESCD 290* ... 27 2
16 May 98 **GOOD HUMOR** *Creation CRECD 225* ... 18 3
20 May 00 ● **TELL ME WHY (THE RIDDLE)** *Deviant DVNT 36CDS* [3] ... 7 5
3 Jun 00 **SOUND OF WATER** *Mantra MNTCD 1018* ... 33 1
24 Jun 00 **HEART FAILED (IN THE BACK OF A TAXI)** *Mantra / Beggars Banquet MNT 54CD* ... 50 1
20 Jan 01 **BOY IS CRYING** *Mantra / Beggars Banquet MNT 60CD* ... 34 2
7 Sep 02 **ACTION** *Mantra / Beggars Banquet MNT 73CD* ... 41 1
19 Oct 02 **FINISTERRE** *Mantra / Beggars Banquet MNTCD 1033* ... 55 1
29 Mar 03 **SOFT LIKE ME** *Mantra MNT 78CD* ... 40 1
18 Jun 05 **SIDE STREETS** *Mantra SANXD 378* ... 36 1
25 Jun 05 **TALES FROM TURNPIKE HOUSE** *Sanctuary SANLP 271* ... 72 1
12 Nov 05 **A GOOD THING** *Sanctuary SANXD 412* ... 70 1

[1] Saint Etienne co-starring Tim Burgess [2] Saint Etienne featuring Etienne Daho [3] Paul Van Dyk featuring Saint Etienne [1] Saint Etienne Daho

ST GERMAIN *France, male producer – Ludovic Navarre (1 Album: 1 Week, 2 Singles: 3 Weeks)*

31 Aug 96 **ALABAMA BLUES (REVISITED)** *F Communications F 050CD* ... 50 1
20 May 00 **TOURIST** *Blue Note 5262012* ... 73 1
10 Mar 01 **ROSE ROUGE** *Blue Note CDROSE 001* ... 54 2

Barry ST JOHN *UK, female vocalist*

9 Dec 65 **COME AWAY MELINDA** *Columbia DB 7783* ... 47 1

ST JOHN'S COLLEGE SCHOOL CHOIR and the Band of the GRENADIER GUARDS *UK, school choir and military band*

3 May 86 **THE QUEEN'S BIRTHDAY SONG** *Columbia Q 1* ... 40 3

ST LOUIS UNION *UK, male vocal / instrumental group*

13 Jan 66 **GIRL** *Decca F 12318* ... 11 10

ST PAUL'S BOYS' CHOIR *UK, choir*

29 Nov 80 **REJOICE** *K-Tel NE 1064* ... 36 8

Crispian ST PETERS *UK, male vocalist – Robin Smith (3 Singles: 31 Weeks)*

6 Jan 66 ● **YOU WERE ON MY MIND** *Decca F 12287* ... 2 14
31 Mar 66 ● **THE PIED PIPER** *Decca F 12359* ... 5 13
15 Sep 66 **CHANGES (re)** *Decca F 12480* ... 47 4

ST PHILIPS CHOIR *UK, choir*

12 Dec 87 **SING FOR EVER** *BBC RESL 222* ... 49 4

ST WINIFRED'S SCHOOL CHOIR (see also BRIAN and MICHAEL; Bill TARMEY) *UK, school choir – lead vocal Dawn Ralph*

22 Nov 80 ★ **THERE'S NO ONE QUITE LIKE GRANDMA** *MFP FP 900* ... 1 11

Buffy SAINTE-MARIE
Canada, female vocalist (1 Album: 2 Weeks, 4 Singles: 29 Weeks)

17 Jul 71 ● **SOLDIER BLUE** *RCA 2081* ... 7 18
18 Mar 72 **I'M GONNA BE A COUNTRY GIRL AGAIN** *Vanguard VRS 35143* ... 34 5
8 Feb 92 **THE BIG ONES GET AWAY** *Ensign ENY 650* ... 39 5
21 Mar 92 **COINCIDENCE (AND LIKELY STORIES)** *Ensign CCD 1920* ... 39 2
4 Jul 92 **FALLEN ANGELS** *Ensign ENY 655* ... 57 1

5 September 1987	12 September 1987	19 September 1987	26 September 1987
NEVER GONNA GIVE YOU UP Rick Astley	NEVER GONNA GIVE YOU UP Rick Astley	NEVER GONNA GIVE YOU UP Rick Astley	NEVER GONNA GIVE YOU UP Rick Astley
HITS 6 Various	BAD Michael Jackson	BAD Michael Jackson	BAD Michael Jackson

KEY: UK No.1 ★ UK Top 10 ● Still on chart + UK entry at No.1 ■ US No.1 ▲ UK million seller £ US million seller $
Singles re-entries are listed as (re), (2re), (3re)... which signifies that the hit re-entered the chart once, twice or three times...
Peak Position / Weeks

The SAINTS *Australia, male vocal / instrumental group*

16 Jul 77 **THIS PERFECT DAY** *Harvest HAR 5130*....34 4

Kyu SAKAMOTO *Japan, male vocalist, b. 10 Nov 1941, d. 12 Aug 1985*

27 Jun 63 ● **SUKIYAKI** *HMV POP 1171* ▲ $....6 13

Ryuichi SAKAMOTO (see also David SYLVIAN) *Japan, male keyboard player*

3 Sep 83 MERRY CHRISTMAS MR LAWRENCE (FILM SOUNDTRACK) *Virgin V 2276*....36 9

SALAD *UK / Holland, male / female vocal / instrumental group (1 Album: 2 Weeks, 5 Singles: 5 Weeks)*

11 Mar 95 **DRINK THE ELIXIR** *Island Red CIRD 104*....66 1
13 May 95 **MOTORBIKE TO HEAVEN** *Island Red CIRD 106*....42 1
27 May 95 DRINK ME *Island Red CIRDX 1002*....16 2
16 Sep 95 **GRANITE STATUE** *Island Red CIRD 108*....50 1
26 Oct 96 **I WANT YOU** *Island CID 646*....60 1
17 May 97 **CARDBOY KING** *Island CID 654*....65 1

The SALFORD JETS *UK, male vocal / instrumental group*

31 May 80 **WHO YOU LOOKING AT?** *RCA PB 5239*....72 2

SALIVA *US, male vocal / instrumental group*

15 Mar 03 **ALWAYS** *Mercury 0637082*....47 1

SALT TANK *UK, male production duo – Malcolm Stanners and David Gates (3 Singles: 4 Weeks)*

11 May 96 **EUGINA** *Internal LIECD 29*....40 2
3 Jul 99 **DIMENSION** *Hooj Choons HOOJ 74CD*....52 1
9 Dec 00 **EUGINA** (re-mix) *Lost Language LOST 004CD*....58 1

SALT-N-PEPA 397 Top 500

Rappers Cheryl "Salt" James, b. 28 Mar 1969, Brooklyn, US, and Sandra "Pepa" Denton, b. 9 Nov 1969, Kingston, Jamaica, backed up by DJ Dee Dee "Spinderella" Roper, are the most commercially successful female rap troupe of all time (6 Albums: 57 Weeks, 17 Singles: 123 Weeks)

26 Mar 88 **PUSH IT / I AM DOWN** *ffrr FFR 2* $....41 6
25 Jun 88 ● **PUSH IT** (re-issue) **/ TRAMP** *Champion CHAMP 51 & ffrr FFR 2*....2 13
6 Aug 88 A SALT WITH A DEADLY PEPA *ffrr FFRLP 3*....19 27
3 Sep 88 **SHAKE YOUR THANG (IT'S YOUR THING)** *ffrr FFR 11* [1]....22 8
12 Nov 88 ● **TWIST AND SHOUT** *ffrr FFR 16*....4 9
14 Apr 90 **EXPRESSION** *ffrr F 127* $....40 6
12 May 90 BLACKS' MAGIC *ffrr 8281641*....70 1
25 May 91 ● **DO YOU WANT ME** *ffrr F 151*....5 12
6 Jul 91 A BLITZ OF SALT-N-PEPA HITS – THE HITS REMIXED *ffrr 8282491*....70 2
31 Aug 91 ● **LET'S TALK ABOUT SEX** *ffrr F 162*....2 13
19 Oct 91 ● GREATEST HITS *ffrr 8282911*....6 20
30 Nov 91 **YOU SHOWED ME** *ffrr F 174* [2]....15 9
28 Mar 92 **EXPRESSION** (re-mix) *ffrr F 182*....23 6
25 Apr 92 RAPPED IN REMIXES *ffrr 8282972*....37 2
3 Oct 92 **START ME UP** *ffrr F 196*....39 3
9 Oct 93 **SHOOP** *ffrr FCD 219*....29 3
19 Mar 94 ● **WHATTA MAN** *ffrr FCD 222* [3] $....7 10
23 Apr 94 VERY NECESSARY *ffrr 8284542*....36 5
28 May 94 **SHOOP** (re-mix) *ffrr FCD 234*....13 8
12 Nov 94 **NONE OF YOUR BUSINESS** (re) *ffrr FCD 244*....19 5
21 Dec 96 **CHAMPAGNE** *MCA MCSTD 48025*....23 6
29 Nov 97 **R U READY** *ffrr FCDP 322*....24 2
11 Dec 99 **THE BRICK TRACK VERSUS GITTY UP** *ffrr FCD 373* [4]....22 4

[1] Salt-N-Pepa featuring EU [2] Additional vocals Joyce Martin & Cari Linger [3] Salt-N-Pepa with En Vogue [4] Saltnpepa

'I Am Down' listed only from 2 Apr 1988. The disc re-entered on 25 Jun when it was made available on Champion with a different flip side. Sales for both discs were amalgamated.

SALVATION ARMY *UK, brass band*

24 Dec 77 BY REQUEST *Warwick WW 5038*....16 5

SAM and DAVE (see also Lou REED)

US, male vocal duo – Sam Moore and Dave Prater, b. 9 May 1937, d. 9 Apr 1998 (3 Albums: 20 Weeks, 4 Singles: 39 Weeks)

21 Jan 67 HOLD ON I'M COMIN' *Atlantic 588045*....35 7
16 Mar 67 **SOOTHE ME** (re) *Stax 601 004*....35 8
22 Apr 67 DOUBLE DYNAMITE *Stax 589003*....28 5
1 Nov 67 **SOUL MAN** *Stax 601 023* $....24 14
13 Mar 68 **I THANK YOU** *Stax 601 030*....34 9
23 Mar 68 SOUL MEN *Stax 589015*....32 8
29 Jan 69 **SOUL SISTER, BROWN SUGAR** *Atlantic 584 237*....15 8

SAM & MARK

UK, male vocal duo – Sam Nixon and Mark Rhodes (2 Singles: 13 Weeks)

21 Feb 04 ★ **WITH A LITTLE HELP FROM MY FRIENDS / MEASURE OF A MAN** *19 19RECS 9* ■....1 10
5 Jun 04 **THE SUN HAS COME YOUR WAY** *19 / UMTV 9866906*....19 3

SAM THE SHAM and The PHARAOHS

US, male vocal / instrumental group (2 Singles: 18 Weeks)

24 Jun 65 **WOOLY BULLY** *MGM 1269* $....11 15
4 Aug 66 **LIL' RED RIDING HOOD** (re) *MGM 1315* $....46 3

Richie SAMBORA (see also BON JOVI)

US, male vocalist / guitarist (2 Albums: 5 Weeks, 3 Singles: 4 Weeks)

7 Sep 91 **BALLAD OF YOUTH** *Mercury MER 350*....59 1
14 Sep 91 STRANGER IN THIS TOWN *Mercury 8488951*....20 3
7 Mar 98 **HARD TIMES COME EASY** *Mercury 5686972*....37 2
14 Mar 98 UNDISCOVERED SOUL *Mercury 5369722*....24 2
1Aug 98 **IN IT FOR LOVE** *Mercury 5660632*....58 1

Michael SAMMES SINGERS (see also Michael HOLLIDAY; Des O'CONNOR; Andy STEWART; Malcolm VAUGHAN; Jimmy YOUNG)

UK, male / female vocal group – leader b. 19 Feb 1928, d. 19 May 2001 (1 Album: 7 Weeks, 2 Singles: 41 Weeks)

27 Feb 59 **THE LITTLE DRUMMER BOY** (re) *Parlophone R 4528* [1]....20 3
15 Sep 66 **SOMEWHERE MY LOVE** (re) *HMV POP 1546*....14 38
19 Jan 76 MUSIC OF AMERICA *Ronco TRD 2016* [1]....18 7

[1] Michael Flanders with the Michael Sammes Singers [1] Richmond Strings / Mike Sammes Singers

'Somewhere My Love' first peaked at No.22 and reached No.14 after re-entry in 1967.

Dave SAMPSON and The HUNTERS

UK, male vocalist and UK group

19 May 60 **SWEET DREAMS** (re) *Columbia DB 4449*....29 6

SAMSON (see also Bruce DICKINSON)

UK, male vocal / instrumental group (1 Album: 6 Weeks, 3 Singles: 6 Weeks)

26 Jul 80 HEAD ON *Gem GEMLP 108*....34 6
4 Jul 81 **RIDING WITH THE ANGELS** *RCA 67*....55 3
24 Jul 82 **LOSING MY GRIP** *Polydor POSP 471*....63 2
5 Mar 83 **RED SKIES** *Polydor POSP 554*....65 1

3 October 1987	10 October 1987	17 October 1987	24 October 1987
UK No.1 SINGLES			
PUMP UP THE VOLUME / ANITINA (THE FIRST TIME I SEE SHE DANCE) M/A/R/R/S	PUMP UP THE VOLUME / ANITINA (THE FIRST TIME I SEE SHE DANCE) M/A/R/R/S	YOU WIN AGAIN The Bee Gees	YOU WIN AGAIN The Bee Gees
UK No.1 ALBUMS			
BAD Michael Jackson	BAD Michael Jackson	TUNNEL OF LOVE Bruce Springsteen	... NOTHING LIKE THE SUN Sting

SAN JOSÉ featuring Rodriguez ARGENTINA
(see also ARGENT; SILSOE) *UK, male instrumental group*

17 Jun 78 **ARGENTINE MELODY (CANCION DE ARGENTINA)** *MCA 369*....14 8

Rodriguez Argentina is Rod Argent.

SAN REMO STRINGS *US, orchestra*

18 Dec 71 **FESTIVAL TIME** *Tamla Motown TMG 795*....39 8

David SANBORN *US, male saxophonist*

14 Mar 87 A CHANGE OF HEART *Warner Bros. 925 4791*....86 1

Junior SANCHEZ featuring DAJAE
US, male DJ / producer and female vocalist – Karen Gordon

16 Oct 99 **B WITH U** *Manifesto FESCD 62*....31 2

Roger SANCHEZ
(see also EL MARIACHI; FUNK JUNKEEZ; TRANSATLANTIC SOUL)
US, male producer (1 Album: 2 Weeks, 5 Singles: 21 Weeks)

3 Oct 98 **BUFFALO GALS STAMPEDE** (re-mix) *Virgin VSCDT 1717* [1] .65 1
20 Feb 99 **I WANT YOUR LOVE** *Perpetual PERPCDS 001* [2] 31 2
29 Jan 00 **I NEVER KNEW** *INCredible INCS 4CDS* [3] 24 2
14 Jul 01 ★ **ANOTHER CHANCE** *Defected DFECT 35CDS* ■....1 12
11 Aug 01 FIRST CONTACT *Defected SMAN 01CD*....34 2
15 Dec 01 **YOU CAN'T CHANGE ME** *Defected DFECT 41CDS* [4] 25 4

[1] Malcolm McLaren and the World's Famous Supreme Team plus Rakim and Roger Sanchez [2] Roger Sanchez presents Twilight [3] Roger Sanchez featuring Cooly's Hot Box [4] Roger Sanchez featuring Armand Van Helden and N'Dea Davenport

Chris SANDFORD *UK, male actor / vocalist*

12 Dec 63 **NOT TOO LITTLE NOT TOO MUCH** *Decca F 11778*....17 9

The SANDPIPERS *US, male vocal group (4 Singles: 33 Weeks)*

15 Sep 66 ● **GUANTANAMERA** *Pye International 7N 25380*....7 17
5 Jun 68 **QUANDO M'INNAMORO (A MAN WITHOUT LOVE)** *A&M AMS 723*....33 6
26 Mar 69 **KUMBAYA (re)** *A&M AMS 744*....38 2
27 Nov 76 **HANG ON SLOOPY** *Satril SAT 114*....32 8

SANDRA *Germany, female vocalist – Sandra Lauer*

17 Dec 88 **EVERLASTING LOVE** *Siren SRN 85*....45 8

Jodie SANDS *US, female vocalist*

17 Oct 58 **SOMEDAY (YOU'LL WANT ME TO WANT YOU)** *HMV POP 533*..14 10

Tommy SANDS *US, male vocalist*

4 Aug 60 **THE OLD OAKEN BUCKET** *Capitol CL 15143*....25 7

SANDSTORM
(see also ABSOLUTE; BASSTOY) *US, male producer – Mark Picchiotti*

13 May 00 **THE RETURN OF NOTHING** *Renaissance Recordings RENCDS 001*....54 1

Samantha SANG *Australia, female vocalist – Cheryl Gray*

4 Feb 78 **EMOTION** *Private Stock PVT 128* $....11 13

SANTA NEW *North Pole, male vocalist – Santa Claus*

10 Dec 05 SANTA SINGS *Brightspark 82876755312*....49 2
31 Dec 05 **IS THIS THE WAY TO AMARILLO? (SANTA'S GROTTO)** *Brightspark 82876767312*....30 1+

SANTA CLAUS and The CHRISTMAS TREES
UK, male vocal / instrumental group (2 Singles: 10 Weeks)

11 Dec 82 **SINGALONG-A-SANTA** *Polydor IVY 1*....19 5
10 Dec 83 **SINGALONG-A-SANTA AGAIN** *Polydor IVY 2*....39 5

SANTA ESMERALDA and Leroy GOMEZ
US / France, male / female vocal / instrumental group

12 Nov 77 **DON'T LET ME BE MISUNDERSTOOD** *Philips 6042 325*....41 5

SANTANA (155 Top 500) *Latin rock band formed in San Francisco in 1966 by Carlos Santana, b. 20 Jul 1947, Autlan de Novarro, Mexico, who peaked in the 21st Century. Their first US No.1 for 28 years, Supernatural, won a record eight Grammy awards in 2000 and sold more than 25 million copies worldwide (27 Albums: 300 Weeks, 8 Singles: 53 Weeks)*

2 May 70 SANTANA *CBS 63815*....26 11
28 Nov 70 ● ABRAXAS *CBS 64807* ▲....7 52
13 Nov 71 ● SANTANA III *CBS 69015* ▲....6 14
26 Aug 72 CARLOS SANTANA AND BUDDY MILES LIVE *CBS 65142* [1] .29 4
25 Nov 72 ● CARAVANSERAI *CBS 65299*....6 11
28 Jul 73 ● LOVE DEVOTION AND SURRENDER *CBS 69037* [2]....7 9
8 Dec 73 ● WELCOME *CBS 69040*....8 6
21 Sep 74 GREATEST HITS *CBS 69081*....14 15
28 Sep 74 **SAMBA PA TI** *CBS 2561*....27 7
2 Nov 74 ILLUMINATIONS *CBS 69063* [3] 40 1
30 Nov 74 BORBOLETTA *CBS 69084*....18 5
10 Apr 76 AMIGOS *CBS 86005*....21 9
8 Jan 77 FESTIVAL *CBS 86020*....27 3
15 Oct 77 **SHE'S NOT THERE** *CBS 5671*....11 12
5 Nov 77 ● MOONFLOWER *CBS 88272*....7 27
11 Nov 78 INNER SECRETS *CBS 86075*....17 16
25 Nov 78 **WELL ALL RIGHT** *CBS 6755*....53 3
24 Mar 79 ONENESS – SILVER DREAMS GOLDEN REALITY *CBS 86037* [4] 55 4
27 Oct 79 MARATHON *CBS 86098*....28 5
22 Mar 80 **ALL I EVER WANTED** *CBS 8160*....57 3
20 Sep 80 THE SWING OF DELIGHT *CBS 22075* [4]....65 2
18 Apr 81 ZEBOP! *CBS 84946*....33 4
14 Aug 82 SHANGO *CBS 85914*....35 7
30 Apr 83 HAVANA MOON *CBS 25350* [4] 84 3
23 Mar 85 BEYOND APPEARANCES *CBS 86307*....58 3
15 Nov 86 VIVA! SANTANA – THE VERY BEST *K-Tel NE 1338*....50 8
14 Jul 90 SPIRITS DANCING IN THE FLESH *CBS 4669131*....68 1
15 Aug 98 THE ULTIMATE COLLECTION *Columbia SONYTV 47CD*....12 26
4 Sep 99 ★ SUPERNATURAL *Arista 7822190802* ▲....1 47
23 Oct 99 **SMOOTH** *Arista 74321709492* [1] ▲ $....75 1
1 Apr 00 ● **SMOOTH** (re-issue) *Arista 74321748762* [1] 3 10
5 Aug 00 ● **MARIA MARIA** *Arista 74321769372* [2] ▲ $....6 9
2 Nov 02 SHAMAN *RCA 74321959382* ▲....15 5
23 Nov 02 **THE GAME OF LOVE** *Arista 74321959442* [3] 16 8
12 Nov 05 ALL THAT I AM *Arista 82876696202*....36 2

[1] Santana featuring Rob Thomas [2] Santana featuring the Product G&B [3] Santana featuring Michelle Branch [1] Carlos Santana and Buddy Miles [2] Carlos Santana and Mahavishnu John McLaughlin [3] Carlos Santana and Alice Coltrane [4] Carlos Santana

SANTO and JOHNNY
US, male guitarists – Santo and Johnny Farina (2 Singles: 5 Weeks)

16 Oct 59 **SLEEP WALK** *Pye International 7N 25037* ▲ $....22 4
31 Mar 60 **TEARDROP** *Parlophone R 4619*....50 1

SANTOS *Italy, male producer – Sante Pucello*

20 Jan 01 ● **CAMELS** *Incentive CENT 15CDS*....9 6

Mike SARNE *UK, male vocalist – Mike Scheuer (4 Singles: 43 Weeks)*

10 May 62 ★ **COME OUTSIDE** *Parlophone R 4902* [1] 1 19
30 Aug 62 **WILL I WHAT** *Parlophone R 4932* [2] 18 10

31 October 1987	7 November 1987	14 November 1987	21 November 1987
YOU WIN AGAIN The Bee Gees	**YOU WIN AGAIN** The Bee Gees	**CHINA IN YOUR HAND** T'Pau	**CHINA IN YOUR HAND** T'Pau
TANGO IN THE NIGHT Fleetwood Mac	**TANGO IN THE NIGHT** Fleetwood Mac	**FAITH** George Michael	**BRIDGE OF SPIES** T'Pau

KEY UK No.1 ★ UK Top 10 ● Still on chart + UK entry at No.1 ■ US No.1 ▲ UK million seller £ US million seller $
Singles re-entries are listed as (re), (2re), (3re)... which signifies that the hit re-entered the chart once, twice or three times...
Peak Position / Weeks

10 Jan 63 **JUST FOR KICKS** *Parlophone R 4974* 22 7
28 Mar 63 **CODE OF LOVE** *Parlophone R 5010* 29 7

[1] Mike Sarne with Wendy Richard [2] Mike Sarne with Billie Davis

Joy SARNEY *UK, female vocalist*

7 May 77 **NAUGHTY NAUGHTY NAUGHTY** *Alaska ALA 2005* 26 6

The SARR BAND
Italy / UK / France, male / female vocal / instrumental group

16 Sep 78 **MAGIC MANDRAKE** *Calendar DAY 111* 68 1

Peter SARSTEDT
UK, male vocalist (1 Album: 4 Weeks, 2 Singles: 25 Weeks)

5 Feb 69 ★ **WHERE DO YOU GO TO (MY LOVELY)** *United Artists UP 2262* 1 16
8 Mar 69 ● PETER SARSTEDT *United Artists SULP 1219* 8 4
4 Jun 69 ● **FROZEN ORANGE JUICE** *United Artists UP 35021* 10 9

Robin SARSTEDT *UK, male vocalist – Clive Sarstedt*

8 May 76 ● **MY RESISTANCE IS LOW** *Decca F 13624* 3 9

SARTORELLO *Italy, male / female vocal / instrumental duo*

10 Aug 96 **MOVE BABY MOVE** *Multiply CDMULTY 12* 56 1

SASH! (431 Top 500)
German pop / dance act named after instrumentalist / producer Sascha (aka Sasha) Lappessen, featuring programmers Thomas Alisson and Ralf Kappmeier. First four hits uniquely featured vocals in different languages (French, Spanish, English, Italian) (4 Albums: 65 Weeks, 10 Singles: 103 Weeks)

1 Mar 97 ● **ENCORE UNE FOIS** *Multiply CDMULTY 18* 2 15
5 Jul 97 ● **ECUADOR** *Multiply CDMULTY 23* [1] 2 12
19 Jul 97 ● IT'S MY LIFE – THE ALBUM *Multiply MULTYCD 1* 6 38
18 Oct 97 ● **STAY** *Multiply CDMULTY 26* [2] 2 14
4 Apr 98 ● **LA PRIMAVERA** *Multiply CXMULTY 32* 3 12
15 Aug 98 ● **MYSTERIOUS TIMES** *Multiply CXMULTY 40* [3] 2 12
5 Sep 98 ● LIFE GOES ON *Multiply MULTYCD 2* 5 19
28 Nov 98 ● **MOVE MANIA** *Multiply CDMULTY 45* [4] 8 10
3 Apr 99 **COLOUR THE WORLD** *Multiply CDMULTY 48* 15 6
12 Feb 00 ● **ADELANTE** *Multiply CDMULTY 60* 2 10
22 Apr 00 ● **JUST AROUND THE HILL** *Multiply CDMULTY 62* [3] 8 7
29 Apr 00 TRILENIUM *Multiply MULTYCD 7* 13 5
23 Sep 00 ● **WITH MY OWN EYES** *Multiply CDMULTY 67* 10 5
11 Nov 00 ENCORE UNE FOIS – THE GREATEST HITS *Multiply MULTYCD 10* 33 3

[1] Sash! featuring Rodriguez [2] Sash! featuring La Trec [3] Sash! featuring Tina Cousins [4] Sash! featuring Shannon

SASHA
UK, male producer – Alexander Coe (4 Albums: 9 Weeks, 7 Singles: 18 Weeks)

31 Jul 93 **TOGETHER** *ffrr FCD 212* [1] 57 1
19 Feb 94 **HIGHER GROUND** *Deconstruction 74321189002* [2] 19 3
12 Mar 94 THE QAT COLLECTION *Deconstruction 74321191962* 55 2
27 Aug 94 **MAGIC** *Deconstruction 74321221862* [2] 32 4
9 Mar 96 **BE AS ONE** *Deconstruction 74321342962* [3] 17 4
17 Jul 99 EXPANDER (EP) *Deconstruction 74321681992* 18 3
23 Sep 00 **SCORCHIO** *Arista 74321788222* [4] 23 3
17 Aug 02 AIRDRAWNDAGGER *Arista 74321947862* 18 3
31 Aug 02 **WAVY GRAVY** *Arista 74321960602* 64 1
26 Jun 04 INVOLVER *Global Underground GUSA 001CDX* 61 1
27 Nov 04 **WATCHING CARS GO BY** *Emperor Norton ENR 532* [5] 49 2

[1] Danny Campbell and Sasha [2] Sasha with Sam Mollison [3] Sasha and Maria [4] Sasha / Emerson [5] Felix Da Housecat vs Sasha and Armand Van Helden

Joe SATRIANI *US, male guitarist (4 Albums: 13 Weeks, 1 Single: 1 Week)*

15 Aug 92 THE EXTREMIST *Epic 4716722* 13 6
13 Feb 93 **THE SATCH EP** *Relativity 6589532* 53 1
6 Nov 93 TIME MACHINE *Relativity 4745152* 32 2
14 Oct 95 JOE SATRIANI *Relativity 4811022* 21 3
14 Mar 98 CRYSTAL PLANET *Epic 4894732* 32 2

Tracks on The Satch EP: The Extremist / Cryin / Banana Bongo / Crazy.

SATURATED SOUL featuring MISS BUNTY
US / UK, male production duo and Holland, female vocalist

14 Aug 04 **GOT TO RELEASE** *Defected DFTD 093* 56 1

SATURDAY NIGHT BAND *US, male vocal / instrumental group*

1 Jul 78 **COME ON, DANCE DANCE** *CBS 6367* 16 9

Anne SAVAGE *UK, female DJ / producer*

19 Apr 03 **HELLRAISER** *Tidy Trax TIDY 186T* 74 1

Chantay SAVAGE *US, female vocalist (1 Album: 1 Week, 2 Singles: 9 Weeks)*

4 May 96 **I WILL SURVIVE** *RCA 74321377682* 12 8
25 May 96 I WILL SURVIVE (DOIN' IT MY WAY) *RCA 74321381622* 66 1
8 Nov 97 **REMINDING ME (OF SEF)** *Relativity 6560762* [1] 59 1

[1] Common featuring Chantay Savage

Edna SAVAGE *UK, female vocalist, b. 21 Apr 1936, d. 31 Dec 2000*

13 Jan 56 **ARRIVEDERCI DARLING** *Parlophone R 4097* 19 1

SAVAGE GARDEN (279 Top 500)
Australian pop vocal / instrumental duo: Darren Hayes and Daniel Jones. Their eponymous debut album earned them 90 platinum albums worldwide and huge critical acclaim followed, with a record-breaking 10 Arias at the 1997 Australian music industry awards. The duo went their separate ways in 2001 and Hayes launched a solo career. Best-selling single: 'Truly Madly Deeply' 657,500 (3 Albums: 138 Weeks, 11 Singles: 101 Weeks)

21 Jun 97 **I WANT YOU** *Columbia 6645452* 11 7
27 Sep 97 **TO THE MOON AND BACK** *Columbia 6648932* 55 1
28 Feb 98 ● **TRULY MADLY DEEPLY** *Columbia 6656022* ▲ 4 23
14 Mar 98 ● SAVAGE GARDEN *Columbia 4871612* 2 68
22 Aug 98 ● **TO THE MOON AND BACK** (re-issue) *Columbia 6662882* 3 16
12 Dec 98 **I WANT YOU '98** (re-mix) *Columbia 6667332* 12 10
10 Jul 99 **THE ANIMAL SONG** *Columbia 6675882* 16 6
13 Nov 99 ● **I KNEW I LOVED YOU** *Columbia 6683102* ▲ 10 12
20 Nov 99 ● AFFIRMATION *Columbia 4949352* 7 64
1 Apr 00 **CRASH AND BURN** *Columbia 6690442* 14 6
29 Jul 00 ● **AFFIRMATION** *Columbia 6696882* 8 10
25 Nov 00 **HOLD ME (re)** *Columbia 6706032* 16 7
31 Mar 01 **THE BEST THING (re)** *Columbia 6709852* 35 3
26 Nov 05 TRULY MADLY COMPLETELY – THE BEST OF SAVAGE GARDEN *Columbia 82876739412* ..... 25 6+

Telly SAVALAS *US, male actor / vocalist – Aristotle Savalas, b. 21 Jan 1924, d. 22 Jan 1994 (1 Album: 10 Weeks, 2 Singles: 12 Weeks)*

22 Feb 75 ★ **IF** *MCA 174* 1 9
22 Mar 75 TELLY *MCA MCF 2699* 12 10
31 May 75 **YOU'VE LOST THAT LOVIN' FEELIN'** *MCA 189* 47 3

SAVANA *UK, male rapper*

24 Jul 04 **PRETTY LADY** *Jetstar JECDS 1805* 48 1

28 November 1987	5 December 1987	12 December 1987	19 December 1987
UK No.1 SINGLES			
CHINA IN YOUR HAND – T'Pau	CHINA IN YOUR HAND – T'Pau	CHINA IN YOUR HAND – T'Pau	ALWAYS ON MY MIND – Pet Shop Boys
UK No.1 ALBUMS			
WHENEVER YOU NEED SOMEBODY – Rick Astley	NOW THAT'S WHAT I CALL MUSIC! 10 – Various	NOW THAT'S WHAT I CALL MUSIC! 10 – Various	NOW THAT'S WHAT I CALL MUSIC! 10 – Various

SAVANNA *UK, male vocal group*

10 Oct 81 **I CAN'T TURN AWAY** *R&B RBS 203* **61** 4

SAVOY BROWN *UK, male vocal / instrumental group*

28 Nov 70 LOOKIN' IN *Decca SKL 5066* 50 1

The SAW DOCTORS *Ireland, male vocal (Davy Carton) / instrumental group (5 Albums: 12 Weeks, 6 Singles: 11 Weeks)*

8 Jun 91 IF THIS IS ROCK AND ROLL I WANT MY OLD JOB BACK *Solid ROCK 7* 69 2
31 Oct 92 ALL THE WAY FROM TUAM *Solid 4509911462* 33 2
12 Nov 94 **SMALL BIT OF LOVE** *Shamtown SAW 001CD* **24** 3
27 Jan 96 **WORLD OF GOOD** *Shamtown SAW 002CD* **15** 3
24 Feb 96 ● SAME OUL' TOWN *Shamtown SAWDOC 004CD* 6 5
13 Jul 96 **TO WIN JUST ONCE** *Shamtown SAW 004CD* **14** 2
6 Dec 97 **SIMPLE THINGS** *Shamtown SAW 006CD* **56** 1
24 Oct 98 SONGS FROM SUN STREET *Shamtown SAWDOC 006CD* 24 2
13 Oct 01 VILLAINS? *Shamtown SAWDOC 008CD* 58 1
1 Jun 02 **THIS IS ME** *Shamtown SAW 012CD* **31** 1
15 Oct 05 **STARS OVER CLOUGHANOVER** *Shamtown SAW 014CD* **69** 1

Nitin SAWHNEY *UK, male multi-instrumentalist / producer (4 Albums: 5 Weeks, 1 Single: 1 Week)*

25 Sep 99 BEYOND SKIN *Outcaste CASTE 9CD* 44 2
30 Jun 01 PROPHESY *V2 VVR 1015912* 40 1
28 Jul 01 **SUNSET** *V2 VVR 5016763* [1] **65** 1
26 Jul 03 HUMAN *V2 VVR 1021852* 54 1
14 May 05 PHILTRE *V2 VVR 1031272* 69 1

[1] Nitin Sawhney featuring Eska

SAXON (462 Top 500)

A key band on the early 1980s British New Wave of Heavy Metal scene, formed in Barnsley in 1977 (originally as Son of a Bitch) and fronted by Peter 'Biff' Byford. In the 1980s, the group's 15 hit singles all missed the Top 10 (9 Albums: 97 Weeks, 15 Singles: 61 Weeks)

22 Mar 80 **WHEELS OF STEEL** *Carrere CAR 143* **20** 11
12 Apr 80 ● WHEELS OF STEEL *Carrere CAL 115* 5 29
21 Jun 80 **747 (STRANGERS IN THE NIGHT)** *Carrere CAR 151* **13** 9
28 Jun 80 **BACKS TO THE WALL** *Carrere HM 6* **64** 2
28 Jun 80 **BIG TEASER / RAINBOW THEME – FROZEN RAINBOW** *Carrere HM 5* **66** 2
15 Nov 80 STRONG ARM OF THE LAW *Carrere CAL 120* 11 13
29 Nov 80 **STRONG ARM OF THE LAW** *Carrere CAR 170* **63** 3
11 Apr 81 **AND THE BANDS PLAYED ON** *Carrere CAR 180* **12** 8
18 Jul 81 **NEVER SURRENDER** *Carrere CAR 204* **18** 6
3 Oct 81 ● DENIM AND LEATHER *Carrere CAL 128* 9 11
31 Oct 81 **PRINCESS OF THE NIGHT** *Carrere CAR 208* **57** 3
22 May 82 ● THE EAGLE HAS LANDED *Carrere CAL 157* 5 19
26 Mar 83 POWER AND THE GLORY *Carrere CAL 147* 15 9
23 Apr 83 **POWER AND THE GLORY** *Carrere SAXON 1* **32** 5
30 Jul 83 **NIGHTMARE** *Carrere CAR 284* **50** 3
11 Feb 84 CRUSADER *Carrere CAL 200* 18 7
31 Aug 85 **BACK ON THE STREETS** *Parlophone R 6103* **75** 1
14 Sep 85 INNOCENCE IS NO EXCUSE *Parlophone SAXON 2* 36 4
29 Mar 86 **ROCK 'N' ROLL GYPSY** *Parlophone R 6112* **71** 1
30 Aug 86 **WAITING FOR THE NIGHT** *EMI EMI 5575* **66** 2
27 Sep 86 ROCK THE NATIONS *EMI EMC 3515* 34 3
5 Mar 88 **RIDE LIKE THE WIND** *EMI EM 43* **52** 4
9 Apr 88 DESTINY *EMI EMC 3543* 49 2
30 Apr 88 **I CAN'T WAIT ANYMORE** *EMI EM 54* **71** 1

Al SAXON *UK, male vocalist – Allan Fowler (4 Singles: 10 Weeks)*

16 Jan 59 **YOU'RE THE TOP CHA** *Fontana H 164* **17** 4
28 Aug 59 **ONLY SIXTEEN** *Fontana H 205* **24** 3
22 Dec 60 **BLUE-EYED BOY** *Fontana H 278* **39** 2
7 Sep 61 **THERE I'VE SAID IT AGAIN** *Piccadilly 7N 35011* **48** 1

Leo SAYER (127 Top 500)

Distinctive singer / songwriter, b. 21 May 1948, Sussex, UK, who was a top singles and album act on both sides of the Atlantic in the late 1970s. His first seven hits all reached the Top 10 – a feat first achieved by his manager, Adam Faith (13 Albums: 238 Weeks, 18 Singles: 151 Weeks)

15 Dec 73 ● **THE SHOW MUST GO ON** *Chrysalis CHS 2023* **2** 13
5 Jan 74 ● SILVER BIRD *Chrysalis CHR 1050* 2 22
15 Jun 74 ● **ONE MAN BAND** *Chrysalis CHS 2045* **6** 9
14 Sep 74 ● **LONG TALL GLASSES** *Chrysalis CHS 2052* **4** 9
26 Oct 74 ● JUST A BOY *Chrysalis CHR 1068* 4 14
30 Aug 75 ● **MOONLIGHTING** *Chrysalis CHS 2076* **2** 8
20 Sep 75 ● ANOTHER YEAR *Chrysalis CHR 1087* 8 9
30 Oct 76 ● **YOU MAKE ME FEEL LIKE DANCING** *Chrysalis CHS 2119* ▲ $. **2** 12
27 Nov 76 ● ENDLESS FLIGHT *Chrysalis CHR 1125* 4 66
29 Jan 77 ★ **WHEN I NEED YOU** *Chrysalis CHS 2127* ▲ $ **1** 13
9 Apr 77 ● **HOW MUCH LOVE** *Chrysalis CHS 2140* **10** 8
10 Sep 77 **THUNDER IN MY HEART** *Chrysalis CHS 2163* **22** 8
22 Oct 77 ● THUNDER IN MY HEART *Chrysalis CDL 1154* 8 16
2 Sep 78 LEO SAYER *Chrysalis CDL 1198* 15 25
16 Sep 78 ● **I CAN'T STOP LOVING YOU (THOUGH I TRY)** *Chrysalis CHS 2240* **6** 11
25 Nov 78 **RAINING IN MY HEART** *Chrysalis CHS 2277* **21** 10
31 Mar 79 ★ THE VERY BEST OF LEO SAYER *Chrysalis CDL 1222* 1 37
13 Oct 79 HERE *Chrysalis CDL 1240* 44 4
5 Jul 80 ● **MORE THAN I CAN SAY** *Chrysalis CHS 2442* $ **2** 11
23 Aug 80 LIVING IN A FANTASY *Chrysalis CDL 1297* 15 9
13 Mar 82 ● **HAVE YOU EVER BEEN IN LOVE** *Chrysalis CHS 2596* **10** 9
8 May 82 WORLD RADIO *Chrysalis CDL 1345* 30 12
19 Jun 82 **HEART (STOP BEATING IN TIME)** *Chrysalis CHS 2616* **22** 10
12 Mar 83 **ORCHARD ROAD** *Chrysalis CHS 2677* **16** 8
15 Oct 83 **TILL YOU COME BACK TO ME** *Chrysalis LEO 01* **51** 3
12 Nov 83 HAVE YOU EVER BEEN IN LOVE *Chrysalis LEOTV 1* 15 18
8 Feb 86 **UNCHAINED MELODY** *Chrysalis LEO 3* **54** 4
13 Feb 93 **WHEN I NEED YOU** (re-issue) *Chrysalis CDCHS 3926* **65** 2
6 Mar 93 ALL THE BEST *Chrysalis CDCHR 1980* 26 4
8 Aug 98 **YOU MAKE ME FEEL LIKE DANCING** *Brothers Org. CDBRUV 8* [1] **32** 3
20 Feb 99 THE DEFINITIVE HITS COLLECTION *PolyGram TV 5471152* 35 2

[1] Groove Generation featuring Leo Sayer

Alexei SAYLE *UK, male comedian / vocalist*

25 Feb 84 **'ULLO JOHN GOT A NEW MOTOR?** *Island IS 162* **15** 8
17 Mar 84 THE FISH PEOPLE TAPES *Island IMA 9* 62 5

The SCAFFOLD (see also Mike McGEAR)

UK, male vocal group (5 Singles: 62 Weeks)

22 Nov 67 ● **THANK U VERY MUCH** *Parlophone R 5643* **4** 12
27 Mar 68 **DO YOU REMEMBER** *Parlophone R 5679* **34** 5
6 Nov 68 ★ **LILY THE PINK** *Parlophone R 5734* **1** 24
1 Nov 69 **GIN GAN GOOLIE (re)** *Parlophone R 5812* **38** 12
1 Jun 74 ● **LIVERPOOL LOU** *Warner Bros. K 16400* **7** 9

Boz SCAGGS *US, male vocalist – William Royce Scaggs (3 Albums: 29 Weeks, 4 Singles: 31 Weeks)*

30 Oct 76 **LOWDOWN** *CBS 4563* $ **28** 4
22 Jan 77 ● **WHAT CAN I SAY** *CBS 4869* **10** 10
12 Mar 77 SILK DEGREES *CBS 81193* 37 24
14 May 77 **LIDO SHUFFLE** *CBS 5136* **13** 9
10 Dec 77 **HOLLYWOOD** *CBS 5836* **33** 8
17 Dec 77 DOWN TWO THEN LEFT *CBS 86036* 55 1
3 May 80 MIDDLE MAN *CBS 86094* 52 4

SCANTY SANDWICH *UK, male DJ / producer – Richard Marshall*

29 Jan 00 ● **BECAUSE OF YOU** *Southern Fried ECB 18CDS* **3** 8

SCARFACE *US, male rapper – Brad Jordan (3 Singles: 6 Weeks)*

11 Mar 95 **HAND OF THE DEAD BODY** *Virgin America VUSCD 88* [1] **41** 2

26 December 1987	2 January 1988	9 January 1988	16 January 1988
ALWAYS ON MY MIND Pet Shop Boys	ALWAYS ON MY MIND Pet Shop Boys	ALWAYS ON MY MIND Pet Shop Boys	HEAVEN IS A PLACE ON EARTH Belinda Carlisle
NOW THAT'S WHAT I CALL MUSIC! 10 Various	NOW THAT'S WHAT I CALL MUSIC! 10 Various	NOW THAT'S WHAT I CALL MUSIC! 10 Various	POPPED IN SOULED OUT Wet Wet Wet

KEY: UK No.1 ★ UK Top 10 ● Still on chart + UK entry at No.1 ■ US No.1 ▲ UK million seller £ US million seller $
Singles re-entries are listed as (re), (2re), (3re)... which signifies that the hit re-entered the chart once, twice or three times...
Peak Position / Weeks

5 Aug 95 **I SEEN A MAN DIE** *Virgin America VUSCD 94* **55** 2
5 Jul 97 **GAME OVER** *Virgin VUSCD 121* **34** 2

[1] Scarface featuring Ice Cube

SCARFO *UK, male vocal / instrumental group (2 Singles: 2 Weeks)*

19 Jul 97 **ALKALINE** *Deceptive BLUFF 044CD* **61** 1
18 Oct 97 **COSMONAUT NO.7** *Deceptive BLUFF 053CD* **67** 1

SCARLET *UK, female vocal / instrumental duo – Cheryl Parker and Joe Youle (1 Album: 2 Weeks, 4 Singles: 18 Weeks)*

21 Jan 95 **INDEPENDENT LOVE SONG** *WEA YZ 820CD* **12** 12
11 Mar 95 NAKED *WEA 4509976432* 59 2
29 Apr 95 **I WANNA BE FREE (TO BE WITH HIM)** *WEA YZ 913CD* **21** 4
5 Aug 95 **LOVE HANGOVER** *WEA YZ 969CD* **54** 1
6 Jul 96 **BAD GIRL** *WEA WEA 046CD* **54** 1

SCARLET FANTASTIC *UK, male / female vocal / instrumental group (2 Singles: 12 Weeks)*

3 Oct 87 **NO MEMORY** *Arista RIS 36* **24** 10
23 Jan 88 **PLUG ME IN (TO THE CENTRAL LOVE LINE)** *Arista 109693* **67** 2

SCARLET PARTY *UK, male vocal / instrumental group*

16 Oct 82 **101 DAM-NATIONS** *Parlophone R 6058* **44** 5

SCARS *UK, male vocal / instrumental group*

18 Apr 81 AUTHOR! AUTHOR! *Pre PREX 5* 67 3

SCATMAN JOHN *US, male vocalist – John Larkin, b. 13 Mar 1942, d. 3 Dec 1999 (2 Singles: 19 Weeks)*

13 May 95 ● **SCATMAN (SKI-BA-BOP-BA-DOP-BOP)** *RCA 74321281712* **3** 12
2 Sep 95 ● **SCATMAN'S WORLD** *RCA 74321289952* **10** 7

SCENT *Italy / Ireland, male / female production / vocal trio*

21 Aug 04 **UP & DOWN** *Positiva CDTIVS 209* **23** 3

Michael SCHENKER GROUP (see also UFO) *Germany / UK, male vocal / instrumental group (7 Albums: 44 Weeks, 3 Singles: 9 Weeks)*

6 Sep 80 ● MICHAEL SCHENKER GROUP *Chrysalis CHR 1302* 8 8
13 Sep 80 **ARMED AND READY** *Chrysalis CHS 2455* **53** 3
8 Nov 80 **CRY FOR THE NATIONS** *Chrysalis CHS 2471* **56** 3
19 Sep 81 MICHAEL SCHENKER GROUP (re-issue) *Chrysalis CHR 1336* 14 8
13 Mar 82 ● ONE NIGHT AT BUDOKAN *Chrysalis CTY 1375* 5 11
11 Sep 82 **DANCER** *Chrysalis CHS 2636* **52** 3
23 Oct 82 ASSAULT ATTACK *Chrysalis CHR 1393* 19 5
10 Sep 83 BUILT TO DESTROY *Chrysalis CHR 1441* 23 5
23 Jun 84 ROCK WILL NEVER DIE *Chrysalis CUX 1470* 24 5
24 Oct 87 PERFECT TIMING *EMI EMC 3539* [1] 65 2

[1] MSG

Lalo SCHIFRIN *Argentina, male orchestra conductor – Boris Schifrin (2 Singles: 11 Weeks)*

9 Oct 76 **JAWS** *CTI CTSP 005* **14** 9
25 Oct 97 **BULLITT** *Warner.esp WESP 002CD* **36** 2

SCHILLER *Germany, male production duo – Christopher von Deylen and Mirko von Schlieffen*

28 Apr 01 **DAS GLOCKENSPIEL** *Data DATA 22CDS* **17** 3

Peter SCHILLING *Germany, male vocalist*

5 May 84 **MAJOR TOM (COMING HOME) (re)** *PSP / WEA X 9438* **42** 6

SCHNAPPI NEW *Egypt / Germany, animated baby crocodile vocalist – Joy Gruttmann*

15 Oct 05 **SCHNAPPI** *UMTV 9873701* **32** 3

Phillip SCHOFIELD *UK, male TV presenter / actor / vocalist*

5 Dec 92 **CLOSE EVERY DOOR** *Really Useful RUR 11* **27** 6

SCHOOL OF EXCELLENCE (see also BLOWING FREE; HARMONIUM; HYPNOSIS; IN TUNE; The JAMES BOYS; RAINDANCE) *UK, male instrumental duo – Bradley and Stewart Palmer*

28 Oct 95 PIANO MOODS *Dino DINCD 114* 47 2

SCHOOL OF ROCK *US, male / female actors / vocalists*

21 Feb 04 **SCHOOL OF ROCK** *Atlantic AT 0172CD* **51** 2

SCIENCE DEPARTMENT featuring ERIRE (see also Danny HOWELLS & Dick TREVOR featuring ERIRE) *UK, male production duo and female vocalist*

10 Nov 01 **BREATHE** *Renaissance Recordings RENCDS 010* **64** 1

SCIENTIST *UK, male producer – Phil Sebastiane (4 Singles: 13 Weeks)*

6 Oct 90 **THE EXORCIST** *Kickin KICK 1* **62** 3
1 Dec 90 **THE EXORCIST** (re-mix) *Kickin KICK 1TR* **46** 3
15 Dec 90 **THE BEE (re)** *Kickin KICK 3S* **47** 6
11 May 91 **SPIRAL SYMPHONY** *Kickin KICK 5* **74** 1

SCISSOR SISTERS *US, male / female vocal (Jake Shears) / instrumental group (1 Album: 90 Weeks, 6 Singles: 41 Weeks)*

8 Nov 03 **LAURA** *Polydor 9812788* **54** 2
31 Jan 04 ● **COMFORTABLY NUMB (re)** *Polydor 9815883* **10** 8
14 Feb 04 ★ SCISSOR SISTERS *Polydor 9866058* 1 90
10 Apr 04 **TAKE YOUR MAMA** *Polydor 9866277* **17** 6
19 Jun 04 **LAURA** (re-issue) *Polydor 9866833* **12** 10
23 Oct 04 **MARY** *Polydor 9868282* **14** 6
15 Jan 05 ● **FILTHY/GORGEOUS** *Polydor 9869799* **5** 9

SCOOBIE *UK, male / female vocal / production / Celtic FC supporters group (2 Singles: 3 Weeks)*

22 Dec 01 **THE MAGNIFICENT 7** *Big Tongue BTR 001CDS* **58** 2
1 Jun 02 **THE MAGNIFICENT 7** (re-mix) *Big Tongue BTR 001CDSX* **71** 1

SCOOCH *UK, male / female vocal group (1 Album: 2 Weeks, 4 Singles: 20 Weeks)*

6 Nov 99 **WHEN MY BABY** *Accolade CDAC 002* **29** 4
22 Jan 00 ● **MORE THAN I NEEDED TO KNOW** *Accolade CDAC 003* **5** 5
6 May 00 **THE BEST IS YET TO COME (re)** *Accolade CDAC 004* **12** 5
5 Aug 00 **FOR SURE** *Accolade CDAS 005* **15** 6
19 Aug 00 FOUR SURE *Accolade 5278190* 41 2

SCOOTER *UK / Germany, male vocal (HP Baxter) / instrumental group (3 Albums: 23 Weeks, 12 Singles: 65 Weeks)*

21 Oct 95 **THE MOVE YOUR ASS EP** *Club Tools 0061675 CLU* **23** 4
17 Feb 96 **BACK IN THE UK** *Club Tools 0061955 CLU* **18** 3
13 Apr 96 OUR HAPPY HARDCORE *Club Tools 0062282 CLU* 24 5
25 May 96 **REBEL YELL** *Club Tools 0062575 CLU* **30** 2
19 Oct 96 **I'M RAVING** *Club Tools 0063015 CLU* **33** 3
17 May 97 **FIRE** *Club Tools 006005 CLU* **45** 2
22 Jun 02 ● **THE LOGICAL SONG** *Sheffield Tunes 0139295 STU* **2** 15
10 Aug 02 ● PUSH THE BEAT FOR THIS JAM (THE SINGLES '94-'02) *Sheffield Tunes 0141172 STU* 6 14
21 Sep 02 ● **NESSAJA** *Sheffield Tunes 0142165 STU* **4** 9

	23 January 1988	30 January 1988	6 February 1988	13 February 1988
UK No.1 SINGLES	HEAVEN IS A PLACE ON EARTH Belinda Carlisle	I THINK WE'RE ALONE NOW Tiffany	I THINK WE'RE ALONE NOW Tiffany	I THINK WE'RE ALONE NOW Tiffany
UK No.1 ALBUMS	TURN BACK THE CLOCK Johnny Hates Jazz	INTRODUCING THE HARDLINE ACCORDING TO TERENCE TRENT D'ARBY Terence Trent D'Arby	INTRODUCING THE HARDLINE ACCORDING TO TERENCE TRENT D'ARBY Terence Trent D'Arby	INTRODUCING THE HARDLINE ACCORDING TO TERENCE TRENT D'ARBY Terence Trent D'Arby

7 Dec 02	**POSSE (I NEED YOU ON THE FLOOR)** *Sheffield Tunes 0143775 STU*	15	7
5 Apr 03	**WEEKEND!** *Sheffield Tunes 0147315 STU*	12	10
26 Apr 03	THE STADIUM TECHNO EXPERIENCE *Sheffield Tunes / Edel UK STU 00147112CD*	20	4
5 Jul 03	**THE NIGHT** *Sheffield Tunes 0149005 STU*	16	5
18 Oct 03	**MARIA (I LIKE IT LOUD)** *Sheffield Tunes 051135 STU* [1]	16	4
10 Jul 04	**JIGGA JIGGA!** *All Around the World CDGLOBE 348*	48	1

[1] Scooter vs Marc Acardipane and Dick Rules

Tracks on The Move Your Ass EP: Move Your Ass / Friends / Endless Summer / Move Your Ass (remix).

SCORPIONS *Germany, male vocal (Klaus Meine) / instrumental group (8 Albums: 56 Weeks, 11 Singles: 35 Weeks)*

21 Apr 79	LOVE DRIVE *Harvest SHSP 4097*	36	11
26 May 79	**IS THERE ANYBODY THERE? / ANOTHER PIECE OF MEAT** *Harvest HAR 5185*	39	4
25 Aug 79	**LOVEDRIVE** *Harvest HAR 5188*	69	2
3 May 80	ANIMAL MAGNETISM *Harvest SHSP 4113*	23	6
31 May 80	**MAKE IT REAL** *Harvest HAR 5206*	72	2
20 Sep 80	**THE ZOO** *Harvest HAR 5212*	75	1
3 Apr 82	**NO ONE LIKE YOU (re)** *Harvest HAR 5219*	64	4
10 Apr 82	BLACKOUT *Harvest SHVL 823*	11	11
17 Jul 82	**CAN'T LIVE WITHOUT YOU** *Harvest HAR 5221*	63	2
24 Mar 84	LOVE AT FIRST STING *Harvest SHSP 2400071*	17	6
29 Jun 85	WORLD WIDE LIVE *Harvest SCORP 1*	18	8
14 May 88	SAVAGE AMUSEMENT *Harvest SHSP 4125*	18	6
4 Jun 88	**RHYTHM OF LOVE** *Harvest HAR 5240*	59	2
18 Feb 89	**PASSION RULES THE GAME** *Harvest 5242*	74	1
17 Nov 90	CRAZY WORLD *Vertigo 8469081*	27	7
1 Jun 91	**WIND OF CHANGE** *Vertigo VER 54*	53	3
28 Sep 91 ●	**WIND OF CHANGE** (re-issue) *Vertigo VER 58*	2	9
30 Nov 91	**SEND ME AN ANGEL (re)** *Vertigo VER 60*	27	5
25 Sep 93	FACE THE HEAT *Mercury 5182802*	51	1

SCOTLAND WORLD CUP SQUAD *UK, male football team vocalists (1 Album: 9 Weeks, 5 Singles: 27 Weeks)*

25 May 74 ●	EASY EASY *Polydor 2383 282*	3	9
22 Jun 74	**EASY EASY** *Polydor 2058 452*	20	4
27 May 78 ●	**OLE OLA (MULHER BRASILEIRA)** *Riva 15* [1]	4	6
1 May 82 ●	**WE HAVE A DREAM** *WEA K 19145* [2]	5	9
9 Jun 90	**SAY IT WITH PRIDE** *RCA PB 43791* [2]	45	3
15 Jun 96	**PURPLE HEATHER** *Warner Bros. W 0354CD* [3]	16	5

[1] Rod Stewart featuring the Scottish World Cup Squad '78 [2] Scottish World Cup Squad [3] Rod Stewart with the Scottish Euro '96 Squad

Band of the SCOTS GUARDS *UK, military band*

28 Jun 69	BAND OF THE SCOTS GUARDS *Fontana SFXL 54*	25	2

Jack SCOTT *Canada, male vocalist – Jack Scafone Jr (2 Albums: 12 Weeks, 4 Singles: 28 Weeks)*

10 Oct 58 ●	**MY TRUE LOVE** *London HLU 8626* **$**	9	10
25 Sep 59	**THE WAY I WALK** *London HLL 8912*	30	1
10 Mar 60	**WHAT IN THE WORLD'S COME OVER YOU** *Top Rank JAR 280* **$**	11	15
7 May 60 ●	I REMEMBER HANK WILLIAMS *Top Rank BUY 034*	7	11
2 Jun 60	**BURNING BRIDGES** *Top Rank JAR 375*	32	2
3 Sep 60	WHAT IN THE WORLD'S COME OVER YOU *Top Rank 25/024*	11	1

Jamie SCOTT *UK, male vocalist (2 Singles: 5 Weeks)*

4 Sep 04	**JUST** *Sony Music 6752282*	29	2
22 Jan 05	**SEARCHING** *Sony Music 6757331*	33	3

Jill SCOTT *US, female vocalist (2 Albums: 6 Weeks, 3 Singles: 5 Weeks)*

29 Jul 00	WHO IS JILL SCOTT? – WORDS AND SOUNDS VOL.1 *Epic 4986252*	69	3
4 Nov 00	**GETTIN' IN THE WAY** *Epic 6705272*	30	3
7 Apr 01	**A LONG WALK** *Epic 6710382*	54	1
11 Sep 04	BEAUTIFULLY HUMAN – WORDS AND SOUNDS VOL.2 *Epic 5176522*	27	3
6 Nov 04	**GOLDEN** *Epic 6751772*	59	1

Linda SCOTT *US, female vocalist – Linda Sampson (2 Singles: 14 Weeks)*

18 May 61 ●	**I'VE TOLD EVERY LITTLE STAR** *Columbia DB 4638* **$**	7	13
14 Sep 61	**DON'T BET MONEY HONEY** *Columbia DB 4692*	50	1

Mike SCOTT (see also The WATERBOYS) *UK, male vocalist / guitarist (2 Albums: 4 Weeks, 4 Singles: 4 Weeks)*

16 Sep 95	**BRING 'EM ALL IN** *Chrysalis CDCHS 5025*	56	1
30 Sep 95	BRING 'EM ALL IN *Chrysalis CDCHR 6108*	23	2
11 Nov 95	**BUILDING THE CITY OF LIGHT** *Chrysalis CDCHS 5026*	60	1
27 Sep 97	**LOVE ANYWAY** *Chrysalis CDCHS 5064*	50	1
11 Oct 97	STILL BURNING *Chrysalis CDCHR 6122*	34	2
14 Feb 98	**RARE, PRECIOUS AND GONE** *Chrysalis CDCHSS 5073*	74	1

Millie SCOTT *US, female vocalist (3 Singles: 11 Weeks)*

12 Apr 86	**PRISONER OF LOVE** *Fourth & Broadway BRW 45*	52	4
23 Aug 86	**AUTOMATIC** *Fourth & Broadway BRW 51*	56	3
21 Feb 87	**EV'RY LITTLE BIT** *Fourth & Broadway BRW 58*	63	4

Simon SCOTT *UK (b. India), male vocalist*

13 Aug 64	**MOVE IT BABY** *Parlophone R 5164*	37	8

Tony SCOTT *Holland, male rapper (2 Singles: 6 Weeks)*

15 Apr 89	**THAT'S HOW I'M LIVING / THE CHIEF** *Champion CHAMP 97* [1]	48	4
10 Feb 90	**GET INTO IT / THAT'S HOW I'M LIVING** (re-issue) *Champion CHAMP 232*	63	2

[1] Toni Scott

'The Chief' listed only from 22 Apr 1989.

SCOTT & LEON *UK, male production duo – Scott Anderson and Leon McCormack (2 Singles: 6 Weeks)*

30 Sep 00	**YOU USED TO HOLD ME** *AM:PM CDAMPM 137*	19	4
19 May 01	**SHINE ON** *AM:PM CDAMPM 143*	34	2

Lisa SCOTT-LEE (see also STEPS) *UK, female vocalist (4 Singles: 17 Weeks)*

24 May 03 ●	**LATELY** *Fontana 9800295*	6	8
20 Sep 03	**TOO FAR GONE** *Fontana 9811642*	11	4
4 Dec 04	**GET IT ON** *Inspired INSPMOS 1CDS* [1]	23	3
22 Oct 05	**ELECTRIC** *Concept CDCON 68X*	13	2

[1] Intenso Project featuring Lisa Scott-Lee

SCOTTISH RUGBY TEAM with Ronnie BROWNE *UK, male rugby team vocalists*

2 Jun 90	**FLOWER OF SCOTLAND** *Greentrax STRAX 1001*	73	1

SCREAMING BLUE MESSIAHS *US / UK, male vocal / instrumental group*

17 May 86	GUN-SHY *WEA WX 41*	90	1
16 Jan 88	**I WANNA BE A FLINTSTONE** *WEA YZ 166*	28	6

SCREAMING TREES *US, male vocal / instrumental group (1 Album: 4 Weeks, 2 Singles: 2 Weeks)*

6 Mar 93	**NEARLY LOST YOU (EP)** *Epic 6582372*	50	1
1 May 93	**DOLLAR BILL** *Epic 6591792*	52	1
20 Jul 96	DUST *Epic 4839802*	32	4

Tracks on Nearly Lost You (EP): E.S.K. / Song of a Baker / Winter Song (acoustic).

SCREEN II *UK, male vocal / instrumental group*

9 Apr 94	LET THE RECORD SPIN *Cleveland City CLE 13015*	36	1

20 February 1988	27 February 1988	5 March 1988	12 March 1988
I SHOULD BE SO LUCKY Kylie Minogue	**I SHOULD BE SO LUCKY** Kylie Minogue	**I SHOULD BE SO LUCKY** Kylie Minogue	**I SHOULD BE SO LUCKY** Kylie Minogue
INTRODUCING THE HARDLINE ACCORDING TO TERENCE TRENT D'ARBY Terence Trent D'Arby	**INTRODUCING THE HARDLINE ACCORDING TO TERENCE TRENT D'ARBY** Terence Trent D'Arby	**INTRODUCING THE HARDLINE ACCORDING TO TERENCE TRENT D'ARBY** Terence Trent D'Arby	**INTRODUCING THE HARDLINE ACCORDING TO TERENCE TRENT D'ARBY** Terence Trent D'Arby

KEY UK No.1 ★ UK Top 10 ● Still on chart + UK entry at No.1 ■ US No.1 ▲ UK million seller £ US million seller $
Singles re-entries are listed as (re), (2re), (3re)... which signifies that the hit re-entered the chart once, twice or three times...
Peak Position / Weeks

SCRITTI POLITTI *UK, male vocal (Green Gartside) / instrumental group (4 Albums: 39 Weeks, 14 Singles: 78 Weeks)*

21 Nov 81 **THE SWEETEST GIRL** *Rough Trade RT 091*....64 3
22 May 82 **FAITHLESS** *Rough Trade RT 101*....56 4
7 Aug 82 **ASYLUMS IN JERUSALEM / JACQUES DERRIDA** *Rough Trade RT 111*....43 5
11 Sep 82 SONGS TO REMEMBER *Rough Trade ROUGH 20*....12 7
10 Mar 84 ● **WOOD BEEZ (PRAY LIKE ARETHA FRANKLIN)** *Virgin VS 657*..10 12
9 Jun 84 **ABSOLUTE** *Virgin VS 680*....17 9
17 Nov 84 **HYPNOTIZE** *Virgin VS 725*....68 2
11 May 85 ● **THE WORD GIRL** *Virgin VS 747*....6 12
22 Jun 85 ● CUPID & PSYCHE 85 *Virgin V 2350*....5 19
7 Sep 85 **PERFECT WAY** *Virgin VS 780*....48 5
7 May 88 **OH PATTI (DON'T FEEL SORRY FOR LOVERBOY)** *Virgin VS 1006*....13 9
18 Jun 88 ● PROVISION *Virgin V 2515*....8 11
27 Aug 88 **FIRST BOY IN THIS TOWN (LOVE SICK)** *Virgin VS 1082*....63 3
12 Nov 88 **BOOM! THERE SHE WAS** *Virgin VS 1143*....55 3
16 Mar 91 **SHE'S A WOMAN** *Virgin VS 1333* [1] 20 7
3 Aug 91 **TAKE ME IN YOUR ARMS AND LOVE ME** *Virgin VS 1346* [2] ..47 3
31 Jul 99 **TINSELTOWN TO THE BOOGIEDOWN** *Virgin VSCDT 1731*....46 1
7 Aug 99 ANOMIE & BONHOMIE *Virgin CDV 2884*....33 2

[1] Scritti Politti featuring Shabba Ranks [2] Scritti Politti and Sweetie Irie

SCUMFROG (see also DUTCH featuring CRYSTAL WATERS) *Holland, male producer – Jesse Houk (2 Singles: 3 Weeks)*

11 May 02 **LOVING THE ALIEN** (re-mix) *Positiva CDTIV 172* [1] 41 1
31 May 03 **MUSIC REVOLUTION** *Positiva CDTIV 191*....46 2

[1] Scumfrog vs Bowie

SEA FRUIT *UK, male vocal / instrumental group*

24 Jul 99 **HELLO WORLD** *Electric Canyon ECCD 3055*....59 1

SEA LEVEL *US, male instrumental group*

17 Feb 79 **FIFTY-FOUR** *Capricorn POSP 28*....63 4

SEAFOOD *UK, male / female vocal / instrumental group (2 Singles: 2 Weeks)*

28 Jul 01 **CLOAKING** *Infectious INFEC 103CDS*....71 1
1 May 04 **GOOD REASON** *Cooking Vinyl FRYCD 189*....65 1

SEAGULLS SKA NEW *UK, male Brighton Football Club supporters*

15 Jan 05 **TOM HARK (WE WANT FALMER!)** *Falmer for All FALMER 001*. 17 3

The SEAHORSES (see also John SQUIRE) *UK, male vocal (Chris Helme) / instrumental group (1 Album: 38 Weeks, 4 Singles: 26 Weeks)*

10 May 97 ● **LOVE IS THE LAW** *Geffen GFSTD 22243*....3 7
7 Jun 97 ● DO IT YOURSELF *Geffen GED 25134*....2 38
26 Jul 97 ● **BLINDED BY THE SUN** *Geffen GFSTD 22266*....7 7
11 Oct 97 **LOVE ME AND LEAVE ME** *Geffen GFSTD 22282*....16 4
13 Dec 97 **YOU CAN TALK TO ME** *Geffen GFSTD 22297*....15 8

SEAL (297 Top 500) (see also ADAMSKI)
Golden-voiced soul artist, b. Sealhenry Samuel, 19 Feb 1963, London, UK. He found fame in 1990 thanks to his Adamski collaboration 'Killer' and has recorded and performed with an impressive array of artists including Queen, Joni Mitchell, Jeff Beck and The Rolling Stones. He married supermodel Heidi Klum in 2005 (5 Albums: 145 Weeks, 15 Singles: 82 Weeks)

8 Dec 90 ● **CRAZY** *ZTT ZANG 8*....2 15
4 May 91 **FUTURE LOVE (EP)** *ZTT ZANG 11*....12 6
1 Jun 91 ★ SEAL *ZTT ZTT 9* ■....1 65
20 Jul 91 **THE BEGINNING** *ZTT ZANG 21*....24 6
16 Nov 91 ● **KILLER (EP)** *ZTT ZANG 23*....8 8
29 Feb 92 **VIOLET** *ZTT ZANG 27*....39 2
21 May 94 **PRAYER FOR THE DYING** *ZTT ZANG 51CD*....14 5
4 Jun 94 ★ SEAL *ZTT 4509962562* ■....1 65
30 Jul 94 **KISS FROM A ROSE** *ZTT ZANG 52CD1*....20 5
5 Nov 94 **NEWBORN FRIEND** *ZTT ZANG 58CD*....45 2
15 Jul 95 ● **KISS FROM A ROSE** (re-issue) **/ I'M ALIVE** *ZTT ZANG 70CD* ▲...4 13
9 Dec 95 **DON'T CRY / PRAYER FOR THE DYING** (re-issue) *ZTT ZANG 75CD*....51 2
29 Mar 97 **FLY LIKE AN EAGLE** *ZTT ZEAL 1CD*....13 5
14 Nov 98 **HUMAN BEINGS** *Warner Bros. W 464CD*....50 1
28 Nov 98 HUMAN BEING *Warner Bros. 9362468282*....44 2
12 Oct 02 ● **MY VISION** *Rulin RULIN 26CDS* [1] 6 8
20 Sep 03 **GET IT TOGETHER** *Warner W 620CD1*....25 3
27 Sep 03 ● IV *Warner Bros. 9362485412*....4 6
22 Nov 03 **LOVE'S DIVINE** *Warner W 629CD*....68 1
20 Nov 04 BEST – 1991-2004 *Warner Bros. 9362489582*....27 7

[1] Jakatta featuring Seal

Tracks on Future Love (EP): Future Love Paradise / A Minor Groove / Violet. Tracks on Killer (EP): Killer / Hey Joe / Come See What Love Has Done. The US No.1 symbol applies to 'Kiss from a Rose' only. The two eponymous albums are different.

Jay SEAN
UK, male vocalist – Kamaljit Jhooti (1 Album: 2 Weeks, 2 Singles: 16 Weeks)

3 Jul 04 ● **EYES ON YOU** *Relentless RELCD 5* [1] 6 10
6 Nov 04 ● **STOLEN** *Relentless RELDX 11*....4 6
20 Nov 04 ME AGAINST MYSELF *Relentless CDREL 05*....29 2

[1] Jay Sean featuring The Rishi Rich Project

The SEARCHERS (319 Top 500)
Infuential Merseybeat combo formed in 1960 and named after the 1956 movie starring John Wayne: Mike Pender (v/g), John McNally (g/v), Tony Jackson (v/b), b. 16 Jul 1940, d. 18 Aug 2003 (left in 1964 – replaced by Frank Allen), Chris Curtis (Chris Crummey) (d), b. 26 Aug 1941, d. 28 Feb 2005. The group was initially tipped to be as big as The Beatles. However, unlike the Fab Four, most of this influential act's early hits were cover versions of US originals (4 Albums: 87 Weeks, 14 Singles: 128 Weeks)

27 Jun 63 ★ **SWEETS FOR MY SWEET** *Pye 7N 15533*....1 16
10 Aug 63 ● MEET THE SEARCHERS *Pye NPL 18086*....2 44
10 Oct 63 **SWEET NOTHINS** *Philips BF 1274*....48 2
24 Oct 63 ● **SUGAR AND SPICE** *Pye 7N 15566*....2 13
16 Nov 63 ● SUGAR AND SPICE *Pye NPL 18089*....5 21
16 Jan 64 ★ **NEEDLES AND PINS** *Pye 7N 15594*....1 15
16 Apr 64 ★ **DON'T THROW YOUR LOVE AWAY** *Pye 7N 15630*....1 11
30 May 64 ● IT'S THE SEARCHERS *Pye NPL 18092*....4 17
16 Jul 64 **SOMEDAY WE'RE GONNA LOVE AGAIN** *Pye 7N 15670*....11 8
17 Sep 64 ● **WHEN YOU WALK IN THE ROOM** *Pye 7N 15694*....3 12
3 Dec 64 **WHAT HAVE THEY DONE TO THE RAIN** *Pye 7N 15739*....13 11
4 Mar 65 ● **GOODBYE MY LOVE** *Pye 7N 15794*....4 11
27 Mar 65 ● SOUNDS LIKE THE SEARCHERS *Pye NPL 18111*....8 5
8 Jul 65 **HE'S GOT NO LOVE** *Pye 7N 15878*....12 10
14 Oct 65 **WHEN I GET HOME** *Pye 7N 15950*....35 3
16 Dec 65 **TAKE ME FOR WHAT I'M WORTH** *Pye 7N 15992*....20 8
21 Apr 66 **TAKE IT OR LEAVE IT** *Pye 7N 17094*....31 6
13 Oct 66 **HAVE YOU EVER LOVED SOMEBODY** *Pye 7N 17170*....48 2

The SEASHELLS *UK, female vocal group*

9 Sep 72 **MAYBE I KNOW** *CBS 8218*....32 5

SEB *UK, male keyboard player – Sebastian Wronski*

18 Feb 95 **SUGAR SHACK** *React CDREACT 50*....61 1

SEBADOH
US, male vocal / instrumental group (4 Albums: 5 Weeks, 2 Singles: 4 Weeks)

8 May 93 BUBBLE AND SCRAPE *Domino WIGCD 4*....63 1

19 March 1988	26 March 1988	2 April 1988	9 April 1988
◂◂ UK No.1 SINGLES ▸▸			
I SHOULD BE SO LUCKY Kylie Minogue	DON'T TURN AROUND Aswad	DON'T TURN AROUND Aswad	HEART Pet Shop Boys
◂◂ UK No.1 ALBUMS ▸▸			
INTRODUCING THE HARDLINE ACCORDING TO TERENCE TRENT D'ARBY Terence Trent D'Arby	VIVA HATE Morrissey	NOW THAT'S WHAT I CALL MUSIC! 11 Various	NOW THAT'S WHAT I CALL MUSIC! 11 Various

3 Sep 94 BAKESALE *Domino WIGCD 11* 40 2
27 Jul 96 **BEAUTY OF THE RIDE** *Domino RUG 47CD* **74** 1
31 Aug 96 HARMACY *Domino Recordings WIGCD 26* 38 1
30 Jan 99 **FLAME** *Domino RUG 80CD1* **30** 3
6 Mar 99 THE SEBADOH *Domino Recordings WIGCD 57* 45 1

Jon SECADA

Cuba, male vocalist – Juan Secada (2 Albums: 16 Weeks, 9 Singles: 42 Weeks)

18 Jul 92 ● **JUST ANOTHER DAY** *SBK SBK 35* **5** 15
5 Sep 92 JON SECADA *SBK SBKCD 19* 20 11
31 Oct 92 **DO YOU BELIEVE IN US** *SBK SBK 37* **30** 4
6 Feb 93 **ANGEL** *SBK CDSBK 39* **23** 5
17 Jul 93 **DO YOU REALLY WANT ME** *SBK CDSBK 41* **30** 4
16 Oct 93 **I'M FREE** *SBK CDSBK 44* **50** 2
14 May 94 **IF YOU GO (re)** *SBK CDSBK 51* **39** 5
4 Jun 94 HEART SOUL AND A VOICE *SBK SBKCD 29* 17 5
4 Feb 95 **MENTAL PICTURE** *SBK CDSBK 54* **44** 2
16 Dec 95 **IF I NEVER KNEW YOU (LOVE THEME FROM 'POCAHONTAS')** *Walt Disney WD 7023C* [1] **51** 4
14 Jun 97 **TOO LATE, TOO SOON** *SBK CDSBK 57* **43** 1

[1] Jon Secada and Shanice

SECCHI featuring Orlando JOHNSON

Italy / US, male vocal / instrumental duo

4 May 91 **I SAY YEAH** *Epic 6568467* **46** 3

Harry SECOMBE (see also The GOONS) *UK, male vocalist / comedian, b. 8 Sep 1921, d. 12 Apr 2001 (8 Albums: 62 Weeks, 3 Singles: 35 Weeks)*

9 Dec 55 **ON WITH THE MOTLEY (VESTA LA GIUBBA)** *Philips PB 523* **16** 3
31 Mar 62 SACRED SONGS *Philips RBL 7501* 16 1
3 Oct 63 **IF I RULED THE WORLD (re)** *Philips BF 1261* **18** 17
18 Apr 64 HOW TO WIN AN ELECTION *Philips AL 3464* [1] 20 1
23 Feb 67 ● **THIS IS MY SONG** *Philips BF 1539* **2** 15
22 Apr 67 ● SECOMBE'S PERSONAL CHOICE *Philips BETS 707* 6 13
7 Aug 71 IF I RULED THE WORLD *Contour 6870 501* 17 20
16 Dec 78 ● 20 SONGS OF JOY *Warwick WW 5052* 8 12
5 Dec 81 GOLDEN MEMORIES *Warwick WW 5107* [2] 46 5
13 Dec 86 HIGHWAY OF LIFE *Telstar STAR 2289* 45 5
30 Nov 91 YOURS SINCERELY *Philips 5107321* 46 5

[1] Harry Secombe, Peter Sellers and Spike Milligan [2] Harry Secombe and Moira Anderson

SECOND CITY SOUND *UK, male instrumental group (2 Singles: 8 Weeks)*

20 Jan 66 **TCHAIKOVSKY ONE** *Decca F 12310* **22** 7
2 Apr 69 **DREAM OF OLWEN** *Major Minor MM 600* **43** 1

SECOND IMAGE

UK, male vocal / instrumental group (1 Album: 1 Week, 5 Singles: 11 Weeks)

24 Jul 82 **STAR** *Polydor POSP 457* **60** 2
2 Apr 83 **BETTER TAKE TIME** *Polydor POSP 565* **67** 2
26 Nov 83 **DON'T YOU** *MCA 848* **68** 2
11 Aug 84 **SING AND SHOUT** *MCA 882* **53** 3
2 Feb 85 **STARTING AGAIN** *MCA 936* **65** 2
30 Mar 85 STRANGE REFLECTIONS *MCA MCF 3255* 100 1

SECOND PHASE (see also BELTRAM) *US, male producer – Joey Beltram*

21 Sep 91 **MENTASM** *R&S RSUK 2* **48** 2

SECOND PROTOCOL *UK, male production duo*

23 Sep 00 **BASSLICK** *East West EW 216CD* **58** 2

SECRET AFFAIR

UK, male vocal / instrumental group (3 Albums: 15 Weeks, 5 Singles: 34 Weeks)

1 Sep 79 **TIME FOR ACTION** *I-Spy SEE 1* **13** 10
10 Nov 79 **LET YOUR HEART DANCE** *I-Spy SEE 3* **32** 6
1 Dec 79 GLORY BOYS *I-Spy 1* 41 8
8 Mar 80 **MY WORLD** *I-Spy SEE 5* **16** 9
23 Aug 80 **SOUND OF CONFUSION** *I-Spy SEE 8* **45** 5
20 Sep 80 BEHIND CLOSED DOORS *I-Spy 2* 48 4
17 Oct 81 **DO YOU KNOW** *I-Spy SEE 10* **57** 4
13 Mar 82 BUSINESS AS USUAL *I-Spy 3* 84 3

SECRET KNOWLEDGE

UK / US, male / female vocal / instrumental duo (2 Singles: 2 Weeks)

27 Apr 96 **LOVE ME NOW** *Deconstruction 74321342432* **66** 1
24 Aug 96 **SUGAR DADDY** *Deconstruction 74321400242* **75** 1

SECRET LIFE *UK, male vocal / production group (5 Singles: 10 Weeks)*

12 Dec 92 **AS ALWAYS** *Cowboy 7RODEO 9* **45** 4
7 Aug 93 **LOVE SO STRONG** *Cowboy RODEO 18CD* **38** 2
7 May 94 **SHE HOLDS THE KEY** *Pulse 8 CDLOSE 58* **63** 1
29 Oct 94 **I WANT YOU** *Pulse 8 CDLOSE 71* **70** 1
28 Jan 95 **LOVE SO STRONG** (re-mix) *Pulse 8 CDLOSE 79* **37** 2

SECRET MACHINES *US, male vocal / instrumental trio (3 Singles: 5 Weeks)*

7 Aug 04 **NOWHERE AGAIN** *Reprise W 648CD* **49** 1
8 Jan 05 **SAD AND LONELY** *679 Recordings 679L0 94CD* **38** 3
23 Apr 05 **THE ROAD LEADS WHERE IT'S LED** *679 Recordings W 669CD2* **56** 1

SECTION-X *France, male instrumental duo*

8 Mar 97 **ATLANTIS** *Perfecto PERF 136* **42** 1

Neil SEDAKA (237 Top 500)

The man who put the 'Tra-La-La' into 1960s pop, b. 13 Mar 1939, New York, US. Ultra-commercial singer / songwriter / pianist who enjoyed two separate chart runs as an artist and wrote many hits for numerous other acts (8 Albums: 80 Weeks, 19 Singles: 190 Weeks)

24 Apr 59 ● **I GO APE** *RCA 1115* **9** 13
13 Nov 59 ● **OH! CAROL** *RCA 1152* **3** 17
14 Apr 60 ● **STAIRWAY TO HEAVEN** *RCA 1178* **8** 15
1 Sep 60 **YOU MEAN EVERYTHING TO ME** *RCA 1198* **45** 3
2 Feb 61 ● **CALENDAR GIRL** *RCA 1220* **8** 14
18 May 61 ● **LITTLE DEVIL** *RCA 1236* **9** 12
21 Dec 61 ● **HAPPY BIRTHDAY, SWEET SIXTEEN** *RCA 1266* **3** 18
19 Apr 62 **KING OF CLOWNS** *RCA 1282* **23** 11
19 Jul 62 ● **BREAKING UP IS HARD TO DO** *RCA 1298* ▲ $ **7** 16
22 Nov 62 **NEXT DOOR TO AN ANGEL** *RCA 1319* **29** 4
30 May 63 **LET'S GO STEADY AGAIN (re)** *RCA 1343* **42** 3
7 Oct 72 **OH CAROL / BREAKING UP IS HARD TO DO / LITTLE DEVIL** (re-issue) *RCA Maximillion 2259* **19** 14
4 Nov 72 **BEAUTIFUL YOU** *RCA 2269* **43** 3
24 Feb 73 **THAT'S WHEN THE MUSIC TAKES ME** *RCA 2310* **18** 10
2 Jun 73 **STANDING ON THE INSIDE** *MGM 2006 267* **26** 9
25 Aug 73 **OUR LAST SONG TOGETHER** *MGM 2006 307* **31** 8
1 Sep 73 THE TRA-LA DAYS ARE OVER *MGM 2315 248* 13 10
9 Feb 74 **A LITTLE LOVIN'** *Polydor 2058 434* **34** 6
22 Jun 74 LAUGHTER IN THE RAIN *Polydor 2383 265* 17 10
22 Jun 74 **LAUGHTER IN THE RAIN** *Polydor 2058 494* ▲ **15** 9
23 Nov 74 LIVE AT THE ROYAL FESTIVAL HALL *Polydor 2383 299* 48 1
1 Mar 75 OVERNIGHT SUCCESS *Polydor 2442 131* 31 6
22 Mar 75 **THE QUEEN OF 1964** *Polydor 2058 546* **35** 5
10 Jul 76 ● LAUGHTER AND TEARS – THE BEST OF NEIL SEDAKA TODAY *Polydor 2383 399* 2 25
2 Nov 91 ● TIMELESS – THE VERY BEST OF NEIL SEDAKA *Polydor 5114421* 10 16
4 Nov 95 CLASSICALLY SEDAKA *Vision VISCD 5* 23 9
19 Jun 99 THE VERY BEST OF NEIL SEDAKA *Universal Music TV 5646452* 33 3

Max SEDGLEY *UK, male producer*

17 Jul 04 **HAPPY** *Sunday Best SBEST C14* **30** 3

16 April 1988	23 April 1988	30 April 1988	7 May 1988
HEART Pet Shop Boys	HEART Pet Shop Boys	THEME FROM S-EXPRESS S-Express	THEME FROM S-EXPRESS S-Express
NOW THAT'S WHAT I CALL MUSIC! 11 Various	SEVENTH SON OF A SEVENTH SON Iron Maiden	THE INNOCENTS Erasure	TANGO IN THE NIGHT Fleetwood Mac

KEY
UK No.1 ★ UK Top 10 ● Still on chart + UK entry at No.1 ■
US No.1 ▲ UK million seller £ US million seller $
Singles re-entries are listed as (re), (2re), (3re)... which signifies that the hit re-entered the chart once, twice or three times...

Peak Position / Weeks

SEDUCTION *US, female vocal group*

21 Apr 90 **HEARTBEAT** *Breakout USA 685*......75 1

The SEEKERS 121 Top 500

First Australian act to top the UK singles or albums charts: Judith Durham (v), Keith Potger (g), Bruce Woodley (g), Athol Guy (b). Their unique harmony vocals were displayed on many of their hits, which were penned and produced by Tom Springfield. Durham went solo in 1967, and Potger later went on to form The New Seekers. Best-selling single: 'The Carnival Is Over' 1,400,000 (7 Albums: 275 Weeks, 9 Singles: 120 Weeks)

7 Jan 65 ★ **I'LL NEVER FIND ANOTHER YOU** *Columbia DB 7431*......1 23
15 Apr 65 ● **A WORLD OF OUR OWN** *Columbia DB 7532*......3 18
3 Jul 65 ● A WORLD OF OUR OWN *Columbia 33SX 1722*......5 37
3 Jul 65 THE SEEKERS *Decca LK 4694*......16 1
28 Oct 65 ★ **THE CARNIVAL IS OVER** *Columbia DB 7711* £......1 17
24 Mar 66 **SOMEDAY ONE DAY** *Columbia DB 7867*......11 11
8 Sep 66 ● **WALK WITH ME** *Columbia DB 8000*......10 12
19 Nov 66 ● COME THE DAY *Columbia SX 6093*......2 67
24 Nov 66 ● **MORNINGTOWN RIDE** *Columbia DB 8060*......2 15
23 Feb 67 ● **GEORGY GIRL** *Columbia DB 8134* $......3 11
20 Sep 67 **WHEN WILL THE GOOD APPLES FALL** *Columbia DB 8273*......11 12
25 Nov 67 SEEKERS – SEEN IN GREEN *Columbia SCX 6193*......15 10
13 Dec 67 **EMERALD CITY** *Columbia DB 8313*......50 1
14 Sep 68 ● LIVE AT THE TALK OF THE TOWN *Columbia SCX 6278*......2 29
16 Nov 68 ★ THE BEST OF THE SEEKERS *Columbia SCX 6268*......1 117
23 Apr 94 ● A CARNIVAL OF HITS *EMI CDEMTV 83* [1]......7 14

[1] Judith Durham and The Seekers

SEELENLUFT featuring Michael SMITH

Switzerland, male producer – Beat Soler and US, male rapper

4 Oct 03 **MANILA** *Back Yard BACK 10CSC 1*......70 1

Bob SEGER and The SILVER BULLET BAND *US, male vocal / instrumental group (7 Albums: 52 Weeks, 9 Singles: 30 Weeks)*

3 Jun 78 STRANGER IN TOWN *Capitol EAST 11698*......31 6
30 Sep 78 **HOLLYWOOD NIGHTS** *Capitol CL 16004*......42 6
3 Feb 79 **WE'VE GOT TONITE** *Capitol CL 16028*......41 6
15 Mar 80 AGAINST THE WIND *Capitol EAST 12041* ▲......26 6
26 Sep 81 NINE TONIGHT *Capitol ESTSP 23*......24 10
24 Oct 81 **HOLLYWOOD NIGHTS** (re-issue) *Capitol CL 223*......49 3
6 Feb 82 **WE'VE GOT TONITE** (re-issue) *Capitol CL 235*......60 4
8 Jan 83 THE DISTANCE *Capitol EST 12254*......45 10
9 Apr 83 **EVEN NOW** *Capitol CL 284*......73 2
26 Apr 86 LIKE A ROCK *Capitol EST 2011*......35 6
21 Sep 91 THE FIRE INSIDE *Capitol EST 2149*......54 2
28 Jan 95 **WE'VE GOT TONIGHT** (2nd re-issue) *Capitol CDCL 734*......22 5
18 Feb 95 ● GREATEST HITS *Capitol CDEST 2241*......6 12
29 Apr 95 **NIGHT MOVES** *Capitol CDCL 741*......45 2
29 Jul 95 **HOLLYWOOD NIGHTS** (2nd re-issue) *Capitol CDCL 749*......52 1
10 Feb 96 **LOCK AND LOAD** *Parlophone CDCL 765*......57 1

Capitol CL 223 and CL 235 were live versions of earlier studio hits. 'We've Got Tonite' and 'We've Got Tonight' are the same single spelt differently.

Shea SEGER *US, female vocalist*

5 May 01 **CLUTCH** *RCA 74321828142*......47 1

SEIKO and Donnie WAHLBERG

(see also NEW KIDS ON THE BLOCK) *Japan / US, female / male vocal duo*

18 Aug 90 **THE RIGHT COMBINATION** *Epic 656203 7*......44 5

SELECTER *UK, male / female vocal (Pauline Black) / instrumental group (2 Albums: 17 Weeks, 4 Singles: 28 Weeks)*

13 Oct 79 ● **ON MY RADIO** *2 Tone CHSTT 4*......8 9
2 Feb 80 **THREE MINUTE HERO** *2 Tone CHSTT 8*......16 6
23 Feb 80 ● TOO MUCH PRESSURE *2 Tone CDLTT 5002*......5 13
29 Mar 80 **MISSING WORDS** *2 Tone CHSTT 10*......23 8
23 Aug 80 **THE WHISPER** *Chrysalis CHSS 1*......36 5
7 Mar 81 CELEBRATE THE BULLET *Chrysalis CHR 1306*......41 4

SELENA vs X MEN *UK, female vocalist and male production duo*

14 Jul 01 **GIVE IT UP** *Go Beat BOBCD 40*......61 1

SELFISH CUNT *UK, male vocal / instrumental group*

17 Jul 04 **AUTHORITY CONFRONTATION** *Horseglue UHU 008*......66 1

Peter SELLERS 491 Top 500 (see also The GOONS)

UK, male actor / vocalist – Richard Sellers, b. 8 Sep 1925, d. 24 Jul 1980 (5 Albums: 113 Weeks, 5 Singles: 39 Weeks)

2 Aug 57 **ANY OLD IRON (re)** *Parlophone R 4337* [1] 00......17 11
14 Feb 59 ● THE BEST OF SELLERS *Parlophone PMD 1069*......3 47
12 Dec 59 ● SONGS FOR SWINGING SELLERS *Parlophone PMC 1111*......3 37
10 Nov 60 ● **GOODNESS GRACIOUS ME** *Parlophone R 4702* [2]......4 14
3 Dec 60 ● PETER AND SOPHIA *Parlophone PMC 1131* [1]......5 18
12 Jan 61 **BANGERS AND MASH** *Parlophone R 4724* [2]......22 5
28 Sep 63 ● FOOL BRITANNIA *Ember CEL 902* [2]......10 10
18 Apr 64 HOW TO WIN AN ELECTION *Philips AL 3464* [3]......20 1
23 Dec 65 **A HARD DAY'S NIGHT** *Parlophone R 5393*......14 7
27 Nov 93 **A HARD DAY'S NIGHT** (re-issue) *EMI CDEMS 293*......52 2

[1] Peter Sellers presents Mate's Skiffle Group featuring Fred Spoons EPNS
[2] Peter Sellers and Sophia Loren [1] Peter Sellers and Sophia Loren
[2] Anthony Newley, Peter Sellers, Joan Collins [3] Harry Secombe, Peter Sellers and Spike Milligan

Michael SEMBELLO *US, male vocalist*

20 Aug 83 **MANIAC** *Casablanca CAN 1017* ▲......43 6

SEMISONIC

US, male vocal / instrumental group (2 Albums: 41 Weeks, 4 Singles: 20 Weeks)

10 Jul 99 **SECRET SMILE** *MCA MCSTD 40210*......13 11
24 Jul 99 FEELING STRANGELY FINE *MCA MCD 11733*......16 37
6 Nov 99 **CLOSING TIME** *MCA MCSTD 40221*......25 5
1 Apr 00 **SINGING IN MY SLEEP** *MCA MCSTD 40227*......39 2
3 Mar 01 **CHEMISTRY** *MCA MCSTD 40248*......35 2
17 Mar 01 ALL ABOUT CHEMISTRY *MCA 1125012*......13 4

SEMPRINI *UK, male pianist – Fernando Riccardo Alberto Semprini, b. 1908, d. 19 Jan 1990, and orchestra*

16 Mar 61 **MAIN THEME FROM 'EXODUS'** *HMV POP 842*......25 8

The SENSATIONAL ALEX HARVEY BAND

UK, male vocal / instrumental group – leader b. 5 Feb 1935, d. 4 Feb 1982 (6 Albums: 42 Weeks, 3 Singles: 25 Weeks)

26 Oct 74 THE IMPOSSIBLE DREAM *Vertigo 6360 112*......16 4
10 May 75 ● TOMORROW BELONGS TO ME *Vertigo 9102 003*......9 10
26 Jul 75 ● **DELILAH** *Vertigo ALEX 001*......7 7
23 Aug 75 NEXT *Vertigo 6360 103*......37 5
27 Sep 75 LIVE *Vertigo 6360 122*......14 7
22 Nov 75 **GAMBLIN' BAR ROOM BLUES** *Vertigo ALEX 002*......38 8
10 Apr 76 PENTHOUSE TAPES *Vertigo 9102 007*......14 7
19 Jun 76 **THE BOSTON TEA PARTY** *Mountain TOP 12*......13 10
31 Jul 76 SAHB STORIES *Mountain TOPS 112*......11 9

SENSELESS THINGS

UK, male vocal / instrumental group (2 Albums: 2 Weeks, 9 Singles: 19 Weeks)

22 Jun 91 **EVERYBODY'S GONE** *Epic 6569807*......73 1
28 Sep 91 **GOT IT AT THE DELMAR** *Epic 6574497*......50 3

14 May 1988	21 May 1988	28 May 1988	4 June 1988
UK No.1 SINGLES			
PERFECTION Fairground Attraction	**WITH A LITTLE HELP FROM MY FRIENDS / SHE'S LEAVING HOME** Wet Wet Wet / Billy Bragg with Cara Tivey	**WITH A LITTLE HELP FROM MY FRIENDS / SHE'S LEAVING HOME** Wet Wet Wet / Billy Bragg with Cara Tivey	**WITH A LITTLE HELP FROM MY FRIENDS / SHE'S LEAVING HOME** Wet Wet Wet / Billy Bragg with Cara Tivey
UK No.1 ALBUMS			
TANGO IN THE NIGHT Fleetwood Mac	**LOVESEXY** Prince	**TANGO IN THE NIGHT** Fleetwood Mac	**NITE FLITE** Various

26 Oct 91	THE FIRST OF TOO MANY *Epic 4691571*	66	1
11 Jan 92	**EASY TO SMILE** *Epic 6576957*	**18**	4
11 Apr 92	**HOLD IT DOWN** *Epic 6579267*	**19**	4
5 Dec 92	**HOMOPHOBIC ASSHOLE** *Epic 6588337*	**52**	2
13 Feb 93	**PRIMARY INSTINCT** *Epic 6589402*	**41**	2
13 Mar 93	EMPIRE OF THE SENSELESS *Epic 4735252*	37	1
12 Jun 93	**TOO MUCH KISSING** *Epic 6592502*	**69**	1
5 Nov 94	**CHRISTINE KEELER** *Epic 6609572*	**56**	1
28 Jan 95	**SOMETHING TO MISS** *Epic 6611162*	**57**	1

SENSER *UK, male / female vocal / instrumental group (2 Albums: 6 Weeks, 4 Singles: 5 Weeks)*

25 Sep 93	**THE KEY** *Ultimate TOPP 019CD*	**47**	1
19 Mar 94	**SWITCH** *Ultimate TOPP 022CD*	**39**	2
7 May 94 ●	STACKED UP *Ultimate TOPPCD 008*	4	5
23 Jul 94	**AGE OF PANIC** *Ultimate TOPP 027CD*	**52**	1
17 Aug 96	**CHARMING DEMONS** *Ultimate TOPP 045CD*	**42**	1
2 May 98	ASYLUM *Ultimate TOPPCD 064*	73	1

SEPULTURA *Brazil, male vocal (Max Cavalera) / instrumental group (4 Albums: 12 Weeks, 6 Singles: 12 Weeks)*

6 Apr 91	ARISE *Roadracer RO 93281*	40	2
2 Oct 93	**TERRITORY** *Roadrunner RR 23823*	**66**	2
23 Oct 93	CHAOS A.D. *Roadrunner RR 90002*	11	4
26 Feb 94	**REFUSE-RESIST** *Roadrunner RR 23773*	**51**	2
4 Jun 94	**SLAVE NEW WORLD** *Roadrunner RR 23745*	**46**	2
24 Feb 96	**ROOTS BLOODY ROOTS** *Roadrunner RR 23205*	**19**	2
9 Mar 96 ●	ROOTS *Roadrunner RR 89002*	4	5
17 Aug 96	**RATAMAHATTA** *Roadrunner RR 23145*	**23**	2
14 Dec 96	**ATTITUDE** *Roadrunner RR 22995*	**46**	2
17 Oct 98	AGAINST *Roadrunner RR 87002*	40	1

SERAFIN *UK, male vocal / instrumental group (2 Singles: 2 Weeks)*

15 May 03	**THINGS FALL APART** *Taste Media TMCDS 5003*	**49**	1
16 Aug 03	**DAY BY DAY** *Taste Media TMCDS 5006*	**49**	1

SERAPHIM SUITE (see also Jeremy HEALY and AMOS; Mica PARIS) *UK, male / female production / vocal trio*

27 Mar 04	**HEART** *Inferno CDFERN 61*	**45**	2

SERIAL DIVA *UK, male / female production group (2 Singles: 3 Weeks)*

18 Jan 97	**KEEP HOPE ALIVE** *Sound of Ministry SOMCD 26*	**57**	1
15 May 99	**PEARL RIVER** *Low Sense SENSECD 24* [1]	**32**	2

[1] Three 'N One presents Johnny Shaker featuring Serial Diva

SERIOUS DANGER *UK, male producer – Richard Phillips (2 Singles: 4 Weeks)*

20 Dec 97	**DEEPER** *Fresh FRSHD 68*	**40**	3
2 May 98	**HIGH NOON** *Fresh FRSHD 69*	**54**	1

SERIOUS INTENTION *US, male vocal / instrumental group (2 Singles: 6 Weeks)*

16 Nov 85	**YOU DON'T KNOW (OH-OH-OH)** *Important TAN 8*	**75**	1
5 Apr 86	**SERIOUS** *Pow Wow LON 93*	**51**	5

SERIOUS ROPE *UK, male / female vocal / production group (2 Singles: 3 Weeks)*

22 May 93	**HAPPINESS** *Rumour RUMACD 64* [1]	**54**	2
1 Oct 94	**HAPPINESS – YOU MAKE ME HAPPY** (re-mix) *Mercury MERCD 407*	**70**	1

[1] Serious Rope presents Sharon Dee Clarke

Erick SERMON *US, male rapper (3 Singles: 8 Weeks)*

6 Oct 01	**MUSIC** *Polydor 4976222* [1]	**36**	2
11 Jan 03	**REACT** *J 74321988492* [2]	**14**	5
19 Apr 03	**LOVE IZ** *J 82876510971*	**72**	1

[1] Erick Sermon featuring Marvin Gaye [2] Erick Sermon featuring Redman

Eric SERRA *France, male composer*

28 Jun 97	THE FIFTH ELEMENT (FILM SOUNDTRACK) *Virgin CDVIRX 63*	58	2

SERTAB *Turkey, female vocalist – Sertab Erener*

21 Jun 03	**EVERY WAY THAT I CAN** *Columbia 6739621*	**72**	1

SET THE TONE *UK, male vocal / instrumental group (2 Singles: 4 Weeks)*

22 Jan 83	**DANCE SUCKER** *Island WIP 6836*	**62**	2
26 Mar 83	**RAP YOUR LOVE** *Island IS 110*	**67**	2

The SETTLERS *UK, male / female vocal / instrumental group*

16 Oct 71	**THE LIGHTNING TREE** *York SYK 505*	**36**	5

Brian SETZER ORCHESTRA (see also The STRAY CATS) *US, male vocal / instrumental group*

3 Apr 99	**JUMP JIVE AN' WAIL** *Interscope IND 95601*	**34**	3

Taja SEVELLE *US, female vocalist (1 Album: 4 Weeks, 2 Singles: 13 Weeks)*

20 Feb 88 ●	**LOVE IS CONTAGIOUS** *Paisley Park W 8257*	**7**	9
26 Mar 88	TAJA SEVELLE *Paisley Park WX 165*	48	4
14 May 88	**WOULDN'T YOU LOVE TO LOVE ME?** *Paisley Park W 8127*	**59**	4

702 *US, female vocal group (4 Singles: 10 Weeks)*

14 Dec 96	**STEELO** *Motown 8606072*	**41**	2
29 Nov 97	**NO DOUBT** *Motown 8607052*	**59**	1
7 Aug 99	**WHERE MY GIRLS AT?** *Motown TMGCD 1500*	**22**	4
27 Nov 99	**YOU DON'T KNOW** *Motown TMGCD 1502*	**36**	3

740 BOYZ *US, male vocal / instrumental duo – Winston and Eddie Rosa (2 Singles: 3 Weeks)*

4 Nov 95	**SHIMMY SHAKE** *MCA MCSTD 40002*	**54**	1
22 Mar 03	**SHAKE YA SHIMMY** *All Around the World CDGLOBE 213* [1]	**28**	2

[1] Porn Kings vs Flip & Fill featuring 740 Boyz

SEVEN GRAND HOUSING AUTHORITY *UK, male producer – Terence Parker*

23 Oct 93	**THE QUESTION** *Olympic ELYCD 010*	**70**	1

7669 *US, female rap group*

18 Jun 94	**JOY** *Motown TMGCD 1429*	**60**	1

7TH HEAVEN *UK, male vocal group*

14 Sep 85	**HOT FUN** *Mercury MER 199*	**47**	5

SEVERINE *France, female vocalist – Josiane Grizeau*

24 Apr 71 ●	**UN BANC, UN ARBRE, UNE RUE** *Philips 6009 135*	**9**	11

David SEVILLE (see also ALFI and HARRY; The CHIPMUNKS) *US, male vocalist – Ross Bagdasarian, b. 27 Jan 1919, d. 16 Jan 1972*

23 May 58	**WITCH DOCTOR** *London HLU 8619* ▲ $	**11**	6

Danny SEWARD NEW *UK, male actor / vocalist*

30 Jul 05	WHERE MY HEART IS *Liberty VTCD 722*	56	1

SEX CLUB featuring BROWN SUGAR *US, male / female vocal / instrumental duo*

28 Jan 95	**BIG DICK MAN** *Club Tools CLU 60775*	**67**	1

11 June 1988	18 June 1988	25 June 1988	2 July 1988
WITH A LITTLE HELP FROM MY FRIENDS / SHE'S LEAVING HOME Wet Wet Wet / Billy Bragg with Cara Tivey	**DOCTORIN' THE TARDIS** The Timelords	**I OWE YOU NOTHING** Bros	**I OWE YOU NOTHING** Bros
NITE FLITE Various	**NITE FLITE** Various	**NITE FLITE** Various	**TRACY CHAPMAN** Tracy Chapman

KEY: UK No.1 ★ UK Top 10 ● Still on chart + UK entry at No.1 ■ US No.1 ▲ UK million seller £ US million seller $
Singles re-entries are listed as (re), (2re), (3re)... which signifies that the hit re-entered the chart once, twice or three times...
Peak Position / Weeks

SEX-O-SONIQUE (see also FULL INTENTION; HUSTLERS CONVENTION featuring Dave LAUDAT and Ondrea DUVERNEY; RONALDO'S REVENGE)

UK, male production / instrumental duo – Michael Gray and Jon Pearn

6 Dec 97 **I THOUGHT IT WAS YOU** *ffrr FCD 321* 32 3

SEX PISTOLS 336 Top 500 (see also PUBLIC IMAGE LTD (PIL))

Provocative and influential quartet who popularised punk, formed in 1975 in London, UK: Johnny Rotten (v) (John Lydon), Steve Jones (g), Paul Cook (d) and Glen Matlock (b) – replaced in 1977 by Sid Vicious, d. 1979. The notorious group, who split up in 1978, reunited for brief and profitable tours in 1996 and 2003, and were added to the Rock and Roll Hall of Fame in 2006. Rotten is now a popular TV personality (7 Albums: 116 Weeks, 14 Singles: 91 Weeks)

18 Dec 76 **ANARCHY IN THE UK** *EMI 2566* 38 4
4 Jun 77 ● **GOD SAVE THE QUEEN** *Virgin VS 181* 2 9
9 Jul 77 ● **PRETTY VACANT** *Virgin VS 184* 6 8
22 Oct 77 ● **HOLIDAYS IN THE SUN** *Virgin VS 191* 8 6
12 Nov 77 ★ **NEVER MIND THE BOLLOCKS HERE'S THE SEX PISTOLS** *Virgin V 2086* ■ 1 58
8 Jul 78 ● **NO ONE IS INNOCENT (A PUNK PRAYER BY RONALD BIGGS) / MY WAY** *Virgin VS 220* [1] 7 10
3 Mar 79 ● **SOMETHING ELSE / FRIGGIN' IN THE RIGGIN'** *Virgin VS 240* [2] 3 12
10 Mar 79 ● **THE GREAT ROCK 'N' ROLL SWINDLE (FILM SOUNDTRACK)** *Virgin VD 2410* 7 33
7 Apr 79 ● **SILLY THING** *Virgin VS 256* 6 8
30 Jun 79 ● **C'MON EVERYBODY** *Virgin VS 272* [3] 3 9
11 Aug 79 ● **SOME PRODUCT – CARRI ON SEX PISTOLS** *Virgin VR 2* 6 10
13 Oct 79 **THE GREAT ROCK 'N' ROLL SWINDLE** *Virgin VS 290* 21 6
16 Feb 80 **FLOGGING A DEAD HORSE** *Virgin V 2142* 23 6
14 Jun 80 **(I'M NOT YOUR) STEPPING STONE** *Virgin VS 339* 21 8
3 Oct 92 **ANARCHY IN THE UK** (re-issue) *Virgin VS 1431* 33 3
17 Oct 92 ● **KISS THIS** *Virgin CDV 2702* 10 4
5 Dec 92 **PRETTY VACANT** (re-issue) *Virgin VS 1448* 56 2
27 Jul 96 **PRETTY VACANT (LIVE)** *Virgin America VUSCD 113* 18 3
10 Aug 96 **FILTHY LUCRE LIVE** *Virgin CDVUS 116* 26 2
8 Jun 02 **GOD SAVE THE QUEEN** (re-issue) *Virgin VSCDT 1832* 15 3
15 Jun 02 **JUBILEE** *Virgin CDV 2961* 29 3

[1] Uncredited vocal by Ronald Biggs [2] Sex Pistols: vocals Sid Vicious / Sex Pistols: vocals Steve Jones [3] Sex Pistols: vocals Sid Vicious

The listed flip side of 'Silly Thing' was 'Who Killed Bambi' by Ten Pole Tudor. The listed flip side of 'The Great Rock 'n' Roll Swindle' was 'Rock Around the Clock', also by Ten Pole Tudor.

Denny SEYTON and The SABRES *UK, male vocal / instrumental group*

17 Sep 64 **THE WAY YOU LOOK TONIGHT** *Mercury MF 824* 48 1

SHABOOM *UK, male instrumental / production group*

31 Jul 99 **SWEET SENSATION** *WEA WEA 218CD1* 64 1

SHACK

UK, male vocal / instrumental group (2 Albums: 3 Weeks, 4 Singles: 4 Weeks)

26 Jun 99 **COMEDY** *London LONCD 427* 44 1
3 Jul 99 **H.M.S. FABLE** *London 5561132* 25 2
14 Aug 99 **NATALIE'S PARTY** *London LONCD 436* 63 1
11 Mar 00 **OSCAR** *London LONCD 445* 67 1
23 Aug 03 **... HERE'S TOM WITH THE WEATHER** *North Country NCCD 002* 55 1
4 Oct 03 **BYRDS TURN TO STONE** *North Country NCCDA 002* 63 1

SHADES *US, female vocal group (2 Singles: 3 Weeks)*

12 Apr 97 **MR BIG STUFF** *Motown 5736572* [1] 31 2
20 Sep 97 **SERENADE** *Motown 8606892* 75 1

[1] Queen Latifah, Shades and Free

SHADES OF LOVE *US, male instrumental / production duo*

22 Apr 95 **KEEP IN TOUCH (BODY TO BODY)** *Vicious Muzik MUZCD 102* 64 1

SHADES OF RHYTHM *UK, male instrumental / production group (1 Album: 3 Weeks, 8 Singles: 25 Weeks)*

2 Feb 91 **HOMICIDE / EXORCIST** *ZTT ZANG 13* 53 3
13 Apr 91 **SWEET SENSATION** *ZTT ZANG 18* 54 4
20 Jul 91 **THE SOUND OF EDEN** *ZTT ZANG 22* 35 5
17 Aug 91 **SHADES** *ZTT ZTT 8* 51 3
30 Nov 91 **EXTACY** *ZTT ZANG 24* 16 7
20 Feb 93 **SWEET REVIVAL (KEEP IT COMIN')** *ZTT ZANG 40CD* 61 1
11 Sep 93 **SOUND OF EDEN** (re-issue) *ZTT ZANG 44CD* 37 3
5 Nov 94 **THE WANDERING DRAGON (EP)** *Public Demand PPDCD 5* 55 1
21 Jun 97 **PSYCHO BASE** *Coalition CRUM 002CD* 57 1

Tracks on The Wandering Dragon (EP): 'My Love' / 'Chicken Flied Lice'

The SHADOWS 7 Top 500

(see also MARVIN, WELCH and FARRAR) *Headliners for five decades until their final tour in 2005 and Britain's most successful instrumental group: Hank Marvin (g), b. Brian Rankin, 28 Oct 1941, Newcastle-upon-Tyne, Bruce Welch OBE (g), b. Bruce Cripps, 2 Nov 1941, Bognor Regis, Terence 'Jet' Harris (b), b. Terence Hawkins, 6 Jul 1939, London, and Tony Meehan (d), b. Daniel Meehan, 2 Mar 1943, London, d. 28 Nov 2005. Bespectacled Marvin and Welch, who started together in The Railroaders skiffle group, first recorded with The Five Chesternuts (1958) before joining Cliff Richard's backing band, The Drifters. The group (with the above line-up) released its first single, 'Feelin' Fine', in early 1959 and later replaced Meehan with drummer Brian Bennett OBE. After another couple of unsuccessful releases and a name change, they started a staggering run of successive hit singles and albums and clocked up more weeks on the 60s EP chart than any other act. They were Britain's most influential and imitated act before The Beatles and the 'Shadows walk', which they say they borrowed from R&B band The Treniers, was aped by hundreds of UK groups. They won countless awards during the 1960s and were named the world's third most successful recording act of 1963 – behind Cliff and Elvis – by Billboard. In addition, they were the first group to top the UK albums chart (a feat they managed before Cliff) and were the first to have a 40 year span of hit albums (49 Albums: 812 Weeks, 63 Singles: 770 Weeks)*

12 Sep 58 ● **MOVE IT!** *Columbia DB 4178* [1] 2 17
21 Nov 58 ● **HIGH CLASS BABY** *Columbia DB 4203* [1] 7 10
30 Jan 59 **LIVIN' LOVIN' DOLL** *Columbia DB 4249* [1] 20 6
18 Apr 59 ● **CLIFF** *Columbia 33SX 1147* [1] 4 31
8 May 59 ● **MEAN STREAK** *Columbia DB 4290 A* [1] 10 9
15 May 59 **NEVER MIND** *Columbia DB 4290 B* [1] 21 2
10 Jul 59 ★ **LIVING DOLL (2re)** *Columbia DB 4306* [1] 1 23
9 Oct 59 ★ **TRAVELLIN' LIGHT** *Columbia DB 4351 B* [2] 1 17
9 Oct 59 **DYNAMITE (re)** *Columbia DB 4351 A* [2] 16 4
14 Nov 59 ● **CLIFF SINGS** *Columbia 33SX 1192* [2] 2 36
15 Jan 60 **EXPRESSO BONGO (EP)** *Columbia SEG 7971* [2] 14 7
22 Jan 60 ● **A VOICE IN THE WILDERNESS (re)** *Columbia DB 4398* [2] 2 16
24 Mar 60 ● **FALL IN LOVE WITH YOU** *Columbia DB 4431* [2] 2 15
30 Jun 60 ★ **PLEASE DON'T TEASE** *Columbia 4479* [2] 1 18
21 Jul 60 ★ **APACHE** *Columbia DB 4484* 1 21
22 Sep 60 ● **NINE TIMES OUT OF TEN** *Columbia DB 4506* [2] 3 12
15 Oct 60 ● **ME AND MY SHADOWS** *Columbia 33SX 1261* [2] 2 33
10 Nov 60 ● **MAN OF MYSTERY / THE STRANGER** *Columbia DB 4530* 5 15
1 Dec 60 ★ **I LOVE YOU** *Columbia DB 4547* [2] 1 16
9 Feb 61 ● **F.B.I.** *Columbia DB 4580* 6 19
2 Mar 61 ● **THEME FOR A DREAM** *Columbia DB 4593* [2] 3 14
30 Mar 61 ● **GEE WHIZ IT'S YOU** *Columbia DC 756* [2] 4 14
11 May 61 ● **THE FRIGHTENED CITY** *Columbia DB 4637* 3 20

22 Jun 61 ● A GIRL LIKE YOU *Columbia DB 4667* [2] 3 14
7 Sep 61 ★ KON-TIKI (re) *Columbia DB 4698* 1 12
16 Sep 61 ★ THE SHADOWS *Columbia 33SX 1374* 1 57
21 Oct 61 ★ 21 TODAY *Columbia 33SX 1368* [3] 1 16
16 Nov 61 ● THE SAVAGE *Columbia DB 4726* 10 8
23 Dec 61 ★ THE YOUNG ONES (FILM SOUNDTRACK) *Columbia 33SX 1384* [4] 1 42
11 Jan 62 ★ THE YOUNG ONES *Columbia DB 4761* [2] ■ £ 1 21
1 Mar 62 ★ WONDERFUL LAND *Columbia DB 4790* 1 19
10 May 62 ● I'M LOOKING OUT THE WINDOW / DO YOU WANT TO DANCE *Columbia DB 4828* [3] 2 17
2 Aug 62 ● GUITAR TANGO *Columbia DB 4870* 4 15
6 Sep 62 ● IT'LL BE ME *Columbia DB 4886* [2] 2 12
29 Sep 62 ● 32 MINUTES AND 17 SECONDS *Columbia 33SX 1431* [2] 3 21
13 Oct 62 ★ OUT OF THE SHADOWS *Columbia 33SX 1458* 1 38
6 Dec 62 ★ THE NEXT TIME / BACHELOR BOY *Columbia DB 4950* [2] 1 18
13 Dec 62 ★ DANCE ON! *Columbia DB 4948* 1 15
26 Jan 63 ★ SUMMER HOLIDAY (FILM SOUNDTRACK) *Columbia 33SX 1472* [2] 1 36
21 Feb 63 ★ SUMMER HOLIDAY *Columbia DB 4977* [2] 1 18
7 Mar 63 ★ FOOT TAPPER *Columbia DB 4984* 1 16
9 May 63 ● LUCKY LIPS *Columbia DB 7034* [2] 4 15
6 Jun 63 ● ATLANTIS *Columbia DB 7047* 2 17
22 Jun 63 ● GREATEST HITS *Columbia 33SX 1522* 2 49
13 Jul 63 ● CLIFF'S HIT ALBUM *Columbia 33SX 1512* [2] 2 19
19 Sep 63 ● SHINDIG *Columbia DB 7106* 6 12
28 Sep 63 ● WHEN IN SPAIN *Columbia 33SX 1541* [2] 8 10
7 Nov 63 ● DON'T TALK TO HIM (re) *Columbia DB 7150* [2] 2 14
5 Dec 63 GERONIMO *Columbia DB 7163* 11 12
6 Feb 64 ● I'M THE LONELY ONE *Columbia DB 7203* [2] 8 10
5 Mar 64 THEME FOR YOUNG LOVERS *Columbia DB 7231* 12 10
7 May 64 ● THE RISE AND FALL OF FLINGEL BUNT *Columbia DB 7261* 5 14
9 May 64 ● DANCE WITH THE SHADOWS *Columbia 33SX 1619* 2 27
2 Jul 64 ● ON THE BEACH *Columbia DB 7305* [2] 7 13
11 Jul 64 ● WONDERFUL LIFE (FILM SOUNDTRACK) *Columbia 33SX 1628* [2] 2 23
3 Sep 64 RHYTHM AND GREENS *Columbia DB 7342* 22 7
3 Dec 64 GENIE WITH THE LIGHT BROWN LAMP *Columbia DB 7416* 17 10
10 Dec 64 ● I COULD EASILY FALL *Columbia DB 7420* [2] 6 11
9 Jan 65 HITS FROM ALADDIN AND HIS WONDERFUL LAMP (PANTOMIME) *Columbia 33SX 1676* [2] 13 5
11 Feb 65 MARY ANNE *Columbia DB 7476* 17 10
17 Apr 65 ● CLIFF RICHARD *Columbia 33SX 1709* [5] 9 5
10 Jun 65 STINGRAY *Columbia DB 7588* 19 7
17 Jul 65 ● THE SOUND OF THE SHADOWS *Columbia 33SX 1736* 4 17
5 Aug 65 ● DON'T MAKE MY BABY BLUE *Columbia DB 7650* 10 10
19 Aug 65 THE TIME IN BETWEEN *Columbia DB 7660* [2] 22 8
25 Nov 65 THE WAR LORD *Columbia DB 7769* 18 9
17 Mar 66 I MET A GIRL *Columbia DB 7853* 22 5
24 Mar 66 BLUE TURNS TO GREY *Columbia DB 7866* [2] 15 9
21 May 66 ● SHADOW MUSIC *Columbia SX 6041* 5 17
7 Jul 66 A PLACE IN THE SUN *Columbia DB 7952* 24 6
13 Oct 66 ● TIME DRAGS BY *Columbia DB 8017* [2] 10 11
3 Nov 66 THE DREAMS I DREAM *Columbia DB 8034* 42 6
15 Dec 66 ● IN THE COUNTRY *Columbia DB 8094* [2] 6 10
17 Dec 66 ● FINDERS KEEPERS (FILM SOUNDTRACK) *Columbia SX 6079* [2] 6 18
7 Jan 67 CINDERELLA (PANTOMIME) *Columbia 33SX 6103* [2] 30 6
13 Apr 67 MAROC 7 *Columbia DB 8170* 24 8
15 Jul 67 ● JIGSAW *Columbia SCX 6148* 8 16
16 Nov 68 ESTABLISHED 1958 *Columbia SCX 6282* [2] 30 4
27 Nov 68 DON'T FORGET TO CATCH ME *Columbia DB 8503* [2] 21 10
24 Oct 70 SHADES OF ROCK *Columbia SCX 6420* 30 4
13 Apr 74 ROCKIN' WITH CURLY LEADS *EMI EMA 762* 45 1
11 May 74 GREATEST HITS (re-issue) *Columbia SCX 1522* 48 6
8 Mar 75 LET ME BE THE ONE *EMI 2269* 12 9
29 Mar 75 SPECS APPEAL *EMI EMC 3066* 30 5
12 Feb 77 ★ 20 GOLDEN GREATS *EMI EMTV 3* 1 43
16 Dec 78 ● DON'T CRY FOR ME ARGENTINA *EMI 2890* 5 14
17 Feb 79 ● THANK YOU VERY MUCH – REUNION CONCERT AT THE LONDON PALLADIUM *EMI EMTV 15* [2] 5 12
28 Apr 79 ● THEME FROM 'THE DEER HUNTER' (CAVATINA) *EMI 2939* 9 14
15 Sep 79 ★ STRING OF HITS *EMI EMC 3310* 1 43
26 Jan 80 RIDERS IN THE SKY *EMI 5027* 12 12
26 Jul 80 ANOTHER STRING OF HITS *EMI EMC 3339* 16 8
23 Aug 80 EQUINOXE (PART V) *Polydor POSP 148* 50 3
13 Sep 80 CHANGE OF ADDRESS *Polydor 2442 179* 17 6
2 May 81 THE THIRD MAN *Polydor POSP 255* 44 4
19 Sep 81 HITS RIGHT UP YOUR STREET *Polydor POLD 5046* 15 16
25 Sep 82 LIFE IN THE JUNGLE / LIVE AT ABBEY ROAD *Polydor SHADS 1* 24 6
22 Oct 83 XXV *Polydor POLD 5120* 34 6
14 Jul 84 20 ORIGINAL GREATS *EMI CRS 1* [2] 43 6
17 Nov 84 GUARDIAN ANGEL *Polydor POLD 5169* 98 1
24 May 86 ● MOONLIGHT SHADOWS *Polydor PROLP 8* 6 19
24 Oct 87 SIMPLY SHADOWS *Polydor SHAD 1* 11 17
20 May 89 STEPPIN' TO THE SHADOWS *Polydor SHAD 30* 11 9
16 Dec 89 AT THEIR VERY BEST *Polydor 8415201* 12 9
13 Oct 90 ● REFLECTION *Roll Over 8471201* 5 15
16 Nov 91 THEMES AND DREAMS *Polydor 5113741* 21 11
15 May 93 SHADOWS IN THE NIGHT – 16 CLASSIC TRACKS *PolyGram TV 8437982* 22 4
22 Oct 94 THE BEST OF HANK MARVIN AND THE SHADOWS *PolyGram TV 5238212* [6] 19 11
22 Nov 97 HANK MARVIN AND THE SHADOWS PLAY THE MUSIC OF ANDREW LLOYD WEBBER AND TIM RICE *PolyGram TV 5394792* [6] 41 6
14 Nov 98 THE VERY BEST OF HANK MARVIN & THE SHADOWS – THE FIRST 40 YEARS *PolyGram TV 5592112* [6] 56 5
12 Aug 00 50 GOLDEN GREATS *EMI 5275862* 35 3
8 May 04 ● LIFE STORY – THE VERY BEST OF THE SHADOWS *Universal TV 9817819* 7 10
27 Aug 05 PLATINUM COLLECTION *EMI 3349382* 30 4

[1] Cliff Richard and The Drifters [2] Cliff Richard and The Shadows [3] Cliff Richard with the Norrie Paramor Orchestra / Cliff Richard / The Shadows

[1] Cliff Richard and The Drifters [2] Cliff Richard and The Shadows [3] Cliff Richard, The Shadows and Norrie Paramor and his Orchestra [4] Cliff Richard – The Shadows with Grazina Frame [5] Cliff Richard with The Shadows [6] Hank Marvin and The Shadows

All The Shadows' hits without Cliff Richard were instrumentals except for 'Mary Anne', 'Don't Make My Baby Blue', 'I Met a Girl', 'The Dreams I Dream' and 'Let Me Be the One'. Tracks on Expresso Bongo (EP): Love / A Voice in the Wilderness / The Shrine on the Second Floor / Bongo Blues. Last track featured The Shadows only.
Only albums where The Shadows are credited in full alongside Cliff Richard, as the named act, on the record sleeve are included where associations with Cliff Richard are concerned. They did collaborate on a number of other albums but without this kind of billing.

SHAFT *UK, male producer – Mark Pritchard (2 Singles: 9 Weeks)*

21 Dec 91 ● ROOBARB AND CUSTARD *Ffrreedom TAB 100* 7 8
25 Jul 92 MONKEY *Ffrreedom TAB 114* 61 1

SHAFT (see also DA MUTTZ)

UK, male production duo – Elliot Ireland and Alex Rizzo (3 Singles: 19 Weeks)

4 Sep 99 ● (MUCHO MAMBO) SWAY *Wonderboy WBOYD 015* 2 12
20 May 00 MAMBO ITALIANO *Wonderboy WBDD 017* 12 6
21 Jul 01 KIKI RIRI BOOM *Wonderboy WBOYD 026* 62 1

SHAGGY 339 Top 500

The world's top-selling Jamaican artist, b. Orville Burrell, 22 Oct 1968, Kingston, who has had more UK and US No.1s than any other West Indian-born act. This US-based artist sold 345,000 copies of 'It Wasn't Me' in the first week in the UK (1,180,700 in total) and Hot Shot sold more than 12 million globally (5 Albums: 61 Weeks, 17 Singles: 145 Weeks)

6 Feb 93 ★ OH CAROLINA *Greensleeves GRECD 361* 1 19
10 Jul 93 SOON BE DONE *Greensleeves GRECD 380* 46 3
24 Jul 93 PURE PLEASURE *Greensleeves GRELCD 184* 67 1
8 Jul 95 ● IN THE SUMMERTIME *Virgin VSCDT 1542* [1] 5 9
23 Sep 95 ★ BOOMBASTIC *Virgin VSCDT 1536* ■ $ 1 12

6 August 1988	13 August 1988	20 August 1988	27 August 1988
THE ONLY WAY IS UP Yazz and The Plastic Population	THE ONLY WAY IS UP Yazz and The Plastic Population	THE ONLY WAY IS UP Yazz and The Plastic Population	THE ONLY WAY IS UP Yazz and The Plastic Population
NOW THAT'S WHAT I CALL MUSIC! 12 Various	NOW THAT'S WHAT I CALL MUSIC! 12 Various	NOW THAT'S WHAT I CALL MUSIC! 12 Various	KYLIE Kylie Minogue

TOP 20 ALBUMS BY MOST WEEKS ON CHART

Pole position in this chart, of non soundtrack albums, was for many years possessed by Meat Loaf's Bat Out of Hell, but Rumours by Fleetwood Mac is now officially the most durable album. Its reappearance in the chart in the 21st century was fuelled by many fans buying the band's 2003 album Say You Will and, at the same time, updating their record collections with a CD copy to replace an old vinyl version of Rumours.

POSITION / ALBUM / ACT - TOTAL WEEKS ON CHART

1. RUMOURS Fleetwood Mac – 478
2. BAT OUT OF HELL Meat Loaf – 474
3. GREATEST HITS Queen – 450
4. DARK SIDE OF THE MOON Pink Floyd – 367
5. GOLD – GREATEST HITS Abba – 352
6. LEGEND – THE BEST OF BOB MARLEY AND THE WAILERS Bob Marley and The Wailers – 339
7. BRIDGE OVER TROUBLED WATER Simon and Garfunkel – 307
8. SIMON AND GARFUNKEL'S GREATEST HITS Simon and Garfunkel – 283
9. TUBULAR BELLS Mike Oldfield – 279
10. JEFF WAYNE'S MUSICAL VERSION OF THE WAR OF THE WORLDS Jeff Wayne's War of the Worlds – 277
11. FACE VALUE Phil Collins – 274
12. MAKING MOVIES Dire Straits – 251
13. BROTHERS IN ARMS Dire Straits – 228
14. THE IMMACULATE COLLECTION Madonna – 213
15. LIVE – UNDER A BLOOD RED SKY U2 – 203
16. THRILLER Michael Jackson – 201
17. LOVE OVER GOLD Dire Straits – 200
18. SGT. PEPPER'S LONELY HEARTS CLUB BAND The Beatles – 198
19. NEVERMIND Nirvana – 196
20=. TRACY CHAPMAN Tracy Chapman – 189
20=. OFF THE WALL Michael Jackson – 189

This list includes all re-issues in addition to the original pressings.

The intended title of Fleetwood Mac's Rumours was Yesterday's Gone, but band member Christine McVie's comment that "the songs all sounded like a bunch of rumours" prompted a change. The band was indeed a rock soap opera of rumour and intrigue. "I think the only ones who didn't have an affair were me and Mick," said a bemused John McVie. The full line-up comprised the two McVies, Lindsey Buckingham, Stevie Nicks (pictured) and Mick Fleetwood (pictured).

14 Oct 95 BOOMBASTIC *Virgin CDV 2782* 37 6
13 Jan 96 WHY YOU TREAT ME SO BAD *Virgin VSCDT 1566* [2] 11 5
23 Mar 96 SOMETHING DIFFERENT / THE TRAIN IS COMING *Virgin VSCDT 1581* [3] 21 5
22 Jun 96 THAT GIRL *Virgin America VUSCDX 106* [4] 15 7
19 Jul 97 ● PIECE OF MY HEART *Virgin VSCDT 1647* [5] 7 6
17 Feb 01 ★ HOT SHOT *MCA 1122932* ▲ 1 47
17 Feb 01 IT WASN'T ME (import) *MCA 1558032* [6] 31 3
10 Mar 01 ★ IT WASN'T ME *MCA 1558022* [6] ■ ▲ £ 1 20
9 Jun 01 ★ ANGEL *MCA MCSTD 40257* [1] ■ ▲ 1 16
29 Sep 01 ● LUV ME LUV ME *MCA MCSTD 40263* 5 10
1 Dec 01 DANCE AND SHOUT / HOPE *MCA MCSTD 40272* 19 7
16 Feb 02 MR. LOVER LOVER – THE BEST OF SHAGGY – PART 1 *Virgin VTCD 429* 20 5
23 Mar 02 ● ME JULIE *Island CID 793* [7] 2 14
9 Nov 02 ● HEY SEXY LADY (re) *MCA MCSTD 40304* [8] 10 7
16 Nov 02 LUCKY DAY *MCA / Uni-Island 1131192* 54 2
3 Jul 04 YOUR EYES *VP VPCD 6415* [9] 57 1
17 Sep 05 WILD 2NITE *Geffen MCSXD 40431* 61 1

[1] Shaggy featuring Rayvon [2] Shaggy featuring Grand Puba [3] Shaggy featuring Wayne Wonder / Shaggy [4] Maxi Priest featuring Shaggy [5] Shaggy featuring Marsha [6] Shaggy featuring Ricardo "Rikrok" Ducent [7] Ali G and Shaggy [8] Shaggy featuring Brian and Tony Gold [9] Rik Rok featuring Shaggy

SHAH *UK, female vocalist – Sarah Morriss*

6 Jun 98 SECRET LOVE *Evocative EVOKE 5CDS* 69 1

SHAI *US, male vocal group*

19 Dec 92 IF I EVER FALL IN LOVE *MCA MCS 1727* $ 36 6

SHAKATAK (461 Top 500)

London-based pop / jazz / funk ensemble who were big in Japan. Their sound was typified by the tinkling piano of Bill Sharpe and Jill Saward's soothing vocals. Sharpe later worked with Gary Numan, while Nigel Wright (k) produced hits for Madonna, Take That, Robson & Jerome, Barbra Streisand, Cliff Richard and Boyzone (7 Albums: 73 Weeks, 14 Singles: 85 Weeks)

8 Nov 80 FEELS LIKE THE RIGHT TIME *Polydor POSP 188* 41 5
7 Mar 81 LIVING IN THE UK *Polydor POSP 230* 52 4
25 Jul 81 BRAZILIAN DAWN *Polydor POSP 282* 48 3
21 Nov 81 EASIER SAID THAN DONE *Polydor POSP 375* 12 17
30 Jan 82 DRIVIN' HARD *Polydor POLS 1030* 35 17
3 Apr 82 ● NIGHT BIRDS *Polydor POSP 407* 9 8
15 May 82 ● NIGHT BIRDS *Polydor POLS 1059* 4 28
19 Jun 82 STREETWALKIN' *Polydor POSP 452* 38 6
4 Sep 82 INVITATIONS *Polydor POSP 502* 24 7
6 Nov 82 STRANGER *Polydor POSP 530* 43 3
27 Nov 82 INVITATIONS *Polydor POLD 5068* 30 11
4 Jun 83 DARK IS THE NIGHT *Polydor POSP 595* 15 8
27 Aug 83 IF YOU COULD SEE ME NOW *Polydor POSP 635* 49 4
22 Oct 83 OUT OF THIS WORLD *Polydor POLD 5115* 30 4
7 Jul 84 ● DOWN ON THE STREET *Polydor POSP 688* 9 11
25 Aug 84 DOWN ON THE STREET *Polydor POLD 5148* 17 9
15 Sep 84 DON'T BLAME IT ON LOVE *Polydor POSP 699* 55 3
23 Feb 85 LIVE! *Polydor POLH 21* 82 3
16 Nov 85 DAY BY DAY *Polydor POSP 770* [1] 53 3
24 Oct 87 MR MANIC AND SISTER COOL *Polydor MANIC 1* 56 3
22 Oct 88 THE COOLEST CUTS *K-Tel NE 1422* 73 1

[1] Shakatak featuring Al Jarreau

SHAKE B4 USE vs Robert PALMER *UK, male production trio and vocalist*

18 Jan 03 ADDICTED TO LOVE *Serious SER 060CD* 42 1

SHAKEDOWN *Switzerland, male DJ / production duo – Stephan and Sebastien Kohler (2 Singles: 10 Weeks)*

11 May 02 ● AT NIGHT *Defected DFECT 50CDS* 6 8
28 Jun 03 DROWSY WITH HOPE *Defected DFTD 071CDS* 46 2

3 September 1988	10 September 1988	17 September 1988	24 September 1988
UK No.1 SINGLES			
THE ONLY WAY IS UP Yazz and The Plastic Population	A GROOVY KIND OF LOVE Phil Collins	A GROOVY KIND OF LOVE Phil Collins	HE AIN'T HEAVY, HE'S MY BROTHER The Hollies
UK No.1 ALBUMS			
KYLIE Kylie Minogue	KYLIE Kylie Minogue	KYLIE Kylie Minogue	HOT CITY NIGHTS Various

SHAKESPEAR'S SISTER (see also BANANARAMA)

UK / US, female vocal / instrumental duo – Siobhan Fahey and Marcella (Detroit) Levy (2 Albums: 63 Weeks, 10 Singles: 52 Weeks)

Date		Title / Label	Pos	Wks
29 Jul 89	●	**YOU'RE HISTORY** *ffrr F 112*	**7**	9
2 Sep 89	●	**SACRED HEART** *London 828131 1*	**9**	8
14 Oct 89		**RUN SILENT** *ffrr F 119*	**54**	3
10 Mar 90		**DIRTY MIND** *ffrr F 128*	**71**	1
12 Oct 91		**GOODBYE CRUEL WORLD** *London LON 309*	**59**	2
25 Jan 92	★	**STAY** *London LON 314*	**1**	16
29 Feb 92	●	**HORMONALLY YOURS** *London 8282262*	**3**	55
16 May 92	●	**I DON'T CARE** *London LON 318*	**7**	7
18 Jul 92		**GOODBYE CRUEL WORLD** (re-issue) *London LON 322*	**32**	4
7 Nov 92		**HELLO (TURN YOUR RADIO ON)** *London LON 330*	**14**	6
27 Feb 93		**MY 16TH APOLOGY (EP)** *London LONCD 337*	**61**	1
22 Jun 96		**I CAN DRIVE** *London LONCD 383*	**30**	3

Tracks on My 16th Apology (EP): My 16th Apology / Catwoman / Dirty Mind (live re-recording) / Hot Love. From 1996 Shakespear's Sister was essentially just vocalist Siobhan Fahey.

The SHAKIN' PYRAMIDS *UK, male vocal / instrumental group*

Date		Title / Label	Pos	Wks
4 Apr 81		**SKIN 'EM UP** *Cuba Libra V 2199*	**48**	4

SHAKIRA *Colombia, female vocalist – Shakira Isabel Mebarek Ripoll (1 Album: 47 Weeks, 3 Singles: 42 Weeks)*

Date		Title / Label	Pos	Wks
9 Mar 02	●	**WHENEVER, WHEREVER** *Epic 6724262*	**2**	19
23 Mar 02	●	**LAUNDRY SERVICE** *Epic 4987202*	**2**	47
3 Aug 02	●	**UNDERNEATH YOUR CLOTHES** *Epic 6729532*	**3**	15
23 Nov 02		**OBJECTION (TANGO)** *Epic 6733402*	**17**	8

SHALAMAR (249 Top 500) (see also BABYFACE)

Influential US dance music vocal trio masterminded by 'Soul Train' TV producer Don Cornelius. Line-up 1979-1983: Jeffrey Daniel, Jody Watley, Howard Hewett. Regarded as fashion icons and trendsetters, they helped to introduce "body-popping" to Britain (4 Albums: 121 Weeks, 18 Singles: 134 Weeks)

Date		Title / Label	Pos	Wks
14 May 77		**UPTOWN FESTIVAL** *Soul Train FB 0885*	**30**	5
9 Dec 78		**TAKE THAT TO THE BANK** *RCA FB 1379*	**20**	12
24 Nov 79		**THE SECOND TIME AROUND** *Solar FB 1709*	**45**	9
9 Feb 80		**RIGHT IN THE SOCKET** *Solar SO 2*	**44**	6
30 Aug 80		**I OWE YOU ONE** *Solar SO 11*	**13**	10
28 Mar 81		**MAKE THAT MOVE** *Solar SO 17*	**30**	10
27 Mar 82	●	**FRIENDS** *Solar K 52345*	**6**	72
27 Mar 82	●	**I CAN MAKE YOU FEEL GOOD** *Solar K 12599*	**7**	11
12 Jun 82	●	**A NIGHT TO REMEMBER** *Solar K 13162*	**5**	12
4 Sep 82	●	**THERE IT IS** *Solar K 13194*	**5**	10
11 Sep 82		**GREATEST HITS** *Solar SOLA 3001*	**71**	5
27 Nov 82		**FRIENDS** *Solar CHUM 1*	**12**	10
11 Jun 83	●	**DEAD GIVEAWAY** *Solar E 9819*	**8**	10
30 Jul 83	●	**THE LOOK** *Solar 960239*	**7**	20
13 Aug 83		**DISAPPEARING ACT** *Solar E 9807*	**18**	8
15 Oct 83		**OVER AND OVER** *Solar E 9792*	**23**	6
24 Mar 84		**DANCING IN THE SHEETS** *CBS A 4171*	**41**	3
31 Mar 84		**DEADLINE USA** *MCA MCA 866*	**52**	3
24 Nov 84		**AMNESIA** *Solar / MCA SHAL 1*	**61**	2
2 Feb 85		**MY GIRL LOVES ME** *MCA SHAL 2*	**45**	3
12 Apr 86	●	**THE GREATEST HITS** *Stylus SMR 8615*	**5**	24
26 Apr 86		**A NIGHT TO REMEMBER** (re-mix) *MCA SHAL 3*	**52**	4

The two Greatest Hits albums are different.

SHAM ROCK *Ireland, male / female vocal / instrumental group*

Date		Title / Label	Pos	Wks
7 Nov 98		**TELL ME MA** *Jive 0522352*	**13**	11

SHAM 69 *UK, male vocal (Jimmy Pursey) / instrumental group (3 Albums: 27 Weeks, 7 Singles: 53 Weeks)*

Date		Title / Label	Pos	Wks
11 Mar 78		**TELL US THE TRUTH** *Polydor 2383 491*	**25**	8
13 May 78		**ANGELS WITH DIRTY FACES** *Polydor 2059 023*	**19**	10
29 Jul 78	●	**IF THE KIDS ARE UNITED** *Polydor 2059 050*	**9**	9
14 Oct 78	●	**HURRY UP HARRY** *Polydor POSP 7*	**10**	8
2 Dec 78		**THAT'S LIFE** *Polydor POLD 5010*	**27**	11
24 Mar 79		**QUESTIONS AND ANSWERS** *Polydor POSP 27*	**18**	9
4 Aug 79	●	**HERSHAM BOYS** *Polydor POSP 64*	**6**	9
29 Sep 79	●	**THE ADVENTURES OF THE HERSHAM BOYS** *Polydor POLD 5025*	**8**	8
27 Oct 79		**YOU'RE A BETTER MAN THAN I** *Polydor POSP 82*	**49**	5
12 Apr 80		**TELL THE CHILDREN** *Polydor POSP 136*	**45**	3

The SHAMEN *UK, male vocal / instrumental duo – Richard West and Colin Angus (6 Albums: 54 Weeks, 15 Singles: 77 Weeks)*

Date		Title / Label	Pos	Wks
7 Apr 90		**PRO-GEN** *One Little Indian 36TP 7*	**55**	4
22 Sep 90		**MAKE IT MINE** *One Little Indian 46TP 7*	**42**	5
2 Nov 90		**EN-TACT** *One Little Indian TPLP 22*	**31**	10
6 Apr 91		**HYPERREAL** *One Little Indian 48TP 7*	**29**	5
27 Jul 91	●	**MOVE ANY MOUNTAIN** (re-mix) *One Little Indian 52TP 7*	**4**	10
28 Sep 91		**PROGENY** *One Little Indian TPLP 32*	**23**	2
18 Jul 92	●	**L.S.I.** *One Little Indian 68TP 7*	**6**	8
5 Sep 92	★	**EBENEEZER GOODE** *One Little Indian 78TP 7*	**1**	10
26 Sep 92	●	**BOSS DRUM / DIFFERENT DRUM** *One Little Indian TPLP 42CD*	**3**	35
7 Nov 92	●	**BOSS DRUM** *One Little Indian 88TP 7*	**4**	7
7 Nov 92		**BOSS DRUM** (re-mix) *One Little Indian 88TP 12*	**58**	1
19 Dec 92	●	**PHOREVER PEOPLE** *One Little Indian 98TP 7*	**5**	10
6 Mar 93		**RE: EVOLUTION** *One Little Indian 118TP 7CD* [1]	**18**	2
6 Nov 93		**THE SOS (EP)** *One Little Indian 108TP 7CD*	**14**	4
20 Nov 93		**ON AIR** *Band of Joy BOJCD 006*	**61**	1
19 Aug 95		**DESTINATION ESCHATON** *One Little Indian 128TP 7CDL*	**15**	4
21 Oct 95		**TRANSAMAZONIA** *One Little Indian 138TP 7CD*	**28**	2
4 Nov 95		**AXIS MUTATIS** *One Little Indian TPLP 52CDL*	**27**	2
10 Feb 96		**HEAL (THE SEPARATION)** *One Little Indian 158TP 7CDL*	**31**	2
21 Dec 96		**MOVE ANY MOUNTAIN '96** (2nd re-mix) *One Little Indian 169TP 7CD*	**35**	3
2 May 98		**THE SHAMEN COLLECTION** *One Little Indian TPLP 72CDE*	**26**	4

[1] The Shamen with Terence McKenna

'Move Any Mountain' is a re-mix of 'Pro-Gen'. Tracks on The SOS (EP): Comin' On / Make It Mine / Possible Worlds (re-mix). From 18 Dec 93 sales of Boss Drum and the re-mix album Different Drum were amalgamated .

SHAMPOO *UK, female vocal duo – Jacqui Blake and Carrie Askew (1 Album: 2 Weeks, 6 Singles: 28 Weeks)*

Date		Title / Label	Pos	Wks
30 Jul 94		**TROUBLE** *Food CDFOOD 51*	**11**	12
15 Oct 94		**VIVA LA MEGABABES** *Food CDFOOD 54*	**27**	4
5 Nov 94		**WE ARE SHAMPOO** *Food FOODCD 12*	**45**	2
18 Feb 95		**DELICIOUS** *Food CDFOOD 58*	**21**	4
5 Aug 95		**TROUBLE** (re-issue) *Food CDFOOD 66*	**36**	3
13 Jul 96		**GIRL POWER** *Food CDFOOD 76*	**25**	4
21 Sep 96		**I KNOW WHAT BOYS LIKE** *Food CDFOOD 83*	**42**	1

Jimmy SHAND BAND *UK, male / female dance band – leader Jimmy Shand – accordion, b. 29 Jan 1908, d. 23 Dec 2000*

Date		Title / Label	Pos	Wks
23 Dec 55		**BLUEBELL POLKA** *Parlophone F 3436*	**20**	2
24 Dec 83		**FIFTY YEARS ON WITH JIMMY SHAND** *Ross WGR 062* [1]	**97**	2

[1] Jimmy Shand, his Band and Guests

Paul SHANE and The YELLOWCOATS

UK, male actor / vocalist and male / female vocal group

Date		Title / Label	Pos	Wks
16 May 81		**HI-DE-HI (HOLIDAY ROCK)** *EMI 5180*	**36**	5

The SHANGRI-LAS

US, female vocal (Mary Weiss, d. 1971) group (4 Singles: 47 Weeks)

Date		Title / Label	Pos	Wks
8 Oct 64		**REMEMBER (WALKIN' IN THE SAND)** *Red Bird RB 10008*	**14**	12
14 Jan 65		**LEADER OF THE PACK** *Red Bird RB 10014* ▲ $	**11**	9
14 Oct 72	●	**LEADER OF THE PACK** (re-issue) *Kama Sutra 2013 024*	**3**	14
5 Jun 76	●	**LEADER OF THE PACK** (2nd re-issue) *Charly CS 1009*	**7**	12

From 19 Jun 1976 until 14 Aug 1976, the last week of the disc's chart run, the Charly and another Contempo release of 'Leader of the Pack' were bracketed together on the chart.

1 October 1988	8 October 1988	15 October 1988	22 October 1988
HE AIN'T HEAVY, HE'S MY BROTHER The Hollies	**DESIRE** U2	**ONE MOMENT IN TIME** Whitney Houston	**ONE MOMENT IN TIME** Whitney Houston
NEW JERSEY Bon Jovi	**NEW JERSEY** Bon Jovi	**FLYING COLOURS** Chris De Burgh	**RATTLE AND HUM** U2

KEY: UK No.1 ★ UK Top 10 ● Still on chart + UK entry at No.1 ■ US No.1 ▲ UK million seller £ US million seller $
Singles re-entries are listed as (re), (2re), (3re)... which signifies that the hit re-entered the chart once, twice or three times...
Peak Position / Weeks

SHANICE
US, female vocalist – Shanice Wilson (1 Album: 4 Weeks, 6 Singles: 24 Weeks)

23 Nov 91 **I LOVE YOUR SMILE** *Motown ZB 44907* 55 4
22 Feb 92 ● **I LOVE YOUR SMILE** (re-mix) *Motown TMG 1401* 2 10
21 Mar 92 **INNER CHILD** *Motown 5300082* 21 4
14 Nov 92 **LOVIN' YOU** *Motown TMG 1409* 54 1
16 Jan 93 **SAVING FOREVER FOR YOU** *Giant W 0148CD* 42 3
13 Aug 94 **I LIKE** *Motown TMGCD 1427* 49 2
16 Dec 95 **IF I NEVER KNEW YOU (LOVE THEME FROM 'POCAHONTAS')** *Walt Disney WD 7023CD* [1] 51 4

[1] Jon Secada and Shanice

SHANKS & BIGFOOT (see also DOOLALLY)
UK, male production duo – Stephen Meade and Daniel Langsman (2 Singles: 24 Weeks)

29 May 99 ★ **SWEET LIKE CHOCOLATE (re)** *Pepper / Jive / Chocolate Boy 0530352* ■ 1 16
29 Jul 00 **SING-A-LONG (re)** *Pepper 9230232* 12 8

SHANNON
US, female vocalist – Brenda Shannon Greene (1 Album: 12 Weeks, 6 Singles: 54 Weeks)

19 Nov 83 **LET THE MUSIC PLAY (re)** *Club LET 1* $ 14 15
10 Mar 84 **LET THE MUSIC PLAY** *Club JABL 1* 52 12
7 Apr 84 **GIVE ME TONIGHT** *Club JAB 1* 24 7
30 Jun 84 **SWEET SOMEBODY** *Club JAB 3* 25 8
20 Jul 85 **STRONGER TOGETHER** *Club JAB 15* 46 6
6 Dec 97 **IT'S OVER LOVE** *Manifesto FESCD 37* [1] 16 8
28 Nov 98 ● **MOVE MANIA** *Multiply CDMULTY 45* [2] 8 10

[1] Todd Terry presents Shannon [2] Sash! featuring Shannon

Del SHANNON (424 Top 500)
Early 1960s chart regular, b. Charles Westover, 30 Dec 1934, Michigan, US, d. 8 Feb 1990. This unmistakable singer / songwriter, who used a falsetto vocal on most hits, topped both the UK and US charts with the first of his many hits (2 Albums: 23 Weeks, 14 Singles: 147 Weeks)

27 Apr 61 ★ **RUNAWAY** *London HLX 9317* ▲ $ 1 22
14 Sep 61 ● **HATS OFF TO LARRY** *London HLX 9402* 6 12
7 Dec 61 ● **SO LONG BABY** *London HLX 9462* 10 11
15 Mar 62 ● **HEY! LITTLE GIRL** *London HLX 9515* 2 15
6 Sep 62 **CRY MYSELF TO SLEEP** *London HLX 9587* 29 6
11 Oct 62 ● **THE SWISS MAID** *London HLX 9609* 2 17
17 Jan 63 ● **LITTLE TOWN FLIRT** *London HLX 9653* 4 13
25 Apr 63 ● **TWO KINDS OF TEARDROPS** *London HLX 9710* 5 13
11 May 63 ● **HATS OFF TO DEL SHANNON** *London HAX 8071* 9 17
22 Aug 63 **TWO SILHOUETTES** *London HLX 9761* 23 8
24 Oct 63 **SUE'S GOTTA BE MINE** *London HLU 9800* 21 8
2 Nov 63 **LITTLE TOWN FLIRT** *London HAX 8091* 15 6
12 Mar 64 **MARY JANE** *Stateside SS 269* 35 5
30 Jul 64 **HANDY MAN** *Stateside SS 317* 36 4
14 Jan 65 ● **KEEP SEARCHIN' (WE'LL FOLLOW THE SUN)** *Stateside SS 368* 3 11
18 Mar 65 **STRANGER IN TOWN** *Stateside SS 395* 40 2

'Sue's Gotta Be Mine' is the correct title of the single, although a label printing error shows 'Sue's Gonna Be Mine' on copies of the record.

Roxanne SHANTE
US, female rapper – Lolita Gooden (5 Singles: 11 Weeks)

1 Aug 87 **HAVE A NICE DAY** *Breakout USA 612* 58 3
4 Jun 88 **GO ON GIRL** *Breakout USA 633* 55 3
29 Oct 88 **SHARP AS A KNIFE** *Club JAB 73* [1] 45 3
14 Apr 90 **GO ON GIRL** (re-mix) *Breakout USA 689* 74 1
23 Sep 00 **WHAT'S GOING ON** *Wall of Sound WALLD 064* [2] 43 1

[1] Brandon Cooke featuring Roxanne Shante [2] Mekon featuring Roxanne Shante

SHAPESHIFTERS
UK / Sweden, male production duo – Simon Marlin and Max Reich and female vocalist (2 Singles: 23 Weeks)

24 Jul 04 ★ **LOLA'S THEME** *Positiva CDTIVS 207* ■ 1 15
26 Mar 05 ● **BACK TO BASICS (re)** *Positiva CDTIVS 216* 10 8

Helen SHAPIRO
UK, female vocalist (1 Album: 25 Weeks, 11 Singles: 119 Weeks)

23 Mar 61 ● **DON'T TREAT ME LIKE A CHILD** *Columbia DB 4589* 3 20
29 Jun 61 ★ **YOU DON'T KNOW** *Columbia DB 4670* 1 23
28 Sep 61 ★ **WALKIN' BACK TO HAPPINESS** *Columbia DB 4715* 1 19
15 Feb 62 ● **TELL ME WHAT HE SAID** *Columbia DB 4782* 2 15
10 Mar 62 ● **'TOPS' WITH ME** *Columbia 33SX 1397* 2 25
3 May 62 **LET'S TALK ABOUT LOVE** *Columbia DB 4824* 23 7
12 Jul 62 ● **LITTLE MISS LONELY** *Columbia DB 4869* 8 11
18 Oct 62 **KEEP AWAY FROM OTHER GIRLS** *Columbia DB 4908* 40 6
7 Feb 63 **QUEEN FOR TONIGHT** *Columbia DB 4966* 33 5
25 Apr 63 **WOE IS ME** *Columbia DB 7026* 35 6
24 Oct 63 **LOOK WHO IT IS** *Columbia DB 7130* 47 3
23 Jan 64 **FEVER** *Columbia DB 7190* 38 4

SHARADA HOUSE GANG
Italy, male / female vocal / instrumental group (3 Singles: 4 Weeks)

12 Aug 95 **KEEP IT UP** *Media MCSTD 2071* 36 2
11 May 96 **LET THE RHYTHM MOVE YOU** *Media MCSTD 40035* 50 1
18 Oct 97 **GYPSY BOY, GYPSY GIRL** *Gut CXGUT 12* 52 1

SHARKEY
UK, male DJ / producer / keyboard player – Jonathan Kneath

8 Mar 97 **REVOLUTIONS (EP)** *React CDREACT 95* 53 1

Tracks on Revolutions (EP): Revolution Part One / Revolution Part Two / Revolution Part Two (re-mix).

Feargal SHARKEY (see also The ASSEMBLY; The UNDERTONES)
UK, male vocalist (2 Albums: 24 Weeks, 7 Singles: 58 Weeks)

13 Oct 84 **LISTEN TO YOUR FATHER** *Zarjazz JAZZ 1* 23 7
29 Jun 85 **LOVING YOU** *Virgin VS 770* 26 10
12 Oct 85 ★ **A GOOD HEART** *Virgin VS 808* 1 16
23 Nov 85 **FEARGAL SHARKEY** *Virgin V 2360* 12 20
4 Jan 86 ● **YOU LITTLE THIEF** *Virgin VS 840* 5 9
5 Apr 86 **SOMEONE TO SOMEBODY** *Virgin VS 828* 64 3
16 Jan 88 **MORE LOVE** *Virgin VS 992* 44 5
16 Mar 91 **I'VE GOT NEWS FOR YOU** *Virgin VS 1294* 12 8
20 Apr 91 **SONGS FROM THE MARDI GRAS** *Virgin V 2642* 27 4

The SHARONETTES
US, female vocal group (2 Singles: 8 Weeks)

26 Apr 75 **PAPA OOM MOW MOW** *Black Magic BM 102* 26 5
12 Jul 75 **GOING TO A GO-GO** *Black Magic BM 104* 46 3

Dee Dee SHARP
US, female vocalist – Dione Larue

25 Apr 63 **DO THE BIRD** *Cameo Parkway C 244* 46 2

Rocky SHARPE and The REPLAYS
UK, male / female vocal group (7 Singles: 41 Weeks)

16 Dec 78 **RAMA LAMA DING DONG** *Chiswick CHIS 104* 17 10
24 Mar 79 **IMAGINATION** *Chiswick CHIS 110* 39 6
25 Aug 79 **LOVE WILL MAKE YOU FAIL IN SCHOOL** *Chiswick CHIS 114* [1] 60 4
9 Feb 80 **MARTIAN HOP** *Chiswick CHIS 121* [1] 55 4
17 Apr 82 **SHOUT SHOUT (KNOCK YOURSELF OUT)** *Chiswick DICE 3* 19 9
7 Aug 82 **CLAP YOUR HANDS** *RAK 345* 54 3
26 Feb 83 **IF YOU WANNA BE HAPPY** *Polydor POSP 560* 46 5

[1] Rocky Sharpe and The Replays featuring The Top Liners

Ben SHAW featuring Adele HOLNESS
UK, male producer and female vocalist

14 Jul 01 **SO STRONG** *Fire Recordings ERIF 009CDS* 72 1

29 October 1988	5 November 1988	12 November 1988	19 November 1988
UK No.1 SINGLES			
ORINOCO FLOW Enya	ORINOCO FLOW Enya	ORINOCO FLOW Enya	THE FIRST TIME Robin Beck
UK No.1 ALBUMS			
MONEY FOR NOTHING Dire Straits	MONEY FOR NOTHING Dire Straits	MONEY FOR NOTHING Dire Straits	KYLIE Kylie Minogue

Mark SHAW (see also THEN JERICO) *UK, male vocalist*

17 Nov 90 **LOVE SO BRIGHT** *EMI EM 161* ... **54** 1

Sandie SHAW 394 Top 500

Barefoot pop princess of the Sixties, b. Sandra Goodrich, 26 Feb 1947, Essex, UK. This distinctive vocalist, who has a 41-year chart span, was the first UK act to win the Eurovision Song Contest (with 'Puppet on a String' in 1967) (3 Albums: 15 Weeks, 20 Singles: 165 Weeks)

8 Oct 64 ★ **(THERE'S) ALWAYS SOMETHING THERE TO REMIND ME** *Pye 7N 15704* ... **1** 11
10 Dec 64 ● **GIRL DON'T COME** *Pye 7N 15743* ... **3** 12
18 Feb 65 ● **I'LL STOP AT NOTHING** *Pye 7N 15783* ... **4** 11
6 Mar 65 ● SANDIE *Pye NPL 18110* ... 3 13
13 May 65 ★ **LONG LIVE LOVE** *Pye 7N 15841* ... **1** 14
23 Sep 65 ● **MESSAGE UNDERSTOOD** *Pye 7N 15940* ... **6** 10
18 Nov 65 **HOW CAN YOU TELL** *Pye 7N 15987* ... **21** 9
27 Jan 66 ● **TOMORROW** *Pye 7N 17036* ... **9** 9
19 May 66 **NOTHING COMES EASY** *Pye 7N 17086* ... **14** 9
8 Sep 66 **RUN** *Pye 7N 17163* ... **32** 5
24 Nov 66 **THINK SOMETIMES ABOUT ME** *Pye 7N 17212* ... **32** 4
19 Jan 67 **I DON'T NEED ANYTHING** *Pye 7N 17239* ... **50** 1
16 Mar 67 ★ **PUPPET ON A STRING** *Pye 7N 17272* ... **1** 18
12 Jul 67 **TONIGHT IN TOKYO** *Pye 7N 17346* ... **21** 6
4 Oct 67 **YOU'VE NOT CHANGED** *Pye 7N 17378* ... **18** 12
7 Feb 68 **TODAY** *Pye 7N 17441* ... **27** 7
12 Feb 69 ● **MONSIEUR DUPONT** *Pye 7N 17675* ... **6** 15
14 May 69 **THINK IT ALL OVER** *Pye 7N 17726* ... **42** 4
21 Apr 84 **HAND IN GLOVE** *Rough Trade RT 130* ... **27** 5
14 Jun 86 **ARE YOU READY TO BE HEARTBROKEN?** *Polydor POSP 793* ... **68** 1
12 Nov 94 **NOTHING LESS THAN BRILLIANT** *Virgin VSCDT 1521* ... **66** 2
19 Nov 94 NOTHING LESS THAN BRILLIANT *Virgin VTCD 34* ... 64 1
12 Mar 05 THE VERY BEST OF SANDIE SHAW *EMI 8661102* ... 60 1

Tracy SHAW *UK, female actor / vocalist*

4 Jul 98 **HAPPENIN' ALL OVER AGAIN** *Recognition CDREC 2* ... **46** 1

Winifred SHAW *US, female vocalist, b. 25 Feb 1899, d. 2 May 1982*

14 Aug 76 **LULLABY OF BROADWAY** *United Artists UP 36131* ... **42** 4

SHE ROCKERS *UK, female rap duo*

13 Jan 90 **JAM IT JAM** *Jive JIVE 233* ... **58** 2

George SHEARING

US (b. UK), male pianist (2 Albums: 13 Weeks, 2 Singles: 15 Weeks)

11 Jun 60 BEAUTY AND THE BEAT *Capitol T 1219* [1] ... 16 6
19 Jul 62 **LET THERE BE LOVE** *Capitol CL 15257* [1] ... **11** 14
4 Oct 62 **BAUBLES, BANGLES AND BEADS** *Capitol CL 15269* [2] ... **49** 1
20 Oct 62 ● NAT 'KING' COLE SINGS / GEORGE SHEARING PLAYS WITH THE QUINTET AND STRING CHOIR *Capitol W 1675* [2] ... 8 7

[1] Nat 'King' Cole with George Shearing [2] George Shearing Quintet [1] Peggy Lee and George Shearing [2] Nat 'King' Cole and the George Shearing Quintet

Gary SHEARSTON *Australia, male vocalist*

5 Oct 74 ● **I GET A KICK OUT OF YOU** *Charisma CB 234* ... **7** 8

SHED SEVEN *UK, male vocal (Rick Witter) / instrumental group (5 Albums: 46 Weeks, 15 Singles: 50 Weeks)*

25 Jun 94 **DOLPHIN** *Polydor YORCD 2* ... **28** 4
27 Aug 94 **SPEAKEASY** *Polydor YORCD 3* ... **24** 3
17 Sep 94 CHANGE GIVER *Polydor 5236152* ... 16 2
12 Nov 94 **OCEAN PIE** *Polydor YORCD 4* ... **33** 2
13 May 95 **WHERE HAVE YOU BEEN TONIGHT** *Polydor YORCD 5* ... **23** 2
27 Jan 96 **GETTING BETTER** *Polydor 5778912* ... **14** 3
23 Mar 96 ● **GOING FOR GOLD** *Polydor 5762152* ... **8** 5
13 Apr 96 ● A MAXIMUM HIGH *Polydor 5310392* ... 8 26
18 May 96 **BULLY BOY** *Polydor 5765972* ... **22** 3
31 Aug 96 **ON STANDBY** *Polydor 5752732* ... **12** 4
23 Nov 96 **CHASING RAINBOWS** *Polydor 5759292* ... **17** 5
14 Mar 98 **SHE LEFT ME ON FRIDAY** *Polydor 5695412* ... **11** 4
23 May 98 **THE HEROES** *Polydor 5699172* ... **18** 3
13 Jun 98 ● LET IT RIDE *Polydor 5573592* ... 9 7
22 Aug 98 **DEVIL IN YOUR SHOES (WALKING ALL OVER)** *Polydor 5672072* ... **37** 2
5 Jun 99 **DISCO DOWN** *Polydor 5638752* ... **13** 6
12 Jun 99 ● GOING FOR GOLD – THE GREATEST HITS *Polydor 5474422* ... 7 10
5 May 01 **CRY FOR HELP** *Artful CD 35ARTFUL* ... **30** 2
19 May 01 TRUTH BE TOLD *Artful ARTFULCD 38* ... 42 1
24 May 03 **WHY CAN'T I BE YOU?** *Taste Media TMCDS 5004* ... **23** 2

SHEEP ON DRUGS *UK, male vocal / instrumental duo – Duncan Gil-Rodriguez and Lee Fraser (1 Album: 1 Week, 3 Singles: 5 Weeks)*

27 Mar 93 **15 MINUTES OF FAME** *Transglobal CID 564* ... **44** 2
10 Apr 93 GREATEST HITS *Transglobal CID 8006* ... 55 1
30 Oct 93 **FROM A TO H AND BACK AGAIN** *Transglobal CID 575* ... **40** 2
14 May 94 **LET THE GOOD TIMES ROLL** *Transglobal CID 576* ... **56** 1

SHEER BRONZE featuring Lisa MILLETT

UK, male / female vocal / instrumental duo

3 Sep 94 **WALKIN' ON** *Go Beat GODCD 115* ... **63** 1

SHEER ELEGANCE *UK, male vocal group (3 Singles: 23 Weeks)*

20 Dec 75 **MILKY WAY** *Pye International 7N 25697* ... **18** 10
3 Apr 76 ● **LIFE IS TOO SHORT GIRL** *Pye International 7N 25703* ... **9** 9
24 Jul 76 **IT'S TEMPTATION** *Pye International 7N 25715* ... **41** 4

SHEILA B DEVOTION *France, female vocalist – Anny Chancel and male vocal trio (3 Singles: 33 Weeks)*

11 Mar 78 **SINGIN' IN THE RAIN PART 1** *Carrere EMI 2751* ... **11** 13
22 Jul 78 **YOU LIGHT MY FIRE** *Carrere EMI 2828* ... **44** 6
24 Nov 79 **SPACER** *Carrere CAR 128* [1] ... **18** 14

[1] Sheila & B Devotion (some pressings credited Sheila B Devotion)

Shade SHEIST featuring Nate DOGG and KURUPT

US, male rappers – leader Tremayne Thompson

25 Aug 01 **WHERE I WANNA BE (re)** *London LONCD 461* ... **14** 7

Doug SHELDON *UK, male vocalist (3 Singles: 15 Weeks)*

9 Nov 61 **RUNAROUND SUE** *Decca F 11398* ... **36** 3
4 Jan 62 **YOUR MA SAID YOU CRIED IN YOUR SLEEP LAST NIGHT** *Decca F 11416* ... **29** 6
7 Feb 63 **I SAW LINDA YESTERDAY** *Decca F 11564* ... **36** 6

Pete SHELLEY (see also The BUZZCOCKS) *UK, male vocalist*

12 Mar 83 **TELEPHONE OPERATOR** *Genetic XX 1* ... **66** 1
2 Jul 83 XL-1 *Genetic XL 1* ... 42 4

Peter SHELLEY *UK, male vocalist – Peter McNeish (2 Singles: 20 Weeks)*

14 Sep 74 ● **GEE BABY** *Magnet MAG 12* ... **4** 10
22 Mar 75 ● **LOVE ME LOVE MY DOG** *Magnet MAG 22* ... **3** 10

Anne SHELTON *UK, female vocalist – Patricia Sibley, b. 10 Nov 1928, d. 31 Jul 1994 (5 Singles: 31 Weeks)*

16 Dec 55 **ARRIVEDERCI DARLING** *HMV POP 146* ... **17** 4
13 Apr 56 **SEVEN DAYS** *Philips PB 567* ... **20** 4
24 Aug 56 ★ **LAY DOWN YOUR ARMS** *Philips PB 616* ... **1** 14
20 Nov 59 **THE VILLAGE OF ST BERNADETTE** *Philips PB 969* ... **27** 1
26 Jan 61 ● **SAILOR** *Philips PB 1096* ... **10** 8

SHÉNA *UK, female vocalist – Shéna McSween (3 Singles: 6 Weeks)*

2 Aug 97 **LET THE BEAT HIT 'EM** *VC VCRD 24* ... **28** 2

26 November 1988	3 December 1988	10 December 1988	17 December 1988
THE FIRST TIME Robin Beck	THE FIRST TIME Robin Beck	MISTLETOE AND WINE Cliff Richard	MISTLETOE AND WINE Cliff Richard
KYLIE Kylie Minogue	NOW THAT'S WHAT I CALL MUSIC! 13 Various	NOW THAT'S WHAT I CALL MUSIC! 13 Various	NOW THAT'S WHAT I CALL MUSIC! 13 Various

KEY: UK No.1 ★ UK Top 10 ● Still on chart + UK entry at No.1 ■ US No.1 ▲ UK million seller £ US million seller $
Singles re-entries are listed as (re), (2re), (3re)… which signifies that the hit re-entered the chart once, twice or three times…
Peak Position / Weeks

1 Sep 01 **I'LL BE WAITING** *Rulin RULIN 17CDS* [1] 44 1
4 Oct 03 **WILDERNESS** *Direction 6742692* [2] 20 3

[1] Full Intention presents Shena [2] Jurgen Vries featuring Shena

Vonda SHEPARD
US, female vocalist (3 Albums: 49 Weeks, 1 Single: 9 Weeks)

17 Oct 98 ● SONGS FROM ALLY MCBEAL *Epic 4911242* 3 34
5 Dec 98 ● **SEARCHIN' MY SOUL** *Epic 6666332* 10 9
12 Jun 99 BY 7:30 *Epic 4945792* 39 2
20 Nov 99 ● HEART & SOUL – NEW SONGS FROM ALLY MCBEAL *Epic 4950912* 9 13

SHEPHERD SISTERS *US, female vocal group*

15 Nov 57 **ALONE (WHY MUST I BE) (re)** *HMV POP 411* 14 6

SHERBET *Australia, male vocal (Daryl Braithwaite) / instrumental group*

25 Sep 76 ● **HOWZAT** *Epic EPC 4574* 4 10

Tony SHERIDAN and The BEATLES
UK, male vocalist and vocal / instrumental group

6 Jun 63 **MY BONNIE** *Polydor NH 66833* 48 1

Allan SHERMAN
US, male vocalist / comedian – Allan Copelon, b. 30 Nov 1924, d. 21 Nov 1973

12 Sep 63 **HELLO MUDDAH! HELLO FADDAH!** *Warner Bros. WB 106* 14 10

Bobby SHERMAN *US, male vocalist*

31 Oct 70 **JULIE DO YA LOVE ME** *CBS 5144* 28 4

SHERRICK *US, male vocalist – F Lamonte-Smith, b. 6 Jul 1957, d. 22 Jan 1999 (1 Album: 6 Weeks, 2 Singles: 10 Weeks)*

1 Aug 87 **JUST CALL** *Warner Bros. W 8380* 23 8
29 Aug 87 SHERRICK *Warner Bros. WX 118* 27 6
21 Nov 87 **LET'S BE LOVERS TONIGHT** *Warner Bros. W 8146* 63 2

Pluto SHERVINGTON *Jamaica, male vocalist (3 Singles: 20 Weeks)*

7 Feb 76 ● **DAT** *Opal Pal 5* 6 8
10 Apr 76 **RAM GOAT LIVER** *Trojan TR 7978* 43 4
6 Mar 82 **YOUR HONOUR** *KR KR 4* [1] 19 8

[1] Pluto

Holly SHERWOOD *US, female vocalist*

5 Feb 72 **DAY BY DAY** *Bell 1182* 29 7

Tony SHEVETON *UK, male vocalist*

13 Feb 64 **A MILLION DRUMS** *Oriole CB 1895* 49 1

SHIFTY
(see also CRAZY TOWN) *US, male rapper – Shifty Shellshock (Steve Brooks)*

11 Sep 04 **SLIDE ALONG SIDE** *Maverick W 649* 29 3

SHIMMON & WOOLFSON
(see also SUNDANCE) *UK, male DJ / production duo*

10 Jan 98 **WELCOME TO THE FUTURE** *React CDREACT 119* 69 1

SHIMON & Andy C
UK, male production duo – Shimon Alcoby and Andy Clarke

15 Sep 01 **BODY ROCK (re)** *Ram RAMM 34CD* 28 5

Brendan SHINE *Ireland, male vocalist (4 Albums: 29 Weeks)*

12 Nov 83 THE BRENDAN SHINE COLLECTION *Play PLAYTV 1* 51 12
3 Nov 84 WITH LOVE *Play PLAYTV 2* 74 4
16 Nov 85 MEMORIES *Play PLAYTV 3* 81 7
18 Nov 89 MAGIC MOMENTS *Stylus SMR 991* 62 6

SHINEHEAD *Jamaica, male vocalist – Edmund Aiken (2 Singles: 6 Weeks)*

3 Apr 93 **JAMAICAN IN NEW YORK** *Elektra EKR 161CD* 30 5
26 Jun 93 **LET 'EM IN** *Elektra EKR 168CD* 70 1

The SHINING
UK, male vocal / instrumental group (1 Album: 1 Week, 2 Singles: 2 Weeks)

6 Jul 02 **I WONDER HOW** *Zuma ZUMAD 002* 58 1
14 Sep 02 **YOUNG AGAIN** *Zuma ZUMASCD 003* 52 1
28 Sep 02 TRUE SKIES *Zuma ZUMACD 001* 73 1

The SHINS *US, male vocal / instrumental group*

13 Mar 04 **SO SAYS I** *Sub Pop SPCD 621* 73 1

The SHIREHORSES *UK, male vocal / instrumental group – includes Mark Radcliffe and Marc 'Lard' Riley (2 Albums: 8 Weeks)*

15 Nov 97 THE WORST ALBUM IN THE WORLD EVER ... EVER! *East West 3984208512* 22 4
26 May 01 OUR KID EH *Columbia 5030492* 20 4

The SHIRELLES
US, female vocal (Shirley Owens) group (3 Singles: 29 Weeks)

9 Feb 61 ● **WILL YOU LOVE ME TOMORROW** *Top Rank JAR 540* ▲ $ 4 15
31 May 62 **SOLDIER BOY** *HMV POP 1019* ▲ $ 23 9
23 May 63 **FOOLISH LITTLE GIRL** *Stateside SS 181* 38 5

SHIRLEY and COMPANY *US, female vocalist – Shirley Pixley Goodman and male vocal / instrumental backing group*

8 Feb 75 ● **SHAME SHAME SHAME** *All Platinum 6146 301* 6 9

SHIVA *UK, male / female vocal / instrumental trio (2 Singles: 5 Weeks)*

13 May 95 **WORK IT OUT** *ffrr FCD 261* 36 2
19 Aug 95 **FREEDOM** *ffrr FCD 263* 18 3

SHIVAREE *US, female / male vocal / instrumental group*

17 Feb 01 **GOODNIGHT MOON** *Capitol CDCL 825* 63 1

SHO NUFF *US, male vocal / instrumental group*

24 May 80 **IT'S ALRIGHT** *Ensign ENY 37* 53 4

Michelle SHOCKED *US, female vocalist – Michelle Johnston (3 Albums: 24 Weeks, 3 Singles: 10 Weeks)*

10 Sep 88 SHORT SHARP SHOCKED *Cooking Vinyl CVLP 1* 33 19
8 Oct 88 **ANCHORAGE** *Cooking Vinyl LON 193* 60 4
14 Jan 89 **IF LOVE WAS A TRAIN** *Cooking Vinyl LON 212* 63 3
11 Mar 89 **WHEN I GROW UP** *Cooking Vinyl LON 219* 67 3
18 Nov 89 CAPTAIN SWING *Cooking Vinyl 838878 1* 31 3
11 Apr 92 ARKANSAS TRAVELER *London 5121892* 46 2

SHOCKING BLUE *Holland, male / female vocal (Mariska Veres) / instrumental group (2 Singles: 14 Weeks)*

17 Jan 70 ● **VENUS** *Penny Farthing PEN 702* ▲ $ 8 11
25 Apr 70 **MIGHTY JOE** *Penny Farthing PEN 713* 43 3

	24 December 1988	31 December 1988	7 January 1989	14 January 1989
UK No.1 SINGLES	MISTLETOE AND WINE – Cliff Richard	MISTLETOE AND WINE – Cliff Richard	ESPECIALLY FOR YOU – Kylie Minogue and Jason Donovan	ESPECIALLY FOR YOU – Kylie Minogue and Jason Donovan
UK No.1 ALBUMS	PRIVATE COLLECTION 1979-1988 – Cliff Richard	PRIVATE COLLECTION 1979-1988 – Cliff Richard	NOW THAT'S WHAT I CALL MUSIC! 13 – Various	THE INNOCENTS – Erasure

SHOLAN *Israel / Germany, male / female production / vocal duo*

5 Apr 03 **CAN YOU FEEL (WHAT I'M GOING THRU)** *Data / Ministry of Sound DATA 39CDS* 47 1

Troy SHONDELL *US, male vocalist – Gary Schelton*

2 Nov 61 **THIS TIME** *London HLG 9432* 22 11

SHOOTING PARTY *UK, male vocal duo*

31 Mar 90 **LET'S HANG ON** *Lisson DOLE 15* 66 2

The SHOP ASSISTANTS *UK, male / female vocal / instrumental group*

29 Nov 86 SHOP ASSISTANTS *Blue Guitar AZLP 2* 100 1

Howard SHORE *US, male composer (3 Albums: 34 Weeks)*

5 Jan 02 ● THE LORD OF THE RINGS – THE FELLOWSHIP OF THE RING (FILM SOUNDTRACK) *Reprise 9362481102* 10 14
11 Jan 03 THE LORD OF THE RINGS – THE TWO TOWERS (FILM SOUNDTRACK) *Reprise 936248212* 28 9
27 Dec 03 THE LORD OF THE RINGS – THE RETURN OF THE KING (FILM SOUNDTRACK) *Reprise 9362486092* 34 11

SHORTIE vs BLACK LEGEND
Italy, male vocalist and production duo – J Reverse and Ferrari

4 Aug 01 **SOMEBODY** *WEA WEA 328CD* 37 2

SHOUT OUT LOUDS NEW
Sweden, male / female vocal / instrumental group

24 Sep 05 **THE COMEBACK** *EMI CDM 668* 63 1

SHOWADDYWADDY 164 Top 500
Rock 'n' roll revival octet from Leicester, UK, who have a 30 year chart span, included vocalists Dave Bartram and Buddy Gask. At the peak of their career, they had seven successive Top 5 entries with rousing revivals of old US rock 'n' roll songs. Best-selling single: 'Under the Moon of Love' 985,000 (11 Albums: 130 Weeks, 23 Singles: 209 Weeks)

18 May 74 ● **HEY ROCK AND ROLL** *Bell 1357* 2 14
17 Aug 74 **ROCK 'N' ROLL LADY** *Bell 1374* 15 9
30 Nov 74 **HEY MR CHRISTMAS** *Bell 1387* 13 8
7 Dec 74 ● SHOWADDYWADDY *Bell BELLS 248* 9 19
22 Feb 75 **SWEET MUSIC** *Bell 1403* 14 9
17 May 75 ● **THREE STEPS TO HEAVEN** *Bell 1426* 2 11
12 Jul 75 ● STEP TWO *Bell BELLS 256* 7 17
6 Sep 75 ● **HEARTBEAT** *Bell 1450* 7 7
15 Nov 75 **HEAVENLY** *Bell 1460* 34 6
29 May 76 TROCADERO *Bell SYBEL 8003* 41 3
29 May 76 **TROCADERO** *Bell 1476* 32 3
6 Nov 76 ★ **UNDER THE MOON OF LOVE** *Bell 1495* 1 15
25 Dec 76 ● GREATEST HITS *Arista ARTY 145* 4 26
5 Mar 77 ● **WHEN** *Arista 91* 3 11
23 Jul 77 ● **YOU GOT WHAT IT TAKES** *Arista 126* 2 10
5 Nov 77 ● **DANCIN' PARTY** *Arista 149* 4 11
3 Dec 77 RED STAR *Arista SPARTY 1023* 20 10
25 Mar 78 ● **I WONDER WHY** *Arista 174* 2 11
24 Jun 78 ● **A LITTLE BIT OF SOAP** *Arista 191* 5 12
4 Nov 78 ● **PRETTY LITTLE ANGEL EYES** *Arista ARIST 222* 5 12
9 Dec 78 ★ GREATEST HITS (1976-1978) *Arista ARTV 1* 1 17
31 Mar 79 **REMEMBER THEN** *Arista 247* 17 8
28 Jul 79 **SWEET LITTLE ROCK 'N' ROLLER** *Arista 278* 15 9
10 Nov 79 ● CREPES AND DRAPES *Arista ARTV 3* 8 14
10 Nov 79 **A NIGHT AT DADDY GEES** *Arista 314* 39 5
27 Sep 80 **WHY DO LOVERS BREAK EACH OTHERS' HEARTS** *Arista ARIST 359* 22 10
29 Nov 80 **BLUE MOON** *Arista ARIST 379* 32 9
20 Dec 80 BRIGHT LIGHTS *Arista SPART 1142* 54 8
13 Jun 81 **MULTIPLICATION** *Arista ARIST 416* 39 4
7 Nov 81 HEY ROCK 'N' ROLL – THE VERY BEST OF SHOWADDYWADDY *Arista SPART 1178* 33 11
28 Nov 81 **FOOTSTEPS** *Bell BELL 1499* 31 9
28 Aug 82 **WHO PUT THE BOMP (IN THE BOMP-A-BOMP-A-BOMP)** *RCA 236* 37 6
5 Dec 87 THE BEST STEPS TO HEAVEN *Tiger SHTV 1* 90 1
27 Nov 04 HEY! ROCK 'N' ROLL – THE VERY BEST OF SHOWADDYWADDY (re-issue) *DMG TV DMGTV 011* 56 4

Hey! Rock 'n' Roll – The Very Best of Showaddywaddy (2004) is a repackaged version of the 1981 album of (almost) the same name, featuring the same tracks but in a different order.

SHOWDOWN *US, male vocal / instrumental group*

17 Dec 77 **KEEP DOIN' IT** *State STAT 63* 41 3

The SHOWSTOPPERS *US, male vocal group (3 Singles: 25 Weeks)*

13 Mar 68 **AIN'T NOTHING BUT A HOUSEPARTY** *Beacon 3-100* 11 15
13 Nov 68 **EENY MEENY** *MGM 1436* 33 7
30 Jan 71 **AIN'T NOTHING BUT A HOUSEPARTY (2re)** (re-issue) *Beacon BEA 100* 33 3

SHRIEKBACK *UK, male vocal / instrumental group*

28 Jul 84 **HAND ON MY HEART** *Arista SHRK 1* 52 4
11 Aug 84 JAM SCIENCE *Arista 206 416* 85 1

SHRINK *Holland, male DJ / production trio (2 Singles: 4 Weeks)*

10 Oct 98 **NERVOUS BREAKDOWN** *VC Recordings VCRD 42* 42 2
19 Aug 00 **ARE YOU READY TO PARTY** *Nulife 74321783772* 39 2

SHUT UP AND DANCE *UK, male vocal / production duo – Smiley and PJ (1 Album: 2 Weeks, 7 Singles: 14 Weeks)*

21 Apr 90 **£20 TO GET IN** *Shut Up and Dance SUAD 3* 56 3
28 Jul 90 **LAMBORGHINI** *Shut Up and Dance SUAD 4* 55 2
8 Feb 92 **AUTOBIOGRAPHY OF A CRACKHEAD / THE GREEN MAN** *Shut Up and Dance SUAD 21* 43 2
30 May 92 ● **RAVING I'M RAVING** *Shut Up and Dance SUAD 30S* [1] 2 2
27 Jun 92 DEATH IS NOT THE END *Shut Up and Dance SUADCD 005* 38 2
15 Aug 92 **THE ART OF MOVING BUTTS** *Shut Up and Dance SUAD 34S* [2] 69 1
1 Apr 95 **SAVE IT 'TIL THE MOURNING AFTER** *Pulse 8 PULS 84CD* 25 3
8 Jul 95 **I LOVE U** *Pulse 8 PULS 90CD* [3] 68 1

[1] Shut Up and Dance featuring Peter Bouncer [2] Shut Up and Dance featuring Erin [3] Shut Up and Dance featuring Richie Davis and Professor T

SHY *UK, male vocal / instrumental group*

19 Apr 80 **GIRL (IT'S ALL I HAVE)** *Gallery GA 1* 60 3
11 Apr 87 EXCESS ALL AREAS *RCA PL 71221* 74 2

SHY FX (see also EBONY DUBSTERS)
UK, male instrumentalist / producer – Andre Williams (6 Singles: 22 Weeks)

1 Oct 94 **ORIGINAL NUTTAH** *Sound of Underground SOUR 008CD* [1] 39 3
20 Mar 99 **BAMBAATA 2012** *Ebony EBR 020CD* 60 1
6 Apr 02 ● **SHAKE UR BODY** *Positiva CDTIV 171* [2] 7 11
23 Nov 02 **DON'T WANNA KNOW** *ffrr FCD 408* [3] 19 4
28 Dec 02 **WOLF** *Ebony Dubs EBD 001* 60 1
7 Jun 03 **FEELIN' U** *London FCD 409* [4] 34 2

[1] UK Apachi with Shy FX [2] Shy FX and T-Power featuring Di [3] Shy FX and T-Power featuring Di and Skibadee [4] Shy FX and T-Power featuring Kele Le Roc

SHYHEIM *US, male rapper – Shyheim Franklin*

8 Jun 96 **THIS IZ REAL** *Noo Trybe VUSCD 105* 61 1

SHYSTIE *UK, female rapper – Chanelle Calica (2 Singles: 3 Weeks)*

17 Jul 04 **ONE WISH** *Polydor 9866875* 40 2
2 Oct 04 **MAKE IT EASY** *Polydor 9867988* 59 1

21 January 1989	28 January 1989	4 February 1989	11 February 1989
ESPECIALLY FOR YOU Kylie Minogue and Jason Donovan	**SOMETHING'S GOTTEN HOLD OF MY HEART** Marc Almond featuring special guest star Gene Pitney	**SOMETHING'S GOTTEN HOLD OF MY HEART** Marc Almond featuring special guest star Gene Pitney	**SOMETHING'S GOTTEN HOLD OF MY HEART** Marc Almond featuring special guest star Gene Pitney
THE LEGENDARY ROY ORBISON Roy Orbison	THE LEGENDARY ROY ORBISON Roy Orbison	THE LEGENDARY ROY ORBISON Roy Orbison	TECHNIQUE New Order

KEY: UK No.1 ★ UK Top 10 ● Still on chart + UK entry at No.1 ■ US No.1 ▲ UK million seller £ US million seller $
Singles re-entries are listed as (re), (2re), (3re)... which signifies that the hit re-entered the chart once, twice or three times...
Peak Position / Weeks

SIA *Australia, female vocalist – Sia Furler (5 Singles: 11 Weeks)*

3 Jun 00 ● **TAKEN FOR GRANTED** *Long Lost Brother S 002CD 1* 10 5
18 Aug 01 **DESTINY** *Ultimate Dilemma UDRCDS 043* [1] 30 3
30 Mar 02 **DISTRACTIONS** *Ultimate Dilemma UDRCDS 046* [2] 45 1
1 May 04 **BREATHE ME** *Go Beat 9866392* 71 1
29 May 04 **SOMERSAULT** *Ultimate Dilemma EW 290CD* [2] 56 1

[1] Zero 7 featuring Sia & Sophie [2] Zero 7 featuring Sia

Labi SIFFRE
UK, male vocalist / guitarist (2 Albums: 2 Weeks, 5 Singles: 44 Weeks)

24 Jul 71 SINGER AND THE SONG *Pye NSPL 28147* 47 1
27 Nov 71 **IT MUST BE LOVE** *Pye International 7N 25572* 14 12
25 Mar 72 **CRYING LAUGHING LOVING LYING** *Pye International 7N 25576* 11 9
29 Jul 72 **WATCH ME** *Pye International 7N 25586* 29 6
14 Oct 72 CRYING LAUGHING LOVING LYING *Pye NSPL 28163* 46 1
4 Apr 87 ● **(SOMETHING INSIDE) SO STRONG** *China WOK 12* 4 13
21 Nov 87 **NOTHIN'S GONNA CHANGE** *China WOK 16* 52 4

SIGNUM *Holland, male production duo – Ronald Hagen and Pascal Minnard (4 Singles: 6 Weeks)*

28 Nov 98 **WHAT YA GOT 4 ME** *Tidy Trax TIDY 118CD* 70 1
31 Jul 99 **COMING ON STRONG** *Tidy Trax TIDY 128T* [1] 66 1
9 Feb 02 **WHAT YA GOT 4 ME** (re-mix) *Tidy Trax TIDY 163CD* 35 3
29 Jun 02 **COMING ON STRONG** (re-mix) *Tidy Two TIDYTWO 104CD* [1] 50 1

[1] Signum featuring Scott Mac

SIGUE SIGUE SPUTNIK *UK, male vocal (Martin Degville) / instrumental group (2 Albums: 7 Weeks, 5 Singles: 20 Weeks)*

1 Mar 86 ● **LOVE MISSILE F1-11** *Parlophone SSS 1* 3 9
7 Jun 86 **21ST CENTURY BOY** *Parlophone SSS 2* 20 5
9 Aug 86 ● FLAUNT IT *Parlophone PCS 7305* 10 6
19 Nov 88 **SUCCESS** *Parlophone SSS 3* 31 3
1 Apr 89 **DANCERAMA** *Parlophone SSS 5* 50 2
15 Apr 89 DRESS FOR EXCESS *Parlophone PCS 7328* 53 1
20 May 89 **ALBINONI VS STAR WARS** *Parlophone SSS 4* 75 1

SIGUR ROS *Iceland, male vocal / instrumental group (3 Albums: 4 Weeks, 2 Singles: 2 Weeks)*

26 Aug 00 AGAETIS BYRJUN *Fat Cat / Pias FATCD 11* 52 1
9 Nov 02 ( ) *Fat Cat FATCD 22* 49 1
24 May 03 **( )** *Pias CD 10FAT 02* 72 1
24 Sep 05 TAKK ... *EMI 3372522* 16 2
10 Dec 05 **HOPPIPOLLA** *EMI CDEM 673* 35 1

SIL *Holland, male DJ / production duo*

11 Apr 98 **WINDOWS '98** *Hooj Choons HOOJCD 60* 58 1

The SILENCERS
UK, male vocal / instrumental group (2 Albums: 3 Weeks, 3 Singles: 7 Weeks)

25 Jun 88 **PAINTED MOON** *RCA HUSH 1* 57 4
27 May 89 **SCOTTISH RAIN** *RCA PB 42701* 71 2
23 Mar 91 DANCE TO THE HOLY MAN *RCA PL 74924* 39 2
15 May 93 **I CAN FEEL IT** *RCA 74321147112* 62 1
5 Jun 93 SECONDS OF PLEASURE *RCA 74321141132* 52 1

SILENT UNDERDOG *UK, male keyboard player – Paul Hardcastle*

16 Feb 85 **PAPA'S GOT A BRAND NEW PIGBAG** *Kaz KAZ 50* 73 1

SILICONE SOUL featuring Louise Clare MARSHALL
UK, male production duo and female vocalist

6 Oct 01 **RIGHT ON! (re)** *VC Recordings / Soma VCRD 96* 15 5

SILJE *Norway, female vocalist – Silje Nergaard*

15 Dec 90 **TELL ME WHERE YOU'RE GOING** *EMI EM 159* 55 6

SILK *US, male vocal group (3 Singles: 10 Weeks)*

24 Apr 93 **FREAK ME (re)** *Elektra EKR 165CD* ▲ $ 46 6
5 Jun 93 **GIRL U FOR ME** *Elektra EKR 167CD* 67 2
9 Oct 93 **BABY IT'S YOU** *Elektra EKR 173CD* 44 2

The SILKIE *UK, male / female vocal / instrumental group*

23 Sep 65 **YOU'VE GOT TO HIDE YOUR LOVE AWAY** *Fontana TF 603* 28 6

SILSOE (see also ARGENT; SAN JOSÉ featuring Rodriguez ARGENTINA)
UK, male keyboard player – Rod Argent

21 Jun 86 **AZTEC GOLD** *CBS A 7231* 48 4

'Aztec Gold' was the ITV theme to the 1986 World Cup.

Lucie SILVAS
UK, female vocalist / keyboard player (1 Album: 31 Weeks, 5 Singles: 19 Weeks)

17 Jun 00 **IT'S TOO LATE** *EMI CDEM 565* 62 1
16 Oct 04 ● **WHAT YOU'RE MADE OF ...** *Mercury 9867463* 7 7
23 Oct 04 BREATHE IN *Mercury 9867025* 11 31
29 Jan 05 ● **BREATHE IN** *Mercury 2103630* 6 7
14 May 05 **THE GAME IS WON** *Mercury 9870820* 38 2
6 Aug 05 **DON'T LOOK BACK** *Mercury 9872943* 34 2

John SILVER *Switzerland / Italy, male production / vocal duo – Dimitri Derisiotis and Gabriel Rizzo*

25 Jan 03 **COME ON OVER** *Cream CREAM 20CD* 35 2

SILVER BULLET
UK, male rapper – Richard Brown (1 Album: 2 Weeks, 3 Singles: 20 Weeks)

2 Sep 89 **BRING FORTH THE GUILLOTINE (re)** *Tam Tam TTT 013* 45 6
9 Dec 89 **20 SECONDS TO COMPLY** *Tam Tam 7TTT 019* 11 10
13 Apr 91 **UNDERCOVER ANARCHIST** *Parlophone R 6284* 33 4
4 May 91 BRING DOWN THE WALLS NO LIMIT SQUAD *Parlophone PCS 7350* 38 2

'Bring Forth the Guillotine' reached its peak position on re-entry in Mar 1990.

SILVER CITY *UK, male / female vocal / instrumental duo*

30 Oct 93 **LOVE INFINITY** *Silver City GFJMCD 1* 62 1

SILVER CONVENTION
Germany / US, female vocal group (1 Album: 3 Weeks, 5 Singles: 35 Weeks)

5 Apr 75 **SAVE ME** *Magnet MAG 26* 30 7
15 Nov 75 **FLY ROBIN FLY** *Magnet MAG 43* ▲ $ 28 8
3 Apr 76 ● **GET UP AND BOOGIE** *Magnet MAG 55* $ 7 11
19 Jun 76 **TIGER BABY / NO NO JOE** *Magnet MAG 69* 41 4
29 Jan 77 **EVERYBODY'S TALKIN' 'BOUT LOVE** *Magnet MAG 81* 25 5
25 Jun 77 GREATEST HITS *Magnet MAG 6001* 34 3

SILVER SUN
UK, male vocal / instrumental group (2 Albums: 2 Weeks, 7 Singles: 13 Weeks)

2 Nov 96 **LAVA** *Polydor 5756872* 54 1
22 Feb 97 **LAST DAY** *Polydor 5732432* 48 1
3 May 97 **GOLDEN SKIN** *Polydor 5738272* 32 2
24 May 97 SILVER SUN *Polydor 5372082* 30 1
5 Jul 97 **JULIA** *Polydor 5711752* 51 1
18 Oct 97 **LAVA** (re-issue) *Polydor 5714242* 35 2
20 Jun 98 **TOO MUCH, TOO LITTLE, TOO LATE** *Polydor 5699152* 20 4
26 Sep 98 **I'LL SEE YOU AROUND** *Polydor 5674532* 26 2
17 Oct 98 NEO WAVE *Polydor 5590852* 74 1

18 February 1989	25 February 1989	4 March 1989	11 March 1989
UK No.1 SINGLES			
SOMETHING'S GOTTEN HOLD OF MY HEART Marc Almond featuring special guest star Gene Pitney	BELFAST CHILD Simple Minds	BELFAST CHILD Simple Minds	TOO MANY BROKEN HEARTS Jason Donovan
UK No.1 ALBUMS			
THE RAW & THE COOKED Fine Young Cannibals	A NEW FLAME Simply Red	A NEW FLAME Simply Red	A NEW FLAME Simply Red

SILVERCHAIR *Australia, male vocal / instrumental group (3 Albums: 5 Weeks, 5 Singles: 8 Weeks)*

Date	Title / Label	Peak	Wks
29 Jul 95	**PURE MASSACRE** *Murmur 6622642*	**71**	1
9 Sep 95	**TOMORROW** *Murmur 6623952*	**59**	2
23 Sep 95	FROGSTOMP *Murmur 4803402*	49	1
15 Feb 97	FREAK SHOW *Columbia 4871032*	38	2
5 Apr 97	**FREAK** *Murmur 6640765*	**34**	2
19 Jul 97	**ABUSE ME** *Murmur 6647907*	**40**	2
27 Mar 99	NEON BALLROOM *Columbia 4933092*	29	2
15 May 99	**ANA'S SONG** *Columbia 6673452*	**45**	1

SILVERFISH *US, male vocal / instrumental group*

Date	Title / Label	Peak	Wks
27 Jun 92	ORGAN FAN *Creation CRECD 118*	65	1

Dooley SILVERSPOON *US, male vocalist*

Date	Title / Label	Peak	Wks
31 Jan 76	**LET ME BE THE NUMBER 1 (LOVE OF YOUR LIFE)** *Seville SEV 1020*	**44**	3

Harry SIMEONE CHORALE

US, choir – leader b. 9 May 1911, d. 22 Feb 2005 (3 Singles: 14 Weeks)

Date	Title / Label	Peak	Wks
13 Feb 59	**LITTLE DRUMMER BOY** *Top Rank JAR 101*	**13**	7
22 Dec 60	**ONWARD CHRISTIAN SOLDIERS (2re)** *Ember EMBS 118*	**35**	5
20 Dec 62	**ONWARD CHRISTIAN SOLDIERS** (re-issue) *Ember EMBS 144*	**38**	2

SIMIAN *UK, male vocal / instrumental group*

Date	Title / Label	Peak	Wks
14 Jun 03	**LA BREEZE** *Source SOURCD 069*	**55**	1

Gene SIMMONS (see also KISS) *US, male vocalist – Chaim Witz*

Date	Title / Label	Peak	Wks
27 Jan 79	RADIOACTIVE *Casablanca CAN 134*	41	4

SIMON *UK, male producer – Simon Pearson*

Date	Title / Label	Peak	Wks
31 Mar 01	**FREE AT LAST** *Positiva CDTIV 152*	**36**	2

Carly SIMON (454 Top 500) (see also Will POWERS)

The winner of a Best New Artist Grammy in 1971, b. 25 Jun 1945, New York, US, first charted Stateside in 1964 as half of folk duo The Simon Sisters with sister Lucy. She was married to fellow singer / songwriter James Taylor from 1972-1983 and elected to the Songwriters' Hall of Fame in 1994 (6 Albums: 74 Weeks, 10 Singles: 85 Weeks)

Date	Title / Label	Peak	Wks
16 Dec 72 ●	**YOU'RE SO VAIN** *Elektra K 12077* ▲ $	**3**	15
20 Jan 73 ●	NO SECRETS *Elektra K 42127* ▲	3	26
31 Mar 73	**THE RIGHT THING TO DO** *Elektra K 12095*	**17**	9
16 Mar 74	HOTCAKES *Elektra K 52005*	19	9
16 Mar 74	**MOCKINGBIRD** *Elektra K 12134* $	**34**	5
6 Aug 77 ●	**NOBODY DOES IT BETTER** *Elektra K 12261* $	**7**	12
21 Aug 82 ●	**WHY** *WEA K 79300*	**10**	13
24 Jan 87 ●	**COMING AROUND AGAIN** *Arista ARIST 687*	**10**	12
9 May 87	COMING AROUND AGAIN *Arista 208 140*	25	20
3 Sep 88	GREATEST HITS LIVE *Arista 209196*	49	6
10 Jun 89	**WHY** (re-issue) *WEA U 7501*	**56**	5
20 Apr 91	**YOU'RE SO VAIN** (re-issue) *Elektra EKR 123*	**41**	5
20 Mar 99	NOBODY DOES IT BETTER – THE VERY BEST OF CARLY SIMON *Warner.esp / Global TV RADCD 103*	22	6
22 Dec 01	**SON OF A GUN (I BETCHA THINK THIS SONG IS ABOUT YOU) (re)** *Virgin VUSCD 232* [1]	**13**	9
12 Jun 04	REFLECTIONS – CARLY SIMON'S GREATEST HITS *Elektra / Rhino 8122789702*	25	7

[1] Janet with Carly Simon featuring Missy Elliott

'Mockingbird' is a duet with uncredited vocals by James Taylor.

Joe SIMON *US, male vocalist*

Date	Title / Label	Peak	Wks
16 Jun 73	**STEP BY STEP** *Mojo 2093 030*	**14**	10

Paul SIMON (135 Top 500)

Acclaimed, award-winning singer / songwriter, b. 13 Oct 1941, New Jersey, US. Recorded under various names in the early 1960s before forming the legendary duo Simon and Garfunkel. He was married to actress Carrie Fisher (1983-85) and wed his current wife, singer Edie Brickell, in 1991. He also helped to popularise world music (13 Albums: 291 Weeks, 11 Singles: 85 Weeks)

Date	Title / Label	Peak	Wks
19 Feb 72 ●	**MOTHER AND CHILD REUNION** *CBS 7793*	**5**	12
26 Feb 72 ★	PAUL SIMON *CBS 69007*	1	26
29 Apr 72	**ME AND JULIO DOWN BY THE SCHOOLYARD** *CBS 7964*	**15**	9
2 Jun 73 ●	THERE GOES RHYMIN' SIMON *CBS 69035*	4	22
16 Jun 73 ●	**TAKE ME TO THE MARDI GRAS** *CBS 1578*	**7**	11
22 Sep 73	**LOVES ME LIKE A ROCK** *CBS 1700* $	**39**	5
1 Nov 75 ●	STILL CRAZY AFTER ALL THESE YEARS *CBS 86001* ▲	6	31
10 Jan 76	**50 WAYS TO LEAVE YOUR LOVER** *CBS 3887* ▲ $	**23**	6
3 Dec 77 ●	GREATEST HITS ETC. *CBS 10007*	6	15
3 Dec 77	**SLIP SLIDIN' AWAY** *CBS 5770*	**36**	5
30 Aug 80	ONE-TRICK PONY *Warner Bros. K 56846*	17	12
6 Sep 80	**LATE IN THE EVENING** *Warner Bros. K 17666*	**58**	4
12 Nov 83	HEARTS AND BONES *Warner Bros. 9239421*	34	8
13 Sep 86 ★	GRACELAND *Warner Bros. WX 52*	1	115
13 Sep 86 ●	**YOU CAN CALL ME AL** *Warner Bros. W 8667*	**4**	13
13 Dec 86	**THE BOY IN THE BUBBLE** *Warner Bros. W 8509*	**26**	8
24 Jan 87	GREATEST HITS ETC. (re-issue) *CBS 450 1661*	73	2
5 Nov 88	NEGOTIATIONS AND LOVE SONGS 1971-1986 *Warner Bros. WX 223*	17	15
6 Oct 90	**THE OBVIOUS CHILD** *Warner Bros. W 9549*	**15**	10
27 Oct 90 ★	THE RHYTHM OF THE SAINTS *Warner Bros. WX 340* ■	1	28
23 Nov 91	PAUL SIMON'S CONCERT IN THE PARK – AUGUST 15TH 1991 *Warner Bros. WX 448*	60	1
9 Dec 95	**SOMETHING SO RIGHT** *RCA 74321332392* [1]	**44**	2
27 May 00 ●	GREATEST HITS – SHINING LIKE A NATIONAL GUITAR *Warner Bros. 9362477212*	6	12
14 Oct 00	YOU'RE THE ONE *Warner Bros. 9362478442*	20	4

[1] Annie Lennox featuring Paul Simon

Ronni SIMON *UK, male vocalist (2 Singles: 2 Weeks)*

Date	Title / Label	Peak	Wks
13 Aug 94	**B GOOD 2 ME** *Network NWKCD 80*	**73**	1
10 Jun 95	**TAKE YOU THERE** *Network NWKCD 85*	**58**	1

Tito SIMON *Jamaica, male vocalist*

Date	Title / Label	Peak	Wks
8 Feb 75	**THIS MONDAY MORNING FEELING** *Horse HOSS 57*	**45**	4

SIMON and GARFUNKEL (15 Top 500)

The most successful recording duo ever: singer / songwriter / guitarist Paul Simon, b. 13 Oct 1941, New Jersey, US, and vocalist Art Garfunkel, b. 5 Nov 1941, New York, US. The pair met at High School and joined doo-wop group The Peptones, but their first US hit was as Tom and Jerry in 1957. They then both recorded solo, with Simon charting as both Jerry Landis and Tico and The Triumphs. The duo reunited and released Wednesday Morning, 3am. When this album flopped, Simon went on a solo UK folk club tour (when he penned 'Homeward Bound'). Producer Tom Wilson re-mixed the album track 'The Sound of Silence', transforming it into a folk-rock song that quickly took off. Paul rushed home, re-united with Art and the rest is history. Before splitting in 1971, they won numerous Grammy awards, became the first duo to top either the UK and US albums chart, and at times had three of America's Top 5 albums in 1968. Their Greatest Hits collection is the world's biggest seller by a duo (13 million in the US alone) and 'Bridge Over Troubled Water' (one of the most performed songs on reality TV pop shows) was voted Best Single of All Time at the BRITs in 1977, while its parent LP – the UK's top seller in 1970 and 1971 – was named Best Album. The duo, who reunited for a successful tour in 2003 / 2004, were inducted into the Rock and Roll Hall of Fame in 1990 and received a Lifetime Achievement Grammy in 2003 (14 Albums: 1114 Weeks, 9 Singles: 87 Weeks)

Date	Title / Label	Peak	Wks
24 Mar 66 ●	**HOMEWARD BOUND** *CBS 202045*	**9**	12
16 Apr 66	SOUNDS OF SILENCE *CBS 62690*	13	104
16 Jun 66	**I AM A ROCK** *CBS 202303*	**17**	10
10 Jul 68 ●	**MRS ROBINSON** *CBS 3443* ▲ $	**4**	12
3 Aug 68 ★	BOOKENDS *CBS 63101* ▲	1	77
31 Aug 68	PARSLEY, SAGE, ROSEMARY AND THYME *CBS 62860*	13	58
26 Oct 68 ●	THE GRADUATE (FILM SOUNDTRACK) *CBS 70042* ▲	3	71

18 March 1989	25 March 1989	1 April 1989	8 April 1989
TOO MANY BROKEN HEARTS Jason Donovan	LIKE A PRAYER Madonna	LIKE A PRAYER Madonna	LIKE A PRAYER Madonna
A NEW FLAME Simply Red	ANYTHING FOR YOU Gloria Estefan and Miami Sound Machine	LIKE A PRAYER Madonna	LIKE A PRAYER Madonna

KEY
UK No.1 ★ UK Top 10 ● Still on chart + UK entry at No.1 ■
US No.1 ▲ UK million seller £ US million seller $
Singles re-entries are listed as (re), (2re), (3re)… which signifies that the hit re-entered the chart once, twice or three times…
Peak Position / Weeks

9 Nov 68 WEDNESDAY MORNING, 3AM *CBS 63370* ... 24 6
8 Jan 69 ● **MRS ROBINSON (EP)** *CBS EP 6400* ... 9 5
30 Apr 69 ● **THE BOXER** *CBS 4162* ... 6 14
21 Feb 70 ★ BRIDGE OVER TROUBLED WATER *CBS 63699* ■ ▲ ... 1 307
21 Feb 70 ★ **BRIDGE OVER TROUBLED WATER (re)** *CBS 4790* [1] ▲ $ ... 1 20
22 Jul 72 ● SIMON AND GARFUNKEL'S GREATEST HITS *CBS 69003* ... 2 283
7 Oct 72 **AMERICA** *CBS 8336* ... 25 7
4 Apr 81 SOUNDS OF SILENCE (re-issue) *CBS 32020* ... 68 1
21 Nov 81 ● THE SIMON AND GARFUNKEL COLLECTION *CBS 10029* ... 4 80
20 Mar 82 ● THE CONCERT IN CENTRAL PARK *Geffen GEF 96008* ... 6 43
30 Nov 91 ● THE DEFINITIVE SIMON AND GARFUNKEL *Columbia MOODCD 21* ... 8 57
7 Dec 91 **A HAZY SHADE OF WINTER / SILENT NIGHT – SEVEN O'CLOCK NEWS** *Columbia 6576537* ... 30 6
15 Feb 92 **THE BOXER** (re-issue) *Columbia 6578067* ... 75 1
5 Feb 00 ● THE VERY BEST OF SIMON AND GARFUNKEL – TALES FROM NEW YORK *Columbia SONYTV 81CD* ... 8 12
6 Dec 03 THE ESSENTIAL SIMON AND GARFUNKEL *Columbia 5134702* ... 25 13
11 Dec 04 OLD FRIENDS – LIVE ON STAGE *Columbia 5191732* ... 61 2

[1] Keyboard: Larry Knechtel

Tracks on Mrs Robinson (EP): Mrs Robinson / Scarborough Fair – Canticle / The Sound of Silence / April Come She Will. This EP would have stayed more than five weeks on chart had a decision to exclude EPs from the chart in Feb 1969 not been taken.

SIMONE *US, female vocalist*

23 Nov 91 **MY FAMILY DEPENDS ON ME** *Strictly Rhythm A 8678* ... 75 1

Nina SIMONE

US, female vocalist / keyboard player – Eunice Waymon, b. 21 Feb 1933, d. 21 Apr 2003 (6 Albums: 33 Weeks, 6 Singles: 46 Weeks)

24 Jul 65 I PUT A SPELL ON YOU *Philips BL 7671* ... 18 3
5 Aug 65 **I PUT A SPELL ON YOU** *Philips BF 1415* ... 49 1
16 Oct 68 ● **AIN'T GOT NO – I GOT LIFE / DO WHAT YOU GOTTA DO** *RCA 1743* ... 2 18
15 Jan 69 ● **TO LOVE SOMEBODY** *RCA 1779* ... 5 9
15 Jan 69 **I PUT A SPELL ON YOU** (re-issue) *Philips BF 1736* ... 28 4
15 Feb 69 NUFF SAID *RCS SF 7979* ... 11 1
31 Oct 87 ● **MY BABY JUST CARES FOR ME** *Charly CYZ 7112* ... 5 11
14 Nov 87 MY BABY JUST CARES FOR ME *Charly CR 30217* ... 56 8
9 Jul 94 **FEELING GOOD** *Mercury MERCD 403* ... 40 3
16 Jul 94 ● FEELING GOOD – THE VERY BEST OF NINA SIMONE *PolyGram TV 5226692* ... 9 8
7 Feb 98 BLUE FOR YOU – THE VERY BEST OF NINA SIMONE *Global Television RADCD 84* ... 12 10
21 Jun 03 GOLD *UCJ 9808087* ... 27 3

'Do What You Gotta Do' was listed only for the first eight weeks of the record's chart run. It peaked at No.7.

Victor SIMONELLI presents SOLUTION *US, male producer*

2 Nov 96 **FEELS SO RIGHT** *Soundproof MCSTD 40068* ... 63 1

SIMPLE KID

UK, male vocalist – Ciaran McFeely (2 Singles: 3 Weeks)

13 Sep 03 **THE AVERAGE MAN** *2M 2M 005CD* ... 72 1
14 Feb 04 **TRUCK ON** *2M 2M 007CD 1* ... 38 2

SIMPLE MINDS (68 Top 500)

The most successful Scottish band of the 1980s, fronted by Jim Kerr, b. 9 Jul 1959, Glasgow, who married Chrissie Hynde, lead singer of The Pretenders. Five of the quintet's albums entered the UK chart at No.1 and world sales topped 30 million (15 Albums: 356 Weeks, 33 Singles: 191 Weeks)

5 May 79 A LIFE IN THE DAY *Zoom ZULP 1* ... 30 6
12 May 79 **LIFE IN A DAY** *Zoom ZUM 10* ... 62 2
27 Sep 80 EMPIRES AND DANCE *Arista SPART 1140* ... 41 3
23 May 81 **THE AMERICAN** *Virgin VS 410* ... 59 3
15 Aug 81 **LOVE SONG** *Virgin VS 434* ... 47 4
12 Sep 81 SONS AND FASCINATIONS / SISTER FEELINGS CALL *Virgin V 2207* ... 11 7
7 Nov 81 **SWEAT IN BULLET** *Virgin VS 451* ... 52 3
27 Feb 82 CELEBRATION *Arista SPART 1183* ... 45 7
10 Apr 82 **PROMISED YOU A MIRACLE** *Virgin VS 488* ... 13 11
28 Aug 82 **GLITTERING PRIZE** *Virgin VS 511* ... 16 11
25 Sep 82 ● NEW GOLD DREAM (81 82 83 84) *Virgin V 2230* ... 3 52
13 Nov 82 **SOMEONE SOMEWHERE (IN SUMMERTIME)** *Virgin VS 538* ... 36 5
26 Nov 83 **WATERFRONT** *Virgin VS 636* ... 13 10
28 Jan 84 **SPEED YOUR LOVE TO ME** *Virgin VS 649* ... 20 4
18 Feb 84 ★ SPARKLE IN THE RAIN *Virgin V 2300* ■ ... 1 57
24 Mar 84 **UP ON THE CATWALK** *Virgin VS 661* ... 27 5
20 Apr 85 ● **DON'T YOU (FORGET ABOUT ME) (4re)** *Virgin VS 749* ▲ ... 7 24
12 Oct 85 ● **ALIVE AND KICKING (re)** *Virgin VS 817* ... 7 11
2 Nov 85 ★ ONCE UPON A TIME *Virgin V 2364* ■ ... 1 83
1 Feb 86 ● **SANCTIFY YOURSELF** *Virgin SM 1* ... 10 7
12 Apr 86 ● **ALL THE THINGS SHE SAID (re)** *Virgin VS 860* ... 9 9
15 Nov 86 **GHOSTDANCING (re)** *Virgin VS 907* ... 13 8
6 Jun 87 ★ LIVE IN THE CITY OF LIGHT *Virgin V SMDL 1* ■ ... 1 26
20 Jun 87 **PROMISED YOU A MIRACLE (LIVE)** *Virgin SM 2* ... 19 7
18 Feb 89 ★ **BELFAST CHILD** *Virgin SMX 3* ... 1 11
22 Apr 89 **THIS IS YOUR LAND** *Virgin SMX 4* ... 13 4
13 May 89 ★ STREET FIGHTING YEARS *Virgin MINDS 1* ■ ... 1 28
29 Jul 89 **KICK IT IN** *Virgin SM 5* ... 15 5
9 Dec 89 **THE AMSTERDAM EP** *Virgin SMX 6* ... 18 6
23 Mar 91 ● **LET THERE BE LOVE** *Virgin VS 1332* ... 6 7
20 Apr 91 ● REAL LIFE *Virgin V 2660* ... 2 25
25 May 91 **SEE THE LIGHTS** *Virgin VS 1343* ... 20 4
31 Aug 91 **STAND BY LOVE** *Virgin VS 1358* ... 13 4
26 Oct 91 **REAL LIFE** *Virgin VS 1382* ... 34 3
10 Oct 92 ● **LOVE SONG / ALIVE AND KICKING** (re-issue) *Virgin VS 1440* ... 6 6
24 Oct 92 ★ GLITTERING PRIZE 81/92 *Virgin SMTVD 1* ■ ... 1 39
28 Jan 95 ● **SHE'S A RIVER** *Virgin VSCDX 1509* ... 9 5
11 Feb 95 ● GOOD NEWS FROM THE NEXT WORLD *Virgin CDV 2760* ... 2 14
8 Apr 95 **HYPNOTISED** *Virgin VSCDX 1534* ... 18 5
14 Mar 98 **GLITTERBALL** *Chrysalis CDCHSS 5078* ... 18 2
28 Mar 98 NEAPOLIS *Chrysalis 4937122* ... 19 3
30 May 98 **WAR BABIES** *Chrysalis CDCHS 5088* ... 43 1
17 Nov 01 THE BEST OF SIMPLE MINDS *Virgin CDVD 2953* ... 34 4
2 Feb 02 **BELFAST TRANCE** *Nebula BELFCD 001* [1] ... 74 1
30 Mar 02 **CRY** *Eagle EAGXS 218* ... 47 1
20 Jul 02 **MONSTER** *Defected DFECT 49* [2] ... 67 1
17 Sep 05 **HOME** *Sanctuary SANXD 388* ... 41 1
24 Sep 05 BLACK & WHITE 050505 *Sanctuary SANCD 390* ... 37 2

[1] John "OO" Fleming vs Simple Minds [2] Liquid People vs Simple Minds

Tracks on The Amsterdam EP: Let It All Come Down / Jerusalem / Sign of the Times.

SIMPLE PLAN *US, male vocal / instrumental group (3 Singles: 4 Weeks)*

5 Jul 03 **ADDICTED** *Lava / Atlantic AT 0158CD* ... 63 1
5 Mar 05 **SHUT UP!** *Lava AT 0195CD* ... 44 2
2 Jul 05 **WELCOME TO MY LIFE** *Lava AT 0206CD2* ... 49 1

SIMPLICIOUS *US, male vocal group (2 Singles: 9 Weeks)*

29 Sep 84 **LET HER FEEL IT** *Fourth & Broadway BRW 13* ... 65 3
2 Feb 85 **LET HER FEEL IT** (re-issue) *Fourth & Broadway BRW 18* ... 34 6

The re-issue of 'Let Her Feel It' was listed with 'Personality' by Eugene Wilde.

SIMPLY RED (27 Top 500)

The unmistakable Mick Hucknall, b. 8 Jun 1960, Manchester, UK, quickly became the representative face and voice of this internationally popular outfit, who have a Top 20 span of 20 years. Their

	15 April 1989	22 April 1989	29 April 1989	6 May 1989
UK No.1 SINGLES	ETERNAL FLAME The Bangles	ETERNAL FLAME The Bangles	ETERNAL FLAME The Bangles	ETERNAL FLAME The Bangles
UK No.1 ALBUMS	WHEN THE WORLD KNOWS YOUR NAME Deacon Blue	WHEN THE WORLD KNOWS YOUR NAME Deacon Blue	A NEW FLAME Simply Red	BLAST Holly Johnson

Stars album sold more than two million copies in the UK and was the biggest British seller in 1991 and 1992. Best-selling single: 'Fairground' 783,000 (14 Albums: 618 Weeks, 36 Singles: 243 Weeks)

15 Jun 85 **MONEY'S TOO TIGHT (TO MENTION)** *Elektra EKR 9*....13 12
21 Sep 85 **COME TO MY AID** *Elektra EKR 19*....66 2
26 Oct 85 ● **PICTURE BOOK** *Elektra EKT 27*....2 130
16 Nov 85 **HOLDING BACK THE YEARS** *Elektra EKR 29* ▲....51 4
8 Mar 86 **JERICHO** *WEA YZ 63*....53 3
17 May 86 ● **HOLDING BACK THE YEARS** (re-issue) *WEA YZ 70*....2 13
9 Aug 86 **OPEN UP THE RED BOX** *WEA YZ 75*....61 4
14 Feb 87 **THE RIGHT THING** *WEA YZ 103*....11 10
21 Mar 87 ● **MEN AND WOMEN** *WEA WX 85*....2 60
23 May 87 **INFIDELITY** *Elektra YZ 114*....31 5
28 Nov 87 **EV'RY TIME WE SAY GOODBYE** *Elektra YZ 161*....11 9
12 Mar 88 **I WON'T FEEL BAD** *Elektra YZ 172*....68 3
28 Jan 89 **IT'S ONLY LOVE** *Elektra YZ 349*....13 8
25 Feb 89 ★ **A NEW FLAME** *Elektra WX 242* ■....1 84
8 Apr 89 ● **IF YOU DON'T KNOW ME BY NOW** *Elektra YZ 377* ▲....2 10
8 Jul 89 **A NEW FLAME** *WEA YZ 404*....17 8
28 Oct 89 **YOU'VE GOT IT** *Elektra YZ 424*....46 3
21 Sep 91 **SOMETHING GOT ME STARTED** *East West YZ 614*....11 8
12 Oct 91 ★ **STARS** *East West WX 427* ■....1 134
30 Nov 91 ● **STARS** *East West YZ 626*....8 10
8 Feb 92 ● **FOR YOUR BABIES** *East West YZ 642*....9 8
2 May 92 **THRILL ME** *East West YZ 671*....33 5
25 Jul 92 **YOUR MIRROR** *East West YZ 689*....17 4
21 Nov 92 **MONTREUX (EP)** *East West YZ 716*....11 10
4 Mar 95 **MEN AND WOMEN** (re-issue) *East West K 2420712*....20 7
30 Sep 95 ★ **FAIRGROUND** *East West EW 001CD1* ■....1 14
21 Oct 95 ★ **LIFE** *East West 0630120692* ■....1 47
16 Dec 95 **REMEMBERING THE FIRST TIME** *East West EW 015CD1*....22 6
24 Feb 96 **A NEW FLAME** (re-issue) *East West K 2446892*....28 6
24 Feb 96 **PICTURE BOOK** (re-issue) *East West 9031769932*....33 5
24 Feb 96 **NEVER NEVER LOVE** *East West EW 029CD1*....18 4
22 Jun 96 **WE'RE IN THIS TOGETHER** *East West EW 046CD1*....11 6
19 Oct 96 ★ **GREATEST HITS** *East West 630165522* ■....1 52
9 Nov 96 ● **ANGEL** *East West EW 074CD1*....4 13
20 Sep 97 **NIGHT NURSE** *East West EW 129CD1* [1]....13 8
16 May 98 ● **SAY YOU LOVE ME** *East West EW 164CD*....7 7
30 May 98 ★ **BLUE** *East West 3984230972* ■....1 26
22 Aug 98 ● **THE AIR THAT I BREATHE** *East West EW 3821CD*....6 7
12 Dec 98 **GHETTO GIRL** *East West EW 191CD1*....34 2
30 Oct 99 **AIN'T THAT A LOT OF LOVE** *East West EW 208CD1*....14 6
13 Nov 99 ● **LOVE AND THE RUSSIAN WINTER** *East West 3984299422*....6 17
19 Feb 00 **YOUR EYES** *East West EW 212CD1*....26 2
25 Nov 00 **IT'S ONLY LOVE** *East West 8573855372*....27 6
29 Mar 03 ● **SUNRISE** *Simplyred.com SRS 001CD1*....7 11
5 Apr 03 ● **HOME** *Simplyred.com SRA 001CD*....2 35
19 Jul 03 **FAKE** *Simplyred.com SRS 002CD1*....21 4
13 Dec 03 ● **YOU MAKE ME FEEL BRAND NEW** *Simplyred.com SRS 003CD1*....7 9
10 Apr 04 **HOME** *Simplyred.com SRS 004CD*....40 2
22 Oct 05 **PERFECT LOVE** *Simplyred.com SRS 005CD2*....30 3
29 Oct 05 ● **SIMPLIFIED** *Simplyred.com SRA 002CD*....3 9

[1] Sly and Robbie featuring Simply Red

Tracks on Montreux (EP): Drowning In My Own Tears / Grandma's Hands / Lady Godiva's Room / Love for Sale.

SIMPLY RED AND WHITE
UK, male Sunderland FC supporters vocal group

6 Apr 96 **DAYDREAM BELIEVER (CHEER UP PETER REID) (re)** *Ropery SHAYISGOD 1D*....41 4

SIMPLY SMOOTH *US, male / female vocal group*

17 Oct 98 **LADY (YOU BRING ME UP)** *Big Bang CDBANG 07*....70 1

Ashlee SIMPSON
US, female vocalist (1 Album: 9 Weeks, 2 Singles: 16 Weeks)

9 Oct 04 ● **PIECES OF ME** *Geffen 9863811*....4 10
16 Oct 04 **AUTOBIOGRAPHY** *Geffen 9863256* ▲....31 9
5 Feb 05 **LA LA** *Geffen 2103875*....11 6

Jessica SIMPSON
US, female vocalist (2 Albums: 7 Weeks, 5 Singles: 42 Weeks)

22 Apr 00 ● **I WANNA LOVE YOU FOREVER (re)** *Columbia 6691272* $....7 11
6 May 00 **SWEET KISSES** *Columbia 4949332*....36 2
15 Jul 00 **I THINK I'M IN LOVE WITH YOU** *Columbia 6695942*....15 7
14 Jul 01 **IRRESISTIBLE** *Columbia 6714102*....11 6
1 May 04 **IN THIS SKIN** *Columbia SNY 865602*....36 5
26 Jun 04 ● **WITH YOU** *Columbia 6748302*....7 8
10 Sep 05 ● **THESE BOOTS ARE MADE FOR WALKIN'** *Columbia 6760652*....4 10

Paul SIMPSON featuring ADEVA
US, male producer / instrumentalist and female vocalist

25 Mar 89 **MUSICAL FREEDOM (MOVING ON UP)** *Cooltempo CDCOOL 182*....22 8

Vida SIMPSON *US, female vocalist*

18 Feb 95 **OOHHH BABY** *Hi-Life HICD 6*....70 1

The SIMPSONS *US, male / female cartoon group – lead vocal Bart Simpson (Nancy Cartwright)* (1 Album: 30 Weeks, 2 Singles: 19 Weeks)

26 Jan 91 ★ **DO THE BARTMAN** *Geffen GEF 87*....1 12
2 Feb 91 ● **THE SIMPSONS SING THE BLUES** *Geffen 7599243081*....6 30
6 Apr 91 ● **DEEP DEEP TROUBLE** *Geffen GEF 88* [1]....7 7

[1] The Simpsons featuring Bart and Homer

Joyce SIMS *US, female vocalist* (2 Albums: 25 Weeks, 6 Singles: 36 Weeks)

19 Apr 86 **ALL AND ALL** *London LON 94*....16 10
13 Jun 87 **LIFETIME LOVE** *London LON 137*....34 6
9 Jan 88 ● **COME INTO MY LIFE** *London LONLP 47*....5 24
9 Jan 88 ● **COME INTO MY LIFE** *London LON 161*....7 9
23 Apr 88 **WALK AWAY** *London LON 176*....24 6
17 Jun 89 **LOOKING FOR A LOVE** *ffrr F 109*....39 4
16 Sep 89 **ALL ABOUT LOVE** *London 828129 1*....64 1
27 May 95 **COME INTO MY LIFE** (re-mix) *Club Tools 0060435 CLU*....72 1

Kym SIMS *US, female vocalist* (1 Album: 2 Weeks, 4 Singles: 23 Weeks)

7 Dec 91 ● **TOO BLIND TO SEE IT** *Atco B 8667*....5 12
28 Mar 92 **TAKE MY ADVICE** *Atco B 8591*....13 7
18 Apr 92 **TOO BLIND TO SEE IT** *Atco 7567921042*....39 2
27 Jun 92 **A LITTLE BIT MORE** *Atco B 8528*....30 3
8 Jun 96 **WE GOTTA LOVE** *Pulse 8 CDLOSE 104*....58 1

SIN WITH SEBASTIAN
Germany, male vocalist – Sebastian Roth (2 Singles: 2 Weeks)

16 Sep 95 **SHUT UP (AND SLEEP WITH ME)** *Sing Sing 74321253592*....44 1
27 Jan 96 **SHUT UP (AND SLEEP WITH ME)** (re-mix) *Sing Sing 74321337972*....46 1

Frank SINATRA 12 Top 500 (see also The RATPACK)

Legendary entertainer regarded by many as the greatest song stylist of the 20th century, b. 12 Dec 1915, New Jersey, US, d. 14 May 1998. The vocalist (with Tommy Dorsey Orchestra) on the first US No.1, 'I'll Never Smile Again' (1940), was the first teen idol. Songs for Swingin' Lovers is the only album to reach the UK Top 20 singles chart and is one of 34 US gold albums amassed by the influential vocalist, who has scored more US Top 10 LPs than any other soloist. Sinatra, the first recipient of a Grammy Lifetime Achievement award (1965), holds the UK chart longevity record with 'My Way'. Total UK single sales: 4,597,630 (65 Albums: 892 Weeks, 38 Singles: 440 Weeks)

9 Jul 54 **YOUNG-AT-HEART** *Capitol CL 14064*....12 1
16 Jul 54 ★ **THREE COINS IN THE FOUNTAIN** *Capitol CL 14120*....1 19
10 Jun 55 **YOU MY LOVE (2re)** *Capitol CL 14240*....13 7
5 Aug 55 ● **LEARNIN' THE BLUES** *Capitol CL 14296* $....2 13

13 May 1989	20 May 1989	27 May 1989	3 June 1989
HAND ON YOUR HEART Kylie Minogue	**FERRY 'CROSS THE MERSEY** The Christians, Holly Johnson, Paul McCartney, Gerry Marsden and Stock Aitken Waterman	**FERRY 'CROSS THE MERSEY** The Christians, Holly Johnson, Paul McCartney, Gerry Marsden and Stock Aitken Waterman	**FERRY 'CROSS THE MERSEY** The Christians, Holly Johnson, Paul McCartney, Gerry Marsden and Stock Aitken Waterman
STREET FIGHTING YEARS Simple Minds	**TEN GOOD REASONS** Jason Donovan	**TEN GOOD REASONS** Jason Donovan	**THE MIRACLE** Queen

KEY
UK No.1 ★ UK Top 10 ● Still on chart + UK entry at No.1 ■
US No.1 ▲ UK million seller £ US million seller $
Singles re-entries are listed as (re), (2re), (3re)... which signifies that the hit re-entered the chart once, twice or three times...
Peak Position / Weeks

2 Sep 55 NOT AS A STRANGER *Capitol CL 14326*..........18 1
13 Jan 56 ● LOVE AND MARRIAGE *Capitol CL 14503*..........3 8
20 Jan 56 ● (LOVE IS) THE TENDER TRAP *Capitol CL 14511*..........2 9
15 Jun 56 SONGS FOR SWINGIN' LOVERS (LP) *Capitol LCT 6106*..........12 8
28 Jul 56 ★ SONGS FOR SWINGIN' LOVERS *Capitol LCT 6106*..........1 34
16 Feb 57 ★ THIS IS SINATRA! *Capitol LCT 6123*..........1 13
25 May 57 ● CLOSE TO YOU *Capitol LCT 6130*..........2 9
20 Jul 57 ● FRANKIE *Philips BBL 7168*..........3 7
7 Sep 57 ★ A SWINGIN' AFFAIR! *Capitol LCT 6135*..........1 19
22 Nov 57 ● ALL THE WAY / CHICAGO (3re) *Capitol CL 14800*..........3 20
7 Feb 58 WITCHCRAFT *Capitol CL 14819*..........12 8
1 Mar 58 ● WHERE ARE YOU? *Capitol LCT 6152*..........3 5
21 Jun 58 ● THIS IS SINATRA (VOL.2) *Capitol LCT 6155*..........3 12
13 Sep 58 ● COME FLY WITH ME *Capitol LCT 6154* ▲..........2 18
14 Nov 58 MR SUCCESS (2re) *Capitol CL 14956*..........25 4
29 Nov 58 ● FRANK SINATRA STORY *Fontana TFL 5030*..........8 1
13 Dec 58 ● FRANK SINATRA SINGS FOR ONLY THE LONELY *Capitol LCT 6168*..........5 13
10 Apr 59 FRENCH FOREIGN LEGION *Capitol CL 14997*..........18 5
15 May 59 COME DANCE WITH ME! (LP) *Capitol LCT 6179* 1..........30 1
16 May 59 ● COME DANCE WITH ME! *Capitol LCT 6179*..........2 30
22 Aug 59 ● LOOK TO YOUR HEART *Capitol LCT 6181*..........5 8
28 Aug 59 ● HIGH HOPES (2re) *Capitol CL 15052* 2..........6 15
7 Apr 60 IT'S NICE TO GO TRAV'LING *Capitol CL 15116*..........48 2
11 Jun 60 ● COME BACK TO SORRENTO *Fontana TFL 5082*..........6 9
16 Jun 60 RIVER STAY 'WAY FROM MY DOOR *Capitol CL 15135*..........18 9
8 Sep 60 NICE 'N' EASY *Capitol CL 15150*..........15 12
29 Oct 60 ● SWING EASY *Capitol W 587*..........5 17
24 Nov 60 OL' MACDONALD *Capitol CL 15168*..........11 8
21 Jan 61 ● NICE 'N EASY *Capitol W 1417* ▲..........4 27
20 Apr 61 MY BLUE HEAVEN *Capitol CL 15193*..........33 7
15 Jul 61 SINATRA SOUVENIR *Fontana TFL 5138*..........18 1
19 Aug 61 ● WHEN YOUR LOVER HAS GONE *Encore ENC 101*..........6 10
23 Sep 61 ● SINATRA'S SWINGIN' SESSION!!! AND MORE *Capitol W 1491*..........6 8
28 Sep 61 GRANADA *Reprise R 20010*..........15 8
28 Oct 61 ● SINATRA SWINGS *Reprise R 1002*..........8 8
23 Nov 61 THE COFFEE SONG *Reprise R 20035*..........39 3
25 Nov 61 ● SINATRA PLUS *Fontana SET 303*..........7 9
16 Dec 61 ● RING-A-DING-DING *Reprise R 1001*..........8 9
17 Feb 62 COME SWING WITH ME *Capitol W 1594*..........13 4
5 Apr 62 EV'RYBODY'S TWISTING *Reprise R 20063*..........22 12
7 Apr 62 ● I REMEMBER TOMMY ... *Reprise R 1003*..........10 12
9 Jun 62 ● SINATRA AND STRINGS *Reprise R 1004*..........6 20
27 Oct 62 GREAT SONGS FROM GREAT BRITAIN *Reprise R 1006*..........12 9
13 Dec 62 ME AND MY SHADOW (re) *Reprise R 20128* 3..........20 9
29 Dec 62 SINATRA WITH SWINGING BRASS *Reprise R 1005*..........14 11
23 Feb 63 ● SINATRA – BASIE *Reprise R 1008* 1..........2 23
7 Mar 63 MY KIND OF GIRL *Reprise R 20148* 4..........35 6
27 Jul 63 ● CONCERT SINATRA *Reprise R 1009*..........8 18
5 Oct 63 ● SINATRA'S SINATRA *Reprise R 1010*..........9 24
19 Sep 64 IT MIGHT AS WELL BE SWING *Reprise R 1012*..........17 4
24 Sep 64 HELLO DOLLY *Reprise R 20351* 4..........47 1
20 Mar 65 SOFTLY AS I LEAVE YOU *Reprise R 1013*..........20 1
22 Jan 66 ● A MAN AND HIS MUSIC *Reprise R 1016*..........9 19
12 May 66 ★ STRANGERS IN THE NIGHT *Reprise R 23052* ▲ $..........1 20
21 May 66 MOONLIGHT SINATRA *Reprise R 1018*..........18 8
2 Jul 66 ● STRANGERS IN THE NIGHT *Reprise R 1017* ▲..........4 18
29 Sep 66 SUMMER WIND *Reprise RS 20509*..........36 5
1 Oct 66 ● SINATRA AT 'THE SANDS' *Reprise RLP 1019*..........7 18
3 Dec 66 FRANK SINATRA SINGS SONGS FOR PLEASURE *MFP 1120*..........26 2
15 Dec 66 THAT'S LIFE *Reprise RS 20531*..........44 5
25 Feb 67 THAT'S LIFE *Reprise RSLP 1020*..........22 12
23 Mar 67 ★ SOMETHIN' STUPID *Reprise RS 23166* 5 ▲ $..........1 18
23 Aug 67 THE WORLD WE KNEW (OVER AND OVER) *Reprise RS 20610*..........33 11
7 Oct 67 FRANK SINATRA *Reprise RSLP 1022*..........28 5
19 Oct 68 ● GREATEST HITS *Reprise RSLP 1025*..........8 38
7 Dec 68 BEST OF FRANK SINATRA *Capitol ST 21140*..........17 10
2 Apr 69 ● MY WAY (8re) *Reprise RS 20817*..........5 122
7 Jun 69 ● MY WAY *Reprise RSLP 1029*..........2 51
4 Oct 69 A MAN ALONE – THE WORDS & MUSIC OF ROD MCKUEN *Reprise RSLP 1030*..........18 7
4 Oct 69 ● LOVE'S BEEN GOOD TO ME *Reprise RS 20852*..........8 18
9 May 70 WATERTOWN *Reprise RSLP 1031*..........14 9
12 Dec 70 ● GREATEST HITS VOLUME 2 *Reprise RSLP 1032*..........6 39
6 Mar 71 I WILL DRINK THE WINE *Reprise RS 23487*..........16 12
5 Jun 71 ● SINATRA AND COMPANY *Reprise RSLP 1033*..........9 9
27 Nov 71 FRANK SINATRA SINGS RODGERS AND HART *Starline SRS 5083*..........35 1
8 Jan 72 GREATEST HITS VOLUME 2 (re-issue) *Reprise K 44018*..........29 3
8 Jan 72 MY WAY (re-issue) *Reprise K 44015*..........35 1
1 Dec 73 OL' BLUE EYES IS BACK *Warner Bros. K 44249*..........12 13
17 Aug 74 SOME NICE THINGS I'VE MISSED *Reprise K 54020*..........35 3
15 Feb 75 THE MAIN EVENT (TV SOUNDTRACK) *Reprise K 54031*..........30 2
14 Jun 75 THE BEST OF OL' BLUE EYES *Reprise K 54042*..........30 3
20 Dec 75 I BELIEVE I'M GONNA LOVE YOU *Reprise K 14400*..........34 7
19 Mar 77 ★ PORTRAIT OF SINATRA *Reprise K 64039*..........1 18
13 May 78 ● 20 GOLDEN GREATS *Capitol EMTV 10*..........4 11
9 Aug 80 ● THEME FROM 'NEW YORK, NEW YORK' (re) *Reprise K 14502*..........4 14
18 Aug 84 L.A. IS MY LADY *Qwest 925145*..........41 8
22 Mar 86 NEW YORK NEW YORK (GREATEST HITS) *Warner Bros. WX 32*..........13 12
4 Oct 86 THE FRANK SINATRA COLLECTION *Capitol EMTV 41*..........40 5
6 Nov 93 ● DUETS *Capitol CDEST 2218*..........5 14
4 Dec 93 ● I'VE GOT YOU UNDER MY SKIN *Island CID 578* 6..........4 9
16 Apr 94 MY WAY (re-issue) *Reprise W 0163CD*..........45 2
26 Nov 94 DUETS II *Capitol CDEST 2245*..........29 6
11 Mar 95 THIS IS FRANK SINATRA 1953-1957 *Music for Pleasure CDDL 1275*..........56 1
2 Dec 95 SINATRA 80TH – ALL THE BEST *Capitol CDESTD 2*..........49 5
16 Aug 97 ● MY WAY – THE BEST OF FRANK SINATRA *Reprise 9362467122*..........7 128
30 Jan 99 THEY ALL LAUGHED *Reprise W 469CD*..........41 1
24 Jun 00 ● CLASSIC SINATRA – HIS GREAT PERFORMANCES 1953-1960 *Capitol 5235022*..........10 7
9 Feb 02 ● A FINE ROMANCE – THE LOVE SONGS OF FRANK SINATRA *Reprise 8122735892*..........6 9
28 Aug 04 THE PLATINUM COLLECTION – THE BEST OF THE ORIGINAL CAPITOL RECORDINGS *Capitol 8647602*..........11 4

1 Frank Sinatra with Billy May and his Orchestra 2 Frank Sinatra with a bunch of kids 3 Frank Sinatra and Sammy Davis Jr 4 Frank Sinatra with Count Basie 5 Nancy Sinatra and Frank Sinatra 6 Frank Sinatra with Bono 1 Frank Sinatra and Count Basie

As a re-entry 'My Way' peaked at No.49, No.30, No.33, No.28 and No.18 in 1970, No.22 and No.39 in 1971 and No.50 in 1972. 'Theme from 'New York, New York' reached its peak position only on re-entry in Feb 1996. 'All the Way' and 'Chicago' were at first billed separately, then together for one week, then 'All the Way' on its own. 'I've Got You Under My Skin' was the flip side of 'Stay (Faraway So Close)' by U2. Songs for Swingin' Lovers was re-released in 1998 with the catalogue number Capitol CDP 7465702.

Nancy SINATRA 499 Top 500

The eldest child of the legendary Frank Sinatra, b. 8 Jun 1940, New Jersey – just days before his first Top 10 entry. She was the subject of his 1945 hit 'Nancy (With the Laughing Eyes)'. After a slow start to her career she had a string of mid-60's hits thanks in part to her producer / songwriter and sometime co-vocalist Lee Hazlewood (6 Albums: 32 Weeks, 10 Singles: 117 Weeks)

27 Jan 66 ★ THESE BOOTS ARE MADE FOR WALKIN' *Reprise R 20432* ▲ $..........1 14
16 Apr 66 BOOTS *Reprise R 6202*..........12 9
28 Apr 66 HOW DOES THAT GRAB YOU DARLIN' *Reprise R 20461*..........19 8
18 Jun 66 HOW DOES THAT GRAB YOU? *Reprise R 6207*..........17 3
19 Jan 67 ● SUGAR TOWN *Reprise RS 20527* $..........8 10
23 Mar 67 ★ SOMETHIN' STUPID *Reprise RS 23166* 1 ▲ $..........1 18

10 June 1989	17 June 1989	24 June 1989	1 July 1989
UK No.1 SINGLES			
SEALED WITH A KISS Jason Donovan	SEALED WITH A KISS Jason Donovan	BACK TO LIFE (HOWEVER DO YOU WANT ME) Soul II Soul featuring Caron Wheeler	FERRY 'CROSS THE MERSEY The Christians, Holly Johnson, Paul McCartney, Gerry Marsden and Stock Aitken Waterman
UK No.1 ALBUMS			
TEN GOOD REASONS Jason Donovan	TEN GOOD REASONS Jason Donovan	FLOWERS IN THE DIRT Paul McCartney	BATMAN (Film Soundtrack) Prince

5 Jul 67 **YOU ONLY LIVE TWICE / JACKSON** *Reprise RS 20595* [2] 11 19
8 Nov 67 **LADYBIRD** *Reprise RS 20629* [3] 47 1
29 Jun 68 **NANCY / LEE 3** *Reprise RSLP 6273* [1] 17 12
29 Nov 69 **THE HIGHWAY SONG** *Reprise RS 20869*......21 10
10 Oct 70 **NANCY'S GREATEST HITS** *Reprise RSLP 6409*......39 3
21 Aug 71 ● **DID YOU EVER** *Reprise K 14093* [4] 2 19
25 Sep 71 **NANCY / LEE 3** (re-issues) *Reprise K 44126* [1] 42 1
29 Jan 72 **DID YOU EVER** *RCA Victor SF 8240* [1] 31 4
23 Oct 04 **LET ME KISS YOU** *Attack ATKXS 005*......46 1
4 Jun 05 ● **SHOT YOU DOWN** *Source SOURCDX 111* [5] 3 17

[1] Nancy Sinatra and Frank Sinatra [2] Nancy Sinatra / Nancy Sinatra and Lee Hazlewood [3] Nancy Sinatra and Lee Hazlewood [4] Nancy and Lee [5] Audio Bullys featuring Nancy Sinatra [1] Nancy Sinatra and Lee Hazlewood

'Jackson' listed with 'You Only Live Twice' from 12 Jul 1967.

SINCLAIR *UK, male vocalist – Mike Sinclair (3 Singles: 8 Weeks)*

21 Aug 93 **AIN'T NO CASANOVA** *Dome CDDOME 1004*......28 5
26 Feb 94 **(I WANNA KNOW) WHY** *Dome CDDOME 1009*......58 2
6 Aug 94 **DON'T LIE** *Dome CDDOME 1010*......70 1

Bob SINCLAR *France, male DJ / producer (6 Singles: 21 Weeks)*

20 Mar 99 **MY ONLY LOVE** *East West EW 196CD* [1] 56 1
19 Aug 00 ● **I FEEL FOR YOU** *Defected DEFECT 18CDS*......9 5
7 Apr 01 **DARLIN'** *Defected DFECT 30CDS* [2] 46 1
25 Jan 03 **THE BEAT GOES ON** *Defected DFTD 062CDS*......33 2
2 Aug 03 **KISS MY EYES** *Defected DFTD 070CDS*......67 1
22 Oct 05 **LOVE GENERATION** *Defected DFTD 111CDX* [3] ......12 11+

[1] Bob Sinclar featuring Lee A Genesis [2] Bob Sinclar featuring James Williams [3] Bob Sinclar featuring Gary Pine

SINDY *UK, female doll vocalist*

5 Oct 96 **SATURDAY NIGHT** *Love This LUVTHISCD 13*......70 1

SINE *US, male / female vocal / instrumental group*

10 Jun 78 **JUST LET ME DO MY THING** *CBS 6351*......33 9

Talvin SINGH *UK, male multi-instrumentalist (2 Albums: 5 Weeks)*

18 Sep 99 **OK** *Island CID 8075*......41 4
7 Apr 01 **HA** *Island CID 8103*......57 1

SINGING CORNER meets DONOVAN
UK, male vocal duo / comedians and vocalist

1 Dec 90 **JENNIFER JUNIPER** *Fontana SYP 1*......68 1

The SINGING NUN (Soeur Sourire)
Belgium, female vocalist – Jeanine Deckers, b. 17 Oct 1933, d. 31 Mar 1985

5 Dec 63 ● **DOMINIQUE** *Philips BF 1293* ▲ $ 7 14

SINGING SHEEP *UK, computerised sheep noises*

18 Dec 82 **BAA BAA BLACK SHEEP** *Sheep BAA 1*......42 5

Maxine SINGLETON *US, female vocalist*

2 Apr 83 **YOU CAN'T RUN FROM LOVE** *Creole CR 50*......57 3

SINITTA *US, female vocalist – Sinitta Malone (2 Albums: 23 Weeks, 12 Singles: 104 Weeks)*

8 Mar 86 ● **SO MACHO / CRUISING (re)** *Fanfare FAN 7*......2 28
11 Oct 86 **FEELS LIKE THE FIRST TIME** *Fanfare FAN 8*......45 5
25 Jul 87 ● **TOY BOY** *Fanfare FAN 12*......4 14
12 Dec 87 **G.T.O.** *Fanfare FAN 14*......15 9
26 Dec 87 **SINITTA!** *Fanfare BOYLP 1*......34 19
19 Mar 88 ● **CROSS MY BROKEN HEART** *Fanfare FAN 15*......6 9
24 Sep 88 **I DON'T BELIEVE IN MIRACLES** *Fanfare FAN 16*......22 8
3 Jun 89 ● **RIGHT BACK WHERE WE STARTED FROM** *Fanfare FAN 18*......4 10
7 Oct 89 **LOVE ON A MOUNTAIN TOP** *Fanfare FAN 21*......20 6
9 Dec 89 **WICKED!** *Fanfare FARE 2*......52 4
21 Apr 90 **HITCHIN' A RIDE** *Fanfare FAN 24*......24 6
22 Sep 90 **LOVE AND AFFECTION** *Fanfare FAN 31*......62 3
4 Jul 92 **SHAME SHAME SHAME** *Arista 74321100327*......28 4
17 Apr 93 **THE SUPREME EP** *Arista 74321139592*......49 2

Tracks on The Supreme EP: Where Did Our Love Go / Stop! In the Name of Love / You Can't Hurry Love / Remember Me.

SINNAMON *US, male vocal / instrumental group*

28 Sep 96 **I NEED YOU NOW** *Worx WORXCD 003*......70 1

SIOUXSIE and The BANSHEES (240 Top 500) (see also GLOVE)

Long-running commercially successful UK punk band included Susan 'Siouxsie' Ballion (v), Steve Severin (b) (also recorded as The Glove), Siouxsie's husband, Peter 'Budgie' Clark (d) (who recorded with Siouxsie as The Creatures) and, at times, Cure front man Robert Smith (g) (14 Albums: 119 Weeks, 30 Singles: 150 Weeks)

26 Aug 78 ● **HONG KONG GARDEN** *Polydor 2059 052*......7 10
2 Dec 78 **THE SCREAM** *Polydor POLD 5009*......12 11
31 Mar 79 **THE STAIRCASE (MYSTERY)** *Polydor POSP 9*......24 8
7 Jul 79 **PLAYGROUND TWIST** *Polydor POSP 59*......28 6
22 Sep 79 **JOIN HANDS** *Polydor POLD 5024*......13 5
29 Sep 79 **MITTAGEISEN (METAL POSTCARD)** *Polydor 2059 151*......47 3
15 Mar 80 **HAPPY HOUSE** *Polydor POSP 117*......17 8
7 Jun 80 **CHRISTINE** *Polydor 2059 249*......22 8
16 Aug 80 ● **KALEIDOSCOPE** *Polydor 2442 177*......5 6
6 Dec 80 **ISRAEL** *Polydor POSP 205*......41 8
30 May 81 **SPELLBOUND** *Polydor POSP 273*......22 8
27 Jun 81 ● **JU JU** *Polydor POLS 1034*......7 17
1 Aug 81 **ARABIAN KNIGHTS** *Polydor POSP 309*......32 7
12 Dec 81 **ONCE UPON A TIME – THE SINGLES** *Polydor POLS 1056*......21 26
29 May 82 **FIRE WORKS** *Polydor POSPG 450*......22 6
9 Oct 82 **SLOWDIVE** *Polydor POSP 510*......41 4
13 Nov 82 **A KISS IN THE DREAMHOUSE** *Polydor POLD 5064*......11 11
4 Dec 82 **MELT / IL EST NE LE DIVIN ENFANT** *Polydor POSP 539*......49 5
1 Oct 83 ● **DEAR PRUDENCE** *Wonderland SHE 4*......3 8
3 Dec 83 **NOCTURNE** *Wonderland SHAH 1*......29 10
24 Mar 84 **SWIMMING HORSES** *Wonderland SHE 6*......28 4
2 Jun 84 **DAZZLE** *Wonderland SHE 7*......33 3
16 Jun 84 **HYAENA** *Wonderland SHELP 2*......15 6
27 Oct 84 **THE THORN EP** *Wonderland SHEEP 8*......47 3
26 Oct 85 **CITIES IN DUST** *Wonderland SHE 9*......21 6
8 Mar 86 **CANDYMAN** *Wonderland SHE 10*......34 5
26 Apr 86 **TINDERBOX** *Wonderland SHELP 3*......13 6
17 Jan 87 **THIS WHEEL'S ON FIRE** *Wonderland SHE 11*......14 6
14 Mar 87 **THROUGH THE LOOKING GLASS** *Wonderland SHELP 4*......15 8
28 Mar 87 **THE PASSENGER** *Wonderland SHE 12*......41 6
25 Jul 87 **SONG FROM THE EDGE OF THE WORLD** *Wonderland SHE 13*..59 3
30 Jul 88 **PEEK-A-BOO** *Wonderland SHE 14*......16 6
17 Sep 88 **PEEPSHOW** *Wonderland SHELP 5*......20 5
8 Oct 88 **THE KILLING JAR** *Wonderland SHE 15*......41 3
3 Dec 88 **THE LAST BEAT OF MY HEART** *Wonderland SHE 16*......44 1
25 May 91 **KISS THEM FOR ME** *Wonderland SHE 19*......32 4
22 Jun 91 **SUPERSTITION** *Wonderland 8477311*......25 4
13 Jul 91 **SHADOWTIME** *Wonderland SHE 20*......57 1
25 Jul 92 **FACE TO FACE** *Wonderland SHE 21*......21 4
17 Oct 92 **TWICE UPON A TIME – THE SINGLES** *Wonderland 5171602*......26 2
20 Aug 94 **INTERLUDE** *Parlophone CDR 6365* [1] 25 2
7 Jan 95 **O BABY** *Wonderland SHECD 22*......34 3
28 Jan 95 **THE RAPTURE** *Wonderland 5237252*......33 2
18 Feb 95 **STARGAZER** *Wonderland SHECD 23*......64 1

[1] Morrissey and Siouxsie

Tracks on The Thorn EP: Overground / Voices / Placebo Effect / Red Over White.

SIR DOUGLAS QUINTET *US, male vocal / instrumental group – leader Doug Sahm, b. 6 Nov 1941, d. 18 Nov 1999*

17 Jun 65 **SHE'S ABOUT A MOVER** *London HLU 9964*......15 10

8 July 1989	15 July 1989	22 July 1989	29 July 1989
BACK TO LIFE (HOWEVER DO YOU WANT ME) Soul II Soul featuring Caron Wheeler	**BACK TO LIFE (HOWEVER DO YOU WANT ME)** Soul II Soul featuring Caron Wheeler	**YOU'LL NEVER STOP ME LOVING YOU** Sonia	**YOU'LL NEVER STOP ME LOVING YOU** Sonia
VELVETEEN Transvision Vamp	**CLUB CLASSICS VOL. ONE** Soul II Soul	**A NEW FLAME** Simply Red	**A NEW FLAME** Simply Red

KEY: UK No.1 ★★ UK Top 10 ●● Still on chart ++ UK entry at No.1 ■■ US No.1 ▲▲ UK million seller £ US million seller $
Singles re-entries are listed as (re), (2re), (3re)... which signifies that the hit re-entered the chart once, twice or three times...
Peak Position / Weeks

SIR KILLALOT vs ROBO BABE
UK, male robot rapper and female vocalist

30 Dec 00 **ROBOT WARS (ANDROID LOVE)** *Polydor 5879362* 51 3

SIR MIX-A-LOT *US, male rapper – Anthony Ray*

8 Aug 92 **BABY GOT BACK** *Def American DEFA 20* ▲ $ 56 2

SIRENS *UK, female vocal group*

28 Aug 04 **BABY (OFF THE WALL)** *Kitchenware SKCD 742* 49 1

SISQO (see also DRU HILL)
US, male vocalist – Mark Andrews (2 Albums: 41 Weeks, 5 Singles: 43 Weeks)

12 Feb 00 **GOT TO GET IT** *Def Soul 5626442* 14 4
26 Feb 00 UNLEASH THE DRAGON *Def Soul 5469392* 15 36
22 Apr 00 ● **THONG SONG** *Def Soul 5688902* 3 14
30 Sep 00 ● **UNLEASH THE DRAGON** *Def Soul 5726422* 6 7
16 Dec 00 **INCOMPLETE** *Def Soul 5727542* ▲ $ 13 8
28 Jul 01 ● **DANCE FOR ME** *Def Soul 5887002* 6 10
4 Aug 01 RETURN OF DRAGON *Def Soul 5864182* 22 5

SISSEL *Norway, female vocalist –*
Sissel Kyrkjebo (2 Albums: 56 Weeks, 1 Single: 7 Weeks)

20 May 95 DEEP WITHIN MY SOUL *Mercury 5267752* 58 1
10 Jan 98 **PRINCE IGOR** *Def Jam 5749652* [1] 15 7
30 Jan 98 ★ TITANIC (FILM SOUNDTRACK) *Sony Classical SK 63213* [1] 1 55

[1] Warren G featuring Sissel [1] James Horner – vocals by Sissel

SISTER BLISS (see also FAITHLESS) *UK, female DJ / producer / multi-instrumentalist – Ayalah Ben-Tovim (5 Singles: 11 Weeks)*

15 Oct 94 **CANTGETAMAN CANTGETAJOB (LIFE'S A BITCH)** *Go Beat GODCD 124* [1] 31 4
15 Jul 95 **OH! WHAT A WORLD** *Go Beat GODCD 126* [1] 40 2
29 Jun 96 **BAD MAN** *Junk Dog JDOGCD 1* 51 1
7 Oct 00 **SISTER SISTER** *Multiply CDMULTY 68* 34 2
24 Mar 01 **DELIVER ME** *Multiply CDMULTY 72* [2] 31 2

[1] Sister Bliss featuring Collette [2] Sister Bliss featuring John Martyn

SISTER SLEDGE (428 Top 500)
Successful US family group from Philadelphia: Kathy, Debra, Joni and Kim Sledge. They found more fame in the UK than in the US, and recorded some of the best-known disco records with noted producers / songwriters Nile Rodgers and Bernard Edwards (4 Albums: 58 Weeks, 14 Singles: 111 Weeks)

21 Jun 75 **MAMA NEVER TOLD ME** *Atlantic K 10619* 20 6
17 Mar 79 ● **HE'S THE GREATEST DANCER** *Atlantic / Cotillion K 11257* 6 11
12 May 79 ● WE ARE FAMILY *Atlantic K 50587* 7 39
26 May 79 ● **WE ARE FAMILY** *Atlantic / Cotillion K 11293* $ 8 10
11 Aug 79 **LOST IN MUSIC** *Atlantic / Cotillion K 11337* 17 10
19 Jan 80 **GOT TO LOVE SOMEBODY** *Atlantic / Cotillion K 11404* 34 4
28 Feb 81 **ALL AMERICAN GIRLS** *Atlantic K 11656* 41 5
26 May 84 **THINKING OF YOU** *Cotillion / Atlantic B 9744* 11 13
8 Sep 84 ● **LOST IN MUSIC** (re-mix) *Cotillion / Atlantic B 9718* 4 12
17 Nov 84 **WE ARE FAMILY** (re-mix) *Cotillion / Atlantic B 9692* 33 4
1 Jun 85 ★ **FRANKIE** *Atlantic A 9547* 1 16
22 Jun 85 WHEN THE BOYS MEET THE GIRLS *Atlantic 7812551* 19 11
31 Aug 85 **DANCING ON THE JAGGED EDGE** *Atlantic A 9520* 50 3
5 Dec 87 FREAK OUT *Telstar STAR 2319* [1] 72 3
23 Jan 93 ● **WE ARE FAMILY** (2nd re-mix) *Atlantic A 4508CD* 5 8
20 Feb 93 THE VERY BEST OF SISTER SLEDGE 1973-1993 *Atlantic 9548318132* 19 5
13 Mar 93 **LOST IN MUSIC** (2nd re-mix) *Atlantic A 4509CD* 14 5
12 Jun 93 **THINKING OF YOU** (re-mix) *Atlantic A 4515CD* 17 4

[1] Chic and Sister Sledge

SISTER 2 SISTER
Australia, female vocal duo – Christine and Sharon Muscat (2 Singles: 5 Weeks)

22 Apr 00 **SISTER** *Mushroom MUSH 70CDS* 18 4
28 Oct 00 **WHAT'S A GIRL TO DO** *Mushroom MUSH 76CDS* 61 1

SISTERHOOD *UK, male vocal / instrumental group*

26 Jul 86 GIFT *Merciful Release SIS 020* 90 1

The SISTERS OF MERCY *UK, male / female vocal / instrumental group – leader Andrew Eldritch (5 Albums: 42 Weeks, 10 Singles: 40 Weeks)*

16 Jun 84 **BODY AND SOUL / TRAIN** *Merciful Release MR 029* 46 3
20 Oct 84 **WALK AWAY** *Merciful Release MR 033* 45 3
9 Mar 85 **NO TIME TO CRY** *Merciful Release MR 035* 63 2
23 Mar 85 FIRST AND LAST AND ALWAYS *Merciful Release MR 337L* 14 8
3 Oct 87 ● **THIS CORROSION** *Merciful Release MR 39* 7 6
28 Nov 87 ● FLOODLAND *Merciful Release MR 441L* 9 20
27 Feb 88 **DOMINION** *Merciful Release MR 43* 13 6
18 Jun 88 **LUCRETIA MY REFLECTION** *Merciful Release MR 45* 20 4
13 Oct 90 **MORE** *Merciful Release MR 47* 14 4
2 Nov 90 VISION THING *Merciful Release 9031726632* 11 4
22 Dec 90 **DOCTOR JEEP** *Merciful Release MR 51* 37 4
2 May 92 ● **TEMPLE OF LOVE** *Merciful Release MR 53* 3 5
9 May 92 ● SOME GIRLS WANDER BY MISTAKE *Merciful Release 9031764762* [1] 5 5
28 Aug 93 **UNDER THE GUN** *Merciful Release MR 59CDX* 19 3
4 Sep 93 GREATEST HITS VOLUME 1 *Merciful Release 4509935792* 14 5

[1] Sisters

Act was male only for first album.

SIVUCA *Brazil, male accordion player – Severino Dias De Oliveira*

28 Jul 84 **AIN'T NO SUNSHINE** *London LON 51* 56 3

SIX BY SEVEN
UK, male vocal / instrumental group (1 Album: 1 Week, 2 Singles: 2 Weeks)

9 May 98 **CANDLELIGHT** *Mantra MNT 34CD* 70 1
2 Mar 02 **I.O.U. LOVE** *Mantra MNT 68CD* 48 1
23 Mar 02 THE WAY I FEEL TODAY *Mantra MNTCD 1027* 69 1

6 BY SIX *UK, male instrumental / production duo*

4 May 96 **INTO YOUR HEART** *Six6 SIXCD 130* 51 1

SIX CHIX *UK, female vocal group*

26 Feb 00 **ONLY THE WOMEN KNOW** *EMI CDCHIX 001* 72 1

666 *Germany, male production duo –*
Thomas Detert and Mike Griesheimer (2 Singles: 5 Weeks)

3 Oct 98 **ALARMA** *Danceteria CDDAN 001* 58 1
25 Nov 00 **DEVIL** *Echo ECSCD 102* 18 4

SIXPENCE NONE THE RICHER *US, male / female vocal (Leigh Nash) / instrumental group (1 Album: 3 Weeks, 2 Singles: 17 Weeks)*

29 May 99 ● **KISS ME** *Elektra E 3750CD* 4 12
26 Jun 99 SIXPENCE NONE THE RICHER *Elektra 7559624202* 27 3
18 Sep 99 **THERE SHE GOES** *Elektra E 3728CD* 14 5

60FT DOLLS
UK, male vocal / instrumental group (1 Album: 2 Weeks, 4 Singles: 4 Weeks)

3 Feb 96 **STAY** *Indolent DOLLS 002CD* 48 1
11 May 96 **TALK TO ME** *Indolent DOLLS 003CD* 37 1
8 Jun 96 THE BIG 3 *Indolent DOLLSCD 004* 36 2

5 August 1989	12 August 1989	19 August 1989	26 August 1989
UK No.1 SINGLES			
SWING THE MOOD Jive Bunny and The Mastermixers	SWING THE MOOD Jive Bunny and The Mastermixers	SWING THE MOOD Jive Bunny and The Mastermixers	SWING THE MOOD Jive Bunny and The Mastermixers
UK No.1 ALBUMS			
CUTS BOTH WAYS Gloria Estefan	CUTS BOTH WAYS Gloria Estefan	CUTS BOTH WAYS Gloria Estefan	CUTS BOTH WAYS Gloria Estefan

20 Jul 96 **HAPPY SHOPPER** *Indolent DOLLS 005CD*....38 1
9 May 98 **ALISON'S ROOM** *Indolent DOLLS 007CD1*....61 1

SIZE 9
(see also Josh WINK) *US, male producer – Josh Wink (2 Singles: 4 Weeks)*

17 Jun 95 **I'M READY** *Virgin America VUSCD 92*....52 1
11 Nov 95 **I'M READY** (re-issue) *VC VCRD 2* [1] 30 3

[1] Josh Wink's Size 9

Roni SIZE / REPRAZENT
UK, male producer – Ryan Williams and male / female vocal / instrumental group (3 Albums: 39 Weeks, 18 Singles: 32 Weeks)

14 Jun 97 **SHARE THE FALL** *Talkin Loud TLCD 21*....37 2
5 Jul 97 ● NEW FORMS *Talkin Loud 5349332*....8 34
13 Sep 97 **HEROES** *Talkin Loud TLCD 25*....31 2
15 Nov 97 **BROWN PAPER BAG** *Talkin Loud TLCD 28*....20 3
14 Mar 98 **WATCHING WINDOWS** *Talkin Loud TLCD 31*....28 2
7 Oct 00 **WHO TOLD YOU** *Talkin Loud TLCD 61*....17 3
21 Oct 00 IN THE MODE *Talkin Loud 5481762*....15 4
24 Mar 01 **DIRTY BEATS** *Talkin Loud TLCDD 63*....32 3
23 Jun 01 **LUCKY PRESSURE** *Talkin Loud TLCD 64*....58 1
19 Oct 02 **SOUND ADVICE** (re-mix) *Full Cycle FCY 044* [1] 69 1
2 Nov 02 TOUCHING DOWN *Full Cycle FCYCDLP 010* [1] 72 1
9 Nov 02 **PLAYTIME** *Full Cycle FCY 045* [1] 53 2
7 Dec 02 **SCRAMBLED EGGS / SWINGS & ROUNDABOUTS** *Full Cycle FCY 046* [1] 57 1
18 Jan 03 **FEEL THE HEAT** *Full Cycle FCY 048* [1] 55 1
22 Feb 03 **SNAPSHOT 3 / SORRY FOR YOU** *Full Cycle FCY 033* [1] 61 1
12 Jul 03 **SIREN SOUNDS / AT THE MOVIES** *Full Cycle FCY 054* [1] 67 1
6 Sep 03 **SOUND ADVICE** (re-issue) **/ FORGET ME NOTS** *Full Cycle FCY 056* [1] 61 1
17 Apr 04 **STRICTLY SOCIAL / AUTUMN** *Liquid V LQD 001* [2] 70 1
24 Apr 04 **BAMBAKITA / FASSY HOLE** *V VO 45* [1] 60 1
9 Oct 04 **OUT OF BREATH** *V VRECUK 002X* [3] 44 2
22 Jan 05 **NO MORE** *V VRECSUK 003CD* [4] 26 4

[1] Roni Size [2] Roni Size and Die [3] Roni Size featuring Rahzel [4] Roni Size featuring Beverley Knight & Dynamite MC [1] Roni Size

'Sound Advice' (6 Sep 2003) is a re-mix of the track from 19 Oct 2002.

SIZZLA *Jamaica, male rapper – Miguel Collins*

17 Apr 99 **RAIN SHOWERS** *Xterminator EXTCDS 76*....51 2

SKANDAL *UK, male vocal group*

14 Oct 00 **CHAMPAGNE HIGHWAY** *Prestige Management CDGING 1*....53 1

SKANDI GIRLS *Sweden / Norway / Finland, female vocal group*

25 Dec 04 **DO THE CAN CAN** *Intelligent IR 001CDX*....38 3

The SKATALITES *Jamaica, male instrumental group*

20 Apr 67 **GUNS OF NAVARONE** *Island WI 168*....36 6

SKEE-LO *US, male rapper – Antoine Roundtree (2 Singles: 10 Weeks)*

9 Dec 95 **I WISH** *Wild Card 5777752*....15 8
27 Apr 96 **TOP OF THE STAIRS** *Wild Card 5763352*....38 2

Peter SKELLERN (see also OASIS)
UK, male vocalist / keyboard player (4 Albums: 31 Weeks, 3 Singles: 24 Weeks)

23 Sep 72 ● **YOU'RE A LADY** *Decca F 13333*....3 11
29 Mar 75 **HOLD ON TO LOVE** *Decca F 13568*....14 9
9 Sep 78 SKELLERN *Mercury 9109 701*....48 3
28 Oct 78 **LOVE IS THE SWEETEST THING** *Mercury 6008 603* [1] 60 4
8 Dec 79 ASTAIRE *Mercury 9102 702*....23 20
4 Dec 82 A STRING OF PEARLS *Mercury MERL 10*....67 5
1 Apr 95 STARDUST MEMORIES *WEA 4509981322*....50 3

[1] Peter Skellern featuring the Grimethorpe Colliery Band

SKID ROW *UK, male vocal / instrumental group*

17 Oct 70 SKID *CBS 63965*....30 3

SKID ROW *US, male vocal (Sebastian Bach) / instrumental group (3 Albums: 28 Weeks, 8 Singles: 27 Weeks)*

2 Sep 89 SKID ROW *Atlantic 781936 1*....30 16
18 Nov 89 **YOUTH GONE WILD** *Atlantic A 8935*....42 3
3 Feb 90 **18 AND LIFE** *Atlantic A 8883*....12 6
31 Mar 90 **I REMEMBER YOU** *East West A 8886*....36 4
15 Jun 91 **MONKEY BUSINESS** *Atlantic A 7673*....19 3
22 Jun 91 ● SLAVE TO THE GRIND *Atlantic WX 423* ▲....5 9
14 Sep 91 **SLAVE TO THE GRIND** *Atlantic A 7603*....43 2
23 Nov 91 **WASTED TIME** *Atlantic A 7570*....20 3
29 Aug 92 **YOUTH GONE WILD** (re-issue) **/ DELIVERING THE GOODS** *Atlantic A 7444*....22 4
8 Apr 95 ● SUBHUMAN RACE *Atlantic 7567827302*....8 3
18 Nov 95 **BREAKIN' DOWN** *Atlantic A 7135CD 1*....48 2

The SKIDS *UK, male vocal (Richard Jobson) / instrumental group (4 Albums: 21 Weeks, 10 Singles: 60 Weeks)*

23 Sep 78 **SWEET SUBURBIA (re)** *Virgin VS 227*....70 3
4 Nov 78 **THE SAINTS ARE COMING** *Virgin VS 232*....48 3
17 Feb 79 ● **INTO THE VALLEY** *Virgin VS 241*....10 11
17 Mar 79 SCARED TO DANCE *Virgin V 2116*....19 10
26 May 79 **MASQUERADE** *Virgin VS 262*....14 9
29 Sep 79 **CHARADE** *Virgin VS 288*....31 6
27 Oct 79 DAYS IN EUROPA *Virgin V 2138*....32 5
24 Nov 79 **WORKING FOR THE YANKEE DOLLAR** *Virgin VS 306*....20 11
1 Mar 80 **ANIMATION** *Virgin VS 323*....56 3
16 Aug 80 **CIRCUS GAMES** *Virgin VS 359*....32 7
27 Sep 80 ● THE ABSOLUTE GAME *Virgin V 2174*....9 5
18 Oct 80 **GOODBYE CIVILIAN** *Virgin VS 373*....52 4
6 Dec 80 **WOMAN IN WINTER** *Virgin VSK 101*....49 3
8 Jun 02 THE GREATEST HITS OF BIG COUNTRY AND THE SKIDS – THE BEST OF STUART ADAMSON *UMTV 5869892* [1] 71 1

[1] Big Country and The Skids

SKIN *UK / Germany, male vocal (Neville MacDonald) / instrumental group (3 Albums: 5 Weeks, 8 Singles: 19 Weeks)*

25 Dec 93 **THE SKIN UP EP** *Parlophone CDR 6363*....67 2
12 Mar 94 **HOUSE OF LOVE** *Parlophone CDR 6374*....45 2
30 Apr 94 **THE MONEY EP** *Parlophone CDR 6381*....18 3
14 May 94 ● SKIN *Parlophone CDPCSD 151*....9 3
23 Jul 94 **TOWER OF STRENGTH** *Parlophone CDR 6387*....19 3
15 Oct 94 **LOOK BUT DON'T TOUCH (EP)** *Parlophone CDRS 6391*....33 3
20 May 95 **TAKE ME DOWN TO THE RIVER** *Parlophone CDR 6409*....26 2
23 Mar 96 **HOW LUCKY YOU ARE** *Parlophone CDR 6426*....32 2
6 Apr 96 LUCKY *Parlophone CDPCSD 168*....38 1
18 May 96 **PERFECT DAY** *Parlophone CDR 6433*....33 2
13 Sep 97 EXPERIENCE ELECTRIC *Reef Recordings SRECD 705*....72 1

Tracks on The Skin Up EP: Look But Don't Touch / Shine Your Light / Monkey. Tracks on The Money EP: Money / Unbelievable / Express Yourself / Funktified. Tracks on Look But Don't Touch (EP): Look But Don't Touch / Should I Stay or Should I Go / Pump It Up / Monkey (re-issue).

SKIN (see also SKUNK ANANSIE)
UK, female vocalist – Deborah Dyer (1 Album: 2 Weeks, 4 Singles: 6 Weeks)

10 Jun 00 **CARMEN QUEASY** *XL Recordings XLS 119CD* [1] 33 2
20 Jul 02 **GOOD TIMES** *Columbia 6727672* [2] 49 1
7 Jun 03 **TRASHED** *EMI CDEM 622*....30 2
14 Jun 03 FLESHWOUNDS *EMI 5841592*....43 2
20 Sep 03 **FAITHFULNESS** *EMI CDEM 624*....64 1

[1] Maxim: vocal by Skin [2] Ed Case featuring Skin

SKIN UP *UK, male producer – Jason Cohen (3 Singles: 9 Weeks)*

7 Sep 91 **IVORY** *Love EVOL 4*....48 3
14 Mar 92 **A JUICY RED APPLE** *Love EVOL 11*....32 4
18 Jul 92 **ACCELERATE** *Love EVOL 17*....45 2

2 September 1989	9 September 1989	16 September 1989	23 September 1989
SWING THE MOOD Jive Bunny and The Mastermixers	**RIDE ON TIME** Black Box	**RIDE ON TIME** Black Box	**RIDE ON TIME** Black Box
CUTS BOTH WAYS Gloria Estefan	**CUTS BOTH WAYS** Gloria Estefan	**ASPECTS OF LOVE** Original London Cast	**WE TOO ARE ONE** Eurythmics

KEY		
UK No.1 ★ UK Top 10 ● Still on chart + UK entry at No.1 ■ US No.1 ▲ UK million seller £ US million seller $ Singles re-entries are listed as (re), (2re), (3re)... which signifies that the hit re-entered the chart once, twice or three times...	Peak Position	Weeks

SKINNY *UK, male vocal / instrumental / production duo – Matt Benbrook and Paul Herman*

11 Apr 98 **FAILURE** *Cheeky CHEKCD 023* **31** 2

SKINNYMAN *UK, male rapper*

21 Aug 04 COUNCIL ESTATE OF MIND *Lowlife LOW 36CD* 65 1

SKIP RAIDERS featuring JADA *UK, male production duo and female vocalist*

15 Jul 00 **ANOTHER DAY** *Perfecto PERF 4CDS* **46** 1

SKIPWORTH & TURNER *US, male vocal duo – Rodney Skipworth and Phil Turner (2 Singles: 12 Weeks)*

27 Apr 85 **THINKING ABOUT YOUR LOVE** *Fourth & Broadway BRW 23* **24** 10
21 Jan 89 **MAKE IT LAST** *Fourth & Broadway BRW 118* **60** 2

SKUNK ANANSIE (see also MAXIM) *UK, female / male vocal (Deborah Dyer aka Skin) / instrumental group (3 Albums: 101 Weeks, 12 Singles: 41 Weeks)*

25 Mar 95 **SELLING JESUS** *One Little Indian 101TP 7CD* **46** 1
17 Jun 95 **I CAN DREAM** *One Little Indian 121TP 7CD* **41** 2
2 Sep 95 **CHARITY** *One Little Indian 131TP 7CD* **40** 2
30 Sep 95 ● PARANOID & SUNBURNT *One Little Indian TPLP 55CD* 8 32
27 Jan 96 **WEAK** *One Little Indian 141TP 7CD* **20** 5
27 Apr 96 **CHARITY** (re-issue) *One Little Indian 151TP 7CD* **20** 3
28 Sep 96 **ALL I WANT** *One Little Indian 161TP 7CD* **14** 4
19 Oct 96 ● STOOSH *One Little Indian TPLP 85CD* 9 55
30 Nov 96 **TWISTED (EVERYDAY HURTS)** *One Little Indian 171TP 7CD* **26** 4
1 Feb 97 **HEDONISM (JUST BECAUSE YOU FEEL GOOD)** *One Little Indian 181TP 7CD* **13** 6
14 Jun 97 **BRAZEN 'WEEP'** *One Little Indian 191TP 7CD1* **11** 5
13 Mar 99 **CHARLIE BIG POTATO** *Virgin VSCDT 1725* **17** 3
3 Apr 99 POST ORGASMIC CHILL *Virgin CDV 2881* 16 14
22 May 99 **SECRETLY** *Virgin VSCDT 1733* **16** 4
7 Aug 99 **LATELY** *Virgin VSCDT 1738* **33** 2

SKY (323 Top 500) *Anglo-Australian jazz-rock fusion quintet with a progressive element. Classical guitarist John Williams OBE was joined by similarly accomplished instrumentalists including Herbie Flowers (b) and Tristan Fry (d). In Feb 1981, Sky gave the only concert ever held in Westminster Abbey (8 Albums: 202 Weeks, 1 Single: 11 Weeks)*

2 Jun 79 ● SKY *Ariola ARLH 5022* 9 56
5 Apr 80 ● **TOCCATA** *Ariola ARO 300* **5** 11
26 Apr 80 ★ SKY 2 *Ariola ADSKY 2* 1 53
28 Mar 81 ● SKY 3 *Ariola ASKY 3* 3 23
3 Apr 82 ● SKY 4 – FORTHCOMING *Ariola ASKY 4* 7 22
22 Jan 83 SKY FIVE LIVE *Ariola 302 171* 14 14
3 Dec 83 CADMIUM *Ariola 205 885* 44 10
12 May 84 MASTERPIECES – THE VERY BEST OF SKY *Telstar STAR 2241* 15 18
13 Apr 85 THE GREAT BALLOON RACE *Epic EPC 26419* 63 6

The SKYHOOKS *Australia, male vocal / instrumental group*

9 Jun 79 **WOMEN IN UNIFORM** *United Artists UP 36508* **73** 1

SKYLARK *UK / France, male DJ / production group*

27 Mar 04 **THAT'S MORE LIKE IT** *Credence CDCRED 042* **62** 1

SKYY *US, male vocal / instrumental group*

21 Jun 86 FROM THE LEFT SIDE *Capitol EST 2014* 85 1

SLACKER (see also RAMP) *UK, male production duo – Shem McCauley and Simon Rogers (2 Singles: 4 Weeks)*

26 Apr 97 **SCARED** *XL XLS 84CD* **36** 2
30 Aug 97 **YOUR FACE** *XL XLS 87CD* **33** 2

SLADE (82 Top 500)

Top UK group of the 1970s: Noddy Holder (v/g), Dave Hill (g), Jimmy Lea (b/p), Don Powell (d). They were the first act to have three singles enter at No.1. All six of the Wolverhampton band's chart-topping stompers were penned by Holder and Lea. Noddy, who is now a popular TV personality, was made an MBE in 2000. Total UK single sales: 6,520,171. Best-selling single: 'Merry Xmas Everybody' 1,006,500 (18 Albums: 216 Weeks, 36 Singles: 279 Weeks)

19 Jun 71 **GET DOWN AND GET WITH IT** *Polydor 2058 112* **16** 14
30 Oct 71 ★ **COZ I LUV YOU** *Polydor 2058 155* **1** 15
5 Feb 72 ● **LOOK WOT YOU DUN** *Polydor 2058 195* **4** 10
8 Apr 72 ● SLADE ALIVE! *Polydor 2383 101* 2 58
3 Jun 72 ★ **TAKE ME BAK 'OME** *Polydor 2058 231* **1** 13
2 Sep 72 ★ **MAMA WEER ALL CRAZEE NOW** *Polydor 2058 274* **1** 10
25 Nov 72 ● **GUDBUY T'JANE** *Polydor 2058 312* **2** 13
9 Dec 72 ★ SLAYED? *Polydor 2383 163* 1 34
3 Mar 73 ★ **CUM ON FEEL THE NOIZE** *Polydor 2058 339* ■ **1** 12
30 Jun 73 ★ **SKWEEZE ME PLEEZE ME** *Polydor 2058 377* ■ **1** 10
6 Oct 73 ★ SLADEST *Polydor 2442 119* ■ 1 24
6 Oct 73 ● **MY FRIEND STAN** *Polydor 2058 407* **2** 8
15 Dec 73 ★ **MERRY XMAS EVERYBODY (4re)** *Polydor 2058 422* ■ £ **1** 25
23 Feb 74 ★ OLD, NEW, BORROWED AND BLUE *Polydor 2383 261* 1 16
6 Apr 74 ● **EVERYDAY** *Polydor 2058 453* **3** 7
6 Jul 74 ● **THE BANGIN' MAN** *Polydor 2058 492* **3** 7
19 Oct 74 ● **FAR FAR AWAY** *Polydor 2058 522* **2** 6
14 Dec 74 ● SLADE IN FLAME *Polydor 2442 126* 6 18
15 Feb 75 **HOW DOES IT FEEL?** *Polydor 2058 547* **15** 7
17 May 75 ● **THANKS FOR THE MEMORY (WHAM BAM THANK YOU MAM)** *Polydor 2058 585* **7** 7
22 Nov 75 **IN FOR A PENNY** *Polydor 2058 663* **11** 8
7 Feb 76 **LET'S CALL IT QUITS** *Polydor 2058 690* **11** 7
27 Mar 76 NOBODY'S FOOL *Polydor 2383 377* 14 4
5 Feb 77 **GYPSY ROADHOG** *Barn 2014 105* **48** 2
29 Oct 77 **MY BABY LEFT ME – THAT'S ALL RIGHT** *Barn 2014 114* **32** 4
18 Oct 80 **SLADE – ALIVE AT READING (EP)** *Cheapskate CHEAP 5* **44** 5
22 Nov 80 SLADE SMASHES *Polydor POLTV 13* 21 15
27 Dec 80 **MERRY XMAS EVERYBODY** (re-recording) *Cheapskate CHEAP 11* [1] **70** 2
31 Jan 81 ● **WE'LL BRING THE HOUSE DOWN** *Cheapskate CHEAP 16* **10** 9
21 Mar 81 WE'LL BRING THE HOUSE DOWN *Cheapskate SKATE 1* 25 4
4 Apr 81 **WHEELS AIN'T COMING DOWN** *Cheapskate CHEAP 21* **60** 3
19 Sep 81 **LOCK UP YOUR DAUGHTERS** *RCA 124* **29** 8
28 Nov 81 TILL DEAF US DO PART *RCA RCALP 6021* 68 2
27 Mar 82 **RUBY RED** *RCA 191* **51** 3
27 Nov 82 **(AND NOW – THE WALTZ) C'EST LA VIE** *RCA 291* **50** 6
18 Dec 82 SLADE ON STAGE *RCA RCALP 3107* 58 3
19 Nov 83 ● **MY OH MY** *RCA 373* **2** 11
24 Dec 83 THE AMAZING KAMIKAZE SYNDROME *RCA PL 70116* 49 13
4 Feb 84 ● **RUN RUNAWAY** *RCA 385* **7** 10
9 Jun 84 SLADE'S GREATS *Polydor SLAD 1* 89 1
17 Nov 84 **ALL JOIN HANDS** *RCA 455* **15** 9
26 Jan 85 **7 YEAR BITCH** *RCA 475* **60** 3
23 Mar 85 **MYZSTERIOUS MIZSTER JONES** *RCA PB 40027* **50** 5
6 Apr 85 ROGUES GALLERY *RCA PL 70604* 60 2
30 Nov 85 CRACKERS – THE CHRISTMAS PARTY ALBUM *Telstar STAR 2271* 34 7
30 Nov 85 **DO YOU BELIEVE IN MIRACLES** *RCA PB 40449* **54** 6
21 Dec 85 **MERRY XMAS EVERYBODY (re)** (re-issue) *Polydor POSP 780* **48** 4
21 Feb 87 **STILL THE SAME** *RCA PB 41137* **73** 2
9 May 87 YOU BOYZ MAKE BIG NOIZE *RCA PL 71260* 98 1
19 Oct 91 **RADIO WALL OF SOUND** *Polydor PO 180* **21** 5
23 Nov 91 WALL OF HITS *Polydor 5116121* 34 5
25 Jan 97 GREATEST HITS – FEEL THE NOIZE *Polydor 5371052* 19 5

26 Dec 98	MERRY XMAS EVERYBODY '98 (2nd re-mix) *Polydor 5633532* [2]	30 3
10 Dec 05	THE VERY BEST OF ... SLADE *Polydor / UMTV 9800715*	39 4+

[1] Slade and the Reading Choir [2] Slade vs Flush

'Merry Xmas Everybody' re-entries peaked at No.32 in 1981, No.67 in 1982, No.20 in 1983, No.47 in 1984 and the re-entry of the 1985 re-issue made No.71 in 1986. Tracks on Slade – Alive at Reading (EP): When I'm Dancin' I Ain't Fightin' / Born to Be Wild / Somethin' Else / Pistol Packin' Mama / Keep a Rollin'.

SLAM
UK, male production duo – Orde Meikle and Stuart McMillan (3 Singles: 4 Weeks)

17 Feb 01	**POSITIVE EDUCATION** *VC Recordings VCRD 84*	44 2
17 Mar 01	**NARCO TOURISTS** *Soma SOMA 100CD* [1]	66 1
7 Jul 01	**LIFETIMES** *Soma SOMA 107CDS* [2]	61 1

[1] Slam vs Unkle [2] Slam featuring Tyrone 'Visionary' Palmer

SLAMM *UK, male vocal / instrumental group (4 Singles: 6 Weeks)*

17 Jul 93	**ENERGIZE** *PWL International PWCD 266*	57 2
23 Oct 93	**VIRGINIA PLAIN** *PWL International PWCD 274*	60 1
22 Oct 94	**THAT'S WHERE MY MIND GOES** *PWL International PWCD 310*	68 1
4 Feb 95	**CAN'T GET BY** *PWL International PWCD 316*	47 2

SLASH'S SNAKEPIT
(see also GUNS N' ROSES) *US, male vocal / instrumental group*

25 Feb 95	IT'S FIVE O'CLOCK SOMEWHERE *Geffen GED 24730*	15 4

Luke SLATER *UK, male producer (2 Singles: 2 Weeks)*

16 Sep 00	**ALL EXHALE** *Novamute CDNOMU 79*	74 1
6 Apr 02	**NOTHING AT ALL** *Mute CDMUTE 261*	70 1

SLAUGHTER
US, male vocal / instrumental group (1 Album: 1 Week, 2 Singles: 2 Weeks)

29 Sep 90	**UP ALL NIGHT** *Chrysalis CHS 3556*	62 1
2 Feb 91	**FLY TO THE ANGELS** *Chrysalis CHS 3634*	55 1
23 May 92	THE WILD LIFE *Chrysalis CCD 1911*	64 1

SLAVE *US, male vocal / instrumental group*

8 Mar 80	**JUST A TOUCH OF LOVE** *Atlantic / Cotillion K 11442*	64 3

SLAYER
US, male vocal / instrumental group (8 Albums: 21 Weeks, 3 Singles: 3 Weeks)

2 May 87	REIGN IN BLOOD *Def Jam LONLP 34*	47 3
13 Jun 87	**CRIMINALLY INSANE** *Def Jam LON 133*	64 1
23 Jul 88	SOUTH OF HEAVEN *London LONLP 63*	25 4
6 Oct 90	SEASONS IN THE ABYSS *Def American 8468711*	18 3
26 Oct 91	**SEASONS IN THE ABYSS** *Def American DEFA 9*	51 1
2 Nov 91	DECADE OF AGGRESSION – LIVE *Def American 5106051*	29 2
15 Oct 94	DIVINE INTERVENTION *American 74321236772*	15 4
9 Sep 95	**SERENITY IN MURDER** *American 74321312482*	50 1
1 Jun 96	UNDISPUTED ATTITUDE *American Recordings 74321357592*	31 2
20 Jun 98	DIABOLUS IN MUSICA *Columbia 4913022*	27 2
22 Sep 01	GOD HATES US ALL *Mercury 5863312*	31 1

SLEAZESISTERS (see also The CANDY GIRLS; CLERGY; DOROTHY; HI-GATE; Paul MASTERSON presents SUSHI; YOMANDA)
UK, male producer – Paul Masterson (3 Singles: 3 Weeks)

29 Jul 95	**SEX** *Pulse 8 CDLOSE 92* [1]	53 1
30 Mar 96	**LET'S WHIP IT UP (YOU GO GIRL)** *Pulse 8 CDLOSE 102* [1]	46 1
26 Sep 98	**WORK IT UP** *Logic 74321616622* [2]	74 1

[1] Sleazesisters with Vikki Shepard [2] Sleaze Sisters

Kathy SLEDGE
(see also SISTER SLEDGE) *US, female vocalist (3 Singles: 7 Weeks)*

16 May 92	**TAKE ME BACK TO LOVE AGAIN** *Epic 6579837*	62 2
18 Feb 95	**ANOTHER STAR** *NRC DEACD 002*	54 1
29 Nov 97	**FREEDOM** *Deconstruction 74321536952* [1]	15 4

[1] Robert Miles featuring Kathy Sledge

Percy SLEDGE *US, male vocalist (1 Album: 4 Weeks, 3 Singles: 34 Weeks)*

12 May 66 ●	**WHEN A MAN LOVES A WOMAN** *Atlantic 584 001* ▲ $	4 17
4 Aug 66	**WARM AND TENDER LOVE** *Atlantic 584 034*	34 7
14 Feb 87 ●	**WHEN A MAN LOVES A WOMAN** (re-issue) *Atlantic YZ 96*	2 10
14 Mar 87	WHEN A MAN LOVES A WOMAN (THE ULTIMATE COLLECTION) *Atlantic WX 89*	36 4

SLEEPER *UK, male / female vocal (Louise Wener) / instrumental group (3 Albums: 48 Weeks, 9 Singles: 29 Weeks)*

21 May 94	**DELICIOUS** *Indolent SLEEP 003CD*	75 1
21 Jan 95	**INBETWEENER** *Indolent SLEEP 006CD*	16 4
25 Feb 95 ●	SMART *Indolent SLEEPCD 007*	5 11
8 Apr 95	**VEGAS** *Indolent SLEEP 008CD*	33 3
7 Oct 95	**WHAT DO I DO NOW** *Indolent SLEEP 009CD1*	14 4
4 May 96 ●	**SALE OF THE CENTURY** *Indolent SLEEP 011CD*	10 5
18 May 96 ●	THE IT GIRL *Indolent SLEEPCD 012*	5 34
13 Jul 96 ●	**NICE GUY EDDIE** *Indolent SLEEP 013CD*	10 5
5 Oct 96	**STATUESQUE** *Indolent SLEEP 014CD1*	17 3
4 Oct 97	**SHE'S A GOOD GIRL** *Indolent SLEEP 015CD*	28 2
25 Oct 97 ●	PLEASED TO MEET YOU *Indolent SLEEPCD 016*	7 3
6 Dec 97	**ROMEO ME** *Indolent SLEEP 17CD1*	39 2

SLEEPY JACKSON
Australia, male vocal / instrumental trio (1 Album: 1 Week, 2 Singles: 2 Weeks)

19 Jul 03	**VAMPIRE RACECOURSE** *Virgin DINSD 261*	50 1
26 Jul 03	LOVERS *Virgin CDVIR 208*	69 1
25 Oct 03	**GOOD DANCERS** *Virgin DINSD 265*	71 1

SLEIGHRIDERS *UK, male vocal / instrumental group*

17 Dec 83	A VERY MERRY DISCO *Warwick WW 5136*	100 1

SLICK *US, male / female vocal / instrumental group (2 Singles: 15 Weeks)*

16 Jun 79	**SPACE BASS** *Fantasy FTC 176*	16 10
15 Sep 79	**SEXY CREAM** *Fantasy FTC 182* [1]	47 5

[1] Slick featuring Doris James

Grace SLICK (see also JEFFERSON AIRPLANE) *US, female vocalist*

24 May 80	**DREAMS** *RCA PB 9534*	50 4
31 May 80	DREAMS *RCA PL 13544*	28 6

SLIK *UK, male vocal (Midge Ure OBE) / instrumental group (1 Album: 1 Week, 2 Singles: 18 Weeks)*

17 Jan 76 ★	**FOREVER AND EVER** *Bell 1464*	1 9
8 May 76	**REQUIEM** *Bell 1478*	24 9
12 Jun 76	SLIK *Bell SYBEL 8004*	58 1

SLIPKNOT *US, male vocal (Corey Taylor) / instrumental group (4 Albums: 18 Weeks, 7 Singles: 20 Weeks)*

10 Jul 99	SLIPKNOT *Roadrunner RR 86552*	37 5
11 Mar 00	**WAIT AND BLEED** *Roadrunner RR 21125*	27 3
16 Sep 00	**SPIT IT OUT** *Roadrunner RR 20903*	28 2
8 Sep 01 ★	IOWA *Roadrunner 12085642* ■	1 7
10 Nov 01	**LEFT BEHIND** *Roadrunner 23203355*	24 4
20 Jul 02	**MY PLAGUE** *Roadrunner RR 20453*	43 2
5 Jun 04 ●	VOL.3: (THE SUBLIMINAL VERSES) *Roadrunner RR 83888*	5 5
26 Jun 04	**DUALITY** (re) *Roadrunner RR 39880*	15 6
30 Oct 04	**VERMILION** *Roadrunner RR 39770*	31 2
25 Jun 05	**BEFORE I FORGET** *Roadrunner RR 39687*	35 1
12 Nov 05	9.0 LIVE *Roadrunner RR 81152*	53 1

SLIPMATT (see also SL2) *UK, male producer – Matt Nelson*

19 Apr 03	**SPACE** *Concept CDCON 37*	41 2

28 October 1989	4 November 1989	11 November 1989	18 November 1989
THAT'S WHAT I LIKE Jive Bunny and The Mastermixers	THAT'S WHAT I LIKE Jive Bunny and The Mastermixers	ALL AROUND THE WORLD Lisa Stansfield	ALL AROUND THE WORLD Lisa Stansfield
WILD! Erasure	WILD! Erasure	THE ROAD TO HELL Chris Rea	THE ROAD TO HELL Chris Rea

KEY
UK No.1 ★★ UK Top 10 ●● Still on chart ++ UK entry at No.1 ■■
US No.1 ▲▲ UK million seller £ US million seller $
Singles re-entries are listed as (re), (2re), (3re)… which signifies that the hit re-entered the chart once, twice or three times…
Peak Position / Weeks

SLIPSTREEM *UK, male vocal group*

19 Dec 92 **WE ARE RAVING – THE ANTHEM** *Boogie Food 7BF 1* 18 7

The SLITS *UK, female vocal / instrumental group*

22 Sep 79 CUT *Island ILPS 9573* 30 5
13 Oct 79 **TYPICAL GIRLS / I HEARD IT THROUGH THE GRAPEVINE** *Island WIP 6505* 60 3

SLK NEW *UK, male / female rap group*

19 Mar 05 **HYPE! HYPE!** *Smoove SMOOVE 01CDS* 22 3

PF SLOAN *US, male vocalist – Philip 'Flip' Sloan*

4 Nov 65 **SINS OF THE FAMILY** *RCA 1482* 38 3

SLO-MOSHUN
UK / US, male / female production / vocal trio (2 Singles: 4 Weeks)

5 Feb 94 **BELLS OF NY** *Six6 SIXCD 108* 29 3
30 Jul 94 **HELP MY FRIEND** *Six6 SIXCD 117* 52 1

SLOWDIVE *UK, male / female vocal / instrumental group (2 Albums: 3 Weeks, 2 Singles: 2 Weeks)*

15 Jun 91 **CATCH THE BREEZE / SHINE** *Creation CRE 112* 52 1
14 Sep 91 JUST FOR A DAY *Creation CRELP 094* 32 2
29 May 93 **OUTSIDE YOUR ROOM (EP)** *Creation CRESCD 119* 69 1
12 Jun 93 SOUVLAKI *Creation CRECD 139* 51 1

Tracks on Outside Your Room (EP): Outside Your Room / Alison / So Tired / Souvlaki Space Station.

SLUSNIK LUNA *Finland, male producer – Niko Nyman*

1 Sep 01 **SUN** *Incentive CENT 29CDS* 40 2

SLY and The FAMILY STONE
US, male / female vocal / instrumental / production group – includes Sly Stone and Larry Graham (1 Album: 2 Weeks, 5 Singles: 42 Weeks)

10 Jul 68 ● **DANCE TO THE MUSIC** *Direction 58 3568* 7 14
2 Oct 68 **M'LADY** *Direction 58 3707* 32 7
19 Mar 69 **EVERYDAY PEOPLE (re)** *Direction 58 3938* ▲ $ 36 5
8 Jan 72 **FAMILY AFFAIR** *Epic EPC 7632* ▲ $ 15 8
5 Feb 72 THERE'S A RIOT GOIN' ON *Epic EPC 64613* ▲ 31 2
15 Apr 72 **RUNNIN' AWAY** *Epic EPC 7810* 17 8

SLY FOX
US, male vocal / instrumental duo – Gary Cooper and Michael Camacho

31 May 86 ● **LET'S GO ALL THE WAY** *Capitol CL 403* 3 16

SLY and ROBBIE *Jamaica, male vocal / instrumental duo – Sly Dunbar and Robbie Shakespeare (1 Album: 5 Weeks, 3 Singles: 23 Weeks)*

4 Apr 87 **BOOPS (HERE TO GO)** *Fourth & Broadway BRW 61* 12 11
9 May 87 RHYTHM KILLERS *Fourth & Broadway BRLP 512* 35 5
25 Jul 87 **FIRE** *Fourth & Broadway BRW 71* 60 4
20 Sep 97 **NIGHT NURSE** *East West EW 129CD1* [1] 13 8

[1] Sly and Robbie featuring Simply Red

The SMALL ADS *UK, male vocal / instrumental group*

18 Apr 81 **SMALL ADS** *Bronze BRO 115* 63 3

The SMALL FACES (334 Top 500)
Revered London-based mod quartet: Steve Marriott (v/g), d. 1991, Ronnie Lane (b), d. 1997, Ian McLagan (k) and Kenney Jones (d). Marriott and Lane penned most of the act's UK hits. Further international fame came when Marriott formed Humble Pie and the other members formed The Faces (6 Albums: 71 Weeks, 14 Singles: 137 Weeks)

2 Sep 65 **WHATCHA GONNA DO ABOUT IT?** *Decca F 12208* 14 12
10 Feb 66 ● **SHA-LA-LA-LA-LEE** *Decca F 12317* 3 11
12 May 66 ● **HEY GIRL** *Decca F 12393* 10 9
14 May 66 ● SMALL FACES *Decca LK 4790* 3 25
11 Aug 66 ★ **ALL OR NOTHING** *Decca F 12470* 1 12
17 Nov 66 ● **MY MIND'S EYE** *Decca F 12500* 4 11
9 Mar 67 **I CAN'T MAKE IT** *Decca F 12565* 26 7
8 Jun 67 **HERE COME THE NICE** *Immediate IM 050* 12 10
17 Jun 67 FROM THE BEGINNING *Decca LK 4879* 17 5
1 Jul 67 SMALL FACES *Immediate IMSP 008* 12 17
9 Aug 67 ● **ITCHYCOO PARK** *Immediate IM 057* 3 14
6 Dec 67 ● **TIN SOLDIER** *Immediate IM 062* 9 12
17 Apr 68 ● **LAZY SUNDAY** *Immediate IM 064* 2 11
15 Jun 68 ★ OGDENS' NUT GONE FLAKE *Immediate IMLP 012* 1 19
10 Jul 68 **UNIVERSAL** *Immediate IM 069* 16 11
19 Mar 69 **AFTERGLOW OF YOUR LOVE** *Immediate IM 077* 36 1
13 Dec 75 ● **ITCHYCOO PARK (re-issue)** *Immediate IMS 102* 9 11
20 Mar 76 **LAZY SUNDAY (re-issue)** *Immediate IMS 106* 39 5
11 May 96 THE DECCA ANTHOLOGY 1965-1967 *Deram 8445832* 66 1
7 Jun 03 ULTIMATE COLLECTION *Sanctuary TDSAN 004* 24 4

The two albums titled Small Faces are different.

Heather SMALL (see also M PEOPLE)
UK, female vocalist (2 Albums: 9 Weeks, 5 Singles: 15 Weeks)

18 Apr 92 **SOMEDAY** *Deconstruction PB 45369* [1] 38 3
20 May 00 **PROUD** *Arista 74321748902* 16 5
10 Jun 00 PROUD *Arista 74321765482* 12 4
19 Aug 00 **HOLDING ON** *Arista 74321781332* 58 1
18 Nov 00 **YOU NEED LOVE LIKE I DO** *GUT CDGUT 36* [2] 24 3
5 Mar 05 ULTIMATE COLLECTION *Sony BMG 82876669192* [1] 17 5
30 Jul 05 **PROUD (re-issue)** *Arista 82876669182* 33 3

[1] M People with Heather Small [2] Tom Jones and Heather Small
[1] M People featuring Heather Small

SMALLER *UK, male vocal / instrumental group (2 Singles: 2 Weeks)*

28 Sep 96 **WASTED** *Better BETSCD 006* 72 1
29 Mar 97 **IS** *Better BETSCD 008* 55 1

SMART E'S *UK, male instrumental / production group*

11 Jul 92 ● **SESAME'S TREET** *Suburban Base SUBBASE 12S* 2 9

S*M*A*S*H
UK, male vocal / instrumental group (2 Albums: 4 Weeks, 1 Single: 1 Week)

2 Apr 94 S*M*A*S*H *Hi-Rise FLATMCD 2* 28 3
6 Aug 94 **(I WANT TO) KILL SOMEBODY** *Hi-Rise FLATSCD 5* 26 1
17 Sep 94 SELF ABUSED *Hi-Rise FLATCD 6* 59 1

SMASH MOUTH *US, male vocal / instrumental group (2 Singles: 9 Weeks)*

25 Oct 97 **WALKIN' ON THE SUN** *Interscope IND 95555* 19 4
31 Jul 99 **ALL STAR** *Interscope 4971172* 24 5

The SMASHING PUMPKINS *US, male / female vocal (Billy Corgan) / instrumental group (5 Albums: 71 Weeks, 14 Singles: 36 Weeks)*

5 Sep 92 **I AM ONE** *Hut HUTT 18* 73 1
3 Jul 93 **CHERUB ROCK** *Hut HUTCD 31* 31 2
31 Jul 93 ● SIAMESE DREAM *Hut CDHUT 11* 4 15
25 Sep 93 **TODAY** *Hut HUTCD 37* 44 2
5 Mar 94 **DISARM** *Hut HUTCD 43* 11 3
28 Oct 95 **BULLET WITH BUTTERFLY WINGS** *Hut HUTCD 63* 20 3

25 November 1989	2 December 1989	9 December 1989	16 December 1989
UK No.1 SINGLES			
YOU GOT IT (THE RIGHT STUFF) New Kids on the Block	YOU GOT IT (THE RIGHT STUFF) New Kids on the Block	YOU GOT IT (THE RIGHT STUFF) New Kids on the Block	LET'S PARTY Jive Bunny and The Mastermixers
UK No.1 ALBUMS			
THE ROAD TO HELL Chris Rea	… BUT SERIOUSLY Phil Collins	… BUT SERIOUSLY Phil Collins	… BUT SERIOUSLY Phil Collins

4 Nov 95 ● MELLON COLLIE AND THE INFINITE SADNESS Hut CDHUTD 30 ▲ 4 37
10 Feb 96 1979 Hut HUTCD 67 ....16 3
18 May 96 ● TONIGHT TONIGHT Hut HUTDX 69 ....7 6
23 Nov 96 THIRTY THREE Hut HUTCD 78 ....21 2
14 Jun 97 ● THE END IS THE BEGINNING IS THE END Warner Bros. W 0404CD 10 4
23 Aug 97 THE END IS THE BEGINNING IS THE END (re-mix) Warner Bros. W 0410CD 72 1
30 May 98 AVA ADORE Hut HUTCD 101 ....11 4
13 Jun 98 ● ADORE Hut CDHUTX 51 ....5 12
19 Sep 98 PERFECT Hut HUTCD 106 ....24 2
4 Mar 00 STAND INSIDE YOUR LOVE Hut HUTCD 127 ....23 2
11 Mar 00 ● MACHINA / THE MACHINES OF GOD Hut CDHUT 59 ....7 4
23 Sep 00 TRY TRY TRY Hut HUTCD 140 ....73 1
1 Dec 01 ROTTEN APPLES – THE SMASHING PUMPKINS GREATEST HITS Hut CDHUTD 70 ....28 3

SMELLS LIKE HEAVEN *Italy, male producer – Fabio Paras*

10 Jul 93 LONDRES STRUTT Deconstruction 74321154312 ....57 1

Steven SMITH and FATHER *UK, male instrumental duo*

13 May 72 STEVEN SMITH AND FATHER AND 16 GREAT SONGS Decca SKL 5128 ....17 3

Brian SMITH and his HAPPY PIANO *UK, male pianist*

19 Sep 81 PLAY IT AGAIN Deram DS 047 ....97 1

SMITH and JONES *UK, male comedy duo – Mel Smith and Griff Rhys Jones*

15 Nov 86 SCRATCH AND SNIFF 10 DIX 51 ....62 8

Ann-Marie SMITH *UK, female vocalist (3 Singles: 5 Weeks)*

23 Jan 93 MUSIC Synthetic CDR 6334 [1] 34 2
18 Mar 95 ROCKIN' MY BODY Media MCSTD 2021 [2] 31 2
15 Jul 95 (YOU'RE MY ONE AND ONLY) TRUE LOVE Media MCSTD 2060 .46 1

[1] Fargetta and Anne-Marie Smith [2] 49ers featuring Ann-Marie Smith

Elliott SMITH *US, male vocalist / guitarist – Steven Smith, b. 6 Aug 1969, d. 21 Oct 2003 (2 Albums: 3 Weeks, 3 Singles: 3 Weeks)*

19 Dec 98 WALTZ #2 (XO) Dreamworks DRMCD 22347 ....52 1
1 May 99 BABY BRITAIN Dreamworks DRMDM 50950 ....55 1
29 Apr 00 FIGURE 8 Dreamworks 4502252 ....37 2
8 Jul 00 SON OF SAM Dreamworks DRMCD 4509492 ....55 1
30 Oct 04 FROM A BASEMENT ON THE HILL Domino WIGCD 147 ....41 1

Hurricane SMITH *UK, male vocalist – Norman Smith (3 Singles: 35 Weeks)*

12 Jun 71 ● DON'T LET IT DIE Columbia DB 8785 ....2 12
29 Apr 72 ● OH BABE, WHAT WOULD YOU SAY? Columbia DB 8878 ....4 16
2 Sep 72 WHO WAS IT Columbia DB 8916 ....23 7

Jimmy SMITH *US, male organist, b. 8 Dec 1925, d. 8 Feb 2005*

28 Apr 66 GOT MY MOJO WORKING (re) Verve VS 536 ....48 3
18 Jun 66 GOT MY MOJO WORKING Verve VLP 912 ....19 3

Keely SMITH *US, female vocalist – Dorothy Smith*

16 Jan 65 LENNON-MCCARTNEY SONGBOOK Reprise R 6142 ....12 9
18 Mar 65 YOU'RE BREAKIN' MY HEART Reprise R 20346 ....14 10

Mandy SMITH *UK, female vocalist*

20 May 89 DON'T YOU WANT ME BABY PWL PWL 37 ....59 2

Mel SMITH (see also NOT THE 9 O'CLOCK NEWS CAST; SMITH and JONES) *UK, male vocalist / comedian (2 Singles: 10 Weeks)*

5 Dec 87 ● ROCKIN' AROUND THE CHRISTMAS TREE 10 TEN 2 [1] 3 7
21 Dec 91 ANOTHER BLOOMING CHRISTMAS Epic 6576877 ....59 3

[1] Mel [Mel Smith] and Kim

Muriel SMITH *US, female vocalist, b. 23 Feb 1923, d. 1985*

15 May 53 ● HOLD ME, THRILL ME, KISS ME Philips PB 122 ....3 17

Hit with Wally Stott and his Orchestra.

OC SMITH *US, male vocalist – Ocie Smith, b. 21 Jun 1936, d. 23 Nov 2001 (1 Album: 1 Week, 2 Singles: 23 Weeks)*

29 May 68 ● THE SON OF HICKORY HOLLER'S TRAMP CBS 3343 ....2 15
17 Aug 68 HICKORY HOLLER REVISITED CBS 63362 ....40 1
26 Mar 77 TOGETHER Caribou CRB 4910 ....25 8

Patti SMITH GROUP *US, female / male vocal / instrumental group (5 Albums: 24 Weeks, 3 Singles: 16 Weeks)*

1 Apr 78 EASTER Arista SPART 1043 ....16 14
29 Apr 78 ● BECAUSE THE NIGHT Arista 181 ....5 12
19 Aug 78 PRIVILEGE (SET ME FREE) Arista 197 ....72 1
19 May 79 WAVE Arista SPART 1086 ....41 6
2 Jun 79 FREDERICK Arista 264 ....63 3
16 Jul 88 DREAM OF LIFE Arista 209172 [1] 70 1
13 Jul 96 GONE AGAIN Arista 7822187472 [1] 44 2
8 May 04 TRAMPIN' Columbia 5152159 [1] 70 1

[1] Patti Smith

Rex SMITH and Rachel SWEET *US, male / female vocalists*

22 Aug 81 EVERLASTING LOVE CBS A 1405 ....35 7

Richard Jon SMITH *South Africa, male vocalist*

16 Jul 83 SHE'S THE MASTER OF THE GAME Jive JIVE 38 ....63 2

Whistling Jack SMITH *UK, male whistler – Billy Moeller*

2 Mar 67 ● I WAS KAISER BILL'S BATMAN Deram DM 112 ....5 12

Will SMITH 291 Top 500

The artist formerly known as The Fresh Prince, b. 25 Sep 1968, Philadelphia, US, was not only one of the 90s' most successful rap stars but also a top TV personality and Oscar-nominated movie actor. The quadruple World Music Award winner (1999) helped to make rap accessible to all ages and was a performer and presenter at the US Live 8 concert. Best-selling single: 'Men in Black' 883,000 (4 Albums: 95 Weeks, 12 Singles: 135 Weeks)

16 Aug 97 ★ MEN IN BLACK Columbia 6648682 ■ 1 16
6 Dec 97 ● BIG WILLIE STYLE Columbia 4886622 ....9 70
13 Dec 97 JUST CRUISIN' Columbia 6653482 ....23 6
7 Feb 98 ● GETTIN' JIGGY WIT IT Columbia 6655605 ▲ 3 10
1 Aug 98 ● JUST THE TWO OF US Columbia 6662092 ....2 10
5 Dec 98 ● MIAMI Columbia 6666782 ....3 14
13 Feb 99 ● BOY YOU KNOCK ME OUT (re) MJJ / Epic 6669372 [1] 3 9
10 Jul 99 ● WILD WILD WEST Columbia 6675962 [2] ▲ 2 16
20 Nov 99 ● WILL 2K Columbia 6684452 ....2 11
27 Nov 99 ● WILLENNIUM Columbia 4949392 ....10 15
25 Mar 00 FREAKIN' IT (re) Columbia 6691052 ....15 8
10 Aug 02 ● BLACK SUITS COMIN' (NOD YA HEAD) Columbia 6730132 [3] .3 10
24 Aug 02 BORN TO REIGN Columbia 5079552 ....24 2
2 Apr 05 ● SWITCH Interscope 9881083 ....4 22
9 Apr 05 LOST AND FOUND Interscope 9880929 ....15 8
5 Nov 05 PARTY STARTER Interscope 9886574 ....19 3

[1] Tatyana Ali featuring Will Smith [2] Will Smith featuring Dru Hill – additional vocals Kool Moe Dee [3] Will Smith featuring Tra-Knox

The SMITHS 178 Top 500

Groundbreaking Mancunian quartet with a loyal fan base: Morrissey (b. Steven Morrissey) (v), Johnny Marr (g), Andy Rourke (b), Mike Joyce (d). Their achievements include monopolising the Top 3 indie chart placings (Feb 1984) and having seven albums simultaneously in the UK chart (Mar 1995) (19 Albums: 210 Weeks, 20 Singles: 105 Weeks)

12 Nov 83 THIS CHARMING MAN Rough Trade RT 136 ....25 12
28 Jan 84 WHAT DIFFERENCE DOES IT MAKE Rough Trade RT 146 ....12 9
3 Mar 84 ● THE SMITHS Rough Trade ROUGH 61 ....2 33

23 December 1989	30 December 1989	6 January 1990	13 January 1990
DO THEY KNOW IT'S CHRISTMAS? Band Aid II	DO THEY KNOW IT'S CHRISTMAS? Band Aid II	DO THEY KNOW IT'S CHRISTMAS? Band Aid II	HANGIN' TOUGH (Re-issue) New Kids on the Block
... BUT SERIOUSLY Phil Collins	... BUT SERIOUSLY Phil Collins	... BUT SERIOUSLY Phil Collins	... BUT SERIOUSLY Phil Collins

KEY UK No.1 ★★ UK Top 10 ●● Still on chart + + UK entry at No.1 ■■ US No.1 ▲▲ UK million seller £ US million seller $
Singles re-entries are listed as (re), (2re), (3re)... which signifies that the hit re-entered the chart once, twice or three times...
Peak Position / Weeks

2 Jun 84 ● HEAVEN KNOWS I'M MISERABLE NOW *Rough Trade RT 156*.10 8
1 Sep 84 WILLIAM, IT WAS REALLY NOTHING *Rough Trade RT 166*......17 6
24 Nov 84 ● HATFUL OF HOLLOW *Rough Trade ROUGH 76*..........7 46
9 Feb 85 HOW SOON IS NOW? *Rough Trade RT 176*..........24 6
23 Feb 85 ★ MEAT IS MURDER *Rough Trade ROUGH 81* ■..........1 13
30 Mar 85 SHAKESPEARE'S SISTER *Rough Trade RT 181*..........26 4
13 Jul 85 THAT JOKE ISN'T FUNNY ANYMORE *Rough Trade RT 186*......49 3
5 Oct 85 THE BOY WITH THE THORN IN HIS SIDE *Rough Trade RT 191*..........23 5
31 May 86 BIG MOUTH STRIKES AGAIN *Rough Trade RT 192*..........26 4
28 Jun 86 ● THE QUEEN IS DEAD *Rough Trade ROUGH 96*..........2 22
2 Aug 86 PANIC *Rough Trade RT 193*..........11 8
1 Nov 86 ASK *Rough Trade RT 194*..........14 5
7 Feb 87 SHOPLIFTERS OF THE WORLD UNITE *Rough Trade RT 195*....12 4
7 Mar 87 ● THE WORLD WON'T LISTEN *Rough Trade ROUGH 101*..........2 15
25 Apr 87 ● SHEILA TAKE A BOW *Rough Trade RT 196*..........10 5
30 May 87 LOUDER THAN BOMBS (import) *Rough Trade ROUGH 255*.....38 5
22 Aug 87 GIRLFRIEND IN A COMA *Rough Trade RT 197*..........13 5
10 Oct 87 ● STRANGEWAYS HERE WE COME *Rough Trade ROUGH 106*......2 17
14 Nov 87 I STARTED SOMETHING I COULDN'T FINISH *Rough Trade RT 198*..........23 4
19 Dec 87 LAST NIGHT I DREAMT THAT SOMEBODY LOVED ME *Rough Trade RT 200*..........30 4
17 Sep 88 ● RANK *Rough Trade ROUGH 126*..........2 7
15 Aug 92 ● THIS CHARMING MAN (re-issue) *WEA YZ 0001*..........8 5
29 Aug 92 ★ BEST ... I *WEA 4509903272* ■..........1 9
12 Sep 92 HOW SOON IS NOW (re-issue) *WEA YZ 0002*..........16 4
24 Oct 92 THERE IS A LIGHT THAT NEVER GOES OUT *WEA YZ 0003*.......25 3
14 Nov 92 BEST ... II *WEA 4509904062*..........29 5
18 Feb 95 ASK (re-issue) *WEA YZ 0004CDX*..........62 1
4 Mar 95 HATFUL OF HOLLOW (re-issue) *WEA 4509918932*..........26 3
4 Mar 95 MEAT IS MURDER (re-issue) *WEA 4509918952*..........39 2
4 Mar 95 ● SINGLES *WEA 4509990902*..........5 13
4 Mar 95 STRANGEWAYS HERE WE COME (re-issue) *WEA 4509918992*.38 4
4 Mar 95 THE QUEEN IS DEAD (re-issue) *WEA 4509918962*..........30 4
4 Mar 95 THE SMITHS (re-issue) *WEA 4509918922*..........42 4
4 Mar 95 THE WORLD WON'T LISTEN (re-issue) *WEA 4509918982*.......52 2
14 Oct 00 LOUDER THAN BOMBS (re-issue) *WEA 4509938332*..........52 2
16 Jun 01 THE VERY BEST OF THE SMITHS *WEA 8573889482*..........30 4

SMOKE *UK, male vocal / instrumental group*

9 Mar 67 MY FRIEND JACK *Columbia DB 8115*..........45 3

SMOKE CITY

UK / Brazil, male / female vocal (Nina Miranda) / instrumental group

12 Apr 97 ● UNDERWATER LOVE *Jive JIVECD 422*..........4 5

SMOKE 2 SEVEN *UK, female vocal trio*

16 Mar 02 BEEN THERE DONE THAT *Curb / London CUBC 077*..........26 2

SMOKIE (426 Top 500) *British group, fronted by vocalist Chris Norman, who became European superstars. Especially popular in Germany, many of their hits were penned by Mike Chapman and Nicky Chinn (5 Albums: 45 Weeks, 13 Singles: 125 Weeks)*

19 Jul 75 ● IF YOU THINK YOU KNOW HOW TO LOVE ME *RAK 206* [1] 3 9
4 Oct 75 ● DON'T PLAY YOUR ROCK 'N ROLL TO ME *RAK 217* [1] 8 7
1 Nov 75 SMOKIE / CHANGING ALL THE TIME *RAK SRAK 517*..........18 5
31 Jan 76 SOMETHING'S BEEN MAKING ME BLUE *RAK 227*..........17 8
25 Sep 76 I'LL MEET YOU AT MIDNIGHT *RAK 241*..........11 9
4 Dec 76 ● LIVING NEXT DOOR TO ALICE *RAK 244*..........5 11
19 Mar 77 LAY BACK IN THE ARMS OF SOMEONE *RAK 251*..........12 9
30 Apr 77 ● GREATEST HITS *RAK SRAK 526*..........6 22
16 Jul 77 ● IT'S YOUR LIFE *RAK 260*..........5 9
15 Oct 77 ● NEEDLES AND PINS *RAK 263*..........10 9
28 Jan 78 FOR A FEW DOLLARS MORE *RAK 267*..........17 6
20 May 78 ● OH CAROL *RAK 276*..........5 13
23 Sep 78 MEXICAN GIRL *RAK 283*..........19 9
4 Nov 78 THE MONTREUX ALBUM *RAK SRAK 6757*..........52 2
19 Apr 80 TAKE GOOD CARE OF MY BABY *RAK 309*..........34 7
11 Oct 80 SMOKIE'S HITS *RAK SRAK 540*..........23 13
13 May 95 ● LIVING NEXT DOOR TO ALICE (WHO THE F**K IS ALICE) (re) (re-recording) *NOW CDWAG 245* [2] 3 19
17 Mar 01 UNCOVERED – THE VERY BEST OF SMOKIE *Universal Music TV 138172*..........63 3

[1] Smokey [2] Smokie featuring Roy 'Chubby' Brown

'Living Next Door to Alice (Who the F**k is Alice)' peaked on re-entry in Aug 1995.

SMOKIN BEATS featuring Lyn EDEN

(see also DJ FLAVOURS; NRG) *UK, male DJ / production duo – Neil Rumney and Paul Landon and female vocalist*

17 Jan 98 DREAMS *AM:PM 5824711*..........23 3

SMOKIN' MOJO FILTERS

UK / US, male / female vocal / instrumental charity group

23 Dec 95 COME TOGETHER (WAR CHILD) *Go Discs GODCD 136*..........19 5

SMOOTH *US, female vocalist – Juanita Stokes (5 Singles: 7 Weeks)*

22 Jul 95 MIND BLOWIN' *Jive JIVECD 379*..........36 2
7 Oct 95 IT'S SUMMERTIME (LET IT GET INTO YOU) *Jive JIVECD 383*..........46 1
16 Mar 96 WE GOT IT *MCA MCSTD 48009* [1] 26 2
16 Mar 96 LOVE GROOVE (GROOVE WITH YOU) *Jive JIVECD 390*..........46 1
6 Jul 96 UNDERCOVER LOVER *Jive JIVECD 397*..........41 1

[1] Immature featuring Smooth

Joe SMOOTH *US, male producer*

4 Feb 89 PROMISED LAND *DJ International DJIN 6*..........56 4

SMOOTH TOUCH *US, male instrumental / production duo*

2 Apr 94 HOUSE OF LOVE (IN MY HOUSE) *Six6 SIXCD 112*..........58 1

Jean Jacques SMOOTHIE *UK, male DJ / producer – Steve Robson*

13 Oct 01 2 PEOPLE *Echo ECSCD 112*..........12 7

SMUJJI *Jamaica, male vocalist – Sean McLeod (2 Singles: 9 Weeks)*

13 Mar 04 MUST BE LOVE *Def Jam 9817508* [1] 13 7
31 Jul 04 K.O. *Def Jam 9867077*..........43 2

[1] Fya featuring Smujji

The SMURFS *Smurfland / Holland, small blue creatures vocal group (6 Albums: 77 Weeks, 5 Singles: 52 Weeks)*

3 Jun 78 ● THE SMURF SONG *Decca F 13759* [1] 2 17
30 Sep 78 DIPPETY DAY *Decca F 13798* [1] 13 12
25 Nov 78 FATHER ABRAHAM IN SMURFLAND *Decca SMURF 1* [1] 19 11
2 Dec 78 CHRISTMAS IN SMURFLAND *Decca F 13819*..........19 7
6 Jul 96 ● THE SMURFS GO POP! *EMI TV CDEMTV 121*..........2 33
7 Sep 96 ● I'VE GOT A LITTLE PUPPY *EMI TV CDSMURF 100*..........4 10
16 Nov 96 ● SMURF'S CHRISTMAS PARTY *EMI TV CDEMTV 140*..........8 9
21 Dec 96 ● YOUR CHRISTMAS WISH *EMI TV CDSMURF 102*..........8 6
22 Feb 97 ● THE SMURFS HITS '97 – VOLUME 1 *EMI TV CDEMTV 150*.........2 11
6 Sep 97 GO POP! AGAIN *EMI CDEMTV 155*..........15 7
18 Apr 98 GREATEST HITS *EMI 4941972*..........28 6

[1] Father Abraham and The Smurfs [1] Father Abraham and The Smurfs

Patty SMYTH with Don HENLEY

(see also EAGLES) *US, female / male vocal duo*

3 Oct 92 SOMETIMES LOVE JUST AIN'T ENOUGH *MCA MCS 1692* 22 6

20 January 1990	27 January 1990	3 February 1990	10 February 1990
UK No.1 SINGLES			
HANGIN' TOUGH (Re-issue) New Kids on the Block	TEARS ON MY PILLOW Kylie Minogue	NOTHING COMPARES 2 U Sinead O'Connor	NOTHING COMPARES 2 U Sinead O'Connor
UK No.1 ALBUMS			
... BUT SERIOUSLY Phil Collins	COLOUR The Christians	... BUT SERIOUSLY Phil Collins	... BUT SERIOUSLY Phil Collins

SNAKEBITE *Italy, male production trio*

9 Aug 97 **THE BIT GOES ON** *Multiply CDMULTY 22*.......**25** 2

SNAP! 388 Top 500

German-based producers Benito Benites (Michael Munzing) and John Garrett Virgo III (Luca Anzilotti) masterminded a string of worldwide dance hits for this act, which featured a host of mostly US vocalists and rappers including Turbo B, Jackie Harris, Penny Ford and Thea Austin. Best-selling single: 'Rhythm is a Dancer' 582,700 (4 Albums: 56 Weeks, 17 Singles: 126 Weeks)

24 Mar 90 ★ **THE POWER** *Arista 113133* $.......**1** 15
26 May 90 ● WORLD POWER *Arista 210682*.......10 39
16 Jun 90 ● **OOOPS UP** *Arista 113296*.......**5** 12
22 Sep 90 ● **CULT OF SNAP!** *Arista 113596*.......**8** 7
8 Dec 90 ● **MARY HAD A LITTLE BOY** *Arista 113831*.......**8** 10
30 Mar 91 ● **SNAP! MEGAMIX** *Arista 114169*.......**10** 6
21 Dec 91 **THE COLOUR OF LOVE** *Arista 114678*.......**54** 3
4 Jul 92 ★ **RHYTHM IS A DANCER** *Arista 115309*.......**1** 19
8 Aug 92 ● THE MADMAN'S RETURN *Logic 262552*.......8 15
9 Jan 93 ● **EXTERMINATE!** *Arista 74321106962* [1].......**2** 11
12 Jun 93 ● **DO YOU SEE THE LIGHT (LOOKING FOR)** *Arista 74321147622* [1].......**10** 8
17 Sep 94 ● **WELCOME TO TOMORROW** (re) *Arista 74321223852* [2].......**6** 14
15 Oct 94 WELCOME TO TOMORROW *Ariola 74321223842*.......69 1
1 Apr 95 **THE FIRST THE LAST ETERNITY (TIL THE END)** *Arista 74321254672* [2].......**15** 7
28 Oct 95 **THE WORLD IN MY HANDS** *Arista 74321314792* [2].......**44** 1
13 Apr 96 **RAME** *Arista 74321368902* [3].......**50** 1
24 Aug 96 **THE POWER 96** *Arista 74321398672* [4].......**42** 1
7 Sep 96 SNAP! ATTACK – THE BEST OF SNAP! / THE REMIXES *Ariola 74321395192*.......47 1
24 Aug 02 **DO YOU SEE THE LIGHT?** (re-mix) *Data MoS DATA 33CDS* [5].......**14** 5
17 May 03 **RHYTHM IS A DANCER** (re-mix) *Data / Mos DATA 47CDS*.......**17** 4
6 Sep 03 **THE POWER (OF BHANGRA)** *Data / MoS DATA 60CDS* [6].......**34** 2

[1] Snap! featuring Niki Haris [2] Snap! featuring Summer [3] Snap! featuring Rukmani [4] Snap! featuring Einstein [5] Snap! vs Plaything [6] Snap! vs Motivo

The Madman's Return changed catalogue number to Arista 74321128512 during its chart run.

SNEAKER PIMPS *UK, male / female vocal (Kelli Dayton) / instrumental group (1 Album: 7 Weeks, 7 Singles: 19 Weeks)*

31 Aug 96 BECOMING X *Clean Up CUP 020CD*.......27 7
19 Oct 96 **6 UNDERGROUND** *Clean Up CUP 023CDS*.......**15** 4
15 Mar 97 **SPIN SPIN SUGAR** *Clean Up CUP 033CDS*.......**21** 3
7 Jun 97 ● **6 UNDERGROUND** (re-mix) *Clean Up CUP 036CDM*.......**9** 4
30 Aug 97 **POST MODERN SLEAZE** *Clean Up CUP 038CDM*.......**22** 3
7 Feb 98 **SPIN SPIN SUGAR** (re-mix) *Clean Up CUP 037X*.......**46** 2
21 Aug 99 **LOW FIVE** *Clean Up CUP 052CDM*.......**39** 2
30 Oct 99 **TEN TO TWENTY** *Clean Up CUP 054CDS*.......**56** 1

David SNEDDON

UK, male vocalist (1 Album: 5 Weeks, 4 Singles: 33 Weeks)

25 Jan 03 ★ **STOP LIVING THE LIE** *Mercury 0637292*.......**1** 18
3 May 03 ● **DON'T LET GO** *Mercury 9800044*.......**3** 10
10 May 03 ● SEVEN YEARS – TEN WEEKS *Mercury 9800063*.......5 5
23 Aug 03 **BEST OF ORDER** *Fontana 9810276*.......**19** 3
8 Nov 03 **BABY GET HIGHER** *Fontana 9813421*.......**38** 2

SNIFF 'N' THE TEARS *UK, male vocal / instrumental group*

23 Jun 79 **DRIVER'S SEAT** *Chiswick CHIS 105*.......**42** 5

SNOOP DOGG 306 Top 500

Ground-breaking g-funk rapper, b. Calvin Broadus, 20 Oct 1972, Long Beach, California, US. Discovered by Dr Dre, he was the first artist to enter the US albums chart at No.1 with his first three albums. The multi-award-winning rap superstar, who was acquitted of murder charges in 1996, performed at Live 8 in London in 2005 (8 Albums: 90 Weeks, 25 Singles: 134 Weeks)

4 Dec 93 **WHAT'S MY NAME?** *Death Row A 8337CD* [1].......**20** 8
11 Dec 93 DOGGYSTYLE *Death Row 6544922792* [1] ▲.......38 27
12 Feb 94 **GIN AND JUICE** *Death Row A 8316CD* [1].......**39** 3
20 Aug 94 **DOGGY DOGG WORLD** *Death Row A 8289CD* [1].......**32** 3
23 Nov 96 THA DOGGFATHER *Interscope INTD 90038* [1] ▲.......15 11
14 Dec 96 **SNOOP'S UPSIDE YA HEAD** *Interscope IND 95520* [2].......**12** 7
26 Apr 97 **WANTED DEAD OR ALIVE** *Def Jam 5744052* [3].......**16** 3
3 May 97 **VAPORS** *Interscope IND 95530* [1].......**18** 2
20 Sep 97 **WE JUST WANNA PARTY WITH YOU** *Columbia 6649902* [4].......**21** 2
24 Jan 98 **THA DOGGFATHER** *Interscope IND 95550* [1].......**36** 2
15 Aug 98 DA GAME IS TO BE SOLD NOT TO BE TOLD *Priority CDPTY 153* ▲.......28 3
12 Dec 98 **COME AND GET WITH ME** *Elektra E 3787CD* [5].......**58** 1
5 Jun 99 TOP DOGG *Priority CDPTY 171*.......48 1
25 Mar 00 ● **STILL D.R.E.** *Interscope 4972742* [6].......**6** 10
3 Feb 01 ● **THE NEXT EPISODE** (re) *Interscope 4974762* [6].......**3** 12
17 Mar 01 **X** *Epic 6709072* [7].......**14** 7
28 Apr 01 **SNOOP DOGG** *Priority PTYCD 134*.......**13** 5
5 May 01 THA LAST MEAL *Priority CDPTY 199*.......62 2
30 Nov 02 **FROM THA CHUUUCH TO DA PALACE** *Priority / Capitol 5516102*.......**27** 6
1 Mar 03 **THE STREETS** *Def Jam 0779852* [8].......**48** 2
5 Apr 03 **BEAUTIFUL** *Priority CDCL 842* [9].......**23** 20
10 May 03 PAID THA COST TO BE DA BO$$ *Priority 5391572*.......64 6
21 Feb 04 **HOLIDAE IN** *Capitol CDCL 852* [10].......**35** 3
14 Aug 04 **I WANNA THANK YA** *J 82876624782* [11].......**31** 3
4 Dec 04 R & G – RHYTHM & GANGSTA – THE MASTERPIECE *Geffen 9864841*.......12 38
11 Dec 04 ● **DROP IT LIKE IT'S HOT** *Geffen 2103461* [12] ▲.......**10** 11
5 Mar 05 **LET'S GET BLOWN** (re) *Geffen 9880425* [12].......**13** 6
7 May 05 ● **SIGNS** *Geffen 9881781* [13].......**2** 16
27 Aug 05 **UPS AND DOWNS** *Geffen 9883732*.......**36** 2
15 Oct 05 THE BEST OF SNOOP DOGG *Capitol 3339572*.......50 2

[1] Snoop Doggy Dogg [2] Snoop Doggy Dogg featuring Charlie Wilson [3] 2Pac and Snoop Doggy Dogg [4] Snoop Doggy Dogg featuring JD [5] Keith Sweat featuring Snoop Dogg [6] Dr Dre featuring Snoop Dogg [7] Xzibit featuring Snoop Dogg [8] WC featuring Snoop Dogg and Nate Dogg [9] Snoop Dogg featuring Pharrell, Uncle Charlie Wilson [10] Chingy featuring Ludacris & Snoop Dogg [11] Angie Stone featuring Snoop Dogg [12] Snoop Dogg featuring Pharrell [13] Snoop Dogg featuring Charlie Wilson and Justin Timberlake [1] Snoop Doggy Dogg

SNOW *Canada, male rapper – Darrin O'Brien (1 Album: 4 Weeks, 3 Singles: 18 Weeks)*

13 Mar 93 ● **INFORMER** *East West America A 8436CD* ▲ $.......**2** 15
17 Apr 93 12 INCHES OF SNOW *East West America 7567922072*.......41 4
5 Jun 93 **GIRL I'VE BEEN HURT** *East West America A 8417CD*.......**48** 2
4 Sep 93 **UHH IN YOU** *Atlantic A 8378CD*.......**67** 1

Mark SNOW *US, male keyboard player*

30 Mar 96 ● **THE X-FILES** *Warner Bros. W 0341CD*.......**2** 15
12 Oct 96 THE TRUTH AND THE LIGHT – MUSIC FROM THE X-FILES *Warner Bros. 9362464482*.......42 2

Phoebe SNOW *US, female vocalist / guitarist – Phoebe Laub*

6 Jan 79 **EVERY NIGHT** *CBS 6842*.......**37** 7

SNOW PATROL *UK, male vocal (Gary Lightbody) / instrumental group (1 Album: 76 Weeks, 5 Singles: 25 Weeks)*

27 Sep 03 **SPITTING GAMES** *Polydor 9809350*.......**54** 1
7 Feb 04 ● **RUN** *Fiction / Polydor 9816353*.......**5** 11
14 Feb 04 ● FINAL STRAW *Fiction / Polydor 9865408*.......3 76
24 Apr 04 **CHOCOLATE** *Fiction / Polydor 9866355*.......**24** 6
24 Jul 04 **SPITTING GAMES** (re-issue) *Fiction / Polydor 9867126*.......**23** 5
6 Nov 04 **HOW TO BE DEAD** *Polydor 9868777*.......**39** 2

The SNOWMEN *UK, male vocal / instrumental group (2 Singles: 12 Weeks)*

12 Dec 81 **HOKEY COKEY** *Stiff ODB 1*.......**18** 8
18 Dec 82 **XMAS PARTY** *Solid STOP 006*.......**44** 4

17 February 1990	24 February 1990	3 March 1990	10 March 1990
NOTHING COMPARES 2 U Sinead O'Connor	**NOTHING COMPARES 2 U** Sinead O'Connor	**DUB BE GOOD TO ME** Beats International featuring Lindy Layton	**DUB BE GOOD TO ME** Beats International featuring Lindy Layton
... BUT SERIOUSLY Phil Collins	**... BUT SERIOUSLY** Phil Collins	**... BUT SERIOUSLY** Phil Collins	**... BUT SERIOUSLY** Phil Collins

UNLUCKIEST No.2 HITS

Massively popular acts such as The Who and Billy Fury are famous for a prodigious output without ever making No.1 in the singles chart. Wham! even managed to sell 1,420,000 copies of their double A-side 'Last Christmas' / 'Everything She Wants' but stalled at No.2. That said, Frank Chacksfield gets our sympathy vote as the unluckiest chart star: together with his orchestra, he spent a frustrating eight weeks at No.2 with 'Terry's Theme from 'Limelight''. This 1950s hit spent a total of 13 unlucky weeks trying to batter Frankie Laine's 'I Believe' into submission. After making No.2 for the first time, its weekly positions ran like this: 2, 2, 5, 4, 2, 2, 2, 3, 2, 2, 3, 5, 2.

All-4-One hold the dubious record of seven consecutive weeks at No.2 when they failed to loosen Wet Wet Wet's hold on the top spot with 'Love Is All Around'. The list of those acts suffering for five weeks or more without registering a chart-topper looks like this:

The New Seekers' 'Never Ending Song of Love' failed to displace T. Rex and Diana Ross chart-toppers in the late summer of 1971

WEEKS AT No.2 / ACT / SINGLE TITLE / DATE OF FIRST WEEK AT No.2

8 FRANK CHACKSFIELD AND HIS ORCHESTRA – Terry's Theme from 'Limelight' (5 Jun 1953)
7 ALL-4-ONE – I Swear (2 Jul 1994)
7 PAT BOONE – Love Letters in the Sand (16 Aug 1957)
6 RIGHT SAID FRED – I'm Too Sexy (17 Aug 1991)
6 FATHER ABRAHAM AND THE SMURFS – The Smurf Song (24 Jun 1978)
6 THE BRIGHOUSE AND RASTRICK BRASS BAND – The Floral Dance (10 Dec 1977)
6 KENNY ROGERS AND THE FIRST EDITION – Ruby, Don't Take Your Love to Town (13 Dec 1969)
6 THE ALLISONS – Are You Sure (9 Mar 1961)
6 FRANKIE LAINE – Blowing Wild (15 Jan 1954)
5 MICHAEL JACKSON – Heal the World (12 Dec 1992)
5 WHAM! – Last Christmas / Everything She Wants (15 Dec 1984)
5 DR HOOK – A Little Bit More (24 Jul 1976)
5 T. REX – Jeepster (27 Nov 1971)
5 THE NEW SEEKERS – Never Ending Song of Love (7 Aug 1971)
5 FREE – All Right Now (4 Jul 1970)
5 SHIRLEY BASSEY – As Long as He Needs Me (27 Oct 1960)
5 JOHNNY OTIS AND HIS ORCHESTRA WITH MARIE ADAMS AND THE THREE TONS OF JOY – Ma (He's Making Eyes at Me) (20 Dec 1957)
5 PAT BOONE – Don't Forbid Me (8 Aug 1957)
5 FRANK SINATRA – Learnin' the Blues (26 Aug 1955)
5 FRANKIE LAINE WITH THE MELLOMEN – Cool Water (5 Aug 1955)
5 DAVID WHITFIELD – Santo Natale (Merry Christmas) (3 Dec 1954)
5 OBERNKIRCHEN CHILDREN'S CHOIR – The Happy Wanderer (19 Feb 1954)
5 NAT 'KING' COLE – Pretend (8 May 1953)

Frank Chacksfield never achieved chart-topping status with the Charlie Chaplin composition 'Terry's Theme from 'Limelight'', or with any other release for that matter

SNUG *UK, male vocal / instrumental group*

18 Apr 98	**BEATNIK GIRL** *WEA WEA 151CDX*	55	1

SO *UK, male vocal / instrumental group*

13 Feb 88	**ARE YOU SURE** *Parlophone R 6173*	62	3

SO SOLID CREW (see also Asher D; HARVEY; Lisa MAFFIA; OXIDE & NEUTRINO; ROMEO) *UK, male / female vocal / rap / production collective (3 Albums: 25 Weeks, 6 Singles: 43 Weeks)*

18 Aug 01 ★	**21 SECONDS (re)** *Relentless RELENT 16CD* ■	1	15
17 Nov 01 ●	**THEY DON'T KNOW** *Relentless RELENT 26CD*	3	9
1 Dec 01 ●	THEY DON'T KNOW *Relentless / Independiente ISOM 27CD*	6	20
19 Jan 02 ●	**HATERS** *Relentless RELENT 23CD* [1]	8	7
26 Jan 02 ●	FUCK IT *Relentless REL 004CD*	3	4
20 Apr 02	**RIDE WID US** *Relentless / Independiente ISOM 55MS*	19	6
27 Sep 03 ●	**BROKEN SILENCE** *Independiente ISOM 71MS*	9	5
11 Oct 03	2ND VERSE *Independiente ISOM 35CD*	70	1
3 Apr 04	**SO GRIMEY** *Independiente ISOM 82MS*	62	1

[1] So Solid Crew presents Mr Shabz featuring MBD and The Reelists

Fuck It appeared only on the Compilation Chart and not on the standard Top 75.

S.O.A.P. *Denmark, female vocal duo – Heidi and Line Sorensen*

25 Jul 98	**THIS IS HOW WE PARTY** *Columbia 6661295*	36	2

SOAPY *UK, male instrumental / production duo – Jak Kaleniuk and Dan Bewick*

14 Sep 96	**HORNY AS FUNK** *WEA WEA 074CD*	35	2

Gino SOCCIO *Canada, male keyboard player*

28 Apr 79	**DANCER** *Warner Bros. K 17357*	46	5

SODA CLUB (see also LOVE TO INFINITY) *UK, male production duo – Andy and Pete Lee (4 Singles: 12 Weeks)*

9 Nov 02	**TAKE MY BREATH AWAY** *Concept CDCON 33* [1]	16	4
8 Mar 03	**HEAVEN IS A PLACE ON EARTH** *Concept CDCON 39* [1]	13	4
23 Aug 03	**KEEP LOVE TOGETHER** *Concept CDCON 44* [2]	31	2
28 Aug 04	**AIN'T NO LOVE (AIN'T NO USE)** *Concept CDCON 58* [3]	40	2

[1] Soda Club featuring Hannah Alethea [2] Soda Club featuring Andrea Anatola [3] Soda Club featuring Ashley Jade

SOFT CELL (322 Top 500) *Successful synth-driven duo from Leeds: Marc Almond (v) and David Ball (k). The visually striking pair's revival of northern soul classic 'Tainted Love' was the top UK single of 1981 and went on to sell 1,135,000. It also broke the longevity record in the US Top 100 (7 Albums: 103 Weeks, 13 Singles: 110 Weeks)*

1 Aug 81 ★	**TAINTED LOVE (3re)** *Some Bizzare BZS 2* £	1	36
14 Nov 81 ●	**BEDSITTER** *Some Bizzare BZS 6*	4	12
5 Dec 81 ●	NON-STOP EROTIC CABARET *Some Bizzare BZLP 2*	5	46
6 Feb 82 ●	**SAY HELLO WAVE GOODBYE** *Some Bizzare BZS 7*	3	9
29 May 82 ●	**TORCH** *Some Bizzare BZS 9*	2	9
26 Jun 82 ●	NON-STOP ECSTATIC DANCING *Some Bizzare BZX 1012*	6	18
21 Aug 82 ●	**WHAT** *Some Bizzare BZS 11*	3	8
4 Dec 82	**WHERE THE HEART IS** *Some Bizzare BZS 16*	21	7
22 Jan 83 ●	THE ART OF FALLING APART *Some Bizzare BIZL 3*	5	10
5 Mar 83	**NUMBERS / BARRIERS** *Some Bizzare BZS 17*	25	4
24 Sep 83	**SOUL INSIDE** *Some Bizzare BZS 20*	16	5
25 Feb 84	**DOWN IN THE SUBWAY** *Some Bizzare BZS 22*	24	6
31 Mar 84	THIS LAST NIGHT IN SODOM *Some Bizzare BIZL 6*	12	5
20 Dec 86	THE SINGLES ALBUM *Some Bizzare BZLP 3*	58	9
23 Mar 91	**SAY HELLO WAVE GOODBYE '91** (re-recording) *Mercury SOFT 1* [1]	38	3
18 May 91 ●	**TAINTED LOVE** (re-issue) *Mercury SOFT 2* [1]	5	8
1 Jun 91 ●	MEMORABILIA – THE SINGLES *Mercury 8485121*	8	13
13 Apr 02	THE VERY BEST OF SOFT CELL *UMTV 5868342*	37	2
28 Sep 02	**MONOCULTURE** *Cooking Vinyl FRYCD 132*	52	1
8 Feb 03	**THE NIGHT** *Cooking Vinyl FRYCD 135*	39	2

[1] Soft Cell / Marc Almond

'Tainted Love' re-entries made No.43 in Jan 1982, No.50 in Jul 1982 and No.43 in Feb 1985.

SOFT MACHINE (see also Robert WYATT) *UK, male vocal / instrumental group (2 Albums: 8 Weeks)*

4 Jul 70	THIRD *CBS 66246*	18	6
3 Apr 71	FOURTH *CBS 64280*	32	2

SOHO *UK, male / female vocal / instrumental group (2 Singles: 11 Weeks)*

5 May 90 ●	**HIPPY CHICK (re)** *Savage 7SAV 106*	8	9
9 Nov 91	**BORN TO BE ALIVE** *MCA MCS 1578* [1]	51	2

[1] Adamski featuring Soho

'Hippy Chick' originally peaked at No.67 and made its peak position only on re-entry in Jan 1991. The listed flip side of 'Born to Be Alive' was 'Never Goin' Down' by Adamski featuring Jimi Polo.

SOHO DOLLS *UK, female / male vocal / instrumental group*

27 Nov 04	**PRINCE HARRY** *Poptones MC 5096SCD*	57	1

SOIL *US, male vocal / instrumental group (2 Singles: 2 Weeks)*

9 Nov 02	**HALO** *J 74321970132*	74	1
5 Jun 04	**REDEFINE** *J 82876618512*	68	1

SOLAR STONE (see also LIQUID STATE featuring Marcella WOODS; Z2) *UK, male DJ / production duo – Rich Mowatt and Andy Bury (3 Singles: 5 Weeks)*

21 Feb 98	**THE IMPRESSIONS EP** *Hooj Choons HOOJCD 57*	75	1
6 Nov 99	**7 CITIES** *Hooj Choons HOOJ 85CD*	39	2
28 Sep 02	**7 CITIES** (re-mix) *Lost Language LOST 018CD*	44	2

Tracks on The Impressions EP: The Calling / Day By Day / So Clear.

SOLID GOLD CHARTBUSTERS *UK, male / female production / vocal group*

25 Dec 99	**I WANNA 1-2-1 WITH YOU** *Virgin VSCDT 1765*	62	1

SOLID HARMONIE *UK / US, female vocal group (4 Singles: 11 Weeks)*

31 Jan 98	**I'LL BE THERE FOR YOU** *Jive JIVECD 437*	18	3
18 Apr 98	**I WANT YOU TO WANT ME** *Jive JIVECD 452*	16	3
15 Aug 98	**I WANNA LOVE YOU** *Jive 0521742*	20	4
21 Nov 98	**TO LOVE ONCE AGAIN** *Jive 0522472*	55	1

The SOLID SENDERS *UK, male vocal / instrumental group*

23 Sep 78	SOLID SENDERS *Virgin V 2105*	42	3

SOLID SESSIONS *Holland, male production duo*

14 Sep 02	**JANEIRO** *Positiva CDTIV 175*	47	1

SOLITAIRE *UK, male production duo (2 Singles: 3 Weeks)*

29 Nov 03	**I LIKE LOVE (I LOVE LOVE)** *Susu CDSUSU 21*	57	2
26 Mar 05	**YOU'VE GOT THE LOVE** *Susu CDSUSU 30*	63	1

SOLO *UK, male producer – Stuart Crichton (3 Singles: 4 Weeks)*

20 Jul 91	**RAINBOW (SAMPLE FREE)** *Reverb RVBT 003*	59	2
18 Jan 92	**COME ON!** *Reverb RVBT 008*	75	1
11 Sep 93	**COME ON!** (re-mix) *Stoatin' STOAT 003CD*	63	1

Sal SOLO (see also CLASSIX NOUVEAUX) *UK, male vocalist (2 Singles: 13 Weeks)*

15 Dec 84	**SAN DAMIANO (HEART AND SOUL)** *MCA MCA 930*	15	10
6 Apr 85	**MUSIC AND YOU** *MCA MCA 946* [1]	52	3

[1] Sal Solo with the London Community Gospel Choir

KEY UK No.1 ★ UK Top 10 ● Still on chart + UK entry at No.1 ■ US No.1 ▲ UK million seller £ US million seller $
Singles re-entries are listed as (re), (2re), (3re)... which signifies that the hit re-entered the chart once, twice or three times...
Peak Position / Weeks

SOLO (US) *US, male vocal group (2 Singles: 3 Weeks)*

3 Feb 96	**HEAVEN** *Perspective 5875212*	35	2
30 Mar 96	**WHERE DO U WANT ME TO PUT IT** *Perspective 5875312*	45	1

Diane SOLOMON *UK, female vocalist*

9 Aug 75	TAKE TWO *Philips 6308 236*	26	6

Martin SOLVEIG *France, male DJ / producer (3 Singles: 9 Weeks)*

24 Apr 04	**ROCKING MUSIC** *Defected DFTD 082CDS*	35	4
26 Jun 04	**I'M A GOOD MAN** *Defected DFTD 091CDS*	57	1
6 Aug 05	**EVERYBODY** *Defected DFTD 107CDS*	22	4

Belouis SOME *UK, male vocalist – Neville Keighley (4 Singles: 26 Weeks)*

27 Apr 85	**IMAGINATION** *Parlophone R 6097*	50	7
18 Jan 86	**IMAGINATION** (re-issue) *Parlophone R 1986*	17	10
12 Apr 86	**SOME PEOPLE** *Parlophone R 6130*	33	7
16 May 87	**LET IT BE WITH YOU** *Parlophone R 6154*	53	2

Jimmy SOMERVILLE (see also BRONSKI BEAT; The COMMUNARDS) *UK, male vocalist (4 Albums: 46 Weeks, 10 Singles: 53 Weeks)*

11 Nov 89	**COMMENT TE DIRE ADIEU** *London LON 241* [1]	14	9
9 Dec 89	READ MY LIPS *London 8281661*	29	14
13 Jan 90 ●	**YOU MAKE ME FEEL (MIGHTY REAL)** *London LON 249*	5	8
17 Mar 90	**READ MY LIPS (ENOUGH IS ENOUGH)** *London LON 254*	26	6
3 Nov 90 ●	**TO LOVE SOMEBODY** *London LON 281*	8	11
24 Nov 90 ●	THE SINGLES COLLECTION 1984/1990 *London 8282261*	4	26
2 Feb 91	**SMALLTOWN BOY** *London LON 287* [2]	32	4
10 Aug 91	**RUN FROM LOVE** *London LON 301*	52	2
28 Jan 95	**HEARTBEAT** *London LONCD 358*	24	4
27 May 95	**HURT SO GOOD** *London LONCD 364*	15	6
24 Jun 95	DARE TO LOVE *London 8285402*	38	2
28 Oct 95	**BY YOUR SIDE** *London LONCD 372*	41	2
13 Sep 97	**DARK SKY** *Gut CXGUT 11*	66	1
22 Sep 01	THE VERY BEST OF JIMMY SOMERVILLE, BRONSKI BEAT AND THE COMMUNARDS *London 927412582* [1]	29	4

[1] Jimmy Somerville featuring June Miles-Kingston [2] Jimmy Somerville with Bronski Beat [1] Jimmy Somerville, Bronski Beat and The Communards

SOMETHIN' FOR THE PEOPLE featuring TRINA and TAMARA *US, male vocal / instrumental group and female vocal duo – Trina and Tamara Powell*

7 Feb 98	**MY LOVE IS THE SHHH!** *Warner Bros. W 0427CD*	64	1

SOMETHING CORPORATE *US, male vocal / instrumental group (2 Singles: 3 Weeks)*

29 Mar 03	**PUNK ROCK PRINCESS** *MCA MCSTD 40315*	33	2
12 Jul 03	**IF YOU C JORDAN** *MCA MCSTD 40324*	68	1

SOMORE featuring Damon TRUEITT *US, male production group and vocalist*

24 Jan 98	**I REFUSE (WHAT YOU WANT)** *XL Recordings XLS 93CD*	21	2

SON OF DORK NEW (see also BUSTED) *UK, male vocal / instrumental group*

19 Nov 05 ●	**TICKET OUTTA LOSERVILLE** *Mercury 9875189*	3	6
3 Dec 05	WELCOME TO LOSERVILLE *Mercury 9875452*	35	2

SONGSTRESS *US, male production / vocal duo*

27 Feb 99	**SEE LINE WOMAN '99** *Locked On LOX 106CD*	64	1

SONIA *UK, female vocalist – Sonia Evans (3 Albums: 14 Weeks, 12 Singles: 78 Weeks)*

24 Jun 89 ★	**YOU'LL NEVER STOP ME LOVING YOU** *Chrysalis CHS 3385*	1	13
7 Oct 89	**CAN'T FORGET YOU** *Chrysalis CHS 3419*	17	6
9 Dec 89 ●	**LISTEN TO YOUR HEART** *Chrysalis CHS 3465*	10	10
7 Apr 90	**COUNTING EVERY MINUTE** *Chrysalis CHS 3492*	16	7
5 May 90 ●	EVERYBODY KNOWS *Chrysalis CHR 1734*	7	10
23 Jun 90	**YOU'VE GOT A FRIEND** *Jive CHILD 90* [1]	14	6
25 Aug 90	**END OF THE WORLD** *Chrysalis / PWL CHS 3557*	18	7
1 Jun 91 ●	**ONLY FOOLS (NEVER FALL IN LOVE)** *IQ ZB 44613*	10	8
31 Aug 91	**BE YOUNG BE FOOLISH BE HAPPY** *IQ ZB 44935*	22	5
19 Oct 91	SONIA *IQ ZL 751675*	33	2
16 Nov 91	**YOU TO ME ARE EVERYTHING** *IQ ZB 45121*	13	5
12 Sep 92	**BOOGIE NIGHTS** *Arista 74321113467*	30	3
1 May 93	**BETTER THE DEVIL YOU KNOW** *Arista 74321146872*	15	7
29 May 93	BETTER THE DEVIL YOU KNOW *Arista 74321149802*	32	2
30 Jul 94	**HOPELESSLY DEVOTED TO YOU** *Cockney COCCD 2*	61	1

[1] Big Fun and Sonia featuring Gary Barnacle

SONIC BOOM *UK, male vocal / instrumental group*

17 Mar 90	SPECTRUM *Silvertone ORELP 56*	65	1

SONIC SOLUTION (see also CJ BOLLAND; RAVESIGNAL III) *Belgium, male production duo – CJ Bolland and Steve Cop*

4 Apr 92	**BEATSTIME** *R&S RSUK 11*	59	1

SONIC SURFERS *Holland, male instrumental / production duo (2 Singles: 2 Weeks)*

20 Mar 93	**TAKE ME UP** *A&M AMCD 210* [1]	61	1
30 Jul 94	**DON'T GIVE IT UP** *Brilliant CDBRIL 6*	54	1

[1] Sonic Surfers featuring Jocelyn Brown

SONIC YOUTH *US, male / female vocal / instrumental group (8 Albums: 14 Weeks, 6 Singles: 14 Weeks)*

29 Oct 88	DAYDREAM NATION *Blast First BFFP 34*	99	1
4 Feb 89	THE WHITEY ALBUM *Blast First BFFP 28* [1]	63	1
7 Jul 90	GOO *DGC 7599242971*	32	2
4 May 91	DIRTY BOOTS – PLUS 5 LIVE TRACKS *DGC DGC 21634*	69	1
11 Jul 92	**100%** *DGC DGCS 11*	28	4
1 Aug 92 ●	DIRTY *DGC DGCD 24485*	6	5
7 Nov 92	**YOUTH AGAINST FASCISM** *Geffen GFS 26*	52	2
3 Apr 93	**SUGAR KANE** *Geffen GFSTD 37*	26	3
7 May 94	**BULL IN THE HEATHER** *Geffen GFSTD 72*	24	2
21 May 94 ●	EXPERIMENTAL JET SET TRASH AND NO STAR *Geffen GED 24632*	10	2
10 Sep 94	**SUPERSTAR** *A&M 5807932*	45	2
14 Oct 95	WASHING MACHINE *Geffen GED 24825*	39	1
23 May 98	A THOUSAND LEAVES *Geffen GED 25203*	38	1
11 Jul 98	**SUNDAY** *Geffen GFSTD 22332*	72	1

[1] Ciccone Youth

The listed flip side of 'Superstar' was 'Yesterday Once More' by Redd Kross.

SONIQUE *UK, female vocalist / DJ – Sonia Clarke (1 Album: 37 Weeks, 7 Singles: 47 Weeks)*

13 Jun 98	**I PUT A SPELL ON YOU** *Serious SERR 001CD*	36	2
5 Dec 98	**IT FEELS SO GOOD** *Serious SERR 004CD*	24	3
3 Jun 00 ★	**IT FEELS SO GOOD** (re-mix) *Universal MCSTD 40233* ■	1	17
24 Jun 00 ●	HEAR MY CRY *Universal 1592302*	6	37
16 Sep 00 ●	**SKY** *Universal MCSTD 40240*	2	10
9 Dec 00 ●	**I PUT A SPELL ON YOU** (re-issue) *Universal MCSTD 40245*	8	10
31 May 03	**CAN'T MAKE UP MY MIND** *Serious 9807217*	17	4
13 Sep 03	**ALIVE** *Serious 9811500*	70	1

SONNY (see also SONNY and CHER) *US, male vocalist – Salvatore Bono, b. 16 Feb 1935, d. 5 Jan 1998 (11 Singles: 11 Weeks)*

19 Aug 65 ●	**LAUGH AT ME** *Atlantic AT 4038*	9	11

12 May 1990	19 May 1990	26 May 1990	2 June 1990
UK No.1 SINGLES			
KILLER Adamski	KILLER Adamski	KILLER Adamski	KILLER Adamski
UK No.1 ALBUMS			
ONLY YESTERDAY - THEIR GREATEST HITS The Carpenters	ONLY YESTERDAY - THEIR GREATEST HITS The Carpenters	ONLY YESTERDAY - THEIR GREATEST HITS The Carpenters	VOLUME II (1990 A NEW DECADE) Soul II Soul

SONNY and CHER *US, male / female vocal / instrumental duo – Sonny (Salvatore Bono), b. 16 Feb 1935, d. 5 Jan 1998, and Cher (Cherilyn Sarkisian LaPierre) (2 Albums: 20 Weeks, 10 Singles: 78 Weeks)*

12 Aug 65 ★ **I GOT YOU BABE** *Atlantic AT 4035* ▲ $ 1 12
16 Sep 65 **BABY DON'T GO** *Reprise R 20309* 11 9
16 Oct 65 ● LOOK AT US *Atlantic ATL 5036* 7 13
21 Oct 65 **BUT YOU'RE MINE** *Atlantic AT 4047* 17 8
17 Feb 66 **WHAT NOW MY LOVE** *Atlantic AT 4069* 13 11
14 May 66 THE WONDROUS WORLD OF SONNY AND CHER *Atlantic 587006* 15 7
30 Jun 66 **HAVE I STAYED TOO LONG** *Atlantic 584 018* 42 3
8 Sep 66 ● **LITTLE MAN** *Atlantic 584 040* 4 10
17 Nov 66 **LIVING FOR YOU** *Atlantic 584 057* 44 4
2 Feb 67 **THE BEAT GOES ON** *Atlantic 584 078* 29 8
15 Jan 72 ● **ALL I EVER NEED IS YOU (2re)** *MCA MU 1145* 8 12
22 May 93 **I GOT YOU BABE** (re-issue) *Epic 6592402* 66 1

SONO *Germany, male production duo*

16 Jun 01 **KEEP CONTROL** *Code Blue BLU 020CD1* 66 1

SONS AND DAUGHTERS *UK, male / female vocal / instrumental group (1 Album: 1 Week, 3 Singles: 3 Weeks)*

16 Oct 04 **JOHNNY CASH** *Domino RUG 186CD* 68 1
4 Jun 05 **DANCE ME IN** *Domino RUG 196CD* 40 1
18 Jun 05 THE REPULSION BOX *Domino Recordings WIGCD 155* 70 1
27 Aug 05 **TASTE THE LAST GIRL** *Domino RUG 206CD* 75 1

SON'Z OF A LOOP DA LOOP ERA *UK, male producer – Daniel Whidett (2 Singles: 4 Weeks)*

15 Feb 92 **FAR OUT** *Suburban Base SUBBASE 008* 36 3
17 Oct 92 **PEACE + LOVEISM** *Suburban Base SUBBASE 14* 60 1

SOOPA HOOPZ featuring QPR MASSIVE *UK, Queens Park Rangers supporters vocal group*

16 Oct 04 **SOOPA HOOPZ** *Sniper Alley SNIPER 001* 54 1

The SORROWS *UK, male vocal / instrumental group*

16 Sep 65 **TAKE A HEART** *Piccadilly 7N 35260* 21 8

Aaron SOUL *UK, male vocalist – Aaron Anyia*

2 Jun 01 **RING RING RING** *Def Soul 5689042* 14 4

David SOUL *US, male actor / vocalist – David Solberg (2 Albums: 51 Weeks, 5 Singles: 56 Weeks)*

27 Nov 76 ● DAVID SOUL *Private Stock PVLP 1012* 2 28
18 Dec 76 ★ **DON'T GIVE UP ON US** *Private Stock PVT 84* ▲ £ $ 1 16
26 Mar 77 ● **GOING IN WITH MY EYES OPEN** *Private Stock PVT 99* 2 8
27 Aug 77 ★ **SILVER LADY** *Private Stock PVT 115* 1 14
17 Sep 77 ● PLAYING TO AN AUDIENCE OF ONE *Private Stock PVLP 1026* ..8 23
17 Dec 77 ● **LET'S HAVE A QUIET NIGHT IN** *Private Stock PVT 130* 8 9
27 May 78 **IT SURE BRINGS OUT THE LOVE IN YOUR EYES** *Private Stock PVT 137* 12 9

Jimmy SOUL *US, male vocalist – James McCleese, b. 24 Aug 1942, d. 25 Jun 1988 (2 Singles: 5 Weeks)*

11 Jul 63 **IF YOU WANNA BE HAPPY** *Stateside SS 178* ▲ $ 39 2
15 Jun 91 **IF YOU WANNA BE HAPPY** (re-issue) *Epic 6569647* 68 3

SOUL ASYLUM *US, male vocal (Dave Pirner) / instrumental group (2 Albums: 29 Weeks, 6 Singles: 33 Weeks)*

19 Jun 93 ● **RUNAWAY TRAIN (re)** *Columbia 6593902* 7 19
31 Jul 93 GRAVE DANCERS UNION *Columbia 4722532* 27 25
4 Sep 93 **SOMEBODY TO SHOVE** *Columbia 6596492* 34 3
22 Jan 94 **BLACK GOLD** *Columbia 6598442* 26 4
26 Mar 94 **SOMEBODY TO SHOVE** (re-issue) *Columbia 6602245* 32 3
1 Jul 95 LET YOUR DIM LIGHT SHINE *Columbia 4803202* 22 4
15 Jul 95 **MISERY** *Columbia 6621092* 30 3
2 Dec 95 **JUST LIKE ANYONE** *Columbia 6624785* 52 1

'Runaway Train' peaked on re-entry in Nov 1993.

SOUL BROTHERS *UK, male vocal / instrumental group*

22 Apr 65 **I KEEP RINGING MY BABY** *Decca F 12116* 42 3

SOUL CENTRAL featuring Kathy BROWN NEW *UK, male production duo – Andy Ward and Paul Timothy and US, female vocalist*

22 Jan 05 ● **STRINGS OF LIFE (STRONGER ON MY OWN)** *Defected DFTD 094CDS* 6 7

SOUL CITY ORCHESTRA *UK, male instrumental / production group*

11 Dec 93 **IT'S JURASSIC** *London JURCD 1* 70 1

SOUL CONTROL *Germany, male vocal / rap duo – Thomas Quella and Leonard Buck*

18 Sep 04 **CHOCOLATE (CHOCO CHOCO)** *Tug CDSNOG 12* 25 3

SOUL FAMILY SENSATION *UK / US, male / female vocal / instrumental group*

11 May 91 **I DON'T EVEN KNOW IF I SHOULD CALL YOU BABY** *One Little Indian 47TP 7* 49 4

SOUL FOR REAL *US, male vocal group (2 Singles: 4 Weeks)*

8 Jul 95 **CANDY RAIN** *Uptown MCSTD 2052* 23 2
23 Mar 96 **EVERY LITTLE THING I DO** *Uptown MCSTD 48005* 31 2

SOUL II SOUL 353 Top 500 (see also PSYCHEDELIC WALTONS) *Enormously influential dance music project led by entrepreneurial producer / DJ Jazzie B (Beresford Romeo). Act featured Nellee Hooper's innovative arrangements and was fronted by a succession of vocalists, most notably Caron Wheeler. Unlike their UK contemporaries, they were equally successful in the US (5 Albums: 108 Weeks, 16 Singles: 89 Weeks)*

21 May 88 **FAIRPLAY** *10 TEN 228* [1] 63 3
17 Sep 88 **FEEL FREE** *10 TEN 236* [2] 64 2
18 Mar 89 ● **KEEP ON MOVING** *10 TEN 263* [3] $ 5 12
22 Apr 89 ★ CLUB CLASSICS VOL. ONE *10 DIX 82* 1 60
10 Jun 89 ★ **BACK TO LIFE (HOWEVER DO YOU WANT ME)** *10 TEN 265* [3] $ 1 14
9 Dec 89 ● **GET A LIFE** *10 TEN 284* 3 13
5 May 90 ● **A DREAM'S A DREAM** *10 TEN 300* 6 6
2 Jun 90 ★ VOLUME II (1990 A NEW DECADE) *10 DIX 90* ■ 1 20
24 Nov 90 **MISSING YOU** *10 TEN 345* [4] 22 7
4 Apr 92 ● **JOY** *Ten TEN 350* 4 7
25 Apr 92 ● VOLUME III JUST RIGHT *Ten DIXCD 100* 3 11
13 Jun 92 **MOVE ME NO MOUNTAIN** *Ten TEN 400* [5] 31 4
26 Sep 92 **JUST RIGHT** *Ten TEN 410* 38 2
6 Nov 93 **WISH** *Virgin VSCDG 1480* 24 4
27 Nov 93 ● VOLUME IV THE CLASSIC SINGLES 88-93 *Virgin CDV 2724* 10 13
22 Jul 95 **LOVE ENUFF** *Virgin VSCDT 1527* 12 6
12 Aug 95 VOLUME V – BELIEVE *Virgin CDV 2739* 13 4
21 Oct 95 **I CARE (SOUL II SOUL)** *Virgin VSCDT 1560* 17 4
19 Oct 96 **KEEP ON MOVIN'** (re-mix) *Virgin VSCDT 1612* 31 2
30 Aug 97 **REPRESENT** *Island CID 668* 39 2
8 Nov 97 **PLEASURE DOME** *Island CID 669* 51 1

[1] Soul II Soul featuring Rose Windross [2] Soul II Soul featuring Do'reen
[3] Soul II Soul featuring Caron Wheeler [4] Soul II Soul featuring Kym Mazelle
[5] Soul II Soul: lead vocals Kofi

SOUL PROVIDERS featuring Michelle SHELLERS *UK, male production duo and US, female vocalist*

14 Jul 01 **RISE** *AM:PM CDAMPM 147* 59 1

S.O.U.L. S.Y.S.T.E.M. introducing Michelle VISAGE (see also C & C MUSIC FACTORY) *US, male / female vocal / instrumental group*

16 Jan 93 **IT'S GONNA BE A LOVELY DAY** *Arista 74321125692* 17 5

9 June 1990	16 June 1990	23 June 1990	30 June 1990
WORLD IN MOTION ... Englandneworder	**WORLD IN MOTION ...** Englandneworder	**SACRIFICE / HEALING HANDS** Elton John	**SACRIFICE / HEALING HANDS** Elton John
VOLUME II (1990 A NEW DECADE) Soul II Soul	**VOLUME II (1990 A NEW DECADE)** Soul II Soul	**THE ESSENTIAL PAVAROTTI** Luciano Pavarotti	**STEP BY STEP** New Kids on the Block

KEY UK No.1 ★★ UK Top 10 ●● Still on chart ++ UK entry at No.1 ■■ US No.1 ▲▲ UK million seller £ US million seller $
Singles re-entries are listed as (re), (2re), (3re)... which signifies that the hit re-entered the chart once, twice or three times...
Peak Position / Weeks

SOUL U*NIQUE *UK, male / female vocal group (2 Singles: 2 Weeks)*

19 Feb 00	**BE MY FRIEND** *M&J MAJCD 2*	53	1
29 Jul 00	**3IL (THRILL)** *M&J MAJCD 3X*	66	1

SOULED OUT *Italy / US / UK, male / female vocal / instrumental group*

9 May 92	**IN MY LIFE** *Columbia 6578367*	75	1

SOULFLY *Brazil / US, male vocal / instrumental group (3 Albums: 4 Weeks)*

2 May 98	**SOULFLY** *Roadrunner RR 87482*	16	2
7 Oct 00	**PRIMITIVE** *Roadrunner RR 85652*	45	1
6 Jul 02	**3** *Roadrunner RR 84552*	61	1

SOULSEARCHER (see also SNAP!)
US, male / female production / vocal (Thea Austin) group (2 Singles: 9 Weeks)

13 Feb 99 ●	**CAN'T GET ENOUGH** *Defected DEFECT 1CDS*	8	7
8 Apr 00	**DO IT TO ME AGAIN** *Defected DFECT 15CDS*	32	2

SOULWAX *Belgium, male vocal / instrumental duo – Stephen and David Dewaele (1 Album: 1 Week, 7 Singles: 11 Weeks)*

25 Mar 00	**CONVERSATION INTERCOM** *Pias Recordings PIASB 018CD*	65	1
24 Jun 00	**MUCH AGAINST EVERYONE'S ADVICE** *Pias Recordings PIASB 026CD*	56	1
30 Sep 00	**TOO MANY DJ'S** *Pias Recordings PIASB 036CD*	40	2
3 Mar 01	**CONVERSATION INTERCOM** (re-mix) *Pias Recordings PIASB 046CD*	50	1
21 Aug 04	**ANY MINUTE NOW** *Pias Recordings PIASB 126CDM*	34	2
4 Sep 04	**ANY MINUTE NOW** *Pias Recordings PIASB 060CD*	53	1
29 Jan 05	**E TALKING** (import) *Pias Recordings PIASB 136CD*	27	2
9 Jul 05	**NY EXCUSE** *Pias Recordings PIASB 156CD*	35	2

SOUND BLUNTZ *Germany, male production / vocal group*

30 Nov 02	**BILLIE JEAN** *Incentive CENT 51CDS*	32	2

SOUND-DE-ZIGN
Holland, male DJ / production duo – Adri Blok and Arjen Rietvink

14 Apr 01	**HAPPINESS** *Nulife / Arista 74321844002*	19	5

SOUND FACTORY *Sweden, male vocal / instrumental duo*

5 Jun 93	**2 THE RHYTHM** *Logic 74321149422*	72	1

SOUND 5 *UK, male vocal / instrumental group*

24 Apr 99	**ALA KABOO** *Gut CDGUT 23*	69	1

SOUND OF ONE featuring GLADEZZ
US, male / female vocal / instrumental duo

20 Nov 93	**AS I AM** *Cooltempo CDCOOL 280*	65	1

SOUNDGARDEN *US, male vocal (Chris Cornell) / instrumental group (3 Albums: 32 Weeks, 10 Singles: 24 Weeks)*

11 Apr 92	**JESUS CHRIST POSE** *A&M AM 862*	30	3
25 Apr 92	**BADMOTORFINGER** *A&M 3953742*	39	2
20 Jun 92	**RUSTY CAGE** *A&M AM 874*	41	1
21 Nov 92	**OUTSHINED** *A&M AM 0102*	50	1
26 Feb 94	**SPOONMAN** *A&M 5805392*	20	3
19 Mar 94 ●	**SUPERUNKNOWN** *A&M 5402152* ▲	4	24
30 Apr 94	**THE DAY I TRIED TO LIVE** *A&M 5805952*	42	2
20 Aug 94	**BLACK HOLE SUN** *A&M 5807532*	12	5
28 Jan 95	**FELL ON BLACK DAYS** *A&M 5809472*	24	2
18 May 96	**PRETTY NOOSE** *A&M 5816202*	14	3
1 Jun 96 ●	**DOWN ON THE UPSIDE** *A&M 5405262*	7	6
28 Sep 96	**BURDEN IN MY HAND** *A&M 5818552*	33	2
28 Dec 96	**BLOW UP THE OUTSIDE WORLD** *A&M 5819862*	40	2

SOUNDMAN and Don LLOYDIE with Elisabeth TROY *UK, male / female vocal / production group*

25 Feb 95	**GREATER LOVE** *Sound of Underground SOURCD 016*	49	2

SOUNDS INCORPORATED (see also Gene VINCENT)
UK, male instrumental group (2 Singles: 11 Weeks)

23 Apr 64	**THE SPARTANS** *Columbia DB 7239*	30	6
30 Jul 64	**SPANISH HARLEM** *Columbia DB 7321*	35	5

SOUNDS NICE featuring Tim MYCROFT
UK, male instrumental group and male, vocalist

6 Sep 69	**LOVE AT FIRST SIGHT (JE T'AIME ... MOI NON PLUS)** *Parlophone R 5797*	18	11

SOUNDS OF BLACKNESS
US, male / female gospel choir (1 Album: 6 Weeks, 11 Singles: 32 Weeks)

22 Jun 91	**OPTIMISTIC** *Perspective PERSS 786*	45	4
28 Sep 91	**THE PRESSURE PART 1** *Perspective PERSS 816*	71	1
15 Feb 92	**OPTIMISTIC** (re-issue) *Perspective PERSS 849*	28	4
25 Apr 92	**THE PRESSURE PART 1** (re-mix) *Perspective PERSS 867*	49	2
8 May 93	**I'M GOING ALL THE WAY** *Perspective 5874252*	27	3
26 Mar 94	**I BELIEVE** *A&M 5874512*	17	4
30 Apr 94	**AFRICA TO AMERICA: THE JOURNEY OF THE DRUM** *A&M 5490092*	28	6
2 Jul 94	**GLORYLAND** *Mercury MERCD 404* [1]	36	4
20 Aug 94	**EVERYTHING IS GONNA BE ALRIGHT** *A&M 5874672*	29	3
14 Jan 95	**I'M GOING ALL THE WAY** (re-issue) *A&M 5874832*	14	4
7 Jun 97	**SPIRIT** *A&M 5822292* [2]	35	2
14 Feb 98	**THE PRESSURE** (re-mix) *AM:PM 5824872*	46	1

[1] Daryl Hall and Sounds of Blackness [2] Sounds of Blackness featuring Craig Mack

SOUNDS ORCHESTRAL
UK, orchestra (1 Album: 1 Week, 2 Singles: 18 Weeks)

3 Dec 64 ●	**CAST YOUR FATE TO THE WIND** *Piccadilly 7N 35206*	5	16
12 Jun 65	**CAST YOUR FATE TO THE WIND** *Piccadilly NPL 38041*	17	1
8 Jul 65	**MOONGLOW** *Piccadilly 7N 35248*	43	2

SOUNDSATION *UK, male producer*

14 Jan 95	**PEACE AND JOY** *Ffrreedom TABCD 224*	48	1

SOUNDSCAPE *UK, male DJ / production group*

14 Feb 98	**DUBPLATE CULTURE** *Satellite 74321552002*	61	1

SOUNDSOURCE *Sweden / UK, male instrumental / production group*

11 Jan 92	**TAKE ME UP** *ffrr FX 177*	62	1

The SOUNDTRACK OF OUR LIVES NEW
Sweden, male vocal / instrumental group

12 Mar 05	**HEADING FOR A BREAKDOWN** *WEA WEA 383CD*	70	1

The SOUP DRAGONS *UK, male vocal (Sean Dickinson) / instrumental group (3 Albums: 17 Weeks, 5 Singles: 23 Weeks)*

20 Jun 87	**CAN'T TAKE NO MORE** *Raw TV RTV 3*	65	1
5 Sep 87	**SOFT AS YOUR FACE** *Raw TV RTV 4*	66	2
7 May 88	**THIS IS OUR ART** *Sire WX 169*	60	1
5 May 90 ●	**LOVEGOD** *Raw TV SOUPLP 2*	7	15
14 Jul 90 ●	**I'M FREE** *Raw TV RTV 9* [1]	5	12
20 Oct 90	**MOTHER UNIVERSE** *Big Life BLR 30*	26	5
11 Apr 92	**DIVINE THING** *Big Life BLR 68*	53	3
16 May 92	**HOTWIRED** *Big Life BLRCD 15*	74	1

[1] The Soup Dragons featuring Junior Reid

7 July 1990	14 July 1990	21 July 1990	28 July 1990
UK No.1 SINGLES			
SACRIFICE / HEALING HANDS Elton John	SACRIFICE / HEALING HANDS Elton John	SACRIFICE / HEALING HANDS Elton John	TURTLE POWER Partners in Kryme
UK No.1 ALBUMS			
THE ESSENTIAL PAVAROTTI Luciano Pavarotti	THE ESSENTIAL PAVAROTTI Luciano Pavarotti	THE ESSENTIAL PAVAROTTI Luciano Pavarotti	SLEEPING WITH THE PAST Elton John

The SOURCE *UK, male producer – John Truelove (5 Singles: 25 Weeks)*

2 Feb 91 ● **YOU GOT THE LOVE** *Truelove TLOVE 7001* [1] **4** 11
26 Dec 92 **ROCK THE HOUSE** *React 12REACT 12* [2] **63** 1
1 Mar 97 ● **YOU GOT THE LOVE** (re-mix) *React CDREACT 89* [1] **3** 8
23 Aug 97 **CLOUDS** *XL Recordings XLS 83CD*....**38** 2
1 Jan 05 **YOU GOT THE LOVE** (import) (2nd re-mix) *ZYX GDC 2221112* [1] **60** 3

[1] The Source featuring Candi Staton [2] The Source featuring Nicole

SOURMASH *UK, male production trio*

23 Dec 00 **PILGRIMAGE / MESCALITO** *Hooj Choons HOOJ 102*....**73** 1

SOUTH *UK, male vocal / instrumental group (4 Singles: 4 Weeks)*

17 Mar 01 **PAINT THE SILENCE** *Mo Wax MWR 134CD*....**69** 1
23 Aug 03 **LOOSEN YOUR HOLD** *Double Dragon DD 2010CD*....**73** 1
3 Apr 04 **COLOURS IN WAVES** *Sanctuary SANXD 249*....**60** 1
14 Aug 04 **MOTIVELESS CRIME** *Sanctuary SANXD 286*....**72** 1

Joe SOUTH *US, male vocalist – Joe Souter*

5 Mar 69 ● **GAMES PEOPLE PLAY** *Capitol CL 15579*....**6** 11

SOUTH BANK ORCHESTRA *UK, orchestra*

2 Dec 78 LILLIE *Sounds MOR 516*....47 6

Album was conducted by Joseph Morovitz and Laurie Holloway.

SOUTH ST. PLAYER *US, male vocalist / producer – Roland Clark*

2 Sep 00 **WHO KEEPS CHANGING YOUR MIND** *Cream CREAM 4CD*....**49** 1

Jeri SOUTHERN
US, female vocalist – Genevieve Hering, b. 5 Aug 1926, d. 4 Aug 1991

21 Jun 57 **FIRE DOWN BELOW** *Brunswick 05665*....**22** 3

The SOUTHLANDERS *Jamaica / UK, male vocal group*

22 Nov 57 **ALONE** *Decca F 10946*....**17** 10

SOUTHSIDE SPINNERS
Holland, male production duo – Marco Verkuylen and Benjamin Kuyten

27 May 00 ● **LUVSTRUCK** *AM:PM CDAMPM 132*....**9** 7

SOUVERNANCE *Holland, male production duo*

31 Aug 02 **HAVIN' A GOOD TIME** *Positiva CDTIV 174*....**63** 1

SOUVLAKI *UK, male producer – Mark Summers (2 Singles: 4 Weeks)*

15 Feb 97 **INFERNO** *Wonderboy WBOYD 003*....**24** 3
8 Aug 98 **MY TIME** *Wonderboy WBOYD 009*....**63** 1

The SOVEREIGN COLLECTION *UK, orchestra*

3 Apr 71 **MOZART 40** *Capitol CL 15676*....**27** 6

Red SOVINE
US, male vocalist – Woodrow Wilson Sovine, b. 17 Jul 1918, d. 4 Apr 1980

13 Jun 81 ● **TEDDY BEAR** *Starday SD 142* **$** **4** 8

SOX *UK, female vocal / instrumental group – lead vocal Samantha Fox*

15 Apr 95 **GO FOR THE HEART** *Living Beat LBECD 33*....**47** 1

Bob B SOXX and The BLUE JEANS *US, male / female vocal group*

31 Jan 63 **ZIP-A-DEE-DOO-DAH** *London HLU 9646*....**45** 2

SPACE *France, male instrumental group*

13 Aug 77 ● **MAGIC FLY** *Pye International 7N 25746*....**2** 12
17 Sep 77 MAGIC FLY *Pye NSPL 28232*....11 9

SPACE *UK, male vocal (Tommy Scott) / instrumental group (2 Albums: 67 Weeks, 11 Singles: 52 Weeks)*

6 Apr 96 **NEIGHBOURHOOD** *Gut CDGUT 1*....**56** 1
8 Jun 96 **FEMALE OF THE SPECIES** *Gut CDGUT 2*....**14** 10
7 Sep 96 ● **ME AND YOU VERSUS THE WORLD** *Gut CDGUT 4*....**9** 6
28 Sep 96 ● SPIDERS *Gut GUTCD 1*....5 42
2 Nov 96 **NEIGHBOURHOOD** (re-issue) *Gut CDGUT 5*....**11** 6
22 Feb 97 **DARK CLOUDS** *Gut CDGUT 6*....**14** 4
10 Jan 98 ● **AVENGING ANGELS** *Gut CDGUT 16*....**6** 8
7 Mar 98 ● **THE BALLAD OF TOM JONES** *Gut CDGUT 018* [1] **4** 8
21 Mar 98 ● TIN PLANET *Gut GUTCD 5*....3 25
4 Jul 98 **BEGIN AGAIN** *Gut CDGUT 19*....**21** 4
5 Dec 98 **THE BAD DAYS (EP)** *Gut CDGUT 22*....**20** 3
8 Jul 00 **DIARY OF A WIMP** *Gut CDGUT 34*....**49** 1
6 Mar 04 **SUBURBAN ROCK 'N' ROLL** *R&M Entertainment RAMCDS 001*. **67** 1

[1] Space with Cerys of Catatonia

Tracks on The Bad Days (EP): Bad Days / We Gotta Get Out of This Place / The Unluckiest Man in the World.

SPACE BABY (see also LOST TRIBE; MDM; MELT featuring LITTLE MS MARCIE; SUNBURST) *UK, male producer – Matt Darey*

8 Jul 95 **FREE YOUR MIND** *Hooj Choons HOOJ 34CD*....**55** 1

SPACE BROTHERS (see also ASCENSION; CHAKRA; ESSENCE; LUSTRAL; OXYGEN featuring Andrea BRITTON) *UK, male production duo – Ricky Simmonds and Stephen Jones (5 Singles: 19 Weeks)*

17 May 97 **SHINE** *Manifesto FESCD 23*....**23** 3
13 Dec 97 **FORGIVEN (I FEEL YOUR LOVE)** *Manifesto FESCD 36*....**27** 7
10 Jul 99 **LEGACY (SHOW ME LOVE)** *Manifesto FESCD 55*....**31** 3
9 Oct 99 **HEAVEN WILL COME** *Manifesto FESCD 61*....**25** 2
5 Feb 00 **SHINE 2000** (re-mix) *Manifesto FESCD 67*....**18** 4

SPACE COWBOY
UK (b. France), male producer – Nick Dresti (2 Singles: 3 Weeks)

6 Jul 02 **I WOULD DIE 4 U** *Southern Fried ECB 29CD*....**55** 2
2 Aug 03 **JUST PUT YOUR HAND IN MINE** *Southern Fried ECB 37CD*....**71** 1

SPACE FROG *Germany, male production duo*

16 Mar 02 **(X RAY) FOLLOW ME** *Tripoli Trax TTRAX 082CD*....**70** 1

SPACE KITTENS *UK, male instrumental / production group*

13 Apr 96 **STORM** *Hooj Choons HOOJCD 41*....**58** 1

SPACE MANOEUVRES *UK, male producer – John Graham*

29 Jan 00 **STAGE ONE** *Hooj Choons HOOJ 79CD*....**25** 2

SPACE MONKEY *UK, male producer – Paul Goodchild*

8 Oct 83 **CAN'T STOP RUNNING** *Innervision A 3742*....**53** 4

SPACE MONKEYZ vs GORILLAZ *UK, male production / instrumental duo and UK, US, animated male vocal / instrumental / production group*

3 Aug 02 **LIL' DUB CHEFIN'** *Parlophone CDR 6584*....**73** 1

SPACE RAIDERS *UK, male production trio*

28 Mar 98 **GLAM RAID** *Skint SKINT 32CD*....**68** 1

SPACE 2000 *UK, male vocal / instrumental duo*

12 Aug 95 **DO U WANNA FUNK** *Wired WIRED 218*....**50** 1

SPACECORN *Sweden, male DJ / producer – Daniel Ellenson*

28 Apr 01 **AXEL F** *69 SN 069CD*....**74** 1

4 August 1990	11 August 1990	18 August 1990	25 August 1990
TURTLE POWER Partners in Kryme	**TURTLE POWER** Partners in Kryme	**TURTLE POWER** Partners in Kryme	**ITSY BITSY TEENY WEENY YELLOW POLKA DOT BIKINI** Bombalurina
SLEEPING WITH THE PAST Elton John	**SLEEPING WITH THE PAST** Elton John	**SLEEPING WITH THE PAST** Elton John	**SLEEPING WITH THE PAST** Elton John

KEY: UK No.1 ★ UK Top 10 ● Still on chart + UK entry at No.1 ■ US No.1 ▲ UK million seller £ US million seller $
Singles re-entries are listed as (re), (2re), (3re)... which signifies that the hit re-entered the chart once, twice or three times...
Peak Position / Weeks

SPACEDUST *UK, male production duo – Paul Glancey and Duncan Glasson (2 Singles: 12 Weeks)*

24 Oct 98 ★ **GYM AND TONIC (re)** *East West EW 188CD* ■ ... 1 10
27 Mar 99 **LET'S GET DOWN** *East West EW 195CD* ... 20 2

SPACEHOG
UK, male vocal / instrumental group (1 Album: 2 Weeks, 2 Singles: 8 Weeks)

11 May 96 **IN THE MEANTIME (re)** *Sire 7559643162* ... 29 7
15 Feb 97 **RESIDENT ALIEN** *Sire 7559618342* ... 40 2
7 Feb 98 **CARRY ON** *Sire W 0428CD* ... 43 1

'In the Meantime' peaked during re-entry in Dec 1996.

SPACEMAID *UK, male vocal / instrumental group*

5 Apr 97 **BABY COME ON** *Big Star STARC 105* ... 70 1

SPACEMEN 3 *UK, male instrumental group*

9 Mar 91 **RECURRING** *Fire FIRELP 23* ... 46 1

SPAGHETTI SURFERS *UK, male instrumental / production duo*

22 Jul 95 **MISIRLOU (THE THEME TO THE MOTION PICTURE 'PULP FICTION')** *Tempo Toons CDTOON 4* ... 55 1

SPAGNA *Italy, female vocalist – Ivana Spagna (3 Singles: 23 Weeks)*

25 Jul 87 ● **CALL ME** *CBS 650279 7* ... 2 12
17 Oct 87 **EASY LADY** *CBS 651169 7* ... 62 3
20 Aug 88 **EVERY GIRL AND BOY** *CBS SPAG 1* ... 23 8

SPAN *Norway, male vocal / instrumental group*

21 Feb 04 **DON'T THINK THE WAY THEY DO** *Island CID 846* ... 52 1

SPANDAU BALLET 104 Top 500
Kilt-clad New Romantic revolutionaries. This London band went on to become smart-suited Top 10 regulars: Tony Hadley (v), Gary Kemp (g), Martin Kemp (b), Steve Norman (g/sax/prc) and John Keeble (d). The Kemp brothers later went into the movies and TV, including lead roles in The Krays (1990), and Martin, who starred in Eastenders and other TV programmes, was voted Best Actor and Sexiest Male at the 2002 Soap Awards. Hadley won 2003 reality TV pop show Reborn in the USA (9 Albums: 274 Weeks, 20 Singles: 159 Weeks)

15 Nov 80 ● **TO CUT A LONG STORY SHORT** *Reformation CHS 2473* ... 5 11
24 Jan 81 **THE FREEZE** *Reformation CHS 2486* ... 17 8
14 Mar 81 ● **JOURNEYS TO GLORY** *Reformation CHR 1331* ... 5 29
4 Apr 81 ● **MUSCLEBOUND / GLOW** *Reformation CHS 2509* ... 10 10
18 Jul 81 ● **CHANT NO.1 (I DON'T NEED THIS PRESSURE ON)** *Reformation CHS 2528* ... 3 10
14 Nov 81 **PAINT ME DOWN** *Chrysalis CHS 2560* ... 30 5
30 Jan 82 **SHE LOVED LIKE DIAMOND** *Chrysalis CHS 2585* ... 49 4
20 Mar 82 **DIAMOND** *Reformation CDL 1353* ... 15 18
10 Apr 82 ● **INSTINCTION** *Chrysalis CHS 2602* ... 10 11
2 Oct 82 ● **LIFELINE** *Chrysalis CHS 2642* ... 7 9
12 Feb 83 **COMMUNICATION** *Reformation CHS 2662* ... 12 10
12 Mar 83 ★ **TRUE** *Reformation CDL 1403* ... 1 90
23 Apr 83 ★ **TRUE** *Reformation SPAN 1* ... 1 12
13 Aug 83 ● **GOLD** *Reformation SPAN 2* ... 2 9
9 Jun 84 ● **ONLY WHEN YOU LEAVE (re)** *Reformation SPAN 3* ... 3 10
7 Jul 84 ● **PARADE** *Reformation CDL 1473* ... 2 39
25 Aug 84 ● **I'LL FLY FOR YOU** *Reformation SPAN 4* ... 9 9
20 Oct 84 **HIGHLY STRUNG** *Reformation SPAN 5* ... 15 5
8 Dec 84 **ROUND AND ROUND** *Reformation SPAN 6* ... 18 8
16 Nov 85 ● **THE SINGLES COLLECTION** *Chrysalis SBTV 1* ... 3 53
26 Jul 86 **FIGHT FOR OURSELVES** *Reformation A 7264* ... 15 7
8 Nov 86 ● **THROUGH THE BARRICADES** *Reformation SPANS 1* ... 6 10
29 Nov 86 ● **THROUGH THE BARRICADES** *Reformation CBS 450 2591* ... 7 19
14 Feb 87 **HOW MANY LIES** *Reformation SPANS 2* ... 34 4
3 Sep 88 **RAW** *CBS SPANS 3* ... 47 3
26 Aug 89 **BE FREE WITH YOUR LOVE** *CBS SPANS 4* ... 42 4
30 Sep 89 **HEART LIKE A SKY** *CBS 463 3181* ... 31 3
28 Sep 91 **THE BEST OF SPANDAU BALLET** *Chrysalis CHR 1894* ... 44 3
16 Sep 00 ● **GOLD – THE BEST OF SPANDAU BALLET** *Chrysalis 5267002* ... 7 20

SPANKOX (see also MOTIVO) *Italy, male producer – Agostino Carollo*

9 Oct 04 **TO THE CLUB** *Inferno CDFERN 62* ... 69 1

SPARKLE *US, female vocalist – Stephanie Edwards (1 Album: 1 Week, 3 Singles: 10 Weeks)*

18 Jul 98 ● **BE CAREFUL (re)** *Jive 0521452* [1] ... 7 7
1 Aug 98 **SPARKLE** *Jive 521462* ... 57 1
7 Nov 98 **TIME TO MOVE ON** *Jive 0522032* ... 40 2
28 Aug 99 **LOVIN' YOU** *Jive 0523450* ... 65 1

[1] Sparkle featuring R Kelly

SPARKLEHORSE
US, male vocal / instrumental group (3 Albums: 4 Weeks, 2 Singles: 2 Weeks)

18 May 96 **VIVADIXIESUBMARINETRANSMISSIONPLOT** *Parlophone CDP 8328162* ... 58 1
31 Aug 96 **RAINMAKER** *Capitol CDCL 777* ... 61 1
1 Aug 98 **GOOD MORNING SPIDER** *Parlophone 4960142* ... 30 2
17 Oct 98 **SICK OF GOODBYES** *Parlophone CDCLS 808* ... 57 1
23 Jun 01 **IT'S A WONDERFUL LIFE** *Capitol 5256162* ... 49 1

SPARKS *US / UK, male vocal / instrumental duo – Russell and Ron Mael (4 Albums: 42 Weeks, 15 Singles: 81 Weeks)*

4 May 74 ● **THIS TOWN AIN'T BIG ENOUGH FOR BOTH OF US** *Island WIP 6193* ... 2 10
1 Jun 74 ● **KIMONO MY HOUSE** *Island ILPS 9272* ... 4 24
20 Jul 74 ● **AMATEUR HOUR** *Island WIP 6203* ... 7 9
19 Oct 74 **NEVER TURN YOUR BACK ON MOTHER EARTH** *Island WIP 6211* ... 13 7
23 Nov 74 ● **PROPAGANDA** *Island ILPS 9312* ... 9 13
18 Jan 75 **SOMETHING FOR THE GIRL WITH EVERYTHING** *Island WIP 6221* ... 17 7
19 Jul 75 **GET IN THE SWING** *Island WIP 6236* ... 27 7
4 Oct 75 **LOOKS, LOOKS, LOOKS** *Island WIP 6249* ... 26 4
18 Oct 75 **INDISCREET** *Island ILPS 9345* ... 18 4
21 Apr 79 **THE NUMBER ONE SONG IN HEAVEN** *Virgin VS 244* ... 14 12
21 Jul 79 ● **BEAT THE CLOCK** *Virgin VS 270* ... 10 9
8 Sep 79 **NUMBER ONE IN HEAVEN** *Virgin V 2115* ... 73 1
27 Oct 79 **TRYOUTS FOR THE HUMAN RACE** *Virgin VS 289* ... 45 5
29 Oct 94 **WHEN DO I GET TO SING 'MY WAY'** *Logic 74321234472* ... 38 3
11 Mar 95 **WHEN I KISS YOU (I HEAR CHARLIE PARKER PLAYING)** *Logic 74321264272* ... 36 2
20 May 95 **WHEN DO I GET TO SING 'MY WAY'** (re-issue) *Logic 74321274002* ... 32 2
9 Mar 96 **NOW THAT I OWN THE BBC** *Logic 74321348672* ... 60 1
25 Oct 97 **THE NUMBER ONE SONG IN HEAVEN** (re-recording) *Roadrunner RR 22692* ... 70 1
13 Dec 97 **THIS TOWN AIN'T BIG ENOUGH FOR BOTH OF US** (re-recording) *Roadrunner RR 22513* [1] ... 40 2

[1] Sparks vs Faith No More

Group was UK / US up to 1975.

Bubba SPARXXX *US, male rapper – Warren Mathis (3 Singles: 13 Weeks)*

24 Nov 01 ● **UGLY** *Interscope / Polydor 4976542* ... 7 10
9 Mar 02 **LOVELY** *Interscope 4976752* ... 24 2
20 Mar 04 **DELIVERANCE** *Interscope 9862013* ... 55 1

1 September 1990	8 September 1990	15 September 1990	22 September 1990
UK No.1 SINGLES			
ITSY BITSY TEENY WEENY YELLOW POLKA DOT BIKINI Bombalurina	**ITSY BITSY TEENY WEENY YELLOW POLKA DOT BIKINI** Bombalurina	**THE JOKER** Steve Miller Band	**THE JOKER** Steve Miller Band
UK No.1 ALBUMS			
GRAFFITI BRIDGE Prince	**IN CONCERT** José Carreras, Placido Domingo and Luciano Pavarotti	**LISTEN WITHOUT PREJUDICE VOLUME 1** George Michael	**IN CONCERT** José Carreras, Placido Domingo and Luciano Pavarotti

SPEAR OF DESTINY *UK, male vocal / instrumental group (6 Albums: 35 Weeks, 10 Singles: 43 Weeks)*

23 Apr 83	GRAPES OF WRATH *Epic EPC 25318*	62	2
21 May 83	THE WHEEL *Epic A 3372*	59	5
21 Jan 84	PRISONER OF LOVE *Epic A 4068*	59	3
14 Apr 84	LIBERATOR *Epic A 4310*	67	2
28 Apr 84	ONE EYED JACKS *Burning Rome EPC 25836*	22	7
15 Jun 85	ALL MY LOVE (ASK NOTHING) *Epic A 6333*	61	3
10 Aug 85	COME BACK *Epic A 6445*	55	3
7 Sep 85	WORLD SERVICE *Burning Rome EPC 26514*	11	7
7 Feb 87	STRANGERS IN OUR TOWN *10 TEN 148*	49	4
4 Apr 87	NEVER TAKE ME ALIVE *10 TEN 162*	14	11
2 May 87	OUTLAND *10 DIX 59*	16	13
16 May 87	S.O.D. – THE EPIC YEARS *Epic 450 8721*	53	3
25 Jul 87	WAS THAT YOU? *10 TEN 173*	55	4
3 Oct 87	THE TRAVELLER *10 TEN 189*	44	3
24 Sep 88	SO IN LOVE WITH YOU *Virgin VS 1123*	36	5
22 Oct 88	THE PRICE YOU PAY *Virgin V 2549*	37	3

SPEARHEAD
US, male vocal / instrumental group (1 Album: 1 Week, 4 Singles: 5 Weeks)

17 Dec 94	OF COURSE YOU CAN *Capitol CDCL 733*	74	1
22 Apr 95	HOLE IN THE BUCKET *Capitol CDCL 742*	55	1
15 Jul 95	PEOPLE IN THA MIDDLE *Capitol CDCLS 752*	49	2
15 Mar 97	WHY OH WHY *Capitol CDCL 785*	45	1
29 Mar 97	CHOCOLATE SUPA HIGHWAY *Capitol CDEST 2293*	68	1

Billie Jo SPEARS
US, female vocalist (3 Albums: 28 Weeks, 4 Singles: 40 Weeks)

12 Jul 75 ●	BLANKET ON THE GROUND *United Artists UP 35805*	6	13
17 Jul 76 ●	WHAT I'VE GOT IN MIND *United Artists UP 36118*	4	13
11 Sep 76	WHAT I'VE GOT IN MIND *United Artists UAS 29955*	47	2
11 Dec 76	SING ME AN OLD FASHIONED SONG *United Artists UP 36179*	34	9
19 May 79 ●	THE BILLIE JO SPEARS SINGLES ALBUM *United Artists UAK 30231*	7	17
21 Jul 79	I WILL SURVIVE *United Artists UP 601*	47	5
21 Nov 81	COUNTRY GIRL *Warwick WW 5109*	17	9

Britney SPEARS (96 Top 500)
One time world's top-selling teen-ager, who sold over 35 million albums before she turned 20, b. 2 Dec 1981, Louisiana, US. She broke the debut act first-week UK sales record with 464,000 for '... Baby One More Time', sales of which went on to total 1,450,154. Britney is the youngest million-selling female in the history of the UK singles chart (5 Albums: 234 Weeks, 18 Singles: 217 Weeks)

27 Feb 99 ★	... BABY ONE MORE TIME *Jive 0522752* ■ ▲ £ $	1	22
20 Mar 99 ●	... BABY ONE MORE TIME *Jive 522172* ▲	2	89
26 Jun 99 ●	SOMETIMES *Jive 0523202*	3	16
2 Oct 99 ●	(YOU DRIVE ME) CRAZY *Jive 0550582*	5	11
29 Jan 00 ★	BORN TO MAKE YOU HAPPY *Jive 9250022* ■	1	12
13 May 00 ★	OOPS! ... I DID IT AGAIN *Jive 9250542* ■	1	14
27 May 00 ●	OOPS! ... I DID IT AGAIN *Jive 9220392* ▲	2	45
26 Aug 00 ●	LUCKY *Jive 9251022*	5	11
16 Dec 00 ●	STRONGER *Jive 9251502*	7	10
7 Apr 01	DON'T LET ME BE THE LAST TO KNOW *Jive 9251982*	12	8
27 Oct 01 ●	I'M A SLAVE 4 U *Jive 9252892*	4	14
17 Nov 01 ●	BRITNEY *Jive 9222532* ▲	4	36
2 Feb 02 ●	OVERPROTECTED *Jive 9253072*	4	12
13 Apr 02 ●	I'M NOT A GIRL, NOT YET A WOMAN *Jive 9253472*	2	10
10 Aug 02 ●	BOYS *Jive 9253912* [1]	7	8
16 Nov 02	I LOVE ROCK 'N' ROLL (re) *Jive 9254202*	13	8
22 Nov 03 ●	ME AGAINST THE MUSIC *Jive 82876576432* [2]	2	12
29 Nov 03	IN THE ZONE *Jive 82876576442* ▲	13	43
13 Mar 04 ★	TOXIC *Jive 82876602092* ■	1	14
26 Jun 04 ★	EVERYTIME *Jive 82876626202* ■	1	14
13 Nov 04 ●	MY PREROGATIVE *Jive 82876652582*	3	12
20 Nov 04 ●	GREATEST HITS: MY PREROGATIVE *Jive 82876666162*	2	21
12 Mar 05 ●	DO SOMETHIN' *Jive 82876681922*	6	9

[1] Britney Spears featuring Pharrell Williams [2] Britney Spears featuring Madonna

SPECIAL D *Germany, male producer and female vocalist – Dennis Horstmann and Laura Nori*

17 Apr 04 ●	COME WITH ME *All Around the World CDGLOBE 340*	6	11

SPECIAL NEEDS *UK, male vocal / instrumental group (2 Singles: 2 Weeks)*

16 Oct 04	FRANCESCA – THAT MADDENING GLARE / THE WINTER GARDENS *Poptones MC 5092SCD*	69	1
25 Jun 05	BLUE SKIES *Mercury 9872234*	56	1

The SPECIALS (384 Top 500)
Midlands-based septet who led the early 1980s ska revival and, under Jerry Dammers (k), founded the trailblazing indie label 2 Tone. In 1981, Terry Hall (v), Neville Staples (v) and Lynval Golding (g) broke away to form Fun Boy Three (5 Albums: 82 Weeks, 12 Singles: 101 Weeks)

28 Jul 79 ●	GANGSTERS *2 Tone CHSTT 1* [1]	6	12
27 Oct 79 ●	A MESSAGE TO YOU RUDY / NITE KLUB *2 Tone CHSTT 5* [2]	10	14
3 Nov 79 ●	SPECIALS *2 Tone CDLTT 5001*	4	45
26 Jan 80 ★	THE SPECIAL A.K.A. LIVE! EP *2 Tone CHSTT 7*	1	10
24 May 80 ●	RAT RACE / RUDE BUOYS OUTA JAIL *2 Tone CHSTT 11*	5	9
20 Sep 80 ●	STEREOTYPE / INTERNATIONAL JET SET *2 Tone CHSTT 13*	6	8
4 Oct 80 ●	MORE SPECIALS *2 Tone CHRTT 5003*	5	19
13 Dec 80 ●	DO NOTHING / MAGGIE'S FARM *2 Tone CHSTT 16*	4	11
20 Jun 81 ★	GHOST TOWN *2 Tone CHSTT 17*	1	14
23 Jan 82	THE BOILER *2 Tone CHSTT 18*	35	5
3 Sep 83	RACIST FRIEND / BRIGHT LIGHTS *2 Tone CHSTT 25* [1]	60	3
17 Mar 84 ●	NELSON MANDELA *2 Tone CHSTT 26* [1]	9	10
23 Jun 84	IN THE STUDIO *2 Tone CHRTT 5008* [1]	34	6
8 Sep 84	WHAT I LIKE MOST ABOUT YOU IS YOUR GIRLFRIEND *2 Tone CHSTT 27* [1]	51	4
7 Sep 91 ●	THE SPECIALS SINGLES *2 Tone CHRTT 5010*	10	9
10 Feb 96	HYPOCRITE *Kuff KUFFD 3*	66	1
7 Jul 01	SPECIALS (re-issue) *Chrysalis CCD 5001*	22	3

[1] The Special AKA [2] The Specials featuring Rico [1] The Special AKA

Tracks on The Special A.K.A. Live! EP: Too Much Too Young / Guns of Navarone / Longshot Kick De Bucket / The Liquidator / Skinhead Moonstomp. 'Maggie's Farm' listed with 'Do Nothing' only from 10 Jan 1981. Group was male / female from 1984.

Phil SPECTOR
US, male producer, featuring various vocal acts (5 Albums: 29 Weeks)

23 Dec 72	PHIL SPECTOR'S CHRISTMAS ALBUM *Apple SAPCOR 24*	21	3
15 Oct 77	PHIL SPECTOR'S ECHOES OF THE 60'S *Phil Spector International 2307 013*	21	10
25 Dec 82	PHIL SPECTOR'S CHRISTMAS ALBUM (re-issue) *Phil Spector International 2307 005*	96	2
10 Dec 83	PHIL SPECTOR'S GREATEST HITS / PHIL SPECTOR'S CHRISTMAS ALBUM (2nd re-issue) *Impression PSLP 1/2*	19	8
12 Dec 87	PHIL SPECTOR'S CHRISTMAS ALBUM (3rd re-issue) *Chrysalis CDL 1625*	69	6

SPECTRUM *UK, male instrumental / production group*

26 Sep 92	TRUE LOVE WILL FIND YOU IN THE END *Silvertone ORE 44*	70	1

Chris SPEDDING (see also NUCLEUS; SOUNDS NICE featuring Tim MYCROFT) *UK, male vocalist / guitarist*

23 Aug 75	MOTOR BIKIN' *RAK 210*	14	8

SPEECH *US, male vocalist – Todd Thomas*

17 Feb 96	LIKE MARVIN GAYE SAID (WHAT'S GOING ON) *Cooltempo CDCOOL 314*	35	2

SPEEDWAY *UK, male / female vocal / instrumental duo – Jill Jackson and Jim Duguid (1 Album: 1 Week, 3 Singles: 10 Weeks)*

6 Sep 03 ●	GENIE IN A BOTTLE / SAVE YOURSELF *Innocent SINCD 47*	10	4
21 Feb 04	CAN'T TURN BACK *Innocent SINCD 55*	12	4
6 Mar 04	SAVE YOURSELF *Innocent CDSIN 12*	42	1
19 Jun 04	IN & OUT *Innocent SINDX 61*	31	2

29 September 1990	6 October 1990	13 October 1990	20 October 1990
SHOW ME HEAVEN Maria McKee	SHOW ME HEAVEN Maria McKee	SHOW ME HEAVEN Maria McKee	SHOW ME HEAVEN Maria McKee
IN CONCERT José Carreras, Placido Domingo and Luciano Pavarotti	IN CONCERT José Carreras, Placido Domingo and Luciano Pavarotti	IN CONCERT José Carreras, Placido Domingo and Luciano Pavarotti	SOME FRIENDLY The Charlatans

KEY: UK No.1 ★ UK Top 10 ● Still on chart + UK entry at No.1 ■ US No.1 ▲ UK million seller £ US million seller $
Singles re-entries are listed as (re), (2re), (3re)... which signifies that the hit re-entered the chart once, twice or three times...

Peak Position / Weeks

SPEEDY *UK, male / female vocal / instrumental group*

9 Nov 96 **BOY WONDER** *Boiler House! BOIL 2CD* **56** 1

SPEEDY J *Holland, male producer – Jochem Paap*

10 Jul 93 GINGER *Warp WARPCD 14* 68 1

SPEKTRUM *UK, male / female vocal / instrumental group*

18 Sep 04 **KINDA NEW** *Non Stop SPEKD 004* **70** 1

SPELLBOUND *India, female vocal duo*

31 May 97 **HEAVEN ON EARTH** *East West EW 098CD* **73** 1

Johnnie SPENCE *UK, orchestra*

1 Mar 62 **THE 'DR KILDARE' THEME** *Parlophone R 4872* **15** 15

Don SPENCER *Australia, male vocalist*

21 Mar 63 **FIREBALL (re)** *HMV POP 1087* **32** 12

Jon SPENCER BLUES EXPLOSION
US, male vocal / instrumental group (2 Albums: 2 Weeks, 3 Singles: 3 Weeks)

12 Oct 96 NOW I GOT WORRY *Mute CDSTUMM 132* 50 1
10 May 97 **WAIL** *Mute CDMUTE 204* **66** 1
31 Oct 98 ACME *Mute CDSTUMM 154* 72 1
6 Apr 02 **SHE SAID** *Mute LCDMUTE 263* **58** 1
6 Jul 02 **SWEET N SOUR** *Mute LCDMUTE 271* **66** 1

Tracie SPENCER *US, female vocalist (2 Singles: 3 Weeks)*

4 May 91 **THIS HOUSE** *Capitol CL 612* **65** 2
6 Nov 99 **IT'S ALL ABOUT YOU (NOT ABOUT ME)** *Parlophone Rhythm Series CDCL 815* **65** 1

SPHINX (see also DUSTED; FAITHLESS; OUR TRIBE / ONE TRIBE; ROLLO) *UK / US, male vocal / instrumental group*

25 Mar 95 **WHAT HOPE HAVE I** *Champion CHAMPCD 318* **43** 2

SPICE GIRLS 179 Top 500
Britain's most successful and influential female vocal group: Geri Halliwell (Ginger Spice, left 1998), Melanie Chisholm (Mel C / Melanie C / Sporty Spice), Emma Bunton (Baby Spice), Victoria Adams, now Victoria Beckham (Posh Spice) and Melanie Brown (Mel B / Mel G / Scary Spice). The ground-breaking girl-power group who made it a Spiceworld was the first act to put its first six singles at No.1 and the only group to spawn five solo hit-makers. Total UK single sales: 7,507,213. Best-selling single: 'Wannabe' 1,269,841 (3 Albums: 135 Weeks, 10 Singles: 179 Weeks)

20 Jul 96 ★ **WANNABE** *Virgin VSCDX 1588* ▲ £ $ **1** 26
26 Oct 96 ★ **SAY YOU'LL BE THERE** *Virgin VSCDT 1601* ■ **1** 17
16 Nov 96 ★ SPICE *Virgin CDV 2812* ■ ▲ 1 72
28 Dec 96 ★ **2 BECOME 1 (re)** *Virgin VSCDT 1607* ■ £ **1** 23
15 Mar 97 ★ **MAMA / WHO DO YOU THINK YOU ARE** *Virgin VSCDT 1623* ■ **1** 15
25 Oct 97 ★ **SPICE UP YOUR LIFE** *Virgin VSCDT 1660* ■ **1** 15
15 Nov 97 ★ SPICEWORLD *Virgin CDV 2850* ■ 1 55
27 Dec 97 ★ **TOO MUCH** *Virgin VSCDR 1669* ■ **1** 15
21 Mar 98 ● **STOP (re)** *Virgin VSCDT 1679* **2** 17
1 Aug 98 ★ **VIVA FOREVER** *Virgin VSCDT 1692* ■ **1** 13
26 Dec 98 ★ **GOODBYE** *Virgin VSCDT 1721* ■ **1** 21
4 Nov 00 ★ **HOLLER / LET LOVE LEAD THE WAY** *Virgin VSCDT 1788* ■ **1** 17
18 Nov 00 ● FOREVER *Virgin CDVX 2928* 2 8

SPIDER
UK, male vocal / instrumental group (2 Albums: 2 Weeks, 2 Singles: 5 Weeks)

23 Oct 82 ROCK 'N' ROLL GYPSIES *RCA RCALP 3101* 75 1
5 Mar 83 **WHY D'YA LIE TO ME** *RCA 313* **65** 2
10 Mar 84 **HERE WE GO ROCK 'N' ROLL** *A&M AM 180* **57** 3
7 Apr 84 ROUGH JUSTICE *A&M AMLX 68563* 96 1

SPILLER (see also Sophie ELLIS-BEXTOR; LAGUNA; THEAUDIENCE)
Italy, male producer – Cristiano Spiller (2 Singles: 26 Weeks)

26 Aug 00 ★ **GROOVEJET (IF THIS AIN'T LOVE)** *Positiva CDTIV 137* ■ **1** 24
2 Feb 02 **CRY BABY** *Positiva CDTIV 167* **40** 2

'Groovejet (If This Ain't Love)' features lead vocals by Sophie Ellis-Bextor.

SPIN CITY *UK / Ireland, male vocal group*

26 Aug 00 **LANDSLIDE** *Epic 6696132* **30** 3

SPIN DOCTORS *US, male vocal (Christopher Barron) / instrumental group (2 Albums: 57 Weeks, 8 Singles: 28 Weeks)*

20 Mar 93 ● POCKET FULL OF KRYPTONITE *Epic 4682502* 2 48
15 May 93 ● **TWO PRINCES** *Epic 6591452* **3** 15
14 Aug 93 **LITTLE MISS CAN'T BE WRONG** *Epic 6584892* **23** 5
9 Oct 93 **JIMMY OLSEN'S BLUES** *Epic 6597582* **40** 2
4 Dec 93 **WHAT TIME IS IT** *Epic 6599552* **56** 1
25 Jun 94 **CLEOPATRA'S CAT** *Epic 6604192* **29** 2
9 Jul 94 ● TURN IT UPSIDE DOWN *Epic 4768862* 3 9
30 Jul 94 **YOU LET YOUR HEART GO TOO FAST** *Epic 6606612* **66** 1
29 Oct 94 **MARY JANE** *Epic 6609772* **55** 1
8 Jun 96 **SHE USED TO BE MINE** *Epic 6632682* **55** 1

SPINAL TAP *US / UK, male vocal / instrumental group (1 Album: 2 Weeks, 2 Singles: 3 Weeks)*

28 Mar 92 **BITCH SCHOOL** *MCA MCS 1624* **35** 2
11 Apr 92 BREAK LIKE THE WIND *MCA MCAD 10514* 51 2
2 May 92 **THE MAJESTY OF ROCK** *MCA MCS 1629* **61** 1

The SPINNERS *UK, male vocal / instrumental group (4 Albums: 24 Weeks)*

5 Sep 70 THE SPINNERS ARE IN TOWN *Fontana 6309 014* 40 5
7 Aug 71 SPINNERS LIVE PERFORMANCE *Contour 6870 502* 14 12
13 Nov 71 THE SWINGING CITY *Philips 6382 002* 20 3
8 Apr 72 LOVE IS TEASING *Columbia SCX 6493* 33 4

SPIRAL TRIBE
UK, male / female vocal / instrumental group (2 Singles: 2 Weeks)

29 Aug 92 **BREACH THE PEACE (EP)** *Butterfly BLRT 79* **66** 1
21 Nov 92 **FORWARD THE REVOLUTION** *Butterfly BLRT 85* **70** 1

Tracks on Breach the Peace (EP): Breach the Peace / Do It / Seven / 25 Minute Warning.

SPIRIT *US, male vocal / instrumental group (2 Albums: 3 Weeks)*

13 Mar 71 TWELVE DREAMS OF DR. SARDONICUS *Epic EPC 64191* 29 1
18 Apr 81 POTATO LAND *Beggars Banquet BEGA 23* 40 2

The SPIRITS *UK, male / female vocal duo – Beverly Thomas and Osmond Wright (2 Singles: 5 Weeks)*

19 Nov 94 **DON'T BRING ME DOWN** *MCA MCSTD 2018* **31** 3
8 Apr 95 **SPIRIT INSIDE** *MCA MCSTD 2045* **39** 2

SPIRITUALIZED *UK, male / female vocal (Jason Pierce) / instrumental group (6 Albums: 26 Weeks, 12 Singles: 19 Weeks)*

30 Jun 90 **ANYWAY THAT YOU WANT ME / STEP INTO THE BREEZE** *Dedicated ZB 43783* **75** 1
17 Aug 91 **RUN** *Dedicated SPIRT 002* **59** 1
11 Apr 92 LAZER GUIDED MELODIES *Dedicated DEDCD 004* 27 2
25 Jul 92 **MEDICATION** *Dedicated SPIRT 005T* **55** 1
23 Oct 93 **ELECTRIC MAINLINE** *Dedicated SPIRT 007CD* **49** 1

	27 October 1990	3 November 1990	10 November 1990	17 November 1990
UK No.1 SINGLES	A LITTLE TIME – The Beautiful South	UNCHAINED MELODY – The Righteous Brothers	UNCHAINED MELODY – The Righteous Brothers	UNCHAINED MELODY – The Righteous Brothers
UK No.1 ALBUMS	THE RHYTHM OF THE SAINTS – Paul Simon	THE RHYTHM OF THE SAINTS – Paul Simon	THE VERY BEST OF ELTON JOHN – Elton John	THE VERY BEST OF ELTON JOHN – Elton John

4 Feb 95	LET IT FLOW *Dedicated SPIRT 009CD* [1]	30	2
18 Feb 95	PURE PHASE *Dedicated DEDCD 0175* [1]	20	2
28 Jun 97 ●	LADIES & GENTLEMEN WE ARE FLOATING IN SPACE *Dedicated DEDCD 034*	4	15
9 Aug 97	ELECTRICITY *Dedicated SPIRT 012CD1*	32	2
14 Feb 98	I THINK I'M IN LOVE *Dedicated SPIRT 014CD*	27	2
6 Jun 98	THE ABBEY ROAD EP *Dedicated SPIRT 015CD*	39	2
7 Nov 98	LIVE AT THE ROYAL ALBERT HALL *Dedicated 74321622852*	38	1
15 Sep 01	STOP YOUR CRYING *Spaceman / Arista OPM 002*	18	3
29 Sep 01 ●	LET IT COME DOWN *Arista OPM 001CD*	3	4
8 Dec 01	OUT OF SIGHT *Spaceman / Arista OPM 005*	65	1
23 Feb 02	DO IT ALL OVER AGAIN *Spaceman / Arista OPM 004*	31	2
13 Sep 03	SHE KISSED ME (IT FELT LIKE A HIT) *Sanctuary SANXD 222*	38	1
20 Sep 03	AMAZING GRACE *Spaceman / Sanctuary SANDCD 214X*	25	2

[1] Spiritualized Electric Mainline [1] Spiritualized Electric Mainline

Tracks on The Abbey Road EP: Come Together / Broken Heart / Broken Heart (instrumental).

SPIRO and WIX *UK, male instrumental duo – Steve Spiro and Paul Wickens*

10 Aug 96	TARA'S THEME *EMI Premier PRESCD 4*	29	2

SPITTING IMAGE
UK, male / female latex puppets (1 Album: 3 Weeks, 2 Singles: 18 Weeks)

10 May 86 ★	THE CHICKEN SONG (re) *Virgin SPIT 1*	1	11
18 Oct 86	SPIT IN YOUR EAR *Virgin V 2403*	55	3
6 Dec 86	SANTA CLAUS IS ON THE DOLE / FIRST ATHEIST TABERNACLE CHOIR *Virgin VS 921*	22	7

SPLINTER *UK, male vocal / instrumental duo – Bill Elliott and Bob Purvis*

2 Nov 74	COSTAFINE TOWN *Dark Horse AMS 7135*	17	10

SPLIT ENZ (see also CROWDED HOUSE; FINN) *New Zealand / UK, male vocal / instrumental group (2 Albums: 9 Weeks, 2 Singles: 15 Weeks)*

16 Aug 80	I GOT YOU *A&M AMS 7546*	12	11
30 Aug 80	TRUE COLOURS *A&M AMLH 64822*	42	8
23 May 81	HISTORY NEVER REPEATS *A&M AMS 8128*	63	4
8 May 82	TIME AND TIDE *A&M AMLH 64894*	71	1

A SPLIT SECOND *Belgium / Italy, male instrumental / production group*

14 Dec 91	FLESH *ffrr FX 178*	68	1

SPLODGENESSABOUNDS *UK, male / female vocal (Max Splodge) / instrumental group (3 Singles: 17 Weeks)*

14 Jun 80 ●	SIMON TEMPLER / TWO PINTS OF LAGER AND A PACKET OF CRISPS PLEASE *Deram BUM 1*	7	8
6 Sep 80	TWO LITTLE BOYS / HORSE *Deram ROLF 1*	26	7
13 Jun 81	COWPUNK MEDLUM *Deram BUM 3*	69	2

SPOILED & ZIGO
Israel, male DJ / production duo – Elad Avnon and Ziv Goland

12 Aug 00	MORE & MORE *Manifesto FESCD 72*	31	3

SPONGE *US, male vocal / instrumental group*

19 Aug 95	PLOWED *Work 6623162*	74	1

SPOOKS *US, male / female vocal (Ming Xia) / rap group (1 Album: 12 Weeks, 3 Singles: 17 Weeks)*

27 Jan 01 ●	THINGS I'VE SEEN *Epic 6706722*	6	10
17 Feb 01	S.I.O.S.O.S. – VOLUME ONE *Epic 4982612*	25	12
5 May 01	KARMA HOTEL *Epic 6709012*	15	6
15 Sep 01	SWEET REVENGE *Epic 6718072*	67	1

SPOOKY *UK, male vocal / instrumental duo*

13 Mar 93	SCHMOO *Guerilla GRRR 45CD*	72	1

SPORTY THIEVZ *US, male rap / vocal group*

10 Jul 99	NO PIGEONS *Columbia / Roc-a-Blok / Ruffhouse 6676022*	21	6

The SPOTNICKS
Sweden, male instrumental group (1 Album: 1 Week, 4 Singles: 37 Weeks)

14 Jun 62	ORANGE BLOSSOM SPECIAL *Oriole CB 1724*	29	10
6 Sep 62	ROCKET MAN *Oriole CB 1755*	38	9
31 Jan 63	HAVA NAGILA *Oriole CB 1790*	13	12
9 Feb 63	OUT-A-SPACE *Oriole PS 40036*	20	1
25 Apr 63	JUST LISTEN TO MY HEART *Oriole CB 1818*	36	6

Dusty SPRINGFIELD 160 Top 500 (see also The SPRINGFIELDS)
One of Britain's leading female vocalists of the 1960s, b. Mary O'Brien, 16 Apr 1939, London, d. 2 Mar 1999. After leaving The Springfields in 1963, she had numerous transatlantic solo hits and during the Sixties was regularly voted the UK's Top Female Singer (13 Albums: 138 Weeks, 26 Singles: 211 Weeks)

21 Nov 63 ●	I ONLY WANT TO BE WITH YOU *Philips BF 1292*	4	18
20 Feb 64	STAY AWHILE *Philips BF 1313*	13	10
25 Apr 64 ●	A GIRL CALLED DUSTY *Philips BL 7594*	6	23
2 Jul 64 ●	I JUST DON'T KNOW WHAT TO DO WITH MYSELF *Philips BF 1348*	3	12
22 Oct 64 ●	LOSING YOU *Philips BF 1369*	9	13
18 Feb 65	YOUR HURTIN' KINDA LOVE *Philips BF 1396*	37	4
1 Jul 65 ●	IN THE MIDDLE OF NOWHERE *Philips BF 1418*	8	10
16 Sep 65 ●	SOME OF YOUR LOVIN' *Philips BF 1430*	8	12
23 Oct 65 ●	EV'RYTHING'S COMING UP DUSTY *Philips RBL 1002*	6	12
27 Jan 66	LITTLE BY LITTLE *Philips BF 1466*	17	9
31 Mar 66 ★	YOU DON'T HAVE TO SAY YOU LOVE ME *Philips BF 1482*	1	13
7 Jul 66 ●	GOIN' BACK *Philips BF 1502*	10	10
15 Sep 66 ●	ALL I SEE IS YOU *Philips BF 1510*	9	12
22 Oct 66 ●	GOLDEN HITS *Philips BL 7737*	2	36
23 Feb 67	I'LL TRY ANYTHING *Philips BF 1553*	13	9
25 May 67	GIVE ME TIME *Philips BF 1577*	24	6
11 Nov 67	WHERE AM I GOING *Philips SBL 7820*	40	1
10 Jul 68 ●	I CLOSE MY EYES AND COUNT TO TEN *Philips BF 1682*	4	12
4 Dec 68 ●	SON-OF-A PREACHER MAN *Philips BF 1730*	9	9
21 Dec 68	DUSTY ... DEFINITELY *Philips SBL 7864*	30	6
20 Sep 69	AM I THE SAME GIRL (re) *Philips BF 1811*	43	4
2 May 70	FROM DUSTY ... WITH LOVE *Philips SBL 7927*	35	2
19 Sep 70	HOW CAN I BE SURE *Philips 6006 045*	36	4
4 Mar 78	IT BEGINS AGAIN *Mercury 9109 607*	41	2
20 Oct 79	BABY BLUE *Mercury DUSTY 4*	61	5
22 Aug 87 ●	WHAT HAVE I DONE TO DESERVE THIS? *Parlophone R 6163* [1]	2	9
30 Jan 88	DUSTY – THE SILVER COLLECTION *Phonogram DUSTV 1*	14	10
25 Feb 89	NOTHING HAS BEEN PROVED *Parlophone R 6207*	16	7
2 Dec 89	IN PRIVATE *Parlophone R 6234*	14	10
26 May 90	REPUTATION *Parlophone R 6253*	38	6
7 Jul 90	REPUTATION *Parlophone PCSD 111*	18	6
24 Nov 90	ARRESTED BY YOU *Parlophone R 6266*	70	2
30 Oct 93	HEART AND SOUL *Columbia 6598562* [2]	75	1
14 May 94 ●	GOIN' BACK – THE VERY BEST OF DUSTY SPRINGFIELD 1962-1994 *Philips 8487892*	5	11
10 Jun 95	WHEREVER WOULD I BE *Columbia 6620592* [3]	44	3
8 Jul 95	A VERY FINE LOVE *Columbia 4785082*	43	1
4 Nov 95	ROLL AWAY *Columbia 6623682*	68	1
7 Nov 98	THE BEST OF DUSTY SPRINGFIELD *Mercury / PolyGram TV 5383452*	19	24
13 Mar 04	THE LOOK OF LOVE *Universal TV 9816495*	25	4

[1] Pet Shop Boys and Dusty Springfield [2] Cilla Black with Dusty Springfield [3] Dusty Springfield and Daryl Hall

From 27 Mar 1999, The Best of Dusty Springfield changed label to Mercury / Universal Music TV.

Rick SPRINGFIELD *Australia, male vocalist / actor – Richard Springthorpe (3 Albums: 8 Weeks, 2 Singles: 13 Weeks)*

14 Jan 84	HUMAN TOUCH / SOULS *RCA RICK 1*	23	7
11 Feb 84	LIVING IN OZ *RCA PL 84660*	41	4

24 November 1990	1 December 1990	8 December 1990	15 December 1990
UNCHAINED MELODY The Righteous Brothers	ICE ICE BABY Vanilla Ice	ICE ICE BABY Vanilla Ice	ICE ICE BABY Vanilla Ice
THE IMMACULATE COLLECTION Madonna	THE IMMACULATE COLLECTION Madonna	THE IMMACULATE COLLECTION Madonna	THE IMMACULATE COLLECTION Madonna

KEY: UK No.1 ★ UK Top 10 ● Still on chart + UK entry at No.1 ■ US No.1 ▲ UK million seller £ US million seller $
Singles re-entries are listed as (re), (2re), (3re)... which signifies that the hit re-entered the chart once, twice or three times...
Peak Position / Weeks

24 Mar 84 **JESSIE'S GIRL** *RCA RICK 2* ▲ $ 43 6
25 May 85 TAO *RCA PL 85370* 68 3
26 Mar 88 ROCK OF LIFE *RCA PL 86620* 80 1

'Souls' listed only from 11 Feb 1984. It peaked at No.24.

The SPRINGFIELDS (see also Dusty SPRINGFIELD)

UK, male / female vocal / instrumental group (5 Singles: 66 Weeks)

31 Aug 61 **BREAKAWAY** *Philips BF 1168* 31 8
16 Nov 61 **BAMBINO** *Philips BF 1178* 16 11
13 Dec 62 ● **ISLAND OF DREAMS** *Philips 326557 BF* 5 26
28 Mar 63 ● **SAY I WON'T BE THERE** *Philips 326577 BF* 5 15
25 Jul 63 **COME ON HOME** *Philips BF 1263* 31 6

Bruce SPRINGSTEEN 48 Top 500

'The Boss', b. 23 Sep 1949, New Jersey, US. Singer / songwriter / guitarist / rock superstar, whose legendary three to four-hour stage performances have packed stadiums worldwide for over 25 years. An insurance valuation of $3 million was once placed on Springsteen's voice. He released the biggest-selling boxed set of all time, Live 1975-85 (22 Albums: 533 Weeks, 25 Singles: 146 Weeks)

1 Nov 75 BORN TO RUN *CBS 69170* 17 50
17 Jun 78 DARKNESS ON THE EDGE OF TOWN *CBS 86061* 16 40
25 Oct 80 ● THE RIVER *CBS 88510* ▲ 2 88
22 Nov 80 **HUNGRY HEART** *CBS 9309* 44 4
13 Jun 81 **THE RIVER** *CBS A 1179* 35 6
2 Oct 82 ● NEBRASKA *CBS 25100* 3 19
26 May 84 ● **DANCING IN THE DARK (re)** *CBS A 4436* $ 4 23
16 Jun 84 ★ BORN IN THE U.S.A. *CBS 86304* ▲ 1 129
6 Oct 84 **COVER ME (re)** *CBS A 4662* 16 13
15 Jun 85 GREETINGS FROM ASBURY PARK N.J. *CBS 32210* 41 10
15 Jun 85 THE WILD, THE INNOCENT & THE E STREET SHUFFLE *CBS 32363* 33 12
15 Jun 85 ● **I'M ON FIRE / BORN IN THE USA** *CBS A 6342* 5 12
3 Aug 85 **GLORY DAYS** *CBS A 6375* 17 6
14 Dec 85 ● **SANTA CLAUS IS COMIN' TO TOWN / MY HOMETOWN** *CBS A 6773* 9 5
22 Nov 86 ● LIVE 1975-85 *CBS 450 2271* [1] ▲ 4 9
29 Nov 86 **WAR** *CBS 650193 7* [1] 18 7
7 Feb 87 **FIRE** *CBS 650381 7* [1] 54 2
23 May 87 **BORN TO RUN** *CBS BRUCE 2* 16 4
3 Oct 87 **BRILLIANT DISGUISE** *CBS 651141 7* 20 5
17 Oct 87 ★ TUNNEL OF LOVE *CBS 460 2701* ■ ▲ 1 33
12 Dec 87 **TUNNEL OF LOVE** *CBS 651295 7* 45 4
18 Jun 88 **TOUGHER THAN THE REST** *CBS BRUCE 3* 13 8
24 Sep 88 **SPARE PARTS** *CBS BRUCE 4* 32 3
21 Mar 92 **HUMAN TOUCH** *Columbia 6578727* 11 5
4 Apr 92 ★ HUMAN TOUCH *Columbia 4714232* ■ 1 17
4 Apr 92 ● LUCKY TOWN *Columbia 4714242* 2 11
23 May 92 **BETTER DAYS** *Columbia 6578907* 34 3
25 Jul 92 **57 CHANNELS (AND NOTHIN' ON)** *Columbia 6581387* 32 4
24 Oct 92 **LEAP OF FAITH** *Columbia 6583697* 46 3
10 Apr 93 **LUCKY TOWN (LIVE)** *Columbia 6592282* 48 3
24 Apr 93 ● IN CONCERT – MTV PLUGGED *Columbia 4738602* 4 7
19 Mar 94 ● **STREETS OF PHILADELPHIA** *Columbia 6600652* 2 12
11 Mar 95 ★ GREATEST HITS *Columbia 4785552* ■ ▲ 1 44
22 Apr 95 **SECRET GARDEN** *Columbia 6612955* 44 3
11 Nov 95 **HUNGRY HEART** (re-issue) *Columbia 6626252* 28 3
25 Nov 95 THE GHOST OF TOM JOAD *Columbia 4816502* 16 14
4 May 96 **THE GHOST OF TOM JOAD** *Columbia 6630315* 26 2
19 Apr 97 **SECRET GARDEN** (re-issue) *Columbia 6643245* 17 4
21 Nov 98 TRACKS *Columbia 4926052* 50 1
24 Apr 99 18 TRACKS *Columbia 4942002* 23 7
14 Apr 01 LIVE IN NEW YORK CITY *Columbia 5000002* [1] 12 6
10 Aug 02 ★ THE RISING *Columbia 5080002* ■ ▲ 1 16
14 Dec 02 **LONESOME DAY** *Columbia 6734082* 39 2
22 Nov 03 THE ESSENTIAL *Columbia 5137009* 28 2
22 Nov 03 THE ESSENTIAL *Columbia 5137002* 32 9
7 May 05 ★ DEVILS & DUST *Columbia 5200002* ■ ▲ 1 8
26 Nov 05 BORN TO RUN – 30TH ANNIVERSARY *Columbia 82876755892* 63 1

[1] Bruce Springsteen and The E Street Band [1] Bruce Springsteen & The E Street Band

'Dancing in the Dark' debuted at No.28 before making its peak position on re-entry in Jan 1985. 'Cover Me' debuted at No.38 before making its peak position on re-entry in Mar 1985. The Essential (Columbia 5137009) is a three-CD set featuring a bonus CD of rare tracks and The Essential (Columbia 5137002) is a double album featuring the same tracks but without the bonus CD. Devils & Dust includes a bonus DVD of live acoustic tracks.

SPRINGWATER

UK, male multi-instrumentalist - Phil Cordell

23 Oct 71 ● **I WILL RETURN** *Polydor 2058 141* 5 12

SPRINKLER

UK / US, male / female vocal / rap group

11 Jul 98 **LEAVE 'EM SOMETHING TO DESIRE** *Island CID 706* 45 2

[SPUNGE]

UK, male vocal / instrumental group (1 Album: 1 Week, 3 Singles: 3 Weeks)

15 Jun 02 **JUMP ON DEMAND** *Rough Trade RTRADSCD 054* 39 2
24 Aug 02 **ROOTS** *B-Unique BUN 030CDS* 52 1
7 Sep 02 THE STORY SO FAR ... *B-Unique 0927487452* 48 1

SPYRO GYRA

US, male instrumental group (2 Albums: 23 Weeks, 1 Single: 10 Weeks)

14 Jul 79 MORNING DANCE *Infinity INS 2003* 11 16
21 Jul 79 **MORNING DANCE** *Infinity INF 111* 17 10
23 Feb 80 CATCHING THE SUN *MCA MCG 4009* 31 7

SQUEEZE 252 Top 500 (see also DIFFORD and TILBROOK)

Critically-acclaimed London band who had several US best-sellers. Featured noted singer / songwriters Glenn Tilbrook (g/v) and Chris Difford (v/g). Fluctuating line-up included Jools Holland (k) and Paul Carrack (v/k), of Ace and Mike and The Mechanics fame (14 Albums: 130 Weeks, 23 Singles: 123 Weeks)

8 Apr 78 **TAKE ME I'M YOURS** *A&M AMS 7335* 19 9
10 Jun 78 **BANG BANG** *A&M AMS 7360* 49 5
18 Nov 78 **GOODBYE GIRL** *A&M AMS 7398* 63 2
24 Mar 79 ● **COOL FOR CATS** *A&M AMS 7426* 2 11
28 Apr 79 COOL FOR CATS *A&M AMLH 68503* 45 11
2 Jun 79 ● **UP THE JUNCTION** *A&M AMS 7444* 2 11
8 Sep 79 **SLAP & TICKLE** *A&M AMS 7466* 24 8
16 Feb 80 ARGY BARGY *A&M AMLH 64802* 32 15
1 Mar 80 **ANOTHER NAIL IN MY HEART** *A&M AMS 7507* 17 9
10 May 80 **PULLING MUSSELS (FROM THE SHELL)** *A&M AMS 7523* 44 6
16 May 81 **IS THAT LOVE** *A&M AMS 8129* 35 8
23 May 81 EAST SIDE STORY *A&M AMLH 64854* 19 26
25 Jul 81 **TEMPTED** *A&M AMS 8147* 41 5
10 Oct 81 ● **LABELLED WITH LOVE** *A&M AMS 8166* 4 10
24 Apr 82 **BLACK COFFEE IN BED** *A&M AMS 8219* 51 4
15 May 82 SWEETS FROM A STRANGER *A&M AMLH 64899* 20 7
23 Oct 82 **ANNIE GET YOUR GUN** *A&M AMS 8259* 43 4
6 Nov 82 ● SINGLES – 45'S AND UNDER *A&M AMLH 68552* 3 29
15 Jun 85 **LAST TIME FOREVER** *A&M AM 255* 45 5
7 Sep 85 COSI FAN TUTTI FRUTTI *A&M AMA 5085* 31 7
8 Aug 87 **HOURGLASS** *A&M AM 400* 16 10
19 Sep 87 BABYLON AND ON *A&M AMA 5161* 14 8
17 Oct 87 **TRUST ME TO OPEN MY MOUTH** *A&M AM 412* 72 1
23 Sep 89 FRANK *A&M AMA 5278* 58 1
7 Apr 90 A ROUND AND A BOUT *IRS DFCLP 1* 50 1
7 Sep 91 PLAY *Reprise WX 428* 41 1
25 Apr 92 **COOL FOR CATS** (re-issue) *A&M AM 860* 62 2
23 May 92 ● GREATEST HITS *A&M 3971812* 6 13
24 Jul 93 **THIRD RAIL** *A&M 5803372* 39 3
11 Sep 93 **SOME FANTASTIC PLACE** *A&M 5803792* 73 1
25 Sep 93 SOME FANTASTIC PLACE *A&M 5401402* 26 4

	22 December 1990	29 December 1990	5 January 1991	12 January 1991
UK No.1 SINGLES	**ICE ICE BABY** Vanilla Ice	**SAVIOUR'S DAY** Cliff Richard	**BRING YOUR DAUGHTER ... TO THE SLAUGHTER** Iron Maiden	**BRING YOUR DAUGHTER ... TO THE SLAUGHTER** Iron Maiden
UK No.1 ALBUMS	**THE IMMACULATE COLLECTION** Madonna	**THE IMMACULATE COLLECTION** Madonna	**THE IMMACULATE COLLECTION** Madonna	**THE IMMACULATE COLLECTION** Madonna

9 Sep 95 **THIS SUMMER** *A&M 5811912* **36** 3
18 Nov 95 **ELECTRIC TRAINS** *A&M 5812692* **44** 2
25 Nov 95 RIDICULOUS *A&M 5404402* 50 1
15 Jun 96 **HEAVEN KNOWS** *A&M 5816052* **27** 2
24 Aug 96 **THIS SUMMER** (re-mix) *A&M 5818372* **32** 2
22 Jun 02 ● BIG SQUEEZE – THE VERY BEST OF SQUEEZE *UMTV 4932532* 8 6

Billy SQUIER *US, male vocalist / guitarist*

3 Oct 81 **THE STROKE** *Capitol CL 214* **52** 3

Chris SQUIRE (see also YES) *UK, male vocalist / bass guitarist*

6 Dec 75 FISH OUT OF WATER *Atlantic K 50203* 25 7

John SQUIRE (see also The SEAHORSES; The STONE ROSES)

UK, male vocalist / guitarist (1 Album: 2 Weeks, 2 Singles: 2 Weeks)

28 Sep 02 TIME CHANGES EVERYTHING *North Country NCCDS 001* 17 2
2 Nov 02 **JOE LOUIS** *North Country NCCDA 001* **43** 1
14 Feb 04 **ROOM IN BROOKLYN** *North Country NCCDA 003* **44** 1

Dorothy SQUIRES *UK, female vocalist – Edna Squires, b. 25 Mar 1915, d. 14 Apr 1998 (5 Singles: 56 Weeks)*

5 Jun 53 **I'M WALKING BEHIND YOU** *Polygon P 1068* **12** 1
24 Aug 61 **SAY IT WITH FLOWERS** *Columbia DB 4665* [1] **23** 10
20 Sep 69 **FOR ONCE IN MY LIFE (re)** *President PT 267* **24** 11
21 Feb 70 **TILL (re)** *President PT 281* **25** 11
8 Aug 70 **MY WAY (2re)** *President PT 305* **25** 23

[1] Dorothy Squires and Russ Conway

STABBS *Finland / US / Cameroon, male instrumental / production group*

24 Dec 94 **JOY AND HAPPINESS** *Hi-Life HICD 3* **65** 1

STACCATO *UK / Holland, male / female vocal / instrumental duo*

20 Jul 96 **I WANNA KNOW** *Multiply CDMULTY 11* **65** 1

Warren STACEY *UK, male vocalist*

23 Mar 02 **MY GIRL MY GIRL** *Def Soul 5889932* **26** 3

Jim STAFFORD *US, male vocalist (2 Singles: 16 Weeks)*

27 Apr 74 **SPIDERS & SNAKES** *MGM 2006 374* $ **14** 8
6 Jul 74 **MY GIRL BILL** *MGM 2006 423* **20** 8

Jo STAFFORD *US, female vocalist (4 Singles: 28 Weeks)*

14 Nov 52 ★ **YOU BELONG TO ME** *Columbia DB 3152* ▲ **1** 19
19 Dec 52 **JAMBALAYA** *Columbia DB 3169* **11** 2
7 May 54 ● **MAKE LOVE TO ME!** *Philips PB 233* ▲ **8** 1
9 Dec 55 **SUDDENLY THERE'S A VALLEY (re)** *Philips PB 509* **12** 6

Terry STAFFORD *US, male vocalist, b. 22 Nov 1941, d. 17 Mar 1996*

7 May 64 **SUSPICION** *London HLU 9871* $ **31** 9

STAGECOACH featuring Penny FOSTER

UK, male / female vocal ensemble

18 Oct 03 **ANGEL LOOKING THROUGH** *Stagecoach Theatre SCR 001* **59** 1

STAIFFI and his MUSTAFAS *France, male vocal / instrumental group*

28 Jul 60 **MUSTAFA CHA CHA CHA** *Pye International 7N 25057* **43** 1

STAIND *US, male vocal (Aaron Lewis) / instrumental group (2 Albums: 29 Weeks, 4 Singles: 11 Weeks)*

1 Sep 01 ★ BREAK THE CYCLE *Elektra 7559626642* ■ ▲ 1 26
15 Sep 01 **IT'S BEEN AWHILE** *Elektra E 7252CD* **15** 6
1 Dec 01 **OUTSIDE** *Elektra E 7277CD* **33** 2
23 Feb 02 **FOR YOU** *Elektra E 7281CD* **55** 1
24 May 03 **PRICE TO PLAY** *Elektra E 7417CD* **36** 2
31 May 03 14 SHADES OF GREY *Elektra 7559628822* ▲ 16 3

STAKKA BO *Sweden, male rap / DJ duo – Johan Renck and Oscar Franzen (2 Singles: 12 Weeks)*

25 Sep 93 **HERE WE GO** *Polydor PZCD 280* **13** 8
18 Dec 93 **DOWN THE DRAIN** *Polydor PZCD 301* **64** 4

Frank STALLONE *US, male vocalist*

22 Oct 83 **FAR FROM OVER** *RSO 95* **68** 2

STAMFORD AMP *UK, male vocal / instrumental group*

12 Oct 02 **ANYTHING FOR YOU** *Mercury 638972* **33** 2

STAMFORD BRIDGE *UK, male Chelsea FC supporters vocal group*

16 May 70 **CHELSEA** *Penny Farthing PEN 715* **47** 1

STAN

UK, male vocal / instrumental duo – Simon Andrew and Kevin Stagg

31 Jul 93 **SUNTAN** *Hug CDBUM 1* **40** 3

The STANDS

UK, male vocal / instrumental group (2 Albums: 3 Weeks, 5 Singles: 8 Weeks)

16 Aug 03 **WHEN THIS RIVER ROLLS OVER YOU** *Echo ECSCD 142* **32** 1
25 Oct 03 **I NEED YOU** *Echo ECSCD 146* **39** 2
21 Feb 04 **HERE SHE COMES AGAIN** *Echo ECSCD 148* **25** 2
6 Mar 04 ALL YEARS LEAVING *Echo ECHCD 50* 28 2
5 Jun 04 **OUTSIDE YOUR DOOR** *Echo ECSCX 151* **49** 1
21 May 05 **DO IT LIKE YOU LIKE** *Echo ECSCD 165* **28** 2
6 Aug 05 HORSE FABULOUS *Echo ECHCD 64* 62 1

Lisa STANSFIELD (251 Top 500)

The only UK act to have three US R&B No.1 hits, b. 11 Apr 1966, Rochdale, Lancashire. Like Yazz, she was a featured vocalist on a Coldcut single before achieving a No.1 in her own right. This multi-BRIT award-winner has sold millions of records all around the world (7 Albums: 126 Weeks, 19 Singles: 127 Weeks)

25 Mar 89 **PEOPLE HOLD ON** *Ahead of Our Time CCUT 5* [1] **11** 9
12 Aug 89 **THIS IS THE RIGHT TIME** *Arista 112512* **13** 8
28 Oct 89 ★ **ALL AROUND THE WORLD** *Arista 112693* $ **1** 14
2 Dec 89 ● AFFECTION *Arista 210379* 2 31
10 Feb 90 ● **LIVE TOGETHER** *Arista 112914* **10** 6
12 May 90 **WHAT DID I DO TO YOU (EP)** *Arista 113168* **25** 4
19 Oct 91 ● **CHANGE** *Arista 114820* **10** 7
23 Nov 91 ● REAL LOVE *Arista 212300* 3 51
21 Dec 91 **ALL WOMAN** *Arista 115000* **20** 8
14 Mar 92 **TIME TO MAKE YOU MINE** *Arista 115113* **14** 8
6 Jun 92 **SET YOUR LOVING FREE** *Arista 74321100587* **28** 4
19 Dec 92 ● **SOMEDAY (I'M COMING BACK)** *Arista 74321123567* **10** 9
1 May 93 ★ **FIVE LIVE (EP) (re)** *Parlophone CDRS 6340* [2] ■ **1** 12
5 Jun 93 ● **IN ALL THE RIGHT PLACES** *MCA MCSTD 1780* **8** 11
23 Oct 93 **SO NATURAL** *Arista 74321169132* **15** 5
20 Nov 93 ● SO NATURAL *Arista 74321172312* 6 14
11 Dec 93 **LITTLE BIT OF HEAVEN** *Arista 74321178202* **32** 4
18 Jan 97 ● **PEOPLE HOLD ON (THE BOOTLEG MIXES)** *Arista 74321452012* [3] **4** 6
22 Mar 97 ● **THE REAL THING** *Arista 74321463222* **9** 7
5 Apr 97 ● LISA STANSFIELD *Arista 74321458512* 2 18
21 Jun 97 **NEVER, NEVER GONNA GIVE YOU UP** *Arista 74321490392* **25** 3
4 Oct 97 **THE LINE** *RCA 74321511372* **64** 1
23 Jun 01 **LET'S JUST CALL IT LOVE** *Arista 74321863422* **48** 1
7 Jul 01 FACE UP *Arista 74321863462* 38 2
15 Feb 03 ● BIOGRAPHY – THE GREATEST HITS *Arista 82876502222* 3 9
9 Oct 04 THE MOMENT *ZTT ZTT 192CD* 57 1

[1] Coldcut featuring Lisa Stansfield [2] George Michael and Queen with Lisa Stansfield [3] Lisa Stansfield vs The Dirty Rotten Scoundrels

Tracks on What Did I Do to You (EP): What Did I Do to You / My Apple Heart / Lay Me Down / Something's Happenin'. Tracks on Five Live (EP): Somebody to Love / These Are the Days of Our Lives / Calling You / Papa Was a Rolling Stone – Killer (medley). Lisa Stansfield appears only on the second track.

19 January 1991	26 January 1991	2 February 1991	9 February 1991
SADNESS PART 1 Enigma	**INNUENDO** Queen	**3:A.M. ETERNAL** The KLF featuring Children of the Revolution	**3:A.M. ETERNAL** The KLF featuring Children of the Revolution
THE IMMACULATE COLLECTION Madonna	**MCMXC A.D. - THE LIMITED EDITION** Enigma	**THE SOUL CAGES** Sting	**DOUBT** Jesus Jones

KEY
UK No.1 ★ UK Top 10 ● Still on chart + UK entry at No.1 ■
US No.1 ▲ UK million seller £ US million seller $
Singles re-entries are listed as (re), (2re), (3re)... which signifies that the hit re-entered the chart once, twice or three times...

Peak Position / Weeks

STANTON WARRIORS *UK, male production duo*

22 Sep 01 DA ANTIDOTE *Mob MOBCD 006* ... 69 1

The STAPLE SINGERS *US, male / female vocal group (2 Singles: 14 Weeks)*

10 Jun 72 I'LL TAKE YOU THERE *Stax 2025 110* ▲ $ ... 30 8
8 Jun 74 IF YOU'RE READY (COME GO WITH ME) *Stax 2025 224* $ ... 34 6

Cyril STAPLETON and his ORCHESTRA
UK, orchestra – leader b. 31 Dec 1914, d. 25 Feb 1974 (5 Singles: 27 Weeks)

27 May 55 ELEPHANT TANGO (2re) *Decca F 10488* ... 19 4
23 Sep 55 ● BLUE STAR (THE MEDIC THEME) *Decca F 10559* [1] ... 2 12
6 Apr 56 THE ITALIAN THEME *Decca F 10703* ... 18 2
1 Jun 56 THE HAPPY WHISTLER *Decca F 10735* [2] ... 22 4
19 Jul 57 FORGOTTEN DREAMS *Decca F 10912* ... 27 5

[1] Cyril Stapleton Orchestra featuring Julie Dawn [2] Cyril Stapleton Orchestra featuring Desmond Lane, penny whistle

The STAR SPANGLES
UK, male vocal / instrumental group (2 Singles: 2 Weeks)

19 Apr 03 STAY AWAY FROM ME *Parlophone CDR 6604* ... 52 1
12 Jul 03 I LIVE FOR SPEED *Parlophone CDR 6609* ... 60 1

STAR TURN ON 45 (PINTS)
UK, male vocalist – Steve O'Donnell, d. 4 Aug 1997 (2 Singles: 9 Weeks)

24 Oct 81 STARTURN ON 45 (PINTS) *V Tone V TONE 003* ... 45 4
30 Apr 88 PUMP UP THE BITTER *Pacific DRINK 1* ... 12 5

STARCHASER *Italy, male DJ / production trio*

22 Jun 02 LOVE WILL SET YOU FREE (JAMBE MYTH) *Rulin RULIN 23CDS* ... 24 4

STARDUST *France, male / female vocal / instrumental group*

8 Oct 77 ARIANA *Satril SAT 120* ... 42 3

STARDUST
France, male vocal (Benjamin Cohen) / production group (2 Singles: 26 Weeks)

1 Aug 98 MUSIC SOUNDS BETTER WITH YOU (import) *Roule ROULE 305* ... 55 3
22 Aug 98 ● MUSIC SOUNDS BETTER WITH YOU *Virgin DINSD 175* ... 2 23

Alvin STARDUST (see also Shane FENTON and The FENTONES) *UK, male vocalist – Bernard Jewry (3 Albums: 17 Weeks, 13 Singles: 119 Weeks)*

3 Nov 73 ● MY COO-CA-CHOO *Magnet MAG 1* ... 2 21
16 Feb 74 ★ JEALOUS MIND *Magnet MAG 5* ... 1 11
16 Mar 74 ● THE UNTOUCHABLE *Magnet MAG 5001* ... 4 12
4 May 74 ● RED DRESS *Magnet MAG 8* ... 7 8
31 Aug 74 ● YOU YOU YOU *Magnet MAG 13* ... 6 10
30 Nov 74 TELL ME WHY *Magnet MAG 19* ... 16 8
21 Dec 74 ALVIN STARDUST *Magnet MAG 5004* ... 37 3
1 Feb 75 GOOD LOVE CAN NEVER DIE *Magnet MAG 21* ... 11 9
12 Jul 75 SWEET CHEATIN' RITA *Magnet MAG 32* ... 37 4
4 Oct 75 ROCK WITH ALVIN *Magnet MAG 5007* ... 52 2
5 Sep 81 ● PRETEND *Stiff BUY 124* ... 4 10
21 Nov 81 A WONDERFUL TIME UP THERE *Stiff BUY 132* ... 56 8
5 May 84 ● I FEEL LIKE BUDDY HOLLY *Chrysalis CHS 2784* ... 7 11
27 Oct 84 ● I WON'T RUN AWAY *Chrysalis CHS 2829* ... 7 13
15 Dec 84 SO NEAR TO CHRISTMAS *Chrysalis CHS 2835* ... 29 4
23 Mar 85 GOT A LITTLE HEARTACHE *Chrysalis CHS 2856* ... 55 2

STARFIGHTER *Belgium, male producer – Philip Dirix*

5 Feb 00 APACHE *Sound of Ministry MOSCDS 136* ... 31 3

STARGARD *US, female vocal group (3 Singles: 14 Weeks)*

28 Jan 78 THEME SONG FROM 'WHICH WAY IS UP' *MCA 346* ... 19 7
15 Apr 78 LOVE IS SO EASY *MCA 354* ... 45 1
9 Sep 78 WHAT YOU WAITIN' FOR *MCA 382* ... 39 6

STARGATE *Norway / US, male / female production / vocal / rap group*

7 Sep 02 EASIER SAID THAN DONE *Telstar CDSTAS 3269* ... 55 1

The STARGAZERS
UK / Australia, male / female vocal group (9 Singles: 68 Weeks)

13 Feb 53 ★ BROKEN WINGS (re) *Decca F 10047* ... 1 12
19 Feb 54 ★ I SEE THE MOON *Decca F 10213* ... 1 15
9 Apr 54 THE HAPPY WANDERER *Decca F 10259* ... 12 1
17 Dec 54 ★ THE FINGER OF SUSPICION *Decca F 10394* [1] ... 1 15
4 Mar 55 SOMEBODY *Decca F 10437* ... 20 1
3 Jun 55 THE CRAZY OTTO RAG *Decca F 10523* ... 18 3
9 Sep 55 ● CLOSE THE DOOR *Decca F 10594* ... 6 9
11 Nov 55 ● TWENTY TINY FINGERS *Decca F 10626* ... 4 11
22 Jun 56 HOT DIGGITY (DOG ZIGGITY BOOM) *Decca F 10731* ... 28 1

[1] Dickie Valentine with The Stargazers

The STARGAZERS *UK, male vocal / instrumental group*

6 Feb 82 GROOVE BABY GROOVE (EP) *Epic EPC A 1924* ... 56 3

Tracks on Groove Baby Groove (EP): Groove Baby Groove / Jump Around / La Rock 'n' Roll (Quelques Uns a la Lune) / Red Light Green Light.

Ed STARINK *US, male instrumentalist - synthesizer (2 Albums: 11 Weeks)*

27 Oct 90 SYNTHESIZER GREATEST *Arcade ARC 938101* [1] ... 22 5
9 Jan 93 SYNTHESIZER GOLD *Arcade ARC 3100012* ... 29 6

[1] Star Inc

The STARJETS *UK, male vocal / instrumental group*

8 Sep 79 WAR STORIES *Epic EPC 7770* ... 51 5

The STARLAND VOCAL BAND *US, male / female vocal group*

7 Aug 76 AFTERNOON DELIGHT *RCA 2716* ▲ $ ... 18 10

STARLIGHT *Italy, male instrumental / production group*

19 Aug 89 ● NUMERO UNO *Citybeat CBE 742* ... 9 11

STARPARTY
(see also ALBION; GENERATOR; GOURYELLA; MOONMAN; SYSTEM F; VERACOCHA) *Holland, male production duo – Ferry Corsten and Robert Smit*

26 Feb 00 I'M IN LOVE *Incentive CENT 5CDS* ... 26 2

Edwin STARR (see also UTAH SAINTS) *US, male vocalist – Charles Hatcher, b. 21 Jan 1942, d. 2 Apr 2003 (10 Singles: 70 Weeks)*

12 May 66 STOP HER ON SIGHT (SOS) *Polydor BM 56 702* ... 35 8
18 Aug 66 HEADLINE NEWS *Polydor 56 717* ... 39 3
11 Dec 68 STOP HER ON SIGHT (SOS) / HEADLINE NEWS (re-issues) *Polydor 56 753* ... 11 11
13 Sep 69 25 MILES *Tamla Motown TMG 672* ... 36 6
24 Oct 70 ● WAR *Tamla Motown TMG 754* ▲ $ ... 3 12
20 Feb 71 STOP THE WAR NOW *Tamla Motown TMG 764* ... 33 1
27 Jan 79 ● CONTACT *20th Century BTC 2396* ... 6 12
26 May 79 ● H.A.P.P.Y. RADIO *RCA TC 2408* ... 9 11
1 Jun 85 IT AIN'T FAIR *Hippodrome HIP 101* ... 56 4
30 Oct 93 WAR (re-recording) *Weekend CDWEEK 103* [1] ... 69 2

[1] Edwin Starr and Shadow

'Headline News' was not listed with 'SOS' from 22 Jan 1969 to 19 Feb 1969 and peaked at No.16. 'War' (1993) was listed with the flip side, 'Wild Thing' by The Troggs and Wolf.

	16 February 1991	23 February 1991	2 March 1991	9 March 1991
UK No.1 SINGLES	DO THE BARTMAN The Simpsons	DO THE BARTMAN The Simpsons	DO THE BARTMAN The Simpsons	SHOULD I STAY OR SHOULD I GO The Clash
UK No.1 ALBUMS	INNUENDO Queen	INNUENDO Queen	CIRCLE OF ONE Oleta Adams	AUBERGE Chris Rea

Freddie STARR *UK, male vocalist / comedian – Fred Smith (2 Albums: 16 Weeks, 2 Singles: 14 Weeks)*

23 Feb 74 ● **IT'S YOU** *Tiffany 6121 501* ... **9** 10
20 Dec 75 **WHITE CHRISTMAS** *Thunderbird THE 102* ... **41** 4
18 Nov 89 ● AFTER THE LAUGHTER *Dover ADD 10* ... 10 9
17 Nov 90 THE WANDERER *Dover ADD 17* ... 33 7

Kay STARR *US, female vocalist – Katherine Starks (1 Album: 1 Week, 5 Singles: 58 Weeks)*

5 Dec 52 ★ **COMES A-LONG A-LOVE** *Capitol CL 13808* ... **1** 16
24 Apr 53 ● **SIDE BY SIDE** *Capitol CL 13871* ... **7** 4
19 Mar 54 ● **CHANGING PARTNERS** *Capitol CL 14050* ... **4** 14
15 Oct 54 **AM I A TOY OR TREASURE (re)** *Capitol CL 14151* ... **17** 4
17 Feb 56 ★ **ROCK AND ROLL WALTZ** *HMV POP 168* ▲ $ ... **1** 20
26 Mar 60 MOVIN' *Capitol 1254* ... 16 1

Ringo STARR (see also The BEATLES) *UK, male vocalist – Richard Starkey (3 Albums: 28 Weeks, 6 Singles: 56 Weeks)*

18 Apr 70 ● SENTIMENTAL JOURNEY *Apple PCS 7101* ... 7 6
17 Apr 71 ● **IT DON'T COME EASY** *Apple R 5898* $ ... **4** 11
1 Apr 72 ● **BACK OFF BOOGALOO** *Apple R 5944* ... **2** 10
27 Oct 73 ● **PHOTOGRAPH** *Apple R 5992* ▲ $ ... **8** 13
8 Dec 73 ● RINGO *Apple PCTC 252* ... 7 20
23 Feb 74 ● **YOU'RE SIXTEEN** *Apple R 5995* ▲ $ ... **4** 10
30 Nov 74 **ONLY YOU** *Apple R 6000* ... **28** 11
7 Dec 74 GOODNIGHT VIENNA *Apple PMC 7168* ... 30 2
6 Jun 92 **WEIGHT OF THE WORLD** *Private Music 115392* ... **74** 1

STARS ON 54 *US, female vocal trio*

28 Nov 98 **IF YOU COULD READ MY MIND** *Tommy Boy TBCD 7497* ... **23** 3

STARSAILOR *UK, male vocal (James Walsh) / instrumental group (3 Albums: 57 Weeks, 9 Singles: 39 Weeks)*

17 Feb 01 **FEVER** *Chrysalis CDCHSS 5123* ... **18** 3
5 May 01 **GOOD SOULS** *Chrysalis CDCHS 5125* ... **12** 6
29 Sep 01 ● **ALCOHOLIC** *Chrysalis CDCHSS 5130* ... **10** 6
20 Oct 01 ● LOVE IS HERE *Chrysalis 5353502* ... 2 41
22 Dec 01 **LULLABY** *Chrysalis CDCHS 5131* ... **36** 4
30 Mar 02 **POOR MISGUIDED FOOL** *Chrysalis CDCHS 5136* ... **23** 3
13 Sep 03 ● **SILENCE IS EASY** *EMI CDEM 625* ... **9** 8
27 Sep 03 ● SILENCE IS EASY *EMI 5900072* ... 2 13
29 Nov 03 **BORN AGAIN** *EMI CDEM 632* ... **40** 2
13 Mar 04 **FOUR TO THE FLOOR** *EMI CDEMS 634* ... **24** 4
15 Oct 05 **IN THE CROSSFIRE** *EMI CDEM 671* ... **22** 3
29 Oct 05 ON THE OUTSIDE *EMI 3422742* ... 13 3

STARSHIP (see also JEFFERSON AIRPLANE) *US, female / male vocal / instrumental group (1 Album: 5 Weeks, 4 Singles: 41 Weeks)*

26 Jan 80 **JANE** *Grunt FB 1750* [1] ... **21** 9
16 Nov 85 **WE BUILT THIS CITY** *RCA PB 49929* ▲ $ ... **12** 12
8 Feb 86 **SARA** *RCA FB 49893* ▲ ... **66** 3
11 Apr 87 ★ **NOTHING'S GONNA STOP US NOW** *Grunt FB 49757* ▲ $ ... **1** 17
18 Jul 87 NO PROTECTION *Grunt FL 86413* ... 26 5

[1] Jefferson Starship

STARSOUND *Holland, male producer – Jaap Eggermont and male / female session singers (3 Albums: 28 Weeks, 4 Singles: 37 Weeks)*

18 Apr 81 ● **STARS ON 45** *CBS A 1102* ▲ $ ... **2** 14
16 May 81 ★ STARS ON 45 *CBS 86132* ... 1 21
4 Jul 81 ● **STARS ON 45 VOLUME 2** *CBS A 1407* ... **2** 10
19 Sep 81 STARS ON 45 VOLUME 2 *CBS 85181* ... 18 6
19 Sep 81 **STARS ON 45 VOLUME 3** *CBS A 1521* ... **17** 6
27 Feb 82 **STARS ON STEVIE** *CBS A 2041* ... **14** 7
3 Apr 82 STARS MEDLEY *CBS 85651* ... 94 1

STARTRAX *UK, male / female vocal group*

1 Aug 81 STARTRAX CLUB DISCO *Picksy KSYA 1001* ... 26 7
1 Aug 81 **STARTRAX CLUB DISCO** *Picksy KSY 1001* ... **18** 8

STARVATION *Multinational, male / female vocal / instrumental charity assembly*

9 Mar 85 **STARVATION / TAM-TAM POUR L'ETHIOPIE** *Zarjazz JAZZ 3* ... **33** 6

STARVING SOULS *UK, male vocal / instrumental group*

21 Oct 95 **I BE THE PROPHET EP** *Durban Poison DPCD 1* ... **66** 1

Tracks on I Be the Prophet EP: I Be the Prophet / If You Want My Love / I Be the Prophet (re-mix). I Be the Prophet features uncredited vocalist Terry Hall.

STATE OF MIND *UK, male / female vocal / production group (2 Singles: 3 Weeks)*

18 Apr 98 **THIS IS IT** *Ministry of Sound MOSCDS 123* ... **30** 2
25 Jul 98 **TAKE CONTROL** *Ministry of Sound MOSCDS 124* ... **46** 1

STATE OF THE HEART *UK, male vocal / instrumental group – includes Dave Lewis – saxophone (2 Albums: 9 Weeks)*

16 Mar 96 PURE SAX *Virgin VTCD 78* ... 18 7
12 Oct 96 SAX AT THE MOVIES *Virgin VTCD 98* ... 62 2

STATE ONE *UK / Germany, male production group*

27 Sep 03 **FOREVER AND A DAY** *Incentive CENT 54CDS* ... **62** 1

STATIC REVENGER *US, male producer – Dennis White*

7 Jul 01 **HAPPY PEOPLE** *Incentive / Rulin CENRUL 1CDS* ... **23** 3

STATIC-X *US, male vocal / instrumental group*

23 Jun 01 MACHINE *Warner Bros. 9362479482* ... 56 2
6 Oct 01 **BLACK AND WHITE** *Warner W 560CD* ... **65** 1

STATLER BROTHERS *US, male vocal group*

24 Feb 66 **FLOWERS ON THE WALL** *CBS 201976* ... **38** 4

Candi STATON *US, female vocalist – Canzata Staton (1 Album: 3 Weeks, 11 Singles: 74 Weeks)*

29 May 76 ● **YOUNG HEARTS RUN FREE** *Warner Bros. K 16730* ... **2** 13
24 Jul 76 YOUNG HEARTS RUN FREE *Warner Bros. K 56259* ... 34 3
18 Sep 76 **DESTINY** *Warner Bros. K 16806* ... **41** 3
23 Jul 77 ● **NIGHTS ON BROADWAY** *Warner Bros. K 16972* ... **6** 12
3 Jun 78 **HONEST I DO LOVE YOU** *Warner Bros. K 17164* ... **48** 5
24 Apr 82 **SUSPICIOUS MINDS** *Sugarhill SH 112* ... **31** 9
31 May 86 **YOUNG HEARTS RUN FREE** (re-mix) *Warner Bros. W 8680* ... **47** 5
2 Feb 91 ● **YOU GOT THE LOVE** *Truelove TLOVE 7001* [1] ... **4** 11
1 Mar 97 ● **YOU GOT THE LOVE** (re-mix) *React CDREACT 89* [1] ... **3** 8
17 Apr 99 **LOVE ON LOVE** *React CDREACT 143* ... **27** 3
7 Aug 99 **YOUNG HEARTS RUN FREE** (re-recording) *React CDREACT 158* ... **29** 2
1 Jan 05 **YOU GOT THE LOVE** (import) (2nd re-mix) *ZYX GDC 2221112* [1] ... **60** 3

[1] The Source featuring Candi Staton

STATUS IV *US, male vocal group*

9 Jul 83 **YOU AIN'T REALLY DOWN** *TMT TMT 4* ... **56** 3

STATUS QUO 26 Top 500

Ever popular London-based three-chord boogie band: Francis Rossi (g/v), Rick Parfitt (g/v), Alan Lancaster (b) and John Coghlan (d). These long-time festival favourites recorded as The Spectres and Traffic Jam before their psychedelic-sounding debut hit introduced them to the UK and US Top 20 (their only major American hit). The Quo hold the record for most

16 March 1991	23 March 1991	30 March 1991	6 April 1991
SHOULD I STAY OR SHOULD I GO The Clash	THE STONK Hale and Pace and The Stonkers	THE ONE AND ONLY Chesney Hawkes	THE ONE AND ONLY Chesney Hawkes
SPARTACUS The Farm	OUT OF TIME R.E.M.	GREATEST HITS Eurythmics	GREATEST HITS Eurythmics

KEY

UK No.1 ★★ UK Top 10 ●● Still on chart ++ UK entry at No.1 ■■
US No.1 ▲▲ UK million seller £ US million seller $
Singles re-entries are listed as (re), (2re), (3re)... which signifies that the hit re-entered the chart once, twice or three times...

Peak Position ▼ Weeks ▼

appearances on Top of the Pops with 106 live perfomances and videos. No group has accumulated more UK hit singles or has a wider Top 20 chart span and only The Beatles and The Rolling Stones can better their tally of Top 20 albums. These heroes of the head-banging set were chosen to open Live Aid in 1985 (36 Albums: 470 Weeks, 62 Singles: 428 Weeks)

Date		Title / Label	Peak	Weeks
24 Jan 68	●	**PICTURES OF MATCHSTICK MEN** *Pye 7N 17449*	7	12
21 Aug 68	●	**ICE IN THE SUN** *Pye 7N 17581*	8	12
28 May 69		**ARE YOU GROWING TIRED OF MY LOVE (re)** *Pye 7N 17728*	46	3
2 May 70		**DOWN THE DUSTPIPE** *Pye 7N 17907*	12	17
7 Nov 70		**IN MY CHAIR** *Pye 7N 17998*	21	14
13 Jan 73	●	**PAPER PLANE** *Vertigo 6059 071*	8	11
20 Jan 73	●	PILEDRIVER *Vertigo 6360 082*	5	37
14 Apr 73		**MEAN GIRL** *Pye 7N 45229*	20	11
9 Jun 73		THE BEST OF STATUS QUO *Pye NSPL 18402*	32	7
8 Sep 73	●	**CAROLINE** *Vertigo 6059 085*	5	13
6 Oct 73	★	HELLO *Vertigo 6360 098*	1	28
4 May 74	●	**BREAK THE RULES** *Vertigo 6059 101*	8	8
18 May 74	●	QUO *Vertigo 9102 001*	2	16
7 Dec 74	★	**DOWN DOWN** *Vertigo 6059 114*	1	11
1 Mar 75	★	ON THE LEVEL *Vertigo 9102 002* ■	1	27
8 Mar 75		DOWN THE DUSTPIPE *Golden Hour CH 604*	20	6
17 May 75	●	**LIVE! (EP)** *Vertigo QUO 13*	9	8
14 Feb 76	●	**RAIN** *Vertigo 6059 133*	7	7
20 Mar 76	★	BLUE FOR YOU *Vertigo 9102 006* ■	1	30
10 Jul 76		**MYSTERY SONG** *Vertigo 6059 146*	11	9
11 Dec 76	●	**WILD SIDE OF LIFE** *Vertigo 6059 163*	9	12
12 Mar 77	●	LIVE *Vertigo 6641 580*	3	14
8 Oct 77	●	**ROCKIN' ALL OVER THE WORLD** *Vertigo 6059 184*	3	16
26 Nov 77	●	ROCKIN' ALL OVER THE WORLD *Vertigo 9102 014*	5	15
2 Sep 78		**AGAIN AND AGAIN** *Vertigo QUO 1*	13	9
11 Nov 78	●	IF YOU CAN'T STAND THE HEAT *Vertigo 9102 027*	3	14
25 Nov 78		**ACCIDENT PRONE** *Vertigo QUO 2*	36	8
22 Sep 79	●	**WHATEVER YOU WANT** *Vertigo 6059 242*	4	9
20 Oct 79	●	WHATEVER YOU WANT *Vertigo 9102 037*	3	14
24 Nov 79		**LIVING ON AN ISLAND** *Vertigo 6059 248*	16	10
22 Mar 80	●	12 GOLD BARS *Vertigo QUO TV 1*	3	48
11 Oct 80	●	**WHAT YOU'RE PROPOSING** *Vertigo QUO 3*	2	11
25 Oct 80	●	JUST SUPPOSIN' *Vertigo 6302 057*	4	18
6 Dec 80		**LIES / DON'T DRIVE MY CAR** *Vertigo QUO 4*	11	10
28 Feb 81	●	**SOMETHING 'BOUT YOU BABY I LIKE** *Vertigo QUO 5*	9	7
28 Mar 81	●	NEVER TOO LATE *Vertigo 6302 104*	2	13
10 Oct 81		FRESH QUOTA *PRT DOW 2*	74	1
28 Nov 81	●	**ROCK 'N' ROLL** *Vertigo QUO 6*	8	11
27 Mar 82	●	**DEAR JOHN** *Vertigo QUO 7*	10	8
24 Apr 82	★	1982 *Vertigo 6302 169* ■	1	20
12 Jun 82		**SHE DON'T FOOL ME** *Vertigo QUO 8*	36	5
30 Oct 82		**CAROLINE (LIVE AT THE N.E.C.)** *Vertigo QUO 10*	13	7
13 Nov 82	●	FROM THE MAKERS OF ... *Vertigo PROLP 1*	4	18
10 Sep 83	●	**OL' RAG BLUES** *Vertigo QUO 11*	9	8
5 Nov 83		**A MESS OF BLUES** *Vertigo QUO 12*	15	6
3 Dec 83	●	BACK TO BACK *Vertigo VERH 10*	9	22
10 Dec 83	●	**MARGUERITA TIME** *Vertigo QUO 14*	3	11
19 May 84		**GOING DOWN TOWN TONIGHT** *Vertigo QUO 15*	20	6
4 Aug 84		LIVE AT THE N.E.C. *Vertigo (Holland) 8189 471*	83	3
27 Oct 84	●	**THE WANDERER** *Vertigo QUO 16*	7	11
1 Dec 84		12 GOLD BARS VOLUME 2 (AND 1) *Vertigo QUO TV 2*	12	18
17 May 86	●	**ROLLIN' HOME** *Vertigo QUO 18*	9	6
26 Jul 86		**RED SKY** *Vertigo QUO 19*	19	8
6 Sep 86	●	IN THE ARMY NOW *Vertigo VERH 36*	7	23
4 Oct 86	●	**IN THE ARMY NOW** *Vertigo QUO 20*	2	14
6 Dec 86		**DREAMIN'** *Vertigo QUO 21*	15	8
26 Mar 88		**AIN'T COMPLAINING** *Vertigo QUO 22*	19	6
21 May 88		**WHO GETS THE LOVE?** *Vertigo QUO 23*	34	4
18 Jun 88		AIN'T COMPLAINING *Vertigo VERH 58*	12	5
20 Aug 88		**RUNNING ALL OVER THE WORLD** *Vertigo QUAID 1*	17	6
3 Dec 88	●	**BURNING BRIDGES (ON AND OFF AND ON AGAIN)** *Vertigo QUO 25*	5	10
28 Oct 89		**NOT AT ALL** *Vertigo QUO 26*	50	2
2 Dec 89		PERFECT REMEDY *Vertigo 842098 1*	49	2
29 Sep 90	●	**THE ANNIVERSARY WALTZ – PART ONE** *Vertigo QUO 28*	2	9
20 Oct 90	●	ROCKING ALL OVER THE YEARS *Vertigo 8467971*	2	25
15 Dec 90		**THE ANNIVERSARY WALTZ – PART TWO** *Vertigo QUO 29*	16	7
7 Sep 91		**CAN'T GIVE YOU MORE** *Vertigo QUO 30*	37	3
5 Oct 91	●	ROCK 'TIL YOU DROP *Vertigo 5103411*	10	7
18 Jan 92		**ROCK 'TIL YOU DROP** *Vertigo QUO 32*	38	3
10 Oct 92		**ROADHOUSE MEDLEY (ANNIVERSARY WALTZ PART 25)** *Polydor QUO 33*	21	4
14 Nov 92		LIVE ALIVE QUO *Polydor 5173672*	37	1
6 Aug 94		**I DIDN'T MEAN IT** *Polydor QUOCD 34*	21	4
3 Sep 94		THIRSTY WORK *Polydor 5236072*	13	3
22 Oct 94		**SHERRI DON'T FAIL ME NOW** *Polydor QUOCD 35*	38	2
3 Dec 94		**RESTLESS** *Polydor QUOCD 36*	39	2
4 Nov 95		**WHEN YOU WALK IN THE ROOM** *PolyGram TV 5775122*	34	2
17 Feb 96	●	DON'T STOP – THE 30TH ANNIVERSARY ALBUM *PolyGram TV 5310352*	2	11
2 Mar 96		**FUN FUN FUN** *PolyGram TV 5762632* [1]	24	4
13 Apr 96		**DON'T STOP** *PolyGram TV 5766352*	35	2
9 Nov 96		**ALL AROUND MY HAT** *PolyGram TV 5759452* [2]	47	1
25 Oct 97		WHATEVER YOU WANT – THE VERY BEST OF STATUS QUO *Mercury / PolyGram TV 5535072*	13	6
20 Mar 99		**THE WAY IT GOES** *Eagle EAGXS 075*	39	2
10 Apr 99		UNDER THE INFLUENCE *Eagle EAGCD 076*	26	2
12 Jun 99		**LITTLE WHITE LIES** *Eagle EAGXS 101*	47	1
2 Oct 99		**TWENTY WILD HORSES** *Eagle EAGXS 105*	53	1
29 Apr 00		FAMOUS IN THE LAST CENTURY *Universal Music TV 1578142*	19	5
13 May 00		**MONY MONY** *Universal TV 1580132*	48	1
17 Aug 02		**JAM SIDE DOWN** *Universal TV 192342*	17	3
5 Oct 02		HEAVY TRAFFIC *Universal TV 0187902*	15	3
9 Nov 02		**ALL STAND UP (NEVER SAY NEVER)** *Universal TV 0194872*	51	1
29 Nov 03		RIFFS *Universal TV 9813909*	44	2
25 Sep 04		**YOU'LL COME 'ROUND** *Universal TV 9868038*	14	3
2 Oct 04		XS ALL AREAS – THE GREATEST HITS *Universal TV 9824883*	16	3
4 Dec 04		**THINKING OF YOU** *Universal TV 9825824*	21	3
25 Jun 05		NOW AND THEN *Crimson 3 CRIMBX 55*	49	1
24 Sep 05		**THE PARTY AIN'T OVER YET ...** *Sanctuary SANXS 400*	11	3
1 Oct 05		THE PARTY AIN'T OVER YET ... *Sanctuary SANCD 389*	18	2
12 Nov 05		**ALL THAT COUNTS IS LOVE** *Sanctuary SANXD 413*	29	2

[1] Status Quo with The Beach Boys [2] Status Quo with Maddy Prior from Steeleye Span

Tracks on Live! EP (17 May 1975): Roll Over Lay Down (live) / Gerundula / Junior's Wailing (live). 'Don't Drive My Car' (6 Dec 1980) was listed from 20 Dec 1980 only. 'Running All Over the World' (20 Aug 1988) is a re-recorded version of 'Rockin' All Over the World' with a slightly changed lyric, released to promote the Race Against Time of 28 Aug 1988. 'The Anniversary Waltz – Part One' (29 Sep 1990) was a medley of: Let's Dance / Red River Rock / No Particular Place to Go / The Wanderer / I Hear You Knocking / Lucille / Great Balls of Fire. 'The Anniversary Waltz – Part Two' (15 Dec 1990) was a medley of: Rock & Roll Music / Lover Please / That'll Be the Day / Singing the Blues / When Will I Be Loved / Let's Work Together / Keep a Knockin' / Long Tall Sally. 'Roadhouse Medley (Anniversary Waltz Part 25)' (10 Oct 1992) was a medley of: The Wanderer / Marguerita Time / Living on an Island / Break the Rules / Something 'Bout You Baby I Like.

STAXX *UK, male / female vocal / instrumental group (3 Singles: 11 Weeks)*

Date	Title / Label	Peak	Weeks
2 Oct 93	**JOY** *Champion CHAMPCD 303*	25	6
20 May 95	**YOU** *Champion CHAMPCD 316*	50	1
13 Sep 97	**JOY** (re-mix) *Champion CHAMPCD 328* [1]	14	4

[1] Staxx featuring Carol Leeming

Carol Leeming appears on the original version of 'Joy' but is only credited on the re-mix.

13 April 1991	20 April 1991	27 April 1991	4 May 1991
◂◂ UK No.1 SINGLES ▸▸			
THE ONE AND ONLY Chesney Hawkes	THE ONE AND ONLY Chesney Hawkes	THE ONE AND ONLY Chesney Hawkes	THE SHOOP SHOOP SONG (IT'S IN HIS KISS) Cher
◂◂ UK No.1 ALBUMS ▸▸			
GREATEST HITS Eurythmics	GREATEST HITS Eurythmics	GREATEST HITS Eurythmics	GREATEST HITS Eurythmics

STEALERS WHEEL
UK, male vocal (Gerry Rafferty) / instrumental group (3 Singles: 22 Weeks)

26 May 73 ● **STUCK IN THE MIDDLE WITH YOU** *A&M AMS 7036*..................8 10
1 Sep 73 **EVERYTHING WILL TURN OUT FINE** *A&M AMS 7079*..................33 6
26 Jan 74 **STAR** *A&M AMS 7094*..................25 6

STEAM *US, male vocal / instrumental group*

31 Jan 70 ● **NA NA HEY HEY KISS HIM GOODBYE** *Fontana TF 1058* ▲ $....9 14

Anthony STEEL and The RADIO REVELLERS
UK, male actor / vocalist, b. 21 May 1920, d. 21 Mar 2001, and vocal group

10 Sep 54 **WEST OF ZANZIBAR** *Polygon P 1114*..................11 6

Act name also credits: 'with Jackie Brown and his Music'.

STEEL PULSE *UK, male vocal (David Hinds) / instrumental group (2 Albums: 18 Weeks, 3 Singles: 12 Weeks)*

1 Apr 78 **KU KLUX KLAN** *Island WIP 6428*..................41 4
8 Jul 78 **PRODIGAL SON** *Island WIP 6449*..................35 6
5 Aug 78 ● HANDSWORTH REVOLUTION *Island EMI ILPS 9502*..................9 12
23 Jun 79 **SOUND SYSTEM** *Island WIP 6490*..................71 2
14 Jul 79 TRIBUTE TO MARTYRS *Island ILPS 9568*..................42 6

Tommy STEELE (392 Top 500)
Britain's first home-grown rock 'n' roll star, b. Thomas Hicks, 17 Dec 1935, London. Just four months after his chart debut he was filming his life story. The singer / songwriter / guitarist, who was the first UK act to have a No.1 album and who topped the singles chart before Elvis, starred in many other movies and musicals (3 Albums: 34 Weeks, 17 Singles: 147 Weeks)

26 Oct 56 **ROCK WITH THE CAVEMAN (re)** *Decca F 10795* [1]..................13 5
14 Dec 56 ★ **SINGING THE BLUES (2re)** *Decca F 10819* [1]..................1 15
15 Feb 57 **KNEE DEEP IN THE BLUES** *Decca F 10849* [1]..................15 9
27 Apr 57 ● TOMMY STEELE STAGE SHOW *Decca LF 1287*..................5 1
3 May 57 ● **BUTTERFINGERS (re)** *Decca F 10877* [1]..................8 18
8 Jun 57 ★ THE TOMMY STEELE STORY *Decca LF 1288*..................1 21
16 Aug 57 ● **WATER WATER / A HANDFUL OF SONGS (re)** *Decca F 10923* [1]..................5 17
30 Aug 57 **SHIRALEE** *Decca F 10896* [1]..................11 4
22 Nov 57 **HEY YOU!** *Decca F 10941* [1]..................28 1
7 Mar 58 ● **NAIROBI** *Decca F 10991*..................3 11
12 Apr 58 ★ THE DUKE WORE JEANS (SOUNDTRACK) *Decca LF 1308*..................1 12
25 Apr 58 **HAPPY GUITAR** *Decca F 10976*..................20 5
18 Jul 58 **THE ONLY MAN ON THE ISLAND** *Decca F 11041* [1]..................16 8
14 Nov 58 ● **COME ON, LET'S GO** *Decca F 11072*..................10 13
14 Aug 59 **TALLAHASSEE LASSIE (re)** *Decca F 11152*..................16 5
28 Aug 59 **GIVE! GIVE! GIVE!** *Decca F 11152*..................28 2
4 Dec 59 ● **LITTLE WHITE BULL (re)** *Decca F 11177*..................6 17
23 Jun 60 ● **WHAT A MOUTH (WHAT A NORTH AND SOUTH)** *Decca F 11245*..5 11
29 Dec 60 **MUST BE SANTA** *Decca F 11299*..................40 1
17 Aug 61 **THE WRITING ON THE WALL** *Decca F 11372*..................30 5

[1] Tommy Steele and The Steelmen

'A Handful of Songs' listed with 'Water Water' from 23 Aug 1957.

STEELEYE SPAN *UK, male / female vocal (Maddy Prior) / instrumental group (7 Albums: 48 Weeks, 2 Singles: 18 Weeks)*

10 Apr 71 PLEASE TO SEE THE KING *B&C CAS 1029*..................45 2
14 Oct 72 BELOW THE SALT *Chrysalis CHR 1008*..................43 1
28 Apr 73 PARCEL OF ROGUES *Chrysalis CHR 1046*..................26 5
8 Dec 73 **GAUDETE** *Chrysalis CHS 2007*..................14 9
23 Mar 74 NOW WE ARE SIX *Chrysalis CHR 1053*..................13 13
15 Feb 75 COMMONER'S CROWN *Chrysalis CHR 1071*..................21 4
25 Oct 75 ● ALL AROUND MY HAT *Chrysalis CHR 1091*..................7 20
15 Nov 75 ● **ALL AROUND MY HAT** *Chrysalis CHS 2078*..................5 9
16 Oct 76 ROCKET COTTAGE *Chrysalis CHR 1123*..................41 3

STEELY DAN *US, male vocal / instrumental group – leaders Donald Fagen and Walter Becker (15 Albums: 92 Weeks, 4 Singles: 21 Weeks)*

30 Mar 74 PRETZEL LOGIC *Probe SPBA 6282*..................37 2
3 May 75 KATY LIED *ABC ABCL 5094*..................13 6
30 Aug 75 **DO IT AGAIN** *ABC 4075*..................39 4
20 Sep 75 CAN'T BUY A THRILL *ABC ABCL 5024*..................38 1
22 May 76 THE ROYAL SCAM *ABC ABCL 5161*..................11 13
11 Dec 76 **HAITIAN DIVORCE** *ABC 4152*..................17 9
8 Oct 77 ● AJA *ABC ABCL 5225*..................5 10
29 Jul 78 **FM (NO STATIC AT ALL) (re)** *MCA 374*..................49 5
2 Dec 78 GREATEST HITS *ABC BLD 616*..................41 18
10 Mar 79 **RIKKI DON'T LOSE THAT NUMBER** *ABC 4241*..................58 3
29 Nov 80 GAUCHO *MCA MCF 3090*..................27 12
3 Jul 82 GOLD *MCA MCF 3145*..................44 6
26 Oct 85 REELIN' IN THE YEARS – THE VERY BEST OF STEELY DAN *MCA DANTV 1*..................43 5
10 Oct 87 DO IT AGAIN – THE VERY BEST OF STEELY DAN *Telstar STAR 2297*..................64 4
20 Nov 93 REMASTERED – THE BEST OF STEELY DAN *MCA MCD 10967*..42 5
28 Oct 95 ALIVE IN AMERICA *Giant 74321286912*..................62 1
11 Mar 00 TWO AGAINST NATURE *Giant 74321621902*..................11 5
21 Jun 03 EVERYTHING MUST GO *Reprise 9362484902*..................21 3
28 May 05 THE STEELY DAN STORY 1972-1980 – SHOWBIZ KIDS *MCA / UMTV 9811741*..................53 1

Wout STEENHUIS *Holland, male guitarist, d. 12 Oct 1996*

21 Nov 81 HAWAIIAN PARADISE / CHRISTMAS *Warwick WW 5106*..................28 7

Gwen STEFANI (see also NO DOUBT)
US, female vocalist (1 Album: 52 Weeks, 7 Singles: 73 Weeks)

25 Aug 01 ● **LET ME BLOW YA MIND** *Interscope / Polydor 4975932* [1]..................4 12
27 Nov 04 ● **WHAT YOU WAITING FOR? (re)** *Interscope 9864986*..................4 15
4 Dec 04 ● LOVE. ANGEL. MUSIC. BABY. *Interscope 2103177*..................4 52
26 Mar 05 ● **RICH GIRL** *Interscope 9880219* [2]..................4 12
4 Jun 05 ● **HOLLABACK GIRL** *Interscope 9882326* ▲ $..................8 14
10 Sep 05 **COOL** *Interscope 9884356*..................11 10
12 Nov 05 ● **CAN I HAVE IT LIKE THAT** *Virgin VUSCD 315* [3]..................3 8+
17 Dec 05 **LUXURIOUS** *Interscope CDRS 9888344*..................44 2

[1] Eve featuring Gwen Stefani [2] Gwen Stefani featuring Eve [3] Pharrell featuring Gwen Stefani

'Hollaback Girl' was the first track to sell one million downloads in the US

Jim STEINMAN
US, male producer (1 Album: 25 Weeks, 2 Singles: 9 Weeks)

9 May 81 ● BAD FOR GOOD *Epic EPC 84361*..................7 25
4 Jul 81 **ROCK AND ROLL DREAMS COME THROUGH** *Epic EPC A 1236* [1]..................52 7
23 Jun 84 **TONIGHT IS WHAT IT MEANS TO BE YOUNG** *MCA MCA 889* [2]..................67 2

[1] Jim Steinman, vocals by Rory Dodd [2] Jim Steinman and Fire Inc

STEINSKI and MASS MEDIA *US, male / female production group*

31 Jan 87 **WE'LL BE RIGHT BACK** *Fourth & Broadway BRW 59*..................63 2

STELLA BROWNE *UK, male production duo (2 Singles: 3 Weeks)*

20 May 00 **EVERY WOMAN NEEDS LOVE** *Perfecto PERF 06*..................55 1
9 Feb 02 **NEVER KNEW LOVE** *Perfecto PERF 26CDS*..................42 2

STELLAR PROJECT featuring Brandi EMMA
Italy, male production trio and US, female vocalist

14 Aug 04 **GET UP STAND UP** *Data DATA 74CDS*..................14 4

STELLASTARR*
US, male / female vocal / instrumental group (3 Singles: 3 Weeks)

31 May 03 **SOMEWHERE ACROSS FOREVER** *Twenty-20 TWENTYCDS 001*.73 1
27 Sep 03 **JENNY** *Twenty-20 TWENTYCDS 002*..................61 1
20 Mar 04 **MY COCO** *RCA 82876599082*..................46 1

11 May 1991	18 May 1991	25 May 1991	1 June 1991
THE SHOOP SHOOP SONG (IT'S IN HIS KISS) Cher	THE SHOOP SHOOP SONG (IT'S IN HIS KISS) Cher	THE SHOOP SHOOP SONG (IT'S IN HIS KISS) Cher	THE SHOOP SHOOP SONG (IT'S IN HIS KISS) Cher
GREATEST HITS Eurythmics	GREATEST HITS Eurythmics	GREATEST HITS Eurythmics	SEAL Seal

KEY: UK No.1 ★ UK Top 10 ● Still on chart + UK entry at No.1 ■ US No.1 ▲ UK million seller £ US million seller $
Singles re-entries are listed as (re), (2re), (3re)... which signifies that the hit re-entered the chart once, twice or three times...
Peak Position / Weeks

Richie STEPHENS *Jamaica, male vocalist (2 Singles: 2 Weeks)*

15 May 93 **LEGACY** *Columbia 6592852* [1] **64** 1
9 Aug 97 **COME GIVE ME YOUR LOVE** *Delirious 74321450442* [2] **61** 1

[1] Mad Cobra featuring Richie Stephens [2] Richie Stephens and General Degree

Martin STEPHENSON and The DAINTEES *UK, male vocal / instrumental group (4 Albums: 11 Weeks, 3 Singles: 7 Weeks)*

17 May 86 BOAT TO BOLIVIA *Kitchenware KWLP 5* 85 3
8 Nov 86 **BOAT TO BOLIVIA** *Kitchenware SL 27* **70** 2
17 Jan 87 **TROUBLE TOWN** *Kitchenware SK 13* [1] **58** 3
16 Apr 88 GLADSOME HUMOUR AND BLUE *Kitchenware KWLP 8* 39 4
19 May 90 SALUTATION ROAD *Kitchenware 8281981* 35 3
27 Jun 92 **BIG SKY NEW LIGHT** *Kitchenware SK 57* **71** 2
25 Jul 92 THE BOY'S HEART *Kitchenware 8283242* 68 1

[1] The Daintees

STEPPENWOLF *US / Canada, male vocal / instrumental group (3 Albums: 20 Weeks, 2 Singles: 14 Weeks)*

11 Jun 69 **BORN TO BE WILD (re)** *Stateside SS 8017* $ **30** 9
28 Feb 70 MONSTER *Stateside SSL 5021* 43 4
25 Apr 70 STEPPENWOLF *Stateside SSL 5020* 59 2
4 Jul 70 STEPPENWOLF LIVE *Stateside SSL 5029* 16 14
27 Feb 99 **BORN TO BE WILD** (re-issue) *MCA MCSTD 48104* **18** 5

STEPS 126 Top 500 (see also H & CLAIRE; Russell WATSON)

Steptacular pop vocal quintet; Lisa Scott-Lee, Claire Richards, Faye Tozer, Lee Latchford-Evans, Ian Watkins (aka H). The hard-working live act's 1999 tour was reportedly the biggest pop arena tour ever in the UK. They bagged 14 consecutive Top 5 singles – the first act since The Beatles to achieve this feat. Having sold more than 12 million records, they announced their split on Boxing Day 2001. Best-selling single: 'Heartbeat / Tragedy' 1,150,285 (5 Albums: 172 Weeks, 16 Singles: 217 Weeks)

22 Nov 97 **5, 6, 7, 8** *Jive JIVECD 438* **14** 17
2 May 98 ● **LAST THING ON MY MIND** *Jive 0518492* **6** 14
5 Sep 98 ● **ONE FOR SORROW** *Jive 0519092* **2** 11
26 Sep 98 ● STEP ONE *Jive 519112* 2 62
21 Nov 98 ★ **HEARTBEAT / TRAGEDY** *Jive 0519142* £ **1** 30
20 Mar 99 ● **BETTER BEST FORGOTTEN (re)** *Ebul / Jive 0519242* **2** 17
10 Apr 99 ● **THANK ABBA FOR THE MUSIC** *Epic ABCD 1* [1] **4** 13
24 Jul 99 ● **LOVE'S GOT A HOLD ON MY HEART (re)** *Ebul / Jive 0519372* **2** 12
23 Oct 99 ● **AFTER THE LOVE HAS GONE (re)** *Ebul / Jive 0519462* **5** 11
6 Nov 99 ★ STEPTACULAR *Jive 519442* ■ 1 62
25 Dec 99 ● **SAY YOU'LL BE MINE / BETTER THE DEVIL YOU KNOW** *Ebul / Jive 9201008* **4** 17
15 Apr 00 ● **DEEPER SHADE OF BLUE** *Ebul / Jive 9201022* **4** 9
15 Jul 00 ● **WHEN I SAID GOODBYE / SUMMER OF LOVE** *Ebul / Jive 9201162* **5** 11
28 Oct 00 ★ **STOMP** *Ebul / Jive 9201212* ■ **1** 11
11 Nov 00 ● BUZZ *Jive 9201172* 4 26
6 Jan 01 ● **IT'S THE WAY YOU MAKE ME FEEL / TOO BUSY THINKING 'BOUT MY BABY** *Ebul / Jive 9201232* **2** 11
16 Jun 01 ● **HERE AND NOW / YOU'LL BE SORRY** *Ebul / Jive 9201322* **4** 10
6 Oct 01 ● **CHAIN REACTION / ONE FOR SORROW** (re-mix) *Ebul / Jive 9201422* **2** 12
27 Oct 01 ★ GOLD – THE GREATEST HITS *Jive 9201412* ■ 1 21
15 Dec 01 ● **WORDS ARE NOT ENOUGH / I KNOW HIM SO WELL** *Ebul / Jive 9201452* **5** 11
7 Dec 02 THE LAST DANCE *Jive 9201522* 57 1

[1] Steps, Tina Cousins, Cleopatra, B*Witched, Billie

STEREO MC's *UK, male / female vocal / rap group (2 Albums: 55 Weeks, 8 Singles: 37 Weeks)*

29 Sep 90 **ELEVATE MY MIND** *Fourth & Broadway BRW 186* **74** 1
9 Mar 91 **LOST IN MUSIC** *Fourth & Broadway BRW 198* **46** 3
26 Sep 92 **CONNECTED** *Fourth & Broadway BRW 262* **18** 6
17 Oct 92 ● CONNECTED *Fourth & Broadway BRCD 589* 2 52
5 Dec 92 **STEP IT UP** *Fourth & Broadway BRW 266* **12** 12
20 Feb 93 **GROUND LEVEL** *Fourth & Broadway BRCD 268* **19** 5
29 May 93 **CREATION** *Fourth & Broadway BRCD 276* **19** 4
26 May 01 **DEEP DOWN & DIRTY (re)** *Island CID 777* **17** 5
9 Jun 01 DEEP DOWN & DIRTY *Island CID 8106* 17 3
1 Sep 01 **WE BELONG IN THIS WORLD TOGETHER** *Island CID 782* **59** 1

STEREO NATION *UK, male vocal duo (2 Singles: 3 Weeks)*

17 Aug 96 **I'VE BEEN WAITING** *EMI Premier PRESCD 5* **53** 1
27 Oct 01 **LAILA** *Wizard WIZ 015* [1] **44** 2

[1] Taz / Stereo Nation

STEREO STAR featuring Mia J NEW *UK, male production group and female vocalist*

23 Apr 05 **UTOPIA (WHERE I WANT TO BE)** *Free 2 Air F2A 5CDX* **66** 1

STEREOLAB *UK / France / Australia, male / female vocal / instrumental group (6 Albums: 11 Weeks, 5 Singles: 6 Weeks)*

18 Sep 93 TRANSIENT RANDOM NOISE BURSTS *Duophonic UHF DUHFCD 02* 62 1
8 Jan 94 **JENNY ONDIOLINE / FRENCH DISCO** *Duophonic UHF DUHFCD 01* **75** 1
30 Jul 94 **PING PONG** *Duophonic UHF DUHFCD 04* **45** 2
20 Aug 94 MARS AUDIAC QUINTET *Duophonic UHF DUHFCD 05X* 16 3
12 Nov 94 **WOW AND FLUTTER** *Duophonic UHF DUHFCD 07* **70** 1
29 Apr 95 MUSIC FOR AMORPHOUS BODY STUDY CENTRE *Duophonic UHF DUHFCD 08* 59 1
16 Sep 95 REFRIED ECTOPLASM (SWITCHED ON VOLUME 2) *Duophonic UHF DUHFCD 09* 30 2
2 Mar 96 **CYBELE'S REVERIE** *Duophonic UHF DUHFCD 10* **62** 1
30 Mar 96 EMPEROR TOMATO KETCHUP *Duophonic UHF DUHFCD 11* 27 2
13 Sep 97 **MISS MODULAR** *Duophonic DUHFCD 16* **60** 1
4 Oct 97 DOTS AND LOOPS *Duophonic UHF DUHFCD 17* 19 2

STEREOPHONICS 71 Top 500 (see also MANCHILD)

Best Newcomer BRIT award-winning (1998) rock trio from Cwmaman, Wales: Kelly Jones (v/g), Richard Jones (b) and Stuart Cable (d). Their 14 hit singles and two chart-topping albums of new material between 1997 and 2001 cannot be bettered by any other group. They performed at Live 8 in London (5 Albums: 378 Weeks, 24 Singles: 155 Weeks)

29 Mar 97 **LOCAL BOY IN THE PHOTOGRAPH** *V2 SPHD 2* **51** 1
31 May 97 **MORE LIFE IN A TRAMP'S VEST** *V2 SPHD 4* **33** 2
23 Aug 97 **A THOUSAND TREES** *V2 VVR 5000443* **22** 3
6 Sep 97 ● WORD GETS AROUND *V2 VVR 1000438* 6 118
8 Nov 97 **TRAFFIC** *V2 VVR 5000948* **20** 3
21 Feb 98 **LOCAL BOY IN THE PHOTOGRAPH** (re-issue) *V2 VVR 5001263* **14** 4
21 Nov 98 ● **THE BARTENDER AND THE THIEF** *V2 VVR 5004653* **3** 12
6 Mar 99 ● **JUST LOOKING (re)** *V2 VVR 5005303* **4** 9
20 Mar 99 ★ PERFORMANCE AND COCKTAILS *V2 VVR 1004498* ■ 1 101
15 May 99 ● **PICK A PART THAT'S NEW** *V2 VVR 5006778* **4** 9
4 Sep 99 **I WOULDN'T BELIEVE YOUR RADIO (re)** *V2 VVR 5008823* **11** 7
20 Nov 99 **HURRY UP AND WAIT (re)** *V2 VVR 5009323* **11** 8
18 Mar 00 ● **MAMA TOLD ME NOT TO COME** *Gut CDGUT 031* [1] **4** 7
31 Mar 01 ● **MR WRITER** *V2 VVR 5015933* **5** 12
21 Apr 01 ★ JUST ENOUGH EDUCATION TO PERFORM *V2 VVR 1015838* ■ 1 87
23 Jun 01 ● **HAVE A NICE DAY** *V2 VVR 5016243* **5** 9
6 Oct 01 **STEP ON MY OLD SIZE NINES** *V2 VVR 5016253* **16** 5
15 Dec 01 ● **HANDBAGS AND GLADRAGS (re)** *V2 VVR 5017753* **4** 15
13 Apr 02 **VEGAS TWO TIMES** *V2 VVR 5019173* **23** 2
31 May 03 ● **MADAME HELGA** *V2 VVR 5021743* **4** 4

8 June 1991	15 June 1991	22 June 1991	29 June 1991
UK No.1 SINGLES			
I WANNA SEX YOU UP Color Me Badd	I WANNA SEX YOU UP Color Me Badd	I WANNA SEX YOU UP Color Me Badd	ANY DREAM WILL DO Jason Donovan
UK No.1 ALBUMS			
SEAL Seal	SEAL Seal	GREATEST HITS Eurythmics	LOVE HURTS Cher

14 Jun 03 ★ YOU GOTTA GO THERE TO COME BACK *V2 VVR 1021902* ■.......1 43
2 Aug 03 ● **MAYBE TOMORROW** *V2 VVR 5021893*......................................**3** 8
22 Nov 03 **SINCE I TOLD YOU IT'S OVER** *V2 VVR 5022623*..........................**16** 4
21 Feb 04 ● **MOVIESTAR** *V2 VVR 5024658*..**5** 5
12 Mar 05 ★ **DAKOTA (re)** *V2 VVR 5031043* ■ **1** 18
26 Mar 05 ★ LANGUAGE. SEX. VIOLENCE. OTHER? *V2 VVR 1031058* ■.........1 29
2 Jul 05 **SUPERMAN** *V2 VVR 5031063*..**13** 4
1 Oct 05 **DEVIL** *V2 VVR 5034053*...**11** 2
3 Dec 05 **REWIND** *V2 VVR 5035043*..**17** 2

[1] Tom Jones and Stereophonics

STEREOPOL featuring NEVADA *Sweden / UK, male production / vocal group and UK, male vocalist – Nevado Cato*

29 Mar 03 **DANCIN' TONIGHT** *Rulin' 28CDS*..**36** 2

STERIOGRAM *New Zealand, male vocal / instrumental group*

20 Nov 04 **WALKIE TALKIE MAN** *EMI CDEMS 652*..**19** 4

STETSASONIC *US, male rap group (2 Singles: 3 Weeks)*

24 Sep 88 **TALKIN' ALL THAT JAZZ** *Breakout USA 640*.............................**73** 2
7 Nov 98 **TALKIN' ALL THAT JAZZ** (re-mix) *Tommy Boy TBCD 7310A*...**54** 1

Cat STEVENS (132 Top 500)

Critically-acclaimed folk-pop singer / songwriter, b. Steven Georgiou, 21 Jul 1947, London, UK, whose songs have been recorded by many top acts. One of the world's biggest album sellers in 1970s. Semi-retired in 1979, he converted to Islam and changed his name to Yusuf Islam. He has received several awards in the 21st century for his humanitarian work, and gave the royalties for Boyzone's version of 'Father and Son', and his re-recording with Ronan Keating, to charity (12 Albums: 275 Weeks, 12 Singles: 107 Weeks)

20 Oct 66 **I LOVE MY DOG** *Deram DM 102*..**28** 7
12 Jan 67 ● **MATTHEW AND SON** *Deram DM 110*..**2** 10
25 Mar 67 ● MATTHEW AND SON *Deram SML 1004*...7 16
30 Mar 67 ● **I'M GONNA GET ME A GUN** *Deram DM 118*..............................**6** 10
2 Aug 67 **A BAD NIGHT** *Deram DM 140*...**20** 8
20 Dec 67 **KITTY** *Deram DM 156*...**47** 1
27 Jun 70 ● **LADY D'ARBANVILLE** *Island WIP 6086*......................................**8** 13
11 Jul 70 MONA BONE JAKON *Island ILPS 9118*...63 4
28 Nov 70 TEA FOR THE TILLERMAN *Island ILPS 9135*.................................20 31
28 Aug 71 **MOON SHADOW** *Island WIP 6092*..**22** 11
2 Oct 71 ● TEASER AND THE FIRECAT *Island ILPS 9154*................................3 93
1 Jan 72 ● **MORNING HAS BROKEN** *Island WIP 6121*...................................**9** 13
7 Oct 72 ● CATCH BULL AT FOUR *Island ILPS 9206* ▲ 2 27
9 Dec 72 **CAN'T KEEP IT IN** *Island WIP 6152*...**13** 12
21 Jul 73 ● FOREIGNER *Island ILPS 9240*...3 10
6 Apr 74 ● BUDDAH AND THE CHOCOLATE BOX *Island ILPS 9274*...............3 15
24 Aug 74 **ANOTHER SATURDAY NIGHT** *Island WIP 6206*.............................**19** 8
19 Jul 75 ● GREATEST HITS *Island ILPS 9310*..2 24
14 May 77 IZITSO *Island ILPS 9451*...18 15
2 Jul 77 **(REMEMBER THE DAYS OF THE) OLD SCHOOL YARD** *Island WIP 6387*..**44** 3
3 Feb 90 ● THE VERY BEST OF CAT STEVENS *Island CATV 1*.........................4 16
27 Nov 99 REMEMBER CAT STEVENS – THE ULTIMATE COLLECTION *Island CID 8079*...31 6
25 Oct 03 ● THE VERY BEST OF CAT STEVENS *Universal TV 9811208*..........6 18
25 Dec 04 ● **FATHER AND SON** *Polydor 9869406* [1] **2** 11

[1] Ronan Keating featuring Yusuf

The two The Very Best of Cat Stevens albums are different.

Connie STEVENS

US, female vocalist / actor – Concetta Ingolia (2 Singles: 20 Weeks)

5 May 60 ● **SIXTEEN REASONS (re)** *Warner Bros. WB 3* $..............................**9** 12
5 May 60 **KOOKIE KOOKIE (LEND ME YOUR COMB)** *Warner Bros. WB 5* [1] $..**27** 8

[1] Edward Byrnes and Connie Stevens

TOP 10

ON THE DAY OF THE MOON LANDING

At 2.56am UK (Earth) time on 21 July 1969, Apollo 11 opened its doors and Neil Armstrong took a giant leap for mankind. Wide-eyed mums and dads, boys and girls watched the poor quality black and white scenes LIVE FROM THE BLOODY MOON! While the Earth stood still and held its breath for the safe return of the astronauts, The Rolling Stones made a giant leap of their own to the No.1 spot for the eighth time.

LW	TW	
3	1	**HONKY TONK WOMEN** The Rolling Stones
4	2	**GIVE PEACE A CHANCE** Plastic Ono Band
1	3	**SOMETHING IN THE AIR** Thunderclap Newman
2	4	**IN THE GHETTO** Elvis Presley
18	5	**SAVED BY THE BELL** Robin Gibb
5	6	**HELLO SUZIE** Amen Corner
7	7	**IT MIEK** Desmond Dekker and The Aces
23	8	**GOODNIGHT MIDNIGHT** Clodagh Rodgers
9	9	**BABY MAKE IT SOON** Marmalade
6	10	**A WAY OF LIFE** Family Dogg

Neil Armstrong and The Rolling Stones

6 July 1991	13 July 1991	20 July 1991	27 July 1991
ANY DREAM WILL DO Jason Donovan	**(EVERYTHING I DO) I DO IT FOR YOU** Bryan Adams	**(EVERYTHING I DO) I DO IT FOR YOU** Bryan Adams	**(EVERYTHING I DO) I DO IT FOR YOU** Bryan Adams
LOVE HURTS Cher	**LOVE HURTS** Cher	**LOVE HURTS** Cher	**LOVE HURTS** Cher

KEY: UK No.1 ★ UK Top 10 ● Still on chart + UK entry at No.1 ■ US No.1 ▲ UK million seller £ US million seller $
Singles re-entries are listed as (re), (2re), (3re)... which signifies that the hit re-entered the chart once, twice or three times...
Peak Position / Weeks

Rachel STEVENS (see also S CLUB 7)
UK, female vocalist (2 Albums: 17 Weeks, 7 Singles: 51 Weeks)

27 Sep 03 ● **SWEET DREAMS MY L.A. EX** *19 / Polydor 9811874* 2 10
11 Oct 03 ● **FUNKY DORY** *19 / Polydor 9865702* 9 15
20 Dec 03 **FUNKY DORY** *Polydor 9614984* 26 4
24 Jul 04 ● **SOME GIRLS** *Polydor 9867433* 2 12
16 Oct 04 ● **MORE MORE MORE** *Polydor 9868325* 3 8
9 Apr 05 ● **NEGOTIATE WITH LOVE** *Polydor 9870784* 10 6
16 Jul 05 ● **SO GOOD** *Polydor 9872236* 10 6
15 Oct 05 **I SAID NEVER AGAIN (BUT HERE WE ARE)** *Polydor 9874240* 12 5
29 Oct 05 **COME AND GET IT** *Polydor 9874712* 28 2

A new version of Funky Dory, with extra tracks, peaked at No.13 in Aug 2004.

Ray STEVENS
US, male vocalist – Ray Ragsdale (2 Albums: 8 Weeks, 7 Singles: 64 Weeks)

16 May 70 ● **EVERYTHING IS BEAUTIFUL** *CBS 4953* ▲ $ 6 16
26 Sep 70 **EVERYTHING IS BEAUTIFUL** *CBS 64074* 62 1
13 Mar 71 ● **BRIDGET THE MIDGET (THE QUEEN OF THE BLUES)** *CBS 7070* 2 14
25 Mar 72 **TURN YOUR RADIO ON** *CBS 7634* 33 4
25 May 74 ★ **THE STREAK** *Janus 6146 201* ▲ $ 1 12
21 Jun 75 ● **MISTY** *Janus 6146 204* 2 10
13 Sep 75 **MISTY** *Janus 9109 401* 23 7
27 Sep 75 **INDIAN LOVE CALL** *Janus 6146 205* 34 4
5 Mar 77 **IN THE MOOD** *Warner Bros. K 16875* 31 4

'In the Mood' features Ray Stevens, not as a conventional vocalist but as a group of chickens.

Ricky STEVENS *UK, male vocalist*

14 Dec 61 **I CRIED FOR YOU** *Columbia DB 4739* 34 7

Shakin' STEVENS (100 Top 500)
With UK single sales totalling 7,108,330, 'Shaky', b. Michael Barratt, 4 Mar 1948, Glamorgan, Wales, performs and records under a broad umbrella of styles from rock and country blues to cajun. He shares with The Beatles (60s) and Elton John (70s) the distinction of being the most successful UK singles chart performer of a decade (80s), and made a comeback in 2005 to win the TV reality show 'Hit Me Baby One More Time' (13 Albums: 168 Weeks, 38 Singles: 280 Weeks)

16 Feb 80 **HOT DOG** *Epic EPC 8090* 24 9
15 Mar 80 **TAKE ONE!** *Epic EPC 83978* 62 2
16 Aug 80 **MARIE MARIE** *Epic EPC 8725* 19 10
28 Feb 81 ★ **THIS OLE HOUSE** *Epic EPC 9555* 1 17
4 Apr 81 ● **THIS OLE HOUSE** *Epic EPC 84985* 2 28
2 May 81 ● **YOU DRIVE ME CRAZY** *Epic A 1165* 2 12
25 Jul 81 ★ **GREEN DOOR** *Epic A 1354* 1 12
8 Aug 81 **SHAKIN' STEVENS** *Hallmark / Pickwick SHM 3065* 34 5
19 Sep 81 ★ **SHAKY** *Epic EPC 10027* 1 28
10 Oct 81 ● **IT'S RAINING** *Epic A 1643* 10 9
16 Jan 82 ★ **OH JULIE** *Epic EPC A 1742* 1 10
24 Apr 82 ● **SHIRLEY** *Epic EPC A 2087* 6 6
21 Aug 82 **GIVE ME YOUR HEART TONIGHT** *Epic EPC A 2656* 11 10
9 Oct 82 ● **GIVE ME YOUR HEART TONIGHT** *Epic EPC 10035* 3 18
16 Oct 82 ● **I'LL BE SATISFIED** *Epic EPC A 2846* 10 8
11 Dec 82 ● **THE SHAKIN' STEVENS EP** *Epic SHAKY 1* 2 7
23 Jul 83 **IT'S LATE** *Epic A 3565* 11 7
5 Nov 83 ● **CRY JUST A LITTLE BIT** *Epic A 3774* 3 12
26 Nov 83 **THE BOP WON'T STOP** *Epic EPC 86301* 21 27
7 Jan 84 ● **A ROCKIN' GOOD WAY** *Epic A 4071* [1] 5 9
24 Mar 84 ● **A LOVE WORTH WAITING FOR** *Epic A 4291* 2 10
15 Sep 84 ● **A LETTER TO YOU** *Epic A 4677* 10 8
17 Nov 84 ● **GREATEST HITS** *Epic EPC 10047* 8 22
24 Nov 84 ● **TEARDROPS** *Epic A 4882* 5 9
2 Mar 85 **BREAKING UP MY HEART** *Epic A 6072* 14 7
12 Oct 85 **LIPSTICK POWDER AND PAINT** *Epic A 6610* 11 9
16 Nov 85 **LIPSTICK POWDER AND PAINT** *Epic EPC 26646* 37 9
7 Dec 85 ★ **MERRY CHRISTMAS EVERYONE** (re) *Epic A 6769* 1 11
8 Feb 86 **TURNING AWAY** *Epic A 6819* 15 7
1 Nov 86 **BECAUSE I LOVE YOU** *Epic SHAKY 2* 14 10
27 Jun 87 **A LITTLE BOOGIE WOOGIE (IN THE BACK OF MY MIND)** *Epic SHAKY 3* 12 10
19 Sep 87 **COME SEE ABOUT ME** *Epic SHAKY 4* 24 6
31 Oct 87 **LET'S BOOGIE** *Epic 460 1261* 59 7
28 Nov 87 ● **WHAT DO YOU WANT TO MAKE THOSE EYES AT ME FOR** *Epic SHAKY 5* 5 8
23 Jul 88 **FEEL THE NEED IN ME** *Epic SHAKY 6* 26 5
15 Oct 88 **HOW MANY TEARS CAN YOU HIDE** *Epic SHAKY 7* 47 4
19 Nov 88 **A WHOLE LOTTA SHAKY** *Epic MOOD 5* 42 8
10 Dec 88 **TRUE LOVE** *Epic SHAKY 8* 23 6
18 Feb 89 **JEZEBEL** *Epic SHAKY 9* 58 2
13 May 89 **LOVE ATTACK** *Epic SHAKY 10* 28 4
24 Feb 90 **I MIGHT** *Epic SHAKY 11* 18 6
12 May 90 **YES I DO** *Epic SHAKY 12* 60 2
18 Aug 90 **PINK CHAMPAGNE** *Epic SHAKY 13* 59 2
13 Oct 90 **MY CUTIE CUTIE** *Epic SHAKY 14* 75 1
20 Oct 90 **THERE'S TWO KINDS OF MUSIC: ROCK 'N' ROLL** *Telstar STAR 2454* 65 2
15 Dec 90 **THE BEST CHRISTMAS OF THEM ALL** *Epic SHAKY 15* 19 4
7 Dec 91 **I'LL BE HOME THIS CHRISTMAS** *Epic 6576507* 34 5
10 Oct 92 **RADIO** *Epic 6584367* [2] 37 3
31 Oct 92 **THE EPIC YEARS** *Epic 4724222* [1] 57 2
23 Apr 05 ● **THE COLLECTION** *Sony 5198822* 4 10
25 Jun 05 **TROUBLE / THIS OLE HOUSE** (re-recording) *EMI Virgin VTSCD 7* 20 3

[1] Shaky and Bonnie [2] Shaky featuring Roger Taylor [1] Shaky

Tracks on The Shakin' Stevens EP (11 Dec 1982): Blue Christmas / Que Sera Sera / Josephine / Lawdy Miss Clawdy. 'Merry Christmas Everyone' re-entered the chart in Dec 1986, peaking at No.58.

STEVENSON'S ROCKET *UK, male vocal / instrumental group*

29 Nov 75 **ALRIGHT BABY** (re) *Magnet MAG 47* 37 5

Al STEWART *UK, male vocalist (5 Albums: 20 Weeks, 1 Single: 6 Weeks)*

11 Apr 70 **ZERO SHE FLIES** *CBS 63848* 40 4
29 Jan 77 **YEAR OF THE CAT** *RCA 2771* 31 6
5 Feb 77 **YEAR OF THE CAT** *RCA RS 1082* 38 7
21 Oct 78 **TIME PASSAGES** *RCA PL 25173* 39 1
6 Sep 80 **24 CARAT** *RCA PL 25306* 55 6
9 Jun 84 **RUSSIANS AND AMERICANS** *RCA PL 70307* 83 2

Amii STEWART *US, female vocalist (8 Singles: 61 Weeks)*

7 Apr 79 ● **KNOCK ON WOOD** *Atlantic / Hansa K 11214* ▲ $ 6 12
16 Jun 79 ● **LIGHT MY FIRE / 137 DISCO HEAVEN (MEDLEY)** *Atlantic / Hansa K 11278* 5 11
3 Nov 79 **JEALOUSY** *Atlantic / Hansa K 11386* 58 3
19 Jan 80 **THE LETTER / PARADISE BIRD** *Atlantic / Hansa K 11424* 39 4
19 Jul 80 **MY GUY – MY GIRL (MEDLEY)** *Atlantic / Hansa K 11550* [1] 39 5
29 Dec 84 **FRIENDS** *RCA 471* 12 11
17 Aug 85 ● **KNOCK ON WOOD / LIGHT MY FIRE** (re-mixes) *Sedition EDIT 3303* 7 12
25 Jan 86 **MY GUY – MY GIRL (MEDLEY)** (re-recordings) *Sedition EDIT 3310* [2] 63 3

[1] Amii Stewart and Johnny Bristol [2] Amii Stewart and Deon Estus

Andy STEWART *UK, male vocalist, b. 20 Dec 1933, d. 11 Oct 1993 (1 Album: 2 Weeks, 5 Singles: 67 Weeks)*

15 Dec 60 **DONALD WHERE'S YOUR TROOSERS** *Top Rank JAR 427* 37 1
12 Jan 61 **A SCOTTISH SOLDIER** (re) *Top Rank JAR 512* 19 40
1 Jun 61 **THE BATTLE'S O'ER** *Top Rank JAR 565* 28 13

	3 August 1991	10 August 1991	17 August 1991	24 August 1991
UK No.1 SINGLES	(EVERYTHING I DO) I DO IT FOR YOU – Bryan Adams	(EVERYTHING I DO) I DO IT FOR YOU – Bryan Adams	(EVERYTHING I DO) I DO IT FOR YOU – Bryan Adams	(EVERYTHING I DO) I DO IT FOR YOU – Bryan Adams
UK No.1 ALBUMS	LOVE HURTS – Cher	ESSENTIAL PAVAROTTI II – Luciano Pavarotti	ESSENTIAL PAVAROTTI II – Luciano Pavarotti	METALLICA – Metallica

3 Feb 62 ANDY STEWART *Top Rank 35116* 13 2
12 Aug 65 **DR FINLAY (re)** *HMV POP 1454* 43 5
9 Dec 89 ● **DONALD WHERE'S YOUR TROOSERS** (re-issue) *Stone SON 2353* 4 8

All hits except 'Dr Finlay' are with the Michael Sammes Singers.

Billy STEWART *US, male vocalist, b. 24 Mar 1937, d. 17 Jan 1970*

8 Sep 66 **SUMMERTIME** *Chess CRS 8040* 39 2

Dave STEWART (see also HATFIELD AND THE NORTH)

UK, male keyboard player (4 Singles: 30 Weeks)

14 Mar 81 **WHAT BECOMES OF THE BROKEN HEARTED** *Stiff BROKEN 1* [1] 13 10
19 Sep 81 ★ **IT'S MY PARTY** *Stiff BROKEN 2* [2] 1 13
13 Aug 83 **BUSY DOING NOTHING** *Broken BROKEN 5* [2] 49 4
14 Jun 86 **THE LOCOMOTION** *Broken BROKEN 8* [2] 70 3

[1] Dave Stewart: Guest vocals: Colin Blunstone [2] Dave Stewart with Barbara Gaskin

David A. STEWART (see also EURYTHMICS; The TOURISTS; VEGAS)

UK, male guitarist (2 Albums: 7 Weeks, 4 Singles: 21 Weeks)

24 Feb 90 ● **LILY WAS HERE** *RCA ZB 43045* [1] 6 12
7 Apr 90 LILY WAS HERE (FILM SOUNDTRACK) *Anxious ZL 74233* 35 5
18 Aug 90 **JACK TALKING** *RCA PB 43907* [2] 69 2
15 Sep 90 DAVE STEWART AND THE SPIRITUAL COWBOYS *RCA OB 74710* [1] 38 2
3 Sep 94 **HEART OF STONE** *East West YZ 845CD* [3] 36 5
6 Nov 04 **OLD HABITS DIE HARD** *Virgin VSCDX 1887* [4] 45 2

[1] David A Stewart featuring Candy Dulfer [2] Dave Stewart and The Spiritual Cowboys [3] Dave Stewart [4] Mick Jagger and Dave Stewart [1] Dave Stewart and the Spiritual Cowboys

Jermaine STEWART *US, male vocalist, b. 7 Sep 1957, d. 17 Mar 1997 (2 Albums: 12 Weeks, 5 Singles: 42 Weeks)*

9 Aug 86 ● **WE DON'T HAVE TO ... TAKE OUR CLOTHES OFF TO HAVE A GOOD TIME** *10 TEN 96* 2 14
4 Oct 86 FRANTIC ROMANTIC *10 DIX 26* 49 4
1 Nov 86 **JODY** *10 TEN 143* 50 4
16 Jan 88 ● **SAY IT AGAIN** *10 TEN 188* 7 12
5 Mar 88 SAY IT AGAIN *Siren SRNLP 14* 32 8
2 Apr 88 **GET LUCKY** *Siren SRN 82* 13 9
24 Sep 88 **DON'T TALK DIRTY TO ME** *Siren SRN 86* 61 3

John STEWART *US, male vocalist*

30 Jun 79 **GOLD** *RSO 35* 43 6

Rod STEWART (11 Top 500)

(see also GLASS TIGER; PYTHON LEE JACKSON) *World-renowned rock superstar, b. 10 Jan 1945, London, UK, of Scottish parents. In the 1960s "Rod the Mod" recorded solo singles for Decca, EMI and Immediate but is best remembered in that period as a member of The Five Dimensions, Hoochie Coochie Men, Steampacket, Shotgun Express and The Jeff Beck Group. Between 1969 and 1975, the gravel-voiced vocalist fronted The Faces as well as having a successful solo career. Over the past 34 years, Stewart has played to packed stadiums worldwide and amassed a vast collection of platinum and gold albums. In the US, he is one of the top selling UK artists of all time with 12 Top 10 albums (and a No.1 span of 23 years) and 16 Top 10 singles. He is also the only UK solo artist to top the US singles or albums charts this century. In Britain, he has scored 28 Top 10 LPs, including seven solo No.1s. His songwriting skills have earned him a Lifetime Ivor Novello Award in the UK. His Great American Songbook set is one of the most successful series of albums in history. Stewart, whose love life also attracts much media attention, earned a Grammy Living Legend Award in 1989 (35 Albums: 927 Weeks, 62 Singles: 477 Weeks)*

3 Oct 70 GASOLINE ALLEY *Vertigo 6360 500* 62 7
24 Jul 71 ★ EVERY PICTURE TELLS A STORY *Mercury 6338 063* ▲ 1 81
4 Sep 71 **REASON TO BELIEVE** *Mercury 6052 097* 19 2
18 Sep 71 ★ **MAGGIE MAY** *Mercury 6052 097* ▲ $ 1 19
5 Aug 72 ★ NEVER A DULL MOMENT *Philips 6499 153* 1 36
12 Aug 72 ★ **YOU WEAR IT WELL** *Mercury 6052 171* 1 12
18 Nov 72 ● **ANGEL / WHAT MADE MILWAUKEE FAMOUS (HAS MADE A LOSER OUT OF ME)** *Mercury 6052 198* 4 11
5 May 73 **I'VE BEEN DRINKING** *RAK RR 4* [1] 27 6
25 Aug 73 ★ SING IT AGAIN ROD *Mercury 6499 484* 1 30
8 Sep 73 ● **OH! NO NOT MY BABY** *Mercury 6052 371* 6 9
26 Jan 74 ● OVERTURE AND BEGINNERS *Mercury 9100 001* [1] 3 7
5 Oct 74 ● **FAREWELL – BRING IT ON HOME TO ME / YOU SEND ME** *Mercury 6167 033* 7 7
19 Oct 74 ★ SMILER *Mercury 9104 011* ■ 1 20
7 Dec 74 **YOU CAN MAKE ME DANCE SING OR ANYTHING (EVEN TAKE THE DOG FOR A WALK, MEND A FUSE, FOLD AWAY THE IRONING BOARD, OR ANY OTHER DOMESTIC SHORT COMINGS)** *Warner Bros. K 16494* [2] 12 9
16 Aug 75 ★ **SAILING (2re)** *Warner Bros. K 16600* 1 34
30 Aug 75 ★ ATLANTIC CROSSING *Warner Bros. K 56151* ■ 1 88
15 Nov 75 ● **THIS OLD HEART OF MINE** *Riva 1* 4 9
5 Jun 76 ● **TONIGHT'S THE NIGHT** *Riva 3* ▲ $ 5 9
3 Jul 76 ★ A NIGHT ON THE TOWN *Riva RVLP 1* 1 47
21 Aug 76 ● **THE KILLING OF GEORGIE** *Riva 4* 2 10
20 Nov 76 **GET BACK** *Riva 6* 11 9
4 Dec 76 **MAGGIE MAY** (re-issue) *Mercury 6160 006* 31 7
23 Apr 77 ★ **I DON'T WANT TO TALK ABOUT IT / FIRST CUT IS THE DEEPEST** *Riva 7* 1 13
16 Jul 77 THE BEST OF ROD STEWART *Mercury 6643 030* 18 22
15 Oct 77 ● **YOU'RE IN MY HEART** *Riva 11* $ 3 10
19 Nov 77 ● FOOT LOOSE & FANCY FREE *Riva RVLP 5* 3 26
21 Jan 78 ATLANTIC CROSSING (re-issue) *Riva RVLP 4* 60 1
28 Jan 78 ● **HOT LEGS / I WAS ONLY JOKING** *Riva 10* 5 8
27 May 78 ● **OLE OLA (MULHER BRASILEIRA)** *Riva 15* [3] 4 6
18 Nov 78 ★ **DA YA THINK I'M SEXY?** *Riva 17* ▲ $ 1 13
9 Dec 78 ● BLONDES HAVE MORE FUN *Riva RVLP 8* ▲ 3 31
3 Feb 79 **AIN'T LOVE A BITCH** *Riva 18* 11 8
5 May 79 **BLONDES (HAVE MORE FUN)** *Riva 19* 63 3
10 Nov 79 ★ GREATEST HITS *Riva ROD TV 1* 1 74
31 May 80 **IF LOVING YOU IS WRONG (I DON'T WANT TO BE RIGHT)** *Riva 23* 23 9
8 Nov 80 **PASSION** *Riva 26* 17 10
22 Nov 80 ● FOOLISH BEHAVIOUR *Riva RVLP 11* 4 13
20 Dec 80 **MY GIRL** *Riva 28* 32 7
17 Oct 81 ● **TONIGHT I'M YOURS (DON'T HURT ME)** *Riva 33* 8 13
14 Nov 81 ● TONIGHT I'M YOURS *Riva RVLP 14* 8 21
12 Dec 81 **YOUNG TURKS** *Riva 34* 11 9
27 Feb 82 **HOW LONG** *Riva 35* 41 4
13 Nov 82 ABSOLUTELY LIVE *Riva RVLP 17* 35 5
4 Jun 83 ★ **BABY JANE** *Warner Bros. W 9608* 1 14
18 Jun 83 ● BODY WISHES *Warner Bros. K 923 8771* 5 27
27 Aug 83 ● **WHAT AM I GONNA DO (I'M SO IN LOVE WITH YOU)** *Warner Bros. W 9564* 3 8
10 Dec 83 **SWEET SURRENDER** *Warner Bros. W 9440* 23 9
26 May 84 **INFATUATION** *Warner Bros. W 9256* 27 7
23 Jun 84 ● CAMOUFLAGE *Warner Bros. 925095* 8 17
28 Jul 84 **SOME GUYS HAVE ALL THE LUCK** *Warner Bros. W 9204* 15 10
24 May 86 **LOVE TOUCH (re)** *Warner Bros. W 8668* 27 8
5 Jul 86 ● EVERY BEAT OF MY HEART *Warner Bros. WX 53* 5 17
12 Jul 86 ● **EVERY BEAT OF MY HEART** *Warner Bros. W 8625* 2 9
20 Sep 86 **ANOTHER HEARTACHE** *Warner Bros. W 8631* 54 2
28 May 88 **LOST IN YOU** *Warner Bros. W 7927* 21 6
4 Jun 88 OUT OF ORDER *Warner Bros. WX 152* 11 8
13 Aug 88 **FOREVER YOUNG** *Warner Bros. W 7796* 57 3
6 May 89 **MY HEART CAN'T TELL YOU NO** *Warner Bros. W 7729* 49 4
11 Nov 89 **THIS OLD HEART OF MINE** *Warner Bros. W 2686* [4] 51 3
25 Nov 89 ● THE BEST OF ROD STEWART *Warner Bros. WX 314* 3 127
13 Jan 90 ● **DOWNTOWN TRAIN** *Warner Bros. W 2647* 10 12
24 Nov 90 ● **IT TAKES TWO** *Warner Bros. ROD 1* [5] 5 8
16 Mar 91 ● **RHYTHM OF MY HEART** *Warner Bros. W 0017* 3 11
6 Apr 91 ● VAGABOND HEART *Warner Bros. WX 408* 2 27
15 Jun 91 ● **THE MOTOWN SONG** *Warner Bros. W 0030* [6] 10 8

31 August 1991	7 September 1991	14 September 1991	21 September 1991
(EVERYTHING I DO) I DO IT FOR YOU Bryan Adams	(EVERYTHING I DO) I DO IT FOR YOU Bryan Adams	(EVERYTHING I DO) I DO IT FOR YOU Bryan Adams	(EVERYTHING I DO) I DO IT FOR YOU Bryan Adams
JOSEPH AND THE AMAZING TECHNICOLOR DREAMCOAT Jason Donovan / cast	JOSEPH AND THE AMAZING TECHNICOLOR DREAMCOAT Jason Donovan / cast	FROM TIME TO TIME - THE SINGLES COLLECTION Paul Young	ON EVERY STREET Dire Straits

UK No.1 ★ UK Top 10 ● Still on chart + UK entry at No.1 ■ US No.1 ▲ UK million seller £ US million seller $
Singles re-entries are listed as (re), (2re), (3re)... which signifies that the hit re-entered the chart once, twice or three times...
Peak Position / Weeks

Date	Title	Peak	Weeks
7 Sep 91	**BROKEN ARROW** *Warner Bros. W 0059*	54	3
7 Mar 92	**PEOPLE GET READY** *Epic 6577567* [1]	49	3
18 Apr 92	**YOUR SONG / BROKEN ARROW** (re-issue) *Warner Bros. W 0104*	41	4
7 Nov 92	THE BEST OF ROD STEWART AND THE FACES 1971-1975 *Mercury 5141802* [1]	58	1
5 Dec 92 ●	**TOM TRAUBERT'S BLUES (WALTZING MATILDA)** *Warner Bros. W 0144*	6	9
20 Feb 93	**RUBY TUESDAY** *Warner Bros. W 0158CD*	11	6
6 Mar 93 ●	ROD STEWART LEAD VOCALIST *Warner Bros. 9362452582*	3	9
17 Apr 93	**SHOTGUN WEDDING** *Warner Bros. W 0171CD*	21	4
5 Jun 93 ●	UNPLUGGED ... AND SEATED *Warner Bros. 9362452892*	2	27
26 Jun 93 ●	**HAVE I TOLD YOU LATELY** *Warner Bros. W 0185CD*	5	9
21 Aug 93	**REASON TO BELIEVE** (re-recording) *Warner Bros. W 0198CD 1*	51	3
18 Dec 93	**PEOPLE GET READY** (re-recording) *Warner Bros. W 0226CD 1*	45	4
15 Jan 94 ●	**ALL FOR LOVE** *A&M 5804772* [7] ▲ $	2	13
20 May 95	**YOU'RE THE STAR** *Warner Bros. W 0296CD*	19	5
10 Jun 95 ●	A SPANNER IN THE WORKS *Warner Bros. 9362458672*	4	12
19 Aug 95	**LADY LUCK** *Warner Bros. W 0310CD 1*	56	1
15 Jun 96	**PURPLE HEATHER** *Warner Bros. W 0354CD* [8]	16	5
16 Nov 96 ●	IF WE FALL IN LOVE TONIGHT *Warner Bros. 9362464672*	8	19
14 Dec 96	**IF WE FALL IN LOVE TONIGHT** *Warner Bros. W 0380CD*	58	1
1 Nov 97 ●	**DA YA THINK I'M SEXY?** *All Around the World CDGLOBE 150* [9]	7	10
30 May 98	**OOH LA LA** *Warner Brothers W 0446CD*	16	5
13 Jun 98 ●	WHEN WE WERE THE NEW BOYS *Warner Bros. 9362467922*	2	11
5 Sep 98	**ROCKS** *Warner Brothers W 0452CD 1*	55	1
17 Apr 99	**FAITH OF THE HEART** *Universal UND 56235*	60	1
24 Mar 01	**I CAN'T DENY IT** *Atlantic AT 0096CD*	26	2
7 Apr 01 ●	HUMAN *Atlantic 7567929742*	9	8
24 Nov 01 ●	THE STORY SO FAR – THE VERY BEST OF ROD STEWART *Warner Bros. 8122735812*	7	43
9 Nov 02 ●	IT HAD TO BE YOU ... THE GREAT AMERICAN SONGBOOK *J 74321968672*	8	18
1 Nov 03 ●	AS TIME GOES BY ... THE GREAT AMERICAN SONGBOOK VOLUME II *J 82876574842*	4	17
1 Nov 03	CHANGING FACES – THE VERY BEST OF ROD STEWART & THE FACES – THE DEFINITIVE COLLECTION 1969-1974 *Universal TV 9812604* [1]	13	5
30 Oct 04 ●	STARDUST ... THE GREAT AMERICAN SONGBOOK VOLUME III *J 82876659282* ▲	3	17
12 Nov 05 ●	THANKS FOR THE MEMORY ... THE GREAT AMERICAN SONGBOOK VOLUME IV *J 82876751902*	3	8+

[1] Jeff Beck and Rod Stewart [2] The Faces / Rod Stewart [3] Rod Stewart featuring the Scottish World Cup Squad '78 [4] Rod Stewart featuring Ronald Isley [5] Rod Stewart and Tina Turner [6] Rod Stewart with backing vocals by The Temptations [7] Bryan Adams, Rod Stewart and Sting [8] Rod Stewart with the Scottish Euro '96 Squad [9] N-Trance featuring Rod Stewart [1] Rod Stewart and The Faces

'Sailing' (16 Aug 1975) re-entries peaked at No.3 in 1976 and No.41 in 1987. The re-recorded 'Reason to Believe' (21 Aug 1993) credits Ronnie Wood on the sleeve. The two The Best of Rod Stewart albums are different. Greatest Hits changed label / number to Warner Bros. K 56744 during its chart run.

STEX *UK, male / female vocal / instrumental group*

Date	Title	Peak	Weeks
19 Jan 91	**STILL FEEL THE RAIN** *Some Bizzare SBZ 7002*	63	2

STICKY featuring MS DYNAMITE

UK, male producer – Richard Forbes and female rapper

Date	Title	Peak	Weeks
23 Jun 01	**BOOO!** *ffrr / Public Demand / Social Circles FCD 399*	12	6

STIFF LITTLE FINGERS *UK, male vocal (Jake Burns) / instrumental group* (6 Albums: 57 Weeks, 8 Singles: 39 Weeks)

Date	Title	Peak	Weeks
3 Mar 79	INFLAMMABLE MATERIAL *Rough Trade ROUGH 1*	14	19
29 Sep 79	**STRAW DOGS** *Chrysalis CHS 2368*	44	4
16 Feb 80	**AT THE EDGE** *Chrysalis CHS 2406*	15	9
15 Mar 80 ●	NOBODY'S HEROES *Chrysalis CHR 1270*	8	10
24 May 80	**NOBODY'S HERO / TIN SOLDIERS** *Chrysalis CHS 2424*	36	5
2 Aug 80	**BACK TO FRONT** *Chrysalis CHS 2447*	49	4
20 Sep 80 ●	HANX! *Chrysalis CHR 1300*	9	5
28 Mar 81	**JUST FADE AWAY** *Chrysalis CHS 2510*	47	6
25 Apr 81	GO FOR IT *Chrysalis CHX 1339*	14	8
30 May 81	**SILVER LINING** *Chrysalis CHS 2517*	68	3
23 Jan 82	**LISTEN (EP)** *Chrysalis CHS 2580*	33	6
18 Sep 82	**BITS OF KIDS** *Chrysalis CHS 2637*	73	2
2 Oct 82	NOW THEN *Chrysalis CHR 1400*	24	6
12 Feb 83	ALL THE BEST *Chrysalis CTY 1414*	19	9

Tracks on Listen (EP): That's When Your Blood Bumps / Two Guitars Clash / Listen / Sad-Eyed People.

Curtis STIGERS

US, male vocalist (2 Albums: 52 Weeks, 6 Singles: 34 Weeks)

Date	Title	Peak	Weeks
18 Jan 92 ●	**I WONDER WHY** *Arista 114716*	5	10
29 Feb 92 ●	CURTIS STIGERS *Arista 261953*	7	50
28 Mar 92 ●	**YOU'RE ALL THAT MATTERS TO ME** *Arista 115273*	6	12
11 Jul 92	**SLEEPING WITH THE LIGHTS ON** *Arista 74321102307*	53	4
17 Oct 92	**NEVER SAW A MIRACLE** *Arista 74321117257*	34	4
3 Jun 95	**THIS TIME** *Arista 74321286962*	28	3
1 Jul 95	TIME WAS *Arista 74321282792*	34	2
2 Dec 95	**KEEP ME FROM THE COLD** *Arista 74321319162*	57	1

The STILLS *Canada, male vocal / instrumental group* (1 Album: 1 Week, 4 Singles: 5 Weeks)

Date	Title	Peak	Weeks
6 Sep 03	**REMEMBERESE (EP)** *679 Recordings 679L 026CD*	75	1
28 Feb 04	**LOLA STARS AND STRIPES** *679 Recordings 679L 036CD*	39	2
6 Mar 04	LOGIC WILL BREAK YOUR HEART *679 Recordings / Vice 7567836742*	66	1
8 May 04	**CHANGES ARE NO GOOD** *679 Recordings / Vice 679L 072CD 1*	51	1
28 Aug 04	**STILL IN LOVE SONG** *679 Recordings / Vice 679L 079CD 2*	45	1

Tracks on Rememberese (EP): Still In Love Song / Killer Bees / Talk To Me

Stephen STILLS (see also CROSBY, STILLS, NASH and YOUNG)

US, male vocalist / guitarist (7 Albums: 27 Weeks, 2 Singles: 8 Weeks)

Date	Title	Peak	Weeks
19 Dec 70 ●	STEPHEN STILLS *Atlantic 2401 004*	8	9
13 Mar 71	**LOVE THE ONE YOU'RE WITH** *Atlantic 2091 046*	37	4
14 Aug 71	STEPHEN STILLS 2 *Atlantic 2401 013*	22	3
20 May 72	MANASSAS *Atlantic K 60021* [1]	30	5
19 May 73	DOWN THE ROAD *Atlantic K 40440* [1]	33	2
26 Jul 75	STILLS *CBS 69146*	31	1
29 May 76	ILLEGAL STILLS *CBS 81330*	54	2
9 Oct 76	LONG MAY YOU RUN *Reprise K 54081* [2]	12	5
6 Jun 98	**HE GOT GAME** *Def Jam 5689852* [1]	16	4

[1] Public Enemy featuring Stephen Stills [1] Stephen Stills Manassas [2] Stills-Young Band

For 1972 and 1973 albums, act was titled Stephen Stills Manassas, a US, male vocal / instrumental group led by Stephen Stills.

STILTSKIN (see also Armin VAN BUUREN) *UK, male vocal (Ray Wilson) / instrumental group* (1 Album: 4 Weeks, 2 Singles: 15 Weeks)

Date	Title	Peak	Weeks
7 May 94 ★	**INSIDE** *White Water LEV 1CD*	1	13
24 Sep 94	**FOOTSTEPS** *White Water WWRD 2*	34	2
29 Oct 94	THE MIND'S EYE *White Water WWD 1*	17	4

STING 66 Top 500

World's best-known ex-Police-man, b. Gordon Sumner, 2 Oct 1951, Newcastle, UK. This singer / songwriter / bass player has amassed more solo hits than as frontman of that top-selling trio. As a soloist, he has won

	28 September 1991	5 October 1991	12 October 1991	19 October 1991
UK No.1 SINGLES	(EVERYTHING I DO) I DO IT FOR YOU Bryan Adams	(EVERYTHING I DO) I DO IT FOR YOU Bryan Adams	(EVERYTHING I DO) I DO IT FOR YOU Bryan Adams	(EVERYTHING I DO) I DO IT FOR YOU Bryan Adams
UK No.1 ALBUMS	USE YOUR ILLUSION II Guns N' Roses	WAKING UP THE NEIGHBOURS Bryan Adams	STARS Simply Red	STARS Simply Red

both BRIT and Grammy awards and reportedly earns £1 a second from touring and royalties. Performed at both Live Aid and Live 8 London concerts (11 Albums: 387 Weeks, 37 Singles: 166 Weeks)

Date		Title	Pos	Wks
14 Aug 82		**SPREAD A LITTLE HAPPINESS** *A&M AMS 8242*	16	8
8 Jun 85		**IF YOU LOVE SOMEBODY SET THEM FREE** *A&M AM 258*	26	7
29 Jun 85	●	**THE DREAM OF THE BLUE TURTLES** *A&M DREAM 1*	3	64
24 Aug 85		**LOVE IS THE SEVENTH WAVE** *A&M AM 272*	41	5
19 Oct 85		**FORTRESS AROUND YOUR HEART** *A&M AM 286*	49	3
7 Dec 85		**RUSSIANS** (re) *A&M AM 292*	12	12
15 Feb 86		**MOON OVER BOURBON STREET** *A&M AM 305*	44	4
28 Jun 86		**BRING ON THE NIGHT** *A&M BRING 1*	16	12
24 Oct 87	★	**... NOTHING LIKE THE SUN** *A&M AMA 6402* ■	1	47
7 Nov 87		**WE'LL BE TOGETHER** *A&M AM 410*	41	4
20 Feb 88		**ENGLISHMAN IN NEW YORK** *A&M AM 431*	51	3
9 Apr 88		**FRAGILE** *A&M AM 439*	70	2
11 Aug 90		**ENGLISHMAN IN NEW YORK** (re-mix) *A&M AM 580*	15	7
12 Jan 91		**ALL THIS TIME** *A&M AM 713*	22	4
2 Feb 91	★	**THE SOUL CAGES** *A&M 3964051* ■	1	16
9 Mar 91		**MAD ABOUT YOU** *A&M AM 721*	56	2
4 May 91		**THE SOUL CAGES** *A&M AM 759*	57	1
29 Aug 92		**IT'S PROBABLY ME** *A&M AM 883* [1]	30	5
13 Feb 93		**IF I EVER LOSE MY FAITH IN YOU** *A&M AMCD 0172*	14	6
13 Mar 93	●	**TEN SUMMONER'S TALES** *A&M 5400752*	2	60
24 Apr 93		**SEVEN DAYS** *A&M 5802232*	25	4
19 Jun 93		**FIELDS OF GOLD** *A&M 5803012*	16	6
4 Sep 93		**SHAPE OF MY HEART** *A&M 5803532*	57	1
20 Nov 93		**DEMOLITION MAN** *A&M 5804512*	21	4
15 Jan 94	●	**ALL FOR LOVE** *A&M 5804772* [2] ▲ $	2	13
26 Feb 94		**NOTHING 'BOUT ME** *A&M 5805292*	32	3
29 Oct 94	●	**WHEN WE DANCE** *A&M 5808612*	9	7
19 Nov 94	●	**FIELDS OF GOLD – THE BEST OF STING 1984-1994** *A&M 5403072*	2	41
11 Feb 95		**THIS COWBOY SONG** *A&M 5809652* [3]	15	6
20 Jan 96		**SPIRITS IN THE MATERIAL WORLD** *MCA MCSTD 2113* [4]	36	2
2 Mar 96		**LET YOUR SOUL BE YOUR PILOT** *A&M 5813312*	15	4
16 Mar 96	●	**MERCURY FALLING** *A&M 5404862*	4	27
11 May 96		**YOU STILL TOUCH ME** *A&M 5815472*	27	3
22 Jun 96		**LIVE AT TFI FRIDAY (EP)** *A&M 5817652*	53	2
14 Sep 96		**I WAS BROUGHT TO MY SENSES** *A&M 5818912*	31	2
30 Nov 96		**I'M SO HAPPY I CAN'T STOP CRYING** *A&M 5820312*	54	1
22 Nov 97	★	**THE VERY BEST OF STING AND THE POLICE** *A&M 5404282* [1]	1	50
20 Dec 97		**ROXANNE '97** (re-mix) *A&M 5824552* [5]	17	6
25 Sep 99		**BRAND NEW DAY** *A&M / Polydor 4971522*	13	5
9 Oct 99	●	**BRAND NEW DAY** *A&M 4904512*	5	44
29 Jan 00		**DESERT ROSE** *A&M / Mercury 4972402* [6]	15	6
22 Apr 00		**AFTER THE RAIN HAS FALLEN** *A&M / Mercury 4973252*	31	4
17 Nov 01	●	**ALL THIS TIME** *A&M 4931802*	3	15
10 May 03	●	**RISE & FALL** *Wildstar CDWILD 45* [7]	2	10
27 Sep 03		**SEND YOUR LOVE** *A&M 9810103*	30	2
4 Oct 03	●	**SACRED LOVE** *A&M 9860619*	3	11
20 Dec 03		**WHENEVER I SAY YOUR NAME** *A&M 9815394* [8]	60	1
29 May 04		**STOLEN CAR (TAKE ME DANCING)** *A&M 9862266*	60	1

[1] Sting with Eric Clapton [2] Bryan Adams, Rod Stewart and Sting [3] Sting featuring Pato Banton [4] Pato Banton with Sting [5] Sting and The Police [6] Sting featuring Cheb Mami [7] Craig David featuring Sting [8] Sting and Mary J Blige [1] Sting and The Police

Tracks on Live at TFI Friday (EP): You Still Touch Me / Lithium Sunset / Message in a Bottle. The Very Best of Sting and The Police originally peaked at No.11. It reached No.1 only when an updated version, containing three new tracks, re-entered the chart in 2002 and sales were combined with the original album.

Byron STINGILY (see also TEN CITY) *US, male vocalist (5 Singles: 14 Weeks)*

Date		Title	Pos	Wks
25 Jan 97		**GET UP (EVERYBODY)** *Manifesto FESCD 19*	14	5
1 Nov 97		**SING A SONG** *Manifesto FESCD 35*	38	2
31 Jan 98		**YOU MAKE ME FEEL (MIGHTY REAL)** *Manifesto FESCD 38*	13	4
13 Jun 98		**TESTIFY** *Manifesto FESCD 42*	48	1
12 Feb 00		**THAT'S THE WAY LOVE IS** *Manifesto FESCD 66*	32	2

STINX *UK, female vocal duo*

Date		Title	Pos	Wks
24 Mar 01		**WHY DO YOU KEEP ON RUNNING** *HEBS HEBS 1*	49	3

STIX 'N' STONED (see also CLERGY; HI-GATE)

UK, male instrumental / production duo – Julius O'Riordan and Jon Kelly

Date		Title	Pos	Wks
20 Jul 96		**OUTRAGEOUS** *Positiva CDTIV 52*	39	2

Catherine STOCK *UK, female vocalist*

Date		Title	Pos	Wks
18 Oct 86		**TO HAVE AND TO HOLD** *Sierra FED 29*	17	6

STOCK AITKEN WATERMAN (see also 14-18; 2 IN A TENT)

UK, male production trio (6 Singles: 36 Weeks)

Date		Title	Pos	Wks
25 Jul 87		**ROADBLOCK** *Breakout USA 611*	13	9
24 Oct 87	●	**MR SLEAZE** *London NANA 14*	3	10
12 Dec 87		**PACKJAMMED (WITH THE PARTY POSSE)** *Breakout USA 620*	41	6
21 May 88		**ALL THE WAY** *MCA GOAL 1* [1]	64	2
3 Dec 88		**SS PAPARAZZI** *PWL PWL 22*	68	2
20 May 89	★	**FERRY 'CROSS THE MERSEY** *PWL PWL 41* [2] ■	1	7

[1] England Football Team and the 'sound' of Stock, Aitken and Waterman [2] The Christians, Holly Johnson, Paul McCartney, Gerry Marsden and Stock Aitken Waterman

The listed flip side of 'Mr Sleaze' was 'Love in the First Degree' by Bananarama.

Rhet STOLLER *UK, male guitarist*

Date		Title	Pos	Wks
12 Jan 61		**CHARIOT** *Decca F 11302*	26	8

Morris STOLOFF *US, orchestra – leader b. 1 Aug 1898, d. 16 Apr 1980*

Date		Title	Pos	Wks
1 Jun 56	●	**MOONGLOW AND THE THEME FROM 'PICNIC'** *Brunswick 05553* $	7	11

Angie STONE

US, female vocalist (2 Albums: 4 Weeks, 6 Singles: 24 Weeks)

Date		Title	Pos	Wks
11 Mar 00		**BLACK DIAMOND** *Arista 74321727752*	62	3
15 Apr 00		**LIFE STORY** *Arista 74321748492*	22	3
16 Dec 00		**KEEP YOUR WORRIES** *Virgin VUSCD 177* [1]	57	1
9 Mar 02		**BROTHA PART II** *J 74321922142* [2]	37	2
27 Jul 02		**WISH I DIDN'T MISS YOU** *J 74321939182*	30	5
27 Dec 03		**SIGNED, SEALED, DELIVERED, I'M YOURS** *Innocent SINCD 50* [3]	11	10
10 Jul 04		**STONE LOVE** *J 82876597922*	56	1
14 Aug 04		**I WANNA THANK YA** *J 82876624782* [4]	31	3

[1] Guru's Jazzmatazz featuring Angie Stone [2] Angie Stone featuring Alicia Keys and Eve [3] Blue featuring Stevie Wonder and Angie Stone [4] Angie Stone featuring Snoop Dogg

Joss STONE *UK, female vocalist – Jocelyn Stoker (2 Albums: 116 Weeks, 6 Singles: 29 Weeks)*

Date		Title	Pos	Wks
17 Jan 04	●	**THE SOUL SESSIONS** *Relentless CDREL 2*	4	70
7 Feb 04		**FELL IN LOVE WITH A BOY** *Relentless / Virgin RELCD 3*	18	5
22 May 04		**SUPER DUPER LOVE (ARE YOU DIGGIN ON ME?)** *Relentless / Virgin RELCD 4*	18	4
25 Sep 04	●	**YOU HAD ME** *Relentless / Virgin RELDX 10*	9	8
9 Oct 04	★	**MIND BODY & SOUL** *Relentless CDREL 04* ■	1	46
11 Dec 04		**RIGHT TO BE WRONG** *Relentless / Virgin RELDX 13*	29	6
26 Mar 05		**SPOILED** *Relentless / Virgin RELCD 16*	32	2
16 Jul 05		**DON'T CHA WANNA RIDE** *Relentless / Virgin RELCD 20*	20	4

R & J STONE

UK / US, male / female vocal duo – Russell and Joanne Stone

Date		Title	Pos	Wks
10 Jan 76	●	**WE DO IT** *RCA 2616*	5	9

The STONE ROSES (278 Top 500)

(see also The SEAHORSES) *'Madchester' 'Baggy' pioneers who successfully combined rock guitar and acid house attitude, inspiring a massive return to guitar-based bands in northern Britain in the 90s: Ian Brown (v), John Squire (g), Mani (Gary Mountfield) (b) and Reni (Alan Wren) (d/v), all from Manchester. Their eponymous debut album, which peaked no higher*

26 October 1991	2 November 1991	9 November 1991	16 November 1991
(EVERYTHING I DO) I DO IT FOR YOU Bryan Adams	THE FLY U2	DIZZY Vic Reeves and The Wonder Stuff	DIZZY Vic Reeves and The Wonder Stuff
CHORUS Erasure	STARS Simply Red	GREATEST HITS II Queen	SHEPHERD MOONS Enya

KEY UK No.1 ★ UK Top 10 ● Still on chart + UK entry at No.1 ■ US No.1 ▲ UK million seller £ US million seller $
Singles re-entries are listed as (re), (2re), (3re)... which signifies that the hit re-entered the chart once, twice or three times...
Peak Position / Weeks

than No.19 in 1989, continues to register in the top five of many all-time best album surveys *(8 Albums: 163 Weeks, 15 Singles: 77 Weeks)*

13 May 89 ● THE STONE ROSES *Silvertone ORELP 502* 9 91
29 Jul 89 SHE BANGS THE DRUMS (re) *Silvertone ORE 6* 34 6
25 Nov 89 ● WHAT THE WORLD IS WAITING FOR / FOOL'S GOLD (re) *Silvertone ORE 13* 8 19
6 Jan 90 SALLY CINNAMON (re) *Revolver REV 36* 46 5
3 Mar 90 ● ELEPHANT STONE *Silvertone ORE 1* 8 6
17 Mar 90 MADE OF STONE *Silvertone ORE 2* 20 4
14 Jul 90 ● ONE LOVE *Silvertone ORE 17* 4 7
14 Sep 91 I WANNA BE ADORED *Silvertone ORE 31* 20 3
11 Jan 92 WATERFALL *Silvertone ORE 35* 27 4
11 Apr 92 I AM THE RESURRECTION *Silvertone ORE 40* 33 2
30 May 92 FOOL'S GOLD (re-issue) *Silvertone ORET 13* 73 1
1 Aug 92 TURNS INTO STONE *Silvertone ORECD 521* 32 3
3 Dec 94 ● LOVE SPREADS *Geffen GFSTD 84* 2 8
17 Dec 94 ● SECOND COMING *Geffen GED 24503* 4 28
11 Mar 95 TEN STOREY LOVE SONG *Geffen GFSTD 87* 11 3
29 Apr 95 FOOL'S GOLD (2nd re-issue) *Silvertone ORECD 71* 25 3
27 May 95 ● THE COMPLETE STONE ROSES *Silvertone ORECD 535* 4 25
11 Nov 95 BEGGING YOU *Geffen GFSTD 22060* 15 3
7 Dec 96 GARAGE FLOWER *Silvertone GARAGECD 1* 58 1
6 Mar 99 FOOL'S GOLD (re-mix) *Jive Electro 0523092* 25 3
16 Oct 99 STONE ROSES – 10TH ANNIVERSARY EDITION *Silvertone 591242* 26 3
11 Nov 00 THE REMIXES *Silvertone 9260152* 41 2
16 Nov 02 THE VERY BEST OF THE STONE ROSES *Silvertone 9260382* 19 10

'She Bangs the Drums' made No.36 on its chart debut and reached its peak position only on re-entry in Mar 1990. 'What the World is Waiting For' / 'Fool's Gold' made No.22 on re-entry in Sep 1990. The Stone Roses reached its peak position in 2004 with a slighty different catalogue number, Silvertone OREZCD 502. The album peaked at No.19 in Sep 2005 with the catalogue number Jive 82876539712.

STONE SOUR
US, male vocal / instrumental group (1 Album: 1 Week, 2 Singles: 3 Weeks)

7 Sep 02 STONE SOUR *Roadrunner RR 84252* 41 1
15 Mar 03 BOTHER *Roadrunner RR 20243* 28 2
19 Jul 03 INHALE *Roadrunner RR 20093* 63 1

STONE TEMPLE PILOTS *US, male vocal (Scott Weiland) / instrumental group (3 Albums: 19 Weeks, 5 Singles: 11 Weeks)*

27 Mar 93 SEX TYPE THING *Atlantic A 5769CD* 60 2
4 Sep 93 CORE *Atlantic 7567824182* 27 8
4 Sep 93 PLUSH *Atlantic A 7349CD* 23 4
27 Nov 93 SEX TYPE THING (re-issue) *Atlantic A 7293CD* 55 2
18 Jun 94 ● PURPLE *Atlantic 7567826072* ▲ 10 9
20 Aug 94 VASOLINE *Atlantic A 5650CD* 48 2
10 Dec 94 INTERSTATE LOVE SONG *Atlantic A 7192CD* 53 1
6 Apr 96 TINY MUSIC ... SONGS FROM THE VATICAN GIFT SHOP *Atlantic 7567828712* 31 2

STONE THE CROWS *UK, female / male vocal / instrumental group*

7 Oct 72 ONTINUOUS PERFORMANCE *Polydor 2391 043* 33 3

STONEBRIDGE
Sweden, male producer – Sten Hollstrom (6 Singles: 17 Weeks)

13 Mar 04 PUT 'EM HIGH (re) *Hed Kandi HEDK 12004* [1] 59 2
28 Aug 04 ● PUT 'EM HIGH (re) (re-issue) *Hed Kandi HEDKCDS 008* 6 13
28 May 05 FREAK ON (re) *Hed Kandi HEDKCDX 10* [2] 37 2

[1] Stonebridge featuring Therese [2] Stonebridge vs Ultra Naté

STONEBRIDGE McGUINNESS *UK, male vocal / instrumental duo*

14 Jul 79 OO-EEH BABY *RCA PB 5163* 54 2

STONEFREE *UK, male vocalist – Tony Stone*

23 May 87 CAN'T SAY 'BYE *Ensign ENY 607* 73 1

STONEPROOF *UK, male producer – John Graham*

15 May 99 EVERYTHING'S NOT YOU *VC Recordings VCRD 47* 68 1

STOP THE VIOLENCE MOVEMENT
US, male / female rap charity ensemble

18 Feb 89 SELF DESTRUCTION *Jive BDPST 1* 75 1

STORM *UK, male / female vocal / instrumental group*

17 Nov 79 IT'S MY HOUSE *Scope SC 10* 36 10

STORM (see also DANCE 2 TRANCE; TOKYO GHETTO PUSSY; JAM & SPOON) *Germany, male production duo – Rolf Ellmer and Markus Löeffel, b. 27 Nov 1966, d. 11 Jan 2006 (4 Singles: 19 Weeks)*

29 Aug 98 STORM *Positiva CDTIV 94* 32 2
12 Aug 00 ● TIME TO BURN *Data DATA 16CDS* 3 10
23 Dec 00 STORM ANIMAL *Data DATA 20CDS* 21 5
26 May 01 STORM (re-mix) *Positiva CDTIV 154* 32 2

Danny STORM *UK, male vocalist*

12 Apr 62 HONEST I DO *Piccadilly 7N 35025* 42 4

Rebecca STORM *UK, female vocalist*

13 Jul 85 THE SHOW (THEME FROM 'CONNIE') *Towerbell TVP 3* 22 13

STORY OF THE YEAR *US, male vocal / instrumental group*

12 Jun 04 UNTIL THE DAY I DIE *Maverick W 634CD* 62 1

Izzy STRADLIN'
(see also GUNS N' ROSES) *US, male vocalist / guitarist – Jeffrey Isbell*

26 Sep 92 PRESSURE DROP *Geffen GFS 25* 45 2
24 Oct 92 IZZY STRADLIN' AND THE JU JU HOUNDS *Geffen GED 24490* [1] 52 1

[1] Izzy Stradlin' and The Ju Ju Hounds

Nick STRAKER BAND
UK, male vocal / instrumental group (2 Singles: 15 Weeks)

2 Aug 80 A WALK IN THE PARK *CBS 8525* 20 12
15 Nov 80 LEAVING ON THE MIDNIGHT TRAIN *CBS 9088* 61 3

Peter STRAKER and The HANDS OF DR TELENY
UK, male vocalist and male vocal / instrumental group

19 Feb 72 THE SPIRIT IS WILLING *RCA 2163* 40 4

STRANGELOVE
UK, male vocal / instrumental group (3 Albums: 3 Weeks, 6 Singles: 8 Weeks)

13 Aug 94 TIME FOR THE REST OF YOUR LIFE *Food FOODCD 11* 69 1
20 Apr 96 LIVING WITH THE HUMAN MACHINES *Food CDFOOD 70* 53 1
15 Jun 96 BEAUTIFUL ALONE *Food CDFOOD 81* 35 2
29 Jun 96 LOVE AND OTHER DEMONS *Food FOODCD 15* 44 1
19 Oct 96 SWAY *Food CDFOOD 82* 47 1
26 Jul 97 THE GREATEST SHOW ON EARTH *Food CDFOODS 97* 36 2
11 Oct 97 FREAK *Food CDFOOD 105* 43 1
18 Oct 97 STRANGELOVE *Food FOODCD 24* 67 1
21 Feb 98 ANOTHER NIGHT IN *Food CDFOOD 110* 46 1

23 November 1991	30 November 1991	7 December 1991	14 December 1991
UK No.1 SINGLES			
BLACK OR WHITE Michael Jackson	BLACK OR WHITE Michael Jackson	DON'T LET THE SUN GO DOWN ON ME George Michael and Elton John	DON'T LET THE SUN GO DOWN ON ME George Michael and Elton John
UK No.1 ALBUMS			
WE CAN'T DANCE Genesis	DANGEROUS Michael Jackson	GREATEST HITS II Queen	GREATEST HITS II Queen

The STRANGLERS 110 Top 500 *The most commercially successful and long-lasting group to emerge from the punk / new wave scene: Hugh Cornwell (v/g up to 1990), Jean-Jacques Burnel (b/v), Dave Greenfield (k), Jet Black (d). More recently, this London-based band has comprised new members Paul Roberts (v 1990 to present), John Ellis (g 1990-2000) and Baz Warne (g 2000 to the present)* (21 Albums: 223 Weeks, 36 Singles: 197 Weeks)

19 Feb 77 **(GET A) GRIP (ON YOURSELF)** *United Artists UP 36211* 44 4
30 Apr 77 ● **STRANGLERS IV (RATTUS NORVEGICUS)** *United Artists UAG 30045* 4 34
21 May 77 ● **PEACHES / GO BUDDY GO** *United Artists UP 36248* 8 14
30 Jul 77 ● **SOMETHING BETTER CHANGE / STRAIGHTEN OUT** *United Artists UP 36277* 9 8
24 Sep 77 ● **NO MORE HEROES** *United Artists UP 36300* 8 9
8 Oct 77 ● **NO MORE HEROES** *United Artists UAG 30200* 2 19
4 Feb 78 **5 MINUTES** *United Artists UP 36350* 11 9
6 May 78 **NICE 'N' SLEAZY** *United Artists UP 36379* 18 8
3 Jun 78 ● **BLACK AND WHITE** *United Artists UAK 30222* 2 18
12 Aug 78 **WALK ON BY** *United Artists UP 36429* 21 8
10 Mar 79 ● **LIVE (X CERT)** *United Artists UAG 30224* 7 10
18 Aug 79 **DUCHESS** *United Artists BP 308* 14 9
6 Oct 79 ● **THE RAVEN** *United Artists UAG 30262* 4 8
20 Oct 79 **NUCLEAR DEVICE (THE WIZARD OF AUS)** *United Artists BP 318* 36 4
1 Dec 79 **DON'T BRING HARRY (EP)** *United Artists STR 1* 41 3
22 Mar 80 **BEAR CAGE** *United Artists BP 344* 36 5
7 Jun 80 **WHO WANTS THE WORLD** *United Artists BP 355* 39 4
31 Jan 81 **THROWN AWAY** *Liberty BP 383* 42 4
21 Feb 81 ● **THEMENINBLACK** *Liberty LBG 30313* 8 5
14 Nov 81 **LET ME INTRODUCE YOU TO THE FAMILY** *Liberty BP 405* 42 3
21 Nov 81 **LA FOLIE** *Liberty LBG 30342* 11 18
9 Jan 82 ● **GOLDEN BROWN** *Liberty BP 407* 2 12
24 Apr 82 **LA FOLIE** *Liberty BP 410* 47 3
24 Jul 82 ● **STRANGE LITTLE GIRL** *Liberty BP 412* 7 9
25 Sep 82 **THE COLLECTION 1977-1982** *Liberty LBS 30353* 12 16
8 Jan 83 ● **EUROPEAN FEMALE** *Epic EPC A 2893* 9 6
22 Jan 83 ● **FELINE** *Epic EPC 25237* 4 11
26 Feb 83 **MIDNIGHT SUMMER DREAM** *Epic EPC A 3167* 35 4
6 Aug 83 **PARADISE** *Epic A 3387* 48 3
6 Oct 84 **SKIN DEEP** *Epic A 4738* 15 7
17 Nov 84 **AURAL SCULPTURE** *Epic EPC 26220* 14 10
1 Dec 84 **NO MERCY** *Epic A 4921* 37 7
16 Feb 85 **LET ME DOWN EASY** *Epic A 6045* 48 4
23 Aug 86 **NICE IN NICE** *Epic 6500557* 30 5
20 Sep 86 **OFF THE BEATEN TRACK** *Liberty LBG 5001* 80 2
18 Oct 86 **ALWAYS THE SUN** *Epic SOLAR 1* 30 5
8 Nov 86 **DREAMTIME** *Epic EPC 26648* 16 6
13 Dec 86 **BIG IN AMERICA** *Epic HUGE 1* 48 6
7 Mar 87 **SHAKIN' LIKE A LEAF** *Epic SHEIK 1* 58 4
9 Jan 88 ● **ALL DAY AND ALL OF THE NIGHT** *Epic VICE 1* 7 7
20 Feb 88 **ALL LIVE AND ALL OF THE NIGHT** *Epic 465259* 12 6
28 Jan 89 **GRIP '89 (GET A) GRIP (ON YOURSELF)** (re-mix) *EMI EM 84* 33 3
18 Feb 89 **THE SINGLES** *EMI EM 1314* 57 2
17 Feb 90 **96 TEARS** *Epic TEARS 1* 17 6
17 Mar 90 **10** *Epic 4664831* 15 4
21 Apr 90 **SWEET SMELL OF SUCCESS** *Epic TEARS 2* 65 2
1 Dec 90 ● **GREATEST HITS 1977-1990** *Epic 4675411* 4 47
5 Jan 91 **ALWAYS THE SUN** (re-mix) *Epic 6564307* 29 5
30 Mar 91 **GOLDEN BROWN** *Epic 6567617* 68 2
22 Aug 92 **HEAVEN OR HELL** *Psycho WOK 2025* 46 2
19 Sep 92 **STRANGLERS IN THE NIGHT** *Psycho WOLCD 1030* 33 1
27 May 95 **ABOUT TIME** *When! WENCD 001* 31 1
8 Feb 97 **WRITTEN IN RED** *When! WENCD 009* 52 1
22 Jun 02 **PEACHES – THE VERY BEST OF THE STRANGLERS** *EMI 5402022* 21 3
14 Feb 04 **BIG THING COMING** *Liberty 5480692* 31 2
28 Feb 04 **NORFOLK COAST** *Liberty 5969512* 70 1
24 Apr 04 **LONG BLACK VEIL** *Liberty 05489062* 51 1

'Go Buddy Go' credited with 'Peaches' from 11 Jun 1977. 'Straighten Out' credited with 'Something Better Change' from 13 Aug 1977. Tracks on Don't Bring Harry (EP): Don't Bring Harry / Wired / Crabs (Live) / In the Shadows (Live).

STRAW *UK, male vocal / instrumental group (3 Singles: 4 Weeks)*

6 Feb 99 **THE AEROPLANE SONG** *WEA WEA 196CD* 37 2
24 Apr 99 **MOVING TO CALIFORNIA** *WEA WEA 205CD1* 50 1
3 Mar 01 **SAILING OFF THE EDGE OF THE WORLD** *Columbia 6708452* 52 1

STRAWBERRY SWITCHBLADE *UK, female vocal duo – Rose McDowell and Jill Bryson* (1 Album: 4 Weeks, 3 Singles: 26 Weeks)

17 Nov 84 ● **SINCE YESTERDAY** *Korova KOW 38* 5 17
23 Mar 85 **LET HER GO** *Korova KOW 39* 59 5
13 Apr 85 **STRAWBERRY SWITCHBLADE** *Korova KODE 11* 25 4
21 Sep 85 **JOLENE** *Korova KOW 42* 53 4

The STRAWBS (see also HUDSON-FORD) *UK, male vocal (Dave Cousins) / instrumental group* (5 Albums: 31 Weeks, 3 Singles: 27 Weeks)

21 Nov 70 **JUST A COLLECTION OF ANTIQUES AND CURIOS** *A&M AMLS 994* 27 2
17 Jul 71 **FROM THE WITCHWOOD** *A&M AMLH 64304* 39 2
26 Feb 72 **GRAVE NEW WORLD** *A&M AMLH 68078* 11 12
28 Oct 72 **LAY DOWN** *A&M AMS 7035* 12 13
27 Jan 73 ● **PART OF THE UNION** *A&M AMS 7047* 2 11
24 Feb 73 ● **BURSTING AT THE SEAMS** *A&M AMLH 68144* 2 12
6 Oct 73 **SHINE ON SILVER SUN** *A&M AMS 7082* 34 3
27 Apr 74 **HERO AND HEROINE** *A&M AMLH 63607* 35 3

The STRAY CATS *US, male vocal (Brian Setzer) / instrumental group* (4 Albums: 32 Weeks, 7 Singles: 49 Weeks)

29 Nov 80 ● **RUNAWAY BOYS** *Arista SCAT 1* 9 10
7 Feb 81 ● **ROCK THIS TOWN** *Arista SCAT 2* 9 8
28 Feb 81 ● **STRAY CATS** *Arista STRAY 1* 6 22
25 Apr 81 **STRAY CAT STRUT** *Arista SCAT 3* 11 10
20 Jun 81 **THE RACE IS ON** *Swansong SSK 19425* [1] 34 6
7 Nov 81 **YOU DON'T BELIEVE ME** *Arista SCAT 4* 57 3
21 Nov 81 **GONNA BALL** *Arista STRAY 2* 48 4
6 Aug 83 **(SHE'S) SEXY AND 17** *Arista SCAT 6* 29 9
3 Sep 83 **RANT 'N' RAVE WITH THE STRAY CATS** *Arista STRAY 3* 51 5
4 Mar 89 **BRING IT BACK AGAIN** *EMI USA MT 62* 64 3
8 Apr 89 **BLAST OFF** *EMI MTL 1040* 58 1

[1] Dave Edmunds and The Stray Cats

STREETBAND (see also Paul YOUNG) *UK, male vocal / instrumental group*

4 Nov 78 **TOAST / HOLD ON** *Logo GO 325* 18 6

The STREETS (see also GRAFITI) *UK, rapper / producer – Mike Skinner* (2 Albums: 96 Weeks, 9 Singles: 51 Weeks)

20 Oct 01 **HAS IT COME TO THIS** (re) *WEA / 679L 001* 18 5
6 Apr 02 ● **ORIGINAL PIRATE MATERIAL** *Locked On / 679 Recordings 927435682* 10 56
27 Apr 02 **LET'S PUSH THINGS FORWARD** *Locked On / 679 Recordings 679L 005CD* 30 3
3 Aug 02 **WEAK BECOME HEROES** *Locked On / 679 Recordings 679L 007CD* 27 3
2 Nov 02 **DON'T MUG YOURSELF** *Locked On / 679 Recordings 679L 008CDX* 21 3
8 May 04 ● **FIT BUT YOU KNOW IT** *Locked On / 679 Recordings 679L 071CD 2* 4 10
22 May 04 ★ **A GRAND DON'T COME FOR FREE** *Locked On / 679 Recordings 2564615342* 1 40
31 Jul 04 ★ **DRY YOUR EYES** *Locked On / 679 Recordings 679L 077CD 1* ■ 1 13
9 Oct 04 ● **BLINDED BY THE LIGHTS** *Locked On / 679 Recordings 679L 085CD* 10 7
11 Dec 04 **COULD WELL BE IN** *Locked On / 679 Recordings 679L 092CD* 30 5
19 Mar 05 **ROUTINE CHECK** *The Beats BEATS 8* [1] 42 2

[1] The Mitchell Brothers featuring Kano and The Streets

Original Pirate Material reached its peak position in 2004.

21 December 1991	28 December 1991	4 January 1992	11 January 1992
BOHEMIAN RHAPSODY (Re-issue) / THESE ARE THE DAYS OF OUR LIVES Queen	BOHEMIAN RHAPSODY (Re-issue) / THESE ARE THE DAYS OF OUR LIVES Queen	BOHEMIAN RHAPSODY (Re-issue) / THESE ARE THE DAYS OF OUR LIVES Queen	BOHEMIAN RHAPSODY (Re-issue) / THESE ARE THE DAYS OF OUR LIVES Queen
GREATEST HITS II Queen	GREATEST HITS II Queen	STARS Simply Red	STARS Simply Red

KEY
UK No.1 ★★ UK Top 10 ●● Still on chart + + UK entry at No.1 ■■
US No.1 ▲▲ UK million seller £ US million seller $
Singles re-entries are listed as (re), (2re), (3re)… which signifies that the hit re-entered the chart once, twice or three times…
Peak Position / Weeks

The STREETWALKERS *UK, male vocal / instrumental group*

12 Jun 76 RED CARD *Vertigo 9102 010* 16 6

Barbra STREISAND 44 Top 500

Acclaimed song stylist who has more gold albums than any other female, b. 24 Apr 1942, Brooklyn, US. This world-renowned MOR vocalist / actress has collected countless awards for her recordings and her stage and film work, and is a recipient of both Grammy Living Legend and Lifetime Achievement awards (26 Albums: 537 Weeks, 18 Singles: 155 Weeks)

20 Jan 66 **SECOND HAND ROSE** *CBS 202025* 14 13
22 Jan 66 ● MY NAME IS BARBRA, TWO ... *CBS BPG 62603* 6 22
4 Apr 70 BARBRA STREISAND'S GREATEST HITS *CBS 63921* 44 2
30 Jan 71 **STONEY END** (re) *CBS 5321* 27 11
17 Apr 71 STONEY END *CBS 64269* 28 2
30 Mar 74 **THE WAY WE WERE** *CBS 1915* ▲ $ 31 6
15 Jun 74 THE WAY WE WERE *CBS 69057* ▲ 49 1
9 Apr 77 ★ A STAR IS BORN *CBS 86021* [1] ▲ 1 54
9 Apr 77 ● **LOVE THEME FROM 'A STAR IS BORN' (EVERGREEN)** *CBS 4855* ▲ $ 3 19
23 Jul 77 STREISAND SUPERMAN *CBS 86030* 32 9
15 Jul 78 SONGBIRD *CBS 86060* 48 2
25 Nov 78 ● **YOU DON'T BRING ME FLOWERS** *CBS 6803* [1] ▲ $ 5 12
17 Mar 79 ★ BARBRA STREISAND'S GREATEST HITS VOLUME 2 *CBS 10012* ▲ 1 30
3 Nov 79 ● **NO MORE TEARS (ENOUGH IS ENOUGH)** *Casablanca CAN 174 / CBS 8000* [2] ▲ $ 3 13
17 Nov 79 WET *CBS 86104* 25 13
4 Oct 80 ★ **WOMAN IN LOVE** *CBS 8966* ▲ $ 1 16
11 Oct 80 ★ GUILTY *CBS 86122* ▲ 1 82
6 Dec 80 **GUILTY** *CBS 9315* [3] $ 34 10
16 Jan 82 ★ LOVE SONGS *CBS 10031* 1 129
30 Jan 82 **COMIN' IN AND OUT OF YOUR LIFE** *CBS A 1789* 66 3
20 Mar 82 **MEMORY** *CBS A 1903* 34 6
19 Nov 83 YENTL (FILM SOUNDTRACK) *CBS 86302* 21 35
27 Oct 84 EMOTION *CBS 86309* 15 12
18 Jan 86 ● THE BROADWAY ALBUM *CBS 86322* ▲ 3 16
30 May 87 ONE VOICE *CBS 450 8901* 27 7
5 Nov 88 **TILL I LOVED YOU (LOVE THEME FROM 'GOYA')** *CBS BARB 2* [4] 16 7
3 Dec 88 TILL I LOVED YOU *CBS 462943 1* 29 13
25 Nov 89 A COLLECTION – GREATEST HITS ... AND MORE *CBS 465845 1* 22 23
7 Mar 92 **PLACES THAT BELONG TO YOU** *Columbia 6577947* 17 5
5 Jun 93 **WITH ONE LOOK** *Columbia 6593422* 30 3
10 Jul 93 ● BACK TO BROADWAY *Columbia 4738802* ▲ 4 17
15 Jan 94 **THE MUSIC OF THE NIGHT** *Columbia 6597382* [5] 54 3
30 Apr 94 **AS IF WE NEVER SAID GOODBYE** *Columbia 6603572* 20 3
29 Oct 94 THE CONCERT *Columbia 4775992* 63 1
8 Feb 97 ● **I FINALLY FOUND SOMEONE** *A&M 5820832* [6] 10 7
15 Nov 97 ● **TELL HIM** *Epic 6653052* [7] 3 15
22 Nov 97 HIGHER GROUND *Columbia 4885322* ▲ 12 12
2 Oct 99 A LOVE LIKE OURS *Columbia 4949342* 12 9
30 Oct 99 **IF YOU EVER LEAVE ME** *Columbia 6681242* [8] 26 3
30 Sep 00 TIMELESS – LIVE IN CONCERT *Columbia 4974352* 54 1
9 Mar 02 ★ THE ESSENTIAL BARBRA STREISAND *Columbia 5062572* 1 22
30 Nov 02 DUETS *Columbia 5098129* 30 6
8 Nov 03 THE MOVIE ALBUM *Columbia 5134213* 25 3
1 Oct 05 ● GUILTY TOO *Columbia 82876732612* [2] 3 14+

[1] Barbra and Neil [Barbra Streisand and Neil Diamond] [2] Donna Summer and Barbra Streisand [3] Barbra Streisand and Barry Gibb [4] Barbra Streisand and Don Johnson [5] Barbra Streisand (duet with Michael Crawford) [6] Barbra Streisand and Bryan Adams [7] Barbra Streisand and Celine Dion [8] Barbra Streisand / Vince Gill [1] Barbra Streisand / Kris Kristofferson [2] Streisand

'No More Tears (Enough Is Enough)' was released simultaneously on two different labels, a 7-inch single on Casablanca and a 12-inch on CBS. Guilty and the sequel, Guilty Too, feature uncredited vocals from Barry Gibb.

STRESS *UK, male vocal / instrumental group*

13 Oct 90 **BEAUTIFUL PEOPLE** *Eternal YZ 495* 74 1

STRETCH *UK, male vocal / instrumental group*

8 Nov 75 **WHY DID YOU DO IT** *Anchor ANC 1021* 16 9

STRETCH 'N' VERN present "MADDOG" *UK, male instrumental / production duo – Stuart Collins and Julian Peake (2 Singles: 14 Weeks)*

14 Sep 96 ● **I'M ALIVE** *ffrr FCD 284* 6 9
9 Aug 97 **GET UP! GO INSANE!** *ffrr FCD 304* 17 5

STRICT INSTRUCTOR *Russia, female vocalist*

24 Oct 98 **STEP-TWO-THREE-FOUR** *All Around the World CDGLOBE 155* 49 1

STRIKE *UK / Australia, male / female vocal (Victoria Newton) / instrumental group (6 Singles: 24 Weeks)*

24 Dec 94 ● **U SURE DO** (re) *Fresh FRSHD 19* 4 14
23 Sep 95 **THE MORNING AFTER (FREE AT LAST)** *Fresh FRSHD 37* 38 1
29 Jun 96 **INSPIRATION** *Fresh FRSHD 45* 27 2
16 Nov 96 **MY LOVE IS FOR REAL** *Fresh FRSHD 46* 35 2
31 May 97 **I HAVE PEACE** *Fresh FRSHCD 58* 17 4
25 Sep 99 **U SURE DO** (re-mix) *Fresh FRSHD 78* 53 1

'U Sure Do' debuted at No.31 and made its peak position only on re-entry in Apr 1995.

The STRIKERS *US, male vocal / instrumental group*

6 Jun 81 **BODY MUSIC** *Epic EPC A 1290* 45 5

The STRING-A-LONGS *US, male instrumental group*

23 Feb 61 ● **WHEELS** *London HLU 9278* $ 8 16

STRINGS FOR PLEASURE *UK, orchestra*

4 Dec 71 THE BEST OF BACHARACH *MFP 1334* 49 1

STRINGS OF LOVE *Italy, male / female vocal / instrumental group*

3 Mar 90 **NOTHING HAS BEEN PROVED** *Breakout USA 688* 59 2

The STROKES *US, male vocal (Julian Casablancas) / instrumental group (2 Albums: 60 Weeks, 8 Singles: 29 Weeks)*

7 Jul 01 **HARD TO EXPLAIN / NEW YORK CITY COPS** *Rough Trade RTRADSCD 023* 16 5
7 Jul 01 **MODERN AGE** (2re) *Rough Trade RTRADSCD 010* 68 3
8 Sep 01 ● IS THIS IT *Rough Trade RTRADCD 030* 2 40
17 Nov 01 **LAST NITE** *Rough Trade RTRADSCD 041* 14 5
5 Oct 02 **SOMEDAY** *Rough Trade RTRADSCD 063* 27 2
18 Oct 03 ● **12:51** *Rough Trade RTRADSCD 140* 7 4
1 Nov 03 ● ROOM ON FIRE *Rough Trade RTRADCD 130* 2 20
21 Feb 04 **REPTILIA** *Rough Trade RTRADSCD 155* 17 5
13 Nov 04 **THE END HAS NO END** *Rough Trade RTRADSCD 205* 27 2
17 Dec 05 ● **JUICEBOX** *Rough Trade RTRADSCDX 282* 5 3+

'Modern Age' is a three-track CD featuring 'Modern Age', 'Last Nite' (later re-recorded and released as the band's next single in 2001) and 'Barely Legal'.

Joe STRUMMER

(see also The CLASH) *UK (b. Turkey), male vocalist – John Mellor, b. 21 Aug 1952, d. 23 Dec 2002 (4 Albums: 4 Weeks, 5 Singles: 17 Weeks)*

2 Aug 86 **LOVE KILLS** *CBS A 7244* 69 1
14 Oct 89 EARTHQUAKE WEATHER *Epic 465347 1* 58 1

18 January 1992	25 January 1992	1 February 1992	8 February 1992
UK No.1 SINGLES			
BOHEMIAN RHAPSODY (Re-issue) / THESE ARE THE DAYS OF OUR LIVES – Queen	GOODNIGHT GIRL – Wet Wet Wet	GOODNIGHT GIRL – Wet Wet Wet	GOODNIGHT GIRL – Wet Wet Wet
UK No.1 ALBUMS			
STARS – Simply Red	STARS – Simply Red	STARS – Simply Red	HIGH ON THE HAPPY SIDE – Wet Wet Wet

23 Dec 95 JUST THE ONE *China WOKCD 2076* [1] 12 8
29 Jun 96 ● ENGLAND'S IRIE *Radioactive RAXTD 25* [2] 6 4
30 Oct 99 ROCK ART AND THE X-RAY STYLE *Mercury 5466542* [1] 71 1
28 Jul 01 GLOBAL A GO GO *Hellcat 4402* [1] 68 1
18 Oct 03 COMA GIRL *Hellcat 11352* [3] 33 2
1 Nov 03 STREETCORE *Hellcat 04542* [1] 50 1
27 Dec 03 REDEMPTION SONG / ARMS ALOFT *Hellcat 11472* [3] 46 2

[1] Levellers, special guest Joe Strummer [2] Black Grape featuring Joe Strummer and Keith Allen [3] Joe Strummer and The Mescaleros [1] Joe Strummer and the Mescaleros

STUART *Holland, male producer – Sjoerd Wijdoogen*

5 Apr 03 FREE (LET IT BE) *Product / Incentive PDT 07CDS* 41 2

Chad STUART and Jeremy CLYDE *UK, male vocal duo*

28 Nov 63 YESTERDAY'S GONE *Ember EMB S 180* 37 7

STUDIO 2 *Jamaica, male vocalist – Errol Jones*

27 Jun 98 TRAVELLING MAN *Multiply CDMULTY 35* 40 1

STUDIO B (see also SO SOLID CREW)
UK, male producer / vocalist – Harry Brooks (2 Singles: 20 Weeks)

6 Dec 03 I SEE GIRLS (CRAZY) *Multiply CDMULTY 109* [1] 52 1
9 Apr 05 I SEE GIRLS (re-mix) (re) *Data BOSSMOS 1CDS* 12 19

[1] Studio B / Romeo and Harry Brooks

STUDIO 45
Germany, male DJ / production duo – Tilo Cielsa and Jens Brachvogel

20 Feb 99 FREAK IT! *Azuli AZNYCD 090* 36 2

Amy STUDT *UK, female vocalist (1 Album: 11 Weeks, 4 Singles: 26 Weeks)*

13 Jul 02 JUST A LITTLE GIRL *Polydor 5708802* 14 6
21 Jun 03 ● MISFIT *Polydor 9800107* 6 10
12 Jul 03 FALSE SMILES *Polydor 9801074* 24 11
11 Oct 03 ● UNDER THE THUMB *Polydor 9811793* 10 6
24 Jan 04 ALL I WANNA DO *Polydor 9815012* 21 4

STUMP *UK, male vocal / instrumental group*

13 Aug 88 CHARLTON HESTON *Ensign ENY 614* 72 1

STUNTMASTERZ *UK, male production duo – Steve Harris and Pete Cook*

3 Mar 01 ● THE LADYBOY IS MINE *East West EW 226CD* 10 9

STUTZ BEARCATS and The Denis KING ORCHESTRA
(see also The KING BROTHERS) *UK, male / female vocal group and orchestra*

24 Apr 82 THE SONG THAT I SING (THEME FROM 'WE'LL MEET AGAIN') *Multi-Media Tapes MMT 6* 36 6

The STYLE COUNCIL 345 Top 500
Eighties chart regulars: Paul Weller (v/g), Mick Talbot (k) and (sometimes) Dee C Lee (v), who was a former Wham! backing vocalist and Weller's ex-wife. As with Weller's previous band, The Jam, most of this London act's hits were in their homeland (9 Albums: 100 Weeks, 18 Singles: 103 Weeks)

19 Mar 83 ● SPEAK LIKE A CHILD *Polydor TSC 1* 4 8
28 May 83 MONEY GO ROUND (PART 1) (re) *Polydor TSC 2* 11 7
13 Aug 83 ● LONG HOT SUMMER / PARIS MATCH *Polydor TSC 3* 3 9
19 Nov 83 SOLID BOND IN YOUR HEART *Polydor TSC 4* 11 8
18 Feb 84 ● MY EVER CHANGING MOODS *Polydor TSC 5* 5 7
24 Mar 84 ● CAFE BLEU *Polydor TSCLP 1* 2 38
26 May 84 ● GROOVIN' (YOU'RE THE BEST THING / THE BIG BOSS GROOVE) *Polydor TSC 6* 5 8
13 Oct 84 ● SHOUT TO THE TOP *Polydor TSC 7* 7 8
11 May 85 ● WALLS COME TUMBLING DOWN! *Polydor TSC 8* 6 7
8 Jun 85 ★ OUR FAVOURITE SHOP *Polydor TSCLP 2* ■ 1 22
6 Jul 85 COME TO MILTON KEYNES *Polydor TSC 9* 23 5
28 Sep 85 THE LODGERS *Polydor TSC 10* 13 6
5 Apr 86 HAVE YOU EVER HAD IT BLUE *Polydor CINE 1* 14 6
17 May 86 ● HOME AND ABROAD *Polydor TSCLP 3* 8 8
17 Jan 87 ● IT DIDN'T MATTER *Polydor TSC 12* 9 5
14 Feb 87 ● THE COST OF LOVING *Polydor TSCLP 4* 2 7
14 Mar 87 WAITING *Polydor TSC 13* 52 3
31 Oct 87 WANTED *Polydor TSC 14* 20 4
28 May 88 LIFE AT A TOP PEOPLE'S HEALTH FARM *Polydor TSC 15* 28 3
2 Jul 88 CONFESSIONS OF A POP GROUP *Polydor TSCMC 5* 15 3
23 Jul 88 HOW SHE THREW IT ALL AWAY (EP) *Polydor TSC 16* 41 2
18 Feb 89 PROMISED LAND *Polydor TSC 17* 27 5
18 Mar 89 ● THE SINGULAR ADVENTURES OF THE STYLE COUNCIL – GREATEST HITS VOL.1 *Polydor TSCTV 1* 3 15
27 May 89 LONG HOT SUMMER 89 (re-mix) *Polydor LHS 1* 48 2
10 Jul 93 HERE'S SOME THAT GOT AWAY *Polydor 5193722* 39 1
2 Mar 96 THE STYLE COUNCIL COLLECTION *Polydor 5294832* 60 1
2 Sep 00 GREATEST HITS *Polydor / Universal TV 5579002* 28 5

'Paris Match' was listed with 'Long Hot Summer' from 3 Sep 1983. It peaked at No.7. Tracks on How She Threw It All Away (EP): How She Threw It All Away / Love the First Time / Long Hot Summer / I Do Like to Be B-Side the A-Side. The version of 'Long Hot Summer' on the EP is a re-recording of their third hit.

Darren STYLES & Mark BREEZE (see also FORCE & STYLES featuring Kelly LLORENNA) *UK, male production duo (3 Singles: 9 Weeks)*

5 Apr 03 LET ME FLY *Nukleuz 0432 CNUK* [1] 59 1
31 Jul 04 YOU'RE SHINING *All Around the World CDGLOBE 333* [2] 19 4
12 Mar 05 HEARTBEATZ *All Around the World CDGLOBE 342* [3] 16 4

[1] Darren Styles & Mark Breeze present Infextious [2] Styles & Breeze [3] Styles & Breeze featuring Karen Danzig

STYLES & Pharoahe MONCH *US, male rappers*

14 Sep 02 THE LIFE *MCA MCSTD 40292* 50 1

The STYLISTICS 215 Top 500
Stylish and smooth vocal group from Philadelphia, US, fronted by falsetto-voiced Russell Thompkins Jr. Their UK hits continued after success in their homeland diminished and they are one of few US acts to have two chart-topping Greatest Hits albums (9 Albums: 142 Weeks, 16 Singles: 143 Weeks)

24 Jun 72 BETCHA BY GOLLY WOW *Avco 6105 011* $ 13 12
4 Nov 72 ● I'M STONE IN LOVE WITH YOU *Avco 6105 015* $ 9 10
17 Mar 73 BREAK UP TO MAKE UP *Avco 6105 020* $ 34 5
30 Jun 73 PEEK-A-BOO *Avco 6105 023* 35 6
19 Jan 74 ● ROCKIN' ROLL BABY *Avco 6105 026* 6 9
13 Jul 74 ● YOU MAKE ME FEEL BRAND NEW *Avco 6105 028* $ 2 14
24 Aug 74 ROCKIN' ROLL BABY *Avco 6466 012* 42 3
21 Sep 74 LET'S PUT IT ALL TOGETHER *Avco 6466 013* 26 14
19 Oct 74 ● LET'S PUT IT ALL TOGETHER *Avco 6105 032* 9 9
25 Jan 75 STAR ON A TV SHOW *Avco 6105 035* 12 8
1 Mar 75 FROM THE MOUNTAIN *Avco 9109 002* 36 1
5 Apr 75 ★ THE BEST OF THE STYLISTICS *Avco 9109 003* 1 63
10 May 75 ● SING BABY SING *Avco 6105 036* 3 10
5 Jul 75 ● THANK YOU BABY *Avco 9109 005* 5 23
26 Jul 75 ★ CAN'T GIVE YOU ANYTHING (BUT MY LOVE) *Avco 6105 039* 1 11
15 Nov 75 ● NA-NA IS THE SADDEST WORD *Avco 6105 041* 5 10
6 Dec 75 YOU ARE BEAUTIFUL *Avco 9109 006* 26 9
14 Feb 76 ● FUNKY WEEKEND *Avco 6105 044* 10 7
24 Apr 76 ● CAN'T HELP FALLING IN LOVE *H&L 6105 050* 4 7
12 Jun 76 FABULOUS *Avco 9109 008* 21 5
7 Aug 76 ● SIXTEEN BARS *H&L 6105 059* 7 9
18 Sep 76 ★ BEST OF THE STYLISTICS VOLUME 2 *H&L 9109 010* 1 21
27 Nov 76 YOU'LL NEVER GET TO HEAVEN (EP) *H&L STYL 001* 24 9
26 Mar 77 $7000 AND YOU *H&L 6105 073* 24 7
17 Oct 92 THE GREATEST HITS OF THE STYLISTICS – LET'S PUT IT ALL TOGETHER *Mercury 5129852* 34 3

Tracks on You'll Never Get to Heaven (EP): You'll Never Get to Heaven / Country Living / You Are Beautiful / The Miracle.

15 February 1992	22 February 1992	29 February 1992	7 March 1992
GOODNIGHT GIRL Wet Wet Wet	STAY Shakespear's Sister	STAY Shakespear's Sister	STAY Shakespear's Sister
HIGH ON THE HAPPY SIDE Wet Wet Wet	STARS Simply Red	STARS Simply Red	STARS Simply Red

KEY
UK No.1 ★ UK Top 10 ● Still on chart + UK entry at No.1 ■
US No.1 ▲ UK million seller £ US million seller $
Singles re-entries are listed as (re), (2re), (3re)… which signifies that the hit re-entered the chart once, twice or three times…
Peak Position / Weeks

STYLUS TROUBLE (see also FIRE ISLAND; HELLER & FARLEY PROJECT) *UK, male producer – Pete Heller*

23 Jun 01 **SPUTNIK** *Junior London BRG 014*....63 1

STYX *US, male vocal (Dennis DeYoung) / instrumental group (4 Albums: 24 Weeks, 3 Singles: 18 Weeks)*

3 Nov 79 CORNERSTONE *A&M AMLK 63711*....36 8
5 Jan 80 ● **BABE** *A&M AMS 7489* ▲ $....6 10
24 Jan 81 ● PARADISE THEATER *A&M AMLH 63719* ▲....8 8
24 Jan 81 **THE BEST OF TIMES** *A&M AMS 8102*....42 5
12 Mar 83 KILROY WAS HERE *A&M AMLX 63734*....67 6
18 Jun 83 **DON'T LET IT END** *A&M AM 120*....56 3
5 May 84 CAUGHT IN THE ACT *A&M AMLM 66704*....44 2

SUB FOCUS NEW *UK, male producer*

19 Mar 05 **X-RAY / SCARECROW** *Ram RAMM 54*....60 1

SUB SUB *UK, male instrumental / production group (2 Singles: 12 Weeks)*

10 Apr 93 ● **AIN'T NO LOVE (AIN'T NO USE)** *Rob's CDROB 9* [1]....3 11
19 Feb 94 **RESPECT** *Rob's CDROB 19*....49 1

[1] Sub Sub featuring Melanie Williams

SUBCIRCUS
Denmark / UK, male vocal / instrumental group (2 Singles: 2 Weeks)

26 Apr 97 **YOU LOVE YOU** *Echo ECSCD 34*....61 1
12 Jul 97 **86'D** *Echo ECSCX 43*....56 1

SUBLIME *US, male vocal / instrumental group*

5 Jul 97 **WHAT I GOT** *Gasoline Alley MCSTD 48045*....71 1

SUBLIMINAL CUTS (see also ARTEMESIA; ETHICS; MOVIN' MELODIES) *Holland, male producer – Patrick Prinz (2 Singles: 3 Weeks)*

15 Oct 94 **LE VOIE LE SOLEIL** *XL XLS 53CD*....69 1
20 Jul 96 **LE VOIE LE SOLEIL** (re-mix) *XL XLSR 53CD*....23 2

SUBMERGE featuring Jan JOHNSTON
(see also ALCATRAZ; LITHIUM and Sonya MADAN)
US, male producer / keyboard player – Victor Imbres and female vocalist

8 Feb 97 **TAKE ME BY THE HAND** *AM:PM 5821012*....28 2

SUBSONIC 2 *UK, male rap duo*

13 Jul 91 **THE UNSUNG HEROES OF HIP HOP** *Unity 6577947*....63 3

SUBTERRANIA featuring Ann CONSUELO
Sweden, male / female vocal / instrumental duo

5 Jun 93 **DO IT FOR LOVE** *Champion CHAMPCD 297*....68 1

The SUBWAYS NEW *UK, male / female vocal / instrumental group (1 Album: 5 Weeks, 4 Singles: 9 Weeks)*

2 Apr 05 **OH YEAH** *WEA WEA 384CD1*....25 3
2 Jul 05 **ROCK & ROLL QUEEN** *Infectious WEA 390CD2*....22 2
16 Jul 05 YOUNG FOR ETERNITY *Infectious 2564624842*....32 5
24 Sep 05 **WITH YOU** *WEA WEA 392DVD*....29 2
24 Dec 05 **NO GOODBYES** *Infectious WEA 398CD*....27 2+

SUEDE 393 Top 500 (see also The TEARS)
London-based Britpop pioneers led by Brett Anderson (v) and featuring co-writer Bernard Butler (g), who left 1994. Melody Maker's 'Best Band in Britain' won the Mercury Music Prize for their 1993 self-titled debut album, which sold more than 100,000 in the first week. Anderson and Butler reunited and recorded together as The Tears in 2005, having reportedly not spoken to each other for a decade (7 Albums: 105 Weeks, 20 Singles: 75 Weeks)

23 May 92 **THE DROWNERS / TO THE BIRDS** *Nude NUD 1S*....49 2
26 Sep 92 **METAL MICKEY** *Nude NUD 3S*....17 3
6 Mar 93 ● **ANIMAL NITRATE** *Nude NUD 4CD*....7 7
10 Apr 93 ★ SUEDE *Nude NUDE 1CD* ■....1 22
29 May 93 **SO YOUNG** *Nude NUD 5CD*....22 3
26 Feb 94 ● **STAY TOGETHER** *Nude NUD 9CD*....3 6
24 Sep 94 **WE ARE THE PIGS** *Nude NUD 10CD*....18 3
22 Oct 94 ● DOG MAN STAR *Nude 4778112*....3 16
19 Nov 94 **THE WILD ONES** *Nude NUD 11CD1*....18 4
11 Feb 95 **NEW GENERATION** (re) *Nude NUD 12CD1*....21 4
10 Aug 96 ● **TRASH** *Nude NUD 21CD1*....3 6
14 Sep 96 ★ COMING UP *Nude NUDE 6CD* ■....1 44
26 Oct 96 ● **BEAUTIFUL ONES** *Nude NUD 23CD1*....8 5
25 Jan 97 ● **SATURDAY NIGHT** *Nude NUD 24CD1*....6 4
19 Apr 97 ● **LAZY** *Nude NUD 27CD1*....9 3
23 Aug 97 ● **FILMSTAR** *Nude NUD 30CD1*....9 4
18 Oct 97 ● SCI-FI LULLABIES *Nude NUDE 9CD*....9 3
24 Apr 99 ● **ELECTRICITY** *Nude NUD 43CD1*....5 5
15 May 99 ★ HEAD MUSIC *Nude NUDE 14CD* ■....1 16
3 Jul 99 **SHE'S IN FASHION** *Nude NUD 44CD1*....13 5
18 Sep 99 **EVERYTHING WILL FLOW** *Nude NUD 45CD1*....24 2
20 Nov 99 **CAN'T GET ENOUGH** *Nude NUD 47CD1*....23 2
28 Sep 02 **POSITIVITY** *Epic 6729492*....16 2
12 Oct 02 A NEW MORNING *Epic 5089569*....24 2
30 Nov 02 **OBSESSIONS** *Epic 6732942*....29 2
18 Oct 03 **ATTITUDE / GOLDEN GUN** *Sony Music 6743582*....14 3
1 Nov 03 SINGLES *Sony Music 5136042*....31 2

SUENO LATINO *Italy, male production duo (2 Singles: 6 Weeks)*

23 Sep 89 **SUENO LATINO** *BCM BCM 323* [1]....47 5
11 Nov 00 **SUENO LATINO** (re-mix) *Distinctive DISNCD 64*....68 1

[1] Sueno Latino featuring Carolina Damas

SUGABABES 282 Top 500
One of the 21st century's most regular UK hitmakers: Keisha Buchanan (London), Liverpudlian Heidi Range, who replaced Siobhan Donaghy and Amelle Berrabah (Aldershot), who replaced Mutya Buena when she left the group in Dec 2005. At 18, these photogenic chart-toppers were the youngest all girl group to reach No.1 (4 Albums: 105 Weeks, 14 Singles: 132 Weeks)

23 Sep 00 ● **OVERLOAD** *London LONCD 449*....6 8
23 Dec 00 ONE TOUCH *London 8573861072*....26 15
30 Dec 00 **NEW YEAR** *London LONCD 455*....12 9
21 Apr 01 **RUN FOR COVER** *London LONCD 459*....13 7
28 Jul 01 **SOUL SOUND** *London LONCD 460*....30 2
4 May 02 ★ **FREAK LIKE ME** (re) *Island CID 798* ■....1 14
24 Aug 02 ★ **ROUND ROUND** *Island CID 804* ■....1 13
7 Sep 02 ● ANGELS WITH DIRTY FACES *Island / Uni-Island CID 8122*....2 40
23 Nov 02 ● **STRONGER / ANGELS WITH DIRTY FACES** *Island CID 813*....7 13
22 Mar 03 **SHAPE** *Island CID 817*....11 9
25 Oct 03 ★ **HOLE IN THE HEAD** *Island CID 836* ■....1 13
8 Nov 03 ● THREE *Island / Uni-Island CID 8137*....3 39
27 Dec 03 ● **TOO LOST IN YOU** *Island CID 844*....10 13
3 Apr 04 ● **IN THE MIDDLE** *Universal / Island MCSXD 40360*....8 8
4 Sep 04 ● **CAUGHT IN A MOMENT** *Universal / Island MCSXD 40371*....8 7
8 Oct 05 ★ **PUSH THE BUTTON** *Island CIDX 911* ■....1 13+
22 Oct 05 ★ TALLER IN MORE WAYS *Island CID 8162* ■....1 11+
17 Dec 05 ● **UGLY** *Island CIDX 918*....3 3+

SUGAR *US, male vocal (Bob Mould) / instrumental group (3 Albums: 19 Weeks, 5 Singles: 7 Weeks)*

19 Sep 92 ● COPPER BLUE *Creation CRECD 129*....10 11

14 March 1992	21 March 1992	28 March 1992	4 April 1992
◂◂ UK No.1 SINGLES ▸▸			
STAY Shakespear's Sister	STAY Shakespear's Sister	STAY Shakespear's Sister	STAY Shakespear's Sister
◂◂ UK No.1 ALBUMS ▸▸			
DIVINE MADNESS Madness	DIVINE MADNESS Madness	DIVINE MADNESS Madness	HUMAN TOUCH Bruce Springsteen

31 Oct 92 **A GOOD IDEA** *Creation CRE 143* **65** 1
30 Jan 93 **IF I CAN'T CHANGE YOUR MIND** *Creation CRESCD 149* 30 2
17 Apr 93 ● BEASTER *Creation CRECD 153* 3 5
21 Aug 93 **TILTED** *Creation CRECD 156* **48** 1
3 Sep 94 **YOUR FAVORITE THING** *Creation CRESCD 186* **40** 2
17 Sep 94 ● FILE UNDER EASY LISTENING *Creation CRECD 172* 7 3
29 Oct 94 **BELIEVE WHAT YOU'RE SAYING** *Creation CRESCD 193* 73 1

SUGAR CANE *US, male / female vocal group*

30 Sep 78 **MONTEGO BAY** *Ariola Hansa AHA 524* **54** 5

SUGAR RAY *US, male vocal (Mark McGrath) / instrumental group (1 Album: 1 Week, 3 Singles: 12 Weeks)*

31 Jan 98 **FLY** *Atlantic AT 0008CD* **58** 1
29 May 99 ● **EVERY MORNING** *Lava / Atlantic AT 0065CD* 10 9
19 Jun 99 14:59 *Atlantic 7567831512* 60 1
20 Oct 01 **WHEN IT'S OVER** *Atlantic AT 0114CD* 32 2

SUGARCOMA *UK, male / female vocal / instrumental group*

13 Apr 02 **YOU DRIVE ME CRAZY / WINDINGS** *Music for Nations CDKUT 190* **57** 1

The SUGARCUBES *Iceland, female / male vocal / instrumental group – leader Björk (4 Albums: 14 Weeks, 7 Singles: 22 Weeks)*

14 Nov 87 **BIRTHDAY** *One Little Indian 7TP 7* **65** 3
30 Jan 88 **COLD SWEAT** *One Little Indian 7TP 9* **56** 4
16 Apr 88 **DEUS** *One Little Indian 7TP 10* **51** 3
7 May 88 LIFE'S TOO GOOD *One Little Indian TPLP 5* 14 6
3 Sep 88 **BIRTHDAY** (re-recording) *One Little Indian 7TP 11* **65** 3
16 Sep 89 **REGINA** *One Little Indian 26TP 7* **55** 2
14 Oct 89 HERE TODAY TOMORROW NEXT WEEK *One Little Indian TPLP 15* 15 3
11 Jan 92 **HIT** *One Little Indian 62TP 7* **17** 6
22 Feb 92 STICK AROUND FOR JOY *One Little Indian TPLP 30CD* 16 4
3 Oct 92 **BIRTHDAY** (re-mix) *One Little Indian 104TP 12* **64** 1
17 Oct 92 IT'S-IT *One Little Indian TPLP 40CD* 47 1

SUGARHILL GANG *US, male rap group (3 Singles: 16 Weeks)*

1 Dec 79 ● **RAPPER'S DELIGHT** *Sugarhill SHL 101* 3 11
11 Sep 82 **THE LOVER IN YOU** *Sugarhill SH 116* **54** 3
25 Nov 89 **RAPPER'S DELIGHT** (re-mix) *Sugarhill SHRD 0007* **58** 2

SUGGS (see also MADNESS) *UK, male vocalist – Graham McPherson (1 Album: 5 Weeks, 7 Singles: 46 Weeks)*

12 Aug 95 ● **I'M ONLY SLEEPING / OFF ON HOLIDAY** *WEA YZ 975CD* 7 6
14 Oct 95 **CAMDEN TOWN** *WEA WEA 019CD* **14** 6
28 Oct 95 THE LONE RANGER *WEA 0630124782* 14 5
16 Dec 95 **THE TUNE** *WEA WEA 031CD* 33 3
13 Apr 96 ● **CECILIA** (2re) *WEA WEA 042CD1* [1] 4 19
21 Sep 96 **NO MORE ALCOHOL** *WEA WEA 065CD1* [1] 24 4
17 May 97 **BLUE DAY** *WEA WEA 112CD* [2] 22 5
5 Sep 98 **I AM** *WEA WEA 174CD* 38 3

[1] Suggs featuring Louchie Lou and Michie One [2] Suggs & Co featuring Chelsea Team

SUICIDAL TENDENCIES *US, male vocal / instrumental group (2 Albums: 2 Weeks)*

9 May 87 JOIN THE ARMY *Virgin V 2424* 81 1
21 Jul 90 LIGHTS ... CAMERA ... REVOLUTION *Epic 4665691* 59 1

SULTANA *Italy, male instrumental / production group*

26 Mar 94 **TE AMO** *Union City UCRD 28* **57** 1

SULTANS OF PING *Ireland, male vocal / instrumental group (2 Albums: 3 Weeks, 7 Singles: 12 Weeks)*

8 Feb 92 **WHERE'S ME JUMPER?** *Divine ATHY 01* [1] **67** 2
9 May 92 **STUPID KID** *Divine ATHY 02* [1] **67** 1
10 Oct 92 **VERONICA** *Divine ATHY 03* [1] **69** 1
9 Jan 93 **YOU TALK TOO MUCH** *Rhythm King 6588872* [1] **26** 3
13 Feb 93 CASUAL SEX IN THE CINEPLEX *Rhythm King 4724952* [1] 26 2
11 Sep 93 **TEENAGE PUNKS** *Epic 6595792* **49** 2
30 Oct 93 **MICHIKO** *Epic 6598222* **43** 2
19 Feb 94 **WAKE UP AND SCRATCH ME** *Epic 6601122* **50** 1
5 Mar 94 TEENAGE DRUG *Epic 4747162* 57 1

[1] Sultans of Ping FC [1] Sultans of Ping FC

SUM 41 *Canada, male vocal (Deryck Whibley) / instrumental group (3 Albums: 50 Weeks, 6 Singles: 40 Weeks)*

11 Aug 01 ● ALL KILLER NO FILLER *Mercury 5486622* 7 43
13 Oct 01 ● **FAT LIP** *Mercury 5888012* 8 9
15 Dec 01 **IN TOO DEEP** *Mercury 5888982* 13 11
6 Apr 02 **MOTIVATION** *Mercury 5889452* 21 7
29 Jun 02 **IT'S WHAT WE'RE ALL ABOUT** *Columbia 6728642* 32 3
30 Nov 02 **STILL WAITING** *Mercury 0638312* **16** 7
7 Dec 02 DOES THIS LOOK INFECTED? *Mercury 0635590* 39 6
22 Feb 03 **THE HELL SONG** *Mercury 0637202* **35** 3
23 Oct 04 CHUCK *Mercury 9864426* 59 1

Donna SUMMER (78 Top 500)

"Queen of disco music", b. LaDonna Gaines, 31 Dec 1948, Massachusetts, US. Germany was the launching pad for this diva, who had eight successive US Top 5 singles in the late 1970s. She was also the first female to score three consecutive US No.1 albums (16 Albums: 204 Weeks, 42 Singles: 299 Weeks)

17 Jan 76 ● **LOVE TO LOVE YOU BABY** *GTO GT 17* $ 4 9
31 Jan 76 LOVE TO LOVE YOU BABY *GTO GTLP 008* 16 9
22 May 76 A LOVE TRILOGY *GTO GTLP 010* 41 10
29 May 76 **COULD IT BE MAGIC** *GTO GT 60* **40** 7
25 Dec 76 **WINTER MELODY** *GTO GT 76* **27** 6
25 Jun 77 ● I REMEMBER YESTERDAY *GTO GTLP 025* 3 23
9 Jul 77 ★ **I FEEL LOVE** *GTO GT 100* $ 1 11
20 Aug 77 ● **DOWN DEEP INSIDE (THEME FROM 'THE DEEP')** *Casablanca CAN 111* 5 10
24 Sep 77 **I REMEMBER YESTERDAY** *GTO GT 107* **14** 7
26 Nov 77 ONCE UPON A TIME *Casablanca CALD 5003* 24 13
3 Dec 77 ● **LOVE'S UNKIND** *GTO GT 113* 3 13
10 Dec 77 ● **I LOVE YOU** *Casablanca CAN 114* 10 9
7 Jan 78 ● GREATEST HITS *GTO GTLP 028* 4 18
25 Feb 78 **RUMOUR HAS IT** *Casablanca CAN 122* **19** 8
22 Apr 78 **BACK IN LOVE AGAIN** *GTO GT 117* **29** 7
10 Jun 78 **LAST DANCE** (re) *Casablanca TGIF 2* $ **51** 9
14 Oct 78 ● **MACARTHUR PARK** *Casablanca CAN 131* ▲ $ 5 10
21 Oct 78 LIVE AND MORE *Casablanca CALD 5006* ▲ 16 16
17 Feb 79 **HEAVEN KNOWS** *Casablanca CAN 141* $ 34 8
12 May 79 **HOT STUFF** *Casablanca CAN 151* ▲ $ 11 10
2 Jun 79 BAD GIRLS *Casablanca CALD 5007* ▲ 23 23
7 Jul 79 **BAD GIRLS** *Casablanca CAN 155* ▲ $ **14** 10
1 Sep 79 **DIM ALL THE LIGHTS** *Casablanca CAN 162* $ 29 9
3 Nov 79 ● **NO MORE TEARS (ENOUGH IS ENOUGH)** *Casablanca CAN 174 / CBS 8000* [1] ▲ $ 3 13
10 Nov 79 ON THE RADIO – GREATEST HITS VOLUMES 1 & 2 *Casablanca CALD 5008* ▲ 24 22
16 Feb 80 **ON THE RADIO** *Casablanca NB 2236* $ 32 6
21 Jun 80 **SUNSET PEOPLE** *Casablanca CAN 198* **46** 5
27 Sep 80 **THE WANDERER** *Geffen K 79180* $ **48** 6
1 Nov 80 THE WANDERER *Geffen K 99124* 55 2
17 Jan 81 **COLD LOVE** *Geffen K 79193* **44** 3
10 Jul 82 **LOVE IS IN CONTROL (FINGER ON THE TRIGGER)** *Warner Bros. K 79302* **18** 11
31 Jul 82 DONNA SUMMER *Warner Bros. K 99163* 13 16
6 Nov 82 **STATE OF INDEPENDENCE** *Warner Bros. K 79344* **14** 11
4 Dec 82 **I FEEL LOVE** (re-mix) *Casablanca FEEL 7* 21 10
5 Mar 83 **THE WOMAN IN ME** *Warner Bros. U 9983* 62 2
18 Jun 83 **SHE WORKS HARD FOR THE MONEY** *Mercury DONNA 1* 25 8
16 Jul 83 SHE WORKS HARD FOR THE MONEY *Mercury MERL 21* 28 5
24 Sep 83 **UNCONDITIONAL LOVE** *Mercury DONNA 2* **14** 12
21 Jan 84 **STOP LOOK AND LISTEN** *Mercury DONNA 3* **57** 2

11 April 1992	18 April 1992	25 April 1992	2 May 1992
STAY Shakespear's Sister	DEEPLY DIPPY Right Said Fred	DEEPLY DIPPY Right Said Fred	DEEPLY DIPPY Right Said Fred
ADRENALIZE Def Leppard	DIVA Annie Lennox	UP Right Said Fred	WISH The Cure

KEY: UK No.1 ★ UK Top 10 ● Still on chart + UK entry at No.1 ■ US No.1 ▲ UK million seller £ US million seller $ Singles re-entries are listed as (re), (2re), (3re)... which signifies that the hit re-entered the chart once, twice or three times... Peak Position / Weeks

15 Sep 84 CATS WITHOUT CLAWS *Warner Bros. 250806* 69 2
24 Oct 87 DINNER WITH GERSHWIN *Warner Bros. U 8237* 13 11
23 Jan 88 ALL SYSTEMS GO *WEA U 8122* 54 3
25 Feb 89 ● THIS TIME I KNOW IT'S FOR REAL *Warner Bros. U 7780* 3 14
25 Mar 89 ANOTHER PLACE AND TIME *Warner Bros. WX 219* 17 28
27 May 89 ● I DON'T WANNA GET HURT *Warner Bros. U 7567* 7 9
26 Aug 89 LOVE'S ABOUT TO CHANGE MY HEART *Warner Bros. U 7494* 20 6
25 Nov 89 WHEN LOVE TAKES OVER YOU *WEA U 7361* 72 1
17 Nov 90 STATE OF INDEPENDENCE (re-issue) *Warner Bros. U 2857* 45 3
24 Nov 90 THE BEST OF DONNA SUMMER *Warner Bros. WX 397* 24 9
12 Jan 91 BREAKAWAY *Warner Bros. U 3308* 49 4
30 Nov 91 WORK THAT MAGIC *Warner Bros. U 5937* 74 1
12 Nov 94 MELODY OF LOVE (WANNA BE LOVED) *Mercury MERCD 418* 21 3
26 Nov 94 ENDLESS SUMMER – GREATEST HITS *Mercury 5262172* 37 2
9 Sep 95 ● I FEEL LOVE (re-recording) *Manifesto FESCD 1* 8 5
6 Apr 96 STATE OF INDEPENDENCE (re-mix) *Manifesto FESCD 7* [2] 13 5
11 Jul 98 CARRY ON *Almighty CDALMY 120* [3] 65 1
30 Oct 99 I WILL GO WITH YOU (CON TE PARTIRO) *Epic 6682092* 44 1
26 Jun 04 ● THE JOURNEY – THE VERY BEST OF DONNA SUMMER *Mercury 9862858* 6 6

[1] Donna Summer and Barbra Streisand [2] Donna Summer featuring the All Star Choir [3] Donna Summer and Giorgio Moroder

'No More Tears (Enough Is Enough)' was released simultaneously on two different labels, a 7-inch single on Casablanca and a 12-inch on CBS. 'Unconditional Love' features the additional vocals of Musical Youth.

SUMMER DAZE *UK, male instrumental / production duo*

26 Oct 96 SAMBA MAGIC *VC VCRD 14* 61 1

Mark SUMMERS (see also SOUVLAKI) *UK, male producer*

26 Jan 91 SUMMER'S MAGIC *Fourth & Broadway BRW 205* 27 6

SUNBURST (see also Matt DAREY; LOST TRIBE; MDM; MELT featuring LITTLE MS MARCIE) *UK, male producer – Matt Darey*

8 Jul 00 EYEBALL (EYEBALL PAUL'S THEME) *Virgin / EMI VTSCD 4* 48 1

SUNDANCE (see also SHIMMON & WOOLFSON) *UK, male production duo – Nick Woolfson and Mark Shimmon (4 Singles: 7 Weeks)*

8 Nov 97 SUNDANCE *React CDREACT 109* 33 2
3 Oct 98 SUNDANCE '98 (re-mix) *React CDREACTX 136* 37 2
27 Feb 99 THE LIVING DREAM *React CDREACT 134* 56 1
5 Feb 00 WON'T LET THIS FEELING GO *Inferno CDFERN 23* 40 2

The SUNDAYS *UK, male / female vocal (Harriet Wheeler) / instrumental group (3 Albums: 15 Weeks, 4 Singles: 12 Weeks)*

11 Feb 89 CAN'T BE SURE *Rough Trade RT 218* 45 5
27 Jan 90 ● READING WRITING AND ARITHMETIC *Rough Trade ROUGH 148* 4 8
3 Oct 92 GOODBYE *Parlophone R 6319* 27 2
31 Oct 92 BLIND *Parlophone CDPCSD 121* 15 3
20 Sep 97 SUMMERTIME *Parlophone CDRS 6475* 15 4
4 Oct 97 ● STATIC & SILENCE *Parlophone CDEST 2300* 10 4
22 Nov 97 CRY *Parlophone CDR 6487* 43 1

SUNDRAGON *UK, male vocal / instrumental duo*

21 Feb 68 GREEN TAMBOURINE *MGM 1380* 50 1

SUNFIRE *US, male vocal / instrumental group*

12 Mar 83 YOUNG, FREE AND SINGLE *Warner Bros. W 9897* 20 11

SUNKIDS featuring CHANCE *US, male production duo and female vocalist*

13 Nov 99 RESCUE ME *AM:PM CDAMPM 126* 50 2

SUNNY *UK, female vocalist – Sunny Leslie*

30 Mar 74 ● DOCTOR'S ORDERS *CBS 2068* 7 10

SUNSCREEM *UK, male / female vocal / instrumental group (2 Albums: 6 Weeks, 12 Singles: 36 Weeks)*

29 Feb 92 PRESSURE *Sony S2 6578017* 60 2
18 Jul 92 LOVE U MORE *Sony S2 6581727* 23 6
17 Oct 92 PERFECT MOTION *Sony S2 6584057* 18 5
9 Jan 93 BROKEN ENGLISH *Sony S2 6589032* 13 5
13 Feb 93 03 *Sony S2 4722182* 33 5
27 Mar 93 PRESSURE US (re-mix) *Sony S2 6591102* 19 5
2 Sep 95 WHEN *Sony S2 6623222* 47 2
18 Nov 95 EXODUS *Sony S2 6625342* 40 2
20 Jan 96 WHITE SKIES *Sony S2 6627425* 25 3
23 Mar 96 SECRETS *Sony S2 6629342* 36 2
30 Mar 96 CHANGE OR DIE *Sony S2 4813132* 53 1
6 Sep 97 CATCH *Pulse-8 CDLOSE 117* 55 1
20 Oct 01 PLEASE SAVE ME *Inferno / Five AM FAMFERN 1CD* [1] 36 2
16 Nov 02 PERFECT MOTION (re-mix) *Five AM FAM 15CD* 71 1

[1] Sunscreem vs Push

SUNSET STRIPPERS NEW *UK, male production trio*

19 Mar 05 ● FALLING STARS *Direction 6758312* 3 13

SUNSHIP featuring MCRB *UK, male producer – Ceri Evans and male rapper – Ricky Benjamin*

1 Apr 00 CHEQUE ONE-TWO *Filter FILT 044* 75 1

SUPAFLY vs FISHBOWL NEW *UK, male production / vocal trio*

17 Sep 05 LET'S GET DOWN *Eye Industries / UMTV 9873464* 22 3

SUPATONIC *UK, male vocal / instrumental duo*

6 Nov 04 I WISH IT WASN'T TRUE *Fluff Alley FLUFFA 001* 69 1

SUPER FURRY ANIMALS *UK, male vocal (Gruff Rhys) / instrumental group (9 Albums: 36 Weeks, 20 Singles: 47 Weeks)*

9 Mar 96 HOMETOWN UNICORN *Creation CRESCD 222* 47 1
11 May 96 GOD! SHOW ME MAGIC *Creation CRESCD 231* 33 2
1 Jun 96 FUZZY LOGIC *Creation CRECD 190* 23 6
13 Jul 96 SOMETHING 4 THE WEEKEND *Creation CRESCD 235* 18 3
12 Oct 96 IF YOU DON'T WANT ME TO DESTROY YOU *Creation CRESCD 243* 18 2
14 Dec 96 THE MAN DON'T GIVE A FUCK *Creation CRESCD 247* 22 2
24 May 97 HERMANN LOVES PAULINE *Creation CRESCD 252* 26 2
26 Jul 97 THE INTERNATIONAL LANGUAGE OF SCREAMING *Creation CRESCD 269* 24 2
6 Sep 97 ● RADIATOR *Creation CRECD 214* 8 3
4 Oct 97 PLAY IT COOL *Creation CRESCD 275* 27 2
6 Dec 97 DEMONS *Creation CRESCD 283* 27 2
6 Jun 98 ICE HOCKEY HAIR EP *Creation CRESCD 288* 12 3
5 Dec 98 OUT SPACED *Creation CRECD 229* 44 1
22 May 99 NORTHERN LITES *Creation CRESCD 314* 11 4
26 Jun 99 ● GUERRILLA *Creation CRECD 242* 10 9
21 Aug 99 FIRE IN MY HEART *Creation CRESCD 323* 25 3
29 Jan 00 DO OR DIE *Creation CRESCD 329* 20 2
27 May 00 MWNG *Placid Casual PLC 03CD* 11 2
21 Jul 01 JUXTAPOZED WITH U *Epic 6712242* 14 4
4 Aug 01 ● RINGS AROUND THE WORLD *Epic 5024132* 3 7
20 Oct 01 (DRAWING) RINGS AROUND THE WORLD *Epic 6719082* 28 2
26 Jan 02 IT'S NOT THE END OF THE WORLD? *Epic 6721752* 30 2
26 Jul 03 GOLDEN RETRIEVER *Epic 6739062* 13 3
2 Aug 03 ● PHANTOM POWER *Epic 5123759* 4 4

	9 May 1992	16 May 1992	23 May 1992	30 May 1992
UK No.1 SINGLES	PLEASE DON'T GO / GAME BOY KWS	PLEASE DON'T GO / GAME BOY KWS	PLEASE DON'T GO / GAME BOY KWS	PLEASE DON'T GO / GAME BOY KWS
UK No.1 ALBUMS	STARS Simply Red	THE LOVE ALBUM Carter - The Unstoppable Sex Machine	FEAR OF THE DARK Iron Maiden	MICHAEL BALL Michael Ball

1 Nov 03 **HELLO SUNSHINE** *Epic 6743602*....31 2
9 Oct 04 **THE MAN DON'T GIVE A FUCK (LIVE)** *Epic 6753041*....16 2
16 Oct 04 SONGBOOK – THE SINGLES – VOLUME ONE *Epic 5176719*....18 2
27 Aug 05 **LAZER BEAM** *Epic 6760111*....28 2
3 Sep 05 LOVE KRAFT *Epic 5205012*....19 2

Tracks on Ice Hockey Hair EP: Smokin' / Ice Hockey Hair / Mu-Tron / Let's Quit Smoking. The band's name is abbreviated to SFA on Guerrilla.

SUPERCAR *Italy, male DJ production duo – Alberto Pizarelli and Ricki Pagano (2 Singles: 6 Weeks)*

13 Feb 99 **TONITE** *Pepper 0530202*....15 5
21 Aug 99 **COMPUTER LOVE** *Pepper 0530392* [1] 67 1

[1] Supercar featuring Mikaela

SUPERCAT *Jamaica, male vocalist – William Maragh (2 Singles: 5 Weeks)*

1 Aug 92 **IT FE DONE** *Columbia 6582737*....66 1
6 May 95 **MY GIRL JOSEPHINE** *Columbia 6614702* [1] 22 4

[1] Supercat featuring Jack Radics

SUPERFUNK *France, male production trio (2 Singles: 2 Weeks)*

4 Mar 00 **LUCKY STAR** *Virgin DINSD 198* [1] 42 1
10 Jun 00 **THE YOUNG MC** *Virgin DINSD 206*....62 1

[1] Superfunk featuring Ron Carroll

SUPERGRASS 403 Top 500 (see also TWISTED X)

Acclaimed power-pop group formed in Oxford in 1994: Gaz Coombes (g/v), Danny Goffey (d/v), Mick Quinn (b/v) and, in 1995, Gaz's brother Rob (k). This popular live band were voted Best British Newcomers at the 1996 BRIT awards. Their first three albums achieved platinum status (6 Albums: 109 Weeks, 18 Singles: 69 Weeks)

29 Oct 94 **CAUGHT BY THE FUZZ** *Parlophone CDR 6396*....43 2
18 Feb 95 **MANSIZE ROOSTER** *Parlophone CDR 6402*....20 3
25 Mar 95 **LOSE IT** *Sub Pop SP 281*....75 1
13 May 95 ● **LENNY** *Parlophone CDR 6410*....10 3
27 May 95 ★ I SHOULD COCO *Parlophone CDPCS 7373*....1 36
15 Jul 95 ● **ALRIGHT / TIME** *Parlophone CDR 6413*....2 10
9 Mar 96 ● **GOING OUT** *Parlophone CDR 6428*....5 6
12 Apr 97 ● **RICHARD III** *Parlophone CDR 6461*....2 5
3 May 97 ● IN IT FOR THE MONEY *Parlophone CDPCS 7388*....2 25
21 Jun 97 ● **SUN HITS THE SKY** *Parlophone CDR 6469*....10 4
18 Oct 97 **LATE IN THE DAY** *Parlophone CDR 6484*....18 4
5 Jun 99 **PUMPING ON YOUR STEREO** (re) *Parlophone CDR 6518*....11 7
18 Sep 99 ● **MOVING** *Parlophone CDR 6524*....9 5
2 Oct 99 ● SUPERGRASS *Parlophone 5220562*....3 25
4 Dec 99 **MARY** (re) *Parlophone CDR 6531*....36 4
13 Jul 02 **NEVER DONE NOTHING LIKE THAT BEFORE** *Parlophone CDR 6563*....75 1
28 Sep 02 **GRACE** *Parlophone CDR 6586*....13 4
12 Oct 02 ● LIFE ON OTHER PLANETS *Parlophone 5418002*....9 6
8 Feb 03 **SEEN THE LIGHT** *Parlophone CDR 6592*....22 3
5 Jun 04 **KISS OF LIFE** *Parlophone CDRS 6638*....23 3
19 Jun 04 ● SUPERGRASS IS 10 – THE BEST OF 94-04 *Parlophone 5708602*....4 13
20 Aug 05 **ST. PETERSBURG** *Parlophone CDR 6670*....22 3
27 Aug 05 ● ROAD TO ROUEN *Parlophone 3333342*....9 4
5 Nov 05 **LOW C** *Parlophone CDR 6675*....52 1

SUPERMEN LOVERS featuring Mani HOFFMAN

France, male producer – Guillaume Atlan and vocalist

15 Sep 01 ● **STARLIGHT** (re) *Independiente ISOM 53MS*....2 16

The SUPERNATURALS *UK, male vocal (James McColl) / instrumental group (2 Albums: 7 Weeks, 8 Singles: 15 Weeks)*

26 Oct 96 **LAZY LOVER** *Food CDFOOD 85*....34 2
8 Feb 97 **THE DAY BEFORE YESTERDAY'S MAN** *Food CDFOODS 88*....25 3
26 Apr 97 **SMILE** *Food CDFOOD 92*....23 2
17 May 97 ● IT DOESN'T MATTER ANYMORE *Food FOODCD 21*....9 4
12 Jul 97 **LOVE HAS PASSED AWAY** *Food CDFOOD 99*....38 2
25 Oct 97 **PREPARE TO LAND** *Food CDFOODS 106*....48 1
1 Aug 98 **I WASN'T BUILT TO GET UP** *Food CDFOOD 112*....25 3
22 Aug 98 A TUNE A DAY *Food 4960662*....21 3
24 Oct 98 **SHEFFIELD SONG** *Food CDFOODS 115*....45 1
13 Mar 99 **EVEREST** *Food CDFOOD 119*....52 1

SUPERNOVA *UK, male / female vocal / instrumental duo*

11 May 96 **SOME MIGHT SAY** *Sing Sing 74321369442*....55 1

SUPERSISTER *UK, female vocal group (3 Singles: 8 Weeks)*

14 Oct 00 **COFFEE** *Gut CDGUT 35*....16 5
25 Aug 01 **SHOPPING** *Gut CDGUT 37*....36 2
17 Nov 01 **SUMMER GONNA COME AGAIN** *Gut CDGUT 38*....51 1

SUPERSTAR *UK, male vocal / instrumental group (2 Singles: 2 Weeks)*

7 Feb 98 **EVERY DAY I FALL APART** *Camp Fabulous CFAB 003CD*....66 1
25 Apr 98 **SUPERSTAR** *Camp Fabulous CFAB 007CD*....49 1

SUPERTRAMP 276 Top 500

Acclaimed Anglo-American group formed in 1969 by UK musicians Rick Davies (v/k) and Roger Hodgson (v/g). A change of sound from progressive rock to more focused pop in the mid-70s was internationally successful: Breakfast in America, their biggest-selling album, shifted 18 million copies worldwide (13 Albums: 190 Weeks, 6 Singles: 52 Weeks)

23 Nov 74 ● CRIME OF THE CENTURY *A&M AMLS 68258*....4 22
15 Feb 75 **DREAMER** *A&M AMS 7132*....13 10
6 Dec 75 CRISIS? WHAT CRISIS? *A&M AMLH 68347*....20 15
23 Apr 77 EVEN IN THE QUIETEST MOMENTS *A&M AMLK 64634*....12 22
25 Jun 77 **GIVE A LITTLE BIT** *A&M AMS 7293*....29 7
31 Jan 79 ● BREAKFAST IN AMERICA *A&M AMLK 63708* ▲....3 53
31 Mar 79 ● **THE LOGICAL SONG** *A&M AMS 7427*....7 11
30 Jun 79 ● **BREAKFAST IN AMERICA** *A&M AMS 7451*....9 10
27 Oct 79 **GOODBYE STRANGER** *A&M AMS 7481*....57 3
4 Oct 80 ● PARIS *A&M AMLM 66702*....7 17
30 Oct 82 **IT'S RAINING AGAIN** *A&M AMS 8255* [1] 26 11
6 Nov 82 ● FAMOUS LAST WORDS *A&M AMLK 63732*....6 16
25 May 85 BROTHER WHERE YOU BOUND *A&M AMA 5014*....20 5
18 Oct 86 ● THE AUTOBIOGRAPHY OF SUPERTRAMP *A&M TRAMP 1*....9 19
31 Oct 87 FREE AS A BIRD *A&M AMA 5181*....93 1
15 Aug 92 THE VERY BEST OF SUPERTRAMP *A&M TRACD 1992*....24 4
3 May 97 SOME THINGS NEVER CHANGE *EMI CDCHR 6121*....74 1
27 Sep 97 ● THE VERY BEST OF SUPERTRAMP (re-issue) *PolyGram TV 3970912*....8 6
5 Nov 05 ● RETROSPECTACLE – THE SUPERTRAMP ANTHOLOGY *A&M 9886928*....9 9+

[1] Supertramp featuring vocals by Roger Hodgson

The SUPREMES 70 Top 500

World's most successful female group: Diana Ross, Mary Wilson, Florence Ballard, b. 1944, d. 1976. Before Ross went solo in 1969, this Detroit-based trio had amassed a dozen US No.1s and became the first female trio to top the UK singles chart. They were inducted into the Rock and Roll Hall of Fame in 1988 (17 Albums: 229 Weeks, 31 Singles: 306 Weeks)

3 Sep 64 ● **WHERE DID OUR LOVE GO** *Stateside SS 327* ▲ $....3 14
22 Oct 64 ★ **BABY LOVE** *Stateside SS 350* ▲ $....1 15
5 Dec 64 ● MEET THE SUPREMES *Stateside SL 10109*....8 6
21 Jan 65 **COME SEE ABOUT ME** *Stateside SS 376* ▲ $....27 6
25 Mar 65 ● **STOP! IN THE NAME OF LOVE** *Tamla Motown TMG 501* ▲ $....7 12
10 Jun 65 **BACK IN MY ARMS AGAIN** *Tamla Motown TMG 516* ▲ $....40 5
9 Dec 65 **I HEAR A SYMPHONY** (re) *Tamla Motown TMG 543* ▲ $....39 5
8 Sep 66 ● **YOU CAN'T HURRY LOVE** *Tamla Motown TMG 575* ▲ $....3 12
1 Dec 66 ● **YOU KEEP ME HANGIN' ON** *Tamla Motown TMG 585* ▲ $....8 10
17 Dec 66 SUPREMES A GO-GO *Tamla Motown STML 11039* ▲....15 21
2 Mar 67 **LOVE IS HERE AND NOW YOU'RE GONE** *Tamla Motown TMG 597* ▲ $....17 10
11 May 67 ● **THE HAPPENING** *Tamla Motown TMG 607* ▲ $....6 12

6 June 1992	13 June 1992	20 June 1992	27 June 1992
PLEASE DON'T GO / GAME BOY KWS	**ABBA-ESQUE (EP)** Erasure	**ABBA-ESQUE (EP)** Erasure	**ABBA-ESQUE (EP)** Erasure
BACK TO FRONT Lionel Richie	**BACK TO FRONT** Lionel Richie	**BACK TO FRONT** Lionel Richie	**BACK TO FRONT** Lionel Richie

KEY
UK No.1 ★ UK Top 10 ● Still on chart + UK entry at No.1 ■ US No.1 ▲ UK million seller £ US million seller $
Singles re-entries are listed as (re), (2re), (3re)... which signifies that the hit re-entered the chart once, twice or three times...
Peak Position / Weeks

13 May 67 THE SUPREMES SING MOTOWN *Tamla Motown STML 11047*..15 16
30 Aug 67 ● **REFLECTIONS** *Tamla Motown TMG 616* [1] $.....5 14
30 Sep 67 THE SUPREMES SING RODGERS & HART *Tamla Motown STML 11054*.....25 7
29 Nov 67 **IN AND OUT OF LOVE** *Tamla Motown TMG 632* [1].....13 13
20 Jan 68 ★ GREATEST HITS *Tamla Motown STML 11063* ▲.....1 60
30 Mar 68 ● LIVE AT THE TALK OF THE TOWN *Tamla Motown STML 11070* [1].....6 18
10 Apr 68 **FOREVER CAME TODAY** *Tamla Motown TMG 650* [1].....28 8
3 Jul 68 **SOME THINGS YOU NEVER GET USED TO** *Tamla Motown TMG 662* [1].....34 6
20 Jul 68 REFLECTIONS *Tamla Motown STML 11073* [1].....30 2
20 Nov 68 **LOVE CHILD** *Tamla Motown TMG 677* [1] ▲ $.....15 14
25 Jan 69 ★ DIANA ROSS AND THE SUPREMES JOIN THE TEMPTATIONS *Tamla Motown STML 11096* [2] ▲.....1 15
29 Jan 69 ● **I'M GONNA MAKE YOU LOVE ME** (re) *Tamla Motown TMG 685* [2] $.....3 12
1 Feb 69 ● LOVE CHILD *Tamla Motown STML 11095* [1].....8 6
23 Apr 69 **I'M LIVIN' IN SHAME** (re) *Tamla Motown TMG 695* [1].....14 10
28 Jun 69 TCB *Tamla Motown STML 11110* [2].....11 12
16 Jul 69 **NO MATTER WHAT SIGN YOU ARE** *Tamla Motown TMG 704* [1].....37 7
20 Sep 69 **I SECOND THAT EMOTION** *Tamla Motown TMG 709* [2].....18 8
13 Dec 69 **SOMEDAY WE'LL BE TOGETHER** *Tamla Motown TMG 721* [1] ▲ $.....13 13
14 Feb 70 TOGETHER *Tamla Motown STML 11122* [2].....28 4
21 Mar 70 **WHY (MUST WE FALL IN LOVE)** *Tamla Motown TMG 730* [2] 31 7
2 May 70 ● **UP THE LADDER TO THE ROOF** *Tamla Motown TMG 735*.....6 15
16 Jan 71 ● **STONED LOVE** *Tamla Motown TMG 760* $.....3 13
29 May 71 ● MAGNIFICENT SEVEN *Tamla Motown STML 11179* [3].....6 11
26 Jun 71 **RIVER DEEP MOUNTAIN HIGH** *Tamla Motown TMG 777* [3]...11 10
21 Aug 71 ● **NATHAN JONES** *Tamla Motown TMG 782*.....5 11
25 Sep 71 TOUCH *Tamla Motown STML 11189*.....40 1
20 Nov 71 **YOU GOTTA HAVE LOVE IN YOUR HEART** *Tamla Motown TMG 793* [3].....25 10
4 Mar 72 ● **FLOY JOY** *Tamla Motown TMG 804*.....9 10
15 Jul 72 ● **AUTOMATICALLY SUNSHINE** *Tamla Motown TMG 821*.....10 9
21 Apr 73 **BAD WEATHER** *Tamla Motown TMG 847*.....37 4
24 Aug 74 **BABY LOVE** (re-issue) *Tamla Motown TMG 915* [1].....12 10
17 Sep 77 ★ 20 GOLDEN GREATS *Motown EMTV 5* [1].....1 34
21 Jan 89 ● LOVE SUPREME *Motown ZL 72701* [1].....10 9
18 Feb 89 **STOP! IN THE NAME OF LOVE** (re-issue) *Motown ZB 41963* [1].....62 1
31 Oct 98 40 GOLDEN MOTOWN GREATS *Motown / PolyGram TV 5309612* [1].....35 4
29 May 04 THE NO 1'S *Motown 9818019* [1].....26 3

[1] Diana Ross and The Supremes [2] Diana Ross and The Supremes and The Temptations [3] The Supremes and The Four Tops [1] Diana Ross and The Supremes [2] Diana Ross and The Supremes with The Temptations [3] The Supremes and The Four Tops

Al B SURE! *US, male vocalist – Al Brown (5 Singles: 13 Weeks)*

16 Apr 88 **NITE AND DAY** *Uptown W 8192*.....44 5
30 Jul 88 **OFF ON YOUR OWN (GIRL)** *Uptown W 7870*.....70 2
10 Jun 89 **IF I'M NOT YOUR LOVER** *Uptown W 2908* [1].....54 3
31 Mar 90 **SECRET GARDEN** *Qwest W 9992* [2].....67 1
12 Jun 93 **BLACK TIE WHITE NOISE** *Arista 74321148682* [3].....36 2

[1] Al B Sure! featuring Slick Rick [2] Quincy Jones featuring Al B Sure!, James Ingram, El DeBarge and Barry White [3] David Bowie featuring Al B Sure!

SUREAL *UK, male / female production / vocal group*

7 Oct 00 **YOU TAKE MY BREATH AWAY** *Cream CREAM 7CD*.....15 4

SURFACE *US, male vocal / instrumental duo (4 Singles: 14 Weeks)*

23 Jul 83 **FALLING IN LOVE** *Salsoul SAL 104*.....67 3
23 Jun 84 **WHEN YOUR 'EX' WANTS YOU BACK** *Salsoul SAL 106*.....52 4
28 Feb 87 **HAPPY** *CBS 650393 7*.....56 5
12 Jan 91 **THE FIRST TIME** *Columbia 6564767* ▲.....60 2

SURFACE NOISE *UK, male instrumental group (2 Singles: 11 Weeks)*

31 May 80 **THE SCRATCH** *WEA K 18291*.....26 8
30 Aug 80 **DANCIN' ON A WIRE** *Groove Production GP 102*.....59 3

The SURFARIS *US, male instrumental group*

25 Jul 63 ● **WIPE OUT** *London HLD 9751* $.....5 14

SURPRISE SISTERS *Australia, female vocal group*

13 Mar 76 **LA BOOGA ROOGA** *Good Earth GD 1*.....38 3

SURVIVOR *US, male vocal (Dave Bickler) / instrumental group (1 Album: 10 Weeks, 2 Singles: 26 Weeks)*

31 Jul 82 ★ **EYE OF THE TIGER** *Scotti Brothers SCT A 2411* ▲ $.....1 15
21 Aug 82 EYE OF THE TIGER *Scotti Brothers SCT 85845*.....12 10
1 Feb 86 ● **BURNING HEART** *Scotti Brothers A 6708*.....5 11

The SUTHERLAND BROTHERS and QUIVER *UK, male vocal / instrumental group (2 Albums: 11 Weeks, 3 Singles: 20 Weeks)*

3 Apr 76 ● **ARMS OF MARY** *CBS 4001*.....5 12
15 May 76 REACH FOR THE SKY *CBS 69191*.....26 8
9 Oct 76 SLIPSTREAM *CBS 81593*.....49 3
20 Nov 76 **SECRETS** *CBS 4668*.....35 4
2 Jun 79 **EASY COME, EASY GO** *CBS 7121* [1].....50 4

[1] The Sutherland Brothers

Pat SUZUKI *US, female vocalist – Chiyoko Suzuki*

14 Apr 60 **I ENJOY BEING A GIRL** *RCA 1171*.....49 1

SVENSON and GIELEN (see also AIRSCAPE; BLUE BAMBOO; CUBIC 22; Johan GIELEN presents ABNEA; TRANSFORMER 2) *Belgium, male production duo – Sven Maes and Johan Gielen*

22 Sep 01 **THE BEAUTY OF SILENCE** *Xtrahard / Xtravaganza X2H 5CDS*.....41 2

Billy SWAN *US, male vocalist (2 Singles: 13 Weeks)*

14 Dec 74 ● **I CAN HELP** *Monument MNT 2752* ▲ $.....6 9
24 May 75 **DON'T BE CRUEL** *Monument MNT 3244*.....42 4

SWAN LAKE (see also BLACK RIOT; The GYPSYMEN; ROYAL HOUSE) *US, male producer – Todd Terry*

17 Sep 88 **IN THE NAME OF LOVE** *Champion CHAMP 86*.....53 4

SWANS WAY *UK, male / female vocal / instrumental group (1 Album: 1 Week, 2 Singles: 12 Weeks)*

4 Feb 84 **SOUL TRAIN** *Exit EXT 3*.....20 7
26 May 84 **ILLUMINATIONS** *Balgier PH 5*.....57 5
3 Nov 84 THE FUGITIVE KIND *Balgier SWAN 1*.....88 1

Patrick SWAYZE featuring Wendy FRASER *US, male / female vocal / actor duo*

26 Mar 88 **SHE'S LIKE THE WIND** *RCA PB 49565*.....17 11

Keith SWEAT *US, male vocalist (5 Albums: 32 Weeks, 9 Singles: 23 Weeks)*

16 Jan 88 MAKE IT LAST FOREVER *Elektra 960763 1*.....41 21
20 Feb 88 **I WANT HER** *Vintertainment EKR 68*.....26 10
14 May 88 **SOMETHING JUST AIN'T RIGHT** *Vintertainment EKR 72*.....55 3

4 July 1992	11 July 1992	18 July 1992	25 July 1992
UK No.1 SINGLES			
ABBA-ESQUE (EP) Erasure	ABBA-ESQUE (EP) Erasure	AIN'T NO DOUBT Jimmy Nail	AIN'T NO DOUBT Jimmy Nail
UK No.1 ALBUMS			
BACK TO FRONT Lionel Richie	BACK TO FRONT Lionel Richie	U.F. ORB The Orb	THE GREATEST HITS 1966-1992 Neil Diamond

23 Jun 90	I'LL GIVE ALL MY LOVE TO YOU *Vintertainment EKT 60*	47	4
14 May 94	**HOW DO YOU LIKE IT** *Elektra EKR 185CD*	**71**	1
9 Jul 94	GET UP ON IT *Elektra 7559615502*	20	4
22 Jun 96	**TWISTED** *Elektra EKR 223CD* $	**39**	2
29 Jun 96	KEITH SWEAT *Elektra 7559617072*	36	2
23 Nov 96	**JUST A TOUCH** *Elektra EKR 227CD*	**35**	2
3 May 97	**NOBODY** *Elektra EKR 233CD* [1] $	**30**	2
6 Dec 97	**I WANT HER** (re-mix) *Elektra E 3887CD*	**44**	1
3 Oct 98	STILL IN THE GAME *Elektra 7559622622*	62	1
12 Dec 98	**COME AND GET WITH ME** *Elektra E 3787CD* [2]	**58**	1
27 Mar 99	**I'M NOT READY** *Elektra E 3767CD*	**53**	1

[1] Keith Sweat featuring Athena Cage [2] Keith Sweat featuring Snoop Dogg

Claire SWEENEY *UK, female actor / vocalist*

27 Jul 02	CLAIRE *T2 TCD 3254*	15	3

Michelle SWEENEY *US, female vocalist*

29 Oct 94	**THIS TIME** *Big Beat A 8229CD*	**57**	1

The SWEET (411 Top 500) *Glam-rock giants: Brian Connolly (v), b. 1944, d. 1997, Andy Scott (g), Steve Priest (b) and Mick Tucker (d), b. 1948, d. 2002. The flamboyantly-attired UK quartet was very popular in Europe and the US. In addition to their No.1 single, they achieved five No.2 hits (4 Albums: 15 Weeks, 17 Singles: 159 Weeks)*

13 Mar 71	**FUNNY FUNNY** *RCA 2051*	**13**	14
12 Jun 71 ●	**CO-CO** *RCA 2087*	**2**	15
16 Oct 71	**ALEXANDER GRAHAM BELL** *RCA 2121*	**33**	5
5 Feb 72	**POPPA JOE** *RCA 2164*	**11**	12
10 Jun 72 ●	**LITTLE WILLY** *RCA 2225* $	**4**	14
9 Sep 72 ●	**WIG-WAM BAM** *RCA 2260*	**4**	13
13 Jan 73 ★	**BLOCKBUSTER!** *RCA 2305*	**1**	15
5 May 73 ●	**HELL RAISER** *RCA 2357*	**2**	11
22 Sep 73 ●	**THE BALLROOM BLITZ** *RCA 2403*	**2**	9
19 Jan 74 ●	**TEENAGE RAMPAGE** *RCA LPBO 5004*	**2**	8
18 May 74	SWEET FANNY ADAMS *RCA LPI 5038*	27	2
13 Jul 74 ●	**THE SIX TEENS** *RCA LPBO 5037*	**9**	7
9 Nov 74	**TURN IT DOWN** *RCA 2480*	**41**	2
15 Mar 75 ●	**FOX ON THE RUN** *RCA 2524* $	**2**	10
12 Jul 75	**ACTION** *RCA 2578*	**15**	6
24 Jan 76	**THE LIES IN YOUR EYES** *RCA 2641*	**35**	4
28 Jan 78 ●	**LOVE IS LIKE OXYGEN** *Polydor POSP 1*	**9**	9
22 Sep 84	SWEET 16 IT'S ... IT'S ... SWEET'S HITS *Anagram GRAM 16*	49	6
26 Jan 85	**IT'S ... IT'S ... THE SWEET MIX** *Anagram ANA 28*	**45**	5
20 Jan 96	BALLROOM HITZ – THE VERY BEST OF SWEET *PolyGram TV 5350012*	15	6
29 Jan 05	THE VERY BEST OF SWEET *BMG 82876668172*	72	1

'It's ... It's ... the Sweet Mix' is a medley of the following songs: Blockbuster / Fox on the Run / Teenage Rampage / Hell Raiser / The Ballroom Blitz.

Rachel SWEET *US, female vocalist (2 Singles: 15 Weeks)*

9 Dec 78	**B-A-B-Y** *Stiff BUY 39*	**35**	8
22 Aug 81	**EVERLASTING LOVE** *CBS A 1405*	**35**	7

SWEET DREAMS (see also Polly BROWN; PICKETTYWITCH; RAGE) *UK, male / female vocal duo – Polly Brown and Tony Jackson*

20 Jul 74 ●	**HONEY HONEY** *Bradley's BRAD 7408*	**10**	12

SWEET DREAMS *UK, male / female vocal group*

9 Apr 83	**I'M NEVER GIVING UP** *Ariola ARO 333*	**21**	7

SWEET FEMALE ATTITUDE *UK, female vocal duo – Leanne Brown and Catherine Cassidy (2 Singles: 14 Weeks)*

15 Apr 00 ●	**FLOWERS** *WEA WEA 267CD*	**2**	12
7 Oct 00	**8 DAYS A WEEK** *WEA WEA 296CD*	**43**	2

SWEET MERCY featuring Joe ROBERTS *UK, male production / instrumental duo and vocalist*

24 Feb 96	**HAPPY DAYS** *Grass Green GRASS 10CD*	**63**	1

The SWEET PEOPLE *France, male vocal / instrumental group*

4 Oct 80 ●	**ET LES OISEAUX CHANTAIENT (AND THE BIRDS WERE SINGING)** (re) *Polydor POSP 179*	**4**	10

Re-entry made No.73 in Aug 1987.

SWEET SENSATION *UK, male vocal (Marcel King, d. 1995) group (2 Singles: 17 Weeks)*

14 Sep 74 ★	**SAD SWEET DREAMER** *Pye 7N 45385*	**1**	10
18 Jan 75	**PURELY BY COINCIDENCE** *Pye 7N 45421*	**11**	7

SWEET TEE *US, female rapper – Toi Jackson (2 Singles: 8 Weeks)*

16 Jan 88	**IT'S LIKE THAT Y'ALL / I GOT DA FEELIN'** *Cooltempo COOL 160*	**31**	6
13 Aug 94	**THE FEELING** *Deep Distraxion OILYCD 029* [1]	**32**	2

[1] Tin Tin Out featuring Sweet Tee

SWEETBACK *UK, male vocal / instrumental group*

29 Mar 97	**YOU WILL RISE** *Epic 6643155*	**64**	1

SWEETBOX *Germany / US, male / female vocal / production duo – Rosan Roberto and Tina Harris*

22 Aug 98 ●	**EVERYTHING'S GONNA BE ALRIGHT** *RCA 74321606842*	**5**	12

SWERVEDRIVER *UK, male vocal / instrumental group (2 Albums: 2 Weeks, 3 Singles: 3 Weeks)*

10 Aug 91	**SANDBLASTED (EP)** *Creation CRE 102*	**67**	1
12 Oct 91	RAISE *Creation CRELP 093*	44	1
30 May 92	**NEVER LOSE THAT FEELING** *Creation CRE 120*	**62**	1
14 Aug 93	**DUEL** *Creation CRESCD 136*	**60**	1
9 Oct 93	MEZCAL HEAD *Creation CCRE 143*	55	1

Tracks on Sandblasted (EP): Sandblaster / Flawed / Out / Laze It Up.

Mampi SWIFT *UK, male producer – Philip Anim*

5 Jun 04	**HI-TEK / DRUNKEN STARS** *Charge CHRG 024*	**72**	1

SWIMMING WITH SHARKS *Germany, female vocal duo*

7 May 88	**CARELESS LOVE** *WEA YZ 173*	**63**	3

SWING featuring DR ALBAN *US, male rapper and Nigeria, male vocalist – Alban Nwapa*

29 Apr 95	**SWEET DREAMS** *Logic 74321251552*	**59**	1

SWING 52 *US, male vocal / instrumental group*

25 Feb 95	**COLOR OF MY SKIN** *ffrr FCD 256*	**60**	1

SWING OUT SISTER *UK, male / female vocal (Corinne Drewery) / instrumental trio (3 Albums: 36 Weeks, 9 Singles: 55 Weeks)*

25 Oct 86 ●	**BREAKOUT** *Mercury SWING 2*	**4**	14
10 Jan 87 ●	**SURRENDER** *Mercury SWING 3*	**7**	8
18 Apr 87	**TWILIGHT WORLD** *Mercury SWING 4*	**32**	6
23 May 87 ★	IT'S BETTER TO TRAVEL *Mercury OUTLP 1* ■	1	21
11 Jul 87	**FOOLED BY A SMILE** *Mercury SWING 5*	**43**	4
8 Apr 89	**YOU ON MY MIND** *Fontana SWING 6*	**28**	9
20 May 89 ●	KALEIDOSCOPE WORLD *Fontana 838293 1*	3	11
8 Jul 89	**WHERE IN THE WORLD** *Fontana SWING 7*	**47**	4
11 Apr 92	**AM I THE SAME GIRL** *Fontana SWING 9*	**21**	6
16 May 92	GET IN TOUCH WITH YOURSELF *Fontana 5122412*	27	4
20 Jun 92	**NOTGONNACHANGE** *Fontana SWING 10*	**49**	2
27 Aug 94	**LA LA (MEANS I LOVE YOU)** *Fontana SWIDD 11*	**37**	2

Act became a male / female duo in 1989.

1 August 1992	8 August 1992	15 August 1992	22 August 1992
AIN'T NO DOUBT Jimmy Nail	RHYTHM IS A DANCER Snap!	RHYTHM IS A DANCER Snap!	RHYTHM IS A DANCER Snap!
THE GREATEST HITS 1966-1992 Neil Diamond	THE GREATEST HITS 1966-1992 Neil Diamond	WELCOME TO WHEREVER YOU ARE INXS	WE CAN'T DANCE Genesis

KEY
UK No.1 ★★ UK Top 10 ●● Still on chart ++ UK entry at No.1 ■■
US No.1 ▲▲ UK million seller £ US million seller $
Singles re-entries are listed as (re), (2re), (3re)... which signifies that the hit re-entered the chart once, twice or three times...
Peak Position / Weeks

The SWINGING BLUE JEANS
UK, male vocal (Ray Ennis) / instrumental group (5 Singles: 57 Weeks)

20 Jun 63	**IT'S TOO LATE NOW** (re) *HMV POP 1170*	30	9
12 Dec 63 ●	**HIPPY HIPPY SHAKE** *HMV POP 1242*	2	17
19 Mar 64	**GOOD GOLLY MISS MOLLY** *HMV POP 1273*	11	10
4 Jun 64 ●	**YOU'RE NO GOOD** *HMV POP 1304*	3	13
20 Jan 66	**DON'T MAKE ME OVER** *HMV POP 1501*	31	8

SWINGLE SINGERS *US / France, male / female vocal group*

1 Feb 64	JAZZ SEBASTIAN BACH *Philips BL 7572*	13	18

SWIRL 360 *US, male vocal duo*

14 Nov 98	**HEY NOW NOW** *Mercury 5665352*	61	1

SWITCH *US, male vocal / instrumental group*

10 Nov 84	**KEEPING SECRETS** *Total Experience RCA XE 502*	61	3

SWITCHFOOT *US, male vocal / instrumental group*

14 Aug 04	**MEANT TO LIVE** *Columbia 6750812*	29	2

SYBIL
US, female vocalist – Sybil Lynch (3 Albums: 12 Weeks, 14 Singles: 69 Weeks)

1 Nov 86	**FALLING IN LOVE** *Champion CHAMP 22*	68	3
25 Apr 87	**LET YOURSELF GO** *Champion CHAMP 42*	32	6
29 Aug 87	**MY LOVE IS GUARANTEED** *Champion CHAMPX 55*	42	5
5 Sep 87	LET YOURSELF GO *Champion CHAMP 1009*	92	1
22 Jul 89	**DON'T MAKE ME OVER** (re) *Champion CHAMP 213*	19	11
27 Jan 90 ●	**WALK ON BY** *PWL PWL 48*	6	9
24 Feb 90	WALK ON BY *PWL HF 10*	21	5
21 Apr 90	**CRAZY FOR YOU** *PWL PWL 53*	71	1
16 Jan 93 ●	**THE LOVE I LOST** *PWL Sanctuary PWCD 253* [1]	3	13
20 Mar 93 ●	**WHEN I'M GOOD AND READY** *PWL International PWCD 260*	5	13
12 Jun 93	GOOD 'N' READY *PWL International HFCD 28*	13	6
26 Jun 93	**BEYOND YOUR WILDEST DREAMS** *PWL International PWCD 265*	41	2
11 Sep 93	**STRONGER TOGETHER** *PWL International PWCD 269*	41	2
11 Dec 93	**MY LOVE IS GUARANTEED** (re-mix) *PWL International PWCD 277*	48	1
9 Mar 96	**SO TIRED OF BEING ALONE** *PWL International PWL 324CD*	53	1
8 Mar 97	**WHEN I'M GOOD AND READY** (re-mix) *Next Plateau NP 14183*	66	1
26 Jul 97	**STILL A THRILL** *Coalition COLA 007CD*	55	1

[1] West End featuring Sybil

SYLK 130 *US, male production duo – King Britt and John Wicks*

25 Apr 98	**LAST NIGHT A DJ SAVED MY LIFE** *Sony S2 SYLK 1CD*	33	2

SYLVER *Belgium, male / female DJ / production / vocal duo*

1 Jun 02	**TURN THE TIDE** *Pepper 9230562*	56	1

SYLVESTER *US, male vocalist – Sylvester James,*
b. 6 Sep 1947, d. 16 Dec 1988 (1 Album: 3 Weeks, 6 Singles: 45 Weeks)

19 Aug 78 ●	**YOU MAKE ME FEEL (MIGHTY REAL)** *Fantasy FTC 160*	8	15
18 Nov 78	**DANCE (DISCO HEAT)** *Fantasy FTC 163*	29	12
31 Mar 79	**I (WHO HAVE NOTHING)** *Fantasy FTC 171*	46	5
23 Jun 79	MIGHTY REAL *Fantasy FTA 3009*	62	3
7 Jul 79	**STARS** *Fantasy FTC 177*	47	3
11 Sep 82	**DO YOU WANNA FUNK** *London LON 13* [1]	32	8
3 Sep 83	**BAND OF GOLD** *London LON 33*	67	2

[1] Sylvester with Patrick Cowley

SYLVIA *US, female vocalist – Sylvia Vanderpool*

23 Jun 73	**PILLOW TALK** *London HL 10415* $	14	11

SYLVIA *Sweden, female vocalist – Sylvia Vrethammer (2 Singles: 33 Weeks)*

10 Aug 74 ●	**Y VIVA ESPANA** (re) *Sonet SON 2037*	4	28
26 Apr 75	**HASTA LA VISTA** *Sonet SON 2055*	38	5

David SYLVIAN (see also JAPAN)
UK, male vocalist – David Batt (7 Albums: 27 Weeks, 12 Singles: 36 Weeks)

7 Aug 82	**BAMBOO HOUSES / BAMBOO MUSIC** *Virgin VS 510* [1]	30	4
2 Jul 83	**FORBIDDEN COLOURS** *Virgin VS 601* [2]	16	8
2 Jun 84	**RED GUITAR** *Virgin VS 633*	17	5
7 Jul 84 ●	BRILLIANT TREES *Virgin V 2290*	4	14
18 Aug 84	**THE INK IN THE WELL** *Virgin VS 700*	36	3
3 Nov 84	**PULLING PUNCHES** *Virgin VS 717*	56	2
14 Dec 85	**WORDS WITH THE SHAMAN** *Virgin VS 835*	72	1
9 Aug 86	**TAKING THE VEIL** *Virgin VS 815*	53	3
13 Sep 86	GONE TO EARTH *Virgin VDL 1*	24	5
17 Jan 87	**BUOY** *Virgin VS 910* [3]	63	2
10 Oct 87	**LET THE HAPPINESS IN** *Virgin VS 1001*	66	1
7 Nov 87	SECRETS OF THE BEEHIVE *Virgin V 2471*	37	2
2 Apr 88	PLIGHT AND PREMONITION *Virgin VE 11* [1]	71	1
13 Jun 92	**HEARTBEAT (TAINAI KAIKI II) RETURNING TO THE WOMB** *Virgin America VUS 57* [4]	58	3
17 Jul 93	THE FIRST DAY *Virgin CDVX 2712* [2]	21	2
28 Aug 93	**JEAN THE BIRDMAN** *Virgin VSCDG 1462* [5]	68	2
27 Mar 99	**I SURRENDER** *Virgin VSCDT 1722*	40	2
10 Apr 99	DEAD BEES ON A CAKE *Virgin CDV 2876*	31	2
21 Oct 00	EVERYTHING AND NOTHING *Virgin CDVD 2897*	57	1

[1] Sylvian Sakamoto [2] David Sylvian and Riuichi Sakamoto [3] Mick Karn featuring David Sylvian [4] David Sylvian / Riuichi Sakamoto featuring Ingrid Chavez [5] David Sylvian and Robert Fripp [1] David Sylvian and Holgar Czukay [2] David Sylvian and Robert Fripp

SYMARIP
(see also The PYRAMIDS) *Jamaica, male vocal / instrumental group*

2 Feb 80	**SKINHEAD MOONSTOMP** *Trojan TRO 9062*	54	3

The SYMBOLS *UK, male vocal / instrumental group (2 Singles: 15 Weeks)*

2 Aug 67	**BYE BYE BABY** *President PT 144*	44	3
3 Jan 68	**(THE BEST PART OF) BREAKING UP** *President PT 173*	25	12

Terri SYMON *UK, female vocalist*

10 Jun 95	**I WANT TO KNOW WHAT LOVE IS** *A&M 5810592*	54	1

SYMPHONIQUE (see also PROJECT D)
UK, male keyboard player – Chris Cozens

1 Apr 95	MOODS SYMPHONIQUE 95 *Vision VISCD 10*	21	4

SYMPOSIUM (see also HELL IS FOR HEROES)
UK, male vocal / instrumental group (2 Albums: 3 Weeks, 6 Singles: 10 Weeks)

22 Mar 97	**FAREWELL TO TWILIGHT** *Infectious INFECT 34CD*	25	2
31 May 97	**THE ANSWER TO WHY I HATE YOU** *Infectious INFECT 37CD*	32	2
30 Aug 97	**FAIRWEATHER FRIEND** *Infectious INFECT 44CD*	25	3
8 Nov 97	ONE DAY AT A TIME *Infectious INFECT 49CD*	29	2
14 Mar 98	**AVERAGE MAN** *Infectious INFECT 52CD*	45	1
16 May 98	**BURY YOU** *Infectious INFECT 55CDS*	41	1
30 May 98	ON THE OUTSIDE *Infectious INFECT 56CD*	32	1
18 Jul 98	**BLUE** *Infectious INFECT 57CD*	48	1

SYNTAX
UK, male production duo – Mike Tournier and Jan Burton (2 Singles: 4 Weeks)

8 Feb 03	**PRAY** *Illustrious CDILL 012*	28	3
28 Feb 04	**BLISS** *Illustrious / Epic CDILLX 020*	69	1

29 August 1992	5 September 1992	12 September 1992	19 September 1992
UK No.1 SINGLES			
RHYTHM IS A DANCER – Snap!	RHYTHM IS A DANCER – Snap!	RHYTHM IS A DANCER – Snap!	EBENEEZER GOODE – The Shamen
UK No.1 ALBUMS			
BEST ... 1 – The Smiths	GREATEST HITS – Kylie	TUBULAR BELLS II – Mike Oldfield	TUBULAR BELLS II – Mike Oldfield

SYNTHPHONIC VARIATIONS *UK, session musicians*

1 Nov 86 SEASONS *CBS 450 1491* 84 1

SYREETA *US, female vocalist – Rita Wright, b. 3 Aug 1946, d. 6 Jul 2004 (5 Singles: 30 Weeks)*

21 Sep 74 SPINNIN' AND SPINNIN' *Tamla Motown TMG 912* 49 3
1 Feb 75 YOUR KISS IS SWEET *Tamla Motown TMG 933* 12 8
12 Jul 75 HARMOUR LOVE *Tamla Motown TMG 954* 32 4
15 Dec 79 ● WITH YOU I'M BORN AGAIN *Motown TMG 1159* [1] 2 11
8 Mar 80 IT WILL COME IN TIME *Motown TMG 1175* [1] 47 4

[1] Billy Preston and Syreeta

The SYSTEM *US, male vocal / instrumental duo*

9 Jun 84 I WANNA MAKE YOU FEEL GOOD *Polydor POSP 685* 73 2

SYSTEM F (see also ALBION; GOURYELLA; MOONMAN; STARPARTY; VERACOCHA) *Holland, male producer – Ferry Corsten (2 Singles: 10 Weeks)*

3 Apr 99 OUT OF THE BLUE *Essential Recordings ESCD 1* 14 6
6 May 00 CRY *Essential Recordings ESCD 14* 19 4

SYSTEM OF A DOWN *US, male vocal / instrumental group (4 Albums: 40 Weeks, 5 Singles: 12 Weeks)*

8 Sep 01 TOXICITY *Columbia 5015346* ▲ 13 27
3 Nov 01 CHOP SUEY! *Columbia 6720342* 17 4
23 Mar 02 TOXICITY *Columbia 6725022* 25 3
27 Jul 02 AERIALS *Columbia 6728692* 34 2
7 Dec 02 STEAL THIS ALBUM! *American Recordings 5102489* 56 1
28 May 05 ● MEZMERIZE *American Recordings / Columbia 5190002* ▲ 2 8
10 Sep 05 QUESTION! *American / Columbia 6760562* 41 1
26 Nov 05 HYPNOTIZE *American / Columbia 82876741302* 48 2
3 Dec 05 HYPNOTIZE *American Recordings / Columbia 82876726122* ▲ 11 4

SYSTEM OF LIFE *UK, production duo*

29 May 04 LUV IS COOL *Freedream CDFDREAM 1* 63 1

SYSTEM presents Kerri B *UK, male production group and female vocalist*

8 Nov 03 IF YOU LEAVE ME NOW *All Around the World CDGLOBE 288* ... 55 1

SYSTEM 7 *UK / France, male / female instrumental duo – Steve Hillage and Miquette Giraudy (2 Albums: 3 Weeks, 2 Singles: 2 Weeks)*

20 Jun 92 ALTITUDE *Ten TENG 403* 75 1
13 Feb 93 7:7 EXPANSION *Butterfly BFLD 2* 39 1
20 Mar 93 777 *Big Life BFLCD 1* 30 2
17 Jul 93 SINBAD / QUEST *Butterfly BFLD 8* 74 1

T

T-BOZ (see also TLC) *US, female vocalist – Tionne Watkins (2 Singles: 2 Weeks)*

23 Nov 96 TOUCH MYSELF *LaFace 74321422882* 48 1
14 Apr 01 MY GETAWAY *Maverick W 549CD* [1] 44 1

[1] Tionne 'T-Boz' Watkins

TC *Italy, male instrumental / production group (3 Singles: 5 Weeks)*

14 Mar 92 BERRY *Union City UCRT 1* [1] 73 1
21 Nov 92 FUNKY GUITAR *Union City UCRT 13* [2] 40 2
10 Jul 93 HARMONY *Union UCRD 20* [3] 51 2

[1] TC 1991 [2] TC 1992 [3] TC 1993

T-CONNECTION *US, male vocal / instrumental group (5 Singles: 27 Weeks)*

18 Jun 77 DO WHAT YOU WANNA DO *TK XC 9109* 11 8
14 Jan 78 ON FIRE *TK TKR 6006* 16 5
10 Jun 78 LET YOURSELF GO *TK TKR 6024* 52 3
24 Feb 79 AT MIDNIGHT *TK TKR 7517* 53 5
5 May 79 SATURDAY NIGHT *TK TKR 7536* 41 6

T-EMPO *UK, male / female vocal / instrumental group (2 Singles: 4 Weeks)*

7 May 94 SATURDAY NIGHT SUNDAY MORNING *ffrr FCD 232* 19 3
9 Nov 96 THE LOOK OF LOVE / THE BLUE ROOM *ffrr FCD 281* 71 1

T-FACTORY *Italy, male production group*

13 Apr 02 MESSAGE IN A BOTTLE *Inferno CDFERN 44* 51 2

THS – THE HORN SECTION *US, male / female vocal / instrumental group*

18 Aug 84 LADY SHINE (SHINE ON) *Fourth & Broadway BRW 10* 54 3

T.I. NEW *US, male rapper – Clifford Harris (2 Singles: 8 Weeks)*

19 Feb 05 ● SOLDIER *Columbia 6757622* [1] 4 7
26 Mar 05 BRING EM OUT *Atlantic AT 0196CD* 59 1

[1] Destiny's Child featuring T.I. and Lil Wayne

TJR featuring XAVIER *UK, male instrumental / production group*

27 Sep 97 JUST GETS BETTER *Multiply CDMULTY 25* 28 2

TLC 390 Top 500 *Multi-award-winning 1990s female trio: Tionne 'T-Boz' Watkins, Lisa 'Left Eye' Lopes, b. 27 May 1971, d. 25 Apr 2002, and Rozonda 'Chilli' Thomas. They have nine US gold singles and The Supremes are the only female group with more US No.1s. Best-selling single: 'No Scrubs' 553,200 (3 Albums: 97 Weeks, 12 Singles: 85 Weeks)*

20 Jun 92 AIN'T 2 PROUD 2 BEG *Arista 115265* $ 13 5
22 Aug 92 BABY-BABY-BABY *LaFace 74321111297* $ 55 3
24 Oct 92 WHAT ABOUT YOUR FRIENDS *LaFace 74321118177* 59 2
21 Jan 95 CREEP *LaFace 74321254212* ▲ $ 22 4
22 Apr 95 RED LIGHT SPECIAL *LaFace 74321273662* 18 4
20 May 95 ● CRAZYSEXYCOOL *LaFace 73008260092* 4 39
5 Aug 95 ● WATERFALLS *LaFace 74321298812* ▲ $ 4 14
4 Nov 95 DIGGIN' ON YOU *LaFace 74321319252* 18 5
13 Jan 96 ● CREEP (re-issue) *LaFace 74321340942* 6 7
6 Mar 99 ● FANMAIL *LaFace 73008260552* ▲ 7 57
3 Apr 99 ● NO SCRUBS *LaFace 74321660952* ▲ 3 19
28 Aug 99 ● UNPRETTY *LaFace 74321695842* ▲ 6 11
18 Dec 99 DEAR LIE *LaFace 74321724012* 31 9
23 Nov 02 3D *Arista 74321981502* 45 1
14 Dec 02 GIRL TALK *Arista 74321983482* 30 2

T99 *Belgium, male instrumental / production group (2 Singles: 10 Weeks)*

11 May 91 ANASTHASIA *XL XLS 19* 14 6
19 Oct 91 NOCTURNE *Emphasis 6574097* 33 4

T-POWER (see also EBONY DUBSTERS) *UK, male producer – Mark Royal (4 Singles: 18 Weeks)*

13 Apr 96 POLICE STATE *Sound of Underground TPOWCD 001* 63 1
6 Apr 02 ● SHAKE UR BODY *Positiva CDTIV 171* [1] 7 11
23 Nov 02 DON'T WANNA KNOW *ffrr FCD 408* [2] 19 4
7 Jun 03 FEELIN' U *London FCD 409* [3] 34 2

[1] Shy FX and T-Power featuring Di [2] Shy FX and T-Power featuring Di and Skibadee [3] Shy FX and T-Power featuring Kele Le Roc

26 September 1992	3 October 1992	10 October 1992	17 October 1992
EBENEEZER GOODE The Shamen	EBENEEZER GOODE The Shamen	EBENEEZER GOODE The Shamen	SLEEPING SATELLITE Tasmin Archer
THE BEST OF BELINDA VOLUME 1 Belinda Carlisle	GOLD - GREATEST HITS Abba	AUTOMATIC FOR THE PEOPLE R.E.M.	SYMBOL Prince and The New Power Generation

KEY UK No.1 ★ UK Top 10 ● Still on chart + UK entry at No.1 ■ US No.1 ▲ UK million seller £ US million seller $ Singles re-entries are listed as (re), (2re), (3re)... which signifies that the hit re-entered the chart once, twice or three times... Peak Position / Weeks

TQ
US, male rapper – Terrance Quaites (2 Albums: 9 Weeks, 6 Singles: 35 Weeks)

30 Jan 99 ● **WESTSIDE** *Epic 6668102*....4 9
1 May 99 ● **BYE BYE BABY** *Epic 6672372*....7 7
8 May 99 THEY NEVER SAW ME COMING *Epic 4914032*....27 7
21 Aug 99 **BETTER DAYS** *Epic 6677532*....32 2
4 Sep 99 ● **SUMMERTIME** *Northwestside 74321694672* [1]....7 7
29 Apr 00 **DAILY** *Epic 6692752*....14 5
20 May 00 THE SECOND COMING *Epic 4977602*....32 2
13 Oct 01 **LET'S GET BACK TO BED ... BOY** *Epic 6718662* [2]....16 5

[1] Another Level featuring TQ [2] Sarah Connor featuring TQ

T. REX 90 Top 500
Highly influential acoustic act turned superstar glam rock boogie duo: singer / songwriter / guitarist Marc Bolan, b. Mark Feld, 30 Sep 1947, London, UK, d. 16 Sep 1977, and percussionist Steve Peregrin Took, b. 28 Jul 1949, d. 27 Oct 1980. Took was replaced by Mickey Finn, b. 3 Jun 1947, d. 12 Jan 2003, in 1969 (23 Albums: 232 Weeks, 30 Singles: 236 Weeks)

8 May 68 **DEBORA** *Regal Zonophone RZ 3008* [1]....34 7
13 Jul 68 MY PEOPLE WERE FAIR AND HAD SKY IN THEIR HAIR BUT NOW THEY'RE CONTENT TO WEAR STARS ON THEIR BROWS *Regal Zonophone SLRZ 1003* [1]....15 9
4 Sep 68 **ONE INCH ROCK** *Regal Zonophone RZ 3011* [1]....28 7
7 Jun 69 UNICORN *Regal Zonophone S 1007* [1]....12 3
9 Aug 69 **KING OF THE RUMBLING SPIRES** *Regal Zonophone RZ 3022* [1]....44 1
14 Mar 70 A BEARD OF STARS *Regal Zonophone SLRZ 1013* [1]....21 6
24 Oct 70 ● **RIDE A WHITE SWAN** *Fly BUG 1*....2 20
16 Jan 71 ● T. REX *Fly HIFLY 2*....7 25
27 Feb 71 ★ **HOT LOVE** *Fly BUG 6*....1 17
27 Mar 71 THE BEST OF T. REX *Flyback TON 2*....21 8
10 Jul 71 ★ **GET IT ON** *Fly BUG 10*....1 13
9 Oct 71 ★ ELECTRIC WARRIOR *Fly HIFLY 6*....1 44
13 Nov 71 ● **JEEPSTER** *Fly BUG 16*....2 15
29 Jan 72 ★ **TELEGRAM SAM** (re) *T. Rex 101*....1 14
29 Mar 72 ★ PROPHETS SEERS & SAGES THE ANGELS OF THE AGES / MY PEOPLE WERE FAIR AND HAD SKY IN THEIR HAIR BUT NOW THEY'RE CONTENT TO WEAR STARS ON THEIR BROWS (re-issues) *Fly Double Back TOOFA 3/4* [1]....1 12
1 Apr 72 ● **DEBORA / ONE INCH ROCK** (re-issues) *Magnifly ECHO 102* [1]....7 10
13 May 72 ★ **METAL GURU** *EMI MARC 1*....1 14
20 May 72 ★ BOLAN BOOGIE *Fly HIFLY 8* ■....1 19
5 Aug 72 ● THE SLIDER *EMI BLN 5001*....4 18
16 Sep 72 ● **CHILDREN OF THE REVOLUTION** *EMI MARC 2*....2 10
9 Dec 72 A BEARD OF STARS / UNICORN (re-issues) *Cube TOOFA 9/10* [1]....44 2
9 Dec 72 ● **SOLID GOLD EASY ACTION** *EMI MARC 3*....2 11
10 Mar 73 ● **20TH CENTURY BOY** *EMI MARC 4*....3 9
31 Mar 73 ● TANX *EMI BLN 5002*....4 12
16 Jun 73 ● **THE GROOVER** *EMI MARC 5*....4 9
10 Nov 73 GREAT HITS *EMI BLN 5003*....32 3
24 Nov 73 **TRUCK ON (TYKE)** *EMI MARC 6*....12 11
9 Feb 74 **TEENAGE DREAM** *EMI MARC 7* [2]....13 5
16 Mar 74 ZINC ALLOY AND THE HIDDEN RIDERS OF TOMORROW *EMI BLNA 7751* [2]....12 3
13 Jul 74 **LIGHT OF LOVE** *EMI MARC 8*....22 5
16 Nov 74 **ZIP GUN BOOGIE** *EMI MARC 9*....41 3
12 Jul 75 **NEW YORK CITY** *EMI MARC 10*....15 8
11 Oct 75 **DREAMY LADY** *EMI MARC 11* [3]....30 5
21 Feb 76 FUTURISTIC DRAGON *EMI BLN 5004*....50 1
6 Mar 76 **LONDON BOYS** *EMI MARC 13*....40 3
19 Jun 76 **I LOVE TO BOOGIE** *EMI MARC 14*....13 9
2 Oct 76 **LASER LOVE** *EMI MARC 15*....41 4
2 Apr 77 **THE SOUL OF MY SUIT** *EMI MARC 16*....42 3
9 Apr 77 DANDY IN THE UNDERWORLD *EMI BLN 5005*....26 3
30 Jun 79 SOLID GOLD *EMI NUT 5*....51 3
9 May 81 **RETURN OF THE ELECTRIC WARRIOR (EP)** *Rarn MBSF 001* [4]....50 4
12 Sep 81 T. REX IN CONCERT *Marc ABOLAN 1*....35 6
19 Sep 81 **YOU SCARE ME TO DEATH** *Cherry Red CHERRY 29* [4]....51 4
7 Nov 81 YOU SCARE ME TO DEATH *Cherry Red ERED 20* [3]....88 1
24 Sep 83 DANCE IN THE MIDNIGHT *Marc on Wax MARCL 501* [3]....83 3
4 May 85 ● BEST OF THE 20TH CENTURY BOY *K-Tel NE 1297* [2]....5 21
18 May 85 **MEGAREX** *Marc on Wax TANX 1* [2]....72 2
9 May 87 **GET IT ON** (re-mix) *Marc on Wax MARC 10* [2]....54 4
24 Aug 91 **20TH CENTURY BOY** (re-issue) *Marc on Wax MARC 501* [2]....13 8
28 Sep 91 ● THE ULTIMATE COLLECTION *Telstar TCD 2539* [2]....4 16
7 Oct 95 THE ESSENTIAL COLLECTION *PolyGram TV 5259612* [2]....24 6
7 Oct 00 **GET IT ON** (re-recording) *All Around the World CDGLOBE 225* [5]....59 1
28 Sep 02 THE ESSENTIAL COLLECTION – 25TH ANNIVERSARY EDITION *Universal TV 4934882* [2]....18 8

[1] Tyrannosaurus Rex [2] Marc Bolan and T. Rex [3] T. Rex Disco Party [4] Marc Bolan [5] Bus Stop featuring T. Rex [1] Tyrannosaurus Rex [2] Marc Bolan and T. Rex [3] Marc Bolan

'Telegram Sam' re-entered the chart in Mar 1982, peaking at No.69. Tracks on Return of the Electric Warrior (EP): Sing Me a Song / Endless Sleep Extended / The Lilac Hand of Menthol Dan. 'Megarex' is a medley of extracts from the following T. Rex hits: Truck On (Tyke) / The Groover / Telegram Sam / Shock Rock / Metal Guru / 20th Century Boy / Children of the Revolution / Hot Love. Prophets ... / My People ... (29 Mar 1972) was a double re-issue, even though Prophets ... had not previously charted. The Essential Collection (1995) returned to the chart in 2000 with a new label, Universal Music TV, but the catalogue number was the same.

TSD
UK, female vocal group (2 Singles: 2 Weeks)

17 Feb 96 **HEART AND SOUL** *Avex UK AVEXCD 21*....69 1
30 Mar 96 **BABY I LOVE YOU** *Avex UK AVEXCD 34*....64 1

T-SHIRT
UK, female vocal duo

13 Sep 97 **YOU SEXY THING** *Eternal WEA 122CD*....63 1

T-SPOON
Holland, male / female vocal / instrumental group (2 Singles: 15 Weeks)

19 Sep 98 ● **SEX ON THE BEACH** *Control 0042395 CON*....2 13
23 Jan 99 **TOM'S PARTY** *Control 0043505 CON*....27 2

T2 featuring Robin S
US, male production duo and female vocalist – Robin Stone

4 Oct 97 **YOU GOT THE LOVE** *Champion CHAMPCD 330*....62 1

TWA
UK, male instrumental / production group

16 Sep 95 **NASTY GIRLS** *Mercury MERCD 441*....51 1

TABERNACLE
UK, male instrumental / production group (2 Singles: 2 Weeks)

4 Mar 95 **I KNOW THE LORD** *Good Groove CDGG 1*....62 1
3 Feb 96 **I KNOW THE LORD** (re-mix) *Good Groove CDGGX 1*....55 1

TACKHEAD
US / UK, male vocal / production / rap group

30 Jun 90 **DANGEROUS SEX** *SBK SBK 7014*....48 3

TAFFY
UK, female vocalist – Catherine Quaye (2 Singles: 14 Weeks)

10 Jan 87 ● **I LOVE MY RADIO (MY DEE JAY'S RADIO)** *Transglobal TYPE 1*....6 10
18 Jul 87 **STEP BY STEP** *Transglobal TYPE 5*....59 4

24 October 1992	31 October 1992	7 November 1992	14 November 1992
UK No.1 SINGLES			
SLEEPING SATELLITE – Tasmin Archer	END OF THE ROAD – Boyz II Men	END OF THE ROAD – Boyz II Men	END OF THE ROAD – Boyz II Men
UK No.1 ALBUMS			
GLITTERING PRIZE 81/92 – Simple Minds	GLITTERING PRIZE 81/92 – Simple Minds	GLITTERING PRIZE 81/92 – Simple Minds	KEEP THE FAITH – Bon Jovi

TAG TEAM

US, male rap duo – Cecil Glenn and Steve Gibson (3 Singles: 8 Weeks)

8 Jan 94	**WHOOMP! (THERE IT IS)** *Club Tools SHXCD 1* $	34	5
29 Jan 94	**ADDAMS FAMILY (WHOOMP!)** *Atlas PZCD 305*	53	1
10 Sep 94	**WHOOMP! (THERE IT IS)** (re-mix) *Club Tools SHXR 1*	48	2

TAIKO

Germany, male DJ / production duo – Oliver Huntemann and Stephan Bodzin

29 Jun 02	**SILENCE** *Nukleuz NUKC 0330*	72	1

TAK TIX *US, male / female vocal / production group*

20 Jan 96	**FEEL LIKE SINGING** *A&M 5813212*	33	2

TAKE 5 *US, male vocal group (2 Singles: 4 Weeks)*

7 Nov 98	**I GIVE** *Edel 0039635 ERE*	70	1
27 Mar 99	**NEVER HAD IT SO GOOD** *Edel 0039355 ERE*	34	3

TAKE THAT (123 Top 500)

Record-breaking British boy band: Gary Barlow (v), Robbie Williams (v), Jason Orange (v), Howard Donald (v) and Mark Owen (v). They were the first artists since The Beatles to score four consecutive chart-toppers and the first act to release eight singles that entered at No.1. Williams departed in July 1995 and Barlow dissolved the band in Feb 1996 having sold nine million albums and 10 million singles. Act re-united (without Williams) in 2005 for a sold-out tour. Best-selling single: 'Back for Good' 959,582 (6 Albums: 234 Weeks, 16 Singles: 158 Weeks)

23 Nov 91	**PROMISES** *RCA PB 45085*	38	2
8 Feb 92	**ONCE YOU'VE TASTED LOVE** *RCA PB 45257*	47	3
6 Jun 92 ●	**IT ONLY TAKES A MINUTE** *RCA 74321101007*	7	8
15 Aug 92	**I FOUND HEAVEN** *RCA 74321108137*	15	6
5 Sep 92 ●	TAKE THAT & PARTY *RCA 74321109232*	2	73
10 Oct 92 ●	**A MILLION LOVE SONGS** *RCA 74321116307*	7	9
12 Dec 92 ●	**COULD IT BE MAGIC** *RCA 74321123137*	3	12
20 Feb 93 ●	**WHY CAN'T I WAKE UP WITH YOU** *RCA 74321133102*	2	10
17 Jul 93 ★	**PRAY** *RCA 74321154502* ■	1	11
9 Oct 93 ★	**RELIGHT MY FIRE** *RCA 74321167722* [1] ■	1	14
23 Oct 93 ★	EVERYTHING CHANGES *RCA 74321169262* ■	1	78
18 Dec 93 ★	**BABE** *RCA 74321182122* ■	1	10
9 Apr 94 ★	**EVERYTHING CHANGES** *RCA 74321167732* ■	1	10
9 Jul 94 ●	**LOVE AIN'T HERE ANYMORE** (re) *RCA 74321214832*	3	12
15 Oct 94 ★	**SURE** *RCA 74321236622* ■	1	15
8 Apr 95 ★	**BACK FOR GOOD** *RCA 74321271462* ■	1	13
13 May 95 ★	NOBODY ELSE *RCA 74321279092* ■	1	33
5 Aug 95 ★	**NEVER FORGET** *RCA 74321299572* ■	1	9
26 Aug 95	NOBODY ELSE (import) *Arista 07822188002*	26	4
9 Mar 96 ★	**HOW DEEP IS YOUR LOVE** (re) *RCA 74321355592* ■	1	14
6 Apr 96 ★	GREATEST HITS *RCA 74321355582* ■	1	40
26 Nov 05 ●	THE ULTIMATE COLLECTION – NEVER FORGET *RCA 82876748522*	2	6+

[1] Take That featuring Lulu

TAKING BACK SUNDAY *US, male vocal / instrumental group*

7 Aug 04	WHERE YOU WANT TO BE *Victory VR 228CD*	71	1
2 Oct 04	**A DECADE UNDER THE INFLUENCE** *Victory VR 236CD*	70	1

TALI *New Zealand, female DJ / producer / rapper – Natalia Scott (3 Singles: 5 Weeks)*

10 Aug 02	**LYRIC ON MY LIP** *Full Cycle FCY 042*	75	1
7 Feb 04	**BLAZIN'** *Full Cycle FCYCDS 059*	42	2
15 May 04	**LYRIC ON MY LIP** (re-issue) *Full Cycle FYCD 065*	39	2

The first issue of 'Lyric on My Lip' was available on 12" only.

TALISMAN P featuring Barrington LEVY

UK, male producer – Philip Larsen and Jamaica, male vocalist

13 Oct 01	**HERE I COME (SING DJ)** (re-recording) *Nulife / Arista 74321895622*	37	2

TALK TALK (449 Top 500) (see also Beth GIBBONS & RUSTIN' MAN)

London-based synth-pop band who rapidly evolved into an organic, reflective rock group: Mark Hollis (v/g/k), Paul Webb (b) and Lee Harris (d). The band, who had several legal wrangles with EMI, also scored four Top 20 singles in Italy (8 Albums: 86 Weeks, 13 Singles: 74 Weeks)

24 Apr 82	**TALK TALK** *EMI 5284*	52	4
24 Jul 82	THE PARTY'S OVER *EMI EMC 3413*	21	25
24 Jul 82	**TODAY** *EMI 5314*	14	13
13 Nov 82	**TALK TALK** (re-mix) *EMI 5352*	23	10
19 Mar 83	**MY FOOLISH FRIEND** *EMI 5373*	57	3
14 Jan 84	**IT'S MY LIFE** *EMI 5443*	46	5
25 Feb 84	IT'S MY LIFE *EMI EMC 2400021*	35	8
7 Apr 84	**SUCH A SHAME** *EMI 5433*	49	6
11 Aug 84	**DUM DUM GIRL** *EMI 5480*	74	1
18 Jan 86	**LIFE'S WHAT YOU MAKE IT** *EMI EMI 5540*	16	9
1 Mar 86 ●	THE COLOUR OF SPRING *EMI EMC 3506*	8	21
15 Mar 86	**LIVING IN ANOTHER WORLD** *EMI EMI 5551*	48	4
17 May 86	**GIVE IT UP** *Parlophone R 6131*	59	3
24 Sep 88	SPIRIT OF EDEN *Parlophone PCSD 105*	19	5
19 May 90	**IT'S MY LIFE** (re-issue) *Parlophone R 6254*	13	9
9 Jun 90 ●	THE VERY BEST OF TALK TALK – NATURAL HISTORY *Parlophone PCSD 109*	3	21
1 Sep 90	**LIFE'S WHAT YOU MAKE IT** (re-issue) *Parlophone R 6264*	23	6
6 Apr 91	HISTORY REVISITED – THE REMIXES *Parlophone PCS 7349*	35	2
28 Sep 91	LAUGHING STOCK *Verve 8477171*	26	2
8 Feb 97	THE VERY BEST OF TALK TALK *EMI CDEMC 3763*	54	2
21 Jun 03	**IT'S MY LIFE** (re-mix) *Nebula NEBCD 045* [1]	64	1

[1] Liquid People vs Talk Talk

TALKING HEADS (208 Top 500)

(see also HEADS with Shaun RYDER) *Unorthodox US 'punk funk' eccentrics formed in 1974 in New York. Tina Weymouth (b) and husband Chris Frantz (d) had a successful side project, Tom Tom Club, while Scottish-born frontman David Byrne (v/g) went solo and won an Oscar for his soundtrack to The Last Emperor (12 Albums: 237 Weeks, 10 Singles: 54 Weeks)*

25 Feb 78	TALKING HEADS '77 *Sire 9103 328*	60	1
29 Jul 78	MORE SONGS ABOUT BUILDINGS AND FOOD *Sire K 56531*	21	3
15 Sep 79	FEAR OF MUSIC *Sire SRK 6076*	33	5
1 Nov 80	REMAIN IN LIGHT *Sire SRK 6095*	21	17
7 Feb 81	**ONCE IN A LIFETIME** *Sire SIR 4048*	14	10
9 May 81	**HOUSES IN MOTION** *Sire SIR 4050*	50	3
10 Apr 82	THE NAME OF THIS BAND IS TALKING HEADS *Sire SRK 23590*	22	5
18 Jun 83	SPEAKING IN TONGUES *Sire K 923 8831*	21	12
21 Jan 84	**THIS MUST BE THE PLACE** *Sire W 9451*	51	3
27 Oct 84	STOP MAKING SENSE *EMI TAH 1*	24	85
3 Nov 84	**SLIPPERY PEOPLE** *EMI 5504*	68	2
29 Jun 85 ●	LITTLE CREATURES *EMI TAH 2*	10	65
12 Oct 85 ●	**ROAD TO NOWHERE** *EMI EMI 5530*	6	16
8 Feb 86	**AND SHE WAS** *EMI EMI 5543*	17	8
6 Sep 86	**WILD WILD LIFE** *EMI EMI 5567*	43	4
27 Sep 86 ●	TRUE STORIES *EMI EU 3511*	7	9
16 May 87	**RADIO HEAD** *EMI EM 1*	52	2
26 Mar 88 ●	NAKED *EMI EMD 1005*	3	15
13 Aug 88	**BLIND** *EMI EM 68*	59	3
10 Oct 92	**LIFETIME PILING UP** *EMI EM 250*	50	3
24 Oct 92 ●	ONCE IN A LIFETIME – THE BEST OF TALKING HEADS / SAND IN THE VASELINE *EMI CDEQ 5010*	7	16
30 Oct 04	THE BEST OF TALKING HEADS *Rhino 8122764882*	30	4

Stop Making Sense re-entered the chart in Jan 2005 with the catalogue number EMI CDFA 3302. It peaked at No.69.

TALL PAUL (see also CAMISRA; ESCRIMA; The GRIFTERS; PARTIZAN)

UK, male DJ / producer – Paul Newman (6 Singles: 15 Weeks)

29 Mar 97	**ROCK DA HOUSE** *VC Recordings VCRD 18*	12	4
29 May 99	**BE THERE** *Duty Free DF 009CD*	45	1
8 Apr 00	**FREEBASE** *Duty Free DF 015CD*	43	2
2 Jun 01	**ROCK DA HOUSE** (re-mix) *VC Recordings VCRD 89*	29	2
18 Aug 01	**PRECIOUS HEART** (re) *Duty Free / Decode DFTELCD 001* [1]	14	5
13 Apr 02	**EVERYBODY'S A ROCKSTAR** *Duty Free / Decode DFTELCD 003*	60	1

[1] Tall Paul vs Inxs

21 November 1992	28 November 1992	5 December 1992	12 December 1992
WOULD I LIE TO YOU Charles and Eddie	WOULD I LIE TO YOU Charles and Eddie	I WILL ALWAYS LOVE YOU Whitney Houston	I WILL ALWAYS LOVE YOU Whitney Houston
GREATEST HITS 1965-1992 Cher	POP! - THE FIRST 20 HITS Erasure	POP! - THE FIRST 20 HITS Erasure	GREATEST HITS 1965-1992 Cher

TOP 100 ACTS

As always, our annual look at the Top 100 acts in chart history is based on the indisputable facts calculated from the weeks each act has spent on the singles and albums charts. Not surprisingly, Elvis is still top as young pretenders Eminem (highest new entry) and Stereophonics (highest climbers) distinguish themselves, while Britney makes her first appearance at No.96 and The Beatles are overtaken by Queen.

In addition to this list you might like to check out the symbols that look like this 422 Top 500 dotted around the book which show the full Top 500 places in the rundown of most successful acts, based on weeks on chart.

www.bibleofpop.com

LAST YEAR	THIS YEAR	ACT	TOTAL WEEKS ON CHART
1	1	ELVIS PRESLEY	2,578
2	2	CLIFF RICHARD	1,985
4	3	QUEEN	1,755
3	4	THE BEATLES	1,749
5	5	MADONNA	1,666
6	6	ELTON JOHN	1,626
7	7	THE SHADOWS	1,582
8	8	MICHAEL JACKSON	1,491
10	9	U2	1,483
9	10	DAVID BOWIE	1,460
11	11	ROD STEWART	1,404
12	12	FRANK SINATRA	1,332
13	13	DIANA ROSS	1,305
14	14	DIRE STRAITS	1,262
15	15	SIMON AND GARFUNKEL	1,201
16	16	THE ROLLING STONES	1,185
17	17	ABBA	1,146
18	18	FLEETWOOD MAC	1,109
19	19	PHIL COLLINS	1,081
20	20	PAUL McCARTNEY	990
21	21	PINK FLOYD	978
22	22	UB40	972
23	23	MEAT LOAF	941
28	24	OASIS	922
24	25	TOM JONES	916
25	26	STATUS QUO	898
26	27	SIMPLY RED	861
27	28	THE BEACH BOYS	855
29	29	STEVIE WONDER	816
30	30	THE CARPENTERS	782
32	31	R.E.M.	778
31	32	THE BEE GEES	771
33	33	BOB DYLAN	764
34	34	TINA TURNER	760
35	35	PRINCE	756
43	36	ROBBIE WILLIAMS	734
36	37	JIM REEVES	730
37	38	NEIL DIAMOND	727
38	39	BOB MARLEY AND THE WAILERS	723
39	40	ERIC CLAPTON	708
40	41	WHITNEY HOUSTON	698
42	42	EURYTHMICS	696
55	43	KYLIE MINOGUE	692
46	44	BARBRA STREISAND	692
44	45	MADNESS	688
45	46	GENESIS	687
41	47	ANDY WILLIAMS	686
47	48	BRUCE SPRINGSTEEN	679
60	49	MARIAH CAREY	674
50	50	BON JOVI	671
48	51	MIKE OLDFIELD	664
51	52	LIONEL RICHIE	663
49	53	CELINE DION	661
54	54	ELECTRIC LIGHT ORCHESTRA	659
52	55	BRYAN ADAMS	657
53	56	DURAN DURAN	653
56	57	GEORGE MICHAEL	631
57	58	SHIRLEY BASSEY	620
58	59	PET SHOP BOYS	596
59	60	ROY ORBISON	593
61	61	ROXY MUSIC	585
62	62	THE FOUR TOPS	574
63	63	JANET JACKSON	567
64	64	THE POLICE	558
66	65	JOHN LENNON	554
65	66	STING	553
69	67	ERASURE	548
67	68	SIMPLE MINDS	547
68	69	CHER	540
70	70	THE SUPREMES	535
84	71	STEREOPHONICS	533
75	72	BLONDIE	530
71	73	BUDDY HOLLY	529
72	74	EAGLES	528
73	75	PERRY COMO	526
74	76	GUNS N' ROSES	525
76	77	ENGELBERT HUMPERDINCK	508
77	78	DONNA SUMMER	503
79	79	LED ZEPPELIN	501
78	80	BILLY JOEL	501
80	81	WET WET WET	498
81	82	SLADE	495
82	83	BARRY MANILOW	492
NEW	84	EMINEM	484
85	85	CHRIS REA	482
83	86	THE WHO	482
89	87	THE CORRS	475
86	88	THE EVERLY BROTHERS	474
87	89	THE HOLLIES	472
88	90	T. REX	468
96	91	KATE BUSH	464
90	92	BRYAN FERRY	462
91	93	RED HOT CHILI PEPPERS	455
92	94	BLUR	454
93	95	THE BEAUTIFUL SOUTH	452
NEW	96	BRITNEY SPEARS	451
94	97	LUTHER VANDROSS	450
95	98	JAMES LAST	450
97	99	THE MOODY BLUES	449
100	100	SHAKIN' STEVENS	448

	19 December 1992	26 December 1992	2 January 1993	9 January 1993
UK No.1 SINGLES	I WILL ALWAYS LOVE YOU Whitney Houston	I WILL ALWAYS LOVE YOU Whitney Houston	I WILL ALWAYS LOVE YOU Whitney Houston	I WILL ALWAYS LOVE YOU Whitney Houston
UK No.1 ALBUMS	GREATEST HITS 1965-1992 Cher	GREATEST HITS 1965-1992 Cher	GREATEST HITS 1965-1992 Cher	GREATEST HITS 1965-1992 Cher

TAMBA TRIO *Argentina, male vocal / instrumental group*

18 Jul 98 **MAS QUE NADA** *Talkin Loud TLCD 34* 34 2

The TAMPERER featuring MAYA (see also FARGETTA) *Italy, male production duo – Alex Farolfi and Mario Fargetta and female vocalist (3 Singles: 38 Weeks)*

25 Apr 98 ★ **FEEL IT** *Pepper 0530032* 1 17
14 Nov 98 ● **IF YOU BUY THIS RECORD YOUR LIFE WILL BE BETTER** *Pepper 0530082* 3 14
12 Feb 00 ● **HAMMER TO THE HEART** (re) *Pepper 9230032* 6 7

The TAMS *US, male vocal (Joseph Pope) group (3 Singles: 31 Weeks)*

14 Feb 70 **BE YOUNG, BE FOOLISH, BE HAPPY** *Stateside SS 2123* 32 7
31 Jul 71 ★ **HEY GIRL DON'T BOTHER ME** *Probe PRO 532* 1 17
21 Nov 87 **THERE AIN'T NOTHING LIKE SHAGGIN'** *Virgin VS 1029* 21 7

Norma TANEGA *US, female vocalist*

7 Apr 66 **WALKIN' MY CAT NAMED DOG** *Stateside SS 496* 22 8

TANGERINE DREAM *Germany, male instrumental group (16 Albums: 77 Weeks)*

20 Apr 74 PHAEDRA *Virgin V 2010* 15 15
5 Apr 75 RUBYCON *Virgin V 2025* 12 14
20 Dec 75 RICOCHET *Virgin V 2044* 40 2
13 Nov 76 STRATOSFEAR *Virgin V 2068* 39 4
23 Jul 77 SORCERER (FILM SOUNDTRACK) *MCA MCF 2806* 25 7
19 Nov 77 ENCORE *Virgin VD 2506* 55 1
1 Apr 78 CYCLONE *Virgin V 2097* 37 4
17 Feb 79 FORCE MAJEURE *Virgin V 2111* 26 7
7 Jun 80 TANGRAM *Virgin V 2147* 36 5
18 Apr 81 THIEF (FILM SOUNDTRACK) *Virgin V 2198* 43 3
19 Sep 81 EXIT *Virgin V 2212* 43 5
10 Apr 82 WHITE EAGLE *Virgin V 2226* 57 5
5 Nov 83 HYPERBOREA *Virgin V 2292* 45 2
10 Nov 84 POLAND *Jive Electro HIP 22* 90 1
26 Jul 86 UNDERWATER SUNLIGHT *Jive Electro HIP 40* 97 1
27 Jun 87 TYGER *Jive Electro HIP 47* 88 1

TANK *UK, male vocal / instrumental group*

13 Mar 82 FILTH HOUNDS OF HADES *Kamaflage KAMLP 1* 33 5

Children of TANSLEY SCHOOL *UK, children's choir*

28 Mar 81 **MY MUM IS ONE IN A MILLION** *EMI 5151* 27 4

Jimmy TARBUCK *UK, male comedian / vocalist*

16 Nov 85 **AGAIN** (re) *Safari SAFE 68* 68 2

Bill TARMEY *UK, male actor / vocalist – Bill Piddington (3 Albums: 25 Weeks, 3 Singles: 9 Weeks)*

3 Apr 93 **ONE VOICE** *Arista 74321140852* 16 4
27 Nov 93 A GIFT OF LOVE *EMI CDEMC 3665* 15 14
19 Feb 94 **WIND BENEATH MY WINGS** *EMI CDEM 304* 40 3
5 Nov 94 TIME FOR LOVE *EMI CDEMTV 85* 28 9
19 Nov 94 **IOU** *EMI CDEM 361* 55 2
18 May 96 AFTER HOURS *EMI Premier PRMTVCD 2* 61 2

'One Voice' features backing vocals by St Winifred's School Choir.

The TARRIERS *US, male vocal / instrumental group (2 Singles: 6 Weeks)*

14 Dec 56 **CINDY, OH CINDY** *London HLN 8340* [1] 26 1
1 Mar 57 **THE BANANA BOAT SONG** *Columbia DB 3891* 15 5

[1] Vince Martin and The Tarriers

TARTAN ARMY *UK, male vocal ensemble*

6 Jun 98 **SCOTLAND BE GOOD** *The Precious JWLCD 33* 54 4

TASTE (see also Rory GALLAGHER) *Ireland, male vocal / instrumental group (3 Albums: 16 Weeks)*

7 Feb 70 ON THE BOARDS *Polydor 583083* 18 11
6 Mar 71 LIVE TASTE *Polydor 2310 082* 14 4
9 Sep 72 LIVE AT THE ISLE OF WIGHT *Polydor 2383 120* 41 1

A TASTE OF HONEY *US, female vocal duo – Janice Marie Johnson and Hazel Payne (2 Singles: 19 Weeks)*

17 Jun 78 ● **BOOGIE OOGIE OOGIE** *Capitol CL 15988* ▲ $ 3 16
18 May 85 **BOOGIE OOGIE OOGIE** (re-mix) *Capitol CL 357* 59 3

TASTE XPERIENCE featuring Natasha PEARL *UK, male instrumental / production group and female vocalist*

6 Nov 99 **SUMMERSAULT** *Manifesto FESCD 64* 66 1

TATA BOX INHIBITORS (see also TRANCESETTERS) *Holland, male production duo*

3 Feb 01 **FREET** *Hooj Choons HOOJ 103CD* 67 1

TATJANA *Croatia, female vocalist – Tatjana Simic*

21 Sep 96 **SANTA MARIA** *Love This LUVTHISCDX 4* 40 2

t.A.T.u. *Russia, female vocal duo – Julia Volkova and Lena Katina (1 Album: 15 Weeks, 4 Singles: 31 Weeks)*

25 Jan 03 200 KMH IN THE WRONG LANE *Interscope / Polydor 0674562* 12 15
25 Jan 03 **ALL THE THINGS SHE SAID** (import) *Interscope 0193332* 44 2
8 Feb 03 ★ **ALL THE THINGS SHE SAID** *Interscope 0196972* ■ 1 15
31 May 03 ● **NOT GONNA GET US** *Interscope 9806961* 7 8
8 Oct 05 ● **ALL ABOUT US** *Interscope 9885763* 8 6

TAVARES *US, male vocal group (2 Albums: 15 Weeks, 10 Singles: 77 Weeks)*

10 Jul 76 ● **HEAVEN MUST BE MISSING AN ANGEL** *Capitol CL 15876* $ 4 11
21 Aug 76 SKY HIGH *Capitol EST 11533* 22 13
9 Oct 76 ● **DON'T TAKE AWAY THE MUSIC** *Capitol CL 15886* 4 10
5 Feb 77 **THE MIGHTY POWER OF LOVE** *Capitol CL 15905* 25 6
9 Apr 77 ● **WHODUNIT** *Capitol CL 15914* 5 10
2 Jul 77 **ONE STEP AWAY** *Capitol CL 15930* 16 7
18 Mar 78 **THE GHOST OF LOVE** *Capitol CL 15968* 29 6
1 Apr 78 THE BEST OF TAVARES *Capitol EST 11701* 39 2
6 May 78 ● **MORE THAN A WOMAN** *Capitol CL 15977* 7 11
12 Aug 78 **SLOW TRAIN TO PARADISE** *Capitol CL 15996* 62 3
22 Feb 86 **HEAVEN MUST BE MISSING AN ANGEL** (re-mix) *Capitol TAV 1* 12 9
3 May 86 **IT ONLY TAKES A MINUTE** *Capitol TAV 2* 46 4

Andy TAYLOR (see also DURAN DURAN) *UK, male vocalist / guitarist*

30 May 87 THUNDER *MCA MCG 6018* 61 1
20 Oct 90 **LOLA** *A&M AM 596* 60 2

Becky TAYLOR *UK, female vocalist*

16 Jun 01 **SONG OF DREAMS** *EMI Classics 8794880* 60 1
23 Jun 01 A DREAM COME TRUE *EMI Classics CDC 5571422* 67 1

Felice TAYLOR *US, female vocalist*

25 Oct 67 **I FEEL LOVE COMIN' ON** *President PT 155* 11 13

James TAYLOR (see also Carly SIMON) *US, male vocalist / instrumentalist – guitar (9 Albums: 122 Weeks, 3 Singles: 18 Weeks)*

21 Nov 70 ● SWEET BABY JAMES *Warner Bros. ES 1843* 6 53
21 Nov 70 **FIRE AND RAIN** *Warner Bros. WB 6104* 42 3
29 May 71 ● MUD SLIDE SLIM AND THE BLUE HORIZON *Warner Bros. WS 2561* 4 41
28 Aug 71 ● **YOU'VE GOT A FRIEND** *Warner Bros. WB 16085* ▲ $ 4 15

16 January 1993	23 January 1993	30 January 1993	6 February 1993
I WILL ALWAYS LOVE YOU Whitney Houston	I WILL ALWAYS LOVE YOU Whitney Houston	I WILL ALWAYS LOVE YOU Whitney Houston	I WILL ALWAYS LOVE YOU Whitney Houston
GREATEST HITS 1965-1992 Cher	LIVE - THE WAY WE WALK VOLUME TWO: THE LONGS Genesis	LIVE - THE WAY WE WALK VOLUME TWO: THE LONGS Genesis	JAM Little Angels

KEY
UK No.1 ★★ UK Top 10 ●● Still on chart ++ UK entry at No.1 ■■
US No.1 ▲▲ UK million seller £ US million seller $
Singles re-entries are listed as (re), (2re), (3re)... which signifies that the hit re-entered the chart once, twice or three times...
Peak Position / Weeks

8 Jan 72 SWEET BABY JAMES (re-issue) *Warner Bros. K 46043* ... 34 6
18 Mar 72 MUD SLIDE SLIM AND THE BLUE HORIZON (re-issue) *Warner Bros. K 46085* ... 49 1
9 Dec 72 ONE MAN DOG *Warner Bros. K 46185* ... 27 5
4 Apr 87 CLASSIC SONGS *CBS / WEA JTV 1* ... 53 5
21 Jun 97 HOURGLASS *Columbia 4877482* ... 46 1
24 Aug 02 OCTOBER ROAD *Columbia 5032922* ... 39 3
13 Sep 03 ● YOU'VE GOT A FRIEND – THE BEST OF JAMES TAYLOR *Warner Bros. 8122738372* ... 4 7

John TAYLOR (see also DURAN DURAN) *UK, male vocalist – Nigel Taylor*

15 Mar 86 **I DO WHAT I DO ... THEME FOR '9 1/2 WEEKS'** *Parlophone R 6125* ... 42 4

Johnnie TAYLOR *US, male vocalist, b. 5 May 1938, d. 31 May 2000*

24 Apr 76 **DISCO LADY** *CBS 4044* ▲ $ ... 25 7

JT TAYLOR
(see also KOOL and The GANG) *US, male vocalist (3 Singles: 5 Weeks)*

24 Aug 91 **LONG HOT SUMMER NIGHT** *MCA MCS 1567* ... 63 2
30 Nov 91 **FEEL THE NEED** *MCA MCS 1592* ... 57 1
18 Apr 92 **FOLLOW ME** *MCA MCS 1617* ... 59 2

Pauline TAYLOR *UK, female vocalist (2 Singles: 3 Weeks)*

8 Jun 96 **LET THIS BE A PRAYER** *Cheeky CHEKCD 013* [1] ... 26 2
9 Nov 96 **CONSTANTLY WAITING** *Cheeky CHEKCD 015* ... 51 1

[1] Rollo Goes Spiritual with Pauline Taylor

R Dean TAYLOR *Canada, male vocalist (5 Singles: 48 Weeks)*

19 Jun 68 **GOTTA SEE JANE** *Tamla Motown TMG 656* ... 17 12
3 Apr 71 ● **INDIANA WANTS ME** *Tamla Motown TMG 763* ... 2 15
11 May 74 ● **THERE'S A GHOST IN MY HOUSE** *Tamla Motown TMG 896* ... 3 12
31 Aug 74 **WINDOW SHOPPING** *Polydor 2058 502* ... 36 5
21 Sep 74 **GOTTA SEE JANE** (re-issue) *Tamla Motown TMG 918* ... 41 4

Roger TAYLOR (see also QUEEN)
UK, male vocalist / drums (4 Albums: 11 Weeks, 8 Singles: 18 Weeks)

18 Apr 81 FUN IN SPACE *EMI EMC 3369* ... 18 5
18 Apr 81 **FUTURE MANAGEMENT** *EMI 5157* ... 49 4
16 Jun 84 **MAN ON FIRE** *EMI 5478* ... 66 2
7 Jul 84 STRANGE FRONTIER *EMI RTA 1* ... 30 4
10 Oct 92 **RADIO** *Epic 6584367* [1] ... 37 3
14 May 94 **NAZIS** *Parlophone CDR 6379* ... 22 2
17 Sep 94 HAPPINESS? *Parlophone CDPCSD 157* ... 22 1
1 Oct 94 **FOREIGN SAND** *Parlophone CDR 6389* [2] ... 26 2
26 Nov 94 **HAPPINESS** *Parlophone CDR 6399* ... 32 2
10 Oct 98 ELECTRIC FIRE *Parlophone 4967242* ... 53 1
10 Oct 98 **PRESSURE ON** *Parlophone CDR 6507* ... 45 1
10 Apr 99 **SURRENDER!** *Parlophone CDR 6517* ... 38 2

[1] Shaky featuring Roger Taylor [2] Roger Taylor and Yoshiki

TAZ *UK, male vocalist (2 Singles: 4 Weeks)*

27 Oct 01 **LAILA** *Wizard WIZ 015* [1] ... 44 2
26 Jun 04 **CAN'T CONTAIN ME** *Def Jam UK / Mercury 9866825* ... 46 2

[1] Taz / Stereo Nation

Kiri TE KANAWA
New Zealand, female vocalist (8 Albums: 53 Weeks, 1 Single: 11 Weeks)

2 Apr 83 CHANTS D'AUVERGNE VOLUME 1 *Decca SXDL 7604* [1] ... 57 1
26 Oct 85 BLUE SKIES *London KTKT 1* [2] ... 40 29
13 Dec 86 CHRISTMAS WITH KIRI *Decca PROLP 12* ... 47 4
17 Dec 88 KIRI *K-Tel NE 1424* ... 70 3
28 Sep 91 ● **WORLD IN UNION** *Columbia 6574817* ... 4 11
29 Feb 92 THE ESSENTIAL KIRI *Decca 4362862* ... 23 10
23 May 92 KIRI SIDETRACKS THE JAZZ ALBUM *Philips 4340922* ... 73 1
9 Apr 94 KIRI! *PolyGram 4436002* ... 16 4
10 Nov 01 KIRI – THE DEFINITIVE COLLECTION *EMI Classics CDC 5572312* ... 73 1

[1] Kiri Te Kanawa with the English Chamber Orchestra [2] Kiri Te Kanawa with the Nelson Riddle Orchestra

TEACH-IN *Holland, male / female vocal / instrumental group*

12 Apr 75 **DING-A-DONG** *Polydor 2058 570* ... 13 7

Clare TEAL *UK, female vocalist*

30 Oct 04 DON'T TALK *Columbia 5186702* ... 20 3

TEAM *UK, male vocal / instrumental group*

1 Jun 85 **WICKI WACKY HOUSE PARTY** *EMI 5519* ... 55 5

TEAM DEEP *Belgium, male production duo*

17 May 97 **MORNINGLIGHT** *Multiply CDMULTY 19* ... 42 1

The TEARDROP EXPLODES (see also Julian COPE) *UK, male vocal / instrumental group (4 Albums: 45 Weeks, 7 Singles: 50 Weeks)*

27 Sep 80 **WHEN I DREAM** *Mercury TEAR 1* ... 47 6
18 Oct 80 KILIMANJARO *Mercury 6359 035* ... 24 35
31 Jan 81 ● **REWARD** *Vertigo TEAR 2* ... 6 13
2 May 81 **TREASON (IT'S JUST A STORY)** *Mercury TEAR 3* ... 18 8
29 Aug 81 **PASSIONATE FRIEND** *Zoo / Mercury TEAR 5* ... 25 10
21 Nov 81 **COLOURS FLY AWAY** *Mercury TEAR 6* ... 54 3
5 Dec 81 WILDER *Mercury 6359 056* ... 29 6
19 Jun 82 **TINY CHILDREN** *Mercury TEAR 7* ... 44 7
19 Mar 83 **YOU DISAPPEAR FROM VIEW** *Mercury TEAR 8* ... 41 3
14 Apr 90 EVERYBODY WANTS TO SHAG ... THE TEARDROP EXPLODES *Fontana 8424391 72* ... 72 1
15 Aug 92 FLOORED GENIUS – THE BEST OF JULIAN COPE AND THE TEARDROP EXPLODES *Island CID 8000* [1] ... 22 3

[1] Julian Cope and The Teardrop Explodes

The TEARS NEW (see also Bernard BUTLER; McALMONT & BUTLER; SUEDE) *UK, male vocal / instrumental duo – Brett Anderson and Bernard Butler (1 Album: 2 Weeks, 2 Singles: 5 Weeks)*

7 May 05 ● **REFUGEES** *Independiente ISOM 92SMS* ... 9 4
18 Jun 05 HERE COME THE TEARS *Independiente ISOM 49CD* ... 15 2
9 Jul 05 **LOVERS** *Independiente ISOM 95SMS* ... 24 1

TEARS FOR FEARS (141 Top 500) *Bath-based duo at the forefront of the mid-1980s 'British Invasion' of the US: Roland Orzabal (v/g/k) and Curt Smith (v/b), who left in 1991 and returned in 2003. The first of their two US No.1s, 'Everybody Wants to Rule the World', won a BRIT award in 1986 for Best Single (8 Albums: 221 Weeks, 22 Singles: 145 Weeks)*

2 Oct 82 ● **MAD WORLD** *Mercury IDEA 3* ... 3 16
5 Feb 83 ● **CHANGE** *Mercury IDEA 4* ... 4 9
19 Mar 83 ★ THE HURTING *Mercury MERS 17* ... 1 65
30 Apr 83 ● **PALE SHELTER** *Mercury IDEA 5* ... 5 8
3 Dec 83 **THE WAY YOU ARE** *Mercury IDEA 6* ... 24 8
18 Aug 84 **MOTHER'S TALK** *Mercury IDEA 7* ... 14 8
1 Dec 84 ● **SHOUT** *Mercury IDEA 8* ▲ $ ... 4 16
9 Mar 85 ● SONGS FROM THE BIG CHAIR *Mercury MERH 58* ▲ ... 2 81
30 Mar 85 ● **EVERYBODY WANTS TO RULE THE WORLD** (re) *Mercury IDEA 9* ▲ ... 2 15
22 Jun 85 **HEAD OVER HEELS** *Mercury IDEA 10* ... 12 9
31 Aug 85 **SUFFER THE CHILDREN** *Mercury IDEA 1* ... 52 4
7 Sep 85 **PALE SHELTER** (re-issue) *Mercury IDEA 2* ... 73 2
12 Oct 85 **I BELIEVE (A SOULFUL RE-RECORDING)** *Mercury IDEA 11* ... 23 4

13 February 1993	20 February 1993	27 February 1993	6 March 1993
UK No.1 SINGLES			
NO LIMIT 2 Unlimited	NO LIMIT 2 Unlimited	NO LIMIT 2 Unlimited	NO LIMIT 2 Unlimited
UK No.1 ALBUMS			
PURE CULT The Cult	WORDS OF LOVE Buddy Holly and The Crickets	WALTHAMSTOW East 17	DIVA Annie Lennox

31 May 86 ● **EVERYBODY WANTS TO RUN THE WORLD** (re-recording) *Mercury RACE 1* ... 5 7
2 Sep 89 ● **SOWING THE SEEDS OF LOVE** *Fontana IDEA 12* ... 5 9
7 Oct 89 ★ **THE SEEDS OF LOVE** *Fontana 838730 1* ■ ... 1 30
18 Nov 89 **WOMAN IN CHAINS** *Fontana IDEA 13* ... 26 8
3 Mar 90 **ADVICE FOR THE YOUNG AT HEART** *Fontana IDEA 14* ... 36 4
22 Feb 92 **LAID SO LOW (TEARS ROLL DOWN)** *Fontana IDEA 17* ... 17 5
14 Mar 92 ● **TEARS ROLL DOWN (GREATEST HITS 1982-1992)** *Fontana 5109392* ... 2 36
25 Apr 92 **WOMAN IN CHAINS** (re-issue) *Fontana IDEA 16* [1] ... 57 1
29 May 93 **BREAK IT DOWN AGAIN** *Mercury IDECD 18* ... 20 5
19 Jun 93 ● **ELEMENTAL** *Mercury 5148752* ... 5 7
31 Jul 93 **COLD** *Mercury IDECD 19* ... 72 1
7 Oct 95 **RAOUL AND THE KINGS OF SPAIN** *Epic 6624765* ... 31 3
28 Oct 95 **RAOUL AND THE KINGS OF SPAIN** *Epic 4809822* ... 41 1
29 Jun 96 **GOD'S MISTAKE** *Epic 6634185* ... 61 1
5 Mar 05 **CLOSEST THING TO HEAVEN** *Gut CDGUT 66* ... 40 2
19 Mar 05 **EVERYBODY LOVES A HAPPY ENDING** *Gut GUTCD 37* ... 45 1

[1] Tears for Fears featuring Oleta Adams

Mercury RACE 1 was a slightly changed version of Mercury IDEA 9, released to promote the Race Against Time of 15 May 1986. Oleta Adams is given no label credit on the original release of 'Woman in Chains'. Tears Roll Down (Greatest Hits 1982-1992) peaked at No.6 when it re-entered the chart in 2004.

TECHNATION *UK, male production duo*

7 Apr 01 **SEA OF BLUE** *Slinky Music SLINKY 012CD* ... 56 1

TECHNICIAN 2 *UK, male instrumental / production group*

14 Nov 92 **PLAYING WITH THE BOY** *MCA MCS 1710* ... 70 1

TECHNIQUE *UK, female vocal / instrumental duo (2 Singles: 2 Weeks)*

10 Apr 99 **SUN IS SHINING** *Creation CRESCD 306* ... 64 1
28 Aug 99 **YOU + ME** *Creation CRESCD 315* ... 56 1

The TECHNO TWINS *UK, male / female vocal duo*

16 Jan 82 **FALLING IN LOVE AGAIN** (re) *PRT 7P 224* ... 70 2

TECHNOCAT featuring Tom WILSON
UK, male producer – Tom Wilson d. 25 Mar 2004

2 Dec 95 **TECHNOCAT** *Pukka CDPUKKA 4* ... 33 3

TECHNOHEAD
(see also GTO; TRICKY DISCO) *UK, male / female production / instrumental duo – Michael Wells and Lee Newman, d. 4 Aug 1995 (3 Singles: 20 Weeks)*

3 Feb 96 ● **I WANNA BE A HIPPY** *Mokum DB 17703* ... 6 14
27 Apr 96 **HAPPY BIRTHDAY** *Mokum DB 17593* ... 18 5
12 Oct 96 **BANANA-NA-NA (DUMB DI DUMB)** *Mokum DB 17473* ... 64 1

Act was Michael Wells only on last two hits.

TECHNOTRONIC (see also HI-TEK 3 featuring YA KID K) *Belgium, male producer – Jo Bogaert (3 Albums: 62 Weeks, 10 Singles: 69 Weeks)*

2 Sep 89 ● **PUMP UP THE JAM** *Swanyard SYR 4* [1] $ ... 2 15
6 Jan 90 ● **PUMP UP THE JAM** *Swanyard SYRLP 1* ... 2 44
3 Feb 90 ● **GET UP (BEFORE THE NIGHT IS OVER)** *Swanyard SYR 8* [2] ... 2 10
7 Apr 90 **THIS BEAT IS TECHNOTRONIC** *Swanyard SYR 9* [3] ... 14 7
14 Jul 90 ● **ROCKIN' OVER THE BEAT** *Swanyard SYR 14* [2] ... 9 9
6 Oct 90 ● **MEGAMIX** *Swanyard SYR 19* ... 6 8
2 Nov 90 ● **TRIP ON THIS – REMIXES** *Telstar STAR 2461* ... 7 14
15 Dec 90 **TURN IT UP** *Swanyard SYD 9* [4] ... 42 4
25 May 91 **MOVE THAT BODY** *ARS 6568377* [5] ... 12 7
15 Jun 91 **BODY TO BODY** *ARS 4683421* ... 27 4
3 Aug 91 **WORK** *ARS 6573317* [5] ... 40 4
14 Dec 96 **PUMP UP THE JAM** (re-mix) *Worx WORXCD 004* ... 36 2
5 Nov 05 **PUMP UP THE JAM** (2nd re-mix) *Data DATA 94CDS* [6] ... 22 3

[1] Technotronic featuring Felly [2] Technotronic featuring Ya Kid K
[3] Technotronic featuring MC Eric [4] Technotronic featuring Melissa and Einstein
[5] Technotronic featuring Reggie [6] D.O.N.S. featuring Technotronic

The TEDDY BEARS *US, male / female vocal (Annette Kleinbard) trio – includes Phil Spector (2 Singles: 17 Weeks)*

19 Dec 58 ● **TO KNOW HIM IS TO LOVE HIM** *London HLN 8733* ▲ $ ... 2 16
14 Apr 79 **TO KNOW HIM IS TO LOVE HIM** (re-issue) *Lightning LIG 9015* ... 66 1

'To Know Him Is to Love Him' re-issue was coupled with 'Endless Sleep' by Jody Reynolds as a double A-side.

TEEBONE featuring MC KIE and MC SPARKS
UK, male producer – Leon Thompson and rap duo

5 Aug 00 **FLY BI** *East West EW 217CD* ... 43 2

TEENAGE FANCLUB *UK, male vocal (Norman Blake) / instrumental group (8 Albums: 25 Weeks, 16 Singles: 23 Weeks)*

24 Aug 91 **STAR SIGN** *Creation CRE 105* ... 44 2
7 Sep 91 **THE KING** *Creation CRELP 096* ... 53 2
2 Nov 91 **THE CONCEPT** *Creation CRE 111* ... 51 1
16 Nov 91 **BANDWAGONESQUE** *Creation CRELP 106* ... 22 7
8 Feb 92 **WHAT YOU DO TO ME (EP)** *Creation CRE 115* ... 31 2
26 Jun 93 **RADIO** *Creation CRESCD 130* ... 31 2
2 Oct 93 **NORMAN 3** *Creation CRESCD 142* ... 50 1
16 Oct 93 **THIRTEEN** *Creation CRECD 144* ... 14 3
2 Apr 94 **FALLIN'** *Epic 6602622* [1] ... 59 1
8 Apr 95 **MELLOW DOUBT** *Creation CRESCD 175* ... 34 2
27 May 95 **SPARKY'S DREAM** *Creation CRESCD 201* ... 40 2
10 Jun 95 ● **GRAND PRIX** *Creation CRECD 173* ... 7 4
2 Sep 95 **NEIL JUNG** *Creation CRESCD 210* ... 62 1
16 Dec 95 **HAVE LOST IT (EP)** *Creation CRESCD 216* ... 53 1
12 Jul 97 **AIN'T THAT ENOUGH** *Creation CRESCD 228* ... 17 3
2 Aug 97 ● **SONGS FROM NORTHERN BRITAIN** *Creation CRECD 196* ... 3 5
30 Aug 97 **I DON'T WANT CONTROL OF YOU** *Creation CRESCD 238* ... 43 1
29 Nov 97 **START AGAIN** *Creation CRESCD 280* ... 54 1
28 Oct 00 **I NEED DIRECTION** *Columbia 6699512* ... 48 1
4 Nov 00 **HOWDY!** *Columbia 5006222* ... 33 2
2 Mar 02 **NEAR TO YOU** (re-mix) *Geographic GEOG 013CD* [2] ... 68 1
8 Feb 03 **FOUR THOUSAND SEVEN HUNDRED & SIXTY SIX** *Poolside POOLS 3CDX* ... 47 1
4 Sep 04 **ASSOCIATION** *Geographic GEOG 29CD* [3] ... 75 1
21 May 05 **MAN-MADE** *Pema PEMA 002CD* ... 34 1

[1] Teenage Fanclub and De La Soul [2] Teenage Fanclub and Jad Fair
[3] International Airport / Teenage Fanclub

Tracks on What You Do to Me (EP): What You Do to Me / B-Side / Life's a Gas / Filler. Tracks on Have Lost It (EP): Don't Look Back / Everything Flows / Star Sign (re-recorded version of the band's first hit) / 120 mins.

Towa TEI featuring Kylie MINOGUE (see also DEEE-LITE)
Japan, male DJ / producer and Australia, female vocalist

31 Oct 98 **GBI** *Athrob ART 021CD* ... 63 1

TEKNO TOO *UK, male producer*

13 Jul 91 **JET-STAR** *D-Zone DANCE 012* ... 56 2

TELEPOPMUSIK *France, male instrumental / production trio and UK, female vocalist - Angela McLuskey*

2 Mar 02 **BREATHE** *Chrysalis CDCHS 5133* ... 42 1

TELETUBBIES *Teletubbyland / UK, male / female cuddly alien vocal group*

13 Dec 97 ★ **TELETUBBIES SAY EH-OH!** (2re) *BBC Worldwide WMXS 00092* ■ £ ... 1 32
4 Apr 98 **THE ALBUM** *BBC Worldwide Music WMXU 00142* ... 31 4

TELEVISION (see also Tom VERLAINE) *US, male vocal / instrumental group (2 Albums: 17 Weeks, 3 Singles: 10 Weeks)*

26 Mar 77 **MARQUEE MOON** *Elektra K 52046* ... 28 13
16 Apr 77 **MARQUEE MOON** *Elektra K 12252* ... 30 4

13 March 1993	20 March 1993	27 March 1993	3 April 1993
NO LIMIT 2 Unlimited	OH CAROLINA Shaggy	OH CAROLINA Shaggy	YOUNG AT HEART (Re-issue) The Bluebells
ARE YOU GONNA GO MY WAY Lenny Kravitz	ARE YOU GONNA GO MY WAY Lenny Kravitz	THEIR GREATEST HITS Hot Chocolate	SONGS OF FAITH AND DEVOTION Depeche Mode

KEY
UK No.1 ★ UK Top 10 ● Still on chart + UK entry at No.1 ■
US No.1 ▲ UK million seller £ US million seller $
Singles re-entries are listed as (re), (2re), (3re)... which signifies that the hit re-entered the chart once, twice or three times...
Peak Position / Weeks

30 Jul 77 **PROVE IT** *Elektra K 12262* 25 4
22 Apr 78 **FOXHOLE** *Elektra K 12287* 36 2
29 Apr 78 ● ADVENTURE *Elektra K 52072* 7 4

TELEX *Belgium, male vocal / instrumental trio*

21 Jul 79 **ROCK AROUND THE CLOCK** *Sire SIR 4020* 34 7

Sebastien TELLIER NEW *France, male producer / multi-instrumentalist*

8 Oct 05 **LA RITOURNELLE** *Lucky Number LUCKY 004CD* 66 1

The TEMPERANCE SEVEN *UK, male vocal (Paul MacDowell) / instrumental group (2 Albums: 10 Weeks, 4 Singles: 45 Weeks)*

30 Mar 61 ★ **YOU'RE DRIVING ME CRAZY** *Parlophone R 4757* 1 16
13 May 61 TEMPERANCE SEVEN PLUS ONE *Argo RG 11* 19 1
15 Jun 61 ● **PASADENA** *Parlophone R 4781* 4 17
28 Sep 61 **HARD HEARTED HANNAH / CHILI BOM BOM** *Parlophone R 4823* 28 4
25 Nov 61 ● TEMPERANCE SEVEN 1961 *Parlophone PMC 1152* 8 9
7 Dec 61 **THE CHARLESTON** *Parlophone R 4851* 22 8

'Chili Bom Bom' listed with 'Hard Hearted Hannah' only for the weeks of 12 and 19 Oct 1961.

TEMPLE CHURCH CHOIR *UK, male vocal / instrumental group*

16 Dec 61 ● CHRISTMAS CAROLS *HMV CLP 1309* 8 3

TEMPLE OF THE DOG *US, male vocal / instrumental group*

24 Oct 92 **HUNGER STRIKE** *A&M AM 0091* 51 2

Nino TEMPO and April STEVENS *US, male / female vocal duo – Antonio and Carol Lo Tempio (2 Singles: 19 Weeks)*

7 Nov 63 **DEEP PURPLE** *London HLK 9782* ▲ $ 17 11
16 Jan 64 **WHISPERING** *London HLK 9829* 20 8

The TEMPTATIONS 161 Top 500

The world's most successful R&B vocal group: Eddie Kendricks, b. 1939, d. 1992, Otis Williams, Paul Williams, b. 1939, d. 1973, Melvin Franklin, b. 1942, d. 1995, and David Ruffin, d. 1991. The Detroit quintet's biggest UK hit, 'My Girl', was a 27-year-old US No.1. The current line-up of the group is still doing well Stateside (18 Albums: 137 Weeks, 29 Singles: 211 Weeks)

18 Mar 65 **MY GIRL** *Stateside SS 378* ▲ $ 43 1
1 Apr 65 **IT'S GROWING** (re) *Tamla Motown TMG 504* 45 2
14 Jul 66 **AIN'T TOO PROUD TO BEG** *Tamla Motown TMG 565* 21 11
6 Oct 66 **BEAUTY IS ONLY SKIN DEEP** *Tamla Motown TMG 578* 18 10
15 Dec 66 **(I KNOW) I'M LOSING YOU** *Tamla Motown TMG 587* 19 9
24 Dec 66 GETTING READY *Tamla Motown STML 11035* 40 1
11 Feb 67 TEMPTATIONS GREATEST HITS *Tamla Motown STML 11042* ..17 40
22 Jul 67 TEMPTATIONS LIVE! *Tamla Motown STML 11053* 20 4
6 Sep 67 **YOU'RE MY EVERYTHING** *Tamla Motown TMG 620* 26 15
18 Nov 67 TEMPTATIONS WITH A LOT OF SOUL *Tamla Motown STML 11057* 19 18
6 Mar 68 **I WISH IT WOULD RAIN** *Tamla Motown TMG 641* 45 1
12 Jun 68 **I COULD NEVER LOVE ANOTHER** *Tamla Motown TMG 658* 47 1
25 Jan 69 ★ DIANA ROSS AND THE SUPREMES JOIN THE TEMPTATIONS *Tamla Motown STML 11096* [1] 1 15
29 Jan 69 ● **I'M GONNA MAKE YOU LOVE ME** (re) *Tamla Motown TMG 685* [1] $ 3 12
5 Mar 69 ● **GET READY** *Tamla Motown TMG 688* 10 9
28 Jun 69 TCB *Tamla Motown STML 11110* [1] 11 12
23 Aug 69 **CLOUD NINE** *Tamla Motown TMG 707* $ 15 10
20 Sep 69 CLOUD NINE *Tamla Motown STML 11109* 32 1
20 Sep 69 **I SECOND THAT EMOTION** *Tamla Motown TMG 709* [1] 18 8
17 Jan 70 **I CAN'T GET NEXT TO YOU** *Tamla Motown TMG 722* ▲ $ 13 9
14 Feb 70 PUZZLE PEOPLE *Tamla Motown STML 11133* 20 4
14 Feb 70 TOGETHER *Tamla Motown STML 11122* [1] 28 4
21 Mar 70 **WHY (MUST WE FALL IN LOVE)** *Tamla Motown TMG 730* [1] 31 7
13 Jun 70 **PSYCHEDELIC SHACK** *Tamla Motown TMG 741* 33 7
11 Jul 70 PSYCHEDELIC SHACK *Tamla Motown STML 11147* 56 1
19 Sep 70 ● **BALL OF CONFUSION (THAT'S WHAT THE WORLD IS TODAY)** (re) *Tamla Motown TMG 749* $ 7 15
26 Dec 70 GREATEST HITS VOLUME 2 *Tamla Motown STML 11170* 28 5
22 May 71 ● **JUST MY IMAGINATION (RUNNING AWAY WITH ME)** *Tamla Motown TMG 773* ▲ $ 8 16
5 Feb 72 **SUPERSTAR (REMEMBER HOW YOU GOT WHERE YOU ARE)** *Tamla Motown TMG 800* 32 5
15 Apr 72 **TAKE A LOOK AROUND** *Tamla Motown TMG 808* 13 10
29 Apr 72 SOLID ROCK *Tamla Motown STML 11202* 34 2
13 Jan 73 **PAPA WAS A ROLLIN' STONE** *Tamla Motown TMG 839* ▲ $ .14 8
20 Jan 73 ALL DIRECTIONS *Tamla Motown STML 11218* 19 7
7 Jul 73 MASTERPIECE *Tamla Motown STML 11229* 28 3
29 Sep 73 **LAW OF THE LAND** *Tamla Motown TMG 866* 41 4
12 Jun 82 **STANDING ON THE TOP (PART 1)** *Motown TMG 1263* [2] 53 3
17 Nov 84 **TREAT HER LIKE A LADY** *Motown TMG 1365* 12 10
8 Dec 84 TRULY FOR YOU *Motown ZL 72342* 75 5
15 Aug 87 **PAPA WAS A ROLLIN' STONE** (re-mix) *Motown ZB 41431* 31 6
6 Feb 88 **LOOK WHAT YOU STARTED** *Motown ZB 41733* 63 2
21 Oct 89 **ALL I WANT FROM YOU** *Motown ZB 43233* 71 1
15 Jun 91 ● **THE MOTOWN SONG** *Warner Bros. W 0030* [3] 10 8
15 Feb 92 ● **MY GIRL** (re-issue) *Epic 6576767* 2 10
22 Feb 92 **THE JONES'** *Motown TMG 1403* 69 1
11 Apr 92 ● MOTOWN'S GREATEST HITS *Motown 5300152* 8 9
27 Jan 01 AT THEIR VERY BEST *Universal Music TV 135782* 28 5
30 Mar 02 AT THEIR VERY BEST – TEMPTATIONS / FOUR TOPS *Universal TV 5830142* 18 1

[1] Diana Ross and The Supremes and The Temptations [2] The Temptations featuring Rick James [3] Rod Stewart with backing vocals by The Temptations
[1] Diana Ross and The Supremes with The Temptations

At Their Very Best – Temptations / Four Tops appeared only in the Compilations Chart and was not listed in the standard Top 75.

10cc 157 Top 500 (see also WAX)

Multi-talented Manchester supergroup: Graham Gouldman (who previously penned hits for The Hollies, The Yardbirds and Herman's Hermits), Eric Stewart (ex-Mindbenders and Hotlegs), Lol Creme and Kevin Godley (both ex-Hotlegs). Godley and Creme went on to have hits as a duo and produced some award-winning videos (13 Albums: 219 Weeks, 14 Singles: 133 Weeks)

23 Sep 72 ● **DONNA** *UK 6* 2 13
19 May 73 ★ **RUBBER BULLETS** *UK 36* 1 15
25 Aug 73 ● **THE DEAN AND I** *UK 48* 10 8
1 Sep 73 10CC *UK UKAL 1005* 36 5
15 Jun 74 ● SHEET MUSIC *UK UKAL 1007* 9 24
15 Jun 74 ● **THE WALL STREET SHUFFLE** *UK 69* 10 10
14 Sep 74 **SILLY LOVE** *UK 77* 24 7
22 Mar 75 ● THE ORIGINAL SOUNDTRACK *Mercury 9102 500* 3 40
5 Apr 75 ● **LIFE IS A MINESTRONE** *Mercury 6008 010* 7 8
31 May 75 ★ **I'M NOT IN LOVE** *Mercury 6008 014* 1 11
7 Jun 75 ● GREATEST HITS OF 10CC *Decca UKAL 1012* 9 18
29 Nov 75 ● **ART FOR ART'S SAKE** *Mercury 6008 017* 5 10
31 Jan 76 ● HOW DARE YOU! *Mercury 9102 501* 5 31
20 Mar 76 ● **I'M MANDY FLY ME** *Mercury 6008 019* 6 9
11 Dec 76 ● **THE THINGS WE DO FOR LOVE** *Mercury 6008 022* $ 6 11
16 Apr 77 ● **GOOD MORNING JUDGE** *Mercury 6008 025* 5 12
14 May 77 ● DECEPTIVE BENDS *Mercury 9102 502* 3 21
10 Dec 77 LIVE AND LET LIVE *Mercury 6641 698* 14 15
12 Aug 78 ★ **DREADLOCK HOLIDAY** *Mercury 6008 035* 1 13
23 Sep 78 ● BLOODY TOURISTS *Mercury 9102 503* 3 15
6 Oct 79 ● GREATEST HITS 1972-1978 *Mercury 9102 504* 5 21
5 Apr 80 LOOK HERE *Mercury 9102 505* 35 5
7 Aug 82 **RUN AWAY** *Mercury MER 113* 50 4

	10 April 1993	17 April 1993	24 April 1993	1 May 1993
UK No.1 SINGLES	YOUNG AT HEART (Re-issue) The Bluebells	YOUNG AT HEART (Re-issue) The Bluebells	YOUNG AT HEART (Re-issue) The Bluebells	FIVE LIVE (EP) George Michael and Queen with Lisa Stansfield
UK No.1 ALBUMS	SUEDE Suede	BLACK TIE WHITE NOISE David Bowie	AUTOMATIC FOR THE PEOPLE R.E.M.	THE ALBUM Cliff Richard

15 Oct 83	WINDOW IN THE JUNGLE *Mercury MERL 28*	70	2
29 Aug 87 ●	CHANGING FACES – THE VERY BEST OF 10CC AND GODLEY AND CREME *ProTV TGCLP 1* [1]	4	18
18 Mar 95	**I'M NOT IN LOVE** (re-recording) *Avex UK AVEXCD 2*	**29**	2
5 Apr 97	THE VERY BEST OF 10CC *Mercury / PolyGram TV 5346122*	37	4

[1] 10cc and Godley and Creme

From 'The Things We do for Love' 10cc were a male vocal / instrumental duo.

TEN CITY *US, male vocal (Byron Stingily) / instrumental group (1 Album: 12 Weeks, 6 Singles: 21 Weeks)*

21 Jan 89 ●	**THAT'S THE WAY LOVE IS** *Atlantic A 8963*	**8**	10
18 Feb 89	FOUNDATION *Atlantic WX 249*	22	12
8 Apr 89	**DEVOTION** *Atlantic A 8916*	**29**	4
22 Jul 89	**WHERE DO WE GO?** *Atlantic A 8864*	**60**	1
27 Oct 90	**WHATEVER MAKES YOU HAPPY** *Atlantic A 7819*	**60**	2
15 Aug 92	**ONLY TIME WILL TELL / MY PEACE OF HEAVEN** *East West America A 8516*	**63**	2
11 Sep 93	**FANTASY** *Columbia 6595042*	**45**	2

10 REVOLUTIONS *UK, male production group*

30 Aug 03	**TIME FOR THE REVOLUTION** *Incentive CENT 53CDS*	**59**	1

TEN SHARP *Holland, male vocal / instrumental duo – Marcel Kapteijn and Niels Hermes (1 Album: 2 Weeks, 2 Singles: 15 Weeks)*

21 Mar 92 ●	**YOU** *Columbia 6566647*	**10**	13
9 May 92	UNDER THE WATER-LINE *Columbia 4690702*	46	2
20 Jun 92	**AIN'T MY BEATING HEART** *Columbia 6580947*	**63**	2

10,000 MANIACS *US, female / male vocal / instrumental group – leader Natalie Merchant (3 Albums: 12 Weeks, 3 Singles: 7 Weeks)*

27 May 89	BLIND MAN'S ZOO *Elektra EKT 57*	18	8
12 Sep 92	**THESE ARE DAYS** *Elektra EKR 156*	**58**	3
10 Oct 92	OUR TIME IN EDEN *Elektra 7559613852*	33	2
10 Apr 93	**CANDY EVERYBODY WANTS** *Elektra EKR 160CD1*	**47**	3
23 Oct 93	**BECAUSE THE NIGHT** *Elektra EKR 175CD*	**65**	1
6 Nov 93	UNPLUGGED *Elektra 7559615692*	40	2

TEN YEARS AFTER *UK, male vocal (Alvin Lee) / instrumental group (8 Albums: 70 Weeks, 1 Single: 18 Weeks)*

21 Sep 68	UNDEAD *Deram SML 1023*	26	7
22 Feb 69 ●	STONEDHENGE *Deram SML 1029*	6	5
4 Oct 69 ●	SSSSH *Deram SML 1052*	4	18
2 May 70 ●	CRICKLEWOOD GREEN *Deram SML 1065*	4	27
6 Jun 70 ●	**LOVE LIKE A MAN** *Deram DM 299*	**10**	18
9 Jan 71 ●	WATT *Deram SML 1078*	5	9
13 Nov 71	A SPACE IN TIME *Chrysalis CHR 1001*	36	1
7 Oct 72	ROCK & ROLL MUSIC TO THE WORLD *Chrysalis CHR 1009*	27	1
28 Jul 73	RECORDED LIVE *Chrysalis CHR 1049*	36	2

TENACIOUS D *US, male vocal / instrumental duo – Jack Black and Kyle Gass*

13 Jul 02	TENACIOUS D *Epic 5077352*	38	35
23 Nov 02	**WONDERBOY** *Epic 6733512*	**34**	2

Danny TENAGLIA *US, male DJ / producer (3 Singles: 5 Weeks)*

5 Sep 98	**MUSIC IS THE ANSWER (DANCIN' AND PRANCIN')** *Twisted UK TWCD 10038* [1]	**36**	3
10 Apr 99	**TURN ME ON** *Twisted UK TWCD 10045* [2]	**53**	1
23 Oct 99	**MUSIC IS THE ANSWER** (re-mix) *Twisted UK TWCD 10052* [1]	**50**	1

[1] Danny Tenaglia and Celeda [2] Danny Tenaglia featuring Liz Torres

TENOR FLY *UK, male vocalist – Jonathan Sutter (5 Singles: 18 Weeks)*

6 Apr 91	**WICKEDEST SOUND** *Desire WANT 40* [1]	**43**	6
15 Jun 91	**TRIBAL BASE** *Desire WANT 44* [2]	**20**	6
7 Jan 95	**BRIGHT SIDE OF LIFE** *Mango CIDM 825*	**51**	2
7 Feb 98	**B-BOY STANCE** *Freskanova FND 7* [3]	**23**	3
9 Jul 05	**TARANTULA / FASTEN YOUR SEATBELT** *Breakbeat Kaos BBK 009SCD* [4]	**60**	1

[1] Rebel MC featuring Tenor Fly [2] Rebel MC featuring Tenor Fly and Barrington Levy [3] Freestylers featuring Tenor Fly [4] Pendulum & Fresh featuring Spyda & Tenor Fly / Pendulum featuring The Freestylers

TENPOLE TUDOR *UK, male vocal (Eddie Tenpole) / instrumental group (1 Album: 8 Weeks, 5 Singles: 40 Weeks)*

7 Apr 79 ●	**WHO KILLED BAMBI** *Virgin VS 256* [1]	**6**	8
13 Oct 79	**ROCK AROUND THE CLOCK** *Virgin VS 290*	**21**	6
25 Apr 81 ●	**SWORDS OF A THOUSAND MEN** *Stiff BUY 109*	**6**	12
9 May 81	EDDIE OLD BOB DICK & GARRY *Stiff SEEZ 31*	44	8
1 Aug 81	**WUNDERBAR** *Stiff BUY 120*	**16**	9
14 Nov 81	**THROWING MY BABY OUT WITH THE BATHWATER** *Stiff BUY 129*	**49**	5

[1] Ten Pole Tudor

The listed flip side of 'Who Killed Bambi' was 'Silly Thing' by Sex Pistols. The listed flip side of 'Rock Around the Clock' was 'The Great Rock 'n' Roll Swindle', also by Sex Pistols.

The TENTH PLANET *UK, male / female vocal / production group*

14 Apr 01	**GHOSTS** *Nebula NEBCD 015*	**59**	1

Bryn TERFEL *UK, male vocalist (5 Albums: 35 Weeks, 1 Single: 3 Weeks)*

16 Nov 96	SOMETHING WONDERFUL *Deutsche Grammophon 4491632*	72	1
23 Oct 99	**WORLD IN UNION** *Universal TV 4669402* [1]	**35**	3
28 Oct 00	WE'LL KEEP A WELCOME – THE WELSH ALBUM *Deutsche Grammophon 4635932*	33	10
3 Nov 01	SOME ENCHANTED EVENING *Deutsche Grammophon 4714252*	49	2
8 Nov 03 ●	BRYN *Deutsche Grammophon 4747032* [1]	6	11
22 Oct 05 ●	SIMPLE GIFTS *Deutsche Grammophon 4775919* [1]	10	11+

[1] Shirley Bassey / Bryn Terfel [1] Bryn

TERRA FERMA *Italy, male producer – Claudio Giussani*

18 May 96	**FLOATING** *Platipus PLAT 21CD*	**64**	1

TERRAPLANE *UK, male vocal / instrumental group*

25 Jan 86	BLACK AND WHITE *Epic EPC 26439*	74	1

TERRIS *UK, male vocal / instrumental group*

17 Mar 01	**FABRICATED LUNACY** *Blanco Y Negro NEG 130CD*	**62**	1

TERROR SQUAD featuring FAT JOE & REMY *US, male / female rap group (2 Singles: 5 Weeks)*

16 Oct 04	**LEAN BACK** *Universal MCSTD 40385* ▲	**24**	5

Hit credit on sleeve: Terror Squad featuring Fat Joe (aka Joey Crack) & Remy.

TERRORIZE *UK, male producer – Shaun Imrei (3 Singles: 6 Weeks)*

2 May 92	**IT'S JUST A FEELING** *Hamster STER 1*	**52**	3
22 Aug 92	**FEEL THE RHYTHM** *Hamster 12STER 2*	**69**	1
14 Nov 92	**IT'S JUST A FEELING** (re-issue) *Hamster STER 8*	**47**	2

TERRORVISION *UK, male vocal (Tony Wright) / instrumental group (5 Albums: 41 Weeks, 16 Singles: 55 Weeks)*

15 May 93	FORMALDEHYDE *Total Vegas VEGASCD 1*	75	1
19 Jun 93	**AMERICAN TV** *Total Vegas CDVEGAS 3*	**63**	1
30 Oct 93	**NEW POLICY ONE** *Total Vegas CDVEGAS 4*	**42**	2
8 Jan 94	**MY HOUSE** *Total Vegas CDVEGAS 5*	**29**	4
9 Apr 94	**OBLIVION** *Total Vegas CDVEGAS 6*	**21**	5
30 Apr 94	HOW TO MAKE FRIENDS AND INFLUENCE PEOPLE *Total Vegas VEGASCD 2*	18	25
25 Jun 94	**MIDDLEMAN** *Total Vegas CDVEGAS 7*	**25**	4

8 May 1993	15 May 1993	22 May 1993	29 May 1993
FIVE LIVE (EP) George Michael and Queen with Lisa Stansfield	**FIVE LIVE (EP)** George Michael and Queen with Lisa Stansfield	**ALL THAT SHE WANTS** Ace of Base	**ALL THAT SHE WANTS** Ace of Base
AUTOMATIC FOR THE PEOPLE R.E.M.	**REPUBLIC** New Order	**AUTOMATIC FOR THE PEOPLE** R.E.M.	**JANET / JANET. REMIXED** Janet Jackson

KEY UK No.1 ★ UK Top 10 ● Still on chart + UK entry at No.1 ■ US No.1 ▲ UK million seller £ US million seller $
Singles re-entries are listed as (re), (2re), (3re)... which signifies that the hit re-entered the chart once, twice or three times...
Peak Position / Weeks

3 Sep 94 **PRETEND BEST FRIEND** *Total Vegas CDVEGAS 8* 25 3
29 Oct 94 **ALICE WHAT'S THE MATTER** *Total Vegas CDVEGAS 9* 24 4
18 Mar 95 **SOME PEOPLE SAY** *Total Vegas CDVEGAS 10* 22 3
2 Mar 96 ● **PERSEVERANCE** *Total Vegas CDVEGAS 11* 5 4
23 Mar 96 ● REGULAR URBAN SURVIVORS *Total Vegas VEGASCD 3* 8 12
4 May 96 **CELEBRITY HIT LIST** *Total Vegas CDVEGAS 12* 20 3
20 Jul 96 ● **BAD ACTRESS** *Total Vegas CDVEGAS 13* 10 3
11 Jan 97 **EASY** *Total Vegas CDVEGAS 14* 12 4
3 Oct 98 **JOSEPHINE** *EMI CDVEGAS 15* 23 2
17 Oct 98 SHAVING PEACHES *Total Vegas 4961322* 34 2
30 Jan 99 ● **TEQUILA** *Total Vegas CDVEGAS 16* 2 10
15 May 99 **III WISHES** *Total Vegas CDVEGAS 17* 42 1
27 Jan 01 **D'YA WANNA GO FASTER** *Papillion BTFLYS 0007* 28 2
17 Feb 01 GOOD TO GO *Papillon BTFLYCD 0011* 48 1

Helen TERRY *UK, female vocalist*

12 May 84 **LOVE LIES LOST** *Virgin VS 678* 34 6

Todd TERRY (see also BLACK RIOT; The GYPSYMEN; ROYAL HOUSE; SWAN LAKE) *US, male producer (1 Album: 1 Week, 7 Singles: 33 Weeks)*

12 Nov 88 **WEEKEND** *Sleeping Bag SBUK 1T* 56 3
5 Aug 95 A DAY IN THE LIFE OF TODD TERRY *Sound of Ministry SOMCD 2* 73 1
14 Oct 95 **WEEKEND** (re-mix) *Ore AG 13CD* 28 3
13 Jul 96 ● **KEEP ON JUMPIN'** *Manifesto FESCD 11* [1] 8 6
12 Jul 97 ● **SOMETHING GOIN' ON** *Manifesto FESCD 25* [1] 5 10
6 Dec 97 **IT'S OVER LOVE** *Manifesto FESCD 37* [2] 16 8
11 Apr 98 **READY FOR A NEW DAY** *Manifesto FESCD 40* [3] 20 2
3 Jul 99 **LET IT RIDE** *Innocent RESTCD 1* 58 1

[1] Todd Terry featuring Martha Wash and Jocelyn Brown [2] Todd Terry presents Shannon [3] Todd Terry featuring Martha Wash

Tony TERRY *US, male vocalist*

27 Feb 88 **LOVEY DOVEY** *Epic TONY 2* 44 6

TESLA

US, male vocal / instrumental group (4 Albums: 6 Weeks, 1 Single: 1 Week)

11 Feb 89 THE GREAT RADIO CONTROVERSY *Geffen WX 244* 34 2
2 Mar 91 FIVE MAN ACOUSTICAL JAM *Geffen 9243111* 59 1
27 Apr 91 **SIGNS** *Geffen GFS 3* 70 1
21 Sep 91 PSYCHOTIC SUPPER *Geffen GEF 24424* 44 2
3 Sep 94 BUST A NUT *Geffen GED 24713* 51 1

TEST ICICLES NEW

UK, male vocal / instrumental trio (1 Album: 1 Week, 2 Singles: 3 Weeks)

13 Aug 05 **BOA VS PYTHON** *Domino Recordings RUG 205CD* 46 1
5 Nov 05 **CIRCLE SQUARE TRIANGLE** *Domino Recordings RUG 210CD* 25 2
12 Nov 05 FOR SCREENING PURPOSES ONLY *Domino Recordings WIGCD 163* 69 1

TESTAMENT *US, male vocal / instrumental group (4 Albums: 6 Weeks)*

28 May 88 THE NEW ORDER *Megaforce 781849 1* 81 1
19 Aug 89 PRACTICE WHAT YOU PREACH *Atlantic WX 297* 40 2
6 Oct 90 SOULS OF BLACK *Megaforce 7567821431* 35 2
30 May 92 THE RITUAL *Atlantic 7567823922* 48 1

Joe TEX *US, male vocalist – Joe Arlington, b. 8 Aug 1933, d. 13 Aug 1982*

23 Apr 77 ● **AIN'T GONNA BUMP NO MORE (WITH NO BIG FAT WOMAN)** *Epic EPC 5035* $ 2 11

TEXAS 130 Top 500

Named after Wim Wenders' movie Paris, Texas the Scots blues turned pop-chart mainstays are: Sharleen Spiteri (v), Ally McErlaine (g), Johnny McElhone (b), Eddie Campbell (k), all from Glasgow. Stuart Kerr, Richard Hynde and Mykey Wilson have all contributed on drums with Tony McGovern (g) the most recent recruit to a band now well established among the multi-million-selling album elite (8 Albums: 243 Weeks, 26 Singles: 143 Weeks)

4 Feb 89 ● **I DON'T WANT A LOVER** *Mercury TEX 1* 8 11
25 Mar 89 ● SOUTHSIDE *Mercury 8381711* 3 30
6 May 89 **THRILL HAS GONE** *Mercury TEX 2* 60 3
5 Aug 89 **EVERYDAY NOW** *Mercury TEX 3* 44 5
2 Dec 89 **PRAYER FOR YOU** *Mercury TEX 4* 73 1
7 Sep 91 **WHY BELIEVE IN YOU** *Mercury TEX 5* 66 1
5 Oct 91 MOTHERS HEAVEN *Mercury 8485781* 32 4
26 Oct 91 **IN MY HEART** *Mercury TEX 6* 74 1
8 Feb 92 **ALONE WITH YOU** *Mercury TEX 7* 32 4
25 Apr 92 **TIRED OF BEING ALONE** *Mercury TEX 8* 19 6
11 Sep 93 **SO CALLED FRIEND** *Vertigo TEXCD 9* 30 3
30 Oct 93 **YOU OWE IT ALL TO ME** *Vertigo TEXCD 10* 39 3
13 Nov 93 RICKS ROAD *Vertigo 5182522* 18 2
12 Feb 94 **SO IN LOVE WITH YOU** *Vertigo TEXCD 11* 28 2
18 Jan 97 ● **SAY WHAT YOU WANT** *Mercury MERCD 480* 3 10
15 Feb 97 ★ WHITE ON BLONDE *Mercury 5343152* ■ 1 102
19 Apr 97 ● **HALO** *Mercury MERCD 482* 10 7
9 Aug 97 ● **BLACK EYED BOY** *Mercury MERCD 490* 5 6
15 Nov 97 ● **PUT YOUR ARMS AROUND ME** (2re) *Mercury MERCD 497* 10 8
21 Mar 98 ● **INSANE / SAY WHAT YOU WANT (ALL DAY EVERY DAY)** (re-mix) *Mercury MERCD 499* [1] 4 7
1 May 99 ● **IN OUR LIFETIME** *Mercury MERCD 517* 4 9
22 May 99 ★ THE HUSH *Mercury 5389722* ■ 1 47
28 Aug 99 ● **SUMMER SON** *Mercury MERCD 520* 5 9
27 Nov 99 **WHEN WE ARE TOGETHER** *Mercury MERCD 525* 12 9
14 Oct 00 ● **IN DEMAND** (re) *Mercury MERCD 528* 6 10
4 Nov 00 ★ THE GREATEST HITS *Mercury 5482622* ■ 1 51
20 Jan 01 ● **INNER SMILE** *Mercury MERCD 531* 6 8
21 Jul 01 **I DON'T WANT A LOVER** (re-mix) *Mercury MERCD 533* 16 4
18 Oct 03 ● **CARNIVAL GIRL** *Mercury 9812253* [2] 9 5
1 Nov 03 ● CAREFUL WHAT YOU WISH FOR *Mercury 9865712* 5 4
20 Dec 03 **I'LL SEE IT THROUGH** *Mercury 9815221* 40 3
13 Aug 05 ● **GETAWAY** *Mercury 9872946* 6 5
12 Nov 05 **CAN'T RESIST** *Mercury 9874784* 13 3
19 Nov 05 RED BOOK *Mercury 9874219* 16 3

[1] Texas featuring Wu-Tang Clan [2] Texas featuring Kardinal Offishall

'Say What You Want (All Day Every Day)' is a new mix of the hit from 18 Jan 1997 with rapping by Method Man and RZA.

THA DOGG POUND (see also KURUPT; SNOOP DOGG)

US, male rap duo – Ricardo Brown and Delmar Amaud

11 Nov 95 DOGG FOOD *Death Row 5241772* ▲ 66 2

THAT KID CHRIS *US, male DJ / producer – Chris Staropoli*

22 Feb 97 **FEEL THA VIBE** *Manifesto FESCD 16* 52 1

THAT PETROL EMOTION *UK / US, male vocal / instrumental group (4 Albums: 8 Weeks, 7 Singles: 24 Weeks)*

10 May 86 MANIC POP THRILL *Demon FIEND 70* 84 2
11 Apr 87 **BIG DECISION** *Polydor TPE 1* 43 7
23 May 87 BABBLE *Polydor TPE LP 1* 30 3
11 Jul 87 **DANCE** *Polydor TPE 2* 64 2
17 Oct 87 **GENIUS MOVE** *Virgin VS 1002* 65 2
24 Sep 88 END OF MILLENNIUM PSYCHOSIS BLUES *Virgin V 2550* 53 2
31 Mar 90 **ABANDON** *Virgin VS 1242* 73 1
21 Apr 90 CHEMICRAZY *Virgin V 2618* 62 1
1 Sep 90 **HEY VENUS** *Virgin VS 1290* 49 4
9 Feb 91 **TINGLE** *Virgin VS 1312* 49 4
27 Apr 91 **SENSITIZE** *Virgin VS 1261* 55 4

	5 June 1993	12 June 1993	19 June 1993	26 June 1993
UK No.1 SINGLES	ALL THAT SHE WANTS Ace of Base	(I CAN'T HELP) FALLING IN LOVE WITH YOU UB40	(I CAN'T HELP) FALLING IN LOVE WITH YOU UB40	DREAMS Gabrielle
UK No.1 ALBUMS	JANET / JANET. REMIXED Janet Jackson	NO LIMITS 2 Unlimited	WHAT'S LOVE GOT TO DO WITH IT (Film Soundtrack) Tina Turner	EMERGENCY ON PLANET EARTH Jamiroquai

The MAGIC NUMBERS *Trinidad / UK, male / female vocal / instrumental group (1 Album: 28 Weeks, 3 Singles: 16 Weeks)*

4 Jun 05	**FOREVER LOST** *Heavenly HVN 151CD*	15	6
25 Jun 05 ●	THE MAGIC NUMBERS *Heavenly HVNLP 53CD*	7	28
20 Aug 05	**LOVE ME LIKE YOU** *Heavenly HVN 153CDS*	12	7
5 Nov 05	**LOVE'S A GAME** *Heavenly HVN 154CD*	24	3

The MARDOUS *UK, male vocal / instrumental trio*

20 Aug 05	**REVOLUTION OVER THE PHONE** *Poptones MC 5102SCD*	74	1

The THE *UK, male vocalist / multi-instrumentalist – Matt Johnson and backing musicians (8 Albums: 53 Weeks, 15 Singles: 52 Weeks)*

4 Dec 82	**UNCERTAIN SMILE** *Epic EPC A 2787*	68	3
17 Sep 83	**THIS IS THE DAY** *Epic A 3710*	71	3
29 Oct 83	SOUL MINING *Some Bizzare EPC 25525*	27	5
9 Aug 86	**HEARTLAND** *Some Bizzare TRUTH 2*	29	10
25 Oct 86	**INFECTED** *Some Bizzare TRUTH 3*	48	5
29 Nov 86	INFECTED *Some Bizzare EPC 26770*	14	30
24 Jan 87	**SLOW TRAIN TO DAWN** *Some Bizzare TENSE 1*	64	2
23 May 87	**SWEET BIRD OF TRUTH** *Epic TENSE 2*	55	2
1 Apr 89	**THE BEAT(EN) GENERATION** *Epic EMU 8*	18	5
27 May 89 ●	MIND BOMB *Epic 463319 1*	4	9
22 Jul 89	**GRAVITATE TO ME** *Epic EMU 9*	63	3
7 Oct 89	**ARMAGEDDON DAYS ARE HERE (AGAIN)** *Epic EMU 10*	70	2
2 Mar 91	**SHADES OF BLUE (EP)** *Epic 6557968*	54	1
16 Jan 93	**DOGS OF LUST** *Epic 6584572*	25	4
6 Feb 93 ●	DUSK *Epic 4724682*	2	4
17 Apr 93	**SLOW EMOTION REPLAY** *Epic 6590772*	35	3
19 Jun 93	BURNING BLUE SOUL *4AD HAD 113CD*	65	1
19 Jun 93	**LOVE IS STRONGER THAN DEATH** *Epic 6593712*	39	3
15 Jan 94	**DIS-INFECTED (EP)** *Epic 6598112*	17	4
4 Feb 95	**I SAW THE LIGHT** *Epic 6610912*	31	2
25 Feb 95	HANKY PANKY *Epic 4781392*	28	2
11 Mar 00	NAKED SELF *Nothing 4905102*	45	1
1 Jun 02	45 RPM – THE SINGLES OF THE THE *Epic 5044699*	60	1

Tracks on Shades of Blue (EP): Jealous of Youth / Another Boy Drowning (live) / Solitude / Dolphins. Tracks on Dis-Infected (EP): This is the Day / Dis-Infected / Helpline Operator (re-mix) / Dogs of Lust (re-mix). 'This is the Day' and 'Dis-Infected' on the EP are re-recordings of earlier hits. Matt Johnson leads The The, an informal group of his studio guests and friends.

THEATRE OF HATE
UK, male vocal / instrumental group (2 Albums: 9 Weeks, 2 Singles: 9 Weeks)

23 Jan 82	**DO YOU BELIEVE IN THE WESTWORLD** *Burning Rome BRR 2*	40	7
13 Mar 82	WESTWORLD *Burning Rome TOH 1*	17	6
29 May 82	**THE HOP** *Burning Rome BRR 3*	70	2
18 Aug 84	REVOLUTION *Burning Rome TOH 2*	67	3

THEAUDIENCE *UK, male / female, vocal / instrumental group – lead vocal Sophie Ellis-Bextor (1 Album: 2 Weeks, 3 Singles: 5 Weeks)*

7 Mar 98	**IF YOU CAN'T DO IT WHEN YOU'RE YOUNG, WHEN CAN YOU DO IT?** *Mercury AUDCD 2*	48	1
23 May 98	**A PESSIMIST IS NEVER DISAPPOINTED** *Mercury AUDCD 3*	27	2
8 Aug 98	**I KNOW ENOUGH (I DON'T GET ENOUGH)** *Elleffe AUDC 4*	25	2
29 Aug 98	THEAUDIENCE *Mercury 5587712*	22	2

THEE UNSTRUNG
UK, male vocal / instrumental group (2 Singles: 2 Weeks)

13 Nov 04	**CONTRARY MARY / YOU** *Poptones MC 5094SCD*	59	1
7 May 05	**PSYCHO** *Poptones 9870969*	41	1

THEM
UK, male vocal (Van Morrison) / instrumental group (3 Singles: 23 Weeks)

7 Jan 65 ●	**BABY PLEASE DON'T GO** *Decca F 12018*	10	9
25 Mar 65 ●	**HERE COMES THE NIGHT** *Decca F 12094*	2	12
9 Feb 91	**BABY PLEASE DON'T GO** (re-issue) *London LON 292*	65	2

THEN JERICO *UK, male vocal (Mark Shaw) / instrumental group (2 Albums: 24 Weeks, 6 Singles: 36 Weeks)*

31 Jan 87	**LET HER FALL** *London LON 97*	65	3
25 Jul 87	**THE MOTIVE (LIVING WITHOUT YOU)** *London LON 145*	18	12
3 Oct 87	FIRST (THE SOUND OF MUSIC) *London LONLP 26*	35	7
24 Oct 87	**MUSCLE DEEP** *London LON 156*	48	4
28 Jan 89	**BIG AREA** *London LON 204*	13	7
4 Mar 89 ●	THE BIG AREA *London 828122 1*	4	17
8 Apr 89	**WHAT DOES IT TAKE?** *London LON 223*	33	4
12 Aug 89	**SUGAR BOX** *London LON 235*	22	6

THERAPY? *UK, male vocal (Andy Cairns) / instrumental group (6 Albums: 24 Weeks, 13 Singles: 33 Weeks)*

8 Feb 92	PLEASURE DEATH *Wiiija WIJ 11*	52	1
31 Oct 92	**TEETHGRINDER** *A&M AM 0097*	30	2
14 Nov 92	NURSE *A&M 5400442*	38	3
20 Mar 93 ●	**SHORTSHARPSHOCK (EP)** *A&M AMCD 208*	9	4
12 Jun 93	**FACE THE STRANGE (EP)** *A&M 5803052*	18	3
28 Aug 93	**OPAL MANTRA** *A&M 5803612*	13	3
29 Jan 94	**NOWHERE** *A&M 5805052*	18	4
19 Feb 94 ●	TROUBLEGUM *A&M 5401962*	5	11
12 Mar 94	**TRIGGER INSIDE** *A&M 5805352*	22	3
11 Jun 94	**DIE LAUGHING** *A&M 5805892*	29	2
27 May 95	**INNOCENT X** *Volume VOLCD 1*	53	1
3 Jun 95	**STORIES** *A&M 5811052*	14	3
24 Jun 95 ●	INFERNAL LOVE *A&M 5403792*	9	7
29 Jul 95	**LOOSE** *A&M 5811652*	25	3
18 Nov 95	**DIANE** *A&M 5812912*	26	2
14 Mar 98	**CHURCH OF NOISE** *A&M 5825392*	29	2
11 Apr 98	SEMI-DETACHED *A&M 5408912*	21	1
30 May 98	**LONELY, CRYIN' ONLY** *A&M 0441212*	32	1
30 Oct 99	SUICIDE PACT – YOU FIRST *Ark 21 1539722*	61	1

Tracks on Shortsharpshock (EP): Screamager / Auto Surgery / Totally Random Man / Accelerator. Tracks on Face the Strange (EP): Turn / Speedball / Bloody Blue / Neckfreak. The listed flip side of 'Innocent X' was 'Belfast' by Orbital.

THESE ANIMAL MEN
UK, male vocal / instrumental group (3 Albums: 4 Weeks, 3 Singles: 3 Weeks)

2 Jul 94	TOO SUSSED *Hi-Rise FLATMCD 4*	39	2
24 Sep 94	**THIS IS THE SOUND OF YOUTH** *Hi-Rise FLATSCD 7*	72	1
8 Oct 94	(COME ON JOIN) THE HIGH SOCIETY *Hi-Rise FLATCD 8*	62	1
25 Mar 95	TAXI FOR THESE ANIMAL MEN *Hi-Rise FLATMCD 14*	64	1
8 Feb 97	**LIFE SUPPORT MACHINE** *Hut HUTCD 76*	62	1
12 Apr 97	**LIGHT EMITTING ELECTRICAL WAVE** *Hut HUTCD 81*	72	1

THEY MIGHT BE GIANTS *US, male vocal / instrumental duo – John Flansburgh and John Linnell (1 Album: 12 Weeks, 3 Singles: 18 Weeks)*

3 Mar 90 ●	**BIRDHOUSE IN YOUR SOUL** *Elektra EKR 104*	6	11
7 Apr 90	FLOOD *Elektra EKT 68*	14	12
2 Jun 90	**ISTANBUL (NOT CONSTANTINOPLE)** *Elektra EKR 110*	61	2
28 Jul 01	**BOSS OF ME** *Pias / Restless PIASREST 001CD*	21	5

THICK D (see also E-SMOOVE featuring Latanza WATERS; PRAISE CATS) *US, male producer – Eric 'E-Smoove' Miller*

12 Oct 02	**INSATIABLE** *Multiply CDMULTY 88*	35	3

THIEVERY CORPORATION NEW
US, male production / DJ duo – Rob Garza and Eric Hilton

5 Mar 05	THE COSMIC GAME *Esl ESL 081*	74	1

THIN LIZZY 128 Top 500 *Accomplished Irish hard-rock group (which at times included noted guitarists Gary Moore, Snowy White and Midge Ure) was built around distinctive singer / bass guitarist Phil Lynott, b. 1951, d. 1986. After a slow start, they wrote their own chapter in British rock history (15 Albums: 261 Weeks, 19 Singles: 128 Weeks)*

20 Jan 73 ●	**WHISKEY IN THE JAR** *Decca F 13355*	6	12
27 Sep 75	FIGHTING *Vertigo 6360 121*	60	1

3 July 1993	10 July 1993	17 July 1993	24 July 1993
DREAMS Gabrielle	**DREAMS** Gabrielle	**PRAY** Take That	**PRAY** Take That
EMERGENCY ON PLANET EARTH Jamiroquai	**EMERGENCY ON PLANET EARTH** Jamiroquai	**ZOOROPA** U2	**PROMISES AND LIES** UB40

KEY
UK No.1 ★ UK Top 10 ● Still on chart + UK entry at No.1 ■
US No.1 ▲ UK million seller £ US million seller $
Singles re-entries are listed as (re), (2re), (3re)... which signifies that the hit re-entered the chart once, twice or three times...

Peak Position / Weeks

10 Apr 76 ● JAILBREAK *Vertigo 9102 008*....10 50
29 May 76 ● THE BOYS ARE BACK IN TOWN *Vertigo 6059 139*....8 10
14 Aug 76 JAILBREAK *Vertigo 6059 150*....31 4
6 Nov 76 JOHNNY THE FOX *Vertigo 9102 012*....11 24
15 Jan 77 DON'T BELIEVE A WORD *Vertigo Lizzy 001*....12 7
13 Aug 77 DANCIN' IN THE MOONLIGHT (IT'S CAUGHT ME IN ITS SPOTLIGHT) *Vertigo 6059 177*....14 8
1 Oct 77 ● BAD REPUTATION *Vertigo 9102 016*....4 9
13 May 78 ROSALIE – (COWGIRLS' SONG) (MEDLEY) *Vertigo LIZZY 2*....20 13
17 Jun 78 ● LIVE AND DANGEROUS *Vertigo 6641 807*....2 62
3 Mar 79 ● WAITING FOR AN ALIBI *Vertigo LIZZY 003*....9 8
5 May 79 ● BLACK ROSE (A ROCK LEGEND) *Vertigo 9102 032*....2 21
16 Jun 79 DO ANYTHING YOU WANT TO *Vertigo LIZZY 004*....14 9
20 Oct 79 SARAH *Vertigo LIZZY 5*....24 13
24 May 80 CHINATOWN *Vertigo LIZZY 6*....21 9
27 Sep 80 ● KILLER ON THE LOOSE *Vertigo LIZZY 7*....10 7
18 Oct 80 ● CHINATOWN *Vertigo 6359 030*....7 7
11 Apr 81 ● THE ADVENTURES OF THIN LIZZY *Vertigo LIZTV 1*....6 13
2 May 81 KILLERS LIVE (EP) *Vertigo LIZZY 8*....19 7
8 Aug 81 TROUBLE BOYS *Vertigo LIZZY 9*....53 4
5 Dec 81 RENEGADE *Vertigo 6359 083*....38 8
6 Mar 82 HOLLYWOOD (DOWN ON YOUR LUCK) *Vertigo LIZZY 10*....53 3
12 Feb 83 COLD SWEAT *Vertigo LIZZY 11*....27 5
12 Mar 83 ● THUNDER AND LIGHTNING *Vertigo VERL 3*....4 11
7 May 83 THUNDER AND LIGHTNING *Vertigo LIZZY 12*....39 2
6 Aug 83 THE SUN GOES DOWN *Vertigo LIZZY 13*....52 3
26 Nov 83 LIFE – LIVE *Vertigo VERD 6*....29 6
14 Nov 87 SOLDIER OF FORTUNE – THE BEST OF PHIL LYNOTT AND THIN LIZZY *Telstar STAR 2300* [1]....55 10
26 Jan 91 DEDICATION *Vertigo LIZZY 14*....35 3
16 Feb 91 ● DEDICATION – THE VERY BEST OF THIN LIZZY *Vertigo 8481921*....8 17
23 Mar 91 THE BOYS ARE BACK IN TOWN (re-issue) *Vertigo LIZZY 15*....63 1
13 Jan 96 WILD ONE – THE VERY BEST OF THIN LIZZY *Vertigo 5281132*....18 11
19 Jun 04 ● GREATEST HITS *Universal TV 9821111*....3 11

[1] Phil Lynott and Thin Lizzy

Tracks on Killers Live (EP): Bad Reputation / Are You Ready / Dear Miss Lonely Hearts.

3RD BASS *US, male rap group (1 Album: 1 Week, 3 Singles: 5 Weeks)*

10 Feb 90 THE GAS FACE *Def Jam 655627 0*....71 1
7 Apr 90 BROOKLYN-QUEENS *Def Jam 655830 7*....61 2
22 Jun 91 POP GOES THE WEASEL *Def Jam 656954 7*....64 2
20 Jul 91 DERELICTS OF DIALECT *Def Jam 4683171*....46 1

THIRD DIMENSION featuring Julie McDERMOTT
UK, male / female vocal / instrumental group

12 Oct 96 DON'T GO *Soundproof MCSTD 40082*....34 2

THIRD EAR BAND *UK, male instrumental group*

27 Jun 70 AIR EARTH FIRE WATER *Harvest SHVL 773*....49 2

3RD EDGE *UK, male production / vocal group (2 Singles: 9 Weeks)*

31 Aug 02 IN AND OUT (re) *Q Zone / Parlophone CDR 6568*....15 5
8 Feb 03 KNOW YA WANNA (re) *Parlophone CDRS 6596*....17 4

THIRD EYE BLIND *US, male vocal / instrumental group (2 Singles: 6 Weeks)*

27 Sep 97 SEMI-CHARMED LIFE *Elektra E 3907CD*....33 5
21 Mar 98 HOW'S IT GOING TO BE *Elektra E 3863CD*....51 1

3RD STOREE *US, male vocal group*

5 Jun 99 IF EVER *Yab Yum / Elektra E 3752CD*....53 1

3RD WISH *US, male vocal trio*

18 Dec 04 OBSESION (SI ES AMOR) *Three8 CXTHREE 8004*....15 6

THIRD WORLD *Jamaica, male vocal (William Clarke) / instrumental group (3 Albums: 18 Weeks, 6 Singles: 53 Weeks)*

23 Sep 78 ● NOW THAT WE'VE FOUND LOVE *Island WIP 6457*....10 9
21 Oct 78 JOURNEY TO ADDIS *Island ILPS 9554*....30 6
6 Jan 79 COOL MEDITATION *Island WIP 6469*....17 10
16 Jun 79 TALK TO ME *Island WIP 6496*....56 5
6 Jun 81 ● DANCING ON THE FLOOR (HOOKED ON LOVE) *CBS A 1214*....10 15
11 Jul 81 ROCKS THE WORLD *CBS 85027*....37 9
17 Apr 82 TRY JAH LOVE *CBS A 2063*....47 6
15 May 82 YOU'VE GOT THE POWER *CBS 85563*....87 3
9 Mar 85 NOW THAT WE'VE FOUND LOVE (re-issue) *Island IS 219*....22 8

THIRST *UK, male vocal / instrumental group*

6 Jul 91 THE ENEMY WITHIN *Ten TEN 379*....61 2

1300 DRUMS featuring the UNJUSTIFIED ANCIENTS OF MU
UK, male instrumental / production group

18 May 96 OOH! AAH! CANTONA *Dynamo DYND 5*....11 4

THIRTEEN SENSES
UK, male vocal / instrumental group (1 Album: 4 Weeks, 4 Singles: 8 Weeks)

12 Jun 04 DO NO WRONG *Vertigo 9866745*....38 2
25 Sep 04 INTO THE FIRE *Vertigo 9867851*....35 2
9 Oct 04 THE INVITATION *Vertigo 9866910*....14 4
22 Jan 05 THRU THE GLASS *Vertigo 9869347*....18 3
9 Apr 05 THE SALT WOUND ROUTINE *Vertigo 9870781*....45 1

The Invitation reached its peak position on re-entry in Jan 2005.

THIS ISLAND EARTH *UK, male / female vocal / instrumental group*

5 Jan 85 SEE THAT GLOW *Magnet MAG 266*....47 5

THIS MORTAL COIL *UK, male / female vocal / instrumental group (3 Albums: 10 Weeks, 1 Single: 3 Weeks)*

22 Oct 83 SONG TO THE SIREN (re) *4AD AD 310*....66 3
20 Oct 84 IT'LL END IN TEARS *4AD CAD 411*....38 4
11 Oct 86 FILIGREE AND SHADOW *4AD DAD 609*....53 3
4 May 91 BLOOD *4AD DAD 1005*....65 3

THIS WAY UP *UK, male vocal / instrumental duo*

22 Aug 87 TELL ME WHY *Virgin VS 954*....72 2

THIS YEAR'S BLONDE
UK, male / female vocal / instrumental group (2 Singles: 8 Weeks)

10 Oct 81 PLATINUM POP *Creole CR 19*....46 5
14 Nov 87 WHO'S THAT MIX *Debut DEBT 3034*....62 3

Sandi THOM NEW *UK, female vocalist / guitarist*

15 Oct 05 I WISH I WAS A PUNK ROCKER (WITH FLOWERS IN MY HAIR) *Viking Legacy VIKINGS 04*....55 1

BJ THOMAS *US, male vocalist – Billy Joe Thomas*

21 Feb 70 RAINDROPS KEEP FALLIN' ON MY HEAD (re) *Wand WN1* ▲ $....38 4

Dante THOMAS featuring PRAS
US, male vocalist – Darin Espinoza and rapper – Prakazrel Michael

1 Sep 01 MISS CALIFORNIA *Elektra E7192CD*....25 3

31 July 1993	7 August 1993	14 August 1993	21 August 1993
UK No.1 SINGLES			
PRAY Take That	PRAY Take That	LIVING ON MY OWN (Re-mix) Freddie Mercury	LIVING ON MY OWN (Re-mix) Freddie Mercury
UK No.1 ALBUMS			
PROMISES AND LIES UB40	PROMISES AND LIES UB40	PROMISES AND LIES UB40	PROMISES AND LIES UB40

Evelyn THOMAS *US, female vocalist (4 Singles: 29 Weeks)*

24 Jan 76 **WEAK SPOT** *20th Century BTC 1014* **26** 7
17 Apr 76 **DOOMSDAY** (re) *20th Century BTC 1017* **41** 2
21 Apr 84 ● **HIGH ENERGY** *Record Shack SOHO 18* **5** 17
25 Aug 84 **MASQUERADE** *Record Shack SOHO 25* **60** 3

Kenny THOMAS
UK, male vocalist (2 Albums: 28 Weeks, 9 Singles: 54 Weeks)

26 Jan 91 **OUTSTANDING** *Cooltempo COOL 227* 12 10
1 Jun 91 ● **THINKING ABOUT YOUR LOVE** *Cooltempo COOL 235* **4** 13
5 Oct 91 **BEST OF YOU** *Cooltempo COOL 243* 11 7
26 Oct 91 ● VOICES *Cooltempo CTLP 24* 3 23
30 Nov 91 **TENDER LOVE** *Cooltempo COOL 247* 26 6
10 Jul 93 **STAY** *Cooltempo CDCOOL 271* 22 6
4 Sep 93 **TRIPPIN' ON YOUR LOVE** *Cooltempo CDCOOL 277* 17 5
25 Sep 93 ● WAIT FOR ME *Cooltempo CTCD 36* 10 5
6 Nov 93 **PIECE BY PIECE** *Cooltempo CDCOOL 283* 36 3
14 May 94 **DESTINY** *Cooltempo CDCOOL 289* **59** 1
2 Sep 95 **WHEN I THINK OF YOU** *Cooltempo CDCOOL 309* 27 3

Lillo THOMAS *US, male vocalist (1 Album: 7 Weeks, 3 Singles: 10 Weeks)*

27 Apr 85 **SETTLE DOWN** *Capitol CL 356* **66** 2
21 Mar 87 **SEXY GIRL** *Capitol CL 445* 23 5
2 May 87 LILLO *Capitol EST 2031* 43 7
30 May 87 **I'M IN LOVE** *Capitol CL 450* **54** 3

Nicky THOMAS *Jamaica, male vocalist – Cecil Thomas*

13 Jun 70 ● **LOVE OF THE COMMON PEOPLE** *Trojan TR 7750* 9 14

Ray THOMAS (see also The MOODY BLUES) *UK, male vocalist*

26 Jul 75 FROM MIGHTY OAKS *Threshold THS 16* 23 3

Rob THOMAS (see also MATCHBOX TWENTY)
US, male vocalist (1 Album: 4 Weeks, 4 Singles: 22 Weeks)

23 Oct 99 **SMOOTH** *Arista 74321709492* [1] ▲ $ **75** 1
1 Apr 00 ● **SMOOTH** (re-issue) *Arista 74321748762* [1] 3 10
28 May 05 **LONELY NO MORE** *Atlantic AT 0203CD* 11 10
11 Jun 05 ... SOMETHING TO BE *Atlantic 7567934352* ▲ 11 4
1 Oct 05 **THIS IS HOW A HEART BREAKS** *Atlantic AT 0219CD* **67** 1

[1] Santana featuring Rob Thomas

Rufus THOMAS *US, male vocalist, b. 26 Mar 1917, d. 15 Dec 2001*

11 Apr 70 **DO THE FUNKY CHICKEN** *Stax 144* 18 12

Tasha THOMAS *US, female vocalist, b. 1950, d. 8 Nov 1984*

20 Jan 79 **SHOOT ME (WITH YOUR LOVE)** *Atlantic LV 4* **59** 3

Timmy THOMAS *US, male vocalist (3 Singles: 20 Weeks)*

24 Feb 73 **WHY CAN'T WE LIVE TOGETHER** *Mojo 2027 012* 12 11
28 Dec 85 **NEW YORK EYES** *Portrait A 6805* [1] **41** 7
14 Jul 90 **WHY CAN'T WE LIVE TOGETHER** (re-mix) *TK TKR 1* **54** 2

[1] Nicole with Timmy Thomas

Jamo THOMAS and his PARTY BROTHERS ORCHESTRA *US, male vocalist and orchestra*

26 Feb 69 **I SPY (FOR THE FBI)** (re) *Polydor 56755* **44** 2

THOMAS and TAYLOR *US, male / female vocal duo*

17 May 86 **YOU CAN'T BLAME LOVE** *Cooltempo COOL 123* 53 5

Chris THOMPSON *UK, male vocalist*

27 Oct 79 **IF YOU REMEMBER ME** *Planet K 12389* 42 5

Richard THOMPSON (see also FAIRPORT CONVENTION)
UK, male vocalist / guitarist (10 Albums: 17 Weeks)

27 Apr 85 ACROSS A CROWDED ROOM *Polydor POLD 5175* 80 2
18 Oct 86 DARING ADVENTURES *Polydor POLD 5202* 92 1
29 Oct 88 AMNESIA *Capitol EST 2075* 89 1
25 May 91 RUMOR AND SIGH *Capitol EST 2142* 32 3
29 Jan 94 MIRROR BLUE *Capitol CDEST 2207* 23 3
20 Apr 96 YOU? ME? US? *Capitol CDEST 2282* 32 2
24 May 97 INDUSTRY *Parlophone CDPCS 7383* [1] 69 1
4 Sep 99 MOCK TUDOR *Capitol 4988602* 28 2
15 Feb 03 THE OLD KIT BAG *Cooking Vinyl COOKCD 251* 52 1
20 Aug 05 FRONT PARLOUR BALLADS *Cooking Vinyl COOKCD 325* 54 1

[1] Richard and Danny Thompson

Sue THOMPSON *US, female vocalist – Eva Sue McKee (2 Singles: 9 Weeks)*

2 Nov 61 **SAD MOVIES (MAKE ME CRY)** (re) *Polydor NH 66967* **46** 2
21 Jan 65 **PAPER TIGER** (re) *Hickory 1284* 30 7

THOMPSON TWINS (280 Top 500) *British-based synth-rock trio: Tom Bailey (v/syn), New Zealand-born Alannah Currie (v/prc/s), Joe Leeway (prc). Named after characters in a Tin Tin cartoon, they were joined on stage at Live Aid by Madonna and were at the forefront of the second so-called 'British Invasion' (6 Albums: 128 Weeks, 16 Singles: 110 Weeks)*

13 Mar 82 SET *Tee TELP 2* 48 3
6 Nov 82 **LIES** *Arista ARIST 486* **67** 3
29 Jan 83 ● **LOVE ON YOUR SIDE** *Arista ARIST 504* 9 12
26 Feb 83 ● QUICK STEP & SIDE KICK *Arista 204 924* 2 56
16 Apr 83 ● **WE ARE DETECTIVE** *Arista ARIST 526* 7 9
16 Jul 83 **WATCHING** *Arista TWINS 1* 33 6
19 Nov 83 ● **HOLD ME NOW** *Arista TWINS 2* **4** 15
4 Feb 84 ● **DOCTOR DOCTOR** *Arista TWINS 3* 3 10
25 Feb 84 ★ INTO THE GAP *Arista 205 971* ■ 1 51
31 Mar 84 ● **YOU TAKE ME UP** *Arista TWINS 4* 2 9
7 Jul 84 **SISTER OF MERCY** (re) *Arista TWINS 5* 11 9
8 Dec 84 **LAY YOUR HANDS ON ME** *Arista TWINS 6* 13 9
31 Aug 85 **DON'T MESS WITH DOCTOR DREAM** *Arista TWINS 9* 15 6
28 Sep 85 ● HERE'S TO FUTURE DAYS *Arista 207 164* 5 9
19 Oct 85 **KING FOR A DAY** *Arista TWINS 7* 22 6
7 Dec 85 **REVOLUTION** (re) *Arista TWINS 10* **56** 4
21 Mar 87 **GET THAT LOVE** (re) *Arista TWINS 12* **66** 3
2 May 87 CLOSE TO THE BONE *Arista 208 143* 90 1
15 Oct 88 **IN THE NAME OF LOVE '88** *Arista 111808* **46** 3
10 Mar 90 GREATEST HITS *Stylus SMR 92* 23 8
28 Sep 91 **COME INSIDE** *Warner Bros. W 0058* **56** 4
25 Jan 92 **THE SAINT** *Warner Bros. W 0080* 53 2

David THORNE *US, male vocalist*

24 Jan 63 **THE ALLEY CAT SONG** *Stateside SS 141* 21 8

Ken THORNE *UK, orchestra*

18 Jul 63 ● **THEME FROM THE FILM 'THE LEGION'S LAST PATROL'** *HMV POP 1176* **4** 15

Trumpet solo by Ray Davies.

The THORNS *US, male vocal / instrumental trio*

14 Jun 03 THE THORNS *Columbia 5113732* 68 1

George THOROGOOD and The DESTROYERS
US, male vocal / instrumental group

2 Dec 78 GEORGE THOROGOOD AND THE DESTROYERS *Sonet SNTF 781* 67 1

THOSE 2 GIRLS (see also DENISE and JOHNNY; Andy WILLIAMS) *UK, female vocal duo – Denise Van Outen and Cathy Warwick (2 Singles: 4 Weeks)*

5 Nov 94 **WANNA MAKE YOU GO ... UUH!** *Final Vinyl 74321233782* **74** 1
4 Mar 95 **ALL I WANT** *Final Vinyl 74321254202* 36 3

28 August 1993	4 September 1993	11 September 1993	18 September 1993
MR VAIN Culture Beat	MR VAIN Culture Beat	MR VAIN Culture Beat	MR VAIN Culture Beat
PROMISES AND LIES UB40	PROMISES AND LIES UB40	MUSIC BOX Mariah Carey	BAT OUT OF HELL II - BACK INTO HELL Meat Loaf

KEY UK No.1 ★ UK Top 10 ● Still on chart + UK entry at No.1 ■ US No.1 ▲ UK million seller £ US million seller $
Singles re-entries are listed as (re), (2re), (3re)... which signifies that the hit re-entered the chart once, twice or three times...

Peak Position / Weeks

THOUSAND YARD STARE

UK, male vocal / instrumental group (1 Album: 2 Weeks, 4 Singles: 5 Weeks)

26 Oct 91 **SEASONSTREAM (EP)** *Stifled Aardvark AARD 5T* 65 1
8 Feb 92 **COMEUPPANCE** *Stifled Aardvark AARD 007* 37 2
11 Jul 92 **SPINDRIFT (EP)** *Stifled Aardvark AARDT 010* 58 1
7 Mar 93 HANDS ON *Polydor 5130012* 38 2
8 May 93 **VERSION OF ME** *Polydor AARDC 012* 57 1

Tracks on Seasonstream (EP): O-O AET / Village End / Keepsake / Worse for Wear. Tracks on Spindrift (EP): Wideshire Two / Hand, Son / Happenstance / Mocca Pune.

THRASHING DOVES *UK, male vocal / instrumental group*

24 Jan 87 **BEAUTIFUL IMBALANCE** *A&M TDOVE 1* 50 3

The THREE AMIGOS *UK, male production trio (2 Singles: 8 Weeks)*

3 Jul 99 **LOUIE LOUIE** *Inferno CDFERN 17* 15 6
24 Mar 01 **25 MILES 2001** *Wonderboy WBOYD 25* 30 2

3 COLOURS RED

UK, male vocal / instrumental group (2 Albums: 4 Weeks, 7 Singles: 17 Weeks)

18 Jan 97 **NUCLEAR HOLIDAY** *Creation CRESCD 250* 22 2
15 Mar 97 **SIXTY MILE SMILE** *Creation CRESCD 254* 20 3
10 May 97 **PURE** *Creation CRESCD 265* 28 1
24 May 97 PURE *Creation CRECD 208* 16 2
12 Jul 97 **COPPER GIRL** *Creation CRESCD 270* 30 2
8 Nov 97 **THIS IS MY HOLLYWOOD** *Creation CRESCD 277* 48 1
23 Jan 99 **BEAUTIFUL DAY** *Creation CRESCD 308* 11 6
20 Feb 99 REVOLT *Creation CRECD 227* 17 2
29 May 99 **THIS IS MY TIME** *Creation CRESCD 313* 36 2

The THREE DEGREES (343 Top 500)

US R&B vocal group who became top UK stars in the 1970s: Sheila Ferguson, Valerie Holiday and Fayette Pinkney. The trio, tagged by the media as "Prince Charles' favourites", were the first girl group to top the UK chart since The Supremes in 1964 (6 Albums: 91 Weeks, 15 Singles: 113 Weeks)

13 Apr 74 **YEAR OF DECISION** *Philadelphia International PIR 2073* 13 10
27 Apr 74 **TSOP (THE SOUND OF PHILADELPHIA)** *Philadelphia International PIR 2289* [1] ▲ $ 22 9
13 Jul 74 ★ **WHEN WILL I SEE YOU AGAIN** *Philadelphia International PIR 2155* $ 1 16
10 Aug 74 THREE DEGREES *Philadelphia International 65858* 12 22
2 Nov 74 **GET YOUR LOVE BACK** *Philadelphia International PIR 2737* 34 4
12 Apr 75 ● **TAKE GOOD CARE OF YOURSELF** *Philadelphia International PIR 3177* 9 9
17 May 75 ● TAKE GOOD CARE OF YOURSELF *Philadelphia International PIR 69137* 6 16
5 Jul 75 **LONG LOST LOVER** *Philadelphia International PIR 3352* 40 4
1 May 76 **TOAST OF LOVE** *Epic EPC 4215* 36 4
7 Oct 78 **GIVING UP, GIVING IN** *Ariola ARO 130* 12 10
13 Jan 79 ● **WOMAN IN LOVE** *Ariola ARO 141* 3 11
24 Feb 79 NEW DIMENSIONS *Ariola ARLH 5012* 34 13
3 Mar 79 ● A COLLECTION OF THEIR 20 GREATEST HITS *Epic EPC 10013* 8 18
24 Mar 79 ● **THE RUNNER** *Ariola ARO 154* 10 10
23 Jun 79 **THE GOLDEN LADY** *Ariola ARO 170* 56 3
29 Sep 79 **JUMP THE GUN** *Ariola ARO 183* 48 5
24 Nov 79 ● **MY SIMPLE HEART** *Ariola ARO 202* 9 11
15 Dec 79 3D *Ariola 3D 1* 61 7
27 Sep 80 ● GOLD *Ariola 3D 2* 9 15
5 Oct 85 **THE HEAVEN I NEED** *Supreme SUPE 102* 42 5
26 Dec 98 **LAST CHRISTMAS** *Wildstar CDWILD 15* [2] 54 2

[1] MFSB featuring The Three Degrees [2] Alien Voices featuring The Three Degrees

THREE DOG NIGHT

US, male vocal / instrumental group (2 Singles: 23 Weeks)

8 Aug 70 ● **MAMA TOLD ME NOT TO COME** *Stateside SS 8052* ▲ $ 3 14
29 May 71 **JOY TO THE WORLD** *Probe PRO 523* ▲ $ 24 9

THREE DRIVES *Holland, male vocal / instrumental duo – Erik De Koning and Tom Van Empel (5 Singles: 9 Weeks)*

27 Jun 98 **GREECE 2000** *Hooj Choons HOOJCD 63* 44 1
30 Jan 99 **GREECE 2000** (re-mix) *Hooj Choons HOOJ 70CD* 12 4
17 Nov 01 **SUNSET ON IBIZA** *Xtravaganza XTRAV 27CDS* [1] 44 2
7 Jun 03 **CARERRA 2** *Nebula NEBCD 043* 57 1
14 Aug 04 **AIR TRAFFIC** *Nebula NEBCD 056* 75 1

[1] Three Drives on a Vinyl

THREE GOOD REASONS *UK, male vocal / instrumental group*

10 Mar 66 **NOWHERE MAN** *Mercury MF 899* 47 3

3 JAYS *UK, male production / vocal trio*

31 Jul 99 **FEELING IT TOO** *Multiply CDMULTY 53* 17 5

3LW *US, female vocal group (1 Album: 1 Week, 3 Singles: 13 Weeks)*

2 Jun 01 ● **NO MORE (BABY I'MA DO RIGHT)** (re) *Epic 6712722* 6 9
16 Jun 01 3LW *Epic 4989142* 75 1
8 Sep 01 **PLAYAS GON' PLAY** *Epic 6717932* 21 3
19 Oct 02 **FEELS GOOD (DON'T WORRY BOUT A THING)** *Island CID 806* [1] 44 1

[1] Naughty By Nature featuring 3LW

THREE 'N ONE (see also Billy HENDRIX) *Germany, male production duo – Sharam Khososi and Andre Straesser (2 Singles: 3 Weeks)*

7 Jun 97 **REFLECT** *ffrr FCD 301* 66 1
15 May 99 **PEARL RIVER** *Low Sense SENSECD 24* [1] 32 2

[1] Three 'N One presents Johnny Shaker featuring Serial Diva

3 OF A KIND *UK, female / male vocal / rap trio*

21 Aug 04 ★ **BABY CAKES** *Relentless RELDX 6* ■ 1 14

3SL *UK, male vocal trio (2 Singles: 10 Weeks)*

20 Apr 02 **TAKE IT EASY** (re) *Epic 6724042* 11 6
7 Sep 02 **TOUCH ME TEASE ME** (re) *Epic 6727872* 16 4

3T *US, male vocal trio (1 Album: 15 Weeks, 5 Singles: 45 Weeks)*

27 Jan 96 ● **ANYTHING** *MJJ 6627152* 2 14
24 Feb 96 BROTHERHOOD *Epic 4816942* 11 15
4 May 96 **24/7** *MJJ 6631995* 11 7
24 Aug 96 ● **WHY** *MJJ 6636482* [1] 2 9
7 Dec 96 ● **I NEED YOU** *Epic 6639912* 3 10
5 Apr 97 ● **GOTTA BE YOU** *Epic 6643645* [2] 10 5

[1] 3T featuring Michael Jackson [2] 3T: rap by Herbie

THRICE *US, male vocal / instrumental group*

18 Oct 03 **ALL THAT'S LEFT** *Island / Mercury 9811957* 69 1

The THRILLS *Ireland, male vocal (Conor Deasy) / instrumental group (2 Albums: 29 Weeks, 7 Singles: 17 Weeks)*

22 Mar 03 **ONE HORSE TOWN** *Virgin VSCDT 1845* 18 3
21 Jun 03 **BIG SUR** *Virgin VSCDT 1852* 17 4
12 Jul 03 ● SO MUCH FOR THE CITY *Virgin CDV 2974* 3 25
6 Sep 03 **SANTA CRUZ (YOU'RE NOT THAT FAR)** *Virgin VSCDT 1862* 33 2
6 Dec 03 **DON'T STEAL OUR SUN** *Virgin VSCDT 1864* 45 1
11 Sep 04 **WHATEVER HAPPENED TO COREY HAIM?** *Virgin VSCDX 1876* 22 4
25 Sep 04 ● LET'S BOTTLE BOHEMIA *Virgin CDV 2986* 9 4
27 Nov 04 **NOT FOR ALL THE LOVE IN THE WORLD** *Virgin VSCDX 1890* 39 2
2 Apr 05 **THE IRISH KEEP GATE-CRASHING** *Virgin VSCDT 1895* 48 1

	25 September 1993	2 October 1993	9 October 1993	16 October 1993
UK No.1 SINGLES	BOOM! SHAKE THE ROOM Jazzy Jeff & The Fresh Prince	BOOM! SHAKE THE ROOM Jazzy Jeff & The Fresh Prince	RELIGHT MY FIRE Take That featuring Lulu	RELIGHT MY FIRE Take That featuring Lulu
UK No.1 ALBUMS	IN UTERO Nirvana	BAT OUT OF HELL II - BACK INTO HELL Meat Loaf	VERY Pet Shop Boys	BAT OUT OF HELL II - BACK INTO HELL Meat Loaf

THRILLSEEKERS
UK, male producer / keyboard player – Steve Helstrip (2 Singles: 3 Weeks)

17 Feb 01 **SYNAESTHESIA (FLY AWAY)** *Neo NEOCD 050* [1] 28 2
7 Sep 02 **DREAMING OF YOU** *Ministry of Sound / Data DATA 36CDS*....48 1

[1] Thrillseekers featuring Sheryl Deane

THROWING MUSES
US, male / female vocal (Kristin Hersh) / instrumental group (7 Albums: 14 Weeks, 4 Singles: 6 Weeks)

4 Feb 89 HUNKPAPA *4AD CAD 901*....59 1
9 Feb 91 **COUNTING BACKWARDS** *4AD AD 1001*....70 2
2 Mar 91 THE REAL RAMONA *4AD CAD 1002*....26 4
1 Aug 92 **FIREPILE (EP)** *4AD BAD 2012*....46 1
22 Aug 92 RED HEAVEN *4AD CAD 2013CD*....13 3
28 Nov 92 THE CURSE *4AD TAD 2019CD*....74 1
24 Dec 94 **BRIGHT YELLOW GUN** *4AD BAD 4018CD*....51 2
28 Jan 95 ● UNIVERSITY *4AD CADD 5002CD*....10 3
10 Aug 96 **SHARK** *4AD BAD 6016CD*....53 1
31 Aug 96 LIMBO *4AD CAD 6014CD*....36 1
29 Mar 03 THROWING MUSES *4AD CAD 2301CD*....75 1

Tracks on Firepile (EP): Firepile / Manic Depression / Snailhead / City of the Dead.

Harry THUMANN (see also WONDER DOG) *Germany, male keyboard player*

21 Feb 81 **UNDERWATER** *Decca F 13901*....41 6

THUNDER
UK, male vocal (Danny Bowes) / instrumental group (8 Albums: 40 Weeks, 20 Singles: 55 Weeks)

17 Feb 90 **DIRTY LOVE** *EMI EM 126*....32 4
17 Mar 90 BACK STREET SYMPHONY *EMI EMC 3570*....21 16
12 May 90 **BACKSTREET SYMPHONY** *EMI EM 137*....25 4
14 Jul 90 **GIMME SOME LOVIN'** *EMI EM 148*....36 3
29 Sep 90 **SHE'S SO FINE** *EMI EM 158*....34 3
23 Feb 91 **LOVE WALKED IN** *EMI EM 175*....21 4
15 Aug 92 **LOW LIFE IN HIGH PLACES** *EMI EM 242*....22 5
5 Sep 92 ● LAUGHING ON JUDGEMENT DAY *EMI CDEMD 1035*....2 10
10 Oct 92 **EVERYBODY WANTS HER** *EMI EM 249*....36 4
13 Feb 93 **A BETTER MAN** *EMI CDBETTER 1*....18 4
19 Jun 93 **LIKE A SATELLITE (EP)** *EMI CDEM 272*....28 2
7 Jan 95 **STAND UP** *EMI CDEM 365*....23 4
4 Feb 95 ● BEHIND CLOSED DOORS *EMI CDEMD 1076*....5 5
25 Feb 95 **RIVER OF PAIN** *EMI CDEM 367*....31 2
6 May 95 **CASTLES IN THE SAND** *EMI CDEM 372*....30 3
23 Sep 95 **IN A BROKEN DREAM** *EMI CDEM 384*....26 2
7 Oct 95 BEST OF THUNDER – THEIR FINEST HOUR (AND A BIT) *EMI CDEMD 1086*....22 3
25 Jan 97 **DON'T WAIT UP** *Raw Power RAWX 1020*....27 2
15 Feb 97 THE THRILL OF IT ALL *Raw Power RAWCD 115*....14 3
5 Apr 97 **LOVE WORTH DYING FOR** *Raw Power RAWX 1043*....60 1
7 Feb 98 **THE ONLY ONE** *Eagle EAGXA 016*....31 2
28 Feb 98 LIVE *Eagle EDGCD 016*....35 1
27 Jun 98 **PLAY THAT FUNKY MUSIC** *Eagle EAGXS 030*....39 2
20 Mar 99 **YOU WANNA KNOW** *Eagle EAGXA 037*....49 1
27 Mar 99 GIVING THE GAME AWAY *Eagle EAGCD 046*....49 1
31 May 03 **LOSER** *STC Recordings STC 20032*....48 1
4 Dec 04 **I LOVE YOU MORE THAN ROCK 'N ROLL** *STC Recordings STC 20044*....27 2
5 Mar 05 THE MAGNIFICENT SEVENTH! *STC STC 20051*....70 1

Tracks on Like a Satellite (EP): Like a Satellite / The Damage Is Done / Like a Satellite (Live) / Gimme Shelter.

THUNDERBUGS
UK / France / Germany, female vocal (Jane Vaughan) / instrumental group (2 Singles: 15 Weeks)

18 Sep 99 ● **FRIENDS FOREVER** (re) *First Avenue / Epic 6676932*....5 10
18 Dec 99 **IT'S ABOUT TIME YOU WERE MINE** *First Avenue / Epic 6683972*....43 5

THUNDERCLAP NEWMAN
UK, male vocal (John "Speedy" Keen) / instrumental group (2 Singles: 13 Weeks)

11 Jun 69 ★ **SOMETHING IN THE AIR** *Track 604-031*....1 12
27 Jun 70 **ACCIDENTS** *Track 2094 001*....46 1

THUNDERTHIGHS *UK, female vocal group*

22 Jun 74 **CENTRAL PARK ARREST** *Philips 6006 386*....30 5

THURSDAY *US, male vocal / instrumental group*

27 Sep 03 WAR ALL THE TIME *Island US / Mercury 9860874*....62 1
25 Oct 03 **SIGNALS OVER THE AIR** *Mercury 9812292*....62 1

Bobby THURSTON *US, male vocalist*

29 Mar 80 ● **CHECK OUT THE GROOVE** *Epic EPC 8348*....10 10

TIFFANY
US, female vocalist – Tiffany Darwish (2 Albums: 27 Weeks, 6 Singles: 45 Weeks)

16 Jan 88 ★ **I THINK WE'RE ALONE NOW** *MCA MCA 1211* ▲....1 13
27 Feb 88 ● TIFFANY *MCA MCF 3415* ▲....5 21
19 Mar 88 ● **COULD'VE BEEN** *MCA TIFF 2* ▲....4 9
4 Jun 88 ● **I SAW HIM STANDING THERE** *MCA TIFF 3*....8 7
6 Aug 88 **FEELINGS OF FOREVER** *MCA TIFF 4*....52 2
12 Nov 88 **RADIO ROMANCE** *MCA TIFF 5*....13 11
17 Dec 88 HOLD AN OLD FRIEND'S HAND *MCA MCF 3437*....56 6
11 Feb 89 **ALL THIS TIME** *MCA TIFF 6*....47 3

TIGA *Canada, male producer – Tiga Sontag (4 Singles: 7 Weeks)*

11 May 02 **SUNGLASSES AT NIGHT** *City Rockers ROCKERS 15CD* [1] 25 3
6 Sep 03 **HOT IN HERRE** *Skint SKINT 90CD*....46 2
19 Jun 04 **PLEASURE FROM THE BASS** *Different DIFB 1028CDM*....57 1
29 Oct 05 **YOU GONNA WANT ME** *Different DIFB 1043CDM*....64 1

[1] Tiga and Zyntherius

TIGER
UK / Ireland, male / female vocal / instrumental group (4 Singles: 5 Weeks)

31 Aug 96 **RACE** *Trade 2 TRDCD 004*....37 2
16 Nov 96 **MY PUPPET PAL** *Trade 2 TRDCD 005*....62 1
22 Feb 97 **ON THE ROSE** *Trade 2 TRDCD 008*....57 1
22 Aug 98 **FRIENDS** *Trade 2 TRDCD 013*....72 1

TIGERTAILZ
US, male vocal / instrumental group (1 Album: 2 Weeks, 2 Singles: 2 Weeks)

24 Jun 89 **LOVE BOMB BABY** *Music for Nations KUT 132*....75 1
7 Apr 90 BEZERK *Music for Nations MFN 96*....36 2
16 Feb 91 **HEAVEN** *Music for Nations KUT 137*....71 1

TIGHT FIT
UK, male / female vocal group (2 Albums: 6 Weeks, 5 Singles: 49 Weeks)

18 Jul 81 ● **BACK TO THE SIXTIES** *Jive JIVE 002*....4 11
26 Sep 81 BACK TO THE SIXTIES *Jive HIP 1*....38 4
26 Sep 81 **BACK TO THE SIXTIES PART 2** *Jive JIVE 005*....33 5
23 Jan 82 ★ **THE LION SLEEPS TONIGHT** *Jive JIVE 9*....1 15
1 May 82 ● **FANTASY ISLAND** *Jive JIVE 13*....5 12
31 Jul 82 **SECRET HEART** *Jive JIVE 20*....41 6
4 Sep 82 TIGHT FIT *Jive HIP 2*....87 2

TIK and TOK *UK, male vocal duo*

8 Oct 83 **COOL RUNNING** *Survival SUR 016*....69 2
4 Aug 84 INTOLERANCE *Survival SURLP 008*....89 2

Tanita TIKARAM
UK, female vocalist (5 Albums: 62 Weeks, 9 Singles: 31 Weeks)

30 Jul 88 ● **GOOD TRADITION** *WEA YZ 196*....10 10
24 Sep 88 ● ANCIENT HEART *WEA WX 210*....3 49
22 Oct 88 **TWIST IN MY SOBRIETY** *WEA YZ 321*....22 8
14 Jan 89 **CATHEDRAL SONG** *WEA YZ 331*....48 3
18 Mar 89 **WORLD OUTSIDE YOUR WINDOW** *WEA YZ 363*....58 2
13 Jan 90 **WE ALMOST GOT IT TOGETHER** *WEA YZ 443*....52 3
10 Feb 90 ● THE SWEET KEEPER *East West WX 330*....3 7
9 Feb 91 **ONLY THE ONES WE LOVE** *East West YZ 558*....69 1

23 October 1993	30 October 1993	6 November 1993	13 November 1993
I'D DO ANYTHING FOR LOVE (BUT I WON'T DO THAT) Meat Loaf	**I'D DO ANYTHING FOR LOVE (BUT I WON'T DO THAT)** Meat Loaf	**I'D DO ANYTHING FOR LOVE (BUT I WON'T DO THAT)** Meat Loaf	**I'D DO ANYTHING FOR LOVE (BUT I WON'T DO THAT)** Meat Loaf
EVERYTHING CHANGES Take That	**BAT OUT OF HELL II - BACK INTO HELL** Meat Loaf	**BAT OUT OF HELL II - BACK INTO HELL** Meat Loaf	**BAT OUT OF HELL II - BACK INTO HELL** Meat Loaf

KEY UK No.1 ★ UK Top 10 ● Still on chart + UK entry at No.1 ■ US No.1 ▲ UK million seller £ US million seller $
Singles re-entries are listed as (re), (2re), (3re)... which signifies that the hit re-entered the chart once, twice or three times...

Peak Position / Weeks

Date	Title	Peak	Weeks
16 Feb 91	EVERYBODY'S ANGEL *East West WX 401*	19	4
4 Feb 95	**I MIGHT BE CRYING** *East West YZ 879CD*	64	2
25 Feb 95	LOVERS IN THE CITY *East West 4509988042*	75	1
6 Jun 98	**STOP LISTENING** *Mother MUMCD 102*	67	1
29 Aug 98	**I DON'T WANNA LOSE AT LOVE** *Mother MUMCD 105*	73	1
19 Sep 98	THE CAPPUCCINO SONGS *Mother MUMCD 9801*	69	1

TILLMANN and REIS
Germany, male production duo – Tillmann Uhrmacher and Peter Reis

Date	Title	Peak	Weeks
16 Sep 00	**BASSFLY** *Liquid Asset ASSETCD 004*	70	1

Johnny TILLOTSON *US, male vocalist (7 Singles: 50 Weeks)*

Date	Title	Peak	Weeks
1 Dec 60 ★	**POETRY IN MOTION** *London HLA 9231* $	1	15
2 Feb 61	**JIMMY'S GIRL** (re) *London HLA 9275*	43	2
12 Jul 62	**IT KEEPS RIGHT ON A HURTIN'** *London HLA 9550*	31	10
4 Oct 62	**SEND ME THE PILLOW YOU DREAM ON** *London HLA 9598*	21	10
27 Dec 62	**I CAN'T HELP IT** (2re) *London HLA 9642*	41	6
9 May 63	**OUT OF MY MIND** *London HLA 9695*	34	5
14 Apr 79	**POETRY IN MOTION** (re-issue) / **PRINCESS PRINCESS** *Lightning LIG 9016*	67	2

TILT *UK, male instrumental / production group (7 Singles: 8 Weeks)*

Date	Title	Peak	Weeks
2 Dec 95	**I DREAM** *Perfecto PERF 112CD*	69	1
10 May 97	**MY SPIRIT** *Perfecto PERF 139CD*	61	1
13 Sep 97	**PLACES** *Perfecto PERF 149CD*	64	1
7 Feb 98	**BUTTERFLY** *Perfecto PERF 154CD1* [1]	41	1
27 Mar 99	**CHILDREN** *Deconstruction 74321648172*	51	1
8 May 99	**INVISIBLE** *Hooj Choons HOOJ 73CD*	20	2
12 Feb 00	**DARK SCIENCE E.P.** *Hooj Choons HOOJ 87*	55	1

[1] Tilt featuring Zee

Tracks on Dark Science E.P.: 36 (two mixes) / Seduction of Orpheus (two mixes).

TIMBALAND *US, male producer / rapper – Tim Mosley (5 Singles: 16 Weeks)*

Date	Title	Peak	Weeks
23 Jan 99	**GET ON THE BUS** *East West E 3780CD* [1]	15	5
13 Mar 99	**HERE WE COME** *Virgin DINSD 179* [2]	43	1
19 Jun 99	**LOBSTER & SCRIMP** *Virgin DINSD 186* [3]	48	1
21 Jul 01	**WE NEED A RESOLUTION** (re) *Blackground VUSCD 206* [4]	20	6
13 Mar 04	**COP THAT SH*T** *Unique Corp TIMBACD 001* [5]	22	3

[1] Destiny's Child featuring Timbaland [2] Timbaland / Missy Elliott and Magoo [3] Timbaland featuring Jay-Z [4] Aaliyah featuring Timbaland [5] Timbaland & Magoo featuring Missy Elliott

Justin TIMBERLAKE (458 Top 500) (see also 'N SYNC)
Mickey Mouse Club favourite-turned boy band idol-turned solo superstar, b. 31 Jan 1981, Memphis, Tennessee. After making his name in the 30 million selling group 'N Sync, the photogenic vocalist had three successive No.2 solo singles and a million selling album (1 Album: 81 Weeks, 7 Singles: 77 Weeks)

Date	Title	Peak	Weeks
2 Nov 02 ●	**LIKE I LOVE YOU** *Jive 9254342*	2	16
16 Nov 02 ★	JUSTIFIED *Jive 9224772*	1	81
15 Feb 03 ●	**CRY ME A RIVER** *Jive 9254612*	2	12
15 Mar 03 ●	**WORK IT** *Universal MCSCD 40312* [1]	7	11
24 May 03	**ROCK YOUR BODY** (import) *Jive 9254962*	46	1
31 May 03 ●	**ROCK YOUR BODY** *Jive 9254952*	2	13
27 Sep 03	**SEÑORITA** *Jive 82876563442*	13	8
7 May 05 ●	**SIGNS** *Geffen 9881781* [2]	2	16

[1] Nelly featuring Justin Timberlake [2] Snoop Dogg featuring Charlie Wilson and Justin Timberlake

TIMBUK 3 *US, male / female vocal / instrumental duo – Pat and Barbara Kooyman MacDonald*

Date	Title	Peak	Weeks
31 Jan 87	**THE FUTURE'S SO BRIGHT I GOTTA WEAR SHADES** *IRS IRM 126*	21	7
14 Feb 87	GREETINGS FROM TIMBUK 3 *IRS MIRF 1015*	51	4

TIME *US, male vocal / instrumental group*

Date	Title	Peak	Weeks
28 Jul 90	PANDEMONIUM *Paisley Park WX 336*	66	1

The TIME FREQUENCY *UK, male / female vocal (Mary Kiani) instrumental / production group (1 Album: 4 Weeks, 7 Singles: 34 Weeks)*

Date	Title	Peak	Weeks
6 Jun 92	**REAL LOVE** *Jive JIVET 307*	60	1
9 Jan 93	**NEW EMOTION** *Internal Affairs KGBCD 009*	36	6
12 Jun 93	**THE POWER ZONE (EP)** *Internal Affairs KGBD 010*	17	11
6 Nov 93 ●	**REAL LOVE** (re) (re-mix) *Internal Affairs KGBCD 011*	8	8
28 May 94	**SUCH A PHANTASY** *Internal Affairs KGBD 013*	25	4
18 Jun 94	DOMINATOR *Internal Affairs KGBD 500*	23	4
8 Oct 94	**DREAMSCAPE '94** *Internal Affairs KGBD 015*	32	3
31 Aug 02	**REAL LOVE** (re-mix) *Jive 9253782*	43	1

Tracks on The Power Zone (EP): The Ultimate High / The Ultimate High (full length) / The Power Zone / Take Me Away.

TIME OF THE MUMPH *UK, male producer – Mark Mumford*

Date	Title	Peak	Weeks
11 Feb 95	**CONTROL** *Fresh FRSHD 24*	69	1

TIME UK *UK, male vocal / instrumental group*

Date	Title	Peak	Weeks
8 Oct 83	**THE CABARET** *Red Bus / Aroadia TIM 123*	63	3

TIME ZONE *UK / US, male vocal / instrumental duo*

Date	Title	Peak	Weeks
19 Jan 85	**WORLD DESTRUCTION** *Virgin VS 743*	44	9

TIMEBOX *UK, male vocal / instrumental group*

Date	Title	Peak	Weeks
24 Jul 68	**BEGGIN'** *Deram DM 194*	38	4

The TIMELORDS (see also JUSTIFIED ANCIENTS OF MU MU; The KLF; 2K) *UK, male vocal / instrumental group*

Date	Title	Peak	Weeks
4 Jun 88 ★	**DOCTORIN' THE TARDIS** *KLF Communications KLF 003*	1	9

TIMEX SOCIAL CLUB *US, male vocal / instrumental group*

Date	Title	Peak	Weeks
13 Sep 86	**RUMORS** *Cooltempo COOL 133*	13	9

TIN MACHINE (see also David BOWIE) *US / UK, male vocal / instrumental group (2 Albums: 12 Weeks, 4 Singles: 10 Weeks)*

Date	Title	Peak	Weeks
3 Jun 89 ●	TIN MACHINE *EMI-USA MTLS 1044*	3	9
1 Jul 89	**UNDER THE GOD** *EMI-USA MT 68*	51	2
9 Sep 89	**TIN MACHINE / MAGGIE'S FARM (LIVE)** *EMI-USA MT 73*	48	2
24 Aug 91	**YOU BELONG IN ROCK 'N' ROLL** *London LON 305*	33	3
14 Sep 91	TIN MACHINE II *London 8282721*	23	3
2 Nov 91	**BABY UNIVERSAL** *London LON 310*	48	3

TIN TIN OUT *UK, male instrumental / production duo – Lindsay Edwards and Darren Stokes (1 Album: 1 Week, 9 Singles: 42 Weeks)*

Date	Title	Peak	Weeks
13 Aug 94	**THE FEELING** *Deep Distraxion OILYCD 029* [1]	32	2
25 Mar 95	**ALWAYS SOMETHING THERE TO REMIND ME** *WEA YZ 91§1CD* [2]	14	5
5 Oct 96	ADVENTURES IN TIN TIN OUT LAND *VC Recordings VCRLPX 1*	65	1
8 Feb 97	**ALL I WANNA DO** *VC VCRD 15*	31	2
10 May 97	**DANCE WITH ME** *VC VCRD 17* [3]	35	2
20 Sep 97	**STRINGS FOR YASMIN** *VC VCRD 20*	31	3
28 Mar 98 ●	**HERE'S WHERE THE STORY ENDS** *VC Recordings VCRD 30* [4]	7	10
12 Sep 98	**SOMETIMES** *VC Recordings VCRD 34* [4]	20	4

	20 November 1993	27 November 1993	4 December 1993	11 December 1993
UK No.1 SINGLES	I'D DO ANYTHING FOR LOVE (BUT I WON'T DO THAT) Meat Loaf	I'D DO ANYTHING FOR LOVE (BUT I WON'T DO THAT) Meat Loaf	I'D DO ANYTHING FOR LOVE (BUT I WON'T DO THAT) Meat Loaf	MR BLOBBY Mr Blobby
UK No.1 ALBUMS	BOTH SIDES Phil Collins	BAT OUT OF HELL II - BACK INTO HELL Meat Loaf	BAT OUT OF HELL II - BACK INTO HELL Meat Loaf	BAT OUT OF HELL II - BACK INTO HELL Meat Loaf

11 Sep 99 **ELEVEN TO FLY** *VC Recordings VCRDX 52* [5] 26 2
13 Nov 99 ● **WHAT I AM** *VC Recordings VCRD 53* [6] 2 12

[1] Tin Tin Out featuring Sweet Tee [2] Tin Tin Out featuring Espiritu
[3] Tin Tin Out featuring Tony Hadley [4] Tin Tin Out featuring Shelley Nelson
[5] Tin Tin Out featuring Wendy Page [6] Tin Tin Out featuring Emma Bunton

TINDERSTICKS
UK, male vocal / instrumental group (6 Albums: 9 Weeks, 7 Singles: 7 Weeks)

23 Oct 93 TINDERSTICKS *This Way Up 5183064* 56 1
5 Feb 94 **KATHLEEN (EP)** *This Way Up WAY 2833CD* 61 1
18 Mar 95 **NO MORE AFFAIRS** *This Way Up WAY 3833* 58 1
15 Apr 95 THE SECOND TINDERSTICKS ALBUM *This Way Up 5263032* 13 3
12 Aug 95 **TRAVELLING LIGHT** *This Way Up WAY 4533* 51 1
28 Oct 95 THE BLOOMSBURY THEATRE 12.3.95 *This Way Up 5285972* 32 1
7 Jun 97 **BATHTIME** *This Way Up WAY 6166* 38 1
21 Jun 97 CURTAINS *This Way Up 5243442* 37 2
1 Nov 97 **RENTED ROOMS** *This Way Up WAY 6566* 56 1
4 Sep 99 **CAN WE START AGAIN?** *Island CID 756* 54 1
18 Sep 99 SIMPLE PLEASURE *Island CID 8085* 36 1
2 Jun 01 CAN OUR LOVE ... *Beggars Banquet BBQCD 222* 47 1
2 Aug 03 **SOMETIMES IT HURTS** *Beggars Banquet BBQ 369CD* 60 1

Tracks on Kathleen (EP): Kathleen / Summat Moon / A Sweet Sweet Man / E-Type Joe.

TINGO TANGO *UK, male instrumental group*

21 Jul 90 **IT IS JAZZ** *Champion CHAMP 250* 68 2

TINMAN *UK, male producer – Paul Dakeyne (2 Singles: 9 Weeks)*

20 Aug 94 ● **EIGHTEEN STRINGS** *ffrr FCD 242* 9 8
3 Jun 95 **GUDVIBE** *ffrr FCD 262* 49 1

TINY TIM
US, male vocalist / banjo – Herbert Khaury, b. 12 Apr 1930, d. 30 Nov 1996

5 Feb 69 **GREAT BALLS OF FIRE** *Reprise RS 20802* 45 1

Rob TISSERA, VINYLGROOVER & The RED HED
UK, male production trio (2 Singles: 1 Week)

10 Jul 04 **STAY** *Tidy Trax TIDYTWO 133C* 61 1

TITANIC *Norway / UK, male instrumental group*

25 Sep 71 ● **SULTANA** *CBS 5365* 5 12

TITIYO *Sweden, female vocalist – Titiyo Jah (3 Singles: 6 Weeks)*

3 Mar 90 **AFTER THE RAIN** *Arista 112722* 60 3
6 Oct 90 **FLOWERS** *Arista 113212* 71 1
5 Feb 94 **TELL ME I'M NOT DREAMING** *Arista 74321185622* 45 2

Art and Dotty TODD
US, male / female vocal duo – Dotty Todd, b. 22 Jun 1913, d. 12 Dec 2000

13 Feb 53 ● **BROKEN WINGS** *HMV B 10399* 6 7

TOGETHER *UK, male vocal / instrumental group*

4 Aug 90 **HARDCORE UPROAR** *ffrr F 143* 12 8

TOGETHER (see also DAFT PUNK) *France, male production duo – Thomas Bangalter and DJ Falcon (Martial Weiss)*

4 Jan 03 **SO MUCH LOVE TO GIVE** (import) *Roule TOGETHER 2* 71 1

The TOKENS *US, male vocal group*

21 Dec 61 **THE LION SLEEPS TONIGHT (WIMOWEH)** *RCA 1263* ▲ $ 11 12

TOKYO DRAGONS
UK, male vocal / instrumental group (3 Singles: 3 Weeks)

26 Jun 04 **TEENAGE SCREAMERS** *Island CID 864* 61 1
23 Oct 04 **GET 'EM OFF!** *Island CID 876* 75 1
5 Mar 05 **WHAT THE HELL** *Island CID 883* 59 1

TOKYO GHETTO PUSSY (see also JAM & SPOON featuring PLAVKA; STORM) *Germany, male instrumental / production duo – Rolf Ellmer and Markus Löeffel, b. 27 Nov 1966, d. 11 Jan 2006 (2 Singles: 4 Weeks)*

16 Sep 95 **EVERYBODY ON THE FLOOR (PUMP IT)** *Epic 6611132* 26 2
16 Mar 96 **I KISS YOUR LIPS** *Epic 6623212* 55 2

TOL and TOL *Holland, male vocal / instrumental duo*

14 Apr 90 **ELENI** *Dover ROJ 5* 73 2

TOM TOM CLUB (see also TALKING HEADS) *US, female / male vocal / instrumental group (1 Album: 1 Week, 3 Singles: 20 Weeks)*

20 Jun 81 ● **WORDY RAPPINGHOOD** *Island WIP 6694* 7 9
10 Oct 81 **GENIUS OF LOVE** *Island WIP 6735* 65 2
24 Oct 81 TOM TOM CLUB *Island ILPS 9686* 78 1
7 Aug 82 **UNDER THE BOARDWALK** *Island WIP 6762* 22 9

TOMBA VIRA (see also CHOCOLATE PUMA; GOODMEN; JARK PRONGO; RHYTHMKILLAZ; RIVA featuring Dannii MINOGUE) *Holland, male production duo – Rene ter Horst and Gaston Steenkist*

16 Jun 01 **THE SOUND OF: OH YEAH** *VC Recordings VCRD 88* 51 1

TOMCAT *UK, male vocal / instrumental group*

14 Oct 00 **CRAZY** *Virgin VSCDT 1785* 48 1

TOMCRAFT
Germany, male producer – Thomas Bruckner (2 Singles: 15 Weeks)

10 May 03 ★ **LONELINESS** *Data / Ministry of Sound DATA 52CDS* ■ 1 13
25 Oct 03 **BRAINWASHED (CALL YOU)** *Data DATA 63CDS* 43 2

TOMITA *Japan, male synthesizer player – Isao Tomita (4 Albums: 33 Weeks)*

7 Jun 75 SNOWFLAKES ARE DANCING *RCA Red Seal ARL 10488* 17 20
16 Aug 75 PICTURES AT AN EXHIBITION *RCA Red Seal ARL 10838* 42 5
7 May 77 HOLST: THE PLANETS *RCA Red Seal RL 11919* 41 6
9 Feb 80 TOMITA'S GREATEST HITS *RCA Red Seal RL 43076* 66 2

Ricky TOMLINSON *UK, male actor / vocalist – Eric Tomlinson*

10 Nov 01 **ARE YOU LOOKIN' AT ME?**
All Around the World CDRICKY 1 ....28 3

TOMMI *UK, female vocal group*

5 Jul 03 **LIKE WHAT** *Sony Music 6739095* 12 8

TOMSKI *UK, male producer – Tom Jankiewicz (2 Singles: 3 Weeks)*

18 Apr 98 **14 HOURS TO SAVE THE EARTH** *Xtravaganza 0091515 EXT* 42 1
12 Feb 00 **LOVE WILL COME** *Xtravaganza XTRAV 6CDS* [1] 31 2

[1] Tomski featuring Jan Johnston

TONE LOC
US, male rapper – Anthony Smith (1 Album: 16 Weeks, 3 Singles: 19 Weeks)

11 Feb 89 **WILD THING / LOC'ED AFTER DARK**
Fourth & Broadway BRW 121 $ 21 8
25 Mar 89 LOC'ED AFTER DARK *Delicious BRLP 526* ▲ 22 16
20 May 89 **FUNKY COLD MEDINA / ON FIRE**
Fourth & Broadway BRW 129 $ 13 9
5 Aug 89 **I GOT IT GOIN' ON** *Fourth & Broadway BRW 140* 55 2

TONGUE 'N' CHEEK *UK, male / female vocal / instrumental group (1 Album: 3 Weeks, 5 Singles: 28 Weeks)*

27 Feb 88 **NOBODY (CAN LOVE ME)** *Criminal BUS 6* [1] 59 6
25 Nov 89 **ENCORE** *Syncopate SY 33* 41 4
14 Apr 90 **TOMORROW** *Syncopate SY 34* 20 7

18 December 1993	25 December 1993	1 January 1994	8 January 1994
BABE Take That	**MR BLOBBY** Mr Blobby	**MR BLOBBY** Mr Blobby	**TWIST AND SHOUT** Chaka Demus and Pliers featuring Jack Radics and Taxi Gang
BAT OUT OF HELL II - BACK INTO HELL Meat Loaf	**BAT OUT OF HELL II - BACK INTO HELL** Meat Loaf	**ONE WOMAN - THE ULTIMATE COLLECTION** Diana Ross	**EVERYTHING CHANGES** Take That

KEY: UK No.1 ★ UK Top 10 ● Still on chart + UK entry at No.1 ■ US No.1 ▲ UK million seller £ US million seller $
Singles re-entries are listed as (re), (2re), (3re)... which signifies that the hit re-entered the chart once, twice or three times...
Peak Position / Weeks

4 Aug 90 **NOBODY** (re-recording) *Syncopate SY 37* 37 5
22 Sep 90 **THIS IS TONGUE 'N' CHEEK** *Syncopate SYLP 6006* 45 3
19 Jan 91 **FORGET ME NOTS** *Syncopate SY 39* 26 6

1 Tongue in Cheek

TONIGHT *UK, male vocal / instrumental group (2 Singles: 10 Weeks)*

28 Jan 78 **DRUMMER MAN** *TDS TDS 1* 14 8
20 May 78 **MONEY THAT'S YOUR PROBLEM** *TDS TDS 2* 66 2

TONY TONI TONÉ (see also Raphael SAADIQ) *US, male vocal group (1 Album: 1 Week, 8 Singles: 12 Weeks)*

30 Jun 90 **OAKLAND STROKE** *Wing WING 7* 1 50 5
9 Mar 91 **IT NEVER RAINS (IN SOUTHERN CALIFORNIA)** *Wing WING 10* 1 69 2
4 Sep 93 **IF I HAD NO LOOT** *Polydor PZCD 292* 44 3
2 Oct 93 **SONS OF SOUL** *Polydor 5149332* 1 66 1
3 May 97 **LET'S GET DOWN** *Mercury MERCD 485* 2 33 2

1 Tony! Toni! Toné! 2 Tony Toni Toné featuring DJ Quick 1 Tony! Toni! Toné!

TOOL *US, male vocal / instrumental group*

26 May 01 **LATERALUS** *Tool Dissectional 9210132* ▲ 16 3

TOP *UK, male vocal / instrumental group*

20 Jul 91 **NUMBER ONE DOMINATOR** *Island IS 496* 67 2

Martina TOPLEY-BIRD *UK, female vocalist*

26 Jul 03 **QUIXOTIC** *Independiente ISOM 34CD* 70 1

TOPLOADER *UK, male vocal (Joseph Washbourn) / instrumental group (2 Albums: 66 Weeks, 8 Singles: 56 Weeks)*

22 May 99 **ACHILLES HEEL** *Sony S2 6671612* 64 1
7 Aug 99 **LET THE PEOPLE KNOW** *Sony S2 6677132* 52 1
4 Mar 00 **DANCING IN THE MOONLIGHT** *Sony S2 6689412* 19 7
13 May 00 ● **ACHILLES HEEL** (re-issue) *Sony S2 6691872* 8 7
3 Jun 00 ● **ONKA'S BIG MOKA** *Sony S2 4947802* 4 61
2 Sep 00 **JUST HOLD ON** *Sony S2 6696242* 20 4
25 Nov 00 ● **DANCING IN THE MOONLIGHT** (re-issue) *Sony S2 6699852* 7 25
21 Apr 01 **ONLY FOR A WHILE** *Sony S2 S2 6708612* 19 4
17 Aug 02 **TIME OF MY LIFE** *Sony S2 S2 6728862* 18 7
31 Aug 02 ● **MAGIC HOTEL** *Sony S2 5084712* 3 5

TOPOL *Israel, male vocalist / actor – Chaim Topol*

20 Apr 67 ● **IF I WERE A RICH MAN** *CBS 202651* 9 20
11 May 85 **TOPOL'S ISRAEL** *BBC REH 529* 80 1

Bernie TORMÉ (see also GILLAN) *Ireland, male vocalist / guitarist*

3 Jul 82 **TURN OUT THE LIGHTS** *Kamaflage KAMLP 2* 50 3

Mel TORMÉ *US, male vocalist, b. 13 Sep 1925, d. 5 Jun 1999 (2 Albums: 8 Weeks, 2 Singles: 32 Weeks)*

27 Apr 56 ● **MOUNTAIN GREENERY** (re) *Vogue / Coral Q 72150* 4 24
28 Jul 56 ● **MEL TORMÉ AT THE CRESCENDO** *Vogue-Coral LVA 9004* 3 4
18 Aug 56 ● **MEL TORMÉ WITH THE MARTY PAICH DEK-TETTE** *London Jazz LTZ N 15009* 3 4
3 Jan 63 **COMIN' HOME BABY** *London HLK 9643* 13 8

The TORNADOS *UK, male instrumental group – includes Heinz (5 Singles: 59 Weeks)*

30 Aug 62 ★ **TELSTAR** *Decca F 11494* ▲ $ 1 25
10 Jan 63 ● **GLOBETROTTER** *Decca F 11562* 5 11
21 Mar 63 **ROBOT** *Decca F 11606* 17 12
6 Jun 63 **THE ICE CREAM MAN** *Decca F 11662* 18 9
10 Oct 63 **DRAGONFLY** *Decca F 11745* 41 2

Mitchell TOROK *US, male vocalist (2 Singles: 19 Weeks)*

28 Sep 56 ● **WHEN MEXICO GAVE UP THE RHUMBA** (re) *Brunswick 05586* 6 18
11 Jan 57 **RED LIGHT, GREEN LIGHT** *Brunswick 05626* 29 1

Emiliana TORRINI *Iceland, female vocalist (3 Singles: 3 Weeks)*

10 Jun 00 **EASY** *One Little Indian 274TP 7CD* 63 1
9 Sep 00 **UNEMPLOYED IN SUMMERTIME** *One Little Indian 275TP 7CDL* 63 1
3 Feb 01 **TO BE FREE** *One Little Indian 276TP 7CD* 44 1

Peter TOSH *Jamaica, male vocalist, b. Winston McIntosh, 9 Oct 1944, d. 11 Sep 1987 (1 Album: 1 Week, 2 Singles: 12 Weeks)*

25 Sep 76 **LEGALIZE IT** *Virgin V 2061* 54 1
21 Oct 78 **(YOU GOTTA WALK) DON'T LOOK BACK** *Rolling Stones 2859* 43 7
2 Apr 83 **JOHNNY B GOODE** *EMI RIC 115* 48 5

TOTAL *US, female vocal group (5 Singles: 11 Weeks)*

15 Jul 95 **CAN'T YOU SEE** *Tommy Boy TBCD 700* 1 43 2
14 Sep 96 **KISSIN' YOU** *Arista 74321404172* 29 2
15 Feb 97 **DO YOU THINK ABOUT US** *Puff Daddy 74321458492* 49 1
18 Apr 98 **WHAT YOU WANT** *Puff Daddy 74321578772* 2 15 5
30 Sep 00 **I WONDER WHY HE'S THE GREATEST DJ** *Tommy Boy TBCD 2100* 3 68 1

1 Total featuring Notorious BIG 2 Ma$e featuring Total 3 Tony Touch featuring Total

TOTAL CONTRAST *UK, male vocal / instrumental duo – Robin Achampong and Delroy Murray (1 Album: 3 Weeks, 4 Singles: 22 Weeks)*

3 Aug 85 **TAKES A LITTLE TIME** *London LON 71* 17 10
19 Oct 85 **HIT AND RUN** *London LON 76* 41 5
1 Mar 86 **THE RIVER** *London LON 83* 44 3
8 Mar 86 **TOTAL CONTRAST** *London LONLP 15* 66 3
10 May 86 **WHAT YOU GONNA DO ABOUT IT** *London LON 95* 63 4

TOTO (see also FAR CORPORATION) *US, male vocal (Bobby Kimball) / instrumental group (5 Albums: 39 Weeks, 5 Singles: 35 Weeks)*

10 Feb 79 **HOLD THE LINE** *CBS 6784* $ 14 11
31 Mar 79 **TOTO** *CBS 83148* 37 5
5 Feb 83 ● **AFRICA** *CBS A 2510* ▲ 3 10
26 Feb 83 ● **TOTO IV** *CBS 85529* 4 30
9 Apr 83 **ROSANNA** *CBS A 2079* 12 8
18 Jun 83 **I WON'T HOLD YOU BACK** *CBS A 3392* 37 5
17 Nov 84 **ISOLATION** *CBS 86305* 67 2
20 Sep 86 **FAHRENHEIT** *CBS 57091* 99 1
9 Apr 88 **THE SEVENTH ONE** *CBS 460465 1* 73 1
18 Nov 95 **I WILL REMEMBER** *Columbia 6626552* 64 1

TOTO COELO *UK, female vocal group (2 Singles: 14 Weeks)*

7 Aug 82 ● **I EAT CANNIBALS PART 1** *Radialchoice TIC 10* 8 10
13 Nov 82 **DRACULA'S TANGO / MUCHO MACHO** *Radialchoice TIC 11* 54 4

TOTTENHAM HOTSPUR FA CUP FINAL SQUAD (see also COCKEREL CHORUS) *UK, male football team vocalists (4 Singles: 23 Weeks)*

9 May 81 ● **OSSIE'S DREAM (SPURS ARE ON THEIR WAY TO WEMBLEY)** *Shelf SHELF 1* 5 8
1 May 82 **TOTTENHAM TOTTENHAM** *Shelf SHELF 2* 19 7
9 May 87 **HOT SHOT TOTTENHAM!** *Rainbow RBR 16* 18 5
11 May 91 **WHEN THE YEAR ENDS IN 1** *A1 A 1324* 44 3

All hits feature the vocal and instrumental talents of Chas and Dave.

	15 January 1994	22 January 1994	29 January 1994	5 February 1994
UK No.1 SINGLES	TWIST AND SHOUT Chaka Demus and Pliers featuring Jack Radics and Taxi Gang	THINGS CAN ONLY GET BETTER (Re-issue) D:ream	THINGS CAN ONLY GET BETTER (Re-issue) D:ream	THINGS CAN ONLY GET BETTER (Re-issue) D:ream
UK No.1 ALBUMS	SO FAR SO GOOD Bryan Adams	ONE WOMAN - THE ULTIMATE COLLECTION Diana Ross	TEASE ME Chaka Demus and Pliers	TEASE ME Chaka Demus and Pliers

TOUCH & GO *UK, male / female vocal (David Lowe) / production group*

7 Nov 98 ● **WOULD YOU ...?** *Oval VVR 5003083* ... 3 12

TOUCH OF SOUL *UK, male / female vocal / instrumental group*

19 May 90 **WE GOT THE LOVE** *Cooltempo COOL 204* ... 46 3

Tony TOUCH featuring TOTAL

US, male producer – Anthony Hernandez and female vocal group

30 Sep 00 **I WONDER WHY HE'S THE GREATEST DJ** *Tommy Boy TBCD 2100* ... 68 1

TOUR DE FORCE *UK, male production trio*

16 May 98 **CATALAN** *East West EW 161CD* ... 71 1

The TOURISTS

(see also EURYTHMICS; Annie LENNOX; David A. STEWART; VEGAS) *UK, male / female vocal / instrumental group (3 Albums: 18 Weeks, 5 Singles: 40 Weeks)*

9 Jun 79 **BLIND AMONG THE FLOWERS** *Logo GO 350* ... 52 5
14 Jul 79 THE TOURISTS *Logo GO 1018* ... 72 1
8 Sep 79 **THE LONELIEST MAN IN THE WORLD** *Logo GO 360* ... 32 7
3 Nov 79 REALITY EFFECT *Logo GO 1019* ... 23 16
10 Nov 79 ● **I ONLY WANT TO BE WITH YOU** *Logo GO 370* ... 4 14
9 Feb 80 ● **SO GOOD TO BE BACK HOME AGAIN** *Logo TOUR 1* ... 8 9
18 Oct 80 **DON'T SAY I TOLD YOU SO** *RCA TOUR 2* ... 40 5
22 Nov 80 LUMINOUS BASEMENT *RCA RCALP 5001* ... 75 1

TOUTES LES FILLES *UK, female vocal group*

4 Sep 99 **THAT'S WHAT LOVE CAN DO** *London LONCD 434* ... 44 1

TOWERS OF LONDON NEW

UK, male vocal / instrumental group (3 Singles: 3 Weeks)

19 Mar 05 **ON A NOOSE** *TVT TOLDCD 01* ... 32 1
9 Jul 05 **FUCK IT UP** *TVT TOLCD 2* ... 46 1
26 Nov 05 **HOW RUDE SHE WAS** *TVT TOLDCD 3* ... 30 1

Carol Lynn TOWNES *US, female vocalist (2 Singles: 7 Weeks)*

4 Aug 84 **99 1/2** *Polydor POSP 693* ... 47 4
19 Jan 85 **BELIEVE IN THE BEAT** *Polydor POSP 720* ... 56 3

Fuzz TOWNSHEND *UK, male producer*

6 Sep 97 **HELLO DARLIN** *Echo ECSCD 46* ... 51 1

Pete TOWNSHEND (see also The WHO)

UK, male vocalist / guitarist (5 Albums: 28 Weeks, 3 Singles: 17 Weeks)

21 Oct 72 WHO CAME FIRST *Track 2408 201* ... 30 2
15 Oct 77 ROUGH MIX *Polydor 2442147* [1] ... 44 3
5 Apr 80 **ROUGH BOYS** *Atco K 11460* ... 39 6
3 May 80 EMPTY GLASS *Atco K 50699* ... 11 14
21 Jun 80 **LET MY LOVE OPEN YOUR DOOR** *Atco K 11486* ... 46 6
3 Jul 82 ALL THE BEST COWBOYS HAVE CHINESE EYES *Atco K 50889* 32 8
21 Aug 82 **UNIFORMS (CORPS D'ESPRIT)** *Atco K 11751* ... 48 5
30 Nov 85 WHITE CITY *Atco 2523921* ... 70 1

[1] Pete Townshend and Ronnie Lane

TOXIC TWO

US, male instrumental / production duo – Ray Love and Damon Wild

7 Mar 92 **RAVE GENERATOR** *PWL International PWL 223* ... 13 6

TOY-BOX *Denmark, male / female vocal duo*

18 Sep 99 **BEST FRIEND** *Edel 0058245 ERE* ... 41 2

The TOY DOLLS *UK, male vocal (Michael Algar) / instrumental group*

1 Dec 84 ● **NELLIE THE ELEPHANT** *Volume VOL 11* ... 4 12
25 May 85 A FAR OUT DISC *Volume VOLP 2* ... 71 1

TOYAH 382 Top 500

Visually striking punk / pop vocalist, b. Toyah Willcox, 16 May 1958, Birmingham, UK. Came to prominence through acting with her first major role in 1977 movie Jubilee. Married King Crimson guitarist Robert Fripp in 1986 (8 Albums: 97 Weeks, 12 Singles: 87 Weeks)

14 Jun 80 THE BLUE MEANING *Safari IEYA 666* ... 40 4
17 Jan 81 TOYAH! TOYAH! TOYAH! *Safari LIVE 2* ... 22 14
14 Feb 81 ● **FOUR FROM TOYAH (EP)** *Safari TOY 1* ... 4 14
16 May 81 ● **I WANT TO BE FREE** *Safari SAFE 34* ... 8 11
30 May 81 ● ANTHEM *Safari VOOR 1* ... 2 46
3 Oct 81 ● **THUNDER IN THE MOUNTAINS** *Safari SAFE 38* ... 4 9
28 Nov 81 **FOUR MORE FROM TOYAH (EP)** *Safari TOY 2* ... 14 9
22 May 82 **BRAVE NEW WORLD** *Safari SAFE 45* ... 21 8
19 Jun 82 ● THE CHANGELING *Safari VOOR 9* ... 6 12
17 Jul 82 **IEYA** *Safari SAFE 28* ... 48 5
9 Oct 82 **BE LOUD BE PROUD (BE HEARD)** *Safari SAFE 52* ... 30 7
13 Nov 82 WARRIOR ROCK – TOYAH ON TOUR *Safari TNT 1* ... 20 6
24 Sep 83 **REBEL RUN** *Safari SAFE 56* ... 24 5
5 Nov 83 LOVE IS THE LAW *Safari VOOR 10* ... 28 7
19 Nov 83 **THE VOW** *Safari SAFE 58* ... 50 5
25 Feb 84 TOYAH! TOYAH! TOYAH! *K-Tel NE 1268* ... 43 4
27 Apr 85 **DON'T FALL IN LOVE (I SAID)** *Portrait A 6160* ... 22 6
29 Jun 85 **SOUL PASSING THROUGH SOUL** *Portrait A 6359* ... 57 3
3 Aug 85 MINX *Portrait PRT 26415* ... 24 4
25 Apr 87 **ECHO BEACH** *EG EGO 31* ... 54 5

Tracks on Four From Toyah (EP): It's a Mystery / Revelations / War Boys / Angels and Demons. Tracks on Four More From Toyah (EP): Good Morning Universe / Urban Tribesman / In the Fairground / The Furious Futures. The two Toyah! Toyah! Toyah! albums are different.

The TOYS *US, female vocal group (2 Singles: 17 Weeks)*

4 Nov 65 ● **A LOVER'S CONCERTO** *Stateside SS 460* $ ... 5 13
27 Jan 66 **ATTACK** *Stateside SS 483* ... 36 4

T'PAU 443 Top 500

Shropshire lads and a lass whose No.1 hit in 1987 had the distinction of being the 600th chart-topper. T'Pau (Mr Spock's Vulcan friend in Star Trek) comprised writers Carol Decker (v) and Ron Rogers (g), plus Michael Chetwood (k), Paul Jackson (b), Tim Burgess (d) and Taj Wyzgowski (g) (4 Albums: 85 Weeks, 11 Singles: 77 Weeks)

8 Aug 87 ● **HEART AND SOUL** *Siren SRN 41* ... 4 13
26 Sep 87 ★ BRIDGE OF SPIES *Siren SIRENLP 8* ... 1 59
24 Oct 87 ★ **CHINA IN YOUR HAND** *Siren SRN 64* ... 1 15
30 Jan 88 ● **VALENTINE** *Siren SRN 69* ... 9 8
2 Apr 88 **SEX TALK (LIVE)** *Siren SRN 80* ... 23 7
25 Jun 88 **I WILL BE WITH YOU** *Siren SRN 87* ... 14 6
1 Oct 88 **SECRET GARDEN** *Siren SRN 93* ... 18 7
5 Nov 88 ● RAGE *Siren SRNLP 20* ... 4 17
3 Dec 88 **ROAD TO OUR DREAM** *Siren SRN 100* ... 42 6
25 Mar 89 **ONLY THE LONELY** *Siren SRN 107* ... 28 6
18 May 91 **WHENEVER YOU NEED ME** *Siren SRN 140* ... 16 6
22 Jun 91 ● THE PROMISE *Siren SRNLP 32* ... 10 7
27 Jul 91 **WALK ON AIR** *Siren SRN 142* ... 62 2
20 Feb 93 **VALENTINE** (re-issue) *Virgin VALEG 1* ... 53 1
27 Feb 93 HEART AND SOUL – THE VERY BEST OF T'PAU *Virgin TPAUD 1* ... 35 2

Ian TRACEY / LIVERPOOL CATHEDRALS' CHOIRS

UK, male conductor and male / female choirs

21 Mar 92 YOUR FAVOURITE HYMNS *Virgin Classics 7912092* ... 62 3

TRACIE

UK, female vocalist – Tracie Young (1 Album: 2 Weeks, 5 Singles: 24 Weeks)

26 Mar 83 ● **THE HOUSE THAT JACK BUILT** *Respond KOB 701* ... 9 8
16 Jul 83 **GIVE IT SOME EMOTION** *Respond KOB 704* ... 24 9
14 Apr 84 **SOUL'S ON FIRE** *Respond KOB 708* ... 73 2
9 Jun 84 **(I LOVE YOU) WHEN YOU SLEEP** *Respond KOB 710* ... 59 3
30 Jun 84 FAR FROM THE HURTING KIND *Respond RRL 502* ... 64 2
17 Aug 85 **I CAN'T LEAVE YOU ALONE** *Respond SBS 1* [1] ... 60 2

[1] Tracie Young

12 February 1994	19 February 1994	26 February 1994	5 March 1994
THINGS CAN ONLY GET BETTER (Re-issue) D:ream	WITHOUT YOU Mariah Carey	WITHOUT YOU Mariah Carey	WITHOUT YOU Mariah Carey
UNDER THE PINK Tori Amos	THE CROSS OF CHANGES Enigma	MUSIC BOX Mariah Carey	MUSIC BOX Mariah Carey

KEY — UK No.1 ★ UK Top 10 ● Still on chart + UK entry at No.1 ■ US No.1 ▲ UK million seller £ US million seller $
Singles re-entries are listed as (re), (2re), (3re)... which signifies that the hit re-entered the chart once, twice or three times...
Peak Position / Weeks

Jeanie TRACY *US, female vocalist (3 Singles: 3 Weeks)*

11 Jun 94 **IF THIS IS LOVE** *Pulse 8 CDLOSE 63* 73 1
5 Nov 94 **DO YOU BELIEVE IN THE WONDER** *Pulse 8 CDLOSE 74* 57 1
13 May 95 **IT'S A MAN'S MAN'S MAN'S WORLD** *Pulse 8 CDLOSE 89* [1] 73 1

[1] Jeanie Tracy and Bobby Womack

TRAFFIC (see also Jim CAPALDI; Steve WINWOOD) *UK, male vocal / instrumental group (6 Albums: 41 Weeks, 4 Singles: 40 Weeks)*

1 Jun 67 ● **PAPER SUN** *Island WIP 6002* 5 10
6 Sep 67 ● **HOLE IN MY SHOE** *Island WIP 6017* 2 14
29 Nov 67 ● **HERE WE GO ROUND THE MULBERRY BUSH** *Island WIP 6025* 8 12
30 Dec 67 ● MR. FANTASY *Island ILP 9061* 8 16
6 Mar 68 **NO FACE, NO NAME, NO NUMBER** *Island WIP 6030* 40 4
26 Oct 68 ● TRAFFIC *Island ILPS 9081T* 9 8
8 Aug 70 JOHN BARLEYCORN MUST DIE *Island ILPS 9116* 11 9
24 Nov 73 ON THE ROAD *Island ISLD 2* 40 3
28 Sep 74 WHEN THE EAGLE FLIES *Island ILPS 9273* 31 1
21 May 94 FAR FROM HOME *Virgin CDV 2727* 29 4

TRAIN *US, male vocal (Patrick Monahan) / instrumental group (1 Album: 9 Weeks, 2 Singles: 10 Weeks)*

11 Aug 01 ● **DROPS OF JUPITER (TELL ME)** *Columbia 6714472* 10 8
18 Aug 01 ● DROPS OF JUPITER *Columbia 5023069* 8 9
2 Mar 02 **SHE'S ON FIRE** *Columbia 6722812* 49 2

TRAMAINE *US, female vocalist – Tramaine Hawkins*

5 Oct 85 **FALL DOWN (SPIRIT OF LOVE)** *A&M AM 281* 60 2

The TRAMMPS *US, male vocal group (8 Singles: 55 Weeks)*

23 Nov 74 **ZING WENT THE STRINGS OF MY HEART** *Buddah BDS 405* 29 10
1 Feb 75 **SIXTY MINUTE MAN** *Buddah BDS 415* 40 4
11 Oct 75 ● **HOLD BACK THE NIGHT** *Buddah BDS 437* 5 8
13 Mar 76 **THAT'S WHERE THE HAPPY PEOPLE GO** *Atlantic K 10703* 35 8
24 Jul 76 **SOUL SEARCHIN' TIME** *Atlantic K 10797* 42 3
14 May 77 **DISCO INFERNO** *Atlantic K 10914* 16 7
24 Jun 78 **DISCO INFERNO** (re-issue) *Atlantic K 11135* 47 10
12 Dec 92 **HOLD BACK THE NIGHT** *Network NWK 65* [1] 30 5

[1] KWS features guest vocal from The Trammps

TRANCESETTERS (see also TATA BOX INHIBITORS) *Holland, male production duo (2 Singles: 2 Weeks)*

4 Mar 00 **ROACHES** *Hooj Choons HOOJ 89CD* 55 1
9 Jun 01 **SYNERGY** *Hooj Choons 107* 72 1

TRANSA *UK, male DJ / production duo (2 Singles: 2 Weeks)*

30 Aug 97 **PROPHASE** *Perfecto PERF 147CD* 65 1
21 Feb 98 **ENERVATE** *Perfecto PERF 155CD* 42 1

TRANSATLANTIC SOUL *US, male producer – Roger Sanchez*

22 Mar 97 **RELEASE YO SELF** *Deconstruction 74321459102* 43 1

TRANSFER *UK, male production duo and female vocalist*

3 Nov 01 **POSSESSION** *Multiply CDMULTY 76* 54 1

TRANSFORMER 2 *Belgium / Holland, male / female vocal / instrumental group*

24 Feb 96 **JUST CAN'T GET ENOUGH** *Positiva CDTIV 49* 45 1

TRANSGLOBAL UNDERGROUND *UK, male / female vocal / instrumental group (3 Albums: 3 Weeks)*

30 Oct 93 DREAM OF 100 NATIONS *Nation NR 021CD* 45 1
29 Oct 94 INTERNATIONAL TIMES *Nation NATCD 38* 40 1
25 May 96 PSYCHIC KARAOKE *Nation NRCD 1067* 62 1

TRANSISTER *UK / US, male / female vocal / instrumental group*

28 Mar 98 **LOOK WHO'S PERFECT NOW** *Virgin VSCDT 1678* 56 1

TRANSPLANTS *US, male vocal / instrumental group (1 Album: 1 Week, 3 Singles: 4 Weeks)*

19 Apr 03 **DIAMONDS AND GUNS** *Hellcat 11082* 27 2
19 Jul 03 **DJ DJ** *Hellcat 11122* 49 1
2 Jul 05 HAUNTED CITIES *Atlantic 7567941042* 72 1
17 Sep 05 **GANGSTERS AND THUGS** *Atlantic AT 0213CD* 35 1

TRANSVISION VAMP *UK, female / male vocal (Wendy James) / instrumental group (2 Albums: 58 Weeks, 10 Singles: 59 Weeks)*

16 Apr 88 **TELL THAT GIRL TO SHUT UP** *MCA TVV 2* 45 3
25 Jun 88 ● **I WANT YOUR LOVE** *MCA TVV 3* 5 13
17 Sep 88 **REVOLUTION BABY** *MCA TVV 4* 30 5
15 Oct 88 ● POP ART *MCA MCF 3421* 4 32
19 Nov 88 **SISTER MOON** *MCA TVV 5* 41 5
1 Apr 89 ● **BABY I DON'T CARE** *MCA TVV 6* 3 11
10 Jun 89 **THE ONLY ONE** *MCA TVV 7* 15 6
8 Jul 89 ★ VELVETEEN *MCA MCG 6050* ■ 1 26
5 Aug 89 **LANDSLIDE OF LOVE** *MCA TVV 8* 14 5
4 Nov 89 **BORN TO BE SOLD** *MCA TVV 9* 22 4
13 Apr 91 **(I JUST WANNA) B WITH U** *MCA TVV 10* 30 4
22 Jun 91 **IF LOOKS COULD KILL** *MCA TVV 11* 41 3

TRANS-X *Canada, male / female vocal (Laurie Gill) / instrumental group*

13 Jul 85 ● **LIVING ON VIDEO** *Boiling Point POSP 650* 9 9

TRASH *UK, male vocal / instrumental group*

25 Oct 69 **GOLDEN SLUMBERS / CARRY THAT WEIGHT** *Apple 17* 35 3

The TRASH CAN SINATRAS *UK, male vocal / instrumental group (2 Albums: 2 Weeks, 1 Single: 1 Week)*

7 Jul 90 CAKE *Go Discs 82820211* 74 1
24 Apr 93 **HAYFEVER** *Go Discs GODCD 98* 61 1
15 May 93 I'VE SEEN EVERYTHING *Go Discs 8284082* 50 1

TRAVEL *France, male producer – Laurent Gutbier*

24 Apr 99 **BULGARIAN** *Tidy Trax TIDY 121CD* 67 2

TRAVELING WILBURYS (see also Bob DYLAN; George HARRISON; Jeff LYNNE; Roy ORBISON; Tom PETTY and The HEARTBREAKERS) *UK / US, male vocal / instrumental group (2 Albums: 44 Weeks, 3 Singles: 19 Weeks)*

29 Oct 88 **HANDLE WITH CARE** *Wilbury W 7732* 21 13
5 Nov 88 THE TRAVELING WILBURYS VOLUME 1 *Wilbury WX 224* 16 35
11 Mar 89 **END OF THE LINE** *Wilbury W 7637* 52 4
30 Jun 90 **NOBODY'S CHILD** *Wilbury W 9773* 44 2
10 Nov 90 THE TRAVELING WILBURYS VOLUME 3 *Wilbury WX 384* 14 9

Pat TRAVERS *Canada, male guitarist*

2 Apr 77 MAKIN' MAGIC *Polydor 2383 436* 40 3

TRAVIS 209 Top 500

Scottish melodic rock merchants named after a character from the 1984 movie Paris, Texas: English-born Fran Healy (v/g) and native Glaswegians Andy Dunlop (g), Dougie Payne (b) and Neil Primrose (d). Among their three BRIT awards is best-selling album by a British act in the UK for The Man Who in 1999. Performed at the London and Edinburgh Live 8 concerts (5 Albums: 198 Weeks, 17 Singles: 92 Weeks)

12 Apr 97 **U16 GIRLS** *Independiente ISOM 1MS* 40 2
28 Jun 97 **ALL I WANT TO DO IS ROCK** *Independiente ISOM 3MS* 39 2

23 Aug 97 TIED TO THE 90'S *Independiente ISOM 5MS* 30 2
20 Sep 97 ● GOOD FEELING *Independiente ISOM 1CD* 9 16
25 Oct 97 HAPPY *Independiente ISOM 6MS* 38 2
11 Apr 98 MORE THAN US (EP) *Independiente ISOM 11MS* 16 3
20 Mar 99 WRITING TO REACH YOU *Independiente ISOM 22MS* 14 5
29 May 99 DRIFTWOOD *Independiente ISOM 27MS* 13 5
5 Jun 99 ★ THE MAN WHO *Independiente ISOM 9CD* 1 102
14 Aug 99 ● WHY DOES IT ALWAYS RAIN ON ME? *Independiente ISOM 33MS* 10 8
20 Nov 99 ● TURN *Independiente ISOM 39MS* 8 11
17 Jun 00 ● COMING AROUND (2re) *Independiente ISOM 45MS* 5 10
9 Jun 01 ● SING *Independiente ISOM 49MS* 3 14
23 Jun 01 ★ THE INVISIBLE BAND *Independiente ISOM 25CD* ■ 1 54
29 Sep 01 SIDE *Independiente ISOM 54MS* 14 8
6 Apr 02 FLOWERS IN THE WINDOW *Independiente ISOM 56MS* 18 7
11 Oct 03 ● RE-OFFENDER *Independiente ISOM 78SMS* 7 4
25 Oct 03 ● 12 MEMORIES *Independiente ISOM 40CD* 3 11
27 Dec 03 THE BEAUTIFUL OCCUPATION *Independiente ISOM 81MS* 48 3
3 Apr 04 LOVE WILL COME THROUGH *Independiente ISOM 84MS* 28 3
30 Oct 04 WALKING IN THE SUN *Independiente ISOM 88MS* 20 3
13 Nov 04 ● SINGLES *Independiente ISOM 46CD* 4 15

Tracks on More Than Us (EP): More Than Us / Give Me Some Truth / All I Want to Do Is Rock / Funny Thing.

Randy TRAVIS *US, male vocalist / guitarist*

21 May 88 FOREVER AND EVER, AMEN *Warner Bros. W 8384* 55 6
6 Aug 88 OLD 8X10 *Warner Bros. WX 162* 64 2

John TRAVOLTA
US, male actor / vocalist (1 Album: 6 Weeks, 7 Singles: 90 Weeks)

20 May 78 ★ YOU'RE THE ONE THAT I WANT *RSO 006* [1] ▲ £ $ 1 26
16 Sep 78 ★ SUMMER NIGHTS *RSO 18* [2] £ $ 1 19
7 Oct 78 ● SANDY *Polydor POSP 6* 2 15
2 Dec 78 GREASED LIGHTNING *Polydor POSP 14* 11 9
23 Dec 78 SANDY *Polydor POLD 5014* 40 6
22 Dec 90 ● THE GREASE MEGAMIX *Polydor PO 114* [1] 3 10
23 Mar 91 GREASE – THE DREAM MIX *PWL / Polydor PO 136* [3] 47 2
25 Jul 98 ● YOU'RE THE ONE THAT I WANT (re-issue) *Polydor 0441332* [1] 4 9

[1] John Travolta and Olivia Newton-John [2] John Travolta, Olivia Newton-John and Cast [3] Frankie Valli, John Travolta and Olivia Newton-John

The TREMELOES (293 Top 500)
Essex-based Brian Poole and The Tremeloes were formed in 1959 and signed by Decca in preference to The Beatles (they auditioned on the same day). They were the first south of England group to top the chart in the Beat Boom era. After supporting Poole on his many hits, The Tremeloes: Len "Chip" Hawkes (v/b), Rick West (g), Alan Blakely (g), b. 1942, d. 1 Jun 1996, and Dave Munden (d) went on to score even more hits in their own right. Hawkes is the father of 1991 chart-topper Chesney Hawkes (1 Album: 7 Weeks, 21 Singles: 222 Weeks)

4 Jul 63 ● TWIST AND SHOUT *Decca F 11694* [1] 4 14
12 Sep 63 ★ DO YOU LOVE ME *Decca F 11739* [1] 1 14
28 Nov 63 I CAN DANCE *Decca F 11771* [1] 31 8
30 Jan 64 ● CANDY MAN *Decca F 11823* [1] 6 13
7 May 64 ● SOMEONE, SOMEONE *Decca F 11893* [1] 2 17
20 Aug 64 TWELVE STEPS TO LOVE *Decca F 11951* [1] 32 7
31 Dec 64 THREE BELLS *Decca F 12037* [1] 17 10
22 Jul 65 I WANT CANDY *Decca F 12197* [1] 25 8
2 Feb 67 ● HERE COMES MY BABY *CBS 202519* 4 11
27 Apr 67 ★ SILENCE IS GOLDEN *CBS 2723* 1 15
3 Jun 67 HERE COME THE TREMELOES – THE COMPLETE 1967 SESSIONS *CBS SBPG 63017* 15 7
2 Aug 67 ● EVEN THE BAD TIMES ARE GOOD *CBS 2930* 4 13
8 Nov 67 BE MINE *CBS 3043* 39 2
17 Jan 68 ● SUDDENLY YOU LOVE ME *CBS 3234* 6 11
8 May 68 HELULE HELULE *CBS 2889* 14 9
18 Sep 68 ● MY LITTLE LADY *CBS 3680* 6 12
11 Dec 68 I SHALL BE RELEASED *CBS 3873* 29 5
19 Mar 69 HELLO WORLD *CBS 4065* 14 8
1 Nov 69 ● (CALL ME) NUMBER ONE *CBS 4582* 2 14
21 Mar 70 BY THE WAY *CBS 4815* 35 6
12 Sep 70 ● ME AND MY LIFE *CBS 5139* 4 18
10 Jul 71 HELLO BUDDY *CBS 7294* 32 7

[1] Brian Poole and The Tremeloes

Jackie TRENT *UK, female vocalist – Yvonne Burgess (3 Singles: 17 Weeks)*

22 Apr 65 ★ WHERE ARE YOU NOW *Pye 7N 15776* 1 11
1 Jul 65 WHEN THE SUMMERTIME IS OVER *Pye 7N 15865* 39 2
2 Apr 69 I'LL BE THERE *Pye 7N 17693* 38 4

Ralph TRESVANT (see also NEW EDITION)
US, male vocalist (1 Album: 3 Weeks, 2 Singles: 21 Weeks)

12 Jan 91 SENSITIVITY *MCA MCS 1462* 18 8
23 Feb 91 RALPH TRESVANT *MCA MCG 6120* 37 3
15 Aug 92 ● THE BEST THINGS IN LIFE ARE FREE *Perspective PERSS 7400* [1] 2 13

[1] Luther Vandross and Janet Jackson with special guests BBD and Ralph Tresvant

TREVOR & SIMON *UK, male production duo – Trevor Reilly and Simon Foy*

10 Jun 00 HANDS UP *Substance SUBS 1CDS* 12 5

TRI *UK, male vocal / instrumental group*

2 Sep 95 WE GOT THE LOVE *Epic 6623642* 61 1

TRIBAL HOUSE *US, male vocal / instrumental group*

3 Feb 90 MOTHERLAND-A-FRI-CA *Cooltempo COOL 198* 57 2

Tony TRIBE *Jamaica, male vocalist*

16 Jul 69 RED RED WINE (re) *Downtown DT 419* 46 2

A TRIBE CALLED QUEST (see also Q-TIP)
US, male rap group (5 Albums: 9 Weeks, 7 Singles: 18 Weeks)

19 May 90 PEOPLE'S INSTINCTIVE TRAVELS AND THE PATHS OF RHYTHM *Jive HIP 96* 54 2
18 Aug 90 BONITA APPLEBUM *Jive JIVE 256* 47 3
19 Jan 91 CAN I KICK IT? *Jive JIVE 265* 15 7
12 Oct 91 THE LOW END THEORY *Jive HIP 117* 58 1
27 Nov 93 MIDNIGHT MARAUDERS *Jive CHIP 143* 70 1
11 Jun 94 OH MY GOD *Jive JIVECD 355* 68 1
13 Jul 96 1NCE AGAIN *Jive JIVECD 399* 34 2
10 Aug 96 BEATS RHYMES AND LIFE *Jive CHIP 170* ▲ 28 4
23 Nov 96 STRESSED OUT *Jive JIVECD 404* [1] 33 2
23 Aug 97 THE JAM EP *Jive JIVECD 427* 61 1
29 Aug 98 FIND A WAY *Jive 0518982* 41 2
10 Oct 98 THE LOVE MOVEMENT *Jive 521032* 38 1

[1] A Tribe Called Quest featuring Faith Evans and Raphael Saadiq

Tracks on The Jam EP: Jam / Get a Hold / Mardi Gras at Midnight / Same Ol' Thing.

TRIBE OF TOFFS *UK, male vocal / instrumental group*

24 Dec 88 JOHN KETTLEY (IS A WEATHERMAN) *Completely Different DAFT 1* 21 5

Obie TRICE *US, male rapper (1 Album: 8 Weeks, 2 Singles: 14 Weeks)*

11 Oct 03 CHEERS *Interscope / Polydor 9860986* 11 8
1 Nov 03 ● GOT SOME TEETH (re) *Interscope 9813061* 8 11
14 Feb 04 THE SET UP (YOU DON'T KNOW) *Interscope 9815333* [1] 32 3

[1] Obie Trice featuring Nate Dogg

TRICK DADDY NEW *US, male rapper – Maurice Young (2 Singles: 3 Weeks)*

26 Feb 05 LET'S GO *Atlantic AT 0193CD* [1] 26 2
28 May 05 SUGAR (GIMME SOME) *Atlantic AT 0202CDX* [2] 61 1

[1] Trick Daddy featuring Twista and Lil' Jon [2] Trick Daddy featuring Ludacris, Lil' Kim & Cee-Lo

9 April 1994	16 April 1994	23 April 1994	30 April 1994
EVERYTHING CHANGES Take That	EVERYTHING CHANGES Take That	THE MOST BEAUTIFUL GIRL IN THE WORLD Symbol (Prince)	THE MOST BEAUTIFUL GIRL IN THE WORLD Symbol (Prince)
THE DIVISION BELL Pink Floyd	THE DIVISION BELL Pink Floyd	THE DIVISION BELL Pink Floyd	THE DIVISION BELL Pink Floyd

STALLED AT No.76

Imagine how much thought, effort, time and money are put into every single released in the hope that it reaches the Top 75, and therefore is regarded as a hit and makes the pages of this book. Consider, then, the frustration when that single enters and peaks just outside the chart at No.76.

It's too late to give these singles a sales plug, but let's give them some overdue acclaim anyway and sound those 76 trombones for these 21st-century releases that so nearly made it.

Date – **SINGLE TITLE** – act – label

2000
5 Feb **ROCK 'N' ROLL / HOLY CALAMITY** – Handsome Boy Modeling School* – Tommy Boy
26 Feb **BLACK BALLOON** – Goo Goo Dolls – Hollywood
1 Apr **CHRISTIAN GIRLS** – Hefner – Too Pure
8 Apr **BREATHE** – Art of Trance – Platipus
3 Jun **GET GONE** – Ideal U.S. – Virgin
24 Jun **PUSH THE LIMITS** – Enigma – Virgin
15 Jul **STAYED** – Smog* – Domino
29 Jul **TOM'S DINER** – Kenny Blake* – Club Tools
9 Sep **BELLS OF REVOLUTION** – Lemon 8* – Tripoli Trax
7 Oct **BAD BOY 2000** - Mark Kavanagh* – Tripoli Trax
21 Oct **WARM WEATHER** – Chris Bangs featuring Rita Campbell* – INCredible
25 Nov **COCKTAILS** – Face* – Indepéndiente
23 Dec **HELSINKI** – Ashtrax* – Deviant

2001
5 May **BABY YOU'RE SO FINE** – Cosmic Rough Riders – Poptones
21 Jul **CLOAKING** – Seafood – Infectious
18 Aug **CRASH THE PARTY** – Kumara – Y2K
13 Oct **IN PRAISE OF THE SUN** – Mr Joshua presents Espiritu – Cream / Parlophone
10 Nov **I STILL WANT YOU** – Mange Le Funk* – Gusto

2002
16 Feb **TURN IT AROUND** – Lee Brennan* – Absolute
27 Apr **TAKE ME HOME** – Wilt – Mushroom
11 May **THE LONELY** – British Sea Power – Rough Trade
1 Jun **MUSIC MAKES ME HAPPY** – Tomy or Zox* – Distinctive
15 Jun **ALL OVER ME** – Aphrodite featuring Barrington Levy – V2
6 Jul **EPIC MONOLITH** – Mirco De Govia* – Xtravaganza
31 Aug **STOP IT (I LIKE IT)** – Rick Guard* – Decca
21 Sep **WHERE HAVE YOU BEEN** – Reel Big Fish – Jive
12 Oct **GOOD GOD! (REMIX)** – JFK – Y2K
26 Oct **NEVER BE ALONE** – Simian – Source
9 Nov **SOME KIND OF WONDERFUL** – Toploader – S2
23 Nov **GATEX** – Umek* – Magic Muzik
21 Dec **COSMOPOLITAN** – Bloodloss* – Glassjaw

2003
1 Mar **KEEP ON RISING** – Jay-J featuring Latrice Barnett* – Defected
8 Mar **70s/80s** – Nightmares on Wax – Warp
15 Mar **SOLARCOASTER** – Solar Stone – Lost Language
12 Apr **THE REVOLUTION EP** – Soul Rebels* – Defected
3 May **IF IT KILLS ME / RUST** – Therapy? – Spitfire
10 May **THE PUSH** – Paul Jackson – Underwater
14 Jun **NEED ONE** – Martina Topley-Bird – Independiente
21 Jun **USER FRIENDLY** – The Blueskins – Domino
5 Jul **THE HIT SONG** – DJ Format featuring Abdominal – Genuine
20 Sep **DEAD MAN WALKING / FORMULA ONE** – Fresh BC – Valve
25 Oct **I JUST WANNA SAY** – Michelle Lawson* – Fontana
15 Nov **HEAVY SOUL / JUST KILLS ME** – Clarkesville – Wildstar
29 Nov **DO YOU LOVE YOURSELF?** – Glitterati – Poptones
20 Dec **MISTY ROWE** – Young Heart Attack – XL Recordings

2004
21 Feb **STUNT 101** – G-Unit – Interscope
13 Mar **PRESSURE / SIGHT BEYOND** – John B – Formation
20 Mar **KNOCK ME DOWN** – My Red Cell – V2
3 Apr **FEVER** – Pink Grease – Muta
17 Apr **BORN TOO SLOW** – The Crystal Method – V2
24 Apr **RAVIN' HELL SAMPLER** – JB & DJ Spice* – Back 2 Basics
1 May **DISCO CLUB** – Black Devil* – Rephlex
15 May **HOT TRANCE EP 6** – Various Artists – Nukleuz
22 May **#1 SOUND** – Total Science* – CIA
5 Jun **TESTIFY** – M.A.S.S.* – There's a Riot Going On
21 Jul **CLEAN AND NEAT** – Cathy Davey* – Regal
18 Sep **SHE WILL ONLY BRING YOU HAPPINESS** – McLusky* – Too Pure
25 Sep **SPANISH EYES** – Fifth Avenue* – Religion Music
9 Oct **ACID HOUSE MIXES BY 808 STATE (1988)** – New Order – Rephlex
16 Oct **NEW HEALTH ROCK** – TV on the Radio* – 4AD
20 Nov **HIT THE CITY** – Mark Lanegan Band – Beggars Banquet
4 Dec **TEN THOUSAND PLACES** – The Polyphonic Spree – Good
25 Dec **LEAVE IT ALL BEHIND** – The Features* – Universal

2005
26 Feb **DEERHUNTER** – Infrasound* – Versity
5 Mar **TIME TO SAY GOODBYE** – Katherine Jenkins – UCJ
19 Mar **HOOLIGANS ON E** – Kill City – Poptones
26 Mar **PEACE AND QUIET** – The Rifles – Blow Up
2 Apr **SANDCASTLES** – Sydenham & Ferrer* – Defected
16 Apr **LOVE'S THEME / WISE UP** – The Chalets* – Setanta
15 Oct **FEELINGS** – Shy FX & T-Power – Soundboy
22 Oct **WHERE DID OUR LOVING GO** – Alfie – Regal
31 Dec **FORGET ME NOT** – Lucie Silvas – Mercury

*Indicates acts that failed to chart with any release at all

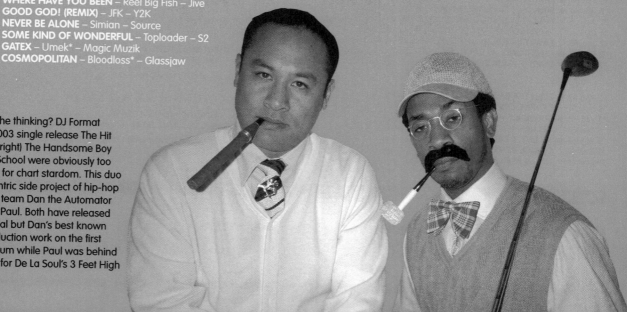

What was he thinking? DJ Format titled his 2003 single release The Hit Song and (right) The Handsome Boy Modeling School were obviously too handsome for chart stardom. This duo is the eccentric side project of hip-hop production team Dan the Automator and Prince Paul. Both have released solo material but Dan's best known for his production work on the first Gorillaz album while Paul was behind the boards for De La Soul's 3 Feet High and Rising

TRICKBABY *UK, female vocal / instrumental group*

12 Oct 96 **INDIE-YARN** *Logic 74321423152* **47** 2

TRICKSTER *UK, male producer – Liam Sullivan*

4 Apr 98 **MOVE ON UP** *AM:PM 5825812* **19** 3

TRICKY (see also NEARLY GOD; Keisha WHITE) *UK, male vocalist / multi-instrumentalist – Adrian Thaws (5 Albums: 43 Weeks, 11 Singles: 29 Weeks)*

5 Feb 94 **AFTERMATH** *Fourth & Broadway BRCD 288* **69** 1
28 Jan 95 **OVERCOME** *Fourth & Broadway BRCD 304* **34** 3
4 Mar 95 ● MAXINQUAYE *Fourth & Broadway BRCD 610* 3 35
15 Apr 95 **BLACK STEEL** *Fourth & Broadway BRCD 320* **28** 3
5 Aug 95 **THE HELL (EP)** *Fourth & Broadway BRCD 326* [1] **12** 3
11 Nov 95 **PUMPKIN** *Fourth & Broadway BRCD 330* **26** 2
9 Nov 96 **CHRISTIANSANDS** *Fourth & Broadway BRCD 340* **36** 2
23 Nov 96 PRE-MILLENNIUM TENSION *Fourth & Broadway BRCDX 623* 30 2
23 Nov 96 ● **MILK** (re) *Mushroom D 1494* [2] **10** 8
11 Jan 97 **TRICKY KID** *Fourth & Broadway BRCD 341* **28** 2
3 May 97 **MAKES ME WANNA DIE** *Fourth & Broadway BRCD 348* **29** 2
30 May 98 **MONEY GREEDY / BROKEN HOMES** *Island CID 701* **25** 2
6 Jun 98 ANGELS WITH DIRTY FACES *Island CID 8071* 23 2
21 Aug 99 **FOR REAL** *Island CID 753* **45** 1
28 Aug 99 JUXTAPOSE *Island CID 8087* [1] 22 2
14 Jul 01 BLOWBACK *Anti 65962* 34 2

[1] Tricky vs The Gravediggaz [2] Garbage featuring Tricky
[1] Tricky with DJ Muggs and Grease

Tracks on The Hell (EP): Hell Is Round the Corner (original) / Hell Is Round the Corner (Hell and Water re-mix) / Psychosis / Tonite Is a Special Nite (Chaos mass confusion re-mix).

TRICKY DISCO (see also GTO; TECHNOHEAD) *UK, male / female instrumental / production duo – Michael Wells and Lee Newman, d. 4 Aug 1995 (2 Singles: 10 Weeks)*

28 Jul 90 **TRICKY DISCO** *Warp WAP 7* **14** 8
20 Apr 91 **HOUSE FLY** *Warp 7WAP 11* **55** 2

The TRIFFIDS *Australia, male vocal / instrumental group*

6 Feb 88 **A TRICK OF THE LIGHT** *Island IS 350* **73** 1
22 Apr 89 THE BLACK SWAN *Island ILPS 9928* 63 1

TRINA *US, female vocalist – Katrina Taylor*

19 Oct 02 **NO PANTIES** *Atlantic AT 0141CD* **45** 1

TRINA and TAMARA *US, female vocal duo – Trina and Tamara Powell (2 Singles: 3 Weeks)*

7 Feb 98 **MY LOVE IS THE SHHH!** *Warner Bros. W 0427CD* **64** 1
12 Jun 99 **WHAT'D YOU COME HERE FOR?** *Columbia 6673382* **46** 2

TRINIDAD OIL COMPANY *Trinidad, male / female vocal / instrumental group*

21 May 77 **THE CALENDAR SONG (JANUARY, FEBRUARY, MARCH, APRIL, MAY)** *Harvest HAR 5122* **34** 5

TRINITY-X *UK, male / female production / vocal trio*

19 Oct 02 **FOREVER** *All Around the World CDGLOBE 255* **19** 3

TRIO *Germany, male vocal / instrumental group*

3 Jul 82 ● **DA DA DA** *Mobile Suit Corporation CORP 5* **2** 10

TRIPLE EIGHT *UK, male vocal group (4 Singles: 10 Weeks)*

3 May 03 ● **KNOCKOUT** *Polydor 9800048* **8** 4
2 Aug 03 ● **GIVE ME A REASON** (re) *Polydor 9809136* **9** 5
11 Jun 05 **GOOD 2 GO** *Osmosis OSMU 8801* **42** 1

TRIPLE X (see also PLAYTHING) *Italy, male production duo – Lucia Moretti and Ricky Romanini*

30 Oct 99 **FEEL THE SAME** *Sound of Ministry MOSCDS 135* **32** 2

TRIPPING DAISY *US, male vocal / instrumental group*

30 Mar 96 **PIRANHA** *Island CID 638* **72** 1

TRISCO *UK, male production duo – Harvey Dawson and Rupert Edwards*

30 Jun 01 **MUSAK** *Positiva CDTIV 155* **28** 2

TRIUMPH *Canada, male vocal / instrumental group (2 Albums: 8 Weeks, 1 Single: 2 Weeks)*

10 May 80 PROGRESSIONS OF POWER *RCA PL 13524* 61 5
22 Nov 80 **I LIVE FOR THE WEEKEND** *RCA 13* **59** 2
3 Oct 81 ALLIED FORCES *RCA RCALP 6002* 64 3

The TROGGS *UK, male vocal (Reg Ball aka Reg Presley) / instrumental group (4 Albums: 35 Weeks, 10 Singles: 86 Weeks)*

5 May 66 ● **WILD THING** *Fontana TF 689* ▲ $ **2** 12
14 Jul 66 ★ **WITH A GIRL LIKE YOU** *Fontana TF 717* **1** 12
30 Jul 66 ● FROM NOWHERE ... THE TROGGS *Fontana TL 5355* 6 16
29 Sep 66 ● **I CAN'T CONTROL MYSELF** *Page One POF 001* **2** 13
15 Dec 66 ● **ANY WAY THAT YOU WANT ME** *Page One POF 010* **8** 10
16 Feb 67 **GIVE IT TO ME** *Page One POF 015* **12** 10
25 Feb 67 ● TROGGLODYNAMITE *Page One POL 001* 10 11
1 Jun 67 **NIGHT OF THE LONG GRASS** *Page One POF 022* **17** 6
26 Jul 67 **HI HI HAZEL** *Page One POF 030* **42** 3
5 Aug 67 THE BEST OF THE TROGGS *Page One FOR 001* 24 5
18 Oct 67 ● **LOVE IS ALL AROUND** *Page One POF 040* **5** 14
28 Feb 68 **LITTLE GIRL** *Page One POF 056* **37** 4
30 Oct 93 **WILD THING** (re-recording) *Weekend CDWEEK 103* [1] **69** 2
16 Jul 94 GREATEST HITS *PolyGram TV 5227392* 27 3

[1] The Troggs and Wolf

'Wild Thing' (1993) was listed with the flip side, 'War', by Edwin Starr and Shadow.

TRONIKHOUSE (see also INNER CITY; REESE PROJECT) *US, male producer – Kevin Saunderson*

14 Mar 92 **UP TEMPO** *KMS UK KMSUK 1* **68** 1

The TROPHY BOYZ NEW *UK, male vocal group*

6 Aug 05 **DU THE DUDEK** *Diablo DIACD 010* **49** 1

TROUBADOURS DU ROI BAUDOUIN *Zaire, male / female vocal group*

19 Mar 69 **SANCTUS (MISSA LUBA)** (re) *Philips BF 1732* **28** 11
22 May 76 MISSA LUBA *Philips SBL 7592* 59 1

TROUBLE FUNK *US, male vocal / instrumental group (2 Albums: 4 Weeks, 1 Single: 3 Weeks)*

8 Nov 86 SAY WHAT! *Fourth & Broadway DCLP 101* 75 2
27 Jun 87 **WOMAN OF PRINCIPLE** *Fourth & Broadway BRW 70* **65** 3
5 Sep 87 TROUBLE OVER HERE TROUBLE OVER THERE *Fourth & Broadway BRLP 513* 54 2

Robin TROWER (see also The PARAMOUNTS; PROCOL HARUM) *UK, male guitarist (5 Albums: 16 Weeks)*

1 Mar 75 FOR EARTH BELOW *Chrysalis CHR 1073* 26 4
13 Mar 76 LIVE! *Chrysalis CHR 1089* 15 6
30 Oct 76 LONG MISTY DAYS *Chrysalis CHR 1107* 31 1
29 Oct 77 IN CITY DREAMS *Chrysalis CHR 1148* 58 1
16 Feb 80 VICTIMS OF THE FURY *Chrysalis CHR 1215* 61 4

Doris TROY *US, female vocalist, b. Doris Higginson, 6 Jan 1937, d. 16 Feb 2004*

19 Nov 64 **WHATCHA GONNA DO ABOUT IT** (re) *Atlantic AT 4011* **37** 12

7 May 1994	14 May 1994	21 May 1994	28 May 1994
THE REAL THING Tony Di Bart	INSIDE Stiltskin	COME ON YOU REDS Manchester United Football Club	COME ON YOU REDS Manchester United Football Club
PARKLIFE Blur	OUR TOWN - THE GREATEST HITS Deacon Blue	OUR TOWN - THE GREATEST HITS Deacon Blue	I SAY I SAY I SAY Erasure

KEY: UK No.1 ★ UK Top 10 ● Still on chart + UK entry at No.1 ■ US No.1 ▲ UK million seller £ US million seller $
Singles re-entries are listed as (re), (2re), (3re)... which signifies that the hit re-entered the chart once, twice or three times...
Peak Position / Weeks

Elisabeth TROY *UK, female vocalist (4 Singles: 8 Weeks)*

25 Feb 95 **GREATER LOVE** *Sound of Underground SOURCD 016* [1] **49** 2
18 Dec 99 **ENOUGH IS ENOUGH** (re) *Northwest 10 NORTHCD 002* [2] **49** 3
2 Dec 00 **HOLD ON TO ME** *Talkin Loud TLCD 62* [3] 35 2
18 May 02 **FOREVER YOUNG** *Botchit & Scarper BOS 2CD 033* [4] **75** 1

[1] Soundman and Don Lloydie with Elisabeth Troy [2] Y-Tribe featuring Elisabeth Troy [3] MJ Cole featuring Elisabeth Troy [4] 4 Vini featuring Elisabeth Troy

TRU FAITH & DUB CONSPIRACY *UK, male production groups*

9 Sep 00 **FREAK LIKE ME** *Public Demand / Positiva CDTIV 138*....12 5

'Freak Like Me' contains uncredited vocal by Imaani.

TRUBBLE *UK, male / female production / vocal trio*

26 Dec 98 **DANCING BABY (OOGA-CHAKA)** *Island YYCD 1*....21 5

TRUCE *UK, female vocal group (4 Singles: 6 Weeks)*

2 Sep 95 **THE FINEST** *Big Life BLRD 118*....**54** 1
30 Mar 96 **CELEBRATION OF LIFE** *Big Life BLRD 126*....**51** 1
29 Nov 97 **NOTHIN' BUT A PARTY** *Big Life BLRD 138*....**71** 1
5 Sep 98 **EYES DON'T LIE** *Big Life BLRD 146*....20 3

TRUCKS *UK / Norway, male vocal / instrumental group*

5 Oct 02 **IT'S JUST PORN MUM** *Gut CDGUT 43*....35 2

Andrea TRUE CONNECTION
US, female vocalist and male instrumental backing group (2 Singles: 16 Weeks)

17 Apr 76 ● **MORE, MORE, MORE** *Buddah BDS 442* $....5 10
4 Mar 78 **WHAT'S YOUR NAME, WHAT'S YOUR NUMBER** *Buddah BDS 467*....34 6

TRUE FAITH and Bridgette GRACE with FINAL CUT
US, male / female vocal / instrumental group

2 Mar 91 **TAKE ME AWAY** *Network NWK 20*....51 4

TRUE PARTY *UK, male production / vocal group*

2 Dec 00 **WHAZZUP** *Positiva CDBUD 001*....13 6

TRUE STEPPERS (see also Jonny L) *UK, male production / instrumental duo – Jonny Linders and Andy Lysandrou (3 Singles: 31 Weeks)*

29 Apr 00 ● **BUGGIN** *Nulife 74321753342* [1] 6 8
26 Aug 00 ● **OUT OF YOUR MIND** (re) *Nulife 74321782942* [2] 2 20
2 Dec 00 **TRUE STEP TONIGHT** *Nulife 74321811312* [3] 25 3

[1] True Steppers featuring Dane Bowers [2] True Steppers and Dane Bowers featuring Victoria Beckham [3] True Steppers featuring Brian Harvey and Donell Jones

TRUMAN & WOLFF featuring STEEL HORSES
UK, male production duo and rap group

22 Aug 98 **COME AGAIN** *Multiply CDMULTY 38*....**57** 1

TRUSSEL *US, male vocal / instrumental group*

8 Mar 80 **LOVE INJECTION** *Elektra K 12412*....43 4

The TRUTH (see also The JAVELLS featuring Nosmo KING)
UK, male vocal duo – Stephen 'Nosmo King' Gold and Francis Aiello

3 Feb 66 **GIRL** *Pye 7N 17035*....27 6

TRUTH *UK, male vocal / instrumental group (3 Singles: 16 Weeks)*

11 Jun 83 **CONFUSION (HITS US EVERY TIME)** *Formation TRUTH 1*....22 7
27 Aug 83 **A STEP IN THE RIGHT DIRECTION** *Formation TRUTH 2*....32 7
4 Feb 84 **NO STONE UNTURNED** *Formation TRUTH 3*....**66** 2

TRUTH HURTS *US, female vocalist – Shari Watson*

24 Aug 02 **TRUTHFULLY SPEAKING** *Interscope 4934592*....61 4
31 Aug 02 ● **ADDICTIVE** *Aftermath / Interscope 4977782* [1] 3 12

[1] Truth Hurts featuring Rakim

TUBBY T *UK, male vocalist – Anthony Robinson (2 Singles: 3 Weeks)*

21 Sep 02 **TALES OF THE HOOD** *Go Beat GOBCD 51*....**47** 1
24 May 03 **BIG N BASHY** *Virgin VSCDT 1847* [1] **45** 2

[1] Fallacy featuring Tubby T

TUBE & BERGER featuring Chrissie HYNDE (see also The PRETENDERS) *Germany, male production duo and US, female vocalist*

7 Feb 04 **STRAIGHT AHEAD** *Direction 6746222*....29 3

The TUBES
US, male vocal / instrumental group (3 Albums: 7 Weeks, 3 Singles: 18 Weeks)

19 Nov 77 **WHITE PUNKS ON DOPE** *A&M AMS 7323*....28 4
4 Mar 78 **WHAT DO YOU WANT FROM LIVE** *A&M AMS 68460*....38 1
28 Apr 79 **PRIME TIME** *A&M AMS 7423*....34 10
2 Jun 79 **REMOTE CONTROL** *A&M AMLH 64751*....40 5
12 Sep 81 **DON'T WANT TO WAIT ANYMORE** *Capitol CL 208*....**60** 4
4 Jun 83 **OUTSIDE INSIDE** *Capitol EST 12260*....77 1

Barbara TUCKER *US, female vocalist (6 Singles: 15 Weeks)*

5 Mar 94 **BEAUTIFUL PEOPLE** *Positiva CDTIV 11*....23 3
26 Nov 94 **I GET LIFTED** *Positiva CDTIV 23*....33 2
23 Sep 95 **STAY TOGETHER** *Positiva CDTIV 39*....**46** 1
8 Aug 98 **EVERYBODY DANCE (THE HORN SONG)** *Positiva CDTIV 96*....28 2
18 Mar 00 **STOP PLAYING WITH MY MIND** *Positiva CDTIV 127* [1] 17 4
14 May 05 **MOST PRECIOUS LOVE** *Defected DFTD 100CDS* [2] **44** 3

[1] Barbara Tucker featuring Darryl D'Bonneau [2] Blaze presents Uda featuring Barbara Tucker

Junior TUCKER *UK, male vocalist*

2 Jun 90 **DON'T TEST** *10 TEN 299*....**54** 2

Louise TUCKER *UK, female vocalist*

9 Apr 83 **MIDNIGHT BLUE** *Ariola ARO 289*....**59** 5

Tommy TUCKER
US, male vocalist, b. Robert Higginbotham, 5 Mar 1939, d. 22 Jan 1982

26 Mar 64 **HI-HEEL SNEAKERS** *Pye International 7N 25238*....23 10

TUFF JAM *UK, male production duo*

10 Oct 98 **NEED GOOD LOVE** *Locked On LOX 99CD*....**44** 1

TUKAN *Denmark, male production duo – Soren Weile and Lars Fredriksen*

15 Dec 01 **LIGHT A RAINBOW** *Incentive CENT 33CDS*....38 3

TUNDE
(see also LIGHTHOUSE FAMILY) *Nigeria, male vocalist – Tunde Baiyewu*

30 Oct 04 **TUNDE** *RCA 82876652262*....32 2

KT TUNSTALL NEW *UK, female vocalist / guitarist – Kate Tunstall (1 Album: 48 Weeks, 4 Singles: 41 Weeks)*

29 Jan 05 ● **EYE TO THE TELESCOPE** *Relentless CDREL 06*....3 48+
5 Mar 05 **BLACK HORSE & THE CHERRY TREE** *Relentless RELDX 14*....28 3

	4 June 1994	11 June 1994	18 June 1994	25 June 1994
UK No.1 SINGLES	LOVE IS ALL AROUND Wet Wet Wet	LOVE IS ALL AROUND Wet Wet Wet	LOVE IS ALL AROUND Wet Wet Wet	LOVE IS ALL AROUND Wet Wet Wet
UK No.1 ALBUMS	SEAL Seal	SEAL Seal	REAL THINGS 2 Unlimited	EVERYBODY ELSE IS DOING IT SO WHY CAN'T WE? The Cranberries

21 May 05 **OTHER SIDE OF THE WORLD** (re) *Relentless RELCD 18*..........13 19
10 Sep 05 **SUDDENLY I SEE** *Relentless RELCD 21*..........12 17+
17 Dec 05 **UNDER THE WEATHER** *Relentless RELCD 23*..........39 2

TURIN BRAKES *UK, male vocal / instrumental duo – Gale Paridjanian and Olly Knight (3 Albums: 33 Weeks, 10 Singles: 18 Weeks)*

3 Mar 01 **THE DOOR** *Source SOURCDS 024*..........67 1
17 Mar 01 THE OPTIMIST LP *Source SOURCD 023*..........27 18
12 May 01 **UNDERDOG (SAVE ME)** *Source SOURCDSE 101*..........39 2
11 Aug 01 **MIND OVER MONEY** *Source SOURCD 038*..........31 2
27 Oct 01 **72** *Source SOURCD 041*..........41 1
2 Nov 02 **LONG DISTANCE** *Source SOURCD 064*..........22 2
1 Mar 03 ● **PAIN KILLER** *Source SOURCD 068*..........5 3
15 Mar 03 ● ETHER SONG *Source CDSOURX 054*..........4 11
7 Jun 03 **AVERAGE MAN** *Source SOURCD 85*..........35 2
11 Oct 03 **5 MILE** *Source SOURCD 089*..........31 2
28 May 05 **FISHING FOR A DREAM** *Source SOURCECD 109*..........32 2
11 Jun 05 ● JACKINABOX *Source CDSOUR 110*..........9 4
13 Aug 05 **OVER AND OVER** *Source SOURCD 114*..........62 1

Ike and Tina TURNER *US, male / female vocal / instrumental duo (1 Album: 1 Week, 5 Singles: 44 Weeks)*

9 Jun 66 ● **RIVER DEEP – MOUNTAIN HIGH** *London HLU 10046*..........3 13
28 Jul 66 **TELL HER I'M NOT HOME** *Warner Bros. WB 5753*..........48 1
1 Oct 66 RIVER DEEP – MOUNTAIN HIGH *London HAU 8298*..........27 1
27 Oct 66 **A LOVE LIKE YOURS (DON'T COME KNOCKING EVERY DAY)** *London HLU 10083*..........16 10
12 Feb 69 **RIVER DEEP MOUNTAIN HIGH** (re-issue) *London HLU 10242*..33 7
8 Sep 73 ● **NUTBUSH CITY LIMITS** *United Artists UP 35582*..........4 13

Ruby TURNER
UK, female vocalist (3 Albums: 19 Weeks, 8 Singles: 31 Weeks)

25 Jan 86 **IF YOU'RE READY (COME GO WITH ME)** *Jive JIVE 109* [1]..........30 7
29 Mar 86 **I'M IN LOVE** *Jive JIVE 118*..........61 4
13 Sep 86 **BYE BABY** *Jive JIVE 126*..........52 3
18 Oct 86 WOMEN HOLD UP HALF THE SKY *Jive HIP 36*..........47 11
14 Mar 87 **I'D RATHER GO BLIND** *Jive RTS 1*..........24 8
16 May 87 **I'M IN LOVE** (re-issue) *Jive RTS 2*..........57 2
8 Oct 88 THE MOTOWN SONGBOOK *Jive HIP 58*..........22 6
13 Jan 90 **IT'S GONNA BE ALRIGHT** *Jive RTS 7*..........57 3
17 Feb 90 PARADISE *Jive HIP 89*..........74 2
5 Feb 94 **STAY WITH ME BABY** *M&G MAGCD 53*..........39 3
9 Dec 95 **SHAKABOOM!** *Telstar HUNTCD 1* [2]..........64 1

[1] Ruby Turner featuring Jonathan Butler [2] Hunter featuring Ruby Turner

Sammy TURNER *US, male vocalist – Samuel Black*

13 Nov 59 **ALWAYS** *London HLX 8963*..........26 2

Tina TURNER (34 Top 500) (see also Ike and Tina TURNER)
Supreme soul singer-cum-rock legend, b. Anna Mae Bullock, 26 Nov 1939, Tennessee, US. After a successful, if stormy, partnership with husband Ike, she reached greater heights as a Grammy-winning soloist and was a hugely popular live act, boasting a 45 year US chart span (9 Albums: 533 Weeks, 37 Singles: 227 Weeks)

19 Nov 83 ● **LET'S STAY TOGETHER** *Capitol CL 316*..........6 13
25 Feb 84 **HELP** *Capitol CL 325*..........40 6
16 Jun 84 ● **WHAT'S LOVE GOT TO DO WITH IT** *Capitol CL 334* ▲ $..........3 16
30 Jun 84 ● PRIVATE DANCER *Capitol TINA 1*..........2 147
15 Sep 84 **BETTER BE GOOD TO ME** *Capitol CL 338*..........45 5
17 Nov 84 **PRIVATE DANCER** *Capitol CL 343*..........26 9
2 Mar 85 **I CAN'T STAND THE RAIN** *Capitol CL 352*..........57 3
20 Jul 85 ● **WE DON'T NEED ANOTHER HERO (THUNDERDOME)** *Capitol CL 364*..........3 12
12 Oct 85 **ONE OF THE LIVING** *Capitol CL 376*..........55 2
2 Nov 85 **IT'S ONLY LOVE** *A&M AM 285* [1]..........29 6
23 Aug 86 **TYPICAL MALE** *Capitol CL 419*..........33 6
20 Sep 86 ● BREAK EVERY RULE *Capitol EST 2018*..........2 49
8 Nov 86 **TWO PEOPLE** *Capitol CL 430*..........43 4
14 Mar 87 **WHAT YOU GET IS WHAT YOU SEE** *Capitol CL 439*..........30 7
13 Jun 87 **BREAK EVERY RULE** *Capitol CL 452*..........43 3
20 Jun 87 **TEARING US APART** *Duck W 8299* [2]..........56 3
19 Mar 88 **ADDICTED TO LOVE (LIVE)** *Capitol CL 484*..........71 2
2 Apr 88 ● LIVE IN EUROPE *Capitol ESTD 1*..........8 13
2 Sep 89 ● **THE BEST** *Capitol CL 543*..........5 12
30 Sep 89 ★ FOREIGN AFFAIR *Capitol ESTU 2103* ■..........1 78
18 Nov 89 ● **I DON'T WANNA LOSE YOU** *Capitol CL 553*..........8 11
17 Feb 90 **STEAMY WINDOWS** *Capitol CL 560*..........13 6
11 Aug 90 **LOOK ME IN THE HEART** *Capitol CL 584*..........31 6
13 Oct 90 **BE TENDER WITH ME BABY** *Capitol CL 593*..........28 4
24 Nov 90 ● **IT TAKES TWO** *Warner Bros. ROD 1* [3]..........5 8
21 Sep 91 **NUTBUSH CITY LIMITS** (re-recording) *Capitol CL 630*..........23 5
12 Oct 91 ● SIMPLY THE BEST *Capitol ESTV 1*..........2 141
23 Nov 91 **WAY OF THE WORLD** *Capitol CL 637*..........13 7
15 Feb 92 **LOVE THING** *Capitol CL 644*..........29 4
6 Jun 92 **I WANT YOU NEAR ME** *Capitol CL 659*..........22 4
22 May 93 ● **I DON'T WANNA FIGHT** *Parlophone CDRS 6346*..........7 9
19 Jun 93 ★ WHAT'S LOVE GOT TO DO WITH IT (FILM SOUNDTRACK) *Parlophone CDPCSD 128* ■..........1 33
28 Aug 93 **DISCO INFERNO** *Parlophone CDR 6357*..........12 6
30 Oct 93 **WHY MUST WE WAIT UNTIL TONIGHT** *Parlophone CDR 6366*...16 4
18 Nov 95 ● **GOLDENEYE** *Parlophone CDR 0071001*..........10 9
23 Mar 96 **WHATEVER YOU WANT** *Parlophone CDR 6429*..........23 6
13 Apr 96 ● WILDEST DREAMS *Parlophone CDEST 2279*..........4 41
8 Jun 96 **ON SILENT WINGS** *Parlophone CDR 6434*..........13 6
27 Jul 96 **MISSING YOU** *Parlophone CDR 6441* [4]..........12 5
19 Oct 96 **SOMETHING BEAUTIFUL REMAINS** *Parlophone CDR 6448*......27 2
21 Dec 96 **IN YOUR WILDEST DREAMS** *Parlophone CDR 6451* [5]..........32 3
30 Oct 99 ● **WHEN THE HEARTACHE IS OVER** *Parlophone CDR 6529* [4] .10 7
13 Nov 99 ● TWENTY FOUR SEVEN *Parlophone 5231802*..........9 19
12 Feb 00 **WHATEVER YOU NEED** *Parlophone CDR 6532* [4]..........27 3
6 Nov 04 **OPEN ARMS** *Parlophone CDCLS 862* [4]..........25 3
13 Nov 04 ● ALL THE BEST *Parlophone 8667172* [1]..........6 12

[1] Bryan Adams and Tina Turner [2] Eric Clapton and Tina Turner [3] Rod Stewart and Tina Turner [4] Tina [5] Tina Turner featuring Barry White [1] Tina

TURNTABLE ORCHESTRA *US, male vocal / instrumental duo*

21 Jan 89 **YOU'RE GONNA MISS ME** *Republic LIC 012*..........52 4

The TURTLES
US, male vocal / instrumental group (1 Album: 9 Weeks, 3 Singles: 39 Weeks)

23 Mar 67 **HAPPY TOGETHER** *London HLU 10115* ▲ $..........12 12
15 Jun 67 ● **SHE'D RATHER BE WITH ME** *London HLU 10135*..........4 15
22 Jul 67 HAPPY TOGETHER *London HAU 8330*..........18 9
30 Oct 68 ● **ELENORE** *London HLU 10223*..........7 12

Shania TWAIN (153 Top 500)
Canadian country and pop music queen whose first three albums have sold 50 million copies worldwide, b. Eileen Regina Edwards, 28 Aug 1965, Ontario. 'Come on Over', written with husband Mutt Lange, sold more than 35 million copies, including two million in the UK and a record-breaking 20 million in the US. She is the only act to have three successive 10 million-selling albums in the US. At the 2004 World Music Awards she was named the World's Top-Selling Female. Best-selling single: 'That Don't Impress Me Much' 763,000 (5 Albums: 227 Weeks, 13 Singles: 128 Weeks)

28 Feb 98 ● **YOU'RE STILL THE ONE** *Mercury 5684932* $..........10 10
21 Mar 98 ★ COME ON OVER *Mercury 5580002*..........1 138
13 Jun 98 **WHEN** *Mercury 5661192*..........18 4
28 Nov 98 ● **FROM THIS MOMENT ON** *Mercury 5665632*..........9 8
22 May 99 ● **THAT DON'T IMPRESS ME MUCH** *Mercury 8708032*..........3 21
2 Oct 99 ● **MAN! I FEEL LIKE A WOMAN!** *Mercury 5623242*..........3 18
26 Feb 00 ● **DON'T BE STUPID (YOU KNOW I LOVE YOU)** (re) *Mercury 1721492*..........5 11
18 Mar 00 ● THE WOMAN IN ME *Mercury 1701292*..........7 25
15 Jul 00 WILD & WICKED *RWP RWPCD 1123*..........62 2
16 Nov 02 ● **I'M GONNA GETCHA GOOD!** *Mercury 1722702*..........4 15
30 Nov 02 ● UP! *Mercury 1703442* ▲..........4 45
22 Mar 03 ● **KA-CHING!** *Mercury 1722862*..........8 8

2 July 1994	9 July 1994	16 July 1994	23 July 1994
LOVE IS ALL AROUND Wet Wet Wet	LOVE IS ALL AROUND Wet Wet Wet	LOVE IS ALL AROUND Wet Wet Wet	LOVE IS ALL AROUND Wet Wet Wet
HAPPY NATION Ace of Base	HAPPY NATION Ace of Base	MUSIC FOR THE JILTED GENERATION The Prodigy	VOODOO LOUNGE The Rolling Stones

KEY: UK No.1 ★ UK Top 10 ● Still on chart + UK entry at No.1 ■ US No.1 ▲ UK million seller £ US million seller $
Singles re-entries are listed as (re), (2re), (3re)... which signifies that the hit re-entered the chart once, twice or three times...
Peak Position / Weeks

14 Jun 03 ● **FOREVER AND FOR ALWAYS** *Mercury 9807733*....6 10
6 Sep 03 **THANK YOU BABY (FOR MAKIN' SOMEDAY COME SO SOON)** *Mercury 9810627*....11 7
29 Nov 03 **WHEN YOU KISS ME / UP!** (re) *Mercury 9814003*....21 5
20 Nov 04 ● GREATEST HITS *Mercury 9863604*....6 17
4 Dec 04 ● **PARTY FOR TWO** *Mercury 2103239* [1]....10 9
12 Mar 05 **DON'T** *Mercury 980434*....30 2

[1] Shania Twain with Mark McGrath

TWEENIES *UK, male / female kiddie TV characters (2 Albums: 9 Weeks, 5 Singles: 58 Weeks)*

11 Nov 00 ● **NO.1** (2re) *BBC Music WMSS 60332*....5 27
25 Nov 00 FRIENDS FOREVER *BBC Music WMSF 60362*....56 4
31 Mar 01 **BEST FRIENDS FOREVER** (re) *BBC Music WMSS 60382*....12 10
4 Aug 01 **DO THE LOLLIPOP** *BBC Music WMSS 60452*....17 8
1 Dec 01 THE CHRISTMAS ALBUM *BBC Music WMSF 60482*....34 5
15 Dec 01 ● **I BELIEVE IN CHRISTMAS** *BBC Music WMSS 60502*....9 6
14 Sep 02 **HAVE FUN, GO MAD!** *BBC Music WMSS 60572*....20 7

TWEET
US, female vocalist – Charlene Keys (1 Album: 5 Weeks, 3 Singles: 13 Weeks)

11 May 02 ● **OOPS (OH MY)** *Elektra E 7306CD*....5 8
25 May 02 SOUTHERN HUMMINGBIRD *Elektra 7559627772*....15 5
7 Sep 02 **CALL ME** *Elektra E 7326CD*....35 2
19 Mar 05 **TURN DA LIGHTS OFF** *Atlantic AT 0200CD* [1]....29 3

[1] Tweet Featuring Missy Elliott

The TWEETS
UK, male feathered vocal / instrumental group (2 Singles: 34 Weeks)

12 Sep 81 ● **THE BIRDIE SONG (BIRDIE DANCE)** (re) *PRT 7P 219*....2 28
5 Dec 81 **LET'S ALL SING LIKE THE BIRDIES SING** *PRT 7P 226*....44 6

'The Birdie Song (Birdie Dance)' re-entered the chart in Dec 1982, peaking at No.48.

TWELFTH NIGHT *UK, male vocal / instrumental group*

27 Oct 84 ART AND ILLUSION *Music for Nations MFN 36*....83 2

20 FINGERS *US, male instrumental / production duo – Charles Babie and Manfred Mohr (3 Singles: 14 Weeks)*

26 Nov 94 **SHORT DICK MAN** *Multiply CDMULT 12* [1]....21 4
30 Sep 95 **SHORT SHORT MAN** (re-mix) *Multiply CXMULTY 7* [1]....11 7
30 Sep 95 **LICK IT** *Zyx ZYX 75908* [2]....48 3

[1] 20 Fingers featuring Gillette [2] 20 Fingers featuring Roula

21ST CENTURY GIRLS *UK, female vocal / instrumental group*

12 Jun 99 **21ST CENTURY GIRLS** *EMI NTNCDS 001*....16 4

24 NEW *US, male producer / musical director – Sean Callery*

12 Feb 05 **THE LONGEST DAY** *Nebula NENCD 064*....56 1

TWEN2Y 4 SE7EN *UK, male vocal group*

12 Jun 04 **HIDE** *Diablo MND 2*....42 1

TWENTY 4 SEVEN featuring CAPTAIN HOLLYWOOD
US / Germany, male / female vocal / instrumental group and US, male rapper (1 Album: 2 Weeks, 6 Singles: 20 Weeks)

22 Sep 90 ● **I CAN'T STAND IT** *BCM BCMR 395* [1]....7 10
24 Nov 90 **ARE YOU DREAMING** *BCM BCM 07504* [1]....17 10
19 Jan 91 STREET MOVES *BCM BCM 3124*....69 2

[1] Twenty 4 Seven featuring Captain Hollywood

29 PALMS *UK, male producer – Pete Lorimar*

25 May 02 **TOUCH THE SKY** *Perfecto PERF 35CDS*....51 1

22-20s
UK, male vocal / instrumental group (1 Album: 1 Week, 4 Singles: 8 Weeks)

17 Apr 04 **WHY DON'T YOU DO IT FOR ME?** *Heavenly HVN 138CD*....41 2
10 Jul 04 **SHOOT YOUR GUN** *Heavenly HVN 141CD*....30 2
25 Sep 04 **22 DAYS** *Heavenly HVN 144CDS*....34 2
2 Oct 04 22-20S *Heavenly HVNLP 51CD*....40 1
12 Feb 05 **SUCH A FOOL** *Heavenly HVN 148CDS*....29 2

TWICE AS MUCH *UK, male vocal duo – David Skinner and Stephen Rose*

16 Jun 66 **SITTIN' ON A FENCE** *Immediate IM 033*....25 9

TWIGGY *UK, female model / vocalist – Lesley Hornby (2 Albums: 11 Weeks, 1 Single: 10 Weeks)*

14 Aug 76 **HERE I GO AGAIN** *Mercury 6007 100*....17 10
21 Aug 76 TWIGGY *Mercury 9102 600*....33 8
30 Apr 77 PLEASE GET MY NAME RIGHT *Mercury 9102 601*....35 3

TWIN HYPE *US, male rap duo*

15 Jul 89 **DO IT TO THE CROWD** *Profile PROF 255*....65 2

TWINKLE *UK, female vocalist – Lynn Ripley (2 Singles: 20 Weeks)*

26 Nov 64 ● **TERRY** *Decca F 12013*....4 15
25 Feb 65 **GOLDEN LIGHTS** *Decca F 12076*....21 5

TWISTA
US, male rapper – Carl Mitchell (1 Album: 22 Weeks, 10 Singles: 45 Weeks)

28 Feb 04 KAMIKAZE *Atlantic 7567835982* ▲....19 22
10 Apr 04 ● **SLOW JAMZ** *Atlantic AT 0174CD* ▲....3 10
3 Jul 04 **OVERNIGHT CELEBRITY** *Atlantic AT 0180CD*....16 7
14 Aug 04 **SUNSHINE** (import) *Atlantic 7567932652* [1]....60 3
11 Sep 04 ● **SUNSHINE** *Atlantic AT 0181CD* [1]....3 10
20 Nov 04 **SO SEXY** *Atlantic AT 0187CD* [2]....28 3
26 Feb 05 **LET'S GO** *Atlantic AT 0193CD* [3]....26 2
9 Apr 05 **HOPE** *Capitol 8694660* [4]....25 5
12 Nov 05 **WHAT WE DO** *Gana / W10 01CDS* [5]....23 3
26 Nov 05 **GIRL TONITE** *Atlantic AT 0225CDX* [6]....47 2

[1] Twista featuring Anthony Hamilton [2] Twista featuring R Kelly [3] Trick Daddy featuring Twista and Lil' Jon [4] Twista featuring Faith Evans [5] Kray Twinz featuring Twista, Lethal B & Gappy Ranks [6] Twista featuring Trey Songz

'Slow Jamz' credits Kanye West and Jamie Foxx on the CD only.

TWISTED INDIVIDUAL *UK, male producer – Lee Greenaway*

9 Aug 03 **BANDWAGON BLUES** *Formation FORM 12102*....51 1

TWISTED SISTER *US, male vocal / instrumental group (5 Albums: 20 Weeks, 5 Singles: 28 Weeks)*

25 Sep 82 UNDER THE BLADE *Secret SECX 9*....70 3
26 Mar 83 **I AM (I'M ME)** *Atlantic A 9854*....18 9
7 May 83 YOU CAN'T STOP ROCK 'N' ROLL *Atlantic A 0074*....14 9
28 May 83 **THE KIDS ARE BACK** *Atlantic A 9827*....32 6
20 Aug 83 **YOU CAN'T STOP ROCK 'N' ROLL** *Atlantic A 9792*....43 4
2 Jun 84 **WE'RE NOT GONNA TAKE IT** *Atlantic A 9657*....58 6
16 Jun 84 STAY HUNGRY *Atlantic 780156*....34 5
14 Dec 85 COME OUT AND PLAY *Atlantic 7812751*....95 1
18 Jan 86 **LEADER OF THE PACK** *Atlantic A 9478*....47 3
25 Jul 87 LOVE IS FOR SUCKERS *Atlantic WX 120*....57 2

TWISTED X *UK, male vocal group – England football fans*

19 Jun 04 ● **BORN IN ENGLAND** *Universal TV 9867021*....9 3

Includes members of Supergrass, The Libertines, Delays and The Wheatleys, Bernard Butler, actor James Nesbitt and XFM DJ Christian O'Connell

30 July 1994	6 August 1994	13 August 1994	20 August 1994
UK No.1 SINGLES			
LOVE IS ALL AROUND Wet Wet Wet	LOVE IS ALL AROUND Wet Wet Wet	LOVE IS ALL AROUND Wet Wet Wet	LOVE IS ALL AROUND Wet Wet Wet
UK No.1 ALBUMS			
END OF PART ONE (THEIR GREATEST HITS) Wet Wet Wet	END OF PART ONE (THEIR GREATEST HITS) Wet Wet Wet	END OF PART ONE (THEIR GREATEST HITS) Wet Wet Wet	END OF PART ONE (THEIR GREATEST HITS) Wet Wet Wet

Conway TWITTY *US, male vocalist, b. Harold Jenkins, 1 Sep 1933, d. 5 Jun 1993 (5 Singles: 36 Weeks)*

14 Nov 58 ★ **IT'S ONLY MAKE BELIEVE** *MGM 992* ▲ $ 1 15
27 Mar 59 **THE STORY OF MY LOVE** *MGM 1003* 30 1
21 Aug 59 ● **MONA LISA** *MGM 1029* 5 14
21 Jul 60 **IS A BLUE BIRD BLUE** *MGM 1082* 43 3
23 Feb 61 **C'EST SI BON** *MGM 1118* 40 3

2 BAD MICE *UK, male instrumental / production group (2 Singles: 4 Weeks)*

15 Feb 92 **HOLD IT DOWN** (re) *Moving Shadow SHADOW 14* 48 3
7 Sep 96 **BOMBSCARE** *Arista 74321397662* 46 1

TWO COWBOYS *Italy, male instrumental / production duo – Roberto Sagotto and Maurizio Braccagni*

9 Jul 94 ● **EVERYBODY GONFI-GON** *3 Beat TABCD 221* 7 11

2 EIVISSA *Germany, female vocal duo – Pascale Jean Louis and Ellen Helbig*

4 Oct 97 **OH LA LA LA** *Club Tools 0063475 CLU* 13 6

2 FOR JOY *UK, male instrumental / production duo (2 Singles: 3 Weeks)*

1 Dec 90 **IN A STATE** *Mercury MER 333* 61 1
9 Nov 91 **LET THE BASS KICK** *All Around the World CDGLOBE 102* 67 2

2 FUNKY 2 starring Kathryn DION *UK, male / female vocal / instrumental group (2 Singles: 4 Weeks)*

6 Nov 93 **BROTHERS AND SISTERS** *Logic 74321170772* 56 2
30 Nov 96 **BROTHERS AND SISTERS** (re-mix) *All Around the World CDGLOBE 138* 36 2

2 HOUSE *US, male instrumental / production duo*

21 Mar 92 **GO TECHNO** *Atlantic A 7519* 65 1

2 IN A ROOM *US, male vocal duo – Roger Pauletta and Rafael Vargas (1 Album: 1 Week, 6 Singles: 15 Weeks)*

18 Nov 89 **SOMEBODY IN THE HOUSE SAY YEAH!** *Big Life BLR 12* 66 1
26 Jan 91 ● **WIGGLE IT** *SBK SBK 19* 3 8
2 Mar 91 WIGGLE IT *SBK SBKLP 11* 73 1
6 Apr 91 **SHE'S GOT ME GOING CRAZY** *SBK SBK 23* 54 2
22 Oct 94 **EL TRAGO (THE DRINK)** *Positiva CDTIV 18* 34 2
8 Apr 95 **AHORA ES (NOW IS THE TIME)** *Positiva CDTIV 32* 43 1
17 Aug 96 **GIDDY-UP** *Encore CDCOR 008* 74 1

2 IN A TENT (see also STOCK AITKEN WATERMAN) *UK, male instrumental / production duo – Mike Stock and Matt Aitken (2 Singles: 7 Weeks)*

17 Dec 94 **WHEN I'M CLEANING WINDOWS (TURNED OUT NICE AGAIN)** (re) *Love This SPONCD 1* 25 6
13 May 95 **BOOGIE WOOGIE BUGLE BOY (DON'T STOP)** *Bald Cat BALDCD 1* [1] 48 1

[1] 2 In a Tank

First hit, which features the sampled vocals of George Formby, re-entered and peaked at No.62 in Jan 1996.

2K (see also JUSTIFIED ANCIENTS OF MU MU; The KLF; The TIMELORDS) *UK, male production duo – Bill Drummond and Jimmy Cauty*

25 Oct 97 *****K THE MILLENNIUM** *Blast First BFFP 146CDK* 28 2

2 MAD *UK, male vocal / instrumental duo*

9 Feb 91 **THINKIN' ABOUT YOUR BODY** *Big Life BLR 37* 43 4

TWO MAN SOUND *Belgium, male vocal / instrumental group*

20 Jan 79 **QUE TAL AMERICA** *Miracle M 1* 46 7

TWO MEN, A DRUM MACHINE AND A TRUMPET (see also FINE YOUNG CANNIBALS) *UK, male instrumental duo – Andy Cox and David Steele (2 Singles: 17 Weeks)*

9 Jan 88 **TIRED OF GETTING PUSHED AROUND** *London LON 141* 18 8
25 Jun 88 **HEAT IT UP** *Jive JIVE 174* [1] 21 9

[1] Wee Papa Girl Rappers featuring Two Men and a Drum Machine

TWO NATIONS *UK, male vocal / instrumental group*

20 Jun 87 **THAT'S THE WAY IT FEELS** *10 TEN 168* 74 1

2PAC (376 Top 500) *Legendary US rapper / actor, b. Tupac Amaru Shakur, New York City, 16 Jun 1971, d. 13 Sep 1996, who achieved more UK and US single and album hits after his death (in a Las Vegas shooting incident) than before. In his homeland, no artist has had more posthumous chart success (12 Albums: 80 Weeks, 18 Singles: 105 Weeks)*

9 Mar 96 ALL EYEZ ON ME *Death Row 5242042* ▲ 32 7
13 Apr 96 ● **CALIFORNIA LOVE** *Death Row DRWCD 3* [1] 6 8
27 Jul 96 **HOW DO YOU WANT IT** *Death Row DRWCD 4* [2] ▲ $ 17 4
16 Nov 96 THE DON KILLUMINATI – THE 7 DAY THEORY *Death Row IND 90039* [1] 53 1
30 Nov 96 **I AIN'T MAD AT CHA** *Death Row DRWCD 5* 13 9
12 Apr 97 ● **TO LIVE & DIE IN LA** *Interscope IND 95529* [3] 10 4
26 Apr 97 **WANTED DEAD OR ALIVE** *Def Jam 5744052* [4] 16 3
9 Aug 97 **TOSS IT UP** *Interscope IND 95521* [3] 15 3
6 Dec 97 R U STILL DOWN? (REMEMBER ME) *Jive CHIP 195* 44 1
10 Jan 98 **I WONDER IF HEAVEN GOT A GHETTO** *Jive JIVECD 446* 21 4
14 Feb 98 **HAIL MARY** *Interscope IND 95575* [3] 43 1
13 Jun 98 **DO FOR LOVE** *Jive 0518512* [5] 12 4
18 Jul 98 **RUNNIN'** *Black Jam BJAM 9005* [6] 15 3
8 Aug 98 IN HIS OWN WORDS *Eagle EAGCD 050* 65 1
28 Nov 98 **HAPPY HOME** *Eagle EAGXS 058* 17 2
12 Dec 98 GREATEST HITS *Jive 522662* 17 35
20 Feb 99 ● **CHANGES** *Jive 0522832* 3 12
3 Jul 99 **DEAR MAMA** *Jive 0523702* $ 27 3
8 Jan 00 STILL I RISE *Interscope 4904172* [2] 75 1
21 Apr 01 UNTIL THE END OF TIME *Interscope 4908402* ▲ 31 17
23 Jun 01 ● **UNTIL THE END OF TIME** *Interscope / Polydor 4975812* 4 11
10 Nov 01 **LETTER 2 MY UNBORN** *Interscope / Polydor 4976142* 21 5
14 Dec 02 BETTER DAYZ *Interscope 4970702* 68 1
22 Feb 03 **THUGZ MANSION** *Interscope / Polydor 4978542* 24 5
22 Nov 03 RESURRECTION (OST) *Interscope / Polydor 9861159* [3] 62 1
31 Jan 04 **RUNNIN' (DYING TO LIVE)** *Interscope / Polydor 9815329* [7] 17 6
28 Aug 04 LIVE *Koch 2357462* 67 1
25 Dec 04 LOYAL TO THE GAME *Interscope 2103291* ▲ 20 13
12 Feb 05 READY 2 DIE *Street Dance SDR 0166882* 70 1
2 Jul 05 ★ **GHETTO GOSPEL** *Interscope 9883248* [8] ■ 1 18

[1] 2Pac featuring Dr Dre [2] 2Pac featuring K-Ci and JoJo [3] Makaveli [4] 2Pac and Snoop Doggy Dogg [5] 2Pac featuring Eric Williams [6] 2Pac and Notorious BIG [7] Tupac featuring Notorious BIG [8] 2Pac (featuring Elton John)
[1] Makaveli [2] 2Pac and Outlawz [3] Tupac

'Ghetto Gospel' samples Elton John's 'Indian Summer' 2Pac does not appear on all the tracks on Ready 2 Die, but the album features re-mixes and tracks from his back catalogue.

TWO PEOPLE *UK, male vocal / instrumental group*

31 Jan 87 **HEAVEN** *Polydor POSP 844* 63 2

2PLAY (see also Thomas JULES-STOCK) *UK, male producer – Wessley Johnson (3 Singles: 23 Weeks)*

24 Jan 04 ● **SO CONFUSED** *2PSL 2PSLCD 002* [1] 6 13
22 May 04 ● **IT CAN'T BE RIGHT** *2PSL / Inferno 2PSLCD 04* [2] 8 7
4 Dec 04 **CARELESS WHISPER** *Inferno 2PSLCD 06* [3] 29 3

[1] 2Play featuring Raghav & Jucxi [2] 2Play featuring Raghav & Naila Boss [3] 2Play featuring Thomas Jules & Jucxi D

27 August 1994	3 September 1994	10 September 1994	17 September 1994
LOVE IS ALL AROUND Wet Wet Wet	**LOVE IS ALL AROUND** Wet Wet Wet	**LOVE IS ALL AROUND** Wet Wet Wet	**SATURDAY NIGHT** Whigfield
COME Prince	**END OF PART ONE (THEIR GREATEST HITS)** Wet Wet Wet	**DEFINITELY MAYBE** Oasis	**THE THREE TENORS IN CONCERT 1994** José Carreras, Placido Domingo and Luciano Pavarotti conducted by Zubin Mehta

KEY
UK No.1 ★ UK Top 10 ● Still on chart + UK entry at No.1 ■
US No.1 ▲ UK million seller £ US million seller $
Singles re-entries are listed as (re), (2re), (3re)… which signifies that the hit re-entered the chart once, twice or three times…

Peak Position / Weeks

2WO THIRD3 *UK, male vocal / instrumental group (4 Singles: 15 Weeks)*

19 Feb 94 **HEAR ME CALLING** *Epic 6600642* 48 3
11 Jun 94 **EASE THE PRESSURE** *Epic 6604782* 45 2
8 Oct 94 **I WANT THE WORLD** *Epic 6608542* 20 5
17 Dec 94 **I WANT TO BE ALONE** *Epic 6610852* 29 5

2-4 FAMILY *UK / US / Korea, male / female rap / vocal group*

29 May 99 **LEAN ON ME (WITH THE FAMILY)** *Epic 6670132* 69 1

2 UNLIMITED (494 Top 500) *The brainchild of Jean-Paul de Coster and Phil Wilde, fronted by Dutch rap / vocalists Ray Slijngaard and Anita Doth. Their youth-aimed, infectious dance tracks sold millions around Europe and gave them 11 successive UK Top 20 hits. Best-selling single: 'No Limit' 531,900 (4 Albums: 38 Weeks, 14 Singles: 112 Weeks)*

5 Oct 91 ● **GET READY FOR THIS** *PWL Continental PWL 206* 2 15
25 Jan 92 ● **TWILIGHT ZONE** *PWL Continental PWL 211* 2 10
7 Mar 92 GET READY *PWL Continental HFCD 23* 37 3
2 May 92 ● **WORKAHOLIC** *PWL Continental PWL 228* 4 7
15 Aug 92 **THE MAGIC FRIEND** *PWL Continental PWL 240* 11 7
30 Jan 93 ★ **NO LIMIT** *PWL Continental PWCD 256* 1 16
8 May 93 ● **TRIBAL DANCE** *PWL Continental PWCD 262* 4 11
22 May 93 ★ NO LIMITS *PWL Continental HFCD 27* 1 21
4 Sep 93 ● **FACES** *PWL Continental PWCD 268* 8 7
20 Nov 93 **MAXIMUM OVERDRIVE** *PWL Continental PWCD 276* 15 8
19 Feb 94 ● **LET THE BEAT CONTROL YOUR BODY** *PWL Continental PWCD 280* 6 9
21 May 94 ● **THE REAL THING** *PWL Continental PWCD 306* 6 7
18 Jun 94 ★ REAL THINGS *PWL Continental HFCD 38* ■ 1 9
1 Oct 94 **NO ONE** *PWL Continental PWCD 314* 17 6
25 Mar 95 **HERE I GO** *PWL Continental PWCD 317* 22 3
21 Oct 95 **DO WHAT'S GOOD FOR ME** *PWL Continental PWL 322CD1* 16 4
11 Nov 95 HITS UNLIMITED *PWL Continental HF 47CD* 27 5
11 Jul 98 **WANNA GET UP** *Big Life BLRD 143* 38 2

For 1998 hit Slijngaard and Anita Doth were replaced by Dutch female duo Romy Van Ooyen and Marjon Van Lwaarden.

TY featuring ROOTS MANUVA *UK, male rappers*

8 May 04 **OH U WANT MORE?** *Big Dada BDCDS 066* 65 1

TYGERS OF PAN TANG *UK, male vocal / instrumental group (4 Albums: 20 Weeks, 4 Singles: 15 Weeks)*

30 Aug 80 WILD CAT *MCA MCF 3075* 18 5
14 Feb 81 **HELLBOUND** *MCA 672* 48 3
18 Apr 81 SPELLBOUND *MCA MCF 3104* 33 4
21 Nov 81 CRAZY NIGHTS *MCA MCF 3123* 51 3
27 Mar 82 **LOVE POTION NO. 9** *MCA 769* 45 6
10 Jul 82 **RENDEZVOUS** *MCA 777* 49 4
28 Aug 82 THE CAGE *MCA MCF 3150* 13 8
11 Sep 82 **PARIS BY AIR** *MCA 790* 63 2

Bonnie TYLER (447 Top 500) *Raspy-voiced vocalist, b. Gaynor Hopkins, 8 Jun 1953, Swansea, Wales. She made the US country Top 10 with 'It's a Heartache' and 'Total Eclipse of the Heart' was the first record by a Welsh artist to top the US pop chart (5 Albums: 79 Weeks, 12 Singles: 81 Weeks)*

30 Oct 76 ● **LOST IN FRANCE** *RCA 2734* 9 10
19 Mar 77 **MORE THAN A LOVER** *RCA PB 5008* 27 6
3 Dec 77 ● **IT'S A HEARTACHE** *RCA PB 5057* $ 4 12
30 Jun 79 **MARRIED MEN** *RCA PB 5164* 35 6
19 Feb 83 ★ **TOTAL ECLIPSE OF THE HEART** *CBS TYLER 1* ▲ $ 1 12
16 Apr 83 ★ FASTER THAN THE SPEED OF NIGHT *CBS 25304* ■ 1 45
7 May 83 **FASTER THAN THE SPEED OF NIGHT** *CBS A 3338* 43 4
25 Jun 83 **HAVE YOU EVER SEEN THE RAIN** *CBS A 3517* 47 3
7 Jan 84 ● **A ROCKIN' GOOD WAY** *Epic A 4071* [1] 5 9
31 Aug 85 ● **HOLDING OUT FOR A HERO** *CBS A 4251* 2 13
14 Dec 85 **LOVING YOU'S A DIRTY JOB BUT SOMEBODY'S GOTTA DO IT** *CBS A 6662* [2] 73 2
17 May 86 SECRET DREAMS AND FORBIDDEN FIRE *CBS 86319* 24 12
29 Nov 86 THE GREATEST HITS *Telstar STAR 2291* 24 17
21 May 88 HIDE YOUR HEART *CBS 460125 1* 78 1
28 Dec 91 **HOLDING OUT FOR A HERO** (re-issue) *Total TYLER 10* 69 2
27 Jan 96 **MAKING LOVE (OUT OF NOTHING AT ALL)** *East West EW 010CD* 45 2
14 Jul 01 GREATEST HITS *Sanctuary / Sony TV SANCD 082* 18 4

[1] Shaky and Bonnie [2] Bonnie Tyler, guest vocals Todd Rundgren

The albums titled The Greatest Hits and Greatest Hits are different.

The TYMES *US, male vocal (George Williams, d. 2004) group (5 Singles: 41 Weeks)*

25 Jul 63 **SO MUCH IN LOVE** *Cameo Parkway P 871* ▲ $ 21 8
15 Jan 69 **PEOPLE** *Direction 58 3903* 16 10
21 Sep 74 **YOU LITTLE TRUSTMAKER** *RCA 2456* 18 9
21 Dec 74 ★ **MS GRACE** *RCA 2493* 1 11
17 Jan 76 **GOD'S GONNA PUNISH YOU** *RCA 2626* 41 3

TYMES 4 *UK, female vocal group (2 Singles: 5 Weeks)*

25 Aug 01 **BODYROCK** *Edel 0118635 ERE* 23 3
15 Dec 01 **SHE GOT GAME** *Blacklist 0133135 ERE* 40 2

TYPE O NEGATIVE *US, male vocal / instrumental group (2 Albums: 2 Weeks)*

14 Sep 96 OCTOBER RUST *Roadrunner RR 88742* 26 1
2 Oct 99 WORLD COMING DOWN *Roadrunner RR 86602* 49 1

TYPICALLY TROPICAL *UK, male vocal / instrumental duo – Jeff Calvert and Max West*

5 Jul 75 ★ **BARBADOS** *Gull GULS 14* 1 11

TYREE *US, male producer – Tyree Cooper (3 Singles: 10 Weeks)*

25 Feb 89 **TURN UP THE BASS** *ffrr FFR 24* [1] 12 7
6 May 89 **HARDCORE HIP HOUSE** *DJ International DJIN 11* 70 2
2 Dec 89 **MOVE YOUR BODY** *CBS 655470 7* [2] 72 1

[1] Tyree featuring Kool Rock Steady [2] Tyree featuring JMD

TYRELL CORPORATION *UK, male vocal / instrumental duo – Joe Watson and Tony Barry (5 Singles: 9 Weeks)*

14 Mar 92 **THE BOTTLE** *Volante TYR 1* 71 1
15 Aug 92 **GOING HOME** *Volante TYR 2* 58 2
10 Oct 92 **WAKING WITH A STRANGER / ONE DAY** *Volante TYRS 3* 59 1
24 Sep 94 **YOU'RE NOT HERE** *Cooltempo CDCOOL 292* 42 2
14 Jan 95 **BETTER DAYS AHEAD** *Cooltempo CDCOOL 303* 29 3

TYRESE *US, male vocalist – Tyrese Gibson (3 Singles: 6 Weeks)*

31 Jul 99 **NOBODY ELSE** *RCA 74321688282* 59 1
25 Sep 99 **SWEET LADY** *RCA 74321700842* 55 1
26 Jul 03 **HOW YOU GONNA ACT LIKE THAT** *J 82876544892* 30 4

TZANT (see also MIRRORBALL; PF PROJECT featuring Ewan McGREGOR) *UK, male rap / instrumental duo – Jamie White and Marcus Thomas (aka ODC MC) (3 Singles: 10 Weeks)*

7 Sep 96 **HOT AND WET (BELIEVE IT)** *Logic 74321376832* 36 2
25 Apr 98 **SOUNDS OF WICKEDNESS** *Logic 74321568842* 11 6
22 Aug 98 **BOUNCE WITH THE MASSIVE** *Logic 74321602102* 39 2

	24 September 1994	1 October 1994	8 October 1994	15 October 1994
UK No.1 SINGLES	SATURDAY NIGHT Whigfield	SATURDAY NIGHT Whigfield	SATURDAY NIGHT Whigfield	SURE Take That
UK No.1 ALBUMS	FROM THE CRADLE Eric Clapton	SONGS Luther Vandross	MONSTER R.E.M.	MONSTER R.E.M.

Judie TZUKE *UK, female vocalist (8 Albums: 61 Weeks, 1 Single: 10 Weeks)*

14 Jul 79 **STAY WITH ME TILL DAWN** *Rocket XPRES 17* **16** 10
4 Aug 79 WELCOME TO THE CRUISE *Rocket TRAIN 7* 14 17
10 May 80 ● SPORTS CAR *Rocket TRAIN 9* 7 11
16 May 81 I AM PHOENIX *Rocket TRAIN 15* 17 10
17 Apr 82 SHOOT THE MOON *Chrysalis CDL 1382* 19 10
30 Oct 82 ROAD NOISE – THE OFFICIAL BOOTLEG *Chrysalis CTY 1405* 39 4
1 Oct 83 RITMO *Chrysalis CDL 1442* 26 5
15 Jun 85 THE CAT IS OUT *Legacy LLP 102* 35 3
29 Apr 89 TURNING STONES *Polydor 839087 1* 57 1

UB40 (22 Top 500)

Reggae's most successful transatlantic group: includes brothers Ali (v/g) and Robin (v/g) Campbell and Earl Falconer (b). Only three groups can claim more chart hits than this Birmingham act, named after the number of the UK unemployment benefit form. The band performed at Live 8 London (24 Albums: 622 Weeks, 51 Singles: 350 Weeks)

8 Mar 80 ● **KING / FOOD FOR THOUGHT** *Graduate GRAD 6* [1] **4** 13
14 Jun 80 ● **MY WAY OF THINKING / I THINK IT'S GOING TO RAIN** *Graduate GRAD 8* [1] **6** 10
6 Sep 80 ● SIGNING OFF *Graduate GRADLP 2* 2 71
1 Nov 80 ● **THE EARTH DIES SCREAMING / DREAM A LIE** *Graduate GRAD 10* **10** 12
23 May 81 **DON'T LET IT PASS YOU BY / DON'T SLOW DOWN** *DEP International DEP 1* **16** 9
6 Jun 81 ● PRESENT ARMS *DEP International LPDEP 1* 2 38
8 Aug 81 ● **ONE IN TEN** *DEP International DEP 2* **7** 10
10 Oct 81 PRESENT ARMS IN DUB *DEP International LPDEP 2* 38 7
13 Feb 82 **I WON'T CLOSE MY EYES** *DEP International DEP 3* **32** 6
15 May 82 **LOVE IS ALL IS ALRIGHT** *DEP International DEP 4* **29** 7
28 Aug 82 THE SINGLES ALBUM *Graduate GRADLSP 3* 17 8
28 Aug 82 **SO HERE I AM** *DEP International DEP 5* **25** 9
9 Oct 82 ● UB 44 *DEP International LPDEP 3* 4 8
5 Feb 83 **I'VE GOT MINE** *DEP International 7 DEP 6* **45** 4
26 Feb 83 UB40 LIVE *DEP International LPDEP 4* 44 5
20 Aug 83 ★ **RED RED WINE** *DEP International 7 DEP 7* ▲ **1** 14
24 Sep 83 ★ LABOUR OF LOVE *DEP International LPDEP 5* ■ 1 76
15 Oct 83 ● **PLEASE DON'T MAKE ME CRY** *DEP International 7 DEP 8* **10** 8
10 Dec 83 **MANY RIVERS TO CROSS** *DEP International 7 DEP 9* **16** 8
17 Mar 84 **CHERRY OH BABY** *DEP International DEP 10* **12** 8
22 Sep 84 ● **IF IT HAPPENS AGAIN** *DEP International DEP 11* **9** 8
20 Oct 84 ● GEFFERY MORGAN *DEP International DEP 6* 3 14
1 Dec 84 **RIDDLE ME** *DEP International DEP 15* **59** 2
3 Aug 85 ★ **I GOT YOU BABE** *DEP International DEP 20* [2] **1** 13
14 Sep 85 BAGGARIDDIM *DEP International LPDEP 10* 14 23
26 Oct 85 ● **DON'T BREAK MY HEART** *DEP International DEP 22* **3** 13
12 Jul 86 ● **SING OUR OWN SONG** *DEP International DEP 23* **5** 9
9 Aug 86 ● RAT IN THE KITCHEN *DEP International LPDEP 11* 8 20
27 Sep 86 **ALL I WANT TO DO** *DEP International DEP 24* **41** 4
17 Jan 87 **RAT IN MI KITCHEN** *DEP International DEP 25* **12** 7
9 May 87 **WATCHDOGS** *DEP International DEP 26* **39** 4
10 Oct 87 **MAYBE TOMORROW** *DEP International DEP 27* **14** 8
7 Nov 87 ● THE BEST OF UB40 – VOLUME ONE *Virgin UBTV 1* 3 133
27 Feb 88 **RECKLESS** *EMI EM 41* [3] **17** 8
18 Jun 88 ● **BREAKFAST IN BED** *DEP International DEP 29* [2] **6** 11
23 Jul 88 UB40 *DEP International LPDEP 13* 12 12
20 Aug 88 **WHERE DID I GO WRONG** *DEP International DEP 30* **26** 6
17 Jun 89 **I WOULD DO FOR YOU** *DEP International DEP 32* **45** 4
18 Nov 89 ● **HOMELY GIRL** *DEP International DEP 33* **6** 10
9 Dec 89 ● LABOUR OF LOVE II *DEP International LPDEP 14* 3 69
27 Jan 90 **HERE I AM (COME AND TAKE ME)** *DEP International DEP 34* **46** 3
31 Mar 90 ● **KINGSTON TOWN** *DEP International DEP 35* **4** 12
28 Jul 90 **WEAR YOU TO THE BALL** *DEP International DEP 36* **35** 6
3 Nov 90 ● **I'LL BE YOUR BABY TONIGHT** *EMI EM 167* [4] **6** 10
1 Dec 90 **IMPOSSIBLE LOVE** *DEP International DEP 37* **47** 2
2 Feb 91 **THE WAY YOU DO THE THINGS YOU DO** *DEP International DEP 38* **49** 3
12 Dec 92 **ONE IN TEN** (re-mix) *ZTT ZANG 39* [5] **17** 8
22 May 93 ★ **(I CAN'T HELP) FALLING IN LOVE WITH YOU** *DEP International DEPDG 40* ▲ $ **1** 16
24 Jul 93 ★ PROMISES AND LIES *DEP International DEPCD 15* ■ 1 37
21 Aug 93 ● **HIGHER GROUND** *DEP International DEPD 41* **8** 9
11 Dec 93 **BRING ME YOUR CUP** *DEP International DEPD 42* **24** 6
2 Apr 94 **C'EST LA VIE** *DEP International DEPD 43* **37** 3
27 Aug 94 **REGGAE MUSIC** *DEP International DEPDG 44* **28** 2
12 Nov 94 ● LABOUR OF LOVE VOLUMES I AND II (re-issues) *DEP International DEPDD 1* 5 15
4 Nov 95 **UNTIL MY DYING DAY** *DEP International DEPD 45* **15** 6
11 Nov 95 THE BEST OF UB40 – VOLUME TWO *DEP International DUBTV 2* 12 11
12 Jul 97 ● GUNS IN THE GHETTO *DEP International DEPCD 16* 7 9
30 Aug 97 **TELL ME IT IS TRUE** *DEP International DEP 48* **14** 4
15 Nov 97 **ALWAYS THERE** *DEP International DEPD 49* **53** 1
10 Oct 98 ● **COME BACK DARLING** *DEP International DEPD 50* **10** 6
24 Oct 98 ● LABOUR OF LOVE III *DEP International DEPCD 18* 8 12
19 Dec 98 **HOLLY HOLY** *DEP International DEPD 51* **31** 3
1 May 99 **THE TRAIN IS COMING** *DEP International DEPD 52* **30** 2
4 Nov 00 ● THE VERY BEST OF UB40 1980-2000 *Virgin DUBTVX 3* 7 23
9 Dec 00 **LIGHT MY FIRE** *DEP International DEPD 53* **63** 1
20 Oct 01 **SINCE I MET YOU LADY / SPARKLE OF MY EYES** *DEP International DEPD 55* [6] **40** 2
3 Nov 01 COVER UP *Virgin DEPCD 19* 29 2
2 Mar 02 **COVER UP** *DEP International DEPD 56* **54** 1
14 Jun 03 ● LABOUR OF LOVE – VOL I II & III *Virgin 5847242* 7 16
8 Nov 03 **SWING LOW** *DEP International DEPD 58* [7] **15** 14
15 Nov 03 HOME GROWN *DEP International DEPCD 22* 49 2
18 Jun 05 **KISS AND SAY GOODBYE** *DEP International DEPDX 59* **19** 4
25 Jun 05 WHO YOU FIGHTING FOR? *DEP International DEPCDX 23* 20 5
10 Sep 05 **REASONS** *DEP International DEPDX 60* [8] **75** 1
26 Nov 05 THE BEST OF – VOLUMES 1 & 2 *DEP International DEPDDX 2* ..... 47 6+

[1] UB40 [2] UB40 featuring Chrissie Hynde [3] Afrika Bambaataa and Family featuring UB40 [4] Robert Palmer and UB40 [5] 808 State vs UB40 [6] UB40 featuring Lady Saw [7] UB40 featuring United Colours of Sound [8] UB40 / Hunterz / The Dhol Blasters

The Best of UB40 – Volume One charted in 2005 with a different catalogue number, DEP International DUBTV 1.

UBM *Germany, male / female vocal / instrumental group*

23 May 98 **LOVIN' YOU** *Logic 74321571692* **46** 1

UD PROJECT
Canada / Germany, male vocal / production group (2 Singles: 10 Weeks)

4 Oct 03 **SUMMER JAM** *Free 2 Air / Kontor 0150345 KON* [1] **14** 6
21 Feb 04 **SATURDAY NIGHT** *Free 2 Air / Kontor 0152955 KON* **19** 4

[1] UD Project vs Sunclub

UFO *UK / Germany, male vocal (Phil Mogg) / instrumental group (9 Albums: 48 Weeks, 7 Singles: 31 Weeks)*

4 Jun 77 LIGHTS OUT *Chrysalis CHR 1127* 54 2
15 Jul 78 OBSESSION *Chrysalis CDL 1182* 26 7
5 Aug 78 **ONLY YOU CAN ROCK ME** *Chrysalis CHS 2241* **50** 4

22 October 1994	29 October 1994	5 November 1994	12 November 1994
SURE Take That	BABY COME BACK Pato Banton	BABY COME BACK Pato Banton	BABY COME BACK Pato Banton
CROSSROAD - THE BEST OF BON JOVI Bon Jovi	CROSSROAD - THE BEST OF BON JOVI Bon Jovi	CROSSROAD - THE BEST OF BON JOVI Bon Jovi	UNPLUGGED IN NEW YORK Nirvana

KEY
UK No.1 ★★ UK Top 10 ●● Still on chart ++ UK entry at No.1 ■■
US No.1 ▲▲ UK million seller £ US million seller $
Singles re-entries are listed as (re), (2re), (3re)... which signifies that the hit re-entered the chart once, twice or three times...

Peak Position / Weeks

27 Jan 79 **DOCTOR DOCTOR** *Chrysalis CHS 2287* 35 6
10 Feb 79 ● STRANGERS IN THE NIGHT *Chrysalis CJT 5* 7 11
31 Mar 79 **SHOOT, SHOOT** *Chrysalis CHS 2318* 48 5
12 Jan 80 **YOUNG BLOOD** *Chrysalis CHS 2399* 36 5
19 Jan 80 NO PLACE TO RUN *Chrysalis CDL 1239* 11 7
17 Jan 81 **LONELY HEART** *Chrysalis CHS 2482* 41 5
24 Jan 81 THE WILD THE WILLING AND THE INNOCENT *Chrysalis CHR 1307* 19 5
30 Jan 82 **LET IT RAIN** *Chrysalis CHS 2576* 62 3
20 Feb 82 ● MECHANIX *Chrysalis CHR 1360* 8 6
12 Feb 83 MAKING CONTACT *Chrysalis CHR 1402* 32 4
19 Mar 83 **WHEN IT'S TIME TO ROCK** *Chrysalis CHS 2672* 70 3
3 Sep 83 HEADSTONE – THE BEST OF UFO *Chrysalis CTY 1437* 39 4
16 Nov 85 MISDEMEANOUR *Chrysalis CHR 1518* 74 2

UHF *US, male instrumental / production group*

14 Dec 91 **UHF / EVERYTHING** *XL Recordings XLS 25* 46 4

U.T.F.O. *US, male vocal group*

16 Mar 85 ROXANNE ROXANNE (6 TRACK VERSION) *Streetwave 6 Track XKHAN 506* 72 1

UGLY DUCKLING *US, male production / rap trio*

13 Oct 01 **A LITTLE SAMBA** *XL Recordings XLS 135CD* 70 1

UGLY KID JOE *US, male vocal (Whitfield Crane) / instrumental group (3 Albums: 42 Weeks, 6 Singles: 28 Weeks)*

16 May 92 ● **EVERYTHING ABOUT YOU** *Mercury MER 367* 3 9
13 Jun 92 ● AS UGLY AS THEY WANNA BE *Mercury 8688232* 9 13
22 Aug 92 **NEIGHBOR** *Mercury MER 374* 28 4
12 Sep 92 AMERICA'S LEAST WANTED *Vertigo 5125712* 11 24
31 Oct 92 **SO DAMN COOL** *Mercury MER 383* 44 2
13 Mar 93 ● **CATS IN THE CRADLE** *Mercury MERCD 385* 7 9
19 Jun 93 **BUSY BEE** *Mercury MERCD 389* 39 2
17 Jun 95 MENACE TO SOBRIETY *Mercury 5282622* 25 5
8 Jul 95 **MILKMAN'S SON** *Mercury MERCD 435* 39 2

Tillmann UHRMACHER

(see also TILLMANN and REIS) *Germany, male producer*

23 Mar 02 **ON THE RUN** *Direction 6721352* 16 3

UK *UK, male vocal / instrumental group*

27 May 78 U.K. *Polydor 2302 080* 43 3
30 Jun 79 **NOTHING TO LOSE** *Polydor POSP 55* 67 2

UK *Canada / Spain, male vocal / instrumental group*

3 Aug 96 **SMALL TOWN BOY** *Media MCSTD 400* 74 1

UK APACHI *UK, male vocalist / rapper / instrumentalist – Abdul Wahab (2 Singles: 4 Weeks)*

1 Oct 94 **ORIGINAL NUTTAH** *Sound of Underground SOUR 008CD* [1] 39 3
28 Jul 01 **SIGNS** *Outcaste OUT 38CD1* [2] 63 1

[1] UK Apachi with Shy FX [2] DJ Badmarsh and Shri featuring UK Apache

UK MIXMASTERS (see also DOCTOR SPIN)

UK, male producer – Nigel Wright (3 Singles: 15 Weeks)

2 Feb 91 **THE NIGHT FEVER MEGAMIX** *IQ ZB 44339* [1] 23 5
27 Jul 91 **LUCKY 7 MEGAMIX** *IQ ZB 44731* 43 3
14 Dec 91 **THE BARE NECESSITIES MEGAMIX** *Connect ZB 35135* 14 7

[1] Mixmasters

The UK PLAYERS *UK, male vocal / instrumental group*

14 May 83 **LOVE'S GONNA GET YOU** *RCA 326* 52 3

UK SUBS *UK, male vocal (David Perez aka Charlie Harper) / instrumental group (4 Albums: 26 Weeks, 7 Singles: 39 Weeks)*

23 Jun 79 **STRANGLEHOLD** *Gem GEMS 5* 26 8
8 Sep 79 **TOMORROW'S GIRLS** *Gem GEMS 10* 28 6
13 Oct 79 ANOTHER KIND OF BLUES *Gem GEMLP 100* 21 6
1 Dec 79 **SHE'S NOT THERE / KICKS (EP)** *Gem GEMS 14* 36 7
8 Mar 80 **WARHEAD** *Gem GEMS 23* 30 4
19 Apr 80 BRAND NEW AGE *Gem GEMLP 106* 18 9
17 May 80 **TEENAGE** *Gem GEMS 30* 32 5
27 Sep 80 ● CRASH COURSE *Gem GEMLP 111* 8 6
25 Oct 80 **PARTY IN PARIS** *Gem GEMS 42* 37 4
21 Feb 81 DIMINISHED RESPONSIBILITY *Gem GEMLP 112* 18 5
18 Apr 81 **KEEP ON RUNNIN' (TILL YOU BURN)** *Gem GEMS 45* 41 5

Tracks on She's Not There / Kicks (EP): She's Not There / Kicks / Victim / The Same Thing.

Tracey ULLMAN

UK, female vocalist / actor (2 Albums: 22 Weeks, 6 Singles: 49 Weeks)

19 Mar 83 ● **BREAKAWAY** *Stiff BUY 168* 4 11
24 Sep 83 ● **THEY DON'T KNOW** *Stiff BUY 180* 2 11
3 Dec 83 YOU BROKE MY HEART IN 17 PLACES *Stiff SEEZ 51* 14 20
3 Dec 83 ● **MOVE OVER DARLING** *Stiff BUY 195* 8 9
3 Mar 84 **MY GUY** *Stiff BUY 197* 23 6
28 Jul 84 **SUNGLASSES** *Stiff BUY 205* 18 9
27 Oct 84 **HELPLESS** *Stiff BUY 211* 61 3
8 Dec 84 YOU CAUGHT ME OUT *Stiff SEEZ 56* 92 2

ULTIMATE KAOS

UK, male vocal group (1 Album: 1 Week, 7 Singles: 28 Weeks)

22 Oct 94 ● **SOME GIRLS** (re) *Wild Card CARDD 12* 9 9
21 Jan 95 **HOOCHIE BOOTY** *Wild Card CARDW 14* 17 4
1 Apr 95 **SHOW A LITTLE LOVE** *Wild Card CARDW 18* 23 5
29 Apr 95 ULTIMATE KAOS *Polydor 5274442* 51 1
1 Jul 95 **RIGHT HERE** *Wild Card 5795832* 18 4
8 Mar 97 **CASANOVA** *Polydor 5759312* 24 3
18 Jul 98 **CASANOVA** (re-issue) *Mercury MERCD 505* 29 2
5 Jun 99 **ANYTHING YOU WANT (I'VE GOT IT)** *Mercury MERCD 510* 52 1

ULTRA *UK, male vocal (James Hearn) / instrumental group (1 Album: 2 Weeks, 4 Singles: 22 Weeks)*

18 Apr 98 **SAY YOU DO** *East West EW 124CD* 11 7
4 Jul 98 **SAY IT ONCE** *East West EW 171CD1* 16 6
10 Oct 98 **THE RIGHT TIME** (re) *East West EW 182CD* 28 3
16 Jan 99 ● **RESCUE ME** *East West EW 193CD1* 8 6
6 Feb 99 ULTRA *East West 3984222452* 37 2

ULTRA HIGH *UK, male vocalist – Michael McCloud (2 Singles: 3 Weeks)*

2 Dec 95 **STAY WITH ME** *MCA MCSTD 40007* 36 2
20 Jul 96 **ARE YOU READY FOR LOVE** *MCA MCSTD 40039* 45 1

ULTRA VIVID SCENE *US, male vocalist – Kurt Ralske*

19 May 90 JOY 1967-1990 *4AD CAD 005* 58 1

ULTRABEAT

UK, male DJ / production / vocal (Mike Di Scala) trio (4 Singles: 33 Weeks)

16 Aug 03 ● **PRETTY GREEN EYES** (re) *All Around the World CDGLOBE 281* 2 15
27 Dec 03 **FEELIN' FINE** *All Around the World CDGLOBE 320* 12 12
11 Sep 04 **BETTER THAN LIFE** *All Around the World CDGLOBE 360* 23 5
1 Oct 05 **FEEL IT WITH ME** *All Around the World CDGLOBE 410* 57 1

ULTRACYNIC

UK, male / female vocal / instrumental group (2 Singles: 3 Weeks)

29 Aug 92 **NOTHING IS FOREVER** *380 PEW 2* 50 2
19 Apr 97 **NOTHING IS FOREVER** (re-mix) *All Around the World CDGLOBE 139* 47 1

	19 November 1994	26 November 1994	3 December 1994	10 December 1994
UK No.1 SINGLES	BABY COME BACK Pato Banton	LET ME BE YOUR FANTASY Baby D	LET ME BE YOUR FANTASY Baby D	STAY ANOTHER DAY East 17
UK No.1 ALBUMS	CROSSROAD - THE BEST OF BON JOVI Bon Jovi	CROSSROAD - THE BEST OF BON JOVI Bon Jovi	CARRY ON UP THE CHARTS - THE BEST OF THE BEAUTIFUL SOUTH The Beautiful South	LIVE AT THE BBC The Beatles

ULTRAMARINE
UK, male instrumental duo (1 Album: 1 Week, 3 Singles: 4 Weeks)

24 Jul 93 **KINGDOM** *Blanco Y Negro NEG 65CD*......46 2
4 Sep 93 **UNITED KINGDOMS** *Blanco Y Negro 4509934252*......49 1
29 Jan 94 **BAREFOOT (EP)** *Blanco Y Negro NEG 67CD*......61 1
27 Apr 96 **HYMN** *Blanco Y Negro NEG 87CD* [1] 65 1

[1] Ultramarine featuring David McAlmont

Tracks on Barefoot (EP): Hooter / The Badger / Urf / Happy Land.

ULTRA-SONIC
UK, male instrumental / production duo (1 Album: 1 Week, 2 Singles: 2 Weeks)

3 Sep 94 **OBSESSION** *Clubscene DCSRT 027*......75 1
11 Nov 95 **GLOBAL TEKNO** *Clubscene DCSR 007*......58 1
21 Sep 96 **DO YOU BELIEVE IN LOVE** *Clubscene DCSRT 070*......47 1

ULTRASOUND
UK, male / female vocal / instrumental group (1 Album: 1 Week, 3 Singles: 5 Weeks)

7 Mar 98 **BEST WISHES** *Nude NUD 33CD*......68 1
13 Jun 98 **STAY YOUNG** *Nude NUD 35CD1*......30 2
10 Apr 99 **FLOODLIT WORLD** *Nude NUD 41CD1*......39 2
1 May 99 **EVERYTHING PICTURE** *Nude NUDE 12CD*......23 1

ULTRAVOX
137 Top 500 *Ground-breaking British electro-rock quartet: Midge Ure (OBE) (v/g) (replaced John Foxx in 1979), Billy Currie (k/syn), Chris Cross (b/syn) and Warren Cann (d). Ex-Slik and Visage vocalist Ure was a driving force behind the Band Aid hits, Live Aid, Live 8 and Nelson Mandela's birthday concerts (8 Albums: 227 Weeks, 18 Singles: 142 Weeks)*

5 Jul 80 **SLEEPWALK** *Chrysalis CHS 2441*......29 11
19 Jul 80 ● **VIENNA** *Chrysalis CHR 1296*......3 72
18 Oct 80 **PASSING STRANGERS** *Chrysalis CHS 2457*......57 4
17 Jan 81 ● **VIENNA** *Chrysalis CHS 2481*......2 14
28 Mar 81 **SLOW MOTION** *Island WIP 6691*......33 4
6 Jun 81 ● **ALL STOOD STILL** *Chrysalis CHS 2522*......8 10
22 Aug 81 **THE THIN WALL** *Chrysalis CHS 2540*......14 8
19 Sep 81 ● **RAGE IN EDEN** *Chrysalis CDL 1338*......4 23
7 Nov 81 **THE VOICE** *Chrysalis CHS 2559*......16 12
25 Sep 82 **REAP THE WILD WIND** *Chrysalis CHS 2639*......12 9
23 Oct 82 ● **QUARTET** *Chrysalis CDL 1394*......6 30
27 Nov 82 **HYMN** *Chrysalis CHS 2657*......11 11
19 Mar 83 **VISIONS IN BLUE** *Chrysalis CHS 2676*......15 6
4 Jun 83 **WE CAME TO DANCE** *Chrysalis VOX 1*......18 7
22 Oct 83 ● **MONUMENT – THE SOUNDTRACK** *Chrysalis CUX 1452*......9 15
11 Feb 84 **ONE SMALL DAY** *Chrysalis VOX 2*......27 6
14 Apr 84 ● **LAMENT** *Chrysalis CDL 1459*......8 26
19 May 84 ● **DANCING WITH TEARS IN MY EYES** (re) *Chrysalis UV 1*......3 11
7 Jul 84 **LAMENT** (re) *Chrysalis UV 2*......22 7
20 Oct 84 **LOVE'S GREAT ADVENTURE** *Chrysalis UV 3*......12 9
10 Nov 84 ● **THE COLLECTION** *Chrysalis UTV 1*......2 53
27 Sep 86 **SAME OLD STORY** *Chrysalis UV 4*......31 4
25 Oct 86 ● **U-VOX** *Chrysalis CDL 1545*......9 6
22 Nov 86 **ALL FALL DOWN** *Chrysalis UV 5*......30 5
6 Feb 93 **VIENNA** (re-issue) *Chrysalis CDCHSS 3936*......13 4
10 Nov 01 **THE VERY BEST OF MIDGE URE & ULTRAVOX** *EMI 5358112*......45 2

UMBOZA
(see also EYE TO EYE featuring Taka BOOM; MUKKAA) *UK, male instrumental / production duo – Bryan Chamberlyn and Stuart Crichton (2 Singles: 9 Weeks)*

23 Sep 95 **CRY INDIA** *Positiva CDTIV 43*......19 4
20 Jul 96 **SUNSHINE** *Positiva CDTIV 47*......14 5

Piero UMILIANI
Italy, orchestra and chorus – leader b. 1926, d. 14 Feb 2001

30 Apr 77 ● **MAH-NA, MAH-NA** *EMI International INT 530*......8 8

UN-CUT
UK, male production duo and female vocalist (2 Singles: 4 Weeks)

29 Mar 03 **MIDNIGHT** *WEA WEA 364CD1*......26 3
28 Jun 03 **FALLIN'** *WEA WEA 368CD1*......63 1

UNA MAS
UK, male production duo

6 Apr 02 **I WILL FOLLOW** *Defected DFECT 47CDS*......55 1

UNATION
UK, male / female vocal / instrumental group (2 Singles: 3 Weeks)

5 Jun 93 **HIGHER AND HIGHER** *MCA MCSTD 1773*......42 2
7 Aug 93 **DO YOU BELIEVE IN LOVE** *MCA MCSTD 1796*......75 1

UNBELIEVABLE TRUTH
UK, male vocal / instrumental group (1 Album: 2 Weeks, 3 Singles: 5 Weeks)

14 Feb 98 **HIGHER THAN REASON** *Virgin VSCDT 1676*......38 2
9 May 98 **SOLVED** *Virgin VSCDT 1684*......39 2
23 May 98 **ALMOST HERE** *Virgin CDV 2849*......21 2
18 Jul 98 **SETTLE DOWN / DUNE SEA** *Virgin VSCDT 1697*......46 1

UNCANNY ALLIANCE
US, male / female vocal / instrumental duo – Brinsley Evans and E.V. Mystique

19 Dec 92 **I GOT MY EDUCATION** *A&M AM 0128*......39 5

UNCLE KRACKER
US, male vocalist – Matt Shafer

8 Sep 01 ● **FOLLOW ME** *Atlantic AT 0108CD*......3 18
22 Sep 01 **DOUBLE WIDE** *Atlantic 7567832792*......40 3

UNCLE SAM
US, male vocalist – Sam Turner

16 May 98 **I DON'T EVER WANT TO SEE YOU AGAIN** *Epic 6656382* **$**......30 2

UNDERCOVER
UK, male vocal (John Matthews) / instrumental group (1 Album: 9 Weeks, 5 Singles: 30 Weeks)

15 Aug 92 ● **BAKER STREET** *PWL International PWL 239*......2 14
14 Nov 92 ● **NEVER LET HER SLIP AWAY** *PWL International PWL 255*......5 11
5 Dec 92 **CHECK OUT THE GROOVE** *PWL International HFCD 26*......26 9
6 Feb 93 **I WANNA STAY WITH YOU** *PWL International PWCD 258*......28 3
14 Aug 93 **LOVESICK** *PWL International PWCD 271* [1] 62 1
3 Jul 04 **VIVA ENGLAND** *MCS MCSRECS 1*......49 1

[1] Undercover featuring John Matthews

The UNDERTAKERS
UK, male vocal / instrumental group

9 Apr 64 **JUST A LITTLE BIT** *Pye 7N 15607*......49 1

The UNDERTONES
(see also Feargal SHARKEY) *UK, male vocal / instrumental group (8 Albums: 52 Weeks, 10 Singles: 67 Weeks)*

21 Oct 78 **TEENAGE KICKS** *Sire SIR 4007*......31 6
3 Feb 79 **GET OVER YOU** *Sire SIR 4010*......57 4
28 Apr 79 **JIMMY JIMMY** *Sire SIR 4015*......16 10
19 May 79 **THE UNDERTONES** *Sire SRK 6071*......13 21
21 Jul 79 **HERE COMES THE SUMMER** *Sire SIR 4022*......34 6
20 Oct 79 **YOU'VE GOT MY NUMBER (WHY DON'T YOU USE IT!)** *Sire SIR 4024*......32 6
5 Apr 80 ● **MY PERFECT COUSIN** *Sire SIR 4038*......9 10
26 Apr 80 ● **HYPNOTISED** *Sire SRK 6088*......6 10
5 Jul 80 **WEDNESDAY WEEK** *Sire SIR 4042*......11 9
2 May 81 **IT'S GOING TO HAPPEN!** *Ardeck ARDS 8*......18 9
16 May 81 **POSITIVE TOUCH** *Ardeck ARD 103*......17 6
25 Jul 81 **JULIE OCEAN** *Ardeck ARDS 9*......41 5
19 Mar 83 **THE SIN OF PRIDE** *Ardeck ARD 104*......43 5
9 Jul 83 **TEENAGE KICKS** (re-issue) *Ardeck ARDS 1*......60 2
10 Dec 83 **ALL WRAPPED UP** *Ardeck ARD 1654281/3*......67 4
14 Jun 86 **CHER O'BOWLIES – PICK OF THE UNDERTONES** *Ardeck EMS 1172*......96 1
25 Sep 93 **THE BEST OF THE UNDERTONES – TEENAGE KICKS** *Castle Communications CTVCD 121*......45 3
13 Sep 03 **TEENAGE KICKS – THE BEST OF THE UNDERTONES** *Sanctuary / Sony TV TVSAN 005*......35 2

17 December 1994	24 December 1994	31 December 1994	7 January 1995
STAY ANOTHER DAY East 17	STAY ANOTHER DAY East 17	STAY ANOTHER DAY East 17	STAY ANOTHER DAY East 17
CARRY ON UP THE CHARTS - THE BEST OF THE BEAUTIFUL SOUTH The Beautiful South	CARRY ON UP THE CHARTS - THE BEST OF THE BEAUTIFUL SOUTH The Beautiful South	CARRY ON UP THE CHARTS - THE BEST OF THE BEAUTIFUL SOUTH The Beautiful South	CARRY ON UP THE CHARTS - THE BEST OF THE BEAUTIFUL SOUTH The Beautiful South

KEY	UK No.1 ★★ UK Top 10 ●● Still on chart ++ UK entry at No.1 ■■ US No.1 ▲▲ UK million seller £ US million seller $ Singles re-entries are listed as (re), (2re), (3re)... which signifies that the hit re-entered the chart once, twice or three times...	Peak Position	Weeks

UNDERWORLD *UK, male instrumental / vocal (Karl Hyde) group (6 Albums: 54 Weeks, 13 Singles: 49 Weeks)*

18 Dec 93	**SPIKEE / DOGMAN GO** *Junior Boy's Own JBO 17CD*	63	1
5 Feb 94	DUBNOBASSWITHMYHEADMAN *Junior Boy's Own JBOCD 1*	12	6
25 Jun 94	**DARK AND LONG** *Junior Boy's Own JBO 19CDS*	57	1
13 May 95	**BORN SLIPPY** *Junior Boy's Own JBO 29CDS*	52	2
23 Mar 96 ●	SECOND TOUGHEST IN THE INFANTS *Junior Boy's Own JBOCD 4*	9	28
18 May 96	**PEARL'S GIRL** *Junior Boy's Own JBO 38CDS 1*	24	2
13 Jul 96 ●	**BORN SLIPPY** (re) (re-mix) *Junior Boy's Own JBO 44CDS*	2	21
9 Nov 96	**PEARL'S GIRL** (re-issue) *Junior Boy's Own JBO 45CDS 1*	22	3
13 Mar 99 ●	BEAUCOUP FISH *JBO JBO 1005438*	3	12
27 Mar 99	**PUSH UPSTAIRS** *Junior Boy's Own JBO 5005443*	12	4
5 Jun 99	**JUMBO** *Junior Boy's Own JBO 5007193*	21	2
28 Aug 99	**KING OF SNAKE** *Junior Boy's Own JBO 5008793*	17	3
2 Sep 00	**COWGIRL** *Junior Boy's Own JBO 5012513*	24	2
16 Sep 00	UNDERWORLD LIVE: EVERYTHING, EVERYTHING *JBO JBO 1012542*	22	3
14 Sep 02	**TWO MONTHS OFF** *Junior Boy's Own JBO 5020093*	12	4
28 Sep 02	A HUNDRED DAYS OFF *JBO JBO 1020102*	16	3
1 Feb 03	**DINOSAUR ADVENTURE 3D** *Junior Boy's Own JBO 5020523*	34	1
8 Nov 03	**BORN SLIPPY NUXX** *Junior Boy's Own JBO 5024703*	27	3
15 Nov 03	1992-2002 *JBO JBO 1024698*	43	2

Act became a duo from 'Two Months Off' onwards.

The UNDISPUTED TRUTH *US, male / female vocal group*

22 Jan 77	**YOU + ME = LOVE** *Warner Bros. K 16804*	43	4

U96 *Germany, male producer – Alex Christiansen (3 Singles: 7 Weeks)*

29 Aug 92	**DAS BOOT** *M&G MAGS 28*	18	5
4 Jun 94	**INSIDE YOUR DREAMS** *Logic 74321209722*	44	1
29 Jun 96	**CLUB BIZARRE** *Urban 5750152*	70	1

UNION
UK / Holland, male instrumental group and UK, rugby team vocalists

12 Oct 91	**SWING LOW (RUN WITH THE BALL)** *Columbia 6575317*	16	7
26 Oct 91	WORLD IN UNION *Columbia 4690471* [1]	17	6

[1] Union featuring the England World Cup Squad

UNIQUE *US, male / female vocal / instrumental group*

10 Sep 83	**WHAT I GOT IS WHAT YOU NEED** *Prelude A 3707*	27	7

UNIQUE 3 *UK, male rap / DJ group (4 Singles: 12 Weeks)*

4 Nov 89	**THE THEME** *10 TEN 285*	61	3
14 Apr 90	**MUSICAL MELODY / WEIGHT FOR THE BASS** *10 TEN 298*	29	5
10 Nov 90	**RHYTHM TAKES CONTROL** *10 TEN 327* [1]	41	3
16 Nov 91	**NO MORE** *10 TEN 387*	74	1

[1] Unique 3 featuring Karin

UNIT FOUR PLUS TWO
UK, male vocal (Peter Moules) / instrumental group (4 Singles: 29 Weeks)

13 Feb 64	**GREEN FIELDS** *Decca F 11821*	48	2
25 Feb 65 ★	**CONCRETE AND CLAY** *Decca F 12071*	1	15
13 May 65	**(YOU'VE) NEVER BEEN IN LOVE LIKE THIS BEFORE** *Decca F 12144*	14	11
17 Mar 66	**BABY NEVER SAY GOODBYE** *Decca F 12333*	49	1

UNITED CITIZEN FEDERATION featuring Sarah BRIGHTMAN
UK, male production duo and female vocalist

14 Feb 98	**STARSHIP TROOPERS** *Coalition COLA 040CD*	58	1

UNITED KINGDOM SYMPHONY *UK, orchestra*

27 Jul 85	**SHADES (THEME FROM THE CROWN PAINT TELEVISION COMMERCIAL)** *Food for Thought YUM 108*	68	4

UNITING NATIONS *UK, male production duo – Paul Keenan and Daz Sampson (3 Singles: 32 Weeks)*

4 Dec 04	**OUT OF TOUCH** (re) *Gusto CDGUS 13*	12	21
6 Aug 05	**YOU AND ME** *Gusto CDGUS 18*	15	7
19 Nov 05	**AI NO CORRIDA** *Gusto CDGUS 25* [1]	18	4

[1] Uniting Nation featuring Laura More

UNITONE ROCKERS featuring STEEL
UK, male vocal / instrumental group

26 Jun 93	**CHILDREN OF THE REVOLUTION** *The Hit Label HLC 4*	60	1

UNITY *UK, male / female vocal / instrumental group*

31 Aug 91	**UNITY** *Cardiac CNY 6*	64	2

UNIVERSAL *Australia, male vocal group (2 Singles: 6 Weeks)*

2 Aug 97	**ROCK ME GOOD** *London LONCD 397*	19	4
18 Oct 97	**MAKE IT WITH YOU** *London LONCD 404*	33	2

UNIVERSAL PROJECT *UK, male vocal group*

1 Jun 02	**VESSEL** *Virus VRS 010*	61	1

'Vessel' shared chart billing with 'Packman' by Ed Rush & Optical

UNKLE (see also DJ SHADOW) *US / UK, male DJ / production duo – Josh Davis and James Lavelle (3 Albums: 12 Weeks, 5 Singles: 13 Weeks)*

21 Jan 95	THE TIME HAS COME (EP) *Mo Wax MW 028P* [1]	73	1
5 Sep 98 ●	PSYENCE FICTION *Mo Wax MW 085CD*	4	9
20 Feb 99 ●	**BE THERE** *Mo Wax MW 108CD1* [1]	8	6
17 Mar 01	**NARCO TOURISTS** *Soma SOMA 100CD* [2]	66	1
6 Sep 03	**EYE FOR AN EYE** *Mo Wax CID 826*	31	2
4 Oct 03	NEVER NEVER LAND *Mo Wax MWU 001CD*	24	2
15 Nov 03	**IN A STATE** *Mo Wax CID 839*	44	2
27 Nov 04	**REIGN** *Mo Wax GUSIN 007CDS* [1]	40	2

[1] Unkle featuring Ian Brown [2] Slam vs Unkle [1] UNKLE

UNO CLIO featuring Martine McCUTCHEON
UK, male instrumental group and female vocalist

18 Nov 95	**ARE YOU MAN ENOUGH** *Avex UK AVEXCD 14*	62	1

The UNTOUCHABLES
US, male vocal / instrumental group (1 Album: 7 Weeks, 2 Singles: 16 Weeks)

6 Apr 85	**FREE YOURSELF** *Stiff BUY 221*	26	11
13 Jul 85	WILD CHILD *Stiff SEEZ 57*	51	7
27 Jul 85	**I SPY FOR THE FBI** *Stiff BUY 227*	59	5

UP YER RONSON featuring Mary PEARCE
UK, male / female vocal / instrumental group (3 Singles: 7 Weeks)

5 Aug 95	**LOST IN LOVE** *Hi-Life 5795572*	27	3
30 Mar 96	**ARE YOU GONNA BE THERE** *Hi-Life 5763272*	27	2
19 Apr 97	**I WILL BE RELEASED** *Hi-Life 5737352*	32	2

Phil UPCHURCH COMBO
US, male instrumental group – leader Phil Upchurch – bass guitar

5 May 66	**YOU CAN'T SIT DOWN** *Sue WI 4005*	39	2

The UPSETTERS
(see also Lee 'Scratch' PERRY) *Jamaica, male instrumental group*

4 Oct 69 ●	**RETURN OF DJANGO / DOLLAR IN THE TEETH** *Upsetter US 301*	5	15

	14 January 1995	21 January 1995	28 January 1995	4 February 1995
UK No.1 SINGLES	COTTON EYE JOE Rednex	COTTON EYE JOE Rednex	COTTON EYE JOE Rednex	THINK TWICE Celine Dion
UK No.1 ALBUMS	CARRY ON UP THE CHARTS - THE BEST OF THE BEAUTIFUL SOUTH The Beautiful South	CARRY ON UP THE CHARTS - THE BEST OF THE BEAUTIFUL SOUTH The Beautiful South	THE COLOUR OF MY LOVE Celine Dion	THE COLOUR OF MY LOVE Celine Dion

Dawn UPSHAW (soprano) / LONDON SINFONIETTA / David ZINMAN (conductor)

US, female vocalist, UK, orchestra and US, male conductor

23 Jan 93 ● GORECKI SYMPHONY NO.3 *Elektra Nonsuch 7559792822*..........6 18

UPSIDE DOWN *UK, male vocal group (4 Singles: 16 Weeks)*

20 Jan 96 **CHANGE YOUR MIND** *World CDWORLD 1A*..........11 7
13 Apr 96 **EVERY TIME I FALL IN LOVE** (re) *World CDWORLD 2A*..........18 4
29 Jun 96 **NEVER FOUND A LOVE LIKE THIS BEFORE** *World CDWORLD 3A*..........19 3
23 Nov 96 **IF YOU LEAVE ME NOW** *World CDWORLD 4A*..........27 2

URBAN ALL STARS (see also BEATS INTERNATIONAL; Norman COOK; FATBOY SLIM; FREAKPOWER; The HOUSEMARTINS; MIGHTY DUB KATZ; PIZZAMAN) *UK, male producer – Norman Cook and US, male / female vocal / instrumental groups*

27 Aug 88 **IT BEGAN IN AFRICA** *Urban URB 23*..........64 2

URBAN BLUES PROJECT presents Michael PROCTER

US, male vocal / instrumental group

10 Aug 96 **LOVE DON'T LIVE** *AM:PM 5817932*..........55 1

URBAN COOKIE COLLECTIVE *UK, male / female vocal (Diane Charlemagne) / instrumental group (1 Album: 2 Weeks, 10 Singles: 40 Weeks)*

10 Jul 93 ● **THE KEY THE SECRET** *Pulse 8 CDLOSE 48*..........2 16
13 Nov 93 ● **FEELS LIKE HEAVEN** *Pulse 8 CDLOSE 55*..........5 9
19 Feb 94 **SAIL AWAY** *Pulse 8 CDLOSE 56*..........18 4
26 Mar 94 HIGH ON A HAPPY VIBE *Pulse 8 PULSE 13CD*..........28 2
23 Apr 94 **HIGH ON A HAPPY VIBE** *Pulse 8 CDLOSE 60*..........31 3
15 Oct 94 **BRING IT ON HOME** *Pulse 8 CDLOSE 73*..........56 1
27 May 95 **SPEND THE DAY** *Pulse 8 CDLOSE 85*..........59 1
9 Sep 95 **REST OF MY LOVE** *Pulse 8 CDLOSE 93*..........67 1
16 Dec 95 **SO BEAUTIFUL** *Pulse 8 CDLOSE 100*..........68 1
24 Aug 96 **THE KEY THE SECRET** (re-mix) *Pulse 8 CDLOSE 109* [1]..........52 1
15 Jan 05 **THE KEY, THE SECRET 2005** (2nd re-mix) *Feverpitch CDFEVS 4*..........31 3

[1] UCC

URBAN DISCHARGE featuring SHE

US, male / female vocal / instrumental group

27 Jan 96 **WANNA DROP A HOUSE (ON THAT BITCH)** *MCA MCSTD 40020*..51 1

URBAN HYPE *UK, male production / instrumental duo – Robert Dibden and Mark Chitty (3 Singles: 12 Weeks)*

11 Jul 92 ● **A TRIP TO TRUMPTON** *Faze 2 FAZE 5*..........6 8
17 Oct 92 **THE FEELING** *Faze 2 FAZE 10*..........67 1
9 Jan 93 **LIVING IN A FANTASY** *Faze 2 CDFAZE 13*..........57 3

Keith URBAN NEW *Australia (b. New Zealand), male vocalist / guitarist*

11 Jun 05 DAYS GO BY *Capitol 4775812*..........40 3

Days Go By features tracks from Urban's previous studio albums, Golden Road and Be Here

URBAN SHAKEDOWN

(see also APHRODITE featuring WILDFLOWER) *UK, male DJ / production duo – Michael Hearn and Gavin King (3 Singles: 8 Weeks)*

27 Jun 92 **SOME JUSTICE** *Urban Shakedown URBST 1*..........23 5
12 Sep 92 **BASS SHAKE** *Urban Shakedown URBST 2* [1]..........59 2
10 Jun 95 **SOME JUSTICE** (re-recording) *Urban Shakedown URBCD 3* [2] 49 1

[1] Urban Shakedown featuring Mickey Finn [2] Urban Shakedown featuring DBO General

URBAN SOUL

UK / US, male / female vocal / production group (4 Singles: 11 Weeks)

30 Mar 91 **ALRIGHT** *Cooltempo COOL 231*..........60 4
21 Sep 91 **ALRIGHT** (re-mix) *Cooltempo COOL 244*..........43 3
28 Mar 92 **ALWAYS** *Cooltempo COOL 251*..........41 3
13 Jun 98 **LOVE IS SO NICE** *VC Recordings VCRD 33*..........75 1

URBAN SPECIES

UK, male vocal / instrumental group (1 Album: 2 Weeks, 4 Singles: 10 Weeks)

12 Feb 94 **SPIRITUAL LOVE** *Talkin Loud TLKCD 45*..........35 4
16 Apr 94 **BROTHER** *Talkin Loud TLKCD 47*..........40 3
7 May 94 LISTEN *Talkin Loud 5186482*..........43 2
20 Aug 94 **LISTEN** *Talkin Loud TLKCD 50* [1]..........47 2
6 Mar 99 **BLANKET** *Talkin Loud TLDD 39* [2]..........56 1

[1] Urban Species featuring MC Solaar [2] Urban Species featuring Imogen Heap

Midge URE (see also The RICH KIDS; SLIK; ULTRAVOX; VISAGE) *UK, male vocalist, received OBE in 2005 (5 Albums: 28 Weeks, 10 Singles: 56 Weeks)*

12 Jun 82 ● **NO REGRETS** *Chrysalis CHS 2618*..........9 10
9 Jul 83 **AFTER A FASHION** *Musicfest FEST 1* [1]..........39 4
14 Sep 85 ★ **IF I WAS** *Chrysalis URE 1*..........1 11
19 Oct 85 ● THE GIFT *Chrysalis CHR 1508*..........2 15
16 Nov 85 **THAT CERTAIN SMILE** *Chrysalis URE 2*..........28 4
8 Feb 86 **WASTELANDS** *Chrysalis URE 3*..........46 3
7 Jun 86 **CALL OF THE WILD** *Chrysalis URE 4*..........27 8
20 Aug 88 **ANSWERS TO NOTHING** *Chrysalis URE 5*..........49 4
10 Sep 88 ANSWERS TO NOTHING *Chrysalis CHR 1649*..........30 3
19 Nov 88 **DEAR GOD** *Chrysalis URE 6*..........55 4
17 Aug 91 **COLD COLD HEART** *Arista 114555*..........17 7
28 Sep 91 PURE *Arista 211922*..........36 2
6 Mar 93 ● IF I WAS: THE VERY BEST OF MIDGE URE & ULTRAVOX *Chrysalis CDCHR 1987* [1]..........10 6
25 May 96 **BREATHE** *Arista 74321371172*..........70 1
10 Nov 01 THE VERY BEST OF MIDGE URE & ULTRAVOX *EMI 5358112* [1]..........45 2

[1] Midge Ure and Mick Karn [1] Midge Ure & Ultravox

If I Was: The Very Best of Midge Ure & Ultravox also includes tracks by Visage, Band Aid and Phil Lynott.

URGE OVERKILL *US, male vocal / instrumental group (3 Singles: 6 Weeks)*

21 Aug 93 **SISTER HAVANA** *Geffen GFSTD 51*..........67 1
16 Oct 93 **POSITIVE BLEEDING** *Geffen GFSTD 57*..........61 1
19 Nov 94 **GIRL, YOU'LL BE A WOMAN SOON** *MCA MCSTD 2024*..........37 4

URIAH HEEP

UK, male vocal (David Byron) / instrumental group (12 Albums: 51 Weeks)

13 Nov 71 LOOK AT YOURSELF *Island ILPS 9169*..........39 1
10 Jun 72 DEMONS AND WIZARDS *Bronze ILPS 9193*..........20 11
2 Dec 72 THE MAGICIAN'S BIRTHDAY *Bronze ILPS 9213*..........28 3
19 May 73 LIVE *Island ISLD 1*..........23 8
29 Sep 73 SWEET FREEDOM *Island ILPS 9245*..........18 3
29 Jun 74 WONDERWORLD *Bronze ILPS 9280*..........23 3
5 Jul 75 ● RETURN TO FANTASY *Bronze ILPS 9335*..........7 6
12 Jun 76 HIGH AND MIGHTY *Island ILPS 9384*..........55 1
22 Mar 80 CONQUEST *Bronze BRON 524*..........37 3
17 Apr 82 ABOMINOG *Bronze BRON 538*..........34 6
18 Jun 83 HEAD FIRST *Bronze BRON 545*..........46 4
6 Apr 85 EQUATOR *Portrait PRT 261414*..........79 2

URUSEI YATSURA *UK, male / female vocal / instrumental group (1 Album: 1 Week, 4 Singles: 4 Weeks)*

22 Feb 97 **STRATEGIC HAMLETS** *Che CHE 67CD*..........64 1
28 Jun 97 **FAKE FUR** *Che CHE 70CD*..........58 1
21 Feb 98 **HELLO TIGER** *Che CHE 75CD1*..........40 1
14 Mar 98 SLAIN BY *Che CHE 76CD*..........64 1
6 Jun 98 **SLAIN BY ELF** *Che CHE 80CD1*..........63 1

11 February 1995	18 February 1995	25 February 1995	4 March 1995
THINK TWICE Celine Dion	THINK TWICE Celine Dion	THINK TWICE Celine Dion	THINK TWICE Celine Dion
THE COLOUR OF MY LOVE Celine Dion	THE COLOUR OF MY LOVE Celine Dion	THE COLOUR OF MY LOVE Celine Dion	THE COLOUR OF MY LOVE Celine Dion

KEY
UK No.1 ★ UK Top 10 ● Still on chart + UK entry at No.1 ■
US No.1 ▲ UK million seller £ US million seller $
Singles re-entries are listed as (re), (2re), (3re)... which signifies that the hit re-entered the chart once, twice or three times...
Peak Position / Weeks

USA FOR AFRICA *US, male / female vocal charity ensemble*

13 Apr 85 ★ WE ARE THE WORLD *CBS USAID 1* ▲ $ 1 9
25 May 85 WE ARE THE WORLD *CBS USAID F1* ▲ 31 5

Soloists: Lionel Richie, Stevie Wonder, Paul Simon, Kenny Rogers, James Ingram, Tina Turner, Billy Joel, Michael Jackson, Diana Ross, Dionne Warwick, Willie Nelson, Al Jarreau, Bruce Springsteen, Kenny Loggins, Steve Perry, Daryl Hall, Huey Lewis, Cyndi Lauper, Kim Carnes, Bob Dylan, Ray Charles. Also credited: Dan Aykroyd, Harry Belafonte, Lindsey Buckingham, Sheila E, Bob Geldof, John Oates, Jackie Jackson, La Toya Jackson, Marlon Jackson, Randy Jackson, Tito Jackson, Waylon Jennings, The News, Bette Midler, Jeffrey Osborne, The Pointer Sisters, Smokey Robinson. Album contains tracks by various artists in addition to the title track.

The USED *US, male vocal / instrumental group (2 Singles: 2 Weeks)*

22 Mar 03 THE TASTE OF INK *Reprise W 601CD* 52 1
5 Feb 05 TAKE IT AWAY *Reprise W 662CD2* 44 1

USHER (271 Top 500)

Multi-award-winning R&B vocalist / composer who first charted at the age of 15, b. Usher Raymond, 14 Oct 1978, Chattanooga, Tennessee, US. In the US in 2004, he had three singles simultaneously in the Top 10, replaced himself at No.1 twice and broke an all-time record by spending 28 weeks at No.1 in a calendar year (3 Albums: 127 Weeks, 13 Singles: 116 Weeks)

18 Mar 95 THINK OF YOU *LaFace 74321269252* 70 1
17 Jan 98 MY WAY *LaFace 73008260432* 16 18
31 Jan 98 ★ YOU MAKE ME WANNA ... (re) *LaFace 74321560652* ■ $ 1 13
2 May 98 NICE & SLOW *LaFace 74321579102* ▲ $ 24 5
3 Feb 01 ● POP YA COLLAR *LaFace 74321828692* 2 9
7 Jul 01 ● U REMIND ME *LaFace 74321863382* ▲ 3 9
21 Jul 01 ★ 8701 *Arista 74321874712* ■ 1 47
20 Oct 01 ● U GOT IT BAD *LaFace 74321898552* ▲ 5 8
20 Apr 02 U-TURN *LaFace 74321934072* 16 6
10 Aug 02 ● I NEED A GIRL (PART ONE) *Puff Daddy / Arista 74321947242* [1] 4 11
27 Mar 04 ★ YEAH! *Arista 82876606002* [2] ■ ▲ 1 14
3 Apr 04 ★ CONFESSIONS *Arista 82876609902* ■ ▲ 1 62
10 Jul 04 ★ BURN *Arista 82876624362* ■ ▲ 1 12
13 Nov 04 ● CONFESSIONS PART II / MY BOO *LaFace / Arista 82876655292* [3] ▲ 5 13
5 Mar 05 ● CAUGHT UP *LaFace 82876679142* 9 8
14 May 05 ● GET LOW / LOVERS & FRIENDS *TVT TVTUKCD 9* [4] 10 7

[1] P Diddy featuring Usher and Loon [2] Usher featuring Lil' Jon & Ludacris [3] Usher / Usher featuring Alicia Keys [4] Lil Jon & The East Side Boyz featuring Ying Yang Twins / featuring Usher and Ludacris

Both 'Confessions Part II' and 'My Boo' were US No.1s separately.

US3 *UK, male instrumental / production / vocal trio (1 Album: 6 Weeks, 4 Singles: 15 Weeks)*

10 Jul 93 RIDDIM *Blue Note CDCL 686* [1] 34 6
31 Jul 93 HAND ON THE TORCH *Capitol CDEST 2195* 40 6
25 Sep 93 CANTALOOP *Blue Note CDCL 696* [2] 23 5
28 May 94 I GOT IT GOIN' ON *Blue Note CDCL 708* [3] 52 2
1 Mar 97 COME ON EVERYBODY (GET DOWN) *Blue Note CDCL 784* 38 2

[1] Us3 featuring Tukka Yoot [2] Us3 featuring Rahsaan [3] Us3 featuring Kobie Powell and Rahsaan

USURA *Italy, male / female vocal / instrumental group (3 Singles: 15 Weeks)*

23 Jan 93 ● OPEN YOUR MIND *Deconstruction 74321128042* 7 9
10 Jul 93 SWEAT *Deconstruction 74321154602* 29 3
6 Dec 97 OPEN YOUR MIND 97 (re-mix) *Malarky MLKD 4* 21 3

UTAH SAINTS *UK, male instrumental / production duo – Jez Willis and Tim Garbutt (1 Album: 15 Weeks, 8 Singles: 39 Weeks)*

24 Aug 91 ● WHAT CAN YOU DO FOR ME *ffrr F 164* 10 11
6 Jun 92 ● SOMETHING GOOD *ffrr F 187* 4 9
8 May 93 ● BELIEVE IN ME *ffrr FCD 209* 8 6
5 Jun 93 ● UTAH SAINTS *ffrr 8283792* 10 15
17 Jul 93 I WANT YOU *ffrr FCD 213* 25 5
25 Jun 94 I STILL THINK OF YOU *ffrr FCD 225* 32 2
2 Sep 95 OHIO *ffrr FCD 264* 42 2
5 Feb 00 LOVE SONG *Echo ECSCD 83* 37 2
20 May 00 FUNKY MUSIC (SHO NUFF TURNS ME ON) *Echo ECSCD 96* 23 2

'Funky Music (Sho Nuff Turns Me On)' features uncredited vocals by Edwin Starr.

UTOPIA *UK, male vocal / instrumental group (2 Albums: 3 Weeks)*

1 Oct 77 OOPS! SORRY WRONG PLANET *Bearsville K 53517* 59 1
16 Feb 80 ADVENTURES IN UTOPIA *Island ILPS 9602* 57 2

U2 (9 Top 500)

The most successful group of the past 20 years: Paul (Bono) Hewson (v), b. 10 May 1960, Dublin, David (The Edge) Evans (g), b. 8 Aug 1961, Barking, Essex, Adam Clayton (b), b. 13 Mar 1960, Chinnor, Oxfordshire, and Larry Mullen Jr (d), b. 31 Oct 1961, Dublin. The Ireland-based act, named after an American spy plane, has come a long way since winning a Guinness-sponsored talent contest in 1978 in Limerick. Their first release, the EP 'U2:3', was an Irish hit but success overseas came slower: their first London show drew nine people and their first few UK releases sold poorly. However, in 1981 they made their UK and US chart debuts and since then have broken countless attendance, sales and concert-grossing records. These arena and stadium-packing giants of rock, whose humanitarian work is legendary, performed at both Live Aid and Live 8 London concerts. The first act to sell a million albums on CDs (The Joshua Tree), U2 have had seven albums simultaneously on both the US and UK charts and scored five consecutive US No.1s. In total, they have sold over 120 million albums and won 22 Grammy awards, a record for a group (this total includes five in 2006). Winners of the Q magazine Icon award in 2004 and founder members of the UK Music Hall of Fame in the same year, they are the only non-UK act to receive a BRIT award for their Outstanding Contribution to British Music and the only musical act in 70 years to receive the Freedom of Dublin (18 Albums: 1165 Weeks, 41 Singles: 318 Weeks)

8 Aug 81 FIRE *Island WIP 6679* 35 6
29 Aug 81 BOY *Island ILPS 9646* 52 31
17 Oct 81 GLORIA *Island WIP 6733* 55 4
24 Oct 81 OCTOBER *Island ILPS 9680* 11 42
3 Apr 82 A CELEBRATION *Island WIP 6770* 47 4
22 Jan 83 ● NEW YEARS DAY *Island WIP 6848* 10 8
12 Mar 83 ★ WAR *Island ILPS 9733* ■ 1 147
2 Apr 83 TWO HEARTS BEAT AS ONE *Island IS 109* 18 5
3 Dec 83 ● LIVE – UNDER A BLOOD RED SKY *Island IMA 3* 2 203
15 Sep 84 ● PRIDE (IN THE NAME OF LOVE) *Island IS 202* 3 11
13 Oct 84 ★ THE UNFORGETTABLE FIRE *Island U 25* ■ 1 130
4 May 85 ● THE UNFORGETTABLE FIRE *Island IS 220* 6 6
27 Jul 85 WIDE AWAKE IN AMERICA (import) *Island 902791 A* 11 16
21 Mar 87 ★ THE JOSHUA TREE *Island U 26* ■ ▲ 1 163
28 Mar 87 ● WITH OR WITHOUT YOU *Island IS 319* ▲ 4 11
6 Jun 87 ● I STILL HAVEN'T FOUND WHAT I'M LOOKING FOR *Island IS 328* ▲ 6 11
12 Sep 87 ● WHERE THE STREETS HAVE NO NAME *Island IS 340* 4 6
26 Dec 87 IN GOD'S COUNTRY (import) *Island 7-99385* 48 4
20 Feb 88 THE JOSHUA TREE SINGLES *Island U 2PK 1* 100 1
1 Oct 88 ★ DESIRE *Island IS 400* 1 8
22 Oct 88 ★ RATTLE AND HUM *Island U 27* ■ ▲ 1 61
17 Dec 88 ● ANGEL OF HARLEM *Island IS 402* 9 6
15 Apr 89 ● WHEN LOVE COMES TO TOWN *Island IS 411* [1] 6 7
24 Jun 89 ● ALL I WANT IS YOU *Island IS 422* 4 6
2 Nov 91 ★ THE FLY (re) *Island IS 500* ■ 1 6
30 Nov 91 ● ACHTUNG BABY *Island U 28* ▲ 2 87
14 Dec 91 MYSTERIOUS WAYS *Island IS 509* 13 7
7 Mar 92 ● ONE *Island IS 515* 7 6
20 Jun 92 EVEN BETTER THAN THE REAL THING *Island IS 525* 12 7

11 March 1995	18 March 1995	25 March 1995	1 April 1995
UK No.1 SINGLES			
THINK TWICE Celine Dion	THINK TWICE Celine Dion	LOVE CAN BUILD A BRIDGE Cher, Chrissie Hynde and Neneh Cherry with Eric Clapton	DON'T STOP (WIGGLE WIGGLE) The Outhere Brothers
UK No.1 ALBUMS			
GREATEST HITS Bruce Springsteen	MEDUSA Annie Lennox	ELASTICA Elastica	THE COLOUR OF MY LOVE Celine Dion

11 Jul 92 ● EVEN BETTER THAN THE REAL THING (re-mix) *Island REALU 2* 8 7
5 Dec 92 WHO'S GONNA RIDE YOUR WILD HORSES *Island IS 550* 14 8
17 Jul 93 ★ ZOOROPA *Island CIDU 29* ■ ▲ 1 31
4 Dec 93 ● STAY (FARAWAY, SO CLOSE) *Island CID 578* 4 9
17 Jun 95 ● HOLD ME THRILL ME KISS ME KILL ME *Atlantic A 7131CD* 2 14
15 Feb 97 ★ DISCOTHEQUE (re) *Island CID 649* ■ 1 11
15 Mar 97 ★ POP *Island CIDU 210* ■ ▲ 1 35
26 Apr 97 ● STARING AT THE SUN *Island CID 658* 3 6
2 Aug 97 ● LAST NIGHT ON EARTH (re) *Island CID 664* 10 5
4 Oct 97 ● PLEASE *Island CID 673* 7 4
20 Dec 97 IF GOD WILL SEND HIS ANGELS *Island CID 684* 12 6
31 Oct 98 ● SWEETEST THING *Island CID 727* 3 13
14 Nov 98 ★ THE BEST OF 1980-1990 & B-SIDES *Island CIDDU 211* ■ 1 12
21 Nov 98 ● THE BEST OF 1980-1990 *Island CIDU 211* 4 71
21 Oct 00 ★ BEAUTIFUL DAY *Island CID 766* ■ 1 16
11 Nov 00 ★ ALL THAT YOU CAN'T LEAVE BEHIND *Island CIDU 212* ■ 1 62
10 Feb 01 ● STUCK IN A MOMENT YOU CAN'T GET OUT OF *Island CID 770* 2 8
2 Jun 01 NEW YEAR'S DUB (re) *Serious SERR 030CD* [2] 15 5
28 Jul 01 ● ELEVATION *Island CID 780* 3 8
1 Dec 01 ● WALK ON *Island CID 788* 5 8
2 Nov 02 ● ELECTRICAL STORM *Island CID 808* 5 13
16 Nov 02 ● THE BEST OF 1990-2000 & B-SIDES *Island / Uni-Island CIDTU 213* 2 21
23 Nov 02 THE BEST OF 1990-2000 *Island / Uni-Island CIDU 213* 37 14
7 Feb 04 ★ TAKE ME TO THE CLOUDS ABOVE *All Around the World CDGLOBE 313* [3] ■ 1 12
20 Nov 04 ★ VERTIGO (re) *Island CIDX 878* ■ 1 13
4 Dec 04 ★ HOW TO DISMANTLE AN ATOMIC BOMB *Island CIDXU 214* ■ ▲ 1 38
19 Feb 05 ALL BECAUSE OF YOU (import) *Island 0249870322CD* 51 1
19 Feb 05 ★ SOMETIMES YOU CAN'T MAKE IT ON YOUR OWN (re) *Island CIDX 886* ■ 1 9
18 Jun 05 ● CITY OF BLINDING LIGHTS *Island CIDX 890* 2 9
22 Oct 05 ● ALL BECAUSE OF YOU *Island CIDX 906* 4 4

[1] U2 with BB King [2] Musique vs U2 [3] LMC vs U2

'Stay (Faraway, So Close)' was listed with 'I've Got You Under My Skin' by Frank Sinatra with Bono, which was featured on some but not all formats. 'Take Me to the Clouds Above' features uncredited vocalist Rachel McFarlane.

V

V *UK, male vocal group (3 Singles: 15 Weeks)*

5 Jun 04 ● BLOOD SWEAT AND TEARS *Universal MCSXD 40362* 6 5
21 Aug 04 ● HIP TO HIP / CAN YOU FEEL IT? *Universal MCSXD 40374* 5 6
20 Nov 04 YOU STOOD UP *Universal MCSXD 40388* 12 4

V.I.M. *UK, male instrumental / production group*

26 Jan 91 MAGGIE'S LAST PARTY *F2 BOZ 1* 68 1

The V.I.P.'s *UK, male vocal / instrumental group*

6 Sep 80 THE QUARTER MOON *Gem GEMS 39* 55 4

Steve VAI *US, male guitarist (4 Albums: 20 Weeks)*

2 Jun 90 ● PASSION AND WARFARE *Food for Thought GRUB 17* 8 10
7 Aug 93 SEX AND RELIGION *Relativity 4729472* [1] 17 6
15 Apr 95 ALIEN LOVE SECRETS *Relativity 4785862* 39 2
28 Sep 96 FIRE GARDEN *Epic 4850622* 41 2

[1] Vai

Holly VALANCE *Australia, female vocalist – Holly Vukadinovic (2 Albums: 12 Weeks, 5 Singles: 49 Weeks)*

11 May 02 ★ KISS KISS *London LONCD 464* ■ 1 16
12 Oct 02 ● DOWN BOY (re) *London LONCD 469* 2 14
26 Oct 02 ● FOOTPRINTS *London 0927493722* 9 11
21 Dec 02 NAUGHTY GIRL *London LONCD 472* 16 9
8 Nov 03 ● STATE OF MIND *London LONCD 482* 8 10
22 Nov 03 STATE OF MIND *London 5046701625* 60 1

Ricky VALANCE *UK, male vocalist – David Spencer*

25 Aug 60 ★ TELL LAURA I LOVE HER *Columbia DB 4493* 1 16

Ritchie VALENS *US, male vocalist / guitarist – Ritchie Valenzuela, b. 13 May 1941, d. 3 Feb 1959 (2 Singles: 5 Weeks)*

6 Mar 59 DONNA *London HL 8803* $ 29 1
1 Aug 87 LA BAMBA *RCA PB 41435* 49 4

Caterina VALENTE with Werner MULLER and the RIAS DANCE ORCHESTRA *France, female vocalist and Germany, orchestra – leader b. 2 Aug 1920, d. 28 Dec 1998*

19 Aug 55 ● THE BREEZE AND I *Polydor BM 6002* 5 14

Brooke VALENTINE featuring BIG BOI & LIL JON NEW *US, female vocalist and male rappers*

16 Jul 05 GIRLFIGHT *Virgin VUSDX 301* 35 2

Dickie VALENTINE *UK, male vocalist – Richard Brice, b. 4 Nov 1929, d. 6 May 1971 (14 Singles: 92 Weeks)*

20 Feb 53 BROKEN WINGS *Decca F 9954* 12 1
13 Mar 53 ● ALL THE TIME AND EVERYWHERE *Decca F 10038* 9 3
5 Jun 53 ● IN A GOLDEN COACH (THERE'S A HEART OF GOLD) *Decca F 10098* 7 1
5 Nov 54 ENDLESS *Decca F 10346* 19 1
17 Dec 54 ● MISTER SANDMAN *Decca F 10415* 5 12
17 Dec 54 ★ THE FINGER OF SUSPICION *Decca F 10394* [1] 1 15
18 Feb 55 ● A BLOSSOM FELL (re) *Decca F 10430* 9 10
3 Jun 55 ● I WONDER *Decca F 10493* 4 15
25 Nov 55 ★ CHRISTMAS ALPHABET *Decca F 10628* 1 7
16 Dec 55 THE OLD PI-ANNA RAG *Decca F 10645* 15 5
7 Dec 56 ● CHRISTMAS ISLAND *Decca F 10798* 8 5
27 Dec 57 SNOWBOUND FOR CHRISTMAS *Decca F 10950* 28 1
13 Mar 59 VENUS (4re) *Pye Nixa 7N 15192* 20 8
23 Oct 59 ONE MORE SUNRISE (MORGEN) *Pye 7N 15221* 14 8

[1] Dickie Valentine with The Stargazers

VALENTINE BROTHERS *US, male vocal duo*

23 Apr 83 MONEY'S TOO TIGHT (TO MENTION) *Energy NRG 1* 73 1

Bobby VALENTINO NEW *US, male vocalist – Bobby Wilson (1 Album: 8 Weeks, 2 Singles: 13 Weeks)*

7 May 05 DISTURBING THA PEACE PRESENTS BOBBY VALENTINO *Def Jam 9880210* 34 8
2 Jul 05 ● SLOW DOWN *Def Jam 9883239* 4 10
8 Oct 05 TELL ME *Def Jam 9885685* 38 3

Joe VALINO *US, male vocalist – Joseph Paolino, b. 9 Mar 1929, d. 26 Dec 1996*

18 Jan 57 THE GARDEN OF EDEN *HMV POP 283* 23 2

8 April 1995	15 April 1995	22 April 1995	29 April 1995
BACK FOR GOOD Take That	BACK FOR GOOD Take That	BACK FOR GOOD Take That	BACK FOR GOOD Take That
WAKE UP! The Boo Radleys	GREATEST HITS Bruce Springsteen	PICTURE THIS Wet Wet Wet	PICTURE THIS Wet Wet Wet

KEY
UK No.1 ★ UK Top 10 ● Still on chart + UK entry at No.1 ■ US No.1 ▲ UK million seller £ US million seller $
Singles re-entries are listed as (re), (2re), (3re)... which signifies that the hit re-entered the chart once, twice or three times...
Peak Position / Weeks

Frankie VALLI (see also The FOUR SEASONS) *US, male vocalist – Francis Castellucio (3 Albums: 28 Weeks, 13 Singles: 117 Weeks)*

27 Aug 64 ● **RAG DOLL** *Philips BF 1347* [1] ▲ 2 13
18 Nov 65 ● **LET'S HANG ON** *Philips BF 1439* [1] 4 16
31 Mar 66 **WORKIN' MY WAY BACK TO YOU** *Philips BF 1474* [2] 50 3
2 Jun 66 **OPUS 17 (DON'T YOU WORRY 'BOUT ME)** *Philips BF 1493* [2] 20 9
29 Sep 66 **I'VE GOT YOU UNDER MY SKIN** *Philips BF 1511* [2] 12 11
12 Dec 70 **YOU'RE READY NOW** *Philips 320226 BF* 11 13
1 Feb 75 ● **MY EYES ADORED YOU** *Private Stock PVT 1* ▲ $ 5 11
19 Apr 75 ● **THE NIGHT** *Mowest MW 3024* [3] 7 9
21 Jun 75 **SWEARIN' TO GOD** *Private Stock PVT 21* 31 5
17 Apr 76 **FALLEN ANGEL** *Private Stock PVT 51* 11 7
26 Aug 78 ● **GREASE** *RSO 012* ▲ $ 3 14
21 May 88 THE COLLECTION *Telstar STAR 2320* [1] 38 9
29 Oct 88 **DECEMBER, 1963 (OH, WHAT A NIGHT)** *BR 45277* [3] 49 4
23 Mar 91 **GREASE – THE DREAM MIX** *PWL / Polydor PO 136* [4] 47 2
7 Mar 92 ● THE VERY BEST OF FRANKIE VALLI AND THE FOUR SEASONS *PolyGram TV 5131192* [1] 7 15
13 Oct 01 THE DEFINITIVE FRANKIE VALLI AND THE FOUR SEASONS *WSM 8122735552* [1] 26 4

[1] The Four Seasons with the sound of Frankie Valli [2] Four Seasons with Frankie Valli [3] Frankie Valli and the Four Seasons [4] Frankie Valli, John Travolta and Olivia Newton-John [1] Frankie Valli and the Four Seasons

Armin VAN BUUREN *Holland, male DJ / producer (6 Singles: 10 Weeks)*

14 Feb 98 **BLUE FEAR** *Xtravaganza 0091485 EXT* [1] 45 1
12 Feb 00 **COMMUNICATION** *AM:PM CDAMPM 129* [1] 18 3
10 May 03 **YET ANOTHER DAY** *Nebula NEBCD 042* [2] 70 1
20 Mar 04 **BURNED WITH DESIRE** *Nebula NEBCD 055* [3] 45 2
28 Aug 04 **BLUE FEAR 2004** *Nebula NEBCD 061* 52 2
2 Jul 05 **SHIVERS / SERENITY** *Nebula NEBCD 069* 72 1

[1] Armin [2] Armin Van Buuren featuring Ray Wilson [3] Armin Van Buuren featuring Justine Suissa

Mark VAN DALE with ENRICO *Belgium, male production duo*

3 Oct 98 **WATER WAVE** *Club Tools 0065815 CLU* 71 1

David VAN DAY (see also DOLLAR; GUYS 'N' DOLLS) *UK, male vocalist*

14 May 83 **YOUNG AMERICANS TALKING** *WEA DAY 1* 43 3

Ron VAN DEN BEUKEN (see also MYSTERY) *Holland, male producer*

19 Jun 04 **TIMELESS (KEEP ON MOVIN')** *Manifesto 9866717* 65 1

VAN DER GRAAF GENERATOR *UK, male vocal / instrumental group*

25 Apr 70 THE LEAST WE CAN DO IS WAVE TO EACH OTHER *Charisma CAS 1007* 47 2

George VAN DUSEN
UK, male vocalist – George Harrington, b. 1905, d. 1992

17 Dec 88 **IT'S PARTY TIME AGAIN** *Bri-Tone 7BT 001* 43 4

Paul VAN DYK
Germany, male DJ / producer (1 Album: 3 Weeks, 10 Singles: 35 Weeks)

17 May 97 **FORBIDDEN FRUIT** *Deviant DVNT 18CDR* 69 1
15 Nov 97 **WORDS** *Deviant DVNT 26CDS* [1] 54 1
5 Sep 98 **FOR AN ANGEL** *Deviant DVT 24CDS* 28 4
20 Nov 99 **ANOTHER WAY / AVENUE** (re) *Deviant DVNT 35CDS* 13 7
20 May 00 ● **TELL ME WHY (THE RIDDLE)** *Deviant DVNT 36CDS* [2] 7 5
17 Jun 00 OUT THERE AND BACK *Deviant DVNT 37CD* 12 3
2 Dec 00 **WE ARE ALIVE** *Deviant DVNT 38CDS* 15 6
12 Jul 03 **NOTHING BUT YOU** *Positiva CDTIVS 192* [3] 14 5
18 Oct 03 **TIME OUT OF LIVES / CONNECTED** *Positiva CDTIVS 196* [4] 28 2
17 Apr 04 **CRUSH** *Positiva CDTIVS 204* [5] 42 3
17 Sep 05 **THE OTHER SIDE** *Positiva CDTIVS 221* [6] 58 1

[1] Paul Van Dyk featuring Toni Halliday [2] Paul Van Dyk featuring Saint Etienne [3] Paul Van Dyk featuring Hemstock [4] Paul Van Dyk featuring Vega 4 [5] Paul Van Dyk featuring Second Sun [6] Paul Van Dyk featuring Wayne Jackson

Leroy VAN DYKE *US, male vocalist (2 Singles: 20 Weeks)*

4 Jan 62 ● **WALK ON BY** *Mercury AMT 1166* 5 17
26 Apr 62 **BIG MAN IN A BIG HOUSE** *Mercury AMT 1173* 34 3

Niels VAN GOGH *Germany, male producer*

10 Apr 99 **PULVERTURM** *Logic 74321649192* 75 1

VAN HALEN (451 Top 500)
Hard rock heroes formed in 1974 in California, US, whose members included Dutch born Eddie (g) and Alex Van Halen (d), David Lee Roth (v), Sammy Hagar (v) and Gary Cherone (v) (ex-Extreme). Their first 12 albums each topped two million sales Stateside, with two passing 10 million (14 Albums: 109 Weeks, 12 Singles: 51 Weeks)

27 May 78 VAN HALEN *Warner Bros. K 56470* 34 11
14 Apr 79 VAN HALEN II *Warner Bros. K 566116* 23 7
5 Apr 80 WOMEN AND CHILDREN FIRST *Warner Bros. K 56793* 15 7
28 Jun 80 **RUNNIN' WITH THE DEVIL** *Warner Bros. HM 10* 52 3
23 May 81 FAIR WARNING *Warner Bros. K 56899* 49 4
1 May 82 DIVER DOWN *Warner Bros. K 57003* 36 5
4 Feb 84 MCMLXXXIV (1984) *Warner Bros. 923985* 15 24
4 Feb 84 ● **JUMP** *Warner Bros. W 9384* ▲ $ 7 13
19 May 84 **PANAMA** *Warner Bros. W 9273* 61 2
5 Apr 86 5150 *Warner Bros. WS 5150* ▲ 16 18
5 Apr 86 ● **WHY CAN'T THIS BE LOVE** *Warner Bros. W 8740* 8 14
12 Jul 86 **DREAMS** *Warner Bros. W 8642* 62 2
4 Jun 88 OU812 *Warner Bros. WX 177* ▲ 16 12
6 Aug 88 **WHEN IT'S LOVE** *Warner Bros. W 7816* 28 7
1 Apr 89 **FEELS SO GOOD** *Warner Bros. W 7565* 63 1
22 Jun 91 **POUNDCAKE** *Warner Bros. W 0045* 74 1
29 Jun 91 FOR UNLAWFUL CARNAL KNOWLEDGE *Warner Bros. WX 420* ▲ 12 5
19 Oct 91 **TOP OF THE WORLD** *Warner Bros. W 0066* 63 1
6 Mar 93 LIVE: RIGHT HERE RIGHT NOW *Warner Bros. 9362451982* 24 3
27 Mar 93 **JUMP (LIVE)** *Warner Bros. W 0155CD* 26 3
21 Jan 95 **DON'T TELL ME** *Warner Bros. W 0280CD* 27 2
4 Feb 95 ● BALANCE *Warner Bros. 9362457602* ▲ 8 3
1 Apr 95 **CAN'T STOP LOVIN' YOU** *Warner Bros. W 0288CD* 33 2
9 Nov 96 THE BEST OF VAN HALEN – VOLUME 1 *Warner Bros. 9362464742* ▲ 45 1
28 Mar 98 VAN HALEN 3 *Warner Bros. 9362466622* 43 1
31 Jul 04 THE BEST OF BOTH WORLDS *Warner Bros. 8122765152* 15 8

Armand VAN HELDEN (see also DEEP CREED '94)
US, male DJ / producer (2 Albums: 7 Weeks, 12 Singles: 55 Weeks)

8 Mar 97 **THE FUNK PHENOMENA** *ZYX ZYX 8523 U8* 38 2
8 Nov 97 **ULTRAFUNKULA** *ffrr FCD 317* 46 1
6 Feb 99 ★ **YOU DON'T KNOW ME** (re) *ffrr FCD 357* [1] ■ 1 12
10 Apr 99 2 FUTURE 4 U *ffrr 5560902* 22 6
1 May 99 **FLOWERZ** *ffrr FCD 361* [2] 18 5
20 May 00 ● **KOOCHY** *ffrr FCD 379* 4 7
10 Jun 00 KILLING PURITANS *ffrr 8573833192* 38 1
3 Nov 01 **WHY CAN'T YOU FREE SOME TIME** *ffrr FCD 402* 34 2
15 Dec 01 **YOU CAN'T CHANGE ME** *Defected DFECT 41CDS* [3] 25 4
1 May 04 **HEAR MY NAME** *Southern Fried ECB 64CDS* [4] 34 2
11 Sep 04 **MY MY MY** (2re) *Southern Fried ECB 67CDS* 15 15
27 Nov 04 **WATCHING CARS GO BY** *Emperor Norton ENR 532* [5] 49 2

6 May 1995	13 May 1995	20 May 1995	27 May 1995
UK No.1 SINGLES			
SOME MIGHT SAY Oasis	**DREAMER (Re-mix)** Livin' Joy	**UNCHAINED MELODY / (THERE'LL BE BLUEBIRDS OVER) THE WHITE CLIFFS OF DOVER** Robson Green and Jerome Flynn	**UNCHAINED MELODY / (THERE'LL BE BLUEBIRDS OVER) THE WHITE CLIFFS OF DOVER** Robson Green and Jerome Flynn
UK No.1 ALBUMS			
PICTURE THIS Wet Wet Wet	**NOBODY ELSE** Take That	**NOBODY ELSE** Take That	**STANLEY ROAD** Paul Weller

2 Jul 05	**INTO YOUR EYES** *Southern Fried ECB 78CDS*	48	2
1 Oct 05	**WHEN THE LIGHTS GO DOWN** *Southern Fried ECB 85CDS*	70	1

[1] Armand Van Helden featuring Duane Harden [2] Armand Van Helden featuring Roland Clark [3] Roger Sanchez featuring Armand Van Helden and N'Dea Davenport [4] Armand Van Helden featuring Spalding Rockwell [5] Felix Da Housecat vs Sasha and Armand Van Helden

Denise VAN OUTEN (see also THOSE 2 GIRLS)

UK, female actor / vocalist (1 Album: 2 Weeks, 2 Singles: 16 Weeks)

26 Dec 98 ●	**ESPECIALLY FOR YOU** (re) *RCA 74321644722* [1]	3	12
29 Jun 02	**CAN'T TAKE MY EYES OFF YOU** *Columbia 6721052* [2]	23	4
26 Apr 03	TELL ME ON A SUNDAY *Really Useful / Polydor 4932922*	34	2

[1] Denise and Johnny [Johnny Vaughan] [2] Andy Williams and Denise Van Outen

VAN TWIST *Zaire / Belgium, male / female vocal / instrumental group*

16 Feb 85	**SHAFT** *Polydor POSP 729*	57	2

Despina VANDI *Greece, female vocalist*

20 Mar 04	**GIA** *Positiva CDTIVS 199*	63	1

Luther VANDROSS (97 Top 500)

Superior soul singer / songwriter and producer, b. 20 Apr 1951, New York, US, d. 1 Jul 2005. The former David Bowie backing vocalist fronted chart group Change before embarking on a solo career that earned him 10 successive US platinum albums and a stack of awards, including four Grammys in 2004 (17 Albums: 298 Weeks, 32 Singles: 152 Weeks)

19 Feb 83	**NEVER TOO MUCH** *Epic EPC A 3101*	44	6
21 Jan 84	BUSY BODY *Epic EPC 25608*	42	8
6 Apr 85	THE NIGHT I FELL IN LOVE *Epic EPC 26387*	19	10
26 Jul 86	**GIVE ME THE REASON** *Epic A 7288*	60	3
1 Nov 86 ●	GIVE ME THE REASON *Epic EPC 4501341*	3	99
21 Feb 87	NEVER TOO MUCH *Epic EPC 32807*	41	30
21 Feb 87	**GIVE ME THE REASON** (re-issue) *Epic 650216 7*	71	2
28 Mar 87	**SEE ME** *Epic LUTH 1*	60	4
4 Jul 87	FOREVER FOR ALWAYS FOR LOVE *Epic EPC 25013*	23	16
11 Jul 87	**I REALLY DIDN'T MEAN IT** *Epic LUTH 3*	16	10
5 Sep 87	**STOP TO LOVE** *Epic LUTH 2*	24	7
7 Nov 87	**SO AMAZING** *Epic LUTH 4*	33	6
23 Jan 88	**GIVE ME THE REASON** (2nd re-issue) *Epic LUTH 5*	26	6
16 Apr 88	BUSY BODY (re-issue) *Epic 460183 1*	78	4
16 Apr 88	**I GAVE IT UP (WHEN I FELL IN LOVE)** *Epic LUTH 6*	28	5
9 Jul 88	**THERE'S NOTHING BETTER THAN LOVE** *Epic LUTH 7* [1]	72	1
8 Oct 88	**ANY LOVE** *Epic LUTH 8*	31	4
29 Oct 88 ●	ANY LOVE *Epic 462908 1*	3	22
4 Feb 89	**SHE WON'T TALK TO ME** *Epic LUTH 9*	34	4
22 Apr 89	**COME BACK** *Epic LUTH 10*	53	3
28 Oct 89	**NEVER TOO MUCH** (re-mix) *Epic LUTH 12*	13	7
11 Nov 89	BEST OF LUTHER VANDROSS – BEST OF LOVE *Epic 4658011*	14	23
6 Jan 90	**HERE AND NOW** *Epic LUTH 13*	43	3
27 Apr 91	**POWER OF LOVE – LOVE POWER** *Epic 6568227*	46	5
25 May 91 ●	POWER OF LOVE *Epic 4680121*	9	9
18 Jan 92	**THE RUSH** *Epic 6577237*	53	3
15 Aug 92 ●	**THE BEST THINGS IN LIFE ARE FREE** *Perspective PERSS 7400* [2]	2	13
22 May 93	**LITTLE MIRACLES (HAPPEN EVERY DAY)** *Epic 6590442*	28	3
12 Jun 93	NEVER LET ME GO *Epic 4735982*	11	5
18 Sep 93	**HEAVEN KNOWS** *Epic 6596522*	34	3
4 Dec 93	**LOVE IS ON THE WAY** *Epic 6599592*	38	2
17 Sep 94 ●	**ENDLESS LOVE** (2re) *Epic 6608062* [3]	3	16
1 Oct 94 ★	SONGS *Epic 4766562* ■	1	28
26 Nov 94	**LOVE THE ONE YOU'RE WITH** *Epic 6610612*	31	4
4 Feb 95	**ALWAYS AND FOREVER** *Epic 6611942*	20	5
15 Apr 95	**AIN'T NO STOPPING US NOW** *Epic 6614242*	22	3
28 Oct 95	GREATEST HITS 1981-1995 *Epic 4811002*	12	14
11 Nov 95	**POWER OF LOVE – LOVE POWER** (re-mix) *Epic 6625902*	31	3
16 Dec 95 ●	**THE BEST THINGS IN LIFE ARE FREE** (re-mix) *A&M 5813092* [4]	7	7
23 Dec 95	**EVERY YEAR EVERY CHRISTMAS** *Epic 6627762*	43	2
12 Oct 96	**YOUR SECRET LOVE** *Epic 6638385*	14	5
19 Oct 96	YOUR SECRET LOVE *Epic 4843832*	14	4
28 Dec 96	**I CAN MAKE IT BETTER** *Epic 6640632*	44	2
11 Oct 97	ONE NIGHT WITH YOU – THE BEST OF LOVE *Epic 4888882*	56	2
22 Aug 98	I KNOW *EMI 8460892*	42	1
20 Oct 01	**TAKE YOU OUT** *J 74321899442*	59	1
16 Feb 02	THE ESSENTIAL LUTHER VANDROSS *Epic 5050252*	18	8
5 Jul 03	DANCE WITH MY FATHER *J 82876540732* ▲	41	15
28 Feb 04	**DANCE WITH MY FATHER** *J 82876569982*	21	4

[1] Luther Vandross, duet with Gregory Hines [2] Luther Vandross and Janet Jackson with special guests BBD and Ralph Tresvant [3] Luther Vandross and Mariah Carey [4] Luther Vandross and Janet Jackson

The Essential Luther Vandross peaked at No.72 in 2002. A repackaged version, with the catalogue number Epic 5133532 and the same track listing, peaked at No.18 in 2003.

VANESSA-MAE *Singapore, female vocalist / violinist – Vanessa-Mae Vanakorn Nicholson (6 Albums: 34 Weeks, 8 Singles: 21 Weeks)*

28 Jan 95	**TOCCATA AND FUGUE** *EMI Classics MAE 8816812*	16	10
25 Feb 95	THE VIOLIN PLAYER *EMI Classics CDC 5550892*	11	21
20 May 95	**RED HOT** *EMI CDMAE 2*	37	2
18 Nov 95	**CLASSICAL GAS** *EMI CDEM 404*	41	2
26 Oct 96	**I'M A DOUN FOR LACK O' JOHNNIE (A LITTLE SCOTTISH FANTASY)** *EMI CDMAE 3*	28	2
2 Nov 96	THE CLASSICAL ALBUM 1 *EMI Classics CDC 5553952*	47	2
25 Oct 97	**STORM** *EMI CDEM 497*	54	1
8 Nov 97	STORM *EMI 8218002*	27	5
20 Dec 97	**I FEEL LOVE** *EMI CDEM 553*	41	2
7 Feb 98	CHINA GIRL – THE CLASSICAL ALBUM 2 *EMI Classics CDC 5564832*	56	3
5 Dec 98	**DEVIL'S TRILL / REFLECTION** *EMI CDEM 530*	53	1
26 May 01	SUBJECT TO CHANGE *EMI 5331002*	58	2
28 Jul 01	**WHITE BIRD** *EMI CDVAN 002*	66	1
30 Oct 04	CHOREOGRAPHY *Sony Classical SK 90895*	66	1

VANGELIS (365 Top 500)

Synthesized soundtrack whizzkid, b. Evangelos Papathanassiou, 29 Mar 1943, Volos, Greece. The Grammy-nominated artist, whose 'Conquest of Paradise' is one of Germany's biggest-selling singles, also had hits in Aphrodite's Child and Jon and Vangelis (12 Albums: 165 Weeks, 3 Singles: 25 Weeks)

10 Jan 76	HEAVEN AND HELL *RCA Victor RS 1025*	31	7
9 Oct 76	ALBEDO 0.39 *RCA Victor RS 1080*	18	6
18 Apr 81 ●	CHARIOTS OF FIRE (FILM SOUNDTRACK) *Polydor POLS 1026*	5	97
9 May 81	**CHARIOTS OF FIRE – TITLES** (re) *Polydor POSP 246* ▲	12	17
11 Jul 81	**HEAVEN AND HELL, THIRD MOVEMENT (THEME FROM THE BBC-TV SERIES 'THE COSMOS')** *BBC 1*	48	6
5 May 84	CHARIOTS OF FIRE (FILM SOUNDTRACK) (re-issue) *Polydor POLD 5160*	39	10
13 Oct 84	SOIL FESTIVITIES *Polydor POLH 11*	55	4
30 Mar 85	MASK *Polydor POLH 19*	69	2
22 Jul 89	THEMES *Polydor VGTV 1*	11	13
24 Oct 92	1492 – THE CONQUEST OF PARADISE (FILM SOUNDTRACK) *East West 4509910142*	33	6
31 Oct 92	**CONQUEST OF PARADISE** *East West YZ 704*	60	2
18 Jun 94	BLADERUNNER (FILM SOUNDTRACK) *East West 4509965742*	20	6
2 Mar 96	VOICES *East West 630127862*	58	1
20 Apr 96	PORTRAIT (SO LONG AGO SO CLEAR) *Polydor 5311512*	14	6
8 Nov 03	ODYSSEY – THE DEFINITIVE COLLECTION *Universal TV 9813149*	20	7

'Chariots of Fire – Titles' re-entered the chart in Apr 1982, peaking at No.41.

VANILLA *UK, female vocal group (2 Singles: 10 Weeks)*

22 Nov 97	**NO WAY NO WAY** (re) *EMI CDEM 487*	14	8
23 May 98	**TRUE TO US** *EMI CDEM 509*	36	2

VANILLA FUDGE *US, male vocal / instrumental group*

9 Aug 67	**YOU KEEP ME HANGIN' ON** *Atlantic 584123*	18	11
4 Nov 67	VANILLA FUDGE *Atlantic 588086*	31	3

3 June 1995	10 June 1995	17 June 1995	24 June 1995
UNCHAINED MELODY / (THERE'LL BE BLUEBIRDS OVER) THE WHITE CLIFFS OF DOVER Robson Green and Jerome Flynn	**UNCHAINED MELODY / (THERE'LL BE BLUEBIRDS OVER) THE WHITE CLIFFS OF DOVER** Robson Green and Jerome Flynn	**UNCHAINED MELODY / (THERE'LL BE BLUEBIRDS OVER) THE WHITE CLIFFS OF DOVER** Robson Green and Jerome Flynn	**UNCHAINED MELODY / (THERE'LL BE BLUEBIRDS OVER) THE WHITE CLIFFS OF DOVER** Robson Green and Jerome Flynn
SINGLES Alison Moyet	PULSE Pink Floyd	PULSE Pink Floyd	HISTORY - PAST PRESENT AND FUTURE BOOK I Michael Jackson

KEY: UK No.1 ★ UK Top 10 ● Still on chart + UK entry at No.1 ■ US No.1 ▲ UK million seller £ US million seller $
Singles re-entries are listed as (re), (2re), (3re)... which signifies that the hit re-entered the chart once, twice or three times...

Peak Position / Weeks

VANILLA ICE

US, male rapper – Robert Van Winkle (2 Albums: 23 Weeks, 5 Singles: 32 Weeks)

24 Nov 90 ★	**ICE ICE BABY** *SBK SBK 18* ▲ $	1	13
15 Dec 90 ●	**TO THE EXTREME** *SBK SBKLP 9* ▲	4	20
2 Feb 91 ●	**PLAY THAT FUNKY MUSIC** *SBK SBK 20*	10	6
30 Mar 91	**I LOVE YOU** *SBK SBK 22*	45	5
29 Jun 91	**ROLLIN' IN MY 5.0** *SBK SBK 27*	27	4
6 Jul 91	**EXTREMELY LIVE** *SBK SBKLP 12*	35	3
10 Aug 91	**SATISFACTION** *SBK SBK 29*	22	4

VANITY FARE

UK, male vocal (Trevor Brice) / instrumental group (3 Singles: 34 Weeks)

28 Aug 68	**I LIVE FOR THE SUN** *Page One POF 075*	20	9
23 Jul 69 ●	**EARLY IN THE MORNING** *Page One POF 142*	8	12
27 Dec 69	**HITCHIN' A RIDE** *Page One POF 158* $	16	13

Joe T VANNELLI PROJECT *Italy, male producer*

17 Jun 95	**SWEETEST DAY OF MAY** *Positiva CDTIV 36*	45	2

Randy VANWARMER

US, male vocalist – Randall Van Wormer, b. 30 Mar 1955, d. 12 Jan 2004

4 Aug 79 ●	**JUST WHEN I NEEDED YOU MOST** *Bearsville WIP 6516* $	8	11

The VAPORS *UK, male vocal (Dave Fenton) / instrumental group (1 Album: 6 Weeks, 3 Singles: 23 Weeks)*

9 Feb 80 ●	**TURNING JAPANESE** *United Artists BP 334*	3	13
7 Jun 80	**NEW CLEAR DAYS** *United Artists UAG 30300*	44	6
5 Jul 80	**NEWS AT TEN** *United Artists BP 345*	44	4
11 Jul 81	**JIMMIE JONES** *Liberty BP 401*	44	6

VARDIS *UK, male vocal / instrumental group*

27 Sep 80	**LET'S GO** *Logo VAR 1*	59	4
1 Nov 80	**100 MPH** *Logo MOGO 4012*	52	1

Halo VARGA *US, male producer*

9 Dec 00	**FUTURE** *Hooj Choons HOOJ 101CD*	67	1

VARIOUS ARTISTS (MONTAGES) *(5 Singles: 31 Weeks)*

17 May 80	**CALIBRE CUTS** *Calibre CAB 502*	75	2
25 Nov 89	**DEEP HEAT '89** *Deep Heat DEEP 10*	12	11
3 Mar 90 ●	**THE BRITS 1990** *RCA PB 43565*	2	7
28 Apr 90	**THE SIXTH SENSE** *Deep Heat DEEP 12*	49	2
10 Nov 90	**TIME TO MAKE THE FLOOR BURN** *Megabass MEGAX 1*	16	9

The following tracks are sampled: Calibre Cuts: Big Apples Rock – Black Ivory; Don't Hold Back – Chanson; The River Drive – Jupiter Beyond; Dancing in the Disco – LAX; Mellow Mellow Right On – Lowrell; Pata Pata – Osibisa; I Like It – The Players Association; We Got the Funk – Positive Force; Holdin' On – Tony Rallo and The Midnite Band; Can You Feel the Force – The Real Thing; Miami Heatwave – Seventh Avenue; Rapper's Delight – Sugarhill Gang; Que Tal America – Two Man Sound; Remakes by session musicians: Ain't No Stoppin' Us Now, Bad Girls, We Are Family. Deep Heat '89 (credited to Latino Rave): Pump Up the Jam – Technotronic; Stakker Humanoid – Humanoid; A Day in the Life – Black Riot; Work it to the Bone – LNR; I Can Make U Dance – DJ 'Fast' Eddie; Voodoo Ray – A Guy Called Gerald; Numero Uno – Starlight; Bango (to the Batmobile) – Todd Terry; Break 4 Love – Raze; Don't Scandalize Mine – Sugar Bear. The BRITs 1990: Street Tuff – Double Trouble and the Rebel MC; Voodoo Ray – A Guy Called Gerald; Theme From S-Express – S-Express; Hey DJ – I Can't Dance (to That Music You're Playing) – The Beatmasters; Eve of the War – Jeff Wayne; Pacific State – 808 State; We Call It Acieed – D Mob; Got to Keep On – The Cookie Crew. The Sixth Sense (credited to Latino Rave): Get Up – Technotronic; The Magic Number – De La Soul; G'Ding G'Ding (Do Wanna Wanna) – Anna G; Show 'M the Bass – MC Miker G; Turn It Out (Go Base) – Rob Base; Eve of the War (War of the Worlds) – Project D; Moments In Love – 2 to the Power. Time to Make the Floor Burn (credited to Megabass): Do This My Way – Kid 'N' Play; Street Tuff – Double Trouble and the Rebel MC; Sex 4 Daze – Lake Eerie; Ride on Time – Black Box; Make My Body Rock – Jomanda; Don't Miss the Partyline – Bizz Nizz; Pump Pump It Up – Hypnotek; Big Fun – Inner City; Pump That Body – Mr Lee; Pump Up the Jam – Technotronic; This Beat Is Technotronic – Technotronic; Get Busy – Mr Lee; Touch Me – 49ers; Thunderbirds Are Go – F A B.

VARIOUS ARTISTS (SINGLES and EPs) *(21 Singles: 76 Weeks)*

15 Jun 56	**CAROUSEL – ORIGINAL SOUNDTRACK (LP)** (re) *Capitol LCT 6105*	26	2
29 Jun 56 ●	**ALL STAR HIT PARADE** *Decca F 10752*	2	9
26 Jul 57	**ALL STAR HIT PARADE NO.2** *Decca F 10915*	15	7
9 Dec 89	**THE FOOD CHRISTMAS EP** *Food FOOD 23*	63	1
20 Jan 90	**THE FURTHER ADVENTURES OF NORTH (EP)** *Deconstruction PT 43372*	64	2
2 Nov 91	**THE APPLE EP** *Apple APP 1*	60	1
11 Jul 92	**FOURPLAY (EP)** *XL XLFP 1*	45	2
7 Nov 92	**THE FRED EP** *Heavenly HVN 19*	26	3
24 Apr 93	**GIMME SHELTER (EP)** *Food CDORDERA 1*	23	4
5 Jun 93	**SUBPLATES VOLUME 1 (EP)** *Suburban Base SUBBASE 24CD*	69	1
9 Oct 93	**THE TWO TONE EP** *2 Tone CHSTT 31*	30	3
4 Nov 95	**HELP (EP)** *Go Discs GODCD 135*	51	2
16 Mar 96	**NEW YORK UNDERCOVER (EP)** *Uptown MCSTD 48002*	39	1
30 Mar 96	**DANGEROUS MINDS (EP)** *MCA MCSTD 48007*	35	1
29 Nov 97 ★	**PERFECT DAY** (re) *Chrysalis CDNEED 01* ■ £	1	21
12 Sep 98	**THE FULL MONTY-MONSTER MIX** *RCA Victor 74321602582*	62	1
26 Sep 98	**TRADE (EP) (DISC 2)** *Tidy Trax TREP 2*	75	1
25 Dec 99	**IT'S ONLY ROCK 'N' ROLL** (re) *Universal TV 1566012*	19	10
17 Jun 00	**PERFECT DAY** (re-recording) *Chrysalis 8887840*	69	1
10 Nov 01	**HARD BEAT EP 19** *Nukleuz NUKP 0369*	71	1
3 Dec 05	**EVER FALLEN IN LOVE (WITH SOMEONE YOU SHOULDN'T'VE)?** *EMI PEELCD 1*	28	2

Tracks and artists on Carousel are as follows: Carousel Waltz – Orchestra conducted by Alfred Newman; You're a Queer One Julie Jordan – Barbara Ruick and Shirley Jones; Mister Snow – Barbara Ruick; If I Loved You – Shirley Jones and Gordon MacRae; June Is Busting Out All Over – Claramae Turner; Soliloquy – Gordon MacRae; Blow High Blow Low – Cameron Mitchell; When the Children Are Asleep – Robert Rounseville and Barbara Ruick; This Was a Real Nice Clambake – Barbara Ruick, Claramae Turner, Robert Rounseville and Cameron Mitchell; Stonecutters Cut It on Stone (There's Nothing So Bad for a Woman) – Cameron Mitchell; What's the Use of Wonderin' – Shirley Jones; You'll Never Walk Alone – Claramae Turner; If I Loved You – Gordon MacRae; You'll Never Walk Alone – Shirley Jones; Tracks on All Star Hit Parade: Theme from The Threepenny Opera – Winifred Atwell; No Other Love – Dave King; My September Love – Joan Regan; A Tear Fell – Lita Roza; Out of Town – Dickie Valentine; It's Almost Tomorrow – David Whitfield. Tracks on All Star Hit Parade No.2: Around the World – Johnston Brothers; Puttin' On the Style – Billy Cotton; When I Fall In Love – Jimmy Young; A White Sport Coat – Max Bygraves; Freight Train – Beverley Sisters; Butterfly – Tommy Steele. Tracks on The Food Christmas EP: Like Princes Do – Crazyhead; I Don't Want That Kind of Love – Jesus Jones; Info Freako – Diesel Park West. Tracks on The Further Adventures of North (EP): Dream 17 – Annette; Carino 90 – T–Coy; The Way I Feel – Frequency 9; Stop This Thing – Dynasty of Two featuring Rowetta. Tracks on The Apple EP: Those Were the Days – Mary Hopkin; That's the Way God Planned It – Billy Preston; Sour Milk Sea – Jackie Lomax; Come and Get It – Badfinger. Tracks on Fourplay (EP): DJs Unite; Alright – Glide; Be Free – Noisy Factory; True Devotion – EQ. Tracks on The Fred EP: Deeply Dippy – Rockingbirds; Don't Talk Just Kiss – Flowered Up; I'm Too Sexy – Saint Etienne. Gimme Shelter EP was available on all four formats, each featuring an interview with the featured artist plus the following artists performing versions of Gimme Shelter: (cassette) Jimmy Somerville and Voice of the Beehive; Heaven 17; (12") Blue Pearl, 808 State and Robert Owens; Pop Will Eat Itself vs Gary Clail; Ranking Roger and the Mighty Diamonds; (CD) Thunder; Little Angels; Hawkwind and Sam Fox; (2nd CD) Cud with Sandie Shaw; Kingmaker; New Model Army and Tom Jones. Tracks on Subplates Volume 1 (EP): Style Warz – Son'z of a Loop Da Loop Era; Funky Dope Track – Q–Bass; The Chopper – DJ Hype; Look No Further – Run Tings. Tracks on The Two Tone EP: Gangsters – Special AKA; The Prince –Madness; On My Radio – Selecter; Tears of a Clown – Beat. Tracks on Help (EP): Lucky – Radiohead; 50ft Queenie (Live) – PJ

1 July 1995	8 July 1995	15 July 1995	22 July 1995
UK No.1 SINGLES			
UNCHAINED MELODY / (THERE'LL BE BLUEBIRDS OVER) THE WHITE CLIFFS OF DOVER Robson Green and Jerome Flynn	**BOOM BOOM BOOM** The Outhere Brothers	**BOOM BOOM BOOM** The Outhere Brothers	**BOOM BOOM BOOM** The Outhere Brothers
UK No.1 ALBUMS			
THESE DAYS Bon Jovi	**THESE DAYS** Bon Jovi	**THESE DAYS** Bon Jovi	**THESE DAYS** Bon Jovi

*Harvey; Momentum – Guru featuring Big Shug; an untitled piece of incidental music. Tracks on New York Undercover (EP): Tell Me What You Like – Guy; Dom Perignon – Little Shawn; I Miss You – Monifah; Jeeps, Lex Coups, Bimax & Menz – Lost Boys. Tracks on Dangerous Minds (EP): Curiosity – Aaron Hall; Gin & Dance – De Vante; It's Alright – Sista featuring Craig Mack. Artists on Perfect Day are as follows: BBC Symphony Orchestra and Andrew Davis, Bono (U2), Boyzone, Brett Anderson (Suede), Brodsky Quartet, Burning Spear, Courtney Pine, David Bowie, Dr John, Elton John, Emmylou Harris, Evan Dando (Lemonheads), Gabrielle, Heather Small (M People), Huey (Fun Lovin' Criminals), Ian Broudie (Lightning Seeds), Joan Armatrading, Laurie Anderson, Lesley Garrett, Lou Reed, Robert Cray, Shane MacGowan, Sheona White, Skye (Morcheeba), Suzanne Vega, Tammy Wynette, Thomas Allen, Tom Jones, Visual Ministry Orchestra. Tracks on The Full Monty – Monster Mix (medley): You Sexy Thing – Hot Chocolate; Hot Stuff – Donna Summer; You Can Leave Your Hat On – Tom Jones. CD also has a full version of 'You Can Leave Your Hat On' by Tom Jones and 'The Stripper' by David Rose. Tracks on Trade (EP) (disc 2): Put Your House in Order – Steve Thomas; The Dawn – Tony De Vit. Artists on 'It's Only Rock 'n' Roll': Keith Richards, Kid Rock, Mary J Blige, Kelly Jones of Stereophonics, Jon Bon Jovi, Kéllé Bryan, Jay Kay of Jamiroquai, Ozzy Osbourne, Womack and Womack, Lionel Richie, Bonnie Raitt, Dolores O'Riordan of The Cranberries, James Brown, Spice Girls (minus Geri), Mick Jagger, Robin Williams, Jackson Browne, Iggy Pop, Chrissie Hynde, Skin of Skunk Anansie, Annie Lennox, Mark Owen, Natalie Imbruglia, Huey of Fun Lovin' Criminals, Dina Carroll, Gavin Rossdale of Bush, BB King, Joe Cocker, The Corrs, Steve Cradock and Simon Fowler of Ocean Colour Scene, Ronan Keating, Ray Barretto, Herbie Hancock, Francis Rossi and Rick Parfitt of Status Quo, S Club 7 and Eric Idle. Tracks on 'Hard Beat EP 19': 'Eternal '99' by Eternal Rhythm and 'Tragic', 'F**k Me' and 'Don't Give Up' all by BK. Artists on the John Peel tribute record 'Ever Fallen in Love 'With Someone You Shouldn't've' are as follows: Roger Daltry, The Datsuns, The Futureheads, David Gilmour, Peter Hook, Elton John, El Presidente, Robert Plant, Pete Shelley, The Soledad Brothers.*

Junior VASQUEZ
US, male DJ / producer – Donald Martin (2 Singles: 5 Weeks)

15 Jul 95 **GET YOUR HANDS OFF MY MAN!** *Positiva CDTIV 37*.....22 3
31 Aug 96 **IF MADONNA CALLS** *Multiply CDMULTY 13*.....24 2

VAST *Australia, male vocal / instrumental group*

16 Sep 00 **FREE** *Mushroom MUSH 79CDS*.....55 1

Sven VATH *Germany, male DJ / producer (3 Singles: 5 Weeks)*

24 Jul 93 **L'ESPERANZA** *Eye Q YZ 757*.....63 2
6 Nov 93 **AN ACCIDENT IN PARADISE** *Eye Q YZ 778CD*.....57 2
22 Oct 94 **HARLEQUIN – THE BEAUTY AND THE BEAST** *Eye Q YZ 857*....72 1

Frankie VAUGHAN (253 Top 500)
High-kicking '50s heart-throb vocalist, b. Frank Abelson, 3 Feb 1928, Liverpool, UK, d. 17 Sep 1999. This variety show veteran was made an OBE in 1965 for his charity work and was one of the most popular performers of the 1950s (4 Albums: 20 Weeks, 31 Singles: 232 Weeks)

29 Jan 54 **ISTANBUL (NOT CONSTANTINOPLE)** *HMV B 10599* [1] 11 1
28 Jan 55 **HAPPY DAYS AND LONELY NIGHTS** *HMV B 10783*.....12 3
22 Apr 55 **TWEEDLE DEE** *Philips PB 423*.....17 1
2 Dec 55 **SEVENTEEN** *Philips PB 511*.....18 3
3 Feb 56 **MY BOY FLAT TOP** *Philips PB 544*.....20 2
9 Nov 56 ● **THE GREEN DOOR** *Philips PB 640*.....2 15
11 Jan 57 ★ **THE GARDEN OF EDEN** *Philips PB 660*.....1 13
4 Oct 57 ● **MAN ON FIRE / WANDERIN' EYES** *Philips PB 729*.....6 12
1 Nov 57 ● **GOT-TA HAVE SOMETHING IN THE BANK, FRANK** *Philips PB 751* [2] 8 11
20 Dec 57 ● **KISSES SWEETER THAN WINE** *Philips PB 775*.....8 11
7 Mar 58 **CAN'T GET ALONG WITHOUT YOU / WE ARE NOT ALONE** *Philips PB 793*.....11 6
9 May 58 ● **KEWPIE DOLL** *Philips PB 825*.....10 12
1 Aug 58 **WONDERFUL THINGS** (re) *Philips PB 834*.....22 6
10 Oct 58 **AM I WASTING MY TIME ON YOU** (re) *Philips PB 865*.....25 4
30 Jan 59 **THAT'S MY DOLL** *Philips PB 895*.....28 2
1 May 59 ● **COME SOFTLY TO ME** *Philips PB 913* [2] 9 9
24 Jul 59 ● **THE HEART OF A MAN** *Philips PB 930*.....5 14
5 Sep 59 ● **FRANKIE VAUGHAN AT THE LONDON PALLADIUM** *Philips BDL 7330*.....6 2
18 Sep 59 **WALKIN' TALL** (re) *Philips PB 931*.....28 2
29 Jan 60 **WHAT MORE DO YOU WANT** *Philips PB 985*.....25 2
22 Sep 60 **KOOKIE LITTLE PARADISE** *Philips PB 1054*.....31 5
27 Oct 60 **MILORD** *Philips PB 1066*.....34 6
9 Nov 61 ★ **TOWER OF STRENGTH** *Philips PB 1195*.....1 13
1 Feb 62 **DON'T STOP – TWIST!** *Philips BF 1219*.....22 7
27 Sep 62 **HERCULES** *Philips 326542 BF*.....42 4
24 Jan 63 ● **LOOP DE LOOP** *Philips 326566 BF*.....5 12
20 Jun 63 **HEY MAMA** *Philips BF 1254*.....21 9
4 Jun 64 **HELLO, DOLLY!** *Philips BF 1339*.....18 11
11 Mar 65 **SOMEONE MUST HAVE HURT YOU A LOT** *Philips BF 1394*......46 1
23 Aug 67 ● **THERE MUST BE A WAY** *Columbia DB 8248*.....7 21
4 Nov 67 **FRANKIE VAUGHAN SONGBOOK** *Philips DBL 001*.....40 1
15 Nov 67 **SO TIRED** *Columbia DB 8298*.....21 9
25 Nov 67 **THERE MUST BE A WAY** *Columbia SCX 6200*.....22 8
28 Feb 68 **NEVERTHELESS** *Columbia DB 8354*.....29 5
12 Nov 77 **100 GOLDEN GREATS** *Ronco RTDX 2021*.....24 9

[1] Frankie Vaughan with The Peter Knight Singers [2] Frankie Vaughan and The Kaye Sisters

Malcolm VAUGHAN
UK, male vocalist – Malcolm Thomas (9 Singles: 106 Weeks)

1 Jul 55 ● **EV'RY DAY OF MY LIFE** *HMV B 10874*.....5 16
27 Jan 56 **WITH YOUR LOVE** (2re) *HMV POP 130*.....18 3
26 Oct 56 ● **ST THERESE OF THE ROSES** (re) *HMV POP 250*.....3 20
12 Apr 57 **THE WORLD IS MINE** (2re) *HMV POP 303*.....26 4
10 May 57 **CHAPEL OF THE ROSES** *HMV POP 325*.....13 8
29 Nov 57 ● **MY SPECIAL ANGEL** *HMV POP 419*.....3 14
21 Mar 58 **TO BE LOVED** *HMV POP 459*.....14 12
17 Oct 58 ● **MORE THAN EVER (COME PRIMA)** *HMV POP 538*.....5 14
27 Feb 59 **WAIT FOR ME / WILLINGLY** (re) *HMV POP 590*.....13 15

'With Your Love' is with The Peter Knight Singers. 'To Be Loved' and 'More Than Ever (Come Prima)' are with The Michael Sammes Singers.

Norman VAUGHAN
UK, male vocalist / comedian, b. 10 Apr 1927, d. 17 May 2002

17 May 62 **SWINGING IN THE RAIN** *Pye 7N 15438*.....34 5

Sarah VAUGHAN *US, female vocalist, b. 27 Mar 1924, d. 3 Apr 1990 (1 Album: 1 Week, 4 Singles: 34 Weeks)*

27 Sep 57 **PASSING STRANGERS** *Mercury MT 164* [1] 22 2
11 Sep 59 ● **BROKEN HEARTED MELODY** *Mercury AMT 1057* **$**.....7 13
26 Mar 60 **NO COUNT – SARAH** *Mercury MMC 14021*.....19 1
29 Dec 60 **LET'S / SERENATA** (re) *Columbia DB 4542*.....37 4
12 Mar 69 **PASSING STRANGERS** (re-issue) *Mercury MF 1082* [1] 20 15

[1] Billy Eckstine and Sarah Vaughan

Stevie Ray VAUGHAN and DOUBLE TROUBLE *US, male vocalist and instrumental group – leader b. 3 Oct 1954, d. 27 Aug 1990*

15 Jul 89 **IN STEP** *Epic 463395 1*.....63 1

The VAUGHAN BROTHERS *US, male vocal / instrumental group*

20 Oct 90 **FAMILY STYLE** *Epic 4670141*.....63 1

Billy VAUGHN and his Orchestra *US, orchestra and chorus – leader b. Richard Vaughn, 12 Apr 1919, d. 26 Sep 1991 (2 Singles: 8 Weeks)*

27 Jan 56 **THE SHIFTING WHISPERING SANDS PART 1** *London HLD 8205* [1] 20 1
23 Mar 56 **THEME FROM 'THE THREEPENNY OPERA'** *London HLD 8238*.. 12 7

[1] Billy Vaughn Orchestra and Chorus, narration by Ken Nordene

The VAULTS *UK, male vocal / instrumental group*

20 Mar 04 **NO SLEEP NO NEED (EP)** *Red Flag RF 09CDS*.....70 1

Tracks on No Sleep No Need (EP): Lady Hell / No Sleep No Need / Leaving Here.

29 July 1995	5 August 1995	12 August 1995	19 August 1995
BOOM BOOM BOOM The Outhere Brothers	**NEVER FORGET** Take That	**NEVER FORGET** Take That	**NEVER FORGET** Take That
I SHOULD COCO Supergrass	**I SHOULD COCO** Supergrass	**I SHOULD COCO** Supergrass	**IT'S GREAT WHEN YOUR'RE STRAIGHT ... YEAH** Black Grape

KEY UK No.1 ★★ UK Top 10 ●● Still on chart ++ UK entry at No.1 ■■ US No.1 ▲▲ UK million seller £ US million seller $
Singles re-entries are listed as (re), (2re), (3re)... which signifies that the hit re-entered the chart once, twice or three times...
Peak Position / Weeks

VBIRDS *UK, female cartoon vocal group*

3 May 03 **VIRTUALITY** *EMI / Liberty CDSVIRT 001* 21 3

Bobby VEE (337 Top 500)

Early 1960s teen idol, b. Robert Velline, 30 Apr 1943, North Dakota, US. This photogenic, Buddy Holly-influenced teenaged vocalist (whose backing band once included Bob Dylan) was rarely away from the UK or US charts in the pre-Beat Boom years (7 Albums: 73 Weeks, 10 Singles: 134 Weeks)

19 Jan 61 ● **RUBBER BALL** *London HLG 9255* 4 11
13 Apr 61 ● **MORE THAN I CAN SAY / STAYIN' IN** *London HLG 9316* 4 16
3 Aug 61 ● **HOW MANY TEARS** *London HLG 9389* 10 13
26 Oct 61 ● **TAKE GOOD CARE OF MY BABY** *London HLG 9438* ▲ $ 3 16
21 Dec 61 ● **RUN TO HIM** *London HLG 9470* $ 6 15
24 Feb 62 ● TAKE GOOD CARE OF MY BABY *London HAG 2428* 7 8
8 Mar 62 **PLEASE DON'T ASK ABOUT BARBARA** *Liberty LIB 55419* 29 9
31 Mar 62 HITS OF THE ROCKIN' 50'S *London HAG 2406* 20 1
7 Jun 62 ● **SHARING YOU** *Liberty LIB 55451* 10 13
27 Sep 62 **A FOREVER KIND OF LOVE** *Liberty LIB 10046* 13 19
27 Oct 62 ● BOBBY VEE MEETS THE CRICKETS *Liberty LBY 1086* [1] 2 27
12 Jan 63 ● A BOBBY VEE RECORDING SESSION *Liberty LBY 1084* 10 11
7 Feb 63 ● **THE NIGHT HAS A THOUSAND EYES** *Liberty LIB 10069* $ 3 12
20 Apr 63 ● BOBBY VEE'S GOLDEN GREATS *Liberty LBY 1112* 10 14
20 Jun 63 **BOBBY TOMORROW** *Liberty LIB 55530* 21 10
5 Oct 63 THE NIGHT HAS A THOUSAND EYES *Liberty LIB 1139* 15 2
19 Apr 80 ● THE BOBBY VEE SINGLES ALBUM *United Artists UAG 30253* 5 10

[1] Bobby Vee and The Crickets

'Stayin' in' listed with 'More Than I Can Say' from 13 Apr to 4 May 1961. It peaked at No.13.

Louie VEGA (see also LIL MO' YIN YANG; MASTERS AT WORK)

US, male producer (4 Singles: 5 Weeks)

5 Oct 91 **RIDE ON THE RHYTHM** *Atlantic A 7602* [1] 71 1
23 May 92 **RIDE ON THE RHYTHM** (re-issue) *Atlantic A 7486* 70 1
31 Jan 98 **RIDE ON THE RHYTHM** (re-mix) *Perfecto PERF 151CD 1* [2] 36 2
23 Nov 02 **DIAMOND LIFE** *Distance DI 2409* [3] 52 1

[1] Little Louie Vega and Marc Anthony [2] Little Louie and Marc Anthony
[3] Louie Vega and Jay 'Sinister' Sealee starring Julie McKnight

Suzanne VEGA (381 Top 500)

Award-winning singer / songwriter / guitarist who started as a fragile folk-pop performer and was educated at New York's High School for Performing Arts, b. 11 Jul 1959, Santa Monica, California, US. The first artist to chart with an accompanied and unaccompanied version of the same song ('Tom's Diner' – inspired by her brother's restaurant) (7 Albums: 132 Weeks, 12 Singles: 52 Weeks)

19 Oct 85 SUZANNE VEGA *A&M AMA 5072* 11 71
18 Jan 86 **SMALL BLUE THING** *A&M AM 294* 65 3
22 Mar 86 **MARLENE ON THE WALL** *A&M AM 309* 21 9
7 Jun 86 **LEFT OF CENTER** *A&M AM 320* [1] 32 9
9 May 87 ● SOLITUDE STANDING *A&M SUZLP 2* 2 39
23 May 87 **LUKA** *A&M VEGA 1* 23 8
18 Jul 87 **TOM'S DINER** *A&M VEGA 2* 58 3
28 Apr 90 ● DAYS OF OPEN HAND *A&M 3952931* 7 7
19 May 90 **BOOK OF DREAMS** *A&M AM 559* 66 1
28 Jul 90 ● **TOM'S DINER** (re-mix) *A&M AM 592* [2] 2 10
22 Aug 92 **IN LIVERPOOL** *A&M AM 0029* 52 2
19 Sep 92 99.9°F *A&M 5400122* 20 4
24 Oct 92 **99.9°F** *A&M AM 0085* 46 2
19 Dec 92 **BLOOD MAKES NOISE** *A&M AM 0112* 60 3
6 Mar 93 **WHEN HEROES GO DOWN** *A&M AMCD 0158* 58 1
22 Feb 97 **NO CHEAP THRILL** *A&M 5818692* 40 1
8 Mar 97 NINE OBJECTS OF DESIRE *A&M 5405832* 43 3
31 Oct 98 TRIED AND TRUE – THE BEST OF SUZANNE VEGA *A&M 5409452* 46 3
19 Jul 03 RETROSPECTIVE – THE BEST OF SUZANNE VEGA *Universal TV 9808884* 27 5

[1] Suzanne Vega featuring Joe Jackson [2] DNA featuring Suzanne Vega

Tata VEGA *US, female vocalist – Carmen Rosa Vega*

26 May 79 **GET IT UP FOR LOVE / I JUST KEEP THINKING ABOUT YOU BABY** *Motown TMG 1140* 52 4

VEGAS (see also EURYTHMICS; FUN BOY THREE; The SPECIALS; The TOURISTS) *UK, male vocal / instrumental duo – David A Stewart and Terry Hall (3 Singles: 10 Weeks)*

19 Sep 92 **POSSESSED** *RCA 74321110437* 32 4
28 Nov 92 **SHE** *RCA 74321124657* 43 4
3 Apr 93 **WALK INTO THE WIND** *RCA 74321122462* 65 2

The VEILS

UK, male vocal / instrumental group (2 Singles: 2 Weeks)

7 Feb 04 **THE WILD SON** *Rough Trade RTRADSCD 154* 74 1
19 Jun 04 **THE TIDE THAT LEFT AND NEVER CAME BACK** *Rough Trade RTRADSCD 164* 63 1

Tom VEK NEW

UK, male vocalist / guitarist (1 Album: 1 Week, 3 Singles: 3 Weeks)

2 Apr 05 **I AIN'T SAYING MY GOODBYES** *Go Beat 9870674* 45 1
16 Apr 05 WE HAVE SOUND *Go Beat 9870389* 73 1
2 Jul 05 **C-C (YOU SET THE FIRE IN ME)** *Go Beat 9871846* 60 1
5 Nov 05 **NOTHING BUT GREEN LIGHTS** *Go Beat 9874748* 59 1

Rosie VELA *US, female vocalist*

17 Jan 87 **MAGIC SMILE** *A&M AM 369* 27 7
31 Jan 87 ZAZU *A&M AMA 5016* 20 11

The VELVELETTES *US, female vocal group*

31 Jul 71 **THESE THINGS WILL KEEP ME LOVING YOU** *Tamla Motown TMG 780* 34 7

VELVET REVOLVER *US, male vocal / instrumental group (1 Album: 16 Weeks, 2 Singles: 5 Weeks)*

19 Jun 04 CONTRABAND *RCA 82876628352* ▲ 11 16
24 Jul 04 **SLITHER** *RCA 8287663312* 35 3
23 Oct 04 **FALL TO PIECES** *RCA 82876647692* 32 2

The VELVET UNDERGROUND (see also Lou REED) *UK / US, male / female vocal / instrumental group (4 Albums: 11 Weeks, 1 Single: 1 Week)*

23 Feb 85 V.U. *Polydor POLD 5167* 47 4
13 Nov 93 LIVE MCMXCIII *Sire 9362454642* 70 1
12 Mar 94 **VENUS IN FURS** *Sire W 0224CD* 71 1
28 Oct 95 THE BEST OF LOU REED & THE VELVET UNDERGROUND *Global Television RADCD 21* [1] 56 4
6 Jul 02 THE VELVET UNDERGROUND & NICO *Polydor 8232902* [2] 59 2

[1] Lou Reed and The Velvet Underground [2] The Velvet Underground & Nico

The VELVETS *US, male vocal group (2 Singles: 2 Weeks)*

11 May 61 **THAT LUCKY OLD SUN** *London HLU 9328* 46 1
17 Aug 61 **TONIGHT (COULD BE THE NIGHT)** *London HLU 9372* 50 1

The VENGABOYS (406 Top 500)

Holland / Trinidad / Brazil, male / female vocal / production dance-pop troupe formed in 1992 by Dutch DJs Danski and Delmundo (Dennis Van Den Drieshen and Wessel Van Diepen). In 1996 they added singers / dancers Kim, Robin (replaced by Yorick in 1999), Roy and Denice to front the group. The first Netherlands-based act to

26 August 1995	2 September 1995	9 September 1995	16 September 1995
UK No.1 SINGLES			
COUNTRY HOUSE Blur	COUNTRY HOUSE Blur	YOU ARE NOT ALONE Michael Jackson	YOU ARE NOT ALONE Michael Jackson
UK No.1 ALBUMS			
IT'S GREAT WHEN YOUR'RE STRAIGHT ... YEAH Black Grape	SAID AND DONE Boyzone	THE CHARLATANS The Charlatans	ZEITGEIST Levellers

score six successive Top 5 singles. Best-selling single: 'Boom, Boom, Boom, Boom!!' 578,900 (2 Albums: 77 Weeks, 10 Singles: 99 Weeks)

28 Nov 98 ● UP AND DOWN Positiva CDTIV 105 ....4 15
13 Mar 99 ● WE LIKE TO PARTY! (THE VENGABUS) Positiva CDTIV 108 ....3 14
3 Apr 99 ● UP & DOWN – THE PARTY ALBUM! Positiva 4993472 ....6 49
26 Jun 99 ★ BOOM, BOOM, BOOM, BOOM!! Positiva CDTIV 114 ■ 1 15
11 Sep 99 WE'RE GOING TO IBIZA (import) Jive 550422 ....69 1
18 Sep 99 ★ WE'RE GOING TO IBIZA! Positiva CDTIV 119 ■ 1 12
18 Dec 99 ● KISS (WHEN THE SUN DON'T SHINE) Positiva CDTIV 122 ....3 18
11 Mar 00 ● SHALALA LALA Positiva CDTIV 126 ....5 10
25 Mar 00 ● THE PLATINUM ALBUM Positiva 5259530 ....9 28
8 Jul 00 ● UNCLE JOHN FROM JAMAICA Positiva CDTIV 135 ....6 7
14 Oct 00 CHEEKAH BOW BOW (THAT COMPUTER SONG) Positiva CDTIV 142 ....19 5
24 Feb 01 FOREVER AS ONE Positiva CDTIV 148 ....28 2

VENOM UK, male vocal / instrumental group (2 Albums: 2 Weeks)

21 Apr 84 AT WAR WITH SATAN Neat NEAT 1015 ....64 1
13 Apr 85 POSSESSED Neat NEAT 1024 ....99 1

VENT 414 UK, male vocal / instrumental group

28 Sep 96 FIXER Polydor 5753292 ....71 1

Anthony VENTURA ORCHESTRA Switzerland, orchestra

20 Jan 79 DREAM LOVER Lotus WH 5007 ....44 4

The VENTURES US, male instrumental group (4 Singles: 31 Weeks)

8 Sep 60 ● WALK DON'T RUN Top Rank JAR 417 $ 8 13
1 Dec 60 ● PERFIDIA London HLG 9232 ....4 13
9 Mar 61 RAM-BUNK-SHUSH London HLG 9292 ....45 1
11 May 61 LULLABY OF THE LEAVES London HLG 9344 ....43 4

VERACOCHA (see also GOURYELLA; MOONMAN; STARPARTY; SYSTEM F) Holland, male production duo – Vincent de Moor and Ferry Corsten

15 May 99 CARTE BLANCHE Positiva CDTIV 110 ....22 4

VERBALICIOUS NEW UK, female rapper – Natalie Keery-Fisher

5 Mar 05 DON'T PLAY NICE All Around the World VERCD 1 ....11 5

Tom VERLAINE (see also TELEVISION) US, male vocalist

14 Mar 87 FLASH LIGHT Fontana SFLP 1 ....99 1

The VERNONS GIRLS UK, female vocal group (4 Singles: 31 Weeks)

17 May 62 LOVER PLEASE / YOU KNOW WHAT I MEAN (3re) Decca F 11450 ....16 20
6 Sep 62 LOCO-MOTION Decca F 11495 ....47 1
3 Jan 63 FUNNY ALL OVER Decca F 11549 ....31 8
18 Apr 63 DO THE BIRD (re) Decca F 11629 ....44 2

'You Know What I Mean' was not coupled with 'Lover Please' on the chart of 23 Aug 1962, but both sides of this record were listed for the following six weeks.

VERNON'S WONDERLAND (see also BRAINCHILD; CYGNUS X) Germany, male producer – Matthias Hoffmann

25 May 96 VERNON'S WONDERLAND Eye-Q Classics EYECL 004CD 59 1

VERTICAL HORIZON US, male vocal / instrumental group

26 Aug 00 EVERYTHING YOU WANT RCA 74321748692 ▲ 42 2

VERUCA SALT US, male / female vocal / instrumental group (1 Album: 2 Weeks, 5 Singles: 5 Weeks)

2 Jul 94 SEETHER Scared Hitless FRET 003CD 61 1
15 Oct 94 AMERICAN THIGHS Hi-Rise FLATCD 9 ....47 2
3 Dec 94 SEETHER (re-issue) Hi-Rise FLATSDG 12 ....73 1
4 Feb 95 NUMBER ONE BLIND Hi-Rise FLATSCD 16 ....68 1
22 Feb 97 VOLCANO GIRLS Outpost OPRCD 22197 ....56 1
30 Aug 97 BENJAMIN Outpost OPRCD 22261 ....75 1

The VERVE 389 Top 500 Anthemic UK indie-rock band formed in 1991 in Wigan and fronted by Richard Ashcroft (v/g). The double BRIT winners' swansong, Urban Hymns, went gold in 17 countries and sold a million in the UK in two successive years (1997/98). Ashcroft went solo when the group split in 1999 (4 Albums: 132 Weeks, 9 Singles: 50 Weeks)

4 Jul 92 SHE'S A SUPERSTAR Hut HUT 16 ....66 1
22 May 93 BLUE Hut HUTCD 29 ....69 1
3 Jul 93 A STORM IN HEAVEN Hut CDHUT 10 [1] 27 2
13 May 95 THIS IS MUSIC Hut HUTCD 54 ....35 3
24 Jun 95 ON YOUR OWN Hut HUTCD 55 ....28 2
15 Jul 95 A NORTHERN SOUL Hut DGHUT 27 ....13 11
30 Sep 95 HISTORY Hut HUTCD 59 ....24 3
28 Jun 97 ● BITTER SWEET SYMPHONY (re) Hut HUTDG 82 ....2 13
13 Sep 97 ★ THE DRUGS DON'T WORK (re) Hut HUTDG 88 ■ 1 13
11 Oct 97 ★ URBAN HYMNS Hut CDHUT 45 ■ 1 109
6 Dec 97 ● LUCKY MAN Hut HUTDG 92 ....7 13
30 May 98 SONNET (import) Hut 8950752 ....74 1
13 Nov 04 THIS IS MUSIC – THE SINGLES 92-98 Virgin CDV 2991 ....15 10

[1] Verve

A VERY GOOD FRIEND OF MINE Italy, male / female vocal / production / instrumental group

3 Jul 99 JUST ROUND Positiva CDTIV 109 ....55 1

VEX RED UK, male vocal / instrumental group

2 Mar 02 CAN'T SMILE Virgin VUSCD 237 ....45 1
16 Mar 02 START WITH A STRONG AND PERSISTENT DESIRE Virgin CDVUS 215 ....48 1

VHS OR BETA NEW US, male vocal / instrumental group (2 Singles: 2 Weeks)

16 Apr 05 THE MELTING MOON Virgin ASW 683202 ....63 1
6 Aug 05 NIGHT ON FIRE Astralwerks ASWCD 12624 ....69 1

The VIBRATORS UK, male vocal / instrumental group (2 Albums: 7 Weeks, 2 Singles: 8 Weeks)

25 Jun 77 THE VIBRATORS Epic EPC 82907 ....49 5
18 Mar 78 AUTOMATIC LOVER Epic EPC 6137 ....35 5
29 Apr 78 V2 Epic EPC 82495 ....33 2
17 Jun 78 JUDY SAYS (KNOCK YOU IN THE HEAD) Epic EPC 6393 ....70 3

The VICE SQUAD UK, male / female vocal / instrumental group (2 Albums: 10 Weeks, 1 Single: 1 Week)

24 Oct 81 NO CAUSE FOR CONCERN Zonophone ZEM 103 ....32 5
13 Feb 82 OUT OF REACH Zonophone Z 26 ....68 1
22 May 82 STAND STRONG STAND PROUD Zonophone ZEM 104 ....47 5

Sid VICIOUS (see also SEX PISTOLS) UK, male vocalist – John Beverley, b. 10 May 1957, d. 2 Feb 1979

15 Dec 79 SID SINGS Virgin V 2144 ....30 8

VICIOUS CIRCLES (see also ART OF TRANCE; POLTERGEIST) UK, male producer – Simon Berry

16 Dec 00 VICIOUS CIRCLES Platipus PLATCD 82 ....68 1

VICIOUS PINK UK, male / female vocal / instrumental duo

15 Sep 84 CCCAN'T YOU SEE Parlophone R 6074 ....67 4

Maria VIDAL US, female vocalist

24 Aug 85 BODY ROCK EMI America EA 189 ....11 13

23 September 1995	30 September 1995	7 October 1995	14 October 1995
BOOMBASTIC Shaggy	FAIRGROUND Simply Red	FAIRGROUND Simply Red	FAIRGROUND Simply Red
THE GREAT ESCAPE Blur	THE GREAT ESCAPE Blur	DAYDREAM Mariah Carey	(WHAT'S THE STORY) MORNING GLORY? Oasis

In our hearts but not topping the charts

In the book of British Hit Singles & Albums, chart placings are quite rightly used as the ultimate guide to success. However, there are many acts in the hallowed pages of the bible of pop that have a relatively small but committed fanbase, whose loyalty gives those acts longevity which many chart-toppers would kill their drummer for.

So hats off to AC/DC, The Fall, Morcheeba and most of all to winsome Welsh psychedelic popsters Gorky's Zygotic Mynci (pronounced Munkee). They may never have troubled the upper echelons of the singles chart, but they have scored a very respectable eight hit singles, which is more than S Club Juniors / S Club 8, Chicago or Aqua can muster.

AC/DC

MOST HITS WITHOUT A TOP 10 SINGLE

28	AC/DC
20	THUNDER
20	SUPER FURRY ANIMALS
19	LEVELLERS
18	DEL AMITRI
18	ADEVA
18	RONI SIZE
17	THE CULT
17	THE MISSION
17	THE ALARM

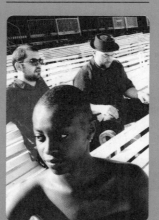

First named artists in act names included only

MOST HITS WITHOUT A TOP 20 SINGLE

16	THE FALL
16	P J HARVEY
14	NEW MODEL ARMY
13	COCTEAU TWINS
12	THE BLACK CROWES

The Fall

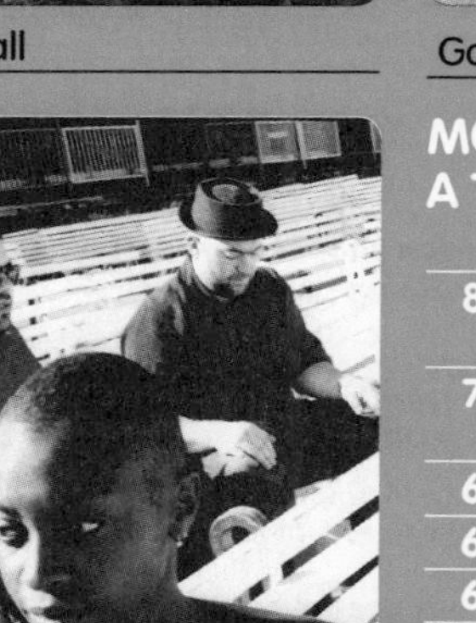

Morcheeba

MOST HITS WITHOUT A TOP 30 SINGLE

10	MORCHEEBA
10	CATHERINE WHEEL
8	BETH ORTON
8	DILLINJA
7	TINDERSTICKS

Gorky's Zygotic Mynci

MOST HITS WITHOUT A TOP 40 SINGLE

8	GORKY'S ZYGOTIC MYNCI
7	THAT PETROL EMOTION
6	TERRY HALL
6	RICK JAMES
6	DEUS
6	DIESEL PARK WEST
6	FRAZIER CHORUS

The VIDEO KIDS *Holland, male / female vocal duo*

5 Oct 85 **WOODPECKERS FROM SPACE** *Epic A 6504*........72 1

VIDEO SYMPHONIC *UK, orchestra*

24 Oct 81 **THE FLAME TREES OF THIKA** *EMI EMI 5222*........42 3

VIENNA PHILHARMONIC ORCHESTRA
Austria, orchestra – conducted by Aram Khatchaturian

18 Dec 71 **THEME FROM 'THE ONEDIN LINE'** *Decca F 13259*........15 14
22 Jan 72 SPARTACUS *Decca SXL 6000* [1] 16 15

[1] Aram Khatchaturian / Vienna Philharmonic Orchestra

VIENNA SYMPHONY ORCHESTRA *Austria, orchestra*

4 Apr 87 SYMPHONIC ROCK WITH THE VIENNA SYMPHONY ORCHESTRA *Stylus SMR 730*........43 4

VIEW FROM THE HILL
UK, male / female vocal / instrumental group (2 Singles: 6 Weeks)

19 Jul 86 **NO CONVERSATION** *EMI EMI 5565*........58 3
21 Feb 87 **I'M NO REBEL** *EMI EM 5580*........59 3

VIKKI *UK, female vocalist – Vikki Watson*

4 May 85 **LOVE IS ...** *PRT 7P 326*........49 3

The VILLAGE PEOPLE
US, male vocal group (3 Albums: 29 Weeks, 9 Singles: 66 Weeks)

3 Dec 77 **SAN FRANCISCO (YOU'VE GOT ME)** *DJM DJS 10817*........45 5
25 Nov 78 ★ **Y.M.C.A.** *Mercury 6007 192* £ $........1 16
27 Jan 79 CRUISIN' *Mercury 9109 614*........24 9
17 Mar 79 ● **IN THE NAVY** *Mercury 6007 209* $........2 9
12 May 79 GO WEST *Mercury 9109 621*........14 19
16 Jun 79 **GO WEST** *Mercury 6007 221*........15 8
9 Aug 80 **CAN'T STOP THE MUSIC** *Mercury MER 16*........11 11
9 Feb 85 **SEX OVER THE PHONE** *Record Shack SOHO 34*........59 5
4 Dec 93 **Y.M.C.A.** (re-mix) *Bell 74321177182*........12 7
18 Dec 93 THE BEST OF THE VILLAGE PEOPLE *Bell 4321178312*........72 1
28 May 94 **IN THE NAVY** (re-mix) *Bell 74321198192*........36 2
27 Nov 99 **Y.M.C.A.** (2nd re-mix) *Wrasse WRASX 002*........35 3

Gene VINCENT *US, male vocalist, b. Eugene Craddock, 11 Feb 1935, d. 12 Oct 1971 (1 Album: 2 Weeks, 8 Singles: 51 Weeks)*

13 Jul 56 **BE-BOP-A-LULA** (2re) *Capitol CL 14599* [1] 16 7
12 Oct 56 **RACE WITH THE DEVIL** *Capitol CL 14628* [1] 28 1
19 Oct 56 **BLUEJEAN BOP** *Capitol CL 14637* [1] 16 5
8 Jan 60 **WILD CAT** (re) *Capitol CL 15099*........21 6
10 Mar 60 **MY HEART** (2re) *Capitol CL 15115*........16 8
16 Jun 60 **PISTOL PACKIN' MAMA** *Capitol CL 15136* [2] 15 9
16 Jul 60 CRAZY TIMES *Capitol T 1342*........12 2
1 Jun 61 **SHE SHE LITTLE SHEILA** (re) *Capitol CL 15202*........22 11
31 Aug 61 **I'M GOING HOME (TO SEE MY BABY)** *Capitol CL 15215* [3] 36 4

[1] Gene Vincent and The Blue Caps [2] Gene Vincent with The Beat Boys
[3] Gene Vincent with Sounds Incorporated

Vinnie VINCENT (see also KISS) *US, male vocalist / guitarist*

28 May 88 ALL SYSTEMS GO *Chrysalis CHR 1626*........51 2

VINDALOO SUMMER SPECIAL
UK, male / female vocal / instrumental group

19 Jul 86 **ROCKIN' WITH RITA (HEAD TO TOE)** *Vindaloo UGH 13*........56 3

The VINES *Australia, male vocal (Craig Nicholls) / instrumental group (2 Albums: 9 Weeks, 5 Singles: 12 Weeks)*

20 Apr 02 **HIGHLY EVOLVED** *Heavenly HVN 112CD*........32 2
29 Jun 02 **GET FREE** *Heavenly HVN 113CD*........24 3
20 Jul 02 ● HIGHLY EVOLVED *Heavenly HVNLP 36CD*........3 7
19 Oct 02 **OUTTATHAWAY** *Heavenly HVN 120CDS*........20 2
20 Mar 04 **RIDE** *Heavenly HVN 137CD*........25 3
3 Apr 04 WINNING DAYS *Heavenly HVNLP 48CD*........29 2
5 Jun 04 **WINNING DAYS** *Heavenly HVN 139CDS*........42 2

Bobby VINTON
US, male vocalist – Stanley Vinton (1 Album: 2 Weeks, 4 Singles: 29 Weeks)

2 Aug 62 **ROSES ARE RED (MY LOVE)** *Columbia DB 4878* ▲ $........15 8
19 Dec 63 **THERE! I'VE SAID IT AGAIN** *Columbia DB 7179* ▲ $........34 10
29 Sep 90 ● **BLUE VELVET** *Epic 6505240* ▲ $........2 10
17 Nov 90 BLUE VELVET *Epic 4675701*........67 2
17 Nov 90 **ROSES ARE RED (MY LOVE)** (re-issue) *Epic 6564677*........71 1

VINYLGROOVER and The RED HED
(see also KONTAKT) *UK, male production duo (2 Singles: 2 Weeks)*

27 Jan 01 **ROK DA HOUSE** *Nukleuz NUKP 0285*........72 1
10 Jul 04 **STAY** *Tidy Trax TIDYTWO 133C* [1] 61 1

[1] Rob Tisseria, Vinylgroover & The Red Hed

VIOLENT DELIGHT
UK, male vocal / instrumental group (3 Singles: 4 Weeks)

1 Mar 03 **I WISH I WAS A GIRL** *WEA WEA 362CD*........25 2
21 Jun 03 **ALL YOU EVER DO** *WEA WEA 367CD 1*........38 1
13 Sep 03 **TRANSMISSION** *WEA WEA 370CD 1*........64 1

VIOLENT FEMMES *US, male / female vocal / instrumental group*

1 Mar 86 THE BLIND LEADING THE NAKED *Slash SLAP 10*........81 1

VIOLINSKI *UK, male instrumental group*

17 Feb 79 **CLOG DANCE** *Jet 136*........17 9
26 May 79 NO CAUSE FOR ALARM *Jet JETLU 219*........49 1

VIPER *Belgium, male production group*

7 Feb 98 **THE TWISTER** *Hooj Choons HOOJCD 59*........55 1

The VIPERS SKIFFLE GROUP *UK, male vocal (Wally Whyton, d. 1997) / instrumental group (3 Singles: 18 Weeks)*

25 Jan 57 ● **DON'T YOU ROCK ME DADDY-O** *Parlophone R 4261*........10 9
22 Mar 57 ● **THE CUMBERLAND GAP** *Parlophone R 4289*........10 6
31 May 57 **STREAMLINE TRAIN** *Parlophone R 4308*........23 3

VIRUS (see also ELEMENTFOUR; OAKENFOLD; PERFECTO ALLSTARZ)
UK, male instrumental / production duo – Paul Oakenfold and Steve Osborne (2 Singles: 3 Weeks)

26 Aug 95 **SUN** *Perfecto PERF 107CD*........62 1
25 Jan 97 **MOON** *Perfecto PERF 134CD*........36 2

VISAGE (see also MIDGE URE) *UK, male vocal (Steve Strange) / instrumental group (4 Albums: 58 Weeks, 8 Singles: 56 Weeks)*

20 Dec 80 ● **FADE TO GREY** *Polydor POSP 194*........8 15
24 Jan 81 VISAGE *Polydor 2490 157*........13 29
14 Mar 81 **MIND OF A TOY** *Polydor POSP 236*........13 8
11 Jul 81 **VISAGE** *Polydor POSP 293*........21 7
13 Mar 82 **DAMNED DON'T CRY** *Polydor POSP 390*........11 8
3 Apr 82 ● THE ANVIL *Polydor POLD 5050*........6 16
26 Jun 82 **NIGHT TRAIN** *Polydor POSP 441*........12 10
13 Nov 82 **PLEASURE BOYS** *Polydor POSP 523*........44 3
19 Nov 83 FADE TO GREY – THE SINGLES COLLECTION *Polydor POLD 5117*........38 11
1 Sep 84 **LOVE GLOVE** *Polydor POSP 691*........54 3
3 Nov 84 BEAT BOY *Polydor POLH 12*........79 2
28 Aug 93 **FADE TO GREY** (re-mix) *Polydor PZCD 282*........39 2

18 November 1995	25 November 1995	2 December 1995	9 December 1995
I BELIEVE / UP ON THE ROOF Robson & Jerome	I BELIEVE / UP ON THE ROOF Robson & Jerome	I BELIEVE / UP ON THE ROOF Robson & Jerome	EARTH SONG Michael Jackson
MADE IN HEAVEN Queen	ROBSON & JEROME Robson & Jerome	ROBSON & JEROME Robson & Jerome	ROBSON & JEROME Robson & Jerome

KEY
UK No.1 ★★ UK Top 10 ●● Still on chart ++ UK entry at No.1 ■■
US No.1 ▲▲ UK million seller £ US million seller $
Singles re-entries are listed as (re), (2re), (3re)... which signifies that the hit re-entered the chart once, twice or three times...
Peak Position / Weeks

The VISCOUNTS *UK, male vocal group (2 Singles: 18 Weeks)*

13 Oct 60 **SHORT'NIN' BREAD** *Pye 7N 15287* 16 8
14 Sep 61 **WHO PUT THE BOMP (IN THE BOMP, BOMP, BOMP)** *Pye 7N 15379* 21 10

VISION *UK, male vocal / instrumental group*

9 Jul 83 **LOVE DANCE** *MVM MVM 2886* 74 1

VISIONMASTERS with Tony KING and Kylie MINOGUE *UK, male DJ / production duo, UK, male DJ / producer and Australia, female vocalist*

30 Nov 91 **KEEP ON PUMPIN' IT** *PWL PWL 207* 49 1

VITAMIN C *US, female vocalist – Colleen Fitzpatrick*

19 Jul 03 **LAST NITE** *V2 VVR 5023283* 70 1

Soraya VIVIAN *UK, female vocalist*

16 Mar 02 **WHEN YOU'RE GONE** *Activ 8 ACT 501* 59 1

VIXEN
US, female vocal / instrumental group (2 Albums: 5 Weeks, 7 Singles: 21 Weeks)

3 Sep 88 **EDGE OF A BROKEN HEART** *Manhattan MT 48* 51 4
8 Oct 88 VIXEN *Manhattan MTL 1028* 66 1
4 Mar 89 **CRYIN'** *EMI Manhattan MT 60* 27 4
3 Jun 89 **LOVE MADE ME** *EMI-USA MT 66* 36 4
2 Sep 89 **EDGE OF A BROKEN HEART** (re-issue) *EMI-USA MT 48* 59 2
28 Jul 90 **HOW MUCH LOVE** *EMI-USA MT 87* 35 3
18 Aug 90 REV IT UP *EMI-USA MTL 1054* 20 4
20 Oct 90 **LOVE IS A KILLER** *EMI-USA MT 91* 41 2
16 Mar 91 **NOT A MINUTE TOO SOON** *EMI-USA MT 93* 37 2

VOGGUE *Canada, male / female production / vocal group*

18 Jul 81 **DANCIN' THE NIGHT AWAY** *Mercury MER 76* 39 6

VOICE OF THE BEEHIVE *US / UK, male / female vocal / instrumental group (2 Albums: 26 Weeks, 8 Singles: 51 Weeks)*

14 Nov 87 **I SAY NOTHING** *London LON 151* 45 5
5 Mar 88 **I WALK THE EARTH** *London LON 169* 42 4
14 May 88 **DON'T CALL ME BABY** *London LON 175* 15 10
2 Jul 88 LET IT BEE *London LONLP 57* 13 13
23 Jul 88 **I SAY NOTHING** (re-issue) *London LON 190* 22 6
22 Oct 88 **I WALK THE EARTH** (re-issue) *London LON 206* 46 4
13 Jul 91 **MONSTERS AND ANGELS** *London LON 302* 17 10
24 Aug 91 HONEY LINGERS *London 8282591* 17 13
28 Sep 91 **I THINK I LOVE YOU** *London LON 308* 25 6
11 Jan 92 **PERFECT PLACE** *London LON 312* 37 6

VOICES OF LIFE (see also JM SILK)
US, male / female vocal / production duo – Sharon Pass and Steve 'Silk' Hurley

21 Mar 98 **THE WORD IS LOVE (SAY THE WORD)** *AM:PM 5825272* 26 2

Sterling VOID *UK, male instrumentalist / vocalist*

4 Feb 89 **RUNAWAY GIRL / IT'S ALL RIGHT** *ffrr FFR 21* 53 3

VOLATILE AGENTS featuring Simone BENN
UK, male production duo and female vocalist

15 Dec 01 **HOOKED ON YOU** *Melting Pot MPRCD 10* 54 3

VOLCANO
Norway / UK, male / female vocal / instrumental group (2 Singles: 4 Weeks)

23 Jul 94 **MORE TO LOVE** *Deconstruction 74321221832* 32 3
18 Nov 95 **THAT'S THE WAY LOVE IS** *EXP EXPCD 002* [1] 72 1

[1] Volcano with Sam Cartwright

The VON BONDIES
US, male vocal / instrumental group (1 Album: 2 Weeks, 2 Singles: 3 Weeks)

14 Feb 04 **C'MON C'MON** *Sire W 635CD* 21 2
21 Feb 04 PAWN SHOPPE HEART *Sire 9362485352* 36 2
15 May 04 **TELL ME WHAT YOU SEE** *Sire W 639CD1* 43 1

Herbert VON KARAJAN
Austria, male conductor, b. 5 Apr 1908, d. 16 Jul 1989 (5 Albums: 18 Weeks)

26 Sep 70 BEETHOVEN TRIPLE CONCERTO *HMV ASD 2582* 51 2
16 Apr 88 THE ESSENTIAL KARAJAN *Deutsche Grammophon HVKTV 1* 51 5
3 Aug 91 HOLST: THE PLANETS *Deutsche Grammophon 4352891* 52 2
7 Oct 95 KARAJAN: ADAGIO *Deutsche Grammophon 4452822* 30 8
13 Apr 96 ADAGIO 2 *Deutsche Grammophon 4495152* [1] 63 1

[1] Berlin Philharmonic Orchestra / Herbert Von Karajan

On Beethoven Triple Concerto the soloists are David Oistrakh (violin), Mstislav Rostropovich (cello) and Sviatoslav Richter (piano). Von Karajan also conducted the Berlin Philharmonic Orchestra.

Anne Sofie VON OTTER meets Elvis COSTELLO
Sweden, female vocalist with UK, male vocalist / guitarist

31 Mar 01 FOR THE STARS *Deutsche Grammophon 4695302* 67 1

VOODOO & SERANO *Germany, male production duo – Reinhard Raith and Tommy Serano (2 Singles: 6 Weeks)*

3 Feb 01 **BLOOD IS PUMPIN'** *Xtrahard / Xtravaganza X2H 2CDS* 19 4
16 Aug 03 **OVERLOAD** *All Around the World CDGLOBE 284* 30 2

VOW WOW *Japan / US, male vocal / instrumental group*

18 Mar 89 HELTER SKELTER *Arista 209691* 75 1

VOYAGE
UK / France, disco aggregation (1 Album: 1 Week, 3 Singles: 27 Weeks)

17 Jun 78 **FROM EAST TO WEST / SCOTS MACHINE** *GTO GT 224* 13 13
9 Sep 78 VOYAGE *GTO GTLP 030* 59 1
25 Nov 78 **SOUVENIRS** *GTO GT 241* 56 7
24 Mar 79 **LET'S FLY AWAY** *GTO GT 245* 38 7

'Scots Machine' credited from 24 Jun 1978 until end of record's chart run.

VOYAGER *UK, male vocal / instrumental group*

26 May 79 **HALFWAY HOTEL** *Mountain VOY 001* 33 8

Jurgen VRIES (see also ANGELIC; CITIZEN CANED; DT8 PROJECT; ORION)
UK, male DJ / producer – Darren Tate (4 Singles: 20 Weeks)

14 Sep 02 **THE THEME** *Direction 6730952* 13 4
1 Feb 03 ● **THE OPERA SONG (BRAVE NEW WORLD)** (re) *Direction 6734642* [1] 3 10
4 Oct 03 **WILDERNESS** *Direction 6742692* [2] 20 3
19 Jun 04 **TAKE MY HAND** *Direction 6749932* [3] 23 3

[1] Jurgen Vries featuring CMC [Charlotte Church] [2] Jurgen Vries featuring Shena [3] Jurgen Vries featuring Andrea Britton

VS *UK, male / female vocal / rap group (3 Singles: 15 Weeks)*

6 Mar 04 ● **LOVE YOU LIKE MAD** *Innocent SINCD 59* 7 7
19 Jun 04 **CALL U SEXY** *Innocent SINDX 62* 11 6
23 Oct 04 **MAKE IT HOT** *Innocent SINDX 66* 29 2

VYBE *US, female vocal group*

7 Oct 95 **WARM SUMMER DAZE** *Fourth & Broadway BRCD 315* 60 1

16 December 1995	23 December 1995	30 December 1995	6 January 1996
◂◂ UK No.1 SINGLES ▸▸			
EARTH SONG Michael Jackson	EARTH SONG Michael Jackson	EARTH SONG Michael Jackson	EARTH SONG Michael Jackson
◂◂ UK No.1 ALBUMS ▸▸			
ROBSON & JEROME Robson & Jerome	ROBSON & JEROME Robson & Jerome	ROBSON & JEROME Robson & Jerome	ROBSON & JEROME Robson & Jerome

Kristine W *US, female vocalist – Kristine Weitz (5 Singles: 8 Weeks)*

21 May 94	**LOVE COME HOME** *Triangle BLUESCD 001* [1]	73	1
25 Jun 94	**FEEL WHAT YOU WANT** *Champion CHAMPCD 304*	33	3
25 May 96	**ONE MORE TRY** *Champion CHAMPCD 317*	41	1
21 Dec 96	**LAND OF THE LIVING** *Champion CHAMPCD 324*	57	1
5 Jul 97	**FEEL WHAT YOU WANT** (re-issue) *Champion CHAMPCD 329*	40	2

[1] Our Tribe with Franke Pharoah and Kristine W

WC featuring SNOOP DOGG & Nate DOGG *US, male rappers (WC is William Calhoun)*

1 Mar 03	**THE STREETS** *Def Jam 0779852*	48	2

W.I.P. featuring EMMIE *UK, male production duo and female vocalist*

16 Feb 02	**I WON'T LET YOU DOWN** *Decode / Telstar CDSTAS 3210*	53	1

Andrew W.K. *US, male vocalist / producer – Andrew Wilkes-Krier (1 Album: 1 Week, 2 Singles: 5 Weeks)*

10 Nov 01	**PARTY HARD** *Mercury 5888132*	19	4
24 Nov 01	I GET WET *Mercury 5865882*	71	1
9 Mar 02	**SHE IS BEAUTIFUL** *Mercury 5889522*	55	1

W.O.S.P. *UK, male / female production / vocal duo*

17 Nov 01	**GETTIN' INTO U** *Data DATA 26CDS*	48	1

WWF SUPERSTARS *US / UK, male wrestling vocalists (1 Album: 5 Weeks, 3 Singles: 15 Weeks)*

12 Dec 92 ●	**SLAM JAM** (re) *Arista 74321124887*	4	9
3 Apr 93	**WRESTLEMANIA** *Arista 74321136832*	14	5
17 Apr 93 ●	WRESTLEMANIA – THE ALBUM *Arista 74321138062*	10	5
10 Jul 93	**USA** *Arista 74321153092* [1]	71	1

[1] WWF Superstars featuring Hacksaw Jim Duggan

Adam WADE *US, male vocalist*

8 Jun 61	**TAKE GOOD CARE OF HER** (re) *HMV POP 843*	38	6

With the George Paxton Orchestra and Chorus.

WAG YA TAIL *UK, male vocal / instrumental group*

3 Oct 92	**XPAND YA MIND (EXPANSIONS)** *PWL International PWL 238*	49	1

WAH! *UK, male vocal (Pete Wylie) / instrumental group (2 Albums: 11 Weeks, 3 Singles: 26 Weeks)*

18 Jul 81	NAH-POO = THE ART OF BLUFF *Eternal CLASSIC 1*	33	5
25 Dec 82 ●	**THE STORY OF THE BLUES** *Eternal JF 1*	3	12
19 Mar 83	**HOPE (I WISH YOU'D BELIEVE ME)** *WEA X 9880*	37	5
30 Jun 84	**COME BACK** *Beggars Banquet BEG 111* [1]	20	9
4 Aug 84	A WORD TO THE WISE GUY *Beggars Banquet BEGA 54* [1]	28	6

[1] Mighty Wah! [1] Mighty Wah!

The WAIKIKIS *Belgium, male instrumental group*

11 Mar 65	**HAWAII TATTOO** *Pye International 7N 25286*	41	2

Martha WAINWRIGHT NEW *Canada, female vocalist*

16 Apr 05	MARTHA WAINWRIGHT *Drowned in Sound DIS 0011*	63	1

Rufus WAINWRIGHT *Canada, male vocalist*

7 Aug 04	**I DON'T KNOW WHAT IT IS** *Dreamworks 9863229*	74	1
19 Mar 05	WANT TWO *Dreamworks 9880444*	21	3

John WAITE (see also The BABYS; BROKEN ENGLISH) *UK, male vocalist (1 Album: 3 Weeks, 2 Singles: 13 Weeks)*

29 Sep 84 ●	**MISSING YOU** *EMI America EA 182* ▲	9	11
10 Nov 84	NO BRAKES *EMI America WAIT 1*	64	3
13 Feb 93	**MISSING YOU** (re-issue) *Chrysalis CDCHS 3938*	56	2

The WAITRESSES *US, male / female vocal / instrumental group*

18 Dec 82	**CHRISTMAS WRAPPING** *Ze / Island WIP 6821*	45	4

Tom WAITS *US, male vocalist (11 Albums: 31 Weeks)*

8 Oct 83	SWORDFISHTROMBONES *Island ILPS 9762*	62	3
19 Oct 85	RAIN DOGS *Island ILPS 9803*	29	5
5 Sep 87	FRANKS WILD YEARS *Island ITW 3*	20	5
8 Oct 88	BIG TIME *Island ITW 4*	84	1
19 Sep 92	BONE MACHINE *Island CID 9993*	26	3
20 Nov 93	THE BLACK RIDER *Island CID 8021*	47	2
27 Jun 98	BEAUTIFUL MALADIES – THE ISLAND YEARS *Island 5245192*	63	1
1 May 99 ●	MULE VARIATIONS *Epitaph 65472*	9	5
18 May 02	ALICE *Anti 66322*	20	2
18 May 02	BLOOD MONEY *Anti 66292*	21	2
16 Oct 04	REAL GONE *Anti 66782*	16	2

Johnny WAKELIN *UK, male vocalist (2 Singles: 20 Weeks)*

18 Jan 75 ●	**BLACK SUPERMAN (MUHAMMAD ALI)** *Pye 7N 45420* [1]	7	10
24 Jul 76 ●	**IN ZAIRE** *Pye 7N 45595*	4	10

[1] Johnny Wakelin and The Kinshasa Band

Rick WAKEMAN (see also ANDERSON BRUFORD WAKEMAN HOWE; The STRAWBS; YES) *UK, male keyboard player (11 Albums: 131 Weeks)*

24 Feb 73 ●	THE SIX WIVES OF HENRY VIII *A&M AMLH 64361*	7	22
18 May 74 ★	JOURNEY TO THE CENTRE OF THE EARTH *A&M AMLH 63621*	1	30
12 Apr 75 ●	THE MYTHS AND LEGENDS OF KING ARTHUR & THE KNIGHTS OF THE ROUND TABLE *A&M AMLH 645150022*	2	28
24 Apr 76 ●	NO EARTHLY CONNECTION *A&M AMLK 64583*	9	9
12 Feb 77	WHITE ROCK *A&M AMLH 64614*	14	9
3 Dec 77	RICK WAKEMAN'S CRIMINAL RECORD *A&M AMLK 64660*	25	5
2 Jun 79	RHAPSODIES *A&M AMLX 68508*	25	10
27 Jun 81	1984 *Charisma CDS 4022*	24	9
13 Oct 84	BEYOND THE PLANETS *Telstar STAR 2244* [1]	64	6
16 May 87	THE GOSPELS *Stylus SMR 729*	94	1
27 Mar 99	RETURN TO THE CENTRE OF THE EARTH *EMI Classics CDC 5567632*	34	2

[1] Kevin Peek and Rick Wakeman

Narada Michael WALDEN *US, male vocalist / producer (1 Albums: 5 Weeks, 3 Singles: 28 Weeks)*

23 Feb 80	**TONIGHT I'M ALRIGHT** *Atlantic K 11437*	34	9
26 Apr 80 ●	**I SHOULDA LOVED YA** *Atlantic K 11413*	8	9
23 Apr 88 ●	**DIVINE EMOTIONS** *Reprise W 7967* [1]	8	10
14 May 88	DIVINE EMOTION *Reprise WX 172* [1]	60	5

[1] Narada [1] Narada

The WALKER BROTHERS 346 Top 500

Unrelated US trio who were top UK teen idols in the mid-60s: Scott Walker (Engel) (v/b/k), John Walker (Maus) (v/g) and Gary Walker (Leeds) (d) all had solo hits after the trio split in 1967, with Scott (who first recorded solo in 1957) creating a large cult following (6 Albums: 109 Weeks, 10 Singles: 93 Weeks)

29 Apr 65	**LOVE HER** *Philips BF 1409*	20	13
19 Aug 65 ★	**MAKE IT EASY ON YOURSELF** *Philips BF 1428*	1	14
2 Dec 65 ●	**MY SHIP IS COMING IN** *Philips BF 1454*	3	12

13 January 1996	20 January 1996	27 January 1996	3 February 1996
EARTH SONG Michael Jackson	JESUS TO A CHILD George Michael	SPACEMAN Babylon Zoo	SPACEMAN Babylon Zoo
(WHAT'S THE STORY) MORNING GLORY? Oasis	(WHAT'S THE STORY) MORNING GLORY? Oasis	(WHAT'S THE STORY) MORNING GLORY? Oasis	(WHAT'S THE STORY) MORNING GLORY? Oasis

KEY

UK No.1 ★★ UK Top 10 ●● Still on chart ++ UK entry at No.1 ■■ US No.1 ▲▲ UK million seller £ US million seller $

Singles re-entries are listed as (re), (2re), (3re)… which signifies that the hit re-entered the chart once, twice or three times…

Peak Position / Weeks

Date		Title	Peak	Weeks
18 Dec 65	●	TAKE IT EASY WITH THE WALKER BROTHERS *Philips BL 7691*	3	36
3 Mar 66	★	THE SUN AIN'T GONNA SHINE ANYMORE *Philips BF 1473*	1	11
14 Jul 66		(BABY) YOU DON'T HAVE TO TELL ME *Philips BF 1497*	13	8
3 Sep 66	●	PORTRAIT *Philips BL 7691*	3	23
22 Sep 66		ANOTHER TEAR FALLS *Philips BF 1514*	12	8
15 Dec 66		DEADLIER THAN THE MALE *Philips BF 1537*	32	6
9 Feb 67		STAY WITH ME BABY *Philips BF 1548*	26	6
18 Mar 67	●	IMAGES *Philips SBL 7770*	6	15
18 May 67		WALKING IN THE RAIN *Philips BF 1576*	26	6
16 Sep 67	●	THE WALKER BROTHERS' STORY *Philips DBL 002*	9	19
17 Jan 76	●	NO REGRETS *GTO GT 42*	7	9
21 Feb 76		NO REGRETS *GTO GTLP 007*	49	3
25 Jan 92	●	NO REGRETS – THE BEST OF SCOTT WALKER AND THE WALKER BROTHERS 1965-1976 *Fontana 5108312* [1]	4	13

[1] Scott Walker and The Walker Brothers

Gary WALKER (see also The WALKER BROTHERS)
US, male vocalist / drums – Gary Leeds (2 Singles: 12 Weeks)

Date		Title	Peak	Weeks
24 Feb 66		YOU DON'T LOVE ME *CBS 202036*	26	6
26 May 66		TWINKIE-LEE *CBS 202081*	26	6

John WALKER (see also The WALKER BROTHERS)
US, male vocalist / guitarist – John Maus

Date		Title	Peak	Weeks
5 Jul 67		ANNABELLA (re) *Philips BF 1593*	24	6

Scott WALKER (see also The WALKER BROTHERS) *US, male vocalist – Scott Engel (7 Albums: 58 Weeks, 3 Singles: 30 Weeks)*

Date		Title	Peak	Weeks
16 Sep 67	●	SCOTT *Philips SBL 7816*	3	17
6 Dec 67		JACKIE *Philips BF 1628*	22	9
20 Apr 68	★	SCOTT 2 *Philips SBL 7840*	1	18
1 May 68	●	JOANNA *Philips BF 1662*	7	11
5 Apr 69	●	SCOTT 3 *Philips S 7882*	3	4
11 Jun 69		LIGHTS OF CINCINNATI *Philips BF 1793*	13	10
5 Jul 69	●	SONGS FROM HIS TV SERIES *Philips SBL 7900*	7	3
31 Mar 84		CLIMATE OF HUNTER *Virgin V 2303*	60	2
25 Jan 92	●	NO REGRETS – THE BEST OF SCOTT WALKER AND THE WALKER BROTHERS 1965-1976 *Fontana 5108312* [1]	4	13
20 May 95		TILT *Fontana 5268592*	27	1

[1] Scott Walker and The Walker Brothers

Terri WALKER *UK, female vocalist (3 Singles: 4 Weeks)*

Date		Title	Peak	Weeks
1 Mar 03		GUESS YOU DIDN'T LOVE ME *Def Soul 779962*	60	1
17 May 03		CHING CHING (LOVIN' YOU STILL) *Def Soul 9800075*	38	2
26 Mar 05		WHOOPSIE DAISY *Mercury 9870690*	41	1

Jr WALKER & The ALL-STARS *US, male instrumental / vocal group – leader b. 14 Jun 1931, d. 23 Nov 1995 (6 Singles: 59 Weeks)*

Date		Title	Peak	Weeks
18 Aug 66		HOW SWEET IT IS (TO BE LOVED BY YOU) *Tamla Motown TMG 571*	22	10
2 Apr 69		ROAD RUNNER *Tamla Motown TMG 691*	12	12
18 Oct 69		WHAT DOES IT TAKE (TO WIN YOUR LOVE) *Tamla Motown TMG 712*	13	12
26 Aug 72		WALK IN THE NIGHT *Tamla Motown TMG 824*	16	11
27 Jan 73		TAKE ME GIRL, I'M READY *Tamla Motown TMG 840*	16	9
30 Jun 73		WAY BACK HOME *Tamla Motown TMG 857*	35	5

The WALKMEN
US, male vocal / instrumental group (1 Album: 1 Week, 2 Singles: 2 Weeks)

Date		Title	Peak	Weeks
1 May 04		THE RAT *WEA W 640CD*	45	1
8 May 04		BOWS + ARROWS *WEA 9362486802*	62	1
10 Jul 04		LITTLE HOUSE OF SAVAGES *Record Collection W 646CD 2*	72	1

WALL OF SOUND featuring Gerald LETHAN
US, male vocal / instrumental group

Date		Title	Peak	Weeks
31 Jul 93		CRITICAL (IF YOU ONLY KNEW) *Positiva CDTIV 4*	73	1

WALL OF VOODOO *US, male vocal / instrumental group*

Date		Title	Peak	Weeks
19 Mar 83		MEXICAN RADIO *Illegal ILS 36*	64	3

Jerry WALLACE *US, male vocalist*

Date		Title	Peak	Weeks
23 Jun 60		YOU'RE SINGING OUR LOVE SONG TO SOMEBODY ELSE *London HLH 9110*	46	1

Rik WALLER *UK, male vocalist (2 Singles: 12 Weeks)*

Date		Title	Peak	Weeks
16 Mar 02	●	I WILL ALWAYS LOVE YOU (re) *EMI / Liberty CDRIK 001*	6	8
6 Jul 02		(SOMETHING INSIDE) SO STRONG *EMI / Liberty CDRIK 002*	25	4

The WALLFLOWERS *US, male vocal / instrumental group*

Date		Title	Peak	Weeks
21 Jun 97		BRINGING DOWN THE HORSE *Interscope IND 90055*	58	2
12 Jul 97		ONE HEADLIGHT *Interscope IND 95532*	54	1

Bob WALLIS and his STORYVILLE JAZZ BAND
UK, male vocalist / trumpet, b. 3 Jun 1934, d. 10 Jan 1991, and jazz band (1 Album: 1 Week, 2 Singles: 7 Weeks)

Date		Title	Peak	Weeks
11 Jun 60		EVERYBODY LOVES SATURDAY NIGHT *Top Rank BUY 023*	20	1
6 Jul 61		I'M SHY MARY ELLEN, I'M SHY *Pye Jazz 7NJ 2043*	44	2
4 Jan 62		COME ALONG PLEASE *Pye Jazz 7NJ 2048*	33	5

Joe WALSH (see also EAGLES)
US, male vocalist / guitarist (2 Albums: 20 Weeks, 2 Singles: 15 Weeks)

Date		Title	Peak	Weeks
17 Apr 76		YOU CAN'T ARGUE WITH A SICK MIND *Anchor ABCL 5156*	28	3
16 Jul 77		ROCKY MOUNTAIN WAY (EP) *ABC ABE 12002*	39	4
10 Jun 78		BUT SERIOUSLY FOLKS *Asylum K 53081*	16	17
8 Jul 78		LIFE'S BEEN GOOD *Asylum K 13129*	14	11

Tracks on Rocky Mountain Way (EP): Rocky Mountain Way / Turn to Stone / Meadows / Walk Away.

Sheila WALSH and Cliff RICHARD *UK, female / male vocal duo*

Date		Title	Peak	Weeks
4 Jun 83		DRIFTING *DJM SHEIL 1*	64	2

Steve WALSH
UK, male DJ / vocalist, b. 1959, d. 3 July 1988 (3 Singles: 18 Weeks)

Date		Title	Peak	Weeks
18 Jul 87	●	I FOUND LOVIN' (re) *A1 A1 299*	9	13
12 Dec 87		LET'S GET TOGETHER TONITE *A1 A1 303*	74	1
30 Jul 88		AIN'T NO STOPPING US NOW (PARTY FOR THE WORLD) *A1 A1 304*	44	4

Trevor WALTERS *UK, male vocalist (3 Singles: 22 Weeks)*

Date		Title	Peak	Weeks
24 Oct 81		LOVE ME TONIGHT *Magnet MAG 198*	27	8
21 Jul 84	●	STUCK ON YOU *Sanity IS 002*	9	12
1 Dec 84		NEVER LET HER SLIP AWAY *Polydor POSP 716*	73	2

WAMDUE PROJECT
US, male producer – Chris Brann (3 Singles: 19 Weeks)

Date		Title	Peak	Weeks
20 Nov 99		KING OF MY CASTLE (import) *Orange ORCDM 53584CD*	61	1
27 Nov 99	★	KING OF MY CASTLE (re) *AM:PM CDAMPM 127* ■	1	16
15 Apr 00		YOU'RE THE REASON *AM:PM CDAMPM 130*	39	2

WANG CHUNG *UK, male vocal / instrumental group*

Date		Title	Peak	Weeks
28 Jan 84		DANCE HALL DAYS *Geffen A 3837*	21	12
21 Apr 84		POINTS ON THE CURVE *Geffen GEF 25589*	34	5

	10 February 1996	17 February 1996	24 February 1996	2 March 1996
UK No.1 SINGLES	SPACEMAN Babylon Zoo	SPACEMAN Babylon Zoo	SPACEMAN Babylon Zoo	DON'T LOOK BACK IN ANGER Oasis
UK No.1 ALBUMS	(WHAT'S THE STORY) MORNING GLORY? Oasis	(WHAT'S THE STORY) MORNING GLORY? Oasis	EXPECTING TO FLY The Bluetones	(WHAT'S THE STORY) MORNING GLORY? Oasis

The WANNADIES *Sweden, male / female vocal / instrumental group (2 Albums: 4 Weeks, 7 Singles: 12 Weeks)*

18 Nov 95 **MIGHT BE STARS** *Indolent DIE 003CD1* 51 2
24 Feb 96 **HOW DOES IT FEEL** *Indolent DIE 004CD1* 53 1
20 Apr 96 **YOU AND ME SONG** *Indolent DIE 005CD* 18 3
7 Sep 96 **SOMEONE SOMEWHERE** *Indolent DIE 006CD* 38 1
26 Apr 97 **HIT** *Indolent DIE 009CD1* 20 2
17 May 97 BAGSY ME *Indolent DIECD 008* 37 3
5 Jul 97 **SHORTY** *Indolent DIE 010CD1* 41 2
4 Mar 00 **YEAH** *RCA 74321745552* 56 1
18 Mar 00 YEAH *RCA 74321687022* 73 1

Dexter WANSELL *US, male keyboard player*

20 May 78 **ALL NIGHT LONG** *Philadelphia International PIR 6255* 59 3

WAR *US / Canada / Denmark, male vocal / instrumental group (2 Albums: 4 Weeks, 6 Singles: 32 Weeks)*

3 Oct 70 ERIC BURDON DECLARES WAR *Polydor 2310041* [1] 50 2
20 Feb 71 BLACKMAN'S BURDON *Liberty LDS 8400* [1] 25 2
24 Jan 76 **LOW RIDER** *Island WIP 6267* 12 7
26 Jun 76 **ME AND BABY BROTHER** *Island WIP 6303* 21 7
14 Jan 78 **GALAXY** *MCA 339* 14 7
15 Apr 78 **HEY SEÑORITA** *MCA 359* 40 2
10 Apr 82 **YOU GOT THE POWER** *RCA 201* 58 4
6 Apr 85 **GROOVIN'** *Bluebird BR 16* 43 5

[1] Eric Burdon and War

Stephen WARBECK *UK, male composer*

19 May 01 CAPTAIN CORELLI'S MANDOLIN (FILM SOUNDTRACK) *Decca 4676782* 30 5

Anita WARD *US, female vocalist*

2 Jun 79 ★ **RING MY BELL** *TK TKR 7543* ▲ $ 1 11

Chrissy WARD *US, female vocalist (2 Singles: 2 Weeks)*

24 Jun 95 **RIGHT AND EXACT** *Ore AG 6CD* 62 1
8 Feb 97 **RIGHT AND EXACT** (re-mix) *Ore AG 21CD* 59 1

Clifford T WARD *UK, male vocalist / keyboard player, b. 10 Feb 1944, d. 18 Dec 2001 (2 Albums: 5 Weeks, 2 Singles: 16 Weeks)*

30 Jun 73 ● **GAYE** *Charisma CB 205* 8 11
21 Jul 73 HOME THOUGHTS *Charisma CAS 1066* 40 3
26 Jan 74 **SCULLERY** *Charisma CB 221* 37 5
16 Feb 74 MANTLE PIECES *Charisma CAS 1077* 42 2

Michael WARD *UK, male vocalist*

29 Sep 73 **LET THERE BE PEACE ON EARTH (LET IT BEGIN WITH ME)** (re) *Philips 6006 340* 15 13
5 Jan 74 INTRODUCING MICHAEL WARD *Philips 6308 189* 26 3

Shayne WARD NEW *UK, male vocalist*

31 Dec 05 ★ **THAT'S MY GOAL** *Syco Music 82876779272* ■ 1 1+

Billy WARD and his DOMINOES *US, male vocal group – leader b. 19 Sep 1921, d. 15 Feb 2002 (2 Singles: 13 Weeks)*

13 Sep 57 **STARDUST** (re) *London HLU 8465* 13 12
29 Nov 57 **DEEP PURPLE** *London HLU 8502* 30 1

WARD BROTHERS *UK, male vocal / instrumental group*

10 Jan 87 **CROSS THAT BRIDGE** *Siren SIREN 37* 32 8

Mathias WARE featuring Rob TAYLOR *Germany, male producer and vocalist*

9 Mar 02 **HEY LITTLE GIRL** *Manifesto FESCD 91* 42 1

WARLOCK *Germany, male / female vocal / instrumental group*

14 Nov 87 TRIUMPH AND AGONY *Vertigo VERH 50* 54 2

WARM JETS *UK / Canada, male vocal / instrumental group (1 Album: 1 Week, 2 Singles: 4 Weeks)*

14 Feb 98 **NEVER NEVER** *Island WAY 6766* 37 2
7 Mar 98 FUTURE SIGNS *Island 5243542* 40 1
25 Apr 98 **HURRICANE** *Island CID 697* 34 2

WARM SOUNDS *UK, male vocal duo – Barry Husband and Denver Gerrard*

4 May 67 **BIRDS AND BEES** *Deram DM 120* 27 6

Toni WARNE *UK, female vocalist*

25 Apr 87 **BEN** *Mint CHEW 110* 50 4

Jennifer WARNES *US, female vocalist (1 Album: 12 Weeks, 3 Singles: 37 Weeks)*

15 Jan 83 ● **UP WHERE WE BELONG** *Island WIP 6830* [1] ▲ $ 7 13
18 Jul 87 FAMOUS BLUE RAINCOAT *RCA PL 90048* 33 12
25 Jul 87 **FIRST WE TAKE MANHATTAN** *Cypress PB 49709* 74 1
31 Oct 87 ● **(I'VE HAD) THE TIME OF MY LIFE** (re) *RCA PB 49625* [2] ▲ $ 6 23

[1] Joe Cocker and Jennifer Warnes [2] Bill Medley and Jennifer Warnes

'(I've Had) the Time of My Life' re-entered the chart in Dec 1990, peaking at No.8.

WARP BROTHERS *Germany, male DJ / production duo – Oliver Goedicke and Jürgen Dohrgroup (4 Singles: 18 Weeks)*

11 Nov 00 **PHATT BASS** (import) *Dos or Die BMSCDM 40009* 58 3
9 Dec 00 ● **PHATT BASS** *Nulife / Arista 74321817102* [1] 9 8
17 Feb 01 **WE WILL SURVIVE** *Nulife / Arista 74321832722* 19 4
29 Dec 01 **BLAST THE SPEAKERS** *Nulife 74321899162* 40 3

[1] Warp Brothers vs Aquagen

WARRANT *US, male vocal / instrumental group (1 Album: 1 Week, 2 Singles: 7 Weeks)*

17 Nov 90 **CHERRY PIE** *CBS 6562587* 59 2
9 Mar 91 **CHERRY PIE** (re-issue) *Columbia 6566867* 35 5
19 Sep 92 DOG EAT DOG *Columbia 4720332* 74 1

Alysha WARREN *UK, female vocalist (3 Singles: 4 Weeks)*

24 Sep 94 **I'M SO IN LOVE** *Wild Card CARDD 10* 61 1
25 Mar 95 **I THOUGHT I MEANT THE WORLD TO YOU** *Wild Card CARDD 16* 40 1
27 Jul 96 **KEEP ON PUSHING OUR LOVE** *Arista 74321390422* [1] 30 2

[1] Nightcrawlers featuring John Reid and Alysha Warren

Nikita WARREN *Italy, female vocalist*

13 Jul 96 **I NEED YOU** *VC VCRD 12* 48 1

WARRIOR *UK, male producer – Michael Woods and female vocalist – Stacey Charles (3 Singles: 7 Weeks)*

21 Oct 00 **WARRIOR** *Incentive CENT 12CDS* 19 4
30 Jun 01 **VOODOO** *Incentive CENT 26CDS* 37 2
4 Oct 03 **X** *Incentive CENT 56CDS* 64 1

Dionne WARWICK (248 Top 500)

Super-stylish soul diva, b. 12 Dec 1940, New Jersey, US, whose classy and unmistakable vocals on songs written by Burt Bacharach and Hal David produced more than 30 US hits for her between 1962 and 1972. She is a cousin of Whitney Houston (14 Albums: 154 Weeks, 14 Singles: 101 Weeks)

13 Feb 64 **ANYONE WHO HAD A HEART** *Pye International 7N 25234* 42 3
16 Apr 64 ● **WALK ON BY** *Pye International 7N 25241* 9 14
23 May 64 PRESENTING DIONNE WARWICK *Pye NPL 28037* 14 10

9 March 1996	16 March 1996	23 March 1996	30 March 1996
HOW DEEP IS YOUR LOVE Take That	HOW DEEP IS YOUR LOVE Take That	HOW DEEP IS YOUR LOVE Take That	FIRESTARTER The Prodigy
(WHAT'S THE STORY) MORNING GLORY? Oasis	(WHAT'S THE STORY) MORNING GLORY? Oasis	FALLING INTO YOU Celine Dion	ANTHOLOGY 2 The Beatles

KEY
UK No.1 ★★ UK Top 10 ●● Still on chart + + UK entry at No.1 ■■
US No.1 ▲▲ UK million seller £ US million seller $
Singles re-entries are listed as (re), (2re), (3re)... which signifies that the hit re-entered the chart once, twice or three times...

Peak Position / Weeks

30 Jul 64 **YOU'LL NEVER GET TO HEAVEN (IF YOU BREAK MY HEART)** *Pye International 7N 25256*....20 8
8 Oct 64 **REACH OUT FOR ME** *Pye International 7N 25265*....23 7
1 Apr 65 **YOU CAN HAVE HIM** *Pye International 7N 25290*....37 5
7 May 66 ● BEST OF DIONNE WARWICK *Pye NPL 28078*....8 11
4 Feb 67 HERE WHERE THERE IS LOVE *Pye NPL 28096*....39 2
13 Mar 68 **(THEME FROM) VALLEY OF THE DOLLS** *Pye International 7N 25445*....28 8
15 May 68 ● **DO YOU KNOW THE WAY TO SAN JOSE** *Pye International 7N 25457*....8 10
18 May 68 ● VALLEY OF THE DOLLS *Pye NSPL 28114*....10 13
23 May 70 GOLDEN HITS VOLUME 1 *Wand WNS 1*....31 26
6 Jun 70 GOLDEN HITS VOLUME 2 *Wand WNS 2*....28 14
19 Oct 74 **THEN CAME YOU** *Atlantic K 10495* [1] ▲ $....29 6
23 Oct 82 ● **HEARTBREAKER** *Arista ARIST 496*....2 13
30 Oct 82 ● HEARTBREAKER *Arista 204 974*....3 33
11 Dec 82 ● **ALL THE LOVE IN THE WORLD** *Arista ARIST 507*....10 10
26 Feb 83 **YOURS** *Arista ARIST 518*....66 2
21 May 83 THE COLLECTION – HER ALL-TIME GREATEST HITS *Arista DIONE 1*....11 17
28 May 83 **I'LL NEVER LOVE THIS WAY AGAIN** *Arista ARIST 530* $....62 3
29 Oct 83 SO AMAZING *Arista 205 755*....60 3
23 Feb 85 WITHOUT YOUR LOVE *Arista 206 571*....86 2
9 Nov 85 **THAT'S WHAT FRIENDS ARE FOR** *Arista ARIST 638* [2] ▲ $16 9
15 Aug 87 **LOVE POWER** *Arista RIS 27* [3]....63 3
6 Jan 90 ● LOVE SONGS *Arista 410441*....6 13
10 Dec 94 CHRISTMAS IN VIENNA II *Sony Classical SK 64304* [1]....60 2
14 Dec 96 THE ESSENTIAL COLLECTION *Global Television RADCD 48*....58 4
3 Aug 02 HEARTBREAKER – THE VERY BEST OF DIONNE WARWICK *BMG TV / WSM WSMCD 101*....32 4

[1] Dionne Warwicke and The Detroit Spinners [2] Dionne Warwick and Friends featuring Elton John, Stevie Wonder and Gladys Knight [3] Dionne Warwick and Jeffrey Osborne [1] Dionne Warwick and Placido Domingo

WAS (NOT WAS) *US, male vocal / instrumental duo – Don Fagenson and David Weiss (3 Albums: 15 Weeks, 10 Singles: 58 Weeks)*

3 Mar 84 **OUT COME THE FREAKS** *Ze / Geffen A 4178*....41 5
18 Jul 87 **SPY IN THE HOUSE OF LOVE** (re) *Fontana WAS 2*....21 15
3 Oct 87 ● **WALK THE DINOSAUR** *Fontana WAS 3*....10 10
9 Apr 88 WHAT UP DOG? *Fontana SFLP 4*....47 6
7 May 88 **OUT COME THE FREAKS (AGAIN)** (re-recording) *Fontana WAS 4*....44 3
16 Jul 88 **ANYTHING CAN HAPPEN** *Fontana WAS 5*....67 3
26 May 90 **PAPA WAS A ROLLING STONE** *Fontana WAS 7*....12 7
21 Jul 90 ARE YOU OKAY? *Fontana 8463511*....35 6
11 Aug 90 **HOW THE HEART BEHAVES** *Fontana WAS 8*....53 3
23 May 92 **LISTEN LIKE THIEVES** *Fontana WAS 10*....58 2
13 Jun 92 HELLO DAD ... I'M IN JAIL *Fontana 5124642*....61 3
11 Jul 92 ● **SHAKE YOUR HEAD** *Fontana WAS 11*....4 9
26 Sep 92 **SOMEWHERE IN AMERICA (THERE'S A STREET NAMED AFTER MY DAD)** *Fontana WAS 12*....57 1

'Spy in the House of Love' first peaked at No.51 and only made its peak position on re-entry in Feb 1988. 'Shake Your Head' features uncredited vocals by Ozzy Osbourne and Kim Basinger. The group dropped the brackets from their name during the chart run of 'Papa Was a Rolling Stone'.

Martha WASH (see also The WEATHER GIRLS) *US, female vocalist (12 Singles: 34 Weeks)*

28 Nov 92 **CARRY ON** *RCA 74321125457*....74 1
6 Mar 93 **GIVE IT TO YOU** *RCA 74321136562*....37 4
10 Jul 93 **RUNAROUND / CARRY ON** (re-mix) *RCA 74321153702*....49 2
18 Feb 95 **I FOUND LOVE** *Columbia 6612112* [1]....26 2
13 Jul 96 ● **KEEP ON JUMPIN'** *Manifesto FESCD 11* [2]....8 6
12 Jul 97 ● **SOMETHING GOIN' ON** *Manifesto FESCD 25* [2]....5 10
25 Oct 97 **CARRY ON** (re-mix) *Delirious DELICD 6*....49 1
28 Feb 98 **IT'S RAINING MEN ... THE SEQUEL** *Logic 74321555412* [3]....21 3
11 Apr 98 **READY FOR A NEW DAY** *Manifesto FESCD 40* [4]....20 2
15 Aug 98 **CATCH THE LIGHT** *Logic 74321587912*....45 1
3 Jul 99 **COME** *Logic 74321653942*....64 1
5 Feb 00 **IT'S RAINING MEN** (re-recording) *Logic 74321726282*....56 1

[1] C & C Music Factory featuring Martha Wash [2] Todd Terry featuring Martha Wash and Jocelyn Brown [3] Martha Wash featuring RuPaul [4] Todd Terry featuring Martha Wash

The listed flip side of 'I Found Love' was 'Take a Toke' by C & C Music Factory.

Dinah WASHINGTON *US, female vocalist – Ruth Jones, b. 29 Aug 1924, d. 14 Dec 1963 (2 Singles: 8 Weeks)*

30 Nov 61 **SEPTEMBER IN THE RAIN** (re) *Mercury AMT 1162*....35 4
4 Apr 92 **MAD ABOUT THE BOY** *Mercury DINAH 1*....41 4

Geno WASHINGTON & The RAM JAM BAND *US, male vocalist and UK, male instrumental backing group (2 Albums: 51 Weeks, 4 Singles: 20 Weeks)*

19 May 66 **WATER** *Piccadilly 7N 35312*....39 8
21 Jul 66 **HI HI HAZEL** (re) *Piccadilly 7N 35329*....45 4
6 Oct 66 **QUE SERA SERA** *Piccadilly 7N 35346*....43 3
10 Dec 66 ● HAND CLAPPIN' FOOT STOMPIN' FUNKY-BUTT ... LIVE! *Piccadilly NPL 38026* [1]....5 38
2 Feb 67 **MICHAEL (HE'S A LOVER)** *Piccadilly 7N 35359*....39 5
23 Sep 67 ● HIPSTERS FLIPSTERS AND FINGER-POPPIN' DADDIES *Piccadilly NSPL 38032* [1]....8 13

[1] Geno Washington

Grover WASHINGTON Jr *US, male saxophone player, b. 12 Dec 1943, d. 17 Dec 1999 (2 Albums: 10 Weeks, 1 Single: 7 Weeks)*

9 May 81 WINELIGHT *Elektra K 52262*....34 9
16 May 81 **JUST THE TWO OF US** *Elektra K 12514*....34 7
19 Dec 81 COME MORNING *Elektra K 52337*....98 1

Although uncredited, Bill Withers sings on 'Just the Two of Us'.

Sarah WASHINGTON *UK, female vocalist (4 Singles: 13 Weeks)*

14 Aug 93 **I WILL ALWAYS LOVE YOU** *Almighty CDALMY 33*....12 7
27 Nov 93 **CARELESS WHISPER** *Almighty CDALMY 43*....45 2
25 May 96 **HEAVEN** *AM:PM 5815352*....28 2
12 Oct 96 **EVERYTHING** *AM:PM 5818872*....30 2

W.A.S.P. *US, male vocal (Steve Duren aka Blackie Lawless) / instrumental group (8 Albums: 24 Weeks, 12 Singles: 38 Weeks)*

8 Sep 84 W.A.S.P. *Capitol EJ 2401951*....51 2
9 Nov 85 THE LAST COMMAND *Capitol WASP 2*....48 1
31 May 86 **WILD CHILD** *Capitol CL 388*....71 2
11 Oct 86 **95 – NASTY** *Capitol CL 432*....70 1
8 Nov 86 INSIDE THE ELECTRIC CIRCUS *Capitol EST 2025*....53 3
29 Aug 87 **SCREAM UNTIL YOU LIKE IT** *Capitol CL 458*....32 5
26 Sep 87 LIVE ... IN THE RAW *Capitol EST 2040*....23 4
31 Oct 87 **I DON'T NEED NO DOCTOR (LIVE)** *Capitol CL 469*....31 5
20 Feb 88 **ANIMAL (F**K LIKE A BEAST)** *Music for Nations KUT 109*....61 3
4 Mar 89 **MEAN MAN** *Capitol CL 521*....21 5
15 Apr 89 ● THE HEADLESS CHILDREN *Capitol EST 2087*....8 10
27 May 89 **THE REAL ME** *Capitol CL 534*....23 5
9 Sep 89 **FOREVER FREE** *Capitol CL 546*....25 5
4 Apr 92 **CHAINSAW CHARLIE (MURDERS IN THE NEW MORGUE)** *Parlophone RS 6308*....17 2
6 Jun 92 **THE IDOL** *Parlophone RPD 6314*....41 2
20 Jun 92 THE CRIMSON IDOL *Parlophone CDPCSD 118*....21 2
31 Oct 92 **I AM ONE** *Parlophone 10RG 6324*....56 1
23 Oct 93 **SUNSET AND BABYLON** *Capitol CDCL 698*....38 2
6 Nov 93 FIRST BLOOD ... LAST CUTS *Capitol CDESTFG 2217*....69 1
1 Jul 95 STILL NOT BLACK ENOUGH *Raw Power RAWCD 103*....52 1

	6 April 1996	13 April 1996	20 April 1996	27 April 1996
UK No.1 SINGLES	FIRESTARTER The Prodigy	FIRESTARTER The Prodigy	RETURN OF THE MACK Mark Morrison	RETURN OF THE MACK Mark Morrison
UK No.1 ALBUMS	GREATEST HITS Take That	GREATEST HITS Take That	GREATEST HITS Take That	GREATEST HITS Take That

The WATER BABIES NEW *UK, male / female vocal / instrumental group*

24 Dec 05 **UNDER THE TREE** *Angel ANGECD 8* ..... 30 2+

The WATERBOYS *UK / Ireland, male vocal (Mike Scott) / instrumental group (8 Albums: 72 Weeks, 7 Singles: 33 Weeks)*

16 Jun 84 A PAGAN PLACE *Ensign ENCL 3* 100 1
28 Sep 85 THIS IS THE SEA *Ensign ENCL 5* 37 18
2 Nov 85 **THE WHOLE OF THE MOON** *Ensign ENY 520* 26 7
29 Oct 88 FISHERMAN'S BLUES *Ensign CHEN 5* 13 19
14 Jan 89 **FISHERMAN'S BLUES** *Ensign ENY 621* 32 6
1 Jul 89 **AND A BANG ON THE EAR** *Ensign ENY 624* 51 4
22 Sep 90 ● ROOM TO ROAM *Ensign CHEN 16* 5 6
6 Apr 91 ● **THE WHOLE OF THE MOON** (re-issue) *Ensign ENY 642* 3 9
11 May 91 ● THE BEST OF THE WATERBOYS '81-'90 *Ensign CHEN 19* 2 16
8 Jun 91 **FISHERMAN'S BLUES** (re-issue) *Ensign ENY 645* 75 1
15 May 93 **THE RETURN OF PAN** *Geffen GFSTD 42* 24 3
5 Jun 93 ● DREAM HARDER *Geffen GED 24476* 5 10
24 Jul 93 **GLASTONBURY SONG** *Geffen GFSTD 49* 29 3
7 Oct 00 A ROCK IN THE WEARY LAND *RCA 74321783052* 47 1
21 Jun 03 UNIVERSAL HALL *Puck PUCK 1* 74 1

WATERFRONT *UK, male vocal / instrumental duo – Phil Cilia and Chris Duffy (1 Album: 3 Weeks, 3 Singles: 19 Weeks)*

15 Apr 89 **BROKEN ARROW** *Polydor WON 3* 63 2
27 May 89 **CRY** *Polydor WON 1* 17 13
12 Aug 89 WATERFRONT *Polydor 837970 1* 45 3
9 Sep 89 **NATURE OF LOVE** *Polydor WON 2* 63 4

WATERGATE

(see also DJ QUICKSILVER) *Turkey, male DJ / producer – Orhan Terzi*

13 May 00 ● **HEART OF ASIA** *Positiva CDTIV 129* 3 10

Dennis WATERMAN *UK, male actor / vocalist (2 Singles: 17 Weeks)*

25 Oct 80 ● **I COULD BE SO GOOD FOR YOU** *EMI 5009* [1] 3 12
17 Dec 83 **WHAT ARE WE GONNA GET 'ER INDOORS** *EMI MIN 101* [2] ..21 5

[1] Dennis Waterman with The Dennis Waterman Band [2] Dennis Waterman and George Cole

Crystal WATERS *US, female vocalist (10 Singles: 39 Weeks)*

18 May 91 ● **GYPSY WOMAN (LA DA DEE)** *A&M AM 772* 2 10
7 Sep 91 **MAKIN' HAPPY** *A&M AM 790* 18 6
11 Jan 92 **MEGAMIX** *A&M AM 843* 39 3
3 Oct 92 **GYPSY WOMAN** (re-mix) *Epic 6584377* 35 2
23 Apr 94 **100% PURE LOVE** *A&M 8586692* 15 7
2 Jul 94 **GHETTO DAY** *A&M 8589592* 40 2
25 Nov 95 **RELAX** *Manifesto FESCD 4* 37 2
24 Aug 96 **IN DE GHETTO** *Manifesto FESCD 12* [1] 35 2
19 Apr 97 **SAY ... IF YOU FEEL ALRIGHT** *Mercury 5742912* 45 1
20 Sep 03 **MY TIME** *Illustrious / Epic CDILL 018* [2] 22 4

[1] David Morales and The Bad Yard Club featuring Crystal Waters and Delta
[2] Dutch featuring Crystal Waters

The listed flip side of 'Gypsy Woman' (re-mix) was 'Peace' (re-mix) by Sabrina Johnston.

Muddy WATERS *US, male vocalist / guitarist, b. 4 Apr 1915, d. 30 Apr 1983*

16 Jul 88 **MANNISH BOY** *Epic MUD 1* 51 6

Roger WATERS (see also PINK FLOYD) *UK, male vocalist / bass guitarist (4 Albums: 25 Weeks, 3 Singles: 8 Weeks)*

12 May 84 THE PROS AND CONS OF HITCH HIKING *Harvest SHVL 240105* 13 11
30 May 87 **RADIO WAVES** *Harvest EM 6* 74 1
27 Jun 87 RADIO K.A.O.S. *EMI KAOS 1* 25 7
26 Dec 87 **THE TIDE IS TURNING (AFTER LIVE AID)** *Harvest EM 37* 54 4
22 Sep 90 THE WALL – LIVE IN BERLIN *Mercury 8466111* 27 3
5 Sep 92 **WHAT GOD WANTS PART 1** *Columbia 6581390* 35 3
19 Sep 92 ● AMUSED TO DEATH *Columbia 4687612* 8 4

Lauren WATERWORTH

UK, female vocalist

1 Jun 02 **BABY NOW THAT I'VE FOUND YOU** *Jive 9253622* 24 3

Michael WATFORD *US, male vocalist*

26 Feb 94 **SO INTO YOU** *East West A 8309CD* 53 2

Adam WATKISS *UK, male vocalist*

15 Dec 01 THIS IS THE MOMENT *UMTV / Decca 166082* 65 3

Jody WATLEY (see also SHALAMAR) *US, female vocalist (2 Albums: 4 Weeks, 8 Singles: 35 Weeks)*

9 May 87 **LOOKING FOR A NEW LOVE** *MCA MCA 1107* 13 11
5 Sep 87 JODY WATLEY *MCA MCG 6024* 62 2
17 Oct 87 **DON'T YOU WANT ME** *MCA MCA 1198* 55 3
8 Apr 89 **REAL LOVE** *MCA MCA 1324* 31 7
27 May 89 LARGER THAN LIFE *MCA MCG 6044* 39 2
12 Aug 89 **FRIENDS** *MCA MCA 1352* [1] 21 6
10 Feb 90 **EVERYTHING** *MCA MCA 1395* 74 2
11 Apr 92 **I'M THE ONE YOU NEED** *MCA MCS 1608* 50 3
21 May 94 **WHEN A MAN LOVES A WOMAN** *MCA MCSTD 1964* 33 2
25 Apr 98 **OFF THE HOOK** *Atlantic AT 0024CD 1* 51 1

[1] Jody Watley with Eric B and Rakim

Johnny 'Guitar' WATSON *US, male vocalist / guitarist, b. 3 Feb 1935, d. 17 May 1996 (2 Singles: 8 Weeks)*

28 Aug 76 **I NEED IT** *DJM DJS 10694* 35 5
23 Apr 77 **A REAL MOTHER FOR YA** *DJM DJS 10762* 44 3

Russell WATSON *UK, male vocalist (4 Albums: 74 Weeks, 4 Singles: 12 Weeks)*

30 Oct 99 **SWING LOW '99** *Decca / Universal TV 4669502* 38 2
22 Jul 00 **BARCELONA (FRIENDS UNTIL THE END)** *Decca 4672772* [1] .. 68 1
7 Oct 00 ● THE VOICE *Decca 4672512* 5 36
10 Nov 01 ● THE VOICE – ENCORE *Decca 4703002* 6 21
18 May 02 ● **SOMEONE LIKE YOU** *Decca 4730002* [2] 10 4
30 Nov 02 THE VOICE – REPRISE *Decca 4731002* 13 8
21 Dec 02 **NOTHING SACRED – A SONG FOR KIRSTY** *Decca 4737402* 17 5
6 Nov 04 ● AMORE MUSICA *Decca 4756294* 10 9

[1] Russell Watson and Shaun Ryder [2] Russell Watson and Faye Tozer

Ben WATT featuring ESTELLE NEW

(see also EVERYTHING BUT THE GIRL) *UK, male producer / multi-instrumentalist and female vocalist – Estelle Swaray*

12 Feb 05 **OUTSPOKEN – PART 1** *Buzzin' Fly 010 BUZZCD* 74 1

A-side features Estelle and B-side features Baby Blak.

Barratt WAUGH *UK, male vocalist*

26 Jul 03 **SKIP A BEAT** *White Elephant BNWCD 02* 56 1

WAVELENGTH *UK, male vocal group*

10 Jul 82 **HURRY HOME** *Ariola ARO 281* 17 12

WAX *US / UK, male vocal / instrumental duo – Andrew Gold and Graham Gouldman (1 Album: 3 Weeks, 2 Singles: 16 Weeks)*

12 Apr 86 **RIGHT BETWEEN THE EYES** *RCA PB 40509* 60 5
1 Aug 87 **BRIDGE TO YOUR HEART** *RCA PB 41405* 12 11
12 Sep 87 AMERICAN ENGLISH *RCA PL 71430* 59 3

4 May 1996	11 May 1996	18 May 1996	25 May 1996
FASTLOVE George Michael	**FASTLOVE** George Michael	**FASTLOVE** George Michael	**OOH AAH ... JUST A LITTLE BIT** Gina G
JAGGED LITTLE PILL Alanis Morissette	**JAGGED LITTLE PILL** Alanis Morissette	**1977** Ash	**OLDER** George Michael

KEY
UK No.1 ★ UK Top 10 ● Still on chart + UK entry at No.1 ■
US No.1 ▲ UK million seller £ US million seller $
Singles re-entries are listed as (re), (2re), (3re)... which signifies that the hit re-entered the chart once, twice or three times...
Peak Position / Weeks

Anthony WAY *UK, male vocalist (4 Albums: 19 Weeks, 1 Single: 2 Weeks)*

8 Apr 95 ● THE CHOIR – MUSIC FROM THE BBC TV SERIES *Decca 4481652* [1] ... 3 12
15 Apr 95 PANIS ANGELICUS *Decca 4481642* ... 55 2
9 Dec 95 THE CHOIRBOY *Permanent PERMCD 41* ... 61 3
14 Dec 96 THE CHOIRBOY'S CHRISTMAS *Decca 4550502* ... 59 3
15 Mar 97 WINGS OF A DOVE *Decca 4556452* ... 69 1

[1] Anthony Way and Stanislas Syrewicz

A WAY OF LIFE *US, male / female vocal / instrumental group*

21 Apr 90 TRIPPIN' ON YOUR LOVE *Eternal YZ 464* ... 55 3

WAY OF THE WEST *UK, male vocal / instrumental group*

25 Apr 81 DON'T SAY THAT'S JUST FOR WHITE BOYS *Mercury MER 66* ... 54 5

WAY OUT WEST *UK, male instrumental / production duo – Nick Warren and Jody Wisternoff (2 Albums: 2 Weeks, 9 Singles: 17 Weeks)*

3 Dec 94 AJARE *Deconstruction 74321243802* ... 52 1
2 Mar 96 DOMINATION *Deconstruction 74321342822* ... 38 2
14 Sep 96 THE GIFT *Deconstruction 74321401912* [1] ... 15 5
30 Aug 97 BLUE *Deconstruction 74321477512* ... 41 2
13 Sep 97 WAY OUT WEST *Deconstruction 74321501952* ... 42 1
29 Nov 97 AJARE (re-mix) *Deconstruction 74321521352* ... 36 2
9 Dec 00 THE FALL *Wow WOW 005CD* ... 61 1
18 Aug 01 INTENSIFY *Distinctive Breaks DISNCD 74* ... 46 1
1 Sep 01 INTENSIFY *Distinctive Breaks DISNCD 76* ... 61 1
30 Mar 02 MINDCIRCUS *Distinctive Breaks DISNCD 80* [2] ... 39 2
21 Sep 02 STEALTH *Distinctive Breaks DISNCD 90* [3] ... 67 1

[1] Way Out West featuring Miss Joanna Law [2] Way Out West featuring Tricia Lee Kelshall [3] Way Out West featuring Kirsty Hawkshaw

Bruce WAYNE *Germany, male DJ / producer (2 Singles: 2 Weeks)*

13 Dec 97 READY *Logic 74321527012* ... 44 1
4 Jul 98 NO GOOD FOR ME *Logic 74321587052* ... 70 1

Jan WAYNE
Germany, male producer – Jan Christiansen (2 Singles: 8 Weeks)

9 Nov 02 BECAUSE THE NIGHT *Product / Incentive PDT 02CDS* ... 14 5
29 Mar 03 TOTAL ECLIPSE OF THE HEART *Product / Incentive PDT 10CDS* ... 28 3

Jeff WAYNE'S 'WAR OF THE WORLDS' (197 Top 500) *Talented New York-born producer / songwriter / arranger and keyboard player who was educated at the prestigious Julliard School of Music. Before unveiling his epic all-star concept album, The War of the Worlds, which originally spent over four years on the chart and returned to No.5 in 2005, he produced a string of David Essex hits (6 Albums: 282 Weeks, 3 Singles: 21 Weeks)*

1 Jul 78 ● JEFF WAYNE'S MUSICAL VERSION OF THE WAR OF THE WORLDS *CBS 96000* ... 5 235
9 Sep 78 THE EVE OF THE WAR *CBS 6496* ... 36 8
10 Jul 82 MATADOR *CBS A 2493* [1] ... 57 3
25 Nov 89 ● EVE OF THE WAR (re-mix) *CBS 6551267* ... 3 10
3 Oct 92 JEFF WAYNE'S MUSICAL VERSION OF SPARTACUS *Columbia 4720302* ... 36 2
6 Jul 96 JEFF WAYNE'S MUSICAL VERSION OF THE WAR OF THE WORLDS (re-issue) *Columbia CDX 96000* ... 23 21
19 Oct 96 HIGHLIGHTS FROM JEFF WAYNE'S MUSICAL VERSION OF THE WAR OF THE WORLDS *Columbia CD 32356* ... 64 2
22 Apr 00 JEFF WAYNE'S MUSICAL VERSION OF THE WAR OF THE WORLDS – ULLADUBULLA – THE REMIX ALBUM *Columbia SONYTV 74CD* ... 64 1
25 Jun 05 ● JEFF WAYNE'S MUSICAL VERSION OF THE WAR OF THE WORLDS (2nd re-issue) *Columbia DPCD 96000* ... 5 21+

[1] Jeff Wayne

All albums feature various artists but are commonly credited to Jeff Wayne, the creator and producer. The 2005 re-issue of Jeff Wayne's Musical Version of the War of the Worlds is a re-mastered edition of the 1978 album.

WAYSTED *UK, male vocal / instrumental group (2 Albums: 5 Weeks)*

8 Oct 83 VICES *Chrysalis CHR 1438* ... 78 3
22 Sep 84 WAYSTED *Music for Nations MFN 31* ... 73 2

WE ARE SCIENTISTS NEW
US, male vocal / instrumental trio (1 Album: 2 Weeks, 2 Singles: 3 Weeks)

9 Jul 05 NOBODY MOVE NOBODY GET HURT *Virgin VUSCD 303* ... 56 1
15 Oct 05 THE GREAT ESCAPE *Virgin VUSDX 308* ... 37 2
29 Oct 05 WITH LOVE AND SQUALOR *Virgin CDVUS 270* ... 45 2

The WEATHER GIRLS *US, female vocal duo – Martha Wash and Izora Rhodes Armstead, b. 1942, d. 16 Sep 2004*

27 Aug 83 ● IT'S RAINING MEN (re) *CBS A 2924* ... 2 14

'It's Raining Men' first peaked at No.73 in 1983 and reached its peak position only on re-entry in Mar 1984.

The WEATHER PROPHETS *UK, male vocal / instrumental group*

28 Mar 87 SHE COMES FROM THE RAIN *Elevation ACID 1* ... 62 2
9 May 87 MAYFLOWER *Elevation ELV 1* ... 67 2

WEATHER REPORT *US, male instrumental group (4 Albums: 12 Weeks)*

23 Apr 77 HEAVY WEATHER *CBS 81775* ... 43 6
11 Nov 78 MR. GONE *CBS 82775* ... 47 3
27 Feb 82 WEATHER REPORT *CBS 85326* ... 88 2
24 Mar 84 DOMINO THEORY *CBS 25839* ... 54 1

Marti WEBB *UK, female vocalist (4 Albums: 33 Weeks, 6 Singles: 42 Weeks)*

9 Feb 80 ● TAKE THAT LOOK OFF YOUR FACE *Polydor POSP 100* ... 3 12
16 Feb 80 ● TELL ME ON A SUNDAY *Polydor POLD 5031* ... 2 23
19 Apr 80 TELL ME ON A SUNDAY *Polydor POSP 111* ... 67 2
20 Sep 80 YOUR EARS SHOULD BE BURNING NOW *Polydor POSP 166* ... 61 4
8 Jun 85 ● BEN *Starblend STAR 6* ... 5 11
28 Sep 85 ENCORE *Starblend BLEND 1* ... 55 4
20 Sep 86 ALWAYS THERE *BBC RESL 190* [1] ... 13 12
6 Dec 86 ALWAYS THERE *BBC REB 619* ... 65 5
6 Jun 87 I CAN'T LET GO *Rainbow RBR 12* ... 65 1
10 Oct 92 THE MAGIC OF THE MUSICALS *Quality Television QTV 013* [1] 55 1

[1] Marti Webb and the Simon May Orchestra [1] Marti Webb and Mark Rattray

WEBB BROTHERS *US, male vocal / instrumental duo*

17 Feb 01 I CAN'T BELIEVE YOU'RE GONE *WEA WEA 320CD* ... 69 1

Simon WEBBE NEW
(see also BLUE) *UK, male vocalist (1 Album: 6 Weeks, 2 Singles: 23 Weeks)*

3 Sep 05 ● LAY YOUR HANDS *Innocent SINCD 76* ... 4 16
19 Nov 05 ● NO WORRIES *Innocent SINDX 77* ... 4 7+
26 Nov 05 SANCTUARY *Innocent CDSIN 20* ... 18 6+

Joan WEBER *US, female vocalist, b. 12 Dec 1935, d. 13 May 1981*

18 Feb 55 LET ME GO LOVER *Philips PB 389* ▲ $ ... 16 1

Nikki WEBSTER *Australia, female vocalist*

8 Jun 02 STRAWBERRY KISSES *Gotham 74321943642* ... 64 1

	1 June 1996	8 June 1996	15 June 1996	22 June 1996
UK No.1 SINGLES	THREE LIONS Baddiel and Skinner and The Lightning Seeds	KILLING ME SOFTLY Fugees	KILLING ME SOFTLY Fugees	KILLING ME SOFTLY Fugees
UK No.1 ALBUMS	OLDER George Michael	OLDER George Michael	LOAD Metallica	18 TIL I DIE Bryan Adams

The WEDDING PRESENT *UK, male vocal (David Gedge) / instrumental group (11 Albums: 22 Weeks, 25 Singles: 42 Weeks)*

24 Oct 87 GEORGE BEST *Reception LEEDS 001* 47 2
5 Mar 88 NOBODY'S TWISTING YOUR ARM *Reception REC 009* 46 2
23 Jul 88 TOMMY *Reception LEEDS 2* 42 3
1 Oct 88 WHY ARE YOU BEING SO REASONABLE NOW? *Reception REC 011* 42 2
29 Apr 89 UKRAINSKI VISTUIP V JOHNA PEELA *RCA PL 74104* 22 3
7 Oct 89 KENNEDY *RCA PB 43117* 33 3
4 Nov 89 BIZARRO *RCA PL 74302* 22 3
17 Feb 90 BRASSNECK *RCA PB 43403* 24 3
29 Sep 90 3 SONGS (EP) *RCA PB 44021* 25 4
11 May 91 DALLIANCE *RCA PB 44495* 29 3
8 Jun 91 SEA MONSTERS *RCA PL 75012* 13 3
27 Jul 91 LOVENEST *RCA PT 44750* 58 1
18 Jan 92 BLUE EYES *RCA PB 45185* 26 2
15 Feb 92 GO-GO DANCER *RCA PB 45183* 20 1
14 Mar 92 THREE *RCA PB 45181* 14 2
18 Apr 92 SILVER SHORTS *RCA PB 45311* 14 1
16 May 92 ● COME PLAY WITH ME *RCA PB 45313* 10 2
13 Jun 92 CALIFORNIA *RCA PB 45315* 16 1
20 Jun 92 HIT PARADE 1 *RCA PD 75343* 22 2
18 Jul 92 FLYING SAUCER *RCA 74321101157* 22 1
15 Aug 92 BOING! *RCA 74321101177* 19 1
19 Sep 92 LOVE SLAVE *RCA 743211101167* 17 1
17 Oct 92 STICKY *RCA 74321116917* 17 1
14 Nov 92 THE QUEEN OF OUTER SPACE *RCA 74321116927* 23 1
19 Dec 92 NO CHRISTMAS *RCA 74321116937* 25 1
16 Jan 93 HIT PARADE 2 *RCA 74321127752* 19 2
10 Sep 94 YEAH YEAH YEAH YEAH YEAH *Island CID 585* 51 2
24 Sep 94 WATUSI *Island CID 8014* 47 1
26 Nov 94 IT'S A GAS *Island CID 591* 71 1
3 Feb 96 MINI *Cooking Vinyl COOKCD 094* 40 1
31 Aug 96 2, 3, GO *Cooking Vinyl FRYCD 048* 67 1
21 Sep 96 SATURNALIA *Cooking Vinyl COOKCD 099* 36 1
25 Jan 97 MONTREAL *Cooking Vinyl FRYCD 053* 40 1
27 Nov 04 INTERSTATE 5 *Scopitones TONECD 18* 62 1
12 Feb 05 I'M FROM FURTHER NORTH THAN YOU *Scopitones TONED 019* 34 3
26 Feb 05 TAKE FOUNTAIN *Scopitones TONECD 020* 68 1

Tracks on 3 Songs (EP): Corduroy / Crawl / Make Me Smile (Come Up and See Me).

Fred WEDLOCK *UK, male vocalist*

31 Jan 81 ● OLDEST SWINGER IN TOWN *Rocket XPRES 46* 6 10

WEE PAPA GIRL RAPPERS *UK, female rap / vocal duo – Samantha and Sandra Lawrence (1 Album: 3 Weeks, 5 Singles: 27 Weeks)*

12 Mar 88 FAITH *Jive JIVE 164* 60 4
25 Jun 88 HEAT IT UP *Jive JIVE 174* [1] 21 9
1 Oct 88 ● WEE RULE *Jive JIVE 185* 6 9
5 Nov 88 THE BEAT THE RHYME AND THE NOISE *Jive HIP 67* 39 3
24 Dec 88 SOULMATE *Jive JIVE 193* 45 4
25 Mar 89 BLOW THE HOUSE DOWN *Jive JIVE 197* 65 1

[1] Wee Papa Girl Rappers featuring Two Men and a Drum Machine

Bert WEEDON *UK, male guitarist (2 Albums: 26 Weeks, 8 Singles: 38 Weeks)*

15 May 59 ● GUITAR BOOGIE SHUFFLE *Top Rank JAR 117* 10 9
20 Nov 59 NASHVILLE BOOGIE *Top Rank JAR 221* 29 2
10 Mar 60 BIG BEAT BOOGIE (re) *Top Rank JAR 300* 37 4
9 Jun 60 TWELFTH STREET RAG *Top Rank JAR 360* 47 2
16 Jul 60 KING SIZE GUITAR *Top Rank BUY 026* 18 1
28 Jul 60 APACHE (re) *Top Rank JAR 415* 24 4
27 Oct 60 SORRY ROBBIE *Top Rank JAR 517* 28 11
2 Feb 61 GINCHY *Top Rank JAR 537* 35 5
4 May 61 MR GUITAR *Top Rank JAR 559* 47 1
23 Oct 76 ★ 22 GOLDEN GUITAR GREATS *Warwick WW 5019* 1 25

WEEKEND *International, male / female vocal / instrumental group*

14 Dec 85 CHRISTMAS MEDLEY / AULD LANG SYNE *Lifestyle XY 1* 47 5

WEEKEND PLAYERS (see also GROOVE ARMADA) *UK, male / female production / vocal duo – Rachel Foster and Andy Cato (2 Singles: 5 Weeks)*

8 Sep 01 21ST CENTURY *Multiply CDMULTY 78* 22 4
16 Mar 02 INTO THE SUN *Multiply CDMULTY 84* 42 1

Michelle WEEKS *US, female vocalist (4 Singles: 7 Weeks)*

2 Aug 97 MOMENT OF MY LIFE *Ministry of Sound MOSCDS 1* [1] 23 3
8 Nov 97 DON'T GIVE UP *Ministry of Sound MOSCDS 2* 28 2
11 Jul 98 GIVE ME LOVE *VC Recordings VCRD 37* [2] 59 1
3 May 03 THE LIGHT *Defected DFTD 064* 69 1

[1] Bobby D'Ambrosio featuring Michelle Weeks [2] DJ Dado vs Michelle Weeks

WEEZER *US, male vocal (Rivers Cuomo) / instrumental group (5 Albums: 22 Weeks, 9 Singles: 26 Weeks)*

11 Feb 95 UNDONE – THE SWEATER SONG *Geffen GFSTD 85* 35 2
4 Mar 95 WEEZER *Geffen GED 24629* 23 11
6 May 95 BUDDY HOLLY *Geffen GFSTD 88* 12 7
22 Jul 95 SAY IT AIN'T SO *Geffen GFSTD 95* 37 2
5 Oct 96 EL SCORCHO *Geffen GFSTD 22167* 50 1
12 Oct 96 PINKERTON *Geffen GED 25007* 43 1
26 May 01 THE GREEN ALBUM *Geffen 4930612* 31 4
14 Jul 01 HASH PIPE *Geffen 4975642* 21 3
3 Nov 01 ISLAND IN THE SUN *Geffen 4976102* 31 2
25 May 02 MALADROIT *Geffen 4933252* 16 3
14 Sep 02 KEEP FISHIN' *Geffen 4977912* 29 2
14 May 05 ● BEVERLEY HILLS *Geffen 9881791* 9 6
21 May 05 MAKE BELIEVE *Geffen 9881718* 11 3
27 Aug 05 WE ARE ALL ON DRUGS *Geffen 9883495* 47 1

Frank WEIR and his Orchestra (see also Vera LYNN) *UK, orchestra – leader d. 12 May 1981*

15 Sep 60 CARIBBEAN HONEYMOON *Oriole CB 1559* 42 4

WEIRD SCIENCE *UK, male DJ / production duo*

1 Jul 00 FEEL THE NEED *Nulife 74321751982* 62 1

Denise WELCH *UK, female actor / vocalist*

4 Nov 95 YOU DON'T HAVE TO SAY YOU LOVE ME / CRY ME A RIVER *Virgin VSCDT 1569* 23 3

Gillian WELCH *UK, female vocalist / guitarist*

14 Jun 03 SOUL JOURNEY *WEA 5046668682* 65 1

Paul WELLER 174 Top 500 (see also COUNCIL COLLECTIVE)

The angry young man reinvented as Britpop's elder statesman, b. John Weller, May 25 1958, Surrey, UK. Vocalist, guitarist and songwriter, 'The Modfather' achieved No.1 albums both solo and as leader of The Jam and The Style Council and has been a regular chart visitor for 28 years. Won the Best Male Solo BRIT in 1995 and 1996, and was awarded the Outstanding Contribution to British Music Award in 2006 (13 Albums: 235 Weeks, 28 Singles: 87 Weeks)

18 May 91 INTO TOMORROW *Freedom High FHP 1* [1] 36 3
15 Aug 92 UH HUH OH YEH *Go Discs GOD 86* 18 5
12 Sep 92 ● PAUL WELLER *Go Discs 8283432* 8 7
10 Oct 92 ABOVE THE CLOUDS *Go Discs GOD 91* 47 2
17 Jul 93 SUNFLOWER *Go Discs GODCD 102* 16 5
4 Sep 93 WILD WOOD *Go Discs GODCD 104* 14 3
18 Sep 93 ● WILD WOOD *Go Discs 8284352* 2 51
13 Nov 93 THE WEAVER (EP) *Go Discs GODCD 107* 18 3
9 Apr 94 HUNG UP *Go Discs GODCD 111* 11 3
24 Sep 94 LIVE WOOD *Go Discs 8285612* 13 5
5 Nov 94 OUT OF THE SINKING *Go Discs GODCD 121* 20 3
6 May 95 ● THE CHANGINGMAN *Go Discs GODCD 127* 7 4

29 June 1996	6 July 1996	13 July 1996	20 July 1996
KILLING ME SOFTLY Fugees	THREE LIONS Baddiel and Skinner and The Lightning Seeds	KILLING ME SOFTLY Fugees	FOREVER LOVE Gary Barlow
JAGGED LITTLE PILL Alanis Morissette	RECURRING DREAM - THE VERY BEST OF CROWDED HOUSE Crowded House	RECURRING DREAM - THE VERY BEST OF CROWDED HOUSE Crowded House	JAGGED LITTLE PILL Alanis Morissette

KEY
UK No.1 ★ UK Top 10 ● Still on chart + UK entry at No.1 ■
US No.1 ▲ UK million seller £ US million seller $
Singles re-entries are listed as (re), (2re), (3re)… which signifies that the hit re-entered the chart once, twice or three times…
Peak Position / Weeks

Date		Title / Label	Peak	Weeks
27 May 95	★	**STANLEY ROAD** *Go Discs / Island 8286192* ■	1	87
22 Jul 95	●	**YOU DO SOMETHING TO ME** *Go Discs GODCD 130*	9	6
30 Sep 95		**BROKEN STONES** *Go Discs GODCD 132*	20	4
9 Mar 96		**OUT OF THE SINKING** (re-recording) *Go Discs GODCD 143*	16	2
17 Aug 96	●	**PEACOCK SUIT** *Go Discs GODCD 149*	5	5
5 Jul 97	●	**HEAVY SOUL** *Go Discs / Island CID 8058*	2	13
9 Aug 97		**BRUSHED** *Island CID 666*	14	3
11 Oct 97		**FRIDAY STREET** *Island CID 676*	21	2
6 Dec 97		**MERMAIDS** *Island CID 683*	30	2
14 Nov 98		**BRAND NEW START** *Island CID 711*	16	3
21 Nov 98	●	**MODERN CLASSICS – THE GREATEST HITS** *Island CID 8080*	7	19
9 Jan 99		**WILD WOOD** (re-issue) *Island CID 734*	22	3
22 Apr 00	●	**HELIOCENTRIC** *Island CID 8093*	2	8
2 Sep 00		**SWEET PEA, MY SWEET PEA** *Island CID 764*	44	1
20 Oct 01	●	**DAYS OF SPEED** *Independiente ISOM 26CD*	3	16
14 Sep 02	●	**IT'S WRITTEN IN THE STARS** *Independiente ISOM 63SMS*	7	3
28 Sep 02	★	**ILLUMINATION** *Independiente ISOM 33CDL* ■	1	7
30 Nov 02		**LEAFY MYSTERIES** *Independiente ISOM 65MS*	23	2
6 Sep 03		**FLY ON THE WALL – B SIDES & RARITIES** *Island 0635272*	22	3
26 Jun 04		**THE BOTTLE** *V2 VVR 5026913*	13	3
11 Sep 04		**WISHING ON A STAR** *V2 VVR 5026923*	11	5
25 Sep 04	●	**STUDIO 150** *V2 VVR 1026908*	2	13
27 Nov 04		**THINKING OF YOU** *V2 VVR 5028463*	18	3
26 Mar 05		**EARLY MORNING RAIN** *V2 VVR 5030597*	40	1
11 Jun 05		**STANLEY ROAD** (re-issue) *Island 9828401*	51	1
30 Jul 05	●	**FROM THE FLOORBOARDS UP** *V2 VVR 5033413*	6	4
8 Oct 05		**COME ON/LET'S GO** *V2 VVR 5033223*	15	2
22 Oct 05	●	**AS IS NOW** *V2 VVR 1033202*	4	5
17 Dec 05		**HERE'S THE GOOD NEWS** *V2 VVR 5034603*	21	2

[1] Paul Weller Movement

Tracks on The Weaver (EP): The Weaver / This is No Time / Another New Day / Ohio (live). Both versions of 'Out of the Sinking' feature uncredited vocals by Carleen Anderson. Modern Classics – The Greatest Hits returned to the chart in Feb 2006. It peaked at No.32. The re-issued Stanley Road is a 'deluxe edition' CD / DVD set featuring demos and alternative versions of tracks from the original Stanley Road album

Brandi WELLS
US, female vocalist – Marguerite J Pinder, b. 13 May 1955, d. 25 Mar 2003

Date		Title / Label	Peak	Weeks
20 Feb 82		**WATCH OUT** *Virgin VS 479*	74	1

Houston WELLS and The MARKSMEN
UK, male vocalist – Andrew Smith and instrumental group

Date		Title / Label	Peak	Weeks
1 Aug 63		**ONLY THE HEARTACHES** *Parlophone R 5031*	22	10

Mary WELLS
US, female vocalist, b. 13 May 1943, d. 26 Jul 1992 (3 Singles: 25 Weeks)

Date		Title / Label	Peak	Weeks
21 May 64	●	**MY GUY** *Stateside SS 288* ▲ $	5	14
30 Jul 64		**ONCE UPON A TIME** *Stateside SS 316* [1]	50	1
8 Jul 72		**MY GUY** (re-issue) *Tamla Motown TMG 820*	14	10

[1] Marvin Gaye and Mary Wells

Terri WELLS *US, female vocalist (2 Singles: 9 Weeks)*

Date		Title / Label	Peak	Weeks
2 Jul 83		**YOU MAKE IT HEAVEN** *Phillyworld PWS 111*	53	2
5 May 84		**I'LL BE AROUND** *Phillyworld LON 48*	17	7

Alex WELSH BAND
UK, male trumpet player and band leader b. 9 Jul 1929, d. 25 Jun 1982

Date		Title / Label	Peak	Weeks
10 Aug 61		**TANSY** *Columbia DB 4686*	45	4

WENDY and LISA *US, female vocal duo – Wendy Melvoin and Lisa Coleman (3 Albums: 7 Weeks, 8 Singles: 31 Weeks)*

Date		Title / Label	Peak	Weeks
5 Sep 87		**WATERFALL** *Virgin VS 999*	66	4
10 Oct 87		**WENDY AND LISA** *Virgin V 2444*	84	2
16 Jan 88		**SIDESHOW** *Virgin VS 1012*	49	5
18 Feb 89		**ARE YOU MY BABY** *Virgin VS 1156*	70	3
28 Mar 89		**FRUIT AT THE BOTTOM** *Virgin V 2580*	45	2
29 Apr 89		**LOLLY LOLLY** *Virgin VS 1175*	64	3
8 Jul 89		**SATISFACTION** *Virgin VS 1194*	27	8
18 Nov 89		**WATERFALL** (re-mix) *Virgin VS 1223*	69	2
30 Jun 90		**STRUNG OUT** *Virgin VS 1272*	44	5
4 Aug 90		**EROICA** *Virgin V 2633*	33	3
10 Nov 90		**RAINBOW LAKE** *Virgin VS 1280*	70	1

WES *Cameroon, male vocalist – Wes Madiko Alane (2 Singles: 7 Weeks)*

Date		Title / Label	Peak	Weeks
14 Feb 98		**ALANE** *Epic 6654682*	11	6
27 Jun 98		**I LOVE FOOTBALL** *Epic 6660772*	75	1

Dodie WEST *UK, female vocalist*

Date		Title / Label	Peak	Weeks
14 Jan 65		**GOING OUT OF MY HEAD** *Decca F 12046*	39	4

Kanye WEST
US, male rapper / producer (2 Albums: 55 Weeks, 7 Singles: 62 Weeks)

Date		Title / Label	Peak	Weeks
28 Feb 04		**THE COLLEGE DROPOUT** *Roc-A-Fella / Def Jam 9861739*	12	38
3 Apr 04	●	**THROUGH THE WIRE** *Roc-A-Fella / Def Jam 9862270*	9	9
19 Jun 04	●	**ALL FALLS DOWN** *Roc-A-Fella 9862670* [1]	10	8
26 Jun 04	●	**TALK ABOUT OUR LOVE** *Atlantic AT 017CD* [2]	6	10
11 Sep 04		**JESUS WALKS** *Roc-A-Fella 9863962*	16	6
16 Jul 05	●	**DIAMONDS FROM SIERRA LEONE** *Roc-A-Fella 9883229*	8	12
10 Sep 05	●	**LATE REGISTRATION** *Roc-A-Fella 9885153* ▲	2	17+
1 Oct 05	●	**GOLD DIGGER** *Roc-A-Fella 9885694* [3] ▲	2	14+
17 Dec 05		**HEARD 'EM SAY** *Roc-A-Fella 9888416* [4]	22	3+

[1] Kanye West featuring Syleena Johnson [2] Brandy featuring Kanye West [3] Kanye West featuring Jamie Foxx [4] Kanye West featuring Adam Levine of Maroon 5

Keith WEST *UK, male vocalist – Keith Hopkins (2 Singles: 18 Weeks)*

Date		Title / Label	Peak	Weeks
9 Aug 67	●	**EXCERPT FROM A TEENAGE OPERA** *Parlophone R 5623*	2	15
22 Nov 67		**SAM** *Parlophone R 5651*	38	3

WEST END *UK, female vocal group*

Date		Title / Label	Peak	Weeks
19 Aug 95		**LOVE RULES** *RCA 74321292702*	44	2

WEST END featuring SYBIL *UK, male production duo and female vocalist*

Date		Title / Label	Peak	Weeks
16 Jan 93	●	**THE LOVE I LOST** *PWL Sanctuary PWCD 253*	3	13

WEST HAM UNITED CUP SQUAD *UK, male football team vocalists*

Date		Title / Label	Peak	Weeks
10 May 75		**I'M FOREVER BLOWING BUBBLES** *Pye 7N 45470*	31	2

WEST STREET MOB *US, male DJs / producers*

Date		Title / Label	Peak	Weeks
8 Oct 83		**BREAK DANCIN' – ELECTRIC BOOGIE** (re) *Sugarhill SH 128*	64	3

WESTBAM *Germany, male producer – Maximillian Lenz (6 Singles: 9 Weeks)*

Date		Title / Label	Peak	Weeks
9 Jul 94		**CELEBRATION GENERATION** *Low Spirit PQCD 5*	48	2
19 Nov 94		**BAM BAM BAM** *Low Spirit PZCD 329*	57	1
3 Jun 95		**WIZARDS OF THE SONIC** *Urban PZCD 344*	32	2
23 Mar 96		**ALWAYS MUSIC** *Low Spirit 5779152* [1]	51	1
13 Jun 98		**WIZARDS OF THE SONIC** (re-mix) *Wonderboy WBOYD 010* [2]	43	2
28 Nov 98		**ROOF IS ON FIRE** *Logic 74321633162*	58	1

[1] Westbam / Koon + Stephenson [2] Westbam vs Red Jerry

	27 July 1996	3 August 1996	10 August 1996	17 August 1996
UK No.1 SINGLES	**WANNABE** Spice Girls	**WANNABE** Spice Girls	**WANNABE** Spice Girls	**WANNABE** Spice Girls
UK No.1 ALBUMS	**JAGGED LITTLE PILL** Alanis Morissette	**JAGGED LITTLE PILL** Alanis Morissette	**JAGGED LITTLE PILL** Alanis Morissette	**JAGGED LITTLE PILL** Alanis Morissette

Hayley WESTENRA *New Zealand, female vocalist (2 Albums: 33 Weeks)*

27 Sep 03 ● PURE *Decca 4753302*....7 26
8 Oct 05 ● ODYSSEY *Decca 4757157*....10 7

Pure returned to the chart at Christmas 2004, with a bonus CD of new songs, with the catalogue number Decca 4756538. It peaked at No.60.

WESTLIFE (108 Top 500)

Record-shattering Irish boy band: Kian Egan, Mark Feehily, Nicky Byrne, Shane Filan and Bryan McFadden (left 2004). The only act to reach No.1 with their first seven releases or enter the chart at No.1 11 times out of their first 13 hits. They are also the first UK-based act to amass four No.1 singles in a year and they average over one million sales for each album release. They are four-time winners of the Record of the Year award (7 Albums: 207 Weeks, 19 Singles: 216 Weeks)

1 May 99 ★ SWEAR IT AGAIN (re) *RCA 74321662062* ■....1 13
21 Aug 99 ★ IF I LET YOU GO *RCA 74321692352* ■....1 11
30 Oct 99 ★ FLYING WITHOUT WINGS *RCA 74321709162* ■....1 13
13 Nov 99 ● WESTLIFE *RCA 74321713212*....2 69
25 Dec 99 ★ I HAVE A DREAM / SEASONS IN THE SUN *RCA 74321726012* ■..1 17
8 Apr 00 ★ FOOL AGAIN (re) *RCA 74321751562* ■....1 12
30 Sep 00 ★ AGAINST ALL ODDS (re) *Columbia 6698872* [1] ■....1 12
11 Nov 00 ★ MY LOVE *RCA 74321802792* ■....1 10
18 Nov 00 ★ COAST TO COAST *RCA 74321808312* ■....1 28
30 Dec 00 ● WHAT MAKES A MAN *RCA 74321826252*....2 13
17 Mar 01 ★ UPTOWN GIRL *RCA 74321841682* ■....1 16
17 Nov 01 ★ QUEEN OF MY HEART *RCA 74321899132* ■....1 15
24 Nov 01 ★ WORLD OF OUR OWN *RCA 74321903082* ■....1 35
2 Mar 02 ★ WORLD OF OUR OWN *S 74321918802* ■....1 13
1 Jun 02 ● BOP BOP BABY *S 74321940452*....5 10
16 Nov 02 ★ UNBREAKABLE (re) *S 74321975182* ■....1 16
23 Nov 02 ★ UNBREAKABLE – THE GREATEST HITS VOL.1 *S 74321975902* ■....1 34
5 Apr 03 ● TONIGHT / MISS YOU NIGHTS *S 74321986792*....3 10
27 Sep 03 ● HEY WHATEVER *S 82876560822*....4 7
29 Nov 03 ★ MANDY *S 82876570732* ■....1 9
6 Dec 03 ★ TURNAROUND *S 82876557412* ■....1 21
6 Mar 04 ● OBVIOUS *S 82876596322*....3 8
20 Nov 04 ● ... ALLOW US TO BE FRANK *S 82876651052*....3 12
5 Nov 05 ★ YOU RAISE ME UP *S 82876739522* ■....1 9+
12 Nov 05 ★ FACE TO FACE *S 82876745382* ■....1 8+
24 Dec 05 ● WHEN YOU TELL ME THAT YOU LOVE ME *S 82876767382* [2] .2 2+

[1] Mariah Carey featuring Westlife [2] Westlife with Diana Ross

WESTMINSTER ABBEY CHOIR

UK, male / female choir – choirmaster Dr Martin Neary (2 Albums: 7 Weeks)

20 Sep 97 JOHN TAVERNER: INNOCENCE *Sony Classical SK 66613*....34 4
12 Sep 98 PERFECT PEACE *Sony Classical SONYTV 49CD*....58 3

WESTWORLD *UK / US, male / female vocal / instrumental group (1 Album: 2 Weeks, 5 Singles: 23 Weeks)*

21 Feb 87 SONIC BOOM BOY *RCA BOOM 1*....11 7
2 May 87 BA-NA-NA-BAM-BOO *RCA BOOM 2*....37 5
25 Jul 87 WHERE THE ACTION IS *RCA BOOM 3*....54 4
5 Sep 87 WHERE THE ACTION IS *RCA PL 71429*....49 2
17 Oct 87 SILVERMAC *RCA BOOM 4*....42 5
15 Oct 88 EVERYTHING GOOD IS BAD *RCA PB 42243*....72 2

WET WET WET (81 Top 500)

Glasgow quartet fronted by vocalist Marti Pellow, b. Mark McLoughlin, 23 Mar 1966. They were voted Best British Newcomers at the 1988 BRIT awards and hold the record for most consecutive weeks at No.1 by a UK act – 15. Best-selling single: 'Love is All Around' 1,783,827 (9 Albums: 286 Weeks, 27 Singles: 212 Weeks)

11 Apr 87 ● WISHING I WAS LUCKY *Precious JEWEL 3*....6 14
25 Jul 87 ● SWEET LITTLE MYSTERY *Precious JEWEL 4*....5 12
3 Oct 87 ★ POPPED IN SOULED OUT *Precious JWWWL 1*....1 72
5 Dec 87 ● ANGEL EYES (HOME AND AWAY) *Precious JEWEL 6*....5 12
19 Mar 88 TEMPTATION *Precious JEWEL 7*....12 8
14 May 88 ★ WITH A LITTLE HELP FROM MY FRIENDS *Childline CHILD 1*....1 11
19 Nov 88 ● THE MEMPHIS SESSIONS *Precious JWWWL 2*....3 13
30 Sep 89 ● SWEET SURRENDER *Precious JEWEL 9*....6 8
11 Nov 89 ● HOLDING BACK THE RIVER *Precious 842011 1*....2 26
9 Dec 89 BROKE AWAY *Precious JEWEL 10*....19 7
10 Mar 90 HOLD BACK THE RIVER *Precious JEWEL 11*....31 4
11 Aug 90 STAY WITH ME HEARTACHE / I FEEL FINE *Precious JEWEL 13*....30 4
14 Sep 91 MAKE IT TONIGHT *Precious JEWEL 15*....37 3
2 Nov 91 PUT THE LIGHT ON *Precious JEWEL 16*....56 2
4 Jan 92 ★ GOODNIGHT GIRL *Precious JEWEL 17*....1 11
8 Feb 92 ★ HIGH ON THE HAPPY SIDE *Precious 5104272* ■....1 25
21 Mar 92 MORE THAN LOVE *Precious JEWEL 18*....19 5
11 Jul 92 LIP SERVICE (EP) *Precious JEWEL 19*....15 5
8 May 93 BLUE FOR YOU / THIS TIME (LIVE) *Precious JWLCD 20*....38 2
29 May 93 ● LIVE AT THE ROYAL ALBERT HALL *Precious 5147742* [1] 10 4
6 Nov 93 SHED A TEAR *Precious JWLCD 21*....22 5
20 Nov 93 ★ END OF PART ONE (THEIR GREATEST HITS) *Precious 5184772*....1 67
8 Jan 94 COLD COLD HEART *Precious JWLCD 22*....20 4
21 May 94 ★ LOVE IS ALL AROUND *Precious JWLCD 23* £....1 37
25 Mar 95 ● JULIA SAYS *Precious JWLDD 24*....3 9
22 Apr 95 ★ PICTURE THIS *Precious 5268512* ■....1 45
17 Jun 95 ● DON'T WANT TO FORGIVE ME NOW *Precious JWLDD 25*....7 8
30 Sep 95 ● SOMEWHERE SOMEHOW *Precious JWLDD 26*....7 7
2 Dec 95 SHE'S ALL ON MY MIND *Precious JWLDD 27*....17 7
30 Mar 96 MORNING *Precious JWLDD 28*....16 4
22 Mar 97 ● IF I NEVER SEE YOU AGAIN (re) *Precious JWLCD 29*....3 9
12 Apr 97 ● 10 *Precious Organisation 5345852*....2 26
14 Jun 97 STRANGE (re) *Precious JWLCD 30*....13 5
16 Aug 97 ● YESTERDAY *Precious JWLCD 31*....4 6
13 Nov 04 ALL I WANT *Mercury 9868448*....14 3
20 Nov 04 THE GREATEST HITS *Mercury 9868751*....13 8

[1] Wet Wet Wet with the Wren Orchestra

The listed A-side of 'With a Little Help from My Friends' was 'She's Leaving Home' by Billy Bragg with Cara Tivey. Tracks on Lip Service (EP): Lip Service / High on the Happy Side / Lip Service (Live) / More than Love (Live).

WE'VE GOT A FUZZBOX AND WE'RE GONNA USE IT *UK, female vocal (Vickie Perks) / instrumental group (1 Album: 6 Weeks, 6 Singles: 39 Weeks)*

26 Apr 86 XX SEX / RULES AND REGULATIONS *Vindaloo UGH 11*....41 7
15 Nov 86 LOVE IS THE SLUG *Vindaloo UGH 14*....31 4
7 Feb 87 WHAT'S THE POINT *Vindaloo YZ 101* [1]....51 2
25 Feb 89 INTERNATIONAL RESCUE *WEA YZ 347*....11 10
20 May 89 PINK SUNSHINE *WEA YZ 401* [1]....14 10
5 Aug 89 SELF! *WEA YZ 408* [1]....24 6
26 Aug 89 ● BIG BANG *WEA WX 282*....5 6

[1] Fuzzbox

WHALE *Sweden, male / female vocal / instrumental group (1 Album: 2 Weeks, 4 Singles: 8 Weeks)*

19 Mar 94 HOBO HUMPIN' SLOBO BABE *East West YZ 798CD*....46 2
15 Jul 95 I'LL DO YA *Hut HUTDG 51*....53 1
12 Aug 95 WE CARE *Hut DGHUT 25*....42 2
25 Nov 95 HOBO HUMPIN' SLOBO BABE (re-issue) *Hut HUTCD 64*....15 4
4 Jul 98 FOUR BIG SPEAKERS *Hut HUTCD 96* [1]....69 1

[1] Whale featuring Bus 75

WHAM! (120 Top 500)

Teen-dream duo with a feel-good, pure pop sound: George Michael (v) and Andrew Ridgeley (g). They were the only British act to have three chart-toppers in the UK and the US during the 1980s, a feat George later equalled as a solo artist. Total UK single sales: 5,298,431. Best-selling single: 'Last Christmas' / 'Everything She Wants' 1,420,000 (4 Albums: 259 Weeks, 12 Singles: 137 Weeks)

16 Oct 82 ● YOUNG GUNS (GO FOR IT) *Innervision IVL A2766*....3 17
15 Jan 83 ● WHAM RAP! *Innervision IVL A2442*....8 11
14 May 83 ● BAD BOYS *Innervision A 3143*....2 14

24 August 1996	31 August 1996	7 September 1996	14 September 1996
WANNABE Spice Girls	WANNABE Spice Girls	WANNABE Spice Girls	FLAVA Peter Andre
JAGGED LITTLE PILL Alanis Morissette	JAGGED LITTLE PILL Alanis Morissette	JAGGED LITTLE PILL Alanis Morissette	COMING UP Suede

KEY: UK No.1 ★ UK Top 10 ● Still on chart + UK entry at No.1 ■ US No.1 ▲ UK million seller £ US million seller $
Singles re-entries are listed as (re), (2re), (3re)... which signifies that the hit re-entered the chart once, twice or three times...
Peak Position / Weeks

9 Jul 83 ★ FANTASTIC *Inner Vision IVL 25328* ■ 1 116
30 Jul 83 ● CLUB TROPICANA *Innervision A 3613* 4 11
3 Dec 83 CLUB FANTASTIC MEGAMIX *Innervision A 3586* 15 8
26 May 84 ★ WAKE ME UP BEFORE YOU GO GO *Epic A 4440* ▲ $ 1 16
13 Oct 84 ★ FREEDOM *Epic A 4743* 1 14
17 Nov 84 ★ MAKE IT BIG *Epic EPC 86311* ■ ▲ 1 72
15 Dec 84 ● LAST CHRISTMAS / EVERYTHING SHE WANTS *Epic GA / QA 4949* ▲ £ 2 13
23 Nov 85 ★ I'M YOUR MAN *Epic A 6716* 1 12
14 Dec 85 ● LAST CHRISTMAS (re-issue) *Epic WHAM 1* 6 7
21 Jun 86 ★ THE EDGE OF HEAVEN / WHERE DID YOUR HEART GO *Epic FIN 1* 1 10
19 Jul 86 ● THE FINAL *Epic EPC 88681* 2 47
20 Dec 86 LAST CHRISTMAS (2nd re-issue) *Epic 650269 7* 45 4
6 Dec 97 ● THE BEST OF WHAM! *Epic 4890202* 4 24

'Last Christmas' / 'Everything She Wants' was first catalogued as GA 4949, but from 5 Jan 1985 the re-mix of 'Everything She Wants' (QA 4949) was listed as the A-side and this was the track that topped the US chart. 'The Edge of Heaven' / 'Where Did Your Heart Go' is a double record set, with 'The Edge of Heaven' / 'Wham Rap 86' (re-mix) on disc one and 'Battlestations' / 'Where Did Your Heart Go' on disc two. 'Where Did Your Heart Go' listed only from 2 Aug 1986. It peaked at No.28.

Sarah WHATMORE *UK, female vocalist (2 Singles: 17 Weeks)*

21 Sep 02 ● WHEN I LOST YOU *RCA 74321965952* 6 9
22 Feb 03 AUTOMATIC *RCA 82876504612* 11 8

Rebecca WHEATLEY *UK, female actor / vocalist*

26 Feb 00 ● STAY WITH ME (BABY) (re) *BBC Music WMSS 60222* 10 8

WHEATUS *US, male vocal (Brendan Brown) / instrumental group (1 Album: 30 Weeks, 4 Singles: 38 Weeks)*

17 Feb 01 ● TEENAGE DIRTBAG *Columbia 6707962* 2 20
3 Mar 01 ● WHEATUS *Columbia 4996052* 7 30
14 Jul 01 ● A LITTLE RESPECT *Columbia 6714282* 3 12
26 Jan 02 WANNABE GANGSTAR / LEROY *Columbia 6721272* 22 5
6 Sep 03 AMERICAN IN AMSTERDAM *Columbia 6741072* 59 1

Caron WHEELER *UK, female vocalist (1 Album: 5 Weeks, 7 Singles: 42 Weeks)*

18 Mar 89 ● KEEP ON MOVING *10 TEN 263* [1] $ 5 12
10 Jun 89 ★ BACK TO LIFE (HOWEVER DO YOU WANT ME) *10 TEN 265* [1] $ 1 14
8 Sep 90 LIVIN' IN THE LIGHT *RCA PB 43939* 14 6
13 Oct 90 UK BLAK *RCA PL 74751* 14 5
10 Nov 90 UK BLAK *RCA PB 43719* 40 4
9 Feb 91 DON'T QUIT *RCA PB 44259* 53 3
7 Nov 92 I ADORE YOU *Perspective PERSS 7407* 59 2
11 Sep 93 BEACH OF THE WAR GODDESS *EMI CDEM 282* 75 1

[1] Soul II Soul featuring Caron Wheeler

Bill WHELAN *Ireland, male composer*

17 Dec 94 ● RIVERDANCE *Son RTEBUACD 1* [1] 9 16
25 Mar 95 MUSIC FROM RIVERDANCE – THE SHOW *Celtic Heartbeat 75678061112* 31 38

[1] Bill Whelan and Anuna featuring the RTE Concert Orchestra

WHEN IN ROME *UK, male vocal / instrumental group*

28 Jan 89 THE PROMISE *10 TEN 244* 58 3

WHIGFIELD *Denmark, female vocalist – Sannia Carlson (1 Album: 7 Weeks, 6 Singles: 52 Weeks)*

17 Sep 94 ★ SATURDAY NIGHT *Systematic SYSCD 3* ■ £ 1 18
10 Dec 94 ● ANOTHER DAY *Systematic SYSCD 4* 7 10
10 Jun 95 ● THINK OF YOU *Systematic SYSCDP 10* 7 11
1 Jul 95 WHIGFIELD *Systematic 8286512* 13 7
9 Sep 95 CLOSE TO YOU *Systematic SYCDP 18* 13 7
16 Dec 95 LAST CHRISTMAS / BIG TIME *Systematic SYSCD 24* 21 5
10 Oct 98 SEXY EYES – REMIXES *ZYX ZYX 8085R 8* 68 1

WHIPPING BOY *Ireland, male vocal / instrumental group (3 Singles: 4 Weeks)*

14 Oct 95 WE DON'T NEED NOBODY ELSE *Columbia 6622205* 51 1
3 Feb 96 WHEN WE WERE YOUNG *Columbia 6628062* 46 2
25 May 96 TWINKLE *Columbia 6632272* 55 1

The WHISPERS *US, male vocal group (2 Albums: 9 Weeks, 9 Singles: 52 Weeks)*

2 Feb 80 ● AND THE BEAT GOES ON *Solar SO 1* $ 2 12
10 May 80 LADY *Solar SO 4* 55 3
12 Jul 80 MY GIRL *Solar SO 8* 26 6
14 Mar 81 IMAGINATION *Solar SOLA 7* 42 5
14 Mar 81 ● IT'S A LOVE THING *Solar SO 16* 9 11
13 Jun 81 I CAN MAKE IT BETTER *Solar SO 19* 44 5
19 Jan 85 CONTAGIOUS *MCA MCA 937* 56 3
28 Mar 87 AND THE BEAT GOES ON (re-issue) *Solar MCA 1126* 45 4
23 May 87 ROCK STEADY *Solar MCA 1152* 38 6
6 Jun 87 JUST GETS BETTER WITH TIME *Solar MCF 3381* 63 4
15 Aug 87 SPECIAL F/X *Solar MCA 1178* 69 2

WHISTLE *US, male rap group*

1 Mar 86 ● (NOTHIN' SERIOUS) JUST BUGGIN' *Champion CHAMP 12* 7 8

Alex WHITCOMBE & BIG C (see also QATTARA) *UK, male production duo*

23 May 98 ICE RAIN *Xtravaganza 0091075 EXT* 44 1

Alan WHITE (see also YES) *UK, male drummer*

13 Mar 76 RAMSHACKLED *Atlantic K 50217* 41 4

Barry WHITE (131 Top 500)

Seventies soul and disco icon, b. 12 Sep 1944, Texas, US, d. 4 Jul 2003. This singer / songwriter / pianist / producer / arranger was behind best-sellers by Love Unlimited and Love Unlimited Orchestra. Lovingly named the "Walrus of Love", his unmistakable deep voice has been heard in the charts for four decades (14 Albums: 247 Weeks, 21 Singles: 138 Weeks)

9 Jun 73 I'M GONNA LOVE YOU JUST A LITTLE MORE BABY *Pye International 7N 25610* $ 23 7
26 Jan 74 NEVER NEVER GONNA GIVE YA UP *Pye International 7N 25633* $ 14 11
9 Mar 74 STONE GON' *Pye NSPL 28186* 18 17
6 Apr 74 RHAPSODY IN WHITE *Pye NSPL 28191* 50 1
17 Aug 74 ● CAN'T GET ENOUGH OF YOUR LOVE, BABE *Pye International 7N 25661* ▲ $ 8 12
2 Nov 74 ● CAN'T GET ENOUGH *20th Century BT 444* ▲ 4 34
2 Nov 74 ★ YOU'RE THE FIRST, THE LAST, MY EVERYTHING *20th Century BTC 2133* $ 1 14
8 Mar 75 ● WHAT AM I GONNA DO WITH YOU *20th Century BTC 2177* 5 8
26 Apr 75 JUST ANOTHER WAY TO SAY I LOVE YOU *20th Century BT 466* 12 15
24 May 75 (FOR YOU) I'LL DO ANYTHING YOU WANT ME TO *20th Century BTC 2208* 20 6
22 Nov 75 GREATEST HITS *20th Century BTH 8000* 18 12
27 Dec 75 ● LET THE MUSIC PLAY *20th Century BTC 2265* 9 8
21 Feb 76 LET THE MUSIC PLAY *20th Century BT 502* 22 14
6 Mar 76 ● YOU SEE THE TROUBLE WITH ME *20th Century BTC 2277* 2 10
21 Aug 76 BABY, WE BETTER TRY TO GET IT TOGETHER *20th Century BTC 2298* 15 7

21 September 1996	28 September 1996	5 October 1996	12 October 1996
UK No.1 SINGLES			
READY OR NOT Fugees	READY OR NOT Fugees	BREAKFAST AT TIFFANY'S (Re-entry) Deep Blue Something	SETTING SUN The Chemical Brothers
UK No.1 ALBUMS			
NEW ADVENTURES IN HI-FI R.E.M.	K Kula Shaker	K Kula Shaker	NATURAL Peter Andre

13 Nov 76 **DON'T MAKE ME WAIT TOO LONG** *20th Century BTC 2309*.......17 8
5 Mar 77 **I'M QUALIFIED TO SATISFY YOU** *20th Century BTC 2328*..........37 5
9 Apr 77 BARRY WHITE'S GREATEST HITS VOLUME 2 *20th Century BTH 8001*..........17 7
15 Oct 77 **IT'S ECSTASY WHEN YOU LAY DOWN NEXT TO ME** *20th Century BTC 2350* $..........40 3
16 Dec 78 **JUST THE WAY YOU ARE** *20th Century BTC 2380*..........12 12
10 Feb 79 THE MAN *20th Century BT 571*..........46 4
24 Mar 79 **SHA LA LA MEANS I LOVE YOU** *20th Century BTC 1041*..........55 6
21 Dec 85 HEART AND SOUL *K-Tel NE 1316*..........34 10
17 Oct 87 THE RIGHT NIGHT AND BARRY WHITE *Breakout AMA 5154*....74 6
7 Nov 87 **SHO' YOU RIGHT** *Breakout USA 614*..........14 7
16 Jan 88 **NEVER NEVER GONNA GIVE YOU UP** (re-mix) *Club JAB 59*....63 2
2 Jul 88 ● THE COLLECTION *Mercury BWTV 1*..........5117
31 Mar 90 **SECRET GARDEN** *Qwest W 9992* [1] 67 1
21 Jan 95 **PRACTICE WHAT YOU PREACH / LOVE IS THE ICON** *A&M 5808992*..........20 4
11 Feb 95 THE ICON IS LOVE *A&M 5402802*..........44 3
8 Apr 95 **I ONLY WANT TO BE WITH YOU** *A&M 5810252*..........36 2
21 Dec 96 **IN YOUR WILDEST DREAMS** *Parlophone CDR 6451* [2] 32 3
4 Nov 00 **LET THE MUSIC PLAY** (re-mix) *Wonderboy WBOYD 020*..........45 2
15 Feb 03 LOVE SONGS *Universal TV 0686422*..........21 4
19 Nov 05 WHITE GOLD – THE VERY BEST OF *UMTV 9834692*..........37 3

[1] Quincy Jones featuring Al B Sure!, James Ingram, El DeBarge and Barry White
[2] Tina Turner featuring Barry White

Chris WHITE *UK, male vocalist*

20 Mar 76 **SPANISH WINE** *Charisma CB 272*..........37 4

Karyn WHITE *US, female vocalist (2 Albums: 30 Weeks, 7 Singles: 38 Weeks)*

5 Nov 88 **THE WAY YOU LOVE ME** *Warner Bros. W 7773*..........42 5
18 Feb 89 **SECRET RENDEZVOUS** *Warner Bros. W 7562*..........52 3
11 Mar 89 KARYN WHITE *Warner Bros. WX 235*..........20 27
10 Jun 89 **SUPERWOMAN** *Warner Bros. W 2920*..........11 13
9 Sep 89 **SECRET RENDEZVOUS** (re-issue) *Warner Bros. W 2855*..........22 9
17 Aug 91 **ROMANTIC** *Warner Bros. W 0028* ▲..........23 5
21 Sep 91 RITUAL OF LOVE *Warner Bros. WX 411*..........31 3
18 Jan 92 **THE WAY I FEEL ABOUT YOU** *Warner Bros. W 0073*..........65 2
24 Sep 94 **HUNGAH** *Warner Bros. W 0264CD*..........69 1

Keisha WHITE

(see also OAKENFOLD) *UK, female vocalist (4 Singles: 6 Weeks)*

22 Feb 03 **THE HARDER THEY COME** *Perfecto PERF 49CDS*..........38 2
1 Mar 03 **BIGGER BETTER DEAL** *Echo ECSCD 129* [1] 67 1
27 Mar 04 **WATCHA GONNA DO** *Radar RAD 005CD*..........53 1
5 Mar 05 **DON'T CARE WHO KNOWS** *Warner Bros. WEA 382CD 2*..........29 2

[1] Desert Eagle Discs featuring Keisha White

'The Harder They Come' credits: Vocals by Keisha White and Tricky.

Tam WHITE *UK, male vocalist*

15 Mar 75 **WHAT IN THE WORLD'S COME OVER YOU** *RAK 193*..........36 4

Tony Joe WHITE *US, male vocalist / guitarist*

6 Jun 70 **GROUPIE GIRL** *Monument MON 1043*..........22 10
26 Sep 70 TONY JOE *CBS 63800*..........63 1

Snowy WHITE (see also THIN LIZZY)

UK, male vocalist / guitarist (2 Albums: 5 Weeks, 2 Singles: 12 Weeks)

24 Dec 83 ● **BIRD OF PARADISE** *Towerbell TOW 42*..........6 10
11 Feb 84 WHITE FLAMES *Towerbell TOWLP 3*..........21 4
9 Feb 85 SNOWY WHITE *Towerbell TOWLP 8*..........88 1
28 Dec 85 **FOR YOU** (re) *R4 FOR 3*..........65 2

WHITE LION *US, male vocal / instrumental group (2 Albums: 3 Weeks)*

1 Jul 89 BIG GAME *Atlantic WX 277*..........47 1
20 Apr 91 MANE ATTRACTION *Atlantic WX 415*..........31 2

WHITE PLAINS

UK, male vocal (Tony Burrows) / instrumental group (5 Singles: 56 Weeks)

7 Feb 70 ● **MY BABY LOVES LOVIN'** *Deram DM 280*..........9 11
18 Apr 70 **I'VE GOT YOU ON MY MIND** *Deram DM 291*..........17 11
24 Oct 70 ● **JULIE DO YA LOVE ME** *Deram DM 315*..........8 14
12 Jun 71 **WHEN YOU ARE A KING** *Deram DM 333*..........13 11
17 Feb 73 **STEP INTO A DREAM** *Deram DM 371*..........21 9

WHITE ROSE MOVEMENT NEW

UK, male / female vocal / instrumental group

12 Nov 05 **ALSATIAN** *Independiente ISOM 99S*..........54 1

The WHITE STRIPES *US, male / female vocal / instrumental duo – Jack and Meg White (3 Albums: 87 Weeks, 10 Singles: 42 Weeks)*

18 Aug 01 WHITE BLOOD CELLS *Sympathy for the Record Industry SFTRI 660CD*..........55 17
24 Nov 01 **HOTEL YORBA** *XL Recordings XLS 139CD*..........26 2
9 Mar 02 **FELL IN LOVE WITH A GIRL** *XL Recordings XLS 142CD*..........21 2
14 Sep 02 **DEAD LEAVES AND THE DIRTY GROUND** *XL Recordings XLS 148CD*..........25 2
12 Apr 03 ★ ELEPHANT *XL XLCD 162* ■..........1 46
3 May 03 ● **7 NATION ARMY** *XL Recordings XLS 162CD*..........7 4
13 Sep 03 **I JUST DON'T KNOW WHAT TO DO WITH MYSELF** *XL Recordings XLS 166CD*..........13 5
29 Nov 03 **THE HARDEST BUTTON TO BUTTON** *XL Recordings XLS 173CD*..........23 3
27 Nov 04 **JOLENE (LIVE)** *XL Recordings XLS 207CD*..........16 4
11 Jun 05 ● **BLUE ORCHID** *XL Recordings XLS 216CD2*..........9 7
18 Jun 05 ● GET BEHIND ME SATAN *XL Recordings XLCD 191*..........3 24
3 Sep 05 ● **MY DOORBELL** (re) *XL Recordings XLS 218CD*..........10 9
26 Nov 05 ● **THE DENIAL TWIST** *XL Recordings XLS 223CD*..........10 4

'Jolene' was recorded 'Live under Blackpool lights'.

WHITE TOWN

UK (b. India), male vocalist / producer – Jyoti Mishra (2 Singles: 10 Weeks)

25 Jan 97 ★ **YOUR WOMAN** *Chrysalis CDCHS 5052* ■..........1 9
24 May 97 **UNDRESSED** *Chrysalis CDCHS 5058*..........57 1

WHITE ZOMBIE (see also Rob ZOMBIE) *US, male vocal / instrumental group (1 Album: 6 Weeks, 2 Singles: 4 Weeks)*

20 May 95 **MORE HUMAN THAN HUMAN** *Geffen GFSTD 92*..........51 2
27 May 95 ASTRO CREEP 2000 / SUPERSEXY SWINGIN' SOUNDS *Geffen GED 24806*..........25 6
18 May 96 **ELECTRIC HEAD PART 2 (THE ECSTASY)** *Geffen GFSXD 22140*..........31 2

Supersexy Swingin' Sounds, a re-mix album, was listed with Astro Creep 2000 from 31 Aug 96 and sales were combined.

WHITE and TORCH *UK, male vocal / instrumental duo*

2 Oct 82 **PARADE** *Chrysalis CHS 2641*..........54 4

WHITEHEAD BROS

US, male vocal duo – Kenny and Johnny Whitehead (2 Singles: 5 Weeks)

14 Jan 95 **YOUR LOVE IS A 187** *Motown TMGCD 1434*..........32 3
13 May 95 **FORGET I WAS A G** *Motown TMGCD 1441*..........40 2

WHITEHOUSE *US / UK, male vocal / instrumental / production duo*

15 Aug 98 **AIN'T NO MOUNTAIN HIGH ENOUGH** *Beautiful Noise BNOISE 2CD*..........60 1

KEY: UK No.1 ★ UK Top 10 ● Still on chart + UK entry at No.1 ■ US No.1 ▲ UK million seller £ US million seller $
Singles re-entries are listed as (re), (2re), (3re)... which signifies that the hit re-entered the chart once, twice or three times...
Peak Position / Weeks

WHITEOUT

UK, male vocal / instrumental group (1 Album: 1 Week, 2 Singles: 2 Weeks)

24 Sep 94 **DETROIT** *Silvertone ORECD 66* 73 1
18 Feb 95 **JACKIE'S RACING** *Silvertone ORECD 68* 72 1
1 Jul 95 BITE IT *Silvertone ORECD 536* 71 1

WHITESNAKE (232 Top 500)

Leading 1980s British rock group founded by ex-Deep Purple vocalist David Coverdale, b. 22 Sep 1949, North Yorkshire, but with an ever-changing line-up. Whitesnake 1987, their most successful album, shifted more than 10 million copies worldwide (12 Albums: 162 Weeks, 21 Singles: 112 Weeks)

24 Jun 78 **SNAKE BITE (EP)** *EMI International INEP 751* [1] 61 3
18 Nov 78 TROUBLE *EMI International INS 3022* 50 2
13 Oct 79 LOVE HUNTER *United Artists UAG 30264* 29 7
10 Nov 79 **LONG WAY FROM HOME** *United Artists BP 324* 55 2
26 Apr 80 **FOOL FOR YOUR LOVING** *United Artists BP 352* 13 9
7 Jun 80 ● READY AND WILLING *United Artists UAG 30302* 6 15
12 Jul 80 **READY AN' WILLING (SWEET SATISFACTION)** *United Artists BP 363* 43 4
8 Nov 80 ● LIVE IN THE HEART OF THE CITY *United Artists SNAKE 1* 5 15
22 Nov 80 **AIN'T NO LOVE IN THE HEART OF THE CITY** *Sunburst / Liberty BP 381* 51 4
11 Apr 81 **DON'T BREAK MY HEART AGAIN** *Liberty BP 395* 17 9
18 Apr 81 ● COME AND GET IT *Liberty LBG 30327* 2 23
6 Jun 81 **WOULD I LIE TO YOU** *Liberty BP 399* 37 6
6 Nov 82 **HERE I GO AGAIN / BLOODY LUXURY** *Liberty BP 416* ▲ 34 10
27 Nov 82 ● SAINTS 'N' SINNERS *Liberty LBG 30354* 9 9
13 Aug 83 **GUILTY OF LOVE** *Liberty BP 420* 31 5
14 Jan 84 **GIVE ME MORE TIME** *Liberty BP 422* 29 4
11 Feb 84 ● SLIDE IT IN *Liberty LBG 2400001* 9 7
28 Apr 84 **STANDING IN THE SHADOW** *Liberty BP 423* 62 2
9 Feb 85 **LOVE AIN'T NO STRANGER** *Liberty BP 424* 44 4
28 Mar 87 **STILL OF THE NIGHT** *EMI EMI 5606* 16 8
11 Apr 87 ● WHITESNAKE 1987 *EMI EMC 3528* 8 57
6 Jun 87 ● **IS THIS LOVE** *EMI EM 3* 9 11
31 Oct 87 ● **HERE I GO AGAIN** (re-mix) *EMI EM 35* 9 11
6 Feb 88 **GIVE ME ALL YOUR LOVE** *EMI EM 23* 18 6
25 Nov 89 ● SLIP OF THE TONGUE *EMI EMD 1013* 10 10
2 Dec 89 **FOOL FOR YOUR LOVING** (re-recording) *EMI EM 123* 43 2
10 Mar 90 **THE DEEPER THE LOVE** *EMI EM 128* 35 3
25 Aug 90 **NOW YOU'RE GONE** *EMI EM 150* 31 4
16 Jul 94 ● GREATEST HITS *EMI CDEMD 1065* 4 12
6 Aug 94 **IS THIS LOVE** (re-issue) **/ SWEET LADY LUCK** *EMI CDEM 329* 25 4
7 Jun 97 **TOO MANY TEARS** *EMI CDEM 471* [2] 46 1
21 Jun 97 RESTLESS HEART *EMI CDEMD 1104* [1] 34 2
5 Apr 03 BEST OF WHITESNAKE *EMI 5812452* 44 3

[1] David Coverdale's Whitesnake [2] David Coverdale and Whitesnake
[1] David Coverdale and Whitesnake

Tracks on Snake Bite (EP): Bloody Mary / Steal Away / Ain't No Love in the Heart of the City / Come On.

WHITEY NEW

UK, male DJ / producer – Nathan Whitey

5 Mar 05 **NONSTOP / A WALK IN THE DARK** *1234 1234CDS 06* 67 1

David WHITFIELD (364 Top 500)

The most successful UK male singer in the US during the pre-rock years, b. 2 Feb 1925, Yorkshire, d. 16 Jan 1980. This operatic-style tenor had a formidable and predominantly female fanbase in the 1950s (19 Singles: 190 Weeks)

2 Oct 53 ● **THE BRIDGE OF SIGHS** *Decca F 10129* 9 1
16 Oct 53 ★ **ANSWER ME** (re) *Decca F 10192* 1 14
11 Dec 53 ● **RAGS TO RICHES** (re) *Decca F 10207* [1] 3 11
19 Feb 54 ● **THE BOOK** (re) *Decca F 10242* 5 15
18 Jun 54 ★ **CARA MIA** *Decca F 10327* $ 1 25
12 Nov 54 ● **SANTO NATALE (MERRY CHRISTMAS)** *Decca F 10399* 2 10
11 Feb 55 ● **BEYOND THE STARS** *Decca F 10458* 8 9
27 May 55 **MAMA** (2re) *Decca F 10515* 12 11
8 Jul 55 ● **EV'RYWHERE** *Decca F 10515* [2] 3 20
25 Nov 55 ● **WHEN YOU LOSE THE ONE YOU LOVE** *Decca F 10627* [3] 7 11
2 Mar 56 ● **MY SEPTEMBER LOVE** (3re) *Decca F 10690* 3 24
24 Aug 56 **MY SON JOHN** *Decca F 10769* 22 4
31 Aug 56 **MY UNFINISHED SYMPHONY** *Decca F 10769* 29 1
25 Jan 57 ● **THE ADORATION WALTZ** *Decca F 10833* [2] 9 11
5 Apr 57 **I'LL FIND YOU** (re) *Decca F 10864* 27 4
14 Feb 58 **CRY MY HEART** *Decca F 10978* [4] 22 3
16 May 58 **ON THE STREET WHERE YOU LIVE** *Decca F 11018* [5] 16 14
8 Aug 58 **THE RIGHT TO LOVE** *Decca F 11039* 30 1
24 Nov 60 **I BELIEVE** *Decca F 11289* 49 1

[1] David Whitfield with Stanley Black and his Orchestra [2] David Whitfield with the Roland Shaw Orchestra [3] David Whitfield with Mantovani, his Orchestra and Chorus [4] David Whitfield with chorus and Mantovani and his Orchestra [5] David Whitfield with Cyril Stapleton and his Orchestra

Slim WHITMAN

US, male vocalist – Otis Whitman Jr (7 Albums: 61 Weeks, 8 Singles: 77 Weeks)

15 Jul 55 ★ **ROSE MARIE** *London HL 8061* 1 19
29 Jul 55 ● **INDIAN LOVE CALL** *London L 1149* 7 12
23 Sep 55 **CHINA DOLL** *London L 1149* 15 2
9 Mar 56 **TUMBLING TUMBLEWEEDS** *London HLU 8230* 19 2
13 Apr 56 **I'M A FOOL** (re) *London HLU 8252* 16 4
22 Jun 56 ● **SERENADE** (re) *London HLU 8287* 8 15
12 Apr 57 ● **I'LL TAKE YOU HOME AGAIN KATHLEEN** *London HLP 8403* 7 13
5 Oct 74 **HAPPY ANNIVERSARY** *United Artists UP 35728* 14 10
14 Dec 74 HAPPY ANNIVERSARY *United Artists UAS 29670* 44 2
31 Jan 76 ★ THE VERY BEST OF SLIM WHITMAN *United Artists UAS 29898* 1 17
15 Jan 77 ★ RED RIVER VALLEY *United Artists UAS 29993* 1 14
15 Oct 77 ● HOME ON THE RANGE *United Artists UATV 30102* 2 13
13 Jan 79 GHOST RIDERS IN THE SKY *United Artists UATV 30202* 27 6
22 Dec 79 SLIM WHITMAN'S 20 GREATEST LOVE SONGS *United Artists UAG 30270* 18 7
27 Sep 97 THE VERY BEST OF SLIM WHITMAN – 50TH ANNIVERSARY COLLECTION *EMI CDEMC 3772* 54 2

Roger WHITTAKER (349 Top 500)

World-renowned vocalist and whistler, b. 22 Mar 1936, Nairobi, Kenya. An easy-listening legend and popular live performer with more than 10 million albums sold in his home base of Germany (12 Albums: 116 Weeks, 7 Singles: 85 Weeks)

8 Nov 69 **DURHAM TOWN (THE LEAVIN')** *Columbia DB 8613* 12 18
11 Apr 70 ● **I DON'T BELIEVE IN IF ANYMORE** *Columbia DB 8664* 8 18
27 Jun 70 I DON'T BELIEVE IN IF ANYMORE *Columbia SCX 6404* 23 1
10 Oct 70 **NEW WORLD IN THE MORNING** *Columbia DB 8718* 17 14
3 Apr 71 NEW WORLD IN THE MORNING *Columbia SCX 6456* 45 2
3 Apr 71 **WHY** *Columbia DB 8752* 47 1
2 Oct 71 **MAMMY BLUE** *Columbia DB 8822* 31 10
26 Jul 75 ● **THE LAST FAREWELL** *EMI 2294* 2 14
6 Sep 75 ● THE VERY BEST OF ROGER WHITTAKER *Columbia SCX 6560* 5 42
15 May 76 THE SECOND ALBUM OF THE VERY BEST OF ROGER WHITTAKER *EMI EMC 3117* 27 7
9 Dec 78 ROGER WHITTAKER SINGS THE HITS *Columbia SCX 6601* 52 5
4 Aug 79 20 ALL TIME GREATS *Polydor POLTV 8* 24 9
7 Feb 81 THE ROGER WHITTAKER ALBUM *K-Tel NE 1105* 18 14
8 Nov 86 ● **THE SKYE BOAT SONG** *Tembo TML 119* [1] 10 10
27 Dec 86 SKYE BOAT SONG AND OTHER GREAT SONGS *Tembo TMB 113* 89 1
23 May 87 HIS FINEST COLLECTION *Tembo RWTV 1* 15 19
23 Sep 89 HOME LOVIN' MAN *Tembo RWTV 2* 20 10
11 May 96 A PERFECT DAY – HIS GREATEST HITS & MORE *RCA 74321371562* 74 1
7 Feb 04 NOW AND THEN – GREATEST HITS 1964-2004 *BMG 82876588332* 21 5

[1] Roger Whittaker and Des O'Connor

	16 November 1996	23 November 1996	30 November 1996	7 December 1996
UK No.1 SINGLES	WHAT BECOMES OF THE BROKENHEARTED / SATURDAY NIGHT AT THE MOVIES / YOU'LL NEVER WALK ALONE Robson & Jerome	BREATHE The Prodigy	BREATHE The Prodigy	I FEEL YOU Peter Andre
UK No.1 ALBUMS	SPICE Spice Girls	TAKE TWO Robson & Jerome	TAKE TWO Robson & Jerome	SPICE Spice Girls

The WHO (86 Top 500) (see also The HIGH NUMBERS)

Legendary live band from London whose Tommy album popularised rock opera: Roger Daltrey CBE (v), Pete Townshend (g), John 'The Ox' Entwistle (b), b. 9 Oct 1944, d. 27 Jun 2002, and Keith Moon (d), b. 23 Aug 1946, d. 7 Sep 1978. These mod to rock giants performed at Woodstock and both Live Aid and Live 8 London concerts. They were inducted into the UK Music Hall of Fame in 2005 (31 Albums: 235 Weeks, 31 Singles: 247 Weeks)

Date		Title / Label	Pos	Wks
18 Feb 65	●	I CAN'T EXPLAIN *Brunswick 05926*	8	13
27 May 65	●	ANYWAY ANYHOW ANYWHERE *Brunswick 05935*	10	12
4 Nov 65	●	MY GENERATION *Brunswick 05944*	2	13
25 Dec 65	●	MY GENERATION *Brunswick LAT 8616*	5	11
10 Mar 66	●	SUBSTITUTE *Reaction 591 001*	5	13
24 Mar 66		A LEGAL MATTER *Brunswick 05956*	32	6
1 Sep 66	●	I'M A BOY *Reaction 591 004*	2	13
1 Sep 66		THE KIDS ARE ALRIGHT (re) *Brunswick 05965*	41	3
15 Dec 66	●	HAPPY JACK *Reaction 591 010*	3	11
17 Dec 66	●	A QUICK ONE *Reaction 593002*	4	17
27 Apr 67	●	PICTURES OF LILY *Track 604 002*	4	10
26 Jul 67		THE LAST TIME / UNDER MY THUMB *Track 604 006*	44	3
18 Oct 67	●	I CAN SEE FOR MILES *Track 604 011*	10	12
13 Jan 68		THE WHO SELL-OUT *Track 613002*	13	11
19 Jun 68		DOGS *Track 604 023*	25	5
23 Oct 68		MAGIC BUS *Track 604 024*	26	6
19 Mar 69	●	PINBALL WIZARD *Track 604 027*	4	13
7 Jun 69	●	TOMMY *Track 613013/4*	2	9
4 Apr 70		THE SEEKER *Track 604 036*	19	11
6 Jun 70	●	LIVE AT LEEDS *Track 2406001*	3	21
8 Aug 70		SUMMERTIME BLUES *Track 2094 002*	38	4
10 Jul 71	●	WON'T GET FOOLED AGAIN *Track 2094 009*	9	12
11 Sep 71	★	WHO'S NEXT *Track 2408102*	1	13
23 Oct 71		LET'S SEE ACTION *Track 2094 012*	16	12
18 Dec 71	●	MEATY BEATY BIG AND BOUNCY *Track 2406006*	9	8
24 Jun 72	●	JOIN TOGETHER *Track 2094 102*	9	9
13 Jan 73		RELAY *Track 2094 106*	21	5
13 Oct 73		5.15 *Track 2094 115*	20	6
17 Nov 73	●	QUADROPHENIA *Track 2647013*	2	13
26 Oct 74	●	ODDS AND SODS *Track 2406116*	10	4
23 Aug 75		TOMMY (FILM SOUNDTRACK) *Track 2657007*	30	2
18 Oct 75	●	THE WHO BY NUMBERS *Polydor 2490129*	7	6
24 Jan 76	●	SQUEEZE BOX *Polydor 2121 275*	10	9
9 Oct 76	●	THE STORY OF THE WHO *Polydor 2683069*	2	18
30 Oct 76	●	SUBSTITUTE (re-issue) *Polydor 2058 803*	7	7
22 Jul 78		WHO ARE YOU *Polydor WHO 1*	18	12
9 Sep 78	●	WHO ARE YOU *Polydor WHOD 5004*	6	9
28 Apr 79		LONG LIVE ROCK *Polydor WHO 2*	48	5
30 Jun 79		THE KIDS ARE ALRIGHT *Polydor 2675 174*	26	13
25 Oct 80		MY GENERATION (re-issue) *Virgin V 2179*	20	7
7 Mar 81	●	YOU BETTER YOU BET *Polydor WHO 004*	9	8
28 Mar 81	●	FACE DANCES *Polydor WHOD 5037*	2	9
9 May 81		DON'T LET GO THE COAT *Polydor WHO 005*	47	4
11 Sep 82		IT'S HARD *Polydor WHOD 5066*	11	6
2 Oct 82		ATHENA *Polydor WHO 6*	40	4
26 Nov 83		READY STEADY WHO (EP) *Polydor WHO 7*	58	2
17 Nov 84		WHO'S LAST *MCA WHO 1*	48	4
12 Oct 85		THE WHO COLLECTION *Impression IMDP 4*	44	6
20 Feb 88		MY GENERATION (re-issue) *Polydor POSP 907*	68	2
19 Mar 88	●	WHO'S BETTER WHO'S BEST *Polydor WTV 1*	10	11
19 Nov 88		THE WHO COLLECTION *Stylus SMR 570*	71	4
24 Mar 90		JOIN TOGETHER *Virgin VDT 102*	59	1
16 Jul 94		30 YEARS OF MAXIMUM R&B *Polydor 5217512*	48	1
4 Mar 95		LIVE AT LEEDS (re-issue) *Polydor 5271692*	59	1
6 Jul 96		QUADROPHENIA (re-issue) *Polydor 5319712*	47	2
27 Jul 96		MY GENERATION (2nd re-issue) *Polydor 8546372*	31	2
24 Aug 96		MY GENERATION – THE VERY BEST OF THE WHO *Polydor 5331502*	11	6
26 Feb 00		BBC SESSIONS *BBC Music / Polydor 5477272*	24	2
21 Sep 02		MY GENERATION (2nd re-issue) *MCA / Uni-Island 1129262*	47	1
2 Nov 02		THE ULTIMATE COLLECTION *Polydor / Universal TV 0653002*	17	6
12 Jul 03		LIVE AT THE ROYAL ALBERT HALL *SPV Recordings SPV 09374882*	72	1
15 May 04	●	THEN AND NOW! – 1964-2004 *Polydor 9866577*	5	12

Tracks on Ready Steady Who (EP): Disguises / Circles / Batman / Bucket 'T' / Barbara Ann. *The two albums titled The Who Collection are different. The 2nd re-issue of My Generation contains a bonus disc of out-takes and rarities.*

WHO DA FUNK *US, male production duo – Alex Alicea and Jorge Jaramillo (3 Singles: 8 Weeks)*

Date		Title / Label	Pos	Wks
26 Oct 02		SHINY DISCO BALLS (import) *White Label SSA 03* [1]	69	1
2 Nov 02		SHINY DISCO BALLS *Cream CREAM 22CD* [1]	15	5
15 Feb 03		STING ME RED (YOU THINK YOU'RE SO CLEVER) *Cream CREAM 19CDS* [2]	32	2

[1] Who Da Funk featuring Jessica Eve [2] Who Da Funk featuring Terra Deva

WHODINI *US, male rap / DJ duo (2 Singles: 10 Weeks)*

Date		Title / Label	Pos	Wks
25 Dec 82		MAGIC'S WAND *Jive JIVE 28*	47	6
17 Mar 84		MAGIC'S WAND (THE WHODINI ELECTRIC EP) *Jive JIVE 61*	63	4

Tracks on 'Magic's Wand (The Whodini Electric EP): Jive Magic Wand / Nasty Lady / Rap Machine / The Haunted House of Rock.

WHOOLIGANZ *US, male rap duo*

Date		Title / Label	Pos	Wks
13 Aug 94		PUT YOUR HANDZ UP *Positiva CDTIV 17*	53	2

WHOOSH *UK, male production trio*

Date		Title / Label	Pos	Wks
13 Sep 97		WHOOSH *Wonderboy WBOYD 006*	72	1

WHYCLIFFE *UK, male vocalist – Bramwell Whycliffe (2 Singles: 2 Weeks)*

Date		Title / Label	Pos	Wks
20 Nov 93		HEAVEN *MCA MCSTD 1944*	56	1
2 Apr 94		ONE MORE TIME *MCA MCSTD 1955*	72	1

WIDEBOYS featuring Dennis G *UK, male production duo and vocalist*

Date		Title / Label	Pos	Wks
27 Oct 01		SAMBUCA *Locked On / 679 Recordings 679L 002CD*	15	6

Jane WIEDLIN (see also GO-GO's) *US, female vocalist (1 Album: 3 Weeks, 2 Singles: 14 Weeks)*

Date		Title / Label	Pos	Wks
6 Aug 88		RUSH HOUR *Manhattan MT 36*	12	11
24 Sep 88		FUR *Manhattan MTL 1029*	48	3
29 Oct 88		INSIDE A DREAM *Manhattan MT 55*	64	3

WIGAN'S CHOSEN FEW *Canada, male vocal / instrumental group and UK, crowd chants*

Date		Title / Label	Pos	Wks
18 Jan 75	●	FOOTSEE *Pye Disco Demand DDS 111*	9	11

WIGAN'S OVATION *UK, male vocal / instrumental group (3 Singles: 19 Weeks)*

Date		Title / Label	Pos	Wks
15 Mar 75		SKIING IN THE SNOW *Spark SRL 1122*	12	10
28 Jun 75		PER-SO-NAL-LY *Spark SRL 1129*	38	6
29 Nov 75		SUPER LOVE *Spark SRL 1133*	41	3

WILCO *US, male vocal / instrumental group (5 Albums: 7 Weeks, 1 Single: 1 Week)*

Date		Title / Label	Pos	Wks
11 Jul 98		MERMAID AVENUE *Elektra 7559622042* [1]	34	2
20 Mar 99		SUMMERTEETH *Reprise 9362472822*	38	2
17 Apr 99		CAN'T STAND IT *Reprise W 475CD1*	67	1
10 Jun 00		MERMAID AVENUE – VOL. 2 *Elektra 7559625222* [1]	61	1
4 May 02		YANKEE HOTEL FOXTROT *Nonesuch 7559796692*	40	1
3 Jul 04		A GHOST IS BORN *Nonesuch 7559798092*	50	1

[1] Billy Bragg and Wilco

Jack WILD *UK, male actor / vocalist*

Date		Title / Label	Pos	Wks
2 May 70		SOME BEAUTIFUL *Capitol CL 15635*	46	2

14 December 1996	21 December 1996	28 December 1996	4 January 1997
A DIFFERENT BEAT Boyzone	KNOCKIN' ON HEAVEN'S DOOR / THROW THESE GUNS AWAY Dunblane	2 BECOME 1 Spice Girls	2 BECOME 1 Spice Girls
SPICE Spice Girls	SPICE Spice Girls	SPICE Spice Girls	SPICE Spice Girls

KEY: UK No.1 ★ UK Top 10 ● Still on chart + UK entry at No.1 ■ US No.1 ▲ UK million seller £ US million seller $
Singles re-entries are listed as (re), (2re), (3re)... which signifies that the hit re-entered the chart once, twice or three times...
Peak Position / Weeks

WILD CHERRY *US, male vocal (Robert Parissi) / instrumental group*

9 Oct 76 ● **PLAY THAT FUNKY MUSIC** *Epic EPC 4593* ▲ $ 7 11

WILD COLOUR *UK, male / female vocal / instrumental group*

14 Oct 95 **DREAMS** *Perfecto PERF 105CD* 25 2

WILD HORSES *UK, male vocal / instrumental group*

26 Apr 80 WILD HORSES *EMI EMC 3324* 38 4

WILD WEEKEND *UK, male vocal / instrumental group (2 Singles: 2 Weeks)*

29 Apr 89 **BREAKIN' UP** *Parlophone R 6204* 74 1
5 May 90 **WHO'S AFRAID OF THE BIG BAD LOVE?** *Parlophone R 6249* ...70 1

WILDCHILD *UK, male producer – Roger McKenzie, b. 1 Jan 1971, d. 25 Nov 1995 (5 Singles: 20 Weeks)*

22 Apr 95 **LEGENDS OF THE DARK BLACK PART** 2 *Hi-Life HICD 9* 34 3
21 Oct 95 **RENEGADE MASTER** (re-issue) *Hi-Life 5771312* 11 4
23 Nov 96 **JUMP TO MY BEAT** *Hi-Life 5757372* 30 2
17 Jan 98 ● **RENEGADE MASTER '98** *Hi-Life 5692792* 3 10
25 Apr 98 **BAD BOY** *Polydor 5716072* [1] 38 1

[1] Wildchild featuring Jomalski

Although titled differently, the first two hits are identical.

Eugene WILDE *US, male vocalist – Ron Broomfield (1 Album: 4 Weeks, 2 Singles: 15 Weeks)*

13 Oct 84 **GOTTA GET YOU HOME TONIGHT** *Fourth & Broadway BRW 15* ..18 9
8 Dec 84 EUGENE WILDE *Fourth & Broadway BRLP 502* 67 4
2 Feb 85 **PERSONALITY** *Fourth & Broadway BRW 18* 34 6

'Personality' was coupled with 'Let Her Feel It' by Simplicious.

Kim WILDE (221 Top 500)

Most charted British female vocalist in the 1980s, b. Kim Smith, 18 Nov 1960, London. Neither Kim nor her father, rock 'n' roll star Marty Wilde, managed a UK No.1, but Kim did top the US chart. She returned in 2003 with a major European hit, 'Any Place, Any Time, Anywhere' (a duet with Nena), and is now a celebrity gardener (10 Albums: 88 Weeks, 30 Singles: 194 Weeks)

21 Feb 81 ● **KIDS IN AMERICA** *RAK 327* 2 13
9 May 81 ● **CHEQUERED LOVE** *RAK 330* 4 9
11 Jul 81 ● KIM WILDE *RAK SRAK 544* 3 14
1 Aug 81 **WATER ON GLASS / BOYS** *RAK 334* 11 8
14 Nov 81 **CAMBODIA** *RAK 336* 12 12
17 Apr 82 **VIEW FROM A BRIDGE** *RAK 342* 16 7
22 May 82 SELECT *RAK SRAK 548* 19 11
16 Oct 82 **CHILD COME AWAY** *RAK 352* 43 4
30 Jul 83 **LOVE BLONDE** *RAK 360* 23 8
12 Nov 83 **DANCING IN THE DARK** *RAK 365* 67 2
26 Nov 83 CATCH AS CATCH CAN *RAK SRAK 165408* 90 1
13 Oct 84 **THE SECOND TIME** *MCA KIM 1* 29 6
17 Nov 84 TEASES AND DARES *MCA MCF 3250* 66 2
8 Dec 84 **THE TOUCH** *MCA KIM 2* 56 3
27 Apr 85 **RAGE TO LOVE** *MCA KIM 3* 19 8
18 May 85 THE VERY BEST OF KIM WILDE *RAK WILDE 1* 78 4
25 Oct 86 ● **YOU KEEP ME HANGIN' ON** *MCA KIM 4* ▲ 2 14
15 Nov 86 ANOTHER STEP *MCA MCF 3339* 73 5
4 Apr 87 ● **ANOTHER STEP (CLOSER TO YOU)** *MCA KIM 5* [1] 6 11
8 Aug 87 **SAY YOU REALLY WANT ME** *MCA KIM 6* 29 5
5 Dec 87 ● **ROCKIN' AROUND THE CHRISTMAS TREE** *10 TEN 2* [2] 3 7
14 May 88 **HEY MISTER HEARTACHE** *MCA KIM 7* 31 5
25 Jun 88 ● CLOSE *MCA MCG 6030* 8 38
16 Jul 88 ● **YOU CAME** *MCA KIM 8* 3 11
1 Oct 88 ● **NEVER TRUST A STRANGER** *MCA KIM 9* 7 9
3 Dec 88 ● **FOUR LETTER WORD** *MCA KIM 10* 6 12
4 Mar 89 **LOVE IN THE NATURAL WAY** *MCA KIM 11* 32 6
14 Apr 90 **IT'S HERE** *MCA KIM 12* 42 4
26 May 90 LOVE MOVES *MCA MCG 6088* 37 3
16 Jun 90 **TIME** *MCA KIM 13* 71 3
15 Dec 90 **I CAN'T SAY GOODBYE** *MCA KIM 14* 51 3
2 May 92 **LOVE IS HOLY** *MCA KIM 15* 16 6
30 May 92 LOVE IS *MCA MCAD 10625* 21 3
27 Jun 92 **HEART OVER MIND** *MCA KIM 16* 34 3
12 Sep 92 **WHO DO YOU THINK YOU ARE** *MCA KIM 17* 49 3
10 Jul 93 **IF I CAN'T HAVE YOU** *MCA KIMTD 18* 12 8
25 Sep 93 THE SINGLES COLLECTION 1981-1993 *MCA MCD 10921* 11 7
13 Nov 93 **IN MY LIFE** *MCA KIMTD 19* 54 1
14 Oct 95 **BREAKIN' AWAY** *MCA KIMTD 21* 43 2
10 Feb 96 **THIS I SWEAR** *MCA KIMTD 22* 46 1

[1] Kim Wilde and Junior [2] Mel [Mel Smith] and Kim

Another Step changed label number to MCA KIML 1 during its chart run.

Marty WILDE *UK, male vocalist – Reginald Smith (13 Singles: 117 Weeks)*

11 Jul 58 ● **ENDLESS SLEEP** *Philips PB 835* [1] 4 14
6 Mar 59 ● **DONNA** (re) *Philips PB 902* 3 18
5 Jun 59 ● **A TEENAGER IN LOVE** *Philips PB 926* 2 17
25 Sep 59 ● **SEA OF LOVE** *Philips PB 959* 3 12
11 Dec 59 ● **BAD BOY** *Philips PB 972* 7 8
10 Mar 60 **JOHNNY ROCCO** *Philips PB 1002* 30 4
19 May 60 **THE FIGHT** *Philips PB 1022* 47 1
22 Dec 60 **LITTLE GIRL** *Philips PB 1078* 16 9
26 Jan 61 ● **RUBBER BALL** *Philips PB 1101* 9 9
27 Jul 61 **HIDE AND SEEK** *Philips PB 1161* 47 2
9 Nov 61 **TOMORROW'S CLOWN** *Philips PB 1191* 33 5
24 May 62 **JEZEBEL** *Philips PB 1240* 19 11
25 Oct 62 **EVER SINCE YOU SAID GOODBYE** *Philips 326546 BF* 31 7

[1] Marty Wilde and The Wildcats

Matthew WILDER *US, male vocalist*

21 Jan 84 ● **BREAK MY STRIDE** *Epic A 3908* 4 11

The WILDHEARTS *UK, male vocal (David Walls) / instrumental group (5 Albums: 9 Weeks, 14 Singles: 32 Weeks)*

11 Sep 93 EARTH VS THE WILDHEARTS *East West 4509932871* 46 1
20 Nov 93 **TV TAN** *Bronze YZ 784CD* 53 2
19 Feb 94 **CAFFEINE BOMB** *Bronze YZ 794CD* 31 3
9 Jul 94 **SUCKERPUNCH** *Bronze YZ 828CD* 38 2
28 Jan 95 **IF LIFE IS LIKE A LOVE BANK I WANT AN OVERDRAFT / GEORDIE IN WONDERLAND** *East West YZ 874CD* 31 3
6 May 95 **I WANNA GO WHERE THE PEOPLE GO** *East West YZ 923CD* ...16 3
3 Jun 95 ● P.H.U.Q. *East West 0630104372* 6 4
29 Jul 95 **JUST IN LUST** *East West YZ 967CD* 28 2
20 Apr 96 **SICK OF DRUGS** *Round WILD 1CD* 14 3
1 Jun 96 FISHING FOR LUCKIES *Round 630148552* 16 2
29 Jun 96 **RED LIGHT – GREEN LIGHT (EP)** *Round WILD 2CD* 30 2
16 Aug 97 **ANTHEM** *Mushroom MUSH 6CD* 21 2
18 Oct 97 **URGE** *Mushroom MUSH 14CD* 26 2
8 Nov 97 ENDLESS NAMELESS *Mushroom MUSH 13CD* 41 1
12 Oct 02 **VANILLA RADIO** *Round / Snapper SMACD 048S* 26 2
1 Feb 03 **STORMY IN THE NORTH – KARMA IN THE SOUTH** *Round SMASCD 049* 17 2
24 May 03 **SO INTO YOU** *Gut / Round CDGUT 49* 22 2
6 Sep 03 THE WILDHEARTS MUST BE DESTROYED *Gut GUTCD 25* 54 1
15 Nov 03 **TOP OF THE WORLD** *Gut CDGUT 54* 26 2

Tracks on Red Light – Green Light (EP): Red Light – Green Light / Got It On Tuesday / Do Anything / The British All-American Homeboy Crowd.

WILEY *UK, male rapper / producer – Richard Cowie (1 Album: 1 Week, 2 Singles: 6 Weeks)*

17 Apr 04 **WOT DO U CALL IT?** *XL Recordings XLS 179CD* 31 4

	11 January 1997	18 January 1997	25 January 1997	1 February 1997
UK No.1 SINGLES	**2 BECOME 1** Spice Girls	**PROFESSIONAL WIDOW (IT'S GOT TO BE BIG) (Re-mix)** Tori Amos	**YOUR WOMAN** White Town	**BEETLEBUM** Blur
UK No.1 ALBUMS	**SPICE** Spice Girls	**SPICE** Spice Girls	**SPICE** Spice Girls	**EVITA (Film Soundtrack)** Madonna / Various

8 May 04	TREDDIN' ON THIN ICE *XL Recordings XLCD 178*	45	1
21 Aug 04	**PIES** *XL Recordings XLS 188CD*	**45**	2

Jonathan WILKES *UK, male vocalist*

17 Mar 01	**JUST ANOTHER DAY** *Innocent SINCD 25*	**24**	2

Colm WILKINSON *Ireland, male vocalist*

10 Jun 89	STAGE HEROES *RCA BL 74105*	27	6

Sue WILKINSON *UK, female vocalist*

2 Aug 80	**YOU GOTTA BE A HUSTLER IF YOU WANNA GET ON** *Cheapskate CHEAP 2*	**25**	8

WILL TO POWER *US, male / female vocal / instrumental duo – Bob Rosenberg and Suzi Carr (2 Singles: 18 Weeks)*

7 Jan 89 ●	**BABY I LOVE YOUR WAY – FREEBIRD** *Epic 6530947* ▲	6	9
22 Dec 90	**I'M NOT IN LOVE** *Epic 6565377*	29	9

Alyson WILLIAMS

US, female vocalist (1 Album: 21 Weeks, 4 Singles: 28 Weeks)

4 Mar 89	**SLEEP TALK** *Def Jam 654656 7*	**17**	9
25 Mar 89	RAW *Def Jam 463293 1*	29	21
6 May 89	**MY LOVE IS SO RAW** *Def Jam 654898 7* [1]	34	5
19 Aug 89 ●	**I NEED YOUR LOVIN'** *Def Jam 655143 7*	8	11
18 Nov 89	**I SECOND THAT EMOTION** *Def Jam 655456 7* [2]	**44**	3

[1] Alyson Williams featuring Nikki D [2] Alyson Williams with Chuck Stanley

Andy WILLIAMS (47 Top 500)

Leading MOR vocalist who hosted a top-rated 1960s TV series, b. 3 Dec 1928, Iowa, US. He left the noted family act The Williams Brothers in 1951 and had an enviable portfolio of smooth UK and US hit singles and albums in the 1950s and 1960s. He had a surprise 1999 re-entry with 'Music to Watch Girls By' following its use in a TV car commercial (29 Albums: 448 Weeks, 23 Singles: 238 Weeks)

19 Apr 57 ★	**BUTTERFLY** (re) *London HLA 8399* $	1	16
21 Jun 57	**I LIKE YOUR KIND OF LOVE** *London HLA 8437*	**16**	10
14 Jun 62	**STRANGER ON THE SHORE** *CBS AAG 103*	**30**	10
21 Mar 63 ●	**CAN'T GET USED TO LOSING YOU** *CBS AAG 138* $	2	18
27 Feb 64	**A FOOL NEVER LEARNS** *CBS AAG 182*	**40**	4
26 Jun 65 ●	ALMOST THERE *CBS BPG 62533*	4	46
7 Aug 65	CAN'T GET USED TO LOSING YOU *CBS BPG 62146*	16	1
16 Sep 65 ●	**ALMOST THERE** *CBS 201813*	2	17
24 Feb 66	**MAY EACH DAY** *CBS 202042*	**19**	8
19 Mar 66	MAY EACH DAY *CBS BPG 62658*	11	6
30 Apr 66	GREAT SONGS FROM MY FAIR LADY *CBS BPG 62430*	30	1
23 Jul 66	SHADOW OF YOUR SMILE *CBS 62633*	24	4
22 Sep 66	**IN THE ARMS OF LOVE** *CBS 202300*	33	7
4 May 67	**MUSIC TO WATCH GIRLS BY** *CBS 2675*	33	6
29 Jul 67	BORN FREE *CBS SBPG 63027*	22	11
2 Aug 67	**MORE AND MORE** *CBS 2886*	**45**	1
13 Mar 68 ●	**CAN'T TAKE MY EYES OFF YOU** *CBS 3298*	5	18
11 May 68 ★	LOVE ANDY *CBS 63167*	1	22
6 Jul 68 ●	HONEY *CBS 63311*	4	17
7 May 69	**HAPPY HEART** (re) *CBS 4062*	**19**	10
26 Jul 69	HAPPY HEART *CBS 63614*	22	9
27 Dec 69	GET TOGETHER WITH ANDY WILLIAMS *CBS 63800*	13	12
24 Jan 70	ANDY WILLIAMS' SOUND OF MUSIC *CBS 66214*	22	10
14 Mar 70 ●	**CAN'T HELP FALLING IN LOVE** *CBS 4818*	3	17
11 Apr 70 ★	GREATEST HITS *CBS 63920*	1	116
20 Jun 70 ●	CAN'T HELP FALLING IN LOVE *CBS 64067*	7	40
1 Aug 70	**IT'S SO EASY** (re) *CBS 5113*	13	14
21 Nov 70 ●	**HOME LOVIN' MAN** *CBS 5267*	7	12
5 Dec 70 ●	ANDY WILLIAMS SHOW *CBS 64127*	10	6
20 Mar 71 ●	**(WHERE DO I BEGIN) LOVE STORY** (re) *CBS 7020*	4	18
27 Mar 71 ★	HOME LOVIN' MAN *CBS 64286*	1	26
31 Jul 71	LOVE STORY *CBS 64467*	11	11
29 Apr 72	THE IMPOSSIBLE DREAM *CBS 67236*	26	3
29 Jul 72	LOVE THEME FROM 'THE GODFATHER' *CBS 64869*	11	16
5 Aug 72	**LOVE THEME FROM 'THE GODFATHER' (SPEAK SOFTLY LOVE)** (2re) *CBS 8166*	42	9
16 Dec 72	GREATEST HITS VOLUME 2 *CBS 65151*	23	10
8 Dec 73 ●	**SOLITAIRE** *CBS 1824*	4	18
22 Dec 73 ●	SOLITAIRE *CBS 65638*	3	26
18 May 74	**GETTING OVER YOU** *CBS 2181*	**35**	5
15 Jun 74 ●	THE WAY WE WERE *CBS 80152*	7	11
31 May 75	**YOU LAY SO EASY ON MY MIND** *CBS 3167*	32	7
11 Oct 75	THE OTHER SIDE OF ME *CBS 69152*	60	1
6 Mar 76	**THE OTHER SIDE OF ME** *CBS 3903*	**42**	3
28 Jan 78 ●	REFLECTIONS *CBS 10006*	2	17
27 Oct 84	GREATEST LOVE CLASSICS *EMI ANDY 1* [1]	22	10
7 Nov 92	THE BEST OF ANDY WILLIAMS *Dino DINCD 50*	51	3
27 Mar 99 ●	**MUSIC TO WATCH GIRLS BY** (re-issue) *Columbia 6671322*	9	6
10 Apr 99	IN THE LOUNGE WITH ... ANDY WILLIAMS *Columbia 4916182*	39	3
19 Feb 00	THE VERY BEST OF ANDY WILLIAMS *Columbia SONYTV 78CD*	27	7
29 Jun 02	**CAN'T TAKE MY EYES OFF YOU** (re-recording) *Columbia 6721052* [1]	23	4
6 Jul 02	THE ESSENTIAL ANDY WILLIAMS *Columbia 5084142*	32	2
9 Jul 05	MUSIC TO WATCH GIRLS BY – THE VERY BEST OF ANDY WILLIAMS *Columbia 5203422*	50	1

[1] Andy Williams and Denise Van Outen [1] Andy Williams and the Royal Philharmonic Orchestra

Andy and David WILLIAMS *US, male vocal duo*

24 Mar 73	**I DON'T KNOW WHY (I JUST DO)** *MCA MUS 1183*	**37**	5

Billy WILLIAMS *US, male vocalist, b. 28 Dec 1910, d. 17 Oct 1972*

2 Aug 57	**I'M GONNA SIT RIGHT DOWN AND WRITE MYSELF A LETTER** (re) *Vogue Coral Q 72266* $	22	9

Danny WILLIAMS *South Africa, male vocalist, b.7 Jan 1942, d.6 Dec 2005 (8 Singles: 74 Weeks)*

25 May 61	**WE WILL NEVER BE AS YOUNG AS THIS AGAIN** *HMV POP 839*	**44**	3
6 Jul 61	**THE MIRACLE OF YOU** *HMV POP 885*	**41**	8
2 Nov 61 ★	**MOON RIVER** *HMV POP 932*	1	19
18 Jan 62	**JEANNIE** *HMV POP 968*	**14**	14
12 Apr 62 ●	**THE WONDERFUL WORLD OF THE YOUNG** *HMV POP 1002*	8	13
5 Jul 62	**TEARS** *HMV POP 1035*	22	7
28 Feb 63	**MY OWN TRUE LOVE** *HMV POP 1112*	**45**	3
30 Jul 77	**DANCIN' EASY** *Ensign ENY 3*	**30**	7

Deniece WILLIAMS *US, female vocalist – Deniece Chandler (2 Albums: 23 Weeks, 6 Singles: 59 Weeks)*

2 Apr 77 ★	**FREE** *CBS 4978*	1	10
21 May 77	THIS IS NIECEY *CBS 81869*	31	12
30 Jul 77 ●	**THAT'S WHAT FRIENDS ARE FOR** *CBS 5432*	8	11
12 Nov 77	**BABY, BABY MY LOVE'S ALL FOR YOU** *CBS 5779*	32	5
25 Mar 78 ●	**TOO MUCH, TOO LITTLE, TOO LATE** *CBS 6164* [1] ▲ $	3	14
29 Jul 78	**YOU'RE ALL I NEED TO GET BY** *CBS 6483* [1]	**45**	6
26 Aug 78	THAT'S WHAT FRIENDS ARE FOR *CBS 86068* [1]	16	11
5 May 84 ●	**LET'S HEAR IT FOR THE BOY** (re) *CBS A 4319* ▲ $	2	13

[1] Johnny Mathis and Deniece Williams [1] Johnny Mathis and Deniece Williams

Diana WILLIAMS *US, female vocalist*

25 Jul 81	**TEDDY BEAR'S LAST RIDE** *Capitol CL 207*	**54**	3

Don WILLIAMS (490 Top 500)

Easy-on-the-ear country singer / songwriter and guitarist, b. 27 May 1939, Floyada, Texas. Member of Pozo-Seco Singers (1964-71), who as a soloist amassed 17 US country No.1s between 1974 and 1986 and was named Country Music Association Vocalist of the Year in 1978 (14 Albums: 136 Weeks, 2 Singles: 16 Weeks)

19 Jun 76	**I RECALL A GYPSY WOMAN** *ABC 4098*	13	10
10 Jul 76	GREATEST HITS VOLUME 1 *ABC ABCL 5147*	29	15
23 Oct 76	**YOU'RE MY BEST FRIEND** *ABC 4144*	**35**	6

8 February 1997	15 February 1997	22 February 1997	1 March 1997
AIN'T NOBODY LL Cool J	DISCOTHEQUE U2	DON'T SPEAK No Doubt	DON'T SPEAK No Doubt
GLOW Reef	WHITE ON BLONDE Texas	BLUR Blur	ATTACK OF THE GREY LANTERN Mansun

KEY: UK No.1 ★ UK Top 10 ● Still on chart + UK entry at No.1 ■ US No.1 ▲ UK million seller £ US million seller $
Singles re-entries are listed as (re), (2re), (3re)... which signifies that the hit re-entered the chart once, twice or three times...
Peak Position / Weeks

19 Feb 77 VISIONS *ABC ABCL 5200* 13 20
15 Oct 77 COUNTRY BOY *ABC ABCL 5233* 27 5
5 Aug 78 ● IMAGES *K-Tel NE 1033* 2 38
5 Aug 78 YOU'RE MY BEST FRIEND *ABC ABCD 5127* 58 1
4 Nov 78 EXPRESSIONS *ABC ABCL 5253* 28 8
22 Sep 79 NEW HORIZONS *K-Tel NE 1048* 29 12
15 Dec 79 PORTRAIT *MCA MCS 3045* 58 4
6 Sep 80 I BELIEVE IN YOU *MCA MCF 3077* 36 5
18 Jul 81 ESPECIALLY FOR YOU *MCA MCF 3114* 33 7
17 Apr 82 LISTEN TO THE RADIO *MCA MCF 3135* 69 3
23 Apr 83 YELLOW MOON *MCA MCF 3159* 52 1
15 Oct 83 LOVE STORIES *K-Tel NE 1252* 22 13
26 May 84 CAFE CAROLINA *MCA MCF 3225* 65 4

Freedom WILLIAMS *US, male rapper (4 Singles: 31 Weeks)*

15 Dec 90 ● **GONNA MAKE YOU SWEAT (EVERYBODY DANCE NOW)** *CBS 6564540* [1] ▲ $ 3 12
30 Mar 91 **HERE WE GO** *Columbia 6567537* [1] 20 7
6 Jul 91 ● **THINGS THAT MAKE YOU GO HMMM ...** *Columbia 6566907* [1] 4 11
5 Jun 93 **VOICE OF FREEDOM** *Columbia 6593342* 62 1

[1] C & C Music Factory (featuring Freedom Williams)

Geoffrey WILLIAMS *UK, male vocalist (4 Singles: 8 Weeks)*

11 Apr 92 **IT'S NOT A LOVE THING** *EMI EM 228* 63 2
22 Aug 92 **SUMMER BREEZE** *EMI EM 245* 56 3
18 Jan 97 **DRIVE** *Hands On CDHOR 11* 52 2
19 Apr 97 **SEX LIFE** *Hands On CDHOR 12* 71 1

Iris WILLIAMS *UK, female vocalist*

27 Oct 79 **HE WAS BEAUTIFUL (CAVATINA) (THE THEME FROM 'THE DEER HUNTER')** *Columbia DB 9070* 18 8
22 Dec 79 HE WAS BEAUTIFUL *Columbia SCX 6627* 69 4

John WILLIAMS
UK, male guitarist (7 Albums: 65 Weeks, 1 Single: 11 Weeks)

3 Oct 70 PLAYS SPANISH MUSIC *CBS 72860* 46 1
8 Feb 76 RODRIGO: CONCERTO DE ARANJUEZ *CBS 79369* [1] 20 9
7 Jan 78 BEST OF FRIENDS *RCA RS 1094* [2] 18 22
17 Jun 78 TRAVELLING *Cube HIFLY 27* 23 5
19 May 79 **CAVATINA** *Cube BUG 80* 13 11
30 Jun 79 ● BRIDGES *Lotus WH 5015* 5 22
4 Aug 79 CAVATINA *Cube HIFLY 32* 64 3
26 Oct 96 JOHN WILLIAMS PLAYS THE MOVIES *Sony Classical S2K 62784* 54 3

[1] John Williams with the English Chamber Orchestra conducted by Daniel Barenboim [2] Cleo Laine and John Williams

John WILLIAMS
US, male orchestra leader (7 Albums: 51 Weeks, 3 Singles: 15 Weeks)

18 Dec 82 **THEME FROM 'E.T.' (THE EXTRA-TERRESTRIAL)** *MCA 800* 17 10
25 Dec 82 E.T. – THE EXTRATERRESTRIAL (FILM SOUNDTRACK) *MCA MCF 3160* 47 10
31 Jul 93 JURASSIC PARK (FILM SOUNDTRACK) *MCA MCD 10859* 42 5
14 Aug 93 **THEME FROM 'JURASSIC PARK'** *MCA MCSTD 1927* 45 2
2 Apr 94 SCHINDLER'S LIST (FILM SOUNDTRACK) *MCA MCD 10969* 59 2
15 May 99 ● STAR WARS – THE PHANTOM MENACE (FILM SOUNDTRACK) *Sony Classical SK 61816* 8 17
10 Nov 01 HARRY POTTER AND THE PHILOSOPHER'S STONE (FILM SOUNDTRACK) *Atlantic 7567930865* 19 7
11 May 02 STAR WARS EPISODE II: ATTACK OF THE CLONES (FILM SOUNDTRACK) *Sony Classical SK 89932* 15 5
14 May 05 STAR WARS EPISODE III – REVENGE OF THE SITH (FILM SOUNDTRACK) *Sony Classical SK 94220* 16 5
4 Jun 05 **BATTLE OF THE HEROES – FROM STAR WARS REVENGE OF THE SITH** *Sony Classical 6759562* [1] 25 3

[1] John Williams / London Symphony Orchestra

All three Star Wars albums feature the London Symphony Orchestra performing music composed and conducted by John Williams. Star Wars Episode III – Revenge of the Sith includes a bonus DVD, Star Wars: A Musical Journey.

Kathryn WILLIAMS *UK, female vocalist / guitarist (2 Albums: 3 Weeks)*

15 Sep 01 LITTLE BLACK NUMBERS *East West 8573899242* 70 1
12 Oct 02 OLD LOW LIGHT *East West 0927475522* 56 2

Kenny WILLIAMS *US, male vocalist*

19 Nov 77 **(YOU'RE) FABULOUS BABE** *Decca FR 13731* 35 7

Larry WILLIAMS *US, male vocalist / pianist, b. 10 May 1935, d. 7 Jan 1980 (2 Singles: 18 Weeks)*

20 Sep 57 **SHORT FAT FANNIE** *London HLN 8472* $ 21 8
17 Jan 58 **BONY MORONIE** *London HLU 8532* 11 10

Lenny WILLIAMS *US, male vocalist (2 Singles: 7 Weeks)*

5 Nov 77 **SHOO DOO FU FU OOH!** *ABC 4194* 38 4
16 Sep 78 **YOU GOT ME BURNING** *ABC 4228* 67 3

Lucinda WILLIAMS *US, female vocalist / guitarist (2 Albums: 2 Weeks)*

16 Jun 01 ESSENCE *Lost Highway 1701972* 63 1
19 Apr 03 WORLD WITHOUT TEARS *Lost Highway 1703552* 48 1

Mason WILLIAMS *US, male guitarist*

28 Aug 68 ● **CLASSICAL GAS** *Warner Bros. WB 7190* $ 9 13

Maurice WILLIAMS and The ZODIACS *US, male vocal group*

5 Jan 61 **STAY** *Top Rank JAR 526* ▲ $ 14 9

Melanie WILLIAMS *UK, female vocalist (5 Singles: 21 Weeks)*

10 Apr 93 ● **AIN'T NO LOVE (AIN'T NO USE)** *Rob's CDROB 9* [1] 3 11
9 Apr 94 **ALL CRIED OUT** *Columbia 6601872* 60 2
11 Jun 94 **EVERYDAY THANG** *Columbia 6604712* 38 3
17 Sep 94 **NOT ENOUGH?** *Columbia 6607752* 65 1
18 Feb 95 **YOU ARE EVERYTHING** *Columbia 6611755* [2] 28 4

[1] Sub Sub featuring Melanie Williams [2] Melanie Williams and Joe Roberts

Robbie WILLIAMS 36 Top 500 (see also 1 GIANT LEAP) *Ex-Take That teen idol who became a multi-award-winning vocalist / songwriter and multi-millionaire after a UK record-breaking 2002 deal with EMI reportedly worth £80 million, b. 13 Feb 1974, Stoke-on-Trent, UK. This energetic and humorous showman has won more BRIT awards (15) than any other artist, including one for the best song from 25 years of the BRITs for 'Angels', amassed 23 solo Top 10 hits (including six No.1s) and attracted record-breaking crowds of 375,000 to Knebworth in 2003. Robbie was inducted into the UK Music Hall of Fame in 2004 and performed at the London Live 8 concert. Best-selling single: 'Angels' 867,999 (8 Albums: 436 Weeks, 24 Singles: 298 Weeks)*

10 Aug 96 ● **FREEDOM** (re) *Chrysalis CDFREE 1* 2 14
26 Apr 97 ● **OLD BEFORE I DIE** (2re) *Chrysalis CDCHS 5055* 2 11
26 Jul 97 ● **LAZY DAYS** *Chrysalis CDCHS 5063* 8 5
27 Sep 97 **SOUTH OF THE BORDER** *Chrysalis CDCHS 5068* 14 4
11 Oct 97 ★ LIFE THRU A LENS *Chrysalis CDCHR 6127* 1 123
13 Dec 97 ● **ANGELS** (4re) *Chrysalis CDCHS 5072* 4 27
28 Mar 98 ● **LET ME ENTERTAIN YOU** *Chrysalis CDCHS 5080* 3 12
19 Sep 98 ★ **MILLENNIUM** (re) *Chrysalis CDCHS 5099* ■ 1 21
7 Nov 98 ★ I'VE BEEN EXPECTING YOU *Chrysalis 4978372* ■ 1 98
12 Dec 98 ● **NO REGRETS** *Chrysalis CDCHS 5100* 4 13
27 Mar 99 ● **STRONG** *Chrysalis CDCHS 5107* 4 9

8 March 1997	15 March 1997	22 March 1997	29 March 1997
UK No.1 SINGLES			
DON'T SPEAK No Doubt	MAMA / WHO DO YOU THINK YOU ARE Spice Girls	MAMA / WHO DO YOU THINK YOU ARE Spice Girls	MAMA / WHO DO YOU THINK YOU ARE Spice Girls
UK No.1 ALBUMS			
SPICE Spice Girls	POP U2	SPICE Spice Girls	SPICE Spice Girls

20 Nov 99 ★ **IT'S ONLY US / SHE'S THE ONE** (re) *Chrysalis CDCHS 5112* ■ 1 20
12 Aug 00 ★ **ROCK DJ** (re) *Chrysalis CDCHS 5118* ■ 1 20
9 Sep 00 ★ SING WHEN YOU'RE WINNING *Chrysalis 5281252* ■ 1 62
21 Oct 00 ● **KIDS** (2re) *Chrysalis CHCHS 5119* [1] 2 19
23 Dec 00 ● **SUPREME** *Chrysalis CDCHS 5120* 4 10
21 Apr 01 ● **LET LOVE BE YOUR ENERGY** (re) *Chrysalis CDCHS 5124* 10 11
21 Jul 01 ★ **ETERNITY / THE ROAD TO MANDALAY** *Chrysalis CDCHS 5126* ■ 1 16
1 Dec 01 ★ SWING WHEN YOU'RE WINNING *Chrysalis 5368262* ■ 1 43
22 Dec 01 ★ **SOMETHIN' STUPID** *Chrysalis CDCHS 5132* [2] ■ 1 12
30 Nov 02 ★ ESCAPOLOGY *EMI 5439942* ■ 1 50
14 Dec 02 ● **FEEL** (re) *Chrysalis CDCHS 5150* 4 15
26 Apr 03 ● **COME UNDONE** *Chrysalis CDCHS 5151* 4 11
9 Aug 03 ● **SOMETHING BEAUTIFUL** *Chrysalis CDCHS 5152* 3 8
11 Oct 03 ● LIVE AT KNEBWORTH *Chrysalis 5946372* 2 21
15 Nov 03 ● **SEXED UP** (re) *Chrysalis CDCHS 5153* 10 10
16 Oct 04 ★ **RADIO** *Chrysalis CDCHSS 5156* ■ 1 8
30 Oct 04 ★ GREATEST HITS *Chrysalis 8668192* ■ ....1 30+
18 Dec 04 ● **MISUNDERSTOOD** *Chrysalis CDCHSS 5157* 8 8
15 Oct 05 ● **TRIPPING** *Chrysalis CDCHSS 5158* ....2 12+
5 Nov 05 ★ INTENSIVE CARE *Chrysalis 3418232* ■ ....1 9+
24 Dec 05 ● **ADVERTISING SPACE** *Chrysalis CDCHSS 5159* ....8 2+

[1] Robbie Williams / Kylie Minogue [2] Robbie Williams and Nicole Kidman

'Angels' re-entered the chart in Jan, Feb and Mar 1999 and again in Jan 2000. 'Millennium' re-entered in Jan 2000.

Vanessa WILLIAMS
US, female vocalist (1 Album: 4 Weeks, 7 Singles: 24 Weeks)

20 Aug 88 **THE RIGHT STUFF** *Wing WING 3* 71 1
25 Mar 89 **DREAMIN'** *Wing WING 4* 74 2
19 Aug 89 **THE RIGHT STUFF** (re-mix) *Wing WINR 3* 62 2
21 Mar 92 ● **SAVE THE BEST FOR LAST** *Polydor PO 192* ▲ 3 11
25 Apr 92 THE COMFORT ZONE *Polydor 5112672* 24 4
8 Apr 95 **THE SWEETEST DAYS** *Mercury MERCD 422* 41 2
8 Jul 95 **THE WAY THAT YOU LOVE** *Mercury MERCD 439* 52 1
18 Sep 95 **COLOURS OF THE WIND** *Walt Disney WD 7677CD* 21 5

Vesta WILLIAMS *US, female vocalist*

20 Dec 86 **ONCE BITTEN TWICE SHY** *A&M AM 362* 14 13

Wendell WILLIAMS *US, male rapper (2 Singles: 6 Weeks)*

6 Oct 90 **EVERYBODY (RAP)** *Deconstruction PB 44701* [1] 30 4
18 May 91 **SO GROOVY** *Deconstruction PB 44567* 74 2

[1] Criminal Element Orchestra and Wendell Williams

Wendy O WILLIAMS
(see also The PLASMATICS) *US, female vocalist, b. 28 May 1949, d. 6 Apr 1998*

30 Jun 84 W.O.W. *Music for Nations MFN 24* 100 1

Ann WILLIAMSON *UK, female vocalist (2 Albums: 13 Weeks)*

15 Feb 86 PRECIOUS MEMORIES *Emerald Gem ERTV 1* 16 9
6 Feb 88 COUNT YOUR BLESSINGS *Emerald Gem ERTV 2* 58 4

Sonny Boy WILLIAMSON
US, male vocalist / guitarist – Rice Miller, b. 5 Dec 1899, d. 25 May 1965

20 Jun 64 DOWN AND OUT BLUES *Pye NPL 28036* 20 1

Bruce WILLIS
US, male actor / vocalist (1 Album: 28 Weeks, 4 Singles: 30 Weeks)

7 Mar 87 ● **RESPECT YOURSELF** *Motown ZB 41117* 7 10
18 Apr 87 ● THE RETURN OF BRUNO *Motown ZL 72571* 4 28
30 May 87 ● **UNDER THE BOARDWALK** *Motown ZB 41349* 2 15
12 Sep 87 **SECRET AGENT MAN – JAMES BOND IS BACK** *Motown ZB 41437* 43 4
23 Jan 88 **COMIN' RIGHT UP** *Motown ZB 41453* 73 1

TOP 10
ON THE DAY DEN GAVE ANGIE A CHRISTMAS PRESENT SHE DIDN'T EXPECT

On Christmas Day 1986, as Dirty Den was passing an envelope containing divorce papers to his wife Angie, Jackie Wilson was the Christmas No.1. Both events proved to be record breakers. The EastEnders BBC broadcast proved to be the biggest audience ever for a TV drama with 30.15 million viewers, and 'Reet Petite' made the slowest journey to No.1 by any chart-topper, 29 years and 42 days after its chart debut.

LW	TW	
2	1	**REET PETITE** Jackie Wilson
1	2	**CARAVAN OF LOVE** The Housemartins
3	3	**THE FINAL COUNTDOWN** Europe
4	4	**OPEN YOUR HEART** Madonna
5	5	**SOMETIMES** Erasure
6	6	**THE RAIN** Oran 'Juice' Jones
10	7	**CRY WOLF** A-Ha
12	8	**IS THIS LOVE?** Alison Moyet
7	9	**SHAKE YOU DOWN** Gregory Abbott
9	10	**LIVIN' ON A PRAYER** Bon Jovi

Angie and Den

Jackie Wilson

5 April 1997	12 April 1997	19 April 1997	26 April 1997
BLOCK ROCKIN' BEATS The Chemical Brothers	**I BELIEVE I CAN FLY** R Kelly	**I BELIEVE I CAN FLY** R Kelly	**I BELIEVE I CAN FLY** R Kelly
SPICE Spice Girls	**SPICE** Spice Girls	**DIG YOUR OWN HOLE** The Chemical Brothers	**ULTRA** Depeche Mode

KEY UK No.1 ★★ UK Top 10 ●● Still on chart + + UK entry at No.1 ■■ US No.1 ▲▲ UK million seller £ US million seller $
Singles re-entries are listed as (re), (2re), (3re)... which signifies that the hit re-entered the chart once, twice or three times...
Peak Position / Weeks

Viola WILLS *US, female vocalist (2 Singles: 16 Weeks)*

6 Oct 79 ● **GONNA GET ALONG WITHOUT YOU NOW** *Ariola / Hansa AHA 546* 8 10
15 Mar 86 **BOTH SIDES NOW / DARE TO DREAM** *Streetwave KHAN 66* 35 6

Maria WILLSON *UK, female vocalist (2 Singles: 3 Weeks)*

9 Aug 03 **CHOOZA LOOZA** *Telstar CDSTAS 3343* 29 2
1 Nov 03 **MR ALIBI** *Telstar CDSTAS 3355* 43 1

Al WILSON *US, male vocalist*

23 Aug 75 **THE SNAKE** *Bell 1436* 41 5

Brian WILSON (see also The BEACH BOYS) *US, male vocalist (4 Albums: 8 Weeks, 3 Singles: 5 Weeks)*

16 Sep 95 I JUST WASN'T MADE FOR THESE TIMES *MCA MCD 11270* 59 1
27 Jun 98 IMAGINATION *Giant 74321573032* 30 2
3 Jul 04 GETTIN IN OVER MY HEAD *Rhino 8122764712* 53 1
2 Oct 04 **WONDERFUL** *Nonesuch / Must Destroy MDA 001X* 29 2
9 Oct 04 ● SMILE *East West 7559798462* 7 4
18 Dec 04 **GOOD VIBRATIONS** *Nonesuch NS 001CD* 30 2
17 Dec 05 **WHAT I REALLY WANT FOR CHRISTMAS** *Arista 82876764802* .. 66 1

Dooley WILSON *US, male vocalist, b. Arthur Wilson, 3 Apr 1894, d. 30 May 1953*

3 Dec 77 **AS TIME GOES BY** *United Artists UP 36331* 15 9

Disc has credit: 'With the voices of Humphrey Bogart and Ingrid Bergman'.

Gretchen WILSON *US, female vocalist*

4 Sep 04 **REDNECK WOMAN** *Epic 6751732* 42 2
11 Sep 04 HERE FOR THE PARTY *Epic 5174312* 60 1

Jackie WILSON *US, male vocalist, b. 9 Jun 1934, d. 21 Jan 1984 (10 Singles: 97 Weeks)*

15 Nov 57 ● **REET PETITE (THE SWEETEST GIRL IN TOWN)** *Coral Q 72290* 6 14
14 Mar 58 **TO BE LOVED** (2re) *Coral Q 72306* 23 8
15 Sep 60 **(YOU WERE MADE FOR) ALL MY LOVE** (re) *Coral Q 72407* 33 7
22 Dec 60 **ALONE AT LAST** *Coral Q 72412* 50 1
14 May 69 **(YOUR LOVE KEEPS LIFTING ME) HIGHER AND HIGHER** *MCA BAG 2* 11 11
29 Jul 72 ● **I GET THE SWEETEST FEELING** *MCA MU 1160* 9 13
3 May 75 **I GET THE SWEETEST FEELING / (YOUR LOVE KEEPS LIFTING ME) HIGHER AND HIGHER** (re-issues) *Brunswick BR 18* 25 8
29 Nov 86 ★ **REET PETITE (THE SWEETEST GIRL IN TOWN)** (re-issue) *SMP SKM 3* 1 17
28 Feb 87 ● **I GET THE SWEETEST FEELING** (2nd re-issue) *SMP SKM 1* 3 11
4 Jul 87 **(YOUR LOVE KEEPS LIFTING ME) HIGHER AND HIGHER** (2nd re-issue) *SMP SKM 10* 15 7

'(Your Love Keeps Lifting Me) Higher and Higher', on Brunswick, was not listed with 'I Get the Sweetest Feeling' until 17 May 1975.

Mari WILSON *UK, female vocalist (1 Album: 9 Weeks, 6 Singles: 34 Weeks)*

6 Mar 82 **BEAT THE BEAT** *Compact PINK 2* 59 3
8 May 82 **BABY IT'S TRUE** *Compact PINK 3* 42 6
11 Sep 82 ● **JUST WHAT I ALWAYS WANTED** *Compact PINK 4* 8 10
13 Nov 82 **(BEWARE) BOYFRIEND** *Compact PINK 5* 51 4
26 Feb 83 SHOW PEOPLE *Compact COMP 2* [1] 24 9
19 Mar 83 **CRY ME A RIVER** *Compact PINK 6* 27 7
11 Jun 83 **WONDERFUL** *Compact PINK 7* [1] 47 4

[1] Mari Wilson and The Wilsations [1] Mari Wilson and The Wilsations

Meri WILSON *US, female vocalist, b. 15 Jun 1949, d. 28 Dec 2002*

27 Aug 77 ● **TELEPHONE MAN** *Pye International 7N 25747* $ 6 10

Mike 'Hitman' WILSON *US, male producer*

22 Sep 90 **ANOTHER SLEEPLESS NIGHT** *Arista 113506* 74 1

Tom WILSON *UK, male producer (2 Singles: 4 Weeks)*

2 Dec 95 **TECHNOCAT** *Pukka CDPUKKA 4* [1] 33 3
16 Mar 96 **LET YOUR BODY GO** *Clubscene DCSRT 050* 60 1

[1] Technocat featuring Tom Wilson

Victoria WILSON JAMES *US, female vocalist*

9 Aug 97 **REACH 4 THE MELODY** *Sony S3 VWJCD 1* 72 1

WILSON PHILLIPS *US, female vocal group (2 Albums: 38 Weeks, 6 Singles: 33 Weeks)*

26 May 90 ● **HOLD ON** *SBK SBK 6* ▲ 6 12
30 Jun 90 ● WILSON PHILLIPS *SBK SBKLP 5* 7 32
18 Aug 90 **RELEASE ME** *SBK SBK 11* ▲ 36 5
10 Nov 90 **IMPULSIVE** *SBK SBK 16* 42 3
11 May 91 **YOU'RE IN LOVE** *SBK SBK 25* ▲ 29 5
23 May 92 **YOU WON'T SEE ME CRY** *SBK SBK 34* 18 5
13 Jun 92 ● SHADOWS AND LIGHT *SBK SBKCD 18* 6 6
22 Aug 92 **GIVE IT UP** *SBK SBK 36* 36 3

WILT *Ireland, male vocal / instrumental group (3 Singles: 3 Weeks)*

8 Apr 00 **RADIO DISCO** *Mushroom MUSH 71CDS* 56 1
8 Jul 00 **OPEN ARMS** *Mushroom MUSH 75CDS* 59 1
13 Jul 02 **DISTORTION** *Mushroom MUSH 103CDS* 66 1

WIMBLEDON CHORAL SOCIETY *UK, choral group (2 Singles: 8 Weeks)*

4 Jul 98 **WORLD CUP '98 – PAVANE** *Telstar CDSTAS 2979* 20 5
12 Dec 98 **IF – READ TO FAURE'S 'PAVANE'** *BBC Worldwide WMSS 60062* [1] 45 3

[1] Des Lynam featuring Wimbledon Choral Society

WIN *UK, male vocal / instrumental group*

4 Apr 87 **SUPER POPOID GROOVE** *Swamplands LON 128* 63 3
25 Apr 87 UH! TEARS BABY *Swamplands LONLP 31* 51 1

The WINANS *US, male vocal group*

30 Nov 85 **LET MY PEOPLE GO (PART 1)** *Qwest W 8874* 71 1

Mario WINANS (see also P DIDDY) *US, male vocalist (1 Album: 20 Weeks, 4 Singles: 21 Weeks)*

20 Nov 99 **BEST FRIEND** *Puff Daddy / Arista 74321712312* [1] 24 4
1 May 04 ● HURT NO MORE *Bad Boy 9862494* 3 20
5 Jun 04 **I DON'T WANNA KNOW** (import) *Universal 9862372 PMI* [2] 71 1
12 Jun 04 ★ **I DON'T WANNA KNOW** *Bad Boy MCSTD 40369* [2] ■ 1 14
11 Sep 04 **NEVER REALLY WAS** *Bad Boy MCSTD 40372* [3] 44 2

[1] Puff Daddy featuring Mario Winans [2] Mario Winans featuring Enya & P Diddy [3] Mario Winans featuring Lil' Flip

WINDJAMMER *US, male vocal / instrumental group*

30 Jun 84 **TOSSING AND TURNING** *MCA MCA 897* 18 12
25 Aug 84 WINDJAMMER II *MCA MCF 3231* 82 1

Barbara WINDSOR *UK, female actor / vocalist*

3 Apr 99 YOU'VE GOT A FRIEND *Telstar TTVCD 3034* 45 2
24 Apr 99 **THE MORE I SEE YOU** *Telstar CDSTAS 3049* [1] 46 2

[1] Barbara Wilson and Mike Reid

	3 May 1997	10 May 1997	17 May 1997	24 May 1997
UK No.1 SINGLES	BLOOD ON THE DANCE FLOOR Michael Jackson	LOVE WON'T WAIT Gary Barlow	YOU'RE NOT ALONE (Re-issue) Olive	YOU'RE NOT ALONE (Re-issue) Olive
UK No.1 ALBUMS	TELLIN' STORIES The Charlatans	TELLIN' STORIES The Charlatans	SPICE Spice Girls	BLOOD ON THE DANCE FLOOR - HISTORY IN THE MIX Michael Jackson

Amy WINEHOUSE
UK, female vocalist (1 Album: 21 Weeks, 4 Singles: 4 Weeks)

18 Oct 03 **STRONGER THAN ME** *Island CID 830* 71 1
1 Nov 03 **FRANK** *Island 9812918* 13 21
24 Jan 04 **TAKE THE BOX** *Island CID 840* 57 1
17 Apr 04 **IN MY BED / YOU SENT ME FLYING** *Island CID 852* 60 1
4 Sep 04 **PUMPS / HELP YOURSELF** *Island CID 865* 65 1

WING AND A PRAYER FIFE AND DRUM CORPS
US, male / female vocal / instrumental group

24 Jan 76 **BABY FACE** *Atlantic K 10705* 12 7

WINGER *US, male vocal / instrumental group*

19 Jan 91 **MILES AWAY** *Atlantic A 7802* 56 3

Pete WINGFIELD *UK, male vocalist / keyboard player*

28 Jun 75 ● **EIGHTEEN WITH A BULLET** *Island WIP 6231* 7 7

Josh WINK (see also SIZE 9) *US, male producer – Joshua Winkelman (1 Album: 1 Week, 5 Singles: 29 Weeks)*

6 May 95 **DON'T LAUGH** *XL XLS 62CD* [1] 38 2
21 Oct 95 ● **HIGHER STATE OF CONSCIOUSNESS** (re) *Manifesto FESCD 3* 8 12
2 Mar 96 **HYPNOTIZIN'** *XL XLS 71CD* [1] 35 2
27 Jul 96 ● **HIGHER STATE OF CONSCIOUSNESS** (re-mix) *Manifesto FESCD 9* [2] 7 10
21 Sep 96 **LEFT ABOVE THE CLOUDS** *XL Recordings XLCD 119* 43 1
12 Aug 00 **HOW'S YOUR EVENING SO FAR** *ffrr FCD 384* [3] 23 3

[1] Winx [2] Wink [3] Josh Wink and Lil' Louis

Kate WINSLET *UK, female actor / vocalist*

8 Dec 01 ● **WHAT IF** *EMI / Liberty CDKATE 001* 6 14

Edgar WINTER GROUP *US, male instrumental group*

26 May 73 **FRANKENSTEIN** *Epic EPC 1440* ▲ $ 18 9

Johnny WINTER
US, male vocal / instrumental group (3 Albums: 12 Weeks)

16 May 70 **SECOND WINTER** *CBS 66321* 59 2
31 Oct 70 **JOHNNY WINTER AND ...** *CBS 64117* 29 4
15 May 71 **JOHNNY WINTER AND LIVE** *CBS 64289* 20 6

Ruby WINTERS
US, female vocalist (2 Albums: 17 Weeks, 4 Singles: 35 Weeks)

5 Nov 77 ● **I WILL!** *Creole CR 141* 4 13
29 Apr 78 **COME TO ME!** *Creole CR 153* 11 12
10 Jun 78 **RUBY WINTERS** *Creole CRLP 512* 27 7
26 Aug 78 **I WON'T MENTION IT AGAIN** *Creole CR 160* 45 5
16 Jun 79 **BABY LAY DOWN** *Creole CR 171* 43 5
23 Jun 79 **SONGBIRD** *K-Tel NE 1045* 31 10

Steve WINWOOD 476 Top 500
R&B vocalist / keyboard player, b. 12 May 1948, Birmingham, UK, whose prodigious talent in The Spencer Davis Group led to supergroup Blind Faith in 1969 and the more enduring Traffic from 1967 to 1974. This Grammy winner became one of the most successful acts Stateside in the late 1980s (8 Albums: 122 Weeks, 7 Singles: 33 Weeks)

9 Jul 77 **STEVE WINWOOD** *Island ILPS 9494* 12 9
10 Jan 81 **ARC OF A DIVER** *Island ILPS 9576* 13 20
17 Jan 81 **WHILE YOU SEE A CHANCE** *Island WIP 6655* 45 5
14 Aug 82 ● **TALKING BACK TO THE NIGHT** *Island ILPS 9777* 6 13
9 Oct 82 **VALERIE** *Island WIP 6818* 51 4
28 Jun 86 **HIGHER LOVE** *Island IS 288* ▲ 13 9
12 Jul 86 ● **BACK IN THE HIGH LIFE** *Island ILPS 9844* 8 42
13 Sep 86 **FREEDOM OVERSPILL** *Island IS 294* 69 1
24 Jan 87 **BACK IN THE HIGH LIFE AGAIN** *Island IS 303* 53 2
19 Sep 87 **VALERIE** (re-mix) *Island IS 336* 19 8
7 Nov 87 **CHRONICLES** *Island SSW 1* 12 17
11 Jun 88 **ROLL WITH IT** *Virgin VS 1085* ▲ 53 4
2 Jul 88 ● **ROLL WITH IT** *Virgin V 2532* ▲ 4 16
17 Nov 90 **REFUGEES OF THE HEART** *Virgin V 2650* 26 3
14 Jun 97 **JUNCTION SEVEN** *Virgin CDV 2832* 32 2

WIRE
UK, male vocal / instrumental group (3 Albums: 3 Weeks, 2 Singles: 4 Weeks)

7 Oct 78 **CHAIRS MISSING** *Harvest SHSP 4093* 48 1
27 Jan 79 **OUTDOOR MINER** *Harvest HAR 5172* 51 3
13 Oct 79 **154** *Harvest SHSP 4105* 39 1
9 May 87 **THE IDEAL COPY** *Mute STUMM 42* 87 1
13 May 89 **EARDRUM BUZZ** *Mute MUTE 87* 68 1

WIRED *Holland / Finland, male production / instrumental duo*

20 Feb 99 **TRANSONIC** *Future Groove CDFGR 001* 73 1

WIRELESS *UK, male vocal / instrumental group (2 Singles: 2 Weeks)*

28 Jun 97 **I NEED YOU** *Chrysalis CDCHS 5059* 68 1
7 Feb 98 **IN LOVE WITH THE FAMILIAR** *Chrysalis CDCHS 5075* 69 1

Norman WISDOM *UK, male actor / vocalist (2 Singles: 20 Weeks)*

19 Feb 54 ● **DON'T LAUGH AT ME ('CAUSE I'M A FOOL)** *Columbia DB 3133* 3 15
15 Mar 57 **THE WISDOM OF A FOOL** *Columbia DB 3903* 13 5

WISD'ME *Italy, male / female production / vocal group*

11 Mar 00 **OFF THE WALL** *Positiva CDTIV 125* 33 2

The WISEGUYS (see also DJ TOUCHÉ)
UK, male DJ / producer – Theo Keating (4 Singles: 13 Weeks)

6 Jun 98 **OOH LA LA** *Wall of Sound WALLD 038* 55 1
12 Sep 98 **START THE COMMOTION** *Wall of Sound WALLD 044* 66 1
5 Jun 99 ● **OOH LA LA** (re-issue) *Wall of Sound WALLD 038X* 2 10
11 Sep 99 **START THE COMMOTION** (re-issue) *Wall of Sound WALLD 059* 47 1

WISHBONE ASH
UK, male vocal / instrumental group (13 Albums: 76 Weeks)

23 Jan 71 **WISHBONE ASH** *MCA MKPS 2014* 29 3
9 Oct 71 **PILGRIMAGE** *MCA MDKS 8004* 14 9
20 May 72 ● **ARGUS** *MCA MDKS 8006* 3 20
26 May 73 **WISHBONE FOUR** *MCA MDKS 8011* 12 10
30 Nov 74 **THERE'S THE RUB** *MCA MCF 2585* 16 5
3 Apr 76 **LOCKED IN** *MCA MCF 2750* 36 2
27 Nov 76 **NEW ENGLAND** *MCA MCG 3523* 22 3
29 Oct 77 **FRONT PAGE NEWS** *MCA MCG 3524* 31 4
28 Oct 78 **NO SMOKE WITHOUT FIRE** *MCA MCG 3528* 43 3
2 Feb 80 **JUST TESTING** *MCA MCF 3052* 41 4
1 Nov 80 **LIVE DATES II** *MCA MCG 4012* 40 3
25 Apr 81 **NUMBER THE BRAVE** *MCA MCF 3103* 61 5
16 Oct 82 **BOTH BARRELS BURNING** *A&M ASH 1* 22 5

Bill WITHERS (see also Grover WASHINGTON Jr)
US, male vocalist / guitarist (3 Albums: 10 Weeks, 4 Singles: 29 Weeks)

12 Aug 72 **LEAN ON ME** *A&M AMS 7004* ▲ $ 18 9
14 Jan 78 ● **LOVELY DAY** *CBS 5773* 7 8
11 Feb 78 **MENAGERIE** *CBS 82265* 27 5
25 May 85 **OH YEAH!** *CBS A 6154* 60 3
15 Jun 85 **WATCHING YOU WATCHING ME** *CBS 26200* 60 1
10 Sep 88 ● **LOVELY DAY** (re-mix) *CBS 6530017* 4 9
17 Sep 88 **GREATEST HITS** *CBS 32343* 90 4

31 May 1997	7 June 1997	14 June 1997	21 June 1997
I WANNA BE THE ONLY ONE Eternal featuring BeBe Winans	MMMBOP Hanson	MMMBOP Hanson	MMMBOP Hanson
BLOOD ON THE DANCE FLOOR - HISTORY IN THE MIX Michael Jackson	OPEN ROAD Gary Barlow	WU-TANG FOREVER Wu-Tang Clan	MIDDLE OF NOWHERE Hanson

KEY		Peak Position	Weeks
	UK No.1 ★★ UK Top 10 ●● Still on chart ++ UK entry at No.1 ■■ US No.1 ▲▲ UK million seller £ US million seller $ Singles re-entries are listed as (re), (2re), (3re)... which signifies that the hit re-entered the chart once, twice or three times...		

WITNESS

UK, male vocal / instrumental group (2 Albums: 2 Weeks, 2 Singles: 2 Weeks)

13 Mar 99 **SCARS** *Island CID 740* ... 71 1
19 Jun 99 **AUDITION** *Island CID 749* ... 71 1
24 Jul 99 BEFORE THE CALM *Island CID 8084* ... 59 1
4 Aug 01 UNDER A SUN *Island CID 8107* ... 62 1

WIZZARD

UK, male vocal / instrumental group – leader Roy Wood (2 Albums: 11 Weeks, 8 Singles: 77 Weeks)

9 Dec 72 ● **BALL PARK INCIDENT** *Harvest HAR 5062* ... 6 12
21 Apr 73 ★ **SEE MY BABY JIVE** *Harvest HAR 5070* [1] ... 1 17
19 May 73 WIZZARD BREW *Harvest SHSP 4025* ... 29 7
1 Sep 73 ★ **ANGEL FINGERS (A TEEN BALLAD)** *Harvest HAR 5076* [2] ... 1 10
8 Dec 73 ● **I WISH IT COULD BE CHRISTMAS EVERYDAY** *Harvest HAR 5079* [3] ... 4 9
27 Apr 74 ● **ROCK 'N' ROLL WINTER (LOONY'S TUNE)** *Warner Bros. K 16497* ... 6 7
10 Aug 74 **THIS IS THE STORY OF MY LOVE (BABY)** *Warner Bros. K 16434* ... 34 4
17 Aug 74 INTRODUCING EDDY AND THE FALCONS *Warner Bros. K 52029* ... 19 4
21 Dec 74 ● **ARE YOU READY TO ROCK** *Warner Bros. K 16357* ... 8 10
19 Dec 81 **I WISH IT COULD BE CHRISTMAS EVERYDAY** (re) (re-issue) *Harvest HAR 5173* [3] ... 23 8

[1] Vocal backing by The Suedettes [2] Vocal backing: The Suedettes and the Bleach Boys [3] Wizzard featuring vocal backing by The Suedettes plus The Stockland Green Bilateral School First Year Choir with additional noises by Miss Snob and Class 3C

The 'I Wish It Could Be Christmas Everyday' re-issue reached No.41 in Dec 1981 before re-entering and peaking at No.23 in Dec 1984.

Jah WOBBLE'S INVADERS of the HEART

UK, male vocalist / multi-instrumentalist – John Wardle (2 Albums: 6 Weeks, 3 Singles: 10 Weeks)

1 Feb 92 **VISIONS OF YOU** *Oval OVAL 103* ... 35 5
30 Apr 94 **BECOMING MORE LIKE GOD** *Island CID 571* ... 36 2
28 May 94 TAKE ME TO GOD *Island CID 8017* ... 13 5
25 Jun 94 **THE SUN DOES RISE** *Island CIDX 587* ... 41 3
14 Oct 95 SPINNER *All Saints ASCD 023* [1] ... 71 1

[1] Brian Eno and Jah Wobble

First hit features the uncredited vocals of Sinead O'Connor.

Terry WOGAN

Ireland, male TV / radio presenter / vocalist

7 Jan 78 **THE FLORAL DANCE** *Philips 6006 592* ... 21 5

Patrick WOLF NEW

Ireland, male vocalist

12 Feb 05 **THE LIBERTINE** *Tomlab TOM 46* ... 67 1

WOLFGANG PRESS

UK, male vocal / instrumental duo

4 Feb 95 FUNKY LITTLE DEMONS *4AD CADD 4016CD* ... 75 1

WOLFMAN

UK, male vocalist / guitarist – Peter Wolfe (3 Singles: 8 Weeks)

24 Apr 04 ● **FOR LOVERS** *Rough Trade RTRADSCD 177* [1] ... 7 6
11 Dec 04 **NAPOLEON** *Beyond Bedlam BEBAD 001CDS* ... 44 1
4 Jun 05 **ICE CREAM GUERILLA** *Beyond Bedlam BEBAD 002CDS* ... 60 1

[1] Wolfman featuring Peter Doherty

WOLFSBANE

UK, male vocal / instrumental group (3 Albums: 3 Weeks, 1 Single: 1 Week)

5 Aug 89 LIVE FAST DIE FAST *Def American 838486 1* ... 48 1
20 Oct 90 ALL HELL'S BREAKING LOOSE ... *Def American 8469671* ... 48 1
5 Oct 91 **EZY** *Def American DEFA 11* ... 68 1
19 Oct 91 DOWN FALL THE GOOD GUYS *Def American 5104131* ... 53 1

WOMACK and WOMACK

US, male / female vocal duo – Linda and Cecil Womack (3 Albums: 52 Weeks, 7 Singles: 51 Weeks)

21 Apr 84 LOVE WARS *Elektra 960293* ... 45 13
28 Apr 84 **LOVE WARS** *Elektra E 9799* ... 14 10
30 Jun 84 **BABY I'M SCARED OF YOU** *Elektra E 9733* ... 72 2
22 Jun 85 RADIO M.U.S.I.C. MAN *Elektra EKT 6* ... 56 2
6 Dec 86 **SOUL LOVE – SOUL MAN** *Manhattan MT 16* ... 58 6
6 Aug 88 ● **TEARDROPS** *Fourth & Broadway BRW 101* ... 3 17
27 Aug 88 ● CONSCIENCE *Fourth & Broadway BRLP 519* ... 4 37
12 Nov 88 **LIFE'S JUST A BALLGAME** *Fourth & Broadway BRW 116* ... 32 5
25 Feb 89 **CELEBRATE THE WORLD** *Fourth & Broadway BRW 125* ... 19 8
5 Feb 94 **SECRET STAR** *Warner Bros. W 0222CD* [1] ... 46 3

[1] House of Zekkariyas aka Womack and Womack

Bobby WOMACK (see also Wilton FELDER)

US, male vocalist / guitarist (2 Albums: 15 Weeks, 7 Singles: 22 Weeks)

28 Apr 84 THE POET II *Motown ZL 72205* ... 31 8
16 Jun 84 **TELL ME WHY** *Motown TMG 1339* ... 60 3
28 Sep 85 SO MANY RIVERS *MCA MCF 3282* ... 28 7
5 Oct 85 **I WISH HE DIDN'T TRUST ME SO MUCH** *MCA MCA 994* ... 64 2
26 Sep 87 **SO THE STORY GOES** *Chrysalis LIB 3* [1] ... 34 8
7 Nov 87 **LIVING IN A BOX** *MCA MCA 1210* ... 70 2
3 Apr 93 **I'M BACK FOR MORE** *Dome CDDOME 1002* [2] ... 27 5
13 May 95 **IT'S A MAN'S MAN'S MAN'S WORLD** *Pulse 8 CDLOSE 89* [3] 73 1
19 Jun 04 **CALIFORNIA DREAMIN'** *EMI WOMACK 001* ... 59 1

[1] Living in a Box featuring Bobby Womack [2] Lulu and Bobby Womack [3] Jeanie Tracy and Bobby Womack

Lee Ann WOMACK

US, female vocalist

9 Jun 01 **I HOPE YOU DANCE** *MCA Nashville MCSTD 40254* $ ... 40 2

The WOMBLES

468 Top 500 *Furriest (and possibly the tidiest) act in the Top 500 are natives of Wimbledon Common, London, and come under the musical guidance of songwriter and producer Mike Batt, b. 6 Feb 1950, Southampton, UK (5 Albums: 58 Weeks, 11 Singles: 98 Weeks)*

26 Jan 74 ● **THE WOMBLING SONG** *CBS 1794* ... 4 23
2 Mar 74 WOMBLING SONGS *CBS 65803* ... 19 17
6 Apr 74 ● **REMEMBER YOU'RE A WOMBLE** *CBS 2241* ... 3 16
22 Jun 74 ● **BANANA ROCK** *CBS 2465* ... 9 13
13 Jul 74 REMEMBER YOU'RE A WOMBLE *CBS 80191* ... 18 31
12 Oct 74 **MINUETTO ALLEGRETTO** *CBS 2710* ... 16 9
7 Dec 74 ● **WOMBLING MERRY CHRISTMAS** *CBS 2842* ... 2 8
21 Dec 74 KEEP ON WOMBLING *CBS 80526* ... 17 6
10 May 75 **WOMBLING WHITE TIE AND TAILS (FOXTROT)** *CBS 3266* ... 22 7
9 Aug 75 **SUPER WOMBLE** *CBS 3480* ... 20 6
13 Dec 75 **LET'S WOMBLE TO THE PARTY TONIGHT** *CBS 3794* ... 34 5
8 Jan 77 20 WOMBLING GREATS *Warwick PR 5022* ... 29 1
21 Mar 98 **REMEMBER YOU'RE A WOMBLE** (re-issue) *Columbia 6656202* 13 5
18 Apr 98 THE BEST WOMBLES ALBUM SO FAR – VOLUME 1 *Columbia 4895622* ... 26 3
13 Jun 98 **THE WOMBLING SONG (UNDERGROUND OVERGROUND)** (re-issue) *Columbia 6660412* ... 27 3
30 Dec 00 **I WISH IT COULD BE A WOMBLING MERRY CHRISTMAS EVERYDAY** *Dramatico DRAMCDS 0001* [1] ... 22 3

[1] The Wombles with Roy Wood

28 June 1997	5 July 1997	12 July 1997	19 July 1997
UK No.1 SINGLES			
I'LL BE MISSING YOU Puff Daddy and Faith Evans featuring 112	**I'LL BE MISSING YOU** Puff Daddy and Faith Evans featuring 112	**I'LL BE MISSING YOU** Puff Daddy and Faith Evans featuring 112	**D'YOU KNOW WHAT I MEAN?** Oasis
UK No.1 ALBUMS			
OK COMPUTER Radiohead	**OK COMPUTER** Radiohead	**THE FAT OF THE LAND** The Prodigy	**THE FAT OF THE LAND** The Prodigy

Stevie WONDER (29 Top 500)

One of the most successful singer / songwriters of all time, b. Steveland Judkins, 13 May 1950, Michigan, US. The youngest artist to top the US singles and albums charts (aged 13) recorded Motown's biggest UK seller, 'I Just Called to Say I Love You'. This popular live performer, who appeared at the US Live 8 concert, has recorded with many of the biggest names in music and has had his songs performed and sampled by countless acts. No one has amassed more No.1 US R&B hits than the blind entertainer, who helped turn Martin Luther King's birthday into a US holiday, and whose charitable work is legendary. Best-selling single: 'I Just Called to Say I Love You' 1,775,000 (21 Albums: 386 Weeks, 57 Singles: 430 Weeks)

Date		Title / Label	Pos	Wks
3 Feb 66		**UPTIGHT (EVERYTHING'S ALRIGHT)** *Tamla Motown TMG 545* $	14	10
18 Aug 66		**BLOWIN' IN THE WIND** *Tamla Motown TMG 570*	36	5
5 Jan 67		**A PLACE IN THE SUN** *Tamla Motown TMG 588*	20	5
26 Jul 67	●	**I WAS MADE TO LOVE HER** *Tamla Motown TMG 613* $	5	15
25 Oct 67		**I'M WONDERING** *Tamla Motown TMG 626*	22	8
8 May 68		**SHOO BE DOO BE DOO DA DAY** *Tamla Motown TMG 653*	46	4
7 Sep 68		STEVIE WONDER'S GREATEST HITS *Tamla Motown STML 11075*	25	10
18 Dec 68	●	**FOR ONCE IN MY LIFE** *Tamla Motown TMG 679* $	3	13
19 Mar 69		**I DON'T KNOW WHY I LOVE YOU** (re) *Tamla Motown TMG 690*	14	11
16 Jul 69	●	**MY CHERIE AMOUR** *Tamla Motown TMG 690* $	4	15
15 Nov 69	●	**YESTER-ME, YESTER-YOU, YESTERDAY** *Tamla Motown TMG 717*	2	13
13 Dec 69		MY CHERIE AMOUR *Tamla Motown STML 11128*	17	2
28 Mar 70	●	**NEVER HAD A DREAM COME TRUE** *Tamla Motown TMG 731*	6	12
18 Jul 70		**SIGNED SEALED DELIVERED I'M YOURS** (re) *Tamla Motown TMG 744* $	15	10
21 Nov 70		**HEAVEN HELP US ALL** *Tamla Motown TMG 757*	29	11
15 May 71		**WE CAN WORK IT OUT** *Tamla Motown TMG 772*	27	7
22 Jan 72		**IF YOU REALLY LOVE ME** *Tamla Motown TMG 798*	20	7
12 Feb 72		GREATEST HITS VOLUME 2 *Tamla Motown STML 11196*	30	4
3 Feb 73		TALKING BOOK *Tamla Motown STMA 8007*	16	48
3 Feb 73		**SUPERSTITION** *Tamla Motown TMG 841* ▲ $	11	9
19 May 73	●	**YOU ARE THE SUNSHINE OF MY LIFE** *Tamla Motown TMG 852* ▲ $	7	11
1 Sep 73	●	INNERVISIONS *Tamla Motown STMA 8011*	8	55
13 Oct 73		**HIGHER GROUND** *Tamla Motown TMG 869*	29	5
12 Jan 74		**LIVING FOR THE CITY** *Tamla Motown TMG 881*	15	9
13 Apr 74	●	**HE'S MISSTRA KNOW IT ALL** *Tamla Motown TMG 892*	10	9
17 Aug 74	●	FULFILLINGNESS' FIRST FINALE *Tamla Motown STMA 8019*	5	16
19 Oct 74		**YOU HAVEN'T DONE NOTHIN'** *Tamla Motown TMG 921* ▲ $	30	5
11 Jan 75		**BOOGIE ON REGGAE WOMAN** *Tamla Motown TMG 928* $	12	8
16 Oct 76	●	SONGS IN THE KEY OF LIFE *Tamla Motown TMSP 6002*	2	54
18 Dec 76	●	**I WISH** *Motown TMG 1054* ▲ $	5	10
9 Apr 77	●	**SIR DUKE** *Motown TMG 1068* ▲ $	2	9
10 Sep 77		**ANOTHER STAR** *Motown TMG 1083*	29	5
24 Feb 79		**POPS, WE LOVE YOU** *Motown TMG 1136* [1]	66	5
10 Nov 79	●	JOURNEY THROUGH THE SECRET LIFE OF PLANTS *Motown TMSP 6009*	8	15
24 Nov 79		**SEND ONE YOUR LOVE** *Motown TMG 1149*	52	3
26 Jan 80		**BLACK ORCHID** *Motown TMG 1173*	63	3
29 Mar 80		**OUTSIDE MY WINDOW** *Motown TMG 1179*	52	4
13 Sep 80	●	**MASTER BLASTER (JAMMIN')** *Motown TMG 1204*	2	10
8 Nov 80	●	HOTTER THAN JULY *Motown STMA 8035*	2	55
27 Dec 80	●	**I AIN'T GONNA STAND FOR IT** *Motown TMG 1215*	10	10
7 Mar 81	●	**LATELY** *Motown TMG 1226*	3	13
25 Jul 81	●	**HAPPY BIRTHDAY** *Motown TMG 1235*	2	11
23 Jan 82		**THAT GIRL** *Motown TMG 1254*	39	6
10 Apr 82	★	**EBONY AND IVORY** *Parlophone R 6054* [2] ▲	1	10
22 May 82	●	ORIGINAL MUSIQUARIUM 1 *Motown TMSP 6012*	8	17
5 Jun 82	●	**DO I DO** *Motown TMG 1269*	10	7
25 Sep 82		**RIBBON IN THE SKY** *Motown TMG 1280*	45	4
25 Aug 84	★	**I JUST CALLED TO SAY I LOVE YOU** (re) *Motown TMG 1349* ▲ £ $	1	26
22 Sep 84	●	THE WOMAN IN RED (FILM SOUNDTRACK) *Motown ZL 72285*	2	19
24 Nov 84		LOVE SONGS – 16 CLASSIC HITS *Telstar STAR 2251*	20	10
1 Dec 84		**LOVE LIGHT IN FLIGHT** *Motown TMG 1364*	44	5
29 Dec 84		**DON'T DRIVE DRUNK** (re) *Motown TMG 1372*	62	3
7 Sep 85	●	**PART-TIME LOVER** *Motown ZB 40351* ▲	3	12
28 Sep 85	●	IN SQUARE CIRCLE *Motown ZL 72005*	5	16
9 Nov 85		**THAT'S WHAT FRIENDS ARE FOR** *Arista ARIST 638* [3] ▲ $	16	9
23 Nov 85		**GO HOME** *Motown ZB 40501*	67	2
8 Mar 86		**OVERJOYED** *Motown ZB 40567*	17	8
15 Nov 86		DIANA ROSS, MICHAEL JACKSON, GLADYS KNIGHT, STEVIE WONDER. THEIR VERY BEST BACK TO BACK *PrioriTyV PTVR 2* [1]	21	10
17 Jan 87		**STRANGER ON THE SHORE OF LOVE** *Motown WOND 2*	55	3
31 Oct 87		**SKELETONS** *Motown ZB 41439*	59	3
28 Nov 87		CHARACTERS *Motown ZL 72001*	33	4
28 May 88		**GET IT** *Motown ZB 41883* [4]	37	4
6 Aug 88	●	**MY LOVE** *CBS JULIO 2* [5]	5	11
20 May 89		**FREE** *Motown ZB 42855*	49	5
8 Jun 91		JUNGLE FEVER (FILM SOUNDTRACK) *Motown ZL 71750*	56	1
12 Oct 91		**FUN DAY** *Motown ZB 44957*	63	1
25 Feb 95		**FOR YOUR LOVE** *Motown TMGCD 1437*	23	4
25 Mar 95	●	CONVERSATION PEACE *Motown 5302382*	8	4
22 Jul 95		**TOMORROW ROBINS WILL SING** *Motown 8603732*	71	1
23 Nov 96		SONG REVIEW – A GREATEST HITS COLLECTION *Motown 5307572*	19	12
19 Jul 97	●	**HOW COME, HOW LONG** *Epic 6646202* [6]	10	5
23 Aug 97		SONGS IN THE KEY OF LIFE (re-issue) *Motown 5300342*	66	1
31 Oct 98		**TRUE TO YOUR HEART** *Motown 8608832* [7]	51	1
9 Nov 02		THE DEFINITIVE COLLECTION *Universal TV 0665022*	16	30
27 Dec 03		**SIGNED, SEALED, DELIVERED, I'M YOURS** *Innocent SINCD 50* [8]	11	10
28 May 05		**SO WHAT THE FUSS** *Motown TMGCDX 1510*	19	4
29 Oct 05		A TIME 2 LOVE *Motown 9882094*	24	3
10 Dec 05		**POSITIVITY** *Motown TMGCD 16* [9]	54	1

[1] Diana Ross, Marvin Gaye, Smokey Robinson and Stevie Wonder [2] Paul McCartney with Stevie Wonder [3] Dionne Warwick and Friends featuring Elton John, Stevie Wonder and Gladys Knight [4] Stevie Wonder and Michael Jackson [5] Julio Iglesias featuring Stevie Wonder [6] Babyface featuring Stevie Wonder [7] 98 Degrees featuring Stevie Wonder [8] Blue featuring Stevie Wonder and Angie Stone [9] Stevie Wonder featuring Aisha Morris [1] Diana Ross / Michael Jackson / Gladys Knight / Stevie Wonder

'You Haven't Done Nothin' included an additional credit on the label: 'Doo Doo Wopsssss by The Jackson 5'. 'I Just Called to Say I Love You' re-entered in Dec 1985.

Wayne WONDER

Jamaica, male vocalist – VonWayne Charles (1 Album: 7 Weeks, 2 Singles: 14 Weeks)

Date		Title / Label	Pos	Wks
28 Jun 03		NO HOLDING BACK *VP / Atlantic 7567836282*	40	7
28 Jun 03	●	**NO LETTING GO** *VP / Atlantic ATO 154CD*	3	8
8 Nov 03		**BOUNCE ALONG** *Atlantic ATO 165CD*	19	6

WONDER DOG

Germany, canine vocalist – Harry Thumann

Date		Title / Label	Pos	Wks
21 Aug 82		**RUFF MIX** *Flip FLIP 001*	31	7

The WONDER STUFF

UK, male vocal (Miles Hunt) / instrumental group (6 Albums: 48 Weeks, 16 Singles: 66 Weeks)

Date		Title / Label	Pos	Wks
30 Apr 88		**GIVE GIVE GIVE ME MORE MORE MORE** *Polydor GONE 3*	72	2
16 Jul 88		**A WISH AWAY** *Polydor GONE 4*	43	5
27 Aug 88		THE EIGHT LEGGED GROOVE MACHINE *Polydor GONLP 1*	18	7
24 Sep 88		**IT'S YER MONEY I'M AFTER BABY** *Polydor GONE 5*	40	3
11 Mar 89		**WHO WANTS TO BE THE DISCO KING?** *Polydor GONE 6*	28	3
23 Sep 89		**DON'T LET ME DOWN GENTLY** *Polydor GONE 7*	19	4
14 Oct 89	●	HUP *Polydor 841187 1*	5	8
11 Nov 89		**GOLDEN GREEN / GET TOGETHER** *Polydor GONE 8*	33	3
12 May 90		**CIRCLESQUARE** *Polydor GONE 10*	20	4
13 Apr 91	●	**THE SIZE OF A COW** *Polydor GONE 11*	5	7
25 May 91		**CAUGHT IN MY SHADOW** *Polydor GONE 12*	18	3
8 Jun 91	●	NEVER LOVED ELVIS *Polydor 8472521*	3	23
7 Sep 91		**SLEEP ALONE** *Polydor GONE 13*	43	2
26 Oct 91	★	**DIZZY** *Sense SIGH 712* [1]	1	12
25 Jan 92	●	**WELCOME TO THE CHEAP SEATS (EP)** *Polydor GONE 14*	8	5
25 Sep 93	●	**ON THE ROPES (EP)** *Polydor GONCD 15*	10	4
16 Oct 93	●	CONSTRUCTION FOR THE MODERN IDIOT *Polydor 5198942*	4	5
27 Nov 93		**FULL OF LIFE (HAPPY NOW)** *Polydor GONCD 16*	28	3
26 Mar 94		**HOT LOVE NOW! (EP)** *Polydor GONCD 17*	19	3
10 Sep 94		**UNBEARABLE** *Polydor GONCD 18*	16	3

26 July 1997	2 August 1997	9 August 1997	16 August 1997
I'LL BE MISSING YOU Puff Daddy and Faith Evans featuring 112	**I'LL BE MISSING YOU** Puff Daddy and Faith Evans featuring 112	**I'LL BE MISSING YOU** Puff Daddy and Faith Evans featuring 112	**MEN IN BLACK** Will Smith
THE FAT OF THE LAND The Prodigy	**THE FAT OF THE LAND** The Prodigy	**THE FAT OF THE LAND** The Prodigy	**THE FAT OF THE LAND** The Prodigy

KEY: UK No.1 ★ UK Top 10 ● Still on chart + UK entry at No.1 ■ US No.1 ▲ UK million seller £ US million seller $
Singles re-entries are listed as (re), (2re), (3re)... which signifies that the hit re-entered the chart once, twice or three times...
Peak Position / Weeks

8 Oct 94 ● IF THE BEATLES HAD READ HUNTER ... THE SINGLES *Polydor 5213972*...8 4
29 Jul 95 LIVE IN MANCHESTER *Windsong WINCD 074X*...74 1

[1] Vic Reeves and The Wonder Stuff

Tracks on Welcome to the Cheap Seats (EP): Welcome to the Cheap Seats / Me, My Mom, My Dad and My Brother / Will the Circle Be Unbroken / That's Entertainment. Tracks on On the Ropes (EP): On the Ropes / Professional Disturber of the Peace / Hank and John / Whites. Tracks on Hot Love Now! (EP): Hot Love Now! / I Think I Must've Had Something Really Useful to Say / Room 512 / All the News That's Fit to Print.

The WONDERS *US, male vocal / instrumental group*

22 Feb 97 THAT THING YOU DO! *Play-Tone 6640552*...22 3

Brenton WOOD *US, male vocalist – Alfred Smith*

27 Dec 67 ● GIMME LITTLE SIGN *Liberty LBF 15021*...8 14

Roy WOOD (see also ELECTRIC LIGHT ORCHESTRA; The MOVE; WIZZARD) *UK, male vocalist / multi-instrumentalist – Ulysses Adrian Wood (2 Albums: 14 Weeks, 7 Singles: 44 Weeks)*

11 Aug 73 DEAR ELAINE *Harvest HAR 5074*...18 8
18 Aug 73 BOULDERS *Harvest SHVL 803*...15 8
1 Dec 73 ● FOREVER *Harvest HAR 5078*...8 13
15 Jun 74 GOIN' DOWN THE ROAD *Harvest HAR 5083*...13 7
31 May 75 OH WHAT A SHAME *Jet 754*...13 7
24 Jul 82 THE SINGLES *Speed SPEED 1000*...37 6
22 Nov 86 WATERLOO *IRS IRM 125* [1] ...45 4
23 Dec 95 I WISH IT COULD BE CHRISTMAS EVERYDAY *Woody WOODY 001CD* [2] ...59 2
30 Dec 00 I WISH IT COULD BE A WOMBLING MERRY CHRISTMAS EVERYDAY *Dramatico DRAMCDS 0001* [3] ...22 3

[1] Doctor and the Medics featuring Roy Wood [2] Roy Wood Big Band [3] The Wombles with Roy Wood

The WOODENTOPS
UK, male vocal / instrumental group (2 Albums: 6 Weeks, 1 Single: 1 Week)

12 Jul 86 GIANT *Rough Trade ROUGH 87*...35 4
11 Oct 86 EVERYDAY LIVING *Rough Trade RT 178*...72 1
5 Mar 88 WOODENFOOT COPS ON THE HIGHWAY *Rough Trade ROUGH 127*...48 2

Michael WOODS
(see also M1; M3; WARRIOR) *UK, male producer (2 Singles: 2 Weeks)*

21 Jun 03 IF YOU WANT ME *Incentive CENT 48CDS* [1] ...46 1
29 Nov 03 SOLEX (CLOSE TO THE EDGE) *Free 2 Air 0150355 F2A*...52 1

[1] Michael Woods featuring Imogen Bailey

Edward WOODWARD
UK, male actor / vocalist (2 Albums: 12 Weeks, 1 Single: 2 Weeks)

6 Jun 70 THE MAN ALONE *DJM DJLPS 405*...53 2
16 Jan 71 THE WAY YOU LOOK TONIGHT (re) *DJM DJS 232*...42 2
19 Aug 72 THE EDWARD WOODWARD ALBUM *Jam JAL 103*...20 10

WOOKIE *UK, male producer / vocalist – Jason Chue (3 Singles: 11 Weeks)*

3 Jun 00 WHAT'S GOING ON *Soul II Soul S2SCD 001*...45 1
12 Aug 00 ● BATTLE *Soul II Soul / Pias S2SPCD 001* [1] ...10 7
12 May 01 BACK UP (TO ME) *Soul II Soul S2SPCD 003* [1] ...38 3

[1] Wookie featuring Lain

Sheb WOOLEY *US, male vocalist / actor, b. 10 Apr 1921, d. 16 Sep 2003*

20 Jun 58 THE PURPLE PEOPLE EATER *MGM 981* ▲ $...12 8

The WOOLPACKERS
UK, male / female actors vocal group (2 Albums: 13 Weeks, 2 Singles: 24 Weeks)

16 Nov 96 ● HILLBILLY ROCK HILLBILLY ROLL *RCA 74321425412*...5 14
14 Dec 96 EMMERDANCE *RCA 74321444052*...26 10
29 Nov 97 THE GREATEST LINE DANCING PARTY ALBUM *RCA 74321512272*...48 3
29 Nov 97 LINE DANCE PARTY *RCA 74321512262*...25 10

WORKING WEEK *UK, male / female vocal / instrumental group (2 Albums: 10 Weeks, 1 Single: 2 Weeks)*

9 Jun 84 VENCEREMOS – WE WILL WIN *Virgin VS 684*...64 2
4 Jun 85 WORKING NIGHTS *Virgin V 2343*...23 9
27 Sep 86 COMPANEROS *Virgin V 2397*...72 1

WORLD OF TWIST *UK, male / female vocal / instrumental group (1 Album: 1 Week, 4 Singles: 12 Weeks)*

24 Nov 90 THE STORM (re) *Circa YR 55*...42 5
23 Mar 91 SONS OF THE STAGE *Circa YR 62*...47 3
12 Oct 91 SWEETS *Circa YR 72*...58 2
9 Nov 91 QUALITY STREET *Circa CIRCA 17*...50 1
22 Feb 92 SHE'S A RAINBOW *Circa YR 82*...62 2

WORLD PARTY *UK / Ireland, male vocal (Karl Wallinger) / instrumental group (5 Albums: 25 Weeks, 8 Singles: 29 Weeks)*

14 Feb 87 SHIP OF FOOLS *Ensign ENY 606*...42 6
21 Mar 87 PRIVATE REVOLUTION *Chrysalis CHEN 4*...56 4
19 May 90 GOODBYE JUMBO *Ensign CHEN 10*...36 10
16 Jun 90 MESSAGE IN THE BOX *Ensign ENY 631*...39 6
15 Sep 90 WAY DOWN NOW *Ensign ENY 634*...66 2
18 May 91 THANK YOU WORLD *Ensign ENY 643*...68 1
10 Apr 93 IS IT LIKE TODAY *Ensign CDENY 658*...19 6
8 May 93 ● BANG! *Ensign CDCHEN 33*...2 8
10 Jul 93 GIVE IT ALL AWAY *Ensign CDENY 659*...43 3
2 Oct 93 ALL I GAVE *Ensign CDENYS 660*...37 3
7 Jun 97 BEAUTIFUL DREAM *Chrysalis CDCHS 5053*...31 2
28 Jun 97 EGYPTOLOGY *Chrysalis CDCHR 6124*...34 2
2 Sep 00 DUMBING UP *Papillon BTFLYCD 0006*...64 1

WORLD PREMIERE *US, male vocal / instrumental group*

28 Jan 84 SHARE THE NIGHT *Epic A 4133*...64 4

WORLD WARRIOR *UK, male producer – Simon Harris*

16 Apr 94 STREET FIGHTER II *Living Beat LBECD 27*...70 1

WORLDS APART *UK, male vocal group (5 Singles: 17 Weeks)*

27 Mar 93 HEAVEN MUST BE MISSING AN ANGEL *Arista 74321139362*..29 3
3 Jul 93 WONDERFUL WORLD *Arista 74321153402*...51 1
25 Sep 93 EVERLASTING LOVE *Bell 74321164802*...20 4
26 Mar 94 COULD IT BE I'M FALLING IN LOVE *Bell 74321189952*...15 6
4 Jun 94 BEGGIN' TO BE WRITTEN *Bell 74321211982*...29 3

WORLD'S FAMOUS SUPREME TEAM (see also Malcolm McLAREN) *US, male vocal / DJ group (4 Singles: 19 Weeks)*

4 Dec 82 ● BUFFALO GALS *Charisma MALC 1* [1] ...9 12
25 Feb 84 HEY DJ *Charisma TEAM 1*...52 5
8 Dec 90 OPERA HOUSE *Virgin VS 1273* [2] ...75 1
3 Oct 98 BUFFALO GALS STAMPEDE (re-mix) *Virgin VSCDT 1717* [3] ..65 1

[1] Malcolm McLaren and the World's Famous Supreme Team [2] World Famous Supreme Team Show [3] Malcolm McLaren and the World's Famous Supreme Team plus Rakim and Roger Sanchez

	23 August 1997	30 August 1997	6 September 1997	13 September 1997
UK No.1 SINGLES	MEN IN BLACK Will Smith	MEN IN BLACK Will Smith	MEN IN BLACK Will Smith	THE DRUGS DON'T WORK The Verve
UK No.1 ALBUMS	WHITE ON BLONDE Texas	BE HERE NOW Oasis	BE HERE NOW Oasis	BE HERE NOW Oasis

WRECKLESS ERIC *UK, male vocalist – Eric Goulden (2 Albums: 5 Weeks)*

1 Apr 78	WRECKLESS ERIC *Stiff SEEZ 6*	46	1
8 Mar 80	BIG SMASH *Stiff SEEZ 21*	30	4

WRECKX-N-EFFECT *US, male vocal group (4 Singles: 18 Weeks)*

13 Jan 90	JUICY *Motown ZB 43295* [1]	29	7
5 Dec 92	RUMP SHAKER *MCA MCS 1725* $	24	7
7 May 94	WRECKX SHOP *MCA MCSTD 1969* [2]	26	2
13 Aug 94	RUMP SHAKER (re-issue) *MCA MCSTD 1989*	40	2

[1] Wrecks-N-Effect [2] Wreckx-N-Effect featuring Apache Indian

Betty WRIGHT
(see also Peter BROWN) *US, female vocalist (4 Singles: 23 Weeks)*

25 Jan 75	SHOORAH! SHOORAH! *RCA 2491*	27	7
19 Apr 75	WHERE IS THE LOVE *RCA 2548*	25	7
8 Feb 86	PAIN *Cooltempo COOL 117*	42	6
9 Sep 89	KEEP LOVE NEW *Sure Delight SD 11*	71	3

Ian WRIGHT *UK, male footballer / vocalist*

28 Aug 93	DO THE RIGHT THING *M&G MAGCD 45*	43	2

Rick WRIGHT
(see also PINK FLOYD) *UK, male vocalist / keyboard player*

19 Oct 96	BROKEN CHINA *EMI CDEMD 1098*	61	1

Ruby WRIGHT
US, female vocalist, b. 8 Jan 1914, d. 9 Mar 2004 (2 Singles: 15 Weeks)

16 Apr 54 ●	BIMBO (re) *Parlophone R 3816*	7	5
22 May 59	THREE STARS *Parlophone R 4556*	19	10

'Three Stars' is narrated by Dick Pike.

Steve WRIGHT *UK, male DJ / vocalist (3 Singles: 10 Weeks)*

27 Nov 82	I'M ALRIGHT *RCA 296* [1]	40	6
15 Oct 83	GET SOME THERAPY *RCA 362* [2]	75	1
1 Dec 84	THE GAY CAVALIEROS (THE STORY SO FAR) *MCA 925*	61	3

[1] Young Steve and The Afternoon Boys [2] Steve Wright and The Sisters of Soul

WUBBLE-U *UK, male production group*

7 Mar 98	PETAL *Indolent DGOL 003CD1*	55	1

Klaus WUNDERLICH
Germany, male organist, b. 18 Jun 1931, d. 28 Oct 1997 (4 Albums: 19 Weeks)

30 Aug 75	THE HIT WORLD OF KLAUS WUNDERLICH *Decca SPA 434*	27	8
20 May 78	THE UNIQUE KLAUS WUNDERLICH SOUND *Decca DBC 5/5*	28	4
26 May 79	THE FANTASTIC SOUND OF KLAUS WUNDERLICH *Lotus LH 5013*	43	5
17 Mar 84	ON THE SUNNY SIDE OF THE STREET *Polydor POLD 5133*	81	2

The WURZELS
UK, male vocal / instrumental group (3 Albums: 29 Weeks, 6 Singles: 31 Weeks)

2 Feb 67	DRINK UP THY ZIDER *Columbia DB 8081* [1]	45	1
11 Mar 67	ADGE CUTLER AND THE WURZELS *Columbia SX 6126* [1]	38	4
15 May 76 ★	THE COMBINE HARVESTER (BRAND NEW KEY) *EMI 2450*	1	13
3 Jul 76	COMBINE HARVESTER *One Up OU 2138*	15	20
11 Sep 76 ●	I AM A CIDER DRINKER (PALOMA BLANCA) *EMI 2520*	3	9
2 Apr 77	GOLDEN DELICIOUS *EMI Note NTS 122*	32	5
25 Jun 77	FARMER BILL'S COWMAN (I WAS KAISER BILL'S BATMAN) *EMI 2637*	32	5
11 Aug 01	COMBINE HARVESTER 2001 (re-mix) *EMI Gold CDWURZ 001*	39	2
12 Oct 02	DON'T LOOK BACK IN ANGER *EMI Gold 5515082*	59	1

[1] Adge Cutler and The Wurzels [1] Adge Cutler and The Wurzels

WU-TANG CLAN
(see also GHOSTFACE KILLAH; METHOD MAN; OL' DIRTY BASTARD; RZA)
US, male rap / instrumental group (2 Albums: 23 Weeks, 3 Singles: 21 Weeks)

14 Jun 97 ★	WU-TANG FOREVER *Loud 74321457682* ■ ▲	1	10
16 Aug 97	TRIUMPH *Loud 74321510212* [1]	46	1
21 Mar 98 ●	SAY WHAT YOU WANT / INSANE *Mercury MERC 499* [2]	4	7
25 Nov 00 ●	GRAVEL PIT *Loud / Epic 67015182*	6	13
2 Dec 00	THE W *Epic 4995762*	19	13

[1] Wu-Tang Clan featuring Cappadonna [2] Texas featuring Wu-Tang Clan (rap by Method Man and RZA)

Robert WYATT (see also SOFT MACHINE)
UK, male vocalist – Robert Wyatt-Ellidge (2 Singles: 11 Weeks)

28 Sep 74	I'M A BELIEVER *Virgin VS 114*	29	5
7 May 83	SHIPBUILDING *Rough Trade RT 115*	35	6

Michael WYCOFF *US, male vocalist*

23 Jul 83	(DO YOU REALLY LOVE ME) TELL ME LOVE *RCA 348*	60	2

Pete WYLIE (see also WAH!) *UK, male vocalist (3 Singles: 18 Weeks)*

3 May 86	SINFUL *Eternal MDM 7*	13	10
13 Sep 86	DIAMOND GIRL *Eternal MDM 12*	57	3
13 Apr 91	SINFUL! (SCARY JIGGIN' WITH DR LOVE) *Siren SRN 138* [1]	28	5

[1] Pete Wylie with The Farm

Bill WYMAN (see also The ROLLING STONES) *UK, male vocalist / bass guitarist – William Perks (3 Albums: 8 Weeks, 2 Singles: 13 Weeks)*

8 Jun 74	MONKEY GRIP *Rolling Stones COC 59102*	39	1
25 Jul 81	(SI SI) JE SUIS UN ROCK STAR *A&M AMS 8144*	14	9
20 Mar 82	A NEW FASHION *A&M AMS 8209*	37	4
10 Apr 82	BILL WYMAN *A&M AMLH 68540*	55	6
27 May 00	GROOVIN' *Papillon BTFLYCD 003* [1]	52	1

[1] Bill Wyman's Rhythm Kings

Tammy WYNETTE
US, female vocalist – Virginia Wynette Pugh, b. 5 May 1942, d. 6 Apr 1998 (5 Albums: 49 Weeks, 4 Singles: 35 Weeks)

26 Apr 75 ★	STAND BY YOUR MAN *Epic EPC 7137*	1	12
17 May 75 ●	THE BEST OF TAMMY WYNETTE *Epic EPC 63578*	4	23
21 Jun 75	STAND BY YOUR MAN *Epic EPC 69141*	13	7
28 Jun 75	D.I.V.O.R.C.E. *Epic EPC 3361*	12	7
12 Jun 76	I DON'T WANNA PLAY HOUSE *Epic EPC 4091*	37	4
17 Dec 77 ●	20 COUNTRY CLASSICS *CBS PR 5040*	3	11
4 Feb 78	COUNTRY GIRL MEETS COUNTRY BOY *Warwick PR 5039*	43	3
6 Jun 87	ANNIVERSARY – 20 YEARS OF HITS *Epic 450 3931*	45	5
7 Dec 91 ●	JUSTIFIED AND ANCIENT *KLF Communications KLF 099* [1]	2	12

[1] The KLF – guest vocals: Tammy Wynette

Mark WYNTER *UK, male vocalist – Terence Lewis (9 Singles: 80 Weeks)*

25 Aug 60	IMAGE OF A GIRL *Decca F 11263*	11	10
10 Nov 60	KICKIN' UP THE LEAVES *Decca F 11279*	24	10
9 Mar 61	DREAM GIRL *Decca F 11323*	27	5
8 Jun 61	EXCLUSIVELY YOURS *Decca F 11354*	32	7
4 Oct 62 ●	VENUS IN BLUE JEANS *Pye 7N 15466*	4	15
13 Dec 62 ●	GO AWAY LITTLE GIRL *Pye 7N 15492*	6	11
6 Jun 63	SHY GIRL *Pye 7N 15525*	28	6
14 Nov 63	IT'S ALMOST TOMORROW *Pye 7N 15577*	12	12
9 Apr 64	ONLY YOU (AND YOU ALONE) *Pye 7N 15626*	38	4

20 September 1997	27 September 1997	4 October 1997	11 October 1997
CANDLE IN THE WIND 1997 / SOMETHING ABOUT THE WAY YOU LOOK TONIGHT Elton John	CANDLE IN THE WIND 1997 / SOMETHING ABOUT THE WAY YOU LOOK TONIGHT Elton John	CANDLE IN THE WIND 1997 / SOMETHING ABOUT THE WAY YOU LOOK TONIGHT Elton John	CANDLE IN THE WIND 1997 / SOMETHING ABOUT THE WAY YOU LOOK TONIGHT Elton John
BE HERE NOW Oasis	MARCHIN' ALREADY Ocean Colour Scene	BE HERE NOW Oasis	URBAN HYMNS The Verve

KEY UK No.1 ★ UK Top 10 ● Still on chart + UK entry at No.1 ■ US No.1 ▲ UK million seller £ US million seller $ Singles re-entries are listed as (re), (2re), (3re)... which signifies that the hit re-entered the chart once, twice or three times... Peak Position Weeks

Malcolm X *US, male orator – Malcolm Little, b. 19 May 1925, d. 21 Feb 1965*

7 Apr 84 **NO SELL OUT** *Tommy Boy IS 165* 60 4

Hit features credit: 'Music by Keith Le Blanc'.

Richard X
UK, male producer – Richard Phillips (1 Album: 2 Weeks, 2 Singles: 16 Weeks)

29 Mar 03 ● **BEING NOBODY** *Virgin RXCD 1* [1] 3 11
23 Aug 03 ● **FINEST DREAMS** *Virgin RXCD 2* [2] 8 5
6 Sep 03 RICHARD X PRESENTS HIS X FACTOR *Virgin CDRICH 1* 31 2

[1] Richard X vs Liberty X [2] Richard X featuring Kelis

X-ECUTIONERS featuring Mike SHINODA and Mr HAHN of LINKIN PARK *US, male DJ / production / rap group and DJ / vocal duo*

13 Apr 02 ● **IT'S GOIN' DOWN** *Epic 6725642* 7 9

X MAL DEUTSCHLAND
UK / Germany, male / female vocal / instrumental group

7 Jul 84 TOCSIN *4AD CAD 407* 86 1

XAVIER *US, male / female vocal / instrumental group*

20 Mar 82 **WORK THAT SUCKER TO DEATH / LOVE IS ON THE ONE** *Liberty UP 651* 53 3

XAVIER NEW *US, male vocalist – Xavier Smith (2 Singles: 1 Week)*

27 Aug 05 **GIVE ME THE NIGHT** *Virgin TENCDX 501* 65 1

XPANSIONS *UK, male producer – Richie Malone (5 Singles: 21 Weeks)*

6 Oct 90 **ELEVATION** *Optimism 113683* 49 5
23 Feb 91 ● **MOVE YOUR BODY (ELEVATION)** *Arista 113 683* 7 9
15 Jun 91 **WHAT YOU WANT** *Arista 114 246* [1] 55 2
26 Aug 95 **MOVE YOUR BODY** (re-mix) *Arista 74321294982* [2] 14 4
30 Nov 02 **ELEVATION (MOVE YOUR BODY) 2002** (re-mix) *RM RMRCD 10* .. 70 1

[1] Xpansions featuring Dale Joyner [2] Xpansions 95

'Move Your Body' is a re-mix of 'Elevation'.

X-PRESS 2 *UK, male instrumental / production group (1 Album: 3 Weeks, 11 Singles: 26 Weeks)*

5 Jun 93 **LONDON X-PRESS** *Junior Boy's Own JBO 12* 59 1
16 Oct 93 **SAY WHAT!** *Junior Boy's Own JBO 16CD* 32 2
30 Jul 94 **ROCK 2 HOUSE / HIP HOUSIN'** *Junior Boy's Own JBO 21CD* [1] 55 2
9 Mar 96 **THE SOUND** *Junior Boy's Own JBO 36* 38 1
12 Oct 96 **TRANZ EURO XPRESS** *Junior Boy's Own JBO 42CD* 45 1
30 Sep 00 **AC / DC** *Skint SKINT 57* 60 1
28 Apr 01 **MUZIKIZUM** *Skint SKINT 65* 52 1
20 Oct 01 **SMOKE MACHINE** *Skint SKINT 69* 43 1
20 Apr 02 ● **LAZY** *Skint SKINT 74CD* [2] 2 13
4 May 02 MUZIKIZUM *Skint BRASSIC 23CD* 15 3
21 Sep 02 **I WANT YOU BACK** *Skint SKINT 81CD* 50 1
8 Oct 05 **GIVE IT** *Skint SKINT 111CD* [3] 33 2

[1] X-Press 2 featuring Lo-Pro [2] X-Press 2 featuring David Byrne
[3] X-Press 2 featuring Kurt Wagner

'I Want You Back' features Dieter Meier.

X-RAY SPEX *UK, male / female vocal / instrumental group (1 Album: 14 Weeks, 4 Singles: 33 Weeks)*

29 Apr 78 **THE DAY THE WORLD TURNED DAYGLO** *EMI International INT 553* 23 8
22 Jul 78 **IDENTITY** *EMI International INT 563* 24 10
4 Nov 78 **GERM FREE ADOLESCENCE** *EMI International INT 573* 19 11
9 Dec 78 GERM FREE ADOLESCENTS *EMI International INS 3023* 30 14
21 Apr 79 **HIGHLY INFLAMMABLE** *EMI International INT 583* 45 4

XSCAPE *US, female vocal group (7 Singles: 15 Weeks)*

20 Nov 93 **JUST KICKIN' IT** *Columbia 6598622* $ 49 2
5 Nov 94 **JUST KICKIN' IT** (re-issue) *Columbia 6608642* 54 2
7 Oct 95 **FEELS SO GOOD** *Columbia 6625022* 34 2
27 Jan 96 **WHO CAN I RUN TO** *Columbia 6628112* 31 3
29 Jun 96 **KEEP ON KEEPIN' ON** *East West A 4287CD* [1] 39 2
19 Apr 97 **KEEP ON KEEPIN' ON** (re-issue) *East West A 3950CD 1* [1] .. 27 2
22 Aug 98 **THE ARMS OF THE ONE WHO LOVES YOU** *Columbia 6662522* .. 46 2

[1] MC Lyte featuring Xscape

XSTASIA *UK, male / female vocal / production duo*

17 Mar 01 **SWEETNESS** *Liquid Asset ASSETCD 005* 65 1

X-STATIC *Italy, male / female vocal / instrumental group*

4 Feb 95 **I'M STANDING (HIGHER)** *Positiva CDTIV 25* 41 2

XTC *UK / Malta, male vocal (Andy Partridge) / instrumental group (14 Albums: 51 Weeks, 12 Singles: 70 Weeks)*

11 Feb 78 WHITE MUSIC *Virgin V 2095* 38 4
28 Oct 78 GO 2 *Virgin V 2108* 21 3
12 May 79 **LIFE BEGINS AT THE HOP** *Virgin VS 259* 54 4
1 Sep 79 DRUMS AND WIRES *Virgin V 2129* 34 7
22 Sep 79 **MAKING PLANS FOR NIGEL** *Virgin VS 282* 17 11
6 Sep 80 **GENERALS AND MAJORS / DON'T LOSE YOUR TEMPER** *Virgin VS 365* 32 8
20 Sep 80 BLACK SEA *Virgin V 2173* 16 7
18 Oct 80 **TOWERS OF LONDON** *Virgin VS 372* 31 5
24 Jan 81 **SGT ROCK (IS GOING TO HELP ME)** *Virgin VS 384* 16 9
23 Jan 82 ● **SENSES WORKING OVERTIME** *Virgin VS 462* 10 9
20 Feb 82 ● ENGLISH SETTLEMENT *Virgin V 2223* 5 11
27 Mar 82 **BALL AND CHAIN** *Virgin VS 482* 58 4
13 Nov 82 WAXWORKS – SOME SINGLES (1977-1982) *Virgin V 2251* 54 3
10 Sep 83 MUMMER *Virgin V 2264* 51 4
15 Oct 83 **LOVE ON A FARMBOY'S WAGES** *Virgin VS 613* 50 4
29 Sep 84 **ALL YOU PRETTY GIRLS** *Virgin VS 709* 55 5
27 Oct 84 THE BIG EXPRESS *Virgin V 2325* 38 2
8 Nov 86 SKYLARKING *Virgin V 2399* 90 1
28 Jan 89 **MAYOR OF SIMPLETON** *Virgin VS 1158* 46 5
11 Mar 89 ORANGES AND LEMONS *Virgin V 2581* 28 3
4 Apr 92 **THE DISAPPOINTED** *Virgin VS 1404* 33 5
9 May 92 NONSUCH *Virgin CDV 2699* 28 2
13 Jun 92 **THE BALLAD OF PETER PUMPKINHEAD** *Virgin VS 1415* 71 1
28 Sep 96 FOSSIL FUEL – THE XTC SINGLES 1977-92 *Virgin CDVD 2811* 33 2
6 Mar 99 APPLE VENUS – VOLUME 1 *Cooking Vinyl COOKCD 172* 42 1
3 Jun 00 WASP STAR (APPLE VENUS VOLUME 2) *Cooking Vinyl COOKCD 194* 40 1

XTM & DJ CHUCKY presents ANNIA *Spain / Japan, male DJ / production trio and female vocalist (2 Singles: 22 Weeks)*

7 Jun 03 ● **FLY ON THE WINGS OF LOVE** *Serious SER 62CD* 8 19
2 Apr 05 **GIVE ME YOUR LOVE** *Wonderboy 9870368* 28 3

18 October 1997	25 October 1997	1 November 1997	8 November 1997
◂◂ UK No.1 SINGLES ▸▸			
CANDLE IN THE WIND 1997 / SOMETHING ABOUT THE WAY YOU LOOK TONIGHT Elton John	**SPICE UP YOUR LIFE** Spice Girls	**BARBIE GIRL** Aqua	**BARBIE GIRL** Aqua
◂◂ UK No.1 ALBUMS ▸▸			
URBAN HYMNS The Verve	**URBAN HYMNS** The Verve	**URBAN HYMNS** The Verve	**URBAN HYMNS** The Verve

XZIBIT
US, male rapper – Alvin Joiner (2 Albums: 13 Weeks, 3 Singles: 16 Weeks)

10 Feb 01	RESTLESS *Epic 4989132*	27	11
17 Mar 01	X *Epic 6709072* [1]	14	7
12 Oct 02	MAN VS MACHINE *Epic 5047539*	43	2
16 Nov 02	MULTIPLY *Epic / Loud 6731552*	39	2
5 Feb 05 ●	HEY NOW (MEAN MUGGIN) *Columbia 6756482*	9	7

[1] Xzibit featuring Snoop Dogg

Y

Y?N-VEE *US, female vocal group*

17 Dec 94	CHOCOLATE *RAL RALCD 2*	65	1

Y & T
US, male vocal / instrumental group (3 Albums: 15 Weeks, 1 Single: 4 Weeks)

11 Sep 82	BLACK TIGER *A&M AMLH 64910*	53	8
13 Aug 83	MEAN STREAK *A&M AM 135*	41	4
10 Sep 83	MEAN STREAK *A&M AMLX 64960*	35	4
18 Aug 84	IN ROCK WE TRUST *A&M AMLX 65007*	33	3

Y-TRAXX
Belgium, male producer – Frederique de Backer (2 Singles: 2 Weeks)

24 May 97	MYSTERY LAND (EP) *ffrr FCD 292*	63	1
20 Sep 03	MYSTERY LAND *Nebula NEBT 047* [1]	70	1

[1] Y-Traxx featuring Neve

Tracks on Mystery Land (EP): Mystery Land (radio edit) / Trance Piano / Kiss the Sound / Mystery Land.

Y-TRIBE featuring Elisabeth TROY
UK, male instrumental / production duo and female vocalist

18 Dec 99	ENOUGH IS ENOUGH (re) *Northwest 10 NORTHCD 002*	49	3

Weird Al YANKOVIC *US, male vocalist (2 Singles: 8 Weeks)*

7 Apr 84	EAT IT *Scotti Bros. / Epic A 4257*	36	7
4 Jul 92	SMELLS LIKE NIRVANA *Scotti Bros. PO 219*	58	1

YANNI *Greece, male keyboard player – Yanni Chryssolmalis*

4 Apr 98	TRIBUTE *Virgin CDVUS 135*	40	2

YARBROUGH and PEOPLES *US, male / female vocal / instrumental duo – Calvin Yarbrough and Alisa Peoples (4 Singles: 20 Weeks)*

27 Dec 80 ●	DON'T STOP THE MUSIC *Mercury MER 53* $	7	12
5 May 84	DON'T WASTE YOUR TIME *Total Experience XE 501*	60	3
11 Jan 86	GUILTY *Total Experience FB 49905*	53	3
5 Jul 86	I WOULDN'T LIE *Total Experience FB 49841*	61	2

The YARDBIRDS (see also Jeff BECK; Eric CLAPTON; CREAM)
UK, male vocal (Keith Relf, b. 22 Mar 1943, d. 14 May 1976) / instrumental group (1 Album: 8 Weeks, 7 Singles: 62 Weeks)

12 Nov 64	GOOD MORNING LITTLE SCHOOLGIRL *Columbia DB 7391*	44	4
18 Mar 65 ●	FOR YOUR LOVE *Columbia DB 7499*	3	12
17 Jun 65 ●	HEART FULL OF SOUL *Columbia DB 7594*	2	13
14 Oct 65 ●	EVIL HEARTED YOU / STILL I'M SAD *Columbia DB 7706*	3	10
3 Mar 66 ●	SHAPES OF THINGS *Columbia DB 7848*	3	9
2 Jun 66 ●	OVER UNDER SIDEWAYS DOWN *Columbia DB 7928*	10	9
23 Jul 66	YARDBIRDS *Columbia SX 6063*	20	8
27 Oct 66	HAPPENINGS TEN YEARS TIME AGO *Columbia DB 8024*	43	5

Tony YAYO NEW (see also G-UNIT) *US, male rapper*

17 Sep 05	THOUGHTS OF A PREDICATE FELON *Interscope 9882806*	41	2
24 Sep 05	SO SEDUCTIVE *Interscope 9884360* [1]	28	3

[1] Tony Yayo featuring 50 Cent

YAZOO (see also The ASSEMBLY; ERASURE)
UK, female / male vocal / instrumental duo – Alison Moyet and Vince Clarke (3 Albums: 86 Weeks, 6 Singles: 55 Weeks)

17 Apr 82 ●	ONLY YOU *Mute MUTE 020*	2	14
17 Jul 82 ●	DON'T GO *Mute YAZ 001*	3	11
4 Sep 82 ●	UPSTAIRS AT ERIC'S *Mute STUMM 7*	2	63
20 Nov 82	THE OTHER SIDE OF LOVE *Mute YAZ 002*	13	9
21 May 83 ●	NOBODY'S DIARY *Mute YAZ 003*	3	11
16 Jul 83 ★	YOU AND ME BOTH *Mute STUMM 12*	1	20
8 Dec 90	SITUATION *Mute YAZ 4*	14	8
4 Sep 99	ONLY YOU (re-mix) *Mute CDYAZ 5*	38	2
18 Sep 99	ONLY YAZOO – THE BEST OF YAZOO *Mute CDMUTEL 6*	22	3

YAZZ *UK, female vocalist – Yasmin Evans*
(1 Album: 32 Weeks, 12 Singles: 69 Weeks)

20 Feb 88 ●	DOCTORIN' THE HOUSE *Ahead of Our Time CCUT 27* [1]	6	9
23 Jul 88 ★	THE ONLY WAY IS UP *Big Life BLR 4* [2]	1	15
29 Oct 88 ●	STAND UP FOR YOUR LOVE RIGHTS *Big Life BLR 5*	2	12
26 Nov 88 ●	WANTED *Big Life YAZZLP 1*	3	32
4 Feb 89 ●	FINE TIME *Big Life BLR 6*	9	8
29 Apr 89	WHERE HAS ALL THE LOVE GONE *Big Life BLR 8*	16	6
23 Jun 90	TREAT ME GOOD *Big Life BLR 24*	20	5
28 Mar 92	ONE TRUE WOMAN *Polydor PO 198*	60	2
31 Jul 93	HOW LONG *Polydor PZCD 252* [3]	31	5
2 Apr 94	HAVE MERCY *Polydor PZCD 309*	42	3
9 Jul 94	EVERYBODY'S GOT TO LEARN SOMETIME *Polydor PZCD 316*	56	2
28 Sep 96	GOOD THING GOING *East West EW 062CD*	53	1
22 Mar 97	NEVER CAN SAY GOODBYE *East West EW 081CD*	61	1

[1] Coldcut featuring Yazz and the Plastic Population [2] Yazz and the Plastic Population [3] Yazz and Aswad

The YEAH YEAH YEAHS *US, male / female vocal / instrumental group (1 Album: 6 Weeks, 5 Singles: 9 Weeks)*

16 Nov 02	MACHINE *Wichita WEBB 036SCD*	37	2
26 Apr 03	DATE WITH THE NIGHT *Dress Up / Polydor 0657442*	16	2
10 May 03	FEVER TO TELL *Dress Up / Polydor 0760612*	13	6
5 Jul 03	PIN *Dress Up / Polydor 9808085*	29	2
4 Oct 03	MAPS *Dress Up / Polydor 9811413*	26	2
13 Nov 04	Y CONTROL *Dress Up / Polydor 9868816*	54	1

Trisha YEARWOOD *US, female vocalist*

9 Aug 97	HOW DO I LIVE *MCA MCSTD 48064*	66	1
25 Jul 98	WHERE YOUR ROAD LEADS *MCA Nashville UMD 80513*	36	2

YELL! *UK, male vocal duo – Paul Varney and Daniel James*

20 Jan 90 ●	INSTANT REPLAY *Fanfare FAN 22*	10	8

YELLO *Switzerland, male vocal / instrumental duo – Dieter Meier and Boris Blank (5 Albums: 15 Weeks, 12 Singles: 42 Weeks)*

21 May 83	YOU GOTTA SAY YES TO ANOTHER EXCESS *Stiff SEEZ 48*	65	2
25 Jun 83	I LOVE YOU *Stiff BUY 176*	41	4
26 Nov 83	LOST AGAIN *Stiff BUY 191*	73	1
6 Apr 85	STELLA *Elektra EKT 1*	92	1
9 Aug 86	GOLDRUSH *Mercury MER 218*	54	3

15 November 1997	22 November 1997	29 November 1997	6 December 1997
BARBIE GIRL Aqua	BARBIE GIRL Aqua	PERFECT DAY Various	PERFECT DAY Various
SPICEWORLD Spice Girls	SPICEWORLD Spice Girls	LET'S TALK ABOUT LOVE Celine Dion	LET'S TALK ABOUT LOVE Celine Dion

KEY: UK No.1 ★★ UK Top 10 ●● Still on chart ++ UK entry at No.1 ■■ US No.1 ▲▲ UK million seller £ US million seller $
Singles re-entries are listed as (re), (2re), (3re)… which signifies that the hit re-entered the chart once, twice or three times…
Peak Position / Weeks

4 Jul 87 ONE SECOND *Mercury MERH 100* ... 48 3
22 Aug 87 **THE RHYTHM DIVINE** *Mercury MER 253* [1] ... 54 2
27 Aug 88 ● **THE RACE** *Mercury YELLO 1* ... 7 11
10 Dec 88 FLAG *Mercury 8367781* ... 56 7
17 Dec 88 **TIED UP** *Mercury YELLO 2* ... 60 5
25 Mar 89 **OF COURSE I'M LYING** *Mercury YELLO 3* ... 23 8
22 Jul 89 **BLAZING SADDLES** *Mercury YELLO 4* ... 47 2
8 Jun 91 **RUBBERBANDMAN** *Mercury YELLO 5* ... 58 2
29 Jun 91 BABY *Mercury 8487911* ... 37 2
5 Sep 92 **JUNGLE BILL** *Mercury MER 376* ... 61 2
7 Nov 92 **THE RACE / BOSTICH** (re-issue) *Mercury MER 382* ... 55 1
15 Oct 94 **HOW HOW** *Mercury MERCD 414* ... 59 1

[1] Yello featuring Shirley Bassey

YELLOW DOG
US / UK, male vocal / instrumental group (2 Singles: 13 Weeks)

4 Feb 78 ● **JUST ONE MORE NIGHT** *Virgin VS 195* ... 8 9
22 Jul 78 **WAIT UNTIL MIDNIGHT** *Virgin VS 217* ... 54 4

YELLOW MAGIC ORCHESTRA *Japan, male instrumental group*

14 Jun 80 **COMPUTER GAME (THEME FROM 'THE INVADERS')** *A&M AMS 7502* ... 17 11

YELLOWCARD *US, male vocal / instrumental group (2 Singles: 2 Weeks)*

12 Jun 04 **WAY AWAY** *Capitol CDCLS 855* ... 63 1
18 Sep 04 **OCEAN AVENUE** *Capitol CDCLS 860* ... 65 1

Bryn YEMM *UK, male vocalist (4 Albums: 14 Weeks)*

9 Jun 84 HOW DO I LOVE THEE *Lifestyle LEG 17* ... 57 2
7 Jul 84 HOW GREAT THOU ART *Lifestyle LEG 15* ... 67 8
22 Dec 84 THE BRYN YEMM CHRISTMAS COLLECTION *Bay BAY 104* ... 95 2
26 Oct 85 MY TRIBUTE – BRYN YEMM INSPIRATIONAL ALBUM *Word WSTR 9665* [1] ... 85 2

[1] Bryn Yemm and the Gwent Chorale

YEOVIL TOWN FC *UK, male football team vocalists*

28 Feb 04 **YEOVIL TRUE** *Yeovil Town FC 188* ... 36 1

YES 242 Top 500 (see also ANDERSON BRUFORD WAKEMAN HOWE; Chris SQUIRE; Alan WHITE)
Seventies progressive rock giants who later flirted successfully with AOR formed in London in 1968. Noted Yes-men include Jon Anderson (v), Bill Bruford (d), Steve Howe (g), Rick Wakeman (k), Patrick Moraz (k) and ex-Buggle Trevor Horn (v/g), who masterminded their 1980s comeback (22 Albums: 226 Weeks, 7 Singles: 39 Weeks)

1 Aug 70 TIME AND A WORD *Atlantic 2400006* ... 45 3
27 Feb 71 ● THE YES ALBUM *Atlantic 2400101* ... 4 34
4 Dec 71 ● FRAGILE *Atlantic 2409019* ... 7 17
23 Sep 72 ● CLOSE TO THE EDGE *Atlantic K 50012* ... 4 13
26 May 73 ● YESSONGS *Atlantic K 60045* ... 7 13
22 Dec 73 ★ TALES FROM TOPOGRAPHIC OCEANS *Atlantic K 80001* ... 1 15
21 Dec 74 ● RELAYER *Atlantic K 50096* ... 4 11
29 Mar 75 YESTERDAYS *Atlantic K 50048* ... 27 7
30 Jul 77 ★ GOING FOR THE ONE *Atlantic K 50379* ... 1 28
17 Sep 77 ● **WONDROUS STORIES** *Atlantic K 10999* ... 7 9
26 Nov 77 **GOING FOR THE ONE** *Atlantic K 11047* ... 24 4
9 Sep 78 **DON'T KILL THE WHALE** *Atlantic K 11184* ... 36 4
7 Oct 78 ● TORMATO *Atlantic K 50518* ... 8 11
30 Aug 80 ● DRAMA *Atlantic K 50736* ... 2 8
10 Jan 81 YESSHOWS *Atlantic K 60142* ... 22 9
12 Nov 83 **OWNER OF A LONELY HEART** *Acto B 9817* ▲ ... 28 9
26 Nov 83 90125 *Atco 790125* ... 16 28
31 Mar 84 **LEAVE IT** *Atco B 9787* ... 56 4
29 Mar 86 9012 LIVE: THE SOLOS *Atco 790 4741* ... 44 3
3 Oct 87 **LOVE WILL FIND A WAY** *Atco A 9449* ... 73 1
10 Oct 87 BIG GENERATOR *Atco WEX 70* ... 17 5
11 May 91 ● UNION *Arista 211558* ... 7 6
2 Apr 94 TALK *London 8284892* ... 20 4
9 Nov 96 KEYS TO ASCENSION *Essential! EDFCD 417* ... 48 1
15 Nov 97 KEYS TO ASCENSION 2 *Essential! EDFCD 457* ... 62 1
2 Oct 99 THE LADDER *Eagle EAGCD 088* ... 36 1
22 Sep 01 MAGNIFICATION *Eagle EAGCD 189* ... 71 1
9 Aug 03 ● THE ULTIMATE YES – 35TH ANNIVERSARY *WSM 8122737022* ... 10 7
28 May 05 ● **OWNER OF A LONELY HEART** (re-mix) *Data 92CDS* [1] ... 9 8

[1] Max Graham vs Yes

Group was UK only for first three hits.

YETI NEW *UK, male vocal / instrumental group (2 Singles: 3 Weeks)*

9 Apr 05 **NEVER LOSE YOUR SENSE OF WONDER** *Moshi Moshi MOSHI 17CD* ... 36 2
10 Sep 05 **KEEP PUSHIN' ON** *Moshi Moshi MOSHI 23CD* ... 57 1

YIN and YAN *UK, male vocal duo – Chris Sanford and Bill Mitchell*

29 Mar 75 **IF** *EMI 2282* ... 25 5

YING YANG TWINS NEW *US, male rap duo – Kaine (Eric Jackson) and D-Roc (D'Angelo Holmes) (2 Singles: 9 Weeks)*

14 May 05 ● **GET LOW / LOVERS & FRIENDS** *TVT TVTUKCD 9* [1] ... 10 7
17 Sep 05 **WAIT (THE WHISPER SONG)** *TVT 12TVTUK 16* ... 47 2

[1] Lil Jon & The East Side Boyz featuring Ying Yang Twins / featuring Usher and Ludacris

Dwight YOAKAM
US, male vocalist / guitarist (2 Albums: 4 Weeks, 1 Single: 2 Weeks)

9 May 87 HILLBILLY DELUXE *Reprise WX 106* ... 51 3
13 Aug 88 BUENAS NOCHES FROM A LONELY ROOM *Reprise WX 193* ... 87 1
10 Jul 99 **CRAZY LITTLE THING CALLED LOVE** *Reprise W 497CD* ... 43 2

YOMANDA (see also The CANDY GIRLS; CLERGY; DOROTHY; HI-GATE; Paul MASTERSON presents SUSHI; SLEAZESISTERS)
UK, male DJ / producer – Paul Masterson (4 Singles: 21 Weeks)

24 Jul 99 ● **SYNTH & STRINGS** *Manifesto FESCD 59* ... 8 10
11 Mar 00 **SUNSHINE** *Manifesto FESCD 68* ... 16 6
2 Sep 00 **ON THE LEVEL** *Manifesto FESCD 73* ... 28 2
26 Jul 03 **YOU'RE FREE** *Incentive CENT 55CDS* ... 22 3

YORK *Germany, male production / instrumental duo – Torsten and Jorg Stenzel (4 Singles: 21 Weeks)*

9 Oct 99 **THE AWAKENING** *Manifesto FESCD 60* ... 11 5
10 Jun 00 ● **ON THE BEACH** *Manifesto FESCD 70* ... 4 10
18 Nov 00 **FAREWELL TO THE MOON** *Manifesto FESCD 76* ... 37 2
27 Jan 01 **THE FIELDS OF LOVE** *Club Tools / Edel 0124095 CLU* [1] ... 16 4

[1] ATB featuring York

YOSH presents LOVEDEEJAY AKEMI
Holland, male producer – Yoshida Rosenboom (3 Singles: 5 Weeks)

29 Jul 95 **IT'S WHAT'S UPFRONT THAT COUNTS** *Limbo LIMB 46CD* ... 69 1
2 Dec 95 **IT'S WHAT'S UPFRONT THAT COUNTS** (re-mix) *Limbo LIMB 50CD* ... 31 2
20 Apr 96 **THE SCREAMER** *Limbo LIMB 54CD* ... 38 2

YOTHU YINDI *Australia, male vocal / instrumental group*

15 Feb 92 **TREATY** *Hollywood HWD 116* ... 72 1

	13 December 1997	20 December 1997	27 December 1997	3 January 1998
UK No.1 SINGLES	TELETUBBIES SAY EH-OH! Teletubbies	TELETUBBIES SAY EH-OH! Teletubbies	TOO MUCH Spice Girls	TOO MUCH Spice Girls
UK No.1 ALBUMS	SPICEWORLD Spice Girls	LET'S TALK ABOUT LOVE Celine Dion	LET'S TALK ABOUT LOVE Celine Dion	URBAN HYMNS The Verve

Faron YOUNG *US, male vocalist, b. 25 Feb 1932, d. 10 Dec 1996*

15 Jul 72 ● **IT'S FOUR IN THE MORNING** *Mercury 6052 140*..............3 23
28 Oct 72 **IT'S FOUR IN THE MORNING** *Mercury 6338 095*..............27 5

Jimmy YOUNG *UK, male vocalist (12 Singles: 88 Weeks)*

9 Jan 53 **FAITH CAN MOVE MOUNTAINS** *Decca F 9986*..............11 1
21 Aug 53 ● **ETERNALLY** *Decca F 10130*..............8 9
6 May 55 ★ **UNCHAINED MELODY** *Decca F 10502*..............1 19
16 Sep 55 ★ **THE MAN FROM LARAMIE** *Decca F 10597*..............1 12
23 Dec 55 **SOMEONE ON YOUR MIND** *Decca F 10640*..............13 5
16 Mar 56 ● **CHAIN GANG** *Decca F 10694*..............9 6
8 Jun 56 **WAYWARD WIND** *Decca F 10736*..............27 1
22 Jun 56 **RICH MAN POOR MAN** *Decca F 10736*..............25 1
28 Sep 56 ● **MORE** *Decca F 10774*..............4 17
3 May 57 **ROUND AND ROUND** *Decca F 10875*..............30 1
10 Oct 63 **MISS YOU** *Columbia DB 7119*..............15 13
26 Mar 64 **UNCHAINED MELODY** (re-recording) *Columbia DB 7234*..............43 3

'Round and Round' and 'Unchained Melody' on Columbia are with the Michael Sammes Singers.

John Paul YOUNG *Australia, male vocalist (3 Singles: 19 Weeks)*

29 Apr 78 ● **LOVE IS IN THE AIR** *Ariola ARO 117*..............5 13
14 Nov 92 **LOVE IS IN THE AIR** (re-mix) *Columbia 6587697*..............49 3
12 Jan 02 **LOVE IS IN THE AIR** (re-recording) *Positiva CDTIV 166* [1]..............25 3

[1] Milk and Sugar vs John Paul Young

Karen YOUNG *UK, female vocalist*

6 Sep 69 ● **NOBODY'S CHILD** *Major Minor MM 625*..............6 21

Karen YOUNG
US, female vocalist, b. 23 Mar 1951, d. 26 Jan 1991 (3 Singles: 9 Weeks)

19 Aug 78 **HOT SHOT** *Atlantic K 11180*..............34 7
24 Feb 79 **HOT SHOT** (re-issue) *Atlantic LV 8*..............75 1
15 Nov 97 **HOT SHOT '97** (re-recording) *Distinctive DISNCD 37*..............68 1

Neil YOUNG 213 Top 500
Single-minded vocalist / guitarist / singer-songwriter, b. 12 Nov 1945, Toronto, Ontario, Canada. Constantly changing musical direction, with country rock as a member of Buffalo Springfield and Crosby Stills Nash and Young, 'Shakey's' solo activity (and with support bands such as The International Harvesters, The Stray Gators and Crazy Horse) has embraced country, punk and rock and resulted in his oft-used title "The Godfather of Grunge". A staunch supporter of Farm Aid, he also appeared at both Live Aid (US) and Live 8 (Canada) (37 Albums: 267 Weeks, 6 Singles: 22 Weeks)

31 Oct 70 ● **AFTER THE GOLD RUSH** *Reprise RSLP 6383*..............7 66
4 Mar 72 ★ **HARVEST** *Reprise K 54005* ▲..............1 35
11 Mar 72 ● **HEART OF GOLD** *Reprise K 14140* ▲ $..............10 11
27 Oct 73 **TIME FADES AWAY** *Warner Bros. K 54010*..............20 2
10 Aug 74 **ON THE BEACH** *Reprise K 54014*..............42 2
5 Jul 75 **TONIGHT'S THE NIGHT** *Reprise K 54040*..............48 1
27 Dec 75 **ZUMA** *Reprise K 54057*..............44 2
9 Oct 76 **LONG MAY YOU RUN** *Reprise K 54081* [1]..............12 5
9 Jul 77 **AMERICAN STARS 'N BARS** *Reprise K 54088*..............17 8
17 Dec 77 **DECADE** *Reprise K 64037*..............46 4
28 Oct 78 **COMES A TIME** *Reprise K 54099*..............42 3
6 Jan 79 **FOUR STRONG WINDS** *Reprise K 14493*..............57 4
14 Jul 79 **RUST NEVER SLEEPS** *Reprise K 54105* [2]..............13 13
1 Dec 79 **LIVE RUST** *Reprise K 64041* [2]..............55 3
15 Nov 80 **HAWKS & DOVES** *Reprise K 54109*..............34 3
14 Nov 81 **RE-AC-TOR** *Reprise K 54116* [2]..............69 3
5 Feb 83 **TRANS** *Geffen GEF 25019*..............29 5
3 Sep 83 **EVERYBODY'S ROCKIN'** *Geffen GEF 25590* [3]..............50 3
14 Sep 85 **OLD WAYS** *Geffen GEF 26377*..............39 3
2 Aug 86 **LANDING ON WATER** *Geffen 924 1091*..............52 2
4 Jul 87 **LIFE** *Geffen WX 109* [2]..............71 1
30 Apr 88 **THIS NOTE'S FOR YOU** *WEA WX 168* [4]..............56 3
21 Oct 89 **FREEDOM** *Reprise WX 257*..............17 5
22 Sep 90 **RAGGED GLORY** *Reprise WX 374*..............15 5
2 Nov 91 **WELD** *Reprise 7599266711*..............20 3
14 Nov 92 ● **HARVEST MOON** *Reprise 9362450572*..............9 18
23 Jan 93 **LUCKY THIRTEEN** *Geffen GED 24452*..............69 1
27 Feb 93 **HARVEST MOON** *Reprise W 0139CD*..............36 3
26 Jun 93 ● **UNPLUGGED** *Reprise 9362453102*..............4 13
17 Jul 93 **THE NEEDLE AND THE DAMAGE DONE** *Reprise W 0191CD*..............75 1
30 Oct 93 **LONG MAY YOU RUN (LIVE)** *Reprise W 0207CD*..............71 1
9 Apr 94 **PHILADELPHIA** *Reprise W 0242CD*..............62 2
27 Aug 94 ● **SLEEPS WITH ANGELS** *Reprise 9362457492* [2]..............2 7
8 Jul 95 ● **MIRROR BALL** *Reprise 9362459342*..............4 9
6 Jul 96 **BROKEN ARROW** *Reprise 9362462912* [2]..............17 5
28 Jun 97 **YEAR OF THE HORSE** *Reprise 9362466522* [2]..............36 2
6 May 00 ● **SILVER AND GOLD** *Reprise 9362473052*..............10 4
20 Apr 02 **ARE YOU PASSIONATE?** *Reprise 9362481112*..............24 3
27 Jul 02 **DECADE** *Reprise 7599272332*..............15 13
26 Jul 03 **ON THE BEACH** *Reprise 9362484972* [2]..............42 1
30 Aug 03 **GREENDALE** *Reprise 9362485432*..............24 3
27 Nov 04 **GREATEST HITS** *Reprise 9362489352*..............45 4
8 Oct 05 **PRAIRIE WIND** *Reprise 9362495932*..............22 4

[1] The Stills-Young Band [2] Neil Young & Crazy Horse [3] Neil and The Shocking Pinks [4] Neil Young and The Blue Notes

Paul YOUNG 139 Top 500
Soulful-sounding pop singer / songwriter, b. 17 Jan 1956, Bedfordshire, UK, who earlier fronted The Q-Tips and chart act Streetband. This multiple BRIT Award-winner sold seven million copies of his No Parlez album, including more than one million in the UK (9 Albums: 232 Weeks, 21 Singles: 134 Weeks)

18 Jun 83 ★ **WHEREVER I LAY MY HAT (THAT'S MY HOME)** *CBS A 3371* [1]..............1 15
30 Jul 83 ★ **NO PARLEZ** *CBS 25521*..............1 119
10 Sep 83 ● **COME BACK AND STAY** *CBS A 3636*..............4 9
19 Nov 83 ● **LOVE OF THE COMMON PEOPLE** *CBS A 3585*..............2 13
13 Oct 84 ● **I'M GONNA TEAR YOUR PLAYHOUSE DOWN** *CBS A 4786*..............9 7
8 Dec 84 ● **EVERYTHING MUST CHANGE** *CBS A 4972*..............9 11
9 Mar 85 ● **EVERYTIME YOU GO AWAY** *CBS A 6300* ▲ $..............4 11
6 Apr 85 ★ **THE SECRET OF ASSOCIATION** *CBS 26234* ■..............1 49
22 Jun 85 **TOMB OF MEMORIES** (re) *CBS A 6321*..............16 8
4 Oct 86 **WONDERLAND** *CBS YOUNG 1*..............24 5
1 Nov 86 ● **BETWEEN TWO FIRES** *CBS 450 1501*..............4 17
29 Nov 86 **SOME PEOPLE** *CBS YOUNG 2*..............56 3
7 Feb 87 **WHY DOES A MAN HAVE TO BE STRONG?** *CBS YOUNG 3*..............63 2
12 May 90 **SOFTLY WHISPERING I LOVE YOU** *CBS YOUNG 4*..............21 6
16 Jun 90 ● **OTHER VOICES** *CBS 4669171*..............4 11
7 Jul 90 **OH GIRL** *CBS YOUNG 5*..............25 6
6 Oct 90 **HEAVEN CAN WAIT** *CBS YOUNG 6*..............71 2
12 Jan 91 **CALLING YOU** *CBS YOUNG 7*..............57 2
30 Mar 91 ● **SENZA UNA DONNA (WITHOUT A WOMAN)** *London LON 294* [2]..............4 12
10 Aug 91 **BOTH SIDES NOW** *MCA MCS 1546* [3]..............74 1
14 Sep 91 ★ **FROM TIME TO TIME – THE SINGLES COLLECTION** *Columbia 4688251* ■..............1 27
26 Oct 91 **DON'T DREAM IT'S OVER** *Columbia 6574117*..............20 5
25 Sep 93 **NOW I KNOW WHAT MADE OTIS BLUE** *Columbia 6596412*..............14 7
23 Oct 93 **THE CROSSING** *Columbia 4739282*..............27 2
27 Nov 93 **HOPE IN A HOPELESS WORLD** *Columbia 6598652*..............42 3
23 Apr 94 **IT WILL BE YOU** *Columbia 6602812*..............34 4
26 Nov 94 **REFLECTIONS** *Vision VISCD 1*..............64 2
17 May 97 **I WISH YOU LOVE** *East West EW 100CD1*..............33 2
31 May 97 **PAUL YOUNG** *East West 630186192*..............39 2
21 Jun 03 **THE ESSENTIAL** *Sony Music 5122992*..............27 3

[1] Paul Young and The Family [2] Zucchero and Paul Young [3] Clannad and Paul Young

Retta YOUNG *US, female vocalist*

24 May 75 **SENDING OUT AN S.O.S.** *All Platinum 6146 305*..............28 7

10 January 1998	17 January 1998	24 January 1998	31 January 1998
PERFECT DAY Various	NEVER EVER All Saints	ALL AROUND THE WORLD Oasis	YOU MAKE ME WANNA … Usher
URBAN HYMNS The Verve	URBAN HYMNS The Verve	URBAN HYMNS The Verve	URBAN HYMNS The Verve

KEY: UK No.1 ★ UK Top 10 ● Still on chart + UK entry at No.1 ■ US No.1 ▲ UK million seller £ US million seller $
Singles re-entries are listed as (re), (2re), (3re)… which signifies that the hit re-entered the chart once, twice or three times…
Peak Position / Weeks

Will YOUNG 387 Top 500

The first and biggest-selling reality pop TV show (Pop Idol) contestant in the UK, b. 20 Jan 1979, Berkshire, UK. Only Elton John's 'Candle in the Wind 1997' topped the 1,108,269 copies his debut single sold in its first week. He was a BRIT award-winner in 2003 and 2005 (3 Albums: 76 Weeks, 8 Singles: 106 Weeks)

9 Mar 02	★	**EVERGREEN / ANYTHING IS POSSIBLE** *S 74321926142* ■ £	1	16
8 Jun 02	★	**LIGHT MY FIRE** (re) *S 74321943002* ■	1	20
5 Oct 02	★	**THE LONG AND WINDING ROAD / SUSPICIOUS MINDS** *S 74321965972* [1] ■	1	18
19 Oct 02	★	FROM NOW ON *S 74321969592* ■	1	25
30 Nov 02	●	**DON'T LET ME DOWN / YOU AND I** (re) *S 74321981262*	2	13
6 Dec 03	★	**LEAVE RIGHT NOW** *S 82876578562* ■	1	18
13 Dec 03	★	FRIDAY'S CHILD *S 82876557462* ■	1	46
27 Mar 04	●	**YOUR GAME** *S 82876603622*	3	9
17 Jul 04	●	**FRIDAY'S CHILD** *S 82876623932*	4	6
26 Nov 05	●	**SWITCH IT ON** *Sony BMG 82876752302*	5	6+
3 Dec 05	●	KEEP ON *Sony BMG 82876749542*	2	5+

[1] Will Young and Gareth Gates / Gareth Gates

YOUNG BUCK *US, male rapper – David Brown*

4 Sep 04	STRAIGHT OUTTA CA$HVILLE *Interscope 9863495*	22	3
23 Oct 04	**LET ME IN** *Interscope 9864517*	62	1

YOUNG DISCIPLES *UK / US, male / female vocal / instrumental group (1 Album: 5 Weeks, 4 Singles: 17 Weeks)*

13 Oct 90	**GET YOURSELF TOGETHER** *Talkin Loud TLK 2*	68	1
23 Feb 91	**APPARENTLY NOTHIN'** (re) *Talkin Loud TLK 5*	13	11
31 Aug 91	ROAD TO FREEDOM *Talkin Loud 5100971*	21	5
5 Oct 91	**GET YOURSELF TOGETHER** (re-issue) *Talkin Loud TLK 15*	65	2
5 Sep 92	**YOUNG DISCIPLES (EP)** *Talkin Loud TLKX 18*	48	3

'Apparently Nothin'' first peaked at No.46 in Feb 1991, making its peak position only on re-entry in Aug 1991. Tracks on Young Disciples (EP): Move On / Freedom / All I Have in Me / Move On (re-mix).

YOUNG RASCALS

US, male vocal / instrumental group (2 Singles: 17 Weeks)

25 May 67	●	**GROOVIN'** *Atlantic 584 111* ▲ $	8	13
16 Aug 67		**A GIRL LIKE YOU** *Atlantic 584 128*	37	4

YOUNG GODS *Switzerland, male vocal / instrumental group*

15 Feb 92	TV SKY *Play it Again Sam BIAS 201CD*	54	1

YOUNG HEART ATTACK *US, male / female vocal / instrumental group (1 Album: 1 Week, 2 Singles: 2 Weeks)*

10 Apr 04	**TOMMY SHOTS** *XL Recordings XLS 183CD*	54	1
24 Apr 04	MOUTHFUL OF LOVE *XL Recordings XLCD 173*	71	1
17 Jul 04	**STARLITE** *XL Recordings XLS 191CD*	69	1

YOUNG and COMPANY

US, male / female vocal / instrumental group

1 Nov 80	**I LIKE (WHAT YOU'RE DOING TO ME)** *Excalibur EXC 501*	20	12

YOUNG AND MOODY BAND *UK, male vocal / instrumental group*

10 Oct 81	**DON'T DO THAT** *Bronze BRO 130*	63	4

YOUNG BLACK TEENAGERS *US, male rap group*

9 Apr 94	**TAP THE BOTTLE** *MCA MCSTD 1967*	39	3

Sydney YOUNGBLOOD

US, male vocalist – Sydney Ford (1 Album: 17 Weeks, 5 Singles: 31 Weeks)

26 Aug 89	●	**IF ONLY I COULD** *Circa YR 34*	3	14
28 Oct 89		FEELING FREE *Circa CIRCA 9*	23	17
9 Dec 89		**SIT AND WAIT** *Circa YR 40*	16	8
31 Mar 90		**I'D RATHER GO BLIND** *Circa YR 43*	44	5
29 Jun 91		**HOOKED ON YOU** *Circa YR 65*	72	2
20 Mar 93		**ANYTHING** *RCA 74321138672*	48	2

YOUNGER YOUNGER 28'S

UK, male / female vocal / instrumental group

5 Jun 99	**WE'RE GOING OUT** *V2 VVR 5006943*	61	1

YOUNG IDEA *UK, male vocal duo – Tony Cox and Douglas MacCrae-Brown*

29 Jun 67	●	**WITH A LITTLE HELP FROM MY FRIENDS** *Columbia DB 8205*	10	6

YOUNG MC *US, male rapper – Marvin Young (3 Singles: 7 Weeks)*

15 Jul 89	**BUST A MOVE** *Delicious Vinyl BRW 137* $	73	2
17 Feb 90	**PRINCIPAL'S OFFICE** *Delicious Vinyl BRW 161*	54	3
17 Aug 91	**THAT'S THE WAY LOVE GOES** *Capitol CL 623*	65	2

YOUNG OFFENDERS *Ireland, male vocal / instrumental group*

7 Mar 98	**THAT'S WHY WE LOSE CONTROL** *Columbia 6651942*	60	1

YOURCODENAMEIS:MILO

UK, male vocal / instrumental group (2 Singles: 2 Weeks)

16 Oct 04	**SCHTEEVE** *Fiction 9868526*	58	1
23 Apr 05	**17** *Fiction 9871093*	65	1

Z FACTOR (see also AKABU featuring Linda CLIFFORD; HED BOYS; IL PADRINOS featuring Jocelyn BROWN; JAKATTA; Li KWAN; Joey NEGRO; PHASE II) *UK, male DJ / producer – Dave Lee (2 Singles: 2 Weeks)*

21 Feb 98	**GOTTA KEEP PUSHIN'** *ffrr FCD 329*	47	1
17 Nov 01	**RIDE THE RHYTHM** *Direction 6718482*	52	1

Z2 (see also LIQUID STATE featuring Marcella WOODS; SOLAR STONE)

UK, male production duo – Rich Mowat and Andy Bury

26 Feb 00	**I WANT YOU** *Platipus PLATCD 67*	61	1

'I Want You' features vocals by Alison Rivers.

Helmut ZACHARIAS ORCHESTRA

Germany, orchestra – leader b. 27 Jan 1920, d. 28 Feb 2002

29 Oct 64	●	**TOKYO MELODY** *Polydor NH 52341*	9	11

Pia ZADORA *US, female vocalist / actor – Pia Schipani (2 Singles: 6 Weeks)*

27 Oct 84	**WHEN THE RAIN BEGINS TO FALL** *Arista ARIST 584* [1]	68	2
12 Nov 88	**DANCE OUT OF MY HEAD** *Epic 6528867* [2]	65	4

[1] Jermaine Jackson and Pia Zadora [2] Pia

	7 February 1998	14 February 1998	21 February 1998	28 February 1998
UK No.1 SINGLES	DOCTOR JONES Aqua	DOCTOR JONES Aqua	MY HEART WILL GO ON Celine Dion	BRIMFUL OF ASHA (Re-mix) Cornershop
UK No.1 ALBUMS	URBAN HYMNS The Verve	TITANIC (Film Soundtrack) James Horner	URBAN HYMNS The Verve	TITANIC (Film Soundtrack) James Horner

ZAGER and EVANS

US, male vocal duo – Denny Zager and Rick Evans

9 Aug 69 ★ **IN THE YEAR 2525 (EXORDIUM AND TERMINUS)** *RCA 1860* ▲ $ 1 13

Michael ZAGER BAND *US, male / female vocal / instrumental group*

1 Apr 78 ● **LET'S ALL CHANT** *Private Stock PVT 143* 8 12

Gheorghe ZAMFIR *Romania, male pan pipes player*

21 Aug 76 ● **(LIGHT OF EXPERIENCE) DOINA DE JALE** *Epic EPC 4310* 4 9

Tommy ZANG *US, male vocalist*

16 Feb 61 **HEY GOOD LOOKING** *Polydor NH 66957* **45** 1

ZAPP *US, male vocal / instrumental group (2 Singles: 6 Weeks)*

25 Jan 86 **IT DOESN'T REALLY MATTER** *Warner Bros. W 8879* **57** 3
24 May 86 **COMPUTER LOVE (PART 1)** *Warner Bros. W 8805* **64** 3

Frank ZAPPA (see also The MOTHERS OF INVENTION) *US, male vocalist / multi-instrumentalist, b. 21 Dec 1940, d. 4 Dec 1993 (13 Albums: 57 Weeks)*

28 Feb 70 ● HOT RATS *Reprise RSLP 6356* 9 27
19 Dec 70 CHUNGA'S REVENGE *Reprise RSLP 2030* 43 1
6 May 78 ZAPPA IN NEW YORK *Discreet K 69204* 55 1
10 Mar 79 SHEIK YERBOUTI *CBS 88339* 32 7
13 Oct 79 JOE'S GARAGE ACT I *CBS 86101* 62 3
19 Jan 80 JOE'S GARAGE ACTS II & III *CBS 88475* 75 1
16 May 81 TINSEL TOWN REBELLION *CBS 88516* 55 4
24 Oct 81 YOU ARE WHAT YOU IS *CBS 88560* 51 2
19 Jun 82 SHIP ARRIVING TOO LATE TO SAVE A DROWNING WITCH *CBS 85804* 61 4
18 Jun 83 THE MAN FROM UTOPIA *CBS 25251* 87 1
27 Oct 84 THEM OR US *EMI FZD 1* 53 2
30 Apr 88 GUITAR *Zappa ZAPPA 6* 82 2
2 Sep 95 STRICTLY COMMERCIAL – THE BEST OF FRANK ZAPPA *Rykodisc RCD 40600* 45 2

Francesco ZAPPALA *Italy, male producer (2 Singles: 3 Weeks)*

10 Aug 91 **WE GOTTA DO IT** *Fourth & Broadway BRW 225* [1] **57** 2
2 May 92 **NO WAY OUT** *PWL Continental PWL 230* **69** 1

[1] DJ Professor featuring Francesco Zappala

Lena ZAVARONI *UK, female vocalist, b. 4 Nov 1963, d. 1 Oct 1999 (1 Album: 5 Weeks, 2 Singles: 14 Weeks)*

9 Feb 74 ● **MA! (HE'S MAKING EYES AT ME)** *Philips 6006 367* **10** 11
23 Mar 74 ● MA *Philips 6308 201* 8 5
1 Jun 74 **(YOU'VE GOT) PERSONALITY** *Philips 6006 391* 33 3

ZED BIAS *UK, male producer – Dave Jones*

15 Jul 00 **NEIGHBOURHOOD** *Locked On / XL Recordings LOX 122CD* 25 4

ZEE *UK, female vocalist – Lesley Cowling (3 Singles: 4 Weeks)*

6 Jul 96 **DREAMTIME** *Perfecto PERF 122CD* 31 2
22 Mar 97 **SAY MY NAME** *Perfecto PERF 135CD* 36 1
7 Feb 98 **BUTTERFLY** *Perfecto PERF 154CD1* [1] 41 1

[1] Tilt featuring Zee

ZENA (see also HONEYZ) *UK, female vocalist – Zena McNally (2 Singles: 2 Weeks)*

19 Jul 03 **LET'S GET THIS PARTY STARTED** *Serious SER 69CD* **69** 1
14 Aug 04 **BEEN AROUND THE WORLD** *Mercury 9867104* [1] **44** 1

[1] Zena featuring Vybz Kartel

The ZEPHYRS *UK, male vocal / instrumental group*

18 Mar 65 **SHE'S LOST YOU** *Columbia DB 7481* **48** 1

ZERO B *UK, male keyboard player – Peter Riding (2 Singles: 6 Weeks)*

22 Feb 92 **THE EP (BRAND NEW MIXES)** *Ffrreedom TAB 102* 32 4
24 Jul 93 **RECONNECTION (EP)** *Internal LIECD 6* **54** 2

Tracks on The EP (Brand New Mixes): Lock Up / Spinning Wheel / Module. Tracks on Reconnection (EP): Love to Be in Love (2 mixes) / Lock Up (re-mix) / Ou est le Spoon.

ZERO 7 *UK, male production duo – Henry Binns and Sam Hardaker (2 Albums: 61 Weeks, 4 Singles: 6 Weeks)*

5 May 01 SIMPLE THINGS *Ultimate Dilemma UDRCD 016* 28 43
18 Aug 01 **DESTINY** *Ultimate Dilemma UDRCDS 043* [1] **30** 3
17 Nov 01 **IN THE WAITING LINE** *Ultimate Dilemma UDRCDS 045* **47** 1
30 Mar 02 **DISTRACTIONS** *Ultimate Dilemma UDRCDS 046* [2] **45** 1
13 Mar 04 ● WHEN IT FALLS *Ultimate Dilemma 5046709875* 3 18
29 May 04 **SOMERSAULT** *Ultimate Dilemma EW 290CD* [2] **56** 1

[1] Zero 7 featuring Sia and Sophie [2] Zero 7 featuring Sia

ZERO VU featuring Lorna B

UK, male / female vocal / production group

15 Mar 97 **FEELS SO GOOD** *Avex UK AVEXCD 53* **69** 1

ZERO ZERO *UK, male instrumental / production duo*

10 Aug 91 **ZEROXED** *Kickin KICK 9* **71** 1

Warren ZEVON

US, male vocalist / keyboard player, b. 24 Jan 1947, d. 7 Sep 2003

27 Sep 03 THE WIND *Rykodisc RCD 17001* 57 1

ZHANÉ *US, female vocal duo – Renee Neufville and Jean Norris (1 Album: 1 Week, 9 Singles: 18 Weeks)*

11 Sep 93 **HEY MR DJ** (re) *Epic 6596102* 26 5
19 Mar 94 **GROOVE THANG** *Motown TMGCD 1423* 34 3
20 Aug 94 **VIBE** *Motown TMGCD 1430* **67** 1
25 Feb 95 **SHAME** *Jive JIVECD 372* **66** 1
21 Sep 96 **IT'S A PARTY** *Elektra EKR 226CD* [1] 23 2
8 Mar 97 **4 MORE** *Tommy Boy TBCD 7779A* [2] **52** 1
26 Apr 97 **REQUEST LINE** *Motown 8606452* 22 3
10 May 97 SATURDAY NIGHT *Motown 5305882* 52 1
30 Aug 97 **CRUSH** *Motown 5716712* **44** 1
11 Sep 99 **JAMBOREE** *Arista 74321692882* [3] **51** 1

[1] Busta Rhymes featuring Zhané [2] De La Soul featuring Zhané [3] Naughty By Nature featuring Zhané

ZIG and ZAG *Zog / Ireland, male puppet duo (2 Singles: 12 Weeks)*

24 Dec 94 ● **THEM GIRLS THEM GIRLS** *RCA 74321251042* **5** 9
1 Jul 95 **HANDS UP! HANDS UP!** *RCA 74321284392* 21 3

Hans ZIMMER *Germany, male composer (4 Albums: 22 Weeks)*

27 May 00 MUSIC FROM THE MOTION PICTURE GLADIATOR (FILM SOUNDTRACK) *Decca 4670942* [1] 17 16
3 Mar 01 HANNIBAL (FILM SOUNDTRACK) *Decca 4676962* 74 2
16 Jun 01 PEARL HARBOR (FILM SOUNDTRACK) *Hollywood / Warner Bros. 9362481132* [2] 50 2
17 Sep 05 MUSIC FROM THE MOTION PICTURE GLADIATOR (FILM SOUNDTRACK) (re-issue) *Decca 4765223* [1] 44 2

[1] Hans Zimmer and Lisa Gerrard [2] Hans Zimmer with orchestra conducted by Gavin Greenaway

Music from the Motion Picture Gladiator features the Lyndhurst Orchestra.

ZION TRAIN *UK, male / female vocal / instrumental group*

13 Jul 96 GROW TOGETHER *China WOLCD 1071* 56 1
27 Jul 96 **RISE** *China WOKCD 2085* **61** 1

7 March 1998	14 March 1998	21 March 1998	28 March 1998
FROZEN Madonna	MY HEART WILL GO ON Celine Dion	IT'S LIKE THAT Run-DMC vs Jason Nevins	IT'S LIKE THAT Run-DMC vs Jason Nevins
TITANIC (Film Soundtrack) James Horner	RAY OF LIGHT Madonna	RAY OF LIGHT Madonna	LET'S TALK ABOUT LOVE Celine Dion

KEY UK No.1 ★ UK Top 10 ● Still on chart + UK entry at No.1 ■ US No.1 ▲ UK million seller £ US million seller $
Singles re-entries are listed as (re), (2re), (3re)... which signifies that the hit re-entered the chart once, twice or three times...
Peak Position / Weeks

ZODIAC MINDWARP and The LOVE REACTION *UK, male vocal / instrumental group (1 Album: 5 Weeks, 3 Singles: 11 Weeks)*

Date	Title / Label	Peak	Weeks
9 May 87	**PRIME MOVER** *Mercury ZOD 1*	18	6
14 Nov 87	**BACKSEAT EDUCATION** *Mercury ZOD 2*	49	3
5 Mar 88	TATTOOED BEAT MESSIAH *Mercury ZODLP 1*	20	5
2 Apr 88	**PLANET GIRL** *Mercury ZOD 3*	63	2

ZOE
UK, female vocalist – Zoe Pollock (1 Album: 1 Week, 4 Singles: 22 Weeks)

Date	Title / Label	Peak	Weeks
10 Nov 90	**SUNSHINE ON A RAINY DAY** *M&G MAGS 6*	53	5
24 Aug 91 ●	**SUNSHINE ON A RAINY DAY** (re-mix) *M&G MAGS 14*	4	11
2 Nov 91	**LIGHTNING** *M&G MAGS 18*	37	4
7 Dec 91	SCARLET RED AND BLUE *M&G 5114431*	67	1
29 Feb 92	**HOLY DAYS** *M&G MAGS 21*	72	2

Rob ZOMBIE
(see also WHITE ZOMBIE) *US, male vocalist – Robert Cummings*

Date	Title / Label	Peak	Weeks
5 Sep 98	HELLBILLY DELUXE *Geffen GED 25212*	37	2
26 Dec 98	**DRAGULA** *Geffen GFSTD 22367*	44	2

ZOMBIE NATION *Germany, male production duo – Florian 'Splank' Senfter and Emanuel 'Mooner' Gunther (2 Singles: 16 Weeks)*

Date	Title / Label	Peak	Weeks
2 Sep 00	**KERNKRAFT 400** (import) *TRANSK TRANSK 002*	61	1
30 Sep 00 ●	**KERNKRAFT 400** *Data DATA 11CDS*	2	15

The ZOMBIES *UK, male vocal / instrumental group – includes Rod Argent and Colin Blunstone (2 Singles: 16 Weeks)*

Date	Title / Label	Peak	Weeks
13 Aug 64	**SHE'S NOT THERE** *Decca F 11940* $	12	11
11 Feb 65	**TELL HER NO** *Decca F 12072*	42	5

ZOO EXPERIENCE featuring DESTRY
UK, male production group and US, male vocalist

Date	Title / Label	Peak	Weeks
22 Aug 92	**LOVE'S GOTTA HOLD ON ME** *Cooltempo COOL 261*	66	1

ZUCCHERO *Italy, male vocalist / guitarist – Adelmo Fornaciari (1 Album: 4 Weeks, 3 Singles: 24 Weeks)*

Date	Title / Label	Peak	Weeks
30 Mar 91 ●	**SENZA UNA DONNA (WITHOUT A WOMAN)** *London LON 294* [1]	4	12
18 May 91	ZUCCHERO *A&M EVERY 1*	29	4
18 Jan 92	**DIAMANTE** *London LON 313* [2]	44	7
24 Oct 92	**MISERERE** *London LON 329* [3]	15	5

[1] Zucchero and Paul Young [2] Zucchero with Randy Crawford [3] Zucchero and Luciano Pavarotti

The ZUTONS *UK, male / female vocal / instrumental group (1 Album: 35 Weeks, 5 Singles: 13 Weeks)*

Date	Title / Label	Peak	Weeks
31 Jan 04	**PRESSURE POINT** ... *Deltasonic DLTCDV 016*	19	3
17 Apr 04	**YOU WILL YOU WON'T** ... *Deltasonic DLTCD 020*	22	3
1 May 04 ●	WHO KILLED ... THE ZUTONS? *Deltasonic DLTCD 019*	6	35
3 Jul 04	**REMEMBER ME** ... *Deltasonic DLTCD 2024*	39	2
30 Oct 04	**DON'T EVER THINK (TOO MUCH)** ... *Deltasonic DLTCD 2026*	15	3
25 Dec 04	**CONFUSION** ... *Deltasonic DLTCD 030*	37	2

ZWAN (see also Billy CORGAN) *US, male vocal / instrumental group (1 Album: 2 Weeks, 2 Singles: 3 Weeks)*

Date	Title / Label	Peak	Weeks
22 Feb 03	MARY STAR OF THE SEA *Reprise WB 484252*	33	2
8 Mar 03	**HONESTLY** *Reprise W 600CD*	28	2
14 Jun 03	**LYRIC** (re-mix) *Reprise W 607*	44	1

ZZ TOP (192 Top 500) *Low-slung, guitar-driven blues-rock trio formed in 1969 in Houston, Texas, US: long-bearded duo Billy Gibbons (v/g) and Dusty Hill (v/b) and clean-shaven Frank Beard (d). Hugely popular stadium-packing festival headliners in the 1980s. The act, who joined the Rock and Roll Hall of Fame in 2004, were named to ensure they would be the last act in record racks and hit books (8 Albums: 211 Weeks, 17 Singles: 94 Weeks)*

Date	Title / Label	Peak	Weeks
12 Jul 75	FANDANGO! *London SHU 8482*	60	1
8 Aug 81	EL LOCO *Warner Bros. K 56929*	88	2
30 Apr 83 ●	ELIMINATOR *Warner Bros. W 3774*	3	137
3 Sep 83 ●	**GIMME ALL YOUR LOVIN'** (re) *Warner Bros. W 9693*	10	18
26 Nov 83	**SHARP DRESSED MAN** (re) *Warner Bros. W 9576*	22	13
31 Mar 84	**TV DINNERS** *Warner Bros. W 9334*	67	3
23 Feb 85	**LEGS** *Warner Bros. W 9272*	16	7
13 Jul 85	**THE ZZ TOP SUMMER HOLIDAY (EP)** *Warner Bros. W 8946*	51	5
19 Oct 85	**SLEEPING BAG** *Warner Bros. W 2001*	27	5
9 Nov 85 ●	AFTERBURNER *Warner Bros. WX 27*	2	40
15 Feb 86	**STAGES** *Warner Bros. W 2002*	43	3
19 Apr 86	**ROUGH BOY** *Warner Bros. W 2003*	23	9
4 Oct 86	**VELCRO FLY** *Warner Bros. W 8650*	54	3
21 Jul 90	**DOUBLEBACK** *Warner Bros. W 9812*	29	6
27 Oct 90 ●	RECYCLER *Warner Bros. WX 390*	8	7
13 Apr 91	**MY HEAD'S IN MISSISSIPPI** *Warner Bros. W 0009*	37	5
11 Apr 92 ●	**VIVA LAS VEGAS** *Warner Bros. W 0098*	10	7
25 Apr 92 ●	GREATEST HITS *Warner Bros. 7599268462*	5	17
20 Jun 92	**ROUGH BOY** (re-issue) *Warner Bros. W 0111*	49	3
29 Jan 94	**PINCUSHION** *RCA 74321184732*	15	3
5 Feb 94 ●	ANTENNA *RCA 74321152602*	3	5
7 May 94	**BREAKAWAY** *RCA 74321192282*	60	1
29 Jun 96	**WHAT'S UP WITH THAT** *RCA 74321394822*	58	1
21 Sep 96	RHYTHMEEN *RCA 74321394662*	32	2
16 Oct 99	**GIMME ALL YOUR LOVIN' 2000** *Riverhorse RIVHCD 2* [1]	28	2

[1] Martay featuring ZZ Top

'Gimme All Your Lovin' debuted at No.61 in 1983, making its peak position only on re-entry in Oct 1984. 'Sharp Dressed Man' debuted at No.53 in Nov 1983, reaching its peak position only on re-entry in Dec 1984. Tracks on The ZZ Top Summer Holiday (EP): Tush / Got Me Under Pressure / Beer Drinkers and Hell Raisers / I'm Bad, I'm Nationwide.

	4 April 1998	11 April 1998	18 April 1998	25 April 1998
UK No.1 SINGLES	IT'S LIKE THAT – Run-DMC vs Jason Nevins	IT'S LIKE THAT – Run-DMC vs Jason Nevins	IT'S LIKE THAT – Run-DMC vs Jason Nevins	IT'S LIKE THAT – Run-DMC vs Jason Nevins
UK No.1 ALBUMS	THE BEST OF – James	THIS IS HARDCORE – Pulp	LIFE THRU A LENS – Robbie Williams	LIFE THRU A LENS – Robbie Williams

A-Z BY SONG TITLE

This section lists every song that has made the singles chart. Use this section when you remember the song title but can't recall which act or acts charted with it.

Professional record hunter Phil Swern is the man with the enviable task of keeping the Broadchart CD and vinyl collection both complete and up to date. Now digitized, this most comprehensive of record collections even has its own sealed air-conditioned vaults
LISTEN TO THE BOOK
In addition to reading this book you will soon be able listen to it! For more information about this Broadchart / British Hit Singles & Albums collaboration, check out our website **www.bibleofpop.com**

HOW TO USE THE SONG TITLE INDEX

This section of the book lists every hit single since 1952 in alphabetical order. The song title is listed first, followed by the act name. No.1 singles are listed in orange.

Songs with the same title but which are completely different in content are listed with a letter in brackets after the title: song [A], song [B], song [C], etc. For example, two different singles with the title 'ABANDON' have charted, [A] by Dare and [B] by That Petrol Emotion.

Cover versions of the same song share the same letter. For example, [A] Pat Boone, [A] Fats Domino and [A] The Four Seasons have all recorded the same song, in this case 'AIN'T THAT A SHAME'. If the original version of a cover was never a chart hit (eg 'AIN'T NO SUNSHINE'), it will not be listed.

2 May 1998	9 May 1998	16 May 1998	23 May 1998
UK No.1 SINGLES			
ALL THAT I NEED Boyzone	**UNDER THE BRIDGE / LADY MARMALADE** All Saints	**TURN BACK TIME** Aqua	**UNDER THE BRIDGE / LADY MARMALADE** All Saints
UK No.1 ALBUMS			
MEZZANINE Massive Attack	**MEZZANINE** Massive Attack	**INTERNATIONAL VELVET** Catatonia	**VERSION 2.0** Garbage

AGNES, QUEEN OF SORROW — BONNIE "PRINCE" BILLY
AHORA ES (NOW IS THE TIME) — 2 IN A ROOM
AI NO CORRIDA [A] — UNITING NATIONS featuring Laura MORE
AI NO CORRIDA (I-NO-KO-REE-DA) [A] — Quincy JONES featuring DUNE
AIKEA-GUINEA — COCTEAU TWINS
AIN'T COMPLAINING — STATUS QUO
AIN'T DOIN' NOTHIN' — Jet BRONX and The FORBIDDEN
AIN'T GOIN' TO GOA — ALABAMA 3
AIN'T GOING DOWN — Garth BROOKS
AIN'T GONNA BE THAT WAY — Marv JOHNSON
AIN'T GONNA BUMP NO MORE (WITH NO BIG FAT WOMAN) — Joe TEX
AIN'T GONNA CRY AGAIN — Peter COX
AIN'T GONNA WASH FOR A WEEK — The BROOK BROTHERS
AIN'T GOT A CLUE — The LURKERS
AIN'T GOT NO - I GOT LIFE — Nina SIMONE
AIN'T IT FUN — GUNS N' ROSES
AIN'T IT FUNNY — Jennifer LOPEZ
AIN'T LOVE A BITCH — Rod STEWART
AIN'T MISBEHAVIN' [A] — Johnnie RAY
AIN'T MISBEHAVIN' [A] — Tommy BRUCE and The BRUISERS
AIN'T MY BEATING HEART — TEN SHARP
AIN'T NO CASANOVA — SINCLAIR
AIN'T NO DOUBT — Jimmy NAIL (92)
AIN'T NO EASY WAY — BLACK REBEL MOTORCYCLE CLUB
AIN'T NO LOVE (AIN'T NO USE) [A] — SUB SUB featuring Melanie WILLIAMS
AIN'T NO LOVE (AIN'T NO USE) [A] — SODA CLUB featuring Ashley JADE
AIN'T NO LOVE IN THE HEART OF THE CITY — WHITESNAKE
AIN'T NO MAN — Dina CARROLL
AIN'T NO MOUNTAIN HIGH ENOUGH [A] — Diana ROSS
AIN'T NO MOUNTAIN HIGH ENOUGH [A] — REMEMBER ME (MEDLEY) — BOYSTOWN GANG
AIN'T NO MOUNTAIN HIGH ENOUGH [A] — Jocelyn BROWN
AIN'T NO MOUNTAIN HIGH ENOUGH [A] — WHITEHOUSE
AIN'T NO NEED TO HIDE — Sandy B
AIN'T NO PLAYA — JAY-Z featuring Foxy BROWN
AIN'T NO PLEASING YOU — CHAS and DAVE
AIN'T NO STOPPIN' US — DJ LUCK & MC NEAT featuring JJ
AIN'T NO STOPPIN' US NOW [A] — McFADDEN and WHITEHEAD
AIN'T NO STOPPIN' US NOW [B] — BIG DADDY KANE
AIN'T NO STOPPING — ENIGMA
AIN'T NO STOPPING US NOW [A] — Luther VANDROSS
AIN'T NO STOPPING US NOW [A] — MOBO ALLSTARS
AIN'T NO STOPPING US NOW (PARTY FOR THE WORLD) — Steve WALSH
AIN'T NO SUNSHINE [A] — Michael JACKSON
AIN'T NO SUNSHINE [A] — SIVUCA
AIN'T NO SUNSHINE [A] — LADYSMITH BLACK MAMBAZO featuring DES'REE
AIN'T NOBODY [A] — RUFUS and Chaka KHAN
AIN'T NOBODY [A] — Jaki GRAHAM
AIN'T NOBODY [A] — Diana KING
AIN'T NOBODY [A] — LL COOL J (97)
AIN'T NOBODY [A] — COURSE
AIN'T NOBODY BETTER — INNER CITY
AIN'T NOBODY (LOVES ME BETTER) — KWS and Gwen DICKEY
AIN'T NOTHIN' GOIN' ON BUT THE RENT — Gwen GUTHRIE
AIN'T NOTHIN' LIKE IT — Michael LOVESMITH
AIN'T NOTHIN' LIKE THE REAL THING [A] — Marvin GAYE and Tammi TERRELL
AIN'T NOTHING BUT A HOUSEPARTY [A] — SHOWSTOPPERS
AIN'T NOTHING BUT A HOUSEPARTY [A] — Phil FEARON
AIN'T NOTHING GONNA KEEP ME FROM YOU — Teri DE SARIO
AIN'T NOTHING LIKE THE REAL THING — Marcella DETROIT and Elton JOHN

AIN'T NOTHING WRONG — HOUSTON
AIN'T SHE SWEET — The BEATLES
AIN'T TALKIN' 'BOUT DUB — APOLLO FOUR FORTY
AIN'T THAT A LOT OF LOVE — SIMPLY RED
AIN'T THAT A SHAME [A] — Pat BOONE
AIN'T THAT A SHAME [A] — Fats DOMINO
AIN'T THAT A SHAME [A] — The FOUR SEASONS
AIN'T THAT ENOUGH — TEENAGE FANCLUB
AIN'T THAT ENOUGH FOR YOU — John DAVIS and The MONSTER ORCHESTRA
AIN'T THAT FUNNY — Jimmy JUSTICE
(AIN'T THAT) JUST LIKE ME — The HOLLIES
AIN'T THAT JUST THE WAY — Lutricia McNEAL
AIN'T THAT LOVING YOU BABY — Elvis PRESLEY
AIN'T THAT THE TRUTH — Frankie KELLY
AIN'T TOO PROUD TO BEG [A] — The TEMPTATIONS
AIN'T 2 PROUD 2 BEG [B] — TLC
AIN'T WE FUNKIN' NOW — The BROTHERS JOHNSON
AIN'T WHAT YOU DO — BIG BROVAZ
AIR HOSTESS — BUSTED
THE AIR THAT I BREATHE [A] — The HOLLIES
THE AIR THAT I BREATHE [A] — SIMPLY RED
AIR TRAFFIC — THREE DRIVES
AIR 2000 — ALBION
AIR WE BREATHE — ALISHA'S ATTIC
THE AIR YOU BREATHE — BOMB THE BASS
AIRHEAD [A] — Thomas DOLBY
AIRHEAD [B] — GIRLS @ PLAY
AIRPLANE GARDENS — FAMILY CAT
AIRPORT — The MOTORS
AIRWAVE — RANK 1
AISHA — DEATH IN VEGAS
AISY WAISY — CARTOONS
AJARE — WAY OUT WEST
AL CAPONE — PRINCE BUSTER
AL DI LA — Emilio PERICOLI
ALA KABOO — SOUND 5
ALABAMA BLUES (REVISITED) — ST GERMAIN
ALABAMA JUBILEE — FERKO STRING BAND
ALABAMA SONG — David BOWIE
ALAN BEAN — HEFNER
ALANE — WES
ALARM CALL — BJÖRK
ALARMA — 666
ALAS AGNES — MYSTERY JETS
ALBATROSS — FLEETWOOD MAC (69)
ALBINONI VS STAR WARS — SIGUE SIGUE SPUTNIK
ALBION — BABYSHAMBLES
ALCOHOLIC — STARSAILOR
ALEXANDER GRAHAM BELL — The SWEET
ALFIE — Cilla BLACK
ALICE I WANT YOU JUST FOR ME — FULL FORCE
ALICE WHAT'S THE MATTER — TERRORVISION
ALICE (WHO THE X IS ALICE) (LIVING NEXT DOOR TO ALICE) — GOMPIE
ALISHA RULES THE WORLD — ALISHA'S ATTIC
ALISON — Linda RONSTADT
ALISON'S ROOM — 60FT DOLLS
ALIVE [A] — PEARL JAM
ALIVE [B] — HELIOTROPIC featuring Verna V
ALIVE [C] — BEASTIE BOYS
ALIVE [D] — P.O.D.
ALIVE [E] — ALIVE featuring D.D. KLEIN
ALIVE [F] — S CLUB
ALIVE [G] — SONIQUE
ALIVE & AMPLIFIED — The MOONEY SUZUKI
ALIVE AND KICKING [A] — SIMPLE MINDS
ALIVE AND KICKING [A] — EAST SIDE BEAT
ALKALINE — SCARFO
ALL ABLAZE — Ian BROWN
ALL ABOUT EVE — MARXMAN
ALL ABOUT LOVIN' YOU — BON JOVI
ALL ABOUT SOUL — Billy JOEL
ALL ABOUT US [A] — Peter ANDRE
ALL ABOUT US [B] — t.A.T.u.
ALL ABOUT YOU — McFLY (05)
ALL ALONE AM I — Brenda LEE
ALL ALONE ON CHRISTMAS — Darlene LOVE
ALL ALONG THE WATCHTOWER — The Jimi HENDRIX EXPERIENCE
ALL ALONG THE WATCHTOWER (EP) — Jimi HENDRIX
THE ALL AMERICAN BOY — Bill PARSONS
ALL AMERICAN GIRLS — SISTER SLEDGE

ALL AND ALL — Joyce SIMS
ALL APOLOGIES — NIRVANA
ALL AROUND MY HAT [A] — STEELEYE SPAN
ALL AROUND MY HAT [A] — STATUS QUO with Maddy PRIOR from STEELEYE SPAN
ALL AROUND THE WORLD [A] — The JAM
ALL AROUND THE WORLD [B] — Lisa STANSFIELD (89)
ALL AROUND THE WORLD [C] — Jason DONOVAN
ALL AROUND THE WORLD [D] — OASIS (98)
ALL AROUND THE WORLD [E] — NORTHERN LINE
ALL BECAUSE OF YOU [A] — GEORDIE
ALL BECAUSE OF YOU [B] — U2
ALL 'BOUT THE MONEY — MEJA
ALL BY MYSELF [A] — Eric CARMEN
ALL BY MYSELF [A] — Celine DION
ALL CRIED OUT [A] — Alison MOYET
ALL CRIED OUT [B] — Melanie WILLIAMS
ALL CRIED OUT [C] — ALLURE featuring 112
ALL DAY ALL NIGHT — Stephanie MILLS
ALL DAY AND ALL OF THE NIGHT [A] — The KINKS
ALL DAY AND ALL OF THE NIGHT [A] — The STRANGLERS
ALL DOWNHILL FROM HERE — NEW FOUND GLORY
ALL EXHALE — Luke SLATER
ALL EYES — CHIKINKI
ALL FALL DOWN [A] — LINDISFARNE
ALL FALL DOWN [B] — FIVE STAR
ALL FALL DOWN [C] — ULTRAVOX
ALL FALL DOWN [D] — MIDGET
ALL FALLS DOWN — Kanye WEST featuring Syleena JOHNSON
ALL FIRED UP — Pat BENATAR
ALL FOR LEYNA — Billy JOEL
ALL FOR LOVE — Bryan ADAMS, Rod STEWART and STING
ALL FOR YOU — JANET
ALL 4 LOVE — COLOR ME BADD
ALL 4 LOVE (BREAK 4 LOVE 1990) — RAZE featuring LADY J and SECRETARY OF ENTERTAINMENT
ALL FUNKED UP — MOTHER
ALL GOD'S CHILDREN — Belinda CARLISLE
ALL GONE AWAY — JOYRIDER
ALL GOOD —DE LA SOUL featuring Chaka KHAN
ALL HOOKED UP — ALL SAINTS
ALL I AM (IS LOVING YOU) — The BLUEBELLS
ALL I ASK — RAE and CHRISTIAN featuring VEBA
ALL I ASK OF MYSELF IS THAT I HOLD TOGETHER — NED'S ATOMIC DUSTBIN
ALL I ASK OF YOU — Cliff RICHARD and Sarah BRIGHTMAN
ALL I DO — CLEPTOMANIACS featuring Bryan CHAMBERS
ALL I EVER NEED IS YOU — SONNY and CHER
ALL I EVER WANTED [A] — SANTANA
ALL I EVER WANTED [B] — HUMAN LEAGUE
ALL I EVER WANTED (DEVOTION) — MYSTERY
ALL I GAVE — WORLD PARTY
ALL I HAVE — Jennifer LOPEZ featuring LL COOL J
ALL I HAVE TO DO IS DREAM [A] — The EVERLY BROTHERS (58)
ALL I HAVE TO DO IS DREAM [A] — Bobbie GENTRY and Glen CAMPBELL
ALL I HAVE TO DO IS DREAM [A] — Cliff RICHARD with Phil EVERLY
ALL I HAVE TO GIVE — BACKSTREET BOYS
(ALL I KNOW) FEELS LIKE FOREVER — Joe COCKER
ALL I NEED — AIR
ALL I NEED IS A MIRACLE — MIKE and The MECHANICS
ALL I NEED IS EVERYTHING — AZTEC CAMERA
ALL I NEED IS YOUR SWEET LOVIN' — Gloria GAYNOR
ALL I REALLY WANT — Alanis MORISSETTE
ALL I REALLY WANT TO DO [A] — The BYRDS
ALL I REALLY WANT TO DO [A] — CHER
ALL I SEE IS YOU — Dusty SPRINGFIELD
ALL I THINK ABOUT IS YOU — NILSSON
ALL I WANNA DO [A] — Sheryl CROW
ALL I WANNA DO [A] — Joanne FARRELL
ALL I WANNA DO [A] — Amy STUDT
ALL I WANNA DO [B] — TIN TIN OUT
ALL I WANNA DO [C] — DANNII

ALL I WANNA DO IS MAKE LOVE TO YOU — HEART
ALL I WANT [A] — Howard JONES
ALL I WANT [B] — THOSE 2 GIRLS
ALL I WANT [C] — SKUNK ANANSIE
ALL I WANT [D] — Susanna HOFFS
ALL I WANT [E] — The OFFSPRING
ALL I WANT [F] — PURESSENCE
ALL I WANT [G] — REEF
ALL I WANT [H] — MIS-TEEQ
ALL I WANT [I] — WET WET WET
ALL I WANT FOR CHRISTMAS IS A BEATLE — Dora BRYAN
ALL I WANT FOR CHRISTMAS IS YOU — Mariah CAREY
ALL I WANT FROM YOU — The TEMPTATIONS
ALL I WANT IS EVERYTHING — DEF LEPPARD
ALL I WANT IS YOU [A] — ROXY MUSIC
ALL I WANT IS YOU [B] — U2
ALL I WANT IS YOU [B] — BELLEFIRE
ALL I WANT IS YOU [C] — Bryan ADAMS
ALL I WANT IS YOU [D] — 911
ALL I WANT TO DO — UB40
ALL I WANT TO DO IS ROCK — TRAVIS
ALL I WANTED — IN TUA NUA
ALL IN MY HEAD — KOSHEEN
ALL IN YOUR HANDS — LAMB
ALL IS FULL OF LOVE — BJÖRK
ALL JOIN HANDS — SLADE
ALL KINDS OF EVERYTHING — DANA (70)
ALL MAPPED OUT — The DEPARTURE
ALL MINE — PORTISHEAD
ALL MY BEST FRIENDS ARE METALHEADS — LESS THAN JAKE
ALL MY LIFE [A] — Major HARRIS
ALL MY LIFE [B] — K-CI & JOJO
ALL MY LIFE [C] — FOO FIGHTERS
ALL MY LOVE [A] — Cliff RICHARD
ALL MY LOVE [B] — HERNANDEZ
ALL MY LOVE [C] — QUEEN PEN featuring Eric WILLIAMS
ALL MY LOVE (ASK NOTHING) — SPEAR OF DESTINY
ALL MY LOVING — DOWLANDS
ALL MY TIME — Lauryn HILL
ALL MY TRIALS — Paul McCARTNEY
ALL 'N' ALL — 187 LOCKDOWN (featuring D'EMPRESS)
ALL N MY GRILL — Missy 'Misdemeanor' ELLIOTT featuring MC SOLAAR
ALL NIGHT ALL RIGHT — Peter ANDRE featuring Warren G
ALL NIGHT DISCO PARTY — BRAKES
ALL NIGHT HOLIDAY — Russ ABBOT
ALL NIGHT LONG [A] — Dexter WANSELL
ALL NIGHT LONG [B] — RAINBOW
ALL NIGHT LONG [C] — CLOUD
ALL NIGHT LONG [D] — MARY JANE GIRLS
ALL NIGHT LONG [D] — Jay MONDI and The LIVING BASS
ALL NIGHT LONG [E] — GANT
ALL NIGHT LONG [F] — Faith EVANS featuring Puff DADDY
ALL NIGHT LONG (ALL NIGHT) — Lionel RICHIE
ALL NITE (DON'T STOP) — JANET
(ALL OF A SUDDEN) MY HEART SINGS — Paul ANKA
ALL OF ME — SABRINA
ALL OF ME FOR ALL OF YOU — 9.9
ALL OF ME LOVES ALL OF YOU — BAY CITY ROLLERS
ALL OF MY HEART — ABC
ALL OF MY LIFE — Diana ROSS
ALL OF THE GIRLS (ALL AI-DI GIRL DEM) — CARNIVAL featuring RIP vs RED RAT
ALL OF YOU [A] — Sammy DAVIS Jr
ALL OF YOU [A] — Julio IGLESIAS and Diana ROSS
ALL OF YOUR DAYS WILL BE BLESSED — Ed HARCOURT
ALL ON BLACK — ALKALINE TRIO
ALL OR NOTHING [A] — The SMALL FACES (66)
ALL OR NOTHING [A] — DOGS D'AMOUR
ALL OR NOTHING [B] — MILLI VANILLI
ALL OR NOTHING [C] — JOE
ALL OR NOTHING [D] — CHER
ALL OR NOTHING [E] — O-TOWN
ALL OUT OF LOVE [A] — AIR SUPPLY
ALL OUT OF LOVE [A] — OTT

30 May 1998	6 June 1998	13 June 1998	20 June 1998
FEEL IT The Tamperer featuring Maya	**C'EST LA VIE** B*Witched	**C'EST LA VIE** B*Witched	**THREE LIONS '98** Baddiel, Skinner and The Lightning Seeds
BLUE Simply Red	**WHERE WE BELONG** Boyzone	**BLUE** Simply Red	**THE GOOD WILL OUT** Embrace

27 June 1998	4 July 1998	11 July 1998	18 July 1998
UK No.1 SINGLES			
THREE LIONS '98 Baddiel, Skinner and The Lightning Seeds	**THREE LIONS '98** Baddiel, Skinner and The Lightning Seeds	**BECAUSE WE WANT TO** Billie	**FREAK ME** Another Level
UK No.1 ALBUMS			
TALK ON CORNERS The Corrs	**FIVE** Five	**TALK ON CORNERS** The Corrs	**HELLO NASTY** Beastie Boys

ANFIELD RAP (RED MACHINE IN FULL EFFECT) — LIVERPOOL FC
ANGEL [A] — Rod STEWART
ANGEL [B] — Aretha FRANKLIN
ANGEL [B] — SIMPLY RED
ANGEL [C] — MADONNA
ANGEL [D] — AEROSMITH
ANGEL [E] — EURYTHMICS
ANGEL [F] — Jon SECADA
ANGEL [G] — A-HA
ANGEL [H] — GOLDIE
ANGEL [I] — MASSIVE ATTACK
ANGEL [J] — Tina COUSINS
ANGEL [K] — Ralph FRIDGE
ANGEL [L] — Lionel RICHIE
ANGEL [M] — SHAGGY featuring RAYVON (01)
ANGEL [N] — Sarah McLACHLAN
ANGEL [O] — The CORRS
THE ANGEL AND THE GAMBLER — IRON MAIDEN
ANGEL EYES [A] — ROXY MUSIC
ANGEL EYES [B] — RAGHAV
ANGEL EYES (HOME AND AWAY) [C] — WET WET WET
ANGEL FACE — GLITTER BAND
ANGEL FINGERS (A TEEN BALLAD) — WIZZARD: Vocal backing: The Suedettes and The Bleach Boys (73)
ANGEL IN BLUE — J GEILS BAND
ANGEL INTERCEPTOR — ASH
ANGEL (LADADI O-HEYO) — JAM & SPOON featuring PLAVKA
ANGEL LOOKING THROUGH — STAGECOACH featuring Penny FOSTER
ANGEL OF HARLEM — U2
ANGEL OF MINE [A] — ETERNAL
ANGEL OF MINE [A] — MONICA
ANGEL OF THE MORNING [A] — PP ARNOLD
ANGEL OF THE MORNING [A] — Juice NEWTON
ANGEL OF THE MORNING [A] — ANY WAY THAT YOU WANT ME (MEDLEY) — Mary MASON
ANGEL STREET — M PEOPLE
ANGELA JONES — Michael COX
ANGELEYES — ABBA
ANGELIA — Richard MARX
ANGELO — BROTHERHOOD OF MAN (77)
ANGELS — Robbie WILLIAMS
THE ANGELS & SHADOWS PROJECT — OMNI TRIO
ANGELS DON'T LIE — Jim REEVES
ANGELS GO BALD: TOO — Howie B
ANGEL'S HEAP — FINN
ANGELS OF THE SILENCES — COUNTING CROWS
ANGEL'S SYMPHONY — RAF
ANGELS WITH DIRTY FACES [A] — SHAM 69
ANGELS WITH DIRTY FACES [B] — SUGABABES
ANGIE — The ROLLING STONES
ANGIE BABY — Helen REDDY
ANGRY AT THE BIG OAK TREE — Frank IFIELD
ANGRY CHAIR — ALICE IN CHAINS
ANGRY SKIES — Maria NAYLER
ANIMAL [A] — DEF LEPPARD
ANIMAL [B] — LOST IT.COM
ANIMAL [C] — R.E.M.
ANIMAL ARMY — BABYLON ZOO
ANIMAL CANNABUS — MULL HISTORICAL SOCIETY
ANIMAL INSTINCT [A] — The COMMODORES
ANIMAL INSTINCT [B] — The CRANBERRIES
ANIMAL NITRATE — SUEDE
THE ANIMAL SONG — SAVAGE GARDEN
ANIMATION — The SKIDS
A9 — ARIEL
ANITINA (THE FIRST TIME I SEE SHE DANCE) — M/A/R/R/S (87)
ANNABELLA — John WALKER
ANNIE GET YOUR GUN — SQUEEZE
ANNIE I'M NOT YOUR DADDY — Kid CREOLE and The COCONUTS
ANNIE'S SONG [A] — John DENVER (74)
ANNIE'S SONG [A] — James GALWAY, flute, NATIONAL PHILHARMONIC ORCHESTRA; Charles Gerhart, conductor
ANNIVERSARY WALTZ — Anita HARRIS
THE ANNIVERSARY WALTZ - PART ONE — STATUS QUO
THE ANNIVERSARY WALTZ - PART TWO — STATUS QUO
ANOMALY — CALLING YOUR NAME — LIBRA presents TAYLOR

ANOTHER BLOOMING CHRISTMAS — Mel SMITH
ANOTHER BODY MURDERED — FAITH NO MORE and BOO-YAA T.R.I.B.E.
ANOTHER BRICK IN THE WALL (PART 2) — PINK FLOYD (79)
ANOTHER CHANCE — Roger SANCHEZ (01)
ANOTHER CUP OF COFFEE — MIKE and The MECHANICS
ANOTHER DAY [A] — Paul McCARTNEY
ANOTHER DAY [B] — WHIGFIELD
ANOTHER DAY [C] — BUCKSHOT LEFONQUE
ANOTHER DAY [D] — SKIP RAIDERS featuring JADA
ANOTHER DAY [E] — LEMAR
ANOTHER DAY (ANOTHER GIRL) — The LAMBRETTAS
ANOTHER DAY IN PARADISE [A] — Phil COLLINS
ANOTHER DAY IN PARADISE [A] — JAM TRONIK
ANOTHER DAY IN PARADISE [A] — BRANDY and RAY J
ANOTHER FINE MESS — Chesney HAWKES
ANOTHER FUNNY HONEYMOON — David DUNDAS
ANOTHER GIRL — ANOTHER PLANET — The ONLY ONES
ANOTHER HEARTACHE — Rod STEWART
ANOTHER KIND OF LOVE — Hugh CORNWELL
ANOTHER LONELY NIGHT IN NEW YORK — Robin GIBB
ANOTHER LOVER — DANE
ANOTHER MAN — Barbara MASON
ANOTHER MONSTERJAM — Simon HARRIS featuring EINSTEIN
ANOTHER MORNING STONER — ... AND YOU WILL KNOW US BY THE TRAIL OF DEAD
ANOTHER NAIL IN MY HEART — SQUEEZE
ANOTHER NIGHT [A] — Aretha FRANKLIN
ANOTHER NIGHT [B] — Jason DONOVAN
ANOTHER NIGHT [C] — (MC SAR &) The REAL McCOY
ANOTHER NIGHT IN — STRANGELOVE
ANOTHER ONE BITES THE DUST [A] — QUEEN
ANOTHER ONE BITES THE DUST [A] — QUEEN with Wyclef JEAN featuring PRAS and FREE
ANOTHER PART OF ME — Michael JACKSON
ANOTHER PEARL — BADLY DRAWN BOY
ANOTHER PIECE OF MEAT — SCORPIONS
ANOTHER PLANET — PENDULUM
ANOTHER ROCK AND ROLL CHRISTMAS — Gary GLITTER
ANOTHER SAD LOVE SONG — Toni BRAXTON
ANOTHER SATURDAY NIGHT [A] — Sam COOKE
ANOTHER SATURDAY NIGHT [A] — Cat STEVENS
ANOTHER SILENT DAY — The ADVENTURES
ANOTHER SLEEPLESS NIGHT [A] — Jimmy CLANTON
ANOTHER SLEEPLESS NIGHT [B] — Mike 'Hitman' WILSON
ANOTHER SLEEPLESS NIGHT [B] — Shawn CHRISTOPHER
ANOTHER STAR [A] — Stevie WONDER
ANOTHER STAR [A] — Kathy SLEDGE
ANOTHER STEP (CLOSER TO YOU) — Kim WILDE and JUNIOR
ANOTHER SUITCASE IN ANOTHER HALL [A] — Barbara DICKSON
ANOTHER SUITCASE IN ANOTHER HALL [A] — MADONNA
ANOTHER TEAR FALLS — The WALKER BROTHERS
ANOTHER TIME, ANOTHER PLACE — Engelbert HUMPERDINCK
ANOTHER WAY — Paul VAN DYK
ANOTHER WEEKEND — FIVE STAR
ANOTHERLOVERHOLENYOHEAD — PRINCE and The REVOLUTION
ANSWER ME [A] — David WHITFIELD (53)
ANSWER ME [A] — Frankie LAINE (53)
ANSWER ME [A] — Ray PETERSON
ANSWER ME [A] — Barbara DICKSON
THE ANSWER TO WHY I HATE YOU — SYMPOSIUM
ANSWERING BELL — Ryan ADAMS
ANSWERS TO NOTHING — Midge URE
ANT RAP — ADAM and The ANTS
ANTE UP — M.O.P. featuring Busta RHYMES
ANTHEM [A] — N-JOI
ANTHEM [B] — The WILDHEARTS
THE ANTHEM — GOOD CHARLOTTE

ANTHEM (ONE DAY IN EVERY WEEK) — The NEW SEEKERS
ANTI-SOCIAL — ANTHRAX
ANTMUSIC — ADAM and The ANTS
THE ANTMUSIC EP (THE B-SIDES) — ADAM and The ANTS
ANY DREAM WILL DO — Jason DONOVAN (91)
ANY MINUTE NOW — SOULWAX
ANY OLD IRON — Peter SELLERS presents Mate's Skiffle Group featuring Fred Spoons E.P.N.S.
ANY OLD TIME — The FOUNDATIONS
ANY ROAD — George HARRISON
ANY TIME ANY PLACE — Janet JACKSON
ANY WAY THAT YOU WANT ME — The TROGGS
ANY WAY YOU LOOK — NORTHERN UPROAR
ANYBODY SEEN MY BABY? — The ROLLING STONES
ANYMORE — Sarah CRACKNELL
ANYONE CAN FALL IN LOVE — Anita DOBSON featuring The Simon MAY ORCHESTRA
ANYONE CAN PLAY GUITAR — RADIOHEAD
ANYONE FOR TENNIS (THE SAVAGE SEVEN THEME) — CREAM
ANYONE OF US (STUPID MISTAKE) — Gareth GATES (02)
ANYONE WHO HAD A HEART [A] — Cilla BLACK (64)
ANYONE WHO HAD A HEART [A] — Dionne WARWICK
ANYONE WHO HAD A HEART [A] — Mary MAY
ANYTHING? [A] — DIRECT DRIVE
ANYTHING [B] — The DAMNED
ANYTHING [C] — Sydney YOUNGBLOOD
ANYTHING [D] — CULTURE BEAT
ANYTHING [E] — SWV
ANYTHING [F] — 3T
ANYTHING [G] — DAMAGE
ANYTHING [H] — JAY-Z
ANYTHING BUT DOWN — Sheryl CROW
ANYTHING CAN HAPPEN — WAS (NOT WAS)
ANYTHING FOR YOU [A] — Gloria ESTEFAN and MIAMI SOUND MACHINE
ANYTHING FOR YOU [B] — STAMFORD AMP
ANYTHING GOES — HARPERS BIZARRE
ANYTHING IS POSSIBLE [A] — Debbie GIBSON
ANYTHING IS POSSIBLE [B] — Will YOUNG (02)
ANYTHING THAT'S ROCK 'N' ROLL — Tom PETTY and The HEARTBREAKERS
ANYTHING YOU WANT — JODIE
ANYTHING YOU WANT (I'VE GOT IT) — ULTIMATE KAOS
ANYTIME [A] — NU-BIRTH
ANYTIME [B] — Brian McKNIGHT
ANYTIME YOU NEED A FRIEND — Mariah CAREY
ANYWAY — HONEYCRACK
ANYWAY ANYHOW ANYWHERE — The WHO
ANYWAY THAT YOU WANT ME — SPIRITUALIZED
ANYWAY YOU DO IT — LIQUID GOLD
ANYWAY YOU WANT IT — Dave CLARK FIVE
ANYWHERE [A] — DUBSTAR
ANYWHERE [B] — Beth ORTON
ANYWHERE FOR YOU — BACKSTREET BOYS
ANYWHERE IS — ENYA
APACHE [A] — The SHADOWS (60)
APACHE [A] — Bert WEEDON
APACHE [B] — STARFIGHTER
APACHE DROPOUT — Edgar BROUGHTON BAND
APEMAN — The KINKS
APHRODITE — PARIS & SHARP
APOCALYPSO — MEW
APOLLO 9 — Adam ANT
APOLOGIES TO INSECT LIFE — BRITISH SEA POWER
APPARENTLY NOTHIN' [A] — YOUNG DISCIPLES
APPARENTLY NOTHING [A] — The BRAND NEW HEAVIES
THE APPLE EP — VARIOUS ARTISTS (Singles and EPs)
APPLE GREEN — The MILLTOWN BROTHERS
APPLE OF MY EYE — Ed HARCOURT
THE APPLE STRETCHING — Grace JONES
APPLE TREE — Erykah BADU
APPLEJACK — Jet HARRIS and Tony MEEHAN
APPLY SOME PRESSURE — MAXIMO PARK
APPRENTICE OF THE UNIVERSE — PURE REASON REVOLUTION
APRIL LOVE — Pat BOONE
APRIL SKIES — JESUS AND MARY CHAIN

AQUARIUS [A] — Paul JONES
AQUARIUS [A] — LET THE SUNSHINE IN (MEDLEY) — 5TH DIMENSION
ARABIAN KNIGHTS — SIOUXSIE and The BANSHEES
ARE EVERYTHING — The BUZZCOCKS
ARE 'FRIENDS' ELECTRIC? — TUBEWAY ARMY (79)
ARE WE HERE — ORBITAL
ARE YOU BEING SERVED — GRACE BROTHERS
ARE YOU BEING SERVED SIR? —John INMAN
ARE YOU BLUE OR ARE YOU BLIND? — The BLUETONES
ARE YOU DREAMING — TWENTY 4 SEVEN featuring CAPTAIN HOLLYWOOD
ARE YOU GETTING ENOUGH OF WHAT MAKES YOU HAPPY — HOT CHOCOLATE
ARE YOU GONNA BE MY GIRL — JET
ARE YOU GONNA BE THERE — UP YER RONSON featuring Mary PEARCE
ARE YOU GONNA GO MY WAY — Lenny KRAVITZ
ARE YOU GROWING TIRED OF MY LOVE — STATUS QUO
ARE YOU HAPPY NOW? — Michelle BRANCH
ARE YOU HEARING (WHAT I HEAR)? — LEVEL 42
ARE YOU IN? — INCUBUS
ARE YOU JIMMY RAY? — Jimmy RAY
ARE YOU LONESOME TO-NIGHT? — Elvis PRESLEY with The JORDANAIRES (61)
ARE YOU LOOKIN' AT ME? — Ricky TOMLINSON
ARE YOU MAN ENOUGH — UNO CLIO featuring Martine McCUTCHEON
ARE YOU MINE? — BROS
ARE YOU MY BABY — WENDY and LISA
ARE YOU OUT THERE — CRESCENDO
ARE YOU READY [A] — Billy OCEAN
ARE YOU READY? [B] — BREAK MACHINE
ARE YOU READY [C] — AC/DC
ARE YOU READY [D] — The GYRES
(ARE YOU READY) DO THE BUS STOP — FATBACK BAND
ARE YOU READY FOR LOVE [A] — Elton JOHN (03)
ARE YOU READY FOR LOVE [B] — ULTRA HIGH
ARE YOU READY FOR SOME MORE — REEL 2 REAL
ARE YOU READY TO BE HEARTBROKEN? — Sandie SHAW
ARE YOU READY TO FLY — ROZALLA
ARE YOU READY TO PARTY — SHRINK
ARE YOU READY TO ROCK — WIZZARD
ARE YOU SATISFIED? (FUNKA NOVA) — RAH BAND
ARE YOU STILL HAVING FUN — Eagle-Eye CHERRY
ARE YOU SURE [A] — The ALLISONS
ARE YOU SURE [B] — SO
ARE YOU THAT SOMEBODY? — AALIYAH
(ARE YOU) THE ONE THAT I'VE BEEN ... — Nick CAVE and The BAD SEEDS
AREA — The FUTUREHEADS
AREA CODES — LUDACRIS featuring Nate DOGG
ARGENTINA — Jeremy HEALY & AMOS
ARGENTINE MELODY (CANCION DE ARGENTINA) — SAN JOSE featuring Rodriguez ARGENTINA
ARIA — Acker BILK, his Clarinet and Strings
ARIANA — STARDUST
ARIENNE — Tasmin ARCHER
ARIZONA SKY — CHINA CRISIS
ARMAGEDDON DAYS ARE HERE (AGAIN) — The THE
ARMAGEDDON IT — DEF LEPPARD
ARMCHAIR ANARCHIST — KINGMAKER
ARMED AND EXTREMELY DANGEROUS — FIRST CHOICE
ARMED AND READY — Michael SCHENKER GROUP
ARMS ALOFT — Joe STRUMMER and The MESCALEROS
ARMS AROUND THE WORLD — LOUISE
ARMS OF LOREN — E'VOKE
ARMS OF MARY — SUTHERLAND BROTHERS and QUIVER
THE ARMS OF ORION — PRINCE with Sheena EASTON
ARMS OF SOLITUDE — OUI 3

25 July 1998	1 August 1998	8 August 1998	15 August 1998
DEEPER UNDERGROUND Jamiroquai	VIVA FOREVER Spice Girls	VIVA FOREVER Spice Girls	NO MATTER WHAT Boyzone
JANE McDONALD Jane McDonald	JANE McDONALD Jane McDonald	JANE McDONALD Jane McDonald	TALK ON CORNERS The Corrs

THE ARMS OF THE ONE WHO LOVES YOU — XSCAPE
ARMY — Ben FOLDS FIVE
ARMY DREAMERS — Kate BUSH
ARMY OF LOVERS — Lee RYAN
ARMY OF ME — BJÖRK
ARMY OF TWO — DUM DUMS
ARNOLD LAYNE — PINK FLOYD
AROUND MY BRAIN — PROGRESS FUNK
AROUND THE WAY GIRL — LL COOL J
AROUND THE WORLD [A] — Ronnie HILTON
AROUND THE WORLD [A] — Bing CROSBY
AROUND THE WORLD [A] — Gracie FIELDS
AROUND THE WORLD [A] — MANTOVANI
AROUND THE WORLD [B] — EAST 17
AROUND THE WORLD [C] — DAFT PUNK
AROUND THE WORLD [D] — RED HOT CHILI PEPPERS
AROUND THE WORLD [E] — AQUA
AROUND THE WORLD (LA LA LA LA LA) — ATC
ARRANGED MARRIAGE — APACHE INDIAN
ARRESTED BY YOU — Dusty SPRINGFIELD
ARRIVEDERCI DARLING [A] — Anne SHELTON
ARRIVEDERCI DARLING [A] — Edna SAVAGE
ARSENAL NUMBER ONE — ARSENAL FC
ART FOR ART'S SAKE — 10cc
THE ART OF DRIVING — BLACK BOX RECORDER
THE ART OF LOSING — AMERICAN HI-FI
ART OF LOVE — ART OF NOISE
THE ART OF MOVING BUTTS — SHUT UP AND DANCE featuring ERIN
THE ART OF PARTIES — JAPAN
ARTHUR DALEY ('E'S ALRIGHT) — The FIRM
ARTHUR'S THEME (BEST THAT YOU CAN DO) — Christopher CROSS
AS — George MICHAEL and Mary J BLIGE
AS ALWAYS [A] — Farley 'Jackmaster' FUNK presents Ricky DILLARD
AS ALWAYS [A] — SECRET LIFE
AS GOOD AS IT GETS — GENE
AS I AM — SOUND OF ONE featuring GLADEZZ
AS I LAY ME DOWN — Sophie B HAWKINS
AS I LOVE YOU — Shirley BASSEY (59)
AS IF WE NEVER SAID GOODBYE — Barbra STREISAND
AS LONG AS HE NEEDS ME — Shirley BASSEY
AS LONG AS THE PRICE IS RIGHT — DR FEELGOOD
AS LONG AS YOU FOLLOW — FLEETWOOD MAC
AS LONG AS YOU LOVE ME — BACKSTREET BOYS
AS LONG AS YOU'RE GOOD TO ME — Judy CHEEKS
AS TEARS GO BY — Marianne FAITHFULL
AS THE RUSH COMES — MOTORCYCLE
AS TIME GOES BY [A] — Richard ALLAN
AS TIME GOES BY [A] — Dooley WILSON
AS TIME GOES BY [A] — Jason DONOVAN
AS TIME GOES BY [B] — FUNKAPOLITAN
AS (UNTIL THE DAY) — KNOWLEDGE
AS USUAL — Brenda LEE
AS WE DO — DJ ZINC
AS YOU LIKE IT — Adam FAITH with John BARRY and his Orchestra
ASCEND — NITZER EBB
ASCENSION DON'T EVER WONDER [A] — MAXWELL
ASCENSION NO ONE'S GONNA LOVE YOU SO DON'T EVER WONDER [A] — MAXWELL
ASHES — EMBRACE
ASHES AND DIAMONDS — Zaine GRIFF
ASHES TO ASHES [A] — The MINDBENDERS
ASHES TO ASHES [B] — David BOWIE (80)
ASHES TO ASHES [C] — FAITH NO MORE
ASIA MINOR — KOKOMO
ASK — The SMITHS
ASK THE LORD — HIPSWAY
ASLEEP IN THE BACK — ELBOW
ASS LIKE THAT — EMINEM
ASSASSIN — The ORB
ASSASSINATOR 13 — CHIKINKI
ASSASSING — MARILLION
ASSESSMENT — The BETA BAND
ASSHOLE — Denis LEARY
ASSOCIATION — INTERNATIONAL AIRPORT / TEENAGE FANCLUB
ASTOUNDED — BRAN VAN 3000 featuring Curtis MAYFIELD
ASTRAL AMERICA — APOLLO 440
ASYLUM — The ORB
ASYLUMS IN JERUSALEM — SCRITTI POLITTI
AT HOME HE'S A TOURIST — GANG OF FOUR
AT MIDNIGHT — T-CONNECTION
AT MY MOST BEAUTIFUL — R.E.M.
AT NIGHT — SHAKEDOWN
AT THE CLUB — The DRIFTERS
AT THE EDGE — STIFF LITTLE FINGERS
AT THE END — IIO
AT THE HOP — DANNY and The JUNIORS
AT THE MOVIES — Roni SIZE
AT THE RIVER — GROOVE ARMADA
AT THE TOP OF THE STAIRS — FORMATIONS
AT THIS TIME OF YEAR — CRAIG
(AT YOUR BEST) YOU ARE LOVE — AALIYAH
ATHEAMA — NEBULA II
ATHENA — The WHO
ATLANTIS [A] — The SHADOWS
ATLANTIS [B] — DONOVAN
ATLANTIS [C] — SECTION-X
ATLANTIS IS CALLING (S.O.S. FOR LOVE) — MODERN TALKING
ATMOSPHERE [A] — Russ ABBOT
ATMOSPHERE [B] — JOY DIVISION
ATMOSPHERE [C] — KAYESTONE
ATMOSPHERIC ROAD — FAMILY CAT
ATOM BOMB — FLUKE
ATOM POWERED ACTION! (EP) — BIS
ATOMIC — BLONDIE (80)
ATOMIC CITY — Holly JOHNSON
ATTACK [A] — TOYS
ATTACK [B] — EXPLOITED
ATTACK ME WITH YOUR LOVE — CAMEO
ATTACK OF THE GHOSTRIDERS — The RAVEONETTES
ATTENTION! — COMMANDER TOM
ATTENTION TO ME — The NOLANS
ATTITUDE [A] — SEPULTURA
ATTITUDE [B] — ALIEN ANT FARM
ATTITUDE [C] — SUEDE
AUBERGE — Chris REA
AUDIO VIDEO — NEWS
AUDITION — WITNESS
AUF WIEDERSEH'N SWEETHEART — Vera LYNN
AUGUST OCTOBER — Robin GIBB
AULD LANG SYNE — WEEKEND
AUSLANDER — LIVING COLOUR
AUSTRALIA — MANIC STREET PREACHERS
AUTHORITY CONFRONTATION — SELFISH CUNT
AUTOBAHN — KRAFTWERK
AUTOBAHN 66 — PRIMAL SCREAM
AUTOBIOGRAPHY OF A CRACKHEAD — SHUT UP AND DANCE
AUTODRIVE — Herbie HANCOCK
AUTOMATIC [A] — POINTER SISTERS
AUTOMATIC [B] — Millie SCOTT
AUTOMATIC [C] — FLOORPLAY
AUTOMATIC [D] — Sarah WHATMORE
AUTOMATIC HIGH — S CLUB JUNIORS
AUTOMATIC LOVER [A] — VIBRATORS
AUTOMATIC LOVER [B] — Dee D JACKSON
AUTOMATIC LOVER (CALL FOR LOVE) — The REAL McCOY
AUTOMATICALLY SUNSHINE — The SUPREMES
AUTOMATIK — BEAT RENEGADES
AUTOPHILIA — The BLUETONES
AUTUMN — Roni SIZE and DIE
AUTUMN ALMANAC — The KINKS
AUTUMN CONCERTO — George MELACHRINO ORCHESTRA
AUTUMN LEAVES — COLDCUT
AUTUMN LOVE — ELECTRA
AUTUMN TACTICS — CHICANE
AVA ADORE — SMASHING PUMPKINS
AVALON [A] — ROXY MUSIC
AVALON [B] — JULIET
AVE MARIA [A] — Shirley BASSEY
AVE MARIA [A] — Lesley GARRETT and Amanda THOMPSON
AVE MARIA [A] — Andrea BOCELLI
AVENGING ANGELS — SPACE
AVENUE [A] — SAINT ETIENNE
AVENUE [B] — Paul VAN DYK
THE AVENUE [C] — ROLL DEEP
AVENUES AND ALLEYWAYS — Tony CHRISTIE
AVERAGE MAN [A] — SYMPOSIUM
AVERAGE MAN [B] — TURIN BRAKES
THE AVERAGE MAN [C] — SIMPLE KID
THE AWAKENING — YORK
AWAY FROM HOME — DR ALBAN
AWAY FROM ME — PUDDLE OF MUDD
AWFUL — HOLE
AXEL F [A] — Harold FALTERMEYER
AXEL F [A] — CLOCK
AXEL F [A] — SPACECORN
AXEL F [A] — CRAZY FROG (05)
AY AY AY AY MOOSEY — MODERN ROMANCE
AYLA — AYLA
AZTEC GOLD — SILSOE
AZTEC LIGHTNING (THEME FROM BBC WORLD CUP GRANDSTAND) — HEADS
B-BOY HUMP — OLD SKOOL ORCHESTRA
B-BOY STANCE — FREESTYLERS featuring TENOR FLY
B GOOD 2 ME — Ronni SIMON
B LINE — LAMB
B O B BOMBS OVER BAGHDAD — OUTKAST
B 2 GETHER — ORIGINAL
B WITH ME — MIS-TEEQ
B WITH U — Junior SANCHEZ featuring DAJAE
BAA BAA BLACK SHEEP — SINGING SHEEP
BAAL'S HYMN (EP) — David BOWIE
BA-BA-BANKROBBERY (ENGLISH VERSION) — EAV
BABALON A.D. (SO GLAD FOR THE MADNESS) — CRADLE OF FILTH
BABARABATIRI — GYPSYMEN
BABE [A] — STYX
BABE [B] — TAKE THAT (93)
BABES IN THE WOOD — MATCHBOX
BABETTE — Tommy BRUCE and The BRUISERS
BABIES — ASHFORD and SIMPSON
BABOOSHKA — Kate BUSH
B-A-B-Y — Rachel SWEET
BABY [A] — HALO JAMES
BABY [B] — ROZALLA
BABY [C] — FABOLOUS featuring Mike SHOREY
THE BABY — The HOLLIES
BABY, BABY [A] — Frankie LYMON and The TEENAGERS
BABY BABY [B] — EIGHTH WONDER
BABY BABY [C] — Amy GRANT
BABY BABY [D] — CORONA
BABY-BABY-BABY — TLC
BABY BABY BYE BYE — Jerry Lee LEWIS
BABY, BABY MY LOVE'S ALL FOR YOU — Deniece WILLIAMS
BABY BE MINE — BLACKSTREET featuring Teddy RILEY
BABY BLUE — Dusty SPRINGFIELD
BABY BOY [A] — BIG BROVAZ
BABY BOY [B] — BEYONCÉ featuring Sean PAUL
BABY BRITAIN — Elliott SMITH
BABY CAKES – 3 OF A KIND (04)
BABY, CAN I GET YOUR NUMBER — OBI PROJECT featuring HARRY, ASHER D & DJ WHAT?
BABY CAN I HOLD YOU — BOYZONE
BABY COME BACK [A] — The EQUALS (68)
BABY COME BACK [A] — Pato BANTON (94)
BABY COME BACK [B] — PLAYER
BABY COME ON — SPACEMAID
BABY COME ON OVER — Samantha MUMBA
BABY COME TO ME [A] — Patti AUSTIN and James INGRAM
BABY COME TO ME [A] — Alexander O'NEAL featuring CHERELLE
BABY DID A BAD BAD THING — Chris ISAAK
BABY DON'T CHANGE YOUR MIND — Gladys KNIGHT and The PIPS
BABY DON'T CRY [A] — Lalah HATHAWAY
BABY DON'T CRY [B] — INXS
BABY DON'T FORGET MY NUMBER — MILLI VANILLI
BABY DON'T GET HOOKED ON ME — Mac DAVIS
BABY DON'T GO [A] — SONNY and CHER
BABY DON'T GO [B] — 4MANDU
BABY FACE [A] — LITTLE RICHARD
BABY FACE [A] — Bobby DARIN
BABY FACE [A] — WING AND A PRAYER FIFE AND DRUM CORPS
BABY GET HIGHER — David SNEDDON
BABY GOODBYE — FRIDAY HILL
BABY GOT BACK — SIR MIX-A-LOT
BABY I DON'T CARE [A] — Buddy HOLLY
BABY I DON'T CARE [A] — Elvis PRESLEY
BABY I DON'T CARE [B] — TRANSVISION VAMP
BABY I DON'T CARE [B] — Jennifer ELLISON
BABY I KNOW — The RUBETTES
BABY I LOVE U — Jennifer LOPEZ
BABY I LOVE YOU [A] — The RONETTES
BABY I LOVE YOU [A] — Dave EDMUNDS
BABY I LOVE YOU [A] — The RAMONES
BABY I LOVE YOU [A] — TSD
BABY I LOVE YOU [B] — Aretha FRANKLIN
BABY I LOVE YOU, OK! — KENNY
BABY I LOVE YOUR WAY [A] — Peter FRAMPTON
BABY I LOVE YOUR WAY [A] — BIG MOUNTAIN
BABY I LOVE YOUR WAY - FREEBIRD — WILL TO POWER
BABY I NEED YOUR LOVIN' — The FOURMOST
BABY I WON'T LET YOU DOWN — PICKETTYWITCH
BABY I'M-A WANT YOU — BREAD
BABY I'M SCARED OF YOU — WOMACK and WOMACK
BABY I'M YOURS [A] — PETER and GORDON
BABY I'M YOURS [A] — Linda LEWIS
BABY, IT'S COLD OUTSIDE — Tom JONES
BABY IT'S TRUE — Mari WILSON
BABY IT'S YOU [A] — Dave BERRY
BABY IT'S YOU [A] — The BEATLES
BABY IT'S YOU [B] — SILK
BABY IT'S YOU [C] — MN8
BABY IT'S YOU [D] — JOJO featuring BOW WOW
BABY JANE — Rod STEWART (83)
BABY JUMP — MUNGO JERRY (71)
BABY LAY DOWN — Ruby WINTERS
BABY LEE — John Lee HOOKER
BABY LET ME TAKE YOU HOME — The ANIMALS
BABY LOVE [A] — The SUPREMES (64)
BABY LOVE [A] — Honey BANE
BABY LOVE [B] — REGINA
BABY LOVE [B] — Dannii MINOGUE
BABY LOVER — Petula CLARK
BABY MAKE IT SOON — MARMALADE
BABY MY HEART — The CRICKETS
BABY NEVER SAY GOODBYE — UNIT FOUR PLUS TWO
BABY NOW I — Dan REED NETWORK
BABY NOW THAT I'VE FOUND YOU [A] — The FOUNDATIONS (67)
BABY NOW THAT I'VE FOUND YOU [A] — Lauren WATERWORTH
BABY OF MINE – Alan PRICE
BABY (OFF THE WALL) – SIRENS
... BABY ONE MORE TIME — Britney SPEARS (99)
BABY PHAT — DE LA SOUL
BABY PLAYS AROUND (EP) — Elvis COSTELLO
BABY PLEASE DON'T GO — THEM
BABY ROO — Connie FRANCIS
BABY SITTIN' — Bobby ANGELO and The TUXEDOS
BABY SITTIN' BOOGIE — Buzz CLIFFORD
BABY STOP CRYING — Bob DYLAN
BABY TAKE A BOW — Adam FAITH
BABY TALK — ALISHA
BABY U LEFT ME (IN THE COLD) — MARILYN
BABY UNIVERSAL — TIN MACHINE
BABY WANTS TO RIDE — HANI
BABY, WE BETTER TRY TO GET IT TOGETHER — Barry WHITE
BABY WE CAN'T GO WRONG — Cilla BLACK
BABY, WHAT A BIG SURPRISE — CHICAGO
BABY WHAT I MEAN — The DRIFTERS
(BABY) YOU DON'T HAVE TO TELL ME — The WALKER BROTHERS
BABY YOU SHOULD KNOW — JOY ZIPPER
BABY YOU'RE DYNAMITE — Cliff RICHARD
BABYLON [A] — BLACK DOG featuring Ofra HAZA
BABYLON [B] — David GRAY
BABYLON'S BURNING — RUTS
BABY'S COMING BACK — JELLYFISH
BABY'S FIRST CHRISTMAS — Connie FRANCIS
BABY'S GOT A TEMPER — The PRODIGY
BABY'S REQUEST — Paul McCARTNEY
BABYSHAMBLES — Peter DOHERTY
BACHELOR BOY — Cliff RICHARD and The SHADOWS (63)
BACHELORETTE — BJÖRK
BACK AND FORTH [A] — CAMEO
BACK AND FORTH [B] — AALIYAH
BACK AROUND — ELEVATOR SUITE
BACK BY DOPE DEMAND — KING BEE

22 August 1998	29 August 1998	5 September 1998	12 September 1998
UK No.1 SINGLES			
NO MATTER WHAT Boyzone	**NO MATTER WHAT** Boyzone	**IF YOU TOLERATE THIS YOUR CHILDREN WILL BE NEXT** Manic Street Preachers	**BOOTIE CALL** All Saints
UK No.1 ALBUMS			
TALK ON CORNERS The Corrs	**TALK ON CORNERS** The Corrs	**WHERE WE BELONG** Boyzone	**WHERE WE BELONG** Boyzone

BACK FOR GOOD [A] — TAKE THAT (95)
BACK FOR GOOD [A] — REAL EMOTION
BACK FOR ME — Candee JAY
BACK FROM THE EDGE — Bruce DICKINSON
BACK HERE — BBMAK
BACK HOME — ENGLAND WORLD CUP SQUAD (70)
BACK IN LOVE AGAIN — Donna SUMMER
BACK IN MY ARMS — Chris PAUL
BACK IN MY ARMS AGAIN — The SUPREMES
BACK IN MY ARMS (ONCE AGAIN) — Hazell DEAN
BACK IN MY LIFE [A] — Joe ROBERTS
BACK IN MY LIFE [B] — ALICE DEEJAY
BACK IN POWER — The GLITTERATI
BACK IN THE DAY [A] — AHMAD
BACK IN THE DAY [B] — ASHER D
BACK IN THE HIGH LIFE AGAIN — Steve WINWOOD
BACK IN THE UK — SCOOTER
BACK IN THE U.S.S.R. — The BEATLES
BACK IT UP — Robin S
THE BACK OF LOVE — ECHO and The BUNNYMEN
BACK OF MY HAND — JAGS
BACK OFF BOOGALOO — Ringo STARR
BACK ON MY FEET AGAIN — The FOUNDATIONS
BACK ON THE CHAIN GANG — The PRETENDERS
BACK ON THE RADIO — The HISS
BACK ON THE ROAD [A] — MARMALADE
BACK ON THE ROAD [B] — EARTH WIND AND FIRE
BACK ON THE STREETS — SAXON
BACK ON TOP — Van MORRISON
BACK SEAT OF MY CAR — Paul and Linda McCARTNEY
BACK STABBERS — The O'JAYS
BACK STREET LUV — CURVED AIR
BACK THEN — MORE FIRE CREW
BACK TO BASICS — SHAPESHIFTERS
BACK TO CALI — Mauro PICOTTO
BACK TO EARTH — Yves DERUYTER
BACK TO FRONT [A] — STIFF LITTLE FINGERS
BACK TO FRONT [B] — ADAMSKI
BACK TO LIFE (HOWEVER DO YOU WANT ME) — SOUL II SOUL featuring Caron WHEELER (89)
BACK TO LOVE [A] — Evelyn 'Champagne' KING
BACK TO LOVE [B] — The BRAND NEW HEAVIES
BACK TO LOVE [C] — E-Z ROLLERS
BACK TO MY ROOTS — RuPAUL
BACK TO REALITY — INTELLIGENT HOODLUM
BACK TO SCHOOL AGAIN — The FOUR TOPS
BACK TO THE LIGHT — Brian MAY
BACK TO THE OLD SCHOOL — BASSHEADS
BACK TO THE SIXTIES — TIGHT FIT
BACK TO THE SIXTIES PART 2 — TIGHT FIT
BACK TO YOU — Bryan ADAMS
BACK TOGETHER — BABYBIRD
BACK TOGETHER AGAIN [A] — Roberta FLACK
BACK TOGETHER AGAIN [A] — INNER CITY
BACK UP (TO ME) — WOOKIE featuring LAIN
BACK WHEN — ALLSTARS
BACK WITH THE BOYS AGAIN — Joe FAGIN
BACK WITH THE KILLER AGAIN — The AUTEURS
BACKCHAT — QUEEN
BACKFIELD IN MOTION — JB's ALL STARS
BACKFIRED [A] — Deborah HARRY
BACKFIRED [B] — MASTERS AT WORK
BACKS TO THE WALL — SAXON
BACKSEAT EDUCATION — ZODIAC MINDWARP and The LOVE REACTION
BACKSTABBERS – Mark MORRISON
BACKSTAGE — Gene PITNEY
BACKSTREET SYMPHONY — THUNDER
BACKSTROKIN' — FATBACK BAND
BACKTOGETHER — HARDSOUL featuring Ron CARROLL
BAD — Michael JACKSON
BAD ACTRESS — TERRORVISION
BAD AMBASSADOR — The DIVINE COMEDY
BAD ASS STRIPPA – JENTINA
BAD BABYSITTER — PRINCESS SUPERSTAR
BAD BAD BOY — NAZARETH
BAD BOY [A] — Marty WILDE
BAD BOY [B] — The ADICTS
BAD BOY [C] — MIAMI SOUND MACHINE
BAD BOY [D] — WILDCHILD
BAD BOY FOR LIFE — P DIDDY featuring BLACK ROB and Mark CURRY
BAD BOYS [A] — WHAM!
BAD BOYS [B] — INNER CIRCLE
BAD BOYS HOLLER BOO — 5050
BAD CASE OF LOVIN' YOU (DOCTOR DOCTOR) — Robert PALMER
BAD COVER VERSION — PULP
BAD DAY [A] — CARMEL
BAD DAY [B] — R.E.M.
BAD DAY [C] — Daniel POWTER
THE BAD DAYS (EP) — SPACE
BAD FEELING — The BEATINGS
BAD GIRL [A] — MADONNA
BAD GIRL [B] — SCARLET
BAD GIRL [C] — DJ RAP
BAD GIRLS [A] — Donna SUMMER
BAD GIRLS [A] — Juliet ROBERTS
BAD HABIT — A.T.F.C. presents ONEPHATDEEVA
BAD HABITS — Jenny BURTON
BAD INTENTIONS — DR DRE featuring KNOC-TURN'AL
BAD LIFE — PUBLIC IMAGE LTD
BAD LOVE — Eric CLAPTON
BAD LUCK — FM
BAD MAN — SISTER BLISS
BAD MEDICINE — BON JOVI
BAD MOON RISING — CREEDENCE CLEARWATER REVIVAL (69)
A BAD NIGHT — Cat STEVENS
BAD OLD DAYS — CO-CO
BAD OLD MAN — BABYBIRD
BAD PENNY BLUES — Humphrey LYTTELTON BAND
THE BAD PHOTOGRAPHER — SAINT ETIENNE
BAD THING — CRY OF LOVE
BAD THINGS — N-JOI
BAD TIME — JAYHAWKS
BAD TO ME — Billy J KRAMER and The DAKOTAS (63)
THE BAD TOUCH — The BLOODHOUND GANG
A BAD TOWN — BIG SOUND AUTHORITY
BAD WEATHER — The SUPREMES
BAD YOUNG BROTHER — Derek B
BADABOOM — B2K featuring FABOLOUS
BADDER BADDER SCHWING — Freddy FRESH featuring FATBOY SLIM
BADDEST RUFFEST — BACKYARD DOG
BADGE — CREAM
BADMAN — COCKNEY REJECTS
THE BADMAN IS ROBBIN' — HIJACK
BAG IT UP — Geri HALLIWELL (00)
BAGGY TROUSERS — MADNESS
THE BAGUIO TRACK — LUZON
BAILAMOS [A] — Enrique IGLESIAS
BAILAMOS [B] — M3
BAILANDO CON LOBOS — CABANA
BAKER STREET [A] — Gerry RAFFERTY
BAKER STREET [A] — UNDERCOVER
BAKERMAN — LAID BACK
BALL AND CHAIN — XTC
BALL OF CONFUSION — The TEMPTATIONS
BALL PARK INCIDENT — WIZZARD
BALLA BABY — CHINGY
BALLAD OF A LANDLORD — Terry HALL
THE BALLAD OF BONNIE AND CLYDE — Georgie FAME (68)
THE BALLAD OF CHASEY LAIN — The BLOODHOUND GANG
BALLAD OF DAVY CROCKETT [A] — Dick JAMES
THE BALLAD OF DAVY CROCKETT [A] — Bill HAYES
THE BALLAD OF DAVY CROCKETT [A] — Max BYGRAVES
THE BALLAD OF DAVY CROCKETT [A] — Tennessee Ernie FORD
THE BALLAD OF JAYNE — L.A. GUNS
THE BALLAD OF JOHN AND YOKO — The BEATLES (69)
THE BALLAD OF LUCY JORDAN — Marianne FAITHFULL
BALLAD OF PALADIN — Duane EDDY and The REBELS
THE BALLAD OF PAUL K — McFLY
THE BALLAD OF PETER PUMPKINHEAD [A] — CRASH TEST DUMMIES
THE BALLAD OF PETER PUMPKINHEAD [A] — XTC
THE BALLAD OF SPOTTY MULDOON — Peter COOK
THE BALLAD OF THE GREEN BERETS — Staff Sergeant Barry SADLER
THE BALLAD OF TOM JONES — SPACE with Cerys of CATATONIA
BALLAD OF YOUTH — Richie SAMBORA
BALLERINA GIRL — Lionel RICHIE
BALLERINA (PRIMA DONNA) — Steve HARLEY and COCKNEY REBEL
BALLOON — CATHERINE WHEEL
THE BALLROOM BLITZ [A] — The SWEET
BALLROOM BLITZ [A] — Tia CARRERE
THE BALLROOM OF ROMANCE — Chris DE BURGH
BALMES — Ian POOLEY featuring ESTHERO
BAM BAM BAM — WESTBAM
BAMA BOOGIE WOOGIE — Cleveland EATON
BAMA LAMA BAMA LOO — LITTLE RICHARD
BAMBAATA 2012 — SHY FX
BAMBAKITA — Roni SIZE
BAMBINO — The SPRINGFIELDS
BAMBOO HOUSES — David SYLVIAN
BAMBOO MUSIC — David SYLVIAN
BAMBOOGIE — BAMBOO
BANANA BANANA — KING KURT
BANANA BOAT SONG [A] — Harry BELAFONTE
BANANA BOAT SONG [A] — TARRIERS
THE BANANA BOAT SONG [A] — Shirley BASSEY
BANANA REPUBLIC — The BOOMTOWN RATS
BANANA ROCK — The WOMBLES
THE BANANA SONG — GSP
BANANA SPLITS (THE TRA LA LA SONG) — The DICKIES
BA-NA-NA-BAM-BOO — WESTWORLD
BANANA-NA-NA (DUMB DI DUMB) — TECHNOHEAD
BAND OF GOLD [A] — Don CHERRY
BAND OF GOLD [B] — Freda PAYNE (70)
BAND OF GOLD [B] — SYLVESTER
BAND ON THE RUN — Paul McCARTNEY
THE BAND PLAYED THE BOOGIE — CCS
BANDAGES — HOT HOT HEAT
BANDWAGON BLUES — TWISTED INDIVIDUAL
BANG [A] — BLUR
BANG [B] — Robbie RIVERA presents RHYTHM BANGERS
BANG AND BLAME — R.E.M.
BANG BANG [A] — SQUEEZE
BANG BANG [B] — B.A. ROBERTSON
BANG BANG (MY BABY SHOT ME DOWN) — CHER
BANG ON! — PROPELLERHEADS
BANG ZOOM (LET'S GO GO) — REAL ROXANNE
BANGERS AND MASH — Peter SELLERS
BANGIN' BASS — DA TECHNO BOHEMIAN
THE BANGIN' MAN — SLADE
BANGLA-DESH — George HARRISON
BANJO BOY [A] — JAN and KJELD
BANJO BOY [A] — George FORMBY
THE BANJO'S BACK IN TOWN — Alma COGAN
BANKROBBER [A] — AUDIOWEB
BANKROBBER [A] — The CLASH
BANKS OF THE OHIO — Olivia NEWTON-JOHN
BANNER MAN — BLUE MINK
BANQUET — BLOC PARTY
BARBADOS — TYPICALLY TROPICAL (75)
BARBARA ANN — The BEACH BOYS
BARBARELLA — ALISHA'S ATTIC
BARBER'S ADAGIO FOR STRINGS — William ORBIT
BARBIE GIRL — AQUA (97)
BARCELONA [A] — Freddie MERCURY
BARCELONA [B] — D KAY & EPSILON featuring STAMINA MC
BARCELONA (FRIENDS UNTIL THE END) — Russell WATSON
BARE NECESSITIES MEGAMIX — UK MIXMASTERS
BAREFOOT (EP) — ULTRAMARINE
BAREFOOT IN THE HEAD — A MAN CALLED ADAM
BAREFOOTIN' — Robert PARKER
BARK AT THE MOON — Ozzy OSBOURNE
BARMY LONDON ARMY — Charlie HARPER
BARNEY (... AND ME) — The BOO RADLEYS
BARREL OF A GUN — DEPECHE MODE
BARRIERS — SOFT CELL
THE BARTENDER AND THE THIEF — STEREOPHONICS
BASEMENT TRACK — HIGH CONTRAST
BASKET CASE [A] — GREEN DAY
BASKET CASE [A] — FREEFALLER
THE BASS EP — FERGIE
BASS (HOW LOW CAN YOU GO) — Simon HARRIS
BASS SHAKE — URBAN SHAKEDOWN
BASSCAD — AUTECHRE
BASSFLY — TILLMAN AND REIS
BASSLICK — SECOND PROTOCOL
BASSLINE — MANTRONIX
BASTARDO — Charlotte HATHERLEY
BAT OUT OF HELL — MEAT LOAF
BATTER UP — NELLY and ST LUNATICS
BATDANCE — PRINCE
BATHTIME — TINDERSTICKS
BATHWATER — NO DOUBT
BATMAN THEME — Neal HEFTI
BATTLE — WOOKIE
BATTLE OF NEW ORLEANS [A] — Johnny HORTON
BATTLE OF NEW ORLEANS [A] — Lonnie DONEGAN
BATTLE OF THE HEROES - FROM STAR WARS REVENGE OF THE SITH — John WILLIAMS / LONDON SYMPHONY ORCHESTRA
BATTLE OF THE SEXES — FAITH, HOPE AND CHARITY
BATTLE OF WHO COULD CARE LESS — Ben FOLDS FIVE
BATTLEFLAG — LO FIDELITY ALLSTARS
THE BATTLE'S O'ER — Andy STEWART
BATTLESHIP CHAINS — GEORGIA SATELLITES
BAUBLES BANGLES AND BEADS — George SHEARING
BAUHAUS — CAPPELLA
BAWITABA — KID ROCK
BBC WORLD CUP GRANDSTAND — ROYAL PHILHARMONIC ORCHESTRA arranged and conducted by Louis CLARK
BE AGGRESSIVE — FAITH NO MORE
BE ALL YOU WANT TO BE — MORNING RUNNER
BE ALONE NO MORE — ANOTHER LEVEL
BE ANGELED — JAM & SPOON featuring REA
BE AS ONE — Maria NAYLER
BE-BOP-A-LULA — Gene VINCENT
BE CAREFUL — SPARKLE featuring R Kelly
BE COOL — PAFFENDORF
BE FAITHFUL — FATMAN SCOOP featuring The CROOKLYN CLAN (03)
BE FREE — LIVE ELEMENT
BE FREE WITH YOUR LOVE — SPANDAU BALLET
BE GOOD TO YOURSELF — Frankie MILLER
BE HAPPY — Mary J BLIGE
BE MINE [A] — Lance FORTUNE
BE MINE [B] — The TREMELOES
BE MINE [C] — CHARLOTTE
BE MINE [D] — David GRAY
BE MINE TONIGHT — JAMMERS
BE MY BABY [A] — The RONETTES
BE MY BABY [B] — Vanessa PARADIS
BE MY BABY [C] — CAPPELLA
BE MY DOWNFALL — DEL AMITRI
BE MY ENEMY — The DEPARTURE
BE MY FRIEND — SOUL U*NIQUE
BE MY GIRL [A] — Jim DALE
BE MY GIRL [B] — DENNISONS
BE MY GUEST — Fats DOMINO
BE MY LIGHT BE MY GUIDE — GENE
BE MY LOVER — LA BOUCHE
BE MY NUMBER TWO — Joe JACKSON
BE MY TWIN — BROTHER BEYOND
BE NEAR ME — ABC
BE PROUD BE LOUD (BE HEARD) — TOYAH
BE QUICK OR BE DEAD — IRON MAIDEN
BE QUIET AND DRIVE (FAR AWAY) — DEFTONES
BE STIFF — DEVO
BE TENDER WITH ME BABY — Tina TURNER
BE THANKFUL FOR WHAT YOU'VE GOT — William DE VAUGHN
BE THE FIRST TO BELIEVE — a1
BE THERE [A] — TALL PAUL
BE THERE [B] — Ian BROWN
BE WITH ME ALWAYS — Cliff RICHARD
BE WITH YOU [A] — The BANGLES
BE WITH YOU [B] — ATOMIC KITTEN
BE WITHOUT YOU — Mary J BLIGE

19 September 1998	26 September 1998	3 October 1998	10 October 1998
MILLENNIUM Robbie Williams	**I WANT YOU BACK** Melanie B featuring Missy 'Misdemeanor' Elliott	**ROLLERCOASTER** B*Witched	**ROLLERCOASTER** B*Witched
TALK ON CORNERS The Corrs	**THIS IS MY TRUTH TELL ME YOURS** Manic Street Preachers	**THIS IS MY TRUTH TELL ME YOURS** Manic Street Preachers	**THIS IS MY TRUTH TELL ME YOURS** Manic Street Preachers

BE YOUNG, BE FOOLISH, BE HAPPY — The TAMS
BE YOUNG BE FOOLISH BE HAPPY — SONIA
BE YOURSELF [A] — CELEDA
BE YOURSELF [B] — AUDIOSLAVE
BEACH BABY — FIRST CLASS
BEACH BOY GOLD — GIDEA PARK
BEACH BOYS MEDLEY — The BEACH BOYS
BEACH BUMP — BABY FORD
BEACH OF THE WAR GODDESS — Caron WHEELER
BEACHBALL — NALIN & KANE
BEACHED — ORBITAL
BEACON LIGHT — WEEN
BEAR CAGE — The STRANGLERS
BEAT BOX — ART OF NOISE
A BEAT CALLED LOVE — GRID
BEAT DIS — BOMB THE BASS
BEAT FOR BEATNIKS — John BARRY ORCHESTRA
THE BEAT GOES ON [A] — SONNY and CHER
BEAT GOES ON [A] — The ALL SEEING I
THE BEAT GOES ON [B] — Bob SINCLAR
BEAT IT — Michael JACKSON
BEAT MAMA — CAST
BEAT STREET BREAKDOWN — GRANDMASTER FLASH, Melle MEL and The FURIOUS FIVE
BEAT SURRENDER — The JAM (82)
BEAT THE BEAT — Mari WILSON
BEAT THE CLOCK — SPARKS
BEAT YOUR HEART OUT — The DISTILLERS
THE BEAT(EN) GENERATION — The THE
BEATIN' THE HEAT — JACK 'N' CHILL
BEATING HEART BABY — HEAD AUTOMATICA
BEATLES AND THE STONES — HOUSE OF LOVE
BEATLES MOVIE MEDLEY — The BEATLES
BEATNIK FLY — JOHNNY and The HURRICANES
BEATNIK GIRL — SNUG
BEATSTIME — SONIC SOLUTION
BEAUTIFUL [A] — MARILLION
BEAUTIFUL [B] — Matt DAREY
BEAUTIFUL [B] — Matt DAREY featuring Marcella WOODS
BEAUTIFUL [C] — ATHLETE
BEAUTIFUL [D] — LEMONESCENT
BEAUTIFUL [E] — BIGFELLA featuring Noel MCCALLA
BEAUTIFUL [F] — SNOOP DOGG featuring PHARRELL, uncle Charlie WILSON
BEAUTIFUL [G] — Christina AGUILERA (03)
BEAUTIFUL ALONE — STRANGELOVE
BEAUTIFUL CHILD (A DEEPER LOVE) — MADELYNE
BEAUTIFUL DAY [A] — 3 COLOURS RED
BEAUTIFUL DAY [B] — U2 (00)
BEAUTIFUL DREAM — WORLD PARTY
THE BEAUTIFUL EXPERIENCE — PRINCE
BEAUTIFUL GIRL — INXS
BEAUTIFUL IMBALANCE — THRASHING DOVES
BEAUTIFUL IN MY EYES — Joshua KADISON
BEAUTIFUL INSIDE — LOUISE
BEAUTIFUL LIFE — ACE OF BASE
BEAUTIFUL LOVE [A] — ADEVA
BEAUTIFUL LOVE [B] — Julian COPE
BEAUTIFUL LOVER — BROTHERHOOD OF MAN
BEAUTIFUL NIGHT — Paul McCARTNEY
BEAUTIFUL NOISE — Neil DIAMOND
THE BEAUTIFUL OCCUPATION — TRAVIS
BEAUTIFUL ONES — SUEDE
BEAUTIFUL PEOPLE [A] — STRESS
BEAUTIFUL PEOPLE [B] — BIG COUNTRY
BEAUTIFUL PEOPLE [C] — Barbara TUCKER
THE BEAUTIFUL PEOPLE [D] — MARILYN MANSON
BEAUTIFUL SON — HOLE
BEAUTIFUL STRANGER — MADONNA
BEAUTIFUL SUNDAY — Daniel BOONE
BEAUTIFUL YOU — Neil SEDAKA
BEAUTY AND THE BEAST [A] — David BOWIE
BEAUTY AND THE BEAST [B] — Celine DION and Peabo BRYSON
BEAUTY DIES YOUNG — LOWGOLD
BEAUTY IS ONLY SKIN DEEP — The TEMPTATIONS
THE BEAUTY OF SILENCE — SVENSON and GIELEN
BEAUTY OF THE RIDE — SEBADOH
BEAUTY ON THE FIRE — Natalie IMBRUGLIA
BEAUTY'S ONLY SKIN DEEP — ASWAD
BECAUSE [A] — Demis ROUSSOS
BECAUSE [B] — Julian LENNON
BECAUSE I GOT HIGH — AFROMAN (01)
BECAUSE I GOT IT LIKE THAT — The JUNGLE BROTHERS
BECAUSE I LOVE YOU [A] — Georgie FAME
BECAUSE I LOVE YOU [B] — Shakin' STEVENS
BECAUSE I LOVE YOU (THE POSTMAN SONG) — Stevie B
BECAUSE OF LOVE [A] — Billy FURY
BECAUSE OF LOVE [B] — Janet JACKSON
BECAUSE OF YOU [A] — DEXY'S MIDNIGHT RUNNERS
BECAUSE OF YOU [B] — GABRIELLE
BECAUSE OF YOU [C] — 98°
BECAUSE OF YOU [D] — SCANTY SANDWICH
BECAUSE OF YOU [E] — Marques HOUSTON
BECAUSE OF YOU [F] — Kelly CLARKSON
BECAUSE THE NIGHT [A] — Patti SMITH GROUP
BECAUSE THE NIGHT [A] — CO-RO featuring TARLISA
BECAUSE THE NIGHT [A] — 10,000 MANIACS
BECAUSE THE NIGHT [A] — Jan WAYNE
BECAUSE THEY'RE YOUNG [A] — Duane EDDY and The REBELS
BECAUSE THEY'RE YOUNG [A] — James DARREN
BECAUSE WE WANT TO — BILLIE
BECAUSE YOU — COSMIC ROUGH RIDERS
BECAUSE YOU LOVED ME (THEME FROM 'UP CLOSE AND PERSONAL') — Celine DION
BECAUSE YOU'RE MINE [A] — Mario LANZA
BECAUSE YOU'RE MINE [A] — Nat 'King' COLE
BECAUSE YOU'RE YOUNG — CLASSIX NOUVEAUX
BECOMING MORE LIKE ALFIE — The DIVINE COMEDY
BECOMING MORE LIKE GOD — Jah WOBBLE'S INVADERS OF THE HEART
BED OF NAILS — Alice COOPER
BED OF ROSES — BON JOVI
BEDS ARE BURNING — MIDNIGHT OIL
THE BED'S TOO BIG WITHOUT YOU — Sheila HYLTON
BEDSHAPED – KEANE
BEDSITTER — SOFT CELL
BEDTIME STORY — MADONNA
THE BEE — SCIENTIST
BEE BOM — Anthony NEWLEY
BEE STING — CAMOUFLAGE featuring MYSTI
BEEF — Gary CLAIL ON-U SOUND SYSTEM
BEEN A LONG TIME — FOG
BEEN AROUND THE WORLD [A] — PUFF DADDY
BEEN AROUND THE WORLD [B] – ZENA featuring Vybz KARTEL
BEEN CAUGHT STEALING — JANE'S ADDICTION
BEEN IT — The CARDIGANS
BEEN THINKING ABOUT YOU — Martine GIRAULT
BEEN THERE DONE THAT — SMOKE 2 SEVEN
BEEN TRAINING DOGS — The COOPER TEMPLE CLAUSE
BEEP ME 911 — Missy 'Misdemeanor' ELLIOTT
BEER DRINKERS AND HELL RAISERS — MOTÖRHEAD
BEETHOVEN (I LOVE TO LISTEN TO) — EURYTHMICS
BEETLEBUM — BLUR (97)
BEFORE — PET SHOP BOYS
BEFORE I FORGET — SLIPKNOT
BEFORE TODAY — EVERYTHING BUT THE GIRL
BEFORE YOU LEAVE — PEPE DELUXÉ
BEFORE YOU LOVE ME — ALSOU
BEFORE YOU WALK OUT OF MY LIFE — MONICA
BEG, STEAL OR BORROW — The NEW SEEKERS
A BEGGAR ON A BEACH OF GOLD — MIKE and The MECHANICS
BEGGIN' — TIMEBOX
BEGGIN' TO BE WRITTEN — WORLDS APART
BEGGING YOU — The STONE ROSES
BEGIN AGAIN — SPACE
BEGIN THE BEGUINE (VOLVER A EMPEZAR) — Julio IGLESIAS (81)
THE BEGINNING — SEAL
BEHIND A PAINTED SMILE — The ISLEY BROTHERS
BEHIND BLUE EYES — LIMP BIZKIT
BEHIND CLOSED DOORS — Charlie RICH
BEHIND THE COUNTER — The FALL
BEHIND THE GROOVE — Teena MARIE
BEHIND THE MASK — Eric CLAPTON
BEHIND THE WHEEL — DEPECHE MODE
BEHIND THESE HAZEL EYES — Kelly CLARKSON
BEIN' AROUND — LEMONHEADS
BEING A GIRL (PART ONE) (EP) — MANSUN
BEING BOILED — HUMAN LEAGUE
BEING BORING — PET SHOP BOYS
BEING BRAVE — MENSWEAR
BEING NOBODY — RICHARD X vs LIBERTY X
BEING WITH YOU — Smokey ROBINSON (81)
BEL AMOUR — BEL AMOUR
BELARUSE — LEVELLERS
BELFAST [A] — BONEY M
BELFAST [B] — BARNBRACK
BELFAST [C] — ENERGY ORCHARD
BELFAST [D] — ORBITAL
BELFAST BOY — Don FARDON
BELFAST CHILD — SIMPLE MINDS (89)
BELFAST TRANCE — John 'OO' FLEMING vs SIMPLE MINDS
BELIEVE [A] — Lenny KRAVITZ
BELIEVE [B] — Q-TEX
BELIEVE [C] — Elton JOHN
BELIEVE [D] — GOLDIE
BELIEVE [E] — CHER (98)
BELIEVE [F] — MINISTERS DA LA FUNK featuring Jocelyn BROWN
BELIEVE [G] — IAN VAN DAHL
BELIEVE [H] — The CHEMICAL BROTHERS
BELIEVE IN ME [A] — UTAH SAINTS
BELIEVE IN ME [B] — QUIVVER
BELIEVE IN ME [C] — MANKEY
BELIEVE IN ME [D] — RAW STYLUS
BELIEVE IN THE BEAT — Carol Lynn TOWNES
BELIEVE IN THE BOOGIE — Mark OWEN
BELIEVE WHAT YOU'RE SAYING — SUGAR
BELIEVER — REAL PEOPLE
BELIEVERS — BAZ
THE BELL — Mike OLDFIELD
BELL BOTTOM BLUES — Alma COGAN
BELL BOTTOMED TEAR — The BEAUTIFUL SOUTH
THE BELLE OF ST MARK — Sheila E
BELLISSIMA — DJ QUICKSILVER
BELLS OF AVIGNON — Max BYGRAVES
BELLS OF NY — SLO-MOSHUN
BELLY DANCER (BANANZA) — AKON
BELO HORIZONTI — HEARTISTS
BEN [A] — Marti WEBB
BEN [A] — Michael JACKSON
BEN [A] — Toni WARNE
BEND IT — Dave DEE, DOZY, BEAKY, MICK and TICH
BEND ME SHAPE ME [A] — AMEN CORNER
BEND ME SHAPE ME [A] — The AMERICAN BREED
BENEDICTUS — BRAINBUG
BENJAMIN — VERUCA SALT
BENNIE AND THE JETS — Elton JOHN
BENNY'S THEME — Paul HENRY and The Mayson GLEN ORCHESTRA
BENTLEY'S GONNA SORT YOU OUT! — BENTLEY RHYTHM ACE
BENZIN — RAMMSTEIN
BERMUDA TRIANGLE — Barry MANILOW
BERNADETTE — The FOUR TOPS
BERRY — TC
BERSERKER — Gary NUMAN
BESAME MUCHO — Jet HARRIS
BESIDE YOU — Iggy POP
THE BEST — Tina TURNER
BEST BIT (EP) — Beth ORTON featuring Terry CALLIER
THE BEST CHRISTMAS OF THEM ALL — Shakin' STEVENS
BEST DAYS — JUICE
THE BEST DAYS OF OUR LIVES — LISBON LIONS featuring Martin O'NEIL & The CELTIC CHOIR
THE BEST DISCO IN TOWN — The RITCHIE FAMILY
BEST FRIEND [A] — The BEAT
BEST FRIEND [B] — Mark MORRISON and Conner REEVES
BEST FRIEND [C] — PUFF DADDY
BEST FRIENDS [A] — TOY-BOX
BEST FRIENDS [B] — ALLSTARS
BEST FRIENDS FOREVER — TWEENIES
BEST FRIEND'S GIRL — ELECTRASY
BEST I CAN — QUEENSRYCHE
BEST IN ME — LET LOOSE
THE BEST IS YET TO COME — SCOOCH
BEST KEPT SECRET — CHINA CRISIS
BEST LOVE — COURSE
THE BEST OF EVERYTHING — Johnny MATHIS
THE BEST OF LOVE — Michael BOLTON
THE BEST OF ME [A] — Cliff RICHARD
THE BEST OF ME [B] — Bryan ADAMS
BEST OF MY LOVE [A] — The EMOTIONS
BEST OF MY LOVE [A] — Dee LEWIS
BEST OF MY LOVE [A] — LOVESTATION
BEST OF MY LOVE [A] — CJ LEWIS
BEST OF MY LOVE [A] — JAVINE
BEST OF ORDER — David SNEDDON
THE BEST OF TIMES — STYX
BEST OF YOU [A] — Kenny THOMAS
BEST OF YOU [B] — FOO FIGHTERS
(THE BEST PART OF) BREAKING UP [A] — The RONETTES
(THE BEST PART OF) BREAKING UP [A] — The SYMBOLS
(THE BEST PART OF) BREAKING UP [A] — Roni GRIFFITH
BEST REGRETS — GENEVA
BEST THING — Adam RICKITT
THE BEST THING — SAVAGE GARDEN
BEST THING IN THE WORLD — OPTIMYSTIC
BEST THING THAT EVER HAPPENED TO ME — Gladys KNIGHT and The PIPS
THE BEST THINGS IN LIFE ARE FREE — Luther VANDROSS and Janet JACKSON
BEST WISHES — ULTRASOUND
THE BEST YEARS OF MY LIFE — Diana ROSS
BEST YEARS OF OUR LIVES — MODERN ROMANCE
BET YER LIFE I DO — HERMAN'S HERMITS
BETA — EMPIRION
BETCHA BY GOLLY WOW [A] — The STYLISTICS
BETCHA BY GOLLY WOW [A] — PRINCE
BETCHA CAN'T LOSE (WITH MY LOVE) — MAGIC LADY
BETCHA CAN'T WAIT — EAST 17
BETCHA' WOULDN'T HURT ME — Quincy JONES
BETTE DAVIS EYES — Kim CARNES
BETTER BE GOOD TO ME — Tina TURNER
BETTER BELIEVE IT (CHILDREN IN NEED) — Sid OWEN
BETTER BEST FORGOTTEN — STEPS
BETTER DAY — OCEAN COLOUR SCENE
BETTER DAYS [A] — GUN
BETTER DAYS [B] — Bruce SPRINGSTEEN
BETTER DAYS [C] — TQ
BETTER DAYS AHEAD — TYRREL CORPORATION
BETTER DO IT SALSA — The GIBSON BROTHERS
BETTER GET READY — LULU
A BETTER LOVE — LONDONBEAT
BETTER LOVE NEXT TIME — DR HOOK
BETTER MADE — HEADSWIM
A BETTER MAN [A] — THUNDER
A BETTER MAN [B] — Brian KENNEDY
BETTER OFF ALONE — DJ JURGEN presents ALICE DEEJAY
BETTER OFF WITH HIM — A
BETTER OFF WITHOUT YOU — Hazell DEAN
BETTER TAKE TIME — SECOND IMAGE
BETTER THAN LIFE — ULTRABEAT
BETTER THAN THEM — NEW MODEL ARMY
BETTER THE DEVIL YOU KNOW [A] — Kylie MINOGUE
BETTER THE DEVIL YOU KNOW [A] — STEPS
BETTER THE DEVIL YOU KNOW [B] — SONIA
BETTER THINGS — The KINKS
BETTER USE YOUR HEAD — LITTLE ANTHONY and The IMPERIALS
BETTER WATCH OUT — ANT & DEC
BETTER WORLD — REBEL MC
BETTY BETTY BETTY — Lonnie DONEGAN
(BETWEEN A) ROCK AND A HARD PLACE — CUTTING CREW
BETWEEN ANGELS & INSECTS — PAPA ROACH
BETWEEN ME AND YOU — JA RULE featuring Christina MILIAN
BETWEEN THE SHEETS — The ISLEY BROTHERS
BETWEEN THE WARS (EP) — Billy BRAGG
BEVERLEY HILLS — WEEZER
BEWARE OF THE BOYS — PANJABI MC featuring JAY-Z

17 October 1998	24 October 1998	31 October 1998	7 November 1998
UK No.1 SINGLES			
GIRLFRIEND Billie	**GYM AND TONIC** Spacedust	**BELIEVE** Cher	**BELIEVE** Cher
UK No.1 ALBUMS			
... HITS Phil Collins	**QUENCH** The Beautiful South	**QUENCH** The Beautiful South	**I'VE BEEN EXPECTING YOU** Robbie Williams

BEWARE — Vivienne McKONE
(BEWARE) BOYFRIEND — Mari WILSON
BEYOND THE INVISIBLE — ENIGMA
BEYOND THE PALE — The MISSION
BEYOND THE REEF — Elvis PRESLEY
BEYOND THE SEA (LA MER) — George BENSON
BEYOND THE STARS — David WHITFIELD
BEYOND TIME — BLANK & JONES
BEYOND YOUR WILDEST DREAMS [A] — Lonnie GORDON
BEYOND YOUR WILDEST DREAMS [A] — SYBIL
THE BHOYS ARE BACK IN TOWN — DANCE TO TIPPERARY
BICYCLE RACE — QUEEN
BIG APPLE — KAJAGOOGOO
BIG AREA — THEN JERICO
BIG BAD EP — LITTLE ANGELS
BIG BAD JOHN — Jimmy DEAN
BIG BAD MAMMA — Foxy BROWN featuring DRU HILL
THE BIG BEAN — PIGBAG
BIG BEAT — CAPPELLA
THE BIG BEAT — Fats DOMINO
BIG BEAT BOOGIE — Bert WEEDON
BIG BIG WORLD — EMILIA
BIG BOSS GROOVE — STYLE COUNCIL
BIG BOY — MINUTEMAN
BIG BOYS DON'T CRY — LOLLY
BIG BROTHER UK TV THEME — ELEMENT FOUR
BIG BUBBLES, NO TROUBLES — ELLIS, BEGGS and HOWARD
BIG CITY — Dandy LIVINGSTONE
BIG CITY LIFE — MATTAFIX
BIG DEAL — Bobby G
BIG DECISION — THAT PETROL EMOTION
BIG DICK MAN — SEX CLUB featuring BROWN SUGAR
BIG EIGHT — JUDGE DREAD
BIG FUN [A] — KOOL and The GANG
BIG FUN [B] — The GAP BAND
BIG FUN [C] — INNER CITY
BIG GAY HEART — LEMONHEADS
BIG GIRL — PRECOCIOUS BRATS featuring KEVIN and PERRY
BIG GIRLS DON'T CRY — The FOUR SEASONS
BIG GREEN CAR — POLECATS
BIG GUN — AC/DC
A BIG HUNK O' LOVE — Elvis PRESLEY
THE BIG HURT [A] — Maureen EVANS
THE BIG HURT [A] — Toni FISHER
BIG IN AMERICA — The STRANGLERS
BIG IN JAPAN — ALPHAVILLE
BIG IRON — Marty ROBBINS
THE BIG L — ROXETTE
BIG LOG — Robert PLANT
BIG LOVE [A] — FLEETWOOD MAC
BIG LOVE [B] — Pete HELLER
BIG LOVE [C] — FRESH BC
BIG MAN — FOUR PREPS
THE BIG MAN AND THE SCREAM TEAM MEET THE BARMY ARMY UPTOWN — PRIMAL SCREAM
BIG MAN IN A BIG HOUSE — Leroy VAN DYKE
BIG ME — FOO FIGHTERS
BIG MISTAKE — Natalie IMBRUGLIA
THE BIG MONEY — RUSH
BIG MOUTH STRIKES AGAIN —The SMITHS
BIG N BASHY — FALLACY featuring TUBBY T
BIG NEW PRINZ — The FALL
BIG NIGHT OUT — FUN LOVIN' CRIMINALS
THE BIG ONE — BLACK
THE BIG ONES GET AWAY — Buffy SAINTE-MARIE
BIG PANTY WOMAN — BAREFOOT MAN
BIG PIMPIN' — JAY-Z
BIG POPPA — NOTORIOUS B.I.G.
BIG PUNK — JUDGE DREAD
BIG RIVER — Jimmy NAIL
BIG SEVEN — JUDGE DREAD
BIG SHIP — Cliff RICHARD
BIG SIX — JUDGE DREAD
THE BIG SKY — Kate BUSH
BIG SKY NEW LIGHT — Martin STEPHENSON and The DAINTEES
BIG SPENDER — Shirley BASSEY
BIG SUR — The THRILLS
BIG TEASER — SAXON
BIG TEN — JUDGE DREAD
BIG THING COMING — The STRANGLERS
BIG TIME [A] — Rick JAMES
BIG TIME [B] — Peter GABRIEL
BIG TIME [C] — WHIGFIELD
BIG TIME OPERATOR — Zoot MONEY and The BIG ROLL BAND
BIG TIME SENSUALITY — BJÖRK
BIG WEDGE — FISH
BIG WHEELS — LLAMA FARMERS
BIG YELLOW TAXI [A] — Amy GRANT
BIG YELLOW TAXI [A] — Joni MITCHELL
BIG YELLOW TAXI [A] — COUNTING CROWS featuring Vanessa CARLTON
BIGAMY AT CHRISTMAS — Tony FERRINO
BIGGEST HORIZON — The Clint BOON EXPERIENCE
BIGGER BETTER DEAL — DESERT EAGLE DISCS featuring Keisha WHITE
BIGGER THAN MY BODY — John MAYER
BIGSCARYANIMAL — Belinda CARLISLE
BIKINI GIRLS WITH MACHINE GUNS — CRAMPS
BIKO — Peter GABRIEL
BILJO — Clodagh RODGERS
BILL BAILEY — Bobby DARIN
BILL McCAI — The CORAL
BILLIE JEAN [A] — Michael JACKSON (83)
BILLIE JEAN [A] — BATES
BILLIE JEAN [A] — SOUND BLUNTZ
BILLS, BILLS, BILLS — DESTINY'S CHILD
BILLS 2 PAY — GLAMMA KID
BILLY BOY — Dick CHARLESWORTH and his CITY GENTS
BILLY DON'T BE A HERO — PAPER LACE (74)
BIMBO — Ruby WRIGHT
BINGO — CATCH
BINGO BANGO — BASEMENT JAXX
BIOLOGY — GIRLS ALOUD
BIONIC — KING ADORA
BIONIC SANTA — Chris HILL
BIRD DOG — The EVERLY BROTHERS
BIRD OF PARADISE — Snowy WHITE
BIRD ON A WIRE — The NEVILLE BROTHERS
BIRD SONG — Lene LOVICH
BIRDHOUSE IN YOUR SOUL — THEY MIGHT BE GIANTS
THE BIRDIE SONG (BIRDIE DANCE) — TWEETS
BIRDMAN — RIDE
BIRDS AND BEES — WARM SOUNDS
THE BIRDS AND THE BEES [A] — Alma COGAN
THE BIRDS AND THE BEES [A] — Jewel AKENS
BIRDS FLY (WHISPER TO A SCREAM) — ICICLE WORKS
BIRDS OF A FEATHER — KILLING JOKE
BIRTH — PEDDLERS
BIRTHDAY [A] — SUGARCUBES
BIRTHDAY [B] — Paul McCARTNEY
BIS VS THE DIY CORPS (EP) — BIS
THE BIT GOES ON — SNAKEBITE
A BIT OF U2 — KISS AMC
BITCH [A] — The ROLLING STONES
BITCH [B] — Meredith BROOKS
BITCH [C] — Dave McCULLEN
THE BITCH — OLYMPIC RUNNERS
THE BITCH IS BACK — Elton JOHN
BITCH SCHOOL — SPINAL TAP
BITCH WITH A PERM — Tim DOG
BITCHES BREW — INSPIRAL CARPETS
BITE YOUR LIP (GET UP AND DANCE) — Elton JOHN
BITES DA DUST — PLANET PERFECTO
THE BITTER END — PLACEBO
BITS + PIECES — ARTEMESIA
BITS AND PIECES — Dave CLARK FIVE
BITS OF KIDS — STIFF LITTLE FINGERS
BITTER FRUIT — LITTLE STEVEN
BITTER SWEET — Marc ALMOND
BITTER SWEET SYMPHONY — The VERVE
BITTER TEARS — INXS
THE BITTEREST PILL (I EVER HAD TO SWALLOW) — The JAM
BITTERSWEET — Billy OCEAN
BITTERSWEET BUNDLE OF MISERY — Graham COXON
BITTERSWEET ME — R.E.M.
BIZARRE LOVE TRIANGLE — NEW ORDER
BIZZI'S PARTY — BIZZI
BJANGO — LUCKY MONKEYS
BLACK AND WHITE [A] — GREYHOUND
BLACK AND WHITE [B] — STATIC-X
BLACK & WHITE ARMY (BRING THE PRIDE BACK HOME) — BLACK & WHITE ARMY
BLACK AND WHITE TOWN — DOVES
BLACK ANGEL — Mica PARIS
BLACK BEAR — Frank CORDELL
BLACK BETTY [A] — RAM JAM
BLACK BETTY [A] — Tom JONES
BLACK BOOK — EYC
BLACK CAT — Janet JACKSON
BLACK CHERRY — GOLDFRAPP
BLACK COFFEE — ALL SAINTS (00)
BLACK COFFEE IN BED — SQUEEZE
BLACK EYED BOY — TEXAS
THE BLACK EYED BOYS — PAPER LACE
BLACK GIRL — The FOUR PENNIES
BLACK GOLD — SOUL ASYLUM
BLACK HEART — Marc ALMOND
THE BLACK HILLS OF DAKOTA — Doris DAY
BLACK HISTORY MONTH — DEATH FROM ABOVE 1979
BLACK HOLE SUN — SOUNDGARDEN
BLACK HORSE & THE CHERRY TREE — KT TUNSTALL
BLACK IS BLACK [A] — LOS BRAVOS
BLACK IS BLACK [A] — LA BELLE EPOQUE
BLACK IS BLACK [B] — The JUNGLE BROTHERS
BLACK JESUS — EVERLAST
BLACK LODGE — ANTHRAX
BLACK MAGIC WOMAN — FLEETWOOD MAC
BLACK MAN RAY — CHINA CRISIS
BLACK MEANING GOOD — REBEL MC
BLACK METALLIC (EP) — CATHERINE WHEEL
BLACK NIGHT — DEEP PURPLE
BLACK NITE CRASH — RIDE
BLACK OR WHITE — Michael JACKSON (91)
BLACK ORCHID — Stevie WONDER
BLACK PEARL — Horace FAITH
BLACK PUDDING BERTHA (THE QUEEN OF NORTHERN SOUL) — The GOODIES
BLACK SABBATH — MAGOO
BLACK SKIN BLUE EYED BOYS — The EQUALS
BLACK STATIONS WHITE STATIONS — M + M
BLACK STEEL — TRICKY
BLACK STOCKINGS — John BARRY ORCHESTRA
BLACK SUITS COMIN' (NOD YA HEAD) — WILL SMITH
BLACK SUPERMAN (MUHAMMAD ALI) — Johnny WAKELIN
BLACK TIE WHITE NOISE — David BOWIE featuring Al B SURE!
BLACK VELVET — Alannah MYLES
BLACK VELVET BAND — DUBLINERS
BLACK WHITE — ASIAN DUB FOUNDATION
BLACKBERRY WAY — The MOVE (69)
BLACKBIRD ON THE WIRE — The BEAUTIFUL SOUTH
BLACKBOARD JUMBLE — The BARRON KNIGHTS
BLACKEN MY THUMB — The DATSUNS
BLACKER THAN BLACK — GOODBYE MR MACKENZIE
BLACKERTHREETRACKER (EP) — CURVE
BLACKWATER [A] — RAIN TREE CROW
BLACKWATER [B] — OCTAVE ONE featuring Ann SAUNDERSON
BLAH — HELTAH SKELTAH and ORIGINOO GUNN CLAPPAZ as The FABULOUS FIVE
BLAME IT ON ME — D:REAM
BLAME IT ON THE BASSLINE — Norman COOK
BLAME IT ON THE BOOGIE [A] — The JACKSONS
BLAME IT ON THE BOOGIE [A] — Mick JACKSON
BLAME IT ON THE BOOGIE [A] — BIG FU
BLAME IT ON THE BOOGIE [A] — CLOCK
BLAME IT ON THE BOSSA NOVA — Eydie GORME
(BLAME IT ON THE) PONY EXPRESS — Johnny JOHNSON and The BANDWAGON
BLAME IT ON THE RAIN — MILLI VANILLI
BLAME IT ON THE WEATHERMAN — B*WITCHED (99)
BLANKET — URBAN SPECIES
BLANKET ON THE GROUND — Billie Jo SPEARS
BLASPHEMOUS RUMOURS — DEPECHE MODE
BLAST THE SPEAKERS — WARP BROTHERS
BLAZE OF GLORY — Jon BON JOVI
BLAZIN' — TALI
BLAZING SADDLES — YELLO
BLEACH — EASYWORLD
BLEED — CATATONIA
BLEED ME WHITE — EAT
BLESS YOU [A] — Tony ORLANDO
BLESS YOU [B] — Martha REEVES and The VANDELLAS
BLIND [A] — TALKING HEADS
BLIND [B] — BAD COMPANY
BLIND AMONG THE FLOWERS — The TOURISTS
BLIND MAN — AEROSMITH
BLIND PILOTS — The COOPER TEMPLE CLAUSE
BLIND VISION — BLANCMANGE
BLINDED BY THE LIGHT — MANFRED MANN
BLINDED BY THE LIGHTS — The STREETS
BLINDED BY THE SUN — The SEAHORSES
BLINDFOLD — MORCHEEBA
THE BLINDFOLD (EP) — CURVE
BLINK — Rosie RIBBONS
BLISS [A] — MUSE
BLISS [B] — SYNTAX
THE BLOCK PARTY — Lisa 'Left Eye' LOPES
BLOCK ROCKIN' BEATS — The CHEMICAL BROTHERS (97)
BLOCKBUSTER! — The SWEET (73)
BLONDE HAIR BLUE JEANS — Chris DE BURGH
BLONDES (HAVE MORE FUN) — Rod STEWART
BLOOD — EDITORS
BLOOD IS PUMPIN' — VOODOO & SERANO
BLOOD MAKES NOISE — Suzanne VEGA
BLOOD MUSIC (EP) — EARTHLING
BLOOD OF EDEN — Peter GABRIEL
BLOOD ON OUR HANDS — DEATH FROM ABOVE 1979
BLOOD ON THE DANCEFLOOR — Michael JACKSON (97)
BLOOD SWEAT AND TEARS — V
THE BLOOD THAT MOVES THE BODY — A-HA
BLOODNOK'S ROCK 'N' ROLL CALL — The GOONS
BLOODSHOT EYES — MILLIE
BLOODSPORTS FOR ALL — CARTER — THE UNSTOPPABLE SEX MACHINE
BLOODY LUXURY — WHITESNAKE
A BLOSSOM FELL [A] — Dickie VALENTINE
A BLOSSOM FELL [A] — Nat 'King' COLE
A BLOSSOM FELL [A] — Ronnie HILTON
BLOSSOMS FALLING — OOBERMAN
BLOW AWAY — George HARRISON
BLOW THE HOUSE DOWN [A] — LIVING IN A BOX
BLOW THE HOUSE DOWN [B] — WEE PAPA GIRL RAPPERS
BLOW UP THE OUTSIDE WORLD — SOUNDGARDEN
BLOW YA MIND — LOCK 'N' LOAD
BLOW YOUR HORNY HORNS — PERFECT PHASE
BLOW YOUR MIND — JAMIROQUAI
BLOW YOUR MIND (I AM THE WOMAN) — Lisa PIN-UP
BLOW YOUR WHISTLE — DJ DUKE
THE BLOWERS DAUGHTER — Damien RICE
BLOWIN' IN THE WIND [A] — Stevie WONDER
BLOWING IN THE WIND [A] — PETER, PAUL and MARY
BLOWIN' ME UP (WITH HER LOVE) — JC CHASEZ
BLOWING WILD — Frankie LAINE
BLUE [A] — FINE YOUNG CANNIBALS
BLUE [B] — The VERVE
BLUE [C] — WAY OUT WEST
BLUE [D] — SYMPOSIUM
BLUE [E] — LeAnn RIMES
BLUE ANGEL [A] — Roy ORBISON
BLUE ANGEL [B] — Gene PITNEY
BLUE ANGELS — Pras MICHEL
BLUE BAYOU [A] — Roy ORBISON
BLUE BAYOU [A] — Linda RONSTADT
BLUE BLUE HEARTACHES — Johnny DUNCAN and The BLUE GRASS BOYS
BLUE CHRISTMAS — Elvis PRESLEY
BLUE (DA BA DEE) — EIFFEL 65 (99)
BLUE DAY — CHELSEA FC
BLUE EMOTION — FIAT LUX
BLUE EYES [A] — Don PARTRIDGE
BLUE EYES [B] — Elton JOHN
BLUE EYES [C] — WEDDING PRESENT
BLUE FEAR [A] — ARMIN
BLUE FEAR 2004 [A] — Armin VAN BUUREN

14 November 1998	21 November 1998	28 November 1998	5 December 1998
BELIEVE Cher	**BELIEVE** Cher	**BELIEVE** Cher	**BELIEVE** Cher
THE BEST OF 1980-1990 & B-SIDES U2	**LADIES & GENTLEMEN - THE BEST OF GEORGE MICHAEL** George Michael	**LADIES & GENTLEMEN - THE BEST OF GEORGE MICHAEL** George Michael	**LADIES & GENTLEMEN - THE BEST OF GEORGE MICHAEL** George Michael

BLUE FLOWERS — DR OCTAGON
BLUE FOR YOU — WET WET WET
BLUE GIRL — The BRUISERS
BLUE GUITAR — Justin HAYWARD
BLUE HAT FOR A BLUE DAY — Nick HEYWARD
BLUE HOTEL — Chris ISAAK
BLUE IS THE COLOUR — CHELSEA FC
BLUE JEAN — David BOWIE
BLUE JEANS — LADYTRON
BLUE JEAN BOP — Gene VINCENT
BLUE LIGHT RED LIGHT (SOMEONE'S THERE) — Harry CONNICK Jr
BLUE LOVE (CALL MY NAME) — DNA
BLUE MONDAY [A] — Fats DOMINO
BLUE MONDAY [B] — NEW ORDER
BLUE MOON [A] — Elvis PRESLEY
BLUE MOON [A] — The MARCELS (61)
BLUE MOON [A] — SHOWADDYWADDY
BLUE MOON [A] — John ALFORD
BLUE MORNING, BLUE DAY — FOREIGNER
BLUE ORCHID — The WHITE STRIPES
BLUE PETER — Mike OLDFIELD
BLUE RIVER — Elvis PRESLEY
BLUE ROOM — The ORB
THE BLUE ROOM — T-EMPO
BLUE SAVANNAH — ERASURE
BLUE SKIES [A] — John DUMMER and Helen APRIL
BLUE SKIES [B] — JETS
BLUE SKIES [C] — BT featuring Tori AMOS
BLUE SKIES [D] — LONGPIGS
BLUE SKIES [E] — SPECIAL NEEDS
BLUE SKY MINE — MIDNIGHT OIL
BLUE SONG — MINT ROYALE
BLUE STAR (THE MEDIC THEME) [A] — Charlie APPLEWHITE
BLUE STAR (THE MEDIC THEME) [A] — Cyril STAPLETON and his Orchestra
BLUE STAR (THE MEDIC THEME) [A] — Ron GOODWIN
BLUE SUEDE SHOES [A] — Carl PERKINS
BLUE SUEDE SHOES [A] — Elvis PRESLEY
BLUE TANGO — Ray MARTIN
BLUE TOMORROW — CHELSEA FC
BLUE TURNS TO GREY — Cliff RICHARD and The SHADOWS
BLUE VELVET — Bobby VINTON
BLUE WATER [A] — FIELDS OF THE NEPHILIM
BLUE WATER [B] — BLACK ROCK featuring Debra ANDREW
BLUE WEEKEND — Karl DENVER
BLUE WORLD — The MOODY BLUES
BLUEBEARD — COCTEAU TWINS
BLUEBELL POLKA — Jimmy SHAND
BLUEBERRY HILL [A] — Fats DOMINO
BLUEBERRY HILL [A] — John BARRY ORCHESTRA
BLUEBIRDS OVER THE MOUNTAIN — The BEACH BOYS
BLUEBOTTLE — POB featuring DJ Patrick REID
BLUEBOTTLE BLUES — The GOONS
BLUE-EYED BOY — Al SAXON
BLUER THAN BLUE — Rolf HARRIS
BLUES BAND (EP) — The BLUES BAND
BLUES FROM A GUN — JESUS AND MARY CHAIN
BLUETONIC — The BLUETONES
BLURRED — PIANOMAN
BLURRY — PUDDLE OF MUDD
BO DIDDLEY — Buddy HOLLY
BOA VS PYTHON — TEST ICICLES
THE BOAT THAT I ROW — LULU
BOAT TO BOLIVIA — Martin STEPHENSON and The DAINTEES
BOBBY TOMORROW — Bobby VEE
BOBBY'S GIRL — Susan MAUGHAN
BODIES — DROWNING POOL
BODY — FUNKY GREEN DOGS
BODY AND SOUL [A] — SISTERS OF MERCY
BODY AND SOUL [B] — MAI TAI
BODY AND SOUL [C] — Anita BAKER
BODY BUMPIN' (YIPPEE-YI-YO) — PUBLIC ANNOUNCEMENT
THE BODY ELECTRIC — RUSH
BODY GROOVE — ARCHITECHS featuring NANA
BODY HEAT — James BROWN
BODY IN MOTION — ATLANTIC OCEAN
BODY LANGUAGE [A] — DETROIT SPINNERS
BODY LANGUAGE [B] — The DOOLEYS
BODY LANGUAGE [C] — QUEEN
BODY LANGUAGE [D] — The ADVENTURES OF STEVIE V
BODY MOVIN' [A] — BEASTIE BOYS
BODY MOVIN' [B] — DRUMSOUND / Simon 'BASSLINE' SMITH
BODY MUSIC — STRIKERS
BODY ROCK [A] — Maria VIDAL
BODY ROCK [B] — SHIMON & Andy C
BODYROCK — TYMES 4
BODY ROCKIN' — Errol BROWN
THE BODY SHINE (EP) — Billy HENDRIX
BODY TALK — IMAGINATION
BODY II BODY — Samantha MUMBA
BODY WORK — HOT STREAK
BODYROCK — MOBY
BODYSHAKIN' — 911
BOG EYED JOG — Ray MOORE
BOHEMIAN LIKE YOU — The DANDY WARHOLS
BOHEMIAN RHAPSODY [A] — QUEEN (75, 91)
BOHEMIAN RHAPSODY [A] — BAD NEWS
BOHEMIAN RHAPSODY [A] — The BRAIDS
BOHEMIAN RHAPSODY [A] — Rolf HARRIS
BOHEMIAN RHAPSODY [A] — G4
BOILER — LIMP BIZKIT
THE BOILER — RHODA with the SPECIAL AKA
BOING! — WEDDING PRESENT
BOLL WEEVIL SONG — Brook BENTON
BOM DIGI BOM (THINK ABOUT THE WAY) — ICE MC
THE BOMB — LOVE CONNECTION
BOMB DIGGY — ANOTHER LEVEL
THE BOMB! (THESE SOUNDS FALL INTO MY MIND) — The BUCKETHEADS
BOMBADIN — 808 STATE
BOMBER — MOTÖRHEAD
BOMBSCARE — 2 BAD MICE
BOMBTRACK — RAGE AGAINST THE MACHINE
BON BON VIE — TS MONK
BOND — 808 STATE
BONE DRIVEN — BUSH
BONEY M MEGAMIX — BONEY M
BONEYARD — LITTLE ANGELS
BONITA APPLEBUM — A TRIBE CALLED QUEST
BONITA MANANA — ESPIRITU
'03 BONNIE & CLYDE — JAY-Z featuring Beyoncé KNOWLES
BONNIE CAME BACK — Duane EDDY and The REBELS
BONY MORONIE — Larry WILLIAMS
BOO! FOREVER — The BOO RADLEYS
BOOGALOO PARTY — The FLAMINGOS
BOOGIE [A] — DIVE
BOOGIE [B] — The BRAND NEW HEAVIES featuring Nicole RUSSO
BOOGIE AT RUSSIAN HILL — John Lee HOOKER
BOOGIE DOWN [A] — Eddie KENDRICKS
BOOGIE DOWN [B] — Al JARREAU
BOOGIE DOWN (BRONX) — Man PARRISH
BOOGIE DOWN (GET FUNKY NOW) — The REAL THING
BOOGIE MAN — MATCH
BOOGIE NIGHTS [A] — HEATWAVE
BOOGIE NIGHTS [A] — La FLEUR
BOOGIE NIGHTS [A] — SONIA
BOOGIE ON REGGAE WOMAN — Stevie WONDER
BOOGIE ON UP — ROKOTTO
BOOGIE OOGIE OOGIE — A TASTE OF HONEY
BOOGIE SHOES — KC and The SUNSHINE BAND
BOOGIE TOWN — FAT LARRY'S BAND
BOOGIE WONDERLAND — EARTH WIND AND FIRE with The EMOTIONS
BOOGIE WOOGIE BUGLE BOY (DON'T STOP) — 2 IN A TENT
THE BOOK — David WHITFIELD
BOOK OF DAYS — ENYA
BOOK OF DREAMS — Suzanne VEGA
BOOK OF LOVE — The MUDLARKS
BOOKS — BELLE & SEBASTIAN
BOOM BANG-A-BANG — LULU
BOOM BLAST — FREESTYLERS featuring MILLION DAN
BOOM BOOM [A] — BLACK SLATE
BOOM BOOM [B] — John Lee HOOKER
BOOM BOOM [C] — DEFINITION OF SOUND
BOOM BOOM [D] — N-TYCE
BOOM BOOM [E] — Basil BRUSH featuring India BEAU
BOOM BOOM BOOM — The OUTHERE BROTHERS (95)
BOOM, BOOM, BOOM, BOOM!! — The VENGABOYS (99)
BOOM BOOM (LET'S GO BACK TO MY ROOM) — Paul LEKAKIS
THE BOOM BOOM ROOM — NATASHA
BOOM, LIKE THAT — Mark KNOPFLER
BOOM ROCK SOUL — BENZ
BOOM SELECTION — GENIUS CRU
BOOM! SHAKE THE ROOM — JAZZY JEFF & The FRESH PRINCE (93)
BOOM! THERE SHE WAS — ROGER
BOOMBASTIC — SHAGGY (95)
BOOO! — STICKY featuring MS DYNAMITE
BOOPS (HERE TO GO) — SLY and ROBBIE
BOOTI CALL — BLACKSTREET
BOOTIE CALL — ALL SAINTS (98)
BOOTY LA LA — BUGZ IN THE ATTIC
BOOTYLICIOUS — DESTINY'S CHILD
BOOTZILLA — BOOTSY'S RUBBER BAND
BOP BOP BABY — WESTLIFE
BOP GUN (ONE NATION) — ICE CUBE featuring George CLINTON
BORA BORA — DA HOOL
BORDERLINE — MADONNA
BORN A WOMAN — Sandy POSEY
BORN AGAIN [A] — The CHRISTIANS
BORN AGAIN [B] — BADLY DRAWN BOY
BORN AGAIN [C] — STARSAILOR
BORN DEAD — BODY COUNT
BORN FREE — Vic REEVES
BORN IN ENGLAND — TWISTED X
BORN IN 69 — ROCKET FROM THE CRYPT
BORN IN THE GHETTO — FUNKY POETS
BORN IN THE 70S — Ed HARCOURT
BORN IN THE USA — Bruce SPRINGSTEEN
BORN OF FRUSTRATION — JAMES
BORN ON THE 5TH OF NOVEMBER — CARTER — THE UNSTOPPABLE SEX MACHINE
BORN SLIPPY — UNDERWORLD
BORN THIS WAY (LET'S DANCE) — COOKIE CREW
BORN TO BE ALIVE [A] — Patrick HERNANDEZ
BORN TO BE ALIVE [B] — ADAMSKI featuring SOHO
BORN TO BE MY BABY — BON JOVI
BORN TO BE SOLD — TRANSVISION VAMP
BORN TO BE WILD — STEPPENWOLF
BORN TO BE WITH YOU [A] — The CHORDETTES
BORN TO BE WITH YOU [A] — Dave EDMUNDS
BORN TO LIVE AND BORN TO DIE — The FOUNDATIONS
BORN TO LOSE — KING ADORA
BORN TO MAKE YOU HAPPY — Britney SPEARS (00)
BORN TO RAISE HELL — MOTÖRHEAD / ICE-T / Whitfield CRANE
BORN TO RUN — Bruce SPRINGSTEEN
BORN TO TRY — Delta GOODREM
BORN TOO LATE — PONI-TAILS
BORN 2 B.R.E.E.D. — Monie LOVE
BORN WITH A SMILE ON MY FACE — Stephanie DE SYKES
BORNE ON THE WIND — Roy ORBISON
BORROWED LOVE — S.O.S. BAND
BORROWED TIME — John LENNON
BORSALINO — Bobby CRUSH
THE BOSS [A] — Diana ROSS
THE BOSS [A] — The BRAXTONS
BOSS DRUM — The SHAMEN
BOSS GUITAR — Duane EDDY and The REBELS
BOSS OF ME — THEY MIGHT BE GIANT
BOSSA NOVA BABY — Elvis PRESLEY
BOSTICH — YELLO
THE BOSTON TEA PARTY — The SENSATIONAL ALEX HARVEY BAND
BOTH ENDS BURNING — ROXY MUSIC
BOTH SIDES NOW [A] — CLANNAD and Paul YOUNG
BOTH SIDES NOW [A] — Judy COLLINS
BOTH SIDES NOW [A] — Viola WILLS
BOTH SIDES OF THE STORY — Phil COLLINS
BOTHER — STONE SOUR
THE BOTTLE [A] — TYRREL CORPORATION
THE BOTTLE [A] — Paul WELLER
THE BOTTLE [B] — The CHRISTIANS
BOTTLE LIVING — Dave GAHAN
BOTTLE ROCKET — The GO! TEAM
BOULEVARD OF BROKEN DREAMS [A] — The BEATMASTERS
BOULEVARD OF BROKEN DREAMS [B] — GREEN DAY
BOUNCE — Sarah CONNOR
BOUNCE ALONG — Wayne WONDER
BOUNCE, ROCK, SKATE, ROLL — BABY DC featuring IMAJIN
BOUNCE WITH THE MASSIVE — TZANT
THE BOUNCER — KICKS LIKE A MULE
BOUNCIN' BACK (BUMPIN' ME AGAINST THE WALL) — MYSTIKAL
BOUNCING FLOW — K2 FAMILY
BOUND 4 DA RELOAD (CASUALTY) — OXIDE & NEUTRINO (00)
BOUNDARIES — Leena CONQUEST and HIP HOP FINGER
BOURGIE, BOURGIE — Gladys KNIGHT and The PIPS
BOUT — JAMELIA featuring Rah DIGGA
BOW DOWN MISTER — JESUS LOVES YOU
BOW WOW (THAT'S MY NAME) — LIL BOW WOW
BOW WOW WOW — FUNKDOOBIEST
THE BOX — ORBITAL
BOX SET GO — HIGH
THE BOXER [A] — SIMON and GARFUNKEL
THE BOXER [B] — The CHEMICAL BROTHERS
BOXER BEAT — JOBOXERS
BOXERS — MORRISSEY
BOY — LULU
THE BOY DONE GOOD — Billy BRAGG
BOY FROM NEW YORK CITY [A] — Alison JORDAN
THE BOY FROM NEW YORK CITY [A] — DARTS
A BOY FROM NOWHERE — Tom JONES
BOY I GOTTA HAVE YOU — RIO and MARS
BOY (I NEED YOU) — Mariah CAREY featuring CAM'RON
THE BOY IN THE BUBBLE — Paul SIMON
BOY IS CRYING — SAINT ETIENNE
THE BOY IS MINE — BRANDY and MONICA
A BOY NAMED SUE — Johnny CASH
BOY NEXT DOOR — JAMELIA
BOY OH BOY — RACEY
BOY ON TOP OF THE NEWS — DIESEL PARK WEST
BOY OR A GIRL — IMPERIAL DRAG
THE BOY RACER — MORRISSEY
THE BOY WHO CAME BACK — Marc ALMOND
THE BOY WITH THE THORN IN HIS SIDE — The SMITHS
THE BOY WITH THE X-RAY EYES — BABYLON ZOO
BOY WONDER — SPEEDY
BOY YOU KNOCK ME OUT — Tatyana ALI featuring Will SMITH
BOYS [A] — Kim WILDE
BOYS [B] — MARY JANE GIRLS
BOYS [C] — BON
BOYS [D] — Britney SPEARS
BOYS AND GIRLS [A] — HUMAN LEAGUE
BOYS AND GIRLS [B] — CHEEKY GIRLS with Andy NEWTON-LEE
THE BOYS ARE BACK IN TOWN [A] — THIN LIZZY
THE BOYS ARE BACK IN TOWN [A] — GLADIATORS
THE BOYS ARE BACK IN TOWN [A] — HAPPY MONDAYS
BOYS BETTER — The DANDY WARHOLS
BOYS CRY — Eden KANE
BOYS DON'T CRY — The CURE
THE BOYS IN THE OLD BRIGHTON BLUE — BRIGHTON AND HOVE ALBION FC
BOYS KEEP SWINGING — David BOWIE
THE BOYS OF SUMMER [A] — Don HENLEY
THE BOYS OF SUMMER [A] — DJ SAMMY
THE BOYS OF SUMMER [A] — The ATARIS
BOYS (SUMMERTIME LOVE) — SABRINA
BOYS WILL BE BOYS [A] — The OSMOND BOYS
BOYS WILL BE BOYS [B] — The ORDINARY BOYS
BOZOS — LEVELLERS
BRACKISH — KITTIE
BRAIN — The JUNGLE BROTHERS
BRAIN STEW — GREEN DAY
BRAINS — NUT
BRAINWASHED (CALL YOU) — TOMCRAFT
BRAND NEW — FINITRIBE
BRAND NEW DAY [A] — DARKMAN
BRAND NEW DAY [B] — MINDS OF MEN

12 December 1998	19 December 1998	26 December 1998	2 January 1999
◂◂ UK No.1 SINGLES ▸▸			
BELIEVE Cher	**TO YOU I BELONG** B*Witched	**GOODBYE** Spice Girls	**CHOCOLATE SALTY BALLS (PS I LOVE YOU)** Chef
◂◂ UK No.1 ALBUMS ▸▸			
LADIES & GENTLEMEN - THE BEST OF GEORGE MICHAEL George Michael	**LADIES & GENTLEMEN - THE BEST OF GEORGE MICHAEL** George Michael	**LADIES & GENTLEMEN - THE BEST OF GEORGE MICHAEL** George Michael	**LADIES & GENTLEMEN - THE BEST OF GEORGE MICHAEL** George Michael

BRAND NEW DAY [C] — STING
BRAND NEW FRIEND — Lloyd COLE
BRAND NEW KEY — MELANIE
BRAND NEW LOVER — DEAD OR ALIVE
BRAND NEW START — Paul WELLER
BRANDY [A] — Scott ENGLISH
BRANDY [B] — O'JAYS
BRAS ON 45 (FAMILY VERSION) — Ivor BIGGUN
BRASS IN POCKET — The PRETENDERS (80)
BRASS: LET THERE BE HOUSE — PARTY FAITHFUL
BRASSNECK — WEDDING PRESENT
BRAVE NEW WORLD [A] — David ESSEX
BRAVE NEW WORLD [B] — TOYAH
BRAVE NEW WORLD [C] — NEW MODEL ARMY
BRAZEN 'WEEP' — SKUNK ANANSIE
BRAZIL [A] — CRISPY AND COMPANY
BRAZIL [A] — RITCHIE FAMILY
BRAZILIAN DAWN — SHAKATAK
BRAZILIAN LOVE AFFAIR — George DUKE
BRAZILIAN LOVE SONG — Nat 'King' COLE
BREACH THE PEACE (EP) — SPIRAL TRIBE
BREAD AND BUTTER — NEWBEATS
BREAK AWAY — The BEACH BOYS
BREAK DANCIN'— ELECTRIC BOOGIE — WEST STREET MOB
BREAK DOWN THE DOORS — MORILLO featuring AUDIO BULLYS
BREAK EVERY RULE — Tina TURNER
BREAK 4 LOVE — RAZE
BREAK FROM THE OLD ROUTINE — OUI 3
BREAK IT DOWN AGAIN — TEARS FOR FEARS
BREAK IT TO ME GENTLY — Brenda LEE
BREAK MY STRIDE — Matthew WILDER
BREAK MY WORLD — DARK GLOBE featuring Amanda GHOST
BREAK OF DAWN — RHYTHM ON THE LOOSE
BREAK ON THROUGH — The DOORS
BREAK THE CHAIN [A] — Elkie BROOKS
BREAK THE CHAIN [B] — MOTIV 8
BREAK THE RULES — STATUS QUO
BREAK UP TO MAKE UP — The STYLISTICS
BREAK UPS 2 MAKE UPS — METHOD MAN featuring D'ANGELO
BREAK YA NECK — Busta RHYMES
BREAK YOU OFF — ROOTS featuring MUSIQ
BREAKADAWN — DE LA SOUL
BREAKAWAY [A] — The SPRINGFIELDS
BREAKAWAY [B] — GALLAGHER and LYLE
BREAKAWAY [C] — Tracey ULLMAN
BREAKAWAY [D] — Donna SUMMER
BREAKAWAY [E] — Kim APPLEBY
BREAKAWAY [F] — ZZ TOP
BREAKBEAT ERA — BREAKBEAT ERA
BREAK DANCE PARTY — BREAK MACHINE
BREAKDOWN [A] — ONE DOVE
BREAKDOWN [B] — DOUBLE SIX
BREAKDOWN [C] — Jack JOHNSON
BREAKFAST — ASSOCIATES
BREAKFAST AT TIFFANY'S — DEEP BLUE SOMETHING (96)
BREAKFAST IN AMERICA — SUPERTRAMP
BREAKFAST IN BED [A] — Sheila HYLTON
BREAKFAST IN BED [A] — UB40 featuring Chrissie HYNDE
BREAKFAST ON PLUTO — Don PARTRIDGE
BREAKIN' — The MUSIC
BREAKIN' AWAY — Kim WILDE
BREAKIN' DOWN — SKID ROW
BREAKIN' DOWN (SUGAR SAMBA) — JULIA and COMPANY
BREAKIN' DOWN THE WALLS OF HEARTACHE — Johnny JOHNSON and The BANDWAGON
BREAKIN' IN A BRAND NEW BROKEN HEART — Connie FRANCIS
BREAKIN' ... THERE'S NO STOPPING US — OLLIE and JERRY
BREAKIN' UP — WILD WEEKEND
BREAKIN' UP IS BREAKIN' MY HEART — Roy ORBISON
BREAKING AWAY — Jaki GRAHAM
BREAKING GLASS (EP) — David BOWIE
BREAKING HEARTS (AIN'T WHAT IT USED TO BE) — Elton JOHN
BREAKING POINT — BOURGIE BOURGIE
BREAKING THE GIRL — RED HOT CHILI PEPPERS
BREAKING THE HABIT — LINKIN PARK
BREAKING THE LAW — JUDAS PRIEST
BREAKING UP IS HARD TO DO [A] — Neil SEDAKA
BREAKING UP IS HARD TO DO [A] — The PARTRIDGE FAMILY
BREAKING UP MY HEART — Shakin' STEVENS
BREAKING UP THE GIRL — GARBAGE
BREAKING US IN TWO — Joe JACKSON
BREAKOUT [A] — SWING OUT SISTER
BREAKOUT [B] — FOO FIGHTERS
THE BREAKS — Kurtis BLOW
BREAKTHRU' — QUEEN
BREATH OF LIFE — ERASURE
BREATH IN — FROU FROU
BREATHE [A] — Maria McKEE
BREATHE [B] — Midge URE
BREATHE [C] — The PRODIGY (96)
BREATHE [D] — Kylie MINOGUE
BREATHE [E] — BLUE AMAZON
BREATHE [F] — Faith HILL
BREATHE [G] — SCIENCE DEPARTMENT featuring ERIRE
BREATHE [H] — TELEPOPMUSIK
BREATHE [I] — Blu CANTRELL featuring Sean PAUL (03)
BREATHE [J] — FABOLOUS
BREATHE [K] — ERASURE
BREATHE (A LITTLE DEEPER) — BLAMELESS
BREATHE A SIGH — DEF LEPPARD
BREATHE AGAIN — Toni BRAXTON
BREATHE AND STOP — Q-TIP
BREATHE, DON'T STOP — MR ON vs The JUNGLE BROTHERS
BREATHE EASY — BLUE
BREATHE IN [A] — FROU FROU
BREATHE IN [B] — Lucie SILVAS
BREATHE LIFE INTO ME — Mica PARIS
BREATHE ME — SIA
BREATHE, STRETCH, SHAKE — MA$E
BREATHING [A] — Kate BUSH
BREATHING [B] — NORTH AND SOUTH
BREATHING IS E-ZEE — E-ZEE POSSEE
BREATHLESS [A] — Jerry Lee LEWIS
BREATHLESS [B] — The CORRS (00)
BREATHLESS [C] — Nick CAVE & The BAD SEEDS
THE BREEZE AND I [A] — Caterina VALENTE
THE BREEZE AND I [A] — FENTONES
BREEZE ON BY — Donny OSMOND
BRIAN WILSON — BARENAKED LADIES
BRICK — Ben FOLDS FIVE
BRICK HOUSE — The COMMODORES
THE BRICK TRACK VERSUS GITTY UP — SALT-N-PEPA
BRIDESHEAD THEME — Geoffrey BURGON
BRIDGE [A] — ORANGE JUICE
BRIDGE [B] — QUEENSRYCHE
THE BRIDGE — CACTUS WORLD NEWS
BRIDGE OF SIGHS — David WHITFIELD
BRIDGE OVER TROUBLED WATER [A] — SIMON and GARFUNKEL: Keyboard: Larry Knechtel (70)
BRIDGE OVER TROUBLED WATER [A] — Linda CLIFFORD
BRIDGE OVER TROUBLED WATER [A] — Hannah JONES
BRIDGE TO YOUR HEART — WAX
BRIDGET THE MIDGET (THE QUEEN OF THE BLUES) — Ray STEVENS
BRIDGING THE GAP — NAS / Olu DARA
THE BRIGHT AMBASSADORS OF MORNING — PURE REASON REVOLUTION
BRIGHT EYES [A] — Art GARFUNKEL (79)
BRIGHT EYES [A] — Stephen GATELY
THE BRIGHT LIGHT — Tanya DONELLY
BRIGHT LIGHTS — The SPECIALS
BRIGHT SIDE OF LIFE — TENOR FLY
BRIGHT SIDE OF THE ROAD — Van MORRISON
BRIGHT YELLOW GUN — THROWING MUSES
BRIGHTER DAY — Kelly LLORENNA
BRIGHTER THAN SUNSHINE — AQUALUNG
BRIGHTEST STAR — DRIZABONE
BRILLIANT DISGUISE — Bruce SPRINGSTEEN
BRILLIANT FEELING — FULL MONTY ALLSTARS featuring TJ DAVIS
BRILLIANT MIND — FURNITURE
BRIMFUL OF ASHA — CORNERSHOP (98)
BRING A LITTLE WATER SYLVIE — Lonnie DONEGAN
BRING 'EM ALL IN — Mike SCOTT
BRING EM OUT — T.I.
BRING FORTH THE GUILLOTINE — SILVER BULLET
BRING IT ALL BACK — S CLUB 7 (99)
BRING IT ALL HOME — Gerry RAFFERTY
BRING IT BACK — McALMONT & BUTLER
BRING IT BACK AGAIN [A] — The STRAY CATS
BRING IT BACK AGAIN [B] — The EARLIES
BRING IT BACK 2 LUV — PROJECT featuring GERIDEAU
BRING IT DOWN (THIS INSANE THING) — REDSKINS
BRING IT ON [A] — N'dea DAVENPORT
BRING IT ON [B] — GOMEZ
BRING IT ON [C] — Nick CAVE & The BAD SEEDS
BRING IT ON [D] — Alistair GRIFFIN
BRING IT ON ... BRING IT ON — James BROWN
BRING IT ON DOWN — JESUS JONES
BRING IT ON HOME — URBAN COOKIE COLLECTIVE
BRING IT ON HOME TO ME — The ANIMALS
BRING IT ON TO MY LOVE — DE NADA
BRING ME CLOSER — ALTERED IMAGES
BRING ME EDELWEISS — EDELWEISS
BRING ME LOVE — Andrea MENDEZ
BRING ME TO LIFE — EVANESCENCE featuring Paul McCOY (03)
BRING ME YOUR CUP — UB40
BRING MY FAMILY BACK — FAITHLESS
BRING ON THE DANCING HORSES — ECHO and The BUNNYMEN
BRING THE FAMILY BACK — Billy PAUL
BRING THE NOISE [A] — PUBLIC ENEMY
BRING THE NOISE [A] — ANTHRAX featuring Chuck D
BRING UP THE MIC SOME MORE — RAGGA TWINS
BRING YOUR DAUGHTER ... TO THE SLAUGHTER — IRON MAIDEN (91)
BRINGING BACK THOSE MEMORIES — Mark JOSEPH
BRINGING ON BACK THE GOOD TIMES — LOVE AFFAIR
BRISTOL STOMP — LATE SHOW
BRITANNIA RAG — Winifred ATWELL
BRITE SIDE — Deborah HARRY
BRITISH HUSTLE — HI TENSION
THE BRITISH WAY OF LIFE — CHORDS
THE BRITS 1990 — VARIOUS ARTISTS (MONTAGES)
BROKE — Cassius HENRY
BROKE AWAY — WET WET WET
BROKE — The BETA BAND
BROKEN ARROW [A] — WATERFRONT
BROKEN ARROW [B] — Rod STEWART
BROKEN BONES — LOVE INC.
BROKEN DOLL — Tommy BRUCE and The BRUISERS
BROKEN DOWN ANGEL — NAZARETH
BROKEN ENGLISH — SUNSCREEM
A BROKEN HEART CAN MEND — Alexander O'NEAL
BROKEN HEART (THIRTEEN VALLEYS) — BIG COUNTRY
BROKEN HEARTED — Ken DODD
BROKEN HEARTED MELODY — Sarah VAUGHAN
BROKEN HOMES — TRICKY
BROKEN LAND — The ADVENTURES
BROKEN NOSE — CATHERINE WHEEL
BROKEN SILENCE — SO SOLID CREW
BROKEN STONES — Paul WELLER
BROKEN WINGS [A] — Art and Dotty TODD
BROKEN WINGS [A] — Dickie VALENTINE
BROKEN WINGS [A] — The STARGAZERS (53)
BROKEN WINGS [B] — MR MISTER
BROKEN WINGS [B] — NETWORK
THE BROKEN YEARS — HIPSWAY
BRONTOSAURUS — The MOVE
BROOKLYN BEATS — Scotti DEEP
BROOKLYN-QUEENS — 3RD BASS
BROTHA PART II — Angie STONE featuring Alicia KEYS & EVE
BROTHER [A] — CCS
BROTHER [B] — URBAN SPECIES
BROTHER BRIGHT — ÇA VA ÇA VA
BROTHER LOUIE [A] — HOT CHOCOLATE
BROTHER LOUIE [A] — QUIREBOYS
BROTHER LOUIE [B] — MODERN TALKING
BROTHER OF MINE — ANDERSON
BRUFORD WAKEMAN HOWE
BROTHERS AND SISTERS — 2 FUNKY 2 starring Kathryn DION
BROTHERS GONNA WORK IT OUT — PUBLIC ENEMY
BROTHERS IN ARMS — DIRE STRAITS
BROWN-EYED HANDSOME MAN [A] — Buddy HOLLY
BROWN EYED HANDSOME MAN [A] — Paul McCARTNEY
BROWN GIRL IN THE RING — BONEY M (78)
BROWN PAPER BAG — Roni SIZE / REPRAZENT
BROWN SKIN — INDIA.ARIE
BROWN SUGAR [A] — The ROLLING STONES
BROWN SUGAR [B] — D'ANGELO
BRUISE PRISTINE — PLACEBO
BRUSHED — Paul WELLER
BRUTAL-8-E — ALTERN 8
BUBBLE — FLUKE
BUBBLING HOT — Pato BANTON
BUBBLIN' — BLUE
BUCCI BAG — Andrea DORIA
BUCK ROGERS — FEEDER
THE BUCKET — KINGS OF LEON
THE BUCKET OF WATER SONG — The FOUR BUCKETEERS
BUDDHA OF SUBURBIA — David BOWIE featuring Lenny KRAVITZ
BUDDY — DE LA SOUL
BUDDY HOLLY — WEEZER
BUDDY X [A] — Neneh CHERRY
BUDDY X 99 [A] — DREEM TEEM vs Neneh CHERRY
BUFFALO BILL'S LAST SCRATCH — The BARRON KNIGHTS
BUFFALO GALS [A] — Malcolm McLAREN and the WORLD'S FAMOUS SUPREME TEAM
BUFFALO GALS STAMPEDE [A] — Malcolm McLAREN
BUFFALO SOLDIER — Bob MARLEY & The WAILERS
BUFFALO STANCE — Neneh CHERRY
THE BUG — DIRE STRAITS
BUG A BOO — DESTINY'S CHILD
BUG IN THE BASSBIN — INNERZONE ORCHESTRA
BUG POWDER DUST — BOMB THE BASS
BUGGIN — TRUE STEPPERS
BUGS — HEPBURN
BUILD [A] — The HOUSEMARTINS
BUILD [B] — INNOCENCE
BUILD ME UP BUTTERCUP [A] — The FOUNDATIONS
BUILD ME UP BUTTERCUP 2003 [A] — PARTY BOYS
BUILD YOUR LOVE — Johnnie RAY
BUILDING THE CITY OF LIGHT — Mike SCOTT
BULGARIAN — TRAVEL
BULL IN THE HEATHER — SONIC YOUTH
BULLDOG NATION — Kevin KENNEDY
BULLET — FLUKE
BULLET COMES — The CHARLATANS
BULLET IN THE GUN — PLANET PERFECTO
BULLET IN THE HEAD — RAGE AGAINST THE MACHINE
BULLET WITH BUTTERFLY WINGS — SMASHING PUMPKINS
BULLETPROOF! — POP WILL EAT ITSELF
BULLETS [A] — CREED
BULLETS [B] — EDITORS
BULLFROG — GTO
BULLITPROOF — BREAKBEAT ERA
BULLITT — Lalo SCHIFRIN
BULLS ON PARADE — RAGE AGAINST THE MACHINE
BULLY BOY — SHED SEVEN
BULLY FOR YOU — Tom ROBINSON
BUMP — FUN LOVIN' CRIMINALS
THE BUMP — KENNY
BUMP, BUMP, BUMP — B2K featuring P DIDDY
BUMP 'N' GRIND — R KELLY
BUMP N GRIND (I AM FEELING HOT TONIGHT) — M DUBS featuring LADY SAW
BUMPED — RIGHT SAID FRED
A BUNCH OF THYME — FOSTER and ALLEN
BUNSEN BURNER — John OTWAY
BUONA SERA [A] — Louis PRIMA
BUONA SERA [A] — Mr Acker BILK and his PARAMOUNT JAZZ BAND

9 January 1999	16 January 1999	23 January 1999	30 January 1999
HEARTBEAT / TRAGEDY Steps	**PRAISE YOU** Fatboy Slim	**A LITTLE BIT MORE** 911	**PRETTY FLY (FOR A WHITE GUY)** The Offspring
LADIES & GENTLEMEN - THE BEST OF GEORGE MICHAEL George Michael	**I'VE BEEN EXPECTING YOU** Robbie Williams	**YOU'VE COME A LONG WAY, BABY** Fatboy Slim	**YOU'VE COME A LONG WAY, BABY** Fatboy Slim

BUONA SERA [A] — BAD MANNERS
BUOY — Mick KARN featuring David SYLVIAN
BURDEN IN MY HAND — SOUNDGARDEN
BURIAL — LEVITICUS
BURIED ALIVE BY LOVE — HIM
BURLESQUE — FAMILY
BURN [A] — DOCTOR and The MEDICS
BURN [B] — Tina ARENA
BURN [C] — USHER (04)
BURN BABY BURN [A] — HUDSON-FORD
BURN BABY BURN [B] — ASH
BURN BURN — LOSTPROPHETS
BURN IT UP — The BEATMASTERS with PP ARNOLD
BURN RUBBER ON ME (WHY YOU WANNA HURT ME) — The GAP BAND
BURN YOUR YOUTH — JOHNNY PANIC
BURNED WITH DESIRE — Armin VAN BUUREN featuring Justine SUISSA
BURNIN' [A] — DAFT PUNK
BURNIN' [B] — K-KLASS
BURNIN' [C] — MIRRORBALL
BURNIN' HOT — Jermaine JACKSON
BURNIN' LOVE — CON FUNK SHUN
BURNING '95 [A] — MK featuring ALANA
BURNING [B] — BABY BUMPS
BURNING BRIDGES — Jack SCOTT
BURNING BRIDGES (ON AND OFF AND ON AGAIN) — STATUS QUO
BURNING CAR — John FOXX
BURNING DOWN ONE SIDE — Robert PLANT
BURNING DOWN THE HOUSE — Tom JONES and The CARDIGANS
BURNING HEART — SURVIVOR
BURNING LOVE — Elvis PRESLEY
BURNING OF THE MIDNIGHT LAMP — The Jimi HENDRIX EXPERIENCE
BURNING THE GROUND — DURAN DURAN
BURNING UP [A] — Tony DE VIT
BURNING UP [B] — BINI & MARTINI
BURNING WHEEL — PRIMAL SCREAM
BURST — DARLING BUDS
BURUCHACCA — MUKKAA
BURUNDI BLACK — BURUNDI STEIPHENSON BLACK
BURUNDI BLUES — BEATS INTERNATIONAL
BURY YOU — SYMPOSIUM
BUS STOP — The HOLLIES
BUSHEL AND A PECK — Vivian BLAINE
BUSHES — Markus NIKOLAI
BUSINESS — EMINEM
THE BUSINESS — Brian MAY
BUST A MOVE — YOUNG MC
BUST THIS HOUSE DOWN — PENTHOUSE 4
BUSTED — Ray CHARLES
BUSY BEE — UGLY KID JOE
BUSY DOING NOTHING — Dave STEWART
BUT I DO — Clarence 'Frogman' HENRY
BUT I DO LOVE YOU — LeAnn RIMES
BUT I FEEL GOOD — GROOVE ARMADA
BUT NOT FOR ME [A] — Ella FITZGERALD
BUT NOT FOR ME [A] — Ketty LESTER
BUT YOU LOVE ME DADDY — Jim REEVES
BUT YOU'RE MINE — SONNY and CHER
BUTCHER BABY — PLASMATICS
BUTTERCUP — Carl ANDERSON
BUTTERFINGERS — Tommy STEELE
BUTTERFLIES & HURRICANES — MUSE
BUTTERFLY [A] — Andy WILLIAMS (57)
BUTTERFLY [A] — Charlie GRACIE
BUTTERFLY [B] — Danyel GERARD
BUTTERFLY [C] — Mariah CAREY
BUTTERFLY [D] — TILT featuring ZEE
BUTTERFLY [E] — CRAZY TOWN
BUTTERFLY KISSES — Bob CARLISLE
BUTTERFLY ON A WHEEL — The MISSION
BUY IT IN BOTTLES — Richard ASHCROFT
BUZZ BUZZ A DIDDLE IT — MATCHBOX
BUZZIN' — ASIAN DUB FOUNDATION
BY MY SIDE — INXS
BY THE DEVIL (I WAS TEMPTED) — BLUE MINK
BY THE FOUNTAINS OF ROME [A] — David HUGHES
BY THE FOUNTAINS OF ROME [A] — Edmund HOCKRIDGE
BY THE LIGHT OF THE SILVERY MOON — LITTLE RICHARD
BY THE TIME THIS NIGHT IS OVER — Kenny G with Peabo BRYSON
BY THE WAY [A] — The BIG THREE
BY THE WAY [B] — The TREMELOES
BY THE WAY [C] — RED HOT CHILI PEPPERS
BY YOUR SIDE [A] — PETERS and LEE
BY YOUR SIDE [B] — Jimmy SOMERVILLE
BY YOUR SIDE [C] — SADE
BYE BABY — Ruby TURNER
BYE BYE BABY [A] — Johnny OTIS SHOW
BYE BYE BABY [B] — SYMBOLS
BYE BYE BABY [B] — BAY CITY ROLLERS (75)
BYE BYE BABY [C] — Tony JACKSON and The VIBRATIONS
BYE BYE BABY [D] — TQ
BYE BYE BLUES — Bert KAEMPFERT
BYE BYE BOY — Jennifer ELLISON
BYE BYE BYE — 'N SYNC
BYE BYE LOVE — The EVERLY BROTHERS
B.Y.O.F. (BRING YOUR OWN FUNK) — FANTASTIC FOUR
BYRDS TURN TO STONE — SHACK
C I AM 15 — KING BISCUIT TIME
C MOON — Paul McCARTNEY
C U WHEN U GET THERE — COOLIO
ÇA PLANE POUR MOI [A] — PLASTIC BERTRAND
ÇA PLANE POUR MOI [A] — Leila K
CABARET — Louis ARMSTRONG ORCHESTRA and Chorus (68)
THE CABARET — TIME UK
CACHARPAYA (ANDES PUMPSA DAESI) — INCANTATION
CAFE DEL MAR — ENERGY 52
CAFFEINE BOMB — The WILDHEARTS
CALEDONIA — Frankie MILLER
CALENDAR GIRL [A] — Neil SEDAKA
CALENDAR GIRL [B] — The NOISE NEXT DOOR
THE CALENDAR SONG (JANUARY, FEBRUARY, MARCH, APRIL, MAY) — TRINIDAD OIL COMPANY
CALIBRE CUTS — VARIOUS ARTISTS (MONTAGES)
CALIFORNIA [A] — WEDDING PRESENT
CALIFORNIA [B] — Belinda CARLISLE
CALIFORNIA [C] — Lenny KRAVITZ
CALIFORNIA [D] — LOW
CALIFORNIA [E] — PHANTOM PLANET
CALIFORNIA DREAMIN' [A] — The MAMAS and The PAPAS
CALIFORNIA DREAMING [A] — COLORADO
CALIFORNIA DREAMIN' [A] — RIVER CITY PEOPLE
CALIFORNIA DREAMIN' [A] — Bobby WOMACK
CALIFORNIA DREAMIN' [B]— ROYAL GIGOLOS
CALIFORNIA GIRLS [A] — The BEACH BOYS
CALIFORNIA GIRLS [A] — David Lee ROTH
CALIFORNIA HERE I COME [A] — Freddy CANNON
CALIFORNIA HERE I COME [B] — Sophie B HAWKINS
CALIFORNIA LOVE — 2PAC featuring Dr DRE
CALIFORNIA MAN — The MOVE
CALIFORNIA SAGA — CALIFORNIA — The BEACH BOYS
CALIFORNIA SCREAMIN' — CARRIE
CALIFORNIA SOUL — RIOT ACT
CALIFORNIA WAITING — KINGS OF LEON
CALIFORNIA'S BLEEDING — AMEN
CALIFORNICATION — RED HOT CHILI PEPPERS
CALINDA – RITMO-DYNAMIC
THE CALL — BACKSTREET BOYS
CALL AND ANSWER — BARENAKED LADIES
CALL HER YOUR SWEETHEART — Frank IFIELD
CALL IT FATE — Richie DAN
CALL IT LOVE — DEUCE
CALL IT ROCK 'N' ROLL — GREAT WHITE
CALL IT WHAT YOU WANT [A] — NEW KIDS ON THE BLOCK
CALL IT WHAT YOU WANT [B] — CREDIT TO THE NATION
CALL ME [A] — BLONDIE (80)
CALL ME [B] — GO WEST
CALL ME [C] — SPAGNA
CALL ME [D] — LE CLICK
CALL ME [E] — JAMELIA
CALL ME [F] — TWEET
(CALL ME) NUMBER ONE — The TREMELOES
CALL ME ROUND — PILOT
CALL MY NAME [A] — ORCHESTRAL MANOEUVRES IN THE DARK
CALL MY NAME [B] — Charlotte CHURCH
CALL OF THE WILD — Midge URE
CALL OFF THE SEARCH — Katie MELUA
CALL ON ME — Eric PRYDZ (04)
CALL OUT THE DOGS — Gary NUMAN
CALL ROSIE ON THE PHONE — Guy MITCHELL
CALL THE MAN — Celine DION
CALL U SEXY — VS
THE CALL UP — The CLASH
CALL UP THE GROUPS — The BARRON KNIGHTS
CALLING — Geri HALLIWELL
CALLING ALL GIRLS — ATL
CALLING ALL THE HEROES — IT BITES
CALLING AMERICA — ELECTRIC LIGHT ORCHESTRA
CALLING ELVIS — DIRE STRAITS
CALLING OCCUPANTS OF INTERPLANETARY CRAFT (THE RECOGNISED ANTHEM OF WORLD CONTACT DAY) — The CARPENTERS
CALLING OUT YOUR NAME — Jimmy NAIL
CALLING YOU — Paul YOUNG
CALLING YOUR NAME — MARILYN
CALLS THE TUNE — Hazel O'CONNOR
CALM DOWN (BASS KEEPS PUMPIN') — CHRIS and JAMES
CALYPSO CRAZY — Billy OCEAN
CAMBODIA — Kim WILDE
CAMDEN TOWN — SUGGS
CAMEL BOBSLED RACE — DJ SHADOW
CAMELS — SANTOS
CAMOUFLAGE — Stan RIDGWAY
CAMPIONE 2000 — E-TYPE
CAN CAN 62 [A] — Peter JAY and The JAYWALKERS
CAN CAN [A] — BAD MANNERS
CAN CAN YOU PARTY — JIVE BUNNY and The MASTERMIXERS
CAN I — CASHMERE
CAN I GET A ... — JAY-Z
CAN I GET A WITNESS — Sam BROWN
CAN I GET OVER — DEFINITION OF SOUND
CAN I HAVE IT LIKE THAT — PHARRELL featuring Gwen STEFANI
CAN I KICK IT — A TRIBE CALLED QUEST
CAN I PLAY WITH MADNESS — IRON MAIDEN
CAN I TAKE YOU HOME LITTLE GIRL — The DRIFTERS
CAN I TOUCH YOU ... THERE — Michael BOLTON
CAN I TRUST YOU — The BACHELORS
CAN THE CAN — Suzi QUATRO (73)
CAN THIS BE LOVE — Matt MONRO
CAN U DANCE — DJ 'FAST' EDDIE
CAN U DIG IT [A] — POP WILL EAT ITSELF
CAN U DIG IT [B] — JAMX & DELEON
CAN U FEEL IT [A] — ELEVATION
CAN U FEEL IT [B] — DEEP CREED '94
CAN WE — SWV
CAN WE FIX IT? — BOB THE BUILDER (00)
CAN WE START AGAIN? — TINDERSTICKS
CAN WE TALK ... — CODE RED
CAN YOU DIG IT? — MOCK TURTLES
CAN YOU DO IT — GEORDIE
CAN YOU FEEL IT [A] — The JACKSONS
CAN YOU FEEL IT? [A] — V
CAN YOU FEEL IT [B] — REEL 2 REAL
CAN YOU FEEL IT [C] — CLS
CAN YOU FEEL IT / CAN YOU FEEL IT — RAZE
CAN YOU FEEL IT (ROCK DA HOUSE) — NYCC
CAN YOU FEEL THE FORCE? — The REAL THING
CAN YOU FEEL THE LOVE TONIGHT — Elton JOHN
(CAN YOU) FEEL THE PASSION — BLUE PEARL
CAN YOU FEEL (WHAT I'M GOING THRU) — SHOLAN
CAN YOU FORGIVE HER — PET SHOP BOYS
CAN YOU FORGIVE ME — Karl DENVER
CAN YOU HANDLE IT [A] — DNA featuring Sharon REDD
CAN YOU HANDLE IT [A] — Sharon REDD
CAN YOU KEEP A SECRET — BROTHER BEYOND
CAN YOU PARTY — ROYAL HOUSE
CAN YOU PLEASE CRAWL OUT YOUR WINDOW — Bob DYLAN
CAN YOUR PUSSY DO THE DOG? — CRAMPS
CANCER FOR THE CURE — EELS
CANDIDA — DAWN
CANDIDATE FOR LOVE — TS MONK
CANDLE IN THE WIND [A] — Elton JOHN
CANDLE IN THE WIND 1997 [A] — Elton JOHN (97)
CANDLEFIRE — DAWN OF THE REPLICANTS
CANDLELAND (THE SECOND COMING) — Ian McCULLOCH
CANDLELIGHT — SIX BY SEVEN
CANDLES — Alex REECE
CANDY [A] — CAMEO
CANDY [B] — Iggy POP
CANDY [C] — Mandy MOORE
CANDY [D] — ASH
CANDY EVERYBODY WANTS — 10,000 MANIACS
CANDY GIRL [A] — NEW EDITION (83)
CANDY GIRL [B] — BABYBIRD
CANDY MAN — Brian POOLE and The TREMELOES
CANDY RAIN — SOUL FOR REAL
CANDY SHOP — 50 CENT
CANDYBAR EXPRESS — LOVE AND MONEY
CANDYMAN — SIOUXSIE and The BANSHEES
CANED AND UNABLE — HI-GATE
CANNED HEAT — JAMIROQUAI
CANNIBALS — Mark KNOPFLER
CANNONBALL [A] — Duane EDDY and The REBELS
CANNONBALL [B] — Damien RICE
CANNONBALL (EP) — The BREEDERS
CAN'T BE SURE — The SUNDAYS
CAN'T BE WITH YOU TONIGHT — Judy BOUCHER
CAN'T BUY ME LOVE [A] — The BEATLES (64)
CAN'T BUY ME LOVE [A] — Ella FITZGERALD
CAN'T CHANGE ME — Chris CORNELL
CAN'T CONTAIN ME — TAZ
CAN'T CRY ANYMORE — Sheryl CROW
CAN'T DO A THING (TO STOP ME) — Chris ISAAK
CAN'T DO NUTTIN' FOR YA MAN — PUBLIC ENEMY
CAN'T DO RIGHT FOR DOING WRONG — Erin ROCHA
CAN'T EXPLAIN — LONGVIEW
CAN'T FAKE THE FEELING — Geraldine HUNT
CAN'T FIGHT THE MOONLIGHT — LeAnn RIMES (00)
CAN'T FIGHT THIS FEELING — REO SPEEDWAGON
CAN'T FORGET YOU — SONIA
CAN'T GET ALONG WITHOUT YOU — Frankie VAUGHAN
CAN'T GET ANY HARDER — James BROWN
CAN'T GET AWAY — MOOD II SWING
CAN'T GET BY — SLAMM
CAN'T GET BY WITHOUT YOU [A] — The REAL THING
CAN'T GET BY WITHOUT YOU (THE SECOND DECADE REMIX) [A] — The REAL THING
CAN'T GET ENOUGH [A] — BAD COMPANY
CAN'T GET ENOUGH [B] — SUEDE
CAN'T GET ENOUGH [C] — SOULSEARCHER
CAN'T GET ENOUGH [D] — RAGHAV
CAN'T GET ENOUGH OF YOU — Eddy GRANT
CAN'T GET ENOUGH OF YOUR LOVE [A] — DARTS
CAN'T GET ENOUGH OF YOUR LOVE [B] — KWS
CAN'T GET ENOUGH OF YOUR LOVE [B] — Taylor DAYNE
CAN'T GET ENOUGH OF YOUR LOVE, BABE [B] — Barry WHITE
CAN'T GET IT BACK — MIS-TEEQ
(CAN'T GET MY) HEAD AROUND YOU — The OFFSPRING
CAN'T GET OUT OF BED — The CHARLATANS
CAN'T GET THE BEST OF ME — CYPRESS HILL
CAN'T GET USED TO LOSING YOU [A] — Andy WILLIAMS
CAN'T GET USED TO LOSING YOU [A] — The BEAT
CAN'T GET USED TO LOSING YOU [A] — COLOUR GIRL
CAN'T GET YOU OFF MY MIND — Lenny KRAVITZ
CAN'T GET YOU OUT OF MY HEAD — Kylie MINOGUE (01)
CAN'T GET YOU OUT OF MY THOUGHTS — DUM DUMS
CAN'T GIVE ME LOVE — PEPSI and SHIRLIE
CAN'T GIVE YOU ANYTHING (BUT MY LOVE) — The STYLISTICS (75)
CAN'T GIVE YOU MORE — STATUS QUO
CAN'T HAPPEN HERE — RAINBOW

6 February 1999	13 February 1999	20 February 1999	27 February 1999
UK No.1 SINGLES			
YOU DON'T KNOW ME Armand Van Helden featuring Duane Harden	**MARIA** Blondie	**FLY AWAY** Lenny Kravitz	**... BABY ONE MORE TIME** Britney Spears
UK No.1 ALBUMS			
YOU'VE COME A LONG WAY, BABY Fatboy Slim	**YOU'VE COME A LONG WAY, BABY** Fatboy Slim	**I'VE BEEN EXPECTING YOU** Robbie Williams	**TALK ON CORNERS** The Corrs

CAN'T HAVE YOU — LYTE FUNKIE ONES
CAN'T HELP FALLING IN LOVE [A] — Elvis PRESLEY with The JORDANAIRES (62)
CAN'T HELP FALLING IN LOVE [A] — Andy WILLIAMS
CAN'T HELP FALLING IN LOVE [A] — The STYLISTICS
CAN'T HELP FALLING IN LOVE [A] — LICK THE TINS
CAN'T HELP IT — HAPPY CLAPPERS
CAN'T HELP MYSELF — LINX
CAN'T HOLD US DOWN — Christina AGUILERA featuring LIL' KIM
CAN'T I — Nat 'King' COLE
CAN'T KEEP IT IN — Cat STEVENS
CAN'T KEEP LIVING THIS WAY — ROOTJOOSE
CAN'T KEEP ME SILENT — ANGELIC
CAN'T KEEP THIS FEELING IN — Cliff RICHARD
CAN'T KNOCK THE HUSTLE — JAY-Z featuring Mary J BLIGE
CAN'T LET GO [A] — EARTH WIND AND FIRE
CAN'T LET GO [B] — Mariah CAREY
CAN'T LET HER GO — BOYZ II MEN
CAN'T LET YOU GO [A] — Barry RYAN
CAN'T LET YOU GO [B] — RAINBOW
CAN'T LET YOU GO [C] — FABOLOUS featuring Mike SHOREY & LIL' MO
CAN'T LIVE WITH YOU (CAN'T LIVE WITHOUT YOU) — The MINDBENDERS
CAN'T LIVE WITHOUT YOU — SCORPIONS
(CAN'T LIVE WITHOUT YOUR) LOVE AND AFFECTION — NELSON
CAN'T MAKE UP MY MIND — SONIQUE
CAN'T NOBODY — Kelly ROWLAND
CAN'T NOBODY HOLD ME DOWN — PUFF DADDY featuring MA$E
CAN'T RESIST — TEXAS
CAN'T SAY 'BYE — STONEFREE
CAN'T SAY GOODBYE — POP!
CAN'T SAY HOW MUCH I LOVE YOU — Demis ROUSSOS
CAN'T SEE ME — Ian BROWN
CAN'T SET RULES ABOUT LOVE — Adam ANT
CAN'T SHAKE LOOSE — Agnetha FALTSKOG
CAN'T SHAKE THE FEELING — BIG FUN
CAN'T SMILE — VEX RED
CAN'T SMILE WITHOUT YOU [A] — Barry MANILOW
CAN'T SMILE WITHOUT YOU [A] — James BULLER
CAN'T STAND IT — WILCO
CAN'T STAND LOSING YOU [A] — The POLICE
CAN'T STAND LOSING YOU [A] — FEEDER
CAN'T STAND ME NOW — The LIBERTINES
CAN'T STAY AWAY FROM YOU — Gloria ESTEFAN and MIAMI SOUND MACHINE
CAN'T STOP [A] — AFTER 7
CAN'T STOP [B] — RED HOT CHILI PEPPERS
CAN'T STOP LOVIN' YOU — VAN HALEN
CAN'T STOP LOVING YOU — Phil COLLINS
CAN'T STOP RUNNING — SPACE MONKEY
CAN'T STOP THE MUSIC — VILLAGE PEOPLE
CAN'T STOP THESE THINGS — CHINA DRUM
CAN'T STOP THIS FEELING — RHYTHM-N-BASS
CAN'T STOP THIS THING WE STARTED — Bryan ADAMS
CAN'T TAKE MY EYES OFF YOU [A] — Andy WILLIAMS
CAN'T TAKE MY EYES OFF YOU [A] — BOYSTOWN GANG
CAN'T TAKE MY EYES OFF YOU [A] — Andy WILLIAMS and Denise VAN OUTEN
CAN'T TAKE NO MORE — SOUP DRAGONS
CAN'T TAKE YOUR LOVE — Pauline HENRY
CAN'T TRUSS IT — PUBLIC ENEMY
CAN'T TURN BACK — SPEEDWAY
CAN'T WAIT ANOTHER MINUTE — FIVE STAR
CAN'T WAIT TO BE WITH YOU — JAZZY JEFF & The FRESH PRINCE
CAN'T YOU HEAR MY HEART — Danny RIVERS
CAN'T YOU HEAR MY HEART BEAT? — GOLDIE and The GINGERBREADS
CAN'T YOU HEAR THE BEAT OF A BROKEN HEART — Iain GREGORY
CAN'T YOU SEE — TOTAL featuring The NOTORIOUS B.I.G.
CAN'T YOU SEE THAT SHE'S MINE — Dave CLARK FIVE
(CAN'T YOU) TRIP LIKE I DO — FILTER and The CRYSTAL METHOD
CANTALOOP — US3
CANTGETAMAN CANTGETAJOB (LIFE'S A BITCH) — SISTER BLISS
CANTO DELLA TERRA — Andrea BOCELLI
CANTON (LIVE) — JAPAN
CANTONESE BOY — JAPAN
CAPOIERA — INFRARED vs Gil FELIX
CAPSTICK COMES HOME — Tony CAPSTICK and The CARLTON MAIN / FRICKLEY COLLIERY BAND
CAPTAIN BEAKY — Keith MICHELL
CAPTAIN DREAD — DREADZONE
CAPTAIN KREMMEN (RETRIBUTION) — Kenny EVERETT
THE CAPTAIN OF HER HEART — DOUBLE
CAPTAIN OF YOUR SHIP — REPARATA and The DELRONS
CAPTAIN SCARLET THEME — Barry GRAY ORCHESTRA
CAPTURE THE FLAG — FRESH
CAPTURE THE HEART (EP) — RUNRIG
CAR BOOT SALE — BILL
CAR 67 — DRIVER 67
CAR SONG — MADDER ROSE
CAR WASH [A] — ROSE ROYCE
CAR WASH [A] — Gwen DICKEY
CAR WASH [A] — ROSE ROYCE featuring Gwen DICKEY
CAR WASH [A] — Christina AGUILERA featuring Missy ELLIOTT
CARA MIA — David WHITFIELD (54)
CARAMEL — CITY HIGH featuring EVE
CARAVAN [A] — Duane EDDY and The REBELS
CARAVAN [B] — INSPIRAL CARPETS
CARAVAN OF LOVE [A] — ISLEY JASPER ISLEY
CARAVAN OF LOVE [A] — The HOUSEMARTINS (86)
CARAVAN SONG — Barbara DICKSON
CARBON KID — ALPINESTARS featuring Brian MOLKO
CARDBOY KING — SALAD
CARDIAC ARREST — MADNESS
CAREFUL — HORSE
CARELESS HANDS — Des O'CONNOR
CARELESS LOVE — SWIMMING WITH SHARKS
CARELESS MEMORIES — DURAN DURAN
CARELESS WHISPER [A] — George MICHAEL (84)
CARELESS WHISPER [A] — Sarah WASHINGTON
CARELESS WHISPER [A] — 2PLAY featuring Thomas JULES & JUCXI D
CARIBBEAN BLUE — ENYA
THE CARIBBEAN DISCO SHOW — LOBO
CARIBBEAN HONEYMOON — Frank WEIR
CARIBBEAN QUEEN (NO MORE LOVE ON THE RUN) — Billy OCEAN
CARMEN QUEASY — MAXIM
CARNATION — Liam GALLAGHER and Steve CRADOCK
CARNAVAL DE PARIS — DARIO G
CARNIVAL [A] — LIONROCK
CARNIVAL [B] — The CARDIGANS
CARNIVAL GIRL — TEXAS featuring Kardinal OFFISHALL
CARNIVAL IN HEAVEN — Malandra BURROWS
THE CARNIVAL IS OVER — The SEEKERS (65)
CAROLINA MOON — Connie FRANCIS (58)
CAROLINE [A] — STATUS QUO
CAROLINE [B] — Kirsty MacCOLL
CAROUSEL — ORIGINAL SOUNDTRACK (LP) — VARIOUS ARTISTS (Singles and EPs)
THE CAROUSEL WALTZ — Ray MARTIN
CARRERA 2 — THREE DRIVES
CARRIE [A] — Cliff RICHARD
CARRIE [B] — EUROPE
CARRIE-ANNE — The HOLLIES
CARRION — BRITISH SEA POWER
CARROT ROPE — PAVEMENT
CARRY ME HOME — GLOWORM
CARRY ON [A] — Martha WASH
CARRY ON [B] — SPACEHOG
CARRY ON [C] — Donna SUMMER and Giorgio MORODER
CARRY ON WAYWARD SON — KANSAS
CARRY THAT WEIGHT — TRASH
CARRY THE BLAME — RIVER CITY PEOPLE
CARRYING A TORCH — Tom JONES
CARS [A] — Gary NUMAN (79)
CARS [A] — FEAR FACTORY
CARS (E REG MODEL) — Gary NUMAN
CARS AND GIRLS — PREFAB SPROUT
CARTE BLANCHE — VERACOCHA
CARTOON HEROES — AQUA
CARTROUBLE — ADAM and The ANTS
CASABLANCA — Kenny BALL and his JAZZMEN
CASANOVA [A] — Petula CLARK
CASANOVA [B] — COFFEE
CASANOVA [B] — BABY D
CASANOVA [C] — LEVERT
CASANOVA [C] — ULTIMATE KAOS
CASCADE — FUTURE SOUND OF LONDON
CASE OF THE EX — MYA
CASINO ROYALE — Herb ALPERT
CASINO ROYALE — DJ Zinc
CASSIUS 1999 — CASSIUS
CAST YOUR FATE TO THE WIND — SOUNDS ORCHESTRAL
CASTLE ROCK — The BLUETONES
CASTLES IN SPAIN — ARMOURY SHOW
CASTLES IN THE AIR [A] — Don McLEAN
CASTLES IN THE AIR [B] — COLOUR FIELD
CASTLES IN THE SAND — THUNDER
CASTLES IN THE SKY — IAN VAN DAHL
CASUAL SUB (BURNING SPEAR) — ETA
CAT AMONG THE PIGEONS — BROS
THE CAT CAME BACK — Sonny JAMES
THE CAT CREPT IN — MUD
CAT PEOPLE (PUTTING OUT FIRE) — David BOWIE
CATALAN — TOUR DE FORCE
CATALYST — OCEANSIZE
CATCH [A] — The CURE
CATCH [B] — SUNSCREEM
CATCH [C] — KOSHEEN
CATCH A FALLING STAR — Perry COMO
CATCH A FIRE — HADDAWAY
CATCH ME — ABSOLUTE
CATCH ME UP — GOMEZ
CATCH MY FALL — Billy IDOL
CATCH THE BREEZE — SLOWDIVE
CATCH THE FIRE — DRIZABONE
CATCH THE LIGHT — Martha WASH
CATCH THE SUN — DOVES
CATCH THE WIND — DONOVAN
CATCH UP TO MY STEP — JUNKIE XL featuring Solomon BURKE
CATCH US IF YOU CAN — Dave CLARK FIVE
CATERINA — Perry COMO
THE CATERPILLAR — The CURE
CATH — The BLUEBELLS
CATHEDRAL PARK — DUBSTAR
CATHEDRAL SONG — Tanita TIKARAM
CATHY'S CLOWN — The EVERLY BROTHERS (60)
CATS IN THE CRADLE [A] — UGLY KID JOE
CATS IN THE CRADLE [A] — Jason DOWNS featuring MILK
CAUGHT A LITE SNEEZE — Tori AMOS
CAUGHT BY THE FUZZ — SUPERGRASS
CAUGHT BY THE RIVER — DOVES
CAUGHT IN A MOMENT — SUGABABES
CAUGHT IN MY SHADOW — The WONDER STUFF
CAUGHT IN THE MIDDLE [A] — Juliet ROBERTS
CAUGHT IN THE MIDDLE [B] — a1
CAUGHT IN THE MIDDLE [C] — Cerys MATTHEWS
CAUGHT OUT THERE — KELIS
CAUGHT UP [A] — USHER
CAUGHT UP [B] — JA RULE featuring LLOYD
CAUGHT UP IN MY HEART — OPTIMYSTIC
CAUGHT UP IN THE RAPTURE — Anita BAKER
CAUSING A COMMOTION — MADONNA
CAVATINA — John WILLIAMS
CAVE — MUSE
C-C (YOU SET THE FIRE IN ME) — Tom VEK
CCCAN'T YOU SEE — VICIOUS PINK
CECILIA — SUGGS featuring Louchie LOU and Michie ONE
THE CEDAR ROOM — DOVES
CELEBRATE [A] — AN EMOTIONAL FISH
CELEBRATE [B] — HORSE
CELEBRATE [C] — LEVELLERS
CELEBRATE OUR LOVE — ALICE DEEJAY
(CELEBRATE) THE DAY AFTER YOU — The BLOW MONKEYS with Curtis MAYFIELD
CELEBRATE THE WORLD — WOMACK and WOMACK
CELEBRATE YOUR MOTHER — The EIGHTIES MATCHBOX B-LINE DISASTER
CELEBRATION [A] — KOOL and The GANG
CELEBRATION [A] — Kylie MINOGUE
A CELEBRATION — U2
CELEBRATION GENERATION — WESTBAM
CELEBRATION OF LIFE — TRUCE
CELEBRITY HIT LIST — TERRORVISION
CELEBRITY SKIN — HOLE
CELL 151 — Steve HACKETT
THE CELTIC SOUL BROTHERS — DEXY'S MIDNIGHT RUNNERS
THE CELTS — ENYA
CEMENT — FEEDER
CEMENTED SHOES — MY VITRIOL
CENTER CITY — FAT LARRY'S BAND
CENTERFOLD [A] — J GEILS BAND
CENTERFOLD [A] — Adam AUSTIN
CENTRAL PARK ARREST — THUNDERTHIGHS
CENTRAL RESERVATION — Beth ORTON
CENTURY — INTASTELLA
CEREMONY — NEW ORDER
CERTAIN PEOPLE I KNOW — MORRISSEY
A CERTAIN SMILE — Johnny MATHIS
THE CERTAINTY OF CHANCE — The DIVINE COMEDY
C'EST LA VIE [A] — Robbie NEVIL
C'EST LA VIE [B] — UB40
C'EST LA VIE [C] — B*WITCHED (98)
C'EST LA VIE [D] — Jean-Michel JARRE
C'EST SI BON — Conway TWITTY
CHA CHA CHA — FLIPMODE SQUAD
CHA CHA HEELS — Eartha KITT and BRONSKI BEAT
CHA CHA SLIDE [A] — MC JIG
CHA CHA SLIDE [A] — DJ CASPER (04)
CHA CHA TWIST — DETROIT COBRAS
CHAIN GANG [A] — Jimmy YOUNG
CHAIN GANG [B] — Sam COOKE
CHAIN-GANG SMILE — BROTHER BEYOND
CHAIN OF FOOLS — Aretha FRANKLIN
CHAIN REACTION [A] — Diana ROSS (86)
CHAIN REACTION [B] — STEPS
CHAIN REACTION [B] — HURRICANE #1
CHAINS [A] — COOKIES
CHAINS [B] — RIVER DETECTIVES
CHAINS [C] — Tina ARENA
CHAINS AROUND MY HEART — Richard MARX
CHAINS OF LOVE — ERASURE
CHAINSAW CHARLIE (MURDERS IN THE NEW MORGUE) — W.A.S.P.
CHAIRMAN OF THE BOARD — CHAIRMEN OF THE BOARD
CHALK DUST - THE UMPIRE STRIKES BACK — BRAT
THE CHAMP — The MOHAWKS
CHAMPAGNE — SALT-N-PEPA
CHAMPAGNE DANCE — PAY AS U GO
CHAMPAGNE HIGHWAY — SKANDAL
THE CHAMPION — Willie MITCHELL
CHANCE — BIG COUNTRY
CHANCES — HOT CHOCOLATE
CHANGE [A] — TEARS FOR FEARS
CHANGE [B] — David GRANT
CHANGE [C] — Lisa STANSFIELD
CHANGE [D] — INCOGNITO
CHANGE [E] — BLIND MELON
CHANGE [F] — The LIGHTNING SEEDS
CHANGE [G] — DAPHNE
CHANGE [H] — PHATS & SMALL
CHANGE CLOTHES — JAY-Z
CHANGE HIS WAYS — Robert PALMER
CHANGE (IN THE HOUSE OF FLIES) — DEFTONES
CHANGE ME — JOCASTA
CHANGE MY MIND — The BLUESKINS
CHANGE OF HEART [A] — CHANGE
CHANGE OF HEART [B] — Cyndi LAUPER
A CHANGE OF HEART [C] — Bernard BUTLER
CHANGE THE WORLD [A] — Eric CLAPTON
CHANGE THE WORLD [B] — Dino LENNY vs The HOUSEMARTINS
CHANGE WITH THE TIMES — Van McCOY
A CHANGE WOULD DO YOU GOOD — Sheryl CROW
CHANGE YOUR MIND [A] — Gary NUMAN
CHANGE YOUR MIND [B] — UPSIDE DOWN
CHANGES [A] — Crispian ST PETERS
CHANGES [B] — IMAGINATION
CHANGES [C] — Alan PRICE
CHANGES [D] — 2PAC
CHANGES [E] — Sandy RIVERA featuring HAZE
CHANGES [F] — Kelly and Ozzy OSBOURNE (03)
CHANGES ARE NO GOOD — The STILLS

6 March 1999	13 March 1999	20 March 1999	27 March 1999
... BABY ONE MORE TIME Britney Spears	WHEN THE GOING GETS TOUGH Boyzone	WHEN THE GOING GETS TOUGH Boyzone	BLAME IT ON THE WEATHERMAN B*Witched
TALK ON CORNERS The Corrs	TALK ON CORNERS The Corrs	PERFORMANCE AND COCKTAILS Stereophonics	13 Blur

CHANGING FOR YOU — CHI-LITES
CHANGING PARTNERS [A] — Bing CROSBY
CHANGING PARTNERS [A] — Kay STARR
THE CHANGINGMAN — Paul WELLER
CHANNEL Z — The B-52's
CHANSON D'AMOUR — MANHATTAN TRANSFER (77)
THE CHANT (WE R) / RIP PRODUCTIONS — RIP PRODUCTIONS
THE CHANT HAS BEGUN — LEVEL 42
THE CHANT HAS JUST BEGUN — The ALARM
CHANT NO.1 (I DON'T NEED THIS PRESSURE ON) — SPANDAU BALLET
CHANTILLY LACE [A] — The BIG BOPPER
CHANTILLY LACE [A] — Jerry Lee LEWIS
CHAPEL OF LOVE [A] — DIXIE CUPS
CHAPEL OF LOVE [B] — LONDON BOYS
CHAPEL OF THE ROSES — Malcolm VAUGHAN
CHAPTER FOUR — RAM TRILOGY
CHAPTER 5 — RAM TRILOGY
CHAPTER 6 — RAM TRILOGY
CHARADE — The SKIDS
CHARIOT [A] — Rhet STOLLER
CHARIOT [B] — Petula CLARK
CHARIOTS OF FIRE - TITLES — VANGELIS
CHARITY — SKUNK ANANSIE
CHARLESTON — TEMPERANCE SEVEN
CHARLIE BIG POTATO — SKUNK ANANSIE
CHARLIE BROWN — The COASTERS
CHARLIE'S ANGELS 2000 — APOLLO FOUR FORTY
CHARLOTTE — KITTIE
CHARLOTTE ANNE — Julian COPE
CHARLOTTE SOMETIMES — The CURE
CHARLTON HESTON — STUMP
CHARLY — The PRODIGY
CHARMAINE — The BACHELORS
CHARMING BILLY — Johnny PRESTON
CHARMING DEMONS — SENSER
CHARMLESS MAN — BLUR
CHASE [A] — Giorgio MORODER
CHASE [A] — MIDI XPRESS
THE CHASE [A] — DJ EMPIRE presents Giorgio MORODER
CHASE THE SUN — PLANET FUNK
CHASING A RAINBOW — Terry HALL
CHASING FOR THE BREEZE — ASWAD
CHASING RAINBOWS — SHED SEVEN
CH-CHECK IT OUT — BEASTIE BOYS
CHEAP THRILLS — PLANET PATROL
CHEATED — PRAYING MANTIS
CHECK IT OUT (EVERYBODY) — BMR featuring FELICIA
CHECK OUT THE GROOVE — Bobby THURSTON
CHECK THE MEANING — Richard ASHCROFT
CHECK THIS OUT — LA MIX
CHECK YO SELF — ICE CUBE featuring DAS EFX
CHEEKAH BOW BOW (THAT COMPUTER SONG) — The VENGABOYS
CHEEKY — BONIFACE
CHEEKY ARMADA — ILLICIT featuring GRAM'MA FUNK
CHEEKY FLAMENCO — CHEEKY GIRLS
CHEEKY SONG (TOUCH MY BUM) — The CHEEKY GIRLS
CHEERS THEN — BANANARAMA
CHELSEA — STAMFORD BRIDGE
CHEMICAL #1 — JESUS JONES
CHEMICAL WORLD — BLUR
THE CHEMICALS BETWEEN US — BUSH
CHEMISTRY [A] — The NOLANS
CHEMISTRY [B] — SEMISONIC
CHEQUE ONE-TWO — SUNSHIP featuring MCRB
CHEQUERED LOVE — Kim WILDE
CHERI BABE — HOT CHOCOLATE
CHERISH [A] — David CASSIDY
CHERISH [B] — KOOL and The GANG
CHERISH [B] — PAPPA BEAR featuring VAN DER TOORN
CHERISH [C] — MADONNA
CHERISH [D] — JODECI
CHERISH THE DAY [A] — SADE
CHERISH THE DAY [B] — PLUMMET
CHERISH WHAT IS DEAR TO YOU (WHILE IT'S NEAR TO YOU) — Freda PAYNE
CHERRY LIPS (DER ERDBEERMUND) — CULTURE BEAT
CHERRY LIPS (GO BABY GO!) — GARBAGE
CHERRY OH BABY — UB40
CHERRY PIE [A] — Jess CONRAD
CHERRY PIE [B] — WARRANT
CHERRY PINK AND APPLE BLOSSOM WHITE [A] — Perez 'Prez' PRADO and his Orchestra, the King of the Mambo (55)
CHERRY PINK AND APPLE BLOSSOM WHITE [A] — Eddie CALVERT (55)
CHERRY PINK AND APPLE BLOSSOM WHITE [A] — MODERN ROMANCE
CHERUB ROCK — SMASHING PUMPKINS
CHERYL'S GOIN' HOME — Adam FAITH
CHESTNUT MARE — The BYRDS
CHEWING GUM — ANNIE
CHI MAI (THEME FROM THE TV SERIES 'THE LIFE AND TIMES OF DAVID LLOYD GEORGE') — Ennio MORRICONE
CHIC MYSTIQUE — CHIC
CHICAGO [A] — Frank SINATRA
CHICAGO [B] — Kiki DEE
CHICK CHICK CHICKEN — Natalie CASEY
CHICKA BOOM — Guy MITCHELL
CHICK-A-BOOM (DON'T YA JES LOVE IT) — Jonathan KING
CHICKEN — The EIGHTIES MATCHBOX B-LINE DISASTER
CHICKEN PAYBACK — The BEES
THE CHICKEN SONG — SPITTING IMAGE (86)
THE CHIEF — Tony SCOTT
CHIEF INSPECTOR — Wally BADAROU
CHIHUAHUA [A] — BOW WOW WOW
CHIHUAHUA [B] — DARE
CHIHUAHUA [B] — DJ BOBO
CHIKKI CHIKKI AHH AHH — BABY FORD
CHILD [A] — DEFINITION OF SOUND
CHILD [B] — Mark OWEN
CHILD COME AWAY — Kim WILDE
CHILD OF LOVE — LEMON TREES
CHILD OF THE UNIVERSE — DJ TAUCHER
CHILD STAR — Marc ALMOND
CHILDREN [A] — EMF
CHILDREN [B] — Robert MILES
CHILDREN [B] — TILT
CHILDREN [C] — 4 CLUBBERS
CHILDREN OF PARADISE — BONEY M
CHILDREN OF THE NIGHT [A] — Richard MARX
CHILDREN OF THE NIGHT [B] — NAKATOMI
CHILDREN OF THE REVOLUTION [A] — BABY FORD
CHILDREN OF THE REVOLUTION [A] — T. REX
CHILDREN OF THE REVOLUTION [A] — UNITONE ROCKERS featuring STEEL
CHILDREN OF THE WORLD – Ana ANN & The LONDON COMMUNITY CHOIR
CHILDREN SAY — LEVEL 42
CHILDREN'S CHILDREN — AGENT BLUE
A CHILD'S PRAYER — HOT CHOCOLATE
CHILI BOM BOM — The TEMPERANCE SEVEN
CHILL OUT (THINGS GONNA CHANGE) — John Lee HOOKER
CHILL TO THE PANIC — DEEP C
CHILLIN' — MODJO
CHILLIN' OUT — Curtis HAIRSTON
CHIME — ORBITAL
CHINA — Tori AMOS
CHINA DOLL [A] — Slim WHITMAN
CHINA DOLL [B] — Julian COPE
CHINA GIRL — David BOWIE
CHINA IN YOUR HAND — T'PAU (87)
CHINA TEA — Russ CONWAY
CHINATOWN [A] — The MOVE
CHINATOWN [B] — THIN LIZZY
CHINESE BAKERY — The AUTEURS
CHINESE BURN — HEAVY STEREO
THE CHINESE WAY — LEVEL 42
CHING CHING (LOVIN' YOU STILL) — Terri WALKER
CHIQUITITA — ABBA
CHIRPY CHIRPY CHEEP CHEEP [A] — Mac and Katie KISSOON
CHIRPY CHIRPY CHEEP CHEEP [A] — MIDDLE OF THE ROAD (71)
CHIRPY CHIRPY CHEEP CHEEP [A] — LINCOLN CITY FC featuring Michael COURTNEY
THE CHISELERS — The FALL
CHOC ICE — LONG AND THE SHORT
CHOCOLATE [A] — Y?N-VEE
CHOCOLATE [B] — SNOW PATROL
CHOCOLATE [C] — KYLIE
CHOCOLATE BOX — BROS
CHOCOLATE CAKE — CROWDED HOUSE
CHOCOLATE (CHOCO CHOCO) — SOUL CONTROL
CHOCOLATE GIRL — DEACON BLUE
CHOCOLATE SALTY BALLS (PS I LOVE YOU) — CHEF (99)
CHOCOLATE SENSATION — Lenny FONTANA & DJ SHORTY
CHOICE? — The BLOW MONKEYS
CHOK THERE — APACHE INDIAN
CHOLI KE PEECHE — Bally SAGOO
CHOOSE — COLOR ME BADD
CHOOSE LIFE — PF PROJECT featuring Ewan McGREGOR
CHOOSE ME (RESCUE ME) — LOOSE ENDS
CHOOZA LOOZA — Maria WILLSON
CHOP SUEY! — SYSTEM OF A DOWN
CHORUS — ERASURE
THE CHOSEN FEW — The DOOLEYS
CHRISTIAN — CHINA CRISIS
CHRISTIANSANDS — TRICKY
CHRISTINE [A] — MISS X
CHRISTINE [B] — SIOUXSIE and The BANSHEES
CHRISTINE KEELER — SENSELESS THINGS
CHRISTMAS ALPHABET — Dickie VALENTINE (55)
CHRISTMAS AND YOU — Dave KING
CHRISTMAS COUNTDOWN — Frank KELLY
CHRISTMAS IN BLOBBYLAND — MR BLOBBY
CHRISTMAS IN DREADLAND — JUDGE DREAD
CHRISTMAS IN HOLLIS — RUN-DMC
CHRISTMAS IN SMURFLAND — The SMURFS
CHRISTMAS IS ALL AROUND — Billy MACK
CHRISTMAS ISLAND — Dickie VALENTINE
A CHRISTMAS KISS — Daniel O'DONNELL
CHRISTMAS MEDLEY — WEEKEND
CHRISTMAS ON 45 — HOLLY and The IVYS
CHRISTMAS RAPPIN' — Kurtis BLOW
CHRISTMAS RAPPING — DIZZY HEIGHTS
CHRISTMAS SLIDE — Basil BRUSH featuring India BEAU
CHRISTMAS SONG — Gilbert O'SULLIVAN
CHRISTMAS SONG (CHESTNUTS ROASTING ON AN OPEN FIRE) [A] — Alexander O'NEAL
THE CHRISTMAS SONG [A] — Nat 'King' COLE
CHRISTMAS SPECTRE — JINGLE BELLES
CHRISTMAS THROUGH YOUR EYES — Gloria ESTEFAN
CHRISTMAS TIME — Bryan ADAMS
CHRISTMAS TIME (DON'T LET THE BELLS END) — The DARKNESS
CHRISTMAS WILL BE JUST ANOTHER LONELY DAY — Brenda LEE
CHRISTMAS WRAPPING — WAITRESSES
THE CHRONICLES OF LIFE AND DEATH — GOOD CHARLOTTE
CHRONOLOGIE PART 4 — Jean-Michel JARRE
CHUCK E'S IN LOVE — Rickie Lee JONES
CHUNG KUO (REVISITED) — ADDAMS and GEE
CHURA LIYA — Bally SAGOO
CHURCH OF FREEDOM — AMOS
CHURCH OF NOISE — THERAPY?
THE CHURCH OF THE HOLY SPOOK — Shane MacGOWAN and The POPES
CHURCH OF THE POISON MIND — CULTURE CLUB
CHURCH OF YOUR HEART — ROXETTE
CIAO CIAO BAMBINA [A] — Domenico MODUGNO
CIAO CIAO BAMBINA [A] — Marino MARINI and his QUARTET
CIGARETTES AND ALCOHOL — OASIS
CINDERELLA — LEMONESCENT
CINDERELLA ROCKEFELLA — Esther and Abi OFARIM (68)
CINDY INCIDENTALLY — The FACES
CINDY, OH CINDY [A] — Eddie FISHER
CINDY, OH CINDY [A] — Tony BRENT
CINDY, OH CINDY [A] — TARRIERS
CINDY'S BIRTHDAY — Shane FENTON and The FENTONES
CINNAMON GIRL — PRINCE
CIRCLE — Edie BRICKELL and The NEW BOHEMIANS
THE CIRCLE — OCEAN COLOUR SCENE
CIRCLE IN THE SAND — Belinda CARLISLE
CIRCLE OF LIFE — Elton JOHN
CIRCLE OF ONE — Oleta ADAMS
CIRCLE SQUARE TRIANGLE — TEST ICICLES
CIRCLES [A] — The NEW SEEKERS
CIRCLES [B] — SAFFRON
CIRCLES [C] — Adam F
CIRCLESQUARE — The WONDER STUFF
CIRCUS [A] — Lenny KRAVITZ
CIRCUS [B] — Eric CLAPTON
THE CIRCUS [C] — ERASURE
CIRCUS GAMES — The SKIDS
CITIES IN DUST — SIOUXSIE and The BANSHEES
THE CITY IS MINE — JAY-Z featuring BLACKSTREET
CITY LIGHTS — David ESSEX
CITY OF BLINDING LIGHTS — U2
CITYSONG — LUSCIOUS JACKSON
THE CIVIL WAR (EP) — GUNS N' ROSES
CLAIR — Gilbert O'SULLIVAN (72)
CLAIRE — Paul and Barry RYAN
THE CLAIRVOYANT — IRON MAIDEN
CLAP BACK — JA RULE
THE CLAP CLAP SOUND — KLAXONS
CLAP YOUR HANDS [A] — Rocky SHARPE and The REPLAYS
CLAP YOUR HANDS [B] — CAMISRA
THE CLAPPING SONG (EP) [A] — Shirley ELLIS
THE CLAPPING SONG [A] — Shirley ELLIS
THE CLAPPING SONG [A] — The BELLE STARS
CLARE — FAIRGROUND ATTRACTION
CLASH CITY ROCKERS — The CLASH
CLASSIC — Adrian GURVITZ
CLASSIC GIRL — JANE'S ADDICTION
CLASSICAL GAS [A] — Mason WILLIAMS
CLASSICAL GAS [A] — VANESSA-MAE
CLASSICAL MUDDLY — PORTSMOUTH SINFONIA
CLAUDETTE — The EVERLY BROTHERS (58)
CLEAN CLEAN — The BUGGLES
CLEAN UP YOUR OWN BACK YARD — Elvis PRESLEY
CLEANIN' OUT MY CLOSET — EMINEM
CLEAR BLUE WATER — OCEANLAB featuring Justine SUISSA
CLEMENTINE [A] — Bobby DARIN
CLEMENTINE [B] — Mark OWEN
CLEOPATRA'S CAT — SPIN DOCTORS
CLEOPATRA'S THEME — CLEOPATRA
CLEVER KICKS — The HISS
THE CLICHES ARE TRUE — MANCHILD featuring Kelly JONES
CLIMB EV'RY MOUNTAIN — Shirley BASSEY (61)
CLINT EASTWOOD — GORILLAZ
CLIPPED — CURVE
CLOAKING — SEAFOOD
CLOCKS — COLDPLAY
CLOG DANCE — VIOLINSKI
CLOSE ... BUT — ECHOBELLY
CLOSE BUT NO CIGAR — Thomas DOLBY
CLOSE COVER — MINIMALISTIX
CLOSE EVERY DOOR — Phillip SCHOFIELD
CLOSE MY EYES — The OPEN
CLOSE MY EYES FOREVER — Lita FORD duet with Ozzy OSBOURNE
CLOSE THE DOOR [A] — The STARGAZERS
CLOSE THE DOOR [B] — Teddy PENDERGRASS
CLOSE TO ME — The CURE
CLOSE TO PERFECTION — Miquel BROWN
CLOSE (TO THE EDIT) — ART OF NOISE
CLOSE TO YOU [A] — Maxi PRIEST
CLOSE TO YOU [B] — The BRAND NEW HEAVIES
CLOSE TO YOU [C] — WHIGFIELD
CLOSE TO YOU [D] — Marti PELLOW
CLOSE TO YOUR HEART — JX
CLOSE YOUR EYES — Tony BENNETT
CLOSED FOR BUSINESS — MANSUN
CLOSER [A] — MR FINGERS
CLOSER [B] — NINE INCH NAILS
CLOSER [C] — LIQUID
THE CLOSER I GET TO YOU — Roberta FLACK
CLOSER THAN CLOSE — Rosie GAINES
CLOSER THAN MOST — The BEAUTIFUL SOUTH
CLOSER TO ALL YOUR DREAMS — RHYTHM QUEST
CLOSER TO ME — FIVE
CLOSER TO THE HEART — RUSH
THE CLOSEST THING TO CRAZY — Katie MELUA
CLOSEST THING TO HEAVEN [A] — KANE GANG
CLOSEST THING TO HEAVEN [B] — Lionel RICHIE
CLOSEST THING TO HEAVEN [C] — TEARS FOR FEARS
CLOSING TIME [A] — DEACON BLUE
CLOSING TIME [B] — SEMISONIC
CLOUD 8 — FRAZIER CHORUS

	3 April 1999	10 April 1999	17 April 1999	24 April 1999
UK No.1 SINGLES	FLAT BEAT Mr Oizo	FLAT BEAT Mr Oizo	PERFECT MOMENT Martine McCutcheon	PERFECT MOMENT Martine McCutcheon
UK No.1 ALBUMS	13 Blur	TALK ON CORNERS The Corrs	GOLD - GREATEST HITS Abba	EQUALLY CURSED AND BLESSED Catatonia

CLOUD LUCKY SEVEN — Guy MITCHELL
CLOUD NINE — The TEMPTATIONS
CLOUD 99 — ST ANDREWS CHORALE
CLOUD NUMBER 9 — Bryan ADAMS
CLOUDBURST [A] — Don LANG
CLOUDBURST [B] — NIAGRA
CLOUDBUSTING — Kate BUSH
CLOUDS — SOURCE
CLOUDS ACROSS THE MOON — RAH BAND
THE CLOUDS WILL SOON ROLL BY — Tony BRENT
CLOWN SHOES — Johnny BURNETTE
CLUB AT THE END OF THE STREET — Elton JOHN
CLUB BIZARRE — U96
CLUB COUNTRY — ASSOCIATES
CLUB FANTASTIC MEGAMIX — WHAM!
CLUB FOOT — KASABIAN
CLUB FOR LIFE '98 — CHRIS and JAMES
CLUB LONELY — GROOVE CONNEKTION 2
CLUB TROPICANA — WHAM!
CLUBBED TO DEATH — Rob DOUGAN
CLUBBIN' — Marques HOUSTON featuring Joe BUDDEN and PIED PIPER
CLUBLAND — Elvis COSTELLO
CLUNK CLINK — LAUREL and HARDY
CLUTCH — SHEA SEGER
C'MERE — INTERPOL
C'MON [A] — MILLIONAIRE HIPPIES
C'MON [A] — MARIO
C'MON AND GET MY LOVE — D MOB with Cathy DENNIS
C'MON BILLY — P J HARVEY
C'MON CHAMELEON — The RESEARCH
C'MON CINCINNATI — DELAKOTA
C'MON C'MON — The VON BONDIES
C'MON EVERY BEATBOX — BIG AUDIO DYNAMITE
C'MON EVERYBODY [A] — Eddie COCHRAN
C'MON EVERYBODY [A] — SEX PISTOLS
C'MON KIDS — The BOO RADLEYS
C'MON LET'S GO — GIRLSCHOOL
C'MON MARIANNE — GRAPEFRUIT
C'MON PEOPLE — Paul McCARTNEY
C'MON PEOPLE (WE'RE MAKING IT NOW) — Richard ASHCROFT
COAST IS CLEAR — CURVE
COCHISE — AUDIOSLAVE
COCK A DOODLE DO IT — EGGS ON LEGS
COCKNEY TRANSLATION — Smiley CULTURE
CO-CO — The SWEET
COCO JAMBOO — MR PRESIDENT
COCOA — CLIPZ
COCOMOTION — EL COCO
COCONUT — NILSSON
COCOON — BJÖRK
CODE OF LOVE — Mike SARNE
CODE RED [A] — CONQUERING LION
CODE RED [B] — BOXER REBELLION
CODED LANGUAGE — KRUST featuring Saul WILLIAMS
COFFEE — SUPERSISTER
COFFEE + TV — BLUR
THE COFFEE SONG — Frank SINATRA
COGNOSCENTI VS INTELLIGENTSIA — CUBAN BOYS
COLD [A] — Annie LENNOX
COLD [B] — TEARS FOR FEARS
COLD AS CHRISTMAS — Elton JOHN
COLD AS ICE [A] — FOREIGNER
COLD AS ICE [A] — M.O.P
COLD COLD HEART [A] — Midge URE
COLD COLD HEART [B] — WET WET WET
COLD DAY IN HELL — Gary MOORE
COLD HARD BITCH — JET
COLD HEARTED — Paula ABDUL
COLD LIGHT OF DAY — HALO
COLD LOVE — Donna SUMMER
COLD ROCK A PARTY — MC LYTE
COLD SHOULDER — CULTURE CLUB
COLD SWEAT [A] — THIN LIZZY
COLD SWEAT [B] — SUGARCUBES
COLD TURKEY — John LENNON
COLD WIND — ARCADE FIRE
COLD WORLD — GENIUS / GZA featuring D'ANGELO
COLDCUT'S CHRISTMAS BREAK — COLDCUT
COLETTE — Billy FURY
COLOR OF MY SKIN — SWING 52
COLOSSAL INSIGHT — ROOTS MANUVA
COLOSSUS — FRESH BC
THE COLOUR FIELD — COLOUR FIELD
COLOUR MY LIFE — M PEOPLE
THE COLOUR OF LOVE [A] — Billy OCEAN
THE COLOUR OF LOVE [B] — SNAP!
THE COLOUR OF LOVE [C] — REESE PROJECT
COLOUR OF MY LOVE — JEFFERSON
COLOUR THE WORLD — SASH!
COLOURBLIND — DARIUS (02)
COLOURED KISSES — MARTIKA
COLOURS — DONOVAN
THE COLOURS — MEN THEY COULDN'T HANG
COLOURS FLY AWAY — TEARDROP EXPLODES
COLOURS IN WAVES — SOUTH
COLOURS OF THE WIND — Vanessa WILLIAMS
COMA AROMA — INAURA
COMA GIRL — Joe STRUMMER & The MESCALEROS
THE COMANCHEROS — Lonnie DONEGAN
THE COMBINE HARVESTER (BRAND NEW KEY) — The WURZELS (76)
COME — Martha WASH
COME AGAIN — TRUMAN & WOLFF featuring STEEL HORSES
COME ALONG PLEASE — Bob WALLIS and his STORYVILLE JAZZ BAND
COME AND GET IT — BADFINGER
COME AND GET ME — CLEOPATRA
COME AND GET SOME — COOKIE CREW
COME AND GET WITH ME — Keith SWEAT
COME AND GET YOUR LOVE — The REAL McCOY
COME AND STAY WITH ME — Marianne FAITHFULL
COME AS YOU ARE [A] — NIRVANA
COME AS YOU ARE [B] — Beverley KNIGHT
COME AWAY MELINDA — Barry ST JOHN
COME BABY COME — K7
COME BACK [A] — WAH!
COME BACK [B] — SPEAR OF DESTINY
COME BACK [C] — Luther VANDROSS
COME BACK [D] — LONDONBEAT
COME BACK [E] — Jessica GARLICK
COME BACK AND FINISH WHAT YOU STARTED — Gladys KNIGHT and The PIPS
COME BACK AND SHAKE ME — Clodagh RODGERS
COME BACK AND STAY — Paul YOUNG
COME BACK AROUND — FEEDER
COME BACK BABY — Dan REED NETWORK
COME BACK BRIGHTER — REEF
COME BACK DARLING — UB40
COME BACK (FOR REAL LOVE) — Alison LIMERICK
COME BACK JONEE — DEVO
COME BACK MY LOVE — DARTS
COME BACK TO ME [A] — Janet JACKSON
COME BACK TO ME [B] — ANGELHEART
COME BACK TO WHAT YOU KNOW — EMBRACE
COME BACK TOMORROW — INSPIRAL CARPETS
COME CLEAN — Hilary DUFF
COME DANCE WITH ME (LP) — Frank SINATRA
COME DANCING [A] — NO DICE
COME DANCING [B] — The KINKS
COME DIG IT — MACHEL
COME GET MY LOVIN' — DIONNE
COME GET SOME — ROOSTER
COME GIVE ME YOUR LOVE — Richie STEPHENS
COME HELL OR WATERS HIGH — DC LEE
COME HOME [A] — Dave CLARK FIVE
COME HOME [B] — JAMES
COME HOME [C] — LIL' DEVIOUS
COME HOME BILLY BIRD — The DIVINE COMEDY
COME HOME WITH ME BABY — DEAD OR ALIVE
COME IN OUT OF THE RAIN — Wendy MOTEN
COME INSIDE — THOMPSON TWINS
COME INTO MY LIFE [A] — Joyce SIMS
COME INTO MY LIFE [B] — GALA
COME INTO MY ROOM — NATHAN
COME INTO MY WORLD — Kylie MINOGUE
COME LIVE WITH ME — HEAVEN 17
COME NEXT SPRING — Tony BENNETT
COME ON [A] — The ROLLING STONES
COME ON [B] — DJ SEDUCTION
COME ON [C] — JESUS AND MARY CHAIN
COME ON [D] — NEW POWER GENERATION
COME ON [E] — LEVELLERS
COME ON! [A] — SOLO
COME ON! [B] — D4
COME ON (AND DO IT) — FPI PROJECT
COME ON AND GET SOME — COOKIE CREW
COME ON, COME ON — BRONSKI BEAT
COME ON DANCE DANCE — SATURDAY NIGHT BAND
COME ON EILEEN [A] — DEXY'S MIDNIGHT RUNNERS with The Emerald Express (82)
COME ON ENGLAND! [A] — ENGLAND'S BARMY ARMY
COME ON ENGLAND [B] — 4-4-2
COME ON EVERYBODY (GET DOWN) — US3
COME ON HOME [A] — The SPRINGFIELDS
COME ON HOME [B] — Wayne FONTANA
COME ON HOME [C] — EVERYTHING BUT THE GIRL
COME ON HOME [D] — Cyndi LAUPER
COME ON LET'S GO [A] — LOS LOBOS
COME ON, LET'S GO [A] — Tommy STEELE
COME ON / LET'S GO — Paul WELLER
COME ON OVER [A] — Kym MARSH
COME ON OVER [B] — John SILVER
COME ON OVER BABY (ALL I WANT IS YOU) — Christina AGUILERA
COME ON OVER TO MY PLACE — The DRIFTERS
COME ON Y'ALL — RHYTHM MASTERS
COME ON YOU REDS — MANCHESTER UNITED FOOTBALL CLUB (94)
COME OUTSIDE [A] — Mike SARNE with Wendy RICHARD (62)
COME OUTSIDE [A] — JUDGE DREAD
COME PLAY WITH ME — The WEDDING PRESENT
COME PRIMA — Marino MARINI and his QUARTET
(COME 'ROUND HERE) I'M THE ONE YOU NEED — The MIRACLES
COME SEE ABOUT ME [A] — The SUPREMES
COME SEE ABOUT ME [A] — Shakin' STEVENS
COME SEE ME — The PRETTY THINGS
COME SOFTLY TO ME [A] — The FLEETWOODS
COME SOFTLY TO ME [A] — Frankie VAUGHAN and The KAYE SISTERS
COME SOFTLY TO ME [A] — The NEW SEEKERS
COME TO DADDY — APHEX TWIN
COME TO ME [A] — Julie GRANT
COME TO ME [B] — Ruby WINTERS
COME TO ME [C] — ATEED
COME TO ME (I AM WOMAN) — Su POLLARD
COME TO MILTON KEYNES — The STYLE COUNCIL
COME TO MY AID — SIMPLY RED
COME TO MY PARTY — Keith HARRIS and ORVILLE
COME TO THE DANCE — The BARRON KNIGHTS
COME TOGETHER [A] — The BEATLES
COME TOGETHER [A] — Michael JACKSON
COME TOGETHER (WAR CHILD) [A] — SMOKIN' MOJO FILTERS
COME TOGETHER [B] — PRIMAL SCREAM
COME TOGETHER [C] — M FACTOR
COME TOGETHER AS ONE — Will DOWNING
COME TOMORROW — MANFRED MANN
COME UNDONE [A] — DURAN DURAN
COME UNDONE [B] — Robbie WILLIAMS
COME WHAT MAY [A] — Vicky LEANDROS
COME WHAT MAY [A] — Nicole KIDMAN & Ewan McGREGOR
COME WITH ME [A] — Jesse GREEN
COME WITH ME [B] — Ronny JORDAN
COME WITH ME [C] — QATTARA
COME WITH ME [D] — PUFF DADDY featuring Jimmy PAGE
COME WITH ME [E] — SPECIAL D
COME WITH US — The CHEMICAL BROTHERS
THE COMEBACK — SHOUT OUT LOUDS
COMEDY — SHACK
COMES A-LONG A-LOVE — Kay STARR (53)
COMEUPPANCE — THOUSAND YARD STARE
COMFORTABLY NUMB — SCISSOR SISTERS
COMFORTING SOUNDS — MEW
COMIN' BACK — CRYSTAL METHOD
COMIN' HOME [A] — DELANEY and BONNIE and FRIENDS featuring Eric CLAPTON
COMIN' HOME [B] — DANGER DANGER
COMIN' IN AND OUT OF YOUR LIFE — Barbra STREISAND
COMIN' ON STRONG [A] — BROKEN ENGLISH
COMIN' ON STRONG [B] — DESIYA featuring Melissa YIANNAKOU
COMING ON STRONG — SIGNUM featuring Scott MAC
COMIN' RIGHT UP — Bruce WILLIS
COMING AROUND — TRAVIS
COMING AROUND AGAIN — Carly SIMON
COMING BACK — DJ DADO
COMING BACK FOR MORE [A] — LA MIX
COMING BACK FOR MORE [B] — JELLYBEAN featuring Richard DARBYSHIRE
COMING DOWN — The CULT
COMING HOME [A] — David ESSEX
COMING HOME [B] — MARSHALL HAIN
COMING HOME [C] — K-WARREN featuring LEE-O
COMING HOME [D] — JJ72
COMING HOME BABY — Mel TORME
COMING HOME NOW — BOYZONE
COMING ON STRONG — SIGNUM
COMING OUT OF THE DARK — Gloria ESTEFAN
COMING SECOND — ELBOW
COMING UP — Paul McCARTNEY
COMING UP ROSES — CURVE
COMMENT TE DIRE ADIEU — Jimmy SOMERVILLE
COMMITMENT — LeAnn RIMES
COMMON PEOPLE — PULP
COMMUNICATION [A] — David McCALLUM
COMMUNICATION [B] — SPANDAU BALLET
COMMUNICATION [C] — POWER STATION
COMMUNICATION [D] — ARMIN
COMMUNICATION BREAKDOWN — JUNIOR
COMMUNICATION (SOMEBODY ANSWER THE PHONE) — Mario PIU
THE COMPASS — Dave CLARKE
COMPLETE — JAIMESON
COMPLETE CONTROL — The CLASH
THE COMPLETE DOMINATOR — HUMAN RESOURCE
THE COMPLETE STELLA — JAM & SPOON featuring PLAVKA
COMPLEX — Gary NUMAN
COMPLICATED — Avril LAVIGNE
COMPLIMENTS ON YOUR KISS — RED DRAGON with Brian and Tony GOLD
COMPUTER GAME (THEME FROM 'THE INVADERS') — YELLOW MAGIC ORCHESTRA
COMPUTER LOVE [A] — KRAFTWERK (82)
COMPUTER LOVE (PART 1) [B] — ZAPP
COMPUTER LOVE [C] — SUPERCAR
CON LOS AÑOS QUE ME QUEDAN — Gloria ESTEFAN
THE CONCEPT — TEENAGE FANCLUB
CONCRETE AND CLAY [A] — Randy EDELMAN
CONCRETE AND CLAY [A] — UNIT FOUR PLUS TWO (65)
CONCRETE SCHOOLYARD — JURASSIC 5
CONDEMNATION — DEPECHE MODE
CONFESSIN' (THAT I LOVE YOU) — Frank IFIELD (63)
CONFESSIONS PART II — USHER
CONFETTI — LEMONHEADS
CONFIDE IN ME — Kylie MINOGUE
CONFUSION [A] — Lee DORSEY
CONFUSION [B] — ELECTRIC LIGHT ORCHESTRA
CONFUSION [C] — NEW ORDER
CONFUSION [C] — Arthur BAKER vs NEW ORDER
CONFUSION ... [D] — The ZUTONS
CONFUSION (HITS US EVERY TIME) — TRUTH
CONGO [A] — BOSS
CONGO [B] — GENESIS
CONGO SQUARE — GREAT WHITE
CONGRATULATIONS — Cliff RICHARD (68)
CONNECTED [A] — STEREO MC's
CONNECTED [B] — Paul VAN DYK featuring VEGA 4
CONNECTION — ELASTICA
CONQUEST OF PARADISE — VANGELIS
CONQUISTADOR [A] — PROCOL HARUM
CONQUISTADOR [B] — ESPIRITU
CONSCIENCE — James DARREN
CONSCIOUS MAN — The JOLLY BROTHERS
CONSIDER YOURSELF — Max BYGRAVES
CONSIDERATION — REEF
A CONSPIRACY — The BLACK CROWES
CONSTANT CRAVING — kd lang
CONSTANTLY — Cliff RICHARD
CONSTANTLY WAITING — Pauline TAYLOR
CONTACT [A] — Edwin STARR
CONTACT ... [B] — EAT STATIC

1 May 1999	8 May 1999	15 May 1999	22 May 1999
SWEAR IT AGAIN Westlife	SWEAR IT AGAIN Westlife	I WANT IT THAT WAY Backstreet Boys	YOU NEEDED ME Boyzone
GOLD - GREATEST HITS Abba	GOLD - GREATEST HITS Abba	HEAD MUSIC Suede	THE HUSH Texas

CONTAGIOUS — WHISPERS
THE CONTINENTAL — Maureen McGOVERN
CONTRARY MARY — THEE UNSTRUNG
CONTRIBUTION — Mica PARIS
CONTROL [A] — Janet JACKSON
CONTROL [B] — TIME OF THE MUMPH
CONTROL [C] — PUDDLE OF MUDD
CONTROLLING ME — OCEANIC
CONTROVERSY — PRINCE
CONVERSATION INTERCOM — SOULWAX
CONVERSATIONS — Cilla BLACK
CONVOY — CW McCALL
CONVOY GB — Laurie LINGO and The DIPSTICKS
CONWAY — REEL 2 REAL
COOCHY COO — EN-CORE featuring Stephen EMMANUEL & ESKA
COOKIN' UP YAH BRAIN — 4 HERO
COOL — Gwen STEFANI
COOL BABY — Charlie GRACIE
COOL FOR CATS — SQUEEZE
COOL JERK — GO-GO's
COOL MEDITATION — THIRD WORLD
COOL OUT TONIGHT — David ESSEX
COOL RUNNING — TIK and TOK
COOL WATER — Frankie LAINE
COP THAT SH*T — TIMBALAND & MAGOO featuring Missy ELLIOTT
COPACABANA (AT THE COPA) — Barry MANILOW
COPPER GIRL — 3 COLOURS RED
COPPERHEAD ROAD — Steve EARLE
CORNER OF THE EARTH — JAMIROQUAI
CORNFLAKE GIRL — Tori AMOS
CORONATION RAG — Winifred ATWELL
CORPSES — Ian BROWN
CORRINE, CORRINA — Ray PETERSON
COSMIC GIRL — JAMIROQUAI
COSMONAUT NO.7 — SCARFO
THE COST OF LIVING (EP) — The CLASH
COSTAFINE TOWN — SPLINTER
COTTON EYE JOE — REDNEX (95)
COTTONFIELDS — The BEACH BOYS
COULD HAVE TOLD YOU SO — HALO JAMES
COULD HEAVEN EVER BE LIKE THIS — Idris MUHAMMAD
COULD I HAVE THIS KISS FOREVER — Whitney HOUSTON and Enrique IGLESIAS
COULD IT BE — JAHEIM
COULD IT BE FOREVER [A] — David CASSIDY
COULD IT BE FOREVER [A] — GEMINI
COULD IT BE I'M FALLING IN LOVE [A] — The DETROIT SPINNERS
COULD IT BE I'M FALLING IN LOVE (EP) [A] — The DETROIT SPINNERS
COULD IT BE I'M FALLING IN LOVE [A] — David GRANT and Jaki GRAHAM
COULD IT BE I'M FALLING IN LOVE [A] — WORLDS APART
COULD IT BE MAGIC [A] — Donna SUMMER
COULD IT BE MAGIC [A] — Barry MANILOW
COULD IT BE MAGIC [A] — TAKE THAT
COULD WELL BE IN — The STREETS
COULD YOU BE LOVED — Bob MARLEY & The WAILERS
COULDN'T GET IT RIGHT — CLIMAX BLUES BAND
COULDN'T HAVE SAID IT BETTER — MEAT LOAF
COULDN'T SAY GOODBYE — Tom JONES
COULD'VE BEEN — TIFFANY
COULD'VE BEEN ME — Billy Ray CYRUS
COULD'VE BEEN YOU — CHER
COUNT ON ME [A] — Julie GRANT
COUNT ON ME [B] — Whitney HOUSTON
COUNT YOUR BLESSINGS — Bing CROSBY
COUNTDOWN — RUSH
COUNTERFEIT — LOWGOLD
COUNTING BACKWARDS — THROWING MUSES
COUNTING DOWN THE DAYS — Natalie IMBRUGLIA
COUNTING EVERY MINUTE — SONIA
COUNTING SHEEP — AIRHEAD
COUNTING TEARDROPS — Emile FORD and The CHECKMATES
COUNTING THE DAYS — ABI
COUNTRY BOY [A] — Fats DOMINO
COUNTRY BOY [B] — HEINZ
COUNTRY BOY [C] — Jimmy NAIL
COUNTRY HOUSE — BLUR (95)
THE COUNTRY OF THE BLIND — The FAITH BROTHERS
COUNTRY ROADS — HERMES HOUSE BAND
COURSE BRUV — GENIUS CRU
COUSIN NORMAN — MARMALADE
COVER FROM THE SKY — DEACON BLUE
COVER GIRL — NEW KIDS ON THE BLOCK
COVER ME — Bruce SPRINGSTEEN
COVER MY EYES (PAIN AND HEAVEN) — MARILLION
(COVER PLUS) WE'RE ALL GROWN UP — Hazel O'CONNOR
COVER UP — UB40
COVERED IN PUNK — PORTOBELLA
COVERS (EP) — EVERYTHING BUT THE GIRL
COWARD OF THE COUNTY — Kenny ROGERS (80)
COWBOY — KID ROCK
COWBOY DREAMS — Jimmy NAIL
COWBOY JIMMY JOE — Alma COGAN
COWBOYS AND ANGELS — George MICHAEL
COWBOYS AND INDIANS — CROSS
COWBOYS & KISSES — ANASTACIA
COWGIRL — UNDERWORLD
COWPUNCHER'S CANTATA — Max BYGRAVES
COWPUNK MEDLUM — SPLODGENESSABOUNDS
COZ I LUV YOU — SLADE (71)
CRACKERS INTERNATIONAL (EP) — ERASURE
CRACKIN' UP [A] — Tommy HUNT
CRACKING UP [B] — Nick LOWE
CRACKING UP — JESUS AND MARY CHAIN
CRACKLIN' ROSIE — Neil DIAMOND
CRADLE — ATOMIC KITTEN
CRADLE OF LOVE [A] — Johnny PRESTON
CRADLE OF LOVE [B] — Billy IDOL
CRANK — CATHERINE WHEEL
CRASH [A] — PRIMITIVES
CRASH [B] — FEEDER
CRASH AND BURN — SAVAGE GARDEN
CRASH! BOOM! BANG! — ROXETTE
CRASH LANDING — ROUTE-1 featuring Jenny FROST
CRASHED THE WEDDING — BUSTED (03)
CRASHIN' A PARTY — LUMIDEE featuring N.O.R.E.
CRASHIN' IN — The CHARLATANS
CRAWL — HEADSWIM
CRAWL HOME — DESERT SESSIONS
CRAWLIN' BACK — Roy ORBISON
CRAWLING — LINKIN PARK
CRAWLING FROM THE WRECKAGE — Dave EDMUNDS
CRAWLING IN THE DARK — HOOBASTANK
CRAWLING UP A HILL— Katie MELUA
CRAYZY MAN — BLAST featuring VDC
CRAZIER — Gary NUMAN vs RICO
CRAZY [A] — MUD
CRAZY [B] — MANHATTANS
CRAZY [C] — ICEHOUSE
CRAZY [D] — The BOYS
CRAZY [E] — Patsy CLINE
CRAZY [E] — Julio IGLESIAS
CRAZY [E] — LeAnn RIMES
CRAZY [F] — SEAL
CRAZY [F] — Alanis MORISSETTE
CRAZY [G] — Bob GELDOF
CRAZY [H] — AEROSMITH
CRAZY [I] — ETERNAL
CRAZY [J] — Mark MORRISON
CRAZY [K] — NUT
CRAZY [L] — AWESOME
CRAZY [M] — The MOFFATTS
CRAZY [N] — LUCID
CRAZY [O] — TOMCAT
CRAZY [P] — K-CI & JOJO
CRAZY [Q] — Andy BELL
CRAZY BEAT — BLUR
CRAZY CHANCE — KAVANA
CRAZY CHICK — Charlotte CHURCH
CRAZY CRAZY NIGHTS — KISS
CRAZY CUTS — GRANDMIXER DST
CRAZY DREAM — Jim DALE
CRAZY (FOR ME) — Freddie JACKSON
CRAZY FOR YOU [A] — MADONNA
CRAZY FOR YOU [B] — SYBIL
CRAZY FOR YOU [C] — INCOGNITO
CRAZY FOR YOU [D] — LET LOOSE
CRAZY HORSES — The OSMONDS
CRAZY IN LOVE — BEYONCÉ (03)
CRAZY LITTLE PARTY GIRL — Aaron CARTER
CRAZY LITTLE THING CALLED LOVE [A] — QUEEN
CRAZY LITTLE THING CALLED LOVE [A] — Dwight YOAKAM
CRAZY LOVE [A] — Paul ANKA
CRAZY LOVE [B] — Maxi PRIEST
CRAZY LOVE [C] — Ce Ce PENISTON
CRAZY LOVE [D] — MJ COLE
CRAZY LOWDOWN WAYS — OCEAN COLOUR SCENE
THE CRAZY OTTO RAG — The STARGAZERS
THE CRAZY PARTY MIXES — JIVE BUNNY and The MASTERMIXERS
CRAZY RAP — AFROMAN
CRAZY SEXY MARVELLOUS — PAFFENDORF
CRAZY TRAIN — Ozzy OSBOURNE
CRAZY WATER — Elton JOHN
CRAZY WORDS CRAZY TUNE — Dorothy PROVINE
CRAZY YOU — GUN
CREAM [A] — PRINCE and The NEW POWER GENERATION
CREAM [B] — BLANK & JONES
CREAM (ALWAYS RISES TO THE TOP) — Gregg DIAMOND BIONIC BOOGIE
CREATION — STEREO MC's
CREATURES OF THE NIGHT — KISS
CREDO — FISH
THE CREEP [A] — Ken MACKINTOSH
CREEP [B] — RADIOHEAD
CREEP [C] — TLC
CREEQUE ALLEY — The MAMAS and The PAPAS
CREOLE JAZZ — Mr Acker BILK and his PARAMOUNT JAZZ BAND
CRESCENT MOON — Lynden David HALL
CRICKETS SING FOR ANAMARIA — EMMA
CRIME OF PASSION — Mike OLDFIELD
CRIMINALLY INSANE — SLAYER
CRIMSON AND CLOVER — Joan JETT and The BLACKHEARTS
CRISPY BACON — Laurent GARNIER
CRITICAL (IF YOU ONLY KNEW) — WALL OF SOUND featuring Gerald LETHAN
CRITICIZE — Alexander O'NEAL
CROCKETT'S THEME — Jan HAMMER
CROCODILE ROCK — Elton JOHN
CROCODILE SHOES — Jimmy NAIL
CROCODILES — ECHO and The BUNNYMEN
CROSS MY BROKEN HEART — SINITTA
CROSS MY HEART — EIGHTH WONDER
CROSS THAT BRIDGE — The WARD BROTHERS
CROSS THE TRACK (WE BETTER GO BACK) — MACEO & The MACKS
CROSSROADS [A] — Tracy CHAPMAN
CROSSROADS [B] — BLAZIN' SQUAD (02)
CROSSTOWN TRAFFIC [A] — Jimi HENDRIX
CROSSTOWN TRAFFIC [A] — The Jimi HENDRIX EXPERIENCE
THE CROWD — Roy ORBISON
THE CROWN — Gary BYRD and The GB EXPERIENCE
CROWS — MODEY LEMON
CRUCIAL —NEW EDITION
CRUCIFIED — ARMY OF LOVERS
CRUCIFY — Tori AMOS
CRUEL — PUBLIC IMAGE LTD
THE CRUEL SEA — DAKOTAS
CRUEL SUMMER [A] — BANANARAMA
CRUEL SUMMER [A] — ACE OF BASE
CRUEL TO BE KIND — Nick LOWE
CRUISE INTO CHRISTMAS MEDLEY — Jane McDONALD
CRUISIN' — D'ANGELO
CRUISING — SINITTA
THE CRUNCH — RAH BAND
CRUSH [A] — ZHANE
CRUSH [B] — Jennifer PAIGE
CRUSH [C] — Paul VAN DYK featuring SECOND SUN
CRUSH ME — HOUSE OF LOVE
CRUSH (1980 ME) [C] — Darren HAYES
CRUSH ON YOU [A] — JETS
CRUSH ON YOU [A] — Aaron CARTER
CRUSH ON YOU [B] — LIL' KIM
CRUSH TONIGHT — FAT JOE featuring GINUWINE
CRUSH WITH EYELINER — R.E.M.
CRUSHED BY THE WHEELS OF INDUSTRY — HEAVEN 17
CRUSHED LIKE FRUIT — INME
CRY [A] — Gerry MONROE
CRY [B] — GODLEY and CREME
CRY [C] — WATERFRONT
CRY [D] — The SUNDAYS
CRY [E] — SYSTEM F
CRY [F] — Michael JACKSON
CRY [G] — SIMPLE MINDS
CRY [H] — Faith HILL
CRY [I] — Kym MARSH
CRY [J] — Alex PARKS
CRY AND BE FREE — MARILYN
CRY BABY [A] — SPILLER
CRY BABY [B] — JEMINI
CRY BOY CRY — BLUE ZOO
CRY DIGNITY — DUB WAR
CRY FOR HELP [A] — Rick ASTLEY
CRY FOR HELP [B] — SHED SEVEN
CRY FOR ME — ROACHFORD
CRY FOR THE NATIONS — Michael SCHENKER GROUP
CRY FOR YOU — JODECI
CRY FREEDOM [A] — George FENTON and Jonas GWANGWA
CRY FREEDOM [B] — MOMBASSA
CRY INDIA — UMBOZA
CRY JUST A LITTLE BIT — Shakin' STEVENS
CRY LIKE A BABY — The BOX TOPS
CRY LITTLE SISTER (I NEED U NOW) — LOST BROTHERS featuring G Tom MAC
CRY ME A RIVER [A] — Julie LONDON
CRY ME A RIVER [A] — Mari WILSON
CRY ME A RIVER [A] — Denise WELCH
CRY ME A RIVER [B] — Justin TIMBERLAKE
CRY MY HEART — David WHITFIELD
CRY MYSELF TO SLEEP — Del SHANNON
CRY TO BE FOUND — DEL AMITRI
CRY TO HEAVEN — Elton JOHN
CRY TO ME — PRETTY THINGS
CRY WOLF — A-HA
CRYIN' [A] — Roy ORBISON
CRYING [A] — Don McLEAN (80)
CRYING [A] — Roy ORBISON (duet with kd lang)
CRYIN' [B] — VIXEN
CRYIN' [C] — AEROSMITH
CRYIN' IN THE RAIN — The EVERLY BROTHERS
CRYIN' MY HEART OUT FOR YOU — Diana ROSS
CRYIN' TIME — Ray CHARLES
CRYING AT THE DISCOTHEQUE — ALCAZAR
THE CRYING GAME [A] — Dave BERRY
THE CRYING GAME [A] — BOY GEORGE
CRYING IN THE CHAPEL [A] — Lee LAWRENCE
CRYING IN THE CHAPEL [A] — Elvis PRESLEY with The JORDANAIRES (65)
CRYING IN THE RAIN [A] — A-HA
CRYING IN THE RAIN [B] — CULTURE BEAT
CRYING LAUGHING LOVING LYING — Labi SIFFRE
CRYING OVER YOU — Ken BOOTHE
THE CRYING SCENE — AZTEC CAMERA
CRYPTIK SOULS CREW — LEN
CRYSTAL — NEW ORDER
CRYSTAL CLEAR — GRID
THE CRYSTAL LAKE — GRANDADDY
C'30, C'60, C'90 GO — BOW WOW WOW
CUBA [A] — The GIBSON BROTHERS
CUBA [A] — EL MARIACHI
CUBAN PETE — Jim CARREY
CUBIK — 808 STATE
CUDDLY TOY — ROACHFORD
THE CUFF OF MY SHIRT — Guy MITCHELL
CULT OF PERSONALITY — LIVING COLOUR
CULT OF SNAP [A] — HI POWER
CULT OF SNAP! [A] — SNAP!
CUM ON FEEL THE NOIZE [A] — SLADE (73)
CUM ON FEEL THE NOIZE [A] — QUIET RIOT
CUMBERLAND GAP [A] — Lonnie DONEGAN and his Skiffle Group (57)
THE CUMBERLAND GAP [A] — VIPERS SKIFFLE GROUP
THE CUP OF LIFE — Ricky MARTIN
CUPBOARD LOVE — John LEYTON
CUPID [A] — Sam COOKE
CUPID [A] — Johnny NASH
CUPID [B] — JC 001
CUPID — I'VE LOVED YOU FOR A LONG TIME (MEDLEY) — The DETROIT SPINNERS
CURIOSITY — The JETS
CURIOUS — LEVERT SWEAT GILL
CURLY — The MOVE
THE CURSE OF VOODOO RAY — Lisa MAY
CURTAIN FALLS — BLUE
CUT CHEMIST SUITE — OZOMATLI
CUT HERE — The CURE

29 May 1999	5 June 1999	12 June 1999	19 June 1999
UK No.1 SINGLES			
SWEET LIKE CHOCOLATE Shanks & Bigfoot	**SWEET LIKE CHOCOLATE** Shanks & Bigfoot	**EVERYBODY'S FREE (TO WEAR SUNSCREEN) - THE SUNSCREEN SONG (CLASS OF '99)** Baz Luhrmann	**BRING IT ALL BACK** S Club 7
UK No.1 ALBUMS			
GOLD - GREATEST HITS Abba	**GOLD - GREATEST HITS** Abba	**... BY REQUEST** Boyzone	**... BY REQUEST** Boyzone

CUT ME DOWN — Lloyd COLE
CUT SOME RUG — The BLUETONES
CUT THE CAKE — AVERAGE WHITE BAND
CUT YOUR HAIR — PAVEMENT
A CUTE SWEET LOVE ADDICTION — Johnny GILL
CUTS ACROSS THE LAND – The DUKE SPIRIT
CUTS BOTH WAYS — Gloria ESTEFAN
CUTT OFF — KASABIAN
THE CUTTER — ECHO and The BUNNYMEN
CUTTY SARK — John BARRY ORCHESTRA
CYANIDE — LURKERS
CYBELE'S REVERIE — STEREOLAB
CYCLONE — DUB PISTOLS
THE CYPHER: PART 3 — Frankie CUTLASS
DA ANTIDOTE — STANTON WARRIORS
DA DA DA — TRIO
DA DOO RON RON — The CRYSTALS
DA-FORCE — BEDLAM
DA FUNK — DAFT PUNK
DA GOODNESS — REDMAN
DA HYPE — JUNIOR JACK featuring Robert SMITH
DA YA THINK I'M SEXY? [A] — Rod STEWART (78)
DA YA THINK I'M SEXY [A] — REVOLTING COCKS
DA YA THINK I'M SEXY [A] — N-TRANCE
DA YA THINK I'M SEXY? [A] — GIRLS OF FHM
D-A-A-ANCE — The LAMBRETTAS
DADDY COOL [A] — BONEY M
DADDY COOL — THE GIRL CAN'T HELP IT [B] — DARTS
DADDY DON'T YOU WALK SO FAST — Daniel BOONE
DADDY'S HOME — Cliff RICHARD
DADDY'S LITTLE GIRL — Nikki D
DAFT PUNK IS PLAYING AT MY HOUSE — LCD SOUNDSYSTEM
DAGENHAM DAVE — MORRISSEY
DAILY — TQ
DAKOTA — STEREOPHONICS (05)
DALICKS — DJ FRESH
DALLIANCE — The WEDDING PRESENT
DAMAGED — PLUMMET
THE DAMBUSTERS MARCH — The Central Band of the ROYAL AIR FORCE, Conductor W/Cdr AE SIMS OBE
DAMN DAMN LEASH — BE YOUR OWN PET
DAMN GOOD — David Lee ROTH
DAMN I WISH I WAS YOUR LOVER — Sophie B HAWKINS
DAMNED DON'T CRY — VISAGE
DAMNED ON 45 — CAPTAIN SENSIBLE
DANCANDO LAMBADA — KAOMA
DANCE — THAT PETROL EMOTION
THE DANCE — Garth BROOKS
DANCE A LITTLE BIT CLOSER — CHARO and The SALSOUL ORCHESTRA
DANCE AND SHOUT — SHAGGY
DANCE AWAY — ROXY MUSIC
DANCE COMMANDER — ELECTRIC SIX
DANCE, DANCE — DESKEE
DANCE DANCE DANCE — The BEACH BOYS
DANCE, DANCE, DANCE (YOWSAH, YOWSAH, YOWSAH) — CHIC
DANCE (DISCO HEAT) — SYLVESTER
DANCE FOR ME [A] — SISQO
DANCE FOR ME [B] — Mary J. BLIGE featuring COMMON
DANCE, GET DOWN (FEEL THE GROOVE) — Al HUDSON
DANCE HALL DAYS — WANG CHUNG
DANCE HALL MOOD — ASWAD
DANCE INTO THE LIGHT — Phil COLLINS
DANCE LADY DANCE — CROWN HEIGHTS AFFAIR
DANCE LITTLE LADY DANCE — Tina CHARLES
DANCE LITTLE SISTER (PART ONE) — Terence Trent D'ARBY
DANCE ME IN — SONS AND DAUGHTERS
DANCE ME UP — Gary GLITTER
DANCE NO MORE — E-LUSTRIOUS
DANCE OF THE CUCKOOS (THE 'LAUREL AND HARDY' THEME) — Band of the BLACK WATCH
DANCE OF THE MAD — POP WILL EAT ITSELF
DANCE ON! [A] — The SHADOWS (63)
DANCE ON [A] — Kathy KIRBY
DANCE ON [B] — MOJO
DANCE OUT OF MY HEAD — Pia ZADORA
DANCE STANCE — DEXY'S MIDNIGHT RUNNERS
DANCE SUCKER — SET THE TONE
DANCE THE BODY MUSIC — OSIBISA
DANCE THE KUNG FU — Carl DOUGLAS
DANCE THE NIGHT AWAY — The MAVERICKS
DANCE TO THE MUSIC [A] — SLY and The FAMILY STONE
DANCE TO THE MUSIC [A] — HUSTLERS CONVENTION featuring Dave LAUDAT and Ondrea DUVERNEY
DANCE TONIGHT — LUCY PEARL
DANCE WIT' ME — Rick JAMES
DANCE WITH ME [A] — The DRIFTERS
DANCE WITH ME [B] — Peter BROWN
DANCE WITH ME [C] — CONTROL
DANCE WITH ME [D] — TIN TIN OUT featuring Tony HADLEY
DANCE WITH ME [E] — Debelah MORGAN
DANCE WITH MY FATHER — Luther VANDROSS
DANCE WITH THE DEVIL — Cozy POWELL
(DANCE WITH THE) GUITAR MAN — Duane EDDY and The REBELS
DANCE (WITH U) — LEMAR
DANCE WITH YOU — Carrie LUCAS
DANCE WITH YOU (NACHNA TERE NAAL) — The RISHI RICH PROJECT featuring Jay SEAN & JUGGY D
DANCE YOURSELF DIZZY — LIQUID GOLD
DANCEHALL MOOD — ASWAD
DANCEHALL QUEEN — BEENIE MAN
DANCER [A] — Gino SOCCIO
DANCER [B] — Michael SCHENKER GROUP
DANCERAMA — SIGUE SIGUE SPUTNIK
DANCIN' EASY — Danny WILLIAMS
DANCIN' IN THE KEY OF LIFE — Steve ARRINGTON
DANCIN' IN THE MOONLIGHT (IT'S CAUGHT ME IN ITS SPOTLIGHT) — THIN LIZZY
DANCIN' ON A WIRE — SURFACE NOISE
DANCIN' PARTY [A] — Chubby CHECKER
DANCIN' PARTY [A] — SHOWADDYWADDY
DANCIN' THE NIGHT AWAY — VOGGUE
DANCIN' TONIGHT — STEREOPOL featuring NEVADA
DANCING BABY (OOGA-CHAKA) — TRUBBLE
DANCING GIRLS — Nik KERSHAW
DANCING IN OUTER SPACE — ATMOSFEAR
DANCING IN THE CITY — MARSHALL HAIN
DANCING IN THE DARK [A] — Kim WILDE
DANCING IN THE DARK [B] — Bruce SPRINGSTEEN
DANCING IN THE DARK (EP) [B] — BIG DADDY
DANCING IN THE DARK [C] — 4TUNE 500
DANCING IN THE MOONLIGHT — TOPLOADER
DANCING IN THE SHEETS — SHALAMAR
DANCING IN THE STREET [A] — Martha REEVES and The VANDELLAS
DANCING IN THE STREET [A] — David BOWIE and Mick JAGGER (85)
DANCING IN THE STREET [B] — MATT BIANCO
DANCIN' (ON A SATURDAY NIGHT) — Barry BLUE
DANCING ON THE CEILING — Lionel RICHIE
DANCING ON THE FLOOR (HOOKED ON LOVE) — THIRD WORLD
DANCING ON THE JAGGED EDGE — SISTER SLEDGE
DANCING QUEEN [A] — ABBA (76)
DANCING QUEEN [A] — ABBACADABRA
DANCING THE NIGHT AWAY — The MOTORS
DANCING TIGHT — Phil FEARON
DANCING WITH MYSELF — GENERATION X
DANCING WITH MYSELF (EP) — GENERATION X
DANCING WITH TEARS IN MY EYES — ULTRAVOX
DANCING WITH THE CAPTAIN — Paul NICHOLAS
DANDELION — The ROLLING STONES
DANGER [A] — AC/DC
DANGER [B] — BLAHZAY BLAHZAY
DANGER (BEEN SO LONG) — MYSTIKAL featuring NIVEA
DANGER GAMES — PINKEES
DANGER! HIGH VOLTAGE — ELECTRIC SIX
THE DANGER OF A STRANGER — Stella PARTON
DANGER ZONE — Kenny LOGGINS
DANGEROUS [A] — Penny FORD
DANGEROUS [B] — ROXETTE
DANGEROUS [C] — Busta RHYMES
DANGEROUS MINDS (EP) — VARIOUS ARTISTS (Singles and EPs)
DANGEROUS SEX — TACK HEAD
DANIEL — Elton JOHN
DARE — GORILLAZ (05)
DARE ME — The POINTER SISTERS
DARE TO DREAM — Viola WILLS
DARK ALAN (AILEIN DUINN) — CAPERCAILLIE
DARK AND LONG — UNDERWORLD
DARK CLOUDS — SPACE
DARK IS LIGHT ENOUGH — DUKE SPIRIT
THE DARK IS RISING — MERCURY REV
DARK IS THE NIGHT [A] — SHAKATAK
DARK IS THE NIGHT [B] — A-HA
DARK LADY — CHER
DARK MOON — Tony BRENT
DARK NIGHT — GORKY'S ZYGOTIC MYNCI
DARK SCIENCE (EP) — TILT
DARK SIDE — ERNESTO vs BASTIAN
DARK SKY — Jimmy SOMERVILLE
DARK THERAPY — ECHOBELLY
DARKHEART — BOMB THE BASS
DARKLANDS — JESUS AND MARY CHAIN
DARKTOWN STRUTTERS BALL — Joe BROWN and The BRUVVERS
DARLIN' [A] — The BEACH BOYS
DARLIN' [A] — David CASSIDY
DARLIN' [B] — Frankie MILLER
DARLIN' [C] — Bob SINCLAIR featuring James WILLIAMS
DARLIN' DARLIN' BABY (SWEET, TENDER, LOVE) — The O'JAYS
DARLING BE HOME SOON [A] — LET LOOSE
DARLING BE HOME SOON [A] — The LOVIN' SPOONFUL
DARLING PRETTY — Mark KNOPFLER
DARTS OF PLEASURE — FRANZ FERDINAND
DAS BOOT — U96
DAS GLOCKENSPIEL — SCHILLER
DAT — Pluto SHERVINGTON
DATE WITH THE NIGHT — The YEAH YEAH YEAHS
DAUGHTER — PEARL JAM
DAUGHTER OF DARKNESS — Tom JONES
DAVID (I STILL HAVE LAST NIGHT IN MY BODY ...) — GUSGUS
DAVID WATTS — The JAM
DAVID'S SONG (MAIN THEME FROM 'KIDNAPPED') — Vladimir COSMA
DAVY'S ON THE ROAD AGAIN — MANFRED MANN
DAWN [A] — FLINTLOCK
DAWN [B] — Tony DE VIT
DAY AFTER DAY [A] — BADFINGER
DAY AFTER DAY [B] — The PRETENDERS
DAY AFTER DAY [C] — Julian LENNON
DAY & NIGHT — Billie PIPER
THE DAY BEFORE YESTERDAY'S MAN — SUPERNATURALS
THE DAY BEFORE YOU CAME [A] — ABBA
THE DAY BEFORE YOU CAME [A] — BLANCMANGE
DAY BY DAY [A] — Holly SHERWOOD
DAY BY DAY [B] — SHAKATAK featuring Al JARREAU
DAY BY DAY [C] — SERAFIN
THE DAY I FALL IN LOVE — Dolly PARTON and James INGRAM
THE DAY I MET MARIE — Cliff RICHARD
THE DAY I TRIED TO LIVE — SOUNDGARDEN
DAY IN DAY OUT — FEEDER
A DAY IN THE LIFE — BLACK RIOT
A DAY IN THE LIFE OF VINCE PRINCE — Russ ABBOT
THE DAY IS ENDED (THE DAY THOU GAVE US LORD, IS ENDED) — The Pipes and Drums and Military Band of the ROYAL SCOTS DRAGOON GUARDS
THE DAY IT RAINED FOREVER — AURORA
THE DAY THAT CURLY BILLY SHOT DOWN CRAZY SAM MCGHEE — The HOLLIES
THE DAY THE EARTH CAUGHT FIRE — CITY BOY
THE DAY THE RAINS CAME — Jane MORGAN (59)
THE DAY THE WORLD TURNED DAY-GLO — X-RAY SPEX
DAY TIME — 4 STRINGS
DAY TRIPPER [A] — The BEATLES (65)
DAY TRIPPER [A] — Otis REDDING
THE DAY WE CAUGHT THE TRAIN — OCEAN COLOUR SCENE
THE DAY WE FIND LOVE — 911
THE DAY WILL COME — QUAKE featuring Marcia RAE
A DAY WITHOUT LOVE — LOVE AFFAIR
DAYDREAM [A] — The LOVIN' SPOONFUL
DAYDREAM [A] — RIGHT SAID FRED
DAYDREAM [B] — BACK TO THE PLANET
DAYDREAM BELIEVER [A] — The MONKEES
DAYDREAM BELIEVER [A] — Anne MURRAY
DAYDREAM BELIEVER (CHEER UP PETER REID) — SIMPLY RED AND WHITE
DAYDREAM IN BLUE — I MONSTER
DAYDREAMER [A] — David CASSIDY (73)
DAYDREAMER [B] — MENSWEAR
DAYDREAMIN' — Tatyana ALI
DAYDREAMING — Penny FORD
DAY-IN DAY-OUT — David BOWIE
DAYLIGHT FADING — COUNTING CROWS
DAYLIGHT KATY — Gordon LIGHTFOOT
DAYS [A] — The KINKS
DAYS [A] — Kirsty MacCOLL
DAYS ARE OK — MOTELS
THE DAYS EP — The KINKS
DAYS GO BY — DIRTY VEGAS
DAYS LIKE THESE — Billy BRAGG
DAYS LIKE THIS [A] — Sheena EASTON
DAYS LIKE THIS [B] — Van MORRISON
DAYS LIKE THIS [C] — Shaun ESCOFFERY
DAYS OF NO TRUST — MAGNUM
DAYS OF OUR LIVEZ — BONE THUGS-N-HARMONY
THE DAYS OF PEARLY SPENCER — Marc ALMOND
DAYS OF YOUTH — LAURNEA
DAYSLEEPER — R.E.M.
DAYTIME FRIENDS — Kenny ROGERS
DAYTONA DEMON — Suzi QUATRO
DAYTRIP TO BANGOR (DIDN'T WE HAVE A LOVELY TIME) — FIDDLER'S DRAM
DAYZ LIKE THAT — FIERCE
DAZZ — BRICK
DAZZLE — SIOUXSIE and The BANSHEES
D-DARLING — Anthony NEWLEY
D-DAYS — Hazel O'CONNOR
DE DAH DAH (SPICE OF LIFE) — Keith MAC PROJECT
DE DO DO DO, DE DA DA DA — The POLICE
DE NIRO — DISCO EVANGELISTS
DEAD A'S — DJ HYPE
DEAD BATTERY — PITCH SHIFTER
DEAD CITIES — EXPLOITED
DEAD END STREET — The KINKS
DEAD FROM THE WAIST DOWN — CATATONIA
DEAD GIVEAWAY — SHALAMAR
THE DEAD HEART — MIDNIGHT OIL
DEAD HUSBAND — DEEJAY PUNK-ROC
DEAD IN HOLLYWOOD — The MURDERDOLLS
DEAD LEAVES AND THE DIRTY GROUND — The WHITE STRIPES
DEAD MAN WALKING — David BOWIE
DEAD OR ALIVE — Lonnie DONEGAN
DEAD POP STARS — ALTERED IMAGES
DEAD RINGER FOR LOVE — MEAT LOAF
DEAD STAR — MUSE
DEADLIER THAN THE MALE — The WALKER BROTHERS
DEADLINE — DUTCH FORCE
DEADLINE USA — SHALAMAR
DEADWEIGHT — BECK
DEAF FOREVER — MOTORHEAD
THE DEAL — Pat CAMPBELL
THE DEAN AND I — 10cc
DEAR ADDY — Kid CREOLE and The COCONUTS
DEAR BOOPSIE — Pam HALL
DEAR DELILAH — GRAPEFRUIT
DEAR ELAINE — Roy WOOD
DEAR GOD — Midge URE
DEAR JESSIE [A] — MADONNA
DEAR JESSIE [A] — ROLLERGIRL
DEAR JOHN [A] — STATUS QUO
DEAR JOHN [B] — Eddi READER
DEAR LIE — TLC
DEAR LONELY HEARTS — Nat 'King' COLE
DEAR MAMA — 2PAC
DEAR MISS LONELY HEARTS — Philip LYNOTT
DEAR MRS APPLEBEE — David GARRICK
DEAR PRUDENCE — SIOUXSIE and The BANSHEES
DEATH DISCO — PUBLIC IMAGE LTD
DEATH OF A CLOWN — Dave DAVIES

26 June 1999	3 July 1999	10 July 1999	17 July 1999
BOOM, BOOM, BOOM, BOOM!! The Vengaboys	9PM (TILL I COME) ATB	9PM (TILL I COME) ATB	LIVIN' LA VIDA LOCA Ricky Martin
SYNKRONIZED Jamiroquai	SURRENDER The Chemical Brothers	... BY REQUEST Boyzone	... BY REQUEST Boyzone

DEBASER — PIXIES
DEBORA — T. REX
A DECADE UNDER THE INFLUENCE — TAKING BACK SUNDAY
DECADENCE DANCE — EXTREME
DECADENT & DESPERATE — MORTIIS
THE DECEIVER — The ALARM
DECEMBER — ALL ABOUT EVE
DECEMBER, 1963 (OH, WHAT A NIGHT) — The FOUR SEASONS (76)
DECEMBER WILL BE MAGIC AGAIN — Kate BUSH
DECENT DAYS AND NIGHTS — The FUTUREHEADS
DECEPTION — FERGIE
DECK OF CARDS [A] — Max BYGRAVES
DECK OF CARDS [A] — Wink MARTINDALE
DEDICATED FOLLOWER OF FASHION — The KINKS
DEDICATED TO THE ONE I LOVE [A] — The MAMAS and The PAPAS
DEDICATED TO THE ONE I LOVE [A] — Bitty McLEAN
DEDICATION — THIN LIZZY
DEEE-LITE THEME — DEEE-LITE
DEEP — EAST 17
THE DEEP — GLOBAL COMMUNICATION
DEEP AND MEANINGLESS — ROOSTER
DEEP AND WIDE AND TALL — AZTEC CAMERA
DEEP DEEP DOWN — HEPBURN
DEEP DEEP TROUBLE — The SIMPSONS
DEEP DOWN & DIRTY — STEREO MC's
DEEP FEELING — Mike SAGAR
DEEP FOREST — DEEP FOREST
DEEP HEAT '89 — VARIOUS ARTISTS (MONTAGES)
DEEP (I'M FALLING DEEPER) — ARIEL
DEEP IN MY HEART — CLUBHOUSE
DEEP IN THE HEART OF TEXAS — Duane EDDY and The REBELS
DEEP IN YOU — LIVIN' JOY
DEEP INSIDE — Mary J BLIGE
DEEP MENACE (SPANK) — D'MENACE
DEEP PURPLE [A] — Billy WARD and his DOMINOES
DEEP PURPLE [A] — Nino TEMPO and April STEVENS
DEEP PURPLE [A] — Donny and Marie OSMOND
DEEP RIVER WOMAN — Lionel RICHIE
DEEP SEA — AQUANAUTS
DEEP SHAG — LUSCIOUS JACKSON
DEEPER [A] — ESCRIMA
DEEPER [B] — DELIRIOUS?
DEEPER [C] — SERIOUS DANGER
DEEPER (EP) — DELIRIOUS?
DEEPER AND DEEPER [A] — Freda PAYNE
DEEPER AND DEEPER [B] — MADONNA
DEEPER LOVE — RUFF DRIVERZ
A DEEPER LOVE [A] — Aretha FRANKLIN
A DEEPER LOVE [A] — C & C MUSIC FACTORY / CLIVILLES & COLE
DEEPER LOVE (SYMPHONIC PARADISE) — BBE
DEEPER SHADE OF BLUE — STEPS
DEEPER THAN THE NIGHT — Olivia NEWTON-JOHN
THE DEEPER THE LOVE — WHITESNAKE
DEEPER UNDERGROUND — JAMIROQUAI (98)
DEEPEST BLUE — DEEPEST BLUE
DEEPLY DIPPY — RIGHT SAID FRED (92)
DEF CON ONE — POP WILL EAT ITSELF
DEFINITE DOOR — The POSIES
DEFINITION OF HOUSE — MINIMAL FUNK
DEGREES — Ian POOLEY
DEJA VU — E-SMOOVE featuring Latanza WATERS
DEJA VU (UPTOWN BABY) — LORD TARIQ and Peter GUNZ
DELAWARE — Perry COMO
DELICATE — Terence Trent D'ARBY featuring DES'REE
DELICIOUS [A] — CATHERINE WHEEL
DELICIOUS [B] — KULAY
DELICIOUS [C] — Deni HINES featuring DON-E
DELICIOUS [D] — PURE SUGAR
DELICIOUS [E] — SLEEPER
DELICIOUS [F] — SHAMPOO
DELILAH [A] — Tom JONES
DELILAH [A] — The SENSATIONAL ALEX HARVEY BAND
DELILAH JONES — The McGUIRE SISTERS
DELIVER ME — SISTER BLISS
DELIVERANCE [A] — The MISSION
DELIVERANCE [B] — Bubba SPARXXX
DELIVERING THE GOODS — SKID ROW
DELLA AND THE DEALER — Hoyt AXTON
DELTA LADY — Joe COCKER
DELTA SUN BOTTLENECK STOMP — MERCURY REV
DEM GIRLS (I DON'T KNOW WHY) — OXIDE & NEUTRINO
DEMOCRACY — KILLING JOKE
DEMOLITION MAN — STING
DEMONS [A] — SUPER FURRY ANIMALS
DEMONS [B] — FATBOY SLIM featuring Macy GRAY
DEMONS [C] — Brian McFADDEN
THE DENIAL TWIST — The WHITE STRIPES
DENIS DENEE — BLONDIE
DENISE — FOUNTAINS OF WAYNE
DER KOMMISSAR — AFTER THE FIRE
DER SCHIEBER — Timo MAAS
DESAFINADO [A] — Ella FITZGERALD
DESAFINADO [A] — Stan GETZ
DESERT DROUGHT — CAST
DESERT SONG — STING
DESIDERATA — Les CRANE
A DESIGN FOR LIFE — MANIC STREET PREACHERS
DESIRE [A] — U2 (88)
DESIRE [B] — NU COLOURS
DESIRE [C] — BBE
DESIRE [D] — DJ ERIC
DESIRE [E] — Ultra NATE
DESIRE [F] — Geri HALLIWELL
DESIRE LINES — LUSH
DESIRE ME — DOLL
DESIREE — Neil DIAMOND
DESPERATE BUT NOT SERIOUS — Adam ANT
DESPERATE DAN — LIEUTENANT PIGEON
THE DESPERATE HOURS — Marc ALMOND
DESTINATION — DT8 featuring Roxanne WILDE
DESTINATION ESCHATON — The SHAMEN
DESTINATION SUNSHINE — BALEARIC BILL
DESTINATION VENUS — REZILLOS
DESTINATION ZULULAND — KING KURT
DESTINY [A] — Anne MURRAY
DESTINY [B] — Candi STATON
DESTINY [C] — The JACKSONS
DESTINY [D] — BABY D
DESTINY [E] — Kenny THOMAS
DESTINY [F] — DEM 2
DESTINY [G] — ZERO 7 featuring SIA and SOPHIE
DESTINY [G] — N-TRANCE
DESTINY CALLING — JAMES
DESTROY EVERYTHING YOU TOUCH — LADYTRON
DESTROY ROCK & ROLL — MYLO
DETROIT — WHITEOUT
DETROIT CITY — Tom JONES
DEUS — SUGARCUBES
DEUTSCHER GIRLS — ADAM and The ANTS
DEVIL [A] — 666
DEVIL [B] — STEREOPHONICS
DEVIL GATE DRIVE — Suzi QUATRO (74)
DEVIL IN YOUR SHOES (WALKING ALL OVER) — SHED SEVEN
DEVIL INSIDE — INXS
DEVIL OR ANGEL — Billy FURY
THE DEVIL WENT DOWN TO GEORGIA — Charlie DANIELS BAND
DEVIL WOMAN [A] — Marty ROBBINS
DEVIL WOMAN [B] — Cliff RICHARD
THE DEVIL YOU KNOW — JESUS JONES
THE DEVIL'S ANSWER — ATOMIC ROOSTER
DEVIL'S BALL — DOUBLE
DEVIL'S GUN — CJ & CO
DEVIL'S HAIRCUT — BECK
DEVIL'S NIGHTMARE — OXIDE & NEUTRINO
DEVIL'S TOY — The ALMIGHTY
DEVIL'S TRILL — VANESSA-MAE
DEVOTED TO YOU — CACIQUE
DEVOTION [A] — TEN CITY
DEVOTION [B] — KICKING BACK with TAXMAN
DEVOTION [C] — David HOLMES
D-FUNKTIONAL — MEKON featuring Afrika BAMBAATAA
DIABLO — GRID
DIAL MY HEART — The BOYS
DIABLA — FUNK D'VOID
DIAMANTE — ZUCCHERO with Randy CRAWFORD
DIAMOND BACK — MEKKA
DIAMOND DEW — GORKY'S ZYGOTIC MYNCI
DIAMOND DOGS — David BOWIE
DIAMOND GIRL — Pete WYLIE
DIAMOND LIFE — Louie VEGA & Jay 'SINISTER' SEALEE featuring Julie MCKNIGHT
DIAMOND LIGHTS — GLENN and CHRIS
DIAMOND SMILES — The BOOMTOWN RATS
DIAMONDS [A] — Jet HARRIS and Tony MEEHAN (63)
DIAMONDS [B] — Chris REA
DIAMONDS [C] — Herb ALPERT
DIAMONDS AND GUNS — TRANSPLANTS
DIAMONDS AND PEARLS — PRINCE and The NEW POWER GENERATION
DIAMONDS ARE FOREVER [A] — David McALMONT
DIAMONDS ARE FOREVER [A] — Shirley BASSEY
DIAMONDS FROM SIERRA LEONE — Kanye WEST
DIANA — Paul ANKA (57)
DIANE [A] — The BACHELORS (64)
DIANE [B] — THERAPY?
DIARY OF A WIMP — SPACE
THE DIARY OF HORACE WIMP — ELECTRIC LIGHT ORCHESTRA
DICK-A-DUM-DUM (KING'S ROAD) — Des O'CONNOR
DID I DREAM (SONG TO THE SIREN) — LOST WITNESS
DID IT AGAIN — Kylie MINOGUE
DID MY TIME — KORN
DID YOU EVER — Nancy SINATRA
DID YOU EVER REALLY LOVE ME — Nicki FRENCH
DID YOU EVER THINK — R KELLY
DID YOU HAVE TO LOVE ME LIKE YOU DID — The COCONUTS
DIDDY — P DIDDY featuring The NEPTUNES
DIDN'T I (BLOW YOUR MIND THIS TIME) [A] — The DELFONICS
DIDN'T I BLOW YOUR MIND [A] — NEW KIDS ON THE BLOCK
DIDN'T I TELL YOU TRUE — Thomas JULES-STOCK
DIDN'T WE ALMOST HAVE IT ALL — Whitney HOUSTON
DIE ANOTHER DAY — MADONNA
DIE LAUGHING — THERAPY?
DIE YOUNG — BLACK SABBATH
DIFFERENCES — GUYVER
DIFFERENT AIR — LIVING IN A BOX
A DIFFERENT BEAT — BOYZONE (96)
A DIFFERENT CORNER — George MICHAEL (86)
DIFFERENT STORY — BOWA featuring MALA
DIFFERENT STROKES — ISOTONIK
DIFFERENT TIME DIFFERENT PLACE — Julia FORDHAM
DIG FOR FIRE — PIXIES
DIGERIDOO — APHEX TWIN
DIGGI LOO-DIGGI LEY — HERREYS
DIGGIN' MY POTATOES — HEINZ
DIGGIN' ON YOU — TLC
DIGGING IN THE DIRT — Peter GABRIEL
DIGGING THE GRAVE — FAITH NO MORE
DIGGING YOUR SCENE — The BLOW MONKEYS
DIGITAL — GOLDIE featuring KRS ONE
DIGITAL LOVE — DAFT PUNK
DIGNITY [A] — DEACON BLUE
DIGNITY [B] — Bob DYLAN
DIL CHEEZ (MY HEART...) — Bally SAGOO
DILEMMA — NELLY featuring Kelly ROWLAND (02)
DIM ALL THE LIGHTS — Donna SUMMER
A DIME AND A DOLLAR — Guy MITCHELL
DIMENSION — SALT TANK
DIMPLES — John Lee HOOKER
DIN DA DA — Kevin AVIANCE
DINAH — BLACKNUSS
DING DONG — George HARRISON
DING DONG SONG — GUNTHER & The SUNSHINE GIRLS
DING-A-DONG — TEACH-IN
DINNER WITH DELORES — PRINCE
DINNER WITH GERSHWIN — Donna SUMMER
DINOSAUR ADVENTURE 3D — UNDERWORLD
DIP IT LOW — Christina MILIAN
DIPPETY DAY — The SMURFS
DIRECT-ME — REESE PROJECT
DIRGE — DEATH IN VEGAS
DIRRTY — Christina AGUILERA featuring REDMAN (02)
DIRT — DEATH IN VEGAS
DIRT OFF YOUR SHOULDER — JAY-Z
DIRTY BEATS — Roni SIZE / REPRAZENT
DIRTY CASH — The ADVENTURES OF STEVIE V
DIRTY DAWG — NEW KIDS ON THE BLOCK
DIRTY DEEDS — Joan JETT and The BLACKHEARTS
DIRTY DEEDS DONE DIRT CHEAP — AC/DC
DIRTY DIANA — Michael JACKSON
DIRTY HARRY — GORILLAZ
DIRTY HARRY'S REVENGE — Adam F featuring BEENIE MAN
DIRTY LAUNDRY — Don HENLEY
DIRTY LOOKS — Diana ROSS
DIRTY LOVE — THUNDER
DIRTY MIND — SHAKESPEAR'S SISTER
DIRTY MIND — The PIPETTES
DIRTY MONEY — Dee FREDRIX
DIRTY MOTHA — QWILO and FELIX DA HOUSECAT
DIRTY OLD TOWN [A] — The POGUES
DIRTY OLD TOWN [A] — BHOYS FROM PARADISE
DIRTY STICKY FLOORS — Dave GAHAN
DIRTY WATER — MADE IN LONDON
DISAPPEAR — INXS
DISAPPEARING ACT — SHALAMAR
DISAPPOINTED [A] — PUBLIC IMAGE LTD
DISAPPOINTED [B] — ELECTRONIC
THE DISAPPOINTED — XTC
DISARM — SMASHING PUMPKINS
DISCIPLINE OF LOVE — Robert PALMER
D.I.S.C.O. [A] — OTTAWAN
D.I.S.C.O. [A] — N-TRANCE
D.I.S.C.O. [A] — JO JINGLES
DISCO BABES FROM OUTER SPACE — BABE INSTINCT
DISCO BEATLEMANIA — DBM
DISCO CONNECTION — Isaac HAYES
DISCO COP — BLUE ADONIS featuring LIL' MISS MAX
DISCO DOWN [A] — SHED SEVEN
DISCO DOWN [B] — HOUSE OF GLASS
DISCO DUCK (PART ONE) — Rick DEES and his CAST OF IDIOTS
DISCO INFERNO [A] — The TRAMMPS
DISCO INFERNO [A] — Tina TURNER
DISCO INFILTRATOR — LCD SOUNDSYSTEM
'DISCO' LA PASSIONE — Chris REA and Shirley BASSEY
DISCO LADY — Johnnie TAYLOR
DISCO MACHINE GUN — LO FIDELITY ALLSTARS
DISCO MUSIC — J.A.L.N. BAND
DISCO NIGHTS - (ROCK FREAK) — G.Q.
DISCO QUEEN — HOT CHOCOLATE
DISCO SCIENCE — MIRWAIS
DISCO STOMP — Hamilton BOHANNON
DISCO 2000 — PULP
DISCOBUG '97 — FREAKYMAN
DISCOHOPPING — KLUBBHEADS
DISCOLAND — FLIP & FILL featuring Karen PARRY
DISCONNECT — ROLLINS BAND
DISCO'S REVENGE — GUSTO
DISCOTHEQUE — U2 (97)
DISCRETION GLOVE — Stephen MALKMUS
DISEASE — MATCHBOX TWENTY
DISENCHANTED — COMMUNARDS
DISILLUSION — BADLY DRAWN BOY
DIS-INFECTED (EP) — The THE
DISPOSABLE TEENS — MARILYN MANSON
DISREMEMBRANCE — Dannii MINOGUE
DISSIDENT — PEARL JAM
THE DISTANCE — CAKE
DISTANT DRUMS — Jim REEVES (66)
DISTANT STAR — Anthony HOPKINS
DISTANT SUN — CROWDED HOUSE
DISTORTION — WILT
DISTRACTIONS — ZERO 7 featuring SIA
DIVA — DANA INTERNATIONAL
DIVE! DIVE! DIVE! — Bruce DICKINSON
DIVE IN — CATCH
DIVE TO PARADISE — EUROGROOVE
DIVEBOMB — NUMBER ONE CUP
DIVINE EMOTIONS — Narada Michael WALDEN

24 July 1999	31 July 1999	7 August 1999	14 August 1999
UK No.1 SINGLES			
LIVIN' LA VIDA LOCA Ricky Martin	LIVIN' LA VIDA LOCA Ricky Martin	WHEN YOU SAY NOTHING AT ALL Ronan Keating	WHEN YOU SAY NOTHING AT ALL Ronan Keating
UK No.1 ALBUMS			
... BY REQUEST Boyzone	... BY REQUEST Boyzone	... BY REQUEST Boyzone	... BY REQUEST Boyzone

DIVINE HAMMER — The BREEDERS
DIVINE THING — The SOUP DRAGONS
DIVING — 4 STRINGS
DIVING FACES — LIQUID CHILD
D.I.V.O.R.C.E. [A] — Tammy WYNETTE
D.I.V.O.R.C.E. [A] — Billy CONNOLLY (75)
DIXIE-NARCO (EP) — PRIMAL SCREAM
DIZZY [A] — Tommy ROE (69)
DIZZY [A] —
Vic REEVES and The WONDER STUFF (91)
DJ [A] — David BOWIE
DJ [B] — RESONANCE featuring The BURRELLS
DJ [C] — H & CLAIRE
DJ [D] — JAMELIA
DJ CULTURE — PET SHOP BOYS
DJ, DJ — TRANSPLANTS
DJ NATION — NUKLEUZ DJS
DJ NATION - BOOTLEG EDITION — NUKLEUZ DJS
DJ NATION - HARDER EDITION —
VARIOUS (NUKLEUZ DJS)
DJ SPINNIN' — PUNK CHIC
DJS FANS & FREAKS — BLANK & JONES
DJS TAKE CONTROL — SL2
DK 50-80 —
John OTWAY and Wild Willy BARRETT
DO AND DON'T FOR LOVE — KIOKA
DO ANYTHING — NATURAL SELECTION
DO ANYTHING YOU WANNA DO —
EDDIE and The HOT RODS
DO ANYTHING YOU WANT TO — THIN LIZZY
DO EVERYTHING I TAUGHT YOU — ALTERKICKS
DO FOR LOVE — 2PAC
DO FRIES GO WITH THAT SHAKE —
George CLINTON
DO I — GIFTED
DO I DO — Stevie WONDER
DO I HAVE TO SAY THE WORDS — Bryan ADAMS
DO I LOVE YOU — The RONETTES
DO I QUALIFY? — Lynden David HALL
DO IT — Tony DI BART
DO IT ALL OVER AGAIN — SPIRITUALIZED
DO IT AGAIN [A] — The BEACH BOYS (68)
DO IT AGAIN [B] — STEELY DAN
DO IT AGAIN [C] — COOKIE
DO IT AGAIN — BILLIE JEAN (MEDLEY) —
CLUBHOUSE
DO IT ANY WAY YOU WANNA —
PEOPLES CHOICE
DO IT, DO IT AGAIN — Raffaella CARRA
DO IT FOR LOVE [A] — Danni'elle GAHA
DO IT FOR LOVE [B] —
SUBTERRANIA featuring Ann CONSUELO
DO IT FOR LOVE [C] — 4MANDU
DO IT LIKE YOU LIKE — The STANDS
DO IT NOW — BRAIN BASHERS
DO IT PROPERLY ('NO WAY BACK') —
ADONIS featuring 2 PUERTO RICANS,
A BLACK MAN AND A DOMINICAN
DO IT TO ME — Lionel RICHIE
DO IT TO ME AGAIN — SOULSEARCHER
DO IT TO THE CROWD — TWIN HYPE
DO IT TO THE MUSIC — RAW SILK
DO IT WITH MADONNA — The ANDROIDS
DO ME — BELL BIV DEVOE
DO ME RIGHT — INNER CITY
DO ME WRONG — Mel BLATT
DO MY THING — Busta RHYMES
DO NO WRONG — THIRTEEN SENSES
DO NOT DISTURB — BANANARAMA
DO NOT PASS ME BY — HAMMER
DO NOTHING — The SPECIALS
DO OR DIE — SUPER FURRY ANIMALS
DO RE ME SO FAR SO GOOD — CARTER —
THE UNSTOPPABLE SEX MACHINE
DO SOMETHIN' — Britney SPEARS
DO SOMETHING — Macy GRAY
DO THAT THING — MASAI
DO THAT TO ME — LISA MARIE EXPERIENCE
DO THAT TO ME ONE MORE TIME —
CAPTAIN and TENNILLE
DO THE BARTMAN — The SIMPSONS (91)
DO THE BIRD [A] — Dee Dee SHARP
DO THE BIRD [A] — VERNONS GIRLS
DO THE CAN CAN — SKANDI GIRLS
DO THE CLAM — Elvis PRESLEY
DO THE CONGA — BLACK LACE
DO THE FUNKY CHICKEN — Rufus THOMAS
(DO) THE HUCKLEBUCK — COAST TO COAST
DO THE LOLLIPOP — TWEENIES
DO THE RIGHT THING [A] —
REDHEAD KINGPIN and The FBI
DO THE RIGHT THING [B] — Ian WRIGHT
(DO THE) SPANISH HUSTLE —
FATBACK BAND
DO THEY KNOW IT'S CHRISTMAS? [A] —
BAND AID (84)
DO THEY KNOW IT'S CHRISTMAS? [A] —
BAND AID II (89)
DO THEY KNOW IT'S CHRISTMAS? [A] —
BAND AID 20 (04)
DO THIS! DO THAT! — FREEFALLER
DO THIS MY WAY — KID 'N' PLAY
DO U FEEL 4 ME — EDEN
DO U KNOW WHERE YOU'RE COMING FROM —
M-BEAT featuring JAMIROQUAI
DO U STILL — EAST 17
DO U WANNA FUNK — SPACE 2000
DO WAH DIDDY DIDDY [A] —
MANFRED MANN (64)
DO WAH DIDDY DIDDY [A] — BLUE MELONS
DO WAH DIDDY [A] — DJ OTZI
DO WATCHA DO — HYPER GO GO and ADEVA
DO WE ROCK — POINT BREAK
DO WHAT YOU DO [A] — Jermaine JACKSON
DO WHAT YOU DO [B] — Annabella LWIN
DO WHAT YOU DO DO WELL — Ned MILLER
DO WHAT YOU DO (EARWORM SONG) —
Clint BOON EXPERIENCE
DO WHAT YOU FEEL [A] — Joey NEGRO
DO WHAT YOU FEEL [B] — JOHNNA
DO WHAT YOU GOTTA DO [A] —
The FOUR TOPS
DO WHAT YOU GOTTA DO [A] — Nina SIMONE
DO WHAT YOU WANNA DO — T-CONNECTION
DO WHAT WE WOULD — ACZESS
DO WHAT'S GOOD FOR ME — 2 UNLIMITED
DO YA — INNER CITY
DO YA DO YA (WANNA PLEASE ME) —
Samantha FOX
DO YA WANNA GET FUNKY WITH ME —
Peter BROWN
DO YOU BELIEVE IN LOVE [A] —
Huey LEWIS and The NEWS
DO YOU BELIEVE IN LOVE [B] — UNATION
DO YOU BELIEVE IN LOVE [C] — ULTRA-SONIC
DO YOU BELIEVE IN MIRACLES — SLADE
DO YOU BELIEVE IN SHAME — DURAN DURAN
DO YOU BELIEVE IN THE WESTWORLD —
THEATRE OF HATE
DO YOU BELIEVE IN THE WONDER —
Jeanie TRACY
DO YOU BELIEVE IN US — Jon SECADA
DO YOU DREAM IN COLOUR? — Bill NELSON
DO YOU FEEL LIKE I FEEL — Belinda CARLISLE
DO YOU FEEL LIKE WE DO — Peter FRAMPTON
DO YOU FEEL ME? (... FREAK YOU) —
MEN OF VIZION
DO YOU FEEL MY LOVE? [A] — Eddy GRANT
DO YOU KNOW [A] — SECRET AFFAIR
DO YOU KNOW [B] — Michelle GAYLE
DO YOU KNOW (I GO CRAZY) —
ANGEL CITY
DO YOU KNOW THE WAY TO SAN JOSE —
Dionne WARWICK
DO YOU KNOW (WHAT IT TAKES) — ROBYN
DO YOU LIKE IT — KINGDOM COME
DO YOU LOVE ME [A] —
Brian POOLE and The TREMELOES (63)
DO YOU LOVE ME [A] — Dave CLARK FIVE
DO YOU LOVE ME [A] — DEEP FEELING
DO YOU LOVE ME [A] — DUKE BAYSEE
DO YOU LOVE ME [B] — MADEMOISELLE
DO YOU LOVE ME [C] —
Nick CAVE and The BAD SEEDS
DO YOU LOVE ME BOY? — KERRI-ANN
DO YOU LOVE ME LIKE YOU SAY —
Terence Trent D'ARBY
DO YOU LOVE WHAT YOU FEEL — INNER CITY
DO YOU MIND — Anthony NEWLEY (60)
DO YOU REALIZE?? — The FLAMING LIPS
DO YOU REALLY LIKE IT — DJ PIED PIPER
and The MASTERS OF CEREMONIES (01)
(DO YOU REALLY LOVE ME) TELL ME LOVE —
Michael WYCOFF
DO YOU REALLY LOVE ME TOO — Billy FURY
DO YOU REALLY WANT ME [A] — Jon SECADA
DO YOU REALLY WANT ME [B] — ROBYN
DO YOU REALLY (WANT MY LOVE) — JUNIOR
DO YOU REALLY WANT TO HURT ME —
CULTURE CLUB (82)
DO YOU REMEMBER — SCAFFOLD
DO YOU REMEMBER HOUSE — BLAZE
DO YOU REMEMBER (LIVE) — Phil COLLINS
DO YOU REMEMBER ROCK 'N' ROLL RADIO? —
The RAMONES
DO YOU REMEMBER THE FIRST TIME — PULP
DO YOU SEE — Warren G
DO YOU SEE THE LIGHT (LOOKING FOR) —
SNAP! featuring Niki HARIS
DO YOU SLEEP? —
Lisa LOEB and NINE STORIES
DO YOU THINK ABOUT US — TOTAL
DO YOU THINK YOU'RE SPECIAL — NIO
DO YOU UNDERSTAND — The ALMIGHTY
DO YOU WANNA DANCE — Barry BLUE
DO YOU WANNA FUNK — SYLVESTER
DO YOU WANNA GET FUNKY —
C&C MUSIC FACTORY / CLIVILLES & COLE
DO YOU WANNA GO OUR WAY??? —
PUBLIC ENEMY
DO YOU WANNA HOLD ME — BOW WOW WOW
DO YOU WANNA PARTY —
DJ SCOTT featuring Lorna B
DO YOU WANNA TOUCH ME? (OH YEAH) —
Gary GLITTER
DO YOU WANT IT RIGHT NOW —
DEGREES OF MOTION featuring BITI
DO YOU WANT ME [A] — SALT-N-PEPA
DO YOU WANT ME [B] — Q-TEX
DO YOU WANT ME? [C] — LEILANI
DO YOU WANT ME TO — The FOUR PENNIES
DO YOU WANT TO — FRANZ FERDINAND
DO YOU WANT TO DANCE —
Cliff RICHARD and The SHADOWS
DO YOU WANT TO KNOW A SECRET? —
Billy J KRAMER and The DAKOTAS
DO YOUR DANCE — ROSE ROYCE
DO YOUR THING — BASEMENT JAXX
DOA — FOO FIGHTERS
THE DOCTOR — The DOOBIE BROTHERS
DR BEAT — MIAMI SOUND MACHINE
DOCTOR DOCTOR [A] — UFO
DOCTOR DOCTOR [B] — THOMPSON TWINS
DR FEELGOOD — MÖTLEY CRÜE
DR FINLAY — Andy STEWART
DR GREENTHUMB — CYPRESS HILL
DR HECKYLL AND MR JIVE — MEN AT WORK
DOCTOR JACKYLL AND MISTER FUNK —
Jackie McLEAN
DOCTOR JEEP — SISTERS OF MERCY
DOCTOR JONES — AQUA (98)
DOCTOR KISS KISS — 5000 VOLTS
DR LOVE — Tina CHARLES
DR MABUSE — PROPAGANDA
DOCTOR MY EYES — The JACKSON FIVE
DOCTOR PRESSURE —
MYLO vs MIAMI SOUND MACHINE
DR STEIN — HELLOWEEN
DR WHO — MANKIND
DOCTORIN' THE HOUSE — COLDCUT featuring
YAZZ and The PLASTIC POPULATION
DOCTORIN' THE TARDIS — The TIMELORDS (88)
DOCTOR'S ORDERS — SUNNY
DOES HE LOVE YOU — Reba McENTIRE
DOES IT FEEL GOOD — BT EXPRESS
DOES IT FEEL GOOD TO YOU — Carl COX
DOES SHE HAVE A FRIEND? — Gene CHANDLER
DOES THAT RING A BELL — DYNASTY
DOES THIS HURT — The BOO RADLEYS
DOES THIS TRAIN STOP ON MERSEYSIDE? —
AMSTERDAM
DOES YOUR CHEWING GUM LOSE ITS FLAVOUR
— Lonnie DONEGAN
DOES YOUR HEART GO BOOM — Helen LOVE
DOES YOUR MOTHER KNOW — ABBA
DOESN'T ANYBODY KNOW MY NAME? —
Vince HILL
DOESN'T REALLY MATTER — Janet JACKSON
DOG — DADA
DOG EAT DOG — ADAM and The ANTS
DOG ON WHEELS — BELLE & SEBASTIAN
DOG TRAIN — LEVELLERS
DOGGY DOGG WORLD — SNOOP DOGG
DOGMAN GO WOOF — UNDERWORLD
DOGMONAUT 2000 (IS THERE ANYONE OUT
THERE?) — FRIGID VINEGAR
DOGS — The WHO
DOGS OF LUST — The THE
DOGS OF WAR — EXPLOITED
DOGS WITH NO TAILS — PALE
DOGZ N SLEDGEZ — MILLION DAN
DOIN' IT [A] — LL COOL J
DOIN' IT [B] — LIBERTY
DOIN' IT IN A HAUNTED HOUSE —
Yvonne GAGE
DOIN' OUR OWN DANG —
The JUNGLE BROTHERS
DOIN' OUR THING — PHOEBE ONE
DOIN' THE DO — Betty BOO
DOING ALRIGHT WITH THE BOYS —
Gary GLITTER
DOLCE VITA — Ryan PARIS
DOLL HOUSE — The KING BROTHERS
DOLL PARTS — HOLE
DOLLAR BILL — SCREAMING TREES
DOLLAR IN THE TEETH — The UPSETTERS
DOLLARS — CJ LEWIS
DOLLARS IN THE HEAVENS — GENEVA
DOLLY MY LOVE — MOMENTS
DOLPHIN — SHED SEVEN
THE DOLPHIN'S CRY — LIVE
DOLPHINS MAKE ME CRY — Martyn JOSEPH
DOLPHINS WERE MONKEYS — Ian BROWN
DOMINATION — WAY OUT WEST
DOMINATOR — HUMAN RESOURCE
DOMINION — SISTERS OF MERCY
DOMINIQUE — SINGING NUN (Soeur Sourire)
DOMINO DANCING — PET SHOP BOYS
DOMINOES — Robbie NEVIL
DOMINOID — MOLOKO
THE DON — 187 LOCKDOWN
DON GARGON COMIN' — PROJECT 1
DON JUAN —
Dave DEE, DOZY, BEAKY, MICK and TICH
DON QUIXOTE — Nik KERSHAW
DONALD WHERE'S YOUR TROOSERS —
Andy STEWART
DONKEY CART — Frank CHACKSFIELD
DONNA [A] — Marty WILDE
DONNA [A] — Ritchie VALENS
DONNA [B] — 10cc
DON'T [A] — Elvis PRESLEY
DON'T [B] — Shania TWAIN
DON'T ANSWER ME [A] — Cilla BLACK
DON'T ANSWER ME [B] —
Alan PARSONS PROJECT
DON'T ARGUE — CABARET VOLTAIRE
DON'T ASK ME — PUBLIC IMAGE LTD
DON'T ASK ME WHY — EURYTHMICS
DON'T BE A DUMMY — John DU CANN
DON'T BE A FOOL — LOOSE ENDS
DON'T BE A STRANGER — Dina CARROLL
DON'T BE AFRAID [A] — Aaron HALL
DON'T BE AFRAID [B] — MOONMAN
DON'T BE CRUEL [A] — Bill BLACK'S COMBO
DON'T BE CRUEL [A] — Billy SWAN
DON'T BE CRUEL [A] — Elvis PRESLEY
DON'T BE CRUEL [B] — Bobby BROWN
DON'T BE STUPID (YOU KNOW I LOVE YOU) —
Shania TWAIN
DON'T BELIEVE A WORD — THIN LIZZY
DON'T BELIEVE THE HYPE [A] — MISTA E
DON'T BELIEVE THE HYPE [B] — PUBLIC ENEMY
DON'T BET MONEY HONEY — Linda SCOTT
DON'T BLAME IT ON LOVE — SHAKATAK
DON'T BLAME IT ON THAT GIRL — MATT BIANCO
DON'T BLAME ME [A] —
The EVERLY BROTHERS
DON'T BLAME ME [A] — Frank IFIELD
DON'T BREAK MY HEART — UB40
DON'T BREAK MY HEART AGAIN —
WHITESNAKE
DON'T BREAK THE HEART THAT LOVES YOU —
Connie FRANCIS
DON'T BRING HARRY (EP) — The STRANGLERS
DON'T BRING LULU — Dorothy PROVINE
DON'T BRING ME DOWN [A] —
The PRETTY THINGS
DON'T BRING ME DOWN [B] — The ANIMALS
DON'T BRING ME DOWN [C] —
ELECTRIC LIGHT ORCHESTRA
DON'T BRING ME DOWN [D] — SPIRITS
DON'T BRING ME YOUR HEARTACHES —
Paul and Barry RYAN
DON'T CALL ME BABY [A] —
VOICE OF THE BEEHIVE

21 August 1999	28 August 1999	4 September 1999	11 September 1999
IF I LET YOU GO Westlife	MI CHICO LATINO Geri Halliwell	MAMBO NO.5 (A LITTLE BIT OF ...) Lou Bega	MAMBO NO.5 (A LITTLE BIT OF...) Lou Bega
... BY REQUEST Boyzone	THE MAN WHO Travis	THE MAN WHO Travis	COME ON OVER Shania Twain

DON'T CALL ME BABY [B] — MADISON AVENUE (00)
DON'T CARE [A] — Klark KENT
DON'T CARE [B] — ANGEL'S REVERSE
DON'T CARE WHO KNOWS — Keisha WHITE
DON'T CHA — PUSSYCAT DOLLS featuring Busta RHYMES (05)
DON'T CHA WANNA RIDE — Joss STONE
DON'T COME AROUND HERE NO MORE — Tom PETTY and The HEARTBREAKERS
DON'T COME CLOSE — The RAMONES
DON'T COME HOME TOO SOON — DEL AMITRI
DON'T COME TO STAY — HOT HOUSE
DON'T CRY [A] — ASIA
DON'T CRY [B] — BOY GEORGE
DON'T CRY [C] — GUNS N' ROSES
DON'T CRY [D] — SEAL
DON'T CRY DADDY — Elvis PRESLEY
DON'T CRY FOR ME ARGENTINA [A] — Julie COVINGTON (77)
DON'T CRY FOR ME ARGENTINA [A] — The SHADOWS
DON'T CRY FOR ME ARGENTINA [A] — MADONNA
DON'T CRY FOR ME ARGENTINA [A] — Mike FLOWERS POPS
DON'T CRY FOR ME ARGENTINA [A] — Sinead O'CONNOR
DON'T CRY OUT LOUD — Elkie BROOKS
DON'T DIE JUST YET — David HOLMES
DON'T DO IT BABY — Mac and Katie KISSOON
DON'T DO THAT [A] — GEORDIE
DON'T DO THAT [B] — YOUNG AND MOODY BAND
DON'T DON'T TELL ME NO — Sophie B HAWKINS
DON'T DREAM — DOVE
DON'T DREAM IT'S OVER [A] — CROWDED HOUSE
DON'T DREAM IT'S OVER [A] — Paul YOUN
DON'T DRIVE DRUNK — Stevie WONDER
DON'T DRIVE MY CAR — STATUS QUO
DON'T DROP BOMBS — Liza MINNELLI
DON'T EVER CHANGE — The CRICKETS
DON'T EVER THINK (TOO MUCH) ... — The ZUTONS
DON'T FALL IN LOVE (I SAID) — TOYAH
DON'T FALTER — MINT ROYALE
(DON'T FEAR) THE REAPER [A] — APOLLO FOUR FORTY
(DON'T FEAR) THE REAPER [A] — BLUE ÖYSTER CULT
DON'T FIGHT IT — Wilson PICKETT
DON'T FIGHT IT FEEL IT — PRIMAL SCREAM featuring Denise JOHNSON
DON'T FORBID ME — Pat BOONE
DON'T FORGET ABOUT US — Mariah CAREY
DON'T FORGET ME (WHEN I'M GONE) — GLASS TIGER
DON'T FORGET TO CATCH ME — Cliff RICHARD and The SHADOWS
DON'T FORGET TO DANCE — The KINKS
DON'T FORGET TO REMEMBER — The BEE GEES
DON'T GET ME WRONG — The PRETENDERS
(DON'T) GIVE HATE A CHANCE — JAMIROQUAI
DON'T GIVE IT UP [A] — SONIC SURFERS
DON'T GIVE IT UP [B] — LEMAR
DON'T GIVE ME UP — Harold MELVIN and The BLUENOTES
DON'T GIVE ME YOUR LIFE — ALEX PARTY
DON'T GIVE UP [A] — Peter GABRIEL and Kate BUSH
DON'T GIVE UP [B] — Michelle WEEKS
DON'T GIVE UP [C] — CHICANE featuring Bryan ADAMS (00)
DON'T GIVE UP 2004 [C] — CHICANE featuring Bryan ADAMS
DON'T GIVE UP [D] — LOUISE
DON'T GIVE UP ON US — David SOUL (77)
DON'T GO [A] — JUDAS PRIEST
DON'T GO [B] — YAZOO
DON'T GO [B] — Lizzy MACK
DON'T GO [C] — HOTHOUSE FLOWERS
DON'T GO [D] — AWESOME 3
DON'T GO [D] — THIRD DIMENSION featuring Julie McDERMOTT
DON'T GO BREAKING MY HEART [A] — Elton JOHN and Kiki DEE (76)
DON'T GO BREAKING MY HEART [A] — Elton JOHN with RuPAUL
DON'T GO MESSIN' WITH MY HEART — MANTRONIX
DON'T HANG UP — ORLONS
DON'T HOLD BACK — CHANSON
DON'T HURT YOURSELF — MARILLION
DON'T IT MAKE MY BROWN EYES BLUE — Crystal GAYLE
DON'T IT MAKE YOU FEEL GOOD — Stefan DENNIS
DON'T JUMP OFF THE ROOF DAD — Tommy COOPER
DON'T KILL IT CAROL — MANFRED MANN
DON'T KILL THE WHALE — YES
DON'T KNOCK IT (UNTIL YOU TRY IT) — Bobby NUNN
DON'T KNOCK THE ROCK — Bill HALEY and his COMETS
DON'T KNOW MUCH — Linda RONSTADT
DON'T KNOW WHAT TO TELL YA — AALIYAH
DON'T KNOW WHAT YOU GOT — CINDERELLA
DON'T KNOW WHY — Norah JONES
DON'T LAUGH — Josh WINK
DON'T LAUGH AT ME (CAUSE I'M A FOOL) — Norman WISDOM
DON'T LEAVE — FAITHLESS
DON'T LEAVE HOME — DIDO
DON'T LEAVE ME [A] — BLACKSTREET
DON'T LEAVE ME [B] — Malandra BURROWS
DON'T LEAVE ME BEHIND — EVERYTHING BUT THE GIRL
DON'T LEAVE ME THIS WAY [A] — COMMUNARDS with Sarah Jane MORRIS (86)
DON'T LEAVE ME THIS WAY [A] — Harold MELVIN and The BLUENOTES
DON'T LEAVE ME THIS WAY [A] — Thelma HOUSTON
DON'T LET 'EM GRIND YOU DOWN — EXPLOITED
DON'T LET GO [A] — MANHATTAN TRANSFER
DON'T LET GO [B] — David SNEDDON
DON'T LET GO (LOVE) — EN VOGUE
DON'T LET GO THE COAT — The WHO
DON'T LET HIM STEAL YOUR HEART AWAY — Phil COLLINS
DON'T LET HIM TOUCH YOU — The ANGELETTES
DON'T LET IT DIE — Hurricane SMITH
DON'T LET IT END — STYX
DON'T LET IT FADE AWAY — DARTS
DON'T LET IT GET YOU DOWN — ECHO and The BUNNYMEN
DON'T LET IT GO TO YOUR HEAD — The BRAND NEW HEAVIES
DON'T LET IT PASS YOU BY — UB40
DON'T LET IT SHOW ON YOUR FACE — ADEVA
DON'T LET LOVE GET YOU DOWN — Archie BELL and The DRELLS
DON'T LET ME BE MISUNDERSTOOD [A] — The ANIMALS
DON'T LET ME BE MISUNDERSTOOD [A] — SANTA ESMERALDA and Leroy GOMEZ
DON'T LET ME BE MISUNDERSTOOD [A] — Elvis COSTELLO
DON'T LET ME BE MISUNDERSTOOD [A] — Joe COCKER
DON'T LET ME BE THE LAST TO KNOW — Britney SPEARS
DON'T LET ME DOWN [A] — The FARM
DON'T LET ME DOWN [B] — Will YOUNG
DON'T LET ME DOWN GENTLY — The WONDER STUFF
DON'T LET ME GET ME — PINK
DON'T LET NOBODY HOLD YOU DOWN — LJ REYNOLDS
DON'T LET THE FEELING GO — NIGHTCRAWLERS featuring John REID
DON'T LET THE RAIN COME DOWN — Ronnie HILTON
DON'T LET THE STARS GET IN YOUR EYES — Perry COMO with The RAMBLERS (53)
DON'T LET THE SUN CATCH YOU CRYING — GERRY and The PACEMAKERS
DON'T LET THE SUN GO DOWN ON ME [A] — Elton JOHN
DON'T LET THE SUN GO DOWN ON ME [A] — Oleta ADAMS
DON'T LET THE SUN GO DOWN ON ME [A] — George MICHAEL and Elton JOHN (91)
DON'T LET THEM — ASHANTI
DON'T LET THIS MOMENT END — Gloria ESTEFAN
DON'T LIE [A] — SINCLAIR
DON'T LIE [B] — The BLACK EYED PEAS
DON'T LOOK ANY FURTHER [A] — Dennis EDWARDS featuring Siedah GARRETT
DON'T LOOK ANY FURTHER [A] — KANE GANG
DON'T LOOK ANY FURTHER [A] — M PEOPLE
DON'T LOOK AT ME THAT WAY — Chaka KHAN
DON'T LOOK BACK [A] — BOSTON
DON'T LOOK BACK [B] — FINE YOUNG CANNIBALS
DON'T LOOK BACK [C] — Lloyd COLE
DON'T LOOK BACK [D] — Lucie SILVAS
DON'T LOOK BACK IN ANGER [A] — OASIS (96)
DON'T LOOK BACK IN ANGER [A] — The WURZELS
DON'T LOOK BACK INTO THE SUN — The LIBERTINES
DON'T LOOK DOWN [A] — PLANETS
DON'T LOOK DOWN [B] — Mick RONSON with Joe ELLIOTT
DON'T LOOK DOWN — THE SEQUEL — GO WEST
DON'T LOSE THE MAGIC — Shawn CHRISTOPHER
DON'T LOSE YOUR TEMPER — XTC
DON'T LOVE ME TOO HARD — The NOLANS
DON'T LOVE YOU NO MORE — Craig DAVID
DON'T MAKE ME (FALL IN LOVE WITH YOU) — Babbity BLUE
DON'T MAKE ME OVER [A] — SWINGING BLUE JEANS
DON'T MAKE ME OVER [A] — SYBIL
DON'T MAKE ME WAIT [A] — PEECH BOYS
DON'T MAKE ME WAIT [B] — LOVELAND featuring the voice of Rachel McFARLANE
DON'T MAKE ME WAIT [C] — 911
DON'T MAKE ME WAIT [D] — BOMB THE BASS
DON'T MAKE ME WAIT TOO LONG [A] — Barry WHITE
DON'T MAKE ME WAIT TOO LONG [B] — Roberta FLACK
DON'T MAKE MY BABY BLUE — The SHADOWS
DON'T MAKE WAVES — The NOLANS
DON'T MARRY HER — The BEAUTIFUL SOUTH
DON'T MESS WITH DOCTOR DREAM — THOMPSON TWINS
DON'T MESS WITH MY MAN [A] — LUCY PEARL
DON'T MESS WITH MY MAN [B] — NIVEA
DON'T MESS WITH THE RADIO — NIVEA
DON'T MISS THE PARTYLINE — BIZZ NIZZ
DON'T MUG YOURSELF — The STREETS
DON'T NEED A GUN — Billy IDOL
DON'T NEED THE SUN TO SHINE (TO MAKE ME SMILE) — GABRIELLE
DON'T PANIC [A] — LIQUID GOLD
DON'T PANIC [B] — LOGO featuring Dawn JOSEPH
DON'T PAY THE FERRYMAN — Chris DE BURGH
DON'T PHUNK WITH MY HEART — The BLACK EYED PEAS
DON'T PLAY NICE — VERBALICIOUS
DON'T PLAY THAT SONG — Aretha FRANKLIN
DON'T PLAY THAT SONG AGAIN — Nicki FRENCH
DON'T PLAY WITH ME — ROZALLA
DON'T PLAY YOUR ROCK 'N ROLL TO ME — SMOKIE
DON'T PULL YOUR LOVE — Sean MAGUIRE
DON'T PUSH IT — Ruth JOY
DON'T PUSH IT DON'T FORCE IT — Leon HAYWOOD
DON'T PUT YOUR SPELL ON ME — Ian McNABB
DON'T QUIT — Caron WHEELER
DON'T RUSH (TAKE LOVE SLOWLY) — K-CI & JOJO
DON'T SAY GOODBYE — Paulina RUBIO
DON'T SAY I TOLD YOU SO — TOURISTS
DON'T SAY IT'S LOVE — JOHNNY HATES JAZZ
DON'T SAY IT'S OVER — GUN
DON'T SAY THAT'S JUST FOR WHITE BOYS — WAY OF THE WEST
DON'T SAY YOU LOVE ME [A] — M2M
DON'T SAY YOU LOVE ME [B] — ERASURE
DON'T SAY YOUR LOVE IS KILLING ME — ERASURE
DON'T SET ME FREE — Ray CHARLES
DON'T SHED A TEAR — Paul CARRACK
DON'T SING — PREFAB SPROUT
DON'T SLEEP IN THE SUBWAY — Petula CLARK
DON'T SLOW DOWN — UB40
DON'T SPEAK [A] — NO DOUBT (97)
DON'T SPEAK [A] — CLUELESS
DON'T STAND SO CLOSE TO ME — The POLICE (80)
DON'T STAY AWAY TOO LONG — PETERS and LEE
DON'T STEAL OUR SUN — The THRILLS
DON'T STOP [A] — FLEETWOOD MAC
DON'T STOP [A] — STATUS QUO
DON'T STOP [B] — K.I.D.
DON'T STOP [C] — MOOD
DON'T STOP [D] — Jeffrey OSBORNE
DON'T STOP [E] — K-KLASS
DON'T STOP [F] — HAMMER
DON'T STOP [G] — RUFF DRIVERZ
DON'T STOP [H] — NO AUTHORITY
DON'T STOP [I] — ATB
DON'T STOP [J] — The ROLLING STONES
DON'T STOP BELIEVIN' — JOURNEY
DON'T STOP (FUNKIN' 4 JAMAICA) — Mariah CAREY
DON'T STOP IT NOW — HOT CHOCOLATE
DON'T STOP (JAMMIN') — LA MIX
DON'T STOP LOVIN' ME BABY — PINKERTON'S ASSORTED COLOURS
DON'T STOP ME NOW — QUEEN
DON'T STOP MOVIN' [A] — LIVIN' JOY
DON'T STOP MOVIN' [B] — S CLUB 7 (01)
DON'T STOP NOW — Gene FARROW and GF BAND
DON'T STOP THAT CRAZY RHYTHM — MODERN ROMANCE
DON'T STOP THE CARNIVAL — Alan PRICE
DON'T STOP THE DANCE — Bryan FERRY
DON'T STOP THE FEELING — Roy AYERS
DON'T STOP THE MUSIC [A] — YARBROUGH and PEOPLES
DON'T STOP THE MUSIC [B] — Lionel RICHIE
DON'T STOP 'TIL YOU GET ENOUGH — Michael JACKSON
DON'T STOP TWIST — Frankie VAUGHAN
DON'T STOP (WIGGLE WIGGLE) — The OUTHERE BROTHERS (95)
DON'T TAKE AWAY THE MUSIC — TAVARES
DON'T TAKE IT LYIN' DOWN — The DOOLEYS
DON'T TAKE IT PERSONAL — Jermaine JACKSON
DON'T TAKE IT PERSONAL (JUST ONE OF DEM DAYS) — MONICA
DON'T TAKE MY KINDNESS FOR WEAKNESS — HEADS with Shaun RYDER
DON'T TAKE MY MIND ON A TRIP — BOY GEORGE
DON'T TAKE NO FOR AN ANSWER — Tom ROBINSON
DON'T TALK [A] — Hank MARVIN
DON'T TALK [B] — Jon B
DON'T TALK ABOUT LOVE — BAD BOYS INC
DON'T TALK DIRTY TO ME — Jermaine STEWART
DON'T TALK JUST KISS — RIGHT SAID FRED Guest vocals: Jocelyn BROWN
DON'T TALK TO HIM — Cliff RICHARD and The SHADOWS
DON'T TALK TO ME ABOUT LOVE — ALTERED IMAGES
DON'T TELL ME [A] — CENTRAL LINE
DON'T TELL ME [B] — BLANCMANGE
DON'T TELL ME [C] — VAN HALEN
DON'T TELL ME [D] — MADONNA
DON'T TELL ME [E] — Avril LAVIGNE
DON'T TELL ME LIES — BREATHE
DON'T TELL ME YOU'RE SORRY — S CLUB 8
DON'T TEST — Junior TUCKER
DON'T THAT BEAT ALL — Adam FAITH
DON'T THINK I'M NOT — KANDI
DON'T THINK IT (FEEL IT) — LANGE featuring LEAH
DON'T THINK THE WAY THEY DO — SPAN
DON'T THINK YOU'RE THE FIRST — The CORAL
DON'T THROW AWAY ALL THOSE TEARDROPS — Frankie AVALON
DON'T THROW IT ALL AWAY — Gary BENSON
DON'T THROW YOUR LOVE AWAY — The SEARCHERS (64)
DON'T TREAT ME BAD — FIREHOUSE

18 September 1999	25 September 1999	2 October 1999	9 October 1999
UK No.1 SINGLES			
WE'RE GOING TO IBIZA! The Vengaboys	**BLUE (DA BA DEE)** Eiffel 65	**BLUE (DA BA DEE)** Eiffel 65	**BLUE (DA BA DEE)** Eiffel 65
UK No.1 ALBUMS			
COME ON OVER Shania Twain	**COME ON OVER** Shania Twain	**RHYTHM AND STEALTH** Leftfield	**RELOAD** Tom Jones

DON'T TREAT ME LIKE A CHILD —
Helen SHAPIRO
DON'T TRY TO CHANGE ME — The CRICKETS
DON'T TRY TO STOP IT — ROMAN HOLLIDAY
DON'T TURN AROUND [A] —
The MERSEYBEATS
DON'T TURN AROUND [B] — ASWAD (88)
DON'T TURN AROUND [B] — ACE OF BASE
DON'T WAIT UP — THUNDER
DON'T WALK [A] — MY LIFE STORY
DON'T WALK [B] — BIG SUPREME
DON'T WALK AWAY [A] —
ELECTRIC LIGHT ORCHESTRA
DON'T WALK AWAY [B] — The FOUR TOPS
DON'T WALK AWAY [C] — Pat BENATAR
DON'T WALK AWAY [D] — Toni CHILDS
DON'T WALK AWAY [E] — JADE
DON'T WALK AWAY [E] — JAVINE
DON'T WALK AWAY TILL I TOUCH YOU —
Elaine PAIGE
DON'T WANNA BE A PLAYER — JOE
DON'T WANNA BE ALONE — Tricia PENROSE
DON'T WANNA FALL IN LOVE — Jane CHILD
DON'T WANNA KNOW — SHY FX & T-POWER
featuring DI and MC SKIBADEE
DON'T WANNA LET YOU GO — FIVE
DON'T WANNA LOSE THIS FEELING —
Dannii MINOGUE
DON'T WANNA LOSE YOU [A] — Gloria ESTEFAN
DON'T WANNA LOSE YOU [B] — Lionel RICHIE
DON'T WANNA SAY GOODNIGHT — KANDIDATE
DON'T WANT TO FORGIVE ME NOW —
WET WET WET
DON'T WANT TO WAIT ANYMORE — TUBES
DON'T WANT YOU BACK — Ellie CAMPBELL
DON'T WASTE MY TIME — Paul HARDCASTLE
DON'T WASTE YOUR TIME —
YARBROUGH and PEOPLES
DON'T WORRY [A] — Johnny BRANDON
DON'T WORRY [B] — Billy FURY
DON'T WORRY [C] — Kim APPLEBY
DON'T WORRY [D] — NEWTON
DON'T WORRY [E] — APPLETON
DON'T WORRY BABY — LOS LOBOS
DON'T WORRY BE HAPPY — Bobby McFERRIN
DON'T YOU — SECOND IMAGE
DON'T YOU (FORGET ABOUT ME) [A] —
SIMPLE MINDS
DON'T YOU FORGET ABOUT ME [A] —
BEST COMPANY
DON'T YOU GET SO MAD — Jeffrey OSBORNE
DON'T YOU JUST KNOW IT — AMAZULU
DON'T YOU KNOW — BUTTERSCOTCH
DON'T YOU KNOW IT — Adam FAITH
DON'T YOU LOVE ME [A] — 49ers
DON'T YOU LOVE ME [B] — ETERNAL
DON'T YOU ROCK ME DADDY-O [A] —
Lonnie DONEGAN
DON'T YOU ROCK ME DADDY-O [A] —
VIPERS SKIFFLE GROUP
DON'T YOU THINK IT'S TIME — Mike BERRY
DON'T YOU WANT ME [A] —
HUMAN LEAGUE (81)
DON'T YOU WANT ME BABY [A] — Mandy SMITH
DON'T YOU WANT ME [A] — The FARM
DON'T YOU WANT ME [B] — Jody WATLEY
DON'T YOU WANT ME [C] — FELIX
DON'T YOU WORRY — MADASUN
DON'T YOU WORRY 'BOUT A THING —
INCOGNITO
DOO WOP (THAT THING) — Lauryn HILL
DOOBEDOOD'NDOOBE DOOBEDOOD'NDOOBE —
Diana ROSS
DOODAH! — CARTOONS
DOOMS NIGHT — Azzido DA BASS
DOOMSDAY — Evelyn THOMAS
DOOP — DOOP (94)
THE DOOR — TURIN BRAKES
THE DOOR IS STILL OPEN TO MY HEART —
Dean MARTIN
DOOR #1 — LEVERT SWEAT GILL
DOORS OF YOUR HEART — The BEAT
DOOT DOOT — FREUR
THE DOPE SHOW — MARILYN MANSON
DOPES TO INFINITY — MONSTER MAGNET
DOUBLE BARREL —
Dave and Ansil COLLINS (71)
DOUBLE DOUBLE DUTCH — DOPE SMUGGLAZ
DOUBLE DROP — FIERCE GIRL

DOUBLE DUTCH [A] — FATBACK BAND
DOUBLE DUTCH [B] — Malcolm McLAREN
DOUBLEBACK — ZZ TOP
DOVE (I'LL BE LOVING YOU) — MOONY
DOVE L'AMORE — CHER
DOWN — BLINK-182
DOWN AND UNDER (TOGETHER) —
KID CRÈME featuring MC SHURAKANO
DOWN AT THE DOCTORS — DR FEELGOOD
DOWN BOY — Holly VALANCE
DOWN BY THE LAZY RIVER — The OSMONDS
DOWN BY THE WATER — P J HARVEY
DOWN DEEP INSIDE (THEME FROM 'THE DEEP')
— Donna SUMMER
DOWN DOWN — STATUS QUO (75)
DOWN DOWN DOWN — GAMBAFREAKS
DOWN FOR THE ONE — Beverley KNIGHT
DOWN 4 U — Irv GOTTI presents JA RULE,
ASHANTI, Charli BALTIMORE & VITA
DOWN 4 WHATEVA — NUTTIN' NYCE
DOWN IN A HOLE — ALICE IN CHAINS
DOWN IN THE BOONDOCKS —
Billy Joe ROYAL
DOWN IN THE SUBWAY — SOFT CELL
DOWN IN THE TUBE STATION AT MIDNIGHT
— The JAM
DOWN LOW (NOBODY HAS TO KNOW) —
R KELLY
DOWN ON THE BEACH TONIGHT —
The DRIFTERS
DOWN ON THE CORNER —
CREEDENCE CLEARWATER REVIVAL
DOWN ON THE STREET — SHAKATAK
DOWN SO LONG — JEWEL
DOWN THAT ROAD — Shara NELSON
DOWN THE DRAIN — STAKKA BO
DOWN THE DUSTPIPE — STATUS QUO
DOWN THE HALL — The FOUR SEASONS
DOWN THE RIVER NILE — John LEYTON
DOWN THE WIRE — ASAP
DOWN TO EARTH [A] — CURIOSITY
DOWN TO EARTH [B] — Monie LOVE
DOWN TO EARTH [C] — GRACE
DOWN TO THE SEA — TIM BOOTH
DOWN TO THE WIRE — GHOST DANCE
DOWN UNDER — MEN AT WORK (83)
DOWN WITH THE CLIQUE — AALIYAH
DOWN WITH THE KING — RUN-DMC
DOWN YONDER —
JOHNNY and The HURRICANES
DOWNHEARTED — Eddie FISHER
DOWNLOAD IT — CLEA
DOWNTOWN [A] — Petula CLARK
DOWNTOWN [B] — ONE 2 MANY
DOWNTOWN [C] — SWV
THE DOWNTOWN LIGHTS — BLUE NILE
DOWNTOWN TRAIN — Rod STEWART
DOWNTOWN VENUS — PM DAWN
DRACULA'S TANGO — TOTO COELO
DRAG ME DOWN — The BOOMTOWN RATS
DRAGGING ME DOWN — INSPIRAL CARPETS
DRAGNET [A] —
Ray ANTHONY and his Orchestra
DRAGNET [A] — Ted HEATH
DRAGNET [A] — ART OF NOISE
DRAGON POWER — JKD BAND
DRAGONFLY — TORNADOS
DRAGOSTEA DIN TEI — O-ZONE
DRAGULA — Rob ZOMBIE
DRAIN THE BLOOD — The DISTILLERS
DRAMA! — ERASURE
DRAW OF THE CARDS — Kim CARNES
(DRAWING) RINGS AROUND THE WORLD —
SUPER FURRY ANIMALS
DRAWING SHAPES — MORNING RUNNER
DRE DAY — DR DRE
DREADLOCK HOLIDAY — 10cc (78)
DREAM — DIZZEE RASCAL
THE DREAM — DREAM FREQUENCY
DREAM A LIE — UB40
DREAM A LITTLE DREAM OF ME [A] —
Anita HARRIS
DREAM A LITTLE DREAM OF ME [A] —
MAMA CASS
DREAM ABOUT YOU — D'BORA
DREAM ANOTHER DREAM — RIALTO
DREAM BABY [A] — Roy ORBISON
DREAM BABY (HOW LONG MUST I DREAM) [A] —
Glen CAMPBELL

DREAM COME TRUE —
The BRAND NEW HEAVIES
DREAM GIRL — Mark WYNTER
DREAM KITCHEN — FRAZIER CHORUS
DREAM LOVER — Bobby DARIN (59)
DREAM OF ME (BASED ON LOVE'S THEME) —
ORCHESTRAL MANOEUVRES IN THE DARK
DREAM OF OLWEN — SECOND CITY SOUND
DREAM ON — DEPECHE MODE
DREAM ON DREAMER —
The BRAND NEW HEAVIES
DREAM ON (IS THIS A DREAM) — LOVE DECADE
DREAM SEQUENCE (ONE) —
Pauline MURRAY and The INVISIBLE GIRLS
DREAM SOME PARADISE — INTASTELLA
DREAM SWEET DREAMS — AZTEC CAMERA
DREAM TALK — Alma COGAN
DREAM TO ME — Dario G
DREAM TO SLEEP — H 20
DREAM UNIVERSE — DJ GARRY
DREAMBOAT [A] — Alma COGAN (55)
DREAMBOAT [B] —
LIMMIE and The FAMILY COOKIN'
DREAMER [A] — SUPERTRAMP
DREAMER [A] — CK & SUPREME DREAM TEAM
DREAMER [B] — The JACKSONS
DREAMER [C] — COLDCUT
DREAMER [D] — LIVIN' JOY (95)
DREAMER [E] — Ozzy OSBOURNE
THE DREAMER — ALL ABOUT EVE
DREAMIN' [A] — Johnny BURNETTE
DREAMIN' [B] — LIVERPOOL EXPRESS
DREAMIN' [C] — Cliff RICHARD
DREAMIN' [D] — STATUS QUO
DREAMIN' [E] — Vanessa WILLIAMS
DREAMIN' [F] — Loleatta HOLLOWAY
DREAMIN' [G] — AMP FIDDLER
DREAMING [A] — BLONDIE
DREAMING [B] —
ORCHESTRAL MANOEUVRES IN THE DARK
DREAMING [C] — Glen GOLDSMITH
DREAMING [D] — MN8
DREAMING [E] — RUFF DRIVERZ
DREAMING [F] — M PEOPLE
DREAMING [G] — BT
DREAMING [H] — AURORA
DREAMING [I] —
I DREAM featuring FRANKIE & CALVIN
THE DREAMING — Kate BUSH
DREAMING OF ME — DEPECHE MODE
DREAMING OF YOU [A] — THRILLSEEKERS
DREAMING OF YOU [B] — The CORAL
DREAMLOVER — Mariah CAREY
DREAMS [A] — FLEETWOOD MAC
DREAMS [A] — WILD COLOUR
DREAMS [A] — The CORRS
DREAMS [B] — Grace SLICK
DREAMS [C] — VAN HALEN
DREAMS [D] — GABRIELLE (93)
DREAMS [E] — The CRANBERRIES
DREAMS [G] — QUENCH
DREAMS [F] —
SMOKIN BEATS featuring Lyn EDEN
DREAMS [H] — MISS SHIVA
DREAMS [I] — KINGS OF TOMORROW
DREAMS [J] — The GAME
A DREAM'S A DREAM — SOUL II SOUL
DREAMS CAN TELL A LIE — Nat 'King' COLE
THE DREAMS I DREAM — The SHADOWS
DREAMS OF CHILDREN — The JAM (80)
DREAMS OF HEAVEN — GROUND LEVEL
DREAMS OF YOU — Ralph McTELL
DREAMS TO REMEMBER — Robert PALMER
DREAMSCAPE '94 — TIME FREQUENCY
DREAMTIME [A] — Daryl HALL
DREAMTIME [B] — ZEE
DREAMY DAYS — Roots MANUVA
DREAMY LADY — T. REX
DRED BASS — DEAD DRED
DRESS YOU UP — MADONNA
DRESSED FOR SUCCESS — ROXETTE
DRIFT AWAY — Michael BOLTON
DRIFTING [A] — Sheila WALSH and Cliff RICHARD
DRIFTING [B] — MOJOLATORS featuring CAMILLA
DRIFTING AWAY — LANGE featuring SKYE
DRIFTWOOD — TRAVIS
THE DRILL — DIRT DEVILS
DRINK THE ELIXIR — SALAD
DRINK UP THY ZIDER — The WURZELS

DRINKING IN L.A. — BRAN VAN 3000
DRINKING SONG — Mario LANZA
DRIP FED FRED —
Ian DURY and The BLOCKHEADS
DRIVE [A] — The CARS
DRIVE [B] — R.E.M.
DRIVE [C] — Geoffrey WILLIAMS
DRIVE [D] — INCUBUS
DRIVE BY CAR — DJ ZINC featuring EKSMAN
DRIVE-IN SATURDAY (SEATTLE - PHOENIX) —
David BOWIE
DRIVE ME CRAZY — PARTIZAN
DRIVE ON — BROTHER BEYOND
DRIVE SAFELY DARLIN' — Tony CHRISTIE
DRIVEN BY YOU — Brian MAY
DRIVER'S SEAT — SNIFF 'N' THE TEARS
DRIVIN' HOME — Duane EDDY and The REBELS
DRIVING — EVERYTHING BUT THE GIRL
DRIVING AWAY FROM HOME (JIM'S TUNE) —
IT'S IMMATERIAL
DRIVING HOME FOR CHRISTMAS (EP) —
Chris REA
DRIVING IN MY CAR [A] — MADNESS
DRIVING IN MY CAR [A] — Maureen REES
DRIVING WITH THE BRAKES ON —
DEL AMITRI
DROP DEAD GORGEOUS — REPUBLICA
DROP IT LIKE IT'S HOT —
SNOOP DOGG featuring PHARRELL
DROP SOME DRUMS — [LOVE] TATTOO
DROP THE BOY — BROS
DROP THE PILOT — Joan ARMATRADING
DROP THE PRESSURE — MYLO
DROP THE ROCK (EP) — D-TEK
DROPS OF JUPITER (TELL ME) — TRAIN
DROWNED WORLD (SUBSTITUTE FOR LOVE)
— MADONNA
THE DROWNERS — SUEDE
DROWNING [A] — The BEAT
DROWNING [B] — BACKSTREET BOYS
DROWNING [C] — CRAZY TOWN
DROWNING IN BERLIN — The MOBILES
DROWNING IN THE SEA OF LOVE —
The ADVENTURES
DROWSY WITH HOPE — SHAKEDOWN
THE DRUGS DON'T WORK — The VERVE (97)
DRUMBEATS — SL2
DRUMMER MAN — TONIGHT
DRUMMIN' UP A STORM — Sandy NELSON
DRUMS ARE MY BEAT — Sandy NELSON
THE DRUMSTRUCK (EP) — N-JOI
DRUNK ON LOVE — BASIA
DRUNKARD LOGIC — FAT LADY SINGS
DRUNKEN FOOL — BURN
DRUNKEN STARS — Mampi SWIFT
DRY COUNTY [A] — BLACKFOOT
DRY COUNTY [B] — BON JOVI
DRY LAND — MARILLION
DRY RISER — KERBDOG
DRY YOUR EYES — The STREETS (04)
DU THE DUDEK — The TROPHY BOYZ
DUALITY — SLIPKNOT
DUB BE GOOD TO ME — BEATS INTERNATIONAL
featuring Lindy LAYTON (90)
DUB WAR — DANCE CONSPIRACY
DUBPLATE CULTURE — SOUNDSCAPE
DUCHESS [A] — The STRANGLERS
DUCHESS [A] — MY LIFE STORY
DUCHESS [B] — GENESIS
DUCK FOR THE OYSTER — Malcolm McLAREN
DUCK TOY — HAMPENBERG
DUDE — BEENIE MAN featuring MS THING
DUDE DESCENDING A STAIRCASE — APOLLO
FOUR FORTY featuring The BEATNUTS
DUDE (LOOKS LIKE A LADY) — AEROSMITH
DUEL [A] — PROPAGANDA
DUEL [B] — SWERVEDRIVER
DUELLING BANJOS —
'DELIVERANCE' SOUNDTRACK
DUI — HAR MAR SUPERSTAR
DUKE OF EARL — DARTS
DUM DUM — Brenda LEE
DUM DUM GIRL — TALK TALK
DUMB [A] — The BEAUTIFUL SOUTH
DUMB [B] — The 411
DUMB WAITERS — PSYCHEDELIC FURS
DUMMY CRUSHER — KERBDOG
DUNE BUGGY — PRESIDENTS OF THE UNITED
STATES OF AMERICA

16 October 1999	23 October 1999	30 October 1999	6 November 1999
GENIE IN A BOTTLE Christina Aguilera	GENIE IN A BOTTLE Christina Aguilera	FLYING WITHOUT WINGS Westlife	KEEP ON MOVIN' Five
COME ON OVER Shania Twain	COME ON OVER Shania Twain	COME ON OVER Shania Twain	STEPTACULAR Steps

DUNE SEA — UNBELIEVABLE TRUTH
DUNNO WHAT IT IS (ABOUT YOU) — The BEATMASTERS
DURHAM TOWN (THE LEAVIN') — Roger WHITTAKER
DUSK TIL DAWN — Danny HOWELLS & Dick TREVOR featuring ERIRE
DUSTED — LEFTFIELD
DW WASHBURN — The MONKEES
D'YA WANNA GO FASTER — TERRORVISION
DYNAMITE [A] — Cliff RICHARD and The SHADOWS
DYNAMITE [B] — Stacy LATTISAW
DYNA-MITE [C] — MUD
DY-NA-MI-TEE — MS DYNAMITE
DYNOMITE (PART 1) — Tony CAMILLO'S BAZUKA
D'YOU KNOW WHAT I MEAN? — OASIS (97)
E — DRUNKEN MUNKY
E=MC2 — BIG AUDIO DYNAMITE
E SAMBA — JUNIOR JACK
E TALKING — SOULWAX
EACH AND EVERY ONE — EVERYTHING BUT THE GIRL
EACH TIME — EAST 17
EACH TIME YOU BREAK MY HEART — Nick KAMEN
EARDRUM BUZZ — WIRE
EARLY IN THE MORNING [A] — Buddy HOLLY
EARLY IN THE MORNING [B] — VANITY FARE
EARLY IN THE MORNING [C] — GAP BAND
EARLY MORNING RAIN — Paul WELLER
EARLY TO BED — PONI-TAILS
EARTH ANGEL [A] — The CREW CUTS
EARTH ANGEL [B] — DREADZONE
THE EARTH DIES SCREAMING — UB40
EARTH SONG — Michael JACKSON (95)
EARTHBOUND — Conner REEVES
EARTHSHAKER — Paul MASTERSON presents SUSHI
EASE MY MIND — ARRESTED DEVELOPMENT
EASE ON BY — BASS-O-MATIC
EASE ON DOWN THE ROAD — Diana ROSS and Michael JACKSON
EASE THE PRESSURE [A] — 2WO THIRD3
EASE THE PRESSURE [B] — The BELOVED
EASE YOUR MIND — GALLIANO
EASIER SAID THAN DONE [A] — ESSEX
EASIER SAID THAN DONE [B] — SHAKATAK
EASIER SAID THAN DONE [C] — STARGATE
EASIER TO LIE — AQUALUNG
EASIER TO WALK AWAY — Elton JOHN
EAST COAST / WEST COAST KILLAS — GROUP THERAPY
EAST EASY RIDER — Julian COPE
EAST OF EDEN — BIG COUNTRY
EAST RIVER — The BRECKER BROTHERS
EAST WEST — HERMAN'S HERMITS
EASTER — MARILLION
EASY [A] — The COMMODORES
EASY [B] — LOUD
EASY [C] — TERRORVISION
EASY [D] — Emiliana TORRINI
EASY [E] — GROOVE ARMADA
EASY [F] — BRIGHT EYES
EASY COME EASY GO — SUTHERLAND BROTHERS and QUIVER
EASY EASY — SCOTLAND WORLD CUP SQUAD
EASY GOING ME — Adam FAITH
EASY LADY — SPAGNA
EASY LIFE [A] — BODYSNATCHERS
EASY LIFE [B] — CABARET VOLTAIRE
EASY LIVIN' — FASTWAY
EASY LOVER — Philip BAILEY (duet with Phil COLLINS) (85)
EASY RIDER — RAIN BAND
EASY TO SMILE — SENSELESS THINGS
EAT IT — Weird Al YANKOVIC
EAT ME DRINK ME LOVE ME — POP WILL EAT ITSELF
EAT MY GOAL — COLLAPSED LUNG
EAT THE RICH — AEROSMITH
EAT YOU ALIVE — LIMP BIZKIT
EAT YOUR HEART OUT — Paul HARDCASTLE
EAT YOURSELF WHOLE — KINGMAKER
EATEN ALIVE — Diana ROSS
EATING ME ALIVE — Diana BROWN and Barrie K SHARPE
EBB TIDE [A] — Frank CHACKSFIELD
EBB TIDE [A] — The RIGHTEOUS BROTHERS
EBENEEZER GOODE — The SHAMEN (92)
EBONY AND IVORY — Paul McCARTNEY with Stevie WONDER (82)
EBONY EYES — The EVERLY BROTHERS (61)
E-BOW THE LETTER — R.E.M.
ECHO BEACH [A] — MARTHA and The MUFFINS
ECHO BEACH [A] — TOYAH
ECHO CHAMBER — BEATS INTERNATIONAL
ECHO MY HEART — Lindy LAYTON
ECHO ON MY MIND PART II — EARTHLING
ECHOES IN A SHALLOW BAY (EP) — COCTEAU TWINS
ECUADOR — SASH!
EDDIE'S GUN — The KOOKS
EDDY VORTEX — Steve GIBBONS BAND
EDELWEISS — Vince HILL
EDEN — Sarah BRIGHTMAN
EDGE OF A BROKEN HEART — VIXEN
EDGE OF DARKNESS — Eric CLAPTON
THE EDGE OF HEAVEN — WHAM! (86)
EDIBLE FLOWERS — The FINN BROTHERS
EDIE (CIAO BABY) — The CULT
ED'S FUNKY DINER (FRIDAY NIGHT, SATURDAY MORNING) — IT'S IMMATERIAL
EENY MEENY — SHOWSTOPPERS
EGG RUSH — FLOWERED UP
EGO — Elton JOHN
EGYPTIAN REGGAE — Jonathan RICHMAN and The MODERN LOVERS
EI — NELLY
EIGHT BY TEN — Ken DODD
8 DAYS A WEEK — SWEET FEMALE ATTITUDE
EIGHT MILES HIGH — The BYRDS
18 AND LIFE — SKID ROW
18 CARAT LOVE AFFAIR — ASSOCIATES
EIGHTEEN STRINGS — TINMAN
18 TIL I DIE — Bryan ADAMS
EIGHTEEN WITH A BULLET — Pete WINGFIELD
EIGHTEEN YELLOW ROSES — Bobby DARIN
EIGHTH DAY — Hazel O'CONNOR
8TH WORLD WONDER — Kimberley LOCKE
808 — BLAQUE IVORY
EIGHTIES — KILLING JOKE
80S ROMANCE — The BELLE STARS
86'D — SUBCIRCUS
EINSTEIN A GO-GO — LANDSCAPE
EL BIMBO — BIMBO JET
EL CAMINOS IN THE WEST — GRANDADDY
EL CAPITAN [A] — OPM
EL CAPITAN [B] — IDLEWILD
EL LUTE — BONEY M
EL NINO — AGNELLI & NELSON
EL PARAISO RICO — DEETAH
EL PASO — Marty ROBBINS
EL PRESIDENT — DRUGSTORE
EL SALVADOR — ATHLETE
EL SCORCHO — WEEZER
EL TRAGO (THE DRINK) — 2 IN A ROOM
EL VINO COLLAPSO — BLACK LACE
ELDORADO — DRUM THEATRE
ELEANOR RIGBY [A] — The BEATLES (66)
ELEANOR RIGBY [A] — Ray CHARLES
ELECTED — Alice COOPER
ELECTION DAY — ARCADIA
ELECTRIC — Lisa SCOTT-LEE
ELECTRIC AVENUE — Eddy GRANT
ELECTRIC BARBARELLA — DURAN DURAN
ELECTRIC BLUE — ICEHOUSE
ELECTRIC BOOGALOO — OLLIE and JERRY
ELECTRIC GUITAR — FLUKE
ELECTRIC GUITARS — PREFAB SPROUT
ELECTRIC HEAD PART 2 (THE ECSTASY) — WHITE ZOMBIE
ELECTRIC LADY — GEORDIE
ELECTRIC MAINLINE — SPIRITUALIZED
ELECTRIC MAN — MANSUN
ELECTRIC TRAINS — SQUEEZE
ELECTRIC YOUTH — Debbie GIBSON
ELECTRICAL STORM — U2
ELECTRICITY [A] — SPIRITUALIZED
ELECTRICITY [B] — SUEDE
ELECTRICITY [C] — Elton JOHN
ELECTROLITE — R.E.M.
ELECTRON BLUE — R.E.M.
ELECTRONIC PLEASURE — N-TRANCE
ELEGANTLY AMERICAN: ONE NIGHT IN HEAVEN — M PEOPLE
ELEGANTLY WASTED — INXS
ELEKTROBANK — The CHEMICAL BROTHERS
ELEMENTS — NEO CORTEX
ELENI — TOL and TOL
ELENORE — The TURTLES
ELEPHANT PAW (GET DOWN TO THE FUNK) — PAN POSITION
ELEPHANT STONE — The STONE ROSES
ELEPHANT TANGO — Cyril STAPLETON and his Orchestra
THE ELEPHANT'S GRAVEYARD (GUILTY) — The BOOMTOWN RATS
ELEVATE MY MIND — STEREO MC's
ELEVATION [A] — XPANSIONS
ELEVATION (MOVE YOUR BODY) 2002 [A] — XPANSIONS
ELEVATION [B] — GTO
ELEVATION [C] — U2
ELEVATION [D] — The OPEN
ELEVATOR SONG — DUBSTAR
ELEVEN TO FLY — TIN TIN OUT
ELISABETH SERENADE — Günter KALLMAN CHOIR
ELIZABETHAN REGGAE — Boris GARDINER
ELLE — DJ GREGORY
ELMO JAMES — CHAIRMEN OF THE BOARD
ELO (EP) — ELECTRIC LIGHT ORCHESTRA
ELOISE [A] — Barry RYAN
ELOISE [A] — The DAMNED
ELSTREE — The BUGGLES
ELUSIVE BUTTERFLY [A] — Bob LIND
ELUSIVE BUTTERFLY [A] — Val DOONICAN
THE ELVIS MEDLEY — Elvis PRESLEY
EMBARRASSMENT — MADNESS
EMBRACE — AGNELLI & NELSON
EMBRACING THE SUNSHINE — BT
EMERALD CITY — The SEEKERS
EMERGE — FISCHERSPOONER
EMERGENCY — KOOL and The GANG
EMERGENCY (DIAL 999) — LOOSE ENDS
EMERGENCY ON PLANET EARTH — JAMIROQUAI
EMILY [A] — BOWLING FOR SOUP
EMILY [B] — Adam GREEN
EMILY [C] — Stephen FRETWELL
EMILY KANE — ART BRUT
EMMA — HOT CHOCOLATE
EMOTIONAL CONTENT — FUNK D'VOID
EMOTIONAL RESCUE — The ROLLING STONES
EMOTIONAL TIME — HOTHOUSE FLOWERS
EMOTION [A] — Samantha SANG
EMOTION [A] — DESTINY'S CHILD
EMOTIONS [A] — Brenda LEE
EMOTIONS [B] — Mariah CAREY
THE EMPEROR'S NEW CLOTHES — Sinead O'CONNOR
EMPIRE — QUEENSRYCHE
EMPIRE LINE — MY LIFE STORY
EMPIRE SONG — KILLING JOKE
EMPIRE STATE HUMAN — HUMAN LEAGUE
EMPTY AT THE END — The ELECTRIC SOFT PARADE
EMPTY GARDEN — Elton JOHN
EMPTY ROOMS — Gary MOORE
EMPTY SKIES — KOSHEEN
EMPTY SOULS — MANIC STREET PREACHERS
EMPTY WORLD — DOGS D'AMOUR
ENCHANTED LADY — PASADENAS
ENCORE [A] — Cheryl LYNN
ENCORE [A] — TONGUE 'N' CHEEK
ENCORE UNE FOIS — SASH!
ENCORES (EP) — DIRE STRAITS
THE END HAS NO END — The STROKES
THE END IS THE BEGINNING IS THE END — SMASHING PUMPKINS
END OF A CENTURY — BLUR
THE END OF THE INNOCENCE — Don HENLEY
END OF THE LINE [A] — TRAVELING WILBURYS
END OF THE LINE [B] — HONEYZ
END OF THE LINE [C] — MOHAIR
END OF THE ROAD — BOYZ II MEN (92)
END OF THE WORLD [A] — Skeeter DAVIS
END OF THE WORLD [A] — SONIA
THE END OF THE WORLD [B] — The CURE
THE END ... OR THE BEGINNING — CLASSIX NOUVEAUX
ENDLESS — Dickie VALENTINE
ENDLESS ART — A HOUSE
ENDLESS LOVE [A] — Diana ROSS and Lionel RICHIE
ENDLESS LOVE [A] — Luther VANDROSS and Mariah CAREY
ENDLESS SLEEP [A] — Marty WILDE
ENDLESS SLEEP [A] — Jody REYNOLDS
ENDLESS SUMMER NIGHTS — Richard MARX
ENDLESSLY [A] — Brook BENTON
ENDLESSLY [B] — John FOXX
ENDS — EVERLAST
ENEMIES — HOPE OF THE STATES
ENEMY MAKER — DUB WAR
THE ENEMY WITHIN — THIRST
ENERGIZE — SLAMM
THE ENERGY (FEEL THE VIBE) — ASTRO TRAX
ENERGY FLASH (EP) — BELTRAM
ENERGY IS EUROBEAT — MAN TO MAN
ENERVATE — TRANSA
ENGINE ENGINE NO.9 — Roger MILLER
ENGINE NO.9 — MIDNIGHT STAR
ENGLAND CRAZY — RIDER & Terry VENABLES
ENGLAND SWINGS — Roger MILLER
ENGLAND, WE'LL FLY THE FLAG — ENGLAND WORLD CUP SQUAD
ENGLAND'S IRIE — BLACK GRAPE featuring Joe STRUMMER and Keith ALLEN
ENGLISH CIVIL WAR (JOHNNY COMES MARCHING HOME) — The CLASH
ENGLISH COUNTRY GARDEN [A] — Jimmie RODGERS
ENGLISH COUNTRY GARDEN [B] — DANDYS
ENGLISH SUMMER RAIN — PLACEBO
ENGLISHMAN IN NEW YORK — STING
ENJOY THE SILENCE [A] — DEPECHE MODE
ENJOY THE SILENCE 04 [A] — DEPECHE MODE
ENJOY YOURSELF [A] — The JACKSONS
ENJOY YOURSELF [B] — A+
ENOLA GAY — ORCHESTRAL MANOEUVRES IN THE DARK
ENOUGH IS ENOUGH [A] — CHUMBAWAMBA and CREDIT TO THE NATION
ENOUGH IS ENOUGH [B] — Y-TRIBE featuring Elisabeth TROY
ENTER SANDMAN — METALLICA
ENTER THE SCENE — DJ SUPREME vs the RHYTHM MASTERS
ENTER YOUR FANTASY (EP) — Joey NEGRO
THE ENTERTAINER — Marvin HAMLISCH
ENTRY OF THE GLADIATORS — NERO and The GLADIATORS
ENVY — ASH
THE EP — ZERO B
EP THREE — HUNDRED REASONS
EP TWO — HUNDRED REASONS
EPIC — FAITH NO MORE
EPLE — RÖYKSOPP
E-PRO — BECK
EQUINOXE PART 5 — Jean-Michel JARRE
EQUINOXE (PART V) — The SHADOWS
ERASE / REWIND — The CARDIGANS
ERASURE-ISH (A LITTLE RESPECT / STOP!) — BJÖRN AGAIN
ERECTION (TAKE IT TO THE TOP) — CORTINA featuring BK & MADAM FRICTION
ERNIE (THE FASTEST MILKMAN IN THE WEST) — Benny HILL (71)
EROTICA — MADONNA
ESCAPADE — Janet JACKSON
ESCAPE [A] — Gary CLAIL ON-U SOUND SYSTEM
ESCAPE [B] — ENRIQUE
ESCAPE ARTISTS NEVER DIE — FUNERAL FOR A FRIEND
ESCAPE (THE PINA COLADA SONG) — Rupert HOLMES
ESCAPING [A] — ASIA BLUE
ESCAPING [A] — Dina CARROLL
E.S.P. — The BEE GEES
ESPECIALLY FOR YOU [A] — Kylie MINOGUE and Jason DONOVAN (89)
ESPECIALLY FOR YOU [A] — DENISE and JOHNNY
THE ESSENTIAL WALLY PARTY MEDLEY — GAY GORDON and The MINCE PIES
ET LES OISEAUX CHANTAIENT (AND THE BIRDS WERE SINGING) — SWEET PEOPLE
ET MÊME — Françoise HARDY
ETERNAL FLAME [A] — The BANGLES (89)
ETERNAL FLAME [A] — ATOMIC KITTEN (01)
ETERNAL LOVE — ANT & DEC
ETERNALLY — Jimmy YOUNG

13 November 1999	20 November 1999	27 November 1999	4 December 1999
UK No.1 SINGLES			
LIFT ME UP Geri Halliwell	**IT'S ONLY US / SHE'S THE ONE** Robbie Williams	**KING OF MY CASTLE** Wamdue Project	**THE MILLENNIUM PRAYER** Cliff Richard
UK No.1 ALBUMS			
STEPTACULAR Steps	**STEPTACULAR** Steps	**ALL THE WAY ... A DECADE OF SONG** Celine Dion	**STEPTACULAR** Steps

ETERNITY [A] — ORION
ETERNITY [B] — Robbie WILLIAMS (01)
ETHER RADIO — CHIKINKI
ETHNIC PRAYER — HAVANA
THE ETON RIFLES — The JAM
EUGINA — SALT TANK
EURODISCO — BIS
EUROPA AND THE PIRATE TWINS — Thomas DOLBY
EUROPE (AFTER THE RAIN) — John FOXX
EUROPEAN FEMALE — The STRANGLERS
EUROPEAN SON — JAPAN
EVANGELINE [A] — ICICLE WORKS
EVANGELINE [B] — COCTEAU TWINS
EVAPOR 8 — ALTERN 8
EVE OF DESTRUCTION — Barry McGUIRE
EVE OF THE WAR — Jeff WAYNE
EVE, THE APPLE OF MY EYE — BELL X1
EVEN AFTER ALL — Finley QUAYE
EVEN BETTER THAN THE REAL THING — U2
EVEN FLOW — PEARL JAM
EVEN GOD CAN'T CHANGE THE PAST — Charlotte CHURCH
EVEN MORE PARTY POPS — Russ CONWAY
EVEN NOW — Bob SEGER and The SILVER BULLET BAND
EVEN THE BAD TIMES ARE GOOD — The TREMELOES
EVEN THE NIGHTS ARE BETTER — AIR SUPPLY
EVEN THOUGH YOU BROKE MY HEART — GEMINI
EVEN THOUGH YOU'VE GONE — The JACKSONS
EVENING FALLS ... — ENYA
EVENING STAR — JUDAS PRIEST
EVER BLAZIN' — Sean PAUL
EVER FALLEN IN LOVE [A] — FINE YOUNG CANNIBALS
EVER FALLEN IN LOVE (WITH SOMEONE YOU SHOULDN'T'VE) [A] — The BUZZCOCKS
EVER FALLEN IN LOVE (WITH SOMEONE YOU SHOULDN'T'VE)? [A] — VARIOUS ARTISTS (Singles and EPs)
EVER REST — MYSTICA
EVER SINCE YOU SAID GOODBYE — Marty WILDE
EVER SO LONELY — MONSOON
EVEREST — SUPERNATURALS
EVERGLADE — L7
EVERGREEN [A] — Hazell DEAN
EVERGREEN [A] — Belle LAWRENCE
EVERGREEN [B] — Will YOUNG (02)
EVERLASTING — Natalie COLE
THE EVERLASTING — MANIC STREET PREACHERS
EVERLASTING LOVE [A] — LOVE AFFAIR (68)
EVERLASTING LOVE [A] — Robert KNIGHT
EVERLASTING LOVE [A] — Rex SMITH and Rachel SWEET
EVERLASTING LOVE [A] — SANDRA
EVERLASTING LOVE [A] — WORLDS APART
EVERLASTING LOVE [A] — Gloria ESTEFAN
EVERLASTING LOVE [A] — CAST FROM CASUALTY
EVERLASTING LOVE [A] — Jamie CULLUM
EVERLASTING LOVE [B] — Howard JONES
EVERLONG — FOO FIGHTERS
EVERLOVIN' — Ricky NELSON
EVERMORE — Ruby MURRAY
EVERY ANGEL — ALL ABOUT EVE
EVERY BEAT OF MY HEART — Rod STEWART
EVERY BEAT OF THE HEART — RAILWAY CHILDREN
EVERY BREATH OF THE WAY — MELANIE
EVERY BREATH YOU TAKE — The POLICE (83)
EVERY DAY — ANTICAPPELLA
EVERY DAY HURTS — SAD CAFE
EVERY DAY I FALL APART — SUPERSTAR
EVERY DAY I LOVE YOU — BOYZONE
EVERY DAY (I LOVE YOU MORE) — Jason DONOVAN
EVERY DAY OF MY LIFE — HOUSE TRAFFIC
EVERY DAY OF THE WEEK — JADE
EVERY DAY SHOULD BE A HOLIDAY — The DANDY WARHOLS
EVERY GIRL AND BOY — SPAGNA
EVERY HEARTBEAT — Amy GRANT
EVERY KINDA PEOPLE [A] — Robert PALMER
EVERY KINDA PEOPLE [A] — MINT JULEPS
EVERY KINDA PEOPLE [A] — Chaka DEMUS and PLIERS
EVERY LITTLE BIT HURTS — Spencer DAVIS GROUP
EVERY LITTLE STEP — Bobby BROWN
EVERY LITTLE TEARDROP — GALLAGHER and LYLE
EVERY LITTLE THING — Jeff LYNNE
EVERY LITTLE THING HE DOES IS MAGIC — Shawn COLVIN
EVERY LITTLE THING I DO — SOUL FOR REAL
EVERY LITTLE THING SHE DOES IS MAGIC [A] — The POLICE (81)
EVERY LITTLE THING SHE DOES IS MAGIC [A] — Chaka DEMUS and PLIERS
EVERY LITTLE TIME [A] — POPPERS presents AURA
EVERY LITTLE TIME [B] — ONYX featuring Gemma J
EVERY LOSER WINS — Nick BERRY (86)
EVERY MAN MUST HAVE A DREAM — LIVERPOOL EXPRESS
EVERY MORNING — SUGAR RAY
EVERY NIGHT — Phoebe SNOW
EVERY NITE'S A SATURDAY NIGHT WITH YOU — The DRIFTERS
EVERY 1'S A WINNER — HOT CHOCOLATE
EVERY OTHER TIME — LYTE FUNKIE ONES
EVERY ROSE HAS ITS THORN — POISON
EVERY SINGLE DAY — DODGY
EVERY TIME — Janet JACKSON
EVERY TIME I FALL — Gina G
EVERY TIME I FALL IN LOVE — UPSIDE DOWN
EVERY TIME YOU TOUCH ME — MOBY
EVERY WHICH WAY BUT LOOSE — Eddie RABBITT
EVERY WOMAN KNOWS — LULU
EVERY WOMAN NEEDS LOVE — STELLA BROWNE
EVERY YEAR EVERY CHRISTMAS — Luther VANDROSS
EVERY YOU EVERY ME — PLACEBO
EVERYBODY [A] — Tommy ROE
EVERYBODY [B] — CAPPELLA
EVERYBODY [C] — ALTERN 8
EVERYBODY [D] — DJ BOBO
EVERYBODY [E] — CLOCK
EVERYBODY [F] — KINKY
EVERYBODY [G] — PROGRESS presents the BOY WUNDA
EVERYBODY [H] — HEAR'SAY
EVERYBODY [I] — Martin SOLVEIG
EVERYBODY (ALL OVER) — FPI PROJECT
EVERYBODY (ALL OVER THE WORLD) — FPI PROJECT
EVERYBODY (BACKSTREET'S BACK) — BACKSTREET BOYS
EVERYBODY BE SOMEBODY — RUFFNECK featuring YAVAHN
EVERYBODY COME DOWN — The DELGADOS
EVERYBODY COME ON (CAN U FEEL IT) — MR REDS vs DJ SKRIBBLE
EVERYBODY CRIES — LIBERTY X
EVERYBODY DANCE [A] — CHIC
EVERYBODY DANCE [A] — EVOLUTION
EVERYBODY DANCE (THE HORN SONG) — Barbara TUCKER
EVERYBODY EVERYBODY — BLACK BOX
(EVERYBODY) GET DANCIN' — The BOMBERS
EVERYBODY GET TOGETHER — Dave CLARK FIVE
EVERYBODY GET UP [A] — FIVE
EVERYBODY GET UP [B] — CAPRICCIO
EVERYBODY GETS A SECOND CHANCE — MIKE and The MECHANICS
EVERYBODY GO HOME THE PARTY'S OVER — Clodagh RODGERS
EVERYBODY GONFI-GON — TWO COWBOYS
EVERYBODY HAVE A GOOD TIME — Archie BELL and The DRELLS
EVERYBODY HERE WANTS YOU — Jeff BUCKLEY
EVERYBODY HURTS — R.E.M.
EVERYBODY IN THE PLACE (EP) — The PRODIGY
EVERYBODY IS A STAR — POINTER SISTERS
EVERYBODY KNOWS [A] — Dave CLARK FIVE
EVERYBODY KNOWS [B] — Dave CLARK FIVE
EVERYBODY KNOWS [C] — The FREE ASSOCIATION
EVERYBODY KNOWS (EXCEPT YOU) — The DIVINE COMEDY
EVERYBODY LET'S SOMEBODY LOVE — Frank K featuring Wiston OFFICE
EVERYBODY LOVES A LOVER — Doris DAY
EVERYBODY LOVES SOMEBODY — Dean MARTIN
EVERYBODY MOVE — Cathy DENNIS
EVERYBODY (MOVE YOUR BODY) — DIVA
EVERYBODY MUST PARTY — GEORGIE PORGIE
EVERYBODY NEEDS A 303 — FATBOY SLIM
EVERYBODY NEEDS SOMEBODY [A] — BIRDLAND
EVERYBODY NEEDS SOMEBODY [B] — Nick HOWARD
EVERYBODY NEEDS SOMEBODY TO LOVE — The BLUES BROTHERS
EVERYBODY ON THE FLOOR (PUMP IT) — TOKYO GHETTO PUSSY
EVERYBODY PUMP — DJ POWER
EVERYBODY (RAP) — Wally JUMP Jr and The CRIMINAL ELEMENT
EVERYBODY SALSA — MODERN ROMANCE
EVERYBODY SAY EVERYBODY DO — LET LOOSE
EVERYBODY THINKS THAT THEY'RE GOING TO GET THEIRS — BIS
EVERYBODY UP! — GLAM METAL DETECTIVES
EVERYBODY WANTS HER — THUNDER
EVERYBODY WANTS TO RULE THE WORLD — TEARS FOR FEARS
EVERYBODY WANTS TO RUN THE WORLD — TEARS FOR FEARS
EVERYBODY'S A ROCKSTAR — TALL PAUL
EVERYBODY'S CHANGING — KEANE
EVERYBODY'S FOOL — EVANESCENCE
EVERYBODY'S FREE — ROZALLA
EVERYBODY'S FREE (TO WEAR SUNSCREEN) – THE SUNSCREEN SONG (CLASS OF '99) — Baz LUHRMANN (99)
EVERYBODY'S GONE — SENSELESS THINGS
EVERYBODY'S GONNA BE HAPPY — The KINKS
EVERYBODY'S GOT SUMMER — ATLANTIC STARR
EVERYBODY'S GOT TO LEARN SOMETIME [A] — KORGIS
EVERYBODY'S GOT TO LEARN SOMETIME [A] — YAZZ
(EVERYBODY'S GOT TO LEARN SOMETIME) I NEED YOUR LOVING [A] — BABY D
EVERYBODY'S GOTTA LEARN SOMETIME [A] — The CANTAMUS GIRLS CHOIR
EVERYBODY'S HAPPY NOWADAYS — The BUZZCOCKS
EVERYBODY'S LAUGHING — Phil FEARON
EVERYBODY'S SOMEBODY'S FOOL — Connie FRANCIS
EVERYBODY'S TALKIN' [A] — NILSSON
EVERYBODY'S TALKIN' [A] — The BEAUTIFUL SOUTH
EVERYBODY'S TALKIN' 'BOUT LOVE — SILVER CONVENTION
EVERYDAY [A] — The MOODY BLUES
EVERYDAY [B] — Don McLEAN
EVERYDAY [C] — SLADE
EVERYDAY [D] — JAM MACHINE
EVERYDAY [E] — ORCHESTRAL MANOEUVRES IN THE DARK
EVERYDAY [F] — Phil COLLINS
EVERYDAY [G] — INCOGNITO
EVERYDAY [H] — Craig McLACHLAN
EVERYDAY [I] — AGNELLI & NELSON
EVERYDAY [J] — BON JOVI
EVERYDAY GIRL — DJ RAP
EVERYDAY I LOVE YOU LESS AND LESS — KAISER CHIEFS
EVERYDAY I WRITE THE BOOK — Elvis COSTELLO
EVERYDAY IS A WINDING ROAD — Sheryl CROW
EVERYDAY IS LIKE SUNDAY — MORRISSEY
EVERYDAY LIVING — WOODENTOPS
EVERYDAY NOW — TEXAS
EVERYDAY PEOPLE [A] — SLY and The FAMILY STONE
EVERYDAY PEOPLE [A] — Aretha FRANKLIN
EVERYDAY SUNSHINE — FISHBONE
EVERYDAY THANG — Melanie WILLIAMS
EVERYONE SAYS "HI" — David BOWIE
EVERYONE SAYS I'M PARANOID — APARTMENT
EVERYONE SAYS YOU'RE SO FRAGILE — IDLEWILD
EVERYONE'S GONE TO THE MOON — Jonathan KING
EVERYTHING [A] — Jody WATLEY
EVERYTHING [B] — KICKING BACK with TAXMAN
EVERYTHING [C] — UHF
EVERYTHING [D] — HYSTERIX
EVERYTHING [E] — Sarah WASHINGTON
EVERYTHING [F] — INXS
EVERYTHING [G] — Mary J BLIGE
EVERYTHING [H] — DUM DUMS
EVERYTHING [I] — Alanis MORISSETTE
EVERYTHING [J] — Fefe DOBSON
EVERYTHING A MAN COULD EVER NEED — Glen CAMPBELL
EVERYTHING ABOUT YOU — UGLY KID JOE
EVERYTHING CHANGES — TAKE THAT (94)
EVERYTHING COUNTS — DEPECHE MODE
EVERYTHING EVENTUALLY — APPLETON
EVERYTHING GOOD IS BAD — WESTWORLD
EVERYTHING I AM — PLASTIC PENNY
(EVERYTHING I DO) I DO IT FOR YOU [A] — Bryan ADAMS (91)
(EVERYTHING I DO) I DO IT FOR YOU [A] — FATIMA MANSIONS
(EVERYTHING I DO) I DO IT FOR YOU [A] — Q
EVERYTHING I HAVE IS YOURS — Eddie FISHER
EVERYTHING I OWN [A] — BREAD
EVERYTHING I OWN [A] — Ken BOOTHE (74)
EVERYTHING I OWN [A] — BOY GEORGE (87)
EVERYTHING I WANTED — Dannii MINOGUE
EVERYTHING IS ALRIGHT (UPTIGHT) — CJ LEWIS
EVERYTHING IS BEAUTIFUL — Ray STEVENS
EVERYTHING IS EVERYTHING [A] — Lauryn HILL
EVERYTHING IS EVERYTHING [A] — PHOENIX
EVERYTHING IS GONNA BE ALRIGHT — SOUNDS OF BLACKNESS
EVERYTHING IS GREAT — INNER CIRCLE
EVERYTHING I'VE GOT IN MY POCKET — Minnie DRIVER
EVERYTHING MUST CHANGE — Paul YOUNG
EVERYTHING MUST GO — MANIC STREET PREACHERS
EVERYTHING MY HEART DESIRES — Adam RICKITT
EVERYTHING SHE WANTS — WHAM!
EVERYTHING STARTS WITH AN 'E' — E-ZEE POSSEE
EVERYTHING TO EVERYONE — EVERCLEAR
EVERYTHING WILL FLOW — SUEDE
EVERYTHING YOU NEED — MADISON AVENUE
EVERYTHING YOU WANT — VERTICAL HORIZON
EVERYTHING WILL TURN OUT FINE — STEALER'S WHEEL
EVERYTHING'S ALRIGHT — MOJOS
EVERYTHING'S COOL — POP WILL EAT ITSELF
EVERYTHING'S GONE GREEN — NEW ORDER
EVERYTHING'S GONNA BE ALRIGHT — SWEETBOX
EVERYTHING'S NOT YOU — STONEPROOF
EVERYTHING'S RUINED — FAITH NO MORE
EVERYTHING'S TUESDAY — CHAIRMEN OF THE BOARD
EVERYTIME [A] — LUSTRAL
EVERYTIME [B] — Tatyana ALI
EVERYTIME [C] — a1
EVERYTIME [D] — Britney SPEARS (04)
EVERYTIME I CLOSE MY EYES — BABYFACE
EVERYTIME I THINK OF YOU — FM
EVERYTIME IT RAINS — ACE OF BASE
EVERYTIME YOU GO AWAY — Paul YOUNG
EVERYTIME YOU NEED ME — FRAGMA featuring Maria RUBIA
EVERYTIME YOU SLEEP — DEACON BLUE
EVERYTIME YOU TOUCH ME — QFX
EVERYWAY THAT I CAN — SERTAB
EVERYWHERE [A] — FLEETWOOD MAC
EVERYWHERE [A] — LNM PROJEKT featuring Bonnie BAILEY
EVERYWHERE [B] — Michelle BRANCH
EVERYWHERE I GO [A] — ISOTONIK
EVERYWHERE I GO [B] — Jackson BROWNE
EVERYWHERE I LOOK — Daryl HALL and John OATES
EVE'S VOLCANO (COVERED IN SIN) — Julian COPE
EVIDENCE — FAITH NO MORE

11 December 1999	18 December 1999	25 December 1999	1 January 2000
THE MILLENNIUM PRAYER Cliff Richard	**THE MILLENNIUM PRAYER** Cliff Richard	**I HAVE A DREAM / SEASONS IN THE SUN** Westlife	**I HAVE A DREAM / SEASONS IN THE SUN** Westlife
COME ON OVER Shania Twain	**COME ON OVER** Shania Twain	**COME ON OVER** Shania Twain	**COME ON OVER** Shania Twain

EVIL [A] — LADYTRON
EVIL [B] — INTERPOL
EVIL HEARTED YOU — YARDBIRDS
EVIL MAN — FATIMA MANSIONS
THE EVIL THAT MEN DO — IRON MAIDEN
EVIL TWIN — LOVE / HATE
EVIL WOMAN — ELECTRIC LIGHT ORCHESTRA
EVOLUTIONDANCE PART ONE (EP) — EVOLUTION
EV'RY DAY OF MY LIFE — Malcolm VAUGHAN
EV'RY LITTLE BIT — Millie SCOTT
EV'RY TIME WE SAY GOODBYE — SIMPLY RED
EV'RYBODY'S TWISTIN' — Frank SINATRA
EV'RYWHERE — David WHITFIELD
THE EX — BILLY TALENT
EX-FACTOR — Lauryn HILL
EX-GIRLFRIEND — NO DOUBT
EXCERPT FROM A TEENAGE OPERA — Keith WEST
EXCITABLE — AMAZULU
EXCITED — M PEOPLE
EXCLUSIVE — APOLLO presents HOUSE OF VIRGINISM
EXCLUSIVELY YOURS — Mark WYNTER
EXCUSE ME BABY — MAGIC LANTERNS
EXCUSE ME MISS — JAY-Z
EXCUSE MY BROTHER — The MITCHELL BROTHERS
EXHALE (SHOOP SHOOP) —Whitney HOUSTON
EXODUS [A] — Bob MARLEY & The WAILERS
EXODUS [B] — SUNSCREEM
EXODUS LIVE [C] — LEVELLERS
EXODUS (THEME FROM 'EXODUS') — FERRANTE and TEICHER
THE EXORCIST [A] — SCIENTIST
EXORCIST [B] — SHADES OF RHYTHM
EXPANDER — FUTURE SOUND OF LONDON
EXPANSIONS '86 (EXPAND YOUR MIND) [A] — Chris PAUL featuring David JOSEPH
EXPANSIONS [A] — Scott GROOVES featuring Roy AYERS
EXPERIENCE — Diana ROSS
EXPERIMENT IV — Kate BUSH
EXPERIMENTS WITH MICE — Johnny DANKWORTH
EXPLAIN THE REASONS — FIRST LIGHT
EXPO 2000 — KRAFTWERK
EXPLORATION OF SPACE — COSMIC GATE
EXPRESS [A] — BT EXPRESS
EXPRESS [B] — Dina CARROLL
EXPRESS YOUR FREEDOM — ANTICAPPELLA
EXPRESS YOURSELF [A] — MADONNA
EXPRESS YOURSELF [B] — NWA
EXPRESS YOURSELF [C] — Jimi POLO
EXPRESSION — SALT-N-PEPA
EXPRESSLY (EP) — Edwyn COLLINS
EXPRESSO BONGO (EP) — Cliff RICHARD and The SHADOWS
EXTACY — SHADES OF RHYTHM
EXTENDED PLAY (EP) — Bryan FERRY
THE EXTENDED PLEASURE OF DANCE (EP) — 808 STATE
EXTERMINATE! — SNAP! featuring Niki HARIS
EXTREME WAYS — MOBY
EXTREMIS — HAL featuring Gillian ANDERSON
EYE BEE M — COMMANDER TOM
EYE FOR AN EYE — UNKLE
EYE HATE U — PRINCE
EYE KNOW — DE LA SOUL
EYE LEVEL (THEME FROM THE TV SERIES 'VAN DER VALK') — The Simon PARK ORCHESTRA (73)
EYE OF THE TIGER [A] — SURVIVOR (82)
EYE OF THE TIGER [A] — Frank BRUNO
EYE TALK — FASHION
EYE TO EYE — Chaka KHAN
EYE WONDER — APPLES
EYEBALL (EYEBALL PAUL'S THEME) — SUNBURST
EYES DON'T LIE — TRUCE
THE EYES HAVE IT — Karel FIALKA
EYES OF A STRANGER — QUEENSRYCHE
EYES OF BLUE — Paul CARRACK
EYES OF SORROW — A GUY CALLED GERALD
THE EYES OF TRUTH — ENIGMA
EYES ON YOU — Jay SEAN featuring The RISHI RICH PROJECT
EYES THAT SEE IN THE DARK — Kenny ROGERS
EYES WITHOUT A FACE — Billy IDOL

EZ PASS — HAR MAR SUPERSTAR
EZY — WOLFSBANE
THE F-WORD — BABYBIRD
FA FA FA FA FA (SAD SONG) — Otis REDDING
FABLE — Robert MILES
FABRICATED LUNACY — TERRIS
FABULOUS [A] — Charlie GRACIE
FABULOUS [B] — JAHEIM
THE FACE — AND WHY NOT?
FACE THE STRANGE EP — THERAPY?
FACE TO FACE — SIOUXSIE and The BANSHEES
FACES — 2 UNLIMITED
THE FACES (EP) — The FACES
FACT OF LIFE — OUI 3
FACTS + FIGURES — Hugh CORNWELL
THE FACTS OF LIFE [A] — Danny MADDEN
THE FACTS OF LIFE [B] — BLACK BOX RECORDER
FACTS OF LOVE — CLIMIE FISHER
FADE — PARIS ANGELS
FADE INTO YOU — MAZZY STAR
FADE TO GREY — VISAGE
FADED — Ben HARPER
FADER — DRUGSTORE
FADING LIKE A FLOWER [A] — ROXETTE
FADING LIKE A FLOWER [A] — DANCING DJs v ROXETTE
FAILING IN LOVE AGAIN — LONDONBEAT
FAILURE [A] — SKINNY
FAILURE [B] — KINGS OF CONVENIENCE
FAILURE'S NOT FLATTERING – NEW FOUND GLORY
FAINT — LINKIN PARK
A FAIR AFFAIR (JE T'AIME) — Misty OLDLAND
FAIR BLOWS THE WIND FOR FRANCE — PELE
FAIR FIGHT — DJ ZINC
FAIRGROUND — SIMPLY RED (95)
FAIRPLAY — SOUL II SOUL
FAIRWEATHER FRIEND — SYMPOSIUM
FAIRYTALE — DANA
FAIRYTALE OF NEW YORK — The POGUES featuring Kirsty MacCOLL
FAIT ACCOMPLI — CURVE
FAITH [A] — George MICHAEL
FAITH [B] — WEE PAPA GIRL RAPPERS
FAITH CAN MOVE MOUNTAINS [A] — Johnnie RAY and The FOUR LADS
FAITH CAN MOVE MOUNTAINS [A] — Jimmy YOUNG
FAITH CAN MOVE MOUNTAINS [A] — Nat 'King' COLE
FAITH HEALER — RECOIL
FAITH IN PEOPLE — The HONEYMOON MACHINE
FAITH (IN THE POWER OF LOVE) — ROZALLA
FAITH OF THE HEART — Rod STEWART
FAITHFUL — GO WEST
THE FAITHFUL HUSSAR (DON'T CRY MY LOVE) [A] — Vera LYNN
THE FAITHFUL HUSSAR [A] — Louis ARMSTRONG
THE FAITHFUL HUSSAR [A] — Ted HEATH
FAITHFULNESS — SKIN
FAITHLESS — SCRITTI POLITTI
FAKE [A] — Alexander O'NEAL
FAKE [B] — SIMPLY RED
FAKE FUR — URUSEI YATSURA
FAKE PLASTIC TREES — RADIOHEAD
THE FAKE SOUND OF PROGRESS — LOSTPROPHETS
FAKER — AUDIOWEB
FALCON — RAH BAND
FALL (EP) — RIDE
THE FALL [A] — MINISTRY
THE FALL [B] — WAY OUT WEST
FALL AT YOUR FEET [A] — CROWDED HOUSE
FALL AT YOUR FEET [A] — CM2 featuring Lisa LAWS
FALL BACK DOWN — RANCID
FALL BEHIND ME — The DONNAS
FALL DOWN (SPIRIT OF LOVE) — TRAMAINE
FALL FROM GRACE — ESKIMOS & EGYPT
FALL IN LOVE WITH ME [A] — EARTH WIND AND FIRE
FALL IN LOVE WITH ME [B] — BOOTH and The BAD ANGEL
FALL IN LOVE WITH YOU — Cliff RICHARD and The SHADOWS
FALL OUT — The POLICE
FALL TO LOVE — DIESEL PARK WEST
FALL TO PIECES — VELVET REVOLVER
FALL VS 2003 — The FALL

FALLEN — Sarah McLACHLAN
FALLEN ANGEL [A] — Frankie VALLI
FALLEN ANGEL [B] — POISON
FALLEN ANGEL [C] — Traci LORDS
FALLEN ANGEL [D] — ELBOW
FALLEN ANGELS — Buffy SAINTE-MARIE
FALLIN' [A] — Connie FRANCIS
FALLIN' [B] — TEENAGE FANCLUB and DE LA SOUL
FALLIN' [C] — Alicia KEYS
FALLIN' [D] — UN-CUT
FALLIN' IN LOVE — HAMILTON, Joe FRANK and REYNOLDS
FALLING [A] — Roy ORBISON
FALLING [B] — Julee CRUISE
FALLING [C] — Cathy DENNIS
FALLING [D] — Alison MOYET
FALLING [E] — ANT & DEC
FALLING [F] — BOOM!
FALLING [G] — LIQUID STATE featuring Marcella WOODS
FALLING [H] — McALMONT & BUTLER
FALLING ANGELS RIDING — David ESSEX
FALLING APART AT THE SEAMS — MARMALADE
FALLING AWAY FROM ME — KORN
FALLING IN AND OUT OF LOVE — FEMME FATALE
FALLING IN LOVE [A] — SURFACE
FALLING IN LOVE [B] — SYBIL
FALLING IN LOVE [C] — LA BOUCHE
FALLING IN LOVE AGAIN [A] — TECHNO TWINS
FALLING IN LOVE AGAIN [B] — Eagle-Eye CHERRY
FALLING IN LOVE (IS HARD ON THE KNEES) — AEROSMITH
FALLING INTO YOU — Celine DION
FALLING STARS — SUNSET STRIPPERS
FALLING TO PIECES — FAITH NO MORE
FALSE ALARM — The BRONX
FALTER — HUNDRED REASONS
FAME [A] — David BOWIE
FAME [B] — Irene CARA (82)
FAMILIAR FEELING — MOLOKO
FAMILIUS HORRIBILUS — POP WILL EAT ITSELF
FAMILY AFFAIR [A] — SLY and The FAMILY STONE
FAMILY AFFAIR [A] — BEF featuring Lalah HATHAWAY
FAMILY AFFAIR [A] — Shabba RANKS featuring PATRA and TERRI & MONICA
FAMILY AFFAIR [B] — Mary J BLIGE
FAMILY MAN [A] — Mike OLDFIELD
FAMILY MAN [A] — Daryl HALL and John OATES
FAMILY MAN [B] — FLEETWOOD MAC
FAMILY MAN [C] — ROACHFORD
FAMILY OF MAN — The FARM
FAMILY PORTRAIT — PINK
FAMINE — Sinead O'CONNOR
FAN MAIL — The DICKIES
FAN THE FLAME — Barbara PENNINGTON
FANCY PANTS — KENNY
FAN'DABI'DOZI — KRANKIES
FANFARE FOR THE COMMON MAN — EMERSON, LAKE and PALMER
FANLIGHT FANNY — Clinton FORD
FANTASTIC DAY — HAIRCUT 100
FANTASTIC VOYAGE — COOLIO
FANTASY [A] — EARTH WIND AND FIRE
FANTASY [A] — BLACK BOX
FANTASY [B] — Gerard KENNY
FANTASY [C] — FANTASY UFO
FANTASY [D] — TEN CITY
FANTASY [E] — Mariah CAREY
FANTASY [F] — LEVELLERS
FANTASY [G] — APPLETONS
FANTASY ISLAND [A] — TIGHT FIT
FANTASY ISLAND [B] — M PEOPLE
FANTASY REAL — Phil FEARON
FAR — LONGPIGS
FAR ABOVE THE CLOUDS — Mike OLDFIELD
FAR AND AWAY — AIDA
FAR AWAY — Shirley BASSEY
FAR FAR AWAY — SLADE
FAR FROM HOME — LEVELLERS
FAR FROM OVER — Frank STALLON
FAR GONE AND OUT — JESUS AND MARY CHAIN
FAR OUT [A] — SON'Z OF A LOOP DA LOOP ERA
FAR OUT [B] — DEEJAY PUNK-ROC
FAR-OUT SON OF LUNG AND THE RAMBLINGS OF A MADMAN — FUTURE SOUND OF LONDON
FARAWAY EYES — The ROLLING STONES

FARAWAY PLACES — The BACHELORS
FAREWELL — Rod STEWART
FAREWELL ANGELINA — Joan BAEZ
FAREWELL IS A LONELY SOUND — Jimmy RUFFIN
FAREWELL MR SORROW — ALL ABOUT EVE
FAREWELL MY SUMMER LOVE [A] — CHAOS
FAREWELL MY SUMMER LOVE [A] — Michael JACKSON
FAREWELL TO THE MOON — YORK
FAREWELL TO TWILIGHT — SYMPOSIUM
FARMER BILL'S COWMAN (I WAS KAISER BILL'S BATMAN) — The WURZELS
FARON YOUNG — PREFAB SPROUT
FASCINATED [A] — Lisa B
FASCINATED [B] — RAVEN MAIZE
FASCINATING RHYTHM — BASS-O-MATIC
FASHION — David BOWIE
FASHION CRISIS HITS NEW YORK — FRANK AND WALTERS
FASHION '98 — GLAMMA KID
FASSY HOLE — Roni SIZE
FAST AS YOU CAN — Fiona APPLE
FAST BOY — The BLUETONES
FAST CAR [A] — Tracy CHAPMAN
FAST CAR [B] — DILLINJA
FAST FOOD SONG — FAST FOOD ROCKERS
FASTEN YOUR SEATBELT — PENDULUM & FRESH featuring SPYDA & TENOR FLY
FASTER — MANIC STREET PREACHERS
FASTER THAN THE SPEED OF NIGHT — Bonnie TYLER
FASTER THE CHASE — INME
FASTLOVE — George MICHAEL (96)
FAT BASTARD — MEDWAY
FAT BLACK HEART — PELE
FAT BOTTOMED GIRLS — QUEEN
FAT LIP — SUM 41
FAT NECK — BLACK GRAPE
FATAL HESITATION — Chris DE BURGH
FATHER [A] — The CHRISTIANS
FATHER [B] — LL COOL J
FATHER AND SON [A] — BOYZONE
FATHER AND SON [A] — Ronan KEATING featuring YUSUF
FATHER CHRISTMAS DO NOT TOUCH ME — The GOODIES
FATHER FIGURE — George MICHAEL
FATTIE BUM BUM [A] — Carl MALCOLM
FATTIE BUM BUM [A] — DIVERSIONS
FAVOURITE SHIRTS (BOY MEETS GIRL) — HAIRCUT 100
FAVOURITE THINGS — BIG BROVAZ
FBI — The SHADOWS
FE' REAL — Maxi PRIEST featuring APACHE INDIAN
F.E.A.R. — Ian BROWN
FEAR LOVES THIS PLACE — Julian COPE
FEAR OF THE DARK [A] — Gordon GILTRAP
FEAR OF THE DARK (LIVE) [B] — IRON MAIDEN
FEAR SATAN — MOGWAI
FEAR: THE MINDKILLER — EON
FEARLESS — The BRAVERY
FED UP — HOUSE OF PAIN
FEDORA (I'LL BE YOUR DAWG) — CARAMBA
FEE FI FO FUM — CANDY GIRLS
FEED MY FRANKENSTEIN — Alice COOPER
FEED THE FEELING — PERCEPTION
FEED THE TREE — BELLY
FEED YOUR ADDICTION — EASTERN LANE
FEEDING TIME — LOOK
FEEL [A] — Ruth JOY
FEEL [B] — HOUSE OF LOVE
FEEL [C] — Robbie WILLIAMS
FEEL EVERY BEAT — ELECTRONIC
FEEL FREE — SOUL II SOUL
FEEL GOOD [A] — PHATS & SMALL
FEEL GOOD [B] — MADASUN
FEEL GOOD INC — GORILLAZ
FEEL GOOD TIME — PINK featuring William ORBIT
FEEL IT [A] — HI-LUX
FEEL IT [B] — Carol BAILEY
FEEL IT [C] — Neneh CHERRY
FEEL IT [D] — The TAMPERER featuring MAYA (98)
FEEL IT [E] — Inaya DAY
FEEL IT BOY — BEENIE MAN
FEEL IT WITH ME — ULTRABEAT
FEEL LIKE CALLING HOME — MR BIG

8 January 2000	15 January 2000	22 January 2000	29 January 2000

UK No.1 SINGLES

I HAVE A DREAM / SEASONS IN THE SUN Westlife	**I HAVE A DREAM / SEASONS IN THE SUN** Westlife	**THE MASSES AGAINST THE CLASSES** Manic Street Preachers	**BORN TO MAKE YOU HAPPY** Britney Spears

UK No.1 ALBUMS

COME ON OVER Shania Twain	**THE MAN WHO** Travis	**THE MAN WHO** Travis	**THE MAN WHO** Travis

FEEL LIKE CHANGE — BLACK
FEEL LIKE MAKIN' LOVE [A] — Roberta FLACK
FEEL LIKE MAKIN' LOVE [A] — George BENSON
FEEL LIKE MAKIN' LOVE [B] — BAD COMPANY
FEEL LIKE MAKING LOVE [B] — Pauline HENRY
FEEL LIKE SINGIN' — Sandy B
FEEL LIKE SINGING — TAK TIX
FEEL ME — BLANCMANGE
FEEL ME FLOW — NAUGHTY BY NATURE
FEEL MY BODY — Frank'o MOIRAGHI featuring AMNESIA
FEEL NO PAIN — SADE
FEEL SO FINE — Johnny PRESTON
FEEL SO GOOD [A] — MA$E
FEEL SO GOOD [B] — JON THE DENTIST vs Ollie JAYE
FEEL SO HIGH — DES'REE
FEEL SO REAL [A] — Steve ARRINGTON
FEEL SO REAL [B] — DREAM FREQUENCY
FEEL SURREAL — FREEFALL featuring PSYCHOTROPIC
FEEL THA VIBE — THAT KID CHRIS
FEEL THE BEAT [A] — CAMISRA
FEEL THE BEAT [B] — DARUDE
FEEL THE DRUM (EP) — PARKS & WILSON
FEEL THE DRUMS — NATIVE
FEEL THE HEAT — Roni SIZE
FEEL THE MUSIC — GURU
FEEL THE NEED [A] — Leif GARRETT
FEEL THE NEED [A] — G NATION featuring ROSIE
FEEL THE NEED [B] — JT TAYLOR
FEEL THE NEED [C] — WEIRD SCIENCE
FEEL THE NEED IN ME [A] — The DETROIT EMERALDS
FEEL THE NEED IN ME [A] — FORREST
FEEL THE NEED IN ME [A] — Shakin' STEVENS
FEEL THE PAIN — DINOSAUR JR
FEEL THE RAINDROPS — The ADVENTURES
FEEL THE REAL — David BENDETH
FEEL THE RHYTHM [A] — Jazzi P
FEEL THE RHYTHM [B] — TERRORIZE
FEEL THE RHYTHM [C] — JINNY
FEEL THE SAME — TRIPLE X
FEEL THE SUNSHINE — Alex REECE
FEEL THE VIBE (TIL THE MORNING COMES) — AXWELL
FEEL TOO BUSY THINKING 'BOUT MY BABY — STEPS
FEEL WHAT YOU WANT — Kristine W
FEELIN' — The LA's
FEELIN' ALRIGHT — EYC
THE FEELIN' (CLAP YOUR HANDS) — RHYTHMATIC JUNKIES
FEELIN' FINE — ULTRABEAT
FEELIN' INSIDE — Bobby BROWN
FEELIN' SO GOOD — Jennifer LOPEZ
FEELIN' THE SAME WAY — Norah JONES
FEELIN' U — SHY FX & T-POWER featuring Kele LE ROC
FEELIN' WAY TOO DAMN GOOD — NICKELBACK
FEELIN' YOU — ALI
THE FEELING [A] — URBAN HYPE
THE FEELING [B] — TIN TIN OUT featuring SWEET TEE
FEELING A MOMENT — FEEDER
FEELING FOR YOU — CASSIUS
FEELING GOOD [A] — Nina SIMONE
FEELING GOOD [A] — HUFF & HERB
FEELING GOOD [A] — MUSE
FEELING IT TOO — 3 JAYS
FEELING SO REAL — MOBY
FEELING THE LOVE — REACTOR
FEELING THIS — BLINK-182
FEELING THIS WAY — CONDUCTOR & The COWBOY
FEELINGS — Morris ALBERT
FEELINGS OF FOREVER — TIFFANY
FEELS GOOD (DON'T WORRY BOUT A THING) — NAUGHTY BY NATURE featuring 3LW
FEELS JUST LIKE IT SHOULD — JAMIROQUAI
(FEELS LIKE) HEAVEN — FICTION FACTORY
FEELS LIKE HEAVEN — URBAN COOKIE COLLECTIVE
FEELS LIKE I'M IN LOVE — Kelly MARIE (80)
FEELS LIKE THE FIRST TIME [A] — FOREIGNER
FEELS LIKE THE FIRST TIME [B] — SINITTA
FEELS LIKE THE RIGHT TIME — SHAKATAK
FEELS SO GOOD [A] — VAN HALEN
FEELS SO GOOD [B] — XSCAPE
FEELS SO GOOD [C] — Lorna B
FEELS SO GOOD [D] — Melanie B
FEELS SO REAL (WON'T LET GO) — Patrice RUSHEN
FEELS SO RIGHT — Victor SIMONELLI presents SOLUTION
FEENIN' — JODECI
FEET UP! — Guy MITCHELL
FELICITY — ORANGE JUICE
FELL IN LOVE WITH A BOY [A] — Joss STONE
FELL IN LOVE WITH A GIRL [A] — The WHITE STRIPES
FELL ON BLACK DAYS — SOUNDGARDEN
FEMALE INTUITION — MAI TAI
FEMALE OF THE SPECIES — SPACE
FERGUS SINGS THE BLUES — DEACON BLUE
FERNANDO — ABBA (76)
FERRIS WHEEL — The EVERLY BROTHERS
FERRY ACROSS THE MERSEY [A] — GERRY and The PACEMAKERS
FERRY 'CROSS THE MERSEY [A] — The CHRISTIANS, Holly JOHNSON, Paul McCARTNEY, Gerry MARSDEN and STOCK AITKEN WATERMAN (89)
FESTIVAL TIME — SAN REMO STRINGS
FEUER FREI — RAMMSTEIN
FEVER [A] — Peggy LEE
FEVER [A] — Helen SHAPIRO
FEVER [A] — McCOYS
FEVER [A] — MADONNA
FEVER [B] — S-J
FEVER [C] — STARSAILOR
FEVER CALLED LOVE — R.H.C.
FEVER FOR THE FLAVA — HOT ACTION COP
FEVER PITCH THE EP — The PRETENDERS, The LA'S, ORLANDO, Neil MacCOLL, Nick HORNBY
FICTION OF LIFE — CHINA DRUM
FIELD OF DREAMS — FLIP & FILL featuring Jo JAMES
FIELDS OF FIRE (400 MILES) — BIG COUNTRY
FIELDS OF GOLD — STING
THE FIELDS OF LOVE — ATB featuring YORK
FIESTA [A] — The POGUES
FIESTA [B] — R KELLY featuring JAY-Z
!FIESTA FATAL! — B-TRIBE
FIFTEEN FEET OF PURE WHITE SNOW — Nick CAVE and The BAD SEEDS
15 MINUTES OF FAME — SHEEP ON DRUGS
15 STEPS (EP) — MONKEY MAFIA
15 WAYS — The FALL
15 YEARS (EP) — LEVELLERS
5TH ANNIVERSARY EP — JUDGE DREAD
A FIFTH OF BEETHOVEN — Walter MURPHY and The BIG APPLE BAND
50/50 — LEMAR
50 FT QUEENIE — P J HARVEY
FIFTY GRAND FOR CHRISTMAS — Paul HOLT
50 TO A £ — The PADDINGTONS
50 WAYS TO LEAVE YOUR LOVER — Paul SIMON
51ST STATE — NEW MODEL ARMY
FIFTY-FOUR — SEA LEVEL
54-46 (WAS MY NUMBER) — ASWAD
59TH STREET BRIDGE SONG (FEELING GROOVY) — HARPERS BIZARRE
57 — Biffy CLYRO
57 CHANNELS (AND NOTHIN' ON) — Bruce SPRINGSTEEN
FIGARO — BROTHERHOOD OF MAN (78)
FIGHT — McKOY
THE FIGHT — Marty WILDE
FIGHT FOR OURSELVES — SPANDAU BALLET
FIGHT FOR YOUR RIGHT (TO PARTY) — NYCC
FIGHT MUSIC — D12
THE FIGHT SONG — MARILYN MANSON
FIGHT TEST — The FLAMING LIPS
FIGHT THE POWER — PUBLIC ENEMY
FIGHT THE YOUTH — FISHBONE
FIGHTER — Christina AGUILERA
FIGHTING FIT — GENE
FIGURE OF EIGHT [A] — Paul McCARTNEY
FIGURE OF 8 [B] — GRID
FIJI — ATLANTIS vs AVATAR
FILL HER UP — GENE
FILL ME IN — Craig DAVID (00)
FILLING UP WITH HEAVEN — HUMAN LEAGUE
A FILM FOR THE FUTURE — IDLEWILD
FILM MAKER — The COOPER TEMPLE CLAUSE
FILMSTAR — SUEDE
FILTHY — SAINT ETIENNE
FILTHY/GORGEOUS — SCISSOR SISTERS
THE FINAL ARREARS — MULL HISTORICAL SOCIETY
THE FINAL COUNTDOWN — EUROPE (86)
FINALLY [A] — Ce Ce PENISTON
FINALLY [B] — KINGS OF TOMORROW featuring Julie McKNIGHT
FINALLY FOUND — HONEYZ
FINCHLEY CENTRAL — NEW VAUDEVILLE BAND
FIND A WAY [A] — COLDCUT featuring QUEEN LATIFAH
FIND A WAY [B] — A TRIBE CALLED QUEST
FIND 'EM, FOOL 'EM, FORGET 'EM — S EXPRESS
FIND ME (ODYSSEY TO ANYOONA) — JAM & SPOON featuring PLAVKA
FIND MY LOVE — FAIRGROUND ATTRACTION
FIND MY WAY BACK HOME — NASHVILLE TEENS
FIND THE ANSWER WITHIN — The BOO RADLEYS
FIND THE COLOUR — FEEDER
FIND THE RIVER — R.E.M.
FIND THE TIME [A] — FIVE STAR
FIND THE TIME (PART ONE) [B] — QUADROPHONIA
FINDERS KEEPERS — CHAIRMEN OF THE BOARD
FINDING OUT TRUE LOVE IS BLIND — LOUIS XIV
FINE DAY [A] — Rolf HARRIS
FINE DAY [B] — KIRSTY HAWKSHAW
FINE LINE — Paul McCARTNEY
FINE TIME [A] — NEW ORDER
FINE TIME [B] — YAZZ
FINER — NIGHTMARES ON WAX
FINER FEELINGS — Kylie MINOGUE
THE FINEST [A] — S.O.S. BAND
THE FINEST [A] — TRUCE
FINEST DREAMS — Richard X featuring KELIS
FINEST WORKSONG — R.E.M.
FINETIME — CAST
THE FINGER OF SUSPICION — Dickie VALENTINE with The STARGAZERS (55)
FINGERS AND THUMBS (COLD SUMMER'S DAY) — ERASURE
FINGERS OF LOVE — CROWDED HOUSE
FINGS AIN'T WOT THEY USED T'BE [A] — Max BYGRAVES
FINGS AIN'T WOT THEY USED T'BE [A] — Russ CONWAY
FINISHED SYMPHONY — HYBRID
FIRE [A] — The Crazy World of Arthur BROWN (68)
FIRE [B] — POINTER SISTERS
FIRE [B] — Bruce SPRINGSTEEN
FIRE [C] — U2
FIRE [D] — SLY and ROBBIE
FIRE [E] — The PRODIGY
FIRE [F] — PRIZNA featuring DEMOLITION MAN
FIRE [G] — SCOOTER
FIRE [H] — Busta RHYMES
FIRE [I] — MOUSSE T
FIRE [J] — LETHAL BIZZLE
FIRE AND RAIN — James TAYLOR
FIRE BRIGADE — The MOVE
FIRE DEPARTMENT — BE YOUR OWN PET
FIRE DOWN BELOW [A] — Jeri SOUTHERN
FIRE DOWN BELOW [A] — Shirley BASSEY
FIRE IN MY HEART — SUPER FURRY ANIMALS
FIRE ISLAND — FIRE ISLAND
FIRE IT UP — Busta RHYMES
FIRE OF LOVE — JUNGLE HIGH with BLUE PEARL
FIRE UP THE SHOESAW — LIONROCK
FIRE WIRE — COSMIC GATE
FIRE WOMAN — The CULT
FIRE WORKS — SIOUXSIE and The BANSHEES
FIREBALL [A] — Don SPENCER
FIREBALL [B] — DEEP PURPLE
FIREFLY — INME
FIRED UP — ELEVATORMAN
FIRED UP! — FUNKY GREEN DOGS
FIREPILE (EP) — THROWING MUSES
FIRES BURNING — RUN TINGS
FIRESTARTER — The PRODIGY (96)
FIREWORKS — ROXETTE
FIREWORKS (EP) — EMBRACE
FIRM BIZ — FIRM featuring Dawn ROBINSON
FIRST ATHEIST TABERNACLE CHOIR — SPITTING IMAGE
FIRST BOY IN THIS TOWN (LOVE SICK) — SCRITTI POLITTI
THE FIRST CUT IS THE DEEPEST [A] — PP ARNOLD
FIRST CUT IS THE DEEPEST [A] — Rod STEWART (77)
THE FIRST CUT IS THE DEEPEST [A] — Sheryl CROW
FIRST DATE — BLINK-182
FIRST DAY [A] — The FUTUREHEADS
FIRST DAY [B] — Timo MAAS
THE FIRST DAY (HORIZON) — MAN WITH NO NAME
FIRST DAY OF MY LIFE [A] — The RASMUS
FIRST DAY OF MY LIFE [B] — BRIGHT EYES
FIRST IMPRESSIONS — The IMPRESSIONS
FIRST IT GIVETH — QUEENS OF THE STONE AGE
1ST MAN IN SPACE — The ALL SEEING I featuring Phil OAKEY
THE FIRST MAN YOU REMEMBER — Michael BALL
THE FIRST NIGHT — MONICA
FIRST OF MAY — The BEE GEES
1ST OF THA MONTH — BONE THUGS-N-HARMONY
FIRST OF THE GANG TO DIE — MORRISSEY
FIRST PICTURE OF YOU — LOTUS EATERS
FIRST TASTE OF LOVE — Ben E KING
THE FIRST THE LAST ETERNITY (TIL THE END) — SNAP! featuring SUMMER
FIRST THING IN THE MORNING — Kiki DEE
THE FIRST TIME [A] — Adam FAITH
THE FIRST TIME [B] — Robin BECK (88)
THE FIRST TIME [C] — SURFACE
FIRST TIME EVER — Joanna LAW
THE FIRST TIME EVER I SAW YOUR FACE [A] — Roberta FLACK
THE FIRST TIME EVER I SAW YOUR FACE [A] — Celine DION
FIRST WE TAKE MANHATTAN — Jennifer WARNES
FISH OUT OF WATER — ONE MINUTE SILENCE
FISHERMAN'S BLUES — The WATERBOYS
FISHING FOR A DREAM — TURIN BRAKES
FIT BUT YOU KNOW IT — The STREETS
5 COLOURS IN HER HAIR — McFLY (04)
FIVE FATHOMS — EVERYTHING BUT THE GIRL
5.15 — The WHO
555 — DELAKOTA
5-5-5 FOR FILMSTARS — DIVE DIVE
5-4-3-2-1 — MANFRED MANN
FIVE GET OVER EXCITED — The HOUSEMARTINS
500 (SHAKE BABY SHAKE) — LUSH
FIVE LITTLE FINGERS — Frankie McBRIDE
FIVE LIVE (EP) — George MICHAEL and QUEEN with Lisa STANSFIELD (93)
5 MILE (THESE ARE THE DAYS) — TURIN BRAKES
FIVE MILES OUT — Mike OLDFIELD
5 MILES TO EMPTY — BROWNSTONE
FIVE MINUTES [A] — The STRANGLERS
5 MINUTES [B] — LIL' MO featuring Missy 'Misdemeanor' ELLIOTT
THE $5.98 EP — GARAGE DAYS RE-REVISITED — METALLICA
5 O'CLOCK — NONCHALANT
5 O'CLOCK WORLD — Julian COPE
5.7.0.5 — CITY BOY
5, 6, 7, 8 — STEPS
5 STEPS — DRU HILL
5000 MINUTES OF PAIN — MINUTEMAN
FIX — BLACKSTREET
FIX MY SINK — DJ SNEAK featuring BEAR WHO?
FIX UP LOOK SHARP — DIZZEE RASCAL
FIX YOU — COLDPLAY
FIXATION — Andy LING
FIXER — VENT 414
FLAGPOLE SITTA — HARVEY DANGER
FLAMBOYANT — PET SHOP BOYS
FLAME — SEBADOH
THE FLAME [A] — ARCADIA
THE FLAME [B] — FINE YOUNG CANNIBALS
THE FLAME STILL BURNS — Jimmy NAIL
THE FLAME TREES OF THIKA — VIDEO SYMPHONIC
FLAMES OF PARADISE — Jennifer RUSH and Elton JOHN

5 February 2000	12 February 2000	19 February 2000	26 February 2000
RISE Gabrielle	RISE Gabrielle	GO LET IT OUT Oasis	PURE SHORES All Saints
THE MAN WHO Travis	THE MAN WHO Travis	RISE Gabrielle	RISE Gabrielle

FLAMING JUNE — BT
FLAMING SWORD — CARE
FLAP YOUR WINGS — NELLY (04)
FLASH [A] — QUEEN
FLASH [A] — QUEEN + VANGUARD
FLASH [B] — BBE
FLASH [B] — BK and Nick SENTIENCE
FLASH [C] — GRIFTERS
FLASHBACK — IMAGINATION
FLASHBACK JACK — ADAMSKI
FLASHDANCE — DEEP DISH
FLASHDANCE ... WHAT A FEELING [A] — Irene CARA
FLASHDANCE ... WHAT A FEELING [A] — BJÖRN AGAIN
THE FLASHER — MISTURA featuring Lloyd MICHELS
FLAT BEAT — MR OIZO (99)
FLATLINERS — NEBULA II
FLAVA [A] — Peter ANDRE (96)
FLAVA [B] — IMAJIN
FLAVA IN YA EAR — Craig MACK
FLAVOUR OF THE OLD SCHOOL — Beverley KNIGHT
FLAVOR OF THE WEAK — AMERICAN HI-FI
FLAWLESS [A] — The ONES
FLAWLESS (GO TO THE CITY) [A] — George MICHAEL
FLEE FLY FLO — FE-M@IL
FLESH [A] — A SPLIT SECOND
FLESH [B] — Jan JOHNSTON
FLESH FOR FANTASY — Billy IDOL
FLESH OF MY FLESH — ORANGE JUICE
FLETCH THEME — Harold FALTERMEYER
FLIGHT OF ICARUS — IRON MAIDEN
FLIGHT 643 — DJ TIESTO
FLIP — Jesse GREEN
FLIP REVERSE — BLAZIN' SQUAD
THE FLIPSIDE — MOLOKO
FLIRT! — Jonathan KING
FLIRTATION WALTZ — Winifred ATWELL
F.L.M. — MEL and KIM
FLOAT ON [A] — The FLOATERS (77)
FLOAT ON [B] — MODEST MOUSE
FLOATATION — GRID
FLOATING — TERRA FIRMA
FLOATING IN THE WIND — HUDSON-FORD
FLOBBADANCE — BILL & BEN
FLOETIC — FLOETRY
FLOODLIT WORLD — ULTRASOUND
THE FLOOR — Johnny GILL
FLOOR-ESSENCE — MAN WITH NO NAME
FLOOR SPACE — OUR HOUSE
THE FLORAL DANCE [A] — The BRIGHOUSE and RASTRICK BRASS BAND
FLORAL DANCE [A] — Terry WOGAN
FLORIBUNDA — MOTHER'S PRIDE
FLOWER DUET (FROM 'LAKMÉ') [A] — Mady MESPLE and Danielle MILLET with the PARIS OPÉRA-COMIQUE ORCHESTRA conducted by Alain LOMBARD
FLOWER DUET [A] — Jonathan PETERS presents LUMINAIRE
FLOWER OF SCOTLAND — SCOTTISH RUGBY TEAM with Ronnie BROWNE
FLOWER OF THE WEST — RUNRIG
FLOWERS [A] — TITIYO
FLOWERS [B] — SWEET FEMALE ATTITUDE
FLOWERS IN DECEMBER — MAZZY STAR
FLOWERS IN THE RAIN — The MOVE
FLOWERS IN THE WINDOW — TRAVIS
FLOWERS OF ROMANCE — PUBLIC IMAGE LTD
FLOWERS ON THE WALL — STATLER BROTHERS
FLOWERZ — Armand VAN HELDEN
FLOWTATION — Vincent DE MOOR
FLOY JOY — The SUPREMES
FLY [A] — SUGAR RAY
FLY [B] — POB featuring DJ Patrick REID
FLY [C] — Mark JOSEPH
FLY [D] — Matt GOSS
THE FLY — U2 (91)
FLY AWAY [A] — HADDAWAY
FLY AWAY [B] — Lenny KRAVITZ (99)
FLY AWAY [C] — Vincent DE MOOR
FLY AWAY (BYE BYE) — EYES CREAM
FLY BI — TEEBONE featuring MC KIE and MC SPARKS
FLY BY II — BLUE
FLY GIRL — QUEEN LATIFAH
FLY LIFE — BASEMENT JAXX
FLY LIKE AN EAGLE — SEAL
FLY ON THE WINGS OF LOVE — XTM & DJ CHUCKY presents ANNIA
FLY ROBIN FLY — SILVER CONVENTION
FLY TO THE ANGELS — SLAUGHTER
FLY TOO HIGH — Janis IAN
FLY WITH ME — COLOURSOUND
FLYING [A] — CAST
FLYING [B] — Bryan ADAMS
FLYING ELVIS — LEILANI
FLYING HIGH [A] — The COMMODORES
FLYING HIGH [B] — FREEEZ
FLYING HIGH [C] — CAPTAIN HOLLYWOOD PROJECT
FLYING MACHINE — Cliff RICHARD
FLYING SAUCER — WEDDING PRESENT
THE FLYING SONG — PQM featuring CICA
FLYING WITHOUT WINGS — WESTLIFE (99)
FLYSWATTER — EELS
FM (NO STATIC AT ALL) — STEELY DAN
FOE-DEE-O-DEE — The RUBETTES
FOG ON THE TYNE (REVISITED) — GAZZA and LINDISFARNE
FOGGY MOUNTAIN BREAKDOWN — Lester FLATT and Earl SCRUGGS
FOGHORN — A
THE FOLK SINGER — Tommy ROE
FOLLOW DA LEADER — NIGEL & MARVIN
FOLLOW ME [A] — JT TAYLOR
FOLLOW ME [B] — ALY-US
FOLLOW ME [C] — ATOMIC KITTEN
FOLLOW ME [D] — UNCLE KRACKER
FOLLOW THAT DREAM (EP) — Elvis PRESLEY
FOLLOW THE LEADER — Eric B and RAKIM
FOLLOW THE LEADERS — KILLING JOKE
FOLLOW THE RULES — LIVIN' JOY
FOLLOW YOU DOWN — GIN BLOSSOMS
FOLLOW YOU FOLLOW ME [A] — GENESIS
FOLLOW YOU FOLLOW ME [A] — Sonny JONES featuring Tara CHASE
FOLLOWED THE WAVES – AUF DER MAUR
FOLLOWING — The BANGLES
THE FOOD CHRISTMAS EP — VARIOUS ARTISTS (Singles and EPs)
FOOD FOR THOUGHT [A] — The BARRON KNIGHTS
FOOD FOR THOUGHT [B] — UB40
FOOL [A] — Elvis PRESLEY
FOOL [B] — Al MATTHEWS
FOOL [C] — MANSUN
FOOL AGAIN — WESTLIFE (00)
A FOOL AM I — Cilla BLACK
FOOL FOR LOVE — RUSSELL
FOOL FOR YOUR LOVING — WHITESNAKE
FOOL (IF YOU THINK IT'S OVER) [A] — Chris REA
FOOL IF YOU THINK IT'S OVER [A] — Elkie BROOKS
A FOOL NEVER LEARNS — Andy WILLIAMS
FOOL NO MORE — S CLUB 8
FOOL NUMBER ONE — Brenda LEE
THE FOOL ON THE HILL — Shirley BASSEY
A FOOL SUCH AS I — Elvis PRESLEY with The JORDANAIRES (59)
FOOL TO CRY — The ROLLING STONES
FOOLED AROUND AND FELL IN LOVE — Elvin BISHOP
FOOLED BY A SMILE — SWING OUT SISTER
FOOLIN' YOURSELF — Paul HARDCASTLE
FOOLISH [A] — ASHANTI
FOOLISH [B] — Tyler JAMES
FOOLISH BEAT — Debbie GIBSON
FOOLISH LITTLE GIRL — SHIRELLES
FOOL'S GOLD — The STONE ROSES
FOOL'S PARADISE — Meli'sa MORGAN
FOOLS RUSH IN [A] — Brook BENTON
FOOLS RUSH IN [A] — Ricky NELSON
FOOT STOMPIN' MUSIC — Hamilton BOHANNON
FOOT TAPPER — The SHADOWS (63)
FOOTLOOSE — Kenny LOGGINS
FOOTPRINT — DISCO CITIZENS
FOOTPRINTS IN THE SNOW — Johnny DUNCAN and The BLUE GRASS BOYS
FOOTSEE — WIGAN'S CHOSEN FEW
FOOTSTEPS [A] — Ronnie CARROLL
FOOTSTEPS [A] — Steve LAWRENCE
FOOTSTEPS [A] — SHOWADDYWADDY
FOOTSTEPS [B] — STILTSKIN
FOOTSTEPS [C] — Daniel O'DONNELL
FOOTSTEPS FOLLOWING ME — Frances NERO
FOR A FEW DOLLARS MORE — SMOKIE
FOR A FRIEND — COMMUNARDS
FOR A PENNY — Pat BOONE
FOR A LIFETIME — ASCENCION featuring Erin LORDAN
FOR ALL THAT YOU WANT — Gary BARLOW
FOR ALL THE COWS — FOO FIGHTERS
FOR ALL TIME — Catherine Zeta JONES
FOR ALL WE KNOW [A] — Nicki FRENCH
FOR ALL WE KNOW [A] — Shirley BASSEY
FOR ALL WE KNOW [A] — The CARPENTERS
FOR AMERICA — RED BOX
FOR AN ANGEL — Paul VAN DYK
FOR BRITAIN ONLY — Alice COOPER
(FOR GOD'S SAKE) GIVE MORE POWER TO THE PEOPLE — CHI-LITES
FOR HER LIGHT — FIELDS OF THE NEPHILIM
FOR LOVE (EP) — LUSH
FOR LOVERS — WOLFMAN featuring Peter DOHERTY
FOR MAMA — Matt MONRO
4 MY PEOPLE — Missy 'Misdemeanor' ELLIOTT
FOR OLD TIME'S SAKE — MILLICAN and NESBITT
FOR ONCE IN MY LIFE [A] — Stevie WONDER
FOR ONCE IN MY LIFE [A] — Dorothy SQUIRES
FOR REAL — TRICKY
FOR SPACIOUS LIES — Norman COOK
FOR SURE — SCOOCH
FOR THE DEAD — GENE
FOR THE GOOD TIMES — Perry COMO
FOR THOSE ABOUT TO ROCK (WE SALUTE YOU) — AC/DC
FOR TOMORROW — BLUR
FOR WHAT IT'S WORTH [A] — OUI 3
FOR WHAT IT'S WORTH [B] — The CARDIGANS
FOR WHAT YOU DREAM OF — BEDROCK
FOR WHOM THE BELL TOLLS [A] — Simon DUPREE and The BIG SOUND
FOR WHOM THE BELL TOLLS [B] — The BEE GEES
FOR YOU [A] — Ricky NELSON
FOR YOU [B] — FARMERS BOYS
FOR YOU [C] — Snowy WHITE
FOR YOU [D] — ELECTRONIC
FOR YOU [E] — STAIND
FOR YOU FOR LOVE — AVERAGE WHITE BAND
FOR YOU I WILL — MONICA
FOR YOU I'LL DO ANYTHING YOU WANT ME TO — Barry WHITE
FOR YOUR BABIES — SIMPLY RED
FOR YOUR BLUE EYES ONLY — Tony HADLEY
FOR YOUR EYES ONLY — Sheena EASTON
FOR YOUR LOVE [A] — The YARDBIRDS
FOR YOUR LOVE [B] — Stevie WONDER
FORBIDDEN CITY — ELECTRONIC
FORBIDDEN COLOURS — David SYLVIAN
FORBIDDEN FRUIT — Paul VAN DYK
FORBIDDEN ZONE — BEDROCK
FORÇA — Nelly FURTADO
THE FORCE BEHIND THE POWER — Diana ROSS
FOREIGN SAND — Roger TAYLOR
FORERUNNER — NATURAL BORN GROOVES
A FOREST — The CURE
FOREST FIRE — Lloyd COLE
FOREVER [A] — Roy WOOD
FOREVER [B] — KISS
FOREVER [C] — DAMAGE
FOREVER [D] — The CHARLATANS
FOREVER [E] — Tina COUSINS
FOREVER [F] — TRINITY-X
FOREVER [G] — N-TRANCE
FOREVER [H] — DEE DEE
FOREVER AND A DAY [A] — BROTHERS IN RHYTHM
FOREVER AND A DAY [B] — STATE ONE
FOREVER AND EVER — SLIK (76)
FOREVER AND EVER, AMEN — Randy TRAVIS
FOREVER AND FOR ALWAYS — Shania TWAIN
FOREVER AS ONE — The VENGABOYS
FOREVER AUTUMN — Justin HAYWARD
FOREVER CAME TODAY — Diana ROSS and The SUPREMES
FOREVER FAILURE — PARADISE LOST
FOREVER FREE — W.A.S.P.
FOREVER GIRL — OTT
FOREVER IN BLUE JEANS — Neil DIAMOND
FOREVER IN LOVE — Kenny G
FOREVER J — Terry HALL
A FOREVER KIND OF LOVE — Bobby VEE
(FOREVER) LIVE AND DIE — ORCHESTRAL MANOEUVRES IN THE DARK
FOREVER LOST — The MAGIC NUMBERS
FOREVER LOVE — Gary BARLOW (96)
FOREVER MAN [A] — Eric CLAPTON
FOREVER MAN (HOW MANY TIMES) [A] — BEATCHUGGERS featuring Eric CLAPTON
FOREVER MORE [A] — Puff JOHNSON
FOREVER MORE [B] — MOLOKO
FOREVER NOW — LEVEL 42
FOREVER REELING — KINESIS
FOREVER TOGETHER — Raven MAIZE
FOREVER YOUNG [A] — Rod STEWART
FOREVER YOUNG [B] — INTERACTIVE
FOREVER YOUNG [C] — 4 VINI featuring Elisabeth TROY
FOREVER YOUR GIRL — Paula ABDUL
FOREVERGREEN — FINITRIBE
FORGET ABOUT THE WORLD — GABRIELLE
FORGET ABOUT TOMORROW — FEEDER
FORGET ABOUT YOU — The MOTORS
FORGET HIM [A] — Bobby RYDELL
FORGET HIM [A] — Billy FURY
FORGET I WAS A G — WHITEHEAD BROS
FORGET ME KNOTS — Roni SIZE
FORGET ME NOT [A] — Eden KANE
FORGET ME NOT [B] — Martha REEVES and The VANDELLAS
FORGET-ME-NOT — Vera LYNN
FORGET ME NOTS [A] — Patrice RUSHEN
FORGET ME NOTS [A] — TONGUE 'N' CHEEK
FORGET MYSELF — ELBOW
FORGIVE ME — Lynden David HALL
FORGIVEN (I FEEL YOUR LOVE) — SPACE BROTHERS
FORGIVENESS — The ENGINEERS
FORGOT ABOUT DRE — DR DRE featuring EMINEM
FORGOTTEN DREAMS [A] — Cyril STAPLETON and his Orchestra
FORGOTTEN DREAMS [A] — Leroy ANDERSON and his POPS CONCERT ORCHESTRA
FORGOTTEN TOWN — The CHRISTIANS
FORMED A BAND — ART BRUT
FORMULAE — JJ72
FORSAKEN DREAMS — DILLINJA
FORT WORTH JAIL — Lonnie DONEGAN
FORTRESS AROUND YOUR HEART — STING
FORTRESS EUROPE — ASIAN DUB FOUNDATION
FORTUNE FADED — RED HOT CHILI PEPPERS
FORTUNES OF WAR — FISH
40 MILES — CONGRESS
FORTY MILES OF BAD ROAD — Duane EDDY and The REBELS
40 YEARS — Paul HARDCASTLE
48 CRASH — Suzi QUATRO
45 R.P.M. — POPPYFIELDS
49 PERCENT — ROYKSOPP
FORWARD THE REVOLUTION — SPIRAL TRIBE
FOUND A CURE — Ultra NATÉ
FOUND LOVE — DOUBLE DEE featuring DANY
FOUND OUT ABOUT YOU — GIN BLOSSOMS
FOUND OUT TOO LATE — 999
FOUND THAT SOUL — MANIC STREET PREACHERS
FOUND YOU — DODGY
FOUNDATION — BEENIE MAN
FOUNTAIN O' YOUTH — CANDYLAND
FOUR BACHARACH AND DAVID SONGS (EP) — DEACON BLUE
FOUR BIG SPEAKERS — WHALE
FOUR FROM TOYAH (EP) — TOYAH
FOUR KICKS — KINGS OF LEON
FOUR LETTER WORD — Kim WILDE
FOUR LITTLE HEELS [A] — The AVONS
FOUR LITTLE HEELS [A] — Brian HYLAND
FOUR MINUTE WARNING — Mark OWEN
4 MORE — DE LA SOUL
FOUR MORE FROM TOYAH (EP) — TOYAH
4 MY PEOPLE — Missy 'Misdemeanor' ELLIOTT
4 PAGE LETTER — AALIYAH
THE 4 PLAY EPS — R KELLY
FOUR SEASONS IN ONE DAY — CROWDED HOUSE
4 SEASONS OF LONELINESS — BOYZ II MEN
FOUR STRONG WINDS — Neil YOUNG
FOUR TO THE FLOOR — STARSAILOR

	4 March 2000	11 March 2000	18 March 2000	25 March 2000
UK No.1 SINGLES	PURE SHORES All Saints	AMERICAN PIE Madonna	DON'T GIVE UP Chicane featuring Bryan Adams	BAG IT UP Geri Halliwell
UK No.1 ALBUMS	RISE Gabrielle	STANDING ON THE SHOULDER OF GIANTS Oasis	THE MAN WHO Travis	THE MAN WHO Travis

4 WORDS (TO CHOKE UPON) — BULLET FOR MY VALENTINE
FOURPLAY (EP) — VARIOUS ARTISTS (Singles and EPs)
FOURTEEN — FORWARD, RUSSIA!
14 HOURS TO SAVE THE EARTH — TOMSKI
FOURTH RENDEZ-VOUS — Jean-Michel JARRE
FOX FORCE FIVE — CHRIS and JAMES
FOX ON THE RUN [A] — MANFRED MANN
FOX ON THE RUN [B] — The SWEET
FOXHOLE — TELEVISION
FOXTROT UNIFORM CHARLIE KILO — The BLOODHOUND GANG
FOXY, FOXY — MOTT THE HOOPLE
'FRAGGLE ROCK' THEME — FRAGGLES
FRAGILE [A] — STING
FRAGILE [A] — Julio IGLESIAS
FRAGILE THING — BIG COUNTRY featuring Eddi READER
FRANCESCA - THAT MADDENING GLARE — SPECIAL NEEDS
THE FRANK SONATA — LONGPIGS
FRANKENSTEIN — Edgar WINTER GROUP
FRANKIE — SISTER SLEDGE (85)
FRANKIE AND JOHNNY [A] — Elvis PRESLEY
FRANKIE AND JOHNNY [A] — Mr Acker BILK and his PARAMOUNT JAZZ BAND
FRANKIE AND JOHNNY [A] — Sam COOKE
FRANTIC — METALLICA
FREAK [A] — Bruce FOXTON
FREAK [B] — SILVERCHAIR
FREAK [C] — STRANGELOVE
FREAK IT! — STUDIO 45
FREAK LIKE ME [A] — Adina HOWARD
FREAK LIKE ME [A] — TRU FAITH & DUB CONSPIRACY
FREAK LIKE ME [A] — SUGABABES (02)
FREAK ME [A] — SILK
FREAK ME [A] — ANOTHER LEVEL (98)
FREAK MODE — The REELISTS
FREAK ON — STONEBRIDGE vs Ultra NATE
FREAK ON A LEASH — KORN
FREAKIN' IT — Will SMITH
FREAKIN' OUT — Graham COXON
FREAKIN' YOU — The JUNGLE BROTHERS
FREAKS — LIVE
FREAKS (LIVE) — MARILLION
THE FREAKS COME OUT — Cevin FISHER
FREAKY BE BEAUTIFUL — MOIST
FREAKYTIME — POINT BREAK
THE FRED EP — VARIOUS ARTISTS (Singles and EPs)
FREDDY KREUGER — REUBEN
FREDERICK — Patti SMITH GROUP
FREE [A] — Deniece WILLIAMS (77)
FREE [A] — Will DOWNING
FREE [A] — Chanté MOORE
FREE [B] — CURIOSITY KILLED THE CAT
FREE [C] — Stevie WONDER
FREE [D] — Ultra NATÉ
FREE [E] — DJ QUICKSILVER
FREE [F] — VAST
FREE [G] — John 'OO' FLEMING
FREE [H] — Claire FREELAND
FREE [I] — MYA
FREE [J] — ESTELLE
FREE [K] — BRIGHT EYES
FREE (EP) — FREE
FREE AS A BIRD — The BEATLES
FREE AT LAST — SIMON
FREE (C'MON) — CATCH
FREE ELECTRIC BAND — Albert HAMMOND
FREE FALLIN' — Tom PETTY and The HEARTBREAKERS
FREE, GAY AND HAPPY — COMING OUT CREW
FREE HUEY — The BOO RADLEYS
FREE (LET IT BE) — STUART
FREE LOVE — Juliet ROBERTS
FREE ME [A] — Roger DALTREY
FREE ME [B] — CAST
FREE ME [C] — EMMA
FREE MY NAME — OCEAN COLOUR SCENE
FREE 'N' EASY — The ALMIGHTY
FREE RANGE — The FALL
FREE SALUTE — LITTLE BARRIE
FREE SATPAL RAM — ASIAN DUB FOUNDATION
FREE SPIRIT — Kim APPLEBY
THE FREE STYLE MEGA-MIX — Bobby BROWN
FREE TO DECIDE — The CRANBERRIES
FREE TO FALL — Deborah HARRY
FREE TO LOVE AGAIN — Suzette CHARLES
FREE WORLD — Kirsty MacCOLL
FREE YOUR BODY — Praga KHAN
FREE YOUR MIND [A] — EN VOGUE
FREE YOUR MIND [B] — SPACE BABY
FREE YOURSELF — UNTOUCHABLES
FREEBASE — TALL PAUL
FREED FROM DESIRE — GALA
FREEDOM [A] — WHAM! (84)
FREEDOM [B] — Alice COOPER
FREEDOM [C] — George MICHAEL
FREEDOM [C] — Robbie WILLIAMS
FREEDOM [D] — A HOMEBOY, a HIPPIE and a FUNKI DREDD
FREEDOM [E] — LONDON BOYS
FREEDOM [F] — Michelle GAYLE
FREEDOM [G] — SHIVA
FREEDOM [H] — Robert MILES featuring Kathy SLEDGE
FREEDOM [I] — ERASURE
FREEDOM (EP) — QFX
FREEDOM COME FREEDOM GO — FORTUNES
FREEDOM FIGHTERS — The MUSIC
FREEDOM GOT AN A.K. — DA LENCH MOB
FREEDOM (MAKE IT FUNKY) — BLACK MAGIC
FREEDOM OVERSPILL — Steve WINWOOD
FREEDOM'S PRISONER — Steve HARLEY and COCKNEY REBEL
FREEEK! — George MICHAEL
FREEFLOATING — Gary CLARK
FREEK 'N YOU — JODECI
FREEK U — BON GARCON
FREELOADER — DRIFTWOOD
FREELOVE — DEPECHE MODE
FREESTYLER — BOMFUNK MC'S
FREET — TATA BOX INHIBITORS
FREEWAY OF LOVE — Aretha FRANKLIN
FREEWHEEL BURNIN' — JUDAS PRIEST
THE FREEZE — SPANDAU BALLET
FREEZE-FRAME — J GEILS BAND
FREEZE THE ATLANTIC — CABLE
FREIGHT TRAIN — Charles McDEVITT SKIFFLE GROUP featuring Nancy WHISKEY
FRENCH DISCO — STEREOLAB
FRENCH FOREIGN LEGION — Frank SINATRA
FRENCH KISS — LIL' LOUIS
FRENCH KISSES — JENTINA
FRENCH KISSIN' IN THE USA — Deborah HARRY
FREQUENCY [A] — RHYTHMATIC
FREQUENCY [B] — ALTERN 8
FRESH [A] — KOOL and The GANG
FRESH! [B] — Gina G
FRIDAY — Daniel BEDINGFIELD
FRIDAY I'M IN LOVE — The CURE
FRIDAY NIGHT (LIVE VERSION) — KIDS FROM 'FAME'
FRIDAY ON MY MIND [A] — The EASYBEATS
FRIDAY ON MY MIND [A] — Gary MOORE
FRIDAY STREET — Paul WELLER
FRIDAY 13TH (EP) — The DAMNED
FRIDAY'S ANGELS — GENERATION X
FRIDAY'S CHILD — Will YOUNG
FRIED MY LITTLE BRAINS — The KILLS
A FRIEND — KRS ONE
FRIEND OF MINE — Kelly PRICE
FRIEND OR FOE — Adam ANT
FRIENDLY PERSUASION [A] — FOUR ACES
FRIENDLY PERSUASION [A] — Pat BOONE
FRIENDLY PRESSURE — JHELISA
FRIENDS [A] — The BEACH BOYS
FRIENDS [B] — ARRIVAL
FRIENDS [C] — SHALAMAR
FRIENDS [D] — Amii STEWART
FRIENDS [E] — Jody WATLEY with Eric B and RAKIM
FRIENDS [F] — TIGER
FRIENDS [G] — HOPE OF THE STATES
THE FRIENDS AGAIN EP — FRIENDS AGAIN
FRIENDS AND NEIGHBOURS — Billy COTTON and his BAND
FRIENDS FOREVER — THUNDERBUGS
FRIENDS IN LOW PLACES — Garth BROOKS
FRIENDS WILL BE FRIENDS — QUEEN
FRIENDSHIP — Sabrina JOHNSTON
FRIGGIN' IN THE RIGGIN' — SEX PISTOLS
FRIGHTENED CITY — The SHADOWS
THE FROG PRINCESS — The DIVINE COMEDY
FROGGY MIX — James BROWN
FROGGY STYLE — NUTTIN' NYCE
FROM A DISTANCE [A] — Bette MIDLER
FROM A DISTANCE [A] — Cliff RICHARD
FROM A JACK TO A KING — Ned MILLER
FROM A LOVER TO A FRIEND — Paul McCARTNEY
FROM A TO H AND BACK AGAIN — SHEEP ON DRUGS
FROM A WINDOW [A] — Billy J KRAMER and The DAKOTAS
FROM A WINDOW [B] — NORTHERN UPROAR
FROM DESPAIR TO WHERE — MANIC STREET PREACHERS
FROM EAST TO WEST — VOYAGE
FROM HEAD TO TOE — Elvis COSTELLO
FROM HERE TO ETERNITY [A] — Giorgio MORODER
FROM HERE TO ETERNITY [B] — IRON MAIDEN
FROM HERE TO ETERNITY [C] — Michael BALL
FROM HERE TO THERE TO YOU — Hank LOCKLIN
FROM ME TO YOU — The BEATLES (63)
FROM NEW YORK TO LA — Patsy GALLANT
FROM NOW ON — Jaki GRAHAM
FROM OUT OF NOWHERE — FAITH NO MORE
FROM RUSH HOUR WITH LOVE — REPUBLICA
FROM RUSSIA WITH LOVE [A] — John BARRY ORCHESTRA
FROM RUSSIA WITH LOVE [A] — Matt MONRO
FROM RUSSIA WITH LOVE [B] — Matt DAREY
FROM THA CHUUUCH TO DA PALACE — SNOOP DOGG
FROM THE BEGINNING — NEW RHODES
FROM THE BENCH AT BELVIDERE — The BOO RADLEYS
FROM THE BOTTOM OF MY HEART — The MOODY BLUES
FROM THE FIRE — FIELDS OF NEPHILIM
FROM THE FLOOR BOARDS UP — Paul WELLER
FROM THE GHETTO — Dread FLIMSTONE and the NEW TONE AGE FAMILY
FROM THE HEART — ANOTHER LEVEL
FROM THE HIP (EP) — Lloyd COLE
FROM THE UNDERWORLD — The HERD
FROM THIS DAY — MACHINE HEAD
FROM THIS MOMENT ON — Shania TWAIN
FRONTIER PSYCHIATRIST — The AVALANCHES
FRONTIN' [A] — PHARRELL WILLIAMS featuring JAY-Z
FRONTIN' [A] — Jamie CULLUM
FROSTY THE SNOWMAN — COCTEAU TWINS
FROZEN — MADONNA (98)
FROZEN HEART — FM
FROZEN METAL HEAD (EP) — BEASTIE BOYS
FROZEN ORANGE JUICE — Peter SARSTEDT
FUCK FOREVER — BABY SHAMBLES
F**K IT (I DON'T WANT YOU BACK) — EAMON (04)
FUCK IT UP — TOWERS OF LONDON
***K THE MILLENNIUM — 2K
FUEL — METALLICA
FU-GEE-LA — The FUGEES
FUGITIVE MOTEL — ELBOW
FULL METAL JACKET (I WANNA BE YOUR DRILL INSTRUCTOR) — Abigail MEAD and Nigel GOULDING
THE FULL MONTY-MONSTER MIX — VARIOUS ARTISTS (Singles and EPs)
FULL OF LIFE (HAPPY NOW) — The WONDER STUFF
FULL MOON — BRANDY
FULL TERM LOVE — Monie LOVE
FULL TIME JOB — Doris DAY and Johnnie RAY
FUN — DA MOB featuring JOCELYN BROWN
FUN DAY — Stevie WONDER
FUN FOR ME — MOLOKO
FUN FUN FUN — STATUS QUO with The BEACH BOYS
THE FUN LOVIN' CRIMINAL — FUN LOVIN' CRIMINALS
THE FUNERAL OF HEARTS — HIM
FUNERAL PYRE — The JAM
THE FUNERAL (SEPTEMBER 25, 1977) — Thuli DUMAKUDE
FUNGI MAMA (BEBOPAFUNKADISCOLYPSO) — Tom BROWNE
FUNK AND DRIVE — ELEVATORMAN
FUNK DAT — SAGAT
FUNK ON AH ROLL — James BROWN
THE FUNK PHENOMENA — Armand VAN HELDEN
FUNK THEORY — ROKOTTO
FUNKATARIUM — JUMP
FUNKDAFIED — DA BRAT
FUNKIN' FOR JAMAICA (N.Y.) — Tom BROWN
FUNKY BROADWAY — Wilson PICKETT
FUNKY COLD MEDINA — Tone LOC
FUNKY DORY — Rachel STEVENS
FUNKY GIBBON — The GOODIES
FUNKY GUITAR — TC
FUNKY JAM — PRIMAL SCREAM
FUNKY LOVE — KAVANA
FUNKY LOVE VIBRATIONS — BASS-O-MATIC
FUNKY MOPED — Jasper CARROTT
FUNKY MUSIC (SHO NUFF TURNS ME ON) — UTAH SAINTS
FUNKY NASSAU — BEGINNING OF THE END
FUNKY PLANET — POWERS THAT BE
FUNKY SENSATION — LADIES CHOICE
FUNKY STREET — Arthur CONLEY
FUNKY TOWN — PSEUDO ECHO
FUNKY WEEKEND — The STYLISTICS
FUNKYTOWN — LIPPS INC
FUNNY ALL OVER — VERNONS GIRLS
FUNNY BREAK (ONE IS ENOUGH) — ORBITAL
FUNNY FAMILIAR FORGOTTEN FEELINGS — Tom JONES
FUNNY FUNNY — The SWEET
FUNNY HOW — AIRHEAD
FUNNY HOW LOVE CAN BE — IVY LEAGUE
FUNNY HOW LOVE IS — FINE YOUNG CANNIBALS
FUNNY HOW TIME FLIES (WHEN YOU'RE HAVING FUN) — Janet JACKSON
FUNNY HOW TIME SLIPS AWAY — Dorothy MOORE
FUNNY WAY OF LAUGHIN' — Burl IVES
FUNTIME — BOY GEORGE
F.U.R.B. — F U RIGHT BACK — FRANKEE (04)
FURIOUS ANGELS — Rob DOUGAN
FURNITURE — FUGAZI
FURNITURE MUSIC — Bill NELSON
FURTHER — LONGVIEW
THE FURTHER ADVENTURES OF NORTH (EP) — VARIOUS ARTISTS (Singles and EPs)
FUTURE — Halo VARGAS
FUTURE LOVE — PRESENCE
FUTURE LOVE (EP) — SEAL
FUTURE MANAGEMENT — Roger TAYLOR
THE FUTURE MUSIC (EP) — LIQUID
THE FUTURE OF THE FUTURE (STAY GOLD) — DEEP DISH with EVERYTHING BUT THE GIRL
FUTURE SHOCK — Herbie HANCOCK
FUTURE SOUND (EP) — PHUTURE ASSASSINS
THE FUTURE'S SO BRIGHT I GOTTA WEAR SHADES — TIMBUK 3
FUZION — PESHAY featuring CO-ORDINATE
FX — A GUY CALLED GERALD
G SPOT — Wayne MARSHALL
GABRIEL — Roy DAVIS Jr featuring Peven EVERETT
GAINESVILLE ROCK CITY — LESS THAN JAKE
GAL WINE — Chaka DEMUS and PLIERS
THE GAL WITH THE YALLER SHOES — Michael HOLLIDAY
GALAXIA — MOONMAN
GALAXIE — BLIND MELON
GALAXY — WAR
GALAXY OF LOVE — CROWN HEIGHTS AFFAIR
GALLOPING HOME — LONDON STRING CHORALE
GALLOWS POLE — Jimmy PAGE and Robert PLANT
GALVANIZE — The CHEMICAL BROTHERS
GALVESTON — Glen CAMPBELL
GALVESTON BAY — Lonnie HILL
GAMBLER — MADONNA
GAMBLIN' BAR ROOM BLUES — The SENSATIONAL ALEX HARVEY BAND
GAMBLIN' MAN — Lonnie DONEGAN and his Skiffle Group (57)
THE GAME [A] — ECHO and The BUNNYMEN
THE GAME [B] — Nichola HOLT
GAME BOY — KWS (92)
THE GAME IS WON — Lucie SILVAS
GAME OF LOVE [A] — Wayne FONTANA and The MINDBENDERS
GAME OF LOVE [B] — Tony HADLEY
THE GAME OF LOVE [C] — SANTANA featuring Michelle BRANCH

1 April 2000	8 April 2000	15 April 2000	22 April 2000
NEVER BE THE SAME AGAIN Melanie C / Lisa 'Left Eye' Lopes	**FOOL AGAIN** Westlife	**FILL ME IN** Craig David	**TOCA'S MIRACLE** Fragma: Vocals by Co Co
SUPERNATURAL Santana	**SUPERNATURAL** Santana	**PLAY** Moby	**PLAY** Moby

29 April 2000	6 May 2000	13 May 2000	20 May 2000
UK No.1 SINGLES			
TOCA'S MIRACLE Fragma: Vocals by Co Co	**BOUND 4 DA RELOAD (CASUALTY)** Oxide & Neutrino	**OOPS! ... I DID IT AGAIN** Britney Spears	**DON'T CALL ME BABY (Re-issue)** Madison Avenue
UK No.1 ALBUMS			
PLAY Moby	**PLAY** Moby	**PLAY** Moby	**RELOAD** Tom Jones

27 May 2000	3 June 2000	10 June 2000	17 June 2000
DAY AND NIGHT Billie Piper	IT FEELS SO GOOD Sonique	IT FEELS SO GOOD Sonique	IT FEELS SO GOOD Sonique
THE GREATEST HITS Whitney Houston	THE GREATEST HITS Whitney Houston	CRUSH Bon Jovi	RELOAD Tom Jones

S Club 7

GOING BACK TO MY HOME TOWN — Hal PAIGE and The WHALERS
GOING BACK TO MY ROOTS [A] — ODYSSEY
GOING BACK TO MY ROOTS [A] — FPI PROJECT
GOING DOWN TO LIVERPOOL — The BANGLES
GOING DOWN TOWN TONIGHT — STATUS QUO
GOING FOR GOLD — SHED SEVEN
GOING FOR THE ONE — YES
GOIN' HOME [A] — The OSMONDS
GOING HOME [B] — TYRREL CORPORATION
GOING HOME (THEME OF 'LOCAL HERO') — Mark KNOPFLER
GOING IN WITH MY EYES OPEN — David SOUL
GOING LEFT RIGHT — DEPARTMENT S
GOING MISSING — MAXIMO PARK
GOING NOWHERE — GABRIELLE
GOING OUT — SUPERGRASS
GOING OUT OF MY HEAD — FATBOY SLIM
GOING OUT WITH GOD — KINKY MACHINE
GOING ROUND — D'BORA
GOING THROUGH THE MOTIONS — HOT CHOCOLATE
GOING TO A GO-GO [A] — The MIRACLES
GOING TO A GO-GO [A] — The SHARONETTES
GOING TO A GO GO [A] — The ROLLING STONES
GOING UNDER — EVANESCENCE
GOING UNDERGROUND [A] — The JAM (80)
GOING UNDERGROUND [A] — BUFFALO TOM
GOING UP THE COUNTRY — CANNED HEAT
GOLD [A] — John STEWART
GOLD [B] — SPANDAU BALLET
GOLD [C] — EAST 17
GOLD [D] — PRINCE
GOLD [E] — Beverley KNIGHT
GOLD DIGGER — Kanye WEST featuring Jamie FOXX
GOLDEN — Jill SCOTT
GOLDEN AGE OF ROCK 'N' ROLL — MOTT THE HOOPLE
GOLDEN BROWN [A] — The STRANGLERS
GOLDEN BROWN [A] — KALEEF
GOLDEN BROWN [A] — OMAR
GOLDEN DAYS — BUCKS FIZZ
GOLDEN GATE BRIDGE — OCEAN COLOUR SCENE
GOLDEN GAZE — Ian BROWN
GOLDEN GREEN — The WONDER STUFF
GOLDEN GUN — SUEDE
THE GOLDEN LADY — The THREE DEGREES
GOLDEN LIGHTS — TWINKLE
THE GOLDEN PATH — The CHEMICAL BROTHERS / The FLAMING LIPS
GOLDEN RETRIEVER — SUPER FURRY ANIMALS
GOLDEN SKIN — SILVER SUN
GOLDEN SLUMBERS - CARRY THAT WEIGHT — TRASH
GOLDEN TOUCH — RAZORLIGHT
GOLDEN YEARS [A] — David BOWIE
GOLDEN YEARS [A] — LOOSE ENDS
THE GOLDEN YEARS (EP) — MOTÖRHEAD
GOLDENBALLS (MR BECKHAM TO YOU) — BELL & SPURLING
GOLDENBOOK — FAMILY CAT
GOLDENEYE — Tina TURNER
GOLDFINGER [A] — Shirley BASSEY
GOLDFINGER [B] — ASH
GOLDRUSH — YELLO
GONE [A] — Shirley BASSEY
GONE [B] — David HOLMES
GONE [C] — The CURE
GONE [D] — 'N SYNC
GONE AWAY — The OFFSPRING
GONE DEAD TRAIN — NAZARETH
GONE GONE GONE [A] — The EVERLY BROTHERS
GONE, GONE, GONE [B] — Johnny MATHIS
GONE TILL NOVEMBER — Wyclef JEAN
GONE TOO SOON — Michael JACKSON
GONE UP IN FLAMES — MORNING RUNNER
GONNA BUILD A MOUNTAIN [A] — Matt MONRO
GONNA BUILD A MOUNTAIN [A] — Sammy DAVIS Jr
GONNA CAPTURE YOUR HEART — BLUE
GONNA CATCH YOU [A] — Lonnie GORDON
GONNA CATCH YOU [A] — The BARKIN BROTHERS featuring Johnnie FIORI
GONNA GET ALONG WITHOUT YA NOW [A] — PATIENCE and PRUDENCE
GONNA GET ALONG WITHOUT YA NOW [A] — Trini LOPEZ
GONNA GET ALONG WITHOUT YOU NOW [A] — Viola WILLS
GONNA GIVE HER ALL THE LOVE I'VE GOT — Jimmy RUFFIN
GONNA MAKE YOU A STAR — David ESSEX (74)
GONNA MAKE YOU AN OFFER YOU CAN'T REFUSE — Jimmy HELMS
GONNA MAKE YOU BLUSH — PAPERDOLLS
GONNA MAKE YOU SWEAT (EVERYBODY DANCE NOW) — C & C MUSIC FACTORY / CLIVILLES & COLE
GONNA WORK IT OUT — HI-GATE
GOO GOO BARABAJAGAL (LOVE IS HOT) — DONOVAN with the Jeff BECK GROUP
GOOD AS GOLD — The BEAUTIFUL SOUTH
GOOD BEAT — DEEE-LITE
GOOD BOYS — BLONDIE
GOOD DANCERS — SLEEPY JACKSON
GOOD DAY — Sean MAGUIRE
GOOD ENOUGH [A] — Bobby BROWN
GOOD ENOUGH [B] — DODGY
GOOD ENOUGH FOR YOU — FREEFALLER
GOOD ENOUGH (LA VACHE) — MILK INCORPORATED
GOOD EVENING FRIENDS — Frankie LAINE and Johnnie RAY
GOOD EVENING PHILADELPHIA — Ricky ROSS
GOOD FEELING — REEF
GOOD FOR ME — Amy GRANT
GOOD FORTUNE — P J HARVEY
GOOD FRIEND — PARIS RED
GOOD FRUIT — HEFNER
GOOD GIRLS — JOE
GOOD GIRLS DON'T — KNACK
GOOD GOD [A] — KORN
GOOD GOD [B] — JFK
GOOD GOLLY MISS MOLLY [A] — LITTLE RICHARD
GOOD GOLLY MISS MOLLY [A] — Jerry Lee LEWIS
GOOD GOLLY MISS MOLLY [A] — SWINGING BLUE JEANS
GOOD GOOD FEELING — ERIC and The GOOD GOOD FEELING
GOOD GRIEF CHRISTINA — CHICORY TIP
A GOOD HEART — Feargal SHARKEY (85)
A GOOD IDEA — SUGAR
GOOD IS GOOD — Sheryl CROW
GOOD LIFE [A] — INNER CITY
GOOD LIFE [B] — E.V.E.
THE GOOD LIFE [A] — Tony BENNETT
THE GOOD LIFE [B] — NEW POWER GENERATION
GOOD LOVE — Meli'sa MORGAN
GOOD LOVE CAN NEVER DIE — Alvin STARDUST
GOOD LOVE REAL LOVE — D'BORA
GOOD LOVER — D'INFLUENCE
GOOD LOVIN' — Regina BELLE
GOOD LOVIN' AIN'T EASY TO COME BY — Marvin GAYE
GOOD LOVIN' GONE BAD — BAD COMPANY
GOOD LUCK — BASEMENT JAXX featuring Lisa KEKAULA
GOOD LUCK CHARM — Elvis PRESLEY with The JORDANAIRES (62)
GOOD MORNING — Leapy LEE
GOOD MORNING BRITAIN — AZTEC CAMERA
GOOD MORNING FREEDOM — BLUE MINK
GOOD MORNING JUDGE — 10cc
GOOD MORNING LITTLE SCHOOLGIRL — The YARDBIRDS
GOOD MORNING STARSHINE — OLIVER
GOOD MORNING SUNSHINE — AQUA
GOOD OLD ARSENAL — ARSENAL FC
GOOD OLD ROCK 'N' ROLL — Dave CLARK FIVE
THE GOOD ONES — The KILLS
GOOD PEOPLE — Jack JOHNSON
GOOD REASON — SEAFOOD
GOOD RHYMES — DA CLICK
GOOD ROCKIN' TONIGHT — MONTROSE
GOOD SIGN — EMILIA
GOOD SONG — BLUR
GOOD SOULS — STARSAILOR
GOOD STUFF [A] — The B-52's
GOOD STUFF [B] — KELIS
GOOD STUFF [C] — CLOR
GOOD SWEET LOVIN' — Louchie LOU and Michie ONE
THE GOOD, THE BAD AND THE UGLY — Hugo MONTENEGRO, his Orchestra and Chorus (68)
GOOD THING [A] — FINE YOUNG CANNIBALS
GOOD THING [B] — ETERNAL
A GOOD THING — SAINT ETIENNE
GOOD THING GOING [A] — Sid OWEN
GOOD THING GOING (WE'VE GOT A GOOD THING GOING) [A] — Sugar MINOTT
GOOD THING GOING [A] — YAZZ
GOOD THINGS — RIVAL SCHOOLS
GOOD TIME [A] — PERAN
GOOD TIME [B] — A
GOOD TIME BABY — Bobby RYDELL
GOOD TIMES [A] — The ANIMALS
GOOD TIMES [B] — CHIC
GOOD TIMES [C] — MATT BIANCO
GOOD TIMES [D] — REID
GOOD TIMES [E] — INXS
GOOD TIMES [F] — Edie BRICKELL and The NEW BOHEMIANS
GOOD TIMES [G] — DREAM FREQUENCY
GOOD TIMES [H] — ED CASE
GOOD TIMES (BETTER TIMES) — Cliff RICHARD
GOOD TIMES GONNA COME — AQUALUNG
GOOD TIMIN' — Jimmy JONES (60)
GOOD TO BE ALIVE — DJ RAP
GOOD 2 GO — TRIPLE EIGHT
GOOD TO GO LOVER — Gwen GUTHRIE
GOOD TRADITION — Tanita TIKARAM
GOOD VIBRATIONS [A] — The BEACH BOYS (66)
GOOD VIBRATIONS [A] — PSYCHIC TV
GOOD VIBRATIONS [A] — Brian WILSON
GOOD VIBRATIONS [B] — MARKY MARK and The FUNKY BUNCH featuring Loleatta HOLLOWAY
GOOD VIBRATIONS [C] — BROTHERS LIKE OUTLAW featuring Alison EVELYN
GOOD WEEKEND — ART BRUT
A GOOD YEAR FOR THE ROSES — Elvis COSTELLO
GOODBYE [A] — Mary HOPKIN
GOODBYE [B] — The SUNDAYS
GOODBYE [C] — AIR SUPPLY
GOODBYE [D] — SPICE GIRLS (98)
GOODBYE [E] — DEF LEPPARD
GOODBYE [F] — The CORAL
A GOODBYE — CAMEO
GOODBYE BABY AND AMEN — LULU
GOODBYE BAD TIMES — Giorgio MORODER
GOODBYE BLUEBIRD — Wayne FONTANA
GOODBYE CIVILIAN — The SKIDS
GOODBYE CRUEL WORLD [A] — James DARREN
GOODBYE CRUEL WORLD [B] — SHAKESPEAR'S SISTER
GOODBYE GIRL [A] — SQUEEZE
GOODBYE GIRL [B] — GO WEST
GOODBYE HEARTBREAK — LIGHTHOUSE FAMILY
GOODBYE IS JUST ANOTHER WORD — The NEW SEEKERS
GOODBYE JIMMY, GOODBYE — Ruby MURRAY
GOODBYE MR MACKENZIE — GOODBYE MR MACKENZIE
GOODBYE MY LOVE [A] — The SEARCHERS
GOODBYE MY LOVE [B] — GLITTER BAND
GOODBYE MY LOVER — James BLUNT
GOODBYE NOTHING TO SAY — The JAVELLS featuring Nosmo KING
GOODBYE SAM HELLO SAMANTHA — Cliff RICHARD
GOODBYE STRANGER [A] — SUPERTRAMP
GOODBYE STRANGER [B] — PEPSI and SHIRLIE
GOODBYE TO LOVE — The CARPENTERS
GOODBYE TO LOVE AGAIN — Maxi PRIEST
GOODBYE TONIGHT — LOSTPROPHETS
GOODBYE YELLOW BRICK ROAD — Elton JOHN
GOODBYE-EE [A] — Peter COOK
GOODBYE-EE [A] — 14-18
GOODBYE'S (THE SADDEST WORD) — Celine DION
GOODGROOVE — Derek B
GOODIES — CIARA featuring Petey PABLO (05)
GOODNESS GRACIOUS ME — Peter SELLERS
GOODNIGHT [A] — Roy ORBISON
GOODNIGHT [B] — BABYBIRD
GOODNIGHT GIRL — WET WET WET (92)
GOODNIGHT GOODNIGHT — HOT HOT HEAT
GOODNIGHT MIDNIGHT — Clodagh RODGERS
GOODNIGHT MOON — SHIVAREE
GOODNIGHT MRS FLINTSTONE — PILTDOWN MEN
GOODNIGHT SAIGON — Billy JOEL
GOODNIGHT SWEET PRINCE — Mr Acker BILK and his PARAMOUNT JAZZ BAND
GOODNIGHT TONIGHT — Paul McCARTNEY
GOODWILL CITY — GOODBYE MR MACKENZIE
GOODY GOODY — Frankie LYMON and The TEENAGERS
GOODY TWO SHOES — Adam ANT (82)
GOOGLE EYE — NASHVILLE TEENS
GORECKI — LAMB
GORGEOUS — GENE LOVES JEZEBEL
GOSP — LWS
GOSPEL OAK (EP) — Sinead O'CONNOR
GOSSIP CALYPSO — Bernard CRIBBINS
GOSSIP FOLKS — Missy ELLIOTT featuring LUDACRIS
GOT A FEELING — Patrick JUVET
GOT A GIRL — The FOUR PREPS
GOT A LITTLE HEARTACHE — Alvin STARDUST
GOT A LOT O' LIVIN' TO DO — Elvis PRESLEY
GOT A LOVE FOR YOU — JOMANDA
GOT A MATCH — Russ CONWAY
GOT FUNK — FUNK JUNKEEZ
GOT IT AT THE DELMAR — SENSELESS THINGS
GOT LOVE TO KILL — JULIETTE and The LICKS
GOT ME A FEELING — Misty OLDLAND
GOT MY MIND MADE UP — INSTANT FUNK
GOT MY MIND SET ON YOU — George HARRISON
GOT MY MOJO WORKING — Jimmy SMITH
GOT MYSELF TOGETHER — The BUCKETHEADS
GOT NO BRAINS — BAD MANNERS
GOT NONE — Robert POST
GOT SOME TEETH — Obie TRICE
GOT THE FEELIN' — FIVE
GOT THE LIFE — KORN
GOT THE TIME — ANTHRAX
GOT 'TIL IT'S GONE — Janet JACKSON
GOT TO BE CERTAIN — Kylie MINOGUE
GOT TO BE FREE — 49ers
GOT TO BE REAL — ERIK
GOT TO BE THERE — Michael JACKSON
GOT TO GET — ROB 'n' RAZ featuring Leila K
GOT TO GET IT [A] — CULTURE BEAT
GOT TO GET IT [B] — SISQO
GOT TO GET UP — Afrika BAMBAATAA
GOT TO GET YOU BACK — Kym MAZELLE
GOT TO GET YOU INTO MY LIFE [A] — Cliff BENNETT and The REBEL ROUSERS
GOT TO GET YOU INTO MY LIFE [A] — EARTH WIND AND FIRE
GOT TO GIVE IT UP [A] — AALIYAH
GOT TO GIVE IT UP (PT.1) [A] — Marvin GAYE
GOT TO GIVE ME LOVE — Dana DAWSON
GOT TO HAVE YOUR LOVE [A] — MANTRONIX
GOT TO HAVE YOUR LOVE [A] — LIBERTY X
GOT TO KEEP ON — COOKIE CREW
GOT TO LOVE SOMEBODY — SISTER SLEDGE
GOT TO RELEASE — SATURATED SOUL featuring MISS BUNTY
GOT UR SELF A ... — NAS
GOT YOU — Pharoahe MONCH
GOT YOU ON MY MIND — Tony BRENT
GOT YOUR MONEY — OL' DIRTY BASTARD featuring KELIS
GOTHAM CITY — R KELLY
GOTTA BE A SIN — Adam ANT
GOTTA BE ... MOVIN' ON UP — PM DAWN
GOTTA BE YOU — 3T
GOTTA CATCH 'EM ALL — 50 GRIND featuring POKEMON ALLSTARS
GOTTA GET A DATE — Frank IFIELD
GOTTA GET AWAY — The OFFSPRING
GOTTA GET IT RIGHT — Lena FIAGBE
GOTTA GET LOOSE — MR and MRS SMITH
GOTTA GET THRU THIS — Daniel BEDINGFIELD (01)
GOTTA GET YOU HOME TONIGHT — Eugene WILDE
GOTTA GETCHA — Jermaine DUPRI
GOTTA GO HOME — BONEY M
GOTTA HAVE HOPE — BLACKOUT

24 June 2000	1 July 2000	8 July 2000	15 July 2000
UK No.1 SINGLES			
YOU SEE THE TROUBLE WITH ME Black Legend	SPINNING AROUND Kylie Minogue	THE REAL SLIM SHADY Eminem	BREATHLESS The Corrs
UK No.1 ALBUMS			
	THE MARSHALL MATHERS LP Eminem	ALONE WITH EVERBODY Richard Ashcroft	THE MARSHALL MATHERS LP Eminem

GOTTA HAVE RAIN — Max BYGRAVES
GOT-TA HAVE SOMETHING IN THE BANK, FRANK — Frankie VAUGHAN and The KAYE SISTERS
GOTTA KEEP PUSHIN' — Z FACTOR
GOTTA KNOW (YOUR NAME) — MALAIKA
GOTTA LOTTA LOVE — ICE-T
GOTTA PULL MYSELF TOGETHER — The NOLANS
GOTTA SEE BABY TONIGHT — Mr Acker BILK and his PARAMOUNT JAZZ BAND
GOTTA SEE JANE — R Dean TAYLOR
GOTTA TELL YOU — Samantha MUMBA
GOURYELLA — GOURYELLA
GOVINDA [A] — RADHA KRISHNA TEMPLE
GOVINDA [B] — KULA SHAKER
GRACE [A] — BAND AKA
GRACE [B] — SUPERGRASS
GRACEADELICA — DARK STAR
GRACELAND — The BIBLE
GRAFFITI — MAXIMO PARK
GRANADA [A] — Frankie LAINE
GRANADA [A] — Frank SINATRA
GRAND COOLIE DAM — Lonnie DONEGAN
GRAND PIANO — MIXMASTER
GRAND UNIFICATION (PART 1) — FIGHTSTAR
GRANDAD — Clive DUNN (71)
GRANDMA'S PARTY — Paul NICHOLAS
GRANDPA'S PARTY — Monie LOVE
GRANITE STATUE — SALAD
GRAPEVYNE — BROWNSTONE
GRATEFUL WHEN YOU'RE DEAD - JERRY WAS THERE — KULA SHAKER
THE GRAVE AND THE CONSTANT — FUN LOVIN' CRIMINALS
GRAVEL PIT — WU-TANG CLAN
GRAVITATE TO ME — The THE
GRAVITY [A] — James BROWN
GRAVITY [B] — EMBRACE
GREASE [A] — Frankie VALLI
GREASE [A] — Craig McLACHLAN
THE GREASE MEGAMIX — John TRAVOLTA and Olivia NEWTON-JOHN
GREASE — THE DREAM MIX — Frankie VALLI, John TRAVOLTA and Olivia NEWTON-JOHN
GREASED LIGHTNIN' — John TRAVOLTA
GREAT BALLS OF FIRE [A] — Jerry Lee LEWIS (58)
GREAT BALLS OF FIRE [A] — TINY TIM
THE GREAT BEYOND — R.E.M.
THE GREAT ESCAPE [A] — ENGLAND SUPPORTERS' BAND
THE GREAT ESCAPE 2000 [A] — ENGLAND SUPPORTERS' BAND
THE GREAT ESCAPE [B] — WE ARE SCIENTISTS
GREAT GOSH A'MIGHTY! (IT'S A MATTER OF TIME) — LITTLE RICHARD
THE GREAT PRETENDER [A] — Jimmy PARKINSON
THE GREAT PRETENDER [A] — Freddie MERCURY
THE GREAT PRETENDER [A] — The PLATTERS
THE GREAT ROCK 'N' ROLL SWINDLE — SEX PISTOLS
THE GREAT SNOWMAN — Bob LUMAN
THE GREAT SONG OF INDIFFERENCE — Bob GELDOF
THE GREAT TEST — HUNDRED REASONS
GREAT THINGS — ECHOBELLY
THE GREAT TRAIN ROBBERY — BLACK UHURU
GREATER LOVE — SOUNDMAN and Don LLOYDIE with Elisabeth TROY
THE GREATEST COCKNEY RIP-OFF — COCKNEY REJECTS
GREATEST DAY — Beverley KNIGHT
THE GREATEST FLAME — RUNRIG
THE GREATEST HIGH — HURRICANE #1
THE GREATEST LOVE OF ALL [A] — George BENSON
GREATEST LOVE OF ALL [A] — Whitney HOUSTON
THE GREATEST LOVE YOU'LL NEVER KNOW — Lutricia McNEAL
THE GREATEST ROMANCE EVER SOLD — PRINCE
THE GREATEST SHOW ON EARTH — STRANGELOVE
THE GREATNESS AND PERFECTION OF LOVE — Julian COPE
GREECE 2000 — THREE DRIVES
GREED — Laurent GARNIER
GREEDY FLY — BUSH
THE GREEDY UGLY PEOPLE — HEFNER
GREEN AND GREY — NEW MODEL ARMY
THE GREEN DOOR [A] — Frankie VAUGHAN
THE GREEN DOOR [A] — Jim LOWE
GREEN DOOR [A] — Glen MASON
GREEN DOOR [A] — Shakin' STEVENS (81)
GREEN FIELDS [A] — The BEVERLEY SISTERS
GREEN FIELDS [A] — UNIT FOUR PLUS TWO
GREEN, GREEN GRASS OF HOME [A] — Tom JONES (66)
GREEN GREEN GRASS OF HOME [A] — Elvis PRESLEY
GREEN JEANS — FLEE-REKKERS
THE GREEN LEAVES OF SUMMER — Kenny BALL and his JAZZMEN
GREEN LIGHT — Cliff RICHARD
THE GREEN MAN— SHUT UP AND DANCE
THE GREEN MANALISHI (WITH THE TWO-PRONG CROWN) — FLEETWOOD MAC
GREEN ONIONS — BOOKER T and The MG's
GREEN RIVER — CREEDENCE CLEARWATER REVIVAL
GREEN SHIRT — Elvis COSTELLO
GREEN STREET GREEN — NEW VAUDEVILLE BAND
GREEN TAMBOURINE [A] — LEMON PIPERS
GREEN TAMBOURINE [A] — SUNDRAGON
GREEN TINTED SIXTIES MIND — MR BIG
GREENBACK DOLLAR — Charles McDEVITT SKIFFLE GROUP featuring Nancy WHISKEY
GREENBANK DRIVE — The CHRISTIANS
GREENFIELDS — The BROTHERS FOUR
GREETINGS TO THE NEW BRUNETTE — Billy BRAGG with Johnny MARR and Kirsty MacCOLL
GREY DAY — MADNESS
GRIEF NEVER GROWS OLD — ONE WORLD PROJECT
GRIMLY FIENDISH — The DAMNED
GRIND — ALICE IN CHAINS
GRIND WITH ME — PRETTY RICKY
GRIP '89 (GET A) GRIP (ON YOURSELF) — The STRANGLERS
GRITTY SHAKER — David HOLMES
THE GROOVE — Rodney FRANKLIN
GROOVE BABY GROOVE (EP) — STARGAZERS
GROOVE IS IN THE HEART — DEEE-LITE
THE GROOVE LINE — HEATWAVE
GROOVE MACHINE — MARVIN and TAMARA
GROOVE OF LOVE — E.V.E.
GROOVE THANG — ZHANE
GROOVE TO MOVE — CHANNEL X
GROOVEBIRD — NATURAL BORN GROOVES
GROOVEJET (IF THIS AIN'T LOVE) — SPILLER (00)
GROOVELINE — BLOCKSTER
THE GROOVER — T. REX
GROOVIN' [A] — YOUNG RASCALS
GROOVIN' [A] — WAR
GROOVIN' [A] — Pato BANTON
GROOVIN' IN THE MIDNIGHT — Maxi PRIEST
GROOVIN' (THAT'S WHAT WE'RE DOIN') — S.O.S. BAND
GROOVIN' WITH MR BLOE — MR BLOE
GROOVY BABY — MICROBE
GROOVY BEAT — D.O.P.
GROOVY FEELING — FLUKE
A GROOVY KIND OF LOVE [A] — The MINDBENDERS
A GROOVY KIND OF LOVE [A] — Les GRAY
A GROOVY KIND OF LOVE [A] — Phil COLLINS (88)
THE GROOVY THANG — MINIMAL FUNK 2
GROOVY TRAIN — The FARM
THE GROUNDBREAKER — FALLACY & FUSION
GROUND LEVEL — STEREO MC's
GROUNDED — MY VITRIOL
GROUPIE GIRL — Tony Joe WHITE
GROWING ON ME — The DARKNESS
THE GRUDGE — MORTIIS
G.T.O. — SINITTA
GUAGLIONE — Perez PRADO
GUANTANAMERA [A] — SANDPIPERS
GUANTANAMERA [A] — The FUGEES
GUARANTEED — LEVEL 42
GUARDIAN ANGEL — Nino DE ANGELO
GUARDIANS OF THE LAND — George BOWYER
GUDBUY T'JANE — SLADE
GUDVIBE — TINMAN
GUERRILLA FUNK — PARIS
GUERRILLA RADIO — RAGE AGAINST THE MACHINE
GUESS I WAS A FOOL — ANOTHER LEVEL
GUESS WHO'S BACK — RAKIM
GUESS YOU DIDN'T LOVE ME — Terri WALKER
GUIDING STAR — CAST
GUILTY [A] — Jim REEVES
GUILTY [B] — PEARLS
GUILTY [C] — Mike OLDFIELD
GUILTY [D] — Barbra STREISAND
GUILTY [E] — CLASSIX NOUVEAUX
GUILTY [F] — Paul HARDCASTLE
GUILTY [G] — YARBROUGH and PEOPLES
GUILTY [H] — BLUE
GUILTY [I] — The RASMUS
GUILTY CONSCIENCE — EMINEM featuring DR. DRE
GUILTY OF LOVE — WHITESNAKE
GUITAR BOOGIE SHUFFLE — Bert WEEDON
GUITAR DATE — The 5.6.7.8'S
GUITAR MAN [A] — Elvis PRESLEY
THE GUITAR MAN [B] — BREAD
GUITAR TANGO — The SHADOWS
GUITARRA G — BANDA SONARA
GUN LAW — KANE GANG
GUNATANAMO — OUTLANDISH
GUNMAN — 187 LOCKDOWN
GUNS AT DAWN — DJ BARON featuring PENDULUM
GUNS DON'T KILL PEOPLE, RAPPERS DO — GOLDIE LOOKIN CHAIN
GUNS FOR HIRE — AC/DC
GUNS OF NAVARONE — SKATALITES
GUNSLINGER — Frankie LAINE
GUNZ AND PIANOZ — BASS BOYZ
GURNEY SLADE — Max HARRIS
THE GUSH — RAGING SPEEDHORN
GYM AND TONIC — SPACEDUST (98)
GYPSY — FLEETWOOD MAC
GYPSY BEAT — PACKABEATS
GYPSY BOY, GYPSY GIRL — SHARADA HOUSE GANG
GYPSY EYES — The Jimi HENDRIX EXPERIENCE
GYPSY ROAD — CINDERELLA
GYPSY ROADHOG — SLADE
GYPSY ROVER — HIGHWAYMEN
GYPSY WOMAN [A] — Brian HYLAND
GYPSY WOMAN [B] — Crystal WATERS
GYPSYS, TRAMPS AND THIEVES — CHER
HA CHA CHA (FUNKTION) — BRASS CONSTRUCTION
HA HA SAID THE CLOWN — MANFRED MANN
HAD TO BE — Cliff RICHARD and Olivia NEWTON-JOHN
HAIL CAESAR — AC/DC
HAIL HAIL ROCK 'N' ROLL — Garland JEFFREYS
HAIL MARY — MAKAVELI
HAITIAN DIVORCE — STEELY DAN
HALCYON — CHICANE
HALE BOPP — DER DRITTE RAUM
HALEY'S GOLDEN MEDLEY — Bill HALEY and his COMETS
HALF A BOY AND HALF A MAN — Nick LOWE
HALF A HEART — H & CLAIRE
HALF A MINUTE — MATT BIANCO
HALF AS MUCH — Rosemary CLOONEY
HALF LIGHT — ATHLETE
HALF MAN HALF MACHINE — GOLDIE LOOKIN CHAIN
HALF OF MY HEART — Emile FORD and The CHECKMATES
HALF ON A BABY — R KELLY
HALF THE DAY'S GONE AND WE HAVEN'T EARNT A PENNY — Kenny LYNCH
HALF THE MAN — JAMIROQUAI
HALF THE WORLD — Belinda CARLISLE
HALFWAY AROUND THE WORLD — A*TEENS
HALFWAY DOWN THE STAIRS — The MUPPETS
HALFWAY HOTEL — VOYAGER
HALFWAY TO HEAVEN — EUROPE
HALFWAY TO PARADISE — Billy FURY
HALFWAY UP HALFWAY DOWN — Dennis BROWN
HALLELUJAH — MILK AND HONEY featuring Gali ATARI
HALLELUJAH DAY — The JACKSON FIVE
HALLELUJAH FREEDOM — Junior CAMPBELL
HALLELUJAH I LOVE HER SO [A] — Dick JORDAN
HALLELUJAH I LOVE HER SO [A] — Eddie COCHRAN
HALLELUIAH MAN — LOVE AND MONEY
HALLELUJAH '92 — INNER CITY
HALLO SPACEBOY — David BOWIE
HALLOWED BE THY NAME (LIVE) — IRON MAIDEN
HALLS OF ILLUSION — INSANE CLOWN POSSE
HALO [A] — TEXAS
HALO [B] — SOIL
(HAMMER HAMMER) THEY PUT ME IN THE MIX — HAMMER
HAMMER HORROR — Kate BUSH
HAMMER TO FALL — QUEEN
HAMMER TO THE HEART — The TAMPERER featuring MAYA
HAND A HANDKERCHIEF TO HELEN — Susan MAUGHAN
HAND HELD IN BLACK AND WHITE — DOLLAR
HAND IN GLOVE — Sandie SHAW
HAND IN HAND — GRACE
HAND IN MY POCKET — Alanis MORISSETTE
HAND IN YOUR HEAD — MONEY MARK
HAND OF THE DEAD BODY — SCARFACE featuring ICE CUBE
HAND ON MY HEART — SHRIEKBACK
HAND ON YOUR HEART — Kylie MINOGUE (89)
THE HAND THAT FEEDS — NINE INCH NAILS
HANDBAGS AND GLADRAGS [A] — Chris FARLOWE
HANDBAGS AND GLADRAGS [A] — STEREOPHONICS
HANDFUL OF PROMISES — BIG FUN
HANDFUL OF SONGS — Tommy STEELE
HANDLE WITH CARE — TRAVELING WILBURYS
HANDS — JEWEL
HANDS ACROSS THE OCEAN — The MISSION
HANDS AROUND MY THROAT — DEATH IN VEGAS
HANDS CLEAN — Alanis MORISSETTE
HANDS DOWN — DASHBOARD CONFESSIONAL
HANDS OFF — SHE'S MINE — The BEAT
HANDS TO HEAVEN — BREATHE
HANDS UP [A] — CLUBZONE
HANDS UP [B] — TREVOR & SIMON
HANDS UP (4 LOVERS) — RIGHT SAID FRED
HANDS UP (GIVE ME YOUR HEART) — OTTAWAN
HANDS UP! HANDS UP! — ZIG and ZAG
HANDY MAN [A] — Jimmy JONES
HANDY MAN [A] — Del SHANNON
HANG 'EM HIGH — Hugo MONTENEGRO
HANG IN LONG ENOUGH — Phil COLLINS
HANG MYSELF ON YOU — The CANDYSKINS
HANG ON IN THERE BABY [A] — Johnny BRISTOL
HANG ON IN THERE BABY [A] — CURIOSITY
HANG ON NOW — KAJAGOOGOO
HANG ON SLOOPY [A] — The McCOYS
HANG ON SLOOPY [A] — The SANDPIPERS
HANG ON TO A DREAM — Tim HARDIN
HANG ON TO YOUR LOVE — Jason DONOVAN
HANG TOGETHER — ODYSSEY
HANG YOUR HEAD — DEACON BLUE
HANGAR 18 — MEGADETH
HANGIN' — CHIC
HANGIN' ON A STRING — LOOSE ENDS
HANGIN' OUT — KOOL and The GANG
HANGIN' TOUGH — NEW KIDS ON THE BLOCK (90)
HANGINAROUND — COUNTING CROWS
HANGING AROUND [A] — Hazel O'CONNOR
HANGING AROUND [B] — ME ME ME
HANGING AROUND [C] — The CARDIGANS
HANGING AROUND [D] — Gemma HAYES
HANGING AROUND [E] — The POLYPHONIC SPREE
HANGING AROUND WITH THE BIG BOYS — BLOOMSBURY SET
HANGING BY A MOMENT — LIFEHOUSE
HANGING GARDEN — The CURE
HANGING ON THE TELEPHONE — BLONDIE
HANGOVER — Betty BOO
HANKY PANKY [A] — Tommy JAMES and The SHONDELLS
HANKY PANKY [B] — MADONNA
HANNA HANNA — CHINA CRISIS
HAPPENIN' ALL OVER AGAIN [A] — Lonnie GORDON

19 August 2000	26 August 2000	2 September 2000	9 September 2000
UK No.1 SINGLES			
I TURN TO YOU Melanie C	GROOVEJET (IF THIS AIN'T LOVE) Spiller	MUSIC Madonna	TAKE ON ME a1
UK No.1 ALBUMS			
…AN …eating	BORN TO DO IT Craig David	BORN TO DO IT Craig David	SING WHEN YOU'RE WINNING Robbie Williams

HEART OF GLASS [A] — BLONDIE (79)
HEART OF GLASS [A] — ASSOCIATES
HEART OF GOLD [A] — Neil YOUNG
HEART OF GOLD [B] — JOHNNY HATES JAZZ
HEART OF GOLD [C] — FORCE & STYLES featuring Kelly LLORENNA
HEART OF GOLD [C] — Kelly LLORENNA
HEART OF LOTHIAN — MARILLION
THE HEART OF ROCK AND ROLL — Huey LEWIS and The NEWS
HEART OF SOUL — The CULT
HEART OF STONE [A] — KENNY
HEART OF STONE [B] — Suzi QUATRO
HEART OF STONE [C] — BUCKS FIZZ
HEART OF STONE [C] — CHER
HEART OF STONE [D] — Dave STEWART
HEART OF THE SUN — RED BOX
HEART OF THE WORLD — BIG COUNTRY
HEART ON MY SLEEVE — GALLAGHER and LYLE
HEART OVER MIND — Kim WILDE
HEART (STOP BEATING IN TIME) — Leo SAYER
HEART USER — Cliff RICHARD
HEARTACHE [A] — Roy ORBISON
HEARTACHE [B] — GENE LOVES JEZEBEL
HEARTACHE [C] — PEPSI and SHIRLIE
HEARTACHE ALL OVER THE WORLD — Elton JOHN
HEARTACHE AVENUE — MAISONETTES
HEARTACHE TONIGHT — EAGLES
HEARTACHES [A] — Patsy CLINE
HEARTACHES [A] — Vince HILL
HEARTACHES BY THE NUMBER — Guy MITCHELL
HEARTBEAT [A] — Ruby MURRAY
HEARTBEAT [B] — Buddy HOLLY
HEARTBEAT [B] — ENGLAND SISTERS
HEARTBEAT [B] — SHOWADDYWADDY
HEARTBEAT [B] — Nick BERRY
HEARTBEAT [B] — HEARTBEAT COUNTRY
HEARTBEAT [C] — Sammy HAGAR
HEARTBEAT [D] — Tippa IRIE
HEARTBEAT [E] — Don JOHNSON
HEARTBEAT [F] — SEDUCTION
HEARTBEAT [G] — GRID
HEARTBEAT [H] — Jimmy SOMERVILLE
HEARTBEAT [I] — KRS ONE
HEARTBEAT [J] — STEPS (99)
HEARTBEAT [K] — ANNIE
A HEARTBEAT AWAY — McGANNS
HEARTBEAT (TAINAI KAIKI II) RETURNING TO THE WOMB — David SYLVIAN
HEARTBEATZ — STYLES & BREEZE featuring Karen DANZIG
HEARTBREAK — MRS WOOD featuring Eve GALLAGHER
HEARTBREAK HOTEL [A] — Elvis PRESLEY
HEARTBREAK HOTEL [A] — Stan FREBERG
HEARTBREAK HOTEL [B] — The JACKSONS
HEARTBREAK HOTEL [C] — Whitney HOUSTON featuring Faith EVANS and Kelly PRICE
HEARTBREAK RADIO — Roy ORBISON
HEARTBREAK STATION — CINDERELLA
HEARTBREAK STROLL — The RAVEONETTES
HEARTBREAKER [A] — Dionne WARWICK
HEARTBREAKER [B] — MUSICAL YOUTH
HEARTBREAKER [C] — COLOR ME BADD
HEARTBREAKER [D] — Mariah CAREY featuring JAY-Z
HEARTBREAKER [E] — The GLITTERATI
HEARTBROKE AND BUSTED — MAGNUM
HEARTHAMMER (EP) — RUNRIG
HEARTLAND — The THE
THE HEARTLESS THEME AKA "THE SUPERGLUE RIDDIM" — HEARTLESS CREW
HEARTLIGHT — Neil DIAMOND
HEARTLINE — Robin GEORGE
THE HEART'S FILTHY LESSON — David BOWIE
THE HEART'S LONE DESIRE — Matthew MARSDEN
HEARTS ON FIRE [A] — Sam HARRIS
HEARTS ON FIRE [B] — Bryan ADAMS
HEART-SHAPED BOX — NIRVANA
HEARTSONG — Gordon GILTRAP
HEARTSPARK DOLLARSIGN — EVERCLEAR
THE HEAT IS ON [A] — Agnetha FALTSKOG
THE HEAT IS ON [B] — Glenn FREY

HEAT IT UP — TWO MEN, A DRUM MACHINE AND A TRUMPET
HEAT OF THE BEAT — Roy AYERS
HEAT OF THE MOMENT — ASIA
HEAT OF THE NIGHT — Bryan ADAMS
HEATHER HONEY — Tommy ROE
HEATSEEKER — AC/DC
HEAVEN [A] — Bryan ADAMS
HEAVEN [A] — DJ SAMMY and YANOU (02)
HEAVEN [B] — TWO PEOPLE
HEAVEN [C] — CHIMES
HEAVEN [D] — Chris REA
HEAVEN [E] — TIGERTAILZ
HEAVEN [F] — WHYCLIFFE
HEAVEN [G] — FITS OF GLOOM
HEAVEN [H] — Sarah WASHINGTON
HEAVEN [I] — KINANE
HEAVEN [J] — PSYCHEDELIC FURS
HEAVEN [K] — SOLO U.S.
HEAVEN & EARTH [A] — RED
HEAVEN AND EARTH [B] — POP!
HEAVEN AND HELL, THIRD MOVEMENT (THEME FROM THE BBC-TV SERIES 'THE COSMOS') — VANGELIS
HEAVEN BESIDE YOU — ALICE IN CHAINS
HEAVEN CAN WAIT — Paul YOUNG
HEAVEN FOR EVERYONE — QUEEN
HEAVEN GIVE ME WORDS — PROPAGANDA
HEAVEN HELP — Lenny KRAVITZ
HEAVEN HELP ME — Deon ESTUS
HEAVEN HELP MY HEART — Tina ARENA
HEAVEN HELP US ALL — Stevie WONDER
THE HEAVEN I NEED — The THREE DEGREES
HEAVEN IN MY HANDS — LEVEL 42
HEAVEN IS — DEF LEPPARD
HEAVEN IS A HALFPIPE — OPM
HEAVEN IS A PLACE ON EARTH [A] — Belinda CARLISLE (88)
HEAVEN IS A PLACE ON EARTH [A] — SODA CLUB featuring Hannah ALETHEA
HEAVEN IS CLOSER (FEELS LIKE HEAVEN) — DARIO G
HEAVEN IS HERE — Julie FELIX
HEAVEN IS IN THE BACK SEAT OF MY CADILLAC — HOT CHOCOLATE
HEAVEN IS MY WOMAN'S LOVE — Val DOONICAN
HEAVEN IS WAITING — DANSE SOCIETY
HEAVEN KNOWS [A] — Donna SUMMER
HEAVEN KNOWS [B] — Jaki GRAHAM
HEAVEN KNOWS [B] — Lalah HATHAWAY
HEAVEN KNOWS [C] — Robert PLANT
HEAVEN KNOWS [D] — COOL DOWN ZONE
HEAVEN KNOWS [E] — Luther VANDROSS
HEAVEN KNOWS [F] — SQUEEZE
HEAVEN KNOWS - DEEP DEEP DOWN — Angel MORAES
HEAVEN KNOWS I'M MISERABLE NOW — The SMITHS
HEAVEN MUST BE MISSING AN ANGEL [A] — TAVARES
HEAVEN MUST BE MISSING AN ANGEL [A] — WORLDS APART
HEAVEN MUST HAVE SENT YOU — ELGINS
HEAVEN MUST HAVE SENT YOU BACK — CICERO
HEAVEN ON EARTH — SPELLBOUND
HEAVEN ON THE 7TH FLOOR — Paul NICHOLAS
HEAVEN OR HELL — The STRANGLERS
HEAVEN SCENT — BEDROCK
HEAVEN SENT [A] — Paul HAIG
HEAVEN SENT [B] — INXS
HEAVEN SENT [C] — M1
HEAVEN WILL COME — SPACE BROTHERS
HEAVENLY — SHOWADDYWADDY
HEAVEN'S EARTH — DELERIUM
HEAVEN'S HERE — Holly JOHNSON
HEAVEN'S ON FIRE — KISS
HEAVEN'S WHAT I FEEL — Gloria ESTEFAN
HEAVY FUEL — DIRE STRAITS
HEAVY MAKES YOU HAPPY — Bobby BLOOM
HEAVY ON MY HEART — ANASTACIA
HEAVY VIBES — MONTANA SEXTET
HEDONISM (JUST BECAUSE YOU FEEL GOOD) — SKUNK ANANSIE
HELEN WHEELS — Paul McCARTNEY
HELENA — MY CHEMICAL ROMANCE
HELICOPTER — BLOC PARTY

HELICOPTER TUNE — DEEP BLUE
HELIOPOLIS BY NIGHT — ABERFELDY
HELIUM — DALLAS SUPERSTARS
HELL HATH NO FURY — Frankie LAINE
HE'LL HAVE TO GO [A] — Jim REEVES
HE'LL HAVE TO GO [A] — Bryan FERRY
HE'LL HAVE TO STAY — Jeanne BLACK
HELL RAISER — The SWEET
HELL YEAH — GINUWINE
THE HELL EP — TRICKY vs the GRAVEDIGGAZ
THE HELL SONG — SUM 41
HELLA GOOD — NO DOUBT
HELLBOUND — TYGERS OF PAN TANG
HELLO [A] — Lionel RICHIE (84)
HELLO [A] — Jhay PALMER featuring MC IMAGE
HELLO [B] — The BELOVED
HELLO AGAIN — Neil DIAMOND
HELLO AMERICA — DEF LEPPARD
HELLO BUDDY — The TREMELOES
HELLO DARLIN — Fuzz TOWNSHEND
HELLO DARLING — Tippa IRIE
HELLO DOLLY! [A] — The BACHELORS
HELLO DOLLY! [A] — Frank SINATRA
HELLO DOLLY! [A] — Frankie VAUGHAN
HELLO DOLLY! [A] — Kenny BALL and his JAZZMEN
HELLO DOLLY! [A] — Louis ARMSTRONG
HELLO, GOODBYE — The BEATLES (67)
HELLO HAPPINESS — The DRIFTERS
HELLO HEARTACHE GOODBYE LOVE — Little Peggy MARCH
HELLO HELLO I'M BACK AGAIN — Gary GLITTER
HELLO HONKY TONKS (ROCK YOUR BODY) — PIZZAMAN
HELLO HOW ARE YOU — The EASYBEATS
HELLO HURRAY — Alice COOPER
HELLO I AM YOUR HEART — Bette BRIGHT
HELLO I LOVE YOU — The DOORS
HELLO? IS THIS THING ON? — !!! (CHK CHK CHK)
HELLO JOSEPHINE — Wayne FONTANA and The MINDBENDERS
HELLO LITTLE GIRL — The FOURMOST
HELLO MARY LOU — Ricky NELSON
HELLO MUDDAH HELLO FADDAH — Allan SHERMAN
HELLO STRANGER — Yvonne ELLIMAN
HELLO SUMMERTIME — Bobby GOLDSBORO
HELLO SUNSHINE — SUPER FURRY ANIMALS
HELLO SUZIE — AMEN CORNER
HELLO, THIS IS JOANNIE (THE TELEPHONE ANSWERING MACHINE SONG) — Paul EVANS
HELLO TIGER — URUSEI YATSURA
HELLO (TURN YOUR RADIO ON) — SHAKESPEAR'S SISTER
HELLO WORLD [A] — The TREMELOES
HELLO WORLD [B] — SEA FRUIT
HELLO YOUNG LOVERS — Paul ANKA
HELLRAISER — Anne SAVAGE
HELL'S PARTY — GLAM
HELP! [A] — The BEATLES (65)
HELP [A] — Tina TURNER
HELP [A] — BANANARAMA
HELP (EP) — VARIOUS ARTISTS (Singles and EPs)
HELP, GET ME SOME HELP! — OTTAWAN
HELP! I'M A FISH — LITTLE TREES
HELP IT ALONG — Cliff RICHARD
HELP ME [A] — Timo MAAS featuring KELIS
HELP ME [B] — Nick CARTER
HELP ME FIND A WAY TO YOUR HEART — Daryl HALL
HELP ME GIRL — The ANIMALS
HELP ME MAKE IT — HUFF AND PUFF
HELP ME MAKE IT THROUGH THE NIGHT [A] — Gladys KNIGHT and The PIPS
HELP ME MAKE IT THROUGH THE NIGHT [A] — John HOLT
HELP ME MAMA — LEMONESCENT
HELP ME RHONDA — The BEACH BOYS
HELP MY FRIEND — SLO-MOSHUN
HELP THE AGED — PULP
HELP YOURSELF [A] — Tom JONES
HELP YOURSELF [A] — Tony FERRINO
HELP YOURSELF [B] — Julian LENNON
HELP YOURSELF [C] — Amy WINEHOUSE
HELPLESS — Tracey ULLMAN
HELULE HELULE — The TREMELOES
HELYOM HALIB — CAPPELLA

HENRY LEE — Nick CAVE and The BAD SEEDS and P J HARVEY
HENRY VIII SUITE (EP) — EARLY MUSIC CONSORT directed by David MUNROW
HER — GUY
HER ROYAL MAJESTY — James DARREN
HERCULES — Frankie VAUGHAN
HERE — LUSCIOUS JACKSON
HERE AND NOW [A] — Luther VANDROSS
HERE AND NOW [B] — DEL AMITRI
HERE AND NOW [C] — STEPS
HERE COME THE GOOD TIMES — A HOUSE
HERE COMES MY BABY — The TREMELOES
HERE COMES SUMMER [A] — Jerry KELLER (59)
HERE COMES SUMMER [A] — Dave CLARK FIVE
HERE COMES THAT FEELING — Brenda LEE
HERE COMES THAT SOUND — Simon HARRIS
HERE COMES THE BIG RUSH — ECHOBELLY
HERE COMES THE HAMMER — HAMMER
HERE COMES THE HOTSTEPPER — Ini KAMOZE
HERE COMES THE JUDGE [A] — Shorty LONG
HERE COMES THE JUDGE [B] — Pigmeat MARKHAM
HERE COMES THE MAN — BOOM BOOM ROOM
HERE COMES THE NICE — The SMALL FACES
HERE COMES THE NIGHT [A] — LULU
HERE COMES THE NIGHT [A] — THEM
HERE COMES THE NIGHT [B] — The BEACH BOYS
HERE COMES THE PAIN — Lee HASLAM
HERE COMES THE RAIN AGAIN — EURYTHMICS
HERE COMES THE STAR —HERMAN'S HERMITS
HERE COMES THE SUMMER — The UNDERTONES
HERE COMES THE SUN — Steve HARLEY and COCKNEY REBEL
HERE COMES THE WAR — NEW MODEL ARMY
HERE COMES YOUR MAN — PIXIES
HERE 4 ONE — BLAZIN' SQUAD
HERE I AM [A] — Bryan ADAMS
HERE I AM [B] — The EXPLOSION
HERE I AM (COME AND TAKE ME) — UB40
HERE I COME — Barrington LEVY
HERE I COME (SING DJ) — TALISMAN P featuring Barrington LEVY
HERE I GO — 2 UNLIMITED
HERE I GO AGAIN [A] — The HOLLIES
HERE I GO AGAIN [B] — Archie BELL and The DRELLS
HERE I GO AGAIN [C] — GUYS and DOLLS
HERE I GO AGAIN [D] — TWIGGY
HERE I GO AGAIN [E] — WHITESNAKE
HERE I GO AGAIN [E] — FRASH
HERE I GO AGAIN [F] — MARIO
HERE I GO IMPOSSIBLE AGAIN — ERASURE
HERE I STAND [A] — The MILLTOWN BROTHERS
HERE I STAND [B] — Bitty McLEAN
HERE IN MY HEART — Al MARTINO (52)
HERE IS THE NEWS — ELECTRIC LIGHT ORCHESTRA
HERE IT COMES — DOVES
HERE IT COMES AGAIN [A] — FORTUNES
HERE IT COMES AGAIN [B] — BLACK
HERE IT COMES AGAIN [C] — Melanie C
HERE SHE COMES AGAIN — The STANDS
HERE, THERE AND EVERYWHERE — Emmylou HARRIS
HERE TO STAY [A] — KORN
HERE TO STAY [B] — NEW ORDER
HERE WE ARE — Gloria ESTEFAN
HERE WE COME — Missy 'Misdemeanor' ELLIOTT
HERE WE GO [A] — EVERTON FOOTBALL CLUB
HERE WE GO [B] — C & C MUSIC FACTORY / CLIVILLES & COLE featuring Freedom WILLIAMS
HERE WE GO [C] — STAKKA BO
HERE WE GO [D] — ARAB STRAP
HERE WE GO [E] — FREESTYLERS
HERE WE GO AGAIN [A] — Ray CHARLES
HERE WE GO AGAIN [B] — PORTRAIT
HERE WE GO AGAIN [C] — A HOMEBOY, a HIPPIE and a FUNKI DREDD
HERE WE GO AGAIN [D] — Aretha FRANKLIN
HERE WE GO ROCK 'N' ROLL — SPIDER
HERE WE GO ROUND THE MULBERRY BUSH — TRAFFIC
HERE WITH ME — DIDO
HERE YOU COME AGAIN — Dolly PARTON
HERE'S MY A — RAPINATION

16 September 2000	23 September 2000	30 September 2000	7 October 2000
LADY (HEAR ME TONIGHT) Modjo	**LADY (HEAR ME TONIGHT)** Modjo	**AGAINST ALL ODDS** Mariah Carey featuring Westlife	**AGAINST ALL ODDS** Mariah Carey featuring Westlife
SING WHEN YOU'RE WINNING Robbie Williams	**SING WHEN YOU'RE WINNING** Robbie Williams	**MUSIC** Madonna	**MUSIC** Madonna

HERE'S THE GOOD NEWS — Paul WELLER
HERE'S TO LOVE (AULD LANG SYNE) — John CHRISTIE
HERE'S WHERE THE STORY ENDS — TIN TIN OUT
HERMANN LOVES PAULINE — SUPER FURRY ANIMALS
HERNANDO'S HIDEAWAY [A] — Johnnie RAY
HERNANDO'S HIDEAWAY [A] — The JOHNSTON BROTHERS (55)
HERO [A] — David CROSBY featuring Phil COLLINS
HERO [B] — Mariah CAREY
HERO [C] — ENRIQUE (02)
HERO [D] — Chad KROEGER featuring Josey SCOTT
HERO OF THE DAY — METALLICA
HEROES [A] — David BOWIE
HEROES [B] — Roni SIZE / REPRAZENT
THE HEROES — SHED SEVEN
HEROES AND VILLAINS — The BEACH BOYS
HERSHAM BOYS — SHAM 69
HE'S A REBEL — CRYSTALS
HE'S A SAINT, HE'S A SINNER — Miquel BROWN
HE'S BACK (THE MAN BEHIND THE MASK) — Alice COOPER
HE'S GONNA STEP ON YOU AGAIN — John KONGOS
HE'S GOT NO LOVE — The SEARCHERS
HE'S GOT THE WHOLE WORLD IN HIS HANDS — Laurie LONDON
HE'S IN TOWN — ROCKIN' BERRIES
HE'S MINE — MOKENSTEF
HE'S MISSTRA KNOW IT ALL — Stevie WONDER
HE'S OLD ENOUGH TO KNOW BETTER — The BROOK BROTHERS
HE'S ON THE PHONE — SAINT ETIENNE
HE'S SO FINE — The CHIFFONS
HE'S THE GREATEST DANCER — SISTER SLEDGE
HE'S THE ONE — Billie DAVIS
HEWLETT'S DAUGHTER — GRANDADDY
HEXAGRAM — DEFTONES
HEY! — Julio IGLESIAS
HEY AMERICA — James BROWN
HEY! BABY [A] — Bruce CHANNEL
HEY BABY (UHH, AHH) [A] — DJ OTZI (01)
HEY BABY (THE UNOFFICIAL WORLD CUP REMIX) [A] — DJ OTZI
HEY BABY [B] — NO DOUBT
HEY BOY HEY GIRL — The CHEMICAL BROTHERS
HEY CHILD — EAST 17
HEY DJ [A] — WORLD'S FAMOUS SUPREME TEAM
HEY DJ [A] — LIGHTER SHADE OF BROWN
HEY DJ – I CAN'T DANCE (TO THAT MUSIC YOU'RE PLAYING) — The BEATMASTERS featuring BETTY BOO
HEY DJ! (PLAY THAT SONG) — N-TYCE
HEY DUDE — KULA SHAKER
HEY GIRL [A] — The SMALL FACES
HEY GIRL [B] — EXPRESSOS
HEY GIRL [C] — DELAYS
HEY GIRL DON'T BOTHER ME — The TAMS (71)
HEY GOD — BON JOVI
HEY GOOD LOOKIN' — Bo DIDDLEY
HEY GOOD LOOKING — Tommy ZANG
HEY JEALOUSY — GIN BLOSSOMS
HEY JOE! [A] — Frankie LAINE (53)
HEY JOE [B] — The Jimi HENDRIX EXPERIENCE
HEY JUDE [A] — The BEATLES (68)
HEY JUDE [A] — Wilson PICKETT
HEY JULIE — FOUNTAINS OF WAYNE
HEY JUPITER — Tori AMOS
HEY LITTLE GIRL [A] — Del SHANNON
HEY LITTLE GIRL [B] — ICEHOUSE
HEY LITTLE GIRL [B] — Mathias WARE featuring Rob TAYLOR
HEY LORD, DON'T ASK ME QUESTIONS — Graham PARKER and The RUMOUR
HEY LOVE — KING SUN-D'MOET
HEY LOVER — LL COOL J featuring BOYZ II MEN
HEY! LUCIANI — The FALL
HEY MA — CAM'RON featuring Juelz SANTANA
HEY MAMA [A] — Frankie VAUGHAN
HEY MAMA [B] — Joe BROWN and The BRUVVERS
HEY MAMA [C] — The BLACK EYED PEAS
HEY MAN (NOW YOU'RE REALLY LIVING) — EELS
HEY MANHATTAN! — PREFAB SPROUT
HEY MATTHEW — Karel FIALKA
HEY MISS PAYNE — CHEQUERS
HEY MR CHRISTMAS — SHOWADDYWADDY
HEY MR DJ [A] — ZHANE
HEY MR DJ [B] — OPEN ARMS featuring ROWETTA
HEY MR DJ [C] — Van MORRISON
HEY MR DREAM MAKER — Cliff RICHARD
HEY MISTER HEARTACHE — Kim WILDE
HEY MR MUSIC MAN — PETERS and LEE
HEY MUSIC LOVER — S EXPRESS
HEY NOW (GIRLS JUST WANT TO HAVE FUN) — Cyndi LAUPER
HEY NOW (MEAN MUGGIN) — XZIBIT
HEY NOW NOW — SWIRL 360
HEY PAPI — Alex CARTAÑA
HEY! PARADISE — FLICKMAN
HEY PAULA — PAUL and PAULA
HEY ROCK AND ROLL — SHOWADDYWADDY
HEY SCENESTERS! — The CRIBS
HEY SENORITA — WAR
HEY SEXY LADY — SHAGGY featuring Brian & Tony GOLD
HEY STOOPID — Alice COOPER
HEY THERE [A] — Johnnie RAY
HEY THERE [A] — Lita ROZA
HEY THERE [A] — Rosemary CLOONEY
HEY THERE [A] — Sammy DAVIS Jr
(HEY THERE) LONELY GIRL [A] — Eddie HOLMAN
HEY THERE LONELY GIRL [A] — BIG FUN
HEY VENUS — THAT PETROL EMOTION
HEY WHATEVER — WESTLIFE
HEY! WHAT'S YOUR NAME — BABY JUNE
HEY WILLY — The HOLLIES
HEY YA! — OUTKAST
HEY YOU [A] — Tommy STEELE
HEY YOU [B] — QUIREBOYS
(HEY YOU) THE ROCKSTEADY CREW — ROCKSTEADY CREW
HEYKEN'S SERENADE (STANDCHEN) — The Pipes and Drums and Military Band of the ROYAL SCOTS DRAGOON GUARDS
HI DE HI, HI DE HO — KOOL and The GANG
HI DE HI (HOLIDAY ROCK) — Paul SHANE and The YELLOWCOATS
HI DE HO — K7
HI HI HAZEL [A] — Geno WASHINGTON and The RAM JAM BAND
HI HI HAZEL [A] — The TROGGS
HI, HI, HI — Paul McCARTNEY
HI HO SILVER — Jim DIAMOND
HI! HOW YA DOIN'? — Kenny G
HI-LILI, HI-LO [A] — Richard CHAMBERLAIN
HI LILI HI LO [A] — Alan PRICE
HI TENSION — HI TENSION
H! VLTG3 — LINKIN PARK
HIBERNACULUM — Mike OLDFIELD
HIDDEN AGENDA — Craig DAVID
HIDDEN PLACE — BJÖRK
HIDE — TWENTY 4 SEVEN
HIDE AND SEEK [A] — Marty WILDE
HIDE AND SEEK [B] — Howard JONES
HIDE U — KOSHEEN
HIDE YOUR HEART — KISS
HIDEAWAY [A] — Dave DEE, DOZY, BEAKY, MICK and TICH
HIDEAWAY [B] — DE'LACY
HIDE-A-WAY — NU SOUL featuring Kelli RICH
HI-FIDELITY — KIDS FROM 'FAME'
HIGH [A] — The CURE
HIGH [B] — HYPER GO GO
HIGH [C] — FEEDER
HIGH [D] — PROPHETS OF SOUND
HIGH [E] — LIGHTHOUSE FAMILY
HIGH [F] — James BLUNT
HIGH AGAIN (HIGH ON EMOTION) — Thomas FALKE
HIGH AND DRY — RADIOHEAD
HIGH AS A KITE — OUR TRIBE / ONE TRIBE
HIGH CLASS BABY — Cliff RICHARD
HIGH ENERGY — Evelyn THOMAS
HIGH FIDELITY — Elvis COSTELLO
HIGH HEAD BLUES — The BLACK CROWES
HIGH HOPES [A] — Frank SINATRA
HIGH HOPES [B] — PINK FLOYD
HIGH HORSE — Evelyn 'Champagne' KING
HIGH IN THE SKY — AMEN CORNER
HIGH LIFE — MODERN ROMANCE
HIGH NOON [A] — DJ SHADOW
HIGH NOON [B] — SERIOUS DANGER
HIGH NOON (DO NOT FORSAKE ME) — Frankie LAINE
HIGH ON A HAPPY VIBE — URBAN COOKIE COLLECTIVE
HIGH ON EMOTION — Chris DE BURGH
HIGH ROLLERS — ICE-T
HIGH SCHOOL CONFIDENTIAL — Jerry Lee LEWIS
HIGH TIME — Paul JONES
HIGH TIMES — JAMIROQUAI
HIGH VOLTAGE [A] — JOHNNY and The HURRICANES
HIGH VOLTAGE (LIVE VERSION) [B] — AC/DC
HIGHER [A] — CREED
HIGHER [B] — David MORALES
HIGHER AND HIGHER — UNATION
HIGHER (FEEL IT) — Erick 'More' MORILLO presents RAW
HIGHER GROUND [A] — Stevie WONDER
HIGHER GROUND [A] — RED HOT CHILI PEPPERS
HIGHER GROUND [B] — GUN
HIGHER GROUND [C] — UB40
HIGHER GROUND [D] — SASHA
HIGHER LOVE — Steve WINWOOD
A HIGHER PLACE — PEYTON
HIGHER STATE OF CONSCIOUSNESS — Josh WINK
HIGHER THAN HEAVEN [A] — AGE OF CHANCE
HIGHER THAN HEAVEN [B] — Kéllé BRYAN
HIGHER THAN REASON — UNBELIEVABLE TRUTH
HIGHER THAN THE SUN — PRIMAL SCREAM
HIGHFLY — John MILES
HIGHLIFE — CYPRESS HILL
HIGHLY EVOLVED — The VINES
HIGHLY INFLAMMABLE — X-RAY SPEX
HIGHLY STRUNG — SPANDAU BALLET
HIGHRISE TOWN — The LANTERNS
HIGHWAY CODE — MASTER SINGERS
HIGHWAY 5 — The BLESSING
HIGHWAY SONG — Nancy SINATRA
HIGHWAY TO HELL — AC/DC
HIGHWAYS OF MY LIFE — The ISLEY BROTHERS
HIGHWIRE [A] — Linda CARR
HIGHWIRE [B] — The ROLLING STONES
HI-HEEL SNEAKERS — Tommy TUCKER
HI-HO SILVER LINING — Jeff BECK
HI-LILI HI-LO — Richard CHAMBERLAIN
HILLBILLY ROCK HILLBILLY ROLL — The WOOLPACKERS
HIM [A] — Rupert HOLMES
HIM [B] — Sarah BRIGHTMAN
THE HINDU TIMES — OASIS (02)
HIP HOP — DEAD PREZ
HIP HOP, BE BOP (DON'T STOP) — Man PARRISH
HIP HOP DON'T YA DROP — HONKY
HIP HOP HOORAY — NAUGHTY BY NATURE
HIP HOUSE — DJ 'FAST' EDDIE
HIP HOUSIN' — X-PRESS 2
HIP TO BE SQUARE — Huey LEWIS and The NEWS
HIP TO HIP — V
HIP TODAY — EXTREME
HIPPY CHICK — SOHO
HIPPY HIPPY SHAKE [A] — SWINGING BLUE JEANS
HIPPY HIPPY SHAKE [A] — The GEORGIA SATELLITES
HIS GIRL — The GUESS WHO
HISTORY [A] — MAI TAI
HISTORY [B] — The VERVE
HISTORY [C] — Michael JACKSON
HISTORY [D] — FUNERAL FOR A FRIEND
HISTORY NEVER REPEATS — SPLIT ENZ
HISTORY OF THE WORLD (PART 1) — The DAMNED
HISTORY REPEATING — PROPELLERHEADS featuring Miss Shirley BASSEY
HIT [A] — SUGARCUBES
HIT [B] — WANNADIES
HIT AND MISS — John BARRY ORCHESTRA
HIT AND RUN [A] — GIRLSCHOOL
HIT AND RUN [B] — TOTAL CONTRAST
HIT BY LOVE — Ce Ce PENISTON
HIT 'EM HIGH (MONSTARS' ANTHEM) — B REAL / BUSTA RHYMES / COOLIO / LL COOL J / METHOD MAN
HIT 'EM UP STYLE (OOPS!) — BLU CANTRELL
HIT 'EM WIT DA HEE — Missy 'Misdemeanor' ELLIOTT featuring LIL' KIM
HIT IT — The BEAT
HIT ME OFF — NEW EDITION
HIT ME WITH YOUR RHYTHM STICK — Ian and The BLOCKHEADS (79)
HIT OR MISS (WAITED TOO LONG) — NEW FOUND GLORY
HIT THAT — The OFFSPRING
HIT THAT PERFECT BEAT — BRONSKI BEAT
HIT THE FREEWAY — Toni BRAXTON featuring LOON
HIT THE GROUND — DARLING BUDS
HIT THE GROUND RUNNING — Tim FINN
HIT THE NORTH — The FALL
HIT THE ROAD JACK — Ray CHARLES
HITCHIN' A RIDE [A] — VANITY FARE
HITCHIN' A RIDE [A] — SINITTA
HITCHIN' A RIDE [B] — GREEN DAY
HI-TEK — Mampi SWIFT
HITMIX (OFFICIAL BOOTLEG MEGA-MIX) — Alexander O'NEAL
HITS MEDLEY — GIPSY KINGS
HITSVILLE UK — The CLASH
HOBART PAVING — SAINT ETIENNE
HOBO HUMPIN' SLOBO BABE — WHALE
HOCUS POCUS — FOCUS
HOGWASH FARM (THE DIESEL HANDS EP) — DAWN OF THE REPLICANTS
HOKEY COKEY [A] — JUDGE DREAD
HOKEY COKEY [A] — SNOWMEN
HOKEY COKEY [A] — BLACK LACE
THE HOKEY COKEY [A] — CAPTAIN SENSIBLE
HOKOYO — ORANGE JUICE
HOKUS POKUS — INSANE CLOWN POSSE
HOLD BACK THE NIGHT [A] — The TRAMMPS
HOLD BACK THE NIGHT [A] — KWS features guest vocal from The TRAMMPS
HOLD BACK THE RIVER — WET WET WET
HOLD BACK TOMORROW — MIKI and GRIFF
HOLD IT — Stephen 'Tin Tin' DUFFY
HOLD IT DOWN [A] — SENSELESS THINGS
HOLD IT DOWN [B] — 2 BAD MICE
HOLD ME [A] — Teddy PENDERGRASS with Whitney HOUSTON
HOLD ME [B] — PJ PROBY
HOLD ME [B] — B.A. ROBERTSON
HOLD ME [C] — SAVAGE GARDEN
HOLD ME CLOSE — David ESSEX (75)
HOLD ME IN YOUR ARMS — Rick ASTLEY
HOLD ME NOW [A] — THOMPSON TWINS
HOLD ME NOW [B] — Johnny LOGAN
HOLD ME NOW [C] — The POLYPHONIC SPREE
HOLD ME THRILL ME KISS ME [A] — Muriel SMITH
HOLD ME THRILL ME KISS ME [A] — Gloria ESTEFAN
HOLD ME THRILL ME KISS ME KILL ME — U2
HOLD ME TIGHT — Johnny NASH
HOLD ME TIGHTER IN THE RAIN — Billy GRIFFIN
HOLD MY BODY TIGHT — EAST 17
HOLD MY HAND [A] — Don CORNELL (54)
HOLD MY HAND [B] — Ken DODD
HOLD MY HAND [C] — HOOTIE & The BLOWFISH
HOLD ON [A] — STREETBAND
HOLD ON [B] — EN VOGUE
HOLD ON [C] — WILSON PHILLIPS
HOLD ON [D] — CB MILTON
HOLD ON [E] — HAPPY CLAPPERS
HOLD ON (EP) [F] — Ann NESBY
HOLD ON [G] — José NUNEZ featuring OCTAHVIA
HOLD ON [H] — GOOD CHARLOTTE
HOLD ON ME — PHIXX
HOLD ON MY HEART — GENESIS
HOLD ON TIGHT [A] — ELECTRIC LIGHT ORCHESTRA
HOLD ON TIGHT [B] — Samantha FOX
HOLD ON TO LOVE [A] — Peter SKELLERN
HOLD ON TO LOVE [B] — Gary MOORE
HOLD ON TO ME — MJ COLE
HOLD ON TO MY LOVE — Jimmy RUFFIN
HOLD ON TO THE NIGHTS — Richard MARX
HOLD ON TO WHAT YOU'VE GOT — Evelyn 'Champagne' KING

14 October 2000	21 October 2000	28 October 2000	4 November 2000

UK No.1 SINGLES

BLACK COFFEE All Saints	BEAUTIFUL DAY U2	STOMP Steps	HOLLER / LET LOVE LEAD THE WAY Spice Girls

UK No.1 ALBUMS

A ad	KID A Radiohead	SAINTS & SINNERS All Saints	THE GREATEST HITS Texas

HOLD ON TO YOUR FRIENDS — MORRISSEY
HOLD ONTO OUR LOVE — James FOX
HOLD THAT SUCKER DOWN — OUR TRIBE / ONE TRIBE
HOLD THE HEART — BIG COUNTRY
HOLD THE LINE — TOTO
HOLD TIGHT [A] — Dave DEE, DOZY, BEAKY, MICK and TICH
HOLD TIGHT [B] — LIVERPOOL EXPRESS
HOLD YOU DOWN — Jennifer LOPEZ featuring FAT JOE
HOLD YOU TIGHT — Tara KEMP
HOLD YOUR HEAD UP — ARGENT
HOLD YOUR HEAD UP HIGH — Boris DLUGOSCH presents BOOOM
HOLD YOUR HORSES, BABE — Celi BEE and The BUZZY BUNCH
HOLDIN' ON — Tony RALLO and The MIDNITE BAND
HOLDING BACK THE YEARS — SIMPLY RED
HOLDING ON [A] — Beverley CRAVEN
HOLDING ON [B] — CLOCK
HOLDING ON [C] — DJ MANTA
HOLDING ON [D] — Heather SMALL
HOLDING ON 4 U [A] — CLOCK
HOLDING ON FOR U [B] — LIBERTY X
HOLDING ON TO NOTHING — AGNELLI & NELSON featuring AUREUS
HOLDING ON TO YOU — Terence Trent D'ARBY
HOLDING ON (WHEN LOVE IS GONE) — L.T.D.
HOLDING OUT FOR A HERO — Bonnie TYLER
HOLE HEARTED — EXTREME
HOLE IN MY SHOE [A] — TRAFFIC
HOLE IN MY SHOE [A] — neil
HOLE IN MY SOUL — AEROSMITH
HOLE IN THE BUCKET [B] — SPEARHEAD
HOLE IN THE GROUND — Bernard CRIBBINS
HOLE IN THE HEAD — SUGABABES (03)
HOLE IN THE ICE — Neil FINN
HOLE IN THE WORLD — EAGLES
HOLIDAE IN — CHINGY featuring LUDACRIS & SNOOP DOGG
HOLIDAY [A] — MADONNA
HOLIDAY [A] — MAD'HOUSE
HOLIDAY [B] — GREEN DAY
HOLIDAY 80 — HUMAN LEAGUE
HOLIDAY RAP — MC MIKER 'G' and Deejay SVEN
HOLIDAYS IN THE SUN — SEX PISTOLS
HOLLABACK GIRL — Gwen STEFANI
HOLLER [A] — GINUWINE
HOLLER [B] — SPICE GIRLS (00)
HOLLIEDAZE (MEDLEY) — The HOLLIES
THE HOLLOW — A PERFECT CIRCLE
HOLLOW HEART — BIRDLAND
THE HOLLOW MAN — MARILLION
HOLLY HOLY — UB40
HOLLYWOOD [A] — Boz SCAGGS
HOLLYWOOD [B] — MADONNA
HOLLYWOOD (DOWN ON YOUR LUCK) — THIN LIZZY
HOLLYWOOD NIGHTS — Bob SEGER and The SILVER BULLET BAND
HOLLYWOOD TEASE — GIRL
THE HOLY CITY — Moira ANDERSON
HOLY COW — Lee DORSEY
HOLY DAYS — ZOE
HOLY DIVER — DIO
HOLY JOE — HAYSI FANTAYZEE
THE HOLY RIVER — PRINCE
HOLY ROLLER — NAZARETH
HOLY ROLLER NOVOCAINE — KINGS OF LEON
HOLY SMOKE — IRON MAIDEN
HOLY WARS ... THE PUNISHMENT DUE — MEGADETH
HOMBURG — PROCOL HARUM
HOME [A] — PUBLIC IMAGE LTD
HOME [B] — GOD MACHINE
HOME [C] — DEPECHE MODE
HOME [D] — CHAKRA
HOME [E] — Sheryl CROW
HOME [F] — COAST 2 COAST featuring DISCOVERY
HOME [G] — Julie MCKNIGHT
HOME [H] — BONE THUGS-N-HARMONY featuring Phil COLLINS
HOME [I] — SIMPLY RED
HOME [J] — Michael BUBLE
HOME [K] — SIMPLE MINDS
HOME ALONE — R KELLY featuring Keith MURRAY
HOME AND AWAY — Karen BODDINGTON and Mark WILLIAMS
HOME AND DRY — PET SHOP BOYS
HOME FOR CHRISTMAS DAY — RED CAR AND THE BLUE CAR
HOME IS WHERE THE HEART IS — Gladys KNIGHT and The PIPS
HOME LOVIN' MAN — Andy WILLIAMS
HOME OF THE BRAVE — Jody MILLER
HOME SWEET HOME — MÖTLEY CRÜE
HOMELY GIRL [A] — The CHI-LITES
HOMELY GIRL [A] — UB40
HOMETOWN UNICORN — SUPER FURRY ANIMALS
HOMEWARD BOUND [A] — SIMON and GARFUNKEL
HOMEWARD BOUND [A] — QUIET FIVE
HOMICIDE [A] — 999
HOMICIDE [B] — SHADES OF RHYTHM
THE HOMING WALTZ — Vera LYNN
HOMOPHOBIC ASSHOLE — SENSELESS THINGS
HONALOOCHIE BOOGIE — MOTT THE HOOPLE
HONDY (NO ACCESS) — HONDY
HONEST I DO — Danny STORM
HONEST I DO LOVE YOU — Candi STATON
HONEST MEN PART TWO — ELECTRIC LIGHT ORCHESTRA
AN HONEST MISTAKE — The BRAVERY
HONESTLY — ZWAN
HONEY [A] — Bobby GOLDSBORO
HONEY [B] — Mariah CAREY
HONEY [C] — MOBY
HONEY [D] — Billie Ray MARTIN
HONEY [E] — R KELLY and JAY-Z
HONEY BE GOOD — The BIBLE
HONEY CHILE [A] — Fats DOMINO
HONEY CHILE [B] — Martha REEVES and The VANDELLAS
HONEY COME BACK — Glen CAMPBELL
HONEY HONEY — SWEET DREAMS
HONEY I — George McCRAE
HONEY I NEED — The PRETTY THINGS
HONEY I'M LOST — The DOOLEYS
HONEY TO THE BEE — Billie PIPER
HONEYCOMB — Jimmie RODGERS
THE HONEYDRIPPER — The JETS
THE HONEYMOON SONG — MANUEL and his MUSIC OF THE MOUNTAINS
THE HONEYTHIEF — HIPSWAY
HONG KONG GARDEN — SIOUXSIE and The BANSHEES
HONKY CAT — Elton JOHN
THE HONKY DOODLE DAY EP — HONKY
HONKY TONK TRAIN BLUES — Keith EMERSON
HONKY TONK WOMEN [A] — The ROLLING STONES (69)
HONKY TONK WOMEN [A] — The POGUES
HOOCHIE BOOTY — ULTIMATE KAOS
HOODED — FRESH BC
HOODIE — LADY SOVEREIGN
HOOKED — 99TH FLOOR ELEVATORS
HOOKED ON A FEELING — Jonathan KING
HOOKED ON CAN-CAN — ROYAL PHILHARMONIC ORCHESTRA arranged and conducted by Louis CLARK
HOOKED ON CLASSICS — ROYAL PHILHARMONIC ORCHESTRA arranged and conducted by Louis CLARK
HOOKED ON LOVE — DEAD OR ALIVE
HOOKED ON YOU [A] — Sydney YOUNGBLOOD
HOOKED ON YOU [B] — VOLATILE AGENTS featuring Simone BENN
HOOKS IN YOU — MARILLION
HOOLIGAN — EMBRACE
HOOLIGAN 69 — RAGGA TWINS
HOOLIGAN'S HOLIDAY — MÖTLEY CRÜE
HOORAY HOORAY, IT'S A HOLI-HOLIDAY [A] — BONEY M
HOORAY HOORAY (IT'S A CHEEKY HOLIDAY) [A] — The CHEEKY GIRLS
HOOTIN' — Nigel GEE
HOOTS MON — Jack Good presents LORD ROCKINGHAM'S XI (58)
HOOVERS & HORNS — FERGIE
HOOVERVILLE (THEY PROMISED US THE WORLD) — The CHRISTIANS
THE HOP — THEATRE OF HATE
HOPE [A] — SHAGGY
HOPE [B] — TWISTA featuring Faith EVANS
HOPE AND WAIT — ORION TOO
HOPE (I WISH YOU'D BELIEVE ME) — WAH!
HOPE IN A HOPELESS WORLD — Paul YOUNG
HOPE (NEVER GIVE UP) — LOVELAND featuring the voice of Rachel McFARLANE
HOPE OF DELIVERANCE — Paul McCARTNEY
HOPE ST — LEVELLERS
HOPE THERE'S SOMEONE — ANTONY & The JOHNSONS
HOPELESS — Dionne FARRIS
HOPELESSLY — Rick ASTLEY
HOPELESSLY DEVOTED TO YOU [A] — Olivia NEWTON-JOHN
HOPELESSLY DEVOTED TO YOU [A] — SONIA
HOPPIPOLLA — SIGUR ROS
THE HORN TRACK — EGYPTIAN EMPIRE
HORNY [A] — Mark MORRISON
HORNY [B] — MOUSSE T
HORNY AS FUNK — SOAPY
HORNY HORNS — PERFECT PHASE
HORROR HEAD (EP) — CURVE
HORSE — SPLODGENESSABOUNDS
HORSE AND CARRIAGE — CAM'RON featuring MA$E
A HORSE WITH NO NAME — AMERICA
HORSEMEN — The BEES
HORSEPOWER — RAVESIGNAL III
HOSPITAL FOOD — David GRAY
HOSTAGE IN A FROCK — CECIL
HOT — IDEAL
HOT AND WET (BELIEVE IT) — TZANT
HOT BLOODED — FOREIGNER
HOT BOYZ — Missy 'Misdemeanour' ELLIOTT
HOT DIGGITY [A] — Perry COMO
HOT DIGGITY (DOG ZIGGITY BOOM) [A] — The STARGAZERS
HOT DIGGITY (DOG ZIGGITY BOOM) [A] — Michael HOLLIDAY
HOT DOG — Shakin' STEVENS
HOT FUN — 7TH HEAVEN
HOT HOT HOT [A] — ARROW
HOT HOT HOT [A] — PAT and MICK
HOT HOT HOT!!! [B] — The CURE
HOT IN HERRE [A] — NELLY
HOT IN HERRE [A] — TIGA
HOT IN THE CITY — Billy IDOL
HOT LEGS — Rod STEWART
HOT LIKE FIRE [A] — AALIYAH
HOT LIKE FIRE [B] — DJ AMS & KHIZA featuring Marlon BINNS & TAFARI
HOT LOVE [A] — T. REX (71)
HOT LOVE [B] — David ESSEX
HOT LOVE [C] — Kelly MARIE
HOT LOVE [D] — FIVE STAR
HOT LOVE NOW — The WONDER STUFF
HOT PEPPER — Floyd CRAMER
HOT ROCKIN' — JUDAS PRIEST
(HOT S**T) COUNTRY GRAMMAR — NELLY
HOT SHOT [A] — Barry BLUE
HOT SHOT [B] — Karen YOUNG
HOT SHOT [C] — Cliff RICHARD
HOT SHOT TOTTENHAM! — TOTTENHAM HOTSPUR FA CUP FINAL SQUAD
HOT SPOT — Foxy BROWN
HOT STUFF [A] — Donna SUMMER
HOT STUFF [A] — ARSENAL FC
HOT SUMMER SALSA — JIVE BUNNY and The MASTERMIXERS
HOT TODDY — Ted HEATH
HOT TRACKS (EP) — NAZARETH
HOT VALVES (EP) — BE BOP DELUXE
HOT WATER — LEVEL 42
HOTEL — CASSIDY featuring R KELLY
HOTEL YORBA — The WHITE STRIPES
HOTEL CALIFORNIA [A] — EAGLES
HOTEL CALIFORNIA [A] — JAM ON THE MUTHA
HOTEL ILLNESS — The BLACK CROWES
HOTEL LOUNGE (BE THE DEATH OF ME) — dEUS
HOTLINE TO HEAVEN — BANANARAMA
HOTNESS — DYNAMITE MC & ORIGIN UNKNOWN
HOUND DOG — Elvis PRESLEY
HOUND DOG MAN — FABIAN
HOUNDS OF LOVE [A] — Kate BUSH
HOUNDS OF LOVE [A] — The FUTUREHEADS
HOURGLASS — SQUEEZE
HOUSE ARREST — KRUSH
HOUSE ENERGY REVENGE — CAPPELLA
HOUSE FLY — TRICKY DISCO
A HOUSE IN THE COUNTRY — The PRETTY THINGS
THE HOUSE IS HAUNTED (BY THE ECHO OF YOUR LAST GOODBYE) — Marc ALMOND
THE HOUSE IS MINE — HYPNOTIST
HOUSE IS NOT A HOME — CHARLES and EDDIE
HOUSE MUSIC — Eddie AMADOR
HOUSE NATION — HOUSEMASTER BOYZ and The RUDE BOY OF HOUSE
HOUSE OF BROKEN LOVE — GREAT WHITE
HOUSE OF FIRE — Alice COOPER
HOUSE OF FUN — MADNESS (82)
HOUSE OF GOD — D.H.S.
HOUSE OF JEALOUS LOVERS — The RAPTURE
HOUSE OF JOY — Vicki Sue ROBINSON
HOUSE OF LOVE [A] — EAST 17
HOUSE OF LOVE [B] — RuPAUL
HOUSE OF LOVE [C] — SKIN
HOUSE OF LOVE [D] — Amy GRANT
HOUSE OF LOVE (IN MY HOUSE) — SMOOTH TOUCH
HOUSE OF THE BLUE DANUBE — Malcolm McLAREN
THE HOUSE OF THE RISING SUN [A] — The ANIMALS (64)
THE HOUSE OF THE RISING SUN [A] — FRIJID PINK
HOUSE OF THE RISING SUN [A] — RAGE
HOUSE ON FIRE [A] — The BOOMTOWN RATS
HOUSE ON FIRE [B] — ARKARNA
HOUSE SOME MORE — LOCK 'N' LOAD
THE HOUSE THAT JACK BUILT [A] — Alan PRICE
THE HOUSE THAT JACK BUILT [B] — TRACIE
A HOUSE WITH LOVE IN IT — Vera LYNN
HOUSECALL — Shabba RANKS featuring Maxi PRIEST
HOUSES IN MOTION — TALKING HEADS
HOW ABOUT THAT — Adam FAITH
HOW AM I SUPPOSED TO LIVE WITHOUT YOU — Michael BOLTON
HOW BIZARRE — OMC
HOW 'BOUT I LOVE YOU MORE — MULL HISTORICAL SOCIETY
HOW 'BOUT US [A] — CHAMPAIGN
HOW 'BOUT US [A] — LULU
HOW CAN I BE SURE [A] — Dusty SPRINGFIELD
HOW CAN I BE SURE [A] — David CASSIDY (72)
HOW CAN I BE SURE? [A] — Darren DAY
HOW CAN I FALL — BREATHE
HOW CAN I FORGET YOU — Elisa FIORILLO
HOW CAN I KEEP FROM SINGING — ENYA
HOW CAN I LOVE YOU MORE — M PEOPLE
HOW CAN I MEET HER — The EVERLY BROTHERS
HOW CAN I TELL HER — The FOURMOST
HOW CAN THIS BE LOVE — Andrew GOLD
HOW CAN WE BE LOVERS — Michael BOLTON
HOW CAN WE EASE THE PAIN — Maxi PRIEST
HOW CAN YOU EXPECT TO BE TAKEN SERIOUSLY — PET SHOP BOYS
HOW CAN YOU TELL — Sandie SHAW
HOW CAN YOU TELL ME IT'S OVER — Lorraine CATO
HOW COME? [A] — Ronnie LANE accompanied by the band SLIM CHANCE
HOW COME [B] — Youssou N'DOUR and CANIBUS
HOW COME [C] — D12
HOW COME, HOW LONG — BABYFACE featuring Stevie WONDER
HOW COME IT NEVER RAINS — DOGS D'AMOUR
HOW COME YOU DON'T CALL ME — Alicia KEYS
HOW COULD AN ANGEL BREAK MY HEART — Toni BRAXTON with Kenny G
HOW COULD I? (INSECURITY) — ROACHFORD
HOW COULD THIS GO WRONG — EXILE
HOW COULD WE DARE TO BE WRONG — Colin BLUNSTONE
HOW DEEP IS YOUR LOVE [A] — The BEE GEES
HOW DEEP IS YOUR LOVE [A] — PORTRAIT
HOW DEEP IS YOUR LOVE [A] — TAKE THAT (96)

11 November 2000	18 November 2000	25 November 2000	2 December 2000
MY LOVE Westlife	**SAME OLD BRAND NEW YOU** a1	**CAN'T FIGHT THE MOONLIGHT** LeAnn Rimes	**INDEPENDENT WOMEN PART 1** Destiny's Child
ALL THAT YOU CAN'T LEAVE BEHIND U2	**COAST TO COAST** Westlife	**1** The Beatles	**1** The Beatles

1 The Be…

HOW DEEP IS YOUR LOVE [B] — DRU HILL featuring REDMAN
HOW DID IT EVER COME TO THIS? — EASYWORLD
HOW DID YOU KNOW — Kurtis MANTRONIK presents CHAMONIX
HOW DO I KNOW? — MARLO
HOW DO I LIVE [A] — Trisha YEARWOOD
HOW DO I LIVE [A] — LeAnn RIMES
HOW DO I SAY GOODBYE — D-RAIL
HOW DO YOU DO [A] — Al HUDSON
HOW DO YOU DO! [B] — ROXETTE
HOW DO YOU DO IT? — GERRY and The PACEMAKERS (63)
HOW DO YOU KNOW IT'S LOVE — Teresa BREWER
HOW DO YOU LIKE IT — Keith SWEAT
HOW DO YOU SAY ... LOVE — DEEE-LITE
HOW DO YOU SPEAK TO AN ANGEL — Dean MARTIN
HOW DO YOU WANT IT — 2PAC
HOW DO YOU WANT ME TO LOVE YOU? — 911
HOW DOES IT FEEL? [A] — SLADE
HOW DOES IT FEEL [B] — ELECTROSET
HOW DOES IT FEEL [C] — WANNADIES
(HOW DOES IT FEEL TO BE) ON TOP OF THE WORLD — ENGLAND UNITED
HOW DOES IT FEEL TO FEEL — RIDE
HOW DOES THAT GRAB YOU DARLIN' — Nancy SINATRA
HOW GEE — BLACK MACHINE
HOW HIGH — The CHARLATANS
HOW HIGH THE MOON [A] — Ella FITZGERALD
HOW HIGH THE MOON [A] — Gloria GAYNOR
HOW HOW — YELLO
HOW I WANNA BE LOVED — Dana DAWSON
HOW I'M COMIN' — LL COOL J
HOW IT IS — BIOHAZARD
HOW IT SHOULD BE — INSPIRAL CARPETS
HOW LONG [A] — ACE
HOW LONG [A] — Rod STEWART
HOW LONG [A] — YAZZ and ASWAD
HOW LONG [A] — Paul CARRACK
HOW LONG DO I GET — RAISSA
HOW LONG HAS IT BEEN — Jim REEVES
HOW LONG'S A TEAR TAKE TO DRY? — The BEAUTIFUL SOUTH
HOW LUCKY YOU ARE — SKIN
HOW MANY LIES — SPANDAU BALLET
HOW MANY TEARS — Bobby VEE
HOW MANY TEARS CAN YOU HIDE — Shakin' STEVENS
HOW MANY TIMES — BROTHER BEYOND
HOW MEN ARE — AZTEC CAMERA
HOW MUCH I FEEL — ALIBI
(HOW MUCH IS) THAT DOGGIE IN THE WINDOW [A] — Lita ROZA (53)
(HOW MUCH IS) THAT DOGGIE IN THE WINDOW [A] — Patti PAGE
HOW MUCH LOVE [A] — Leo SAYER
HOW MUCH LOVE [B] — VIXEN
HOW MUSIC CAME ABOUT (BOP B DA B DA DA) — The GAP BAND
HOW RUDE SHE WAS — TOWERS OF LONDON
HOW SHE THREW IT ALL AWAY (EP) — The STYLE COUNCIL
HOW SOON — Henry MANCINI
HOW SOON IS NOW [A] — The SMITHS
HOW SOON IS NOW [A] — INNER SANCTUM
HOW SOON IS NOW? [A] — HUNDRED REASONS
HOW SOON WE FORGET — Colonel ABRAMS
HOW SWEET IT IS [A] — Marvin GAYE
HOW SWEET IT IS [A] — Junior WALKER and The ALL-STARS
HOW THE HEART BEHAVES — WAS (NOT WAS)
HOW TO BE A MILLIONAIRE — ABC
HOW TO BE DEAD — SNOW PATROL
HOW TO FALL IN LOVE PART 1 — The BEE GEES
HOW TO WIN YOUR LOVE — Engelbert HUMPERDINCK
HOW U LIKE BASS — Norman BASS
HOW WAS IT FOR YOU — JAMES
HOW WE DO — The GAME featuring 50 CENT
HOW WILL I KNOW — Whitney HOUSTON
HOW WILL I KNOW (WHO YOU ARE) — JESSICA
HOW WONDERFUL TO KNOW — Pearl CARR and Teddy JOHNSON
HOW WONDERFUL YOU ARE — Gordon HASKELL
HOW WOULD U FEEL — David MORALES featuring Lea LORIEN
HOW YOU GONNA ACT LIKE THAT — TYRESE
HOW YOU GONNA SEE ME NOW — Alice COOPER
HOW YOU REMIND ME — NICKELBACK
HOW'D I DO DAT — BENTLEY RHYTHM ACE
HOW'S IT GOING TO BE — THIRD EYE BLIND
HOW'S YOUR EVENING SO FAR — Josh WINK and Lil' LOUIS
HOWARD'S WAY — Simon MAY
HOWZAT — SHERBET
HUBBLE BUBBLE TOIL AND TROUBLE — MANFRED MANN
HUDSON STREET — AGNELLI & NELSON
HUG MY SOUL — SAINT ETIENNE
HUMAN [A] — HUMAN LEAGUE
HUMAN [B] — The PRETENDERS
HUMAN BEHAVIOUR — BJÖRK
HUMAN BEING — The BETA BAND
HUMAN BEINGS — SEAL
HUMAN NATURE [A] — Gary CLAIL ON-U SOUND SYSTEM
HUMAN NATURE [B] — MADONNA
HUMAN RACING — Nik KERSHAW
HUMAN TOUCH [A] — Rick SPRINGFIELD
HUMAN TOUCH [B] — Bruce SPRINGSTEEN
HUMAN WORK OF ART [A] — Maxi PRIEST
HUMAN WORK OF ART [A] — Cliff RICHARD
HUMANISTIC — KAWALA
HUMANITY — REBEL MC
HUMMING BIRD — Frankie LAINE
HUMPIN' — GAP BAND
HUMPIN' AROUND — Bobby BROWN
HUNDRED MILE HIGH CITY — OCEAN COLOUR SCENE
A HUNDRED POUNDS OF CLAY — Craig DOUGLAS
HUNG UP [A] — Paul WELLER
HUNG UP [B] — MADONNA (05)
HUNGAH — Karyn WHITE
THE HUNGER — The DISTILLERS
HUNGER STRIKE — TEMPLE OF THE DOG
HUNGRY — KOSHEEN
HUNGRY EYES — EYEOPENER
HUNGRY FOR HEAVEN — DIO
HUNGRY FOR LOVE — Johnny KIDD and The PIRATES
HUNGRY HEART — Bruce SPRINGSTEEN
HUNGRY LIKE THE WOLF — DURAN DURAN
HUNT — Barry RYAN
HUNTER [A] — BJÖRK
HUNTER [B] — DIDO
HUNTING HIGH AND LOW — A-HA
HURDY GURDY MAN — DONOVAN
HURRICANE [A] — Bob DYLAN
HURRICANE [B] — WARM JETS
HURRY HOME — WAVELENGTH
HURRY UP AND WAIT — STEREOPHONICS
HURRY UP HARRY — SHAM 69
HURT [A] — Elvis PRESLEY
HURT [A] — MANHATTANS
HURT [B] — Johnny CASH
HURT BY LOVE — Inez FOXX
HURT ME SO BAD — LULU
HURT SO GOOD [A] — Susan CADOGAN
HURT SO GOOD [A] — Jimmy SOMERVILLE
HURTING KIND (I'VE GOT MY EYES ON YOU) — Robert PLANT
HUSAN — BHANGRA KNIGHTS vs HUSAN
HUSBAND — FLUFFY
HUSH [A] — DEEP PURPLE
HUSH [A] — KULA SHAKER
HUSH [B] — LL COOL J featuring 7 AURELIUS
HUSH ... NOT A WORD TO MARY — John ROWLES
THE HUSTLE — Van McCOY
HUSTLE! (TO THE MUSIC ...) — FUNKY WORM
HYBRID — EAT STATIC
HYMN [A] — ULTRAVOX
HYMN [B] — MOBY
HYMN [C] — ULTRAMARINE featuring David McALMONT
HYMN TO HER — The PRETENDERS
HYMNE À L'AMOUR (IF YOU LOVE ME) — Elaine PAIGE
HYPE! HYPE! — SLK
HYPER MUSIC — MUSE
HYPERACTIVE — Thomas DOLBY
HYPERBALLAD — BJÖRK
HYPERREAL — The SHAMEN
HYPNOSIS — MUD
HYPNOTIC ST-8 — ALTERN 8
HYPNOTIC TANGO — MASTER BLASTER
HYPNOTISED [A] — CABARET VOLTAIRE
HYPNOTISED [B] — SIMPLE MINDS
HYPNOTISED [C] — Paul OAKENFOLD
HYPNOTISING — KID CREME featuring CHARLISE
HYPNOTIZE [A] — SCRITTI POLITTI
HYPNOTIZE [B] — D'INFLUENCE
HYPNOTIZE [C] — NOTORIOUS B.I.G.
HYPNOTIZE [D] — SYSTEM OF A DOWN
HYPNOTIZIN' — Josh WINK
HYPOCRITE [A] — LUSH
HYPOCRITE [B] — The SPECIALS
HYSTERIA [A] — DEF LEPPARD
HYSTERIA [B] — MUSE
I — Petey PABLO
I ADORE MI AMOR — COLOR ME BADD
I ADORE YOU — Caron WHEELER
I AIN'T GOIN' OUT LIKE THAT — CYPRESS HILL
I AIN'T GONNA CRY — LITTLE ANGELS
I AIN'T GONNA STAND FOR IT — Stevie WONDER
I AIN'T GOT TIME ANYMORE — Cliff RICHARD
I AIN'T LYIN' — George McCRAE
I AIN'T MAD AT CHA — 2PAC
I AIN'T MOVIN' — DES'REE
I AIN'T NEW TA THIS — ICE-T
I AIN'T SAYING MY GOODBYES — Tom VEK
I ALMOST FELT LIKE CRYING — Craig McLACHLAN
I ALMOST LOST MY MIND — Pat BOONE
I ALONE — LIVE
I AM [A] — CHAKRA
I AM [B] — SUGGS
I AM A CIDER DRINKER (PALOMA BLANCA) — The WURZELS
I AM A CLOWN — David CASSIDY
I AM A ROCK — SIMON and GARFUNKEL
I AM BLESSED — ETERNAL
I AM DOWN — SALT-N-PEPA
I AM I — QUEENSRYCHE
I AM I FEEL — ALISHA'S ATTIC
I AM ... I SAID — Neil DIAMOND
I AM (I'M ME) — TWISTED SISTER
I AM IN LOVE WITH THE WORLD — CHICKEN SHED THEATRE
I AM MINE — PEARL JAM
I AM LV — LV
I AM ONE [A] — SMASHING PUMPKINS
I AM ONE [B] — W.A.S.P.
I AM THE BEAT — LOOK
I AM THE BLACK GOLD OF THE SUN — NUYORICAN SOUL featuring Jocelyn BROWN
I AM THE LAW — ANTHRAX
I AM THE MOB — CATATONIA
I AM THE MUSIC HEAR ME! — MILLIONAIRE HIPPIES
I AM THE MUSIC MAN — BLACK LACE
I AM THE NEWS — OCEAN COLOUR SCENE
I AM THE ONE — CRACKOUT
I AM THE RESURRECTION — The STONE ROSES
I AM THE SUN — DARK STAR
I AM WHAT I AM [A] — GREYHOUND
I AM WHAT I AM [B] — Mark OWEN
I AM WHAT I AM (FROM 'LA CAGE AUX FOLLES') — Gloria GAYNOR
I APOLOGISE — PJ PROBY
I BE THE PROPHET — STARVING SOULS
I BEG YOUR PARDON — KON KAN
I BEGIN TO WONDER — Dannii MINOGUE
I BELIEVE [A] — Frankie LAINE (53)
I BELIEVE [A] — David WHITFIELD
I BELIEVE [A] — The BACHELORS
I BELIEVE [A] — ROBSON & JEROME (95)
I BELIEVE [B] — EMF
I BELIEVE [C] — REESE PROJECT
I BELIEVE [D] — BON JOVI
I BELIEVE [E] — Robert PLANT
I BELIEVE [F] — Marcella DETROIT
I BELIEVE [G] — SOUNDS OF BLACKNESS
I BELIEVE [H] — BLESSID UNION OF SOULS
I BELIEVE [I] — HAPPY CLAPPERS
I BELIEVE [J] — BOOTH and The BAD ANGEL
I BELIEVE [K] — ABSOLUTE
I BELIEVE [L] — LANGE featuring SARAH DWYER
I BELIEVE [M] — JAMESTOWN featuring JOCELYN BROWN
I BELIEVE [N] — Stephen GATELY
I BELIEVE (A SOULFUL RERECORDING) — TEARS FOR FEARS
I BELIEVE I CAN FLY — R KELLY (97)
I BELIEVE I'M GONNA LOVE YOU — Frank SINATRA
I BELIEVE IN A THING CALLED LOVE — The DARKNESS
I BELIEVE IN CHRISTMAS — TWEENIES
I BELIEVE IN FATHER CHRISTMAS — Greg LAKE
I BELIEVE (IN LOVE) — HOT CHOCOLATE
I BELIEVE IN LOVE — COOPER
I BELIEVE IN MIRACLES [A] — The JACKSON SISTERS
I BELIEVE IN MIRACLES [A] — The PASADENAS
I BELIEVE IN THE SPIRIT — Tim BURGESS
I BELIEVE IN YOU [A] — OUR TRIBE / ONE TRIBE
I BELIEVE IN YOU [B] — AMP FIDDLER
I BELIEVE IN YOU [C] — KYLIE
I BELIEVE IN YOU AND ME — Whitney HOUSTON
(I BELIEVE) LOVE'S A PRIMA DONNA — Steve HARLEY and COCKNEY REBEL
I BELIEVE MY HEART — Duncan JAMES & KEEDIE
I BELIEVE YOU — Dorothy MOORE
I BELONG — Kathy KIRBY
I BELONG TO YOU [A] — Whitney HOUSTON
I BELONG TO YOU [B] — Gina G
I BELONG TO YOU [C] — Lenny KRAVITZ
I BET YOU LOOK GOOD ON THE DANCEFLOOR — ARCTIC MONKEYS (05)
I BREATHE AGAIN — Adam RICKITT
I BRUISE EASILY — Natasha BEDINGFIELD
I CALL YOUR NAME — A-HA
I CALLED U — LIL' LOUIS
I CAN — NAS
I CAN BUY YOU — A CAMP
I CAN CALL YOU — PORTRAIT
I CAN CAST A SPELL — DISCO TEX presents CLOUDBURST
I CAN CLIMB MOUNTAINS — HELL IS FOR HEROES
I CAN DANCE [A] — Brian POOLE and The TREMELOES
I CAN DANCE [B] — DJ 'FAST' EDDIE
I CAN DO IT — The RUBETTES
I CAN DO THIS — Monie LOVE
I CAN DREAM — SKUNK ANANSIE
I CAN DREAM ABOUT YOU — Dan HARTMAN
I CAN DRIVE — SHAKESPEAR'S SISTER
I CAN FEEL IT — The SILENCERS
I CAN HEAR MUSIC — The BEACH BOYS
I CAN HEAR THE GRASS GROW — The MOVE
I CAN HEAR VOICES — HI-GATE
I CAN HEAR YOUR HEARTBEAT — Chris REA
I CAN HELP [A] — Billy SWAN
I CAN HELP [A] — Elvis PRESLEY
I CAN LOVE YOU LIKE THAT — ALL-4-ONE
I CAN MAKE IT BETTER [A] — The WHISPERS
I CAN MAKE IT BETTER [B] — Luther VANDROSS
I CAN MAKE YOU FEEL GOOD [A] — SHALAMAR
I CAN MAKE YOU FEEL GOOD [A] — KAVANA
I CAN MAKE YOU FEEL LIKE — MAXX
I CAN ONLY DISAPOINT U — MANSUN
I CAN PROVE IT [A] — Tony ETORIA
I CAN PROVE IT [A] — Phil FEARON
I CAN SEE CLEARLY NOW [A] — Johnny NASH
I CAN SEE CLEARLY NOW [A] — HOTHOUSE FLOWERS
I CAN SEE CLEARLY NOW [A] — Jimmy CLIFF
I CAN SEE CLEARLY NOW [B] — Deborah HARRY
I CAN SEE FOR MILES — The WHO
I CAN SEE HER NOW — DRAMATIS
I CAN SEE IT — BLANCMANGE
I CAN SING A RAINBOW - LOVE IS BLUE (MEDLEY) — The DELLS
I CAN TAKE OR LEAVE YOUR LOVING — HERMAN'S HERMITS
I CANNOT GIVE YOU MY LOVE — Cliff RICHARD
I CAN'T ASK FOR ANYTHING MORE THAN YOU — Cliff RICHARD

9 December 2000	16 December 2000	23 December 2000	30 December 2000

◂◂ UK No.1 SINGLES ▸▸

NEVER HAD A DREAM COME TRUE S Club 7	STAN Eminem	CAN WE FIX IT? Bob the Builder	CAN WE FIX IT? Bob the Builder

◂ UK No.1 ALBUMS ▸▸

...les	1 The Beatles	1 The Beatles	1 The Beatles

I CAN'T BE WITH YOU — The CRANBERRIES
I CAN'T BELIEVE YOU'RE GONE — The WEBB BROTHERS
I CAN'T BREAK DOWN — Sinead QUINN
I CAN'T CONTROL MYSELF — The TROGGS
I CAN'T DANCE — GENESIS
I CAN'T DENY IT — Rod STEWART
I CAN'T EXPLAIN — The WHO
I CAN'T FACE THE WORLD — LEMON TREES
I CAN'T GET NEXT TO YOU — The TEMPTATIONS
(I CAN'T GET NO) SATISFACTION [A] — The ROLLING STONES (65)
(I CAN'T GET NO) SATISFACTION [A] — Jonathan KING
I CAN'T GET NO SLEEP — INDIA
I CAN'T GET YOU OUT OF MY MIND — Yvonne ELLIMAN
I CAN'T GO FOR THAT (NO CAN DO) — Daryl HALL and John OATES
(I CAN'T HELP) FALLING IN LOVE WITH YOU — UB40 (93)
I CAN'T HELP IT [A] — Johnny TILLOTSON
I CAN'T HELP IT [C] — JUNIOR
I CAN'T HELP IT [B] — BANANARAMA
I CAN'T HELP MYSELF [A] — The FOUR TOPS
I CAN'T HELP MYSELF [A] — Donnie ELBERT
I CAN'T HELP MYSELF [B] — ORANGE JUICE
I CAN'T HELP MYSELF [C] — Joey LAWRENCE
I CAN'T HELP MYSELF [D] — Julia FORDHAM
I CAN'T HELP MYSELF [E] — LUCID
I CAN'T IMAGINE THE WORLD WITHOUT ME — ECHOBELLY
I CAN'T LEAVE YOU ALONE [A] — George McCRAE
I CAN'T LEAVE YOU ALONE [A] — TRACIE
I CAN'T LET GO [A] — The HOLLIES
I CAN'T LET GO [B] — Marti WEBB
I CAN'T LET MAGGIE GO — HONEYBUS
I CAN'T LET YOU GO [A] — HAYWOODE
I CAN'T LET YOU GO [B] — 52ND STREET
I CAN'T LET YOU GO [C] — MACK VIBE featuring JACQUELINE
I CAN'T LET YOU GO [D] — IAN VAN DAHL
I CAN'T LIVE A DREAM — The OSMONDS
I CAN'T MAKE A MISTAKE — MC LYTE
I CAN'T MAKE IT — The SMALL FACES
I CAN'T MAKE IT ALONE [A] — PJ PROBY
I CAN'T MAKE IT ALONE [A] — Maria McKEE
I CAN'T MAKE YOU LOVE ME [A] — Bonnie RAITT
I CAN'T MAKE YOU LOVE ME [B] — George MICHAEL
(I CAN'T GET ME NO) SATISFACTION — DEVO
I CAN'T READ — David BOWIE
I CAN'T READ YOU — Daniel BEDINGFIELD
I CAN'T SAY GOODBYE — Kim WILDE
I CAN'T SAY GOODBYE TO YOU — Helen REDDY
I CAN'T SEE — Nicole RAY
I CAN'T STAND MY BABY — REZILLOS
I CAN'T STAND IT [A] — Spencer DAVIS GROUP
I CAN'T STAND IT [B] — CAPTAIN HOLLYWOOD PROJECT
I CAN'T STAND THE RAIN [A] — Ann PEEBLES
I CAN'T STAND THE RAIN [A] — ERUPTION
I CAN'T STAND THE RAIN [A] — Tina TURNER
I CAN'T STAND UP FOR FALLING DOWN — Elvis COSTELLO
I CAN'T STOP [A] — The OSMONDS
I CAN'T STOP [B] — Gary NUMAN
I CAN'T STOP [C] — Sandy RIVERA
I CAN'T STOP LOVIN' YOU (THOUGH I TRY) — Leo SAYER
I CAN'T STOP LOVING YOU — Ray CHARLES (62)
I CAN'T TAKE THE POWER — OFF-SHORE
I CAN'T TELL A WALTZ FROM A TANGO — Alma COGAN
I CAN'T TELL THE BOTTOM FROM THE TOP — The HOLLIES
I CAN'T TELL YOU WHY — BROWNSTONE
I CAN'T TURN AROUND — JM SILK
I CAN'T TURN AWAY — SAVANNA
I CAN'T TURN YOU LOOSE — Otis REDDING
I CAN'T WAIT [A] — Stevie NICKS
I CAN'T WAIT [B] — NU SHOOZ
I CAN'T WAIT [B] — LADIES FIRST
I CAN'T WAIT ANYMORE — SAXON
I CARE (SOUL II SOUL) — SOUL II SOUL

I CAUGHT YOU OUT — Rebecca DE RUVO
I CLOSE MY EYES AND COUNT TO TEN — Dusty SPRINGFIELD
I COME FROM ANOTHER PLANET BABY — Julian COPE
I CONFESS — The BEAT
I COULD BE AN ANGLE — The EIGHTIES MATCHBOX B-LINE DISASTER
I COULD BE HAPPY — ALTERED IMAGES
I COULD BE SO GOOD FOR YOU — Dennis WATERMAN
I COULD BE THE ONE — Stacie ORRICO
I COULD EASILY FALL — Cliff RICHARD and The SHADOWS
I COULD HAVE BEEN A DREAMER — DIO
I COULD NEVER LOVE ANOTHER — The TEMPTATIONS
I COULD NEVER MISS YOU (MORE THAN I DO) — LULU
I COULD NEVER TAKE THE PLACE OF YOUR MAN — PRINCE
I COULD NOT LOVE YOU MORE — The BEE GEES
I COULD SING OF YOUR LOVE FOREVER — DELIRIOUS?
I COULDN'T LIVE WITHOUT YOUR LOVE — Petula CLARK
I COUNT THE TEARS — The DRIFTERS
I CRIED FOR YOU [A] — Ricky STEVENS
I CRIED FOR YOU [B] — Katie MELUA
I DID WHAT I DID FOR MARIA — Tony CHRISTIE
I DIDN'T KNOW I LOVED YOU (TILL I SAW YOU ROCK 'N' ROLL) [A] — Gary GLITTER
I DIDN'T KNOW I LOVED YOU (TILL I SAW YOU ROCK 'N' ROLL) [A] — ROCK GODDESS
I DIDN'T KNOW I WAS LOOKING FOR LOVE (EP) — EVERYTHING BUT THE GIRL
I DIDN'T MEAN IT — STATUS QUO
I DIDN'T MEAN TO HURT YOU — The ROCKIN' BERRIES
I DIDN'T MEAN TO TURN YOU ON — Robert PALMER
I DIDN'T WANT TO NEED YOU — HEART
I DIE: YOU DIE — Gary NUMAN
I DIG YOU BABY — Marvin RAINWATER
I DISAPPEAR — METALLICA
I DO — JAMELIA
I DO, I DO, I DO, I DO, I DO — ABBA
I DO WHAT I DO ... THEME FOR '9 1/2 WEEKS' — John TAYLOR
I DON'T BELIEVE IN IF ANYMORE — Roger WHITTAKER
I DON'T BELIEVE IN MIRACLES [A] — Colin BLUNSTONE
I DON'T BELIEVE IN MIRACLES [B] — SINITTA
I DON'T BLAME YOU AT ALL — MIRACLES
I DON'T CARE [A] — LIBERACE
I DON'T CARE [B] — LOS BRAVOS
I DON'T CARE [C] — SHAKESPEAR'S SISTER
I DON'T CARE [D] — Tony De VIT
I DON'T CARE [E] — Ricky MARTIN
I DON'T CARE IF THE SUN DON'T SHINE — Elvis PRESLEY
I DON'T EVEN KNOW IF I SHOULD CALL YOU BABY — SOUL FAMILY SENSATION
I DON'T EVER WANT TO SEE YOU AGAIN — UNCLE SAM
I DON'T KNOW [A] — RUTH
I DON'T KNOW [B] — HONEYZ
I DON'T KNOW ANYBODY ELSE — BLACK BOX
I DON'T KNOW HOW TO LOVE HIM [A] — Petula CLARK
I DON'T KNOW HOW TO LOVE HIM [A] — Yvonne ELLIMAN
I DON'T KNOW IF IT'S RIGHT — Evelyn 'Champagne' KING
I DON'T KNOW WHAT IT IS — Rufus WAINWRIGHT
I DON'T KNOW WHAT IT IS BUT I LOVE IT — Chris REA
I DON'T KNOW WHAT YOU WANT BUT I CAN'T GIVE IT ANYMORE — PET SHOP BOYS
I DON'T KNOW WHERE IT COMES FROM — RIDE
I DON'T KNOW WHY [A] — Eden KANE
I DON'T KNOW WHY [B] — Shawn COLVIN
I DON'T KNOW WHY (I JUST DO) — Andy and David WILLIAMS

(I DON'T KNOW WHY) BUT I DO — Clarence 'Frogman' HENRY
I DON'T KNOW WHY I LOVE YOU — HOUSE OF LOVE
I DON'T KNOW WHY (I LOVE YOU) — Stevie WONDER
I DON'T LIKE MONDAYS — The BOOMTOWN RATS (79)
I DON'T LOVE YOU ANYMORE — QUIREBOYS
I DON'T LOVE YOU BUT I THINK I LIKE YOU — Gilbert O'SULLIVAN
I DON'T MIND — The BUZZCOCKS
I DON'T MIND AT ALL — BOURGEOIS TAGG
I DON'T NEED ANYTHING — Sandie SHAW
I DON'T NEED NO DOCTOR (LIVE) — W.A.S.P.
I DON'T NEED TO TELL HER — LURKERS
I DON'T REALLY CARE — K-GEE
I DON'T REMEMBER — Peter GABRIEL
I DON'T SMOKE — DJ DEE KLINE
I DON'T THINK SO — DINOSAUR JR
I DON'T THINK THAT MAN SHOULD SLEEP ALONE — Ray PARKER Jr
I DON'T WANNA BE A STAR — CORONA
I DON'T WANNA DANCE — Eddy GRANT (82)
I DON'T WANNA FIGHT — Tina TURNER
I DON'T WANNA GET HURT — Donna SUMMER
I DON'T WANNA GO ON WITH YOU LIKE THAT — Elton JOHN
I DON'T WANNA KNOW [A] — Mario WINANS featuring ENYA & P DIDDY (04)
I DON'T WANNA KNOW [B] — NEW FOUND GLORY
I DON'T WANNA LOSE AT LOVE — Tanita TIKARAM
I DON'T WANNA LOSE MY WAY — DREAMCATCHER
I DON'T WANNA LOSE YOU [A] — KANDIDATE
I DON'T WANNA LOSE YOU [B] — Tina TURNER
I DON'T WANNA LOSE YOUR LOVE — The EMOTIONS
I DON'T WANNA PLAY HOUSE — Tammy WYNETTE
I DON'T WANNA TAKE THIS PAIN — Dannii MINOGUE
I DON'T WANT A LOVER — TEXAS
I DON'T WANT CONTROL OF YOU — TEENAGE FANCLUB
I DON'T WANT NOBODY (TELLIN' ME WHAT TO DO) — Cherie AMORE
I DON'T WANT OUR LOVING TO DIE — The HERD
I DON'T WANT TO — Toni BRAXTON
I DON'T WANT TO BE — Gavin DEGRAW
I DON'T WANT TO BE A FREAK (BUT I CAN'T HELP MYSELF) — DYNASTY
I DON'T WANT TO BE A HERO — JOHNNY HATES JAZZ
I DON'T WANT TO GO ON WITHOUT YOU — The MOODY BLUES
(I DON'T WANT TO GO TO) CHELSEA — Elvis COSTELLO
I DON'T WANT TO HURT YOU (EVERY SINGLE TIME) — Frank BLACK
I DON'T WANT TO KNOW (IF YOU DON'T WANT ME) — The DONNAS
I DON'T WANT TO MISS A THING — AEROSMITH
I DON'T WANT TO PUT A HOLD ON YOU — Berni FLINT
I DON'T WANT TO TALK ABOUT IT [A] — Rod STEWART (77)
I DON'T WANT TO TALK ABOUT IT [A] — EVERYTHING BUT THE GIRL
I DON'T WANT TO WAIT — Paula COLE
I DON'T WANT YOUR LOVE — DURAN DURAN
I DREAM — TILT
I DREAMED — The BEVERLEY SISTERS
I DROVE ALL NIGHT [A] — Cyndi LAUPER
I DROVE ALL NIGHT [A] — Roy ORBISON
I EAT CANNIBALS PART 1 — TOTO COELO
I ENJOY BEING A GIRL — Pat SUZUKI
I FEEL A CRY COMING ON — Hank LOCKLIN
I FEEL DIVINE — S-J
I FEEL FINE [A] — The BEATLES (64)
I FEEL FINE [A] — WET WET WET
I FEEL FOR YOU [A] — Chaka KHAN (84)
I FEEL FOR YOU [B] — Bob SINCLAR
I FEEL FREE — CREAM

I FEEL GOOD THINGS FOR YOU — DADDY'S FAVOURITE
I FEEL IT — MOBY
I FEEL JUST LIKE A CHILD — Devendra BANHART
I FEEL LIKE BUDDY HOLLY — Alvin STARDUST
I FEEL LIKE WALKIN' IN THE RAIN — Millie JACKSON
I FEEL LOVE [A] — Donna SUMMER (77)
I FEEL LOVE (MEDLEY) [A] — BRONSKI BEAT and Marc ALMOND
I FEEL LOVE [A] — MESSIAH
I FEEL LOVE [A] — VANESSA-MAE
I FEEL LOVE [B] — CRW
I FEEL LOVE COMIN' ON [A] — Felice TAYLOR
I FEEL LOVE COMIN' ON [A] — DANA
I FEEL LOVED — DEPECHE MODE
I FEEL SO — BOX CAR RACER
I FEEL SO BAD — Elvis PRESLEY
I FEEL SO FINE — KMC featuring DHANY
I FEEL SOMETHING IN THE AIR — CHER
I FEEL STEREO — Dino LENNY
I FEEL THE EARTH MOVE — MARTIKA
I FEEL YOU [A] — LOVE DECADE
I FEEL YOU [B] — DEPECHE MODE
I FEEL YOU [C] — Peter ANDRE (96)
I FINALLY FOUND SOMEONE — Barbra STREISAND and Bryan ADAMS
I FORGOT [A] — COOLNOTES
I FORGOT [B] — Lionel RICHIE
I FOUGHT THE LAW [A] — Bobby FULLER FOUR
I FOUGHT THE LAW [A] — The CLASH
I FOUND HEAVEN — TAKE THAT
I FOUND LOVE [A] — Darlene DAVIS
I FOUND LOVE [B] — LONE JUSTICE
I FOUND LOVE [C] — C & C MUSIC FACTORY / CLIVILLES & COLE featuring Martha WASH
I FOUND LOVIN' [A] — FATBACK BAND
I FOUND LOVIN' [A] — Steve WALSH
I FOUND OUT — The CHRISTIANS
I FOUND OUT THE HARD WAY — FOUR PENNIES
I FOUND SOMEONE [A] — CHER
I FOUND SOMEONE [B] — Billy and Sarah GAINES
I FOUND SUNSHINE — CHI-LITES
I (FRIDAY NIGHT) — DUBSTAR
I GAVE IT UP (WHEN I FELL IN LOVE) — Luther VANDROSS
I GAVE MY EYES TO STEVIE WONDER — MILLION DEAD
I GAVE YOU EVERYTHING — CODE RED
I GAVE YOU MY HEART (DIDN'T I) — HOT CHOCOLATE
I GET A KICK OUT OF YOU — Gary SHEARSTON
I GET A LITTLE SENTIMENTAL OVER YOU — The NEW SEEKERS
I GET ALONG — PET SHOP BOYS
I GET AROUND — The BEACH BOYS
I GET LIFTED — Barbara TUCKER
I GET LONELY — Janet JACKSON
I GET SO EXCITED — The EQUALS
I GET THE SWEETEST FEELING — Jackie WILSON
I GET WEAK — Belinda CARLISLE
I GIVE — TAKE 5
I GIVE IT ALL TO YOU — Mary KIANI
I GIVE YOU MY HEART — MR PRESIDENT
I GO APE — Neil SEDAKA
I GO TO EXTREMES — Billy JOEL
I GO TO PIECES (EVERYTIME) — Gerri GRANGER
I GO TO SLEEP — The PRETENDERS
I GO WILD — The ROLLING STONES
I GOT A FEELING — Ricky NELSON
I GOT A GIRL — Lou BEGA
I GOT A LITTLE SONG — OFF-SHORE
I GOT A MAN — POSITIVE K
I GOT DA FEELIN' — SWEET TEE
I GOT 5 ON IT — LUNIZ
I GOT ID — PEARL JAM
I GOT IT GOIN' ON [A] — Tone LOC
I GOT IT GOIN' ON [B] — US3
I GOT MINE — MOTÖRHEAD
I GOT MY EDUCATION — UNCANNY ALLIANCE
I GOT RHYTHM — HAPPENINGS
I GOT SOMEBODY ELSE — CHANGING FACES
I GOT STUNG — Elvis PRESLEY (59, 05)
I GOT THE VIBRATION — BLACK BOX
I GOT THIS FEELING — BABY BUMPS
I GOT TO SING — J.A.L.N. BAND

6 January 2001	13 January 2001	20 January 2001	27 January 2001
CAN WE FIX IT? Bob the Builder	TOUCH ME Rui Da Silva featuring Cassandra	LOVE DON'T COST A THING Jennifer Lopez	ROLLIN' Limp Bizkit
1 The Beatles	1 The Beatles	1 The Beatles	THE GREATEST HITS Texas

I GOT YOU [A] — James BROWN
I GOT YOU [B] — SPLIT ENZ
I GOT YOU BABE [A] — SONNY and CHER (65)
I GOT YOU BABE [A] — UB40 featuring Chrissie HYNDE (85)
I GOT YOU BABE [A] — CHER
I GOT YOU BABE [A] — MERRION, McCALL & KENSIT
I GUESS I'LL ALWAYS LOVE YOU — The ISLEY BROTHERS
I GUESS THAT'S WHY THEY CALL IT THE BLUES — Elton JOHN
I HAD TOO MUCH TO DREAM LAST NIGHT — The ELECTRIC PRUNES
I HATE MYSELF FOR LOVING YOU — Joan JETT and The BLACKHEARTS
I HATE ... PEOPLE — ANTI-NOWHERE LEAGUE
I HATE ROCK 'N' ROLL — JESUS AND MARY CHAIN
I HAVE A DREAM [A] — ABBA
I HAVE A DREAM [A] — WESTLIFE (99)
I HAVE FORGIVEN JESUS — MORRISSEY
I HAVE NOTHING — Whitney HOUSTON
I HAVE PEACE — STRIKE
I HAVEN'T STOPPED DANCING YET — PAT and MICK
I HEAR A SYMPHONY — The SUPREMES
I HEAR TALK — BUCKS FIZZ
I HEAR YOU KNOCKING — Dave EDMUNDS' ROCKPILE (70)
I HEAR YOU NOW — JON and VANGELIS
I HEAR YOUR NAME — INCOGNITO
I HEARD A HEART BREAK LAST NIGHT — Jim REEVES
I HEARD A RUMOUR — BANANARAMA
I HEARD IT THROUGH THE GRAPEVINE [A] — Gladys KNIGHT and The PIPS
I HEARD IT THROUGH THE GRAPEVINE [A] — Marvin GAYE (69)
I HEARD IT THROUGH THE GRAPEVINE [A] — The SLITS
I HONESTLY LOVE YOU — Olivia NEWTON-JOHN
I HOPE YOU DANCE [A] — Lee Ann WOMACK
I HOPE YOU DANCE [A] — Ronan KEATING
I IMAGINE — Mary KIANI
I JUST CALLED TO SAY I LOVE YOU — Stevie WONDER (84)
I JUST CAN'T BE HAPPY TODAY — The DAMNED
(I JUST CAN'T) FORGIVE AND FORGET — BLUE ZOO
I JUST CAN'T GET ENOUGH — HERD & FITZ featuring Abigail BAILEY
I JUST CAN'T HELP BELIEVING — Elvis PRESLEY
I JUST CAN'T STOP LOVING YOU — Michael JACKSON (87)
(I JUST) DIED IN YOUR ARMS [A] — CUTTING CREW
(I JUST) DIED IN YOUR ARMS [A] — RESOURCE
I JUST DON'T HAVE THE HEART — Cliff RICHARD
I JUST DON'T KNOW WHAT TO DO WITH MYSELF [A] — Dusty SPRINGFIELD
I JUST DON'T KNOW WHAT TO DO WITH MYSELF [A] — The WHITE STRIPES
I JUST FALL IN LOVE AGAIN — Anne MURRAY
I JUST GO FOR YOU — Jimmy JONES
I JUST HAD TO HEAR YOUR VOICE — Oleta ADAMS
I JUST KEEP THINKING ABOUT YOU BABY — Tata VEGA
I JUST NEED MYSELF — OCEAN COLOUR SCENE
(I JUST WANNA) B WITH U — TRANSVISION VAMP
I JUST WANNA BE LOVED — CULTURE CLUB
I JUST WANNA BE YOUR EVERYTHING — Andy GIBB
I JUST WANNA LIVE — GOOD CHARLOTTE
I JUST WANNA LOVE U (GIVE IT 2 ME) — JAY-Z
I JUST WANNA (SPEND SOME TIME WITH YOU) — Alton EDWARDS
I JUST WANT TO DANCE WITH YOU — Daniel O'DONNELL
I JUST WANT TO MAKE LOVE TO YOU — Etta JAMES
I JUST WANT YOU — Ozzy OSBOURNE
I KEEP FORGETTIN' — Michael McDONALD
I KEEP RINGING MY BABY — The SOUL BROTHERS
I KISS YOUR LIPS — TOKYO GHETTO PUSSY
I KNEW I LOVED YOU — SAVAGE GARDEN
I KNEW THE BRIDE — Dave EDMUNDS
I KNEW YOU WERE WAITING (FOR ME) — Aretha FRANKLIN and George MICHAEL (87)
I KNOW [A] — Perry COMO
I KNOW [B] — Paul KING
I KNOW [C] — NEW ATLANTIC
I KNOW [D] — Dionne FARRIS
I KNOW A PLACE [A] — Petula CLARK
I KNOW A PLACE [B] — Kim ENGLISH
I KNOW ENOUGH (I DON'T GET ENOUGH) — THEAUDIENCE
I KNOW HIM SO WELL [A] — Elaine PAIGE and Barbara DICKSON (85)
I KNOW HIM SO WELL [A] — STEPS
(I KNOW) I'M LOSING YOU — The TEMPTATIONS
I KNOW MY LOVE — The CHIEFTAINS featuring The CORRS
I KNOW THE LORD — TABERNACLE
I KNOW THERE'S SOMETHING GOING ON — FRIDA
I KNOW WHAT BOYS LIKE — SHAMPOO
I KNOW WHAT I LIKE (IN YOUR WARDROBE) — GENESIS
I KNOW WHAT I'M HERE FOR — JAMES
I KNOW WHAT YOU WANT — Busta RHYMES and Mariah CAREY
I KNOW WHERE I'M GOING [A] — George HAMILTON IV
I KNOW WHERE I'M GOING [A] — COUNTRYMEN
I KNOW WHERE IT'S AT — ALL SAINTS
I KNOW YOU DON'T LOVE ME — ROACHFORD
I KNOW YOU GOT SOUL — Eric B and RAKIM
I KNOW YOU'RE OUT THERE SOMEWHERE — The MOODY BLUES
I LEARNED FROM THE BEST — Whitney HOUSTON
I LEFT MY HEART IN SAN FRANCISCO — Tony BENNETT
I LIFT MY CUP — GLOWORM
I LIKE [A] — SHANICE
I LIKE [B] — KUT KLOSE
I LIKE [C] — Montell JORDAN
I LIKE [D] — Juliet ROBERTS
I LIKE GIRLS — HOUND DOGS
I LIKE IT [A] — GERRY and The PACEMAKERS (63)
I LIKE IT [B] — J.A.L.N. BAND
I LIKE IT [C] — DJH featuring STEFY
I LIKE IT [D] — Ce Ce PENISTON
I LIKE IT [E] — D:REAM
I LIKE IT [F] — JOMANDA
I LIKE IT [G] — Angel MORAES
I LIKE IT [H] — NARCOTIC THRUST
I LIKE LOVE (I LOVE LOVE) — SOLITAIRE
I LIKE THAT — HOUSTON featuring CHINGY, NATE DOGG & I-20
I LIKE THE WAY [A] — Deni HINES
I LIKE THE WAY [B] — BODYROCKERS
I LIKE THE WAY (THE KISSING GAME) [A] — HI-FIVE
I LIKE THE WAY (THE KISSING GAME) [A] — KALEEF
I LIKE TO MOVE IT — REEL 2 REAL
I LIKE TO ROCK — APRIL WINE
I LIKE (WHAT YOU'RE DOING TO ME) — YOUNG and COMPANY
I LIKE YOUR KIND OF LOVE — Andy WILLIAMS
I LIVE FOR SPEED — STAR SPANGLES
I LIVE FOR THE SUN — VANITY FARE
I LIVE FOR THE WEEKEND — TRIUMPH
I LIVE FOR YOUR LOVE — Natalie COLE
I LOST MY HEART TO A STARSHIP TROOPER — Sarah BRIGHTMAN
I LOVE A MAN IN UNIFORM — GANG OF FOUR
I LOVE A RAINY NIGHT — Eddie RABBITT
I LOVE AMERICA — Patrick JUVET
I LOVE BEING IN LOVE WITH YOU — Adam FAITH
I LOVE CHRISTMAS — FAST FOOD ROCKERS
I LOVE FOOTBALL — WES
I LOVE HER — Paul and Barry RYAN
I LOVE HOW YOU LOVE ME [A] — Jimmy CRAWFORD
I LOVE HOW YOU LOVE ME [A] — Maureen EVANS
I LOVE HOW YOU LOVE ME [A] — Paul and Barry RYAN
I LOVE I HATE — Neil ARTHUR
I LOVE IT WHEN WE DO — Ronan KEATING
I LOVE LAKE TAHOE — A
I LOVE MEN — Eartha KITT
I LOVE MUSIC [A] — O'JAYS
I LOVE MUSIC [A] — ENIGMA
I LOVE MUSIC [A] — ROZALLA
I LOVE MY DOG — Cat STEVENS
I LOVE MY RADIO (MY DEE JAY'S RADIO) — TAFFY
I LOVE ROCK 'N' ROLL [A] — Joan JETT and The BLACKHEARTS
I LOVE ROCK 'N' ROLL [A] — Britney SPEARS
I LOVE SATURDAY — ERASURE
I LOVE THE NIGHT LIFE (DISCO ROUND) — Alicia BRIDGES
I LOVE THE SOUND OF BREAKING GLASS — Nick LOWE
I LOVE THE WAY YOU LOVE — Marv JOHNSON
I LOVE THE WAY YOU LOVE ME — BOYZONE
I LOVE TO BOOGIE — T. REX
I LOVE TO LOVE (BUT MY BABY LOVES TO DANCE) — Tina CHARLES (76)
I LOVE YOU [A] — Cliff RICHARD and The SHADOWS (60)
I LOVE YOU [B] — Donna SUMMER
I LOVE YOU [C] — YELLO
I LOVE YOU [D] — VANILLA ICE
I LOVE YOU [E] — FLESH & BONES
I LOVE YOU ALWAYS FOREVER — Donna LEWIS
I LOVE YOU BABY [A] — FREDDIE and The DREAMERS
I LOVE YOU, BABY [A] — Paul ANKA
I LOVE YOU BECAUSE [A] — Al MARTINO
I LOVE YOU BECAUSE [A] — Jim REEVES
I LOVE YOU, BUT — The RESEARCH
I LOVE YOU 'CAUSE I HAVE TO — DOGS DIE IN HOT CARS
I LOVE YOU GOODBYE — Thomas DOLBY
I LOVE YOU LOVE ME LOVE — Gary GLITTER (73)
I LOVE YOU MORE THAN ROCK 'N ROLL — THUNDER
I LOVE YOU ... STOP! — RED 5
I LOVE YOU SO MUCH IT HURTS — Charlie GRACIE
(I LOVE YOU) WHEN YOU SLEEP — TRACIE
I LOVE YOU, YES I DO — The MERSEYBEATS
I LOVE YOU, YES I LOVE YOU — Eddy GRANT
I LOVE YOUR SMILE — SHANICE
I LUV U [A] — SHUT UP AND DANCE
I LUV U [B] — DIZZEE RASCAL
I LUV U BABY — ORIGINAL
I MADE IT THROUGH THE RAIN — Barry MANILOW
I MAY NEVER PASS THIS WAY AGAIN [A] — Perry COMO
I MAY NEVER PASS THIS WAY AGAIN [A] — Robert EARL
I MAY NEVER PASS THIS WAY AGAIN [A] — Ronnie HILTON
I MET A GIRL — The SHADOWS
I MIGHT — Shakin' STEVENS
I MIGHT BE CRYING — Tanita TIKARAM
I MIGHT BE LYING — EDDIE and The HOT RODS
I MISS YOU [A] — BJÖRK
I MISS YOU [B] — 4 OF US
I MISS YOU [C] — HADDAWAY
I MISS YOU [D] — Darren HAYES
I MISS YOU [E] — BLINK-182
I MISS YOU BABY — Marv JOHNSON
I MISSED AGAIN — Phil COLLINS
I MISSED THE BUS — KRIS KROSS
I MUST BE IN LOVE — RUTLES
I MUST BE SEEING THINGS — Gene PITNEY
I MUST STAND — ICE-T
I NEED — Meredith BROOKS
I NEED A GIRL — GROUNDED
I NEED A GIRL (PART ONE) — P DIDDY
I NEED A LOVER TONIGHT — Ken DOH
I NEED A MAN [A] — MAN TO MAN
I NEED A MAN [B] — EURYTHMICS
I NEED A MAN [C] — Li KWAN
I NEED A MIRACLE — COCO
I NEED ANOTHER (EP) — DODGY
I NEED DIRECTION — TEENAGE FANCLUB
I NEED IT — Johnny 'Guitar' WATSON
I NEED LOVE [A] — LL COOL J
I NEED LOVE [B] — Olivia NEWTON-JOHN
I NEED SOME FINE WINE AND YOU, YOU NEED TO BE NICER — The CARDIGANS
I NEED SOMEBODY — LOVELAND featuring the voice of Rachel McFARLANE
I NEED THE KEY — MINIMAL CHIC featuring Matt GOSS
I NEED TO BE IN LOVE — The CARPENTERS
I NEED TO KNOW — Marc ANTHONY
I NEED YOU [A] — Joe DOLAN
I NEED YOU [B] — POINTER SISTERS
I NEED YOU [C] — BVSMP
I NEED YOU [D] — DEUCE
I NEED YOU [E] — Nikita WARREN
I NEED YOU [F] — 3T
I NEED YOU [G] — WIRELESS
I NEED YOU [H] — LeAnn RIMES
I NEED YOU [I] — Dave GAHAN
I NEED YOU [J] — The STANDS
I NEED YOU NOW [A] — Eddie FISHER
I NEED YOU NOW [B] — SINNAMON
I NEED YOU TONIGHT — JUNIOR M.A.F.I.A. featuring AALIYAH
I NEED YOUR LOVE TONIGHT — Elvis PRESLEY with The JORDANAIRES (59)
I NEED YOUR LOVIN' [A] — Teena MARIE
I NEED YOUR LOVIN' [A] — CURIOSITY
I NEED YOUR LOVIN' [B] — Alyson WILLIAMS
I NEED YOUR LOVIN' (LIKE THE SUNSHINE) — MARC et CLAUDE
I NEED YOUR LOVING — HUMAN LEAGUE
I NEVER FELT LIKE THIS BEFORE — Mica PARIS
I NEVER GO OUT IN THE RAIN — HIGH SOCIETY
I NEVER KNEW — Roger SANCHEZ
I NEVER LOVED YOU ANYWAY — The CORRS
I NEVER WANT AN EASY LIFE IF ME AND HE WERE EVER TO GET THERE — The CHARLATANS
I ONLY HAVE EYES FOR YOU — Art GARFUNKEL (75)
I ONLY LIVE TO LOVE YOU — Cilla BLACK
I ONLY WANNA BE WITH YOU [A] — BAY CITY ROLLERS
I ONLY WANNA BE WITH YOU [A] — Samantha FOX
I ONLY WANT TO BE WITH YOU [A] — Dusty SPRINGFIELD
I ONLY WANT TO BE WITH YOU [A] — TOURISTS
I ONLY WANT TO BE WITH YOU [B] — Barry WHITE
I OWE YOU NOTHING — BROS (88)
I OWE YOU ONE — SHALAMAR
I PREDICT A RIOT — KAISER CHIEFS
I PRETEND — Des O'CONNOR (68)
I PROMISE — Stacie ORRICO
I PROMISE YOU (GET READY) — Samantha FOX
I PROMISED MYSELF — Nick KAMEN
I PRONOUNCE YOU — MADNESS
I PUT A SPELL ON YOU [A] — Alan PRICE
I PUT A SPELL ON YOU [A] — Nina SIMONE
I PUT A SPELL ON YOU [A] — Bryan FERRY
I PUT A SPELL ON YOU [A] — SONIQUE
I QUIT [A] — BROS
I QUIT [B] — HEPBURN
I RAN — A FLOCK OF SEAGULLS
I REALLY DIDN'T MEAN IT — Luther VANDROSS
I RECALL A GYPSY WOMAN — Don WILLIAMS
I REFUSE — HUE AND CRY
I REFUSE (WHAT YOU WANT) — SOMORE featuring DAMON TRUEITT
I REMEMBER — COOLIO
I REMEMBER ELVIS PRESLEY (THE KING IS DEAD) — Danny MIRROR
I REMEMBER YESTERDAY — Donna SUMMER
I REMEMBER YOU [A] — Frank IFIELD (62)
I REMEMBER YOU [B] — SKID ROW
I ROCK — Tom NOVY
I SAID I LOVE YOU — Raul MALO
I SAID NEVER AGAIN (BUT HERE WE ARE) — Rachel STEVENS
I SAID PIG ON FRIDAY — EASTERN LANE
I SAVED THE WORLD TODAY — EURYTHMICS
I SAW HER AGAIN — The MAMAS and The PAPAS
I SAW HER STANDING THERE [A] — Elton JOHN BAND featuring John LENNON and the MUSCLE SHOALS HORNS

3 February 2001	10 February 2001	17 February 2001	24 February 2001
UK No.1 SINGLES			
ROLLIN' Limp Bizkit	WHOLE AGAIN Atomic Kitten	WHOLE AGAIN Atomic Kitten	WHOLE AGAIN Atomic Kitten
UK No.1 ALBUMS			
…COLATE STARFISH AND THE HOT …VORED WATER Limp Bizkit	NO ANGEL Dido	NO ANGEL Dido	NO ANGEL Dido

I SAW HIM STANDING THERE [A] — TIFFANY
I SAW LINDA YESTERDAY — Doug SHELDON
I SAW MOMMY KISSING SANTA CLAUS [A] — The BEVERLEY SISTERS
I SAW MOMMY KISSING SANTA CLAUS [A] — Billy COTTON and his BAND
I SAW MOMMY KISSING SANTA CLAUS [A] — Jimmy BOYD
I SAW THE LIGHT [A] — Todd RUNDGREN
I SAW THE LIGHT [B] — The THE
I SAY A LITTLE PRAYER [A] — Aretha FRANKLIN
I SAY A LITTLE PRAYER [A] — Diana KING
I SAY NOTHING — VOICE OF THE BEEHIVE
I SAY YEAH — SECCHI featuring Orlando JOHNSON
I SCARE MYSELF — Thomas DOLBY
I SECOND THAT EMOTION [A] — MIRACLES
I SECOND THAT EMOTION [A] — Diana ROSS and The SUPREMES and The TEMPTATIONS
I SECOND THAT EMOTION [A] — JAPAN
I SECOND THAT EMOTION [A] — Alyson WILLIAMS
I SEE A STAR — MOUTH and MACNEAL
I SEE GIRLS (CRAZY) — STUDIO B / ROMEO and Harry BROOKS
I SEE ONLY YOU — NOOTROPIC
I SEE THE MOON — The STARGAZERS (54)
I SEE YOU BABY — GROOVE ARMADA featuring GRAM'MA FUNK
I SEE YOUR SMILE — Gloria ESTEFAN
I SEEN A MAN DIE — SCARFACE
I SHALL BE RELEASED — The TREMELOES
I SHALL BE THERE — B*WITCHED featuring LADYSMITH BLACK MAMBAZO
I SHOT THE SHERIFF [A] — Eric CLAPTON
I SHOT THE SHERIFF [A] — LIGHT OF THE WORLD
I SHOT THE SHERIFF [A] — Warren G
I SHOT THE SHERIFF [A] — Bob MARLEY & The WAILERS
I SHOULD BE SO LUCKY — Kylie MINOGUE (88)
I SHOULD CARE — Frank IFIELD
I SHOULD HAVE KNOWN BETTER [A] — NATURALS
I SHOULD HAVE KNOWN BETTER [B] — Jim DIAMOND (84)
I SHOULDA LOVED YA — Narada Michael WALDEN
I SHOULD'VE KNOWN — Aimee MANN
I SINGS — MARY MARY
I SLEEP ALONE AT NIGHT — Jim DIAMOND
I SPEAKA DA LINGO — BLACK LACE
I SPECIALIZE IN LOVE [A] — Sharon BROWN
I SPECIALIZE IN LOVE [A] — ARIZONA featuring ZEITIA
I SPY FOR THE FBI [A] — Jamo THOMAS
I SPY FOR THE FBI [A] — UNTOUCHABLES
I STAND ACCUSED — The MERSEYBEATS
I STAND ALONE — E-MOTION
I STARTED A JOKE — FAITH NO MORE
I STARTED SOMETHING I COULDN'T FINISH — The SMITHS
I STILL BELIEVE [A] — Ronnie HILTON
I STILL BELIEVE [B] — Mariah CAREY
I STILL BELIEVE IN YOU — Cliff RICHARD
I STILL HAVEN'T FOUND WHAT I'M LOOKING FOR [A] — U2
I STILL HAVEN'T FOUND WHAT I'M LOOKING FOR [A] — The CHIMES
I STILL LOVE YOU ALL — Kenny BALL and his JAZZMEN
I STILL REMEMBER — Gary NUMAN
I STILL THINK ABOUT YOU — DANGER DANGER
I STILL THINK OF YOU — UTAH SAINTS
I SURRENDER [A] — RAINBOW
I SURRENDER [B] — Rosie GAINES
I SURRENDER [C] — David SYLVIAN
I SURRENDER (TO THE SPIRIT OF THE NIGHT) — Samantha FOX
I SURRENDER TO YOUR LOVE — BY ALL MEANS
I SWEAR — ALL-4-ONE
I TALK TO THE TREES — Clint EASTWOOD
I TALK TO THE WIND — OPUS III
I THANK YOU [A] — SAM and DAVE
I THANK YOU [B] — ADEVA
I THINK I LOVE YOU [A] — PARTRIDGE FAMILY
I THINK I LOVE YOU [A] — VOICE OF THE BEEHIVE
I THINK I LOVE YOU [A] — KACI
I THINK I WANT TO DANCE WITH YOU — RUMPLE-STILTS-SKIN
I THINK I'M IN LOVE — SPIRITUALIZED
I THINK I'M IN LOVE WITH YOU — Jessica SIMPSON
I THINK I'M PARANOID — GARBAGE
I THINK IT'S GOING TO RAIN TODAY — UB40
I THINK OF YOU [A] — The MERSEYBEATS
I THINK OF YOU [B] — Perry COMO
I THINK OF YOU [C] — DETROIT EMERALDS
I THINK OF YOU [D] — Bryan POWELL
I THINK WE'RE ALONE NOW [A] — TIFFANY (88)
I THINK WE'RE ALONE NOW [A] — PASCAL featuring Karen PARRY
I THOUGHT I MEANT THE WORLD TO YOU — Alysha WARREN
I THOUGHT IT TOOK A LITTLE TIME (BUT TODAY I FELL IN LOVE) — Diana ROSS
I THOUGHT IT WAS YOU [A] — Herbie HANCOCK
I THOUGHT IT WAS YOU [A] — SEX-O-SONIQUE
I THOUGHT IT WAS YOU [B] — Julia FORDHAM
I THREW IT ALL AWAY — Bob DYLAN
I TOLD YOU SO — Jimmy JONES
I TOUCH MYSELF — DIVINYLS
I TRY [A] — Macy GRAY
I TRY [B] — Talib KWELI featuring Mary J BLIGE
I TURN TO YOU [A] — Melanie C (00)
I TURN TO YOU [B] — Christina AGUILERA
I UNDERSTAND [A] — G-CLEFS
I UNDERSTAND [A] — FREDDIE and The DREAMERS
I UNDERSTAND IT — IDLEWILD
I WALK THE EARTH — VOICE OF THE BEEHIVE
I WANNA BE A FLINTSTONE — SCREAMING BLUE MESSIAHS
I WANNA BE A HIPPY — TECHNOHEAD
I WANNA BE A WINNER — BROWN SAUCE
I WANNA BE ADORED — The STONE ROSES
I WANNA BE DOWN — BRANDY
I WANNA BE FREE — MINTY
I WANNA BE FREE (TO BE WITH HIM) — SCARLET
I WANNA BE IN LOVE AGAIN — BEIJING SPRING
I WANNA BE LOVED [A] — Ricky NELSON
I WANNA BE LOVED [B] — Elvis COSTELLO
I WANNA BE THE ONLY ONE — ETERNAL featuring BeBe WINANS (97)
I WANNA BE WITH YOU [A] — COFFEE
I WANNA BE WITH YOU [B] — MAZE featuring Frankie BEVERLY
I WANNA BE WITH YOU [C] — Mandy MOORE
I WANNA BE U — CHOCOLATE PUMA
I WANNA BE YOUR LADY — Hinda HICKS
I WANNA BE YOUR LOVER — PRINCE
I WANNA BE YOUR MAN [A] — The ROLLING STONES
I WANNA BE YOUR MAN [A] — REZILLOS
I WANNA BE YOUR MAN [B] — Chaka DEMUS and PLIERS
I WANNA DANCE WIT' CHOO (DOO DAT DANCE) - PART 1 — DISCO TEX and The SEX-O-LETTES
I WANNA DANCE WITH SOMEBODY (WHO LOVES ME) [A] — Whitney HOUSTON (87)
I WANNA DANCE WITH SOMEBODY [A] — FLIP & FILL
I WANNA DO IT WITH YOU — Barry MANILOW
I WANNA GET NEXT TO YOU — ROSE ROYCE
(I WANNA GIVE YOU) DEVOTION — NOMAD
I WANNA GO BACK — The NEW SEEKERS
I WANNA GO HOME — Lonnie DONEGAN
I WANNA GO WHERE THE PEOPLE GO — The WILDHEARTS
I WANNA HAVE SOME FUN — Samantha FOX
I WANNA HOLD ON TO YOU — Mica PARIS
I WANNA HOLD YOU — McFLY
I WANNA HOLD YOUR HAND — DOLLAR
I WANNA KNOW [A] — STACCATO
I WANNA KNOW [B] — JOE
I WANNA KNOW [C] — The BLUESKINS
(I WANNA KNOW) WHY — SINCLAIR
(I WANNA) LOVE MY LIFE AWAY — Gene PITNEY
I WANNA LOVE YOU [A] — JADE
I WANNA LOVE YOU [B] — SOLID HARMONIE
I WANNA LOVE YOU FOREVER — Jessica SIMPSON
I WANNA MAKE YOU FEEL GOOD — SYSTEM
I WANNA 1-2-1 WITH YOU — SOLID GOLD CHARTBUSTERS
I WANNA SEX YOU UP — COLOR ME BADD (91)
I WANNA SING — Sabrina JOHNSTON
I WANNA STAY HOME — JELLYFISH
I WANNA STAY WITH YOU [A] — GALLAGHER and LYLE
I WANNA STAY WITH YOU [A] — UNDERCOVER
I WANNA THANK YA — Angie STONE featuring SNOOP DOGG
I WANT AN ALIEN FOR CHRISTMAS — FOUNTAINS OF WAYNE
I WANT CANDY [A] — Brian POOLE and The TREMELOES
I WANT CANDY [A] — BOW WOW WOW
I WANT CANDY [A] — CANDY GIRLS
I WANT CANDY [A] — Aaron CARTER
I WANT HER — Keith SWEAT
I WANT IT ALL — QUEEN
I WANT IT THAT WAY — BACKSTREET BOYS (99)
I WANT LOVE — Elton JOHN
I WANT MORE [A] — CAN
I WANT MORE [B] — FAITHLESS
I WANT OUT — HELLOWEEN
I WANT OUT (I CAN'T BELIEVE) — Harry 'Choo-Choo' ROMERO
I WANT THAT MAN — Deborah HARRY
I WANT THE WORLD — 2WO THIRD3
I WANT TO BE ALONE — 2WO THIRD3
(I WANT TO BE) ELECTED — Bruce DICKINSON
I WANT TO BE FREE — TOYAH
I WANT TO BE STRAIGHT — Ian DURY and The BLOCKHEADS
I WANT TO BE THERE WHEN YOU COME — ECHO and The BUNNYMEN
I WANT TO BE WANTED — Brenda LEE
I WANT TO BE YOUR MAN — ROGER
I WANT TO BE YOUR PROPERTY — BLUE MERCEDES
I WANT TO BREAK FREE — QUEEN
I WANT TO GIVE — Perry COMO
I WANT TO GO WITH YOU — Eddy ARNOLD
I WANT TO HEAR IT FROM YOU — GO WEST
I WANT TO HOLD YOUR HAND — The BEATLES (63)
(I WANT TO) KILL SOMEBODY — S*M*A*S*H
I WANT TO KNOW WHAT LOVE IS [A] — FOREIGNER (85)
I WANT TO KNOW WHAT LOVE IS [A] — Terri SYMON
I WANT TO LIVE — GRACE
I WANT TO STAY HERE [A] — Eydie GORME
I WANT TO STAY HERE [A] — MIKI and GRIFF
I WANT TO THANK YOU — Robin S
I WANT TO TOUCH YOU — CATHERINE WHEEL
I WANT TO WAKE UP WITH YOU — Boris GARDINER (86)
I WANT TO WALK YOU HOME — Fats DOMINO
I WANT U — Rosie GAINES
I WANT YOU [A] — Bob DYLAN
I WANT YOU [A] — Sophie B HAWKINS
I WANT YOU [B] — Gary LOW
I WANT YOU [C] — UTAH SAINTS
I WANT YOU [D] — Juliet ROBERTS
I WANT YOU [E] — SECRET LIFE
I WANT YOU [F] — SALAD
I WANT YOU [G] — INSPIRAL CARPETS
I WANT YOU [H] — SAVAGE GARDEN
I WANT YOU [I] — Z2
I WANT YOU [J] — CZR featuring DELANO
I WANT YOU [K] — JANET
I WANT YOU (ALL TONIGHT) — Curtis HAIRSTON
I WANT YOU BACK [A] — The JACKSON FIVE
I WANT YOU BACK [A] — Michael JACKSON with The JACKSON FIVE
I WANT YOU BACK [A] — CLEOPATRA
I WANT YOU BACK [B] — BANANARAMA
I WANT YOU BACK [C] — 'N SYNC
I WANT YOU BACK [D] — Melanie B featuring Missy 'Misdemeanor' ELLIOTT (98)
I WANT YOU BACK [E] — XPRESS-2
I WANT YOU FOR MYSELF — ANOTHER LEVEL / GHOSTFACE KILLAH
I WANT YOU (FOREVER) — Carl COX
I WANT YOU I NEED YOU I LOVE YOU — Elvis PRESLEY
I WANT YOU NEAR ME — Tina TURNER
I WANT YOU TO BE MY BABY — Billie DAVIS
I WANT YOU TO WANT ME [A] — CHEAP TRICK
I WANT YOU TO WANT ME [B] — SOLID HARMONIE
I WANT YOUR LOVE [A] — CHIC
I WANT YOUR LOVE [A] — Roger SANCHEZ
I WANT YOUR LOVE [B] — TRANSVISION VAMP
I WANT YOUR LOVE [C] — ATOMIC KITTEN
I WANT YOUR LOVIN' (JUST A LITTLE BIT) — Curtis HAIRSTON
I WANT YOUR SEX — George MICHAEL
I WAS A KING — Shabba RANKS
I WAS BORN ON CHRISTMAS DAY — SAINT ETIENNE
I WAS BORN TO BE ME — Tom JONES
I WAS BORN TO LOVE YOU — Freddie MERCURY
I WAS BROUGHT TO MY SENSES — STING
I WAS KAISER BILL'S BATMAN — Whistling Jack SMITH
I WAS MADE FOR DANCIN' — Leif GARRETT
I WAS MADE FOR LOVIN' YOU — KISS
I WAS MADE TO LOVE HER — Stevie WONDER
I WAS MADE TO LOVE YOU — Lorraine CATO
I WAS ONLY JOKING — Rod STEWART
I WAS RIGHT AND YOU WERE WRONG — DEACON BLUE
I WAS THE ONE — Elvis PRESLEY
I WAS TIRED OF BEING ALONE — Patrice RUSHEN
I WASN'T BUILT TO GET UP — The SUPERNATURALS
I WEAR MY SKIN — ONE MINUTE SILENCE
I (WHO HAVE NOTHING) [A] — Shirley BASSEY
I (WHO HAVE NOTHING) [A] — Tom JONES
I (WHO HAVE NOTHING) [A] — SYLVESTER
I WILL [A] — Billy FURY
I WILL [A] — Ruby WINTERS
I WILL ALWAYS LOVE YOU [A] — Whitney HOUSTON (92)
I WILL ALWAYS LOVE YOU [A] — Sarah WASHINGTON
I WILL ALWAYS LOVE YOU [A] — Rik WALLER
I WILL BE RELEASED — UP YER RONSON featuring Mary PEARCE
I WILL BE WITH YOU — T'PAU
I WILL BE YOUR GIRLFRIEND — DUBSTAR
I WILL COME TO YOU — HANSON
I WILL DRINK THE WINE — Frank SINATRA
I WILL FOLLOW — UNA MAS
I WILL GO WITH YOU (CON TE PARTIRO) — Donna SUMMER
I WILL LOVE AGAIN — LARA FABIAN
I WILL LOVE YOU ALL MY LIFE — FOSTER and ALLEN
I WILL LOVE YOU (EV'RY TIME WHEN WE ARE GONE) — The FUREYS
I WILL REMEMBER — TOTO
I WILL RETURN — SPRINGWATER
I WILL SURVIVE [A] — ARRIVAL
I WILL SURVIVE [B] — Gloria GAYNOR (79)
I WILL SURVIVE [B] — Billie Jo SPEARS
I WILL SURVIVE [B] — Chantay SAVAGE
I WILL SURVIVE [B] — Diana ROSS
I WILL SURVIVE [B] — CAKE
I WILL WAIT — HOOTIE & The BLOWFISH
I WISH [A] — Stevie WONDER
I WISH [B] — GABRIELLE
I WISH [C] — SKEE-LO
I WISH [D] — R KELLY
I WISH HE DIDN'T TRUST ME SO MUCH — Bobby WOMACK
I WISH I COULD SHIMMY LIKE MY SISTER KATE — OLYMPICS
(I WISH I KNEW HOW IT WOULD FEEL TO BE) FREE [A] — LIGHTHOUSE FAMILY
I WISH I KNEW HOW IT WOULD FEEL TO BE FREE [A] — Sharlene HECTOR with the NEW INSPIRATIONAL CHOIR
I WISH I WAS A GIRL — VIOLENT DELIGHT
I WISH I WAS A PUNK ROCKER (WITH FLOWERS IN MY HAIR) — Sandi THOM
I WISH I WAS YOU — NEW RHODES
I WISH IT COULD BE CHRISTMAS EVERYDAY [A] — WIZZARD

3 March 2001	10 March 2001	17 March 2001	24 March 2001
WHOLE AGAIN Atomic Kitten	**IT WASN'T ME** Shaggy featuring Ricardo 'Rikrok' Ducent	**UPTOWN GIRL** Westlife	**PURE AND SIMPLE** Hear'Say
NO ANGEL Dido	**NO ANGEL** Dido	**NO ANGEL** Dido	**SONGBIRD** Eva Cassidy

I WISH IT COULD BE CHRISTMAS EVERYDAY [A] — Roy WOOD
I WISH IT COULD BE A WOMBLING MERRY CHRISTMAS EVERYDAY [A] — The WOMBLES with Roy WOOD
I WISH IT WASN'T TRUE — SUPATONIC
I WISH IT WOULD RAIN [A] — The TEMPTATIONS
I WISH IT WOULD RAIN [A] — The FACES
I WISH IT WOULD RAIN DOWN — Phil COLLINS
I WISH U HEAVEN — PRINCE
I WISH YOU LOVE — Paul YOUNG
I WISH YOU WOULD — Jocelyn BROWN
I WONDER [A] — Dickie VALENTINE
I WONDER [A] — Jane FROMAN
I WONDER [B] — Brenda LEE
I WONDER [C] — CRYSTALS
I WONDER HOW — SHINING
I WONDER IF HEAVEN GOT A GHETTO — 2PAC
I WONDER IF I TAKE YOU HOME — LISA LISA and CULT JAM with FULL FORCE
I WONDER WHO'S KISSING HER NOW — Emile FORD and The CHECKMATES
I WONDER WHY [A] — SHOWADDYWADDY
I WONDER WHY [B] — Curtis STIGERS
I WONDER WHY HE'S THE GREATEST DJ — TONY TOUCH featuring TOTAL
I WON'T BACK DOWN — Tom PETTY and The HEARTBREAKERS
I WON'T BLEED FOR YOU — CLIMIE FISHER
I WON'T CHANGE YOU — Sophie ELLIS-BEXTOR
I WON'T CLOSE MY EYES — UB40
I WON'T COME IN WHILE HE'S THERE — Jim REEVES
I WON'T CRY — Glen GOLDSMITH
I WON'T FEEL BAD — SIMPLY RED
I WON'T FORGET YOU — Jim REEVES
I WON'T HOLD YOU BACK — TOTO
I WON'T LAST A DAY WITHOUT YOU — The CARPENTERS
I WON'T LET THE SUN GO DOWN ON ME — Nik KERSHAW
I WON'T LET YOU DOWN [A] — PhD
I WON'T LET YOU DOWN [A] — W.I.P. featuring EMMIE
I WON'T MENTION IT AGAIN — Ruby WINTERS
I WON'T RUN AWAY — Alvin STARDUST
I WOULD DIE 4 U [A] — PRINCE
I WOULD DIE 4 U [A] — SPACE COWBOY
I WOULD DO FOR YOU — UB40
I WOULD FIX YOU — KENICKIE
I WOULD NEVER — BLUE NILE
I WOULDN'T BELIEVE YOUR RADIO — STEREOPHONICS
I WOULDN'T LIE — YARBROUGH and PEOPLES
I WOULDN'T NORMALLY DO THIS KIND OF THING — PET SHOP BOYS
I WOULDN'T TRADE YOU FOR THE WORLD — The BACHELORS
I WOULDN'T WANNA HAPPEN TO YOU — EMBRACE
I WRITE THE SONGS — David CASSIDY
I WROTE YOU A SONG — Misty OLDLAND
IBIZA — MAXIMA featuring LILY
ICE CREAM GUERILLA — WOLFMAN
THE ICE CREAM MAN — TORNADOS
ICE HOCKEY HAIR — SUPER FURRY ANIMALS
ICE ICE BABY — VANILLA ICE (90)
ICE IN THE SUN — STATUS QUO
ICE RAIN — Alex WHITCOMBE & BIG C
ICEBLINK LUCK — COCTEAU TWINS
ICH BIN EIN AUSLANDER — POP WILL EAT ITSELF
ICH WILL — RAMMSTEIN
ICING ON THE CAKE — Stephen 'Tin Tin' DUFFY
I'D BE SURPRISINGLY GOOD FOR YOU — Linda LEWIS
I'D DIE WITHOUT YOU — PM DAWN
I'D DO ANYTHING — Mike PRESTON
I'D DO ANYTHING FOR LOVE (BUT I WON'T DO THAT) — MEAT LOAF (93)
I'D LIE FOR YOU (AND THAT'S THE TRUTH) — MEAT LOAF
I'D LIKE TO TEACH THE WORLD TO SING (IN PERFECT HARMONY) [A] — The NEW SEEKERS (72)
I'D LIKE TO TEACH THE WORLD TO SING [A] — NO WAY SIS
I'D LIKE TO TEACH THE WORLD TO SING [A] — Demi HOLBORN
I'D LOVE YOU TO WANT ME — LOBO
I'D NEVER FIND ANOTHER YOU — Billy FURY
I'D RATHER DANCE WITH YOU — KINGS OF CONVENIENCE
I'D RATHER GO BLIND [A] — CHICKEN SHACK
I'D RATHER GO BLIND [A] — Ruby TURNER
I'D RATHER GO BLIND [A] — Sydney YOUNGBLOOD
I'D RATHER JACK — REYNOLDS GIRLS
I'D REALLY LOVE TO SEE YOU TONIGHT — ENGLAND DAN and John Ford COLEY
THE IDEAL HEIGHT — BIFFY CLYRO
IDEAL WORLD — The CHRISTIANS
IDENTITY — X-RAY SPEX
IDIOTS AT THE WHEEL (EP) — KINGMAKER
IDLE GOSSIP — Perry COMO
IDLE ON PARADE (EP) — Anthony NEWLEY
IDOL — Amanda GHOST
THE IDOL [A] — W.A.S.P.
THE IDOL [B] — Marc ALMOND
IEYA — TOYAH
IF [A] — Telly SAVALAS (75)
IF [A] — Dolly PARTON
IF [A] — YIN and YAN
IF [A] — John ALFORD
IF [B] — Janet JACKSON
IF ... [C] — The BLUETONES
IF — READ TO FAURÉ'S 'PAVANE' [D] — WIMBLEDON CHORAL SOCIETY
IF A MAN ANSWERS — Bobby DARIN
IF ANYONE FINDS THIS, I LOVE YOU — Ruby MURRAY
IF DREAMS CAME TRUE — Pat BOONE
IF EVER — 3RD STOREE
IF EVERY DAY WAS LIKE CHRISTMAS — Elvis PRESLEY
IF EVERYBODY LOOKED THE SAME — GROOVE ARMADA
IF EYE LOVE U 2 NIGHT — MAYTE
IF GOD WILL SEND HIS ANGELS — U2
IF HE TELLS YOU — Adam FAITH
IF I AIN'T GOT YOU — Alicia KEYS
IF I CAN DREAM — Elvis PRESLEY
IF I CAN DREAM (EP) — Michael BALL
IF I CAN'T — 50 CENT & G-UNIT
IF I CAN'T CHANGE YOUR MIND — SUGAR
IF I CAN'T HAVE YOU [A] — Yvonne ELLIMAN
IF I CAN'T HAVE YOU [A] — Kim WILDE
IF I COULD [A] — David ESSEX
IF I COULD [B] — HUNDRED REASONS
IF I COULD BUILD MY WHOLE WORLD AROUND YOU — Marvin GAYE
IF I COULD (EL CONDOR PASA) — Julie FELIX
IF I COULD FLY — GRACE
IF I COULD GIVE ALL MY LOVE — COUNTING CROWS
IF I COULD GO! — Angie MARTINEZ featuring LIL' MO & SACARIO
IF I COULD ONLY MAKE YOU CARE — Mike BERRY
IF I COULD ONLY SAY GOODBYE — David HASSELHOFF
IF I COULD TALK I'D TELL YOU — LEMONHEADS
IF I COULD TURN BACK THE HANDS OF TIME — R KELLY
IF I COULD TURN BACK TIME — CHER
IF I DIDN'T CARE — David CASSIDY
IF I DIE TOMORROW — MOTLEY CRUE
IF I EVER FALL IN LOVE — SHAI
IF I EVER LOSE MY FAITH IN YOU — STING
IF I FALL — Alice MARTINEAU
IF I GIVE MY HEART TO YOU [A] — Doris DAY
IF I GIVE MY HEART TO YOU [A] — Joan REGAN
IF I GIVE YOU MY NUMBER — ANT & DEC
IF I HAD A HAMMER — Trini LOPEZ
IF I HAD NO LOOT — TONY TONI TONÉ
IF I HAD WORDS — Scott FITZGERALD
IF I HAD YOU — KORGIS
IF I HAVE TO GO AWAY — JIGSAW
IF I HAVE TO STAND ALONE — Lonnie GORDON
IF I KNEW THEN WHAT I KNOW NOW — Val DOONICAN
IF I LET YOU GO — WESTLIFE (99)
IF I LOVE U 2 NITE — Mica PARIS
IF I LOVE YA THEN I NEED YA IF I NEED YA THEN I WANT YOU AROUND — Eartha KITT
IF I LOVED YOU — Richard ANTHONY
IF I NEEDED SOMEONE — The HOLLIES
IF I NEVER FEEL BETTER — PHOENIX
IF I NEVER KNEW YOU (LOVE THEME FROM 'POCAHONTAS') — Jon SECADA and SHANICE
IF I NEVER SEE YOU AGAIN — WET WET WET
IF I ONLY HAD TIME — John ROWLES
IF I ONLY KNEW — Tom JONES
IF I REMEMBER — BENZ
IF I RULED THE WORLD [A] — Harry SECOMBE
IF I RULED THE WORLD [A] — Tony BENNETT
IF I RULED THE WORLD [B] — Kurtis BLOW
IF I RULED THE WORLD [B] — NAS
IF I SAID YOU HAVE A BEAUTIFUL BODY WOULD YOU HOLD IT AGAINST ME — The BELLAMY BROTHERS
IF I SAY YES — FIVE STAR
IF I SHOULD FALL FROM GRACE WITH GOD — The POGUES
IF I SHOULD LOVE AGAIN — Barry MANILOW
IF I SURVIVE — HYBRID featuring Julee CRUISE
IF I THOUGHT YOU'D EVER CHANGE YOUR MIND [A] — Cilla BLACK
IF I THOUGHT YOU'D EVER CHANGE YOUR MIND [A] — Agnetha FALTSKOG
IF I TOLD YOU THAT — Whitney HOUSTON / George MICHAEL
IF I WAS [A] — Midge URE (85)
IF I WAS [B] — ASWAD
IF I WAS A RIVER — Tina ARENA
IF I WAS YOUR GIRLFRIEND — PRINCE
IF I WERE A CARPENTER [A] — Bobby DARIN
IF I WERE A CARPENTER [A] — The FOUR TOPS
IF I WERE A CARPENTER [A] — Robert PLANT
IF I WERE A RICH MAN — TOPOL
IF I WERE YOU [A] — kd lang
IF I WERE YOU [B] — Candee JAY
IF I'M NOT YOUR LOVER — Al B SURE!
IF IT DON'T FIT DON'T FORCE IT — Kellee PATTERSON
IF IT HAPPENS AGAIN — UB40
IF IT MAKES YOU HAPPY — Sheryl CROW
IF IT WASN'T FOR THE REASON THAT I LOVE YOU — Miki ANTHONY
IF IT'S ALRIGHT WITH YOU BABY — KORGIS
IF IT'S LOVE THAT YOU WANT — Donny OSMOND
IF IT'S LOVIN' THAT YOU WANT — RIHANNA
IF LEAVING ME IS EASY — Phil COLLINS
IF LIFE IS LIKE A LOVE BANK I WANT AN OVERDRAFT — The WILDHEARTS
IF LOOKS COULD KILL — TRANSVISION VAMP
IF LOVE WAS A TRAIN — Michelle SHOCKED
IF LOVE WAS LIKE GUITARS — Ian McNABB
IF LOVING YOU IS WRONG (I DON'T WANT TO BE RIGHT) — Rod STEWART
IF MADONNA CALLS — Junior VASQUEZ
IF MY FRIENDS COULD SEE ME NOW — Linda CLIFFORD
IF NOT FOR YOU — Olivia NEWTON-JOHN
IF NOT YOU — DR HOOK
IF ONLY — HANSON
IF ONLY I COULD — Sydney YOUNGBLOOD
IF ONLY I COULD LIVE MY LIFE AGAIN — Jane MORGAN
IF ONLY TOMORROW — Ronnie CARROLL
(IF PARADISE IS) HALF AS NICE — AMEN CORNER (69)
IF SHE KNEW WHAT SHE WANTS — The BANGLES
IF SHE SHOULD COME TO YOU — Anthony NEWLEY
IF 60S WERE 90S — BEAUTIFUL PEOPLE
IF THAT WERE ME — Melanie C
IF THAT'S YOUR BOYFRIEND (HE WASN'T LAST NIGHT) — Me'Shell NDEGEOCELLO
IF THE KIDS ARE UNITED — SHAM 69
IF THE RIVER CAN BEND — Elton JOHN
IF THE WHOLE WORLD STOPPED LOVING — Val DOONICAN
IF THERE WAS A MAN — The PRETENDERS
IF THERE'S ANY JUSTICE — LEMAR
IF THIS IS IT — Huey LEWIS and The NEWS
IF THIS IS LOVE [A] — JJ
IF THIS IS LOVE [B] — Jeanie TRACY
IF TOMORROW NEVER COMES — Ronan KEATING (02)
IF U WANT ME — Michael WOODS featuring Imogen BAILEY
IF WE FALL IN LOVE TONIGHT — Rod STEWART
IF WE HOLD ON TOGETHER — Diana ROSS
IF WE TRY — Karen RAMIREZ
IF WE WERE LOVERS — Gloria ESTEFAN
IF YA GETTIN' DOWN — FIVE
IF YOU ASKED ME TO — Celine DION
IF YOU BELIEVE — Johnnie RAY
IF YOU BUY THIS RECORD YOUR LIFE WILL BE BETTER — The TAMPERER featuring MAYA
IF YOU C JORDAN — SOMETHING CORPORATE
IF YOU CAN WANT — Smokey ROBINSON and The MIRACLES
IF YOU CAN'T DO IT WHEN YOU'RE YOUNG, WHEN CAN YOU DO IT? — THEAUDIENCE
IF YOU CAN'T GIVE ME LOVE — Suzi QUATRO
IF YOU CAN'T SAY NO — Lenny KRAVITZ
IF YOU CAN'T STAND THE HEAT — BUCKS FIZZ
IF YOU CARED — Kim APPLEBY
IF YOU COME BACK — BLUE (01)
IF YOU COME TO ME — ATOMIC KITTEN
IF YOU COULD READ MY MIND [A] — Gordon LIGHTFOOT
IF YOU COULD READ MY MIND [A] — STARS ON 54
IF YOU COULD SEE ME NOW — SHAKATAK
IF YOU DON'T KNOW ME BY NOW [A] — Harold MELVIN and The BLUENOTES
IF YOU DON'T KNOW ME BY NOW [A] — SIMPLY RED
IF YOU DON'T LOVE ME — PREFAB SPROUT
IF YOU DON'T WANT ME TO DESTROY YOU — SUPER FURRY ANIMALS
IF YOU DON'T WANT MY LOVE — Robert JOHN
IF YOU EVER — EAST 17 featuring GABRIELLE
IF YOU EVER LEAVE ME — Barbra STREISAND
IF YOU FEEL IT — Thelma HOUSTON
IF YOU GO — Jon SECADA
IF YOU GO AWAY [A] — Terry JACKS
IF YOU GO AWAY [B] — NEW KIDS ON THE BLOCK
IF YOU GOTTA GO GO NOW — MANFRED MANN
IF YOU GOTTA MAKE A FOOL OF SOMEBODY — FREDDIE and The DREAMERS
IF YOU HAD MY LOVE — Jennifer LOPEZ
IF YOU HAVE TO GO — GENEVA
IF YOU KNEW SOUSA (AND FRIENDS) — ROYAL PHILHARMONIC ORCHESTRA arranged and conducted by Louis CLARK
IF YOU KNOW WHAT I MEAN — Neil DIAMOND
IF YOU LEAVE — ORCHESTRAL MANOEUVRES IN THE DARK
IF YOU LEAVE ME NOW [A] — CHICAGO (76)
IF YOU LEAVE ME NOW [A] — UPSIDE DOWN
IF YOU LEAVE ME NOW [A] — SYSTEM presents KERRI B
IF YOU LET ME STAY — Terence Trent D'ARBY
IF YOU LOVE HER — Dick EMERY
IF YOU LOVE ME (I WON'T CARE) — Mary HOPKIN
IF YOU LOVE ME — BROWNSTONE
IF YOU LOVE SOMEBODY SET THEM FREE — STING
IF YOU ONLY LET ME IN — MN8
IF YOU REALLY CARED — GABRIELLE
IF YOU REALLY LOVE ME — Stevie WONDER
IF YOU REALLY WANNA KNOW — Marc DORSEY
IF YOU REALLY WANT TO — MEAT LOAF
IF YOU REMEMBER ME — Chris THOMPSON
IF YOU SHOULD NEED A FRIEND — FIRE ISLAND
IF YOU TALK IN YOUR SLEEP — Elvis PRESLEY
IF YOU THINK YOU KNOW HOW TO LOVE ME — SMOKIE
(IF YOU THINK YOU'RE) GROOVY — PP ARNOLD
IF YOU TOLERATE THIS YOUR CHILDREN WILL BE NEXT — MANIC STREET PREACHERS (98)
IF YOU WALK AWAY — Peter COX
IF YOU WANNA BE HAPPY [A] — Jimmy SOUL

	31 March 2001	7 April 2001	14 April 2001	21 April 2001
UK No.1 SINGLES	PURE AND SIMPLE Hear'Say	PURE AND SIMPLE Hear'Say	WHAT TOOK YOU SO LONG Emma Bunton	WHAT TOOK YOU SO LONG Emma Bunton
UK No.1 ALBUMS	ONGBIRD Cassidy	POPSTARS Hear'Say	POPSTARS Hear'Say	JUST ENOUGH EDUCATION TO PERFORM Stereophonics

IF YOU WANNA BE HAPPY [A] — Rocky SHARPE and The REPLAYS
IF YOU WANNA PARTY — MOLELLA featuring The OUTHERE BROTHERS
IF YOU WANT — LUCIANA
IF YOU WANT ME — Hinda HICKS
IF YOU WANT MY LOVE — CHEAP TRICK
IF YOU WANT MY LOVIN' — Evelyn 'Champagne' KING
IF YOU WERE HERE TONIGHT [A] — Alexander O'NEAL
IF YOU WERE HERE TONIGHT [A] — Matt GOSS
IF YOU WERE MINE MARY — Eddy ARNOLD
IF YOU WERE THE ONLY BOY IN THE WORLD — Stevie MARSH
IF YOU WERE WITH ME NOW — Kylie MINOGUE and Keith WASHINGTON
IF YOU'LL BE MINE — BABYBIRD
IF YOUR GIRL ONLY KNEW — AALIYAH
IF YOUR HEART ISN'T IN IT — ATLANTIC STARR
IF YOU'RE GONE — MATCHBOX 20
IF YOU'RE LOOKIN' FOR A WAY OUT — ODYSSEY
IF YOU'RE NOT THE ONE — Daniel BEDINGFIELD (02)
IF YOU'RE READY (COME GO WITH ME) [A] — STAPLE SINGERS
IF YOU'RE READY (COME GO WITH ME) [A] — Ruby TURNER featuring Jonathan BUTLER
IF YOU'RE THINKING OF ME — DODGY
IGGIN' ME — Chico DeBARGE
IGNITION — R KELLY (03)
IGNORANCE — OCEANIC
IGUANA — Mauro PICOTTO
IKO IKO [A] — DIXIE CUPS
IKO IKO [A] — The BELLE STARS
IKO IKO [A] — NATASHA
IL ADORE — BOY GEORGE
IL EST NÉ LE DIVIN ENFANT — SIOUXSIE and The BANSHEES
IL NOSTRO CONCERTO — Umberto BINDI
IL SILENZIO — Nini ROSSO
I'LL ALWAYS BE AROUND — C&C MUSIC FACTORY / CLIVILLES & COLE
I'LL ALWAYS BE IN LOVE WITH YOU — Michael HOLLIDAY
I'LL ALWAYS LOVE MY MAMA — The INTRUDERS
I'LL ALWAYS LOVE YOU — Taylor DAYNE
I'LL BE — Foxy BROWN featuring JAY-Z
(I'LL BE A) FREAK FOR YOU — ROYALLE DELITE
I'LL BE AROUND [A] — Terri WELLS
I'LL BE AROUND [A] — The DETROIT SPINNERS
I'LL BE BACK — ARNEE and The TERMINATERS
I'LL BE GOOD — RENE and ANGELA
I'LL BE GOOD TO YOU — Quincy JONES featuring Ray CHARLES and Chaka KHAN
I'LL BE HOME — Pat BOONE (56)
I'LL BE HOME THIS CHRISTMAS — Shakin' STEVENS
I'LL BE LOVING YOU (FOREVER) — NEW KIDS ON THE BLOCK
I'LL BE MISSING YOU — PUFF DADDY and Faith EVANS featuring 112 (97)
I'LL BE OK — McFLY (05)
I'LL BE SATISFIED — Shakin' STEVENS
I'LL BE THERE [A] — GERRY and The PACEMAKERS
I'LL BE THERE [B] — Jackie TRENT
I'LL BE THERE [C] — The JACKSON FIVE
I'LL BE THERE [C] — Mariah CAREY
I'LL BE THERE [D] — INNOCENCE
I'LL BE THERE [E] — 99TH FLOOR ELEVATORS featuring Tony DE VIT
I'LL BE THERE [F] — EMMA
I'LL BE THERE FOR YOU [A] — BON JOVI
I'LL BE THERE FOR YOU [B] — SOLID HARMONIE
I'LL BE THERE FOR YOU (DOYA DODODO DOYA) — HOUSE OF VIRGINISM
I'LL BE THERE FOR YOU (THEME FROM 'FRIENDS') — REMBRANDTS
I'LL BE THERE FOR YOU - YOU'RE ALL I NEED TO GET BY — METHOD MAN featuring Mary J BLIGE
I'LL BE WAITING [A] — Clive GRIFFIN
I'LL BE WAITING [B] — FULL INTENTION presents SHENA
(I'LL BE WITH YOU) IN APPLE BLOSSOM TIME — Rosemary JUNE
I'LL BE YOUR ANGEL — KIRA
I'LL BE YOUR BABY TONIGHT [A] — Robert PALMER and UB40
I'LL BE YOUR BABY TONIGHT [A] — Norah JONES
I'LL BE YOUR EVERYTHING — Tommy PAGE
I'LL BE YOUR FRIEND — Robert OWENS
I'LL BE YOUR SHELTER — Taylor DAYNE
I'LL COME RUNNIN' — JUICE
I'LL COME RUNNING — Cliff RICHARD
I'LL COME WHEN YOU CALL — Ruby MURRAY
I'LL CRY FOR YOU — EUROPE
I'LL CUT YOUR TAIL OFF — John LEYTON
I'LL DO ANYTHING — TO MAKE YOU MINE — HOLLOWAY & CO.
I'LL DO YA — WHALE
I'LL FIND MY WAY HOME — JON and VANGELIS
I'LL FIND YOU [A] — David WHITFIELD
I'LL FIND YOU [B] — Michelle GAYLE
I'LL FLY FOR YOU — SPANDAU BALLET
I'LL GET BY [A] — Connie FRANCIS
I'LL GET BY [A] — Shirley BASSEY
I'LL GIVE YOU THE EARTH (TOUS LES BATEAUX, TOUS LES OISEAUX) — Keith MICHELL
I'LL GO ON HOPING — Des O'CONNOR
I'LL GO WHERE YOUR MUSIC TAKES ME [A] — Jimmy JAMES and The VAGABONDS
I'LL GO WHERE YOUR MUSIC TAKES ME [A] — Tina CHARLES
I'LL HOUSE YOU — Richie RICH meets The JUNGLE BROTHERS
I'LL KEEP ON LOVING YOU — PRINCESS
I'LL KEEP YOU SATISFIED — Billy J KRAMER and The DAKOTAS
I'LL KEEP YOUR DREAMS ALIVE — George BENSON and Patti AUSTIN
I'LL LOVE YOU FOREVER TODAY — Cliff RICHARD
I'LL MAKE LOVE TO YOU — BOYZ II MEN
I'LL MANAGE SOMEHOW — MENSWEAR
I'LL MEET YOU AT MIDNIGHT — SMOKIE
I'LL NEVER BREAK YOUR HEART — BACKSTREET BOYS
I'LL NEVER FALL IN LOVE AGAIN [A] — Johnnie RAY
I'LL NEVER FALL IN LOVE AGAIN [B] — Tom JONES
I'LL NEVER FALL IN LOVE AGAIN [C] — Bobbie GENTRY (69)
I'LL NEVER FIND ANOTHER YOU — The SEEKERS (65)
I'LL NEVER GET OVER YOU [A] — Johnny KIDD and The PIRATES
I'LL NEVER GET OVER YOU [B] — The EVERLY BROTHERS
I'LL NEVER GET OVER YOU (GETTING OVER ME) — EXPOSÉ
I'LL NEVER LOVE THIS WAY AGAIN — Dionne WARWICK
I'LL NEVER QUITE GET OVER YOU — Billy FURY
I'LL NEVER STOP — 'N SYNC
I'LL NEVER STOP LOVING YOU — Doris DAY
I'LL PICK A ROSE FOR MY ROSE — Marv JOHNSON
I'LL PUT YOU TOGETHER AGAIN (FROM DEAR ANYONE) — HOT CHOCOLATE
I'LL REMEMBER — MADONNA
I'LL REMEMBER TONIGHT — Pat BOONE
I'LL SAIL THIS SHIP ALONE — The BEAUTIFUL SOUTH
I'LL SAY FOREVER MY LOVE — Jimmy RUFFIN
I'LL SEE IT THROUGH — TEXAS
I'LL SEE YOU ALONG THE WAY — Rick CLARKE
I'LL SEE YOU AROUND — SILVER SUN
I'LL SEE YOU IN MY DREAMS — Pat BOONE
I'LL SET YOU FREE — The BANGLES
I'LL SLEEP WHEN I'M DEAD — BON JOVI
I'LL STAND BY YOU [A] — The PRETENDERS
I'LL STAND BY YOU [A] — GIRLS ALOUD (04)
I'LL STAY BY YOU — Kenny LYNCH
I'LL STAY SINGLE — Jerry LORDAN
I'LL STEP DOWN — Garry MILLS
I'LL STICK AROUND — FOO FIGHTERS
I'LL STOP AT NOTHING — Sandie SHAW
I'LL TAKE THE RAIN — R.E.M.
I'LL TAKE YOU HOME [A] — The DRIFTERS
I'LL TAKE YOU HOME [A] — Cliff BENNETT and The REBEL ROUSERS
I'LL TAKE YOU HOME AGAIN KATHLEEN — Slim WHITMAN
I'LL TAKE YOU THERE [A] — STAPLE SINGERS
I'LL TAKE YOU THERE [A] — GENERAL PUBLIC
I'LL TRY ANYTHING — Dusty SPRINGFIELD
I'LL WAIT — Taylor DAYNE
I'LL WALK WITH GOD — Mario LANZA
ILLEGAL ALIEN — GENESIS
ILLEGAL GUNSHOT — RAGGA TWINS
ILLUMINATIONS — SWANS WAY
ILLUSIONS — CYPRESS HILL
ILOVEROCKNROLL — JESUS AND MARY CHAIN
I'M A BELIEVER [A] — The MONKEES (67)
I'M A BELIEVER [A] — Robert WYATT
I'M A BELIEVER [A] — EMF
I'M A BETTER MAN (FOR HAVING LOVED YOU) — Engelbert HUMPERDINCK
I'M A BITCH — OLGA
I'M A BOY — The WHO
I'M A CUCKOO — BELLE & SEBASTIAN
I'M A DISCO DANCER — Christopher JUST
I'M A DOUN FOR LACK O' JOHNNIE (A LITTLE SCOTTISH FANTASY) — VANESSA-MAE
(I'M A) DREAMER — B B and Q BAND
I'M A FOOL — Slim WHITMAN
I'M A FOOL TO CARE — Joe BARRY
I'M A GOOD MAN — Martin SOLVEIG
I'M A LITTLE CHRISTMAS CRACKER — BOUNCING CZECKS
I'M A MAN [A] — Spencer DAVIS GROUP
I'M A MAN [A] — CHICAGO
I'M A MAN NOT A BOY [A] — Chesney HAWKES
I'M A MAN NOT A BOY [B] — NORTH AND SOUTH
I'M A MAN — YE KE YE KE (MEDLEY) — CLUBHOUSE
I'M A MESSAGE — IDLEWILD
I'M A MIDNIGHT MOVER — Wilson PICKETT
I'M A MOODY GUY — Shane FENTON and The FENTONES
I'M A SLAVE 4 U — Britney SPEARS
I'M A SUCKER FOR YOUR LOVE — Teena MARIE, co-lead vocals Rick JAMES
I'M A TIGER — LULU
(I'M A) TV SAVAGE — BOW WOW WOW
I'M A WONDERFUL THING, BABY — Kid CREOLE and The COCONUTS
I'M ALIVE [A] — The HOLLIES (65)
I'M ALIVE [B] — ELECTRIC LIGHT ORCHESTRA
I'M ALIVE [C] — CUT 'N' MOVE
I'M ALIVE [D] — SEAL
I'M ALIVE [E] — STRETCH 'N' VERN present MADDOG
I'M ALIVE [F] — Celine DION
I'M ALL ABOUT YOU — DJ LUCK & MC NEAT featuirng Ari GOLD
I'M ALL YOU NEED — Samantha FOX
I'M ALRIGHT [A] — Steve WRIGHT
I'M ALRIGHT [B] — Katherine E
(I'M ALWAYS HEARING) WEDDING BELLS — Eddie FISHER
(I'M ALWAYS TOUCHED BY YOUR) PRESENCE DEAR — BLONDIE
I'M AN UPSTART — ANGELIC UPSTARTS
I'M BACK FOR MORE — LULU and Bobby WOMACK
I'M BAD — LL COOL J
I'M BLUE — The 5.6.7.8'S
I'M BORN AGAIN — BONEY M
I'M BROKEN — PANTERA
I'M CHILLIN' — Kurtis BLOW
I'M COMIN' HARDCORE — M.A.N.I.C.
I'M COMING HOME — Tom JONES
I'M COMING HOME CINDY — Trini LOPEZ
I'M COMING OUT — Diana ROSS
I'M COMING WITH YA — Matt GOSS
I'M COUNTING ON YOU — Petula CLARK
I'M CRYING — The ANIMALS
I'M DOIN' FINE — DAY ONE
I'M DOING FINE — Jason DONOVAN
I'M DOIN' FINE NOW [A] — NEW YORK CITY
I'M DOING FINE NOW [A] — PASADENAS
I'M EASY — FAITH NO MORE
I'M EVERY WOMAN [A] — Chaka KHAN
I'M EVERY WOMAN [A] — Whitney HOUSTON
I'M FALLING — The BLUEBELLS
I'M FOR REAL — NIGHTMARES ON WAX
I'M FOREVER BLOWING BUBBLES [A] — WEST HAM UNITED CUP SQUAD
I'M FOREVER BLOWING BUBBLES [A] — COCKNEY REJECTS
I'M FREE [A] — Roger DALTREY
I'M FREE [B] — SOUP DRAGONS
I'M FREE [C] — Jon SECADA
I'M FROM FURTHER NORTH THAN YOU — The WEDDING PRESENT
I'M GLAD — Jennifer LOPEZ
I'M GOIN' DOWN — Mary J BLIGE
I'M GOING ALL THE WAY — SOUNDS OF BLACKNESS
I'M GOING HOME — Gene VINCENT
I'M GOING SLIGHTLY MAD — QUEEN
I'M GONE — Diana ROSS
I'M GONNA BE A COUNTRY GIRL AGAIN — Buffy SAINTE-MARIE
I'M GONNA BE ALRIGHT — Jennifer LOPEZ
I'M GONNA BE (500 MILES) — The PROCLAIMERS
I'M GONNA BE STRONG [A] — Gene PITNEY
I'M GONNA BE STRONG [A] — Cyndi LAUPER
I'M GONNA BE WARM THIS WINTER — Connie FRANCIS
I'M GONNA CHANGE EVERYTHING — Jim REEVES
(I'M GONNA) CRY MYSELF BLIND — PRIMAL SCREAM
I'M GONNA GET MARRIED — Lloyd PRICE
I'M GONNA GET ME A GUN — Cat STEVENS
I'M GONNA GET THERE SOMEHOW — Val DOONICAN
I'M GONNA GET YA BABY — BLACK CONNECTION
I'M GONNA GET YOU — BIZARRE INC
I'M GONNA GETCHA GOOD! — Shania TWAIN
I'M GONNA GIT YOU SUCKA — GAP BAND
I'M GONNA KNOCK ON YOUR DOOR [A] — Eddie HODGES
I'M GONNA KNOCK ON YOUR DOOR [A] — Little Jimmy OSMOND
I'M GONNA LOVE HER FOR BOTH OF US — MEAT LOAF
I'M GONNA LOVE YOU FOREVER — CROWN HEIGHTS AFFAIR
I'M GONNA LOVE YOU A LITTLE BIT MORE BABY — Barry WHITE
I'M GONNA MAKE YOU LOVE ME — Diana ROSS and The SUPREMES and The TEMPTATIONS
I'M GONNA MAKE YOU MINE [A] — Lou CHRISTIE
I'M GONNA MAKE YOU MINE [B] — Tanya BLOUNT
I'M GONNA MISS YOU FOREVER — Aaron CARTER
I'M GONNA RUN AWAY FROM YOU — Tami LYNN
I'M GONNA SIT RIGHT DOWN AND WRITE MYSELF A LETTER [A] — Billy WILLIAMS
I'M GONNA SIT RIGHT DOWN AND WRITE MYSELF A LETTER [A] — Barry MANILOW
I'M GONNA SOOTHE YOU — Maria McKEE
I'M GONNA TEAR YOUR PLAYHOUSE DOWN — Paul YOUNG
I'M IN A DIFFERENT WORLD — The FOUR TOPS
I'M IN A PHILLY MOOD — Daryl HALL
I'M IN FAVOUR OF FRIENDSHIP — FIVE SMITH BROTHERS
I'M IN HEAVEN [A] — Jason NEVINS presents UKNY / Holly JAMES
I'M IN HEAVEN [B] — N-TRANCE
I'M IN IT FOR LOVE — Donny OSMOND
I'M IN LOVE [A] — The FOURMOST
I'M IN LOVE [B] — Evelyn 'Champagne' KING
I'M IN LOVE [C] — Ruby TURNER
I'M IN LOVE [D] — Lillo THOMAS
I'M IN LOVE [E] — STARPARTY
I'M IN LOVE [F] — AUDIO BULLYS
I'M IN LOVE AGAIN [A] — Fats DOMINO
I'M IN LOVE AGAIN [B] — SAD CAFE
I'M IN LOVE (AND I LOVE THE FEELING) — ROSE ROYCE
I'M IN LOVE WITH A GERMAN FILM STAR — The PASSIONS

28 April 2001	5 May 2001	12 May 2001	19 May 2001
SURVIVOR Destiny's Child	**DON'T STOP MOVIN'** S Club 7	**IT'S RAINING MEN** Geri Halliwell	**IT'S RAINING MEN** Geri Halliwell
JUST ENOUGH EDUCATION TO PERFORM Stereophonics	**FREE ALL ANGELS** Ash	**SURVIVOR** Destiny's Child	**SURVIVOR** Destiny's Child

26 May 2001	2 June 2001	9 June 2001	16 June 2001
UK No.1 SINGLES			
DON'T STOP MOVIN' S Club 7	**DO YOU REALLY LIKE IT** DJ Pied Piper and The Masters of Ceremonies	**ANGEL** Shaggy featuring Rayvon	**ANGEL** Shaggy featuring Rayvon
UK No.1 ALBUMS			
REVEAL R.E.M.	**REVEAL** R.E.M.	**HOT SHOT** Shaggy	**AMNESIAC** Radiohead

IN THE MIDDLE OF THE HOUSE [A] — The JOHNSTON BROTHERS
IN THE MIDDLE OF THE HOUSE [A] — Jimmy PARKINSON
IN THE MIDDLE OF THE NIGHT — MAGIC AFFAIR
IN THE MIDNIGHT HOUR — Wilson PICKETT
IN THE MOOD [A] — Ernie FIELDS
IN THE MOOD [A] — Jonathan KING
IN THE MOOD [A] — Glenn MILLER
IN THE MOOD [A] — Ray STEVENS
IN THE MORNING — The CORAL
IN THE NAME OF LOVE [A] — Sharon REDD
IN THE NAME OF LOVE [B] — SWAN LAKE
IN THE NAME OF LOVE '88 [B] — THOMPSON TWINS
IN THE NAME OF THE FATHER [A] — BONO
IN THE NAME OF THE FATHER [B] — BLACK GRAPE
IN THE NAVY — VILLAGE PEOPLE
IN THE NIGHT — Barbara DICKSON
IN THE ONES YOU LOVE — Diana ROSS
IN THE REALM OF THE SENSES — BASS-O-MATIC
IN THE SHADOWS — The RASMUS
IN THE SHAPE OF A HEART — Jackson BROWNE
IN THE SPRINGTIME — Maxi PRIEST
IN THE STILL OF THE NITE (I'LL REMEMBER) — BOYZ II MEN
IN THE STONE — EARTH WIND AND FIRE
IN THE SUMMERTIME [A] — MUNGO JERRY (70)
IN THE SUMMERTIME [A] — SHAGGY
IN THE SUMMERTIME [A] — JUNGLE BOYS
IN THE THICK OF IT — Brenda RUSSELL
IN THE VALLEY — MIDNIGHT OIL
IN THE WAITING LINE — ZERO 7
IN THE YEAR 2525 (EXORDIUM AND TERMINUS) — ZAGER and EVANS (69)
IN THESE ARMS — BON JOVI
IN THIS WORLD — MOBY
IN THOUGHTS OF YOU — Billy FURY
IN TOO DEEP [A] — DEAD OR ALIVE
IN TOO DEEP [B] — GENESIS
IN TOO DEEP [C] — Belinda CARLISLE
IN TOO DEEP [D] — SUM 41
IN WALKED LOVE — LOUISE
IN YER FACE — 808 STATE
IN YOUR ARMS (RESCUE ME) — NU GENERATION
IN YOUR BONES — FIRE ISLAND
IN YOUR CAR [A] — COOLNOTES
IN YOUR CAR [B] — KENICKIE
IN YOUR CARE — Tasmin ARCHER
IN YOUR DANCE — E-LUSTRIOUS
IN YOUR EYES [A] — George BENSON
IN YOUR EYES [B] — Niamh KAVANAGH
IN YOUR EYES [C] — Kylie MINOGUE
IN YOUR HANDS — REDD SQUARE featuring Tiff LACEY
IN YOUR ROOM [A] — The BANGLES
IN YOUR ROOM [B] — DEPECHE MODE
IN YOUR WILDEST DREAMS — Tina TURNER featuring Barry WHITE
IN YOUR WORLD — MUSE
IN ZAIRE [A] — Johnny WAKELIN
IN ZAIRE [A] — AFRICAN BUSINESS
INBETWEENER — SLEEPER
THE INBETWEENIES — The GOODIES
THE INCIDENTALS — ALISHA'S ATTIC
INCOMMUNICADO — MARILLION
INCOMPLETE [A] — SISQO
INCOMPLETE [B] — BACKSTREET BOYS
INCREDIBLE [A] — M-BEAT featuring GENERAL LEVY
INCREDIBLE [B] — Keith MURRAY featuring LL COOL J
INCREDIBLE (WHAT I MEANT TO SAY) — DARIUS
INDEPENDENCE — LULU
INDEPENDENCE DAY — COMSAT ANGELS
INDEPENDENT LOVE SONG — SCARLET
INDEPENDENT WOMEN PART 1 — DESTINY'S CHILD (00)
INDESCRIBABLY BLUE — Elvis PRESLEY
INDESTRUCTIBLE [A] — The FOUR TOPS featuring Smokey ROBINSON
INDESTRUCTIBLE [B] — ALISHA'S ATTIC

INDIAN LOVE CALL [A] — Slim WHITMAN
INDIAN LOVE CALL [A] — Karl DENVER
INDIAN LOVE CALL [A] — Ray STEVENS
INDIAN RESERVATION [A] — Don FARDON
INDIAN RESERVATION [A] — 999
INDIAN ROPE — The CHARLATANS
INDIAN SUMMER — The BELLE STARS
INDIANA — Freddy CANNON
INDIANA WANTS ME — R Dean TAYLOR
INDIANS — ANTHRAX
INDICA — MOVIN' MELODIES
INDIE-YARN — TRICKBABY
INDIGO — MOLOKO
INDUSTRIAL STRENGTH (EP) — KROKUS
INERTIATIC ESP — The MARS VOLTA
INFATUATION — Rod STEWART
INFECTED [A] — The THE
INFECTED [B] — BARTHEZZ
INFERNO — SOUVLAKI
INFIDELITY — SIMPLY RED
INFILTRATE 202 — ALTERN 8
INFINITE DREAMS — IRON MAIDEN
INFINITY — GURU JOSH
INFO-FREAKO — JESUS JONES
INFORMER — SNOW
INHALE — STONE SOUR
INHERIT THE WIND — Wilton FELDER
INJECTED WITH A POISON — Praga KHAN
THE INK IN THE WELL — David SYLVIAN
INKANYEZI NEZAZI (THE STAR AND THE WISEMAN) — LADYSMITH BLACK MAMBAZO
INNA CITY MAMMA — Neneh CHERRY
INNAMORATA — Dean MARTIN
INNER CITY LIFE — GOLDIE
INNER LIFE — DECOY and ROY
INNER SMILE — TEXAS
INNOCENT — ADDIS BLACK WIDOW
INNOCENT EYES — Delta GOODREM
INNOCENT X — THERAPY?
INNOCENTE (FALLING IN LOVE) — DELERIUM featuring Leigh NASH
INNUENDO — QUEEN (91)
INS — DJ ZINC featuring EKSMAN
INSANE [A] — TEXAS featuring WU-TANG CLAN
INSANE [B] — DARK MONKS
INSANE IN THE BRAIN — CYPRESS HILL
INSANIA — Peter ANDRE
INSANITY — OCEANIC
INSATIABLE [A] — Darren HAYES
INSATIABLE [B] — THICK D
INSENSITIVE — Jann ARDEN
INSIDE — STILTSKIN (94)
INSIDE A DREAM — Jane WIEDLIN
INSIDE AMERICA — Juggy JONES
INSIDE LOOKING OUT — GRAND FUNK RAILROAD
INSIDE — LOOKING OUT — The ANIMALS
INSIDE LOVE (SO PERSONAL) — George BENSON
INSIDE OF LOVE — NADA SURF
INSIDE OUT [A] — ODYSSEY
INSIDE OUT [B] — MIGHTY LEMON DROPS
INSIDE OUT [C] — GUN
INSIDE OUT [D] — Shara NELSON
INSIDE OUT [E] — CULTURE BEAT
INSIDE OUTSIDE — CLASSIX NOUVEAUX
INSIDE THAT I CRIED — Ce Ce PENISTON
INSIDE YOUR DREAMS — U96
INSOMNIA [A] — FAITHLESS
INSOMNIA 2005 [A] — FAITHLESS
INSOMNIA [B] — FEEDER
INSOMNIAC — ECHOBELLY
INSPECTOR GADGET — KARTOON KREW
'INSPECTOR MORSE' THEME — Barrington PHELOUNG
INSPIRATION — STRIKE
INSSOMNIAK — DJPC
INSTANT KARMA — John LENNON
INSTANT REPLAY [A] — Dan HARTMAN
INSTANT REPLAY [A] — YELL!
INSTANT REPLAY [A] — GAMBAFREAKS
INSTANT STREET — dEUS
INSTINCT — CROWDED HOUSE
INSTINCTION — SPANDAU BALLET
INSTINCTUAL — IMAGINATION INSTRUMENTS OF DARKNESS (ALL OF US ARE ONE PEOPLE) — ART OF NOISE
INTACT — NED'S ATOMIC DUSTBIN

INTENSIFY — WAY OUT WEST
INTERCEPTOR — EAT STATIC
INTERESTING DRUG — MORRISSEY
INTERGALACTIC — BEASTIE BOYS
INTERLUDE — MORRISSEY
INTERNAL EXILE — FISH
INTERNATIONAL — BRASS CONSTRUCTION
INTERNATIONAL BRIGHT YOUNG THING — JESUS JONES
INTERNATIONAL JET SET — The SPECIALS
THE INTERNATIONAL LANGUAGE OF SCREAMING — SUPER FURRY ANIMALS
INTERNATIONAL RESCUE — WE'VE GOT A FUZZBOX AND WE'RE GONNA USE IT
INTERSTATE 5 — WEDDING PRESENT
INTERSTATE LOVE SONG — STONE TEMPLE PILOTS
INTERVENTION — Lavine HUDSON
INTO MY ARMS — Nick CAVE and The BAD SEEDS
INTO MY WORLD — AUDIOWEB
INTO SPACE — PLAYTHING
INTO THE BLUE [A] — The MISSION
INTO THE BLUE [B] — MOBY
INTO THE BLUE [C] — GENEVA
INTO THE FIRE — THIRTEEN SENSES
INTO THE FUTURE — NEW ATLANTIC
INTO THE GROOVE — MADONNA (85)
INTO THE MOTION — COOLNOTES
INTO THE NIGHT — LOVE INC.
INTO THE SUN — WEEKEND PLAYERS
INTO THE VALLEY — The SKIDS
INTO TOMORROW — Paul WELLER
INTO YOU — FABOLOUS featuring TAMIA
INTO YOUR ARMS — LEMONHEADS
INTO YOUR EYES — Armand VAN HELDEN
INTO YOUR HEAD — The HONEYMOON MACHINE
INTO YOUR HEART — 6 BY SIX
INTOXICATION — REACT 2 RHYTHM
INTRO — Alan BRAXE and Fred FALKE
INTUITION [A] — LINX
INTUITION [B] — JEWEL
INVALID LITTER DEPT — AT THE DRIVE-IN
INVINCIBLE (THEME FROM 'THE LEGEND OF BILLIE JEAN') — Pat BENATAR
INVISIBLE [A] — Alison MOYET
INVISIBLE [B] — PUBLIC DEMAND
INVISIBLE [C] — TILT
INVISIBLE [D] — D-SIDE
INVISIBLE BALLOON — MIDGET
INVISIBLE GIRL — Minnie DRIVER
INVISIBLE MAN — 98°
THE INVISIBLE MAN — QUEEN
INVISIBLE SUN — The POLICE
INVISIBLE TOUCH — GENESIS
INVITATIONS — SHAKATAK
I.O.I.O. — The BEE GEES
I.O.U. [A] — Jane KENNAWAY and STRANGE BEHAVIOUR
I.O.U. [B] — FREEEZ
IOU [C] — Bill TARMEY
I.O.U. LOVE — SIX BY SEVEN
IRE FEELINGS (SKANGA) — Rupie EDWARDS
IRENE — PHOTOS
IRIE — LUCK & NEAT
IRIS — GOO GOO DOLLS
IRISH BLOOD, ENGLISH HEART — MORRISSEY
IRISH BLUE — FLIP & FILL featuring JUNIOR
THE IRISH KEEP GATE-CRASHING — The THRILLS
THE IRISH ROVER — The POGUES and The DUBLINERS
IRISH SON — Brian McFADDEN
IRON FIST — MOTÖRHEAD
IRON HORSE — CHRISTIE
IRON LION ZION — Bob MARLEY & The WAILERS
IRON SKY — MEGA CITY FOUR
IRONIC — Alanis MORISSETTE
IRRESISTIBLE [A] — Cathy DENNIS
IRRESISTIBLE [B] — The CORRS
IRRESISTIBLE [C] — Jessica SIMPSON
IS — SMALLER
IS A BLUE BIRD BLUE — Conway TWITTY
IS IT A CRIME — SADE
IS IT A DREAM [A] — CLASSIX NOUVEAUX
IS IT A DREAM [B] — The DAMNED
IS IT A SIN — DEEPEST BLUE
IS IT BECAUSE — The HONEYCOMBS

IS IT COS I'M COOL? — MOUSSE T featuring Emma LANFORD
IS IT GOOD TO YOU [A] — HEAVY D and The BOYZ
IS IT GOOD TO YOU [A] — Teddy RILEY
IS IT LIKE TODAY — WORLD PARTY
IS IT LOVE? — CHILI HI FLY
IS IT LOVE — BASEMENT BOYS present Ultra NATÉ
IS IT LOVE YOU'RE AFTER — ROSE ROYCE
IS IT REALLY OVER — Jim REEVES
IS IT TRUE — Brenda LEE
IS NOTHING SACRED — MEAT LOAF
IS SHE REALLY GOING OUT WITH HIM? — Joe JACKSON
IS THAT LOVE — SQUEEZE
IS THAT YOUR FINAL ANSWER? (WHO WANTS TO BE A MILLIONAIRE — THE SINGLE) — AMOURE
IS THERE ANY LOVE IN YOUR HEART — Lenny KRAVITZ
IS THERE ANYBODY OUT THERE —BASSHEADS
IS THERE ANYBODY THERE — SCORPIONS
IS THERE SOMEONE OUT THERE? — CODE RED
IS THERE SOMETHING I SHOULD KNOW? [A] — DURAN DURAN (83)
IS THERE SOMETHING I SHOULD KNOW [A] — ALLSTARS
IS THIS A DREAM — LOVE DECADE
IS THIS A LOVE THING — RAYDIO
IS THIS LOVE [A] — Bob MARLEY & The WAILERS
IS THIS LOVE? [B] — Alison MOYET
IS THIS LOVE [C] — WHITESNAKE
IS THIS LOVE [D] — CLAP YOUR HANDS SAY YEAH
(IS THIS THE WAY TO) AMARILLO [A] — Tony CHRISTIE
(IS THIS THE WAY TO) AMARILLO [A] — Tony CHRISTIE featuring Peter KAY (05)
IS THIS THE WAY TO AMARILLO? (SANTA'S GROTTO) [A] — SANTA
IS THIS WHAT I GET FOR LOVING YOU — Marianne FAITHFULL
IS VIC THERE? — DEPARTMENT S
IS YOUR LOVE IN VAIN? — Bob DYLAN
IS YOUR LOVE STRONG ENOUGH? — Bryan FERRY
ISLAND GIRL — Elton JOHN
ISLAND HEAD (EP) — INSPIRAL CARPETS
ISLAND IN THE SUN [A] — Harry BELAFONTE
ISLAND IN THE SUN [A] — The RIGHTEOUS BROTHERS
ISLAND IN THE SUN [B] — WEEZER
ISLAND OF DREAMS — The SPRINGFIELDS
ISLAND OF LOST SOULS — BLONDIE
ISLANDS IN THE STREAM — Kenny ROGERS and Dolly PARTON
ISLE OF INNISFREE — Bing CROSBY
ISMS — DOG EAT DOG
ISN'T IT A WONDER — BOYZONE
ISN'T IT AMAZING — HOTHOUSE FLOWERS
ISN'T IT MIDNIGHT — FLEETWOOD MAC
ISN'T IT TIME — The BABYS
ISN'T LIFE STRANGE — The MOODY BLUES
ISN'T SHE LOVELY — David PARTON
ISOBEL — BJÖRK
ISRAEL — SIOUXSIE and The BANSHEES
ISRAELITES — Desmond DEKKER and The ACES (69)
ISTANBUL NOT CONSTANTINOPLE [A] — Frankie VAUGHAN
ISTANBUL (NOT CONSTANTINOPLE) [A] — THEY MIGHT BE GIANTS
IT AIN'T A CRIME — HOUSE OF PAIN
IT AIN'T ENOUGH — DREEM TEEM vs ARTFUL DODGER featuring MZ MAY and MC ALISTAIR
IT AIN'T FAIR — Edwin STARR
IT AIN'T GONNA BE ME — CJ BOLLAND
IT AIN'T HARD TO TELL — NAS
IT AIN'T ME BABE — Johnny CASH
IT AIN'T NECESSARILY SO — BRONSKI BEAT
IT AIN'T OVER TIL IT'S OVER — Lenny KRAVITZ
IT AIN'T WHAT YOU DO IT'S THE WAY THAT YOU DO IT — FUN BOY THREE and BANANARAMA
IT BEGAN IN AFRICA — URBAN ALL STARS
IT BEGAN IN AFRIKA — The CHEMICAL BROTHERS

23 June 2001	30 June 2001	7 July 2001	14 July 2001
ANGEL Shaggy featuring Rayvon	**LADY MARMALADE** Christina Aguilera, Lil' Kim, Mya and Pink	**THE WAY TO YOUR LOVE** Hear'Say	**ANOTHER CHANCE** Roger Sanchez
THE INVISIBLE BAND Travis	**THE INVISIBLE BAND** Travis	**THE INVISIBLE BAND** Travis	**THE INVISIBLE BAND** Travis

IT CAN'T BE RIGHT — 2PLAY featuring RAGHAV & Naila BOSS
IT COULD HAPPEN TO YOU — Robert PALMER
IT DIDN'T MATTER — STYLE COUNCIL
IT DOESN'T HAVE TO BE — ERASURE
IT DOESN'T HAVE TO BE THIS WAY — The BLOW MONKEYS
IT DOESN'T MATTER — Wyclef JEAN featuring THE ROCK and MELKY SEDECK
IT DOESN'T MATTER ANYMORE [A] — Buddy HOLLY (59)
IT DOESN'T MATTER ANYMORE [B] — PURESSENCE
IT DOESN'T REALLY MATTER — ZAPP
IT DON'T COME EASY — Ringo STARR
IT ENDED ON AN OILY STAGE — BRITISH SEA POWER
IT FE DONE — SUPERCAT
IT FEELS SO GOOD — SONIQUE (00)
IT HAD TO BE YOU — Harry CONNICK Jr
IT HURTS SO MUCH — Jim REEVES
IT HURTS TO BE IN LOVE — Gene PITNEY
IT IS JAZZ — TINGO TANGO
IT IS TIME TO GET FUNKY — D MOB
IT ISN'T RIGHT — The PLATTERS
IT ISN'T, IT WASN'T, IT AIN'T NEVER GONNA BE — Aretha FRANKLIN and Whitney HOUSTON
IT JUST WON'T DO — Tim DELUXE featuring SAM OBERNIK
IT KEEPS RAININ' [A] — Fats DOMINO
IT KEEP RAININ' (TEARS FROM MY EYES) [A] — Bitty McLEAN
IT KEEPS RIGHT ON A HURTIN' — Johnny TILLOTSON
IT LOOKS LIKE YOU — Evan DANDO
IT MAKES ME WONDER — Bruce FOXTON
IT MAKES YOU FEEL LIKE DANCIN' — ROSE ROYCE
IT MAY BE WINTER OUTSIDE (BUT IN MY HEART IT'S SPRING) — LOVE UNLIMITED
IT MIEK — Desmond DEKKER and The ACES
IT MIGHT AS WELL RAIN UNTIL SEPTEMBER — Carole KING
IT MUST BE HIM (SEUL SUR SON ÉTOILE) — Vikki CARR
IT MUST BE LOVE [A] — Labi SIFFRE
IT MUST BE LOVE [A] — MADNESS
IT MUST BE LOVE [B] — Robin S
IT MUST BE LOVE [C] — MERO
IT MUST BE SANTA — Joan REGAN
IT MUST HAVE BEEN LOVE [A] — MAGNUM
IT MUST HAVE BEEN LOVE [B] — ROXETTE
IT NEVER RAINS (IN SOUTHERN CALIFORNIA) — TONY TONI TONÉ
IT ONLY TAKES A MINUTE [A] — Jonathan KING
IT ONLY TAKES A MINUTE [A] — TAVARES
IT ONLY TAKES A MINUTE [A] — TAKE THAT
IT ONLY TOOK A MINUTE — Joe BROWN and The BRUVVERS
IT OUGHTA SELL A MILLION — Lyn PAUL
IT SEEMS TO HANG ON [A] — ASHFORD and SIMPSON
IT SEEMS TO HANG ON [A] — KWS
IT SHOULD HAVE BEEN ME [A] — Yvonne FAIR
IT SHOULD'VE BEEN ME [A] — ADEVA
IT STARTED ALL OVER AGAIN — Brenda LEE
IT STARTED WITH A KISS — HOT CHOCOLATE / Errol BROWN
IT SURE BRINGS OUT THE LOVE IN YOUR EYES — David SOUL
IT TAKES ALL NIGHT LONG — Gary GLITTER
IT TAKES MORE — MS DYNAMITE
IT TAKES SCOOP — FATMAN SCOOP featuring The CROOKLYN CLAN
IT TAKES TWO [A] — Marvin GAYE
IT TAKES TWO BABY [A] — Liz KERSHAW and Bruno BROOKES
IT TAKES TWO [A] — Rod STEWART and Tina TURNER
IT TAKES TWO [B] — Rob BASE and DJ E-Z ROCK
IT TAKES TWO TO TANGO — Richard MYHILL
IT WAS A GOOD DAY — ICE CUBE
IT WAS EASIER TO HURT HER — Wayne FONTANA
IT WASN'T ME — SHAGGY featuring Ricardo 'Rikrok' DUCENT (01)
IT WILL BE ALRIGHT — ODYSSEY
IT WILL BE YOU — Paul YOUNG
IT WILL COME IN TIME — Billy PRESTON and SYREETA
IT WILL MAKE ME CRAZY — FELIX
IT WON'T BE LONG — Alison MOYET
IT WON'T SEEM LIKE CHRISTMAS (WITHOUT YOU) — Elvis PRESLEY
THE ITALIAN THEME — Cyril STAPLETON and his Orchestra
ITALO HOUSE MIX — ROCOCO
ITCHYCOO PARK [A] — The SMALL FACES
ITCHYCOO PARK [A] — M PEOPLE
IT'LL BE ME — Cliff RICHARD and The SHADOWS
IT'S A BEAUTIFUL THING — OCEAN COLOUR SCENE
IT'S A BETTER THAN GOOD TIME — Gladys KNIGHT and The PIPS
IT'S A DISCO NIGHT (ROCK DON'T STOP) — The ISLEY BROTHERS
IT'S A FINE DAY [A] — OPUS III
IT'S A FINE DAY [A] — MISS JANE
IT'S A GAME — BAY CITY ROLLERS
IT'S A GAS — The WEDDING PRESENT
IT'S A GIRL THING — MY LIFE STORY
IT'S A GOOD LIFE — Cevin FISHER featuring Romona KELLY
IT'S A HARD LIFE — QUEEN
IT'S A HEARTACHE — Bonnie TYLER
IT'S A LONG WAY TO THE TOP (IF YOU WANNA ROCK 'N' ROLL) — AC/DC
IT'S A LOVE THING — The WHISPERS
IT'S A LOVING THING — CB MILTON
IT'S A MAN'S MAN'S MAN'S WORLD [A] — James BROWN
IT'S A MAN'S MAN'S MAN'S WORLD [A] — BRILLIANT
IT'S A MAN'S MAN'S MAN'S WORLD [A] — Jeanie TRACY and Bobby WOMACK
IT'S A MIRACLE — CULTURE CLUB
IT'S A MISTAKE — MEN AT WORK
IT'S A PARTY [A] — Busta RHYMES featuring ZHANE
IT'S A PARTY [B] — BOUNTY KILLER
IT'S A RAGGY WALTZ — Dave BRUBECK QUARTET
IT'S A RAINBOW — RAINBOW
IT'S A RAINY DAY — ICE MC
IT'S A SHAME [A] — The DETROIT SPINNERS
IT'S A SHAME [B] — KRIS KROSS
IT'S A SHAME ABOUT RAY — The LEMONHEADS
IT'S A SHAME (MY SISTER) — Monie LOVE
IT'S A SIN — PET SHOP BOYS (87)
IT'S A SIN TO TELL A LIE — Gerry MONROE
IT'S A TRIP (TUNE IN, TURN ON, DROP OUT) — CHILDREN OF THE NIGHT
IT'S ABOUT TIME — The LEMONHEADS
IT'S ABOUT TIME YOU WERE MINE — THUNDERBUGS
IT'S ALL ABOUT THE BENJAMINS — PUFF DADDY
IT'S ALL ABOUT U — SWV
IT'S ALL ABOUT YOU — JUSTIN
IT'S ALL ABOUT YOU (NOT ABOUT ME) — Tracie SPENCER
IT'S ALL BEEN DONE — BARENAKED LADIES
IT'S ALL COMING BACK TO ME NOW [A] — PANDORA'S BOX
IT'S ALL COMING BACK TO ME NOW [A] — Celine DION
IT'S ALL GONE — Chris REA
IT'S ALL GOOD [A] — HAMMER
IT'S ALL GOOD [B] — DA MOB featuring JOCELYN BROWN
IT'S ALL GRAVY — ROMEO featuring Christina MILIAN
IT'S ALL IN THE GAME [A] — Tommy EDWARDS (58)
IT'S ALL IN THE GAME [A] — Cliff RICHARD
IT'S ALL IN THE GAME [A] — The FOUR TOPS
IT'S ALL OVER — Cliff RICHARD
IT'S ALL OVER NOW [A] — Shane FENTON and The FENTONES
IT'S ALL OVER NOW [B] — The ROLLING STONES (64)
IT'S ALL OVER NOW BABY BLUE [A] — Joan BAEZ
IT'S ALL OVER NOW BABY BLUE [A] — The MILLTOWN BROTHERS
IT'S ALL THE WAY LIVE (NOW) — COOLIO
IT'S ALL RIGHT — Sterling VOID
IT'S ALL TRUE — LEMONHEADS
IT'S ALL UP TO YOU — Jim CAPALDI
IT'S ALL VAIN — MAGNOLIA
IT'S ALL YOURS — MC LYTE
IT'S ALMOST TOMORROW [A] — The DREAMWEAVERS (56)
IT'S ALMOST TOMORROW [A] — Mark WYNTER
IT'S ALRIGHT [A] — SHO NUFF
IT'S ALRIGHT [B] — PET SHOP BOYS
IT'S ALRIGHT [B] — HYPER GO GO
IT'S ALRIGHT [C] — EAST 17
IT'S ALRIGHT [D] — Bryan POWELL
IT'S ALRIGHT [E] — Deni HINES
IT'S ALRIGHT [F] — ECHO and The BUNNYMEN
IT'S ALRIGHT (BABY'S COMING BACK) — EURYTHMICS
IT'S ALRIGHT, I FEEL IT! — NUYORICAN SOUL featuring Jocelyn BROWN
IT'S ALRIGHT NOW — The BELOVED
IT'S AN OPEN SECRET — JOY STRINGS
IT'S BEEN AWHILE — STAIND
IT'S BEEN NICE — The EVERLY BROTHERS
IT'S BEEN SO LONG — George McCRAE
IT'S BETTER TO HAVE (AND DON'T NEED) — Don COVAY
IT'S CALLED A HEART — DEPECHE MODE
IT'S DIFFERENT FOR GIRLS — Joe JACKSON
IT'S ECSTASY WHEN YOU LAY DOWN NEXT TO ME — Barry WHITE
IT'S FOR YOU — Cilla BLACK
IT'S FOUR IN THE MORNING — Faron YOUNG
IT'S GETTING BETTER — MAMA CASS
IT'S GOIN DOWN — X-ECUTIONERS featuring Mike SHINODA & Mr HAHN of LINKIN PARK
IT'S GOING TO HAPPEN! — The UNDERTONES
IT'S GONNA BE A COLD COLD CHRISTMAS — DANA
IT'S GONNA BE A LOVELY DAY — S.O.U.L. S.Y.S.T.E.M. introducing Michelle VISAGE
IT'S GONNA BE ... (A LOVELY DAY) — BRANCACCIO & AISHER
IT'S GONNA BE ALL RIGHT — GERRY and The PACEMAKERS
IT'S GONNA BE ALRIGHT [A] — Ruby TURNER
IT'S GONNA BE ALRIGHT [B] — PUSSY 2000
IT'S GONNA BE ME — 'N SYNC
IT'S GONNA BE MY WAY — PRECIOUS
IT'S GOOD NEWS WEEK — HEDGEHOPPERS ANONYMOUS
IT'S GREAT WHEN WE'RE TOGETHER — Finley QUAYE
IT'S GRIM UP NORTH — JUSTIFIED ANCIENTS OF MU MU
IT'S GROWING — The TEMPTATIONS
IT'S HAPPENIN' — PLUS ONE featuring SIRRON
IT'S HARD SOMETIMES — Frankie KNUCKLES
IT'S HARD TO BE HUMBLE — Mac DAVIS
IT'S HERE — Kim WILDE
IT'S IMPOSSIBLE — Perry COMO
IT'S IN EVERY ONE OF US — Cliff RICHARD
IT'S IN HIS KISS (THE SHOOP SHOOP SONG) [A] — Betty EVERETT
IT'S IN HIS KISS [A] — Linda LEWIS
IT'S IN OUR HANDS — BJÖRK
IT'S IN YOUR EYES — Phil COLLINS
IT'S ... IT'S ... THE SWEET MIX — The SWEET
IT'S JURASSIC — SOUL CITY ORCHESTRA
IT'S JUST A FEELING — TERRORIZE
IT'S JUST PORN MUM — TRUCKS
(IT'S JUST) THE WAY THAT YOU LOVE ME — Paula ABDUL
IT'S LATE [A] — Ricky NELSON
IT'S LATE [A] — Shakin' STEVENS
(IT'S LIKE A) SAD OLD KINDA MOVIE — PICKETTYWITCH
IT'S LIKE THAT [A] — RUN-DMC vs Jason NEVINS (98)
IT'S LIKE THAT [A] — Mariah CAREY
IT'S LIKE THAT Y'ALL — SWEET TEE
IT'S LOVE — Ken DODD
IT'S LOVE THAT REALLY COUNTS — The MERSEYBEATS
IT'S LOVE (TRIPPIN') — GOLDTRIX presents Andrea BROWN
IT'S LULU — The BOO RADLEYS
IT'S ME — Alice COOPER
IT'S MY HOUSE [A] — Diana ROSS
IT'S MY HOUSE [A] — STORM
IT'S MY LIFE [A] — The ANIMALS
IT'S MY LIFE [B] — TALK TALK
IT'S MY LIFE [B] — LIQUID PEOPLE vs TALK TALK
IT'S MY LIFE [B] — NO DOUBT
IT'S MY LIFE [C] — DR ALBAN
IT'S MY LIFE [D] — BON JOVI
IT'S MY PARTY [A] — Lesley GORE
IT'S MY PARTY [A] — Dave STEWART with Barbara GASKIN (81)
IT'S MY PARTY [B] — Chaka KHAN
IT'S MY TIME — The EVERLY BROTHERS
IT'S MY TURN [A] — Diana ROSS
IT'S MY TURN [B] — ANGELIC
IT'S NATURE'S WAY (NO PROBLEM) — DOLLAR
IT'S NEVER TOO LATE — Diana ROSS
IT'S NICE TO GO TRAV'LING — Frank SINATRA
IT'S NO GOOD — DEPECHE MODE
IT'S NOT A LOVE THING — Geoffrey WILLIAMS
IT'S NOT RIGHT BUT (IT'S OK) — Whitney HOUSTON
IT'S NOT THE END OF THE WORLD? — SUPER FURRY ANIMALS
IT'S NOT UNUSUAL — Tom JONES (65)
IT'S NOW OR NEVER — Elvis PRESLEY (60, 05)
IT'S OH SO QUIET — BJÖRK
IT'S OK [A] — DELIRIOUS?
IT'S OK [B] — ATOMIC KITTEN
IT'S OKAY — DES'REE
IT'S ON [A] — FLOWERED UP
IT'S ON [B] — NAUGHTY BY NATURE
IT'S ON YOU (SCAN ME) — EUROGROOVE
IT'S ONE OF THOSE NIGHTS (YES LOVE) — PARTRIDGE FAMILY
IT'S ONLY LOVE [A] — Tony BLACKBURN
IT'S ONLY LOVE [A] — Elvis PRESLEY
IT'S ONLY LOVE [B] — Gary 'US' BONDS
IT'S ONLY LOVE [C] — Bryan ADAMS
IT'S ONLY LOVE [C] — Tina TURNER
IT'S ONLY LOVE [D] — SIMPLY RED
IT'S ONLY MAKE BELIEVE [A] — Billy FURY
IT'S ONLY MAKE BELIEVE [A] — CHILD
IT'S ONLY MAKE BELIEVE [A] — Conway TWITTY (58)
IT'S ONLY MAKE BELIEVE [A] — Glen CAMPBELL
IT'S ONLY NATURAL — CROWDED HOUSE
IT'S ONLY ROCK AND ROLL [A] — The ROLLING STONES
IT'S ONLY ROCK 'N' ROLL [A] — VARIOUS ARTISTS (Singles and EPs)
IT'S ONLY US — Robbie WILLIAMS (99)
IT'S 'ORRIBLE BEING IN LOVE (WHEN YOU'RE 8 1/2) — CLAIRE and FRIENDS
IT'S OVER [A] — Roy ORBISON (64)
IT'S OVER [B] — FUNK MASTER
IT'S OVER [C] — LEVEL 42
IT'S OVER [B] — CLOCK
IT'S OVER [D] — RIMES featuring Shaila PROSPERE
IT'S OVER [E] — KURUPT
IT'S OVER (DISTORTION) — PIANOHEADZ
IT'S OVER LOVE — Todd TERRY PROJECT presents SHANNON
IT'S OVER NOW [A] — Ultra NATÉ
IT'S OVER NOW [B] — Deborah COX
IT'S OVER NOW [C] — 112
IT'S OVER NOW [D] — BIG ANG featuring SIOBHAN
IT'S PARTY TIME AGAIN — George VAN DUSEN
IT'S PROBABLY ME — STING with Eric CLAPTON
IT'S RAINING [A] — DARTS
IT'S RAINING [B] — Shakin' STEVENS
IT'S RAINING AGAIN — SUPERTRAMP
IT'S RAINING MEN [A] — WEATHER GIRLS
IT'S RAINING MEN [A] — Martha WASH
IT'S RAINING MEN [A] — Geri HALLIWELL (01)
IT'S SO EASY — Andy WILLIAMS
IT'S SO HIGH — Matt FRETTON
IT'S SO NICE (TO HAVE YOU HOME) — The NEW SEEKERS

21 July 2001	28 July 2001	4 August 2001	11 August 2001
UK No.1 SINGLES			
ETERNITY / THE ROAD TO MANDALAY Robbie Williams	ETERNITY / THE ROAD TO MANDALAY Robbie Williams	ETERNAL FLAME Atomic Kitten	ETERNAL FLAME Atomic Kitten
UK No.1 ALBUMS			
701 her	SURVIVOR Destiny's Child	SURVIVOR Destiny's Child	WHITE LADDER David Gray

IT'S STILL ROCK AND ROLL TO ME — Billy JOEL
IT'S STILL YOU — Michael BALL
IT'S SUMMERTIME (LET IT GET INTO YOU) — SMOOTH
IT'S TEMPTATION — SHEER ELEGANCE
IT'S THE END OF THE WORLD AS WE KNOW IT — R.E.M.
IT'S THE SAME OLD SONG [A] — The FOUR TOPS
IT'S THE SAME OLD SONG [A] — Jonathan KING
IT'S THE SAME OLD SONG [A] — KC and The SUNSHINE BAND
IT'S THE WAY YOU MAKE ME FEEL — STEPS
IT'S TIME [A] — Elvis COSTELLO
IT'S TIME [B] — Ferry CORSTEN
IT'S TIME FOR LOVE — CHI-LITES
IT'S TIME TO CRY — Paul ANKA
IT'S TOO LATE [A] — Carole KING
IT'S TOO LATE [A] — QUARTZ introducing Dina CARROLL
IT'S TOO LATE [B] — Luci SILVAS
IT'S TOO LATE NOW [A] — SWINGING BLUE JEANS
IT'S TOO LATE NOW [B] — Long John BALDRY
IT'S TOO SOON TO KNOW — Pat BOONE
IT'S TRICKY [A] — RUN-DMC
IT'S TRICKY 2003 [A] — RUN-DMC featuring Jacknife LEE
IT'S TRUE — QUEEN PEN
IT'S UP TO YOU — Ricky NELSON
IT'S UP TO YOU PETULA — EDISON LIGHTHOUSE
IT'S UP TO YOU (SHINING THROUGH) — LAYO & BUSHWACKA!
IT'S WHAT'S UPFRONT THAT COUNTS — YOSH presents LOVEDEEJAY AKEMI
IT'S WHAT WE'RE ALL ABOUT — SUM 41
IT'S WONDERFUL (TO BE LOVED BY YOU) — Jimmy RUFFIN
IT'S WRITTEN IN THE STARS — Paul WELLER
IT'S WRITTEN ON YOUR BODY — Ronnie BOND
IT'S YER MONEY I'M AFTER BABY — The WONDER STUFF
IT'S YOU [A] — Freddie STARR
IT'S YOU [B] — MANHATTANS
IT'S YOU [C] — EMF
IT'S YOU ONLY YOU (MEIN SCHMERZ) — Lene LOVICH
IT'S YOUR DAY TODAY — PJ PROBY
IT'S YOUR DESTINY — ELECTRA
IT'S YOUR LIFE — SMOKIE
IT'S YOUR THING — The ISLEY BROTHERS
IT'S YOUR TIME — Arthur BAKER
IT'S YOURS — Jon CUTLER featuring E-MAN
ITSY BITSY TEENIE WEENIE YELLOW POLKA DOT BIKINI [A] — Brian HYLAND
ITSY BITSY TEENY WEENY YELLOW POLKA DOT BIKINI [A] — BOMBALURINA (90)
ITZA TRUMPET THING — MONTANO vs THE TRUMPET MAN
I'VE BEEN A BAD BAD BOY — Paul JONES
I'VE BEEN AROUND THE WORLD — Marti PELLOW
I'VE BEEN DRINKING — Jeff BECK and Rod STEWART
I'VE BEEN HURT — Guy DARRELL
I'VE BEEN IN LOVE BEFORE — CUTTING CREW
I'VE BEEN LONELY SO LONG — Frederick KNIGHT
I'VE BEEN LOSING YOU — A-HA
I'VE BEEN THINKING ABOUT YOU — LONDONBEAT
I'VE BEEN TO A MARVELLOUS PARTY — The DIVINE COMEDY
I'VE BEEN WAITING — STEREO NATION
I'VE BEEN WATCHIN' — JOE PUBLIC
I'VE BEEN WRONG BEFORE — Cilla BLACK
I'VE DONE EVERYTHING FOR YOU — Sammy HAGAR
I'VE FOUND LOVE AGAIN — Richard CARTRIDGE
I'VE GOT A LIFE — EURYTHMICS
I'VE GOT A LITTLE PUPPY — The SMURFS
I'VE GOT A LITTLE SOMETHING FOR YOU — MN8
I'VE GOT A THING ABOUT YOU BABY — Elvis PRESLEY
I'VE GOT MINE — UB40
I'VE GOT NEWS FOR YOU — Feargal SHARKEY
I'VE GOT SOMETHING TO SAY — REEF
I'VE GOT THE MUSIC IN ME — Kiki DEE
I'VE GOT THIS FEELING — MAVERICKS
I'VE GOT TO LEARN TO SAY NO — Richard 'Dimples' FIELDS
I'VE GOT TO MOVE — Calvin RICHARDSON
I'VE GOT YOU — Martine McCUTCHEON
I'VE GOT YOU ON MY MIND [A] — Dorian GRAY
I'VE GOT YOU ON MY MIND [A] — The WHITE PLAINS
I'VE GOT YOU UNDER MY SKIN [A] — The FOUR SEASONS
I'VE GOT YOU UNDER MY SKIN [A] — Neneh CHERRY
I'VE GOT YOU UNDER MY SKIN [A] — Frank SINATRA with BONO
(I'VE GOT YOUR) PLEASURE CONTROL — Simon HARRIS featuring Lonnie GORDON
I'VE GOTTA GET A MESSAGE TO YOU — The BEE GEES (68)
I'VE HAD ENOUGH [A] — Paul McCARTNEY
I'VE HAD ENOUGH [B] — EARTH WIND AND FIRE
I'VE HAD ENOUGH [C] — Ivan MATIAS
I'VE HAD ENOUGH [D] — HILLMAN MINX
(I'VE HAD) THE TIME OF MY LIFE — Bill MEDLEY and Jennifer WARNES
I'VE JUST BEGUN TO LOVE YOU — DYNASTY
I'VE LOST YOU — Elvis PRESLEY
I'VE NEVER BEEN IN LOVE — Suzi QUATRO
I'VE NEVER BEEN TO ME — CHARLENE (82)
I'VE PASSED THIS WAY BEFORE — Jimmy RUFFIN
I'VE SEEN THE WORD — BLANCMANGE
I'VE TOLD EVERY LITTLE STAR — Linda SCOTT
I'VE WAITED SO LONG — Anthony NEWLEY
IVORY — SKIN UP
IVORY TOWER — KAYE SISTERS
IZ U — NELLY
IZZO (H.O.V.A.) — JAY-Z
JACK AND DIANE — John Cougar MELLENCAMP
JACK AND JILL — RAYDIO
JACK AND JILL PARTY — Pete BURNS
JACK IN THE BOX [A] — Clodagh RODGERS
JACK IN THE BOX [B] — MOMENTS
JACK LE FREAK — CHIC
JACK MIX II/III — MIRAGE
JACK MIX IV — MIRAGE
JACK MIX VII — MIRAGE
JACK O' DIAMONDS — Lonnie DONEGAN
JACK TALKING — Dave STEWART
THE JACK THAT HOUSE BUILT — JACK 'N' CHILL
JACK THE GROOVE — RAZE
JACK THE RIPPER [A] — LL COOL J
JACK THE RIPPER [B] — Nick CAVE and The BAD SEEDS
JACK TO THE SOUND OF THE UNDERGROUND — HITHOUSE
JACK YOUR BODY — Steve 'Silk' HURLEY (87)
JACK'S HEROES — The POGUES and The DUBLINERS
JACKET HANGS — The BLUE AEROPLANES
JACKIE — Scott WALKER
JACKIE WILSON SAID (I'M IN HEAVEN WHEN YOU SMILE) — DEXY'S MIDNIGHT RUNNERS
JACKIE'S RACING — WHITEOUT
JACKSON — Nancy SINATRA
JACKY — Marc ALMOND
JACQUELINE — Bobby HELMS
JACQUES DERRIDA — SCRITTI POLITTI
JACQUES YOUR BODY (MAKE ME SWEAT) — LES RYTHMES DIGITALES
JA-DA — JOHNNY and The HURRICANES
JADED [A] — GREEN DAY
JADED [B] — AEROSMITH
JAGGED END — LINCOLN CITY FC featuring Michael COURTNEY
JAGUAR — DJ ROLANDO AKA AZTEC MYSTIC
JAIL HOUSE RAP — FAT BOYS
JAILBIRD — PRIMAL SCREAM
JAILBREAK [A] — THIN LIZZY
JAILBREAK [B] — PARADOX
JAILHOUSE ROCK — Elvis PRESLEY (58, 05)
JAILHOUSE ROCK (EP) — Elvis PRESLEY
JAM — Michael JACKSON
THE JAM EP — A TRIBE CALLED QUEST
JAM IT JAM — SHE ROCKERS
JAM J — JAMES
JAM, JAM, JAM (ALL NIGHT LONG) — PEOPLES CHOICE
JAM ON REVENGE (THE WIKKI WIKKI SONG) — NEWCLEUS
JAM SIDE DOWN — STATUS QUO
JAMAICAN IN NEW YORK — SHINEHEAD
JAMBALAYA [A] — Jo STAFFORD
JAMBALAYA [A] — Fats DOMINO
JAMBALAYA (ON THE BAYOU) [A] — The CARPENTERS
JAMBOREE — NAUGHTY BY NATURE featuring ZHANÉ
JAMES BOND THEME [A] — John BARRY ORCHESTRA
JAMES BOND THEME [A] — MOBY
JAMES DEAN (I WANNA KNOW) — Daniel BEDINGFIELD
JAMES HAS KITTENS — BLU PETER
JAMMIN' IN AMERICA — GAP BAND
JAMMING — Bob MARLEY & The WAILERS
JANA — KILLING JOKE
JANE [A] — STARSHIP
JANE [B] — PERFECT DAY
JANE FALLS DOWN — The MODERN
JANEIRO — SOLID SESSIONS
JANIE, DON'T TAKE YOUR LOVE TO TOWN — Jon BON JOVI
JANUARY — PILOT (75)
JANUARY FEBRUARY — Barbara DICKSON
JAPANESE BOY — ANEKA (81)
JARROW SONG — Alan PRICE
JAWS — Lalo SCHIFRIN
JAYOU — JURASSIC 5
JAZZ CARNIVAL — AZYMUTH
JAZZ IT UP — REEL 2 REAL
JAZZ RAP — Kim CARNEGIE
JAZZ THING — GANG STARR
JAZZIN' THE WAY YOU KNOW — JAZZY M
JCB SONG — NIZLOPI (05)
JE NE SAIS PAS POURQUOI — Kylie MINOGUE
JE SUIS MUSIC — CERRONE
JE T'AIME ... MOI NON PLUS [A] — Jane BIRKIN and Serge GAINSBOURG (69)
JE T'AIME (MOI NON PLUS) [A] — JUDGE DREAD
JE T'AIME (ALLO ALLO) [A] — RENÉ and YVETTE
JE VOULAIS (TE DIRE QUE JE T'ATTENDS) — MANHATTAN TRANSFER
JEALOUS AGAIN — The BLACK CROWES
JEALOUS GUY [A] — ROXY MUSIC (81)
JEALOUS GUY [A] — John LENNON
JEALOUS HEART [A] — CADETS with Eileen READ
JEALOUS HEART [A] — Connie FRANCIS
JEALOUS LOVE [A] — JOBOXERS
JEALOUS LOVE [B] — Hazell DEAN
JEALOUS MIND — Alvin STARDUST (74)
JEALOUSY [A] — Billy FURY
JEALOUSY [B] — Amii STEWART
JEALOUSY [C] — The ADVENTURES OF STEVIE V
JEALOUSY [D] — PET SHOP BOYS
JEALOUSY [E] — OCTOPUS
THE JEAN GENIE — David BOWIE
JEAN THE BIRDMAN — David SYLVIAN
JEANETTE — The BEAT
JEANNIE — Danny WILLIAMS
JEANNIE, JEANNIE, JEANNIE — Eddie COCHRAN
JEANNY — FALCO
JEANS ON — David DUNDAS
JEDI WANNABE — BELLATRIX
JEEPSTER [A] — T. REX
JEEPSTER [A] — POLECATS
JELLYHEAD — CRUSH
JENNIFER ECCLES — The HOLLIES
JENNIFER JUNIPER [A] — DONOVAN
JENNIFER JUNIPER [A] — SINGING CORNER meets DONOVAN
JENNIFER SHE SAID — Lloyd COLE
JENNY — STELLASTARR*
JENNY FROM THE BLOCK — Jennifer LOPEZ
JENNY JENNY — LITTLE RICHARD
JENNY ONDIOLINE — STEREOLAB
JENNY TAKE A RIDE — Mitch RYDER and The DETROIT WHEELS
JENNY WREN — Paul McCARTNEY
JEOPARDY — Greg KIHN BAND
JEREMY — PEARL JAM
JERICHO [A] — SIMPLY RED
JERICHO [B] — The PRODIGY
JERK IT OUT — CAESARS
JERUSALEM [A] — The FALL
JERUSALEM [A] — FAT LES
JERUSALEM [A] — KEEDIE & The ENGLAND CRICKET TEAM
JERUSALEM [B] — Herb ALPERT
JESAMINE — CASUALS
JESSE HOLD ON — B*WITCHED
JESSICA — Adam GREEN
JESSIE — Joshua KADISON
JESSIE'S GIRL — Rick SPRINGFIELD
JESUS — Cliff RICHARD
JESUS CHRIST — LONGPIGS
JESUS CHRIST POSE — SOUNDGARDEN
JESUS HAIRDO — The CHARLATANS
JESUS HE KNOWS ME — GENESIS
JESUS OF SUBURBIA — GREEN DAY
JESUS SAYS — ASH
JESUS TO A CHILD — George MICHAEL (96)
JESUS WALKS — Kanye WEST
JET — Paul McCARTNEY
JET CITY WOMAN — QUEENSRŸCHE
JET-STAR — TEKNO TOO
JETSTREAM — NEW ORDER featuring Ana MATRONIC
JEWEL — CRANES
JEZEBEL [A] — Marty WILDE
JEZEBEL [A] — Shakin' STEVENS
JIBARO — ELECTRA
JIG-A-JIG — EAST OF EDEN
JIGGA JIGGA! — SCOOTER
JIGGY — CLIPZ
JILTED JOHN — JILTED JOHN
JIMMIE JONES — VAPORS
JIMMY — PURPLE HEARTS
JIMMY JIMMY — The UNDERTONES
JIMMY LEE — Aretha FRANKLIN
JIMMY MACK — Martha REEVES and The VANDELLAS
JIMMY OLSEN'S BLUES — SPIN DOCTORS
JIMMY UNKNOWN — Lita ROZA
JIMMY'S GIRL — Johnny TILLOTSON
JINGLE BELL ROCK [A] — Max BYGRAVES
JINGLE BELL ROCK [A] — Chubby CHECKER and Bobby RYDELL
JINGLE BELLS [A] — JUDGE DREAD
JINGLE BELLS [B] — CRAZY FROG
JINGLE BELLS LAUGHING ALL THE WAY — HYSTERICS
JINGO [A] — CANDIDO
JINGO [A] — JELLYBEAN
JINGO [A] — FKW
JITTERBUGGIN' — HEATWAVE
JIVE TALKIN' [A] — The BEE GEES
JIVE TALKIN' [A] — BOOGIE BOX HIGH
JJ TRIBUTE — ASHA
JOAN OF ARC — ORCHESTRAL MANOEUVRES IN THE DARK
JOANNA [A] — Scott WALKER
JOANNA [B] — KOOL and The GANG
JOANNA [C] — MRS WOOD
JOCELYN SQUARE — LOVE AND MONEY
JOCK MIX 1 — MAD JOCKS featuring JOCKMASTER B.A.
JOCKO HOMO — DEVO
JODY — Jermaine STEWART
JOE — INSPIRAL CARPETS
JOE LE TAXI — Vanessa PARADIS
JOE LOUIS — John SQUIRE
JOE 90 (THEME) — Barry GRAY ORCHESTRA
JOGI — PANJABI MC featuring JAY-Z
JOHN AND JULIE — Eddie CALVERT
JOHN, I'M ONLY DANCING [A] — David BOWIE
JOHN I'M ONLY DANCING [A] — POLECATS
JOHN KETTLEY (IS A WEATHERMAN) — TRIBE OF TOFFS
JOHN WAYNE IS BIG LEGGY — HAYSI FANTAYZEE
JOHNNY AND MARY — Robert PALMER
JOHNNY ANGEL [A] — Shelley FABARES
JOHNNY ANGEL [A] — Patti LYNN
JOHNNY B GOODE [A] — Jimi HENDRIX
JOHNNY B GOODE [A] — Peter TOSH

18 August 2001	25 August 2001	1 September 2001	8 September 2001
21 SECONDS So Solid Crew	**LET'S DANCE** Five	**LET'S DANCE** Five	**TOO CLOSE** Blue
RIGHT NOW (Re-issue) Atomic Kitten	**WHITE LADDER** David Gray	**BREAK THE CYCLE** Staind	**IOWA** Slipknot

JOHNNY B GOODE [A] — JUDAS PRIEST
JOHNNY CASH — SONS AND DAUGHTERS
JOHNNY COME HOME — FINE YOUNG CANNIBALS
JOHNNY COME LATELY — Steve EARLE
JOHNNY DAY — Rolf HARRIS
JOHNNY FRIENDLY — JOBOXERS
JOHNNY GET ANGRY — Carol DEENE
JOHNNY JOHNNY — PREFAB SPROUT
JOHNNY MATHIS' FEET — AMERICAN MUSIC CLUB
JOHNNY PANIC AND THE BIBLE OF DREAMS — Johnny PANIC and The BIBLE OF DREAMS
JOHNNY REGGAE — PIGLETS
JOHNNY REMEMBER ME [A] — John LEYTON (61)
JOHNNY REMEMBER ME [A] — METEORS
JOHNNY ROCCO — Marty WILDE
JOHNNY THE HORSE — MADNESS
JOHNNY WILL — Pat BOONE
JOIN IN AND SING AGAIN — The JOHNSTON BROTHERS
JOIN IN AND SING (NO.3) — The JOHNSTON BROTHERS
JOIN ME — LIGHTFORCE
JOIN OUR CLUB — SAINT ETIENNE
JOIN THE PARTY — HONKY
JOIN TOGETHER — The WHO
JOINING YOU — Alanis MORISSETTE
JOINTS & JAMS — BLACK EYED PEAS
JOJO ACTION — MR PRESIDENT
JOKE (I'M LAUGHING) — Eddi READER
THE JOKER [A] — Steve MILLER BAND (90)
THE JOKER [A] — FATBOY SLIM
THE JOKER (THE WIGAN JOKER) — ALLNIGHT BAND
JOLE BLON — Gary 'US' BONDS
JOLENE [A] — Dolly PARTON
JOLENE [A] — STRAWBERRY SWITCHBLADE
JOLENE (LIVE) [A] — The WHITE STRIPES
JONAH — BREATHE
JONATHAN DAVID — BELLE & SEBASTIAN
THE JONES' — The TEMPTATIONS
JONES VS JONES — KOOL and The GANG
JONESTOWN MIND — The ALMIGHTY
JOOK GAL — ELEPHANT MAN
JORDAN: THE EP — PREFAB SPROUT
JOSEPH MEGA REMIX — Jason DONOVAN
JOSEPHINE [A] — Chris REA
JOSEPHINE [B] — TERRORVISION
JOSEY — DEEP BLUE SOMETHING
JOURNEY — Duncan BROWNE
THE JOURNEY [A] — 911
THE JOURNEY [B] — CITIZEN CANED
THE JOURNEY [C] — AMSTERDAM
JOURNEY TO THE MOON — BIDDU
JOURNEY TO THE PAST — AALIYAH
JOY [A] — BAND AKA
JOY [B] — Teddy PENDERGRASS
JOY [C] — SOUL II SOUL
JOY [D] — STAXX featuring Carol LEEMING
JOY [E] — 7669
JOY [F] — BLACKSTREET
JOY [G] — Deni HINES
JOY [H] — Kathy BROWN
JOY! [I] — GAY DAD
JOY [J] — Mark RYDER
JOY AND HAPPINESS — STABBS
JOY AND HEARTBREAK — MOVEMENT 98 featuring Carroll THOMPSON
JOY AND PAIN [A] — Donna ALLEN
JOY AND PAIN [[B] — MAZE featuring Frankie BEVERLY
JOY AND PAIN [A] — Rob BASE and DJ E-Z ROCK
JOY AND PAIN [C] — ANGELLE
(JOY) I KNOW IT — ODYSSEY
JOY OF LIVING [A] — Cliff RICHARD
JOY OF LIVING [B] — OUI 3
JOY TO THE WORLD — THREE DOG NIGHT
JOYBRINGER — MANFRED MANN
JOYENERGIZER — Joy KITIKONTI
JOYRIDE — ROXETTE
JOYRIDER (YOU'RE PLAYING WITH FIRE) — COLOUR GIRL
JOYS OF CHRISTMAS — Chris REA
JOYS OF LIFE — David JOSEPH
JUDGE FUDGE — HAPPY MONDAYS
JUDGEMENT DAY — MS DYNAMITE
THE JUDGEMENT IS THE MIRROR — DALI'S CAR
JUDY IN DISGUISE (WITH GLASSES) — John FRED and The PLAYBOY BAND
JUDY OVER THE RAINBOW — ORANGE
JUDY SAYS (KNOCK YOU IN THE HEAD) — VIBRATORS
JUDY TEEN — Steve HARLEY and COCKNEY REBEL
JUGGLING — RAGGA TWINS
JUICEBOX — The STROKES
JUICY [A] — WRECKX-N-EFFECT
JUICY [A] — NOTORIOUS B.I.G.
JUICY FRUIT — MTUME
A JUICY RED APPLE — SKIN UP
JUKE BOX BABY — Perry COMO
JUKE BOX GYPSY — LINDISFARNE
JUKE BOX HERO — FOREIGNER
JUKE BOX JIVE — The RUBETTES
JULIA [A] — EURYTHMICS
JULIA [B] — Chris REA
JULIA [C] — SILVER SUN
JULIA SAYS — WET WET WET
JULIE ANNE — KENNY
JULIE DO YA LOVE ME [A] — Bobby SHERMAN
JULIE DO YA LOVE ME [A] — WHITE PLAINS
JULIE (EP) — LEVELLERS
JULIE OCEAN — The UNDERTONES
JULIET — The FOUR PENNIES (64)
JULIET (KEEP THAT IN MIND) — Thea GILMORE
JULY — OCEAN COLOUR SCENE
JUMBO [A] — The BEE GEES
JUMBO [B] — UNDERWORLD
JUMP [A] — VAN HALEN
JUMP [A] — AZTEC CAMERA
JUMP [A] — BUS STOP
JUMP [B] — KRIS KROSS
JUMP! [C] — MOVEMENT
JUMP [D] — GIRLS ALOUD
JUMP [E] — The FADERS
JUMP AROUND — HOUSE OF PAIN
JUMP BACK (SET ME FREE) — Dhar BRAXTON
JUMP DOWN — B*WITCHED
JUMP (FOR MY LOVE) — POINTER SISTERS
JUMP JIVE AN' WAIL — Brian SETZER ORCHESTRA
JUMP 'N SHOUT — BASEMENT JAXX
THE JUMP OFF — LIL' KIM featuring MR. CHEEKS
JUMP ON DEMAND — [SPUNGE]
JUMP START — Natalie COLE
JUMP THE GUN — The THREE DEGREES
JUMP THEY SAY — David BOWIE
JUMP TO IT — Aretha FRANKLIN
JUMP TO MY BEAT — WILDCHILD
JUMP TO MY LOVE — INCOGNITO
JUMP TO THE BEAT [A] — Stacy LATTISAW
JUMP TO THE BEAT [A] — Dannii MINOGUE
JUMP UP — JUST 4 JOKES featuring MC RB
JUMPIN' — LIBERTY X
JUMPIN' JACK FLASH [A] — The ROLLING STONES (68)
JUMPIN' JACK FLASH [A] — Aretha FRANKLIN
JUMPIN' JIVE — Joe JACKSON
JUMPIN' JUMPIN' — DESTINY'S CHILD
JUNE AFTERNOON — ROXETTE
JUNE JULY — APARTMENT
JUNEAU — FUNERAL FOR A FRIEND
JUNGLE BILL — YELLO
THE JUNGLE BOOK GROOVE — JUNGLE BOOK
JUNGLE BROTHER — The JUNGLE BROTHERS
JUNGLE FEVER — CHAKACHAS
JUNGLE HIGH — JUNO REACTOR
JUNGLE ROCK [A] — Hank MIZELL
JUNGLE ROCK [A] — JUNGLE BOYS
JUNGLIST — DRUMSOUND & Simon 'BASSLINE' SMITH
JUNIOR'S FARM — Paul McCARTNEY
JUNKIES — EASYWORLD
JUPITER — EARTH WIND AND FIRE
JUS' A RASCAL — DIZZEE RASCAL
JUS' COME — COOL JACK
JUS 1 KISS — BASEMENT JAXX
JUS' REACH (RECYCLED) — GALLIANO
JUST [A] — RADIOHEAD
JUST [B] — Jamie SCOTT
JUST A DAY — FEEDER
JUST A DAY AWAY — BARCLAY JAMES HARVEST
JUST A DREAM [A] — NENA
JUST A DREAM [B] — Donna DE LORY
JUST A FEELING — BAD MANNERS
JUST A FEW THINGS THAT I AIN'T — The BEAUTIFUL SOUTH
JUST A FRIEND [A] — Biz MARKIE
JUST A FRIEND [B] — MARIO
JUST A GIRL — NO DOUBT
JUST A GROOVE — NOMAD
JUST A LIL BIT — 50 CENT
JUST A LITTLE — LIBERTY X (02)
JUST A LITTLE BIT — UNDERTAKERS
JUST A LITTLE BIT BETTER — HERMAN'S HERMITS
JUST A LITTLE BIT LONGER (EP) — Maxi PRIEST
JUST A LITTLE BIT OF LOVE — Rebekah RYAN
JUST A LITTLE BIT TOO LATE — Wayne FONTANA and The MINDBENDERS
JUST A LITTLE MISUNDERSTANDING — CONTOURS
JUST A LITTLE GIRL — Amy STUDT
JUST A LITTLE MORE — DELUXE
JUST A LITTLE MORE LOVE — David GUETTA featuring Chris WILLIS
JUST A LITTLE TOO MUCH — Ricky NELSON
JUST A LITTLE WHILE — JANET
JUST A MAN — Mark MORRISON
JUST A MIRAGE — JELLYBEAN
JUST A RIDE — JEM
JUST A SHADOW — BIG COUNTRY
JUST A SMILE — PILOT
JUST A STEP FROM HEAVEN — ETERNAL
JUST A TOUCH — Keith SWEAT
JUST A TOUCH OF LOVE — SLAVE
JUST A TOUCH OF LOVE (EVERYDAY) — C & C MUSIC FACTORY / CLIVILLES & COLE
JUST AN ILLUSION — IMAGINATION
JUST ANOTHER BROKEN HEART — Sheena EASTON
JUST ANOTHER DAY [A] — Jon SECADA
JUST ANOTHER DAY [B] — Jonathan WILKES
JUST ANOTHER DREAM — Cathy DENNIS
JUST ANOTHER GROOVE — MIGHTY DUB KATZ
JUST ANOTHER ILLUSION — HURRICANE #1
JUST ANOTHER NIGHT — Mick JAGGER
JUST AROUND THE HILL — SASH!
JUST AS LONG AS YOU ARE THERE — Vanessa PARADIS
JUST AS MUCH AS EVER — Nat 'King' COLE
JUST BE — TIESTO featuring Kirsty HAWKSHAW
JUST BE DUB TO ME [A] — REVELATION
JUST BE GOOD TO ME [A] — S.O.S. BAND
JUST BE TONIGHT — BBG
JUST BECAUSE — JANE'S ADDICTION
JUST BEFORE YOU LEAVE — DEL AMITRI
JUST BETWEEN YOU AND ME — APRIL WINE
JUST BORN — Jim DALE
JUST CALL — SHERRICK
JUST CALL ME — GOOD GIRLS
JUST CAN'T GET ENOUGH [A] — DEPECHE MODE
JUST CAN'T GET ENOUGH [B] — TRANSFORMER 2
JUST CAN'T GET ENOUGH [C] — Harry 'Choo Choo' ROMERO presents Inaya DAY
JUST CAN'T GET ENOUGH (NO NO NO NO) — EYE TO EYE featuring Taka BOOM
JUST CAN'T GIVE YOU UP — MYSTIC MERLIN
JUST CAN'T STAND IT — MATT BIANCO
JUST CAN'T WAIT (SATURDAY) — ONEHUNDREDPERCENT featuring Jennifer JOHN
JUST CHECKIN' — The BEAUTIFUL SOUTH
JUST CRUISIN' — Will SMITH
JUST DON'T WANT TO BE LONELY [A] — MAIN INGREDIENT
JUST DON'T WANT TO BE LONELY [A] — Freddie McGREGOR
JUST FADE AWAY — STIFF LITTLE FINGERS
JUST FOR KICKS — Mike SARNE
JUST FOR MONEY — Paul HARDCASTLE
JUST FOR OLD TIME'S SAKE — FOSTER and ALLEN
JUST FOR ONE DAY (HEROES) — David GUETTA vs BOWIE
JUST FOR YOU [A] — FREDDIE and The DREAMERS
JUST FOR YOU [B] — GLITTER BAND
JUST FOR YOU [C] — Alan PRICE
JUST FOR YOU [D] — M PEOPLE
JUST FOR YOU [E] — Lionel RICHIE
JUST FRIENDS — NINE BLACK ALPS
JUST FUCK — Tom NEVILLE
JUST GET UP AND DANCE — Afrika BAMBAATAA
JUST GETS BETTER — TJR featuring XAVIER
JUST GIVE THE DJ A BREAK — DYNAMIX II featuring TOO TOUGH TEE
JUST GOOD FRIENDS — FISH featuring Sam BROWN
JUST GOT LUCKY — JOBOXERS
JUST GOT PAID — Johnny KEMP
JUST HOLD ON — TOPLOADER
JUST IN CASE — JAHEIM
JUST IN LUST — The WILDHEARTS
JUST IN TIME — RAW SILK
JUST KEEP IT UP — Dee CLARK
JUST KEEP ME MOVING — kd LANG
JUST KEEP ROCKIN' — DOUBLE TROUBLE and The REBEL MC
JUST KICK — COHEN vs DELUXE
JUST KICKIN' IT — XSCAPE
JUST LET ME DO MY THING — SINE
JUST LIKE A MAN — DEL AMITRI
JUST LIKE A PILL — PINK (02)
JUST LIKE A WOMAN — MANFRED MANN
JUST LIKE ANYONE — SOUL ASYLUM
JUST LIKE BRUCE LEE — KILL CITY
JUST LIKE EDDIE — HEINZ
JUST LIKE FRED ASTAIRE — JAMES
JUST LIKE HEAVEN [A] — The CURE
JUST LIKE HEAVEN [B] — Katie MELUA
JUST LIKE HONEY — JESUS AND MARY CHAIN
JUST LIKE JESSE JAMES — CHER
JUST LIKE PARADISE — David Lee ROTH
(JUST LIKE) STARTING OVER — John LENNON (80)
JUST LISTEN TO MY HEART — SPOTNICKS
JUST LOOKIN' — The CHARLATANS
JUST LOOKING — STEREOPHONICS
JUST LOSE IT — EMINEM (04)
JUST LOVING YOU — Anita HARRIS
JUST MELLOW — RUTHLESS RAP ASSASSINS
JUST MY IMAGINATION (RUNNING AWAY WITH ME) [A] — The TEMPTATIONS
JUST MY IMAGINATION [A] — The McGANNS
JUST MY SOUL RESPONDING — Smokey ROBINSON
JUST ONE LOOK [A] — The HOLLIES
JUST ONE LOOK [A] — FAITH, HOPE AND CHARITY
JUST ONE MORE KISS — RENÉE and RENATO
JUST ONE MORE NIGHT — YELLOW DOG
JUST ONE SMILE — Gene PITNEY
JUST OUT OF REACH (OF MY TWO EMPTY ARMS) — Ken DODD
JUST OUTSIDE OF HEAVEN — H 20
JUST PLAY MUSIC — BIG AUDIO DYNAMITE
JUST PLAYIN' — JT PLAYAZ
JUST PUT YOUR HAND IN MINE — SPACE COWBOY
JUST RIGHT — SOUL II SOUL
JUST ROUND — A VERY GOOD FRIEND OF MINE
JUST SAY NO — GRANGE HILL CAST
JUST SAY YOU LOVE ME — MALACHI
JUST SEVEN NUMBERS (CAN STRAIGHTEN OUT MY LIFE) — The FOUR TOPS
JUST SHOW ME HOW TO LOVE YOU — Sarah BRIGHTMAN & The LONDON SYMPHONY ORCHESTRA featuring José CURA
JUST SO YOU KNOW — AMERICAN HEAD CHARGE
JUST TAH LET YOU KNOW — EAZY-E
JUST TAKE MY HEART — MR BIG
JUST THE ONE — LEVELLERS, special guest Joe STRUMMER
JUST THE TWO OF US [A] — Grover WASHINGTON Jr
JUST THE TWO OF US [A] — Will SMITH
JUST THE WAY — Alfonzo HUNTER
JUST THE WAY I'M FEELING — FEEDER
JUST THE WAY IT IS — Lisa MOORISH
JUST THE WAY YOU ARE [A] — Billy JOEL
JUST THE WAY YOU ARE [A] — Barry WHITE
JUST THE WAY YOU ARE [B] — MILKY
JUST THE WAY YOU LIKE IT — S.O.S. BAND
JUST THIRTEEN — The LURKERS
JUST THIS SIDE OF LOVE — Malandra BURROWS

	15 September 2001	22 September 2001	29 September 2001	6 October 2001
UK No.1 SINGLES	MAMBO NO.5 Bob the Builder	HEY BABY (UHH, AHH) DJ Otzi	CAN'T GET YOU OUT OF MY HEAD Kylie	CAN'T GET YOU OUT OF MY HEAD Kylie
UK No.1 ALBUMS	A FUNK ODYSSEY Jamiroquai	A FUNK ODYSSEY Jamiroquai	THE ID Macy Gray	NO ANGEL Dido

JUST TO BE CLOSE TO YOU — The COMMODORES
JUST TO SEE HER — Smokey ROBINSON
JUST WALK IN MY SHOES — Gladys KNIGHT and The PIPS
JUST WALKING IN THE RAIN — Johnnie RAY (56)
JUST WANNA KNOW — Maxi PRIEST
JUST WANNA TOUCH ME — FIDELFATTI featuring RONNETTE
JUST WANT TO LIVE — The OPEN
JUST WANT YOU TO KNOW — BACKSTREET BOYS
JUST WAVE HELLO — Charlotte CHURCH
JUST WHAT I ALWAYS WANTED — Mari WILSON
JUST WHAT I NEEDED — The CARS
JUST WHEN I NEEDED YOU MOST [A] — Randy VANWARMER
JUST WHEN I NEEDED YOU MOST [A] — Barbara JONES
JUST WHEN YOU'RE THINKIN' THINGS OVER — The CHARLATANS
JUST WHO IS THE FIVE O'CLOCK HERO — The JAM
(JUST) YOU AND ME — NEW VISION
JUSTIFIED AND ANCIENT — The KLF guest vocals: Tammy WYNETTE
JUSTIFY MY LOVE — MADONNA
JUSTIFY THE RAIN — COSMIC ROUGH RIDERS
JUXTAPOZED WITH U — SUPER FURRY ANIMALS
KA-CHING! — Shania TWAIN
KALEIDOSCOPE SKIES — JAM & SPOON featuring PLAVKA
KAMICHI — HELL IS FOR HEROES
KAMIKAZE — KING ADORA
KANSAS CITY [A] — LITTLE RICHARD
KANSAS CITY [A] — Trini LOPEZ
KANSAS CITY STAR — Roger MILLER
KARA-KARA — NEW WORLD
KARAOKE QUEEN — CATATONIA
KARAOKE SOUL — Tom McRAE
KARMA CHAMELEON — CULTURE CLUB (83)
KARMA HOTEL — SPOOKS
KARMA POLICE — RADIOHEAD
KARMACOMA — MASSIVE ATTACK
KARMADROME — POP WILL EAT ITSELF
KATE — Ben FOLDS FIVE
KATHLEEN — ROACHFORD
KATHLEEN (EP) — TINDERSTICKS
KAYLEIGH — MARILLION
KEEEP YOUR BODY WORKIN' — KLEEER
KEEP A KNOCKIN' — LITTLE RICHARD
KEEP AWAY FROM OTHER GIRLS — Helen SHAPIRO
KEEP COMING BACK — Richard MARX
KEEP CONTROL — SONO
KEEP DOIN' IT — SHOWDOWN
KEEP EACH OTHER WARM — BUCKS FIZZ
(KEEP FEELING) FASCINATION — HUMAN LEAGUE
KEEP FISHIN' — WEEZER
KEEP GIVIN' ME YOUR LOVE — Ce Ce PENISTON
KEEP GIVING ME LOVE [A] — D TRAIN
KEEP GIVING ME LOVE [B] — BOMB THE BASS
KEEP HOPE ALIVE [A] — SERIAL DIVA
KEEP HOPE ALIVE [B] — CRYSTAL METHOD
KEEP IN TOUCH — FREEEZ
KEEP IN TOUCH (BODY TO BODY) — SHADES OF LOVE
KEEP IT CLEAR — DTI
KEEP IT COMIN' (DANCE TILL YOU CAN'T DANCE NO MORE) — C & C MUSIC FACTORY / CLIVILLES & COLE
KEEP IT COMIN' LOVE — KC and The SUNSHINE BAND
KEEP IT DARK — GENESIS
KEEP IT ON — Hannah JONES
KEEP IT OUT OF SIGHT — Paul and Barry RYAN
KEEP IT TO YOURSELF — REUBEN
KEEP IT TOGETHER — David GRANT
KEEP IT UP — SHARADA HOUSE GANG
KEEP LOVE NEW — Betty WRIGHT
KEEP LOVE TOGETHER [A] — LOVE TO INFINITY
KEEP LOVE TOGETHER [B] — SODA CLUB featuring Andrea ANATOLA
KEEP ME A SECRET — Ainslie HENDERSON
KEEP ME FROM THE COLD — Curtis STIGERS
KEEP ME IN MIND — BOY GEORGE
KEEP ON [A] — Bruce CHANNEL
KEEP ON [B] — CABARET VOLTAIRE
KEEP ON BELIEVING — GRAND PRIX
KEEP ON BURNING — Edwyn COLLINS
KEEP ON DANCIN' — GARY'S GANG
KEEP ON DANCIN' (LET'S GO) — PERPETUAL MOTION
KEEP ON DANCING — BAY CITY ROLLERS
KEEP ON JAMMIN' — Willie HUTCH
KEEP ON JUMPIN' [A] — LISA MARIE EXPERIENCE
KEEP ON JUMPIN' [A] — Todd TERRY featuring Martha WASH and Jocelyn BROWN
KEEP ON KEEPIN' ON [A] — REDSKINS
KEEP ON KEEPIN' ON [B] — MC LYTE featuring XSCAPE
KEEP ON LOVING YOU — REO SPEEDWAGON
KEEP ON MOVIN' [A] — SOUL II SOUL
KEEP ON MOVIN' [B] — FIVE (99)
KEEP ON MOVING [C] — Bob MARLEY & The WAILERS
KEEP ON PUMPIN' IT — VISIONMASTERS with Tony KING and Kylie MINOGUE
KEEP ON PUSHING OUR LOVE — NIGHTCRAWLERS featuring John REID and Alysha WARREN
KEEP ON RUNNIN' (TILL YOU BURN) — UK SUBS
KEEP ON RUNNING [A] — Spencer DAVIS GROUP (66)
KEEP ON RUNNING [A] — John ALFORD
(KEEP ON) SHINING — LOVELAND featuring the voice of Rachel McFARLANE
KEEP ON TRUCKIN' — Eddie KENDRICKS
KEEP ON WALKIN' — Ce Ce PENISTON
KEEP PUSHIN' [A] — CLOCK
KEEP PUSHIN' [B] — Boris DLUGOSCH presents BOOOM
KEEP PUSHIN' ON — YETI
KEEP REACHING OUT FOR LOVE — LINER
KEEP SEARCHIN' (WE'LL FOLLOW THE SUN) — Del SHANNON
KEEP STEPPIN' — OMAR
KEEP TALKING — PINK FLOYD
KEEP THE CUSTOMER SATISFIED — Marsha HUNT
KEEP THE FAITH — BON JOVI
KEEP THE FIRE BURNIN' — Dan HARTMAN starring Loleatta HOLLOWAY
KEEP THE FIRES BURNING — CLOCK
KEEP THE HOME FIRES BURNING — The BLUETONES
KEEP THE MUSIC STRONG — BIZARRE INC
KEEP THEIR HEADS RINGIN' — DR DRE
KEEP THIS FIRE BURNING — Beverley KNIGHT
KEEP THIS FREQUENCY CLEAR — DTI
KEEP WARM — JINNY
KEEP WHAT YA GOT — Ian BROWN
KEEP YOUR EYE ON ME — Herb ALPERT
KEEP YOUR HANDS OFF MY BABY — LITTLE EVA
KEEP YOUR HANDS TO YOURSELF — GEORGIA SATELLITES
KEEP YOUR LOVE — PARTIZAN
KEEP YOUR WORRIES — GURU'S JAZZMATAZZ featuring Angie STONE
KEEPER OF THE CASTLE — The FOUR TOPS
KEEPIN' LOVE NEW — Howard JOHNSON
KEEPIN' THE FAITH — DE LA SOUL
KEEPING A RENDEZVOUS — BUDGIE
KEEPING SECRETS — SWITCH
KEEPING THE DREAM ALIVE — FREIHEIT
KEEPS ME WONDERING WHY — Steve MILLER BAND
KEINE LUST — RAMMSTEIN
KELLY — Wayne GIBSON
KELLY WATCH THE STARS — AIR
KELLY'S HEROES — BLACK GRAPE
KENNEDY — WEDDING PRESENT
KENTUCKY RAIN — Elvis PRESLEY
KERNKRAFT 400 — ZOMBIE NATION
KERRY KERRY — CINERAMA
THE KETCHUP SONG (ASEREJE) — LAS KETCHUP (02)
KEVIN CARTER — MANIC STREET PREACHERS
KEWPIE DOLL [A] — Frankie VAUGHAN
KEWPIE DOLL [A] — Perry COMO
THE KEY [A] — SENSER
THE KEY [B] — Matt GOSS
KEY LARGO — Bertie HIGGINS
THE KEY THE SECRET — URBAN COOKIE COLLECTIVE
KEY TO MY LIFE — BOYZONE
KICK IN THE EYE — BAUHAUS
KICK IN THE EYE (EP) — BAUHAUS
A KICK IN THE MOUTH — REUBEN
KICK IT [A] — NITZER EBB
KICK IT [B] — REGGAE BOYZ
KICK IT [C] — PEACHES featuring Iggy POP
KICK IT IN — SIMPLE MINDS
KICKIN' HARD — KLUBBHEADS
KICKIN' IN THE BEAT — Pamela FERNANDEZ
KICKIN' UP DUST — LITTLE ANGELS
KICKING MY HEART AROUND — The BLACK CROWES
KICKIN' UP THE LEAVES — Mark WYNTER
KICKS (EP) — UK SUBS
KID [A] — The PRETENDERS
KID 2000 [A] — HYBRID featuring Chrissie HYNDE
KIDDIO — Brook BENTON
KIDS — Robbie WILLIAMS / Kylie MINOGUE
THE KIDS ARE ALRIGHT — The WHO
THE KIDS ARE BACK — TWISTED SISTER
THE KIDS AREN'T ALRIGHT — The OFFSPRING
KIDS IN AMERICA — Kim WILDE
THE KID'S LAST FIGHT — Frankie LAINE
KIDS OF THE CENTURY — HELLOWEEN
KIDS ON THE STREET — ANGELIC UPSTARTS
KIKI RIRI BOOM — SHAFT
KILLAMANGIRO – BABY SHAMBLES
KILL ALL HIPPIES — PRIMAL SCREAM
KILL THE KING — RAINBOW
KILL THE POOR — DEAD KENNEDYS
KILL YOUR TELEVISION — NED'S ATOMIC DUSTBIN
KILLED BY DEATH — MOTÖRHEAD
KILLER [A] — ADAMSKI (90)
KILLER (EP) [A] — SEAL
KILLER [A] — ATB
KILLER ON THE LOOSE — THIN LIZZY
KILLER QUEEN — QUEEN
KILLERS LIVE (EP) — THIN LIZZY
KILLIN' TIME — Tina COUSINS
KILLING IN THE NAME — RAGE AGAINST THE MACHINE
THE KILLING JAR — SIOUXSIE and The BANSHEES
KILLING ME SOFTLY WITH HIS SONG [A] — Roberta FLACK
KILLING ME SOFTLY [A] — FUGEES (96)
THE KILLING MOON — ECHO and The BUNNYMEN
THE KILLING OF GEORGIE — Rod STEWART
A KIND OF CHRISTMAS CARD — Morten HARKET
A KIND OF MAGIC — QUEEN
KINDA LOVE — DARIUS
KINDA NEW — SPEKTRUM
KINETIC — GOLDEN GIRLS
KINETIC '99 — GOLDEN GIRLS
KING — UB40
THE KING AND QUEEN OF AMERICA — EURYTHMICS
KING CREOLE — Elvis PRESLEY
KING FOR A DAY [A] — THOMPSON TWINS
KING FOR A DAY [B] — JAMIROQUAI
KING IN A CATHOLIC STYLE (WAKE UP) — CHINA CRISIS
THE KING IS DEAD — GO WEST
THE KING IS HALF UNDRESSED — JELLYFISH
THE KING IS HERE — 45 KING
KING KONG — Terry LIGHTFOOT and his NEW ORLEANS JAZZMEN
KING MIDAS IN REVERSE — The HOLLIES
KING OF CLOWNS — Neil SEDAKA
KING OF DREAMS — DEEP PURPLE
KING OF EMOTION — BIG COUNTRY
KING OF KINGS — Ezz RECO and the LAUNCHERS with Boysie GRANT
THE KING OF KISSINGDOM — MY LIFE STORY
KING OF LOVE — Dave EDMUNDS
KING OF MISERY — HONEYCRACK
KING OF MY CASTLE — WAMDUE PROJECT (99)
KING OF NEW YORK — FUN LOVIN' CRIMINALS
KING OF PAIN — The POLICE
THE KING OF ROCK 'N' ROLL — PREFAB SPROUT
KING OF SNAKE — UNDERWORLD
KING OF SORROW — SADE
KING OF THE COPS — Billy HOWARD
KING OF THE DANCEHALL — BEENIE MAN
KING OF THE KERB — ECHOBELLY
KING OF THE MOUNTAIN — Kate BUSH
KING OF THE NEW YORK STREET — DION
KING OF THE ROAD — Roger MILLER (65)
KING OF THE ROAD (EP) — The PROCLAIMERS
KING OF THE RODEO — KINGS OF LEON
KING OF THE RUMBLING SPIRES — T. REX
THE KING OF WISHFUL THINKING — GO WEST
KING ROCKER — GENERATION X
KING WITHOUT A CROWN — ABC
KINGDOM — ULTRAMARINE
KINGS AND QUEENS — KILLING JOKE
KING'S CALL — Philip LYNOTT
KINGS OF THE WILD FRONTIER — ADAM and The ANTS
KINGSTON TOWN — UB40
KINKY AFRO — HAPPY MONDAYS
KINKY BOOTS — Patrick MacNEE and Honor BLACKMAN
KINKY LOVE — PALE SAINTS
KIKI RIRI BOOM — SHAFT
KISS [A] — Dean MARTIN
KISS [B] — PRINCE
KISS [B] — AGE OF CHANCE
KISS [B] — ART OF NOISE featuring Tom JONES
KISS AND SAY GOODBYE [A] — The MANHATTANS
KISS AND SAY GOODBYE [A] — UB40
KISS AND TELL [A] — Bryan FERRY
KISS AND TELL [B] — BROWNSTONE
KISS FROM A ROSE — SEAL
KISS KISS — Holly VALANCE (02)
KISS LIKE ETHER — Claudia BRÜCKEN
KISS ME [A] — Stephen 'Tin Tin' DUFFY
KISS ME [B] — SIXPENCE NONE THE RICHER
KISS ME ANOTHER — Georgia GIBBS
KISS ME DEADLY — Lita FORD
KISS ME GOODBYE — Petula CLARK
KISS ME HONEY HONEY, KISS ME — Shirley BASSEY
KISS ME QUICK — Elvis PRESLEY
KISS MY EYES — Bob SINCLAR
KISS OF LIFE [A] — SADE
KISS OF LIFE [B] — SUPERGRASS
KISS ON MY LIST — Daryl HALL and John OATES
KISS ON THE LIPS — The DUALERS
KISS THAT FROG — Peter GABRIEL
KISS THE BRIDE — Elton JOHN
KISS THE DIRT (FALLING DOWN THE MOUNTAIN) — INXS
KISS THE GIRL — Peter ANDRE
KISS THE RAIN — Billie MYERS
KISS THEM FOR ME — SIOUXSIE and The BANSHEES
KISS THIS THING GOODBYE — DEL AMITRI
KISS (WHEN THE SUN DON'T SHINE) — The VENGABOYS
KISS YOU ALL OVER [A] — EXILE
KISS YOU ALL OVER [A] — NO MERCY
KISSES IN THE MOONLIGHT — George BENSON
KISSES ON THE WIND — Neneh CHERRY
KISSES SWEETER THAN WINE [A] — Jimmie RODGERS
KISSES SWEETER THAN WINE [A] — Frankie VAUGHAN
KISSIN' COUSINS — Elvis PRESLEY
KISSIN' IN THE BACK ROW OF THE MOVIES — The DRIFTERS
KISSIN' YOU — TOTAL
KISSING A FOOL — George MICHAEL
KISSING GATE — Sam BROWN
KISSING WITH CONFIDENCE — Will POWERS
KITE — Nick HEYWARD
KITES — Simon DUPREE and The BIG SOUND
KITSCH — Barry RYAN
KITTY — Cat STEVENS

13 October 2001	20 October 2001	27 October 2001	3 November 2001
CAN'T GET YOU OUT OF MY HEAD Kylie	CAN'T GET YOU OUT OF MY HEAD Kylie	BECAUSE I GOT HIGH Afroman	BECAUSE I GOT HIGH Afroman
FEVER Kylie	FEVER Kylie	GOLD - THE GREATEST HITS Steps	GOLD - THE GREATEST HITS Steps

10 November 2001	17 November 2001	24 November 2001	1 December 2001
UK No.1 SINGLES			
BECAUSE I GOT HIGH Afroman	**QUEEN OF MY HEART** Westlife	**IF YOU COME BACK** Blue	**HAVE YOU EVER** S Club 7
UK No.1 ALBUMS			
INVINCIBLE Michael Jackson	**GOLD - THE GREATEST HITS** Steps	**WORLD OF OUR OWN** Westlife	**SWING WHEN YOU'RE WINNING** Robbie Williams

LEAN ON ME (AH-LI-AYO) — RED BOX
LEAN ON ME I WON'T FALL OVER — CARTER — THE UNSTOPPABLE SEX MACHINE
LEAN ON YOU — Cliff RICHARD
LEAN PERIOD — ORANGE JUICE
LEAP OF FAITH — Bruce SPRINGSTEEN
LEAP UP AND DOWN (WAVE YOUR KNICKERS IN THE AIR) — ST CECILIA
LEARN CHINESE — JIN
LEARN TO FLY — FOO FIGHTERS
LEARNIN' THE BLUES — Frank SINATRA
LEARNIN' THE GAME — Buddy HOLLY
LEARNING TO FLY [A] — Tom PETTY and The HEARTBREAKERS
LEARNING TO FLY [B] — MOTHER'S PRIDE
LEAVE A LIGHT ON — Belinda CARLISLE
LEAVE A LITTLE LOVE — LULU
LEAVE A TENDER MOMENT ALONE — Billy JOEL
LEAVE 'EM SOMETHING TO DESIRE — SPRINKLER
LEAVE (GET OUT) — JOJO
LEAVE HOME — The CHEMICAL BROTHERS
LEAVE IN SILENCE — DEPECHE MODE
LEAVE IT [A] — Mike McGEAR
LEAVE IT [B] — YES
LEAVE IT ALONE — LIVING COLOUR
LEAVE IT UP TO ME — Aaron CARTER
LEAVE ME ALONE — Michael JACKSON
LEAVE RIGHT NOW — Will YOUNG (03)
LEAVE THEM ALL BEHIND — RIDE
LEAVIN' [A] — Tony RICH PROJECT
LEAVIN' [B] — Shelby LYNNE
LEAVIN' ON A JET PLANE — PETER, PAUL and MARY
LEAVING HERE — The BIRDS
LEAVING LAS VEGAS — Sheryl CROW
LEAVING ME NOW — LEVEL 42
LEAVING NEW YORK – R.E.M.
LEAVING ON A JET PLANE — Chantal KREVIAZUK
LEAVING ON THE MIDNIGHT TRAIN — Nick STRAKER BAND
THE LEAVING SONG PT.2 — AFI
THE LEBANON — HUMAN LEAGUE
LEEDS, LEEDS, LEEDS — LEEDS UNITED FC
LEEDS UNITED — LEEDS UNITED FC
LEFT BANK — Winifred ATWELL
LEFT BEHIND — SLIPKNOT
LEFT OF CENTER — Suzanne VEGA featuring Joe JACKSON
LEFT OUTSIDE ALONE — ANASTACIA
LEFT TO MY OWN DEVICES — PET SHOP BOYS
LEGACY — Mad COBRA featuring Richie STEPHENS
THE LEGACY — PUSH
LEGACY (EP) — MANSUN
LEGACY (SHOW ME LOVE) — SPACE BROTHERS
LEGAL MAN — BELLE & SEBASTIAN
A LEGAL MATTER — The WHO
LEGEND OF A COWGIRL — Imani COPPOLA
LEGEND OF THE GOLDEN SNAKE — DEPTH CHARGE
THE LEGEND OF XANADU — Dave DEE, DOZY, BEAKY, MICK and TICH (68)
LEGENDS OF THE DARK BLACK PART 2 — WILDCHILD
LEGO SKANGA — Rupie EDWARDS
LEGS [A] — ART OF NOISE
LEGS [B] — ZZ TOP
LEMMINGS — SFX
LEMON TREE — FOOL'S GARDEN
LENINGRAD — Billy JOEL
LENNY — SUPERGRASS
LENNY AND TERENCE — CARTER — THE UNSTOPPABLE SEX MACHINE
LENNY VALENTINO — The AUTEURS
LEONARD NIMOY — FREAKY REALISTIC
LEROY — WHEATUS
LES BICYCLETTES DE BELSIZE — Engelbert HUMPERDINCK
LES FLEUR — 4 HERO
L'ESPERANZA [A] — Sven VATH
L'ESPERANZA [B] — AIRSCAPE
LESS TALK MORE ACTION — Tim DELUXE
LESSON ONE — Russ CONWAY
LESSONS IN LOVE [A] — The ALLISONS
LESSONS IN LOVE [B] — LEVEL 42
LESSONS LEARNED FROM ROCKY I TO ROCKY III — CORNERSHOP
LET A BOY CRY — GALA
LET A GOOD THING GO — Gemma HAYES
LET 'EM IN [A] — Paul McCARTNEY
LET 'EM IN [A] — Billy PAUL
LET 'EM IN [A] — SHINEHEAD
LET FOREVER BE — The CHEMICAL BROTHERS
LET GO WITH THE FLOW — The BEAUTIFUL SOUTH
LET HER CRY — HOOTIE & The BLOWFISH
LET HER DOWN EASY — Terence Trent D'ARBY
LET HER FALL — THEN JERICO
LET HER FEEL IT — SIMPLICIOUS
LET HER GO — STRAWBERRY SWITCHBLADE
LET IT ALL BLOW — DAZZ BAND
LET IT ALL HANG OUT — Jonathan KING
LET IT BE [A] — The BEATLES
LET IT BE [A] — FERRY AID (87)
LET IT BE ME [A] — The EVERLY BROTHERS
LET IT BE ME [A] — JUSTIN
LET IT BE WITH YOU — BELOUIS SOME
LET IT FLOW — SPIRITUALIZED
LET IT LAST — Carleen ANDERSON
LET IT LIVE — HAVEN
LET IT LOOSE — LEMON TREES
LET IT RAIN [A] — UFO
LET IT RAIN [B] — EAST 17
LET IT RAIN [C] — 4 STRINGS
LET IT REIGN — INNER CITY
LET IT RIDE — Todd TERRY PROJECT
LET IT ROCK [A] — Chuck BERRY
LET IT ROCK [A] — The ROLLING STONES
LET IT ROLL — RAZE presents Doug LAZY
LET IT SLIDE [A] — MUDHONEY
LET IT SLIDE [B] — ARIEL
LET IT SWING — The BOBBYSOCKS
LET LOVE BE THE LEADER — FM
LET LOVE BE YOUR ENERGY — Robbie WILLIAMS
LET LOVE LEAD THE WAY — SPICE GIRLS (00)
LET LOVE RULE — Lenny KRAVITZ
LET LOVE SHINE — AMOS
LET LOVE SPEAK UP ITSELF — The BEAUTIFUL SOUTH
LET ME BE — BLACK DIAMOND
LET ME BE THE NUMBER 1 (LOVE OF YOUR LIFE) — Dooley SILVERSPOON
LET ME BE THE ONE [A] — The SHADOWS
LET ME BE THE ONE [B] — FIVE STAR
LET ME BE THE ONE [C] — BLESSID UNION OF SOULS
LET ME BE THE ONE [D] — MINT CONDITION
LET ME BE THE ONE [E] — Cliff RICHARD
LET ME BE YOUR FANTASY — BABY D (94)
(LET ME BE YOUR) TEDDY BEAR — Elvis PRESLEY
LET ME BE YOUR UNDERWEAR — CLUB 69
LET ME BE YOUR WINGS — Barry MANILOW
LET ME BE YOURS — FIVE STAR
LET ME BLOW YA MIND — EVE featuring Gwen STEFANI
LET ME CLEAR MY THROAT [A] — DJ KOOL
LET ME CLEAR MY THROAT [B] — PUBLIC DOMAIN
LET ME COME ON HOME — Otis REDDING
LET ME CRY ON YOUR SHOULDER — Ken DODD
LET ME DOWN EASY — The STRANGLERS
LET ME ENTERTAIN YOU — Robbie WILLIAMS
LET ME FLY — Darren STYLES & Mark BREEZE present INFEXTIOUS
LET ME GO — HEAVEN 17
LET ME GO HOME — ALL ABOUT EVE
LET ME GO LOVER [A] — Teresa BREWER
LET ME GO LOVER [A] — Dean MARTIN
LET ME GO LOVER [A] — Ruby MURRAY
LET ME GO LOVER [A] — Joan WEBER
LET ME GO LOVER [A] — Kathy KIRBY
LET ME HEAR YOU SAY 'OLE OLE' — The OUTHERE BROTHERS
LET ME HOLD YOU — BOW WOW featuring OMARION
LET ME IN [A] — The OSMONDS
LET ME IN [A] — OTT
LET ME IN [B] — YOUNG BUCK
LET ME INTRODUCE YOU TO THE FAMILY — The STRANGLERS
LET ME KISS YOU [A] — MORRISSEY
LET ME KISS YOU [A] — Nancy SINATRA
LET ME KNOW [A] — JUNIOR
LET ME KNOW [B] — Maxi PRIEST
LET ME KNOW (I HAVE A RIGHT) — Gloria GAYNOR
LET ME LET GO — Faith HILL
LET ME LIVE — QUEEN
LET ME LOVE YOU — MARIO
LET ME LOVE YOU FOR TONIGHT — KARIYA
LET ME MOVE ON — GENE
LET ME RIDE — DR DRE
LET ME ROCK YOU — KANDIDATE
LET ME SEE — MORCHEEBA
LET ME SHOW YOU [A] — K-KLASS
LET ME SHOW YOU [B] — CAMISRA
LET ME SHOW YOU [C] — Tony MOMRELLE
LET ME TAKE YOU THERE — Betty BOO
LET ME TALK — EARTH WIND AND FIRE
LET ME TRY AGAIN — Tammy JONES
LET ME WAKE UP IN YOUR ARMS — LULU
LET MY LOVE OPEN YOUR DOOR — Pete TOWNSHEND
LET MY NAME BE SORROW — Mary HOPKIN
LET MY PEOPLE GO (PART 1) — WINANS
LET MY PEOPLE GO-GO — RAINMAKERS
LET ROBESON SING — MANIC STREET PREACHERS
LET SOMEBODY LOVE YOU — Keni BURKE
LET THE BASS KICK — 2 FOR JOY
LET THE BEAT CONTROL YOUR BODY — 2 UNLIMITED
LET THE BEAT HIT 'EM [A] — LISA LISA
LET THE BEAT HIT 'EM [A] — SHENA
LET THE DAY BEGIN — CALL
LET THE DRUMS SPEAK — MIGHTY DUB KATS
LET THE FLAME BURN BRIGHTER — Graham KENDRICK
LET THE FREAK — BIG RON
LET THE GOOD TIMES ROLL — SHEEP ON DRUGS
LET THE HAPPINESS IN — David SYLVIAN
LET THE HEALING BEGIN — Joe COCKER
LET THE HEARTACHES BEGIN — Long John BALDRY (67)
LET THE LITTLE GIRL DANCE — Billy BLAND
LET THE LOVE — Q-TEX
LET THE MUSIC HEAL YOUR SOUL — BRAVO ALL STARS
LET THE MUSIC (LIFT YOU UP) — Darlene LEWIS
LET THE MUSIC MOVE U — RAZE
LET THE MUSIC PLAY [A] — Barry WHITE
LET THE MUSIC PLAY [B] — Charles EARLAND
LET THE MUSIC PLAY [C] — SHANNON
LET THE MUSIC PLAY [C] — BBG
LET THE MUSIC PLAY [C] — Mary KIANI
LET THE MUSIC TAKE CONTROL — JM SILK
LET THE MUSIC USE YOU — NIGHTWRITERS
LET THE PEOPLE KNOW — TOPLOADER
LET THE RHYTHM MOVE YOU — SHARADA HOUSE GANG
LET THE RHYTHM PUMP — Doug LAZY
LET THE SUNSHINE IN [A] — PEDDLERS
LET THE SUNSHINE IN [A] — MILK & SUGAR featuring Lizzy PATTINSON
LET THE WATER RUN DOWN — PJ PROBY
LET THE YOUNG GIRL DO WHAT SHE WANTS — Ian McNABB
LET THEM ALL TALK — Elvis COSTELLO
LET THERE BE DRUMS — Sandy NELSON
LET THERE BE HOUSE — DESKEE
LET THERE BE LIGHT — Mike OLDFIELD
LET THERE BE LOVE [A] — Nat 'King' COLE with George SHEARING
LET THERE BE LOVE [B] — SIMPLE MINDS
LET THERE BE LOVE [C] — OASIS
LET THERE BE PEACE ON EARTH (LET IT BEGIN WITH ME) — Michael WARD
LET THERE BE ROCK — ONSLAUGHT
LET THIS BE A PRAYER — ROLLO GOES SPIRITUAL with Pauline TAYLOR
LET THIS FEELING — Simone ANGEL
LET TRUE LOVE BEGIN — Nat 'King' COLE
LET U GO — ATB
LET YOUR BODY GO — Tom WILSON
LET YOUR BODY GO DOWNTOWN — Martyn FORD ORCHESTRA
LET YOUR HEAD GO — Victoria BECKHAM
LET YOUR HEART DANCE — SECRET AFFAIR
LET YOUR LOVE FLOW — BELLAMY BROTHERS
LET YOUR SOUL BE YOUR PILOT — STING
LET YOUR YEAH BE YEAH [A] — PIONEERS
LET YOUR YEAH BE YEAH [A] — Ali CAMPBELL
LET YOURSELF GO [A] — T-CONNECTION
LET YOURSELF GO [B] — SYBIL
LETHAL INDUSTRY — DJ TIESTO
LETITGO — PRINCE
LETS — Sarah VAUGHAN
LET'S ALL CHANT [A] — Michael ZAGER BAND
LET'S ALL CHANT [A] — PAT and MICK
LET'S ALL CHANT [A] — GUSTO
(LET'S ALL GO BACK) DISCO NIGHTS — JAZZ and The BROTHERS GRIMM
LET'S ALL (GO TO THE FIRE DANCES) — KILLING JOKE
LET'S ALL GO TOGETHER — MARION
LET'S ALL SING LIKE THE BIRDIES SING — The TWEETS
LET'S BE FRIENDS — Johnny NASH
LET'S BE LOVERS TONIGHT — SHERRICK
LET'S CALL IT QUITS — SLADE
LET'S CELEBRATE — NEW YORK SKYY
LET'S CLEAN UP THE GHETTO — PHILADELPHIA INTERNATIONAL ALL-STARS
LET'S DANCE [A] — Chris MONTEZ
LET'S DANCE [A] — Liz KERSHAW and Bruno BROOKES
LET'S DANCE [B] — The BOMBERS
LET'S DANCE [C] — David BOWIE (83)
LET'S DANCE [D] — MIDDLESBROUGH FC
LET'S DANCE [D] — Chris REA
LET'S DANCE [E] — FIVE (01)
LET'S DO IT AGAIN [A] — George BENSON
LET'S DO IT AGAIN [B] — Lynden David HALL
LET'S DO ROCK STEADY — BODYSNATCHERS
LET'S DO THE LATIN HUSTLE [A] — Eddie DRENNON and B.B.S. UNLIMITED
LET'S DO THE LATIN HUSTLE [A] — M and O BAND
LET'S FACE THE MUSIC AND DANCE — Nat 'King' COLE
LET'S FLY AWAY — VOYAGE
LET'S FUNK TONIGHT — BLUE FEATHER
LET'S GET BACK TO BED ... BOY — Sarah CONNOR featuring TQ
LET'S GET BLOWN — SNOOP DOGG featuring PHARRELL
LET'S GET BRUTAL — NITRO DELUXE
LET'S GET DOWN [A] — ISOTONIK
LET'S GET DOWN [B] — Mark MORRISON
LET'S GET DOWN [C] — TONY TONI TONÉ
LET'S GET DOWN [D] — JT PLAYAZ
LET'S GET DOWN [E] — SPACEDUST
LET'S GET DOWN [F] — SUPAFLY vs FISHBOWL
LET'S GET FUNKTIFIED — BOILING POINT
LET'S GET HAPPY — MASS ORDER
LET'S GET ILL — P DIDDY featuring KELIS
LET'S GET IT ON [A] — Marvin GAYE
LET'S GET IT ON [B] — Shabba RANKS
LET'S GET IT ON [C] — BIG BOSS STYLUS presents RED VENOM
LET'S GET IT STARTED — BLACK EYED PEAS
LET'S GET IT UP — AC/DC
LET'S GET MARRIED — The PROCLAIMERS
LET'S GET READY TO RHUMBLE — ANT & DEC
LET'S GET ROCKED — DEF LEPPARD
LET'S GET SERIOUS — Jermaine JACKSON
LET'S GET TATTOOS — CARTER — THE UNSTOPPABLE SEX MACHINE
LET'S GET THIS PARTY STARTED — ZENA
LET'S GET THIS STRAIGHT (FROM THE START) — DEXY'S MIDNIGHT RUNNERS
LET'S GET TOGETHER [A] — Hayley MILLS
LET'S GET TOGETHER [B] — Alexander O'NEAL
LET'S GET TOGETHER AGAIN [A] — BIG BEN BANJO BAND
LET'S GET TOGETHER AGAIN [B] — GLITTER BAND
LET'S GET TOGETHER (IN OUR MINDS) — GORKY'S ZYGOTIC MYNCI
LET'S GET TOGETHER NO.1 — BIG BEN BANJO BAND
LET'S GET TOGETHER (SO GROOVY NOW) — KRUSH PERSPECTIVE
LET'S GET TOGETHER TONITE — Steve WALSH

8 December 2001	15 December 2001	22 December 2001	29 December 2001
GOTTA GET THRU THIS Daniel Bedingfield	GOTTA GET THRU THIS Daniel Bedingfield	SOMETHIN' STUPID Robbie Williams and Nicole Kidman	SOMETHIN' STUPID Robbie Williams and Nicole Kidman
SWING WHEN YOU'RE WINNING Robbie Williams	SWING WHEN YOU'RE WINNING Robbie Williams	SWING WHEN YOU'RE WINNING Robbie Williams	SWING WHEN YOU'RE WINNING Robbie Williams

LET'S GO [A] — ROUTERS
LET'S GO [B] — The CARS
LET'S GO [C] — VARDIS
LET'S GO [D] — TRICK DADDY featuring TWISTA & LIL' JON
LET'S GO ALL THE WAY — SLY FOX
LET'S GO CRAZY — PRINCE
LET'S GO DISCO — The REAL THING
LET'S GO ROUND AGAIN [A] — AVERAGE WHITE BAND
LET'S GO ROUND AGAIN [A] — LOUISE
LET'S GO ROUND THERE — DARLING BUDS
LET'S GO STEADY AGAIN — Neil SEDAKA
LET'S GO TO BED — The CURE
LET'S GO TO SAN FRANCISCO — FLOWERPOT MEN
LET'S GO TOGETHER — CHANGE
LET'S GROOVE [A] — EARTH WIND AND FIRE
LET'S GROOVE [A] — PHAT 'N' PHUNKY
LET'S GROOVE [B] — George MOREL featuring Heather WILDMAN
LET'S HANG ON [A] — The FOUR SEASONS
LET'S HANG ON [A] — Johnny JOHNSON and The BANDWAGON
LET'S HANG ON [A] — DARTS
LET'S HANG ON [A] — Barry MANILOW
LET'S HANG ON [A] — SHOOTING PARTY
LET'S HAVE A BALL — Winifred ATWELL
LET'S HAVE A DING DONG — Winifred ATWELL
LET'S HAVE A PARTY [A] — Winifred ATWELL
LET'S HAVE A PARTY [B] — Wanda JACKSON
LET'S HAVE A QUIET NIGHT IN — David SOUL
LET'S HAVE ANOTHER PARTY — Winifred ATWELL (54)
LET'S HEAR IT FOR THE BOY — Deniece WILLIAMS
LET'S JUMP THE BROOMSTICK [A] — Brenda LEE
LET'S JUMP THE BROOMSTICK [A] — COAST TO COAST
LET'S JUST CALL IT LOVE — Lisa STANSFIELD
LET'S KILL MUSIC — The COOPER TEMPLE CLAUSE
LET'S LIVE IT UP (NITE PEOPLE) — David JOSEPH
LET'S LOVEDANCE TONIGHT — GARY'S GANG
LET'S MAKE A BABY — Billy PAUL
LET'S MAKE A NIGHT TO REMEMBER — Bryan ADAMS
LET'S PARTY — JIVE BUNNY and The MASTERMIXERS (89)
LET'S PLAY HOUSE — KRAZE
LET'S PRETEND — LULU
LET'S PUSH IT [A] — INNOCENCE
LET'S PUSH IT [B] — NIGHTCRAWLERS featuring John REID
LET'S PUSH THINGS FORWARD — The STREETS
LET'S PUT IT ALL TOGETHER — The STYLISTICS
LET'S RIDE — Montell JORDAN
LET'S ROCK — E-TRAX
LET'S ROCK 'N' ROLL — Winifred ATWELL
LET'S SEE ACTION — The WHO
LET'S SLIP AWAY — Cleo LAINE
LET'S SPEND THE NIGHT TOGETHER [A] — The ROLLING STONES
LET'S SPEND THE NIGHT TOGETHER [A] — MASH!
LET'S START OVER — Pamela FERNANDEZ
LET'S START THE DANCE — Hamilton BOHANNON
LET'S START TO DANCE AGAIN — Hamilton BOHANNON
LET'S STAY HOME TONIGHT — JOE
LET'S STAY TOGETHER [A] — Al GREEN
LET'S STAY TOGETHER [A] — Bobby M featuring Jean CARN
LET'S STAY TOGETHER [A] — Tina TURNER
LET'S STAY TOGETHER [A] — PASADENAS
LET'S STICK TOGETHER — Bryan FERRY
LET'S SWING AGAIN — JIVE BUNNY and The MASTERMIXERS
LET'S TALK ABOUT SHHH — ONE WAY
LET'S TALK ABOUT LOVE — Helen SHAPIRO
LET'S TALK ABOUT SEX — SALT-N-PEPA
LET'S THINK ABOUT LIVING — Bob LUMAN
LET'S TRY AGAIN — NEW KIDS ON THE BLOCK
LET'S TURKEY TROT — LITTLE EVA
LET'S TWIST AGAIN [A] — Chubby CHECKER
LET'S TWIST AGAIN [A] — John ASHER
LET'S WAIT AWHILE — Janet JACKSON
LET'S WALK THAT-A-WAY — Doris DAY and Johnnie RAY
LET'S WHIP IT UP (YOU GO GIRL) — SLEAZESISTERS
LET'S WOMBLE TO THE PARTY TONIGHT — The WOMBLES
LET'S WORK — Mick JAGGER
LET'S WORK IT OUT — RAGHAV featuring JAHAZIEL
LET'S WORK TOGETHER — CANNED HEAT
THE LETTER [A] — LONG AND THE SHORT
THE LETTER [B] — The BOX TOPS
THE LETTER [B] — The MINDBENDERS
THE LETTER [B] — Joe COCKER
THE LETTER [B] — Amii STEWART
THE LETTER [C] — PJ HARVEY
LETTER FROM AMERICA — The PROCLAIMERS
LETTER FULL OF TEARS — Billy FURY
LETTER TO A SOLDIER — Barbara LYON
A LETTER TO ELISE — The CURE
LETTER TO LUCILLE — Tom JONES
LETTER 2 MY UNBORN — 2PAC
A LETTER TO YOU — Shakin' STEVENS
LETTERS TO YOU — FINCH
LETTIN' YA MIND GO — DESERT
LETTING GO — Paul McCARTNEY
LETTING THE CABLES SLEEP — BUSH
LEVI STUBBS' TEARS — Billy BRAGG
LFO — LFO
LIAR [A] — Graham BONNET
LIAR [B] — ROLLINS BAND
LIAR LIAR — CREDIT TO THE NATION
LIARS' BAR — The BEAUTIFUL SOUTH
LIBERATE — Lee HASLAM
LIBERATION [A] — LIBERATION
LIBERATION [B] — PET SHOP BOYS
LIBERATION [C] — Lippy LOU
LIBERATION (TEMPTATION — FLY LIKE AN EAGLE) — Matt DAREY
LIBERATOR — SPEAR OF DESTINY
LIBERIAN GIRL — Michael JACKSON
THE LIBERTINE — Patrick WOLF
LIBERTY TOWN — PERFECT DAY
LIBIAMO — José CARRERAS featuring Placido DOMINGO and Luciano PAVAROTTI with MEHTA
LICENCE TO KILL — Gladys KNIGHT and The PIPS
LICK A SHOT — CYPRESS HILL
LICK A SMURP FOR CHRISTMAS (ALL FALL DOWN) — Jonathan KING
LICK IT — 20 FINGERS
LICK IT UP — KISS
LIDO SHUFFLE — Boz SCAGGS
LIE TO ME — BON JOVI
LIES [A] — STATUS QUO
LIES [B] — THOMPSON TWINS
LIES [C] — Jonathan BUTLER
LIES [D] — EN VOGUE
LIES [E] — EMF
THE LIES IN YOUR EYES — The SWEET
LIFE [A] — HADDAWAY
LIFE? [B] — BLAIR
LIFE [C] — DES'REE
THE LIFE [D] — STYLES & Pharoahe MONCH
LIFE AIN'T EASY — CLEOPATRA
LIFE AT A TOP PEOPLE'S HEALTH FARM — STYLE COUNCIL
LIFE BECOMING A LANDSLIDE — MANIC STREET PREACHERS
LIFE BEGINS AT THE HOP — XTC
LIFE FOR RENT — DIDO
LIFE GOES ON — GEORGIE PORGIE
LIFE GOES ON — LeAnn RIMES
LIFE GOT COLD — GIRLS ALOUD
LIFE IN A DAY [A] — SIMPLE MINDS
LIFE IN A DAY [B] — I AM KLOOT
LIFE IN A NORTHERN TOWN — DREAM ACADEMY
LIFE IN MONO — MONO
LIFE IN ONE DAY — Howard JONES
LIFE IN TOKYO — JAPAN
LIFE IS A FLOWER — ACE OF BASE
LIFE IS A HIGHWAY — Tom COCHRANE
LIFE IS A LONG SONG — JETHRO TULL
LIFE IS A MINESTRONE — 10cc
LIFE IS A ROCK (BUT THE RADIO ROLLED ME) — REUNION
LIFE IS A ROLLERCOASTER — Ronan KEATING (00)
LIFE IS FOR LIVING — BARCLAY JAMES HARVEST
LIFE IS SWEET — The CHEMICAL BROTHERS
LIFE IS TOO SHORT GIRL — SHEER ELEGANCE
A LIFE LESS ORDINARY — ASH
LIFE, LOVE AND HAPPINESS — Brian KENNEDY
LIFE LOVE AND UNITY — DREADZONE
THE LIFE OF RILEY — The LIGHTNING SEEDS
LIFE OF SURPRISES — PREFAB SPROUT
LIFE ON MARS? — David BOWIE
LIFE ON YOUR OWN — HUMAN LEAGUE
LIFE STORY — Angie STONE
LIFE SUPPORT MACHINE — THESE ANIMAL MEN
LIFE WILL BE THE DEATH OF ME — The ORDINARY BOYS
LIFEBOAT — Terry NEASON
THE LIFEBOAT PARTY — Kid CREOLE and The COCONUTS
LIFEFORMS — FUTURE SOUND OF LONDON
LIFELINE — SPANDAU BALLET
LIFE'S A CINCH — MUNDY
LIFE'S BEEN GOOD — Joe WALSH
LIFE'S JUST A BALLGAME — WOMACK and WOMACK
LIFE'S TOO SHORT [A] — HOLE IN ONE
LIFE'S TOO SHORT [B] — The LIGHTNING SEEDS
LIFE'S WHAT YOU MAKE IT — TALK TALK
LIFESAVER — GURU
LIFESTYLES OF THE RICH AND FAMOUS — GOOD CHARLOTTE
LIFETIME LOVE — Joyce SIMS
LIFETIME PILING UP — TALKING HEADS
LIFETIMES — SLAM featuring Tyrone PALMER
LIFT — 808 STATE
LIFT EVERY VOICE (TAKE ME AWAY) — MASS ORDER
LIFT IT HIGH (ALL ABOUT BELIEF) — MANCHESTER UNITED FOOTBALL CLUB
LIFT ME UP [A] — Howard JONES
LIFT ME UP [B] — RED 5
LIFT ME UP [C] — Geri HALLIWELL (99)
LIFT ME UP [D] — REEL
LIFT ME UP [E] — MOBY
LIFTED — LIGHTHOUSE FAMILY
LIFTING ME HIGHER — GEMS FOR JEM
LIGHT — Pharoahe MONCH
THE LIGHT [A] — COMMON
THE LIGHT [B] — Michelle WEEKS
LIGHT A CANDLE — Daniel O'DONNELL
LIGHT A RAINBOW — TUKAN
LIGHT AIRCRAFT ON FIRE — The AUTEURS
LIGHT AND DAY — The POLYPHONIC SPREE
THE LIGHT COMES FROM WITHIN — Linda McCARTNEY
LIGHT EMITTING ELECTRICAL WAVE — THESE ANIMAL MEN
LIGHT FLIGHT — PENTANGLE
LIGHT IN YOUR EYES — Sheryl CROW
LIGHT MY FIRE [A] — The DOORS
LIGHT MY FIRE [A] — José FELICIANO
LIGHT MY FIRE [A] — Mike FLOWERS POPS
LIGHT MY FIRE [A] — UB40
LIGHT MY FIRE [A] — Will YOUNG (02)
LIGHT MY FIRE [B] — CLUBHOUSE
LIGHT MY FIRE — 137 DISCO HEAVEN (MEDLEY) — Amii STEWART
(LIGHT OF EXPERIENCE) DOINA DE JALE — Gheorghe ZAMFIR
LIGHT OF LOVE — T. REX
LIGHT OF MY LIFE — LOUISE
LIGHT OF THE WORLD — Kim APPLEBY
LIGHT UP THE FIRE — PARCHMENT
LIGHT UP THE NIGHT — The BROTHERS JOHNSON
LIGHT UP THE WORLD FOR CHRISTMAS — LAMPIES
LIGHT YEARS — PEARL JAM
LIGHT YOUR ASS ON FIRE — Busta RHYMES featuring PHARRELL
LIGHTER — DJ SS
LIGHTERS UP — LIL' KIM
LIGHTNIN' STRIKES — Lou CHRISTIE
LIGHTNING — ZOE
LIGHTNING CRASHES — LIVE
LIGHTNING FLASH — BROTHERHOOD OF MAN
LIGHTNING STRIKES — Ozzy OSBOURNE
THE LIGHTNING TREE — SETTLERS
LIGHTS OF CINCINNATI — Scott WALKER
LIGHTS OUT — Lisa Marie PRESLEY
LIKE A BABY — Len BARRY
LIKE A BUTTERFLY — Mac and Katie KISSOON
LIKE A CAT — CRW featuring VERONIKA
LIKE A CHILD — Julie ROGERS
LIKE A CHILD AGAIN — The MISSION
LIKE A FEATHER — Nikka COSTA
LIKE A HURRICANE — The MISSION
LIKE A MOTORWAY — SAINT ETIENNE
LIKE A PLAYA — LA GANZ
LIKE A PRAYER [A] — MADONNA (89)
LIKE A PRAYER [A] — MAD'HOUSE
LIKE A ROLLING STONE [A] — Bob DYLAN
LIKE A ROLLING STONE [A] — The ROLLING STONES
LIKE A ROSE — A1
LIKE A SATELLITE (EP) — THUNDER
LIKE A STAR — Corinne BAILEY RAE
LIKE A VIRGIN — MADONNA
LIKE A WOMAN — Tony RICH PROJECT
LIKE A YO-YO — SABRINA
LIKE AN ANIMAL — GLOVE
LIKE AN OLD TIME MOVIE — Scott McKENZIE
LIKE CLOCKWORK — The BOOMTOWN RATS
LIKE DREAMERS DO [A] — The APPLEJACKS
LIKE DREAMERS DO [B] — Mica PARIS featuring Courtney PINE
LIKE FLAMES — BERLIN
LIKE GLUE — Sean PAUL
LIKE I DO [A] — Maureen EVANS
LIKE I DO [B] — FOR REAL
LIKE I LIKE IT — AURRA
LIKE I LOVE YOU — Justin TIMBERLAKE
LIKE IT OR LEAVE IT — CHIKINKI
LIKE I'VE NEVER BEEN GONE — Billy FURY
LIKE LOVERS DO — Lloyd COLE
LIKE MARVIN GAYE SAID (WHAT'S GOING ON) — SPEECH
LIKE PRINCES DO — DIESEL PARK WEST
LIKE SISTER AND BROTHER — The DRIFTERS
LIKE STRANGERS — The EVERLY BROTHERS
LIKE THIS AND LIKE THAT [A] — MONICA
LIKE THIS AND LIKE THAT [B] — LaKiesha BERRI
LIKE THIS LIKE THAT — Mauro PICOTTO
LIKE TO GET TO KNOW YOU WELL — Howard JONES
LIKE TOY SOLDIERS — EMINEM (05)
LIKE WE USED TO BE — Georgie FAME
A LIL' AIN'T ENOUGH — David Lee ROTH
LIL' BIG MAN — Omera MUMBA
LIL' DEVIL — The CULT
LIL' DUB — SPACE MONKEYZ vs GORILLAZ
LIL' RED RIDING HOOD [A] — SAM THE SHAM and The PHARAOHS
LIL RED RIDING HOOD [A] — 999
LILAC WINE — Elkie BROOKS
LILY THE PINK — SCAFFOLD (68)
LILY WAS HERE — Candy DULFER
LIMBO ROCK — Chubby CHECKER
LINDA LU — Johnny KIDD and The PIRATES
THE LINE — Lisa STANSFIELD
LINE DANCE PARTY — WOOLPACKERS
LINE UP — ELASTICA
LINES — PLANETS
LINGER — The CRANBERRIES
LION RIP — The DUKE SPIRIT
THE LION SLEEPS TONIGHT (WIMOWEH) [A] — TOKENS
THE LION SLEEPS TONIGHT [A] — Dave NEWMAN
THE LION SLEEPS TONIGHT [A] — TIGHT FIT (82)
LIONROCK — LIONROCK
THE LION'S MOUTH — KAJAGOOGOO
LIP GLOSS — PULP
LIP SERVICE (EP) — WET WET WET
LIP UP FATTY — BAD MANNERS
LIPS LIKE SUGAR — ECHO and The BUNNYMEN
LIPSMACKIN' ROCK 'N' ROLLIN' — Peter BLAKE
LIPSTICK — ROCKET FROM THE CRYPT
LIPSTICK ON YOUR COLLAR — Connie FRANCIS
LIPSTICK POWDER AND PAINT — Shakin' STEVENS

5 January 2002	12 January 2002	19 January 2002	26 January 2002
UK No.1 SINGLES			
SOMETHIN' STUPID Robbie Williams and Nicole Kidman	**GOTTA GET THRU THIS** Daniel Bedingfield	**MORE THAN A WOMAN** Aaliyah	**MY SWEET LORD (Re-issue)** George Harrison
UK No.1 ALBUMS			
SWING WHEN YOU'RE WINNING Robbie Williams	**SWING WHEN YOU'RE WINNING** Robbie Williams	**JUST ENOUGH EDUCATION TO PERFORM** Stereophonics	**JUST ENOUGH EDUCATION TO PERFORM** Stereophonics

LIQUID COOL — APOLLO FOUR FORTY
LIQUID DREAMS — O-TOWN
LIQUID LIPS — The BLUETONES
LIQUIDATOR — HARRY J ALL STARS
LISTEN — URBAN SPECIES
LISTEN (EP) — STIFF LITTLE FINGERS
LISTEN LIKE THIEVES [A] — INXS
LISTEN LIKE THIEVES [A] — WAS (NOT WAS)
LISTEN LITTLE GIRL — Keith KELLY
LISTEN TO ME [A] — Buddy HOLLY
LISTEN TO ME [B] — The HOLLIES
LISTEN TO THE MUSIC — The DOOBIE BROTHERS
LISTEN TO THE OCEAN — NINA and FREDERICK
LISTEN TO THE RADIO: ATMOSPHERICS — Tom ROBINSON
LISTEN TO THE RHYTHM — K3M
LISTEN TO THE RHYTHM FLOW — GTO
LISTEN TO WHAT THE MAN SAID — Paul McCARTNEY
LISTEN TO YOUR FATHER — Feargal SHARKEY
LISTEN TO YOUR HEART [A] — ROXETTE
LISTEN TO YOUR HEART [A] — D.H.T. featuring EDMEE
LISTEN TO YOUR HEART [B] — SONIA
LITHIUM — NIRVANA
LITTLE ARITHMETICS — dEUS
LITTLE ARROWS — Leapy LEE
LITTLE BABY NOTHING — MANIC STREET PREACHERS
LITTLE BAND OF GOLD — James GILREATH
LITTLE BERNADETTE — Harry BELAFONTE
LITTLE BIRD — Annie LENNOX
A LITTLE BIT — Rosie RIBBONS
A LITTLE BIT FURTHER AWAY — KOKOMO
A LITTLE BIT ME A LITTLE BIT YOU — The MONKEES
A LITTLE BIT MORE [A] — DR HOOK
A LITTLE BIT MORE [A] — 911 (99)
A LITTLE BIT MORE [B] — Kym SIMS
A LITTLE BIT OF ACTION — NADIA
LITTLE BIT OF HEAVEN — Lisa STANSFIELD
LITTLE BIT OF LOVE — FREE
LITTLE BIT OF LOVIN' — Kele LE ROC
A LITTLE BIT OF LUCK — DJ LUCK & MC NEAT
A LITTLE BIT OF SNOW — Howard JONES
A LITTLE BIT OF SOAP — SHOWADDYWADDY
A LITTLE BITTY TEAR [A] — Burl IVES
LITTLE BITTY TEAR [A] — MIKI and GRIFF
LITTLE BLACK BOOK [A] — Jimmy DEAN
LITTLE BLACK BOOK [B] — Belinda CARLISLE
LITTLE BLUE BIRD — Vince HILL
A LITTLE BOOGIE WOOGIE IN THE BACK OF MY MIND [A] — Gary GLITTER
A LITTLE BOOGIE WOOGIE (IN THE BACK OF MY MIND) [A] — Shakin' STEVENS
LITTLE BOY LOST — Michael HOLLIDAY
LITTLE BOY SAD — Johnny BURNETTE
LITTLE BRITAIN — DREADZONE
LITTLE BROTHER — BLUE PEARL
LITTLE BROWN JUG — Glenn MILLER
LITTLE BY LITTLE [A] — Dusty SPRINGFIELD
LITTLE BY LITTLE [B] — OASIS
LITTLE CHILD — DES'REE
LITTLE CHILDREN — Billy J KRAMER and The DAKOTAS (64)
LITTLE CHRISTINE — Dick JORDAN
LITTLE DARLIN' [A] — DIAMONDS
LITTLE DARLIN' [B] — Marvin GAYE
LITTLE DARLING — The RUBETTES
LITTLE DEVIL — Neil SEDAKA
LITTLE DISCOURAGE — IDLEWILD
LITTLE DOES SHE KNOW — KURSAAL FLYERS
LITTLE DONKEY [A] — The BEVERLEY SISTERS
LITTLE DONKEY [A] — Gracie FIELDS
LITTLE DONKEY [A] — NINA and FREDERICK
LITTLE DROPS OF SILVER — Gerry MONROE
LITTLE DRUMMER BOY [A] — The BEVERLEY SISTERS
LITTLE DRUMMER BOY [A] — Harry SIMEONE CHORALE
LITTLE DRUMMER BOY [A] — Michael FLANDERS
LITTLE DRUMMER BOY [A] — PIPES and DRUMS and MILITARY BAND of the ROYAL SCOTS DRAGOON GUARDS
LITTLE DRUMMER BOY [A] — RuPAUL
LITTLE 15 — DEPECHE MODE
LITTLE FLUFFY CLOUDS — The ORB
LITTLE GIRL [A] — Marty WILDE
LITTLE GIRL [B] — The TROGGS
LITTLE GIRL [C] — BANNED
LITTLE GIRL LOST — ICICLE WORKS
LITTLE GREEN APPLES — Roger MILLER
LITTLE HOUSE OF SAVAGES — The WALKMEN
A LITTLE IN LOVE — Cliff RICHARD
LITTLE JEANNIE — Elton JOHN
LITTLE L — JAMIROQUAI
LITTLE LADY — ANEKA
A LITTLE LESS CONVERSATION — ELVIS vs JXL (02)
LITTLE LIES — FLEETWOOD MAC
LITTLE LOST SOMETIMES — The ALMIGHTY
LITTLE LOVE — LIL' LOVE
A LITTLE LOVE A LITTLE KISS — Karl DENVER
A LITTLE LOVE AND UNDERSTANDING — Gilbert BECAUD
A LITTLE LOVIN' — Neil SEDAKA
A LITTLE LOVING — The FOURMOST
LITTLE MAN — SONNY and CHER
LITTLE MIRACLES (HAPPEN EVERY DAY) — Luther VANDROSS
LITTLE MISS CAN'T BE WRONG — SPIN DOCTORS
LITTLE MISS LONELY — Helen SHAPIRO
LITTLE MISS PERFECT — Summer MATTHEWS
A LITTLE MORE LOVE — Olivia NEWTON-JOHN
A LITTLE PEACE — NICOLE (82)
A LITTLE PIECE OF LEATHER — Donnie ELBERT
LITTLE PINK STARS — RADISH
LITTLE RED CORVETTE — PRINCE
LITTLE RED MONKEY — Frank CHACKSFIELD
LITTLE RED ROOSTER — The ROLLING STONES (64)
A LITTLE RESPECT [A] — ERASURE
A LITTLE RESPECT [A] — WHEATUS
LITTLE RHYMES — MERCURY REV
A LITTLE SAMBA — UGLY DUCKLING
LITTLE SERENADE — Eddie CALVERT
THE LITTLE SHOEMAKER — Petula CLARK
LITTLE SISTER [A] — Elvis PRESLEY (61)
LITTLE SISTER [B] — QUEENS OF THE STONE AGE
A LITTLE SOUL — PULP
LITTLE STAR [A] — ELEGANTS
LITTLE STAR [B] — MADONNA
LITTLE THINGS [A] — Dave BERRY
LITTLE THINGS [B] — INDIA.ARIE
LITTLE THINGS MEAN A LOT [A] — Alma COGAN
LITTLE THINGS MEAN A LOT [A] — Kitty KALLEN (54)
LITTLE THOUGHTS — BLOC PARTY
A LITTLE TIME — The BEAUTIFUL SOUTH (90)
LITTLE TOWN — Cliff RICHARD
LITTLE TOWN FLIRT — Del SHANNON
LITTLE TRAIN — Max BYGRAVES
LITTLE WHITE BERRY — Roy CASTLE
LITTLE WHITE BULL — Tommy STEELE
LITTLE WHITE LIES — STATUS QUO
LITTLE WILLY — The SWEET
LITTLE WONDER — David BOWIE
A LITTLE YOU — FREDDIE and The DREAMERS
LIVE AND LEARN — JOE PUBLIC
LIVE AND LET DIE [A] — Paul McCARTNEY
LIVE AND LET DIE [A] — GUNS N' ROSES
LIVE ANIMAL (F**K LIKE A BEAST) — W.A.S.P.
LIVE ANOTHER LIFE — PLASTIC BOY featuring ROZALLA
LIVE AT TFI FRIDAY (EP) — STING
LIVE AT THE MARQUEE (EP) — EDDIE and The HOTRODS
LIVE EP — BARCLAY JAMES HARVEST
THE LIVE EP — Gary NUMAN
LIVE FOR LOVING YOU — Gloria ESTEFAN
LIVE FOR THE ONE I LOVE — Tina ARENA
LIVE FOREVER — OASIS
LIVE IN A HIDING PLACE — IDLEWILD
LIVE IN MANCHESTER (PARTS 1 + 2) — N-JOI
LIVE IN THE SKY — Dave CLARK FIVE
LIVE IN TROUBLE — The BARRON KNIGHTS
LIVE IS LIFE [A] — OPUS
LIVE IS LIFE [B] — HERMES HOUSE BAND & DJ OTZI
LIVE IT UP — MENTAL AS ANYTHING
LIVE LIKE HORSES — Elton JOHN and Luciano PAVAROTTI
LIVE MY LIFE — BOY GEORGE
LIVE OR DIE — DILLINJA
LIVE TO TELL — MADONNA
LIVE TOGETHER — Lisa STANSFIELD
LIVE TWICE — DARIUS
LIVE YOUR LIFE BE FREE — Belinda CARLISLE
LIVELY — Lonnie DONEGAN
LIVERPOOL (ANTHEM) — LIVERPOOL FC
LIVERPOOL LOU — SCAFFOLD
LIVERPOOL (WE'RE NEVER GONNA ...) — LIVERPOOL FC
LIVIN' IN THE LIGHT — Caron WHEELER
LIVIN' IT UP [A] — NORTHERN UPROAR
LIVIN' IT UP [B] — JA RULE featuring CASE
LIVIN' IT UP (FRIDAY NIGHT) — BELL and JAMES
LIVIN' LA VIDA LOCA — Ricky MARTIN (99)
LIVIN' LOVIN' DOLL — Cliff RICHARD
LIVIN' ON A PRAYER — BON JOVI
LIVIN' ON THE EDGE — AEROSMITH
LIVIN' ON THE EDGE OF THE NIGHT — Iggy POP
LIVIN' THING [A] — ELECTRIC LIGHT ORCHESTRA
LIVIN' THING [A] — The BEAUTIFUL SOUTH
LIVIN' IN THIS WORLD — GURU
LIVING AFTER MIDNIGHT — JUDAS PRIEST
LIVING BY NUMBERS — NEW MUSIK
THE LIVING DAYLIGHTS — A-HA
LIVING DOLL [A] — Cliff RICHARD and The DRIFTERS (59)
LIVING DOLL [A] — Cliff RICHARD and The YOUNG ONES featuring Hank B MARVIN (86)
THE LIVING DREAM — SUNDANCE
LIVING FOR THE CITY [A] — Stevie WONDER
LIVING FOR THE CITY [A] — GILLAN
LIVING FOR THE WEEKEND — HARD-FI
LIVING FOR YOU — SONNY and CHER
LIVING IN A BOX [A] — LIVING IN A BOX
LIVING IN A BOX [A] — Bobby WOMACK
LIVING IN A FANTASY — URBAN HYPE
LIVING IN A WORLD (TURNED UPSIDE DOWN) — PRIVATE LIVES
LIVING IN AMERICA — James BROWN
LIVING IN ANOTHER WORLD — TALK TALK
LIVING IN DANGER — ACE OF BASE
LIVING IN HARMONY — Cliff RICHARD
LIVING IN SIN — BON JOVI
LIVING IN THE PAST [A] — JETHRO TULL
LIVING IN THE PAST [B] — DRUM THEATRE
LIVING IN THE ROSE (THE BALLADS EP) — NEW MODEL ARMY
LIVING IN THE (SLIGHTLY MORE RECENT) PAST — JETHRO TULL
LIVING IN THE SUNSHINE — CLUBHOUSE
LIVING IN THE UK — SHAKATAK
LIVING NEXT DOOR TO ALICE — SMOKIE featuring Roy 'Chubby' BROWN
LIVING ON AN ISLAND — STATUS QUO
LIVING ON MY OWN — Freddie MERCURY (93)
LIVING ON THE CEILING — BLANCMANGE
LIVING ON THE FRONT LINE — Eddy GRANT
LIVING ON VIDEO — TRANS-X
LIVING THE DREAM — MILLION DEAD
LIVING WITH THE HUMAN MACHINES — STRANGELOVE
THE LIVING YEARS — MIKE and The MECHANICS
LIZARD (GONNA GET YOU) — Mauro PICOTTO
LK (CAROLINA CAROL BELA) — DJ MARKY & XRS featuring STAMINA MC
L'L'LUCY — MUD
LO MISMO QUE YO (IF ONLY) — Alex CUBA BAND featuring Ron SEXSMITH
LOADED [A] — PRIMAL SCREAM
LOADED [B] — Ricky MARTIN
LOADED GUN — The DEAD 60s
LOADSAMONEY (DOIN' UP THE HOUSE) — Harry ENFIELD
LOBSTER & SCRIMP — TIMBALAND featuring JAY-Z
LOC'ED AFTER DARK — Tone LOC
LOCAL BOY — The RIFLES
LOCAL BOY IN THE PHOTOGRAPH — STEREOPHONICS
LOCK AND LOAD — Bob SEGER and The SILVER BULLET BAND
LOCK UP YA DAUGHTERS — The NOISE NEXT DOOR
LOCK UP YOUR DAUGHTERS — SLADE
LOCKED OUT — CROWDED HOUSE
LOCKED UP [A] — AKON (2005) / AKON featuring STYLES P (2004)
LOCO — FUN LOVIN' CRIMINALS
LOCO IN ACAPULCO — The FOUR TOPS
LOCOMOTION — ORCHESTRAL MANOEUVRES IN THE DARK
LOCO-MOTION [A] — VERNONS GIRLS
THE LOCO-MOTION [A] — LITTLE EVA
THE LOCOMOTION [A] — Dave STEWART
THE LOCO-MOTION [A] — Kylie MINOGUE
L.O.D. (LOVE ON DELIVERY) — Billy OCEAN
THE LODGERS — STYLE COUNCIL
THE LOGICAL SONG [A] — SUPERTRAMP
THE LOGICAL SONG [A] — SCOOTER
L'OISEAU ET L'ENFANT — Marie MYRIAM
LOLA [A] — The KINKS
LOLA [A] — Andy TAYLOR
LOLA STARS AND STRIPES — The STILLS
LOLA'S THEME [A] — SHAPESHIFTERS (04)
LOLLIPOP [A] — The CHORDETTES
LOLLIPOP [A] — MUDLARKS
LOLLY LOLLY — WENDY and LISA
LONDINIUM — CATATONIA
LONDON BOYS — T. REX
LONDON CALLING — The CLASH
LONDON GIRLS — CHAS and DAVE
LONDON KID — Jean-Michel JARRE featuring Hank MARVIN
LONDON NIGHTS — LONDON BOYS
A LONDON THING — Scott GARCIA featuring MC STYLES
LONDON TIMES — RADIO HEART featuring Gary NUMAN
LONDON TONIGHT — COLLAPSED LUNG
LONDON TOWN [A] — Paul McCARTNEY
LONDON TOWN [B] — LIGHT OF THE WORLD
LONDON TOWN [C] — BUCKS FIZZ
LONDON TOWN [D] — JDS
LONDON X-PRESS — X-PRESS 2
LONDON'S BRILLIANT — Wendy JAMES
LONDON'S BRILLIANT PARADE — Elvis COSTELLO
LONDRES STRUTT — SMELLS LIKE HEAVEN
THE LONE RANGER — QUANTUM JUMP
LONE RIDER — John LEYTON
THE LONELIEST MAN IN THE WORLD — TOURISTS
LONELINESS [A] — Des O'CONNOR
LONELINESS [B] — TOMCRAFT (03)
LONELINESS [C] — Ed HARCOURT
LONELINESS IS GONE — NINE YARDS
LONELY [A] — Eddie COCHRAN
LONELY [B] — Mr Acker BILK and his PARAMOUNT JAZZ BAND
LONELY [C] — Peter ANDRE
LONELY [D] — AKON (05)
LONELY BALLERINA — MANTOVANI
LONELY BOY [A] — Paul ANKA
LONELY BOY [B] — Andrew GOLD
LONELY BOY LONELY GUITAR — Duane EDDY and The REBELS
THE LONELY BULL — Herb ALPERT
LONELY CITY — John LEYTON
LONELY, CRYIN' ONLY — THERAPY?
LONELY DAYS — The BEE GEES
LONELY DAYS, LONELY NIGHTS — Don DOWNING
LONELY (HAVE WE LOST OUR LOVE) — Lance ELLINGTON
LONELY HEART — UFO
THE LONELY MAN THEME — Cliff ADAMS ORCHESTRA
LONELY NIGHT — MAGNUM
LONELY NO MORE — Rob THOMAS
THE LONELY ONE — ALICE DEEJAY
LONELY PUP (IN A CHRISTMAS SHOP) — Adam FAITH
LONELY STREET — Clarence 'Frogman' HENRY
LONELY SYMPHONY — Frances RUFFELLE
LONELY TEENAGER — DION
LONELY THIS CHRISTMAS — MUD (74)
LONELY TOGETHER — Barry MANILOW
THE LONER — Gary MOORE
LONESOME — Adam FAITH

2 February 2002	9 February 2002	16 February 2002	23 February 2002
HERO Enrique	HERO Enrique	HERO Enrique	HERO Enrique
JUST ENOUGH EDUCATION TO PERFORM Stereophonics	COME WITH US The Chemical Brothers	ESCAPE Enrique Iglesias	ESCAPE Enrique Iglesias

LONESOME DAY — Bruce SPRINGSTEEN
LONESOME NUMBER ONE — Don GIBSON
LONESOME (SI TU VOIS MA MÈRE) — Chris BARBER'S JAZZ BAND
LONESOME TRAVELLER — Lonnie DONEGAN
LONG AFTER TONIGHT IS ALL OVER — Jimmy RADCLIFFE
LONG AND LASTING LOVE (ONCE IN A LIFETIME) — Glenn MEDEIROS
THE LONG AND WINDING ROAD [A] — Ray MORGAN
THE LONG AND WINDING ROAD [A] — Will YOUNG and Gareth GATES (02)
LONG AS I CAN SEE THE LIGHT [A] — CREEDENCE CLEARWATER REVIVAL
LONG AS I CAN SEE THE LIGHT [A] — MONKEY MAFIA
LONG BLACK VEIL — The STRANGLERS
LONG COOL WOMAN IN A BLACK DRESS — The HOLLIES
A LONG DECEMBER — COUNTING CROWS
LONG DISTANCE — TURIN BRAKES
THE LONG GOODBYE — Ronan KEATING
LONG HAIRED LOVER FROM LIVERPOOL — Little Jimmy OSMOND with The Mike CURB CONGREGATION (72)
LONG HOT SUMMER [A] — STYLE COUNCIL
LONG HOT SUMMER [B] — GIRLS ALOUD
LONG HOT SUMMER NIGHT — JT TAYLOR
LONG LEGGED GIRL (WITH THE SHORT DRESS ON) — Elvis PRESLEY
LONG LEGGED WOMAN DRESSED IN BLACK — MUNGO JERRY
LONG LIVE LOVE [A] — Sandie SHAW (65)
LONG LIVE LOVE [A] — Nick BERRY
LONG LIVE LOVE [B] — Olivia NEWTON-JOHN
LONG LIVE ROCK — The WHO
LONG LIVE ROCK 'N' ROLL — RAINBOW
LONG LIVE THE UK MUSIC SCENE — Helen LOVE
LONG LONG WAY TO GO — DEF LEPPARD
LONG LOST LOVER — The THREE DEGREES
LONG MAY YOU RUN (LIVE) — Neil YOUNG
LONG NIGHT — The CORRS
THE LONG RUN — EAGLES
LONG SHOT KICK DE BUCKET — PIONEERS
LONG TALL GLASSES — Leo SAYER
LONG TALL SALLY [A] — Pat BOONE
LONG TALL SALLY [A] — LITTLE RICHARD
LONG TERM LOVERS OF PAIN (EP) — HUE AND CRY
LONG TIME — ARROW
LONG TIME COMING [A] — BUMP & FLEX
LONG TIME COMING [B] — DELAYS
LONG TIME GONE — GALLIANO
LONG TRAIN RUNNING [A] — BANANARAMA
LONG TRAIN RUNNIN' [A] — The DOOBIE BROTHERS
A LONG WALK — Jill SCOTT
LONG WAY — ROOTJOOSE
LONG WAY AROUND — Eagle-Eye CHERRY featuring Neneh CHERRY
LONG WAY FROM HOME — WHITESNAKE
LONG WAY SOUTH — JJ72
LONG WAY TO GO — Stevie NICKS
LONG WHITE CAR — HIPSWAY
LONGER — Dan FOGELBERG
THE LONGEST DAY — 24
THE LONGEST TIME — Billy JOEL
LONGTIME BOY — NINA and FREDERICK
LONGVIEW — GREEN DAY
LONNIE DONEGAN SHOWCASE (LP) — Lonnie DONEGAN
LONNIE'S SKIFFLE PARTY — Lonnie DONEGAN
LOO-BE-LOO — CHUCKS
THE LOOK — ROXETTE
LOOK AROUND — Vince HILL
LOOK AT ME — Geri HALLIWELL
LOOK AT ME (I'M IN LOVE) — MOMENTS
LOOK AT ME NOW — JESSY
LOOK AT THAT GIRL — Guy MITCHELL (53)
LOOK AT US — NORTHERN HEIGHTZ
LOOK AT YOURSELF — David McALMONT
LOOK AWAY — BIG COUNTRY
LOOK BEFORE YOU LEAP — Dave CLARK FIVE
LOOK BUT DON'T TOUCH (EP) — SKIN
LOOK FOR A STAR — Garry MILLS
LOOK HOMEWARD ANGEL — Johnnie RAY
LOOK INTO MY EYES — BONE THUGS-N-HARMONY
LOOK MAMA — Howard JONES
LOOK ME IN THE HEART — Tina TURNER
THE LOOK OF LOVE [A] — Gladys KNIGHT and The PIPS
THE LOOK OF LOVE [A] — T-EMPO
THE LOOK OF LOVE [B] — ABC
THE LOOK OF LOVE [C] — MADONNA
LOOK ON THE FLOOR (HYPNOTIC TANGO) — BANANARAMA
LOOK THROUGH ANY WINDOW — The HOLLIES
LOOK THROUGH MY EYES — Phil COLLINS
LOOK UP TO THE LIGHT — EVOLUTION
LOOK WHAT YOU DONE FOR ME — Al GREEN
LOOK WHAT YOU STARTED — The TEMPTATIONS
LOOK WHAT YOU'VE DONE — JET
LOOK WHO IT IS — Helen SHAPIRO
LOOK WHO'S DANCING — Ziggy MARLEY and The MELODY MAKERS
LOOK WHO'S PERFECT NOW — TRANSISTER
LOOK WHO'S TALKING — DR ALBAN
LOOK WOT YOU DUN — SLADE
LOOKIN' AT YOU — Warren G featuring TOI
LOOKIN' THROUGH THE WINDOWS — The JACKSON FIVE
LOOKING AFTER NO.1 — The BOOMTOWN RATS
LOOKING AS YOU ARE — EMBRACE
LOOKING AT MIDNIGHT — IMAGINATION
LOOKING FOR A LOVE — Joyce SIMS
LOOKING FOR A NEW LOVE — Jody WATLEY
LOOKING FOR A PLACE — MANIA
LOOKING FOR A SONG — BIG AUDIO DYNAMITE
LOOKING FOR ATLANTIS — PREFAB SPROUT
LOOKING FOR CLUES — Robert PALMER
LOOKING FOR LEWIS AND CLARK — LONG RYDERS
LOOKING FOR LINDA — HUE AND CRY
LOOKING FOR LOVE — Karen RAMIREZ
LOOKING FOR LOVE TONIGHT — FAT LARRY'S BAND
LOOKING FOR THE SUMMER — Chris REA
LOOKING HIGH HIGH HIGH — Bryan JOHNSON
LOOKING THROUGH PATIENT EYES — PM DAWN
LOOKING THROUGH THE EYES OF LOVE [A] — Gene PITNEY
LOOKING THRU THE EYES OF LOVE [A] — PARTRIDGE FAMILY
LOOKING THROUGH YOUR EYES — LeAnn RIMES
LOOKING UP — Michelle GAYLE
LOOKS LIKE I'M IN LOVE AGAIN — ERIK
LOOKS, LOOKS, LOOKS — SPARKS
LOOP-DE-LOOP — Frankie VAUGHAN
LOOP DI LOVE — Jonathan KING
LOOPS OF FURY (EP) — The CHEMICAL BROTHERS
LOOPS OF INFINITY — COSMIC BABY
LOOPZILLA — George CLINTON
LOOSE — THERAPY?
LOOSE CANNON — KILLING JOKE
LOOSE FIT — HAPPY MONDAYS
LOOSEN YOUR HOLD — SOUTH
LOPEZ — 808 STATE
LORDS OF THE NEW CHURCH — Tasmin ARCHER
LORELEI — Lonnie DONEGAN
LORRAINE — BAD MANNERS
LOS ANGELES IS BURNING — BAD RELIGION
LOS AMERICANOS — ESPIRITU
LOSE CONTROL [A] — JAMES
LOSE CONTROL [B] — Missy ELLIOTT featuring CIARA & FAT MAN SCOOP
LOSE IT — SUPERGRASS
LOSE MY BREATH — DESTINY'S CHILD
LOSE YOURSELF — EMINEM (02)
LOSER [A] — BECK
LOSER [B] — THUNDER
LOSING GRIP — Avril LAVIGNE
LOSING MY GRIP — SAMSON
LOSING MY MIND — Liza MINNELLI
LOSING MY RELIGION — R.E.M.
LOSING YOU [A] — Brenda LEE
LOSING YOU [B] — Dusty SPRINGFIELD
LOST AGAIN — YELLO
LOST AND FOUND — D*NOTE
THE LOST ART OF KEEPING A SECRET — QUEENS OF THE STONE AGE
LOST CAT — CATATONIA
LOST FOR WORDS — Ronan KEATING
LOST IN A MELODY — DELAYS
LOST IN AMERICA — Alice COOPER
LOST IN EMOTION [A] — LISA LISA
LOST IN EMOTION [B] — John 'OO' FLEMING
LOST IN FRANCE — Bonnie TYLER
LOST IN LOVE [A] — UP YER RONSON featuring Mary PEARCE
LOST IN LOVE [B] — LEGEND B
LOST IN MUSIC [A] — SISTER SLEDGE
LOST IN MUSIC [B] — STEREO MC's
LOST IN SPACE [A] — APOLLO FOUR FORTY
LOST IN SPACE [B] — ELECTRASY
LOST IN SPACE [C] — LIGHTHOUSE FAMILY
LOST IN THE PLOT — The DEARS
LOST IN THE TRANSLATION — PACIFICA
LOST IN YOU [A] — Rod STEWART
LOST IN YOU [B] — Garth BROOKS as Chris GAINES
LOST IN YOUR EYES — Debbie GIBSON
LOST IN YOUR LOVE — Tony HADLEY
LOST JOHN — Lonnie DONEGAN
LOST MYSELF — LONGPIGS
LOST WEEKEND — Lloyd COLE
LOST WITHOUT EACH OTHER — HANSON
LOST WITHOUT YOU [A] — Jayn HANNA
LOST WITHOUT YOU [B] — Delta GOODREM
LOST WITHOUT YOUR LOVE — BREAD
LOST YOU SOMEWHERE — CHICANE
A LOT OF LOVE — Marti PELLOW
LOTUS — R.E.M.
LOUIE LOUIE [A] — KINGSMEN
LOUIE LOUIE [A] — MOTÖRHEAD
LOUIE LOUIE [A] — FAT BOYS
LOUIE LOUIE [A] — THREE AMIGOS
LOUIS QUATORZE — BOW WOW WOW
LOUISE [A] — Phil EVERLY
LOUISE [B] — HUMAN LEAGUE
LOUNGER — DOGS DIE IN HOT CARS
LOUNGIN' — LL COOL J
L.O.V.E. — Al GREEN
LOVE [A] — John LENNON
LOVE [A] — Jimmy NAIL
LOVE ACTION (I BELIEVE IN LOVE) — HUMAN LEAGUE
LOVE AIN'T GONNA WAIT FOR YOU — S CLUB
LOVE AIN'T HERE ANYMORE — TAKE THAT
LOVE AIN'T NO STRANGER — WHITESNAKE
LOVE ALL DAY — Nick HEYWARD
LOVE ALL THE HURT AWAY — Aretha FRANKLIN and George BENSON
LOVE AND AFFECTION [A] — Joan ARMATRADING
LOVE AND AFFECTION [A] — SINITTA
LOVE & AFFECTION [A] — MR PINK presents the PROGRAM
LOVE AND ANGER — Kate BUSH
LOVE AND DESIRE (PART 1) — ARPEGGIO
LOVE AND DEVOTION — (MC SAR &) The REAL McCOY
LOVE AND HAPPINESS (YEMAYA Y OCHUN) — RIVER OCEAN featuring INDIA
LOVE AND KISSES — Dannii MINOGUE
LOVE AND LONELINESS — The MOTORS
LOVE AND MARRIAGE — Frank SINATRA
LOVE AND MONEY — LOVE AND MONEY
LOVE AND PAIN [A] — CARLTON
LOVE & PAIN [B] — CLOR
LOVE AND PRIDE — KING
LOVE AND REGRET — DEACON BLUE
LOVE AND TEARS — Naomi CAMPBELL
LOVE AND UNDERSTANDING — CHER
LOVE ANYWAY — Mike SCOTT
LOVE AT FIRST SIGHT [A] — Kylie MINOGUE
LOVE @ 1ST SIGHT [B] — Mary J BLIGE featuring METHOD MAN
LOVE AT FIRST SIGHT (JE T'AIME ... MOI NON PLUS) — SOUNDS NICE featuring Tim MYCROFT
LOVE ATTACK — Shakin' STEVENS
LOVE BALLAD — George BENSON
LOVE BE MY LOVER (PLAYA SOL) — NOVOCANE vs NO ONE DRIVING
LOVE BITES — DEF LEPPARD
LOVE BLONDE — Kim WILDE
LOVE BOMB BABY — TIGERTAILZ
LOVE BREAKDOWN — ROZALLA
LOVE BUG — RAMSEY and FEN featuring Lynsey MOORE
LOVE BUG — SWEETS FOR MY SWEET (MEDLEY) — Tina CHARLES
LOVE BURNS — BLACK REBEL MOTORCYCLE CLUB
LOVE CAN BUILD A BRIDGE [A] — CHILDREN FOR RWANDA
LOVE CAN BUILD A BRIDGE [A] — CHER, Chrissie HYNDE and Neneh CHERRY with Eric CLAPTON (95)
LOVE CAN MOVE MOUNTAINS — Celine DION
LOVE CAN'T TURN AROUND [A] — Farley 'Jackmaster' FUNK with Darryl PANDY
LOVE CAN'T TURN AROUND [A] — HEAVY WEATHER
THE LOVE CATS — The CURE
LOVE CHANGES (EVERYTHING) [A] — CLIMIE FISHER
LOVE CHANGES EVERYTHING [B] — Michael BALL
LOVE CHILD [A] — Diana ROSS and The SUPREMES
LOVE CHILD [B] — GOODBYE MR MACKENZIE
LOVE CITY GROOVE — LOVE CITY GROOVE
LOVE COME DOWN [A] — Evelyn 'Champagne' KING
LOVE COME DOWN [A] — Alison LIMERICK
LOVE COME DOWN [B] — Eve GALLAGHER
LOVE COME HOME — OUR TRIBE with Franke PHAROAH and Kristine W
LOVE COME RESCUE ME — LOVESTATION
LOVE COMES AGAIN — TIESTO featuring BT
LOVE COMES QUICKLY — PET SHOP BOYS
LOVE COMES TO MIND — CHIMES
LOVE COMMANDMENTS — Gisele JACKSON
LOVE CONQUERS ALL [A] — DEEP PURPLE
LOVE CONQUERS ALL [B] — ABC
LOVE DANCE — VISION
LOVE DETECTIVE — ARAB STRAP
LOVE DISCO STYLE — EROTIC DRUM BAND
LOVE DOESN'T HAVE TO HURT — ATOMIC KITTEN
LOVE DON'T COME EASY — The ALARM
LOVE DON'T COST A THING — Jennifer LOPEZ (01)
LOVE DON'T LET ME GO — David GUETTA featuring Chris WILLIS
LOVE DON'T LIVE — URBAN BLUES PROJECT presents Michael PROCTER
LOVE DON'T LIVE HERE ANYMORE [A] — ROSE ROYCE
LOVE DON'T LIVE HERE ANYMORE [A] — Jimmy NAIL
LOVE DON'T LIVE HERE ANYMORE [A] — DOUBLE TROUBLE
LOVE DON'T LOVE YOU — EN VOGUE
LOVE ENOUGH FOR TWO — PRIMA DONNA
LOVE ENUFF — SOUL II SOUL
LOVE EVICTION — Lonnie GORDON
LOVE FOOLOSOPHY — JAMIROQUAI
LOVE FOR LIFE — Lisa MOORISH
THE LOVE GAME — MUDLARKS
LOVE GAMES [A] — The DRIFTERS
LOVE GAMES [B] — LEVEL 42
LOVE GAMES [C] — BELLE and The DEVOTIONS
LOVE GENERATION — Bob SINCLAR featuring Gary PINE
LOVE GLOVE — VISAGE
LOVE GROOVE (GROOVE WITH YOU) — SMOOTH
LOVE GROWS (WHERE MY ROSEMARY GOES) — EDISON LIGHTHOUSE (70)
LOVE GUARANTEED — DAMAGE
LOVE HANGOVER [A] — Diana ROSS
LOVE HANGOVER [A] — ASSOCIATES
LOVE HANGOVER [A] — Pauline HENRY
LOVE HANGOVER [B] — SCARLET
LOVE HAS COME AGAIN — HUMAN MOVEMENT featuring Sophie MOLETA
LOVE HAS COME AROUND — Donald BYRD
LOVE HAS FOUND ITS WAY — Dennis BROWN
LOVE HAS PASSED AWAY — SUPERNATURALS
LOVE HER — The WALKER BROTHERS
LOVE HERE I COME — BAD BOYS INC
LOVE HIT ME — Maxine NIGHTINGALE
LOVE HOUSE — Samantha FOX
LOVE HOW YOU FEEL — Sharon REDD

2 March 2002	9 March 2002	16 March 2002	23 March 2002
UK No.1 SINGLES			
WORLD OF OUR OWN Westlife	**EVERGREEN / ANYTHING IS POSSIBLE** Will Young	**EVERGREEN / ANYTHING IS POSSIBLE** Will Young	**EVERGREEN / ANYTHING IS POSSIBLE** Will Young
UK No.1 ALBUMS			
THE VERY BEST OF STING AND THE POLICE Sting and The Police	**THE VERY BEST OF STING AND THE POLICE** Sting and The Police	**THE ESSENTIAL BARBRA STREISAND** Barbra Streisand	**SILVER SIDE UP** Nickelback

LOVE HURTS [A] — Jim CAPALDI
LOVE HURTS [A] — CHER
LOVE HURTS [B] — Peter POLYCARPOU
THE LOVE I LOST [A] — Harold MELVIN and The BLUENOTES
THE LOVE I LOST [A] — WEST END featuring SYBIL
LOVE IN A PEACEFUL WORLD — LEVEL 42
LOVE IN A TRASHCAN — The RAVEONETTES
LOVE IN AN ELEVATOR — AEROSMITH
LOVE IN ANGER — ARMOURY SHOW
LOVE IN C MINOR — CERRONE
LOVE IN ITSELF — DEPECHE MODE
LOVE IN THE FIRST DEGREE — BANANARAMA
LOVE IN THE KEY OF C — Belinda CARLISLE
LOVE IN THE NATURAL WAY — Kim WILDE
LOVE IN THE SUN — GLITTER BAND
THE LOVE IN YOUR EYES [A] — Vicky LEANDROS
THE LOVE IN YOUR EYES [A] — Daniel O'DONNELL
LOVE INFINITY — SILVER CITY
LOVE INJECTION — TRUSSEL
LOVE INSIDE — Sharon FORRESTER
LOVE IS ... [A] — VIKKI
LOVE IS [B] — Alannah MYLES
LOVE IS A BATTLEFIELD — Pat BENATAR
LOVE IS A BEAUTIFUL THING — Al GREEN
LOVE IS A DESERTER — The KILLS
LOVE IS A GOLDEN RING — Frankie LAINE
LOVE IS A KILLER — VIXEN
LOVE IS A MANY SPLENDORED THING — FOUR ACES
LOVE IS A STRANGER — EURYTHMICS
LOVE IS A WONDERFUL COLOUR — ICICLE WORKS
LOVE IS A WONDERFUL THING — Michael BOLTON
LOVE IS ALL [A] — Malcolm ROBERTS
LOVE IS ALL [A] — Engelbert HUMPERDINCK
LOVE IS ALL [B] — The RAPTURE
LOVE IS ALL AROUND [A] — The TROGGS
LOVE IS ALL AROUND [A] — WET WET WET (94)
LOVE IS ALL AROUND [B] — DJ BOBO
LOVE IS ALL IS ALRIGHT — UB40
LOVE IS ALL THAT MATTERS — HUMAN LEAGUE
LOVE IS ALL WE NEED — Mary J BLIGE
LOVE IS AN ARROW — ABERFELDY
LOVE IS AN UNFAMILIAR NAME — The DUKE SPIRIT
LOVE IS BLUE [A] — Jeff BECK
LOVE IS BLUE (L'AMOUR EST BLEU) [A] — Paul MAURIAT
LOVE IS BLUE [B] — Edward BALL
LOVE IS CONTAGIOUS — Taja SEVELLE
LOVE IS EVERYWHERE — CICERO
LOVE IS FOREVER — Billy OCEAN
LOVE IS HERE AND NOW YOU'RE GONE — The SUPREMES
LOVE IS HOLY — Kim WILDE
LOVE IS IN CONTROL (FINGER ON THE TRIGGER) — Donna SUMMER
LOVE IS IN THE AIR [A] — John Paul YOUNG
LOVE IS IN THE AIR [A] — MILK & SUGAR vs John Paul YOUNG
LOVE IS IN YOUR EYES — LEMON TREES
LOVE IS JUST THE GREAT PRETENDER — ANIMAL NIGHTLIFE
LOVE IS LIFE — HOT CHOCOLATE
LOVE IS LIKE A VIOLIN — Ken DODD
LOVE IS LIKE OXYGEN — The SWEET
LOVE IS LOVE — Barry RYAN
LOVE IS NOT A GAME — J MAJIK featuring Kathy BROWN
LOVE IS ON THE ONE — XAVIER
LOVE IS ON THE WAY — Luther VANDROSS
LOVE IS ONLY A FEELING — The DARKNESS
LOVE IS SO EASY — STARGARD
LOVE IS SO NICE — URBAN SOUL
LOVE IS STRANGE — The EVERLY BROTHERS
LOVE IS STRONG — The ROLLING STONES
LOVE IS STRONGER THAN DEATH — The THE
LOVE IS STRONGER THAN PRIDE — SADE
LOVE IS THE ANSWER — ENGLAND DAN and John Ford COLEY
LOVE IS THE ART — LIVING IN A BOX
LOVE IS THE DRUG [A] — ROXY MUSIC
LOVE IS THE DRUG [A] — Grace JONES
LOVE IS THE GOD — Maria NAYLER
LOVE IS THE GUN — BLUE MERCEDES
LOVE IS THE ICON — Barry White
LOVE IS THE KEY — The CHARLATANS
LOVE IS THE LAW — The SEAHORSES
LOVE IS THE MESSAGE — LOVE INCORPORATED featuring MC NOISE
LOVE IS THE SEVENTH WAVE — STING
LOVE IS THE SLUG — WE'VE GOT A FUZZBOX AND WE'RE GONNA USE IT
LOVE IS THE SWEETEST THING — Peter SKELLERN
(LOVE IS) THE TENDER TRAP — Frank SINATRA
LOVE IS WAR — BRILLIANT
LOVE IZ — Erick SERMON
LOVE KILLS [A] — Freddie MERCURY
LOVE KILLS [B] — Joe STRUMMER
LOVE KISSES AND HEARTACHES — Maureen EVANS
LOVE LADY — DAMAGE
LOVE LETTER — Marc ALMOND
LOVE LETTERS [A] — Ketty LESTER
LOVE LETTERS [A] — Elvis PRESLEY
LOVE LETTERS [A] — Alison MOYET
LOVE LETTERS [B] — ALI
LOVE LETTERS IN THE SAND [A] — Pat BOONE
LOVE LETTERS IN THE SAND [A] — Vince HILL
LOVE LIES LOST — Helen TERRY
LOVE LIGHT IN FLIGHT — Stevie WONDER
LOVE LIKE A FOUNTAIN — Ian BROWN
LOVE LIKE A MAN — TEN YEARS AFTER
LOVE LIKE A RIVER — CLIMIE FISHER
LOVE LIKE A ROCKET — Bob GELDOF
LOVE LIKE BLOOD — KILLING JOKE
LOVE LIKE THIS — Faith EVANS
LOVE LIKE YOU AND ME — Gary GLITTER
A LOVE LIKE YOURS — Ike and Tina TURNER
L.O.V.E. ... LOVE — ORANGE JUICE
LOVE LOVE LOVE — Bobby HEBB
LOVE LOVE LOVE — HERE I COME — ROLLO
LOVE LOVES TO LOVE LOVE — LULU
LOVE MACHINE [A] — Elvis PRESLEY
LOVE MACHINE [B] — MIRACLES
LOVE MACHINE [C] — GIRLS ALOUD
LOVE MADE ME — VIXEN
LOVE MAKES NO SENSE — Alexander O'NEAL
LOVE MAKES THE WORLD GO ROUND [A] — Perry COMO
LOVE MAKES THE WORLD GO ROUND [A] — JETS
LOVE MAKES THE WORLD GO ROUND [B] — DON-E
LOVE MAN — Otis REDDING
LOVE ME [A] — Yvonne ELLIMAN
LOVE ME [A] — Martine McCUTCHEON
LOVE ME [B] — Diana ROSS
LOVE ME [C] — PATRIC
LOVE ME AND LEAVE ME — The SEAHORSES
LOVE ME AS THOUGH THERE WERE NO TOMORROW — Nat 'King' COLE
LOVE ME BABY — Susan CADOGAN
LOVE ME DO — The BEATLES
LOVE ME FOR A REASON [A] — The OSMONDS (74)
LOVE ME FOR A REASON [A] — BOYZONE
LOVE ME FOREVER [A] — FOUR ESQUIRES
LOVE ME FOREVER [A] — Eydie GORME
LOVE ME FOREVER [A] — Marion RYAN
LOVE ME LIKE A LOVER — Tina CHARLES
LOVE ME LIKE I LOVE YOU — BAY CITY ROLLERS
LOVE ME LIKE THIS — REAL TO REEL
LOVE ME LIKE YOU — The MAGIC NUMBERS
LOVE ME LOVE MY DOG — Peter SHELLEY
LOVE ME NOW [A] — Briana CORRIGAN
LOVE ME NOW [B] — SECRET KNOWLEDGE
LOVE ME OR LEAVE ME [A] — Sammy DAVIS Jr
LOVE ME OR LEAVE ME [A] — Doris DAY
LOVE ME RIGHT NOW — ROSE ROYCE
LOVE ME RIGHT (OH SHEILA) — ANGEL CITY
LOVE ME TENDER [A] — Elvis PRESLEY
LOVE ME TENDER [A] — Richard CHAMBERLAIN
LOVE ME TENDER [A] — Roland RAT SUPERSTAR
LOVE ME THE RIGHT WAY — RAPINATION featuring Kym MAZELLE
LOVE ME TO SLEEP — HOT CHOCOLATE
LOVE ME TONIGHT [A] — Tom JONES
LOVE ME TONIGHT [B] — Trevor WALTERS
LOVE ME WARM AND TENDER — Paul ANKA
LOVE ME WITH ALL YOUR HEART — Karl DENVER
LOVE MEETING LOVE — LEVEL 42
LOVE MISSILE F1-11 — SIGUE SIGUE SPUTNIK
LOVE MOVES (IN MYSTERIOUS WAYS) — Julia FORDHAM
LOVE MY WAY — PSYCHEDELIC FURS
LOVE NEEDS NO DISGUISE — Gary NUMAN and DRAMATIS
LOVE NEVER DIES ... — Belinda CARLISLE
LOVE OF A LIFETIME [A] — Chaka KHAN
LOVE OF A LIFETIME [B] — HONEYZ
LOVE OF MY LIFE [A] — The DOOLEYS
LOVE OF MY LIFE [B] — QUEEN
THE LOVE OF RICHARD NIXON — MANIC STREET PREACHERS
LOVE OF THE COMMON PEOPLE [A] — Nicky THOMAS
LOVE OF THE COMMON PEOPLE [A] — Paul YOUNG
LOVE OF THE LOVED — Cilla BLACK
LOVE OH LOVE — Lionel RICHIE
LOVE ON A FARMBOY'S WAGES — XTC
LOVE ON A MOUNTAIN TOP [A] — Robert KNIGHT
LOVE ON A MOUNTAIN TOP [A] — SINITTA
LOVE ON A SUMMER NIGHT — McCRARYS
LOVE ON LOVE [A] — E-ZEE POSSEE
LOVE ON LOVE [A] — Candi STATON
LOVE ON MY MIND — FREEMASONS featuring Amanda WILSON
LOVE ON THE LINE [A] — BARCLAY JAMES HARVEST
LOVE ON THE LINE [B] — BLAZIN' SQUAD
LOVE ON THE NORTHERN LINE — NORTHERN LINE
LOVE ON THE ROCKS — Neil DIAMOND
LOVE ON THE RUN — CHICANE featuring Peter CUNNAH
LOVE ON THE SIDE — BROKEN ENGLISH
LOVE ON YOUR SIDE — THOMPSON TWINS
LOVE OR MONEY [A] — The BLACKWELLS
LOVE OR MONEY [A] — Jimmy CRAWFORD
LOVE OR MONEY [A] — Billy FURY
LOVE OR MONEY [B] — Sammy HAGAR
LOVE OR NOTHING — Diana BROWN and Barrie K SHARPE
LOVE OVER GOLD (LIVE) — DIRE STRAITS
LOVE OVERBOARD — Gladys KNIGHT and The PIPS
LOVE PAINS [A] — Hazell DEAN
LOVE PAINS [A] — Liza MINNELLI
THE LOVE PARADE — DREAM ACADEMY
LOVE PATROL — The DOOLEYS
LOVE, PEACE & GREASE — BT
LOVE PEACE AND HARMONY — DREAM FREQUENCY
LOVE, PEACE & NAPPINESS — LOST BOYZ
LOVE PLUS ONE — HAIRCUT 100
LOVE POTION NO.9 — TYGERS OF PAN TANG
LOVE POWER — Dionne WARWICK and Jeffrey OSBORNE
LOVE PROFUSION — MADONNA
LOVE REACTION — DIVINE
LOVE REALLY HURTS WITHOUT YOU — Billy OCEAN
LOVE REARS ITS UGLY HEAD — LIVING COLOUR
LOVE REMOVAL MACHINE — The CULT
LOVE RENDEZVOUS — M PEOPLE
LOVE RESURRECTION [A] — Alison MOYET
LOVE RESURRECTION [A] — D'LUX
LOVE REVOLUTION — PHIXX
LOVE ROLLERCOASTER — RED HOT CHILI PEPPERS
LOVE RULES — WEST END
THE LOVE SCENE — JOE
LOVE SCENES — Beverley CRAVEN
LOVE SEE NO COLOUR — The FARM
LOVE SENSATION — 911
LOVE SHACK — The B-52's
LOVE SHADOW — FASHION
LOVE SHINE — RHYTHM SOURCE
LOVE SHINE A LIGHT — KATRINA and The WAVES
LOVE SHINES THROUGH — CHAKRA
LOVE SHOULD BE A CRIME — O-TOWN
LOVE SHOULDA BROUGHT YOU HOME — Toni BRAXTON
LOVE SHY — Kristine BLOND
LOVE SICK — Bob DYLAN
LOVE SITUATION — Mark FISHER featuring Dotty GREEN
LOVE SLAVE — WEDDING PRESENT
LOVE SNEAKIN' UP ON YOU — Bonnie RAITT
A LOVE SO BEAUTIFUL — Michael BOLTON
LOVE SO BRIGHT — Mark SHAW
LOVE SO RIGHT — The BEE GEES
LOVE SO STRONG — SECRET LIFE
LOVE SONG [A] — The DAMNED
LOVE SONG [B] — SIMPLE MINDS
LOVE SONG [C] — UTAH SAINTS
LOVE SONG FOR A VAMPIRE — Annie LENNOX
LOVE SONGS ARE BACK AGAIN (MEDLEY) — BAND OF GOLD
THE LOVE SONGS EP — Daniel O'DONNELL
LOVE SPREADS — The STONE ROSES
LOVE STEALS US FROM LONELINESS — IDLEWILD
LOVE STIMULATION — HUMATE
LOVE STORY [A] — JETHRO TULL
LOVE STORY [B] — LAYO & BUSHWACKA!
LOVE STORY (VS FINALLY) [B] — LAYO & BUSHWACKA!
LOVE STRAIN — Kym MAZELLE
A LOVE SUPREME — Will DOWNING
LOVE TAKE OVER — FIVE STAR
LOVE TAKES TIME — Mariah CAREY
LOVE THE LIFE — JTQ
LOVE THE ONE YOU'RE WITH [A] — Stephen STILLS
LOVE THE ONE YOU'RE WITH [A] — BUCKS FIZZ
LOVE THE ONE YOU'RE WITH [A] — Luther VANDROSS
LOVE THEM — EAMON featuring GHOSTFACE
LOVE THEME FROM 'A STAR IS BORN' (EVERGREEN) — Barbra STREISAND
LOVE THEME FROM SPARTACUS — Terry CALLIER
LOVE THEME FROM 'THE GODFATHER' (SPEAK SOFTLY LOVE) — Andy WILLIAMS
LOVE THEME FROM 'THE THORN BIRDS' — Juan MARTIN
LOVE THING [A] — PASADENAS
LOVE THING [B] — Tina TURNER
LOVE THING [C] — EVOLUTION
LOVE ... THY WILL BE DONE — MARTIKA
LOVE TIMES LOVE — HEAVY PETTIN'
LOVE X LOVE — George BENSON
LOVE TO HATE YOU — ERASURE
LOVE II LOVE — DAMAGE
LOVE TO LOVE YOU — The CORRS
LOVE TO LOVE YOU BABY — Donna SUMMER
LOVE TO SEE YOU CRY — Enrique IGLESIAS
LOVE TO STAY — ALTERED IMAGES
LOVE TOGETHER — LA MIX
LOVE TOUCH — Rod STEWART
LOVE TOWN — Booker NEWBERRY III
LOVE TRAIN [A] — O'JAYS
LOVE TRAIN [B] — Holly JOHNSON
LOVE TRIAL — Kelly MARIE
LOVE, TRUTH AND HONESTY — BANANARAMA
LOVE U 4 LIFE — JODECI
LOVE U MORE — SUNSCREEM
LOVE UNLIMITED — FUN LOVIN' CRIMINALS
LOVE WALKED IN — THUNDER
LOVE WARS — WOMACK AND WOMACK
LOVE WASHES OVER — ART OF TRANCE
LOVE WHAT YOU DO — The DIVINE COMEDY
LOVE WILL COME — TOMSKI
LOVE WILL COME THROUGH — TRAVIS
LOVE WILL CONQUER ALL — Lionel RICHIE
LOVE WILL FIND A WAY [A] — David GRANT
LOVE WILL FIND A WAY [B] — YES
LOVE WILL KEEP US ALIVE — EAGLES
LOVE WILL KEEP US TOGETHER [A] — CAPTAIN and TENNILLE
LOVE WILL KEEP US TOGETHER [B] — JTQ featuring Alison LIMERICK
LOVE WILL LEAD YOU BACK — Taylor DAYNE
LOVE WILL MAKE YOU FAIL IN SCHOOL — Rocky SHARPE and The REPLAYS

30 March 2002	6 April 2002	13 April 2002	20 April 2002
UNCHAINED MELODY Gareth Gates	UNCHAINED MELODY Gareth Gates	UNCHAINED MELODY Gareth Gates	UNCHAINED MELODY Gareth Gates
SILVER SIDE UP Nickelback	A NEW DAY HAS COME Celine Dion	A NEW DAY HAS COME Celine Dion	A NEW DAY HAS COME Celine Dion

LOVE WILL NEVER DO (WITHOUT YOU) — Janet JACKSON
LOVE WILL SAVE THE DAY — Whitney HOUSTON
LOVE WILL SET YOU FREE (JAMBE MYTH) — STARCHASER
LOVE WILL TEAR US APART [A] — JOY DIVISION
LOVE WILL TEAR US APART [A] — HONEYROOT
LOVE WON'T LET ME WAIT — Major HARRIS
LOVE WON'T WAIT — Gary BARLOW (97)
LOVE WORTH DYING FOR — THUNDER
A LOVE WORTH WAITING FOR — Shakin' STEVENS
LOVE YOU ALL MY LIFETIME — Chaka KHAN
LOVE YOU ANYWAY — DE NADA
LOVE YOU DOWN — READY FOR THE WORLD
LOVE YOU INSIDE OUT — The BEE GEES
LOVE YOU LIKE MAD — VS
LOVE YOU MORE — The BUZZCOCKS
LOVE YOU SOME MORE — Cevin FISHER featuirng Sheila SMITH
THE LOVE YOU SAVE — The JACKSON FIVE
LOVE YOU TOO MUCH — HOUSE OF LOVE
LOVE YOUR MONEY — DAISY CHAINSAW
LOVE YOUR SEXY ... !! — BYKER GROOOVE!
LOVE ZONE — Billy OCEAN
LOVEBIRDS — DODGY
LOVEDRIVE — SCORPIONS
LOVEFOOL — The CARDIGANS
LOVELIGHT (RIDE ON A LOVE TRAIN) — Jayn HANNA
LOVELY — Bubba SPARXXX
LOVELY DAUGHTER — MERZ
LOVELY DAY — Bill WITHERS
LOVELY DAZE — JAZZY JEFF & The FRESH PRINCE
LOVELY MONEY — The DAMNED
LOVELY ONE — The JACKSONS
LOVELY THING — REGGAE PHILHARMONIC ORCHESTRA
LOVENEST — WEDDING PRESENT
LOVER [A] — Dan REED NETWORK
LOVER [B] — Joe ROBERTS
LOVER [C] — Rachel McFARLANE
LOVER COME BACK TO ME — DEAD OR ALIVE
THE LOVER IN ME — Sheena EASTON
THE LOVER IN YOU — SUGARHILL GANG
LOVER LOVER LOVER — Ian McCULLOCH
LOVER PLEASE — VERNONS GIRLS
A LOVER SPURNED — Marc ALMOND
THE LOVER THAT YOU ARE — PULSE featuring Antoinette ROBERSON
LOVERBOY [A] — Billy OCEAN
LOVER BOY [B] — The CHAIRMEN OF THE BOARD
LOVERBOY [C] — MARIAH featuring CAMEO
LOVERIDE — NUANCE featuring Vikki LOVE
THE LOVERS — Alexander O'NEAL
LOVERS — The TEARS
LOVERS & FRIENDS — LIL JON & The EAST SIDE BOYZ
A LOVER'S CONCERTO — TOYS
A LOVER'S HOLIDAY — CHANGE
LOVER'S LANE — GEORGIO
LOVERS OF THE WORLD UNITE — DAVID and JONATHAN
THE LOVERS WE WERE — Michael BALL
LOVE'S A GAME — The MAGIC NUMBERS
LOVE'S A LOADED GUN — Alice COOPER
LOVE'S ABOUT TO CHANGE MY HEART — Donna SUMMER
LOVE'S BEEN GOOD TO ME — Frank SINATRA
LOVE'S COMIN' AT YA — Melba MOORE
LOVE'S CRASHING WAVES — DIFFORD and TILBROOK
LOVE'S DIVINE — SEAL
LOVE'S EASY TEARS — COCTEAU TWINS
LOVE'S GONNA GET YOU [A] — UK PLAYERS
LOVE'S GONNA GET YOU [B] — Jocelyn BROWN
LOVE'S GOT A HOLD ON MY HEART — STEPS
LOVE'S GOT ME — LOOSE ENDS
LOVE'S GOT ME ON A TRIP SO HIGH — Loni CLARK
LOVE'S GOTTA HOLD ON ME [A] — DOLLAR
LOVE'S GOTTA HOLD ON ME [B] — ZOO EXPERIENCE featuring DESTRY
LOVE'S GREAT ADVENTURE — ULTRAVOX
LOVE'S JUST A BROKEN HEART — Cilla BLACK
LOVE'S MADE A FOOL OF YOU [A] — The CRICKETS
LOVE'S MADE A FOOL OF YOU [A] — Buddy HOLLY
LOVE'S MADE A FOOL OF YOU [A] — MATCHBOX
LOVES ME LIKE A ROCK — Paul SIMON
LOVE'S ON EVERY CORNER — Dannii MINOGUE
LOVE'S SUCH A WONDERFUL THING — The REAL THING
LOVE'S SWEET EXILE — MANIC STREET PREACHERS
LOVE'S TAKEN OVER — Chanté MOORE
LOVE'S THEME — LOVE UNLIMITED ORCHESTRA
LOVE'S UNKIND [A] — Donna SUMMER
LOVE'S UNKIND [A] — Sophie LAWRENCE
LOVESICK [A] — GANG STARR
LOVESICK [B] — UNDERCOVER
LOVESICK BLUES — Frank IFIELD (62)
LOVESONG — The CURE
LOVESTRUCK — MADNESS
LOVETOWN — Peter GABRIEL
LOVEY DOVEY — Tony TERRY
LOVIN' — CRW
LOVIN' EACH DAY — Ronan KEATING
LOVIN' IS EASY — HEAR'SAY
LOVIN' (LET ME LOVE YOU) — APACHE INDIAN
LOVIN', LIVIN' AND GIVIN' — Diana ROSS
LOVIN' ON THE SIDE — REID
LOVIN' THINGS — MARMALADE
LOVIN' UP A STORM — Jerry Lee LEWIS
LOVIN' YOU [A] — SHANICE
LOVIN' YOU [A] — UBM
LOVIN' YOU [A] — SPARKLE
LOVIN' YOU [B] — POKER PETS featuring Nate JAMES
LOVIN' YOU MORE (THAT BIG TRACK) — Steve MAC vs MOSQUITO featuring Steve SMITH
LOVING AND FREE — Kiki DEE
LOVING ARMS — Elvis PRESLEY
LOVING EVERY MINUTE — LIGHTHOUSE FAMILY
LOVING JUST FOR FUN — Kelly MARIE
LOVING ON THE LOSING SIDE — Tommy HUNT
LOVING THE ALIEN — David BOWIE
LOVING YOU [A] — Elvis PRESLEY
LOVIN' YOU [B] — Minnie RIPERTON
LOVING YOU '03 [B] — MARC et CLAUDE
LOVING YOU [B] — MASSIVO featuring TRACY
LOVING YOU [C] — Donald BYRD
LOVING YOU [D] — Chris REA
LOVING YOU [E] — Feargal SHARKEY
LOVING YOU AGAIN — Chris REA
LOVIN' YOU AIN'T EASY — PAGLIARO
LOVING YOU HAS MADE ME BANANAS — Guy MARKS
LOVING YOU IS SWEETER THAN EVER [A] — The FOUR TOPS
LOVING YOU IS SWEETER THAN EVER [A] — Nick KAMEN
LOVING YOU MORE — BT
LOVING YOU (OLE OLE OLE) — Brian HARVEY and The REFUGEE CREW
LOVING YOU'S A DIRTY JOB BUT SOMEBODY'S GOTTA DO IT — Bonnie TYLER, guest vocals Todd RUNDGREN
LOW [A] — CRACKER
LOW [B] — FOO FIGHTERS
LOW [C] — Kelly CLARKSON
LOW C — SUPERGRASS
LOW FIVE — SNEAKER PIMPS
LOW LIFE IN HIGH PLACES — THUNDER
LOW RIDER — WAR
LOWDOWN [A] — Boz SCAGGS
LOWDOWN [A] — HINDSIGHT
LOWDOWN [B] — ELECTRAFIXION
LOWRIDER — CYPRESS HILL
THE LOYALISER — FATIMA MANSIONS
LSD (EP) — KAOTIC CHEMISTRY
L.S.F. — KASABIAN
LSI — The SHAMEN
LUCAS WITH THE LID OFF — LUCAS
LUCHINI AKA (THIS IS IT) — CAMP LO
LUCILLE [A] — LITTLE RICHARD
LUCILLE [A] — The EVERLY BROTHERS
LUCILLE [B] — Kenny ROGERS (77)
LUCKY [A] — Britney SPEARS
LUCKY [B] — BRIGHT EYES
LUCKY DEVIL [A] — Carl DOBKINS Jr
LUCKY DEVIL [A] — Frank IFIELD
LUCKY FIVE — Russ CONWAY
LUCKY LIPS — Cliff RICHARD and The SHADOWS
LUCKY LOVE — ACE OF BASE
LUCKY LUCKY ME — Marvin GAYE
LUCKY MAN — The VERVE
LUCKY NUMBER — Lene LOVICH
LUCKY ONE — Amy GRANT
THE LUCKY ONE — Laura BRANIGAN
LUCKY PRESSURE — Roni SIZE / REPRAZENT
LUCKY 7 MEGAMIX — UK MIXMASTERS
LUCKY STAR [A] — MADONNA
LUCKY STAR [B] — SUPERFUNK
LUCKY STAR [C] — BASEMENT JAXX featuring DIZZEE RASCAL
LUCKY STARS — Dean FRIEDMAN
LUCKY TOWN (LIVE) — Bruce SPRINGSTEEN
LUCKY YOU — The LIGHTNING SEEDS
LUCRETIA MY REFLECTION — SISTERS OF MERCY
LUCY — HABIT
LUCY IN THE SKY WITH DIAMONDS — Elton JOHN
LUDI — DREAM WARRIORS
LUKA — Suzanne VEGA
LULLABY [A] — The CURE
LULLABY [B] — Shawn MULLINS
LULLABY [C] — Melanie B
LULLABY [D] — STARSAILOR
LULLABY [E] — LEMAR
LULLABY OF BROADWAY — Winifred SHAW
LULLABY OF THE LEAVES — VENTURES
LUMBERED — Lonnie DONEGAN
LUMP — PRESIDENTS OF THE UNITED STATES OF AMERICA
LUMP IN MY THROAT — The DEPARTURE
THE LUNATICS (HAVE TAKEN OVER THE ASYLUM) — FUN BOY THREE
LUNCH OR DINNER — Sunshine ANDERSON
LUSH — ORBITAL
LUST FOR LIFE — Iggy POP
LUTON AIRPORT — CATS UK
LUV DA SUNSHINE — INTENSO PROJECT
LUV DUP — HIGH FIDELITY
LUV 4 LUV — Robin S
LUV IS COOL — SYSTEM OF LIFE
LUV ME LUV ME — SHAGGY
LUV U BETTER — LL COOL J
LUV'D UP — CRUSH
LUVSTRUCK — SOUTHSIDE SPINNERS
LUVSTUFF — SAGAT
LUXURIOUS — Gwen STEFANI
L'VIA L'VIAQUEZ — The MARS VOLTA
LYDIA — Dean FRIEDMAN
LYIN' EYES — EAGLES
LYLA — OASIS (05)
LYRIC — ZWAN
LYRIC ON MY LIP — TALI
MA BAKER — BONEY M
MA BAKER — SOMEBODY SCREAM — BONEY M
MA! (HE'S MAKING EYES AT ME) [A] — Johnny OTIS SHOW
MA HE'S MAKING EYES AT ME [A] — Lena ZAVARONI
MA, I DON'T LOVE HER — CLIPSE featuring Faith EVANS
MA SAYS, PA SAYS — Doris DAY and Johnnie RAY
MA SOLITUDA — CATHERINE WHEEL
MACARENA [A] — LOS DEL MAR featuring Wil VELOZ
MACARENA [A] — LOS DEL RIO
MACARENA [A] — CHIPMUNKS
MACARTHUR PARK [A] — Richard HARRIS
MACARTHUR PARK [A] — Donna SUMMER
MACH 5 — PRESIDENTS OF THE UNITED STATES OF AMERICA
MACHINE — The YEAH YEAH YEAHS
MACHINE + SOUL — Gary NUMAN
MACHINE GUN — The COMMODORES
MACHINE SAYS YES — FC KAHUNA
MACHINEHEAD — BUSH
MACHINERY — Sheena EASTON
MACK THE KNIFE [A] — Louis ARMSTRONG
MACK THE KNIFE [A] — Bobby DARIN (59)
MACK THE KNIFE [A] — Ella FITZGERALD
MACK THE KNIFE [A] — KING KURT
MACUSHLA — Bernie NOLAN
MAD ABOUT THE BOY — Dinah WASHINGTON
MAD ABOUT YOU [A] — Bruce RUFFIN
MAD ABOUT YOU [B] — Belinda CARLISLE
MAD ABOUT YOU [C] — STING
MAD DOG — ELASTICA
MAD EYED SCREAMER — CREATURES
MAD IF YA DON'T — GAYLE & GILLIAN
MAD LOVE (EP) — LUSH
MAD PASSIONATE LOVE — Bernard BRESSLAW
MAD WORLD [A] — TEARS FOR FEARS
MAD WORLD [A] — Michael ANDREWS featuring Gary JULES (03)
MADAGASCAR — ART OF TRANCE
MADAM BUTTERFLY (UN BEL DI VEDREMO) — Malcolm McLAREN
MADAME HELGA — STEREOPHONICS
MADCHESTER RAVE ON (EP) — HAPPY MONDAYS
MADE FOR LOVIN' YOU — ANASTACIA
MADE IN ENGLAND — Elton JOHN
MADE IN HEAVEN — Freddie MERCURY
MADE IN 2 MINUTES — BUG KANN and The PLASTIC JAM
MADE IT BACK — Beverley KNIGHT featuring REDMAN
MADE IT BACK 99 — Beverley KNIGHT
MADE IT LAST — HIGH CONTRAST
MADE OF STONE — The STONE ROSES
MADE YOU — Adam FAITH
MADE YOU LOOK — NAS
THE MADISON — Ray ELLINGTON
MADLY IN LOVE — BROS
MADNESS (IS ALL IN THE MIND) — MADNESS
MADNESS THING — LEILANI
MAGGIE — FOSTER and ALLEN
MAGGIE MAY — Rod STEWART (71)
MAGGIE'S FARM [A] — Bob DYLAN
MAGGIE'S FARM [A] — The SPECIALS
MAGGIE'S FARM (LIVE) [A] — TIN MACHINE
MAGGIE'S LAST PARTY — V.I.M.
MAGIC [A] — PILOT
MAGIC [B] — Olivia NEWTON-JOHN
MAGIC [C] — SASHA
MAGIC [D] — D'INFLUENCE
MAGIC [E] — Nick DRAKE
MAGIC BUS — The WHO
MAGIC CARPET RIDE — MIGHTY DUB KATZ
MAGIC FLY [A] — SPACE
MAGIC FLY [A] — MINIMALISTIX
THE MAGIC FRIEND — 2 UNLIMITED
MAGIC HOUR [A] — HALO JAMES
MAGIC HOUR [B] — CAST
THE MAGIC IS THERE — Daniel O'DONNELL
MAGIC MANDRAKE — SARR BAND
MAGIC MIND — EARTH WIND AND FIRE
MAGIC MOMENTS [A] — Perry COMO (58)
MAGIC MOMENTS [A] — Ronnie HILTON
THE MAGIC NUMBER — DE LA SOUL
THE MAGIC PIPER (OF LOVE) — Edwyn COLLINS
MAGIC ROUNDABOUT — Jasper CARROTT
MAGIC SMILE — Rosie VELA
MAGIC STYLE — BADMAN
MAGIC TOUCH [A] — ODYSSEY
MAGIC TOUCH [B] — ROSE ROYCE
MAGIC TOUCH [C] — LOOSE ENDS
MAGICAL — BUCKS FIZZ
MAGICAL MYSTERY TOUR (DOUBLE EP) — The BEATLES
MAGICAL SPIEL — Barry RYAN
MAGIC'S BACK (THEME FROM 'THE GHOSTS OF OXFORD STREET') — Malcolm McLAREN featuring Alison LIMERICK
MAGIC'S WAND — WHODINI
THE MAGNIFICENT — AGENT 00
THE MAGNIFICENT SEVEN [A] — John BARRY ORCHESTRA
THE MAGNIFICENT SEVEN [A] — Al CAIOLA
THE MAGNIFICENT 7 [A] — SCOOBIE
THE MAGNIFICENT SEVEN [B] — The CLASH
MAGNUM — MAGNUM
MAH-NA, MAH-NA — Piero UMILIANI
MAID OF ORLEANS (THE WALTZ JOAN OF ARC) — ORCHESTRAL MANOEUVRES IN THE DARK
MAIDEN JAPAN (EP) — IRON MAIDEN

27 April 2002	4 May 2002	11 May 2002	18 May 2002
UK No.1 SINGLES			
THE HINDU TIMES Oasis	FREAK LIKE ME Sugababes	KISS KISS Holly Valance	IF TOMORROW NEVER COMES Ronan Keating
UK No.1 ALBUMS			
A NEW DAY HAS COME Celine Dion	ALL RISE Blue	THE LAST BROADCAST Doves	THE LAST BROADCAST Doves

MAIDS, WHEN YOU'RE YOUNG NEVER WED AN OLD MAN — DUBLINERS
THE MAIGRET THEME — Joe LOSS
THE MAIN ATTRACTION — Pat BOONE
MAIN OFFENDER — The HIVES
MAIN THEME FROM 'EXODUS' — SEMPRINI
MAIN THEME FROM 'THE THORN BIRDS' — Henry MANCINI
MAIN TITLE THEME FROM 'MAN WITH THE GOLDEN ARM' [A] — Billy MAY
MAIN TITLE THEME FROM 'MAN WITH THE GOLDEN ARM' [A] — Jet HARRIS
MAINSTREAM — Thea GILMORE
MAIS OUI — The KING BROTHERS
THE MAJESTY OF ROCK — SPINAL TAP
MAJOR TOM (COMING HOME) — Peter SCHILLING
MAJORCA — Petula CLARK
MAKE A DAFT NOISE FOR CHRISTMAS — The GOODIES
MAKE A FAMILY — Gary CLARK
MAKE A MOVE ON ME — Olivia NEWTON-JOHN
MAKE BELIEVE IT'S YOUR FIRST TIME — The CARPENTERS
MAKE HER MINE — Nat 'King' COLE
MAKE IT A PARTY — Winifred ATWELL
MAKE IT CLAP — Busta RHYMES featuring SPLIFF STAR
MAKE IT EASY — SHYSTIE
MAKE IT EASY ON YOURSELF — The WALKER BROTHERS (65)
MAKE IT GOOD — a1
MAKE IT HAPPEN — Mariah CAREY
MAKE IT HOT [A] — Nicole RAY featuring Missy 'Misdemeanor' ELLIOTT
MAKE IT HOT [B] — VS
MAKE IT LAST [A] — SKIPWORTH and TURNER
MAKE IT LAST [B] — EMBRACE
MAKE IT MINE — The SHAMEN
MAKE IT ON MY OWN — Alison LIMERICK
MAKE IT REAL — SCORPIONS
MAKE IT RIGHT — Christian FALK featuring DEMETREUS
MAKE IT SOON — Tony BRENT
MAKE IT TONIGHT — WET WET WET
MAKE IT UP WITH LOVE — ATL
MAKE IT WITH YOU [A] — BREAD
MAKE IT WITH YOU [A] — PASADENAS
MAKE IT WITH YOU [A] — LET LOOSE
MAKE IT WITH YOU [B] — UNIVERSAL
MAKE LOVE EASY — Freddie JACKSON
MAKE LOVE LIKE A MAN — DEF LEPPARD
MAKE LOVE TO ME! [A] — Jo STAFFORD
MAKE LOVE TO ME [A] — John LEYTON
MAKE LOVE TO ME [B] — Jill FRANCIS
MAKE LUV — ROOM 5 featuring Oliver CHEATHAM (03)
MAKE ME AN ISLAND — Joe DOLAN
MAKE ME BAD — KORN
MAKE ME LAUGH — ANTHRAX
MAKE ME SMILE (COME UP AND SEE ME) [A] — Steve HARLEY and COCKNEY REBEL (75)
MAKE ME SMILE (COME UP AND SEE ME) [A] — ERASURE
MAKE ME WANNA SCREAM — Blu CANTRELL
MAKE MY BODY ROCK — JOMANDA
MAKE MY DAY — Buju BANTON
MAKE MY HEART FLY — The PROCLAIMERS
MAKE MY LOVE — Shawn CHRISTOPHER
MAKE SOMEONE HAPPY — Jimmy DURANTE
MAKE THAT MOVE — SHALAMAR
MAKE THE DEAL — OCEAN COLOUR SCENE
MAKE THE WORLD GO AWAY [A] — Eddy ARNOLD
MAKE THE WORLD GO AWAY [A] — Donny and Marie OSMOND
MAKE THE WORLD GO ROUND [A] — Sandy B
MAKE THE WORLD GO ROUND 2004 [A] — Sandy B
MAKE THINGS RIGHT — LEMON JELLY
MAKE U HAPPY — The LEVELLERS
MAKE UP YOUR MIND — BASS JUMPERS
MAKE WAY FOR NODDY — NODDY
MAKE WAY FOR THE INDIAN — APACHE INDIAN and TIM DOG
MAKE YOURS A HAPPY HOME — Gladys KNIGHT and The PIPS
MAKES ME LOVE YOU — ECLIPSE
MAKES ME WANNA DIE — TRICKY
MAKIN' HAPPY — Crystal WATERS
MAKIN' IT — David NAUGHTON
MAKIN' LOVE — Floyd ROBINSON
MAKIN' OUT — Mark OWEN
MAKIN' WHOOPEE — Ray CHARLES
MAKING LOVE (OUT OF NOTHING AT ALL) — Bonnie TYLER
MAKING PLANS FOR NIGEL — XTC
MAKING THE MOST OF — DODGY
MAKING TIME — CREATION
MAKING UP AGAIN — GOLDIE
MAKING YOUR MIND UP — BUCKS FIZZ (81)
MALE STRIPPER — Man PARRISH
MALIBU — HOLE
MALT AND BARLEY BLUES — McGUINNESS FLINT
MAMA [A] — David WHITFIELD
MAMA [A] — Connie FRANCIS
MAMA [B] — Dave BERRY
MAMA [C] — GENESIS
MAMA [D] — Kim APPLEBY
MAMA [E] — SPICE GIRLS (97)
MAMA GAVE BIRTH TO THE SOUL CHILDREN — QUEEN LATIFAH + DE LA SOUL
MAMA I'M COMING HOME — Ozzy OSBOURNE
MA-MA-MA-BELLE — ELECTRIC LIGHT ORCHESTRA
MAMA NEVER TOLD ME — SISTER SLEDGE
MAMA SAID [A] — Carleen ANDERSON
MAMA SAID [B] — METALLICA
MAMA SAID KNOCK YOU OUT — LL COOL J
MAMA TOLD ME NOT TO COME [A] — THREE DOG NIGHT
MAMA TOLD ME NOT TO COME [A] — Tom JONES and STEREOPHONICS
MAMA USED TO SAY [A] — JUNIOR
MAMA USED TO SAY [A] — AZURE
MAMA WEER ALL CRAZEE NOW — SLADE (72)
MAMA — WHO DA MAN? — Richard BLACKWOOD
MAMA'S BOY — Suzi QUATRO
MAMA'S PEARL — The JACKSON FIVE
MAMBO ITALIANO [A] — Rosemary CLOONEY and The MELLOMEN (55)
MAMBO ITALIANO [A] — Dean MARTIN
MAMBO ITALIANO [A] — SHAFT
MAMBO NO.5 (A LITTLE BIT OF ...) [A] — Lou BEGA (99)
MAMBO NO.5 [A] — BOB THE BUILDER (01)
MAMBO ROCK — Bill HALEY and his COMETS
MAMMA GAVE BIRTH TO THE SOUL CHILDREN — QUEEN LATIFAH + DE LA SOUL
MAMMA MIA [A] — ABBA (76)
MAMMA MIA [A] — A*TEENS
MAMOUNA — Bryan FERRY
MAMY BLUE [A] — LOS POP TOPS
MAMY BLUE [A] — Roger WHITTAKER
MAN — Rosemary CLOONEY
MAN BEHIND THE MUSIC — QUEEN PEN
THE MAN DON'T GIVE A FUCK — SUPER FURRY ANIMALS
THE MAN FROM LARAMIE [A] — Al MARTINO
THE MAN FROM LARAMIE [A] — Jimmy YOUNG (55)
MAN FROM MADRID — Tony OSBORNE SOUND
THE MAN FROM NAZARETH — John Paul JOANS
MAN! I FEEL LIKE A WOMAN! — Shania TWAIN
THE MAN I LOVE — Kate BUSH
THE MAN IN BLACK — Cozy POWELL
MAN IN THE MIRROR — Michael JACKSON
MAN IN THE MOON — CSILLA
MAN LIKE ME — NO REASON
A MAN NEEDS TO BE TOLD — The CHARLATANS
MAN OF MYSTERY — The SHADOWS
MAN OF STEEL — MEAT LOAF
MAN OF THE WORLD — FLEETWOOD MAC
MAN ON FIRE [A] — Frankie VAUGHAN
MAN ON FIRE [B] — Roger TAYLOR
MAN ON THE CORNER — GENESIS
MAN ON THE EDGE — IRON MAIDEN
MAN ON THE MOON — R.E.M.
MAN OUT OF TIME — Elvis COSTELLO
MAN SHORTAGE — LOVINDEER
THE MAN THAT GOT AWAY — Judy GARLAND
MAN TO MAN — HOT CHOCOLATE
THE MAN WHO PLAYS THE MANDOLINO — Dean MARTIN
THE MAN WHO SOLD THE WORLD [A] — LULU
THE MAN WHO SOLD THE WORLD (LIVE) [A] — David BOWIE
THE MAN WHO TOLD EVERYTHING — DOVES
THE MAN WITH THE CHILD IN HIS EYES — Kate BUSH
MAN WITH THE RED FACE — Laurent GARNIER
A MAN WITHOUT LOVE [A] — Kenneth McKELLAR
A MAN WITHOUT LOVE [A] — Engelbert HUMPERDINCK
MANCHESTER UNITED — MANCHESTER UNITED FOOTBALL CLUB
MANCHILD — Neneh CHERRY
MANDINKA — Sinead O'CONNOR
MANDOLIN RAIN — Bruce HORNSBY and The RANGE
MANDOLINS IN THE MOONLIGHT — Perry COMO
MANDY [A] — Barry MANILOW
MANDY [A] — WESTLIFE (03)
MANDY (LA PANSE) — Eddie CALVERT
MANEATER — Daryl HALL and John OATES
MANGOS — Rosemary CLOONEY
MANHATTAN SKYLINE — A-HA
MANHATTAN SPIRITUAL — Reg OWEN
MANIAC — Michael SEMBELLO
MANIC MINDS — MANIX
MANIC MONDAY — The BANGLES
MANILA — SEELENLUFT featuring Michael SMITH
MANNEQUIN — KIDS FROM 'FAME'
MANNISH BOY — Muddy WATERS
MAN-SIZE — P J HARVEY
MANSIZE ROOSTER — SUPERGRASS
MANTRA FOR A STATE OF MIND — S EXPRESS
MANY RIVERS TO CROSS [A] — UB40
MANY RIVERS TO CROSS [A] — CHER
MANY TEARS AGO — Connie FRANCIS
MANY TOO MANY — GENESIS
MANY WEATHERS APART — MERZ
MAPS — The YEAH YEAH YEAHS
MARBLE BREAKS IRON BENDS — Peter FENTON
MARBLEHEAD JOHNSON — The BLUETONES
MARBLES — BLACK GRAPE
MARCH OF THE MODS — Joe LOSS
MARCH OF THE PIGS — NINE INCH NAILS
MARCH OF THE SIAMESE CHILDREN — Kenny BALL and his JAZZMEN
MARCHETA — Karl DENVER
MARGATE — CHAS and DAVE
MARGIE — Fats DOMINO
MARGO — Billy FURY
MARGUERITA TIME — STATUS QUO
MARIA [A] — PJ PROBY
MARIA [B] — BLONDIE (99)
MARIA ELENA [A] — LOS INDIOS TABAJARAS
MARIA ELENA [B] — Gene PITNEY
MARIA (I LIKE IT LOUD) — SCOOTER vs Marc ACARDIPANE & Dick RULES
MARIA MARIA — SANTANA
MARIANA — The GIBSON BROTHERS
MARIANNE [A] — HILLTOPPERS
MARIANNE [B] — Cliff RICHARD
MARIE — The BACHELORS
MARIE CELESTE — POLECATS
MARIE MARIE — Shakin' STEVENS
(MARIE'S THE NAME) HIS LATEST FLAME — Elvis PRESLEY (61)
MARJORINE — Joe COCKER
MARKET SQUARE HEROES — MARILLION
MARLENE ON THE WALL — Suzanne VEGA
MAROC 7 — The SHADOWS
MARQUEE MOON — TELEVISION
MARQUIS — LINOLEUM
MARRAKESH EXPRESS — CROSBY, STILLS, NASH and YOUNG
MARRIED MEN — Bonnie TYLER
MARRY ME — Mike PRESTON
MARTA — The BACHELORS
MARTA'S SONG — DEEP FOREST
MARTELL — The CRIBS
MARTHA'S HARBOUR — ALL ABOUT EVE
MARTIAN HOP — Rocky SHARPE and The REPLAYS
MARTIKA'S KITCHEN — MARTIKA
MARVELLOUS — The LIGHTNING SEEDS
MARVIN — MARVIN THE PARANOID ANDROID
MARY [A] — SUPERGRASS
MARY [B] — SCISSOR SISTERS
MARY ANN — BLACK LACE
MARY ANNE — The SHADOWS
MARY HAD A LITTLE BOY — SNAP!
MARY HAD A LITTLE LAMB — Paul McCARTNEY
MARY JANE [A] — Del SHANNON
MARY JANE [B] — MEGADETH
MARY JANE [C] — SPIN DOCTORS
MARY JANE (ALL NIGHT LONG) — Mary J BLIGE
MARY JANE'S LAST DANCE — Tom PETTY and The HEARTBREAKERS
MARY OF THE 4TH FORM — The BOOMTOWN RATS
MARY'S BOY CHILD [A] — Harry BELAFONTE (57)
MARY'S BOY CHILD [A] — NINA and FREDERICK
MARY'S BOY CHILD – OH MY LORD [A] — BONEY M (78)
MARY'S PRAYER — DANNY WILSON
MAS QUE MANCADA — RONALDO'S REVENGE
MAS QUE NADA [A] — ECHOBEATZ
MAS QUE NADA [A] — TAMBA TRIO
MAS QUE NADA [A] — COLOUR GIRL featuring PSG
MASH IT UP — MDM
MASQUERADE [A] — The SKIDS
MASQUERADE [B] — Evelyn THOMAS
MASQUERADE [C] — The FALL
MASQUERADE [D] — GERIDEAU
MASS DESTRUCTION — FAITHLESS
THE MASSES AGAINST THE CLASSES — MANIC STREET PREACHERS (00)
MASSIVE ATTACK (EP) — MASSIVE ATTACK
MASTER AND SERVANT — DEPECHE MODE
MASTER BLASTER (JAMMIN') [A] — Stevie WONDER
THE MASTER HAS COME BACK — Damian "Jr. Gong" MARLEY
MASTERBLASTER 2000 [A] — DJ LUCK & MC NEAT
THE MASTERPLAN — Diana BROWN and Barrie K SHARPE
MATADOR — Jeff WAYNE
MATCHSTALK MEN AND MATCHSTALK CATS AND DOGS (LOWRY'S SONG) — BRIAN and MICHAEL (78)
MATED — David GRANT and Jaki GRAHAM
MATERIAL GIRL — MADONNA
MATHAR — INDIAN VIBES
MATINÉE — FRANZ FERDINAND
A MATTER OF FACT — INNOCENCE
MATTER OF TIME — NINE YARDS
A MATTER OF TRUST — Billy JOEL
MATTHEW AND SON — Cat STEVENS
MATT'S MOOD [A] — MATT BIANCO
MATT'S MOOD [A] — BREEKOUT KREW
MAX DON'T HAVE SEX WITH YOUR EX — E-ROTIC
THE MAXI PRIEST EP — Maxi PRIEST
MAXIMUM (EP) — DREADZONE
MAXIMUM OVERDRIVE — 2 UNLIMITED
MAY EACH DAY — Andy WILLIAMS
MAY I HAVE THE NEXT DREAM WITH YOU — Malcolm ROBERTS
MAY IT BE — ENYA
MAY THE SUNSHINE — NAZARETH
MAY YOU ALWAYS [A] — The McGUIRE SISTERS
MAY YOU ALWAYS [A] — Joan REGAN
MAYBE [A] — Thom PACE
MAYBE [B] — ENRIQUE
MAYBE [C] — EMMA
MAYBE [D] — N*E*R*D
MAYBE BABY — The CRICKETS
MAYBE I KNOW [A] — Lesley GORE
MAYBE I KNOW [A] — SEASHELLS
MAYBE I'M AMAZED [A] — Paul McCARTNEY
MAYBE I'M AMAZED [A] — Carleen ANDERSON
MAYBE I'M DEAD — MONEY MARK
MAYBE LOVE — Stevie NICKS
MAYBE THAT'S WHAT IT TAKES — Alex PARKS
MAYBE TOMORROW [A] — Billy FURY
MAYBE TOMORROW [B] — CHORDS
MAYBE TOMORROW [C] — UB40
MAYBE TOMORROW [D] — STEREOPHONICS
MAYBE (WE SHOULD CALL IT A DAY) — Hazell DEAN
MAYOR OF SIMPLETON — XTC
McDONALD'S CAVE — The PILTDOWN MEN

25 May 2002	1 June 2002	8 June 2002	15 June 2002
JUST A LITTLE Liberty X	WITHOUT ME Eminem	LIGHT MY FIRE Will Young	LIGHT MY FIRE Will Young
18 Moby	DESTINATION Ronan Keating	THE EMINEM SHOW Eminem	THE EMINEM SHOW Eminem

ME AGAINST THE MUSIC — Britney SPEARS featuring MADONNA
ME AND BABY BROTHER — WAR
ME AND JULIO DOWN BY THE SCHOOLYARD — Paul SIMON
ME AND MR SANCHEZ — BLUE RONDO A LA TURK
ME AND MRS JONES [A] — Billy PAUL
ME AND MRS JONES [A] — Freddie JACKSON
ME AND MY GIRL (NIGHT-CLUBBING) — David ESSEX
ME AND MY LIFE — The TREMELOES
ME AND MY SHADOW — Frank SINATRA and Sammy DAVIS Jr
ME AND THE FARMER — The HOUSEMARTINS
ME AND YOU AND A DOG NAMED BOO — LOBO
ME AND YOU VERSUS THE WORLD — SPACE
ME. IN TIME — The CHARLATANS
ME' ISRAELITES — CHOPS-EMC + EXTENSIVE
ME JULIE — Ali G & SHAGGY
ME MYSELF AND I [A] — DE LA SOUL
ME, MYSELF AND I [B] — BEYONCÉ
ME MYSELF I — Joan ARMATRADING
ME NO POP I — Kid CREOLE and The COCONUTS
ME OR YOU? — KILLING JOKE
ME THE PEACEFUL HEART — LULU
MEA CULPA PART II — ENIGMA
MEAN GIRL — STATUS QUO
MEAN MAN — W.A.S.P.
MEAN MEAN MAN — Wanda JACKSON
MEAN STREAK [A] — Cliff RICHARD
MEAN STREAK [B] — Y & T
MEAN TO ME — Shaye COGAN
MEAN WOMAN BLUES — Roy ORBISON
THE MEANING OF CHRISTMAS — Boris GARDINER
THE MEANING OF LOVE [A] — DEPECHE MODE
THE MEANING OF LOVE [B] — MICHELLE
MEANT TO LIVE — SWITCHFOOT
MEANTIME — The FUTUREHEADS
MEASURE OF A MAN — SAM & MARK (04)
MEAT PIE SAUSAGE ROLL — GRANDAD ROBERTS and his SON ELVIS
MECCA — CHEETAHS
MECHANICAL WONDER — OCEAN COLOUR SCENE
THE MEDAL SONG — CULTURE CLUB
MEDICATION — SPIRITUALIZED
MEDICINE SHOW — BIG AUDIO DYNAMITE
THE MEDICINE SONG — Stephanie MILLS
MEET EL PRESIDENTE — DURAN DURAN
MEET HER AT THE LOVE PARADE — DA HOOL
MEET ME ON THE CORNER [A] — Max BYGRAVES
MEET ME ON THE CORNER [B] — LINDISFARNE
(MEET) THE FLINTSTONES — The B-52's
MEGABLAST — BOMB THE BASS
MEGACHIC — CHIC MEDLEY — CHIC
MEGALOMANIA — PELE
MEGALOMANIAC — INCUBUS
MEGAMIX [A] — TECHNOTRONIC
MEGAMIX [B] — Crystal WATERS
MEGAMIX [C] — CORONA
MEGAMIX [D] — BONEY M
MEGAREX — T. REX
MEIN TEIL — RAMMSTEIN
MEISO — DJ KRUSH
MELANCHOLY ROSE — Marc ALMOND
MELLOW DOUBT — TEENAGE FANCLUB
MELLOW MELLOW RIGHT ON — LOWRELL
MELLOW YELLOW — DONOVAN
THE MELOD-EP — DODGY
MELODY OF LOVE — INK SPOTS
MELODY OF LOVE (WANNA BE LOVED) — Donna SUMMER
MELT [A] — SIOUXSIE and The BANSHEES
MELT [B] — MELANIE C
THE MELTING MOON — VHS OR BETA
MELTING POT — BLUE MINK
MEMO FROM TURNER — Mick JAGGER
MEMORIES [A] — PUBLIC IMAGE LTD
MEMORIES [B] — Mike BERRY
MEMORIES [C] — Beverley CRAVEN
MEMORIES ARE MADE OF THIS [A] — Dave KING
MEMORIES ARE MADE OF THIS [A] — Dean MARTIN (56)
MEMORIES ARE MADE OF THIS [A] — Val DOONICAN
MEMORY [A] — Elaine PAIGE
MEMORY [A] — Barbra STREISAND
MEMORY [A] — Aled JONES
THE MEMORY REMAINS — METALLICA
MEMPHIS — Lonnie MACK
MEMPHIS TENNESSEE [A] — Chuck BERRY
MEMPHIS TENNESSEE [A] — Dave BERRY
MEN IN BLACK [A] — Frank BLACK
MEN IN BLACK [B] — Will SMITH (97)
MENTAL — MANIC MCs featuring Sara CARLSON
MENTAL PICTURE — Jon SECADA
MENTASM — SECOND PHASE
MERCEDES BOY — PEBBLES
MERCI CHERI — Vince HILL
MERCURY — LOWGOLD
MERCURY AND SOLACE — BT
MERCY ME — ALKALINE TRIO
MERCY MERCY ME — I WANT YOU — Robert PALMER
MERMAIDS — Paul WELLER
MERRY CHRISTMAS DARLING — The CARPENTERS
MERRY CHRISTMAS EVERYONE — Shakin' STEVENS (85)
MERRY GENTLE POPS — The BARRON KNIGHTS
A MERRY JINGLE — GREEDIES
THE MERRY PLOUGHBOY — Dermot O'BRIEN
MERRY XMAS EVERYBODY [A] — SLADE (73)
MERRY XMAS EVERYBODY [A] — METAL GURUS
MERRY XMAS EVERYBODY [A] — Tony CHRISTIE
MERRY X-MESS — ROTTERDAM TERMINATION SOURCE
MERSEYBEAST — Ian McNABB
MESCALITO — SOURMASH
MESMERISE [A] — CHAPTERHOUSE
MESMERIZE [B] — JA RULE featuring ASHANTI
MESMERIZED — Faith EVANS
A MESS OF BLUES [A] — Elvis PRESLEY
A MESS OF BLUES [A] — STATUS QUO
THE MESSAGE [A] — GRANDMASTER FLASH, Melle MEL and The FURIOUS FIVE
THE MESSAGE [B] — 49ers
MESSAGE IN A BOTTLE [A] — The POLICE (79)
MESSAGE IN A BOTTLE [A] — DANCE FLOOR VIRUS
MESSAGE IN A BOTTLE [A] — T-FACTORY
MESSAGE IN THE BOX — WORLD PARTY
THE MESSAGE IS LOVE — Arthur BAKER and The BACKBEAT DISCIPLES featuring Al GREEN
MESSAGE OF LOVE [A] — The PRETENDERS
MESSAGE OF LOVE [B] — LOVEHAPPY
MESSAGE TO MARTHA (KENTUCKY BLUEBIRD) [A] — Adam FAITH
MESSAGE TO MARTHA [A] — Lou JOHNSON
A MESSAGE TO YOU RUDY — The SPECIALS
A MESSAGE TO YOUR HEART — Samantha JANUS
MESSAGE II (SURVIVAL) — GRANDMASTER FLASH, Melle MEL and The FURIOUS FIVE
MESSAGE UNDERSTOOD — Sandie SHAW
MESSAGES — ORCHESTRAL MANOEUVRES IN THE DARK
MESSAGES FROM THE STARS — RAH BAND
MESSED UP — The BEAT UP
MESSIN' — LADIES FIRST
METAFORCE — ART OF NOISE
METAL GURU — T. REX (72)
METAL HEALTH — QUIET RIOT
METAL MICKEY — SUEDE
METEOR MAN — Dee D JACKSON
METHOD OF MODERN LOVE — Daryl HALL and John OATES
METROSOUND — Adam F & J MAJIK
METROPOLIS — Oliver LIEB presents SMOKED
MEXICALI ROSE — Karl DENVER
THE MEXICAN — FENTONES
MEXICAN GIRL — SMOKIE
MEXICAN RADIO — WALL OF VOODOO
MEXICAN WAVE — KERBDOG
MEXICO — Long John BALDRY
MF FROM HELL — The DATSUNS
MFEO — KAVANA
MI CHICO LATINO — Geri HALLIWELL (99)
MI TIERRA — Gloria ESTEFAN
MIAMI — Will SMITH
MIAMI HIT MIX — Gloria ESTEFAN
MIAMI VICE THEME — Jan HAMMER
MICHAEL [A] — The HIGHWAYMEN (61)
MICHAEL [B] — Geno WASHINGTON and The RAM JAM BAND
MICHAEL [C] — FRANZ FERDINAND
MICHAEL AND THE SLIPPER TREE — The EQUALS
MICHAEL CAINE — MADNESS
MICHAEL JACKSON MEDLEY — ASHAYE
MICHAEL ROW THE BOAT — Lonnie DONEGAN
MICHELLE [A] — DAVID and JONATHAN
MICHELLE [A] — The OVERLANDERS (66)
MICHIKO — SULTANS OF PING
MICKEY [A] — Toni BASIL
MICKEY [A] — LOLLY
MICRO KID — LEVEL 42
THE MICROPHONE FIEND — Eric B and RAKIM
MICROWAVED — PITCHSHIFTER
MIDAS TOUCH — MIDNIGHT STAR
THE MIDDLE — JIMMY EAT WORLD
MIDDLE OF NOWHERE — HOT HOT HEAT
MIDDLE OF THE NIGHT — BROTHERHOOD OF MAN
MIDDLEMAN — TERRORVISION
MIDLIFE CRISIS — FAITH NO MORE
MIDNIGHT [A] — Paul ANKA
MIDNIGHT [B] — UN-CUT
MIDNIGHT AT THE LOST AND FOUND — MEAT LOAF
MIDNIGHT AT THE OASIS [A] — Maria MULDAUR
MIDNIGHT AT THE OASIS [A] — The BRAND NEW HEAVIES
MIDNIGHT BLUE — Louise TUCKER
MIDNIGHT COWBOY — MIDNIGHT COWBOY SOUNDTRACK
MIDNIGHT FLYER — Nat 'King' COLE
MIDNIGHT GROOVIN' — LIGHT OF THE WORLD
MIDNIGHT IN A PERFECT WORLD — DJ SHADOW
MIDNIGHT IN CHELSEA — Jon BON JOVI
MIDNIGHT IN MOSCOW — Kenny BALL and his JAZZMEN
MIDNIGHT RIDER — Paul DAVIDSON
MIDNIGHT SHIFT — Buddy HOLLY
MIDNIGHT SUMMER DREAM — The STRANGLERS
MIDNIGHT TO SIX MAN — PRETTY THINGS
MIDNIGHT TRAIN TO GEORGIA — Gladys KNIGHT and The PIPS
MIDNITE — D'INFLUENCE
MIDNITE DYNAMOS — MATCHBOX
MIDNITE SPECIAL — Paul EVANS
MIDSUMMER MADNESS (EP) — RHYTHM SECTION
MIGHT BE STARS — WANNADIES
THE MIGHTY HIGH — REVIVAL 3000
MIGHTY JOE — SHOCKING BLUE
THE MIGHTY POWER OF LOVE — TAVARES
MIGHTY QUINN — MANFRED MANN (68)
MIG29 — MIG29
MIKE OLDFIELD'S SINGLE (THEME FROM TUBULAR BELLS) — Mike OLDFIELD
MILES AWAY [A] — John FOXX
MILES AWAY [B] — WINGER
MILES FROM HOME — PESHAY
MILK — GARBAGE featuring TRICKY
MILK AND ALCOHOL — DR FEELGOOD
MILKMAN'S SON — UGLY KID JOE
MILKSHAKE — KELIS
MILKY WAY — SHEER ELEGANCE
THE MILL HILL SELF HATE CLUB — Edward BALL
MILLENNIUM [A] — KILLING JOKE
MILLENNIUM [B] — Robbie WILLIAMS (98)
MILLENNIUM CHIMES — BIG BEN
THE MILLENNIUM PRAYER — Cliff RICHARD (99)
MILLION DOLLAR LOVE — DUB WAR
MILLION DRUMS — Tony SHEVETON
A MILLION LOVE SONGS — TAKE THAT
MILLION MILES AWAY — The OFFSPRING
MILLION SUNS — OOBERMAN
MILLIONAIRE — KELIS featuring ANDRE 3000
MILLIONAIRE SWEEPER — KENICKIE
MILLIONS LIKE US — PURPLE HEARTS
MILLY MOLLY MANDY — Glyn POOLE
MILORD [A] — Edith PIAF
MILORD [A] — Frankie VAUGHAN
MIND — The FARM
MIND ADVENTURES — DES'REE
MIND BLOWIN' — SMOOTH
MIND BLOWING DECISIONS — HEATWAVE
MIND BODY SOUL — FANTASY UFO
MIND GAMES — John LENNON
MIND OF A TOY — VISAGE
A MIND OF ITS OWN — Victoria BECKHAM
THE MIND OF LOVE (WHERE IS YOUR HEAD, KATHRYN?) — kd LANG
THE MIND OF THE MACHINE — N-TRANCE
MIND OVER MONEY — TURIN BRAKES
MIND TRICK — Jamie CULLUM
MIND UP TONIGHT — Melba MOORE
MINDCIRCUS — WAY OUT WEST featuring Tricia LEE
MINDLESS BOOGIE — HOT CHOCOLATE
MINDSTREAM — MEAT BEAT MANIFESTO
MINE — EVERYTHING BUT THE GIRL
MINE ALL MINE — CA$HFLOW
MINE TO GIVE — PHOTEK featuring Robert J OWENS
MINEFIELD — I-LEVEL
MINERVA — DEFTONES
MINISTRY OF LOVE — HYSTERIC EGO
MINISTRY OF MAYHEM — The NOISE NEXT DOOR
MINNIE THE MOOCHER — REGGAE PHILHARMONIC ORCHESTRA
MINORITY — GREEN DAY
MINORITY OF ONE — JOHNNY PANIC
MINT CAR — The CURE
MINUETTO ALLEGRETTO — The WOMBLES
MINUTE BY MINUTE — The DOOBIE BROTHERS
A MINUTE OF YOUR TIME — Tom JONES
THE MINUTE YOU'RE GONE — Cliff RICHARD (65)
MIRACLE [A] — Jon BON JOVI
MIRACLE [B] — OLIVE
A MIRACLE — HIDDEN CAMERAS
THE MIRACLE [A]— QUEEN
THE MIRACLE [B]— Cliff RICHARD
MIRACLE GOODNIGHT — David BOWIE
THE MIRACLE OF LOVE — EURYTHMICS
THE MIRACLE OF YOU — Danny WILLIAMS
MIRACLES [A] — Gary NUMAN
MIRACLES [B] — PET SHOP BOYS
MIRROR IN THE BATHROOM — The BEAT
MIRROR KISSERS — The CRIBS
MIRROR MAN — HUMAN LEAGUE
MIRROR MIRROR [A] — PINKERTON'S ASSORTED COLOURS
MIRROR MIRROR [B] — Diana ROSS
MIRROR MIRROR (MON AMOUR) — DOLLAR
MIRRORS — Sally OLDFIELD
MIS-SHAPES — PULP
MISERERE — ZUCCHERO with Luciano PAVAROTTI
MISERY [A] — SOUL ASYLUM
MISERY [B] — The MOFFATTS
MISFIT [A] — CURIOSITY KILLED THE CAT
MISFIT [B] — Amy STUDT
MISGUIDED — DYVERSE
MISIRLOU (THE THEME TO THE MOTION PICTURE 'PULP FICTION') — SPAGHETTI SURFERS
MISLED [A] — KOOL and The GANG
MISLED [B] — QUIREBOYS
MISLED [C] — Celine DION
MISS AMERICA — BIG DISH
MISS CALIFORNIA — Dante THOMAS featuring PRAS
MISS CHATELAINE — kd LANG
MISS FAT BOOTY — PART II — MOS DEF featuring GHOSTFACE KILLAH
MISS HIT AND RUN — Barry BLUE
MISS INDEPENDENT — Kelly CLARKSON
MISS LUCIFER — PRIMAL SCREAM
MISS MODULAR — STEREOLAB
MISS PARKER [A] — BENZ
MISS PARKER [B] — MORGAN
MISS PERFECT — ABS featuring NODESHA
MISS SARAJEVO — PASSENGERS
MISS THE GIRL — CREATURES
MISS WORLD — HOLE
MISS YOU [A] — Jimmy YOUNG
MISS YOU [B] — The ROLLING STONES
MISS YOU LIKE CRAZY — Natalie COLE
MISS YOU MUCH — Janet JACKSON
MISS YOU NIGHTS [A] — Cliff RICHARD
MISS YOU NIGHTS [A] — WESTLIFE
MISSING [A] — Terry HALL

	22 June 2002	29 June 2002	6 July 2002	13 July 2002
UK No.1 SINGLES	A LITTLE LESS CONVERSATION Elvis vs JXL	A LITTLE LESS CONVERSATION Elvis vs JXL	A LITTLE LESS CONVERSATION Elvis vs JXL	A LITTLE LESS CONVERSATION Elvis vs JXL
UK No.1 ALBUMS	THE EMINEM SHOW Eminem	THE EMINEM SHOW Eminem	THE EMINEM SHOW Eminem	HEATHEN CHEMISTRY Oasis

MISSING [B] — EVERYTHING BUT THE GIRL
MISSING WORDS — SELECTER
MISSING YOU [A] — Chris DE BURGH
MISSING YOU [B] — John WAITE
MISSING YOU [B] — Tina TURNER
MISSING YOU [C] — Mary J BLIGE
MISSING YOU [C] — SOUL II SOUL featuring Kym MAZELLE
MISSING YOU [D] — Lucy CARR
MISSING YOU NOW — Michael BOLTON featuring Kenny G
MISSION OF LOVE — Jason DONOVAN
MISSIONARY MAN — EURYTHMICS
MISSISSIPPI — PUSSYCAT (76)
MISSY MISSY — Paul and Barry RYAN
MISTI BLU — AMILLIONSONS
MISTAKES AND REGRETS — ... AND YOU WILL KNOW US BY THE TRAIL OF DEAD
MR ALIBI — Maria WILLSON
MR BACHELOR — LOOSE ENDS
MR BASS MAN — Johnny CYMBAL
MR BIG STUFF [A] — HEAVY D and The BOYZ
MR BIG STUFF [B] — QUEEN LATIFAH, SHADES and FREE
MR BLOBBY — MR BLOBBY (93)
MR BLUE [A] — David MacBETH
MR BLUE [A] — Mike PRESTON
MR BLUE SKY — ELECTRIC LIGHT ORCHESTRA
MR BRIGHTSIDE — The KILLERS
MR CABDRIVER — Lenny KRAVITZ
MR CROWLEY — Ozzy OSBOURNE
MR CUSTER — Charlie DRAKE
MR DEVIL — BIG TIME CHARLIE
MR DJ [A] — CONCEPT
MR DJ [B] — BLACKOUT
MR E'S BEAUTIFUL BLUES — EELS
MR FIXIT — ROOTJOOSE
MR FRIDAY NIGHT — Lisa MOORISH
MR GUDER — The CARPENTERS
MR GUITAR — Bert WEEDON
MR HANKEY THE CHRISTMAS POO — MR HANKEY
MISTER JONES — OUT OF MY HAIR
MR JONES — COUNTING CROWS
MR KIRK'S NIGHTMARE — 4 HERO
MR LEE — Diana ROSS
MR LOVERMAN — Shabba RANKS
MR MANIC AND SISTER COOL — SHAKATAK
MISTER MENTAL — The EIGHTIES MATCHBOX B-LINE DISASTER
MR PHARMACIST — The FALL
MR PORTER — Mickie MOST
MR PRESIDENT — D, B, M and T
MR RAFFLES (MAN, IT WAS MEAN) — Steve HARLEY and COCKNEY REBEL
MR SANDMAN [A] — The CHORDETTES
MR SANDMAN [A] — Dickie VALENTINE
MISTER SANDMAN [A] — Max BYGRAVES
MISTER SANDMAN [A] — FOUR ACES
MR SECOND CLASS — Spencer DAVIS GROUP
MR SLEAZE — STOCK AITKEN WATERMAN
MR SOFT — Steve HARLEY and COCKNEY REBEL
MR SOLITAIRE — ANIMAL NIGHTLIFE
MR SUCCESS — Frank SINATRA
MR TAMBOURINE MAN — The BYRDS (65)
MR TELEPHONE MAN — NEW EDITION
MR VAIN — CULTURE BEAT (93)
MR WENDAL — ARRESTED DEVELOPMENT
MR WONDERFUL — Peggy LEE
MR WRITER — STEREOPHONICS
MR ZERO — Keith RELF
MISTLETOE AND WINE — Cliff RICHARD (88)
MISTY [A] — Johnny MATHIS
MISTY [A] — Ray STEVENS
MISTY BLUE — Dorothy MOORE
MISTY MORNING, ALBERT BRIDGE — The POGUES
MISUNDERSTANDING — GENESIS
MISUNDERSTOOD [A] — BON JOVI
MISUNDERSTOOD [B] — Robbie WILLIAMS
MISUNDERSTOOD MAN — Cliff RICHARD
MITCH — BISCUIT BOY
MITTAGEISEN (METAL POSTCARD) — SIOUXSIE and The BANSHEES
MIX IT UP — Dan REED NETWORK
MIXED BIZNESS — BECK
MIXED EMOTIONS — The ROLLING STONES
MIXED TRUTH — RAGGA TWINS
MIXED UP WORLD — Sophie ELLIS-BEXTOR
MIYAKO HIDEAWAY — MARION
M'LADY — SLY and The FAMILY STONE
MMM MMM MMM MMM — CRASH TEST DUMMIES
MMMBOP — HANSON (97)
MO' FIRE — BAD COMPANY
MO MONEY MO PROBLEMS — NOTORIOUS B.I.G. featuring PUFF DADDY and MA$E
MOAN & GROAN — Mark MORRISON
MOANIN' — Chris FARLOWE
MOB RULES — BLACK SABBATH
MOBILE — Ray BURNS
MOBSCENE — MARILYN MANSON
MOCKINGBIRD [A] — Inez FOXX
MOCKINGBIRD [A] — Carly SIMON
MOCKINGBIRD [A] — The BELLE STARS
MOCKINGBIRD [B] — EMINEM
MOCKINGBIRD HILL — MIGIL FIVE
THE MODEL — KRAFTWERK (82)
MODEL LIFE — CHOCOLATE MONDAY
MODELS FOR THE PROGRAMME — HELL IS FOR HEROES
MODERN AGE — The STROKES
MODERN ART — ART BRUT
MODERN FEELING — IKARA COLT
MODERN GIRL [A] — Sheena EASTON
MODERN GIRL [B] — MEAT LOAF
MODERN LOVE — David BOWIE
MODERN ROMANCE (I WANT TO FALL IN LOVE AGAIN) — Francis ROSSI
MODERN WAY — KAISER CHIEFS
A MODERN WAY OF LETTING GO — IDLEWILD
THE MODERN WORLD — The JAM
MODUS OPERANDI — PHOTEK
MOI ... LOLITA — ALIZÉE
MOIRA JANE'S CAFE — DEFINITION OF SOUND
MOLLIE'S SONG — Beverley CRAVEN
MOLLY — CARRIE
MOLLY'S CHAMBERS — KINGS OF LEON
MOMENT OF MY LIFE — Bobby D'AMBROSIO featuring Michelle WEEKS
MOMENTS IN LOVE — ART OF NOISE
MOMENTS IN SOUL — JT and The BIG FAMILY
MOMENTS OF PLEASURE — Kate BUSH
MON AMI — GIRESSE
MON AMOUR TOKYO — PIZZICATO FIVE
MONA — Craig McLACHLAN
MONA LISA — Conway TWITTY
MONDAY MONDAY — The MAMAS and The PAPAS
MONDAY MORNING — The CANDYSKINS
MONDAY MORNING 5:19 — RIALTO
MONEY [A] — Bern ELLIOTT and The FENMEN
MONEY [A] — FLYING LIZARDS
MONEY [A] — BACKBEAT BAND
MONEY [B] — Dan REED NETWORK
MONEY [C] — SKIN
MONEY [D] — Charli BALTIMORE
MONEY [E] — JAMELIA
(MONEY CAN'T) BUY ME LOVE — BLACKSTREET
MONEY DON'T MATTER 2 NIGHT — PRINCE and The NEW POWER GENERATION
MONEY (EVERYBODY LOVES HER) — GUN
MONEY FOR NOTHING — DIRE STRAITS
MONEY GO ROUND (PART 1) — STYLE COUNCIL
MONEY GREEDY — TRICKY
MONEY HONEY — BAY CITY ROLLERS
MONEY IN MY POCKET — Dennis BROWN
MONEY LOVE — Neneh CHERRY
MONEY, MONEY, MONEY — ABBA
MONEY THAT'S YOUR PROBLEM — TONIGHT
MONEY TO BURN — Richard ASHCROFT
MONEY'S TOO TIGHT (TO MENTION) [A] — The VALENTINE BROTHERS
MONEY'S TOO TIGHT (TO MENTION) [A] — SIMPLY RED
MONEYTALKS — AC/DC
MONIE IN THE MIDDLE — Monie LOVE
THE MONKEES — RAMPAGE
THE MONKEES EP — The MONKEES
MONKEY [A] — George MICHAEL
MONKEY [B] — SHAFT
MONKEY BUSINESS [A] — SKID ROW
MONKEY BUSINESS [B] — DANGER DANGER
MONKEY CHOP — DAN-I
MONKEY GONE TO HEAVEN — PIXIES
MONKEY MAN [A] — The MAYTALS
MONKEY MAN [A] — GENERAL LEVY
MONKEY SPANNER — Dave and Ansil COLLINS
MONKEY WAH — RADICAL ROB
MONKEY WRENCH — FOO FIGHTERS
MONO — Courtney LOVE
MONOCULTURE — SOFT CELL
MONSIEUR DUPONT — Sandie SHAW
MONSTER — L7
MONSTER — LIQUID PEOPLE vs SIMPLE MINDS
MONSTER MASH — Bobby 'Boris' PICKETT and The CRYPT-KICKERS
MONSTERS — FUNERAL FOR A FRIEND
MONSTERS AND ANGELS — VOICE OF THE BEEHIVE
MONTEGO BAY [A] — Freddie NOTES and The RUDIES
MONTEGO BAY [A] — Bobby BLOOM
MONTEGO BAY [A] — SUGAR CANE
MONTEGO BAY [A] — AMAZULU
MONTREAL — WEDDING PRESENT
MONTREUX (EP) — SIMPLY RED
MONTUNO — Gloria ESTEFAN
MONY MONY [A] — Tommy JAMES and The SHONDELLS (68)
MONY MONY [A] — AMAZULU
MONY MONY [A] — Billy IDOL
MONY MONY [A] — STATUS QUO
THE MOOD CLUB — FIRSTBORN
MOODSWINGS — MY VITRIOL
MOODY BLUE — Elvis PRESLEY
MOODY PLACES — NORTHSIDE
MOODY RIVER — Pat BOONE
MOOG ERUPTION — DIGITAL ORGASM
MOON — VIRUS
MOON HOP — Derrick MORGAN
MOON OVER BOURBON STREET — STING
MOON RIVER [A] — Henry MANCINI
MOON RIVER [A] — Danny WILLIAMS (61)
MOON RIVER [A] — GREYHOUND
MOON SHADOW — Cat STEVENS
MOON TALK — Perry COMO
MOONCHILD — FIELDS OF THE NEPHILIM
MOONGLOW [A] — Morris STOLOFF
MOONGLOW [A] — SOUNDS ORCHESTRAL
MOONLIGHT AND MUZAK — M
MOONLIGHT & ROSES — Jim REEVES
MOONLIGHT GAMBLER — Frankie LAINE
MOONLIGHT SERENADE — Glenn MILLER
MOONLIGHT SHADOW — Mike OLDFIELD
MOONLIGHTING — Leo SAYER
'MOONLIGHTING' THEME — Al JARREAU
MOONSHINE SALLY — MUD
MOR — BLUR
MORE [A] — Jimmy YOUNG
MORE [A] — Perry COMO
MORE [B] — SISTERS OF MERCY
MORE ... [C] — HIGH
MORE & MORE — SPOILED & ZIGO
MORE AND MORE [A] — Andy WILLIAMS
MORE AND MORE [B] — CAPTAIN HOLLYWOOD PROJECT
MORE & MORE [C] — JOE featuring G-UNIT
MORE AND MORE PARTY POPS — Russ CONWAY
MORE BEATS & PIECES — COLDCUT
MORE GOOD OLD ROCK 'N' ROLL — Dave CLARK FIVE
MORE HUMAN THAN HUMAN — WHITE ZOMBIE
THE MORE I GET THE MORE I WANT — KWS featuring Teddy PENDERGRASS
THE MORE I SEE (THE LESS I BELIEVE) — FUN BOY THREE
THE MORE I SEE YOU [A] — Joy MARSHALL
THE MORE I SEE YOU [A] — Chris MONTEZ
THE MORE I SEE YOU [A] — Barbara WINDSOR and Mike REID
MORE LIFE IN A TRAMP'S VEST — STEREOPHONICS
MORE LIKE THE MOVIES — DR HOOK
MORE LOVE [A] — Feargal SHARKEY
MORE LOVE [B] — NEXT OF KIN
MORE MONEY FOR YOU AND ME (MEDLEY) — FOUR PREPS
MORE, MORE, MORE [A] — Andrea TRUE CONNECTION
MORE MORE MORE [A] — BANANARAMA
MORE MORE MORE [A] — Rachel STEVENS
MORE, MORE, MORE [B] — CARMEL
MORE PARTY POPS — Russ CONWAY
MORE THAN A FEELING — BOSTON
MORE THAN A LOVER — Bonnie TYLER
MORE THAN A WOMAN [A] — TAVARES
MORE THAN A WOMAN [A] — 911
MORE THAN A WOMAN [B] — AALIYAH (02)
MORE THAN EVER (COME PRIMA) [A] — Malcolm VAUGHAN
MORE THAN EVER (COME PRIMA) [A] — Robert EARL
MORE THAN I CAN BEAR — MATT BIANCO
MORE THAN I CAN SAY [A] — The CRICKETS
MORE THAN I CAN SAY [A] — Bobby VEE
MORE THAN I CAN SAY [A] — Leo SAYER
MORE THAN I NEEDED TO KNOW — SCOOCH
MORE THAN IN LOVE — Kate ROBBINS and BEYOND
MORE THAN LIKELY — PM DAWN featuring BOY GEORGE
MORE THAN LOVE [A] — Ken DODD
MORE THAN LOVE [B] — WET WET WET
MORE THAN ONE KIND OF LOVE — Joan ARMATRADING
MORE THAN PHYSICAL — BANANARAMA
MORE THAN THAT — BACKSTREET BOYS
MORE THAN THIS [A] — ROXY MUSIC
MORE THAN THIS [A] — EMMIE
MORE THAN THIS [B] — Peter GABRIEL
MORE THAN US (EP) — TRAVIS
MORE THAN WORDS — EXTREME
MORE THAN YOU KNOW — MARTIKA
THE MORE THEY KNOCK, THE MORE I LOVE YOU — Gloria D BROWN
MORE TO LIFE — Cliff RICHARD
MORE TO LOVE — VOLCANO
MORE TO THIS WORLD — BAD BOYS INC
THE MORE YOU IGNORE ME THE CLOSER I GET — MORRISSEY
THE MORE YOU LIVE, THE MORE YOU LOVE — A FLOCK OF SEAGULLS
MORGEN — Ivo ROBIC
MORNIN' — Al JARREAU
MORNING [A] — Val DOONICAN
MORNING [B] — WET WET WET
THE MORNING AFTER (FREE AT LAST) — STRIKE
MORNING AFTERGLOW — ELECTRASY
MORNING ALWAYS COMES TOO SOON — Brad CARTER
MORNING DANCE — SPYRO GYRA
MORNING GLORY — James and Bobby PURIFY
MORNING HAS BROKEN [A] — Cat STEVENS
MORNING HAS BROKEN [A] — Neil DIAMOND
MORNING HAS BROKEN [A] — Daniel O'DONNELL
THE MORNING OF OUR LIVES — Jonathan RICHMAN and The MODERN LOVERS
THE MORNING PAPERS — PRINCE and The NEW POWER GENERATION
MORNING SIDE OF THE MOUNTAIN — Donny and Marie OSMOND
MORNING WONDER — The EARLIES
MORNINGLIGHT — TEAM DEEP
MORNINGTOWN RIDE — The SEEKERS
THE MOST BEAUTIFUL GIRL — Charlie RICH
THE MOST BEAUTIFUL GIRL IN THE WORLD — SYMBOL (PRINCE) (94)
MOST GIRLS — PINK
MOST HIGH — Jimmy PAGE
MOST PRECIOUS LOVE — BLAZE presents UDA featuring Barbara TUCKER
THE MOST TIRING DAY — CECIL
MOTHER — DANZIG
MOTHER — M FACTOR
MOTHER AND CHILD REUNION — Paul SIMON
MOTHER DAWN — BLUE PEARL
MOTHER FIXATION — MINUTEMAN
MOTHER NATURE AND FATHER TIME — Nat 'King' COLE
MOTHER OF MINE — Neil REID
MOTHER UNIVERSE — SOUP DRAGONS
MOTHER-IN-LAW — Ernie K-DOE
MOTHERLAND-A-FRI-CA — TRIBAL HOUSE
MOTHERLESS CHILD — Eric CLAPTON
MOTHER'S TALK — TEARS FOR FEARS
MOTHERSHIP RECONNECTION — Scott GROOVES featuring PARLIAMENT / FUNKADELIC
THE MOTION OF LOVE — GENE LOVES JEZEBEL

20 July 2002	27 July 2002	3 August 2002	10 August 2002
ANYONE OF US (STUPID MISTAKE) Gareth Gates	ANYONE OF US (STUPID MISTAKE) Gareth Gates	ANYONE OF US (STUPID MISTAKE) Gareth Gates	COLOURBLIND Darius
BY THE WAY Red Hot Chili Peppers	BY THE WAY Red Hot Chili Peppers	BY THE WAY Red Hot Chili Peppers	THE RISING Bruce Springsteen

17 August 2002	24 August 2002	31 August 2002	7 September 2002
UK No.1 SINGLES			
COLOURBLIND Darius	ROUND ROUND Sugababes	CROSSROADS Blazin' Squad	THE TIDE IS HIGH (GET THE FEELING) Atomic Kitten
UK No.1 ALBUMS			
BY THE WAY Red Hot Chili Peppers	BY THE WAY Red Hot Chili Peppers	IMAGINE Eva Cassidy	A RUSH OF BLOOD TO THE HEAD Coldplay

MY JAMAICAN GUY — Grace JONES
MY KIND OF GIRL [A] — Matt MONRO
MY KIND OF GIRL [A] — Frank SINATRA
MY KINDA LIFE — Cliff RICHARD
MY KINGDOM — FUTURE SOUND OF LONDON
MY LAST NIGHT WITH YOU — The ARROWS
MY LIFE — Billy JOEL
MY LIFE IS IN YOUR HANDS — MELTDOWN
MY LITTLE BABY — Mike BERRY
MY LITTLE BROTHER — ART BRUT
MY LITTLE CORNER OF THE WORLD — Anita BRYANT
MY LITTLE GIRL [A] — The CRICKETS
MY LITTLE GIRL [B] — AUTUMN
MY LITTLE LADY — The TREMELOES
MY LITTLE ONE — MARMALADE
MY LOVE [A] — Petula CLARK
MY LOVE [B] — Paul McCARTNEY
MY LOVE [C] — Lionel RICHIE
MY LOVE [D] — Julio IGLESIAS featuring Stevie WONDER
MY LOVE [E] — LONDON BOYS
MY LOVE [F] — Mary J BLIGE
MY LOVE [G] — Kele LE ROC
MY LOVE [H] — WESTLIFE (00)
MY LOVE [I] — KLUSTER featuring Ron CARROLL
MY LOVE AND DEVOTION [A] — Doris DAY
MY LOVE AND DEVOTION [A] — Matt MONRO
MY LOVE FOR YOU — Johnny MATHIS
MY LOVE IS A FIRE — Donny OSMOND
MY LOVE IS ALWAYS — SAFFRON HILL featuring Ben ONONO
MY LOVE IS DEEP — Sara PARKER
MY LOVE IS FOR REAL [A] — Paula ABDUL featuring Ofra HAZA
MY LOVE IS FOR REAL [A] — STRIKE
MY LOVE IS GUARANTEED — SYBIL
MY LOVE IS LIKE ... WO — MYA
MY LOVE IS MAGIC — BAS NOIR
MY LOVE IS SO RAW — Alyson WILLIAMS featuring Nikki D
MY LOVE IS THE SHHH! — SOMETHIN' FOR THE PEOPLE featuring TRINA and TAMARA
MY LOVE IS WAITING — Marvin GAYE
MY LOVE IS YOUR LOVE — Whitney HOUSTON
MY LOVE LIFE — MORRISSEY
MY LOVER'S PRAYER [A] — Otis REDDING
MY LOVER'S PRAYER [B] — Alistair GRIFFIN
MY LOVIN' — EN VOGUE
MY MAGIC MAN — ROCHELLE
MY MAMMY — HAPPENINGS
MY MAN, A SWEET MAN — Millie JACKSON
MY MAN AND ME — Lynsey DE PAUL
MY MARIE — Engelbert HUMPERDINCK
MY MATE PAUL — David HOLMES
MY MELANCHOLY BABY [A] — Tommy EDWARDS
MY MELANCHOLY BABY [A] — CHAS and DAVE
MY MIND'S EYE — The SMALL FACES
MY MUM IS ONE IN A MILLION — Children of TANSLEY SCHOOL
MY MY MY — Armand VAN HELDEN
MY NAME IS — EMINEM
MY NAME IS JACK — MANFRED MANN
MY NAME IS NOT SUSAN — Whitney HOUSTON
MY NAME IS PRINCE — PRINCE and The NEW POWER GENERATION
MY NECK, MY BACK (LICK IT) — KHIA
MY OH MY [A] — SAD CAFE
MY OH MY [B] — SLADE
MY OH MY [C] — AQUA
MY OLD MAN'S A DUSTMAN — Lonnie DONEGAN and his Group (60)
MY OLD PIANO — Diana ROSS
MY ONE SIN — Nat 'King' COLE
MY ONE TEMPTATION — Mica PARIS
MY ONE TRUE FRIEND — Bette MIDLER
MY ONLY LOVE — Bob SINCLAR
MY OWN SUMMER (SHOVE IT) — DEFTONES
MY OWN TRUE LOVE — Danny WILLIAMS
MY OWN WAY — DURAN DURAN
MY OWN WORST ENEMY — LIT
MY PEACE OF HEAVEN — TEN CITY
MY PERFECT COUSIN — The UNDERTONES
MY PERSONAL POSSESSION — Nat 'King' COLE
MY PHILOSOPHY — BOOGIE DOWN PRODUCTIONS
MY PLACE — NELLY (04)
MY PLAGUE — SLIPKNOT
MY PRAYER [A] — The PLATTERS
MY PRAYER [A] — Gerry MONROE
MY PREROGATIVE [A] — Bobby BROWN
MY PREROGATIVE [A] — Britney SPEARS
MY PRETTY ONE — Cliff RICHARD
MY PUPPET PAL — TIGER
MY RECOVERY INJECTION — BIFFY CLYRO
MY REMEDY — Hinda HICKS
MY RESISTANCE IS LOW — Robin SARSTEDT
MY RISING STAR — NORTHSIDE
MY SACRIFICE — CREED
MY SALT HEART — HUE AND CRY
MY SENTIMENTAL FRIEND — HERMAN'S HERMITS
MY SEPTEMBER LOVE — David WHITFIELD
MY SHARONA — KNACK
MY SHIP IS COMING IN — The WALKER BROTHERS
MY SIDE OF THE BED — Susanna HOFFS
MY SIMPLE HEART — The THREE DEGREES
MY SISTER — Juliana HATFIELD
MY 16TH APOLOGY (EP) — SHAKESPEAR'S SISTER
MY SON JOHN — David WHITFIELD
MY SON, MY SON — Vera LYNN with Frank WEIR, his Saxophone, his Orchestra and Chorus (54)
MY SPECIAL ANGEL [A] — Bobby HELMS
MY SPECIAL ANGEL [A] — Malcolm VAUGHAN
MY SPECIAL CHILD — Sinead O'CONNOR
MY SPECIAL DREAM — Shirley BASSEY
MY SPIRIT — TILT
MY STAR — Ian BROWN
MY SUNDAY BABY — DALE SISTERS
MY SUPERSTAR — DIMESTARS
MY SWEET JANE — GUN
MY SWEET LORD — George HARRISON (71, 02)
MY SWEET ROSALIE — BROTHERHOOD OF MAN
MY TELEPHONE — COLDCUT
MY TIME — SOUVLAKI
MY TOOT TOOT — Denise LA SALLE
MY TOWN — GLASS TIGER
MY TRUE LOVE — Jack SCOTT
MY UKULELE — Max BYGRAVES
MY UNFINISHED SYMPHONY — David WHITFIELD
MY UNKNOWN LOVE — COUNT INDIGO
MY VISION — JAKATTA featuring SEAL
MY WAY [A] — Eddie COCHRAN
MY WAY [B] — Frank SINATRA
MY WAY [B] — Dorothy SQUIRES
MY WAY [B] — Elvis PRESLEY
MY WAY [B] — SEX PISTOLS
MY WAY [B] — Shane MacGOWAN
MY WAY [C] — LIMP BIZKIT
MY WAY OF GIVING IN — Chris FARLOWE
MY WAY OF THINKING — UB40
MY WEAKNESS IS NONE OF YOUR BUSINESS — EMBRACE
MY WHITE BICYCLE — NAZARETH
MY WOMAN'S MAN — Dave DEE
MY WORLD [A] — CUPID'S INSPIRATION
MY WORLD [B] — The BEE GEES
MY WORLD [C] — SECRET AFFAIR
MY WORLD OF BLUE — Karl DENVER
MYFANWY — David ESSEX
MYSTERIES OF LOVE — LA MIX
MYSTERIES OF THE WORLD — MFSB
MYSTERIOUS GIRL — Peter ANDRE (04)
MYSTERIOUS TIMES — SASH! featuring Tina COUSINS
MYSTERIOUS WAYS — U2
MYSTERY [A] — DIO
MYSTERY [B] — MYSTERY
MYSTERY GIRL [A] — Jess CONRAD
MYSTERY GIRL [B] — DUKES
MYSTERY LADY — Billy OCEAN
MYSTERY LAND (EP) [A] — Y-TRAXX
MYSTERY LAND [B] — Y-TRAXX featuring NEVE
MYSTERY SONG — STATUS QUO
MYSTERY TRAIN — Elvis PRESLEY
MYSTICAL MACHINE GUN — KULA SHAKER
MYSTIFY — INXS
MYZSTERIOUS MIZSTER JONES — SLADE
N DEY SAY — NELLY
NA NA HEY HEY KISS HIM GOODBYE [A] — STEAM
NA NA HEY HEY KISS HIM GOODBYE [A] — BANANARAMA
NA NA IS THE SADDEST WORD — The STYLISTICS
NA NA NA — Cozy POWELL
NADINE (IS IT YOU) — Chuck BERRY
NAGASAKI BADGER — DISCO CITIZENS
NAILS IN MY FEET — CROWDED HOUSE
NAIROBI — Tommy STEELE
NAIVE SONG — MIRWAIS
NAKASAKI EP (I NEED A LOVER TONIGHT) — Ken DOH
NAKED [A] — REEF
NAKED [B] — LOUISE
NAKED AND SACRED [A] — Chynna PHILLIPS
NAKED AND SACRED [A] — Maria NAYLER
NAKED EYE — LUSCIOUS JACKSON
NAKED IN THE RAIN — BLUE PEARL
NAKED LOVE (JUST SAY YOU WANT ME) — QUARTZ and Dina CARROLL
NAKED WITHOUT YOU — ROACHFORD
NAME AND NUMBER — CURIOSITY
THE NAME OF THE GAME — ABBA (77)
THE NAMELESS ONE — Wendy JAMES
NANCY BOY — PLACEBO
A NANNY IN MANHATTAN — LILYS
NAPOLEON — WOLFMAN
NAPPY LOVE — The GOODIES
NARCO TOURISTS — SLAM vs UNKLE
NARCOTIC INFLUENCE — EMPIRION
NASHVILLE BOOGIE — Bert WEEDON
NASHVILLE CATS — LOVIN' SPOONFUL
NASTRADAMUS — NAS
NASTY — Janet JACKSON
NASTY BREAKS — CLIPZ
NASTY GIRL — Inaya DAY
NASTY GIRLS — TWA
NATALIE'S PARTY — SHACK
NATHAN JONES [A] — The SUPREMES
NATHAN JONES [A] — BANANARAMA
NATIONAL EXPRESS — The DIVINE COMEDY
NATIVE BOY (UPTOWN) — ANIMAL NIGHTLIFE
NATIVE LAND — EVERYTHING BUT THE GIRL
NATIVE NEW YORKER [A] — ODYSSEY
NATIVE NEW YORKER [A] — BLACK BOX
NATURAL [A] — Bryan POWELL
NATURAL [B] — Peter ANDRE
NATURAL [C] — S CLUB 7
NATURAL BLUES — MOBY
NATURAL BORN BUGIE — HUMBLE PIE
NATURAL BORN KILLAZ — DR DRE and ICE CUBE
NATURAL HIGH [A] — BLOODSTONE
NATURAL HIGH [B] — Bitty McLEAN
NATURAL LIFE — NATURAL LIFE
NATURAL ONE — FOLK IMPLOSION
NATURAL SINNER — FAIR WEATHER
NATURAL THING — INNOCENCE
NATURAL WORLD — RODEO JONES
NATURE BOY [A] — Bobby DARIN
NATURE BOY [A] — George BENSON
NATURE BOY [A] — CENTRAL LINE
NATURE BOY [B] — Nick CAVE & The BAD SEEDS
NATURE OF LOVE — WATERFRONT
NATURE'S TIME FOR LOVE — Joe BROWN and The BRUVVERS
NAUGHTY CHRISTMAS (GOBLIN IN THE OFFICE) — FAT LES
NAUGHTY GIRL [A] — Holly VALANCE
NAUGHTY GIRL [B] — BEYONCÉ
NAUGHTY GIRLS (NEED LOVE TOO) — Samantha FOX featuring FULL FORCE
THE NAUGHTY LADY OF SHADY LANE [A] — The AMES BROTHERS
THE NAUGHTY LADY OF SHADY LANE [A] — Dean MARTIN
NAUGHTY NAUGHTY — John PARR
NAUGHTY NAUGHTY NAUGHTY — Joy SARNEY
THE NAUGHTY NORTH AND THE SEXY SOUTH — E-MOTION
NAZIS — Roger TAYLOR
NEANDERTHAL MAN — HOTLEGS
NEAR TO YOU — TEENAGE FANCLUB and JAD FAIR
NEAR WILD HEAVEN — R.E.M.
NEAR YOU — MIGIL FIVE
NEARER THAN HEAVEN — DELAYS
NEARLY LOST YOU — SCREAMING TREES
NECESSARY EVIL — BODY COUNT
NEED GOOD LOVE — TUFF JAM
NEED TO FEEL LOVED — REFLEKT featuring Delline BASS
NEED YOU TONIGHT — INXS
NEED YOUR LOVE SO BAD [A] — FLEETWOOD MAC
NEED YOUR LOVE SO BAD [A] — Gary MOORE
NEEDIN' U [A] — David MORALES
NEEDIN' U II [A] — David MORALES presents the FACE featuring Juliet ROBERTS
THE NEEDLE AND THE DAMAGE DONE — Neil YOUNG
NEEDLES AND PINS [A] — The SEARCHERS (64)
NEEDLES AND PINS [A] — SMOKIE
NEGASONIC TEENAGE WARHEAD — MONSTER MAGNET
NEGATIVE — MANSUN
NEGOTIATE WITH LOVE — Rachel STEVENS
NEHEMIAH — HOPE OF THE STATES
NEIGHBOR — UGLY KID JOE
NEIGHBOURHOOD [A] — SPACE
NEIGHBOURHOOD [B] — ZED BIAS
NEIGHBOURHOOD #3 (POWER OUT) — ARCADE FIRE
NEIGHBOURHOOD #2 (LAIKA) — ARCADE FIRE
NEIL JUNG — TEENAGE FANCLUB
NEITHER ONE OF US (WANTS TO BE THE FIRST TO SAY GOODBYE) — Gladys KNIGHT and The PIPS
NELLIE THE ELEPHANT — TOY DOLLS
NELSON MANDELA — The SPECIALS
NE-NE NA-NA NA-NA NU-NU — BAD MANNERS
NEON KNIGHTS — BLACK SABBATH
NEON LIGHTS — KRAFTWERK
NEPTUNE — INME
NERVOUS — MATT BIANCO
NERVOUS BREAKDOWN [A] — Carleen ANDERSON
NERVOUS BREAKDOWN [B] — SHRINK
NERVOUS SHAKEDOWN — AC/DC
NERVOUS WRECK — RADIO STARS
NESSAJA — SCOOTER
NESSUN DORMA [A] — Luciano PAVAROTTI
NESSUN DORMA FROM 'TURANDOT' [A] — Luis COBOS featuring Placido DOMINGO
NETHERWORLD — LSG
NEUROTICA — CUD
NEUTRON DANCE — POINTER SISTERS
NEVER [A] — HEART
NEVER [B] — HOUSE OF LOVE
NEVER [C] — JOMANDA
NEVER [D] — ELECTRAFIXION
NEVER 'AD NOTHIN' — ANGELIC UPSTARTS
NEVER AGAIN [A] — DISCHARGE
NEVER AGAIN [B] — The MISSION
NEVER AGAIN [C] — JC 001
NEVER AGAIN [D] — HAPPY CLAPPERS
NEVER AGAIN [E] — NICKELBACK
NEVER AGAIN (THE DAYS TIME ERASED) — CLASSIX NOUVEAUX
NEVER BE ANYONE ELSE BUT YOU — Ricky NELSON
NEVER BE THE SAME AGAIN — Melanie C / Lisa 'Left Eye' LOPES (00)
NEVER BEFORE — DEEP PURPLE
NEVER CAN SAY GOODBYE [A] — The JACKSON FIVE
NEVER CAN SAY GOODBYE [A] — Gloria GAYNOR
NEVER CAN SAY GOODBYE [A] — The COMMUNARDS
NEVER CAN SAY GOODBYE [A] — YAZZ
NEVER CAN TELL — I KAMANCHI
NEVER DO A TANGO WITH AN ESKIMO — Alma COGAN
NEVER DO YOU WRONG — Stephanie MILLS
NEVER DONE NOTHING LIKE THAT BEFORE — SUPERGRASS
NEVER ENDING SONG OF LOVE — The NEW SEEKERS
NEVER ENDING STORY — LIMAHL
NEVER ENOUGH [A] — JESUS JONES
NEVER ENOUGH [B] — The CURE
NEVER ENOUGH [C] — Boris DLUGOSCH featuring Roisin MURPHY
NEVER ENOUGH [D] — The OPEN
NEVER EVER — ALL SAINTS (98)
NEVER FELT LIKE THIS BEFORE — Shaznay LEWIS
NEVER FELT THIS WAY — HI-LUX
NEVER FORGET — TAKE THAT (95)

14 September 2002	21 September 2002	28 September 2002	5 October 2002
THE TIDE IS HIGH (GET THE FEELING) Atomic Kitten	THE TIDE IS HIGH (GET THE FEELING) Atomic Kitten	JUST LIKE A PILL Pink	THE LONG AND WINDING ROAD / SUSPICIOUS MINDS Will Young and Gareth Gates / Gareth Gates
A RUSH OF BLOOD TO THE HEAD Coldplay	FEELS SO GOOD Atomic Kitten	ILLUMINATION Paul Weller	ELVIS - 30 #1 HITS Elvis Presley

NEVER FOUND A LOVE LIKE THIS BEFORE — UPSIDE DOWN
NEVER GIVE UP — Monie LOVE
NEVER GIVE UP ON A GOOD THING — George BENSON
NEVER GIVE YOU UP — Sharon REDD
NEVER GOIN' DOWN — ADAMSKI and Jimi POLO
NEVER GOING NOWHERE — The BLUETONES
NEVER GONNA BE THE SAME — DANNY WILSON
NEVER GONNA CHANGE MY MIND — Joey LAWRENCE
NEVER GONNA COME BACK DOWN — BT
NEVER GONNA CRY AGAIN — EURYTHMICS
NEVER GONNA FALL IN LOVE AGAIN — DANA
NEVER GONNA GIVE YOU UP [A] — MUSICAL YOUTH
NEVER GONNA GIVE YOU UP [B] — Rick ASTLEY (87)
NEVER GONNA (GIVE YOU UP) [B] — FKW
NEVER GONNA GIVE YOU UP (WON'T LET YOU BE) — Patrice RUSHEN
NEVER GONNA LEAVE YOUR SIDE — Daniel BEDINGFIELD (03)
NEVER GONNA LET YOU GO [A] — Sergio MENDES
NEVER GONNA LET YOU GO [B] — Tina MOORE
NEVER GOODBYE — Karl DENVER
NEVER HAD A DREAM COME TRUE [A] — Stevie WONDER
NEVER HAD A DREAM COME TRUE [B] — S CLUB 7 (00)
NEVER HAD IT SO GOOD — TAKE 5
NEVER IN A MILLION YEARS — The BOOMTOWN RATS
NEVER KNEW LOVE [A] — Rick ASTLEY
NEVER KNEW LOVE [B] — Oleta ADAMS
NEVER KNEW LOVE [C] — NIGHTCRAWLERS featuring John REID
NEVER KNEW LOVE [D] — Stella BROWNE
NEVER KNEW LOVE LIKE THIS [A] — Alexander O'NEAL and CHERRELLE
NEVER KNEW LOVE LIKE THIS [A] — Pauline HENRY featuring Wayne MARSHALL
NEVER KNEW LOVE LIKE THIS BEFORE — Stephanie MILLS
NEVER LEAVE YOU - UH OOH, UH OOOH! — LUMIDEE
NEVER LEFT HIS HARDCORE — NRG
NEVER LET GO [A] — John BARRY ORCHESTRA
NEVER LET GO [B] — HYPER GO GO
NEVER LET GO [C] — Cliff RICHARD
NEVER LET HER SLIP AWAY [A] — Andrew GOLD
NEVER LET HER SLIP AWAY [A] — Trevor WALTERS
NEVER LET HER SLIP AWAY [A] — UNDERCOVER
NEVER LET ME DOWN — David BOWIE
NEVER LET ME DOWN AGAIN — DEPECHE MODE
NEVER LET YOU DOWN — HONEYZ
NEVER LET YOU GO — NEW KIDS ON THE BLOCK
NEVER LOOK BACK — DUMONDE
NEVER LOSE THAT FEELING — SWERVEDRIVER
NEVER LOSE YOUR SENSE OF WONDER — YETI
NEVER LOST HIS HARDCORE — NRG
NEVER MIND — Cliff RICHARD
NEVER MIND THE PRESENTS — The BARRON KNIGHTS
NEVER MISS THE WATER — Chaka KHAN and Me'Shell NDEGEOCELLO
NEVER MY LOVE — Sugar MINOTT
NEVER NEVER [A] — The ASSEMBLY
NEVER NEVER [B] — WARM JETS
NEVER NEVER GONNA GIVE YA UP [A] — Barry WHITE
NEVER, NEVER GONNA GIVE YOU UP [A] — Lisa STANSFIELD
NEVER NEVER LOVE — SIMPLY RED
NEVER, NEVER, NEVER (GRANDE, GRANDE, GRANDE) — Shirley BASSEY
NEVER ON SUNDAY [A] — CHAQUITO
NEVER ON SUNDAY [A] — Lynn CORNELL
NEVER ON SUNDAY [A] — Don COSTA
NEVER ON SUNDAY [A] — MAKADOPOULOS and his GREEK SERENADERS
NEVER ON SUNDAY [A] — MANUEL and his MUSIC OF THE MOUNTAINS
NEVER (PAST TENSE) — ROC PROJECT featuring Tina ARENA
NEVER REALLY WAS — Mario WINANS featuring LIL' FLIP
NEVER SAW A MIRACLE — Curtis STIGERS
NEVER SAY DIE [A] — BLACK SABBATH
NEVER SAY DIE [B] — MONKEY HANGERZ
NEVER SAY DIE (GIVE A LITTLE BIT MORE) — Cliff RICHARD
NEVER SAY GOODBYE — BON JOVI
NEVER STOP [A] — ECHO and The BUNNYMEN
NEVER STOP [B] — The BRAND NEW HEAVIES
NEVER SURRENDER — SAXON
NEVER TAKE ME ALIVE — SPEAR OF DESTINY
NEVER TEAR US APART — INXS
NEVER THERE — CAKE
NEVER TOO FAR — Mariah CAREY
NEVER TOO LATE — Kylie MINOGUE
NEVER TOO MUCH — Luther VANDROSS
NEVER TRUST A STRANGER — Kim WILDE
NEVER TURN AWAY — ORCHESTRAL MANOEUVRES IN THE DARK
NEVER TURN YOUR BACK ON MOTHER EARTH — SPARKS
NEVER UNDERSTAND — JESUS AND MARY CHAIN
NEVER WIN — FISCHERSPOONER
NEVERENDING — HALO
NEVERTHELESS — Frankie VAUGHAN
NEVERTHELESS (I'M IN LOVE WITH YOU) — The NEW SEEKERS
NEW — NO DOUBT
NEW AMSTERDAM — Elvis COSTELLO
NEW ANGER — Gary NUMAN
NEW BEGINNING [A] — Stephen GATELY
NEW BEGINNING [B] — PRECIOUS
NEW BEGINNING (MAMBA SEYRA) — BUCKS FIZZ
NEW BIRD — REEF
NEW BORN — MUSE
NEW DAWN — PROPHETS OF SOUND
NEW DAY [A] — Wyclef JEAN featuring BONO
A NEW DAY [B] — KILLING JOKE
A NEW DAY HAS COME — Celine DION
NEW DIMENSION — IMAGINATION
NEW DIRECTION — FREAKPOWER
NEW DIRECTION — S CLUB JUNIORS
NEW EMOTION — TIME FREQUENCY
A NEW ENGLAND — Kirsty MacCOLL
A NEW FASHION — Bill WYMAN
A NEW FLAME — SIMPLY RED
NEW GENERATION — SUEDE
NEW GRANGE — CLANNAD
NEW GUITAR IN TOWN — LURKERS
NEW HOME NEW LIFE — The ALARM
NEW KICKS — JOHANN
NEW KID IN TOWN — EAGLES
NEW KIND OF MEDICINE — Ultra NATÉ
NEW LIFE — DEPECHE MODE
NEW LIVE AND RARE (EP) — DEEP PURPLE
NEW LIVE AND RARE II (EP) — DEEP PURPLE
NEW LIVE AND RARE III (EP) — DEEP PURPLE
NEW MISTAKE — JELLYFISH
NEW MOON ON MONDAY — DURAN DURAN
NEW ORLEANS [A] — Gary 'US' BONDS
NEW ORLEANS [A] — Bern ELLIOTT and The FENMEN
NEW ORLEANS [A] — HARLEY QUINNE
NEW ORLEANS [A] — GILLAN
NEW POLICY ONE — TERRORVISION
THE NEW POLLUTION — BECK
NEW POWER GENERATION — PRINCE
NEW SENSATION — INXS
NEW SONG — Howard JONES
A NEW SOUTH WALES — The ALARM
NEW THING FROM LONDON TOWN — Gary NUMAN
NEW TOY — Lene LOVICH
NEW WAY, NEW LIFE — ASIAN DUB FOUNDATION
NEW WORLD IN THE MORNING — Roger WHITTAKER
NEW WORLD MAN — RUSH
NEW WORLD MAN (LIVE) — RUSH
NEW YEAR — SUGABABES
NEW YEARS DAY [A] — U2
NEW YEAR'S DUB [A] — MUSIQUE vs U2
NEW YORK AFTERNOON — MONDO KANE
NEW YORK CITY — T. REX
NEW YORK CITY BOY — PET SHOP BOYS
NEW YORK CITY COPS — The STROKES
NEW YORK EYES — NICOLE with Timmy THOMAS
NEW YORK GROOVE — HELLO
NEW YORK MINING DISASTER 1941 — The BEE GEES
NEW YORK, NEW YORK [A] — Gerard KENNY
NEW YORK NEW YORK [B] — Ryan ADAMS
NEW YORK UNDERCOVER (EP) — VARIOUS ARTISTS (Singles and EPs)
NEWBORN — ELBOW
NEWBORN FRIEND — SEAL
NEWS AT TEN — VAPORS
NEWS OF THE WORLD — The JAM
NEXT BEST SUPERSTAR — Melanie C
THE NEXT BIG THING — JESUS JONES
NEXT DOOR TO AN ANGEL — Neil SEDAKA
THE NEXT EPISODE — DR DRE featuring SNOOP DOGG
NEXT LEVEL — ILS
NEXT LIFETIME — Erykah BADU
THE NEXT TIME — Cliff RICHARD and The SHADOWS (63)
NEXT TIME YOU FALL IN LOVE — Reva RICE and Greg ELLIS
NEXT TO YOU — ASWAD
NEXT YEAR — FOO FIGHTERS
NHS (EP) — DJ Doc SCOTT
NIALL QUINN'S DISCO PANTS — A LOVE SUPREME
NICE GUY EDDIE — SLEEPER
NICE IN NICE — The STRANGLERS
NICE LEGS SHAME ABOUT HER FACE —MONKS
NICE 'N' EASY — Frank SINATRA
NICE 'N SLEAZY — The STRANGLERS
NICE 'N' SLOW — Freddie JACKSON
NICE ONE CYRIL — COCKEREL CHORUS
NICE AND SLOW [A] — Jesse GREEN
NICE & SLOW [B] — USHER
NICE WEATHER FOR DUCKS — LEMON JELLY
NIGHT [A] — The FOUR SEASONS
THE NIGHT [A] — INTASTELLA
THE NIGHT [B] — SCOOTER
THE NIGHT [C] — SOFT CELL
A NIGHT AT DADDY GEE'S — SHOWADDYWADDY
A NIGHT AT THE APOLLO LIVE! — Daryl HALL and John OATES featuring David RUFFIN and Eddie KENDRICK
NIGHT BIRDS — SHAKATAK
NIGHT BOAT TO CAIRO — MADNESS
THE NIGHT CHICAGO DIED — PAPER LACE
NIGHT CRAWLER — JUDAS PRIEST
NIGHT DANCING — Joe FARRELL
NIGHT FEVER [A] — FATBACK BAND
NIGHT FEVER [B] — The BEE GEES (78)
NIGHT FEVER [B] — Carol DOUGLAS
NIGHT FEVER [B] — Adam GARCIA
THE NIGHT FEVER MEGAMIX — UK MIXMASTERS
THE NIGHTFLY — BLANK & JONES
NIGHT GAMES — Graham BONNET
THE NIGHT HAS A THOUSAND EYES — Bobby VEE
NIGHT IN MOTION — CUBIC 22
NIGHT IN MY VEINS — The PRETENDERS
A NIGHT IN NEW YORK — Elbow BONES and The RACKETEERS
THE NIGHT IS YOUNG — Gary MILLER
NIGHT LADIES — CRUSADERS
NIGHT LIFE — David Lee ROTH
NIGHT LINE — Randy CRAWFORD
NIGHT MOVES — Bob SEGER and The SILVER BULLET BAND
NIGHT NURSE — SLY and ROBBIE featuring SIMPLY RED
NIGHT OF FEAR — The MOVE
NIGHT OF THE LIVING BASEHEADS — PUBLIC ENEMY
NIGHT OF THE LONG GRASS — The TROGGS
NIGHT OF THE VAMPIRE — MOONTREKKERS
NIGHT ON FIRE — VHS OR BETA
NIGHT OWL — Gerry RAFFERTY
NIGHT PORTER — JAPAN
THE NIGHT THE EARTH CRIED — GRAVEDIGGAZ
(THE NIGHT THE LIGHTS WENT OUT IN) MASSACHUSETTS — The BEE GEES (67)
THE NIGHT THE WINE AND THE ROSES — LIQUID GOLD
THE NIGHT THEY DROVE OLD DIXIE DOWN — Joan BAEZ
A NIGHT TO REMEMBER [A] — SHALAMAR
A NIGHT TO REMEMBER [A] — LIBERTY X
NIGHT TO REMEMBER [A] — 911
NIGHT TRAIN [A] — Buddy MORROW
NIGHT TRAIN [B] — VISAGE
NIGHT VISION — HELL IS FOR HEROES
THE NIGHT YOU MURDERED LOVE — ABC
NIGHTBIRD — CONVERT
NIGHTLIFE — KENICKIE
NIGHTMARE [A] — GILLAN
NIGHTMARE [B] — SAXON
NIGHTMARE [C] — KID UNKNOWN
NIGHTMARE [D] — BRAINBUG
NIGHTMARES — A FLOCK OF SEAGULLS
NIGHTRAIN — GUNS N' ROSES
NIGHTS IN WHITE SATIN [A] — The MOODY BLUES
NIGHTS IN WHITE SATIN [A] — The DICKIES
NIGHTS IN WHITE SATIN [A] — Elkie BROOKS
NIGHTS OF PLEASURE — LOOSE ENDS
NIGHTS ON BROADWAY — Candi STATON
NIGHTS OVER EGYPT — INCOGNITO
NIGHTSHIFT — The COMMODORES
NIGHTSWIMMING — R.E.M.
NIGHTTRAIN — PUBLIC ENEMY
THE NIGHTTRAIN — KADOC
NIKITA — Elton JOHN
NIKKE DOES IT BETTER — NIKKE? NICOLE!
NIMBUS — 808 STATE
9 AM (THE COMFORT ZONE) — LONDONBEAT
NINE MILLION BICYCLES — Katie MELUA
9PM (TILL I COME) — ATB (99)
NINE TIMES OUT OF TEN — Cliff RICHARD and The SHADOWS
9 TO 5 [A] — Sheena EASTON
9 TO 5 [B] — Dolly PARTON
9 TO 5 [C] — LADY SOVEREIGN
NINE WAYS — JDS
900 NUMBER — 45 KING
911 — Wyclef JEAN featuring Mary J BLIGE
911 IS A JOKE — PUBLIC ENEMY
977 — The PRETENDERS
19 — Paul HARDCASTLE (85)
1980 — ESTELLE
1985 — BOWLING FOR SOUP
1998 — BINARY FINARY
1999 [A] — PRINCE
1999 [B] — BINARY FINARY
1979 — SMASHING PUMPKINS
NINETEEN63 — NEW ORDER
1962 — GRASS-SHOW
NINETEENTH NERVOUS BREAKDOWN — The ROLLING STONES
19/2000 — GORILLAZ
90'S GIRL — BLACKGIRL
98.6 [A] — The BYSTANDERS
98.6 [A] — KEITH
95 — NASTY — W.A.S.P.
99 1/2 — Carol Lynn TOWNES
99.9°F — Suzanne VEGA
99 PROBLEMS — JAY-Z
99 RED BALLOONS — NENA (84)
NINETY-NINE WAYS — Tab HUNTER
96 TEARS [A] — ? (QUESTION MARK) and The MYSTERIANS
96 TEARS [A] — The STRANGLERS
92°F — POP WILL EAT ITSELF
'92 TOUR (EP) — MOTÖRHEAD
NIPPLE TO THE BOTTLE — Grace JONES
NITE AND DAY — Al B SURE!
NITE AND FOG — MERCURY REV
NITE KLUB — The SPECIALS
NITE LIFE — Kim ENGLISH
NITE NITE — KANO
NI-TEN-ICHI-RYU (TWO SWORDS TECHNIQUE) — PHOTEK
NITRO — PALE X
N-N-NINETEEN NOT OUT — COMMENTATORS
NO — Chuck D
NO ALIBIS — Eric CLAPTON
NO ARMS CAN EVER HOLD YOU — The BACHELORS
NO BLUE SKIES — Lloyd COLE
NO CHARGE [A] — JJ BARRIE (76)
NO CHANCE (NO CHARGE) [A] — Billy CONNOLLY
NO CHEAP THRILL — Suzanne VEGA
NO CHRISTMAS — The WEDDING PRESENT

12 October 2002	19 October 2002	26 October 2002	2 November 2002
UK No.1 SINGLES			
THE LONG AND WINDING ROAD / SUSPICIOUS MINDS Will Young and Gareth Gates / Gareth Gates	**THE KETCHUP SONG (ASEREJE)** Las Ketchup	**DILEMMA** Nelly featuring Kelly Rowland	**DILEMMA** Nelly featuring Kelly Rowland
UK No.1 ALBUMS			
ELVIS - 30 #1 HITS Elvis Presley	**FROM NOW ON** Will Young	**FROM NOW ON** Will Young	**ONE BY ONE** Foo Fighters

NO CLASS — MOTÖRHEAD
NO CLAUSE 28 — BOY GEORGE
NO CONVERSATION — VIEW FROM THE HILL
NO DIGGITY — BLACKSTREET featuring DR DRE
NO DISTANCE LEFT TO RUN — BLUR
NO DOUBT [A] — 702
NO DOUBT [B] — IMAJIN
NO DOUBT ABOUT IT — HOT CHOCOLATE
NO DREAM IMPOSSIBLE — LINDSAY
NO EDUCATION NO FUTURE (F**K THE CURFEW) — MOGWAI
NO ESCAPIN' THIS — The BEATNUTS
NO FACE, NO NAME, NO NUMBER — TRAFFIC
NO FEAR — The RASMUS
NO FLOW — Lisa ROXANNE
NO FOOL (FOR LOVE) — Hazell DEAN
NO FRONTS — DOG EAT DOG
NO GETTING OVER YOU — PARIS
NO GOOD — DA FOOL
NO GOOD ADVICE — GIRLS ALOUD
NO GOOD FOR ME — Bruce WAYNE
NO GOOD 4 ME — OXIDE & NEUTRINO
NO GOOD (START THE DANCE) — The PRODIGY
NO GOODBYES [A] — Curtis MAYFIELD
NO GOODBYES [B] — The SUBWAYS
NO GOVERNMENT — NICOLETTE
NO HIDING PLACE — Ken MACKINTOSH
NO HONESTLY — Lynsey DE PAUL
NO LAUGHING IN HEAVEN — GILLAN
NO LETTING GO — Wayne WONDER
NO LIES — S.O.S. BAND
NO LIMIT [A] — 2 UNLIMITED (93)
NO LIMITS [A] — BAKSHELF DOG
NO LOVE — Joan ARMATRADING
NO MAN'S LAND [A] — Gerard KENNY
NO MAN'S LAND [B] — Billy JOEL
(NO MATTER HOW HIGH I GET) I'LL STILL BE LOOKIN' UP TO YOU — Wilton FELDER
NO MATTER HOW I TRY — Gilbert O'SULLIVAN
NO MATTER WHAT [A] — BADFINGER
NO MATTER WHAT [B] — BOYZONE (98)
NO MATTER WHAT I DO — Will MELLOR
NO MATTER WHAT SIGN YOU ARE — Diana ROSS and The SUPREMES
NO MATTER WHAT THEY SAY — LIL' KIM
NO MATTER WHAT YOU DO — Benny BENASSI presents The BIZ
NO MEMORY — SCARLET FANTASTIC
NO MERCY — The STRANGLERS
NO MILK TODAY — HERMAN'S HERMITS
NO MORE [A] — The McGUIRE SISTERS
NO MORE [B] — UNIQUE 3
NO MORE [C] — RUFF ENDZ
NO MORE [D] — a1
NO MORE [E] — Roni SIZE featuring Beverley KNIGHT & DYNAMITE MC
NO MORE AFFAIRS — TINDERSTICKS
NO MORE ALCOHOL — SUGGS featuring Louchie LOU and Michie ONE
NO MORE (BABY I'MA DO RIGHT) — 3LW
NO MORE DRAMA — Mary J BLIGE
NO MORE HEROES — The STRANGLERS
NO MORE (I CAN'T STAND IT) — MAXX
NO MORE 'I LOVE YOU'S' [A] — LOVER SPEAKS
NO MORE 'I LOVE YOU'S' [A] — Annie LENNOX
NO MORE LIES — Gary NUMAN
NO MORE LONELY NIGHTS (BALLAD) — Paul McCARTNEY
(NO MORE) LOVE AT YOUR CONVENIENCE — Alice COOPER
NO MORE MR NICE GUY [A] — Alice COOPER
NO MORE MR NICE GUY [A] — MEGADETH
NO MORE RAINY DAYS — FREE SPIRIT
NO MORE TALK — DUBSTAR
NO MORE TEARS [A] — HOLLYWOOD BEYOND
NO MORE TEARS [B] — Jaki GRAHAM
NO MORE TEARS [C] — Ozzy OSBOURNE
NO MORE TEARS (ENOUGH IS ENOUGH) [A] — Barbra STREISAND and Donna SUMMER
NO MORE TEARS (ENOUGH IS ENOUGH) [A] — Jocelyn BROWN and Kym MAZELLE
NO MORE THE FOOL — Elkie BROOKS
NO MORE TOMORROWS — Paul JOHNSON
NO MORE TURNING BACK — GITTA
NO MULE'S FOOL — FAMILY
NO NEED — ALFIE
NO NO JOE — SILVER CONVENTION
NO, NO, NO [A] — Nancy NOVA
NO, NO, NO [B] — DESTINY'S CHILD
NO NO NO [C] — MANIJAMA featuring MUKUPA & L'IL T
NO, NOT NOW — HOT HOT HEAT
NO ONE [A] — Ray CHARLES
NO ONE [B] — 2 UNLIMITED
NO ONE BUT YOU [A] — Billy ECKSTINE
NO-ONE BUT YOU [B] — QUEEN
NO ONE CAN — MARILLION
NO ONE CAN BREAK A HEART LIKE YOU — Dave CLARK FIVE
NO ONE CAN LOVE YOU MORE THAN ME — Kym MAZELLE
NO ONE CAN MAKE MY SUNSHINE SMILE — The EVERLY BROTHERS
NO ONE CAN STOP US NOW — CHELSEA FC
NO ONE DRIVING — John FOXX
NO ONE ELSE COMES CLOSE — JOE
NO ONE GETS THE PRIZE — Diana ROSS
NO ONE IS INNOCENT — SEX PISTOLS
NO ONE IS TO BLAME — Howard JONES
NO ONE KNOWS — QUEENS OF THE STONE AGE
NO ONE LIKE YOU — SCORPIONS
NO ONE SPEAKS — GENEVA
NO ONE TO CRY TO — Ray CHARLES
NO ONE WILL EVER KNOW — Frank IFIELD
NO ONE'S DRIVING — Dave CLARKE
NO ORDINARY LOVE — SADE
NO ORDINARY MORNING — CHICANE
NO OTHER BABY [A] — Bobby HELMS
NO OTHER BABY [A] — Paul McCARTNEY
NO OTHER LOVE [A] — Ronnie HILTON (56)
NO OTHER LOVE [A] — Edmund HOCKRIDGE
NO OTHER LOVE [A] — The JOHNSTON BROTHERS
NO PANTIES — TRINA
NO PARTICULAR PLACE TO GO — Chuck BERRY
NO PIGEONS — SPORTY THIEVZ
NO PLACE TO HIDE — KORN
NO PROMISES — ICEHOUSE
NO RAIN — BLIND MELON
NO REGRETS [A] — Shirley BASSEY
NO REGRETS [B] — The WALKER BROTHERS
NO REGRETS [B] — Midge URE
NO REGRETS [C] — Robbie WILLIAMS
NO RELIGION — Van MORRISON
NO REST — NEW MODEL ARMY
NO SCRUBS — TLC
NO SELF CONTROL — Peter GABRIEL
NO SELL OUT — Malcolm X
NO SENSE — NEW MODEL ARMY
NO SLEEP NO NEED (EP) — VAULTS
NO SLEEP TILL BROOKLYN — BEASTIE BOYS
NO SLEEP TONIGHT — The FADERS
NO SON OF MINE — GENESIS
NO STONE UNTURNED — TRUTH
NO STRESS — CYCLEFLY
NO SUCH THING — John MAYER
NO SURPRISES — RADIOHEAD
NO SURRENDER — DEUCE
NO SURVIVORS — GBH
NO SWEAT '98 — NORTH AND SOUTH
NO TENGO DINERO — LOS UMBRELLOS
NO TIME — LIL' KIM featuring PUFF DADDY
NO TIME TO BE 21 — The ADVERTS
NO TIME TO CRY — SISTERS OF MERCY
NO TIME TO PLAY — GURU featuring DC LEE
NO TREND — KOOPA
NO WAY — FREAKPOWER
NO WAY BACK — ADONIS featuring 2 PUERTO RICANS, A BLACK MAN AND A DOMINICAN
NO WAY NO WAY — VANILLA
NO WAY OUT — Francesco ZAPPALA
NO WOMAN NO CRY [A] — Bob MARLEY & The WAILERS
NO WOMAN NO CRY [A] — LONDONBEAT
NO WOMAN, NO CRY [A] — The FUGEES
NO WORRIES — Simon WEBBE
NO WOW — The KILLS
THE NOBODIES — MARILYN MANSON
NOBODY [A] — Toni BASIL
NOBODY [B] — TONGUE 'N' CHEEK
NOBODY [C] — Shara NELSON
NOBODY [D] — Keith SWEAT
NOBODY BETTER — Tina MOORE
NOBODY BUT YOU — Gladys KNIGHT and The PIPS
NOBODY DOES IT BETTER — Carly SIMON
NOBODY ELSE [A] — Nick KAMEN
NOBODY ELSE [B] — TYRESE
NOBODY I KNOW — PETER and GORDON
NOBODY KNOWS [A] — Nik KERSHAW
NOBODY KNOWS [B] — Tony RICH PROJECT
NOBODY MADE ME — Randy EDELMAN
NOBODY MOVE NOBODY GET HURT — WE ARE SCIENTISTS
NOBODY NEEDS YOUR LOVE — Gene PITNEY
NOBODY TOLD ME — John LENNON
NOBODY WANTS TO BE LONELY — Ricky MARTIN and Christina AGUILERA
NOBODY WINS — Elton JOHN
NOBODY'S BUSINESS [A] — H2o
NOBODY'S BUSINESS [B] — PEACE BY PIECE
NOBODY'S CHILD [A] — Karen YOUNG
NOBODY'S CHILD [A] — TRAVELING WILBURYS
NOBODY'S DARLIN' BUT MINE — Frank IFIELD
NOBODY'S DIARY — YAZOO
NOBODY'S FOOL [A] — Jim REEVES
NOBODY'S FOOL [B] — HAIRCUT 100
NOBODY'S HERO — STIFF LITTLE FINGERS
NOBODY'S HOME — Avril LAVIGNE
NOBODY'S SUPPOSED TO BE HERE — Deborah COX
NOBODY'S TWISTING YOUR ARM — WEDDING PRESENT
NOCTURNE — T99
NOMANSLAND (DAVID'S SONG) — DJ SAKIN & FRIENDS
NOMZAMO (ONE PEOPLE ONE CAUSE) — LATIN QUARTER
NON HO L'ETA PER AMARTI — Gigliola CINQUETTI
NONE OF YOUR BUSINESS — SALT-N-PEPA
NONSTOP — WHITEY
(NONSTOPOPERATION) — DUST JUNKYS
NOOKIE — JAMESY P
NORA MALONE — Teresa BREWER
NORMAN — Carol DEENE
NORMAN BATES — LANDSCAPE
NORMAN 3 — TEENAGE FANCLUB
NORTH COUNTRY BOY — The CHARLATANS
NORTH, SOUTH, EAST, WEST — MARVIN and TAMARA
NORTH TO ALASKA — Johnny HORTON
NORTHERN LIGHTS — RENAISSANCE
NORTHERN LITES — SUPER FURRY ANIMALS
NORTHERN STAR — Melanie C
NOT A DRY EYE IN THE HOUSE — MEAT LOAF
NOT A JOB — ELBOW
NOT A MINUTE TOO SOON — VIXEN
NOT ABOUT US — GENESIS
NOT ALONE — Bernard BUTLER
NOT ANYONE — BLACK BOX
NOT AS A STRANGER — Frank SINATRA
NOT AT ALL — STATUS QUO
NOT ENOUGH? — Melanie WILLIAMS
NOT ENOUGH LOVE IN THE WORLD — CHER
NOT EVEN GONNA TRIP — HONEYZ
NOT EVERYONE — NINE BLACK ALPS
NOT FADE AWAY — The ROLLING STONES
NOT FOR ALL THE LOVE IN THE WORLD — The THRILLS
NOT FOR YOU — PEARL JAM
NOT GON' CRY — Mary J BLIGE
NOT GONNA GET US — t.A.T.u.
NOT IF YOU WERE THE LAST JUNKIE ON EARTH — The DANDY WARHOLS
NOT IN LOVE — ENRIQUE featuring KELIS
NOT ME, NOT I — Delta GOODREM
NOT NOW — BLINK-182
NOT NOW JOHN — PINK FLOYD
NOT OVER YET [A] — GRACE
NOT OVER YET 99 [A] — Planet PERFECTO featuring GRACE
NOT OVER YOU YET — Diana ROSS
NOT RESPONSIBLE — Tom JONES
NOT SLEEPING AROUND — NED'S ATOMIC DUSTBIN
NOT SO MANIC NOW — DUBSTAR
NOT SUCH AN INNOCENT GIRL — Victoria BECKHAM
NOT THAT KIND — ANASTACIA
NOT THE GIRL YOU THINK YOU ARE — CROWDED HOUSE
(NOT THE) GREATEST RAPPER — 1000 CLOWNS
NOT TODAY — Mary J. BLIGE featuring EVE
NOT TONIGHT — LIL' KIM
NOT TOO LATE FOR LOVE — Beverley KNIGHT
NOT TOO LITTLE NOT TOO MUCH — Chris SANDFORD
NOT UNTIL THE NEXT TIME — Jim REEVES
NOT WHERE IT'S AT — DEL AMITRI
NOTGONNACHANGE — SWING OUT SISTER
NOTHIN' — N.O.R.E.
NOTHIN' AT ALL — HEART
NOTHIN' BUT A GOOD TIME — POISON
NOTHIN' BUT A PARTY — TRUCE
NOTHIN' MY LOVE CAN'T FIX — Joey LAWRENCE
NOTHIN' PERSONAL — DUST JUNKYS
(NOTHIN' SERIOUS) JUST BUGGIN' — WHISTLE
NOTHIN' (THAT COMPARES 2 U) — The JACKSONS
NOTHIN' TO DO — Michael HOLLIDAY
NOTHING [A] — FRAZIER CHORUS
NOTHING [B] — FLUFFY
NOTHING [C] — A
NOTHING [D] — HOLDEN & THOMPSON
NOTHING AS IT SEEMS — PEARL JAM
NOTHING AT ALL — Luke SLATER
NOTHING 'BOUT ME — STING
NOTHING BUT GREEN LIGHTS — Tom VEK
NOTHING BUT LOVE — OPTIMYSTIC
NOTHING CAN CHANGE THIS LOVE — Bitty McLEAN
NOTHING CAN DIVIDE US — Jason DONOVAN
NOTHING CAN STOP ME — Gene CHANDLER
NOTHING CAN STOP US — SAINT ETIENNE
NOTHING COMES EASY — Sandie SHAW
NOTHING COMPARES 2 U [A] — Sinead O'CONNOR (90)
NOTHING COMPARES 2 U [A] — MXM
NOTHING ELSE MATTERS — METALLICA
NOTHING EVER HAPPENS — DEL AMITRI
NOTHING HAS BEEN PROVED [A] — Dusty SPRINGFIELD
NOTHING HAS BEEN PROVED [A] — STRINGS OF LOVE
NOTHING HURTS LIKE LOVE — Daniel BEDINGFIELD
NOTHING IN PARTICULAR — The BROTHERHOOD
NOTHING IS FOREVER — ULTRACYNIC
NOTHING IS REAL BUT THE GIRL — BLONDIE
NOTHING LASTS FOREVER — ECHO and The BUNNYMEN
NOTHING LEFT — ORBITAL
NOTHING LEFT TOULOUSE — SAD CAFE
NOTHING LESS THAN BRILLIANT — Sandie SHAW
NOTHING NATURAL — LUSH
NOTHING REALLY MATTERS — MADONNA
NOTHING RHYMED — Gilbert O'SULLIVAN
NOTHING SACRED – A SONG FOR KIRSTY — RUSSELL WATSON
NOTHING TO DECLARE — LAPTOP
NOTHING TO FEAR — Chris REA
NOTHING TO LOSE [A] — UK
NOTHING TO LOSE [B] — S EXPRESS
NOTHING WITHOUT ME — MANCHILD
NOTHING WRONG WITH YOU — FINN BROTHERS
NOTHING'S GONNA CHANGE MY LOVE FOR YOU — Glenn MEDEIROS (88)
NOTHING'S GONNA STOP ME NOW — Samantha FOX
NOTHING'S GONNA STOP US NOW — STARSHIP (87)
NOTHIN'S GONNA CHANGE — Labi SIFFRE
NOTORIOUS — DURAN DURAN
NOTORIOUS B.I.G. — NOTORIOUS B.I.G.
NOVELTY WAVES — BIOSPHERE
NOVEMBER RAIN — GUNS N' ROSES
NOVEMBER SPAWNED A MONSTER — MORRISSEY
NOVOCAINE FOR THE SOUL — EELS
NOW [A] — Al MARTINO
NOW [B] — Val DOONICAN
NOW [C] — DEF LEPPARD
NOW ALWAYS AND FOREVER — GAY DAD
NOW AND FOREVER — Richard MARX
NOW I KNOW WHAT MADE OTIS BLUE — Paul YOUNG
NOW I'M HERE — QUEEN
NOW IS THE TIME — Jimmy JAMES and The VAGABONDS
NOW IS TOMORROW — DEFINITION OF SOUND
NOW IT'S GONE — CHORDS
NOW IT'S ON — GRANDADDY

9 November 2002	16 November 2002	23 November 2002	30 November 2002
HEAVEN DJ Sammy and Yanou featuring Do	**UNBREAKABLE** Westlife	**DIRRTY** Christina Aguilera featuring Redman	**DIRRTY** Christina Aguilera featuring Redman
A NEW DAY AT MIDNIGHT David Gray	**ONE LOVE** Blue	**UNBREAKABLE – THE GREATEST HITS VOL.1** Westlife	**ESCAPOLOGY** Robbie Williams

NOW I'VE FOUND YOU — Sean MAGUIRE
NOW OR NEVER — Tom NOVY featuring LIMA
NOW THAT I OWN THE BBC — SPARKS
NOW THAT THE MAGIC HAS GONE — Joe COCKER
NOW THAT WE'VE FOUND LOVE [A] — THIRD WORLD
NOW THAT WE FOUND LOVE [A] — HEAVY D and The BOYZ
NOW THAT YOU LOVE ME — The ALICE BAND
NOW THAT YOU'VE GONE — MIKE and The MECHANICS
NOW THEY'LL SLEEP — BELLY
NOW THOSE DAYS ARE GONE — BUCKS FIZZ
NOW WE ARE FREE — GLADIATOR featuring IZZY
NOW WE'RE THRU — POETS
NOW YOU'RE GONE [A] — BLACK
NOW YOU'RE GONE [B] — WHITESNAKE
NOW YOU'RE IN HEAVEN — Julian LENNON
NOWHERE [A] — THERAPY?
NOWHERE [B] — LONGVIEW
NOWHERE AGAIN — SECRET MACHINES
NOWHERE FAST — MEAT LOAF
NOWHERE GIRL — B-MOVIE
NOWHERE LAND — CLUBHOUSE
NOWHERE MAN — THREE GOOD REASONS
NOWHERE TO RUN [A] — Martha REEVES and The VANDELLAS
NOWHERE TO RUN 2000 [A] — NU GENERATION
N-R-G — ADAMSKI
NU FLOW — BIG BROVAZ
NUCLEAR — Ryan ADAMS
NUCLEAR DEVICE (THE WIZARD OF AUS) — The STRANGLERS
NUCLEAR HOLIDAY — 3 COLOURS RED
NUFF VIBES EP — APACHE INDIAN
NUMB [A] — LINKIN PARK
NUMB [A] / ENCORE — JAY-Z / LINKIN PARK
#9 DREAM — John LENNON
THE NUMBER OF THE BEAST — IRON MAIDEN
NUMBER ONE [A] — EYC
NUMBER ONE [B] — A
NUMBER ONE [C] — PLAYGROUP
NUMBER 1 [D] — TWEENIES
NUMBER 1 [E] — EBONY DUBSTERS
NUMBER ONE [F] — John LEGEND
NUMBER 1 [G] — GOLDFRAPP
NUMBER ONE BLIND — VERUCA SALT
NUMBER ONE DEE JAY — GOODY GOODY
NUMBER ONE DOMINATOR — TOP
NUMBER ONE RAT FAN — Roland RAT SUPERSTAR
THE NUMBER ONE SONG IN HEAVEN — SPARKS
NUMBER ONE SPOT — LUDACRIS
NUMBERS — SOFT CELL
NUMERO UNO — STARLIGHT
NUNC DIMITTIS — Paul PHOENIX
NURSERY RHYMES — ICEBERG SLIMM
NURTURE — LFO
NUT ROCKER — B BUMBLE and The STINGERS (62)
NUTBUSH CITY LIMITS [A] — Ike and Tina TURNER
NUTBUSH CITY LIMITS [A] — Tina TURNER
NUTHIN' BUT A 'G' THANG — DR DRE
NWO — MINISTRY
NY EXCUSE — SOULWAX
NYC — INTERPOL
N.Y.C. (CAN YOU BELIEVE THIS CITY) — CHARLES and EDDIE
O — OMARION
O BABY — SIOUXSIE and The BANSHEES
O L'AMOUR [A] — DOLLAR
OH L'AMOUR [A] — ERASURE
O' MY FATHER HAD A RABBIT — Ray MOORE
O-O-O — ADRENALIN M.O.D.
O SUPERMAN — Laurie ANDERSON
OAKLAND STROKE — TONY TONI TONÉ
OBJECT OF MY DESIRE — Dana RAYNE
OBJECTION (TANGO) — SHAKIRA
OBJECTS IN THE REAR VIEW MIRROR MAY APPEAR CLOSER THAN THEY ARE — MEAT LOAF
OB-LA-DI OB-LA-DA [A] — BEDROCKS
OB-LA-DI, OB-LA-DA [A] — MARMALADE (69)
OBLIVION — TERRORVISION
OBLIVION (HEAD IN THE CLOUDS) (EP) — MANIX
OBLIVIOUS — AZTEC CAMERA
THE OBOE SONG — CLERGY
OBSESION (SI ES AMOR) — 3RD WISH
OBSESSED — 999
OBSESSION [A] — Reg OWEN
OBSESSION [B] — ANIMOTION
OBSESSION [C] — ARMY OF LOVERS
OBSESSION [D] — ULTRA-SONIC
OBSESSION [E] — TIESTO & JUNKIE XL
OBSESSION (NO ES AMOR) — Frankie J featuring BABY BASH
OBSESSIONS — SUEDE
OBSTACLE 1 — INTERPOL
OBVIOUS — WESTLIFE
THE OBVIOUS CHILD — Paul SIMON
OBVIOUSLY — McFLY (04)
OCEAN AVENUE — YELLOWCARD
OCEAN BLUE — ABC
OCEAN DEEP — Cliff RICHARD
OCEAN DRIVE — LIGHTHOUSE FAMILY
OCEAN OF ETERNITY — FUTURE BREEZE
OCEAN PIE — SHED SEVEN
OCEAN SPRAY — MANIC STREET PREACHERS
OCTOBER SWIMMER — JJ72
ODE TO BILLY JOE — Bobbie GENTRY
ODE TO BOY — Alison MOYET
ODE TO JOY (FROM BEETHOVEN'S SYMPHONY NO.9) — BBC CONCERT ORCHESTRA, BBC SYMPHONY CHORUS cond. Stephen JACKSON
ODE TO MY FAMILY — The CRANBERRIES
THE ODYSSEY — DRUMSOUND / Simon 'BASSLINE' SMITH
OF COURSE I'M LYING — YELLO
OF COURSE YOU CAN — SPEARHEAD
OFF ON HOLIDAY — SUGGS
OFF ON YOUR OWN (GIRL) — Al B SURE!
OFF THE HOOK — Jody WATLEY
OFF THE WALL [A] — Michael JACKSON
OFF THE WALL [A] — WISDOME
OFF 2 WORK — DIZZEE RASCAL
OFFICIAL SECRETS — M
OFFSHORE — CHICANE
OFFSHORE BANKING BUSINESS — MEMBERS
OH — CIARA featuring LUDACRIS
OH BABE, WHAT WOULD YOU SAY? — Hurricane SMITH
OH BABY — RHIANNA
OH BABY I ... — ETERNAL
(OH BABY MINE) I GET SO LONELY — FOUR KNIGHTS
OH BOY [A] — The CRICKETS
OH BOY [A] — MUD (75)
OH BOY [B] — FABULOUS BAKER BOYS
OH BOY [C] — CAM'RON
OH BOY (THE MOOD I'M IN) — BROTHERHOOD OF MAN
OH CAROL [A] — Neil SEDAKA
OH CAROL! [A] — Clint EASTWOOD and General SAINT
OH CAROL [B] — SMOKIE
OH CAROLINA — SHAGGY (93)
OH DIANE — FLEETWOOD MAC
OH FATHER — MADONNA
OH GIRL [A] — CHI-LITES
OH GIRL [A] — Paul YOUNG
OH, HAPPY DAY [A] — The JOHNSTON BROTHERS
OH HAPPY DAY [B] — Edwin HAWKINS SINGERS
OH HOW I MISS YOU — The BACHELORS
OH JIM — GAY DAD
OH JULIE — Shakin' STEVENS (82)
OH LA LA LA — 2 EIVISSA
OH LONESOME ME — Craig DOUGLAS
OH, LORI — ALESSI
OH LOUISE — JUNIOR
OH ME OH MY (I'M A FOOL FOR YOU BABY) — LULU
OH, MEIN PAPA — Eddie CALVERT (54)
OH MILLWALL — MILLWALL FC
OH MY GOD [A] — A TRIBE CALLED QUEST
OH MY GOD [B] — KAISER CHIEFS
OH MY GOSH — BASEMENT JAXX
OH MY PAPA (OH, MEIN PAPA) — Eddie FISHER
OH NO [A] — The COMMODORES
OH NO [B] — MOS DEF and Nate DOGG featuring Pharoahe MONCH
OH NO NOT MY BABY [A] — MANFRED MANN
OH! NO NOT MY BABY [A] — Rod STEWART
OH NO NOT MY BABY [A] — CHER
OH NO WON'T DO (EP) — CUD
OH-OH, I'M FALLING IN LOVE AGAIN — Jimmie RODGERS
OH PATTI (DON'T FEEL SORRY FOR LOVERBOY) — SCRITTI POLITTI
OH, PEOPLE — Patti LaBELLE
OH, PRETTY WOMAN [A] — Roy ORBISON (64)
OH PRETTY WOMAN [B] — Gary MOORE
OH ROMEO — Mindy McCREADY
OH SHEILA — READY FOR THE WORLD
OH THE GUILT — NIRVANA
OH U WANT MORE? — TY featuring Roots MANUVA
OH WELL [A] — FLEETWOOD MAC
OH WELL [A] — OH WELL
OH WHAT A CIRCUS — David ESSEX
OH! WHAT A DAY — Craig DOUGLAS
OH WHAT A FEELING — CHANGE
OH WHAT A NIGHT — CLOCK
OH WHAT A SHAME — Roy WOOD
OH! WHAT A WORLD — SISTER BLISS
OH WORLD — Paul RUTHERFORD
OH YEAH! [A] — Bill WITHERS
OH YEAH [B] — ASH
OH YEAH [C] — CAPRICE
OH YEAH [D] — Foxy BROWN
OH YEAH [E] — The SUBWAYS
OH YEAH, BABY — DWEEB
OH YEAH (ON THE RADIO) — ROXY MUSIC
OH YES! YOU'RE BEAUTIFUL — Gary GLITTER
OH YOU PRETTY THING — Peter NOONE
OHIO — UTAH SAINTS
OI! — PLATINUM 45 featuring MORE FIRE CREW
OK — BIG BROVAZ
OK? — Julie COVINGTON, Rula LENSKA, Charlotte CORNWELL and Sue JONES-DAVIES
OK FRED — Errol DUNKLEY
OKAY! — Dave DEE, DOZY, BEAKY, MICK and TICH
OL' MACDONALD — Frank SINATRA
OL' RAG BLUES — STATUS QUO
OLD [A] — DEXY'S MIDNIGHT RUNNERS
OLD [B] — MACHINE HEAD
OLD AND WISE — Alan PARSONS PROJECT
OLD BEFORE I DIE — Robbie WILLIAMS
THE OLD FASHIONED WAY (LES PLAISIRS DÉMODÉS) — Charles AZNAVOUR
OLD FLAMES — FOSTER and ALLEN
OLD FOLKS — A
OLD HABITS DIE HARD — Mick JAGGER and Dave STEWART
OLD MAN AND ME (WHEN I GET TO HEAVEN) — HOOTIE & The BLOWFISH
THE OLD MAN AND THE ANGEL — IT BITES
OLD OAKEN BUCKET — Tommy SANDS
THE OLD PAYOLA ROLL BLUES — Stan FREBERG
OLD PI-ANNA RAG — Dickie VALENTINE
OLD POP IN AN OAK — REDNEX
OLD RED EYES IS BACK — The BEAUTIFUL SOUTH
OLD RIVERS — Walter BRENNAN
THE OLD RUGGED CROSS — Ethna CAMPBELL
OLD SHEP — Clinton FORD
OLD SIAM SIR — Paul McCARTNEY
OLD SMOKEY — JOHNNY and The HURRICANES
THE OLD SONGS — Barry MANILOW
OLD TOWN — The CORRS
OLDER — George MICHAEL
OLDEST SWINGER IN TOWN — Fred WEDLOCK
OLE OLA (MULHER BRASILEIRA) — Rod STEWART
OLIVE TREE — Judith DURHAM
OLIVER'S ARMY — Elvis COSTELLO
OLYMPIAN — GENE
OLYMPIC — 808 STATE
THE OMD REMIXES EP — ORCHESTRAL MANOEUVRES IN THE DARK
OMEN — ORBITAL
THE OMEN — BELTRAM
OMEN III — MAGIC AFFAIR
ON — APHEX TWIN
ON A CAROUSEL — The HOLLIES
ON A CROWDED STREET — Barbara PENNINGTON
ON A DAY LIKE TODAY — Bryan ADAMS
ON A GOOD THING — C-SIXTY FOUR
ON A LITTLE STREET IN SINGAPORE — MANHATTAN TRANSFER
ON A MISSION — ALOOF
ON A NIGHT LIKE THIS — Kylie MINOGUE
ON A NOOSE — TOWERS OF LONDON
ON A RAGGA TIP — SL2
ON A ROPE — ROCKET FROM THE CRYPT
ON A SATURDAY NIGHT — Terry DACTYL and The DINOSAURS
ON A SLOW BOAT TO CHINA — Emile FORD and The CHECKMATES
ON A SUNDAY — Nick HEYWARD
ON A SUN-DAY — BENZ
ON AND ON [A] — ASWAD
ON AND ON [B] — LONGPIGS
ON & ON [C] — Erykah BADU
ON BENDED KNEE — BOYZ II MEN
ON EVERY STREET — DIRE STRAITS
ON FIRE [A] — T-CONNECTION
ON FIRE [B] — Tone LOC
ON FIRE [C] — Lloyd BANK$
ON HER MAJESTY'S SECRET SERVICE — PROPELLERHEADS
ON HORSEBACK — Mike OLDFIELD
ON MOTHER KELLY'S DOORSTEP — Danny LA RUE
ON MY KNEES — The 411 featuring GHOSTFACE KILLAH
ON MY MIND — FUTURESHOCK featuring Ben ONONO
ON MY OWN [A] — Patti LaBELLE and Michael McDONALD
ON MY OWN [B] — Craig McLACHLAN
ON MY OWN [C] — PEACH
ON MY RADIO — SELECTER
ON MY WAY [A] — MR FINGERS
ON MY WAY [B] — Mike KOGLIN
ON MY WAY HOME — ENYA
ON MY WORD — Cliff RICHARD
ON OUR OWN (FROM GHOSTBUSTERS II) — Bobby BROWN
ON POINT — HOUSE OF PAIN
ON SILENT WINGS — Tina TURNER
ON STAGE (EP) — Kate BUSH
ON STANDBY — SHED SEVEN
ON THE BEACH [A] — Cliff RICHARD and The SHADOWS
ON THE BEACH [B] — Chris REA
ON THE BEACH [B] — YORK
ON THE BEAT — B B and Q BAND
ON THE BIBLE — DEUCE
ON THE DANCEFLOOR — DJ DISCIPLE
ON THE HORIZON — Melanie C
ON THE INSIDE (THEME FROM 'PRISONER CELL BLOCK H') — Lynne HAMILTON
ON THE LEVEL — YOMANDA
ON THE MOVE — BARTHEZZ
ON THE NIGHT — PAT and MICK
ON THE ONE — LUKK featuring Felicia COLLINS
ON THE RADIO [A] — Donna SUMMER
ON THE RADIO [A] — Martine McCUTCHEON
ON THE RADIO (REMEMBER THE DAYS) — Nelly FURTADO
ON THE REBOUND — Floyd CRAMER (61)
ON THE ROAD AGAIN — CANNED HEAT
ON THE ROPES (EP) — The WONDER STUFF
ON THE ROSE — TIGER
ON THE RUN [A] — DE BOS
ON THE RUN [B] — OMC
ON THE RUN [C] — BIG TIME CHARLIE
ON THE RUN [D] — The CRESCENT
ON THE RUN [E] — Tillman UHRMACHER
ON THE STREET WHERE YOU LIVE [A] — Vic DAMONE (58)
ON THE STREET WHERE YOU LIVE [A] — David WHITFIELD
ON THE TOP OF THE WORLD — DIVA SURPRISE featuring Georgia JONES
ON THE TRAIL — PRIME MOVERS
ON THE TURNING AWAY — PINK FLOYD
ON THE WINGS OF A NIGHTINGALE — The EVERLY BROTHERS
ON THE WINGS OF LOVE — Jeffrey OSBORNE
ON WITH THE MOTLEY — Harry SECOMBE
ON YA WAY — HELICOPTER
ON YOUR OWN [A] — The VERVE
ON YOUR OWN [B] — BLUR
ONCE — GENEVIEVE
ONCE AGAIN [A] — CUD
1NCE AGAIN [A] — A TRIBE CALLED QUEST

7 December 2002	14 December 2002	21 December 2002	28 December 2002
UK No.1 SINGLES			
IF YOU'RE NOT THE ONE Daniel Bedingfield	**LOSE YOURSELF** Eminem	**SORRY SEEMS TO BE THE HARDEST WORD** Blue featuring Elton John	**SOUND OF THE UNDERGROUND** Girls Aloud
UK No.1 ALBUMS			
ESCAPOLOGY Robbie Williams	**ESCAPOLOGY** Robbie Williams	**ESCAPOLOGY** Robbie Williams	**ESCAPOLOGY** Robbie Williams

ONCE AROUND THE BLOCK —
BADLY DRAWN BOY
ONCE AROUND THE SUN — CAPRICE
ONCE BITTEN TWICE SHY [A] — Ian HUNTER
ONCE BITTEN TWICE SHY [B] —
Vesta WILLIAMS
ONCE I HAD A SWEETHEART — PENTANGLE
ONCE IN A LIFETIME — TALKING HEADS
ONCE IN A WHILE — The BLACK VELVETS
ONCE IN EVERY LIFETIME — Ken DODD
ONCE MORE — The ORB
ONCE THERE WAS A TIME — Tom JONES
ONCE UPON A DREAM — Billy FURY
ONCE UPON A LONG AGO — Paul McCARTNEY
ONCE UPON A TIME [A] —
Marvin GAYE and Mary WELLS
ONCE UPON A TIME [B] — Tom JONES
ONCE UPON A TIME [C] — The POGUES
ONCE UPON A TIME IN AMERICA —
The JEEVAS
ONCE YOU'VE TASTED LOVE — TAKE THAT
ONE [A] — METALLICA
ONE [B] — The BEE GEES
ONE [C] — U2
ONE [C] — Mica PARIS
ONE [C] — LIGHTHOUSE FAMILY
ONE [D] — Busta RHYMES featuring Erykah BADU
ONE [E] — JOY ZIPPER
ONE (EP) — MANSUN
THE ONE [A] — Elton JOHN
THE ONE [B] — BACKSTREET BOYS
THE ONE [C] — DEE DEE
THE ONE [D] — Cassius HENRY featuring FREEWAY
ONE & ONE —
Robert MILES featuring Maria NAYLER
ONE AND ONE IS ONE — MEDICINE HEAD
THE ONE AND ONLY [A] —
Gladys KNIGHT and The PIPS
THE ONE AND ONLY [B] —
Chesney HAWKES (91)
ONE ARMED SCISSOR — AT THE DRIVE-IN
ONE BETTER DAY — MADNESS
ONE BETTER WORLD — ABC
ONE BIG FAMILY E.P. — EMBRACE
ONE BROKEN HEART FOR SALE — Elvis PRESLEY
ONE BY ONE — CHER
ONE CALL AWAY — CHINGY featuring J WEAV
ONE COOL REMOVE —
Shawn COLVIN with Mary-Chapin CARPENTER
ONE DANCE WON'T DO — Audrey HALL
ONE DAY [A] — TYRREL CORPORATION
ONE DAY [B] — D MOB
ONE DAY AT A TIME [A] — Lena MARTELL (79)
ONE DAY AT A TIME [B] — The ALICE BAND
ONE DAY I'LL FLY AWAY — Randy CRAWFORD
ONE DAY IN YOUR LIFE [A] —
Michael JACKSON (81)
ONE DAY IN YOUR LIFE [B] — ANASTACIA
ONE DRINK TOO MANY — SAILOR
ONE FINE DAY [A] — CHIFFONS
ONE FINE DAY [B] — OPERA BABES
ONE FINE DAY [C] — JAKATTA
ONE FINE MORNING — Tommy HUNT
ONE FOOT IN THE GRAVE —
Eric IDLE featuring Richard WILSON
THE ONE FOR ME — JOE
ONE FOR SORROW — STEPS
ONE FOR THE MOCKINGBIRD — CUTTING CREW
ONE FOR THE MONEY — Horace BROWN
ONE FOR YOU, ONE FOR ME [A] —
Jonathan KING
ONE FOR YOU ONE FOR ME [A] — La BIONDA
ONE GIANT LOVE — CUD
ONE GIFT OF LOVE — DEAR JON
ONE GOODBYE IN TEN — Shara NELSON
ONE GREAT THING — BIG COUNTRY
ONE HEADLIGHT — WALLFLOWERS
ONE HEART — Celine DION
ONE HEART BETWEEN TWO — Dave BERRY
ONE HELLO — Randy CRAWFORD
ONE HORSE TOWN — The THRILLS
100 MILES AND RUNNIN' — NWA
100 MPH — EL PRESIDENTE
101 — Sheena EASTON
101 DAM-NATIONS — SCARLET PARTY
138 TREK — DJ ZINC
100% — Mary KIANI
100% PURE LOVE — Crystal WATERS

THE ONE I GAVE MY HEART TO — AALIYAH
THE ONE I LOVE [A] — R.E.M.
THE ONE I LOVE [B] — David GRAY
ONE IN A MILLION — AALIYAH
ONE IN TEN [A] — UB40
ONE IN TEN [A] — 808 STATE vs UB40
ONE INCH ROCK — T. REX
ONE KISS FROM HEAVEN — LOUISE
ONE LAST BREATH — CREED
ONE LAST KISS — J GEILS BAND
ONE LAST LOVE SONG —
The BEAUTIFUL SOUTH
ONE LOVE [A] — ATLANTIC STARR
ONE LOVE [B] — Pat BENATAR
ONE LOVE [C] — The STONE ROSES
ONE LOVE [D] — DR ALBAN
ONE LOVE [E] — The PRODIGY
ONE LOVE [F] — BLUE
ONE LOVE FAMILY — LIQUID
ONE LOVE IN MY LIFETIME — INNOCENCE
ONE LOVE — PEOPLE GET READY —
Bob MARLEY & The WAILERS
ONE LOVER AT A TIME — ATLANTIC STARR
ONE LOVER (DON'T STOP THE SHOW) — FORREST
ONE MAN — CHANELLE
ONE MAN ARMY — OUR LADY PEACE
ONE MAN BAND — Leo SAYER
ONE MAN IN MY HEART — HUMAN LEAGUE
ONE MAN WOMAN — Sheena EASTON
ONE MAN'S BITCH — PHOEBE ONE
ONE MIND, TWO HEARTS — PARADISE
ONE MINUTE MAN — Missy 'Misdemeanor'
ELLIOTT featuring LUDACRIS
ONE MIRROR TOO MANY — The BLACK CROWES
ONE MOMENT IN TIME —
Whitney HOUSTON (88)
ONE MORE — HAZIZA
ONE MORE CHANCE [A] — Diana ROSS
ONE MORE CHANCE [B] — Maxi PRIEST
ONE MORE CHANCE [C] — EYC
ONE MORE CHANCE [D] — MADONNA
ONE MORE CHANCE [E] — The ONE
ONE MORE CHANCE [F] — Michael JACKSON
ONE MORE CHANCE – STAY WITH ME —
NOTORIOUS B.I.G.
ONE MORE DANCE — Esther and Abi OFARIM
ONE MORE GOOD NIGHT WITH THE BOYS —
Tasmin ARCHER
ONE MORE NIGHT — Phil COLLINS
ONE MORE RIVER — LUCIANA
ONE MORE SATURDAY NIGHT — MATCHBOX
ONE MORE SUNRISE (MORGEN) —
Dickie VALENTINE
ONE MORE TIME [A] — WHYCLIFFE
ONE MORE TIME [B] — DAFT PUNK
ONE MORE TRY [A] — George MICHAEL
ONE MORE TRY [B] — Kristine W
ONE NATION — MASQUERADE
ONE NATION UNDER A GROOVE (PART 1) —
FUNKADELIC
ONE NIGHT [A] — Elvis PRESLEY (59, 05)
ONE NIGHT [A] — MUD
ONE NIGHT IN BANGKOK — Murray HEAD
ONE NIGHT IN HEAVEN — M PEOPLE
ONE NIGHT STAND [A] — LET LOOSE
ONE NIGHT STAND [B] — ALOOF
ONE NINE FOR SANTA —
Fogwell FLAX and The ANKLEBITERS
from FREEHOLD JUNIOR SCHOOL
ONE OF THE LIVING — Tina TURNER
ONE OF THE LUCKY ONES — Joan REGAN
ONE OF THE PEOPLE — ADAMSKI
ONE OF THESE DAYS — AMBASSADOR
ONE OF THESE NIGHTS — EAGLES
ONE OF THOSE NIGHTS — BUCKS FIZZ
ONE OF US [A] — ABBA
ONE OF US [B] — Joan OSBORNE
ONE OF US [C] — HELL IS FOR HEROES
ONE OF US MUST KNOW (SOONER OR LATER) —
Bob DYLAN
ONE ON ONE — Daryl HALL and John OATES
ONE PERFECT SUNRISE — ORBITAL
ONE PIECE AT A TIME — Johnny CASH
ONE REASON WHY — Craig McLACHLAN
ONE ROAD — LOVE AFFAIR
ONE RULE FOR YOU — AFTER THE FIRE
ONE SHINING MOMENT — Diana ROSS
ONE SHOT — The BROTHERHOOD

ONE SLIP — PINK FLOYD
ONE SMALL DAY — ULTRAVOX
ONE STEP — KILLAH PRIEST
ONE STEP AHEAD — Nik KERSHAW
ONE STEP AWAY — TAVARES
ONE STEP BEYOND... — MADNESS
ONE STEP CLOSER [A] — LINKIN PARK
ONE STEP CLOSER [B] — S CLUB JUNIORS
ONE STEP CLOSER (TO LOVE) — George McCRAE
ONE STEP FURTHER — BARDO
ONE STEP OUT OF TIME — Michael BALL
ONE STEP TOO FAR —
FAITHLESS featuring DIDO
ONE SWEET DAY —
Mariah CAREY and BOYZ II MEN
1 THING — AMERIE
1000 % — FATIMA MANSIONS
1000 YEARS (JUST LEAVE ME NOW) —
JUPITER ACE featuring SHEENA
ONE TO ANOTHER — The CHARLATANS
THE ONE TO CRY — ESCORTS
1 TO 1 RELIGION —
BOMB THE BASS featuring CARLTON
THE ONE TO SING THE BLUES — MOTÖRHEAD
ONE TONGUE — HOTHOUSE FLOWERS
ONE TRUE WOMAN — YAZZ
1, 2 STEP — CIARA featuring Missy ELLIOTT
1-2-3 [A] — Len BARRY
1-2-3 [B] — PROFESSIONALS
1-2-3 [C] —
Gloria ESTEFAN and MIAMI SOUND MACHINE
1-2-3 [D] — CHIMES
ONE, TWO, THREE [E] — Dina CARROLL
1-2-3 O'LEARY — Des O'CONNOR
1234 — MRS WOOD
1234 (SUMPIN' NEW) — COOLIO
ONE VISION — QUEEN
ONE VOICE — Bill TARMEY
ONE WAY — LEVELLERS
ONE WAY LOVE —
Cliff BENNETT and The REBEL ROUSERS
ONE WAY MIRROR — KINESIS
ONE WAY OUT — REID
ONE WAY TICKET [A] — ERUPTION
ONE WAY TICKET [A] — The DARKNESS
ONE WEEK — BARENAKED LADIES
ONE WILD NIGHT — BON JOVI
ONE WISH [A] — SHYSTIE
ONE WISH [B] — Ray J
ONE WOMAN — JADE
ONE WORD — Kelly OSBOURNE
THE ONES YOU LOVE — Rick ASTLEY
ONION SONG — Marvin GAYE
ONLY [A] — ANTHRAX
ONLY [B] — NINE INCH NAILS
ONLY A BOY — Tim BURGESS
ONLY CRYING — Keith MARSHALL
THE ONLY FLAME IN TOWN — Elvis COSTELLO
ONLY FOOLS (NEVER FALL IN LOVE) — SONIA
ONLY FOR A WHILE — TOPLOADER
ONLY FOR LOVE — LIMAHL
ONLY HAPPY WHEN IT RAINS — GARBAGE
ONLY HUMAN — Dina CARROLL
ONLY IF ... — ENYA
ONLY IN MY DREAMS — Debbie GIBSON
THE ONLY LIVING BOY IN NEW CROSS — CARTER
— THE UNSTOPPABLE SEX MACHINE
THE ONLY LIVING BOY IN NEW YORK (EP) —
EVERYTHING BUT THE GIRL
ONLY LOVE — Nana MOUSKOURI
ONLY LOVE CAN BREAK YOUR HEART [A] —
Elkie BROOKS
ONLY LOVE CAN BREAK YOUR HEART [A] —
MINT JULEPS
ONLY LOVE CAN BREAK YOUR HEART [A] —
SAINT ETIENNE
ONLY LOVE REMAINS — Paul McCARTNEY
ONLY LOVING DOES IT — GUYS and DOLLS
THE ONLY MAN ON THE ISLAND [A] —
Vic DAMONE
THE ONLY MAN ON THE ISLAND [A] —
Tommy STEELE
ONLY ME — HYPERLOGIC
ONLY ONE — Peter ANDRE
THE ONLY ONE [A] — TRANSVISION VAMP
THE ONLY ONE [B] — GUN
THE ONLY ONE [C] — THUNDER
THE ONLY ONE I KNOW — The CHARLATANS

ONLY ONE ROAD — Celine DION
ONLY ONE WOMAN — MARBLES
ONLY ONE WORD — PROPAGANDA
ONLY ONE WORD COMES TO MIND —
BIFFY CLYRO
THE ONLY RHYME THAT BITES —
MC TUNES versus 808 STATE
ONLY SAW TODAY – INSTANT KARMA — AMOS
ONLY SIXTEEN [A] — Sam COOKE
ONLY SIXTEEN [A] — Craig DOUGLAS (59)
ONLY SIXTEEN [A] — Al SAXON
ONLY TENDER LOVE — DEACON BLUE
ONLY THE HEARTACHES — Houston WELLS
ONLY THE LONELY (KNOW HOW I FEEL) [A] —
Roy ORBISON (60)
ONLY THE LONELY [A] — PRELUDE
ONLY THE LONELY [B] — T'PAU
ONLY THE LOOT CAN MAKE ME HAPPY —
R KELLY
ONLY THE MOMENT — Marc ALMOND
ONLY THE ONES WE LOVE — Tanita TIKARAM
ONLY THE STRONG SURVIVE [A] — Billy PAUL
ONLY THE STRONG SURVIVE [B] — DJ KRUSH
ONLY THE STRONGEST WILL SURVIVE —
HURRICANE #1
ONLY THE WOMEN KNOW — SIX CHIX
THE ONLY THING THAT LOOKS GOOD ON ME
IS YOU — Bryan ADAMS
ONLY THIS MOMENT — ROYKSOPP
ONLY TIME — ENYA
ONLY TIME WILL TELL [A] — ASIA
ONLY TIME WILL TELL [B] — TEN CITY
ONLY TO BE WITH YOU — ROACHFORD
ONLY U — ASHANTI
ONLY WANNA KNOW U COS URE FAMOUS —
OXIDE & NEUTRINO
THE ONLY WAY IS UP —
YAZZ and The PLASTIC POPULATION (88)
THE ONLY WAY OUT — Cliff RICHARD
ONLY WHEN I LOSE MYSELF — DEPECHE MODE
ONLY WHEN I SLEEP — The CORRS
ONLY WHEN YOU LEAVE — SPANDAU BALLET
ONLY WITH YOU —
CAPTAIN HOLLYWOOD PROJECT
ONLY WOMEN BLEED — Julie COVINGTON
ONLY YESTERDAY — The CARPENTERS
ONLY YOU [A] — HILLTOPPERS
ONLY YOU [A] — The PLATTERS
ONLY YOU [A] — Mark WYNTER
ONLY YOU [A] — Jeff COLLINS
ONLY YOU [A] — Ringo STARR
ONLY YOU [A] — John ALFORD
ONLY YOU (AND YOU ALONE) [A] — CHILD
ONLY YOU [B] — Teddy PENDERGRASS
ONLY YOU [C] — YAZOO
ONLY YOU [C] — The FLYING PICKETS (83)
ONLY YOU [D] — PRAISE
ONLY YOU [E] — PORTISHEAD
ONLY YOU [F] — CASINO
ONLY YOU CAN — FOX
ONLY YOU CAN ROCK ME — UFO
ONLY YOUR LOVE — BANANARAMA
ONWARD CHRISTIAN SOLDIERS —
Harry SIMEONE CHORALE
OO ... AH ... CANTONA — OO LA LA
OOCHIE WALLY —
QB FINEST featuring NAS and BRAVEHEARTS
OOCHY KOOCHY (F.U. BABY, YEAH YEAH) —
BABY FORD
OO-EEH BABY — STONEBRIDGE McGUINNESS
OOH! AAH! CANTONA — 1300 DRUMS
featuring the UNJUSTIFIED ANCIENTS OF MU
OOH AAH (G-SPOT) — Wayne MARSHALL
OOH-AH-AA (I FEEL IT) — EYC
OOH AAH ... JUST A LITTLE BIT — Gina G (96)
OOH BABY — Gilbert O'SULLIVAN
OOH BOY — ROSE ROYCE
OOH I DO — Lynsey DE PAUL
OOH I LIKE IT — Jonny L
OOH! LA! LA! [A] — Joe 'Mr Piano' HENDERSON
OOH LA LA [B] — COOLIO
OOH LA LA [C] — Rod STEWART
OOH LA LA [D] — WISEGUYS
OOH LA LA [E] — GOLDFRAPP
OOH LA LA LA — RED RAW featuring 007
OOH LA LA LA (LET'S GO DANCIN') —
KOOL and The GANG
OOH! MY SOUL — LITTLE RICHARD

4 January 2003	11 January 2003	18 January 2003	25 January 2003
SOUND OF THE UNDERGROUND Girls Aloud	**SOUND OF THE UNDERGROUND** Girls Aloud	**SOUND OF THE UNDERGROUND** Girls Aloud	**STOP LIVING THE LIE** David Sneddon
ESCAPOLOGY Robbie Williams	**LET GO** Avril Lavigne	**LET GO** Avril Lavigne	**LET GO** Avril Lavigne

OOH STICK YOU! — DAPHNE & CELESTE
OOH TO BE AH — KAJAGOOGOO
OOHHH BABY — Vida SIMPSON
OOH-WAKKA-DOO-WAKKA-DAY — Gilbert O'SULLIVAN
OOH WEE — Mark RONSON featuring GHOSTFACE KILLAH & Nate DOGG
OOH! WHAT A LIFE — The GIBSON BROTHERS
OOO LA LA LA — Teena MARIE
OOOH — DE LA SOUL featuring REDMAN
OOOIE, OOOIE, OOOIE — PRICKLY HEAT
OOOPS — 808 STATE featuring BJÖRK
OOOPS UP — SNAP!
OOPS! ... I DID IT AGAIN — Britney SPEARS (00)
OOPS (OH MY) — TWEET
OOPS UP SIDE YOUR HEAD [A] — The GAP BAND
OOPS UPSIDE YOUR HEAD [A] — DJ CASPER featuring The GAP BAND
007 [A] — Desmond DEKKER and The ACES
007 [A] — MUSICAL YOUTH
OPAL MANTRA — THERAPY?
OPEN ARMS [A] — Mariah CAREY
OPEN ARMS [B] — WILT
OPEN ARMS [C] — TINA
OPEN HEART ZOO — Martin GRECH
AN OPEN LETTER TO NYC — BEASTIE BOYS
OPEN ROAD [A] — Gary BARLOW
OPEN ROAD [B] — Bryan ADAMS
OPEN SESAME — Leila K
OPEN UP [A] — MUNGO JERRY
OPEN UP [B] — LEFTFIELD
OPEN UP THE RED BOX — SIMPLY RED
OPEN UP YOUR HEART — Joan REGAN
OPEN UP YOUR MIND (LET ME IN) — REAL PEOPLE
OPEN YOUR EYES [A] — BLACK BOX
OPEN YOUR EYES [B] — GOLDFINGER
OPEN YOUR HEART [A] — HUMAN LEAGUE
OPEN YOUR HEART [B] — MADONNA
OPEN YOUR HEART [C] — M PEOPLE
OPEN YOUR MIND [A] — 808 STATE
OPEN YOUR MIND [B] — USURA
THE OPERA HOUSE — Jack E MAKOSSA
THE OPERA SONG (BRAVE NEW WORLD) — Jurgen VRIES featuring CMC
OPERAA HOUSE — WORLD'S FAMOUS SUPREME TEAM
OPERATION BLADE (BASS IN THE PLACE) — PUBLIC DOMAIN
OPERATOR [A] — MIDNIGHT STAR
OPERATOR [B] — LITTLE RICHARD
OPIUM SCUMBAGZ — Olav BASOSKI
O.P.P. — NAUGHTY BY NATURE
OPPORTUNITIES (LET'S MAKE LOTS OF MONEY) — PET SHOP BOYS
OPPOSITES ATTRACT — Paula ABDUL
OPTIMISTIC — SOUNDS OF BLACKNESS
OPUS 40 — MERCURY REV
OPUS 17 (DON'T YOU WORRY 'BOUT ME) — The FOUR SEASONS
ORANGE BLOSSOM SPECIAL — The SPOTNICKS
ORANGE CRUSH — R.E.M.
THE ORANGE THEME — CYGNUS X
ORCHARD ROAD — Leo SAYER
ORCHESTRAL MANOEUVRES IN THE DARKNESS — DIFF'RENT DARKNESS
ORDINARY ANGEL — HUE AND CRY
ORDINARY DAY [A] — CURIOSITY
ORDINARY DAY [B] — Vanessa CARLTON
ORDINARY GIRL — Alison MOYET
ORDINARY LIVES — The BEE GEES
ORDINARY PEOPLE — John LEGEND
ORDINARY WORLD [A] — DURAN DURAN
ORDINARY WORLD [A] — AURORA
ORIGINAL — LEFTFIELD
ORIGINAL BIRD DANCE — ELECTRONICAS
ORIGINAL NUTTAH — UK APACHI with SHY FX
ORIGINAL PRANKSTER — The OFFSPRING
ORIGINAL SIN — Elton JOHN
ORIGINAL SIN (THEME FROM 'THE SHADOW') — Taylor DAYNE
ORINOCO FLOW — ENYA (88)
ORLANDO DAWN — LIQUID
ORPHEUS — ASH
ORVILLE'S SONG — Keith HARRIS and ORVILLE
OSCAR — SHACK
OSSIE'S DREAM (SPURS ARE ON THEIR WAY TO WEMBLEY) — TOTTENHAM HOTSPUR FA CUP FINAL SQUAD
THE OTHER MAN'S GRASS (IS ALWAYS GREENER) — Petula CLARK
THE OTHER SIDE [A] — AEROSMITH
THE OTHER SIDE [B] — David GRAY
THE OTHER SIDE [C] — Paul VAN DYK featuring Wayne JACKSON
THE OTHER SIDE OF LOVE — YAZOO
THE OTHER SIDE OF ME — Andy WILLIAMS
THE OTHER SIDE OF SUMMER — Elvis COSTELLO
THE OTHER SIDE OF THE SUN — Janis IAN
OTHER SIDE OF THE WORLD — KT TUNSTALL
THE OTHER SIDE OF YOU — MIGHTY LEMON DROPS
THE OTHER WOMAN, THE OTHER MAN — Gerard KENNY
OTHERNESS (EP) — COCTEAU TWINS
OTHERSIDE — RED HOT CHILI PEPPERS
OTHERWISE — MORCHEEBA
OUIJA BOARD OUIJA BOARD — MORRISSEY
OUR DAY WILL COME — RUBY and The ROMANTICS
OUR FAVOURITE MELODIES — Craig DOUGLAS
OUR FRANK — MORRISSEY
OUR GOAL — ARSENAL FC
OUR HOUSE — MADNESS
OUR KIND OF LOVE — HANNAH
OUR LAST SONG TOGETHER — Neil SEDAKA
OUR LIPS ARE SEALED [A] — GO-GO's
OUR LIPS ARE SEALED [A] — FUN BOY THREE
OUR LIVES — The CALLING
OUR LOVE — Elkie BROOKS
(OUR LOVE) DON'T THROW IT ALL AWAY — Andy GIBB
OUR RADIO ROCKS — ANT & DEC
OUR WORLD — BLUE MINK
OUT COME THE FREAKS — WAS (NOT WAS)
OUT COME THE FREAKS (AGAIN) — WAS (NOT WAS)
OUT DEMONS OUT — Edgar BROUGHTON BAND
OUT HERE — PENDULUM
OUT HERE ON MY OWN — Irene CARA
OUT IN THE DARK — LURKERS
OUT IN THE FIELDS — Gary MOORE and Phil LYNOTT
OUT IS THROUGH — Alanis MORISSETTE
OUT OF BREATH — Roni SIZE featuring RAHZEL
OUT OF CONTROL [A] — ANGELIC UPSTARTS
OUT OF CONTROL [B] — The ROLLING STONES
OUT OF CONTROL [C] — The CHEMICAL BROTHERS
OUT OF CONTROL (BACK FOR MORE) — DARUDE
OUT OF HAND — MIGHTY LEMON DROPS
OUT OF MY HEAD — MARRADONA
OUT OF MY HEART — BBMAK
OUT OF MY MIND [A] — Johnny TILLOTSON
OUT OF MY MIND [B] — DURAN DURAN
OUT OF OUR MINDS — CRACKOUT
OUT OF REACH [A] — VICE SQUAD
OUT OF REACH [B] — PRIMITIVES
OUT OF REACH [C] — GABRIELLE
OUT OF SEASON — The ALMIGHTY
OUT OF SIGHT [A] — BABYBIRD
OUT OF SIGHT [B] — SPIRITUALIZED
OUT OF SIGHT, OUT OF MIND — LEVEL 42
OUT OF SPACE — The PRODIGY
OUT OF TEARS — The ROLLING STONES
OUT OF THE BLUE [A] — Debbie GIBSON
OUT OF THE BLUE [B] — SYSTEM F
OUT OF THE BLUE [C] — Delta GOODREM
OUT OF THE SILENT PLANET — IRON MAIDEN
OUT OF THE SINKING — Paul WELLER
OUT OF THE STORM — INCOGNITO
OUT OF THE VOID — GRASS-SHOW
OUT OF THIS WORLD — Tony HATCH
OUT OF TIME [A] — Chris FARLOWE and The THUNDERBIRDS (66)
OUT OF TIME [A] — Dan McCAFFERTY
OUT OF TIME [A] — The ROLLING STONES
OUT OF TIME [B] — BLUR
OUT OF TOUCH [A] — Daryl HALL and John OATES
OUT OF TOUCH [A] — UNITING NATIONS
OUT OF TOWN — Max BYGRAVES
OUT OF YOUR MIND — TRUE STEPPERS and Dane BOWERS featuring Victoria BECKHAM
OUT ON THE FLOOR — Dobie GRAY
OUT THERE [A] — DINOSAUR JR
OUT THERE [B] — FRIENDS OF MATTHEW
OUT WITH HER — The BLOW MONKEYS
OUTA SPACE — Billy PRESTON
OUTTATHAWAY — The VINES
OUTDOOR MINER — WIRE
OUTERSPACE GIRL — The BELOVED
OUTLAW — OLIVE
OUTLINES — CLOR
OUTRAGEOUS — STIX 'N' STONED
OUTSHINED — SOUNDGARDEN
OUTSIDE [A] — OMAR
OUTSIDE [B] — George MICHAEL
OUTSIDE [C] — STAIND
OUT-SIDE [D] — The BETA BAND
OUTSIDE IN THE RAIN — Gwen GUTHRIE
OUTSIDE MY WINDOW — Stevie WONDER
OUTSIDE OF HEAVEN — Eddie FISHER (53)
OUTSIDE YOUR DOOR — The STANDS
OUTSIDE YOUR ROOM (EP) — SLOWDIVE
OUTSPOKEN - PART 1 — Ben WATT featuring ESTELLE / BABY BLAK
OUTSTANDING [A] — GAP BAND
OUTSTANDING [A] — Kenny THOMAS
OUTSTANDING [A] — Andy COLE
OUTTA CONTROL — 50 CENT featuring MOBB DEEP
OUTTA SPACE — MELLOW TRAX
OVER [A] — PORTISHEAD
OVER [B] — Lindsay LOHAN
OVER AND OVER [A] — Dave CLARK FIVE
OVER AND OVER [B] — JAMES BOYS
OVER AND OVER [C] — SHALAMAR
OVER AND OVER [D] — PLUX featuring Georgia JONES
OVER AND OVER [E] — Puff JOHNSON
OVER AND OVER [F] — NELLY featuring Tim McGRAW (05)
OVER AND OVER [G] — TURIN BRAKES
OVER MY HEAD — LIT
OVER MY SHOULDER [A] — MIKE and The MECHANICS
OVER MY SHOULDER [B] — I AM KLOOT
OVER RISING — The CHARLATANS
OVER THE EDGE — The ALMIGHTY
OVER THE HILLS AND FAR AWAY — Gary MOORE
OVER THE RAINBOW [A] - YOU BELONG TO ME (MEDLEY) — MATCHBOX
OVER THE RAINBOW [A] — Sam HARRIS
OVER THE RAINBOW [A] — Eva CASSIDY
OVER THE RIVER — Bitty McLEAN
OVER THE SEA — Jesse RAE
OVER THE WEEKEND — Nick HEYWARD
OVER THERE — BABE TEAM
OVER THERE (I DON'T CARE) — HOUSE OF PAIN
OVER TO YOU JOHN (HERE WE GO AGAIN) — JIVE BUNNY and The MASTERMIXERS
OVER UNDER SIDEWAYS DOWN — The YARDBIRDS
OVER YOU [A] — FREDDIE and The DREAMERS
OVER YOU [B] — ROXY MUSIC
OVER YOU [C] — Ray PARKER Jr
OVER YOU [D] — JUSTIN
OVER YOU [E] — Warren CLARKE featuring Kathy BROWN
OVERCOME — TRICKY
OVERDRIVE — DJ SANDY vs HOUSETRAP
OVERJOYED — Stevie WONDER
OVERKILL [A] — MOTÖRHEAD
OVERKILL [B] — MEN AT WORK
OVERLOAD [A] — SUGABABES
OVERLOAD [B] — VOODOO & SERANO
OVERNIGHT CELEBRITY — TWISTA
OVERPROTECTED — Britney SPEARS
OVERRATED — Siobhan DONAGHY
OVERTHROWN — LIBIDO
OVERTIME — LEVEL 42
OWNER OF A LONELY HEART [A] — YES
OWNER OF A LONELY HEART [A] — Max GRAHAM vs YES
OXBOW LAKES — The ORB
OXYGEN [A] — BLAGGERS I.T.A.
OXYGEN [B] — JJ72
OXYGEN [C] — Willy MASON
OXYGENE 8 — Jean-Michel JARRE
OXYGENE PART IV — Jean-Michel JARRE
OXYGENE 10 — Jean-Michel JARRE
OYE — Gloria ESTEFAN
OYE COMA VA — Tito PUENTE Jr and The LATIN RHYTHM featuring Tito PUENTE, INDIA and Cali ALEMAN
OYE MI CANTO (HEAR MY VOICE) — Gloria ESTEFAN
P MACHINERY — PROPAGANDA
PABLO — Russ CONWAY
PACIFIC — 808 STATE
PACIFIC MELODY — AIRSCAPE
PACK OF WOLVES — NIGHTBREED
PACK UP YOUR SORROWS — Joan BAEZ
PACKET OF PEACE — LIONROCK
PACKJAMMED (WITH THE PARTY POSSE) — STOCK AITKEN WATERMAN
PAC-MAN — POWERPILL
PACMAN — Ed RUSH & OPTICAL
THE PADDLE — DJ TOUCHE
PAGAN POETRY — BJÖRK
PAID IN FULL — Eric B and RAKIM
PAID MY DUES — ANASTACIA
PAIN [A] — Betty WRIGHT
PAIN [B] — JIMMY EAT WORLD
THE PAIN INSIDE — COSMIC ROUGH RIDERS
PAIN KILLER [A] — TURIN BRAKES
A PAIN THAT I'M USED TO — DEPECHE MODE
PAINKILLER [B] — JUDAS PRIEST
PAINT A PICTURE — MAN WITH NO NAME
PAINT IT BLACK [A] — The ROLLING STONES (66)
PAINT IT BLACK [A] — MODETTES
PAINT ME DOWN — SPANDAU BALLET
PAINT THE SILENCE — SOUTH
PAINT THE TOWN RED — DELIRIOUS?
PAINT YOUR TARGET — FIGHTSTAR
PAINTED MOON — The SILENCERS
PAINTER MAN [A] — CREATION
PAINTER MAN [A] — BONEY M
A PAIR OF BROWN EYES — The POGUES
PAISLEY PARK — PRINCE
PAL OF MY CRADLE DAYS — Ann BREEN
PALE BLUE EYES — Paul QUINN and Edwyn COLLINS
PALE MOVIE — SAINT ETIENNE
PALE RED — Jerry BURNS
PALE SHELTER — TEARS FOR FEARS
PALISADES PARK — Freddy CANNON
PALOMA BLANCA — George BAKER SELECTION
PAMELA PAMELA — Wayne FONTANA
PANAMA — VAN HALEN
THE PANDEMONIUM SINGLE — KILLING JOKE
PANDORA'S BOX [A] — PROCOL HARUM
PANDORA'S BOX [B] — ORCHESTRAL MANOEUVRES IN THE DARK
PANDORA'S KISS — LOUISE
PANIC — The SMITHS
PANIC ATTACK — The PADDINGTONS
PANIC ON — MADDER ROSE
PANINARO — PET SHOP BOYS
PANIS ANGELICUS — Anthony WAY
PANTHER PARTY — MAD MOSES
PAPA DON'T PREACH [A] — MADONNA (86)
PAPA DON'T PREACH [A] — Kelly OSBOURNE
PAPA LOVES MAMA — Joan REGAN
PAPA LOVES MAMBO — Perry COMO
PAPA OOM MOW MOW [A] — Gary GLITTER
PAPA OOM MOW MOW [A] — SHARONETTES
PAPA WAS A ROLLIN' STONE [A] — The TEMPTATIONS
PAPA WAS A ROLLING STONE [A] — WAS (NOT WAS)
PAPA'S GOT A BRAND NEW BAG — James BROWN
PAPA'S GOT A BRAND NEW PIGBAG [A] — PIGBAG
PAPA'S GOT A BRAND NEW PIGBAG [A] — SILENT UNDERDOG
PAPER DOLL [A] — Windsor DAVIES and Don ESTELLE
PAPER DOLL [B] — PM DAWN
PAPER HOUSE — FOOLPROOF
PAPER PLANE — STATUS QUO
PAPER ROSES [A] — Anita BRYANT
PAPER ROSES [A] — Maureen EVANS
PAPER ROSES [A] — KAYE SISTERS
PAPER ROSES [A] — Marie OSMOND
PAPER SUN — TRAFFIC
PAPER TIGER — Sue THOMPSON
PAPERBACK WRITER — The BEATLES (66)

1 February 2003	8 February 2003	15 February 2003	22 February 2003
UK No.1 SINGLES			
STOP LIVING THE LIE David Sneddon	ALL THE THINGS SHE SAID t.A.T.u.	ALL THE THINGS SHE SAID t.A.T.u.	ALL THE THINGS SHE SAID t.A.T.u.
UK No.1 ALBUMS			
JUSTIFIED Justin Timberlake	JUSTIFIED Justin Timberlake	SIMPLY DEEP Kelly Rowland	100TH WINDOW Massive Attack

PAPERCUT — LINKIN PARK
PAPERFACES — FEEDER
PAPILLON — N-JOI
PAPUA NEW GUINEA —
FUTURE SOUND OF LONDON
PARA MI — MOTIVATION
PARADE — WHITE and TORCH
PARADISE [A] — Frank IFIELD
PARADISE [B] — The STRANGLERS
PARADISE [C] — BLACK
PARADISE [D] — SADE
PARADISE [E] — BIRDLAND
PARADISE [F] — Diana ROSS
PARADISE [G] — Ralph FRIDGE
PARADISE [H] — KACI
PARADISE [I] — LL COOL J featuring AMERIE
PARADISE BIRD — Amii STEWART
PARADISE CITY [A] — GUNS N' ROSES
PARADISE CITY [A] — N-TRANCE
PARADISE LOST — The HERD
PARADISE SKIES — MAX WEBSTER
PARALYZED — Elvis PRESLEY
PARANOID [A] — BLACK SABBATH
PARANOID [A] — The DICKIES
PARANOID ANDROID — RADIOHEAD
PARANOIMIA — ART OF NOISE
PARDON ME — INCUBUS
PARIS BY AIR — TYGERS OF PAN TANG
PARIS IS ONE DAY AWAY — MOOD
PARIS MATCH — STYLE COUNCIL
PARISIENNE GIRL — INCOGNITO
PARISIENNE WALKWAYS — Gary MOORE
PARKLIFE — BLUR
PART OF THE PROCESS — MORCHEEBA
PART OF THE UNION — STRAWBS
PART TIME LOVE [A] —
Gladys KNIGHT and The PIPS
PART TIME LOVE [B] — Elton JOHN
PART-TIME LOVER — Stevie WONDER
PARTAY FEELING — B-CREW
PARTY — Elvis PRESLEY
THE PARTY — KRAZE
THE PARTY AIN'T OVER YET ... — STATUS QUO
PARTY ALL NIGHT [A] — KREUZ
PARTY ALL NIGHT [B] — MYTOWN
PARTY CRASHERS — RADIO 4
PARTY DOLL [A] — Buddy KNOX
PARTY DOLL [A] — JETS
PARTY FEARS TWO — ASSOCIATES
PARTY FOR TWO —
Shania TWAIN with Mark McGRATH
PARTY FOUR (EP) —
MAD JOCKS featuring JOCKMASTER B.A.
PARTY FREAK — CA$HFLOW
PARTY HARD [A] — PULP
PARTY HARD [B] — Andrew W.K.
PARTY IN PARIS — UK SUBS
PARTY LIGHTS — GAP BAND
PARTY PARTY — Elvis COSTELLO
PARTY PEOPLE (LIVE YOUR LIFE BE FREE) —
PIANOMAN
PARTY PEOPLE ... FRIDAY NIGHT — 911
PARTY POPS — Russ CONWAY
PARTY STARTER — Will SMITH
PARTY TIME — FATBACK BAND
PARTY TIME (THE GO-GO EDIT) — Kurtis BLOW
PARTY UP THE WORLD — D:REAM
PARTY ZONE —
DAFFY DUCK featuring the GROOVE GANG
PARTYLINE — BRASS CONSTRUCTION
PARTYMAN — PRINCE
THE PARTY'S OVER — Lonnie DONEGAN
PASADENA — TEMPERANCE SEVEN
PASILDA — AFRO MEDUSA
PASS AND MOVE (IT'S THE LIVERPOOL GROOVE)
— LIVERPOOL FC
PASS IT ON [A] — Bitty McLEAN
PASS IT ON [B] — The CORAL
PASS THAT DUTCH — Missy ELLIOTT
PASS THE COURVOISIER – PART II — Busta
RHYMES featuring P DIDDY & PHARRELL
PASS THE DUTCHIE — MUSICAL YOUTH (82)
PASS THE MIC — BEASTIE BOYS
PASS THE VIBES — DEFINITION OF SOUND
A PASSAGE TO BANGKOK — RUSH
THE PASSENGER [A] —
SIOUXSIE and The BANSHEES
THE PASSENGER [A] — Iggy POP

PASSENGERS — Elton JOHN
PASSIN' ME BY — The PHARCYDE
PASSING BREEZE — Russ CONWAY
PASSING STRANGERS [A] —
Billy ECKSTINE and Sarah VAUGHAN
PASSING STRANGERS [A] — Joe LONGTHORNE
PASSING STRANGERS [B] — ULTRAVOX
PASSION [A] — Rod STEWART
PASSION [B] — GAT DECOR
PASSION [C] — JON OF THE PLEASED WIMMIN
PASSION [D] — AMEN! UK
P.A.S.S.I.O.N. — RYTHM SYNDICATE
PASSION IN DARK ROOMS — MOOD
PASSION KILLER — ONE THE JUGGLER
THE PASSION OF LOVERS — BAUHAUS
PASSION RULES THE GAME — SCORPIONS
PASSIONATE FRIEND — TEARDROP EXPLODES
PAST, PRESENT AND FUTURE —
CINDY and The SAFFRONS
PAST THE MISSION — Tori AMOS
PATCHES — Clarence CARTER
PATHS — Robert MILES featuring Nina MIRANDA
PATHS OF PARADISE — Johnnie RAY
PATHWAY TO THE MOON — MN8
PATIENCE [A] — GUNS N' ROSES
PATIENCE [B] — Nerina PALLOT
PATIENCE OF ANGELS — Eddi READER
PATIO SONG — GORKY'S ZYGOTIC MYNCI
PATRICIA — Perez PRADO
THE PAY OFF — Kenny BALL and his JAZZMEN
PAY TO THE PIPER —
The CHAIRMEN OF THE BOARD
PAYBACK TIME —
DYSFUNCTIONAL PSYCHEDELIC WALTONS
THE PAYBACK MIX — James BROWN
PAYING THE PRICE OF LOVE — The BEE GEES
PCP — MANIC STREET PREACHERS
P.E. 2000 — PUFF DADDY
PEACE — Sabrina JOHNSTON
PEACE AND JOY — SOUNDSATION
PEACE + LOVEISM —
SON'Z OF A LOOP DA LOOP ERA
PEACE IN OUR TIME [A] — Elvis COSTELLO
PEACE IN OUR TIME [B] — BIG COUNTRY
PEACE IN OUR TIME [C] — Cliff RICHARD
PEACE IN THE WORLD — DON-E
PEACE ON EARTH — HI TENSION
PEACE ON EARTH — LITTLE DRUMMER BOY —
David BOWIE and Bing CROSBY
PEACE THROUGHOUT THE WORLD — Maxi PRIEST
PEACEFUL — Georgie FAME
PEACH — PRINCE
PEACHES [A] — The STRANGLERS
PEACHES [B] — DARTS
PEACHES [C] — PRESIDENTS OF
THE UNITED STATES OF AMERICA
PEACHES [D] — PINK GREASE
PEACHES & CREAM — 112
PEACOCK SUIT — Paul WELLER
PEAKIN' — BLEACHIN'
PEARL — CHAPTERHOUSE
PEARL IN THE SHELL — Howard JONES
PEARL RIVER — THREE 'N ONE presents
JOHNNY SHAKER featuring SERIAL DIVA
PEARL'S A SINGER — Elkie BROOKS
PEARL'S GIRL — UNDERWORLD
PEARLY-DEWDROPS' DROPS — COCTEAU TWINS
PEEK-A-BOO [A] — NEW VAUDEVILLE BAND
PEEK-A-BOO [B] — The STYLISTICS
PEEK-A-BOO [C] —
SIOUXSIE and The BANSHEES
THE PEEL SESSIONS (1ST JUNE 1982) —
NEW ORDER
PEGGY SUE — Buddy HOLLY
PEGGY SUE GOT MARRIED — Buddy HOLLY
PENNIES FROM HEAVEN — INNER CITY
PENNY & ME — HANSON
PENNY ARCADE — Roy ORBISON
PENNY LANE — The BEATLES
PENNY LOVER — Lionel RICHIE
PENTHOUSE AND PAVEMENT — HEAVEN 17
PEOPLE [A] — TYMES
PEOPLE [B] — INTASTELLA
PEOPLE [C] — ALFIE
PEOPLE ARE PEOPLE — DEPECHE MODE
PEOPLE ARE STILL HAVING SEX — LATOUR
PEOPLE ARE STRANGE —
ECHO and The BUNNYMEN

PEOPLE EVERYDAY —
ARRESTED DEVELOPMENT
PEOPLE GET READY [A] —
Jeff BECK and Rod STEWART
PEOPLE GET READY [A] — Rod STEWART
PEOPLE GET REAL — SAINT ETIENNE
PEOPLE HOLD ON —
COLDCUT featuring Lisa STANSFIELD
PEOPLE IN THA MIDDLE — SPEARHEAD
PEOPLE LIKE YOU AND PEOPLE LIKE ME —
The GLITTER BAND
PEOPLE OF LOVE — AMEN UK
PEOPLE OF THE SUN —
RAGE AGAINST THE MACHINE
PEPE [A] — Duane EDDY and The REBELS
PEPE [A] — Russ CONWAY
PEPPER — BUTTHOLE SURFERS
PEPPER BOX — PEPPERS
PEPPERMINT TWIST [A] —
Joey DEE and The STARLITERS
PEPPERMINT TWIST [B] —
Danny PEPPERMINT and The JUMPING JACKS
PER SEMPRE AMORE (FOREVER IN LOVE) —
LOLLY
PERFECT [A] — FAIRGROUND ATTRACTION (88)
PERFECT [B] — The LIGHTNING SEEDS
PERFECT [C] — ANT & DEC
PERFECT [D] — SMASHING PUMPKINS
PERFECT BLISS — BELLEFIRE
PERFECT DAY [A] — EMF
PERFECT DAY [B] — DURAN DURAN
PERFECT DAY [B] — Kirsty MacCOLL
PERFECT DAY [B] —
VARIOUS ARTISTS (Singles and EPs) (97)
PERFECT DAY [C] — SKIN
A PERFECT DAY ELISE — P J HARVEY
THE PERFECT DRUG — NINE INCH NAILS
PERFECT GENTLEMEN — Wyclef JEAN
THE PERFECT KISS — NEW ORDER
PERFECT LOVE — SIMPLY RED
PERFECT LOVESONG — The DIVINE COMEDY
PERFECT MOMENT — Martine McCUTCHEON (99)
PERFECT MOTION — SUNSCREEM
PERFECT PLACE — VOICE OF THE BEEHIVE
PERFECT SKIN — Lloyd COLE
PERFECT STRANGERS — DEEP PURPLE
PERFECT 10 — The BEAUTIFUL SOUTH
PERFECT TIMING — Kiki DEE
PERFECT WAY — SCRITTI POLITTI
PERFECT WORLD — Huey LEWIS and The NEWS
THE PERFECT YEAR — Dina CARROLL
PERFECTION —
Dannii MINOGUE & The SOUL SEEKERZ
PERFIDIA — The VENTURES
PERFUME — PARIS ANGELS
PERFUMED GARDEN — RAH BAND
PERHAPS LOVE —
Placido DOMINGO with John DENVER
PERMANENT TEARS — Eagle-Eye CHERRY
PERPETUAL DAWN — The ORB
PERRY MASON — Ozzy OSBOURNE
PERSEVERANCE — TERRORVISION
PERSONAL FEELING — AUDIOWEB
PERSONAL JESUS [A] — DEPECHE MODE
PERSONAL JESUS [A] — Johnny CASH
PERSONAL JESUS [A] — MARILYN MANSON
PERSONAL TOUCH — Errol BROWN
PERSONALITY [A] — Anthony NEWLEY
PERSONALITY [A] — Lloyd PRICE
PERSONALITY [B] — Eugene WILDE
PER-SO-NAL-LY — WIGAN'S OVATION
PERSUASION — Tim FINN
A PESSIMIST IS NEVER DISAPPOINTED —
THEAUDIENCE
PETAL — WUBBLE-U
PETER AND THE WOLF —
CLYDE VALLEY STOMPERS
PETER GUNN [A] —
Duane EDDY and The REBELS
PETER GUNN [A] — ART OF NOISE
PETER PIPER — RUN-DMC
PETITE FLEUR — Chris BARBER'S JAZZ BAND
PETS — PORNO FOR PYROS
THE PHANTOM OF THE OPERA —
Sarah BRIGHTMAN
PHASED (EP) — ALL ABOUT EVE
PHAT GIRLS — IGNORANTS
PHATT BASS — WARP BROTHERS

PHENOMENON — LL COOL J
PHEW WOW — FARMERS BOYS
PHILADELPHIA — Neil YOUNG
PHILADELPHIA FREEDOM — Elton JOHN
PHOBIA — FLOWERED UP
PHONE HOME — Jonny CHINGAS
PHOREVER PEOPLE — The SHAMEN
PHOTOGRAPH [A] — Ringo STARR
PHOTOGRAPH [B] — DEF LEPPARD
PHOTOGRAPH [C] — NICKELBACK
PHOTOGRAPH OF MARY — Trey LORENZ
PHUTURE 2000 — Carl COX
PHYSICAL — Olivia NEWTON-JOHN
PIANISSIMO — Ken DODD
PIANO IN THE DARK — Brenda RUSSELL
PIANO LOCO — DJ LUCK & MC NEAT
PIANO MEDLEY NO. 114 — Charlie KUNZ
PIANO PARTY — Winifred ATWELL
PICCADILLY PALARE — MORRISSEY
PICK A BALE OF COTTON — Lonnie DONEGAN
PICK A PART THAT'S NEW — STEREOPHONICS
PICK ME UP, I'LL DANCE — Melba MOORE
PICK UP THE PIECES [A] — HUDSON-FORD
PICK UP THE PIECES [B] —
AVERAGE WHITE BAND
PICKIN' A CHICKEN — Eve BOSWELL
PICKNEY GAL —
Desmond DEKKER and The ACES
PICNIC IN THE SUMMERTIME — DEEE-LITE
PICTURE OF YOU — BOYZONE
A PICTURE OF YOU —
Joe BROWN and The BRUVVERS
PICTURE THIS — BLONDIE
PICTURES IN THE DARK —
Mike OLDFIELD featuring Aled JONES,
Anita HEGERLAND and Barry PALMER
PICTURES OF LILY — The WHO
PICTURES OF MATCHSTICK MEN —
STATUS QUO
PICTURES OF YOU — The CURE
PIE JESU — Sarah BRIGHTMAN
PIECE BY PIECE [A] — Kenny THOMAS
PIECE BY PIECE [B] — FEEDER
PIECE OF MY HEART [A] — Sammy HAGAR
PIECE OF MY HEART [A] — SHAGGY
PIECE OF THE ACTION [A] — BUCKS FIZZ
PIECE OF THE ACTION [B] — MEAT LOAF
PIECES — MY VITRIOL
PIECES OF A DREAM [A] — INCOGNITO
PIECES OF A DREAM [A] — ANASTACIA
PIECES OF ICE — Diana ROSS
PIECES OF ME — Ashlee SIMPSON
PIED PIPER [A] — Crispian ST PETERS
PIED PIPER [A] — BOB and MARCIA
PIED PIPER (THE BEEJE) — Steve RACE
PIES — WILEY
PIHA — Ian POOLEY & MAGIK J
PILGRIMAGE — SOURMASH
PILLOW TALK — SYLVIA
PILLS AND SOAP — Elvis COSTELLO
PILOT OF THE AIRWAVES — Charlie DORE
PILOTS — GOLDFRAPP
PILTDOWN RIDES AGAIN — PILTDOWN MEN
P.I.M.P. — 50 CENT
PIN — The YEAH YEAH YEAHS
PINBALL — Brian PROTHEROE
PINBALL WIZARD [A] — The WHO
PINBALL WIZARD [A] — Elton JOHN
PINBALL WIZARD [A] — SEE ME, FEEL ME
(MEDLEY) — The NEW SEEKERS
PINCUSHION — ZZ TOP
PINEAPPLE HEAD — CROWDED HOUSE
PING ONE DOWN — GOMEZ
PING PONG — STEREOLAB
PINK — AEROSMITH
PINK CADILLAC — Natalie COLE
PINK CHAMPAGNE [A] — Shakin' STEVENS
PINK CHAMPAGNE [B] — RHYTHM ETERNITY
PINK FLOWER — DAISY CHAINSAW
THE PINK G.R.EASE — PINK GREASE
THE PINK PARKER EP —
Graham PARKER and The RUMOUR
PINK SUNSHINE — WE'VE GOT A
FUZZBOX AND WE'RE GONNA USE IT
PINKY BLUE — ALTERED IMAGES
THE PIONEERS — BLOC PARTY
PIPELINE [A] — CHANTAYS
PIPELINE [A] — Bruce JOHNSTON

1 March 2003	8 March 2003	15 March 2003	22 March 2003
ALL THE THINGS SHE SAID t.A.T.u.	BEAUTIFUL Christina Aguilera	BEAUTIFUL Christina Aguilera	SPIRIT IN THE SKY Gareth Gates featuring The Kumars
JUSTIFIED Justin Timberlake	COME AWAY WITH ME Norah Jones	COME AWAY WITH ME Norah Jones	COME AWAY WITH ME Norah Jones

PIPES OF PEACE — Paul McCARTNEY (84)
PIRANHA — TRIPPING DAISY
PISSING IN THE WIND — BADLY DRAWN BOY
PISTOL PACKIN' MAMA — Gene VINCENT
PISTOL WHIP — Joshua RYAN
PITCHIN' (IN EVERY DIRECTION) — HI-GATE
A PLACE CALLED HOME — PJ HARVEY
A PLACE IN THE SUN [A] — The SHADOWS
A PLACE IN THE SUN [B] — Stevie WONDER
PLACE IN YOUR HEART — NAZARETH
PLACE YOUR HANDS — REEF
PLACES — TILT
PLACES THAT BELONG TO YOU — Barbra STREISAND
PLAN A — The DANDY WARHOLS
PLAN B — DEXY'S MIDNIGHT RUNNERS
PLAN 9 — 808 STATE
PLAN OF MY OWN — DEEYAH
PLANET CARAVAN — PANTERA
PLANET CLAIRE — The B-52's
THE PLANET DANCE (MOVE YA BODY) — LIQUID OXYGEN
PLANET E — KC FLIGHTT
PLANET EARTH — DURAN DURAN
PLANET GIRL — ZODIAC MINDWARP and The LOVE REACTION
PLANET LOVE — DJ QUICKSILVER
THE PLANET OF LOVE — Carl COX
PLANET OF SOUND — PIXIES
PLANET ROCK [A] — Afrika BAMBAATAA
PLANET ROCK [A] — Paul OAKENFOLD presents Afrika BAMBAATAA
PLANET ROCK [A] — POWERS THAT BE
PLANET TELEX — RADIOHEAD
PLANET VIOLET — NALIN I.N.C.
PLANETARY SIT-IN (EVERY GIRL HAS YOUR NAME) — Julian COPE
THE PLASTIC AGE — The BUGGLES
PLASTIC DREAMS — JAYDEE
PLASTIC MAN — The KINKS
PLATINUM BLONDE — PRELUDE
PLATINUM POP — THIS YEAR'S BLONDE
PLAY — Jennifer LOPEZ
PLAY (EP) — RIDE
PLAY DEAD — BJÖRK
PLAY IT COOL — SUPER FURRY ANIMALS
PLAY ME LIKE YOU PLAY YOUR GUITAR — Duane EDDY and The REBELS
PLAY THAT FUNKY MUSIC [A] — WILD CHERRY
PLAY THAT FUNKY MUSIC [A] — VANILLA ICE
PLAY THAT FUNKY MUSIC [A] — THUNDER
PLAY THE GAME — QUEEN
PLAY THE HITS — HAL
PLAY TO WIN — HEAVEN 17
PLAYA HATA — LUNIZ
PLAYA NO MO' — LINA
PLAYAS GON' PLAY — 3LW
PLAYA'S ONLY — R KELLY featuring The GAME
PLAYAZ CLUB — RAPPIN' 4-TAY
PLAYED-A-LIVE (THE BONGO SONG) — SAFRI DUO
THE PLAYER — Carl COX
PLAYGROUND — Anita HARRIS
PLAYGROUND LOVE — AIR
PLAYGROUND SUPERSTAR — HAPPY MONDAYS
PLAYGROUND TWIST — SIOUXSIE and The BANSHEES
PLAYING WITH KNIVES — BIZARRE INC
PLAYING WITH THE BOY — TECHNICIAN 2
PLAYTHING — LINX
PLAYTIME — Roni SIZE
PLEASANT VALLEY SUNDAY — The MONKEES
PLEASE [A] — Elton JOHN
PLEASE [B] — U2
PLEASE [C] — Robin GIBB
PLEASE BE CRUEL — INSPIRAL CARPETS
PLEASE COME HOME FOR CHRISTMAS [A] — EAGLES
PLEASE COME HOME FOR CHRISTMAS [A] — BON JOVI
PLEASE DON'T ASK ABOUT BARBARA — Bobby VEE
PLEASE DON'T BE SCARED — Barry MANILOW
PLEASE DON'T FALL IN LOVE — Cliff RICHARD
PLEASE DON'T GO [A] — Donald PEERS
PLEASE DON'T GO [B] — DOUBLE YOU?
PLEASE DON'T GO [B] — KC and The SUNSHINE BAND
PLEASE DON'T GO [B] — KWS (92)
PLEASE DON'T GO [C] — NO MERCY
PLEASE DON'T MAKE ME CRY — UB40
PLEASE DON'T TEASE — Cliff RICHARD and The SHADOWS (60)
PLEASE DON'T TOUCH — Johnny KIDD and The PIRATES
PLEASE DON'T TURN ME ON — ARTFUL DODGER
PLEASE FORGIVE ME [A] — Bryan ADAMS
PLEASE FORGIVE ME [B] — David GRAY
PLEASE HELP ME, I'M FALLING — Hank LOCKLIN
PLEASE MR POSTMAN [A] — BACKBEAT BAND
PLEASE MR POSTMAN [A] — The CARPENTERS
PLEASE PLEASE ME [A] — The BEATLES
PLEASE PLEASE ME [A] — David CASSIDY
PLEASE RELEASE ME — Mike FLOWERS POPS
PLEASE SAVE ME — SUNSCREEM vs PUSH
PLEASE SIR — Martyn JOSEPH
PLEASE STAND UP — BRITISH SEA POWER
PLEASE STAY [A] — CRYIN' SHAMES
PLEASE STAY [B] — Kylie MINOGUE
PLEASE TELL HIM THAT I SAID HELLO — DANA
PLEASE (YOU GOT THAT ...) — INXS
PLEASE YOURSELF — BIG SUPREME
PLEASURE BOYS — VISAGE
PLEASURE DOME — SOUL II SOUL
PLEASURE FROM THE BASS — TIGA
PLEASURE LOVE — DE FUNK featuring F45
PLEASURE PRINCIPLE — Janet JACKSON
PLENTY GOOD LOVIN' — Connie FRANCIS
PLOWED — SPONGE
PLUG ME IN (TO THE CENTRAL LOVE LINE) — SCARLET FANTASTIC
PLUG IN BABY — MUSE
PLUG IT IN — BASEMENT JAXX featuring JC CHASEZ
PLUS — ECHELON
PLUSH — STONE TEMPLE PILOTS
THE POACHER — Ronnie LANE
POCKET CALCULATOR — KRAFTWERK
POEMS — NEARLY GOD
POETRY IN MOTION — Johnny TILLOTSON (61)
POGUETRY IN MOTION (EP) — The POGUES
POING — ROTTERDAM TERMINATION SOURCE
POINT OF NO RETURN [A] — NU SHOOZ
POINT OF NO RETURN [B] — CENTORY
POINT OF VIEW (SQUEEZE A LITTLE LOVIN) — MATUMBI
POINT OF VIEW — DB BOULEVARD
POISON [A] — Alice COOPER
POISON [B] — BELL BIV DEVOE
POISON [C] — The PRODIGY
POISON [D] — BARDOT
POISON [E] — GROOVE COVERAGE
POISON ARROW — ABC
POISON HEART — The RAMONES
POISON IVY [A] — The COASTERS
POISON IVY [A] — PARAMOUNTS
POISON IVY [A] — LAMBRETTAS
POISON STREET — NEW MODEL ARMY
POLICE AND THIEVES — Junior MURVIN
POLICE OFFICER — Smiley CULTURE
POLICE STATE — T-POWER
POLICEMAN SKANK ... (THE STORY OF MY LIFE) — AUDIOWEB
POLICY OF TRUTH — DEPECHE MODE
THE POLITICS OF DANCING — RE-FLEX
POLK SALAD ANNIE — Elvis PRESLEY
POLYESTERDAY — GUS GUS
PON DE REPLAY — RIHANNA
PON DE RIVER, PON DE BANK — ELEPHANT MAN
PONY — GINUWINE
PONY TIME — Chubby CHECKER
POODLE ROCKIN' — GORKY'S ZYGOTIC MYNCI
POOL HALL RICHARD — The FACES
POOR JENNY — The EVERLY BROTHERS
POOR LENO — RÖYKSOPP
POOR LITTLE FOOL — Ricky NELSON
POOR MAN'S SON — ROCKIN' BERRIES
POOR ME — Adam FAITH (60)
POOR MISGUIDED FOOL — STARSAILOR
THE POOR PEOPLE OF PARIS — Winifred ATWELL (56)
POP — 'N SYNC
POP COP — The GYRES
POP GO THE WORKERS — The BARRON KNIGHTS
POP GOES MY LOVE — FREEEZ
POP GOES THE WEASEL [A] — Anthony NEWLEY
POP GOES THE WEASEL [B] — 3RD BASS
POP IS DEAD — RADIOHEAD
POP LIFE — PRINCE
POP MUZIK [A] — M
POP MUZIK [A] — ALL SYSTEMS GO
THE POP SINGER'S FEAR OF THE POLLEN COUNT — The DIVINE COMEDY
POP THAT BOOTY — Marques HOUSTON featuring Jermaine "JD" DUPRI
POP YA COLLAR — USHER
POPCORN [A] — HOT BUTTER
POPCORN [A] — CRAZY FROG
POPCORN LOVE — NEW EDITION
POPPA JOE — The SWEET
POPPA PICCOLINO — Diana DECKER
POPPED!! — FOOL BOONA
POPS WE LOVE YOU — Diana ROSS, Marvin GAYE, Smokey ROBINSON and Stevie WONDER
POPSCENE — BLUR
POP!ULAR — Darren HAYES
PORCELAIN — MOBY
PORNOGRAPHY — CLIENT
PORT-AU-PRINCE — Winifred ATWELL and Frank CHACKSFIELD
PORTRAIT OF MY LOVE — Matt MONRO
PORTSMOUTH — Mike OLDFIELD
PORTUGUESE WASHERWOMAN — Joe 'Fingers' CARR
POSITIVE BLEEDING — URGE OVERKILL
POSITIVE EDUCATION — SLAM
POSITIVE TENSION — BLOC PARTY
A POSITIVE VIBRATION — BLACK BOX
POSITIVELY FOURTH STREET — Bob DYLAN
POSITIVITY [A] — SUEDE
POSITIVITY [B] — Stevie WONDER featuring Aisha MORRIS
POSSEE (I NEED YOU ON THE FLOOR) — SCOOTER
POSSESSED — VEGAS
POSSESSION — TRANSFER
POSSIBLY MAYBE — BJÖRK
POST MODERN SLEAZE — SNEAKER PIMPS
POSTCARD FROM HEAVEN — LIGHTHOUSE FAMILY
POSTMAN PAT — Ken BARRIE
POUNDCAKE — VAN HALEN
POUNDING — DOVES
POUR SOME SUGAR ON ME — DEF LEPPARD
POW! (FORWARD) — LETHAL BIZZLE
POW POW POW — FONTANA featuring Darryl D'BONNEAU
POWDER BLUE — ELBOW
THE POWER [A] — SNAP! (90)
THE POWER 96 [A] — SNAP! featuring EINSTEIN
THE POWER (OF BHANGRA) [A] — SNAP! vs MOTIVO
POWER [B] — NU COLOURS
THE POWER [B] — Monie LOVE
POWER AND THE GLORY — SAXON
THE POWER IS YOURS — REDSKINS
POWER OF A WOMAN — ETERNAL
THE POWER (OF ALL THE LOVE IN THE WORLD) — D:REAM
P.OWER OF A.MERICAN N.ATIVES — DANCE 2 TRANCE
THE POWER OF GOODBYE — MADONNA
POWER OF LOVE [A] — DEEE-LITE
POWER OF LOVE [B] — Q-TEX
POWER OF LOVE - LOVE POWER — Luther VANDROSS
THE POWER OF LOVE [A] — FRANKIE GOES TO HOLLYWOOD (84)
THE POWER OF LOVE [A] — Holly JOHNSON
THE POWER OF LOVE [B] — Celine DION
THE POWER OF LOVE [B] — FITS OF GLOOM featuring Lizzy MACK
THE POWER OF LOVE [B] — Jennifer RUSH (85)
THE POWER OF LOVE [C] — Huey LEWIS and The NEWS
POWER RANGERS — MIGHTY MORPH'N POWER RANGERS
POWER TO ALL OUR FRIENDS — Cliff RICHARD
POWER TO THE PEOPLE — John LENNON
POWERGEN (ONLY YOUR LOVE) — PKA
POWERLESS (SAY WHAT YOU WANT) — Nelly FURTADO
POWERTRIP — MONSTER MAGNET
THE POWER ZONE — TIME FREQUENCY
PRACTICE WHAT YOU PREACH — Barry WHITE
PRAISE — INNER CITY
PRAISE YOU — FATBOY SLIM (99)
PRANCE ON — Eddie HENDERSON
PRAY [A] — HAMMER
PRAY [B] — TAKE THAT (93)
PRAY [C] — Tina COUSINS
PRAY [D] — LASGO
PRAY [E] — SYNTAX
PRAY FOR LOVE — LOVE TO INFINITY
PRAYER — DISTURBED
PRAYER FOR THE DYING — SEAL
PRAYER FOR YOU — TEXAS
A PRAYER TO THE MUSIC — MARCO POLO
PRAYER TOWER — PARADISE ORGANISATION
PRAYING FOR TIME — George MICHAEL
PREACHER MAN — BANANARAMA
PREACHER, PREACHER — ANIMAL NIGHTLIFE
PRECIOUS [A] — The JAM (82)
PRECIOUS [B] — Annie LENNOX
PRECIOUS [C] — DEPECHE MODE
PRECIOUS HEART — TALL PAUL vs INXS
PRECIOUS ILLUSIONS — Alanis MORISSETTE
PRECIOUS LIFE — CRW presents VERONIKA
PRECIOUS TIME — Van MORRISON
PREDICTABLE — GOOD CHARLOTTE
PREGNANT FOR THE LAST TIME — MORRISSEY
PREPARE TO LAND — SUPERNATURALS
PRESENCE OF LOVE (LAUGHERNE) — The ALARM
PRESS — Paul McCARTNEY
PRESSURE [A] — SUNSCREEM
PRESSURE [B] — Billy OCEAN
PRESSURE [C] — DRIZABONE
THE PRESSURE — SOUNDS OF BLACKNESS
PRESSURE COOKER — G CLUB presents BANDA SONORA
PRESSURE DROP — Izzy STRADLIN'
PRESSURE ON — Roger TAYLOR
PRESSURE POINT ... — The ZUTONS
PRESSURE US — SUNSCREEM
PRETEND [A] — Nat 'King' COLE
PRETEND [A] — Alvin STARDUST
PRETEND BEST FRIEND — TERRORVISION
PRETEND WE'RE DEAD — L7
PRETENDER GOT MY HEART — ALISHA'S ATTIC
PRETENDER TO THE THRONE — The BEAUTIFUL SOUTH
PRETTIEST EYES — The BEAUTIFUL SOUTH
PRETTY BLUE EYES — Craig DOUGLAS
PRETTY BROWN EYES — Jim REEVES
PRETTY DEEP — Tanya DONELLY
PRETTY FLAMINGO — MANFRED MANN (66)
PRETTY FLY (FOR A WHITE GUY) — The OFFSPRING (99)
PRETTY GOOD YEAR — Tori AMOS
PRETTY GREEN EYES — ULTRABEAT
PRETTY IN PINK — PSYCHEDELIC FURS
PRETTY JENNY — Jess CONRAD
PRETTY LADY — SAVANA
PRETTY LITTLE ANGEL EYES [A] — Curtis LEE
PRETTY LITTLE ANGEL EYES [A] — SHOWADDYWADDY
PRETTY LITTLE BLACK-EYED SUSIE — Guy MITCHELL
PRETTY NOOSE — SOUNDGARDEN
PRETTY PAPER — Roy ORBISON
PRETTY THING — Bo DIDDLEY
PRETTY VACANT — SEX PISTOLS
PRETTY WOMAN — JUICY LUCY
THE PRICE OF LOVE [A] — The EVERLY BROTHERS
THE PRICE OF LOVE [A] — Bryan FERRY
PRICE TO PLAY — STAIND
PRICE YOU PAY — QUESTIONS
PRIDE (IN THE NAME OF LOVE) [A] — U2
PRIDE (IN THE NAME OF LOVE) [A] — C & C MUSIC FACTORY / CLIVILLES & COLE
PRIDE'S PARANOIA — FUTURESHOCK
PRIMAL SCREAM — MÖTLEY CRÜE
PRIMARY — The CURE
PRIMARY INSTINCT — SENSELESS THINGS
PRIMARY RHYMING — MC TUNES
PRIME MOVER [A] — RUSH

	29 March 2003	5 April 2003	12 April 2003	19 April 2003
UK No.1 SINGLES	SPIRIT IN THE SKY Gareth Gates featuring The Kumars	MAKE LUV Room 5 featuring Oliver Cheatham	MAKE LUV Room 5 featuring Oliver Cheatham	MAKE LUV Room 5 featuring Oliver Cheatham
UK No.1 ALBUMS	COME AWAY WITH ME Norah Jones	METEORA Linkin Park	ELEPHANT The White Stripes	ELEPHANT The White Stripes

PRIME MOVER [B] —
ZODIAC MINDWARP and The LOVE REACTION
PRIME TIME [A] — TUBES
PRIME TIME [B] — HAIRCUT 100
PRIME TIME [C] — MTUME
PRIMITIVE (THE WAY I TREAT YOU) —
AMBULANCE LTD
PRIMROSE LANE — Dickie PRIDE
THE PRINCE — MADNESS
A PRINCE AMONG ISLANDS (EP) —
CAPERCAILLIE
PRINCE CHARMING — ADAM and The ANTS (81)
PRINCE HARRY — SOHO DOLLS
PRINCE IGOR — Warren G
PRINCE OF DARKNESS — BOW WOW WOW
PRINCE OF PEACE — GALLIANO
PRINCES OF THE NIGHT — BLAST featuring VDC
PRINCESS IN RAGS — Gene PITNEY
PRINCESS OF THE NIGHT — SAXON
PRINCIPAL'S OFFICE — YOUNG MC
PRINCIPLES OF LUST — ENIGMA
PRISONER — ALL BLUE
THE PRISONER — FAB
PRISONER OF LOVE [A] — SPEAR OF DESTINY
PRISONER OF LOVE [B] — Millie SCOTT
A PRISONER OF THE PAST — PREFAB SPROUT
PRIVATE DANCER — Tina TURNER
PRIVATE EMOTION —
Ricky MARTIN featuring MEJA
PRIVATE EYE — ALKALINE TRIO
PRIVATE EYES — Daryl HALL and John OATES
PRIVATE INVESTIGATIONS — DIRE STRAITS
PRIVATE LIFE — Grace JONES
PRIVATE NUMBER [A] — William BELL
PRIVATE NUMBER [A] — 911
PRIVATE PARTY —
Wally JUMP Jr and The CRIMINAL ELEMENT
PRIVILEGE (SET ME FREE) —
Patti SMITH GROUP
PRIX CHOC REMIXES — Etienne DE CRECY
PRIZE OF GOLD — Joan REGAN
PROBABLY A ROBBERY —
RENEGADE SOUNDWAVE
PROBLEM IS —
DUB PISTOLS featuring Terry HALL
PROBLEMS — The EVERLY BROTHERS
PROCESS OF ELIMINATION — Eric GABLE
PROCESSED BEATS — KASABIAN
PROCESSION — NEW ORDER
PRODIGAL BLUES — Billy IDOL
PRODIGAL SON — STEEL PULSE
PRODUCT OF THE WORKING CLASS —
LITTLE ANGELS
PROFESSIONAL WIDOW (IT'S GOT TO BE BIG) —
Tori AMOS (97)
PROFIT IN PEACE — OCEAN COLOUR SCENE
PROFOUNDLY IN LOVE WITH PANDORA —
Ian DURY and The BLOCKHEADS
PROFOUNDLY YOURS — HUE AND CRY
PRO-GEN — The SHAMEN
THE PROGRAM — David MORALES
PROMISE — DELIRIOUS?
A PROMISE — ECHO and The BUNNYMEN
THE PROMISE [A] — ARCADIA
THE PROMISE [B] — WHEN IN ROME
THE PROMISE [C] — Michael NYMAN
THE PROMISE [D] — ESSENCE
PROMISE ME — Beverley CRAVEN
THE PROMISE OF A NEW DAY — Paula ABDUL
THE PROMISE YOU MADE — COCK ROBIN
PROMISED LAND [A] — Chuck BERRY
PROMISED LAND [A] — Elvis PRESLEY
PROMISED LAND [B] — Joe SMOOTH
PROMISED LAND [B] — STYLE COUNCIL
PROMISED YOU A MIRACLE — SIMPLE MINDS
PROMISES [A] — Ken DODD
PROMISES [B] — Eric CLAPTON
PROMISES [C] — The BUZZCOCKS
PROMISES [D] — BASIA
PROMISES [E] — TAKE THAT
PROMISES [F] — PARIS RED
PROMISES [G] — The CRANBERRIES
PROMISES [H] — DEF LEPPARD
PROMISES PROMISES —
The COOPER TEMPLE CLAUSE
PROPER CRIMBO — BO SELECTA
PROPHASE — TRANSA
THE PROPHET — CJ BOLLAND
PROTECT YOUR MIND (FOR THE LOVE OF A
PRINCESS) — DJ SAKIN & FRIENDS
PROTECTION — MASSIVE ATTACK
PROUD — Heather SMALL
PROUD MARY [A] — CHECKMATES LTD
PROUD MARY [A] —
CREEDENCE CLEARWATER REVIVAL
THE PROUD ONE — The OSMONDS
PROUD TO FALL — Ian McCULLOCH
PROVE IT — TELEVISION
PROVE YOUR LOVE — Taylor DAYNE
PROVIDER — N*E*R*D
PSYCHE ROCK — Pierre HENRY
PSYCHEDELIC SHACK — The TEMPTATIONS
PSYCHO — THEE UNSTRUNG
PSYCHO BASE — SHADES OF RHYTHM
PSYCHONAUT — FIELDS OF THE NEPHILIM
PSYCHOSIS SAFARI —
The EIGHTIES MATCHBOX B-LINE DISASTER
PSYKO FUNK — BOO-YAA T.R.I.B.E.
PTS.OF.ATHRTY — LINKIN PARK
A PUB WITH NO BEER — Slim DUSTY
PUBLIC ENEMY NO:1 — HYPO PSYCHO
PUBLIC IMAGE — PUBLIC IMAGE LTD
PUCKWUDGIE — Charlie DRAKE
PUFF — Kenny LYNCH
PULL THE WIRES FROM THE WALL —
The DELGADOS
PULL UP TO THE BUMPER [A] — Grace JONES
PULL UP TO THE BUMPER [A] — PATRA
PULLING MUSSELS (FROM THE SHELL) —
SQUEEZE
PULLING PUNCHES — David SYLVIAN
PULSAR 2002 — Mauro PICOTTO
PULS(T)AR — Ben LIEBRAND
PULVERTURM — Niels VAN GOGH
PUMP IT UP [A] — Elvis COSTELLO
PUMP IT UP [B] — Joe BUDDEN
PUMP IT UP [C] — DANZEL
PUMP ME UP — GRANDMASTER FLASH,
Melle MEL and The FURIOUS FIVE
PUMP UP LONDON — MR LEE
PUMP UP THE BITTER —
STARTURN ON 45 (PINTS)
PUMP UP THE JAM [A] — TECHNOTRONIC
PUMP UP THE JAM [A] —
D.O.N.S. featuring TECHNOTRONIC
PUMP UP THE VOLUME [A] — M/A/R/R/S (87)
PUMP UP THE VOLUME [A] —
GREED featuring Ricardo Da FORCE
PUMPIN — Tom NOVY
PUMPING ON YOUR STEREO — SUPERGRASS
PUMPKIN — TRICKY
PUMPS — Amy WINEHOUSE
PUNCH AND JUDY — MARILLION
PUNK — Ferry CORSTEN
PUNK ROCK 101 — BOWLING FOR SOUP
PUNK ROCK PRINCESS —
SOMETHING CORPORATE
PUNKA — KENICKIE
PUNKY REGGAE PARTY —
Bob MARLEY & The WAILERS
PUPPET MAN — Tom JONES
PUPPET ON A STRING — Sandie SHAW (67)
PUPPY LOVE [A] — Paul ANKA
PUPPY LOVE [A] — Donny OSMOND (72)
PUPPY LOVE [A] — S CLUB JUNIORS
THE PUPPY SONG — David CASSIDY (73)
PURE [A] — The LIGHTNING SEEDS
PURE [B] — GTO
PURE [C] — 3 COLOURS RED
PURE AND SIMPLE — HEAR'SAY (01)
PURE MASSACRE — SILVERCHAIR
PURE MORNING — PLACEBO
PURE PLEASURE — DIGITAL EXCITATION
PURE PLEASURE SEEKER — MOLOKO
PURE SHORES — ALL SAINTS (00)
PURELY BY COINCIDENCE —
SWEET SENSATION
PURGATORY — IRON MAIDEN
PURITY — NEW MODEL ARMY
PURPLE HAZE [A] —
The Jimi HENDRIX EXPERIENCE
PURPLE HAZE [B] — GROOVE ARMADA
PURPLE HEATHER — Rod STEWART
PURPLE LOVE BALLOON — CUD
PURPLE MEDLEY — PRINCE
PURPLE PEOPLE EATER [A] — Jackie DENNIS
THE PURPLE PEOPLE EATER [A] —
Sheb WOOLEY
PURPLE PILLS — D12
PURPLE RAIN — PRINCE
PUSH [A] — MOIST
PUSH [B] — MATCHBOX 20
PUSH [C] — GHOSTFACE featuring Missy ELLIOTT
THE PUSH (FAR FROM HERE) —
Paul JACKSON / Steve SMITH
PUSH IT [A] — SALT-N-PEPA
PUSH IT [B] — GARBAGE
PUSH IT ALL ASIDE — ALISHA'S ATTIC
PUSH THE BEAT [A] — CAPPELLA
PUSH THE BEAT [A] — MIRAGE
PUSH THE BUTTON — SUGABABES (05)
PUSH THE FEELING ON —
NIGHTCRAWLERS featuring John REID
PUSH UP — FREESTYLERS
PUSH UPSTAIRS — UNDERWORLD
THE PUSHBIKE SONG — MIXTURES
PUSHIN' ME OUT — D-SIDE
PUSHING THE SENSES — FEEDER
PUSS — JESUS LIZARD
PUSS 'N BOOTS — Adam ANT
PUSSYCAT — MULU
PUT A LIGHT IN THE WINDOW —
The KING BROTHERS
PUT A LITTLE LOVE IN YOUR HEART [A] —
Dave CLARK FIVE
PUT A LITTLE LOVE IN YOUR HEART [A] —
Annie LENNOX and Al GREEN
PUT 'EM HIGH —
STONEBRIDGE featuring THERESE
PUT HIM OUT — MS DYNAMITE
PUT HIM OUT OF YOUR MIND — DR FEELGOOD
PUT IT THERE — Paul McCARTNEY
PUT MY ARMS AROUND YOU — Kevin KITCHEN
PUT OUR HEADS TOGETHER — O'JAYS
PUT THE LIGHT ON — WET WET WET
PUT THE MESSAGE IN THE BOX —
Brian KENNEDY
PUT THE NEEDLE ON IT — Dannii MINOGUE
PUT THE NEEDLE TO THE RECORD —
Wally JUMP Jr and The CRIMINAL ELEMENT
PUT YOU ON THE GAME — The GAME
PUT YOUR ARMS AROUND ME [A] — TEXAS
PUT YOUR ARMS AROUND ME [B] — NATURAL
PUT YOUR FAITH IN ME — Alison LIMERICK
PUT YOUR HANDS TOGETHER — D MOB
PUT YOUR HANDS WHERE MY EYES COULD SEE
— Busta RHYMES
PUT YOUR HANDS UP —
REFLEX featuring MC VIPER
PUT YOUR HANDZ UP — WHOOLIGANZ
PUT YOUR HEAD ON MY SHOULDER —
Paul ANKA
PUT YOUR LOVE IN ME — HOT CHOCOLATE
PUT YOUR MONEY WHERE YOUR MOUTH IS —
ROSE ROYCE
PUT YOURSELF IN MY PLACE [A] —
The ISLEY BROTHERS
PUT YOURSELF IN MY PLACE [A] — ELGINS
PUT YOURSELF IN MY PLACE [B] —
Kylie MINOGUE
PUTTIN' ON THE STYLE —
Lonnie DONEGAN and his Skiffle Group (57)
PYJAMARAMA — ROXY MUSIC
PYRAMID SONG — RADIOHEAD
P.Y.T. (PRETTY YOUNG THING) —
Michael JACKSON
QUADROPHONIA — QUADROPHONIA
QUANDO M'INNAMORO (A MAN WITHOUT LOVE)
— The SANDPIPERS
QUANDO QUANDO QUANDO [A] — Pat BOONE
QUANDO QUANDO QUANDO [A] —
Engelbert HUMPERDINCK
THE QUARTER MOON — VIPs
QUARTER TO THREE — Gary 'US' BONDS
QUE SERA — Chris REA
QUE SERA MI VIDA (IF YOU SHOULD GO) —
The GIBSON BROTHERS
QUE SERA SERA [A] — Doris DAY
QUE SERA SERA [A] —
Geno WASHINGTON and The RAM JAM BAND
QUE SERA SERA [A] — HERMES HOUSE BAND
QUE TAL AMERICA — TWO MAN SOUND
QUEEN FOR TONIGHT — Helen SHAPIRO
QUEEN JANE — KINGMAKER
QUEEN OF CLUBS —
KC and The SUNSHINE BAND
QUEEN OF HEARTS [A] — Dave EDMUNDS
QUEEN OF HEARTS [B] — CHARLOTTE
QUEEN OF MY HEART — WESTLIFE (01)
QUEEN OF MY SOUL — AVERAGE WHITE BAND
QUEEN OF NEW ORLEANS — Jon BON JOVI
THE QUEEN OF 1964 — Neil SEDAKA
THE QUEEN OF OUTER SPACE —
The WEDDING PRESENT
QUEEN OF RAIN — ROXETTE
QUEEN OF THE HOP — Bobby DARIN
QUEEN OF THE NEW YEAR — DEACON BLUE
QUEEN OF THE NIGHT — Whitney HOUSTON
QUEEN OF THE RAPPING SCENE (NOTHING EVER
GOES THE WAY YOU PLAN) —
MODERN ROMANCE
THE QUEEN'S BIRTHDAY SONG —
ST JOHN'S COLLEGE SCHOOL CHOIR and
the Band of the GRENADIER GUARDS
QUEEN'S FIRST EP — QUEEN
QUEER — GARBAGE
QUEST — SYSTEM 7
QUESTION [A] — The MOODY BLUES
QUESTION! [B] — SYSTEM OF A DOWN
THE QUESTION —
SEVEN GRAND HOUSING AUTHORITY
QUESTION OF FAITH — LIGHTHOUSE FAMILY
A QUESTION OF LUST — DEPECHE MODE
A QUESTION OF TIME — DEPECHE MODE
QUESTIONS AND ANSWERS [A] — SHAM 69
QUESTIONS & ANSWERS [B] — BIFFY CLYRO
QUESTIONS I CAN'T ANSWER — HEINZ
QUESTIONS (MUST BE ASKED) —
David FORBES
QUICK JOEY SMALL (RUN JOEY RUN) —
KASENETZ-KATZ SINGING ORCHESTRAL
CIRCUS
QUIEREME MUCHO (YOURS) — Julio IGLESIAS
QUIET LIFE — JAPAN
THE QUIET THINGS THAT NO ONE EVER KNOWS
— BRAND NEW
QUIT PLAYING GAMES (WITH MY HEART)
— BACKSTREET BOYS
QUIT THIS TOWN — EDDIE and The HOT RODS
QUITE A PARTY — FIREBALLS
QUITE RIGHTLY SO — PROCOL HARUM
QUOTE GOODBYE QUOTE — Carolyne MAS
QUOTH — POLYGON WINDOW
R 'N' B — GOLDIE LOOKIN CHAIN
R.R. EXPRESS — ROSE ROYCE
R TO THE A — CJ LEWIS
R U READY — SALT-N-PEPA
R U SLEEPING — INDO
RABBIT — CHAS and DAVE
THE RACE [A] — YELLO
RACE [B] — TIGER
RACE [C] — The LEAVES
RACE FOR THE PRIZE — The FLAMING LIPS
THE RACE IS ON [A] — Suzi QUATRO
THE RACE IS ON [B] —
Dave EDMUNDS and The STRAY CATS
RACE WITH THE DEVIL [A] — Gene VINCENT
RACE WITH THE DEVIL [B] — GIRLSCHOOL
RACE WITH THE DEVIL [B] — GUN
RACHEL — Al MARTINO
RACHMANINOFF'S 18TH VARIATION ON A THEME
BY PAGANINI (THE STORY OF THREE LOVES)
— Winifred ATWELL
RACING GREEN — HIGH CONTRAST
RACIST FRIEND — The SPECIALS
RADANCER — MARMALADE
RADAR LOVE [A] — GOLDEN EARRING
RADAR LOVE [A] — OH WELL
RADIATION VIBE — FOUNTAINS OF WAYNE
RADICAL YOUR LOVER — LITTLE ANGELS
RADICCIO (EP) — ORBITAL
RADIO [A] — Roger TAYLOR
RADIO [B] — TEENAGE FANCLUB
RADIO [C] — The CORRS
RADIO [D] — CLIENT
RADIO [E] — Robbie WILLIAMS (04)
RADIO [F] — LUDES
RADIO AFRICA — LATIN QUARTER
RADIO DISCO — WILT
RADIO GAGA [A] — QUEEN
RADIO GAGA [A] — ELECTRIC SIX
RADIO HEAD — TALKING HEADS

26 April 2003	3 May 2003	10 May 2003	17 May 2003
MAKE LUV Room 5 featuring Oliver Cheatham	**YOU SAID NO** Busted	**LONELINESS** Tomcraft	**IGNITION** R Kelly
A RUSH OF BLOOD TO THE HEAD Coldplay	**AMERICAN LIFE** Madonna	**JUSTIFIED** Justin Timberlake	**THINK TANK** Blur

RADIO HEART — RADIO HEART featuring Gary NUMAN
RADIO MUSICOLA — Nik KERSHAW
RADIO #1 — AIR
RADIO ON — Ricky ROSS
RADIO RADIO — Elvis COSTELLO
RADIO ROMANCE — TIFFANY
RADIO SONG — R.E.M.
RADIO WALL OF SOUND — SLADE
RADIO WAVES — Roger WATERS
RADIOACTIVE — Gene SIMMONS
RADIOACTIVITY — KRAFTWERK
RAG DOLL [A] — The FOUR SEASONS
RAG DOLL [B] — AEROSMITH
RAG MAMA RAG — The BAND
RAGAMUFFIN MAN — MANFRED MANN
RAGE HARD — FRANKIE GOES TO HOLLYWOOD
RAGE TO LOVE — Kim WILDE
RAGGA HOUSE (ALL NIGHT LONG) — Simon HARRIS
RAGGAMUFFIN GIRL — APACHE INDIAN
RAGING (EP) [A] — BEYOND
RAGING [B] — COSMIC GATE
RAGS TO RICHES [A] — David WHITFIELD
RAGS TO RICHES [A] — Elvis PRESLEY
RAGTIME COWBOY JOE — CHIPMUNKS
RAIN [A] — Bruce RUFFIN
RAIN [B] — STATUS QUO
RAIN [C] — The CULT
RAIN [D] — MADONNA
RAIN [E] — GROOVE CORPORATION
THE RAIN — Oran 'Juice' JONES
THE RAIN (SUPA DUPA FLY) — Missy 'Misdemeanor' ELLIOTT
RAIN AND TEARS — APHRODITE'S CHILD
RAIN DOWN ON ME — KANE
RAIN FALL DOWN — The ROLLING STONES
RAIN FALLS — Frankie KNUCKLES
RAIN FOREST [A] — BIDDU
RAIN FOREST [B] — Paul HARDCASTLE
RAIN IN THE SUMMERTIME — The ALARM
RAIN KING — COUNTING CROWS
RAIN ON ME — ASHANTI
RAIN OR SHINE — FIVE STAR
RAIN RAIN RAIN — Frankie LAINE and The FOUR LADS
RAIN SHOWERS — SIZZLA
RAINBOW [A] — MARMALADE
RAINBOW [B] — PETERS and LEE
RAINBOW CHASER — NIRVANA
RAINBOW CHILD — Dan REED NETWORK
RAINBOW COUNTRY — Bob MARLEY & The WAILERS
RAINBOW IN THE DARK — DIO
RAINBOW LAKE — WENDY and LISA
RAINBOW PEOPLE — MANIX
RAINBOW (SAMPLE FREE) — SOLO
RAINBOW THEME - FROZEN RAINBOW — SAXON
RAINBOW VALLEY — LOVE AFFAIR
RAINBOWS OF COLOUR — GROOVERIDER
RAINCLOUD — LIGHTHOUSE FAMILY
THE RAINDANCE — DARE
RAINDROPS KEEP FALLIN' ON MY HEAD [A] — Bobbie GENTRY
RAINDROPS KEEP FALLIN' ON MY HEAD [A] — BJ THOMAS
RAINDROPS KEEP FALLING ON MY HEAD [A] — Sacha DISTEL
RAINFOREST — DILLINJA
RAININ' THROUGH MY SUNSHINE — The REAL THING
RAINING ALL OVER THE WORLD — The ADVENTURES
RAINING IN MY HEART — Leo SAYER
RAINMAKER [A] — SPARKLEHORSE
RAINMAKER [B] — IRON MAIDEN
RAINY DAY WOMEN NOS. 12 & 35 — Bob DYLAN
RAINY DAYS AND MONDAYS — The CARPENTERS
RAINY DAYZ — Mary J. BLIGE
RAINY NIGHT IN GEORGIA — Randy CRAWFORD
A RAINY NIGHT IN SOHO — The POGUES
RAISE — HYPER GO GO
RAISE YOUR HAND — Eddie FLOYD
RAISE YOUR HANDS [A] — REEL 2 REAL
RAISE YOUR HANDS [B] — BIG ROOM GIRL featuring Darryl PANDY
RAISED ON ROCK — Elvis PRESLEY
RAM GOAT LIVER — Pluto SHERVINGTON
RAMA LAMA DING DONG — Rocky SHARPE and The REPLAYS
RAMBLIN' ROSE — Nat 'King' COLE
RAM-BUNK-SHUSH — VENTURES
RAME — SNAP! featuring RUKMANI
RAMONA — The BACHELORS
RANDOM — LADY SOVEREIGN
RANDY — BLUE MINK
RANKING FULL STOP — The BEAT
RAOUL AND THE KINGS OF SPAIN — TEARS FOR FEARS
RAP DIS (U DON'T KNOW THIS SHIT) — OXIDE & NEUTRINO
RAP SCHOLAR — DAS EFX featuring REDMAN
RAP SUMMARY — BIG DADDY KANE
(RAP) SUPERSTAR — CYPRESS HILL
RAP YOUR LOVE — SET THE TONE
RAPE ME — NIRVANA
RAPID HOPE LOSS — DASHBOARD CONFESSIONAL
RAPP PAYBACK (WHERE IZ MOSES?) — James BROWN
RAPPAZ R N DAINJA — KRS ONE
RAPPER'S DELIGHT — SUGARHILL GANG
RAPTURE [A] — BLONDIE
RAPTURE [B] — IIO
RARE, PRECIOUS AND GONE — Mike SCOTT
THE RASCAL KING — MIGHTY MIGHTY BOSSTONES
RASPBERRY BERET — PRINCE
RASPUTIN — BONEY M
THE RAT — The WALKMEN
RAT IN MI KITCHEN — UB40
RAT RACE — The SPECIALS
RAT RAPPING — Roland RAT SUPERSTAR
RAT TRAP — The BOOMTOWN RATS (78)
RATAMAHATTA — SEPULTURA
THE RATTLER — GOODBYE MR MACKENZIE
RATTLESNAKES — Lloyd COLE
RAUNCHY [A] — Bill JUSTIS
RAUNCHY [A] — Ken MACKINTOSH
RAVE ALERT — Praga KHAN
THE RAVE DIGGER — MC LETHAL
RAVE GENERATOR — TOXIC TWO
RAVE ON — Buddy HOLLY
RAVEL'S PAVANE POUR UNE INFANTE DEFUNTE — William ORBIT
RAVING I'M RAVING — SHUT UP AND DANCE
RAW [A] — SPANDAU BALLET
RAW [B] — The ALARM
RAW [C] — MELKY SEDECK
RAW POWER — APOLLO FOUR FORTY
RAWHIDE — Frankie LAINE
RAY OF LIGHT — MADONNA
RAYS OF THE RISING SUN [A] — Denise JOHNSON
RAYS OF THE RISING SUN [A] — MOZAIC
RAZOR'S EDGE — MEAT LOAF
RAZZAMATAZZ — Quincy JONES
RAZZLE DAZZLE [A] — Bill HALEY and his COMETS
RAZZLE DAZZLE [B] — HEATWAVE
RE: EVOLUTION — The SHAMEN
RE-REWIND THE CROWD SAY BO SELECTA — ARTFUL DODGER featuring Craig DAVID
REACH [A] — Judy CHEEKS
REACH [B] — LIL MO' YIN YANG
REACH [C] — Gloria ESTEFAN
REACH [D] — S CLUB 7
REACH 4 THE MELODY — Victoria WILSON JAMES
REACH FOR THE STARS — Shirley BASSEY (61)
REACH OUT — MIDFIELD GENERAL featuring LINDA LEWIS
REACH OUT AND TOUCH — Diana ROSS
REACH OUT FOR ME — Dionne WARWICK
REACH OUT I'LL BE THERE [A] — The FOUR TOPS (66)
REACH OUT I'LL BE THERE [A] — Gloria GAYNOR
REACH OUT I'LL BE THERE [A] — Michael BOLTON
REACH UP — Toney LEE
(REACH UP FOR THE) SUNRISE — DURAN DURAN
REACH UP (PAPA'S GOT A BRAND NEW PIG BAG) — PERFECTO ALLSTARZ
REACHIN' [A] — PHASE II
REACHIN' [A] — Joey NEGRO
REACHIN [A] — HOUSE OF VIRGINISM
REACHING FOR THE BEST — The EXCITERS
REACHING FOR THE WORLD — Harold MELVIN and The BLUENOTES
REACHOUT — DJ ZINC
REACT — Erick SERMON featuring REDMAN
READ 'EM AND WEEP — Barry MANILOW
READ MY LIPS [A] — DSK
READ MY LIPS [B] — ALEX PARTY
READ MY LIPS (ENOUGH IS ENOUGH) — Jimmy SOMERVILLE
READ MY MIND — Conner REEVES
READY — Bruce WAYNE
READY AN' WILLING (SWEET SATISFACTION) — WHITESNAKE
READY FOR A NEW DAY — Martha WASH
READY FOR LOVE [A] — Jimmy JONES
READY FOR LOVE [B] — Gary MOORE
READY OR NOT [A] — The LIGHTNING SEEDS
READY OR NOT [B] — DJ DADO
READY OR NOT [C] — FUGEES (96)
READY OR NOT [C] — COURSE
READY OR NOT [D] — a1
READY OR NOT HERE I COME (CAN'T HIDE FROM YOUR LOVE) — The DELFONICS
READY STEADY GO [A] — GENERATION X
READY STEADY GO [B] — OAKENFOLD
READY STEADY WHO (EP) — The WHO
READY TO GO — REPUBLICA
READY TO RECEIVE — ANIMALHOUSE
READY TO RUN — DIXIE CHICKS
READY, WILLING AND ABLE — Doris DAY
READY2WEAR — FELIX DA HOUSECAT
REAL [A] — Donna ALLEN
REAL [B] — PLUMB
REAL A LIE — AUF DER MAUR
REAL COOL WORLD — David BOWIE
REAL EMOTION — REID
REAL FASHION REGGAE STYLE — Carey JOHNSON
REAL GONE KID — DEACON BLUE
REAL GOOD — DOUBLE SIX
REAL GOOD TIME — ALDA
REAL GREAT BRITAIN — ASIAN DUB FOUNDATION
REAL LIFE [A] — SIMPLE MINDS
REAL LIFE [B] — BON JOVI
THE REAL LIFE — RAVEN MAIZE
REAL LOVE [A] — Ruby MURRAY
REAL LOVE [B] — Jody WATLEY
REAL LOVE [C] — DRIZABONE
REAL LOVE [D] — DARE
REAL LOVE [D] — TIME FREQUENCY
REAL LOVE [E] — Mary J BLIGE
REAL LOVE [F] — The BEATLES
THE REAL ME — W.A.S.P.
A REAL MOTHER FOR YA — Johnny 'Guitar' WATSON
REAL PEOPLE — APACHE INDIAN
REAL REAL REAL — JESUS JONES
THE REAL SLIM SHADY — EMINEM (00)
THE REAL THING [A] — JELLYBEAN featuring Steven DANTE
THE REAL THING [B] — BROTHERS JOHNSON
THE REAL THING [C] — ABC
THE REAL THING [D] — Tony DI BART (94)
THE REAL THING [E] — Lisa STANSFIELD
THE REAL THING [F] — 2 UNLIMITED
REAL THINGS — JAVINE
REAL TO ME — Brian McFADDEN (04)
REAL VIBRATION (WANT LOVE) — EXPRESS OF SOUND
REAL WILD CHILD (WILD ONE) — Iggy POP
THE REAL WILD HOUSE — Raul ORELLANA
REAL WORLD — D-SIDE
REALITY USED TO BE A FRIEND OF MINE — PM DAWN
REALLY DOE — ICE CUBE
REALLY FREE — John OTWAY and Wild Willy BARRETT
REALLY SAYING SOMETHING — BANANARAMA with FUN BOY THREE
REAP THE WILD WIND — ULTRAVOX
REASON — IAN VAN DAHL
THE REASON [A] — Celine DION
THE REASON [B] — HOOBASTANK
REASON FOR LIVING — Roddy FRAME
REASON TO BELIEVE — Rod STEWART
REASON TO LIVE — KISS
REASONS [A] — KLESHAY
REASONS [B] — UB40 / HUNTERZ / The DHOL BLASTERS
REASONS TO BE CHEERFUL (PT. 3) — Ian DURY and The BLOCKHEADS
REBEL MUSIC — REBEL MC
REBEL NEVER GETS OLD — David BOWIE
REBEL REBEL — David BOWIE
REBEL ROUSER — Duane EDDY and The REBELS
REBEL RUN — TOYAH
REBEL WITHOUT A PAUSE — PUBLIC ENEMY
REBEL WOMAN — DNA featuring Jazzi P
REBEL YELL [A] — Billy IDOL
REBEL YELL [A] — SCOOTER
REBELLION (LIES) — ARCADE FIRE
REBIRTH OF SLICK (COOL LIKE DAT) — DIGABLE PLANETS
RECIPE FOR LOVE — Harry CONNICK Jr
RECKLESS — AFRIKA BAMBAATAA and FAMILY featuring UB40
RECKLESS GIRL — BEGINERZ
RECONNECTION (EP) — ZERO B
RECOVER YOUR SOUL — Elton JOHN
RECOVERY — Fontella BASS
RED — ELBOW
RED ALERT — BASEMENT JAXX
RED BALLOON — Dave CLARK FIVE
RED BLOODED WOMAN — Kylie MINOGUE
RED DRESS — Alvin STARDUST
RED FRAME WHITE LIGHT — ORCHESTRAL MANOEUVRES IN THE DARK
RED GUITAR — David SYLVIAN
RED HOT [A] — PRINCESS
RED HOT [B] — VANESSA-MAE
A RED LETTER DAY — PET SHOP BOYS
RED LIGHT GREEN, LIGHT — Mitchell TOROK
RED LIGHT — GREEN LIGHT (EP) — The WILDHEARTS
RED LIGHT SPECIAL — TLC
RED LIGHT SPELLS DANGER — Billy OCEAN
RED RAIN — Peter GABRIEL
RED RED WINE [A] — Jimmy JAMES and The VAGABONDS
RED RED WINE [A] — Tony TRIBE
RED RED WINE [A] — UB40 (83)
RED RIVER ROCK — JOHNNY and The HURRICANES
RED SAILS IN THE SUNSET — Fats DOMINO
THE RED SHOES — Kate BUSH
RED SKIES [A] — FIXX
RED SKIES [B] — SAMSON
RED SKY — STATUS QUO
THE RED STROKES — Garth BROOKS
RED SUN RISING — LOST WITNESS
THE RED THE WHITE THE BLACK THE BLUE — HOPE OF THE STATES
RED THREE: THUNDER — Dave CLARKE
REDEFINE — SOIL
REDEMPTION SONG — Joe STRUMMER and The MESCALEROS
REDHEAD — BARON
REDNECK WOMAN — Gretchen WILSON
REDONDO BEACH — MORRISSEY
REDUNDANT — GREEN DAY
REELIN' AND ROCKIN' [A] — Dave CLARK FIVE
REELIN' AND ROCKIN' [A] — Chuck BERRY
REELING — PASADENAS
REET PETITE (THE SWEETEST GIRL IN TOWN) [A] — Jackie WILSON (86)
REET PETITE [A] — DARTS
REET PETITE [A] — PINKY and PERKY
REFLECT — THREE 'N ONE
REFLECTION — VANESSA-MAE
REFLECTIONS — Diana ROSS and The SUPREMES
REFLECTIONS OF MY LIFE — MARMALADE
THE REFLEX — DURAN DURAN (84)
REFUGEES — The TEARS
REFUSE-RESIST — SEPULTURA
REGGAE FOR IT NOW — Bill LOVELADY
REGGAE LIKE IT USED TO BE — Paul NICHOLAS
REGGAE MUSIC — UB40

24 May 2003	31 May 2003	7 June 2003	14 June 2003
UK No.1 SINGLES			
IGNITION R Kelly	**IGNITION** R Kelly	**IGNITION** R Kelly	**BRING ME TO LIFE** Evanescence featuring Paul McCoy
UK No.1 ALBUMS			
JUSTIFIED Justin Timberlake	**JUSTIFIED** Justin Timberlake	**JUSTIFIED** Justin Timberlake	**YOU GOTTA GO THERE TO COME BACK** Stereophonics

21 June 2003	28 June 2003	5 July 2003	12 July 2003
BRING ME TO LIFE Evanescence featuring Paul McCoy	**BRING ME TO LIFE** Evanescence featuring Paul McCoy	**BRING ME TO LIFE** Evanescence featuring Paul McCoy	**CRAZY IN LOVE** Beyoncé
HAIL TO THE THIEF Radiohead	**FALLEN** Evanescence	**DANGEROUSLY IN LOVE** Beyoncé	**DANGEROUSLY IN LOVE** Beyoncé

RIP — Gary NUMAN
RIP IT UP [A] — LITTLE RICHARD
RIP IT UP [A] — Bill HALEY and his COMETS
RIP IT UP [A] — Elvis PRESLEY
RIP IT UP [B] — ORANGE JUICE
RIP IT UP [C] — RAZORLIGHT
RIP PRODUCTIONS — RIP PRODUCTIONS
RIPGROOVE — DOUBLE 99
RIPPED IN 2 MINUTES — A vs B
RIPPIN KITTIN — GOLDEN BOY with MISS KITTIN
RISE [A] — Herb ALPERT
RISE [B] — PUBLIC IMAGE LTD
RISE [C] — ZION TRAIN
RISE [D] — Eddie AMADOR
RISE [E] — GABRIELLE (00)
RISE [F] — SOUL PROVIDERS featuring Michelle SHELLERS
THE RISE AND FALL OF FLINGEL BUNT — The SHADOWS
RISE & FALL — Craig DAVID featuring STING
RISE AND SHINE — The CARDIGANS
RISE 'IN — Steve LAWLER
RISE OF THE EAGLES — The EIGHTIES MATCHBOX B-LINE DISASTER
RISE TO THE OCCASION — CLIMIE FISHER
RISE UP — JAMAICA UNITED
RISIN' TO THE TOP — Keni BURKE
RISING FREE (EP) — Tom ROBINSON BAND
RISING SIGN — HURRICANE #1
RISING SUN [A] — MEDICINE HEAD
RISING SUN [B] — The FARM
RISINGSON — MASSIVE ATTACK
THE RITUAL — EBONY DUBSTERS
THE RIVER [A] — Bruce SPRINGSTEEN
THE RIVER [B] — KING TRIGGER
THE RIVER [C] — TOTAL CONTRAST
THE RIVER [D] — The BEAUTIFUL SOUTH
THE RIVER [E] — BREED 77
RIVER BELOW — BILLY TALENT
RIVER DEEP MOUNTAIN HIGH [A] — Ike and Tina TURNER
RIVER DEEP MOUNTAIN HIGH [A] — The SUPREMES and The FOUR TOPS
THE RIVER (LE COLLINE SONO IN FIORE) — Ken DODD
RIVER MAN — Nick DRAKE
THE RIVER OF DREAMS — Billy JOEL
RIVER OF PAIN — THUNDER
RIVER STAY 'WAY FROM MY DOOR — Frank SINATRA
THE RIVERBOAT SONG — OCEAN COLOUR SCENE
RIVERDANCE — Bill WHELAN featuring ANUNA and The RTE CONCERT ORCHESTRA
RIVERS OF BABYLON — BONEY M (78)
THE RIVERS OF BELIEF — ENIGMA
THE RIVER'S RUN DRY — Vince HILL
ROACHES — TRANCESETTERS
THE ROAD LEADS WHERE IT'S LEAD — SECRET MACHINES
ROAD RAGE — CATATONIA
ROAD RUNNER — Junior WALKER and The ALL-STARS
THE ROAD TO HELL (PART 2) — Chris REA
THE ROAD TO MANDALAY — Robbie WILLIAMS (01)
ROAD TO NOWHERE — TALKING HEADS
ROAD TO OUR DREAM — T'PAU
THE ROAD TO PARADISE — BHOYS FROM PARADISE
ROAD TO YOUR SOUL — ALL ABOUT EVE
ROAD TRIPPIN' — RED HOT CHILI PEPPERS
ROADBLOCK — STOCK AITKEN WATERMAN
ROADHOUSE MEDLEY (ANNIVERSARY WALTZ PART 25) — STATUS QUO
ROADRUNNER — Jonathan RICHMAN and The MODERN LOVERS
ROAM — The B-52's
ROBERT DE NIRO'S WAITING — BANANARAMA
ROBIN HOOD [A] — Dick JAMES
ROBIN HOOD [A] — Gary MILLER
ROBIN (THE HOODED MAN) — CLANNAD
ROBIN'S RETURN — Neville DICKIE
ROBOT — TORNADOS
ROBOT MAN — Connie FRANCIS
ROBOT ROCK — DAFT PUNK
ROBOT WARS (ANDROID LOVE) — SIR KILLALOT vs ROBO BABE
THE ROBOTS — KRAFTWERK
ROC YA BODY 'MIC CHECK 1,2' — M.V.P.
ROCCO — DEATH IN VEGAS
ROCHDALE COWBOY — Mike HARDING
ROC-IN-IT — Deejay PUNK-ROC vs ONYX
THE ROCK [A] — DELAKOTA
THE ROCK [B] — The ALARM
THE ROCK [C] — PUNX
ROCK AND A HARD PLACE — The ROLLING STONES
ROCK AND ROLL DREAMS COME THROUGH — MEAT LOAF
ROCK AND ROLL IS DEAD — Lenny KRAVITZ
ROCK AND ROLL (IS GONNA SET THE NIGHT ON FIRE) — PRETTY BOY FLOYD
ROCK AND ROLL MUSIC — The BEACH BOYS
ROCK AND ROLL (PARTS 1 & 2) — Gary GLITTER
ROCK & ROLL QUEEN — The SUBWAYS
ROCK AND ROLL WALTZ — Kay STARR (56)
ROCK AROUND THE CLOCK [A] — Bill HALEY and his COMETS (55)
ROCK AROUND THE CLOCK [A] — TELEX
ROCK AROUND THE CLOCK [A] — TEN POLE TUDOR
ROCK BOTTOM [A] — Lynsey DE PAUL
ROCK BOTTOM [B] — BABYFACE
ROCK DA FUNKY BEATS — PUBLIC DOMAIN featuring Chuck D
ROCK DA HOUSE — TALL PAUL
ROCK DJ — Robbie WILLIAMS (00)
ROCK HARD — Suzi QUATRO
R.O.C.K. IN THE USA — John Cougar MELLENCAMP
ROCK IS DEAD — MARILYN MANSON
ROCK ISLAND LINE [A] — Lonnie DONEGAN
ROCK ISLAND LINE [A] — Stan FREBERG
ROCK LOBSTER — The B-52's
ROCK ME AMADEUS — FALCO (86)
ROCK ME BABY [A] — David CASSIDY
ROCK ME BABY [B] — Johnny NASH
ROCK ME BABY [C] — BABY ROOTS
ROCK ME GENTLY — Andy KIM
ROCK ME GOOD — UNIVERSAL
ROCK ME STEADY — DJ PROFESSOR
ROCK ME TONIGHT (FOR OLD TIME'S SAKE) — Freddie JACKSON
ROCK MY HEART — HADDAWAY
ROCK MY WORLD — FIVE STAR
ROCK 'N' ME — Steve MILLER BAND
ROCK 'N' ROLL [A] — John McENROE and Pat CASH with the FULL METAL RACKETS
ROCK 'N' ROLL [B] — STATUS QUO
ROCK 'N' ROLL AIN'T NOISE POLLUTION — AC/DC
ROCK 'N' ROLL CHILDREN — DIO
ROCK 'N' ROLL DAMNATION — AC/DC
ROCK 'N' ROLL DANCE PARTY — JIVE BUNNY and The MASTERMIXERS
ROCK 'N' ROLL (DOLE) — J PAC
ROCK 'N' ROLL DREAMS COME THROUGH — Jim STEINMAN
ROCK 'N' ROLL GYPSY — SAXON
ROCK 'N' ROLL HIGH SCHOOL — The RAMONES
ROCK 'N' ROLL (I GAVE YOU THE BEST YEARS OF MY LIFE) — Kevin JOHNSON
ROCK 'N' ROLL IS KING — ELECTRIC LIGHT ORCHESTRA
ROCK 'N' ROLL LADY — SHOWADDYWADDY
ROCK 'N' ROLL LIES — RAZORLIGHT
ROCK 'N' ROLL MERCENARIES — MEAT LOAF featuring John PARR
ROCK 'N' ROLL NIGGER — BIRDLAND
ROCK 'N' ROLL OUTLAW — ROSE TATTOO
ROCK 'N ROLL STAGE SHOW (LP) — Bill HALEY and his COMETS
ROCK 'N' ROLL SUICIDE — David BOWIE
ROCK 'N' ROLL WINTER (LOONY'S TUNE) — WIZZARD
ROCK OF AGES — DEF LEPPARD
ROCK ON — David ESSEX
ROCK ON BROTHER — CHEQUERS
THE ROCK SHOW — BLINK-182
ROCK STAR — N*E*R*D
ROCK STEADY [A] — WHISPERS
ROCK STEADY [B] — Bonnie RAITT and Bryan ADAMS
(ROCK) SUPERSTAR — CYPRESS HILL
ROCK THE BELLS — KADOC
ROCK THE BOAT [A] — HUES CORPORATION
ROCK THE BOAT [A] — FORREST
ROCK THE BOAT [A] — DELAGE
ROCK THE BOAT [B] — AALIYAH
ROCK THE CASBAH — The CLASH
ROCK THE DISCOTEK — RAMP
ROCK THE FUNKY BEATS — NATURAL BORN CHILLERS
ROCK THE HOUSE [A] — The SOURCE featuring NICOLE
ROCK THE HOUSE [B] — GORILLAZ
ROCK THE JOINT — Bill HALEY and his COMETS
ROCK THE MIDNIGHT — David GRANT
ROCK THE NIGHT — EUROPE
ROCK THIS TOWN — STRAY CATS
ROCK 'TIL YOU DROP — STATUS QUO
ROCK 2 HOUSE — X-PRESS 2
ROCK WIT U (AWWW BABY) — ASHANTI
ROCK WIT'CHA — Bobby BROWN
ROCK WITH THE CAVEMAN — Tommy STEELE
ROCK WITH YOU [A] — D'INFLUENCE
ROCK WITH YOU [A] — Michael JACKSON
ROCK YOUR BABY [A] — George McCRAE (74)
ROCK YOUR BABY [A] — KWS
ROCK YOUR BODY [A] — CLOCK
ROCK YOUR BODY [B] — Justin TIMBERLAKE
ROCK YOUR BODY ROCK — Ferry CORSTEN
ROCK-A-BEATIN' BOOGIE — Bill HALEY and his COMETS
ROCK-A-BILLY — Guy MITCHELL (57)
ROCKABILLY BOB — COLUMBO featuring OOE
ROCKABILLY GUY — POLECATS
ROCKABILLY REBEL — MATCHBOX
ROCK-A-BYE YOUR BABY (WITH A DIXIE MELODY) — Jerry LEWIS
ROCK-A-DOODLE-DOO — Linda LEWIS
THE ROCKAFELLER SKANK — FATBOY SLIM
ROCK-A-HULA BABY — Elvis PRESLEY with The JORDANAIRES (62)
ROCKALL — MEZZOFORTE
ROCKARIA! — ELECTRIC LIGHT ORCHESTRA
ROCKER — ALTER EGO
ROCKET [A] — MUD
ROCKET [B] — DEF LEPPARD
ROCKET [C] — EL PRESIDENTE
ROCKET (A NATURAL GAMBLER) — BRAUND REYNOLDS
ROCKET MAN — SPOTNICKS
ROCKET MAN (I THINK IT'S GOING TO BE A LONG LONG TIME) [A] — Elton JOHN
ROCKET MAN (I THINK IT'S GOING TO BE A LONG LONG TIME) [A] — Kate BUSH
ROCKET RIDE — FELIX DA HOUSECAT
ROCKET 2 U — JETS
ROCKIN' ALL OVER THE WORLD — STATUS QUO
ROCKIN' ALONE — MIKI and GRIFF
ROCKIN' AROUND THE CHRISTMAS TREE [A] — Brenda LEE
ROCKIN' AROUND THE CHRISTMAS TREE [A] — The JETS
ROCKIN' AROUND THE CHRISTMAS TREE [A] — Kim WILDE
ROCKIN' BACK INSIDE MY HEART — Julee CRUISE
ROCKIN' CHAIR — MAGNUM
ROCKIN' FOR MYSELF — MOTIV 8
ROCKIN' GOOD CHRISTMAS — Roy 'Chubby' BROWN
A ROCKIN' GOOD WAY — Bonnie TYLER
ROCKIN' ME — DJ PROFESSOR
ROCKIN' MY BODY — 49ers featuring Ann-Marie SMITH
ROCKIN' OVER THE BEAT — TECHNOTRONIC
ROCKIN' RED WING — Sammy MASTERS
ROCKIN' ROBIN [A] — Bobby DAY
ROCKIN' ROBIN [A] — Michael JACKSON
ROCKIN' ROBIN [A] — LOLLY
ROCKIN' ROLL BABY — The STYLISTICS
ROCKIN' SOUL — HUES CORPORATION
ROCKIN' THE SUBURBS — Ben FOLDS
ROCKIN' THROUGH THE RYE — Bill HALEY and his COMETS
ROCKIN' TO THE MUSIC — BLACK BOX
ROCKIN' TO THE RHYTHM — CONVERT
ROCKIN' WITH RITA (HEAD TO TOE) — VINDALOO SUMMER SPECIAL
ROCKING GOOSE — JOHNNY and The HURRICANES
ROCKING MUSIC — Martin SOLVEIG
ROCKIT — Herbie HANCOCK
ROCKS [A] — PRIMAL SCREAM
ROCKS [A] — Rod STEWART
ROCKS ON THE ROAD — JETHRO TULL
ROCKSTAR — BIZARRE
ROCKY — Austin ROBERTS
ROCKY MOUNTAIN WAY (EP) — Joe WALSH
THE RODEO SONG — Garry LEE and SHOWDOWN
RODRIGO'S GUITAR CONCERTO DE ARANJUEZ (THEME FROM 2ND MOVEMENT) — MANUEL and his MUSIC OF THE MOUNTAINS
ROFO'S THEME — ROFO
ROK DA HOUSE [A] — The BEATMASTERS featuring The COOKIE CREW
ROK DA HOUSE [B] — VINYLGROOVER and The RED HED
ROK THE NATION — ROB 'N' RAZ featuring Leila K
ROLL AWAY — Dusty SPRINGFIELD
ROLL AWAY THE STONE — MOTT THE HOOPLE
ROLL ON — MIS-TEEQ
ROLL ON DOWN THE HIGHWAY — BACHMAN-TURNER OVERDRIVE
ROLL OVER BEETHOVEN — ELECTRIC LIGHT ORCHESTRA
ROLL OVER LAY DOWN — STATUS QUO
ROLL THE BONES — RUSH
ROLL TO ME — DEL AMITRI
ROLL WID US — AKALA
ROLL WITH IT [A] — Steve WINWOOD
ROLL WITH IT [B] — OASIS
A ROLLER SKATING JAM NAMED 'SATURDAYS' — DE LA SOUL
ROLLERBLADE [A] — Nick HEYWARD
ROLLERBLADE [B] — MOVIN' MELODIES
ROLLERCOASTER (EP) [A] — JESUS AND MARY CHAIN
ROLLERCOASTER (EP) [B] — EVERYTHING BUT THE GIRL
ROLLERCOASTER [C] — GRID
ROLLERCOASTER [D] — NORTHERN UPROAR
ROLLERCOASTER [E] — B*WITCHED (98)
ROLLIN' — LIMP BIZKIT (01)
ROLLIN' HOME — STATUS QUO
ROLLIN' IN MY 5.0 — VANILLA ICE
ROLLIN' ON — CIRRUS
ROLLING STONE — David ESSEX
ROLLOUT (MY BUSINESS) — LUDACRIS
ROLLOVER DJ — JET
ROLODEX PROPAGANDA — AT THE DRIVE-IN
ROMAN P — PSYCHIC TV
ROMANCE (LET YOUR HEART GO) — David CASSIDY
ROMANCING THE STONE — Eddy GRANT
ROMANTIC — Karyn WHITE
ROMANTIC RIGHTS — DEATH FROM ABOVE 1979
ROMANTICA — Jane MORGAN
ROME WASN'T BUILT IN A DAY — MORCHEEBA
ROMEO [A] — Petula CLARK
ROMEO [B] — MR BIG
ROMEO [C] — BASEMENT JAXX
ROMEO AND JULIET — DIRE STRAITS
ROMEO DUNN — ROMEO
ROMEO ME — SLEEPER
ROMEO WHERE'S JULIET? — COLLAGE
RONDO — Kenny BALL and his JAZZMEN
RONI — Bobby BROWN
ROOBARB AND CUSTARD — SHAFT
ROOF IS ON FIRE — WESTBAM
ROOFTOP SINGING — NEW WORLD
ROOM AT THE TOP — Adam ANT
ROOM ELEVEN — DAISY CHAINSAW
ROOM IN BROOKLYN — John SQUIRE
ROOM IN YOUR HEART — LIVING IN A BOX
ROOMS ON FIRE — Stevie NICKS
ROOM ON THE 3RD FLOOR — McFLY
ROOTS — [SPUNGE]
ROOTS BLOODY ROOTS — SEPULTURA
ROSALIE — COWGIRLS' SONG (MEDLEY) — THIN LIZZY
ROSALYN — PRETTY THINGS
ROSANNA — TOTO
THE ROSE [A] — Heather PEACE

19 July 2003	26 July 2003	2 August 2003	9 August 2003
UK No.1 SINGLES			
CRAZY IN LOVE Beyoncé	**CRAZY IN LOVE** Beyoncé	**NEVER GONNA LEAVE YOUR SIDE** Daniel Bedingfield	**BREATHE** Blu Cantrell featuring Sean Paul
UK No.1 ALBUMS			
DANGEROUSLY IN LOVE Beyoncé	**DANGEROUSLY IN LOVE** Beyoncé	**DANGEROUSLY IN LOVE** Beyoncé	**MAGIC AND MEDICINE** The Coral

THE ROSE [A] — Michael BALL
ROSE GARDEN [A] — Lynn ANDERSON
ROSE GARDEN [A] — NEW WORLD
A ROSE HAS TO DIE — The DOOLEYS
A ROSE IS STILL A ROSE — Aretha FRANKLIN
ROSE MARIE — Slim WHITMAN (55)
ROSE ROUGE — ST GERMAIN
ROSEABILITY — IDLEWILD
ROSES [A] — HAYWOODE
ROSES [B] — RHYTHM-N-BASS
ROSES [C] — dEUS
ROSES [D] — OUTKAST
ROSES ARE RED [A] — Ronnie CARROLL
ROSES ARE RED [A] — Bobby VINTON
ROSES ARE RED [B] — MAC BAND featuring The McCAMPBELL BROTHERS
ROSES IN THE HOSPITAL — MANIC STREET PREACHERS
ROSES OF PICARDY — Vince HILL
ROSETTA — Alan PRICE
ROSIE [A] — Don PARTRIDGE
ROSIE [B] — Joan ARMATRADING
ROTATION — Herb ALPERT
ROTTERDAM — The BEAUTIFUL SOUTH
ROUGH BOY — ZZ TOP
ROUGH BOYS [A] — Pete TOWNSHEND
ROUGH BOYS [B] — NORTHERN UPROAR
ROUGH JUSTICE [A] — BANANARAMA
ROUGH JUSTICE [B] — The ROLLING STONES
ROUGH WITH THE SMOOTH — Shara NELSON
ROUGH NECK (EP) — PROJECT 1
ROULETTE — Russ CONWAY (59)
ROUND AND ROUND [A] — Jimmy YOUNG
ROUND AND ROUND [B] — SPANDAU BALLET
ROUND AND ROUND [C] — Jaki GRAHAM
ROUND AND ROUND [D] — NEW ORDER
ROUND & ROUND [E] — HI-TEK featuring JONELL
ROUND EVERY CORNER — Petula CLARK
ROUND HERE [A] — COUNTING CROWS
ROUND HERE [B] — George MICHAEL
ROUND ROUND — SUGABABES (02)
THE ROUSSOS PHENOMENON (EP) — Demis ROUSSOS (76)
ROUTINE CHECK — The MITCHELL BROTHERS featuring KANO and The STREETS
ROXANNE — The POLICE
ROYAL EVENT — Russ CONWAY
ROYAL MILE — Gerry RAFFERTY
ROY'S KEEN — MORRISSEY
RSVP [A] — FIVE STAR
RSVP [B] — Jason DONOVAN
RSVP [C] — POP WILL EAT ITSELF
RUB A DUB DUB — The EQUALS
RUB-A-DUB — DOUBLE TROUBLE
RUBBER BALL [A] — The AVONS
RUBBER BALL [A] — Bobby VEE
RUBBER BALL [A] — Marty WILDE
RUBBER BULLETS — 10cc (73)
RUBBERBAND GIRL — Kate BUSH
THE RUBBERBAND MAN — The DETROIT SPINNERS
RUBBERBANDMAN — YELLO
RUBBERNECKIN' — Elvis PRESLEY
RUBBISH — CARTER — THE UNSTOPPABLE SEX MACHINE
THE RUBETTES — The AUTEURS
RUBY ANN — Marty ROBBINS
RUBY DON'T TAKE YOUR LOVE TO TOWN — Kenny ROGERS
RUBY RED [A] — SLADE
RUBY RED [B] — Marc ALMOND
RUBY TUESDAY [A] — MELANIE
RUBY TUESDAY [A] — Rod STEWART
RUBY TUESDAY [A] — The ROLLING STONES
RUDD — IKARA COLT
RUDE BOY ROCK — LIONROCK
RUDE BUOYS OUTA JAIL — The SPECIALS
RUDI GOT MARRIED — Laurel AITKEN and The UNITONE
RUDI'S IN LOVE — LOCOMOTIVE
RUDY'S ROCK — Bill HALEY and his COMETS
RUFF IN THE JUNGLE BIZNESS — The PRODIGY
RUFF MIX — WONDER DOG
RUFFNECK — MC LYTE
RUGGED AND MEAN, BUTCH AND ON SCREEN — PEE BEE SQUAD
RUINED IN A DAY — NEW ORDER

RULES AND REGULATIONS — WE'VE GOT A FUZZBOX AND WE'RE GONNA USE IT
RULES OF THE GAME — BUCKS FIZZ
RUMBLE IN THE JUNGLE — The FUGEES
RUMORS — TIMEX SOCIAL CLUB
RUMOUR HAS IT — Donna SUMMER
RUMOURS [A] — HOT CHOCOLATE
RUMOURS [B] — AWESOME
RUMOURS [C] — DAMAGE
RUMP SHAKER — WRECKX-N-EFFECT
RUN [A] — Sandie SHAW
RUN [B] — SPIRITUALIZED
RUN [C] — LIGHTHOUSE FAMILY
RUN [D] — SNOW PATROL
RUN AWAY [A] — 10cc
RUN AWAY [B] — (MC SAR &) The REAL McCOY
RUN AWAY (I WANNA BE WITH YOU) — NIVEA
RUN BABY RUN [A] — NEWBEATS
RUN BABY RUN [B] — Sheryl CROW
RUN BACK — Carl DOUGLAS
RUN DADDY RUN — FUN LOVIN' CRIMINALS
RUN FOR COVER — SUGABABES
RUN FOR HOME — LINDISFARNE
RUN FOR YOUR LIFE [A] — BUCKS FIZZ
RUN FOR YOUR LIFE [B] — NORTHERN LINE
RUN FROM LOVE — Jimmy SOMERVILLE
RUN ON — MOBY
RUN RUDOLPH RUN — Chuck BERRY
RUN RUN RUN [A] — JO JO GUNNE
RUN RUN RUN [B] — PHOENIX
RUN RUNAWAY — SLADE
RUN SILENT — SHAKESPEAR'S SISTER
RUN TO HIM — Bobby VEE
RUN TO ME — The BEE GEES
RUN TO MY LOVIN' ARMS — Billy FURY
RUN TO THE DOOR — Clinton FORD
RUN TO THE HILLS — IRON MAIDEN
RUN TO THE SUN — ERASURE
RUN TO YOU [A] — Bryan ADAMS
RUN TO YOU [A] — RAGE
RUN TO YOU [B] — Whitney HOUSTON
RUN TO YOU [C] — ROXETTE
RUN 2 — NEW ORDER
RUNAGROUND — JAMES
RUNAROUND — Martha WASH
RUNAROUND SUE [A] — DION
RUNAROUND SUE [A] — Doug SHELDON
RUNAROUND SUE [A] — RACEY
RUNAWAY [A] — Del SHANNON (61)
RUNAWAY [B] — DEEE-LITE
RUNAWAY [C] — Janet JACKSON
RUNAWAY [D] — E'VOKE
RUNAWAY [E] — The CORRS
RUNAWAY [F] — NUYORICAN SOUL featuring INDIA
THE RUNAWAY — Elkie BROOKS
RUNAWAY BOYS — STRAY CATS
RUNAWAY GIRL — Sterling VOID
RUNAWAY HORSES — Belinda CARLISLE
RUNAWAY LOVE — EN VOGUE
RUNAWAY SKIES — CELETIA
RUNAWAY TRAIN [A] — Elton JOHN and Eric CLAPTON
RUNAWAY TRAIN [B] — SOUL ASYLUM
THE RUNNER — The THREE DEGREES
RUNNIN [A] — BASSTOY
RUNNIN' [A] — Mark PICCHIOTTI presents BASSTOY featuring DANA
RUNNIN' [B] — BASS BUMPERS
RUNNIN' [C] — 2PAC and NOTORIOUS B.I.G.
RUNNIN' [D] — The PHARCYDE
RUNNIN' AWAY [A] — SLY and The FAMILY STONE
RUNNIN' AWAY [A] — NICOLE
RUNNIN' DOWN A DREAM — Tom PETTY and The HEARTBREAKERS
RUNNIN' (DYING TO LIVE) — TUPAC featuring NOTORIOUS B.I.G.
RUNNIN' FOR THE RED LIGHT (I GOTTA LIFE) — MEAT LOAF
RUNNIN' WITH THE DEVIL — VAN HALEN
RUNNING ALL OVER THE WORLD — STATUS QUO
RUNNING AROUND TOWN — Billie Ray MARTIN
RUNNING BEAR — Johnny PRESTON (60)
RUNNING FREE — IRON MAIDEN
RUNNING FROM PARADISE — Daryl HALL and John OATES
RUNNING IN THE FAMILY — LEVEL 42

RUNNING OUT OF TIME — DIGITAL ORGASM
RUNNING SCARED — Roy ORBISON
RUNNING UP THAT HILL — Kate BUSH
RUNNING WITH THE NIGHT — Lionel RICHIE
RUN'S HOUSE — RUN-DMC
RUPERT — Jackie LEE
RUSH [A] — FREAKPOWER
RUSH [B] — KLESHAY
THE RUSH — Luther VANDROSS
RUSH HOUR [A] — Jane WIEDLIN
RUSH HOUR [A] — JOYRIDER
RUSH HOUR [B] — BAD COMPANY
RUSH RUSH — Paula ABDUL
RUSH SONG — A
RUSHES — DARIUS
RUSHING — Loni CLARK
RUSSIANS — STING
RUST — ECHO and The BUNNYMEN
RUSTY CAGE — SOUNDGARDEN
S CLUB PARTY — S CLUB 7
SABOTAGE — BEASTIE BOYS
SABRE DANCE — LOVE SCULPTURE
SACRAMENTO (A WONDERFUL TOWN) — MIDDLE OF THE ROAD
SACRED CYCLES — Peter LAZONBY
SACRED TRUST — ONE TRUE VOICE
SACRIFICE — Elton JOHN (90)
SAD AND LONELY — SECRET MACHINES
SAD BUT TRUE — METALLICA
SAD EYES — Robert JOHN
SAD MOVIES (MAKE ME CRY) [A] — Carol DEENE
SAD MOVIES MAKE ME CRY [A] — Sue THOMPSON
SAD SONGS (SAY SO MUCH) — Elton JOHN
SAD SWEET DREAMER — SWEET SENSATION (74)
SADDLE UP — David CHRISTIE
SADIE'S SHAWL — Frank CORDELL
SADNESS PART 1 — ENIGMA (91)
SAFARI (EP) — The BREEDERS
SAFE FROM HARM [A] — MASSIVE ATTACK
SAFE FROM HARM [A] — NARCOTIC THRUST
THE SAFETY DANCE — MEN WITHOUT HATS
SAFFRON — EASTERN LANE
SAID I LOVED YOU BUT I LIED — Michael BOLTON
SAID SHE WAS A DANCER — JETHRO TULL
SAIL AWAY [A] — LITTLE ANGELS
SAIL AWAY [B] — URBAN COOKIE COLLECTIVE
SAIL AWAY [C] — David GRAY
SAIL ON — The COMMODORES
SAILING [A] — Rod STEWART (75)
SAILING [B] — Christopher CROSS
SAILING OFF THE EDGE OF THE WORLD — STRAW
SAILING ON THE SEVEN SEAS — ORCHESTRAL MANOEUVRES IN THE DARK
SAILOR [A] — Anne SHELTON
SAILOR [A] — Petula CLARK (61)
SAILORTOWN — ENERGY ORCHARD
THE SAINT [A] — THOMPSON TWINS
THE SAINT [B] — ORBITAL
ST ANGER — METALLICA
ST ELMO'S FIRE (MAN IN MOTION) — John PARR
SAINT OF ME — The ROLLING STONES
ST PETERSBURG — SUPERGRASS
ST TERESA — Joan OSBORNE
ST THERESE OF THE ROSES — Malcolm VAUGHAN
ST VALENTINE'S DAY MASSACRE (EP) — MOTÖRHEAD and GIRLSCHOOL (also known as HEADGIRL)
THE SAINTS ARE COMING — The SKIDS
THE SAINTS ROCK 'N ROLL — Bill HALEY and his COMETS
SALE OF THE CENTURY — SLEEPER
SALLY [A] — Gerry MONROE
SALLY [B] — CARMEL
SALLY [C] — KERBDOG
SALLY ANN — Joe BROWN and The BRUVVERS
SALLY CINNAMON — The STONE ROSES
SALLY DON'T YOU GRIEVE — Lonnie DONEGAN
SALLY MACLENNANE — The POGUES
SAL'S GOT A SUGAR LIP — Lonnie DONEGAN
SALSA HOUSE — Richie RICH
SALSOUL NUGGET (IF U WANNA) — M&S presents GIRL NEXT DOOR

SALT IN THE WOUND — CARPET BOMBERS FOR PEACE
SALT SWEAT SUGAR — JIMMY EAT WORLD
THE SALT WOUND ROUTINE — THIRTEEN SENSES
SALTWATER [A] — Julian LENNON
SALTWATER [B] — CHICANE featuring Maire BRENNAN of CLANNAD
SALTY — Dylan RHYMES featuring K ELLIS
SALTY DOG — PROCOL HARUM
SALVA MEA — FAITHLESS
SALVATION — The CRANBERRIES
SAM [A] — Keith WEST
SAM [B] — Olivia NEWTON-JOHN
SAMANTHA — Kenny BALL and his JAZZMEN
SAMBA DE JANEIRO — BELLINI
SAMBA MAGIC — SUMMER DAZE
SAMBA PA TI — SANTANA
SAMBUCA — WIDEBOYS featuring Dennis G
SAME OLD BRAND NEW YOU — a1 (00)
THE SAME OLD SCENE — ROXY MUSIC
SAME OLD STORY — ULTRAVOX
SAME PICTURE — GOLDRUSH
SAME SONG — DIGITAL UNDERGROUND
SAME TEMPO — CHANGING FACES
SAME THING IN REVERSE — BOY GEORGE
SAMSON AND DELILAH [A] — MIDDLE OF THE ROAD
SAMSON AND DELILAH [B] — BAD MANNERS
SAN ANTONIO ROSE — Floyd CRAMER
SAN BERNADINO — CHRISTIE
SAN DAMIANO (HEART AND SOUL) — Sal SOLO
SAN FRANCISCAN NIGHTS — The ANIMALS
SAN FRANCISCO (BE SURE TO WEAR SOME FLOWERS IN YOUR HAIR) — Scott McKENZIE (67)
SAN FRANCISCO DAYS — Chris ISAAK
SAN FRANCISCO (YOU'VE GOT ME) — VILLAGE PEOPLE
SAN MIGUEL [A] — KINGSTON TRIO
SAN MIGUEL [A] — Lonnie DONEGAN
SANCTIFIED LADY — Marvin GAYE
SANCTIFY YOURSELF — SIMPLE MINDS
SANCTIMONIOUS — HALO
SANCTUARY [A] — IRON MAIDEN
SANCTUARY [B] — NEW MUSIK
SANCTUARY [C] — DEJURE
SANCTUS (MISSA LUBA) — TROUBADOURS DU ROI BAUDOUIN
SAND IN MY SHOES — DIDO
SANDBLASTED (EP) — SWERVEDRIVER
SANDCASTLES — BOMB THE BASS
SANDMAN — BLUE BOY
SANDS OF TIME — KALEEF
SANDSTORM [A] — CAST
SANDSTORM [B] — DARUDE
SANDWICHES — DETROIT GRAND PU BAHS
SANDY — John TRAVOLTA
SANITY — KILLING JOKE
SANTA BRING MY BABY BACK (TO ME) — Elvis PRESLEY
SANTA CLAUS IS BACK IN TOWN — Elvis PRESLEY
SANTA CLAUS IS COMING TO TOWN [A] — The JACKSON FIVE
SANTA CLAUS IS COMIN' TO TOWN [A] — The CARPENTERS
SANTA CLAUS IS COMIN' TO TOWN [A] — Bruce SPRINGSTEEN
SANTA CLAUS IS COMING TO TOWN [A] — BJÖRN AGAIN
SANTA CLAUS IS ON THE DOLE — SPITTING IMAGE
SANTA CRUZ (YOU'RE NOT THAT FAR) — The THRILLS
SANTA MARIA [A] — TATJANA
SANTA MARIA [A] — DJ MILANO featuring SAMANTHA FOX
SANTA MONICA (WATCH THE WORLD DIE) — EVERCLEAR
SANTA'S LIST — Cliff RICHARD
SANTO NATALE (MERRY CHRISTMAS) — David WHITFIELD
SARA [A] — FLEETWOOD MAC
SARA [B] — STARSHIP
SARAH — THIN LIZZY
SARTORIAL ELOQUENCE — Elton JOHN
SAT IN YOUR LAP — Kate BUSH

16 August 2003	23 August 2003	30 August 2003	6 September 2003
BREATHE Blu Cantrell featuring Sean Paul	BREATHE Blu Cantrell featuring Sean Paul	BREATHE Blu Cantrell featuring Sean Paul	ARE YOU READY FOR LOVE Elton John
ESCAPOLOGY Robbie Williams	AMERICAN TUNE Eva Cassidy	AMERICAN TUNE Eva Cassidy	PERMISSION TO LAND The Darkness

SATAN — ORBITAL
SATAN REJECTED MY SOUL — MORRISSEY
THE SATCH EP — Joe SATRIANI
SATELLITE [A] — HOOTERS
SATELLITE [B] — The BELOVED
SATELLITE [C] — OCEANLAB
SATELLITE KID — DOGS D'AMOUR
SATELLITE OF LOVE '04— Lou REED
SATIN SHEETS — The BELLAMY BROTHERS
SATISFACTION [A] — Aretha FRANKLIN
SATISFACTION [A] — Otis REDDING
SATISFACTION [A] — VANILLA ICE
SATISFACTION [B] — WENDY and LISA
SATISFACTION [C] — EVE
SATISFACTION [D] — Benny BENASSI presents The BIZ
SATISFACTION GUARANTEED (OR TAKE YOUR LOVE BACK) — Harold MELVIN and The BLUENOTES
SATISFIED — Richard MARX
SATISFIED (TAKE ME HIGHER) — H2o
SATISFY MY LOVE [A] — EXOTERIX
SATISFY MY LOVE [B] — Sabrina JOHNSTON
SATISFY MY LOVE [C] — PESHAY
SATISFY MY SOUL — Bob MARLEY & The WAILERS
SATISFY YOU — PUFF DADDY
SATURDAY [A] — Joey NEGRO
SATURDAY [A] — EAST 57th STREET featuring Donna ALLEN
SATURDAY [B] — OMAR
SATURDAY GIG — MOTT THE HOOPLE
SATURDAY LOVE [A] — CHERELLE with Alexander O'NEAL
SATURDAY LOVE [A] —ILLEGAL MOTION featuring Simone CHAPMAN
SATURDAY NIGHT [A] — T-CONNECTION
SATURDAY NIGHT [B] — BLUE NILE
SATURDAY NIGHT [C] — SINDY
SATURDAY NIGHT [C] — WHIGFIELD (94)
SATURDAY NIGHT [D] — SUEDE
SATURDAY NIGHT [E] — UD PROJECT
SATURDAY NIGHT AT THE MOVIES [A] — The DRIFTERS
SATURDAY NIGHT AT THE MOVIES [A] — ROBSON & JEROME (96)
SATURDAY NIGHT (BENEATH THE PLASTIC PALM TREES) — LEYTON BUZZARDS
SATURDAY NIGHT PARTY (READ MY LIPS) — ALEX PARTY
SATURDAY NIGHT SUNDAY MORNING — T-EMPO
SATURDAY NIGHT'S ALRIGHT FOR FIGHTING — Elton JOHN
SATURDAY NITE [A] — EARTH WIND AND FIRE
SATURDAY NITE [B] — The BRAND NEW HEAVIES
SATURDAY NITE AT THE DUCK-POND — The COUGARS
SATURDAY (OOOH OOOH) — LUDACRIS
SATURDAY'S NOT WHAT IT USED TO BE — KINGMAKER
SATURN 5 — INSPIRAL CARPETS
THE SAVAGE — The SHADOWS
SAVANNA DANCE — DEEP FOREST
SAVE A LITTLE BIT — Glen GOLDSMITH
SAVE A PRAYER [A] — DURAN DURAN
SAVE A PRAYER [A] — 56K featuring BEJAY
SAVE IT FOR LATER — The BEAT
SAVE IT 'TIL THE MOURNING AFTER — SHUT UP AND DANCE
SAVE ME [A] — Dave DEE, DOZY, BEAKY, MICK and TICH
SAVE ME [B] — SILVER CONVENTION
SAVE ME [C] — QUEEN
SAVE ME [D] — FLEETWOOD MAC
SAVE ME [E] — BIG COUNTRY
SAVE ME [F] — EMBRACE
SAVE ME [G] — MEEKER
SAVE ME [H] — REMY ZERO
SAVE OUR LOVE — ETERNAL
SAVE THE BEST FOR LAST — Vanessa WILLIAMS
SAVE THE CHILDREN — Marvin GAYE
SAVE THE LAST DANCE FOR ME [A] — The DRIFTERS
SAVE THE LAST DANCE FOR ME [A] — Ben E KING
SAVE THE LAST DANCE FOR ME [A] — GENERAL SAINT
SAVE TONIGHT — Eagle-Eye CHERRY
SAVE UP ALL YOUR TEARS — CHER
SAVE US — Philip JAP
SAVE YOUR KISSES FOR ME — BROTHERHOOD OF MAN (76)
SAVE YOUR LOVE — RENÉE and RENATO (82)
SAVE YOUR LOVE (FOR #1) — RENÉ and ANGELA featuring Kurtis BLOW
SAVE YOURSELF — SPEEDWAY
SAVED [A] — MR ROY
SAVED [B] — OCTOPUS
SAVED BY THE BELL — Robin GIBB
SAVED MY LIFE — LIL' LOUIS
SAVING ALL MY LOVE FOR YOU — Whitney HOUSTON (85)
SAVING FOREVER FOR YOU — SHANICE
SAVIOUR'S DAY — Cliff RICHARD (90)
SAXUALITY — Candy DULFER
SAXY LADY — QUIVVER
SAY — CREATURES
SAY A LITTLE PRAYER — BOMB THE BASS featuring MAUREEN
SAY A PRAYER — Taylor DAYNE
SAY CHEESE (SMILE PLEASE) — FAST FOOD ROCKERS
SAY GOODBYE — S CLUB
SAY, HAS ANYBODY SEEN MY SWEET GYPSY ROSE — DAWN
SAY HELLO — DEEP DISH
SAY HELLO TO THE ANGELS — INTERPOL
SAY HELLO WAVE GOODBYE [A] — SOFT CELL
SAY HELLO WAVE GOODBYE [A] — David GRAY
SAY HOW I FEEL — Rhian BENSON
SAY I WON'T BE THERE — The SPRINGFIELDS
SAY ... IF YOU FEEL ALRIGHT — Crystal WATERS
SAY I'M YOUR NUMBER ONE — PRINCESS
SAY IT [A] — ABC
SAY IT [B] — Maria RUBIA
SAY IT AGAIN [A] — Jermaine STEWART
SAY IT AGAIN [B] — PRECIOUS
SAY IT AIN'T SO — WEEZER
SAY IT ISN'T SO [A] — Daryl HALL and John OATES
SAY IT ISN'T SO [B] — BON JOVI
SAY IT ISN'T SO [C] — Gareth GATES
SAY IT ONCE — ULTRA
SAY IT WITH FLOWERS — Dorothy SQUIRES and Russ CONWAY
SAY IT WITH PRIDE — SCOTLAND WORLD CUP SQUAD
SAY JUST WORDS — PARADISE LOST
SAY MY NAME [A] — ZEE
SAY MY NAME [B] — DESTINY'S CHILD
SAY NO GO — DE LA SOUL
SAY NOTHIN' — OMAR
SAY SAY SAY — Paul McCARTNEY and Michael JACKSON
SAY SOMETHING [A] — JAMES
SAY SOMETHING [B] — HAVEN
SAY SOMETHING ANYWAY — BELLEFIRE
SAY THAT YOU'RE HERE — FRAGMA
SAY WHAT! — X-PRESS 2
SAY WHAT YOU WANT — TEXAS
SAY WHEN — Lene LOVICH
SAY WONDERFUL THINGS — Ronnie CARROLL
SAY YEAH [A] — LIMIT
SAY YEAH [B] — BULLETPROOF
SAY YES — The BLOOD ARM
SAY YOU DO — ULTRA
SAY YOU DON'T MIND — Colin BLUNSTONE
SAY YOU LOVE ME [A] — FLEETWOOD MAC
SAY YOU LOVE ME [B] — SIMPLY RED
SAY YOU LOVE ME [C] — JOHNSON
SAY YOU REALLY WANT ME — Kim WILDE
SAY YOU, SAY ME — Lionel RICHIE
SAY YOU WILL — FOREIGNER
SAY YOU'LL BE MINE [A] — Amy GRANT
SAY YOU'LL BE MINE [B] — STEPS
SAY YOU'LL BE MINE [C] — QFX
SAY YOU'LL BE THERE — SPICE GIRLS (96)
SAY YOU'LL STAY UNTIL TOMORROW — Tom JONES
SAY YOU'RE MINE AGAIN — June HUTTON
(SAY) YOU'RE MY GIRL — Roy ORBISON
SAY YOU'RE WRONG — Julian LENNON
SCALES OF JUSTICE — LIVING IN A BOX
SCANDAL — QUEEN
SCANDALOUS [A] — CLICK
SCANDALOUS [B] — MIS-TEEQ
SCAR TISSUE — RED HOT CHILI PEPPERS
SCARECROW — SUB FOCUS
SCARED — SLACKER
SCARLET — ALL ABOUT EVE
SCARLET RIBBONS — Harry BELAFONTE
SCARLETT O'HARA — Jet HARRIS and Tony MEEHAN
SCARS — WITNESS
SCARY MONSTERS (AND SUPER CREEPS) — David BOWIE
SCARY MOVIES — BAD MEETS EVIL featuring EMINEM and ROYCE DA 5'9
THE SCARY-GO-ROUND EP — JELLYFISH
SCATMAN (SKI-BA-BOP-BA-DOP-BOP) — SCATMAN JOHN
SCATMAN'S WORLD — SCATMAN JOHN
SCATTER & SWING — LIONROCK
SCATTERLINGS OF AFRICA [A] — JULUKA
SCATTERLINGS OF AFRICA [A] — Johnny CLEGG and SAVUKA
SCHEMING — MAXIM
SCHMOO — SPOOKY
SCHNAPPI — SCHNAPPI
SCHONEBERG — MARMION
SCHOOL DAY [A] — Chuck BERRY
SCHOOL DAY [A] — Don LANG
SCHOOL LOVE — Barry BLUE
SCHOOL OF ROCK — SCHOOL OF ROCK
SCHOOL'S OUT [A] — Alice COOPER (72)
SCHOOL'S OUT [A] — DAPHNE & CELESTE
SCHOOLTIME CHRONICLE — Smiley CULTURE
SCHTEEVE — YOURCODENAMEIS:MILO
SCIENCE OF SILENCE — Richard ASHCROFT
THE SCIENTIST — COLDPLAY
SCOOBY DOO [A] — DWEEB
SCOOBY DOO [B] — J MAJIK and WICKAMAN
SCOOBY SNACKS — FUN LOVIN' CRIMINALS
SCOPE — PARIS ANGELS
SCORCHIO — SASHA
SCORPIO RISING — DEATH IN VEGAS with Liam GALLAGHER
SCOTCH ON THE ROCKS — Band of the BLACK WATCH
SCOTLAND BE GOOD — TARTAN ARMY
SCOTLAND FOR EVER (EP) — Sidney DEVINE
SCOTS MACHINE — VOYAGE
SCOTTISH RAIN — The SILENCERS
A SCOTTISH SOLDIER — Andy STEWART
SCRAMBLED EGGS — Roni SIZE
THE SCRATCH — SURFACE NOISE
SCREAM [A] — DISCO ANTHEM
SCREAM [B] — Michael JACKSON and Janet JACKSON
SCREAM [C] — NUT
SCREAM IF YOU WANNA GO FASTER — Geri HALLIWELL
SCREAM (PRIMAL SCREAM) — MANTRONIX
SCREAM UNTIL YOU LIKE IT — W.A.S.P.
THE SCREAMER — YOSH presents LOVEDEEJAY AKEMI
SCULLERY — Clifford T WARD
SE A VIDE É (THAT'S THE WAY LIFE IS) — PET SHOP BOYS
SEA OF BLUE — TECHNATION
SEA OF HEARTBREAK — Don GIBSON
SEA OF LOVE [A] — Marty WILDE
SEA OF LOVE [A] — HONEYDRIPPERS
SEAGULL — RAINBOW COTTAGE
THE SEAGULL'S NAME WAS NELSON — Peter E BENNETT with the CO-OPERATION CHOIR
SEAL MY FATE — BELLY
SEAL OUR FATE — Gloria ESTEFAN
SEALED WITH A KISS [A] — Brian HYLAND
SEALED WITH A KISS [A] — Jason DONOVAN (89)
SEANCE — NEBULA II
SEARCH AND DESTROY — DICTATORS
SEARCH FOR THE HERO — M PEOPLE
SEARCHIN' [A] — The COASTERS
SEARCHIN' [A] — The HOLLIES
SEARCHIN' FOR MY RIZLA — RATPACK
SEARCHIN' (I GOTTA FIND A MAN) — Hazell DEAN
SEARCHIN' MY SOUL — Vonda SHEPARD
SEARCHING [A] — CHANGE
SEARCHING [B] — CHINA BLACK
SEARCHING [C] — Jamie SCOTT
SEARCHING FOR A SOUL — Conner REEVES
SEARCHING FOR THE GOLDEN EYE — MOTIV 8 and Kym MAZELLE
SEASIDE — The ORDINARY BOYS
SEASIDE SHUFFLE — Terry DACTYL and The DINOSAURS
SEASON NO.5 — BEDLAM AGO GO
SEASONS IN THE ABYSS — SLAYER
SEASONS IN THE SUN [A] — Terry JACKS (74)
SEASONS IN THE SUN [A] — WESTLIFE (99)
SEASONS OF GOLD — GIDEA PARK
SEASONSTREAM (EP) — THOUSAND YARD STARE
SEATTLE — PUBLIC IMAGE LTD
2ND AMENDMENT — EASYWORLD
SECOND CHANCE — Phillip LEO
SECOND HAND ROSE — Barbra STREISAND
SECOND NATURE [A] — Dan HARTMAN
SECOND NATURE [B] — ELECTRONIC
SECOND ROUND KO — CANIBUS
THE SECOND SUMMER OF LOVE — DANNY WILSON
THE SECOND TIME — Kim WILDE
THE SECOND TIME AROUND — SHALAMAR
THE SECOND TIME (THEME FROM 'BILITIS') — Elaine PAIGE
SECRET [A] — ORCHESTRAL MANOEUVRES IN THE DARK
SECRET [B] — MADONNA
SECRET AGENT MAN - JAMES BOND IS BACK — Bruce WILLIS
SECRET COMBINATION — Randy CRAWFORD
SECRET GARDEN [A] — T'PAU
SECRET GARDEN [B] — Quincy JONES featuring Al B SURE!, James INGRAM, El DeBARGE and Barry WHITE
SECRET GARDEN [C] — Bruce SPRINGSTEEN
SECRET HEART — TIGHT FIT
SECRET KISS — The CORAL
SECRET LOVE [A] — Doris DAY (54)
SECRET LOVE [A] — Kathy KIRBY
SECRET LOVE [A] — Daniel O'DONNELL
SECRET LOVE [B] — The BEE GEES
SECRET LOVE [C] — Danni'elle GAHA
SECRET LOVE [D] — SHAH
SECRET LOVE [E] — Kelly PRICE
SECRET LOVERS — ATLANTIC STARR
SECRET MESSAGES — ELECTRIC LIGHT ORCHESTRA
SECRET RENDEZVOUS [A] — RENÉ and ANGELA
SECRET RENDEZVOUS [B] — Karyn WHITE
SECRET SMILE — SEMISONIC
SECRET STAR — WOMACK and WOMACK
THE SECRET VAMPIRE SOUNDTRACK (EP) — BIS
SECRETLY — SKUNK ANANSIE
SECRETS [A] — SUTHERLAND BROTHERS and QUIVER
SECRETS [B] — FIAT LUX
SECRETS [C] — PRIMITIVES
SECRETS [D] — SUNSCREEM
SECRETS [E] — ETERNAL
SECRETS [F] — MUTINY UK
SECRETS IN THE STREET — Nils LOFGREN
SECRETS (OF SUCCESS) — COOKIE CREW
SECRETS OF THE HEART — Chesney HAWKES
THE SECOND LINE — CLINIC
THE SECRETS THAT YOU KEEP — MUD
THE SEDUCTION (LOVE THEME) — James LAST BAND
SEE A BRIGHTER DAY — JTQ
SEE EMILY PLAY — PINK FLOYD
SEE IT IN A BOY'S EYES — JAMELIA
SEE JUNGLE! (JUNGLE BOY) — BOW WOW WOW
SEE LINE WOMAN' '99 — SONGSTRESS
SEE ME — Luther VANDROSS
SEE MY BABY JIVE — WIZZARD: Vocal backing by The Suedettes (73)
SEE MY FRIEND — The KINKS
SEE THAT GLOW — THIS ISLAND EARTH
SEE THE DAY — Dee C LEE
SEE THE DAY [A] — GIRLS ALOUD
SEE THE LIGHT — PARADISE
SEE THE LIGHTS — SIMPLE MINDS
SEE THE STAR — DELIRIOUS?
SEE THOSE EYES — ALTERED IMAGES

	13 September 2003	20 September 2003	27 September 2003	4 October 2003
UK No.1 SINGLES	WHERE IS THE LOVE? The Black Eyed Peas	WHERE IS THE LOVE? The Black Eyed Peas	WHERE IS THE LOVE? The Black Eyed Peas	WHERE IS THE LOVE? The Black Eyed Peas
UK No.1 ALBUMS	PERMISSION TO LAND The Darkness	PERMISSION TO LAND The Darkness	PERMISSION TO LAND The Darkness	ABSOLUTION Muse

SEE THRU IT —
APHRODITE featuring WILDFLOWER
SEE WANT MUST HAVE — BLUE MERCEDES
SEE YA — ATOMIC KITTEN
SEE YOU — DEPECHE MODE
SEE YOU LATER — REGENTS
SEE YOU LATER ALLIGATOR —
Bill HALEY and his COMETS
THE SEED (2.0) —
ROOTS featuring Cody CHESTNUTT
SEEING THINGS — The BLACK CROWES
THE SEEKER — The WHO
SEEMS FINE — The CONCRETES
SEEN THE LIGHT — SUPERGRASS
SEETHER — VERUCA SALT
SEIZE THE DAY — FKW
SELA — Lionel RICHIE
SELECTA (URBAN HEROES) — JAMESON & VIPER
SELF! — WE'VE GOT A FUZZBOX AND WE'RE GONNA USE IT
SELF CONTROL — Laura BRANIGAN
SELF DESTRUCTION —
STOP THE VIOLENCE MOVEMENT
SELF ESTEEM — The OFFSPRING
SELF SUICIDE — GOLDIE LOOKIN CHAIN
SELFISH — The OTHER TWO
SELFISH WAYS — DOGS
SELLING JESUS — SKUNK ANANSIE
SELLING THE DRAMA — LIVE
SEMI-CHARMED LIFE — THIRD EYE BLIND
SEMI-DETACHED SUBURBAN MR JAMES —
MANFRED MANN
SEND HIS LOVE TO ME — P J HARVEY
SEND IN THE CLOWNS — Judy COLLINS
SEND ME AN ANGEL [A] — BLACKFOOT
SEND ME AN ANGEL [B] — SCORPIONS
SEND ME THE PILLOW YOU DREAM ON —
Johnny TILLOTSON
SEND MY HEART — The ADVENTURES
SEND ONE YOUR LOVE — Stevie WONDER
SEND YOUR LOVE — STING
SENDING OUT AN S.O.S. — Retta YOUNG
SEÑORITA — Justin TIMBERLAKE
SENSATION — ELECTROSET
SENSATIONAL — Michelle GAYLE
SENSE [A] — The LIGHTNING SEEDS
SENSE [A] — Terry HALL
SENSE OF DANGER —
PRESENCE featuring Shara NELSON
SENSES WORKING OVERTIME — XTC
SENSITIVITY — Ralph TRESVANT
SENSITIZE — THAT PETROL EMOTION
SENSUAL SOPHIS-TI-CAT — Carl COX
THE SENSUAL WORLD — Kate BUSH
SENSUALITY — LOVESTATION
SENTIMENTAL [A] — Alexander O'NEAL
SENTIMENTAL [B] — Deborah COX
SENTIMENTAL [C] — Kym MARSH
SENTIMENTAL FOOL — Lloyd COLE
SENTINEL — Mike OLDFIELD
SENZA UNA DONNA (WITHOUT A WOMAN)
— ZUCCHERO and Paul YOUNG
SEPARATE LIVES — Phil COLLINS
SEPARATE TABLES — Chris DE BURGH
SEPARATE WAYS — Gary MOORE
SEPTEMBER — EARTH WIND AND FIRE
SEPTEMBER IN THE RAIN —
Dinah WASHINGTON
SEPTEMBER SONG — Ian McCULLOCH
SERENADE [A] — Mario LANZA
SERENADE [B] — Mario LANZA
SERENADE [B] — Slim WHITMAN
SERENADE [C] — SHADES
SERENATA — Sarah VAUGHAN
SERENITY — Armin VAN BUUREN
SERENITY IN MURDER — SLAYER
SERIOUS [A] — Billy GRIFFIN
SERIOUS [B] — SERIOUS INTENTION
SERIOUS [C] — Donna ALLEN
SERIOUS [D] — DEJA
SERIOUS [E] — DURAN DURAN
SERIOUS [F] — Maxwell D
SERIOUS [G] — POP!
SERIOUS MIX — MIRAGE
SERPENTS KISS — The MISSION
SESAME'S TREET — SMART E'S
SET ADRIFT ON MEMORY BLISS — PM DAWN
SET FIRE TO ME — Willie COLON
SET IN STONE — BEDROCK
SET IT OFF [A] — HARLEQUIN 4s / BUNKER KRU
SET IT OFF [B] — PEACHES
SET ME FREE [A] — KINKS
SET ME FREE [B] — Jaki GRAHAM
SET ME FREE [C] — BRIT PACK
SET THE RECORD STRAIGHT — REEF
SET THE TONE — Nate JAMES
SET THEM FREE — ASWAD
THE SET UP (YOU DON'T KNOW) —
Obie TRICE featuring NATE DOGG
SET YOU FREE — N-TRANCE
SET YOUR LOVING FREE — Lisa STANSFIELD
SETTING SUN — The CHEMICAL BROTHERS (96)
SETTLE DOWN [A] — Lillo THOMAS
SETTLE DOWN [B] — UNBELIEVABLE TRUTH
7 [A] —
PRINCE and The NEW POWER GENERATION
SEVEN [B] — David BOWIE
SEVEN (EP) — JAMES
SEVEN AND SEVEN IS (LIVE VERSION) —
Alice COOPER
SEVEN CITIES — SOLAR STONE
7 COLOURS — LOST WITNESS
SEVEN DAFFODILS [A] — CHEROKEES
SEVEN DAFFODILS [A] — MOJOS
SEVEN DAYS [A] — Anne SHELTON
SEVEN DAYS [B] — STING
SEVEN DAYS [C] —
Mary J BLIGE featuring George BENSON
7 DAYS [D] — Craig DAVID (00)
SEVEN DAYS AND ONE WEEK — BBE
SEVEN DAYS IN SUNNY JUNE — JAMIROQUAI
SEVEN DAYS IN THE SUN — FEEDER
SEVEN DRUNKEN NIGHTS — DUBLINERS
747 — KENT
747 (STRANGERS IN THE NIGHT) — SAXON
SEVEN LITTLE GIRLS SITTING IN THE BACK SEAT
[A] — The AVONS
SEVEN LITTLE GIRLS SITTING IN THE BACK SEAT
[A] — Paul EVANS
SEVEN LITTLE GIRLS SITTING IN THE BACKSEAT
[A] — BOMBALURINA
SEVEN LONELY DAYS — Gisele MacKENZIE
7 NATION ARMY — The WHITE STRIPES
7 O'CLOCK — QUIREBOYS
SEVEN ROOMS OF GLOOM — The FOUR TOPS
SEVEN SEAS — ECHO and The BUNNYMEN
SEVEN SEAS OF RHYE — QUEEN
7 SECONDS —
Youssou N'DOUR (featuring Neneh CHERRY)
7:7 EXPANSION — SYSTEM 7
7-6-5-4-3-2-1 (BLOW YOUR WHISTLE) —
The RIMSHOTS
SEVEN TEARS — GOOMBAY DANCE BAND (82)
7 TEEN — REGENTS
$7000 AND YOU — The STYLISTICS
7 WAYS TO LOVE — COLA BOY
7 WEEKS — INME
SEVEN WONDERS — FLEETWOOD MAC
7 YEAR BITCH — SLADE
SEVEN YEARS IN TIBET — David BOWIE
SEVENTEEN [A] —
Boyd BENNETT and his ROCKETS
SEVENTEEN [A] — Frankie VAUGHAN
SEVENTEEN [B] — LET LOOSE
SEVENTEEN [C] — LADYTRON
17 [D] — YOURCODENAMEIS:MILO
17 AGAIN — EURYTHMICS
SEVENTH SON — Georgie FAME
78 STONE WOBBLE — GOMEZ
74-75 — CONNELLS
77 STRINGS —
Kurtis MANTRONIK presents CHAMONIX
SEVENTY-SIX TROMBONES —
The KING BROTHERS
72 — TURIN BRAKES
SEVERINA — The MISSION
SEX [A] — SLEAZESISTERS
SEX [B] — Robbie RIVERA featuring Billy Paul W
SEX [C] — GA GAS
SEX AND CANDY — MARCY PLAYGROUND
SEX AS A WEAPON — Pat BENATAR
SEX BOMB — Tom JONES & Mousse T
SEX, DRUGS AND ROCKS THROUGH YOUR
WINDOW — AGENT BLUE
SEX IS NOT THE ENEMY — GARBAGE
SEX LIFE — Geoffrey WILLIAMS
SEX ME —
R KELLY and Public ANNOUNCEMENT
THE SEX OF IT —
Kid CREOLE and The COCONUTS
SEX ON THE BEACH — T-SPOON
SEX ON THE STREETS — PIZZAMAN
SEX OVER THE PHONE — VILLAGE PEOPLE
SEX TALK (LIVE) — T'PAU
SEX TYPE THING — STONE TEMPLE PILOTS
SEXCRIME (NINETEEN EIGHTY FOUR) —
EURYTHMICS
SEXED UP — Robbie WILLIAMS
SEXOMATIC — The BAR-KAYS
SEXIEST MAN IN JAMAICA — MINT ROYALE
SEXUAL [A] — Maria ROWE
SEXUAL [B] — AMBER
SEXUAL GUARANTEE — ALCAZAR
(SEXUAL) HEALING — Marvin GAYE
SEXUAL REVOLUTION — Macy GRAY
SEXUALITY — Billy BRAGG
SEXX LAWS — BECK
SEXY — MFSB
SEXY BOY — AIR
SEXY CINDERELLA — Lynden David HALL
SEXY CREAM — SLICK
SEXY EYES — DR HOOK
SEXY EYES — REMIXES — WHIGFIELD
SEXY GIRL — Lillo THOMAS
SEXY MF —
PRINCE and The NEW POWER GENERATION
SGT. PEPPER'S LONELY HEARTS CLUB BAND
– WITH A LITTLE HELP FROM MY FRIENDS
— The BEATLES
SGT ROCK (IS GOING TO HELP ME) — XTC
SHA LA LA LA LEE [A] — PLASTIC BERTRAND
SHA LA LA LA LEE [A] — The SMALL FACES
SHA LA LA — MANFRED MANN
SHA LA LA MEANS I LOVE YOU — Barry WHITE
SHACKLES (PRAISE YOU) — MARY MARY
SHADDAP YOU FACE —
Joe DOLCE MUSIC THEATRE (81)
SHADES OF BLUE (EP) — The THE
SHADES OF GREEN — The MISSION
SHADES OF PARANOIMIA — ART OF NOISE
SHADES OF SUMMER — RODEO JONES
SHADES (THEME FROM THE CROWN PAINT
TELEVISION COMMERCIAL) —
UNITED KINGDOM SYMPHONY
SHADOW DANCING — Andy GIBB
THE SHADOW OF LOVE — The DAMNED
SHADOWS — BREED 77
SHADOWS OF THE NIGHT — Pat BENATAR
SHADOWTIME —
SIOUXSIE and The BANSHEES
SHADY LADY — Gene PITNEY
SHADY LANE — PAVEMENT
SHAFT — VAN TWIST
SHAKE [A] — Otis REDDING
SHAKE [B] — Andrew RIDGELEY
SHAKE A LEG — ROLL DEEP
SHAKE! (HOW ABOUT A SAMPLING, GENE?) —
GENE AND JIM ARE INTO SHAKES
SHAKE IT BABY —
DJD presents HYDRAULIC DOGS
SHAKE IT DOWN — MUD
SHAKE IT (NO TE MUEVAS TANTO) [A] —
LEE-CABRERA
SHAKE IT (MOVE A LITTLE CLOSER) [A] —
LEE-CABRERA featuring Alex CARTAÑA
SHAKE IT OFF — Mariah CAREY
SHAKE ME I RATTLE — The KAYE SISTERS
SHAKE RATTLE AND ROLL —
Bill HALEY and his COMETS
(SHAKE, SHAKE, SHAKE) SHAKE YOUR BOOTY —
KC and The SUNSHINE BAND
SHAKE THE DISEASE — DEPECHE MODE
SHAKE THIS MOUNTAIN — HORSE
SHAKE UR BODY —
SHY FX and T-POWER featuring DI
SHAKE (WHAT YA MAMA GAVE YA) — GENERAL
LEVY vs ZEUS featuring Bally JAGPAL
SHAKE YA ASS — MYSTIKAL
SHAKE YA BODY — N-TRANCE
SHAKE YA SHIMMY — PORN KINGS vs
FLIP & FILL featuring 740 BOYZ
SHAKE YA TAILFEATHER —
NELLY, P DIDDY and Murphy LEE
SHAKE YOU DOWN — Gregory ABBOTT
SHAKE YOUR BODY (DOWN TO THE GROUND) [A]
— FULL INTENTION
SHAKE YOUR BODY (DOWN TO THE GROUND) [A]
— The JACKSONS
SHAKE YOUR BON-BON — Ricky MARTIN
SHAKE YOUR FOUNDATIONS — AC/DC
SHAKE YOUR GROOVE THING —
PEACHES and HERB
SHAKE YOUR HEAD — WAS (NOT WAS)
SHAKE YOUR LOVE — Debbie GIBSON
SHAKE YOUR RUMP TO THE FUNK —
The BAR-KAYS
SHAKE YOUR THANG (IT'S YOUR THING) —
SALT-N-PEPA
SHAKERMAKER — OASIS
SHAKESPEARE'S SISTER — The SMITHS
SHAKESPEARE'S (WAY WITH) WORDS —
ONE TRUE VOICE
SHAKIN' ALL OVER —
Johnny KIDD and The PIRATES (60)
SHAKIN' LIKE A LEAF — The STRANGLERS
THE SHAKIN' STEVENS EP — Shakin' STEVENS
SHAKING THE TREE —
Youssou N'DOUR and Peter GABRIEL
SHAKTI (THE MEANING OF WITHIN) —
MONSOON
SHAKALAKA BABY — Preeya KALIDAS
SHALALA LALA — The VENGABOYS
SHA-LA-LA (MAKE ME HAPPY) — Al GREEN
SHALL WE TAKE A TRIP — NORTHSIDE
SHAME [A] — Alan PRICE
SHAME [B] — Evelyn 'Champagne' KING
SHAME [B] — ALTERN 8
SHAME [B] — ZHANÉ
SHAME [B] — RUFF DRIVERZ
SHAME [C] —
ORCHESTRAL MANOEUVRES IN THE DARK
SHAME [D] — EURYTHMICS
SHAME [E] — PJ HARVEY
SHAME & SCANDAL [A] — MADNESS
SHAME AND SCANDAL IN THE FAMILY [A] —
Lance PERCIVAL
SHAME ON ME — Alexander O'NEAL
SHAME ON YOU — GUN
SHAME SHAME SHAME [A] — Jimmy REED
SHAME SHAME SHAME [B] —
SHIRLEY and COMPANY
SHAME SHAME SHAME [B] — SINITTA
SHAMELESS — Garth BROOKS
SHAMROCKS AND SHENANIGANS —
HOUSE OF PAIN
SHANG-A-LANG — BAY CITY ROLLERS
SHANGHAI'D IN SHANGHAI — NAZARETH
SHANGRI-LA — The RUTLES
SHANNON — Henry GROSS
SHANTE — MASS PRODUCTION
SHAPE — SUGABABES
SHAPE OF MY HEART [A] — STING
SHAPE OF MY HEART [B] — BACKSTREET BOYS
THE SHAPE OF THINGS TO COME —
HEADBOYS
THE SHAPE YOU'RE IN — Eric CLAPTON
SHAPES OF THINGS — YARDBIRDS
SHAPES THAT GO TOGETHER — A-HA
SHARE MY LIFE — INNER CITY
SHARE THE FALL — Roni SIZE / REPRAZENT
SHARE THE NIGHT — WORLD PREMIERE
SHARE YOUR LOVE (NO DIGGITY) — PASSION
SHARING THE NIGHT TOGETHER — DR HOOK
SHARING YOU — Bobby VEE
SHARK — THROWING MUSES
SHARP AS A KNIFE — Brandon COOKE featuring
Roxanne SHANTE
SHARP DRESSED MAN — ZZ TOP
SHATTER — FEEDER
SHATTERED DREAMS — JOHNNY HATES JAZZ
SHATTERED GLASS — DTOX
SHAZAM! — Duane EDDY and The REBELS
SH-BOOM [A] — The CREW CUTS
SH-BOOM [A] — Stan FREBERG
SH-BOOM (LIFE COULD BE A DREAM) [A] —
DARTS
SHE [A] — Charles AZNAVOUR (74)
SHE [A] — Elvis COSTELLO
SHE [A] — VEGAS
SHE AIN'T WORTH IT — Glenn MEDEIROS
featuring Bobby BROWN
SHE BANGS — Ricky MARTIN

11 October 2003	18 October 2003	25 October 2003	1 November 2003
WHERE IS THE LOVE? The Black Eyed Peas	**WHERE IS THE LOVE?** The Black Eyed Peas	**HOLE IN THE HEAD** Sugababes	**BE FAITHFUL** Fatman Scoop featuring The Crooklyn Clan
LIFE FOR RENT Dido	**LIFE FOR RENT** Dido	**LIFE FOR RENT** Dido	**LIFE FOR RENT** Dido

SHE BANGS THE DRUMS — The STONE ROSES
SHE BELIEVES IN ME [A] — Kenny ROGERS
SHE BELIEVES (IN ME) [A] — Ronan KEATING
SHE BLINDED ME WITH SCIENCE — Thomas DOLBY
SHE BOP — Cyndi LAUPER
SHE CAME HOME FOR CHRISTMAS — MEW
SHE CAN ROCK IT — POWER STATION
SHE COMES FROM THE RAIN — WEATHER PROPHETS
SHE COMES IN THE FALL — INSPIRAL CARPETS
SHE CRIES YOUR NAME — Beth ORTON
SHE DON'T FOOL ME — STATUS QUO
SHE DON'T LET NOBODY — Chaka DEMUS and PLIERS
SHE DRIVES ME CRAZY — FINE YOUNG CANNIBALS
SHE DROVE ME TO DAYTIME TELEVISION — FUNERAL FOR A FRIEND
SHE GOT GAME — TYMES 4
SHE GOT ME ON — Paul JOHNSON
SHE GOT SOUL — Jocelyn BROWN
SHE HATES ME — PUDDLE OF MUDD
SHE HITS ME — 4 OF US
SHE HOLDS THE KEY — SECRET LIFE
SHE IS BEAUTIFUL — Andrew W.K.
SHE IS LOVE — OASIS
SHE IS SUFFERING — MANIC STREET PREACHERS
SHE KISSED ME — Terence Trent D'ARBY
SHE KISSED ME (IT FELT LIKE A HIT) — SPIRITUALIZED
SHE KNOWS — BALAAM and The ANGEL
SHE LEFT ME ON FRIDAY — SHED SEVEN
SHE LOVED LIKE DIAMOND — SPANDAU BALLET
SHE LOVES ME NOT — PAPA ROACH
SHE LOVES YOU — The BEATLES (63)
SHE MAKES MY DAY — Robert PALMER
SHE MAKES MY NOSE BLEED — MANSUN
SHE MEANS NOTHING TO ME — Phil EVERLY and Cliff RICHARD
SHE MIGHT — The NOISE NEXT DOOR
SHE MOVES (LA LA LA) — KARAJA
SHE NEEDS LOVE — Wayne FONTANA and The MINDBENDERS
SHE SAID [A] — LONGPIGS
SHE SAID [B] — The PHARCYDE
SHE SAID [C] — Jon SPENCER BLUES EXPLOSION
SHE SELLS — BANDERAS
SHE SELLS SANCTUARY — The CULT
SHE SHE LITTLE SHEILA — Gene VINCENT
SHE SOLD ME MAGIC — Lou CHRISTIE
SHE TALKS TO ANGELS — The BLACK CROWES
SHE TAUGHT ME HOW TO YODEL — Frank IFIELD featuring The BACKROOM BOYS
SHE USED TO BE MINE — SPIN DOCTORS
SHE WAITS FOR ME — PROTOCOL
SHE WANTS TO DANCE WITH ME — Rick ASTLEY
SHE WANTS TO MOVE — N*E*R*D
SHE WANTS YOU — Billie PIPER
SHE WAS HOT — The ROLLING STONES
SHE WEARS MY RING — Solomon KING
SHE WEARS RED FEATHERS — Guy MITCHELL (53)
SHE WILL BE LOVED — MAROON5
SHE WILL HAVE HER WAY — Neil FINN
SHE WON'T TALK TO ME — Luther VANDROSS
SHE WORKS HARD FOR THE MONEY — Donna SUMMER
SHED A TEAR — WET WET WET
SHED MY SKIN — D*NOTE
SHE'D RATHER BE WITH ME — The TURTLES
SHEELA-NA-GIG — P J HARVEY
SHEENA IS A PUNK ROCKER — The RAMONES
SHEEP — The HOUSEMARTINS
THE SHEFFIELD GRINDER — Tony CAPSTICK and The CARLTON MAIN / FRICKLEY COLLIERY BAND
SHEFFIELD SONG — SUPERNATURALS
SHEILA — Tommy ROE
SHEILA TAKE A BOW — The SMITHS
SHELLSHOCK — NEW ORDER
SHELTER — The BRAND NEW HEAVIES
SHELTER ME [A] — CINDERELLA
SHELTER ME [B] — CIRCUIT
THE SHEPHERD'S SONG — Tony OSBORNE SOUND
SHERIFF FATMAN — CARTER — THE UNSTOPPABLE SEX MACHINE
SHERRI DON'T FAIL ME NOW — STATUS QUO
SHERRY [A] — The FOUR SEASONS
SHERRY [A] — Adrian BAKER
SHE'S A BAD MAMA JAMA (SHE'S BUILT, SHE'S STACKED) — Carl CARLTON
SHE'S A GIRL AND I'M A MAN — Lloyd COLE
SHE'S A GOOD GIRL — SLEEPER
SHE'S A GROOVY FREAK — The REAL THING
SHE'S A LADY — Tom JONES
SHE'S A LITTLE ANGEL — LITTLE ANGELS
SHE'S A MYSTERY TO ME — Roy ORBISON
SHE'S A RAINBOW — WORLD OF TWIST
SHE'S A RIVER — SIMPLE MINDS
SHE'S A STAR — JAMES
SHE'S A SUPERSTAR — The VERVE
SHE'S A VISION — ALL EYES
SHE'S A WIND UP — DR FEELGOOD
SHE'S A WOMAN — SCRITTI POLITTI featuring Shabba RANKS
SHE'S ABOUT A MOVER — SIR DOUGLAS QUINTET
SHE'S ALL ON MY MIND — WET WET WET
SHE'S ALRIGHT — Bitty McLEAN
SHE'S ALWAYS A WOMAN — Billy JOEL
SHE'S CRAFTY — BEASTIE BOYS
SHE'S EVERY WOMAN — Garth BROOKS
SHE'S GONE [A] — Buddy KNOX
SHE'S GONE [B] — Daryl HALL and John OATES
SHE'S GONE [B] — Matthew MARSDEN featuring DESTINY'S CHILD
SHE'S GONNA BREAK SOON — LESS THAN JAKE
SHE'S GONNA WIN — BILBO
SHE'S GOT A REASON — DOGS
SHE'S GOT CLAWS — Gary NUMAN
SHE'S GOT ISSUES — The OFFSPRING
SHE'S GOT IT — LITTLE RICHARD
SHE'S GOT ME GOING CRAZY — 2 IN A ROOM
SHE'S GOT THAT VIBE — R KELLY
SHE'S GOT YOU — Patsy CLINE
SHE'S IN FASHION — SUEDE
SHE'S IN LOVE WITH YOU — Suzi QUATRO
SHE'S IN PARTIES — BAUHAUS
SHE'S LEAVING HOME — Billy BRAGG with Cara TIVEY (88)
SHE'S LIKE THE WIND — Patrick SWAYZE featuring Wendy FRASER
SHE'S LOST YOU — ZEPHYRS
SHE'S MINE — CAMEO
SHE'S MY EVERYTHING — FREEFALLER
SHE'S MY MACHINE — David Lee ROTH
SHE'S NEW TO YOU — Susan MAUGHAN
SHE'S NOT LEAVING — The RESEARCH
SHE'S NOT THERE [A] — ZOMBIES
SHE'S NOT THERE [A] — Neil MacARTHUR
SHE'S NOT THERE [A] — SANTANA
SHE'S NOT YOU — Elvis PRESLEY with The JORDANAIRES (62)
SHE'S ON FIRE [A] — TRAIN
SHE'S ON FIRE [B] — CUBAN HEELS
SHE'S ON IT — BEASTIE BOYS
SHE'S OUT OF MY LIFE — Michael JACKSON
SHE'S PLAYING HARD TO GET — HI-FIVE
(SHE'S) SEXY AND 17 — STRAY CATS
SHE'S SO BEAUTIFUL — Cliff RICHARD
SHE'S SO COLD — The ROLLING STONES
SHE'S SO FINE — THUNDER
SHE'S SO HIGH [A] — BLUR
SHE'S SO HIGH [B] — Tal BACHMAN
SHE'S SO HIGH [B] — Kurt NILSEN
SHE'S SO MODERN — The BOOMTOWN RATS
SHE'S STRANGE — CAMEO
SHE'S THE MASTER OF THE GAME — Richard Jon SMITH
SHE'S THE ONE [A] — James BROWN
SHE'S THE ONE [B] — Robbie WILLIAMS (99)
SHIFTING WHISPERING SANDS [A] — Billy VAUGHN
THE SHIFTING WHISPERING SANDS (PARTS 1 & 2) [A] — Eamonn ANDREWS
SHIMMY SHAKE — 740 BOYZ
SHINDIG — The SHADOWS
SHINE [A] — Joe BROWN and The BRUVVERS
SHINE [B] — MOTÖRHEAD
SHINE [C] — ASWAD
SHINE [D] — MOLLY HALF HEAD
SHINE [E] — SPACE BROTHERS
SHINE [F] — MONTROSE AVENUE
SHINE [G] — SLOWDIVE
SHINE [H] — The LOVEFREEKZ
SHINE A LITTLE LOVE — ELECTRIC LIGHT ORCHESTRA
SHINE EYE — RAGGA TWINS
SHINE EYE GAL — Shabba RANKS
SHINE IT ALL AROUND — Robert PLANT & The STRANGE SENSATION
SHINE LIKE A STAR — BERRI
SHINE ON [A] — HOUSE OF LOVE
SHINE ON [B] — DEGREES OF MOTION featuring BITI
SHINE ON ME — LOVESTATION
SHINE ON SILVER SUN — STRAWBS
SHINE SO HARD (EP) — ECHO and The BUNNYMEN
SHINE (SOMEONE WHO NEEDS ME) — MONACO
SHINED ON ME — PRAISE CATS
SHINEON — SCOTT & LEON
SHINING [A] — DOUBLE DEE
SHINING [B] — Kristian LEONTIOU
SHINING LIGHT — ASH
SHINING ROAD — CRANES
SHINING STAR — MANHATTANS
SHINING STAR (EP) — INXS
SHINOBI VS DRAGON NINJA — LOSTPROPHETS
SHINY DISCO BALLS — WHO DA FUNK featuring Jessica EVE
SHINY HAPPY PEOPLE — R.E.M.
SHINY SHINY — HAYSI FANTAYZEE
SHIP AHOY — MARXMAN
SHIP OF FOOLS [A] — WORLD PARTY
SHIP OF FOOLS [B] — ERASURE
SHIPBUILDING [A] — Robert WYATT
SHIPBUILDING [A] — Tasmin ARCHER
SHIPS IN THE NIGHT — BE BOP DELUXE
SHIPS (WHERE WERE YOU?) — BIG COUNTRY
SHIPWRECKED — GENESIS
SHIRALEE — Tommy STEELE
SHIRLEY — Shakin' STEVENS
SH!T ON YOU — D12
SHIVER [A] — George BENSON
SHIVER [B] — S-J
SHIVER [C] — COLDPLAY
SHIVER [D] — Natalie IMBRUGLIA
SHIVERING SAND — MEGA CITY FOUR
SHIVERS — Armin VAN BUUREN
SHO' YOU RIGHT — Barry WHITE
SHOCK THE MONKEY — Peter GABRIEL
SHOCK TO THE SYSTEM — Billy IDOL
SHOCK YOUR MAMA — Debbie GIBSON
SHOCKAHOLIC — KINKY MACHINE
SHOCKED — Kylie MINOGUE
SHOES — REPARATA and The DELRONS
SHOO BE DOO BE DOO DA DAY — Stevie WONDER
SHOO DOO FU FU OOH! — Lenny WILLIAMS
SHOOP — SALT-N-PEPA
THE SHOOP SHOOP SONG (IT'S IN HIS KISS) — CHER (91)
SHOORAH! SHOORAH! — Betty WRIGHT
SHOOT ALL THE CLOWNS — Bruce DICKINSON
SHOOT ME (WITH YOUR LOVE) — Tasha THOMAS
SHOOT ME WITH YOUR LOVE — D:REAM
SHOOT SHOOT — UFO
SHOOT THE DOG — George MICHAEL
SHOOT YOUR GUN — 22-20S
SHOOTING FROM MY HEART — BIG BAM BOO
SHOOTING FROM THE HEART — Cliff RICHARD
SHOOTING STAR [A] — BOYZONE
SHOOTING STAR [B] — DOLLAR
SHOOTING STAR [C] — FLIP & FILL
SHOOTING STAR [D] — DEEPEST BLUE
SHOPLIFTERS OF THE WORLD UNITE — The SMITHS
SHOPPING — SUPERSISTER
SHORLEY WALL — OOBERMAN
SHORT CUT TO SOMEWHERE — FISH
SHORT DICK MAN — 20 FINGERS
SHORT FAT FANNIE — Larry WILLIAMS
SHORT SHORT MAN — 20 FINGERS
SHORT SKIRT LONG JACKET — CAKE
SHORT'NIN' BREAD — VISCOUNTS
SHORT'NIN' BREAD ROCK — Tony CROMBIE and his ROCKETS
SHORTSHARPSHOCK (EP) — THERAPY?
SHORTY — WANNADIES
SHORTY (GOT HER EYES ON ME) — Donell JONES
SHORTY (YOU KEEP PLAYING WITH MY MIND) — IMAJIN featuring Keith MURRAY
SHOT BY BOTH SIDES — MAGAZINE
SHOT DOWN — NINE BLACK ALPS
SHOT DOWN IN THE NIGHT — HAWKWIND
SHOT IN THE DARK [A] — Ozzy OSBOURNE
SHOT IN THE DARK [B] — DJ HYPE
SHOT OF POISON — Lita FORD
SHOT OF RHYTHM AND BLUES — Johnny KIDD and The PIRATES
SHOT SHOT — GOMEZ
SHOT YOU DOWN — AUDIO BULLYS featuring Nancy SINATRA
SHOTGUN WEDDING [A] — Roy C
SHOTGUN WEDDING [A] — Rod STEWART
SHOULD I DO IT? — POINTER SISTERS
SHOULD I EVER (FALL IN LOVE) — NIGHTCRAWLERS featuring John REID
SHOULD I STAY — GABRIELLE
SHOULD I STAY OR SHOULD I GO — The CLASH (91)
SHOULDER HOLSTER — MORCHEEBA
SHOULDN'T DO THAT — KAJAGOOGOO
SHOULD'VE KNOWN BETTER — Richard MARX
SHOUT [A] — LULU
SHOUT [A] — Louchie LOU and Michie ONE
SHOUT [B] — TEARS FOR FEARS
SHOUT [C] — ANT & DEC
SHOUT SHOUT (KNOCK YOURSELF OUT) — Rocky SHARPE and The REPLAYS
SHOUT TO THE TOP [A] — STYLE COUNCIL
SHOUT TO THE TOP [A] — Fire ISLAND featuring Loleatta HOLLOWAY
SHOUTING FOR THE GUNNERS — ARSENAL FC
THE SHOUTY TRACK — LEMON JELLY
THE SHOW [A] — Doug E FRESH and The GET FRESH CREW
THE SHOW [B] — GIRLS ALOUD
SHOW A LITTLE LOVE — ULTIMATE KAOS
SHOW ME [A] — DEXY'S MIDNIGHT RUNNERS
SHOW ME [B] — Lindy LAYTON
SHOW ME [C] — Ultra NATÉ
SHOW ME [D] — Dana DAWSON
SHOW ME A SIGN — KONTAKT
SHOW ME GIRL — HERMAN'S HERMITS
SHOW ME HEAVEN [A] — Maria McKEE (90)
SHOW ME HEAVEN [A] — Tina ARENA
SHOW ME HEAVEN [A] — CHIMIRA
SHOW ME HEAVEN [A] — SAINT featuring Suzanna DEE
SHOW ME LOVE [A] — Robin S
SHOW ME LOVE [B] — ROBYN
SHOW ME LOVE [C] — INDIEN
SHOW ME MARY — CATHERINE WHEEL
SHOW ME THE MEANING OF BEING LONELY — BACKSTREET BOYS
SHOW ME THE MONEY — ARCHITECHS
SHOW ME THE WAY [A] — Peter FRAMPTON
SHOW ME THE WAY [B] — OSMOND BOYS
SHOW ME YOUR MONKEY — PERCY FILTH
SHOW ME YOUR SOUL — Lenny KRAVITZ / P DIDDY / LOON / Pharrell WILLIAMS
SHOW ME YOU'RE A WOMAN — MUD
THE SHOW MUST GO ON [A] — Leo SAYER
THE SHOW MUST GO ON [B] — QUEEN
THE SHOW (THEME FROM 'CONNIE') — Rebecca STORM
SHOW YOU THE WAY TO GO [A] — The JACKSONS (77)
SHOW YOU THE WAY TO GO [A] — Dannii MINOGUE
SHOWDOWN [A] — ELECTRIC LIGHT ORCHESTRA
SHOWDOWN [B] — Jody LEI
SHOWER YOUR LOVE — KULA SHAKER
SHOWING OUT (GET FRESH AT THE WEEKEND) — MEL and KIM
SHOWROOM DUMMIES — KRAFTWERK
THE SHUFFLE — Van McCOY
SHUGGIE LOVE — MONKEY BARS featuring Gabrielle WIDMAN

8 November 2003	15 November 2003	22 November 2003	29 November 2003
UK No.1 SINGLES			
BE FAITHFUL Fatman Scoop featuring The Crooklyn Clan	**SLOW** Kylie Minogue	**CRASHED THE WEDDING** Busted	**MANDY** Westlife
UK No.1 ALBUMS			
THE BEST OF R.E.M. - IN TIME - 1988-2003 R.E.M.	**GUILTY** Blue	**LIFE FOR RENT** Dido	**NUMBER ONES** Michael Jackson

SHUT 'EM DOWN — PUBLIC ENEMY
SHUT UP [A] — MADNESS
SHUT UP [B] — Kelly OSBOURNE
SHUT UP [C] — The BLACK EYED PEAS
SHUT UP! [D] — SIMPLE PLAN
SHUT UP AND DANCE — AEROSMITH
SHUT UP AND FORGET ABOUT IT — DANE
SHUT UP AND KISS ME — Mary-Chapin CARPENTER
SHUT UP (AND SLEEP WITH ME) — SIN WITH SEBASTIAN
SHUT YOUR MOUTH [A] — MADE IN LONDON
SHUT YOUR MOUTH [B] — GARBAGE
SHUTDOWN — PITCHSHIFTER
SHY BOY — BANANARAMA
SHY GIRL — Mark WYNTER
SHY GUY [A] — Diana KING
SHY GUY [A] — ASWAD
(SI SI) JE SUIS UN ROCK STAR — Bill WYMAN
SI TU DOIS PARTIR — FAIRPORT CONVENTION
SIC TRANSIT GLORIA GLORY FADES — BRAND NEW
SICK AND TIRED [A] — Fats DOMINO
SICK AND TIRED [B] — The CARDIGANS
SICK AND TIRED [C] — ANASTACIA
SICK MAN BLUES — The GOODIES
SICK OF DRUGS — The WILDHEARTS
SICK OF GOODBYES — SPARKLEHORSE
SICK OF IT — PRIMITIVES
SIDE — TRAVIS
SIDE BY SIDE — Kay STARR
SIDE SADDLE — Russ CONWAY (59)
SIDE STREETS — SAINT ETIENNE
THE SIDEBOARD SONG (GOT MY BEER IN THE SIDEBOARD HERE) — CHAS and DAVE
SIDESHOW [A] — CHANTER SISTERS
SIDESHOW [A] — Barry BIGGS
SIDEWALK TALK — JELLYBEAN
SIDEWALKING — JESUS AND MARY CHAIN
THE SIDEWINDER SLEEPS TONITE — R.E.M.
SIGHT FOR SORE EYES — M PEOPLE
THE SIGN — ACE OF BASE
SIGN 'O' THE TIMES — PRINCE
SIGN OF THE TIMES [A] — Bryan FERRY
SIGN OF THE TIMES [B] — The BELLE STARS
SIGN OF THE TIMES [C] — GRANDMASTER FLASH, Melle MEL and The FURIOUS FIVE
A SIGN OF THE TIMES — Petula CLARK
SIGN YOUR NAME — Terence Trent D'ARBY
SIGNAL [A] — JD aka 'DREADY'
SIGNAL [B] — FRESH BC
SIGNALS OVER THE AIR — THURSDAY
THE SIGNATURE TUNE OF 'THE ARMY GAME' — Michael MEDWIN, Bernard BRESSLAW, Alfie BASS and Leslie FYSON
SIGNED SEALED DELIVERED I'M YOURS [A] — Stevie WONDER
SIGNED SEALED DELIVERED (I'M YOURS) [A] — BOYSTOWN GANG
SIGNED, SEALED, DELIVERED, I'M YOURS [A] — BLUE featuring Stevie WONDER and Angie STONE
SIGNS [A] — TESLA
SIGNS ... [B] — BLAMELESS
SIGNS [C] — DJ BADMARSH & SHRI featuring UK APACHE
SIGNS [D] — SNOOP DOGG featuring Charlie WILSON and Justin TIMBERLAKE
SILENCE [A] — DELERIUM
SILENCE 2004 [A] — DELERIUM featuring Sarah McLACHLAN
SILENCE [B] — TAIKO
SILENCE [C] — GOMEZ
THE SILENCE — Mike KOGLIN
SILENCE IS EASY — STARSAILOR
SILENCE IS GOLDEN — The TREMELOES (67)
SILENCE WHEN YOU'RE BURNING — HAPPYLIFE
SILENT ALL THESE YEARS — Tori AMOS
SILENT LUCIDITY — QUEENSRŸCHE
SILENT NIGHT [A] — Bing CROSBY
SILENT NIGHT [A] — The DICKIES
SILENT NIGHT [A] — BROS
SILENT NIGHT [A] — Sinead O'CONNOR
SILENT NIGHT — SEVEN O'CLOCK NEWS [A] — SIMON and GARFUNKEL
SILENT RUNNING — MIKE and The MECHANICS
SILENT SCREAM — Richard MARX
SILENT SIGH — BADLY DRAWN BOY
SILENT TO THE DARK II — The ELECTRIC SOFT PARADE
SILENT VOICE — INNOCENCE
SILENT WORDS — Jan JOHNSTON
SILENTLY BAD MINDED — PRESSURE DROP
SILHOUETTES [A] — HERMAN'S HERMITS
SILHOUETTES [A] — Cliff RICHARD
SILK PYJAMAS — Thomas DOLBY
SILLY GAMES [A] — Janet KAY
SILLY GAMES [A] — Lindy LAYTON featuring Janet KAY
SILLY LOVE — 10cc
SILLY LOVE SONGS — Paul McCARTNEY
SILLY THING — SEX PISTOLS
SILVER [A] — ECHO and The BUNNYMEN
SILVER [B] — MOIST
SILVER [C] — HUNDRED REASONS
SILVER AND GOLD — ASAP
SILVER DREAM MACHINE (PART 1) — David ESSEX
SILVER LADY — David SOUL (77)
SILVER LINING — STIFF LITTLE FINGERS
SILVER MACHINE — HAWKWIND
SILVER SCREEN SHOWER SCENE — FELIX DA HOUSECAT
SILVER SHADOW — ATLANTIC STARR
SILVER SHORTS — WEDDING PRESENT
SILVER STAR — The FOUR SEASONS
SILVER THUNDERBIRD — Marc COHN
SILVERMAC — WESTWORLD
SILVERY RAIN — Cliff RICHARD
SIMBA GROOVE — HI POWER
SIMON SAYS [A] — Pharoahe MONCH
SIMON SAYS [B] — 1910 FRUITGUM CO
SIMON SMITH AND HIS AMAZING DANCING BEAR — Alan PRICE
SIMON TEMPLER — SPLODGENESSABOUNDS
SIMPLE AS THAT — Huey LEWIS and The NEWS
SIMPLE GAME — The FOUR TOPS
SIMPLE KIND OF LIFE — NO DOUBT
SIMPLE LIFE — Elton JOHN
SIMPLE SIMON (YOU GOTTA REGARD) — MANTRONIX
SIMPLE SINCERITY — RADISH
SIMPLE THINGS — SAW DOCTORS
THE SIMPLE THINGS — Joe COCKER
THE SIMPLE TRUTH (A CHILD IS BORN) — Chris DE BURGH
SIMPLY IRRESISTABLE — Robert PALMER
SIN — NINE INCH NAILS
SINBAD — SYSTEM 7
SINCE DAY ONE — Teena MARIE
SINCE I DON'T HAVE YOU [A] — Art GARFUNKEL
SINCE I DON'T HAVE YOU [A] — GUNS N' ROSES
SINCE I LEFT YOU — The AVALANCHES
SINCE I MET YOU BABY [A] — Gary MOORE and BB KING
SINCE I MET YOU BABY [B] — UB40 and LADY SAW
SINCE I TOLD YOU IT'S OVER — STEREOPHONICS
SINCE U BEEN GONE — Kelly CLARKSON
SINCE YESTERDAY — STRAWBERRY SWITCHBLADE
SINCE YOU'RE GONE — The CARS
SINCE YOU'VE BEEN GONE [A] — Aretha FRANKLIN
SINCE YOU'VE BEEN GONE [B] — RAINBOW
SINCERE — MJ COLE
SINCERELY — The McGUIRE SISTERS
SINFUL — Pete WYLIE
SING — TRAVIS
SING A HAPPY SONG [A] — George McCRAE
SING A HAPPY SONG [B] — O'JAYS
SING A LITTLE SONG — Desmond DEKKER and The ACES
SING-A-LONG [A] — A
SING-A-LONG [B] — SHANKS & BIGFOOT
SING A SONG — Byron STINGILY
SING A SONG (BREAK IT DOWN) — MANTRONIX
SING A SONG OF FREEDOM — Cliff RICHARD
SING AND SHOUT — SECOND IMAGE
SING BABY SING — The STYLISTICS
SING DON'T SPEAK — BLACKFOOT SUE
SING FOR ABSOLUTION — MUSE
SING FOR EVER — ST PHILIPS CHOIR
SING FOR THE MOMENT — EMINEM
SING HALLELUJAH! — DR ALBAN
SING IT AGAIN WITH JOE — Joe 'Mr Piano' HENDERSON
SING IT BACK — MOLOKO
SING IT (THE HALLELUJAH SONG) — MOZAIC
SING IT TO YOU (DEE-DOOB-DEE-DOO) — Lavinia JONES
SING IT WITH JOE — Joe 'Mr Piano' HENDERSON
SING LIKE AN ANGEL — Jerry LORDAN
SING LITTLE BIRDIE — Pearl CARR and Teddy JOHNSON
SING ME — The BROTHERS
SING ME AN OLD FASHIONED SONG — Billie Jo SPEARS
SING (OOH-EE-OOH) — Vivienne McKONE
SING OUR OWN SONG — UB40
SING SING — GAZ
SING UP FOR THE CHAMPIONS — REDS UNITED
SING YOUR LIFE — MORRISSEY
SINGALONG-A-SANTA — SANTA CLAUS and The CHRISTMAS TREES
SINGALONG-A-SANTA AGAIN — SANTA CLAUS and The CHRISTMAS TREES
THE SINGER SANG HIS SONG — The BEE GEES
SINGIN' IN THE RAIN [A] — MINT ROYALE
SINGIN' IN THE RAIN PART 1 [A] — Sheila B DEVOTION
THE SINGING DOGS (MEDLEY) — SINGING DOGS
SINGING IN MY SLEEP — SEMISONIC
SINGING THE BLUES [A] — Guy MITCHELL (57)
SINGING THE BLUES [A] — Tommy STEELE and The STEELMEN (57)
SINGING THE BLUES [A] — Dave EDMUNDS
SINGING THE BLUES [A] — Daniel O'DONNELL
SINGLE [A] — EVERYTHING BUT THE GIRL
SINGLE [B] — PET SHOP BOYS
SINGLE [C] — Natasha BEDINGFIELD
THE SINGLE — RISE
SINGLE AGAIN — FIERY FURNACES
SINGLE GIRL [A] — Sandy POSEY
SINGLE GIRL [B] — LUSH
SINGLE LIFE — CAMEO
THE SINGLES 1981-83 — BAUHAUS
SINK THAT SHIP — KAISER CHIEFS
SINK THE BISMARCK — Don LANG
SINK TO THE BOTTOM — FOUNTAINS OF WAYNE
SINNER — Neil FINN
SINS OF THE FAMILY — PF SLOAN
SIPPIN' SODA — Guy MITCHELL
SIR DANCEALOT — OLYMPIC RUNNERS
SIR DUKE — Stevie WONDER
SIREN SOUNDS — Roni SIZE
SISSYNECK — BECK
SISTA SISTA — Beverley KNIGHT
SISTER [A] — BROS
SISTER [B] — SISTER 2 SISTER
SISTER DEW — dEUS
SISTER FRICTION — HAYSI FANTAYZEE
SISTER HAVANA — URGE OVERKILL
SISTER JANE — NEW WORLD
SISTER MOON — TRANSVISION VAMP
SISTER OF MERCY — THOMPSON TWINS
SISTER PAIN — ELECTRAFIXION
SISTER SAVIOUR — RAPTURE
SISTER SISTER — SISTER BLISS
SISTER SURPRISE — Gary NUMAN
THE SISTERS (EP) — PULP
SISTERS ARE DOIN' IT FOR THEMSELVES — EURYTHMICS and Aretha FRANKLIN
SIT AND WAIT — Sydney YOUNGBLOOD
SIT DOWN — JAMES
SIT DOWN AND CRY — Errol DUNKLEY
THE SIT SONG — The BARRON KNIGHTS
SITTIN' ON A FENCE — TWICE AS MUCH
(SITTIN' ON) THE DOCK OF THE BAY — Otis REDDING
SITTIN' UP IN MY ROOM — BRANDY
SITTING AT HOME — HONEYCRACK
SITTING DOWN HERE — Lene MARLIN
SITTING IN THE PARK — Georgie FAME
SITTING ON THE TOP OF THE WORLD — LIVERPOOL FC
SITUATION — YAZOO
SIX — MANSUN
SIX DAYS — DJ SHADOW
SIX FEET DEEP (EP) — GRAVEDIGGAZ
643 (LOVE'S ON FIRE) — DJ TIESTO featuring Suzanne PALMER
SIX MILLION STEPS (WEST RUNS SOUTH) — Rahni HARRIS and F.L.O.
SIX PACK — The POLICE
THE SIX TEENS — The SWEET
634-5789 — Wilson PICKETT
6 UNDERGROUND — SNEAKER PIMPS
SIXTEEN — MUSICAL YOUTH
SIXTEEN BARS — The STYLISTICS
SIXTEEN REASONS — Connie STEVENS
SIXTEEN TONS [A] — Frankie LAINE
SIXTEEN TONS [A] — Tennessee Ernie FORD (56)
THE 6TH SENSE — COMMON
THE SIXTH SENSE — VARIOUS ARTISTS (MONTAGES)
68 GUNS — The ALARM
SIXTY MILE SMILE — 3 COLOURS RED
60 MILES AN HOUR — NEW ORDER
SIXTY MINUTE MAN — The TRAMMPS
69 POLICE — David HOLMES
THE SIZE OF A COW — The WONDER STUFF
SKA — DJ ZINC
SKA TRAIN — The BEATMASTERS featuring Betty BOO
SKAT STRUT — MC SKAT KAT and The STRAY MOB
SKATEAWAY — DIRE STRAITS
SK8ER BOI — Avril LAVIGNE
SKELETONS — Stevie WONDER
SKIFFLE SESSION (EP) — Lonnie DONEGAN
SKIING IN THE SNOW — WIGAN'S OVATION
SKIN — CHARLOTTE
SKIN DEEP [A] — Duke ELLINGTON
SKIN DEEP [A] — Ted HEATH
SKIN DEEP [B] — The STRANGLERS
THE SKIN GAME — Gary NUMAN
SKIN O' MY TEETH — MEGADETH
SKIN ON SKIN — GRACE
SKIN TRADE — DURAN DURAN
THE SKIN UP EP — SKIN
SKINHEAD MOONSTOMP — SYMARIP
SKIP A BEAT — Barrett WAUGH
SKIP TO MY LU — LISA LISA
SKUNK FUNK — GALLIANO
SKWEEZE ME PLEEZE ME — SLADE (73)
SKY — SONIQUE
A SKY BLUE SHIRT AND A RAINBOW TIE — Norman BROOKS
SKY HIGH [A] — JIGSAW
SKY HIGH [A] — NEWTON
SKY PILOT — The ANIMALS
SKY PLUS — NYLON MOON
SKY STARTS FALLING — DOVES
SKYDIVE — FREEFALL featuring Jan JOHNSTON
THE SKYE BOAT SONG — Roger WHITTAKER and Des O'CONNOR
SKYLARK — Michael HOLLIDAY
SKY'S THE LIMIT — NOTORIOUS B.I.G.
SKYWRITER — The JACKSON FIVE
SLADE – ALIVE AT READING (EP) — SLADE
SLAIN BY ELF — URUSEI YATSURA
SLAIN THE TRUTH (AT THE ROADHOUSE) — The BASEMENT
SLAM [A] — HUMANOID
SLAM [B] — ONYX
SLAM [C] — PENDULUM
SLAM DUNK (DA FUNK) — FIVE
SLAM JAM — WWF SUPERSTARS
SLANG — DEF LEPPARD
SLAP AND TICKLE — SQUEEZE
SLASH 'N' BURN — MANIC STREET PREACHERS
SLASHDOTDASH — FATBOY SLIM
SLAVE NEW WORLD — SEPULTURA
SLAVE TO LOVE — Bryan FERRY
SLAVE TO THE GRIND — SKID ROW
SLAVE TO THE RHYTHM — Grace JONES
SLAVE TO THE VIBE — AFTERSHOCK
SLAVE TO THE WAGE — PLACEBO
SLAVES NO MORE — The BLOW MONKEYS

6 December 2003	13 December 2003	20 December 2003	27 December 2003
LEAVE RIGHT NOW Will Young	**LEAVE RIGHT NOW** Will Young	**CHANGES** Kelly and Ozzy Osbourne	**MAD WORLD** Michael Andrews featuring Gary Jules
TURNAROUND Westlife	**FRIDAY'S CHILD** Will Young	**LIFE FOR RENT** Dido	**LIFE FOR RENT** Dido

SLEAZY BED TRACK — The BLUETONES
SLEDGEHAMMER — Peter GABRIEL
SLEDGER — PORN KINGS
SLEEP [A] — MARION
SLEEP [B] — CONJURE ONE
SLEEP ALONE — The WONDER STUFF
SLEEP FREAK — HEAVY STEREO
SLEEP NOW IN THE FIRE — RAGE AGAINST THE MACHINE
SLEEP ON THE LEFT SIDE — CORNERSHOP
SLEEP TALK — Alyson WILLIAMS
SLEEP TALK — A.T.F.C. featuring Lisa Millett
SLEEP WALK — SANTO and JOHNNY
SLEEP WELL TONIGHT — GENE
SLEEP WITH ME — BIRDLAND
SLEEPER — AUDIOWEB
SLEEPING AWAKE — P.O.D.
SLEEPING BAG — ZZ TOP
SLEEPING IN — MENSWEAR
SLEEPING IN MY CAR — ROXETTE
SLEEPING ON THE JOB — GILLAN
SLEEPING SATELLITE — Tasmin ARCHER (92)
SLEEPING WITH THE LIGHT ON — BUSTED
SLEEPING WITH THE LIGHTS ON — Curtis STIGERS
SLEEPING WITH VICTOR — Lynden David HALL
SLEEPWALK — ULTRAVOX
SLEEPWALKERS — MODEY LEMON
SLEEPY JOE — HERMAN'S HERMITS
SLEEPY SHORES — Johnny PEARSON
SLEIGH RIDE — S CLUB JUNIORS
SLICE OF DA PIE — Monie LOVE
SLID — FLUKE
SLIDE [A] — RAH BAND
SLIDE [B] — GOO GOO DOLLS
SLIDE ALONG SIDE — SHIFTY
SLIDING — Ian McCULLOCH
SLIGHT RETURN — The BLUETONES
THE SLIGHTEST TOUCH — FIVE STAR
SLIP AND DIP — COFFEE
SLIP AND SLIDE — MEDICINE HEAD
(SLIP & SLIDE) SUICIDE — KOSHEEN
SLIP SLIDIN' AWAY — Paul SIMON
SLIP YOUR DISC TO THIS — HEATWAVE
SLIPPERY PEOPLE — TALKING HEADS
SLIPPERY SLOPES — CLIPZ
SLIPPIN' — DMX
SLIPPING AWAY [A] — Dave EDMUNDS
SLIPPING AWAY [B] — MANSUN
SLITHER — VELVET REVOLVER
SLOGANS — Bob MARLEY & The WAILERS
SLOOP JOHN B — The BEACH BOYS
SLOPPY HEART — FRAZIER CHORUS
SLOW — KYLIE (03)
SLOW AND SEXY — Shabba RANKS featuring Johnny GILL
SLOW DOWN [A] — John MILES
SLOW DOWN [B] — LOOSE ENDS
SLOW DOWN [C] — Bobby VALENTINO
SLOW EMOTION REPLAY — The THE
SLOW FLOW — The BRAXTONS
SLOW HANDS — INTERPOL
SLOW IT DOWN — EAST 17
SLOW JAMZ — TWISTA
SLOW MOTION — ULTRAVOX
SLOW RIVERS — Elton JOHN and Cliff RICHARD
SLOW TRAIN TO DAWN — The THE
SLOW TRAIN TO PARADISE — TAVARES
SLOW TWISTIN' — Chubby CHECKER
SLOWDIVE — SIOUXSIE and The BANSHEES
SLOWHAND — POINTER SISTERS
SLY — MASSIVE ATTACK
SMACK MY BITCH UP — The PRODIGY
SMALL ADS — SMALL ADS
SMALL BIT OF LOVE — SAW DOCTORS
SMALL BLUE THING — Suzanne VEGA
SMALL SAD SAM — Phil McLEAN
SMALL TOWN — John Cougar MELLENCAMP
SMALL TOWN BOY — UK
A SMALL VICTORY — FAITH NO MORE
SMALLTOWN BOY — BRONSKI BEAT
SMALLTOWN CREED — KANE GANG
SMARTY PANTS — FIRST CHOICE
SMASH IT UP — The DAMNED
SMASH SUMTHIN' — REDMAN featuring Adam F
S.M.D.U. — BROCK LANDARS

SMELLS LIKE NIRVANA — Weird Al YANKOVIC
SMELLS LIKE TEEN SPIRIT [A] — NIRVANA
SMELLS LIKE TEEN SPIRIT [A] — ABIGAIL
SMILE [A] — Nat 'King' COLE
SMILE [A] — Robert DOWNEY Jr
SMILE [B] — PUSSYCAT
SMILE [C] — Audrey HALL
SMILE [D] — ASWAD
SMILE [E] — SUPERNATURALS
SMILE [F] — LONESTAR
SMILE [G] — FUTURE BREEZE
SMILE [H] — MONROE
THE SMILE — David ESSEX
A SMILE IN A WHISPER — FAIRGROUND ATTRACTION
SMILE LIKE YOU MEAN IT — The KILLERS
SMILER — HEAVY STEREO
SMOKE — Natalie IMBRUGLIA
SMOKE GETS IN YOUR EYES [A] — The PLATTERS (59)
SMOKE GETS IN YOUR EYES [A] — BLUE HAZE
SMOKE GETS IN YOUR EYES [A] — Bryan FERRY
SMOKE GETS IN YOUR EYES [A] — John ALFORD
SMOKE IT — The DANDY WARHOLS
SMOKE MACHINE — X-PRESS 2
SMOKE ON THE WATER [A] — DEEP PURPLE
SMOKE ON THE WATER [A] — ROCK AID ARMENIA
SMOKEBELCH II — SABRES OF PARADISE
SMOKESTACK LIGHTNIN' — HOWLIN' WOLF
SMOKEY BLUE'S AWAY — A NEW GENERATION
SMOKIN' IN THE BOYS' ROOM [A] — BROWNSVILLE STATION
SMOKIN' IN THE BOYS ROOM [A] — MÖTLEY CRÜE
SMOKIN' ME OUT — Warren G
SMOOTH — SANTANA
SMOOTH CRIMINAL [A] — Michael JACKSON
SMOOTH CRIMINAL [A] — ALIEN ANT FARM
SMOOTH OPERATOR [A] — SADE
SMOOTH OPERATOR [B] — BIG DADDY KANE
SMOOTHIN' GROOVIN' — INGRAM
SMOULDER — KING ADORA
SMUGGLER'S BLUES — Glenn FREY
THE SMURF — Tyrone BRUNSON
THE SMURF SONG — The SMURFS
SNAKE — R KELLY featuring BIG TIGGER
THE SNAKE — Al WILSON
SNAKE BITE (EP) — WHITESNAKE
SNAKE IN THE GRASS — Dave DEE, DOZY, BEAKY, MICK and TICH
SNAP! MEGAMIX — SNAP!
SNAP YOUR FINGAZ — KUMARA
SNAPPED IT — KRUST
SNAPPINESS — BBG
SNAPSHOT 3 — Roni SIZE
SNEAKIN' SUSPICION — DR FEELGOOD
SNEAKING OUT THE BACK DOOR — MATT BIANCO
SNOBBERY AND DECAY — ACT
SNOOKER LOOPY — CHAS and DAVE
SNOOP DOGG — SNOOP DOGGY DOGG
SNOOP'S UPSIDE YA HEAD — SNOOP DOGGY DOGG featuring Charlie WILSON
SNOOPY VS THE RED BARON [A] — HOTSHOTS
SNOOPY VS THE RED BARON [A] — ROYAL GUARDSMEN
SNOT RAP — Kenny EVERETT
SNOW [A] — ORN
SNOW [B] — JJ72
SNOW COACH — Russ CONWAY
SNOWBIRD — Anne MURRAY
SNOWBOUND FOR CHRISTMAS — Dickie VALENTINE
SNOWDEN — DOVES
THE SNOWS OF NEW YORK — Chris DE BURGH
SO ALIVE — Ryan ADAMS
SO AMAZING — Luther VANDROSS
SO BEAUTIFUL [A] — URBAN COOKIE COLLECTIVE
SO BEAUTIFUL [B] — Chris DE BURGH
SO BEAUTIFUL [C] — DJ INNOCENCE featuring ALEX CHARLES
SO BEAUTIFUL [D] — Darren HAYES
SO CALLED FRIEND — TEXAS

SO CLOSE [A] — Diana ROSS
SO CLOSE [B] — Daryl HALL and John OATES
SO CLOSE [C] — Dina CARROLL
SO CLOSE TO LOVE — Wendy MOTEN
SO COLD THE NIGHT — COMMUNARDS
SO CONFUSED — 2PLAY featuring RAGHAV & JUCXI
SO DAMN BEAUTIFUL — POLOROID
SO DAMN COOL — UGLY KID JOE
SO DEEP — REESE PROJECT
SO DEEP IS THE NIGHT — Ken DODD
SO DO I — Kenny BALL and his JAZZMEN
SO EASY — RÖYKSOPP
SO EMOTIONAL — Whitney HOUSTON
SO FAR AWAY — DIRE STRAITS
SO FINE [A] — Howard JOHNSON
SO FINE [B] — KINANE
SO FRESH, SO CLEAN — OUTKAST
SO GOOD [A] — Roy ORBISON
SO GOOD [B] — ETERNAL
SO GOOD [C] — BOYZONE
SO GOOD [D] — Juliet ROBERTS
SO GOOD [E] — Rachel STEVENS
SO GOOD [F] — BRATZ ROCK ANGELZ
SO GOOD SO RIGHT — Brenda RUSSELL
SO GOOD TO BE BACK HOME AGAIN — The TOURISTS
SO GOOD (TO COME HOME TO) — Ivan MATIAS
SO GRIMEY — SO SOLID CREW
SO GROOVY — Wendell WILLIAMS
SO HARD — PET SHOP BOYS
SO HELP ME GIRL — Gary BARLOW
SO HERE I AM — UB40
SO HERE WE ARE — BLOC PARTY
SO HOT — JC
SO I BEGIN — GALLEON
SO IN LOVE — ORCHESTRAL MANOEUVRES IN THE DARK
SO IN LOVE (THE REAL DEAL) — Judy CHEEKS
SO IN LOVE WITH YOU [A] — Freddy BRECK
SO IN LOVE WITH YOU [B] — SPEAR OF DESTINY
SO IN LOVE WITH YOU [C] — TEXAS
SO IN LOVE WITH YOU [D] — DUKE
SO INTO YOU [A] — Michael WATFORD
SO INTO YOU [B] — The WILDHEARTS
SO IT WILL ALWAYS BE — The EVERLY BROTHERS
SO LET ME GO FAR — DODGY
SO LITTLE TIME — ARKARNA
SO LONELY [A] — The POLICE
SO LONELY [B] — JAKATTA
SO LONG [A] — FISCHER-Z
SO LONG [B] — FIERCE
SO LONG [C] — Willy MASON
SO LONG BABY — Del SHANNON
SO LOW — OCEAN COLOUR SCENE
SO MACHO — SINITTA
SO MANY TIMES — GADJO featuring Alexandra PRINCE
SO MANY WAYS [A] — The BRAXTONS
SO MANY WAYS [B] — Ellie CAMPBELL
SO MUCH IN LOVE [A] — TYMES
SO MUCH IN LOVE [A] — ALL-4-ONE
SO MUCH IN LOVE [B] — MIGHTY AVENGERS
SO MUCH LOVE — Tony BLACKBURN
SO MUCH LOVE TO GIVE [A] — TOGETHER
SO MUCH LOVE TO GIVE [B] — FREELOADERS featuring The REAL THING
SO MUCH TROUBLE IN THE WORLD — Bob MARLEY & The WAILERS
SO NATURAL — Lisa STANSFIELD
SO NEAR TO CHRISTMAS — Alvin STARDUST
SO PURE [A] — BABY D
SO PURE [B] — Alanis MORISSETTE
SO REAL [A] — LOVE DECADE
SO REAL [B] — HARRY
SO RIGHT [A] — RAILWAY CHILDREN
SO RIGHT [B] — K-KLASS
SO ROTTEN — BLAK TWANG featuring JAHMALI
SO SAD THE SONG — Gladys KNIGHT and The PIPS
SO SAD (TO WATCH GOOD LOVE GO BAD) — The EVERLY BROTHERS
SO SAYS I — The SHINS
SO SEDUCTIVE — Tony YAYO featuring 50 CENT

SO SEXY — TWISTA featuring R KELLY
SO SORRY I SAID — Liza MINNELLI
SO STRONG — Ben SHAW featuring Adele HOLNESS
SO TELL ME WHY — POISON
SO THE STORY GOES — LIVING IN A BOX featuring Bobby WOMACK
SO THIS IS ROMANCE — LINX
SO TIRED [A] — Frankie VAUGHAN
SO TIRED [B] — Ozzy OSBOURNE
SO TIRED OF BEING ALONE — SYBIL
SO WHAT [A] — Gilbert O'SULLIVAN
SO WHAT! [B] — Ronny JORDAN
SO WHAT THE FUSS — Stevie WONDER
SO WHATCHA GONNA DO NOW — PUBLIC ENEMY
SO WHAT IF I — DAMAGE
SO WHY SO SAD — MANIC STREET PREACHERS
SO YESTERDAY — Hilary DUFF
SO YOU KNOW — INME
SO YOU WIN AGAIN — HOT CHOCOLATE (77)
SO YOU'D LIKE TO SAVE THE WORLD — Lloyd COLE
SO YOUNG [A] — SUEDE
SO YOUNG [B] — The CORRS
SOAK UP THE SUN — Sheryl CROW
SOAPBOX — LITTLE ANGELS
SOBER [A] — DRUGSTORE
SOBER [B] — Jennifer PAIGE
SOC IT TO ME — BADFELLAS featuring CK
SOCKIT2ME — Missy 'Misdemeanor' ELLIOTT featuring DA BRAT
SODA POP — MERRION, McCALL & KENSIT
SOFA SONG — The KOOKS
SOFT AS YOUR FACE — SOUP DRAGONS
SOFT LIKE ME — SAINT ETIENNE
SOFT TOP HARD SHOULDER — Chris REA
SOFTLY AS I LEAVE YOU — Matt MONRO
SOFTLY, SOFTLY [A] — Ruby MURRAY (55)
SOFTLY SOFTLY [B] — The EQUALS
SOFTLY WHISPERING I LOVE YOU [A] — CONGREGATION
SOFTLY WHISPERING I LOVE YOU [A] — Paul YOUNG
SOLACE OF YOU — LIVING COLOUR
SOLD — BOY GEORGE
SOLD ME DOWN THE RIVER — The ALARM
SOLD MY ROCK 'N' ROLL (GAVE IT FOR FUNKY SOUL) — Linda CARR
SOLD OUT (EP) — REEL BIG FISH
SOLDIER — DESTINY'S CHILD featuring T.I. & LIL WAYNE
SOLDIER BLUE — Buffy SAINTE-MARIE
SOLDIER BOY [A] — SHIRELLES
SOLDIER BOY [A] — CHEETAHS
SOLDIER GIRL — The POLYPHONIC SPREE
SOLDIER OF LOVE — Donny OSMOND
SOLDIER'S SONG — The HOLLIES
SOLEX (CLOSE TO THE EDGE) — Michael WOODS
SOLEY SOLEY — MIDDLE OF THE ROAD
SOLID — ASHFORD and SIMPSON
SOLID BOND IN YOUR HEART — The STYLE COUNCIL
SOLID GOLD EASY ACTION — T. REX
SOLID ROCK (LIVE) — DIRE STRAITS
SOLID WOOD — Alison MOYET
SOLITAIRE [A] — Andy WILLIAMS
SOLITAIRE [A] — The CARPENTERS
SOLITARY MAN — HIM
SOLOMON BITES THE WORM — The BLUETONES
SOLSBURY HILL [A] — Peter GABRIEL
SOLSBURY HILL [A] — ERASURE
(SOLUTION TO) THE PROBLEM — MASQUERADE
SOLVED — UNBELIEVABLE TRUTH
SOME BEAUTIFUL — Jack WILD
SOME CANDY TALKING — JESUS AND MARY CHAIN
SOME FANTASTIC PLACE — SQUEEZE
SOME FINER DAY — ALL ABOUT EVE
SOME GIRLS [A] — RACEY
SOME GIRLS [B] — ULTIMATE KAOS
SOME GIRLS [C] — Rachel STEVENS
SOME GIRLS (DANCE WITH WOMEN) — JC CHASEZ

3 January 2004	10 January 2004	17 January 2004	24 January 2004
UK No.1 SINGLES			
MAD WORLD Michael Andrews featuring Gary Jules	**MAD WORLD** Michael Andrews featuring Gary Jules	**ALL THIS TIME** Michelle	**ALL THIS TIME** Michelle
UK No.1 ALBUMS			
LIFE FOR RENT Dido	**FRIDAY'S CHILD** Will Young	**LIFE FOR RENT** Dido	**LIFE FOR RENT** Dido

SOME GUYS HAVE ALL THE LUCK [A] — Robert PALMER
SOME GUYS HAVE ALL THE LUCK [A] — Rod STEWART
SOME GUYS HAVE ALL THE LUCK [A] — Maxi PRIEST
SOME JUSTICE — URBAN SHAKEDOWN
SOME KIND OF A SUMMER — David CASSIDY
SOME KIND OF BLISS — Kylie MINOGUE
SOME KIND OF FRIEND — Barry MANILOW
SOME KIND OF HEAVEN — BBG
SOME KIND OF WONDERFUL — The BLOW MONKEYS
SOME KINDA EARTHQUAKE — Duane EDDY and The REBELS
SOME KINDA FUN — Chris MONTEZ
SOME LIE 4 LOVE — L.A. GUNS
SOME LIKE IT HOT — POWER STATION
SOME MIGHT SAY [A] — OASIS (95)
SOME MIGHT SAY [A] — DE-CODE featuring Beverli SKEETE
SOME MIGHT SAY [A] — SUPERNOVA
SOME OF YOUR LOVIN' — Dusty SPRINGFIELD
SOME OLD GIRL — PADDINGTONS
SOME OTHER GUY — The BIG THREE
SOME OTHER SUCKER'S PARADE — DEL AMITRI
SOME PEOPLE [A] — Carol DEENE
SOME PEOPLE [B] — BELOUIS SOME
SOME PEOPLE [C] — Paul YOUNG
SOME PEOPLE [D] — Cliff RICHARD
SOME PEOPLE SAY — TERRORVISION
SOME SAY — Kristian LEONTIOU
SOME THINGS YOU NEVER GET USED TO — Diana ROSS and The SUPREMES
SOME VELVET MORNING — PRIMAL SCREAM & Kate MOSS
SOMEBODY [A] — The STARGAZERS
SOMEBODY [B] — JUNIOR
SOMEBODY [C] — DEPECHE MODE
SOMEBODY [D] — Bryan ADAMS
SOMEBODY [E] — BRILLIANT
SOMEBODY [F] — SHORTIE vs BLACK LEGEND
SOMEBODY ELSE'S GIRL — Billy FURY
SOMEBODY ELSE'S GUY [A] — Ce Ce PENISTON
SOMEBODY ELSE'S GUY [A] — Jocelyn BROWN
SOMEBODY ELSE'S GUY [A] — Louchie LOU and Michie ONE
SOMEBODY HELP ME — Spencer DAVIS GROUP (66)
(SOMEBODY) HELP ME OUT — BEGGAR and CO
SOMEBODY IN THE HOUSE SAY YEAH! — 2 IN A ROOM
SOMEBODY LIKE YOU — ELATE
SOMEBODY LOVES YOU — Nik KERSHAW
SOMEBODY PUT SOMETHING IN MY DRINK — The RAMONES
SOMEBODY SCREAM — BONEY M
SOMEBODY STOLE MY GAL — Johnnie RAY
SOMEBODY TO LOVE [A] — Brad NEWMAN
SOMEBODY TO LOVE [A] — JETS
SOMEBODY TO LOVE [B] — QUEEN
SOMEBODY TO LOVE [C] — BOOGIE PIMPS
SOMEBODY TO SHOVE — SOUL ASYLUM
SOMEBODY TOLD ME — The KILLERS
SOMEBODY'S BABY — Pat BENATAR
SOMEBODY'S WATCHING ME — ROCKWELL
SOMEDAY [A] — Ricky NELSON
SOMEDAY [B] — GAP BAND
SOMEDAY [C] — GLASS TIGER
SOMEDAY [D] — Mariah CAREY
SOMEDAY [D] — REZONANCE Q
SOMEDAY [E] — M PEOPLE
SOMEDAY [F] — EDDY
SOMEDAY [G] — LOVE TO INFINITY
SOMEDAY [H] — ETERNAL
SOMEDAY [I] — CHARLOTTE
SOMEDAY [J] — The STROKES
SOMEDAY [K] — NICKELBACK
SOMEDAY I'LL BE SATURDAY NIGHT — BON JOVI
SOMEDAY I'LL FIND YOU — Shola AMA and Craig ARMSTRONG / The DIVINE COMEDY
SOMEDAY (I'M COMING BACK) — Lisa STANSFIELD
SOMEDAY MAN — The MONKEES
SOMEDAY ONE DAY — The SEEKERS
SOMEDAY WE'LL BE TOGETHER — Diana ROSS and The SUPREMES
SOMEDAY WE'LL KNOW — NEW RADICALS
SOMEDAY WE'RE GONNA LOVE AGAIN — The SEARCHERS
SOMEDAY (YOU'LL BE SORRY) — Kenny BALL and his JAZZMEN
SOMEDAY (YOU'LL COME RUNNING) — FM
SOMEDAY (YOU'LL WANT ME TO WANT YOU) — Jodie SANDS
SOMEHOW SOMEWHERE — DEEP SENSATION
SOMEONE [A] — Johnny MATHIS
SOMEONE [B] — ASCENSION
SOMEONE [C] — SWV featuring Puff DADDY
SOMEONE ALWAYS GETS THERE FIRST — BENNET
SOMEONE BELONGING TO SOMEONE — The BEE GEES
SOMEONE ELSE NOT ME — DURAN DURAN
SOMEONE ELSE'S BABY — Adam FAITH
SOMEONE ELSE'S ROSES — Joan REGAN
SOMEONE LIKE ME — ATOMIC KITTEN
SOMEONE LIKE YOU [A] — Dina CARROLL
SOMEONE LIKE YOU [B] — Russell WATSON and Faye TOZER
SOMEONE LOVES YOU HONEY — Lutricia McNEAL
SOMEONE MUST HAVE HURT YOU A LOT — Frankie VAUGHAN
SOMEONE ON YOUR MIND — Jimmy YOUNG
SOMEONE SAVED MY LIFE TONIGHT — Elton JOHN
SOMEONE SHOULD TELL HER — MAVERICKS
SOMEONE SOMEONE — Brian POOLE and The TREMELOES
SOMEONE SOMEWHERE — WANNADIES
SOMEONE SOMEWHERE (IN SUMMERTIME) — SIMPLE MINDS
SOMEONE THERE FOR ME — Richard BLACKWOOD
SOMEONE TO CALL MY LOVER — JANET
SOMEONE TO HOLD — Trey LORENZ
SOMEONE TO LOVE [A] — Sean MAGUIRE
SOMEONE TO LOVE [B] — EAST 17
SOMEONE TO SOMEBODY — Feargal SHARKEY
SOMEONE'S DAUGHTER — Beth ORTON
SOMEONE'S LOOKING AT YOU — The BOOMTOWN RATS
SOMEONE'S TAKEN MARIA AWAY — Adam FAITH
SOMERSAULT — ZERO 7 featuring SIA
SOMETHIN' ELSE — Eddie COCHRAN
SOMETHIN' 4 DA HONEYZ — Montell JORDAN
SOMETHIN' IS GOIN' ON — Cliff RICHARD
SOMETHIN' STUPID [A] — Nancy SINATRA and Frank SINATRA (67)
SOMETHIN' STUPID [A] — Ali CAMPBELL
SOMETHING STUPID [A] — Amanda BARRIE and Johnny BRIGGS
SOMETHIN' STUPID [A] — Robbie WILLIAMS and Nicole KIDMAN (01)
SOMETHING [A] — Georgie FAME
SOMETHING [B] — The BEATLES
SOMETHING [B] — Shirley BASSEY
SOMETHING [C] — LASGO
SOMETHING ABOUT THE MUSIC — DA SLAMMIN' PHROGZ
SOMETHING ABOUT THE WAY YOU LOOK TONIGHT — Elton JOHN (97)
SOMETHING ABOUT U (CAN'T BE BEAT) — MR ROY
SOMETHING ABOUT YOU [A] — LEVEL 42
SOMETHING ABOUT YOU [B] — MR ROY
SOMETHING ABOUT YOU [C] — NEW EDITION
SOMETHING BEAUTIFUL — Robbie WILLIAMS
SOMETHING BEAUTIFUL REMAINS — Tina TURNER
SOMETHING BETTER BEGINNING — The HONEYCOMBS
SOMETHING BETTER CHANGE — The STRANGLERS
SOMETHING 'BOUT YOU BABY I LIKE [A] — Tom JONES
SOMETHING 'BOUT YOU BABY I LIKE [A] — STATUS QUO
SOMETHING CHANGED — PULP
SOMETHING DEEP INSIDE — Billie PIPER
SOMETHING DIFFERENT — SHAGGY
SOMETHING ELSE [A] — SEX PISTOLS
SOMETHING ELSE [B] — AGENT BLUE
SOMETHING FOR THE GIRL WITH EVERYTHING — SPARKS
SOMETHING FOR THE PAIN — BON JOVI
SOMETHING FOR THE WEEKEND [A] — The DIVINE COMEDY
SOMETHING FOR THE WEEKEND [B] — FRED & ROXY
SOMETHING 4 THE WEEKEND [C] — SUPER FURRY ANIMALS
SOMETHING GOIN' ON — Todd TERRY featuring Martha WASH and Jocelyn BROWN
SOMETHING GOOD — UTAH SAINTS
SOMETHING GOT ME STARTED — SIMPLY RED
SOMETHING HAPPENED ON THE WAY TO HEAVEN — Phil COLLINS
SOMETHING HERE IN MY HEART (KEEPS A-TELLIN' ME NO) — PAPER DOLLS
SOMETHING IN COMMON — Bobby BROWN and Whitney HOUSTON
SOMETHING IN MY HOUSE — DEAD OR ALIVE
SOMETHING IN THE AIR [A] — THUNDERCLAP NEWMAN (69)
SOMETHING IN THE AIR [A] — FISH
SOMETHING IN THE AIR [A] — Tom PETTY and The HEARTBREAKERS
SOMETHING IN YOUR EYES [A] — BELL BIV DEVOE
SOMETHING IN YOUR EYES [B] — Ed CASE
SOMETHING INSIDE OF ME — The CORAL
(SOMETHING INSIDE) SO STRONG [A] — Labi SIFFRE
(SOMETHING INSIDE) SO STRONG [A] — Michael BALL
(SOMETHING INSIDE) SO STRONG [A] — Rik WALLER
SOMETHING JUST AIN'T RIGHT — Keith SWEAT
SOMETHING MISSING — Petula CLARK
SOMETHING OLD, SOMETHING NEW — FANTASTICS
SOMETHING ON MY MIND — Chris ANDREWS
SOMETHING OUTA NOTHING — Letitia DEAN and Paul MEDFORD
SOMETHING SO GOOD — RAILWAY CHILDREN
SOMETHING SO REAL (CHINHEADS THEME) — LOVE DECREE
SOMETHING SO RIGHT — Annie LENNOX featuring Paul SIMON
SOMETHING SPECIAL [A] — Steve HARVEY
SOMETHING SPECIAL [B] — NOMAD
SOMETHING TELLS ME (SOMETHING IS GONNA HAPPEN TONIGHT) — Cilla BLACK
SOMETHING THAT I SAID — RUTS
SOMETHING THAT YOU SAID — The BANGLES
SOMETHING TO BELIEVE IN [A] — POISON
SOMETHING TO BELIEVE IN [B] — The RAMONES
SOMETHING TO DO – DEPECHE MODE
SOMETHING TO MISS — SENSELESS THINGS
SOMETHING WILD — RARE
SOMETHING WORTHWHILE — GUN
SOMETHING YOU GOT — AND WHY NOT?
SOMETHING'S BEEN MAKING ME BLUE — SMOKIE
SOMETHING'S BURNING — Kenny ROGERS
SOMETHING'S COOKIN' IN THE KITCHEN — DANA
SOMETHING'S GOIN' ON [A] — MYSTIC 3
SOMETHING'S GOING ON [B] — A
SOMETHING'S GOTTA GIVE — Sammy DAVIS Jr
SOMETHING'S GOTTEN HOLD OF MY HEART [A] — Gene PITNEY
SOMETHING'S GOTTEN HOLD OF MY HEART [A] — Marc ALMOND featuring special guest star Gene PITNEY (89)
SOMETHING'S HAPPENING — HERMAN'S HERMITS
SOMETHING'S JUMPIN' IN YOUR SHIRT — Malcolm McLAREN
SOMETHING'S MISSING — CHORDS
SOMETIMES [A] — ERASURE
SOMETIMES [B] — MAX Q
SOMETIMES [C] — JAMES
SOMETIMES [D] — The BRAND NEW HEAVIES
SOMETIMES [E] — TIN TIN OUT
SOMETIMES [F] — LES RYTHMES DIGITALES featuring Nik KERSHAW
SOMETIMES [G] — Britney SPEARS
SOMETIMES [H] — ASH
SOMETIMES ALWAYS — JESUS AND MARY CHAIN
SOMETIMES I MISS YOU SO MUCH — PM DAWN
SOMETIMES IT HURTS — TINDERSTICKS
SOMETIMES IT SNOWS IN APRIL — AMAR
SOMETIMES IT'S A BITCH — Stevie NICKS
SOMETIMES LOVE JUST AIN'T ENOUGH — Don HENLEY
SOMETIMES (THEME FROM 'CHAMPIONS') — Elaine PAIGE
SOMETIMES WHEN WE TOUCH [A] — Dan HILL
SOMETIMES WHEN WE TOUCH [A] — NEWTON
SOMETIMES YOU CAN'T MAKE IT ON YOUR OWN — U2 (05)
SOMEWHERE [A] — PJ PROBY
SOMEWHERE [A] — PET SHOP BOYS
SOMEWHERE [B] — EFUA
SOMEWHERE ACROSS FOREVER — STELLASTARR*
SOMEWHERE ALONG THE WAY — Nat 'King' COLE
SOMEWHERE DOWN THE CRAZY RIVER — Robbie ROBERTSON
SOMEWHERE ELSE [A] — CHINA DRUM
SOMEWHERE ELSE [B] — RAZORLIGHT
SOMEWHERE I BELONG — LINKIN PARK
SOMEWHERE IN AMERICA (THERE'S A STREET NAMED AFTER MY DAD) — WAS (NOT WAS)
SOMEWHERE IN MY HEART — AZTEC CAMERA
SOMEWHERE IN THE COUNTRY — Gene PITNEY
SOMEWHERE IN THE NIGHT — Barry MANILOW
SOMEWHERE MY LOVE [A] — MANUEL and his MUSIC OF THE MOUNTAINS
SOMEWHERE MY LOVE [A] — Mike SAMMES SINGERS
SOMEWHERE ONLY WE KNOW — KEANE
SOMEWHERE OUT THERE — Linda RONSTADT and James INGRAM
SOMEWHERE OVER THE RAINBOW — Cliff RICHARD
SOMEWHERE SOMEBODY — FIVE STAR
SOMEWHERE SOMEHOW — WET WET WET
SON OF A GUN — JX
SON OF A GUN (I BET YOU THINK THIS SONG IS ABOUT YOU) — Janet JACKSON with Carly SIMON featuring Missy ELLIOTT
SON-OF-A PREACHER MAN — Dusty SPRINGFIELD
SON OF HICKORY HOLLER'S TRAMP — OC SMITH
SON OF MARY — Harry BELAFONTE
SON OF MY FATHER — CHICORY TIP (72)
SON OF SAM — Elliott SMITH
SON OF THREE — The BREEDERS
SON THIS IS SHE — John LEYTON
(SONG FOR A) FUTURE GENERATION — The B-52's
SONG FOR GUY — Elton JOHN
SONG FOR LOVE — EXTREME
SONG 4 LOVERS — LIBERTY X featuring REV RUN from RUN DMC
A SONG FOR MAMA — BOYZ II MEN
SONG FOR SHELTER — FATBOY SLIM
A SONG FOR THE LOVERS — Richard ASHCROFT
SONG FOR WHOEVER — The BEAUTIFUL SOUTH
SONG FOR YOU — Michael BUBLE
SONG FROM THE EDGE OF THE WORLD — SIOUXSIE and The BANSHEES
THE SONG FROM THE MOULIN ROUGE — MANTOVANI (53)
SONG OF DREAMS — Becky TAYLOR
SONG OF JOY — Miguel RIOS
SONG OF LIFE — LEFTFIELD
SONG OF MEXICO — Tony MEEHAN COMBO
THE SONG OF MY LIFE — Petula CLARK
SONG OF THE DREAMER — Johnnie RAY
SONG SUNG BLUE — Neil DIAMOND
THE SONG THAT I SING (THEME FROM 'WE'LL MEET AGAIN') — STUTZ BEARCATS and the Denis KING ORCHESTRA
SONG TO THE SIREN — THIS MORTAL COIL
SONG 2 — BLUR
SONGBIRD [A] — Kenny G
SONGBIRD [B] — OASIS
SONGS FOR CHRISTMAS '87 (EP) — MINI POPS

31 January 2004	7 February 2004	14 February 2004	21 February 2004
ALL THIS TIME Michelle	**TAKE ME TO THE CLOUDS ABOVE** LMC vs U2	**TAKE ME TO THE CLOUDS ABOVE** LMC vs U2	**WITH A LITTLE HELP FROM MY FRIENDS / MEASURE OF A MAN** Sam & Mark
CALL OFF THE SEARCH Katie Melua	**CALL OFF THE SEARCH** Katie Melua	**CALL OFF THE SEARCH** Katie Melua	**FEELS LIKE HOME** Norah Jones

SONGS FOR SWINGING LOVERS (LP) — Frank SINATRA
SONIC BOOM BOY — WESTWORLD
SONIC BOOM (LIFE'S TOO SHORT) — QUO VADIS
SONIC EMPIRE — MEMBERS OF MAYDAY
SONNET — The VERVE
'SONS AND DAUGHTERS' THEME — KERRI and MICK
SONS OF THE STAGE — WORLD OF TWIST
SOON — MY BLOODY VALENTINE
SOON BE DONE — SHAGGY
SOONER OR LATER — Larry GRAHAM
SOOPA HOOPZ — SOOPA HOOPZ featuring QPR MASSIVE
SOOTHE ME — SAM and DAVE
SORRENTO MOON (I REMEMBER) — Tina ARENA
SORROW [A] — MERSEYS
SORROW [A] — David BOWIE
SORRY [A] — Ben ADAMS
SORRY [B] — The PADDINGTONS
SORRY BUT I'M GONNA HAVE TO PASS — The COASTERS
SORRY DOESN'T ALWAYS MAKE IT RIGHT — Diana ROSS
SORRY FOR YOU — Roni SIZE
SORRY (I DIDN'T KNOW) — MONSTA BOY featuring DENZIE
SORRY (I RAN ALL THE WAY HOME) — The IMPALAS
SORRY I'M A LADY — BACCARA
SORRY ROBBIE — Bert WEEDON
SORRY SEEMS TO BE THE HARDEST WORD [A] — Elton JOHN
SORRY SEEMS TO BE THE HARDEST WORD [A] — BLUE featuring Elton JOHN (02)
THE SORRY SUITOR — DIVE DIVE
SORRY SUZANNE — The HOLLIES
A SORTA FAIRYTALE — Tori AMOS
SORTED FOR E'S AND WIZZ — PULP
S.O.S. [A] — ABBA
S.O.S. [B] — ABC
THE SOS EP — The SHAMEN
SOUL BEAT CALLING — I KAMANCHI
SOUL BOSSA NOVA — COOL, The FAB, and The GROOVY present Quincy JONES
THE SOUL CAGES — STING
SOUL CHA CHA — Van McCOY
THE SOUL CITY WALK — Archie BELL and The DRELLS
SOUL CLAP '69 — BOOKER T and The MG's
SOUL COAXING — Raymond LEFEVRE
SOUL DEEP [A] — The BOX TOPS
SOUL DEEP [A] — Gary 'US' BONDS
SOUL DEEP (PART 1) — COUNCIL COLLECTIVE
SOUL DRACULA — HOT BLOOD
SOUL FINGER — The BAR-KAYS
SOUL FREEDOM — FREE YOUR SOUL — DEGREES OF MOTION featuring BITI
SOUL HEAVEN — GOODFELLAS featuring Lisa MILLETT
SOUL INSIDE — SOFT CELL
SOUL INSPIRATION — Simon CLIMIE
SOUL LIMBO — BOOKER T and The MG's
SOUL LOVE — The BLESSING
SOUL LOVE — SOUL MAN — WOMACK and WOMACK
SOUL MAN [A] — SAM and DAVE
SOUL MAN [A] — Sam MOORE and Lou REED
SOUL OF MY SOUL — Michael BOLTON
THE SOUL OF MY SUIT — T. REX
SOUL PASSING THROUGH SOUL — TOYAH
SOUL PROVIDER — Michael BOLTON
SOUL SEARCHIN' TIME — The TRAMMPS
SOUL SERENADE — Willie MITCHELL
SOUL SISTER, BROWN SUGAR — SAM and DAVE
SOUL SOUND — SUGABABES
SOUL TRAIN — SWANS WAY
SOULJACKER PART 1 — EELS
SOULMATE — WEE PAPA GIRL RAPPERS
SOULS — Rick SPRINGFIELD
THE SOULSHAKER — MAX LINEN
SOUL'S ON FIRE — TRACIE
SOUND — JAMES
THE SOUND — X-PRESS 2
SOUND ADVICE — Roni SIZE
SOUND AND VISION — David BOWIE
SOUND BWOY BURIAL — GANT
SOUND CLASH (CHAMPION SOUND) — KICK SQUAD
THE SOUND OF BAMBOO — FLICKMAN
THE SOUND OF BLUE — JFK
SOUND OF CONFUSION — SECRET AFFAIR
THE SOUND OF CRYING — PREFAB SPROUT
SOUND OF DRUMS — KULA SHAKER
SOUND OF EDEN [A] — SHADES OF RHYTHM
SOUND OF EDEN [A] — CASINO
THE SOUND OF MUSIC — DAYTON
THE SOUND OF MUSIK — FALCO
THE SOUND OF: OH YEAH — TOMBA VIRA
THE SOUND OF SILENCE — The BACHELORS
SOUND OF SOUNDS — GOMEZ
SOUND OF SPEED (EP) — JESUS AND MARY CHAIN
THE SOUND OF THE CROWD — HUMAN LEAGUE
THE SOUND OF THE SUBURBS — MEMBERS
SOUND OF THE UNDERGROUND — GIRLS ALOUD (02)
THE SOUND OF VIOLENCE — CASSIUS
THE SOUND OF YOUR CRY — Elvis PRESLEY
SOUND SYSTEM [A] — STEEL PULSE
SOUND SYSTEM [B] — DRUM CLUB
SOUND YOUR FUNKY HORN — KC and The SUNSHINE BAND
SOUNDS OF EDEN (EVERYTIME I SEE THE GIRL) — DEEP COVER
SOUNDS OF WICKEDNESS — TZANT
SOUR TIMES — PORTISHEAD
SOUTH AFRICAN MAN — Hamilton BOHANNON
SOUTH MANZ — DILLINJA
SOUTH OF THE BORDER — Robbie WILLIAMS
SOUTH OF THE RIVER — Mica PARIS
SOUTH PACIFIC — DJ ZINC
SOUTHAMPTON BOYS — RED 'N' WHITE MACHINES
SOUTHERN COMFORT — Berni FLINT
SOUTHERN FREEEZ — FREEEZ
SOUTHERN NIGHTS — Glen CAMPBELL
SOUTHERN SUN — OAKENFOLD
SOUTHSIDE — Dave CLARKE
SOUVENIR — ORCHESTRAL MANOEUVRES IN THE DARK
SOUVENIRS — VOYAGE
SOWETO [A] — Malcolm McLAREN
SOWETO [B] — Jeffrey OSBORNE
SOWING THE SEEDS OF HATRED — CREDIT TO THE NATION
SOWING THE SEEDS OF LOVE — TEARS FOR FEARS
SPACE [A] — NEW MODEL ARMY
SPACE [B] — SLIPMATT
SPACE AGE LOVE SONG — A FLOCK OF SEAGULLS
SPACE BASS — SLICK
THE SPACE BETWEEN — Dave MATTHEWS Band
SPACE COWBOY — JAMIROQUAI
SPACE JAM — QUAD CITY DJs
THE SPACE JUNGLE — ADAMSKI
SPACE LORD — MONSTER MAGNET
SPACE OASIS — Billie Ray MARTIN
SPACE ODDITY — David BOWIE (75)
SPACE RIDER — Shaun ESCOFFERY
SPACE STATION NO.5 [A] — Sammy HAGAR
SPACE STATION NUMBER 5 [A] — MONTROSE
SPACE WALK — LEMON JELLY
SPACED INVADER — HATIRAS featuring SLARTA JOHN
SPACEHOPPER — BAD COMPANY
SPACEMAN [A] — 4 NON BLONDES
SPACEMAN [B] — BABYLON ZOO (96)
A SPACEMAN CAME TRAVELLING — Chris DE BURGH
SPACER — Sheila B DEVOTION
SPANISH — Craig DAVID
SPANISH DANCE TROUPE — GORKY'S ZYGOTIC MYNCI
SPANISH EYES — Al MARTINO
SPANISH FLEA — Herb ALPERT
SPANISH HARLEM [A] — Jimmy JUSTICE
SPANISH HARLEM [A] — SOUNDS INCORPORATED
SPANISH HARLEM [A] — Aretha FRANKLIN
SPANISH HORSES — AZTEC CAMERA
SPANISH STROLL — MINK DeVILLE
SPANISH WINE — Chris WHITE
SPARE PARTS — Bruce SPRINGSTEEN
SPARK — Tori AMOS
SPARKLE — MY LIFE STORY
SPARKLE OF MY EYES — UB40 and LADY SAW
SPARKS — RÖYKSOPP
SPARKY'S DREAM — TEENAGE FANCLUB
THE SPARROW — The RAMBLERS (from the Abbey Hey Junior School)
THE SPARTANS — SOUNDS INCORPORATED
SPEAK LIKE A CHILD — STYLE COUNCIL
SPEAK TO ME PRETTY — Brenda LEE
SPEAK TO ME SOMEONE — GENE
SPEAKEASY — SHED SEVEN
SPECIAL [A] — GARBAGE
SPECIAL [B] — MEW
SPECIAL 2003 [C] — LEE-CABRERA
THE SPECIAL A.K.A. LIVE! EP — The SPECIALS (80)
SPECIAL BREW — BAD MANNERS
SPECIAL CASES — MASSIVE ATTACK
SPECIAL F/X — WHISPERS
SPECIAL KIND OF LOVE — Dina CARROLL
SPECIAL KIND OF LOVER — NU COLOURS
SPECIAL KIND OF SOMETHING — KAVANA
SPECIAL NEEDS — PLACEBO
SPECIAL WAY — RIVER CITY PEOPLE
THE SPECIAL YEARS — Val DOONICAN
SPECTACULAR — Graham COXON
SPEECHLESS — D-SIDE
SPEED — Billy IDOL
SPEED (CAN YOU FEEL IT) — Azzido DA BASS featuring Roland CLARK
SPEED OF SOUND — COLDPLAY
SPEED OF THE SOUND OF LONELINESS — ALABAMA 3
SPEED YOUR LOVE TO ME — SIMPLE MINDS
SPEEDWELL — SAINT ETIENNE
SPEEDY GONZALES — Pat BOONE
THE SPELL! — FUNKY WORM
SPELL (UNDER HER) — Hugh CORNWELL
SPELLBOUND — SIOUXSIE and The BANSHEES
SPEND SOME TIME — The BRAND NEW HEAVIES
SPEND THE DAY — URBAN COOKIE COLLECTIVE
SPEND THE NIGHT [A] — The COOLNOTES
SPEND THE NIGHT [B] — Danny J LEWIS
SPENDING MY TIME — ROXETTE
SPICE OF LIFE — MANHATTAN TRANSFER
SPICE UP YOUR LIFE — SPICE GIRLS (97)
SPIDERS — MOBY
SPIDERS & SNAKES — Jim STAFFORD
SPIDERWEBS — NO DOUBT
SPIES LIKE US — Paul McCARTNEY
SPIKEE — UNDERWORLD
SPILLER FROM RIO (DO IT EASY) — LAGUNA
SPIN SPIN SUGAR — SNEAKER PIMPS
SPIN THAT WHEEL (TURTLES GET REAL) — HI-TEK 3 featuring YA KID K
SPIN THE BLACK CIRCLE — PEARL JAM
SPIN THE WHEEL — BELLEFIRE
SPINDRIFT (EP) — THOUSAND YARD STARE
SPINNIN' AND SPINNIN' — SYREETA
SPINNING — CLARKESVILLE
SPINNING AROUND — Kylie MINOGUE (00)
SPINNING ROCK BOOGIE — Hank C BURNETTE
SPINNING THE WHEEL — George MICHAEL
SPINNIN' WHEELS — The CRESCENT
SPIRAL SCRATCH (EP) — The BUZZCOCKS
SPIRAL SYMPHONY — SCIENTIST
SPIRIT [A] — BAUHAUS
SPIRIT [B] — Wayne MARSHALL
SPIRIT [C] — SOUNDS OF BLACKNESS
SPIRIT [D] — Craig MACK
SPIRIT BODY AND SOUL — The NOLANS
SPIRIT IN THE SKY [A] — Norman GREENBAUM (70)
SPIRIT IN THE SKY [A] — DOCTOR and The MEDICS (86)
SPIRIT IN THE SKY [A] — Gareth GATES featuring The KUMARS (03)
SPIRIT INSIDE — SPIRITS
THE SPIRIT IS WILLING — Peter STRAKER and The HANDS OF DR TELENY
SPIRIT OF RADIO — RUSH
SPIRIT OF '76 — The ALARM
SPIRITS (HAVING FLOWN) — The BEE GEES
SPIRITS IN THE MATERIAL WORLD [A] — The POLICE
SPIRITS IN THE MATERIAL WORLD [A] — Pato BANTON with STING
SPIRITUAL HIGH (STATE OF INDEPENDENCE) — MOODSWINGS / CHRISSIE HYNDE
SPIRITUAL LOVE — URBAN SPECIES
SPIRITUAL THANG — Eric BENET
SPIRITUALIZED — Finley QUAYE
SPIT IN THE RAIN — DEL AMITRI
SPIT IT OUT [A] — SLIPKNOT
SPIT IT OUT [B] — Brendan BENSON
SPITTING GAMES — SNOW PATROL
SPLIFFHEAD — RAGGA TWINS
SPLISH SPLASH [A] — Bobby DARIN
SPLISH SPLASH [A] — Charlie DRAKE
SPOILED — Joss STONE
SPOOKY [A] — CLASSICS IV
SPOOKY [A] — ATLANTA RHYTHM SECTION
SPOOKY [B] — NEW ORDER
SPOONMAN — SOUNDGARDEN
SPOT THE PIGEON (EP) — GENESIS
SPREAD A LITTLE HAPPINESS — STING
SPREAD LOVE — FIGHT CLUB featuring Laurent KONRAD
SPREAD YOUR WINGS — QUEEN
SPRING IN MY STEP — NU-MATIC
SPRINGTIME FOR THE WORLD — The BLOW MONKEYS
SPUTNIK — STYLUS TROUBLE
SPY IN THE HOUSE OF LOVE — WAS (NOT WAS)
SPYBREAK! — PROPELLERHEADS
SPYCATCHER — J MAJIK and WICKAMAN
(SQUARE ROOT OF) 231 — ANTICAPPELLA
SQUARES — The BETA BAND
SQUEEZE BOX — The WHO
SQUIRT — FLUKE
SS PAPARAZZI — STOCK AITKEN WATERMAN
S-S-S-SINGLE BED — FOX
SSSST (LISTEN) — JONAH
STABBED IN THE BACK — MIND OF KANE
STACCATO'S THEME — Elmer BERNSTEIN
STACY'S MOM — FOUNTAINS OF WAYNE
STAGE ONE — SPACE MANOEVRES
STAGES — ZZ TOP
STAGGER LEE — Lloyd PRICE
STAINSBY GIRLS — Chris REA
THE STAIRCASE (MYSTERY) — SIOUXSIE and The BANSHEES
STAIRWAY OF LOVE [A] — Michael HOLLIDAY
STAIRWAY OF LOVE [A] — Terry DENE
STAIRWAY TO HEAVEN [A] — Neil SEDAKA
STAIRWAY TO HEAVEN [B] — FAR CORPORATION
STAIRWAY TO HEAVEN [B] — DREAD ZEPPELIN
STAIRWAY TO HEAVEN [B] — Rolf HARRIS
STAKES IS HIGH — DE LA SOUL
STAKKER HUMANOID — HUMANOID
STALEMATE — MAC BAND featuring The McCAMPBELL BROTHERS
STAMP! — AMOS
STAN — EMINEM (00)
STAN BOWLES — The OTHERS
STAND [A] — R.E.M.
STAND [B] — POISON
STAND ABOVE ME — ORCHESTRAL MANOEUVRES IN THE DARK
STAND AND DELIVER — ADAM and The ANTS (81)
STAND AND FIGHT — PACK featuring Nigel BENN
STAND BACK — LINUS LOVES featuring Sam OBERNIK
STAND BY — ROMAN HOLLIDAY
STAND BY LOVE — SIMPLE MINDS
STAND BY ME [A] — Ben E KING (87)
STAND BY ME [A] — John LENNON
STAND BY ME [A] — Kenny LYNCH
STAND BY ME [A] — 4 THE CAUSE
STAND BY ME [B] — OASIS
STAND BY MY WOMAN — Lenny KRAVITZ
STAND BY YOUR MAN — Tammy WYNETTE (75)
STAND CLEAR — ADAM F featuring M.O.P.
STAND DOWN MARGARET (DUB) — The BEAT
STAND INSIDE YOUR LOVE — SMASHING PUMPKINS
STAND OR FALL — FIXX

28 February 2004	6 March 2004	13 March 2004	20 March 2004
UK No.1 SINGLES			
WHO'S DAVID Busted	MYSTERIOUS GIRL (2nd Re-issue) Peter Andre	TOXIC Britney Spears	CHA CHA SLIDE DJ Casper
UK No.1 ALBUMS			
FEELS LIKE HOME Norah Jones	CALL OFF THE SEARCH Katie Melua	CALL OFF THE SEARCH Katie Melua	CALL OFF THE SEARCH Katie Melua

STAND TOUGH — POINT BREAK
STAND UP [A] — David Lee ROTH
STAND UP [B] — Loleatta HOLLOWAY
STAND UP [C] — THUNDER
STAND UP [D] — LOVE TRIBE
STAND UP [E] — LUDACRIS
STAND UP FOR YOUR LOVE RIGHTS — YAZZ
STAND UP JAMROCK — Bob MARLEY & The WAILERS
STAND UP TALL — DIZZEE RASCAL
STANDING — Silvio ECOMO
STANDING HERE ALL ALONE — MICHELLE
STANDING IN THE NEED OF LOVE — RIVER CITY PEOPLE
STANDING IN THE ROAD — BLACKFOOT SUE
STANDING IN THE SHADOW — WHITESNAKE
STANDING IN THE SHADOWS OF LOVE — The FOUR TOPS
STANDING ON THE CORNER [A] — FOUR LADS
STANDING ON THE CORNER [A] — The KING BROTHERS
STANDING ON THE INSIDE — Neil SEDAKA
STANDING ON THE TOP (PART 1) — The TEMPTATIONS featuring Rick JAMES
STANDING ON THE VERGE (OF GETTING IT ON) — PLATINUM HOOK
STANDING OUTSIDE A BROKEN PHONE BOOTH WITH MONEY IN MY HAND — PRIMITIVE RADIO GODS
STANDING OUTSIDE THE FIRE — Garth BROOKS
STANDING THERE — CREATURES
STANDING WATCHING — CHERRYFALLS
STANLEY (HERE I AM) — AIRHEADZ
STAR [A] — STEALER'S WHEEL
STAR [B] — EARTH WIND AND FIRE
STAR [C] — NAZARETH
STAR [D] — Kiki DEE
STAR [E] — SECOND IMAGE
STAR [F] — ERASURE
STAR [G] — D:REAM
STAR [H] — The CULT
STAR [I] — Bryan ADAMS
STAR [J] — PRIMAL SCREAM
THE STAR AND THE WISEMAN — LADYSMITH BLACK MAMBAZO
STAR CATCHING GIRL — BROTHER BROWN featuring FRANK'EE
STAR CHASERS — 4 HERO
STAR FLEET — Brian MAY
STAR GUITAR — The CHEMICAL BROTHERS
STAR ON A TV SHOW — The STYLISTICS
STAR PEOPLE '97 — George MICHAEL
STAR SIGN — TEENAGE FANCLUB
STAR 69 — FATBOY SLIM
STAR TO FALL — CABIN CREW
STAR TREKKIN' — The FIRM (87)
STAR WARS THEME - CANTINA BAND — MECO
STARBRIGHT — Johnny MATHIS
STARCHILD — LEVEL 42
STARCROSSED — ASH
STARDATE 1990 — Dan REED NETWORK
STARDUST [A] — Billy WARD and his DOMINOES
STARDUST [A] — Nat 'King' COLE
STARDUST [B] — David ESSEX
STARDUST [B] — Martin L. GORE
STARDUST [C] — MENSWEAR
STARGAZER — SIOUXSIE and The BANSHEES
STARING AT THE RUDE BOYS — RUTS
STARING AT THE SUN [A] — U2
STARING AT THE SUN [B] — ROOSTER
STARLIGHT [A] — DESIDERIO
STARLIGHT [B] — SUPERMEN LOVERS
STARLITE — YOUNG HEART ATTACK
STARLOVERS — GUS GUS
STARMAKER — KIDS FROM 'FAME'
STARMAN [A] — David BOWIE
STARMAN [A] — CULTURE CLUB
STARRY EYED — Michael HOLLIDAY with The Michael SAMMES SINGERS (60)
STARRY EYED SURPRISE — OAKENFOLD
A STARRY NIGHT — JOY STRINGS
STARS [A] — SYLVESTER
STARS [B] — FELIX
STARS [C] — HEAR 'N' AID
STARS [D] — SIMPLY RED
STARS [E] — CHINA BLACK
STARS [F] — DUBSTAR
STARS [G] — ROXETTE
STARS [H] — MORJAC featuring Raz CONWAY
STARS AND STRIPES FOREVER — Mr Acker BILK and his PARAMOUNT JAZZ BAND
STARS ON 45 — STARSOUND
STARS ON 45 VOL.3 — STARSOUND
STARS ON 45 VOL.2 — STARSOUND
STARS ON STEVIE — STARSOUND
STARS OVER CLOUGHANOVER — The SAW DOCTORS
STARS OVER 45 — CHAS and DAVE
STARS SHINE IN YOUR EYES — Ronnie HILTON
STARSHIP – ICEBERG SLIMM featuring COREE
STARSHIP TROOPERS — Sarah BRIGHTMAN
STARSKY & HUTCH - THE THEME — Andy G's STARSKY & HUTCH ALL STARS
START — The JAM (80)
START A BRAND NEW LIFE (SAVE ME) — BASSHEADS
START AGAIN [A] — TEENAGE FANCLUB
START AGAIN [B] — MONTROSE AVENUE
START CHOPPIN' — DINOSAUR JR
START ME UP [A] — The ROLLING STONES
START ME UP [B] — SALT-N-PEPA
START MOVIN' [A] — Sal MINEO
START MOVIN' [A] — Terry DENE
START TALKING LOVE — MAGNUM
START THE COMMOTION — WISEGUYS
STARTING AGAIN — SECOND IMAGE
STARTING OVER AGAIN — Natalie COLE
STARTING TOGETHER — Su POLLARD
STARTOUCHERS — DIGITAL ORGASM
STARTRAX CLUB DISCO — STARTRAX
STARTURN ON 45 (PINTS) — STAR TURN ON 45 (PINTS)
STARVATION — STARVATION
STATE OF INDEPENDENCE [A] — Donna SUMMER
STATE OF INDEPENDENCE [A] — JON and VANGELIS
STATE OF LOVE — IMAGINATION
STATE OF MIND [A] — FISH
STATE OF MIND [B] — Holly VALANCE
STATE OF SHOCK — The JACKSONS, lead vocals Mick JAGGER and Michael JACKSON
STATE OF THE NATION — NEW ORDER
STATUESQUE — SLEEPER
STATUS ROCK — HEADBANGERS
STAY [A] — Maurice WILLIAMS and The ZODIACS
STAY [A] — The HOLLIES
STAY [A] — Jackson BROWNE
STAY [A] — DREAMHOUSE
STAY [B] — Barry MANILOW
STAY [C] — SHAKESPEAR'S SISTER (92)
STAY [D] — Kenny THOMAS
STAY [E] — ETERNAL
STAY [F] — 60FT DOLLS
STAY [G] — 18 WHEELER
STAY [H] — SASH!
STAY [I] — Bernard BUTLER
STAY [J] — Mica PARIS
STAY [K] — Stephen GATELY
STAY [L] — Rob TISSERA, VINYLGROOVER & The RED HED
STAY A LITTLE WHILE, CHILD — LOOSE ENDS
STAY A WHILE — RAKIM
STAY ANOTHER DAY — EAST 17 (94)
STAY AWAY FROM ME — STAR SPANGLES
STAY AWHILE — Dusty SPRINGFIELD
STAY BEAUTIFUL — MANIC STREET PREACHERS
STAY (FARAWAY, SO CLOSE) — U2
STAY FOREVER — Joey LAWRENCE
STAY GOLD — DEEP DISH
STAY (I MISSED YOU) — Lisa LOEB and NINE STORIES
STAY IN THE SUN — KENICKIE
STAY ON THESE ROADS — A-HA
STAY OUT OF MY LIFE — FIVE STAR
STAY RIGHT HERE — AKIN
STAY THE SAME [A] — BENT
STAY THE SAME [B] — GABRIELLE
STAY THIS WAY — The BRAND NEW HEAVIES
STAY TOGETHER [A] — SUEDE
STAY TOGETHER [B] — Barbara TUCKER
STAY (TONIGHT) — ISHA-D
STAY WHERE YOU ARE — AMBULANCE LTD
STAY WITH ME [A] — The FACES
STAY WITH ME [B] — BLUE MINK
STAY WITH ME [C] — EIGHTH WONDER
STAY WITH ME [D] — The MISSION
STAY WITH ME [E] — John O'KANE
STAY WITH ME [F] — ERASURE
STAY WITH ME [G] — ULTRA HIGH
STAY WITH ME [H] — Richie RICH
STAY WITH ME [I] — ANGELIC
STAY WITH ME BABY [A] — The WALKER BROTHERS
STAY WITH ME BABY [A] — David ESSEX
STAY WITH ME BABY [A] — Ruby TURNER
STAY WITH ME (BABY) [A] — Rebecca WHEATLEY
STAY WITH ME HEARTACHE — WET WET WET
STAY WITH ME TILL DAWN [A] — Judie TZUKE
STAY WITH ME TILL DAWN [A] — LUCID
STAY WITH ME TONIGHT [A] — Jeffrey OSBORNE
STAY WITH ME TONIGHT [B] — HUMAN LEAGUE
STAY WITH YOU — LEMON JELLY
STAY YOUNG — ULTRASOUND
STAYIN' ALIVE [A] — The BEE GEES
STAYIN' ALIVE [A] — Richard ACE
STAYIN' ALIVE [A] — N-TRANCE featuring Ricardo DA FORCE
STAYING ALIVE 95 [A] — FEVER featuring Tippa IRIE
STAYING FAT — BLOC PARTY
STAYING IN — Bobby VEE
STAYING OUT FOR THE SUMMER — DODGY
STAYING TOGETHER — Debbie GIBSON
STEAL MY SUNSHINE — LEN
STEAL YOUR FIRE — GUN
STEAL YOUR LOVE AWAY — GEMINI
STEALTH — WAY OUT WEST
STEAM [A] — Peter GABRIEL
STEAM [B] — EAST 17
STEAMY WINDOWS — Tina TURNER
STEEL BARS — Michael BOLTON
A STEEL GUITAR AND A GLASS OF WINE — Paul ANKA
STEELO — 702
STEM — DJ SHADOW
STEP BACK IN TIME — Kylie MINOGUE
STEP BY STEP [A] — Steve PERRY
STEP BY STEP [B] — Joe SIMON
STEP BY STEP [C] — TAFFY
STEP BY STEP [D] — NEW KIDS ON THE BLOCK
STEP BY STEP [E] — Whitney HOUSTON
STEP IN THE NAME OF LOVE — R KELLY
A STEP IN THE RIGHT DIRECTION — TRUTH
STEP INSIDE LOVE — Cilla BLACK
STEP INTO A DREAM — WHITE PLAINS
STEP INTO A WORLD (RAPTURE'S DELIGHT) — KRS ONE
STEP INTO CHRISTMAS — Elton JOHN
STEP INTO MY OFFICE BABY — BELLE & SEBASTIAN
STEP INTO MY WORLD — HURRICANE #1
STEP INTO THE BREEZE — SPIRITUALIZED
STEP IT UP — STEREO MC's
STEP OFF — JUNIOR
STEP OFF (PART 1) — GRANDMASTER FLASH, Melle MEL and The FURIOUS FIVE
STEP ON — HAPPY MONDAYS
STEP ON MY OLD SIZE NINES — STEREOPHONICS
STEP RIGHT UP — Jaki GRAHAM
STEP TO ME (DO ME) — MANTRONIX
STEPPIN' OUT [A] — KOOL and The GANG
STEPPIN' OUT [B] — Joe JACKSON
STEPPIN STONES — DJ ZINC
STEPPING STONE [A] — The FARM
STEPPING STONE [A] — ANT & DEC
STEPTOE AND SON AT BUCKINGHAM PALACE — Wilfrid BRAMBELL and Harry H CORBETT
STEP-TWO-THREE-FOUR — STRICT INSTRUCTOR
STEREO — PAVEMENT
STEREOTYPE — The SPECIALS
STEREOTYPES — BLUR
STEVE MCQUEEN — Sheryl CROW
STEWBALL — Lonnie DONEGAN
STICK IT OUT — RIGHT SAID FRED
STICKS AND STONES — CUD
STICKWITU — The PUSSYCAT DOLLS (05)
STICKY — WEDDING PRESENT
STIFF UPPER LIP — AC/DC
STILL [A] — Karl DENVER
STILL [A] — Ken DODD
STILL [B] — The COMMODORES
STILL [C] — Macy GRAY
STILL A FRIEND OF MINE — INCOGNITO
STILL A THRILL — SYBIL
STILL BE LOVIN' YOU — DAMAGE
STILL BELIEVE — Shola AMA
STILL D.R.E. — DR DRE
STILL FEEL THE RAIN — STEX
STILL GOT THE BLUES (FOR YOU) — Gary MOORE
STILL I'M SAD — YARDBIRDS
STILL IN LOVE [A] — GO WEST
STILL IN LOVE [B] — Lionel RICHIE
STILL IN LOVE SONG — The STILLS
STILL OF THE NIGHT — WHITESNAKE
STILL ON YOUR SIDE — BBMAK
STILL THE SAME — SLADE
STILL TOO YOUNG TO REMEMBER — IT BITES
STILL WAITING — SUM 41
STILL WATER (LOVE) — The FOUR TOPS
STILL WATERS (RUN DEEP) — The BEE GEES
STILLNESS IN TIME — JAMIROQUAI
THE STING — RAGTIMERS
STING ME — The BLACK CROWES
STING ME RED (YOU THINK YOU'RE SO CLEVER) — WHO DA FUNK featuring TERRA DEVA
STINGRAY — The SHADOWS
THE STINGRAY MEGAMIX — FAB
STINKIN THINKIN — HAPPY MONDAYS
STIR IT UP — Johnny NASH
STOLE — Kelly ROWLAND
STOLEN — Jay SEAN
STOLEN CAR — Beth ORTON
STOLEN CAR (TAKE ME DANCING) — STING
STOMP [A] — The BROTHERS JOHNSON
STOMP [A] — Quincy JONES
STOMP [B] — GOD'S PROPERTY
STOMP [C] — STEPS (00)
STONE BY STONE — CATATONIA
STONE COLD — RAINBOW
STONE LOVE — KOOL and The GANG
STONED LOVE — The SUPREMES
STONEY END — Barbra STREISAND
STONEY GROUND — GUYS and DOLLS
THE STONK — HALE and PACE and The STONKERS (91)
STOOD ON GOLD — GORKY'S ZYGOTIC MYNCI
STOOD UP — Ricky NELSON
STOOL PIGEON — Kid CREOLE and The COCONUTS
STOP [A] — Sam BROWN
STOP [A] — JAMELIA
STOP [B] — SPICE GIRLS
STOP [C] — BLACK REBEL MOTORCYCLE CLUB
STOP (EP) — MEGA CITY FOUR
STOP AND GO — David GRANT
STOP BAJON ... PRIMAVERA — Tullio DE PISCOPO
STOP BREAKING MY HEART — INNER CIRCLE
STOP BY — Rahsaan PATTERSON
STOP DRAGGIN' MY HEART AROUND — Stevie NICKS with Tom PETTY and The HEARTBREAKERS
STOP FEELING SORRY FOR YOURSELF — Adam FAITH
STOP HER ON SIGHT (SOS) — Edwin STARR
STOP! IN THE NAME OF LOVE — Diana ROSS and The SUPREMES
STOP KNOCKING THE WALLS DOWN — RICKY
STOP LISTENING — Tanita TIKARAM
STOP LIVING THE LIE — David SNEDDON (03)
STOP LOOK AND LISTEN [A] — Wayne FONTANA and The MINDBENDERS
STOP LOOK AND LISTEN [B] — Donna SUMMER
STOP LOOK LISTEN (TO YOUR HEART) — Diana ROSS and Marvin GAYE
STOP LOVING ME STOP LOVING YOU — Daryl HALL
STOP ME (IF YOU'VE HEARD IT ALL BEFORE) — Billy OCEAN
STOP MY HEAD — Evan DANDO
STOP PLAYING WITH MY MIND — Barbara TUCKER
STOP SIGN — ABS

27 March 2004	3 April 2004	10 April 2004	17 April 2004
YEAH! Usher featuring Lil' Jon & Ludacris	YEAH! Usher featuring Lil' Jon & Ludacris	5 COLOURS IN HER HAIR McFly	5 COLOURS IN HER HAIR McFly
PATIENCE George Michael	CONFESSIONS Usher	ANASTACIA Anastacia	ANASTACIA Anastacia

24 April 2004	1 May 2004	8 May 2004	15 May 2004
UK No.1 SINGLES			
F**K IT (I DON'T WANT YOU BACK) Eamon	F**K IT (I DON'T WANT YOU BACK) Eamon	F**K IT (I DON'T WANT YOU BACK) Eamon	F**K IT (I DON'T WANT YOU BACK) Eamon
UK No.1 ALBUMS			
GREATEST HITS Guns N' Roses	GREATEST HITS Guns N' Roses	D12 WORLD D12	GREATEST HITS Guns N' Roses

SUMMER BREEZE [A] — The ISLEY BROTHERS
SUMMER BREEZE [A] — Geoffrey WILLIAMS
SUMMER BUNNIES — R KELLY
SUMMER EDITION — DJ NATION
SUMMER '89 — CALIFORNIA SUNSHINE
SUMMER FUN — The BARRACUDAS
SUMMER GIRLS — LYTE FUNKIE ONES
SUMMER GONNA COME AGAIN — SUPERSISTER
SUMMER HOLIDAY [A] — Cliff RICHARD and The SHADOWS (63)
SUMMER HOLIDAY [A] — KEVIN THE GERBIL
SUMMER HOLIDAY (EP) — ZZ TOP
SUMMER HOLIDAY MEDLEY — Darren DAY
SUMMER IN SIAM — The POGUES
SUMMER IN SPACE — COSMOS
SUMMER IN THE CITY — LOVIN' SPOONFUL
THE SUMMER IS MAGIC — EXOTICA featuring Itsy FOSTER
SUMMER IS OVER — Frank IFIELD
SUMMER JAM — UD PROJECT vs SUNCLUB
SUMMER MADNESS — KOOL and The GANG
SUMMER MOVED ON — A-HA
SUMMER NIGHT CITY — ABBA
SUMMER NIGHTS [A] — Marianne FAITHFULL
SUMMER NIGHTS [B] — John TRAVOLTA, Olivia NEWTON-JOHN and Cast (78)
SUMMER OF '42 — BIDDU
SUMMER OF LOVE [A] — LONYO - COMME CI COMME ÇA
SUMMER OF LOVE [B] — STEPS
THE SUMMER OF MY LIFE — Simon MAY
SUMMER OF '69 — Bryan ADAMS
SUMMER OF THE SEVENTEENTH DOLL — Winifred ATWELL
SUMMER ON THE UNDERGROUND — A
SUMMER RAIN — Belinda CARLISLE
SUMMER SET — Mr Acker BILK and his PARAMOUNT JAZZ BAND
SUMMER SON — TEXAS
SUMMER SONG — BEDAZZLED
SUMMER SUNSHINE — The CORRS
SUMMER (THE FIRST TIME) — Bobby GOLDSBORO
SUMMER WIND — Frank SINATRA
SUMMERLANDS — BEIJING SPRING
SUMMERLOVE SENSATION — BAY CITY ROLLERS
SUMMER'S MAGIC — Mark SUMMERS
SUMMER'S OVER — RIALTO
SUMMERSAULT — TASTE XPERIENCE featuring NATASHA PEARL
SUMMERTIME [A] — Al MARTINO
SUMMERTIME [A] — MARCELS
SUMMERTIME [A] — Billy STEWART
SUMMERTIME [A] — FUN BOY THREE
SUMMERTIME [B] — JAZZY JEFF & The FRESH PRINCE
SUMMERTIME [C] — The SUNDAYS
SUMMERTIME [D] — ANOTHER LEVEL featuring TQ
SUMMERTIME BLUES [A] — Eddie COCHRAN
SUMMERTIME BLUES [A] — The WHO
SUMMERTIME CITY — Mike BATT with The NEW EDITION
SUMMERTIME HEALING — EUSEBE
SUMMERTIME OF OUR LIVES — a1
SUMTHIN' SUMTHIN' THE MANTRA — MAXWELL
SUN [A] — VIRUS
SUN [B] — John LYDON
SUN [C] — SLUSNIK LUNA
THE SUN AIN'T GONNA SHINE ANYMORE [A] — The WALKER BROTHERS (66)
THE SUN AIN'T GONNA SHINE ANYMORE [A] — CHER
THE SUN ALWAYS SHINES ON TV [A] — A-HA (86)
THE SUN ALWAYS SHINES ON TV [A] — DIVA
THE SUN AND THE RAIN — MADNESS
SUN ARISE — Rolf HARRIS
SUN CITY — ARTISTS UNITED AGAINST APARTHEID
THE SUN DOES RISE — Jah WOBBLE'S INVADERS of the HEART
THE SUN DOESN'T SHINE — BEATS INTERNATIONAL
THE SUN GOES DOWN — THIN LIZZY
THE SUN GOES DOWN (LIVING IT UP) — LEVEL 42
THE SUN HAS COME YOUR WAY — SAM & MARK
SUN HITS THE SKY — SUPERGRASS
SUN IS SHINING [A] — TECHNIQUE
SUN IS SHINING [B] — Bob MARLEY vs FUNKSTAR DE LUXE
THE SUN IS SHINING (DOWN ON ME) — DT8 PROJECT
SUN KING — The CULT
THE SUN MACHINE — E-ZEE POSSEE
SUN OF JAMAICA — GOOMBAY DANCE BAND
THE SUN RISING — The BELOVED
SUN SHINING DOWN — CIRCA featuring DESTRY
SUN STREET — KATRINA and The WAVES
SUN WORSHIPPERS (POSITIVE THINKING) — Diana BROWN and Barrie K SHARPE
SUNBURN [A] — Graham GOULDMAN
SUNBURN [B] — Michelle COLLINS
SUNBURN [C] — MUSE
SUNCHYME — DARIO G
SUNDANCE — SUNDANCE
SUNDAY [A] — BUSTER
SUNDAY [B] — SONIC YOUTH
SUNDAY GIRL — BLONDIE (79)
SUNDAY MONDAYS — Vanessa PARADIS
SUNDAY MORNING [A] — NO DOUBT
SUNDAY MORNING [B] — MAROON5
SUNDAY MORNING CALL — OASIS
SUNDAY SHINING — Finley QUAYE
SUNDAY SHOUTIN' — JOHNNY CORPORATE
SUNDAY SUNDAY — BLUR
SUNDOWN [A] — Gordon LIGHTFOOT
SUNDOWN [A] — ELWOOD
SUNDOWN [B] — S CLUB 8
SUNFLOWER — Paul WELLER
SUNGLASSES — Tracey ULLMAN
SUNGLASSES AT NIGHT — TIGA and ZYNTHERIUS
SUNLIGHT — DJ SAMMY
SUNMACHINE — Dario G
SUNNY [A] — CHER
SUNNY [A] — Georgie FAME
SUNNY [A] — Bobby HEBB
SUNNY [A] — BONEY M
SUNNY [A] — BOOGIE PIMPS
SUNNY [B] — MORRISSEY
SUNNY AFTERNOON — The KINKS (66)
SUNNY CAME HOME — Shawn COLVIN
SUNNY DAY — PIGBAG
SUNNY HONEY GIRL — Cliff RICHARD
SUNRISE [A] — GOLDENSCAN
SUNRISE [B] — MOVEMENT 98 featuring Carroll THOMPSON
SUNRISE [C] — PULP
SUNRISE [D] — SIMPLY RED
SUNRISE [E] — Norah JONES
SUNRISE [F] — ANGEL CITY
SUNSET — Nitin SAWHNEY featuring ESKA
SUNSET AND BABYLON — W.A.S.P.
SUNSET (BIRD OF PREY) — FATBOY SLIM
SUNSET BOULEVARD — Michael BALL
SUNRISE (HERE I AM) — RATTY
SUNSET NOW — HEAVEN 17
SUNSET ON IBIZA — THREE DRIVES ON A VINYL
SUNSET PEOPLE — Donna SUMMER
SUNSHINE [A] — Warren MILLS
SUNSHINE [B] — JAY-Z featuring BABYFACE and Foxy BROWN
SUNSHINE [C] — GABRIELLE
SUNSHINE [D] — UMBOZA
SUNSHINE [E] — Alexander O'NEAL
SUNSHINE [F] — YOMANDA
SUNSHINE [G] — Gareth GATES
SUNSHINE [H] — HOLIDAY PLAN
SUNSHINE [I] — TWISTA featuring Anthony HAMILTON
SUNSHINE [J] — LIL' FLIP
SUNSHINE AFTER THE RAIN [A] — Elkie BROOKS
THE SUNSHINE AFTER THE RAIN [A] — BERRI
SUNSHINE & HAPPINESS — Darryl PANDY
SUNSHINE AND LOVE — HAPPY MONDAYS
SUNSHINE DAY [A] — OSIBISA
SUNSHINE DAY [A] — CLOCK
SUNSHINE GIRL — HERMAN'S HERMITS
SUNSHINE OF LOVE — Louis ARMSTRONG
SUNSHINE OF YOUR LOVE [A] — CREAM
SUNSHINE OF YOUR LOVE [A] — CREAM vs The HOXTONS
THE SUNSHINE OF YOUR SMILE — Mike BERRY
SUNSHINE ON A RAINY DAY [A] — ZOE
SUNSHINE ON A RAINY DAY [A] — REAL & RICHARDSON featuring JOBABE
SUNSHINE ON LEITH — The PROCLAIMERS
SUNSHINE PLAYROOM — Julian COPE
SUNSHINE SUPERMAN — DONOVAN
SUNSTORM — HURLEY & TODD
SUNSTROKE — CHICANE
SUNTAN — STAN
SUPER BOWL SUNDAE — OZOMATLI
SUPER DJ — DILLINJA
SUPER DUPER LOVE (ARE YOU DIGGIN ON ME?) — Joss STONE
SUPER GRAN — Billy CONNOLLY
SUPER LOVE — WIGAN'S OVATION
SUPER POPOID GROOVE — WIN
SUPER TROUPER [A] — ABBA (80)
SUPER TROUPER [A] — A*TEENS
SUPER WOMBLE — The WOMBLES
SUPERBAD SUPERSLICK — REDHEAD KINGPIN and The FBI
SUPERFLY GUY — S EXPRESS
SUPERFLY 1990 — Curtis MAYFIELD and ICE-T
SUPERFREAKON — Missy 'Misdemeanor' ELLIOTT
SUPERGIRL — Graham BONNEY
SUPERHERO — REEF
SUPERMAN — STEREOPHONICS
SUPERMAN (GIOCA JOUER) — BLACK LACE
SUPERMAN (IT'S NOT EASY) — FIVE FOR FIGHTING
SUPERMAN'S BIG SISTER — Ian DURY and The BLOCKHEADS
SUPERMARIOLAND — AMBASSADORS OF FUNK featuring MC MARIO
SUPERMARKET SWEEP — MC DALE & The BAR-CODES featuring Alison BROWN
SUPERMODEL — RuPAUL
SUPERNATURAL — Kim ENGLISH
SUPERNATURAL GIVER — KINKY MACHINE
SUPERNATURAL THING — FREELAND
SUPERNATURE [A] — CERRONE
SUPERNATURE [B] — BARON & FRESH
SUPERNOVA — FIVE THIRTY
SUPERSHIP — George BENSON
SUPERSONIC [A] — HWA featuring SONIC THE HEDGEHOG
SUPERSONIC [B] — OASIS
SUPERSONIC [C] — JAMIROQUAI
SUPERSONIC ROCKET SHIP — The KINKS
SUPERSTAR [A] — The CARPENTERS
SUPERSTAR [A] — SONIC YOUTH
SUPERSTAR [B] — Murray HEAD
SUPERSTAR [C] — Lydia MURDOCK
SUPERSTAR [D] — Tom NOVY
SUPERSTAR [E] — SUPERSTAR
SUPERSTAR [F] — The ONES
SUPERSTAR [G] — JAMELIA
SUPERSTAR (REMEMBER HOW YOU GOT WHERE YOU ARE) — The TEMPTATIONS
SUPERSTITION — Stevie WONDER
SUPERSTITION — GOOD TIMES (MEDLEY) — CLUBHOUSE
SUPERSTITIOUS — EUROPE
SUPERSTRING — CYGNUS X
SUPERSTYLIN' — GROOVE ARMADA
SUPERWOMAN — Karyn WHITE
SUPPORT THE TOON — IT'S YOUR DUTY (EP) — MUNGO JERRY
SUPREME — Robbie WILLIAMS
THE SUPREME EP — SINITTA
SURE — TAKE THAT (94)
SURE SHOT — BEASTIE BOYS
SURE THING — DARLING BUDS
SURF CITY — JAN and DEAN
SURFIN' USA [A] — The BEACH BOYS
SURFIN' USA [A] — Aaron CARTER
SURPRISE — BIZARRE INC
SURPRISE SURPRISE — CENTRAL LINE
SURRENDER [A] — Elvis PRESLEY with The JORDANAIRES (61)
SURRENDER [B] — Diana ROSS
SURRENDER [C] — SWING OUT SISTER
SURRENDER [D] — Roger TAYLOR
SURRENDER [E] — LASGO
SURRENDER YOUR LOVE [A] — NIGHTCRAWLERS featuring John REID
SURRENDER (YOUR LOVE) [B] — JAVINE
SURROUND YOURSELF WITH SORROW — Cilla BLACK
SURVIVAL CAR — FOUNTAINS OF WAYNE
SURVIVE — David BOWIE
SURVIVOR — DESTINY'S CHILD (01)
SUSANNA — ART COMPANY
SUSANNAH'S STILL ALIVE — Dave DAVIES
SUSAN'S HOUSE — EELS
SUSIE DARLIN' [A] — Robin LUKE
SUSIE DARLIN' [A] — Tommy ROE
SUSPICION [A] — Terry STAFFORD
SUSPICION [A] — Elvis PRESLEY
SUSPICIOUS MINDS [A] — Elvis PRESLEY
SUSPICIOUS MINDS [A] — Candi STATON
SUSPICIOUS MINDS [A] — FINE YOUNG CANNIBALS
SUSPICIOUS MINDS [A] — Gareth GATES (02)
SUSSUDIO — Phil COLLINS
SUZANNE BEWARE OF THE DEVIL — Dandy LIVINGSTONE
SVEN SVEN SVEN — BELL & SPURLING
SW LIVE (EP) — Peter GABRIEL
SWALLOW MY PRIDE — The RAMONES
SWALLOWED — BUSH
SWAMP THING — GRID
SWAN LAKE — CATS
SWASTIKA EYES — PRIMAL SCREAM
SWAY [A] — Dean MARTIN
SWAY [A] — Bobby RYDELL
SWAY [B] — STRANGELOVE
SWEAR IT AGAIN — WESTLIFE (99)
SWEARIN' TO GOD — Frankie VALLI
SWEAT — USURA
SWEAT (A LA LA LA LA LONG) — INNER CIRCLE
SWEAT IN BULLET — SIMPLE MINDS
SWEATING BULLETS — MEGADETH
SWEDISH RHAPSODY [A] — MANTOVANI
SWEDISH RHAPSODY [A] — Ray MARTIN
SWEET AND LOW — Deborah HARRY
SWEET BABY — Macy GRAY featuring Erykah BADU
SWEET BIRD OF TRUTH — The THE
SWEET CAROLINE — Neil DIAMOND
SWEET CATATONIA — CATATONIA
SWEET CHEATIN' RITA — Alvin STARDUST
SWEET CHILD O' MINE [A] — GUNS N' ROSES
SWEET CHILD O' MINE [A] — Sheryl CROW
SWEET DANGER — ANGELWITCH
SWEET DREAM — JETHRO TULL
SWEET DREAMS [A] — Dave SAMPSON
SWEET DREAMS (ARE MADE OF THIS) [B] — EURYTHMICS
SWEET DREAMS [B] — DJ SCOTT featuring Lorna B
SWEET DREAMS [B] — SWING featuring Dr ALBAN
SWEET DREAMS [C] — Tommy McLAIN
SWEET DREAMS [C] — Roy BUCHANAN
SWEET DREAMS [C] — Elvis COSTELLO
SWEET DREAMS [D] — LA BOUCHE
SWEET DREAMS MY L.A. EX — Rachel STEVENS
SWEET EMOTION — AEROSMITH
SWEET FREEDOM [A] — Michael McDONALD
SWEET FREEDOM [A] — SAFRI DUO featuring Michael McDONALD
SWEET FREEDOM [B] — POSITIVE GANG
SWEET FREEDOM PART 2 — POSITIVE GANG
SWEET HARMONY [A] — LIQUID
SWEET HARMONY [B] — The BELOVED
SWEET HEART CONTRACT — MAGAZINE
SWEET HITCH-HIKER — CREEDENCE CLEARWATER REVIVAL
SWEET HOME ALABAMA — LYNYRD SKYNYRD
SWEET ILLUSION — Junior CAMPBELL
SWEET IMPOSSIBLE YOU — Brenda LEE
SWEET INSPIRATION — Johnny JOHNSON and The BANDWAGON
SWEET INVISIBILITY — HUE AND CRY
SWEET JOHNNY — GORKY'S ZYGOTIC MYNCI
SWEET LADY — TYRESE
SWEET LADY LUCK — WHITESNAKE
SWEET LEAF — MOGWAI
SWEET LIES [A] — Robert PALMER
SWEET LIES [B] — Ellie CAMPBELL
SWEET LIKE CHOCOLATE — SHANKS & BIGFOOT (99)
SWEET LIPS — MONACO
SWEET LITTLE MYSTERY — WET WET WET

22 May 2004	29 May 2004	5 June 2004	12 June 2004
F.U.R.B. - F U RIGHT BACK Frankee	**F.U.R.B. - F U RIGHT BACK** Frankee	**F.U.R.B. - F U RIGHT BACK** Frankee	**I DON'T WANNA KNOW** Mario Winans featuring Enya & P Diddy
HOPES AND FEARS Keane	**HOPES AND FEARS** Keane	**UNDER MY SKIN** Avril Lavigne	**HOPES AND FEARS** Keane

SWEET LITTLE ROCK 'N' ROLLER — SHOWADDYWADDY
SWEET LITTLE SIXTEEN [A] — Chuck BERRY
SWEET LITTLE SIXTEEN [A] — Jerry Lee LEWIS
SWEET LOVE [A] — The COMMODORES
SWEET LOVE [B] — Anita BAKER
SWEET LOVE [B] — M-BEAT
SWEET LOVE 2K [B] — FIERCE
SWEET LUI-LOUISE — IRONHORSE
SWEET LULLABY — DEEP FOREST
SWEET MEMORY — The BELLE STARS
SWEET MUSIC — SHOWADDYWADDY
SWEET 'N' SOUR — Jon SPENCER BLUES EXPLOSION
SWEET NOTHIN'S [A] — Brenda LEE
SWEET NOTHINS [A] — The SEARCHERS
A SWEET OLD FASHIONED GIRL — Teresa BREWER
SWEET PEA — MANFRED MANN
SWEET PEA, MY SWEET PEA — Paul WELLER
SWEET POTATOE PIE — DOMINO
SWEET REVENGE — SPOOKS
SWEET REVIVAL (KEEP IT COMIN') — SHADES OF RHYTHM
SWEET SENSATION [A] — MELODIANS
SWEET SENSATION [B] — SHADES OF RHYTHM
SWEET SENSATION [C] — SHABOOM
SWEET SENSUAL LOVE — BIG MOUNTAIN
SWEET SHOP AVENGERZ — BIS
SWEET SISTER — PEACE BY PIECE
SWEET SIXTEEN — Billy IDOL
SWEET SMELL OF SUCCESS — The STRANGLERS
SWEET SOMEBODY — SHANNON
SWEET SOUL MUSIC — Arthur CONLEY
SWEET SOUL SISTER — The CULT
SWEET STUFF — Guy MITCHELL
SWEET SUBURBIA — The SKIDS
SWEET SURRENDER [A] — Rod STEWART
SWEET SURRENDER [B] — WET WET WET
SWEET, SWEET SMILE — The CARPENTERS
SWEET TALKIN' GUY — CHIFFONS
SWEET TALKIN' WOMAN — ELECTRIC LIGHT ORCHESTRA
SWEET THANG — JONESTOWN
SWEET THING — Mick JAGGER
SWEET TOXIC LOVE — JESUS LOVES YOU
SWEET UNDERSTANDING LOVE — The FOUR TOPS
SWEET WILLIAM — MILLIE
SWEETER THAN THE MIDNIGHT RAIN — Luke GOSS and The BAND OF THIEVES
SWEETER THAN WINE — Dionne RAKEEM
SWEETER THAN YOU — Ricky NELSON
SWEETEST CHILD — Maria McKEE
SWEETEST DAY OF MAY — Joe T VANNELLI PROJECT
THE SWEETEST DAYS — Vanessa WILLIAMS
THE SWEETEST GIRL [A] — SCRITTI POLITTI
SWEETEST GIRL [A] — MADNESS
SWEETEST SMILE — BLACK
SWEETEST SOUL SENSATIONS — The LIGHTNING SEEDS
THE SWEETEST SURRENDER — FACTORY OF UNLIMITED RHYTHM
SWEETEST SWEETEST — Jermaine JACKSON
THE SWEETEST TABOO — SADE
SWEETEST THING [A] — GENE LOVES JEZEBEL
SWEETEST THING [B] — U2
THE SWEETEST THING [C] — The FUGEES
SWEETHEART — Engelbert HUMPERDINCK
SWEETIE PIE — Eddie COCHRAN
SWEETNESS [A] — Michelle GAYLE
SWEETNESS [B] — XSATSIA
SWEETNESS [C] — JIMMY EAT WORLD
SWEETNESS AND LIGHT — LUSH
SWEETS — WORLD OF TWIST
SWEETS FOR MY SWEET [A] — The SEARCHERS (63)
SWEETS FOR MY SWEET [A] — CJ LEWIS
SWEETSMOKE — MR SCRUFF
SWEETY — REEF
SWIM — FISHBONE
SWIMMING HORSES — SIOUXSIE and The BANSHEES
SWING LOW [A] — UB40 featuring UNITED COLOURS OF SOUND
SWING LOW '99 [A] — Russell WATSON
SWING LOW (RUN WITH THE BALL) [A] — UNION featuring the ENGLAND WORLD CUP SQUAD
SWING LOW SWEET CHARIOT [A] — Eric CLAPTON
SWING LOW SWEET CHARIOT [A] — LADYSMITH BLACK MAMBAZO featuring CHINA BLACK
SWING MY WAY — KP & ENVYI
SWING MY HIPS (SEX DANCE) — LEMONESCENT
SWING, SWING — The ALL-AMERICAN REJECTS
SWING THAT HAMMER — Mike COTTON'S JAZZMEN
SWING THE MOOD — JIVE BUNNY and The MASTERMIXERS (89)
SWING YOUR DADDY — Jim GILSTRAP
SWINGIN' — LIGHT OF THE WORLD
SWINGIN' LOW — OUTLAWS
SWINGIN' SHEPHERD BLUES [A] — Ella FITZGERALD
SWINGIN' SHEPHERD BLUES [A] — Moe KOFFMAN QUARTETTE
SWINGIN' SHEPHERD BLUES [A] — Ted HEATH
SWINGING IN THE RAIN — Norman VAUGHAN
SWINGING ON A STAR — Big Dee IRWIN
SWINGING SCHOOL — Bobby RYDELL
SWINGS AND ROUNDABOUTS — Roni SIZE
SWISS MAID — Del SHANNON
SWITCH [A] — BENELUX and Nancy DEE
SWITCH [B] — SENSER
SWITCH [C] — Howie B
SWITCH [D] — PESHAY
SWITCH [E] — Will SMITH
THE SWITCH — PLANET FUNK
SWITCH IT ON — Will YOUNG
SWITCHED ON SWING — KINGS OF SWING ORCHESTRA
SWOON — The MISSION
SWORDS OF A THOUSAND MEN — TEN POLE TUDOR
SYLVIA — FOCUS
SYLVIA'S MOTHER — DR HOOK
SYLVIE — SAINT ETIENNE
SYMMETRY C — BRAINCHILD
SYMPATHY [A] — RARE BIRD
SYMPATHY [B] — MARILLION
SYMPATHY FOR THE DEVIL [A] — GUNS N' ROSES
SYMPATHY FOR THE DEVIL [A] — The ROLLING STONES
SYMPHONY — Donell RUSH
SYMPHONY OF DESTRUCTION — MEGADETH
SYNAESTHESIA (FLY AWAY) — THRILLSEEKERS featuring SHERYL DEANE
SYNCHRONICITY II — The POLICE
SYNERGY — TRANCESETTERS
SYNTH & STRINGS — YOMANDA
SYSTEM ADDICT — FIVE STAR
SYSTEM CHECK — BROCKIE & Ed SOLO
SYSTEM OF SURVIVAL — EARTH WIND AND FIRE
THE TABLE — The BEAUTIFUL SOUTH
TABOO — GLAMMA KID featuring Shola AMA
TACKY LOVE SONG — CREDIT TO THE NATION
TAHITI (FROM 'MUTINY ON THE BOUNTY') — David ESSEX
TAINTED LOVE [A] — SOFT CELL (81)
TAINTED LOVE [A] — IMPEDANCE
TAINTED LOVE [A] — ICON
TAINTED LOVE [A] — MARILYN MANSON
TAKE — COLOUR FIELD
TAKE A BOW — MADONNA
TAKE A CHANCE ON ME — ABBA (78)
TAKE A CHANCE WITH ME — ROXY MUSIC
TAKE A FREE FALL — DANCE 2 TRANCE
TAKE A HEART — SORROWS
(TAKE A LITTLE) PIECE OF MY HEART — Erma FRANKLIN
TAKE A LITTLE TIME — Gary MOORE
TAKE A LOOK — LEVEL 42
TAKE A LOOK AROUND — The TEMPTATIONS
TAKE A LOOK AROUND (THEME FROM 'MI:2') — LIMP BIZKIT
TAKE A LOOK AT YOURSELF — COVERDALE PAGE
TAKE A MESSAGE TO MARY — The EVERLY BROTHERS
TAKE A PICTURE — FILTER
TAKE A REST — GANG STARR
TAKE A RUN AT THE SUN — DINOSAUR JR
TAKE A TOKE — C & C MUSIC FACTORY / CLIVILLES & COLE
TAKE CALIFORNIA — PROPELLERHEADS
TAKE CARE OF YOURSELF — LEVEL 42
TAKE CONTROL [A] — STATE OF MIND
TAKE CONTROL [B] — John B
TAKE CONTROL [C] — JAIMESON featuring Angel BLU and CK
TAKE CONTROL OF THE PARTY — BG THE PRINCE OF RAP
TAKE DOWN THE UNION JACK — Billy BRAGG and The BLOKES
TAKE FIVE [A] — Dave BRUBECK QUARTET
TAKE 5 [B] — NORTHSIDE
TAKE 4 (EP) — Mike OLDFIELD
TAKE GOOD CARE OF HER — Adam WADE
TAKE GOOD CARE OF MY BABY [A] — Bobby VEE
TAKE GOOD CARE OF MY BABY [A] — SMOKIE
TAKE GOOD CARE OF MY HEART — MICHAELA
TAKE GOOD CARE OF YOURSELF — The THREE DEGREES
TAKE IT — FLOWERED UP
TAKE IT AND RUN — The BANDITS
TAKE IT AWAY [A] — Paul McCARTNEY
TAKE IT AWAY [B] — The USED
TAKE IT BACK — PINK FLOYD
TAKE IT EASY [A] — LET LOOSE
TAKE IT EASY [B] — MINT ROYALE
TAKE IT EASY [C] — 3SL
TAKE IT EASY ON ME — A HOUSE
TAKE IT FROM ME [A] — Roger CHRISTIAN
TAKE IT FROM ME [B] — GIRLFRIEND
TAKE IT OFF — The DONNAS
TAKE IT ON THE RUN — REO SPEEDWAGON
TAKE IT OR LEAVE IT — The SEARCHERS
TAKE IT SATCH (EP) — Louis ARMSTRONG
TAKE IT TO THE LIMIT — EAGLES
TAKE IT TO THE STREETS — RAMPAGE featuring Billy LAWRENCE
TAKE IT TO THE TOP [A] — KOOL and The GANG
TAKE IT TO THE TOP [B] — CLOUD
TAKE ME — DREAM FREQUENCY
TAKE ME AWAY [A] — TRUE FAITH with FINAL CUT
TAKE ME AWAY [A] — CAPPELLA featuring Loleatta HOLLOWAY
TAKE ME AWAY [B] — D:REAM
TAKE ME AWAY [C] — CULTURE BEAT
TAKE ME AWAY [D] — STONEBRIDGE featuring THERESE
TAKE ME AWAY (I'LL FOLLOW YOU) — BAD BOYS INC
TAKE ME AWAY (INTO THE NIGHT) — 4 STRINGS
TAKE ME AWAY (PARADISE) — MIX FACTORY
TAKE ME BACK — RHYTHMATIC
TAKE ME BACK TO LOVE AGAIN — Kathy SLEDGE
TAKE ME BAK 'OME — SLADE (72)
TAKE ME BY THE HAND — SUBMERGE featuring Jan JOHNSTON
TAKE ME DOWN TO THE RIVER — SKIN
TAKE ME FOR A LITTLE WHILE — COVERDALE PAGE
TAKE ME FOR WHAT I'M WORTH — The SEARCHERS
TAKE ME GIRL I'M READY — Junior WALKER and The ALL-STARS
TAKE ME HIGH — Cliff RICHARD
TAKE ME HIGHER [A] — R.A.F.
TAKE ME HIGHER [B] — Diana ROSS
TAKE ME HIGHER [C] — GEORGIE PORGIE
TAKE ME HOME [A] — Phil COLLINS
TAKE ME HOME [B] — Joe COCKER
TAKE ME HOME (A GIRL LIKE ME) — Sophie ELLIS-BEXTOR
TAKE ME HOME COUNTRY ROADS — Olivia NEWTON-JOHN
TAKE ME I'M YOURS — SQUEEZE
TAKE ME IN YOUR ARMS (ROCK ME A LITTLE WHILE) — The DOOBIE BROTHERS
TAKE ME IN YOUR ARMS AND LOVE ME [A] — Gladys KNIGHT and The PIPS
TAKE ME IN YOUR ARMS AND LOVE ME [A] — SCRITTI POLITTI
TAKE ME NOW — Tammy PAYNE
TAKE ME OUT — FRANZ FERDINAND
TAKE ME OVER — McKAY
TAKE ME THERE — BLACKSTREET and MYA featuring MA$E and BLINKY BLINK
TAKE ME TO HEAVEN — BABY D
TAKE ME TO THE CLOUDS ABOVE — LMC vs U2 (04)
TAKE ME TO THE MARDI GRAS — Paul SIMON
TAKE ME TO THE NEXT PHASE — The ISLEY BROTHERS
TAKE ME TO YOUR HEART — Rick ASTLEY
TAKE ME TO YOUR HEART AGAIN — Vince HILL
TAKE ME TO YOUR HEAVEN — Charlotte NILSSON
TAKE ME UP [A] — SOUNDSOURCE
TAKE ME UP [B] — SONIC SURFERS featuring Jocelyn BROWN
TAKE ME WITH U [A] — PRINCE
TAKE ME WITH YOU [B] — COSMOS
TAKE MY ADVICE — Kym SIMS
TAKE MY BREATH AWAY (LOVE THEME FROM 'TOP GUN') [A] — BERLIN (86)
TAKE MY BREATH AWAY [A] — SODA CLUB featuring Hannah ALETHEA
TAKE MY BREATH AWAY [B] — Emma BUNTON
TAKE MY HAND — Jurgen VRIES featuring Andrea BRITTON
TAKE MY HEART — Al MARTINO
TAKE MY HEART (YOU CAN HAVE IT IF YOU WANT IT) — KOOL and The GANG
TAKE MY SCARS — MACHINE HEAD
TAKE MY TIME — Sheena EASTON
TAKE OFF SOME TIME — NEW ATLANTIC
TAKE ON ME [A] — A-HA
TAKE ON ME [A] — a1 (00)
TAKE ON THE WORLD — JUDAS PRIEST
TAKE THAT LOOK OFF YOUR FACE — Marti WEBB
TAKE THAT SITUATION — Nick HEYWARD
TAKE THAT TO THE BANK — SHALAMAR
TAKE THE BOX — Amy WINEHOUSE
TAKE THE LONG ROAD AND WALK IT — The MUSIC
TAKE THE LONG WAY HOME — FAITHLESS
TAKE THESE CHAINS FROM MY HEART — Ray CHARLES
TAKE THIS HEART — Richard MARX
TAKE THIS TIME — Sean MAGUIRE
TAKE TO THE MOUNTAINS — Richard BARNES
TAKE YOU OUT — Luther VANDROSS
TAKE YOU THERE — Ronni SIMON
TAKE YOUR MAMA — SCISSOR SISTERS
TAKE YOUR MAMA FOR A RIDE — LULU
TAKE YOUR PARTNER BY THE HAND — Howie B featuring Robbie ROBERTSON
TAKE YOUR SHOES OFF — CHEEKY GIRLS
TAKE YOUR TIME [A] — HIGH
TAKE YOUR TIME [B] — MANTRONIX
TAKE YOUR TIME [C] — LOVE BITE
TAKE YOUR TIME (DO IT RIGHT) PART 1 — S.O.S. BAND
TAKEN FOR GRANTED — SIA
TAKES A LITTLE TIME — TOTAL CONTRAST
TAKES TWO TO TANGO — Louis ARMSTRONG
TAKIN' A CHANCE ON YOU — DOLLAR
TAKIN' HOLD — Sam LA MORE
TAKING OFF — The CURE
TAKING ON THE WORLD — GUN
TAKING THE VEIL — David SYLVIAN
TALES FROM A DANCEOGRAPHIC OCEAN EP — JAM & SPOON featuring PLAVKA
TALES FROM THE HARD SIDE — BIOHAZARD
TALES OF THE HOOD — TUBBY T
TALK — COLDPLAY
TALK ABOUT IT IN THE MORNING — Martyn JOSEPH
TALK ABOUT OUR LOVE — BRANDY featuring Kanye WEST
TALK BACK — DOUBLE TROUBLE
TALK DIRTY TO ME — POISON
TALK OF THE TOWN — The PRETENDERS
TALK SHOWS ON MUTE — INCUBUS
TALK TALK [A] — TALK TALK
TALK TALK TALK — The ORDINARY BOYS
TALK TO ME [A] — THIRD WORLD
TALK TO ME [B] — Stevie NICKS
TALK TO ME [C] — Anita BAKER
TALK TO ME [D] — 60FT DOLLS
TALKIN' ALL THAT JAZZ — STETSASONIC
TALKING IN YOUR SLEEP [A] — Crystal GAYLE

TALKING IN YOUR SLEEP [A] — Martine McCUTCHEON
TALKING IN YOUR SLEEP [B] — BUCKS FIZZ
TALKING LOUD AND CLEAR — ORCHESTRAL MANOEUVRES IN THE DARK
TALKING OF LOVE — Anita DOBSON
TALKING WITH MYSELF — ELECTRIBE 101
TALL DARK STRANGER — Rose BRENNAN
TALL 'N' HANDSOME — OUTRAGE
TALLAHASSEE LASSIE [A] — Freddy CANNON
TALLAHASSEE LASSIE [A] — Tommy STEELE
TALLYMAN — Jeff BECK
TALULA — Tori AMOS
TAM-TAM POUR L'ÉTHIOPIE — STARVATION
TAMMY — Debbie REYNOLDS
TANGERINE — FEEDER
TANGO IN MONO — EXPRESSOS
TANSY — Alex WELSH
TANTALISE (WO WO EE YEH YEH) — JIMMY THE HOOVER
TAP THE BOTTLE — YOUNG BLACK TEENAGERS
TAP TURNS ON THE WATER — CCS
TAPE LOOP — MORCHEEBA
TARANTINO'S NEW STAR — NORTH AND SOUTH
TARANTULA [A] — FAITHLESS
TARANTULA [B] — PENDULUM & FRESH featuring SPYDA & TENOR FLY
TARA'S THEME [A] — SPIRO and WIX
TARA'S THEME FROM 'GONE WITH THE WIND' [A] — ROSE OF ROMANCE ORCHESTRA
TARRED & FEATHERED — DOGS
TARZAN BOY — BALTIMORA
TASTE IN MEN — PLACEBO
TASTE IT — INXS
A TASTE OF AGGRO — The BARRON KNIGHTS
TASTE OF BITTER LOVE — Gladys KNIGHT and The PIPS
A TASTE OF HONEY — Acker BILK and his PARAMOUNT JAZZ BAND
THE TASTE OF INK — The USED
THE TASTE OF YOUR TEARS — KING
TASTE THE LAST GIRL — SONS AND DAUGHTERS
TASTE THE PAIN — RED HOT CHILI PEPPERS
TASTE YOU — AUF DER MAUR
TASTE YOUR LOVE — Horace BROWN
TASTY FISH — The OTHER TWO
TASTY LOVE — Freddie JACKSON
TATTOO — Mike OLDFIELD
TATTOOED MILLIONAIRE — Bruce DICKINSON
TATTVA — KULA SHAKER
TAVERN IN THE TOWN — Terry LIGHTFOOT and his NEW ORLEANS JAZZMEN
TAXI — J BLACKFOOT
TAXLOSS — MANSUN
TCHAIKOVSKY ONE — SECOND CITY SOUND
TE AMO — SULTANA
TEA FOR TWO CHA CHA — Tommy DORSEY ORCHESTRA starring Warren COVINGTON
TEACH ME TO TWIST — Chubby CHECKER and Bobby RYDELL
TEACH ME TONIGHT — DE CASTRO SISTERS
TEACH YOU TO ROCK — Tony CROMBIE and his ROCKETS
TEACHER [A] — JETHRO TULL
TEACHER [B] — I-LEVEL
THE TEACHER — BIG COUNTRY
TEACHER, TEACHER — Johnny MATHIS
TEAR AWAY — DROWNING POOL
TEAR DOWN THE WALLS — NO SWEAT
A TEAR FELL — Teresa BREWER
TEAR ME APART — Suzi QUATRO
TEAR OFF YOUR OWN HEAD (IT'S A DOLL REVOLUTION) — Elvis COSTELLO
TEAR SOUP — QUESTIONS
TEARDROP [A] — SANTO and JOHNNY
TEARDROP [B] — MASSIVE ATTACK
TEARDROP CITY — The MONKEES
TEARDROPS [A] — Shakin' STEVENS
TEARDROPS [B] — WOMACK and WOMACK
TEARDROPS [B] — LOVESTATION
TEARDROPS [C] — The 411
TEARIN' UP MY HEART — 'N SYNC
TEARING — ROLLINS BAND
TEARING US APART — Eric CLAPTON and Tina TURNER
TEARS [A] — Danny WILLIAMS
TEARS [B] — Ken DODD (65)
TEARS [C] — Frankie KNUCKLES
TEARS [C] — NU COLOURS
TEARS ARE FALLING — KISS
TEARS ARE NOT ENOUGH — ABC
TEARS DON'T LIE — MARK 'OH
TEARS FROM A WILLOW — OOBERMAN
TEARS FROM HEAVEN — HEARTBEAT
TEARS FROM THE MOON — CONJURE ONE
THE TEARS I CRIED — GLITTER BAND
TEARS IN HEAVEN [A] — Eric CLAPTON
TEARS IN HEAVEN [A] — The CHOIRBOYS
TEARS IN THE RAIN — N-TRANCE
TEARS IN THE WIND — CHICKEN SHACK
THE TEARS OF A CLOWN [A] — Smokey ROBINSON and The MIRACLES (70)
TEARS OF A CLOWN [A] — The BEAT
TEARS OF THE DRAGON — Bruce DICKINSON
TEARS ON MY PILLOW [A] — Johnny NASH (75)
TEARS ON MY PILLOW [B] — Kylie MINOGUE (90)
TEARS ON THE TELEPHONE [A] — Claude FRANÇOIS
TEARS ON THE TELEPHONE [B] — HOT CHOCOLATE
TEARS RUN RINGS — Marc ALMOND
TEARS WON'T WASH AWAY THESE HEARTACHES — Ken DODD
TEARY EYED — Missy ELLIOTT
TEASE ME — Chaka DEMUS and PLIERS
TEASER — George BENSON
TECHNARCHY — CYBERSONIK
TECHNO FUNK — LOST
TECHNO TRANCE — D-SHAKE
TECHNOCAT — Tom WILSON
TECHNOLOGIC — DAFT PUNK
TEDDY BEAR [A] — Red SOVINE
TEDDY BEAR [B] — Booker NEWBURY III
TEDDY BEAR'S LAST RIDE — Diana WILLIAMS
TEEN ANGEL — Mark DINNING
TEEN BEAT — Sandy NELSON
TEENAGE — UK SUBS
TEENAGE ANGST — PLACEBO
TEENAGE DEPRESSION — EDDIE and The HOT RODS
TEENAGE DIRTBAG — WHEATUS
TEENAGE DREAM — T. REX
TEENAGE IDOL — Ricky NELSON
TEENAGE KICKS — The UNDERTONES
TEENAGE LAMENT '74 — Alice COOPER
TEENAGE PUNKS — SULTANS OF PING
TEENAGE RAMPAGE — The SWEET
TEENAGE SCREAMERS — TOKYO DRAGONS
TEENAGE SENSATION — CREDIT TO THE NATION
TEENAGE TURTLES — BACK TO THE PLANET
TEENAGE WARNING — ANGELIC UPSTARTS
A TEENAGER IN LOVE [A] — Craig DOUGLAS
A TEENAGER IN LOVE [A] — DION
A TEENAGER IN LOVE [A] — Marty WILDE
TEENSVILLE — Chet ATKINS
TEETHGRINDER — THERAPY?
TELEFUNKIN' — N-TYCE
TELEGRAM SAM — T. REX (72)
TELEGRAPH — ORCHESTRAL MANOEUVRES IN THE DARK
THE TELEPHONE ALWAYS RINGS — FUN BOY THREE
TELEPHONE LINE — ELECTRIC LIGHT ORCHESTRA
TELEPHONE MAN — Meri WILSON
TELEPHONE OPERATOR — Pete SHELLEY
TELEPHONE THING — The FALL
TELEPORT — MAN WITH NO NAME
TELETUBBIES SAY EH-OH! — TELETUBBIES (97)
TELEVATORS — The MARS VOLTA
TELEVISION THE DRUG OF THE NATION — DISPOSABLE HEROES OF HIPHOPRISY
TELL HER ABOUT IT — Billy JOEL
TELL HER I'M NOT HOME — Ike and Tina TURNER
TELL HER NO — ZOMBIES
TELL HER THIS — DEL AMITRI
TELL HIM [A] — Billie DAVIS
TELL HIM [A] — EXCITERS
TELL HIM [A] — HELLO
TELL HIM [A] — QUENTIN and ASH
TELL HIM [B] — Barbra STREISAND and Celine DION
TELL IT LIKE IT T-I-IS — The B-52's
TELL IT ON THE MOUNTAIN — PETER, PAUL and MARY
TELL IT TO MY HEART [A] — Taylor DAYNE
TELL IT TO MY HEART [A] — Q-CLUB
TELL IT TO MY HEART [A] — Kelly LLORENNA
TELL IT TO THE RAIN — The FOUR SEASONS
TELL LAURA I LOVE HER — Ricky VALANCE (60)
TELL ME [A] — Nick KAMEN
TELL ME [B] — GROOVE THEORY
TELL ME [C] — DRU HILL
TELL ME [D] — Billie MYERS
TELL ME [E] — Melanie B
TELL ME [F] — Bobby VALENTINO
TELL ME A STORY — Jimmy BOYD and Frankie LAINE
TELL ME DO U WANNA — GINUWINE
TELL ME (HOW IT FEELS) — 52ND STREET
TELL ME I'M NOT DREAMING — TITIYO
TELL ME IT IS TRUE — UB40
TELL ME IT'S REAL — K-CI & JOJO
TELL ME MA — SHAM ROCK
TELL ME ON A SUNDAY — Marti WEBB
TELL ME THAT YOU LOVE ME — Paul ANKA
TELL ME THE WAY — CAPPELLA
TELL ME THERE'S A HEAVEN — Chris REA
TELL ME TO MY FACE — KEITH
TELL ME TOMORROW [A] — Smokey ROBINSON
TELL ME TOMORROW [B] — PRINCESS
TELL ME WHAT HE SAID — Helen SHAPIRO
TELL ME WHAT YOU SEE — The VON BONDIES
TELL ME WHAT YOU WANT [A] — Jimmy RUFFIN
TELL ME WHAT YOU WANT [B] — LOOSE ENDS
TELL ME WHAT YOU WANT [C] — BLU PETER
TELL ME WHAT YOU WANT ME TO DO — Tevin CAMPBELL
TELL ME WHEN [A] — The APPLEJACKS
TELL ME WHEN [B] — HUMAN LEAGUE
TELL ME WHEN THE FEVER ENDED — ELECTRIBE 101
TELL ME WHERE YOU'RE GOING — SILJE
TELL ME WHY [A] — Elvis PRESLEY
TELL ME WHY [B] — Alvin STARDUST
TELL ME WHY [C] — MUSICAL YOUTH
TELL ME WHY [D] — Bobby WOMACK
TELL ME WHY [E] — THIS WAY UP
TELL ME WHY [F] — GENESIS
TELL ME WHY [G] — DECLAN featuring YOUNG VOICES CHOIR
TELL ME WHY (THE RIDDLE) — Paul VAN DYK featuring SAINT ETIENNE
TELL THAT GIRL TO SHUT UP — TRANSVISION VAMP
TELL THE CHILDREN — SHAM 69
TELLIN' STORIES — The CHARLATANS
TELSTAR — The TORNADOS (62)
TEMMA HARBOUR — Mary HOPKIN
TEMPERAMENTAL — EVERYTHING BUT THE GIRL
TEMPERATURE RISING — PKA
TEMPERTEMPER — GOLDIE
TEMPLE OF DOOM — DJ FRESH
TEMPLE OF DREAMS [A] — MESSIAH
TEMPLE OF DREAMS [B] — FUTURE BREEZE
TEMPLE OF LOVE — SISTERS OF MERCY
TEMPO FIESTA (PARTY TIME) — ITTY BITTY BOOZY WOOZY
TEMPORARY BEAUTY — Graham PARKER and The RUMOUR
TEMPTATION [A] — The EVERLY BROTHERS (61)
TEMPTATION [B] — NEW ORDER
TEMPTATION [C] — HEAVEN 17
TEMPTATION [D] — Joan ARMATRADING
TEMPTATION [E] — WET WET WET
TEMPTED — SQUEEZE
TEMPTED TO TOUCH — RUPEE
10 A.M. AUTOMATIC — The BLACK KEYS
10538 OVERTURE — ELECTRIC LIGHT ORCHESTRA
10 IN 01 — MEMBERS OF MAYDAY
TEN MILES HIGH — LITTLE ANGELS
10 SECOND BIONIC MAN — KINKY MACHINE
TEN STOREY LOVE SONG — The STONE ROSES
TEN THOUSAND MILES — Michael HOLLIDAY
10 X 10 — 808 STATE
TEN TO TWENTY — SNEAKER PIMPS
10 YEARS ASLEEP — KINGMAKER
TEN YEARS TIME — GABRIELLE
TENDER [A] — BLUR
TENDER [B] — FEEDER
TENDER HANDS — Chris DE BURGH
TENDER HEART — Lionel RICHIE
TENDER LOVE [A] — FORCE M.D.s
TENDER LOVE [A] — Kenny THOMAS
TENDERLY — Nat 'King' COLE
TENDERNESS — Diana ROSS
TENNESSEE — ARRESTED DEVELOPMENT
TENNESSEE WIG WALK — Bonnie LOU
TENSHI — GOURYELLA
THE TENTH PLANET — DISTORTED MINDS
TEQUILA [A] — CHAMPS
TEQUILA [A] — Ted HEATH
TEQUILA [A] — NO WAY JOSÉ
TEQUILA [B] — TERRORVISION
TEQUILA SUNRISE — CYPRESS HILL
TERESA — Joe DOLAN
TERRITORY — SEPULTURA
TERRY — TWINKLE
TERRY'S THEME FROM 'LIMELIGHT' [A] — Frank CHACKSFIELD
TERRY'S THEME FROM 'LIMELIGHT' [A] — Ron GOODWIN
TESLA GIRLS — ORCHESTRAL MANOEUVRES IN THE DARK
THE TEST — The CHEMICAL BROTHERS
TEST OF TIME [A] — Will DOWNING
TEST OF TIME [A] — The CRESCENT
TEST THE THEORY — AUDIOWEB
TESTAMENT 4 — Chubby CHUNKS
TESTIFY [A] — M PEOPLE
TESTIFY [B] — Byron STINGILY
TETRIS — DOCTOR SPIN
TEXAS — Chris REA
TEXAS COWBOYS — GRID
THA CROSSROADS — BONE THUGS-N-HARMONY
THA DOGGFATHER — SNOOP DOGG
THA HORNS OF JERICHO — DJ SUPREME
THA WILD STYLE — DJ SUPREME
THANK ABBA FOR THE MUSIC — VARIOUS ARTISTS (Singles and EPs)
THANK GOD I FOUND YOU — 98°
THANK GOD IT'S CHRISTMAS — QUEEN
THANK GOD IT'S FRIDAY — R KELLY
THANK U — Alanis MORISSETTE
THANK U VERY MUCH — SCAFFOLD
THANK YOU [A] — PALE FOUNTAINS
THANK YOU [B] — BOYZ II MEN
THANK YOU [C] — DIDO
THANK YOU [D] — JAMELIA
THANK YOU BABY (FOR MAKIN' SOMEDAY COME SO SOON) — Shania TWAIN
THANK YOU FOR A GOOD YEAR — Alexander O'NEAL
THANK YOU FOR BEING A FRIEND — Andrew GOLD
THANK YOU FOR HEARING ME — Sinead O'CONNOR
THANK YOU FOR LOVING ME — BON JOVI
THANK YOU FOR THE MUSIC — ABBA
THANK YOU FOR THE PARTY — DUKES
THANK YOU FOR THE VENOM — MY CHEMICAL ROMANCE
THANK YOU MY LOVE — IMAGINATION
THANK YOU WORLD — WORLD PARTY
THANKS A LOT — Brenda LEE
THANKS FOR MY CHILD — Cheryl Pepsii RILEY
THANKS FOR SAVING MY LIFE — Billy PAUL
THANKS FOR THE MEMORY (WHAM BAM THANK YOU MAM) — SLADE
THANKS FOR THE NIGHT — The DAMNED
THAT CERTAIN SMILE — Midge URE
THAT DAY — Natalie IMBRUGLIA
THAT DON'T IMPRESS ME MUCH — Shania TWAIN
THAT EXTRA MILE — RICKY
THAT FEELING — DJ CHUS presents GROOVE FOUNDATION
THAT GIRL [A] — Stevie WONDER
THAT GIRL [B] — Maxi PRIEST featuring SHAGGY
THAT GIRL [C] — McFLY
THAT GIRL BELONGS TO YESTERDAY — Gene PITNEY
THAT GIRL (GROOVY SITUATION) — Freddie McGREGOR

17 July 2004	24 July 2004	31 July 2004	7 August 2004
BURN Usher	**LOLA'S THEME** Shapeshifters	**DRY YOUR EYES** The Streets	**THUNDERBIRDS / 3AM** Busted
ROOM ON THE 3RD FLOOR McFly	**SCISSOR SISTERS** Scissor Sisters	**A GRAND DON'T COME FOR FREE** The Streets	**LIVE IN HYDE PARK** Red Hot Chili Peppers

REAT LOVE SOUND — The RAVEONETTES
AT JOKE ISN'T FUNNY ANYMORE — The SMITHS
THAT LADY — The ISLEY BROTHERS
THAT LOOK — DE'LACY
THAT LOOK IN YOUR EYE — Ali CAMPBELL
THAT LOVING FEELING — CICERO
THAT LUCKY OLD SUN — VELVETS
THAT MAN (HE'S ALL MINE) — INNER CITY
THAT MAN WILL NOT HANG — McLUSKEY
THAT MEANS A LOT — PJ PROBY
THAT NOISE — Anthony NEWLEY
THAT OLD BLACK MAGIC — Sammy DAVIS Jr
THAT OLE DEVIL CALLED LOVE — Alison MOYET
THAT SAME OLD FEELING — PICKETTYWITCH
THAT SOUND — Michael MOOG
THAT SOUNDS GOOD TO ME — JIVE BUNNY and The MASTERMIXERS
THAT THING YOU DO! — The WONDERS
THAT WAS MY VEIL — John PARISH and Polly Jean HARVEY
THAT WAS THEN THIS IS NOW [A] — ABC
THAT WAS THEN, THIS IS NOW [B] — The MONKEES
THAT WAS YESTERDAY — FOREIGNER
THAT WOMAN'S GOT ME DRINKING — Shane MacGOWAN and The POPES
THAT ZIPPER TRACK — DJ DAN presents NEEDLE DAMAGE
THAT'LL BE THE DAY [A] — The CRICKETS (57)
THAT'LL BE THE DAY [A] — The EVERLY BROTHERS
THAT'LL DO NICELY — BAD MANNERS
THAT'S ALL — GENESIS
THAT'S ALL RIGHT — Elvis PRESLEY
THAT'S AMORE — Dean MARTIN
THAT'S ENTERTAINMENT — The JAM
THAT'S HOW A LOVE SONG WAS BORN — Ray BURNS with The CORONETS
THAT'S HOW GOOD YOUR LOVE IS — IL PADRINOS featuring JOCELYN BROWN
THAT'S HOW I FEEL ABOUT YOU — LONDONBEAT
THAT'S HOW I'M LIVING [A] — Tony SCOTT
THAT'S HOW I'M LIVIN' [B] — ICE-T
THAT'S HOW STRONG MY LOVE IS — The IN CROWD
THAT'S JUST THE WAY IT IS — Phil COLLINS
THAT'S LIFE — Frank SINATRA
THAT'S LIVIN' ALRIGHT — Joe FAGIN
THAT'S LOVE — Billy FURY
THAT'S LOVE, THAT IT IS — BLANCMANGE
THAT'S MORE LIKE IT — SKYLARK
THAT'S MY DOLL — Frankie VAUGHAN
THAT'S MY GOAL — Shayne WARD (05)
THAT'S MY HOME — Mr Acker BILK and his PARAMOUNT JAZZ BAND
THAT'S NICE — Neil CHRISTIAN
THAT'S RIGHT — DEEP RIVER BOYS
THAT'S THE WAY — HONEYCOMBS
THAT'S THE WAY GOD PLANNED IT — Billy PRESTON
THAT'S THE WAY I LIKE IT [A] — KC and The SUNSHINE BAND
THAT'S THE WAY (I LIKE IT) [A] — DEAD OR ALIVE
THAT'S THE WAY (I LIKE IT) [A] — CLOCK
THAT'S THE WAY I WANNA ROCK 'N' ROLL — AC/DC
THAT'S THE WAY IT FEELS — TWO NATIONS
THAT'S THE WAY IT IS [A] — MEL and KIM
THAT'S THE WAY IT IS [B] — Celine DION
THAT'S THE WAY LOVE GOES [A] — Charles DICKENS
THAT'S THE WAY LOVE GOES [B] — YOUNG MC
THAT'S THE WAY LOVE GOES [C] — Janet JACKSON
THAT'S THE WAY LOVE IS [A] — TEN CITY
THAT'S THE WAY LOVE IS [A] — VOLCANO
THAT'S THE WAY LOVE IS [A] — Byron STINGILY
THAT'S THE WAY LOVE IS [B] — Bobby BROWN
THAT'S THE WAY OF THE WORLD — D MOB with Cathy DENNIS
THAT'S THE WAY THE MONEY GOES — M
THAT'S THE WAY YOU DO IT — PURPLE KINGS
THAT'S WHAT FRIENDS ARE FOR [A] — Deniece WILLIAMS
THAT'S WHAT FRIENDS ARE FOR [B] — Dionne WARWICK and FRIENDS featuring Elton JOHN, Stevie WONDER and Gladys KNIGHT
THAT'S WHAT I LIKE — JIVE BUNNY and The MASTERMIXERS (89)
THAT'S WHAT I THINK — Cyndi LAUPER
THAT'S WHAT I WANT — MARAUDERS
THAT'S WHAT I WANT TO BE — Neil REID
THAT'S WHAT LIFE IS ALL ABOUT — Bing CROSBY
THAT'S WHAT LOVE CAN DO — TOUTES LES FILLES
THAT'S WHAT LOVE IS FOR — Amy GRANT
THAT'S WHAT LOVE WILL DO — Joe BROWN and The BRUVVERS
THAT'S WHEN I REACH FOR MY REVOLVER — MOBY
THAT'S WHEN I THINK OF YOU — 1927
THAT'S WHEN THE MUSIC TAKES ME — Neil SEDAKA
THAT'S WHERE MY MIND GOES — SLAMM
THAT'S WHERE THE HAPPY PEOPLE GO — The TRAMMPS
THAT'S WHY I LIE — Ray J
THAT'S WHY I'M CRYING — IVY LEAGUE
THAT'S WHY WE LOSE CONTROL — YOUNG OFFENDERS
THAT'S YOU — Nat 'King' COLE
THEIR WAY — LITTLE'ANS featuring Peter DOHERTY
THEM BONES — ALICE IN CHAINS
THEM GIRLS THEM GIRLS — ZIG and ZAG
... THEM THANGS — 50 CENT & G-UNIT
THEM THERE EYES — Emile FORD and The CHECKMATES
THEME — SABRES OF PARADISE
THE THEME [A] — UNIQUE 3
THE THEME [B] — Tracey LEE
THE THEME [C] — DREEM TEEM
THE THEME [D] — Jurgen VRIES
THEME FOR A DREAM — Cliff RICHARD and The SHADOWS
THEME FOR YOUNG LOVERS — The SHADOWS
THEME FROM 'A SUMMER PLACE' [A] — Norrie PARAMOR
THE THEME FROM 'A SUMMER PLACE' [A] — Percy FAITH
THEME FROM 'CADE'S COUNTY' — Henry MANCINI
THEME FROM 'CHEERS' — Gary PORTNOY
THEME FROM 'COME SEPTEMBER' — Bobby DARIN
THEME FROM DIXIE — Duane EDDY and The REBELS
THEME FROM 'DR KILDARE' [A] — Johnnie SPENCE
THEME FROM 'DR KILDARE' (THREE STARS WILL SHINE TONIGHT) [A] — Richard CHAMBERLAIN
THEME FROM 'E.T.' (THE EXTRA-TERRESTRIAL) — John WILLIAMS
THEME FROM GUTBUSTER — BENTLEY RHYTHM ACE
THEME FROM 'HARRY'S GAME' — CLANNAD
THEME FROM 'HILL STREET BLUES' — Mike POST
THEME FROM 'JURASSIC PARK' — John WILLIAMS
THEME FROM 'MAHOGANY' (DO YOU KNOW WHERE YOU'RE GOING TO) — Diana ROSS
THEME FROM M*A*S*H (SUICIDE IS PAINLESS) [A] — MASH (80)
THEME FROM M.A.S.H. (SUICIDE IS PAINLESS) [A] — MANIC STREET PREACHERS
THEME FROM 'MISSION: IMPOSSIBLE' — Adam CLAYTON and Larry MULLEN
THEME FROM 'NEW YORK, NEW YORK' — Frank SINATRA
THEME FROM PICNIC — Morris STOLOFF
THEME FROM P.O.P. — PERFECTLY ORDINARY PEOPLE
THEME FROM 'RANDALL & HOPKIRK (DECEASED)' — Nina PERSSON and David ARNOLD
THEME FROM S-EXPRESS — S EXPRESS (88)
THEME FROM 'SHAFT' [A] — Isaac HAYES
THEME FROM 'SHAFT' [A] — EDDY and The SOUL BAND
THEME FROM SPARTA FC #2 — The FALL
THEME FROM 'SUPERMAN' (MAIN TITLE) — LONDON SYMPHONY ORCHESTRA
THEME FROM 'THE APARTMENT' — FERRANTE and TEICHER
THEME FROM 'THE DEER HUNTER' (CAVATINA) — The SHADOWS
THEME FROM THE FILM 'THE LEGION'S LAST PATROL' — Ken THORNE
THEME FROM 'HONG KONG BEAT' — Richard DENTON and Martin COOK
THEME FROM 'THE ONEDIN LINE' — VIENNA PHILHARMONIC ORCHESTRA
THEME FROM 'THE PERSUADERS' — John BARRY ORCHESTRA
THEME FROM 'THE PROFESSIONALS' — Laurie JOHNSON
THEME FROM 'THE THREEPENNY OPERA' [A] — Louis ARMSTRONG
THEME FROM 'THE THREEPENNY OPERA' [A] — Dick HYMAN TRIO
THEME FROM 'THE THREEPENNY OPERA' [A] — Billy VAUGHN
THEME FROM 'THE TRAVELLING MAN' — Duncan BROWNE
THEME FROM 'THE VALLEY OF THE DOLLS' [A] — Dionne WARWICK
THEME FROM TURNPIKE (EP) — dEUS
THEME FROM 'VIETNAM' (CANON IN D) — Orchestre de Chambre Jean-François PAILLARD
THEME FROM 'WHICH WAY IS UP' — STARGARD
THEME FROM 'Z CARS' [A] — Norrie PARAMOR
THEME FROM 'Z CARS' JOHNNY TODD [A] — Johnny KEATING
THEME ONE — Cozy POWELL
THEN — The CHARLATANS
THEN CAME YOU [A] — Dionne WARWICK and The DETRIOT SPINNERS
THEN CAME YOU [A] — JUNIOR
THEN HE KISSED ME — CRYSTALS
THEN I FEEL GOOD — Katherine E
THEN I KISSED HER — The BEACH BOYS
THEN YOU CAN TELL ME GOODBYE — CASINOS
THEN YOU TURN AWAY — ORCHESTRAL MANOEUVRES IN THE DARK
THERE AIN'T NOTHIN' LIKE THE LOVE — MONTAGE
THERE AIN'T NOTHING LIKE SHAGGIN' — The TAMS
THERE ARE MORE QUESTIONS THAN ANSWERS — Johnny NASH
THERE ARE MORE SNAKES THAN LADDERS — CAPTAIN SENSIBLE
THERE BUT FOR FORTUNE — Joan BAEZ
THERE BUT FOR THE GRACE OF GOD — FIRE ISLAND
THERE BY THE GRACE OF GOD — MANIC STREET PREACHERS
THERE GOES MY EVERYTHING [A] — Engelbert HUMPERDINCK
THERE GOES MY EVERYTHING [A] — Elvis PRESLEY
THERE GOES MY FIRST LOVE — The DRIFTERS
THERE GOES THAT SONG AGAIN — Gary MILLER
THERE GOES THE FEAR — DOVES
THERE GOES THE NEIGHBORHOOD — Sheryl CROW
THERE I GO — Vikki CARR
THERE I GO AGAIN — POWER OF DREAMS
THERE IS A LIGHT THAT NEVER GOES OUT [A] — The SMITHS
THERE IS A LIGHT THAT NEVER GOES OUT [A] — MORRISSEY
THERE IS A MOUNTAIN — DONOVAN
THERE IS A STAR — PHARAO
THERE IS ALWAYS SOMETHING THERE TO REMIND ME — The HOUSEMARTINS
THERE IS NO LOVE BETWEEN US ANYMORE — POP WILL EAT ITSELF
THERE IT IS — SHALAMAR
THERE I'VE SAID IT AGAIN [A] — Al SAXON
THERE I'VE SAID IT AGAIN [A] — Bobby VINTON
THERE MUST BE A REASON — Frankie LAINE
THERE MUST BE A WAY [A] — Joni JAMES
THERE MUST BE A WAY [A] — Frankie VAUGHAN
THERE MUST BE AN ANGEL (PLAYING WITH MY HEART) — EURYTHMICS (85)
THERE MUST BE THOUSANDS — QUADS
THERE SHE GOES [A] — The LA's
THERE SHE GOES [A] — SIXPENCE NONE THE RICHER
THERE SHE GOES AGAIN — QUIREBOYS
THERE SHE GOES, MY BEAUTIFUL WORLD — Nick CAVE and The BAD SEEDS
THERE THERE — RADIOHEAD
THERE THERE MY DEAR — DEXY'S MIDNIGHT RUNNERS
THERE WILL NEVER BE ANOTHER TONIGHT — Bryan ADAMS
THERE WILL NEVER BE ANOTHER YOU [A] — Chris MONTEZ
THERE WILL NEVER BE ANOTHER YOU [B] — Jimmy RUFFIN
THERE WON'T BE MANY COMING HOME — Roy ORBISON
THERE YOU GO — PINK
THERE YOU'LL BE — Faith HILL
(THERE'LL BE BLUEBIRDS OVER) THE WHITE CLIFFS OF DOVER — Robson GREEN and Jerome FLYNN (95)
THERE'LL BE SAD SONGS (TO MAKE YOU CRY) — Billy OCEAN
THERE'S A BRAND NEW WORLD — FIVE STAR
THERE'S A GHOST IN MY HOUSE [A] — R Dean TAYLOR
THERE'S A GHOST IN MY HOUSE [A] — The FALL
THERE'S A GOLDMINE IN THE SKY — Pat BOONE
THERE'S A GUY WORKS DOWN THE CHIPSHOP SWEARS HE'S ELVIS — Kirsty MacCOLL
THERE'S A HEARTACHE FOLLOWING ME — Jim REEVES
THERE'S A HOLE IN MY BUCKET — Harry BELAFONTE
THERE'S A KIND OF HUSH [A] — HERMAN'S HERMITS
THERE'S A KIND OF HUSH (ALL OVER THE WORLD) [A] — The CARPENTERS
THERE'S A SILENCE — The ELECTRIC SOFT PARADE
THERE'S A STAR — ASH
THERE'S A WHOLE LOT OF LOVING — GUYS & DOLLS
THERE'S ALWAYS ROOM ON THE BROOM — The LIARS
(THERE'S) ALWAYS SOMETHING THERE TO REMIND ME — Sandie SHAW (64)
(THERE'S GONNA BE A) SHOWDOWN — Archie BELL and The DRELLS
THERE'S GOT TO BE A WAY — Mariah CAREY
(THERE'S GOTTA BE) MORE TO LIFE — Stacie ORRICO
THERE'S MORE TO LOVE — The COMMUNARDS
THERE'S NO LIVING WITHOUT YOU — Will DOWNING
THERE'S NO ONE QUITE LIKE GRANDMA — ST WINIFRED'S SCHOOL CHOIR (80)
THERE'S NO OTHER WAY — BLUR
THERE'S NOTHING BETTER THAN LOVE — Luther VANDROSS
THERE'S NOTHING I WON'T DO — JX
THERE'S NOTHING LIKE THIS — OMAR
THERE'S SOMETHING WRONG IN PARADISE — Kid CREOLE and The COCONUTS
THERE'S THE GIRL — HEART
THERE'S YOUR TROUBLE — DIXIE CHICKS
THESE ARE DAYS — 10,000 MANIACS
THESE ARE THE DAYS [A] — O-TOWN
THESE ARE THE DAYS [B] — Jamie CULLUM
THESE ARE THE DAYS OF OUR LIVES — QUEEN (91)
THESE ARE THE TIMES — DRU HILL
THESE ARMS OF MINE — The PROCLAIMERS
THESE BOOTS ARE MADE FOR WALKIN' [A] — Nancy SINATRA (66)
THESE BOOTS ARE MADE FOR WALKIN' [A] — Billy Ray CYRUS
THESE BOOTS ARE MADE FOR WALKIN' [A] — Jessica SIMPSON
THESE DAYS — BON JOVI
THESE DREAMS — HEART

	14 August 2004	21 August 2004	28 August 2004	4 September 2004
UK No.1 SINGLES	THUNDERBIRDS / 3AM Busted	BABY CAKES 3 of a Kind	THESE WORDS Natasha Bedingfield	THESE WORDS Natasha Bedingfield
UK No.1 ALBUMS	LIVE IN HYDE PARK Red Hot Chili Peppers	ANASTACIA Anastasia	SONGS ABOUT JANE Maroon5	ALWAYS OUTNUMBERED NEVER OUTGUNNED The Prodigy

THESE EARLY DAYS — EVERYTHING BUT THE GIRL
THESE THINGS ARE WORTH FIGHTING FOR — Gary CLAIL ON-U SOUND SYSTEM
THESE THINGS WILL KEEP ME LOVING YOU — The VELVELETTES
THESE WOODEN IDEAS — IDLEWILD
THESE WORDS — Natasha BEDINGFIELD (04)
THEY — JEM
THEY ALL LAUGHED — Frank SINATRA
(THEY CALL HER) LA BAMBA — The CRICKETS
THEY DON'T CARE ABOUT US — Michael JACKSON
THEY DON'T KNOW [A] — Tracey ULLMAN
THEY DON'T KNOW [B] — Jon B
THEY DON'T KNOW [C] — SO SOLID CREW
THEY GLUED YOUR HEAD ON UPSIDE DOWN — The BELLRAYS
(THEY LONG TO BE) CLOSE TO YOU [A] — The CARPENTERS
(THEY LONG TO BE) CLOSE TO YOU [A] — Gwen GUTHRIE
THEY SAY IT'S GONNA RAIN — Hazell DEAN
THEY SHOOT HORSES DON'T THEY? — RACING CARS
THEY WILL KILL US ALL — The BRONX
THEY'RE COMING TO TAKE ME AWAY HA-HAAA! — NAPOLEON XIV
THEY'RE HERE — EMF
THIEVES IN THE TEMPLE — PRINCE
THIEVES LIKE US — NEW ORDER
THIGHS HIGH (GRIP YOUR HIPS AND MOVE) — Tom BROWNE
THIN LINE BETWEEN LOVE AND HATE — The PRETENDERS
THE THIN WALL — ULTRAVOX
A THING CALLED LOVE — Johnny CASH
THE THING I LIKE — AALIYAH
THINGS — Bobby DARIN
THE THINGS — AUDIO BULLYS
THINGS CAN ONLY GET BETTER [A] — Howard JONES
THINGS CAN ONLY GET BETTER [B] — D:REAM (94)
THINGS FALL APART — SERAFIN
THINGS GET BETTER — Eddie FLOYD
THINGS HAVE CHANGED — Bob DYLAN
THINGS I'VE SEEN — SPOOKS
THINGS THAT ARE — RUNRIG
THINGS THAT MAKE YOU GO HMMM ... — C & C MUSIC FACTORY / CLIVILLES & COLE
THE THINGS THE LONELY DO — AMAZULU
THINGS THAT GO BUMP IN THE NIGHT — ALLSTARS
THE THINGS WE DO FOR LOVE [A] — 10cc
THINGS WILL GO MY WAY — The CALLING
THINGS WE DO FOR LOVE [B] — Horace BROWN
THINK [A] — Brenda LEE
THINK [B] — Chris FARLOWE
THINK [C] — Aretha FRANKLIN
THINK ABOUT ... — DJH featuring STEFY
THINK ABOUT ME — ARTFUL DODGER featuring Michelle ESCOFFERY
THINK ABOUT THAT — Dandy LIVINGSTONE
THINK ABOUT THE WAY (BOM DIGI DIGI BOM ...) — ICE MC
THINK ABOUT YOUR CHILDREN — Mary HOPKIN
THINK FOR A MINUTE — The HOUSEMARTINS
THINK I'M GONNA FALL IN LOVE WITH YOU — The DOOLEYS
THINK IT ALL OVER — Sandie SHAW
THINK IT OVER — The CRICKETS
THINK OF ME (WHEREVER YOU ARE) — Ken DODD
THINK OF YOU [A] — USHER
THINK OF YOU [B] — WHIGFIELD
THINK SOMETIMES ABOUT ME — Sandie SHAW
THINK TWICE — Celine DION (95)
THINKIN' ABOUT YOUR BODY — Bobby McFERRIN
THINKIN' AIN'T FOR ME — Paul JONES
THINKING ABOUT TOMORROW — Beth ORTON
THINKING ABOUT YOUR BODY — 2 MAD
THINKING ABOUT YOUR LOVE [A] — SKIPWORTH and TURNER
THINKING ABOUT YOUR LOVE [A] — Phillip LEO
THINKING ABOUT YOUR LOVE [B] — Kenny THOMAS
THINKING IT OVER — LIBERTY
THINKING OF YOU [A] — SISTER SLEDGE
THINKING OF YOU [A] — MAUREEN
THINKING OF YOU [A] — Curtis LYNCH Jr featuring Kele LE ROC and RED RAT
THINKING OF YOU [A] — Paul WELLER
THINKING OF YOU [B] — COLOUR FIELD
THINKING OF YOU [C] — HANSON
THINKING OF YOU [D] — STATUS QUO
THINKING OF YOU BABY — Dave CLARK FIVE
THINKING OVER — Dana GLOVER
THIRD FINGER, LEFT HAND — PEARLS
THE THIRD MAN — The SHADOWS
THIRD RAIL — SQUEEZE
THIRTEEN — FORWARD, RUSSIA!
13 STEPS LEAD DOWN — Elvis COSTELLO
THE 13TH — The CURE
13TH DISCIPLE — FIVE THIRTY
30 CENTURY MAN — CATHERINE WHEEL
36D — The BEAUTIFUL SOUTH
THIRTY THREE — SMASHING PUMPKINS
THIS AIN'T A LOVE SONG — BON JOVI
THIS AND THAT — Tom JONES
THIS BEAT IS MINE — Vicky D
THIS BEAT IS TECHNOTRONIC — TECHNOTRONIC
THIS BOY [A] — JUSTIN
THIS BOY [A] — Tom BAXTER
THIS BRUTAL HOUSE — NITRO DELUXE
THIS CAN BE REAL — CANDY FLIP
THIS CHARMING MAN — The SMITHS
THIS CORROSION — SISTERS OF MERCY
THIS COWBOY SONG — STING featuring Pato BANTON
THIS DAY SHOULD LAST FOREVER — OCEAN COLOUR SCENE
THIS DJ — Warren G
THIS DOOR SWINGS BOTH WAYS — HERMAN'S HERMITS
THIS FEELIN' — Frank HOOKER and POSITIVE PEOPLE
THIS FEELING — PURESSENCE
THIS FLIGHT TONIGHT — NAZARETH
THIS GARDEN — LEVELLERS
THIS GENERATION — ROACHFORD
THIS GIVEN LINE — The ELECTRIC SOFT PARADE
THIS GOLDEN RING — FORTUNES
THIS GROOVE — Victoria BECKHAM
THIS GUY'S IN LOVE WITH YOU — Herb ALPERT
THIS HERE GIRAFFE — The FLAMING LIPS
THIS HOUSE [A] — Tracie SPENCER
THIS HOUSE [B] — Alison MOYET
THIS HOUSE IS NOT A HOME — REMBRANDTS
THIS HOUSE (IS WHERE YOUR LOVE STANDS) — BIG SOUND AUTHORITY
THIS I PROMISE YOU — 'N SYNC
THIS I SWEAR [A] — Richard DARBYSHIRE
THIS I SWEAR [B] — Kim WILDE
THIS IS A CALL — FOO FIGHTERS
THIS IS A REBEL SONG — Sinead O'CONNOR
THIS IS A WARNING — DILLINJA
THIS IS ENGLAND — The CLASH
THIS IS FOR REAL — David DEVANT & his SPIRIT WIFE
THIS IS FOR THE LOVER IN YOU — BABYFACE
THIS IS FOR THE POOR — The OTHERS
THIS IS GOODBYE — Lucy CARR
THIS IS HARDCORE — PULP
THIS IS HOW A HEART BREAKS — Rob THOMAS
THIS IS HOW IT FEELS — INSPIRAL CARPETS
THIS IS HOW WE DO IT [A] — Montell JORDAN
THIS IS HOW WE DO IT [A] — MIS-TEEQ
THIS IS HOW WE PARTY — S.O.A.P.
THIS IS IT! [A] — Adam FAITH
THIS IS IT [B] — Melba MOORE
THIS IS IT [B] — Dannii MINOGUE
THIS IS IT [C] — Dan HARTMAN
THIS IS IT [D] — 4MANDU
THIS IS IT [E] — STATE OF MIND
THIS IS IT (YOUR SOUL) — HOTHOUSE FLOWERS
THIS IS LOVE [A] — Gary NUMAN
THIS IS LOVE [B] — George HARRISON
THIS IS LOVE [C] — PJ HARVEY
THIS IS ME [A] — CLIMIE FISHER
THIS IS ME [B] — SAW DOCTORS
THIS IS MINE — HEAVEN 17
THIS IS MUSIC — The VERVE
THIS IS MY HOLLYWOOD — 3 COLOURS RED
THIS IS MY LIFE — Eartha KITT
THIS IS MY NIGHT — Chaka KHAN
THIS IS MY SONG [A] — Harry SECOMBE
THIS IS MY SONG [A] — Petula CLARK (67)
THIS IS MY SOUND — DJ SHOG
THIS IS MY TIME — 3 COLOURS RED
THIS IS NOT A LOVE SONG — PUBLIC IMAGE LTD
THIS IS NOT A SONG — FRANK AND WALTERS
THIS IS NOT AMERICA (THE THEME FROM 'THE FALCON AND THE SNOWMAN') — David BOWIE
THIS IS OUR SONG — CODE RED
THIS IS RADIO CLASH — The CLASH
THIS IS SKA — Longsy D
THIS IS THE DAY — The THE
THIS IS THE LAST TIME — KEANE
THIS IS THE NEW *HIT — MARILYN MANSON
THIS IS THE PLACE — Zeitia MASSIAH
THIS IS THE RIGHT TIME — Lisa STANSFIELD
THIS IS THE SOUND OF YOUTH — THESE ANIMAL MEN
THIS IS THE STORY OF MY LOVE (BABY) — WIZZARD
THIS IS THE WAY [A] — Bruce FOXTON
THIS IS THE WAY [B] — Dannii MINOGUE
THIS IS THE WAY [C] — FKW
THIS IS THE WAY [D] — E-TYPE
THIS IS THE WORLD CALLING — Bob GELDOF
THIS IS THE WORLD WE LIVE IN — ALCAZAR
THIS IS TOMORROW — Bryan FERRY
THIS IS WHAT WE DO — CRACKOUT
THIS IS WHERE I CAME IN — The BEE GEES
THIS IS YOUR LAND — SIMPLE MINDS
THIS IS YOUR LIFE [A] — The BLOW MONKEYS
THIS IS YOUR LIFE [B] — BANDERAS
THIS IS YOUR LIFE [C] — DUST BROTHERS
THIS IS YOUR NIGHT [A] — HEAVY D and The BOYZ
THIS IS YOUR NIGHT [B] — ANOTHERSIDE
THIS IZ REAL — SHYHEIM
THIS KIND OF LOVE — Phil FEARON
THIS KISS — Faith HILL
THIS LITTLE BIRD [A] — Marianne FAITHFULL
THIS LITTLE BIRD [A] — NASHVILLE TEENS
THIS LITTLE GIRL — Gary 'US' BONDS
THIS LOVE [A] — LeAnn RIMES
THIS LOVE [B] — MAROON5
THIS LOVE AFFAIR — Stefan DENNIS
THIS LOVE I HAVE FOR YOU — Lance FORTUNE
THIS MONDAY MORNING FEELING — Tito SIMON
THIS MORNING — NORTHERN UPROAR
THIS MUST BE THE PLACE — TALKING HEADS
THIS NEW YEAR — Cliff RICHARD
THIS OLD HEART OF MINE [A] — The ISLEY BROTHERS
THIS OLD HEART OF MINE [A] — Rod STEWART
THIS OLD SKIN — The BEAUTIFUL SOUTH
THIS OLE HOUSE [A] — Billie ANTHONY
THIS OLE HOUSE [A] — Rosemary CLOONEY (54)
THIS OLE HOUSE [A] — Shakin' STEVENS (81)
THIS ONE — Paul McCARTNEY
THIS ONE'S FOR THE CHILDREN — NEW KIDS ON THE BLOCK
THIS ONE'S FOR YOU — Ed HARCOURT
THIS PARTY SUCKS! — FUSED
THIS PERFECT DAY — SAINTS
THIS PICTURE — PLACEBO
THIS PLANET'S ON FIRE (BURN IN HELL) — Sammy HAGAR
THIS STRANGE EFFECT — Dave BERRY
THIS SUMMER — SQUEEZE
THIS TIME [A] — Troy SHONDELL
THIS TIME [B] — Bryan ADAMS
THIS TIME [C] — Dina CARROLL
THIS TIME [D] — Michelle SWEENEY
THIS TIME [E] — Judy CHEEKS
THIS TIME [F] — Curtis STIGERS
THIS TIME (LIVE) [G] — WET WET WET
THIS TIME AROUND — PHATS & SMALL
THIS TIME (WE'LL GET IT RIGHT) — ENGLAND WORLD CUP SQUAD
THIS TIME BABY — Jackie MOORE
THIS TIME I FOUND LOVE — ROZALLA
THIS TIME I KNOW IT'S FOR REAL [A] — Donna SUMMER
THIS TIME I KNOW IT'S FOR REAL [A] — Kelly LLORENNA
THIS TIME OF YEAR — RUNRIG
THIS TOWN AIN'T BIG ENOUGH FOR BOTH OF US [A] — SPARKS
THIS TOWN AIN'T BIG ENOUGH FOR BOTH OF US [A] — BRITISH WHALE
THIS TRAIN DON'T STOP THERE ANYMORE — Elton JOHN
THIS USED TO BE MY PLAYGROUND — MADONNA
THIS WAITING HEART — Chris DE BURGH
THIS WAY — DILATED PEOPLES
THIS WHEEL'S ON FIRE [A] — Julie DRISCOLL, Brian AUGER and The TRINITY
THIS WHEEL'S ON FIRE [A] — SIOUXSIE and The BANSHEES
THIS WILL BE — Natalie COLE
THIS WILL BE OUR YEAR — The BEAUTIFUL SOUTH
THIS WOMAN'S WORK — Kate BUSH
THIS WORLD IS NOT MY HOME — Jim REEVES
THIS WORLD OF WATER — NEW MUSIK
THIS WRECKAGE — Gary NUMAN
THIS YEAR'S LOVE — David GRAY
THOIA THOING — R KELLY
THONG SONG — SISQO
THE THORN EP — SIOUXSIE and The BANSHEES
THORN IN MY SIDE — EURYTHMICS
THOSE FIRST IMPRESSIONS — ASSOCIATES
THOSE SIMPLE THINGS — RIGHT SAID FRED
THOSE WERE THE DAYS — Mary HOPKIN (68)
THOU SHALT NOT STEAL — FREDDIE and The DREAMERS
THOUGHT I'D DIED AND GONE TO HEAVEN — Bryan ADAMS
THE THOUGHT OF IT — Louie LOUIE
THOUGHT U WERE THE ONE FOR ME — Joey B ELLIS
THOUGHTLESS — KORN
A THOUSAND MILES — Vanessa CARLTON
A THOUSAND STARS — Billy FURY
A THOUSAND TREES — STEREOPHONICS
THREE — WEDDING PRESENT
3AM [A] — MATCHBOX 20
3 AM [B] — Bobby BLANCO & Mikki MOTO
3AM [C] — BUSTED (04)
3:A.M. ETERNAL — The KLF featuring CHILDREN OF THE REVOLUTION (91)
THREE BABIES — Sinead O'CONNOR
THE THREE BELLS [A] — The BROWNS
THE THREE BELLS (THE JIMMY BROWN SONG) [A] — COMPAGNONS DE LA CHANSON
THREE BELLS [A] — Brian POOLE and The TREMELOES
THE THREE BELLS [A] — Daniel O'DONNELL
THREE COINS IN THE FOUNTAIN [A] — The FOUR ACES
THREE COINS IN THE FOUNTAIN [A] — Frank SINATRA (54)
3 FEET TALL — I AM KLOOT
3 IS FAMILY — Dana DAWSON
3 LIBRAS — A PERFECT CIRCLE
THREE LIONS (THE OFFICIAL SONG OF THE ENGLAND FOOTBALL TEAM) [A] — BADDIEL and SKINNER and The LIGHTNING SEEDS (96)
THREE LIONS '98 [A] — BADDIEL and SKINNER and The LIGHTNING SEEDS (98)
THREE LITTLE BIRDS — Bob MARLEY & The WAILERS
THREE LITTLE PIGS — GREEN JELLY
THREE LITTLE WORDS — The APPLEJACKS
3 MC'S & 1 DJ — BEASTIE BOYS
THREE MINUTE HERO — SELECTER
THREE NIGHTS A WEEK — Fats DOMINO
THREE RING CIRCUS — Barry BIGGS
3 ... 6 ... 9 SECONDS OF LIGHT (EP) — BELLE & SEBASTIAN
3 SONGS (EP) — WEDDING PRESENT
THREE STARS — Ruby WRIGHT

11 September 2004
MY PLACE / FLAP YOUR WINGS
Nelly
THE LIBERTINES
The Libertines

18 September 2004
REAL TO ME
Brian McFadden
UNWRITTEN
Natasha Bedingfield

25 September 2004
CALL ON ME
Eric Prydz
OUT OF NOTHING
Embrace

2 October 2004
CALL ON ME
Eric Prydz
AMERICAN IDIOT
Green Day

…TEPS TO HEAVEN [A] — …die COCHRAN (60)
…E STEPS TO HEAVEN [A] — SHOWADDYWADDY
THREE TIMES A LADY — The COMMODORES (78)
THREE TIMES A MAYBE — K CREATIVE
3 X 3 (EP) — GENESIS
III WISHES — TERRORVISION
THREESOME — FENIX TX
3345 — The BLACK VELVETS
3IL (THRILL) — SOUL U*NIQUE
THRILL HAS GONE — TEXAS
THRILL ME [A] — SIMPLY RED
THRILL ME [B] — JUNIOR JACK
THRILLER — Michael JACKSON
THROUGH — KINGS OF TOMORROW
THROUGH THE BARRICADES — SPANDAU BALLET
THROUGH THE GATE — ARTIFICIAL INTELLIGENCE
THROUGH THE RAIN — Mariah CAREY
THROUGH THE ROOF — CUD
THROUGH THE STORM — Aretha FRANKLIN and Elton JOHN
THROUGH THE WIRE — Kanye WEST
THROUGH THE YEARS [A] — Gary GLITTER
THROUGH THE YEARS [B] — Cilla BLACK
THROW AWAY THE KEY — LINX
THROW DOWN A LINE — Cliff RICHARD
THROW THESE GUNS AWAY — DUNBLANE (96)
THROW YA GUNZ — ONYX
THROW YOUR HANDS UP — LV
THROW YOUR SET IN THE AIR — CYPRESS HILL
THROWING IT ALL AWAY — GENESIS
THROWING MY BABY OUT WITH THE BATHWATER — TEN POLE TUDOR
THROWN AWAY — The STRANGLERS
THRU — KINGS OF TOMORROW featuring HAZE
THRU THE GLASS — THIRTEEN SENSES
THRU' THESE WALLS — Phil COLLINS
THUG LOVIN' — JA RULE featuring Bobby BROWN
THUGGED OUT BITCH — DILLINJA
THUGZ MANSION — 2PAC
THUNDER [A] — PRINCE and The NEW POWER GENERATION
THUNDER [B] — EAST 17
THUNDER AND LIGHTNING — THIN LIZZY
THUNDER IN MY HEART — Leo SAYER
THUNDER IN THE MOUNTAINS — TOYAH
THUNDERBALL — Tom JONES
THUNDERBIRDS [A] — Barry GRAY ORCHESTRA
THUNDERBIRDS [A] — BUSTED (04)
THUNDERBIRDS ARE GO [A] — FAB
THUNDERDOME — MESSIAH
THUNDERSTRUCK — AC/DC
THURSDAY'S CHILD — David BOWIE
THUS SPAKE ZARATHUSTRA — PHILHARMONIA ORCHESTRA, conductor Lorin MAAZEL
TI AMO — Gina G
TIC, TIC TAC — CHILLI featuring CARRAPICHO
TIC TOC — KLEA
TICKET OUTTA LOSERVILLE — SON OF DORK
TICKET TO RIDE — The BEATLES (65)
TICKET TO THE MOON — ELECTRIC LIGHT ORCHESTRA
THE TIDE IS HIGH [A] — BLONDIE (80)
THE TIDE IS HIGH (GET THE FEELING) [A] — ATOMIC KITTEN (02)
THE TIDE IS TURNING (AFTER LIVE AID) — Roger WATERS
THE TIDE THAT LEFT AND NEVER CAME BACK — The VEILS
TIE A YELLOW RIBBON ROUND THE OLE OAK TREE — DAWN (73)
TIE ME KANGAROO DOWN SPORT — Rolf HARRIS
TIE YOUR MOTHER DOWN — QUEEN
TIED TO THE 90'S — TRAVIS
TIED UP — YELLO
TIED UP TOO TIGHT — HARD-FI
TIGER BABY — SILVER CONVENTION
TIGER FEET — MUD (74)
TIGHTEN UP — I JUST CAN'T STOP DANCING — Wally JUMP Jr and The CRIMINAL ELEMENT
TIJUANA TAXI — Herb ALPERT
TIL I HEAR IT FROM YOU — GIN BLOSSOMS
('TIL) I KISSED YOU — The EVERLY BROTHERS
... TIL THE COPS COME KNOCKIN' — MAXWELL
'TIL THE DAY — EASYWORLD
TILL [A] — Tony BENNETT
TILL [A] — Dorothy SQUIRES
TILL [A] — Tom JONES
TILL I CAN'T TAKE LOVE NO MORE — Eddy GRANT
TILL I GET MY WAY — The BLACK KEYS
TILL I LOVED YOU (LOVE THEME FROM 'GOYA') [A] — Barbra STREISAND and Don JOHNSON
TILL I LOVED YOU [A] — Placido DOMINGO and Jennifer RUSH
TILL THE END — HAVEN
TILL THE END OF THE DAY — The KINKS
TILL TEARS DO US PART — HEAVENS CRY
TILL THERE WAS YOU — Peggy LEE
TILL WE MEET AGAIN [A] — INNER CITY
TILL WE MEET AGAIN [B] — PUSH
TILL YOU COME BACK TO ME — Leo SAYER
TILT YA HEAD BACK — NELLY & Christina AGUILERA
TILTED — SUGAR
TIME [A] — Craig DOUGLAS
TIME [B] — LIGHT OF THE WORLD
TIME [C] — B.A. ROBERTSON
TIME [D] — Freddie MERCURY
TIME [E] — Kim WILDE
TIME [F] — SUPERGRASS
TIME [G] — MARION
TIME AFTER TIME [A] — Cyndi LAUPER
TIME AFTER TIME [A] — HYPERSTATE
TIME AFTER TIME [A] — CHANGING FACES
TIME AFTER TIME [A] — DISTANT SOUNDZ
TIME AFTER TIME [A] — NOVASPACE
TIME AFTER TIME [B] — The BELOVED
TIME ALONE WILL TELL — Malcolm ROBERTS
TIME AND CHANCE — COLOR ME BADD
A TIME AND PLACE — MIKE and The MECHANICS
TIME AND THE RIVER — Nat 'King' COLE
TIME AND TIDE — BASIA
TIME AND TIME AGAIN — PAPA ROACH
TIME BOMB [A] — 808 STATE
TIME BOMB [B] — RANCID
TIME (CLOCK OF THE HEART) — CULTURE CLUB
TIME DRAGS BY — Cliff RICHARD and The SHADOWS
TIME FOR ACTION — SECRET AFFAIR
TIME FOR DELIVERANCE — DO ME BAD THINGS
TIME FOR HEROES — The LIBERTINES
TIME FOR LIVIN' — The ASSOCIATION
TIME FOR LOVE — Kim ENGLISH
TIME FOR THE REVOLUTION — 10 REVOLUTIONS
THE TIME HAS COME [A] — Adam FAITH
THE TIME HAS COME [A] — PP ARNOLD
TIME HAS TAKEN ITS TOLL ON YOU — CRAZYHEAD
THE TIME IN BETWEEN — Cliff RICHARD and The SHADOWS
TIME IS MY EVERYTHING — Ian BROWN
THE TIME IS NOW — MOLOKO
TIME IS ON MY SIDE — The ROLLING STONES
TIME IS RUNNING OUT — MUSE
TIME IS TIGHT — BOOKER T and The MG's
A TIME LIKE THIS — HAYWOODE
TIME LOVE AND TENDERNESS — Michael BOLTON
TIME OF MY LIFE — TOPLOADER
TIME OF OUR LIVES [A] — Alison LIMERICK
TIME OF OUR LIVES [B] — Paul VAN DYK featuring VEGA 4
TIME OF YOUR LIFE (GOOD RIDDANCE) — GREEN DAY
TIME SELLER — Spencer DAVIS GROUP
TIME STAND STILL — RUSH with Aimee MANN
TIME TO BURN — STORM
TIME TO GET BACK — HYSTERIC EGO
TIME TO GET UP — LIQUID
TIME TO GROW — LEMAR
TIME TO MAKE THE FLOOR BURN — VARIOUS ARTISTS (MONTAGES)
TIME TO MAKE YOU MINE — Lisa STANSFIELD
TIME TO MOVE ON — SPARKLE
TIME TO SAY GOODBYE (CON TE PARTIRO) — Sarah BRIGHTMAN and Andrea BOCELLI
TIME TO WASTE — ALKALINE TRIO
THE TIME WARP — DAMIAN
TIME WILL CRAWL — David BOWIE
TIMEBOMB — CHUMBAWAMBA
TIMELESS — Daniel O'DONNELL
TIMELESS (KEEP ON MOVIN') — Ron VAN DEN BEUKEN
TIMELESS MELODY — The LA's
TIMES LIKE THESE — FOO FIGHTERS
THE TIMES THEY ARE A-CHANGIN' [A] — PETER, PAUL and MARY
TIMES THEY ARE A-CHANGIN' [A] — Bob DYLAN
THE TIMES THEY ARE A-CHANGIN' [A] — Ian CAMPBELL FOLK GROUP
THE TIMEWARP — CAST OF THE NEW ROCKY HORROR SHOW
TIN MACHINE — TIN MACHINE
TIN SOLDIER — The SMALL FACES
TIN SOLDIERS — STIFF LITTLE FINGERS
TINA MARIE — Perry COMO
TINGLE — THAT PETROL EMOTION
TINSEL TOWN — Ronny JORDAN
TINSELTOWN TO THE BOOGIEDOWN — SCRITTI POLITTI
TINY CHILDREN — TEARDROP EXPLODES
TINY DYNAMITE (EP) — COCTEAU TWINS
TINY MACHINE — DARLING BUDS
TIPP CITY — The AMPS
THE TIPS OF MY FINGERS — Des O'CONNOR
TIPSY — J-KWON
TIRED OF BEING ALONE [A] — Al GREEN
TIRED OF BEING ALONE [A] — TEXAS
TIRED OF TOEIN' THE LINE — Rocky BURNETTE
TIRED OF WAITING FOR YOU — The KINKS (65)
TISHBITE — COCTEAU TWINS
TKO — LE TIGRE
T.N.T. FOR THE BRAIN — ENIGMA
TO A BRIGHTER DAY (O' HAPPY DAY) — BEAT SYSTEM
TO ALL THE GIRLS I'VE LOVED BEFORE — Julio IGLESIAS and Willie NELSON
TO BE A LOVER — Billy IDOL
TO BE FREE — Emiliana TORRINI
TO BE IN LOVE — INDIA
TO BE LOVED [A] — Jackie WILSON
TO BE LOVED [A] — Malcolm VAUGHAN
TO BE OR NOT TO BE — B.A. ROBERTSON
TO BE OR NOT TO BE (THE HITLER RAP) — Mel BROOKS
TO BE REBORN — BOY GEORGE
TO BE WITH YOU — MR BIG
TO BE WITH YOU AGAIN — LEVEL 42
TO CUT A LONG STORY SHORT — SPANDAU BALLET
TO DIE FOR — Luke GALLIANA
TO EARTH WITH LOVE — GAY DAD
TO FRANCE — Mike OLDFIELD
TO GET DOWN — Timo MAAS
TO HAVE AND TO HOLD — Catherine STOCK
TO HERE KNOWS WHEN — MY BLOODY VALENTINE
TO KNOW HIM IS TO LOVE HIM — TEDDY BEARS
TO KNOW SOMEONE DEEPLY IS TO KNOW SOMEONE SOFTLY — Terence Trent D'ARBY
TO KNOW YOU IS TO LOVE YOU — PETER and GORDON
TO LIVE & DIE IN LA — MAKAVELI
TO LOVE A WOMAN — Lionel RICHIE featuring Enrique IGLESIAS
TO LOVE ONCE AGAIN — SOLID HARMONIE
TO LOVE SOMEBODY [A] — The BEE GEES
TO LOVE SOMEBODY [A] — Nina SIMONE
TO LOVE SOMEBODY [A] — Jimmy SOMERVILLE
TO LOVE SOMEBODY [A] — Michael BOLTON
TO MAKE A BIG MAN CRY — PJ PROBY
TO THE BEAT OF THE DRUM (LA LUNA) — ETHICS
TO THE BIRDS — SUEDE
TO THE CLUB — SPANKOX
TO THE END — BLUR
TO THE LIMIT — Tony DE VIT
TO THE MOON AND BACK — SAVAGE GARDEN
TO THE WORLD — O.R.G.A.N.
TO WHOM IT CONCERNS — Chris ANDREWS
TO WIN JUST ONCE — SAW DOCTORS
TO YOU I BELONG — B*WITCHED (98)
TO YOU I BESTOW — MUNDY
TOAST — STREETBAND
TOAST OF LOVE — The THREE DEGREES
TOBACCO ROAD — NASHVILLE TEENS
TOCA ME — FRAGMA
TOCA'S MIRACLE — FRAGMA: Vocals by Co Co (00)
TOCCATA — SKY
TOCCATA AND FUGUE — VANESSA-MAE
TODAY [A] — Sandie SHAW
TODAY [B] — TALK TALK
TODAY [C] — SMASHING PUMPKINS
TODAY [D] — Melanie BROWN
TODAY FOREVER — RIDE
TODAY'S THE DAY — Sean MAGUIRE
TODAY'S YOUR LUCKY DAY — Harold MELVIN and The BLUENOTES
TOGETHER [A] — Connie FRANCIS
TOGETHER [A] — PJ PROBY
TOGETHER [B] — OC SMITH
TOGETHER [C] — Danny CAMPBELL and SASHA
TOGETHER [D] — ARTIFICIAL FUNK featuring Nellie ETTISON
TOGETHER AGAIN [A] — Ray CHARLES
TOGETHER AGAIN [B] — Janet JACKSON
TOGETHER FOREVER — Rick ASTLEY
TOGETHER IN ELECTRIC DREAMS — Giorgio MORODER
TOGETHER WE ARE BEAUTIFUL [A] — Steve ALLAN
TOGETHER WE ARE BEAUTIFUL [A] — Fern KINNEY (80)
TOGETHERNESS — Mike PRESTON
TOKOLOSHE MAN — John KONGOS
TOKYO — CLASSIX NOUVEAUX
TOKYO JOE — Bryan FERRY
TOKYO MELODY — Helmut ZACHARIAS
TOKYO STEALTH FIGHTER — Dave ANGEL
TOKYO STORM WARNING — Elvis COSTELLO
TOLEDO — Elvis COSTELLO / Burt BACHARACH
TOM DOOLEY [A] — KINGSTON TRIO
TOM DOOLEY [A] — Lonnie DONEGAN
TOM HARK [A] — ELIAS and his ZIGZAG JIVE FLUTES
TOM HARK [A] — Ted HEATH
TOM HARK [A] — PIRANHAS
TOM HARK (WE WANT FALMER!) [A] — SEAGULLS SKA
TOM JONES INTERNATIONAL — Tom JONES
TOM PILLIBI — Jacqueline BOYER
TOM SAWYER — RUSH
TOM THE MODEL — Beth GIBBONS & RUSTIN MAN
TOM THE PEEPER — ACT ONE
TOM-TOM TURNAROUND — NEW WORLD
TOM TRAUBERT'S BLUES (WALTZING MATILDA) — Rod STEWART
TOMB OF MEMORIES — Paul YOUNG
TOMBOY — Perry COMO
TOMMY GUN — The CLASH
TOMMY SHOTS — YOUNG HEART ATTACK
TOMORROW [A] — Johnny BRANDON
TOMORROW [B] — Sandie SHAW
TOMORROW [C] — COMMUNARDS
TOMORROW [D] — TONGUE 'N' CHEEK
TOMORROW [E] — SILVERCHAIR
TOMORROW [F] — JAMES
TOMORROW [G] — DUMONDE
TOMORROW COMES TODAY — GORILLAZ
TOMORROW NEVER DIES — Sheryl CROW
TOMORROW NIGHT — ATOMIC ROOSTER
TOMORROW PEOPLE — Ziggy MARLEY and The MELODY MAKERS
TOMORROW RISING — Cliff RICHARD
TOMORROW ROBINS WILL SING — Stevie WONDER
TOMORROW TOMORROW — The BEE GEES
TOMORROW'S CLOWN — Marty WILDE
TOMORROW'S GIRLS [A] — UK SUBS
TOMORROW'S GIRLS [B] — Donald FAGEN
TOMORROW'S (JUST ANOTHER DAY) — MADNESS
TOM'S DINER [A] — Suzanne VEGA
TOM'S DINER [A] — DNA featuring Suzanne VEGA
TOM'S PARTY — T-SPOON
TONES OF HOME (EP) — BLIND MELON
TONGUE — R.E.M.
TONGUE TIED — The CAT

9 October 2004	16 October 2004	23 October 2004	30 October 2004
UK No.1 SINGLES			
CALL ON ME Eric Prydz	RADIO Robbie Williams	CALL ON ME Eric Prydz	CALL ON ME Eric Prydz
UK No.1 ALBUMS			
MIND BODY & SOUL Joss Stone	AROUND THE SUN R.E.M.	10 YEARS OF HITS Ronan Keating	GREATEST HITS Robbie Williams

TONIGHT [A] — Shirley BASSEY
TONIGHT [B] — The MOVE
TONIGHT [C] — The RUBETTES
TONIGHT [D] — Zaine GRIFF
TONIGHT [E] — MODETTES
TONIGHT [F] — Steve HARVEY
TONIGHT [G] — KOOL and The GANG
TONIGHT [H] — The BOOMTOWN RATS
TONIGHT [I] — David BOWIE
TONIGHT [J] — NEW KIDS ON THE BLOCK
TONIGHT [K] — DEF LEPPARD
TONIGHT [L] — BAD COMPANY
TONIGHT [M] — WESTLIFE
TONIGHT (COULD BE THE NIGHT) — The VELVETS
TONIGHT I CELEBRATE MY LOVE — Peabo BRYSON and Roberta FLACK
TONIGHT I'M ALRIGHT — Narada Michael WALDEN
TONIGHT I'M FREE — ANT & DEC
TONIGHT I'M GONNA LET GO — Syleena JOHNSON
TONIGHT I'M GONNA LOVE YOU ALL OVER — The FOUR TOPS
TONIGHT I'M YOURS (DON'T HURT ME) — Rod STEWART
TONIGHT IN TOKYO — Sandie SHAW
TONIGHT IS WHAT IT MEANS TO BE YOUNG — Jim STEINMAN
TONIGHT TONIGHT — SMASHING PUMPKINS
TONIGHT TONIGHT TONIGHT — GENESIS
TONIGHT YOU BELONG TO ME — PATIENCE and PRUDENCE
TONIGHT'S THE NIGHT — Rod STEWART
TONITE [A] — PHATS & SMALL
TONITE [B] — SUPERCAR
TOO BEAUTIFUL TO LAST — Engelbert HUMPERDINCK
TOO BAD — NICKELBACK
TOO BIG — Suzi QUATRO
TOO BLIND TO SEE IT — Kym SIMS
TOO BUSY THINKING 'BOUT MY BABY [A] — Marvin GAYE
TOO BUSY THINKING ABOUT MY BABY [A] — MARDI GRAS
TOO BUSY THINKING 'BOUT MY BABY [A] — STEPS
TOO CLOSE [A] — NEXT
TOO CLOSE [A] — BLUE (01)
TOO COLD — ROOTS MANUVA
TOO DRUNK TO FUCK — DEAD KENNEDYS
TOO FAR GONE — Lisa SCOTT-LEE
TOO FUNKY — George MICHAEL
TOO GONE, TOO LONG — EN VOGUE
TOO GOOD — LITTLE TONY
TOO GOOD TO BE FORGOTTEN [A] — CHI-LITES
TOO GOOD TO BE FORGOTTEN [A] — AMAZULU
TOO GOOD TO BE TRUE — Tom PETTY and The HEARTBREAKERS
TOO HARD TO BE FREE — AMEN
TOO HOT [A] — KOOL and The GANG
TOO HOT [B] — COOLIO
TOO HOT [C] — FUN LOVIN' CRIMINALS
TOO HOT [D] — FYA
TOO HOT TA TROT — The COMMODORES
TOO HOT TO HANDLE — HEATWAVE
TOO LATE — JUNIOR
TOO LATE FOR GOODBYES — Julian LENNON
TOO LATE TO SAY GOODBYE — Richard MARX
TOO LATE, TOO SOON — Jon SECADA
TOO LOST IN YOU — SUGABABES
TOO MANY BEAUTIFUL GIRLS — Clinton FORD
TOO MANY BROKEN HEARTS — Jason DONOVAN (89)
TOO MANY DJ'S — SOULWAX
TOO MANY FISH — Frankie KNUCKLES featuring ADEVA
TOO MANY GAMES — MAZE featuring Frankie BEVERLY
TOO MANY MC'S — PUBLIC DOMAIN
TOO MANY PEOPLE — Pauline HENRY
TOO MANY RIVERS — Brenda LEE
TOO MANY TEARS — David COVERDALE and WHITESNAKE
TOO MANY WALLS — Cathy DENNIS
TOO MUCH [A] — Elvis PRESLEY
TOO MUCH [B] — BROS
TOO MUCH [C] — SPICE GIRLS (97)
TOO MUCH FOR ONE HEART — Michael BARRYMORE
TOO MUCH HEAVEN — The BEE GEES
TOO MUCH INFORMATION — DURAN DURAN
TOO MUCH KISSING — SENSELESS THINGS
TOO MUCH LOVE WILL KILL YOU [A] — Brian MAY
TOO MUCH LOVE WILL KILL YOU [A] — QUEEN
TOO MUCH TEQUILA — CHAMPS
TOO MUCH TOO LITTLE TOO LATE [A] — Johnny MATHIS and Deniece WILLIAMS
TOO MUCH, TOO LITTLE, TOO LATE [A] — SILVER SUN
TOO MUCH TOO YOUNG — LITTLE ANGELS
TOO MUCH TROUBLE — LIMAHL
TOO NICE TO TALK TO — The BEAT
TOO REAL — LEVELLERS
TOO RIGHT TO BE WRONG — The CARTER TWINS
TOO RISKY — Jim DAVIDSON
TOO SHY — KAJAGOOGOO (83)
TOO SOON TO KNOW — Roy ORBISON
TOO TIRED — Gary MOORE
TOO WICKED (EP) — ASWAD
TOO YOUNG [A] — Bill FORBES
TOO YOUNG [A] — Donny OSMOND
TOO YOUNG TO DIE — JAMIROQUAI
TOO YOUNG TO GO STEADY — Nat 'King' COLE
TOOK MY LOVE — BIZARRE INC
TOOK THE LAST TRAIN — David GATES
TOP O' THE MORNING TO YA — HOUSE OF PAIN
TOP OF THE POPS — REZILLOS
TOP OF THE STAIRS — SKEE-LO
TOP OF THE WORLD [A] — The CARPENTERS
TOP OF THE WORLD [B] — VAN HALEN
TOP OF THE WORLD [C] — BRANDY featuring MA$E
TOP OF THE WORLD [D] — The WILDHEARTS
TOP OF THE WORLD (OLE, OLE, OLE) — CHUMBAWAMBA
TOP TEEN BABY — Garry MILLS
TOPKNOT — CORNERSHOP presents Bubbley KAUR
TOPSY (PARTS 1 AND 2) — Cozy COLE
TORCH — SOFT CELL
TORERO [A] — Julius LAROSA
TORERO — CHA CHA CHA [A] — Renato CAROSONE and his SEXTET
TORN — Natalie IMBRUGLIA
TORN BETWEEN TWO LOVERS — Mary MacGREGOR
TORTURE [A] — The JACKSONS
TORTURE [B] — KING
TOSH — FLUKE
TOSS IT UP — MAKAVELI
TOSSING AND TURNING [A] — The IVY LEAGUE
TOSSING AND TURNING [B] — WINDJAMMER
TOSSING AND TURNING [C] — CHAKKA BOOM BANG
TOTAL CONFUSION — A HOMEBOY, a HIPPIE and a FUNKI DREDD
TOTAL ECLIPSE OF THE HEART [A] — Bonnie TYLER (83)
TOTAL ECLIPSE OF THE HEART [A] — Nicki FRENCH
TOTAL ECLIPSE OF THE HEART [A] — Jan WAYNE
TOTAL ERASURE — Philip JAP
THE TOTAL MIX — BLACK BOX
TOTTENHAM TOTTENHAM — TOTTENHAM HOTSPUR FA CUP FINAL SQUAD
TOUCH [A] — LORI and The CHAMELEONS
TOUCH [B] — AMERIE
THE TOUCH — Kim WILDE
TOUCH BY TOUCH — Diana ROSS
TOUCH IT — MONIFAH
TOUCH ME [A] — 49ers
TOUCH ME [B] — Rui DA SILVA featuring CASSANDRA (01)
TOUCH ME (ALL NIGHT LONG) — Cathy DENNIS
TOUCH ME — ANGEL CITY
TOUCH ME (I WANT YOUR BODY) — Samantha FOX
TOUCH ME IN THE MORNING — Diana ROSS
TOUCH ME TEASE ME [A] — CASE featuring Foxxy BROWN
TOUCH ME TEASE ME [A] — 3SL
TOUCH ME TOUCH ME — Dave DEE, DOZY, BEAKY, MICK and TICH
TOUCH ME WITH YOUR LOVE — Beth ORTON
TOUCH MY FIRE — JAVINE
TOUCH MYSELF — T-BOZ
A TOUCH OF EVIL — JUDAS PRIEST
A TOUCH OF LOVE — CLEOPATRA
A TOUCH OF VELVET – A STING OF BRASS — Ron GRAINER ORCHESTRA
TOUCH THE SKY — 29 PALMS
TOUCH TOO MUCH — AC/DC
A TOUCH TOO MUCH — The ARROWS
TOUCH YOU — KATOI
TOUCHED BY GOD — KATCHA
TOUCHED BY THE HAND OF CICCIOLINA — POP WILL EAT ITSELF
TOUCHED BY THE HAND OF GOD — NEW ORDER
TOUCHY! — A-HA
TOUGHER THAN THE REST — Bruce SPRINGSTEEN
TOUR DE FRANCE — KRAFTWERK
TOURIST — ATHLETE
TOURNIQUET [A] — MARILYN MANSON
TOURNIQUET [B] — HEADSWIM
TOUS LES GARÇONS ET LES FILLES — Françoise HARDY
TOWER OF STRENGTH [A] — Frankie VAUGHAN (61)
TOWER OF STRENGTH [A] — Gene McDANIELS
TOWER OF STRENGTH [B] — The MISSION
TOWER OF STRENGTH [C] — SKIN
TOWERS OF LONDON — XTC
TOWN — NORTHERN UPROAR
TOWN CALLED MALICE — The JAM (82)
TOWN CLOWNS — BLAMELESS
TOWN CRIER — Craig DOUGLAS
TOWN OF PLENTY — Elton JOHN
TOWN TO TOWN — MICRODISNEY
TOWN WITHOUT PITY [A] — Gene PITNEY
TOWN WITHOUT PITY [A] — Eddi READER
TOXIC — Britney SPEARS (04)
TOXIC GIRL — KINGS OF CONVENIENCE
TOXICITY — SYSTEM OF A DOWN
TOXYGENE — The ORB
TOY — CASUALS
TOY BALLOONS — Russ CONWAY
TOY BOY — SINITTA
TOY SOLDIERS — MARTIKA
TOYS FOR BOYS — MARION
TRACEY IN MY ROOM — EBTG vs SOUL VISION
TRACIE — LEVEL 42
TRACKIN' — Billy CRAWFORD
TRACKS OF MY TEARS [A] — MIRACLES
TRACKS OF MY TEARS [A] — Linda RONSTADT
TRACKS OF MY TEARS [A] — Colin BLUNSTONE
TRACKS OF MY TEARS [A] — GO WEST
TRACY — CUFFLINKS
TRADE (EP) (DISC 2) — VARIOUS ARTISTS (Singles and EPs)
TRAFFIC [A] — STEREOPHONICS
TRAFFIC [B] — TIESTO
TRAGEDY [A] — ARGENT
TRAGEDY [B] — The BEE GEES (79)
TRAGEDY [B] — STEPS (99)
TRAGEDY AND MYSTERY — CHINA CRISIS
TRAGIC COMIC — EXTREME
TRAIL OF TEARS — DOGS D'AMOUR
THE TRAIL OF THE LONESOME PINE — LAUREL and HARDY with The AVALON BOYS featuring Chill WILLS
TRAILER LOAD A GIRLS — Shabba RANKS
TRAIN [A] — SISTERS OF MERCY
TRAIN [B] — GOLDFRAPP
THE TRAIN IS COMING [A] — SHAGGY
THE TRAIN IS COMING [A] — UB40
TRAIN OF CONSEQUENCES — MEGADETH
TRAIN OF LOVE — Alma COGAN
TRAIN OF THOUGHT [A] — A-HA
TRAIN OF THOUGHT [B] — ESCRIMA
TRAIN ON A TRACK — Kelly ROWLAND
TRAIN TO SKAVILLE — ETHIOPIANS
TRAIN TOUR TO RAINBOW CITY — PYRAMIDS
TRAINS AND BOATS AND PLANES [A] — Billy J KRAMER and The DAKOTAS
TRAINS AND BOATS AND PLANES [A] — Burt BACHARACH
TRAMBONE — KREW-KATS
TRAMP [A] — Otis REDDING
TRAMP [B] — SALT-N-PEPA
TRAMPOLENE — Julian COPE
TRAMPS AND THIEVES — QUIREBOYS
TRANCESCRIPT — HARDFLOOR
TRANQUILLIZER — GENEVA
TRANSAMAZONIA — The SHAMEN
TRANSATLANTIC — ROACH MOTEL
TRANSFER AFFECTION — A FLOCK OF SEAGULLS
TRANSISTOR RADIO — Benny HILL
TRANSMISSION [A] — GAY DAD
TRANSMISSION [B] — VIOLENT DELIGHT
TRANSONIC — WIRED
TRANZ EURO XPRESS — X-PRESS 2
TRANZY STATE OF MIND — PUSH
TRAPPED [A] — Colonel ABRAMS
TRAPPED [B] — GUYVER
TRASH [A] — ROXY MUSIC
TRASH [B] — SUEDE
TRASHED — SKIN
TRAVELIN' BAND — CREEDENCE CLEARWATER REVIVAL
TRAVELIN' HOME — Vera LYNN
TRAVELIN' MAN — Ricky NELSON
THE TRAVELLER — SPEAR OF DESTINY
TRAVELLERS TUNE — OCEAN COLOUR SCENE
TRAVELLIN' LIGHT — Cliff RICHARD and The SHADOWS (59)
TRAVELLING LIGHT — TINDERSTICKS
TRAVELLING MAN — STUDIO 2
TREASON (IT'S JUST A STORY) — TEARDROP EXPLODES
TREASURE OF LOVE — Clyde McPHATTER
TREAT 'EM RIGHT — Chubb ROCK
TREAT HER LIKE A LADY [A] — The TEMPTATIONS
TREAT HER LIKE A LADY [B] — Celine DION
TREAT HER LIKE A LADY [C] — JOE
TREAT HER RIGHT — Roy HEAD
TREAT INFAMY — REST ASSURED
TREAT ME GOOD — YAZZ
TREAT ME LIKE A LADY [A] — FIVE STAR
TREAT ME LIKE A LADY [B] — Zoe BIRKETT
TREAT ME RIGHT — ADEVA
TREATY — YOTHU YINDI
TREBLE CHANCE — Joe 'Mr Piano' HENDERSON
TREE FROG — HOPE A.D.
TREES — PULP
TREMBLE — MARC et CLAUDE
TREMELO SONG (EP) — The CHARLATANS
THE TRIAL OF HISSING SID — Keith MICHELL
TRIALS OF LIFE — KALEEF
TRIBAL BASE — REBEL MC featuring TENOR FLY and Barrington LEVY
TRIBAL DANCE — 2 UNLIMITED
TRIBULATIONS — LCD SOUNDSYSTEM
TRIBUTE (RIGHT ON) — PASADENAS
TRIBUTE TO A KING — William BELL
TRIBUTE TO BUDDY HOLLY — Mike BERRY
TRIBUTE TO JIM REEVES — LARRY CUNNINGHAM and The MIGHTY AVONS
TRIBUTE TO OUR ANCESTORS — RUBBADUBB
TRICK ME — KELIS
A TRICK OF THE LIGHT — TRIFFIDS
TRICK OF THE NIGHT — BANANARAMA
TRICKY DISCO — TRICKY DISCO
TRICKY KID — TRICKY
TRIGGER HIPPIE — MORCHEEBA
TRIGGER INSIDE — THERAPY?
TRINI TRAX — Trini LOPEZ
TRIP II THE MOON — ACEN
A TRIP TO TRUMPTON — URBAN HYPE
TRIPLE TROUBLE — BEASTIE BOYS
TRIPPIN' [A] — Mark MORRISON
TRIPPIN' [B] — Oris JAY presents DELSENA
TRIPPIN' ON SUNSHINE — PIZZAMAN
TRIPPIN' ON YOUR LOVE [A] — A WAY OF LIFE
TRIPPIN' ON YOUR LOVE [A] — Kenny THOMAS
TRIPPING — Robbie WILLIAMS
TRIPPY — ARAB STRAP
TRIPWIRE — LIONROCK
TRIUMPH [A] — WU-TANG CLAN
TRIUMPH [B] — The HISS
TRIUMPH OF A HEART — BJORK
TRIXSTAR — BLAK TWANG featuring EST'ELLE
TROCADERO — SHOWADDYWADDY
THE TROOPER — IRON MAIDEN
TROPIC ISLAND HUM — Paul McCARTNEY

6 November 2004	13 November 2004	20 November 2004	27 November 2004
WONDERFUL Ja Rule featuring R Kelly & Ashanti	**JUST LOSE IT** Eminem	**VERTIGO** U2	**I'LL STAND BY YOU** Girls Aloud
GREATEST HITS Robbie Williams	**IL DIVO** Il Divo	**ENCORE** Eminem	**ENCORE** Eminem

4 December 2004	11 December 2004	18 December 2004	25 December 2004
UK No.1 SINGLES			
I'LL STAND BY YOU Girls Aloud	DO THEY KNOW IT'S CHRISTMAS? Band Aid 20	DO THEY KNOW IT'S CHRISTMAS? Band Aid 20	DO THEY KNOW IT'S CHRISTMAS? Band Aid 20
UK No.1 ALBUMS			
HOW TO DISMANTLE AN ATOMIC BOMB U2	HOW TO DISMANTLE AN ATOMIC BOMB U2	HOW TO DISMANTLE AN ATOMIC BOMB U2	GREATEST HITS Robbie Williams

1 January 2005	8 January 2005	15 January 2005	22 January 2005
DO THEY KNOW IT'S CHRISTMAS? Band Aid 20	**AGAINST ALL ODDS** Steve Brookstein	**JAILHOUSE ROCK (3rd Re-issue)** Elvis Presley	**ONE NIGHT (Re-issue) / I GOT STUNG (Re-issue)** Elvis Presley
GREATEST HITS Robbie Williams	**AMERICAN IDIOT** Green Day	**SCISSOR SISTERS** Scissor Sisters	**HOT FUSS** The Killers

VAMOS A LA PLAYA — RIGHEIRA
VAMP — OUTLANDER
VAMPIRE RACECOURSE — SLEEPY JACKSON
VANESSA — Ted HEATH
VANILLA RADIO — The WILDHEARTS
VANITY KILLS — ABC
VAPORIZER — LUPINE HOWL
VAPORS — SNOOP DOGG
VASOLINE — STONE TEMPLE PILOTS
VAVOOM! — MAN WITH NO NAME
VAYA CON DIOS (MAY GOD BE WITH YOU) [A] — Les PAUL and Mary FORD
VAYA CON DIOS (MAY GOD BE WITH YOU) [A] — MILLICAN and NESBITT
VEGAS [A] — SLEEPER
VEGAS [B] — AGNELLI & NELSON
VEGAS TWO TIMES — STEREOPHONICS
VEHICLE — IDES OF MARCH
VELCRO FLY — ZZ TOP
VELOURIA — PIXIES
VELVET MOODS — Johan GIELEN presents ABNEA
VENCEREMOS — WE WILL WIN — WORKING WEEK
VENI VIDI VICI — Ronnie HILTON
VENTOLIN — APHEX TWIN
VENTURA HIGHWAY — AMERICA
VENUS [A] — Dickie VALENTINE
VENUS [A] — Frankie AVALON
VENUS [B] — SHOCKING BLUE
VENUS [B] — BANANARAMA
VENUS [B] — DON PABLO'S ANIMALS
VENUS AND MARS — Jo BREEZER
VENUS AS A BOY — BJÖRK
VENUS IN BLUE JEANS — Mark WYNTER
VENUS IN FURS — VELVET UNDERGROUND
VERMILION — SLIPKNOT
VERNON'S WONDERLAND —
VERNON'S WONDERLAND
VERONICA [A] — Elvis COSTELLO
VERONICA [B] — SULTANS OF PING
VERDI — Mauro PICOTTO
VERSION OF ME — THOUSAND YARD STARE
VERTIGO — U2 (04)
VERY BEST FRIEND — PROUD MARY
VERY METAL NOISE POLLUTION (EP) — POP WILL EAT ITSELF
A VERY PRECIOUS LOVE — Doris DAY
THE VERY THOUGHT OF YOU [A] — Tony BENNETT
THE VERY THOUGHT OF YOU [A] — Natalie COLE
VESSEL — Ed RUSH & OPTICAL / UNIVERSAL PROJECT
VIBE — ZHANÉ
VIBEOLOGY — Paula ABDUL
VIBRATOR — Terence Trent D'ARBY
VICE — RAZORLIGHT
VICIOUS CIRCLES [A] — POLTERGEIST
VICIOUS CIRCLES [A] — VICIOUS CIRCLES
VICTIM OF LOVE [A] — ERASURE
VICTIM OF LOVE [B] — Bryan ADAMS
VICTIMS — CULTURE CLUB
VICTIMS OF SUCCESS — DOGS D'AMOUR
VICTORIA [A] — The KINKS
VICTORIA [A] — The FALL
VICTORY — KOOL and The GANG
VIDEO — INDIA.ARIE
VIDEO KILLED THE RADIO STAR [A] — The BUGGLES (79)
VIDEO KILLED THE RADIO STAR [A] — PRESIDENTS OF THE UNITED STATES OF AMERICA
VIDEO KILLED THE RADIO STAR [A] — DRAGONHEART
VIDEOTHEQUE — DOLLAR
VIENNA — ULTRAVOX
VIENNA CALLING — FALCO
VIETNAM — Jimmy CLIFF
VIEW FROM A BRIDGE — Kim WILDE
A VIEW TO A KILL — DURAN DURAN
VILLAGE OF ST BERNADETTE — Anne SHELTON
VINCENT — Don McLEAN (72)
VINDALOO — FAT LES
VIOLA — MOOGWAI
VIOLAINE — COCTEAU TWINS
VIOLENCE OF SUMMER (LOVE'S TAKING OVER) — DURAN DURAN
VIOLENTLY (EP) — HUE AND CRY
VIOLENTLY HAPPY — BJÖRK
VIOLET [A] — SEAL
VIOLET [B] — HOLE
V.I.P. — The JUNGLE BROTHERS
VIRGIN MARY — Lonnie DONEGAN
VIRGINIA PLAIN [A] — ROXY MUSIC
VIRGINIA PLAIN [A] — SLAMM
VIRTUAL INSANITY — JAMIROQUAI
VIRTUALITY — VBIRDS
VIRUS [A] — IRON MAIDEN
VIRUS [B] — MUTINY UK
VISAGE — VISAGE
THE VISION — Mario PIU presents DJ ARABESQUE
VISION INCISION — LO FIDELITY ALLSTARS
VISION OF LOVE — Mariah CAREY
VISION OF YOU — Belinda CARLISLE
VISIONARY — REDD KROSS
VISIONS [A] — Cliff RICHARD
VISIONS [B] — Lena FIAGBE
VISIONS IN BLUE — ULTRAVOX
VISIONS OF CHINA — JAPAN
VISIONS OF PARADISE — Mick JAGGER
VISIONS OF YOU — Jah WOBBLE'S INVADERS of the HEART
VITAL SIGNS — RUSH
VITO SATAN — CAMPAG VELOCET
VIVA BOBBY JOE — The EQUALS
VIVA EL FULHAM — Tony REES and The COTTAGERS
VIVA ENGLAND — UNDERCOVER
VIVA FOREVER — SPICE GIRLS (98)
VIVA LA MEGABABES — SHAMPOO
VIVA LA RADIO — LOLLY
VIVA LAS VEGAS [A] — Elvis PRESLEY
VIVA LAS VEGAS [A] — ZZ TOP
VIVE LE ROCK — Adam ANT
VIVID — ELECTRONIC
VIVRANT THING — Q-TIP
VOGUE — MADONNA (90)
THE VOICE [A] — ULTRAVOX
THE VOICE [B] — Eimear QUINN
VOICE IN THE WILDERNESS — Cliff RICHARD and The SHADOWS
VOICE OF FREEDOM — Freedom WILLIAMS
THE VOICE WITHIN — Christina AGUILERA
VOICES [A] — DARIO G
VOICES [B] — BEDROCK
VOICES [C] — Ann LEE
VOICES [D] — DISTURBED
VOICES [E] — KC FLIGHTT vs FUNKY JUNCTION
VOICES IN THE SKY — The MOODY BLUES
VOID — EXOTERIX
VOLARE [A] — Charlie DRAKE
VOLARE [A] — Dean MARTIN
VOLARE [A] — Domenico MODUGNO
VOLARE [A] — Marino MARINI and his QUARTET
VOLARE [A] — Bobby RYDELL
VOLCANO — Damien RICE
VOLCANO GIRLS — VERUCA SALT
VOLUME 1 (WHAT YOU WANT WHAT YOU NEED) — INDUSTRY STANDARD
VOODOO — WARRIOR
VOODOO CHILE — The Jimi HENDRIX EXPERIENCE (70)
VOODOO LOVE — LEE-CABRERA presents PHASE 2
VOODOO PEOPLE — The PRODIGY
VOODOO RAY — A GUY CALLED GERALD
VOODOO VOODOO — Den HEGARTY
VOULEZ-VOUS — ABBA
THE VOW — TOYAH 3
VOYAGE VOYAGE — DESIRELESS
VOYAGER — PENDULUM
VOYEUR — Kim CARNES
VULNERABLE — ROXETTE
WACK ASS MF — RHYTHMKILLAZ
WADE IN THE WATER — Ramsey LEWIS
WAGES DAY — DEACON BLUE
THE WAGON — DINOSAUR JR
WAIL — Jon SPENCER BLUES EXPLOSION
WAIT — Kym MAZELLE
WAIT A MINUTE — Ray J featuring LIL' KIM
WAIT AND BLEED — SLIPKNOT
WAIT FOR ME — Malcolm VAUGHAN
WAIT FOR ME, DARLING — Joan REGAN with The JOHNSTON BROTHERS
WAIT FOR ME MARY-ANNE — MARMALADE
WAIT (THE WHISPER SONG) — YING YANG TWINS
WAIT UNTIL MIDNIGHT — YELLOW DOG
WAIT UNTIL TONIGHT (MY LOVE) — Phil FEARON
WAITING [A] — STYLE COUNCIL
WAITING [B] — GREEN DAY
THE WAITING 18 — AMEN
WAITING FOR A GIRL LIKE YOU — FOREIGNER
WAITING FOR A STAR TO FALL — BOY MEETS GIRL
WAITIN' FOR A SUPERMAN — The FLAMING LIPS
WAITING FOR A TRAIN — FLASH and The PAN
WAITING FOR AN ALIBI — THIN LIZZY
WAITING FOR SUMMER — DELIRIOUS?
WAITING FOR THAT DAY — George MICHAEL
(WAITING FOR) THE GHOST TRAIN — MADNESS
WAITING FOR THE GREAT LEAP FORWARDS — Billy BRAGG
WAITING FOR THE LOVEBOAT — ASSOCIATES
WAITING FOR THE NIGHT — SAXON
WAITING FOR THE SIRENS' CALL — NEW ORDER
WAITING FOR THE SUN — RUFF DRIVERZ
WAITING FOR TONIGHT — Jennifer LOPEZ
WAITING HOPEFULLY — D*NOTE
WAITING IN VAIN [A] — Bob MARLEY & The WAILERS
WAITING IN VAIN [A] — Lee RITENOUR and Maxi PRIEST
WAITING IN VAIN [A] — Annie LENNOX
WAITING ON A FRIEND — The ROLLING STONES
WAKE IN THE CITY — IKARA COLT
WAKE ME UP — GIRLS ALOUD
WAKE ME UP BEFORE YOU GO GO — WHAM! (84)
WAKE ME UP WHEN SEPTEMBER ENDS — GREEN DAY
WAKE UP [A] — DANSE SOCIETY
WAKE UP [B] — Hilary DUFF
WAKE UP [C] — ARCADE FIRE
WAKE UP AND SCRATCH ME — SULTANS OF PING
WAKE UP BOO! — The BOO RADLEYS
WAKE UP DEAD — MEGADETH
WAKE UP EVERYBODY — Harold MELVIN and The BLUENOTES
WAKE UP LITTLE SUSIE [A] — The EVERLY BROTHERS
WAKE UP LITTLE SUSIE [A] — The KING BROTHERS
WAKE UP (MAKE A MOVE) — LOSTPROPHETS
WAKE UP SUSAN — The DETROIT SPINNERS
WAKING UP — ELASTICA
WAKING WITH A STRANGER — TYRREL CORPORATION
WALHALLA — GOURYELLA
WALK — PANTERA
THE WALK [A] — INMATES
THE WALK [B] — The CURE
WALK AWAY [A] — Shane FENTON and The FENTONES
WALK AWAY [B] — Matt MONRO
WALK AWAY [C] — SISTERS OF MERCY
WALK AWAY [D] — Joyce SIMS
WALK AWAY [E] — FRANZ FERDINAND
WALK AWAY FROM LOVE — David RUFFIN
WALK AWAY RENEE — The FOUR TOPS
WALK DON'T RUN [A] — John BARRY ORCHESTRA
WALK DON'T RUN [A] — VENTURES
WALK — MY LIFE STORY
WALK HAND IN HAND [A] — Jimmy PARKINSON
WALK HAND IN HAND [A] — Ronnie CARROLL
WALK HAND IN HAND [A] — Tony MARTIN
WALK HAND IN HAND [A] — GERRY and The PACEMAKERS
WALK IDIOT WALK — The HIVES
WALK IN LOVE — MANHATTAN TRANSFER
A WALK IN THE BLACK FOREST — Horst JANKOWSKI
A WALK IN THE DARK — WHITEY
WALK IN THE NIGHT [A] — Junior WALKER and The ALL-STARS
WALK IN THE NIGHT [A] — Paul HARDCASTLE
A WALK IN THE PARK — Nick STRAKER BAND
WALK INTO THE SUN — DIRTY VEGAS
WALK INTO THE WIND — VEGAS
WALK LIKE A CHAMPION — KALEEF
WALK LIKE A MAN [A] — The FOUR SEASONS
WALK LIKE A MAN [A] — DIVINE
WALK LIKE A PANTHER '98 — The ALL SEEING I featuring Tony CHRISTIE
WALK LIKE AN EGYPTIAN — The BANGLES
WALK OF LIFE [A] — DIRE STRAITS
WALK OF LIFE [B] — Billie PIPER
WALK ON [A] — Roy ORBISON
WALK ON [B] — U2
WALK ON AIR — T'PAU
WALK ON BY [A] — Leroy VAN DYKE
WALK ON BY [B] — Dionne WARWICK
WALK ON BY [B] — The STRANGLERS
WALK ON BY [B] — AVERAGE WHITE BAND
WALK ON BY [B] — D TRAIN
WALK ON BY [B] — SYBIL
WALK ON BY [B] — GABRIELLE
WALK ON GILDED SPLINTERS — Marsha HUNT
WALK ON THE WILD SIDE [A] — Lou REED
WALK ON THE WILD SIDE [A] — BEAT SYSTEM
WALK ON THE WILD SIDE [A] — Jamie J MORGAN
WALK ON WATER — MILK INC
WALK OUT TO WINTER — AZTEC CAMERA
WALK RIGHT BACK [A] — The EVERLY BROTHERS (61)
WALK RIGHT BACK [A] — Perry COMO
WALK RIGHT IN — ROOFTOP SINGERS
WALK RIGHT NOW — The JACKSONS
WALK TALL — Val DOONICAN
WALK THE DINOSAUR — WAS (NOT WAS)
WALK ... (THE DOG) LIKE AN EGYPTIAN — JODE featuring YO-HANS
WALK THIS LAND — E-Z ROLLERS
WALK THIS WAY — RUN-DMC
WALK THIS WORLD — Heather NOVA
WALK THROUGH THE FIRE — Peter GABRIEL
WALK THROUGH THE WORLD — Marc COHN
WALK WITH FAITH IN YOUR HEART — The BACHELORS
WALK WITH ME — The SEEKERS
WALK WITH ME MY ANGEL — Don CHARLES
WALK WITH ME TALK WITH ME DARLING — The FOUR TOPS
WALKAWAY — CAST
WALKED OUTTA HEAVEN — JAGGED EDGE
WALKIE TALKIE MAN — STERIOGRAM
WALKIN' — CCS
WALKIN' BACK TO HAPPINESS — Helen SHAPIRO (61)
WALKIN IN THE NAME — FUNKSTAR DE LUXE
WALKIN' IN THE RAIN WITH THE ONE I LOVE — LOVE UNLIMITED
A WALKIN' MIRACLE — LIMMIE and The FAMILY COOKIN'
WALKIN' ON — SHEER BRONZE featuring Lisa MILLETT
WALKIN' ON THE SUN — SMASH MOUTH
WALKIN' ON UP — DJ PROFESSOR
WALKIN' TALL [A] — Frankie VAUGHAN
WALKIN' TALL [B] — Adam FAITH
WALKIN' THE DOG — DENNISONS
WALKIN' THE LINE — BRASS CONSTRUCTION
WALKIN' TO MISSOURI — Tony BRENT
WALKING AFTER YOU: BEACON LIGHT — FOO FIGHTERS
WALKING ALONE — Richard ANTHONY
WALKING AWAY — Craig DAVID
WALKING BY MYSELF — Gary MOORE
WALKING DEAD — PURESSENCE
WALKING DOWN MADISON — Kirsty MacCOL
WALKING DOWN YOUR STREET — The BANGLES
WALKING IN MEMPHIS [A] — Marc COHN
WALKING IN MEMPHIS [A] — CHER
WALKING IN MY SHOES — DEPECHE MODE
WALKING IN MY SLEEP — Roger DALTREY
WALKING IN RHYTHM — The BLACKBYRDS
WALKING IN THE AIR [A] — Aled JONES
WALKING IN THE AIR [A] — Peter AUTY and The SINFONIA OF LONDON conducted by Howard BLAKE
WALKING IN THE AIR [A] — DIGITAL DREAM BABY
WALKING IN THE RAIN [A] — The WALKER BROTHERS

29 January 2005	5 February 2005	12 February 2005	19 February 2005
UK No.1 SINGLES			
GOODIES Ciara featuring Petey Pablo	**IT'S NOW OR NEVER (2nd Re-issue)** Elvis Presley	**LIKE TOY SOLDIERS** Eminem	**SOMETIMES YOU CAN'T MAKE IT ON YOUR OWN** U2
UK No.1 ALBUMS			
HOT FUSS The Killers	**PUSH THE BUTTON** The Chemical Brothers	**TOURIST** Athlete	**HOPES AND FEARS** Keane

26 February 2005	5 March 2005	12 March 2005	19 March 2005
GET RIGHT Jennifer Lopez	**OVER AND OVER** Nelly featuring Tim McGraw	**DAKOTA** Stereophonics	**ALL ABOUT YOU / YOU'VE GOT A FRIEND** McFly
SCISSOR SISTERS Scissor Sisters	**SOME CITIES** Doves	**G4** G4	**THE MASSACRE** 50 Cent

WE GOT THE LOVE [B] — ERIK
WE GOT THE LOVE [C] — TRI
WE GOTTA DO IT — DJ PROFESSOR featuring Francesco ZAPPALA
WE GOTTA GET OUT OF THIS PLACE [A] — The ANIMALS
WE GOTTA GET OUT OF THIS PLACE [A] — ANGELIC UPSTARTS
WE GOTTA LOVE — Kym SIMS
WE HATE IT WHEN OUR FRIENDS BECOME SUCCESSFUL — MORRISSEY
WE HAVE A DREAM — SCOTLAND WORLD CUP SQUAD
WE HAVE ALL THE TIME IN THE WORLD — Louis ARMSTRONG
WE HAVE EXPLOSIVE — FUTURE SOUND OF LONDON
WE HAVEN'T TURNED AROUND — GOMEZ
WE JUST BE DREAMIN' — BLAZIN' SQUAD
WE JUST WANNA PARTY WITH YOU — SNOOP DOGG
WE KILL THE WORLD (DON'T KILL THE WORLD) — BONEY M
WE KNOW SOMETHING YOU DON'T KNOW — DJ FORMAT featuring CHALI 2NA & AKIL
WE LAUGHED — ROSETTA LIFE featuring Billy BRAGG
WE LET THE STARS GO — PREFAB SPROUT
WE LIKE TO PARTY! (THE VENGABUS) — The VENGABOYS
WE LOVE EACH OTHER — Charlie RICH
WE LOVE YOU [A] — The ROLLING STONES
WE LOVE YOU [B] — ORCHESTRAL MANOEUVRES IN THE DARK
WE LOVE YOU [C] — MENSWEAR
WE LUV U — GRAND THEFT AUDIO
WE NEED A RESOLUTION — AALIYAH featuring TIMBALAND
WE NEED LOVE — CASHMERE
WE ROCK — DIO
WE SAIL ON THE STORMY WATERS — Gary CLARK
WE SHALL OVERCOME — Joan BAEZ
WE SHOULD BE TOGETHER — Cliff RICHARD
WE SHOULDN'T HOLD HANDS IN THE DARK — LA MIX
WE TAKE MYSTERY (TO BED) — Gary NUMAN
WE THUGGIN' — FAT JOE
WE TRYING TO STAY ALIVE — The FUGEES
WE USED TO BE FRIENDS — The DANDY WARHOLS
WE WAIT AND WE WONDER — Phil COLLINS
WE WALKED IN LOVE — DOLLAR
WE WANNA THANK YOU (THE THINGS YOU DO) — BIG BROVAZ
(WE WANT) THE SAME THING — Belinda CARLISLE
WE WANT YOUR SOUL — FREELAND
WE WILL — Gilbert O'SULLIVAN
WE WILL MAKE LOVE — Russ HAMILTON
WE WILL MEET AGAIN — Oleta ADAMS
WE WILL NEVER BE AS YOUNG AS THIS AGAIN — Danny WILLIAMS
WE WILL ROCK YOU — FIVE and QUEEN (00)
WE WILL SURVIVE — WARP BROTHERS
WEAK [A] — SWV
WEAK [B] — SKUNK ANANSIE
WEAK BECOME HEROES — The STREETS
WEAK IN THE PRESENCE OF BEAUTY — Alison MOYET
WEAK SPOT — Evelyn THOMAS
WEAR MY HAT — Phil COLLINS
WEAR MY RING AROUND YOUR NECK — Elvis PRESLEY
WEAR YOU TO THE BALL — UB40
WEAR YOUR LOVE LIKE HEAVEN — DEFINITION OF SOUND
WEATHER FORECAST — MASTER SINGERS
WEATHER WITH YOU — CROWDED HOUSE
WEAVE YOUR SPELL — LEVEL 42
THE WEAVER (EP) — Paul WELLER
THE WEDDING [A] — Julie ROGERS
THE WEDDING [B] — Cliff RICHARD
WEDDING BELL BLUES — 5TH DIMENSION
WEDDING BELLS — GODLEY and CREME
WEDDING RING — Russ HAMILTON
WEDNESDAY WEEK — The UNDERTONES
WEE RULE — WEE PAPA GIRL RAPPERS
WEE TOM — LORD ROCKINGHAM'S XI
WEEK IN WEEK OUT — The ORDINARY BOYS
WEEKEND [A] — Eddie COCHRAN
WEEKEND [B] — Mick JACKSON
WEEKEND [C] — CLASS ACTION featuring Chris WILTSHIRE
WEEKEND [C] — Todd TERRY PROJECT
WEEKEND [D] — BAD HABIT BOYS
WEEKEND! [E] — SCOOTER
THE WEEKEND — Michael GRAY
WEEKEND GIRL — S.O.S. BAND
THE WEEKEND HAS LANDED — MINKY
WEEKENDER — FLOWERED UP
THE WEIGHT — The BAND
WEIGHT FOR THE BASS — UNIQUE 3
WEIGHT OF THE WORLD — Ringo STARR
WEIRD [A] — REEF
WEIRD [B] — HANSON
WEIRDO — The CHARLATANS
WELCOME — Gino LATINO
WELCOME BACK — MA$E
WELCOME HOME — PETERS and LEE (73)
WELCOME HOME BABY — The BROOK BROTHERS
WELCOME TO CHICAGO EP — Gene FARRIS
WELCOME TO JAMROCK — Damian 'Jr. Gong' MARLEY
WELCOME TO MY LIFE — SIMPLE PLAN
WELCOME TO MY TRUTH — ANASTACIA
WELCOME TO MY WORLD — Jim REEVES
WELCOME TO OUR WORLD (OF MERRY MUSIC) — MASS PRODUCTION
WELCOME TO PARADISE — GREEN DAY
WELCOME TO THE CHEAP SEATS (EP) — The WONDER STUFF
WELCOME TO THE FUTURE — SHIMMON & WOOLFSON
WELCOME TO THE JUNGLE — GUNS N' ROSES
WELCOME TO THE PLEASURE DOME — FRANKIE GOES TO HOLLYWOOD
WELCOME TO THE REAL WORLD — GUN
WELCOME TO THE TERRORDOME — PUBLIC ENEMY
WELCOME TO TOMORROW — SNAP! featuring SUMMER
WELL ALL RIGHT — SANTANA
WE'LL BE RIGHT BACK — STEINSKI and MASS MEDIA
WE'LL BE TOGETHER — STING
WE'LL BE WITH YOU — POTTERS
WE'LL BRING THE HOUSE DOWN — SLADE
WELL DID YOU EVAH! — Deborah HARRY and Iggy POP
WE'LL FIND OUR DAY — Stephanie DE SYKES
WE'LL GATHER LILACS — ALL MY LOVING (MEDLEY) — Simon MAY
WELL I ASK YOU — Eden KANE (61)
WE'LL SING IN THE SUNSHINE — The LANCASTRIANS
WE'RE ALL ALONE — Rita COOLIDGE
WE'RE ALL IN LOVE — BLACK REBEL MOTORCYCLE CLUB
WE'RE ALMOST THERE — Michael JACKSON
WE'RE COMIN' AT YA — QUARTZ
WE'RE COMING OVER — MR SMASH & FRIENDS
WE'RE GOING OUT — YOUNGER YOUNGER 28'S
WE'RE GOING TO IBIZA! — The VENGABOYS (99)
WE'RE GOING TO MISS YOU — JAMES
WE'RE GONNA DO IT AGAIN — MANCHESTER UNITED FOOTBALL CLUB
WE'RE GONNA GO FISHIN' — Hank LOCKLIN
WE'RE IN THIS LOVE TOGETHER — Al JARREAU
WE'RE IN THIS TOGETHER [A] — SIMPLY RED
WE'RE IN THIS TOGETHER [B] — NINE INCH NAILS
WE'RE NOT ALONE — HHC
WE'RE NOT GONNA SLEEP TONIGHT — Emma BUNTON
WE'RE NOT GONNA TAKE IT — TWISTED SISTER
WE'RE ON THE BALL — ANT & DEC
WE'RE ONLY YOUNG ONCE — The AVONS
WE'RE REALLY SAYING SOMETHING — BUFFALO G
WE'RE THROUGH — The HOLLIES
WEST END GIRLS [A] — PET SHOP BOYS (86)
WEST END GIRLS [A] — EAST 17
WEST END PAD — Cathy DENNIS
WEST OF ZANZIBAR — Anthony STEEL and The RADIO REVELLERS
WEST ONE (SHINE ON ME) — RUTS
WESTERN MOVIES — OLYMPICS
WESTSIDE [A] — TQ
WESTSIDE [B] — ATHLETE
WET DREAM — Max ROMEO
WET MY WHISTLE — MIDNIGHT STAR
WE'VE GOT IT GOIN' ON — BACKSTREET BOYS
WE'VE GOT THE JUICE — Derek B
WE'VE GOT THE WHOLE WORLD AT OUR FEET — ENGLAND WORLD CUP SQUAD
WE GOT THE WHOLE WORLD IN OUR HANDS — NOTTINGHAM FOREST FC with PAPER LACE
WE'VE GOT TO LIVE TOGETHER — R.A.F.
WE'VE GOT TO WORK IT OUT — BEL CANTO
WE'VE GOT TONITE [A] — Bob SEGER and The SILVER BULLET BAND
WE'VE GOT TONIGHT [A] — Kenny ROGERS and Sheena EASTON
WE'VE GOT TONIGHT [A] — Elkie BROOKS
WE'VE GOT TONIGHT [A] — Bob SEGER and The SILVER BULLET BAND
WE'VE GOT TONIGHT [A] — Ronan KEATING featuring LULU
WE'VE HAD ENOUGH — ALKALINE TRIO
WE'VE ONLY JUST BEGUN [A] — The CARPENTERS
WE'VE ONLY JUST BEGUN [A] — Bitty McLEAN
WFL — HAPPY MONDAYS
WHADDA U WANT (FROM ME) — Frankie KNUCKLES featuring ADEVA
WHADDA WE LIKE? — ROUND SOUND presents ONYX STONE & MC MALIBU
WHAM BAM — CANDY GIRLS
WHAM RAP! — WHAM!
WHAT — SOFT CELL
WHAT A BEAUTIFUL DAY — LEVELLERS
WHAT A CRAZY WORLD WE'RE LIVING IN — Joe BROWN and The BRUVVERS
WHAT A DIFFERENCE A DAY MADE — Esther PHILLIPS
WHAT A FOOL BELIEVES [A] — The DOOBIE BROTHERS
WHAT A FOOL BELIEVES [A] — Aretha FRANKLIN
WHAT A FOOL BELIEVES [A] — Peter COX
WHAT A GIRL WANTS — Christina AGUILERA
WHAT A LOVELY DANCE — HAL
WHAT A MOUTH — Tommy STEELE
WHAT A NIGHT — CITY BOY
WHAT A PARTY — Fats DOMINO
WHAT A WASTE! — Ian DURY and The BLOCKHEADS
WHAT A WASTER — The LIBERTINES
WHAT A WOMAN IN LOVE WON'T DO — Sandy POSEY
WHAT A WONDERFUL WORLD [A] — Louis ARMSTRONG ORCHESTRA and Chorus (68)
WHAT A WONDERFUL WORLD [A] — Nick CAVE and Shane MacGOWAN
WHAT A WONDERFUL WORLD [A] — Cliff RICHARD
(WHAT A) WONDERFUL WORLD — Johnny NASH
WHAT ABOUT LOVE — HEART
WHAT ABOUT ME — The CRIBS
WHAT ABOUT THIS LOVE — MR FINGERS
WHAT ABOUT US [A] — POINT BREAK
WHAT ABOUT US? [B] — BRANDY
WHAT ABOUT YOUR FRIENDS — TLC
WHAT AM I GONNA DO — Emile FORD and The CHECKMATES
WHAT AM I GONNA DO (I'M SO IN LOVE WITH YOU) — Rod STEWART
WHAT AM I GONNA DO WITH YOU — Barry WHITE
WHAT AM I TO YOU — Kenny LYNCH
WHAT ARE WE GONNA DO ABOUT IT? — MERCY MERCY
WHAT ARE WE GONNA GET 'ER INDOORS — Dennis WATERMAN
WHAT ARE YOU DOING SUNDAY — DAWN
WHAT BECAME OF THE LIKELY LADS — The LIBERTINES
WHAT BECOMES OF THE BROKENHEARTED [A] — Jimmy RUFFIN
WHAT BECOMES OF THE BROKEN HEARTED [A] — Dave STEWART: Guest vocals: Colin BLUNSTONE
WHAT BECOMES OF THE BROKENHEARTED [A] — ROBSON & JEROME (96)
WHAT CAN I DO — The CORRS
WHAT CAN I SAY — Boz SCAGGS
(WHAT CAN I SAY) TO MAKE YOU LOVE ME — Alexander O'NEAL
WHAT CAN YOU DO FOR ME [A] — UTAH SAINTS
WHAT CAN YOU DO 4 ME? [B] — Lisa LASHES
WHAT CAR — Cliff RICHARD
WHAT 'CHA GONNA DO — ETERNAL
WHAT DID I DO TO YOU (EP) — Lisa STANSFIELD
WHAT DIFFERENCE DOES IT MAKE — The SMITHS
WHAT DO I DO — Phil FEARON
WHAT DO I DO NOW — SLEEPER
WHAT DO I GET? — The BUZZCOCKS
WHAT DO I HAVE TO DO — Kylie MINOGUE
WHAT DO YA SAY — Chubby CHECKER
WHAT DO YOU WANT? [A] — Adam FAITH (59)
WHAT DO YOU WANT [B] — MORILLO featuring Terra DEVA
WHAT DO YOU WANT FROM ME? — MONACO
WHAT DO YOU WANT TO MAKE THOSE EYES AT ME FOR? [A] — Emile FORD and The CHECKMATES (59)
WHAT DO YOU WANT TO MAKE THOSE EYES AT ME FOR [A] — Shakin' STEVENS
WHAT DOES IT FEEL LIKE? — FELIX DA HOUSECAT
WHAT DOES IT TAKE — THEN JERICO
WHAT DOES IT TAKE (TO WIN YOUR LOVE) [A] — Junior WALKER and The ALL-STARS
WHAT DOES IT TAKE (TO WIN YOUR LOVE) [A] — Kenny G
WHAT DOES YOUR SOUL LOOK LIKE — DJ SHADOW
WHAT ELSE IS THERE? — ROYKSOPP
WHAT EVER HAPPENED TO OLD FASHIONED LOVE — Daniel O'DONNELL
WHAT GOD WANTS PART 1 — Roger WATERS
WHAT GOES AROUND [A] — Bitty McLEAN
WHAT GOES AROUND [B] — LUCIANA
WHAT GOES AROUND COMES AROUND — Bob MARLEY & The WAILERS
WHAT GOES ON — Bryan FERRY
WHAT GOOD AM I — Cilla BLACK
WHAT HAPPENED TO THE MUSIC — Joey NEGRO
WHAT HAPPENS TOMORROW — DURAN DURAN
WHAT HAVE I DONE TO DESERVE THIS — PET SHOP BOYS and Dusty SPRINGFIELD
WHAT HAVE THEY DONE TO MY SONG MA [A] — The NEW SEEKERS
WHAT HAVE THEY DONE TO MY SONG MA [A] — MELANIE
WHAT HAVE THEY DONE TO THE RAIN — The SEARCHERS
WHAT HAVE YOU DONE FOR ME LATELY — Janet JACKSON
WHAT HAVE YOU DONE (IS THIS ALL) — OUR TRIBE / ONE TRIBE
WHAT HOPE HAVE I — SPHINX
WHAT HURTS THE MOST — Jo O'MEARA
WHAT I AM [A] — Edie BRICKELL and The NEW BOHEMIANS
WHAT I AM [A] — TIN TIN OUT featuring Emma BUNTON
WHAT I CAN DO FOR YOU — Sheryl CROW
WHAT I DO BEST — Robin S
WHAT I GO TO SCHOOL FOR — BUSTED
WHAT I GOT — SUBLIME
WHAT I GOT IS WHAT YOU NEED — UNIQUE
WHAT I LIKE MOST ABOUT YOU IS YOUR GIRLFRIEND — The SPECIALS
WHAT I MEAN — MODJO
WHAT I MISS THE MOST — ALOOF
WHAT I REALLY WANT FOR CHRISTMAS — Brian WILSON
WHAT I SAW — KINGS OF LEON
WHAT IF ... — The LIGHTNING SEEDS
WHAT IF — Kate WINSLET
WHAT IF A WOMAN — JOE

26 March 2005	2 April 2005	9 April 2005	16 April 2005
UK No.1 SINGLES			
(IS THIS THE WAY TO) AMARILLO Tony Christie featuring Peter Kay	(IS THIS THE WAY TO) AMARILLO Tony Christie featuring Peter Kay	(IS THIS THE WAY TO) AMARILLO Tony Christie featuring Peter Kay	(IS THIS THE WAY TO) AMARILLO Tony Christie featuring Peter Kay
UK No.1 ALBUMS			
LANGUAGE. SEX. VIOLENCE. OTHER? Stereophonics	DEFINITIVE COLLECTION Tony Christie	DEFINITIVE COLLECTION Tony Christie	COUNTING DOWN THE DAYS Natalie Imbruglia

WHAT IN THE WORLD — NU COLOURS
WHAT IN THE WORLD'S COME OVER YOU [A] — Jack SCOTT
WHAT IN THE WORLD'S COME OVER YOU [A] — The ROCKIN' BERRIES
WHAT IN THE WORLD'S COME OVER YOU [A] — Tam WHITE
WHAT IS A MAN — The FOUR TOPS
WHAT IS HOUSE (EP) — LFO
WHAT IS LIFE [A] — Olivia NEWTON-JOHN
WHAT IS LIFE [A] — Shawn MULLINS
WHAT IS LIFE? [B] — BLACK UHURU
WHAT IS LOVE [A] — Howard JONES
WHAT IS LOVE [B] — DEEE-LITE
WHAT IS LOVE [C] — HADDAWAY
WHAT IS THE PROBLEM? — GRAFITI
WHAT IS THIS THING CALLED LOVE — Alexander O'NEAL
WHAT IS TRUTH — Johnny CASH
WHAT IT FEELS LIKE FOR A GIRL — MADONNA
WHAT IT IS [A] — Garnet MIMMS and TRUCKIN' CO
WHAT IT IS [B] — Freddy FRESH
WHAT IT'S LIKE — EVERLAST
WHAT I'VE GOT IN MIND — Billie Jo SPEARS
WHAT KIND OF FOOL — ALL ABOUT EVE
WHAT KIND OF FOOL AM I? [A] — Anthony NEWLEY
WHAT KIND OF FOOL AM I? [A] — Sammy DAVIS Jr
WHAT KIND OF FOOL AM I? [A] — Shirley BASSEY
WHAT KIND OF FOOL (HEARD ALL THAT BEFORE) — Kylie MINOGUE
WHAT KIND OF MAN WOULD I BE — MINT CONDITION
WHAT KINDA BOY YOU LOOKING FOR (GIRL) — HOT CHOCOLATE
WHAT MADE MILWAUKEE FAMOUS (HAS MADE A LOSER OUT OF ME) — Rod STEWART
WHAT MAKES A GIRL FIERCE — FIERCE GIRL
WHAT MAKES A MAN — WESTLIFE
WHAT MAKES A MAN A MAN (LIVE) — Marc ALMOND
WHAT MAKES YOU CRY — The PROCLAIMERS
WHAT MORE DO YOU WANT — Frankie VAUGHAN
WHAT MY HEART WANTS TO SAY — Gareth GATES
WHAT NOW — Adam FAITH
WHAT NOW MY LOVE [A] — Shirley BASSEY
WHAT NOW MY LOVE [A] — SONNY and CHER
WHAT PRESENCE? — ORANGE JUICE
WHAT THE HELL — TOKYO DRAGONS
WHAT THE WORLD IS WAITING FOR — The STONE ROSES
WHAT THEY DO — ROOTS
WHAT TIME IS IT — SPIN DOCTORS
WHAT TIME IS IT? — DUST JUNKYS
WHAT TIME IS LOVE (LIVE AT TRANCENTRAL) — The KLF
WHAT TO DO — Buddy HOLLY
WHAT TOOK YOU SO LONG — Emma BUNTON (01)
WHAT U DO — COLOURS featuring EMMANUEL & ESKA
WHAT 'U' WAITIN' '4' — The JUNGLE BROTHERS
WHAT WAS HER NAME? — Dave CLARKE featuring CHICKS ON SPEED
WHAT WE DO — KRAY TWINS featuring TWISTA, LETHAL B & Gappy RANKS
WHAT WILL BE WILL BE (DESTINY) — DIVINE INSPIRATION
WHAT WILL I DO WITHOUT YOU — Lene LOVICH
WHAT WILL MARY SAY — Johnny MATHIS
WHAT WOULD HAPPEN — Meredith BROOKS
WHAT WOULD I BE — Val DOONICAN
WHAT WOULD WE DO? — DSK
WHAT WOULD YOU DO? — CITY HIGH
WHAT WOULD YOU DO IF ...? — CODE RED
WHAT YA GOT 4 ME — SIGNUM
WHAT YA LOOKIN' AT — CROW
WHAT YOU DO — BIG BASS vs Michelle NARINE
WHAT YOU DO TO ME (EP) — TEENAGE FANCLUB
WHAT YOU GET — HUNDRED REASONS
WHAT YOU GET IS WHAT YOU SEE — Tina TURNER
WHAT YOU GONNA DO ABOUT IT — TOTAL CONTRAST
WHAT YOU GOT — ABS
WHAT YOU NEED [A] — INXS
WHAT YOU NEED [B] — POWERHOUSE
WHAT YOU NEED IS ... — Sinead QUINN
WHAT YOU NEED (TONIGHT) — NU CIRCLES featuring EMMA B
WHAT YOU SAY — The LIGHTNING SEEDS
WHAT YOU SEE IS WHAT YOU GET — Glen GOLDSMITH
WHAT YOU THINK OF THAT — JAY-Z
WHAT YOU WAITING FOR [A] — STARGARD
WHAT YOU WAITING FOR? [B] — Gwen STEFANI
WHAT YOU WANT [A] — XPANSIONS
WHAT YOU WANT [C] — FUTURE FORCE
WHAT YOU WANT [B] — MA$E / TOTAL
WHAT YOU WON'T DO FOR LOVE — GO WEST
WHAT YOU'RE MADE OF ... — Lucie SILVAS
WHAT YOU'RE MISSING — K-KLASS
WHAT YOU'RE PROPOSING — STATUS QUO
WHATCHA GONE DO? — LINK
WHAT'CHA GONNA DO — Shabba RANKS featuring Queen LATIFAH
WHATCHA GONNA DO WITH MY LOVIN' — INNER CITY
WHATCHA GONNA DO ABOUT IT [A] — Doris TROY
WHATCHA GONNA DO ABOUT IT? [B] — The SMALL FACES
WHATCHA GONNA DO NOW — Chris ANDREWS
WHATCHULOOKINAT — Whitney HOUSTON
WHAT'D I SAY — Jerry Lee LEWIS
WHAT'D YOU COME HERE FOR? — TRINA and TAMARA
WHATEVER [A] — OASIS
WHATEVER [B] — EN VOGUE
WHATEVER [C] — IDEAL US featuring LIL' MO
WHATEVER GETS YOU THRU' THE NIGHT — John LENNON
WHATEVER HAPPENED TO COREY HAIM? — The THRILLS
WHATEVER HAPPENED TO MY ROCK 'N' ROLL (PUNK SONG) — BLACK REBEL MOTORCYCLE CLUB
WHATEVER HAPPENED TO YOU ('LIKELY LADS' THEME) — HIGHLY LIKELY
WHATEVER I DO (WHEREVER I GO) — Hazell DEAN
WHATEVER IT TAKES — OLYMPIC RUNNERS
WHATEVER LOLA WANTS — Alma COGAN
WHATEVER MAKES YOU HAPPY — TEN CITY
WHATEVER U WANT — Christina MILIAN featuring Joe BUDDEN
WHATEVER WILL BE, WILL BE (QUE SERA, SERA) — Doris DAY (56)
WHATEVER YOU NEED — Tina TURNER
WHATEVER YOU WANT [A] — STATUS QUO
WHATEVER YOU WANT [B] — Tina TURNER
WHAT'LL I DO — Janet JACKSON
WHAT'S A GIRL TO DO — SISTER 2 SISTER
WHAT'S ANOTHER YEAR — Johnny LOGAN (80)
WHAT'S GOIN DOWN — HONKY
WHAT'S GOING ON [A] — MEKON featuring Roxanne SHANTE
WHAT'S GOING ON [B] — Cyndi LAUPER
WHAT'S GOING ON [B] — MUSIC RELIEF '94
WHAT'S GOING ON [B] — ARTISTS AGAINST AIDS WORLDWIDE
WHAT'S GOING ON [C] — WOOKIE
WHAT'S HAPPENIN' — METHOD MAN featuring Busta RHYMES
WHAT'S HIDEOUS — DO ME BAD THINGS
WHAT'S IN A KISS — Gilbert O'SULLIVAN
WHAT'S IN A WORD — The CHRISTIANS
WHAT'S IN THE BOX? (SEE WATCHA GOT) — The BOO RADLEYS
WHAT'S IT ALL ABOUT — RUN-DMC
WHAT'S IT GONNA BE?! — Janet JACKSON / Busta RHYMES
WHAT'S IT LIKE TO BE BEAUTIFUL — Lena FIAGBE
WHAT'S LUV? — FAT JOE featuring ASHANTI
WHAT'S LOVE GOT TO DO WITH IT [A] — Tina TURNER
WHAT'S LOVE GOT TO DO WITH IT [A] — Warren G featuring Adina HOWARD
WHAT'S MY AGE AGAIN? — BLINK-182
WHAT'S MY NAME? — SNOOP DOGG
WHAT'S NEW PUSSYCAT — Tom JONES
WHAT'S ON YOUR MIND — George BENSON
WHAT'S SO DIFFERENT? — GINUWINE
WHAT'S THAT TUNE (DOO DOO DOO DOO DOO-DOO-DOO-DOO-DOO-DOO) — DOROTHY
WHAT'S THE COLOUR OF MONEY? — HOLLYWOOD BEYOND
WHAT'S THE FREQUENCY, KENNETH — R.E.M.
WHAT'S THE POINT — WE'VE GOT A FUZZBOX AND WE'RE GONNA USE IT
WHAT'S UP [A] — 4 NON BLONDES
WHAT'S UP [A] — DJ MIKO
WHAT'S UP WITH THAT — ZZ TOP
(WHAT'S WRONG WITH) DREAMING — RIVER CITY PEOPLE
WHAT'S WRONG WITH THIS PICTURE — Chesney HAWKES
WHAT'S YOUR FANTASY — LUDACRIS
WHAT'S YOUR FLAVA? — Craig DAVID
WHAT'S YOUR NAME — CHICORY TIP
WHAT'S YOUR NAME? — Angel LEE
WHAT'S YOUR NAME, WHAT'S YOUR NUMBER — Andrea TRUE CONNECTION
WHAT'S YOUR NUMBER? — CYPRESS HILL
WHAT'S YOUR PROBLEM? — BLANCMANGE
WHAT'S YOUR SIGN? — DES'REE
WHAT'S YOUR SIGN GIRL — Barry BIGGS
WHATTA MAN — SALT-N-PEPA with EN VOGUE
WHAZZUP — TRUE PARTY
THE WHEEL — SPEAR OF DESTINY
WHEEL OF FORTUNE — ACE OF BASE
WHEELS — STRING-A-LONGS
WHEELS AIN'T COMING DOWN — SLADE
WHEELS CHA CHA — Joe LOSS
WHEELS OF STEEL — SAXON
THE WHEELS ON THE BUS — MAD DONNA
WHEN [A] — The KALIN TWINS (58)
WHEN [A] — SHOWADDYWADDY
WHEN [B] — SUNSCREEM
WHEN [C] — Shania TWAIN
WHEN A CHILD IS BORN (SOLEADO) [A] — Johnny MATHIS (76)
WHEN A CHILD IS BORN [A] — Gladys KNIGHT and The PIPS
WHEN A HEART BEATS — Nik KERSHAW
WHEN A MAN LOVES A WOMAN [A] — Percy SLEDGE
WHEN A MAN LOVES A WOMAN [A] — Michael BOLTON
WHEN A MAN LOVES A WOMAN [B] — Jody WATLEY
WHEN A WOMAN — GABRIELLE
WHEN AM I GONNA MAKE A LIVING — SADE
WHEN BOUZOUKIS PLAYED — Vicky LEANDROS
WHEN BOYS TALK — INDEEP
WHEN CAN I SEE YOU — BABYFACE
WHEN CHILDREN RULE THE WORLD — RED HILL CHILDREN
WHEN DO I GET TO SING 'MY WAY' — SPARKS
WHEN DOVES CRY [A] — PRINCE
WHEN DOVES CRY [A] — GINUWINE
WHEN DREAMS TURN TO DUST — Cathy DENNIS
WHEN FOREVER HAS GONE — Demis ROUSSOS
WHEN HE SHINES — Sheena EASTON
WHEN HEROES GO DOWN — Suzanne VEGA
WHEN I ARGUE I SEE SHAPES — IDLEWILD
WHEN I CALL YOUR NAME — Mary KIANI
WHEN I COME AROUND — GREEN DAY
WHEN I COME HOME — Spencer DAVIS GROUP
WHEN I DREAM [A] — TEARDROP EXPLODES
WHEN I DREAM [B] — Carol KIDD featuring Terry WAITE
WHEN I FALL IN LOVE [A] — Nat 'King' COLE
WHEN I FALL IN LOVE [A] — Donny OSMOND
WHEN I FALL IN LOVE [A] — Rick ASTLEY
WHEN I FALL IN LOVE [B] — ANT & DEC
WHEN I GET HOME — The SEARCHERS
WHEN I GROW UP [A] — Michelle SHOCKED
WHEN I GROW UP [B] — GARBAGE
WHEN I GROW UP (TO BE A MAN) — The BEACH BOYS
WHEN I KISS YOU (I HEAR CHARLIE PARKER PLAYING) — SPARKS
WHEN I LEAVE THE WORLD BEHIND — Rose MARIE
WHEN I LOOK INTO YOUR EYES [A] — FIREHOUSE
WHEN I LOOK INTO YOUR EYES [B] — MAXEE
WHEN I LOST YOU — Sarah WHATMORE
WHEN I NEED YOU [A] — Leo SAYER (77)
WHEN I NEED YOU [A] — Will MELLOR
WHEN I SAID GOODBYE — STEPS
WHEN I SEE YOU — Macy GRAY
WHEN I SEE YOU SMILE — BAD ENGLISH
WHEN I THINK OF YOU [A] — Janet JACKSON
WHEN I THINK OF YOU [B] — Kenny THOMAS
WHEN I THINK OF YOU [C] — Chris DE BURGH
WHEN I WAS YOUNG [A] — The ANIMALS
WHEN I WAS YOUNG [B] — RIVER CITY PEOPLE
WHEN I'M ALONE — The RIFLES
WHEN I'M AWAY FROM YOU — Frankie MILLER
WHEN I'M BACK ON MY FEET AGAIN — Michael BOLTON
WHEN I'M CLEANING WINDOWS (TURNED OUT NICE AGAIN) — 2 IN A TENT
WHEN I'M DEAD AND GONE — McGUINNESS FLINT
WHEN I'M GONE — EMINEM
WHEN I'M GOOD AND READY — SYBIL
WHEN I'M SIXTY FOUR — Kenny BALL and his JAZZMEN
WHEN IT'S LOVE — VAN HALEN
WHEN IT'S OVER — SUGAR RAY
WHEN IT'S TIME TO ROCK — UFO
WHEN JOHNNY COMES MARCHING HOME — Adam FAITH
WHEN JULIE COMES AROUND — The CUFFLINKS
WHEN LOVE AND HATE COLLIDE — DEF LEPPARD
WHEN LOVE BREAKS DOWN — PREFAB SPROUT
WHEN LOVE COMES ALONG — Matt MONRO
WHEN LOVE COMES CALLING — Paul JOHNSON
WHEN LOVE COMES ROUND AGAIN (L'ARCA DI NOE) — Ken DODD
WHEN LOVE COMES TO TOWN — U2 with BB KING
WHEN LOVE TAKES OVER YOU — Donna SUMMER
WHEN MEXICO GAVE UP THE RHUMBA — Mitchell TOROK
WHEN MY BABY — SCOOCH
WHEN MY LITTLE GIRL IS SMILING [A] — Craig DOUGLAS
WHEN MY LITTLE GIRL IS SMILING [A] — The DRIFTERS
WHEN MY LITTLE GIRL IS SMILING [A] — Jimmy JUSTICE
WHEN ONLY LOVE WILL DO — Richard DARBYSHIRE
WHEN ROCK 'N ROLL CAME TO TRINIDAD — Nat 'King' COLE
WHEN SHE WAS MY GIRL — The FOUR TOPS
WHEN SMOKEY SINGS — ABC
WHEN THE BOYS TALK ABOUT THE GIRLS — Valerie CARR
WHEN THE DAWN BREAKS — NARCOTIC THRUST
WHEN THE FINGERS POINT — The CHRISTIANS
WHEN THE GIRL IN YOUR ARMS IS THE GIRL IN YOUR HEART — Cliff RICHARD
WHEN THE GOING GETS TOUGH [A] — BOYZONE (99)
WHEN THE GOING GETS TOUGH, THE TOUGH GET GOING [A] — Billy OCEAN (86)
WHEN THE HEARTACHE IS OVER — Tina TURNER
WHEN THE HOODOO COMES — DIESEL PARK WEST
WHEN THE LAST TIME — CLIPSE
WHEN THE LIGHTS GO DOWN — Armand VAN HELDEN
WHEN THE LIGHTS GO OUT — FIVE
WHEN THE MORNING COMES — LOVE DECADE
WHEN THE MORNING SUN DRIES THE DEW — QUIET FIVE
WHEN THE NIGHT COMES — Joe COCKER
WHEN THE NIGHT FEELS MY SONG — BEDOUIN SOUNDCLASH
WHEN THE RAIN BEGINS TO FALL — Jermaine JACKSON and Pia ZADORA

23 April 2005	30 April 2005	7 May 2005	14 May 2005
(IS THIS THE WAY TO) AMARILLO Tony Christie featuring Peter Kay	**(IS THIS THE WAY TO) AMARILLO** Tony Christie featuring Peter Kay	**(IS THIS THE WAY TO) AMARILLO** Tony Christie featuring Peter Kay	**LONELY** Akon
THE SINGLES Basement Jaxx	**TROUBLE** Akon	**DEVILS & DUST** Bruce Springsteen	**TROUBLE** Akon

WHEN THE RIVER ROLLS OVER YOU — The STANDS
WHEN THE SH.. GOES DOWN — CYPRESS HILL
WHEN THE SUMMERTIME IS OVER — Jackie TRENT
WHEN THE SUN COMES SHININ' THRU — Long John BALDRY
WHEN THE SUN GOES DOWN — DJ FRESH featuring Adam F
WHEN THE TIGERS BROKE FREE — PINK FLOYD
WHEN THE WIND BLOWS — David BOWIE
WHEN THE WORLD IS RUNNING DOWN — DIFFERENT GEAR vs The POLICE
WHEN THE YEAR ENDS IN 1 — TOTTENHAM HOTSPUR FA CUP FINAL SQUAD
WHEN TOMORROW COMES — EURYTHMICS
WHEN TWO WORLDS COLLIDE — Jim REEVES
WHEN TWO WORLDS DRIFT APART — Cliff RICHARD
WHEN WE ARE FAR FROM HOME — ENGLAND WORLD CUP SQUAD
WHEN WE ARE GONE — FALLOUT TRUST
WHEN WE ARE TOGETHER — TEXAS
WHEN WE DANCE — STING
WHEN WE WAS FAB — George HARRISON
WHEN WE WERE YOUNG [A] — Solomon KING
WHEN WE WERE YOUNG [B] — BUCKS FIZZ
WHEN WE WERE YOUNG [C] — WHIPPING BOY
WHEN WE WERE YOUNG [D] — HUMAN NATURE
WHEN WILL I BE FAMOUS — BROS
WHEN WILL I BE LOVED — The EVERLY BROTHERS
WHEN WILL I SEE YOU AGAIN [A] — The THREE DEGREES (74)
WHEN WILL I SEE YOU AGAIN [A] — BROTHER BEYOND
WHEN WILL I SEE YOU AGAIN [A] — Sheila FERGUSON
WHEN WILL THE GOOD APPLES FALL — The SEEKERS
WHEN WILL YOU BE MINE — AVERAGE WHITE BAND
WHEN WILL YOU MAKE MY TELEPHONE RING — DEACON BLUE
WHEN WILL YOU SAY I LOVE YOU — Billy FURY
WHEN YOU ARE A KING — WHITE PLAINS
WHEN YOU ASK ABOUT LOVE [A] — The CRICKETS
WHEN YOU ASK ABOUT LOVE [A] — MATCHBOX
WHEN YOU BELIEVE — Mariah CAREY & Whitney HOUSTON
WHEN YOU COME BACK TO ME — Jason DONOVAN
WHEN YOU GET RIGHT DOWN TO IT — Ronnie DYSON
WHEN YOU GONNA LEARN — JAMIROQUAI
WHEN YOU KISS ME — Shania TWAIN
WHEN YOU LOOK AT ME — Christina MILIAN
WHEN YOU LOSE THE ONE YOU LOVE — David WHITFIELD
WHEN YOU MADE THE MOUNTAIN — OPUS III
WHEN YOU SAY NOTHING AT ALL — Ronan KEATING (99)
(WHEN YOU SAY YOU LOVE SOMEBODY) IN THE HEART — KOOL and The GANG
WHEN YOU SLEEP — LONGVIEW
WHEN YOU TELL ME THAT YOU LOVE ME [A] — Diana ROSS
WHEN YOU TELL ME THAT YOU LOVE ME [A] — WESTLIFE with Diana ROSS
WHEN YOU WALK IN THE ROOM [A] — The SEARCHERS
WHEN YOU WALK IN THE ROOM [A] — CHILD
WHEN YOU WALK IN THE ROOM [A] — Paul CARRACK
WHEN YOU WALK IN THE ROOM [A] — STATUS QUO
WHEN YOU WALK IN THE ROOM [A] — Agnetha FALTSKOG
WHEN YOU WERE SWEET SIXTEEN — The FUREYS
WHEN YOU WERE YOUNG — DEL AMITRI
WHEN YOUR 'EX' WANTS YOU BACK — SURFACE
WHEN YOUR OLD WEDDING RING WAS NEW — Jimmy ROSELLI
WHEN YOU'RE GONE [A] — Bryan ADAMS featuring Melanie C
WHEN YOU'RE GONE [B] — Soraya VIVIAN
WHEN YOU'RE IN LOVE WITH A BEAUTIFUL WOMAN — DR HOOK (79)
WHEN YOU'RE NUMBER 1 — Gene CHANDLER
WHEN YOU'RE YOUNG — The JAM
WHEN YOU'RE YOUNG AND IN LOVE [A] — The MARVELETTES
WHEN YOU'RE YOUNG AND IN LOVE [A] — The FLYING PICKETS
WHENEVER GOD SHINES HIS LIGHT — Van MORRISON with Cliff RICHARD
WHENEVER I SAY YOUR NAME — STING and Mary J BLIGE
WHENEVER, WHEREVER — SHAKIRA
WHENEVER YOU NEED ME — T'PAU
WHENEVER YOU NEED SOMEBODY — Rick ASTLEY
WHENEVER YOU NEED SOMEONE — BAD BOYS INC
WHENEVER YOU WANT MY LOVE — The REAL THING
WHENEVER YOU'RE NEAR — CHER
WHENEVER YOU'RE READY — FIVE STAR
WHENEVER I STOP — MIKE and The MECHANICS
WHERE ARE THEY NOW? — GENE
WHERE ARE YOU [A] — KAVANA
WHERE ARE YOU [B] — IMAANI
WHERE ARE YOU BABY — Betty BOO
WHERE ARE YOU GOING TO MY LOVE — BROTHERHOOD OF MAN
WHERE ARE YOU NOW [A] — Jackie TRENT (65)
WHERE ARE YOU NOW? [B] — GENERATOR
WHERE CAN I FIND LOVE — LIVIN' JOY
WHERE DID ALL THE GOOD TIMES GO — Donny OSMOND
WHERE DID I GO WRONG — UB40
WHERE DID OUR LOVE GO [A] — The SUPREMES
WHERE DID OUR LOVE GO? [A] — Donnie ELBERT
WHERE DID OUR LOVE GO [A] — MANHATTAN TRANSFER
WHERE DID OUR LOVE GO [A] — Tricia PENROSE
WHERE DID WE GO WRONG — LIQUID GOLD
WHERE DID YOUR HEART GO — WHAM! (86)
WHERE DO BROKEN HEARTS GO — Whitney HOUSTON
(WHERE DO I BEGIN) LOVE STORY [A] — Andy WILLIAMS
(WHERE DO I BEGIN) LOVE STORY [A] — Shirley BASSEY
WHERE DO I STAND? — MONTROSE AVENUE
WHERE DO U WANT ME TO PUT IT — SOLO U.S.
WHERE DO WE GO — TEN CITY
WHERE DO WE GO FROM HERE — Cliff RICHARD
WHERE DO YOU GO — NO MERCY
WHERE DO YOU GO TO (MY LOVELY) — Peter SARSTEDT (69)
WHERE DOES MY HEART BEAT NOW — Celine DION
WHERE DOES THE TIME GO — Julia FORDHAM
WHERE EAGLES FLY — CRYSTAL PALACE
WHERE HAS ALL THE LOVE GONE [A] — YAZZ
WHERE HAS ALL THE LOVE GONE [B] — MAUREEN
WHERE HAS LOVE GONE — Holly JOHNSON
WHERE HAVE ALL THE COWBOYS GONE? — Paula COLE
WHERE HAVE YOU BEEN TONIGHT — SHED SEVEN
WHERE I FIND MY HEAVEN — GIGOLO AUNTS
WHERE I WANNA BE — Shade SHEIST featuring Nate DOGG and KURUPT
WHERE I'M HEADED — Lene MARLIN
WHERE IN THE WORLD [A] — SWING OUT SISTER
WHERE IN THE WORLD [B] — BBM
WHERE IS MY MAN — Eartha KITT
WHERE IS THE FEELING — Kylie MINOGUE
WHERE IS THE LOVE [A] — Roberta FLACK
WHERE IS THE LOVE [A] — Betty WRIGHT
WHERE IS THE LOVE [A] — Mica PARIS and Will DOWNING
WHERE IS THE LOVE? [B] — ADEVA
WHERE IS THE LOVE? [C] — The BLACK EYED PEAS (03)
WHERE IS THE LOVE (WE USED TO KNOW) — DELEGATION
WHERE IS TOMORROW — Cilla BLACK
WHERE IT'S AT — BECK
WHERE LOVE LIVES — Alison LIMERICK
WHERE MY GIRLS AT? — 702
WHERE THE ACTION IS — WESTWORLD
WHERE THE BOYS ARE — Connie FRANCIS
WHERE THE HEART IS — SOFT CELL
WHERE THE HOOD AT — DMX
WHERE THE PARTY AT? — JAGGED EDGE featuring NELLY
WHERE THE POOR BOYS DANCE — LULU
WHERE THE ROSE IS SOWN — BIG COUNTRY
WHERE THE STORY ENDS — BLAZIN' SQUAD
WHERE THE STREETS HAVE NO NAME — U2
WHERE THE STREETS HAVE NO NAME - CAN'T TAKE MY EYES OFF YOU — PET SHOP BOYS
WHERE THE WILD ROSES GROW — Nick CAVE and Kylie MINOGUE
WHERE THE WINDS BLOW — Frankie LAINE
WHERE WERE YOU — ADULT NET
WHERE WERE YOU HIDING WHEN THE STORM BROKE — The ALARM
WHERE WERE YOU (ON OUR WEDDING DAY)? — Lloyd PRICE
WHERE WILL THE DIMPLE BE? — Rosemary CLOONEY
WHERE WILL YOU BE — Sue NICHOLLS
WHERE YOU ARE — Rahsaan PATTERSON
WHERE YOU GONNA BE TONIGHT? — Willie COLLINS
WHERE'S JACK THE RIPPER — GROOVERIDER
WHERE'S ME JUMPER — SULTANS OF PING FC
WHERE'S MY ...? — Adam F featuring LIL' MO
WHERE'S ROMEO — ÇA VA ÇA VA
WHERE'S THE LOVE — HANSON
WHERE'S YOUR HEAD AT? — BASEMENT JAXX
WHERE'S YOUR LOVE BEEN — HELIOCENTRIC WORLD
WHEREVER I LAY MY HAT (THAT'S MY HOME) — Paul YOUNG (83)
WHEREVER I MAY ROAM — METALLICA
WHEREVER WOULD I BE — Dusty SPRINGFIELD and Daryl HALL
WHEREVER YOU ARE — Neil FINN
WHEREVER YOU WILL GO — The CALLING
WHICH WAY SHOULD I JUMP — The MILLTOWN BROTHERS
WHICH WAY YOU GOIN' BILLY? — The POPPY FAMILY
WHIGGLE IN LINE — BLACK DUCK
WHILE I LIVE — Kenny DAMON
WHILE YOU SEE A CHANCE — Steve WINWOOD
WHINE AND GRINE — PRINCE BUSTER
WHIP IT — DEVO
WHIPLASH — JFK
WHIPPIN' PICCADILLY — GOMEZ
WHISKEY IN THE JAR [A] — THIN LIZZY
WHISKEY IN THE JAR [A] — DUBLINERS
WHISKEY IN THE JAR [A] — The POGUES
WHISKEY IN THE JAR [A] — METALLICA
THE WHISPER — SELECTER
WHISPER A PRAYER — Mica PARIS
WHISPER YOUR NAME — HUMAN NATURE
WHISPERING [A] — The BACHELORS
WHISPERING [A] — Nino TEMPO and April STEVENS
WHISPERING GRASS — Windsor DAVIES as BSM Williams and Don ESTELLE as Gunner Sugden (Lofty) (75)
WHISPERING HOPE — Jim REEVES
WHISPERING YOUR NAME — Alison MOYET
WHISPERS — Elton JOHN
WHISPERS — Ian BROWN
WHISTLE DOWN THE WIND [A] — Nick HEYWARD
WHISTLE DOWN THE WIND [B] — Tina ARENA
THE WHISTLE SONG [A] — Frankie KNUCKLES
THE WHISTLE SONG (BLOW MY WHISTLE BITCH) [B] — DJ ALIGATOR PROJECT
THE WHISTLER — HONKY
WHITE BIRD — VANESSA-MAE
WHITE BOY WITH A FEATHER — Jason DOWNS featuring MILK
WHITE BOYS AND HEROES — Gary NUMAN
WHITE CHRISTMAS [A] — MANTOVANI
WHITE CHRISTMAS [A] — Pat BOONE
WHITE CHRISTMAS [A] — Freddie STARR
WHITE CHRISTMAS [A] — Bing CROSBY
WHITE CHRISTMAS [A] — DARTS
WHITE CHRISTMAS [A] — Jim DAVIDSON
WHITE CHRISTMAS [A] — Keith HARRIS and ORVILLE
WHITE CHRISTMAS [A] — Max BYGRAVES
WHITE CLIFFS OF DOVER [A] — Mr Acker BILK and his PARAMOUNT JAZZ BAND
WHITE CLIFFS OF DOVER [A] — The RIGHTEOUS BROTHERS
WHITE COATS (EP) — NEW MODEL ARMY
WHITE FLAG — DIDO
WHITE HORSES — Jackie LEE
WHITE LIE — FOREIGNER
WHITE LIGHT, WHITE HEAT — David BOWIE
WHITE LIGHTNING — The FALL
WHITE LINES (DON'T DON'T DO IT) [A] — GRANDMASTER FLASH, Melle MEL and The FURIOUS FIVE
WHITE LINES (DON'T DO IT) [A] — DURAN DURAN
WHITE LOVE — ONE DOVE
(WHITE MAN) IN HAMMERSMITH PALAIS — The CLASH
WHITE NO SUGAR — The Clint BOON EXPERIENCE
WHITE PUNKS ON DOPE — TUBES
WHITE RIBBON DAY — DELIRIOUS?
WHITE RIOT — The CLASH
WHITE ROOM — CREAM
WHITE SILVER SANDS — Bill BLACK'S COMBO
WHITE SKIES — SUNSCREEM
A WHITE SPORT COAT [A] — The KING BROTHERS
A WHITE SPORT COAT [A] — Terry DENE
WHITE WEDDING [A] — Billy IDOL
WHITE WEDDING [A] — The MURDERDOLLS
A WHITER SHADE OF PALE [A] — PROCOL HARUM (67)
A WHITER SHADE OF PALE [A] — MUNICH MACHINE
A WHITER SHADE OF PALE [A] — Annie LENNOX
WHO? — Ed CASE and SWEETIE IRIE
WHO AM I [A] — Adam FAITH
WHO AM I "SIM SIMMA" — BEENIE MAN
WHO ARE WE [A] — Ronnie HILTON
WHO ARE WE [A] — Vera LYNN
WHO ARE YOU — The WHO
WHO CAN I RUN TO — XSCAPE
WHO CAN IT BE NOW? — MEN AT WORK
WHO CAN MAKE ME FEEL GOOD — BASSHEADS
WHO COMES TO BOOGIE — LITTLE BENNY and The MASTERS
WHO COULD BE BLUER — Jerry LORDAN
WHO DO U LOVE — Deborah COX
WHO DO YOU LOVE [A] — JUICY LUCY
WHO DO YOU LOVE? [B] — INTRUDERS
WHO DO YOU LOVE [C] — José PADILLA featuring Angela JOHN
WHO DO YOU LOVE NOW (STRINGER) — RIVA featuring Dannii MINOGUE
WHO DO YOU THINK YOU ARE [A] — CANDLEWICK GREEN
WHO DO YOU THINK YOU ARE [A] — SAINT ETIENNE
WHO DO YOU THINK YOU ARE [B] — Kim WILDE
WHO DO YOU THINK YOU ARE [C] — SPICE GIRLS (97)
WHO DO YOU WANT FOR YOUR LOVE — The ICICLE WORKS
WHO FEELS LOVE? — OASIS
WHO FOUND WHO — JELLYBEAN featuring Elisa FIORILLO
WHO GETS THE LOVE — STATUS QUO
WHO INVITED YOU? — The DONNAS
WHO IS IT [A] — MANTRONIX
WHO IS IT [B] — Michael JACKSON
WHO IS IT [C] — BJÖRK
WHO IS SHE 2 U — BRANDY
WHO KEEPS CHANGING YOUR MIND — SOUTH ST PLAYER
WHO KILLED BAMBI — TEN POLE TUDOR
WHO LET IN THE RAIN — Cyndi LAUPER
WHO LET THE DOGS OUT — BAHA MEN
WHO LOVES YOU — The FOUR SEASONS
WHO MADE WHO — AC/DC
WHO NEEDS ENEMIES — The COOPER TEMPLE CLAUSE
WHO NEEDS LOVE (LIKE THAT) — ERASURE
WHO PAYS THE FERRYMAN? — Yannis MARKOPOULOS

	21 May 2005	28 May 2005	4 June 2005	11 June 2005
UK No.1 SINGLES	**LONELY** Akon	**LYLA** Oasis	**AXEL F** Crazy Frog	**AXEL F** Crazy Frog
UK No.1 ALBUMS	**HEART & SOUL** Steve Brookstein	**FOREVER FAITHLESS - THE GREATEST HITS** Faithless	**DEMON DAYS** Gorillaz	**DON'T BELIEVE THE TRUTH** Oasis

WHO PAYS THE PIPER —
Gary CLAIL ON-U SOUND SYSTEM
WHO PUT THE BOMP (IN THE BOMP, BOMP, BOMP) [A] — The VISCOUNTS
WHO PUT THE BOMP (IN THE BOMP-A-BOMP-A-BOMP) [A] — SHOWADDYWADDY
WHO PUT THE LIGHTS OUT — DANA
WHO SAID (STUCK IN THE UK) — PLANET FUNK
WHO THE HELL ARE YOU — MADISON AVENUE
WHO TOLD YOU — Roni SIZE / REPRAZENT
WHO WANTS THE WORLD — The STRANGLERS
WHO WANTS TO BE THE DISCO KING? — The WONDER STUFF
WHO WANTS TO LIVE FOREVER [A] — QUEEN
WHO WANTS TO LIVE FOREVER [A] — Sarah BRIGHTMAN
WHO WAS IT — Hurricane SMITH
WHO WE BE — DMX
WHO WEARS THESE SHOES — Elton JOHN
WHO WERE YOU WITH IN THE MOONLIGHT — DOLLAR
WHO, WHAT, WHEN, WHERE, WHY — MANHATTAN TRANSFER
WHO WHERE WHY — JESUS JONES
WHO WILL SAVE YOUR SOUL — JEWEL
WHO WILL YOU RUN TO — HEART
WHO YOU ARE — PEARL JAM
WHO YOU LOOKING AT — SALFORD JETS
WHO YOU WIT — JAY-Z
WHOA — BLACK ROB
WHO'D SEE COO — OHIO PLAYERS
WHODUNIT — TAVARES
WHOLE AGAIN — ATOMIC KITTEN (01)
WHOLE LOTTA LOVE [A] — CCS
WHOLE LOTTA LOVE [A] — GOLDBUG
WHOLE LOTTA LOVE [A] — LED ZEPPELIN
WHOLE LOTTA ROSIE — AC/DC
WHOLE LOTTA SHAKIN' GOIN' ON — Jerry Lee LEWIS
WHOLE LOTTA TROUBLE — Stevie NICKS
WHOLE LOTTA WOMAN — Marvin RAINWATER (58)
WHOLE NEW WORLD — IT BITES
A WHOLE NEW WORLD (ALADDIN'S THEME) — Regina BELLE and Peabo BRYSON
THE WHOLE OF THE MOON [A] — WATERBOYS
THE WHOLE OF THE MOON [A] — LITTLE CAESAR
THE WHOLE TOWN'S LAUGHING AT ME — Teddy PENDERGRASS
THE WHOLE WORLD — OUTKAST featuring KILLER MIKE
THE WHOLE WORLD LOST ITS HEAD — GO-GO's
WHOOMP! (THERE IT IS) [A] — TAG TEAM
WHOOMPH! (THERE IT IS) [A] — CLOCK
WHOOMP THERE IT IS [A] — BM DUBS present MR RUMBLE
WHOOPS NOW — Janet JACKSON
WHOOPSIE DAISY — Terri WALKER
WHOOSH — WHOOSH
WHO'S AFRAID OF THE BIG BAD LOVE — WILD WEEKEND
WHO'S AFRAID OF THE BIG BAD NOISE! — AGE OF CHANCE
WHO'S COMING ROUND — 5050
WHO'S CRYING NOW — JOURNEY
WHO'S DAVID — BUSTED (04)
WHO'S GONNA LOVE ME — IMPERIALS
WHO'S GONNA RIDE YOUR WILD HORSES — U2
WHO'S GONNA ROCK YOU — The NOLANS
WHO'S IN THE HOUSE — The BEATMASTERS
WHO'S IN THE STRAWBERRY PATCH WITH SALLY — DAWN
WHO'S JOHNNY ('SHORT CIRCUIT' THEME) — El DeBARGE
WHO'S LEAVING WHO — Hazell DEAN
WHO'S LOVING MY BABY — Shola AMA
WHO'S SORRY NOW [A] — Johnnie RAY
WHO'S SORRY NOW? [A] — Connie FRANCIS (58)
WHO'S THAT GIRL? [A] — EURYTHMICS
WHO'S THAT GIRL [A] — The FLYING PICKETS
WHO'S THAT GIRL [B] — MADONNA (87)
WHO'S THAT GIRL [C] — EVE
WHO'S THAT GIRL (SHE'S GOT IT) — A FLOCK OF SEAGULLS
WHO'S THAT MIX — THIS YEAR'S BLONDE
WHO'S THE BAD MAN? — Dee PATTEN
WHO'S THE DADDY — LOVEBUG
WHO'S THE DARKMAN — DARKMAN
WHO'S THE MACK! — Mark MORRISON
WHO'S THE MAN — HOUSE OF PAIN
WHO'S ZOOMIN' WHO — Aretha FRANKLIN
WHOSE FIST IS THIS ANYWAY (EP) — PRONG
WHOSE LAW (IS IT ANYWAY) — GURU JOSH
WHOSE PROBLEM? — MOTELS
WHY [A] — Anthony NEWLEY (60)
WHY [A] — Frankie AVALON
WHY [A] — Donny OSMOND
WHY [B] — Roger WHITTAKER
WHY [C] — Carly SIMON
WHY [C] — GLAMMA KID
WHY? [D] — BRONSKI BEAT
WHY [E] — Annie LENNOX
WHY [E] — DJ SAMMY
WHY [F] — D MOB with Cathy DENNIS
WHY [G] — Ricardo DA FORCE
WHY [H] — 3T
WHY [I] — MIS-TEEQ
WHY? [J] — AGENT SUMO
WHY ARE PEOPLE GRUDGEFUL — The FALL
WHY ARE YOU BEING SO REASONABLE NOW — The WEDDING PRESENT
WHY BABY WHY — Pat BOONE
WHY BELIEVE IN YOU — TEXAS
WHY CAN'T YOU — Clarence 'Frogman' HENRY
WHY CAN'T I BE YOU [A] — The CURE
WHY CAN'T I BE YOU? [B] — SHED SEVEN
WHY CAN'T I WAKE UP WITH YOU — TAKE THAT
WHY CAN'T THIS BE LOVE — VAN HALEN
WHY CAN'T WE BE LOVERS — HOLLAND-DOZIER featuring Lamont DOZIER
WHY CAN'T WE LIVE TOGETHER — Timmy THOMAS
WHY CAN'T YOU FREE SOME TIME — Armand VAN HELDEN
WHY DID YA — Tony DI BART
WHY DID YOU DO IT — STRETCH
WHY DIDN'T YOU CALL ME — Macy GRAY
WHY DO FOOLS FALL IN LOVE [A] — Alma COGAN
WHY DO FOOLS FALL IN LOVE? [A] — TEENAGERS featuring Frankie LYMON (56)
WHY DO FOOLS FALL IN LOVE [A] — Diana ROSS
WHY DO I ALWAYS GET IT WRONG — LIVE REPORT
WHY DO I DO? — Tyler JAMES
WHY DO LOVERS BREAK EACH OTHER'S HEARTS — SHOWADDYWADDY
WHY DO YOU KEEP ON RUNNING — STINX
WHY DO YOU LOVE ME — GARBAGE
WHY DOES A MAN HAVE TO BE STRONG — Paul YOUNG
WHY DOES IT ALWAYS RAIN ON ME? — TRAVIS
WHY DOES MY HEART FEEL SO BAD? — MOBY
WHY DON'T THEY UNDERSTAND — George HAMILTON IV
WHY DON'T WE FALL IN LOVE — AMERIE featuring LUDACRIS
WHY DON'T WE TRY AGAIN — Brian MAY
WHY DON'T YOU — RAGE
WHY DON'T YOU BELIEVE ME — Joni JAMES
WHY DON'T YOU DANCE WITH ME — FUTURE BREEZE
WHY DON'T YOU DO IT FOR ME? — 22-20s
WHY DON'T YOU GET A JOB? — The OFFSPRING
WHY DON'T YOU TAKE ME — ONE DOVE
WHY D'YA LIE TO ME — SPIDER
WHY GO? — FAITHLESS featuring ESTELLE
WHY (LOOKING BACK) — HEARTLESS CREW
WHY ME [A] — Linda MARTIN
WHY ME [B] — A HOUSE
WHY ME [C] — ANT & DEC
WHY ME [D] — ASHER D
WHY (MUST WE FALL IN LOVE) — Diana ROSS and The SUPREMES and The TEMPTATIONS
WHY MUST WE WAIT UNTIL TONIGHT — Tina TURNER
WHY NOT NOW — Matt MONRO
WHY NOT TONIGHT — MOJOS
WHY OH WHY — SPEARHEAD
WHY, OH WHY, OH WHY — Gilbert O'SULLIVAN
WHY SHE'S A GIRL FROM THE CHAINSTORE — The BUZZCOCKS
WHY SHOULD I — Bob MARLEY & The WAILERS
WHY SHOULD I BE LONELY — Tony BRENT
WHY SHOULD I CRY — Nona HENDRYX
WHY SHOULD I LOVE YOU — DES'REE
WHY WHY BYE BYE — Bob LUMAN
WHY WHY WHY — DEJA VU
WHY YOU FOLLOW ME — Eric BENET
WHY YOU TREAT ME SO BAD — SHAGGY featuring GRAND PUBA
WHY'D YOU LIE TO ME — ANASTACIA
WHY'S EVERYBODY ALWAYS PICKIN' ON ME? — The BLOODHOUND GANG
WIBBLING RIVALRY (INTERVIEWS WITH NOEL AND LIAM GALLAGHER) — OASIS
WICHITA LINEMAN — Glen CAMPBELL
WICKED — ICE CUBE
WICKED GAME — Chris ISAAK
WICKED LOVE — OCEANIC
WICKED SOUL — KUBB
WICKED WAYS — The BLOW MONKEYS
WICKEDEST SOUND — REBEL MC featuring TENOR FLY
THE WICKER MAN — IRON MAIDEN
WICKI WACKY HOUSE PARTY — TEAM
WIDE AWAKE IN A DREAM — Barry BIGGS
WIDE BOY — Nik KERSHAW
WIDE EYED AND LEGLESS — Andy FAIRWEATHER-LOW
WIDE EYED ANGEL — ORIGIN
WIDE OPEN SKY — GOLDRUSH
WIDE OPEN SPACE — MANSUN
WIDE PRAIRIE — Linda McCARTNEY
THE WIDOW — The MARS VOLTA
WIFEY — NEXT
WIG WAM BAM [A] — BLACK LACE
WIG WAM BAM [A] — DAMIAN
WIGGLE IT — 2 IN A ROOM
WIGGLY WORLD — MR JACK
WIG-WAM BAM — The SWEET
WIKKA WRAP — EVASIONS
THE WILD AMERICA (EP) — Iggy POP
WILD AND WONDERFUL — The ALMIGHTY
WILD AS ANGELS EP — LEVELLERS
WILD BOYS [A] — PHIXX
THE WILD BOYS [A] — DURAN DURAN
WILD CAT — Gene VINCENT
WILD CHILD [A] — W.A.S.P.
WILD CHILD [B] — ENYA
WILD DANCES — RUSLANA
WILD FLOWER — The CULT
WILD FRONTIER — Gary MOORE
WILD HEARTED SON — The CULT
WILD HEARTED WOMAN — ALL ABOUT EVE
WILD HONEY — The BEACH BOYS
WILD IN THE COUNTRY — Elvis PRESLEY
WILD IS THE WIND — David BOWIE
WILD LOVE — MUNGO JERRY
WILD LUV — ROACH MOTEL
WILD 'N FREE — REDNEX
WILD NIGHT — John Cougar MELLENCAMP
WILD ONE — Bobby RYDELL
THE WILD ONE — Suzi QUATRO
THE WILD ONES — SUEDE
WILD SIDE — MÖTLEY CRÜE
WILD SIDE OF LIFE [A] — Tommy QUICKLY
WILD SIDE OF LIFE [A] — STATUS QUO
THE WILD SON — The VEILS
WILD SURF — ASH
WILD THING [A] — The TROGGS
WILD THING [A] — The GOODIES
WILD THING [B] — Tone LOC
WILD 2NITE — SHAGGY
WILD WEST HERO — ELECTRIC LIGHT ORCHESTRA
WILD WILD LIFE — TALKING HEADS
WILD WILD WEST [A] — GET READY
WILD WILD WEST [B] — Will SMITH featuring DRU HILL – additional vocals Kool Moe DEE
WILD WIND — John LEYTON
WILD WOMEN DO — Natalie COLE
WILD WOOD — Paul WELLER
WILD WORLD [A] — Jimmy CLIFF
WILD WORLD [A] — Maxi PRIEST
WILD WORLD [A] — MR BIG
WILDERNESS — Jurgen VRIES featuring SHENA
WILDEST DREAMS — IRON MAIDEN
WILDLIFE (EP) — GIRLSCHOOL
WILDSIDE — MARKY MARK and The FUNKY BUNCH
WILDWOOD — Paul WELLER
WILFRED THE WEASEL — Keith MICHELL
WILL I — IAN VAN DAHL
WILL I EVER — ALICE DEEJAY
WILL I WHAT — Mike SARNE with Billie DAVIS
WILL THE WOLF SURVIVE — LOS LOBOS
WILL 2K — Will SMITH
WILL WE BE LOVERS — DEACON BLUE
WILL YOU [A] — Hazel O'CONNOR
WILL YOU [B] — P.O.D.
WILL YOU BE MY BABY — GRAND PUBA
WILL YOU BE THERE — Michael JACKSON
WILL YOU BE THERE (IN THE MORNING) — HEART
WILL YOU BE WITH ME — Maria NAYLER
WILL YOU LOVE ME TOMORROW [A] — The SHIRELLES
WILL YOU LOVE ME TOMORROW [A] — MELANIE
WILL YOU LOVE ME TOMORROW [A] — Bryan FERRY
WILL YOU MARRY ME — Paula ABDUL
WILL YOU SATISFY? — CHERRELLE
WILL YOU WAIT FOR ME — KAVANA
WILLIAM — The OTHERS
WILLIAM, IT WAS REALLY NOTHING — The SMITHS
WILLIE CAN [A] — Alma COGAN
WILLIE CAN [A] — The BEVERLEY SISTERS
WILLING TO FORGIVE — Aretha FRANKLIN
WILLINGLY — Malcolm VAUGHAN
WILLOW TREE — The IVY LEAGUE
WILMOT — SABRES OF PARADISE
WIMMIN' — Ashley HAMILTON
WIMOWEH — Karl DENVER
WIN PLACE OR SHOW (SHE'S A WINNER) — The INTRUDERS
WINCHESTER CATHEDRAL — NEW VAUDEVILLE BAND
THE WIND — P J HARVEY
THE WIND BENEATH MY WINGS [A] — Lee GREENWOOD
WIND BENEATH MY WINGS [A] — Bette MIDLER
WIND BENEATH MY WINGS [A] — Bill TARMEY
WIND BENEATH MY WINGS [A] — Steven HOUGHTON
THE WIND CRIES MARY — The Jimi HENDRIX EXPERIENCE
WIND IT UP (REWOUND) — The PRODIGY
WIND ME UP (LET ME GO) — Cliff RICHARD
WIND OF CHANGE — SCORPIONS
WIND THE BOBBIN UP! — Jo JINGLES
WINDINGS — SUGARCOMA
A WINDMILL IN OLD AMSTERDAM — Ronnie HILTON
WINDMILLS OF YOUR MIND — Noel HARRISON
WINDOW PANE (EP) — REAL PEOPLE
WINDOW SHOPPER — 50 CENT
WINDOW SHOPPING — R Dean TAYLOR
WINDOWLICKER — APHEX TWIN
WINDOWS '98 — SIL
WINDPOWER — Thomas DOLBY
THE WINDSOR WALTZ — Vera LYNN
WINDSWEPT — Bryan FERRY
WINGS OF A BUTTERFLY — HIM
WINGS OF A DOVE — MADNESS
WINGS OF LOVE — BONE
THE WINKER'S SONG (MISPRINT) — Ivor BIGGUN
THE WINKLE MAN — JUDGE DREAD
THE WINNER [A] — HEARTBEAT
THE WINNER [B] — COOLIO
THE WINNER TAKES IT ALL — ABBA (80)
WINNING DAYS — The VINES
WINTER [A] — LOVE AND MONEY
WINTER [B] — Tori AMOS
WINTER [C] — DT8 PROJECT featuring Andrea BRITTON
WINTER CEREMONY (TOR-CHENEY-NAHANA) — SACRED SPIRIT
THE WINTER GARDENS — SPECIAL NEEDS
WINTER IN JULY — BOMB THE BASS
WINTER MELODY — Donna SUMMER
WINTER SONG — Chris REA
A WINTER STORY — Aled JONES
WINTER WONDERLAND [A] — Johnny MATHIS
WINTER WONDERLAND [A] — COCTEAU TWINS
WINTER WORLD OF LOVE — Engelbert HUMPERDINCK
A WINTER'S TALE [A] — David ESSEX
A WINTER'S TALE [B] — QUEEN

18 June 2005	25 June 2005	2 July 2005	9 July 2005
AXEL F Crazy Frog	**AXEL F** Crazy Frog	**GHETTO GOSPEL** 2Pac (featuring Elton John)	**GHETTO GOSPEL** 2Pac (featuring Elton John)
X&Y Coldplay	**X&Y** Coldplay	**X&Y** Coldplay	**X&Y** Coldplay

WIPE OUT [A] — SURFARIS
WIPE OUT [A] — ANIMAL
WIPE THE NEEDLE — RAGGA TWINS
WIPEOUT — FAT BOYS and The BEACH BOYS
WIRED FOR SOUND — Cliff RICHARD
WIRES — ATHLETE
THE WISDOM OF A FOOL [A] — Norman WISDOM
THE WISDOM OF A FOOL [A] — Ronnie CARROLL
WISE UP! SUCKER — POP WILL EAT ITSELF
WISEMEN — James BLUNT
WISER TIME — The BLACK CROWES
WISH — SOUL II SOUL
A WISH AWAY — The WONDER STUFF
WISH I — JEM
WISH I COULD FLY — ROXETTE
WISH I DIDN'T MISS YOU — Angie STONE
WISH I HAD AN ANGEL — NIGHTWISH
WISH I WAS SKINNY — The BOO RADLEYS
WISH I WERE YOU — ALISHA'S ATTIC
WISH THE WORLD AWAY — AMERICAN MUSIC CLUB
WISH YOU WERE HERE [A] — Eddie FISHER
WISH YOU WERE HERE [B] — FIRST LIGHT
WISH YOU WERE HERE ... [C] — ALOOF
WISH YOU WERE HERE [D] — Wyclef JEAN
WISH YOU WERE HERE [E] — INCUBUS
WISHES — HUMAN NATURE
WISHES OF HAPPINESS AND PROSPERITY (YEHA-NOHA) — SACRED SPIRIT
WISHFUL THINKING — CHINA CRISIS
WISHIN' AND HOPIN' — The MERSEYBEATS
WISHING — Buddy HOLLY
WISHING I WAS LUCKY — WET WET WET
WISHING I WAS THERE — Natalie IMBRUGLIA
WISHING (IF I HAD A PHOTOGRAPH OF YOU) — A FLOCK OF SEAGULLS
WISHING ON A STAR [A] — ROSE ROYCE
WISHING ON A STAR [A] — FRESH 4 featuring Lizz E
WISHING ON A STAR [A] — The COVER GIRLS
WISHING ON A STAR [A] — Lisa MAY
WISHING ON A STAR [A] — JAY-Z featuring Gwen DICKEY
WISHING ON A STAR [A] — Paul WELLER
WISHING WELL [A] — FREE
WISHING WELL [B] — Terence Trent D'ARBY
THE WISHING WELL — G.O.S.H.
WISHING YOU WERE HERE — Alison MOYET
WISHING YOU WERE SOMEHOW HERE AGAIN — Sarah BRIGHTMAN
WISHLIST — PEARL JAM
THE WITCH — RATTLES
WITCH DOCTOR [A] — David SEVILLE
WITCH DOCTOR [A] — Don LANG
WITCH DOCTOR [A] — CARTOONS
THE WITCH QUEEN OF NEW ORLEANS — REDBONE
THE WITCH'S PROMISE — JETHRO TULL
WITCHCRAFT [A] — Frank SINATRA
WITCHCRAFT [A] — Robert PALMER
WITCHES' BREW — Janie JONES
WITH A GIRL LIKE YOU — The TROGGS (66)
WITH A LITTLE HELP FROM MY FRIENDS [A] — Joe BROWN and The BRUVVERS
WITH A LITTLE HELP FROM MY FRIENDS [A] — YOUNG IDEA
WITH A LITTLE HELP FROM MY FRIENDS [A] — Joe COCKER (68)
WITH A LITTLE HELP FROM MY FRIENDS [A] — WET WET WET (88)
WITH A LITTLE HELP FROM MY FRIENDS [A] — SAM & MARK (04)
WITH A LITTLE LOVE — Sam BROWN
WITH A LITTLE LUCK — Paul McCARTNEY
WITH ALL MY HEART — Petula CLARK
WITH ARMS WIDE OPEN — CREED
WITH EVERY BEAT OF MY HEART — Taylor DAYNE
WITH EVERY HEARTBEAT — FIVE STAR
WITH GOD ON OUR SIDE — The NEVILLE BROTHERS
WITH ME — DESTINY'S CHILD
WITH MY OWN EYES — SASH!
WITH ONE LOOK — Barbra STREISAND
WITH OR WITHOUT YOU [A] — U2
WITH OR WITHOUT YOU [A] — Mary KIANI
WITH PEN IN HAND — Vikki CARR
WITH THE EYES OF A CHILD — Cliff RICHARD
WITH THE WIND AND THE RAIN IN YOUR HAIR — Pat BOONE
WITH THESE HANDS [A] — Shirley BASSEY
WITH THESE HANDS [A] — Tom JONES
WITH YOU [A] — Jessica SIMPSON
WITH YOU [B] — The SUBWAYS
WITH YOU I'M BORN AGAIN — Billy PRESTON and SYREETA
WITH YOUR LOVE — Malcolm VAUGHAN
WITHOUT A DOUBT — BLACK SHEEP
WITHOUT HER — Herb ALPERT
WITHOUT LOVE [A] — Tom JONES
WITHOUT LOVE [B] — Donna LEWIS
WITHOUT LOVE [C] — Dina CARROLL
WITHOUT ME — EMINEM (02)
WITHOUT YOU [A] — Matt MONRO
WITHOUT YOU [B] — NILSSON (72)
WITHOUT YOU [B] — Mariah CAREY (94)
WITHOUT YOU [C] — MÖTLEY CRÜE
WITHOUT YOU [D] — LUCY PEARL
WITHOUT YOU [E] — EL PRESIDENTE
WITHOUT YOU (ONE AND ONE) — Lindy LAYTON
WITHOUT YOUR LOVE — Roger DALTREY
WITNESS (EP) — Ann NESBY
WITNESS FOR THE WORLD — CRY BEFORE DAWN
WITNESS (1 HOPE) — ROOTS MANUVA
THE WIZARD — Paul HARDCASTLE
WIZARDS OF THE SONIC [A] — WESTBAM
WIZZY WOW — BLACKSTREET
WOE IS ME — Helen SHAPIRO
W.O.L.D. — Harry CHAPIN
WOLF — SHY FX
WOMAN (UH-HUH) [A] — Jose FERRER
WOMAN [B] — PETER and GORDON
WOMAN [C] — John LENNON (81)
WOMAN [D] — ANTI-NOWHERE LEAGUE
WOMAN [E] — Neneh CHERRY
WOMAN FROM LIBERIA — Jimmie RODGERS
THE WOMAN I LOVE — The HOLLIES
WOMAN IN CHAINS [A] — TEARS FOR FEARS
A WOMAN IN LOVE [A] — The FOUR ACES
A WOMAN IN LOVE [A] — Ronnie HILTON
A WOMAN IN LOVE [A] — Frankie LAINE (56)
WOMAN IN LOVE [A] — The THREE DEGREES
WOMAN IN LOVE [B] — Barbra STREISAND (80)
WOMAN IN LOVE [B] — Rebekah RYAN
WOMAN IN ME — Carleen ANDERSON
THE WOMAN IN ME [A] — Donna SUMMER
THE WOMAN IN ME [B] — KINANE
WOMAN IN WINTER — The SKIDS
WOMAN OF MINE — Dean FRIEDMAN
WOMAN OF PRINCIPLE — TROUBLE FUNK
WOMAN TO WOMAN — Beverley CRAVEN
WOMAN TROUBLE — ARTFUL DODGER and Robbie CRAIG featuring Craig DAVID
WOMAN, WOMAN — Gary PUCKETT and The UNION GAP
WOMANKIND — LITTLE ANGELS
A WOMAN'S PLACE — Gilbert O'SULLIVAN
A WOMAN'S STORY — Marc ALMOND
WOMAN'S WORLD — The JAGS
A WOMAN'S WORTH — Alicia KEYS
WOMBLING MERRY CHRISTMAS — The WOMBLES
THE WOMBLING SONG — The WOMBLES
WOMBLING WHITE TIE AND TAILS (FOX TROT) — The WOMBLES
WOMEN BEAT THEIR MEN — Junior CARTIER
WOMEN IN UNIFORM [A] — SKYHOOKS
WOMEN IN UNIFORM [A] — IRON MAIDEN
WOMEN OF IRELAND — Mike OLDFIELD
WON — The BETA BAND
WONDER — EMBRACE
WONDERBOY — TENACIOUS D
THE WONDER OF LOVE — LOVELAND featuring the voice of Rachel McFARLANE
THE WONDER OF YOU [A] — Ronnie HILTON
THE WONDER OF YOU [A] — Ray PETERSON
THE WONDER OF YOU [A] — Elvis PRESLEY (70)
WONDERBOY — The KINKS
WONDERFUL [A] — Mari WILSON
WONDERFUL [B] — RUNRIG
WONDERFUL [C] — Adam ANT
WONDERFUL [D] — EVERCLEAR
WONDERFUL [E] — Brian WILSON
WONDERFUL [F] — JA RULE featuring R KELLY & ASHANTI (04)
WONDERFUL CHRISTMASTIME — Paul McCARTNEY
WONDERFUL COPENHAGEN — Danny KAYE
WONDERFUL DREAM — Anne-Marie DAVID
WONDERFUL EXCUSE — The FAMILY CAT
WONDERFUL LAND — The SHADOWS (62)
WONDERFUL LIFE [A] — BLACK
WONDERFUL LIFE [A] — TJ DAVIS
WONDERFUL LIFE [A] — Tina COUSINS
A WONDERFUL NIGHT — FATBOY SLIM
THE WONDERFUL SECRET OF LOVE — Robert EARL
WONDERFUL THINGS — Frankie VAUGHAN
A WONDERFUL TIME UP THERE [A] — Pat BOONE
A WONDERFUL TIME UP THERE [A] — Alvin STARDUST
WONDERFUL TONIGHT [A] — DAMAGE
WONDERFUL TONIGHT (LIVE) [A] — Eric CLAPTON
WONDERFUL! WONDERFUL! [A] — Ronnie HILTON
WONDERFUL, WONDERFUL [A] — Gary MILLER
WONDERFUL WORLD [A] — Sam COOKE
WONDERFUL WORLD [A] — HERMAN'S HERMITS
WONDERFUL WORLD [B] — WORLDS APART
WONDERFUL WORLD BEAUTIFUL PEOPLE — Jimmy CLIFF
WONDERFUL WORLD OF THE YOUNG — Danny WILLIAMS
WONDERING WHY — MJ COLE
WONDERLAND [A] — The COMMODORES
WONDERLAND [B] — BIG COUNTRY
WONDERLAND [C] — Paul YOUNG
WONDERLAND [D] — 911
WONDERLAND [E] — PSYCHEDELIC WALTONS featuring Roisin MURPHY
WONDERMAN — RIGHT SAID FRED
WONDERWALL [A] — OASIS
WONDERWALL [A] — Mike FLOWERS POPS
WONDERWALL [A] — DE-CODE featuring Beverli SKEETE
WONDERWALL [A] — Ryan ADAMS
WONDROUS PLACE — Billy FURY
WONDROUS STORIES — YES
WON'T GET FOOLED AGAIN — The WHO
WON'T GIVE IN — The FINN BROTHERS
WON'T LET THIS FEELING GO — SUNDANCE
WON'T SOMEBODY DANCE WITH ME — Lynsey DE PAUL
WON'T STOP LOVING YOU — A CERTAIN RATIO
WON'T TALK ABOUT IT [A] — Billy BRAGG
WON'T TALK ABOUT IT [A] — Norman COOK
WON'T TALK ABOUT IT [A] — BEATS INTERNATIONAL
WON'T YOU HOLD MY HAND NOW — KING
WON'T YOU SAY — Christian FRY
WOO HOO — The 5.6.7.8'S
WOOD BEEZ (PRAY LIKE ARETHA FRANKLIN) — SCRITTI POLITTI
WOODEN HEART — Elvis PRESLEY (61)
WOODPECKERS FROM SPACE — The VIDEO KIDS
WOODSTOCK — MATTHEWS' SOUTHERN COMFORT (70)
WOO-HAH!! GOT YOU ALL IN CHECK — Busta RHYMES
WOOLY BULLY — SAM THE SHAM and The PHARAOHS
WOPBABALUBOP — FUNKDOOBIEST
THE WORD — DOPE SMUGGLAZ
THE WORD GIRL — SCRITTI POLITTI
A WORD IN YOUR EAR — ALFIE
THE WORD IS LOVE (SAY THE WORD) — VOICES OF LIFE
WORD IS OUT — Kylie MINOGUE
WORD LOVE — RHIANNA
WORD OF MOUTH — MIKE and The MECHANICS
WORD PERFECT — KRS ONE
WORD UP [A] — CAMEO
WORD UP [A] — GUN
WORD UP [A] — Melanie B
WORDS [A] — The ALLISONS
WORDS [B] — The BEE GEES
WORDS [B] — Rita COOLIDGE
WORDS [B] — BOYZONE (96)
WORDS [C] — FR DAVID
WORDS [D] — The CHRISTIANS
WORDS [E] — Paul VAN DYK
WORDS ARE NOT ENOUGH — STEPS
WORDS OF LOVE — The MAMAS and The PAPAS
WORDS THAT SAY — MEGA CITY FOUR
WORDS WITH THE SHAMAN — David SYLVIAN
WORDY RAPPINGHOOD [A] — TOM TOM CLUB
WORDY RAPPINGHOOD [A] — CHICKS ON SPEED
WORK [A] — TECHNOTRONIC
WORK [B] — Barrington LEVY
WORK [C] — JIMMY EAT WORLD
WORK ALL DAY — Barry BIGGS
WORK IT [A] — Missy ELLIOTT
WORK IT [B] — NELLY featuring Justin TIMBERLAKE
WORK IT OUT [A] — SHIVA
WORK IT OUT [B] — DEF LEPPARD
WORK IT OUT [C] — BEYONCÉ
WORK IT TO THE BONE — LNR
WORK IT UP — SLEAZESISTERS
WORK MI BODY — MONKEY MAFIA featuring PATRA
W.O.R.K. (N.O. NAH NO NO MY DADDY DON'T) — BOW WOW WOW
WORK REST AND PLAY (EP) — MADNESS
WORK THAT BODY — Diana ROSS
WORK THAT MAGIC — Donna SUMMER
WORK THAT SUCKER TO DEATH — XAVIER
WORK, WORK, WORK (PUB, CLUB, SLEEP) — The RAKES
WORKAHOLIC — 2 UNLIMITED
THE WORKER — FISCHER-Z
WORKIN' FOR THE MAN — Roy ORBISON
WORKIN' MY WAY BACK TO YOU — The FOUR SEASONS
WORKIN' OVERTIME — Diana ROSS
WORKIN' UP A SWEAT — FULL CIRCLE
WORKING FOR THE YANKEE DOLLAR — The SKIDS
WORKING IN A GOLDMINE — AZTEC CAMERA
WORKING IN THE COALMINE — Lee DORSEY
WORKING MAN — Rita MacNEIL
WORKING MOTHER — Martyn JOSEPH
WORKING MY WAY BACK TO YOU — FORGIVE ME GIRL (MEDLEY) — The DETROIT SPINNERS (80)
WORKING ON A BUILDING OF LOVE — CHAIRMEN OF THE BOARD
WORKING ON IT — Chris REA
WORKING WITH FIRE AND STEEL — CHINA CRISIS
WORLD — The BEE GEES
THE WORLD — Nick HEYWARD
WORLD CUP '98 — PAVANE — WIMBLEDON CHORAL SOCIETY
WORLD DESTRUCTION — TIME ZONE
WORLD FILLED WITH LOVE — Craig DAVID
WORLD IN MOTION ... — ENGLANDNEWORDER (90)
THE WORLD IN MY ARMS — Nat 'King' COLE
WORLD IN MY EYES — DEPECHE MODE
THE WORLD IN MY HANDS — SNAP! featuring SUMMER
WORLD IN UNION [A] — Kiri TE KANAWA
WORLD IN UNION [A] — Shirley BASSEY
WORLD IN UNION '95 — LADYSMITH BLACK MAMBAZO
WORLD IN YOUR HANDS — CULTURE BEAT
THE WORLD IS A GHETTO — GETO BOYS featuring FLAJ
THE WORLD IS FLAT — ECHOBELLY
THE WORLD IS MINE [A] — Malcolm VAUGHAN
THE WORLD IS MINE [B] — ICE CUBE
THE WORLD IS MINE [C] — David GUETTA featuring JD DAVIS
THE WORLD IS NOT ENOUGH — GARBAGE
THE WORLD IS STONE — Cyndi LAUPER
THE WORLD IS WHAT YOU MAKE IT — Paul BRADY
WORLD LOOKING AWAY — MORCHEEBA
WORLD OF BROKEN HEARTS — AMEN CORNER
WORLD OF GOOD — The SAW DOCTORS
A WORLD OF OUR OWN [A] — The SEEKERS
WORLD OF OUR OWN [B] — WESTLIFE (02)
WORLD ON FIRE — Sarah McLACHLAN
THE WORLD OUTSIDE [A] — Russ CONWAY
THE WORLD OUTSIDE [A] — Ronnie HILTON
THE WORLD OUTSIDE [A] — The FOUR ACES
WORLD OUTSIDE YOUR WINDOW — Tanita TIKARAM
THE WORLD SHE KNOWS — DMAC
WORLD SHUT YOUR MOUTH — Julian COPE

16 July 2005	23 July 2005	30 July 2005	6 August 2005
UK No.1 SINGLES			
GHETTO GOSPEL 2Pac (featuring Elton John)	YOU'RE BEAUTIFUL James Blunt	YOU'RE BEAUTIFUL James Blunt	YOU'RE BEAUTIFUL James Blunt
UK No.1 ALBUMS			
BACK TO BEDLAM James Blunt	BACK TO BEDLAM James Blunt	BACK TO BEDLAM James Blunt	BACK TO BEDLAM James Blunt

WORLD (THE PRICE OF LOVE) — NEW ORDER
THE WORLD TONIGHT — Paul McCARTNEY
THE WORLD WE KNEW (OVER AND OVER) — Frank SINATRA
A WORLD WITHOUT HEROES — KISS
A WORLD WITHOUT LOVE — PETER and GORDON (64)
WORLD WITHOUT YOU — Belinda CARLISLE
WORLDS APART — CACTUS WORLD NEWS
THE WORLD'S GREATEST — R KELLY
WORLD'S ON FIRE — BREED 77
WORRY ABOUT THE WIND — HAL
WORST COMES TO WORST — DILATED PEOPLES
WORZEL'S SONG — Jon PERTWEE
WOT! — CAPTAIN SENSIBLE
WOT DO U CALL IT? — WILEY
WOT'S IT TO YA — Robbie NEVIL
WOULD — ALICE IN CHAINS
WOULD I LIE TO YOU [A] — WHITESNAKE
WOULD I LIE TO YOU? [B] — EURYTHMICS
WOULD I LIE TO YOU [C] — CHARLES and EDDIE (92)
WOULD YOU ...? — TOUCH & GO
WOULD YOU BE HAPPIER? — The CORRS
WOULDN'T CHANGE A THING [A] — Kylie MINOGUE
WOULDN'T CHANGE A THING [B] — HAVEN
WOULDN'T IT BE GOOD — Nik KERSHAW
WOULDN'T IT BE NICE — The BEACH BOYS
WOULDN'T YOU LOVE TO LOVE ME — Taja SEVELLE
WOW — Kate BUSH
WOW AND FLUTTER — STEREOLAB
WOW WOW — NA NA — GRAND PLAZ
WOZ NOT WOZ — Eric PRYDZ & Steve ANGELLO
WRAP HER UP — Elton JOHN
WRAP ME UP — ALEX PARTY
WRAP MY WORDS AROUND YOU — Daniel BEDINGFIELD
WRAP MY BODY TIGHT — Johnny GILL
WRAP YOUR ARMS AROUND ME — Agnetha FALTSKOG
WRAPPED AROUND HER — Joan ARMATRADING
WRAPPED AROUND YOUR FINGER — The POLICE
WRAPPING PAPER — CREAM
WRATH CHILD — IRON MAIDEN
WRATH OF KANE — BIG DADDY KANE
WRECK OF THE ANTOINETTE — Dave DEE, DOZY, BEAKY, MICK and TICH
THE WRECK OF THE EDMUND FITZGERALD — Gordon LIGHTFOOT
THE WRECKONING — BOOMKAT
WRECKX SHOP — WRECKZ-N-EFFECT featuring APACHE INDIAN
WRENCH — The ALMIGHTY
WRESTLEMANIA — WWF SUPERSTARS
WRITING ON THE WALL — Tommy STEELE
WRITING TO REACH YOU — TRAVIS
WRITTEN IN THE STARS — Elton JOHN and LeAnn RIMES
WRITTEN ON THE WIND — Roger DALTREY
WRONG — EVERYTHING BUT THE GIRL
WRONG IMPRESSION — Natalie IMBRUGLIA
WRONG NUMBER — The CURE
WRONG OR RIGHT — SABRE featuring PRESIDENT BROWN
WUNDERBAR — TEN POLE TUDOR
WUTHERING HEIGHTS — Kate BUSH (78)
X [A] — SNOOP DOGG
X [B] — WARRIOR
X GON' GIVE IT TO YA — DMX
X RAY FOLLOW ME — SPACE FROG
X Y & ZEE — POP WILL EAT ITSELF
XANADU — Olivia NEWTON-JOHN and ELECTRIC LIGHT ORCHESTRA (80)
X-FILES [A] — DJ DADO
THE X-FILES [A] — Mark SNOW
XMAS PARTY — SNOWMEN
X-MAS TIME — DJ OTZI
XPAND YA MIND (EXPANSIONS) — WAG YA TAIL
XPRESS YOURSELF — FAMILY FOUNDATION
X-RATED — DJ NATION
X-RAY — SUB FOCUS
XX SEX — WE'VE GOT A FUZZBOX AND WE'RE GONNA USE IT
Y CONTROL — The YEAH YEAH YEAHS
Y (HOW DEEP IS YOUR LOVE) — DJ SCOT PROJECT
Y VIVA ESPAÑA — SYLVIA
Y VIVA SUSPENDERS — JUDGE DREAD
YA DON'T SEE THE SIGNS — Mark B & BLADE
YA MAMA — FATBOY SLIM
YA PLAYIN YASELF — JERU THE DAMAJA
YA YA TWIST — Petula CLARK
YAAAH — D-SHAKE
YABBA DABBA DOO — DARKMAN
YAH MO B THERE — James INGRAM with Michael McDONALD
YAKETY YAK — The COASTERS
YEAH [A] — AUDIOWEB
YEAH [B] — WANNADIES
YEAH! [C] — USHER featuring LIL' JON & LUDACRIS (04)
YEAH! BUDDY — ROYAL HOUSE
YEAH, YEAH, YEAH, YEAH, YEAH [A] — The POGUES
YEAH YEAH YEAH YEAH YEAH [B] — The WEDDING PRESENT
YEAR OF DECISION — The THREE DEGREES
YEAR OF THE CAT — Al STEWART
YEAR OF THE RAT — BADLY DRAWN BOY
YEAR 3000 — BUSTED
YEARNING FOR YOUR LOVE — The GAP BAND
YEARS FROM NOW — DR HOOK
YEARS GO BY — Stan CAMPBELL
YEARS LATER — CACTUS WORLD NEWS
YEARS MAY COME, YEARS MAY GO — HERMAN'S HERMITS
YEBO — ART OF NOISE
YEH, YEH [A] — Georgie FAME and The BLUE FLAMES (65)
YEH YEH [A] — MATT BIANCO
YEH YEH YEH — MELANIE C
YEHA-NOHA (WISHES OF HAPPINESS AND PROSPERITY) — SACRED SPIRIT
YEKE YEKE — Mory KANTE
YELLOW — COLDPLAY
YELLOW PEARL — Philip LYNOTT
YELLOW RIVER — CHRISTIE (70)
THE YELLOW ROSE OF TEXAS [A] — Ronnie HILTON
THE YELLOW ROSE OF TEXAS [A] — Gary MILLER
THE YELLOW ROSE OF TEXAS [A] — Mitch MILLER
YELLOW SUBMARINE — The BEATLES (66)
YEOVIL TRUE — YEOVIL TOWN FC
YEP — Duane EDDY and The REBELS
YER OLD — REEF
YES [A] — Merry CLAYTON
YES [B] — Bernard BUTLER
YES I DO — Shakin' STEVENS
YES I WILL — The HOLLIES
YES MY DARLING DAUGHTER — Eydie GORME
YES SIR, I CAN BOOGIE — BACCARA (77)
YES TONIGHT, JOSEPHINE [A] — Johnnie RAY (57)
YES TONIGHT JOSEPHINE [A] — JETS
YESTERDAY [A] — The BEATLES
YESTERDAY [A] — Ray CHARLES
YESTERDAY [A] — Marianne FAITHFULL
YESTERDAY [A] — Matt MONRO
YESTERDAY [A] — WET WET WET
YESTERDAY HAS GONE [A] — CUPID'S INSPIRATION
YESTERDAY HAS GONE [A] — PJ PROBY and Marc ALMOND featuring the MY LIFE STORY ORCHESTRA
YESTERDAY MAN — Chris ANDREWS
YESTERDAY ONCE MORE [A] — The CARPENTERS
YESTERDAY ONCE MORE [A] — REDD KROSS
YESTERDAY TODAY — OCEAN COLOUR SCENE
YESTERDAY WENT TOO SOON — FEEDER
YESTERDAY WHEN I WAS MAD — PET SHOP BOYS
YESTERDAYS — GUNS N' ROSES
YESTERDAY'S DREAMS — The FOUR TOPS
YESTERDAY'S GONE — Chad STUART and Jeremy CLYDE
YESTERDAY'S MEN — MADNESS
YESTER-ME, YESTER-YOU, YESTERDAY — Stevie WONDER
YET ANOTHER DAY — Armin VAN BUUREN featuring Ray WILSON
YIM — JEZ & CHOOPIE
YING TONG SONG [A] — The GOONS
YIPPIE-I-OH — BARNDANCE BOYS
Y.M.C.A. — VILLAGE PEOPLE (79)
YO!! SWEETNESS — HAMMER
YO YO GET FUNKY — DJ 'FAST' EDDIE
THE YODELLING SONG — Frank IFIELD
YOSHIMI BATTLES THE PINK ROBOTS PT.1 — The FLAMING LIPS
YOU [A] — Johnny JOHNSON and The BANDWAGON
YOU [B] — George HARRISON
YOU [C] — Randy EDELMAN
YOU [D] — TEN SHARP
YOU [E] — Bonnie RAITT
YOU [F] — STAXX featuring Carol LEEMING
YOU [G] — POINT BREAK
YOU [H] — S CLUB 7
YOU [I] — Shaznay LEWIS
YOU [J] — THEE UNSTRUNG
YOU (EP) — FIVE THIRTY
YOU AIN'T GOING NOWHERE — The BYRDS
YOU AIN'T LIVIN' TILL YOU'RE LOVIN' — Marvin GAYE
YOU AIN'T REALLY DOWN — STATUS IV
YOU AIN'T SEEN NOTHIN' YET [A] — BUS STOP
YOU AIN'T SEEN NOTHING YET [A] — BACHMAN-TURNER OVERDRIVE
YOU ALL DAT — BAHA MEN
YOU ALWAYS HURT THE ONE YOU LOVE [A] — Connie FRANCIS
YOU ALWAYS HURT THE ONE YOU LOVE [A] — Clarence 'Frogman' HENRY
YOU AND I [A] — Rick JAMES
YOU AND I [B] — Will YOUNG
YOU AND I WILL NEVER SEE THINGS EYE TO EYE — KINGMAKER
YOU AND ME [A] — LINER
YOU AND ME [B] — DJ SEDUCTION
YOU AND ME [C] — Lisa B
YOU AND ME [C] — EASYWORLD
YOU + ME [D] — TECHNIQUE
YOU AND ME [E] — UNITING NATIONS
YOU AND ME SONG — The WANNADIES
YOU AND ME TONIGHT [A] — AURRA
YOU AND ME (TONIGHT) [B] — Alistair GRIFFIN
YOU AND YOUR HEART SO BLUE — BUCKS FIZZ
YOU ANGEL YOU — MANFRED MANN
YOU ARE — Lionel RICHIE
YOU ARE ALIVE — FRAGMA
YOU ARE AWFUL — Dick EMERY
YOU ARE BEAUTIFUL — Johnny MATHIS
YOU ARE EVERYTHING [A] — The PEARLS
YOU ARE EVERYTHING [A] — Diana ROSS and Marvin GAYE
YOU ARE EVERYTHING [A] — Melanie WILLIAMS and Joe ROBERTS
YOU ARE IN MY SYSTEM — Robert PALMER
YOU ARE MY DESTINY — Paul ANKA
YOU ARE MY FIRST LOVE — Ruby MURRAY
YOU ARE MY HIGH — DEMON vs HEARTBREAKER
YOU ARE MY LADY — Freddie JACKSON
YOU ARE MY LOVE — LIVERPOOL EXPRESS
YOU ARE MY MELODY — CHANGE
YOU ARE MY SISTER — ANTONY & The JOHNSONS
YOU ARE MY WORLD — The COMMUNARDS
YOU ARE NOT ALONE — Michael JACKSON (95)
YOU ARE SOMEBODY — FULL INTENTION
YOU ARE THE GENERATION THAT BOUGHT MORE SHOES AND YOU GET WHAT YOU DESERVE — JOHNNY BOY
YOU ARE THE ONE — A-HA
YOU ARE THE SUNSHINE OF MY LIFE — Stevie WONDER
YOU ARE THE UNIVERSE — The BRAND NEW HEAVIES
YOU ARE THE WAY — The PRIMITIVES
YOU ARE THE WEAKEST LINK — ECHOBASS
YOU BE ILLIN' — RUN-DMC
YOU BELONG IN ROCK 'N' ROLL — TIN MACHINE
YOU BELONG TO ME [A] — Jo STAFFORD (53)
YOU BELONG TO ME [B] — Gary GLITTER
YOU BELONG TO ME [C] — JX
YOU BELONG TO ME [D] — Michael MOOG
YOU BET YOUR LOVE — Herbie HANCOCK
YOU BETTER — MOUNT RUSHMORE presents The KNACK
YOU BETTER COME HOME — Petula CLARK
YOU BETTER YOU BET — The WHO
YOU BLOW ME AWAY — Robert PALMER
YOU BRING ME JOY [A] — MEECHIE
YOU BRING ME JOY [B] — RHYTHM FACTOR
YOU BRING ME UP — K-CI & JOJO
YOU BRING ON THE SUN — LONDONBEAT
YOU BROKE MY HEART — LOVE BITES
YOU CAME — Kim WILDE
YOU CAME, YOU SAW, YOU CONQUERED — The PEARLS
YOU CAN CALL ME AL — Paul SIMON
YOU CAN COUNT ON ME — Jaki GRAHAM
YOU CAN DANCE (IF YOU WANT TO) — GO GO LORENZO and The DAVIS PINCKNEY PROJECT
YOU CAN DO IT [A] — Al HUDSON
YOU CAN DO IT [B] — ICE CUBE featuring MACK 10 + MS TOI
YOU CAN DO MAGIC [A] — LIMMIE and The FAMILY COOKIN'
YOU CAN DO MAGIC [B] — AMERICA
YOU CAN GET IT — MAXX
YOU CAN GET IT IF YOU REALLY WANT — Desmond DEKKER and The ACES
YOU CAN GO YOUR OWN WAY — Chris REA
YOU CAN HAVE HIM — Dionne WARWICK
YOU CAN HAVE IT ALL [A] — George McCRAE
YOU CAN HAVE IT ALL [B] — Eve GALLAGHER
YOU CAN HAVE IT (TAKE MY HEART) — Robert PALMER
YOU CAN LOVE ME NOW — HOTHOUSE FLOWERS
YOU CAN MAKE ME DANCE SING OR ANYTHING (EVEN TAKE THE DOG FOR A WALK, MEND A FUSE, FOLD AWAY THE IRONING BOARD, OR ANY OTHER DOMESTIC SHORT COMINGS) — The FACES / Rod STEWART
YOU CAN NEVER STOP ME LOVING YOU — Kenny LYNCH
YOU CAN TALK TO ME — The SEAHORSES
YOU CAN WIN IF YOU WANT — MODERN TALKING
YOU CAN'T BE TRUE TO TWO — Dave KING
YOU CAN'T BLAME LOVE — THOMAS and TAYLOR
YOU CAN'T CHANGE ME — Roger SANCHEZ featuring Armand VAN HELDEN and N'Dea DAVENPORT
YOU CAN'T FOOL ME DENNIS — MYSTERY JETS
YOU CAN'T GO HOME AGAIN — DJ SHADOW
YOU CAN'T HIDE (YOUR LOVE FROM ME) — David JOSEPH
YOU CAN'T HURRY LOVE [A] — The SUPREMES
YOU CAN'T HURRY LOVE [A] — Phil COLLINS (83)
YOU CAN'T HURRY LOVE [B] — The CONCRETES
YOU CAN'T RUN FROM LOVE — Maxine SINGLETON
YOU CAN'T SIT DOWN — Phil UPCHURCH COMBO
YOU CAN'T STEAL MY LOVE — MANDO DIAO
YOU CAN'T STOP ROCK 'N' ROLL — TWISTED SISTER
YOU CAN'T STOP THE REIGN — Shaquille O'NEAL
YOU CAUGHT MY EYE — Judy BOUCHER
YOU COME FROM EARTH — Lena FIAGBE
YOU COME THROUGH — PJ HARVEY
YOU COULD BE MINE — GUNS N' ROSES
YOU COULD BE MY EVERYTHING — Mikey GRAHAM
YOU COULD HAVE BEEN A LADY — HOT CHOCOLATE
YOU COULD HAVE BEEN WITH ME — Sheena EASTON
YOU DID CUT ME — CHINA CRISIS
YOU DIDN'T EXPECT THAT — Billy CRAWFORD
YOU DISAPPEAR FROM VIEW — The TEARDROP EXPLODES
YOU DO — Bernard BUTLER
YOU DO SOMETHING TO ME [A] — Paul WELLER
YOU DO SOMETHING TO ME [B] — DUM DUMS
YOU DON'T BELIEVE ME — The STRAY CATS
YOU DON'T BRING ME FLOWERS — Barbra STREISAND
YOU DON'T CARE ABOUT US — PLACEBO
YOU DON'T FOOL ME — QUEEN
YOU DON'T HAVE TO BE A BABY TO CRY — The CARAVELLES

13 August 2005	20 August 2005	27 August 2005	3 September 2005
YOU'RE BEAUTIFUL James Blunt	**YOU'RE BEAUTIFUL** James Blunt	**I'LL BE OK** McFly	**THE IMPORTANCE OF BEING IDLE** Oasis
BACK TO BEDLAM James Blunt	**BACK TO BEDLAM** James Blunt	**BACK TO BEDLAM** James Blunt	**BACK TO BEDLAM** James Blunt

YOU DON'T HAVE TO BE A STAR (TO BE IN MY SHOW) — Marilyn McCOO and Billy DAVIS Jr
YOU DON'T HAVE TO BE IN THE ARMY TO FIGHT IN THE WAR — MUNGO JERRY
YOU DON'T HAVE TO GO — The CHI-LITES
YOU DON'T HAVE TO SAY YOU LOVE ME [A] — Dusty SPRINGFIELD (66)
YOU DON'T HAVE TO SAY YOU LOVE ME [A] — Elvis PRESLEY
YOU DON'T HAVE TO SAY YOU LOVE ME [A] — GUYS 'n' DOLLS
YOU DON'T HAVE TO SAY YOU LOVE ME [A] — Denise WELCH
YOU DON'T HAVE TO WORRY — Mary J BLIGE
YOU DON'T KNOW [A] — Helen SHAPIRO (61)
YOU DON'T KNOW [B] — BERLIN
YOU DON'T KNOW [C] — Cyndi LAUPER
YOU DON'T KNOW [D] — MASS SYNDICATE featuring Su Su BOBIEN
YOU DON'T KNOW [E] — 702
(YOU DON'T KNOW) HOW GLAD I AM — Kiki DEE
YOU DON'T KNOW ME [A] — Ray CHARLES
YOU DON'T KNOW ME [B] — Armand VAN HELDEN featuring Duane HARDEN (99)
YOU DON'T KNOW MY NAME — Alicia KEYS
YOU DON'T KNOW NOTHIN' — FOR REAL
YOU DON'T KNOW (OH-OH-OH) — SERIOUS INTENTION
YOU DON'T KNOW WHAT YOU'VE GOT (UNTIL YOU LOSE IT) — Ral DONNER
YOU DON'T LOVE ME [A] — Gary WALKER
YOU DON'T LOVE ME [B] — MARILYN
YOU DON'T LOVE ME [C] — JAGGED EDGE
YOU DON'T LOVE ME (NO, NO, NO) — Dawn PENN
YOU DON'T MISS YOUR WATER ('TIL THE WELL RUNS DRY) — Craig DAVID
YOU DON'T NEED A REASON — Phil FEARON
YOU DON'T NEED SOMEONE NEW — LOTUS EATERS
YOU DON'T OWE ME A THING — Johnnie RAY
YOU DON'T UNDERSTAND — HOUSE OF LOVE
YOU DON'T UNDERSTAND ME — ROXETTE
YOU DREAMER — BIG COUNTRY
YOU DRIVE ME CRAZY [A] — Shakin' STEVENS
(YOU DRIVE ME) CRAZY [B] — Britney SPEARS
YOU DRIVE ME CRAZY [B] — SUGARCOMA
YOU DROVE ME TO IT — HELL IS FOR HEROES
YOU GAVE ME LOVE — CROWN HEIGHTS AFFAIR
YOU GAVE ME SOMEBODY TO LOVE — MANFRED MANN
YOU GET THE BEST FROM ME (SAY, SAY, SAY) — Alicia MYERS
YOU GET WHAT YOU GIVE — NEW RADICALS
YOU GIVE LOVE A BAD NAME — BON JOVI
YOU GIVE ME SOMETHING — JAMIROQUAI
YOU GO TO MY HEAD — Bryan FERRY
YOU GONNA WANT ME — TIGA
YOU GOT IT — Roy ORBISON
YOU GOT IT (THE RIGHT STUFF) — NEW KIDS ON THE BLOCK (89)
YOU GOT ME [A] — Christian FRY
YOU GOT ME [B] — ROOTS featuring Erykah BADU
YOU GOT ME BURNING [A] — Lenny WILLIAMS
YOU GOT ME BURNING [B] — PESHAY featuring CO-ORDINATE
(YOU GOT ME) BURNING UP — Cevin FISHER / Loleatta HOLLOWAY
YOU GOT ME ROCKING — The ROLLING STONES
YOU GOT NOTHING ON ME — The GLITTERATI
YOU GOT SOUL — Johnny NASH
YOU GOT THE FLOOR — Arthur ADAMS
YOU GOT THE LOVE [A] — The SOURCE featuring Candi STATON
YOU GOT THE LOVE [B] — Robin S
YOU GOT THE POWER [A] — WAR
YOU GOT THE POWER [B] — QFX
YOU GOT THE STYLE — ATHLETE
YOU GOT TO BE THERE — KADOC
YOU GOT WHAT IT TAKES [A] — Marv JOHNSON
YOU GOT WHAT IT TAKES [A] — Johnny KIDD and The PIRATES
YOU GOT WHAT IT TAKES [A] — The Dave CLARK FIVE
YOU GOT WHAT IT TAKES [A] — SHOWADDYWADDY
YOU GOTTA BE — DES'REE
YOU GOTTA BE A HUSTLER IF YOU WANNA GET ON — Sue WILKINSON
YOU GOTTA BELIEVE — MARKY MARK and The FUNKY BUNCH
(YOU GOTTA) FIGHT FOR YOUR RIGHT (TO PARTY) — BEASTIE BOYS
YOU GOTTA HAVE LOVE IN YOUR HEART — The SUPREMES and The FOUR TOPS
YOU GOTTA LOVE SOMEONE — Elton JOHN
YOU GOTTA STOP — Elvis PRESLEY
(YOU GOTTA WALK) DON'T LOOK BACK — Peter TOSH
YOU HAD ME — Joss STONE
YOU HAVE — Marc ALMOND
YOU HAVE BEEN LOVED — George MICHAEL
YOU HAVE PLACED A CHILL IN MY HEART — EURYTHMICS
YOU HAVEN'T DONE NOTHIN' — Stevie WONDER
YOU HELD THE WORLD IN YOUR ARMS — IDLEWILD
YOU JUST MIGHT SEE ME CRY — OUR KID
YOU KEEP IT ALL IN — The BEAUTIFUL SOUTH
YOU KEEP ME HANGIN' ON [A] — The SUPREMES
YOU KEEP ME HANGIN' ON [A] — VANILLA FUDGE
YOU KEEP ME HANGIN' ON [A] — Kim WILDE
YOU KEEP ME HANGIN' ON [A] - STOP IN THE NAME OF LOVE — Roni HILL
(YOU KEEP ME) HANGIN' ON [B] — Cliff RICHARD
YOU KEEP RUNNING AWAY — The FOUR TOPS
YOU KNOW HOW TO LOVE ME — Phyllis HYMAN
YOU KNOW HOW WE DO IT — ICE CUBE
YOU KNOW I LOVE YOU ... DON'T YOU? — Howard JONES
YOU KNOW THAT I LOVE YOU — Donell JONES
YOU KNOW WHAT I MEAN — VERNONS GIRLS
(YOU KNOW) YOU CAN DO IT — CENTRAL LINE
YOU KNOWS I LOVES YOU BABY — GOLDIE LOOKIN CHAIN
YOU LAY SO EASY ON MY MIND — Andy WILLIAMS
YOU LEARN — Alanis MORISSETTE
YOU LET YOUR HEART GO TOO FAST — SPIN DOCTORS
YOU LIED TO ME — Cathy DENNIS
YOU LIFT ME UP — Rebekah RYAN
YOU LIGHT MY FIRE — Sheila B DEVOTION
YOU LIGHT UP MY LIFE — Debby BOONE
YOU LIKE ME DON'T YOU — Jermaine JACKSON
YOU LITTLE FOOL — Elvis COSTELLO
YOU LITTLE THIEF — Feargal SHARKEY
YOU LITTLE TRUSTMAKER — The TYMES
YOU LOOK SO FINE — GARBAGE
YOU LOVE US — MANIC STREET PREACHERS
YOU LOVE YOU — SUBCIRCUS
YOU MADE ME BELIEVE IN MAGIC — BAY CITY ROLLERS
YOU MADE ME LOVE YOU — Nat 'King' COLE
YOU MADE ME THE THIEF OF YOUR HEART — Sinead O'CONNOR
YOU MAKE IT HEAVEN — Terri WELLS
YOU MAKE IT MOVE — Dave DEE, DOZY, BEAKY, MICK and TICH
YOU MAKE LOVING FUN — FLEETWOOD MAC
YOU MAKE ME FEEL BRAND NEW [A] — The STYLISTICS
YOU MAKE ME FEEL BRAND NEW [A] — SIMPLY RED
(YOU MAKE ME FEEL LIKE A) NATURAL WOMAN — Mary J BLIGE
YOU MAKE ME FEEL LIKE DANCING [A] — Leo SAYER
YOU MAKE ME FEEL LIKE DANCING [A] — GROOVE GENERATION featuring Leo SAYER
YOU MAKE ME FEEL (MIGHTY REAL) [A] — SYLVESTER
YOU MAKE ME FEEL (MIGHTY REAL) [A] — Jimmy SOMERVILLE
YOU MAKE ME FEEL MIGHTY REAL [A] — DREAM FREQUENCY
YOU MAKE ME FEEL (MIGHTY REAL) [A] — Byron STINGILY
YOU MAKE ME GO OOOH — Kristine BLOND
YOU MAKE ME SICK — PINK
YOU MAKE ME WANNA ... — USHER (98)
YOU MAKE ME WANT TO SCREAM — DANDYS
YOU MAKE ME WORK — CAMEO
YOU MAKE NO BONES — ALFIE
YOU ME AND US — Alma COGAN
YOU MEAN EVERYTHING TO ME — Neil SEDAKA
YOU MEAN THE WORLD TO ME — Toni BRAXTON
YOU MIGHT NEED SOMEBODY [A] — Randy CRAWFORD
YOU MIGHT NEED SOMEBODY [A] — Shola AMA
YOU MUST BE PREPARED TO DREAM — Ian McNABB
YOU MUST GO ON — Bernard BUTLER
YOU MUST HAVE BEEN A BEAUTIFUL BABY — Bobby DARIN
YOU MUST LOVE ME — MADONNA
YOU MY LOVE — Frank SINATRA
YOU NEED HANDS — Max BYGRAVES
YOU NEED LOVE LIKE I DO — Tom JONES and Heather SMALL
YOU NEED WHEELS — MERTON PARKAS
YOU NEEDED ME [A] — Anne MURRAY
YOU NEEDED ME [A] — BOYZONE (99)
YOU NEVER CAN TELL — Chuck BERRY
YOU NEVER DONE IT LIKE THAT — CAPTAIN and TENNILLE
YOU NEVER KNOW — MARLY
YOU NEVER KNOW WHAT YOU'VE GOT — ME AND YOU featuring WE THE PEOPLE BAND
YOU NEVER LOVE THE SAME WAY TWICE — ROZALLA
YOU ON MY MIND — SWING OUT SISTER
YOU ONLY LIVE TWICE — Nancy SINATRA
YOU ONLY TELL ME YOU LOVE ME WHEN YOU'RE DRUNK — PET SHOP BOYS
YOU ONLY YOU — Rita PAVONE
YOU OUGHTA KNOW — Alanis MORISSETTE
YOU OWE IT ALL TO ME — TEXAS
YOU PLAYED YOURSELF — ICE-T
YOU + ME = LOVE — UNDISPUTED TRUTH
YOU PUT ME IN HEAVEN WITH YOUR TOUCH — RHYTHM OF LIFE
YOU RAISE ME UP [A] — Daniel O'DONNELL
YOU RAISE ME UP [A] — WESTLIFE (05)
YOU REALLY GOT ME — The KINKS (64)
YOU REMIND ME — Mary J BLIGE
YOU REMIND ME OF SOMETHING — R KELLY
YOU ROCK MY WORLD — Michael JACKSON
YOU SAID NO — BUSTED (03)
(YOU SAID) YOU'D GIMME SOME MORE — KC and The SUNSHINE BAND
YOU SCARE ME TO DEATH — T. REX
YOU SEE THE TROUBLE WITH ME [A] — Barry WHITE
YOU SEE THE TROUBLE WITH ME [A] — BLACK LEGEND (00)
YOU SEND ME [A] — Sam COOKE
YOU SEND ME [A] — Rod STEWART
YOU SENT ME FLYING — Amy WINEHOUSE
YOU SEXY DANCER — ROCKFORD FILES
YOU SEXY SUGAR PLUM (BUT I LIKE IT) — Rodger COLLINS
YOU SEXY THING [A] — HOT CHOCOLATE
YOU SEXY THING [A] — T-SHIRT
YOU SHOOK ME ALL NIGHT LONG — AC/DC
YOU SHOULD BE [A] — BLOCKSTER
YOU SHOULD BE DANCING [A] — The BEE GEES
YOU SHOULD BE MINE — Brian McKNIGHT
YOU SHOULD HAVE KNOWN BETTER — TC CURTIS
YOU SHOULD REALLY KNOW — PIRATES featuring ENYA, Shola AMA, Naila BOSS & ISHANI
YOU SHOWED ME [A] — SALT-N-PEPA
YOU SHOWED ME [A] — The LIGHTNING SEEDS
YOU SPIN ME ROUND (LIKE A RECORD) — DEAD OR ALIVE (85)
YOU STILL TOUCH ME — STING
YOU STOLE THE SUN FROM MY HEART — MANIC STREET PREACHERS
YOU STOOD UP — V
YOU SURE LOOK GOOD TO ME — Phyllis HYMAN
YOU SURROUND ME — ERASURE
YOU TAKE ME AWAY — REEL
YOU TAKE ME UP — THOMPSON TWINS
YOU TAKE MY BREATH AWAY [A] — SUREAL
YOU TAKE MY BREATH AWAY [B] — Eva CASSIDY
YOU TAKE MY HEART AWAY — De Etta LITTLE and Nelson PIGFORD
YOU TALK TOO MUCH — SULTANS OF PING
YOU THINK YOU OWN ME — Hinda HICKS
YOU THINK YOU'RE A MAN — DIVINE
YOU TO ME ARE EVERYTHING [A] — The REAL THING (76)
YOU TO ME ARE EVERYTHING [A] — SONIA
YOU TO ME ARE EVERYTHING [A] — Sean MAGUIRE
YOU TO ME ARE EVERYTHING (THE DECADE REMIX 76-86) [A] — The REAL THING
YOU TOOK THE WORDS RIGHT OUT OF MY MOUTH — MEAT LOAF
YOU TRIP ME UP — JESUS AND MARY CHAIN
YOU USED TO HOLD ME — SCOTT & LEON
YOU USED TO HOLD ME SO TIGHT — Thelma HOUSTON
YOU USED TO LOVE ME — Faith EVANS
YOU USED TO SALSA — Richie RICH
YOU WANNA KNOW — THUNDER
YOU WANT IT, YOU GOT IT — The DETROIT EMERALDS
YOU WANT THIS — Janet JACKSON
YOU WEAR IT WELL [A] — Rod STEWART (72)
YOU WEAR IT WELL [B] — DeBARGE
YOU WERE ALWAYS THE ONE — The CRIBS
(YOU WERE MADE FOR) ALL MY LOVE — Jackie WILSON
YOU WERE MADE FOR ME — FREDDIE and The DREAMERS
YOU WERE MEANT FOR ME — JEWEL
YOU WERE RIGHT — BADLY DRAWN BOY
YOU WERE ON MY MIND — Crispian ST PETERS
YOU WERE THE LAST HIGH — DANDY WARHOLS
YOU WERE THERE — HEINZ
YOU WEREN'T IN LOVE WITH ME — Billy FIELD
YOU WEREN'T THERE — Lene MARLIN
YOU WILL RISE — SWEETBACK
YOU WILL YOU WON'T ... — The ZUTONS
YOU WIN AGAIN — The BEE GEES (87)
YOU WOKE UP MY NEIGHBOURHOOD — Billy BRAGG
YOU WON'T BE LEAVING — HERMAN'S HERMITS
YOU WON'T FIND ANOTHER FOOL LIKE ME — The NEW SEEKERS featuring Lyn PAUL (74)
YOU WON'T FORGET ABOUT ME — Dannii MINOGUE vs FLOWER POWER
YOU WON'T SEE ME CRY — WILSON PHILLIPS
YOU WOULDN'T KNOW LOVE — CHER
YOU YOU ROMEO — Shirley BASSEY
YOU YOU YOU — Alvin STARDUST
YOU'LL ALWAYS BE A FRIEND — HOT CHOCOLATE
YOU'LL ALWAYS FIND ME IN THE KITCHEN AT PARTIES — Jona LEWIE
YOU'LL ANSWER TO ME — Cleo LAINE
YOU'LL BE IN MY HEART — Phil COLLINS
YOU'LL BE MINE (PARTY TIME) — Gloria ESTEFAN
YOU'LL BE SORRY — STEPS
YOU'LL COME 'ROUND — STATUS QUO
YOU'LL NEVER BE ALONE — ANASTACIA
YOU'LL NEVER BE SO WRONG — HOT CHOCOLATE
YOU'LL NEVER FIND ANOTHER LOVE LIKE MINE — Lou RAWLS
YOU'LL NEVER GET TO HEAVEN — Dionne WARWICK
YOU'LL NEVER GET TO HEAVEN (EP) — The STYLISTICS
YOU'LL NEVER KNOW [A] — Shirley BASSEY
YOU'LL NEVER KNOW [B] — HI GLOSS
YOU'LL NEVER KNOW WHAT YOU'RE MISSING — The REAL THING
YOU'LL NEVER KNOW WHAT YOU'RE MISSING ('TIL YOU TRY) — Emile FORD and The CHECKMATES
YOU'LL NEVER NEVER KNOW — The PLATTERS
YOU'LL NEVER STOP ME LOVING YOU — SONIA (89)
YOU'LL NEVER WALK ALONE [A] — Gerry and The PACEMAKERS (63)
YOU'LL NEVER WALK ALONE [A] — Elvis PRESLEY
YOU'LL NEVER WALK ALONE [A] — The CROWD (85)
YOU'LL NEVER WALK ALONE [A] — ROBSON & JEROME (96)
YOU'LL NEVER WALK ALONE [A] — José CARRERAS, Placido DOMINGO and Luciano PAVAROTTI with MEHTA

10 September 2005	17 September 2005	24 September 2005	1 October 2005
UK No.1 SINGLES			
DARE Gorillaz	DON'T CHA Pussycat Dolls featuring Busta Rhymes	DON'T CHA Pussycat Dolls featuring Busta Rhymes	DON'T CHA Pussycat Dolls featuring Busta Rhymes
UK No.1 ALBUMS			
WONDERLAND McFly	BACK TO BEDLAM James Blunt	LIFE IN SLOW MOTION David Gray	LIFE IN SLOW MOTION David Gray

YOU'LL SEE — MADONNA
YOUNG AGAIN — SHINING
YOUNG AMERICANS — David BOWIE
YOUNG AMERICANS TALKING — David VAN DAY
YOUNG AND FOOLISH [A] — Ronnie HILTON
YOUNG AND FOOLISH [A] — Edmund HOCKRIDGE
YOUNG AND FOOLISH [A] — Dean MARTIN
THE YOUNG AND THE HOPELESS — GOOD CHARLOTTE
YOUNG AT HEART [A] — Frank SINATRA
YOUNG AT HEART [B] — The BLUEBELLS (93)
YOUNG BLOOD — UFO
YOUNG BOY — Paul McCARTNEY
YOUNG DISCIPLES (EP) — YOUNG DISCIPLES
YOUNG EMOTIONS — Ricky NELSON
YOUNG, FREE AND SINGLE — SUNFIRE
YOUNG FRESH N' NEW — KELIS
YOUNG, GIFTED AND BLACK — BOB and MARCIA
YOUNG GIRL [A] — UNION GAP featuring Gary PUCKETT (68)
YOUNG GIRL [A] — Darren DAY
YOUNG GIRL [A] — Joe LONGTHORNE
YOUNG GIRLS & HAPPY ENDINGS — GORKY'S ZYGOTIC MYNCI
YOUNG GODS — LITTLE ANGELS
YOUNG GUNS (GO FOR IT) — WHAM!
YOUNG HEARTS [A] — KINGS OF TOMORROW
YOUNG HEARTS [B] — KUJAY DADA
YOUNG HEARTS RUN FREE [A] — Candi STATON
YOUNG HEARTS RUN FREE [A] — Kym MAZELLE
YOUNG LIVERS — ROCKET FROM THE CRYPT
YOUNG LOVE [A] — Tab HUNTER (57)
YOUNG LOVE [A] — Sonny JAMES
YOUNG LOVE [A] — Donny OSMOND (73)
YOUNG LOVERS — PAUL and PAULA
THE YOUNG MC — SUPERFUNK
THE YOUNG NEW MEXICAN PUPPETEER — Tom JONES
THE YOUNG OFFENDER'S MUM — CARTER — THE UNSTOPPABLE SEX MACHINE
THE YOUNG ONES — Cliff RICHARD and The SHADOWS (62)
YOUNG PARISIANS — ADAM and The ANTS
YOUNG SOUL REBELS — Mica PARIS
YOUNG TURKS — Rod STEWART
YOUNG WORLD — Ricky NELSON
YOUNGER GIRL — The CRITTERS
YOUR BABY AIN'T YOUR BABY ANYMORE — Paul DA VINCI
YOUR BABY'S GONE SURFIN' — Duane EDDY and The REBELS
YOUR BODY — Tom NOVY featuring Michael MARSHALL
YOUR BODY'S CALLIN' — R KELLY
YOUR CARESS (ALL I NEED) — DJ FLAVOURS
YOUR CASSETTE PET (EP) — BOW WOW WOW
YOUR CHEATING HEART — Ray CHARLES
YOUR CHRISTMAS WISH — The SMURFS
YOUR DREAM — Adrian GURVITZ
YOUR DRESS — John FOXX
YOUR EARS SHOULD BE BURNING NOW — Marti WEBB
YOUR EYES [A] — SIMPLY RED
YOUR EYES [B] — RIK ROK featuring SHAGGY
YOUR FACE — SLACKER
YOUR FASCINATION — Gary NUMAN
YOUR FAVORITE THING — SUGAR
YOUR GAME — Will YOUNG
YOUR GENERATION — GENERATION X
YOUR GHOST — Kristin HERSH
YOUR HONOUR — Pluto SHERVINGTON
YOUR HURTIN' KIND OF LOVE — Dusty SPRINGFIELD
YOUR KISS IS SWEET — SYREETA
YOUR KISSES ARE CHARITY — CULTURE CLUB
YOUR LATEST TRICK — DIRE STRAITS
YOUR LOSS MY GAIN — OMAR
YOUR LOVE [A] — HIPSWAY
YOUR LOVE [B] — Frankie KNUCKLES
YOUR LOVE [C] — Diana ROSS
YOUR LOVE [D] — INNER CITY
YOUR LOVE GETS SWEETER — Finley QUAYE
(YOUR LOVE HAS LIFTED ME) HIGHER AND HIGHER — Rita COOLIDGE
YOUR LOVE IS A 187 — WHITEHEAD BROS
YOUR LOVE IS CALLING — EVOLUTION
YOUR LOVE IS KING — SADE
YOUR LOVE IS LIFTING ME — NOMAD
(YOUR LOVE KEEPS LIFTING ME) HIGHER AND HIGHER — Jackie WILSON
YOUR LOVE TAKES ME HIGHER — The BELOVED
YOUR LOVING ARMS — Billie Ray MARTIN
YOUR LUCKY DAY IN HELL — EELS
YOUR MA SAID YOU CRIED IN YOUR SLEEP LAST NIGHT — Doug SHELDON
YOUR MAGIC PUT A SPELL ON ME — LJ JOHNSON
YOUR MAMA DON'T DANCE — POISON
YOUR MAMMA WON'T LIKE ME — Suzi QUATRO
YOUR MIRROR — SIMPLY RED
YOUR MISSUS IS A NUTTER — GOLDIE LOOKIN CHAIN
YOUR MOTHER'S GOT A PENIS — GOLDIE LOOKIN CHAIN
YOUR MUSIC — INTENSO PROJECT featuring Laura JAYE
YOUR NEW CUCKOO — The CARDIGANS
YOUR OWN RELIGION — ALFIE
YOUR OWN SPECIAL WAY — GENESIS
YOUR PAINTED SMILE — Bryan FERRY
YOUR PERSONAL TOUCH — Evelyn 'Champagne' KING
YOUR PLACE OR MINE — CHOCOLATE MONDAY
YOUR SECRET LOVE — Luther VANDROSS
YOUR SMILE — OCTOPUS
YOUR SONG [A] — Elton JOHN
YOUR SONG [A] — Billy PAUL
YOUR SONG [A] — Rod STEWART
YOUR SWAYING ARMS — DEACON BLUE
YOUR TENDER LOOK — Joe BROWN and The BRUVVERS
YOUR TIME HASN'T COME YET BABY — Elvis PRESLEY
YOUR TIME IS GONNA COME — DREAD ZEPPELIN
YOUR TOWN — DEACON BLUE
YOUR WOMAN [A] — WHITE TOWN (97)
YOUR WOMAN [A] — Tyler JAMES
YOU'RE A BETTER MAN THAN I — SHAM 69
YOU'RE A LADY — Peter SKELLERN
YOU'RE A STAR — AQUARIAN DREAM
YOU'RE A SUPERSTAR — LOVE INC.
YOU'RE ALL I NEED — MÖTLEY CRÜE
YOU'RE ALL I NEED TO GET BY [A] — Marvin GAYE
YOU'RE ALL I NEED TO GET BY [A] — Johnny MATHIS and Deniece WILLIAMS
YOU'RE ALL THAT MATTERS TO ME — Curtis STIGERS
YOU'RE BEAUTIFUL — James BLUNT (05)
YOU'RE BREAKIN' MY HEART — Keely SMITH
YOU'RE DRIVING ME CRAZY — The TEMPERANCE SEVEN (61)
YOU'RE EVERYTHING TO ME — Boris GARDINER
(YOU'RE) FABULOUS BABE — Kenny WILLIAMS
YOU'RE FREE — YOMANDA
YOU'RE FREE TO GO — Jim REEVES
YOU'RE GONE — MARILLION
YOU'RE GONNA GET NEXT TO ME — Bo KIRKLAND and Ruth DAVIS
YOU'RE GONNA LOSE US — The CRIBS
YOU'RE GONNA MISS ME — TURNTABLE ORCHESTRA
YOU'RE GORGEOUS — BABYBIRD
(YOU'RE) HAVING MY BABY — Paul ANKA
YOU'RE HISTORY — SHAKESPEAR'S SISTER
YOU'RE IN A BAD WAY — SAINT ETIENNE
YOU'RE IN LOVE — WILSON PHILLIPS
YOU'RE IN MY HEART [A] — Rod STEWART
YOU'RE IN MY HEART [B] — David ESSEX
YOU'RE INVITED (BUT YOUR FRIEND CAN'T COME) — Vince NEIL
YOU'RE LOOKING HOT TONIGHT — Barry MANILOW
YOU'RE LYING — LINX
YOU'RE MAKIN' ME HIGH — Toni BRAXTON
YOU'RE MORE THAN A NUMBER IN MY LITTLE RED BOOK — The DRIFTERS
YOU'RE MOVING OUT TODAY — Carole Bayer SAGER
YOU'RE MY ANGEL — Mikey GRAHAM
YOU'RE MY BEST FRIEND [A] — QUEEN
YOU'RE MY BEST FRIEND [B] — Don WILLIAMS
YOU'RE MY EVERYTHING [A] — The TEMPTATIONS
YOU'RE MY EVERYTHING [B] — Max BYGRAVES
YOU'RE MY EVERYTHING [C] — EAST SIDE BEAT
YOU'RE MY EVERYTHING [C] — Lee GARRETT
YOU'RE MY GIRL — ROCKIN' BERRIES
YOU'RE MY HEART, YOU'RE MY SOUL — MODERN TALKING
YOU'RE MY LAST CHANCE — 52ND STREET
YOU'RE MY LIFE — Barry BIGGS
YOU'RE MY MATE — RIGHT SAID FRED
YOU'RE MY NUMBER ONE — S CLUB 7
(YOU'RE MY ONE AND ONLY) TRUE LOVE — Ann-Marie SMITH
(YOU'RE MY) SOUL AND INSPIRATION — The RIGHTEOUS BROTHERS
YOU'RE MY WORLD [A] — Cilla BLACK (64)
YOU'RE MY WORLD [B] — Nick HEYWARD
YOU'RE NEVER TOO YOUNG — COOLNOTES
YOU'RE NO GOOD [A] — SWINGING BLUE JEANS
YOU'RE NO GOOD [B] — ASWAD
YOU'RE NOT ALONE [A] — OLIVE (97)
YOU'RE NOT ALONE [B] — EMBRACE
YOU'RE NOT HERE — TYRREL CORPORATION
YOU'RE OK [A] — OTTAWAN
YOU'RE OK [B] — kd LANG
YOU'RE ONE — IMPERIAL TEEN
(YOU'RE PUTTIN') A RUSH ON ME — Stephanie MILLS
YOU'RE READY NOW — Frankie VALLI
YOU'RE SHINING — STYLES & BREEZE
YOU'RE SINGING OUR LOVE SONG TO SOMEBODY ELSE — Jerry WALLACE
YOU'RE SIXTEEN [A] — Johnny BURNETTE
YOU'RE SIXTEEN [A] — Ringo STARR
YOU'RE SO RIGHT FOR ME [A] — EASTSIDE CONNECTION
YOU'RE SO RIGHT FOR ME [B] — ROOSTER
YOU'RE SO VAIN — Carly SIMON
YOU'RE SPEAKING MY LANGUAGE — JULIETTE & The LICKS
YOU'RE STILL THE ONE — Shania TWAIN
YOU'RE SUCH A GOOD LOOKING WOMAN — Joe DOLAN
YOU'RE THE BEST THING — STYLE COUNCIL
(YOU'RE THE) DEVIL IN DISGUISE — Elvis PRESLEY with The JORDANAIRES (63)
YOU'RE THE FIRST, THE LAST, MY EVERYTHING [A] — Barry WHITE (74)
YOU'RE THE FIRST, THE LAST, MY EVERYTHING [A] — Howard BROWN
YOU'RE THE GREATEST LOVER — Jonathan KING
YOU'RE THE INSPIRATION — CHICAGO
YOU'RE THE ONE [A] — Kathy KIRBY
YOU'RE THE ONE [B] — Petula CLARK
YOU'RE THE ONE [C] — BANG
YOU'RE THE ONE [D] — SWV
YOU'RE THE ONE FOR ME — D TRAIN
YOU'RE THE ONE FOR ME - DAYBREAK - AM — Paul HARDCASTLE
YOU'RE THE ONE FOR ME, FATTY — MORRISSEY
YOU'RE THE ONE I LOVE — Shola AMA
YOU'RE THE ONE THAT I WANT [A] — John TRAVOLTA and Olivia NEWTON-JOHN (78)
YOU'RE THE ONE THAT I WANT [A] — Hylda BAKER and Arthur MULLARD
YOU'RE THE ONE THAT I WANT [A] — Craig McLACHLAN and Debbie GIBSON
YOU'RE THE ONLY GOOD THING — Jim REEVES
YOU'RE THE ONLY ONE — Val DOONICAN
YOU'RE THE REASON — WAMDUE PROJECT
YOU'RE THE REASON WHY — The RUBETTES
YOU'RE THE STAR — Rod STEWART
YOU'RE THE STORM — The CARDIGANS
YOU'RE THE STORY OF MY LIFE — Judy CHEEKS
YOU'RE THE TOP CHA — Al SAXON
YOU'RE THE VOICE [A] — John FARNHAM
YOU'RE THE VOICE [A] — HEART
YOU'RE WALKING — ELECTRIBE 101
YOURS — Dionne WARWICK
YOURS FATALLY — BIG BROVAZ
YOURS UNTIL TOMORROW — Gene PITNEY
YOUTH AGAINST FASCISM — SONIC YOUTH
YOUTH GONE WILD — SKID ROW
YOUTH OF NATION ON FIRE — Bill NELSON
YOUTH OF THE NATION — P.O.D.
YOUTH OF TODAY — MUSICAL YOUTH
YOU'VE BEEN DOING ME WRONG — DELEGATION
YOU'VE BEEN GONE — CROWN HEIGHTS AFFAIR
YOU'VE COME BACK — PJ PROBY
YOU'VE GIVEN ME SOMETHING THAT I CAN'T GIVE BACK — NEW RHODES
YOU'VE GOT A FRIEND [A] — James TAYLOR
YOU'VE GOT A FRIEND [A] — The BRAND NEW HEAVIES
YOU'VE GOT A FRIEND [A] — McFLY (05)
YOU'VE GOT A FRIEND [B] — BIG FUN and SONIA featuring Gary BARNACLE
YOU'VE GOT A LOT TO ANSWER FOR — CATATONIA
YOU'VE GOT ANOTHER THING COMIN' — JUDAS PRIEST
YOU'VE GOT IT — SIMPLY RED
YOU'VE GOT IT BAD — OCEAN COLOUR SCENE
YOU'VE GOT LOVE — Buddy HOLLY and The CRICKETS
YOU'VE GOT ME DANGLING ON A STRING — CHAIRMEN OF THE BOARD
YOU'VE GOT ME THINKING — The BELOVED
YOU'VE GOT MY NUMBER (WHY DON'T YOU USE IT?) — The UNDERTONES
(YOU'VE GOT) PERSONALITY [A] — Lena ZAVARONI
YOU'VE GOT THAT SOMETHIN' — ROBYN
YOU'VE GOT THE LOVE — SOLITAIRE
YOU'VE GOT TO CHOOSE — The DARLING BUDS
YOU'VE GOT TO GIVE ME ROOM — Oleta ADAMS
YOU'VE GOT TO HIDE YOUR LOVE AWAY — SILKIE
YOU'VE GOT YOUR TROUBLES — The FORTUNES
YOU'VE LOST THAT LOVIN' FEELIN' [A] — Cilla BLACK
YOU'VE LOST THAT LOVIN' FEELIN' [A] — The RIGHTEOUS BROTHERS (65)
YOU'VE LOST THAT LOVIN' FEELIN' [A] — Telly SAVALAS
YOU'VE LOST THAT LOVIN' FEELIN' [A] — Daryl HALL and John OATES
YOU'VE MADE ME SO VERY HAPPY — BLOOD SWEAT AND TEARS
(YOU'VE) NEVER BEEN IN LOVE LIKE THIS BEFORE — UNIT FOUR PLUS TWO
YOU'VE NOT CHANGED — Sandie SHAW
YOU'VE SAID ENOUGH — CENTRAL LINE
YOYO BOY — ALBERTA
YUM, YUM (GIMME SOME) — FATBACK BAND
YUMMY YUMMY YUMMY — OHIO EXPRESS
ZABADAK! — Dave DEE, DOZY, BEAKY, MICK and TICH
ZAMBESI [A] — Lou BUSCH and his Orchestra
ZAMBESI [A] — Eddie CALVERT
ZAMBESI [A] — PIRANHAS featuring Boring Bob Grover
ZEPHYR — ELECTRAFIXION
THE ZEPHYR SONG — RED HOT CHILI PEPPERS
ZEROES & ONES — JESUS JONES
ZEROTONINE — JUNKIE XL
ZEROX — ADAM and The ANTS
ZEROXED — ZERO ZERO
ZIGGY STARDUST — BAUHAUS
ZING A LITTLE ZONG — Bing CROSBY and Jane Wyman
ZING WENT THE STRINGS OF MY HEART — The TRAMMPS
ZION YOUTH — DREADZONE
ZIP - LOCK — LIT
ZIP GUN BOOGIE — T. REX
ZIP-A-DEE-DOO-DAH — Bob B SOXX and The BLUE JEANS
ZODIACS — Roberta KELLY
ZOE — PAGANINI TRAXX
ZOMBIE [A] — The CRANBERRIES
ZOMBIE [A] — A.D.A.M. featuring AMY
THE ZOO — SCORPIONS
THE ZOO (THE HUMAN ZOO) — The COMMODORES
ZOOM [A] — The COMMODORES
ZOOM [B] — FAT LARRY'S BAND
ZOOM [B] — Scott BRADLEY
ZOOM [C] — DR DRE and LL COOL J
ZORBA'S DANCE [A] — Marcello MINERBI
ZORBA'S DANCE [A] — LCD
ZUNGA ZENG — K7 and The Swing Kids

8 October 2005	15 October 2005	22 October 2005	29 October 2005
PUSH THE BUTTON Sugababes	**PUSH THE BUTTON** Sugababes	**PUSH THE BUTTON** Sugababes	**I BET YOU LOOK GOOD ON THE DANCEFLOOR** Arctic Monkeys
PIECE BY PIECE Katie Melua	**YOU COULD HAVE IT SO MUCH BETTER** Franz Ferdinand	**TALLER IN MORE WAYS** Sugababes	**THEIR LAW - THE SINGLES 1990-2005** The Prodigy

PICTURE CREDITS

PAGE 1 Left to right: Rex Features; Empics; David Roberts; ITV-Granada
PAGE 5 Left: Angela Lubrano; right: Getty Images
PAGE 6 Top: Tim Graham Picture Library / Getty Images; bottom: Rex Features
PAGE 7 ITV-Granada
PAGE 8 Right: Atlantic Records
PAGE 9 Betty Halvagi
PAGE 28 David Roberts
PAGE 46 Left to right: Corbis; Rex Features; Rex Features
PAGE 47 Corbis
PAGE 65 Left: Redferns; right: Corbis
PAGE 84 Left: Rex Features; right: Redferns
PAGE 121 Chris Clunn / Idols
PAGE 134 ©A.M.P.A.S.®
PAGE 135 Left: Corbis; right: Rex Features
PAGE 137 Time & Life Pictures / Getty Images
PAGE 153 Dave Breese
PAGE 185 Left: Getty Images; right: Redferns
PAGE 202 Dave McAleer
PAGE 203 Redferns
PAGE 220 Getty Images
PAGE 240 Left: Redferns; Right: © POPPERFOTO / Alamy
PAGE 257 Getty Images
PAGE 275 Left and right: Getty Images
PAGE 292 Left: Getty Images; right: AFP/Getty Images
PAGE 311 Left: Getty Images; right: Tim Graham Picture Library / Getty Images
PAGE 329 Empics
PAGE 346 Left: Corbis; right: Getty Images
PAGE 364 Outside Organisation
PAGE 365 Getty Images
PAGE 383 Left: Getty Images; right: Corbis
PAGE 437 Left: Rex Features; right: Getty Images
PAGE 456 Getty Images
PAGE 475 Left: © POPPERFOTO / Alamy; right: Time & Life Pictures / Getty Images
PAGE 492 Redferns
PAGE 512 Top: Corbis; bottom: Redferns
PAGE 529 Top: NASA Kennedy Space Center; bottom: Redferns
PAGE 566 Atlantic Records
PAGE 586 Left: Redferns; centre: Kevin Cummins; right: Empics; lower: Atlantic Records
PAGE 605 Left: Rex Features; right: Rich Stenner
PAGE 619 Betty Halvagi

	5 November 2005	12 November 2005	19 November 2005	26 November 2005
UK No.1 SINGLES	YOU RAISE ME UP Westlife	YOU RAISE ME UP Westlife	HUNG UP Madonna	HUNG UP Madonna
UK No.1 ALBUMS	INTENSIVE CARE Robbie Williams	FACE TO FACE Westlife	ANCORA Il Divo	CONFESSIONS ON A DANCE FLOOR Madonna

31 December 2005

UK No.1 SINGLES

THAT'S MY GOAL
Shayne Ward

UK No.1 ALBUMS

CURTAIN CALL - THE HITS
Eminem